5-

The National Hockey League

Official Guide & Record Book

2004

THE NATIONAL HOCKEY LEAGUE
Official Guide & Record Book/2004

Copyright © 2003 by the National Hockey League.
Compiled by the NHL Public Relations Department and the 30 NHL Club Public Relations Directors.

Printed in Canada. All rights reserved under the Pan-American and International Copyright Conventions.

Published in Canada by:
Dan Diamond and Associates, Inc, 194 Dovercourt Road, Toronto, Ontario M6J 3C8 Canada
   ISBN in Canada 0-920445-84-5

Published in the United States by:
Triumph Books, 601 South LaSalle, Suite 500, Chicago, Illinois 60605
   ISBN in USA 1-57243-603-4

Staff
For the NHL: Dave McCarthy, George Puro; Supervising Editor: Greg Inglis; Statistician: Benny Ercolani;
Editorial Staff: John Halligan, David Keon, Dave Baker, Jackie Rinaldi, Kelley Rosset, Julie Young.

Senior Managing Editor: Ralph Dinger   **Player Register Editor:** James Duplacey

Photo Editor: Eric Zweig   **Production Editors:** John Pasternak, Alex Dubiel

Assistant Editor: Paul Bontje   **Contributing Editor:** Jonathan Zweig

Contributors: Ken Anderson, Craig Baines, Heiko Behrens, Aaron Bell (OHL), Steven M. Black, Case and Nellie Bontje; Bob Borgen, Craig Campbell, Jack Carnefix (ECHL), Paul R. Carroll Jr., Steve Cherwonak (CHL), Diana Danforth (ECHL), Bob Duff, Peter Fillman, Ernie Fitzsimmons, Mel Foster, Kelli Frank (WCHL), Pierre Genest, Hockey Hall of Fame, Patrick Houda, Peter Jagla, Len Kotylo, Roger Leblond, Al Mason, Leroy McKinnon (WHL), Herb Morell (OHL), NHL Broadcasters' Association, NHL Central Registry, NHL Officiating, NHL Players' Association, Joseph Nieforth, Randy Novac, Becky Pasternak, Brenda Pasternak, Stephanie Pasternak, John Paton, Gary J. Pearce, Lisa Peppin (UHL), Phil Pritchard, Valentina Riazanova, Frank and Rita Rocys, Mrs. Claude Rompré (QMJHL), Minako Saki, Chuck Scott, Ralph Slate, Bret Stothart (AHL), Toronto Star/Pages of the Past, Toronto Young Nats, U.S. Hockey Hall of Fame, Bob Waterman, Terry Weir, Ian Wilson, Tyler Wolosewich.
Special thanks to NCAA Conference and School Sports Information Departments.

Publisher: Dan Diamond

Data Management and Typesetting: Caledon Data Management, Hillsburgh, Ontario
Film Output and Scanning: Stafford Graphics, Toronto, Ontario
Printing: Fidelity National Information Solutions Canada, Scarborough, Ontario
Production Management: Dan Diamond and Associates, Inc., Toronto, Ontario

Photo Credits
NHL Images: Anita Cechowski.
Photographers: Graig Abel, Toronto; Scott Audette, Tampa; Steve Babineau, Boston; Bruce Bennett Studios, New York/New Jersey; Andrew D. Bernstein Associates, Los Angeles; Mark Buckner, St. Louis; Scott Cunningham, Atlanta; Tim Defrisco, Colorado; Gregg Forwerck, Carolina; Bob Fisher, Montreal; Freestyle Photography, Ottawa; Getty Images/NHLI (Scott Cunningham, Elsa, Craig Jones, Tom Pigeon, Dave Sandford, Jamie Squire, Jeff Vinnick); Barry Gossage, Phoenix; Hockey Hall of Fame Collections; Glenn James, Dallas; Bruce Kluckhohn, Minnesota; Mitchell Layton, Washington: Richard Lewis, Florida; Dale McMillan, Edmonton; Matt Polk, Pittsburgh; Deborah Robinson, Anaheim; John Russell, Nashville; Jamie Sabau, Columbus; Bill Smith, Chicago; Don Smith, San Jose; Kent Smith, Carolina; Gerry Thomas, Calgary and Edmonton; Jeff Vinnick, Vancouver; Rocky Widner, San Jose; Bill Wippert, Buffalo;

Distribution
Trade sales and distribution in Canada by:
North 49 Books, 35 Prince Andrew Drive, Toronto, Ontario M3C 2H2
416/449-4000; FAX 416/449-9924
Dan Diamond and Associates, Inc., 194 Dovercourt Road, Toronto, Ontario M6J 3C8
416/531-6535; FAX 416/531-3939   e-mail: dda.nhl@sympatico.ca

Trade sales and distribution in the United States by:
Triumph Books, 601 South LaSalle, Suite 500, Chicago, Illinois 60605
312/939-3330; FAX 312/663-3557

International representatives:
Barkers Worldwide Publications, Unit 6/7 The Elms Centre, Glaziers Lane, Normandy, Guildford, Surrey GU3 2DF England
Tel: 011/441/483/811-971 and FAX: 011/441/483/811-972 e-mail: sales@bwpu.demon.co.uk website: www.bwpu.demon.co.uk

Dan Diamond and Associates books may be purchased for educational, business or sales promotional use.
For information please write to: Dan Diamond and Associates, 194 Dovercourt Road, Toronto, Ontario M6J 3C8 Canada
e-mail: dda.nhl@sympatico.ca

Licensed by the National Hockey League.

The National Hockey League
1251 Avenue of the Americas, 47th Floor, New York, New York 10020-1198
1800 McGill College Ave., Suite 2600, Montreal, Quebec H3A 3J6
50 Bay Street, 11th Floor, Toronto, Ontario M5J 2X8

Table of Contents

13 CLUBS   records, rosters, management

133 FINAL STATISTICS 2002-03

Table of Contents *continued*

(2003-04 NHL Schedule begins inside front cover)

Introduction

WELCOME TO *THE NHL OFFICIAL GUIDE & RECORD BOOK 2004.* This is the 72nd edition of a book that began as a twenty-five cent staple-bound pocket book of 140 pages. The book grew steadily, paralleling the addition of more teams, larger rosters and more sophisticated statistical tracking of on-ice events. The book acquired its current editors and received a significant redesign with the 1984-85 edition when today's big-page photo-illustrated format and the name "NHL Official Guide & Record Book" made its debut. That make this 2004 edition the 20th produced by the same crew.

As people who enjoy hockey statistics as much as the next person, this 20th anniversary leaves us appropriately humbled if only for the sheer number of times the Zamboni has scraped the ice since we began work on the *Guide.* How long ago was 1984-85? It was Mario Lemieux's rookie season. The first edition of the new-style guide featured Wayne Gretzky, Mark Messier and Paul Coffey lifting the Stanley Cup for the first time in their eventual Hall of Fame careers. In fact, watching an NHL game from 1984-85 is somewhat of a revelation: those games look more like hockey of the six-team era than they do the hockey of today. And almost every player drafted at the 2003 NHL Entry Draft in Nashville was born since we began the perpetual facet-polishing that characterizes our efforts to provide fans of the game, media on the hockey beat and club and League personnel with the best annual guide book in sports.

A great many of our readers make the *Official Guide & Record Book* an annual part of their connection to the NHL, its franchises and players. You have our thanks. Your support, loyalty, sharp eyes and suggestions have mattered and continue to do so. Stick with us: there's more where the first 20 years came from! Further thanks to our colleagues at the National Hockey League, both off-ice and on. It literally couldn't be done without you.

The 2002-03 season and playoffs provided their share of exceptional performances: two old friends from Ornskoldsvik, a small city in northern Sweden, found themselves finalists for the Hart Trophy as the NHL's most valuable player. Colorado's Peter Forsberg won the award as well as the Art Ross Trophy as the League's scoring leader with 106 points (29G–77A). Fellow finalist Markus Naslund of the Vancouver Canucks finished the season with 104 points (48G–56A). Martin Brodeur became the first goaltender to record four 40-win seasons, shared the Jennings Trophy for fewest team goals-against and won the Vezina Trophy as the NHL's outstanding goaltender. Vezina finalist Marty Turco of the Dallas Stars finished the season with a superb goals-against average of 1.72, the lowest recorded by an NHL goaltender since 1940. In the postseason, two Western Conference clubs, the Mighty Ducks of Anaheim and the third-year Minnesota Wild reached the third round of the playoffs by upsetting accomplished playoff teams that finished ahead of them in the standings. Anaheim prevailed, backed by spectacular goaltending from Jean-Sebastien Giguere, and reached the Stanley Cup Finals for the first time in franchise history. In the East, the seven-game Eastern Conference final between the eventual Cup champion New Jersey Devils and the Ottawa Senators was a magnificent series, decided on a goal by Jeff Friesen with less than two minutes to play in the third period of game seven. Seven games were required in the Cup Finals as well. The Devils prevailed, but Anaheim's J-S Giguere was awarded the Conn Smythe Trophy as playoff MVP. (2003 playoff coverage begins on page 233. Trophies and Awards begin on page 199.)

For 2003–04, the first regular-season NHL game ever played outdoors will take place in Commonwealth Stadiium when the Montreal Canadiens face off against the hometown Edmonton Oilers on Saturday, November 22, 2003, the anniversary date of the founding of the NHL at the old WIndsor Hotel in Montreal in 1917. (The 2003-04 NHL Schedule is found on the inside covers and on the first page of each club's section.)

Records, rosters and management for each NHL club begin on page 13. Note that in each club's section, overtime losses (abbreviated OL or, elsewhere where space permits, OTL) are not included in a team's loss total. Therefore W+L+T+OTL=GP. Overtime losses are only reflected in team statistics. Goaltender and coaching statistics do not include OTLs.

Expanded coverage of the NHL's Amateur/Entry Draft since 1969 begins on page 207 with a revamped Draft Summary table. Individual data panels on drafted forwards and defensemen are found in the *Guide's* Prospect Register (page 267). Players in the Prospect Register are active, but have yet to play in the NHL. They have been drafted, signed as free agents or invited to training camp by NHL clubs. Players who will make their NHL debut in 2003-04 are found here.

The NHL Player Register begins on page 336. It includes active forwards and defensemen who have appeared in an NHL regular-season or playoff game at any time. In addition to the standard GP-G-A-Pts-PIM, an NHLer's player panel includes the following statistical categories, listed from left to right as they appear in the book: power-play goals (PP), shorthand goals (SH), game-winning goals (GW), shots on goal (S), percentage of shots that score (%), plus-minus rating (+/–), total face-offs taken (TF*), face-off winning percentage (F%*), and average time-on-ice per game played (Min*). Categories marked with an asterisk (*) are NHL Real-Time statistics gathered by teams of trained spotters who, working with laptop computers and specialized software, record shots, ice-time, face-off wins, etc. "on-the-fly" at each game. New this year is the addition of time-on-ice per game played in the playoffs. These statistics were kept officially for the first time in 1998-99, so no player in this year's *NHL Guide* has more than five years of Real-Time statistics. Career totals in these Real-Time categories reflect only the past five seasons.

The order of the Registers is as follows: Prospect, NHL Player, Goaltender (page 574), Retired Player (598) and Retired Goaltender (632). Note that the Goaltender Register combines prospects and NHL goaltenders in the same section.

A key to the abbreviations and symbols used in individual player and goaltender data panels, along with useful information on how to use the Registers, is found on page 266. Late additions to the Registers are found on page 335 along with a list of abbreviations used for league names. Each NHL club's minor-pro affiliates are found on page 220 at the end of the *NHL Guide's* Entry Draft coverage.

As always, our thanks to readers, correspondents and members of the media who take the time to comment on the *Guide & Record Book.* Thanks as well to the people working in the communications departments of the NHL's member clubs and to their counterparts in minor pro, junior, college and European hockey.

Best wishes for an enjoyable 2003-04 NHL season.

ACCURACY REMAINS THE *GUIDE & RECORD BOOK'*S TOP PRIORITY.

We appreciate comments and clarification from our readers. Please direct these to:

- Ralph Dinger   Senior Managing Editor, 194 Dovercourt Road, Toronto, Ontario M6J 3C8. e-mail: ralph.dda@sympatico.ca.
- Greg Inglis   47th floor, 1251 Avenue of the Americas, New York, New York 10020-1198 . . . or . . .
- David Keon   50 Bay Street, 11th Floor, Toronto, Ontario, M5J 2X8

Your involvement makes a better book.

NATIONAL HOCKEY LEAGUE

Established November 22, 1917

New York, 1251 Avenue of the Americas, 47th Floor, New York, NY 10020-1198, 212/789-2000, Fax: 212/789-2020, PR Fax: 212/789-2080
Montréal, 1800 McGill College Avenue, Suite 2600, Montréal, Québec, H3A 3J6, 514/841-9220, Fax: 514/841-1070
Toronto, 50 Bay Street, 11th Floor, Toronto, Ontario, M5J 2X8, 416/981-2777, Fax: 416/981-2779
NHL Enterprises, L.P. — 1251 Avenue of the Americas, 47th Floor, New York, NY 10020-1198, 212/789-2000, Fax: 212/789-2020
NHL Enterprises Canada, L.P. — 50 Bay Street, 11th Floor, Toronto, Ontario, M5J 2X8, 416/981-2777, Fax: 416/981-2779
NHL Productions/NHL Images — 240 Pegasus Avenue, Northvale, NJ 07647, 201/750-5800, Fax: 201/750-5850

Executive

Commissioner	Gary B. Bettman
Executive Vice President & Chief Legal Officer	William Daly
Executive Vice President & Director of Hockey Operations	Colin Campbell
Executive Vice President & Chief Operating Officer	Jon Litner
Executive Vice President & Chief Financial Officer	Craig Harnett
Director, Administration & Executive Assistant to the Commissioner	Debbie Jordan

Administration

Director of Administration	Debbie Jordan
Director, Human Resources	Janet Meyers
Director, Offices & Facilities	Andrew Crawford
Manager, Human Resources	Patrice Distler

Broadcasting/Scheduling

Vice President, Broadcasting & Programming	Adam Acone
Director, Television Production & Technology	Onnie Bose
Director, NHL Radio	Brian G. Hamilton
Manager, Business & Special Events	Phyllis DeCongilio
Manager, Television Production & Operations	Stacie Watkins
Vice President, Scheduling, Operations & Research (Montreal)	Steve Hatze Petros
Director, Research & Scheduling	Mark Erlichson
Manager, Scheduling & Operations	William Bredin

NHL Productions

Executive Producer	Ken Rosen
Vice President	Patti Fallick
Coordinating Producer	Darryl Lepik
Director, Operations/Footage	Peg Walsh
Producers	Janice Arbour, Michele Giordano-Moore, Robert Lekhwani, Gary Waksman
Senior Editor	Chip Swain
Associate Producer	Nick Mascolo
Sr. Production Manager	Christine Cortez
Manager, Video Services	Chris Cesa

NHL Images

Director	Anita Cechowski

Communications

Group Vice President, Communications	Bernadette Mansur
Vice President, Media Relations	Frank Brown
Vice President, Public Relations & Media Services (Toronto)	Gary Meagher
Chief Statistician (Toronto)	Benny Ercolani
Director, Communications	Jamey Horan
Director, Community and Diversity Programming	Ken Martin
Director, Media Relations	Amy Early
Director, News Services	Greg Inglis
Director, Player Publicity	Sandra John
Director, Youth Development, NHL Diversity	Willie O'Ree
Director, Corporate Communications	Brian Walker
Manager, Community Relations	Ann Marie Lynch
Manager, Corporate Communications	Veronique Marchal
Manager, NHL Diversity	Nirva Milord
Manager, News Services	Adam Schwartz
Managers, Public Relations (Toronto)	David Keon, Julie Young

Events and Entertainment

Group Vice President	Frank Supovitz
Vice President	Ken Chin
Directors	Sammy Choi, Bill Miller
Senior Managers	Susan Aglietti, Danny Frank, Dean Matsuzaki, Greta Palmer
Managers	Eileen Murphy, Chie Sakuma

Finance

Executive Vice President & Chief Financial Officer	Craig Harnett
Senior Vice President, Finance	Joseph DeSousa
Vice President, Finance and Office Manager (Montreal)	Olivia Pietrantonio
Director, Financial Systems	Belinda Haeberlein
Director, Finance	Lowell Heit
Corporate Controller	Kenneth Cartisano

Hockey Operations

Executive Vice President & Director of Hockey Operations	Colin Campbell
Senior Vice President, Hockey Operations (Toronto)	Jim Gregory
Vice President, Hockey Operations (Toronto)	Mike Murphy
Director of Officiating (Toronto)	Andy VanHellemond
Associate Director of Hockey Operations	Claude Loiselle
Consultant (Toronto)	Kris King
Vice President & Managing Director, Central Registry (Toronto)	Stephen Pellegrini
Director of Systems, Central Registry (Montreal)	Madeleine Supino
Director of Projects, Central Registry (Toronto)	Sean MacLeod
Director, Central Scouting (Toronto)	Frank Bonello
Director of Alumni Relations (Toronto)	Patrick Flatley
Video Director	Damian Echevarrieta
Video Technologies Consultant	Jed Dole
Video Coordinator (Toronto)	Paul Brighty
Facilities Operation Manager	Dan Craig
Consultant (Toronto)	Dave Dryden

Information Technology

Group Vice President, Information Technology	Peter DelGiacco
Assistant Director (Montreal)	Luc Coulombe
Senior Director	Carol Dann
Director, Network Services	Patrick Powers
Director, Technical Services	John Ho
Manager, Technical Support	Dan O'Neill

Legal

Executive Vice President & Chief Legal Officer	William Daly
Senior Vice President, General Counsel	David Zimmerman
Vice President, Deputy General Counsel	Julie Grand
Associate Counsel	Daniel Ages

Pension

Vice President and Managing Director, Pension (Montreal)	Yvon Chamberland
Controller, Pension (Montreal)	Mary Skiadopoulos
Manager, Pension (Montreal)	Lise de Jocas

Security

Senior Vice President, Security	Dennis Cunningham
Senior Director, Security	Joseph Caporicci
Manager, Security	Al Young

Television and Media Ventures

Senior Vice President, Television & Media Ventures	Doug Perlman
Vice President, Television & Business Affairs	Leslie Gittess
Director, Team Television & Business Affairs	John Tortora
Director, NHL Center Ice & Program Development	Ken Gelman
Manager, NHL Center Ice & Media Ventures	Peter Aquilone
Manager, Television & Business Affairs	Bridget DeMouy

NHL Interactive CyberEnterprises (NHL ICE)

President, NHL ICE & Senior Vice President, New Business Development	Keith Ritter
Group Vice President, Business Operations	Ken Nova
Vice President, Editorial & Production	Richard Libero
Senior Director, Web Operations	Grant Nodine

NHL Enterprises

President, NHL Enterprises	Ed Horne

Consumer Products Marketing

Group Vice President, Consumer Products Marketing	Brian Jennings
Vice President, Consumer Products Marketing	James Haskins
Vice President, Consumer Products Marketing, Canada (Toronto)	Glenn Wakefield
Senior Director, Retail Sales & Marketing, Canada (Toronto)	Barry Monaghan
Director, Center Ice Program and Sporting Goods	Lloyd Haymes
Director, Consumer Products Marketing, Canada (Toronto)	Karen Hanson
Director, Entertainment Products	Dave McCarthy
Director, Non-Apparel	Judith Salsberg
Director, Retail Sales & Marketing	Cathy Groves
Manager, Youth Licensing	Rachel Podradchik
Manager, Printed Products & Publishing	George Puro
Manager, Apparel, Non-Apparel, & Trade Shows	John Gulla
Manager, Entertainment Products	Linda M. Santiago
Manager, Center Ice & Sporting Goods	Richard Villani

Club Marketing

Vice President, Club Marketing	Scott Carmichael
Manager	Tammy Levine

Corporate Marketing

Group Vice President, Corporate Marketing	Andrew Judelson
Senior Director, Canada (Toronto)	Laurie Kepron
Directors	Eustace King, Susan Rosenfeld
Managers	Jean Marie Cesare, David Levy, Lauren Ordower
Manager, Canada (Toronto)	Jeff Rockwell

Creative Services

Associate Director, Creative Services	Kathy Drew

Fan Development

Vice President, Fan Development	Alysse Soll
Managers	Felicia Sass, Suzanne Sherman

Finance

Vice President, Finance – NHL Enterprises	Mary McCarthy
Director, Finance	Scott Weinfeld
Director, Accounting Operations	Deborah Corletta

International

Group Vice President & Managing Director, NHL International	Ken Yaffe
Senior Director, International Business Operations	Frank Nakano
Director, International Broadcasting	Susanna Mandel-Mantello
Director, International Marketing	Kamini Sharma
Director, International Licensing & Special Projects	Lynn White
Manager, International Marketing & Special Projects	Michael Rolnick

NHLE Legal and Business Affairs

Executive Vice President & General Counsel	Richard Zahnd
Vice President, Licensing and Trademark Compliance	Ruth Gruhin
Vice President & Corporate Counsel	Robert Hawkins
Vice President, Legal & Business Affairs	Tom Prochnow
Associate Counsels	Jason Camhi, Michael Gold, Matthew Kline
Staff Attorney	Lisa Stancati
Director, Contract Administration	Heather Atria
Director, Quality Control	Catherine O'Brien
Senior Manager, Intellectual Property	Alison Nunez

Strategic Development

Vice President, Strategic Development	Susan Cohig

BOARD OF GOVERNORS

Chairman of the Board – Harley N. Hotchkiss

Mighty Ducks of Anaheim

Jay Rasulo.....................................Governor
Michael D. Eisner ....Alternate Governor
Al Coates ....Alternate Governor

Atlanta Thrashers

Stan Kasten ....Governor
Don Waddell ....Alternate Governor

Boston Bruins

Jeremy M. Jacobs ....Governor
Jeremy M. Jacobs, Jr. ....Alternate Governor
Louis Jacobs ....Alternate Governor
Charles M. Jacobs ....Alternate Governor
Harry J. Sinden ....Alternate Governor
Mike O'Connell ....Alternate Governor

Buffalo Sabres

B. Thomas Golisano .... Governor
Lawrence Quinn ....Alternate Governor

Calgary Flames

Harley N. Hotchkiss........................Governor
N. Murray Edwards ....Alternate Governor
Alvin Libin ....Alternate Governor
Ken King ....Alternate Governor

Carolina Hurricanes

Peter Karmanos, Jr. ....Governor
Jim Rutherford ....Alternate Governor
Jason Karmanos ....Alternate Governor
Ken Lehner ....Alternate Governor

Chicago Blackhawks

William W. Wirtz ....Governor
Robert J. Pulford ....Alternate Governor
John A. Ziegler, Jr. ....Alternate Governor
Peter R. Wirtz ....Alternate Governor

Colorado Avalanche

E. Stanley Kroenke..........................Governor
Donald M. Elliman, Jr. ....Alternate Governor
Pierre Lacroix ....Alternate Governor

Columbus Blue Jackets

John H. McConnell ....Governor
John P. McConnell..........................Alternate Governor
John S. Christie ....Alternate Governor
Doug MacLean ....Alternate Governor

Dallas Stars

Thomas O. Hicks.............................Governor
James R. Lites.................................Alternate Governor
Doug Armstrong ....Alternate Governor

Detroit Red Wings

Michael Ilitch ....Governor
Jim Devellano................................Alternate Governor
Christopher Ilitch...........................Alternate Governor
Denise Ilitch ....Alternate Governor
Ken Holland ....Alternate Governor

Edmonton Oilers

Cal Nichols ....Governor
Patrick R. LaForge ....Alternate Governor
Kevin Lowe ....Alternate Governor
William K. Butler ....Alternate Governor

Florida Panthers

Alan Cohen ....Governor
Jeff Cogen ....Alternate Governor
Steven Cohen ....Alternate Governor
Richard Lehman ....Alternate Governor
William A. Torrey...........................Alternate Governor
Jordan Zimmerman ....Alternate Governor

Los Angeles Kings

Timothy J. Leiweke ....Governor
Philip F. Anschutz ....Alternate Governor
David Taylor ....Alternate Governor

Minnesota Wild

Robert O. Naegele, Jr. ....Governor
Jac Sperling....................................Alternate Governor
Doug Risebrough ....Alternate Governor

Montréal Canadiens

George N. Gillett, Jr. ....Governor
Pierre Boivin ....Alternate Governor
Fred Steer......................................Alternate Governor
Bob Gainey ....Alternate Governor
Jeff Joyce ....Alternate Governor
Foster Gillett..................................Alternate Governor

Nashville Predators

Craig Leipold ....Governor
Jack Diller......................................Alternate Governor
David Poile ....Alternate Governor

New Jersey Devils

Lou Lamoriello...............................Governor
Michael Gilfillan ....Alternate Governor

New York Islanders

Charles B. Wang ....Governor
Sanjay Kumar ....Alternate Governor
Mike Milbury.................................Alternate Governor
Michael J. Picker............................Alternate Governor
Roy E. Reichbach ....Alternate Governor

New York Rangers

James L. Dolan .... Governor
Glen Sather...................................Alternate Governor
Steve Mills....................................Alternate Governor

Ottawa Senators

Eugene Melnyk...............................Governor
Roy Mlakar....................................Alternate Governor

Philadelphia Flyers

Edward M. Snider...........................Governor
Ronald K. Ryan ....Alternate Governor
Philip I. Weinberg ....Alternate Governor
Bob Clarke ....Alternate Governor

Phoenix Coyotes

Steve Ellman..................................Governor
Wayne Gretzky...............................Alternate Governor
Doug Moss ....Alternate Governor
Mike Barnett ....Alternate Governor

Pittsburgh Penguins

Kenneth Sawyer ....Governor
Craig Patrick ....Alternate Governor
Ronald Burkle................................Alternate Governor
Anthony Liberati ....Alternate Governor

St. Louis Blues

William J. Laurie ....Governor
Richard C. Thomas ....Alternate Governor
Brent P. Karasiuk ....Alternate Governor
Mark Sauer ....Alternate Governor
Larry Pleau ....Alternate Governor

San Jose Sharks

Greg Jamison..................................Governor
Kevin Compton ....Alternate Governor
Doug Wilson ....Alternate Governor

Tampa Bay Lightning

Thomas S. Wilson ....Governor
Ronald J. Campbell ....Alternate Governor
Jay H. Feaster ....Alternate Governor

Toronto Maple Leafs

Larry Tanenbaum ....Governor
Dean Metcalf ....Alternate Governor
Dale Lastman ....Alternate Governor
Richard Peddie ....Alternate Governor
Ken Dryden....................................Alternate Governor

Vancouver Canucks

John E. McCaw, Jr. ....Governor
Brian P. Burke ....Alternate Governor
Stanley B. McCammon....................Alternate Governor
David Cobb....................................Alternate Governor
David M. Nonis ....Alternate Governor

Washington Capitals

Richard M. Patrick ....Governor
Ted Leonsis....................................Alternate Governor
George McPhee ....Alternate Governor

Commissioner and League Presidents

Gary B. Bettman

Gary B. Bettman took office as the NHL's first Commissioner on February 1, 1993. Since the League was formed in 1917, there have been five League Presidents.

NHL President	Years in Office
Frank Calder	1917-1943
Mervyn "Red" Dutton	1943-1946
Clarence Campbell	1946-1977
John A. Ziegler, Jr.	1977-1992
Gil Stein	1992-1993

Hockey Hall of Fame

BCE Place
30 Yonge Street
Toronto, Ontario M5E 1X8
Phone: 416/360-7735
Executive Fax: 416/360-1501
Resource Centre Fax: 416/360-1316
www.hhof.com

Bill Hay – Chairman and Chief Executive Officer
Jeff Denomme – President, Chief Operating Officer
    and Treasurer
Craig Baines – Vice President, Marketing and Facility Services
Phil Pritchard – Vice President, Hockey Operations and Curator
Ron Ellis – Director, Public Affairs and Assistant to the President
Ray Paquet – Creative Director, Exhibit Development
Sandra Walters – Controller and Office Manager
Peter Jagla – Producer, New Media and E-Business
Craig Campbell – Manager, Resource Centre and Archives
Steve Ozimec – Manager, Special Events and Hospitality
Kelly Massé – Manager, Corporate and Media Relations
Craig Beckim – Manager, Merchandising and Retail Operations
Jackie Boughazale – Manager, Promotions and
    Attractions Services
Anthony Fusco – Manager, Information Systems
Pearl Rajwanth – Executive Assistant to the President

National Hockey League Players' Association

777 Bay Street, Suite 2400
Toronto, Ontario M5G 2C8
Phone: 416/313-2300
Fax: 416/313-2301
www.nhlpa.com

Robert W. Goodenow – Executive Director and General Counsel
Ted Saskin – Senior Director, Business Affairs and Licensing
Mike Gartner – Director, Business Relations
Kenneth Kim – Director, Marketing
Ian Pulver, Ian Penny, Roland Lee – Associate Counsel, Labour
Mike Ouellet – Associate Counsel, Licensing
Eric Weisz – Manager, Licensing and International Business
Steve Larmer – Player Relations
Greg Dick – Senior Manager, Finance and Business Administration
Kim Murdoch – Manager, Pensions and Benefits
Devin Smith – Program Manager, Goals & Dreams Fund
Dave Tredgett – Executive Producer-Television
Jonathan Weatherdon – Manager, Media Relations

NHL On-Ice Officials

Total NHL Games and 2002-03 Games columns count regular-season games only.

Referees

#	Name	Birthplace	Birthdate	First NHL Game	Total NHL Games	2002-03 Games
9	Blaine Angus	Shawville, Que.	9/25/61	10/17/92	390	72
15	Stephane Auger	Montreal, Que.	12/9/70	4/1/00	168	70
10	Paul Devorski	Guelph, Ont.	8/18/58	10/14/89	823	72
44	Harry Dumas	Mount Laurel, N.J.	7/7/73	12/27/00	14	6
39	Gord Dwyer	Halifax, N.S.	5/18/77			
2	Kerry Fraser	Sarnia, Ont.	5/30/52	4/6/75	1479	72
27	Eric Furlatt	Cap de la Madelaine, Que.	12/2/71	10/8/01	95	65
4	Terry Gregson	Erin, Ont.	11/7/53	12/19/81	1361	71
30	Mike Hasenfratz	Regina, Sask.	7/19/66	10/21/00	177	71
17	Shane Heyer	Summerland, B.C.	2/7/64	*10/1/99	¹242	72
46	Scott Hoberg	Windsor, Ont.	1/23/71			0
8	Dave Jackson	Montreal, Que.	11/28/64	12/23/90	682	72
25	Marc Joannette	Verdun, Que.	11/3/68	10/27/99	217	72
18	Greg Kimmerly	Toronto, Ont.	12/8/64	11/30/96	304	72
12	Don Koharski	Halifax, N.S.	12/2/55	10/14/77	²1362	72
48	Tom Kowal	Vernon, B.C.	11/2/67	10/29/99	149	9
40	Steve Kozari	Penticton, B.C.	6/20/73			
37	Bob Langdon	Woodstock, Ont.	3/11/71	11/11/01	28	18
14	Dennis LaRue	Savannah, GA	7/14/59	3/26/91	501	71
28	Chris Lee	Saint John, N.B.	7/7/70	4/2/00	75	53
3	Mike Leggo	North Bay, Ont.	10/7/64	3/3/98	296	69
6	Dan Marouelli	Edmonton, Alta.	7/16/55	11/2/84	1194	72
26	Rob Martell	Winnipeg, Man.	10/21/63	3/14/84	³217	72
41	Wes McCauley	Georgetown, Ont.	1/11/72	1/20/03	5	5
7	Bill McCreary	Guelph, Ont.	11/17/55	11/3/84	1233	72
19	Mick McGeough	Regina, Sask.	6/20/57	1/19/89	804	65
34	Brad Meier	Dayton, OH	4/11/67	10/23/99	219	69
36	Dean Morton	Peterborough, Ont.	2/27/68	11/11/00	31	22
13	Dan O'Halloran	Essex, Ont.	3/25/64	10/14/95	374	72
42	Dan O'Rourke	Calgary, Alta.	8/31/72	10/2/99	⁴2	2
20	Tim Peel	Toronto, Ont.	4/27/66	10/21/99	226	72
43	Brian Pochmara	Detroit, MI	11/27/76			0
33	Kevin Pollock	Kincardine, Ont.	2/7/70	3/28/00	223	72
21	Chris Rooney	Boston, MA	5/26/74	11/22/00	120	67
38	Francois St. Laurent	Greenfield Park, Que.	6/26/77			
45	Justin St. Pierre`	Dolbeau, Que.	2/17/72			
22	Jay Sharrers	Jamaica, West Indies	7/3/67	*4/3/01	⁵67	37
16	Rob Shick	Port Alberni, B.C.	12/4/57	4/6/86	930	72
49	Jeff Smith	Hamilton, Ont.	9/2/69			0
31	Craig Spada	Welland, Ont.	9/7/71	3/28/02	19	13
11	Kelly Sutherland	Victoria, B.C.	4/18/71	12/19/00	160	71
5	Don Van Massenhoven	London, Ont.	7/17/60	11/11/93	620	72
24	Stephen Walkom	North Bay, Ont.	8/8/63	10/18/92	621	73
29	Ian Walsh	Philadelphia, PA	5/9/72	10/14/00	64	24
35	Dean Warren	Toronto, Ont.	7/22/63	10/8/99	221	72
23	Brad Watson	Regina, Sask.	10/4/61	2/5/94	324	72

¹ plus 785 games as a linesman. ² plus 163 games as a linesman. ³ plus 1 game as a linesman. ⁴ plus 120 games as a linesman.
⁵ plus 642 games as a linesman. * Date of first game as a referee. Previously worked as a linesman.

Linesmen

#	Name	Birthplace	Birthdate	First NHL Game	Total NHL Games	2002-03 Games
75	Derek Amell	Port Colborne, Ont.	9/16/68	10/13/97	360	70
59	Steve Barton	Ottawa, Ont.	12/27/71	11/1/00	139	68
96	David Brisebois	Sudbury, Ont.	4/14/76	10/11/99	136	20
74	Lonnie Cameron	Victoria, B.C.	7/15/64	10/5/96	475	71
67	Pierre Champoux	Ville St-Pierre, Que.	4/18/63	10/8/88	937	66
50	Kevin Collins	Springfield, MA	12/15/50	10/13/77	1893	65
76	Michel Cormier	Trois-Rivieres, Que.	5/28/74			
88	Mike Cvik	Calgary, Alta.	7/6/62	10/8/87	1063	62
83	Angelo D'Amico	Etobicoke, Ont.	5/29/74	11/27/00	70	19
60	Pat Dapuzzo	Hoboken, NJ	12/29/58	12/5/84	1336	64
54	Greg Devorski	Guelph, Ont.	8/3/69	10/9/93	644	67
68	Scott Driscoll	Seaforth, Ont.	5/2/68	10/10/92	713	67
82	Ryan Galloway	Winnipeg, Man.	7/12/72	10/17/02	25	25
66	Darren Gibbs	Edmonton, Alta.	9/30/66	10/1/97	335	66
91	Don Henderson	Calgary, Alta.	9/23/68	3/10/95	463	67
71	Brad Kovachik	Woodstock, Ont.	3/7/71	10/10/96	449	70
86	Brad Lazarowich	Vancouver, B.C.	8/4/62	10/9/86	1156	69
78	Brian Mach	Little Falls, MN	4/15/74	10/7/00	203	66
51	Dan McCourt	Falconbridge, Ont.	8/14/54	12/27/80	1558	70
90	Andy McElman	Chicago Heights, IL	8/4/61	10/7/93	647	68
89	Steve Miller	Stratford, Ont.	6/22/72	10/7/00	196	62
98	Randy Mitton	Fredericton, N.B.	9/22/50	2/2/74	2040	67
97	Jean Morin	Sorel, Que.	8/10/63	10/5/91	767	65
93	Brian Murphy	Dover, NH	12/13/64	10/7/88	⁶88	69
95	Jonny Murray	Beauport, Que.	8/10/74	10/7/00	203	67
70	Derek Nansen	Ottawa, Ont.	12/6/71	10/11/02	65	65
80	Thor Nelson	Westminister, CA	1/6/68	2/16/95	376	64
77	Tim Nowak	Buffalo, NY	9/6/67	10/8/93	655	66
79	Mark Paré	Windsor, Ont.	7/26/57	10/11/79	1746	62
72	Stephane Provost	Montreal, Que.	5/5/67	1/25/95	623	66
65	Pierre Racicot	Verdun, Que.	2/15/67	10/12/93	676	62
73	Vaughan Rody	Winnipeg, Man.	12/13/68	10/8/00	209	65
81	Troy Sartison	Swift Current, Sask.	2/25/70	10/6/99	262	67
53	Ray Scapinello	Guelph, Ont.	11/5/46	10/17/71	2434	69
52	Dan Schachte	Madison, WI	7/13/58	10/6/82	1467	69
61	Lyle Seitz	Brooks, Alta.	1/22/69	10/6/92	⁷323	69
84	Anthony Sericolo	Troy, NY	7/17/68	10/21/98	300	66
92	Mark Shewchuk	hamilton, Ont.	6/1/75			
56	Mark Wheler	North Battleford, Sask.	9/20/65	10/10/92	740	71

⁶ Murphy also worked 88 games as a referee. ⁷ Seitz also worked 10 games as a referee.

NHL History

1917 — National Hockey League organized November 22 in Montreal following suspension of operations by the National Hockey Association of Canada Limited (NHA). Montreal Canadiens, Montreal Wanderers, Ottawa Senators and Quebec Bulldogs attended founding meeting. Delegates decided to use NHA rules.

Toronto Arenas were later admitted as fifth team; Quebec decided not to operate during the first season. Quebec players allocated to remaining four teams.

Frank Calder elected president and secretary-treasurer.

First NHL games played December 19, with Toronto only arena with artificial ice. Clubs played 22-game split schedule.

1918 — Emergency meeting held January 3 due to destruction by fire of Montreal Arena which was home ice for both Canadiens and Wanderers.

Wanderers withdrew, reducing the NHL to three teams; Canadiens played remaining home games at 3,250-seat Jubilee rink.

Quebec franchise sold to P.J. Quinn of Toronto on October 18 on the condition that the team operate in Quebec City for 1918-19 season. Quinn did not attend the November League meeting and Quebec did not play in 1918-19.

1919-20 — NHL reactivated Quebec Bulldogs franchise. Former Quebec players returned to the club. New Mount Royal Arena became home of Canadiens. Toronto Arenas changed name to St. Patricks. Clubs played 24-game split schedule.

1920-21 — H.P. Thompson of Hamilton, Ontario made application for the purchase of an NHL franchise. Quebec franchise shifted to Hamilton with other NHL teams providing players to strengthen the club.

1921-22 — Split schedule abandoned. First and second place teams at the end of full schedule to play for championship.

1922-23 — Clubs agreed that players could not be sold or traded to clubs in any other league without first being offered to all other clubs in the NHL. In March, Foster Hewitt broadcasts radio's first hockey game.

1923-24 — Ottawa's new 10,000-seat arena opened. First U.S. franchise granted to Boston for following season.

Dr. Cecil Hart Trophy donated to NHL to be awarded to the player judged most useful to his team.

1924-25 — Canadian Arena Company of Montreal granted a franchise to operate Montreal Maroons. NHL now six team league with two clubs in Montreal. Inaugural game in new Montreal Forum played November 29, 1924 as Canadiens defeated Toronto 7-1. Forum was home rink for the Maroons, but no ice was available in the Canadiens arena November 29, resulting in shift to Forum.

Hamilton finished first in the standings, receiving a bye into the finals. But Hamilton players, demanding $200 each for additional games in the playoffs, went on strike. The NHL suspended all players, fining them $200 each. Stanley Cup finalist to be the winner of NHL semi-final between Toronto and Canadiens.

Prince of Wales and Lady Byng trophies donated to NHL.

Clubs played 30-game schedule.

1925-26 — Hamilton club dropped from NHL. Players signed by new New York Americans franchise. Pittsburgh Pirates granted franchise.

Clubs played 36-game schedule.

1926-27 — New York Rangers granted franchise May 15, 1926. Chicago Black Hawks and Detroit Cougars granted franchises September 25, 1926. NHL now ten-team league with an American and a Canadian Division.

Stanley Cup came under the control of NHL. In previous seasons, winners of the now-defunct Western or Pacific Coast leagues would play NHL champion in Cup finals.

Toronto franchise sold to a new company controlled by Hugh Aird and Conn Smythe. Name changed from St. Patricks to Maple Leafs.

Clubs played 44-game schedule.

The Montreal Canadiens donated the Vezina Trophy to be awarded to the team allowing the fewest goals-against in regular season play. The winning team would, in turn, present the trophy to the goaltender playing in the greatest number of games during the season.

1930-31 — Detroit franchise changed name from Cougars to Falcons. Pittsburgh transferred to Philadelphia for one season. Pirates changed name to Philadelphia Quakers. Trading deadline for teams set at February 15 of each year. NHL approved operation of farm teams by Rangers, Americans, Falcons and Bruins. Four-sided electric arena clock first demonstrated.

1931-32 — Philadelphia dropped out. Ottawa withdrew for one season. New Maple Leaf Gardens completed.

Clubs played 48-game schedule

1932-33 — Detroit franchise changed name from Falcons to Red Wings. Franchise application received from St. Louis but refused because of additional travel costs. Ottawa team resumed play.

1933-34 — First All-Star Game played as a benefit for injured player Ace Bailey. Leafs defeated All-Stars 7-3 in Toronto.

1934-35 — Ottawa franchise transferred to St. Louis. Team called St. Louis Eagles and consisted largely of Ottawa's players.

1935-36 — Ottawa-St. Louis franchise terminated. Montreal Canadiens finished season with very poor record. To strengthen the club, NHL gave Canadiens first call on the services of all French-Canadian players for three seasons.

1937-38 — Second benefit All-Star game staged November 2 in Montreal in aid of the family of the late Canadiens star Howie Morenz.

Montreal Maroons withdrew from the NHL on June 22, 1938, leaving seven clubs in the League.

1938-39 — Expenses for each club regulated at $5 per man per day for meals and $2.50 per man per day for accommodation.

1939-40 — Benefit All-Star Game played October 29, 1939 in Montreal for the children of the late Albert (Babe) Siebert.

1940-41 — Ross-Tyer puck adopted as the official puck of the NHL. Early in the season it was apparent that this puck was too soft. The Spalding puck was adopted in its place.

On May 16, 1941, Arthur Ross, NHL governor from Boston, donated a perpetual trophy to be awarded annually to the player voted outstanding in the league. Due to wartime restrictions, the trophy was never awarded.

1941-42 — New York Americans changed name to Brooklyn Americans.

1942-43 — Brooklyn Americans withdrew from NHL, leaving six teams: Boston, Chicago, Detroit, Montreal, New York and Toronto. Playoff format saw first-place team play third-place team and second play fourth.

Clubs played 50-game schedule.

Frank Calder, president of the NHL since its inception, died in Montreal. Meryn "Red" Dutton, former manager of the New York Americans, became president. The NHL commissioned the Calder Memorial Trophy to be awarded to the League's outstanding rookie each year.

1945-46 — Philadelphia, Los Angeles and San Francisco applied for NHL franchises.

The Philadelphia Arena Company of the American Hockey League applied for an injunction to prevent the possible operation of an NHL franchise in that city.

1946-47 — Mervyn Dutton retired as president of the NHL prior to the start of the season. He was succeeded by Clarence S. Campbell.

Individual trophy winners and all-star team members to receive $1,000 awards.

Playoff guarantees for players introduced.

Clubs played 60-game schedule.

1947-48 — The first annual All-Star Game for the benefit of the players' pension fund was played when the All-Stars defeated the Stanley Cup Champion Toronto Maple Leafs 4-3 in Toronto on October 13, 1947.

Criteria for awarding Art Ross Trophy changed. Now awarded to top scorer. Elmer Lach was its first winner.

Philadelphia and Los Angeles franchise applications refused.

National Hockey League Pension Society formed.

1949-50 — Clubs played 70-game schedule. First intra-league draft held April 30, 1950. Clubs allowed to protect 30 players. Remaining players available for $25,000 each.

1951-52 — Referees included in the League's pension plan.

1952-53 — In May of 1952, City of Cleveland applied for NHL franchise. Application denied. In March of 1953, the Cleveland Barons of the AHL challenged the NHL champions for the Stanley Cup. The NHL governors did not accept this challenge.

1953-54 — The James Norris Memorial Trophy presented to the NHL for annual presentation to the League's best defenseman.

Intra-league draft rules amended to allow teams to protect 18 skaters and two goaltenders, claiming price reduced to $15,000.

1954-55 — Each arena to operate an "out-of-town" scoreboard. Referees and linesmen to wear shirts of black and white vertical stripes.

1956-57 — Standardized signals for referees and linesmen introduced.

1960-61 — Canadian National Exhibition, City of Toronto and NHL reach agreement for the construction of a Hockey Hall of Fame on the CNE grounds. Hall opens on August 26, 1961.

1963-64 — Player development league established with clubs operated by NHL franchises located in Minneapolis, St. Paul, Indianapolis, Omaha and, beginning in 1964-65, Tulsa. First universal amateur draft took place. All players of qualifying age (17) unaffected by sponsorship of junior teams available to be drafted.

1964-65 — Conn Smythe Trophy presented to the NHL to be awarded annually to the outstanding player in the Stanley Cup playoffs.

Minimum age of players subject to amateur draft changed to 18.

1965-66 — NHL announced expansion plans for a second six-team division to begin play in 1967-68.

1966-67 — Fourteen applications for NHL franchises received.

Lester Patrick Trophy presented to the NHL to be awarded annually for outstanding service to hockey in the United States.

NHL sponsorship of junior teams ceased, making all players of qualifying age not already on NHL-sponsored lists eligible for the amateur draft.

1967-68 — Six new teams added: California Seals, Los Angeles Kings, Minnesota North Stars, Philadelphia Flyers, Pittsburgh Penguins, St. Louis Blues. New teams to play in West Division. Remaining six teams to play in East Division.

Minimum age of players subject to amateur draft changed to 20.

Clubs played 74-game schedule.

Clarence S. Campbell Trophy awarded to team finishing the regular season in first place in West Division.

California Seals change name to Oakland Seals on December 8, 1967.

1968-69 — Clubs played 76-game schedule. Amateur draft expanded to cover any amateur player of qualifying age throughout the world.

1970-71 — Two new teams added: Buffalo Sabres and Vancouver Canucks. These teams joined East Division: Chicago switched to West Division. Oakland Seals change name to California Golden Seals prior to season.

Clubs played 78-game schedule.

1971-72 — Playoff format amended. In each division, first to play fourth; second to play third.

1972-73 — Soviet Nationals and Canadian NHL stars play eight-game pre-season series. Canadians win 4-3-1.

Two new teams added. Atlanta Flames join West Division; New York Islanders join East Division.

1974-75 — Two new teams added: Kansas City Scouts and Washington Capitals. Teams realigned into two nine-team conferences, the Prince of Wales made up of the Norris and Adams Divisions, and the Clarence Campbell made up of the Smythe and Patrick Divisions.

Clubs played 80-game schedule.

1976-77 — California franchise transferred to Cleveland. Team named Cleveland Barons. Kansas City franchise transferred to Denver. Team named Colorado Rockies.

1977-78 — Clarence S. Campbell retires as NHL president. Succeeded by John A. Ziegler, Jr.

1978-79 — Cleveland and Minnesota franchises merge, leaving NHL with 17 teams. Merged team placed in Adams Division, playing home games in Minnesota.

Minimum age of players subject to amateur draft changed to 19.

1979-80 — Four new teams added: Edmonton Oilers, Hartford Whalers, Quebec Nordiques and Winnipeg Jets.

Minimum age of players subject to entry draft changed to 18.

1980-81 — Atlanta franchise shifted to Calgary, retaining "Flames" name.

1981-82 — Teams realigned within existing divisions. New groupings based on geographical areas. Unbalanced schedule adopted.

1982-83 — Colorado Rockies franchise shifted to East Rutherford, New Jersey. Team named New Jersey Devils. Franchise moved to Patrick Division from Smythe; Winnipeg moved to Smythe Division from Norris.

NHL History — continued

1991-92 — San Jose Sharks added, making the NHL a 22-team league. NHL celebrates 75th Anniversary Season. The 1991-92 regular season suspended due to a strike by members of the NHL Players' Association on April 1, 1992. Play resumed April 12, 1992.

1992-93 — Gil Stein named NHL president (October, 1992). Gary Bettman named first NHL Commissioner (February, 1993). Ottawa Senators and Tampa Bay Lightning added, making the NHL a 24-team league. NHL celebrates Stanley Cup Centennial. Clubs played 84-game schedule.

1993-94 — Mighty Ducks of Anaheim and Florida Panthers added, making the NHL a 26-team league. Minnesota franchise shifted to Dallas, team named Dallas Stars. Prince of Wales and Clarence Campbell Conferences renamed Eastern and Western. Adams, Patrick, Norris and Smythe Divisions renamed Northeast, Atlantic, Central and Pacific. Winnipeg moved to Central Division from Pacific; Tampa Bay moved to Atlantic Division from Central; Pittsburgh moved to Northeast Division from Atlantic.

1994-95 — The National Hockey League locked out the members of the NHL Players' Association, forcing the cancellation of 468 games from October 1, 1994 to January 19, 1995. Clubs played a 48-game schedule that began January 20, 1995 and ended May 3, 1995. No inter-conference games were played.

1995-96 — Quebec franchise transferred to Denver. Team named Colorado Avalanche and placed in Pacific Division of Western Conference. Clubs to play 82-game schedule.

1996-97 — Winnipeg franchise transferred to Phoenix. Team named Phoenix Coyotes and placed in Central Division of Western Conference.

1997-98 — Hartford franchise transferred to Raleigh. Team named Carolina Hurricanes and remains in Northeast Division of Eastern Conference.

1998-99 — The addition of the Nashville Predators made the NHL a 27-team league and brought about the creation of two new divisions and a League-wide realignment in preparation for further expansion to 30 teams by 2000-2001. Nashville was added to the Central Division of the Western Conference, while Toronto moved into the Northeast Division of the Eastern Conference. Pittsburgh was shifted from the Northeast to the Atlantic, while Carolina left the Northeast for the newly created Southeast Division of the Eastern Conference. Florida, Tampa Bay and Washington also joined the Southeast. In the Western Conference, Calgary, Colorado, Edmonton and Vancouver make up the new Northwest Division. Dallas and Phoenix moved from the Central to the Pacific Division.

The NHL retired uniform number 99 in honor of all-time scoring leader Wayne Gretzky who retired at the end of the season.

1999-2000 — Atlanta Thrashers added, making the NHL a 28-team league.

2000-01 — Columbus Blue Jackets and Minnesota Wild added, making the NHL a 30-team league.

Major Rule Changes

1910-11 — Game changed from two 30-minute periods to three 20-minute periods.

1911-12 — National Hockey Association (forerunner of the NHL) originated six-man hockey, replacing seven-man game.

1917-18 — Goalies permitted to fall to the ice to make saves. Previously a goaltender was penalized for dropping to the ice.

1918-19 — Penalty rules amended. For minor fouls, substitutes not allowed until penalized player had served three minutes. For major fouls, no substitutes for five minutes. For match fouls, no substitutes allowed for the remainder of the game.

With the addition of two lines painted on the ice twenty feet from center, three playing zones were created, producing a forty-foot neutral center ice area in which forward passing was permitted. Kicking the puck was permitted in this neutral zone.

Tabulation of assists began.

1921-22 — Goaltenders allowed to pass the puck forward up to their own blue line.

Overtime limited to twenty minutes.

Minor penalties changed from three minutes to two minutes.

1923-24 — Match foul defined as actions deliberately injuring or disabling an opponent. For such actions, a player was fined not less than $50 and ruled off the ice for the balance of the game. A player assessed a match penalty may be replaced by a substitute at the end of 20 minutes. Match penalty recipients must meet with the League president who can assess additional punishment.

1925-26 — Delayed penalty rules introduced. Each team must have a minimum of four players on the ice at all times.

Two rules were amended to encourage offense: No more than two defensemen permitted to remain inside a team's own blue line when the puck has left the defensive zone. A faceoff to be called for ragging the puck unless short-handed.

Team captains only players allowed to talk to referees.

Goaltender's leg pads limited to 12-inch width.

Timekeeper's gong to mark end of periods rather than referee's whistle. Teams to dress a maximum of 12 players for each game from a roster of no more than 14 players.

1926-27 — Blue lines repositioned to sixty feet from each goal-line, thereby enlarging the neutral zone and standardizing distance from blueline to goal.

Uniform goal nets adopted throughout NHL with goal posts securely fastened to the ice.

1927-28 — To further encourage offense, forward passes allowed in defending and neutral zones and goaltender's pads reduced in width from 12 to 10 inches.

Game standardized at three twenty-minute periods of stop-time separated by ten-minute intermissions. Teams to change ends after each period.

Ten minutes of sudden-death overtime to be played if the score is tied after regulation time.

Minor penalty to be assessed to any player other than a goaltender for deliberately picking up the puck while it is in play. Minor penalty to be assessed for deliberately shooting the puck out of play.

The Art Ross goal net adopted as the official net of the NHL.

Maximum length of hockey sticks limited to 53 inches measured from heel of blade to end of handle. No minimum length stipulated.

Home teams given choice of end to defend at start of game.

1928-29 — Forward passing permitted in defensive and neutral zones and into attacking zone if pass receiver is in neutral zone when pass is made. No forward passing allowed inside attacking zone.

Minor penalty to be assessed to any player who delays the game by passing the puck back into his defensive zone.

Ten-minute overtime without sudden-death provision to be played in games tied after regulation time. Games tied after this overtime period declared a draw.

Exclusive of goaltenders, team to dress at least 8 and no more than 12 skaters.

NHL Attendance

Season	Games	Regular Season Attendance	Games	Playoffs Attendance	Total Attendance
1960-61	210	2,317,142	17	242,000	2,559,142
1961-62	210	2,435,424	18	277,000	2,712,424
1962-63	210	2,590,574	16	220,906	2,811,480
1963-64	210	2,732,642	21	309,149	3,041,791
1964-65	210	2,822,635	20	303,859	3,126,494
1965-66	210	2,941,164	16	249,000	3,190,184
1966-67	210	3,084,759	16	248,336	3,333,095
1967-68[1]	444	4,938,043	40	495,089	5,433,132
1968-69	456	5,550,613	33	431,739	5,982,352
1969-70	456	5,992,065	34	461,694	6,453,759
1970-71[2]	546	7,257,677	43	707,633	7,965,310
1971-72	546	7,609,368	36	582,666	8,192,034
1972-73[3]	624	8,575,651	38	624,637	9,200,288
1973-74	624	8,640,978	38	600,442	9,241,420
1974-75[4]	720	9,521,536	51	784,181	10,305,717
1975-76	720	9,103,761	48	726,279	9,830,040
1976-77	720	8,563,890	44	646,279	9,210,169
1977-78	720	8,526,564	45	686,634	9,213,198
1978-79	680	7,758,053	45	694,521	8,452,574
1979-80[5]	840	10,533,623	63	976,699	11,510,322
1980-81	840	10,726,198	68	966,390	11,692,588
1981-82	840	10,710,894	71	1,058,948	11,769,842
1982-83	840	11,020,610	66	1,088,222	12,028,832
1983-84	840	11,359,386	70	1,107,400	12,466,786
1984-85	840	11,633,730	70	1,107,500	12,741,230
1985-86	840	11,621,000	72	1,152,503	12,773,503
1986-87	840	11,855,880	87	1,383,967	13,239,847
1987-88	840	12,117,512	83	1,336,901	13,454,413
1988-89	840	12,417,969	83	1,327,214	13,745,183
1989-90	840	12,579,651	85	1,355,593	13,935,244
1990-91	840	12,343,897	92	1,442,203	13,786,100
1991-92[6]	880	12,769,676	86	1,327,920	14,097,596
1992-93[7]	1,008	14,158,177[8]	83	1,346,034	15,504,211
1993-94[9]	1,092	16,105,604[10]	90	1,440,095	17,545,699
1994-95	624[11]	9,233,884	81	1,329,130	10,563,014
1995-96	1,066	17,041,614	86	1,540,140	18,581,754
1996-97	1,066	17,640,529	82	1,494,878	19,135,407
1997-98	1,066	17,264,678	82	1,507,416	18,772,094
1998-99[12]	1,107	18,001,741	86	1,509,411	19,511,152
1999-2000[13]	1,148	18,800,139	83	1,524,629	20,324,768
2000-01[14]	1,230	20,373,379	86	1,584,011	21,957,390
2001-02	1,230	20,614,613	90	1,691,174	22,305,787
2002-03	1,230	20,408,704	89	1,636,120	22,044,824

[1] First expansion: Los Angeles, Pittsburgh, California (Cleveland),Philadelphia, St. Louis and Minnesota (Dallas)
[2] Second expansion: Buffalo and Vancouver
[3] Third expansion: Atlanta (Calgary) and New York Islanders
[4] Fourth expansion: Kansas City (Colorado, New Jersey) and Washington
[5] Fifth expansion: Edmonton, Hartford, Quebec (Colorado) and Winnipeg
[6] Sixth expansion: San Jose
[7] Seventh expansion: Ottawa and Tampa Bay
[8] Includes 24 neutral site games
[9] Eighth expansion: Anaheim and Florida
[10] Includes 26 neutral site games
[11] Lockout resulted in the cancellation of 468 regular-season games.
[12] Ninth expansion: Nashville
[13] Tenth expansion: Atlanta
[14] Eleventh expansion: Columbus and Minnesota

Major Rule Changes — *continued*

1929-30 — Forward passing permitted inside all three zones but not permitted across either blue line.

Kicking the puck allowed, but a goal cannot be scored by kicking the puck in.

No more than three players including the goaltender may remain in their defensive zone when the puck has gone up ice. Minor penalties to be assessed for the first two violations of this rule in a game; major penalties thereafter.

Goaltenders forbidden to hold the puck. Pucks caught must be cleared immediately. For infringement of this rule, a faceoff to be taken ten feet in front of the goal with no player except the goaltender standing between the faceoff spot and the goal-line.

Highsticking penalties introduced.

Maximum number of players in uniform increased from 12 to 15.

December 21, 1929 — Forward passing rules instituted at the beginning of the 1929-30 season more than doubled number of goals scored. Partway through the season, these rules were further amended to read, "No attacking player allowed to precede the play when entering the opposing defensive zone." This is similar to modern offside rule.

1930-31 — A player without a complete stick ruled out of play and forbidden from taking part in further action until a new stick is obtained. A player who has broken his stick must obtain a replacement at his bench.

A further refinement of the offside rule stated that the puck must first be propelled into the attacking zone before any player of the attacking side can enter that zone; for infringement of this rule a faceoff to take place at the spot where the infraction took place.

1931-32 — Though there is no record of a team attempting to play with two goaltenders on the ice, a rule was instituted which stated that each team was allowed only one goaltender on the ice at one time.

Attacking players forbidden to impede the movement or obstruct the vision of opposing goaltenders.

Defending players with the exception of the goaltender forbidden from falling on the puck within 10 feet of the net.

1932-33 — Each team to have captain on the ice at all times.

If the goaltender is removed from the ice to serve a penalty, the manager of the club to appoint a substitute.

Match penalty with substitution after five minutes instituted for kicking another player.

1933-34 — Number of players permitted to stand in defensive zone restricted to three including goaltender.

Visible time clocks required in each rink.

Two referees replace one referee and one linesman.

1934-35 — Penalty shot awarded when a player is tripped and thus prevented from having a clear shot on goal, having no player to pass to other than the offending player. Shot taken from inside a 10-foot circle located 38 feet from the goal. The goaltender must not advance more than one foot from his goal-line when the shot is taken.

1937-38 — Rules introduced governing icing the puck.

Penalty shot awarded when a player other than a goaltender falls on the puck within 10 feet of the goal.

1938-39 — Penalty shot modified to allow puck carrier to skate in before shooting.

One referee and one linesman replace two referee system.

Blue line widened to 12 inches.

Maximum number of players in uniform increased from 14 to 15.

1939-40 — A substitute replacing a goaltender removed from ice to serve a penalty may use a goaltender's stick and gloves but no other goaltending equipment.

1940-41 — Flooding ice surface between periods made obligatory.

1941-42 — Penalty shots classified as minor and major. Minor shot to be taken from a line 28 feet from the goal. Major shot, awarded when a player is tripped with only the goaltender to beat, permits the player taking the penalty shot to skate right into the goalkeeper and shoot from point-blank range.

One referee and two linesmen employed to officiate games.

For playoffs, standby minor league goaltenders employed by NHL as emergency substitutes.

1942-43 — Because of wartime restrictions on train scheduling, regular-season overtime was discontinued on November 21, 1942.

Player limit reduced from 15 to 14. Minimum of 12 men in uniform abolished.

1943-44 — Red line at center ice introduced to speed up the game and reduce offside calls. This rule is considered to mark the beginning of the modern era in the NHL.

1945-46 — Goal indicator lights synchronized with official time clock required at all rinks.

1946-47 — System of signals by officials to indicate infractions introduced.

Linesmen from neutral cities employed for all games.

1947-48 — Goal awarded when a player with the puck has an open net to shoot at and a thrown stick prevents the shot on goal. Major penalty to any player who throws his stick in any zone other than defending zone. If a stick is thrown by a player in his defending zone but the thrown stick is not considered to have prevented a goal, a penalty shot is awarded.

All playoff games played until a winner determined, with 20-minute sudden-death overtime periods separated by 10-minute intermissions.

1949-50 — Ice surface painted white.

Clubs allowed to dress 17 players exclusive of goaltenders.

Major penalties incurred by goaltenders served by a member of the goaltender's team instead of resulting in a penalty shot.

1950-51 — Each team required to provide an emergency goaltender in attendance with full equipment at each game for use by either team in the event of illness or injury to a regular goaltender.

1951-52 — Home teams to wear basic white uniforms; visiting teams basic colored uniforms.

Goal crease enlarged from 3 × 7 feet to 4 × 8 feet.

Number of players in uniform reduced to 15 plus goaltenders.

Faceoff circles enlarged from 10-foot to 15-foot radius.

1952-53 — Teams permitted to dress 15 skaters on the road and 16 at home.

1953-54 — Number of players in uniform set at 16 plus goaltenders.

1954-55 — Number of players in uniform set at 18 plus goaltenders up to December 1 and 16 plus goaltenders thereafter. Teams agree to wear colored uniforms at home and white uniforms on the road.

1956-57 — Player serving a minor penalty allowed to return to ice when a goal is scored by opposing team.

1959-60 — Players prevented from leaving their benches to enter into an altercation. Substitutions permitted providing substitutes do not enter into altercation.

1960-61 — Number of players in uniform set at 16 plus goaltenders.

1961-62 — Penalty shots to be taken by the player against whom the foul was committed. In the event of a penalty shot called in a situation where a particular player hasn't been fouled, the penalty shot to be taken by any player on the ice when the foul was committed.

1964-65 — No bodily contact on faceoffs.

In playoff games, each team to have its substitute goaltender dressed in his regular uniform except for leg pads and body protector. All previous rules governing standby goaltenders terminated.

1965-66 — Teams required to dress two goaltenders for each regular-season game. Maximum stick length increased to 55 inches.

1966-67 — Substitution allowed on coincidental major penalties.

Between-periods intermissions fixed at 15 minutes.

1967-68 — If a penalty incurred by a goaltender is a co-incident major, the penalty to be served by a player of the goaltender's team on the ice at the time the penalty was called. Limit of curvature of hockey stick blade set at 1-½ inches.

1969-70 — Limit of curvature of hockey stick blade set at 1 inch.

1970-71 — Home teams to wear basic white uniforms; visiting teams basic colored uniforms.

Limit of curvature of hockey stick blade set at ½ inch.

Minor penalty for deliberately shooting the puck out of the playing area.

1971-72 — Number of players in uniform set at 17 plus 2 goaltenders.

Third man to enter an altercation assessed an automatic game misconduct penalty.

1972-73 — Minimum width of stick blade reduced to 2 inches from 2-½ inches.

1974-75 — Bench minor penalty imposed if a penalized player does not proceed directly and immediately to the penalty box.

1976-77 — Rule dealing with fighting amended to provide a major and game misconduct penalty for any player who is clearly the instigator of a fight.

1977-78 — Teams requesting a stick measurement to be assessed a minor penalty in the event that the measured stick does not violate the rules.

1979-80 — Wearing of helmets made mandatory for players entering the NHL.

1980-81 — Maximum stick length increased to 58 inches.

1981-82 — If both of a team's listed goaltenders are incapacitated, the team can dress and play any eligible goaltender who is available.

1982-83 — Number of players in uniform set at 18 plus 2 goaltenders.

1983-84 — Five-minute sudden-death overtime to be played in regular-season games that are tied at the end of regulation time.

1985-86 — Substitutions allowed in the event of co-incidental minor penalties. Maximum stick length increased to 60 inches.

1986-87 — Delayed off-side is no longer in effect once the players of the offending team have cleared the opponents' defensive zone.

1989-90 — Maximum width of goaltender's pads increased from 10 to 12 inches.

1990-91 — The goal lines, blue lines, defensive zone face-off circles and markings all moved one foot out from the end boards, creating 11 feet of room behind the nets and shrinking the neutral zone from 60 to 58 feet.

1991-92 — Video replays employed to assist referees in goal/no goal situations. Size of goal crease increased. Crease changed to semi-circular configuration. Time clock to record tenths of a second in last minute of each period and overtime. Major and game misconduct penalty for checking from behind into boards. Penalties added for crease infringement and unnecessary contact with goaltender. Goal disallowed if puck enters net while a player of the attacking team is standing on the goal crease line, is in the goal crease or places his stick in the goal crease.

1992-93 — No substitutions allowed in the event of coincidental minor penalties called when both teams are at full strength. Wearing of helmets made optional for forwards and defensemen. Minor penalty for attempting to draw a penalty ("diving"). Major and game misconduct penalty for checking from behind into goal frame. Game misconduct penalty for instigating a fight. Highsticking redefined to include any use of the stick above waist-height. Previous rule stipulated shoulder-height.

1993-94 — High sticking redefined to allow goals scored with a high stick below the height of the crossbar of the goal frame.

1996-97 — Maximum stick length increased to 63 inches.

1998-99 — The league instituted a two-referee system with each team to play 20 regular-season games with two referees and a pair of linesmen. Also, the goal lines, blue lines, defensive zone face-off circles and markings all moved two feet closer to center, creating 13 feet of room behind the nets and cutting the neutral zone from 58 to 54 feet. The goal crease was altered so that it extends only one foot beyond each goal post (eight feet across in total) and has square sides for the first 4'6". Only the top of the crease remains rounded.

1999-2000 — Each team to play 25 home and 25 road games using the two-referee system. Crease rule revised to implement a "no harm, no foul, no video review" standard. An attacking player's position, whether inside or outside the crease, does not, in itself, determine whether a goal should be allowed or disallowed. The on-ice judgement of the referee(s) — instead of video review — will determine if a goal is "good" or not. Also, regular-season games tied at the end of three periods will result in each team being awarded one point in the standings. As before, there will be a five-minute sudden death overtime when the score is tied after three periods, but each team will play "four on four," with four skaters and a goalkeeper. In the event that penalties dictate that one team has a two-man advantage, the penalized team plays with three skaters while the team with the two-man advantage adds a fifth skater. A team that scores a goal in regular-season overtime is credited with a win and earns two points in the standings. A team scored upon in regular-season overtime is credited with an overtime loss and earns one point in the standings.

2000-01 — All games to be played using the two-referee system.

2002-03 — "Hurry-up" faceoff and line-change rules implemented.

2003-04 — Home teams to wear basic colored uniforms; visiting teams basic white uniforms. Maximum length of goaltender's pads set at 38 inches.

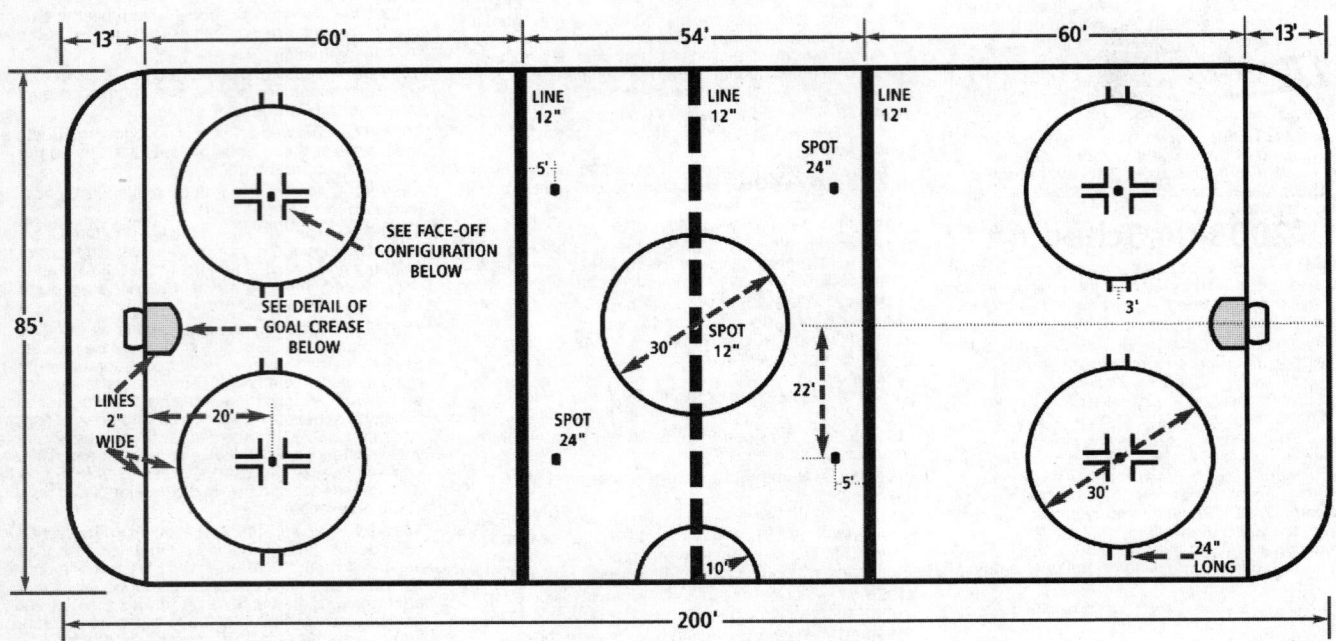

NHL RINK DIMENSIONS

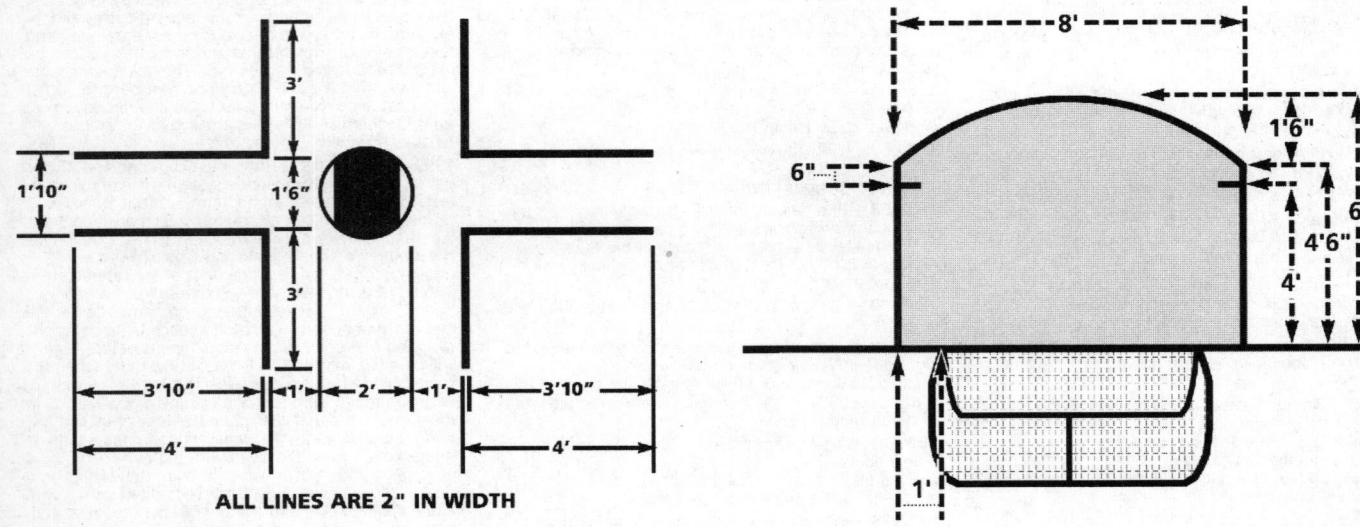

FACEOFF CONFIGURATION

ALL LINES ARE 2" IN WIDTH

CREASE DIMENSIONS

Mighty Ducks of Anaheim

2002-03 Results: 40w-27L-9T-6OTL 95PTS.
Second, Pacific Division

Year-by-Year Record

Season	GP	Home W	L	T	OL	Road W	L	T	OL	Overall W	L	T	OL	GF	GA	Pts.	Finished	Playoff Result
2002-03	82	22	10	7	2	18	17	2	4	40	27	9	6	203	193	95	2nd, Pacific Div.	Lost Final
2001-02	82	15	19	5	2	14	23	3	1	29	42	8	3	175	198	69	5th, Pacific Div.	Out of Playoffs
2000-01	82	15	20	4	2	10	21	7	3	25	41	11	5	188	245	66	5th, Pacific Div.	Out of Playoffs
1999-2000	82	19	13	7	2	15	20	5	1	34	33	12	3	217	227	83	5th, Pacific Div.	Out of Playoffs
1998-99	82	21	14	6	...	14	20	7	...	35	34	13	...	215	206	83	3rd, Pacific Div.	Lost Conf. Quarter-Final
1997-98	82	12	23	6	...	14	20	7	...	26	43	13	...	205	261	65	6th, Pacific Div.	Out of Playoffs
1996-97	82	23	12	6	...	13	21	7	...	36	33	13	...	245	233	85	2nd, Pacific Div.	Lost Conf. Semi-Final
1995-96	82	22	15	4	...	13	24	4	...	35	39	8	...	234	247	78	4th, Pacific Div.	Out of Playoffs
1994-95	48	11	9	4	...	5	18	1	...	16	27	5	...	125	164	37	6th, Pacific Div.	Out of Playoffs
1993-94	84	14	26	2	...	19	20	3	...	33	46	5	...	229	251	71	4th, Pacific Div.	Out of Playoffs

2003-04 Schedule

Oct.	Wed.	8	at Dallas	Fri.	9	Vancouver
	Thu.	9	at Nashville	Sun.	11	Columbus*
	Sun.	12	Phoenix*	Tue.	13	at Colorado
	Fri.	17	Ottawa	Thu.	15	at Edmonton
	Sun.	19	Boston*	Sat.	17	at Vancouver
	Tue.	21	at San Jose	Mon.	19	Calgary*
	Wed.	22	Philadelphia	Wed.	21	Detroit
	Fri.	24	Buffalo	Fri.	23	Minnesota
	Sun.	26	Chicago*	Sat.	24	at Los Angeles
	Tue.	28	at NY Rangers	Wed.	28	Los Angeles
	Wed.	29	at Washington	Fri.	30	Colorado
Nov.	Sat.	1	at NY Islanders*	**Feb.** Sun.	1	at Calgary
	Sun.	2	at Chicago	Mon.	2	at Edmonton
	Tue.	4	at St. Louis	Wed.	4	Carolina
	Sat.	8	at Phoenix	Wed.	11	Phoenix
	Sun.	9	Phoenix*	Fri.	13	at Calgary
	Wed.	12	Toronto	Sat.	14	at Vancouver
	Sun.	16	St. Louis*	Mon.	16	Dallas*
	Tue.	18	at Colorado	Wed.	18	Columbus
	Wed.	19	at Dallas	Fri.	20	Nashville
	Fri.	21	Nashville	Sun.	22	at Dallas*
	Wed.	26	New Jersey	Mon.	23	at Phoenix
	Fri.	28	Chicago*	Wed.	25	Edmonton
	Sun.	30	at Minnesota*	Sat.	28	at Los Angeles*
Dec.	Tue.	2	at Columbus	Sun.	29	Los Angeles*
	Wed.	3	at Detroit	**Mar.** Wed.	3	Minnesota
	Fri.	5	at Atlanta	Fri.	5	at Chicago
	Sun.	7	Dallas*	Sat.	6	at Pittsburgh
	Wed.	10	San Jose	Mon.	8	Montreal
	Sat.	13	at San Jose	Fri.	12	NY Islanders
	Sun.	14	Edmonton*	Sun.	14	at Los Angeles*
	Fri.	19	Colorado	Tue.	16	at Phoenix
	Sun.	21	San Jose*	Wed.	17	St. Louis
	Mon.	22	at San Jose	Fri.	19	San Jose
	Sat.	27	at Florida	Sun.	21	Detroit*
	Mon.	29	at Tampa Bay	Tue.	23	at Nashville
	Wed.	31	at Carolina	Thu.	25	at St. Louis
Jan.	Fri.	2	at Buffalo	Fri.	26	at Columbus
	Sat.	3	at Detroit	Sun.	28	at Minnesota*
	Mon.	5	Dallas	Wed.	31	Vancouver
	Wed.	7	Los Angeles	**Apr.** Sun.	4	Calgary*

Denotes afternoon game.

Franchise date: June 15, 1993

PACIFIC DIVISION

11th NHL Season

Steve Rucchin rebounded from two injury-filled seasons to play in all 82 regular-season games in 2002-03. He had 20 goals and 38 assists. Rucchin also played in all 21 Ducks postseason games and led the team with seven playoff goals.

2003-04 Player Personnel

FORWARDS	HT	WT	S	Place of Birth	Date	2002-03 Club
BURNETT, Garrett	6-3	230	L	Coquitlam, B.C.	9/23/75	Hartford
BYLSMA, Dan	6-2	212	L	Grand Haven, MI	9/19/70	Anaheim
CHISTOV, Stanislav	5-10	178	R	Chelyabinsk, USSR	4/17/83	Anaheim
FEDOROV, Sergei	6-1	200	L	Pskov, USSR	12/13/69	Detroit
GETZLAF, Ryan	6-2	195	R	Regina, Sask.	5/10/85	Calgary (WHL)
GORNICK, Brian	6-5	210	L	St. Paul, MN	3/17/80	Cincinnati (AHL)
HANKINSON, Casey	6-1	187	L	Edina, MN	5/8/76	Norfolk
HEDSTROM, Jonathan	6-0	200	L	Skelleftea, Sweden	12/27/77	Anaheim-Cincinnati (AHL)
HOLMQVIST, Mikael	6-3	189	L	Stockholm, Sweden	6/8/79	TPS Turku
KJELLBERG, Patric	6-2	210	L	Trelleborg, Sweden	6/17/69	Anaheim
KROG, Jason	5-11	191	R	Fernie, B.C.	10/9/75	Anaheim-Cincinnati (AHL)
KUNITZ, Chris	6-0	186	L	Regina, Sask.	9/26/79	Ferris State
LECLERC, Mike	6-2	208	L	Winnipeg, Man.	11/10/76	Anaheim
MARTENSSON, Tony	6-0	189	L	Upplands Vasby, Sweden	6/23/80	Cincinnati (AHL)
McDONALD, Andy	5-10	186	L	Strathroy, Ont.	8/25/77	Anaheim
NIEDERMAYER, Rob	6-2	204	L	Cassiar, B.C.	12/28/74	Calgary-Anaheim
PAHLSSON, Samuel	5-11	212	L	Ornskoldsvik, Sweden	12/17/77	Anaheim-Cincinnati (AHL)
PECKER, Cory	6-0	195	R	Montreal, Que.	3/20/81	Cincinnati (AHL)
PROSPAL, Vaclav	6-2	195	L	Ceske Budejovice, Czech.	2/17/75	Tampa Bay
RUCCHIN, Steve	6-2	211	L	Thunder Bay, Ont.	7/4/71	Anaheim
SEVERSON, Cam	6-1	215	L	Canora, Sask.	1/15/78	Cincinnati (AHL)-Anaheim
SMIRNOV, Alexei	6-3	211	L	Tver, USSR	1/28/82	Anaheim-Cincinnati (AHL)
SMITH, Nick	6-2	196	L	Hamilton, Ont.	3/23/79	Cincinnati (AHL)
SYKORA, Petr	6-0	190	L	Plzen, Czech.	11/19/76	Anaheim
DEFENSEMEN						
BROOKBANK, Sheldon	6-2	200	R	Lanigan, Sask.	10/3/80	Grand Rapids
CARNEY, Keith	6-2	211	L	Providence, RI	2/3/70	Anaheim
HAVELID, Niclas	5-11	196	L	Stockholm, Sweden	4/12/73	Anaheim
MOTTAU, Mike	6-0	192	L	Quincy, MA	3/19/78	Hartford-Calgary-Saint John
OZOLINSH, Sandis	6-3	215	L	Riga, Latvia	8/3/72	Florida-Anaheim
POPOVIC, Mark	6-1	191	L	Stoney Creek, Ont.	10/11/82	Cincinnati (AHL)
REIRDEN, Todd	6-5	225	L	Deerfield, IL	6/25/71	Cincinnati (AHL)
SALEI, Ruslan	6-1	205	L	Minsk, USSR	11/2/74	Anaheim
SAUER, Kurt	6-4	225	L	St. Cloud, MN	1/16/81	Anaheim
TABACEK, Jan	5-11	169	L	Martin, Czech.	4/7/80	Cincinnati (AHL)-Dayton
VISHNEVSKI, Vitaly	6-2	206	L	Kharkov, USSR	3/18/80	Anaheim
WARD, Lance	6-3	220	L	Lloydminster, Alta.	6/2/78	Florida-Anaheim

GOALTENDERS	HT	WT	C	Place of Birth	Date	2002-03 Club
BRYZGALOV, Ilya	6-3	198	L	Togliatti, USSR	6/22/80	Cincinnati (AHL)
FERHI, Eddie	6-3	181	L	Charenton, France	11/26/79	Sacred Heart-Cincinnati (AHL)
GERBER, Martin	6-0	185	L	Burgdorf, Switz.	9/3/74	Anaheim-Cincinnati (AHL)
GIGUERE, Jean-Sebastien	6-1	199	L	Montreal, Que.	5/16/77	Anaheim

Coach

BABCOCK, MIKE
Coach, Mighty Ducks of Anaheim.
Born in Manitouwadge, Ont., April 29, 1963.

The Mighty Ducks of Anaheim announced Mike Babcock as the club's head coach on May 22, 2002. In his first season behind the bench in 2002-03, he led the team to the seventh game of the Stanley Cup Finals. Babcock spent the previous two seasons as head coach of the Cincinnati Mighty Ducks, Anaheim's primary development affiliate in the American Hockey League. While with Cincinnati, he led the club to a franchise-best 41 wins and 95 points in 2000-01.

Babcock earned the honor of coaching the Canadian World Junior team in 1997, leading the club to its fifth consecutive gold medal in the tournament. Prior to joining the Mighty Ducks, Babcock had a successful six-year run as the head coach of the Spokane Chiefs of the Western Hockey League. While with Spokane, he had a regular-season record of 224-175-29 (.557 winning percentage, the highest in the WHL in that span). He was twice named WHL coach of the year (1996 & 2000) after taking the franchise to the league finals both seasons. Additionally, he was the head coach of the 2000 WHL West Division All-Star team.

In 1988, Babcock was named head coach at Red Deer College in Red Deer, Alberta. He spent three seasons at the school, winning the Alberta college championship and coach of the year honors in 1989. Babcock won a national championship and was again named the coach of the year while with the University of Lethbridge in 1993-94. He began his WHL career as head coach of the Moose Jaw Warriors from 1991 to 1993.

Coaching Record

		Regular Season				Playoffs		
Season	Team	Games	W	L	T	Games	W	L
1991-92	Moose Jaw (WHL)	72	33	36	3	4	0	4
1992-93	Moose Jaw (WHL)	72	27	42	3	....	....	....
1993-94	U. of Lethbridge (CIAU)	28	19	7	2	....	....	....
1994-95	Spokane (WHL)	72	32	36	4	11	6	5
1995-96	Spokane (WHL)	72	50	18	4	9	3	6
1996-97	Spokane (WHL)	65	31	30	4	9	4	5
1997-98	Spokane (WHL)	72	45	23	4	18	10	8
1998-99	Spokane (WHL)	72	19	44	9	....	....	....
1999-2000	Spokane (WHL)	72	47	21	4	20	15	5
2000-01	Cincinnati (WHL)	80	41	26	13	4	1	3
2001-02	Cincinnati (WHL)	80	33	33	14	3	1	2
2002-03	**Anaheim (NHL)**	**82**	**40**	**33**	**9**	**21**	**15**	**6**
	NHL Totals	**82**	**40**	**33**	**9**	**21**	**15**	**6**

2002-03 Scoring

* – rookie

Regular Season

Pos	#	Player	Team	GP	G	A	Pts	+/–	PIM	PP	SH	GW	GT	S	%
L	9	Paul Kariya	ANA	82	25	56	81	–3	48	11	1	2	1	257	9.7
R	39	Petr Sykora	ANA	82	34	25	59	–7	24	15	1	5	1	299	11.4
C	20	Steve Rucchin	ANA	82	20	38	58	–14	12	6	1	4	0	194	10.3
C	77	Adam Oates	ANA	67	9	36	45	–1	16	4	0	2	0	67	13.4
D	8	Sandis Ozolinsh	FLA	51	7	19	26	–16	40	5	0	2	0	83	8.4
			ANA	31	5	13	18	10	16	1	0	1	0	54	9.3
			TOTAL	82	12	32	44	–6	56	6	0	3	0	137	8.8
D	28	Niclas Havelid	ANA	82	11	22	33	5	30	4	0	5	0	169	6.5
R	32	Steve Thomas	CHI	69	4	13	17	0	51	0	0	1	0	91	4.4
			ANA	12	10	3	13	10	2	1	0	3	0	27	37.0
			TOTAL	81	14	16	30	10	53	1	0	4	0	118	11.9
L	23 *	Stanislav Chistov	ANA	79	12	18	30	4	54	3	0	2	0	114	10.5
L	12	Mike Leclerc	ANA	57	9	19	28	–8	34	1	0	4	0	122	7.4
L	10	Jason Krog	ANA	67	10	15	25	1	12	0	1	1	0	92	10.9
C	44	Rob Niedermayer	CGY	54	8	10	18	–13	42	2	0	1	0	104	7.7
			ANA	12	2	2	4	3	15	1	0	0	0	21	9.5
			TOTAL	66	10	12	22	–10	57	3	0	1	0	125	8.0
D	3	Keith Carney	ANA	81	4	18	22	8	65	0	0	1	2	87	4.6
C	19	Andy McDonald	ANA	46	10	11	21	–1	14	3	0	1	0	92	10.9
R	18	Patric Kjellberg	ANA	76	8	11	19	–9	16	2	1	2	0	95	8.4
C	26	Samuel Pahlsson	ANA	34	4	11	15	10	18	0	1	2	0	28	14.3
D	24	Ruslan Salei	ANA	61	4	8	12	2	78	0	0	0	0	93	4.3
D	2	Fredrik Olausson	ANA	44	2	6	8	0	22	2	0	1	0	38	5.3
D	5	Vitaly Vishnevski	ANA	80	2	6	8	–8	76	0	1	0	0	65	3.1
C	11	Marc Chouinard	ANA	70	3	4	7	–9	40	0	1	0	0	52	5.8
L	22 *	Alexei Smirnov	ANA	44	3	2	5	–1	18	0	0	1	0	46	6.5
D	4	Lance Ward	FLA	36	3	1	4	–4	78	0	0	1	0	34	8.8
			ANA	29	0	1	1	–2	43	0	0	0	0	18	0.0
			TOTAL	65	3	2	5	–6	121	0	0	1	0	52	5.8
R	21	Dan Bylsma	ANA	39	1	4	5	–1	12	0	0	0	0	23	4.3
L	25	Kevin Sawyer	ANA	31	2	1	3	–2	115	0	0	0	0	11	18.2
D	34 *	Kurt Sauer	ANA	80	1	2	3	–23	74	0	0	0	0	50	2.0
L	44 *	Mike Brown	ANA	16	1	1	2	0	44	0	0	1	0	8	12.5
R	38	Rob Valicevic	ANA	10	1	0	1	1	2	0	0	1	0	7	14.3
D	37	Chris O'Sullivan	ANA	2	0	1	1	0	0	0	0	0	0	3	0.0
L	14 *	Cam Severson	ANA	2	0	0	0	0	8	0	0	0	0	1	0.0
R	51 *	Jonathan Hedstrom	ANA	4	0	0	0	–1	0	0	0	0	0	3	0.0

Goaltending

No.	Goaltender	GPI	Mins	Avg	W	L	T	EN	SO	GA	SA	S%	G	A	PIM
29	Martin Gerber	22	1203	1.95	6	11	3	4	1	39	548	.929	0	1	0
35	J-S Giguere	65	3775	2.30	34	22	6	5	8	145	1820	.920	0	0	8
	Totals	**82**	**4997**	**2.32**	**40**	**33**	**9**	**9**	**9**	**193**	**2377**	**.919**			

Playoffs

Pos	#	Player	Team	GP	G	A	Pts	+/–	PIM	PP	SH	GW	GT	S	%
C	77	Adam Oates	ANA	21	4	9	13	2	6	3	0	1	0	18	22.2
R	39	Petr Sykora	ANA	21	4	9	13	3	12	1	0	2	2	58	6.9
L	9	Paul Kariya	ANA	21	6	6	12	0	6	0	0	1	1	53	11.3
L	12	Mike Leclerc	ANA	21	2	9	11	3	12	1	0	2	1	55	3.6
C	20	Steve Rucchin	ANA	21	7	3	10	–2	2	1	0	2	1	46	15.2
C	44	Rob Niedermayer	ANA	21	3	7	10	–5	18	0	2	0	0	41	7.3
R	32	Steve Thomas	ANA	21	4	4	8	2	8	2	0	3	1	40	10.0
D	8	Sandis Ozolinsh	ANA	21	2	6	8	8	10	0	0	1	0	39	5.1
L	23 *	Stanislav Chistov	ANA	21	4	2	6	4	8	0	0	1	0	33	12.1
C	26	Samuel Pahlsson	ANA	21	2	4	6	1	12	0	0	0	0	24	8.3
D	24	Ruslan Salei	ANA	21	2	3	5	3	26	0	0	1	1	33	6.1
L	10	Jason Krog	ANA	21	3	1	4	3	4	0	0	0	0	23	13.0
D	3	Keith Carney	ANA	21	0	4	4	3	16	0	0	0	0	26	0.0
D	28	Niclas Havelid	ANA	21	0	4	4	0	2	0	0	0	0	29	0.0
D	34 *	Kurt Sauer	ANA	21	1	1	2	3	6	0	1	1	0	8	12.5
C	11	Marc Chouinard	ANA	15	1	0	1	1	0	0	0	0	0	11	9.1
R	21	Dan Bylsma	ANA	11	0	1	1	3	2	0	0	0	0	12	0.0
D	5	Vitaly Vishnevski	ANA	21	0	1	1	–3	6	0	0	0	0	8	0.0
D	2	Fredrik Olausson	ANA	1	0	0	0	0	0	0	0	0	0	0	0.0
L	14 *	Cam Severson	ANA	1	0	0	0	0	0	0	0	0	0	0	0.0
L	22 *	Alexei Smirnov	ANA	4	0	0	0	0	2	0	0	0	0	3	0.0
R	18	Patric Kjellberg	ANA	10	0	0	0	–2	0	0	0	0	0	6	0.0

Goaltending

No.	Goaltender	GPI	Mins	Avg	W	L	EN	SO	GA	SA	S%	G	A	PIM
35	J-S Giguere	21	1407	1.62	15	6	1	5	38	697	.945	0	1	0
29	Martin Gerber	2	20	3.00	0	0	0	0	1	6	.833	0	0	0
	Totals	**21**	**1428**	**1.68**	**15**	**6**	**1**	**5**	**40**	**704**	**.943**			

Club Records

Team

(Figures in brackets for season records are games played; records for fewest points, wins, ties, losses, goals, goals against are for 70 or more games)

Most Points	95	2002-03 (82)
Most Wins	40	2002-03 (82)
Most Ties	13	1996-97 (82); 1997-98 (82); 1998-99 (82)
Most Losses	46	1993-94 (84)
Most Goals	245	1996-97 (82)
Most Goals Against	261	1997-98 (82)
Fewest Points	65	1997-98 (82)
Fewest Wins	25	2000-01 (82)
Fewest Ties	5	1993-94 (84)
Fewest Losses	27	2002-03 (82)
Fewest Goals	175	2001-02 (82)
Fewest Goals Against	193	2002-03 (82)

Longest Winning Streak
Overall	7	Feb. 20-Mar. 7/99
Home	5	Three times
Away	5	Nov. 26-Dec. 26/99

Longest Undefeated Streak
Overall	12	Feb. 22-Mar. 19/97 (7 wins, 5 ties)
Home	14	Feb. 12-Apr. 9/97 (10 wins, 4 ties)
Away	5	Five times

Longest Losing Streak
Overall	8	Oct. 12-30/96
Home	8	Jan. 10-Feb. 9/01
Away	6	Three times

Longest Winless Streak
Overall	9	Twice
Home	11	Jan. 5-Feb. 14/01 (8 losses, 3 ties)
Away	10	Mar. 26-Oct. 11/95 (9 losses, 1 tie)

Most Shutouts, Season	9	2002-03 (82)
Most PIM, Season	1,843	1997-98 (82)
Most Goals, Game	8	Jan. 21/98 (Ana. 8, Fla. 3)

Individual

Most Seasons	9	Paul Kariya
Most Games	606	Paul Kariya
Most Goals, Career	300	Paul Kariya
Most Assists, Career	369	Paul Kariya
Most Points, Career	669	Paul Kariya (300G, 369A)
Most PIM, Career	788	Dave Karpa
Most Shutouts, Career	27	Guy Hebert
Longest Consecutive Games Streak	237	Oleg Tverdovsky (Oct. 2/99-Mar. 24/02)
Most Goals, Season	52	Teemu Selanne (1997-98)
Most Assists, Season	62	Paul Kariya (1998-99)
Most Points, Season	109	Teemu Selanne (1996-97; 51G, 58A)
Most PIM, Season	285	Todd Ewen (1995-96)
Most Points, Defenseman, Season	56	Fredrik Olausson (1998-99; 16G, 40A)
Most Points, Center, Season	67	Steve Rucchin (1996-97; 19G, 48A)
Most Points, Right Wing, Season	109	Teemu Selanne (1996-97; 51G, 58A)
Most Points, Left Wing, Season	108	Paul Kariya (1995-96; 50G, 58A)
Most Points, Rookie, Season	39	Paul Kariya (1994-95; 18G, 21A)
Most Shutouts, Season	8	Jean-Sebastien Giguere (2002-03)
Most Goals, Game	3	Thirteen times
Most Assists, Game	5	Dmitri Mironov (Dec. 12/97)
Most Points, Game	5	Six times

General Managers' History

Jack Ferreira, 1993-94 to 1997-98; Pierre Gauthier, 1998-99 to 2001-02; Bryan Murray, 2002-03 to date.

Coaching History

Ron Wilson, 1993-94 to 1996-97; Pierre Page, 1997-98; Craig Hartsburg, 1998-99, 1999-2000; Craig Hartsburg and Guy Charron, 2000-01; Bryan Murray, 2001-02; Mike Babcock, 2002-03 to date.

Captains' History

Troy Loney, 1993-94; Randy Ladouceur, 1994-95, 1995-96; Paul Kariya, 1996-97; Paul Kariya and Teemu Selanne, 1997-98; Paul Kariya, 1998-99 to 2002-03.

All-time Record vs. Other Clubs

Regular Season

	At Home								On Road								Total							
	GP	W	L	T	OL	GF	GA	PTS	GP	W	L	T	OL	GF	GA	PTS	GP	W	L	T	OL	GF	GA	PTS
Atlanta	4	2	2	0	0	12	9	4	3	3	0	0	0	14	4	6	7	5	2	0	0	26	13	10
Boston	8	2	3	2	1	15	20	7	8	4	4	0	0	24	23	8	16	6	7	2	1	39	43	15
Buffalo	8	2	6	0	0	13	25	4	8	2	3	3	0	18	20	7	16	4	9	3	0	31	45	11
Calgary	24	11	7	6	0	77	63	28	23	9	13	1	0	56	64	19	47	20	20	7	0	133	127	47
Carolina	8	4	3	1	0	26	24	9	8	2	5	1	0	16	22	5	16	6	8	2	0	42	46	14
Chicago	20	11	7	2	0	53	43	24	22	9	11	2	0	52	62	20	42	20	18	4	0	105	105	44
Colorado	19	5	10	3	1	43	50	14	19	6	9	4	0	51	60	16	38	11	19	7	1	94	110	30
Columbus	6	4	2	0	0	19	13	8	6	2	4	0	0	13	18	4	12	6	6	0	0	32	31	12
Dallas	24	9	13	2	0	52	63	20	24	5	17	1	1	48	90	12	48	14	30	3	1	100	153	32
Detroit	20	6	11	3	0	42	57	15	20	2	13	3	2	46	73	9	40	8	24	6	2	88	130	24
Edmonton	24	14	8	2	0	65	59	30	23	8	14	0	1	49	54	17	47	22	22	2	1	114	113	47
Florida	9	4	5	1	0	27	30	7	7	2	2	2	1	15	20	7	16	5	7	3	1	42	50	14
Los Angeles	27	12	6	6	3	87	69	33	27	9	14	4	0	68	78	22	54	21	20	10	3	155	147	55
Minnesota	6	3	2	0	1	11	15	7	6	3	2	1	0	12	10	7	12	6	4	1	1	23	25	14
Montreal	7	3	4	0	0	23	22	6	8	2	4	2	0	19	24	6	15	5	8	2	0	42	46	12
Nashville	10	9	1	0	0	28	13	18	10	4	4	2	0	23	20	10	20	13	5	2	0	51	33	28
New Jersey	9	4	5	0	0	23	23	8	8	1	6	0	1	14	31	3	17	5	11	0	1	37	54	11
NY Islanders	8	2	3	3	0	17	21	7	7	3	3	1	1	22	20	7	15	5	6	4	0	39	41	14
NY Rangers	8	6	1	0	1	32	25	13	8	4	2	1	1	23	22	10	16	10	3	1	2	55	47	23
Ottawa	8	4	2	2	0	21	15	10	8	3	4	1	0	19	24	7	16	7	6	3	0	40	39	17
Philadelphia	8	3	3	2	0	26	25	8	8	2	3	3	0	17	22	7	16	5	6	5	0	43	47	15
Phoenix	24	13	8	3	0	67	61	29	23	12	10	1	0	70	68	25	47	25	18	4	0	137	129	54
Pittsburgh	8	5	3	0	0	29	24	10	8	2	4	2	0	26	27	6	16	7	7	2	0	55	51	16
St. Louis	20	6	13	1	0	49	61	13	20	7	9	3	1	53	62	18	40	13	22	4	1	102	123	31
San Jose	27	10	15	2	0	72	91	22	27	13	11	2	1	77	80	29	54	23	26	4	1	149	171	51
Tampa Bay	8	4	3	1	0	24	20	9	8	4	4	0	0	21	17	8	16	8	7	1	0	45	37	17
Toronto	10	4	5	1	0	29	27	9	15	2	9	4	0	30	50	8	25	6	14	5	0	59	77	17
Vancouver	23	7	8	7	1	56	67	22	24	6	16	2	0	55	89	14	47	13	24	9	1	111	156	36
Washington	9	6	2	1	0	29	22	13	8	4	4	0	0	18	14	8	17	10	6	1	0	47	36	21
Totals	**394**	**174**	**161**	**51**	**8**	**1067**	**1057**	**407**	**394**	**135**	**204**	**46**	**9**	**969**	**1168**	**325**	**788**	**309**	**365**	**97**	**17**	**2036**	**2225**	**732**

Playoffs

	Series	W	L	GP	W	L	T	GF	GA	Last Mtg.	Rnd.	Result
Dallas	1	1	0	6	4	2	0	14	14	2003	CSF	W 4-2
Detroit	3	1	2	12	4	8	0	24	36	2003	CQF	W 4-0
Minnesota	1	1	0	4	4	0	0	9	1	2003	CF	W 4-0
New Jersey	1	0	1	7	3	4	0	12	19	2003	F	L 3-4
Phoenix	1	1	0	7	4	3	0	17	17	1997	CQF	W 4-3
Totals	**7**	**4**	**3**	**36**	**19**	**17**	**0**	**76**	**87**			

Playoff Results 2003-1999

Year	Round	Opponent	Result	GF	GA
2003	F	New Jersey	L 3-4	12	19
	CF	Minnesota	W 4-0	9	1
	CSF	Dallas	W 4-2	14	14
	CQF	Detroit	W 4-0	10	6
1999	CQF	Detroit	L 0-4	6	17

Abbreviations: Round: F - Final; **CF** – conference final; **CSF** – conference quarter-final; **CQF** – conference quarter-final

Carolina totals include Hartford, 1993-94 to 1996-97.
Colorado totals include Quebec, 1993-94 to 1994-95.
Phoenix totals include Winnipeg, 1993-94 to 1995-96.

2002-03 Results

Oct.	10	at St. Louis	4-3		9	at Colorado	5-3
	11	at Dallas	2-4		12	St. Louis	2-1
	13	Detroit	2-4		15	at Columbus	4-3
	16	Los Angeles	2-4		16	at Ottawa	1-3
	18	Vancouver	2-2		18	at Minnesota	1-0
	20	Colorado	3-2*		20	Minnesota	1-2*
	24	at Vancouver	2-2		22	Los Angeles	6-5
	26	at Edmonton	3-4		24	New Jersey	1-3
	28	at Toronto	2-5		29	Ottawa	3-2
	29	at Montreal	2-2		30	at San Jose	4-3
	31	at Boston	4-1	Feb.	4	at Calgary	3-2
Nov.	3	San Jose	3-4		5	at Edmonton	1-2
	6	Nashville	2-1		7	Phoenix	3-2
	8	at Colorado	3-2*		9	Carolina	2-1
	10	Minnesota	1-0		12	Calgary	4-3*
	12	at New Jersey	2-3*		14	at Dallas	4-2
	14	at Columbus	3-2		15	at Nashville	1-2
	15	at Detroit	1-2*		17	NY Islanders	2-2
	17	at Atlanta	5-1		19	Columbus	2-0
	19	at NY Rangers	2-3*		21	NY Rangers	2-6
	22	Dallas	0-4		23	at Carolina	4-0
	24	Florida	4-4		25	at Tampa Bay	0-2
	27	Phoenix	2-2		26	at Florida	2-1
	29	Los Angeles	2-2		28	at Phoenix	1-3
Dec.	1	Chicago	3-2	Mar.	2	Atlanta	1-4
	3	at Detroit	1-2		4	at Los Angeles	2-1
	4	at Buffalo	0-4		5	Montreal	3-1
	6	at Chicago	4-3		7	Edmonton	1-4
	8	Nashville	3-0		9	Detroit	4-1
	11	Washington	3-0		12	Chicago	5-2
	15	Pittsburgh	5-0		13	San Jose	3-2*
	18	St. Louis	5-2		15	at Phoenix	2-4
	19	at Los Angeles	4-5		16	Calgary	2-2
	22	Phoenix	4-0		19	at Chicago	4-3
	26	at San Jose	1-4		20	at St. Louis	2-3*
	28	at Vancouver	3-7		22	at San Jose	3-2*
	29	at Calgary	2-2		24	Columbus	5-0
	31	at Minnesota	1-4		30	Vancouver	3-1
Jan.	3	Philadelphia	0-1	Apr.	1	at Nashville	2-1*
	5	Dallas	1-1		2	at Dallas	1-2
	8	Edmonton	0-1		4	Colorado	3-4*

* – Overtime

Entry Draft
Selections 2003-1993

2003
Pick
19 Ryan Getzlaf
28 Corey Perry
86 Shane Hynes
90 Juha Alen
119 Nathan Saunders
186 Andrew Miller
218 Dirk Southern
250 Shane O'Brien
280 Ville Mantymaa

2002
Pick
7 Joffrey Lupul
37 Tim Brent
71 Brian Lee
103 Joonas Vihko
140 George Davis
173 Luke Fritshaw
261 Francois Caron
267 Chris Petrow

2001
Pick
5 Stanislav Chistov
35 Mark Popovic
69 Joel Stepp
102 Timo Parssinen
105 Vladimir Korsunov
118 Brandon Rogers
137 Joel Perreault
170 Jan Tabacek
224 Tony Martensson
232 Martin Gerber
264 Pierre Parenteau

2000
Pick
12 Alexei Smirnov
44 Ilya Bryzgalov
98 Jonas Ronnqvist
134 Peter Podhradsky
153 Bill Cass

1999
Pick
44 Jordan Leopold
83 Niclas Havelid
105 Alexandr Chagodayev
141 Maxim Rybin
173 Jan Sandstrom
230 Petr Tenkrat
258 Brian Gornick

1998
Pick
5 Vitaly Vishnevski
32 Stephen Peat
112 Viktor Wallin
150 Trent Hunter
178 Jesse Fibiger
205 David Bernier
233 Pelle Prestberg
245 Andreas Andersson

1997
Pick
18 Mikael Holmqvist
45 Maxim Balmochnykh
72 Jay Legault
125 Luc Vaillancourt
178 Tony Mohagen
181 Mat Snesrud
209 Rene Stussi
235 Tommi Degerman

1996
Pick
9 Ruslan Salei
35 Matt Cullen
117 Brendan Buckley
149 Blaine Russell
172 Timo Ahmaoja
198 Kevin Kellett
224 Tobias Johansson

1995
Pick
4 Chad Kilger
29 Brian Wesenberg
55 Mike Leclerc
107 Igor Nikulin
133 Peter LeBoutillier
159 Mike LaPlante
185 Igor Karpenko

1994
Pick
2 Oleg Tverdovsky
28 Johan Davidsson
67 Craig Reichert
80 Byron Briske
106 Pavel Trnka
132 Bates Battaglia
158 Rocky Welsing
184 Brad Englehart
236 Tommi Miettinen
262 Jeremy Stevenson

1993
Pick
4 Paul Kariya
30 Nikolai Tsulygin
56 Valeri Karpov
82 Joel Gagnon
108 Mikhail Shtalenkov
134 Antti Aalto
160 Matt Peterson
186 Tom Askey
212 Vitali Kozel
238 Anatoli Fedotov
264 David Penney

Vice President and General Manager

MURRAY, BRYAN
Senior Vice President/General Manager, Mighty Ducks of Anaheim.
Born in Shawville, Que., December 5, 1942.

After serving behind the bench during the 2001-02 season, Bryan Murray stepped down as head coach on May 2, 2002 in order to become the team's new general manager. In his first season in the front office, Anaheim reached the Stanley Cup Finals. Prior to joining the Mighty Ducks in 2001, Murray had served most recently as the Florida Panthers' vice president and general manager from 1994 to 2001. He also assumed head coaching duties with Florida during the 1997-98 season, prior to naming his brother Terry Murray as head coach before the 1998-99 season. Bryan joined the Panthers on August 1, 1994 and assembled a team that went to the Stanley Cup Finals in just its third year of existence (1996).

Prior to joining the Panthers, Murray was the general manager of the Detroit Red Wings from 1990 to 1994, also taking on head coaching duties for the first three seasons. He earned his first NHL head coaching job with the Washington Capitals, taking over on November 11, 1981. He spent the next eight and a half seasons with the Capitals, winning the Jack Adams Award as coach of the year in 1983-84. Murray led Washington to the postseason seven times during his tenure, including the club's first division title in 1988-89.

A graduate of McGill University, Murray spent four years as the athletic director and coach at the school. He left that post to become the coach of the Regina Pats (WHL) in 1979-80. Murray took over as coach of the Hershey Bears (AHL) the next season and was named the Minor League Coach of the Year by *The Hockey News* after leading Hershey to its best mark in 40 years.

NHL Coaching Record

Season	Team	Games	Regular Season W	L	T	Playoffs Games	W	L
1981-82	Washington	66	25	28	13			
1982-83	Washington	80	39	25	16	4	1	3
1983-84	Washington	80	48	27	5	8	4	4
1984-85	Washington	80	46	25	9	5	2	3
1985-86	Washington	80	50	23	7	9	5	4
1986-87	Washington	80	38	32	10	7	3	4
1987-88	Washington	80	38	33	9	14	7	7
1988-89	Washington	80	41	29	10	6	2	4
1989-90	Washington	46	18	24	4	....	....	....
1990-91	Detroit	80	34	38	8	7	3	4
1991-92	Detroit	80	43	25	12	11	4	7
1992-93	Detroit	84	47	28	9	7	3	4
1997-98	Florida	59	17	31	11	....	....	....
2001-02	Anaheim	82	29	45	8	....	....	....
	NHL Totals	**1057**	**513**	**413**	**131**	**78**	**34**	**44**

Club Directory

Arrowhead Pond of Anaheim

Mighty Ducks of Anaheim
Arrowhead Pond of Anaheim
2695 Katella Ave.
Anaheim, CA 92806
Phone 714/940-2900
FAX 714/940-2953
Ticket Information 877/WILDWING
www.mightyducks.com
Capacity: 17,174

Executive Management
President and Governor. . . . . Jay Rasulo
Senior Vice President and General Manager . . . . Bryan Murray
Senior Vice President, Business Operations . . . . Al Coates
Assistant General Manager . . . . David McNab
Administrative Assistant, Senior Vice President
   and General Manager . . . . Maureen Nyeholt
Sr. Paralegal . . . . Tia Wood

Coaching Staff
Head Coach . . . . Mike Babcock
Assistant Coaches . . . . Lorne Henning, Paul MacLean
Goaltending Consultant . . . . François Allaire
Video/Scouting Coordinator . . . . Greg Carvel

Hockey Club Operations
Director, Hockey Operations . . . . Chuck Fletcher
Director of Player Personnel. . . . . Tim Murray
Director of Amateur Scouting . . . . Alain Chainey
Scouting Staff . . . . Jeff Crisp, Jan-Åke Danielson, Brent Flahr, Todd Hearty, Konstantin Krylov, Donald Marier, Wayne Meier, Pavel Routa, Floyd Smith, Tom Watt
Head Athletic Trainer . . . . Chris Phillips
Strength and Conditioning Coach . . . . Sean Skahan
Equipment Manager . . . . Mark O'Neill
Assistant Equipment Manager . . . . John Allaway
Cincinnati Mighty Ducks (AHL) Head Coach . . . . . . Brad Shaw
Cincinnati Assistant Coach . . . . Darryl Williams
Team Physicians . . . . Dr. Ronald Glousman, Dr. Craig Milhouse
Oral Surgeon. . . . . Dr. Jeff Pulver
Visiting Team Equipment Attendant . . . . Chris Kincaid

Communications Department
Communications and Team Services Manager . . . . . Alex Gilchrist
Sr. Media Relations Representative . . . . Merit Tully
Publications & Media Relations Representative . . . Scott Johnson
Team Photographer . . . . V.J. Lovero (Lovero Group)

Finance and Administration Department
Sr. Financial Analyst . . . . TBA
Director, Human Resources . . . . Pat Navarro
Sr. EUCS Analyst . . . . Kevin Ramirez
Assistant Controller . . . . Melody Martin
Accountant . . . . Rosanna Sitzman
Accounting Assistant . . . . Rob Dumlao
Event Services Representative . . . . Jason Davis
Sr. Travel Consultant . . . . Taki Papadatos
General Manager, Disney ICE . . . . Art Trottier

Sales and Marketing Department
Director, Ticket Sales & Customer Service . . . . Bill Chapin
Director, Marketing and Promotions . . . . Michael Williams
Premium Ticket Services Specialist . . . . Mandi Van Eps
Sr. Marketing Representative . . . . TBA
Marketing and Promotions Assistant . . . . Sara Heri
Marketing/Database Manager . . . . Veronica Tarnofsky
Premium Account Managers . . . . Ron Campbell, Bob Ruiz
Account Executives . . . . Bill Schaeffer, Ben Plaisted, Mike Morrow, Justin Sheppard
Group Sales Account Executives . . . . Ken Bamberg, Pati Perez-Freund, Casey Norvall
Ticketing Representative . . . . Jessica Doebler
Sales Secretary . . . . Roxanne Gandara
Group Secretary . . . . Jayme Johnson
Receptionist . . . . Christina Cruz, Erin Jones

Ticketing Department
Ticketing Operations Manager . . . . Christa Richards
Ticketing Supervisor . . . . Jonas Calicdan
Ticketing Representative . . . . Gina Bulgheroni

Publicity and Community Development Department
Director, Publicity and Community Development . . . Charles Harris
Manager, Community Development . . . . Erin Bickmeier
Website Editor . . . . Terry Crowley

Broadcasting and Entertainment Department
Telecast Producer . . . . Aaron Teats
Telecast Director . . . . Mike Levy
Entertainment Manager . . . . Rod Murray
T.V., KCAL (Ch. 9) & Fox Sports West 2 (Cable) . . . . John Ahlers, Brian Hayward
Radio, Flagship TBA & Mighty Ducks Radio Network . Steve Carroll

Advertising Sales and Broadcasting Department
Director, Advertising Sales . . . . John Covarrubias
Sponsorship Services Manager . . . . Tamara Goddard
Advertising Sales Managers . . . . Matt Vicelja, Alex Grant
Executive Secretary, Advertising Sales . . . . Jacklyn Perkins

Miscellaneous
Practice Facilities . . . . Disney ICE (300 W. Lincoln Ave.) and the Arrowhead Pond (2695 Katella Ave.)
Primary Developmental Affiliate . . . . Cincinnati Mighty Ducks (AHL)
Home Starting Times. . . . . Weeknights - 7:35 p.m.; Sundays - 5:05 p.m.
Founded 1993
Press Box Phone 714/704-2623
Press Room . . . . 714/704-2514 or 2517

Atlanta Thrashers

2002-03 Results: 31w-39L-7T-5OTL 74PTS.
Third, Southeast Division

Year-by-Year Record

Season	GP	Home				Road				Overall				GF	GA	Pts.	Finished	Playoff Result
		W	L	T	OL	W	L	T	OL	W	L	T	OL					
2002-03	82	15	19	4	3	16	20	3	2	31	39	7	5	226	284	74	3rd, Southeast Div.	Out of Playoffs
2001-02	82	11	21	9	0	8	26	2	5	19	47	11	5	187	288	54	5th, Southeast Div.	Out of Playoffs
2000-01	82	10	23	6	2	13	22	6	0	23	45	12	2	211	289	60	4th, Southeast Div.	Out of Playoffs
1999-2000	82	9	26	3	3	5	31	4	1	14	57	7	4	170	313	39	5th, Southeast Div.	Out of Playoffs

2003-04 Schedule

Oct. Thu. 9 Columbus
Sat. 11 at Washington
Tue. 14 NY Islanders
Thu. 16 at NY Rangers
Sat. 18 Chicago
Tue. 21 at Tampa Bay
Thu. 23 Nashville
Sat. 25 Florida
Mon. 27 at Toronto
Thu. 30 at Minnesota
Fri. 31 at Washington
Nov. Sun. 2 San Jose
Wed. 5 at Buffalo
Fri. 7 at Columbus
Sat. 8 at NY Islanders
Tue. 11 Ottawa
Thu. 13 at Carolina
Sat. 15 at Philadelphia
Sun. 16 Florida*
Wed. 19 Boston
Fri. 21 at Florida
Sun. 23 Phoenix*
Tue. 25 Ottawa
Thu. 27 Toronto
Sat. 29 Tampa Bay
Dec. Mon. 1 at Pittsburgh
Wed. 3 Boston
Fri. 5 Anaheim
Sat. 6 at Florida
Wed. 10 Los Angeles
Fri. 12 Pittsburgh
Sat. 13 at NY Islanders
Tue. 16 Washington
Thu. 18 New Jersey
Sat. 20 at Pittsburgh
Sun. 21 Philadelphia
Fri. 26 Tampa Bay
Sun. 28 at Ottawa*
Mon. 29 Montreal
Wed. 31 at Detroit
Jan. Sat. 3 at Montreal*

Thu. 8 at Dallas
Sat. 10 at San Jose*
Sun. 11 at Phoenix*
Wed. 14 Montreal
Fri. 16 Carolina
Sun. 18 at Carolina*
Tue. 20 Buffalo
Thu. 22 Colorado
Sat. 24 NY Islanders
Sun. 25 at New Jersey
Wed. 28 St. Louis
Fri. 30 Toronto
Sat. 31 at Tampa Bay
Feb. Tue. 3 at Boston
Thu. 5 Philadelphia
Tue. 10 at Calgary
Wed. 11 at Edmonton
Fri. 13 at Vancouver
Mon. 16 at Buffalo*
Tue. 17 at Montreal
Thu. 19 at Ottawa
Sat. 21 at Philadelphia*
Wed. 25 Tampa Bay
Fri. 27 at New Jersey
Sun. 29 NY Rangers*
Mar. Tue. 2 at NY Rangers
Fri. 5 Carolina
Sat. 6 at Boston
Tue. 9 NY Rangers
Fri. 12 at Carolina
Sat. 13 Washington
Mon. 15 Carolina
Wed. 17 Buffalo
Fri. 19 Florida
Sat. 20 at Washington
Wed. 24 Washington
Fri. 26 New Jersey
Sat. 27 at Florida
Mon. 29 at Toronto
Apr. Fri. 2 Pittsburgh
Sat. 3 at Tampa Bay

* Denotes afternoon game.

Franchise date: June 25, 1997

SOUTHEAST DIVISION

5th NHL Season

There was no sophomore jinx for Calder Trophy winner Dany Heatley in 2002-03. Heatley was the hottest player in the NHL over the final quarter of the season and finished the year with 41 goals and 48 assists. He was ninth in the NHL in scoring.

2003-04 Player Personnel

FORWARDS	HT	WT	S	Place of Birth	Date	2002-03 Club
AQUINO, Anthony	5-10	175	R	Mississauga, Ont.	8/1/82	Oshawa-Chicago (AHL)
BABY, Stephen	6-5	235	R	Chicago, IL	1/31/80	Cornell
BLATNY, Zdenek	6-1	190	L	Brno, Czech.	1/14/81	Atlanta-Chicago (AHL)
COWAN, Jeff	6-2	210	L	Scarborough, Ont.	9/27/76	Atlanta
GAMACHE, Simon	5-9	185	L	Thetford Mines, Que.	1/3/81	Atlanta-Chicago (AHL)
HEALEY, Eric	5-11	200	L	Hull, MA	1/20/75	Manchester
HEATLEY, Dany	6-3	215	L	Freiburg, West Germany	1/21/81	Atlanta
KACZOWKA, David	6-3	235	L	Regina, Sask.	7/5/81	Greenville
KOVALCHUK, Ilya	6-2	235	R	Tver, USSR	4/15/83	Atlanta
KOZLOV, Vyacheslav	5-10	185	L	Voskresensk, USSR	5/3/72	Atlanta
LESSARD, Francis	6-2	220	R	Montreal, Que.	5/30/79	Atlanta-Chicago (AHL)
LINDSAY, Bill	6-0	195	L	Fernie, B.C.	5/17/71	Montreal-Hamilton
MacKENZIE, Derek	5-11	175	L	Sudbury, Ont.	6/11/81	Chicago (AHL)
MALONEY, Brian	6-1	205	L	Bassano, Alta.	9/27/78	Michigan State-Chi (AHL)
McEACHERN, Shawn	5-11	200	L	Waltham, MA	2/28/69	Atlanta
PIROS, Kamil	6-0	190	L	Most, Czech.	11/20/78	Atlanta-Chicago (AHL)
ROBITAILLE, Randy	5-11	200	L	Ottawa, Ont.	10/12/75	Pittsburgh-NY Islanders
SANTALA, Tommi	6-2	205	R	Helsinki, Finland	6/27/79	HPK
SAVARD, Marc	5-10	190	L	Ottawa, Ont.	7/17/77	Calgary-Atlanta
SNYDER, Dan	6-0	190	L	Elmira, Ont.	2/23/78	Atlanta-Chicago (AHL)
STEFAN, Patrik	6-2	210	L	Pribram, Czech.	9/16/80	Atlanta
STEWART, Karl	5-10	175	L	Aurora, Ont.	6/30/83	Plymouth
SWANSON, Brian	5-10	185	L	Eagle River, AK	3/24/76	Edmonton
TAPPER, Brad	6-0	185	R	Scarborough, Ont.	4/28/78	Atlanta-Chicago (AHL)
VIGIER, J.P.	6-0	205	R	Notre Dame de Lourdes, Man.	9/11/76	Atlanta-Chicago (AHL)

DEFENSEMEN						
DiPENTA, Joe	6-2	235	L	Barrie, Ont.	2/25/79	Atlanta-Chicago (AHL)
EXELBY, Garnet	6-1	210	L	Craik, Sask.	8/16/81	Chicago (AHL)-Atlanta
FLACHE, Paul	6-5	215	R	Toronto, Ont.	3/4/82	Greenville
FOSTER, Kurtis	6-5	230	R	Carp, Ont.	11/24/81	Atlanta-Chicago (AHL)
KABERLE, Frantisek	6-1	190	L	Kladno, Czech.	11/8/73	Atlanta
MAJESKY, Ivan	6-5	225	R	Banska Bystrica, Czech.	9/2/76	Florida
SAFRONOV, Kirill	6-2	215	L	Leningrad, USSR	2/26/81	Chicago (AHL)-Atlanta
SELLARS, Luke	6-1	205	L	Toronto, Ont.	5/21/81	Chicago (AHL)-Greenville
SUTTON, Andy	6-6	245	L	Kingston, Ont.	3/10/75	Atlanta
TAMER, Chris	6-2	205	L	Dearborn, MI	11/17/70	Atlanta
TJARNQVIST, Daniel	6-2	195	L	Umea, Sweden	10/14/76	Atlanta
TREMBLAY, Yannick	6-2	200	R	Pointe-aux-Trembles, Que.	11/15/75	Atlanta
USTRNUL, Libor	6-5	230	L	Sterubeck, Czech.	2/20/82	Chicago (AHL)
WEAVER, Mike	5-9	180	L	Bramalea, Ont.	5/2/78	Atlanta-Chicago (AHL)

GOALTENDERS	HT	WT	C	Place of Birth	Date	2002-03 Club
CASSIVI, Frederic	6-4	215	L	Sorel, Que.	6/12/75	Chicago (AHL)-Atlanta
DAFOE, Byron	5-11	200	L	Sussex, England	2/25/71	Atlanta
GARNETT, Michael	6-1	200	L	Saskatoon, Sask.	11/25/82	Chicago (AHL)-Greenville
HNILICKA, Milan	6-1	190	L	Pardubice, Czech.	6/25/73	Chicago (AHL)-Atlanta
LEHTONEN, Kari	6-3	190	L	Helsinki, Finland	11/16/83	Jokerit
NURMINEN, Pasi	5-10	210	L	Lahti, Finland	12/17/75	Atlanta

2002-03 Scoring

* - rookie

Regular Season

Pos	#	Player	Team	GP	G	A	Pts	+/-	PIM	PP	SH	GW	GT	S	%
R	15	Dany Heatley	ATL	77	41	48	89	-8	58	19	1	6	0	252	16.3
R	13	Vyacheslav Kozlov	ATL	79	21	49	70	-10	66	9	1	2	0	185	11.4
L	17	Ilya Kovalchuk	ATL	81	38	29	67	-24	57	9	0	3	0	257	14.8
C	9	Marc Savard	CGY	10	1	2	3	-3	8	0	0	0	0	21	4.8
			ATL	57	16	31	47	-11	77	6	0	4	0	127	12.6
			TOTAL	67	17	33	50	-14	85	6	0	4	0	148	11.5
C	27	Patrik Stefan	ATL	71	13	21	34	-10	12	3	0	2	1	96	13.5
D	38	Yannick Tremblay	ATL	75	8	22	30	-27	32	5	0	1	0	151	5.3
L	19	Shawn McEachern	ATL	46	10	16	26	-27	28	4	1	1	0	120	8.3
C	12	Tony Hrkac	ATL	80	9	17	26	-16	14	2	0	2	0	86	10.5
D	8	Frantisek Kaberle	ATL	79	7	19	26	-19	32	3	1	2	0	105	6.7
D	25	Andy Sutton	ATL	53	3	18	21	-8	114	1	1	0	0	65	4.6
R	23	Lubos Bartecko	ATL	37	7	9	16	3	8	0	0	1	0	54	13.0
D	36	Daniel Tjarnvist	ATL	75	3	12	15	-20	26	1	0	0	0	65	4.6
R	18	Brad Tapper	ATL	35	10	4	14	-2	23	1	0	3	1	68	14.7
C	37 *	Dan Snyder	ATL	36	10	4	14	-4	34	0	1	1	1	41	24.4
D	4	Chris Tamer	ATL	72	1	9	10	-10	118	0	0	0	0	53	1.9
L	16	Jeff Cowan	ATL	66	3	5	8	-15	115	0	0	0	0	52	5.8
L	39	Per Svartvadet	ATL	62	1	7	8	-11	8	0	0	0	0	47	2.1
C	3 *	Mark Hartigan	ATL	23	5	2	7	-8	6	1	0	0	0	25	20.0
R	20	Jeff Odgers	ATL	74	2	4	6	-13	171	0	0	1	0	48	4.2
L	7	Chris Herperger	ATL	27	4	1	5	-11	7	0	0	0	0	26	15.4
L	22 *	Kamil Piros	ATL	3	3	2	5	4	2	0	0	1	0	8	37.5
D	43 *	Mike Weaver	ATL	40	0	5	5	-5	20	0	0	0	0	21	0.0
D	29 *	Kirill Safronov	ATL	32	2	2	4	-10	14	0	0	0	0	21	9.5
C	10	Yuri Butsayev	ATL	16	2	0	2	-5	8	0	0	0	0	21	9.5
D	50 *	Joe Dipenta	ATL	3	1	1	2	3	0	0	0	0	0	2	50.0
D	2 *	Garnet Exelby	ATL	15	0	2	2	0	41	0	0	0	0	9	0.0
R	6 *	Francis Lessard	ATL	18	0	2	2	1	61	0	0	0	0	7	0.0
C	45 *	Ben Simon	ATL	10	0	1	1	0	9	0	0	0	0	1	0.0
D	47 *	Kurtis Foster	ATL	2	0	0	0	-2	0	0	0	0	0	3	0.0
L	41 *	Simon Gamache	ATL	2	0	0	0	-1	0	0	0	0	0	3	0.0
C	28 *	Jeff Farkas	ATL	3	0	0	0	-1	0	0	0	0	1	0	0.0
D	44	Uwe Krupp	ATL	2	0	0	0	-2	10	0	0	0	0	0	0.0
L	49 *	Zdenek Blatny	ATL	4	0	0	0	-1	0	0	0	0	0	2	0.0
R	11	Jean-Pierre Vigier	ATL	13	0	0	0	-13	4	0	0	0	0	21	0.0

Goaltending

No.	Goaltender	GPI	Mins	Avg	W	L	T	EN	SO	GA	SA	S%	G	A	PIM
31	Pasi Nurminen	52	2856	2.88	21	19	5	6	2	137	1452	.906	0	3	4
33	Milan Hnilicka	21	1097	3.56	4	13	1	0	0	65	605	.893	0	0	2
34	Byron Dafoe	17	895	4.36	5	11	1	0	0	65	472	.862	0	0	0
35	Frederic Cassivi	2	123	5.37	1	1	0	0	0	11	58	.810	0	0	0
	Totals	82	4993	3.41	31	44	7	6	2	284	2593	.890			

Vice President and General Manager

WADDELL, DON
Vice President/General Manager, Atlanta Thrashers.
Born in Detroit, MI, August 19, 1958.

Don Waddell serves as vice president and general manager of the Atlanta Thrashers. He also went behind the bench briefly as an interim coach in 2002-03. Waddell came to the Thrashers on June 23, 1998, — almost a year to the day after the NHL granted Atlanta a franchise — bringing with him more than 20 years experience in professional hockey as a player, coach and general manager. During his tenure in Atlanta, he has used a combination of intelligent draft picks, shrewd trades and astute free agent signings to work towards the long-term success of the Thrashers. Previously, he built two professional hockey franchises, the San Diego Gulls and the Orlando Solar Bears of the International Hockey League. He's also no stranger to winning through his role as assistant general manager for the NHL's Stanley Cup champion Detroit Red Wings during the 1997-98 season.

Prior to Detroit, Waddell was vice president of RDV Sports, where he served on the executive committee which oversaw operations of the National Basketball Association's Orlando Magic, the International Hockey League's Orlando Solar Bears, Magic Fanattics (retail) and Magic Carpet Aviation. While at RDV Sports, Waddell was vice president and general manager of the IHL's Orlando Solar Bears from 1995 to 1997. Prior to the Solar Bears, he held the same role with the IHL's San Diego Gulls from 1990 to 1995. He also served as the club's head coach for the 1991-92 season, guiding the team to the franchise's first playoff berth. He spent two seasons with the IHL's Flint Spirits where he served as head coach and general manager in 1988-89, and general manager in 1989-90.

Waddell's playing experience includes being player/coach for the Flint Spirits from 1986 to 1988, and the Goaldiggers hockey club in Toledo, Ohio for the 1985-86 season. He was drafted by the NHL's Los Angeles Kings back in 1978, and spent three years with the organization from 1980 to 1983. He was a member of the 1983 U.S. national team and had been a member of the 1980 gold medal Olympic hockey team, but was injured prior to play.

Waddell played Division I hockey at Northern Michigan University from 1976 to 1980, where he majored in business management. He was inducted into the Northern Michigan University Sports Hall of Fame in 1992.

NHL Coaching Record

Season	Team	Games	Regular Season			Playoffs			
			W	L	T	Games	W	L	
2002-03	Atlanta	10	4	5	1	....	....	....	
	NHL Totals	10	4	5	1	....	....	....	

General Managers' History

Don Waddell, 1999-2000 to date.

Captains' History

Kelly Buchberger, 1999-2000; Steve Staios, 2000-01; Ray Ferraro, 2001-02.

Coaching History

Curt Fraser, 1999-2000 to 2001-02; Curt Fraser, Don Waddell and Bob Hartley, 2002-03; Bob Hartley, 2003-04.

Club Records

Team

(Figures in brackets for season records are games played.)

Most Points 74	2002-03 (82)	
Most Wins 31	2002-03 (82)	
Most Ties 12	2000-01 (82)	
Most Losses 57	1999-2000 (82)	
Most Goals 226	2002-03 (82)	
Most Goals Against 313	1999-2000 (82)	
Fewest Points 39	1999-2000 (82)	
Fewest Wins 14	1999-2000 (82)	
Fewest Ties 7	1999-2000 (82), 2002-03 (82)	
Fewest Losses. 39	2002-03 (82)	
Fewest Goals 170	1999-2000 (82)	
Fewest Goals Against 284	2002-03 (82)	

Longest Winning Streak
Overall. . . . . 3 Three times
Home. . . . . 2 Eight times
Away. 4 Jan. 13-Feb. 7/03

Longest Undefeated Streak
Overall. . . . . 4 Three times
Home. . . . . 3 Three times
Away. 7 Oct. 21-Nov. 13/00
(3 wins, 4 ties)

Longest Losing Streak
Overall. . . . . 12 Jan. 24-Feb. 20/00
Home. . . . . *11 Jan. 24-Mar. 16/00
Away. 10 Oct. 6-Nov. 18/01

Longest Winless Streak
Overall. . . . . 16 Jan. 16-Feb. 20/00
(2 ties, 14 losses)
Home. . . . . *17 Jan. 19-Mar. 29/00
(2 ties, 15 losses)
Away. 10 Oct. 6-Nov. 18/01
(10 losses)

Most Shutouts, Season 3 2001-02 (82)
Most PIM, Season 1,500 2000-01 (82)
Most Goals, Game . . . . 8 Twice

Individual

Most Seasons . . . . 4 Five players
Most Games . . . . 301 Chris Tamer
Most Goals, Career . . . . 67 Dany Heatley
Most Assists, Career . . . . 91 Ray Ferraro
Most Points, Career . . . . 156 Dany Heatley
(67G, 89A)
Most PIM, Career . . . . 532 Jeff Odgers
Most Shutouts, Career. . . . . 5 Milan Hnilicka
Longest Consecutive
Games Streak . . . . 110 Dany Heatley
(Oct. 4/01-Dec. 13/02)
Most Goals, Season . . . . 41 Dany Heatley
(2002-03)
Most Assists, Season . . . . 49 Vyachaslev Kozlov
(2002-03)
Most Points, Season . . . . 89 Dany Heatley
(2002-03; 41G, 48A)
Most PIM, Season . . . . 226 Jeff Odgers
(2000-01)

Most Points, Defenseman,
Season. . . . . 31 Yannick Tremblay
(1999-2000; 10G, 21A)

Most Points, Center,
Season. . . . . 76 Ray Ferraro
(2000-01; 29G, 47A)

Most Points, Right Wing,
Season. . . . . 89 Dany Heatley
(2002-03; 41G, 48A)

Most Points, Left Wing,
Season. . . . . 67 Ilya Kovalchuk
(2002-03; 38G, 29A)

Most Points, Rookie,
Season. . . . . 67 Dany Heatley
(2001-02; 26G, 41A)

Most Shutouts, Season . . . . 3 Milan Hnilicka
(2001-02)

Most Goals, Game . . . . 4 Pascal Rheaume
(Jan. 19/02)

Most Assists, Game . . . . 4 Andrew Brunette
(Dec. 19/00),
Ilya Kovalchuk
(Jan. 19/02)

Most Points, Game. . . . . 5 Ilya Kovalchuk
(Jan. 19/02; 1G, 4A),
Pascal Rheaume
(Jan. 19/02; 4G, 1A)

* NHL Record.

Ilya Kovalchuk, sitting in the middle of the Thrashers bench, stayed healthy for the whole season in 2002-03. He played in 81 games and improved from 29 goals to 38.

All-time Record vs. Other Clubs

Regular Season

	At Home								On Road								Total							
	GP	W	L	T	OL	GF	GA	PTS	GP	W	L	T	OL	GF	GA	PTS	GP	W	L	T	OL	GF	GA	PTS
Anaheim	3	0	3	0	0	4	14	0	4	2	0	0	9	12	4	7	2	5	0	0	13	26	4	
Boston	8	3	5	0	0	19	20	6	8	3	2	1	2	32	29	9	16	6	7	1	2	51	49	15
Buffalo	8	5	2	1	0	24	26	11	8	3	5	0	0	20	32	6	16	8	7	1	0	44	58	17
Calgary	4	3	0	1	0	8	5	7	2	0	2	0	0	4	9	0	6	3	2	1	0	12	14	7
Carolina	10	1	5	3	1	24	31	6	10	1	6	1	2	23	36	5	20	2	11	4	3	47	67	11
Chicago	3	1	2	0	0	7	8	2	2	0	2	0	0	0	6	0	5	1	4	0	0	7	14	2
Colorado	3	1	1	0	1	6	7	3	4	2	2	0	0	10	17	4	7	3	3	0	1	16	24	7
Columbus	2	1	1	0	0	3	5	2	3	2	0	0	1	9	8	5	5	3	1	0	1	12	13	7
Dallas	4	0	3	0	1	9	16	1	3	0	3	0	0	3	7	0	7	0	6	0	1	12	23	1
Detroit	3	0	3	0	0	7	19	0	3	0	2	0	1	3	11	1	6	0	5	0	1	10	30	1
Edmonton	3	1	2	0	0	3	8	2	3	1	1	1	0	10	9	3	6	2	3	1	0	13	17	5
Florida	10	3	2	4	1	30	33	11	10	5	4	1	0	31	25	11	20	8	6	5	1	61	58	22
Los Angeles	3	0	3	0	0	3	13	0	4	1	3	0	0	9	18	2	7	1	6	0	0	12	31	2
Minnesota	2	0	2	0	0	6	10	0	2	0	1	1	0	3	5	1	4	0	3	1	0	9	15	1
Montreal	8	1	5	2	0	10	27	4	8	2	6	0	0	19	28	4	16	3	11	2	0	29	55	8
Nashville	3	1	0	1	1	8	8	4	3	1	2	0	0	6	12	2	6	2	2	1	1	14	20	6
New Jersey	8	1	5	2	0	13	28	4	8	2	5	1	0	15	28	5	16	3	10	3	0	28	56	9
NY Islanders	8	2	5	1	0	25	32	5	8	4	4	0	0	21	29	8	16	6	9	1	0	46	61	13
NY Rangers	8	2	6	0	0	25	30	4	8	5	3	0	0	30	25	10	16	7	9	0	0	55	55	14
Ottawa	8	2	5	1	0	25	34	5	8	2	5	1	0	21	40	5	16	4	10	2	0	46	74	10
Philadelphia	8	1	5	1	1	19	28	4	8	1	5	2	0	24	37	4	16	2	10	3	1	43	65	8
Phoenix	3	0	3	0	0	5	12	0	4	0	4	0	0	6	15	0	7	0	7	0	0	11	27	0
Pittsburgh	8	0	7	0	1	16	33	1	8	1	6	0	1	15	31	3	16	1	13	0	2	31	64	4
St. Louis	3	1	2	0	0	13	15	2	3	0	3	0	0	1	11	0	6	1	5	0	0	14	26	2
San Jose	3	1	2	0	0	5	9	2	3	0	2	1	0	5	11	1	6	1	4	1	0	10	20	3
Tampa Bay	10	6	1	3	0	41	28	15	10	2	7	1	0	23	40	5	20	8	8	4	0	64	68	20
Toronto	7	3	3	0	1	14	24	7	8	4	4	0	0	16	27	5	14	5	7	1	1	30	51	12
Vancouver	3	1	2	0	0	11	12	2	3	0	2	1	0	1	9	1	5	1	3	1	0	12	21	3
Washington	10	4	4	2	0	20	29	10	10	0	7	2	1	22	43	2	20	4	11	4	1	42	72	13
Totals	**164**	**45**	**89**	**22**	**8**	**403**	**564**	**120**	**164**	**42**	**99**	**15**	**8**	**391**	**610**	**107**	**328**	**87**	**188**	**37**	**16**	**794**	**1174**	**227**

2002-03 Results

Oct.	11	at Carolina	3-5		11	at NY Islanders	3-7
	12	Florida	4-5*		13	at Philadelphia	7-4
	16	at Pittsburgh	2-3		15	Montreal	1-0
	18	at Tampa Bay	5-8		17	Boston	3-1
	19	NY Islanders	4-5		19	NY Islanders	1-4
	21	at Florida	2-3		21	St. Louis	8-4
	23	New Jersey	1-2		23	Ottawa	3-3
	26	at Boston	3-4		25	at NY Rangers	4-1
	29	Los Angeles	0-4		28	NY Rangers	5-2
	31	at Toronto	3-3		30	Toronto	2-5
Nov.	2	at Florida	3-1	Feb.	4	at Montreal	4-3
	7	at Chicago	0-5		7	at New Jersey	4-2
	9	at Buffalo	6-4		8	at Ottawa	1-3
	11	Calgary	2-1		12	Washington	1-5
	13	San Jose	3-2*		14	Tampa Bay	2-2
	15	Phoenix	1-5		15	Detroit	2-6
	17	Anaheim	1-5		17	Buffalo	4-3*
	19	Florida	4-3*		19	at Tampa Bay	0-2
	22	Pittsburgh	1-3		23	at Edmonton	3-3
	23	at Washington	3-6		25	at Vancouver	0-8
	26	at Montreal	2-3		27	at Colorado	4-3*
	28	NY Rangers	7-4	Mar.	1	at Los Angeles	1-4
Dec.	1	Washington	5-4		2	at Anaheim	4-1
	5	at Boston	3-4*		6	at Washington	4-4
	6	at Washington	6-7*		7	Florida	1-2
	8	Edmonton	0-3		9	Minnesota	4-6
	11	at Phoenix	2-4		11	at New Jersey	3-2
	13	at Dallas	1-3		13	Montreal	2-4
	14	at St. Louis	0-4		15	Buffalo	5-3
	16	Toronto	1-0		17	Columbus	3-2
	18	Philadelphia	1-3		19	Dallas	4-5*
	20	Carolina	2-3*		21	Ottawa	1-5
	23	at Toronto	1-5		22	at Columbus	3-2
	27	at Carolina	3-3		24	at Philadelphia	2-6
	28	Boston	0-1		26	Carolina	5-1
	30	at Pittsburgh	3-2*		28	New Jersey	1-1
Jan.	2	at Ottawa	1-8		29	at Nashville	3-2
	3	Pittsburgh	1-4		31	at NY Rangers	4-3*
	5	Philadelphia	4-5	Apr.	2	at Buffalo	3-4
	7	Carolina	3-3		5	at NY Islanders	3-2
	9	at Tampa Bay	3-2*		6	Tampa Bay	6-2

* – Overtime

Entry Draft Selections 2003-1999

2003

Pick	
8	Braydon Coburn
110	James Sharrow
116	Guillaume Desbiens
136	Michael Vannelli
145	Brett Sterling
175	Mike Hamilton
203	Denis Loginov
239	Tobias Enstrom
269	Rylan Kaip

2002

Pick	
2	Kari Lehtonen
30	Jim Slater
116	Patrick Dwyer
124	Lane Manson
144	Paul Flache
167	Brad Schell
198	Nathan Oystrick
230	Colton Fretter
236	Tyler Boldt
257	Pauli Levokari

2001

Pick	
1	Ilya Kovalchuk
80	Michael Garnett
100	Brian Sipotz
112	Milan Gajic
135	Colin Stuart
189	Pasi Nurminen
199	Matt Suderman
201	Colin FitzRandolph
262	Mario Cartelli

2000

Pick	
2	Dany Heatley
31	Ilja Nikulin
42	Libor Ustrnul
107	Carl Mallette
108	Blake Robson
147	Matt McRae
168	Zdenek Smid
178	Jeff Dwyer
180	Darcy Hordichuk
230	Samu Isosalo
242	Evan Nielsen
244	Eric Bowen
288	Mark McRae
290	Simon Gamache

1999

Pick	
1	Patrik Stefan
30	Luke Sellars
68	Zdenek Blatny
98	David Kaczowka
99	Rob Zepp
128	Derek MacKenzie
159	Yuri Dobryshkin
188	Stephan Baby
217	Garnet Exelby
245	Tommi Santala
246	Raymond DiLauro

Coach

HARTLEY, BOB
Coach, Atlanta Thrashers. Born in Hawkesbury, Ont., September 7, 1960.

Bob Hartley brought an impressive track record of winning to the Atlanta Thrashers when he was hired as the second head coach in franchise history on January 14, 2003. Just a few weeks later, on February 7, he became the seventh-fastest coach in NHL history to reach 200 wins as Atlanta beat New Jersey 4-2 in Hartley's 369th game as a head coach.

Prior to joining the Thrashers, Hartley had guided the Colorado Avalanche to the 2001 Stanley Cup championship. In the 2002 playoffs, he became the first NHL coach to lead his team to the Conference Final in his first four seasons with the same club. In his first 14 seasons as a head coach at the professional and amateur levels (prior to joining the Thrashers), Hartley's teams all qualified for the postseason and won five league championships, while capturing 40 or more victories eight times and 30 or more wins 13 times. His Avalanche teams won at least 42 games in four consecutive seasons from 1998 to 2002.

Hartley became the second head coach of the Avalanche, and the 11th in franchise history, when he was named to the position on June 30, 1998. He served there until December 18, 2002 and is Colorado's all-time coaching victory leader (193), having guided the Avalanche to four consecutive Northwest Division titles and four straight trips to the Western Conference Final. Hartley guided the 2000-01 Avalanche to its most successful season in franchise history. Colorado established team records for points (118), wins (52) and goals against (192).

Hartley has been a proven winner at every level he has coached. Prior to joining Colorado, Hartley coached four seasons in the American Hockey League from 1994 to 1998, posting a 151-136-33 regular-season record and making four consecutive trips to the playoffs with Cornwall (1994 to 1996) and Hershey (1996 to 1998). He guided Hershey to the 1997 Calder Cup championship. After serving as an assistant coach for Cornwall in 1993-94, Hartley guided the Aces to the Southern Division title in 1994-95, and a trip to the Southern Division Final again in 1995-96. He led Laval to the Quebec Major Junior Hockey League championship and the Memorial Cup in 1993, and compiled an 81-52-7 record in two seasons with Laval from 1991 to 1993.

From 1987 to 1991, Hartley served as head coach for Hawkesbury of the Canadian Junior Hockey League. After enduring an 18-point season his rookie term behind the Hawks' bench, he guided the club to an impressive 117-45-5 mark during the next three seasons, including CJHL championships in 1990 and 1991. His teams dropped just three postseason games in 1990 and 1991, going 24-3 in that span. Overall, his teams in Hawkesbury advanced to the playoffs four consecutive seasons and finished 31-13 in the postseason during that span.

Throughout his coaching career, Hartley has shared a strong sense of dedication with his community. He was honored in his hometown of Hawkesbury, where the local ice arena was renamed Complex Bob Hartley in August 1998 in recognition of his service to the community where he grew up and coached. He has been involved in hockey camps and charitable endeavors throughout his career.

Coaching Record

		Regular Season				Playoffs		
Season	**Team**	**Games**	**W**	**L**	**T**	**Games**	**W**	**L**
1991-92	Laval (QMJHL)	70	38	27	5	10	4	6
1992-93	Laval (QMJHL)	70	43	25	2	13	12	1
1994-95	Cornwall (AHL)	80	38	33	9	15	8	7
1995-96	Cornwall (AHL)	80	34	39	7	8	3	5
1996-97	Hershey (AHL)	80	43	27	10	23	15	8
1997-98	Hershey (AHL)	80	36	37	7	7	3	4
1998-99	**Colorado (NHL)**	**82**	**44**	**28**	**10**	**19**	**11**	**8**
1999-2000	**Colorado (NHL)**	**82**	**42**	**29**	**11**	**17**	**11**	**6**
2000-01	**Colorado (NHL)**	**82**	**52**	**20**	**10**	**23**	**16**	**7***
2001-02	**Colorado (NHL)**	**82**	**45**	**29**	**8**	**21**	**11**	**10**
2002-03	**Colorado (NHL)**	**31**	**10**	**12**	**9**	....	....	....
	Atlanta (NHL)	**39**	**19**	**15**	**5**	....	....	....
	NHL Totals	**398**	**212**	**133**	**53**	**80**	**49**	**31**

* Stanley Cup win.

Club Directory

Philips Arena

Atlanta Thrashers
One CNN Center
12 South, South Tower
Atlanta, GA 30303
Phone **404/827-5300**
FAX 404/827-5769
www.atlantathrashers.com
Capacity: 18,545

Executive Management

President and Governor	Stan Kasten
Vice President & G.M./Alternate Governor	Don Waddell
Vice President of Sales and Marketing	Derek Schiller

Hockey Operations

Director of Player Personnel	Jack Ferreira
Dir. of Amateur Scouting & Player Development	Dan Marr
Head Coach	Bob Hartley
Assistant Coaches	Brad McCrimmon and Steve Weeks
Head Scout	Marcel Comeau
Full-Time Scouts	Mark Dobson, Bernd Freimuller, Mark Hillier, Peter Mahovlich, Bob Owen, John Perpich, Normand Poisson
Part-Time Scouts	Evgeny Bogdanovich, Terry Brennan, Pat Carmichael, Pentti Katainen, Terho Koskela, Jan Lindegren
Director of Hockey Administration	Larry Simmons
Director of Team Services	Michele Zarzaca
Strength and Conditioning Coach	Ray Bear
Head Athletic Trainer	Scott Green
Assistant Athletic Trainer	Craig Brewer
Massage Therapist	Inar Treiguts
Head Equipment Manager	Bobby Stewart
Assistant Equipment Manager	Joe Guilmet
Team Physician	Dr. Scott Gillogly
Team Internist	Dr. William Whaley
Team Dentists	Dr. Gary Saban, Dr. Lawrence Saltzman, Dr. Brett Silverman
Video and Hockey Operations Coordinator	Tony Borgford

Administration

Executive Assistant to Stan Kasten/Office Manager	Carole Harding
Assistant to Don Waddell/ Practice Facility office manager	Leisa Strickland

Corporate Sales (Philips Arena Sports Marketing)

Vice President of Broadcast and Corporate Sales	Tracy White
Director of Broadcast and Corporate Sales	Terri Scalcucci-Cameron
Director of Broadcast and Corporate Sales	Bill Abercrombie
Senior Manager of Broadcast and Corporate Sales	Stewart Tanner
Broadcast and Corporate Sales Managers	Chris Beaudin, Tamara Gehris, Arden Robbins, Maggie Spurlin
Manager of Broadcast Operations	Diana Corbin
Manager of Promotions/Sponsor Services	Chris Carter
Sponsor Services Coordinators	Kory Burke, Amanda Cooper, Cari Powell, Adam Ragsdale

Finance/Accounting

Controller	David Kane
Assistant Controller	Darius Nixon
Senior Financial Analyst	Lonna Donaldson
Staff Accountants	Raiford Hodges and Julia Yoon

Human Resources

Vice President of Management Company/Turner Sports/ Sports Teams/Philips Arena/Ad Sales	Tim Goodly
HR Director of Sports/Teams/Philips Arena	Ginni Siler
Human Resources Coordinator	Tomeka Cherry

Legal

Team Counsel	John Cooper
Assistant Team Counsels	T. Scott Wilkinson, Greg Heller

Marketing

Director of Marketing	Jim Pfeifer
Senior Manager of Game Presentation and Special Events	Peter Sorckoff
Marketing Manager	Kimberly Hartley
Manager of Special Events	Connie Zaleski
Manager of Community Relations	Terri Hickman
Interactive Marketing Manager	Wes Taft
Marketing Coordinators	Reagan Carey, Ralph Humphlett
Fan Development Coordinator	David Porter
Game Operations Coordinator	Scott Brooks

Media Relations

Director of Media Relations	Tom Hughes
Senior Manager of Media Relations	Rob Koch
Senior Manager of Publications and Web Site	Matt Musgrove
Team Information Specialist	John Heid
Web site Specialist	Kevin McCormack
Junior Publicist	Katie McLennan
Team Photographer	Scott Cunningham

Television/Radio Broadcasting

Sr. V.P./Coordinating Television Producer	Jeff Behnke
Television Producer	C.J. Bottitta
Television Director	Jim Allen
TV Analyst/Director of Hockey Programs	Darren Eliot
TV Play-by-play Announcer	TBD
Director of Radio Operations/ Radio Play by Play Broadcaster	Dan Kamal
Radio Analyst	Billy Jaffe

Ticket Sales

Director of Ticket Sales	Dan Froehlich
Director of Ticket Operations	Wendell Byrne
New Account Sales, Senior Manager	Keith Brennan
New Account Sales Managers	John Farrell, Larry Jones, Jacque Murdoch, Michael Simmons, William Stephens
Client Services, Senior Manager	Scott Fillmore
Client Services Managers	Grady Landis, Jonathan Tillman
Group Sales Managers	Evan Kellner, Sasha Trendley, Kenan Woods
Ticket Operations Coordinator	Phil Kvidt

Glen Murray had 44 goals and 48 assists.

Boston Bruins

2002-03 Results: 36W-31L-6T-4OTL 87PTS.
Third, Northeast Division

2003-04 Schedule

Oct.	Wed.	8	New Jersey		Thu.	8	Pittsburgh
	Fri.	10	at Tampa Bay		Sat.	10	Detroit*
	Sat.	11	at Florida		Mon.	12	Buffalo
	Wed.	15	at Dallas		Thu.	15	at Buffalo
	Sat.	18	at Los Angeles		Sat.	17	at Ottawa
	Sun.	19	at Anaheim*		Mon.	19	NY Rangers*
	Tue.	21	at Colorado		Tue.	20	at NY Rangers
	Thu.	23	Carolina		Thu.	22	Buffalo
	Sat.	25	at New Jersey		Sat.	24	Florida
	Tue.	28	at Montreal		Tue.	27	at NY Islanders
	Thu.	30	Montreal		Thu.	29	NY Islanders
Nov.	Sat.	1	at Pittsburgh*		Sat.	31	at Montreal*
	Thu.	6	San Jose	**Feb.**	Sun.	1	Pittsburgh*
	Sat.	8	Dallas		Tue.	3	Atlanta
	Tue.	11	Edmonton		Thu.	5	at Buffalo
	Fri.	14	at Columbus		Tue.	10	at Pittsburgh
	Sat.	15	Vancouver		Thu.	12	at Ottawa
	Wed.	19	at Atlanta		Sat.	14	at Chicago*
	Thu.	20	Washington		Tue.	17	at Toronto
	Sat.	22	at Philadelphia		Thu.	19	at Philadelphia
	Tue.	25	at St. Louis		Sat.	21	at Carolina
	Fri.	28	Nashville*		Mon.	23	Florida
	Sun.	30	Phoenix		Tue.	24	at NY Islanders
Dec.	Wed.	3	at Atlanta		Thu.	26	Montreal
	Thu.	4	Toronto		Sat.	28	Philadelphia*
	Sat.	6	Philadelphia	**Mar.**	Tue.	2	at Toronto
	Mon.	8	Ottawa		Thu.	4	NY Rangers
	Wed.	10	at Florida		Sat.	6	Atlanta
	Thu.	11	at Washington		Tue.	9	at Nashville
	Sat.	13	at Ottawa		Thu.	11	at Buffalo
	Tue.	16	at Montreal		Sat.	13	Buffalo*
	Thu.	18	Calgary		Tue.	16	at Toronto
	Sat.	20	Carolina*		Thu.	18	Minnesota
	Mon.	22	at NY Rangers		Sat.	20	Tampa Bay*
	Tue.	23	Tampa Bay		Tue.	23	Ottawa
	Sat.	27	at Tampa Bay		Thu.	25	Toronto
	Mon.	29	at Washington		Sat.	27	Montreal
	Tue.	30	Ottawa		Tue.	30	at Carolina
Jan.	Thu.	1	Toronto	**Apr.**	Thu.	1	Washington
	Sat.	3	NY Islanders		Sat.	3	New Jersey*
	Wed.	7	at Detroit		Sun.	4	at New Jersey*

* Denotes afternoon game.

Franchise date: November 1, 1924

EASTERN CONFERENCE
NORTHEAST DIVISION

80th NHL Season

Year-by-Year Record

		Home				Road				Overall								
Season	GP	W	L	T	OL	W	L	T	OL	W	L	T	OL	GF	GA	Pts.	Finished	Playoff Result
2002-03	82	23	11	5	2	13	20	6	2	36	31	11	4	245	237	87	3rd, Northeast Div.	Lost Conf. Quarter-Final
2001-02	82	23	11	2	5	20	13	4	4	43	24	6	9	236	201	101	1st, Northeast Div.	Lost Conf. Quarter-Final
2000-01	82	21	12	5	3	15	18	3	5	36	30	8	8	227	249	88	4th, Northeast Div.	Out of Playoffs
1999-2000	82	12	17	11	1	12	16	8	5	24	33	19	6	210	248	73	5th, Northeast Div.	Out of Playoffs
1998-99	82	22	10	9	...	17	20	4	...	39	30	13	...	214	181	91	3rd, Northeast Div.	Lost Conf. Semi-Final
1997-98	82	19	16	6	...	20	14	7	...	39	30	13	...	221	194	91	2nd, Northeast Div.	Lost Conf. Quarter-Final
1996-97	82	14	20	7	...	12	27	2	...	26	47	9	...	234	300	61	6th, Northeast Div.	Out of Playoffs
1995-96	82	22	14	5	...	18	17	6	...	40	31	11	...	282	269	91	2nd, Northeast Div.	Lost Conf. Quarter-Final
1994-95	48	15	7	2	...	12	11	1	...	27	18	3	...	150	127	57	3rd, Northeast Div.	Lost Conf. Quarter-Final
1993-94	84	20	14	8	...	22	15	5	...	42	29	13	...	289	252	97	2nd, Northeast Div.	Lost Conf. Semi-Final
1992-93	84	29	10	3	...	22	16	4	...	51	26	7	...	332	268	109	1st, Adams Div.	Lost Div. Semi-Final
1991-92	80	23	11	6	...	13	21	6	...	36	32	12	...	270	275	84	2nd, Adams Div.	Lost Conf. Championship
1990-91	80	26	9	5	...	18	15	7	...	44	24	12	...	299	264	100	1st, Adams Div.	Lost Conf. Championship
1989-90	80	23	13	4	...	23	12	5	...	46	25	9	...	289	232	101	1st, Adams Div.	Lost Final
1988-89	80	17	15	8	...	20	14	6	...	37	29	14	...	289	256	88	2nd, Adams Div.	Lost Div. Final
1987-88	80	24	13	3	...	20	17	3	...	44	30	6	...	300	251	94	2nd, Adams Div.	Lost Final
1986-87	80	25	11	4	...	14	23	3	...	39	34	7	...	301	276	85	3rd, Adams Div.	Lost Div. Semi-Final
1985-86	80	24	9	7	...	13	22	5	...	37	31	12	...	311	288	86	3rd, Adams Div.	Lost Div. Semi-Final
1984-85	80	21	15	4	...	15	19	6	...	36	34	10	...	303	287	82	4th, Adams Div.	Lost Div. Semi-Final
1983-84	80	25	12	3	...	24	13	3	...	49	25	6	...	336	261	104	1st, Adams Div.	Lost Div. Semi-Final
1982-83	80	28	6	6	...	22	14	4	...	50	20	10	...	327	228	110	1st, Adams Div.	Lost Conf. Championship
1981-82	80	24	12	4	...	19	15	6	...	43	27	10	...	323	285	96	2nd, Adams Div.	Lost Div. Final
1980-81	80	26	10	4	...	11	20	9	...	37	30	13	...	316	272	87	2nd, Adams Div.	Lost Prelim. Round
1979-80	80	27	9	4	...	19	12	9	...	46	21	13	...	310	234	105	2nd, Adams Div.	Lost Quarter-Final
1978-79	80	25	10	5	...	18	13	9	...	43	23	14	...	316	270	100	1st, Adams Div.	Lost Semi-Final
1977-78	80	29	6	5	...	22	12	6	...	51	18	11	...	333	218	113	1st, Adams Div.	Lost Final
1976-77	80	27	7	6	...	22	16	2	...	49	23	8	...	312	240	106	1st, Adams Div.	Lost Final
1975-76	80	27	5	8	...	21	10	9	...	48	15	17	...	313	237	113	1st, Adams Div.	Lost Semi-Final
1974-75	80	29	5	6	...	11	21	8	...	40	26	14	...	345	245	94	2nd, Adams Div.	Lost Prelim. Round
1973-74	78	33	4	2	...	19	13	7	...	52	17	9	...	349	221	113	1st, East Div.	Lost Final
1972-73	78	27	10	2	...	24	12	3	...	51	22	5	...	330	235	107	2nd, East Div.	Lost Quarter-Final
1971-72	**78**	**28**	**4**	**7**	**...**	**26**	**9**	**4**	**...**	**54**	**13**	**11**	**...**	**330**	**204**	**119**	**1st, East Div.**	**Won Stanley Cup**
1970-71	78	33	4	2	...	24	10	5	...	57	14	7	...	399	207	121	1st, East Div.	Lost Quarter-Final
1969-70	**76**	**27**	**3**	**8**	**...**	**13**	**14**	**11**	**...**	**40**	**17**	**19**	**...**	**277**	**216**	**99**	**2nd, East Div.**	**Won Stanley Cup**
1968-69	76	29	3	6	...	13	15	10	...	42	18	16	...	303	221	100	2nd, East Div.	Lost Semi-Final
1967-68	74	22	9	6	...	15	18	4	...	37	27	10	...	259	216	84	3rd, East Div.	Lost Quarter-Final
1966-67	70	10	21	4	...	7	22	6	...	17	43	10	...	182	253	44	6th,	Out of Playoffs
1965-66	70	15	17	3	...	6	26	3	...	21	43	6	...	174	275	48	5th,	Out of Playoffs
1964-65	70	12	17	6	...	9	26	0	...	21	43	6	...	166	253	48	6th,	Out of Playoffs
1963-64	70	13	15	7	...	5	25	5	...	18	40	12	...	170	212	48	6th,	Out of Playoffs
1962-63	70	7	18	10	...	7	21	7	...	14	39	17	...	198	281	45	6th,	Out of Playoffs
1961-62	70	9	22	4	...	6	25	4	...	15	47	8	...	177	306	38	6th,	Out of Playoffs
1960-61	70	13	17	5	...	2	25	8	...	15	42	13	...	176	254	43	6th,	Out of Playoffs
1959-60	70	21	11	3	...	7	23	5	...	28	34	8	...	220	241	64	5th,	Out of Playoffs
1958-59	70	21	11	3	...	11	18	6	...	32	29	9	...	205	215	73	2nd,	Lost Semi-Final
1957-58	70	15	14	6	...	12	14	9	...	27	28	15	...	199	194	69	4th,	Lost Final
1956-57	70	20	9	6	...	14	15	6	...	34	24	12	...	195	174	80	3rd,	Lost Final
1955-56	70	14	14	7	...	9	20	6	...	23	34	13	...	147	185	59	5th,	Out of Playoffs
1954-55	70	16	10	9	...	7	16	12	...	23	26	21	...	169	188	67	4th,	Lost Semi-Final
1953-54	70	22	8	5	...	10	20	5	...	32	28	10	...	177	181	74	4th,	Lost Semi-Final
1952-53	70	19	10	6	...	9	19	7	...	28	29	13	...	152	172	69	3rd,	Lost Final
1951-52	70	15	12	8	...	10	17	8	...	25	29	16	...	162	176	66	4th,	Lost Semi-Final
1950-51	70	13	12	10	...	9	18	8	...	22	30	18	...	178	197	62	4th,	Lost Semi-Final
1949-50	70	15	12	8	...	7	20	8	...	22	32	16	...	198	228	60	5th,	Out of Playoffs
1948-49	60	18	10	2	...	11	13	6	...	29	23	8	...	178	163	66	2nd,	Lost Semi-Final
1947-48	60	12	8	10	...	11	16	3	...	23	24	13	...	167	168	59	3rd,	Lost Semi-Final
1946-47	60	18	7	5	...	8	16	6	...	26	23	11	...	190	175	63	3rd,	Lost Semi-Final
1945-46	50	11	5	4	...	13	13	4	...	24	18	8	...	167	156	56	2nd,	Lost Final
1944-45	50	11	12	2	...	5	18	2	...	16	30	4	...	179	219	36	4th,	Lost Semi-Final
1943-44	50	15	8	2	...	4	18	3	...	19	26	5	...	223	268	43	5th,	Out of Playoffs
1942-43	50	17	3	5	...	7	14	4	...	24	17	9	...	195	176	57	2nd,	Lost Final
1941-42	48	17	4	3	...	8	13	3	...	25	17	6	...	160	118	56	3rd,	Lost Semi-Final
1940-41	**48**	**15**	**4**	**5**	**...**	**12**	**4**	**8**	**...**	**27**	**8**	**13**	**...**	**168**	**102**	**67**	**1st,**	**Won Stanley Cup**
1939-40	48	20	3	1	...	11	9	4	...	31	12	5	...	170	98	67	1st,	Lost Semi-Final
1938-39	**48**	**20**	**2**	**2**	**...**	**16**	**8**	**0**	**...**	**36**	**10**	**2**	**...**	**156**	**76**	**74**	**1st,**	**Won Stanley Cup**
1937-38	48	18	3	3	...	12	8	4	...	30	11	7	...	142	89	67	1st, Amn. Div.	Lost Semi-Final
1936-37	48	9	11	4	...	14	7	3	...	23	18	7	...	120	110	53	2nd, Amn. Div.	Lost Quarter-Final
1935-36	48	15	8	1	...	7	12	5	...	22	20	6	...	92	83	50	2nd, Amn. Div.	Lost Quarter-Final
1934-35	48	17	7	0	...	9	9	6	...	26	16	6	...	129	112	58	1st, Amn. Div.	Lost Semi-Final
1933-34	48	11	11	2	...	7	14	3	...	18	25	5	...	111	130	41	4th, Amn. Div.	Out of Playoffs
1932-33	48	19	2	3	...	6	13	5	...	25	15	8	...	124	88	58	1st, Amn. Div.	Lost Semi-Final
1931-32	48	11	10	3	...	4	11	9	...	15	21	12	...	122	117	42	4th, Amn. Div.	Out of Playoffs
1930-31	44	16	1	5	...	12	9	1	...	28	10	6	...	143	90	62	1st, Amn. Div.	Lost Semi-Final
1929-30	44	21	1	0	...	17	4	1	...	38	5	1	...	179	98	77	1st, Amn. Div.	Lost Final
1928-29	**44**	**15**	**6**	**1**	**...**	**11**	**7**	**4**	**...**	**26**	**13**	**5**	**...**	**89**	**52**	**57**	**1st, Amn. Div.**	**Won Stanley Cup**
1927-28	44	13	4	5	...	7	9	6	...	20	13	11	...	77	70	51	1st, Amn. Div.	Lost Semi-Final
1926-27	44	15	7	0	...	6	13	3	...	21	20	3	...	97	89	45	2nd, Amn. Div.	Lost Final
1925-26	36	10	7	1	...	7	8	3	...	17	15	4	...	92	85	38	4th,	Out of Playoffs
1924-25	30	3	12	0	...	3	12	0	...	6	24	0	...	49	119	12	6th,	Out of Playoffs

2003-04 Player Personnel

FORWARDS	HT	WT	S	Place of Birth	Date	2002-03 Club
AXELSSON, P.J.	6-1	184	L	Kungalv, Sweden	2/26/75	Boston
BARBER, Greg	6-0	185	R	Dawson Creek, B.C.	5/26/80	U. of Denver
CORAZZINI, Carl	5-10	182	R	Framingham, MA	4/21/79	Providence (AHL)-Atlantic City
DONATO, Ted	5-10	180	L	Boston, MA	4/28/69	NY Rangers-Hartford
DOULL, Doug	6-2	216	L	Green Bay, N.S.	5/31/74	St. John's
GELLARD, Mike	6-1	193	L	Markham, Ont.	10/10/78	Providence (AHL)
GROSEK, Michal	6-2	207	R	Vyskov, Czech.	6/1/75	Boston
HERR, Matt	6-2	204	L	Hackensack, NJ	5/26/76	Boston-Providence (AHL)
HILBERT, Andy	5-11	190	L	Lansing, MI	2/6/81	Boston-Providence (AHL)
HUML, Ivan	6-2	195	L	Kladno, Czech.	9/6/81	Boston-Providence (AHL)
KNUBLE, Mike	6-3	228	R	Toronto, Ont.	7/4/72	Boston
LAPOINTE, Martin	5-11	215	R	Ville St-Pierre, Que.	9/12/73	Boston
LEAHY, Patrick	6-3	190	R	Brighton, MA	6/9/79	Providence (AHL)
McCARTHY, Sandy	6-3	222	R	Toronto, Ont.	6/15/72	NY Rangers
MURRAY, Glen	6-3	225	R	Halifax, N.S.	11/1/72	Boston
ORR, Colton	6-3	210	R	Winnipeg, Man.	3/3/82	Kamlps-Regn-Prov (AHL)
PARADISE, Chris	6-2	200	R	St. Paul, MN	8/6/77	Providence (AHL)-Atlantic City
ROLSTON, Brian	6-2	210	L	Flint, MI	2/21/73	Boston
SAMSONOV, Sergei	5-8	194	R	Moscow, USSR	10/27/78	Boston
SAMUELSSON, Martin	6-2	200	L	Upplands Vasby, Sweden	1/25/82	Boston-Providence (AHL)
STOCK, P.J.	5-10	197	L	Montreal, Que.	5/26/75	Boston
THORNTON, Joe	6-4	220	L	London, Ont.	7/2/79	Boston
VAN OENE, Darren	6-4	216	L	Edmonton, Alta.	1/18/78	Providence (AHL)
VERNARSKY, Kris	6-3	201	L	Detroit, MI	4/5/82	Boston-Providence (AHL)
ZAMUNER, Rob	6-3	203	L	Oakville, Ont.	9/17/69	Boston
DEFENSEMEN						
BOYNTON, Nick	6-2	210	R	Nobleton, Ont.	1/14/79	Boston
BRENNAN, Rich	6-2	200	R	Schenectady, NY	11/26/72	Boston-Providence (AHL)
CAMPBELL, Ed	6-2	204	L	Worcester, MA	11/26/74	Grand Rapids
DALLMAN, Kevin	5-11	195	R	Niagara Falls, Ont.	2/26/81	Providence (AHL)
GILL, Hal	6-7	250	L	Concord, MA	4/6/75	Boston
GIRARD, Jonathan	5-11	201	R	Joliette, Que.	5/27/80	Boston
JILLSON, Jeff	6-3	220	R	North Smithfield, RI	7/24/80	S.J.-Cleveland-Prov (AHL)
JURCINA, Milan	6-4	198	R	Liptovsky Mikulas, Czech.	6/7/83	Halifax
KUTLAK, Zdenek	6-3	221	L	Budejovice, Czech.	2/13/80	Boston-Providence (AHL)
McGILLIS, Dan	6-2	230	L	Hawkesbury, Ont.	7/1/72	Philadelphia-San Jose-Boston
METCALF, Peter	6-0	200	L	Steamboat Springs, CO	2/25/79	Providence (AHL)-Atlantic City
MORAN, Ian	6-0	200	R	Cleveland, OH	8/24/72	Pittsburgh-Boston
MORRISONN, Shaone	6-3	205	L	Vancouver, B.C.	12/23/82	Boston-Providence (AHL)
O'DONNELL, Sean	6-3	230	L	Ottawa, Ont.	10/13/71	Boston
GOALTENDERS	**HT**	**WT**	**C**	**Place of Birth**	**Date**	**2002-03 Club**
HAMERLIK, Peter	6-1	194	L	Myjava, Czech.	1/2/82	King-Prov (AHL)-Cin (ECHL)
RAYCROFT, Andrew	6-0	174	L	Belleville, Ont.	5/4/80	Boston-Providence (AHL)
SHIELDS, Steve	6-3	215	L	Toronto, Ont.	7/19/72	Boston
TOIVONEN, Hannu	6-2	191	L	Kalvola, Finland	5/18/84	HPK

Coach

SULLIVAN, MIKE
Coach, Boston Bruins. Born in Marshfield, MA, February 27, 1968.

The Boston Bruins named Mike Sullivan their head coach on June 23, 2003. He is the 25th head coach in team history. At the age of 35, he becomes the youngest coach in the NHL. Sullivan began his coaching career with Providence of the AHL when he was hired on July 29, 2002. Under his watch, the Providence Bruins won the North Division with a 44-20-11-5 record and 104 points. The club established a new franchise record with a 19-game home unbeaten streak (16 wins, three ties) from December 6 to February 23. Sullivan's record behind the Providence bench was 41-17-9-4 through March 20, when he was promoted to Boston as an assistant coach under Mike O'Connell. Boston went 3-3-3-0 in the nine remaining regular season games and was eliminated by the eventual Stanley Cup champion New Jersey Devils in five games during the opening round of the playoffs. Sullivan returned to Providence following the NHL playoffs, and was behind the bench for the final three games of Providence's four-game series loss to Manitoba in their AHL playoff series.

Sullivan played four seasons of college hockey at Boston University from 1986-87 through 1989-90 with 61 goals, 77 assists and 104 penalty minutes in 141 career college games. The New York Rangers drafted the center as their fourth pick, 69th overall, in the 1987 NHL Entry Draft, but he never signed with the Rangers. He turned professional in 1990, playing the 1990-91 season with San Diego of the International Hockey League before signing with the San Jose Sharks as a free agent in August, 1991 and beginning his 11-year NHL career. He played in San Jose, Calgary, Boston and Phoenix before retiring after the 2001-02 season. His career NHL playing totals were 54 goals and 82 assists for 136 points with 203 penalty minutes in 709 games.

Coaching Record

		Regular Season				Playoffs		
Season	Team	Games	W	L	T	Games	W	L
2002-03	Providence (AHL)	71	41	21	9	3	1	2

2002-03 Scoring

* - rookie

Regular Season

Pos	#	Player	Team	GP	G	A	Pts	+/–	PIM	PP	SH	GW	GT	S	%
C	19	Joe Thornton	BOS	77	36	65	101	12	109	12	2	4	1	196	18.4
R	27	Glen Murray	BOS	82	44	48	92	9	64	12	0	5	2	331	13.3
R	26	Mike Knuble	BOS	75	30	29	59	18	45	9	0	4	1	185	16.2
C	12	Brian Rolston	BOS	81	27	32	59	1	32	6	5	5	1	281	9.6
C	16	Jozef Stumpel	BOS	78	14	37	51	0	12	4	0	2	1	110	12.7
D	34	Bryan Berard	BOS	80	10	28	38	–4	64	4	0	1	0	205	4.9
L	11	P.J. Axelsson	BOS	66	17	19	36	8	24	2	2	1	0	122	13.9
D	44	Nick Boynton	BOS	78	7	17	24	8	99	0	1	2	0	160	4.4
D	46	Jonathan Girard	BOS	73	6	16	22	4	21	2	0	2	0	123	4.9
D	6	Dan McGillis	PHI	24	0	3	3	7	20	0	0	0	0	41	0.0
			S.J.	37	3	13	16	–6	30	2	0	0	1	71	4.2
			BOS	10	0	1	1	2	10	0	0	0	0	18	0.0
			TOTAL	71	3	17	20	3	60	2	0	0	1	130	2.3
L	22	Michal Grosek	BOS	63	2	18	20	2	71	0	0	1	0	74	2.7
R	10	Marty McInnis	BOS	77	9	10	19	–11	38	0	0	1	0	121	7.4
R	20	Martin Lapointe	BOS	59	8	10	18	–19	87	1	0	1	0	110	7.3
L	36	* Ivan Huml	BOS	41	6	11	17	3	30	0	0	2	0	75	8.0
D	25	Hal Gill	BOS	76	4	13	17	21	56	0	0	0	0	114	3.5
L	17	Rob Zamuner	BOS	55	10	6	16	2	18	3	0	1	0	94	10.6
D	21	Sean O'Donnell	BOS	70	1	15	16	8	76	0	0	1	0	61	1.6
L	14	Sergei Samsonov	BOS	8	5	6	11	8	2	1	0	3	0	23	21.7
C	42	P.J. Stock	BOS	71	1	9	10	–5	160	1	0	0	0	38	2.6
D	32	Don Sweeney	BOS	67	3	5	8	–1	24	0	0	0	1	55	5.5
D	18	Ian Moran	PIT	70	0	7	7	–17	46	0	0	0	0	85	0.0
			BOS	8	0	1	1	–1	2	0	0	0	0	11	0.0
			TOTAL	78	0	8	8	–18	48	0	0	0	0	96	0.0
D	23	Sean Brown	BOS	69	1	5	6	–6	117	0	0	0	0	39	2.6
R	37	* Lee Goren	BOS	14	2	1	3	–2	7	2	0	0	0	15	13.3
C	29	* Andy Hilbert	BOS	14	0	3	3	–1	7	0	0	0	0	22	0.0
D	39	* Zdenek Kutlak	BOS	4	1	0	1	0	0	0	0	0	0	1	100.0
C	76	* Kris Vernarsky	BOS	14	1	0	1	–2	2	0	0	0	0	18	5.6
D	59	Rich Brennan	BOS	7	0	1	1	3	6	0	0	0	0	12	0.0
L	43	* Martin Samuelsson	BOS	8	0	1	1	–1	2	0	0	0	0	3	0.0
R	55	Brantt Myhres	BOS	1	0	0	0	0	31	0	0	0	0	0	0.0
D	64	Jarno Kultanen	BOS	2	0	0	0	1	0	0	0	0	0	3	0.0
C	63	Matt Herr	BOS	3	0	0	0	0	0	0	0	0	0	1	0.0
D	28	* Shaone Morrisonn	BOS	11	0	0	0	0	8	0	0	0	0	4	0.0
L	33	Krzysztof Oliwa	NYR	9	0	0	0	1	51	0	0	0	0	3	0.0
			BOS	33	0	0	0	–4	110	0	0	0	0	11	0.0
			TOTAL	42	0	0	0	–3	161	0	0	0	0	14	0.0

Goaltending

No.	Goaltender	GPI	Mins	Avg	W	L	T	EN	SO	GA	SA	S%	G	A	PIM
1	* Andrew Raycroft	5	300	2.40	2	3	0	0	0	12	146	.918	0	0	0
47	John Grahame	23	1352	2.71	11	9	2	0	1	61	625	.902	0	2	2
31	Steve Shields	36	2112	2.76	12	13	9	2	0	97	930	.896	0	0	8
70	Tim Thomas	4	220	3.00	3	1	0	0	0	11	118	.907	0	0	0
30	Jeff Hackett	18	991	3.21	8	9	0	1	1	53	500	.894	0	0	2
	Totals	**82**	**4993**	**2.85**	**36**	**35**	**11**	**3**	**2**	**237**	**2322**	**.898**			

Playoffs

Pos	#	Player	Team	GP	G	A	Pts	+/–	PIM	PP	SH	GW	GT	S	%
D	6	Dan McGillis	BOS	5	3	0	3	–2	2	2	0	1	0	9	33.3
C	19	Joe Thornton	BOS	5	1	2	3	–5	4	1	0	0	0	12	8.3
R	27	Glen Murray	BOS	5	1	1	2	–5	4	0	0	0	0	12	8.3
C	12	Brian Rolston	BOS	5	0	2	2	–1	0	0	0	0	0	6	0.0
C	16	Jozef Stumpel	BOS	5	0	2	2	0	0	0	0	0	0	9	0.0
R	26	Mike Knuble	BOS	5	0	2	2	–2	2	0	0	0	0	8	0.0
L	14	Sergei Samsonov	BOS	5	0	2	2	–1	0	0	0	0	0	10	0.0
D	34	Bryan Berard	BOS	3	1	0	1	–1	2	0	0	0	0	5	20.0
R	10	Marty McInnis	BOS	5	1	0	1	1	2	0	0	0	0	6	16.7
R	20	Martin Lapointe	BOS	5	1	0	1	–2	14	0	0	0	0	6	16.7
D	46	Jonathan Girard	BOS	2	0	1	1	–1	0	0	0	0	0	4	0.0
D	32	Don Sweeney	BOS	5	0	1	1	0	0	0	0	0	0	4	0.0
D	18	Ian Moran	BOS	5	0	1	1	–2	4	0	0	0	0	2	0.0
D	44	Nick Boynton	BOS	5	0	1	1	–2	4	0	0	0	0	12	0.0
L	17	Rob Zamuner	BOS	5	0	0	0	0	4	0	0	0	0	9	0.0
L	22	Michal Grosek	BOS	5	0	0	0	–1	13	0	0	0	0	3	0.0
D	25	Hal Gill	BOS	5	0	0	0	–1	4	0	0	0	0	10	0.0
L	11	P.J. Axelsson	BOS	5	0	0	0	–2	6	0	0	0	0	10	0.0
R	37	* Lee Goren	BOS	5	0	0	0	–1	5	0	0	0	0	3	0.0

Goaltending

No.	Goaltender	GPI	Mins	Avg	W	L	EN	SO	GA	SA	S%	G	A	PIM
30	Jeff Hackett	3	179	1.68	1	2	2	0	5	76	.934	0	0	0
31	Steve Shields	2	119	3.03	0	2	0	0	6	58	.897	0	0	0
	Totals	**5**	**300**	**2.60**	**1**	**4**	**2**	**0**	**13**	**136**	**.904**			

Captains' History

No captain, 1924-25 to 1926-27; Lionel Hitchman, 1927-28 to 1930-31; George Owen, 1931-32; Dit Clapper, 1932-33 to 1937-38; Cooney Weiland, 1938-39; Dit Clapper, 1939-40 to 1945-46; Dit Clapper and John Crawford, 1946-47; John Crawford 1947-48 to 1949-50; Milt Schmidt, 1950-51 to 1953-54; Milt Schmidt, Ed Sanford, 1954-55; Fern Flaman, 1955-56 to 1960-61; Don McKenney, 1961-62, 1962-63; Leo Boivin, 1963-64 to 1965-66; John Bucyk, 1966-67; no captain, 1967-68 to 1972-73; John Bucyk, 1973-74 to 1976-77; Wayne Cashman, 1977-78 to 1982-83; Terry O'Reilly, 1983-84, 1984-85; Raymond Bourque, Rick Middleton (co-captains) 1985-86 to 1987-88; Raymond Bourque, 1988-89 to 1999-2000; Jason Allison, 2000-01; no captain, 2001-02; Joe Thornton, 2002-03 to date.

Club Records

Team

(Figures in brackets for season records are games played; records for fewest points, wins, ties, losses, goals, goals against are for 70 or more games)

Most Points	121	1970-71 (78)
Most Wins	57	1970-71 (78)
Most Ties	21	1954-55 (70)
Most Losses	47	1961-62 (70), 1996-97 (82)
Most Goals	399	1970-71 (78)
Most Goals Against	306	1961-62 (70)
Fewest Points	38	1961-62 (70)
Fewest Wins	14	1962-63 (70)
Fewest Ties	5	1972-73 (78)
Fewest Losses	13	1971-72 (78)
Fewest Goals	147	1955-56 (70)
Fewest Goals Against	172	1952-53 (70)
Longest Winning Streak		
Overall	14	Dec. 3/29-Jan. 9/30
Home	*20	Dec. 3/29-Mar. 18/30
Away	8	Feb. 17-Mar. 8/72, Mar. 15-Apr. 14/93
Longest Undefeated Streak		
Overall	23	Dec. 22/40-Feb. 23/41 (15 wins, 8 ties)
Home	27	Nov. 22/70-Mar. 20/71 (26 wins, 1 tie)
Away	15	Dec. 22/40-Mar. 16/41 (9 wins, 6 ties)
Longest Losing Streak		
Overall	11	Dec. 3/24-Jan. 5/25
Home	*11	Dec. 8/24-Feb. 17/25
Away	14	Dec. 27/64-Feb. 21/65
Longest Winless Streak		
Overall	20	Jan. 28-Mar. 11/62 (16 losses, 4 ties)
Home	11	Dec. 8/24-Feb. 17/25 (11 losses)
Away	14	Three times
Most Shutouts, Season	15	1927-28 (44)
Most PIM, Season	2,443	1987-88 (80)
Most Goals, Game	14	Jan. 21/45 (NYR 3 at Bos. 14)

Individual

Most Seasons	21	John Bucyk, Raymond Bourque
Most Games	1,518	Raymond Bourque
Most Goals, Career	545	John Bucyk
Most Assists, Career	1,111	Raymond Bourque
Most Points, Career	1,506	Raymond Bourque (395G, 1,111A)
Most PIM, Career	2,095	Terry O'Reilly
Most Shutouts, Career	74	Tiny Thompson
Longest Consecutive Games Streak	418	John Bucyk (Jan. 23/69-Mar. 2/75)
Most Goals, Season	76	Phil Esposito (1970-71)
Most Assists, Season	102	Bobby Orr (1970-71)
Most Points, Season	152	Phil Esposito (1970-71; 76G, 76A)
Most PIM, Season	302	Jay Miller (1987-88)
Most Points, Defenseman, Season	*139	Bobby Orr (1970-71; 37G, 102A)
Most Points, Center, Season	152	Phil Esposito (1970-71; 76G, 76A)
Most Points, Right Wing, Season	105	Ken Hodge (1970-71; 43G, 62A), (1973-74; 50G, 55A), Rick Middleton (1983-84; 47G, 58A)
Most Points, Left Wing, Season	116	John Bucyk (1970-71; 51G, 65A)
Most Points, Rookie, Season	102	Joe Juneau (1992-93; 32G, 70A)
Most Shutouts, Season	15	Hal Winkler (1927-28)
Most Goals, Game	4	Twenty times
Most Assists, Game	6	Ken Hodge (Feb. 9/71), Bobby Orr (Jan. 1/73)
Most Points, Game	7	Bobby Orr (Nov. 15/73; 3G, 4A), Phil Esposito (Dec. 19/74; 3G, 4A), Barry Pederson (Apr. 4/82; 3G, 4A), Cam Neely (Oct. 16/88; 3G, 4A)

* NHL Record.

Retired Numbers

2	Eddie Shore	1926-1940
3	Lionel Hitchman	1925-1934
4	Bobby Orr	1966-1976
5	Dit Clapper	1927-1947
7	Phil Esposito	1967-1975
9	John Bucyk	1957-1978
15	Milt Schmidt	1936-1955
24	Terry O'Reilly	1971-1985
77	Raymond Bourque	1979-2000

All-time Record vs. Other Clubs

Regular Season

	At Home								On Road								Total							
	GP	W	L	T	OL	GF	GA	PTS	GP	W	L	T	OL	GF	GA	PTS	GP	W	L	T	OL	GF	GA	PTS
Anaheim	8	4	4	0	0	23	24	8	8	4	2	2	0	20	15	10	16	8	6	2	0	43	39	18
Atlanta	8	4	2	1	1	29	32	10	8	5	3	0	0	20	19	10	16	9	5	1	1	49	51	20
Buffalo	104	59	31	14	0	391	303	132	105	37	52	15	1	312	382	90	209	96	83	29	1	703	685	222
Calgary	46	28	11	6	1	165	125	63	44	22	18	4	0	154	160	48	90	50	29	10	1	319	285	111
Carolina	76	46	23	7	0	273	203	99	74	35	31	8	0	257	247	78	150	81	54	15	0	530	450	177
Chicago	284	161	89	34	0	1023	808	356	285	94	145	45	1	766	924	234	569	255	234	79	1	1789	1732	590
Colorado	62	31	21	9	1	240	192	72	65	35	24	6	0	267	233	76	127	66	45	15	1	507	425	148
Columbus	2	1	1	0	0	8	7	2	2	1	0	0	1	10	3	3	4	2	1	0	1	18	10	5
Dallas	59	40	9	10	0	254	145	90	60	29	17	13	1	218	175	72	119	69	26	23	1	472	320	162
Detroit	286	153	89	43	1	1005	760	350	284	78	153	52	1	717	952	209	570	231	242	95	2	1722	1712	559
Edmonton	29	20	6	3	0	122	77	43	29	15	11	3	0	97	98	33	58	35	17	6	0	219	175	76
Florida	20	8	8	4	0	55	53	20	19	10	8	0	1	56	55	21	39	18	16	4	1	111	108	41
Los Angeles	61	44	11	6	0	287	169	94	60	32	21	7	0	220	207	71	121	76	32	13	0	507	376	165
Minnesota	2	0	2	0	0	4	11	0	2	0	2	0	0	2	7	0	4	0	4	0	0	6	18	0
Montreal	332	154	122	56	0	985	898	364	331	96	189	46	0	786	1119	238	663	250	311	102	0	1771	2017	602
Nashville	4	2	1	1	0	13	7	5	5	3	1	0	1	13	11	7	9	5	2	1	1	26	18	12
New Jersey	54	31	14	7	2	213	163	71	51	25	13	11	2	164	136	63	105	56	27	18	4	377	299	134
NY Islanders	57	31	15	10	1	215	160	73	59	27	24	8	0	197	200	62	116	58	39	18	1	412	360	135
NY Rangers	296	158	95	42	1	1068	831	359	300	115	130	55	0	847	916	285	596	273	225	97	1	1915	1747	644
Ottawa	30	18	8	4	0	117	85	40	28	14	7	3	4	88	69	35	58	32	15	7	4	205	154	75
Philadelphia	74	45	18	10	1	279	208	101	71	30	31	10	0	205	235	70	145	75	49	20	1	484	443	171
Phoenix	29	22	4	3	0	133	89	47	30	14	13	3	0	102	101	31	59	36	17	6	0	235	190	78
Pittsburgh	76	54	16	6	0	336	216	114	78	32	31	15	0	278	267	79	154	86	47	21	0	614	483	193
St. Louis	59	35	14	9	1	247	161	80	58	23	24	9	2	195	184	57	117	58	38	18	3	442	345	137
San Jose	9	7	0	2	0	34	21	16	11	5	4	2	0	38	30	12	20	12	4	4	0	72	51	28
Tampa Bay	21	15	1	5	0	78	44	35	21	10	8	3	0	63	61	23	42	25	9	8	0	141	105	58
Toronto	295	160	87	47	1	964	775	368	296	90	155	51	0	760	999	231	591	250	242	98	1	1724	1774	599
Vancouver	51	37	7	7	0	215	123	81	51	27	16	8	0	209	166	62	102	64	23	15	0	424	289	143
Washington	54	31	15	8	0	203	146	70	53	25	15	12	1	183	148	63	107	56	30	20	1	386	294	133
Defunct Clubs	164	112	39	13	0	525	306	237	164	79	67	18	0	496	440	176	328	191	106	31	0	1021	746	413
Totals	**2652**	**1511**	**763**	**367**	**11**	**9504**	**7142**	**3400**	**2652**	**1012**	**1215**	**409**	**16**	**7740**	**8559**	**2449**	**5304**	**2523**	**1978**	**776**	**27**	**17244**	**15701**	**5849**

Playoffs

	Series	W	L	GP	W	L	T	GF	GA	Last Mtg.	Rnd.	Result
Buffalo	7	5	2	39	21	18	0	139	130	1999	CSF	L 2-4
Carolina	3	3	0	19	12	7	0	63	48	1999	CQF	W 4-2
Chicago	6	5	1	22	16	5	1	97	63	1978	QF	W 4-0
Colorado	2	1	1	11	6	5	0	37	36	1983	DSF	W 3-1
Dallas	1	0	1	3	0	3	0	13	20	1981	PRE	L 0-3
Detroit	7	4	3	33	19	14	0	96	98	1957	SF	W 4-1
Edmonton	2	0	2	9	1	8	0	20	41	1990	F	L 1-4
Florida	1	0	1	5	1	4	0	16	22	1996	CQF	L 1-4
Los Angeles	2	2	0	13	8	5	0	56	38	1977	QF	W 4-2
Montreal	29	7	22	145	54	91	0	357	450	2002	CQF	L 2-4
New Jersey	4	1	3	23	8	15	0	60	68	2003	CQF	L 1-4
NY Islanders	2	0	2	11	3	8	0	35	49	1983	CF	L 2-4
NY Rangers	9	6	3	42	22	18	2	114	104	1973	QF	L 1-4
Philadelphia	4	2	2	20	11	9	0	60	57	1978	SF	W 4-1
Pittsburgh	4	2	2	19	9	10	0	62	67	1992	CF	L 0-4
St. Louis	2	2	0	8	8	0	0	48	15	1972	SF	W 4-0
Toronto	13	5	8	62	30	31	1	153	150	1974	QF	W 4-0
Washington	2	1	1	10	6	4	0	28	21	1998	CQF	L 2-4
Defunct Clubs	3	1	2	11	4	5	2	20	20			
Totals	**103**	**47**	**56**	**505**	**239**	**260**	**6**	**1474**	**1497**			

Calgary totals include Atlanta Flames, 1972-73 to 1979-80. Carolina totals include Hartford, 1979-80 to 1996-97.
Colorado totals include Quebec, 1979-80 to 1994-95. Dallas totals include Minnesota North Stars, 1967-68 to 1992-93.
New Jersey totals include Kansas City, 1974-75 to 1975-76, and Colorado Rockies, 1976-77 to 1981-82.
Phoenix totals include Winnipeg, 1979-80 to 1995-96.

Playoff Results 2003-1999

Year	Round	Opponent	Result	GF	GA
2003	CQF	New Jersey	L 1-4	8	13
2002	CQF	Montreal	L 2-4	18	20
1999	CSF	Buffalo	L 2-4	14	17
	CQF	Carolina	W 4-2	16	10

Abbreviations: Round: F - Final;
CF - conference final; **CSF** - conference semi-final;
CQF - conference quarter-final;
DSF - division semi-final; **SF** - semi-final;
QF - quarter-final; **PRE** - preliminary round.

2002-03 Results

Oct.	11	at Minnesota	1-5
	14	at Colorado	2-1
	16	at Vancouver	6-3
	17	at Calgary	3-3
	19	at Edmonton	4-3
	21	at Toronto	4-1
	24	Ottawa	2-2
	26	Atlanta	4-3
	30	at Washington	7-2
	31	Anaheim	1-4
Nov.	2	NY Rangers	3-2
	7	at Detroit	1-2*
	9	Ottawa	7-1
	11	Edmonton	6-1
	12	at Buffalo	4-3
	14	NY Islanders	4-1
	16	at Philadelphia	2-2
	19	at Toronto	0-2
	21	Carolina	3-1
	23	Buffalo	4-1
	26	Calgary	7-2
	29	Montreal	4-2
	30	at Pittsburgh	3-2
Dec.	3	St. Louis	0-4
	5	Atlanta	4-3*
	7	Tampa Bay	3-2*
	8	at NY Rangers	4-1
	10	Montreal	2-4
	12	Ottawa	2-5
	14	at Montreal	2-4
	18	at Buffalo	2-4
	19	at Washington	3-5
	21	Florida	3-3
	23	San Jose	5-2
	27	at Tampa Bay	2-5
	28	at Atlanta	1-0
	30	New Jersey	0-1
Jan.	3	at NY Islanders	4-8
	4	Carolina	2-4
	7	at Toronto	2-5
	10	at Buffalo	2-4
	11	Toronto	6-2
	13	Pittsburgh	1-2
	15	at Florida	0-3
	17	at Atlanta	1-3
	18	Columbus	7-2
	20	Washington	3-3
	23	at Pittsburgh	4-1
	25	Philadelphia	1-0*
	28	Nashville	2-1
	30	Chicago	1-3
Feb.	4	Colorado	2-3*
	6	Montreal	6-3
	8	Pittsburgh	2-5
	11	at Montreal	1-3
	14	at Florida	6-5*
	15	at Tampa Bay	2-5
	17	at Nashville	1-5
	19	at Carolina	1-1
	21	at New Jersey	2-3
	23	at NY Islanders	4-4
	25	Dallas	5-5
	27	at NY Rangers	1-4
Mar.	1	Philadelphia	2-3*
	3	Vancouver	4-6
	4	at Carolina	4-2
	6	NY Islanders	4-1
	8	Washington	5-4*
	9	at Chicago	5-8
	11	at Ottawa	3-4*
	13	New Jersey	4-3
	15	Florida	4-1
	18	at Phoenix	1-2
	21	at San Jose	2-3
	22	at Los Angeles	4-3*
	24	Toronto	3-2
	27	at Philadelphia	2-2
	29	NY Rangers	1-3
	31	Tampa Bay	2-2
Apr.	1	at Ottawa	2-3
	3	at New Jersey	1-1
	5	Buffalo	8-5

* – Overtime

Entry Draft
Selections 2003-1989

2003
Pick
21	Mark Stuart
45	Patrice Bergeron
66	Masi Marjamaki
107	Byron Bitz
118	Frank Rediker
129	Patrik Valcak
153	Mike Brown
183	Nate Thompson
247	Benoit Mondou
277	Kevin Regan

2002
Pick
29	Hannu Toivonen
56	Vladislav Yevseyev
130	Jan Kubista
153	Peter Hamerlik
228	Dmitri Utkin
259	Yan Stastny
290	Pavel Frolov

2001
Pick
19	Shaone Morrisonn
77	Darren McLachlan
111	Matti Kaltiainen
147	Jiri Jakes
179	Andrew Alberts
209	Jordan Sigalet
241	Milan Jurcina
282	Marcel Rodman

2000
Pick
7	Lars Jonsson
27	Martin Samuelsson
37	Andy Hilbert
59	Ivan Huml
66	Tuukka Makela
73	Sergei Zinovjev
102	Brett Nowak
174	Jarno Kultanen
204	Chris Berti
237	Zdenek Kutlak
268	Pavel Kolarik
279	Andreas Lindstrom

1999
Pick
21	Nick Boynton
56	Matt Zultek
89	Kyle Wanvig
118	Jaakko Harikkala
147	Seamus Kotyk
179	Donald Choukalos
207	Greg Barber
236	John Cronin
247	Mikko Eloranta
264	Georgy Pujacs

1998
Pick
48	Jonathan Girard
52	Bobby Allen
78	Peter Nordstrom
135	Andrew Raycroft
165	Ryan Milanovic

1997
Pick
1	Joe Thornton
8	Sergei Samsonov
27	Ben Clymer
54	Mattias Karlin
63	Lee Goren
81	Karol Bartanus
135	Denis Timofeev
162	Joel Trottier
180	Jim Baxter
191	Antti Laaksonen
218	Eric Van Acker
246	Jay Henderson

1996
Pick
8	Johnathan Aitken
45	Henry Kuster
53	Eric Naud
80	Jason Doyle
100	Trent Whitfield
132	Elias Abrahamsson
155	Chris Lane
182	Thomas Brown
208	Bob Prier
234	Anders Soderberg

1995
Pick
9	Kyle McLaren
21	Sean Brown
47	Paxton Schafer
73	Bill McCauley
99	Cameron Mann
151	Yevgeny Shaldybin
177	P.J. Axelsson
203	Sergei Zhukov
229	Jonathon Murphy

1994
Pick
21	Evgeni Ryabchikov
47	Daniel Goneau
99	Eric Nickulas
125	Darren Wright
151	Andre Roy
177	Jeremy Schaefer
229	John Grahame
255	Neil Savary
281	Andrei Yakhanov

1993
Pick
25	Kevyn Adams
51	Matt Alvey
88	Charles Paquette
103	Shawn Bates
129	Andrei Sapozhnikov
155	Milt Mastad
181	Ryan Golden
207	Hal Gill
233	Joel Prpic
259	Joakim Persson

1992
Pick
16	Dmitri Kvartalnov
55	Sergei Zholtok
112	Scott Bailey
133	Jiri Dopita
136	Grigori Panteleev
184	Kurt Seher
208	Mattias Timander
232	Chris Crombie
256	Denis Chervyakov
257	Evgeny Pavlov

1991
Pick
18	Glen Murray
40	Jozef Stumpel
62	Marcel Cousineau
84	Brad Tiley
106	Mariusz Czerkawski
150	Gary Golczewski
172	Jay Moser
194	Daniel Hodge
216	Steve Norton
238	Stephen Lombardi
260	Torsten Kienass

1990
Pick
21	Bryan Smolinski
63	Cam Stewart
84	Jerome Buckley
105	Mike Bales
126	Mark Woolf
147	Jim Mackey
168	John Gruden
189	Darren Wetherill
210	Dean Capuano
231	Andy Bezeau
252	Ted Miskolczi

1989
Pick
17	Shayne Stevenson
38	Mike Parson
57	Wes Walz
80	Jackson Penney
101	Mark Montanari
122	Stephen Foster
143	Otto Hascak
164	Rick Allain
185	James Lavish
206	Geoff Simpson
227	David Franzosa

Vice President and General Manager

O'CONNELL, MIKE
Vice President/General Manager, Boston Bruins.
Born in Chicago, IL, November 25, 1955.

Mike O'Connell was named the general manager of the Boston Bruins on November 1, 2000, becoming just the sixth man in club history to hold that position. He was involved in all aspects of the on-ice operation of the hockey team over the previous six seasons as the team's assistant general manager and was instrumental in bringing much of the young talent into the organization.

O'Connell's experience as both a player and assistant coach in the National Hockey League, and as a head coach in both the American and International Hockey Leagues, dates back to the 1977-78 season. Raised in Cohasset, MA, he played two years of high school hockey at Archbishop Williams High School in Braintree, MA. He then made what at the time was an unusual move for an American player, jumping to the Ontario Hockey League to play Canadian major junior hockey at the suggestion of Harry Sinden and Tom Johnson. The move proved beneficial as, after two seasons with Kingston of the OHL, he was drafted by Chicago 43rd overall in the 1975 NHL Amateur Draft.

He turned professional with the Blackhawks organization in 1975 and played five-plus seasons with Chicago and their Central Hockey League affiliate in Dallas before coming to Boston on December 18, 1980, in a trade for Al Secord. He enjoyed his best NHL seasons during his six years in a Bruins uniform, recording 50+ point campaigns for three straight years from 1982 to 1985 and representing the team in the 1984 NHL All-Star Game in New Jersey. He was traded to Detroit for Reed Larson on March 10, 1986 and concluded his playing career with the Red Wings at the end of the 1989-90 season.

O'Connell then moved into the coaching ranks, assuming the head coaching position for the IHL's San Diego Gulls in 1990-91. He then returned to the NHL, with Boston as an assistant coach. On June 12, 1992, he was named as the head coach of Boston's American Hockey League affiliate in Providence. Working with many players who also wore a Boston uniform during his tenure, he compiled a 74-71-15 record over a two-year span and won a Northern Division title in 1992-93. He then returned to Boston when he was named the club's assistant general manager on July 5, 1994. He was named as a vice president of the team in 1998. During the 2002-03 season, O'Connell took over behind the bench late in the season.

NHL Coaching Record

Season	Team	Games	Regular Season W	L	T	Playoffs Games	W	L
2002-03	Boston	9	3	3	3	5	1	4
	NHL Totals	9	3	3	3	5	1	4

Club Directory

FleetCenter

Boston Bruins
One FleetCenter Place, Suite 250
Boston, MA 02114
Phone **617/624-1900**
FAX 617/523-7184
www.bostonbruins.com
Capacity: 17,565

Executive
Owner and Governor	Jeremy M. Jacobs
Alternate Governor	Louis Jacobs, Charles Jacobs, Jeremy Jacobs Jr.
President and Alternate Governor	Harry Sinden
Senior Assistant to the President	Nate Greenberg
Chief Legal Officer	Michael Wall
Chief Financial Officer	Jessica Rahuba
Vice President, General Manager and Alternate Governor	Mike O'Connell
Assistant General Manager	Jeff Gorton
Executive Vice President	Charles Jacobs
Executive Vice President	Richard Krezwick
Director of Administration	Dale Hamilton-Powers
Assistant to the President	Joe Curnane
Assistant Director of Administration/ Travel Coordinator	Carol Gould
Executive Secretary	Rita Brandano
Administrative Assistant	Karen Ondo

Coaching Staff
Head Coach	Mike Sullivan
Assistant Coaches	Wayne Cashman, Norm Maciver
Video Coordinator	Brant Berglund
Team Road Services Coordinator	John Bucyk
Coach, Providence Bruins	Scott Gordon

Scouting Staff
Director of Pro Scouting & Player Development	Sean Coady
Director of Amateur Scouting	Scott Bradley
Scouting Staff	Nikolai Bobrov, Adam Creighton, Gerry Cheevers, Daniel Dore, Don Matheson, Mike McGraw, Tom McVie, Tom Songin, Svenake Svensson

Medical & Training Staff
Strength and Conditioning Coach	John Whitesides
Athletic Trainer	Don DelNegro
Physical Therapist	Scott Waugh
Equipment Manager	Peter Henderson
Assistant Equipment Managers	Chris "Muggsy" Aldrich, Keith Robinson

Communications & Marketing Staff
Director of Media Relations	Heidi Holland
Media Relations Manager	Ryan Nadeau
Director of Marketing & Community Relations	Sue Byrne
Promotions Manager	Dave Murray
Community Relations Coordinator	TBA
Game Presentation and Marketing Coordinator	TBA
Administrative Assistant, Alumni Office	Mal Viola

Ticketing & Finance Staff
Director of Ticket Operations	Matt Brennan
Assistant Director of Ticket Operations	Jim Foley
Ticket Office Receptionist	Jo-Ann Connolly-White
Controller	Rick McGlinchey
Accountant, Payroll & Benefits	Audrey Horgan
Accounts Payable	Linda Bartlett

General Managers' History

Art Ross, 1924-25 to 1953-54; Lynn Patrick, 1954-55 to 1964-65; Hap Emms, 1965-66, 1966-67; Milt Schmidt, 1967-68 to 1971-72; Harry Sinden, 1972-73 to 1999-2000; Harry Sinden and Mike O'Connell, 2000-01; Mike O'Connell, 2001-02 to date.

Coaching History

Art Ross, 1924-25 to 1927-28; Cy Denneny, 1928-29; Art Ross, 1929-30 to 1933-34; Frank Patrick, 1934-35, 1935-36; Art Ross, 1936-37 to 1938-39; Cooney Weiland, 1939-40, 1940-41; Art Ross, 1941-42 to 1944-45; Dit Clapper, 1945-46 to 1948-49; Georges Boucher, 1949-50; Lynn Patrick, 1950-51 to 1953-54; Lynn Patrick and Milt Schmidt, 1954-55; Milt Schmidt, 1955-56 to 1960-61; Phil Watson, 1961-62; Phil Watson and Milt Schmidt, 1962-63; Milt Schmidt, 1963-64 to 1965-66; Harry Sinden, 1966-67 to 1969-70; Tom Johnson, 1970-71, 1971-72; Tom Johnson and Bep Guidolin, 1972-73; Bep Guidolin, 1973-74; Don Cherry, 1974-75 to 1978-79; Fred Creighton and Harry Sinden, 1979-80; Gerry Cheevers, 1980-81 to 1983-84; Gerry Cheevers and Harry Sinden, 1984-85; Butch Goring, 1985-86; Butch Goring and Terry O'Reilly, 1986-87; Terry O'Reilly, 1987-88, 1988-89; Mike Milbury, 1989-90, 1990-91; Rick Bowness, 1991-92; Brian Sutter, 1992-93 to 1994-95; Steve Kasper, 1995-96, 1996-97; Pat Burns, 1997-98 to 1999-2000; Pat Burns and Mike Keenan, 2000-01; Robbie Ftorek, 2001-02; Robbie Ftorek and Mike O'Connell, 2002-03; Mike Sullivan, 2003-04.

Buffalo Sabres

2002-03 Results: 27w-37L-10T-8OTL 72PTS.
Fifth, Northeast Division

2003-04 Schedule

Oct.	Thu.	9	at Philadelphia		Wed.	7	Philadelphia
	Sat.	11	NY Islanders		Fri.	9	Ottawa
	Mon.	13	Dallas*		Mon.	12	at Boston
	Thu.	16	at Edmonton		Tue.	13	Philadelphia
	Sat.	18	at Calgary		Thu.	15	Boston
	Mon.	20	at Vancouver		Sat.	17	at NY Islanders
	Thu.	23	at Los Angeles		Tue.	20	at Atlanta
	Fri.	24	at Anaheim		Thu.	22	at Boston
	Sun.	26	at Colorado		Sat.	24	at Philadelphia*
	Tue.	28	Minnesota		Sun.	25	at Carolina*
	Thu.	30	Toronto		Tue.	27	Montreal
Nov.	Sat.	1	at Ottawa		Fri.	30	at NY Rangers
	Wed.	5	Atlanta		Sat.	31	NY Rangers
	Fri.	7	Montreal	**Feb.**	Thu.	5	Boston
	Sat.	8	at Montreal		Tue.	10	San Jose
	Wed.	12	New Jersey		Fri.	13	Los Angeles
	Fri.	14	Pittsburgh		Sat.	14	at Toronto
	Mon.	17	at Ottawa		Mon.	16	Atlanta*
	Wed.	19	at New Jersey		Wed.	18	Florida
	Fri.	21	Carolina		Fri.	20	Tampa Bay
	Sat.	22	at Tampa Bay		Sat.	21	at NY Islanders
	Mon.	24	at Florida		Wed.	25	at New Jersey
	Wed.	26	Washington		Fri.	27	NY Islanders
	Fri.	28	Florida		Sat.	28	at Ottawa
	Sat.	29	at Nashville	**Mar.**	Wed.	3	Ottawa
Dec.	Wed.	3	at Chicago		Sat.	6	at Toronto
	Thu.	4	Phoenix		Sun.	7	St. Louis
	Sat.	6	Tampa Bay		Wed.	10	at Washington
	Wed.	10	Detroit		Thu.	11	Boston
	Fri.	12	NY Rangers		Sat.	13	at Boston*
	Sat.	13	at Minnesota		Mon.	15	Toronto
	Tue.	16	at Pittsburgh		Wed.	17	at Atlanta
	Fri.	19	New Jersey		Thu.	18	at Tampa Bay
	Tue.	23	Ottawa		Sat.	20	at Florida
	Fri.	26	Carolina		Wed.	24	Montreal
	Sat.	27	at Washington		Fri.	26	Pittsburgh
	Mon.	29	at Carolina		Sat.	27	at Pittsburgh
	Wed.	31	Washington		Mon.	29	Columbus
Jan.	Fri.	2	Anaheim		Wed.	31	at NY Rangers
	Sat.	3	at Toronto	**Apr.**	Fri.	2	Toronto
	Tue.	6	at Montreal		Sat.	3	at Montreal

Denotes afternoon game.

Franchise date: May 22, 1970

NORTHEAST DIVISION

34th NHL Season

In his first season with the Sabres, Jochen Hecht played just 49 games but still finished seventh in team scoring with 10 goals and 16 assists. Hecht has represented Germany nine times in international play, including the Olympics in 1998 and 2002.

Year-by-Year Record

		Home				Road				Overall								
Season	GP	W	L	T	OL	W	L	T	OL	W	L	T	OL	GF	GA	Pts.	Finished	Playoff Result
2002-03	82	18	16	5	2	9	21	5	6	27	37	10	8	190	219	72	5th, Northeast Div.	Out of Playoffs
2001-02	82	20	16	5	0	15	19	6	1	35	35	11	1	213	200	82	5th, Northeast Div.	Out of Playoffs
2000-01	82	26	12	3	0	20	18	2	1	46	30	5	1	218	184	98	2nd, Northeast Div.	Lost Conf. Semi-Final
1999-2000	82	21	14	5	1	14	18	6	3	35	32	11	4	213	204	85	3rd, Northeast Div.	Lost Conf. Quarter-Final
1998-99	82	23	12	6	...	14	16	11	...	37	28	17	...	207	175	91	4th, Northeast Div.	Lost Final
1997-98	82	20	13	8	...	16	16	9	...	36	29	17	...	211	187	89	3rd, Northeast Div.	Lost Conf. Final
1996-97	82	24	11	6	...	16	19	6	...	40	30	12	...	237	208	92	1st, Northeast Div.	Lost Conf. Semi-Final
1995-96	82	19	17	5	...	14	25	2	...	33	42	7	...	247	262	73	5th, Northeast Div.	Out of Playoffs
1994-95	48	15	8	1	...	7	11	6	...	22	19	7	...	130	119	51	4th, Northeast Div.	Lost Conf. Quarter-Final
1993-94	84	22	17	3	...	21	15	6	...	43	32	9	...	282	218	95	4th, Northeast Div.	Lost Conf. Quarter-Final
1992-93	84	24	15	2	...	13	21	8	...	38	36	10	...	335	297	86	4th, Adams Div.	Lost Div. Final
1991-92	80	22	13	5	...	9	24	7	...	31	37	12	...	289	299	74	3rd, Adams Div.	Lost Div. Semi-Final
1990-91	80	15	13	12	...	16	17	7	...	31	30	19	...	292	278	81	3rd, Adams Div.	Lost Div. Semi-Final
1989-90	80	27	11	2	...	18	16	6	...	45	27	8	...	286	248	98	2nd, Adams Div.	Lost Div. Semi-Final
1988-89	80	25	12	3	...	13	23	4	...	38	35	7	...	291	299	83	3rd, Adams Div.	Lost Div. Semi-Final
1987-88	80	19	14	7	...	18	18	4	...	37	32	11	...	283	305	85	3rd, Adams Div.	Lost Div. Semi-Final
1986-87	80	18	18	4	...	10	26	4	...	28	44	8	...	280	308	64	5th, Adams Div.	Out of Playoffs
1985-86	80	23	16	1	...	14	21	5	...	37	37	6	...	296	291	80	5th, Adams Div.	Out of Playoffs
1984-85	80	23	10	7	...	15	18	7	...	38	28	14	...	290	237	90	3rd, Adams Div.	Lost Div. Semi-Final
1983-84	80	25	9	6	...	23	16	1	...	48	25	7	...	315	257	103	2nd, Adams Div.	Lost Div. Semi-Final
1982-83	80	25	7	8	...	13	22	5	...	38	29	13	...	318	285	89	3rd, Adams Div.	Lost Div. Final
1981-82	80	23	8	9	...	16	18	6	...	39	26	15	...	307	273	93	3rd, Adams Div.	Lost Div. Semi-Final
1980-81	80	21	7	12	...	18	13	9	...	39	20	21	...	327	250	99	1st, Adams Div.	Lost Quarter-Final
1979-80	80	27	5	8	...	20	12	8	...	47	17	16	...	318	201	110	1st, Adams Div.	Lost Semi-Final
1978-79	80	19	13	8	...	17	15	8	...	36	28	16	...	280	263	88	2nd, Adams Div.	Lost Prelim. Round
1977-78	80	25	7	8	...	19	12	9	...	44	19	17	...	288	215	105	2nd, Adams Div.	Lost Quarter-Final
1976-77	80	27	8	5	...	21	16	3	...	48	24	8	...	301	220	104	2nd, Adams Div.	Lost Quarter-Final
1975-76	80	28	7	5	...	18	14	8	...	46	21	13	...	339	240	105	2nd, Adams Div.	Lost Quarter-Final
1974-75	80	28	6	6	...	21	10	9	...	49	16	15	...	354	240	113	1st, Adams Div.	Lost Final
1973-74	78	23	10	6	...	9	24	6	...	32	34	12	...	242	250	76	5th, East Div.	Out of Playoffs
1972-73	78	30	6	3	...	7	21	11	...	37	27	14	...	257	219	88	4th, East Div.	Lost Quarter-Final
1971-72	78	11	19	9	...	5	24	10	...	16	43	19	...	203	289	51	6th, East Div.	Out of Playoffs
1970-71	78	16	13	10	...	8	26	5	...	24	39	15	...	217	291	63	5th, East Div.	Out of Playoffs

2003-04 Player Personnel

FORWARDS	HT	WT	S	Place of Birth	Date	2002-03 Club
AFINOGENOV, Maxim	6-0	190	L	Moscow, USSR	9/4/79	Buffalo
BEGIN, Steve	5-11	190	L	Trois-Rivieres, Que.	6/14/78	Calgary
BOTTERILL, Jason	6-4	220	L	Edmonton, Alta.	5/19/76	Buffalo-Rochester
BOULTON, Eric	6-0	222	L	Halifax, N.S.	8/17/76	Buffalo
BRIERE, Daniel	5-10	178	R	Gatineau, Que.	10/6/77	Phoenix-Buffalo
BROWN, Curtis	6-0	197	L	Unity, Sask.	2/12/76	Buffalo
CONNOLLY, Tim	6-1	182	R	Syracuse, NY	5/7/81	Buffalo
DRURY, Chris	5-10	180	R	Trumbull, CT	8/20/76	Calgary
DUMONT, J.P.	6-1	205	L	Montreal, Que.	4/1/78	Buffalo
HECHT, Jochen	6-1	200	L	Mannheim, W. Germany	6/21/77	Buffalo
KOTALIK, Ales	6-1	217	R	Jindrichuv Hradec, Czech.	12/23/78	Buffalo-Rochester
MAIR, Adam	6-2	215	R	Hamilton, Ont.	2/15/79	Buffalo
MROZIK, Rick	6-2	185	L	Duluth, MN	1/2/75	Calgary-Saint John
PYATT, Taylor	6-4	222	L	Thunder Bay, Ont.	8/19/81	Buffalo
ROY, Derek	5-9	186	L	Ottawa, Ont.	5/4/83	Kitchener
SATAN, Miroslav	6-3	190	L	Topolcany, Czech.	10/22/74	Buffalo
TAYLOR, Chris	6-2	192	L	Stratford, Ont.	3/6/72	Buffalo-Rochester

DEFENSEMEN	HT	WT	S	Place of Birth	Date	2002-03 Club
BOUCHARD, Joel	6-1	209	L	Montreal, Que.	1/23/74	NY Rangers-Hartford-Pittsburgh
CAMPBELL, Brian	6-0	190	L	Strathroy, Ont.	5/23/79	Buffalo
CHAPMAN, Brian	6-1	195	L	Brockville, Ont.	2/10/68	Manitoba
DELMORE, Andy	6-1	200	R	LaSalle, Ont.	12/26/76	Nashville
FITZPATRICK, Rory	6-2	215	R	Rochester, NY	1/11/75	Buffalo-Rochester
KALININ, Dmitri	6-3	215	L	Chelyabinsk, USSR	7/22/80	Buffalo-Rochester
McKEE, Jay	6-4	212	L	Kingston, Ont.	9/8/77	Buffalo
PATRICK, James	6-2	202	R	Winnipeg, Man.	6/14/63	Buffalo
TALLINDER, Henrik	6-3	210	L	Stockholm, Sweden	1/10/79	Buffalo
ZHITNIK, Alexei	5-11	215	L	Kiev, USSR	10/10/72	Buffalo

GOALTENDERS	HT	WT	C	Place of Birth	Date	2002-03 Club
BIRON, Martin	6-2	168	L	Lac-St-Charles, Que.	8/15/77	Buffalo
MILLER, Ryan	6-2	150	L	East Lansing, MI	7/17/80	Rochester-Buffalo
NORONEN, Mika	6-2	196	L	Tampere, Finland	6/17/79	Buffalo-Rochester

Coaching History

Punch Imlach, 1970-71; Punch Imlach, Floyd Smith and Joe Crozier, 1971-72; Joe Crozier, 1972-73, 1973-74; Floyd Smith, 1974-75 to 1976-77; Marcel Pronovost, 1977-78; Marcel Pronovost and Billy Inglis, 1978-79; Scotty Bowman, 1979-80; Roger Neilson, 1980-81; Jim Roberts and Scotty Bowman, 1981-82; Scotty Bowman 1982-83 to 1984-85; Jim Schoenfeld and Scotty Bowman, 1985-86; Scotty Bowman, Craig Ramsay and Ted Sator, 1986-87; Ted Sator, 1987-88, 1988-89; Rick Dudley, 1989-90, 1990-91; Rick Dudley and John Muckler, 1991-92; John Muckler, 1992-93 to 1994-95; Ted Nolan, 1995-96, 1996-97; Lindy Ruff, 1997-98 to date.

Head Coach

RUFF, LINDY
Head Coach, Buffalo Sabres. Born in Warburg, Alta., February, 17, 1960.
A former captain of the Sabres, Lindy Ruff was appointed as the club's 15th head coach on July 21, 1997. In 1999, he led the Sabres to the Stanley Cup Finals for just the second time in club history. With 216 victories in six seasons behind the bench, Ruff has surpassed Scotty Bowman (210) as the winningest coach in Sabres history. As a player, Ruff was drafted 32nd overall by the Sabres in the 1979 Entry Draft. He played both defense and left wing in an NHL career that spanned 12 seasons including 608 regular-season games with Buffalo. He became a playing assistant coach with Rochester of the AHL in 1991-92 and San Diego of the IHL in 1992-93. Ruff's San Diego club set a pro hockey record with 62 wins. In 1993-94 he became an NHL assistant coach with the Florida Panthers.

Coaching Record

Season	Team	Games	Regular Season W	L	T	Playoffs Games	W	L
1997-98	Buffalo (NHL)	82	36	29	17	15	10	5
1998-99	Buffalo (NHL)	82	37	28	17	21	14	7
1999-2000	Buffalo (NHL)	82	35	36	11	5	1	4
2000-01	Buffalo (NHL)	82	46	31	5	13	7	6
2001-02	Buffalo (NHL)	82	35	36	11	....	....	....
2002-03	Buffalo (NHL)	82	27	45	10	....	....	....
	NHL Totals	492	216	205	71	54	32	22

2002-03 Scoring
* - rookie

Regular Season

Pos	#	Player	Team	GP	G	A	Pts	+/−	PIM	PP	SH	GW	GT	S	%
R	81	Miroslav Satan	BUF	79	26	49	75	−3	20	11	1	3	1	240	10.8
C	48	Daniel Briere	PHX	68	17	29	46	−21	50	4	0	3	1	142	12.0
			BUF	14	7	5	12	1	12	5	0	1	0	39	17.9
			TOTAL	82	24	34	58	−20	62	9	0	4	1	181	13.3
R	12 *	Ales Kotalik	BUF	68	21	14	35	−2	30	4	0	2	2	138	15.2
R	17	Jean-Pierre Dumont	BUF	76	14	21	35	−14	44	2	0	2	0	135	10.4
C	37	Curtis Brown	BUF	74	15	16	31	4	40	3	4	4	0	144	10.4
L	24	Taylor Pyatt	BUF	78	14	14	28	−8	38	2	0	0	0	110	12.7
L	71	Jochen Hecht	BUF	49	10	16	26	4	30	2	0	2	0	145	6.9
C	18	Tim Connolly	BUF	80	12	13	25	−28	32	6	0	2	0	159	7.5
D	45	Dmitri Kalinin	BUF	65	8	13	21	−7	57	3	1	0	1	83	9.6
D	44	Alexei Zhitnik	BUF	70	3	18	21	−5	85	0	0	1	0	138	2.2
D	51	Brian Campbell	BUF	65	2	19	21	−8	20	0	0	1	0	90	2.2
C	22	Adam Mair	BUF	79	6	11	17	−4	146	0	1	1	0	83	7.2
D	3	James Patrick	BUF	69	4	12	16	−3	26	2	0	1	0	63	6.3
D	10 *	Henrik Tallinder	BUF	46	3	10	13	−3	28	1	0	0	0	37	8.1
R	61	Maxim Afinogenov	BUF	35	5	6	11	−12	21	2	0	2	0	77	6.5
D	4	Rhett Warrener	BUF	50	0	9	9	1	63	0	0	0	0	47	0.0
L	26	Eric Boulton	BUF	58	1	5	6	1	178	0	0	0	0	33	3.0
L	28	Jason Botterill	BUF	17	1	4	5	1	14	1	0	0	0	20	5.0
D	74	Jay McKee	BUF	59	0	5	5	−16	49	0	0	0	0	44	0.0
C	16	Chris Taylor	BUF	11	1	3	4	−1	2	0	0	0	0	10	10.0
R	8	Rory Fitzpatrick	BUF	36	1	3	4	−7	16	0	0	0	0	29	3.4
R	55	Denis Hamel	BUF	25	2	0	2	−4	17	0	0	1	0	41	4.9
R	19 *	Norman Milley	BUF	8	0	2	2	−2	6	0	0	0	0	8	0.0
R	15 *	Milan Bartovic	BUF	3	1	0	1	0	0	0	0	0	0	5	20.0
D	6	Doug Houda	BUF	1	0	0	0	−2	2	0	0	0	0	1	0.0
C	60 *	Paul Gaustad	BUF	1	0	0	0	0	0	0	0	0	0	0	0.0
R	23 *	Sean McMorrow	BUF	1	0	0	0	0	0	0	0	0	0	0	0.0
R	29 *	Jaroslav Kristek	BUF	6	0	0	0	−2	4	0	0	0	0	4	0.0
D	33 *	Doug Janik	BUF	6	0	0	0	1	2	0	0	0	0	0	0.0
D	21	Radoslav Hecl	BUF	14	0	0	0	0	2	0	0	0	0	3	0.0

Goaltending

No.	Goaltender	GPI	Mins	Avg	W	L	T	EN	SO	GA	SA	S%	G	A	PIM
35	* Mika Noronen	16	891	2.42	4	9	3	2	1	36	411	.912	0	0	0
43	Martin Biron	54	3170	2.56	17	28	6	5	4	135	1468	.908	0	1	12
30	* Ryan Miller	15	912	2.63	6	8	1	1	1	40	410	.902	0	0	0
	Totals	82	5002	2.63	27	45	10	8	6	219	2297	.905			

Miroslav Satan led the Sabres in goals, assists, points and power-play goals for the second straight season. Satan has been the Sabres' top scorer four times in his six full seasons with Buffalo.

Captains' History

Floyd Smith, 1970-71; Gerry Meehan, 1971-72 to 1973-74; Gerry Meehan and Jim Schoenfeld, 1974-75; Jim Schoenfeld, 1975-76, 1976-77; Danny Gare, 1977-78 to 1980-81; Danny Gare and Gilbert Perreault, 1981-82; Gilbert Perreault, 1982-83 to 1985-86; Gilbert Perreault and Lindy Ruff, 1986-87; Lindy Ruff and Mike Foligno, 1988-89; Mike Foligno, 1989-90; Mike Foligno and Mike Ramsey, 1990-91; Mike Ramsey, 1991-92; Mike Ramsey and Pat LaFontaine, 1992-93; Pat LaFontaine and Alexander Mogilny, 1993-94; Pat LaFontaine, 1994-95 to 1996-97; Donald Audette and Michael Peca, 1997-98; Michael Peca, 1998-99, 1999-2000; no captain, 2000-01; Stu Barnes. 2001-02, 2002-03.

Club Records

Team

(Figures in brackets for season records are games played; records for fewest points, wins, ties, losses, goals, goals against are for 70 or more games)

Most Points .... 113 — 1974-75 (80)
Most Wins .... 49 — 1974-75 (80)
Most Ties .... 21 — 1980-81 (80)
Most Losses .... 44 — 1986-87 (80)
Most Goals .... 354 — 1974-75 (80)
Most Goals Against .... 308 — 1986-87 (80)
Fewest Points .... 51 — 1971-72 (78)
Fewest Wins .... 16 — 1971-72 (78)
Fewest Ties .... 5 — 2000-01 (82)
Fewest Losses .... 16 — 1974-75 (80)
Fewest Goals .... 190 — 2002-03 (82)
Fewest Goals Against .... 175 — 1998-99 (82)

Longest Winning Streak
Overall .... 10 — Jan. 4-23/84
Home .... 12 — Nov. 12/72-Jan. 7/73, Oct. 13-Dec. 10/89
Away .... *10 — Dec. 10/83-Jan. 23/84

Longest Undefeated Streak
Overall .... 14 — Mar. 6-Apr. 6/80 (8 wins, 6 ties)
Home .... 21 — Oct. 8/72-Jan. 7/73 (18 wins, 3 ties)
Away .... 10 — Dec. 10/83-Jan. 23/84 (10 wins)

Longest Losing Streak
Overall .... 7 — Oct. 25-Nov. 8/70, Apr. 3-15/93, Oct. 9-22/93
Home .... 6 — Oct. 10-Nov. 10/93, Mar. 3-Apr. 3/96
Away .... 7 — Oct. 14-Nov. 7/70, Feb. 6-27/71, Jan. 10-Feb. 3/96

Longest Winless Streak
Overall .... 12 — Nov. 23-Dec. 20/91 (8 losses, 4 ties)
Home .... 12 — Jan. 27-Mar. 10/91 (7 losses, 5 ties)
Away .... 23 — Oct. 30/71-Feb. 19/72 (15 losses, 8 ties)

Most Shutouts, Season .... 13 — 1997-98 (82)
Most PIM, Season .... *2,713 — 1991-92 (80)
Most Goals, Game .... 14 — Jan. 21/75 (Wsh. 2 at Buf. 14), Mar. 19/81 (Tor. 4 at Buf. 14)

Individual

Most Seasons .... 17 — Gilbert Perreault
Most Games .... 1,191 — Gilbert Perreault
Most Goals, Career .... 512 — Gilbert Perreault
Most Assists, Career .... 814 — Gilbert Perreault
Most Points, Career .... 1,326 — Gilbert Perreault (512G, 814A)
Most PIM, Career .... 3,189 — Rob Ray
Most Shutouts, Career .... 55 — Dominik Hasek
Longest Consecutive Games Streak .... 776 — Craig Ramsay (Mar. 27/73-Feb. 10/83)
Most Goals, Season .... 76 — Alexander Mogilny (1992-93)
Most Assists, Season .... 95 — Pat LaFontaine (1992-93)
Most Points, Season .... 148 — Pat LaFontaine (1992-93; 53G, 95A)
Most PIM, Season .... 354 — Rob Ray (1991-92)
Most Points, Defenseman, Season .... 81 — Phil Housley (1989-90; 21G, 60A)
Most Points, Center, Season .... 148 — Pat LaFontaine (1992-93; 53G, 95A)
Most Points, Right Wing, Season .... 127 — Alexander Mogilny (1992-93; 76G, 51A)
Most Points, Left Wing, Season .... 95 — Rick Martin (1974-75; 52G, 43A)
Most Points, Rookie, Season .... 74 — Rick Martin (1971-72; 44G, 30A)
Most Shutouts, Season .... 13 — Dominik Hasek (1997-98)
Most Goals, Game .... 5 — Dave Andreychuk (Feb. 6/86)
Most Assists, Game .... 5 — Gilbert Perreault (Feb. 1/76, Mar. 9/80, Jan. 4/84), Dale Hawerchuk (Jan. 15/92), Pat LaFontaine (Dec. 31/92, Feb. 10/93)
Most Points, Game .... 7 — Gilbert Perreault (Feb. 1/76; 2G, 5A)

* NHL Record.

Retired Numbers

2	Tim Horton	1972-1974
7	Rick Martin	1971-1981
11	Gilbert Perreault	1970-1987
14	Rene Robert	1971-1979

All-time Record vs. Other Clubs

Regular Season

	At Home								On Road								Total							
	GP	W	L	T	OL	GF	GA	PTS	GP	W	L	T	OL	GF	GA	PTS	GP	W	L	T	OL	GF	GA	PTS
Anaheim	8	3	2	3	0	20	18	9	8	6	2	0	0	25	13	12	16	9	4	3	0	45	31	21
Atlanta	8	5	3	0	0	32	20	10	8	2	4	1	1	26	24	6	16	7	7	1	1	58	44	16
Boston	105	53	37	15	0	382	312	121	104	31	59	14	0	303	391	76	209	84	96	29	0	685	703	197
Calgary	45	27	13	5	0	189	131	59	45	17	17	11	0	144	152	45	90	44	30	16	0	333	283	104
Carolina	75	44	23	7	1	301	225	96	76	34	31	11	0	225	223	79	151	78	54	18	1	526	448	175
Chicago	53	32	14	7	0	199	138	71	50	17	27	6	0	136	162	40	103	49	41	13	0	335	300	111
Colorado	63	36	18	9	0	247	204	81	63	21	31	11	0	194	226	53	126	57	49	20	0	441	430	134
Columbus	3	1	2	0	0	7	9	2	2	0	1	1	0	4	5	1	5	1	3	1	0	11	14	3
Dallas	51	27	13	11	0	184	136	65	54	21	27	6	0	156	173	48	105	48	40	17	0	340	309	113
Detroit	51	33	10	8	0	224	146	74	55	18	31	5	1	159	203	42	106	51	41	13	1	383	349	116
Edmonton	30	10	13	7	0	109	112	27	28	5	20	3	0	73	116	13	58	15	33	10	0	182	228	40
Florida	21	14	5	2	0	59	33	30	19	9	9	1	0	60	56	19	40	23	14	3	0	119	89	49
Los Angeles	52	27	16	9	0	209	154	63	53	22	22	9	0	182	184	53	105	49	38	18	0	391	338	116
Minnesota	2	1	1	0	0	6	5	2	2	2	0	0	0	5	1	4	4	3	1	0	0	11	6	6
Montreal	99	51	29	19	0	309	265	121	100	34	54	12	0	302	380	80	199	85	83	31	0	611	645	201
Nashville	4	0	3	1	0	9	16	1	4	3	1	0	0	8	6	6	8	3	4	1	0	17	22	7
New Jersey	52	31	14	7	0	209	158	69	52	26	16	9	1	174	150	62	104	57	30	16	1	383	308	131
NY Islanders	59	32	17	9	1	195	154	74	59	25	24	9	1	163	164	60	118	57	41	18	2	358	318	134
NY Rangers	66	38	18	10	0	275	208	86	64	21	27	15	1	173	210	58	130	59	45	25	1	448	418	144
Ottawa	28	19	7	2	0	90	41	40	30	15	8	6	1	82	67	37	58	34	15	8	1	172	108	77
Philadelphia	61	31	23	7	0	202	173	69	65	15	37	12	1	161	224	43	126	46	60	19	1	363	397	112
Phoenix	30	20	5	5	0	125	77	45	29	14	13	2	0	92	87	30	59	34	18	7	0	217	164	75
Pittsburgh	69	33	18	17	1	268	187	84	69	17	35	17	0	214	262	51	138	50	53	34	1	482	449	135
St. Louis	51	29	16	6	0	199	159	64	50	14	28	7	1	125	180	36	101	43	44	13	1	324	339	100
San Jose	10	10	0	0	0	50	26	20	10	1	4	4	1	33	36	7	20	11	4	4	1	83	62	27
Tampa Bay	21	12	7	2	0	58	57	26	21	14	4	3	0	68	44	31	42	26	11	5	0	126	101	57
Toronto	66	42	18	6	0	269	173	90	64	25	26	11	2	214	195	63	130	67	44	17	2	483	368	153
Vancouver	52	26	18	8	0	186	152	60	51	16	24	11	0	161	187	43	103	42	42	19	0	347	339	103
Washington	54	33	15	6	0	204	143	72	54	30	15	9	0	187	139	69	108	63	30	15	0	391	282	141
Defunct Clubs	23	13	5	5	0	94	63	31	23	12	8	3	0	97	76	27	46	25	13	8	0	191	139	58
Totals	**1312**	**733**	**383**	**193**	**3**	**4910**	**3695**	**1662**	**1312**	**487**	**605**	**209**	**11**	**3946**	**4336**	**1194**	**2624**	**1220**	**988**	**402**	**14**	**8856**	**8031**	**2856**

Playoffs

	Series	W	L	GP	W	L	T	GF	GA	Last Mtg.	Rnd.	Result
Boston	7	2	5	39	18	21	0	130	139	1999	CSF	W 4-2
Chicago	2	2	0	9	8	1	0	36	17	1980	QF	W 4-0
Colorado	2	0	2	8	2	6	0	27	35	1985	DSF	L 2-3
Dallas	3	1	2	13	5	8	0	37	39	1999	F	L 2-4
Montreal	7	3	4	35	17	18	0	111	124	1998	CSF	W 4-0
New Jersey	1	0	1	7	3	4	0	14	14	1994	CQF	L 3-4
NY Islanders	3	0	3	16	4	12	0	45	59	1980	SF	L 2-4
NY Rangers	1	1	0	3	2	1	0	11	6	1978	PRE	W 2-1
Ottawa	2	2	0	11	8	3	0	26	19	1999	CQF	W 4-0
Philadelphia	7	2	5	37	14	23	0	96	110	2001	CQF	W 4-2
Pittsburgh	2	0	2	10	4	6	0	26	26	2001	CSF	L 3-4
St. Louis	1	1	0	3	2	1	0	7	8	1976	PRE	W 2-1
Toronto	1	1	0	5	4	1	0	21	16	1999	CF	W 4-1
Vancouver	2	2	0	7	6	1	0	28	14	1981	PRE	W 3-0
Washington	1	0	1	6	2	4	0	11	13	1998	CF	L 2-4
Totals	**42**	**17**	**25**	**209**	**99**	**110**	**0**	**626**	**639**			

Playoff Results 2003-1999

Year	Round	Opponent	Result	GF	GA
2001	CSF	Pittsburgh	L 3-4	17	17
	CQF	Philadelphia	W 4-2	21	13
2000	CQF	Philadelphia	L 1-4	8	14
1999	F	Dallas	L 2-4	9	13
	CF	Toronto	W 4-1	21	16
	CSF	Boston	W 4-2	17	14
	CQF	Ottawa	W 4-0	12	6

Abbreviations: Round: F - Final; **CF** - conference final; **CSF** - conference semi-final; **CQF** - conference quarter-final; **DSF** - division semi-final; **SF** - semi-final; **QF** - quarter-final; **PRE** - preliminary round.

Calgary totals include Atlanta Flames, 1972-73 to 1979-80.
Colorado totals include Quebec, 1979-80 to 1994-95.
New Jersey totals include Kansas City, 1974-75 to 1975-76, and Colorado Rockies, 1976-77 to 1981-82.
Phoenix totals include Winnipeg, 1979-80 to 1995-96.
Carolina totals include Hartford, 1979-80 to 1996-97.
Dallas totals include Minnesota North Stars, 1970-71 to 1992-93.

2002-03 Results

Oct.	10	NY Islanders	5-1
	12	at Montreal	6-1
	13	at Chicago	0-3
	17	NY Rangers	4-4
	19	Phoenix	2-3
	22	Philadelphia	2-1
	25	New Jersey	1-2
	26	at Pittsburgh	2-5
	29	at Vancouver	1-1
	31	at Calgary	0-3
Nov.	1	at Edmonton	1-1
	3	at Columbus	2-3
	7	at Carolina	0-2
	9	Atlanta	4-6
	12	Boston	3-4
	15	Toronto	2-3
	16	at Ottawa	1-4
	19	at New Jersey	3-4*
	22	Columbus	5-4
	23	at Boston	1-4
	27	Tampa Bay	1-1
	29	Pittsburgh	1-4
	30	at Toronto	1-3
Dec.	4	Anaheim	4-0
	6	at NY Rangers	4-1
	7	Washington	4-3
	10	Ottawa	2-4
	13	Chicago	1-1
	14	at Philadelphia	0-2
	18	Boston	4-2
	20	Florida	0-3
	21	at Montreal	2-6
	23	at Pittsburgh	2-5
	26	Ottawa	2-3
	28	Minnesota	3-4
	30	at Washington	3-4
	31	NY Islanders	0-1*
Jan.	3	Carolina	6-3
	4	at Ottawa	2-1*
	7	at Philadelphia	2-3
	10	Boston	4-2
	11	at Montreal	3-2
	14	at Minnesota	1-0
	16	at San Jose	2-2
	18	at Phoenix	1-0
	21	Pittsburgh	0-0
	24	Toronto	4-0
	25	at Ottawa	3-4*
	27	Nashville	1-5
	30	at St. Louis	1-2*
Feb.	4	at New Jersey	1-4
	7	Vancouver	2-4
	8	at NY Islanders	1-3
	11	St. Louis	2-3
	13	at Detroit	2-4
	15	NY Rangers	5-4
	17	at Atlanta	3-4*
	19	Montreal	2-1*
	21	Los Angeles	1-4
	23	at Tampa Bay	4-1
	24	at Florida	2-2
	26	at Washington	2-3
	28	Dallas	5-3
Mar.	1	at NY Islanders	1-2*
	4	Washington	1-2
	6	Toronto	4-2
	8	at Florida	4-0
	9	at Tampa Bay	1-1
	12	Carolina	2-3*
	14	Tampa Bay	2-4
	15	at Atlanta	3-5
	18	Philadelphia	5-2
	19	at NY Rangers	0-3
	22	at Toronto	2-3*
	24	Colorado	4-3*
	26	Florida	2-1
	28	Montreal	4-1
	29	at Carolina	3-1
	31	at Dallas	0-3
Apr.	2	Atlanta	4-3
	5	at Boston	5-8
	6	New Jersey	2-2

* – Overtime

Entry Draft
Selections 2003-1989

2003 Pick		1999 Pick		1995 Pick		1991 Pick	
5	Thomas Vanek	20	Barrett Heisten	14	Jay McKee	13	Philippe Boucher
65	Branislav Fabry	35	Milan Bartovic	16	Martin Biron	35	Jason Dawe
74	Clarke MacArthur	55	Doug Janik	42	Mark Dutiaume	57	Jason Young
106	Jan Hejda	64	Mike Zigomanis	68	Mathieu Sunderland	72	Peter Ambroziak
114	Denis Ezhov	73	Tim Preston	94	Matt Davidson	101	Steve Shields
150	Thomas Morrow	117	Karel Mosovsky	111	Marian Menhart	123	Sean O'Donnell
172	Pavel Voroshnin	138	Ryan Miller	119	Kevin Popp	124	Brian Holzinger
202	Nathan Paetsch	146	Matt Kinch	123	Daniel Bienvenue	145	Chris Snell
235	Jeff Weber	178	Seneque Hyacinthe	172	Brian Scott	162	Jiri Kuntos
266	Louis Philippe Martin	206	Bret DeCecco	198	Mike Zanutto	189	Tony Iob
		235	Brad Self	224	Rob Skrlac	211	Spencer Meany
2002 Pick		263	Craig Brunel			233	Mikhail Volkov
11	Keith Ballard			1994 Pick		255	Michael Smith
20	Dan Paille	1998 Pick		17	Wayne Primeau		
76	Michael Tessier	18	Dmitri Kalinin	43	Curtis Brown	1990 Pick	
82	John Adams	34	Andrew Peters	69	Rumun Ndur	14	Brad May
108	Jakub Hulva	47	Norm Milley	121	Sergei Klimentiev	82	Brian McCarthy
121	Marty Magers	50	Jaroslav Kristek	147	Cal Benazic	97	Richard Smehlik
178	Maxim Schejev	77	Mike Pandolfo	168	Steve Plouffe	100	Todd Bojcun
208	Radoslav Hecl	137	Aaron Goldade	173	Shane Hnidy	103	Brad Pascall
241	Dennis Wideman	164	Ales Kotalik	176	Steve Webb	142	Viktor Gordiouk
271	Martin Cizek	191	Brad Moran	199	Bob Westerby	166	Milan Nedoma
		218	David Moravec	225	Craig Millar	187	Jason Winch
2001 Pick		249	Edo Terglav	251	Mark Polak	208	Sylvain Naud
22	Jiri Novotny			277	Shayne Wright	229	Kenneth Martin
32	Derek Roy	1997 Pick				250	Brad Rubachuk
50	Chris Thorburn	21	Mika Noronen	1993 Pick			
55	Jason Pominville	48	Henrik Tallinder	38	Denis Tsygurov	1989 Pick	
155	Michal Vondrka	69	Maxim Afinogenov	64	Ethan Philpott	14	Kevin Haller
234	Calle Aslund	75	Jeff Martin	116	Richard Safarik	56	Scott Thomas
247	Marek Dubec	101	Luc Theoret	142	Kevin Pozzo	77	Doug MacDonald
279	Ryan Jorde	128	Torrey DiRoberto	168	Sergei Petrenko	98	Ken Sutton
		156	Brian Campbell	194	Mike Barrie	107	Bill Pye
2000 Pick		184	Jeremy Adduono	220	Barrie Moore	119	Mike Barkley
15	Artem Kryukov	212	Kamil Piros	246	Chris Davis	161	Derek Plante
48	Gerard Dicaire	238	Dylan Kemp	272	Scott Nichol	183	Donald Audette
111	Ghyslain Rousseau					194	Mark Astley
149	Denis Denisov	1996 Pick		1992 Pick		203	John Nelson
213	Vasili Bizyayev	7	Erik Rasmussen	11	David Cooper	224	Todd Henderson
220	Paul Gaustad	27	Cory Sarich	35	Jozef Cierny	245	Michael Bavis
258	Sean McMorrow	33	Darren Van Oene	59	Ondrej Steiner		
277	Ryan Courtney	54	Francois Methot	80	Dean Melanson		
		87	Kurt Walsh	83	Matthew Barnaby		
		106	Mike Martone	107	Markus Ketterer		
		115	Alexei Tezikov	108	Yuri Khmylev		
		142	Ryan Davis	131	Paul Rushforth		
		161	Darren Mortier	179	Dean Tiltgen		
		222	Scott Buhler	203	Todd Simon		
				227	Rick Kowalsky		
				251	Chris Clancy		

General Managers' History

Punch Imlach, 1970-71 to 1977-78; John Anderson, 1978-79; Scotty Bowman, 1979-80 to 1985-86; Scotty Bowman and Gerry Meehan, 1986-87; Gerry Meehan, 1987-88 to 1992-93; John Muckler, 1993-94 to 1996-97; Darcy Regier, 1997-98 to date.

General Manager

REGIER, DARCY
General Manager, Buffalo Sabres. Born in Swift Current, Sask., Nov. 27, 1957.

Darcy Regier became the sixth general manager of the Buffalo Sabres on June 11, 1997 after a lengthy management apprenticeship in the New York Islanders organization. As a player, Regier played eight pro seasons, including part of the 1977-78 season with the Cleveland Barons and parts of the 1982-83 and 1983-84 campaigns with the New York Islanders.

He began his career as an administrator with the Islanders in 1984-85 and went on to serve in a variety of capacities including director of administration, assistant director of hockey operations, assistant coach and assistant general manager. He also served as an assistant coach with Hartford in 1991-92.

While with the Islanders, Regier benefitted from working with talented managers and coaches including Bill Torrey and Al Arbour. As a minor pro player with Indianapolis of the CHL he became associated with another important influence on his hockey career, current Detroit Red Wing executive Jim Devellano.

Club Directory

HSBC Arena

Buffalo Sabres
HSBC Arena
One Seymour H. Knox III Plaza
Buffalo, NY 14203
Phone **716/855-4100**
Fax 716/855-4110
Tickets, U.S.: **888/GO-SABRES**
Capacity: 18,690

Executive
Owner . . . . B. Thomas Golisano
Managing Partner . . . . Larry Quinn
Chief Operating Officer . . . . Dan DiPofi
Vice President Sales & Marketing . . . . Jim Leahy

Hockey Department
General Manager . . . . Darcy Regier
Assistant to the General Manager . . . . Larry Carriere
Director of Player Personnel . . . . Don Luce
Hockey Operations Assistant . . . . Scott Schranz
Director of Pro Scouting . . . . Terry Martin
Director of Amateur Scouting . . . . Jim Benning
Professional Scout . . . . Kevin Devine
Scouting Staff . . . . Don Barrie, Bo Berglund, Iouri Khmylev, Paul Merritt, Rudy Migay, Darryl Plandowski, Mike Racicot, David Volek
Head Coach . . . . Lindy Ruff
Assistant Coaches . . . . Scott Arniel, Brian McCutcheon
Strength & Conditioning Coach . . . . Doug McKenney
Assistant Strength Coach . . . . Dennis Cole
Goaltender Coach . . . . Jim Corsi
Head Trainer/Message Therapist . . . . Jim Pizzutelli
Head Equipment Manager . . . . Rip Simonick
Assistant Equipment Manager . . . . George Babcock
Equipment Assistant . . . . Encil "Porky" Palmer
Travel Coordinator . . . . Neil Herman

Medical
Club Doctor . . . . Les Bisson, M.D.
Doctors . . . . Nicholas Aquino, M.D., William Hartrich, M.D.
Oral Surgeon . . . . Steven Jenson, DDS
Club Dentist . . . . Daniel Yustin, DDS, M.S.
Physical Therapist . . . . Joe Aquino
Club Doctor Emeritus . . . . John L. Butsch, M.D.

Legal
Sr. VP/Legal & Business Affairs . . . . Kevin Billet
Director of Legal Affairs/Human Resources . . . . Richard Mugel
Executive Assistant . . . . Eleanore MacKenzie

Administration
Management Information Systems Manager . . . . Marc Wittman
Special Consultant . . . . Joe Crozier
Executive Assistant . . . . Donna Webb-Smith

Broadcast Production
Staff Producer . . . . Joe Pinter
Staff Director . . . . Eric Grossman
Feature Producer/Editor . . . . Jeff Hill
Broadcast Coordinator . . . . Lisa Tzetzo
Broadcast Team . . . . Rick Jeanneret (Play-By-Play), Jim Lorentz (Color Commentary), Danny Gare (Reporter)

Public Relations
Director of Public Relations . . . . Mike Gilbert
Manager of Media Relations . . . . Gregg Huller
Media Relations Assistant . . . . Matt Schmidt
Public Relations Assistant . . . . Brian Wheeler
Manager of Community Development . . . . Peter Hassen
Youth Hockey Manager . . . . Patrick Fisher
Team Photographer . . . . Bill Wippert
Director of Alumni Relations . . . . Larry Playfair
Corporate & Community Relations Liaison . . . . . Gilbert Perreault

Merchandise
Director of Merchandise . . . . Mike Kaminska
Store Manager . . . . Tammy John

Sponsorship Sales/Service
Director of Sales . . . . John Livsey
Director of Suite Sales . . . . Jody Ulrich
Local Sales Manager . . . . Steve Cuccia
Sales Support Account Executive . . . . Lauren Hartmayer

Finance
VP/Finance . . . . John Marsh
Accounting Manager . . . . Christine Ivansitz
Payroll Manager . . . . Birgid Haensel

Marketing
Director of Advertising & Promotions . . . . Rob Kopacz
Director of Game Presentation . . . . Rich Wall
Director of Creative Services . . . . Frank Cravotta

Ticket Sales & Operations
Director of Ticket Operations & Services . . . . . . John Sinclair
Director of Ticket Sales . . . . Dan Carroll
Box Office Manager . . . . Michael Tout

HSBC Arena
Director of Arena Operations . . . . Stan Makowski, Jr.
Director of Event Booking . . . . Jennifer Van Rysdam
Director of Lacrosse & Amateur Athletics . . . . . Kurt Silcott
Director of Technical Operations . . . . Al Weissman
Chief Engineer . . . . Barry Becker
Ice Technician . . . . Brian Harszlak

Calgary Flames

2002-03 Results: 29w-36L-13T-4OTL 75PTS.
Fifth, Northwest Division

2003-04 Schedule

Oct.	Thu.	9	at Vancouver	Tue.	13	at Toronto
	Sat.	11	San Jose	Wed.	14	at Washington
	Tue.	14	Edmonton	Sat.	17	Dallas
	Sat.	18	Buffalo	Mon.	19	at Anaheim*
	Tue.	21	at Minnesota	Tue.	20	at Los Angeles
	Fri.	24	St. Louis	Thu.	22	Nashville
	Sat.	25	at Edmonton	Sat.	24	Tampa Bay
	Tue.	28	at Colorado	Tue.	27	at Phoenix
	Wed.	29	at Dallas	Wed.	28	at San Jose
Nov.	Sat.	1	Columbus	Fri.	30	Chicago
	Tue.	4	Detroit	Feb. Sun.	1	Anaheim
	Fri.	7	Minnesota	Tue.	3	Los Angeles
	Sun.	9	at Columbus*	Thu.	5	St. Louis
	Wed.	12	at Chicago	Tue.	10	Atlanta
	Thu.	13	at Nashville	Wed.	11	at Vancouver
	Sat.	15	at Edmonton	Fri.	13	Anaheim
	Tue.	18	Toronto	Sun.	15	at Minnesota*
	Thu.	20	Montreal	Thu.	19	at Montreal
	Sat.	22	Chicago	Sat.	21	at Ottawa*
	Thu.	27	Colorado	Sun.	22	at New Jersey
	Sat.	29	Vancouver	Tue.	24	at Colorado
Dec.	Tue.	2	San Jose	Thu.	26	Detroit
	Thu.	4	at Vancouver	Sun.	29	Phoenix
	Fri.	5	Minnesota	Mar. Tue.	2	at St. Louis
	Sun.	7	Pittsburgh	Wed.	3	at Detroit
	Tue.	9	at Minnesota	Fri.	5	at Dallas
	Thu.	11	Carolina	Sun.	7	at Colorado*
	Sat.	13	Colorado	Tue.	9	Edmonton
	Tue.	16	at Philadelphia	Thu.	11	Ottawa
	Thu.	18	at Boston	Sat.	13	at Nashville
	Fri.	19	at Columbus	Sun.	14	at St. Louis
	Tue.	23	Edmonton	Tue.	16	at Detroit
	Fri.	26	Vancouver	Thu.	18	Columbus
	Sun.	28	at Edmonton	Sat.	20	Nashville
	Mon.	29	Minnesota	Mon.	22	Dallas
	Wed.	31	Colorado	Wed.	24	at Phoenix
Jan.	Sat.	3	Vancouver	Thu.	25	at San Jose
	Mon.	5	at NY Rangers	Sat.	27	Los Angeles*
	Tue.	6	at NY Islanders	Wed.	31	Phoenix
	Thu.	8	at Chicago	Apr. Fri.	2	at Los Angeles
	Sat.	10	Florida	Sun.	4	at Anaheim*

Denotes afternoon game.

Year-by-Year Record

		Home				Road				Overall							
Season	GP	W	L	T	OL	W	L	T	OL	W	L	T	OL	GF	GA	Pts.	Finished	Playoff Result
2002-03	82	14	16	10	1	15	20	3	3	29	36	13	4	186	228	75	5th, Northwest Div.	Out of Playoffs
2001-02	82	20	14	5	2	12	21	7	1	32	35	12	3	201	220	79	4th, Northwest Div.	Out of Playoffs
2000-01	82	12	18	9	2	15	18	6	2	27	36	15	4	197	236	73	4th, Northwest Div.	Out of Playoffs
1999-2000	82	20	14	6	1	11	22	4	4	31	36	10	5	211	256	77	4th, Northwest Div.	Out of Playoffs
1998-99	82	15	20	6	...	15	20	6	...	30	40	12	...	211	234	72	3rd, Northwest Div.	Out of Playoffs
1997-98	82	18	17	6	...	8	24	9	...	26	41	15	...	217	252	67	5th, Pacific Div.	Out of Playoffs
1996-97	82	21	18	2	...	11	23	7	...	32	41	9	...	214	239	73	5th, Pacific Div.	Out of Playoffs
1995-96	82	18	18	5	...	16	19	6	...	34	37	11	...	241	240	79	2nd, Pacific Div.	Lost Conf. Quarter-Final
1994-95	48	15	7	2	...	9	10	5	...	24	17	7	...	163	135	55	1st, Pacific Div.	Lost Conf. Quarter-Final
1993-94	84	25	12	5	...	17	17	8	...	42	29	13	...	302	256	97	1st, Pacific Div.	Lost Conf. Quarter-Final
1992-93	84	23	14	5	...	20	16	6	...	43	30	11	...	322	282	97	2nd, Smythe Div.	Lost Div. Semi-Final
1991-92	80	19	14	7	...	12	23	5	...	31	37	12	...	296	305	74	5th, Smythe Div.	Out of Playoffs
1990-91	80	29	8	3	...	17	18	5	...	46	26	8	...	344	263	100	2nd, Smythe Div.	Lost Div. Semi-Final
1989-90	80	28	7	5	...	14	16	10	...	42	23	15	...	348	265	99	1st, Smythe Div.	Lost Div. Semi-Final
1988-89	**80**	**32**	**4**	**4**	**...**	**22**	**13**	**5**	**...**	**54**	**17**	**9**	**...**	**354**	**226**	**117**	**1st, Smythe Div.**	**Won Stanley Cup**
1987-88	80	26	11	3	...	22	12	6	...	48	23	9	...	397	305	105	1st, Smythe Div.	Lost Div. Final
1986-87	80	25	13	2	...	21	18	1	...	46	31	3	...	318	289	95	2nd, Smythe Div.	Lost Div. Semi-Final
1985-86	80	23	11	6	...	17	20	3	...	40	31	9	...	354	315	89	2nd, Smythe Div.	Lost Final
1984-85	80	23	11	6	...	18	16	6	...	41	27	12	...	363	302	94	3rd, Smythe Div.	Lost Div. Semi-Final
1983-84	80	22	11	7	...	12	21	7	...	34	32	14	...	311	314	82	2nd, Smythe Div.	Lost Div. Final
1982-83	80	21	12	7	...	11	22	7	...	32	34	14	...	321	317	78	2nd, Smythe Div.	Lost Div. Final
1981-82	80	20	11	9	...	9	23	8	...	29	34	17	...	334	345	75	3rd, Smythe Div.	Lost Div. Semi-Final
1980-81	80	25	5	10	...	14	22	4	...	39	27	14	...	329	298	92	3rd, Patrick Div.	Lost Semi-Final
1979-80*	80	25	11	4	...	16	20	4	...	35	32	13	...	282	269	83	4th, Patrick Div.	Lost Prelim. Round
1978-79*	80	25	11	4	...	16	20	4	...	41	31	8	...	327	280	90	4th, Patrick Div.	Lost Prelim. Round
1977-78*	80	20	13	7	...	14	14	12	...	34	27	19	...	274	252	87	3rd, Patrick Div.	Lost Prelim. Round
1976-77*	80	22	11	7	...	12	23	5	...	34	34	12	...	264	265	80	3rd, Patrick Div.	Lost Prelim. Round
1975-76*	80	19	14	7	...	16	19	5	...	35	33	12	...	262	237	82	3rd, Patrick Div.	Lost Prelim. Round
1974-75*	80	24	9	7	...	10	22	8	...	34	31	15	...	243	233	83	4th, Patrick Div.	Out of Playoffs
1973-74*	78	17	15	7	...	13	19	7	...	30	34	14	...	214	238	74	4th, West Div.	Lost Quarter-Final
1972-73*	78	16	16	7	...	9	22	8	...	25	38	15	...	191	239	65	7th, West Div.	Out of Playoffs

* Atlanta Flames

A large presence on the Flames blueline, Robyn Regehr stands 6'3" and weighs 226 pounds. He averaged 22:45 of ice time in 2002-03, second to Toni Lydman among Flames defensemen. Though he had no goals, his 12 assists were a career high.

Franchise date: June 6, 1972
Transferred from Atlanta to Calgary, June 24, 1980.

NORTHWEST DIVISION

32nd NHL Season

2003-04 Player Personnel

FORWARDS	HT	WT	S	Place of Birth	Date	2002-03 Club
BEMBRIDGE, Garrett	6-0	180	R	Melfort, Sask.	7/6/81	Saint John
BETTS, Blair	6-1	200	L	Edmonton, Alta.	2/16/80	Calgary-Saint John
CLARK, Chris	6-0	200	R	South Windsor, CT	3/8/76	Calgary
CONROY, Craig	6-2	197	R	Potsdam, NY	9/4/71	Calgary
DAVIDSON, Matt	6-3	196	R	Flin Flon, Man.	8/9/77	Columbus-Syracuse
DOME, Robert	6-0	210	L	Skalica, Czech.	1/29/79	Calgary-Saint John
DONOVAN, Shean	6-2	200	R	Timmins, Ont.	1/22/75	Pittsburgh-Calgary
GELINAS, Martin	5-11	195	L	Shawinigan, Que.	6/5/70	Calgary
GREEN, Josh	6-4	212	L	Camrose, Alta.	11/16/77	Edmonton-NY Rangers-Washington
IGINLA, Jarome	6-1	208	R	Edmonton, Alta.	7/1/77	Calgary
KOBASEW, Chuck	5-11	195	L	Osoyoos, B.C.	4/17/82	Calgary-Saint John
LOMBARDI, Matthew	5-11	191	L	Montreal, Que.	3/18/82	Saint John
LYNCH, Darren	5-11	175	R	Regina, Sask.	7/7/83	Vancouver (WHL)
McAMMOND, Dean	5-11	193	L	Grand Cache, Alta.	6/15/73	Colorado
MORGAN, Jason	6-1	200	L	St. John's, Nfld.	10/9/76	Saint John
NYSTROM, Eric	6-1	195	L	Syosset, NY	2/14/83	U. of Michigan
OLIWA, Krzysztof	6-5	245	L	Tychy, Poland	4/12/73	NY Rangers-Hartford-Boston
REINPRECHT, Steve	6-0	190	L	Edmonton, Alta.	5/7/76	Colorado
SAPRYKIN, Oleg	6-0	195	L	Moscow, USSR	2/12/81	Calgary-Saint John
SONNENBERG, Martin	6-0	197	L	Wetaskiwin, Alta.	1/23/78	Saint John
YELLE, Stephane	6-1	190	L	Ottawa, Ont.	5/9/74	Calgary

DEFENSEMEN	HT	WT	S	Place of Birth	Date	2002-03 Club
BUZEK, Petr	6-1	220	L	Jihlava, Czech.	4/26/77	Calgary
COMMODORE, Mike	6-4	230	R	Fort Saskatchewan, Alta.	11/7/79	Cin (AHL)-Cgy-Saint Jn
FERENCE, Andrew	5-10	196	L	Edmonton, Alta.	3/17/79	Pit-Wilkes-Barre-Cgy
GAUTHIER, Denis	6-2	224	L	Montreal, Que.	10/1/76	Calgary
LEOPOLD, Jordan	6-0	193	L	Golden Valley, MN	8/3/80	Calgary-Saint John
LYDMAN, Toni	6-1	202	L	Lahti, Finland	9/25/77	Calgary
MONTADOR, Steve	6-0	210	R	Vancouver, B.C.	12/21/79	Calgary-Saint John
PHANEUF, Dion	6-2	205	L	Edmonton, Alta.	4/10/85	Red Deer
REGEHR, Robyn	6-2	226	L	Recife, Brazil	4/19/80	Calgary
ROZAKOV, Roman	6-1	198	L	Murmansk, USSR	3/29/81	Togliatti-Cherepovets
WALLIN, Jesse	6-2	190	L	Saskatoon, Sask.	3/10/78	Detroit
WARRENER, Rhett	6-2	217	L	Shaunavon, Sask.	1/27/76	Buffalo

GOALTENDERS	HT	WT	C	Place of Birth	Date	2002-03 Club
KRAHN, Brent	6-4	200	L	Winnipeg, Man.	4/2/82	Calgary (WHL)-Seattle
McLENNAN, Jamie	6-0	190	L	Edmonton, Alta.	6/30/71	Calgary
SABOURIN, Dany	6-2	182	L	Val-d'Or, Que.	9/2/80	Saint John
TUREK, Roman	6-3	220	R	Strakonice, Czech.	5/21/70	Calgary

2002-03 Scoring
* - rookie

Regular Season

Pos	#	Player	Team	GP	G	A	Pts	+/−	PIM	PP	SH	GW	GT	S	%
R	12	Jarome Iginla	CGY	75	35	32	67	−10	49	11	3	6	1	316	11.1
C	22	Craig Conroy	CGY	79	22	37	59	−4	36	5	0	2	0	143	15.4
C	18	Chris Drury	CGY	80	23	30	53	−9	33	5	1	5	2	224	10.3
L	23	Martin Gelinas	CGY	81	21	31	52	−3	51	6	0	3	1	152	13.8
D	32	Toni Lydman	CGY	81	6	20	26	−7	28	3	0	0	0	143	4.2
C	11	Stephane Yelle	CGY	82	10	15	25	−10	50	3	0	3	0	121	8.3
L	19	Oleg Saprykin	CGY	52	8	15	23	5	46	1	0	1	0	116	6.9
R	17	Chris Clark	CGY	81	10	12	22	−11	126	2	0	2	1	156	6.4
L	10	Dave Lowry	CGY	34	5	14	19	4	22	1	0	0	0	40	12.5
D	6	Bob Boughner	CGY	69	3	14	17	5	126	0	0	1	0	62	4.8
D	4 *	Jordan Leopold	CGY	58	4	10	14	−15	12	3	0	0	0	78	5.1
R	16	Shean Donovan	PIT	52	4	5	9	−6	30	0	1	0	0	66	6.1
			CGY	13	1	2	3	−2	7	0	0	1	0	22	4.5
			TOTAL	65	5	7	12	−8	37	0	1	1	0	88	5.7
D	3	Denis Gauthier	CGY	72	1	11	12	5	99	0	0	1	0	50	2.0
D	28	Robyn Regehr	CGY	76	0	12	12	−9	87	0	0	0	0	109	0.0
C	40	Scott Nichol	CGY	68	5	5	10	−7	149	0	1	0	0	66	7.6
R	24	Blake Sloan	CGY	67	2	8	10	−5	28	0	0	0	0	56	3.6
D	8	Petr Buzek	CGY	44	3	5	8	−6	14	3	0	0	0	48	6.3
D	21	Andrew Ference	PIT	22	1	3	4	−16	36	1	0	0	0	22	4.5
			CGY	16	0	4	4	1	6	0	0	0	0	17	0.0
			TOTAL	38	1	7	8	−15	42	1	0	0	0	39	2.6
R	7 *	Chuck Kobasew	CGY	23	4	2	6	−3	8	1	0	1	0	29	13.8
L	27	Craig Berube	CGY	55	2	4	6	−6	100	0	0	0	0	21	9.5
C	26	Steve Begin	CGY	50	3	1	4	−7	51	0	0	1	0	59	5.1
C	15 *	Blair Betts	CGY	9	1	3	4	3	0	0	0	0	0	16	6.3
D	42 *	Micki DuPont	CGY	16	1	2	3	−5	4	0	0	0	0	27	3.7
D	5 *	Steve Montador	CGY	50	1	1	2	−9	114	0	0	0	0	64	1.6
R	43	Ladislav Kohn	CGY	3	0	1	1	1	2	0	0	0	0	3	0.0
D	2	Mike Commodore	CGY	6	0	1	1	2	19	0	0	0	0	5	0.0
C	38	Robert Dome	CGY	1	0	0	0	0	0	0	0	0	0	0	0.0
D	51	Rick Mrozik	CGY	2	0	0	0	0	0	0	0	0	0	2	0.0
D	36 *	Mike Mottau	CGY	2	0	0	0	−1	0	0	0	0	0	0	0.0

Goaltending

No.	Goaltender	GPI	Mins	Avg	W	L	T	EN	SO	GA	SA	S%	G	A	PIM
1	Roman Turek	65	3822	2.57	27	29	9	4	4	164	1679	.902	0	4	14
33	Jamie McLennan	22	1165	2.99	2	11	4	2	0	58	537	.892	0	0	14
	Totals	**82**	**5012**	**2.73**	**29**	**40**	**13**	**6**	**4**	**228**	**2222**	**.897**			

Coach and General Manager

SUTTER, DARRYL
Coach/General Manager, Calgary Flames.
Born in Vikings, Alta., August 19, 1958.

Darryl Sutter was named general manager of the Calgary Flames on April 11, 2003 adding the portfolio to his head coaching position. He had joined the Flames as coach on December 28, 2002. Before joining the Flames, Sutter was the San Jose Sharks franchise leader in regular-season games coached (434) and wins (192). Through the 2001-02 season, Sutter became only the second coach in NHL history (Al Arbour, New York Islanders) to improve his team's point total for five consecutive years.

Prior to San Jose, Sutter coached Chicago for three years (1992 to 1995) and spent two seasons (1995 to 1997) with the Blackhawks as a consultant for special assignments. He spent the 1987-88 campaign as a Blackhawks assistant coach to Bob Murdoch and served as an associate coach for Mike Keenan during the 1990-91 and 1991-92 seasons. During his final season as associate coach, the Blackhawks advanced to the Stanley Cup Finals. Sutter spent two seasons coaching the Blackhawks top development affiliate in the IHL, which played in Saginaw (1988-89) and in Indianapolis (1989-90). Under his leadership, the Indianapolis Ice stormed through the regular season with 114 points and won the Turner Cup championship. He was named IHL coach of the year.

As a player, Sutter was selected by Chicago in the ninth round, 179th overall, in the 1978 NHL Entry Draft. During his eight-year career with the Blackhawks from 1979 to 1987, he scored 279 points (161 goals, 118 assists) with 288 penalty minutes in 406 NHL career games. Sutter served as team captain with the Blackhawks for five seasons, beginning in the 1982-83 season through 1986-87 when he was forced to retire prematurely due to a series of injuries.

Darryl is a member of the famous Sutter hockey family, who had six brothers that played in the NHL. They were all inducted into the Alberta Sports Hall of Fame in May 2000 under the Lifetime Achievement category. Along with his brothers, Darryl is very involved in the Sutter Foundation, started by he and his family in Alberta, which raises money for non-profit organizations.

Coaching Record

			Regular Season				Playoffs		
Season	Team	Games	W	L	T		Games	W	L
1988-89	Saginaw (IHL)	82	46	26	10		6	2	4
1989-90	Indianapolis (IHL)	82	53	21	8		14	12	2
1992-93	Chicago (NHL)	84	47	25	12		4	0	4
1993-94	Chicago (NHL)	84	39	36	9		6	2	4
1994-95	Chicago (NHL)	48	24	19	5		16	9	7
1997-98	San Jose (NHL)	82	34	38	10		6	2	4
1998-99	San Jose (NHL)	82	31	33	18		6	2	4
1999-2000	San Jose (NHL)	82	35	37	10		12	5	7
2000-01	San Jose (NHL)	82	40	30	12		6	2	4
2001-02	San Jose (NHL)	82	44	30	8		12	7	5
2002-03	San Jose (NHL)	24	8	14	2		....	....	....
	Calgary (NHL)	46	19	19	8		....	....	....
	NHL Totals	**696**	**321**	**281**	**94**		**68**	**29**	**39**

Captains' History

Keith McCreary, 1972-73 to 1974-75; Pat Quinn, 1975-76, 1976-77; Tom Lysiak, 1977-78, 1978-79; Jean Pronovost, 1979-80; Brad Marsh, 1980-81; Phil Russell, 1981-82, 1982-83; Lanny McDonald, Doug Risebrough (co-captains), 1983-84; Lanny McDonald, Doug Risebrough, Jim Peplinski (tri-captains), 1984-85 to 1986-87; Lanny McDonald, Jim Peplinski (co-captains), 1987-88; Lanny McDonald, Jim Peplinski, Tim Hunter (tri-captains), 1988-89; Brad McCrimmon, 1989-90; alternating captains, 1990-91; Joe Nieuwendyk, 1991-92 to 1994-95; Theoren Fleury, 1995-96, 1996-97; Todd Simpson, 1997-98, 1998-99; Steve Smith, 1999-2000; Steve Smith and Dave Lowry, 2000-01; Dave Lowry; Bob Boughner and Craig Conroy (co-captains), 2001-02; Bob Boughner and Craig Conroy (co-captains), 2002-03; Craig Conroy, 2003-04.

General Managers' History

Cliff Fletcher, 1972-73 to 1990-91; Doug Risebrough, 1991-92 to 1994-95; Doug Risebrough and Al Coates, 1995-96; Al Coates, 1996-97 to 1999-2000; Craig Button, 2000-01 to 2001-02; Craig Button and Darryl Sutter, 2002-03; Darryl Sutter, 2003-04.

Coaching History

Bernie Geoffrion, 1972-73, 1973-74; Bernie Geoffrion and Fred Creighton, 1974-75; Fred Creighton, 1975-76 to 1978-79; Al MacNeil, 1979-80 to 1981-82; Bob Johnson, 1982-83 to 1986-87; Terry Crisp, 1987-88 to 1989-90; Doug Risebrough, 1990-91; Doug Risebrough and Guy Charron, 1991-92; Dave King, 1992-93 to 1994-95; Pierre Page, 1995-96, 1996-97; Brian Sutter, 1997-98 to 1999-2000; Don Hay and Greg Gilbert, 2000-01; Greg Gilbert, 2001-02; Greg Gilbert, Al MacNeil and Darryl Sutter, 2002-03; Darryl Sutter, 2003-04.

Club Records

Team

(Figures in brackets for season records are games played; records for fewest points, wins, ties, losses, goals, goals against are for 70 or more games)

Most Points .... 117 — 1988-89 (80)
Most Wins .... 54 — 1988-89 (80)
Most Ties .... 19 — 1977-78 (80)
Most Losses .... 41 — 1996-97 (82), 1997-98 (82), 1999-2000 (82)
Most Goals .... 397 — 1987-88 (80)
Most Goals Against .... 345 — 1981-82 (80)
Fewest Points .... 65 — 1972-73 (78)
Fewest Wins .... 25 — 1972-73 (78)
Fewest Ties .... 3 — 1986-87 (80)
Fewest Losses .... 17 — 1988-89 (80)
Fewest Goals .... 186 — 2002-03 (82)
Fewest Goals Against .... 220 — 2001-02 (82)

Longest Winning Streak
Overall .... 10 — Oct. 14-Nov. 3/78
Home .... 9 — Oct. 17-Nov. 15/78, Jan. 3-Feb. 5/89, Mar. 3-Apr. 1/90, Feb. 21-Mar. 14/91
Away .... 7 — Nov. 10-Dec. 4/88

Longest Undefeated Streak
Overall .... 13 — Nov. 10-Dec. 8/88 (12 wins, 1 tie)
Home .... 18 — Dec. 29/90-Mar. 14/91 (17 wins, 1 tie)
Away .... 9 — Feb. 20-Mar. 21/88 (6 wins, 3 ties), Nov. 11-Dec. 16/90 (6 wins, 3 ties)

Longest Losing Streak
Overall .... 11 — Dec. 14/85-Jan. 7/86
Home .... 6 — Dec. 5-31/98
Away .... 9 — Dec. 1/85-Jan. 12/86

Longest Winless Streak
Overall .... 11 — Dec. 14/85-Jan. 7/86 (11 losses), Jan. 5-26/93 (9 losses, 2 ties)
Home .... 10 — Oct. 21-Dec. 4/00 (6 losses, 4 ties)
Away .... 13 — Feb. 3-Mar. 29/73 (10 losses, 3 ties)

Most Shutouts, Season .... 8 — 1974-75 (80), 2000-01 (82)
Most PIM, Season .... 2,643 — 1991-92 (80)
Most Goals, Game .... 13 — Feb. 10/93 (S.J. 1 at Cgy. 13)

Individual

Most Seasons .... 13 — Al MacInnis
Most Games .... 803 — Al MacInnis
Most Goals, Career .... 364 — Theoren Fleury
Most Assists, Career .... 609 — Al MacInnis
Most Points, Career .... 830 — Theoren Fleury (364G, 466A)
Most PIM, Career .... 2,405 — Tim Hunter
Most Shutouts, Career .... 20 — Dan Bouchard
Longest Consecutive Games Streak .... 257 — Brad Marsh (Oct. 11/78-Nov. 10/81)
Most Goals, Season .... 66 — Lanny McDonald (1982-83)
Most Assists, Season .... 82 — Kent Nilsson (1980-81)
Most Points, Season .... 131 — Kent Nilsson (1980-81; 49G, 82A)
Most PIM, Season .... 375 — Tim Hunter (1988-89)
Most Points, Defenseman, Season .... 103 — Al MacInnis (1990-91; 28G, 75A)
Most Points, Center, Season .... 131 — Kent Nilsson (1980-81; 49G, 82A)
Most Points, Right Wing, Season .... 110 — Joe Mullen (1988-89; 51G, 59A)
Most Points, Left Wing, Season .... 90 — Gary Roberts (1991-92; 53G, 37A)
Most Points, Rookie, Season .... 92 — Joe Nieuwendyk (1987-88; 51G, 41A)
Most Shutouts, Season .... 5 — Dan Bouchard (1973-74), Phil Myre (1974-75), Fred Brathwaite (1999-2000, 2000-01), Roman Turek (2001-02)
Most Goals, Game .... 5 — Joe Nieuwendyk (Jan. 11/89)
Most Assists, Game .... 6 — Guy Chouinard (Feb. 25/81), Gary Suter (Apr. 4/86)
Most Points, Game .... 7 — Sergei Makarov (Feb. 25/90; 2G, 5A)

Records include Atlanta Flames, 1972-73 through 1979-80.

Retired Numbers

9	Lanny McDonald	1981-1989

All-time Record vs. Other Clubs

Regular Season

	At Home								On Road								Total							
	GP	W	L	T	OL	GF	GA	PTS	GP	W	L	T	OL	GF	GA	PTS	GP	W	L	T	OL	GF	GA	PTS
Anaheim	23	13	9	1	0	64	56	27	24	7	9	6	2	63	77	22	47	20	18	7	2	127	133	49
Atlanta	2	2	0	0	0	9	4	4	4	0	3	1	0	5	8	1	6	2	3	1	0	14	12	5
Boston	44	18	22	4	0	160	154	40	46	12	28	6	0	125	165	30	90	30	50	10	0	285	319	70
Buffalo	45	17	17	11	0	152	144	45	45	13	26	5	1	131	189	32	90	30	43	16	1	283	333	77
Carolina	28	20	6	2	0	139	92	42	28	13	10	5	0	103	91	31	56	33	16	7	0	242	183	73
Chicago	61	28	20	13	0	196	182	69	59	21	25	13	0	172	191	55	120	49	45	26	0	368	373	124
Colorado	44	20	16	8	0	153	132	48	44	16	16	11	1	143	160	44	88	36	32	19	1	296	292	92
Columbus	6	3	3	0	0	19	18	6	6	1	5	0	0	11	21	2	12	4	8	0	0	30	39	8
Dallas	60	33	13	14	0	206	148	80	60	21	28	11	0	192	219	53	120	54	41	25	0	398	367	133
Detroit	58	34	18	6	0	227	174	74	57	17	30	10	0	169	212	44	115	51	48	16	0	396	386	118
Edmonton	78	41	29	8	0	320	273	90	78	27	41	10	0	258	301	64	156	68	70	18	0	578	574	154
Florida	7	3	3	1	0	17	18	7	9	4	3	2	0	22	21	10	16	7	6	3	0	39	39	17
Los Angeles	92	54	27	11	0	406	304	119	89	35	44	9	1	312	332	80	181	89	71	20	1	718	636	199
Minnesota	7	4	0	2	1	19	15	11	8	3	3	1	1	14	19	8	15	7	3	3	2	33	34	19
Montreal	48	15	26	7	0	144	163	37	45	12	25	8	0	111	159	32	93	27	51	15	0	255	322	69
Nashville	10	5	1	3	1	30	23	14	11	4	7	0	0	20	31	8	21	9	8	3	1	50	54	22
New Jersey	42	28	6	8	0	184	111	64	44	27	14	3	0	161	125	57	86	55	20	11	0	345	236	121
NY Islanders	49	24	14	11	0	172	145	59	50	16	25	9	0	140	189	41	99	40	39	20	0	312	334	100
NY Rangers	49	27	11	10	1	216	148	65	51	22	22	5	2	179	178	51	100	49	33	15	3	395	326	116
Ottawa	10	5	4	1	0	34	23	11	9	2	4	3	0	23	25	7	19	7	8	4	0	57	48	18
Philadelphia	52	25	18	9	0	208	172	59	50	14	33	3	0	134	197	31	102	39	51	12	0	342	369	90
Phoenix	69	37	22	9	1	290	225	84	68	23	33	11	1	232	263	58	137	60	55	20	2	522	488	142
Pittsburgh	45	26	11	8	0	198	139	60	44	10	24	10	0	133	167	30	89	36	35	18	0	331	306	90
St. Louis	60	29	24	5	2	199	176	65	62	22	31	9	0	188	227	53	122	51	55	14	2	387	403	118
San Jose	30	16	10	4	0	110	84	36	32	17	11	4	0	99	93	38	62	33	21	8	0	209	177	74
Tampa Bay	9	6	3	0	0	30	18	12	10	4	5	1	0	32	31	9	19	10	8	1	0	62	49	21
Toronto	60	33	22	5	0	236	193	71	52	18	27	7	0	188	198	43	112	51	49	12	0	424	391	114
Vancouver	95	57	24	14	0	387	274	128	96	43	34	18	1	319	328	105	191	100	58	32	1	706	602	233
Washington	38	24	7	7	0	157	93	55	40	14	21	5	0	136	150	33	78	38	28	12	0	293	243	88
Defunct Clubs	13	8	4	1	0	51	34	17	13	7	3	3	0	43	33	17	26	15	7	4	0	94	67	34
Totals	**1234**	**655**	**390**	**183**	**6**	**4733**	**3735**	**1499**	**1234**	**445**	**590**	**189**	**10**	**3858**	**4400**	**1089**	**2468**	**1100**	**980**	**372**	**16**	**8591**	**8135**	**2588**

Playoffs

	Series	W	L	GP	W	L	T	GF	GA	Last Mtg.	Rnd.	Result
Chicago	3	2	1	12	7	5	0	37	33	1996	CQF	L 0-4
Dallas	1	0	1	6	2	4	0	18	25	1981	SF	L 2-4
Detroit	1	0	1	2	0	2	0	5	8	1978	PRE	L 0-2
Edmonton	5	1	4	30	11	19	0	96	132	1991	DSF	L 3-4
Los Angeles	6	2	4	26	13	13	0	102	105	1993	DSF	L 2-4
Montreal	2	1	1	11	5	6	0	32	31	1989	F	W 4-2
NY Rangers	1	0	1	4	1	3	0	8	14	1980	PRE	L 1-3
Philadelphia	2	1	1	11	4	7	0	28	43	1981	QF	W 4-3
St. Louis	1	1	0	7	4	3	0	28	22	1986	CF	W 4-3
San Jose	1	0	1	7	3	4	0	35	26	1995	CQF	L 3-4
Toronto	1	0	1	2	0	2	0	5	9	1979	PRE	L 0-2
Vancouver	5	3	2	25	13	12	0	82	80	1994	CQF	L 3-4
Winnipeg	3	1	2	13	6	7	0	43	45	1987	DSF	L 2-4
Totals	**32**	**12**	**20**	**156**	**69**	**87**	**0**	**519**	**573**			

Playoff Results 2003-1999

(Last playoff appearance: 1996)

Abbreviations: Round: F - Final;
CF - conference final; **CQF** - conference quarter-final;
DSF - division semi-final; **SF** - semi-final;
QF - quarter-final; **PRE** - preliminary round.

Carolina totals include Hartford, 1979-80 to 1996-97.
Colorado totals include Quebec, 1979-80 to 1994-95.
Dallas totals include Minnesota North Stars, 1972-73 to 1992-93.
New Jersey totals include Kansas City, 1974-75 to 1975-76, and Colorado Rockies, 1976-77 to 1981-82.
Phoenix totals include Winnipeg, 1979-80 to 1995-96.

2002-03 Results

Oct.	10	Vancouver	0-3		9	Ottawa	0-1
	12	Philadelphia	4-5		11	Columbus	2-7
	14	at Vancouver	3-2		13	at Montreal	2-4
	17	Boston	3-3		14	at Toronto	2-3
	19	at Chicago	5-2		16	Nashville	2-2
	21	at Detroit	0-4		18	Los Angeles	2-1*
	22	at Minnesota	3-4*		20	Edmonton	4-3
	24	Dallas	3-3		23	Phoenix	1-7
	26	St. Louis	3-4*		25	Detroit	4-1
	31	Buffalo	3-0		28	at Phoenix	3-4
Nov.	2	Colorado	4-4		29	at Dallas	1-4
	4	at NY Islanders	4-2	Feb.	4	Anaheim	2-3
	5	at New Jersey	3-2		6	Chicago	2-2
	7	at NY Rangers	0-1*		7	at Edmonton	4-3
	9	at Florida	0-3		9	at Colorado	2-4
	11	at Atlanta	1-2		12	at Anaheim	3-4*
	14	NY Rangers	1-2		13	at Los Angeles	2-4
	16	St. Louis	0-1		15	Vancouver	2-2
	19	Detroit	0-5		17	at St. Louis	3-5
	21	Edmonton	1-3		19	at Dallas	1-1
	23	Chicago	3-1		20	at Nashville	1-4
	26	at Boston	2-7		23	at Phoenix	4-2
	27	at Washington	2-4		24	at San Jose	2-5
	29	at St. Louis	2-7	Mar.	1	San Jose	4-3
Dec.	1	at Detroit	2-4		5	New Jersey	5-4*
	3	at Colorado	2-1		7	at Chicago	2-0
	5	Minnesota	1-1		8	at Columbus	3-2*
	9	at Vancouver	2-1		11	Edmonton	2-5
	12	Carolina	3-4		13	Toronto	4-3*
	14	Colorado	1-3		15	at San Jose	2-3
	15	at Vancouver	3-3		16	at Anaheim	2-2
	17	at Nashville	3-0		18	at Los Angeles	4-1
	19	at Columbus	0-3		20	Washington	1-4
	21	at Pittsburgh	0-2		22	Nashville	1-1
	23	at Minnesota	3-2		24	Phoenix	2-0
	27	Toronto	3-4		27	Dallas	2-1*
	29	Anaheim	4-2		29	Columbus	4-6
	31	Montreal	1-1		31	at Minnesota	0-3
Jan.	2	Tampa Bay	4-1	Apr.	2	San Jose	2-2
	4	Minnesota	3-2		4	Los Angeles	2-1*
	7	at Colorado	4-2		5	at Edmonton	4-1

* – Overtime

Entry Draft
Selections 2003-1989

2003		1999		1995		1991	
Pick		**Pick**		**Pick**		**Pick**	
9	Dion Phaneuf	11	Oleg Saprykin	20	Denis Gauthier	19	Niklas Sundblad
39	Tim Ramholt	38	Dan Cavanaugh	46	Pavel Smirnov	41	Francois Groleau
97	Ryan Donally	77	Craig Anderson	72	Rocky Thompson	52	Sandy McCarthy
112	Jamie Tardif	106	Roman Rozakov	98	Jan Labraaten	63	Brian Caruso
143	Greg Moore	135	Matt Doman	150	Clarke Wilm	85	Steven Magnusson
173	Tyler Johnson	153	Jesse Cook	176	Ryan Gillis	107	Jerome Butler
206	Thomas Bellemare	166	Cory Pecker	233	Steve Shirreffs	129	Bobby Marshall
240	Cam Cunning	170	Matt Underhill			140	Matt Hoffman
270	Kevin Harvey	190	Blair Stayzer	**1994**		151	Kelly Harper
		252	Dmitri Kirilenko	**Pick**		173	David St-Pierre
2002				19	Chris Dingman	195	David Struch
Pick		**1998**		45	Dmitri Ryabykin	217	Sergei Zolotov
10	Eric Nystrom	**Pick**		77	Chris Clark	239	Marko Jantunen
39	Brian McConnell	6	Rico Fata	91	Ryan Duthie	261	Andrei Trefilov
90	Matthew Lombardi	33	Blair Betts	97	Johan Finnstrom		
112	Yuri Artemenkov	62	Paul Manning	107	Nils Ekman	**1990**	
141	Jiri Cetkovsky	102	Shaun Sutter	123	Frank Appel	**Pick**	
142	Emanuel Peter	108	Dany Sabourin	149	Patrick Haltia	11	Trevor Kidd
146	Viktor Bobrov	120	Brent Gauvreau	175	Ladislav Kohn	26	Nicolas Perreault
159	Kristofer Persson	192	Radek Duda	201	Keith McCambridge	32	Vesa Viitakoski
176	Curtis McElhinney	206	Jonas Frogren	227	Jorgen Jonsson	41	Etienne Belzile
206	David Van Der Gulik	234	Kevin Mitchell	253	Mike Peluso	62	Glen Mears
207	Pierre Johnsson			279	Pavel Torgaev	83	Paul Kruse
238	Jyri Marttinen	**1997**				125	Chris Tschupp
		Pick		**1993**		146	Dimitri Frolov
2001		6	Daniel Tkaczuk	**Pick**		167	Shawn Murray
Pick		32	Evan Lindsay	18	Jesper Mattsson	188	Mike Murray
14	Chuck Kobasew	42	John Tripp	44	Jamie Allison	209	Rob Sumner
41	Andrei Taratukhin	51	Dimitri Kokorev	70	Dan Tompkins	230	invalid pick
56	Andrei Medvedev	60	Derek Schutz	95	Jason Smith	251	Leo Gudas
108	Tomi Maki	70	Erik Andersson	96	Marty Murray		
124	Yegor Shastin	92	Chris St. Croix	121	Darryl Lafrance	**1989**	
145	James Hakewill	100	Ryan Ready	122	John Emmons	**Pick**	
164	Yuri Trubachev	113	Martin Moise	148	Andreas Karlsson	24	Kent Manderville
207	Garrett Bembridge	140	Ilja Demidov	200	Derek Sylvester	42	Ted Drury
220	David Moss	167	Jeremy Rondeau	252	German Titov	50	Veli-Pekka Kautonen
233	Joe Campbell	223	Dustin Paul	278	Burke Murphy	63	Corey Lyons
251	Ville Hamalainen					70	Robert Reichel
		1996		**1992**		84	Ryan O'Leary
2000		**Pick**		**Pick**		105	Toby Kearney
Pick		13	Derek Morris	6	Cory Stillman	147	Alex Nikolic
9	Brent Krahn	39	Travis Brigley	30	Chris O'Sullivan	168	Kevin Wortman
40	Kurtis Foster	40	Steve Begin	54	Mathias Johansson	189	Sergei Gomolyako
46	Jarret Stoll	73	Dmitri Vlasenkov	78	Robert Svehla	210	Dan Sawyer
116	Levente Szuper	89	Toni Lydman	102	Sami Helenius	231	Alexander Yudin
141	Wade Davis	94	Christian Lefebvre	126	Ravil Yakubov	252	Kenneth Kennholt
155	Travis Moen	122	Josef Straka	129	Joel Bouchard		
176	Jukka Hentunen	202	Ryan Wade	150	Pavel Rajnoha		
239	David Hajek	228	Ronald Petrovicky	174	Ryan Mulhern		
270	Micki DuPont			198	Brandon Carper		
				222	Jonas Hoglund		
				246	Andrei Potaichuk		

Stephane Yelle had spent seven seasons in Colorado before being traded to Calgary just prior to the 2002-03 season. He was the only Flame to play in all 82 games last year.

Club Directory

Pengrowth Saddledome

Calgary Flames
Pengrowth Saddledome
P.O. Box 1540 Station M
Calgary, Alberta T2P 3B9
Phone 403/777-2177
FAX 403/777-2199
www.calgaryflames.com
Capacity: 17,448

Owners: N. Murray Edwards, Harley N. Hotchkiss, Alvin G. Libin, Allan P. Markin, J.R. (Bud) McCaig, Byron J. Seaman, Daryl K. Seaman

Executive
President & Chief Executive Officer . . . . Ken King
General Manager & Head Coach . . . . Darryl Sutter
Vice President, Hockey Administration . . . . Michael Holditch
Vice-President, Building Operations . . . . Libby Raines
Vice-President, Advertising,
   Sponsorship & Marketing . . . . Jim Bagshaw
Vice-President, Sales . . . . Rollie Cyr
Vice-President, Business Development . . . . Jim Peplinski

Hockey Club Personnel
General Manager & Head Coach . . . . Darryl Sutter
Vice-President, Hockey Administration . . . . Michael Holditch
Director, Hockey Administration . . . . Mike Burke
Special Assistant to the GM. . . . . Al MacNeil
Assistant Coaches . . . . Jim Playfair, Rich Preston, Rob Cookson
Development Coach . . . . Jamie Hislop
Goaltending Coach . . . . David Marcoux
Exec. Asst. to GM and Hockey Operations . . . . Brenda Koyich
Team Services Manager . . . . Kelly Chesla
Director of Scouting . . . . Tod Button
Director of Amateur Scouting . . . . Mike Sands
Western Pro Scout . . . . Ron Sutter
Eastern Pro Scout . . . . Tom Webster
Scouts . . . . Bob Atrill, Pertti Hasanen, Tomas Jelinek,
                     Larry Johnston, Sergei Samoylov, Al Tuer

Medical/Training Staff
Athletic Therapist . . . . Morris Boyer
Assistant Athletic Therapist . . . . Gerry Kurylowich
Strength & Conditioning Coach . . . . Rich Hesketh
Equipment Manager . . . . Gus Thorson
Assistant Equipment Manager . . . . Les Jarvis
Sport Medicine Physician . . . . TBA
Internal Medicine . . . . TBA
Team Dentist . . . . TBA
Dressing Room Attendant . . . . Jules Carriere

Communications
Director, Communications . . . . Peter Hanlon
Manager, Media Relations . . . . Sean O'Brien
Administrative Assistant, Communications . . . . Bernie Hargrave
Community Relations Coordinator . . . . Trevor Elgar
Community Relations Ambassador . . . . Jim "Bearcat" Murray

Administration
Controller . . . . Karen Kingham
Assistant Controllers . . . . Trudy McInnes, Kelly Shillington
Exec. Asst. to President/CEO . . . . Judy O'Brien
Exec. Asst. to Finance & Administration . . . . Judith Virag

Marketing
Senior Director, Advertising . . . . Pat Halls
Director, Retail/FanAttic . . . . Kip Reghenas
Director, Executive Suites . . . . Bob White
Business Development Manager . . . . Kevin Gross
Sales Manager . . . . Mike Franco
Director, Game Presentation . . . . Dave Imbach
Director/Producer, Jumbotron . . . . Carlo Petrini
Publishing . . . . Laurie Wheeler
Exec. Asst. to VP, Advertising,
   Sponsorship & Marketing . . . . Yvette Mutcheson
Mascot . . . . Harvey the Hound

Pengrowth Saddledome
Operations Manager . . . . George Greenwood
Food Services Manager . . . . Art Hernandez
Concessions Manager . . . . Sheila Parisien
Security/Parking Manager . . . . Bob Godun

Calgary Hitmen (WHL)
General Manager . . . . Kelly Kisio
Asst. General Manager . . . . Blaine Forsythe
Head Coach . . . . Richard Kromm
Assistant Coach . . . . Bruno Campese

Miscellaneous Data
Home ice (capacity) . . . . Pengrowth Saddledome (17,448)
Website . . . . www.calgaryflames.com
Practice Facility . . . . Pengrowth Saddledome
Training Camp . . . . Pengrowth Saddledome
Club Colours . . . . Red, white, gold and black
Radio Affiliate . . . . The FAN 960 (960 AM)
TV Affiliate . . . . Rogers Sportsnet, CBC-TV, TSN
AHL Affiliate . . . . Lowell Lock Monsters
ECHL Affiliate . . . . Las Vegas Wranglers

Carolina Hurricanes

2002-03 Results: 22w-43l-11t-6otl 61pts.
Fifth, Southeast Division

2003-04 Schedule

Oct.	Thu.	9	at Florida
	Sat.	11	New Jersey
	Mon.	13	Florida
	Sat.	18	at NY Rangers
	Wed.	22	at Pittsburgh
	Thu.	23	at Boston
	Sat.	25	at Philadelphia
	Tue.	28	San Jose
	Thu.	30	at NY Rangers
Nov.	Sat.	1	at Tampa Bay
	Sun.	2	Toronto*
	Thu.	6	NY Rangers
	Sat.	8	Los Angeles
	Sun.	9	Tampa Bay*
	Wed.	12	at Washington
	Thu.	13	Atlanta
	Sat.	15	Washington
	Tue.	18	Philadelphia
	Thu.	20	at Ottawa
	Fri.	21	at Buffalo
	Sun.	23	Tampa Bay
	Wed.	26	at NY Islanders
	Fri.	28	at Philadelphia*
	Sat.	29	Pittsburgh
Dec.	Wed.	3	Nashville
	Fri.	5	Montreal
	Sat.	6	at Montreal
	Tue.	9	at Edmonton
	Thu.	11	at Calgary
	Sun.	14	at Vancouver
	Thu.	18	Pittsburgh
	Sat.	20	at Boston*
	Mon.	22	Dallas
	Fri.	26	at Buffalo
	Sat.	27	Montreal
	Mon.	29	Buffalo
	Wed.	31	Anaheim
Jan.	Fri.	2	Detroit
	Sun.	4	Phoenix*
	Tue.	6	St. Louis
	Thu.	8	NY Rangers

	Fri.	9	at Washington
	Sun.	11	Ottawa*
	Thu.	15	at Tampa Bay
	Fri.	16	at Atlanta
	Sun.	18	Atlanta*
	Tue.	20	Ottawa
	Wed.	21	at New Jersey
	Fri.	23	NY Islanders
	Sun.	25	Buffalo*
	Tue.	27	at Toronto
	Thu.	29	Washington
	Sat.	31	at Detroit
Feb.	Tue.	3	at Colorado
	Wed.	4	at Anaheim
	Thu.	12	Washington
	Sat.	14	at New Jersey*
	Mon.	16	Florida
	Thu.	19	Toronto
	Sat.	21	Boston
	Mon.	23	at Toronto
	Wed.	25	at Washington
	Sat.	28	at Montreal
	Sun.	29	at Minnesota
Mar.	Tue.	2	Columbus
	Fri.	5	at Atlanta
	Sat.	6	New Jersey
	Mon.	8	at Columbus
	Wed.	10	Tampa Bay
	Fri.	12	Atlanta
	Sat.	13	at Tampa Bay
	Mon.	15	at Atlanta
	Wed.	17	at Chicago
	Fri.	19	at Pittsburgh
	Sat.	20	at Ottawa
	Tue.	23	Philadelphia
	Thu.	25	Florida
	Sat.	27	at NY Islanders
	Mon.	29	at Florida
	Tue.	30	Boston
Apr.	Fri.	2	NY Islanders
	Sun.	4	at Florida*

* Denotes afternoon game.

Year-by-Year Record

Season	GP	Home				Road				Overall						Pts.	Finished	Playoff Result
		W	L	T	OL	W	L	T	OL	W	L	T	OL	GF	GA			
2002-03	82	12	17	9	3	10	26	2	3	22	43	11	6	171	240	61	5th, Southeast Div.	Out of Playoffs
2001-02	82	15	13	11	2	20	13	5	3	35	26	16	5	217	217	91	1st, Southeast Div.	Lost Final
2000-01	82	23	15	3	0	15	17	6	3	38	32	9	3	212	225	88	2nd, Southeast Div.	Lost Conf. Quarter-Final
1999-2000	82	20	16	5	0	17	19	5	0	37	35	10	0	217	216	84	3rd, Southeast Div.	Out of Playoffs
1998-99	82	20	12	9	...	14	18	9	...	34	30	18	...	210	202	86	1st, Southeast Div.	Lost Conf. Quarter-Final
1997-98	82	16	18	7	...	17	23	1	...	33	41	8	...	200	219	74	6th, Northeast Div.	Out of Playoffs
1996-97*	82	23	15	3	...	9	24	8	...	32	39	11	...	226	256	75	5th, Northeast Div.	Out of Playoffs
1995-96*	82	22	15	4	...	12	24	5	...	34	39	9	...	237	259	77	4th, Northeast Div.	Out of Playoffs
1994-95*	48	12	10	2	...	7	14	3	...	19	24	5	...	127	141	43	5th, Northeast Div.	Out of Playoffs
1993-94*	84	14	22	6	...	13	26	3	...	27	48	9	...	227	288	63	6th, Northeast Div.	Out of Playoffs
1992-93*	84	12	25	5	...	14	27	1	...	26	52	6	...	284	369	58	5th, Adams Div.	Out of Playoffs
1991-92*	80	13	17	10	...	13	24	3	...	26	41	13	...	247	283	65	4th, Adams Div.	Lost Div. Semi-Final
1990-91*	80	18	16	6	...	13	22	5	...	31	38	11	...	238	276	73	4th, Adams Div.	Lost Div. Semi-Final
1989-90*	80	17	18	5	...	21	15	4	...	38	33	9	...	275	268	85	4th, Adams Div.	Lost Div. Semi-Final
1988-89*	80	21	17	2	...	16	21	3	...	37	38	5	...	299	290	79	4th, Adams Div.	Lost Div. Semi-Final
1987-88*	80	21	14	5	...	14	24	2	...	35	38	7	...	249	267	77	4th, Adams Div.	Lost Div. Semi-Final
1986-87*	80	26	9	5	...	17	21	2	...	43	30	7	...	287	270	93	1st, Adams Div.	Lost Div. Semi-Final
1985-86*	80	21	17	2	...	19	19	2	...	40	36	4	...	332	302	84	4th, Adams Div.	Lost Div. Final
1984-85*	80	17	18	5	...	13	23	4	...	30	41	9	...	268	318	69	5th, Adams Div.	Out of Playoffs
1983-84*	80	19	16	5	...	9	26	5	...	28	42	10	...	288	320	66	5th, Adams Div.	Out of Playoffs
1982-83*	80	13	22	5	...	6	32	2	...	19	54	7	...	261	403	45	5th, Adams Div.	Out of Playoffs
1981-82*	80	13	17	10	...	8	24	8	...	21	41	18	...	264	351	60	5th, Adams Div.	Out of Playoffs
1980-81*	80	14	17	9	...	7	24	9	...	21	41	18	...	292	372	60	4th, Norris Div.	Out of Playoffs
1979-80	80	22	12	6	...	5	22	13	...	27	34	19	...	303	312	73	4th, Norris Div.	Lost Prelim. Round

* Hartford Whalers

Franchise date: June 22, 1979
Transferred from Hartford to Carolina, June 25, 1997.

EASTERN CONFERENCE

SOUTHEAST DIVISION

25th NHL Season

After a solid rookie season, injuries limited Erik Cole to just 53 games played in 2002-03. Still, he nearly matched his first-year totals with 14 goals. Cole had a career-high four points (three goals, one assist) versus Montreal on November 23, 2002.

2003-04 Player Personnel

FORWARDS

	HT	WT	S	Place of Birth	Date	2002-03 Club
ADAMS, Craig	6-0	200	R	Seria, Brunei	4/26/77	Carolina
ADAMS, Kevyn	6-1	195	R	Washington, DC	10/8/74	Carolina
BAYDA, Ryan	5-11	185	L	Saskatoon, Sask.	12/9/80	Carolina-Lowell
BOULERICE, Jesse	6-2	203	R	Plattsburgh, NY	8/10/78	Carolina
BRENDL, Pavel	6-1	206	R	Opocno, Czech.	3/23/81	Philadelphia-Carolina
BRIND'AMOUR, Rod	6-1	200	L	Ottawa, Ont.	8/9/70	Carolina
COLE, Erik	6-2	200	L	Oswego, NY	11/6/78	Carolina
DANIELS, Jeff	6-1	200	L	Oshawa, Ont.	6/24/68	Carolina
DEFAUW, Brad	6-2	220	L	Edina, MN	11/10/77	Carolina-Lowell
FRANCIS, Ron	6-3	200	L	Sault Ste. Marie, Ont.	3/1/63	Carolina
HEEREMA, Jeff	6-1	190	R	Thunder Bay, Ont.	1/17/80	Carolina-Lowell
KURKA, Tomas	5-11	190	L	Most, Czech.	12/14/81	Carolina-Lowell
MURRAY, Marty	5-9	180	L	Lylton, Man.	2/16/75	Philadelphia
O'NEILL, Jeff	6-1	195	R	Richmond Hill, Ont.	2/23/76	Carolina
STAAL, Eric	6-3	182	L	Thunder Bay, Ont.	10/29/84	Peterborough
SURMA, Damian	5-10	200	L	Lincoln Park, MI	1/22/81	Carolina-Lowell
SVOBODA, Jaroslav	6-2	190	L	Cervenka, Czech.	6/1/80	Carolina-Lowell
TETARENKO, Joey	6-2	215	R	Prince Albert, Sask.	3/3/78	Fla-San Antonio-Ott-Binghamton
VASICEK, Josef	6-4	200	L	Havlickuv Brod, Czech.	9/12/80	Carolina
VRBATA, Radim	6-1	190	R	Mlada Boleslav, Czech.	6/13/81	Colorado-Carolina
ZIGOMANIS, Mike	6-1	189	R	North York, Ont.	1/17/81	Carolina-Lowell

DEFENSEMEN

	HT	WT	S	Place of Birth	Date	2002-03 Club
BOUGHNER, Bob	6-0	203	R	Windsor, Ont.	3/8/71	Calgary
CURRY, Sean	6-4	230	R	Burnsville, MN	4/29/82	Lowell-Florida (ECHL)
HEDICAN, Bret	6-2	205	L	St. Paul, MN	8/10/70	Carolina
HILL, Sean	6-0	205	R	Duluth, MN	2/14/70	Carolina
MALEC, Tomas	6-2	195	L	Skalica, Czech.	5/13/82	Carolina-Lowell
MARKOV, Danny	6-1	190	L	Moscow, USSR	7/30/76	Phoenix
ROURKE, Allan	6-1	214	L	Mississauga, Ont.	3/6/80	St. John's
ST. JACQUES, Bruno	6-2	204	L	Montreal, Que.	8/22/80	Phi-Phi (AHL)-Car-Lowell (AHL)
WALLIN, Niclas	6-3	220	L	Boden, Sweden	2/20/75	Carolina
WARD, Aaron	6-2	225	R	Windsor, Ont.	1/17/73	Carolina
WESLEY, Glen	6-1	205	L	Red Deer, Alta.	10/2/68	Carolina-Toronto

GOALTENDERS

	HT	WT	C	Place of Birth	Date	2002-03 Club
DesROCHERS, Patrick	6-3	209	L	Penetanguishene, Ont.	10/27/79	Phx-Sprfld-Car-Lowell (AHL)
WEEKES, Kevin	6-0	195	L	Toronto, Ont.	4/4/75	Carolina
ZEPP, Rob	6-1	181	L	Scarborough, Ont.	9/7/81	Lowell-Florida (ECHL)

Coaching History

Don Blackburn, 1979-80; Don Blackburn and Larry Pleau, 1980-81; Larry Pleau, 1981-82; Larry Kish, Larry Pleau and John Cuniff, 1982- 83; Jack Evans, 1983-84 to 1986-87; Jack Evans and Larry Pleau, 1987-88; Larry Pleau, 1988-89; Rick Ley, 1989-90, 1990-91; Jim Roberts, 1991-92; Paul Holmgren, 1992-93; Paul Holmgren and Pierre Maguire, 1993-94; Paul Holmgren, 1994-95; Paul Holmgren and Paul Maurice, 1995-96; Paul Maurice, 1996-97 to date.

Coach

MAURICE, PAUL
Coach, Carolina Hurricanes. Born in Sault Ste. Marie, Ont., January 30, 1967.

Paul Maurice became the tenth coach in franchise history on November 6, 1995 and is the only man to serve as head coach since the club moved to Carolina in 1997. He was the youngest coach in the NHL when he first stepped behind the bench 12 games into the 1995-96 season and is now the second youngest despite having the longest tenure among current NHL head coaches. He ranks as the club's all-time leader in wins and games coached, and guided the team to the Stanley Cup Finals for the first time in franchise history in 2002.

Maurice joined the Whalers in June of 1995 as an assistant coach after serving as the head coach of the Detroit Junior Red Wings for two seasons. The Junior Wings won the OHL Western Division regular-season title and played for the 1995 Memorial Cup by winning the OHL playoffs. The Wings lost in the Cup finals to Kamloops. For his efforts, Maurice was the runner-up for OHL coach of the year honors in 1995. In the 1993-94 season, Maurice's squad won the OHL Hap Emms Division title and advanced to the finals of the OHL playoffs before losing in seven games to North Bay.

Maurice began his coaching career in 1986 as an assistant coach for the Detroit Junior Red Wings after an eye injury ended his junior playing career. He served six seasons in that capacity before taking over the head coaching responsibilities in the 1993-94 season.

Coaching Record

			Regular Season			Playoffs		
Season	Team	Games	W	L	T	Games	W	L
1993-94	Detroit (OHL)	66	42	20	4	17	11	6
1994-95	Detroit (OHL)	66	44	18	4	21	16	5
1995-96	Hartford (NHL)	70	29	33	8	....	....	....
1996-97	Hartford (NHL)	82	32	39	11	....	....	....
1997-98	Carolina (NHL)	82	33	41	8	....	....	....
1998-99	Carolina (NHL)	82	34	30	18	6	2	4
1999-2000	Carolina (NHL)	82	37	35	10	....	....	....
2000-01	Carolina (NHL)	82	38	35	9	6	2	4
2001-02	Carolina (NHL)	82	35	31	16	23	13	10
2002-03	Carolina (NHL)	82	22	49	11	....	....	....
	NHL Totals	644	260	293	91	35	17	18

2002-03 Scoring

* - rookie

Regular Season

Pos	#	Player	Team	GP	G	A	Pts	+/-	PIM	PP	SH	GW	GT	S	%
R	92	Jeff O'Neill	CAR	82	30	31	61	-21	38	11	0	7	2	316	9.5
C	10	Ron Francis	CAR	82	22	35	57	-22	30	8	1	1	0	156	14.1
C	17	Rod Brind'Amour	CAR	48	14	23	37	-9	37	7	1	0	0	110	12.7
R	19	Radim Vrbata	COL	66	11	19	30	0	16	3	0	4	1	171	6.4
			CAR	10	5	0	5	-7	2	3	0	0	0	44	11.4
			TOTAL	76	16	19	35	-7	18	6	0	4	1	215	7.4
D	22	Sean Hill	CAR	82	5	24	29	4	141	1	0	0	0	188	2.7
L	26	Erik Cole	CAR	53	14	13	27	1	72	6	2	3	0	125	11.2
L	20	Jan Hlavac	VAN	9	1	1	2	-1	6	0	0	0	0	7	14.3
			CAR	52	9	15	24	-9	22	6	0	1	1	116	7.8
			TOTAL	61	10	16	26	-10	28	6	0	1	1	123	8.1
C	63	Josef Vasicek	CAR	57	10	10	20	-19	33	4	0	1	0	87	11.5
C	14	Kevyn Adams	CAR	77	9	9	18	-8	57	0	0	0	0	169	5.3
R	27	Craig Adams	CAR	81	6	12	18	-11	71	0	0	1	0	107	5.6
D	6	Bret Hedican	CAR	72	3	14	17	-24	75	1	0	1	0	113	2.7
L	47	* Ryan Bayda	CAR	25	4	10	14	-5	16	0	0	1	0	49	8.2
R	62	* Jaroslav Svoboda	CAR	48	3	11	14	-5	32	1	0	0	0	63	4.8
R	55	* Pavel Brendl	PHI	42	5	7	12	8	4	1	0	1	0	80	6.3
			CAR	8	0	1	1	-3	2	0	0	0	0	14	0.0
			TOTAL	50	5	8	13	5	6	1	0	1	0	94	5.3
D	21	David Tanabe	CAR	68	3	10	13	-27	24	2	0	0	0	104	2.9
D	7	Niclas Wallin	CAR	77	2	8	10	-19	71	0	0	2	0	69	2.9
D	4	Aaron Ward	CAR	77	3	6	9	-23	90	0	0	1	0	66	4.5
D	25	* Bruno St. Jacques	PHI	6	0	0	0	-1	2	0	0	0	0	5	0.0
			CAR	18	2	5	7	-3	12	0	0	0	0	14	14.3
			TOTAL	24	2	5	7	-4	14	0	0	0	0	19	10.5
L	37	* Tomas Kurka	CAR	14	3	2	5	1	2	0	0	0	0	22	13.6
C	15	Harold Druken	VAN	3	1	1	2	-1	0	0	0	0	0	3	33.3
			CAR	10	0	1	1	-1	2	0	0	0	0	3	0.0
			TOR	5	0	2	2	1	2	0	0	0	0	8	0.0
			CAR	4	0	0	0	0	0	0	0	0	0	2	0.0
			TOTAL	22	1	4	5	-1	4	0	0	0	0	16	6.3
C	12	Craig MacDonald	CAR	35	1	3	4	-3	20	0	0	0	0	43	2.3
L	11	Jeff Daniels	CAR	59	0	4	4	-9	8	0	0	0	0	41	0.0
L	39	* Brad Defauw	CAR	9	3	0	3	-2	2	1	0	1	0	19	15.8
R	42	* Jeff Heerema	CAR	10	3	0	3	-2	2	0	0	0	0	16	18.8
C	46	* Mike Zigomanis	CAR	19	2	1	3	-4	0	1	1	0	0	19	10.5
R	36	* Jesse Boulerice	CAR	48	2	1	3	-2	108	0	0	0	1	12	16.7
D	71	* Tomas Malec	CAR	41	0	2	2	-5	43	0	0	0	0	30	0.0
L	52	* Damian Surma	CAR	1	1	0	1	0	0	0	0	0	0	1	100.0
L	16	Tommy Westlund	CAR	3	0	0	0	0	0	0	0	0	0	0	0.0
L	29	Mike Watt	CAR	5	0	0	0	-1	0	0	0	0	0	2	0.0
D	28	Steven Halko	CAR	6	0	0	0	1	0	0	0	0	0	5	0.0

Goaltending

No.	Goaltender	GPI	Mins	Avg	W	L	T	EN	SO	GA	SA	S%	G	A	PIM
80	Kevin Weekes	51	2965	2.55	14	24	9	2	5	126	1438	.912	0	0	2
1	Arturs Irbe	34	1884	3.18	7	24	2	5	0	100	816	.877	0	0	4
30	* Patrick DesRochers	2	122	3.44	1	1	0	0	0	7	71	.901	0	0	0
	Totals	82	5003	2.88	22	49	11	7	5	240	2332	.897			

General Managers' History

Jack Kelly, 1979-80, 1980-81; Larry Pleau, 1981-82, 1982-83; Emile Francis, 1983-84 to 1988-89; Eddie Johnston, 1989-90 to 1991-92; Brian Burke, 1992-93; Paul Holmgren, 1993-94; Jim Rutherford, 1994-95 to date.

Captains' History

Rick Ley, 1979-80; Rick Ley and Mike Rogers, 1980-81; Dave Keon, 1981-82; Russ Anderson, 1982-83; Mark Johnson, 1983-84; Mark Johnson and Ron Francis, 1984-85; Ron Francis, 1985-86 to 1990-91; Randy Ladouceur, 1991-92; Pat Verbeek, 1992-93 to 1994-95; Brendan Shanahan, 1995-96; Kevin Dineen, 1996-97, 1997-98; Keith Primeau, 1998-99; Keith Primeau and Ron Francis, 1999-2000; Ron Francis, 2000-01 to date.

Club Records

Team

(Figures in brackets for season records are games played; records for fewest points, wins, ties, losses, goals, goals against are for 70 or more games)

Most Points	93	1986-87 (80)
Most Wins	43	1986-87 (80)
Most Ties	19	1979-80 (80)
Most Losses	54	1982-83 (80)
Most Goals	332	1985-86 (80)
Most Goals Against	403	1982-83 (80)
Fewest Points	45	1982-83 (80)
Fewest Wins	19	1982-83 (80)
Fewest Ties	4	1985-86 (80)
Fewest Losses	26	2001-02 (82)
Fewest Goals	171	2002-03 (82)
Fewest Goals Against	202	1998-99 (82)

Longest Winning Streak
Overall................7 Mar. 16-29/85
Home.................5 Mar. 17-29/85
Away.................6 Nov. 10-Dec. 7/90

Longest Undefeated Streak
Overall...............10 Jan. 20-Feb. 10/82
(6 wins, 4 ties)
Home.................9 Dec. 15/00-Jan. 18/01
(8 wins, 1 tie)
Away.................8 Nov. 11-Dec. 5/96
(4 wins, 4 ties)

Longest Losing Streak
Overall................9 Feb. 19-Mar. 8/83
Home.................6 Feb. 19-Mar. 12/83,
Feb. 10-Mar. 3/85
Away................13 Dec. 18/82-Feb. 5/83

Longest Winless Streak
Overall...............14 Jan. 4-Feb. 9/92
(8 losses, 6 ties)
Home................13 Jan. 15-Mar. 10/85
(11 losses, 2 ties)
Away................15 Nov. 11/79-Jan. 9/80
(11 losses, 4 ties)

Most Shutouts, Season.......8 1998-99 (82)
Most PIM, Season........2,354 1992-93 (84)
Most Goals, Game..........11 Feb. 12/84
(Edm. 0 at Hfd. 11),
Oct. 19/85
(Mtl. 6 at Hfd. 11),
Jan. 17/86
(Que. 6 at Hfd. 11),
Mar. 15/86
(Chi. 4 at Hfd. 11)

Individual

Most Seasons..............15 Ron Francis
Most Games...........1,118 Ron Francis
Most Goals, Career........372 Ron Francis
Most Assists, Career.......773 Ron Francis
Most Points, Career......1,145 Ron Francis
(372G, 773A)
Most PIM, Career........1,439 Kevin Dineen
Most Shutouts, Career.......20 Arturs Irbe
Longest Consecutive
Games Streak...........419 Dave Tippett
(Mar. 3/84-Oct. 7/89)
Most Goals, Season.........56 Blaine Stoughton
(1979-80)
Most Assists, Season........69 Ron Francis
(1989-90)
Most Points, Season.......105 Mike Rogers
(1979-80; 44G, 61A),
(1980-81; 40G, 65A)
Most PIM, Season.........358 Torrie Robertson
(1985-86)

Most Points, Defenseman,
Season..................69 Dave Babych
(1985-86; 14G, 55A)
Most Points, Center,
Season.................105 Mike Rogers
(1979-80; 44G, 61A),
(1980-81; 40G, 65A)
Most Points, Right Wing,
Season.................100 Blaine Stoughton
(1979-80; 56G, 44A)
Most Points, Left Wing,
Season..................89 Geoff Sanderson
(1992-93; 46G, 43A)
Most Points, Rookie,
Season..................72 Sylvain Turgeon
(1983-84; 40G, 32A)
Most Shutouts, Season.......6 Arturs Irbe
(1998-99, 2000-01)
Most Goals, Game...........4 Jordy Douglas
(Feb. 3/80),
Ron Francis
(Feb. 12/84)
Most Assists, Game...........6 Ron Francis
(Mar. 5/87)
Most Points, Game...........6 Paul Lawless
(Jan. 4/87; 2G, 4A),
Ron Francis
(Mar. 5/87; 6A)
(Oct. 8/89; 3G, 3A)

Records include Hartford Whalers, 1979-80 through 1996-97.

All-time Record vs. Other Clubs
Regular Season

	At Home								On Road								Total							
	GP	W	L	T	OL	GF	GA	PTS	GP	W	L	T	OL	GF	GA	PTS	GP	W	L	T	OL	GF	GA	PTS
Anaheim	8	5	2	1	0	22	16	11	8	3	4	1	0	24	26	7	16	8	6	2	0	46	42	18
Atlanta	10	8	1	1	0	36	23	17	10	6	1	3	0	31	24	15	20	14	2	4	0	67	47	32
Boston	74	31	35	8	0	247	257	70	76	23	46	7	0	203	273	53	150	54	81	15	0	450	530	123
Buffalo	76	31	34	11	0	223	225	73	75	24	43	7	1	225	301	56	151	55	77	18	1	448	526	129
Calgary	28	10	13	5	0	91	103	25	28	6	20	2	0	92	139	14	56	16	33	7	0	183	242	39
Chicago	30	14	12	4	0	97	93	32	28	9	16	3	0	80	115	21	58	23	28	7	0	177	208	53
Colorado	62	24	25	12	1	203	214	61	64	17	38	9	0	190	271	43	126	41	63	21	1	393	485	104
Columbus	3	3	0	0	0	13	8	6	2	1	1	0	0	5	5	2	5	4	1	0	0	18	13	8
Dallas	31	13	14	4	0	100	107	30	29	10	16	2	1	86	115	23	60	23	30	6	1	186	222	53
Detroit	29	17	11	1	0	103	82	35	30	7	16	6	1	82	115	21	59	24	27	7	1	185	197	56
Edmonton	29	11	11	7	0	112	98	29	30	6	19	5	0	89	119	17	59	17	30	12	0	201	217	46
Florida	22	11	9	2	0	65	58	24	23	7	8	7	1	47	62	22	45	18	17	9	1	112	120	46
Los Angeles	30	14	11	5	0	111	113	33	30	10	17	3	0	113	129	23	60	24	28	8	0	224	242	56
Minnesota	2	2	0	0	0	3	0	4	3	1	1	1	0	9	6	3	5	3	1	1	0	12	6	7
Montreal	76	28	36	12	0	221	266	68	73	18	48	7	0	212	305	43	149	46	84	19	0	433	571	111
Nashville	4	2	1	1	0	13	11	5	4	1	3	0	0	7	9	2	8	3	4	1	0	20	20	7
New Jersey	42	18	16	8	0	135	126	44	43	15	23	4	1	137	153	35	85	33	39	12	1	272	279	79
NY Islanders	43	21	16	5	1	146	139	48	42	18	19	4	1	116	130	41	85	39	35	9	2	262	269	89
NY Rangers	41	22	16	3	0	136	132	47	43	14	26	3	0	112	166	31	84	36	42	6	0	248	298	78
Ottawa	25	16	6	3	0	78	60	35	27	12	11	4	0	74	73	28	52	28	17	7	0	152	133	63
Philadelphia	42	13	20	8	1	136	152	35	41	9	26	4	2	101	154	24	83	22	46	12	3	237	306	59
Phoenix	29	14	9	6	0	103	86	34	31	15	14	2	0	112	110	32	60	29	23	8	0	215	196	66
Pittsburgh	46	20	21	5	0	172	173	45	44	17	22	5	0	166	180	39	90	37	43	10	0	338	353	84
St. Louis	30	11	17	2	0	90	97	24	31	9	18	3	1	94	119	22	61	20	35	5	1	184	216	46
San Jose	10	5	5	0	0	31	23	10	11	4	7	0	0	31	50	8	21	9	12	0	0	62	73	18
Tampa Bay	24	15	3	5	1	78	60	36	23	8	12	3	0	55	63	19	47	23	15	8	1	133	123	55
Toronto	35	18	11	6	0	142	115	42	34	16	13	5	0	122	119	37	69	34	24	11	0	264	234	79
Vancouver	29	12	12	5	0	94	100	29	29	10	13	6	0	80	103	26	58	22	25	11	0	174	203	55
Washington	46	15	21	9	1	121	142	40	44	13	27	4	0	114	151	30	90	28	48	13	1	235	293	70
Totals	**956**	**424**	**388**	**139**	**5**	**3122**	**3079**	**992**	**956**	**309**	**528**	**110**	**9**	**2809**	**3585**	**737**	**1912**	**733**	**916**	**249**	**14**	**5931**	**6664**	**1729**

Playoffs

	Series	W	L	GP	W	L	T	GF	GA	Last Mtg.
Boston	3	0	3	19	7	12	0	48	63	1999
Colorado	2	1	1	9	5	4	0	35	34	1987
Detroit	1	0	1	5	1	4	0	7	14	2002
Montreal	6	1	5	33	12	21	0	91	108	2002
New Jersey	2	1	1	12	6	6	0	17	31	2002
Toronto	1	1	0	6	4	2	0	10	6	2002
Totals	**15**	**4**	**11**	**84**	**35**	**49**	**0**	**208**	**256**	

Playoff Results 2003-1999

Year	Round	Opponent	Result	GF	GA
2002	F	Detroit	L 1-4	7	14
	CF	Toronto	W 4-2	10	6
	CSF	Montreal	W 4-2	21	12
	CQF	New Jersey	W 4-2	9	11
2001	CQF	New Jersey	L 2-4	8	20
1999	CQF	Boston	L 2-4	10	16

Abbreviations: Round: F - Final; **CF** - conference final; **CSF** - conference semi-final; **CQF** - conference quarter-final; **DSF** - division semi-final.

Calgary totals include Atlanta Flames, 1979-80.
Dallas totals include Minnesota North Stars, 1979-80 to 1992-93.
Phoenix totals include Winnipeg, 1979-80 to 1995-96.

Colorado totals include Quebec, 1979-80 to 1994-95.
New Jersey totals include Colorado Rockies, 1979-80 to 1981-82.

2002-03 Results

Oct.	9	NY Rangers	1-4		8	at NY Rangers	1-5
	11	Atlanta	5-3		10	Washington	1-4
	12	at Tampa Bay	1-5		12	Colorado	2-3*
	15	at St. Louis	1-2*		15	Pittsburgh	0-2
	17	Washington	1-2		17	New Jersey	1-2
	19	New Jersey	3-1		18	at New Jersey	2-5
	22	at NY Islanders	4-1		20	St. Louis	3-5
	23	at Ottawa	1-4		22	at Washington	3-5
	26	Chicago	3-3		24	Florida	3-1
	29	at New Jersey	2-1		25	at Florida	2-3*
	30	NY Islanders	4-2		29	Toronto	2-3
Nov.	1	Montreal	2-2		30	at Tampa Bay	1-3
	5	Philadelphia	1-2*	Feb.	5	at San Jose	2-6
	7	Buffalo	2-0		7	at Los Angeles	2-8
	9	Pittsburgh	3-2		9	at Anaheim	1-2
	12	Phoenix	3-2		11	at Dallas	1-2*
	15	Philadelphia	1-1		14	Washington	3-2
	17	Tampa Bay	1-2*		15	at Philadelphia	2-2
	19	Ottawa	4-4		18	at Toronto	3-4
	21	at Boston	1-3		19	Boston	1-1
	23	at Montreal	7-3		21	Tampa Bay	2-2
	25	at NY Rangers	1-3		23	Anaheim	0-4
	27	Vancouver	2-3		26	at Phoenix	2-4
	29	Detroit	6-4	Mar.	1	at Toronto	1-4
	30	at Columbus	4-2		2	at Washington	0-2
Dec.	3	at Nashville	2-1		4	Boston	2-4
	4	at Florida	2-4		6	at Pittsburgh	4-0
	6	Florida	0-2		7	Minnesota	1-0
	7	at Ottawa	2-5		10	Columbus	6-5
	11	at Edmonton	1-4		12	at Buffalo	3-2*
	12	at Calgary	4-3		13	at Philadelphia	3-5
	15	at Minnesota	1-2		15	Los Angeles	0-0
	18	Tampa Bay	1-1		18	Ottawa	5-6
	20	at Atlanta	3-2*		22	at Montreal	3-5
	22	Dallas	1-0		25	Toronto	3-3
	27	Atlanta	3-5		26	at Atlanta	1-5
	28	at NY Islanders	0-3		29	Buffalo	1-3
	31	NY Rangers	0-2		31	Montreal	0-4
Jan.	3	at Buffalo	3-6	Apr.	2	at Pittsburgh	2-3
	4	at Boston	4-2		4	at Florida	1-4
	7	at Atlanta	3-3		6	NY Islanders	1-2

* – Overtime

Entry Draft
Selections 2003-1989

2003
Pick
2	Eric Staal
31	Danny Richmond
102	Aaron Dawson
126	Kevin Nastiuk
130	Matej Trojovsky
137	Tyson Strachan
198	Shay Stephenson
230	Jamie Hoffmann
262	Ryan Rorabeck

2002
Pick
25	Cam Ward
91	Jesse Lane
160	Daniel Manzato
224	Adam Taylor

2001
Pick
15	Igor Knyazev
46	Mike Zigomanis
91	Kevin Estrada
110	Rob Zepp
181	Daniel Boisclair
211	Sean Curry
244	Carter Trevisani
274	Peter Reynolds

2000
Pick
32	Tomas Kurka
80	Ryan Bayda
97	Niclas Wallin
110	Jared Newman
181	J.D. Forrest
212	Magnus Kahnberg
235	Craig Kowalski
276	Troy Ferguson

1999
Pick
16	David Tanabe
49	Brett Lysak
84	Brad Fast
113	Ryan Murphy
174	Damian Surma
202	Jim Baxter
231	David Evans
237	Antti Jokela
259	Yevgeny Kurilin

1998
Pick
11	Jeff Heerema
70	Kevin Holdridge
71	Erik Cole
91	Josef Vasicek
93	Tommy Westlund
97	Chris Madden
184	Don Smith
208	Jaroslav Svoboda
211	Mark Kosick
239	Brent McDonald

1997
Pick
22	Nikos Tselios
28	Brad DeFauw
80	Francis Lessard
88	Shane Willis
142	Kyle Dafoe
169	Andrew Merrick
195	Niklas Nordgren
199	Randy Fitzgerald
225	Kent McDonell

1996
Pick
34	Trevor Wasyluk
61	Andrei Petrunin
88	Craig MacDonald
104	Steve Wasylko
116	Mark McMahon
143	Aaron Baker
171	Greg Kuznik
197	Kevin Marsh
223	Craig Adams
231	Ashkat Rakhmatullin

1995
Pick
13	Jean-Sebastien Giguere
35	Sergei Fedotov
85	Ian MacNeil
87	Sami Kapanen
113	Hugh Hamilton
165	Byron Ritchie
191	Milan Kostolny
217	Mike Rucinski

1994
Pick
5	Jeff O'Neill
83	Hnat Domenichelli
109	Ryan Risidore
187	Tom Buckley
213	Ashlin Halfnight
230	Matt Ball
239	Brian Regan
265	Steve Nimigon

1993
Pick
2	Chris Pronger
72	Marek Malik
84	Trevor Roenick
115	Nolan Pratt
188	Manny Legace
214	Dmitri Gorenko
240	Wes Swinson
266	Igor Chibirev

1992
Pick
9	Robert Petrovicky
47	Andrei Nikolishin
57	Jan Vopat
79	Kevin Smyth
81	Jason McBain
143	Jarrett Reid
153	Ken Belanger
177	Konstantin Korotkov
201	Greg Zwakman
225	Steven Halko
249	Joacim Esbjors

1991
Pick
9	Patrick Poulin
31	Martin Hamrlik
53	Todd Hall
59	Michael Nylander
75	Jim Storm
119	Mike Harding
141	Brian Mueller
163	Steve Yule
185	Chris Belanger
207	Jason Currie
229	Mike Santonelli
251	Rob Peters

1990
Pick
15	Mark Greig
36	Geoff Sanderson
57	Mike Lenarduzzi
78	Chris Bright
120	Cory Keenan
141	Jergus Baca
162	Martin D'Orsonnens
183	Corey Osmak
204	Espen Knutsen
225	Tommie Eriksen
246	Denis Chalifoux

1989
Pick
10	Bobby Holik
52	Blair Atcheynum
73	Jim McKenzie
94	James Black
115	Jerome Bechard
136	Scott Daniels
157	Raymond Saumier
178	Michel Picard
199	Trevor Buchanan
220	John Battice
241	Peter Kasowski

Club Directory

RBC Center

Carolina Hurricanes
1400 Edwards Mill Rd.
Raleigh, NC 27607
Phone **919/861-2300**
FAX 919/462-0123
www.carolinahurricanes.com
Capacity: 18,730

Carolina Hurricanes Directory
CEO/Owner/Governor	Peter Karmanos Jr.
President/General Manager	Jim Rutherford
Vice President/Assistant General Manager	Jason Karmanos
Head Coach	Paul Maurice
Assistant Coach	Randy Ladouceur
Assistant Coach	Kevin McCarthy
Goaltending Consultant	Don Edwards
Director of Media Relations	Mike Sundheim
Manager of Media Relations	Kyle Hanlin
Head Athletic Therapist/ Strength Conditioning Coach	Peter Friesen
Associate Athletic Therapist	Stu Lempke
Equipment Managers	Wally Tatomir, Bob Gorman, Skip Cunningham
RBC Center Capacity	18,730
Public Relations Phone	(919) 861-5477 or (919) 861-5429
Public Relations Fax	(919) 462-0123
Press Box Phone	(919) 861-2300 ext. 6561, 6562, 6563, 6564
Practice Facility Phone	(919) 754-0441
Practice Facility	Rec Zone, 912 Hodges St., Raleigh
Radio	WKXU-FM (101.1) WKIX-FM (102.3) WDTF-AM (570)
Television	FOX Sports South FOX 50 Digital

Jeff O'Neill led the Hurricanes in goals (30) and points (61) last season. It was the fourth straight year he led the team in goals and the second time in three years he topped the team in points.

President and General Manager

RUTHERFORD, JIM
President/General Manager, Carolina Hurricanes.
Born in Beeton, Ont., February 17, 1949.

Jim Rutherford, a former NHL goaltender, is the franchise's seventh general manager and the only general manager of the Carolina Hurricanes. Named to his position on June 28, 1994, Rutherford has always taken an aggressive approach towards improving the fortunes of the franchise through trades and the NHL draft. In 2002, the team reached the Stanley Cup Finals for the first time in history.

A veteran of 13 NHL seasons, Rutherford began his professional goaltending career in 1969 as a first-round selection of the Detroit Red Wings. While playing for Detroit, Pittsburgh, Toronto and Los Angeles, Rutherford collected 14 career shutouts. For five seasons he also served as the Red Wings' player representative. Rutherford also played for Team Canada at the World Championships in Vienna in 1977 and Moscow in 1979.

After his playing days with the Red Wings, Rutherford joined Compuware to serve as the director of hockey operations for Compuware Sports Corporation. Rutherford gained a wealth of experience in youth hockey and junior programs. As a former player, coach, and general manager, his ability to develop players and produce winning programs is widely respected throughout the hockey community.

He started his management career by guiding Compuware Sports Corporation's purchase of the Windsor Spitfires of the Ontario Hockey League in April of 1984. During the next four years, Rutherford acted as general manager of the Spitfires. After the Spitfires advanced to the 1988 Memorial Cup finals, Rutherford led Compuware's efforts to bring the first American-based OHL franchise to Detroit on December 11, 1989. Rutherford was voted the 1987 executive of the year in both the OHL and the Canadian Hockey League and won the OHL executive of the year award again in 1988.

Jocelyn Thibault had eight shutouts last season.

Chicago Blackhawks

2002-03 Results: 30W-33L-13T-6OTL 79PTS.
Third, Central Division

2003-04 Schedule

Oct.	Wed.	8	Minnesota		Wed.	7	at Minnesota
	Fri.	10	at Colorado		Thu.	8	Calgary
	Sun.	12	Los Angeles		Sun.	11	Colorado
	Thu.	16	at Columbus		Mon.	12	at St. Louis
	Sat.	18	at Atlanta		Wed.	14	at Detroit
	Sun.	19	Nashville		Sun.	18	Los Angeles
	Thu.	23	at San Jose		Wed.	21	at Minnesota
	Sat.	25	at Los Angeles		Thu.	22	Columbus
	Sun.	26	at Anaheim*		Sat.	24	at Columbus
	Tue.	28	at Phoenix		Tue.	27	at Vancouver
	Thu.	30	Pittsburgh		Thu.	29	at Edmonton
Nov.	Sat.	1	at St. Louis		Fri.	30	at Calgary
	Sun.	2	Anaheim	**Feb.**	Sun.	1	at Montreal*
	Fri.	7	at Nashville		Tue.	3	at Toronto
	Sun.	9	Colorado		Wed.	11	Nashville
	Mon.	10	at Detroit		Sat.	14	Boston*
	Wed.	12	Calgary		Sun.	15	Washington*
	Fri.	14	Detroit		Thu.	19	San Jose
	Sun.	16	NY Rangers		Sun.	22	St. Louis*
	Tue.	18	at Edmonton		Tue.	24	at Philadelphia
	Thu.	20	at Vancouver		Wed.	25	at Columbus
	Sat.	22	at Calgary		Fri.	27	Columbus
	Wed.	26	at San Jose		Sun.	29	Florida*
	Fri.	28	at Anaheim*	**Mar.**	Mon.	1	at Nashville
	Sat.	29	at Los Angeles*		Wed.	3	Tampa Bay
Dec.	Wed.	3	Buffalo		Fri.	5	Anaheim
	Sat.	6	at NY Islanders		Sun.	7	Edmonton*
	Sun.	7	Phoenix		Thu.	11	at New Jersey
	Thu.	11	Detroit		Fri.	12	at Washington
	Fri.	12	at Dallas		Sun.	14	Dallas*
	Sun.	14	Dallas		Wed.	17	Carolina
	Thu.	18	at Ottawa		Fri.	19	Vancouver
	Fri.	19	at Detroit		Sun.	21	Phoenix*
	Sun.	21	New Jersey		Tue.	23	at Colorado
	Tue.	23	St. Louis		Thu.	25	Minnesota
	Fri.	26	Columbus		Sat.	27	at St. Louis*
	Sun.	28	Detroit		Sun.	28	St. Louis*
	Mon.	29	at Pittsburgh		Tue.	30	at Nashville
	Wed.	31	Vancouver	**Apr.**	Thu.	1	Nashville
Jan.	Fri.	2	San Jose		Sat.	3	at Phoenix*
	Sun.	4	Edmonton		Sun.	4	at Dallas*

* Denotes afternoon game.

Franchise date: September 25, 1926

CENTRAL DIVISION

78th NHL Season

Year-by-Year Record

		Home				Road				Overall								
Season	GP	W	L	T	OL	W	L	T	OL	W	L	T	OL	GF	GA	Pts.	Finished	Playoff Result
2002-03	82	17	15	7	2	13	18	6	4	30	33	13	6	207	226	79	3rd, Central Div.	Out of Playoffs
2001-02	82	28	7	5	1	13	20	8	0	41	27	13	1	216	207	96	3rd, Central Div.	Lost Conf. Quarter-Final
2000-01	82	14	21	4	2	15	19	4	3	29	40	8	5	210	246	71	4th, Central Div.	Out of Playoffs
1999-2000	82	16	19	5	1	17	18	5	1	33	37	10	2	242	245	78	3rd, Central Div.	Out of Playoffs
1998-99	82	20	17	4	...	9	24	8	...	29	41	12	...	202	248	70	3rd, Central Div.	Out of Playoffs
1997-98	82	14	19	8	...	16	20	5	...	30	39	13	...	192	199	73	5th, Central Div.	Out of Playoffs
1996-97	82	16	21	4	...	18	14	9	...	34	35	13	...	223	210	81	5th, Central Div.	Lost Conf. Quarter-Final
1995-96	82	22	13	6	...	18	15	8	...	40	28	14	...	273	220	94	2nd, Central Div.	Lost Conf. Semi-Final
1994-95	48	11	10	3	...	13	9	2	...	24	19	5	...	156	115	53	3rd, Central Div.	Lost Conf. Championship
1993-94	84	21	16	5	...	18	20	4	...	39	36	9	...	254	240	87	5th, Central Div.	Lost Conf. Quarter-Final
1992-93	84	25	11	6	...	22	14	6	...	47	25	12	...	279	230	106	1st, Norris Div.	Lost Div. Semi-Final
1991-92	80	23	9	8	...	13	20	7	...	36	29	15	...	257	236	87	2nd, Norris Div.	Lost Final
1990-91	80	28	8	4	...	21	15	4	...	49	23	8	...	284	211	106	1st, Norris Div.	Lost Div. Semi-Final
1989-90	80	25	13	2	...	16	20	4	...	41	33	6	...	316	294	88	1st, Norris Div.	Lost Conf. Championship
1988-89	80	16	14	10	...	11	27	2	...	27	41	12	...	297	335	66	4th, Norris Div.	Lost Conf. Championship
1987-88	80	21	17	2	...	9	24	7	...	30	41	9	...	284	328	69	3rd, Norris Div.	Lost Div. Semi-Final
1986-87	80	18	13	9	...	11	24	5	...	29	37	14	...	290	310	72	3rd, Norris Div.	Lost Div. Semi-Final
1985-86	80	23	12	5	...	16	21	3	...	39	33	8	...	351	349	86	1st, Norris Div.	Lost Div. Semi-Final
1984-85	80	22	16	2	...	16	19	5	...	38	35	7	...	309	299	83	2nd, Norris Div.	Lost Conf. Championship
1983-84	80	25	13	2	...	5	29	6	...	30	42	8	...	277	311	68	4th, Norris Div.	Lost Div. Semi-Final
1982-83	80	29	8	3	...	18	15	7	...	47	23	10	...	338	268	104	1st, Norris Div.	Lost Conf. Championship
1981-82	80	20	13	7	...	10	25	5	...	30	38	12	...	332	363	72	4th, Norris Div.	Lost Conf. Championship
1980-81	80	21	11	8	...	10	22	8	...	31	33	16	...	304	315	78	2nd, Smythe Div.	Lost Prelim. Round
1979-80	80	21	12	7	...	13	15	12	...	34	27	19	...	241	250	87	1st, Smythe Div.	Lost Quarter-Final
1978-79	80	18	12	10	...	11	24	5	...	29	36	15	...	244	277	73	1st, Smythe Div.	Lost Quarter-Final
1977-78	80	20	9	11	...	12	20	8	...	32	29	19	...	230	220	83	1st, Smythe Div.	Lost Quarter-Final
1976-77	80	19	16	5	...	7	27	6	...	26	43	11	...	240	298	63	3rd, Smythe Div.	Lost Prelim. Round
1975-76	80	17	15	8	...	15	15	10	...	32	30	18	...	254	261	82	1st, Smythe Div.	Lost Quarter-Final
1974-75	80	24	12	4	...	13	23	4	...	37	35	8	...	268	241	82	3rd, Smythe Div.	Lost Quarter-Final
1973-74	78	20	6	13	...	21	8	10	...	41	14	23	...	272	164	105	2nd, West Div.	Lost Semi-Final
1972-73	78	26	9	4	...	16	18	5	...	42	27	9	...	284	225	93	1st, West Div.	Lost Final
1971-72	78	28	3	8	...	18	14	7	...	46	17	15	...	256	166	107	1st, West Div.	Lost Semi-Final
1970-71	78	30	6	3	...	19	14	6	...	49	20	9	...	277	184	107	1st, West Div.	Lost Final
1969-70	76	26	7	5	...	19	15	4	...	45	22	9	...	250	170	99	1st, East Div.	Lost Semi-Final
1968-69	76	20	14	4	...	14	19	5	...	34	33	9	...	280	246	77	6th, East Div.	Out of Playoffs
1967-68	74	20	13	4	...	12	13	12	...	32	26	16	...	212	222	80	4th, East Div.	Lost Semi-Final
1966-67	70	24	5	6	...	17	12	6	...	41	17	12	...	264	170	94	1st,	Lost Semi-Final
1965-66	70	21	8	6	...	16	17	2	...	37	25	8	...	240	187	82	2nd,	Lost Semi-Final
1964-65	70	20	13	2	...	14	15	6	...	34	28	8	...	224	176	76	3rd,	Lost Final
1963-64	70	26	4	5	...	10	18	7	...	36	22	12	...	218	169	84	2nd,	Lost Semi-Final
1962-63	70	17	9	9	...	15	12	8	...	32	21	17	...	194	178	81	2nd,	Lost Semi-Final
1961-62	70	20	10	5	...	11	16	8	...	31	26	13	...	217	186	75	3rd,	Lost Final
1960-61	**70**	**20**	**6**	**9**	**...**	**9**	**18**	**8**	**...**	**29**	**24**	**17**	**...**	**198**	**180**	**75**	**3rd,**	**Won Stanley Cup**
1959-60	70	18	11	6	...	10	18	7	...	28	29	13	...	191	180	69	3rd,	Lost Semi-Final
1958-59	70	14	12	9	...	14	17	4	...	28	29	13	...	197	208	69	3rd,	Lost Semi-Final
1957-58	70	15	17	3	...	9	22	4	...	24	39	7	...	163	202	55	5th,	Out of Playoffs
1956-57	70	12	15	8	...	4	24	7	...	16	39	15	...	169	225	47	6th,	Out of Playoffs
1955-56	70	9	19	7	...	10	20	5	...	19	39	12	...	155	216	50	6th,	Out of Playoffs
1954-55	70	6	21	8	...	7	19	9	...	13	40	17	...	161	235	43	6th,	Out of Playoffs
1953-54	70	8	21	6	...	4	30	1	...	12	51	7	...	133	242	31	6th,	Out of Playoffs
1952-53	70	14	11	10	...	13	17	5	...	27	28	15	...	169	175	69	4th,	Lost Semi-Final
1951-52	70	9	19	7	...	8	25	2	...	17	44	9	...	158	241	43	6th,	Out of Playoffs
1950-51	70	8	22	5	...	5	25	5	...	13	47	10	...	171	280	36	6th,	Out of Playoffs
1949-50	70	13	18	4	...	9	20	6	...	22	38	10	...	203	244	54	6th,	Out of Playoffs
1948-49	60	13	12	5	...	8	19	3	...	21	31	8	...	173	211	50	5th,	Out of Playoffs
1947-48	60	10	17	3	...	10	17	3	...	20	34	6	...	195	225	46	6th,	Out of Playoffs
1946-47	60	10	17	3	...	9	20	1	...	19	37	4	...	193	274	42	6th,	Out of Playoffs
1945-46	50	15	5	5	...	8	15	2	...	23	20	7	...	200	178	53	3rd,	Lost Semi-Final
1944-45	50	9	14	2	...	4	16	5	...	13	30	7	...	141	194	33	5th,	Out of Playoffs
1943-44	50	15	6	4	...	7	17	1	...	22	23	5	...	178	187	49	4th,	Lost Final
1942-43	50	14	3	8	...	3	15	7	...	17	18	15	...	179	180	49	5th,	Out of Playoffs
1941-42	48	15	8	1	...	7	15	2	...	22	23	3	...	145	155	47	4th,	Lost Quarter-Final
1940-41	48	11	10	3	...	5	15	4	...	16	25	7	...	112	139	39	5th,	Lost Semi-Final
1939-40	48	15	7	2	...	8	12	4	...	23	19	6	...	112	120	52	4th,	Lost Quarter-Final
1938-39	48	5	13	6	...	7	15	2	...	12	28	8	...	91	132	32	7th,	Out of Playoffs
1937-38	**48**	**10**	**10**	**4**	**...**	**4**	**15**	**5**	**...**	**14**	**25**	**9**	**...**	**97**	**139**	**37**	**3rd, Amn. Div.**	**Won Stanley Cup**
1936-37	48	8	13	3	...	6	14	4	...	14	27	7	...	99	131	35	4th, Amn. Div.	Out of Playoffs
1935-36	48	15	7	2	...	6	12	6	...	21	19	8	...	93	92	50	3rd, Amn. Div.	Lost Quarter-Final
1934-35	48	12	9	3	...	14	8	2	...	26	17	5	...	118	88	57	2nd, Amn. Div.	Lost Quarter-Final
1933-34	**48**	**13**	**4**	**7**	**...**	**7**	**13**	**4**	**...**	**20**	**17**	**11**	**...**	**88**	**83**	**51**	**2nd, Amn. Div.**	**Won Stanley Cup**
1932-33	48	12	7	5	...	4	13	7	...	16	20	12	...	88	101	44	4th, Amn. Div.	Out of Playoffs
1931-32	48	13	5	6	...	5	14	5	...	18	19	11	...	86	101	47	2nd, Amn. Div.	Lost Quarter-Final
1930-31	44	13	8	1	...	11	9	2	...	24	17	3	...	108	78	51	2nd, Amn. Div.	Lost Final
1929-30	44	12	9	1	...	9	9	4	...	21	18	5	...	117	111	47	2nd, Amn. Div.	Lost Quarter-Final
1928-29	44	3	13	6	...	4	16	2	...	7	29	8	...	33	85	22	5th, Amn. Div.	Out of Playoffs
1927-28	44	2	18	2	...	5	16	1	...	7	34	3	...	68	134	17	5th, Amn. Div.	Out of Playoffs
1926-27	44	12	8	2	...	7	14	1	...	19	22	3	...	115	116	41	3rd, Amn. Div.	Lost Quarter-Final

2003-04 Player Personnel

FORWARDS

	HT	WT	S	Place of Birth	Date	2002-03 Club
ARNASON, Tyler	5-11	198	L	Oklahoma City, OK	3/16/79	Chicago
BAINES, Ajay	5-10	178	L	Kamloops, B.C.	3/25/78	Norfolk
BELL, Mark	6-3	205	L	St. Paul's, Ont.	8/5/80	Chicago
CALDER, Kyle	5-11	180	L	Mannville, Alta.	1/5/79	Chicago
DAZE, Eric	6-6	234	L	Montreal, Que.	7/2/75	Chicago
ELLISON, Matt	6-0	192	R	Duncan, B.C.	12/8/83	Red Deer
FLEURY, Theoren	5-6	182	R	Oxbow, Sask.	6/29/68	Chicago
KEITH, Matt	6-2	194	R	Edmonton, Alta.	4/11/83	Spokane-Red Deer
KOJEVNIKOV, Alexander	6-0	185	L	Moscow, USSR	4/12/84	Krylja Sovetov
KOROLEV, Igor	6-1	190	L	Moscow, USSR	9/6/70	Chicago-Norfolk
McLEAN, Brett	5-11	194	L	Comox, B.C.	8/14/78	Chicago-Norfolk
MOEN, Travis	6-2	210	L	Stewart Valley, Sask.	4/6/82	Norfolk
NICHOL, Scott	5-8	173	R	Edmonton, Alta.	12/31/74	Calgary
NIEMINEN, Ville	6-0	200	L	Tampere, Finland	4/6/77	Pittsburgh
RADULOV, Igor	6-1	186	L	Nizhny Tagil, USSR	8/23/82	Chicago-Norfolk
RUUTU, Tuomo	6-0	201	L	Vantaa, Finland	2/16/83	HIFK Helsinki
SULLIVAN, Steve	5-9	155	R	Timmins, Ont.	7/6/74	Chicago
THORNTON, Shawn	6-1	203	R	Oshawa, Ont.	7/23/77	Chicago-Norfolk
VANDENBUSSCHE, Ryan	6-0	200	R	Simcoe, Ont.	2/28/73	Norfolk-Chicago
VOROBIEV, Pavel	6-0	183	L	Karaganda, USSR	5/5/82	Yaroslavl
YAKUBOV, Mikhail	6-3	204	L	Barnaul, USSR	2/16/82	Norfolk
ZHAMNOV, Alexei	6-1	204	L	Moscow, USSR	10/1/70	Chicago

DEFENSEMEN

	HT	WT	S	Place of Birth	Date	2002-03 Club
AITKEN, Johnathan	6-4	230	L	Edmonton, Alta.	5/24/78	Norfolk
BABCHUK, Anton	6-5	202	R	Kiev, USSR	5/6/84	Kazan-St. Petersburg
BARINKA, Michal	6-3	200	L	Vyskov, Czech.	6/12/84	Ceske Budejovice-C. Budejovice Jr.
DEMPSEY, Nathan	6-0	190	R	Spruce Grove, Alta.	7/14/74	Chicago
GUSEV, Vladimir	6-2	205	L	Novosibirsk, USSR	11/24/82	Novosibirsk 2
HENRY, Burke	6-3	206	L	Ste. Rose, Man.	1/21/79	Norfolk-Chicago
KARPOVTSEV, Alexander	6-3	221	R	Moscow, USSR	4/7/70	Chicago
KEITH, Duncan	6-0	168	L	Winnipeg, Man.	7/16/83	Michigan State-Kelowna
KLEMM, Jon	6-2	200	R	Cranbrook, B.C.	1/8/70	Chicago
KUKKONEN, Lasse	6-0	187	L	Oulu, Finland	9/18/81	Karpat
McCARTHY, Steve	6-1	197	L	Trail, B.C.	2/3/81	Chicago-Norfolk
POAPST, Steve	6-0	200	L	Cornwall, Ont.	1/3/69	Chicago
QUINT, Deron	6-2	219	L	Durham, NH	3/12/76	Phoenix-Springfield
SEABROOK, Brent	6-3	220	R	Richmond, B.C.	4/20/85	Lethbridge
STRUDWICK, Jason	6-3	210	L	Edmonton, Alta.	7/17/75	Chicago

GOALTENDERS

	HT	WT	C	Place of Birth	Date	2002-03 Club
ANDERSON, Craig	6-2	174	L	Park Ridge, IL	5/21/81	Chicago-Norfolk
LEIGHTON, Michael	6-2	175	L	Petrolia, Ont.	5/19/81	Chicago-Norfolk
PASSMORE, Steve	5-9	165	L	Thunder Bay, Ont.	1/29/73	Chicago-Norfolk
THIBAULT, Jocelyn	5-11	170	L	Montreal, Que.	1/12/75	Chicago

Coach

SUTTER, BRIAN
Coach, Chicago Blackhawks. Born in Viking, Alta., October 7, 1956.

Brian Sutter was hired as the head coach in Chicago on May 3, 2001. In his first year behind the bench in 2001-02, Sutter guided the club into the playoffs for the first time since 1997 and was rewarded with a nomination for the Jack Adams Award as coach of the year. He is the second member of this storied family to have coached the Blackhawks (Darryl Sutter was the head coach of the Blackhawks from 1992 to 1995). The Sutter name has always been synonymous with intensity, honesty, tenacity and hard work.

Following a 12-year playing career with the St. Louis Blues from 1976 to 1988, Sutter immediately joined the NHL coaching ranks by taking over the reigns of the team he had captained for nine of his 12 seasons. He spent four seasons as the coach of the Blues, posting a mark of 153-124-43 which then exceeded Scotty Bowman's club record for coaching victories. Sutter captured the Jack Adams Award in 1990-91.

Sutter became the head coach of the Boston Bruins in the 1992-93 season and immediately led the club to its first 50-win season in ten years. In his three seasons as the Bruins' chief mentor, Sutter had a coaching record of 120-73-23. After leaving the coaching ranks for two seasons, Sutter returned behind the bench in his native province of Alberta as the head coach of the Calgary Flames for the 1997-98 season. He coached the Flames for three seasons.

As a player, Sutter was drafted by the St. Louis Blues with their second pick, 20th overall, in the 1976 Entry Draft. He wound up playing his entire 12-year NHL career with the Blues. A three-time NHL All-Star Game selection, Sutter played 779 games and had 303 goals and 333 assists for 636 points. A great leader and an outstanding performer on the ice, Sutter's #11 was retired by the Blues on December 30, 1988.

Coaching Record

			Regular Season			Playoffs		
Season	Team	Games	W	L	T	Games	W	L
1988-89	St. Louis (NHL)	80	33	35	12	10	5	5
1989-90	St. Louis (NHL)	80	37	34	9	12	7	5
1990-91	St. Louis (NHL)	80	47	22	11	13	6	7
1991-92	St. Louis (NHL)	80	36	33	11	6	2	4
1992-93	Boston (NHL)	84	51	26	7	4	0	4
1993-94	Boston (NHL)	84	42	29	13	13	6	7
1994-95	Boston (NHL)	48	27	18	3	5	1	4
1997-98	Calgary (NHL)	82	26	41	15	....	....	....
1998-99	Calgary (NHL)	82	30	40	12	....	....	....
1999-2000	Calgary (NHL)	82	31	41	10	....	....	....
2001-02	Chicago (NHL)	82	41	28	13	5	1	4
2002-03	Chicago (NHL)	82	30	39	13			
	NHL Totals	**946**	**431**	**386**	**129**	**68**	**28**	**40**

2002-03 Scoring
* - rookie

Regular Season

Pos	#	Player	Team	GP	G	A	Pts	+/-	PIM	PP	SH	GW	GT	S	%
R	26	Steve Sullivan	CHI	82	26	35	61	15	42	4	2	3	0	190	13.7
C	13	Alexei Zhamnov	CHI	74	15	43	58	0	70	2	3	1	0	166	9.0
L	55	Eric Daze	CHI	54	22	22	44	10	14	3	0	5	0	170	12.9
L	19	Kyle Calder	CHI	82	15	27	42	-6	40	7	0	2	0	164	9.1
C	39 *	Tyler Arnason	CHI	82	19	20	39	7	20	3	0	6	0	178	10.7
R	14	Theoren Fleury	CHI	54	12	21	33	-7	77	1	0	3	1	124	9.7
L	28	Mark Bell	CHI	82	14	15	29	0	113	0	2	0	0	127	11.0
D	43	Nathan Dempsey	CHI	67	5	23	28	-7	26	1	0	2	0	124	4.0
C	11	Andrei Nikolishin	CHI	60	6	15	21	-3	26	0	1	0	0	73	8.2
L	17	Chris Simon	WSH	10	0	2	2	-3	23	0	0	0	0	16	0.0
			CHI	61	12	6	18	-4	125	2	0	2	1	72	16.7
			TOTAL	71	12	8	20	-7	148	2	0	2	1	88	13.6
C	20	Mike Eastwood	STL	17	1	3	4	1	8	1	0	0	0	7	14.3
			CHI	53	2	10	12	-6	24	0	0	0	0	32	6.3
			TOTAL	70	3	13	16	-5	32	1	0	0	0	39	7.7
D	42	Jon Klemm	CHI	70	2	14	16	-9	44	1	0	1	0	74	2.7
D	25	Alexander Karpovtsev	CHI	40	4	10	14	-8	12	3	0	1	0	36	11.1
D	8	Steve Poapst	CHI	75	2	11	13	14	50	0	0	0	0	49	4.1
C	22	Igor Korolev	CHI	48	4	5	9	-1	30	1	0	1	0	32	12.5
L	50 *	Igor Radulov	CHI	7	5	0	5	-3	4	3	0	0	0	14	35.7
L	34	Jason Strudwick	CHI	48	2	3	5	-4	87	0	0	0	0	19	10.5
D	5	Steve McCarthy	CHI	57	1	4	5	-1	23	0	0	0	0	55	1.8
L	49 *	Shawn Thornton	CHI	13	1	1	2	-4	31	0	0	0	0	15	6.7
D	44 *	Burke Henry	CHI	16	0	2	2	-13	9	0	0	0	0	25	0.0
D	46	Todd Gill	CHI	5	0	1	1	3	0	0	0	0	0	9	0.0
C	16	Peter White	CHI	6	0	1	1	0	0	0	0	0	0	2	0.0
D	4	Sami Helenius	DAL	5	0	0	0	0	6	0	0	0	0	2	0.0
			CHI	10	0	1	1	3	28	0	0	0	0	5	0.0
			TOTAL	15	0	1	1	3	34	0	0	0	0	7	0.0
R	15	Garry Valk	CHI	16	0	1	1	0	6	0	0	0	0	9	0.0
C	53 *	Brett McLean	CHI	2	0	0	0	-1	0	0	0	0	0	1	0.0
L	33	Louie DeBrusk	CHI	9	0	0	0	0	7	0	0	0	0	0	0.0
R	23	Ryan Vandenbussche	CHI	22	0	0	0	0	58	0	0	0	0	0	0.0

Goaltending

No.	Goaltender	GPI	Mins	Avg	W	L	T	EN	SO	GA	SA	S%	G	A	PIM
41	Jocelyn Thibault	62	3650	2.37	26	28	7	4	8	144	1690	.915	0	0	4
30	* Michael Leighton	8	447	2.82	2	3	2	1	1	21	241	.913	0	0	0
29	Steve Passmore	11	617	3.70	2	5	2	0	0	38	284	.866	0	0	4
31	* Craig Anderson	6	270	4.00	0	3	2	0	0	18	125	.856	0	0	0
	Totals	**82**	**5007**	**2.71**	**30**	**39**	**13**	**5**	**9**	**226**	**2345**	**.904**			

Tiny but talented, 5'9" Steve Sullivan led the Blackhawks in scoring last season for the second time in three years. He also topped the team in plus-minus.

Captains' History

Dick Irvin, 1926-27 to 1928-29; Duke Dukowski, 1929-30; Ty Arbour, 1930-31; Cy Wentworth, 1931-32; Helge Bostrom, 1932-33; Charlie Gardiner, 1933-34; no captain, 1934-35; Johnny Gottselig, 1935-36 to 1939-40; Earl Seibert, 1940-41, 1941-42; Doug Bentley, 1942-43, 1943-44; Clint Smith 1944-45; John Mariucci, 1945-46; Red Hamill, 1946-47; John Mariucci, 1947-48; Gaye Stewart, 1948-49; Doug Bentley, 1949-50; Jack Stewart, 1950-51, 1951-52; Bill Gadsby, 1952-53, 1953-54; Gus Mortson, 1954-55 to 1956-57; no captain, 1957-58; Ed Litzenberger, 1958-59 to 1960-61; Pierre Pilote, 1961-62 to 1967-68, no captain, 1968-69; Pat Stapleton, 1969-70; no captain, 1970-71 to 1974-75; Stan Mikita and Pit Martin, 1975-76; Stan Mikita, Pit Martin and Keith Magnuson, 1976-77; Keith Magnuson, 1977-78, 1978-79; Keith Magnuson and Terry Ruskowski, 1979-80; Terry Ruskowski, 1980-81, 1981-82; Darryl Sutter, 1982-83 to 1984-85; Darryl Sutter and Bob Murray, 1985-86; Darryl Sutter, 1986-87; no captain, 1987-88; Denis Savard and Dirk Graham, 1988-89; Dirk Graham, 1989-90 to 1994-95; Chris Chelios, 1995-96 to 1998-99; Doug Gilmour, 1999-2000; Tony Amonte, 2000-01, 2001-02; Alexei Zhamnov, 2002-03 to date.

Club Records

Team

(Figures in brackets for season records are games played; records for fewest points, wins, ties, losses, goals, goals against are for 70 or more games)

Most Points	**107**	1970-71 (78), 1971-72 (78)
Most Wins	**49**	1970-71 (78), 1990-91 (80)
Most Ties	**23**	1973-74 (78)
Most Losses	**51**	1953-54 (70)
Most Goals	**351**	1985-86 (80)
Most Goals Against	**363**	1981-82 (80)
Fewest Points	**31**	1953-54 (70)
Fewest Wins	**12**	1953-54 (70)
Fewest Ties	**6**	1989-90 (80)
Fewest Losses	**14**	1973-74 (78)
Fewest Goals	***133**	1953-54 (70)
Fewest Goals Against	**164**	1973-74 (78)
Longest Winning Streak		
Overall	**8**	Dec. 9-26/71, Jan. 4-21/81
Home	**13**	Nov. 11-Dec. 20/70
Away	**7**	Dec. 9-29/64
Longest Undefeated Streak		
Overall	**15**	Jan. 14-Feb. 16/67 (12 wins, 3 ties)
Home	**18**	Oct. 11-Dec. 20/70 (16 wins, 2 ties)
Away	**12**	Nov. 2-Dec. 16/67 (6 wins, 6 ties)
Longest Losing Streak		
Overall	**12**	Feb. 25-Mar. 25/51
Home	**9**	Feb. 8-Mar. 21/28
Away	**16**	Jan. 2-Mar. 21/54
Longest Winless Streak		
Overall	**21**	Dec. 17/50-Jan. 28/51 (18 losses, 3 ties)
Home	**15**	Dec. 16/28-Feb. 28/29 (11 losses, 4 ties)
Away	**22**	Dec. 19/50-Mar. 25/51 (20 losses, 2 ties)
Most Shutouts, Season	**15**	1969-70 (76)
Most PIM, Season	**2,663**	1991-92 (80)
Most Goals, Game	**12**	Jan. 30/69 (Chi. 12 at Phi. 0)

Individual

Most Seasons	**22**	Stan Mikita
Most Games	**1,394**	Stan Mikita
Most Goals, Career	**604**	Bobby Hull
Most Assists, Career	**926**	Stan Mikita
Most Points, Career	**1,467**	Stan Mikita (541G, 926A)
Most PIM, Career	**1,495**	Chris Chelios
Most Shutouts, Career	**74**	Tony Esposito
Longest Consecutive Games Streak	**884**	Steve Larmer (Oct. 6/82-Apr. 15/93)
Most Goals, Season	**58**	Bobby Hull (1968-69)
Most Assists, Season	**87**	Denis Savard (1981-82, 1987-88)
Most Points, Season	**131**	Denis Savard (1987-88; 44G, 87A)
Most PIM, Season	**408**	Mike Peluso (1991-92)
Most Points, Defenseman, Season	**85**	Doug Wilson (1981-82; 39G, 46A)
Most Points, Center, Season	**131**	Denis Savard (1987-88; 44G, 87A)
Most Points, Right Wing, Season	**101**	Steve Larmer (1990-91; 44G, 57A)
Most Points, Left Wing, Season	**107**	Bobby Hull (1968-69; 58G, 49A)
Most Points, Rookie, Season	**90**	Steve Larmer (1982-83; 43G, 47A)
Most Shutouts, Season	**15**	Tony Esposito (1969-70)
Most Goals, Game	**5**	Grant Mulvey (Feb. 3/82)
Most Assists, Game	**6**	Pat Stapleton (Mar. 30/69)
Most Points, Game	**7**	Max Bentley (Jan. 28/43; 4G, 3A), Grant Mulvey (Feb. 3/82; 5G, 2A)

* NHL Record.

Retired Numbers

1	Glenn Hall	1957-1967
9	Bobby Hull	1957-1972
18	Denis Savard	1980-1990, 1995-1997
21	Stan Mikita	1958-1980
35	Tony Esposito	1969-1984

All-time Record vs. Other Clubs

Regular Season

	At Home								On Road								Total							
	GP	W	L	T	OL	GF	GA	PTS	GP	W	L	T	OL	GF	GA	PTS	GP	W	L	T	OL	GF	GA	PTS
Anaheim	22	11	9	2	0	62	52	24	20	7	11	2	0	43	53	16	42	18	20	4	0	105	105	40
Atlanta	2	2	0	0	0	6	0	4	3	2	1	0	0	8	7	4	5	4	1	0	0	14	7	8
Boston	285	146	94	45	0	924	766	337	284	89	161	34	0	808	1023	212	569	235	255	79	0	1732	1789	549
Buffalo	50	27	16	6	1	162	136	61	53	14	32	7	0	138	199	35	103	41	48	13	1	300	335	96
Calgary	59	25	21	13	0	191	172	63	61	20	27	13	1	182	196	54	120	45	48	26	1	373	368	117
Carolina	28	16	8	3	1	115	80	36	30	12	14	4	0	93	97	28	58	28	22	7	1	208	177	64
Colorado	39	21	14	3	1	137	121	46	37	12	20	5	0	122	151	29	76	33	34	8	1	259	272	75
Columbus	7	6	0	1	0	19	7	13	8	3	3	1	1	26	23	8	15	9	3	2	1	45	30	21
Dallas	108	64	30	14	0	411	284	142	110	44	49	16	1	338	371	105	218	108	79	30	1	749	655	247
Detroit	335	153	130	51	1	1005	944	358	332	99	199	33	1	829	1134	232	667	252	329	84	2	1834	2078	590
Edmonton	42	21	14	7	0	161	144	49	43	18	20	5	0	143	155	41	85	39	34	12	0	304	299	90
Florida	9	5	3	1	0	32	28	11	8	5	2	1	0	30	18	11	17	10	5	2	0	62	46	22
Los Angeles	73	35	29	9	0	258	215	79	72	32	32	8	0	242	240	72	145	67	61	17	0	500	455	151
Minnesota	6	2	3	1	0	14	17	5	6	2	3	0	1	14	17	5	12	4	6	1	1	28	34	10
Montreal	273	93	125	55	0	731	761	241	275	54	172	48	1	649	1061	157	548	147	297	103	1	1380	1822	398
Nashville	14	8	4	1	1	40	33	18	13	5	5	2	1	37	40	13	27	13	9	3	2	77	73	31
New Jersey	45	24	12	9	0	174	125	57	46	16	19	11	0	138	141	43	91	40	31	20	0	312	266	100
NY Islanders	48	26	17	5	0	162	162	57	46	14	17	15	0	139	158	43	94	40	34	20	0	301	320	100
NY Rangers	285	128	115	42	0	868	790	298	285	113	117	55	0	807	841	281	570	241	232	97	0	1675	1631	579
Ottawa	8	4	2	2	0	18	18	10	9	6	3	0	0	29	25	12	17	10	5	2	0	47	43	22
Philadelphia	60	26	15	19	0	205	170	71	61	16	34	11	0	161	201	43	121	42	49	30	0	366	371	114
Phoenix	46	26	12	8	0	180	124	60	48	18	26	4	0	151	160	40	94	44	38	12	0	331	284	100
Pittsburgh	59	39	10	10	0	236	156	88	58	23	28	7	0	190	209	53	117	62	38	17	0	426	365	141
St. Louis	115	63	34	18	0	426	343	144	112	40	55	17	0	346	375	97	227	103	89	35	0	772	718	241
San Jose	23	12	8	2	1	71	70	27	24	10	11	2	1	65	66	23	47	22	19	4	2	136	136	50
Tampa Bay	13	8	3	2	0	42	30	18	11	4	4	3	0	28	26	11	24	12	7	5	0	70	56	29
Toronto	318	156	120	42	0	968	831	354	314	96	164	54	0	817	1070	246	632	252	284	96	0	1785	1901	600
Vancouver	69	46	16	7	0	260	157	99	70	22	33	15	0	206	212	59	139	68	49	22	0	466	369	158
Washington	39	22	11	6	0	151	116	50	40	14	21	5	0	123	142	33	79	36	32	11	0	274	258	83
Defunct Clubs	139	79	40	20	0	408	268	178	140	52	67	21	0	316	346	125	279	131	107	41	0	724	614	303
Totals	**2619**	**1294**	**915**	**404**	**6**	**8437**	**7120**	**2998**	**2619**	**862**	**1350**	**399**	**8**	**7218**	**8757**	**2131**	**5238**	**2156**	**2265**	**803**	**14**	**15655**	**15877**	**5129**

Playoffs

	Series	W	L	GP	W	L	T	GF	GA	Last Mtg.	Rnd.	Result
Boston	6	1	5	22	5	16	1	63	97	1978	QF	L 0-4
Buffalo	2	0	2	9	1	8	0	17	36	1980	QF	L 0-4
Calgary	3	1	2	12	5	7	0	33	37	1996	CQF	W 4-0
Colorado	2	0	2	12	4	8	0	28	49	1997	CQF	L 2-4
Dallas	6	4	2	33	19	14	0	120	118	1991	DSF	L 2-4
Detroit	14	8	6	69	38	31	0	210	190	1995	CF	L 1-4
Edmonton	4	1	3	20	8	12	0	77	102	1992	CF	W 4-0
Los Angeles	1	1	0	5	4	1	0	10	7	1974	QF	W 4-1
Montreal	17	5	12	81	29	50	2	185	261	1976	QF	L 0-4
NY Islanders	2	0	2	6	0	6	0	6	21	1979	QF	L 0-4
NY Rangers	5	4	1	24	14	10	0	66	54	1973	SF	W 4-1
Philadelphia	1	1	0	4	4	0	0	20	8	1971	QF	W 4-0
Pittsburgh	2	1	1	8	4	4	0	24	23	1992	F	L 0-4
St. Louis	10	7	3	50	28	22	0	171	142	2002	CQF	L 1-4
Toronto	9	3	6	38	15	22	1	89	111	1995	CQF	W 4-3
Vancouver	2	1	1	9	5	4	0	24	24	1995	CSF	W 4-0
Defunct Clubs	4	2	2	9	5	3	1	16	15			
Totals	**90**	**40**	**50**	**411**	**188**	**218**	**5**	**1159**	**1295**			

Calgary totals include Atlanta Flames, 1972-73 to 1979-80. Carolina totals include Hartford, 1979-80 to 1996-97.
Colorado totals include Quebec, 1979-80 to 1994-95. Dallas totals include Minnesota North Stars, 1967-68 to 1992-93.
New Jersey totals include Kansas City, 1974-75 to 1975-76, and Colorado Rockies, 1976-77 to 1981-82.
Phoenix totals include Winnipeg, 1979-80 to 1995-96.

Playoff Results 2003-1999

Year	Round	Opponent	Result	GF	GA
2002	CQF	St. Louis	L 1-4	5	13

Abbreviations: Round: F - Final; **CF** - conference final; **CSF** - conference semi-final; **CQF** - conference quarter-final; **DSF** - division semi-final; **SF** - semi-final; **QF** - quarter-final.

2002-03 Results

Oct.	10	at Columbus	1-2
	13	Buffalo	3-0
	17	Florida	4-1
	19	Calgary	2-5
	24	Minnesota	2-3
	26	at Carolina	3-3
	27	San Jose	3-2
	29	Columbus	3-2
	31	Los Angeles	2-1*
Nov.	2	at New Jersey	1-5
	3	Edmonton	1-4
	5	at Detroit	2-0
	7	Atlanta	5-0
	9	at Tampa Bay	3-2*
	11	at Florida	2-2
	15	Washington	2-2
	17	Nashville	4-2
	19	at Edmonton	1-3
	20	at Vancouver	3-5
	23	at Calgary	1-3
	25	at Colorado	0-1
	28	at Phoenix	4-2
	30	at Los Angeles	1-4
Dec.	1	at Anaheim	2-3
	4	Ottawa	1-0
	6	Anaheim	3-4
	8	Tampa Bay	3-1
	10	at NY Islanders	3-2
	11	at NY Rangers	4-3
	13	at Buffalo	1-1
	15	Dallas	0-5
	17	Vancouver	3-2
	20	Columbus	3-1
	22	Los Angeles	3-1
	26	Minnesota	2-2
	28	at San Jose	3-3
	30	at Los Angeles	2-0
Jan.	2	at St. Louis	4-1
	4	at Nashville	3-3
	5	Detroit	3-4*
	8	Phoenix	0-0
	9	at Dallas	3-4*
	12	Nashville	2-0
	13	at Detroit	4-5*
	15	Detroit	4-1
	17	Vancouver	2-4
	18	at St. Louis	2-4
	20	at Columbus	1-5
	23	St. Louis	3-3
	25	at Pittsburgh	3-5
	26	at Montreal	3-4
	30	at Boston	3-1
Feb.	5	at Minnesota	1-2
	6	at Calgary	2-2
	8	at Edmonton	3-0
	10	at Vancouver	1-2
	12	Toronto	1-3
	14	San Jose	2-4
	15	at Columbus	7-1
	17	Colorado	4-5
	20	Phoenix	1-2
	23	Dallas	0-3
	25	Philadelphia	0-2
	27	at Philadelphia	2-5
Mar.	1	at Nashville	4-5*
	2	Colorado	2-3*
	5	at Dallas	4-7
	7	Calgary	0-2
	9	Boston	8-5
	12	at Anaheim	2-5
	14	at Phoenix	4-0
	17	at San Jose	3-2*
	19	Anaheim	3-4
	22	at Colorado	1-8
	23	Pittsburgh	1-1
	25	NY Islanders	2-9
	27	Nashville	4-1
	28	at Minnesota	3-4*
	30	Edmonton	4-4
Apr.	3	at St. Louis	6-4
	4	St. Louis	2-2
	6	Detroit	4-3*

* – Overtime

Entry Draft
Selections 2003-1989

2003
Pick
14 Brent Seabrook
52 Corey Crawford
59 Michal Barinka
151 Lasse Kukkonen
156 Alexei Ivanov
181 Johan Andersson
211 Mike Brodeur
245 Dustin Byfuglien
275 Karel Grenzy
282 Chris Porter

2002
Pick
21 Anton Babchuk
54 Duncan Keith
93 Alexander Kojevnikov
128 Matt Ellison
156 James Wisniewski
188 Kevin Kantee
219 Tyson Kellerman
251 Jason Kostadine
282 Adam Burish

2001
Pick
9 Tuomo Ruutu
29 Adam Munro
59 Matt Keith
73 Craig Anderson
104 Brent MacLellan
115 Vladimir Gusev
119 Alexei Zotkin
142 Tommi Jaminki
174 Alexander Golovin
186 Pavel Puncochar
205 Teemu Jaaskelainen
216 Oleg Minakov
268 Jeff Miles

2000
Pick
10 Mikhail Yakubov
11 Pavel Vorobiev
49 Jonas Nordqvist
74 Igor Radulov
106 Scott Balan
117 Olli Malmivaara
151 Alexander Barkunov
177 Michael Ayers
193 Joey Martin
207 Cliff Loya
225 Vladislav Luchkin
240 Adam Berkhoel
262 Peter Flache
271 Reto Von Arx
291 Arne Ramholt

1999
Pick
23 Steve McCarthy
46 Dimitri Levinski
63 Stepan Mokhov
134 Michael Jacobsen
165 Michael Leighton
194 Mattias Wennerberg
195 Yorick Treille
223 Andrew Carver

1998
Pick
8 Mark Bell
94 Matthias Trattnig
156 Kent Huskins
158 Jari Viuhkola
166 Jonathan Pelletier
183 Tyler Arnason
210 Sean Griffin
238 Alexandre Couture
240 Andrei Yershov

1997
Pick
13 Daniel Cleary
16 Ty Jones
39 Jeremy Reich
67 Mike Souza
110 Ben Simon
120 Peter Gardiner
130 Kyle Calder
147 Heath Gordon
174 Jerad Smith
204 Sergei Shikhanov
230 Chris Feil

1996
Pick
31 Remi Royer
42 Jeff Paul
46 Geoff Peters
130 Andy Johnson
184 Mike Vellinga
210 Chris Twerdun
236 Andrei Kozyrev

1995
Pick
19 Dmitri Nabokov
45 Christian Laflamme
71 Kevin McKay
82 Chris Van Dyk
97 Pavel Kriz
146 Marc Magliarditi
149 Marty Wilford
175 Steve Tardif
201 Casey Hankinson
227 Mike Pittman

1994
Pick
14 Ethan Moreau
40 Jean-Yves Leroux
85 Steve McLaren
118 Marc Dupuis
144 Jim Enson
170 Tyler Prosofsky
196 Mike Josephson
222 Lubomir Jandera
248 Lars Weibel
263 Rob Mara

1993
Pick
24 Eric Lecompte
50 Eric Manlow
54 Bogdan Savenko
76 Ryan Huska
90 Eric Daze
102 Patrik Pysz
128 Jonni Vauhkonen
180 Tom White
206 Sergei Petrov
232 Mike Rusk
258 Mike McGhan
284 Tom Noble

1992
Pick
12 Sergei Krivokrasov
36 Jeff Shantz
41 Sergei Klimovich
89 Andy MacIntyre
113 Tim Hogan
137 Gerry Skrypec
161 Mike Prokopec
185 Layne Roland
209 David Hymovitz
233 Richard Raymond

1991
Pick
22 Dean McAmmond
39 Michael Pomichter
44 Jamie Matthews
66 Bobby House
71 Igor Kravchuk
88 Zac Boyer
110 Maco Balkovec
112 Kevin St. Jacques
132 Jacques Auger
154 Scott Kirton
176 Roch Belley
198 Scott MacDonald
220 Alexander Andrievski
242 Mike Larkin
264 Scott Dean

1990
Pick
16 Karl Dykhuis
37 Ivan Droppa
79 Chris Tucker
121 Brett Stickney
124 Derek Edgerly
163 Hugo Belanger
184 Owen Lessard
205 Erik Peterson
226 Steve Dubinsky
247 Dino Grossi

1989
Pick
6 Adam Bennett
27 Michael Speer
48 Bob Kellogg
111 Tommi Pullola
132 Tracy Egeland
153 Milan Tichy
174 Jason Greyerbiehl
195 Matt Saunders
216 Mike Kozak
237 Michael Doneghey

Coaching History

Pete Muldoon, 1926-27; Barney Stanley and Hugh Lehman, 1927-28; Herb Gardiner and Dick Irvin, 1928-29; Tom Shaughnessy and Bill Tobin, 1929-30; Dick Irvin, 1930-31; Bill Tobin, 1931-32; Emil Iverson, Godfrey Matheson and Tommy Gorman, 1932-33; Tommy Gorman, 1933-34; Clem Loughlin, 1934-35 to 1936-37; Bill Stewart, 1937-38; Bill Stewart and Paul Thompson, 1938-39; Paul Thompson, 1939-40 to 1943-44; Paul Thompson and Johnny Gottselig, 1944-45; Johnny Gottselig, 1945-46, 1946-47; Johnny Gottselig and Charlie Conacher, 1947-48; Charlie Conacher, 1948-49, 1949-50; Ebbie Goodfellow, 1950-51, 1951-52; Sid Abel, 1952-53, 1953-54; Frank Eddolls, 1954-55; Dick Irvin, 1955-56; Tommy Ivan, 1956-57; Tommy Ivan and Rudy Pilous, 1957-58; Rudy Pilous, 1958-59 to 1962-63; Billy Reay, 1963-64 to 1975-76; Billy Reay and Bill White, 1976-77; Bob Pulford, 1977-78, 1978-79; Eddie Johnston, 1979-80; Keith Magnuson, 1980-81; Keith Magnuson and Bob Pulford, 1981-82; Orval Tessier, 1982-83, 1983-84; Orval Tessier and Bob Pulford, 1984-85; Bob Pulford, 1985-86, 1986-87; Bob Murdoch, 1987-88; Mike Keenan, 1988-89 to 1991-92; Darryl Sutter, 1992-93 to 1994-95; Craig Hartsburg, 1995-96 to 1997-98; Dirk Graham and Lorne Molleken, 1998-99; Lorne Molleken and Bob Pulford, 1999-2000; Alpo Suhonen, 2000-01; Brian Sutter, 2001-02 to date.

General Managers' History

Major Frederic McLaughlin, 1926-27 to 1941-42; Bill Tobin, 1942-43 to 1953-54; Tommy Ivan, 1954-55 to 1976-77; Bob Pulford, 1977-78 to 1989-90; Mike Keenan, 1990-91, 1991-92; Mike Keenan and Bob Pulford, 1992-93; Bob Pulford, 1993-94 to 1996-97; Bob Murray, 1997-98, 1998-99; Bob Murray and Bob Pulford, 1999-2000; Mike Smith, 2000-01 to date.

General Manager

SMITH, MIKE
General Manager, Chicago Blackhawks.
Born in Potsdam, NY, August 31, 1945.

Mike Smith joined the Chicago Blackhawks as manager of hockey operations on December 12, 1999, and was officially named the club's general manager on September 22, 2000. Smith served as associate general manager of the Toronto Maple Leafs for two seasons (1997-98 and 1998-99) before joining the Blackhawks. Previously, he had served as a consultant under Bob Pulford with Chicago from 1995 to 1997. Smith held a variety of positions with the Winnipeg Jets from 1979 to

Club Directory

United Center

Chicago Blackhawks
United Center
1901 W. Madison Street
Chicago, IL 60612
Phone **312/455-7000**
FAX 312/455-7041
www.chicagoblackhawks.com
Capacity: 20,500

President . . . . William W. Wirtz
Senior Vice President . . . . Robert J. Pulford
Vice President . . . . Peter R. Wirtz
Vice President . . . . Jack Davison
General Manager . . . . Mike Smith
Assistant General Manager . . . . Nick Beverley
Director of Player Evaluation . . . . Marshall Johnston
Director of Amateur Scouting . . . . Bill Lesuk
Head Coach . . . . Brian Sutter
Assistant Coach . . . . Denis Savard
Assistant Coach . . . . Al MacAdam
Asst. Coach, Strength & Cond. . . . . Phil Walker
Goaltending Consultant . . . . Vladislav Tretiak
Chief Amateur Scout . . . . Michel Dumas
Amateur Scouts . . . . Bruce Franklin, Tim Higgins, Rob Pulford, Ron Anderson, Gord Donnelly, Joe Yannetti
European Scouting Coordinator . . . . Sakari Pietela
European Amateur Scouts . . . . Matti Kautto, Karl Pavlik, Ruslan Shabanov
Amateur Scouting Analyst . . . . Brad Hornung
Executive Assistant . . . . Cindy Brueck
Special Assistant to G.M . . . . Stan Bowman
Manager of Team Services . . . . Matt Colleran
Video Coordinator . . . . Ike Rhodes

Medical Staff
Team Physicians . . . . Mark Bowen, Gordon Nuber, Greg Ewert
Team Dentists . . . . Daniel Mackey, Dean Sana
Oral Surgeon . . . . Eric Pulver
Eye Doctor . . . . Robert Stein
Head Trainer . . . . Michael Gapski
Assistant Trainer . . . . Jeff Thomas
Massage Therapist . . . . Pawel Prylinski
Equipment Manager . . . . Troy Parchman
Asst. Equipment Manager . . . . Bill Stehle
Equipment Assistant . . . . Mark DePasquale

Public Relations/Marketing
Exec. Dir. of Communications . . . . Jim De Maria
Dir. of Comm. Relations/PR Asst . . . . Barbara Davidson
Manager of Public Relations . . . . Tony Ommen
Exec. Dir. of Marketing &
  New Business Development . . . . Jim Sofranko
Dir. of Corporate Sponsorships . . . . Steve Waight
Acct. Exec., Corp. Sponsorship . . . . David Stensby
Manager, Client Services . . . . Kelly Bodnarchuk
Ex. Dir. of Fan Dev., Oper., Charities . . . . . Carol Czaplicki
Mgr., Youth and Fan Development . . . . Drew Stevenson
Manager, Game Operations . . . . Mike Sullivan
Website Producer . . . . Adam Kempenaar
Manager of Promotions . . . . Maxine Olhava
Marketing Associate . . . . Alison Finley
Administrative Assistant . . . . Angela Armbruster

Finance
Controller . . . . Tracy Hernandez
Treasurer . . . . Robert Rinkus
Accounting Manager . . . . Deb Kulir
Accounting Clerk . . . . Rita Loretto

Ticketing
Director, Ticket Operations . . . . James K. Bare
Director, Ticket Sales . . . . Doug Ryan
Season Ticket Sales Manager . . . . Steve Rigney
Account Executives . . . . Brad Bober, Shannon Burney, Adam Collopy, Ildegardo Esparza, Evan Hall, Erin Hoffman, Dustin Sublett
Ticket Operations Manager . . . . Kathie Raimondi
Customer Service Representative . . . . Holly Manthei

Miscellaneous Information
Team Photographer . . . . Bill Smith
Organist . . . . Frank Pellico
Public Address Announcer . . . . Gene Honda
Website Contributor . . . . Harvey Wittenberg
Radio Station . . . . WSCR (AM 670)
Television Station . . . . Fox Sports Net
Broadcaster . . . . Pat Foley
Broadcaster . . . . Dale Tallon

1994, including general manager. Under Smith, the Jets entered into a formal agreement with Sokol Kiev in 1989, the first of its kind for any NHL team.

Smith has a doctorate in Political Science and Russian Studies from Syracuse University. He has authored 10 books, mostly on coaching hockey.

NHL Coaching Record

| Season | Team | | Regular Season | | | | Playoffs | | |
		Games	W	L	T		Games	W	L
1980-81	Winnipeg	23	2	17	4		....	....	....
	NHL Totals	**23**	**2**	**17**	**4**		....	....	....

Colorado Avalanche

2002-03 Results: 42W-19L-13T-8OTL 105PTS.
First, Northwest Division

2003-04 Schedule

Oct.	Fri.	10	Chicago
	Sun.	12	St. Louis
	Thu.	16	at Minnesota
	Sat.	18	at Edmonton
	Tue.	21	Boston
	Thu.	23	Edmonton
	Sat.	25	at Nashville
	Sun.	26	Buffalo
	Tue.	28	Calgary
Nov.	Sat.	1	at New Jersey*
	Sun.	2	at NY Rangers*
	Tue.	4	Minnesota
	Thu.	6	Phoenix
	Sun.	9	at Chicago
	Tue.	11	at San Jose
	Thu.	13	at Phoenix
	Sat.	15	Dallas
	Tue.	18	Anaheim
	Thu.	20	NY Rangers
	Sat.	22	Los Angeles
	Mon.	24	Nashville
	Thu.	27	at Calgary
	Fri.	28	at Edmonton
	Sun.	30	New Jersey
Dec.	Thu.	4	at San Jose
	Sat.	6	Columbus
	Mon.	8	Washington
	Thu.	11	at Vancouver
	Sat.	13	at Calgary
	Wed.	17	Minnesota
	Fri.	19	at Anaheim
	Sat.	20	at Los Angeles
	Fri.	26	at St. Louis
	Sat.	27	Philadelphia
	Mon.	29	Vancouver
	Wed.	31	at Calgary
Jan.	Fri.	2	at Vancouver
	Sun.	4	Minnesota
	Tue.	6	Columbus
	Thu.	8	at Nashville
	Sat.	10	at Dallas*

	Sun.	11	at Chicago
	Tue.	13	Anaheim
	Thu.	15	Dallas
	Sat.	17	San Jose
	Mon.	19	at Tampa Bay
	Wed.	21	at Florida
	Thu.	22	at Atlanta
	Sat.	24	at Pittsburgh
	Tue.	27	Edmonton
	Thu.	29	at Los Angeles
	Fri.	30	at Anaheim
Feb.	Tue.	3	Carolina
	Thu.	5	Detroit
	Tue.	10	NY Islanders
	Thu.	12	at St. Louis
	Sat.	14	at Detroit*
	Mon.	16	Vancouver
	Wed.	18	Edmonton
	Fri.	20	at Dallas
	Sun.	22	at Minnesota
	Tue.	24	Calgary
	Thu.	26	St. Louis
	Sat.	28	at Columbus
Mar.	Mon.	1	Tampa Bay
	Wed.	3	Vancouver
	Fri.	5	San Jose
	Sun.	7	Calgary*
	Mon.	8	at Vancouver
	Wed.	10	at Edmonton
	Fri.	12	at Phoenix
	Sun.	14	Phoenix*
	Tue.	16	at Montreal
	Thu.	18	at Ottawa
	Sat.	20	at Toronto
	Tue.	23	Chicago
	Thu.	25	Detroit
	Sat.	27	at Detroit*
	Mon.	29	Los Angeles
	Wed.	31	at Minnesota
Apr.	Fri.	2	at Columbus
	Sun.	4	Nashville*

* Denotes afternoon game.

Franchise date: June 22, 1979
Transferred from Quebec to Denver, June 21, 1995

**NORTHWEST
DIVISION**

**25th
NHL
Season**

In addition to leading the NHL with 50 goals, Milan Hejduk kept Colorado in contention for its record ninth straight division title with an overtime game-winner at Anaheim with 10 seconds remaining in their second-last game of the season.

Year-by-Year Record

Season	GP	Home W	L	T	OL	Road W	L	T	OL	Overall W	L	T	OL	GF	GA	Pts.	Finished	Playoff Result
2002-03	82	21	9	8	3	21	10	5	5	42	19	13	8	251	194	105	1st, Northwest Div.	Lost Conf. Quarter-Final
2001-02	82	24	12	4	1	21	16	4	0	45	28	8	1	212	169	99	1st, Northwest Div.	Lost Conf. Championship
2000-01	**82**	**28**	**6**	**5**	**2**	**24**	**10**	**5**	**2**	**52**	**16**	**10**	**4**	**270**	**192**	**118**	**1st, Northwest Div.**	**Won Stanley Cup**
1999-2000	82	25	12	4	0	17	16	7	1	42	28	11	1	233	201	96	1st, Northwest Div.	Lost Conf. Championship
1998-99	82	21	14	6	...	23	14	4	...	44	28	10	...	239	205	98	1st, Northwest Div.	Lost Conf. Championship
1997-98	82	21	10	10	...	18	16	7	...	39	26	17	...	231	205	95	1st, Pacific Div.	Lost Conf. Quarter-Final
1996-97	82	26	10	5	...	23	14	4	...	49	24	9	...	277	205	107	1st, Pacific Div.	Lost Conf. Championship
1995-96	**82**	**24**	**10**	**7**	**...**	**23**	**15**	**3**	**...**	**47**	**25**	**10**	**...**	**326**	**240**	**104**	**1st, Pacific Div.**	**Won Stanley Cup**
1994-95*	48	19*	1	4	...	11	12	1	...	30	13	5	...	185	134	65	1st, Northeast Div.	Lost Conf. Quarter-Final
1993-94*	84	19	17	6	...	15	25	2	...	34	42	8	...	277	292	76	5th, Northeast Div.	Out of Playoffs
1992-93*	84	23	17	2	...	24	10	8	...	47	27	10	...	351	300	104	2nd, Adams Div.	Lost Div. Semi-Final
1991-92*	80	18	19	3	...	2	29	9	...	20	48	12	...	255	318	52	5th, Adams Div.	Out of Playoffs
1990-91*	80	9	23	8	...	7	27	6	...	16	50	14	...	236	354	46	5th, Adams Div.	Out of Playoffs
1989-90*	80	8	26	6	...	4	35	1	...	12	61	7	...	240	407	31	5th, Adams Div.	Out of Playoffs
1988-89*	80	16	20	4	...	11	26	3	...	27	46	7	...	269	342	61	5th, Adams Div.	Out of Playoffs
1987-88*	80	15	23	2	...	17	20	3	...	32	43	5	...	271	306	69	5th, Adams Div.	Out of Playoffs
1986-87*	80	20	13	7	...	11	26	3	...	31	39	10	...	267	276	72	4th, Adams Div.	Lost Div. Final
1985-86*	80	23	13	4	...	20	18	2	...	43	31	6	...	330	289	92	1st, Adams Div.	Lost Div. Semi-Final
1984-85*	80	24	12	4	...	17	18	5	...	41	30	9	...	323	275	91	2nd, Adams Div.	Lost Conf. Championship
1983-84*	80	24	11	5	...	18	17	5	...	42	28	10	...	360	278	94	3rd, Adams Div.	Lost Div. Final
1982-83*	80	23	10	7	...	11	24	5	...	34	34	12	...	343	336	80	4th, Adams Div.	Lost Div. Semi-Final
1981-82*	80	24	13	3	...	9	18	13	...	33	31	16	...	356	345	82	4th, Adams Div.	Lost Conf. Championship
1980-81*	80	18	11	11	...	12	21	7	...	30	32	18	...	314	318	78	4th, Adams Div.	Lost Prelim. Round
1979-80*	80	17	16	7	...	8	28	4	...	25	44	11	...	248	313	61	5th, Adams Div.	Out of Playoffs

* Quebec Nordiques

2003-04 Player Personnel

FORWARDS	HT	WT	S	Place of Birth	Date	2002-03 Club
BATTAGLIA, Bates	6-2	205	L	Chicago, IL	12/13/75	Carolina-Colorado
FORSBERG, Peter	6-0	205	L	Ornskoldsvik, Sweden	7/20/73	Colorado
HAHL, Riku	6-0	190	L	Hameenlinna, Finland	11/1/80	Colorado-Hershey
HEJDUK, Milan	5-11	185	R	Usti-nad-Labem, Czech.	2/14/76	Colorado
HINOTE, Dan	6-0	190	R	Leesburg, FL	1/30/77	Colorado
KARIYA, Paul	5-10	176	L	Vancouver, B.C.	10/16/74	Anaheim
KRESTANOVICH, Jordan	6-1	170	L	Langley, B.C.	6/14/81	Hershey
LARSEN, Brad	6-0	200	L	Nakusp, B.C.	6/28/77	Colorado-Hershey
MOORE, Steve	6-2	205	R	Windsor, Ont.	9/22/78	Colorado-Hershey
NIKOLISHIN, Andrei	6-0	213	L	Vorkuta, USSR	3/25/73	Chicago
SAKIC, Joe	5-11	195	L	Burnaby, B.C.	7/7/69	Colorado
SELANNE, Teemu	6-0	204	R	Helsinki, Finland	7/3/70	San Jose
STEPHENS, Charlie	6-3	225	R	London, Ont.	4/5/81	Colorado-Hershey
TANGUAY, Alex	6-0	190	L	Ste-Justine, Que.	11/21/79	Colorado
WILLSIE, Brian	6-1	195	R	London, Ont.	3/16/78	Colorado-Hershey
WORRELL, Peter	6-6	235	L	Pierrefonds, Que.	8/18/77	Florida

DEFENSEMEN	HT	WT	S	Place of Birth	Date	2002-03 Club
BLAKE, Rob	6-4	225	R	Simcoe, Ont.	12/10/69	Colorado
BOYCHUK, Johnny	6-2	205	R	Edmonton, Alta.	1/19/84	Calgary (WHL)-Moose Jaw
CLARK, Brett	6-1	195	L	Wapella, Sask.	12/23/76	Hershey
FOOTE, Adam	6-2	215	R	Toronto, Ont.	7/10/71	Colorado
LILES, John-Michael	5-10	185	L	Zionsville, IN	11/25/80	Hershey-Michigan State
McALLISTER, Chris	6-8	240	L	Saskatoon, Sask.	6/16/75	Phi (AHL)-Phi-Col
MORRIS, Derek	5-11	210	R	Edmonton, Alta.	8/24/78	Colorado
SKOULA, Martin	6-2	195	L	Litomerice, Czech.	10/28/79	Colorado
SKRASTINS, Karlis	6-1	212	L	Riga, USSR	7/9/74	Nashville
SLOVAK, Tomas	6-1	203	R	Kosice, Czech.	4/5/83	Kelowna
SMITH, D.J.	6-2	205	L	Windsor, Ont.	5/13/77	Colorado-Hershey

GOALTENDERS	HT	WT	C	Place of Birth	Date	2002-03 Club
AEBISCHER, David	6-1	190	L	Fribourg, Switz.	2/7/78	Colorado
BUDAJ, Peter	6-0	200	L	Bystrica, Czech.	9/18/82	Hershey
LAWSON, Tom	6-5	200	L	Whitby, Ont.	8/15/79	Fort Wayne
SAUVE, Philippe	6-0	180	L	Buffalo, NY	2/27/80	Hershey

Captains' History

Marc Tardif, 1979-80, 1980-81; Robbie Ftorek and Andre Dupont, 1981-82; Mario Marois, 1982-83 to 1984-85; Mario Marois and Peter Stastny, 1985-86; Peter Stastny, 1986-87 to 1989-90; Joe Sakic and Steven Finn, 1990-91; Mike Hough, 1991-92; Joe Sakic, 1992-93 to date.

Coaching History

Jacques Demers, 1979-80; Maurice Filion and Michel Bergeron, 1980-81; Michel Bergeron, 1981-82 to 1986-87; Andre Savard and Ron Lapointe, 1987-88; Ron Lapointe and Jean Perron, 1988-89; Michel Bergeron, 1989-90; Dave Chambers, 1990-91; Dave Chambers and Pierre Page, 1991-92; Pierre Page, 1992-93, 1993-94; Marc Crawford, 1994-95 to 1997-98; Bob Hartley, 1998-99 to 2001-02; Bob Hartley and Tony Granato, 2002-03; Tony Granato, 2003-04.

Coach

GRANATO, TONY
Coach, Colorado Avalanche. Born in Downers Grove, IL, July 25, 1964.

Tony Granato was named head coach of the Colorado Avalanche on December 18, 2002 after having joined the organization as an assistant coach on June 18, 2002. Regarded as a feisty, two-way winger, Granato enjoyed a playing career that spanned 13 seasons in the National Hockey League. He skated in 773 regular-season games with the New York Rangers, Los Angeles Kings, and San Jose Sharks. He posted 248 goals and 244 assists with 1,425 penalty minutes.

Originally drafted by the New York Rangers 120th overall in the 1982 Entry Draft, Granato spent a season and a half with the Rangers before being dealt to the Los Angeles Kings, where he played six-and-a-half seasons, cracking the 30-goal barrier three times. He concluded his playing career in 2000-01 with San Jose after five seasons in Silicon Valley, signing with the Sharks as a free agent for the 1996-97 campaign.

Granato received several accolades during his career. He was named to the NHL All-Rookie Team in 1989, played in the NHL All-Star Game in 1997, and won the Bill Masterton Memorial Trophy, given for perseverance, sportsmanship, and dedication to hockey, in 1997.

Prior to joining the professional ranks, Granato played for four years at the University of Wisconsin, where he was named to the WCHA Second All-Star Team for 1985 and 1987 and to the NCAA West Second All-Star Team in the same years. He is a member of the University of Wisconsin's Hall of Fame. Granato was also a member of the 1988 U.S. national and Olympic hockey teams. His sister, Cammi, served as captain of the gold medal-winning U.S. women's hockey team at the 1998 Olympics and was a silver medalist in Salt Lake City in 2002.

Coaching Record

Season	Team	Games	Regular Season			Playoffs		
			W	L	T	Games	W	L
2002-03	Colorado (NHL)	51	32	15	4	7	3	4
	NHL Totals	51	32	15	4	7	3	4

2002-03 Scoring

* - rookie

Regular Season

Pos	#	Player	Team	GP	G	A	Pts	+/-	PIM	PP	SH	GW	GT	S	%
C	21	Peter Forsberg	COL	75	29	77	106	52	70	8	0	2	0	166	17.5
R	23	Milan Hejduk	COL	82	50	48	98	52	32	18	0	4	1	244	20.5
L	40	Alex Tanguay	COL	82	26	41	67	34	36	3	0	5	2	142	18.3
C	19	Joe Sakic	COL	58	26	32	58	4	24	8	0	1	0	190	13.7
C	28	Steve Reinprecht	COL	77	18	33	51	-6	18	2	1	1	0	146	12.3
D	53	Derek Morris	COL	75	11	37	48	16	68	9	0	7	0	191	5.8
D	4	Rob Blake	COL	79	17	28	45	20	57	8	2	3	0	269	6.3
D	7	Greg de Vries	COL	82	6	26	32	15	70	0	0	2	0	112	5.4
D	52	Adam Foote	COL	78	11	20	31	30	88	3	0	2	0	106	10.4
L	44	Bates Battaglia	CAR	70	5	14	19	-17	90	0	1	1	0	96	5.2
			COL	13	1	5	6	-2	10	1	0	1	0	27	3.7
			TOTAL	83	6	19	25	-19	100	1	1	2	0	123	4.9
D	41	Martin Skoula	COL	81	4	21	25	11	68	2	0	0	0	93	4.3
C	37	Dean McAmmond	COL	41	10	8	18	1	10	2	0	2	0	72	13.9
L	29	Eric Messier	COL	72	4	10	14	-2	16	0	1	1	0	52	7.7
D	20	Bryan Marchment	S.J.	67	2	9	11	-2	108	0	0	0	0	66	3.0
			COL	14	0	3	3	4	33	0	0	0	0	18	0.0
			TOTAL	81	2	12	14	2	141	0	0	0	0	84	2.4
R	13	Dan Hinote	COL	60	6	4	10	4	49	0	0	3	0	65	9.2
L	12	Mike Keane	COL	65	5	5	10	0	34	0	1	1	0	35	14.3
L	10	Serge Aubin	COL	66	4	6	10	-2	64	0	0	1	0	62	6.5
C	22 *	Vaclav Nedorost	COL	42	4	5	9	8	20	1	0	0	0	35	11.4
C	11	Jeff Shantz	COL	74	3	6	9	-12	35	0	0	2	0	68	4.4
C	32 *	Riku Hahl	COL	42	3	4	7	3	12	0	0	0	0	61	4.9
R	27	Scott Parker	COL	43	1	3	4	6	82	0	0	0	0	20	5.0
L	9	Brad Larsen	COL	6	0	3	3	3	2	0	0	0	0	6	0.0
D	2	Bryan Muir	COL	32	0	2	2	3	19	0	0	0	0	9	0.0
D	6 *	D.J. Smith	COL	34	1	0	1	2	55	0	0	0	0	7	14.3
R	50	Brian Willsie	COL	12	0	1	1	0	15	0	0	0	0	12	0.0
D	24	Chris McAllister	PHI	19	0	0	0	-2	21	0	0	0	0	9	0.0
			COL	14	0	1	1	6	26	0	0	0	0	4	0.0
			TOTAL	33	0	1	1	4	47	0	0	0	0	13	0.0
R	45	Steve Brule	COL	2	0	0	0	0	0	0	0	0	0	2	0.0
D	39 *	Jeff Paul	COL	2	0	0	0	0	7	0	0	0	0	0	0.0
C	38 *	Charlie Stephens	COL	2	0	0	0	0	0	0	0	0	0	1	0.0
C	36 *	Steve Moore	COL	4	0	0	0	0	0	0	0	0	0	0	0.0

Goaltending

No.	Goaltender	GPI	Mins	Avg	W	L	T	EN	SO	GA	SA	S%	G	A	PIM
33	Patrick Roy	63	3769	2.18	35	15	13	3	5	137	1723	.920	0	0	20
1	David Aebischer	22	1235	2.43	7	12	0	4	1	50	593	.916	0	0	4
	Totals	82	5026	2.32	42	27	13	7	6	194	2323	.916			

Playoffs

Pos	#	Player	Team	GP	G	A	Pts	+/-	PIM	PP	SH	GW	GT	S	%
C	19	Joe Sakic	COL	7	6	3	9	1	2	2	0	1	0	26	23.1
C	21	Peter Forsberg	COL	7	2	6	8	3	6	1	0	0	0	23	8.7
R	23	Milan Hejduk	COL	7	2	2	4	4	2	1	0	0	0	21	9.5
D	4	Rob Blake	COL	7	1	2	3	2	8	0	0	0	0	27	3.7
R	13	Dan Hinote	COL	7	1	2	3	0	2	0	0	0	0	9	11.1
L	40	Alex Tanguay	COL	7	1	2	3	-2	4	0	0	0	0	10	10.0
C	28	Steve Reinprecht	COL	7	1	2	3	1	0	0	0	0	0	9	11.1
D	53	Derek Morris	COL	7	0	3	3	2	6	0	0	0	0	12	0.0
D	7	Greg de Vries	COL	7	2	0	2	2	0	0	0	0	0	12	16.7
C	32 *	Riku Hahl	COL	6	0	2	2	2	2	0	0	0	0	11	0.0
L	44	Bates Battaglia	COL	7	0	2	2	1	4	0	0	0	0	14	0.0
R	50	Brian Willsie	COL	6	1	0	1	1	0	0	0	1	0	7	14.3
D	52	Adam Foote	COL	7	0	1	1	2	8	0	0	0	0	3	0.0
D	41	Martin Skoula	COL	7	0	1	1	1	0	0	0	0	0	4	0.0
D	24	Chris McAllister	COL	1	0	0	0	0	0	0	0	0	0	0	0.0
R	27	Scott Parker	COL	5	0	0	0	0	4	0	0	0	0	0	0.0
L	29	Eric Messier	COL	5	0	0	0	0	0	0	0	0	0	4	0.0
L	10	Serge Aubin	COL	5	0	0	0	0	4	0	0	0	0	1	0.0
L	12	Mike Keane	COL	6	0	0	0	0	2	0	0	0	0	1	0.0
C	11	Jeff Shantz	COL	6	0	0	0	-1	0	0	0	0	0	1	0.0
D	20	Bryan Marchment	COL	7	0	0	0	1	4	0	0	0	0	3	0.0

Goaltending

No.	Goaltender	GPI	Mins	Avg	W	L	EN	SO	GA	SA	S%	G	A	PIM
33	Patrick Roy	7	423	2.27	3	4	0	1	16	177	.910	0	0	0
	Totals	7	428	2.24	3	4	0	1	16	177	.910			

Club Records

Team

(Figures in brackets for season records are games played; records for fewest points, wins, ties, losses, goals, goals against are for 70 or more games)

Most Points	**118**	2000-01 (82)
Most Wins	**52**	2000-01 (82)
Most Ties	**18**	1980-81 (80)
Most Losses	**61**	1989-90 (80)
Most Goals	**360**	1983-84 (80)
Most Goals Against	**407**	1989-90 (80)
Fewest Points	**31**	1989-90 (80)
Fewest Wins	**12**	1989-90 (80)
Fewest Ties	**5**	1987-88 (80)
Fewest Losses	**16**	2000-01 (82)
Fewest Goals	**212**	2001-02 (82)
Fewest Goals Against	**169**	2001-02 (82)
Longest Winning Streak		
Overall	**12**	Jan. 10-Feb. 7/99
Home	**10**	Nov. 26/83-Jan. 10/84, Mar. 6-Apr. 16/95
Away	**7**	Jan. 10-Feb. 7/99
Longest Undefeated Streak		
Overall	**12**	Dec. 23/96-Jan. 20/97 (9 wins, 3 ties), Jan. 10-Feb. 7/99 (12 wins)
Home	**14**	Nov. 19/83-Jan. 21/84 (11 wins, 3 ties)
Away	**10**	Jan. 10-Mar. 3/99 (8 wins, 2 ties)
Longest Losing Streak		
Overall	**14**	Oct. 21-Nov. 19/90
Home	**8**	Oct. 21-Nov. 24/90
Away	**18**	Jan. 18-Apr. 1/90
Longest Winless Streak		
Overall	**17**	Oct. 21-Nov. 25/90 (15 losses, 2 ties)
Home	**11**	Nov. 14-Dec. 26/89 (7 losses, 4 ties)
Away	**33**	Oct. 8/91-Feb. 27/92 (25 losses, 8 ties)
Most Shutouts, Season	**11**	2001-02 (82)
Most PIM, Season	**2,104**	1989-90 (80)
Most Goals, Game	**12**	Three times

Individual

Most Seasons	**15**	Joe Sakic
Most Games	**1,074**	Joe Sakic
Most Goals, Career	**509**	Joe Sakic
Most Assists, Career	**806**	Joe Sakic
Most Points, Career	**1,315**	Joe Sakic (509G, 806A)
Most PIM, Career	**1,562**	Dale Hunter
Most Shutouts, Career	**37**	Patrick Roy
Longest Consecutive Games Streak	**312**	Dale Hunter (Oct. 9/80-Mar. 13/84)
Most Goals, Season	**57**	Michel Goulet (1982-83)
Most Assists, Season	**93**	Peter Stastny (1981-82)
Most Points, Season	**139**	Peter Stastny (1981-82; 46G, 93A)
Most PIM, Season	**301**	Gord Donnelly (1987-88)
Most Points, Defenseman, Season	**82**	Steve Duchesne (1992-93; 20G, 62A)
Most Points, Center, Season	**139**	Peter Stastny (1981-82; 46G, 93A)
Most Points, Right Wing, Season	**103**	Jacques Richard (1980-81; 52G, 51A)
Most Points, Left Wing, Season	**121**	Michel Goulet (1983-84; 56G, 65A)
Most Points, Rookie, Season	**109**	Peter Stastny (1980-81; 39G, 70A)
Most Shutouts, Season	**9**	Patrick Roy (2001-02)
Most Goals, Game	**5**	Mats Sundin (Mar. 5/92), Mike Ricci (Feb. 17/94)
Most Assists, Game	**5**	Six times
Most Points, Game	**8**	Peter Stastny (Feb. 22/81; 4G, 4A), Anton Stastny (Feb. 22/81; 3G, 5A)

Records include Quebec Nordiques, 1979-80 through 1994-95.

Retired Numbers

3	J.C. Tremblay*	1972-1979
8	Marc Tardif*	1979-1983
16	Michel Goulet*	1979-1990
77	Raymond Bourque	2000-2001

* Quebec Nordiques

All-time Record vs. Other Clubs

Regular Season

	At Home								On Road								Total							
	GP	W	L	T	OL	GF	GA	PTS	GP	W	L	T	OL	GF	GA	PTS	GP	W	L	T	OL	GF	GA	PTS
Anaheim	19	9	5	4	1	60	51	23	19	11	4	3	1	50	43	26	38	20	9	7	2	110	94	49
Atlanta	4	2	1	0	1	17	10	5	3	2	1	0	0	7	6	4	7	4	2	0	1	24	16	9
Boston	65	24	35	6	0	233	267	54	62	22	31	9	0	192	240	53	127	46	66	15	0	425	507	107
Buffalo	63	31	20	11	1	226	194	74	63	18	35	9	1	204	247	46	126	49	55	20	2	430	441	120
Calgary	44	17	16	11	0	160	143	45	44	16	20	8	0	132	153	40	88	33	36	19	0	292	296	85
Carolina	64	38	17	9	0	271	190	85	62	26	24	12	0	214	203	64	126	64	41	21	0	485	393	149
Chicago	37	20	12	5	0	151	122	45	39	15	21	3	0	121	137	33	76	35	33	8	0	272	259	78
Columbus	6	6	0	0	0	27	9	12	6	5	0	1	0	23	6	11	12	11	0	1	0	50	15	23
Dallas	39	21	11	7	0	143	102	49	39	14	19	5	1	110	124	34	78	35	30	12	1	253	226	83
Detroit	40	20	16	4	0	145	136	44	38	14	22	1	1	115	138	30	78	34	38	5	1	260	274	74
Edmonton	44	22	18	4	0	169	162	48	43	15	23	4	1	127	177	35	87	37	41	8	1	296	339	83
Florida	11	4	4	3	0	30	27	11	10	9	1	0	0	42	25	18	21	13	5	3	0	72	52	29
Los Angeles	40	22	15	3	0	167	137	47	41	13	25	3	0	131	170	29	81	35	40	6	0	298	307	76
Minnesota	8	7	0	1	0	27	14	15	7	4	1	1	1	24	13	10	15	11	1	2	1	51	27	25
Montreal	63	32	26	5	0	216	222	69	63	16	37	10	0	196	257	42	126	48	63	15	0	412	479	111
Nashville	10	6	2	2	0	29	19	14	10	5	2	3	0	37	29	13	20	11	4	5	0	66	48	27
New Jersey	34	18	13	3	0	123	97	39	35	13	18	4	0	118	143	30	69	31	31	7	0	241	240	69
NY Islanders	33	20	11	2	0	122	96	42	32	13	18	1	0	109	129	27	65	33	29	3	0	231	225	69
NY Rangers	34	18	13	3	0	139	127	39	33	10	19	4	0	96	132	24	67	28	32	7	0	235	259	63
Ottawa	15	12	2	1	0	70	41	25	17	7	7	3	0	64	51	17	32	19	9	4	0	134	92	42
Philadelphia	34	11	10	12	1	121	120	35	34	10	21	2	1	91	122	23	68	21	31	14	2	212	242	58
Phoenix	39	19	15	5	0	136	131	43	38	16	15	7	0	137	139	39	77	35	30	12	0	273	270	82
Pittsburgh	32	17	13	2	0	142	122	36	36	16	15	5	0	147	142	37	68	33	28	7	0	289	264	73
St. Louis	39	20	12	6	1	135	107	47	38	13	22	3	0	117	145	29	77	33	34	9	1	252	252	76
San Jose	21	13	3	4	1	76	39	31	22	15	7	0	0	83	60	30	43	28	10	4	1	159	99	61
Tampa Bay	12	8	2	2	0	50	25	18	11	2	8	1	0	27	35	5	23	10	10	3	0	77	60	23
Toronto	29	17	7	5	0	111	87	39	34	15	15	4	0	131	113	34	63	32	22	9	0	242	200	73
Vancouver	44	22	15	7	0	150	124	51	44	21	16	6	1	167	148	49	88	43	31	13	1	317	272	100
Washington	33	14	14	5	0	101	115	33	33	11	18	4	0	105	131	26	66	25	32	9	0	206	246	59
Totals	**956**	**490**	**328**	**132**	**6**	**3547**	**3036**	**1118**	**956**	**367**	**465**	**116**	**8**	**3117**	**3458**	**858**	**1912**	**857**	**793**	**248**	**14**	**6664**	**6494**	**1976**

Playoffs

	Series	W	L	GP	W	L	T	GF	GA	Last Mtg.	Rnd.	Result
Boston	2	1	1	11	5	6	0	36	37	1983	DSF	L 1-3
Buffalo	2	2	0	8	6	2	0	35	27	1985	DSF	W 3-2
Chicago	2	2	0	12	8	4	0	49	28	1997	CQF	W 4-2
Dallas	2	0	2	14	6	8	0	29	37	2000	CF	L 3-4
Detroit	5	3	2	30	17	13	0	79	76	2002	CF	L 3-4
Edmonton	2	1	1	12	7	5	0	35	30	1998	CQF	L 3-4
Florida	1	1	0	4	4	0	0	15	4	1996	F	W 4-0
Hartford	2	1	1	9	4	5	0	34	35	1987	DSF	W 4-2
Los Angeles	2	2	0	14	8	6	0	33	23	2002	CQF	W 4-3
Minnesota	1	0	1	7	3	4	0	17	16	2003	CQF	L 3-4
Montreal	5	2	3	31	14	17	0	85	105	1993	DSF	L 2-4
New Jersey	1	1	0	7	4	3	0	19	11	2001	F	W 4-3
NY Islanders	1	0	1	4	0	4	0	9	18	1982	CF	L 0-4
NY Rangers	1	0	1	6	2	4	0	19	25	1995	CQF	L 2-4
Philadelphia	2	0	2	11	4	7	0	29	39	1985	CF	L 2-4
Phoenix	1	1	0	5	4	1	0	17	10	2000	CQF	W 4-1
St. Louis	1	1	0	5	4	1	0	17	11	2001	CF	W 4-1
San Jose	2	2	0	13	8	5	0	44	38	2002	CSF	W 4-3
Vancouver	2	2	0	10	8	2	0	40	26	2001	CQF	W 4-0
Totals	**37**	**22**	**15**	**213**	**116**	**97**	**0**	**641**	**596**			

Calgary totals include Atlanta Flames, 1979-80.
Dallas totals include Minnesota North Stars, 1979-80 to 1992-93.
Phoenix totals include Winnipeg, 1979-80 to 1995-96.
Carolina totals include Hartford, 1979-80 to 1996-97.
New Jersey totals include Colorado Rockies, 1979-80 to 1981-82.

Playoff Results 2003-1999

Year	Round	Opponent	Result	GF	GA
2003	CQF	Minnesota	L 3-4	17	16
2002	CF	Detroit	L 3-4	13	22
	CSF	San Jose	W 4-3	25	21
	CQF	Los Angeles	W 4-3	16	13
2001	**F**	**New Jersey**	**W 4-3**	**19**	**11**
	CF	St. Louis	W 4-1	17	11
	CSF	Los Angeles	W 4-3	17	10
	CQF	Vancouver	W 4-0	16	9
2000	CF	Dallas	L 3-4	13	14
	CSF	Detroit	W 4-1	13	8
	CQF	Phoenix	W 4-1	17	10
1999	CF	Dallas	L 3-4	16	23
	CSF	Detroit	W 4-2	21	14
	CQF	San Jose	W 4-2	19	17

Abbreviations: Round: F - Final; **CF** - conference final; **CSF** - conference semi-final; **CQF** - conference quarter-final; **DSF** - division semi-final.

2002-03 Results

Oct.	9	Dallas	1-1
	14	Boston	1-2
	17	at Los Angeles	4-1
	19	at San Jose	3-1
	20	at Anaheim	2-3*
	22	Edmonton	3-3
	24	at Phoenix	3-2
	27	Minnesota	3-3
	29	at Minnesota	2-3*
	31	at Vancouver	5-1
Nov.	2	at Calgary	4-4
	4	Vancouver	2-4
	6	Ottawa	2-5
	8	Anaheim	2-3*
	10	Nashville	3-4
	12	Columbus	5-4
	14	at Nashville	3-1
	15	at Dallas	2-4
	17	at Phoenix	4-4
	21	Nashville	1-1
	23	at St. Louis	3-1
	25	Chicago	1-0
	27	St. Louis	4-4
	29	at Minnesota	2-2
	30	at Edmonton	0-1
Dec.	3	Calgary	1-2
	6	Montreal	7-6*
	11	at Vancouver	1-3
	13	at Edmonton	3-4*
	14	at Calgary	3-1
	16	Washington	2-2
	19	Edmonton	2-1
	21	Minnesota	4-2
	23	Vancouver	5-3
	26	at St. Louis	2-3
	27	Philadelphia	1-2*
	29	Los Angeles	6-1
Jan.	1	at Nashville	7-3
	2	Florida	1-4
	4	at San Jose	6-1
	7	Calgary	2-4
	9	Anaheim	3-5
	11	at Dallas	3-6
	12	at Carolina	3-2*
	16	Detroit	2-4
	20	Dallas	1-1
	23	Columbus	5-0
	25	at Toronto	3-0
	28	at Columbus	2-2
	30	at NY Rangers	4-3*
Feb.	4	at Boston	3-2*
	6	at Detroit	1-0
	8	Detroit	5-3
	9	Calgary	4-2
	11	New Jersey	3-1
	13	at Vancouver	1-2*
	15	Minnesota	3-2
	17	at Chicago	5-4
	20	at Pittsburgh	5-2
	21	at NY Islanders	1-4
	23	NY Rangers	4-1
	25	Edmonton	4-2
	27	Atlanta	3-4*
Mar.	1	Pittsburgh	4-1
	2	at Chicago	3-2*
	5	at Florida	3-1
	7	at Tampa Bay	3-4
	8	at Philadelphia	2-1*
	10	Phoenix	2-2
	13	at Columbus	5-1
	15	at Detroit	3-5
	16	at Washington	1-2
	20	San Jose	2-0
	22	Chicago	8-1
	24	at Buffalo	3-4*
	25	at Ottawa	2-2
	27	Los Angeles	3-0
	29	Phoenix	6-1
	31	San Jose	3-1
Apr.	2	at Los Angeles	3-5
	4	at Anaheim	4-3*
	6	St. Louis	5-2

* – Overtime

Entry Draft
Selections 2003-1989

2003 Pick		1999 Pick		1995 Pick		1991 Pick	
63	David Liffiton	25	Mikhail Kuleshov	25	Marc Denis	1	Eric Lindros
131	David Svagrovsky	45	Martin Grenier	51	Nic Beaudoin	24	Rene Corbet
146	Mark McCutcheon	93	Branko Radivojevic	77	John Tripp	46	Rich Brennan
163	Brad Richardson	112	Sanny Lindstrom	81	Tomi Kallio	68	Dave Karpa
204	Linus Videll	122	Kristian Kovac	129	Brent Johnson	90	Patrick Labrecque
225	Brett Hemingway	142	Will Magnuson	155	John Cirjak	103	Bill Lindsay
257	Darryl Yacboski	152	Jordan Krestanovich	181	Dan Smith	134	Mikael Johansson
288	David Jones	158	Anders Lovdahl	207	Tomi Hirvonen	156	Janne Laukkanen
		183	Riku Hahl	228	Chris George	157	Aaron Asp
2002 Pick		212	Radim Vrbata			178	Adam Bartell
28	Jonas Johansson	240	Jeff Finger	**1994 Pick**		188	Brent Brekke
61	Johnny Boychuk			12	Wade Belak	200	Paul Koch
94	Eric Lundberg	**1998 Pick**		22	Jeffrey Kealty	222	Doug Friedman
107	Mikko Kalteva	12	Alex Tanguay	35	Josef Marha	244	Eric Meloche
129	Tom Gilbert	17	Martin Skoula	61	Sebastien Bety		
164	Tyler Weiman	19	Robyn Regehr	72	Chris Drury	**1990 Pick**	
195	Taylor Christie	20	Scott Parker	87	Milan Hejduk	1	Owen Nolan
227	Ryan Steeves	28	Ramzi Abid	113	Tony Tuzzolino	22	Ryan Hughes
258	Sergei Shemetov	38	Philippe Sauve	139	Nicholas Windsor	43	Brad Zavisha
289	Sean Collins	53	Steve Moore	165	Calvin Elfring	106	Jeff Parrott
		79	Yevgeny Lazarev	191	Jay Bertsch	127	Dwayne Norris
2001 Pick		141	K.C. Timmons	217	Tim Thomas	148	Andrei Kovalenko
63	Peter Budaj	167	Alexander Riazantsev	243	Chris Pittman	158	Alexander Karpovtsev
97	Danny Bois			285	Steven Low	169	Pat Mazzoli
130	Colt King	**1997 Pick**				190	Scott Davis
143	Frantisek Skladany	26	Kevin Grimes	**1993 Pick**		211	Mika Stromberg
144	Cody McCormick	53	Graham Belak	10	Jocelyn Thibault	232	Wade Klippenstein
149	Mikko Viitanen	55	Rick Berry	14	Adam Deadmarsh		
165	Pierre-Luc Emond	78	Ville Nieminen	49	Ashley Buckberger	**1989 Pick**	
184	Scott Horvath	87	Brad Larsen	75	Bill Pierce	1	Mats Sundin
196	Charlie Stephens	133	Aaron Miskovich	101	Ryan Tocher	22	Adam Foote
227	Marek Svatos	161	David Aebischer	127	Anders Myrvold	43	Stephane Morin
		217	Doug Schmidt	137	Nicholas Checco	54	John Tanner
2000 Pick		243	Kyle Kidney	153	Christian Matte	68	Niklas Andersson
14	Vaclav Nedorost	245	Stephen Lafleur	179	David Ling	76	Eric Dubois
47	Jared Aulin			205	Petr Franek	85	Kevin Kaiser
50	Sergei Soin	**1996 Pick**		231	Vincent Auger	106	Dan Lambert
63	Agris Saviels	25	Peter Ratchuk	257	Mark Pivetz	127	Sergei Mylnikov
88	Kurt Sauer	51	Yuri Babenko	283	John Hillman	148	Paul Krake
92	Sergei Klyazmin	79	Mark Parrish			169	Vyacheslav Bykov
119	Brian Fahey	98	Ben Storey	**1992 Pick**		190	Andrei Khomutov
159	John-Michael Liles	107	Randy Petruk	4	Todd Warriner	211	Byron Witkowski
189	Chris Bahen	134	Luke Curtin	28	Paul Brousseau	232	Noel Rahn
221	Aaron Molnar	146	Brian Willsie	29	Tuomas Gronman		
252	Darryl Bootland	160	Kai Fischer	52	Manny Fernandez		
266	Sean Kotary	167	Dan Hinote	76	Ian McIntyre		
285	Blake Ward	176	Samuel Pahlsson	100	Charlie Wasley		
		188	Roman Pylner	124	Paxton Schulte		
		214	Matt Scorsune	148	Martin Lepage		
		240	Justin Clark	172	Mike Jickling		
				196	Steve Passmore		
				220	Anson Carter		
				244	Aaron Ellis		

General Managers' History

Maurice Filion, 1979-80 to 1987-88; Martin Madden, 1988-89; Martin Madden and Maurice Filion, 1989-90; Pierre Page, 1990-91 to 1993-94; Pierre Lacroix, 1994-95 to date.

President and General Manager

LACROIX, PIERRE
President/General Manager, Colorado Avalanche.
Born in Montreal, Que., August 3, 1948.

Pierre Lacroix was appointed to the general manager's post on May 24, 1994 after 21 years as a respected player agent. In his first season as general manager, his leadership was instrumental in moving the team from 11th to second place in the NHL. Lacroix's second season began with the club's move to Denver. The revamped Avs finished atop the Pacific Division and went on to win the Stanley Cup. He was named NHL executive of the year by *The Hockey News* and became president of the club's hockey operations in August, 1995. The Avalanche have continued to rank among the NHL's top teams, and won the Stanley Cup again in 2001. Colorado won its record-setting ninth consecutive division title in 2002-03.

Club Directory

Pepsi Center

Colorado Avalanche
Pepsi Center
1000 Chopper Circle
Denver, CO 80204
Phone **303/405-1100**
FAX 303/893-0614
Press Box 303/575-1926
www.coloradoavalanche.com
Capacity: 18,007

Owner & Governor	E. Stanley Kroenke
Alternate Governor, President & General Manager	Pierre Lacroix
Head Coach	Tony Granato
Assistant Coaches	Jacques Cloutier, Rick Tocchet
Vice President of Player Personnel	Michel Goulet
Assistant to the General Manager	Greg Sherman
Director of Hockey Operations	Eric Lacroix
Director of Player Development/Goaltending Coach	Craig Billington
Director of Hockey Administration	Charlotte Grahame
Video Coordinator	Mike McCready
Team Services Assistant	Ronnie Jameson
Hockey Administration Assistant	Andrea Furness
Chief Scout	Jim Hammett
Pro Scouts	Brad Smith, Garth Joy
Scouts	Glen Cochrane, Yvon Gendron, Alan Hepple, Chris O'Sullivan, Don Paarup, Richard Pracey
European Scouts	Kirill Ladygin, Joni Lehto
Computer Research Consultant	John Donohue
Strength and Conditioning Coach	Paul Goldberg
Head Athletic Trainer	Pat Karns
Assistant Athletic Trainer	Matt Sokolowski
Massage Therapist	Gregorio Pradera
Inventory Manager	Wayne Flemming
Head Equipment Manager	Mark Miller
Assistant Equipment Managers	Terry Geer, Cliff Halstead

Communications Department

Senior Vice President, Communications & Team Services	Jean Martineau
Director of Special Projects/Communications	Hayne Ellis
Assistant Director of Media Relations	Damen Zier

Team Information

Press Box Location	West Side - Level 6
Practice Facility	South Suburban Family Sports Center
Minor League Affiliate	Hershey Bears (AHL)
Television Outlets	Fox Sports Net Rocky Mountain, KTVD UPN-20
Radio Flagship	KKFN AM-950

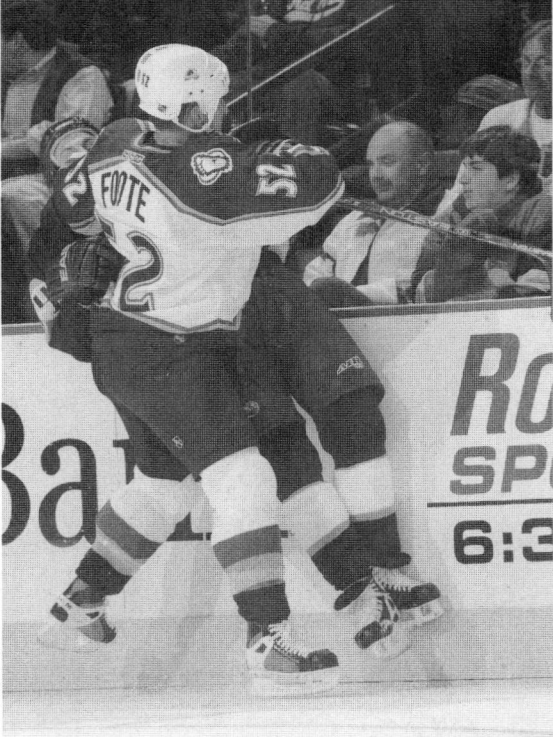

Adam Foote more than doubled his previous career high with 11 goals last season. His 31 assists and 42 points were also personal bests. Still as defensively sound as ever, Foote's +30 rating tied him for third among NHL blueliners.

Columbus Blue Jackets

2002-03 Results: 29w-42L-8T-3OTL 69PTS.
Fifth, Central Division

Year-by-Year Record

Season	GP	Home				Road				Overall						Finished	Playoff Result
		W	L	T	OL	W	L	T	OL	W	L	T	OL	GF	GA	Pts.		
2002-03	82	20	14	5	2	9	28	3	1	29	42	8	3	213	263	69	5th, Central Div.	Out of Playoffs
2001-02	82	14	18	5	4	8	29	3	1	22	47	8	5	164	255	57	5th, Central Div.	Out of Playoffs
2000-01	82	19	15	4	3	9	24	5	3	28	39	9	6	190	233	71	5th, Central Div.	Out of Playoffs

2003-04 Schedule

Oct.	Thu.	9	at Atlanta	Sat.	10	at Los Angeles
	Sat.	11	NY Rangers	Sun.	11	at Anaheim*
	Mon.	13	Vancouver	Thu.	15	at St. Louis
	Thu.	16	Chicago	Fri.	16	Los Angeles
	Sat.	18	at Nashville	Sun.	18	Edmonton
	Wed.	22	at Detroit	Wed.	21	St. Louis
	Thu.	23	Tampa Bay	Thu.	22	at Chicago
	Sat.	25	Dallas	Sat.	24	Chicago
	Tue.	28	at Vancouver	Tue.	27	New Jersey
	Thu.	30	at Edmonton	Thu.	29	Nashville
Nov.	Sat.	1	at Calgary	Sat.	31	Minnesota
	Fri.	7	Atlanta	Feb. Mon.	2	at Phoenix
	Sun.	9	Calgary*	Wed.	4	at Dallas
	Tue.	11	at Montreal	Wed.	11	Los Angeles
	Thu.	13	at Ottawa	Thu.	12	at Toronto
	Fri.	14	Boston	Sat.	14	San Jose
	Sun.	16	Phoenix*	Mon.	16	Nashville
	Wed.	19	at Detroit	Wed.	18	at Anaheim
	Thu.	20	Detroit	Fri.	20	at Phoenix
	Sat.	22	NY Islanders	Sat.	21	at Los Angeles
	Tue.	25	Edmonton	Mon.	23	at San Jose
	Wed.	26	at Nashville	Wed.	25	Chicago
	Sat.	29	Washington	Fri.	27	at Chicago
Dec.	Tue.	2	Anaheim	Sat.	28	Colorado
	Thu.	4	Nashville	Mar. Tue.	2	at Carolina
	Sat.	6	at Colorado	Wed.	3	at Dallas
	Wed.	10	Philadelphia	Sat.	6	Vancouver
	Fri.	12	St. Louis	Mon.	8	Carolina
	Sat.	13	at Pittsburgh	Thu.	11	Detroit
	Tue.	16	at St. Louis	Sat.	13	at St. Louis
	Fri.	19	Calgary	Sun.	14	at Minnesota
	Sat.	20	at Minnesota	Tue.	16	at Edmonton
	Tue.	23	Phoenix	Thu.	18	at Calgary
	Fri.	26	at Chicago	Sun.	21	at Vancouver
	Sat.	27	Dallas	Wed.	24	Minnesota
	Mon.	29	St. Louis	Fri.	26	Anaheim
	Wed.	31	San Jose	Sat.	27	at Nashville
Jan.	Fri.	2	at Tampa Bay*	Mon.	29	at Buffalo
	Sat.	3	at Florida	Wed.	31	Detroit
	Tue.	6	at Colorado	Apr. Fri.	2	Colorado
	Thu.	8	at San Jose	Sat.	3	at Detroit

* Denotes afternoon game.

Franchise date: June 25, 1997

CENTRAL DIVISION

4th NHL Season

In his third NHL season, David Vyborny set career highs in goals (20), assists (26) and points (46). He was one of four Columbus players to score at least 20 goals and his plus-minus rating of +12 was the best in the brief history of the Blue Jackets.

2003-04 Player Personnel

FORWARDS	HT	WT	S	Place of Birth	Date	2002-03 Club
CASSELS, Andrew	6-1	185	L	Bramalea, Ont.	7/23/69	Columbus
HARTIGAN, Mark	6-0	200	L	Fort St. John, B.C.	10/15/77	Atlanta-Chicago (AHL)
JACKMAN, Tim	6-3	190	R	Minot, ND	11/14/81	Syracuse
KNOPP, Ben	6-1	190	R	Calgary, Alta.	4/8/82	Syracuse-Dayton
KNUTSEN, Espen	5-11	188	L	Oslo, Norway	1/12/72	Columbus
LETOWSKI, Trevor	5-10	176	R	Thunder Bay, Ont.	4/5/77	Vancouver
LING, David	5-10	204	R	Halifax, N.S.	1/9/75	Columbus-Syracuse
MacLEAN, Don	6-2	199	L	Sydney, N.S.	1/14/77	Syracuse
MARCHANT, Todd	5-10	178	L	Buffalo, NY	8/12/73	Edmonton
McDONELL, Kent	6-2	205	R	Williamstown, Ont.	3/1/79	Columbus-Syracuse
MORAN, Brad	5-11	187	L	Abbotsford, B.C.	3/20/79	Syracuse
MOTZKO, Joe	6-0	180	R	Bemidji, MN	3/14/80	St. Cloud State-Syracuse
NASH, Rick	6-3	188	L	Brampton, Ont.	6/16/84	Columbus
NEDOROST, Andrej	6-0	192	L	Trencin, Czech.	4/30/80	Columbus-Syracuse
PANDOLFO, Mike	6-3	221	L	Winchester, MA	9/15/79	Syracuse
PIRJETA, Lasse	6-3	222	L	Oulu, Finland	4/4/74	Columbus
PRONGER, Sean	6-3	209	L	Thunder Bay, Ont.	11/30/72	Columbus
REICH, Jeremy	6-1	204	L	Craik, Sask.	2/11/79	Syracuse
SANDERSON, Geoff	6-0	190	L	Hay River, N.W.T.	2/1/72	Columbus
SHELLEY, Jody	6-4	225	L	Thompson, Man.	2/7/76	Columbus
VYBORNY, David	5-10	189	L	Jihlava, Czech.	6/2/75	Columbus
WRIGHT, Tyler	6-0	190	R	Kamsack, Sask.	4/6/73	Columbus
ZHERDEV, Nikolai	6-0	176	R	Kiev, USSR	11/5/84	CSKA Moscow

DEFENSEMEN						
GRAND-PIERRE, Jean-Luc	6-3	223	R	Montreal, Que.	2/2/77	Columbus-Syracuse
GUSKOV, Alexander	6-2	202	L	Gorky, USSR	11/26/76	Yaroslavl
JOHNSON, Aaron	6-0	186	L	Port Hawkesbury, N.S.	4/30/83	Rimouski-Quebec (QMJHL)
KLESLA, Rostislav	6-3	206	L	Novy Jicin, Czech.	3/21/82	Columbus
LACHANCE, Scott	6-1	215	L	Charlottesville, VA	10/22/72	Columbus
LEVOKARI, Pauli	6-7	260	L	Luvia, Finland	4/7/79	Chi (AHL)-G'ville-Syr
RICHARDSON, Luke	6-4	210	L	Ottawa, Ont.	3/26/69	Columbus
SCOVILLE, Darrel	6-3	215	L	Swift Current, Sask.	10/13/75	Syracuse-Columbus
SPACEK, Jaroslav	5-11	206	L	Rokycany, Czech.	2/11/74	Columbus
SYDOR, Darryl	6-1	205	L	Edmonton, Alta.	5/13/72	Dallas
WALSER, Derrick	5-10	196	L	New Glasgow, N.S.	5/12/78	Columbus-Syracuse
WESTCOTT, Duvie	5-11	192	L	Winnipeg, Man.	10/30/77	Columbus-Syracuse

GOALTENDERS	HT	WT	C	Place of Birth	Date	2002-03 Club
BRATHWAITE, Fred	5-7	175	L	Ottawa, Ont.	11/24/72	St. Louis
DENIS, Marc	6-1	190	L	Montreal, Que.	8/1/77	Columbus
LECLAIRE, Pascal	6-2	185	L	Repentigny, Que.	11/7/82	Syracuse

Mark Denis started all but five of Columbus's games in 2002-03. His total of more than 4,510 minutes played set a new NHL record. Denis faced a league-high 2,404 shots and made a league-leading 2,172 saves for a percentage of .903.

2002-03 Scoring
* - rookie

Regular Season

Pos	#	Player	Team	GP	G	A	Pts	+/-	PIM	PP	SH	GW	GT	S	%
L	14	Ray Whitney	CBJ	81	24	52	76	-26	22	8	2	2	1	235	10.2
C	25	Andrew Cassels	CBJ	79	20	48	68	-4	30	9	1	5	0	113	17.7
L	8	Geoff Sanderson	CBJ	82	34	33	67	-4	34	15	2	2	0	286	11.9
R	9	David Vyborny	CBJ	79	20	26	46	12	16	4	1	4	0	125	16.0
D	3	Jaroslav Spacek	CBJ	81	9	36	45	-23	70	5	0	1	0	166	5.4
C	16	Mike Sillinger	CBJ	75	18	25	43	-21	52	9	3	3	0	128	14.1
L	61 *	Rick Nash	CBJ	74	17	22	39	-27	78	6	0	2	0	154	11.0
C	28	Tyler Wright	CBJ	70	19	11	30	-25	113	3	2	3	0	108	17.6
L	20	Lasse Pirjeta	CBJ	51	11	10	21	-4	12	2	0	2	0	80	13.8
C	23 *	Derrick Walser	CBJ	53	4	13	17	-9	34	3	0	2	0	86	4.7
D	44	Rostislav Klesla	CBJ	72	2	14	16	-22	71	0	0	0	0	89	2.2
C	19	Sean Pronger	CBJ	78	7	6	13	-26	72	1	0	0	0	67	10.4
D	22	Luke Richardson	CBJ	82	0	13	13	-16	73	0	0	0	0	56	0.0
C	21	Espen Knutsen	CBJ	31	5	4	9	-15	20	3	0	1	0	28	17.9
R	41 *	Matt Davidson	CBJ	34	4	5	9	-12	18	0	0	0	0	28	14.3
R	24	Hannes Hyvonen	CBJ	36	4	5	9	-11	22	0	0	0	0	48	8.3
D	42 *	Duvie Westcott	CBJ	39	0	7	7	-3	77	0	0	0	0	27	0.0
R	43	David Ling	CBJ	35	3	2	5	-6	86	0	0	0	0	37	8.1
L	45	Jody Shelley	CBJ	68	1	4	5	-5	249	0	0	0	0	39	2.6
D	27	Darren Van Impe	CBJ	14	1	1	2	-6	10	0	1	0	1	11	9.1
D	34	Jean-Luc Grand-Pierre	CBJ	41	1	0	1	-6	64	0	0	0	0	32	3.1
C	26 *	Andrej Nedorost	CBJ	12	0	1	1	-6	4	0	0	0	0	10	0.0
D	33	Jamie Allison	CBJ	48	0	1	1	-15	99	0	0	0	0	23	0.0
D	7	Scott Lachance	CBJ	61	0	1	1	-20	46	0	0	0	0	35	0.0
L	12	Mathieu Darche	CBJ	1	0	0	0	-1	0	0	0	0	0	1	0.0
D	37	Darrel Scoville	CBJ	2	0	0	0	0	4	0	0	0	0	1	0.0
R	15 *	Kent McDonell	CBJ	3	0	0	0	-1	0	0	0	0	0	4	0.0
C	38 *	Blake Bellefeuille	CBJ	3	0	0	0	0	0	0	0	0	0	3	0.0
R	11	Kevin Dineen	CBJ	4	0	0	0	0	12	0	0	0	0	7	0.0
D	17 *	Paul Manning	CBJ	8	0	0	0	0	2	0	0	0	0	4	0.0

Goaltending

No.	Goaltender	GPI	Mins	Avg	W	L	T	EN	SO	GA	SA	S%	G	A	PIM
30	Marc Denis	77	4511	3.09	27	41	8	3	5	232	2404	.903	0	0	6
35	Jean-Francois Labbe	11	451	3.59	2	4	0	1	0	27	233	.884	0	0	2
	Totals	82	4984	3.17	29	45	8	4	5	263	2641	.900			

Coaching History

Dave King, 2000-01 to 2001-02; Dave King and Doug MacLean, 2002-03; Doug MacLean, 2003-04.

General Managers' History

Doug MacLean, 2000-01 to date.

Coach and General Manager

MacLEAN, DOUG
President/Coach/General Manager, Columbus Blue Jackets.
Born in Summerside, PEI, April 12, 1954.

Doug MacLean was named the first general manager of the Blue Jackets on February 11, 1998. A month later he was named president of the organization and as its top executive, he holds the dual role of overseeing both the business and hockey operations of the franchise as well as the management of Nationwide Arena. On January 7, 2003, MacLean also assumed the club's coaching duties, taking over from Dave King on an interim basis. It was announced officially on June 6, 2003, that he would remain on as the team's head coach. Under MacLean's guidance, the Blue Jackets have established themselves as one of the most successful business franchises in the NHL while continuing to build on the ice. Now, with MacLean behind the bench, other members of the front office will take on a greater role in the club's business interests.

MacLean began his NHL coaching career in 1986 as an assistant to Jacques Martin in St. Louis. He spent two seasons with the Blues before joining the Washington Capitals in 1988, assisting Bryan Murray behind the bench. He was named coach of the Capitals' American Hockey League affiliate in Baltimore for the final 35 games of the 1989-90 season.

The following season, MacLean joined Murray on the Detroit Red Wings, serving as an assistant coach for two years. In 1992, MacLean was named assistant general manager of the Red Wings and also served as general manager of the team's AHL affiliate in Adirondack for two years. MacLean followed Murray to the Panthers in 1994, becoming the expansion club's director of player development. He was named head coach on July 24, 1995.

A collegiate hockey player at the University of Prince Edward Island, MacLean graduated with a bachelor's degree in education. He also played for the Montreal Jr. Canadiens and was invited to training camp with the St. Louis Blues in 1974. Following his playing career, MacLean enrolled at the University of Western Ontario, where he received a master's degree in educational psychology. While attending Western, MacLean began his coaching career as an assistant with London of the Ontario Hockey League.

NHL Coaching Record

		Regular Season				Playoffs		
Season	Team	Games	W	L	T	Games	W	L
1995-96	Florida	82	41	31	10	22	12	10
1996-97	Florida	82	35	28	19	5	1	4
1997-98	Florida	23	7	12	4	....	....	....
2002-03	Columbus	42	15	23	4	....	....	....
	NHL Totals	229	98	94	37	27	13	14

Club Records

Team

(Figures in brackets for season records are games played.)

Most Points . . . . 71 — 2000-01 (82)
Most Wins . . . . 29 — 2002-03 (82)
Most Ties . . . . 9 — 2000-01 (82)
Most Losses . . . . 47 — 2001-02 (82)
Most Goals . . . . 213 — 2002-03 (82)
Most Goals Against . . . . 263 — 2002-03 (82)
Fewest Points . . . . 57 — 2001-02 (82)
Fewest Wins . . . . 22 — 2001-02 (82)
Fewest Ties . . . . 8 — 2001-02 (82), 2002-03 (82)
Fewest Losses . . . . 39 — 2000-01 (82)
Fewest Goals . . . . 164 — 2001-02 (82)
Fewest Goals Against . . . . . . 233 — 2000-01 (82)

Longest Winning Streak
Overall . . . . 4 — Nov. 9-Nov. 16/00
Home . . . . 4 — Mar. 24-Apr. 8/01, Dec. 31/01-Jan. 16/02
Away . . . . 3 — Jan. 8-11/03

Longest Undefeated Streak
Overall . . . . 4 — Nov. 9-Nov. 16/00 (4 wins)
Home . . . . 6 — Jan. 20-Feb. 12/03 (4 wins, 2 ties)
Away . . . . 4 — Jan. 3-11/03 (3 wins, 1 tie)

Longest Losing Streak
Overall . . . . 8 — Nov. 17-Dec. 3/00
Home . . . . 6 — Oct. 12-Nov. 9/01
Away . . . . 11 — Mar. 25-Oct. 29/02

Longest Winless Streak
Overall . . . . 8 — Nov. 17-Dec. 3/00 (8 losses)
Home . . . . 8 — Oct. 4-Nov. 9/01 (6 losses, 2 ties)
Away . . . . 10 — Dec. 15/01-Jan. 30/02 (9 losses, 1 tie)

Most Shutouts, Season . . . . 5 — 2002-03 (82)
Most PIM, Season . . . . 1,505 — 2002-03 (82)
Most Goals, Game . . . . 7 — Three times

Individual

Most Seasons . . . . 3 — Many players
Most Games . . . . 233 — David Vyborny
Most Goals, Career . . . . 75 — Geoff Sanderson
Most Assists, Career . . . . 95 — Ray Whitney
Most Points, Career . . . . 140 — Ray Whitney (45G, 95A)
Most PIM, Career . . . . 465 — Jody Shelley
Most Shutouts, Career . . . . 6 — Ron Tugnutt / Marc Denis

Longest Consecutive Games Streak . . . . 82 — Geoff Sanderson, Luke Richardson (Oct. 10/02 to date)
Most Goals, Season . . . . 34 — Geoff Sanderson (2002-03)

Most Assists, Season . . . . 52 — Ray Whitney (2002-03)
Most Points, Season . . . . 76 — Ray Whitney (2002-03; 24G, 52A)
Most PIM, Season . . . . 249 — Jody Shelley (2002-03)
Most Points, Defenseman, Season . . . . 45 — Jaroslav Spacek (2002-03; 9G, 36A)
Most Points, Center, Season . . . . 68 — Andrew Cassels (2002-03; 20G, 48A)
Most Points, Right Wing, Season . . . . 46 — David Vyborny (2002-03; 20G, 26A)
Most Points, Left Wing, Season . . . . 76 — Ray Whitney (2002-03; 24G, 52A)
Most Points, Rookie, Season . . . . 39 — Rick Nash (2002-03; 17G, 22A)
Most Shutouts, Season . . . . 5 — Marc Denis (2002-03)
Most Goals, Game . . . . 4 — Geoff Sanderson (Jan. 11/03)
Most Assists, Game . . . . 5 — Espen Knutsen (Mar. 24/01)
Most Points, Game . . . . 5 — Espen Knutsen (Mar. 24/01; 5A), Geoff Sanderson (Jan. 11/03; 4G, 1A), Andrew Cassels (Jan. 11/03; 1G, 4A)

Captains' History

Lyle Odelein, 2000-01 to 2001-02; Ray Whitney, 2002-03.

All-time Record vs. Other Clubs

Regular Season

| | At Home | | | | | | | On Road | | | | | | | Total | | | | | | |
	GP	W	L	T	OL	GF	GA	PTS	GP	W	L	T	OL	GF	GA	PTS	GP	W	L	T	OL	GF	GA	PTS
Anaheim	6	4	2	0	0	18	13	8	6	2	3	0	1	13	19	5	12	6	5	0	1	31	32	13
Atlanta	3	1	2	0	0	8	9	2	2	1	1	0	0	5	3	2	5	2	3	0	0	13	12	4
Boston	2	1	1	0	0	3	10	2	2	1	1	0	0	7	8	2	4	2	2	0	0	10	18	4
Buffalo	2	1	0	1	0	5	4	3	3	2	1	0	0	9	7	4	5	3	1	1	0	14	11	7
Calgary	6	5	0	0	1	21	11	11	6	3	3	0	0	18	19	6	12	8	3	0	1	39	30	17
Carolina	2	1	1	0	0	5	5	2	3	0	3	0	0	8	13	0	5	1	4	0	0	13	18	2
Chicago	8	4	3	1	0	23	26	9	7	0	6	1	0	7	19	1	15	4	9	2	0	30	45	10
Colorado	6	0	5	1	0	6	23	1	6	0	6	0	0	9	27	0	12	0	11	1	0	15	50	1
Dallas	6	2	4	0	0	14	19	4	6	0	5	0	1	7	21	1	12	2	9	0	1	21	40	5
Detroit	8	1	2	1	4	14	19	7	7	1	6	0	0	16	29	2	15	2	8	1	4	30	48	9
Edmonton	6	1	4	1	0	13	20	3	6	1	5	0	0	12	24	2	12	2	9	1	0	25	44	5
Florida	2	1	1	0	0	4	4	2	2	1	1	0	0	7	8	2	4	2	2	0	0	11	12	4
Los Angeles	6	3	3	0	0	15	22	6	6	3	3	0	0	11	12	6	12	6	6	0	0	26	34	12
Minnesota	5	3	1	1	0	15	6	7	6	2	3	0	1	12	17	5	11	5	4	1	1	27	23	12
Montreal	1	0	1	0	0	1	3	0	3	2	1	0	0	5	5	4	4	2	2	0	0	6	8	4
Nashville	7	4	2	0	1	13	15	9	8	2	5	1	0	17	20	5	15	6	7	1	1	30	35	14
New Jersey	3	2	1	0	0	10	9	4	2	0	1	0	1	4	5	1	5	2	2	0	1	14	14	5
NY Islanders	3	2	0	1	0	11	6	5	2	2	0	0	0	11	7	4	5	4	0	1	0	22	13	9
NY Rangers	3	2	1	0	0	11	7	4	2	0	2	0	0	5	7	1	5	2	3	0	0	16	14	5
Ottawa	2	0	1	1	0	7	9	1	2	0	1	1	0	4	7	1	4	0	2	2	0	11	16	2
Philadelphia	2	0	1	1	0	5	6	1	2	0	1	1	0	3	7	1	4	0	2	2	0	8	13	2
Phoenix	6	4	2	0	0	16	10	8	6	0	4	2	0	10	18	2	12	4	6	2	0	26	28	10
Pittsburgh	3	1	0	0	2	10	9	4	2	1	1	0	0	6	7	2	5	2	1	0	2	16	16	6
St. Louis	7	3	2	2	0	15	19	8	8	1	6	1	0	16	33	3	15	4	8	3	0	31	52	11
San Jose	6	3	3	0	0	20	17	6	6	0	5	0	1	7	26	1	12	3	8	0	1	27	43	7
Tampa Bay	2	1	0	1	0	5	3	3	2	0	2	0	0	1	5	0	4	1	2	1	0	6	8	3
Toronto	1	0	1	0	0	4	3	0	2	1	0	0	1	3	2	3	3	1	1	0	1	7	5	3
Vancouver	6	1	3	2	0	14	23	4	6	1	4	0	1	15	24	3	12	2	7	2	1	29	47	7
Washington	3	1	1	0	1	8	10	3	2	0	1	1	0	5	8	1	5	1	2	1	1	13	18	4
Totals	**123**	**53**	**47**	**14**	**9**	**314**	**340**	**129**	**123**	**26**	**81**	**11**	**5**	**253**	**411**	**68**	**246**	**79**	**128**	**25**	**14**	**567**	**751**	**197**

2002-03 Results

Oct.	10	Chicago	2-1		10	at Vancouver	3-2
	12	at New Jersey	2-3		11	at Calgary	7-2
	14	Phoenix	2-4		13	at Edmonton	5-8
	17	at St. Louis	1-7		15	Anaheim	3-4
	19	Florida	4-1		18	at Boston	2-7
	23	Tampa Bay	2-2		20	Chicago	5-1
	25	San Jose	4-5		22	at Dallas	2-4
	27	Los Angeles	5-1		23	at Colorado	0-5
	29	at Chicago	2-3		25	NY Islanders	4-1
Nov.	1	Dallas	4-2		28	Colorado	2-2
	3	Buffalo	3-2		30	Nashville	2-1
	5	Washington	3-4*	Feb.	5	Vancouver	4-4
	7	at St. Louis	5-2		8	at Nashville	2-3
	9	NY Rangers	6-3		12	San Jose	1-0
	12	at Colorado	4-5		13	at Montreal	2-1*
	14	Anaheim	2-3		15	Chicago	1-7
	16	at Nashville	1-1		18	at Phoenix	2-5
	17	at Dallas	2-3*		19	at Anaheim	0-2
	20	St. Louis	3-2		21	at San Jose	0-6
	22	at Buffalo	4-5		23	at Vancouver	2-7
	23	at Ottawa	2-4		25	at Nashville	0-5
	27	Edmonton	1-3		27	Los Angeles	3-1
	29	at NY Islanders	4-2	Mar.	1	Edmonton	3-3
	30	Carolina	2-4		3	Detroit	2-3
Dec.	3	at NY Rangers	3-5		6	Vancouver	5-4*
	6	at San Jose	4-2		8	Calgary	2-3*
	7	at Los Angeles	4-2		10	at Carolina	5-6
	9	at Phoenix	3-3		11	Dallas	0-2
	12	New Jersey	4-2		13	Colorado	1-5
	14	at Detroit	4-6		15	Minnesota	5-0
	19	Calgary	3-0		17	at Atlanta	2-3
	20	at Chicago	1-3		20	Toronto	4-3*
	23	Detroit	0-1		22	Atlanta	2-3
	26	at Detroit	2-4		24	at Anaheim	0-5
	28	St. Louis	1-6		25	at Los Angeles	2-1*
	29	at St. Louis	2-5		28	at Edmonton	0-4
	31	Pittsburgh	5-2		29	at Calgary	6-4
Jan.	3	at Washington	2-2	Apr.	1	at Philadelphia	0-4
	4	Phoenix	2-0		2	Minnesota	3-0
	6	Nashville	1-5		4	Detroit	5-5
	8	at Minnesota	2-1		6	at Minnesota	3-4

* – Overtime

Entry Draft
Selections 2003-2000

2003 Pick		2002 Pick		2001 Pick		2000 Pick	
4	Nikolai Zherdev	1	Rick Nash	8	Pascal Leclaire	4	Rostislav Klesla
46	Dan Fritsche	41	Joakim Lindstrom	38	Tim Jackman	69	Ben Knopp
71	Dimitri Kosmachev	65	Ole-Kristian Tollefsen	53	Kiel McLeod	133	Petteri Nummelin
103	Kevin Jarman	96	Jeff Genovy	85	Aaron Johnson	138	Scott Heffernan
104	Philippe Dupuis	98	Ivan Tkachenko	87	Per Mars	150	Tyler Kolarik
138	Arsi Piispanen	119	Jekabs Redlihs	141	Cole Jarrett	169	Shane Bendera
168	Marc Methot	133	Lasse Pirjeta	173	Justin Aikins	200	Janne Jokila
200	Alexander Guskov	168	Tim Konsorada	187	Artem Vostrikov	231	Peter Zingoni
233	Mathieu Gravel	184	Jaroslav Balastik	204	Raffaele Sannitz	278	Martin Paroulek
283	Trevor Hendrikx	199	Greg Mauldin	236	Ryan Bowness	286	Andrej Nedorost
		225	Steve Goertzen	242	Andrew Murray	292	Louis Mandeville
		231	Jaroslav Kracik				
		263	Sergei Mozyakin				

In his first season with the Blue Jackets, Andrew Cassels reached the 20-goal plateau for the fourth time in his career. His five game-winning goals were tops on the team.

Club Directory

Nationwide Arena

Columbus Blue Jackets
Nationwide Arena
200 W. Nationwide Blvd.
Columbus, Ohio 43215
Phone **614/246-4625**
FAX 614/246-4007
www.BlueJackets.com
Capacity: 18,136

Ownership
Majority Owner/Governor . . . . John H. McConnell
Alternate Governor . . . . John P. McConnell

Executive Staff
President/General Manager/Alternate Governor . . . Doug MacLean
Executive Vice-President/Assistant General Manager . Jim Clark
Senior Vice-President of Business Operations . . . . . Michael Humes
Vice-President of Marketing . . . . David Paitson
Vice-President of Ticket Sales . . . . Todd Taylor
Chief Financial Officer . . . . T.J. LaMendola
General Counsel . . . . Greg Kirstein

Hockey Operations
Head Coach . . . . Doug MacLean
Associate Coach . . . . Newell Brown
Assistant Coach . . . . Gerard Gallant
Assistant Coach . . . . Gord Murphy
Goaltending Coach, Pro Scout . . . . Rick Wamsley
Director of Amateur Scouting . . . . Don Boyd
Director of Pro Scouting . . . . Bob Strumm
Director of Player Development . . . . Paul Castron
Manager of Hockey Operations . . . . Chris MacFarland
Manager of Team Services . . . . Jim Rankin
Video Coordinator . . . . Dan Singleton
Administrative Assistant, Hockey Operations . . . . . Julie Uhler
Amateur Scouts . . . . Sam McMaster, Wayne Smith, John Williams
Pro Scout . . . . Peter Dineen
European Scout . . . . Kjell Larsson
Regional Scouts . . . . Brian Bates, Scott Fitzgerald, Jukka Holtari, Denis LeBlanc, John McNamara, Artem Telepin Nicholaevich, Bryan Raymond, Andrew Shaw, Milan Tichy
Head Athletic Trainer . . . . Chris Mizer
Strength and Conditioning Coach . . . . Mark Casterline
Equipment Manager . . . . Tim LeRoy
Assistant Equipment Manager . . . . Jamie Healy
Equipment Assistant . . . . Andre Szucko

Business Operations
Executive Director of Sales . . . . Paul D'Aiuto
Director of Communications . . . . Todd Sharrock
Director of Advertising and Promotions . . . . Marc Gregory
Director of Client Services . . . . Brent Baker
Director of Event Presentation/Production . . . . . . Kimberly Kershaw
Director of Fan Development . . . . J.D. Kershaw
Director of Community Development . . . . Wendy Peterson
Director of Retail Operations . . . . Chris Weller
Business Development Manager . . . . Scott Klein
Business Development Manager . . . . Scott Shepherd
Assistant Director of Communications . . . . Jason Rothwell
Manager of Multimedia . . . . Jay Levin
Graphic Designer/Manager of Print Production . . . . Will Bennett
Client Services Manager . . . . Heather Popa
Manager of Advertising and Promotions . . . . Chris Sprague
Managers of Production . . . . David Bakalik, Jonny Greco
Manager of Event Presentation . . . . Matt Bettinger
Manager of Fan Development . . . . Joel Siegman
Mascot Coordinator . . . . Jason Zumpano
Community Development Coordinator . . . . Tracey Vogelpohl
Corporate Development Representative . . . . Brice Clark
Marketing Coordinator . . . . Kylie Rimer
Executive Assistant to Doug MacLean . . . . Kari Pitzer
Administrative Assistant to Michael Humes . . . . . . Michelle LeVeque
Administrative Assistant to Greg Kirstein . . . . Nikki Ward
Administrative Assistant to David Paitson . . . . Jennifer Pritz
Legal/Immigration Associate . . . . Kelley Walton

Finance
Controller . . . . Rich Gross
Financial Analyst . . . . Dana Fletcher
Staff Accountants . . . . Nora Ludwig, Pete Nyikes
Accounts Payable . . . . Rose Phillips, Malika Dickerson
Accounts Receivable . . . . Shelly Phillips
MIS Manager . . . . Jim Connolly
Office Manager . . . . Rachel Durham
Receptionist . . . . Beth Carlisle

Ticket Operations
Director of Ticket Operations/Customer Service . . . Mark Morris
Manager of Ticket Operations/Customer Service . . . Karen Bierley
Asst. Manager of Ticket Operations/
  Customer Service . . . . Mark Metz
Account Executives - PSL . . . . Celeste Wilson, Ted Hritz, David Melfi
Ticket Sales Development Manager . . . . John Motto
Account Executives - Group Sales . . . . Heather Bardocz, Adam Russell
Premium and Suite Services Coordinator . . . . Melissa DeGraw
Database Coordinator . . . . Krista Romano
Season Ticket Service Coordinator . . . . Liz Burri

Broadcasting
Director of Broadcasting . . . . Russ Mollohan
Fox Sports Net Play-By-Play Announcer . . . . Dan Kelly
Fox Sports Net Color Analyst . . . . Steve Konroyd
Radio Play-By-Play Announcer . . . . George Matthews
Radio Color Analyst . . . . Bill Davidge

Dallas Stars

2002-03 Results: 46w-17L-15T-4OTL 111PTS.
First, Pacific Division

2003-04 Schedule

Oct.	Wed.	8	Anaheim	Mon.	5	at Anaheim
	Sat.	11	at Nashville	Thu.	8	Atlanta
	Mon.	13	at Buffalo*	Sat.	10	Colorado*
	Wed.	15	Boston	Tue.	13	at San Jose
	Fri.	17	Washington	Thu.	15	at Colorado
	Sun.	19	Minnesota	Sat.	17	at Calgary
	Wed.	22	Toronto	Mon.	19	at Vancouver
	Fri.	24	at Detroit	Tue.	20	at Edmonton
	Sat.	25	at Columbus	Fri.	23	St. Louis
	Wed.	29	Calgary	Sat.	24	at St. Louis
Nov.	Sat.	1	at Nashville	Mon.	26	Detroit
	Sun.	2	Nashville	Wed.	28	Ottawa
	Tue.	4	at NY Rangers	Fri.	30	San Jose
	Thu.	6	at NY Islanders	Sat.	31	at Phoenix
	Sat.	8	at Boston	Feb. Wed.	4	Columbus
	Wed.	12	Detroit	Wed.	11	NY Islanders
	Fri.	14	Phoenix	Sat.	14	at Phoenix
	Sat.	15	at Colorado	Mon.	16	at Anaheim*
	Wed.	19	Anaheim	Wed.	18	at Los Angeles
	Fri.	21	Los Angeles	Fri.	20	Colorado
	Sat.	22	at St. Louis	Sun.	22	Anaheim*
	Mon.	24	Phoenix	Wed.	25	Los Angeles
	Wed.	26	at Minnesota	Fri.	27	Minnesota
	Fri.	28	New Jersey	Sun.	29	Edmonton*
	Sun.	30	Los Angeles	Mar. Wed.	3	Columbus
Dec.	Thu.	4	at Los Angeles	Fri.	5	Calgary
	Sat.	6	at San Jose	Sun.	7	San Jose*
	Sun.	7	at Anaheim*	Tue.	9	at Pittsburgh
	Wed.	10	at Phoenix	Thu.	11	at Philadelphia
	Fri.	12	Chicago	Sat.	13	at Detroit*
	Sun.	14	at Chicago	Sun.	14	at Chicago*
	Wed.	17	Vancouver	Tue.	16	San Jose
	Fri.	19	at Florida	Thu.	18	Vancouver
	Sat.	20	at Tampa Bay	Sat.	20	St. Louis*
	Mon.	22	at Carolina	Mon.	22	at Calgary
	Fri.	26	Nashville	Wed.	24	at Edmonton
	Sat.	27	at Columbus	Sat.	27	at Vancouver
	Mon.	29	Philadelphia	Sun.	28	at San Jose
	Wed.	31	Montreal	Wed.	31	Edmonton
Jan.	Fri.	2	Phoenix	Apr. Fri.	2	at Minnesota
	Sat.	3	at Los Angeles	Sun.	4	Chicago*

Denotes afternoon game.

Franchise date: June 5, 1967
Transferred from Minnesota to Dallas, June 9, 1993.

PACIFIC DIVISION

37th NHL Season

Marty Turco responded to the challenge of becoming the Stars' number-one goaltender with a record of 31-10-10 and a 1.72 goals-against average that was the lowest in the NHL since 1939-40. His .932 save percentage also led the league.

Year-by-Year Record

		Home				Road				Overall							
Season	GP	W	L	T	OL	W	L	T	OL	W	L	T	OL	GF	GA	Pts.	Finished	Playoff Result
2002-03	82	28	5	6	2	18	12	9	2	46	17	15	4	245	169	111	1st, Pacific Div.	Lost Conf. Semi-Final
2001-02	82	18	13	6	4	18	15	7	1	36	28	13	5	215	213	90	4th, Pacific Div.	Out of Playoffs
2000-01	82	26	10	5	0	22	14	3	2	48	24	8	2	241	187	106	1st, Pacific Div.	Lost Conf. Semi-Final
1999-2000	82	21	11	5	4	22	12	5	2	43	23	10	6	211	184	102	1st, Pacific Div.	Lost Final
1998-99	**82**	**29**	**8**	**4**	**...**	**22**	**11**	**8**	**...**	**51**	**19**	**12**	**...**	**236**	**168**	**114**	**1st, Pacific Div.**	**Won Stanley Cup**
1997-98	82	26	8	7	...	23	14	4	...	49	22	11	...	242	167	109	1st, Central Div.	Lost Conf. Final
1996-97	82	25	13	3	...	23	13	5	...	48	26	8	...	252	198	104	1st, Central Div.	Lost Conf. Quarter-Final
1995-96	82	14	18	9	...	12	24	5	...	26	42	14	...	227	280	66	6th, Central Div.	Out of Playoffs
1994-95	48	9	10	5	...	8	13	3	...	17	23	8	...	136	135	42	5th, Central Div.	Lost Conf. Quarter-Final
1993-94	84	23	12	7	...	19	17	6	...	42	29	13	...	286	265	97	3rd, Central Div.	Lost Conf. Semi-Final
1992-93*	84	18	17	7	...	18	21	3	...	36	38	10	...	272	293	82	5th, Norris Div.	Out of Playoffs
1991-92*	80	20	16	4	...	12	26	2	...	32	42	6	...	246	278	70	4th, Norris Div.	Lost Div. Semi-Final
1990-91*	80	19	15	6	...	8	24	8	...	27	39	14	...	256	266	68	4th, Norris Div.	Lost Final
1989-90*	80	26	12	2	...	10	28	2	...	36	40	4	...	284	291	76	4th, Norris Div.	Lost Div. Semi-Final
1988-89*	80	17	15	8	...	10	22	8	...	27	37	16	...	258	278	70	3rd, Norris Div.	Lost Div. Semi-Final
1987-88*	80	10	24	6	...	9	24	7	...	19	48	13	...	242	349	51	5th, Norris Div.	Out of Playoffs
1986-87*	80	17	20	3	...	13	20	7	...	30	40	10	...	296	314	70	5th, Norris Div.	Out of Playoffs
1985-86*	80	21	15	4	...	17	18	5	...	38	33	9	...	327	305	85	2nd, Norris Div.	Lost Div. Semi-Final
1984-85*	80	14	19	7	...	11	24	5	...	25	43	12	...	268	321	62	4th, Norris Div.	Lost Div. Final
1983-84*	80	22	14	4	...	17	17	6	...	39	31	10	...	345	344	88	1st, Norris Div.	Lost Conf. Championship
1982-83*	80	23	6	11	...	17	18	5	...	40	24	16	...	321	290	96	2nd, Norris Div.	Lost Div. Final
1981-82*	80	21	7	12	...	16	16	8	...	37	23	20	...	346	288	94	1st, Norris Div.	Lost Div. Semi-Final
1980-81*	80	23	10	7	...	12	18	10	...	35	28	17	...	291	263	87	3rd, Adams Div.	Lost Final
1979-80*	80	25	8	7	...	11	20	9	...	36	28	16	...	311	253	88	3rd, Adams Div.	Lost Semi-Final
1978-79*	80	19	15	6	...	9	25	6	...	28	40	12	...	257	289	68	4th, Adams Div.	Out Of Playoffs
1977-78*	80	12	24	4	...	6	29	5	...	18	53	9	...	218	325	45	5th, Smythe Div.	Out of Playoffs
1976-77*	80	17	14	9	...	6	25	9	...	23	39	18	...	240	310	64	2nd, Smythe Div.	Lost Prelim. Round
1975-76*	80	15	22	3	...	5	31	4	...	20	53	7	...	195	303	47	4th, Smythe Div.	Out of Playoffs
1974-75*	80	17	20	3	...	6	30	4	...	23	50	7	...	221	341	53	4th, Smythe Div.	Out of Playoffs
1973-74*	78	18	15	6	...	5	23	11	...	23	38	17	...	235	275	63	7th, West Div.	Out of Playoffs
1972-73*	78	26	8	5	...	11	22	6	...	37	30	11	...	254	230	85	3rd, West Div.	Lost Quarter-Final
1971-72*	78	22	11	6	...	15	18	6	...	37	29	12	...	212	191	86	2nd, West Div.	Lost Quarter-Final
1970-71*	78	16	15	8	...	12	19	8	...	28	34	16	...	191	223	72	4th, West Div.	Lost Semi-Final
1969-70*	76	11	16	11	...	8	19	11	...	19	35	22	...	224	257	60	3rd, West Div.	Lost Quarter-Final
1968-69*	76	11	21	6	...	7	22	9	...	18	43	15	...	189	270	51	6th, West Div.	Out of Playoffs
1967-68*	74	17	12	8	...	10	20	7	...	27	32	15	...	191	226	69	4th, West Div.	Lost Semi-Final

*Minnesota North Stars

2003-04 Player Personnel

FORWARDS	HT	WT	S	Place of Birth	Date	2002-03 Club
ARNOTT, Jason	6-4	225	R	Collingwood, Ont.	10/11/74	Dallas
BARARUK, David	6-0	175	L	Moose Jaw, Sask.	5/26/83	Moose Jaw
BARNES, Stu	5-11	180	R	Spruce Grove, Alta.	12/25/70	Buffalo-Dallas
BATEMAN, Jeff	5-11	184	L	Belleville, Ont.	8/29/81	Utah-Lexington
COX, Justin	6-0	173	R	Merritt, B.C.	3/13/81	Utah
DiMAIO, Rob	5-10	190	R	Calgary, Alta.	2/19/68	Dallas
DOWNEY, Aaron	6-1	216	R	Shelburne, Ont.	8/27/74	Dallas
DRANEY, Brett	6-1	195	L	Merritt, B.C.	3/12/81	Utah-Lexington
GAINEY, Steve	6-1	192	L	Montreal, Que.	1/26/79	Utah
GOSSELIN, David	6-1	205	R	Levis, Que.	6/22/77	Utah
GUERIN, Bill	6-2	210	R	Worcester, MA	11/9/70	Dallas
HEISTEN, Barrett	6-1	200	L	Anchorage, AK	3/19/80	Utah
KAPANEN, Niko	5-9	180	L	Hattula, Finland	4/29/78	Dallas
KRISTOFFERSSON, Marcus	6-3	217	L	Ostersund, Sweden	1/22/79	Utah
LEHTINEN, Jere	6-0	200	R	Espoo, Finland	6/24/73	Dallas
LEMIEUX, Claude	6-1	227	R	Buckingham, Que.	7/16/65	Phoenix-Dallas
MALHOTRA, Manny	6-2	215	L	Mississauga, Ont.	5/18/80	Dallas
MIETTINEN, Antti	5-11	180	R	Hameenlinna, Finland	7/3/80	HPK
MODANO, Mike	6-3	205	L	Livonia, MI	6/7/70	Dallas
MORGAN, Gavin	5-11	191	R	Scarborough, Ont.	7/9/76	Utah
MORROW, Brenden	5-11	200	L	Carlyle, Sask.	1/16/79	Dallas
OLIVER, David	6-0	190	R	Sechelt, B.C.	4/17/71	Dallas-Utah
OTT, Steve	6-0	160	L	Summerside, P.E.I.	8/19/82	Dallas-Utah
SKALDE, Jarrod	6-0	185	L	Niagara Falls, Ont.	2/26/71	Lausanne
TJARNQVIST, Mathias	6-1	183	L	Umea, Sweden	4/15/79	Djurgarden
TURGEON, Pierre	6-1	199	L	Rouyn, Que.	8/28/69	Dallas
YOUNG, Scott	6-1	200	R	Clinton, MA	10/1/67	Dallas

DEFENSEMEN						
BERENZWEIG, Bubba	6-1	217	L	Arlington Heights, IL	8/8/77	Nashville-Milwaukee-Utah
BOUCHER, Philippe	6-2	221	R	Ste-Apollinaire, Que.	3/24/73	Dallas
DALEY, Trevor	5-9	197	L	Toronto, Ont.	10/9/83	Sault Ste. Marie
ERSKINE, John	6-4	215	L	Kingston, Ont.	6/26/80	Dallas-Utah
JANCEVSKI, Dan	6-3	212	L	Windsor, Ont.	6/15/81	Utah
KOMAROV, Alexei	6-4	194	L	Moscow, USSR	6/11/78	Utah
MacMILLAN, Jeff	6-3	206	L	Durham, Ont.	3/30/79	Utah
MATVICHUK, Richard	6-2	215	L	Edmonton, Alta.	2/5/73	Dallas
NUMMINEN, Teppo	6-2	197	R	Tampere, Finland	7/3/68	Phoenix
ROBIDAS, Stephane	5-11	189	R	Sherbrooke, Que.	3/3/77	Dallas
SWEENEY, Don	5-10	185	L	St. Stephen, N.B.	8/17/66	Boston
WOTTON, Mark	6-1	195	L	Foxwarren, Man.	11/16/73	Utah
ZUBOV, Sergei	6-1	200	R	Moscow, USSR	7/22/70	Dallas

GOALTENDERS	HT	WT	C	Place of Birth	Date	2002-03 Club
BACASHIHUA, Jason	5-11	175	L	Garden City, MI	9/20/82	Utah
SMITH, Mike	6-3	189	L	Kingston, Ont.	3/22/82	Utah-Lexington
TUGNUTT, Ron	5-11	160	L	Scarborough, Ont.	10/22/67	Dallas
TURCO, Marty	5-11	183	L	Sault Ste. Marie, Ont.	8/13/75	Dallas

Coach

TIPPETT, DAVE
Coach, Dallas Stars. Born in Moosomin, Sask., August 25, 1961.

Dallas Stars general manager Doug Armstrong announced the hiring of Dave Tippett as the club's head coach on May 16, 2002. In his first season behind the bench in 2002-03, he led the Stars to the best record in the Western Conference and the second best in the NHL. Tippett had spent the previous three seasons as an assistant coach with the Los Angeles Kings. He served a five-game stint as interim head coach in 2002 while head coach Andy Murray recovered from an auto accident. In all three seasons Tippett was in Los Angeles the Kings qualified for the playoffs. They had reached the postseason just once out of the previous six seasons.

Under Tippett's direction, the Kings power-play led the NHL in 2001-02 with a 20.7 percent success rate. The year before Tippett came aboard the Kings, in 1998-99, the Kings power-play unit ranked 24th in the league. As a highly regarded minor league coach with tremendous work ethic, Tippett posted two 50-win seasons at Houston (International Hockey League) and led the Aeros to the 1999 Turner Cup championship while serving as general manager/head coach. He was also named IHL coach of the year.

Prior to becoming a coach, Tippett played 11 years as a forward in the National Hockey League with the Hartford Whalers, Washington Capitals, Pittsburgh Penguins and Philadelphia Flyers. He ended his playing career in 1995 as a player-assistant coach with the Houston Aeros (IHL). Internationally, he captained the 1984 Canadian Olympic team in Sarajevo, Yugoslavia, and he earned a silver medal as a member of the Canadian Olympic team in Albertville, France, in 1992. He was a member of the 1982 NCAA Division I championship squad at the University of North Dakota with former Stars defenseman Craig Ludwig.

Coaching Record

		Regular Season				Playoffs		
Season	Team	Games	W	L	T	Games	W	L
1995-96	Houston (IHL)	42	17	18	7	....	....	....
1996-97	Houston (IHL)	82	44	30	8	13	8	5
1997-98	Houston (IHL)	82	50	22	10	4	1	3
1998-99	Houston (IHL)	82	54	15	13	19	11	8
2002-03	**Dallas (NHL)**	**82**	**46**	**21**	**15**	**12**	**6**	**6**
	NHL Totals	**82**	**46**	**21**	**15**	**12**	**6**	**6**

2002-03 Scoring

* - rookie

Regular Season

Pos	#	Player	Team	GP	G	A	Pts	+/–	PIM	PP	SH	GW	GT	S	%
C	9	Mike Modano	DAL	79	28	57	85	34	30	5	2	6	0	193	14.5
D	56	Sergei Zubov	DAL	82	11	44	55	21	26	8	0	2	0	158	7.0
R	13	Bill Guerin	DAL	64	25	25	50	5	113	11	0	2	1	229	10.9
R	26	Jere Lehtinen	DAL	80	31	17	48	39	20	5	0	3	2	238	13.0
C	44	Jason Arnott	DAL	72	23	24	47	9	51	7	0	6	1	169	13.6
L	10	Brenden Morrow	DAL	71	21	22	43	20	134	2	3	4	2	105	20.0
R	48	Scott Young	DAL	79	23	19	42	24	30	5	1	4	1	237	9.7
C	77	Pierre Turgeon	DAL	65	12	30	42	4	18	3	0	5	1	76	15.8
C	14	Stu Barnes	BUF	68	11	21	32	–13	20	2	1	2	0	124	8.9
			DAL	13	2	5	7	2	8	2	0	1	0	25	8.0
			TOTAL	81	13	26	39	–11	28	4	1	3	0	149	8.7
R	11	Ulf Dahlen	DAL	63	17	20	37	11	14	9	0	1	0	100	17.0
D	5	Darryl Sydor	DAL	81	5	31	36	22	40	2	0	1	0	132	3.8
C	39 *	Niko Kapanen	DAL	82	5	29	34	25	44	0	1	1	0	80	6.3
D	2	Derian Hatcher	DAL	82	8	22	30	37	106	1	1	2	0	159	5.0
D	43	Philippe Boucher	DAL	80	7	20	27	28	94	1	1	3	1	137	5.1
R	32	Claude Lemieux	PHX	36	6	8	14	–3	30	1	1	0	1	74	8.1
			DAL	32	2	4	6	–9	14	0	0	0	0	45	4.4
			TOTAL	68	8	12	20	–12	44	1	1	0	1	119	6.7
R	18	Rob DiMaio	DAL	69	10	9	19	18	76	0	0	2	0	81	12.3
D	4	Lyle Odelein	CHI	65	7	4	11	7	76	0	0	0	0	77	9.1
			DAL	3	0	0	0	0	6	0	0	0	0	1	0.0
			TOTAL	68	7	4	11	7	82	0	0	0	0	78	9.0
L	27	Manny Malhotra	DAL	59	3	7	10	–2	42	0	0	1	0	62	4.8
D	17	Stephane Robidas	DAL	76	3	7	10	15	35	0	0	1	0	47	6.4
C	29 *	Steve Ott	DAL	26	3	4	7	6	31	0	0	0	0	25	12.0
C	22	Kirk Muller	DAL	55	1	5	6	–6	18	0	0	0	0	48	2.1
D	24	Richard Matvichuk	DAL	68	1	5	6	1	58	0	0	1	0	59	1.7
R	28	David Oliver	DAL	6	0	3	3	1	2	0	0	0	0	5	0.0
D	3	John Erskine	DAL	16	2	0	2	1	29	0	0	0	0	12	16.7
R	47	Aaron Downey	DAL	43	1	1	2	1	69	0	0	0	0	14	7.1
C	32	Jim Montgomery	DAL	1	0	0	0	0	0	0	0	0	0	0	0.0

Goaltending

No.	Goaltender	GPI	Mins	Avg	W	L	T	EN	SO	GA	SA	S%	G	A	PIM
35	Marty Turco	55	3203	1.72	31	10	10	3	7	92	1359	.932	0	3	16
30	Corey Hirsch	2	97	2.47	0	1	0	0	0	4	39	.897	0	0	0
31	Ron Tugnutt	31	1701	2.47	15	10	5	0	4	70	672	.896	0	0	0
	Totals	**82**	**5020**	**2.02**	**46**	**21**	**15**	**3**	**11**	**169**	**2073**	**.918**			

Playoffs

Pos	#	Player	Team	GP	G	A	Pts	+/–	PIM	PP	SH	GW	GT	S	%
C	9	Mike Modano	DAL	12	5	10	15	2	4	1	0	2	0	30	16.7
D	56	Sergei Zubov	DAL	12	4	10	14	2	4	2	0	0	0	27	14.8
L	10	Brenden Morrow	DAL	12	3	5	8	3	16	2	0	0	0	28	10.7
R	48	Scott Young	DAL	10	4	3	7	5	6	2	0	1	0	32	12.5
C	39 *	Niko Kapanen	DAL	12	4	3	7	4	12	0	1	0	0	20	20.0
D	5	Darryl Sydor	DAL	12	0	6	6	–3	6	0	0	0	0	18	0.0
C	44	Jason Arnott	DAL	11	3	2	5	–2	6	1	0	0	0	18	16.7
R	26	Jere Lehtinen	DAL	12	3	2	5	1	0	1	0	1	0	42	7.1
C	14	Stu Barnes	DAL	12	2	3	5	0	0	0	0	2	0	22	9.1
R	18	Rob DiMaio	DAL	12	1	4	5	2	10	0	0	0	0	26	3.8
R	11	Ulf Dahlen	DAL	11	1	3	4	–3	0	1	0	0	0	19	5.3
D	2	Derian Hatcher	DAL	11	1	2	3	8	33	0	0	0	0	22	4.5
D	43	Philippe Boucher	DAL	11	1	2	3	1	11	0	0	0	0	19	5.3
D	24	Richard Matvichuk	DAL	12	0	3	3	1	8	0	0	0	0	12	0.0
C	22	Kirk Muller	DAL	12	1	1	2	0	8	0	0	0	0	14	7.1
L	27	Manny Malhotra	DAL	5	1	0	1	1	0	0	0	0	0	3	33.3
C	77	Pierre Turgeon	DAL	5	0	1	1	1	0	0	0	0	0	8	0.0
R	32	Claude Lemieux	DAL	7	0	1	1	–1	10	0	0	0	0	6	0.0
D	17	Stephane Robidas	DAL	12	0	1	1	1	20	0	0	0	0	10	0.0
C	29 *	Steve Ott	DAL	1	0	0	0	–1	0	0	0	0	0	0	0.0
D	4	Lyle Odelein	DAL	2	0	0	0	–1	0	0	0	0	0	2	0.0
R	13	Bill Guerin	DAL	4	0	0	0	–1	4	0	0	0	0	3	0.0
R	28	David Oliver	DAL	6	0	0	0	–2	2	0	0	0	0	1	0.0

Goaltending

No.	Goaltender	GPI	Mins	Avg	W	L	EN	SO	GA	SA	S%	G	A	PIM
35	Marty Turco	12	798	1.88	6	6	0	0	25	310	.919	0	0	8
	Totals	**12**	**803**	**1.87**	**6**	**6**	**0**	**0**	**25**	**310**	**.919**			

Coaching History

Wren Blair, 1967-68; Wren Blair and John Muckler, 1968-69; Wren Blair and Charlie Burns, 1969-70; Jack Gordon, 1970-71 to 1972-73; Jack Gordon and Parker MacDonald, 1973-74; Jack Gordon and Charlie Burns, 1974-75; Ted Harris, 1975-76, 1976-77; Ted Harris, André Beaulieu and Lou Nanne, 1977-78; Harry Howell and Glen Sonmor, 1978-79; Glen Sonmor, 1979-80 to 1981-82; Glen Sonmor and Murray Oliver, 1982-83; Bill Mahoney, 1983-84, 1984-85; Lorne Henning, 1985-86; Lorne Henning and Glen Sonmor, 1986-87; Herb Brooks, 1987-88; Pierre Page, 1988-89, 1989-90; Bob Gainey, 1990-91 to 1994-95; Bob Gainey and Ken Hitchcock, 1995-96; Ken Hitchcock, 1996-97 to 2000-01; Ken Hitchcock and Rick Wilson, 2001-02; Dave Tippett, 2002-03 to date.

Club Records

Team

(Figures in brackets for season records are games played; records for fewest points, wins, ties, losses, goals, goals against are for 70 or more games)

Most Points	**114**	1998-99 (82)
Most Wins	**51**	1998-99 (82)
Most Ties	**22**	1969-70 (76)
Most Losses	**53**	1975-76, 1977-78 (80)
Most Goals	**346**	1981-82 (80)
Most Goals Against	**349**	1987-88 (80)
Fewest Points	**45**	1977-78 (80)
Fewest Wins	**18**	1968-69 (76), 1977-78 (80)
Fewest Ties	**4**	1989-90 (80)
Fewest Losses	**17**	2002-03 (82)
Fewest Goals	**189**	1968-69 (76)
Fewest Goals Against	**167**	1997-98 (82)
Longest Winning Streak		
Overall	**7**	Mar. 16-28/80, Mar. 16-Apr. 2/97, Nov. 22-Dec. 5/97
Home	**11**	Nov. 4-Dec. 27/72
Away	**7**	Three times
Longest Undefeated Streak		
Overall	**15**	Dec. 6/98-Jan. 6/99 (12 wins, 3 ties)
Home	**13**	Oct. 28-Dec. 27/72 (12 wins, 1 tie), Nov. 21/79-Jan. 9/80 (10 wins, 3 ties), Jan. 17-Mar. 17/91 (11 wins, 2 ties)
Away	**10**	Jan. 12-Mar. 4/99 (8 wins, 2 ties)
Longest Losing Streak		
Overall	**10**	Feb. 1-20/76
Home	**6**	Jan. 17-Feb. 4/70
Away	**8**	Oct. 19-Nov. 13/75, Jan. 28-Mar. 3/88
Longest Winless Streak		
Overall	**20**	Jan. 15-Feb. 28/70 (15 losses, 5 ties)
Home	**12**	Jan. 17-Feb. 25/70 (8 losses, 4 ties)
Away	**23**	Oct. 25/74-Jan. 28/75 (19 losses, 4 ties)
Most Shutouts, Season	**11**	2000-01 (82), 2002-03 (82)
Most PIM, Season	**2,313**	1987-88 (80)
Most Goals, Game	**15**	Nov. 11/81 (Wpg. 2 at Min. 15)

Individual

Most Seasons	**16**	Neal Broten
Most Games	**992**	Neal Broten
Most Goals, Career	**444**	Mike Modano
Most Assists, Career	**618**	Mike Modano
Most Points, Career	**1,062**	Mike Modano (444G, 618A)
Most PIM, Career	**1,883**	Shane Churla
Most Shutouts, Career	**27**	Ed Belfour
Longest Consecutive Games Streak	**442**	Danny Grant (Dec. 4/68-Apr. 7/74)
Most Goals, Season	**55**	Dino Ciccarelli (1981-82), Brian Bellows (1989-90)
Most Assists, Season	**76**	Neal Broten (1985-86)
Most Points, Season	**114**	Bobby Smith (1981-82; 43G, 71A)
Most PIM, Season	**382**	Basil McRae (1987-88)
Most Points, Defenseman, Season	**77**	Craig Hartsburg (1981-82; 17G, 60A)
Most Points, Center, Season	**114**	Bobby Smith (1981-82; 43G, 71A)
Most Points, Right Wing, Season	**106**	Dino Ciccarelli (1981-82; 55G, 51A)
Most Points, Left Wing, Season	**99**	Brian Bellows (1989-90; 55G, 44A)
Most Points, Rookie, Season	**98**	Neal Broten (1981-82; 38G, 60A)
Most Shutouts, Season	**9**	Ed Belfour (1997-98)
Most Goals, Game	**5**	Tim Young (Jan. 15/79)
Most Assists, Game	**5**	Murray Oliver (Oct. 24/71), Larry Murphy (Oct. 17/89)
Most Points, Game	**7**	Bobby Smith (Nov. 11/81; 4G, 3A)

Records include Minnesota North Stars, 1967-68 through 1992-93.

Retired Numbers

7	Neal Broten	1980-1995, 1996-1997
8	Bill Goldsworthy*	1967-1976
19	Bill Masterton*	1967-1968

* Minnesota North Stars

All-time Record vs. Other Clubs

Regular Season

	At Home								On Road								Total							
	GP	W	L	T	OL	GF	GA	PTS	GP	W	L	T	OL	GF	GA	PTS	GP	W	L	T	OL	GF	GA	PTS
Anaheim	24	18	5	1	0	90	48	37	24	13	9	2	0	63	52	28	48	31	14	3	0	153	100	65
Atlanta	3	3	0	0	0	7	3	6	4	4	0	0	0	16	9	8	7	7	0	0	0	23	12	14
Boston	60	18	29	13	0	175	218	49	59	9	40	10	0	145	254	28	119	27	69	23	0	320	472	77
Buffalo	54	27	21	6	0	173	156	60	51	13	27	11	0	136	184	37	105	40	48	17	0	309	340	97
Calgary	60	28	20	11	1	219	192	68	60	13	31	14	2	148	206	42	120	41	51	25	3	367	398	110
Carolina	29	17	10	2	0	115	86	36	31	14	13	4	0	107	100	32	60	31	23	6	0	222	186	68
Chicago	110	50	43	16	1	371	338	117	108	30	64	14	0	284	411	74	218	80	107	30	1	655	749	191
Colorado	39	20	12	5	2	124	110	47	39	11	20	7	1	102	143	30	78	31	32	12	3	226	253	77
Columbus	6	6	0	0	0	21	7	12	6	4	2	0	0	19	14	8	12	10	2	0	0	40	21	20
Detroit	104	51	35	17	1	366	311	120	104	37	51	16	0	336	399	90	208	88	86	33	1	702	710	210
Edmonton	43	23	13	7	0	157	119	53	42	14	19	8	1	141	170	37	85	37	32	15	1	298	289	90
Florida	8	3	2	2	1	25	22	9	9	5	3	1	0	28	21	11	17	8	5	3	1	53	43	20
Los Angeles	81	51	18	12	0	318	214	114	79	27	34	18	0	228	269	72	160	78	52	30	0	546	483	186
Minnesota	6	2	2	1	1	21	16	6	6	3	3	0	0	14	18	6	12	5	5	1	1	35	34	12
Montreal	58	17	30	11	0	152	202	45	58	12	37	9	0	144	250	33	116	29	67	20	0	296	452	78
Nashville	10	8	2	0	0	27	10	16	10	4	6	0	0	19	26	8	20	12	8	0	0	46	36	24
New Jersey	44	25	13	6	0	162	117	56	43	19	21	3	0	132	146	41	87	44	34	9	0	294	263	97
NY Islanders	46	18	20	7	1	135	166	44	47	14	24	8	1	133	172	37	93	32	44	15	2	268	338	81
NY Rangers	61	20	30	11	0	187	221	51	61	15	35	11	0	165	210	41	122	35	65	22	0	352	431	92
Ottawa	10	6	4	0	0	39	25	12	9	5	3	0	1	24	22	11	19	11	7	0	1	63	47	23
Philadelphia	65	27	23	15	0	214	210	69	66	9	42	15	0	148	253	33	131	36	65	30	0	362	463	102
Phoenix	52	26	18	8	0	191	155	60	51	26	21	4	0	174	161	56	103	52	39	12	0	365	316	116
Pittsburgh	64	37	21	6	0	246	213	80	62	19	37	6	0	178	232	44	126	56	58	12	0	424	445	124
St. Louis	113	51	39	22	1	378	333	125	115	31	62	21	1	326	420	84	228	82	101	43	2	704	753	209
San Jose	26	13	10	3	0	71	60	29	27	17	9	1	0	80	64	35	53	30	19	4	0	151	124	64
Tampa Bay	11	7	3	1	0	39	27	15	12	9	1	2	0	35	19	20	23	16	4	3	0	74	46	35
Toronto	96	50	35	11	0	364	303	111	101	35	49	17	0	319	356	87	197	85	84	28	0	683	659	198
Vancouver	69	35	22	12	0	253	210	82	69	29	30	10	0	213	247	68	138	64	52	22	0	466	457	150
Washington	40	20	11	8	1	148	108	49	40	17	15	8	0	129	120	42	80	37	26	16	1	277	228	91
Defunct Clubs	33	19	8	6	0	123	86	44	32	10	16	6	0	84	105	26	65	29	24	12	0	207	191	70
Totals	**1425**	**696**	**499**	**220**	**10**	**4911**	**4286**	**1622**	**1425**	**468**	**724**	**226**	**7**	**4070**	**5053**	**1169**	**2850**	**1164**	**1223**	**446**	**17**	**8981**	**9339**	**2791**

Playoffs

	Series	W	L	GP	W	L	T	GF	GA	Last Mtg.	Rnd.	Result
Anaheim	1	0	1	6	2	4	0	14	14	2003	CSF	L 2-4
Boston	1	1	0	3	3	0	0	20	13	1981	PRE	W 3-0
Buffalo	3	2	1	13	8	5	0	39	37	1999	F	W 4-2
Calgary	1	1	0	6	4	2	0	25	18	1981	SF	W 4-2
Chicago	6	2	4	33	14	19	0	118	120	1991	DSF	W 4-2
Colorado	2	2	0	14	8	6	0	37	29	2000	CF	W 4-3
Detroit	3	0	3	18	6	12	0	40	55	1998	CF	L 2-4
Edmonton	8	6	2	42	27	15	0	118	104	2003	CQF	W 4-2
Los Angeles	1	1	0	7	4	3	0	26	21	1968	QF	W 4-3
Montreal	2	1	1	13	6	7	0	37	48	1980	QF	W 4-3
New Jersey	1	0	1	6	2	4	0	9	15	2000	F	L 2-4
NY Islanders	1	0	1	5	1	4	0	16	26	1981	F	L 1-4
Philadelphia	2	0	2	11	3	8	0	26	41	1980	SF	L 1-4
Pittsburgh	1	0	1	6	2	4	0	16	28	1991	F	L 2-4
St. Louis	12	6	6	66	34	32	0	197	187	2001	CSF	L 0-4
San Jose	2	2	0	11	8	3	0	31	19	2000	CSF	W 4-1
Toronto	2	2	0	7	6	1	0	35	26	1983	DSF	W 3-1
Vancouver	1	0	1	5	1	4	0	11	18	1994	CSF	L 1-4
Totals	**50**	**26**	**24**	**272**	**139**	**133**	**0**	**815**	**819**			

Calgary totals include Atlanta Flames, 1972-73 to 1979-80. Carolina totals include Hartford, 1979-80 to 1996-97.
Colorado totals include Quebec, 1979-80 to 1994-95.
New Jersey totals include Kansas City, 1974-75 to 1975-76, and Colorado Rockies, 1976-77 to 1981-82.
Phoenix totals include Winnipeg, 1979-80 to 1995-96.

Playoff Results 2003-1999

Year	Round	Opponent	Result	GF	GA
2003	CSF	Anaheim	L 2-4	14	14
	CQF	Edmonton	W 4-2	20	11
2001	CSF	St. Louis	L 0-4	6	13
	CQF	Edmonton	W 4-2	16	13
2000	F	New Jersey	L 2-4	9	15
	CF	Colorado	W 4-3	14	13
	CSF	San Jose	W 4-1	15	7
	CQF	Edmonton	W 4-1	14	11
1999	**F**	**Buffalo**	**W 4-2**	**13**	**9**
	CF	Colorado	W 4-3	23	16
	CSF	St. Louis	W 4-2	17	12
	CQF	Edmonton	W 4-0	11	7

Abbreviations: Round: F - Final; **CF** - conference final; **CSF** - conference semi-final; **CQF** - conference quarter-final; **DSF** - division semi-final; **SF** - semi-final; **QF** - quarter-final; **PRE** - preliminary round.

2002-03 Results

Oct.	9	at Colorado	1-1
	11	Anaheim	4-2
	12	at Phoenix	5-2
	15	Edmonton	3-0
	17	at Minnesota	1-3
	19	at St. Louis	3-5
	20	Washington	5-2
	24	at Calgary	3-3
	26	at Vancouver	4-1
	28	at Edmonton	4-3*
	30	Florida	2-3*
Nov.	1	at Columbus	2-4
	3	at Detroit	3-3
	6	Vancouver	4-0
	8	Toronto	2-1
	10	at NY Islanders	2-3
	12	at Montreal	4-2
	13	at Washington	6-1
	15	Colorado	4-2
	17	Columbus	3-2*
	20	at Phoenix	2-2
	22	at Anaheim	4-0
	23	at Los Angeles	0-2
	25	Phoenix	5-1
	27	Minnesota	5-0
	29	NY Rangers	3-3
	30	at Nashville	2-5
Dec.	4	Montreal	5-1
	6	Detroit	3-3
	11	Los Angeles	0-3
	13	Atlanta	3-1
	15	at Chicago	5-0
	17	at Philadelphia	2-2
	19	at Detroit	1-1
	21	at New Jersey	3-5
	22	at Carolina	0-1
	26	at Nashville	1-3
	27	at Florida	4-0
	29	Detroit	2-2
	31	Edmonton	4-1
Jan.	2	at San Jose	3-1
	4	at Los Angeles	3-2
	5	at Anaheim	1-1
	7	Los Angeles	7-4
	9	Chicago	4-3*
	11	Colorado	6-3
	18	at San Jose	3-1
	20	at Colorado	1-1
	22	Columbus	4-2
	24	Tampa Bay	1-4
	25	at St. Louis	4-2
	27	Ottawa	5-3
	29	Calgary	4-1
Feb.	5	St. Louis	2-2
	8	at Phoenix	3-1
	9	Los Angeles	3-1
	11	Carolina	2-1*
	14	Anaheim	2-4
	16	San Jose	3-1
	19	Calgary	1-1
	21	Phoenix	2-2
	23	at Chicago	3-0
	25	at Boston	5-5
	27	at Ottawa	2-3*
	28	at Buffalo	3-5
Mar.	2	Pittsburgh	3-1
	5	Chicago	7-4
	7	Nashville	1-2
	9	San Jose	3-0
	11	at Columbus	2-0
	12	at Minnesota	2-4
	15	at Edmonton	3-4
	17	Vancouver	2-4
	19	at Atlanta	5-4*
	21	Minnesota	2-3*
	23	St. Louis	3-1
	25	at Vancouver	4-3
	27	at Calgary	1-2*
	29	at San Jose	4-3
	31	Buffalo	3-0
Apr.	2	Anaheim	2-1
	6	Nashville	2-0

* – Overtime

Entry Draft
Selections 2003-1989

2003 Pick		1999 Pick		1995 Pick		1991 Pick	
33	Loui Eriksson	32	Michael Ryan	11	Jarome Iginla	8	Richard Matvichuk
36	Vojtech Polak	66	Dan Jancevski	37	Patrick Cote	74	Mike Torchia
54	Brandon Crombeen	96	Mathias Tjarnqvist	63	Petr Buzek	97	Mike Kennedy
99	Matt Nickerson	126	Jeff Bateman	69	Sergey Gusev	118	Mark Lawrence
134	Alexander Naurov	156	Gregor Baumgartner	115	Wade Strand	137	Geoff Finch
144	Eero Kilpelainen	184	Justin Cox	141	Dominic Marleau	174	Michael Burkett
165	Gino Guyer	186	Brett Draney	173	Jeff Dewar	184	Derek Herlofsky
185	Francis Wathier	215	Jeff MacMillan	193	Anatoli Koveshnikov	206	Tom Nemeth
195	Drew Bagnall	243	Brian Sullivan	202	Sergei Luchinkin	228	Shayne Green
196	Elias Granath	265	Jamie Chamberlain	219	Stephen Lowe	250	Jukka Suomalainen
259	Niko Vainio	272	Mikhail Donika				

2002 Pick		1998 Pick		1994 Pick		1990 Pick	
26	Martin Vagner	39	John Erskine	20	Jason Botterill	8	Derian Hatcher
32	Janos Vas	57	Tyler Bouck	46	Lee Jinman	50	Laurie Billeck
34	Tobias Stephan	86	Gabriel Karlsson	98	Jamie Wright	70	Cal McGowan
42	Marius Holtet	153	Pavel Patera	124	Marty Turco	71	Frank Kovacs
43	Trevor Daley	173	Niko Kapanen	150	Evgeny Petrochinin	92	Enrico Ciccone
78	Geoff Waugh	200	Scott Perry	228	Marty Flichel	113	Roman Turek
110	Jarkko A. Immonen			254	Jimmy Roy	134	Jeff Levy
147	David Bararuk	**1997 Pick**		280	Chris Szysky	155	Doug Barrault
180	Kirill Sidorenko	25	Brenden Morrow			176	Joe Biondi
210	Bryan Hamm	52	Roman Lyashenko	**1993 Pick**		197	Troy Binnie
243	Tuomas Mikkonen	77	Steve Gainey	9	Todd Harvey	218	Ole-Eskild Dahlstrom
273	Ned Havern	105	Marcus Kristoffersson	35	Jamie Langenbrunner	239	John McKersie
		132	Teemu Elomo	87	Chad Lang		
2001 Pick		160	Alexei Timkin	136	Rick Mrozik	**1989 Pick**	
26	Jason Bacashihua	189	Jeff McKercher	139	Per Svartvadet	7	Doug Zmolek
70	Yared Hagos	216	Alexei Komarov	165	Jeremy Stasiuk	28	Mike Craig
92	Anthony Aquino	242	Brett McLean	191	Rob Lurtsema	60	Murray Garbutt
126	Daniel Volrab			243	Jordan Willis	75	Jean-Francois Quintin
161	Mike Smith	**1996 Pick**		249	Bill Lang	87	Pat MacLeod
167	Michal Blazek	5	Richard Jackman	269	Cory Peterson	91	Bryan Schoen
192	Jussi Jokinen	70	Jon Sim			97	Rhys Hollyman
255	Marco Rosa	90	Mike Hurley	**1992 Pick**		112	Scott Cashman
265	Dale Sullivan	112	Ryan Christie	34	Jarkko Varvio	154	Jonathon Pratt
285	Marek Tomica	113	Yevgeny Tsybuk	58	Jeff Bes	175	Kenneth Blum
		166	Eoin McInerney	88	Jere Lehtinen	196	Arturs Irbe
2000 Pick		194	Joel Kwiatkowski	130	Michael Johnson	217	Tom Pederson
25	Steve Ott	220	Nick Bootland	154	Kyle Peterson	238	Helmut Balderis
60	Dan Ellis			178	Juha Lind		
68	Joel Lundqvist			202	Lars Edstrom		
91	Alexei Tereschenko			226	Jeff Romfo		
123	Vadim Khomitsky			250	Jeffrey Moen		
139	Ruslan Bernikov						
162	Artem Chernov						
192	Ladislav Vlcek						
219	Marco Tuokko						
224	Antti Miettinen						

Captains' History

Bob Woytowich, 1967-68; Moose Vasko, 1968-69; Claude Larose, 1969-70; Ted Harris, 1970-71 to 1973-74; Bill Goldsworthy, 1974-75, 1975-76; Bill Hogaboam, 1976-77; Nick Beverley, 1977-78; J.P. Parise, 1978-79; Paul Shmyr, 1979-80, 1980-81; Tim Young, 1981-82; Craig Hartsburg, 1982-83; Craig Hartsburg and Brian Bellows, 1983-84; Craig Hartsburg, 1984-85 to 1987-88; Curt Fraser, Bob Rouse and Curt Giles, 1988-89; Curt Giles, 1989-90, 1990-91; Mark Tinordi, 1991-92 to 1993-94; Neal Broten and Derian Hatcher, 1994-95; Derian Hatcher, 1995-96 to 2002-03; Mike Modano, 2003-04.

General Managers' History

Wren Blair, 1967-68 to 1973-74; Jack Gordon, 1974-75 to 1976-77; Lou Nanne, 1977-78 to 1987-88; Jack Ferreira, 1988-89, 1989-90; Bob Clarke 1990-91, 1991-92; Bob Gainey, 1992-93 to 2000-01; Bob Gainey and Doug Armstrong, 2001-02; Doug Armstrong, 2002-03 to date.

General Manager

ARMSTRONG, DOUG
General Manager, Dallas Stars. Born in Sarnia, Ont., September 24, 1964.
Doug Armstrong was in his ninth season as an assistant to Bob Gainey when he was elevated to the position of general manager on January 25, 2002. In his first full season on the job in 2002-03, the Stars had the best record in the Western Conference and the second best in the NHL. Armstrong originally joined the club in 1991. As Gainey's assistant, he worked on contract information and season scheduling and handled the day-to-day operations of the hockey department. In five seasons from 1996 to 2001, he helped Gainey build a team that won five straight division championships, as well as the Presidents' Trophy for the best regular-season record in the NHL twice, and the 1999 Stanley Cup. At the international level, Armstrong served as Team Canada's assistant general manger at the 2002 World Championships in Sweden.

A native of Sarnia, Ontario, Armstrong attended Western Michigan University for two years before transferring to Florida State University in Tallahassee, where he earned his B.S. in Business Administration with a major in marketing.

Club Directory

American Airlines Center

Dallas Stars
2601 Ave. of the Stars
Frisco, TX 75034
Office Address:
Dr Pepper StarCenter
211 Cowboys Parkway
Irving, TX 75063
Phone **214/387-5600**
FAX 214/387-5610
Ticket Information 214/GO STARS
www.dallasstars.com
Capacity: 18,532

Chairman of the Board & Owner	Thomas O. Hicks
President	James R. Lites
Executive Vice President, Business Operations	Geoff Moore
Executive Vice President, Marketing & Communications	Bryan M. Perez
Executive Vice President, Finance & CFO	Robert Hutson
Executive Vice President, Corporate Sales	Tom Fireoved
Assistant to the President	Cheryl Hocker

Hockey Operations
General Manager	Doug Armstrong
Assistant General Manager	Francois Giguere
Director, Hockey Operations	Les Jackson
Special Assistant to General Manager	Guy Carbonneau
Head Coach	Dave Tippett
Associate Coach	Rick Wilson
Assistant Coaches	Mark Lamb, Andy Moog
Coaching Assistant/Video Coordinator	Derrick MacKinnon
Director, Hockey Administration and Team Services	Lesa Moake
Community Liaison/Alumni Director	Craig Ludwig
Director, Amateur Scouting	Tim Bernhardt
Director, Professional Scouting	Doug Overton
Scout	Bob Gernander
Professional Scout	Paul McIntosh
Regional Scouts	Shannon Currie, Hans Edlund, Jack Foley, Jiri Hrdina, Dennis Holland, Jimmy Johnston, Jim Pedersen, Brad Robson, Karri Takko
Head Athletic Trainer	Dave Surprenant
Head Equipment Manager	Dave Smith
Strength and Conditioning Coach	J.J. McQueen
Assistant Equipment Manager	Steve Sumner
Assistant Athletic Trainer	Craig Lowry
Equipment Assistant	Anthony Addeo
Administrative Assistant, Hockey Operations	Pam Wenzel

Communications
Senior Director, Hockey Communications	Rob Scichili
Director, Media Relations	Mark Janko
Director, Community Relations	Julie Berkhouse
Manager of Publications and Media Relations	Jason Rademan
Assistant Director, Community Relations	Kim Stricklin
Website Editor	Doug Foster
Desktop/LAN Support	Bill Jennings
Office Manager	Genia Mezzenga

Broadcasting
Director of Broadcasting	Kevin Spivey
Announcers, TV/Radio	Ralph Strangis, Daryl Reaugh
Arena Announcer	Bill Oellermann

Business Operations
Director, Food and Beverage	Barbara Altom
Director, Event Operations	Ben Marthaler
Department Analyst	Christy Norton

Corporate Sales
Vice President, Sponsorship Sales	Ronnie Davis
Director, Corporate Sales	Jeff Tummonds
Director, Advertising Sales	Gina Owen
Broadcast and Sales Services Manager	Brooke Fendrick
Sponsorship Manager	Ben Young

Finance & Accounting
Vice President, Finance	Kellie Fischer
Assistant Controllers	Melissa Embry, Starr Pritchard, Christie Steblein
Payroll Manager	Donna Blaylock
Senior Accountant	Donna Kee
Staff Accountant	Brent Jasper
Treasury Accountant	Becky Robbins
Purchasing Manager	Chelle Jezek

Marketing
Vice President, Marketing	Christy Martinez
Director, Promotions & Game Entertainment	Tina Miller
Promotions Coordinator	Scott Robertson

Merchandising
Vice President, Merchandising	Steve Shilts
District Manager, Merchandise	Jason Atkinson
Director, Merchandising Equipment	Jason Maxwell
Merchandising Analyst and Buyer	Jill Moore
Inventory Controller	Gary Peterson
Warehouse Manager	Oscar Garza
Manager, Arena Operations	Aaron Perez

Ticket Operations
Director, Ticket Operations	Stacey Marthaler
Assistant Director, Ticket Operations	Matt McKee

Ticket Sales
Vice President, Ticket Sales	Jamie Norman
Assistant Vice President, Luxury Suite Sales	Paige Jackson
Manager, Stars Season Tickets Sales	Colin Faulkner
Senior Account Executive	Megan O'Sullivan
Account Executives	Ben Cahalane, Michelle Donis, Nick Ralston, Jessica Tomlinson
Manager, Sales and Marketing Programs	Ashley House
Manager, Special Projects	Lane Pate

Brett Hull (with Pavel Datsyuk) topped 700 goals.

Detroit Red Wings

2002-03 Results: 48W-20L-10T-4OTL 110PTS.
First, Central Division

2003-04 Schedule

Month	Day	Date	Opponent
Oct.	Thu.	9	Los Angeles
	Sat.	11	at Ottawa
	Thu.	16	Vancouver
	Sat.	18	at Pittsburgh
	Mon.	20	at Montreal
	Wed.	22	Columbus
	Fri.	24	Dallas
	Sat.	25	at NY Rangers
	Wed.	29	St. Louis
	Thu.	30	at Nashville
Nov.	Sat.	1	at Edmonton
	Mon.	3	at Vancouver
	Tue.	4	at Calgary
	Sat.	8	Nashville
	Mon.	10	Chicago
	Wed.	12	at Dallas
	Fri.	14	at Chicago
	Sat.	15	at Minnesota
	Wed.	19	Columbus
	Thu.	20	at Columbus
	Sat.	22	at Minnesota
	Mon.	24	Washington
	Wed.	26	Edmonton
	Fri.	28	NY Islanders
	Sat.	29	at St. Louis
Dec.	Wed.	3	Anaheim
	Thu.	4	at St. Louis
	Sat.	6	at Toronto
	Mon.	8	Los Angeles
	Wed.	10	at Buffalo
	Thu.	11	at Chicago
	Sat.	13	at Washington
	Mon.	15	Florida
	Wed.	17	San Jose
	Fri.	19	Chicago
	Sat.	20	at Nashville
	Mon.	22	St. Louis
	Fri.	26	Minnesota
	Sun.	28	at Chicago
	Wed.	31	Atlanta
Jan.	Fri.	2	at Carolina
	Sat.	3	Anaheim
	Mon.	5	Nashville
	Wed.	7	Boston
	Sat.	10	at Boston*
	Wed.	14	Chicago
	Fri.	16	Phoenix
	Mon.	19	at San Jose*
	Wed.	21	at Anaheim
	Thu.	22	at Los Angeles
	Sat.	24	at Phoenix
	Mon.	26	at Dallas
	Thu.	29	New Jersey
	Sat.	31	Carolina
Feb.	Tue.	3	at Nashville
	Thu.	5	at Colorado
	Wed.	11	San Jose
	Sat.	14	Colorado*
	Mon.	16	Edmonton
	Wed.	18	Phoenix
	Fri.	20	St. Louis
	Mon.	23	at Edmonton
	Tue.	24	at Vancouver
	Thu.	26	at Calgary
	Sun.	29	Philadelphia
Mar.	Wed.	3	Calgary
	Fri.	5	Vancouver
	Mon.	8	Tampa Bay
	Thu.	11	at Columbus
	Sat.	13	Dallas*
	Sun.	14	Nashville
	Tue.	16	Calgary
	Thu.	18	at Phoenix
	Sat.	20	at Los Angeles
	Sun.	21	at Anaheim*
	Tue.	23	at San Jose
	Thu.	25	at Colorado
	Sat.	27	Colorado*
	Mon.	29	Minnesota
	Wed.	31	at Columbus
Apr.	Thu.	1	at St. Louis
	Sat.	3	Columbus

* Denotes afternoon game.

Year-by-Year Record

Season	GP	Home W	Home L	Home T	Home OL	Road W	Road L	Road T	Road OL	Overall W	Overall L	Overall T	Overall OL	GF	GA	Pts.	Finished	Playoff Result
2002-03	82	28	6	5	2	20	14	5	2	48	20	10	4	269	203	110	1st, Central Div.	Lost Conf. Quarter-Final
2001-02	**82**	**28**	**7**	**5**	**1**	**23**	**10**	**5**	**3**	**51**	**17**	**10**	**4**	**251**	**187**	**116**	**1st, Central Div.**	**Won Stanley Cup**
2000-01	82	27	9	3	2	22	11	6	2	49	20	9	4	253	202	111	1st, Central Div.	Lost Conf. Quarter-Final
1999-2000	82	28	9	3	1	20	13	7	1	48	22	10	2	278	210	108	2nd, Central Div.	Lost Conf. Semi-Final
1998-99	82	27	12	2	...	16	20	5	...	43	32	7	...	245	202	93	1st, Central Div.	Lost Conf. Semi-Final
1997-98	**82**	**25**	**8**	**8**	**...**	**19**	**15**	**7**	**...**	**44**	**23**	**15**	**...**	**250**	**196**	**103**	**2nd, Central Div.**	**Won Stanley Cup**
1996-97	**82**	**20**	**12**	**9**	**...**	**18**	**14**	**9**	**...**	**38**	**26**	**18**	**...**	**253**	**197**	**94**	**2nd, Central Div.**	**Won Stanley Cup**
1995-96	82	36	3	2	...	26	10	5	...	62	13	7	...	325	181	131	1st, Central Div.	Lost Conf. Championship
1994-95	48	17	4	3	...	16	7	1	...	33	11	4	...	180	117	70	1st, Central Div.	Lost Final
1993-94	84	23	13	6	...	23	17	2	...	46	30	8	...	356	275	100	1st, Central Div.	Lost Conf. Quarter-Final
1992-93	84	25	14	3	...	22	14	6	...	47	28	9	...	369	280	103	2nd, Norris Div.	Lost Div. Semi-Final
1991-92	80	24	12	4	...	19	13	8	...	43	25	12	...	320	256	98	1st, Norris Div.	Lost Div. Final
1990-91	80	26	14	0	...	8	24	8	...	34	38	8	...	273	298	76	3rd, Norris Div.	Lost Div. Semi-Final
1989-90	80	20	14	6	...	8	24	8	...	28	38	14	...	288	323	70	5th, Norris Div.	Out of Playoffs
1988-89	80	20	14	6	...	14	20	6	...	34	34	12	...	313	316	80	1st, Norris Div.	Lost Div. Semi-Final
1987-88	80	24	10	6	...	17	18	5	...	41	28	11	...	322	269	93	1st, Norris Div.	Lost Conf. Championship
1986-87	80	20	14	6	...	14	22	4	...	34	36	10	...	260	274	78	2nd, Norris Div.	Lost Conf. Championship
1985-86	80	10	26	4	...	7	31	2	...	17	57	6	...	266	415	40	5th, Norris Div.	Out of Playoffs
1984-85	80	19	14	7	...	8	27	5	...	27	41	12	...	313	357	66	3rd, Norris Div.	Lost Div. Semi-Final
1983-84	80	18	20	2	...	13	22	5	...	31	42	7	...	298	323	69	3rd, Norris Div.	Lost Div. Semi-Final
1982-83	80	14	19	7	...	7	25	8	...	21	44	15	...	263	344	57	5th, Norris Div.	Out of Playoffs
1981-82	80	15	19	6	...	6	28	6	...	21	47	12	...	270	351	54	6th, Norris Div.	Out of Playoffs
1980-81	80	16	15	9	...	3	28	9	...	19	43	18	...	252	339	56	5th, Norris Div.	Out of Playoffs
1979-80	80	14	21	5	...	12	22	6	...	26	43	11	...	268	306	63	5th, Norris Div.	Out of Playoffs
1978-79	80	15	17	8	...	8	24	8	...	23	41	16	...	252	295	62	5th, Norris Div.	Out of Playoffs
1977-78	80	22	11	7	...	10	23	7	...	32	34	14	...	252	266	78	2nd, Norris Div.	Lost Quarter-Final
1976-77	80	12	22	6	...	4	33	3	...	16	55	9	...	183	309	41	5th, Norris Div.	Out of Playoffs
1975-76	80	17	15	8	...	9	29	2	...	26	44	10	...	226	300	62	4th, Norris Div.	Out of Playoffs
1974-75	80	17	17	6	...	6	28	6	...	23	45	12	...	259	335	58	4th, Norris Div.	Out of Playoffs
1973-74	78	21	12	6	...	8	27	4	...	29	39	10	...	255	319	68	6th, East Div.	Out of Playoffs
1972-73	78	22	12	5	...	15	17	7	...	37	29	12	...	265	243	86	5th, East Div.	Out of Playoffs
1971-72	78	25	11	3	...	8	24	7	...	33	35	10	...	261	262	76	5th, East Div.	Out of Playoffs
1970-71	78	17	15	7	...	5	30	4	...	22	45	11	...	209	308	55	7th, East Div.	Out of Playoffs
1969-70	76	20	11	7	...	20	10	8	...	40	21	15	...	246	199	95	3rd, East Div.	Lost Quarter-Final
1968-69	76	23	8	7	...	10	23	5	...	33	31	12	...	239	221	78	5th, East Div.	Out of Playoffs
1967-68	74	18	15	4	...	9	20	8	...	27	35	12	...	245	257	66	6th, East Div.	Out of Playoffs
1966-67	70	21	11	3	...	6	28	1	...	27	39	4	...	212	241	58	5th,	Out of Playoffs
1965-66	70	20	8	7	...	11	19	5	...	31	27	12	...	221	194	74	4th,	Lost Final
1964-65	70	25	7	3	...	15	16	4	...	40	23	7	...	224	175	87	1st,	Lost Semi-Final
1963-64	70	23	9	3	...	7	20	8	...	30	29	11	...	191	204	71	4th,	Lost Final
1962-63	70	19	10	6	...	13	15	7	...	32	25	13	...	200	194	77	4th,	Lost Final
1961-62	70	17	11	7	...	6	22	7	...	23	33	14	...	184	219	60	5th,	Out of Playoffs
1960-61	70	15	13	7	...	10	16	9	...	25	29	16	...	195	215	66	4th,	Lost Final
1959-60	70	18	14	3	...	8	15	12	...	26	29	15	...	186	197	67	4th,	Lost Semi-Final
1958-59	70	13	17	5	...	12	20	3	...	25	37	8	...	167	218	58	6th,	Out of Playoffs
1957-58	70	16	11	8	...	13	18	4	...	29	29	12	...	176	207	70	3rd,	Lost Semi-Final
1956-57	70	23	7	5	...	15	13	7	...	38	20	12	...	198	157	88	1st,	Lost Semi-Final
1955-56	70	21	6	8	...	9	18	8	...	30	24	16	...	183	148	76	2nd,	Lost Final
1954-55	**70**	**25**	**5**	**5**	**...**	**17**	**12**	**6**	**...**	**42**	**17**	**11**	**...**	**204**	**134**	**95**	**1st,**	**Won Stanley Cup**
1953-54	**70**	**24**	**4**	**7**	**...**	**13**	**15**	**7**	**...**	**37**	**19**	**14**	**...**	**191**	**132**	**88**	**1st,**	**Won Stanley Cup**
1952-53	70	20	5	10	...	16	11	8	...	36	16	18	...	222	133	90	1st,	Lost Semi-Final
1951-52	**70**	**24**	**7**	**4**	**...**	**20**	**7**	**8**	**...**	**44**	**14**	**12**	**...**	**215**	**133**	**100**	**1st,**	**Won Stanley Cup**
1950-51	70	25	3	7	...	19	10	6	...	44	13	13	...	236	139	101	1st,	Lost Semi-Final
1949-50	**70**	**19**	**9**	**7**	**...**	**18**	**10**	**7**	**...**	**37**	**19**	**14**	**...**	**229**	**164**	**88**	**1st,**	**Won Stanley Cup**
1948-49	60	21	6	3	...	13	13	4	...	34	19	7	...	195	145	75	1st,	Lost Final
1947-48	60	16	9	5	...	14	9	7	...	30	18	12	...	187	148	72	2nd,	Lost Final
1946-47	60	14	10	6	...	8	17	5	...	22	27	11	...	190	193	55	4th,	Lost Semi-Final
1945-46	50	16	5	4	...	4	15	6	...	20	20	10	...	146	159	50	4th,	Lost Semi-Final
1944-45	50	19	5	1	...	12	9	4	...	31	14	5	...	218	161	67	2nd,	Lost Final
1943-44	50	18	5	2	...	8	13	4	...	26	18	6	...	214	177	58	2nd,	Lost Semi-Final
1942-43	**50**	**16**	**4**	**5**	**...**	**9**	**10**	**6**	**...**	**25**	**14**	**11**	**...**	**169**	**124**	**61**	**1st,**	**Won Stanley Cup**
1941-42	48	14	7	3	...	5	18	1	...	19	25	4	...	140	147	42	5th,	Lost Final
1940-41	48	14	5	5	...	7	11	6	...	21	16	11	...	112	102	53	3rd,	Lost Final
1939-40	48	11	10	3	...	5	16	3	...	16	26	6	...	91	126	38	5th,	Lost Semi-Final
1938-39	48	14	8	2	...	4	16	4	...	18	24	6	...	107	128	42	5th,	Lost Semi-Final
1937-38	48	8	10	6	...	4	15	5	...	12	25	11	...	99	133	35	4th, Amn. Div.	Out of Playoffs
1936-37	**48**	**14**	**5**	**5**	**...**	**11**	**9**	**4**	**...**	**25**	**14**	**9**	**...**	**128**	**102**	**59**	**1st, Amn. Div.**	**Won Stanley Cup**
1935-36	**48**	**14**	**5**	**5**	**...**	**10**	**11**	**3**	**...**	**24**	**16**	**8**	**...**	**124**	**103**	**56**	**1st, Amn. Div.**	**Won Stanley Cup**
1934-35	48	11	8	5	...	8	14	2	...	19	22	7	...	127	114	45	4th, Amn. Div.	Out of Playoffs
1933-34	48	15	5	4	...	9	9	6	...	24	14	10	...	113	98	58	1st, Amn. Div.	Lost Final
1932-33*	48	17	3	4	...	8	12	4	...	25	15	8	...	111	93	58	2nd, Amn. Div.	Lost Semi-Final
1931-32	48	15	3	6	...	3	17	4	...	18	20	10	...	95	108	46	3rd, Amn. Div.	Lost Quarter-Final
1930-31**	44	10	7	5	...	6	14	2	...	16	21	7	...	102	105	39	4th, Amn. Div.	Out of Playoffs
1929-30	44	9	10	3	...	5	14	3	...	14	24	6	...	117	133	34	4th, Amn. Div.	Out of Playoffs
1928-29	44	11	6	5	...	8	10	4	...	19	16	9	...	72	63	47	3rd, Amn. Div.	Lost Quarter-Final
1927-28	44	9	10	3	...	10	9	3	...	19	19	6	...	88	79	44	4th, Amn. Div.	Out of Playoffs
1926-27***	44	5	16	0	...	7	12	4	...	12	28	4	...	76	105	28	5th, Amn. Div.	Out of Playoffs

* Team name changed to Red Wings. ** Team name changed to Falcons. *** Team named Cougars.

Franchise date: September 25, 1926

CENTRAL DIVISION

78th NHL Season

2003-04 Player Personnel

FORWARDS

	HT	WT	S	Place of Birth	Date	2002-03 Club
BARNES, Ryan	6-1	201	L	Dunnville, Ont.	1/30/80	Grand Rapids
DANDENAULT, Mathieu	6-0	200	R	Sherbrooke, Que.	2/3/76	Detroit
DATSYUK, Pavel	5-11	180	L	Sverdlovsk, USSR	7/20/78	Detroit
DEVEREAUX, Boyd	6-2	195	L	Seaforth, Ont.	4/16/78	Detroit
DRAPER, Kris	5-11	190	L	Toronto, Ont.	5/24/71	Detroit
HOLMSTROM, Tomas	6-0	200	L	Pitea, Sweden	1/23/73	Detroit
HUDLER, Jiri	5-9	178	L	Olomouc, Czech.	1/4/84	Vsetin-Kazan
HULL, Brett	5-11	203	R	Belleville, Ont.	8/9/64	Detroit
KING, Derek	6-1	203	L	Hamilton, Ont.	2/11/67	Grand Rapids
KOPECKY, Tomas	6-3	187	L	Ilava, Czech.	2/5/82	Grand Rapids
LARIONOV, Igor	5-9	170	L	Voskresensk, USSR	12/3/60	Detroit
MALTBY, Kirk	6-0	180	R	Guelph, Ont.	12/22/72	Detroit
McCARTY, Darren	6-1	210	R	Burnaby, B.C.	4/1/72	Detroit
MOWERS, Mark	5-11	187	R	Whitesboro, NY	2/16/74	Grand Rapids
PICARD, Michel	5-11	190	L	Beauport, Que.	11/7/69	Grand Rapids
SHANAHAN, Brendan	6-3	218	R	Mimico, Ont.	1/23/69	Detroit
WHITNEY, Ray	5-10	175	R	Fort Saskatchewan, Alta.	5/8/72	Columbus
WILLIAMS, Jason	5-11	185	R	London, Ont.	8/11/80	Detroit-Grand Rapids
YZERMAN, Steve	5-11	185	R	Cranbrook, B.C.	5/9/65	Detroit
ZETTERBERG, Henrik	5-11	176	L	Njurunda, Sweden	10/9/80	Detroit

DEFENSEMEN

	HT	WT	S	Place of Birth	Date	2002-03 Club
BALLANTYNE, Paul	6-3	200	R	Waterloo, Ont.	7/16/82	Toledo-Grand Rapids
CHELIOS, Chris	6-1	190	R	Chicago, IL	1/25/62	Detroit
FISCHER, Jiri	6-5	225	L	Horovice, Czech.	7/31/80	Detroit
GROULX, Danny	6-0	205	L	LaSalle, Que.	6/23/81	Grand Rapids
HATCHER, Derian	6-5	235	L	Sterling Hts., MI	6/4/72	Dallas
KRONWALL, Niklas	5-11	165	L	Stockholm, Sweden	1/12/81	Djurgarden
LIDSTROM, Nicklas	6-2	185	L	Vasteras, Sweden	4/28/70	Detroit
RIVERS, Jamie	6-0	195	L	Ottawa, Ont.	3/16/75	Florida-San Antonio
SCHNEIDER, Mathieu	5-10	192	L	New York, NY	6/12/69	Los Angeles-Detroit
WOOLLEY, Jason	6-0	203	L	Toronto, Ont.	7/27/69	Buffalo-Detroit

GOALTENDERS

	HT	WT	C	Place of Birth	Date	2002-03 Club
HASEK, Dominik	5-11	180	L	Pardubice, Czech.	1/29/65	did not play
JOSEPH, Curtis	5-11	190	L	Keswick, Ont.	4/29/67	Detroit
LAMOTHE, Marc	6-2	210	L	New Liskeard, Ont.	2/27/74	Grand Rapids
LEGACE, Manny	5-9	162	L	Toronto, Ont.	2/4/73	Detroit

Coach

LEWIS, DAVE
Coach, Detroit Red Wings. Born in Kindersley, Sask,. July 3, 1953.

A member of the Red Wings coaching staff since retiring as a player on November 6, 1987, Dave Lewis was officially named to replace Scotty Bowman as Detroit's head coach on July 17, 2002. He guided the club to the Central Division title and the second-best record in the Western Conference in 2002-03. In his 14 seasons as an assistant coach, Lewis worked under Jacques Demers, Bryan Murray and Bowman. He served as an associate coach alongside Barry Smith during Bowman's nine-year tenure as head coach. Lewis excelled as both a motivator and a tactician. Besides the ability to shape the young talent on the Red Wings roster, Lewis also earned the respect of the Wings veterans like Steve Yzerman, Chris Chelios, Nicklas Lidstrom and Brett Hull. His primary focus was the team's defensive corps. His other duties included extensive video work used in scouting opponents.

Lewis joined the Red Wings organization as a player when he was signed as a free agent on July 27, 1986. He played his 1,000th NHL game with Detroit on April 1, 1987. Lewis was originally selected 33rd overall by the New York Islanders in the 1973 Amateur Draft and entered the NHL for the 1973-74 season directly out of junior hockey with the Saskatoon Blades. He never played a game in the minor leagues. In all, Lewis played 1,008 games with the Islanders, Los Angeles, New Jersey and Detroit. He recorded 36 goals, 187 assists and 953 penalty minutes. He was never a Stanley Cup winner during 15 years as a player, but he helped the Red Wings win the championship three times (1997, 1998 and 2002) as an assistant coach.

Off the ice, Lewis has been actively involved with the Make-A-Wish Foundation. He has organized the Dave Lewis Detroit Red Wings Fantasy Camp and celebrity auctions to raise funds for the charitable organization.

Coaching Record

		Regular Season				Playoffs		
Season	Team	Games	W	L	T	Games	W	L
1998-99	Detroit (NHL)	5	4	1	0			
2002-03	Detroit (NHL)	82	48	24	10	4	0	4
	NHL Totals	87	52	25	10	4	0	4

Shared a 4-1-0 record with associate coach Barry Smith while serving as co-head coaches until Scotty Bowman received medical clearance and returned to coaching on October 23, 1998.

2002-03 Scoring

*- rookie

Regular Season

Pos	#	Player	Team	GP	G	A	Pts	+/−	PIM	PP	SH	GW	GT	S	%
C	91	Sergei Fedorov	DET	80	36	47	83	15	52	10	2	11	0	281	12.8
R	17	Brett Hull	DET	82	37	39	76	11	22	12	1	4	1	262	14.1
L	14	Brendan Shanahan	DET	78	30	38	68	5	103	13	0	6	0	260	11.5
D	5	Nicklas Lidstrom	DET	82	18	44	62	40	38	8	1	4	0	175	10.3
C	13	Pavel Datsyuk	DET	64	12	39	51	20	16	1	0	1	1	82	14.6
D	23	Mathieu Schneider	L.A.	65	9	29	43	0	57	10	0	1	0	162	8.6
			DET	13	2	5	7	2	16	1	0	0	0	37	5.4
			TOTAL	78	11	34	50	2	73	11	0	1	0	199	8.0
L	40	* Henrik Zetterberg	DET	79	22	22	44	6	8	5	1	4	0	135	16.3
C	8	Igor Larionov	DET	74	10	33	43	-7	48	5	0	3	0	50	20.0
L	96	Tomas Holmstrom	DET	74	20	20	40	11	62	12	0	2	0	109	18.3
L	18	Kirk Maltby	DET	82	14	23	37	17	91	0	4	1	0	116	12.1
C	33	Kris Draper	DET	82	14	21	35	6	82	0	1	2	0	142	9.9
L	20	Luc Robitaille	DET	81	11	20	31	4	50	3	0	0	1	148	7.4
D	15	Jason Woolley	BUF	14	0	3	3	-1	29	0	0	0	0	29	0.0
			DET	62	6	17	23	12	22	1	0	2	0	52	11.5
			TOTAL	76	6	20	26	11	51	1	0	2	0	81	7.4
R	25	Darren McCarty	DET	73	13	9	22	10	138	1	0	2	0	129	10.1
D	11	Mathieu Dandenault	DET	74	4	15	19	25	64	1	0	0	0	74	5.4
D	24	Chris Chelios	DET	66	2	17	19	4	78	0	1	1	0	92	2.2
C	21	Boyd Devereaux	DET	61	3	9	12	4	16	0	0	1	0	72	4.2
D	55	* Dmitri Bykov	DET	71	2	10	12	1	43	1	0	0	0	58	3.4
C	19	Steve Yzerman	DET	16	2	6	8	6	8	1	0	1	0	13	15.4
D	27	Patrick Boileau	DET	25	2	6	8	0	14	0	0	1	0	18	11.1
C	29	* Jason Williams	DET	16	3	3	6	3	2	1	0	1	0	20	15.0
D	2	Jiri Fischer	DET	15	1	5	6	0	16	0	0	0	0	19	5.3
D	3	* Jesse Wallin	DET	32	0	1	1	-2	19	0	0	0	0	23	0.0
R	23	Stacy Roest	DET	2	0	0	0	0	0	0	0	0	0	2	0.0

Goaltending

No.	Goaltender	GPI	Mins	Avg	W	L	T	EN	SO	GA	SA	S%	G	A	PIM
34	Manny Legace	25	1406	2.18	14	5	4	1	0	51	681	.925	0	1	2
31	Curtis Joseph	61	3566	2.49	34	19	6	3	5	148	1676	.912	0	0	4
	Totals	82	4993	2.44	48	24	10	4	5	203	2361	.914			

Playoffs

Pos	#	Player	Team	GP	G	A	Pts	+/−	PIM	PP	SH	GW	GT	S	%
C	91	Sergei Fedorov	DET	4	1	2	3	-1	2	0	0	0	0	14	7.1
L	14	Brendan Shanahan	DET	4	1	1	2	-1	4	1	0	0	0	17	5.9
L	96	Tomas Holmstrom	DET	4	1	1	2	-1	4	1	0	0	0	7	14.3
D	5	Nicklas Lidstrom	DET	4	0	2	2	-1	0	0	0	0	0	15	0.0
L	20	Luc Robitaille	DET	4	1	0	1	1	0	0	0	0	0	12	8.3
D	15	Jason Woolley	DET	4	1	0	1	-2	0	0	0	0	0	3	33.3
L	40	* Henrik Zetterberg	DET	4	1	0	1	-4	0	0	0	0	0	10	10.0
R	17	Brett Hull	DET	4	0	1	1	-4	0	0	0	0	0	15	0.0
C	8	Igor Larionov	DET	4	0	1	1	-1	0	0	0	0	0	6	0.0
C	19	Steve Yzerman	DET	4	0	1	1	0	2	0	0	0	0	10	0.0
D	24	Chris Chelios	DET	4	0	0	0	-3	2	0	0	0	0	4	0.0
C	33	Kris Draper	DET	4	0	0	0	-2	4	0	0	0	0	8	0.0
D	23	Mathieu Schneider	DET	4	0	0	0	-4	6	0	0	0	0	12	0.0
R	25	Darren McCarty	DET	4	0	0	0	-3	6	0	0	0	0	9	0.0
L	18	Kirk Maltby	DET	4	0	0	0	-2	4	0	0	0	0	7	0.0
D	11	Mathieu Dandenault	DET	4	0	0	0	-1	2	0	0	0	0	9	0.0
C	13	Pavel Datsyuk	DET	4	0	0	0	-4	2	0	0	0	0	5	0.0
D	55	* Dmitri Bykov	DET	4	0	0	0	-2	0	0	0	0	0	4	0.0

Goaltending

No.	Goaltender	GPI	Mins	Avg	W	L	EN	SO	GA	SA	S%	G	A	PIM
31	Curtis Joseph	4	289	2.08	0	4	0	0	10	120	.917	0	0	0
	Totals	4	290	2.07	0	4	0	0	10	120	.917			

Coaching History

Art Duncan, 1926-27; Jack Adams, 1927-28 to 1946-47; Tommy Ivan, 1947-48 to 1953-54; Jimmy Skinner, 1954-55 to 1956-57; Jimmy Skinner and Sid Abel, 1957-58; Sid Abel, 1958-59 to 1967-68; Bill Gadsby, 1968-69; Bill Gadsby and Sid Abel, 1969-70; Ned Harkness and Doug Barkley, 1970-71; Doug Barkley and Johnny Wilson, 1971-72; Johnny Wilson, 1972-73; Ted Garvin and Alex Delvecchio, 1973-74; Alex Delvecchio, 1974-75; Doug Barkley and Alex Delvecchio, 1975-76; Alex Delvecchio and Larry Wilson, 1976-77; Bobby Kromm, 1977-78, 1978-79; Bobby Kromm and Ted Lindsay, 1979-80; Ted Lindsay and Wayne Maxner, 1980-81; Wayne Maxner and Billy Dea, 1981-82; Nick Polano, 1982-83 to 1984-85; Harry Neale and Brad Park, 1985-86; Jacques Demers, 1986-87 to 1989-90; Bryan Murray, 1990-91 to 1992-93; Scotty Bowman, 1993-94 to 1997-98; Dave Lewis, Barry Smith (co-coaches) and Scotty Bowman, 1998-99; Scotty Bowman, 1999-2000 to 2001-02; Dave Lewis, 2002-03 to date.

Club Records

Team

(Figures in brackets for season records are games played; records for fewest points, wins, ties, losses, goals, goals against are for 70 or more games)

Most Points 131 1995-96 (82)
Most Wins *62 1995-96 (82)
Most Ties 18 1952-53 (70), 1980-81 (80), 1996-97 (82)
Most Losses 57 1985-86 (80)
Most Goals 369 1992-93 (84)
Most Goals Against 415 1985-86 (80)
Fewest Points 40 1985-86 (80)
Fewest Wins 16 1976-77 (80)
Fewest Ties 4 1966-67 (70)
Fewest Losses 13 1950-51 (70), 1995-96 (82)
Fewest Goals 167 1958-59 (70)
Fewest Goals Against 132 1953-54 (70)
Longest Winning Streak
Overall .... 9 Mar. 3-21/51, Feb. 27-Mar. 20/55, Dec. 12-31/95, Mar. 3-22/96
Home .... 14 Jan. 21-Mar. 25/65
Away .... 7 Mar. 25-Apr. 14/95, Feb. 18-Mar. 20/96
Longest Undefeated Streak
Overall .... 15 Nov. 27-Dec. 28/52 (8 wins, 7 ties)
Home .... 19 Dec. 31/00-Apr.7/01 (17 wins, 2 ties)
Away .... 15 Oct. 18-Dec. 20/51 (10 wins, 5 ties)
Longest Losing Streak
Overall .... 14 Feb. 24-Mar. 25/82
Home .... 7 Feb. 20-Mar. 25/82
Away .... 14 Oct. 19-Dec. 21/66
Longest Winless Streak
Overall .... 19 Feb. 26-Apr. 3/77 (18 losses, 1 tie)
Home .... 10 Dec. 11/85-Jan. 18/86 (9 losses, 1 tie)
Away .... 26 Dec. 15/76-Apr. 3/77 (23 losses, 3 ties)
Most Shutouts, Season 13 1953-54 (70)
Most. PIM, Season 2,393 1985-86 (80)
Most Goals, Game .... 15 Jan. 23/44 (NYR 0 at Det. 15)

Individual

Most Seasons .... 25 Gordie Howe
Most Games .... 1,687 Gordie Howe
Most Goals, Career .... 786 Gordie Howe
Most Assists, Career .... 1,023 Gordie Howe
Most Points, Career .... 1,809 Gordie Howe (786G, 1,023A)
Most PIM, Career .... 2,090 Bob Probert
Most Shutouts, Career .... 85 Terry Sawchuk
Longest Consecutive Games Streak .... 548 Alex Delvecchio (Dec. 13/56-Nov. 11/64)
Most Goals, Season .... 65 Steve Yzerman (1988-89)
Most Assists, Season .... 90 Steve Yzerman (1988-89)
Most Points, Season .... 155 Steve Yzerman (1988-89; 65G, 90A)
Most PIM, Season .... 398 Bob Probert (1987-88)
Most Points, Defenseman, Season .... 77 Paul Coffey (1993-94; 14G, 63A)
Most Points, Center, Season .... 155 Steve Yzerman (1988-89; 65G, 90A)
Most Points, Right Wing, Season .... 103 Gordie Howe (1968-69; 44G, 59A)
Most Points, Left Wing, Season .... 105 John Ogrodnick (1984-85; 55G, 50A)
Most Points, Rookie, Season .... 87 Steve Yzerman (1983-84; 39G, 48A)
Most Shutouts, Season .... 12 Terry Sawchuk (1951-52, 1953-54, 1954-55), Glenn Hall (1955-56)
Most Goals, Game .... 6 Syd Howe (Feb. 3/44)
Most Assists, Game .... *7 Billy Taylor (Mar. 16/47)
Most Points, Game .... 7 Carl Liscombe (Nov. 5/42; 3G, 4A), Don Grosso (Feb. 3/44; 1G, 6A), Billy Taylor (Mar. 16/47; 7A)

* NHL Record.

Retired Numbers

1	Terry Sawchuk	1949-55, 57-64, 68-69
7	Ted Lindsay	1944-57, 64-65
9	Gordie Howe	1946-1971
10	Alex Delvecchio	1951-1973
12	Sid Abel	1938-43, 45-52

All-time Record vs. Other Clubs

Regular Season

	At Home								On Road								Total							
	GP	W	L	T	OL	GF	GA	PTS	GP	W	L	T	OL	GF	GA	PTS	GP	W	L	T	OL	GF	GA	PTS
Anaheim	20	15	2	3	0	73	46	33	20	11	6	3	0	57	42	25	40	26	8	6	0	130	88	58
Atlanta	3	3	0	0	0	11	3	6	3	3	0	0	0	19	7	6	6	6	0	0	0	30	10	12
Boston	284	154	78	52	0	952	717	360	286	90	153	43	0	760	1005	223	570	244	231	95	0	1712	1722	583
Buffalo	55	32	18	5	0	203	159	69	51	10	33	8	0	146	224	28	106	42	51	13	0	349	383	97
Calgary	57	30	17	10	0	212	169	70	58	18	34	6	0	174	227	42	115	48	51	16	0	386	396	112
Carolina	30	17	7	6	0	115	82	40	29	11	17	1	0	82	103	23	59	28	24	7	0	197	185	63
Chicago	332	200	98	33	1	1134	829	434	335	131	151	51	2	944	1005	315	667	331	249	84	3	2078	1834	749
Colorado	38	23	14	1	0	138	115	47	40	16	20	4	0	136	145	36	78	39	34	5	0	274	260	83
Columbus	7	6	1	0	0	29	16	12	8	6	1	1	0	19	14	13	15	12	2	1	0	48	30	25
Dallas	104	51	37	16	0	399	336	118	104	36	51	17	0	311	366	89	208	87	88	33	0	710	702	207
Edmonton	42	23	15	3	1	163	144	50	42	14	19	8	1	150	163	37	84	37	34	11	2	313	307	87
Florida	7	3	1	3	0	26	20	9	9	6	1	2	0	27	17	14	16	9	2	5	0	53	37	23
Los Angeles	77	34	30	13	0	294	267	81	78	22	41	14	1	237	315	59	155	56	71	27	1	531	582	140
Minnesota	6	4	2	0	0	25	15	8	6	3	1	1	1	15	15	8	12	7	3	1	1	40	30	16
Montreal	280	130	97	53	0	805	717	313	281	67	171	43	0	635	992	177	561	197	268	96	0	1440	1709	490
Nashville	14	11	0	2	1	57	32	25	13	6	4	2	1	38	33	15	27	17	4	4	2	95	65	40
New Jersey	39	24	13	2	0	159	127	50	40	10	21	9	0	103	138	29	79	34	34	11	0	262	265	79
NY Islanders	44	25	17	2	0	159	135	52	46	19	23	4	0	137	164	42	90	44	40	6	0	296	299	94
NY Rangers	285	164	76	45	0	1004	699	373	283	92	133	58	0	737	865	242	568	256	209	103	0	1741	1564	615
Ottawa	9	6	3	0	0	33	19	12	9	5	3	1	0	26	26	11	18	11	6	1	0	59	45	23
Philadelphia	58	30	18	10	0	206	180	70	58	13	34	11	0	168	230	37	116	43	52	21	0	374	410	107
Phoenix	49	24	18	7	0	192	165	55	47	18	16	13	0	150	143	49	96	42	34	20	0	342	308	104
Pittsburgh	65	40	13	12	0	253	178	92	64	17	43	4	0	192	277	38	129	57	56	16	0	445	455	130
St. Louis	107	50	40	17	0	392	328	117	107	32	54	19	2	299	368	85	214	82	94	36	2	691	696	202
San Jose	23	20	2	1	0	97	41	41	24	14	7	3	0	97	76	31	47	34	9	4	0	194	117	72
Tampa Bay	11	10	1	0	0	46	20	20	14	9	4	1	0	61	43	19	25	19	5	1	0	107	63	39
Toronto	322	168	106	46	2	968	792	384	315	105	163	47	0	844	1040	257	637	273	269	93	2	1812	1832	641
Vancouver	64	39	16	8	1	269	185	87	63	26	27	10	0	207	226	62	127	65	43	18	1	476	411	149
Washington	46	21	14	11	0	160	131	53	45	19	21	5	0	142	167	43	91	40	35	16	0	302	298	96
Defunct Clubs	141	76	40	25	0	430	307	177	141	49	63	29	0	364	375	127	282	125	103	54	0	794	682	304
Totals	**2619**	**1433**	**794**	**386**	**6**	**9004**	**6974**	**3258**	**2619**	**878**	**1315**	**418**	**8**	**7277**	**8811**	**2182**	**5238**	**2311**	**2109**	**804**	**14**	**16281**	**15785**	**5440**

Playoffs

	Series	W	L	GP	W	L	T	GF	GA	Last Mtg.	Rnd.	Result
Anaheim	3	2	1	12	8	4	0	36	24	2003	CQF	L 0-4
Boston	7	3	4	33	14	19	0	98	96	1957	SF	L 1-4
Calgary	1	1	0	2	2	0	0	8	5	1978	PRE	W 2-0
Carolina	1	1	0	5	4	1	0	14	7	2002	F	W 4-1
Chicago	14	6	8	69	31	38	0	190	210	1995	CF	W 4-1
Colorado	5	2	3	30	13	17	0	76	79	2002	CF	W 4-3
Dallas	3	3	0	18	12	6	0	55	40	1998	CF	W 4-2
Edmonton	2	0	2	10	2	8	0	26	39	1988	CF	L 1-4
Los Angeles	2	1	1	10	6	4	0	32	21	2001	CQF	L 2-4
Montreal	12	7	5	62	29	33	0	149	161	1978	QF	L 1-4
New Jersey	1	0	1	4	0	4	0	7	16	1995	F	L 0-4
NY Rangers	5	4	1	23	13	10	0	57	49	1950	F	W 4-3
Philadelphia	1	1	0	4	4	0	0	16	6	1997	F	W 4-0
Phoenix	2	2	0	12	8	4	0	44	28	1998	CQF	W 4-2
St. Louis	7	5	2	40	24	16	0	125	103	2002	CSF	W 4-1
San Jose	2	1	1	11	7	4	0	51	27	1995	CSF	W 4-0
Toronto	23	11	12	117	59	58	0	321	311	1993	DSF	L 3-4
Vancouver	1	1	0	6	4	2	0	22	16	2002	CQF	W 4-2
Washington	1	1	0	4	4	0	0	13	7	1998	F	W 4-0
Defunct Clubs	4	3	1	10	7	2	1	21	13			
Totals	**97**	**55**	**42**	**482**	**251**	**230**	**1**	**1361**	**1258**			

Playoff Results 2003-1999

Year	Round	Opponent	Result	GF	GA
2003	CQF	Anaheim	L 0-4	6	10
2002	**F**	**Carolina**	**W 4-1**	**14**	**7**
	CF	Colorado	W 4-3	22	13
	CSF	St. Louis	W 4-1	14	11
	CQF	Vancouver	W 4-2	22	16
2001	CQF	Los Angeles	L 2-4	17	15
2000	CSF	Colorado	L 1-4	8	13
	CQF	Los Angeles	W 4-0	15	6
1999	CSF	Colorado	L 2-4	14	21
	CQF	Anaheim	W 4-0	17	6

Abbreviations: Round: F - Final; **CF** - conference final; **CSF** - conference semi-final; **CQF** - conference quarter-final; **DSF** - division semi-final; **SF** - semi-final; **QF** - quarter-final; **PRE** - preliminary round.

Calgary totals include Atlanta Flames, 1972-73 to 1979-80.
Carolina totals include Hartford, 1979-80 to 1996-97.
Colorado totals include Quebec, 1979-80 to 1994-95.
Dallas totals include Minnesota North Stars, 1967-68 to 1992-93.
New Jersey totals include Kansas City, 1974-75 to 1975-76, and Colorado Rockies, 1976-77 to 1981-82.
Phoenix totals include Winnipeg, 1979-80 to 1995-96.

2002-03 Results

Month	Day	Opponent	Score	Month	Day	Opponent	Score
Oct.	10	at San Jose	6-3		8	at Florida	2-1*
	12	at Los Angeles	2-3		11	at Philadelphia	2-3
	13	at Anaheim	4-2		13	Chicago	5-4*
	17	Montreal	2-3		15	at Chicago	1-4
	19	at Minnesota	5-3		16	at Colorado	4-2
	21	Calgary	4-0		19	Vancouver	1-4
	23	Los Angeles	3-3		22	at Edmonton	3-4*
	25	Pittsburgh	7-3		24	at Vancouver	5-2
	26	at Nashville	1-3		25	at Calgary	1-4
	29	San Jose	3-2		28	at New Jersey	0-1
Nov.	2	at Ottawa	2-5		30	Florida	2-2
	3	Dallas	3-3	**Feb.**	4	Nashville	5-5
	5	Chicago	0-2		6	Colorado	0-1
	7	Boston	2-1*		8	at Colorado	3-5
	12	Nashville	4-1		10	San Jose	5-4
	15	Anaheim	2-1*		13	Buffalo	4-2
	16	at Toronto	2-1		15	at Atlanta	6-2
	19	at Calgary	5-0		18	Vancouver	3-4*
	22	at Vancouver	1-4		20	Edmonton	6-2
	23	at Edmonton	1-1		22	at Washington	5-1
	25	Edmonton	4-5*		24	Los Angeles	5-4
	27	New Jersey	3-2*		27	Toronto	7-2
	29	at Carolina	4-6	**Mar.**	2	Phoenix	5-2
Dec.	1	Calgary	4-2		3	at Columbus	3-2
	3	Anaheim	2-1		5	Tampa Bay	3-2
	5	at Phoenix	5-3		7	St. Louis	7-2
	6	at Dallas	3-3		9	at Anaheim	1-4
	8	St. Louis	4-3*		10	at Los Angeles	3-2
	12	Minnesota	2-3		12	at Phoenix	3-2
	14	Columbus	6-4		15	Colorado	5-3
	17	at NY Islanders	2-2		16	Ottawa	6-2
	19	Dallas	1-1		18	at Pittsburgh	5-1
	21	NY Rangers	3-2		22	at St. Louis	4-2
	23	at Columbus	1-0		23	at Minnesota	0-4
	26	Columbus	4-2		25	Minnesota	4-0
	28	at Nashville	4-2		27	at San Jose	0-3
	29	at Dallas	2-2		29	at St. Louis	6-2
	31	St. Louis	5-1		31	Nashville	3-0
Jan.	3	Phoenix	1-4	**Apr.**	3	NY Islanders	5-2
	5	at Chicago	4-3*		4	at Columbus	5-5
	7	at Tampa Bay	0-1		6	at Chicago	3-4*

* – Overtime

Entry Draft
Selections 2003-1989

2003	1999	1995	1991
Pick	**Pick**	**Pick**	**Pick**
64 James Howard	120 Jari Tolsa	26 Maxim Kuznetsov	10 Martin Lapointe
132 Kyle Quincey	149 Andrei Maximenko	52 Philippe Audet	32 Jamie Pushor
164 Ryan Oulahen	181 Kent McDonell	58 Darryl Laplante	54 Chris Osgood
170 Andreas Sundin	210 Henrik Zetterberg	104 Anatoli Ustyugov	76 Mike Knuble
194 Stefan Blom	238 Anton Borodkin	125 Chad Wilchynski	98 Dimitri Motkov
226 Tomas Kollar	266 Ken Davis	126 David Arsenault	142 Igor Malykhin
258 Vladimir Kutny		156 Tyler Perry	186 Jim Bermingham
289 Mikael Johansson	**1998**	182 Per Eklund	208 Jason Firth
	Pick	208 Andrei Samokhvalov	230 Bart Turner
2002	25 Jiri Fischer	234 David Engblom	252 Andrew Miller
Pick	55 Ryan Barnes		
58 Jiri Hudler	56 Tomek Valtonen	**1994**	**1990**
63 Tomas Fleischmann	84 Jake McCracken	**Pick**	**Pick**
95 Valtteri Filppula	111 Brent Hobday	23 Yan Golubovsky	3 Keith Primeau
131 Johan Berggren	142 Calle Steen	49 Mathieu Dandenault	45 Vyacheslav Kozlov
166 Logan Koopmans	151 Adam DeLeeuw	75 Sean Gillam	66 Stewart Malgunas
197 James Cuddihy	171 Pavel Datsyuk	114 Frederic Deschenes	87 Tony Burns
229 Derek Meech	198 Jeremy Goetzinger	127 Doug Battaglia	108 Claude Barthe
260 Pierre-Olivier Beaulieu	226 David Petrasek	153 Pavel Agarkov	129 Jason York
262 Christian Soderstrom	256 Petja Pietilainen	205 Jason Elliot	150 Wes McCauley
291 Jonathan Ericsson		231 Jeff Mikesch	171 Anthony Gruba
	1997	257 Tomas Holmstrom	192 Travis Tucker
2001	**Pick**	283 Toivo Suursoo	213 Brett Larson
Pick	49 Yuri Butsayev		234 John Hendry
62 Igor Grigorenko	76 Petr Sykora	**1993**	
121 Drew MacIntyre	102 Quintin Laing	**Pick**	**1989**
129 Miroslav Blatak	129 John Wikstrom	5 Benoit Larose	**Pick**
157 Andreas Jamtin	157 B.J. Young	22 Anders Eriksson	11 Mike Sillinger
195 Nick Pannoni	186 Mike Laceby	48 Jon Coleman	32 Bob Boughner
258 Dmitri Bykov	213 Steve Willejto	74 Kevin Hilton	53 Nicklas Lidstrom
288 Francois Senez	239 Greg Willers	97 John Jakopin	74 Sergei Fedorov
		126 Norm Maracle	95 Shawn McCosh
2000	**1996**	152 Tim Spitzig	116 Dallas Drake
Pick	**Pick**	178 Yuri Yeresko	137 Scott Zygulski
29 Niklas Kronwall	26 Jesse Wallin	204 Vitezslav Skuta	158 Andy Suhy
38 Tomas Kopecky	52 Aren Miller	230 Ryan Shanahan	179 Bob Jones
102 Stefan Liv	108 Johan Forsander	256 James Kosecki	200 Greg Bignell
127 Dmitri Semenov	135 Michal Podolka	282 Gordon Hunt	204 Rick Judson
128 Alexander Seluyanov	144 Magnus Nilsson		221 Vladimir Konstantinov
130 Aaron Van Leusen	162 Alexandre Jacques	**1992**	242 Joseph Frederick
187 Per Backer	189 Colin Beardsmore	**Pick**	246 Jason Glickman
196 Paul Ballantyne	215 Craig Stahl	22 Curtis Bowen	
228 Jimmie Svensson	241 Eugeny Afanasiev	46 Darren McCarty	
251 Todd Jackson		70 Sylvain Cloutier	
260 Yevgeny Bumagin		118 Mike Sullivan	
		142 Jason MacDonald	
		166 Greg Scott	
		183 Justin Krall	
		189 C. J. Denomme	
		214 Jeff Walker	
		238 Dan McGillis	
		262 Ryan Bach	

Club Directory

Joe Louis Arena

Detroit Red Wings
Joe Louis Arena
600 Civic Center Drive
Detroit, MI 48226
Phone **313/396-7544**
FAX PR: 313/567-0296
Media Hotline: 313/396-7599
www.detroitredwings.com
Capacity: 20,058

Owner/Governor	Mike Ilitch
Owner/Secretary-Treasurer	Marian Ilitch
Senior Vice-President/Alternate Governor	Jim Devellano
Vice-President, Red Wings/President, Ilitch Holdings, Inc./Alternate Governor	Christopher Ilitch
President, Ilitch Holdings, Inc./Alternate Governor	Denise Ilitch
General Counsel	Rob Carr
General Manager/Alternate Governor	Ken Holland
Assistant General Manager	Jim Nill
Head Coach	Dave Lewis
Associate Coach	Barry Smith
Assistant Coach	Joe Kocur
Consultant	Scotty Bowman
Goaltending Coach	Jim Bedard
NHL Scout	Dan Belisle
NHL Scout	Mark Howe
NHL Scout	Bob McCammon
Amateur Scout	Glenn Merkosky
Amateur Scout	Joe McDonnell
Amateur Scout	Bruce Haralson
Amateur Scout	Mark Leach
Part-Time Scout	Marty Stein
Director of European Scouting	Hakan Andersson
European Scout	Vladimir Havluj
Part-Time European Scout	Evgeni Erfilov
Vice-President of Finance	Paul MacDonald
Executive Assistant	Nancy Beard
Administrative and Scouting Coordinator	David Kolb
Accounting Assistant	Bridget Merritt
Athletic Therapist	Piet Van Zant
Assistant Athletic Therapist	Russ Baumann
Equipment Manager	Paul Boyer
Assistant Equipment Manager	Tim Abbott
Team Masseur	Sergei Tchekmarev
Senior Director of Communications	John Hahn
Media Relations Manager	Michael Kuta
Community Relations Manager	Anne Marie Krappmann
Team Photographer	Steve Kovich
Medical Director	David Collon, M.D.
Team Physician	Anthony Colucci, D.O., F.A.C.E.P.
Team Dentist	C.J. Regula, D.M.D.
Radio Broadcasters, AM 1270 - WXYT	Ken Kal, Paul Woods
Television Broadcasters, FOX Sports Net Detroit	Ken Daniels, Mickey Redmond

General Manager

HOLLAND, KEN
General Manager, Detroit Red Wings. Born in Vernon, B.C., Nov. 10, 1955.
Ken Holland is entering his seventh season as a general manager and his 21st year with the Red Wings organization. In his six seasons as Detroit's general manager, Holland has established himself as one of the most innovative and aggressive GMs in the National Hockey League. Detroit's Stanley Cup victory in 2002 marked the team's second championship under his leadership. Holland began his tenure as the club's general manager after serving as assistant general manager for the previous three seasons. He was elevated to his present position July 18, 1997.

Holland oversees all aspects of hockey operations including all matters relating to player personnel, development, contract negotiations and player movements. He also continues to be Detroit's point person at the NHL Entry Draft, as he has been for the past 13 years.

Holland has deftly handled several different front-office duties for the club over the past 20 years. At the conclusion of his playing days as a goaltender, spending most of his pro career at the American Hockey League level, Holland began his off-ice career in 1985 as a western Canada scout followed by five years as an amateur scouting director before promotions led to his current position as general manager.

A native of Vernon, BC, Holland played in the junior ranks for Medicine Hat (WHL) in 1974-75. He was Toronto's 13th pick (188th overall) in the 1975 draft but never saw action with the Maple Leafs. Holland twice signed with NHL teams as a free agent — in 1980 with Hartford and 1983 with Detroit. He spent most of his pro career with AHL clubs in Binghamton and Springfield, along with Adirondack, but did appear in four NHL games, making his debut with Hartford in 1980-81 and playing three contests for Detroit in 1983-84.

General Managers' History

Art Duncan and Duke Keats, 1926-27; Jack Adams, 1927-28 to 1961-62; Sid Abel, 1962-63 to 1969-70; Sid Abel and Ned Harkness, 1970-71; Ned Harkness, 1971-72 to 1973-74; Alex Delvecchio, 1974-75, 1975-76; Alex Delvecchio and Ted Lindsay, 1976-77; Ted Lindsay, 1977-78 to 1979-80; Jimmy Skinner, 1980-81, 1981-82; Jim Devellano, 1982-83 to 1989-90; Bryan Murray, 1990-91 to 1993-94; Jim Devellano (Senior Vice President), 1994-95 to 1996-97; Ken Holland, 1997-98 to date.

Captains' History

Art Duncan, 1926-27; Reg Noble, 1927-28 to 1929-30; George Hay, 1930-31; Carson Cooper, 1931-32; Larry Aurie, 1932-33; Herbie Lewis, 1933-34; Ebbie Goodfellow, 1934-35; Doug Young, 1935-36 to 1937-38; Ebbie Goodfellow, 1938-39 to 1940-41; Ebbie Goodfellow and Syd Howe, 1941-42; Sid Abel, 1942-43; Mud Bruneteau, Flash Hollett (co-captains), 1943-44; Flash Hollett, 1944-45; Flash Hollett and Sid Abel, 1945-46; Sid Abel, 1946-47 to 1951-52; Ted Lindsay, 1952-53 to 1955-56; Red Kelly, 1956-57, 1957-58; Gordie Howe, 1958-59 to 1961-62; Alex Delvecchio, 1962-63 to 1972-73; Alex Delvecchio, Nick Libett, Red Berenson, Gary Bergman, Ted Harris, Mickey Redmond and Larry Johnston, 1973-74; Marcel Dionne, 1974-75; Danny Grant and Terry Harper, 1975-76; Danny Grant and Dennis Polonich, 1976-77; Dan Maloney and Dennis Hextall, 1977-78; Dennis Hextall, Nick Libett and Paul Woods, 1978-79; Dale McCourt, 1979-80; Errol Thompson and Reed Larson, 1980-81; Reed Larson, 1981-82; Danny Gare, 1982-83 to 1985-86; Steve Yzerman, 1986-87 to date.

Edmonton Oilers

2002-03 Results: 36w-26L-11T-9OTL 92PTS.
Fourth, Northwest Division

2003-04 Schedule

Oct.	Thu.	9	San Jose	Sat.	10	at Philadelphia
	Sat.	11	at Vancouver	Sun.	11	at Washington
	Tue.	14	at Calgary	Tue.	13	Florida
	Thu.	16	Buffalo	Thu.	15	Anaheim
	Sat.	18	Colorado	Sat.	17	at Nashville
	Tue.	21	St. Louis	Sun.	18	at Columbus
	Thu.	23	at Colorado	Tue.	20	Dallas
	Sat.	25	Calgary	Thu.	22	Tampa Bay
	Thu.	30	Columbus	Sat.	24	Nashville
Nov.	Sat.	1	Detroit	Tue.	27	at Colorado
	Tue.	4	at Montreal	Thu.	29	Chicago
	Thu.	6	at Ottawa	Sat.	31	Los Angeles
	Sat.	8	at Toronto	Feb. Mon.	2	Anaheim
	Mon.	10	at NY Rangers	Wed.	4	St. Louis
	Tue.	11	at Boston	Wed.	11	Atlanta
	Thu.	13	at Minnesota	Fri.	13	at Minnesota
	Sat.	15	Calgary	Sun.	15	at Nashville*
	Tue.	18	Chicago	Mon.	16	at Detroit
	Thu.	20	Toronto	Wed.	18	at Colorado
	Sat.	22	Montreal*	Sat.	21	Vancouver
	Tue.	25	at Columbus	Mon.	23	Detroit
	Wed.	26	at Detroit	Wed.	25	at Anaheim
	Fri.	28	Colorado	Fri.	27	at Phoenix
	Sun.	30	San Jose	Sun.	29	at Dallas*
Dec.	Wed.	3	Minnesota	Mar. Tue.	2	Phoenix
	Sat.	6	Pittsburgh	Thu.	4	at St. Louis
	Tue.	9	Carolina	Sun.	7	at Chicago*
	Thu.	11	at San Jose	Tue.	9	at Calgary
	Fri.	12	at Phoenix	Wed.	10	Colorado
	Sun.	14	at Anaheim*	Fri.	12	Vancouver
	Tue.	16	at Los Angeles	Sun.	14	Ottawa
	Thu.	18	Minnesota	Tue.	16	Columbus
	Sat.	20	Vancouver	Fri.	19	Nashville
	Tue.	23	at Calgary	Sun.	21	at San Jose*
	Sat.	27	at Vancouver	Mon.	22	at Los Angeles
	Sun.	28	Calgary	Wed.	24	Dallas
	Tue.	30	Minnesota	Fri.	26	Los Angeles
Jan.	Fri.	2	at Minnesota	Sun.	28	Phoenix*
	Sun.	4	at Chicago	Tue.	30	at St. Louis
	Mon.	5	at New Jersey	Wed.	31	at Dallas
	Thu.	8	at NY Islanders	Apr. Sat.	3	at Vancouver

* Denotes afternoon game.

Year-by-Year Record

		Home				Road				Overall							
Season	GP	W	L	T	OL	W	L	T	OL	W	L	T	OL	GF	GA	Pts.	Finished	Playoff Result
2002-03	82	20	12	5	4	16	14	6	5	36	26	11	9	231	230	92	4th, Northwest Div.	Lost Conf. Quarter-Final
2001-02	82	23	14	4	0	15	14	8	4	38	28	12	4	205	182	92	3rd, Northwest Div.	Out of Playoffs
2000-01	82	23	9	7	2	16	19	5	1	39	28	12	3	243	222	93	2nd, Northwest Div.	Lost Conf. Quarter-Final
1999-2000	82	18	11	9	3	14	15	7	5	32	26	16	8	226	212	88	2nd, Northwest Div.	Lost Conf. Quarter-Final
1998-99	82	17	19	5	...	16	18	7	...	33	37	12	...	230	226	78	2nd, Northwest Div.	Lost Conf. Quarter-Final
1997-98	82	20	16	5	...	15	21	5	...	35	37	10	...	215	224	80	3rd, Pacific Div.	Lost Conf. Semi-Final
1996-97	82	21	16	4	...	15	21	5	...	36	37	9	...	252	247	81	3rd, Pacific Div.	Lost Conf. Semi-Final
1995-96	82	15	21	5	...	15	23	3	...	30	44	8	...	240	304	68	5th, Pacific Div.	Out of Playoffs
1994-95	48	11	12	1	...	6	15	3	...	17	27	4	...	136	183	38	5th, Pacific Div.	Out of Playoffs
1993-94	84	17	22	3	...	8	23	11	...	25	45	14	...	261	305	64	6th, Pacific Div.	Out of Playoffs
1992-93	84	16	21	5	...	10	29	3	...	26	50	8	...	242	337	60	5th, Smythe Div.	Out of Playoffs
1991-92	80	22	13	5	...	14	21	5	...	36	34	10	...	295	297	82	3rd, Smythe Div.	Lost Conf. Championship
1990-91	80	22	15	3	...	15	22	3	...	37	37	6	...	272	272	80	3rd, Smythe Div.	Lost Conf. Championship
1989-90	**80**	**23**	**11**	**6**	...	**15**	**17**	**8**	...	**38**	**28**	**14**	...	**315**	**283**	**90**	**2nd, Smythe Div.**	**Won Stanley Cup**
1988-89	80	21	16	3	...	17	18	5	...	38	34	8	...	325	306	84	3rd, Smythe Div.	Lost Div. Semi-Final
1987-88	**80**	**28**	**8**	**4**	...	**16**	**17**	**7**	...	**44**	**25**	**11**	...	**363**	**288**	**99**	**2nd, Smythe Div.**	**Won Stanley Cup**
1986-87	**80**	**29**	**6**	**5**	...	**21**	**18**	**1**	...	**50**	**24**	**6**	...	**372**	**284**	**106**	**1st, Smythe Div.**	**Won Stanley Cup**
1985-86	80	32	6	2	...	24	11	5	...	56	17	7	...	426	310	119	1st, Smythe Div.	Lost Div. Final
1984-85	**80**	**26**	**7**	**7**	...	**23**	**13**	**4**	...	**49**	**20**	**11**	...	**401**	**298**	**109**	**1st, Smythe Div.**	**Won Stanley Cup**
1983-84	**80**	**31**	**5**	**4**	...	**26**	**13**	**1**	...	**57**	**18**	**5**	...	**446**	**314**	**119**	**1st, Smythe Div.**	**Won Stanley Cup**
1982-83	80	25	9	6	...	22	12	6	...	47	21	12	...	424	315	106	1st, Smythe Div.	Lost Final
1981-82	80	31	5	4	...	17	12	11	...	48	17	15	...	417	295	111	1st, Smythe Div.	Lost Div. Semi-Final
1980-81	80	17	13	10	...	12	22	6	...	29	35	16	...	328	327	74	4th, Smythe Div.	Lost Quarter-Final
1979-80	80	17	14	9	...	11	25	4	...	28	39	13	...	301	322	69	4th, Smythe Div.	Lost Prelim. Round

Franchise date: June 22, 1979

NORTHWEST DIVISION

25th NHL Season

With 22 goals last season, Mike York reached the 20-goal plateau for the third time in four seasons in the NHL. He was one of four Oilers to score at least 20 goals in 2002-03.

2003-04 Player Personnel

FORWARDS	HT	WT	S	Place of Birth	Date	2002-03 Club
BISHAI, Mike	5-11	185	L	Edmonton, Alta.	5/30/79	Hamilton-Columbus (ECHL)
CHIMERA, Jason	6-2	204	L	Edmonton, Alta.	5/2/79	Edmonton
COMRIE, Mike	5-9	178	L	Edmonton, Alta.	9/11/80	Edmonton
CULLEN, Joe	6-1	210	L	Virginia, MN	2/14/81	Colorado College
DiCASMIRRO, Nate	5-11	205	L	Burnsville, MN	9/27/78	Hamilton
DVORAK, Radek	6-2	200	R	Tabor, Czech.	3/9/77	NY Rangers-Edmonton
HEMSKY, Ales	6-0	192	R	Pardubice, Czech.	8/13/83	Edmonton
HENRICH, Michael	6-2	206	R	Thornhill, Ont.	3/3/80	Hamilton-Mora-Hershey
HINZ, Chad	5-10	190	R	Saskatoon, Sask.	3/21/79	Hamilton
HORCOFF, Shawn	6-1	204	L	Trail, B.C.	9/17/78	Edmonton
HUNTER, J.J.	6-1	185	L	Shaunavon, Sask.	7/6/80	Hamilton-Columbus (ECHL)
ISBISTER, Brad	6-4	220	R	Edmonton, Alta.	5/7/77	NY Islanders-Edmonton
LARAQUE, Georges	6-3	245	R	Montreal, Que.	12/7/76	Edmonton
McASLAN, Sean	6-1	190	R	Okotoks, Alta.	1/12/80	Columbus (ECHL)-Hamilton
MOREAU, Ethan	6-2	209	L	Huntsville, Ont.	9/22/75	Edmonton
NIINIMAKI, Jesse	6-2	183	L	Tampere, Finland	8/19/83	Ilves-Ilves Jr.-Sport
PISANI, Fernando	6-1	203	L	Edmonton, Alta.	12/27/76	Edmonton-Hamilton
POULIOT, Marc-Antoine	6-1	195	R	Quebec City, Que.	5/22/85	Rimouski
REASONER, Marty	6-1	190	L	Honeoye Falls, NY	2/26/77	Edmonton-Hamilton
RITA, Jani	6-1	206	L	Helsinki, Finland	7/25/81	Edmonton-Hamilton
SALMELAINEN, Tony	5-9	185	R	Espoo, Finland	8/8/81	Hamilton
SARNO, Peter	5-11	185	L	Toronto, Ont.	7/26/79	Blues Espoo
SMYTH, Ryan	6-1	190	L	Banff, Alta.	2/21/76	Edmonton
STOLL, Jarret	6-1	200	R	Melville, Sask.	6/25/82	Edmonton-Hamilton
TORRES, Raffi	6-0	210	L	Toronto, Ont.	10/8/81	NYI-Bridgeport-Hamilton
WINCHESTER, Brad	6-5	215	L	Madison, WI	3/1/81	U. of Wisconsin
WRIGHT, Jamie	6-0	195	L	Kitchener, Ont.	5/13/76	Cgy-Saint Jn-Phi-Phi (AHL)
YORK, Mike	5-10	185	R	Waterford, MI	1/3/78	Edmonton
DEFENSEMEN						
ALLEN, Bobby	6-1	205	L	Braintree, MA	11/14/78	Edmonton-Hamilton
BERGERON, Marc-Andre	5-9	190	L	St-Louis-de-France, Que.	10/13/80	Edmonton-Hamilton
BREWER, Eric	6-3	220	L	Vernon, B.C.	4/17/79	Edmonton
CROSS, Cory	6-5	220	L	Lloydminster, Alta.	1/3/71	Hartford-NY Rangers-Edmonton
FERGUSON, Scott	6-1	195	L	Camrose, Alta.	1/6/73	Edmonton
HORACEK, Jan	6-4	221	R	Benesov, Czech.	5/22/79	Liberec-Vsetin-Slavia Praha-Havirov
LUOMA, Mikko	6-3	207	L	Jyvaskyla, Finland	6/22/76	Tappara
LYNCH, Doug	6-3	214	L	North Vancouver, B.C.	4/4/83	Red Deer-Spokane
ROY, Mathieu	6-2	214	R	St-Georges, Que.	8/10/83	Val-d'Or
SEMENOV, Alexei	6-6	210	L	Murmansk, USSR	4/10/81	Edmonton-Hamilton
SMITH, Dan	6-2	200	L	Fernie, B.C.	10/19/76	Springfield
SMITH, Jason	6-3	212	R	Calgary, Alta.	11/2/73	Edmonton
STAIOS, Steve	6-1	200	R	Hamilton, Ont.	7/28/73	Edmonton
THOMPSON, Rocky	6-2	205	R	Calgary, Alta.	8/8/77	San Antonio
GOALTENDERS	HT	WT	C	Place of Birth	Date	2002-03 Club
ANTILA, Kristian	6-3	207	L	Vammala, Finland	1/10/80	Hamilton-Wichita
CONKLIN, Ty	6-0	180	L	Anchorage, AK	3/30/76	Hamilton
MORRISON, Mike	6-3	194	R	Medford, MA	7/11/79	Columbus (ECHL)
SALO, Tommy	5-11	182	L	Surahammar, Sweden	2/1/71	Edmonton
VALIQUETTE, Steve	6-5	205	L	Etobicoke, Ont.	8/20/77	Bridgeport

Coaching History
Glen Sather, 1979-80; Bryan Watson and Glen Sather, 1980-81; Glen Sather, 1981-82 to 1988-89; John Muckler, 1989-90; Ted Green, 1991-92; 1992-93; Ted Green and Glen Sather, 1993-94; George Burnett and Ron Low, 1994-95; Ron Low, 1995-96 to 1998-99; Kevin Lowe, 1999-2000; Craig MacTavish, 2000-01 to date.

Coach

MacTAVISH, CRAIG
Coach, Edmonton Oilers. Born in London, Ont., August 15, 1958.
The Edmonton Oilers named Craig MacTavish as their head coach on June 22, 2000. He became the eighth person in the club's NHL history to hold the position. MacTavish joined Kevin Lowe and Glen Sather as head coaches who were former captains of the Oilers. The team has reached the playoffs twice in his three years behind the bench.

MacTavish played for 18 seasons in the NHL, including eight-and-three-quarter campaigns with the Oilers. He was instrumental in helping his teams win four Stanley Cup titles; three with Edmonton and one with the New York Rangers. Although he was the last player in the NHL to play without a helmet, MacTavish was known for his aggressive style, combined with above average skills.

MacTavish retired as a player in 1997 and was immediately named an assistant coach with the New York Rangers. He was with the Rangers for two seasons prior to joining the Oilers' coaching staff as an assistant under Kevin Lowe in 1999-2000.

Coaching Record

			Regular Season			Playoffs		
Season	Team	Games	W	L	T	Games	W	L
2000-01	Edmonton (NHL)	82	39	31	12	6	2	4
2001-02	Edmonton (NHL)	82	38	32	12	.....	.....	.....
2002-03	Edmonton (NHL)	82	36	35	11	6	2	4
NHL Totals		**246**	**113**	**98**	**35**	**12**	**4**	**8**

2002-03 Scoring
* - rookie

Regular Season

Pos	#	Player	Team	GP	G	A	Pts	+/-	PIM	PP	SH	GW	GT	S	%
L	94	Ryan Smyth	EDM	66	27	34	61	5	67	10	0	3	1	199	13.6
C	26	Todd Marchant	EDM	77	20	40	60	13	48	7	1	3	1	146	13.7
L	16	Mike York	EDM	71	22	29	51	-8	10	7	2	4	0	177	12.4
C	89	Mike Comrie	EDM	69	20	31	51	-18	90	8	0	6	0	170	11.8
R	20	Radek Dvorak	NYR	63	6	21	27	-3	16	2	0	0	0	134	4.5
			EDM	12	4	4	8	-3	14	1	0	0	1	32	12.5
			TOTAL	75	10	25	35	-6	30	3	0	0	1	166	6.0
C	10	Shawn Horcoff	EDM	78	12	21	33	10	55	2	0	3	0	98	12.2
L	18	Ethan Moreau	EDM	78	14	17	31	-7	112	2	3	2	1	137	10.2
C	19	Marty Reasoner	EDM	70	11	20	31	19	28	2	2	0	0	102	10.8
R	83 *	Ales Hemsky	EDM	59	6	24	30	5	14	0	0	1	0	50	12.0
D	2	Eric Brewer	EDM	80	8	21	29	-11	45	1	0	1	0	147	5.4
L	15	Brad Isbister	NYI	53	10	13	23	-9	34	2	0	1	1	90	11.1
			EDM	13	3	2	5	0	9	0	0	1	0	29	10.3
			TOTAL	66	13	15	28	-9	43	2	0	2	1	119	10.9
D	24	Steve Staios	EDM	76	5	21	26	13	96	1	3	0	0	126	4.0
L	28 *	Jason Chimera	EDM	66	14	9	23	-2	36	0	1	4	1	90	15.6
R	7	Daniel Cleary	EDM	58	4	13	17	5	31	0	0	1	0	89	4.5
R	34 *	Fernando Pisani	EDM	35	8	5	13	9	10	0	1	0	0	32	25.0
R	27	Georges Laraque	EDM	64	6	7	13	-4	110	0	0	2	0	46	13.0
D	21	Jason Smith	EDM	68	4	8	12	5	64	0	0	1	0	93	4.3
C	37	Brian Swanson	EDM	44	2	10	12	-7	10	1	0	1	0	67	3.0
D	23	Cory Cross	NYR	26	0	4	4	13	16	0	0	0	0	18	0.0
			EDM	11	2	3	5	3	8	1	0	1	0	11	18.2
			TOTAL	37	2	7	9	16	24	1	0	1	0	29	6.9
D	32	Scott Ferguson	EDM	78	3	5	8	11	120	0	0	0	0	45	6.7
D	5 *	Alexei Semenov	EDM	46	1	6	7	-7	58	0	0	0	0	33	3.0
C	33	Jiri Dopita	EDM	21	1	5	6	-4	11	0	0	1	0	23	4.3
L	14 *	Jani Rita	EDM	12	3	1	4	2	0	0	0	0	0	18	16.7
D	47 *	Marc-Andre Bergeron	EDM	5	1	1	2	2	9	0	0	0	0	5	20.0
C	36 *	Jarret Stoll	EDM	4	0	1	1	-3	0	0	0	0	0	4	0.0
D	12 *	Bobby Allen	EDM	9	0	0	0	0	0	0	0	0	0	4	0.0
D	29	Kari Haakana	EDM	13	0	0	0	-2	4	0	0	0	0	2	0.0

Goaltending

No.	Goaltender	GPI	Mins	Avg	W	L	T	EN	SO	GA	SA	S%	G	A	PIM
30	Jussi Markkanen	22	1180	2.59	7	8	3	3	5	51	533	.904	0	1	2
35	Tommy Salo	65	3814	2.71	29	27	8	4	4	172	1708	.899	0	0	4
	Totals	82	5020	2.75	36	35	11	7	7	230	2248	.898			

Playoffs

Pos	#	Player	Team	GP	G	A	Pts	+/-	PIM	PP	SH	GW	GT	S	%
C	10	Shawn Horcoff	EDM	6	3	1	4	1	6	0	0	1	0	7	42.9
R	27	Georges Laraque	EDM	6	1	3	4	2	4	0	0	0	0	8	12.5
D	2	Eric Brewer	EDM	6	1	3	4	1	6	0	0	0	0	9	11.1
L	94	Ryan Smyth	EDM	6	2	0	2	-1	16	0	1	0	0	12	16.7
C	28 *	Jason Chimera	EDM	2	0	2	2	2	0	0	0	0	0	3	0.0
C	26	Todd Marchant	EDM	6	0	2	2	-1	2	0	0	0	0	5	0.0
L	16	Mike York	EDM	6	0	2	2	2	2	0	0	0	0	4	0.0
R	20	Radek Dvorak	EDM	4	1	0	1	0	0	0	0	0	0	10	10.0
C	19	Marty Reasoner	EDM	6	1	0	1	-2	1	0	0	0	0	8	12.5
R	34 *	Fernando Pisani	EDM	6	1	0	1	-2	2	0	0	0	0	8	12.5
C	89	Mike Comrie	EDM	6	1	0	1	-1	10	0	0	0	0	9	11.1
D	47 *	Marc-Andre Bergeron	EDM	1	0	1	1	1	0	0	0	0	0	3	0.0
D	23	Cory Cross	EDM	6	0	1	1	-3	20	0	0	0	0	10	0.0
L	18	Ethan Moreau	EDM	6	0	1	1	-4	16	0	0	0	0	10	0.0
L	15	Brad Isbister	EDM	6	0	1	1	-1	12	0	0	0	0	5	0.0
D	32	Scott Ferguson	EDM	6	0	0	0	0	4	0	0	0	0	7	0.0
D	24	Steve Staios	EDM	6	0	0	0	2	10	0	0	0	0	4	0.0
D	21	Jason Smith	EDM	6	0	0	0	-2	19	0	0	0	0	6	0.0
D	5 *	Alexei Semenov	EDM	6	0	0	0	-1	0	0	0	0	0	4	0.0
R	83 *	Ales Hemsky	EDM	6	0	0	0	-5	2	0	0	0	0	7	0.0

Goaltending

No.	Goaltender	GPI	Mins	Avg	W	L	EN	SO	GA	SA	S%	G	A	PIM
35	Tommy Salo	6	343	3.15	2	4	1	0	18	161	.888	0	1	0
30	Jussi Markkanen	1	14	4.29	0	0	0	1	1	12	.917	0	0	0
	Totals	6	360	3.33	2	4	1	0	20	174	.885			

Club Records

Team

(Figures in brackets for season records are games played; records for fewest points, wins, ties, losses, goals, goals against are for 70 or more games)

Most Points .... 119 — 1983-84 (80), 1985-86 (80)
Most Wins .... 57 — 1983-84 (80)
Most Ties .... 16 — 1980-81 (80), 1999-2000 (82)
Most Losses .... 50 — 1992-93 (84)
Most Goals .... *446 — 1983-84 (80)
Most Goals Against .... 337 — 1992-93 (84)
Fewest Points .... 60 — 1992-93 (84)
Fewest Wins .... 25 — 1993-94 (84)
Fewest Ties .... 5 — 1983-84 (80)
Fewest Losses .... 17 — 1981-82 (80), 1985-86 (80)
Fewest Goals .... 205 — 2001-02 (82)
Fewest Goals Against .... 182 — 2001-02 (82)
Longest Winning Streak
Overall .... 9 — Feb. 20-Mar. 13/01
Home .... 8 — Jan. 19-Feb. 22/85, Feb. 24-Apr. 2/86
Away .... 8 — Dec. 9/86-Jan. 17/87
Longest Undefeated Streak
Overall .... 15 — Oct. 11-Nov. 9/84 (12 wins, 3 ties)
Home .... 14 — Nov. 15/89-Jan. 6/90 (11 wins, 3 ties)
Away .... 9 — Jan. 17-Mar. 2/82 (6 wins, 3 ties), Nov. 23/82-Jan. 18/83 (7 wins, 2 ties)
Longest Losing Streak
Overall .... 11 — Oct. 16-Nov. 7/93
Home .... 9 — Oct. 16-Nov. 24/93
Away .... 9 — Nov. 25-Dec. 30/80
Longest Winless Streak
Overall .... 14 — Oct. 11-Nov. 7/93 (13 losses, 1 tie)
Home .... 9 — Oct. 16-Nov. 24/93 (9 losses)
Away .... 11 — Dec. 18/01-Feb. 8/02 (7 losses, 4 ties)
Most Shutouts, Season .... 8 — 1997-98 (82); 2000-01 (82); 2001-02 (82)
Most PIM, Season .... 2,173 — 1987-88 (80)
Most Goals, Game .... 13 — Nov. 19/83 (N.J. 4 at Edm. 13), Nov. 8/85 (Van. 0 at Edm. 13)

Individual

Most Seasons .... 15 — Kevin Lowe
Most Games .... 1,037 — Kevin Lowe
Most Goals, Career .... 583 — Wayne Gretzky
Most Assists, Career ..... 1,086 — Wayne Gretzky
Most Points, Career ...... 1,669 — Wayne Gretzky (583G, 1,086A)
Most PIM, Career .... 1,747 — Kelly Buchberger
Most Shutouts, Career .... 20 — Tommy Salo
Longest Consecutive Games Streak ... 519 — Craig MacTavish (Oct. 11/86-Jan. 2/93)
Most Goals, Season .... *92 — Wayne Gretzky (1981-82)
Most Assists, Season ...... *163 — Wayne Gretzky (1985-86)
Most Points, Season .... *215 — Wayne Gretzky (1985-86; 52G, 163A)
Most PIM, Season .... 286 — Steve Smith (1987-88)
Most Points, Defenseman, Season ... 138 — Paul Coffey (1985-86; 48G, 90A)
Most Points, Center, Season ... *215 — Wayne Gretzky (1985-86; 52G, 163A)
Most Points, Right Wing, Season ... 135 — Jari Kurri (1984-85; 71G, 64A)
Most Points, Left Wing, Season ... 106 — Mark Messier (1982-83; 48G, 58A)
Most Points, Rookie, Season ... 75 — Jari Kurri (1980-81; 32G, 43A)
Most Shutouts, Season .... 8 — Curtis Joseph (1997-98), Tommy Salo (2000-01)
Most Goals, Game .... 5 — Wayne Gretzky (Feb. 18/81, Dec. 30/81, Dec. 15/84, Dec. 6/87), Jari Kurri (Nov. 19/83), Pat Hughes (Feb. 3/84)
Most Assists, Game .... *7 — Wayne Gretzky (Feb. 15/80, Dec. 11/85, Feb. 14/86)
Most Points, Game .... 8 — Wayne Gretzky (Nov. 19/83; 3G, 5A), (Jan. 4/84; 4G, 4A), Paul Coffey (Mar. 14/86; 2G, 6A)

* NHL Record.

Retired Numbers

3	Al Hamilton	1972-1980
17	Jari Kurri	1980-1990
31	Grant Fuhr	1981-1991
99	Wayne Gretzky	1979-1988

Captains' History

Ron Chipperfield, 1979-80; Blair MacDonald and Lee Fogolin, Jr., 1980-81; Lee Fogolin, Jr., 1981-82, 1982-83; Wayne Gretzky, 1983-84 to 1987-88; Mark Messier, 1988-89 to 1990-91; Kevin Lowe, 1991-92; Craig MacTavish, 1992-93, 1993-94; Shayne Corson, 1994-95; Kelly Buchberger, 1995-96 to 1998-99; Doug Weight, 1999-2000, 2000-01; Jason Smith, 2001-02 to date.

All-time Record vs. Other Clubs

Regular Season

	At Home								On Road								Total							
	GP	W	L	T	OL	GF	GA	PTS	GP	W	L	T	OL	GF	GA	PTS	GP	W	L	T	OL	GF	GA	PTS
Anaheim	23	15	8	0	0	54	49	30	24	8	14	2	0	59	65	18	47	23	22	2	0	113	114	48
Atlanta	3	1	1	1	0	9	10	3	3	2	1	0	0	8	3	4	6	3	2	1	0	17	13	7
Boston	29	11	15	3	0	98	97	25	29	6	19	3	1	77	122	16	58	17	34	6	1	175	219	41
Buffalo	28	20	5	3	0	116	73	43	30	13	10	7	0	112	109	33	58	33	15	10	0	228	182	76
Calgary	78	41	26	10	1	301	258	93	78	29	41	8	0	273	320	66	156	70	67	18	1	574	578	159
Carolina	30	19	6	5	0	119	89	43	29	11	11	7	0	98	112	29	59	30	17	12	0	217	201	72
Chicago	43	20	18	5	0	155	143	45	42	14	21	7	0	144	161	35	85	34	39	12	0	299	304	80
Colorado	43	24	15	4	0	177	127	52	44	18	22	4	0	162	169	40	87	42	37	8	0	339	296	92
Columbus	6	5	1	0	0	24	12	10	6	4	1	1	0	20	13	9	12	9	2	1	0	44	25	19
Dallas	42	20	13	8	1	170	141	49	43	13	23	7	0	119	157	33	85	33	36	15	1	289	298	82
Detroit	42	20	14	8	0	163	150	48	42	16	21	3	2	144	163	37	84	36	35	11	2	307	313	85
Florida	6	3	2	1	0	20	14	7	9	2	5	2	0	24	24	6	15	5	7	3	0	44	38	13
Los Angeles	75	38	22	15	0	341	270	91	75	33	26	15	1	314	293	82	150	71	48	30	1	655	563	173
Minnesota	8	6	0	1	1	21	10	14	7	5	0	1	1	25	18	12	15	11	0	2	2	46	28	26
Montreal	34	18	16	0	0	114	109	36	29	9	16	4	0	91	103	22	63	27	32	4	0	205	212	58
Nashville	10	5	3	0	2	28	26	12	11	6	3	2	0	34	28	14	21	11	6	2	2	62	54	26
New Jersey	31	14	10	6	1	136	114	35	32	16	13	3	0	110	108	35	63	30	23	9	1	246	222	70
NY Islanders	29	16	8	5	0	107	87	37	30	7	14	9	0	108	125	23	59	23	22	14	0	215	212	60
NY Rangers	28	12	13	3	0	101	94	27	29	13	9	6	1	108	108	33	57	25	22	9	1	209	202	60
Ottawa	10	6	2	2	0	36	24	14	9	5	3	1	0	23	16	11	19	11	5	3	0	59	40	25
Philadelphia	28	14	8	6	0	98	83	34	30	8	20	2	0	82	128	18	58	22	28	8	0	180	211	52
Phoenix	70	44	20	6	0	304	228	94	69	36	26	4	3	304	279	79	139	80	46	10	3	608	507	173
Pittsburgh	29	21	7	1	0	144	95	43	30	12	14	3	1	127	117	28	59	33	21	4	1	271	212	71
St. Louis	42	22	16	4	0	152	135	48	42	16	19	6	1	152	155	39	84	38	35	10	1	304	290	87
San Jose	31	18	6	7	0	106	67	43	30	10	14	4	2	93	108	26	61	28	20	11	2	199	175	69
Tampa Bay	9	7	2	0	0	24	18	14	11	6	3	2	0	35	31	14	20	13	5	2	0	59	49	28
Toronto	42	22	13	6	1	175	136	51	36	15	19	2	0	153	150	32	78	37	32	8	1	328	286	83
Vancouver	78	48	21	7	2	349	246	105	79	37	28	12	2	312	285	88	157	85	49	19	4	661	531	193
Washington	29	15	10	4	0	120	91	34	28	9	17	2	0	93	117	20	57	24	27	6	0	213	208	54
Totals	**956**	**525**	**301**	**121**	**9**	**3762**	**2996**	**1180**	**956**	**379**	**433**	**129**	**15**	**3404**	**3587**	**902**	**1912**	**904**	**734**	**250**	**24**	**7166**	**6583**	**2082**

Playoffs

	Series	W	L	GP	W	L	T	GF	GA	Last Mtg.	Rnd.	Result
Boston	2	2	0	9	8	1	0	41	20	1990	F	W 4-1
Calgary	5	4	1	30	19	11	0	132	96	1991	DSF	W 4-3
Chicago	4	3	1	20	12	8	0	102	77	1992	CF	L 0-4
Colorado	2	1	1	12	5	7	0	30	35	1998	CQF	W 4-3
Dallas	8	2	6	42	15	27	0	104	118	2003	CQF	L 2-4
Detroit	2	2	0	10	8	2	0	39	26	1988	CF	W 4-1
Los Angeles	7	5	2	36	24	12	0	154	127	1992	DSF	W 4-2
Montreal	1	1	0	3	3	0	0	15	6	1981	PRE	W 3-0
NY Islanders	3	1	2	15	6	9	0	47	58	1984	F	W 4-1
Philadelphia	3	2	1	15	8	7	0	49	44	1987	F	W 4-3
Vancouver	2	2	0	9	7	2	0	35	20	1992	DF	W 4-2
Winnipeg	6	6	0	26	22	4	0	120	75	1990	DSF	W 4-3
Totals	**45**	**31**	**14**	**227**	**137**	**90**	**0**	**868**	**702**			

Playoff Results 2003-1999

Year	Round	Opponent	Result	GF	GA
2003	CQF	Dallas	L 2-4	11	20
2001	CQF	Dallas	L 2-4	13	16
2000	CQF	Dallas	L 1-4	11	14
1999	CQF	Dallas	L 0-4	7	11

Abbreviations: Round: F - Final; **CF** - conference final; **CQF** - conference quarter-final; **DF** - division final; **DSF** - division semi-final; **PRE** - preliminary round.

Calgary totals include Atlanta Flames, 1979-80.
Colorado totals include Quebec, 1979-80 to 1994-95.
New Jersey totals include Colorado Rockies, 1979-80 to 1981-82.
Carolina totals include Hartford, 1979-80 to 1996-97.
Dallas totals include Minnesota North Stars, 1979-80 to 1992-93.
Phoenix totals include Winnipeg, 1979-80 to 1995-96.

2002-03 Results

Oct.	10	Philadelphia	2-2		8	at Anaheim	1-0
	12	at Nashville	3-2		9	at Los Angeles	5-4
	15	at Dallas	0-3		11	Ottawa	0-2
	17	at San Jose	3-4		13	Columbus	8-5
	19	Boston	3-4		16	Los Angeles	2-0
	22	at Colorado	3-3		18	Nashville	2-3*
	24	St. Louis	1-2		20	at Calgary	3-4
	26	Anaheim	4-3		22	Detroit	4-3*
	28	Dallas	3-4*		24	Phoenix	1-5
Nov.	1	Buffalo	1-1		29	Minnesota	5-1
	3	at Chicago	4-1		30	at Vancouver	3-3
	5	at NY Rangers	2-5	Feb.	5	Anaheim	2-1
	8	at NY Islanders	2-4		7	Calgary	3-4
	9	at New Jersey	6-3		8	Chicago	0-3
	11	at Boston	1-6		11	at Toronto	5-4
	12	at Minnesota	3-2		13	at Ottawa	0-2
	15	St. Louis	5-0		15	at Montreal	2-3
	16	Los Angeles	1-4		18	at Pittsburgh	3-4*
	19	Chicago	3-1		20	at Detroit	2-6
	21	at Calgary	3-1		22	Vancouver	2-3*
	23	Detroit	1-1		23	Atlanta	3-3
	25	at Detroit	5-4*		25	at Colorado	2-4
	27	at Columbus	3-1		27	at St. Louis	1-4
	30	Colorado	1-0	Mar.	1	at Columbus	3-3
Dec.	3	Minnesota	2-1*		4	San Jose	2-1
	5	at Tampa Bay	2-3		6	at Los Angeles	2-1
	7	at Florida	4-0		7	at Anaheim	4-1
	8	at Atlanta	3-0		10	Toronto	2-3
	11	Carolina	4-1		11	at Calgary	5-2
	13	Colorado	4-3*		13	NY Islanders	2-5
	14	Vancouver	3-6		15	Dallas	4-3
	17	at Minnesota	3-4*		17	at Nashville	5-3
	19	at Colorado	1-2		20	at Phoenix	2-3*
	21	at Vancouver	3-4*		22	Washington	5-3
	26	Vancouver	2-4		23	Nashville	3-2*
	28	Toronto	3-2*		26	Phoenix	4-3
	30	at Phoenix	3-4*		28	Columbus	4-0
	31	at Dallas	1-4		30	at Chicago	4-4
Jan.	2	Minnesota	1-2*		31	at St. Louis	5-5
	4	Montreal	5-4*	Apr.	3	San Jose	3-3
	6	at San Jose	5-5		5	Calgary	1-4

* – Overtime

Entry Draft
Selections 2003-1989

2003
Pick
22	Marc-Antoine Pouliot
51	Colin McDonald
68	Jean-Francois Jacques
72	Mishail Joukov
94	Zachery Stortini
147	Kalle Olsson
154	David Rohlfs
184	Dragan Umicevic
214	Kyle Brodziak
215	Mathieu Roy
248	Josef Hrabal
278	Troy Bodie

2002
Pick
15	Jesse Niinimaki
31	Jeff Deslauriers
36	Jarret Stoll
44	Matt Greene
79	Brock Radunske
106	Ivan Koltsov
111	Jonas Almtorp
123	invalid pick
148	Glenn Fisher
181	Mikko Luoma
205	J.F. Dufort
211	Patrick Murphy
244	Dwight Helminen
245	Tomas Micka
274	Fredrik Johansson

2001
Pick
13	Ales Hemsky
43	Doug Lynch
52	Ed Caron
84	Kenny Smith
133	Jussi Markkanen
154	Jake Brenk
185	Mikael Svensk
215	Dan Baum
248	Kari Haakana
272	Ales Pisa
278	Shay Stephenson

2000
Pick
17	Alexei Mikhnov
35	Brad Winchester
83	Alexander Liubimov
113	Lou Dickenson
152	Paul Flache
184	Shaun Norrie
211	Joe Cullen
215	Matthew Lombardi
247	Jason Platt
274	Yevgeny Muratov

1999
Pick
13	Jani Rita
36	Alexei Semenov
41	Tony Salmelainen
81	Adam Hauser
91	Mike Comrie
139	Jonathan Fauteux
171	Chris Legg
199	Chris Chartier
256	Tamas Groschl

1998
Pick
13	Michael Henrich
67	Alex Henry
99	Shawn Horcoff
113	Kristian Antila
128	Paul Elliott
144	Oleg Smirnov
159	Trevor Ettinger
186	Mike Morrison
213	Christian Lefebvre
241	Maxim Spiridonov

1997
Pick
14	Michel Riesen
41	Patrick Dovigi
68	Sergei Yerkovich
94	Jonas Elofsson
121	Jason Chimera
141	Peter Sarno
176	Kevin Bolibruck
187	Chad Hinz
205	Chris Kerr
231	Alexander Fomitchev

1996
Pick
6	Boyd Devereaux
19	Matthieu Descoteaux
32	Chris Hajt
59	Tom Poti
114	Brian Urick
141	Bryan Randall
168	David Bernier
170	Brandon Lafrance
195	Fernando Pisani
221	John Hultberg

1995
Pick
6	Steve Kelly
31	Georges Laraque
57	Lukas Zib
83	Mike Minard
109	Jan Snopek
161	Martin Cerven
187	Stephen Douglas
213	Jiri Antonin

1994
Pick
4	Jason Bonsignore
6	Ryan Smyth
32	Mike Watt
53	Corey Neilson
60	Brad Symes
79	Adam Copeland
95	Jussi Tarvainen
110	Jon Gaskins
136	Terry Marchant
160	Curtis Sheptak
162	Dmitri Shulga
179	Chris Wickenheiser
185	Rob Guinn
188	Jason Reid
214	Jeremy Jablonski
266	Ladislav Benysek

1993
Pick
7	Jason Arnott
16	Nick Stajduhar
33	David Vyborny
59	Kevin Paden
60	Alexander Kerch
111	Miroslav Satan
163	Alexander Zhurik
189	Martin Bakula
215	Brad Norton
241	Oleg Maltsev
267	Ilja Byakin

1992
Pick
13	Joe Hulbig
37	Martin Reichel
61	Simon Roy
65	Kirk Maltby
96	Ralph Intranuovo
109	Joaquin Gage
157	Steve Gibson
181	Kyuin Shim
190	Colin Schmidt
205	Marko Tuomainen
253	Bryan Rasmussen

1991
Pick
12	Tyler Wright
20	Martin Rucinsky
34	Andrew Verner
56	George Breen
78	Mario Nobili
93	Ryan Haggerty
144	David Oliver
166	Gary Kitching
210	Vegar Barlie
232	Yevgeny Belosheikin
254	Juha Riihijarvi

1990
Pick
17	Scott Allison
38	Alexandre Legault
59	Joe Crowley
67	Joel Blain
101	Greg Louder
122	Keijo Sailynoja
143	Mike Power
164	Roman Mejzlik
185	Richard Zemlicka
206	Petr Korinek
227	invalid pick
248	Sami Nuutinen

1989
Pick
15	Jason Soules
36	Richard Borgo
78	Josef Beranek
92	Peter White
120	Anatoli Semenov
140	Davis Payne
141	Sergei Yashin
162	Darcy Martini
225	Roman Bozek

General Managers' History

Larry Gordon, 1979-80; Glen Sather, 1980-81 to 1999-2000; Kevin Lowe, 2000-01 to date.

Vice President and General Manager

LOWE, KEVIN
Executive Vice President/General Manager, Edmonton Oilers.
Born in Lachute, Que., April 15, 1959.

The Edmonton Oilers named Kevin Lowe as their general manager on June 9, 2000, filling the position left vacant when Glen Sather resigned on May 19th. Lowe moved into the front office after spending the 1999-2000 season as coach of the Oilers.

After a brilliant 19-year playing career with the Edmonton Oilers and New York Rangers, Kevin Lowe announced his retirement on July 30, 1998 and joined the Edmonton Oilers coaching staff. He replaced Ron Low as head coach on June 18, 1999. The team reached the playoffs that season and has qualified twice in his three seasons as general manager.

Lowe was the Oilers' first-ever draft pick when he was selected 1st overall in the 1979 NHL Entry Draft. He went on to play in 1,254 regular-season games and 214 playoff games, winning six Stanley Cup championships; the first five with Edmonton (1984, 1985, 1987, 1988, 1990) followed by a sixth title with the Rangers in 1994.

Besides being the first draft choice in Oilers history, Lowe also scored the first goal in team history on October 10, 1979. He holds the Oilers' record for most games played in both the regular season (1,037) and playoffs (172), and became the sixth captain in team history in 1990-91. He was no less a leader off the ice, becoming the only player to win the King Clancy Memorial Trophy and the Budweiser/NHL Man of the Year Award in the same season (1989-90). Both awards are presented for leadership qualities and humanitarian contributions. His work with the Edmonton Christmas Bureau has set the standard for the Oilers' commitment to community involvement.

NHL Coaching Record

Season	Team	Games	Regular Season W	L	T	Playoffs Games	W	L
1999-2000	Edmonton	82	32	34	16	5	1	4
	NHL Totals	**82**	**32**	**34**	**16**	**5**	**1**	**4**

Club Directory

Skyreach Centre

Edmonton Oilers
11230 – 110 Street
Edmonton, Alberta T5G 3H7
Phone **780/414-4000**
Press Box 780/414-4235
Ticketing 780/414-4400
Media Lounge 780/414-4173
FAX 780/414-4659
www.edmontonoilers.com
Capacity: 16,839

Owner	Edmonton Investors Group Ltd.
Governor	Cal Nichols
Alternate Governors	Patrick R. LaForge, Kevin Lowe and Bill Butler
President and Chief Executive Officer	Patrick R. LaForge
Executive Vice-President and General Manager	Kevin Lowe
Vice-President, Hockey Operations	Kevin Prendergast
Assistant General Manager	Scott Howson
Head Coach	Craig MacTavish
Assistant Coaches	Charlie Huddy, Bill Moores, Craig Simpson
Goaltending Coach	Pete Peeters
Video Coach	Brian Ross
European Scout/Development Coach	Frank Musil
Vice President, Public Relations	Bill Tuele
Information Coordinator	Steve Knowles
Public Relations Coordinator, Hockey	J.J. Hebert
Dir. of Research, Analysis & Software Dev.	Sean Draper
Scouting Staff	Bob Brown, Bill Dandy, Brad Davis, Lorne Davis, Morey Gare, Stu MacGregor, Bob Mancini, Chris McCarthy, Kent Nilsson, Dave Semenko, John Stevenson
Executive Assistant to the President	Donna Perman
Executive Assistant to the General Manager	Valerie Rendell
Security Advisor	Gary Goulet

Medical and Training Staff
Head Medical Trainer	Ken Lowe
Assistant Medical Trainer	Ryan McInnes
Head Equipment Manager	Barrie Stafford
Equipment Manager	Lyle Kulchisky
Assistant Equipment Manager	Jeff Lang
Massage Therapist	Stewart Poirier
Team Medical Chief of Staff/Director of Glen Sather Sports Medicine Clinic	Dr. David C. Reid
Team Physicians	Dr. John Clarke
Team Dermatologist	Dr. Don Groot
Team Dentists	Dr. Ben Eastwood, Dr. Tony Sneazwell
Fitness Consultants	Dr. Art Quinney, Dr. Gordon Bell
Physical Therapy Consultant	Dr. Dave Magee
Team Optometrist	Dr. Brent Saik
Strength and Conditioning Consultant	Daryl Duke

Finance and Administration
Vice-President of Finance and CFO	Darryl Boessenkool
Controller	Jason Quilley
Facilities Manager	Craig Tkachuk
Senior Accounting Manager	Colleen Rolston
Legal	Antoinette Mongillo
IT Manager	Terry Rhoades
IT Administrators	Rod Pruden, Tuan Nguyen
Payroll and Human Resource Manager	Michelle Schwendeman
Payroll Manager	Shawna Quigley
Financial Staff	Donna Chizen, Corinne McGregor, Trisha Rendflesh, Sherry Smith and Cheryl Thomas

Marketing and Communications
Vice-President, Marketing and Communications	Allan Watt
Director, Corp. Communications and Marketing	Natalie Minckler
Marketing Coordinators	Darren Krill, Stacey Brockhoff
Director of Broadcast	Don Metz
Game Night	Glenn Wiun, Marilyn Riddell
Director, Licensing and Merchandising	Nick Wilson
Manager, New Media and Website	Andreas Schwabe
Publications Coordinator	Steve Sandor
Receptionist	Lisa Saskiw

Community Relations
Director Community Relations and Executive Director, Edmonton Oilers Community Foundation	Gillian Andries
Community Relations Coordinators	Heidi Lippert, Christopher Field
ICE School Coordinator	Sandy VanRiper

Sales
Director of Sales	Eric Upton

Sponsorships Sales
Manager, Corporate Sponsorships	Brad MacGregor
National Accounts Managers	Matt Cummings, Michael Lake and Sean Price
Sponsorship Coordinators	Kristie Brown, Connie Lloyd

Suite Sales
Manager, Luxury Suite Operations	Bob Haromy
Suite Coordinator	Chella Barott

Ticket Sales
Director of Ticket Sales	Ken Brown
Ticket Sales Department Coordinator	Erin Lewyk
Corporate Account Executives	Damon Bunting, Scott Jacques, Randy Keller and Jeff Tetz
Group Account Executive	Janice Wimberly
Inside Sales Representatives	Brad Bistritz and Jamie Schenknecht
Credit	Deborah Barnes, Candace Lega
Payroll Deduction Clerk/Group Sales Assistant	Krista Keen

Ticket Operations
Box Office Manager	Christine Dmytryshyn
Customer Service Coordinator	Layna Mulligan
Ticketing Services Representatives	Chris Gosse, Sandy Langley, Sheila McCaskill and Jaclyn Wilkie

Team Information
Training Camp Site	Skyreach Centre; Edmonton, Alberta and Millennium Place; Sherwood Park, Alberta
Television Outlets	Sportsnet, CBXT TV and TSN
Radio Flagship Station	630 CHED (AM); Rod Phillips (Play-by-play) and Morley Scott (colour)

Florida Panthers

2002-03 Results: 24W-36L-13T-9OTL 70PTS.
Fourth, Southeast Division

2003-04 Schedule

Oct.	Thu.	9	Carolina		Thu.	8	at Philadelphia
	Sat.	11	Boston		Sat.	10	at Calgary
	Mon.	13	at Carolina		Sun.	11	at Vancouver
	Wed.	15	Phoenix		Tue.	13	at Edmonton
	Sat.	18	at NY Islanders		Sat.	17	Tampa Bay
	Mon.	20	at NY Rangers		Mon.	19	St. Louis*
	Wed.	22	at New Jersey		Wed.	21	Colorado
	Fri.	24	Minnesota		Fri.	23	Washington
	Sat.	25	at Atlanta		Sat.	24	at Boston
	Wed.	29	at Philadelphia		Mon.	26	at NY Rangers
	Thu.	30	at Ottawa		Wed.	28	Philadelphia
Nov.	Sat.	1	San Jose		Sat.	31	at NY Islanders
	Wed.	5	Los Angeles	Feb.	Tue.	3	at San Jose
	Fri.	7	Pittsburgh		Wed.	4	at Phoenix
	Sat.	8	at St. Louis		Tue.	10	Montreal
	Tue.	11	Tampa Bay		Thu.	12	Pittsburgh
	Thu.	13	at New Jersey		Sat.	14	at Tampa Bay
	Sat.	15	at Pittsburgh		Mon.	16	at Carolina
	Sun.	16	at Atlanta*		Wed.	18	at Buffalo
	Wed.	19	NY Islanders		Fri.	20	at Pittsburgh
	Fri.	21	Atlanta		Sat.	21	at Washington
	Sat.	22	at Washington		Mon.	23	at Boston
	Mon.	24	Buffalo		Wed.	25	Toronto
	Wed.	26	NY Rangers		Fri.	27	Washington
	Fri.	28	at Buffalo		Sun.	29	at Chicago*
	Sat.	29	at Montreal	Mar.	Tue.	2	at Washington
Dec.	Wed.	3	Ottawa		Wed.	3	New Jersey
	Sat.	6	Atlanta		Sat.	6	Tampa Bay
	Wed.	10	Boston		Tue.	9	at Toronto
	Fri.	12	Montreal		Thu.	11	at Montreal
	Sat.	13	at Nashville		Sat.	13	NY Rangers
	Mon.	15	at Detroit		Wed.	17	NY Islanders
	Wed.	17	Washington		Fri.	19	at Atlanta
	Fri.	19	Dallas		Sat.	20	Buffalo
	Mon.	22	at Ottawa		Tue.	23	New Jersey
	Tue.	23	at Toronto		Thu.	25	at Carolina
	Sat.	27	Anaheim		Sat.	27	Atlanta
	Mon.	29	Toronto		Mon.	29	Carolina
	Wed.	31	at Tampa Bay*		Wed.	31	Ottawa
Jan.	Fri.	2	Philadelphia*	Apr.	Thu.	1	at Tampa Bay
	Sat.	3	Columbus		Sun.	4	Carolina*

Denotes afternoon game.

Year-by-Year Record

		Home				Road				Overall							
Season	GP	W	L	T	OL	W	L	T	OL	W	L	T	OL	GF	GA	Pts.	Finished	Playoff Result
2002-03	82	8	21	7	5	16	15	6	4	24	36	13	9	176	237	70	4th, Southeast Div.	Out of Playoffs
2001-02	82	11	23	3	4	11	21	7	2	22	44	10	6	180	250	60	4th, Southeast Div.	Out of Playoffs
2000-01	82	12	18	7	4	10	20	6	5	22	38	13	9	200	246	66	3rd, Southeast Div.	Out of Playoffs
1999-2000	82	26	9	4	2	17	18	2	4	43	27	6	6	244	209	98	2nd, Southeast Div.	Lost Conf. Quarter-Final
1998-99	82	17	17	7	...	13	17	11	...	30	34	18	...	210	228	78	2nd, Southeast Div.	Out of Playoffs
1997-98	82	11	24	6	...	13	19	9	...	24	43	15	...	203	256	63	6th, Atlantic Div.	Out of Playoffs
1996-97	82	21	12	8	...	14	16	11	...	35	28	19	...	221	201	89	3rd, Atlantic Div.	Lost Conf. Quarter-Final
1995-96	82	25	12	4	...	16	19	6	...	41	31	10	...	254	234	92	3rd, Atlantic Div.	Lost Final
1994-95	48	9	12	3	...	11	10	3	...	20	22	6	...	115	127	46	5th, Atlantic Div.	Out of Playoffs
1993-94	84	15	18	9	...	18	16	8	...	33	34	17	...	233	233	83	5th, Atlantic Div.	Out of Playoffs

Olli Jokinen had never scored more than 11 goals in a season before exploding for 36 last year. He also set career highs (and led the Panthers) with 29 assists, 65 points, 13 power-play goals, three shorthand goals, six game winners and 240 shots.

Franchise date: June 14, 1993

SOUTHEAST DIVISION

11th NHL Season

2003-04 Player Personnel

FORWARDS	HT	WT	S	Place of Birth	Date	2002-03 Club
BEAUDOIN, Eric	6-5	210	L	Ottawa, Ont.	5/3/80	Florida-San Antonio
BEDNAR, Jaroslav	6-0	198	R	Prague, Czech.	11/8/76	Los Angeles-Florida
BURE, Valeri	5-10	185	R	Moscow, USSR	6/13/74	Florida-St. Louis
CAMPBELL, Gregory	6-0	191	L	London, Ont.	12/17/83	Kitchener
CULLEN, Matt	6-2	199	L	Virginia, MN	11/2/76	Anaheim-Florida
GOREN, Lee	6-3	207	R	Winnipeg, Man.	12/26/77	Boston-Providence (AHL)
GREEN, Mike	5-11	192	R	Calgary, Alta.	8/23/79	San Antonio
HAGMAN, Niklas	6-0	200	L	Espoo, Finland	12/5/79	Florida
HORDICHUK, Darcy	6-1	215	L	Kamsack, Sask.	8/10/80	Phoenix-Springfield-Florida
HORTON, Nathan	6-2	201	R	Welland, Ont.	5/29/85	Oshawa
HUSELIUS, Kristian	6-1	190	L	Osterhaninge, Sweden	11/10/78	Florida
JOKINEN, Olli	6-3	205	L	Kuopio, Finland	12/5/78	Florida
KOLNIK, Juraj	5-10	190	R	Nitra, Czech.	11/13/80	Florida-San Antonio
KOZLOV, Viktor	6-5	225	R	Togliatti, USSR	2/14/75	Florida
MacDONALD, Craig	6-1	195	L	Antigonish, N.S.	4/7/77	Carolina-Lowell
MESSIER, Eric	6-2	195	L	Drummondville, Que.	10/29/73	Colorado
NEDOROST, Vaclav	6-1	190	L	Budejovice, Czech.	3/16/82	Colorado-Hershey
NILSON, Marcus	6-2	195	R	Balsta, Sweden	3/1/78	Florida
NOVOSELTSEV, Ivan	6-1	210	L	Golitsino, USSR	1/23/79	Florida
RITCHIE, Byron	5-10	195	L	Burnaby, B.C.	4/24/77	Florida-San Antonio
SAMUELSSON, Mikael	6-2	211	R	Mariefred, Sweden	12/23/76	NY Rangers-Pittsburgh
SHVIDKI, Denis	6-0	195	L	Kharkov, USSR	11/21/80	Florida-San Antonio
STEWART, Anthony	6-1	225	R	Lasalle, Que.	1/5/85	Kingston
TATICEK, Petr	6-3	195	L	Rakovnik, Czech.	9/22/83	Sault Ste. Marie
TOMS, Jeff	6-5	200	L	Swift Current, Sask.	6/4/74	San Antonio-Florida
WEISS, Stephen	5-11	185	L	Toronto, Ont.	4/3/83	Florida

DEFENSEMEN	HT	WT	S	Place of Birth	Date	2002-03 Club
BIRON, Mathieu	6-6	220	R	Lac-St-Charles, Que.	4/29/80	San Antonio-Florida
BOUWMEESTER, Jay	6-4	210	L	Edmonton, Alta.	9/27/83	Florida
GILL, Todd	6-0	180	L	Cardinal, Ont.	11/9/65	Springfield-Chicago-Norfolk
KADLEC, Petr	5-11	180	L	Prague, Czech.	1/5/77	Slavia Praha
KRAJICEK, Lukas	6-2	185	L	Prostejov, Czech.	3/11/83	Peterborough-San Antonio
KUDROC, Kristian	6-7	255	R	Michalovce, Czech.	5/21/81	Springfield
LAUS, Paul	6-1	215	R	Beamsville, Ont.	9/26/70	did not play
LILJA, Andreas	6-3	228	L	Landskrona, Sweden	7/13/75	Los Angeles-Florida
McNEILL, Grant	6-2	210	L	Vermillion, Alta.	6/8/83	Prince Albert
MEZEI, Branislav	6-5	236	L	Nitra, Czech.	10/8/80	Florida-San Antonio
NOVAK, Filip	6-1	185	L	Ceske Budejovice, Czech.	5/7/82	San Antonio
PAUL, Jeff	6-3	200	R	London, Ont.	3/1/78	Colorado-Hershey
ROSSITER, Kyle	6-3	217	L	Edmonton, Alta.	6/9/80	Florida-San Antonio
TRNKA, Pavel	6-2	206	L	Plzen, Czech.	7/27/76	Anaheim-Florida
VAN RYN, Mike	6-1	202	R	London, Ont.	5/14/79	StL-Wor-San Antonio

GOALTENDERS	HT	WT	C	Place of Birth	Date	2002-03 Club
HURME, Jani	6-0	180	L	Turku, Finland	1/7/75	Florida
LUONGO, Roberto	6-3	205	L	Montreal, Que.	4/4/79	Florida
MASON, Chris	6-0	195	L	Red Deer, Alta.	4/20/76	San Antonio
SCOTT, Travis	6-2	185	L	Kanata, Ont.	9/14/75	Manchester

General Manager

DUDLEY, RICK
General Manager, Florida Panthers. Born in Toronto, Ont., January 31, 1949.
The Florida Panthers named Rick Dudley as their general manager on May 10, 2002. Dudley's career in hockey has been successful at all levels as a player, coach and general manager. Prior to joining the Panthers, he served as senior vice president of hockey operations and general manager of the Tampa Bay Lightning from 1999-2000 to the 2001-02 season. Before that, Dudley served one season as the general manager of the Ottawa Senators in 1998-99, where his team finished with a mark of 44-23-15 and 103 points. The Senators improved by 20 points in the standings and finished with the third best overall record in the NHL during Dudley's tenure.

Before serving with Ottawa, Dudley spent four successful seasons with the Detroit Vipers of the International Hockey League. He began his tenure in Detroit as general manager and head coach in 1994-95, the team's inaugural year. Midway through the 1995-96 season, he stepped down as coach to concentrate on his g.m. duties. Under Dudley's direction, the Vipers finished with more than 100 points in each of their first four seasons and won the 1996-97 Turner Cup championship. While with Detroit, Dudley developed future NHL stars such as Petr Sykora and Miroslav Satan and imported a 17-year-old Sergei Samsonov.

Dudley's minor league coaching career also includes stints with the IHL's Phoenix Roadrunners (1993-94), San Diego Gulls (1992-93) and Flint Spirits (1986-88), the AHL's New Haven Nighthawks (1988-89) and the ECHL's Carolina Thunderbirds (1981-86). He spent two-and-a-half seasons as an NHL coach with the Buffalo Sabres between 1989 and 1992. As a coach, Dudley amassed a lifetime record of 476-196-51, and while with San Diego he set marks for the best start in professional hockey (25-0-1) and the most wins in a season in professional hockey history (62). As a general manager, he has led his teams to the finals eight times in three different leagues (IHL, American Hockey League and East Coast Hockey League), winning four championships.

As a player, Dudley skated six seasons in the NHL with the Sabres from 1972-73 to 1974-75 and 1978-79 to 1980-81. He finished ninth in Hart Trophy voting after posting 70 points (31 goals, 39 assists) in the 1974-75 season. Dudley posted back-to-back 40-goal seasons with Cincinnati of the World Hockey Association in 1975-76 and 1976-77 and played briefly with the Winnipeg Jets and Fredericton of the AHL before retiring early in the 1981-82 season.

NHL Coaching Record

Season	Team	Games	Regular Season W	L	T	Playoffs Games	W	L
1989-90	Buffalo	80	45	27	8	6	2	4
1990-91	Buffalo	80	31	30	9	6	2	4
1991-92	Buffalo	28	9	15	4	....	....	....
	NHL Totals	**188**	**85**	**72**	**31**	**12**	**4**	**8**

2002-03 Scoring
* - rookie

Regular Season

Pos	#	Player	Team	GP	G	A	Pts	+/−	PIM	PP	SH	GW	GT	S	%
C	12	Olli Jokinen	FLA	81	36	29	65	−17	79	13	3	6	0	240	15.0
R	25	Viktor Kozlov	FLA	74	22	34	56	−8	18	7	1	1	1	232	9.5
L	22	Kristian Huselius	FLA	78	20	23	43	−6	20	3	0	3	3	187	10.7
L	18	Marcus Nilson	FLA	82	15	19	34	2	31	7	1	0	0	187	8.0
C	16	Matt Cullen	ANA	50	7	14	21	−4	12	1	0	1	0	77	9.1
			FLA	30	6	6	12	−4	22	2	1	1	0	54	11.1
			TOTAL	80	13	20	33	−8	34	3	1	2	0	131	9.9
R	39	Ivan Novoseltsev	FLA	78	10	17	27	−16	30	1	0	0	1	115	8.7
L	27	* Jaroslav Bednar	L.A.	15	0	9	9	3	4	0	0	0	0	29	0.0
			FLA	52	5	13	18	−2	14	2	0	1	2	66	7.6
			TOTAL	67	5	22	27	1	18	2	0	1	2	95	5.3
L	14	Niklas Hagman	FLA	80	8	15	23	−8	20	2	0	0	0	132	6.1
C	9	* Stephen Weiss	FLA	77	6	15	21	−13	17	0	0	2	0	87	6.9
D	4	* Jay Bouwmeester	FLA	82	4	12	16	−29	14	2	0	0	2	110	3.6
D	6	Andreas Lilja	L.A.	17	0	3	3	5	14	0	0	0	0	13	0.0
			FLA	56	4	8	12	8	56	0	0	0	0	59	6.8
			TOTAL	73	4	11	15	13	70	0	0	0	0	72	5.6
D	56	Ivan Majesky	FLA	82	4	8	12	−18	92	0	0	2	0	52	7.7
D	7	Pavel Trnka	ANA	24	3	6	9	2	6	1	0	0	0	33	9.1
			FLA	22	0	3	3	−1	24	0	0	0	0	25	0.0
			TOTAL	46	3	9	12	1	30	1	0	0	0	58	5.2
D	34	Mathieu Biron	FLA	34	1	8	9	−18	14	0	1	0	0	52	1.9
L	32	Stephane Matteau	FLA	52	4	4	8	−9	27	0	0	0	0	47	8.5
R	21	Denis Shvidki	FLA	23	4	2	6	−7	12	2	0	1	0	29	13.8
L	8	Peter Worrell	FLA	63	2	3	5	−14	193	0	0	0	0	52	3.8
C	29	Jeff Toms	FLA	8	2	2	4	2	4	0	0	1	0	12	16.7
C	19	Byron Ritchie	FLA	30	0	3	3	−4	19	0	0	0	0	29	0.0
D	5	Branislav Mezei	FLA	11	2	0	2	−2	10	0	0	1	0	10	20.0
D	55	Igor Ulanov	FLA	56	1	1	2	7	39	0	0	0	0	20	5.0
D	29	Igor Kravchuk	FLA	7	0	1	1	−3	4	0	0	0	0	8	0.0
R	23	Juraj Kolnik	FLA	10	0	1	1	1	0	0	0	0	0	14	0.0
L	38	* Eric Beaudoin	FLA	15	0	1	1	−7	25	0	0	0	0	11	0.0
R	15	Jim Campbell	FLA	1	0	0	0	0	0	0	0	0	0	3	0.0
D	28	Jamie Rivers	FLA	1	0	0	0	−2	2	0	0	0	0	1	0.0
D	33	* Kyle Rossiter	FLA	3	0	0	0	−2	0	0	0	0	0	4	0.0
L	26	Pierre Dagenais	FLA	9	0	0	0	−1	4	0	0	0	0	5	0.0
L	24	Darcy Hordichuk	PHX	25	0	0	0	−1	82	0	0	0	0	5	0.0
			FLA	3	0	0	0	−1	15	0	0	0	0	2	0.0
			TOTAL	28	0	0	0	−2	97	0	0	0	0	7	0.0

Goaltending

No.	Goaltender	GPI	Mins	Avg	W	L	T	EN	SO	GA	SA	S%	G	A	PIM
1	Roberto Luongo	65	3627	2.71	20	34	7	7	6	164	2011	.918	0	0	4
30	Jani Hurme	28	1376	2.88	4	11	6	0	1	66	707	.907	0	0	2
	Totals	**82**	**5021**	**2.83**	**24**	**45**	**13**	**7**	**7**	**237**	**2725**	**.913**			

General Managers' History
Bob Clarke, 1993-94; Bryan Murray, 1994-95 to 1999-2000; Bryan Murray and Bill Torrey, 2000-01; Bill Torrey and Chuck Fletcher, 2001-02; Rick Dudley, 2002-03 to date.

Marcus Nilson enters his sixth NHL season, all with the Florida Panthers. His 82 games, 15 goals and 34 points last year were all one more than his previous career high.

Club Records

Team

(Figures in brackets for season records are games played; records for fewest points, wins, ties, losses, goals, goals against are for 70 or more games)

Most Points	98	1999-2000 (82)
Most Wins	43	1999-2000 (82)
Most Ties	19	1996-97 (82)
Most Losses	44	2001-02 (82)
Most Goals	254	1995-96 (82)
Most Goals Against	256	1997-98 (82)
Fewest Points	60	2001-02 (82)
Fewest Wins	22	2000-01 (82), 2001-02 (82)
Fewest Ties	6	1999-2000 (82)
Fewest Losses	27	1999-2000 (82)
Fewest Goals	176	2002-03 (82)
Fewest Goals Against	201	1996-97 (82)

Longest Winning Streak
Overall................... 7 Nov. 2-14/95
Home..................... 5 Nov. 5-14/95
Away..................... 4 Four times

Longest Undefeated Streak
Overall................... 12 Oct. 5-30/96 (8 wins, 4 ties)
Home..................... 8 Nov. 5-26/95 (7 wins, 1 tie)
Away..................... 7 Twice

Longest Losing Streak
Overall................... 13 Feb. 7-Mar. 23/98
Home..................... 6 Feb. 25-Mar. 23/98
Away..................... 9 Feb. 9-Mar. 25/02

Longest Winless Streak
Overall................... 15 Feb. 1-Mar. 23/98 (14 losses, 1 tie)
Home..................... 13 Feb. 5-Mar. 24/03 (11 losses, 2 ties)
Away..................... 16 Jan. 2-Mar. 21/98 (12 losses, 4 ties)

Most Shutouts, Season........ 7 2002-03 (82)
Most PIM, Season........ 1,994 2001-02 (82)
Most Goals, Game.......... 10 Nov. 26/97 (Bos. 5 at Fla. 10)

Individual

Most Seasons................. 9 Paul Laus
Most Games.............. 573 Robert Svehla
Most Goals, Career........ 157 Scott Mellanby
Most Assists, Career........ 229 Robert Svehla
Most Points, Career........ 354 Scott Mellanby (157G, 197A)
Most PIM, Career........ 1,702 Paul Laus
Most Shutouts, Career........ 15 Roberto Luongo

Longest Consecutive
Games Streak........... 300 Robert Svehla (Dec. 23/98-Apr. 14/02)

Most Goals, Season.......... 59 Pavel Bure (2000-01)
Most Assists, Season........ 53 Viktor Kozlov (1999-2000)
Most Points, Season........ 94 Pavel Bure (1999-2000; 58G, 36A)
Most PIM, Season .... 354 Peter Worrell (2001-02)

Most Points, Defenseman, Season................... 57 Robert Svehla (1995-96; 8G, 49A)
Most Points, Center, Season................... 70 Viktor Kozlov (1999-2000; 17G, 53A)
Most Points, Right Wing, Season................... 94 Pavel Bure (1999-2000; 58G, 36A)
Most Points, Left Wing, Season................... 71 Ray Whitney (1999-2000; 29G, 42A)
Most Points, Rookie, Season................... 50 Jesse Belanger (1993-94; 17G, 33A)
Most Shutouts, Season........ 6 Roberto Luongo (2002-03)
Most Goals, Game............ 4 Mark Parrish (Oct. 30/98); Pavel Bure (Jan. 1/00, Feb. 10/01)
Most Assists, Game........... 4 Scott Mellanby (Nov. 26/97); Ray Whitney (Oct. 30/00)
Most Points, Game............ 5 Pavel Bure (Feb. 10/01; 4G, 1A)

Coaching History

Roger Neilson, 1993-94, 1994-95; Doug MacLean, 1995-96, 1996-97; Doug MacLean and Bryan Murray, 1997-98; Terry Murray, 1998-99, 1999-2000; Terry Murray and Duane Sutter, 2000-01; Duane Sutter and Mike Keenan, 2001-02; Mike Keenan, 2002-03 to date.

Captains' History

Brian Skrudland, 1993-94 to 1996-97; Scott Mellanby, 1997-98 to 2000-01; Pavel Bure, 2001-02; no captain, 2002-03.

All-time Record vs. Other Clubs

Regular Season

	At Home					GF	GA	PTS	On Road					GF	GA	PTS	Total					GF	GA	PTS
	GP	W	L	T	OL				GP	W	L	T	OL				GP	W	L	T	OL			
Anaheim	7	3	2	0	0	20	15	8	9	5	2	1	1	30	27	12	16	8	4	3	1	50	42	20
Atlanta	10	4	5	1	0	25	31	9	10	3	1	4	2	33	30	12	20	7	6	5	2	58	61	21
Boston	19	9	9	0	1	55	56	19	20	8	8	4	0	53	55	20	39	17	17	4	1	108	111	39
Buffalo	19	9	9	1	0	56	60	19	21	5	13	2	1	33	59	13	40	14	22	3	1	89	119	32
Calgary	9	3	3	2	1	21	22	9	7	3	3	1	0	18	17	7	16	6	6	3	1	39	39	16
Carolina	23	9	5	7	2	62	47	27	22	9	10	2	1	58	65	21	45	18	15	9	3	120	112	48
Chicago	8	2	5	1	0	18	30	5	9	3	5	1	0	28	32	7	17	5	10	2	0	46	62	12
Colorado	10	1	9	0	0	25	42	2	11	4	4	3	0	27	30	11	21	5	13	3	0	52	72	13
Columbus	2	1	0	0	1	8	7	3	2	1	1	0	0	4	4	2	4	2	1	0	1	12	11	5
Dallas	9	3	5	1	0	21	28	7	8	3	3	2	0	22	25	8	17	6	8	3	0	43	53	15
Detroit	9	1	4	2	2	17	27	6	7	1	3	3	0	20	26	5	16	2	7	5	2	37	53	11
Edmonton	9	5	2	2	0	24	24	12	6	2	3	1	0	14	20	5	15	7	5	3	0	38	44	17
Los Angeles	7	4	0	3	0	21	11	11	9	4	5	0	0	29	27	8	16	8	5	3	0	50	38	19
Minnesota	2	1	1	0	0	3	4	2	3	0	2	1	0	1	10	1	5	1	3	1	0	4	14	3
Montreal	20	9	8	3	0	62	58	21	19	9	7	2	1	45	51	21	39	18	15	5	1	107	109	42
Nashville	4	2	0	1	1	11	8	6	4	1	1	0	0	8	6	5	8	4	1	2	1	19	14	11
New Jersey	23	7	12	4	0	48	57	18	22	6	11	3	2	46	68	17	45	13	23	7	2	94	125	35
NY Islanders	23	10	7	6	0	69	66	26	23	11	9	2	1	62	58	25	46	21	16	8	1	131	124	51
NY Rangers	23	9	12	1	1	58	64	20	22	8	10	4	0	56	66	20	45	17	22	5	1	114	130	40
Ottawa	20	9	9	1	1	60	58	20	20	9	8	2	1	55	56	21	40	18	17	3	2	115	114	41
Philadelphia	22	5	16	0	1	53	83	11	23	8	9	6	0	55	57	22	45	13	25	6	1	108	140	33
Phoenix	7	3	4	0	0	22	19	6	9	3	2	3	1	26	21	10	16	6	6	3	1	48	40	16
Pittsburgh	20	11	8	1	0	53	46	23	21	6	10	3	2	63	70	17	41	17	18	4	2	116	116	40
St. Louis	8	2	4	2	0	16	18	6	8	1	6	1	0	12	23	3	16	3	10	3	0	28	41	9
San Jose	8	2	1	5	0	23	21	9	8	2	4	2	0	17	23	6	16	4	5	7	0	40	44	15
Tampa Bay	25	14	5	4	2	72	56	34	25	12	8	5	0	70	51	29	50	26	13	9	2	142	107	63
Toronto	15	4	7	4	0	40	47	12	13	4	7	2	0	32	43	10	28	8	14	6	0	72	90	22
Vancouver	8	3	3	1	1	21	27	8	8	1	3	4	0	17	23	6	16	4	6	5	1	38	50	14
Washington	25	10	11	3	1	63	64	24	25	6	13	4	2	55	82	18	50	16	24	7	3	118	146	42
Totals	394	155	166	58	15	1047	1096	383	394	139	171	69	15	989	1125	362	788	294	337	127	30	2036	2221	745

Playoffs

	Series	W	L	GP	W	L	T	GF	GA	Last Mtg.	Rnd.	Result
Boston	1	1	0	5	4	1	0	22	16	1996	CQF	W 4-1
Colorado	1	0	1	4	0	4	0	4	15	1996	F	L 0-4
New Jersey	1	0	1	4	0	4	0	6	12	2000	CQF	L 0-4
NY Rangers	1	0	1	5	1	4	0	10	13	1997	CQF	L 1-4
Philadelphia	1	1	0	6	4	2	0	15	11	1996	CSF	W 4-2
Pittsburgh	1	1	0	7	4	3	0	20	15	1996	CF	W 4-3
Totals	6	3	3	31	13	18	0	77	82			

Colorado totals include Quebec, 1993-94 to 1994-95.
Phoenix totals include Winnipeg, 1993-94 to 1995-96.

Carolina totals include Hartford, 1993-94 to 1996-97.

Playoff Results 2003-1999

Year	Round	Opponent	Result	GF	GA
2000	CQF	New Jersey	L 0-4	6	12

Abbreviations: Round: F - Final;
CF - conference final; CSF - conference semi-final;
CQF - conference quarter-final.

2002-03 Results

Oct.	10	Tampa Bay	3-4*		10	New Jersey	1-2
	12	at Atlanta	5-4*		11	at Washington	2-12
	15	at Minnesota	1-4		13	at New Jersey	2-6
	17	at Chicago	1-4		15	Boston	3-0
	19	at Columbus	1-4		18	Pittsburgh	3-0
	21	Atlanta	3-2		20	Montreal	2-3
	23	at Toronto	4-1		22	Ottawa	1-2
	24	at NY Islanders	3-5		24	at Carolina	1-3
	26	Washington	1-1		25	Carolina	3-2*
	28	Tampa Bay	1-6		28	at Montreal	3-6
	30	at Dallas	3-2*		30	at Detroit	2-2
Nov.	2	Atlanta	1-3	Feb.	5	Toronto	0-6
	6	Pittsburgh	4-3*		6	at Pittsburgh	6-0
	7	at Washington	1-2*		8	Tampa Bay	4-4
	9	Calgary	3-0		12	NY Rangers	1-3
	11	Chicago	2-2		14	Boston	5-6*
	13	at Philadelphia	1-1		15	at Washington	1-3
	14	at Ottawa	2-3*		18	at Montreal	3-0
	16	San Jose	3-7		20	at Ottawa	4-3
	19	at Atlanta	3-4*		22	at Philadelphia	4-3
	20	NY Islanders	3-3		24	Buffalo	2-2
	22	at Phoenix	3-3		26	Anaheim	1-2
	24	at Anaheim	4-4		27	at Tampa Bay	1-3
	27	at Los Angeles	5-2	Mar.	1	at NY Rangers	2-5
	30	Vancouver	2-5		3	at Toronto	2-1
Dec.	4	Carolina	4-2		5	Colorado	1-3
	6	at Carolina	2-0		7	at Atlanta	2-1
	7	Edmonton	0-4		8	Buffalo	0-4
	10	Philadelphia	2-5		10	at NY Rangers	1-3
	13	NY Islanders	3-3		12	Montreal	0-4
	18	Toronto	2-2		15	at Boston	1-4
	20	at Buffalo	3-0		16	at Pittsburgh	4-2
	21	at Boston	3-3		19	Minnesota	1-3
	23	Nashville	2-3*		22	Ottawa	1-3
	27	Dallas	0-4		24	New Jersey	1-4
	28	NY Rangers	1-2*		26	at Buffalo	1-2
	30	at NY Islanders	1-2*		27	at St. Louis	1-2
Jan.	1	at New Jersey	2-1		29	at Tampa Bay	1-1
	2	at Colorado	4-1	Apr.	1	at Washington	0-3
	4	at Vancouver	2-3		4	Carolina	4-1
	8	Detroit	1-2*		6	Philadelphia	2-6

* – Overtime

Entry Draft
Selections 2003-1993

2003		2001		1998		1995	
Pick		**Pick**		**Pick**		**Pick**	
3	Nathan Horton	4	Stephen Weiss	30	Kyle Rossiter	10	Radek Dvorak
25	Anthony Stewart	24	Lukas Krajicek	61	Joe DiPenta	36	Aaron MacDonald
38	Kamil Kreps	34	Greg Watson	63	Lance Ward	62	Mike O'Grady
55	Stefan Meyer	64	Tomas Malec	89	Ryan Jardine	80	Dave Duerden
105	Martin Lojek	68	Grant McNeill	117	Jaroslav Spacek	88	Daniel Tjarnqvist
124	James Pemberton	117	Mike Woodford	148	Chris Ovington	114	Francois Cloutier
141	Dan Travis	136	Billy Thompson	176	B.J. Ketcheson	166	Peter Worrell
162	Martin Tuma	169	Dustin Johner	203	Ian Jacobs	192	Filip Kuba
171	Denis Stasyuk	200	Toni Koivisto	231	Adrian Wichser	218	David Lemanowicz
223	Dany Roussin	231	Kyle Bruce				
234	Petr Kadlec	263	Jan Blanar	**1997**		**1994**	
264	John Hecimovic	267	Ivan Majesky	**Pick**		**Pick**	
265	Tanner Glass			20	Mike Brown	1	Ed Jovanovski
		2000		47	Kristian Huselius	27	Rhett Warrener
2002		**Pick**		56	Vratislav Cech	31	Jason Podollan
Pick		58	Vladimir Sapozhnikov	74	Nick Smith	36	Ryan Johnson
3	Jay Bouwmeester	77	Robert Fried	95	Ivan Novoseltsev	84	David Nemirovsky
9	Petr Taticek	82	Sean O'Connor	127	Pat Parthenais	105	Dave Geris
40	Rob Globke	115	Chris Eade	155	Keith Delaney	157	Matt O'Dette
67	Gregory Campbell	120	Davis Parley	183	Tyler Palmer	183	Jason Boudrias
134	Topi Jaakola	190	Josh Olson	211	Doug Schueller	235	Tero Lehtera
158	Vince Bellissimo	234	Janis Sprukts	237	Benoit Cote	261	Per Gustafsson
169	Jeremy Swanson	253	Mathew Sommerfeld				
196	Mikael Vuorio			**1996**		**1993**	
200	Denis Yachmenev	**1999**		**Pick**		**Pick**	
232	Peter Hafner	**Pick**		20	Marcus Nilson	5	Rob Niedermayer
		12	Denis Shvidki	60	Chris Allen	41	Kevin Weekes
		40	Alexander Auld	65	Oleg Kvasha	57	Chris Armstrong
		70	Niklas Hagman	82	Joey Tetarenko	67	Mikael Tjallden
		80	Jean-Francois Laniel	129	Andrew Long	78	Steve Washburn
		103	Morgan McCormick	156	Gaetan Poirier	83	Bill McCauley
		109	Rod Sarich	183	Alexandre Couture	109	Todd MacDonald
		169	Brad Woods	209	Denis Khloptonov	135	Alain Nasreddine
		198	Travis Eagles	235	Russell Smith	161	Trevor Doyle
		227	Jonathon Charron			187	Briane Thompson
						213	Chad Cabana
						239	John Demarco
						265	Eric Montreuil

Coach

KEENAN, MIKE
Coach, Florida Panthers. Born in Bowmanville, Ont., October 21, 1949.

Mike Keenan became the sixth head coach in Panthers history on December 3, 2001. The veteran coach has guided six other NHL franchises — Philadelphia Flyers (1984-88), Chicago Blackhawks (1988-92), New York Rangers (1993-94), St. Louis Blues (1994-96), Vancouver Canucks (1997-98) and Boston Bruins (2000-01) — and ranks among the NHL's all-time coaching leaders in both games coached and victories. In addition to his coaching duties, Keenan has acted as interim general manager for Vancouver, and as general manager in Chicago and St. Louis.

Keenan led the New York Rangers to the Stanley Cup championship in 1994, the team's first championship in 54 years. The Rangers went 52-24-8 under Keenan in 1993-94, going from a non-playoff team to the Presidents' Trophy winner and Stanley Cup champion in just one year. The Keenan-led Rangers won a thrilling seven-game Stanley Cup final over the Vancouver Canucks that year. During his four years in Chicago, the team made the playoffs every year and reached the Stanley Cup finals in 1992. Keenan's NHL coaching career began in Philadelphia, where his team made two appearances in the Stanley Cup finals (1985 and 1987) in four years. He also won the Jack Adams Award as the NHL's coach of the year in 1985. His resume includes three Presidents' Trophy wins (1985, 1991 and 1994), and six division titles (1985, 1986, 1987, 1990, 1991 and 1994). He led Team Canada to victory at the Canada Cup in 1987 and 1991. His international career also includes head coaching jobs with Team Canada at the 1980 World Junior Championships and the World Championships in 1993.

An accomplished coach at all levels of hockey, Keenan guided the Peterborough Petes (OHL) to the Memorial Cup finals in 1980. He took the Rochester Americans (AHL) from a non-playoff team to a Calder Cup winner in just three seasons, taking over in 1980-81 and winning the AHL championship in 1983. He also led the University of Toronto to a CIAU championship, winning the University Cup in 1984.

Coaching Record

			Regular Season				Playoffs		
Season	Team	Games	W	L	T	Games	W	L	
1979-80	Peterborough (OHL)	68	47	20	1	18	15	3	
1980-81	Rochester (AHL)	80	30	42	8	....	....	....	
1981-82	Rochester (AHL)	80	40	31	9	9	4	5	
1982-83	Rochester (AHL)	80	46	25	9	16	12	4	
1983-84	U. of Toronto (CIAU)	49	41	5	3	....	....	....	
1984-85	Philadelphia (NHL)	80	53	20	7	19	12	7	
1985-86	Philadelphia (NHL)	80	53	23	4	5	2	3	
1986-87	Philadelphia (NHL)	80	46	26	8	26	15	11	
1987-88	Philadelphia (NHL)	80	38	33	9	7	3	4	
1988-89	Chicago (NHL)	80	27	41	12	16	9	7	
1989-90	Chicago (NHL)	80	41	33	6	20	10	10	
1990-91	Chicago (NHL)	80	49	23	8	6	2	4	
1991-92	Chicago (NHL)	80	36	29	15	18	12	6	
1993-94	NY Rangers (NHL)	84	52	24	8	23	16	7*	
1994-95	St. Louis (NHL)	48	28	15	5	7	3	4	
1995-96	St. Louis (NHL)	82	32	34	16	13	7	6	
1996-97	St. Louis (NHL)	33	15	17	1	....	....	....	
1997-98	Vancouver (NHL)	63	21	30	12	....	....	....	
1998-99	Vancouver (NHL)	45	15	24	6	....	....	....	
2000-01	Boston (NHL)	74	33	34	7	....	....	....	
2001-02	Florida (NHL)	56	16	32	8	....	....	....	
2002-03	Florida (NHL)	82	24	45	13	....	....	....	
	NHL Totals	1207	579	483	145	160	91	69	

* Stanley Cup win.

Club Directory

Office Depot Center

Florida Panthers
Office Depot Center
One Panthers Parkway
Sunrise, FL 33323
Phone **954/835-7000**
FAX 954/835-7600
www.floridapanthers.com
Capacity: 19,250

Executive
General Partner and Chairman of the Board/
  Chief Executive Officer/Governor . . . . Alan Cohen
Partner/President, Panthers Hockey LLLP
  & Alternate Governor . . . . Jordan Zimmerman
Partners . . . . Steve Cohen, David Epstein, Dr. Elliott Hahn, H. Wayne Huizenga, Bernie Kosar,
        Richard C. Lehman, M.D., Al Maroone, Michael Maroone, Cliff Viner
Alternate Governor . . . . William A. Torrey
Chief Operating Officer & Alternate Governor . . . . Jeff Cogen
Chief Financial Officer . . . . Bill Duffy
Chief Marketing Officer & Exec. VP, Business Ops . . Chris Overholt
Sr. VP & GM, Office Depot Center . . . . Steve Dangerfield
Regional Vice President, SMG . . . . Ned Collett
Executive Assistant to Chairman of the Board/CEO . Athena Melfi
Executive Assistant to COO & CMO/EVP . . . . Janine Shea
Executive Assistant to Alternate Governor & CFO . . Cathy Stevenson

Hockey Operations
General Manager . . . . Rick Dudley
Assistant General Manager . . . . Grant Sonier
Head Coach . . . . Mike Keenan
Assistant Coach . . . . John Torchetti
Goaltending Coach . . . . Clint Malarchuk
Director of Player Development . . . . Duane Sutter
Director of Scouting . . . . Scott Luce
Skating & Skills Instructor and Scout . . . . Paul Vincent
Head Amateur Scout . . . . Darwin Bennett
Amateur Scouts . . . . Erin Ginnell, Ron Harris
Pro Scouts . . . . Billy Dea, Craig Muni
Part-Time Scouts . . . . Fred Bandel, Lou Clare, Dale Degray,
        Richard Rothermel, Buck Steele
European Scouts . . . . Niklas Blomgren, Jari Kekalainen
Part-Time European Scout . . . . Vadim Podrezov
Executive Assistant to General Manager . . . . Vanessa Rey-Fischel
Strength & Conditioning Coach . . . . Chris Reichart
Head Medical Trainer . . . . Dave Boyer
Head Equipment Manager . . . . Mark Brennan
Associate Equipment Manager . . . . Scott Tinkler
Assistant Equipment Manager . . . . Jon Korman
Massage Therapist . . . . Mikhail Manchik
Team Services Coordinator . . . . Austin Guhl
Video Coach . . . . Scott Masters
Coordinator of Hockey Operations . . . . Rhonda Larocque
Director of Hockey Operations, San Antonio . . . . . Bobby Jay
Head Coach, San Antonio . . . . Steve Ludzik
Assistant Coach, San Antonio . . . . Scott Allen
Orthopedic Surgeon . . . . Lex Simpson, M.D.
Internist . . . . Howard Bush, M.D.
Team Dentist . . . . Martin Robins, D.D.S.
Neuropsychologist . . . . Kathleen Knee, PSY.D.
Laser Eye Surgeon . . . . Cory Lessner, M.D.

Community Development
Director of Community Dev. & Youth Hockey . . . . . Randy Moller
Community Development Manager . . . . Jean Marshall
Youth & Amateur Hockey Coordinator . . . . Andee Boiman

Corporate Sales
Vice President, Corporate Partnerships . . . . Jason Camp
Corporate Marketing Manager . . . . Susan Ferro
Account Executives . . . . Meagan Bradley, Kevin Rooney
Corporate Sales Manager . . . . Bob Ohrablo

Finance & Administration
Senior Director of Finance/Controller . . . . Evelyn Lopez
Director of Human Resources/Payroll . . . . Carol Duncanson
Director of Accounting . . . . Michele Gilbert
Director of Information Technology . . . . Kelly Moyer
Office Manager . . . . Laura Barrera
Human Resources Manager . . . . Cheryl Udrich

Event Presentation/Promotions
Director, Game Presentation & Events . . . . Matthew Coppola
Coordinator, Game/Event Presentation . . . . Kristen Hewitt
Special Events & Mascot . . . . Phil Crowhurst
Special Events Coordinator . . . . Eric Wasser

Marketing
Director, Marketing . . . . Gabrielle Valdez
Director of Marketing Partnerships . . . . Brette Sadler
Marketing Partnerships Managers . . . . Heather Germano, Lauren Hannan

Media Relations Department
Director of Media Relations . . . . Randy Sieminski
Publications & Media Relations Coordinator . . . . . Michael Citro
Media Relations Coordinator . . . . Justin Copertino
Website Coordinator . . . . Mary Lou Veroline

Ticket Operations & Sales
Director of Sales . . . . Chris Gargani
Director of Suite & Club Level Services . . . . Steve Woznick
Manager of Ticket Operations . . . . Matt Coyne
Manager of Account Services . . . . Carrie Rubin

General Information
Television . . . . FOX Sports Net
Television Announcers . . . . Jeff Rimer, Denis Potvin
Radio Flagship . . . . WQAM 560 AM
Radio Announcers . . . . Jiggs McDonald, Randy Moller, Steve Goldstein
Practice Facility . . . . incredible ICE

Los Angeles Kings

2002-03 Results: 33w-37L-6T-6OTL 78PTS.
Third, Pacific Division

2003-04 Schedule

Oct.	Thu.	9	at Detroit
	Fri.	10	at Pittsburgh
	Sun.	12	at Chicago
	Wed.	15	Ottawa
	Sat.	18	Boston
	Tue.	21	Philadelphia
	Thu.	23	Buffalo
	Sat.	25	Chicago
	Thu.	30	Vancouver
Nov.	Sat.	1	Phoenix
	Wed.	5	at Florida
	Thu.	6	at Tampa Bay
	Sat.	8	at Carolina
	Mon.	10	at Washington
	Thu.	13	Toronto
	Sat.	15	St. Louis*
	Wed.	19	Nashville
	Fri.	21	at Dallas
	Sat.	22	at Colorado
	Tue.	25	New Jersey
	Thu.	27	at Phoenix
	Sat.	29	Chicago*
	Sun.	30	at Dallas
Dec.	Tue.	2	at St. Louis
	Thu.	4	Dallas
	Sat.	6	Washington
	Mon.	8	at Detroit
	Wed.	10	at Atlanta
	Thu.	11	at Nashville
	Sat.	13	at St. Louis
	Tue.	16	Edmonton
	Thu.	18	Phoenix
	Sat.	20	Colorado
	Mon.	22	at Vancouver
	Fri.	26	at San Jose
	Sat.	27	San Jose
	Tue.	30	NY Rangers
	Wed.	31	at Phoenix
Jan.	Sat.	3	Dallas
	Wed.	7	at Anaheim
	Thu.	8	Vancouver

	Sat.	10	Columbus
	Tue.	13	at Nashville
	Wed.	14	at Minnesota
	Fri.	16	at Columbus
	Sun.	18	at Chicago
	Tue.	20	Calgary
	Thu.	22	Detroit
	Sat.	24	Anaheim
	Mon.	26	Minnesota
	Wed.	28	at Anaheim
	Thu.	29	Colorado
	Sat.	31	at Edmonton
Feb.	Tue.	3	at Calgary
	Tue.	10	at Minnesota
	Wed.	11	at Columbus
	Fri.	13	at Buffalo
	Sun.	15	at New Jersey*
	Mon.	16	at NY Islanders*
	Wed.	18	Dallas
	Sat.	21	Columbus
	Mon.	23	Nashville
	Wed.	25	at Dallas
	Sat.	28	Anaheim*
	Sun.	29	at Anaheim*
Mar.	Thu.	4	Minnesota
	Sat.	6	Montreal
	Tue.	9	Phoenix
	Wed.	10	at Phoenix
	Sat.	13	at San Jose*
	Sun.	14	Anaheim*
	Tue.	16	St. Louis
	Thu.	18	San Jose
	Sat.	20	Detroit
	Mon.	22	Edmonton
	Wed.	24	at Vancouver
	Fri.	26	at Edmonton
	Sat.	27	at Calgary*
	Mon.	29	at Colorado
	Wed.	31	San Jose
Apr.	Fri.	2	Calgary
	Sun.	4	at San Jose*

* Denotes afternoon game.

Franchise date: June 5, 1967

PACIFIC DIVISION

37th NHL Season

Kings captain Mattias Norstrom was one of only two Los Angeles players to take part in all 82 games last season. He was named the Kings' best defenseman for the fourth time in his seven full seasons with the club.

Year-by-Year Record

Season	GP	Home W	L	T	OL	Road W	L	T	OL	Overall W	L	T	OL	GF	GA	Pts.	Finished	Playoff Result
2002-03	82	19	19	2	1	14	18	4	5	33	37	6	6	203	221	78	3rd, Pacific Div.	Out of Playoffs
2001-02	82	22	12	6	1	18	15	5	3	40	27	11	4	214	190	95	3rd, Pacific Div.	Lost Conf. Quarter-Final
2000-01	82	20	12	8	1	18	16	5	2	38	28	13	3	252	228	92	3rd, Pacific Div.	Lost Conf. Semi-Final
1999-2000	82	21	13	5	2	18	14	7	2	39	27	12	4	245	228	94	2nd, Pacific Div.	Lost Conf. Quater-Final
1998-99	82	18	20	3	...	14	25	2	...	32	45	5	...	189	222	69	5th, Pacific Div.	Out of Playoffs
1997-98	82	22	16	3	...	16	17	8	...	38	33	11	...	227	225	87	2nd, Pacific Div.	Lost Conf. Quater-Final
1996-97	82	18	16	7	...	10	27	4	...	28	43	11	...	214	268	67	6th, Pacific Div.	Out of Playoffs
1995-96	82	16	16	9	...	8	24	9	...	24	40	18	...	256	302	66	6th, Pacific Div.	Out of Playoffs
1994-95	48	7	11	6	...	9	12	3	...	16	23	9	...	142	174	41	4th, Pacific Div.	Out of Playoffs
1993-94	84	18	19	5	...	9	26	7	...	27	45	12	...	294	322	66	5th, Pacific Div.	Out of Playoffs
1992-93	84	22	15	5	...	17	20	5	...	39	35	10	...	338	340	88	3rd, Smythe Div.	Lost Final
1991-92	80	20	11	9	...	15	20	5	...	35	31	14	...	287	296	84	2nd, Smythe Div.	Lost Div. Semi-Final
1990-91	80	26	9	5	...	20	15	5	...	46	24	10	...	340	254	102	1st, Smythe Div.	Lost Div. Final
1989-90	80	21	16	3	...	13	23	4	...	34	39	7	...	338	337	75	4th, Smythe Div.	Lost Div. Final
1988-89	80	25	12	3	...	17	19	4	...	42	31	7	...	376	335	91	2nd, Smythe Div.	Lost Div. Final
1987-88	80	19	18	3	...	11	24	5	...	30	42	8	...	318	359	68	4th, Smythe Div.	Lost Div. Semi-Final
1986-87	80	20	17	3	...	11	24	5	...	31	41	8	...	318	341	70	4th, Smythe Div.	Lost Div. Semi-Final
1985-86	80	9	27	4	...	14	22	4	...	23	49	8	...	284	389	54	5th, Smythe Div.	Out of Playoffs
1984-85	80	20	14	6	...	14	18	8	...	34	32	14	...	339	326	82	4th, Smythe Div.	Lost Div. Semi-Final
1983-84	80	13	19	8	...	10	25	5	...	23	44	13	...	309	376	59	5th, Smythe Div.	Out of Playoffs
1982-83	80	20	13	7	...	7	28	5	...	27	41	12	...	308	365	66	5th, Smythe Div.	Out of Playoffs
1981-82	80	19	15	6	...	5	26	9	...	24	41	15	...	314	369	63	4th, Smythe Div.	Lost Div. Final
1980-81	80	22	11	7	...	21	13	6	...	43	24	13	...	337	290	99	2nd, Norris Div.	Lost Prelim. Round
1979-80	80	18	13	9	...	12	23	5	...	30	36	14	...	290	313	74	2nd, Norris Div.	Lost Prelim. Round
1978-79	80	20	13	7	...	14	21	5	...	34	34	12	...	292	286	80	3rd, Norris Div.	Lost Prelim. Round
1977-78	80	18	16	6	...	13	18	9	...	31	34	15	...	243	245	77	3rd, Norris Div.	Lost Prelim. Round
1976-77	80	20	13	7	...	14	18	8	...	34	31	15	...	271	241	83	2nd, Norris Div.	Lost Quarter-Final
1975-76	80	22	13	5	...	16	20	4	...	38	33	9	...	263	265	85	2nd, Norris Div.	Lost Quarter-Final
1974-75	80	22	7	11	...	20	10	10	...	42	17	21	...	269	185	105	2nd, Norris Div.	Lost Prelim. Round
1973-74	78	22	13	4	...	11	20	8	...	33	33	12	...	233	231	78	3rd, West Div.	Lost Quarter-Final
1972-73	78	21	11	7	...	10	25	4	...	31	36	11	...	232	245	73	6th, West Div.	Out of Playoffs
1971-72	78	14	23	2	...	6	26	7	...	20	49	9	...	206	305	49	7th, West Div.	Out of Playoffs
1970-71	78	17	14	8	...	8	26	5	...	25	40	13	...	239	303	63	5th, West Div.	Out of Playoffs
1969-70	76	12	22	4	...	2	30	6	...	14	52	10	...	168	290	38	6th, West Div.	Out of Playoffs
1968-69	76	19	14	5	...	5	28	5	...	24	42	10	...	185	260	58	4th, West Div.	Lost Semi-Final
1967-68	74	20	13	4	...	11	20	6	...	31	33	10	...	200	224	72	2nd, West Div.	Lost Quarter-Final

2003-04 Player Personnel

FORWARDS

	HT	WT	S	Place of Birth	Date	2002-03 Club
ALLISON, Jason	6-3	215	R	North York, Ont.	5/29/75	Los Angeles
ARMSTRONG, Derek	6-0	195	R	Ottawa, Ont.	4/23/73	Los Angeles-Manchester
AULIN, Jared	6-0	192	R	Calgary, Alta.	3/15/82	Los Angeles-Manchester
AVERY, Sean	5-10	185	L	Pickering, Ont.	4/10/80	Det-Grand Rapids-L.A.-Manchester
BARNEY, Scott	6-4	208	R	Oshawa, Ont.	3/27/79	Los Angeles
BELANGER, Eric	6-0	185	L	Sherbrooke, Que.	12/16/77	Los Angeles
BRENNAN, Kip	6-4	228	L	Kingston, Ont.	8/27/80	Los Angeles-Manchester
BROWN, Dustin	6-0	195	R	Ithaca, NY	11/4/84	Guelph
CAMMALLERI, Michael	5-9	180	L	Richmond Hill, Ont.	6/8/82	Los Angeles-Manchester
CHARTRAND, Brad	5-11	185	L	Winnipeg, Man.	12/14/74	Los Angeles
CLARKE, Noah	5-9	175	L	LaVerne, CA	6/11/79	Colorado College-Manchester
DEADMARSH, Adam	6-0	205	R	Trail, B.C.	5/10/75	Los Angeles
FLINN, Ryan	6-5	248	L	Halifax, N.S.	4/20/80	Los Angeles-Manchester
FROLOV, Alexander	6-4	195	R	Moscow, USSR	6/19/82	Los Angeles
KANKO, Petr	5-9	195	L	Pribram, Czech.	2/7/84	Kitchener
KELLY, Steve	6-2	205	L	Vancouver, B.C.	10/26/76	Los Angeles-Manchester
KLATT, Trent	6-1	210	R	Robbinsdale, MN	1/30/71	Vancouver
LAPERRIERE, Ian	6-1	201	R	Montreal, Que.	1/19/74	Los Angeles
LEHOUX, Yanick	6-1	200	R	Montreal, Que.	4/8/82	Manchester
PALFFY, Ziggy	5-10	183	L	Skalica, Czech.	5/5/72	Los Angeles
PIRNES, Esa	6-0	189	L	Oulu, Finland	4/1/77	Tappara
ROBITAILLE, Luc	6-1	215	L	Montreal, Que.	2/17/66	Detroit
ROSA, Pavel	5-11	188	R	Most, Czech.	6/7/77	Los Angeles-Manchester
SCHMIDT, Chris	6-3	212	L	Beaver Lodge, Alta.	3/1/76	Los Angeles-Manchester
SIM, Jon	5-10	190	L	New Glasgow, N.S.	9/29/77	Utah-Dal-Nsh-L.A.
SMITHSON, Jerred	6-2	197	R	Vernon, B.C.	2/4/79	Los Angeles-Manchester
STUMPEL, Jozef	6-3	225	R	Nitra, Czech.	7/20/72	Boston
TRIPP, John	6-2	215	R	Kingston, Ont.	5/4/77	NY Rangers-Hartford

DEFENSEMEN

	HT	WT	S	Place of Birth	Date	2002-03 Club
CORVO, Joe	6-1	205	R	Oak Park, IL	6/20/77	Manchester-Los Angeles
GLEASON, Tim	6-1	202	L	Southfield, MI	1/29/83	Windsor
GREBESHKOV, Denis	6-0	190	L	Yaroslavl, USSR	10/11/83	Yaroslavl
HOLLAND, Jason	6-3	219	R	Morinville, Alta.	4/30/76	Los Angeles-Manchester
KUZNETSOV, Maxim	6-5	230	L	Pavlodar, USSR	3/24/77	Detroit-Los Angeles
MILLER, Aaron	6-4	200	R	Buffalo, NY	8/11/71	Los Angeles
MODRY, Jaroslav	6-2	220	L	Ceske Budejovice, Czech.	2/27/71	Los Angeles
MUIR, Bryan	6-4	220	L	Winnipeg, Man.	6/8/73	Hershey-Colorado
NORSTROM, Mattias	6-2	201	L	Stockholm, Sweden	1/2/72	Los Angeles
NORTON, Brad	6-4	235	L	Cambridge, MA	2/13/75	Los Angeles
STRBAK, Martin	6-2	200	L	Presov, Czech.	1/15/75	Hameenlinna-Yaroslavl
VISNOVSKY, Lubomir	5-10	183	L	Topolcany, Czech.	8/11/76	Los Angeles
ZIZKA, Tomas	6-1	198	L	Sternberk, Czech.	10/10/79	Los Angeles-Manchester

GOALTENDERS

	HT	WT	C	Place of Birth	Date	2002-03 Club
CECHMANEK, Roman	6-3	187	L	Gottwaldov, Czech.	3/2/71	Philadelphia
CHOUINARD, Mathieu	6-1	211	L	Laval, Que.	4/11/80	Binghamton-Peoria
HUET, Cristobal	6-0	194	L	St. Martin D'Heres, France	9/3/75	Los Angeles-Manchester

2002-03 Scoring

* - rookie

Regular Season

Pos	#	Player	Team	GP	G	A	Pts	+/–	PIM	PP	SH	GW	GT	S	%
R	33	Ziggy Palffy	L.A.	76	37	48	85	22	47	10	2	5	0	277	13.4
D	44	Jaroslav Modry	L.A.	82	13	25	38	–13	68	8	0	1	0	205	6.3
C	32	Derek Armstrong	L.A.	66	12	26	38	5	30	2	0	1	0	106	11.3
C	25	Eric Belanger	L.A.	62	16	19	35	–5	26	0	3	1	0	114	14.0
L	24	* Alexander Frolov	L.A.	79	14	17	31	12	34	1	0	3	0	141	9.9
C	41	Jason Allison	L.A.	26	6	22	28	9	22	2	0	3	1	46	13.0
D	17	Lubomir Visnovsky	L.A.	57	8	16	24	2	28	1	0	1	0	85	9.4
R	22	Ian Laperriere	L.A.	73	7	12	19	–9	122	1	1	1	0	85	8.2
D	28	Adam Deadmarsh	L.A.	20	13	4	17	2	21	4	0	1	0	55	23.6
L	42	Mikko Eloranta	L.A.	75	5	12	17	–15	56	1	0	1	0	96	5.2
L	27	Erik Rasmussen	L.A.	57	4	12	16	–1	28	0	0	1	0	75	5.3
C	19	Sean Avery	DET	39	5	6	11	7	120	0	0	2	0	40	12.5
			L.A.	12	1	3	4	0	33	0	0	0	0	19	5.3
			TOTAL	51	6	9	15	7	153	0	0	2	0	59	10.2
C	29	Brad Chartrand	L.A.	62	8	6	14	–10	33	0	1	2	0	64	12.5
R	57	Steve Heinze	L.A.	27	5	7	12	–5	12	1	0	0	0	44	11.4
D	26	* Joe Corvo	L.A.	50	5	7	12	2	14	2	0	0	0	84	6.0
L	23	Craig Johnson	L.A.	70	3	6	9	–13	22	0	0	0	0	87	3.4
C	13	* Michael Cammalleri	L.A.	28	5	3	8	–4	22	2	0	2	0	40	12.5
D	63	Brad Norton	L.A.	53	3	3	6	1	97	0	0	0	0	19	15.8
D	3	Aaron Miller	L.A.	49	1	5	6	–7	24	0	0	0	0	34	2.9
D	14	Mattias Norstrom	L.A.	82	0	6	6	0	49	0	0	0	0	63	0.0
C	11	Steve Kelly	L.A.	15	2	3	5	–6	0	0	0	1	0	14	14.3
C	31	* Jared Aulin	L.A.	17	2	2	4	–3	0	1	0	0	0	21	9.5
L	43	Jon Sim	DAL	4	0	0	0	–1	0	0	0	0	0	7	0.0
			NSH	4	1	0	1	0	0	0	0	0	0	3	33.3
			L.A.	14	0	2	2	–3	19	0	0	0	0	29	0.0
			TOTAL	22	1	2	3	–4	19	0	0	0	0	39	2.6
D	5	* Tomas Zizka	L.A.	10	0	3	3	–4	4	0	0	0	0	12	0.0
D	6	Maxim Kuznetsov	DET	53	0	3	3	0	54	0	0	0	0	32	0.0
			L.A.	3	0	0	0	1	0	0	0	0	0	1	0.0
			TOTAL	56	0	3	3	1	54	0	0	0	0	33	0.0
C	51	Chris Schmidt	L.A.	10	0	2	2	–1	5	0	0	0	0	10	0.0
D	38	Chris McAlpine	L.A.	21	0	2	2	–4	24	0	0	0	0	15	0.0
C	52	* Jerred Smithson	L.A.	22	0	2	2	–5	21	0	0	0	0	9	0.0
D	49	* Ryan Flinn	L.A.	19	1	0	1	0	28	0	0	0	0	13	7.7
D	53	Jason Holland	L.A.	2	0	1	1	1	0	0	0	0	0	4	0.0
R	55	Pavel Rosa	L.A.	2	0	1	1	–1	0	0	0	0	0	4	0.0
L	12	Ken Belanger	L.A.	4	0	0	0	0	17	0	0	0	0	0	0.0
C	62	* Scott Barney	L.A.	5	0	0	0	–1	0	0	0	0	0	5	0.0
C	58	Derek Bekar	L.A.	6	0	0	0	–1	4	0	0	0	0	4	0.0
L	37	* Kip Brennan	L.A.	19	0	0	0	0	57	0	0	0	0	6	0.0

Goaltending

No.	Goaltender	GPI	Mins	Avg	W	L	T	EN	SO	GA	SA	S%	G	A	PIM
35	Cristobal Huet	12	541	2.33	4	4	1	2	1	21	241	.913	0	0	0
1	Jamie Storr	39	2027	2.55	12	19	2	4	3	86	904	.905	0	1	8
39	Felix Potvin	42	2367	2.66	17	20	3	3	3	105	987	.894	0	0	4
	Totals	**82**	**4986**	**2.66**	**33**	**43**	**6**	**9**	**7**	**221**	**2141**	**.897**			

Vice President and General Manager

TAYLOR, DAVE
Senior Vice President/General Manager, Los Angeles Kings.
Born in Levack, Ont., December 4, 1955.

No player in the history of the Kings ever wore the uniform with more distinction and class than Dave Taylor. For 17 seasons, Taylor gave his all, both on and off the ice, receiving All-Star status for his outstanding play.

Fittingly, after finishing his illustrious career during the 1993-94 season, Taylor remains a key part of the Kings organization, now serving as vice president and general manager for the NHL club. Taylor assumed his current responsibilities on April 22, 1997, becoming the seventh g.m. in team history. He joined the Kings front office four years earlier as an assistant to his predecessor, Sam McMaster.

An All-American hockey player while at Clarkson College, Taylor was relatively unknown when the Kings picked him in the 15th round of the 1975 draft. His grit and work ethic kept him around long enough to hook up with a center named Marcel Dionne, who virtually ignited Taylor's career. As a member of the renowned Triple Crown line with Dionne and left winger Charlie Simmer, Taylor became a prolific scorer and a fearsome checker. Taylor's NHL career stats include a Kings-record 1,111 games, 431 goals, 638 assists and 1,069 points.

A four-time NHL All-Star Game selection, Taylor served as the Kings captain for four seasons (1985-89). After posting career highs in goals (47) and points (112) during the 1980-81 season, Taylor earned a spot on the NHL Second All-Star Team. On April 3, 1995, Taylor's jersey No. 18 was retired, joining Rogie Vachon (No. 30) and Marcel Dionne (No. 16). For all his individual accomplishments in hockey, his crowning glory was reaching the Stanley Cup Finals with the 1992-93 Kings.

Away from the ice, Taylor has worked tirelessly for numerous charities throughout the years. Each year he hosts the Dave Taylor Golf Classic benefiting the Cystic Fibrosis Foundation, which annually raises more than $125,000. In 1991, the NHL honored Taylor's contributions to hockey and the community by awarding him both the Bill Masterton and King Clancy trophies.

General Managers' History

Larry Regan, 1967-68 to 1972-73; Larry Regan and Jake Milford, 1973-74; Jake Milford, 1974-75 to 1976-77; George Maguire, 1977-78 to 1982-83; George Maguire and Rogie Vachon, 1983-84; Rogie Vachon, 1984-85 to 1991-92; Nick Beverley, 1992-93, 1993-94; Sam McMaster, 1994-95 to 1996-97; Dave Taylor, 1997-98 to date.

Captains' History

Bob Wall, 1967-68, 1968-69; Larry Cahan, 1969-70, 1970-71; Bob Pulford, 1971-72, 1972-73; Terry Harper, 1973-74, 1974-75; Mike Murphy, 1975-76 to 1980-81; Dave Lewis, 1981-82, 1982-83; Terry Ruskowski, 1983-84, 1984-85; Dave Taylor, 1985-86 to 1988-89; Wayne Gretzky, 1989-90 to 1991-92; Wayne Gretzky and Luc Robitaille, 1992-93; Wayne Gretzky, 1993-94, 1994-95; Wayne Gretzky and Rob Blake, 1995-96; Rob Blake, 1996-97 to 2000-01; Mattias Norstrom, 2001-02 to date.

Club Records

Team

(Figures in brackets for season records are games played; records for fewest points, wins, ties, losses, goals, goals against are for 70 or more games)

Most Points	**105**	1974-75 (80)
Most Wins	**46**	1990-91 (80)
Most Ties	**21**	1974-75 (80)
Most Losses	**52**	1969-70 (76)
Most Goals	**376**	1988-89 (80)
Most Goals Against	**389**	1985-86 (80)
Fewest Points	**38**	1969-70 (76)
Fewest Wins	**14**	1969-70 (76)
Fewest Ties	**5**	1998-99 (82)
Fewest Losses	**17**	1974-75 (80)
Fewest Goals	**168**	1969-70 (76)
Fewest Goals Against	**185**	1974-75 (80)
Longest Winning Streak		
Overall	**8**	Oct. 21-Nov. 7/72, Feb. 23-Mar. 9/92
Home	**12**	Oct. 10-Dec. 5/92
Away	**8**	Dec. 18/74-Jan. 16/75
Longest Undefeated Streak		
Overall	**11**	Feb. 28-Mar. 24/74 (9 wins, 2 ties)
Home	**13**	Oct. 10-Dec. 8/92 (12 wins, 1 tie)
Away	**11**	Oct. 10-Dec. 11/74 (6 wins, 5 ties)
Longest Losing Streak		
Overall	**10**	Feb. 22-Mar. 9/84
Home	**9**	Feb. 8-Mar. 12/86
Away	**12**	Jan. 11-Feb. 15/70
Longest Winless Streak		
Overall	**17**	Jan. 29-Mar. 5/70 (13 losses, 4 ties)
Home	**9**	Jan. 29-Mar. 5/70 (8 losses, 1 tie), Feb. 8-Mar. 12/86 (9 losses)
Away	**21**	Jan. 11-Apr. 3/70 (17 losses, 4 ties)
Most Shutouts, Season	**10**	2000-01 (82)
Most PIM, Season	**2,247**	1992-93 (84)
Most Goals, Game	**12**	Nov. 29/84 (Van. 1 at L.A. 12)

Individual

Most Seasons	**17**	Dave Taylor
Most Games	**1,111**	Dave Taylor
Most Goals, Career	**550**	Marcel Dionne
Most Assists, Career	**757**	Marcel Dionne
Most Points Career	**1,307**	Marcel Dionne (550G, 757A)
Most PIM, Career	**1,846**	Marty McSorley
Most Shutouts, Career	**32**	Rogie Vachon
Longest Consecutive Games Streak	**324**	Marcel Dionne (Jan. 7/78-Jan. 9/82)
Most Goals, Season	**70**	Bernie Nicholls (1988-89)
Most Assists, Season	**122**	Wayne Gretzky (1990-91)
Most Points, Season	**168**	Wayne Gretzky (1988-89; 54G, 114A)
Most PIM, Season	**399**	Marty McSorley (1992-93)
Most Points, Defenseman, Season	**76**	Larry Murphy (1980-81; 16G, 60A)
Most Points, Center, Season	**168**	Wayne Gretzky (1988-89; 54G, 114A)
Most Points, Right Wing, Season	**112**	Dave Taylor (1980-81; 47G, 65A)
Most Points, Left Wing, Season	***125**	Luc Robitaille (1992-93; 63G, 62A)
Most Points, Rookie, Season	**84**	Luc Robitaille (1986-87; 45G, 39A)
Most Shutouts, Season	**8**	Rogie Vachon (1976-77)
Most Goals, Game	**4**	Sixteen times
Most Assists, Game	**6**	Bernie Nicholls (Dec. 1/88), Tomas Sandstrom (Oct. 9/93)
Most Points, Game	**8**	Bernie Nicholls (Dec. 1/88; 2G, 6A)

* NHL Record.

Coaching History

Red Kelly, 1967-68, 1968-69; Hal Laycoe and Johnny Wilson, 1969-70; Larry Regan, 1970-71; Larry Regan and Fred Glover, 1971-72; Bob Pulford, 1972-73 to 1976-77; Ron Stewart, 1977-78; Bob Berry, 1978-79 to 1980-81; Parker MacDonald and Don Perry, 1981-82; Don Perry, 1982-83; Don Perry, Rogie Vachon and Roger Neilson, 1983-84; Pat Quinn, 1984-85, 1985-86; Pat Quinn and Mike Murphy 1986-87; Mike Murphy, Rogie Vachon and Robbie Ftorek, 1987-88; Robbie Ftorek, 1988-89; Tom Webster, 1989-90 to 1991-92; Barry Melrose, 1992-93, 1993-94; Barry Melrose and Rogie Vachon, 1994-95; Larry Robinson, 1995-96 to 1998-99; Andy Murray, 1999-2000 to date.

Retired Numbers

16	Marcel Dionne	1975-1987
18	Dave Taylor	1977-1994
30	Rogie Vachon	1971-1978
99	Wayne Gretzky	1988-1996

All-time Record vs. Other Clubs

Regular Season

	At Home								On Road								Total							
	GP	W	L	T	OL	GF	GA	PTS	GP	W	L	T	OL	GF	GA	PTS	GP	W	L	T	OL	GF	GA	PTS
Anaheim	27	14	9	4	0	78	68	32	27	9	12	6	0	69	87	24	54	23	21	10	0	147	155	56
Atlanta	4	3	0	0	1	18	9	7	3	3	0	0	0	13	3	6	7	6	0	0	1	31	12	13
Boston	60	21	31	7	1	207	220	50	61	11	44	6	0	169	287	28	121	32	75	13	1	376	507	78
Buffalo	53	22	22	9	0	184	182	53	52	16	27	9	0	154	209	41	105	38	49	18	0	338	391	94
Calgary	89	45	35	9	0	332	312	99	92	27	52	11	2	304	406	67	181	72	87	20	2	636	718	166
Carolina	30	17	10	3	0	129	113	37	30	11	13	5	1	113	111	28	60	28	23	8	1	242	224	65
Chicago	72	32	32	8	0	240	242	72	73	29	34	9	1	215	258	68	145	61	66	17	1	455	500	140
Colorado	41	25	13	3	0	170	131	53	40	15	22	3	0	137	167	33	81	40	35	6	0	307	298	86
Columbus	6	3	3	0	0	12	11	6	6	3	3	0	0	22	15	6	12	6	6	0	0	34	26	12
Dallas	79	34	27	18	0	269	228	86	81	18	49	12	2	214	318	50	160	52	76	30	2	483	546	136
Detroit	78	42	22	14	0	315	237	98	77	30	34	13	0	267	294	73	155	72	56	27	0	582	531	171
Edmonton	75	27	33	15	0	293	314	69	75	22	38	15	0	270	341	59	150	49	71	30	0	563	655	128
Florida	9	5	4	0	0	27	29	10	7	0	4	3	0	11	21	3	16	5	8	3	0	38	50	13
Minnesota	6	2	4	0	0	14	18	4	6	3	1	2	0	16	10	8	12	5	5	2	0	30	28	12
Montreal	64	19	36	9	0	197	252	47	64	8	45	11	0	160	289	27	128	27	81	20	0	357	541	74
Nashville	10	5	4	0	1	30	28	11	10	7	1	2	0	27	15	16	20	12	5	2	1	57	43	27
New Jersey	41	28	7	6	0	201	126	62	42	19	18	5	0	146	139	43	83	47	25	11	0	347	265	105
NY Islanders	45	21	17	7	0	163	143	49	43	15	24	4	0	122	155	34	88	36	41	11	0	285	298	83
NY Rangers	59	23	26	10	0	197	213	56	58	17	35	6	0	172	233	40	117	40	61	16	0	369	446	96
Ottawa	9	7	1	1	0	42	18	15	9	4	4	1	0	28	30	9	18	11	5	2	0	70	48	24
Philadelphia	65	20	37	8	0	189	223	48	63	16	40	7	0	156	244	39	128	36	77	15	0	345	467	87
Phoenix	71	26	31	13	1	280	279	66	73	26	35	11	1	243	290	64	144	52	66	24	2	523	569	130
Pittsburgh	69	44	17	8	0	265	183	96	72	24	38	10	0	230	265	58	141	68	55	18	0	495	448	154
St. Louis	76	35	29	12	0	258	220	82	76	18	47	10	1	193	287	47	152	53	76	22	1	451	507	129
San Jose	34	23	8	3	0	109	76	49	34	12	17	3	2	98	116	29	68	35	25	6	2	207	192	78
Tampa Bay	11	1	8	2	0	24	36	4	9	4	5	0	0	21	23	8	20	5	13	2	0	45	59	12
Toronto	64	34	21	9	0	230	187	77	68	22	34	11	1	223	266	56	132	56	55	20	1	453	453	133
Vancouver	97	51	30	16	0	391	304	118	95	31	48	15	1	296	360	78	192	82	78	31	1	687	664	196
Washington	46	26	13	6	1	180	141	59	45	20	18	7	0	168	183	47	91	46	31	13	1	348	324	106
Defunct Clubs	35	27	6	2	0	141	76	56	34	11	14	9	0	91	109	31	69	38	20	11	0	232	185	87
Totals	**1425**	**682**	**536**	**202**	**5**	**5185**	**4619**	**1571**	**1425**	**451**	**756**	**206**	**12**	**4348**	**5531**	**1120**	**2850**	**1133**	**1292**	**408**	**17**	**9533**	**10150**	**2691**

Playoffs

	Series	W	L	GP	W	L	T	GF	GA	Last Mtg.	Rnd.	Result
Boston	2	0	2	13	5	8	0	38	56	1977	QF	L 2-4
Calgary	6	4	2	26	13	13	0	105	102	1993	DSF	W 4-2
Chicago	1	0	1	5	1	4	0	7	10	1974	QF	L 1-4
Colorado	2	0	2	14	6	8	0	23	33	2002	CQF	L 3-4
Dallas	1	0	1	7	3	4	0	21	26	1968	QF	L 3-4
Detroit	2	1	1	10	4	6	0	21	32	2001	CQF	W 4-2
Edmonton	7	2	5	36	12	24	0	127	154	1992	DSF	L 2-4
Montreal	1	0	1	5	1	4	0	12	15	1993	F	L 1-4
NY Islanders	1	0	1	4	1	3	0	10	21	1980	PRE	L 1-3
NY Rangers	2	0	2	6	1	5	0	14	32	1981	PRE	L 1-3
St. Louis	2	0	2	8	0	8	0	13	32	1998	CQF	L 0-4
Toronto	3	1	2	12	5	7	0	31	41	1993	CF	W 4-3
Vancouver	3	2	1	17	9	8	0	66	60	1993	DF	W 4-2
Defunct Clubs	1	1	0	7	4	3	0	23	25			
Totals	**34**	**11**	**23**	**170**	**65**	**105**	**0**	**511**	**639**			

Calgary totals include Atlanta Flames, 1972-73 to 1979-80.
Colorado totals include Quebec, 1979-80 to 1994-95.
New Jersey totals include Kansas City, 1974-75 to 1975-76, and Colorado Rockies, 1976-77 to 1981-82.
Phoenix totals include Winnipeg, 1979-80 to 1995-96.
Carolina totals include Hartford, 1979-80 to 1996-97.
Dallas totals include Minnesota North Stars, 1967-68 to 1992-93.

Playoff Results 2003-1999

Year	Round	Opponent	Result	GF	GA
2002	CQF	Colorado	L 3-4	13	16
2001	CSF	Colorado	L 3-4	10	17
	CQF	Detroit	W 4-2	15	17
2000	CQF	Detroit	L 0-4	6	15

Abbreviations: Round: F - Final;
CF - conference final; **CSF** - conference semi-final;
CQF - conference quarter-final; **DF** - division final;
DSF - division semi-final; **QF** - quarter-final;
PRE - preliminary round.

2002-03 Results

Month	Day		Opponent	Score
Oct.	9		Phoenix	4-1
	12		Detroit	3-2
	16	at	Anaheim	4-2
	17		Colorado	1-4
	19		Vancouver	2-2
	23	at	Detroit	3-3
	25	at	NY Rangers	6-2
	27	at	Columbus	1-5
	29	at	Atlanta	4-0
	31	at	Chicago	1-2*
Nov.	2		Nashville	6-5*
	4		Minnesota	2-5
	5	at	San Jose	2-5
	8	at	Ottawa	3-2
	9	at	Montreal	1-3
	12	at	Toronto	3-4*
	14	at	Vancouver	2-3
	16	at	Edmonton	4-1
	19	at	Minnesota	2-2
	21	at	St. Louis	2-3*
	23		Dallas	2-0
	27		Florida	2-5
	29	at	Anaheim	2-2
	30		Chicago	4-1
Dec.	5		Nashville	2-3
	7		Columbus	2-4
	10	at	Nashville	3-0
	11	at	Dallas	3-0
	14		Pittsburgh	3-2*
	15	at	Phoenix	1-2
	17		St. Louis	6-2
	19		Anaheim	5-4
	22	at	Chicago	1-3
	23	at	St. Louis	0-5
	26		Phoenix	4-3*
	29	at	Colorado	1-6
	30		Chicago	0-2
Jan.	2		Philadelphia	1-4
	4		Dallas	2-3
	6	at	Minnesota	3-2
	7	at	Dallas	4-7
	9		Edmonton	4-5
	11		St. Louis	1-2
	13		San Jose	3-2*
	16	at	Edmonton	0-2
	18	at	Calgary	1-2*
	22	at	Anaheim	5-6
	23		Minnesota	1-2
	25		New Jersey	2-1*
	27		San Jose	0-3
	28	at	San Jose	1-3
	30		Ottawa	3-0
Feb.	5		Phoenix	4-3
	7		Carolina	8-2
	9	at	Dallas	1-3
	11	at	Nashville	3-2
	13		Calgary	4-2
	15		NY Islanders	2-3
	17		San Jose	3-2
	20	at	Philadelphia	0-5
	21	at	Buffalo	4-1
	24	at	Detroit	4-5
	25	at	Pittsburgh	5-3
	27	at	Columbus	1-3
Mar.	1		Atlanta	4-1
	4		Anaheim	1-2
	6		Edmonton	1-2
	8		Montreal	2-1
	10		Detroit	2-3
	12	at	Tampa Bay	2-4
	14	at	Washington	3-1
	15	at	Carolina	0-0
	18		Calgary	1-4
	20		Tampa Bay	2-2
	22		Boston	3-4*
	25		Columbus	1-2**
	27	at	Colorado	0-3
	29		Vancouver	1-5
	31	at	Phoenix	5-4*
Apr.	2		Colorado	5-3
	4	at	Calgary	1-2*
	6	at	Vancouver	2-0

* – Overtime
** – Lost in overtime after having removed the goaltender for an extra attacker. No point awarded

Entry Draft
Selections 2003-1989

2003
Pick
13	Dustin Brown
26	Brian Boyle
27	Jeff Tambellini
44	Konstantin Pushkaryov
82	Ryan Munce
152	Brady Murray
174	Esa Pirnes
231	Matt Zaba
244	Mike Sullivan
274	Martin Guerin

2002
Pick
18	Denis Grebeshkov
50	Sergei Anshakov
66	Petr Kanko
104	Aaron Rome
115	Mark Rooneem
152	Greg Hogeboom
157	Joel Andresen
185	Ryan Murphy
215	Mikhail Lyubushin
248	Tuukka Pulliainen
279	Connor James

2001
Pick
18	Jens Karlsson
30	Dave Steckel
49	Michael Cammalleri
51	Jaroslav Bednar
83	Henrik Juntunen
116	Richard Petiot
152	Terry Denike
153	Tuukka Mantyla
214	Cristobal Huet
237	Mike Gabinet
277	Sebastien Laplante

2000
Pick
20	Alexander Frolov
54	Andreas Lilja
86	Yanick Lehoux
118	Lubomir Visnovsky
165	Nathan Marsters
201	Yevgeny Fedorov
206	Tim Eriksson
218	Craig Olynick
245	Dan Welch
250	Flavien Conne
282	Carl Grahn

1999
Pick
43	Andrei Shefer
74	Jason Crain
76	Frantisek Kaberle
92	Cory Campbell
104	Brian McGrattan
125	Daniel Johansson
133	Jean-Francois Nogues
193	Kevin Baker
222	George Parros
250	Noah Clarke

1998
Pick
21	Mathieu Biron
46	Justin Papineau
76	Alexei Volkov
103	Kip Brennan
133	Joe Rullier
163	Tomas Zizka
190	Tommi Hannus
217	Jim Henkel
248	Matthew Yeats

1997
Pick
3	Olli Jokinen
15	Matt Zultek
29	Scott Barney
83	Joe Corvo
99	Sean Blanchard
137	Richard Seeley
150	Jeff Katcher
193	Jay Kopischke
220	Konrad Brand

1996
Pick
30	Josh Green
37	Marian Cisar
57	Greg Phillips
84	Mikael Simons
96	Eric Belanger
120	Jesse Black
123	Peter Hogan
190	Steve Valiquette
193	Kai Nurminen
219	Sebastien Simard

1995
Pick
3	Aki Berg
33	Don MacLean
50	Pavel Rosa
59	Vladimir Tsyplakov
118	Jason Morgan
137	Igor Melyakov
157	Benoit Larose
163	Juha Vuorivirta
215	Brian Stewart

1994
Pick
7	Jamie Storr
33	Matt Johnson
59	Vitali Yachmenev
111	Chris Schmidt
163	Luc Gagne
189	Andrew Dale
215	Jan Nemecek
241	Sergei Shalomai

1993
Pick
42	Shayne Toporowski
68	Jeff Mitchell
94	Bob Wren
105	Frederick Beaubien
117	Jason Saal
120	Tomas Vlasak
146	Jere Karalahti
172	Justin Martin
198	John-Tra Dillabough
224	Martin Strbak
250	Kimmo Timonen
276	Patrick Howald

1992
Pick
39	Justin Hocking
63	Sandy Allan
87	Kevin Brown
111	Jeff Shevalier
135	Rem Murray
207	Magnus Wernblom
231	Ryan Pisiak
255	Jukka Tiilikainen

1991
Pick
42	Guy Leveque
79	Keith Redmond
81	Alexei Zhitnik
108	Pauli Jaks
130	Brett Seguin
152	Kelly Fairchild
196	Craig Brown
218	Mattias Olsson
240	Andre Bouliane
262	Mike Gaul

1990
Pick
7	Darryl Sydor
28	Brandy Semchuk
49	Bill Berg
91	David Goverde
112	Erik Andersson
133	Robert Lang
154	Dean Hulett
175	Denis Leblanc
196	Patrik Ross
217	K.J.(Kevin) White
238	Troy Mohns

1989
Pick
39	Brent Thompson
81	Jim Maher
102	Eric Ricard
103	Thomas Newman
123	Daniel Rydmark
144	Ted Kramer
165	Sean Whyte
182	Jim Giacin
186	Martin Maskarinec
207	Jim Hiller
228	Steve Jaques
249	Kevin Sneddon

Club Directory

STAPLES Center

Los Angeles Kings
STAPLES Center
1111 South Figueroa Street
Los Angeles, CA 90015
Phone **213/742-7100**
GM FAX 310/535-4507
www.lakings.com
Capacity: 18,118

Executive
Owner . . . . Philip F. Anschutz
Owner . . . . Edward P. Roski
President . . . . Timothy J. Lieweke

Hockey Operations
Senior Vice President/General Manager . . . . Dave Taylor
Vice President, Hockey Operations/
   Assistant General Manager . . . . Kevin Gilmore
Assistant to the General Manager . . . . John Wolf
Executive Assistant to the General Manager . . . . . . Marcia Galloway
Head Coach . . . . Andy Murray
Assistant Coach . . . . Mark Hardy, Ray Bennett, John Van Boxmeer
Video Coordinator . . . . Bill Gurney
Pro Scout - Director of European Evaluation . . . . . . Rob Laird
Scouts . . . . Vaclav Nedomansky, Brian Putnam, Parrry
                  Shockey, John Stanton, Jan Vopar, Ari Vuori,
                  Glen Williamson, Michel Boucher, Jim Cassidy,
                  Mike Donnelly, Viacheslav Golovin, Gary
                  Harker, Jerry Sodomlak, Victor Tjumenev

Medical
Athletic Trainer . . . . Peter Demers
Assistant Athletic Trainer . . . . Rick Burrill
Rehabilitation Trainer . . . . Robert Zolg
Head Strength and Conditioning Coach . . . . Mike Kadar

Equipment Staff
Equipment Manager . . . . Peter Millar
Assistant Equipment Manager . . . . Rick Garcia, Dan Del Vecchio

Media Relations/Team Services
Director, Media Relations/Team Services . . . . Mike Altieri
Manager, Media Relations/Team Services . . . . Jeff Moeller
Assistant Manager, Media Relations/Team Services . . Lee Callans

Broadcasters
TV Play-by-Play Announcer . . . . Bob Miller
Radio Play-by-Play Announcer . . . . Nick Nickson
TV Color Commentator . . . . Jim Fox
Radio Color Commentator . . . . Daryl Evans
Training Center . . . . HealthSouth Training Center
Team Colors . . . . Purple, Silver, Black, White
Television . . . . Fox Sports Net
Radio Flagship . . . . ESPN Radio - KSPN 710
Minor League Affiliates . . . . Manchester Monarchs (AHL),
                  Reading Royals (ECHL)

Coach

MURRAY, ANDY
Coach, Los Angeles Kings. Born in Gladstone, Man., March 3, 1951.

Andy Murray became the 19th head coach in Kings history on June 14, 1999. His coaching experience dates back to 1974 and includes seven seasons as an NHL assistant or associate coach with the Winnipeg Jets (1993 to 1995), Minnesota North Stars (1990 to 1992) and Philadelphia Flyers (1988 to 1990). As an assistant coach in Minnesota, Murray reached the Stanley Cup Finals in 1991.

In addition to his NHL service, Murray brings to the Kings a tremendous amount of international coaching experience. As head coach of the Canadian national team, he guided his team to a 77-29-14 record and the gold medal in the 1997 World Championships.

From 1976 to 1978, Murray served his first head coaching position with the Brandon Travelers of the Manitoba Junior Hockey League. He moved on to become head coach for Brandon University from 1978 to 1981, leading the Bobcats to the #1 ranking in Canadian university hockey during his final year. In 1981-82, Murray moved to Switzerland, where for the next seven years he coached several Swiss-A Division teams.

Murray returned to North America as an assistant coach for the Hershey Bears of the American Hockey League in 1987 and helped guide the Bears to the 1988 Calder Cup championship. In 1992, Murray returned to Europe to coach Lugano in Switzerland and then Eisbaren Berlin in Germany a year later. Most recently, Murray served as the head coach for Shattuck-St. Mary's in Faribault, Minnesota, where he led the prep school to a 70-9-2 record and the Midget Triple A USA Hockey national championship in 1998-99.

Coaching Record

Season	Team	Games	Regular Season W	L	T	Playoffs Games	W	L
1999-2000	Los Angeles (NHL)	82	39	31	12	4	0	4
2000-01	Los Angeles (NHL)	82	38	31	13	13	7	6
2001-02	Los Angeles (NHL)	82	40	31	11	7	3	4
2002-03	Los Angeles (NHL)	82	33	43	6	....	....	....
	NHL Totals	**328**	**150**	**136**	**42**	**24**	**10**	**14**

Assistant coach Dave Tippett posted a 2-2-1 record as replacement coach when Murray was sidelined following a car accident, February 26 to March 6, 2002. All games are credited to Murray's coaching record.

Adam Deadmarsh was just one of several key players the Kings lost to injury last season. Though he played just 20 games, he scored 13 goals.

Minnesota Wild

2002-03 Results: 42w-29L-10T-1OTL 95PTS.
Third, Northwest Division

2003-04 Schedule

Oct.	Wed.	8	at Chicago
	Fri.	10	NY Rangers
	Sun.	12	San Jose
	Thu.	16	Colorado
	Sat.	18	Vancouver
	Sun.	19	at Dallas
	Tue.	21	Calgary
	Fri.	24	at Florida
	Sat.	25	at Tampa Bay
	Tue.	28	at Buffalo
	Thu.	30	Atlanta
Nov.	Sat.	1	Washington
	Tue.	4	at Colorado
	Fri.	7	at Calgary
	Sat.	8	at Vancouver
	Tue.	11	Vancouver
	Thu.	13	Edmonton
	Sat.	15	Detroit
	Wed.	19	at Pittsburgh
	Thu.	20	at Philadelphia
	Sat.	22	Detroit
	Wed.	26	Dallas
	Fri.	28	San Jose*
	Sun.	30	Anaheim*
Dec.	Wed.	3	at Edmonton
	Fri.	5	at Calgary
	Sat.	6	at Vancouver
	Tue.	9	Calgary
	Thu.	11	Toronto
	Sat.	13	Buffalo
	Mon.	15	at Phoenix
	Wed.	17	at Colorado
	Thu.	18	at Edmonton
	Sat.	20	Columbus
	Tue.	23	Nashville
	Fri.	26	at Detroit
	Mon.	29	at Calgary
	Tue.	30	at Edmonton
Jan.	Fri.	2	Edmonton
	Sun.	4	at Colorado
	Mon.	5	at St. Louis

	Wed.	7	Chicago
	Fri.	9	Phoenix
	Mon.	12	Nashville
	Wed.	14	Los Angeles
	Fri.	16	Pittsburgh
	Sat.	17	at St. Louis
	Mon.	19	at Nashville
	Wed.	21	Chicago
	Fri.	23	at Anaheim
	Sat.	24	at San Jose
	Mon.	26	at Los Angeles
	Thu.	29	Montreal
	Sat.	31	at Columbus
Feb.	Mon.	2	St. Louis
	Wed.	4	at NY Rangers
	Tue.	10	Los Angeles
	Fri.	13	Edmonton
	Sun.	15	Calgary*
	Tue.	17	at New Jersey
	Thu.	19	Vancouver
	Sun.	22	Colorado
	Thu.	26	at Nashville
	Fri.	27	at Dallas
	Sun.	29	Carolina
Mar.	Wed.	3	at Anaheim
	Thu.	4	at Los Angeles
	Sun.	7	at Phoenix*
	Tue.	9	at San Jose
	Wed.	10	at Vancouver
	Sun.	14	Columbus
	Tue.	16	Ottawa
	Thu.	18	at Boston
	Fri.	19	at NY Islanders
	Mon.	22	Phoenix
	Wed.	24	at Columbus
	Thu.	25	at Chicago
	Sun.	28	Anaheim*
	Mon.	29	at Detroit
	Wed.	31	Colorado
Apr.	Fri.	2	Dallas
	Sun.	4	St. Louis*

* Denotes afternoon game.

Franchise date: June 25, 1997

**NORTHWEST
DIVISION**

**4th
NHL
Season**

Year-by-Year Record

| | | Home | | | Road | | | | Overall | | | | | | |
Season	GP	W	L	T	OL	W	L	T	OL	W	L	T	OL	GF	GA	Pts.	Finished	Playoff Result
2002-03	82	25	13	3	0	17	16	7	1	42	29	10	1	198	178	95	3rd, Northwest Div.	Lost Conf. Championship
2001-02	82	14	14	8	5	12	21	4	4	26	35	12	9	195	238	73	5th, Northwest Div.	Out of Playoffs
2000-01	82	14	13	10	4	11	26	3	1	25	39	13	5	168	210	68	5th, Northwest Div.	Out of Playoffs

Andrew Brunette was a playoff hero, scoring the series winner at 3:25 of overtime in game seven to complete Minnesota's comeback against Colorado. He scored two goals in game six against Vancouver as Minnesota again rallied from a 3-1 deficit.

2003-04 Player Personnel

FORWARDS	HT	WT	S	Place of Birth	Date	2002-03 Club
BALA, Chris	6-1	196	L	Alexandria, VA	9/24/78	Binghamton
BERZINS, Armands	6-3	218	L	Riga, Latvia	12/27/83	Shawinigan
BOUCHARD, Pierre-Marc	5-10	165	L	Sherbrooke, Que.	4/27/84	Minnesota
BRANDNER, Christoph	6-4	224	L	Bruck an der Mur, Austria	7/5/75	Krefeld
BRUNETTE, Andrew	6-1	210	L	Sudbury, Ont.	8/24/73	Minnesota
CAVANAUGH, Dan	6-1	190	R	Springfield, MA	3/3/80	Houston
CAVOSIE, Marc	6-0	173	L	Albany, NY	8/6/81	Houston
CHOUINARD, Marc	6-5	218	R	Charlesbourg, Que.	5/6/77	Anaheim
CULLEN, Mark	5-11	175	L	Moorhead, MN	10/28/78	Houston
DOWD, Jim	6-1	190	R	Brick, NJ	12/25/68	Minnesota
DUPUIS, Pascal	6-0	196	L	Laval, Que.	4/7/79	Minnesota
GABORIK, Marian	6-1	190	L	Trencin, Czech.	2/14/82	Minnesota
HANNULA, Mika	5-11	180	L	Huddinge, Sweden	4/2/79	Malmo
HENDRICKSON, Darby	6-1	195	L	Richfield, MN	8/28/72	Minnesota
HOGGAN, Jeff	6-0	200	R	Hope, B.C.	2/1/78	Houston
JOHNSON, Matt	6-5	235	L	Welland, Ont.	11/23/75	Minnesota
LAAKSONEN, Antti	6-0	180	L	Tammela, Finland	10/3/73	Minnesota
MUCKALT, Bill	6-1	200	R	Surrey, B.C.	7/15/74	Minnesota
PARK, Richard	5-11	190	R	Seoul, South Korea	5/27/76	Minnesota
STEVENSON, Jeremy	6-1	215	L	San Bernardino, CA	7/28/74	Minnesota-Houston
VEILLEUX, Stephane	6-1	187	L	Beaureville, Que.	11/16/81	Minnesota-Houston
WALLIN, Rickard	6-2	185	L	Stockholm, Sweden	4/19/80	Minnesota-Houston
WALZ, Wes	5-10	180	R	Calgary, Alta.	5/15/70	Minnesota
WANVIG, Kyle	6-2	219	R	Calgary, Alta.	1/29/81	Minnesota-Houston
ZHOLTOK, Sergei	6-2	197	R	Riga, Latvia	12/2/72	Minnesota
DEFENSEMEN						
BECKETT, Jason	6-3	218	R	Lethbridge, Alta.	7/23/80	Milwaukee
BOMBARDIR, Brad	6-1	205	L	Powell River, B.C.	5/5/72	Minnesota
BROWN, Brad	6-4	220	R	Baie Verte, Nfld.	12/27/75	Minnesota
DYMENT, Chris	6-3	207	R	Reading, MA	10/24/79	Houston
HEID, Chris	6-2	205	L	Langley, B.C.	3/14/83	Spokane
KUBA, Filip	6-3	205	L	Ostrava, Czech.	12/29/76	Minnesota
MARSHALL, Jason	6-2	200	R	Cranbrook, B.C.	2/22/71	Minnesota
MICHALEK, Zbynek	6-1	199	R	Jindrichuv Hradec, Czech.	12/23/82	Houston
MITCHELL, Willie	6-3	205	L	Port McNeill, B.C.	4/23/77	Minnesota
REITZ, Erik	6-1	210	R	Detroit, MI	7/29/82	Houston
ROCHE, Travis	6-1	190	R	Grand Cache, Alta	6/17/78	Houston
SCHULTZ, Nick	6-1	207	L	Strasbourg, Sask.	8/25/82	Minnesota
ZYUZIN, Andrei	6-1	215	L	Ufa, USSR	1/21/78	New Jersey-Minnesota

GOALTENDERS	HT	WT	C	Place of Birth	Date	2002-03 Club
CLOUTIER, Frederic	6-0	165	R	St-Georges, Que.	5/14/81	Houston-Louisiana
FERNANDEZ, Manny	6-0	180	L	Etobicoke, Ont.	8/27/74	Minnesota
HOLMQVIST, Johan	6-3	195	L	Tolfta, Sweden	5/24/78	NYR-Hart-Char-Houston
KETTLES, Kyle	6-3	180	L	Lac du Bonnet, Man.	2/19/81	Louisiana
ROLOSON, Dwayne	6-1	178	L	Simcoe, Ont.	10/12/69	Minnesota

Coach

LEMAIRE, JACQUES
Coach, Minnesota Wild. Born in LaSalle, Que., September 7, 1945.

The Minnesota Wild announced the signing of Jacques Lemaire as the club's first head coach on June 19, 2000. In 2002-03, he led Minnesota into the playoffs after just three seasons and all the way to the Western Conference Final. He also won the Jack Adams Award as coach of the year. Prior to joining the Wild, Lemaire had spent parts of the previous two seasons as a senior consultant to the general manager for the Montreal Canadiens, the franchise with which he captured eight Stanley Cup championships as a player.

Lemaire spent five seasons behind the New Jersey Devils bench and compiled a 199-122-57 mark. In 1994-95, he coached the Devils to their first Stanley Cup championship. In his first season with the team (1993-94), he was awarded the Jack Adams Award for the first time.

Lemaire began his NHL coaching career with the Montreal Canadiens in 1983-84. He stepped aside as head coach following the 1984-85 campaign and moved to the front office where he held the position of assistant to the managing director. In that role, Lemaire played a part in Montreal's Stanley Cup championships of 1986 and 1993.

Lemaire spent his entire NHL playing career with Montreal from 1967 to 1979 winning the Stanley Cup eight times. He then began his coaching career in Switzerland where he served as player/coach of the Sierre club. He returned to North America in 1981 and was named the first head coach of the Quebec Major Junior Hockey League's expansion Longueuil Chevaliers. In his only season at the helm (1982-83), Lemaire guided the team to the QMJHL finals.

Coaching Record

		Regular Season				Playoffs		
Season	Team	Games	W	L	T	Games	W	L
1979-80	Sierre (Switzerland)				UNAVAILABLE			
1980-81	Sierre (Switzerland)				UNAVAILABLE			
1982-83	Longueuil (QMJHL)	70	37	29	4	15	9	6
1983-84	**Montreal (NHL)**	**17**	**7**	**10**	**0**	**15**	**9**	**6**
1984-85	**Montreal (NHL)**	**80**	**41**	**27**	**12**	**12**	**6**	**6**
1993-94	**New Jersey (NHL)**	**84**	**47**	**25**	**12**	**20**	**11**	**9**
1994-95	**New Jersey (NHL)**	**48**	**22**	**18**	**8**	**20**	**16**	**4***
1995-96	**New Jersey (NHL)**	**82**	**37**	**33**	**12**	....	....	....
1996-97	**New Jersey (NHL)**	**82**	**45**	**23**	**14**	**10**	**5**	**5**
1997-98	**New Jersey (NHL)**	**82**	**48**	**23**	**11**	**6**	**2**	**4**
2000-01	**Minnesota (NHL)**	**82**	**25**	**44**	**13**	....	....	....
2001-02	**Minnesota (NHL)**	**82**	**26**	**44**	**12**	....	....	....
2002-03	**Minnesota (NHL)**	**82**	**42**	**30**	**10**	**18**	**8**	**10**
	NHL Totals	**721**	**340**	**277**	**104**	**101**	**57**	**44**

* Stanley Cup win.

2002-03 Scoring

* - rookie

Regular Season

Pos	#	Player	Team	GP	G	A	Pts	+/–	PIM	PP	SH	GW	GT	S	%
R	10	Marian Gaborik	MIN	81	30	35	65	12	46	5	1	8	0	280	10.7
L	11	Pascal Dupuis	MIN	80	20	28	48	17	44	6	0	4	1	183	10.9
C	7	Cliff Ronning	MIN	80	17	31	48	–6	24	8	0	5	0	171	9.9
L	15	Andrew Brunette	MIN	82	18	28	46	–10	30	9	0	2	3	97	18.6
R	33	Sergei Zholtok	MIN	78	16	26	42	1	18	3	0	2	2	153	10.5
C	37	Wes Walz	MIN	80	13	19	32	11	63	0	0	4	0	115	11.3
L	24	Antti Laaksonen	MIN	82	15	16	31	4	26	1	2	4	2	106	14.2
D	17	Filip Kuba	MIN	78	8	21	29	0	29	4	2	1	0	129	6.2
C	34	Jim Dowd	MIN	78	8	17	25	–1	31	3	1	2	0	78	10.3
R	18	Richard Park	MIN	81	14	10	24	–3	16	2	2	3	1	149	9.4
C	96 *	Pierre-Marc Bouchard	MIN	50	7	13	20	1	18	5	0	1	0	53	13.2
D	20	Andrei Zyuzin	N.J.	1	0	1	1	–1	2	0	0	0	0	0	0.0
			MIN	66	4	12	16	–7	34	2	0	0	0	113	3.5
			TOTAL	67	4	13	17	–8	36	2	0	0	0	113	3.5
D	5	Brad Bombardir	MIN	58	1	14	15	15	16	1	0	0	0	55	1.8
D	2	Willie Mitchell	MIN	69	2	12	14	13	84	0	1	1	0	67	3.0
L	28	Jeremy Stevenson	MIN	32	5	6	11	6	69	1	0	1	0	29	17.2
D	77	Lubomir Sekeras	MIN	60	2	9	11	–12	30	1	0	1	0	50	4.0
D	55	Nick Schultz	MIN	75	3	7	10	11	23	0	0	1	0	70	4.3
R	16	Bill Muckalt	MIN	8	5	3	8	5	6	0	0	0	0	13	38.5
L	12	Matt Johnson	MIN	60	3	5	8	–8	201	0	0	1	0	24	12.5
C	14	Darby Hendrickson	MIN	28	1	5	6	–3	8	0	0	0	0	34	2.9
L	23	Jason Marshall	MIN	45	1	5	6	4	69	0	0	0	0	40	2.5
C	19 *	Stephane Veilleux	MIN	38	3	2	5	–6	23	1	0	0	0	52	5.8
C	25 *	Rickard Wallin	MIN	4	1	0	1	1	0	0	0	1	0	1	100.0
R	27 *	Kyle Wanvig	MIN	7	1	0	1	0	13	0	0	0	0	5	20.0
D	4	Brad Brown	MIN	57	0	1	1	–1	90	0	0	0	0	10	0.0
L	9	Hnat Domenichelli	MIN	1	0	0	0	0	0	0	0	0	0	1	0.0
L	6	Jean-Guy Trudel	MIN	1	0	0	0	0	2	0	0	0	0	0	0.0
D	38	Curtis Murphy	MIN	1	0	0	0	0	0	0	0	0	0	0	0.0
D	3	Ladislav Benysek	MIN	14	0	0	0	–3	8	0	0	0	0	7	0.0

Goaltending

No.	Goaltender	GPI	Mins	Avg	W	L	T	EN	SO	GA	SA	S%	G	A	PIM
30	Dwayne Roloson	50	2945	2.00	23	16	8	1	4	98	1334	.927	0	1	4
35	Manny Fernandez	35	1979	2.24	19	13	2	0	2	74	972	.924	0	1	6
31	Dieter Kochan	1	60	5.00	0	1	0	0	0	5	28	.821	0	0	0
	Totals	**82**	**4997**	**2.14**	**42**	**30**	**10**	**1**	**6**	**178**	**2335**	**.924**			

Playoffs

Pos	#	Player	Team	GP	G	A	Pts	+/–	PIM	PP	SH	GW	GT	S	%
R	10	Marian Gaborik	MIN	18	9	8	17	2	6	4	0	0	0	52	17.3
C	37	Wes Walz	MIN	18	7	6	13	5	14	0	2	2	0	29	24.1
L	15	Andrew Brunette	MIN	18	7	6	13	–3	4	4	0	1	1	33	21.2
R	33	Sergei Zholtok	MIN	18	2	11	13	–7	0	1	0	0	0	34	5.9
C	7	Cliff Ronning	MIN	17	2	7	9	–3	4	1	0	0	0	37	5.4
L	11	Pascal Dupuis	MIN	16	4	4	8	0	8	2	0	1	0	36	11.1
D	17	Filip Kuba	MIN	18	3	5	8	–8	24	3	0	0	0	21	14.3
R	18	Richard Park	MIN	18	3	3	6	–2	4	0	0	1	1	26	11.5
C	14	Darby Hendrickson	MIN	17	2	3	5	1	4	0	0	1	0	22	9.1
L	28	Jeremy Stevenson	MIN	14	0	5	5	0	12	0	0	0	0	17	0.0
L	24	Antti Laaksonen	MIN	16	1	3	4	–3	4	0	0	0	0	25	4.0
D	2	Willie Mitchell	MIN	18	1	3	4	5	14	0	0	0	0	18	5.6
R	23	Jason Marshall	MIN	15	1	1	2	–1	16	0	0	1	0	12	8.3
D	77	Lubomir Sekeras	MIN	15	1	1	2	–2	6	1	0	1	0	13	7.7
C	34	Jim Dowd	MIN	15	0	2	2	–1	0	0	0	0	0	24	0.0
C	96 *	Pierre-Marc Bouchard	MIN	5	0	1	1	–1	2	0	0	0	0	8	0.0
D	20	Andrei Zyuzin	MIN	18	0	1	1	–3	14	0	0	0	0	30	0.0
D	55	Nick Schultz	MIN	18	0	1	1	5	10	0	0	0	0	5	0.0
D	5	Brad Bombardir	MIN	4	0	0	0	–1	0	0	0	0	0	1	0.0
R	16	Bill Muckalt	MIN	5	0	0	0	–3	0	0	0	0	0	4	0.0
D	4	Brad Brown	MIN	11	0	0	0	–1	16	0	0	0	0	0	0.0
L	12	Matt Johnson	MIN	12	0	0	0	0	25	0	0	0	0	2	0.0

Goaltending

No.	Goaltender	GPI	Mins	Avg	W	L	EN	SO	GA	SA	S%	G	A	PIM
35	Manny Fernandez	9	552	1.96	3	4	0	0	18	253	.929	0	0	0
30	Dwayne Roloson	11	579	2.59	5	6	0	0	25	257	.903	0	0	4
	Totals	**18**	**1135**	**2.27**	**8**	**10**	**0**	**0**	**43**	**510**	**.916**			

TM

Club Records

Team
(Figures in brackets for season records are games played.)

Most Points 95   2002-03 (82)
Most Wins 42   2002-03 (82)
Most Ties 13   2000-01 (82)
Most Losses 39   2000-01 (82)
Most Goals 198   2002-03 (82)
Most Goals Against 238   2001-02 (82)
Fewest Points 68   2000-01 (82)
Fewest Wins 25   2000-01 (82)
Fewest Ties 10   2002-03 (82)
Fewest Losses 29   2002-03 (82)
Fewest Goals 168   2000-01 (82)
Fewest Goals Against 178   2002-03 (82)

Longest Winning Streak
Overall 3   Eight times
Home 5   Feb. 23-Mar. 23/03
Away 2   Ten times

Longest Undefeated Streak
Overall 8   Dec. 17/00-Jan. 5/01
                      (5 wins, 3 ties)
Home 9   Dec. 13/00-Jan. 10/01
                      (5 wins, 4 ties)
Away 5   Oct. 12-Nov. 4/02
                      (3 wins, 2 ties)

Longest Losing Streak
Overall 5   Mar. 11-19/01,
                      Jan. 28-Feb. 8/02,
                      Mar. 29-Apr. 5/02
Home 4   Oct. 29-Nov. 15/00
Away 5   Mar. 15-Apr. 2/01,
                      Jan. 19-Feb. 6/02

Longest Winless Streak
Overall 12   Mar. 11-Apr. 4/01
                      (9 losses, 3 ties)
Home 8   Feb. 26-Mar. 28/01
                      (5 losses, 3 ties)
Away 6   Six times
Most Shutouts, Season 6   2000-01 (82), 2001-02 (82),
                      2002-03 (82)
Most PIM, Season 1,209   2000-01 (82)
Most Goals, Game 6   Eight times

Individual
Most Seasons 3   Many players
Most Games 246   Antti Laaksonen
Most Goals, Career 78   Marian Gaborik
Most Assists, Career 90   Marian Gaborik
Most Points, Career 168   Marian Gaborik
                      (78G, 90A)
Most PIM, Career 521   Matt Johnson
Most Shutouts, Career 9   Dwayne Roloson

Longest Consecutive Games Streak 246   Antti Laaksonen
                      (Oct. 6/00-to date)
Most Goals, Season 30   Marian Gaborik
                      (2001-02, 2002-03)
Most Assists, Season 48   Andrew Brunette
                      (2001-02)
Most Points, Season 69   Andrew Brunette
                      (2001-02; 21G, 48A)
Most PIM, Season 201   Matt Johnson
                      (2002-03)

Most Points, Defenseman,
  Season 34   Lubomir Sekeras
                      (2000-01; 11G, 23A)
Most Points, Center,
  Season 48   Cliff Ronning
                      (2002-03; 17G, 31A)
Most Points, Right Wing,
  Season 67   Marian Gaborik
                      (2001-02; 30G, 37A)
Most Points, Left Wing,
  Season 69   Andrew Brunette
                      (2001-02; 21G, 48A)
Most Points, Rookie,
  Season 36   Marian Gaborik
                      (2000-01; 18G, 18A)
Most Shutouts, Season 5   Dwayne Roloson
                      (2001-02)
Most Goals, Game 3   Antti Laaksonen
                      (Nov. 26/00),
                      Marian Gaborik
                      (Five times)
Most Assists, Game 4   Andrew Brunette
                      (Mar. 10/02),
                      Marian Gaborik
                      (Oct. 26/02)
Most Points, Game 6   Marian Gaborik
                      (Oct. 26/02; 2G, 4A)

General Managers' History
Doug Risebrough, 2000-01 to date.

Coaching History
Jacques Lemaire, 2000-01 to date.

Captains' History
Sean O'Donnell, Scott Pellerin, Wes Walz, Brad Bombardir, Darby Hendrickson, 2000-01; Jim Dowd, Filip Kuba, Brad Brown, Andrew Brunette, 2001-02; Brad Bombardir, Matt Johnson, Sergei Zholtok, 2002-03.

All-time Record vs. Other Clubs
Regular Season

	At Home							On Road							Total						
	GP	W	L	T	OL	GF	GA	PTS	GP	W	L	T	OL	GF	GA	PTS	GP	W	L	T	OL	GF	GA	PTS
Anaheim	6	2	1		1	10	12	6	6	3	0		1	15	11	7	12	5	4	1	2	25	23	13
Atlanta	2	1	0	1	0	5	3	3	2	2	0	0	0	10	6	4	4	3	0	1	0	15	9	7
Boston	2	2	0	0	0	7	2	4	2	2	0	0	0	11	4	4	4	4	0	0	0	18	6	8
Buffalo	2	0	2	0	0	1	5	0	2	1	1	0	0	5	6	2	4	1	3	0	0	6	11	2
Calgary	8	4	2	1	1	19	14	10	7	1	4	2	0	15	19	4	15	5	6	3	1	34	33	14
Carolina	3	1	1	1	0	6	9	3	2	0	2	0	0	0	3	0	5	1	3	1	0	6	12	3
Chicago	6	4	2	0	0	17	14	8	6	3	2	1	0	17	14	7	12	7	4	1	0	34	28	15
Colorado	7	2	3	1	1	13	24	6	8	0	7	1	0	14	27	1	15	2	10	2	1	27	51	7
Columbus	6	4	2	0	0	17	12	8	5	1	3	1	0	6	15	3	11	5	5	1	0	23	27	11
Dallas	6	3	3	0	0	18	14	6	6	3	2	1	0	16	21	7	12	6	5	1	0	34	35	13
Detroit	6	2	2	1	1	15	15	6	6	2	4	0	0	15	25	4	12	4	6	1	1	30	40	10
Edmonton	7	1	4	1	1	18	25	4	8	1	4	1	2	10	21	5	15	2	8	2	3	28	46	9
Florida	3	2	0	1	0	10	1	5	2	1	1	0	0	4	3	2	5	3	1	1	0	14	4	7
Los Angeles	6	1	3	2	0	10	16	4	6	4	2	0	0	18	14	8	12	5	5	2	0	28	30	12
Montreal	1	1	0	0	0	4	2	2	3	1	1	1	0	8	9	3	4	2	1	1	0	12	11	5
Nashville	6	3	3	1	0	14	12	7	6	1	3	2	0	11	15	4	12	4	5	3	0	25	27	11
New Jersey	3	1	1	1	0	7	8	3	2	0	2	0	0	4	9	0	5	1	3	1	0	11	17	3
NY Islanders	3	2	1	0	0	9	9	4	2	1	1	0	0	5	3	2	5	3	2	0	0	14	12	6
NY Rangers	3	0	2	0	1	6	10	1	2	0	2	0	0	3	7	0	5	0	4	0	1	9	17	1
Ottawa	2	0	0	1	1	5	6	2	2	1	1	0	0	4	4	2	4	1	1	1	1	9	10	4
Philadelphia	2	1	0	1	0	5	3	3	3	1	2	0	0	2	8	2	5	2	2	1	0	7	11	5
Phoenix	6	2	2	2	0	13	12	6	6	1	1	0	0	10	20	3	12	3	6	2	1	23	32	9
Pittsburgh	2	1	0	1	0	5	3	3	2	1	1	0	0	6	4	2	4	2	1	1	0	11	7	5
St. Louis	6	1	1	2	2	12	13	6	6	2	3	1	0	8	12	5	12	3	4	3	2	20	25	11
San Jose	6	4	1	1	0	16	12	9	6	2	3	1	0	10	14	5	12	6	4	2	0	26	26	14
Tampa Bay	3	3	0	0	0	13	8	6	2	1	1	0	0	7	5	3	5	4	0	0	0	20	13	9
Toronto	0	0	0	0	0	0	0	0	3	0	3	0	0	3	11	0	3	0	3	0	0	3	11	0
Vancouver	8	3	4	1	0	18	23	7	7	3	1	1	2	21	22	9	15	6	5	2	2	39	45	16
Washington	2	2	0	0	0	4	0	4	3	1	2	0	0	6	7	2	5	3	2	0	0	10	7	6
Totals	**123**	**53**	**40**	**21**	**9**	**297**	**287**	**136**	**123**	**40**	**63**	**14**	**6**	**264**	**339**	**100**	**246**	**93**	**103**	**35**	**15**	**561**	**626**	**236**

Playoffs

	Series	W	L	GP	W	L	T	GF	GA	Last Mtg.	Rnd.	Result
Anaheim	1	0	1	4	0	4	0	1	9	2003	CF	L 0-4
Colorado	1	1	0	7	4	3	0	16	17	2003	CQF	W 4-3
Vancouver	1	1	0	7	4	3	0	26	17	2003	CSF	W 4-3
Totals	**3**	**2**	**1**	**18**	**8**	**10**	**0**	**43**	**43**			

Playoff Results 2003-1999

Year	Round	Opponent	Result	GF	GA
2003	CF	Anaheim	L 0-4	1	9
	CSF	Vancouver	W 4-3	26	17
	CQF	Colorado	W 4-3	16	17

Abbreviations: Round: CF – conference final; **CSF** – conference semi-final; **CQF** – conference quarter-final.

2002-03 Results

Oct.	11	Boston	5-1	6	Los Angeles	2-3
	12	at St. Louis	2-2	8	Columbus	1-2
	15	Florida	4-1	10	Phoenix	2-1
	17	Dallas	3-1	14	Buffalo	0-1
	19	Detroit	3-5	16	Vancouver	5-2
	22	Calgary	4-3*	18	Anaheim	0-1
	24	at Chicago	3-2	20	at Anaheim	2-1*
	26	at Phoenix	6-1	23	at Los Angeles	2-1
	27	at Colorado	3-3	25	at San Jose	1-4
	29	Colorado	3-2*	28	at Vancouver	2-2
	31	San Jose	2-1*	29	at Edmonton	1-5
Nov.	2	Vancouver	2-4	**Feb.** 5	Chicago	2-1
	4	at Los Angeles	5-2	7	San Jose	4-3
	7	at Phoenix	1-4	9	at New Jersey	1-0
	9	at San Jose	4-2	10	at Philadelphia	1-0
	10	at Anaheim	0-1	12	Philadelphia	2-0
	12	Edmonton	2-3	14	Phoenix	2-3
	14	Pittsburgh	1-1	15	at Colorado	2-3
	16	Washington	1-0	19	NY Rangers	2-4
	19	Los Angeles	2-2	23	St. Louis	3-1
	21	at Washington	4-3	25	at Ottawa	3-0
	23	Nashville	4-2	27	at Montreal	6-3
	25	Vancouver	1-2	**Mar.** 1	at St. Louis	0-2
	27	at Dallas	0-5	4	New Jersey	3-2
	29	Colorado	2-2	6	at Nashville	2-2
Dec.	3	at Edmonton	1-2*	7	at Carolina	0-1
	5	at Calgary	1-1	9	at Atlanta	6-4
	7	at Vancouver	4-2	12	Dallas	4-2
	10	Tampa Bay	5-3	14	Nashville	3-1
	12	at Detroit	3-2	15	at Columbus	0-5
	14	at Nashville	1-3	17	at Tampa Bay	3-3
	15	Carolina	2-1	19	at Florida	3-1
	17	Edmonton	4-3*	21	at Dallas	3-2*
	19	NY Islanders	2-4	23	Detroit	2-0
	21	at Colorado	2-4	25	at Detroit	0-4
	23	Calgary	2-3	26	St. Louis	0-1
	26	at Chicago	2-2	28	Chicago	4-3*
	28	at Buffalo	4-3	31	Calgary	3-0
	31	Anaheim	4-1	**Apr.** 2	at Columbus	0-3
Jan.	2	at Edmonton	2-1*	3	at Toronto	1-2
	4	at Calgary	2-3	6	Columbus	4-3

* – Overtime

Entry Draft
Selections 2003-2000

2003 Pick		**2002** Pick		**2001** Pick		**2000** Pick	
20	Brent Burns	8	Pierre-Marc Bouchard	6	Mikko Koivu	3	Marian Gaborik
56	Patrick O'Sullivan	38	Josh Harding	36	Kyle Wanvig	33	Nick Schultz
78	Danny Irmen	72	Mike Erickson	74	Chris Heid	99	Marc Cavosie
157	Marcin Kolusz	73	Barry Brust	93	Stephane Veilleux	132	Maxim Sushinsky
187	Miroslav Kopriva	155	Armands Berzins	103	Tony Virta	170	Erik Reitz
207	Grigory Misharin	175	Matt Foy	202	Derek Boogaard	199	Brian Passmore
219	Adam Courchaine	204	Niklas Eckerblom	239	Jake Riddle	214	Peter Bartos
251	Mathieu Melanson	237	Christoph Brandner			232	Lubomir Sekeras
281	Jean-Michel Bolduc	268	Mikhail Tyulyapkin			255	Eric Johansson
		269	Mika Hannula				

After a second straight 30-goal season, Marian Gaborik performed brilliantly in the playoffs, ranking third among postseason performers with nine goals and 17 points.

President and General Manager

RISEBROUGH, DOUG
President/General Manager, Minnesota Wild.
Born in Guelph, Ont., January 29, 1954.

Doug Risebrough was hired as the first executive vice president and general manager of the Minnesota Wild on September 2, 1999. He is responsible for the club's overall hockey operations. His efforts to build a winner through the draft has been exemplified by the success of Martin Gaborik, the club's first-round choice in 2000. The Wild qualified for the playoffs after just three seasons, going all the way to the 2003 Western Conference Final.

After ending his 13-year NHL playing career with the Flames in 1987, Risebrough was named as assistant coach with Calgary and joined Terry Crisp behind the bench. Risebrough was appointed head coach of the Flames on May 18, 1990 and on May 16, 1991, he also assumed the role of general manager. Late in the 1991-92 campaign he directed his energies full-time to general manager, handing the coaching responsibilities over to Guy Charron for the balance of the season. Risebrough served as g.m. in Calgary through the start of the 1995-96 season. He was vice president of hockey operations for the Edmonton Oilers from 1996 to 1999.

Risebrough was Montreal's first selection, seventh overall, in the 1974 Amateur Draft. During his nine years with the Canadiens, he helped his club to four consecutive Stanley Cup championships between 1976 and 1979. He joined the Flames prior to the start of the club's 1982 training camp. During his NHL career, his clubs have won five Stanley Cup titles (1976-1979 as a player and 1989 as an assistant coach with Calgary) and two Presidents' Trophies (1987-88 and 1988-89 as an assistant coach).

NHL Coaching Record

		Regular Season				Playoffs		
Season	Team	Games	W	L	T	Games	W	L
1990-91	Calgary	80	46	26	8	7	3	4
1991-92	Calgary	64	25	30	9	....	....	....
	NHL Totals	**144**	**71**	**56**	**17**	**7**	**3**	**4**

Club Directory

Xcel Energy Center

Minnesota Wild
317 Washington Street
St. Paul, MN 55102
Phone **651/602-6000**
FAX 651/222-1055
Tickets 651/222-9453
www.wild.com
Capacity: 18,064

Executive Management
Chairman	Bob Naegele, Jr.
Chief Executive Officer	Jac Sperling
President and General Manager	Doug Risebrough
Senior V.P. of Business Operations	Matt Majka
Senior V.P. and Chief Financial Officer	Pamela Wheelock
V.P. of Customer Sales and Service	Steve Griggs
V.P./General Manager of RiverCentre	Jim Ibister
V.P. of Information Technology	Brian Jore
V.P./General Manager of Xcel Energy Center	Jack Larson
V.P. of Finance and Corporate Controller	Mike Nealy
V.P. of Administration	Mike Reeves
V.P. of Communications and Broadcasting	Bill Robertson
Manager of Special Projects	Kris Parod
Executive Assistant to Chief Executive Officer	Heather Bernier
Executive Assistant to President and G.M.	Stephanie Huseby
Executive Assistant to Chief Financial Officer	Patti Marquardt

Hockey Operations
Head Coach	Jacques Lemaire
Assistant Coaches	Mike Ramsey, Mario Tremblay
Strength and Conditioning Coach	Kirk Olson
Goaltending Consultant	Bob Mason
Director of Strength and Conditioning Programs	George Kinnear
Assistant General Manager/Hockey Operations	Tom Lynn
Assistant General Manager/Player Personnel	Tom Thompson
Coordinator of Amateur Scouting	Guy Lapointe
Coordinator of Player Development	Barry MacKenzie
Scouts	Yuri Agureikin, Marc Chamard, Paul Charles, Frank Effinger, Branislav Gaborik, Herb Hammond, Ken Hoodikoff, Jiri Koluch, Doug Mosher, Darryl Porter, Glen Sonmor, Bruce Southern, Thomas Steen, Rich Sutter, Tim Sweeney, Matti Vaisanen, Ernie Vargas
Head Athletic Therapist	Don Fuller
Head Equipment Manager	Tony DaCosta
Assistant Athletic Trainer	Mike Vogt
Assistant Equipment Manager	Brent Proulx
Assistant Equipment Manager	Matt Benz
Video Coordinator	Todd Woodcroft
Hockey Operations Assistant	Tobin Wright
Hockey Operations Administrator	Cindy Sweiger
Hockey Operations Coordinator	Denny Scanlon
Medical Director	Dr. Sheldon Burns
Orthopedic Surgeon	Dr. Joel Boyd

Customer Sales And Service
Director of Customer Sales and Service	Jamie Spencer
Director of Group and Event Suite Sales	Kelly Harens
Director of Retail Operations	Chris Poitras
Director of Premium Service/Operation	Rachael Johnson
Coordinator, Xcel Energy Center Group Sales	Karen Reisinger

Communications And Broadcasting
Manager of Media Relations and Team Services	Brad Smith
Director of Broadcasting	Pat O'Connor
Manager of Arena Communications	Chris Kelleher
Communications Manager	Aaron Sickman
Communications Coordinator	Jason Ball
Director of Community Relations	Marlene Wall
Coordinator of Community Relations	Kendra Christensen
Broadcast Coordinator	Maggie Kukar
Associate Radio Producer	Kevin Falness
Radio Play-by-Play	Bob Kurtz
Radio Analyst	Tom Reid
TV Play-by-Play	Matt McConnell
TV Analyst	Mike Greenlay

Finance
Executive Assistant	Maggie Hobbs
Director of Accounting Operations	Dean Harris
Senior Staff Accountant	Lisa Merry
Senior Staff Accountant	Mindee Mills
Staff Accountant	Melissa Webb
Executive Director of 10K Rinks Foundation	Heather McGinty

Marketing & Corporate Partnerships
Team Curator	Roger Godin
Director of Corporate Services	Carin Anderson
Director of Advertising and Promotion	Wayne Petersen
Senior Director of Creative Services	John Maher
Director of Graphic Services and Publications	Brian Israel

Information Technology
Director of Technology Services	Chris Monicatti
Director of Internet Services	Brian Hutchinson

Administration
Employment and Benefits Manager	Timothy Case
317 Facilities Manager	Tim Wolfgram

Miscellaneous
Training Site	Parade Ice Garden and Xcel Energy Center
Radio Network Flagship	WCCO (830 AM)
T.V. Networks	KMSP 9 (over-the-air), FOX Sports Net (Cable)
Team Photographer	Bruce Kluckhohn
Public Address Announcer	Adam Abrams

Saku Koivu had 71 points in 82 games.

Montreal Canadiens

2002-03 Results: 30W-35L-8T-9OTL 77PTS.
Fourth, Northeast Division

Year-by-Year Record

Season	GP	Home W	L	T	OL	Road W	L	T	OL	Overall W	L	T	OL	GF	GA	Pts	Finished	Playoff Result
2002-03	82	16	16	5	4	14	19	3	5	30	35	8	9	206	234	77	4th, Northeast Div.	Out of Playoffs
2001-02	82	21	13	6	1	15	18	6	2	36	31	12	3	207	209	87	4th, Northeast Div.	Lost Conf. Semi-Final
2000-01	82	15	20	4	2	13	20	4	4	28	40	8	6	206	232	70	5th, Northeast Div.	Out of Playoffs
1999-2000	82	18	17	5	1	17	17	4	3	35	34	9	4	196	194	83	4th, Northeast Div.	Out of Playoffs
1998-99	82	21	15	5	...	11	24	6	...	32	39	11	...	184	209	75	5th, Northeast Div.	Out of Playoffs
1997-98	82	15	17	9	...	22	15	4	...	37	32	13	...	235	208	87	4th, Northeast Div.	Lost Conf. Semi-Final
1996-97	82	17	17	7	...	14	19	8	...	31	36	15	...	249	276	77	4th, Northeast Div.	Lost Conf. Quarter-Final
1995-96	82	23	12	6	...	17	20	4	...	40	32	10	...	265	248	90	3rd, Northeast Div.	Lost Conf. Quarter-Final
1994-95	48	15	5	4	...	3	18	3	...	18	23	7	...	125	148	43	6th, Northeast Div.	Out of Playoffs
1993-94	84	26	12	4	...	15	17	10	...	41	29	14	...	283	248	96	3rd, Northeast Div.	Lost Conf. Quarter-Final
1992-93	84	27	13	2	...	21	17	4	...	48	30	6	...	326	280	102	3rd, Adams Div.	Won Stanley Cup
1991-92	80	27	8	5	...	14	20	6	...	41	28	11	...	267	207	93	1st, Adams Div.	Lost Div. Final
1990-91	80	23	12	5	...	16	18	6	...	39	30	11	...	273	249	89	2nd, Adams Div.	Lost Div. Final
1989-90	80	26	8	6	...	15	20	5	...	41	28	11	...	288	234	93	3rd, Adams Div.	Lost Div. Final
1988-89	80	30	6	4	...	23	12	5	...	53	18	9	...	315	218	115	1st, Adams Div.	Lost Final
1987-88	80	26	8	6	...	19	14	7	...	45	22	13	...	298	238	103	1st, Adams Div.	Lost Div. Final
1986-87	80	27	9	4	...	14	20	6	...	41	29	10	...	277	241	92	2nd, Adams Div.	Lost Conf. Championship
1985-86	80	25	11	4	...	15	22	3	...	40	33	7	...	330	280	87	2nd, Adams Div.	Won Stanley Cup
1984-85	80	24	10	6	...	17	17	6	...	41	27	12	...	309	262	94	1st, Adams Div.	Lost Div. Final
1983-84	80	19	19	2	...	16	21	3	...	35	40	5	...	286	295	75	4th, Adams Div.	Lost Conf. Championship
1982-83	80	25	6	9	...	17	18	5	...	42	24	14	...	350	286	98	2nd, Adams Div.	Lost Div. Semi-Final
1981-82	80	25	6	9	...	21	11	8	...	46	17	17	...	360	223	109	1st, Adams Div.	Lost Div. Semi-Final
1980-81	80	31	7	2	...	14	15	11	...	45	22	13	...	332	232	103	1st, Norris Div.	Lost Prelim. Round
1979-80	80	30	7	3	...	17	13	10	...	47	20	13	...	328	240	107	1st, Norris Div.	Lost Quarter-Final
1978-79	80	29	6	5	...	23	11	6	...	52	17	11	...	337	204	115	1st, Norris Div.	Won Stanley Cup
1977-78	80	32	4	4	...	27	6	7	...	59	10	11	...	359	183	129	1st, Norris Div.	Won Stanley Cup
1976-77	80	33	1	6	...	27	7	6	...	60	8	12	...	387	171	132	1st, Norris Div.	Won Stanley Cup
1975-76	80	32	3	5	...	26	8	6	...	58	11	11	...	337	174	127	1st, Norris Div.	Won Stanley Cup
1974-75	80	27	8	5	...	20	6	14	...	47	14	19	...	374	225	113	1st, Norris Div.	Lost Semi-Final
1973-74	78	24	12	3	...	21	12	6	...	45	24	9	...	293	240	99	2nd, East Div.	Lost Quarter-inal
1972-73	78	29	4	6	...	23	6	10	...	52	10	16	...	329	184	120	1st, East Div.	Won Stanley Cup
1971-72	78	29	3	7	...	17	13	9	...	46	16	16	...	307	205	108	3rd, East Div.	Lost Quarter-Final
1970-71	78	29	7	3	...	13	16	10	...	42	23	13	...	291	216	97	3rd, East Div.	Won Stanley Cup
1969-70	76	21	9	8	...	17	13	8	...	38	22	16	...	244	201	92	5th, East Div.	Out of Playoffs
1968-69	76	26	7	5	...	20	12	6	...	46	19	11	...	271	202	103	1st, East Div.	Won Stanley Cup
1967-68	74	26	5	6	...	16	17	4	...	42	22	10	...	236	167	94	1st, East Div.	Won Stanley Cup
1966-67	70	19	9	7	...	13	16	6	...	32	25	13	...	202	188	77	2nd,	Lost Final
1965-66	70	23	11	1	...	18	10	7	...	41	21	8	...	239	173	90	1st,	Won Stanley Cup
1964-65	70	20	8	7	...	16	15	4	...	36	23	11	...	211	185	83	2nd,	Won Stanley Cup
1963-64	70	22	7	6	...	14	14	7	...	36	21	13	...	209	167	85	1st,	Lost Semi-Final
1962-63	70	15	10	10	...	13	9	13	...	28	19	23	...	225	183	79	3rd,	Lost Semi-Final
1961-62	70	26	2	7	...	16	12	7	...	42	14	14	...	259	166	98	1st,	Lost Semi-Final
1960-61	70	24	6	5	...	17	13	5	...	41	19	10	...	254	188	92	1st,	Lost Semi-Final
1959-60	70	23	4	8	...	17	14	4	...	40	18	12	...	255	178	92	1st,	Won Stanley Cup
1958-59	70	21	8	6	...	18	10	7	...	39	18	13	...	258	158	91	1st,	Won Stanley Cup
1957-58	70	23	8	4	...	20	9	6	...	43	17	10	...	250	158	96	1st,	Won Stanley Cup
1956-57	70	23	6	6	...	12	17	6	...	35	23	12	...	210	158	82	2nd,	Won Stanley Cup
1955-56	70	29	5	1	...	16	10	9	...	45	15	10	...	222	131	100	1st,	Won Stanley Cup
1954-55	70	26	5	4	...	15	13	7	...	41	18	11	...	228	157	93	2nd,	Lost Final
1953-54	70	27	5	3	...	8	19	8	...	35	24	11	...	195	141	81	2nd,	Lost Final
1952-53	70	18	12	5	...	10	11	14	...	28	23	19	...	155	148	75	2nd,	Won Stanley Cup
1951-52	70	22	8	5	...	12	18	5	...	34	26	10	...	195	164	78	2nd,	Lost Final
1950-51	70	17	10	8	...	8	20	7	...	25	30	15	...	173	184	65	3rd,	Lost Final
1949-50	70	17	8	10	...	12	14	9	...	29	22	19	...	172	150	77	2nd,	Lost Semi-Final
1948-49	60	19	8	3	...	9	15	6	...	28	23	9	...	152	126	65	3rd,	Lost Semi-Final
1947-48	60	13	13	4	...	7	16	7	...	20	29	11	...	147	169	51	5th,	Out of Playoffs
1946-47	60	19	6	5	...	15	10	5	...	34	16	10	...	189	138	78	1st,	Lost Final
1945-46	50	16	6	3	...	12	11	2	...	28	17	5	...	172	134	61	1st,	Won Stanley Cup
1944-45	50	21	2	2	...	17	6	2	...	38	8	4	...	228	121	80	1st,	Lost Semi-Final
1943-44	50	22	0	3	...	16	5	4	...	38	5	7	...	234	109	83	1st,	Won Stanley Cup
1942-43	50	14	4	7	...	5	15	5	...	19	19	12	...	181	191	50	4th,	Lost Semi-Final
1941-42	48	12	10	2	...	6	17	1	...	18	27	3	...	134	173	39	6th,	Lost Quarter-Final
1940-41	48	11	9	4	...	5	17	2	...	16	26	6	...	121	147	38	6th,	Lost Quarter-Final
1939-40	48	5	14	5	...	5	19	0	...	10	33	5	...	90	167	25	7th,	Out of Playoffs
1938-39	48	8	11	5	...	7	13	4	...	15	24	9	...	115	146	39	6th,	Lost Quarter-Final
1937-38	48	13	4	7	...	5	13	6	...	18	17	13	...	123	128	49	3rd, Cdn. Div.	Lost Quarter-Final
1936-37	48	16	8	0	...	8	10	6	...	24	18	6	...	115	111	54	1st, Cdn. Div.	Lost Semi-Final
1935-36	48	5	11	8	...	6	15	3	...	11	26	11	...	82	123	33	4th, Cdn. Div.	Out of Playoffs
1934-35	48	11	11	2	...	8	12	4	...	19	23	6	...	110	145	44	3rd, Cdn. Div.	Lost Quarter-Final
1933-34	48	16	6	2	...	6	14	4	...	22	20	6	...	99	101	50	2nd, Cdn. Div.	Lost Quarter-Final
1932-33	48	15	5	4	...	3	20	1	...	18	25	5	...	92	115	41	3rd, Cdn. Div.	Lost Quarter-Final
1931-32	48	18	3	3	...	7	13	4	...	25	16	7	...	128	111	57	1st, Cdn. Div.	Lost Semi-Final
1930-31	44	15	3	4	...	11	7	4	...	26	10	8	...	129	89	60	1st, Cdn. Div.	Won Stanley Cup
1929-30	44	13	5	4	...	8	9	5	...	21	14	9	...	142	114	51	2nd, Cdn. Div.	Won Stanley Cup
1928-29	44	12	4	6	...	10	3	9	...	22	7	15	...	71	43	59	1st, Cdn. Div.	Lost Semi-Final
1927-28	44	12	7	3	...	14	4	4	...	26	11	7	...	116	48	59	1st, Cdn. Div.	Lost Semi-Final
1926-27	44	15	5	2	...	13	9	0	...	28	14	2	...	99	67	58	2nd, Cdn. Div.	Lost Semi-Final
1925-26	36	5	12	1	...	6	12	0	...	11	24	1	...	79	108	23	7th,	Out of Playoffs
1924-25	30	10	5	0	...	7	6	2	...	17	11	2	...	93	56	36	3rd,	Lost Final
1923-24	24	10	2	0	...	3	9	0	...	13	11	0	...	59	48	26	2nd,	Won Stanley Cup
1922-23	24	10	2	0	...	3	7	2	...	13	9	2	...	73	61	28	2nd,	Lost NHL Final
1921-22	24	8	3	1	...	4	8	0	...	12	11	1	...	88	94	25	3rd,	Out of Playoffs
1920-21	24	9	3	0	...	4	8	0	...	13	11	0	...	112	99	26	3rd and 2nd*	Out of Playoffs
1919-20	24	8	4	0	...	5	7	0	...	13	11	0	...	129	113	26	2nd and 3rd*	Out of Playoffs
1918-19	18	7	2	0	...	3	6	0	...	10	8	0	...	88	78	20	1st and 2nd*	Cup Final but no Decision
1917-18	22	8	3	0	...	5	6	0	...	13	9	0	...	115	84	26	1st and 3rd*	Lost NHL Final

* Season played in two halves with no combined standing at end.
From 1917-18 through 1925-26, NHL champions played against PCHA/WCHL champions for Stanley Cup.

2003-04 Schedule

Oct.	Thu.	9	at Ottawa		Tue.	6	Buffalo	
	Sat.	11	at Toronto		Thu.	8	Tampa Bay	
	Tue.	14	Washington		Sat.	10	at Pittsburgh*	
	Thu.	16	Pittsburgh		Tue.	13	St. Louis	
	Sat.	18	Toronto		Wed.	14	at Atlanta	
	Mon.	20	Detroit		Sat.	17	NY Rangers	
	Thu.	23	NY Islanders		Tue.	20	at Philadelphia	
	Sat.	25	Ottawa		Fri.	23	at New Jersey	
	Mon.	27	at Philadelphia		Sat.	24	Toronto	
	Tue.	28	Boston		Tue.	27	at Buffalo	
	Thu.	30	at Boston		Thu.	29	at Minnesota	
Nov.	Sat.	1	NY Rangers		Sat.	31	Boston*	
	Tue.	4	Edmonton	Feb.	Sun.	1	Chicago*	
	Fri.	7	at Buffalo		Tue.	3	at Pittsburgh	
	Sat.	8	Buffalo		Thu.	5	NY Islanders	
	Tue.	11	Columbus		Tue.	10	at Florida	
	Thu.	13	at NY Islanders		Thu.	12	at Tampa Bay	
	Sat.	15	at Ottawa		Sat.	14	at Ottawa	
	Tue.	18	at Vancouver		Tue.	17	Atlanta	
	Thu.	20	at Calgary		Thu.	19	Colorado	
	Sat.	22	at Edmonton*		Sat.	21	at Toronto	
	Tue.	25	Vancouver		Mon.	23	at NY Rangers	
	Fri.	28	at Washington		Tue.	24	Ottawa	
	Sat.	29	Florida		Thu.	26	at Boston	
Dec.	Tue.	2	Tampa Bay		Sat.	28	Carolina	
	Fri.	5	at Carolina	Mar.	Mon.	1	New Jersey	
	Sat.	6	Carolina		Wed.	3	at San Jose	
	Mon.	8	Philadelphia		Fri.	5	at Phoenix	
	Wed.	10	at NY Rangers		Sat.	6	at Los Angeles	
	Fri.	12	at Florida		Mon.	8	at Anaheim	
	Sat.	13	at Tampa Bay		Thu.	11	Florida	
	Tue.	16	Boston		Sat.	13	Toronto	
	Thu.	18	Nashville		Tue.	16	Colorado	
	Sat.	20	at Toronto		Fri.	19	at New Jersey	
	Mon.	22	Pittsburgh		Sat.	20	New Jersey	
	Tue.	23	at Washington		Wed.	24	at Buffalo	
	Sat.	27	at Carolina		Thu.	25	Ottawa	
	Mon.	29	at Atlanta		Sat.	27	at Boston	
	Wed.	31	at Dallas		Wed.	31	at NY Islanders	
Jan.	Sat.	3	Atlanta*	Apr.	Thu.	1	at Philadelphia	
	Sun.	4	Washington*		Sat.	3	Buffalo	

* Denotes afternoon game.

Franchise date: November 22, 1917

NORTHEAST DIVISION

87th NHL Season

2003-04 Player Personnel

FORWARDS	HT	WT	S	Place of Birth	Date	2002-03 Club
AUDETTE, Donald	5-8	190	R	Laval, Que.	9/23/69	Montreal-Hamilton
BLOUIN, Sylvain	6-2	215	L	Montreal, Que.	5/21/74	Minnesota-Montreal-Hamilton
BULIS, Jan	6-2	201	L	Pardubice, Czech.	3/18/78	Montreal
DACKELL, Andreas	5-11	194	R	Gavle, Sweden	12/29/72	Montreal
DAGENAIS, Pierre	6-5	215	L	Blainville, Que.	3/4/78	Florida-San Antonio
DWYER, Gordie	6-3	215	L	Dalhousie, N.B.	1/25/78	NY Rangers-Hartford-Montreal
GRATTON, Benoit	5-11	194	L	Montreal, Que.	12/28/76	Hamilton
HOSSA, Marcel	6-2	211	L	Ilava, Czech.	10/12/81	Montreal-Hamilton
JUNEAU, Joe	6-0	195	L	Pont-Rouge, Que.	1/5/68	Montreal
KILGER, Chad	6-4	224	L	Cornwall, Ont.	11/27/76	Montreal
KOIVU, Saku	5-10	181	L	Turku, Finland	11/23/74	Montreal
PERREAULT, Yanic	5-11	185	L	Sherbrooke, Que.	4/4/71	Montreal
RIBEIRO, Mike	6-0	177	L	Montreal, Que.	2/10/80	Montreal-Hamilton
RYDER, Michael	6-1	195	R	St. John's, Nfld.	3/31/80	Hamilton
SUNDSTROM, Niklas	6-0	195	L	Ornskoldsvik, Sweden	6/6/75	San Jose-Montreal
WARD, Jason	6-3	200	R	Chapleau, Ont.	1/16/79	Montreal-Hamilton
ZEDNIK, Richard	6-0	200	L	Bystrica, Czech.	1/6/76	Montreal
DEFENSEMEN						
BEAUCHEMIN, Francois	6-0	206	L	Sorel, Que.	6/4/80	Montreal-Hamilton
BOUILLON, Francis	5-8	194	L	New York, NY	10/17/75	Nashville-Montreal-Hamilton
BRISEBOIS, Patrice	6-2	203	R	Montreal, Que.	1/27/71	Montreal
DYKHUIS, Karl	6-3	214	L	Sept-Iles, Que.	7/8/72	Montreal
HAINSEY, Ron	6-3	200	L	Bolton, CT	3/24/81	Montreal-Hamilton
KOMISAREK, Mike	6-4	240	R	Islip Terrace, NY	1/19/82	Montreal-Hamilton
MARKOV, Andrei	6-0	208	L	Voskresensk, USSR	12/20/78	Montreal
QUINTAL, Stephane	6-3	231	R	Boucherville, Que.	10/22/68	Montreal
RIVET, Craig	6-2	207	R	North Bay, Ont.	9/13/74	Montreal
SOURAY, Sheldon	6-4	223	L	Elk Point, Alta.	7/13/76	did not play
TRAVERSE, Patrick	6-4	207	L	Montreal, Que.	3/14/74	Montreal
GOALTENDERS	**HT**	**WT**	**C**	**Place of Birth**	**Date**	**2002-03 Club**
DAMPHOUSSE, Jean-Francois	6-0	180	L	St-Alexis-des-Monts, Que.	7/21/79	Cincinnati (AHL)-Saint John
FICHAUD, Eric	5-11	179	L	Anjou, Que.	11/4/75	Hamilton
GARON, Mathieu	6-2	192	R	Chandler, Que.	1/9/78	Montreal-Hamilton
MICHAUD, Olivier	5-11	160	L	Beloeil, Que.	9/14/83	Shawinigan-Baie-Comeau
THEODORE, Jose	5-11	182	R	Laval, Que.	9/13/76	Montreal

2002-03 Scoring

* - rookie

Regular Season

Pos	#	Player	Team	GP	G	A	Pts	+/–	PIM	PP	SH	GW	GT	S	%
C	11	Saku Koivu	MTL	82	21	50	71	5	72	5	1	5	0	147	14.3
R	20	Richard Zednik	MTL	80	31	19	50	4	79	9	0	2	1	250	12.4
C	94	Yanic Perreault	MTL	73	24	22	46	–11	30	7	0	4	0	145	16.6
C	38	Jan Bulis	MTL	82	16	24	40	9	30	0	0	2	0	160	10.0
D	79	Andrei Markov	MTL	79	13	24	37	13	34	3	0	2	0	159	8.2
D	43	Patrice Brisebois	MTL	73	4	25	29	–14	32	1	0	1	0	105	3.8
R	37	Niklas Sundstrom	S.J.	47	2	10	12	–4	22	0	0	0	0	36	5.6
			MTL	33	5	9	14	3	8	0	0	1	0	35	14.3
			TOTAL	80	7	19	26	–1	30	0	0	1	0	71	9.9
R	24	Andreas Dackell	MTL	73	7	18	25	–5	24	0	0	1	0	74	9.5
R	82	Donald Audette	MTL	54	11	12	23	–7	19	4	0	4	1	118	9.3
D	52	Craig Rivet	MTL	82	7	15	22	1	71	3	0	2	0	118	5.9
C	90	Joe Juneau	MTL	72	6	16	22	–10	20	0	0	2	0	88	6.8
R	21	Randy McKay	MTL	75	6	13	19	–14	72	2	0	0	1	52	11.5
C	71	Mike Ribeiro	MTL	52	5	12	17	–3	6	2	0	0	0	57	8.8
L	25	Chad Kilger	MTL	60	9	7	16	–4	21	0	0	1	0	60	15.0
R	27	Mariusz Czerkawski	MTL	43	5	9	14	–7	16	1	0	0	0	77	6.5
L	81	* Marcel Hossa	MTL	34	6	7	13	3	14	2	0	1	0	51	11.8
D	54	Patrick Traverse	MTL	65	0	13	13	–9	24	0	0	0	0	63	0.0
D	5	Stephane Quintal	MTL	67	5	5	10	–4	70	0	0	0	0	73	6.8
R	17	Jason Ward	MTL	8	3	2	5	3	0	0	0	0	0	10	30.0
D	28	Karl Dykhuis	MTL	65	1	4	5	–5	34	0	0	0	0	24	4.2
D	51	Francis Bouillon	NSH	4	0	0	0	–1	2	0	0	0	0	0	0.0
			MTL	20	3	1	4	–1	2	0	1	0	0	30	10.0
			TOTAL	24	3	1	4	–2	4	0	1	0	0	30	10.0
L	22	Bill Lindsay	MTL	19	0	2	2	–1	23	0	0	0	0	7	0.0
D	8	* Mike Komisarek	MTL	21	0	1	1	–6	28	0	0	0	0	26	0.0
L	32	Gordie Dwyer	NYR	17	0	1	1	–1	50	0	0	0	0	8	0.0
			MTL	11	0	0	0	–2	46	0	0	0	0	2	0.0
			TOTAL	28	0	1	1	–3	96	0	0	0	0	10	0.0
D	36	* Francois Beauchemin	MTL	1	0	0	0	–1	0	0	0	0	0	1	0.0
L	26	Sylvain Blouin	MIN	2	0	0	0	0	4	0	0	0	0	1	0.0
			MTL	17	0	0	0	–3	43	0	0	0	0	3	0.0
			TOTAL	19	0	0	0	–3	47	0	0	0	0	4	0.0
D	65	* Ron Hainsey	MTL	21	0	0	0	–1	2	0	0	0	0	12	0.0

Goaltending

No.	Goaltender	GPI	Mins	Avg	W	L	T	EN	SO	GA	SA	S%	G	A	PIM
30	* Mathieu Garon	8	482	1.99	3	5	0	1	2	16	267	.940	0	0	0
30	Jeff Hackett	18	1063	2.54	7	8	2	1	0	45	606	.926	0	0	0
60	Jose Theodore	57	3419	2.90	20	31	6	6	2	165	1797	.908	0	2	6
	Totals	**82**	**4988**	**2.81**	**30**	**44**	**8**	**8**	**4**	**234**	**2678**	**.913**			

Vice President and General Manager

GAINEY, BOB
Executive Vice President/General Manager, Montreal Canadiens.
Born in Peterborough, Ont., December 13, 1953.

On June 2, 2003, Canadiens president Pierre Boivin announced the appointment of Bob Gainey as executive vice president and general manager, effective July 1, 2003. Gainey replaced Andre Savard, who remained with the club as assistant g.m.

Described as the world's best all-around player by legendary Soviet national team coach Viktor Tikhonov, Bob Gainey brought many elements to the Montreal Canadiens during his 16-year NHL playing career. The left winger was a tenacious competitor, relentless checker and a respected team leader. His presence on the Canadiens' roster helped the team win the Stanley Cup five times in the decade between 1976 and 1986. He won the Conn Smythe Trophy as playoff MVP in 1979 and was a four-time winner of the Selke Trophy as the NHL's best defensive forward. Gainey was captain of the Canadiens from 1981 until his retirement in 1989. He was elected to the Hockey Hall of Fame in 1992.

After leaving the NHL, Gainey signed on for a year as player-coach of the Epinal franchise in French hockey's first division. He returned from France to become coach of the Minnesota North Stars in 1990-91 and led the team to the Stanley Cup Final that season. Gainey was given the g.m.'s job in 1992 and was in the dual role when the Stars relocated to Dallas in 1993.

In Texas, Gainey helped build the team into a powerhouse. He stepped down as coach on January 8, 1996 to focus solely on the duties of general manager and masterminded the acquisition of key performers such as Joe Nieuwendyk, Pat Verbeek, Brett Hull and Ed Belfour, who augmented homegrown talent like Derian Hatcher and Jamie Langenbrunner. Under Gainey's leadership, the Stars won five straight division titles from 1996-97 to 2000-01, the Presidents' Trophy in 1998 and 1999, and the Stanley Cup in 1999.

NHL Coaching Record

		Regular Season				Playoffs		
Season	Team	Games	W	L	T	Games	W	L
1990-91	Minnesota	80	27	39	14	23	14	9
1991-92	Minnesota	80	32	42	6	7	3	4
1992-93	Minnesota	84	36	38	10	....	....	....
1993-94	Dallas	84	42	29	13	9	5	4
1994-95	Dallas	48	17	23	8	5	1	4
1995-96	Dallas	39	11	19	9	....	....	....
	NHL Totals	**415**	**165**	**190**	**60**	**44**	**23**	**21**

Coaching History

Jack Laviolette, 1909-10; Adolphe Lecours, 1910-11; Napoleon Dorval, 1911-12, 1912-13; Jimmy Gardner, 1913-14, 1914-15; Newsy Lalonde, 1915-16 to 1920-21; Newsy Lalonde and Léo Dandurand, 1921-22; Léo Dandurand, 1922-23 to 1925-26; Cecil Hart, 1926-27 to 1931-32; Newsy Lalonde, 1932-33, 1933-34; Newsy Lalonde and Léo Dandurand, 1934-35; Sylvio Mantha, 1935-36; Cecil Hart, 1936-37, 1937-38; Cecil Hart and Jules Dugal, 1938-39; Babe Siebert, 1939*; Pit Lepine, 1939-40; Dick Irvin 1940-41 to 1954-55; Toe Blake, 1955-56 to 1967-68; Claude Ruel, 1968-69, 1969-70; Claude Ruel and Al MacNeil, 1970-71; Scotty Bowman, 1971-72 to 1978-79; Bernie Geoffrion and Claude Ruel, 1979-80; Claude Ruel, 1980-81; Bob Berry, 1981-82, 1982-83; Bob Berry and Jacques Lemaire, 1983-84; Jacques Lemaire, 1984-85; Jean Perron, 1985-86 to 1987-88; Pat Burns, 1988-89 to 1991-92; Jacques Demers, 1992-93 to 1994-95; Jacques Demers and Mario Tremblay, 1995-96; Mario Tremblay, 1996-97; Alain Vigneault, 1997-98 to 1999-2000; Alain Vigneault and Michel Therrien, 2000-01; Michel Therrien, 2001-02; Michel Therrien and Claude Julien, 2002-03; Claude Julien, 2003-04.

* Named coach in summer but died before 1939-40 season began.

General Managers' History

Jack Laviolette and Joseph Cattarinich, 1909-1910; George Kennedy, 1910-11 to 1920-21; Leo Dandurand, 1921-22 to 1934-35; Ernest Savard, 1935-36; Cecil Hart, 1936-37 to 1938-39; Jules Dugal, 1939-40; Tom P. Gorman, 1940-41 to 1945-46; Frank J. Selke, 1946-47 to 1963-64; Sam Pollock, 1964-65 to 1977-78; Irving Grundman, 1978-79 to 1982-83; Serge Savard, 1983-84 to 1994-95; Serge Savard and Réjean Houle, 1995-96; Réjean Houle, 1996-97 to 1999-2000; Réjean Houle and Andre Savard, 2000-01; Andre Savard, 2001-02 to 2002-03; Bob Gainey, 2003-04.

Captains' History

Jack Laviolette, 1909-10; Newsy Lalonde, 1910-11; Jack Laviolette, 1911-12; Newsy Lalonde, 1912-13; Jimmy Gardner, 1913-14, 1914-15; Howard McNamara, 1915-16; Newsy Lalonde, 1916-17 to 1921-22; Sprague Cleghorn, 1922-23 to 1924-25; Bill Coutu, 1925-26; Sylvio Mantha, 1926-27 to 1931-32; George Hainsworth, 1932-33; Sylvio Mantha, 1933-34 to 1935-36; Babe Siebert, 1936-37 to 1938-39; Walt Buswell, 1939-40; Toe Blake, 1940-41 to 1946-47; Toe Blake and Bill Durnan, 1947-48; Butch Bouchard, 1948-49 to 1955-56; Maurice Richard, 1956-57 to 1959-60; Doug Harvey, 1960-61; Jean Béliveau, 1961-62 to 1970-71; Henri Richard, 1971-72 to 1974-75; Yvan Cournoyer, 1975-76 to 1978-79; Serge Savard, 1979-80, 1980-81; Bob Gainey, 1981-82 to 1988-89; Guy Carbonneau and Chris Chelios (co-captains), 1989-90; Guy Carbonneau, 1990-91 to 1993-94; Kirk Muller and Mike Keane, 1994-95; Mike Keane and Pierre Turgeon, 1995-96; Pierre Turgeon and Vincent Damphousse, 1996-97; Vincent Damphousse, 1997-98, 1998-99; Saku Koivu, 1999-2000 to date.

Club Records

Team

(Figures in brackets for season records are games played; records for fewest points, wins, ties, losses, goals, goals against are for 70 or more games)

Most Points	*132	1976-77 (80)
Most Wins	60	1976-77 (80)
Most Ties	23	1962-63 (70)
Most Losses	40	1983-84 (80), 2000-01 (82)
Most Goals	387	1976-77 (80)
Most Goals Against	295	1983-84 (80)
Fewest Points	65	1950-51 (70)
Fewest Wins	25	1950-51 (70)
Fewest Ties	5	1983-84 (80)
Fewest Losses	*8	1976-77 (80)
Fewest Goals	155	1952-53 (70)
Fewest Goals Against	*131	1955-56 (70)
Longest Winning Streak		
Overall	12	Jan. 6-Feb. 3/68
Home	13	Nov. 2/43-Jan. 8/44, Jan. 30-Mar. 26/77
Away	8	Dec. 18/77-Jan. 18/78, Jan. 21-Feb. 21/82
Longest Undefeated Streak		
Overall	28	Dec. 18/77-Feb. 23/78 (23 wins, 5 ties)
Home	*34	Nov. 1/76-Apr. 2/77 (28 wins, 6 ties)
Away	*23	Nov. 27/74-Mar. 12/75 (14 wins, 9 ties)
Longest Losing Streak		
Overall	12	Feb. 13-Mar. 13/26
Home	7	Dec. 16/39-Jan. 18/40, Oct. 28-Nov. 25/00
Away	10	Jan. 16-Mar. 13/26
Longest Winless Streak		
Overall	12	Feb. 13-Mar. 13/26 (12 losses), Nov. 28-Dec. 29/35 (8 losses, 4 ties)
Home	15	Dec. 16/39-Mar. 7/40 (12 losses, 3 ties)
Away	12	Nov. 26/33-Jan. 28/34 (8 losses, 4 ties), Oct. 20/50-Dec. 13/51 (8 losses, 4 ties)
Most Shutouts, Season	*22	1928-29 (44)
Most PIM, Season	1,847	1995-96 (82)
Most Goals, Game	*16	Mar. 3/20 (Mtl. 16 at Que. 3)

Individual

Most Seasons	20	Henri Richard, Jean Béliveau
Most Games	1,256	Henri Richard
Most Goals, Career	544	Maurice Richard
Most Assists, Career	728	Guy Lafleur
Most Points, Career	1,246	Guy Lafleur (518G, 728A)
Most PIM, Career	2,248	Chris Nilan
Most Shutouts, Career	75	George Hainsworth
Longest Consecutive Games Streak	560	Doug Jarvis (Oct. 8/75-Apr. 4/82)
Most Goals, Season	60	Steve Shutt (1976-77), Guy Lafleur (1977-78)
Most Assists, Season	82	Pete Mahovlich (1974-75)
Most Points, Season	136	Guy Lafleur (1976-77; 56G, 80A)
Most PIM, Season	358	Chris Nilan (1984-85)
Most Points, Defenseman, Season	85	Larry Robinson (1976-77; 19G, 66A)
Most Points, Center, Season	117	Pete Mahovlich (1974-75; 35G, 82A)
Most Points, Right Wing, Season	136	Guy Lafleur (1976-77; 56G, 80A)
Most Points, Left Wing, Season	110	Mats Naslund (1985-86; 43G, 67A)
Most Points, Rookie, Season	71	Mats Naslund (1982-83; 26G, 45A), Kjell Dahlin (1985-86; 32G, 39A)
Most Shutouts, Season	*22	George Hainsworth (1928-29)
Most Goals, Game	6	Newsy Lalonde (Jan. 10/20)
Most Assists, Game	6	Elmer Lach (Feb. 6/43)
Most Points, Game	8	Maurice Richard (Dec. 28/44; 5G, 3A), Bert Olmstead (Jan. 9/54; 4G, 4A)

* NHL Record.

Retired Numbers

1	Jacques Plante	1952-1963
2	Doug Harvey	1947-1961
4	Jean Béliveau	1950-1971
7	Howie Morenz	1923-1937
9	Maurice Richard	1942-1960
10	Guy Lafleur	1971-1984
16	Henri Richard	1955-1975

All-time Record vs. Other Clubs

Regular Season

	At Home								On Road								Total							
	GP	W	L	T	OL	GF	GA	PTS	GP	W	L	T	OL	GF	GA	PTS	GP	W	L	T	OL	GF	GA	PTS
Anaheim	8	4	2	2	0	24	19	10	7	4	3	0	0	22	23	8	15	8	5	2	0	46	42	18
Atlanta	8	6	2	0	0	28	19	12	8	5	1	2	0	27	10	12	16	11	3	2	0	55	29	24
Boston	331	189	95	46	1	1119	786	425	332	122	152	56	2	898	985	302	663	311	247	102	3	2017	1771	727
Buffalo	100	54	34	12	0	380	302	120	99	29	50	19	1	265	309	78	199	83	84	31	1	645	611	198
Calgary	45	25	12	8	0	159	111	58	48	26	14	7	1	163	144	60	93	51	26	15	1	322	255	118
Carolina	73	48	17	7	1	305	212	104	76	36	27	12	1	266	221	85	149	84	44	19	2	571	433	189
Chicago	275	173	54	48	0	1061	649	394	273	125	93	55	0	761	731	305	548	298	147	103	0	1822	1380	699
Colorado	63	37	15	10	1	257	196	85	63	26	31	5	1	222	216	58	126	63	46	15	2	479	412	143
Columbus	3	1	1	0	1	5	5	3	1	1	0	0	0	3	1	2	4	2	1	0	1	8	6	5
Dallas	58	37	12	9	0	250	144	83	58	30	17	11	0	202	152	71	116	67	29	20	0	452	296	154
Detroit	281	171	67	43	0	992	635	385	280	97	129	53	1	717	805	248	561	268	196	96	1	1709	1440	633
Edmonton	29	16	8	4	1	103	91	37	34	16	16	0	2	109	114	34	63	32	24	4	3	212	205	71
Florida	19	8	9	2	0	51	45	18	20	8	9	3	0	58	62	19	39	16	18	5	0	109	107	37
Los Angeles	64	45	8	11	0	289	160	101	64	36	19	9	0	252	197	81	128	81	27	20	0	541	357	182
Minnesota	3	1	1	1	0	9	8	3	1	0	1	0	0	2	4	0	4	1	2	1	0	11	12	3
Nashville	3	3	0	0	0	10	5	6	4	1	2	1	0	7	14	3	7	4	2	1	0	17	19	9
New Jersey	52	31	15	6	0	177	131	68	52	25	24	3	0	189	157	53	104	56	39	9	0	366	288	121
NY Islanders	58	34	15	9	0	212	167	77	58	24	26	6	2	165	179	56	116	58	41	15	2	377	346	133
NY Rangers	288	190	59	39	0	1122	662	419	288	116	117	54	1	838	833	287	576	306	176	93	1	1960	1495	706
Ottawa	30	16	10	4	0	91	83	36	28	14	12	1	1	80	78	30	58	30	22	5	1	171	161	66
Philadelphia	72	34	23	14	1	252	224	83	71	27	28	16	0	211	217	70	143	61	51	30	1	463	441	153
Phoenix	29	24	3	2	0	142	66	50	28	12	9	7	0	108	91	31	57	36	12	9	0	250	157	81
Pittsburgh	80	60	10	10	0	375	201	130	80	39	28	13	0	278	235	91	160	99	38	23	0	653	436	221
St. Louis	58	40	11	7	0	250	159	87	57	28	14	15	0	195	147	71	115	68	25	22	0	445	306	158
San Jose	11	7	2	2	0	36	20	16	10	4	3	2	1	25	29	11	21	11	5	4	1	61	49	27
Tampa Bay	20	10	9	1	0	55	47	21	21	8	8	5	0	53	48	21	41	18	17	6	0	108	95	42
Toronto	330	197	89	43	1	1157	819	438	330	115	170	45	0	855	998	275	660	312	259	88	1	2012	1817	713
Vancouver	52	38	9	5	0	242	130	81	54	33	13	8	0	198	141	74	106	71	22	13	0	440	271	155
Washington	58	33	16	8	1	220	125	75	57	23	25	9	0	170	157	55	115	56	41	17	1	390	282	130
Defunct Clubs	231	148	58	25	0	779	469	321	230	98	97	35	0	586	606	231	461	246	155	60	0	1365	1075	552
Totals	**2732**	**1680**	**666**	**378**	**8**	**10152**	**6690**	**3746**	**2732**	**1128**	**1138**	**452**	**14**	**7925**	**7904**	**2722**	**5464**	**2808**	**1804**	**830**	**22**	**18077**	**14594**	**6468**

Playoffs

	Series	W	L	GP	W	L	T	GF	GA	Last Mtg.	Rnd.	Result
Boston	29	22	7	145	91	54	0	450	357	2002	CQF	W 4-2
Buffalo	7	4	3	35	18	17	0	124	111	1998	CSF	L 0-4
Calgary	2	1	1	11	6	5	0	31	32	1989	F	L 2-4
Carolina	6	5	1	33	21	12	0	108	91	2002	CSF	L 2-4
Chicago	17	12	5	81	50	29	2	261	185	1976	QF	W 4-0
Colorado	5	3	2	31	17	14	0	105	85	1993	DSF	W 4-2
Dallas	2	1	1	13	7	6	0	48	37	1980	QF	L 3-4
Detroit	12	5	7	62	33	29	0	161	149	1978	QF	W 4-1
Edmonton	1	0	1	3	0	3	0	6	15	1981	PRE	L 0-3
Los Angeles	1	1	0	5	4	1	0	15	12	1993	F	W 4-1
New Jersey	1	0	1	5	1	4	0	11	22	1997	CQF	L 1-4
NY Islanders	4	3	1	22	14	8	0	64	55	1993	CF	W 4-1
NY Rangers	14	7	7	61	34	25	2	188	158	1996	CQF	L 2-4
Philadelphia	4	3	1	21	14	7	0	72	52	1989	CF	W 4-2
Pittsburgh	1	1	0	6	4	2	0	18	15	1998	CQF	W 4-2
St. Louis	3	3	0	12	12	0	0	42	14	1977	QF	W 4-0
Toronto	15	8	7	71	42	29	0	215	160	1979	QF	W 4-0
Vancouver	1	1	0	5	4	1	0	20	9	1975	QF	W 4-1
Defunct Clubs	11*	6	4	28	15	9	4	70	71			
Totals	**136***	**86**	**49**	**650**	**387**	**255**	**8**	**2009**	**1630**			

* 1919 Final incomplete due to influenza epidemic.

Playoff Results 2003-1999

Year	Round	Opponent	Result	GF	GA
2002	CSF	Carolina	L 2-4	12	21
	CQF	Boston	W 4-2	20	18

Abbreviations: Round: F - Final; **CF** - conference final; **CSF** - conference semi-final; **CQF** - conference quarter-final; **DSF** - division semi-final; **QF** - quarter-final; **PRE** - preliminary round.

Calgary totals include Atlanta Flames, 1972-73 to 1979-80. Carolina totals include Hartford, 1979-80 to 1996-97.
Colorado totals include Quebec, 1979-80 to 1994-95. Dallas totals include Minnesota North Stars, 1967-68 to 1992-93.
New Jersey totals include Kansas City, 1974-75 to 1975-76, and Colorado Rockies, 1976-77 to 1981-82.
Phoenix totals include Winnipeg, 1979-80 to 1995-96.

2002-03 Results

Oct.	11	at NY Rangers	4-1
	12	Buffalo	1-6
	15	Philadelphia	2-6
	17	at Detroit	3-2
	19	Toronto	2-2
	22	Pittsburgh	3-3
	24	at Philadelphia	2-6
	26	Ottawa	5-3
	29	Anaheim	2-2
Nov.	1	at Carolina	2-2
	2	at Toronto	5-2
	5	St. Louis	2-5
	7	NY Islanders	3-0
	9	Los Angeles	3-1
	12	Dallas	2-4
	15	at New Jersey	1-5
	16	New Jersey	3-1
	18	Pittsburgh	5-4*
	20	at Pittsburgh	3-2*
	21	at Ottawa	2-3
	23	Carolina	3-7
	26	Atlanta	3-2
	29	at Boston	2-4
	30	Philadelphia	1-2*
Dec.	4	at Dallas	1-5
	6	at Colorado	6-7*
	7	at Phoenix	4-2
	10	at Boston	4-2
	12	Tampa Bay	2-3
	14	Boston	4-2
	16	at Ottawa	3-2
	17	San Jose	1-3
	19	at NY Rangers	3-1
	21	Buffalo	6-2
	23	at NY Islanders	1-3
	27	at Ottawa	2-3*
	28	at Pittsburgh	2-3
	31	at Calgary	1-1
Jan.	2	at Vancouver	2-3
	4	at Edmonton	4-5*
	7	at New Jersey	2-3
	9	NY Rangers	3-2
	11	Buffalo	2-3
	13	Calgary	4-2
	15	at Atlanta	0-1
	16	at Philadelphia	1-4
	18	Toronto	2-3*
	20	at Florida	3-2
	22	at Tampa Bay	2-2
	25	Washington	1-1
	26	Chicago	4-3
	28	Florida	6-3
	30	at NY Islanders	1-3
Feb.	4	Atlanta	3-4
	6	at Boston	3-6
	8	at Toronto	1-3
	9	at Washington	2-0
	11	Boston	3-1
	13	Columbus	1-2*
	15	Edmonton	3-2
	18	Florida	0-3
	19	at Buffalo	1-2*
	22	Toronto	3-5
	24	at Washington	1-4
	27	Minnesota	3-6
Mar.	1	Vancouver	1-1
	5	at Anaheim	1-3
	6	at San Jose	3-4*
	8	at Los Angeles	1-2
	10	at Nashville	3-1
	12	at Florida	4-0
	13	at Atlanta	4-2
	15	Tampa Bay	1-2
	18	New Jersey	0-1
	20	NY Islanders	3-6
	22	Carolina	5-3
	25	Washington	3-4*
	28	at Buffalo	1-4
	29	Ottawa	1-3
	31	at Carolina	4-0
Apr.	2	at Tampa Bay	1-2
	5	NY Rangers	5-4

* – Overtime

Entry Draft
Selections 2003-1989

2003
Pick
10	Andrei Kastitsyn
40	Cory Urquhart
61	Maxim Lapierre
79	Ryan O'Byrne
113	Corey Locke
123	Danny Stewart
177	Christopher Heino-Lindberg
188	Mark Flood
217	Oskari Korpikari
241	Jimmy Bonneau
271	Jaroslav Halak

2002
Pick
14	Christopher Higgins
45	Tomas Linhart
99	Michael Lambert
182	Andre Deveaux
212	Jonathan Ferland
275	Konstantin Korneev

2001
Pick
7	Mike Komisarek
25	Alexander Perezhogin
37	Duncan Milroy
71	Tomas Plekanec
109	Martti Jarventie
171	Eric Himelfarb
203	Andrew Archer
266	Viktor Ujcik

2000
Pick
13	Ron Hainsey
16	Marcel Hossa
78	Josef Balej
79	Tyler Hanchuck
109	Johan Eneqvist
114	Christian Larrivee
145	Ryan Glenn
172	Scott Selig
182	Petr Chvojka
243	Joni Puurula
275	Jonathan Gauthier

1999
Pick
39	Alexander Buturlin
58	Matt Carkner
97	Chris Dyment
107	Evan Lindsay
136	Dusty Jamieson
145	Marc-Andre Thinel
150	Matt Shasby
167	Sean Dixon
196	Vadim Tarasov
225	Mikko Hyytia
253	Jerome Marois

1998
Pick
16	Eric Chouinard
45	Mike Ribeiro
75	Francois Beauchemin
132	Andrei Bashkirov
152	Gordie Dwyer
162	Andrei Markov
189	Andrei Kruchinin
201	Craig Murray
216	Michael Ryder
247	Darcy Harris

1997
Pick
11	Jason Ward
37	Gregor Baumgartner
65	Ilkka Mikkola
91	Daniel Tetrault
118	Konstantin Sidulov
122	Gennady Razin
145	Jonathan Desroches
172	Ben Guite
197	Petr Kubos
202	Andrei Sidyakin
228	Jarl Espen Ygranes

1996
Pick
18	Matt Higgins
44	Mathieu Garon
71	Arron Asham
92	Kim Staal
99	Etienne Drapeau
127	Daniel Archambault
154	Brett Clark
181	Timo Vertala
207	Mattia Baldi
233	Michel Tremblay

1995
Pick
8	Terry Ryan
60	Miloslav Guren
74	Martin Hohenberger
86	Jonathan Delisle
112	Niklas Anger
138	Boyd Olson
164	Stephane Robidas
190	Greg Hart
216	Eric Houde

1994
Pick
18	Brad Brown
44	Jose Theodore
54	Chris Murray
70	Marko Kiprusoff
74	Martin Belanger
96	Arto Kuki
122	Jimmy Drolet
148	Joel Irving
174	Jessie Rezansoff
200	Peter Strom
226	Tomas Vokoun
252	Chris Aldous
278	Ross Parsons

1993
Pick
21	Saku Koivu
47	Rory Fitzpatrick
73	Sebastien Bordeleau
85	Adam Wiesel
99	Jean-Francois Houle
113	Jeff Lank
125	Dion Darling
151	Darcy Tucker
177	David Ruhly
203	Alan Letang
229	Alexandre Duchesne
255	Brian Larochelle
281	Russell Guzior

1992
Pick
20	David Wilkie
33	Valeri Bure
44	Keli Corpse
68	Craig Rivet
82	Louis Bernard
92	Marc Lamothe
116	Don Chase
140	Martin Sychra
164	Christian Proulx
188	Michael Burman
212	Earl Cronan
236	Trent Cavicchi
260	Hiroyuki Miura

1991
Pick
17	Brent Bilodeau
28	Jim Campbell
43	Craig Darby
61	Yves Sarault
73	Vladimir Vujtek
83	Sylvain Lapointe
100	Brad Layzell
105	Tony Prpic
127	Oleg Petrov
149	Brady Kramer
171	Brian Savage
193	Scott Fraser
215	Greg MacEachern
237	Paul Lepler
259	Dale Hooper

1990
Pick
12	Turner Stevenson
39	Ryan Kuwabara
58	Charles Poulin
60	Robert Guillet
81	Gilbert Dionne
102	Paul Di Pietro
123	Craig Conroy
144	Stephen Rohr
165	Brent Fleetwood
186	Derek Maguire
207	Mark Kettelhut
228	John Uniac
249	Sergei Martynyuk

1989
Pick
13	Lindsay Vallis
30	Patrice Brisebois
41	Steve Larouche
51	Pierre Sevigny
83	Andre Racicot
104	Marc Deschamps
146	Craig Ferguson
167	Patrick Lebeau
188	Roy Mitchell
209	Ed Henrich
230	Justin Duberman
251	Steve Cadieux

Coach

JULIEN, CLAUDE
Coach, Montreal Canadiens. Born in Blind River, Ont., April 23, 1960.

Claude Julien became head coach of the Montreal Canadiens on January 17, 2003. At the time, Julien was in his third season as head coach of the Hamilton Bulldogs, the Canadiens' affiliate team in the American Hockey League.

Julien started his coaching career at the helm of the Ottawa Senators of the Central Junior Hockey League in 1993-94. He later became an assistant coach with the Hull Olympiques of the QMJHL and was promoted to head coach in 1996-97, leading Hull to the Memorial Cup championship that year. He also had success at the international level, winning a bronze medal as head coach of the Canadian team at the World Junior Championship in 2000 and a silver medal as assistant coach at the same tournament a year earlier. Julien also coached the Under-18 team to the gold medal at the 3 Nations Tournament held in 1997 in the Czech Republic.

Julien suited up for a total of 14 games as a player in the NHL with the Quebec Nordiques in 1984-85 and 1985-86. Playing defense, he played in 409 games in the American Hockey League, recording 40 goals and 206 assists for a total of 246 points.

Coaching Record

			Regular Season				Playoffs		
Season	Team	Games	W	L	T	Games	W	L	
1996-97	Hull (QMJHL)	70	48	19	3	14	12	2	
1997-98	Hull (QMJHL)	70	32	37	1	11	6	5	
1998-99	Hull (QMJHL)	70	23	38	9	23	15	8	
1999-00	Hull (QMJHL)	72	42	24	6	15	9	6	
2000-01	Hamilton (AHL)	80	28	46	6	....	....	....	
2001-02	Hamilton (AHL)	80	37	33	10	15	10	5	
2002-03	Hamilton (AHL)	45	33	9	3	....	....	....	
2002-03	**Montreal (NHL)**	**36**	**12**	**21**	**3**	....	....	....	
	NHL Totals	**36**	**12**	**21**	**3**	....	....	....	

Club Directory

Bell Centre

Bell Centre
1260 de La Gauchetière Street W.
Montréal, QC H3B 5E8
Phone: **514/932-2582**
Media Hotline: 514/989-2835
Fax Lines (all area code 514):
  Communications 932-8285
  Hockey 989-2717
  Press Lounge 932-5258
  Marketing 925-2145
  Community Relations 925-2144
www.canadiens.com
Capacity: 21,273

Executive Management
Chairman and Governor	George N. Gillett Jr.
Vice-Chairman	Jeff Joyce
President, Club de hockey Canadien and Bell Centre & Alternate Governor	Pierre Boivin
Assistant to the President & Alternate Governor	Foster Gillett
Administrative Assistant to the President	Lise Beaudry
Exec. V.P. Hockey, G.M. & Alternate Governor	Bob Gainey
Chief Financial Officer & Alternate Governor	Fred Steer
Vice-President, Marketing and Sales	Ray Lalonde
Vice-President, Communications and Community Relations	Donald Beauchamp
Vice-President, Operations, Bell Centre	Alain Gauthier
President, Gillett Entertainment Group	Aldo Giampaolo

Hockey
Assistant General Manager	André Savard
Director of Hockey Operations and Legal Affairs	Julien BriseBois
Director of Player Personnel	Trevor Timmins
Director of Professional Scouting	Pierre Gauthier
Head Coach	Claude Julien
Assistant Coaches	Guy Charron, Rick Green, Roland Melanson
Professional Scouts	Richard Green, Gordie Roberts
Amateur Scouting Coordinator	Pierre Dorion
Scouting Staff	Patrik Allvin, Elmer Benning, William A. Berglund, Hannu Laine, Dave Mayville, Trent McCleary, Antonin Routa, Nikolai Vakourov
Team Services & Hockey Administration Manager	Claudine Crépin
Administrative Assistant to the General Manager	Suzanne Charlebois

Medical and Training Staff
Club Physician and Chief Surgeon	Dr. David Mulder
Consultant Orthopedic Surgeon	Dr. Eric Lenczner
Dentist	Dr. Pierre Desautels
Consultant Ophthalmologist	Dr. John Little
Head Athletic Therapist	Graham Rynbend
Assistant to the the Athletic Therapist	Jody Van Rees
Strength & Conditioning Coordinator	Scott Livingston
Video Supervisor	Mario Leblanc
Equipment Manager	Pierre Gervais
Assistants to the Equipment Manager	Robert Boulanger, Pierre Ouellette
Visiting team Coordinator	Richard Généreux

Communications
Director of Media Relations	Dominick Saillant
Administrative Assistant to VP Communications	Sylvie Lambert
Communications Coordinator	Frédéric Daigle

Community Relations
President, Canadiens Alumni	Réjean Houle
CEO, Canadiens Children's Foundation	Robert Sirois
Manager of Community Relations	Frédérique Cardinal
Community Relations Coordinator	Geneviève Paquette
Coordinator, CHC Foundation	Normande Herget
Coordinator, Community Relations	Suzanne Lafranchise

Marketing and Sales
Executive Director, Premium Sales and Services	Richard Primeau
Group Manager, Marketing	Paul-André Côté
Group Manager, Game Day Sales and Promo	Vincent Lucier
Administrative Asst. to VP Marketing & Sales	Nicole Malboeuf
Manager, Game Presentation	Chantal Bunnett
Manager, Internet Services	Jon Trzcienski
Manager, Editorial	Carl Lavigne
Manager, Consumer Products	Luc Rocheleau
Manager, Group Sales	Pierre Constant
Manager, Sponsor Promotions	Marc Fisher
Manager, Fan Development	Matt Zalkowitz
Team Photographer	Bob Fisher

Advertising and Sponsorship Sales
Effix Inc.	François-Xavier Seigneur

Ticket Sales and Building Operations
Director of Ticket Office	Cathy D'Ascoli
Assistant Director of Ticket Office	Lucie Masse
Director of Building Operations	Xavier Luydlin
Administrative Assistant to VP Operations	Maryse Cartwright

Finances
Executive Director, Finance	Jacques Aubé
Controller, Budgeting & Analysis	Dennis McKinley
Director of Information Technology	Pierre-Éric Belzile
Administrative Assistant, Chief Financial Officer	Christine Ouellette

AHL Affiliation
Hamilton Bulldogs	www.hamiltonbulldogs.com
Arena	Copps Coliseum, 85 York Blvd, Hamilton, ON L8R 3L4 (905) 529-8500 info@hamiltonbulldogs.com
President	Steve Katzman
General Manager	André Savard
Head Coach	Doug Jarvis
Assistant Coach	Ron Wilson
Equipment Manager	Patrick Langlois
Assistant to Equipment Manager	Stéphane Gauthier
Head Athletic Therapist	Luc Leblanc
Director of Public Relations	Craig Downey

Team Information
Play-by-play - Radio/TV	Pierre Houde (RDS & SRC), TBA (CKAC), Dino Sisto (CJAD)
Colormen - Radio/TV	Yvon Pedneault (RDS & SRC), Dany Dubé (CKAC), Murray Wilson (CJAD)
Radio/TV Flagship Stations	RDS (Cable 33), CKAC (730 AM), CJAD (800 AM)

Nashville Predators

2002-03 Results: 27w-35L-13T-7OTL 74PTS.
Fourth, Central Division

2003-04 Schedule

Oct.	Thu.	9	Anaheim
	Sat.	11	Dallas
	Thu.	16	St. Louis
	Sat.	18	Columbus
	Sun.	19	at Chicago
	Thu.	23	at Atlanta
	Sat.	25	Colorado
	Tue.	28	at St. Louis
	Thu.	30	Detroit
Nov.	Sat.	1	Dallas
	Sun.	2	at Dallas
	Wed.	5	Vancouver
	Fri.	7	Chicago
	Sat.	8	at Detroit
	Thu.	13	Calgary
	Sat.	15	NY Islanders
	Wed.	19	at Los Angeles
	Fri.	21	at Anaheim
	Sat.	22	at San Jose
	Mon.	24	at Colorado
	Wed.	26	Columbus
	Fri.	28	at Boston*
	Sat.	29	Buffalo
Dec.	Wed.	3	at Carolina
	Thu.	4	at Columbus
	Sat.	6	at St. Louis
	Thu.	11	Los Angeles
	Sat.	13	Florida
	Tue.	16	Vancouver
	Thu.	18	at Montreal
	Sat.	20	Detroit
	Mon.	22	Phoenix
	Tue.	23	at Minnesota
	Fri.	26	at Dallas
	Sat.	27	at Phoenix
	Mon.	29	at San Jose
Jan.	Thu.	1	Pittsburgh*
	Sat.	3	New Jersey
	Mon.	5	at Detroit
	Tue.	6	at Toronto
	Thu.	8	Colorado

	Sat.	10	St. Louis
	Mon.	12	at Minnesota
	Tue.	13	Los Angeles
	Thu.	15	Phoenix
	Sat.	17	Edmonton
	Mon.	19	Minnesota
	Thu.	22	at Calgary
	Sat.	24	at Edmonton
	Sun.	25	at Vancouver
	Thu.	29	at Columbus
	Sat.	31	San Jose
Feb.	Tue.	3	Detroit
	Thu.	5	Tampa Bay
	Wed.	11	at Chicago
	Fri.	13	Washington
	Sun.	15	Edmonton*
	Mon.	16	at Columbus
	Wed.	18	San Jose
	Fri.	20	at Anaheim
	Sat.	21	at Phoenix
	Mon.	23	at Los Angeles
	Thu.	26	Minnesota
	Sat.	28	NY Rangers*
Mar.	Mon.	1	Chicago
	Wed.	3	at Philadelphia
	Thu.	4	at Pittsburgh
	Sat.	6	at Ottawa
	Tue.	9	Boston
	Thu.	11	at St. Louis
	Sat.	13	Calgary
	Sun.	14	at Detroit
	Tue.	16	at Vancouver
	Fri.	19	at Edmonton
	Sat.	20	at Calgary
	Tue.	23	Anaheim
	Thu.	25	at NY Rangers
	Sat.	27	Columbus
	Tue.	30	Chicago
Apr.	Thu.	1	at Chicago
	Sat.	3	St. Louis*
	Sun.	4	at Colorado*

Denotes afternoon game.

Year-by-Year Record

Season	GP	Home				Road				Overall					GF	GA	Pts.	Finished	Playoff Result
		W	L	T	OL	W	L	T	OL	W	L	T	OL						
2002-03	82	18	17	5	1	9	18	8	6	27	35	13	7		183	206	74	4th, Central Div.	Out of Playoffs
2001-02	82	17	16	8	0	11	25	5	0	28	41	13	0		196	230	69	4th, Central Div.	Out of Playoffs
2000-01	82	16	18	7	0	18	18	2	3	34	36	9	3		186	200	80	3rd, Central Div.	Out of Playoffs
1999-2000	82	15	21	3	2	13	19	4	5	28	40	7	7		199	240	70	4th, Central Div.	Out of Playoffs
1998-99	82	15	22	4	...	13	25	3	...	28	47	7	...		190	261	63	4th, Central Div.	Out of Playoffs

Tomas Vokoun established franchise records and career highs in games played (69), wins (25), consecutive starts (38) and goals-against average (2.20). His games played ranked him third in the NHL, while his average tied him for eighth.

Franchise date: June 25, 1997

CENTRAL DIVISION

6th NHL Season

2003-04 Player Personnel

FORWARDS	HT	WT	S	Place of Birth	Date	2002-03 Club
ANDERSSON, Jonas	6-3	202	L	Stockholm, Sweden	2/24/81	Milwaukee
ARKHIPOV, Denis	6-3	214	L	Kazan, USSR	5/19/79	Nashville
CLASSEN, Greg	6-1	200	L	Aylsham, Sask.	8/24/77	Nashville-Milwaukee
ERAT, Martin	6-0	195	L	Trebic, Czech.	8/28/81	Nashville-Milwaukee
FARRELL, Mike	6-0	222	R	Edina, MN	10/20/78	Washington-Portland (AHL)
FIDDLER, Vernon	5-11	197	L	Edmonton, Alta.	5/9/80	Nashville-Milwaukee
HALL, Adam	6-3	205	R	Kalamazoo, MI	8/14/80	Nashville-Milwaukee
HARTNELL, Scott	6-2	205	L	Regina, Sask.	4/18/82	Nashville
HAYDAR, Darren	5-9	170	L	Toronto, Ont.	10/22/79	Nashville-Milwaukee
JOHANSSON, Andreas	6-0	202	L	Hofors, Sweden	5/19/73	Nashville
JOHNSON, Greg	5-11	200	L	Thunder Bay, Ont.	3/16/71	Nashville
LEGWAND, David	6-2	190	L	Detroit, MI	8/17/80	Nashville
McKENZIE, Jim	6-4	230	L	Gull Lake, Sask.	11/3/69	New Jersey
MURRAY, Rem	6-2	200	L	Stratford, Ont.	10/9/72	NY Rangers-Nashville
ORSZAGH, Vladimir	5-11	195	L	Banska Bystrica, Czech.	5/24/77	Nashville
PIVKO, Libor	6-2	195	L	Novy Vicin, Czech.	3/29/80	Zlin
PLATONOV, Denis	6-3	202	L	Saratov, USSR	11/6/81	Kazan
SHISHKANOV, Timofei	6-1	213	R	Moscow, USSR	6/10/83	Quebec
SIMON, Ben	6-0	195	L	Shaker Heights, OH	6/14/78	Atlanta-Chicago (AHL)
SMITH, Wyatt	5-11	200	L	Thief River Falls, MN	2/13/77	Nashville-Milwaukee
TOOTOO, Jordin	5-9	195	R	Churchill, Man.	2/2/83	Brandon
UPSHALL, Scottie	6-0	187	L	Fort McMurray, Alta.	10/7/83	Nashville-Kamloops-Milwaukee
WALKER, Scott	5-10	196	R	Cambridge, Ont.	7/19/73	Nashville

DEFENSEMEN						
EATON, Mark	6-2	208	L	Wilmington, DE	5/6/77	Nashville-Milwaukee
HAMHUIS, Dan	6-0	205	L	Smithers, B.C.	12/13/82	Milwaukee
HELBLING, Timo	6-3	209	R	Basel, Switz.	7/21/81	Milwaukee-Toledo
HUTCHINSON, Andrew	6-2	204	R	Evanston, IL	3/24/80	Toledo-Milwaukee
KLOUCEK, Tomas	6-3	225	L	Prague, Czech.	3/7/80	Hartford-Nashville-Milwaukee
MURPHY, Curtis	5-8	185	R	Kerrobert, Sask.	12/3/75	Minnesota-Houston
SCHNABEL, Robert	6-5	230	L	Prague, Czech.	11/10/78	Nashville-Milwaukee
SCHULTZ, Ray	6-2	215	L	Red Deer, Alta.	11/14/76	NY Islanders-Bridgeport
TIMONEN, Kimmo	5-10	196	L	Kuopio, Finland	3/18/75	Nashville
YORK, Jason	6-1	208	R	Nepean, Ont.	5/20/70	Nashville-Cincinnati (AHL)
ZIDLICKY, Marek	5-11	187	L	Most, Czech.	2/3/77	HIFK Helsinki

GOALTENDERS	HT	WT	C	Place of Birth	Date	2002-03 Club
FINLEY, Brian	6-3	205	R	Sault Ste. Marie, Ont.	7/13/81	Nashville-Milwaukee-Toledo
FLAHERTY, Wade	6-0	185	L	Terrace, B.C.	1/11/68	Nashville-San Antonio
LASAK, Jan	6-1	200	L	Zvolen, Czech.	4/10/79	Nashville-Milwaukee
VOKOUN, Tomas	6-0	195	R	Karlovy Vary, Czech.	7/2/76	Nashville

Scott Walker is one of three current Predators (along with Tomas Vokoun and Greg Johnson) who were selected by Nashville in the 1998 Expansion Draft.

2002-03 Scoring

* - rookie

Regular Season

Pos	#	Player	Team	GP	G	A	Pts	+/–	PIM	PP	SH	GW	GT	S	%
C	11	David Legwand	NSH	64	17	31	48	-2	34	3	1	4	1	167	10.2
C	44	Kimmo Timonen	NSH	72	6	34	40	-3	46	4	0	0	0	144	4.2
L	21	Andreas Johansson	NSH	56	20	17	37	-4	22	10	0	1	1	124	16.1
C	25	Denis Arkhipov	NSH	79	11	24	35	-18	32	3	0	1	1	148	7.4
D	5	Andy Delmore	NSH	71	18	16	34	-17	28	14	0	6	0	149	12.1
L	17	Scott Hartnell	NSH	82	12	22	34	-3	101	2	0	2	0	221	5.4
R	24	Scott Walker	NSH	60	15	18	33	2	58	7	0	5	0	124	12.1
R	33	Vladimir Orszagh	NSH	78	16	16	32	-1	38	3	0	3	0	152	10.5
C	15	Rem Murray	NYR	32	6	6	12	-3	4	1	1	1	0	62	9.7
			NSH	53	6	13	19	1	18	1	0	0	0	81	7.4
			TOTAL	85	12	19	31	-2	22	2	1	1	0	143	8.4
R	18 *	Adam Hall	NSH	79	16	12	28	-8	31	8	0	2	0	146	11.0
R	14	Oleg Petrov	MTL	53	7	16	23	-2	16	2	0	2	0	87	8.0
			NSH	17	2	2	4	-4	2	0	0	0	0	37	5.4
			TOTAL	70	9	18	27	-6	18	2	0	2	0	124	7.3
L	43	Vitali Yachmenev	NSH	62	5	15	20	7	12	0	0	1	0	68	7.4
D	27	Jason York	NSH	74	4	15	19	13	52	2	0	0	1	107	3.7
C	22	Greg Johnson	VAN	38	6	9	17	7	22	0	0	0	0	55	14.5
L	20	Todd Warriner	VAN	30	4	6	10	0	22	0	0	0	0	53	7.5
			PHI	13	2	3	5	2	6	0	1	0	0	13	15.4
			NSH	6	0	1	1	-1	4	0	0	0	0	6	0.0
			TOTAL	49	6	10	16	1	32	0	1	0	0	72	8.3
C	10	Clarke Wilm	NSH	82	5	11	16	-11	36	0	0	1	0	108	4.6
D	3	Karlis Skrastins	NSH	82	3	10	13	-18	44	0	1	0	0	86	3.5
C	16	Denis Pederson	NSH	43	4	6	10	2	39	0	0	1	0	64	6.3
D	4	Mark Eaton	NSH	50	2	7	9	1	22	0	0	0	0	52	3.8
D	32	Cale Hulse	NSH	80	2	6	8	-11	121	0	0	1	0	82	2.4
L	19	Martin Erat	NSH	27	1	7	8	-9	14	1	0	0	0	39	2.6
C	38 *	Vernon Fiddler	NSH	19	4	2	6	2	14	0	0	1	0	20	20.0
D	23	Bill Houlder	NSH	82	2	4	6	-2	46	0	0	1	0	51	3.9
L	41	Brent Gilchrist	NSH	41	1	2	3	-11	14	0	0	0	0	41	2.4
R	7 *	Scottie Upshall	NSH	8	1	0	1	2	0	0	0	1	0	6	16.7
C	46	Wyatt Smith	NSH	11	1	0	1	-1	0	0	0	0	0	8	12.5
L	12	Reid Simpson	NSH	26	0	1	1	-4	56	0	0	0	0	11	0.0
D	27	Pascal Trepanier	NSH	1	0	0	0	0	0	0	0	0	0	1	0.0
R	20 *	Nathan Perrott	NSH	1	0	0	0	-1	0	0	0	0	0	0	0.0
D	36 *	Robert Schnabel	NSH	1	0	0	0	0	0	0	0	0	0	1	0.0
C	39	Domenic Pittis	NSH	2	0	0	0	0	2	0	0	0	0	1	0.0
R	54 *	Darren Haydar	NSH	2	0	0	0	-1	0	0	0	0	0	4	0.0
D	28	Tomas Kloucek	NSH	3	0	0	0	1	2	0	0	0	0	1	0.0
R	28	Cameron Mann	NSH	4	0	0	0	0	0	0	0	0	0	5	0.0
D	26	Bubba Berenzweig	NSH	4	0	0	0	0	0	0	0	0	0	5	0.0
C	9	Greg Classen	NSH	8	0	0	0	-3	4	0	0	0	0	2	0.0

Goaltending

No.	Goaltender	GPI	Mins	Avg	W	L	T	EN	SO	GA	SA	S%	G	A	PIM
29	Tomas Vokoun	69	3974	2.20	25	31	11	5	3	146	1771	.918	0	1	28
30	Mike Dunham	15	819	3.15	2	9	2	0	0	43	397	.892	0	0	0
35	* Jan Lasak	3	90	3.33	0	1	0	0	0	5	39	.872	0	0	0
31	* Brian Finley	1	47	3.83	0	0	0	0	0	3	13	.769	0	0	0
34	Wade Flaherty	1	51	4.71	0	1	0	0	0	4	27	.852	0	1	0
	Totals	82	5015	2.46	27	42	13	5	3	206	2252	.909			

Vice President and General Manager

POILE, DAVID
Executive Vice President/General Manager, Nashville Predators.
Born in Toronto, Ont., February 14, 1949.

Since joining the Predators as general manager on July 9, 1997, David Poile has made a commitment to building for the future, surrounding himself with one of the youngest and most talented staffs in the National Hockey League. Poile has an impressive reputation as an NHL leader and in 2001 he received the Lester Patrick Trophy for his contributions to hockey in the United States. His father, Norman "Bud" Poile, had won the honor in 1989.

Prior to joining Nashville, Poile spent 15 seasons as vice president/general manager of the Washington Capitals. During his tenure in Washington, the Capitals made 14 postseason appearances, winning their only Patrick Division title in 1989 and advancing to the Conference Finals in 1990. During Poile's 15 years in Washington, the Capitals compiled a record of 594-454-132, finished second in the Patrick Division seven times and recorded 90-or-more points seven different seasons.

Poile started his professional hockey career as an administrative assistant for the Atlanta Flames in 1972, shortly after graduating from Northeastern University in Boston. At Northeastern, he was hockey team captain, leading scorer and most valuable player for two years.

In 1977, he was named assistant general manager of the Atlanta Flames (who moved to Calgary in 1980), serving as the manager and coordinator of the Flames farm club.

Poile is a member of the NHL's general managers committee and was instrumental in the NHL's adoption of the instant replay rule in 1991. He was awarded *Inside Hockey's* man of the year for his leadership on the issue. He was also twice honored as *The Sporting News* NHL executive of the year following the 1982-83 and 1983-84 seasons. Poile served as general manager of the 1998 and 1999 U.S. national team for the World Championships.

Poile was introduced to hockey by watching his father play seven seasons in the NHL. Bud Poile later became general manager for the Vancouver Canucks and the Philadelphia Flyers, both NHL expansion franchises at the time. He was inducted into the Hockey Hall of Fame in 1990.

Club Records

Team

(Figures in brackets for season records are games played; records for fewest points, wins, ties, losses, goals, goals against are for 70 or more games)

Most Points	80	2000-01 (82)
Most Wins	34	2000-01 (82)
Most Ties	13	2001-02 (82), 2002-03 (82)
Most Losses	47	1998-99 (82)
Most Goals	199	1999-2000 (82)
Most Goals Against	261	1998-99 (82)
Fewest Points	63	1998-99 (82)
Fewest Wins	27	2002-03 (82)
Fewest Ties	7	1998-99 (82)
		1999-2000 (82)
Fewest Losses	35	2002-03 (82)
Fewest Goals	183	2002-03 (82)
Fewest Goals Against	200	2000-01 (82)

Longest Winning Streak

Overall	4	Four times
Home	7	Feb. 13-Mar. 1/03
Away	3	Feb. 12-24/99, Jan. 29-Feb. 1/01, Jan. 30-Feb. 28/02

Longest Undefeated Streak

Overall	8	Dec. 18/99-Jan. 1/00 (5 wins, 3 ties)
Home	11	Nov. 3-Dec. 23/01 (8 wins, 3 ties)
Away	3	Ten times

Longest Losing Streak

Overall	7	Nov. 20-Dec. 2/99
Home	6	Jan. 21-Feb. 15/99, Feb. 26-Mar. 21/02
Away	5	Five times

Longest Winless Streak

Overall	15	Mar. 10-Apr. 6/03 (12 losses (2 in OT), 3 ties)
Home	9	Jan. 21-Mar. 2/99 (8 losses, 1 tie)
Away	9	Three times
Most Shutouts, Season	6	2000-01 (82)
Most PIM, Season	1,420	1998-99 (82)
Most Goals, Game	7	Nov. 26/00 (Nsh. 7 at Car. 4)

Individual

Most Seasons	5	Many players
Most Games	352	Greg Johnson
Most Goals, Career	81	Cliff Ronning
Most Assists, Career	145	Cliff Ronning
Most Points, Career	226	Cliff Ronning (81G, 145A)
Most PIM, Career	370	Cale Hulse
Most Shutouts, Career	9	Tomas Vokoun
Longest Consecutive Games Streak	269	Karlis Skrastins (Feb. 21/00-Apr. 6/03)
Most Goals, Season	26	Cliff Ronning (1999-2000)
Most Assists, Season	43	Cliff Ronning (2000-01)
Most Points, Season	62	Cliff Ronning (1999-2000; 26G, 36A) (2000-01; 19G, 43A)
Most PIM, Season	242	Patrick Cote (1999-2000)
Most Points, Defenseman, Season	42	Kimmo Timonen (2001-02; 13G, 29A)
Most Points, Center, Season	62	Cliff Ronning (1999-2000; 26G, 36A) (2000-01; 19G, 43A)
Most Points, Right Wing, Season	54	Scott Walker (2000-01; 25G, 29A)
Most Points, Left Wing, Season	41	Scott Hartnell (2001-02; 14G, 27A)
Most Points, Rookie, Season	33	Martin Erat (2001-02; 9G, 24A)
Most Shutouts, Season	4	Mike Dunham (2000-01)
Most Goals, Game	3	Rob Valicevic (Nov. 10/99), Scott Walker (Dec. 26/00), Petr Tenkrat (Dec. 15/01), Andreas Johansson (Nov. 27/02)
Most Assists, Game	3	Twelve times
Most Points, Game	4	Seven times

General Managers' History

David Poile, 1998-99 to date.

Coaching History

Barry Trotz, 1998-99 to date.

Captains' History

Tom Fitzgerald, 1998-99 to 2001-02; Greg Johnson, 2002-03 to date.

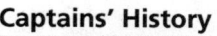

All-time Record vs. Other Clubs

Regular Season

	At Home								On Road								Total							
	GP	W	L	T	OL	GF	GA	PTS	GP	W	L	T	OL	GF	GA	PTS	GP	W	L	T	OL	GF	GA	PTS
Anaheim	10	4	3	2	1	20	23	11	10	1	8	0	1	13	28	3	20	5	11	2	2	33	51	14
Atlanta	3	2	1	0	0	12	6	4	3	1	1	1	0	8	8	3	6	3	2	1	0	20	14	7
Boston	5	2	3	0	0	11	13	4	4	1	2	1	0	7	13	3	9	3	5	1	0	18	26	7
Buffalo	4	1	2	0	1	6	8	3	4	3	0	1	0	16	9	7	8	4	2	1	1	22	17	10
Calgary	11	7	4	0	0	31	20	14	10	2	3	3	2	23	30	9	21	9	7	3	2	54	50	23
Carolina	4	3	1	0	0	9	7	6	4	1	2	1	0	11	13	3	8	4	3	1	0	20	20	9
Chicago	13	6	5	2	0	40	37	14	14	5	8	1	0	33	40	11	27	11	13	3	0	73	77	25
Colorado	10	2	5	3	0	29	37	7	10	2	5	2	1	19	29	7	20	4	10	5	1	48	66	14
Columbus	8	5	2	1	0	20	17	11	7	3	4	0	0	15	13	6	15	8	6	1	0	35	30	17
Dallas	10	6	4	0	0	26	19	12	10	2	7	0	1	10	27	5	20	8	11	0	1	36	46	17
Detroit	13	5	6	2	0	33	38	12	14	1	10	2	1	32	57	5	27	6	16	4	1	65	95	17
Edmonton	11	3	6	2	0	28	34	8	10	5	4	0	1	26	28	11	21	8	10	2	1	54	62	19
Florida	4	1	2	1	0	6	8	3	4	1	2	1	0	8	11	3	8	2	4	2	0	14	19	6
Los Angeles	10	1	7	2	0	15	27	4	10	5	3	0	2	28	30	12	20	6	10	2	2	43	57	16
Minnesota	6	3	1	2	0	15	11	8	6	2	3	1	0	12	14	5	12	5	4	3	0	27	25	13
Montreal	4	2	1	1	0	14	7	5	3	0	3	0	0	5	10	0	7	2	4	1	0	19	17	5
New Jersey	4	0	4	0	0	6	12	0	5	3	1	1	0	14	15	7	9	3	5	1	0	20	27	7
NY Islanders	4	2	2	0	0	10	13	4	4	2	1	0	1	12	11	5	8	4	3	0	1	22	24	9
NY Rangers	3	1	2	0	0	11	13	2	5	2	2	1	0	11	16	5	8	3	4	1	0	22	29	7
Ottawa	4	2	2	0	0	8	11	4	4	1	3	0	0	5	11	2	8	3	5	0	0	13	22	6
Philadelphia	4	0	2	2	0	4	7	2	4	2	1	0	1	7	12	5	8	2	3	2	1	11	19	7
Phoenix	10	4	5	1	0	25	28	9	10	3	6	0	1	24	30	7	20	7	11	1	1	49	58	16
Pittsburgh	5	3	2	0	0	18	8	6	4	1	1	2	0	8	10	4	9	4	3	2	0	26	18	10
St. Louis	14	5	8	3	0	27	40	9	13	3	8	0	2	21	47	8	27	6	16	3	2	48	87	17
San Jose	10	3	6	1	0	19	29	7	10	5	4	1	0	28	22	11	20	8	10	2	0	47	51	18
Tampa Bay	5	2	3	0	0	10	11	4	4	1	1	2	0	10	11	4	9	3	4	2	0	20	22	8
Toronto	1	1	0	0	0	3	2	2	5	1	3	1	0	17	11	7	6	2	3	1	0	20	13	9
Vancouver	11	5	4	1	1	31	34	12	10	1	7	0	2	17	11	7	21	6	11	1	3	56	76	16
Washington	4	2	1	0	1	11	9	5	4	1	3	0	0	8	10	2	8	3	4	1	1	19	19	7
Totals	**205**	**81**	**94**	**27**	**3**	**498**	**529**	**192**	**205**	**64**	**105**	**22**	**14**	**456**	**608**	**164**	**410**	**145**	**199**	**49**	**17**	**954**	**1137**	**356**

2002-03 Results

Date		Opponent	Score			Opponent	Score
Oct.	11	at Washington	4-5		11	Phoenix	4-3*
	12	Edmonton	2-3		12	at Chicago	0-2
	15	at NY Islanders	3-4*		14	at Vancouver	3-4
	18	at New Jersey	2-3*		16	at Calgary	2-2
	19	at NY Rangers	2-2		18	at Edmonton	3-2*
	22	Phoenix	1-2		21	Vancouver	3-2
	24	San Jose	1-2		23	NY Rangers	2-4
	26	Detroit	3-1		25	Tampa Bay	3-2
	30	at St. Louis	0-7		27	at Buffalo	5-1
Nov.	2	at Los Angeles	5-6*		28	at Boston	1-2
	3	at Phoenix	1-2*		30	at Columbus	1-2
	6	at Anaheim	1-2	Feb.	4	at Detroit	5-5
	7	at San Jose	2-2		8	Columbus	3-2
	10	at Colorado	4-3		11	Los Angeles	2-3
	12	at Detroit	1-4		13	NY Islanders	2-0
	14	Colorado	1-3		15	Anaheim	2-1
	16	Columbus	1-1		17	Boston	5-1
	17	at Chicago	2-4		20	Calgary	4-1
	21	at Colorado	1-1		22	at Ottawa	0-4
	23	at Minnesota	2-4		23	at Toronto	5-2
	27	San Jose	4-2		25	Columbus	5-0
	29	New Jersey	1-2	Mar.	1	Chicago	5-4*
	30	Dallas	5-2		4	at St. Louis	1-2*
Dec.	3	Carolina	1-2		6	Minnesota	2-2
	5	at Los Angeles	3-2		7	at Dallas	2-1
	7	at San Jose	4-2		10	Montreal	1-3
	8	at Anaheim	0-3		12	at Pittsburgh	2-2
	10	Los Angeles	0-3		14	at Minnesota	1-3
	12	St. Louis	2-2		15	St. Louis	0-1
	14	Minnesota	3-1		17	Edmonton	3-5
	17	Calgary	0-3		20	at Vancouver	3-7
	19	Vancouver	1-3		22	at Calgary	1-1
	21	at Tampa Bay	2-2		23	at Edmonton	2-3*
	23	at Florida	3-2*		25	Philadelphia	1-1
	26	Dallas	3-1		27	at Chicago	1-4
	28	Detroit	2-4		29	Atlanta	2-3
	30	Ottawa	3-2		31	at Detroit	1-3
Jan.	1	Colorado	3-7	Apr.	1	Anaheim	1-2*
	4	Chicago	3-3		4	at Phoenix	0-1
	6	at Columbus	5-1		6	at Dallas	0-2
	7	St. Louis	2-1*				

* – Overtime

Entry Draft
Selections 2003-1998

2003
Pick
7	Ryan Suter
35	Konstantin Glazachev
37	Kevin Klein
49	Shea Weber
76	Richard Stehlik
89	Paul Brown
92	Alexander Sulzer
98	Grigory Shafigulin
117	Teemu Lassila
133	Rustam Sidikov
210	Andrei Mukhachev
213	Miroslav Hanuljak
268	Lauris Darzins

2002
Pick
6	Scottie Upshall
102	Brandon Segal
138	Patrick Jarrett
172	Mike McKenna
203	Josh Morrow
235	Kaleb Betts
264	Matt Davis
266	Steve Spencer

2001
Pick
12	Dan Hamhuis
33	Timofei Shishkanov
42	Tomas Slovak
75	Denis Platonov
76	Oliver Setzinger
98	Jordin Tootoo
178	Anton Lavrentiev
240	Gustav Grasberg
271	Mikko Lehtonen

2000
Pick
6	Scott Hartnell
36	Daniel Widing
72	Mattias Nilsson
89	Libor Pivko
131	Matt Hendricks
137	Mike Stuart
154	Matt Koalska
173	Tomas Harant
197	Zbynek Irgl
203	Jure Penko
236	Mats Christeen
284	Martin Hohener

1999
Pick
6	Brian Finley
33	Jonas Andersson
52	Adam Hall
54	Andrew Hutchinson
61	Ed Hill
65	Jan Lasak
72	Brett Angel
121	Yevgeny Pavlov
124	Alexandre Krevsun
131	Konstantin Panov
162	Timo Helbling
191	Martin Erat
205	Kyle Kettles
220	Miroslav Durak
248	Darren Haydar

1998
Pick
2	David Legwand
60	Denis Arkhipov
85	Geoff Koch
88	Kent Sauer
138	Martin Beauchesne
147	Craig Brunel
202	Martin Bartek
230	Karlis Skrastins

A hot streak in February had Nashville in playoff contention last year, but an injury to David Legwand hurt the team's chances. Legwand played just 64 games but was still the team's top scorer.

Coach

TROTZ, BARRY
Coach, Nashville Predators. Born in Winnipeg, Man., July 15, 1962.

Barry Trotz realized his dream of becoming an NHL head coach on August 6, 1997, after serving four seasons as head coach and director of hockey operations for the American Hockey League's Portland Pirates. He and assistant Paul Gardner spent the 1997-98 season scouting in preparation for the inaugural season of the Nashville Predators.

Trotz began his coaching career in 1984 as assistant coach with the University of Manitoba for one season, before serving two seasons as the head coach and general manager of the Dauphin Kings Junior Hockey Club from 1985 to 1987. He became head coach of the University of Manitoba the 1987 season and also served as a scout for the Spokane Chiefs of the Western Hockey League that season. Trotz joined the Washington Capitals organization as their chief western scout during the 1988 season. The Winnipeg, Manitoba native was appointed an assistant coach of the Capitals' American Hockey League affiliate in Baltimore prior to the 1991 season before being named head coach prior to the 1992 season. When the franchise relocated to Portland, he guided the Pirates to two AHL Calder Cup Final appearances in the club's first four seasons. He led the Pirates to a league-best 43-27-10 record, captured the Calder Cup championship and was named the American Hockey League coach of the year following the 1994-95 season.

In 1995, Trotz guided Portland to a new North American professional hockey league record 17-game unbeaten streak (14-0-3) to start the season. He was named head coach for the U.S. team at the American Hockey League All-Star Game in 1996.

Prior to his coaching career, Trotz played junior hockey for the Western Hockey League's Regina Pats from 1979-83. During that time, he recorded 39 goals, 121 assists for 160 points, along with 490 penalty minutes in 204 games.

Coaching Record

Season	Team	Games	Regular Season W	L	T	Playoffs Games	W	L
1992-93	Baltimore (AHL)	80	28	40	12	7	3	4
1993-94	Portland (AHL)	80	43	27	10	8	6	2
1994-95	Portland (AHL)	80	46	22	12	7	3	4
1995-96	Portland (AHL)	80	32	38	10	24	14	10
1996-97	Portland (AHL)	80	37	33	10	5	2	3
1998-99	Nashville (NHL)	82	28	47	7	....	....	....
1999-2000	Nashville (NHL)	82	28	47	7	....	....	....
2000-01	Nashville (NHL)	82	34	39	9	....	....	....
2001-02	Nashville (NHL)	82	28	41	13	....	....	....
2002-03	Nashville (NHL)	82	27	42	13	....	....	....
	NHL Totals	410	145	216	49			

Club Directory

Gaylord Entertainment Center

Nashville Predators
Gaylord Entertainment Center
501 Broadway
Nashville, TN 37203
Phone **615/770-2300**
FAX 615/770-2309
Ticket Information 615/770-PUCK
www.nashvillepredators.com
Capacity: 17,113

Owner, Chairman and Governor . . . . Craig Leipold
General Partner . . . . Nashville Predators, LLC
Limited Partner . . . . Gaylord Entertainment Company
President, COO and Alternate Governor . . . . Jack Diller
Exec. V.P./G.M and Alternate Governor . . . . David Poile
Exec. V.P. of Finance & Administration/CFO . . . . . Ed Lang
Senior V.P./Communications & Development . . . . . Gerry Helper

Hockey Operations
Assistant General Manager . . . . Ray Shero
Head Coach . . . . Barry Trotz
Assistant Coach . . . . Peter Horachek
Associate Coach . . . . Brent Peterson
Strength and Conditioning Coach . . . . Mark Nemish
Goaltending Coach . . . . Mitch Korn
Video Coach . . . . Robert Bouchard
Director of Player Personnel . . . . Paul Fenton
Assistant Directors of Amateur Scouting . . . . Rick Knickle, Greg Royce
Professional Scouts . . . . Paul Gardner, Dan MacKinnon
Quebec/Ontario Scout . . . . Luc Gauthier
New England Scout . . . . Jeff Kealty
Western Amateur Scout . . . . Mike Rooney
Western Collegiate Scout . . . . Dennis Schueller
Amateur Scouts - Europe . . . . Lucas Bergman, Alexei Dementiev,
Martin Divis, Janne Kekalainen
Head Athletic Trainer . . . . Dan Redmond
Assistant Athletic Trainer . . . . Eric Claas
Equipment Manager . . . . Pete Rogers
Assistant Equipment Manager . . . . Chris Scoppetto
Equipment Assistant . . . . Chris Moody
Locker Room Attendant . . . . Craig "Partner" Baugh
Director of Team Services . . . . Gregory Harvey
Executive Assistant . . . . Jessica Halperin
Hockey Operations Coordinator . . . . Brandon Walker

Team Doctors
Dr. Michael J. Pagnani, MD, Dr. Blake Garside, MD, Dr. James W. McPherson Jr., DDS, Dr. Daniel Weikert, MD, Dr. Bryan D. Oslin, MD, Dr. Donald Griffin, MD, Dr. Gary S. Solomon, Ph. D., Dr. Carl Hampf, MD, Dr. Richard W. Garman, MD

Communications/Development
Director of Communications . . . . Ken Anderson
Communications Coordinator . . . . Tim Darling
Corporate Communications Coordinator . . . . Cathy Lewandowski
Senior Director of Community Relations/
Executive Director of Predators Foundation . . . . . Polly Pearce
Community Relations & Amateur Hockey Mgr. . . . . Alexis Herbster
Manager, Amateur Hockey . . . . Marc Spigel
Graphic Artist, Communications & Development . . . Maggie Bizwell
Team Photographer . . . . John Russell

Business/Marketing/Corporate Sales
Vice President of Corporate Partnerships . . . . David Nivison
Account Executives - Corporate Partnerships . . . . . David Morse,
Tom Moulton
Senior Sponsor Services Account Manager . . . . . . Kristin Fricke
Sponsor Services Account Manager . . . . Tiffany Williams
Premium Seating Manager . . . . Britt Kincheloe
Premium Seating Account Manager . . . . Myron Murray
Vice President of Marketing . . . . Randy Campbell
Marketing and Special Events Manager . . . . Christel Foley
Advertising Manager . . . . Carrie Poss
Entertainment Coordinator . . . . Adam DeVault
Database Marketing Manager . . . . Michael Vivelo
Graphic Artist, Marketing . . . . Jennifer Sheets
Executive Assistant . . . . Linda Adams
Sponsorship Department Coordinator . . . . Kelly Preuett

Finance/Human Resources
Vice President of Business Administration . . . . Susie Masotti
Senior Director of Finance . . . . Beth Snider
Senior Director of Human Resources . . . . Stephanie Ditenhafer
Payroll Manager . . . . Susan Charnley
Senior Accountant, Gaylord Entertainment Center . Tracy Hardes
Senior Accountant, Predators . . . . Sjar Toney
Accounts Payable Clerk . . . . Bill Brown
Finance and Human Resources Coordinator . . . . . . Jonathan Norris
Manager, Internet Development . . . . Scott Pilkinton
Information Systems Manager . . . . Jeff Beck
Computer Support Technician . . . . Wesley Green
Human Resources/Finance Assistant . . . . Andrea Hyde
Executive Assistant . . . . Elaine Lewis
Office Coordinator . . . . Erin Hart

Broadcast/Game Presentation Department
Director of Broadcasting . . . . Erik Barnhart
Director of Game Operations . . . . Bryan Shaffer
Director of Technical Operations . . . . Blake Grant
Associate Producer . . . . Bill Filipiak
Technical Operations Assistant . . . . Robert Hill
Play-by-Play Announcer . . . . Pete Weber
Color Analyst . . . . Terry Crisp

Ticket Operations
Vice President of Ticket Sales . . . . Scott Wampold
Ticket Operations Manager . . . . Gene Connelly
Ticket Operations Coordinators . . . . Brad MacLachlan, Joe Donovan
Season Ticket Sales Manager . . . . Nat Harden
Suite and Group Sales Manager . . . . Chris Junghans
Account Executives . . . . Dan Bauchiero, Ed Chamberlain, Betsy Rose Gunselman,
Bob Milhizer, Sean Mahoney, Jason Mott, Bill Walker
Ticket Sales Administrative Assistant . . . . Annie Snelgrove
Fan Relations Supervisor . . . . Brad Gillispie
Radio Flagship . . . . WTN-FM (99.7 FM)
TV Flagship . . . . Fox Sports Net

New Jersey Devils

2002-03 Results: 46w-20l-10t-6otl 108pts.
First, Atlantic Division

Year-by-Year Record

Season	GP	Home W	L	T	OL	Road W	L	T	OL	Overall W	L	T	OL	GF	GA	Pts	Finished	Playoff Result
2002-03	82	25	11	3	2	21	9	7	4	46	20	10	6	216	166	108	1st, Atlantic Div.	Won Stanley Cup
2001-02	82	22	13	4	2	19	15	5	2	41	28	9	4	205	187	95	3rd, Atlantic Div.	Lost Conf. Quarter-Final
2000-01	82	24	11	6	0	24	8	6	3	48	19	12	3	295	195	111	1st, Atlantic Div.	Lost Final
1999-2000	82	28	9	3	1	17	15	5	4	45	24	8	5	251	203	103	2nd, Atlantic Div.	Won Stanley Cup
1998-99	82	19	14	8	...	28	10	3	...	47	24	11	...	248	196	105	1st, Atlantic Div.	Lost Conf. Quarter-Final
1997-98	82	29	10	2	...	19	13	9	...	48	23	11	...	225	166	107	1st, Atlantic Div.	Lost Conf. Quarter-Final
1996-97	82	23	9	9	...	22	14	5	...	45	23	14	...	231	182	104	1st, Atlantic Div.	Lost Conf. Semi-Final
1995-96	82	22	17	2	...	15	16	10	...	37	33	12	...	215	202	86	6th, Atlantic Div.	Out of Playoffs
1994-95	48	14	4	6	...	8	14	2	...	22	18	8	...	136	121	52	2nd, Atlantic Div.	Won Stanley Cup
1993-94	84	29	11	2	...	18	14	10	...	47	25	12	...	306	220	106	2nd, Atlantic Div.	Lost Conf. Championship
1992-93	84	24	14	4	...	16	23	3	...	40	37	7	...	308	299	87	4th, Patrick Div.	Lost Div. Semi-Final
1991-92	80	24	12	4	...	14	19	3	...	38	31	11	...	289	259	87	4th, Patrick Div.	Lost Div. Semi-Final
1990-91	80	23	10	7	...	9	23	8	...	32	33	15	...	272	264	79	4th, Patrick Div.	Lost Div. Semi-Final
1989-90	80	22	15	3	...	15	19	6	...	37	34	9	...	295	288	83	2nd, Patrick Div.	Lost Div. Semi-Final
1988-89	80	17	18	5	...	10	23	7	...	27	41	12	...	281	325	66	5th, Patrick Div.	Out of Playoffs
1987-88	80	23	16	1	...	15	20	5	...	38	36	6	...	295	296	82	4th, Patrick Div.	Lost Conf. Championship
1986-87	80	20	17	3	...	9	28	3	...	29	45	6	...	293	368	64	6th, Patrick Div.	Out of Playoffs
1985-86	80	17	21	2	...	11	28	1	...	28	49	3	...	300	374	59	6th, Patrick Div.	Out of Playoffs
1984-85	80	13	21	6	...	9	27	4	...	22	48	10	...	264	346	54	5th, Patrick Div.	Out of Playoffs
1983-84	80	10	28	2	...	7	28	5	...	17	56	7	...	231	350	41	5th, Patrick Div.	Out of Playoffs
1982-83	80	11	20	9	...	6	29	5	...	17	49	14	...	230	338	48	5th, Patrick Div.	Out of Playoffs
1981-82**	80	14	21	5	...	4	28	8	...	18	49	13	...	241	362	49	5th, Smythe Div.	Out of Playoffs
1980-81**	80	15	16	9	...	7	29	4	...	22	45	13	...	258	344	57	5th, Smythe Div.	Out of Playoffs
1979-80**	80	12	20	8	...	7	28	5	...	19	48	13	...	234	308	51	6th, Smythe Div.	Out of Playoffs
1978-79**	80	8	24	8	...	7	29	4	...	15	53	12	...	210	331	42	4th, Smythe Div.	Out of Playoffs
1977-78**	80	17	14	9	...	2	26	12	...	19	40	21	...	257	305	59	2nd, Smythe Div.	Lost Prelim. Round
1976-77**	80	12	20	8	...	8	26	6	...	20	46	14	...	226	307	54	5th, Smythe Div.	Out of Playoffs
1975-76*	80	8	24	8	...	4	32	4	...	12	56	12	...	190	351	36	5th, Smythe Div.	Out of Playoffs
1974-75*	80	12	20	8	...	3	34	3	...	15	54	11	...	184	328	41	5th, Smythe Div.	Out of Playoffs

* Kansas City Scouts. ** Colorado Rockies.

2003-04 Schedule

Oct.
Wed. 8 at Boston
Sat. 11 at Carolina
Thu. 16 Toronto
Sat. 18 Tampa Bay
Wed. 22 Florida
Fri. 24 at Pittsburgh
Sat. 25 Boston
Tue. 28 at NY Islanders
Thu. 30 Philadelphia

Nov.
Sat. 1 Colorado*
Wed. 5 San Jose
Fri. 7 Toronto
Sat. 8 at Ottawa
Wed. 12 at Buffalo
Thu. 13 Florida
Sat. 15 NY Rangers*
Wed. 19 Buffalo
Fri. 21 Pittsburgh
Tue. 25 at Los Angeles
Wed. 26 at Anaheim
Fri. 28 at Dallas
Sun. 30 at Colorado

Dec.
Tue. 2 Phoenix
Thu. 4 Washington
Sat. 6 at Ottawa
Wed. 10 NY Islanders
Fri. 12 Philadelphia
Sat. 13 at Philadelphia
Tue. 16 at NY Islanders
Thu. 18 at Atlanta
Fri. 19 at Buffalo
Sun. 21 at Chicago
Fri. 26 NY Islanders
Sat. 27 at Pittsburgh
Mon. 29 at NY Islanders

Jan.
Thu. 1 at Washington
Sat. 3 at Nashville
Mon. 5 Edmonton
Wed. 7 Pittsburgh
Fri. 9 Tampa Bay
Sat. 10 at Toronto

Tue. 13 Ottawa
Thu. 15 at NY Rangers
Sat. 17 Washington*
Tue. 20 at Pittsburgh
Wed. 21 Carolina
Fri. 23 Montreal
Sun. 25 Atlanta
Tue. 27 at Columbus
Thu. 29 at Detroit
Sat. 31 at St. Louis

Feb.
Tue. 3 Ottawa
Thu. 5 Vancouver
Tue. 10 at Philadelphia
Wed. 11 NY Rangers
Sat. 14 Carolina*
Sun. 15 Los Angeles*
Tue. 17 Minnesota
Thu. 19 at Washington
Sat. 21 at NY Rangers*
Sun. 22 Calgary*
Wed. 25 Buffalo
Fri. 27 Atlanta
Sat. 28 at Toronto

Mar.
Mon. 1 at Montreal
Wed. 3 at Florida
Fri. 5 at Tampa Bay
Sat. 6 at Carolina
Tue. 9 Philadelphia
Thu. 11 Chicago
Sat. 13 at Philadelphia*
Mon. 15 at NY Rangers
Wed. 17 Pittsburgh
Fri. 19 Montreal
Sat. 20 at Montreal
Tue. 23 at Florida
Thu. 25 at Tampa Bay
Fri. 26 at Atlanta
Sun. 28 NY Islanders*
Tue. 30 NY Rangers

Apr.
Sat. 3 at Boston*
Sun. 4 Boston*

Denotes afternoon game.

Franchise date: June 11, 1974
Transferred from Denver to New Jersey, June 30, 1982.
Previously transferred from Kansas City to Denver.

EASTERN NHL **CONFERENCE**

ATLANTIC DIVISION

30th NHL Season

With 28 goals and 29 assists last season, Patrik Elias led the Devils in scoring for the fourth straight season in 2002-03. No one else in franchise history has ever led the team in scoring more than twice.

2003-04 Player Personnel

FORWARDS	HT	WT	S	Place of Birth	Date	2002-03 Club
BALMOCHNYKH, Maxim	6-1	210	L	Lipetsk, USSR	3/7/79	Cherepovets
BERGLUND, Christian	5-11	190	L	Orebro, Sweden	3/12/80	New Jersey-Albany
BICEK, Jiri	5-10	195	L	Kosice, Czech.	12/3/78	New Jersey-Albany
BRYLIN, Sergei	5-10	190	L	Moscow, USSR	1/13/74	New Jersey
CAMERON, Scott	6-0	195	L	Sudbury, Ont.	4/11/81	Albany
CLOUTHIER, Brett	6-5	225	L	Ottawa, Ont.	6/9/81	Albany
CROZIER, Greg	6-3	200	L	Calgary, Alta.	7/6/76	Houston-Albany
DARBY, Craig	6-4	205	R	Oneida, NY	9/26/72	New Jersey-Albany
ELIAS, Patrik	6-1	195	L	Trebic, Czech.	4/13/76	New Jersey
FOSTER, Adrian	6-1	205	L	Lethbridge, Alta.	1/15/82	Albany
FRIESEN, Jeff	6-0	215	L	Meadow Lake, Sask.	8/5/76	New Jersey
GIONTA, Brian	5-7	175	R	Rochester, NY	1/18/79	New Jersey
GOMEZ, Scott	5-11	200	L	Anchorage, AK	12/23/79	New Jersey
GUOLLA, Steve	6-0	190	L	Scarborough, Ont.	3/15/73	New Jersey-Albany
HARTSBURG, Chris	6-0	200	R	Edina, MN	5/30/80	Albany
HULBIG, Joe	6-3	215	L	Norwood, MA	9/29/73	Albany
JANSSEN, Cam	5-11	210	R	St. Louis, MO	4/15/84	Windsor
JENSEN, Erik	6-1	195	R	Madison, WI	9/4/79	U. of Wisconsin
JOHANSSON, Eric	6-0	195	L	Edmonton, Alta.	1/7/82	Albany
KARIYA, Steve	5-8	170	R	North Vancouver, B.C.	12/22/77	Manitoba-Albany
KHOMUTOV, Ivan	6-2	200	L	Saratov, USSR	3/11/85	Elektrostal
KINKEL, Bill	6-5	225	L	Buffalo, NY	2/27/84	Kitchener-Kingston
LANGENBRUNNER, Jamie	6-1	200	R	Duluth, MN	7/24/75	New Jersey
MADDEN, John	5-11	190	L	Barrie, Ont.	5/4/73	New Jersey
MARSHALL, Grant	6-1	195	R	Mississauga, Ont.	6/9/73	Columbus-New Jersey
MURPHY, Ryan	6-1	195	L	Van Nuys, CA	3/21/79	Florida (ECHL)-Lowell
NITTEL, Ahren	6-3	225	L	Waterloo, Ont.	12/6/83	Windsor-Oshawa
PANDOLFO, Jay	6-1	190	L	Winchester, MA	12/27/74	New Jersey
PIHLMAN, Thomas	6-2	205	L	Espoo, Finland	11/13/82	JYP Jyvaskyla
PIKKARAINEN, Ilkka	6-2	190	R	Sonkajarvi, Finland	4/19/81	HIFK Helsinki
RASMUSSEN, Erik	6-3	210	L	Minneapolis, MN	3/28/77	Los Angeles
RUPP, Mike	6-5	230	L	Cleveland, OH	1/13/80	New Jersey-Albany
STEVENSON, Turner	6-3	220	R	Prince George, B.C.	5/18/72	New Jersey
SUGLOBOV, Aleksander	6-0	175	L	Elektrostal, USSR	1/15/82	Nizhnekamsk-Yaroslavl
TENUTE, Joey	5-10	175	L	Hamilton, Ont.	4/2/83	Sarnia
VRANA, Petr	5-10	175	L	Sternberk, Czech.	3/29/85	Halifax
DEFENSEMEN						
ALBELIN, Tommy	6-2	195	L	Stockholm, Sweden	5/21/64	New Jersey
BROOKS, Alex	6-1	195	R	Madison, WI	8/21/76	Albany
BROWN, Sean	6-3	210	L	Oshawa, Ont.	11/5/76	Boston
CHVATAL, Marek	6-1	180	L	Pardubice, Czech.	1/27/84	Sarnia
COLE, Phil	6-4	205	L	Winnipeg, Man.	9/6/82	Albany-Columbus (ECHL)
DeMARCHI, Matt	6-3	180	L	Bemidji, MN	5/4/81	U. of Minnesota
GIROUX, Raymond	6-1	190	L	North Bay, Ont.	7/20/76	New Jersey-Albany
HALE, David	6-2	210	L	Colorado Springs, CO	6/18/81	North Dakota
KADEYKIN, Anton	6-3	200	L	Elektrostal, USSR	5/17/84	Sarnia
MARTIN, Paul	6-2	195	L	Minneapolis, MN	3/5/81	U. of Minnesota
MATTEUCCI, Mike	6-3	210	L	Trail, B.C.	12/27/71	Albany
NIEDERMAYER, Scott	6-1	200	L	Edmonton, Alta.	8/31/73	New Jersey
RAFALSKI, Brian	5-9	190	R	Dearborn, MI	9/28/73	New Jersey
REDLIHS, Krisjanis	6-2	190	L	Riga, Latvia	1/15/81	Albany
STEVENS, Scott	6-2	215	L	Kitchener, Ont.	4/1/64	New Jersey
UCHEVATOV, Victor	6-4	225	L	Angarsk, USSR	2/10/83	Albany
WHITE, Colin	6-4	215	L	New Glasgow, N.S.	12/12/77	New Jersey

GOALTENDERS	HT	WT	C	Place of Birth	Date	2002-03 Club
AHONEN, Ari	6-1	195	L	Jyvaskyla, Finland	2/6/81	Albany
BRODEUR, Martin	6-2	210	L	Montreal, Que.	5/6/72	New Jersey
CLEMMENSEN, Scott	6-2	205	L	Des Moines, IA	7/23/77	Albany
KOSTUR, Matus	6-1	190	L	Banska Bystrica, Czech.	3/28/80	Columbus (ECHL)
SCHWAB, Corey	6-0	180	L	North Battleford, Sask.	11/4/70	New Jersey

General Managers' History

Sid Abel, 1974-75, 1975-76; Ray Miron, 1976-77 to 1980-81; Bill MacMillan, 1981-82, 1982-83; Bill MacMillan and Max McNab, 1983-84; Max McNab 1984-85 to 1986-87; Lou Lamoriello, 1987-88 to date.

President and General Manager

LAMORIELLO, LOU
CEO/President/General Manager, New Jersey Devils.
Born in Providence, RI, October 21, 1942.

Lou Lamoriello's life-long dedication to the game of hockey was rewarded in 1992 when he was named a recipient of the Lester Patrick Trophy for outstanding service to hockey in the United States. Lamoriello is entering his 17th season as president and general manager of the Devils following more than 20 years with Providence College as a player, coach and administrator. His trades, signings and draft choices helped lead the Devils to their first Stanley Cup championship in 1995 and was followed by victories again in 2000 and 2003. A member of the varsity hockey Friars during his undergraduate days, he became an assistant coach with the college club after graduating in 1963. Lamoriello was later named head coach and in the ensuing 15 years, led his teams to a 248-179-13 record and appearances in 10 post-season tournaments, including the 1983 NCAA Final Four. Lamoriello also served a five-year term as athletic director at Providence and was a co-founder of Hockey East, one of the strongest collegiate hockey conferences in the U.S. He remained as athletic director until he was hired as president of the Devils on April 30, 1987. He assumed the responsibility of general manager on September 10, 1987. He was g.m. of Team USA for the first World Cup of Hockey in 1996 as the U.S. captured the championship. He was also the g.m. for the 1998 U.S. Olympic team.

2002-03 Scoring

* - rookie

Regular Season

Pos	#	Player	Team	GP	G	A	Pts	+/–	PIM	PP	SH	GW	GT	S	%
C	26	Patrik Elias	N.J.	81	28	29	57	17	22	6	0	4	1	255	11.0
R	15	Jamie Langenbrunner	N.J.	78	22	33	55	17	65	5	1	5	0	197	11.2
C	23	Scott Gomez	N.J.	80	13	42	55	17	48	2	0	4	1	205	6.3
L	12	Jeff Friesen	N.J.	81	23	28	51	23	26	3	0	4	1	179	12.8
C	25	Joe Nieuwendyk	N.J.	80	17	28	45	10	56	3	0	4	0	201	8.5
C	11	John Madden	N.J.	80	19	22	41	13	26	2	2	3	0	207	9.2
D	28	Brian Rafalski	N.J.	79	3	37	40	18	14	2	0	0	0	178	1.7
D	27	Scott Niedermayer	N.J.	81	11	28	39	23	62	3	0	3	0	164	6.7
R	29	Grant Marshall	CBJ	66	8	20	28	–8	71	3	0	2	0	96	8.3
			N.J.	10	1	3	4	–3	7	0	0	0	0	17	5.9
			TOTAL	76	9	23	32	–11	78	3	0	2	0	113	8.0
R	14	Brian Gionta	N.J.	58	12	13	25	5	23	2	0	3	0	129	9.3
R	24	Turner Stevenson	N.J.	77	7	13	20	7	115	0	0	0	0	85	8.2
D	4	Scott Stevens	N.J.	81	4	16	20	18	41	0	0	2	0	113	3.5
C	18	Sergei Brylin	N.J.	52	11	8	19	–2	16	3	1	1	0	86	12.8
C	21	Pascal Rheaume	ATL	56	4	9	13	–8	24	0	2	1	0	70	5.7
			N.J.	21	4	1	5	3	8	0	1	1	0	23	17.4
			TOTAL	77	8	10	18	–5	32	0	3	2	0	93	8.6
L	20	Jay Pandolfo	N.J.	68	6	11	17	12	23	0	1	4	0	92	6.5
D	10	Oleg Tverdovsky	N.J.	50	5	8	13	2	22	2	0	1	0	76	6.6
D	5	Colin White	N.J.	72	5	8	13	19	98	0	0	1	0	81	6.2
D	2	Richard Smehlik	ATL	43	2	9	11	–4	16	0	0	0	0	38	5.3
			N.J.	12	0	2	2	–1	0	0	0	0	0	11	0.0
			TOTAL	55	2	11	13	–5	16	0	0	0	0	49	4.1
L	19	Jim McKenzie	N.J.	76	4	8	12	3	88	0	0	2	0	42	9.5
R	9	* Jiri Bicek	N.J.	44	5	6	11	7	25	1	0	1	0	63	7.9
L	17	* Christian Berglund	N.J.	38	4	5	9	3	20	0	0	0	0	50	8.0
D	3	Ken Daneyko	N.J.	69	2	7	9	6	33	0	0	0	0	38	5.3
R	16	* Mike Rupp	N.J.	26	5	3	8	0	21	2	0	3	0	34	14.7
D	6	Tommy Albelin	N.J.	37	1	6	7	10	6	0	1	0	0	30	3.3
C	8	Stephen Guolla	N.J.	12	2	0	2	1	2	0	0	0	0	6	33.3
C	22	Mike Danton	N.J.	17	2	0	2	0	35	0	0	0	0	18	11.1
C	9	Craig Darby	N.J.	3	0	1	1	–1	0	0	0	0	0	1	0.0
D	7	Raymond Giroux	N.J.	11	0	1	1	–2	6	0	0	0	0	20	0.0

Goaltending

No.	Goaltender	GPI	Mins	Avg	W	L	T	EN	SO	GA	SA	S%	G	A	PIM
35	Corey Schwab	11	614	1.47	5	3	1	0	1	15	223	.933	0	0	0
30	Martin Brodeur	73	4374	2.02	41	23	9	4	9	147	1706	.914	0	0	10
	Totals	**82**	**5009**	**1.99**	**46**	**26**	**10**	**4**	**10**	**166**	**1933**	**.914**			

Playoffs

Pos	#	Player	Team	GP	G	A	Pts	+/–	PIM	PP	SH	GW	GT	S	%
R	15	Jamie Langenbrunner	N.J.	24	11	7	18	11	16	1	0	4	1	53	20.8
D	27	Scott Niedermayer	N.J.	24	2	16	18	11	16	1	0	0	0	40	5.0
C	11	John Madden	N.J.	24	6	10	16	10	2	2	1	1	0	77	7.8
L	12	Jeff Friesen	N.J.	24	10	4	14	10	6	1	0	4	0	46	21.7
C	26	Patrik Elias	N.J.	24	5	8	13	5	26	2	0	2	0	59	8.5
L	20	Jay Pandolfo	N.J.	24	6	6	12	9	2	0	0	1	0	38	15.8
C	23	Scott Gomez	N.J.	24	3	9	12	3	2	0	0	0	0	56	5.4
D	28	Brian Rafalski	N.J.	23	2	9	11	7	8	2	0	0	0	36	5.6
C	25	Joe Nieuwendyk	N.J.	17	3	6	9	–2	4	1	0	0	0	24	12.5
D	4	Scott Stevens	N.J.	24	3	6	9	14	14	1	0	1	0	33	9.1
R	14	Brian Gionta	N.J.	24	1	8	9	5	6	0	0	0	0	59	1.7
R	29	Grant Marshall	N.J.	24	6	2	8	3	8	2	0	1	1	47	12.8
D	5	Colin White	N.J.	24	0	5	5	3	29	0	0	0	0	21	0.0
R	16	* Mike Rupp	N.J.	4	1	3	4	4	0	0	0	1	0	2	50.0
C	18	Sergei Brylin	N.J.	19	1	3	4	–4	8	0	0	1	0	25	4.0
C	21	Pascal Rheaume	N.J.	24	1	2	3	–2	13	0	0	0	0	30	3.3
D	10	Oleg Tverdovsky	N.J.	15	0	3	3	–4	0	0	0	0	0	5	0.0
R	24	Turner Stevenson	N.J.	14	1	1	2	2	26	0	0	0	0	20	5.0
D	6	Tommy Albelin	N.J.	16	1	0	1	3	2	0	0	0	0	6	16.7
D	2	Richard Smehlik	N.J.	5	0	0	0	–2	2	0	0	0	0	2	0.0
L	9	* Jiri Bicek	N.J.	5	0	0	0	–2	0	0	0	0	0	2	0.0
D	3	Ken Daneyko	N.J.	13	0	0	0	2	2	0	0	0	0	2	0.0
L	19	Jim McKenzie	N.J.	13	0	0	0	–2	14	0	0	0	0	3	0.0

Goaltending

No.	Goaltender	GPI	Mins	Avg	W	L	EN	SO	GA	SA	S%	G	A	PIM
35	Corey Schwab	2	28	0.00	0	0	0	0	0	8	1.000	0	0	0
30	Martin Brodeur	24	1491	1.65	16	8	0	7	41	622	.934	0	1	6
	Totals	**24**	**1520**	**1.62**	**16**	**8**	**0**	**7**	**41**	**630**	**.935**			

Coaching History

Bep Guidolin, 1974-75; Bep Guidolin, Sid Abel and Eddie Bush, 1975-76; Johnny Wilson, 1976-77; Pat Kelly, 1977-78; Pat Kelly and Aldo Guidolin, 1978-79; Don Cherry, 1979-80; Bill MacMillan, 1980-81; Bert Marshall and Marshall Johnston, 1981-82; Bill MacMillan, 1982-83; Bill MacMillan and Tom McVie, 1983-84; Doug Carpenter, 1984-85 to 1986-87; Doug Carpenter and Jim Schoenfeld, 1987-88; Jim Schoenfeld, 1988-89; Jim Schoenfeld and John Cunniff, 1989-90; John Cunniff and Tom McVie, 1990-91; Tom McVie, 1991-92; Herb Brooks, 1992-93; Jacques Lemaire, 1993-94 to 1997-98; Robbie Ftorek, 1998-99; Robbie Ftorek and Larry Robinson, 1999-2000; Larry Robinson, 2000-01; Larry Robinson and Kevin Constantine, 2001-02; Pat Burns, 2002-03 to date.

Club Records

Team

(Figures in brackets for season records are games played; records for fewest points, wins, ties, losses, goals, goals against are for 70 or more games)

Record		
Most Points	**111**	2000-01 (82)
Most Wins	**48**	1997-98 (82), 2000-01 (82)
Most Ties	**21**	1977-78 (80)
Most Losses	**56**	1975-76 (80), 1983-84 (80)
Most Goals	**308**	1992-93 (84)
Most Goals Against	**374**	1985-86 (80)
Fewest Points	***36**	1975-76 (80)
	41	1983-84 (80)
Fewest Wins	***12**	1975-76 (80)
	17	1982-83 (80), 1983-84 (80)
Fewest Ties	**3**	1985-86 (80)
Fewest Losses	**19**	2000-01 (82)
Fewest Goals	***184**	1974-75 (80)
	205	2001-02 (82)
Fewest Goals Against	**166**	1997-98 (82), 2002-03 (82)
Longest Winning Streak		
Overall	**13**	Feb. 26-Mar. 23/01
Home	**8**	Oct. 9-Nov. 7/87
Away	****10**	Feb. 27-Apr. 7/01
Longest Undefeated Streak		
Overall	**13**	Three times
Home	**15**	Jan. 8-Mar. 15/97 (9 wins, 6 ties)
Away	**10**	Feb. 27-Apr. 7/01 (10 wins)
Longest Losing Streak		
Overall	***14**	Dec. 30/75-Jan. 29/76
	10	Oct. 14-Nov. 4/83
Home	**9**	Dec. 22/85-Feb. 6/86
Away	**12**	Oct. 19-Dec. 1/83
Longest Winless Streak		
Overall	***27**	Feb. 12-Apr. 4/76 (21 losses, 6 ties)
	18	Oct. 20-Nov. 26/82 (14 losses 4 ties)
Home	***14**	Feb. 12-Mar. 30/76 (10 losses, 4 ties), Feb. 4-Mar. 31/79 (12 losses, 2 ties)
	9	Dec. 22/85-Feb. 6/86 (9 losses)
Away	***32**	Nov. 12/77-Mar. 15/78 (22 losses, 10 ties)
	14	Dec. 26/82-Mar. 5/83 (13 losses, 1 tie)
Most Shutouts, Season	**13**	1996-97 (82)
Most PIM, Season	**2,494**	1988-89 (80)
Most Goals, Game	**9**	Nine times

Individual

Record		
Most Seasons	**20**	Ken Daneyko
Most Games	**1,283**	Ken Daneyko
Most Goals, Career	**347**	John MacLean
Most Assists, Career	**354**	John MacLean
Most Points, Career	**701**	John MacLean (347G, 354A)
Most PIM, Career	**2,519**	Ken Daneyko
Most Shutouts, Career	**64**	Martin Brodeur
Longest Consecutive Games Streak	**388**	Ken Daneyko (Nov. 4/89-Mar. 29/94)
Most Goals, Season	**46**	Pat Verbeek (1987-88)
Most Assists, Season	**60**	Scott Stevens (1993-94)
Most Points, Season	**96**	Patrik Elias (2000-01; 40G, 56A)
Most PIM, Season	**295**	Krzysztof Oliwa (1997-98)
Most Points, Defenseman, Season	**78**	Scott Stevens (1993-94; 18G, 60A)
Most Points, Center, Season	**94**	Kirk Muller (1987-88; 37G, 57A)
Most Points, Right Wing, Season	***87**	Wilf Paiement (1977-78; 31G, 56A)
	87	John MacLean (1988-89; 42G, 45A)
Most Points, Left Wing, Season	**96**	Patrik Elias (2000-01; 40G, 56A)
Most Points, Rookie, Season	**70**	Scott Gomez (1999-2000; 19G, 51A)
Most Shutouts, Season	**10**	Martin Brodeur (1996-97, 1997-98)
Most Goals, Game	**4**	Five times
Most Assists, Game	**5**	Greg Adams (Oct. 10/85), Kirk Muller (Mar. 25/87), Tom Kurvers (Feb. 13/89), Scott Gomez (Mar. 30/03)
Most Points, Game	**6**	Kirk Muller (Nov. 29/86; 3G, 3A)

* Records include Kansas City Scouts and Colorado Rockies, 1974-75 through 1981-82.

** NHL Record.

Captains' History

Simon Nolet, 1974-75 to 1976-77; Wilf Paiement, 1977-78; Gary Croteau, 1978-79; Mike Christie, Rene Robert and Lanny McDonald, 1979-80; Lanny McDonald, 1980-81; Lanny McDonald and Rob Ramage, 1981-82; Don Lever, 1982-83; Don Lever and Mel Bridgman, 1983-84; Mel Bridgman, 1984-85 to 1986-87; Kirk Muller, 1987-88 to 1990-91; Bruce Driver, 1991-92; Scott Stevens, 1992-93 to date.

All-time Record vs. Other Clubs

Regular Season

	At Home								On Road								Total							
	GP	W	L	T	OL	GF	GA	PTS	GP	W	L	T	OL	GF	GA	PTS	GP	W	L	T	OL	GF	GA	PTS
Anaheim	8	7	1	0	0	31	14	14	9	5	4	0	0	23	23	10	17	12	5	0	0	54	37	24
Atlanta	8	5	2	1	0	28	15	11	8	5	1	2	0	28	13	12	16	10	3	3	0	56	28	23
Boston	51	15	25	11	0	136	164	41	54	16	29	7	2	163	213	41	105	31	54	18	2	299	377	82
Buffalo	52	17	26	9	0	150	174	43	52	14	31	7	0	158	209	35	104	31	57	16	0	308	383	78
Calgary	44	14	27	3	0	125	161	31	42	6	27	8	1	111	184	21	86	20	54	11	1	236	345	52
Carolina	43	24	15	4	0	153	137	52	42	16	17	8	1	126	135	41	85	40	32	12	1	279	272	93
Chicago	46	19	16	11	0	141	138	49	45	12	24	9	0	125	174	33	91	31	40	20	0	266	312	82
Colorado	35	18	13	4	0	143	118	40	34	13	18	3	0	97	123	29	69	31	31	7	0	240	241	69
Columbus	2	1	0	1	0	5	4	3	3	1	2	0	0	9	10	2	5	2	2	1	0	14	14	5
Dallas	43	21	19	3	0	146	132	45	44	13	24	6	1	117	162	33	87	34	43	9	1	263	294	78
Detroit	40	21	10	9	0	138	103	51	39	13	23	2	1	127	159	29	79	34	33	11	1	265	262	80
Edmonton	32	13	16	3	0	108	110	29	31	11	14	6	0	114	136	28	63	24	30	9	0	222	246	57
Florida	22	13	6	3	0	68	46	29	23	12	7	4	0	57	48	28	45	25	13	7	0	125	94	57
Los Angeles	42	18	19	5	0	139	146	41	41	7	27	6	1	126	201	21	83	25	46	11	1	265	347	62
Minnesota	2	2	0	0	0	9	4	4	3	1	1	1	0	8	7	3	5	3	1	1	0	17	11	7
Montreal	52	24	25	3	0	157	189	51	52	15	30	6	1	131	177	37	104	39	55	9	1	288	366	88
Nashville	5	2	3	0	0	15	14	4	4	4	0	0	0	12	6	8	9	6	3	0	0	27	20	12
NY Islanders	81	34	36	11	0	274	283	79	82	18	53	11	0	238	347	47	163	52	89	22	0	512	630	126
NY Rangers	83	43	33	7	0	290	277	93	81	22	39	19	1	242	316	64	164	65	72	26	1	532	593	157
Ottawa	21	12	7	2	0	64	49	26	22	13	5	3	1	57	46	30	43	25	12	5	1	121	95	56
Philadelphia	80	41	32	7	0	276	277	89	82	23	49	10	0	210	316	56	162	64	81	17	0	486	593	145
Phoenix	28	12	10	6	0	94	84	30	31	7	21	3	0	81	114	17	59	19	31	9	0	175	198	47
Pittsburgh	78	37	28	13	0	285	263	87	76	32	39	4	1	262	288	69	154	69	67	17	1	547	551	156
St. Louis	46	22	17	7	0	146	128	51	45	11	26	7	1	139	191	30	91	33	43	14	1	285	319	81
San Jose	11	6	4	1	0	41	22	13	10	6	2	1	1	32	24	14	21	12	6	2	1	73	46	27
Tampa Bay	24	18	3	2	1	90	37	39	23	12	6	5	0	72	54	29	47	30	9	7	1	162	91	68
Toronto	44	17	13	13	1	152	133	48	46	11	30	5	0	137	179	27	90	28	43	18	1	289	312	75
Vancouver	48	20	20	6	2	151	155	48	47	9	27	11	0	130	175	29	95	29	47	17	2	281	330	77
Washington	77	37	32	7	1	235	225	82	77	24	48	5	0	220	303	53	154	61	80	12	1	455	528	135
Defunct Clubs	8	4	2	2	0	25	19	10	8	2	3	3	0	19	27	7	16	6	5	5	0	44	46	17
Totals	**1156**	**537**	**460**	**154**	**5**	**3815**	**3621**	**1233**	**1156**	**354**	**627**	**162**	**13**	**3371**	**4360**	**883**	**2312**	**891**	**1087**	**316**	**18**	**7186**	**7981**	**2116**

Playoffs

	Series	W	L	GP	W	L	T	GF	GA	Last Mtg.	Rnd.	Result
Anaheim	1	1	0	7	4	3	0	19	12	2003	F	W 4-3
Boston	4	3	1	23	15	8	0	68	60	2003	CQF	W 4-1
Buffalo	1	1	0	7	4	3	0	14	14	1994	CQF	W 4-3
Carolina	2	1	1	12	6	6	0	31	17	2002	CQF	L 2-4
Colorado	1	0	1	7	3	4	0	11	19	2001	F	L 3-4
Dallas	1	1	0	6	4	2	0	15	9	2000	F	W 4-2
Detroit	1	1	0	4	4	0	0	16	7	1995	F	W 4-0
Florida	1	1	0	4	4	0	0	12	6	2000	CQF	W 4-0
Montreal	1	1	0	5	4	1	0	22	11	1997	CQF	W 4-1
NY Islanders	1	1	0	6	4	2	0	23	18	1988	DSF	W 4-2
NY Rangers	3	0	3	19	7	12	0	46	56	1997	CSF	L 1-4
Ottawa	2	1	1	13	6	7	0	29	26	2003	CF	W 4-3
Philadelphia	3	2	1	15	8	7	0	41	35	2000	CF	W 4-3
Pittsburgh	5	2	3	29	15	14	0	86	80	2001	CF	W 4-1
Tampa Bay	1	1	0	5	4	1	0	14	8	2003	CSF	W 4-1
Toronto	2	2	0	13	8	5	0	37	27	2001	CSF	W 4-3
Washington	2	1	1	13	6	7	0	43	44	1990	DSF	L 2-4
Totals	**32**	**20**	**12**	**188**	**106**	**82**	**0**	**527**	**449**			

Calgary totals include Atlanta Flames, 1974-75 to 1979-80.
Colorado totals include Quebec, 1979-80 to 1994-95.
Phoenix totals include Winnipeg, 1979-80 to 1995-96.

Playoff Results 2003-1999

Year	Round	Opponent	Result	GF	GA
2003	**F**	**Anaheim**	**W 4-3**	**19**	**12**
	CF	Ottawa	W 4-3	17	13
	CSF	Tampa Bay	W 4-1	14	8
	CQF	Boston	W 4-1	13	8
2002	CQF	Carolina	L 2-4	11	9
2001	F	Colorado	L 3-4	11	19
	CF	Pittsburgh	W 4-1	17	7
	CSF	Toronto	W 4-3	21	18
	CQF	Carolina	W 4-2	20	8
2000	**F**	**Dallas**	**W 4-2**	**15**	**9**
	CF	Philadelphia	W 4-3	18	15
	CSF	Toronto	W 4-2	16	9
	CQF	Florida	W 4-0	12	6
1999	CQF	Pittsburgh	L 3-4	18	21

Abbreviations: Round: F – Final; **CF** – conference final; **CSF** – conference semi-final; **CQF** – conference quarter-final; **DSF** – division semi-final.

Carolina totals include Hartford, 1979-80 to 1996-97.
Dallas totals include Minnesota North Stars, 1974-75 to 1992-93.

2002-03 Results

Month	Day		Opponent	Score
Oct.	10	at	Ottawa	2-1
	12		Columbus	3-2
	18		Nashville	3-2*
	19	at	Carolina	1-3
	23	at	Atlanta	2-1
	25	at	Buffalo	2-1
	26		Tampa Bay	5-1
	29		Carolina	1-2
Nov.	2		Chicago	5-1
	5		Calgary	2-3
	7	at	Philadelphia	1-0
	9		Edmonton	3-6
	12		Anaheim	3-2*
	15		Montreal	5-1
	16	at	Montreal	1-3
	19		Buffalo	4-3*
	21		NY Rangers	4-4
	23		Tampa Bay	1-3
	27	at	Detroit	2-3*
	29	at	Nashville	2-1
	30	at	St. Louis	5-4*
Dec.	2	at	Philadelphia	1-0*
	4		Vancouver	2-3*
	6		Pittsburgh	3-1
	7	at	Toronto	0-1
	10		St. Louis	2-0
	12	at	Columbus	2-4
	14	at	Ottawa	3-4*
	18		Ottawa	0-3
	19	at	Pittsburgh	3-1
	21		Dallas	5-3
	23	at	NY Rangers	2-2
	27	at	Washington	2-3
	28		Washington	2-1*
	30	at	Boston	1-0
Jan.	1		Florida	1-2
	3		Toronto	2-0
	4	at	Toronto	1-2
	7		Montreal	3-2
	10	at	Florida	2-1
	11	at	Tampa Bay	3-3
	13		Florida	6-2
	15		NY Islanders	5-0
	17	at	Carolina	2-1
	18		Carolina	5-2
	22	at	San Jose	5-4*
	24	at	Anaheim	3-1
	25	at	Los Angeles	1-2*
	28		Detroit	1-0
	30		Philadelphia	5-1
Feb.	4		Buffalo	4-1
	5	at	Washington	4-1
	7		Atlanta	2-4
	9		Minnesota	3-2
	11	at	Colorado	1-3
	12	at	Phoenix	3-0
	15		Pittsburgh	1-4
	18	at	Philadelphia	2-2
	19		Ottawa	3-5
	21		Boston	3-2
	23	at	Pittsburgh	4-3
	25		NY Rangers	3-3
	27	at	NY Islanders	3-3
Mar.	1		Washington	2-1*
	4	at	Minnesota	2-3
	5	at	Calgary	4-5*
	8	at	NY Islanders	4-2
	11		Atlanta	2-3
	13	at	Boston	3-4
	15		NY Rangers	3-1
	17		Philadelphia	2-4
	18	at	Montreal	1-0
	21		Pittsburgh	3-1
	22	at	NY Islanders	4-2
	24	at	Florida	4-1
	27	at	Tampa Bay	2-2
	28	at	Atlanta	1-1
	30		NY Islanders	6-0
Apr.	1		Toronto	2-3*
	3		Boston	1-1
	4	at	NY Rangers	2-1
	6	at	Buffalo	2-2

* – Overtime

Entry Draft
Selections 2003-1989

2003 Pick
17 Zach Parise
42 Petr Vrana
93 Ivan Khomutov
167 Zach Tarkir
197 Jason Smith
261 Joey Tenute
292 Arseny Bondarev

2002 Pick
51 Anton Kadeykin
53 Barry Tallackson
64 Jason Ryznar
84 Marek Chvatal
85 Ahren Nittel
117 Cam Janssen
154 Krisjanis Redlihs
187 Eric Johansson
218 Ilkka Pikkarainen
250 Dan Glover
281 Bill Kinkel

2001 Pick
28 Adrian Foster
44 Igor Pohanka
48 Thomas Pihlman
60 Victor Uchevatov
67 Robin Leblanc
72 Brandon Nolan
128 Andrei Posnov
163 Andreas Salomonsson
194 James Massen
229 Aaron Voros
257 Yevgeny Gamalei

2000 Pick
22 David Hale
39 Teemu Laine
56 Alexander Suglobov
57 Matt DeMarchi
62 Paul Martin
67 Max Birbraer
76 Mike Rupp
125 Phil Cole
135 Mike Danton
164 Matus Kostur
194 Deryk Engelland
198 Ken Magowan
257 Warren McCutcheon

1999 Pick
27 Ari Ahonen
42 Mike Commodore
50 Brett Clouthier
95 Andre Lakos
100 Teemu Kesa
185 Scott Cameron
214 Chris Hartsburg
242 Justin Dziama

1998 Pick
26 Mike Van Ryn
27 Scott Gomez
37 Christian Berglund
82 Brian Gionta
96 Mikko Jokela
105 Pierre Dagenais
119 Anton But
143 Ryan Flinn
172 Jacques Lariviere
199 Erik Jensen
227 Marko Ahosilta
257 Ryan Held

1997 Pick
24 Jean-Francois Damphousse
38 Stanislav Gron
104 Lucas Nehrling
131 Jiri Bicek
159 Sascha Goc
188 Mathieu Benoit
215 Scott Clemmensen
241 Jan Srdinko

1996 Pick
10 Lance Ward
38 Wes Mason
41 Josh DeWolf
47 Pierre Dagenais
49 Colin White
63 Scott Parker
91 Josef Boumedienne
101 Josh MacNevin
118 Glenn Crawford
145 Sean Ritchlin
173 Daryl Andrews
199 Willie Mitchell
205 Jay Bertsch
225 Pasi Petrilainen

1995 Pick
18 Petr Sykora
44 Nathan Perrott
70 Sergei Vyshedkevich
78 David Gosselin
79 Alyn McCauley
96 Henrik Rehnberg
122 Chris Mason
148 Adam Young
174 Richard Rochefort
200 Frederic Henry
226 Colin O'Hara

1994 Pick
25 Vadim Sharifijanov
51 Patrik Elias
71 Sheldon Souray
103 Zdenek Skorepa
129 Christian Gosselin
134 Ryan Smart
155 Luciano Caravaggio
181 Jeff Williams
207 Eric Bertrand
233 Steve Sullivan
259 Scott Swanjord
269 Mike Hanson

1993 Pick
13 Denis Pederson
32 Jay Pandolfo
39 Brendan Morrison
65 Krzysztof Oliwa
110 John Guirestante
143 Steve Brule
169 Nikolai Zavarukhin
195 Thomas Cullen
221 Judd Lambert
247 Jimmy Provencher
273 Mike Legg

1992 Pick
18 Jason Smith
42 Sergei Brylin
66 Cale Hulse
90 Vitali Tomilin
94 Scott McCabe
114 Ryan Black
138 Dan Trebil
162 Geordie Kinnear
186 Stephane Yelle
210 Jeff Toms
234 Heath Weenk
258 Vladislav Yakovenko

1991 Pick
3 Scott Niedermayer
11 Brian Rolston
33 Donevan Hextall
55 Fredrik Lindquist
77 Bradley Willner
121 Curt Regnier
143 David Craievich
165 Paul Wolanski
187 Daniel Reimann
231 Kevin Riehl
253 Jason Hehr

1990 Pick
20 Martin Brodeur
24 David Harlock
29 Chris Gotziaman
53 Mike Dunham
56 Brad Bombardir
64 Mike Bodnarchuk
95 Dean Malkoc
104 Petr Kuchyna
116 Lubomir Kolnik
137 Chris McAlpine
179 Jaroslav Modry
200 Corey Schwab
221 Valeri Zelepukin
242 Todd Reirden

1989 Pick
5 Bill Guerin
18 Jason Miller
26 Jarrod Skalde
47 Scott Pellerin
89 Mike Heinke
110 David Emma
152 Sergei Starikov
173 Andre Faust
215 Jason Simon
236 Peter Larsson

Coach

BURNS, PAT
Coach, New Jersey Devils. Born in St-Henri, Que., April 4, 1952.

Pat Burns was hired as head coach of the New Jersey Devils on June 13, 2002. In his first season with the club, he guided the Devils to the 2003 Stanley Cup title. Before joining New Jersey, Burns had been out of coaching for more than a year after being fired by Boston early in 2000-01. He had joined the Bruins in 1997-98 and won the Jack Adams Award as coach of the year in 1998 after his Bruins showed a 30-point improvement over the previous season. He became the first man in NHL history to win the award three times, having won it previously with Toronto (1993) and Montreal (1989).

Burns began his coaching career with the Hull Olympiques of the QMJHL in 1983. He spent four seasons with the club, guiding them to a berth in the Memorial Cup finals in 1986. He moved into the professional ranks in 1987 with Montreal's AHL affiliate and took over the Canadiens the following year. Burns was the winningest coach in the NHL during his four-year tenure with the Canadiens, posting a record of 174-104-42. He was hired by the Toronto Maple Leafs on May 29, 1992, and promptly led the team to a club-record 32-point improvement on their 1991-92 record with a mark of 44-29-11 and 99 points.

Coaching Record

			Regular Season			Playoffs		
Season	Team	Games	W	L	T	Games	W	L
1983-84	Hull (QMJHL)	70	25	45	0	....	....	....
1984-85	Hull (QMJHL)	68	33	34	1	5	1	4
1985-86	Hull (QMJHL)	72	54	18	0	15	15	0
1986-87	Hull (QMJHL)	70	26	39	5	8	4	4
1987-88	Sherbrooke (AHL)	80	42	34	4	6	2	4
1988-89	Montreal (NHL)	80	53	18	9	21	14	7
1989-90	Montreal (NHL)	80	41	28	11	11	5	6
1990-91	Montreal (NHL)	80	39	30	11	13	7	6
1991-92	Montreal (NHL)	80	41	28	11	11	4	7
1992-93	Toronto (NHL)	84	44	29	11	21	11	10
1993-94	Toronto (NHL)	84	43	29	12	18	9	9
1994-95	Toronto (NHL)	48	21	19	8	7	3	4
1995-96	Toronto (NHL)	65	25	30	10	....	....	....
1997-98	Boston (NHL)	82	39	30	13	6	2	4
1998-99	Boston (NHL)	82	39	30	13	12	6	6
1999-2000	Boston (NHL)	82	24	39	19	....	....	....
2000-01	Boston (NHL)	8	3	4	1	....	....	....
2002-03	New Jersey (NHL)	82	46	26	10	24	16	8*
NHL Totals		**937**	**458**	**340**	**139**	**144**	**77**	**67**

* Stanley Cup win.

Club Directory

Continental Airlines Arena

New Jersey Devils
Continental Airlines Arena
50 Route 120 North
P.O. Box 504
East Rutherford, NJ 07073
Phone **201/935-6050**
FAX 201/935-2127
www.newjerseydevils.com
Capacity: 19,040

Chairman . . . . Peter Simon
CEO/President/General Manager . . . . Louis A. Lamoriello
Executive Vice President . . . . Peter S. McMullen
Executive Vice President . . . . Chris Modrzynski
Vice President, Community Dev./Broadcasting . . . . Glenn Adamo
Vice President, General Counsel . . . . . . Joseph C. Benedetti
Vice President, Ticket Operations . . . . . . Terry Farmer
Vice President, Corporate Partnerships . . . . Kenneth F. Ferriter
Vice President, Sales/Marketing . . . . . . Jason Siegel
Vice President, Finance . . . . Scott Struble

Hockey Club Personnel
Head Coach . . . . Pat Burns
Assistant Coaches . . . . Jacques Laperriere, Bob Carpenter, John MacLean
Goaltending Coach . . . . Jacques Caron
Special Assignment Coach . . . . . . Larry Robinson
Director, Scouting . . . . David Conte
Assistant Director, Scouting . . . . . . Claude Carrier
Scouting Staff . . . . Glen Dirk, Milt Fisher, Ferny Flaman, Dan Labraaten, Chris Lamoriello, Vladimir Lokotko, Joe Mahoney, Larry Perris, Marcel Pronovost, Lou Reycroft, Vaclav Slansky, Jr., Geoff Stevens, Ed Thomlinson, Les Widdifield
Pro Scouting Staff . . . . Andre Boudrias, Bob Hoffmeyer, Jan Ludvig
Special Assignment Scout . . . . . . Kurt Kleinendorst
Hockey Operations Video Coordinator . . . . Taran Singleton
Scouting Staff Assistant . . . . . . Callie A. Smith
Medical Trainer . . . . Bill Murray
Strength/Conditioning Coordinator . . . . Michael Vasalani
Equipment Manager . . . . Rich Matthews
Assistant Equipment Manager . . . . . . Alex Abasto
Massage Therapist . . . . Juergen Merz
Team Cardiologist . . . . Dr. Joseph Niznik
Team Dentist . . . . Dr. H. Hugh Gardy
Team Optometrist . . . . Dr. Paul Berman
Team Orthopedists . . . . . . Dr. Barry Fisher, Dr. Len Jaffe
Fitness Consultant . . . . Vladimir Bure
Exercise Physiologist . . . . . . Dr. Garret Caffrey
Physical Therapist . . . . David Feniger
Video Consultant . . . . Mitch Kaufman
Head Coach, Albany . . . . Dennis Gendron
Assistant Coaches, Albany . . . . Chris Terreri, Geordie Kinnear, Gates Orlando
Athletic Trainer, Albany . . . . . . Curtis Bell
Equipment Manager, Albany . . . . . . Jason McGrath

Administration
Hockey Operations Executive Assistant to
the CEO/President/General Manager . . . . Marie Carnevale
Corporate Executive Assistant to
the CEO/President/General Manager . . . . Mary K. Morrison
Receptionists . . . . . . Jelsa Belotta, Pat Maione
Operations Staff Assistant . . . . . . John Gerba

Ticket Operations
Director, Ticket Operations . . . . . . Tom Bates
Director, Customer Service/Season Ticket Accounts . Dave Beck
Customer Service Representative . . . . . Andrea Marchesani
Director, Group Sales . . . . . . Neil Desormeaux
Group Account Manager . . . . . . Rich Davis

Corporate Partnerships
Director, Corporate Accounts . . . . . . Michael DeMartino
Account Manager, Corporate Partnerships . . . . Michael Merolla
Staff Assistant, Corporate Partner Services . . . . Matt Dugan

Marketing
Director, Season Ticket Sales . . . . . . Todd Hyland
Account Managers . . . . John Baier, Chris Brehm, Michael Dilworth, David Forrest, Scott Hollingshead, Peter Juncaj, Seth Kohn, Louie Leone, Brian Propfe
Receptionist, Sales/Marketing . . . . . . Stacy Holand
Merchandise Manager . . . . . . David Perricone
Merchandise Assistants . . . . Adam Manger, Don Gleeson
Assistant Director, Community Development . . . . Paul Viola
Coordinator, Game Entertainment . . . . . . Bruce Cohn

Communications
Director, Information/Publications . . . . Mike Levine
Director, Public Relations . . . . . . Jeff Altstadter
Staff Assistants . . . . Erica Luthman, Pete Albietz

Finance
Assistant Controller . . . . Craig S. Wolman
Staff Accountants . . . . Jill Bach, Matt Courtney, Marc Glasser
Administrative Assistant . . . . . . Eileen Howell

Computer Operations
Director, Programming/Computer Operations . . . . Jack Skelley
Programmer/Analyst . . . . Joseph Wyks
Systems Administrator . . . . . . Mike Tukes
Director, Website Operations . . . . . . Antonio Barrera
Coordinator, Website Operations . . . . Anthony Bovasso

Nets/Devils Foundation
Executive Director . . . . Shané Harris
Program/Grants Manager . . . . . . Daniel McNeal

Television/Radio
Television Outlet . . . . FOX Sports Net
Broadcasters . . . . . . Mike Emrick, Play-by-Play
Glenn Resch, Color
Radio Outlet . . . . WABC 770 AM
Broadcasters . . . . John Hennessy, Play-by-Play
Randy Velischek, Color

New York Islanders

2002-03 Results: 35w-34L-11T-2OTL 83PTS.
Third, Atlantic Division

2003-04 Schedule

Oct.	Thu.	9	at Washington
	Sat.	11	at Buffalo
	Tue.	14	at Atlanta
	Sat.	18	Florida
	Mon.	20	Toronto
	Thu.	23	at Montreal
	Sat.	25	Pittsburgh
	Tue.	28	New Jersey
	Wed.	29	at Pittsburgh
Nov.	Sat.	1	Anaheim*
	Mon.	3	Ottawa
	Thu.	6	Dallas
	Sat.	8	Atlanta
	Tue.	11	at Philadelphia
	Thu.	13	Montreal
	Sat.	15	at Nashville
	Wed.	19	at Florida
	Thu.	20	at Tampa Bay
	Sat.	22	at Columbus
	Wed.	26	Carolina
	Fri.	28	at Detroit
	Sat.	29	Philadelphia
Dec.	Tue.	2	Washington
	Thu.	4	NY Rangers
	Sat.	6	Chicago
	Tue.	9	Tampa Bay
	Wed.	10	at New Jersey
	Sat.	13	Atlanta
	Tue.	16	New Jersey
	Thu.	18	at NY Rangers
	Sat.	20	at Philadelphia*
	Sun.	21	at Washington
	Tue.	23	Philadelphia
	Fri.	26	at New Jersey
	Sat.	27	Toronto
	Mon.	29	New Jersey
	Wed.	31	at Pittsburgh*
Jan.	Thu.	1	at Ottawa
	Sat.	3	at Boston
	Tue.	6	Calgary
	Thu.	8	Edmonton

	Sat.	10	NY Rangers*
	Tue.	13	at NY Rangers
	Thu.	15	at Ottawa
	Sat.	17	Buffalo
	Mon.	19	Ottawa*
	Tue.	20	at Toronto
	Fri.	23	at Carolina
	Sat.	24	at Atlanta
	Tue.	27	Boston
	Thu.	29	at Boston
	Sat.	31	Florida
Feb.	Tue.	3	Vancouver
	Thu.	5	at Montreal
	Tue.	10	at Colorado
	Wed.	11	at Dallas
	Fri.	13	at Phoenix
	Mon.	16	Los Angeles*
	Wed.	18	Pittsburgh
	Thu.	19	at NY Rangers
	Sat.	21	Buffalo
	Tue.	24	Boston
	Thu.	26	NY Rangers
	Fri.	27	at Buffalo
	Sun.	29	Pittsburgh*
Mar.	Tue.	2	at Pittsburgh
	Thu.	4	at Toronto
	Sat.	6	St. Louis
	Tue.	9	at St. Louis
	Thu.	11	at San Jose
	Fri.	12	at Anaheim
	Tue.	16	at Tampa Bay
	Wed.	17	at Florida
	Fri.	19	Minnesota
	Sun.	21	Tampa Bay*
	Tue.	23	Washington
	Thu.	25	at Philadelphia
	Sat.	27	Carolina
	Sun.	28	at New Jersey*
	Wed.	31	Montreal
Apr.	Fri.	2	at Carolina
	Sun.	4	Philadelphia*

Denotes afternoon game.

Franchise date: June 6, 1972

EASTERN CONFERENCE
ATLANTIC DIVISION

32nd NHL Season

Rumors around the trade deadline seemed to have Janne Niinimaa headed from Edmonton to Toronto. Instead, he wound up with the Islanders who sent Brad Isbister and Raffi Torres to the Oilers to get him.

Year-by-Year Record

		Home				Road				Overall							
Season	GP	W	L	T	OL	W	L	T	OL	W	L	T	OL	GF	GA	Pts.	Finished	Playoff Result
2002-03	82	18	18	5	0	17	16	6	2	35	34	11	2	224	231	83	3rd, Atlantic Div.	Lost Conf. Quarter-Final
2001-02	82	21	13	5	2	21	15	3	2	42	28	8	4	239	220	96	2nd, Atlantic Div.	Lost Conf. Quarter-Final
2000-01	82	12	27	1	1	9	24	6	2	21	51	7	3	185	268	52	5th, Atlantic Div.	Out of Playoffs
1999-2000	82	10	25	5	1	14	23	4	0	24	48	9	1	194	275	58	5th, Atlantic Div.	Out of Playoffs
1998-99	82	11	23	7	...	13	25	3	...	24	48	10	...	194	244	58	5th, Atlantic Div.	Out of Playoffs
1997-98	82	17	20	4	...	13	21	7	...	30	41	11	...	212	225	71	4th, Atlantic Div.	Out of Playoffs
1996-97	82	19	18	4	...	10	23	8	...	29	41	12	...	240	250	70	7th, Atlantic Div.	Out of Playoffs
1995-96	82	14	21	6	...	8	29	4	...	22	50	10	...	229	315	54	7th, Atlantic Div.	Out of Playoffs
1994-95	48	10	11	3	...	5	17	2	...	15	28	5	...	126	158	35	7th, Atlantic Div.	Out of Playoffs
1993-94	84	23	15	4	...	13	21	8	...	36	36	12	...	282	264	84	4th, Atlantic Div.	Lost Conf. Quarter-Final
1992-93	84	20	19	3	...	20	18	4	...	40	37	7	...	335	297	87	3rd, Patrick Div.	Lost Conf. Championship
1991-92	80	20	15	5	...	14	20	6	...	34	35	11	...	291	299	79	5th, Patrick Div.	Out of Playoffs
1990-91	80	15	19	6	...	10	26	4	...	25	45	10	...	223	290	60	6th, Patrick Div.	Out of Playoffs
1989-90	80	15	17	8	...	16	21	3	...	31	38	11	...	281	288	73	4th, Patrick Div.	Lost Div. Semi-Final
1988-89	80	19	18	3	...	9	29	2	...	28	47	5	...	265	325	61	6th, Patrick Div.	Out of Playoffs
1987-88	80	24	10	6	...	15	21	4	...	39	31	10	...	308	267	88	1st, Patrick Div.	Lost Div. Semi-Final
1986-87	80	20	15	5	...	15	18	7	...	35	33	12	...	279	281	82	3rd, Patrick Div.	Lost Div. Final
1985-86	80	22	11	7	...	17	18	5	...	39	29	12	...	327	284	90	3rd, Patrick Div.	Lost Div. Semi-Final
1984-85	80	26	11	3	...	14	23	3	...	40	34	6	...	345	312	86	3rd, Patrick Div.	Lost Div. Final
1983-84	80	28	11	1	...	22	15	3	...	50	26	4	...	357	269	104	1st, Patrick Div.	Lost Final
1982-83	**80**	**26**	**11**	**3**	...	**16**	**15**	**9**	...	**42**	**26**	**12**	...	**302**	**226**	**96**	**2nd, Patrick Div.**	**Won Stanley Cup**
1981-82	**80**	**33**	**3**	**4**	...	**21**	**13**	**6**	...	**54**	**16**	**10**	...	**385**	**250**	**118**	**1st, Patrick Div.**	**Won Stanley Cup**
1980-81	**80**	**23**	**6**	**11**	...	**25**	**12**	**3**	...	**48**	**18**	**14**	...	**355**	**260**	**110**	**1st, Patrick Div.**	**Won Stanley Cup**
1979-80	**80**	**26**	**9**	**5**	...	**13**	**19**	**8**	...	**39**	**28**	**13**	...	**281**	**247**	**91**	**2nd, Patrick Div.**	**Won Stanley Cup**
1978-79	80	31	3	6	...	20	12	8	...	51	15	14	...	358	214	116	1st, Patrick Div.	Lost Semi-Final
1977-78	80	29	3	8	...	19	14	7	...	48	17	15	...	334	210	111	1st, Patrick Div.	Lost Quarter-Final
1976-77	80	24	11	5	...	23	10	7	...	47	21	12	...	288	193	106	2nd, Patrick Div.	Lost Semi-Final
1975-76	80	24	8	8	...	18	13	9	...	42	21	17	...	297	190	101	2nd, Patrick Div.	Lost Semi-Final
1974-75	80	22	6	12	...	11	19	10	...	33	25	22	...	264	221	88	3rd, Patrick Div.	Lost Semi-Final
1973-74	78	13	17	9	...	6	24	9	...	19	41	18	...	182	247	56	8th, East Div.	Out of Playoffs
1972-73	78	10	25	4	...	2	35	2	...	12	60	6	...	170	347	30	8th, East Div.	Out of Playoffs

2003-04 Player Personnel

FORWARDS	HT	WT	S	Place of Birth	Date	2002-03 Club
ASHAM, Arron	5-11	209	R	Portage La Prairie, Man.	4/13/78	NY Islanders
BATES, Shawn	6-0	205	R	Melrose, MA	4/3/75	NY Islanders
BLAKE, Jason	5-10	180	L	Moorhead, MN	9/2/73	NY Islanders
CZERKAWSKI, Mariusz	6-0	200	L	Radomsko, Poland	4/13/72	Montreal-Hamilton
GODARD, Eric	6-4	227	R	Vernon, B.C.	3/7/80	NY Islanders-Bridgeport
HUNTER, Trent	6-3	191	R	Red Deer, Alta.	7/5/80	NY Islanders-Bridgeport
KRAFT, Ryan	5-9	181	L	Bottineau, ND	11/7/75	San Jose-Cleveland
KVASHA, Oleg	6-5	230	R	Moscow, USSR	7/26/78	NY Islanders
MANLOW, Eric	6-0	180	L	Belleville, Ont.	4/7/75	NY Islanders-Bridgeport
MAPLETOFT, Justin	6-1	180	L	Lloydminster, Sask.	1/11/81	NY Islanders-Bridgeport
PAPINEAU, Justin	5-10	178	L	Ottawa, Ont.	1/15/80	StL-Wor-NYI-Bridgeport
PARRISH, Mark	5-11	200	R	Edina, MN	2/2/77	NY Islanders
PECA, Michael	5-11	190	R	Toronto, Ont.	3/26/74	NY Islanders
SCATCHARD, Dave	6-2	224	R	Hinton, Alta.	2/20/76	NY Islanders
WEINHANDL, Mattias	6-0	183	R	Ljungby, Sweden	6/1/80	NY Islanders-Bridgeport
WIEMER, Jason	6-1	225	L	Kimberley, B.C.	4/14/76	NY Islanders
YASHIN, Alexei	6-3	225	R	Sverdlovsk, USSR	11/5/73	NY Islanders
DEFENSEMEN						
AUCOIN, Adrian	6-2	214	R	Ottawa, Ont.	7/3/73	NY Islanders
BUTENSCHON, Sven	6-4	215	L	Itzehoe, West Germany	3/22/76	NY Islanders-Bridgeport
CAIRNS, Eric	6-6	230	L	Oakville, Ont.	6/27/74	NY Islanders
HAMRLIK, Roman	6-2	200	L	Zlin, Czech.	4/12/74	NY Islanders
JONSSON, Kenny	6-3	217	L	Angelholm, Sweden	10/6/74	NY Islanders
LETANG, Alan	6-1	201	L	Renfrew, Ont.	9/4/75	NY Islanders-Bridgeport
MARTINEK, Radek	6-1	200	R	Havlickuv Brod, Czech.	8/31/76	NY Islanders-Bridgeport
NASREDDINE, Alain	6-1	201	L	Montreal, Que.	7/10/75	NY Islanders-Bridgeport
NIINIMAA, Janne	6-1	220	L	Raahe, Finland	5/22/75	Edmonton-NY Islanders
SMITH, Brandon	6-1	209	L	Hazelton, B.C.	2/25/73	NY Islanders-Bridgeport
TIMANDER, Mattias	6-2	230	L	Solleftea, Sweden	4/16/74	NY Islanders

GOALTENDERS	HT	WT	C	Place of Birth	Date	2002-03 Club
DiPIETRO, Rick	5-11	185	R	Winthrop, MA	9/19/81	NY Islanders-Bridgeport
SNOW, Garth	6-3	200	L	Wrentham, MA	7/28/69	NY Islanders

Coach

STIRLING, STEVE
Coach, New York Islanders. Born in Clarkson, Ont., November 19, 1949.

The New York Islanders introduced Steve Stirling as the franchise's head coach on June 3, 2003. Stirling had spent the previous two seasons as the coach of the Islanders' top minor-league affiliate in Bridgeport and had spent six seasons in various roles throughout the organization. He was *The Hockey News* minor pro coach of the year in 2001-02.

Stirling joined the Islanders' organization as a scout in 1997. He served as an assistant coach for the Lowell Lock Monsters, the Islanders' AHL affiliate, from 1998 through 2000 and for the Islanders themselves during the 2000-01 season. He was named the first head coach of the Sound Tigers on July 26, 2001 and led Bridgeport to the AHL's 2001-02 Kilpatrick Trophy regular-season championship and Eastern Conference playoff championship before losing to the Chicago Wolves in the 2002 Calder Cup Final.

Stirling first moved into the coaching ranks with the NCAA's Babson College Beavers from 1978 through 1983 and 1985 through 1993. He was the NCAA Division II/III coach of the year in 1980 and again in 1982 and also served as Babson's athletic director from 1986 through 1997. Stirling coached Division I Providence College from 1983 though 1985, leading the Friars to an appearance in the 1985 NCAA National Championship Game.

As a player, Stirling led the Boston University Terriers to appearances in the Beanpot Tournament during each of his three seasons at the school, 1968 to 1971, winning the tournament in 1970 and 1971. As a senior and BU's team captain in 1970-71, he was named Beanpot Most Valuable Player and led the Terriers to the NCAA National Championship. Stirling was inducted into the Beanpot Hall of Fame in February 2003.

Stirling played six seasons, (1971 to 1977), of professional hockey in the AHL and North American Hockey League, as well as in Austria. He spent the bulk of his professional playing career in the AHL with the Boston Braves (1971 to 1974) and Rochester Americans (1974 to 1977).

Coaching Record

		Regular Season				Playoffs		
Season	Team	Games	W	L	T	Games	W	L
2001-02	Bridgeport (AHL)	80	43	29	8	20	12	8
2002-03	Bridgeport (AHL)	80	40	29	11	9	5	4

2002-03 Scoring

* - rookie

Regular Season

Pos	#	Player	Team	GP	G	A	Pts	+/–	PIM	PP	SH	GW	GT	S	%
C	79	Alexei Yashin	NYI	81	26	39	65	–12	32	14	0	7	1	274	9.5
C	55	Jason Blake	NYI	81	25	30	55	16	58	3	1	4	0	253	9.9
R	37	Mark Parrish	NYI	81	23	25	48	–11	28	9	0	5	0	147	15.6
C	38	Dave Scatchard	NYI	81	27	18	45	9	108	5	0	2	1	165	16.4
C	27	Michael Peca	NYI	66	13	29	42	–4	43	4	2	2	0	117	11.1
C	17	Shawn Bates	NYI	74	13	29	42	–9	52	1	6	1	1	126	10.3
D	4	Roman Hamrlik	NYI	73	9	32	41	21	87	3	0	2	0	151	6.0
D	3	Adrian Aucoin	NYI	73	8	27	35	–5	70	5	0	1	0	175	4.6
R	45	Arron Asham	NYI	78	15	19	34	1	57	4	0	1	0	114	13.2
D	44	Janne Niinimaa	EDM	63	4	24	28	–7	66	2	0	0	0	90	4.4
			NYI	13	1	5	6	–2	14	1	0	0	0	11	9.1
			TOTAL	76	5	29	34	–9	80	3	0	0	0	101	5.0
C	28	Jason Wiemer	NYI	81	9	19	28	5	116	0	1	2	0	139	6.5
L	12	Oleg Kvasha	NYI	69	12	14	26	4	44	0	1	2	0	121	9.9
D	29	Kenny Jonsson	NYI	71	8	18	26	–8	24	3	1	0	1	108	7.4
R	11	* Mattias Weinhandl	NYI	47	6	17	23	–2	10	1	0	0	0	66	9.1
C	25	Randy Robitaille	PIT	41	5	12	17	5	8	1	0	2	0	61	8.2
			NYI	10	1	2	3	0	2	1	0	0	0	8	12.5
			TOTAL	51	6	14	20	5	10	2	0	2	0	69	8.7
D	2	Mattias Timander	NYI	80	3	13	16	–2	24	0	0	1	0	83	3.6
D	24	Radek Martinek	NYI	66	2	11	13	15	26	0	0	1	0	67	3.0
C	16	* Justin Papineau	STL	11	2	1	3	–1	0	0	0	1	0	15	13.3
			NYI	5	1	2	3	1	4	0	0	1	0	8	12.5
			TOTAL	16	3	3	6	0	4	0	0	2	0	23	13.0
D	33	Eric Cairns	NYI	60	1	4	5	–7	124	0	0	0	0	31	3.2
L	16	* Raffi Torres	NYI	17	0	5	5	0	10	0	0	0	0	12	0.0
C	26	* Justin Mapletoft	NYI	11	2	2	4	–1	2	1	0	0	0	12	16.7
R	21	* Trent Hunter	NYI	8	0	4	4	5	4	0	0	0	0	19	0.0
D	44	Sven Butenschon	NYI	37	0	4	4	–6	26	0	0	0	0	19	0.0
C	10	Eric Manlow	NYI	8	2	1	3	2	4	1	0	0	0	7	28.6
R	20	Steve Webb	NYI	49	1	0	1	–5	75	0	0	0	0	27	3.7
D	8	* Tomi Pettinen	NYI	2	0	0	0	1	0	0	0	0	0	0	0.0
D	6	Brandon Smith	NYI	3	0	0	0	–2	0	0	0	0	0	1	0.0
D	59	Alain Nasreddine	NYI	3	0	0	0	0	2	0	0	0	0	0	0.0
D	32	Alan Letang	NYI	4	0	0	0	–1	0	0	0	0	0	2	0.0
D	36	Ray Schultz	NYI	4	0	0	0	–1	28	0	0	0	0	1	0.0
R	49	* Eric Godard	NYI	19	0	0	0	–3	48	0	0	0	0	6	0.0

Goaltending

No.	Goaltender	GPI	Mins	Avg	W	L	T	EN	SO	GA	SA	S%	G	A	PIM
30	Garth Snow	43	2390	2.31	16	17	5	8	1	92	1120	.918	0	0	24
30	Chris Osgood	37	1993	2.92	17	14	4	4	2	97	912	.894	0	0	12
39	* Rick Dipietro	10	585	2.97	2	5	2	1	0	29	273	.894	0	0	2
	Totals	**82**	**4992**	**2.78**	**35**	**36**	**11**	**13**	**3**	**231**	**2318**	**.900**			

Playoffs

Pos	#	Player	Team	GP	G	A	Pts	+/–	PIM	PP	SH	GW	GT	S	%
C	79	Alexei Yashin	NYI	5	2	2	4	–1	2	0	0	0	0	20	10.0
D	3	Adrian Aucoin	NYI	5	1	2	3	–1	4	0	0	0	0	19	5.3
C	25	Randy Robitaille	NYI	5	1	1	2	–1	0	1	0	0	0	8	12.5
D	4	Roman Hamrlik	NYI	5	0	2	2	–2	2	0	0	0	0	9	0.0
C	17	Shawn Bates	NYI	5	1	0	1	–2	0	1	0	0	0	7	14.3
C	38	Dave Scatchard	NYI	5	1	0	1	–3	6	0	0	1	0	3	33.3
R	37	Mark Parrish	NYI	5	1	0	1	–1	4	1	0	0	0	4	25.0
R	49	* Eric Godard	NYI	2	0	1	1	1	4	0	0	0	0	0	0.0
D	29	Kenny Jonsson	NYI	5	0	1	1	–2	0	0	0	0	0	11	0.0
D	44	Janne Niinimaa	NYI	5	0	1	1	–4	12	0	0	0	0	5	0.0
L	12	Oleg Kvasha	NYI	5	0	1	1	–1	2	0	0	0	0	11	0.0
C	55	Jason Blake	NYI	5	0	1	1	–2	2	0	0	0	0	12	0.0
D	2	Mattias Timander	NYI	1	0	0	0	1	0	0	0	0	0	0	0.0
C	16	* Justin Papineau	NYI	1	0	0	0	0	0	0	0	0	0	0	0.0
C	26	* Justin Mapletoft	NYI	2	0	0	0	0	0	0	0	0	0	1	0.0
D	24	Radek Martinek	NYI	4	0	0	0	–1	4	0	0	0	0	0	0.0
C	27	Michael Peca	NYI	5	0	0	0	–1	4	0	0	0	0	7	0.0
D	33	Eric Cairns	NYI	5	0	0	0	–1	13	0	0	0	0	3	0.0
C	28	Jason Wiemer	NYI	5	0	0	0	–3	23	0	0	0	0	9	0.0
R	20	Steve Webb	NYI	5	0	0	0	–2	10	0	0	0	0	3	0.0
R	45	Arron Asham	NYI	5	0	0	0	–1	16	0	0	0	0	4	0.0

Goaltending

No.	Goaltender	GPI	Mins	Avg	W	L	EN	SO	GA	SA	S%	G	A	PIM
39	* Rick Dipietro	1	15	0.00	0	0	0	0	0	3	1.000	0	0	0
30	Garth Snow	5	305	2.36	1	4	1	1	12	134	.910	0	0	0
	Totals	**5**	**322**	**2.42**	**1**	**4**	**1**	**1**	**13**	**138**	**.906**			

Coaching History

Phil Goyette and Earl Ingarfield, 1972-73; Al Arbour, 1973-74 to 1985-86; Terry Simpson, 1986-87, 1987-88; Terry Simpson and Al Arbour, 1988-89; Al Arbour, 1989-90 to 1993-94; Lorne Henning, 1994-95; Mike Milbury, 1995-96; Mike Milbury and Rick Bowness, 1996-97; Rick Bowness and Mike Milbury, 1997-98; Mike Milbury and Bill Stewart, 1998-99; Butch Goring, 1999-2000; Butch Goring and Lorne Henning, 2000-01; Peter Laviolette, 2001-02, 2002-03; Steve Stirling, 2003-04.

Club Records

Team

(Figures in brackets for season records are games played; records for fewest points, wins, ties, losses, goals, goals against are for 70 or more games)

Most Points **118** 1981-82 (80)
Most Wins **54** 1981-82 (80)
Most Ties **22** 1974-75 (80)
Most Losses **60** 1972-73 (78)
Most Goals **385** 1981-82 (80)
Most Goals Against **347** 1972-73 (78)
Fewest Points **30** 1972-73 (78)
Fewest Wins **12** 1972-73 (78)
Fewest Ties **4** 1983-84 (80)
Fewest Losses **15** 1978-79 (80)
Fewest Goals **170** 1972-73 (78)
Fewest Goals Against **190** 1975-76 (80)
Longest Winning Streak
Overall .... **15** Jan. 21-Feb. 20/82
Home .... **14** Jan. 2-Feb. 25/82
Away .... **8** Feb. 27-Mar. 29/81
Longest Undefeated Streak
Overall .... **15** Three times
Home .... **23** Oct. 17/78-Jan. 27/79 (19 wins, 4 ties), Jan. 2-Apr. 3/82 (21 wins, 2 ties)
Away .... **8** Three times
Longest Losing Streak
Overall .... **12** Dec. 27/72-Jan. 16/73, Nov. 22-Dec. 15/88
Home .... **7** Nov. 13-Dec. 14/99
Away .... **15** Jan. 20-Mar. 31/73
Longest Winless Streak
Overall .... **15** Nov. 22-Dec. 21/72 (12 losses, 3 ties)
Home .... **9** Mar. 2-Apr. 6/99 (7 losses, 2 ties)
Away .... **20** Nov. 3/72-Jan. 13/73 (19 losses, 1 tie)
Most Shutouts, Season **10** 1975-76 (80)
Most PIM, Season **1,857** 1986-87 (80)
Most Goals, Game .... **11** Dec. 20/83 (Pit. 3 at NYI 11), Mar. 3/84 (NYI 11 at Tor. 6)

Individual

Most Seasons .... **17** Billy Smith
Most Games .... **1,123** Bryan Trottier
Most Goals, Career .... **573** Mike Bossy
Most Assists, Career .... **853** Bryan Trottier
Most Points, Career .... **1,353** Bryan Trottier (500G, 853A)
Most PIM, Career .... **1,879** Mick Vukota
Most Shutouts, Career .... **25** Glenn Resch
Longest Consecutive Games Streak .... **576** Billy Harris (Oct. 7/72-Nov. 30/79)
Most Goals, Season .... **69** Mike Bossy (1978-79)
Most Assists, Season .... **87** Bryan Trottier (1978-79)
Most Points, Season .... **147** Mike Bossy (1981-82; 64G, 83A)
Most PIM, Season .... **356** Brian Curran (1986-87)
Most Points, Defenseman, Season .... **101** Denis Potvin (1978-79; 31G, 70A)
Most Points, Center, Season .... **134** Bryan Trottier (1978-79; 47G, 87A)
Most Points, Right Wing, Season .... **147** Mike Bossy (1981-82; 64G, 83A)
Most Points, Left Wing, Season .... **100** John Tonelli (1984-85; 42G, 58A)
Most Points, Rookie, Season .... **95** Bryan Trottier (1975-76; 32G, 63A)
Most Shutouts, Season .... **7** Glenn Resch (1975-76)
Most Goals, Game .... **5** Bryan Trottier (Dec. 23/78, Feb. 13/82), John Tonelli (Jan. 6/81)
Most Assists, Game .... **6** Mike Bossy (Jan. 6/81)
Most Points, Game .... **8** Bryan Trottier (Dec. 23/78; 5G, 3A)

Captains' History

Ed Westfall, 1972-73 to 1975-76; Ed Westfall and Clark Gillies, 1976-77; Clark Gillies, 1977-78, 1978-79; Denis Potvin, 1979-80 to 1986-87; Brent Sutter, 1987-88 to 1990-91; Brent Sutter and Pat Flatley, 1991-92; Pat Flatley, 1992-93 to 1995-96; no captain, 1996-97; Bryan McCabe and Trevor Linden, 1997-98; Trevor Linden, 1998-99; Kenny Jonsson, 1999-2000, 2000-01; Michael Peca, 2001-02 to date.

Retired Numbers

5	Denis Potvin	1973-1988
9	Clark Gillies	1974-1986
19	Bryan Trottier	1975-1990
22	Mike Bossy	1977-1987
23	Bob Nystrom	1972-1986
31	Billy Smith	1972-1989

All-time Record vs. Other Clubs

Regular Season

	At Home								On Road								Total							
	GP	W	L	T	OL	GF	GA	PTS	GP	W	L	T	OL	GF	GA	PTS	GP	W	L	T	OL	GF	GA	PTS
Anaheim	7	3	3	1	0	20	22	7	8	3	2	3	0	21	17	9	15	6	5	4	0	41	39	16
Atlanta	8	4	4	0	0	29	21	8	8	5	2	1	0	32	25	11	16	9	6	1	0	61	46	19
Boston	59	24	27	8	0	200	197	56	57	16	31	10	0	160	215	42	116	40	58	18	0	360	412	98
Buffalo	59	25	25	9	0	164	163	59	59	18	31	9	1	154	195	46	118	43	56	18	1	318	358	105
Calgary	50	25	16	9	0	189	140	59	49	14	24	11	0	145	172	39	99	39	40	20	0	334	312	98
Carolina	42	20	18	4	0	130	116	44	43	17	21	5	0	139	146	39	85	37	39	9	0	269	262	83
Chicago	46	17	14	15	0	158	139	49	48	17	26	5	0	162	162	39	94	34	40	20	0	320	301	88
Colorado	32	18	13	1	0	129	109	37	33	11	20	2	0	96	122	24	65	29	33	3	0	225	231	61
Columbus	2	0	2	0	0	7	11	0	3	0	2	1	0	6	11	1	5	0	4	1	0	13	22	1
Dallas	47	25	14	8	0	172	133	58	46	21	18	7	0	166	135	49	93	46	32	15	0	338	268	107
Detroit	46	23	18	4	1	164	137	51	44	17	25	2	0	135	159	36	90	40	43	6	1	299	296	87
Edmonton	30	14	7	9	0	125	108	37	29	8	16	5	0	87	107	21	59	22	23	14	0	212	215	58
Florida	23	10	11	2	0	58	62	22	23	7	10	6	0	66	69	20	46	17	21	8	0	124	131	42
Los Angeles	43	24	15	4	0	155	122	52	45	17	21	7	0	143	163	41	88	41	36	11	0	298	285	93
Minnesota	2	1	1	0	0	3	5	2	3	1	2	0	0	9	9	2	5	2	3	0	0	12	14	4
Montreal	58	28	24	6	0	179	165	62	58	15	34	9	0	167	212	39	116	43	58	15	0	346	377	101
Nashville	4	2	2	0	0	11	12	4	4	2	2	0	0	13	10	4	8	4	4	0	0	24	22	8
New Jersey	82	53	18	11	0	347	238	117	81	36	33	11	1	283	274	84	163	89	51	22	1	630	512	201
NY Rangers	93	54	30	8	1	364	293	117	93	30	52	11	0	278	344	71	186	84	82	19	1	642	637	188
Ottawa	22	3	12	6	1	67	84	13	21	5	12	4	0	58	73	14	43	8	24	10	1	125	157	27
Philadelphia	95	49	32	14	0	348	279	112	92	28	53	11	0	262	333	67	187	77	85	25	0	610	612	179
Phoenix	30	13	9	8	0	113	91	34	29	14	11	4	0	100	94	32	59	27	20	12	0	213	185	66
Pittsburgh	83	44	30	8	1	335	277	97	85	33	39	12	1	297	321	79	168	77	69	20	2	632	598	176
St. Louis	48	25	12	11	0	181	127	61	46	20	17	9	0	151	163	49	94	45	29	20	0	332	290	110
San Jose	11	5	4	2	0	40	35	12	11	6	4	1	0	36	25	13	22	11	8	3	0	76	60	25
Tampa Bay	23	11	11	1	0	70	67	23	24	11	10	2	1	75	63	25	47	22	21	3	1	145	130	48
Toronto	51	28	20	3	0	200	152	59	53	23	25	4	1	182	181	51	104	51	45	7	1	382	333	110
Vancouver	46	25	11	10	0	169	125	60	47	21	23	3	0	153	155	45	93	46	34	13	0	322	280	105
Washington	79	41	36	2	0	294	251	84	79	29	38	11	1	245	257	70	158	70	74	13	1	539	508	154
Defunct Clubs	13	11	0	2	0	75	33	24	13	4	5	4	0	35	41	12	26	15	5	6	0	110	74	36
Totals	**1234**	**625**	**439**	**166**	**4**	**4496**	**3714**	**1420**	**1234**	**449**	**609**	**170**	**6**	**3856**	**4253**	**1074**	**2468**	**1074**	**1048**	**336**	**10**	**8352**	**7967**	**2494**

Playoffs

	Series	W	L	GP	W	L	T	GF	GA	Last Mtg.	Rnd.	Result
Boston	2	2	0	11	8	3	0	49	35	1983	CF	W 4-2
Buffalo	3	3	0	16	12	4	0	59	45	1980	SF	W 4-2
Chicago	2	2	0	6	6	0	0	21	6	1979	QF	W 4-0
Colorado	1	1	0	4	4	0	0	18	9	1982	CF	W 4-0
Dallas	1	1	0	5	4	1	0	26	16	1981	F	W 4-1
Edmonton	3	2	1	15	9	6	0	58	47	1984	F	L 1-4
Los Angeles	1	1	0	4	3	1	0	21	10	1980	PRE	W 3-1
Montreal	4	1	3	22	8	14	0	55	64	1993	CF	L 1-4
New Jersey	1	0	1	6	2	4	0	18	23	1988	DSF	L 2-4
NY Rangers	8	5	3	39	20	19	0	129	132	1994	CQF	L 0-4
Ottawa	1	0	1	5	1	4	0	7	13	2003	CQF	L 1-4
Philadelphia	4	1	3	25	11	14	0	69	83	1987	DF	L 3-4
Pittsburgh	3	3	0	19	11	8	0	67	58	1993	DF	W 4-3
Toronto	3	1	2	17	9	8	0	54	42	2002	CQF	L 3-4
Vancouver	2	2	0	6	6	0	0	26	14	1982	F	W 4-0
Washington	6	5	1	30	18	12	0	99	88	1993	DSF	W 4-2
Totals	**45**	**30**	**15**	**230**	**132**	**98**	**0**	**776**	**685**			

Calgary totals include Atlanta Flames, 1972-73 to 1979-80.
Carolina totals include Hartford, 1979-80 to 1996-97.
Colorado totals include Quebec, 1979-80 to 1994-95.
Dallas totals include Minnesota North Stars, 1972-73 to 1992-93.
New Jersey totals include Kansas City, 1974-75 to 1975-76, and Colorado Rockies, 1976-77 to 1981-82.
Phoenix totals include Winnipeg, 1979-80 to 1995-96.

Playoff Results 2003-1999

Year	Round	Opponent	Result	GF	GA
2003	CQF	Ottawa	L 1-4	7	13
2002	CQF	Toronto	L 3-4	21	22

Abbreviations: Round: F – Final; **CF** – conference final; **CQF** – conference quarter-final; **DF** – division final; **DSF** – division semi-final; **SF** – semi-final; **QF** – quarter-final; **PRE** – preliminary round.

2002-03 Results

Oct.	10	at Buffalo	1-5
	12	Washington	1-2
	15	Nashville	4-3*
	17	at Philadelphia	3-3
	19	at Atlanta	5-4
	22	Carolina	1-4
	24	Florida	5-3
	26	Philadelphia	2-6
	29	Phoenix	2-3
	30	at Carolina	2-4
Nov.	2	St. Louis	1-6
	4	Calgary	2-4
	7	at Montreal	0-3
	8	Edmonton	4-2
	10	Dallas	3-2
	12	Ottawa	3-5
	14	at Boston	1-4
	16	at Pittsburgh	3-2
	20	at Florida	3-3
	21	at Tampa Bay	7-2
	23	at NY Rangers	3-1
	27	Ottawa	2-2
	29	Columbus	2-4
	30	at Ottawa	2-4
Dec.	3	Vancouver	2-1
	6	Toronto	4-2
	7	at Pittsburgh	6-3
	10	Chicago	2-3
	13	at Florida	3-3
	14	at Tampa Bay	3-4
	17	Detroit	2-2
	19	at Minnesota	4-2
	21	Washington	1-3
	23	Montreal	3-1
	28	Carolina	3-0
	30	Florida	2-1*
	31	at Buffalo	1-0*
Jan.	3	Boston	8-4
	4	at Pittsburgh	2-3*
	7	Pittsburgh	6-3
	9	Philadelphia	0-4
	11	Atlanta	7-3
	13	at Washington	3-4*
	15	at New Jersey	0-5
	16	at St. Louis	3-2*
	19	at Atlanta	4-1
	21	NY Rangers	0-5
	24	at Philadelphia	3-1
	25	at Columbus	1-4
	28	Pittsburgh	5-2
	30	Montreal	3-1
Feb.	4	Philadelphia	1-2
	7	at Washington	0-3
	8	Buffalo	3-1
	11	Tampa Bay	6-2
	13	at Nashville	0-2
	15	at Los Angeles	3-2
	17	at Anaheim	2-2
	19	at San Jose	3-0
	21	Colorado	4-1
	23	Boston	4-4
	25	at Toronto	2-5
	27	New Jersey	3-3
Mar.	1	Buffalo	2-1*
	3	at NY Rangers	1-1
	4	Tampa Bay	1-3
	6	at Boston	1-4
	8	New Jersey	2-4
	11	at Vancouver	3-4
	13	at Edmonton	5-2
	15	at Ottawa	5-2
	17	at NY Rangers	0-1
	18	at Toronto	3-3
	20	at Montreal	6-3
	22	New Jersey	2-4
	25	at Chicago	9-2
	28	Toronto	2-5
	30	at New Jersey	0-6
Apr.	1	NY Rangers	2-2
	3	at Detroit	2-5
	5	Atlanta	2-3
	6	at Carolina	2-1

* – Overtime

Entry Draft
Selections 2003-1989

2003
Pick
15	Robert Nilsson
48	Dimitri Chernykh
53	Evgeni Tunik
58	Jeremy Colliton
120	Stefan Blaho
182	Bruno Gervais
212	Denis Rehak
238	Cody Blanshan
246	Igor Volkov

2002
Pick
22	Sean Bergenheim
87	Frans Nielsen
149	Marcus Paulsson
189	Alexei Stonkus
220	Brad Topping
252	Martin Chabada
283	Per Braxenholm

2001
Pick
101	Cory Stillman
132	Dusan Salficky
166	Andy Chiodo
197	Jan Holub
228	Mike Bray
260	Bryan Perez
280	Roman Kuhtinov
287	Juha-Pekka Ketola

2000
Pick
1	Rick DiPietro
5	Raffi Torres
101	Arto Tukio
105	Vladimir Gorbunov
136	Dmitri Upper
148	Kristofer Ottosson
202	Ryan Caldwell
264	Dmitri Altarev
267	Tomi Pettinen

1999
Pick
5	Tim Connolly
8	Taylor Pyatt
10	Branislav Mezei
28	Kristian Kudroc
78	Mattias Weinhandl
87	Brian Collins
101	Juraj Kolnik
102	Johan Halvardsson
130	Justin Mapletoft
140	Adam Johnson
163	Bjorn Melin
228	Radek Martinek
255	Brett Henning
268	Tyler Scott

1998
Pick
9	Mike Rupp
36	Chris Nielsen
95	Andy Burnham
123	Jiri Dopita
155	Kevin Clauson
182	Evgeny Korolev
209	Frederik Brindamour
237	Ben Blais
242	Jason Doyle
250	Radek Matejovsky

1997
Pick
4	Roberto Luongo
9	Eric Brewer
31	Jeff Zehr
59	Jarrett Smith
79	Robert Schnabel
85	Petr Mika
115	Adam Edinger
139	Bobby Leavins
166	Kris Knoblauch
196	Jeremy Symington
222	Ryan Clark

1996
Pick
3	J.P. Dumont
29	Dan LaCouture
56	Zdeno Chara
83	Tyrone Garner
109	Bubba Berenzweig
128	Petr Sachl
138	Todd Miller
165	J.R. Prestifilippo
192	Evgeny Korolev
218	Mike Muzechka

1995
Pick
2	Wade Redden
28	Jan Hlavac
41	D.J. Smith
106	Vladimir Orszagh
158	Andrew Taylor
210	David MacDonald
211	Mike Broda

1994
Pick
9	Brett Lindros
38	Jason Holland
63	Jason Strudwick
90	Brad Lukowich
112	Mark McArthur
116	Albert O'Connell
142	Jason Stewart
194	Mike Loach
203	Peter Hogardh
220	Gord Walsh
246	Kirk Dewaele
272	Dick Tarnstrom

1993
Pick
23	Todd Bertuzzi
40	Bryan McCabe
66	Vladimir Chebaturkin
92	Warren Luhning
118	Tommy Salo
144	Peter LeBoutillier
170	Darren Van Impe
196	Rod Hinks
222	Daniel Johansson
248	Stephane Larocque
274	Carl Charland

1992
Pick
5	Darius Kasparaitis
56	Jarrett Deuling
104	Thomas Klimt
105	Ryan Duthie
128	Derek Armstrong
152	Vladimir Grachev
159	Steve O'Rourke
176	Jason Widmer
200	Daniel Paradis
224	David Wainwright
248	Andrei Vasilyev

1991
Pick
4	Scott Lachance
26	Ziggy Palffy
48	Jamie McLennan
70	Milan Hnilicka
92	Steve Junker
114	Rob Valicevic
136	Andreas Johansson
158	Todd Sparks
180	John Johnson
202	Robert Canavan
224	Marcus Thuresson
246	Marty Schriner

1990
Pick
6	Scott Scissons
27	Chris Taylor
48	Dan Plante
90	Chris Marinucci
111	Joni Lehto
132	Michael Guilbert
153	Sylvain Fleury
174	John Joyce
195	Richard Enga
216	Martin Lacroix
237	Andy Shier

1989
Pick
2	Dave Chyzowski
23	Travis Green
44	Jason Zent
65	Brent Grieve
86	Jace Reed
90	Steve Young
99	Kevin O'Sullivan
128	Jon Larson
133	Brett Harkins
149	Phil Huber
170	Matthew Robbins
191	Vladimir Malakhov
212	Kelly Ens
233	Iain Fraser

General Managers' History

Bill Torrey, 1972-73 to 1991-92; Don Maloney, 1992-93 to 1994-95; Don Maloney and Mike Milbury, 1995-96; Mike Milbury, 1996-97 to date.

General Manager

MILBURY, MIKE
General Manager, New York Islanders. Born in Walpole, MA, June 17, 1952.

Mike Milbury came to the Islanders with 20 years of professional hockey experience with the Boston Bruins — as a player, assistant coach, assistant general manager, general manager and coach on both the NHL and AHL levels. Milbury took over as general manager from Don Maloney on December 12, 1995.

His recent trades have brought the Islanders established stars like Alexei Yashin and Michael Peca as well as an abundance of young talent. In 2001-02, the Islanders returned to the playoffs for the first time since 1994. They made it again in 2002-03.

Milbury joined the Boston organization after graduating from Colgate University with a degree in urban sociology and enjoyed a 10-year playing career with the team. He retired May 6, 1985 and took over as assistant coach. He returned to the ice late in the 1985-86 season when injuries decimated the Bruins defense.

Milbury's playing career concluded after the 1986-87 season and on July 16, 1987 he took over as coach of the Maine Mariners, Boston's top AHL affiliate. In his first year with the team he guided the Mariners to the AHL's Northern Division title and was named both AHL coach of the year and *The Hockey News* minor league coach of the year.

NHL Coaching Record

Season	Team	Games	Regular Season W	L	T	Games	Playoffs W	L
1989-90	Boston	80	46	25	9	21	13	8
1990-91	Boston	80	44	24	12	19	10	9
1995-96	NY Islanders	82	22	50	10	....	....	....
1996-97	NY Islanders	45	13	23	9	....	....	....
1997-98	NY Islanders	19	8	9	2	....	....	....
	NHL Totals	**306**	**133**	**131**	**42**	**40**	**23**	**17**

Club Directory

Nassau Veterans' Memorial Coliseum

New York Islanders Executive Office
1535 Old Country Rd.
Plainview, NY 11803
Phone **516/501-6700**
FAX 516/501-6762
www.newyorkislanders.com
Arena
Nassau Veterans'
Memorial Coliseum
Uniondale, NY 11553
Capacity: 16,234

Owner and Governor	Charles B. Wang
Owner and Alternate Governor	Sanjay Kumar
Senior V.P. of Operations and Alternate Governor	Michael J. Picker
Senior Vice President of Sales and Marketing	Paul Lancey
Alternate Governor and General Counsel	Roy E. Reichbach
Senior Vice President/CFO	Arthur McCarthy
Executive Assistant	Theresa Dewar

Hockey Staff
General Manager and Alternate Governor	Mike Milbury
Head Coach	Steve Stirling
Assistant Coaches	Curt Fraser, Jeff Jackson
Goaltending Consultant/Scout	Bill Smith
Goaltending Consultant	Sudarshan Maharaj
Manager, Hockey Administration	Joanne Holewa
Assistant Manager, Hockey Administration	Kerry Gwydir
Head Amateur Scout	Tony Feltrin
Director of Pro Scouting	Ken Morrow
Assistant Director of Pro Scouting	Kevin Maxwell
Western Scouts	Earl Ingarfield, Harkie Singh, Al MacPherson
Sweden/Finland Amateur Scout	Anders Kallur
Russian Amateur Scout	Yuri Karmanov
U.S. Amateur Scouts	Jay Heinbuck, Jim Madigan, Brian Hunter, Todd Stirling
Ontario Scouts	Doug Gibson, Dave McNamara
Quebec Amateur Scout	Mario Saraceno
Czech Republic Amateur Scout	Karel Pavlick
Finnish Amateur Scout	Harri Rindell
Chief European Amateur Head Scout	Ryan Jankowski
Slovakian Scout	Miroslav Hlinka
Video Coordinator	Bob Smith

Medical Staff
Director of Medical Services	Dr. Elliot Pellman
Internist	Dr. Clifford Cooper
Team Orthopedists	Dr. David Gazzaniga, Dr. Elliot Hershman, Dr. Kenneth Montgomery
Team Dentists	Dr. Bruce Michnick, Dr. Jan Sherman

Training/Equipment Staff
Head Athletic Trainer	Rich Campbell
Assistant Athletic Trainer	Andy Wetstein
Head Equipment Manager	Scott Moon
Assistant Equipment Managers	Vinny Ferraiuolo, Tom Kitz

Sales and Administration
Vice President of Communications	Chris Botta
Vice President of Corporate and Community Relations	Bill Kain
Vice President of Marketing and Game Operations	Tim Beach
Vice President of Ticket Sales and Customer Service	Larry Fitzpatrick
Assistant General Counsel	Jaimie Wolf
Director of Corporate Relations	Bob Nystrom
Director of Corporate Sponsorships	Ted Van Zelst
Director of Executive Suites	Mary Dolan Grippo
Director of Community Relations/Fan Development	Heather Umen
Director of Merchandise	Jessica Rotoli
Controller	Ralph Sellitti
Assistant Controller	Ginna Cotton
Customer Service Manager	Kerry Cornils
Payroll Manager	Christine Bowler
Senior Accountant	Heather Jabick
Manager of Human Resources and Administration	Trish Turtell
Manager of Ticket Sales	Brian Reynolds
Manager of Corporate Ticket Sales	Erik Scheibe
Manager of Media Relations	Jamie R. Fabos
Arena Manager, Merchandise	Danny DiPierri
Creative Services Manager	Tim Gilroy
Manager of Executive Suite Services	Jennifer Meilan
Marketing Manager	Jessica Sousa
Manager of Game Operations and Events	Brad Preston
Community Relations Manager	Heather Cozzens
Team Store Manager	Mary Anne Steves
Group Sales Manager	Cliff Gault
Corporate Account Executives	Anthony Mercogliano, Rob Olenchak, Steven Bromberg
Staff Accountants	Laura Ferretti, Teressa Farino
Group Ticket Sales Representatives	Emily Derkasch, Kevin Schwab
Corporate Sales Account Executive	Jennifer Frusci, Larry Sragow
Account Executives	Mike Bellinzoni, Mike Clough, Steven Beisel
Customer Service Representatives	Jesse Mones, Jennifer Maskel
Graphic Designers	Bill Averso, Therese Burns
Media Relations Coordinator	Howie Wirtheim
Creative Services Avid Editor	Nima Foroush
Ticket Coordinator	Maria Corvino
Assistant Ticket Coordinator	Adam Ortiz
Community Relations Coordinator	Erin Leavy
Sponsor Services Coordinators	Rainbow Kirby, Kate Larson
Administrative Services Coordinator	Sheriene Ahmed
Accounts Payable Bookkeeper	Janet Nelson
Receptionist	Bonnie Dreher
Office Attendant	Todd Aronovitch

Team Information
Television Coverage	FOX Sports New York
TV Announcers	Howie Rose, Joe Micheletti
Radio	1050 AM ESPN Radio
Radio Announcers	John Wiedeman, Chris King

New York Rangers

Mike Dunham joined the Rangers on December 12, 2002.

2002-03 Results: 32W-36L-10T-4OTL 78PTS.
Fourth, Atlantic Division

2003-04 Schedule

Oct.	Fri.	10	at Minnesota		Sun.	11	Tampa Bay*
	Sat.	11	at Columbus		Tue.	13	NY Islanders
	Thu.	16	Atlanta		Thu.	15	New Jersey
	Sat.	18	Carolina		Sat.	17	at Montreal
	Mon.	20	Florida		Mon.	19	at Boston*
	Sat.	25	Detroit		Tue.	20	Boston
	Tue.	28	Anaheim		Thu.	22	Philadelphia
	Thu.	30	Carolina		Sat.	24	at Ottawa
Nov.	Sat.	1	at Montreal		Mon.	26	Florida
	Sun.	2	Colorado*		Wed.	28	Washington
	Tue.	4	Dallas		Fri.	30	Buffalo
	Thu.	6	at Carolina		Sat.	31	at Buffalo
	Sat.	8	Philadelphia*	**Feb.**	Mon.	2	Vancouver
	Mon.	10	Edmonton		Wed.	4	Minnesota
	Wed.	12	Pittsburgh		Wed.	11	at New Jersey
	Sat.	15	at New Jersey*		Thu.	12	Philadelphia
	Sun.	16	at Chicago		Sat.	14	at Philadelphia*
	Tue.	18	at San Jose		Mon.	16	Ottawa*
	Thu.	20	at Colorado		Thu.	19	NY Islanders
	Sun.	23	Ottawa*		Sat.	21	New Jersey*
	Tue.	25	at Tampa Bay		Mon.	23	Montreal
	Wed.	26	at Florida		Thu.	26	at NY Islanders
	Fri.	28	at Pittsburgh		Sat.	28	at Nashville*
	Sun.	30	Toronto		Sun.	29	at Atlanta*
Dec.	Tue.	2	at Toronto	**Mar.**	Tue.	2	Atlanta
	Thu.	4	at NY Islanders		Thu.	4	at Boston
	Sun.	7	Tampa Bay*		Fri.	5	Washington
	Wed.	10	Montreal		Sun.	7	Pittsburgh*
	Fri.	12	at Buffalo		Tue.	9	at Atlanta
	Sat.	13	at Toronto		Fri.	12	at Tampa Bay
	Thu.	18	NY Islanders		Sat.	13	at Florida
	Sat.	20	at Ottawa		Mon.	15	New Jersey
	Mon.	22	Boston		Thu.	18	at Washington
	Fri.	26	Toronto		Sat.	20	at Philadelphia*
	Mon.	29	at Phoenix		Sun.	21	at Pittsburgh*
	Tue.	30	at Los Angeles		Tue.	23	Pittsburgh
Jan.	Thu.	1	at St. Louis		Thu.	25	Nashville
	Sat.	3	at Pittsburgh*		Sat.	27	at Philadelphia*
	Mon.	5	Calgary		Tue.	30	at New Jersey
	Thu.	8	at Carolina		Wed.	31	Buffalo
	Sat.	10	at NY Islanders*	**Apr.**	Sat.	3	at Washington*

* Denotes afternoon game.

Franchise date: May 15, 1926

ATLANTIC DIVISION

78th NHL Season

Year-by-Year Record

		Home				Road				Overall								
Season	**GP**	**W**	**L**	**T**	**OL**	**W**	**L**	**T**	**OL**	**W**	**L**	**T**	**OL**	**GF**	**GA**	**Pts.**	**Finished**	**Playoff Result**
2002-03	82	17	18	4	2	15	18	6	2	32	36	10	4	210	231	78	4th, Atlantic Div.	Out of Playoffs
2001-02	82	19	19	2	1	17	19	2	3	36	38	4	4	227	258	80	4th, Atlantic Div.	Out of Playoffs
2000-01	82	17	20	3	1	16	23	2	0	33	43	5	1	250	290	72	4th, Atlantic Div.	Out of Playoffs
1999-2000	82	15	20	5	1	14	18	7	2	29	38	12	3	218	246	73	4th, Atlantic Div.	Out of Playoffs
1998-99	82	17	19	5	...	16	19	6	...	33	38	11	...	217	227	77	4th, Atlantic Div.	Out of Playoffs
1997-98	82	14	18	9	...	11	21	9	...	25	39	18	...	197	231	68	5th, Atlantic Div.	Out of Playoffs
1996-97	82	21	14	6	...	17	20	4	...	38	34	10	...	258	231	86	4th, Atlantic Div.	Lost Conf. Final
1995-96	82	22	10	9	...	19	17	5	...	41	27	14	...	272	237	96	2nd, Atlantic Div.	Lost Conf. Semi-Final
1994-95	48	11	10	3	...	11	13	0	...	22	23	3	...	139	134	47	4th, Atlantic Div.	Lost Conf. Semi-Final
1993-94	**84**	**28**	**8**	**6**	**...**	**24**	**16**	**2**	**...**	**52**	**24**	**8**	**...**	**299**	**231**	**112**	**1st, Atlantic Div.**	**Won Stanley Cup**
1992-93	84	20	17	5	...	14	22	6	...	34	39	11	...	304	308	79	6th, Patrick Div.	Out of Playoffs
1991-92	80	28	8	4	...	22	17	1	...	50	25	5	...	321	246	105	1st, Patrick Div.	Lost Div. Final
1990-91	80	22	11	7	...	14	20	6	...	36	31	13	...	297	265	85	2nd, Patrick Div.	Lost Div. Semi-Final
1989-90	80	20	11	9	...	16	20	4	...	36	31	13	...	279	267	85	1st, Patrick Div.	Lost Div. Final
1988-89	80	21	17	2	...	16	18	6	...	37	35	8	...	310	307	82	3rd, Patrick Div.	Lost Div. Semi-Final
1987-88	80	22	13	5	...	14	21	5	...	36	34	10	...	300	283	82	5th, Patrick Div.	Out of Playoffs
1986-87	80	18	18	4	...	16	20	4	...	34	38	8	...	307	323	76	4th, Patrick Div.	Lost Div. Semi-Final
1985-86	80	20	18	2	...	16	20	4	...	36	38	6	...	280	276	78	4th, Patick Div.	Lost Conf. Championship
1984-85	80	16	18	6	...	10	26	4	...	26	44	10	...	295	345	62	4th, Patrick Div.	Lost Div. Semi-Final
1983-84	80	27	12	1	...	15	17	8	...	42	29	9	...	314	304	93	4th, Patrick Div.	Lost Div. Semi-Final
1982-83	80	24	13	3	...	11	22	7	...	35	35	10	...	306	287	80	4th, Patrick Div.	Lost Div. Final
1981-82	80	19	15	6	...	20	12	8	...	39	27	14	...	316	306	92	2nd, Patrick Div.	Lost Div. Final
1980-81	80	17	13	10	...	13	23	4	...	30	36	14	...	312	317	74	4th, Patrick Div.	Lost Semi-Final
1979-80	80	22	10	8	...	16	22	2	...	38	32	10	...	308	284	86	3rd, Patrick Div.	Lost Quarter-Final
1978-79	80	19	13	8	...	21	16	3	...	40	29	11	...	316	292	91	3rd, Patrick Div.	Lost Final
1977-78	80	18	15	7	...	12	22	6	...	30	37	13	...	279	280	73	4th, Patrick Div.	Lost Prelim. Round
1976-77	80	17	18	5	...	12	19	9	...	29	37	14	...	272	310	72	4th, Patrick Div.	Out of Playoffs
1975-76	80	16	16	8	...	13	26	1	...	29	42	9	...	262	333	67	4th, Patrick Div.	Out of Playoffs
1974-75	80	21	11	8	...	16	18	6	...	37	29	14	...	319	276	88	2nd, Patrick Div.	Lost Prelim. Round
1973-74	78	26	7	6	...	14	17	8	...	40	24	14	...	300	251	94	3rd, East Div.	Lost Semi-Final
1972-73	78	26	8	5	...	21	15	3	...	47	23	8	...	297	208	102	3rd, East Div.	Lost Semi-Final
1971-72	78	26	6	7	...	22	11	6	...	48	17	13	...	317	192	109	2nd, East Div.	Lost Final
1970-71	78	30	2	7	...	19	16	4	...	49	18	11	...	259	177	109	2nd, East Div.	Lost Semi-Final
1969-70	76	22	8	8	...	16	14	8	...	38	22	16	...	246	189	92	4th, East Div.	Lost Quarter-Final
1968-69	76	27	7	4	...	14	19	5	...	41	26	9	...	231	196	91	3rd, East Div.	Lost Quarter-Final
1967-68	74	22	8	7	...	17	15	5	...	39	23	12	...	226	183	90	2nd, East Div.	Lost Quarter-Final
1966-67	70	18	12	5	...	12	16	7	...	30	28	12	...	188	189	72	4th,	Lost Semi-Final
1965-66	70	12	16	7	...	6	25	4	...	18	41	11	...	195	261	47	6th,	Out of Playoffs
1964-65	70	8	19	8	...	12	19	4	...	20	38	12	...	179	246	52	5th,	Out of Playoffs
1963-64	70	14	13	8	...	8	25	2	...	22	38	10	...	186	242	54	5th,	Out of Playoffs
1962-63	70	12	17	6	...	10	19	6	...	22	36	12	...	211	233	56	5th,	Out of Playoffs
1961-62	70	16	11	8	...	10	21	4	...	26	32	12	...	195	207	64	4th,	Lost Semi-Final
1960-61	70	15	15	5	...	7	23	5	...	22	38	10	...	204	248	54	5th,	Out of Playoffs
1959-60	70	10	15	10	...	7	23	5	...	17	38	15	...	187	247	49	6th,	Out of Playoffs
1958-59	70	14	16	5	...	12	16	7	...	26	32	12	...	201	217	64	5th,	Out of Playoffs
1957-58	70	14	15	6	...	18	10	7	...	32	25	13	...	195	188	77	2nd,	Lost Semi-Final
1956-57	70	15	12	8	...	11	18	6	...	26	30	14	...	184	227	66	4th,	Lost Semi-Final
1955-56	70	20	7	8	...	12	21	2	...	32	28	10	...	204	203	74	3rd,	Lost Semi-Final
1954-55	70	10	12	13	...	7	23	5	...	17	35	18	...	150	210	52	5th,	Out of Playoffs
1953-54	70	18	12	5	...	11	19	5	...	29	31	10	...	161	182	68	5th,	Out of Playoffs
1952-53	70	11	14	10	...	6	23	6	...	17	37	16	...	152	211	50	6th,	Out of Playoffs
1951-52	70	16	13	6	...	7	21	7	...	23	34	13	...	192	219	59	5th,	Out of Playoffs
1950-51	70	14	11	10	...	6	18	11	...	20	29	21	...	169	201	61	5th,	Out of Playoffs
1949-50	70	19	12	4	...	9	19	7	...	28	31	11	...	170	189	67	4th,	Lost Final
1948-49	60	13	12	5	...	5	19	6	...	18	31	11	...	133	172	47	6th,	Out of Playoffs
1947-48	60	11	12	7	...	10	14	6	...	21	26	13	...	176	201	55	4th,	Lost Semi-Final
1946-47	60	11	14	5	...	11	18	1	...	22	32	6	...	167	186	50	5th,	Out of Playoffs
1945-46	50	8	12	5	...	5	16	4	...	13	28	9	...	144	191	35	6th,	Out of Playoffs
1944-45	50	7	11	7	...	4	18	3	...	11	29	10	...	154	247	32	6th,	Out of Playoffs
1943-44	50	4	17	4	...	2	22	1	...	6	39	5	...	162	310	17	6th,	Out of Playoffs
1942-43	50	7	13	5	...	4	18	3	...	11	31	8	...	161	253	30	6th,	Out of Playoffs
1941-42	48	15	8	1	...	14	9	1	...	29	17	2	...	177	143	60	1st,	Lost Semi-Final
1940-41	48	13	7	4	...	8	12	4	...	21	19	8	...	143	125	50	4th,	Lost Quarter-Final
1939-40	**48**	**17**	**4**	**3**	**...**	**10**	**7**	**7**	**...**	**27**	**11**	**10**	**...**	**136**	**77**	**64**	**2nd,**	**Won Stanley Cup**
1938-39	48	13	8	3	...	13	8	3	...	26	16	6	...	149	105	58	2nd,	Lost Semi-Final
1937-38	48	15	5	4	...	12	10	2	...	27	15	6	...	149	96	60	2nd, Amn. Div.	Lost Quarter-Final
1936-37	48	9	7	8	...	10	13	1	...	19	20	9	...	117	106	47	3rd, Amn. Div.	Lost Final
1935-36	48	11	6	7	...	8	11	5	...	19	17	12	...	91	96	50	4th, Amn. Div.	Out of Playoffs
1934-35	48	11	8	5	...	11	12	1	...	22	20	6	...	137	139	50	3rd, Amn. Div.	Lost Semi-Final
1933-34	48	11	7	6	...	10	12	2	...	21	19	8	...	120	113	50	3rd, Amn. Div.	Lost Quarter-Final
1932-33	**48**	**12**	**7**	**5**	**...**	**11**	**10**	**3**	**...**	**23**	**17**	**8**	**...**	**135**	**107**	**54**	**3rd, Amn. Div.**	**Won Stanley Cup**
1931-32	48	13	7	4	...	10	10	4	...	23	17	8	...	134	112	54	1st, Amn. Div.	Lost Final
1930-31	44	10	9	3	...	9	7	6	...	19	16	9	...	106	87	47	3rd, Amn. Div.	Lost Semi-Final
1929-30	44	11	5	6	...	6	12	4	...	17	17	10	...	136	143	44	3rd, Amn. Div.	Lost Semi-Final
1928-29	44	12	6	4	...	9	7	6	...	21	13	10	...	72	65	52	2nd, Amn. Div.	Lost Final
1927-28	**44**	**10**	**8**	**4**	**...**	**9**	**8**	**5**	**...**	**19**	**16**	**9**	**...**	**94**	**79**	**47**	**2nd, Amn. Div.**	**Won Stanley Cup**
1926-27	44	13	5	4	...	12	8	2	...	25	13	6	...	95	72	56	1st, Amn. Div.	Lost Quarter-Final

2003-04 Player Personnel

FORWARDS	HT	WT	S	Place of Birth	Date	2002-03 Club
ANDREWS, Bobby	6-1	200	L	Birtle, Man.	1/5/78	Hartford
BARNABY, Matthew	6-0	189	L	Ottawa, Ont.	5/4/73	NY Rangers
BURE, Pavel	5-10	189	L	Moscow, USSR	3/31/71	NY Rangers
CARTER, Anson	6-1	200	R	Toronto, Ont.	6/6/74	Edmonton-NY Rangers
DUSABLON, Benoit	6-1	207	L	Ste Anne de la Perad, Que.	8/1/79	Hartford
GERNANDER, Ken	5-10	175	L	Coleraine, MN	6/30/69	Hartford
HEALEY, Paul	6-2	198	R	Edmonton, Alta.	3/20/75	St. John's-Toronto
HOLIK, Bobby	6-4	230	R	Jihlava, Czech.	1/1/71	NY Rangers
KOVALEV, Alex	6-1	220	L	Togliatti, USSR	2/24/73	Pittsburgh-NY Rangers
LaCOUTURE, Dan	6-2	208	L	Hyannis, MA	4/18/77	Pittsburgh-NY Rangers
LAROSE, Cory	6-0	188	L	Campbellton, N.B.	5/14/75	Houston-Hartford
LAWSON, Lucas	6-1	195	L	Braeside, Ont.	8/10/79	U. of Maine-Hartford
LINDROS, Eric	6-4	240	R	London, Ont.	2/28/73	NY Rangers
LUNDMARK, Jamie	6-0	174	R	Edmonton, Alta.	1/16/81	NY Rangers-Hartford
MOORE, Dominic	6-0	180	L	Thornhill, Ont.	8/3/80	Harvard
MURRAY, Garth	6-1	205	L	Regina, Sask.	9/17/82	Hartford
NEDVED, Petr	6-3	195	L	Liberec, Czech.	12/9/71	NY Rangers
ORTMEYER, Jed	6-1	186	R	Omaha, NE	9/3/78	U. of Michigan
PETROVICKY, Ronald	5-11	190	R	Zilina, Czech.	2/15/77	NY Rangers
SCOTT, Richard	6-2	195	L	Orillia, Ont.	8/1/78	Hartford-Charlotte
SIMON, Chris	6-4	235	L	Wawa, Ont.	1/30/72	Washington-Chicago
ULMER, Layne	6-1	205	L	North Battleford, Sask.	9/14/80	Hartford
WISEMAN, Chad	6-0	190	L	Burlington, Ont.	3/25/81	San Jose-Cleveland
DEFENSEMEN						
de VRIES, Greg	6-3	215	L	Sundridge, Ont.	1/4/73	Colorado
JAKOPIN, John	6-5	239	R	Toronto, Ont.	5/16/75	San Jose-Cleveland
KASPARAITIS, Darius	5-11	212	L	Elektrenai, USSR	10/16/72	NY Rangers
KINCH, Matt	6-0	195	L	Red Deer, Alta.	2/17/80	Hartford
LEETCH, Brian	6-1	190	L	Corpus Christi, TX	3/3/68	NY Rangers
MALAKHOV, Vladimir	6-4	230	L	Sverdlovsk, USSR	8/30/68	NY Rangers
MIRONOV, Boris	6-3	223	R	Moscow, USSR	3/21/72	Chicago-NY Rangers
NYCHOLAT, Lawrence	6-0	192	L	Calgary, Alta.	5/7/79	Houston-Hartford
POTI, Tom	6-3	215	L	Worcester, MA	3/22/77	NY Rangers
PURINTON, Dale	6-3	214	L	Fort Wayne, IN	10/11/76	NY Rangers
RAWLYK, Rory	6-3	175	R	Edmonton, Alta.	9/9/83	Van (WHL)-P.A.-R.Deer
STATE, Jeff	6-6	235	R	Tonowanda, NY	9/17/79	Hartford-Charlotte
TJUTIN, Fedor	6-2	196	L	Izhevsk, USSR	7/19/83	St. Petersburg-Kazan
WELLER, Craig	6-3	195	R	Calgary, Alta.	1/17/81	Hartford-Charlotte

GOALTENDERS	HT	WT	C	Place of Birth	Date	2002-03 Club
BLACKBURN, Dan	6-0	180	L	Montreal, Que.	5/20/83	NY Rangers
DUNHAM, Mike	6-3	200	L	Johnson City, NY	6/1/72	Nashville-NY Rangers
LABARBERA, Jason	6-2	205	L	Prince George, B.C.	1/18/80	Hartford
MARKKANEN, Jussi	5-11	183	L	Imatra, Finland	5/8/75	Edmonton
MEYER, Scott	6-0	185	L	White Bear Lake, MN	4/10/76	Charlotte-Hartford
RICHTER, Mike	5-11	185	L	Abington, PA	9/22/66	NY Rangers

2002-03 Scoring

* - rookie

Regular Season

Pos	#	Player	Team	GP	G	A	Pts	+/–	PIM	PP	SH	GW	GT	S	%
R	27	Alex Kovalev	PIT	54	27	37	64	–11	50	8	0	1	0	212	12.7
			NYR	24	10	3	13	2	20	3	0	2	1	59	16.9
			TOTAL	78	37	40	77	–9	70	11	0	3	1	271	13.7
R	22	Anson Carter	EDM	68	25	30	55	–11	20	10	0	1	1	176	14.2
			NYR	11	1	4	5	0	6	0	0	0	0	17	5.9
			TOTAL	79	26	34	60	–11	26	10	0	1	1	193	13.5
C	93	Petr Nedved	NYR	78	27	31	58	–4	64	8	3	4	1	205	13.2
C	88	Eric Lindros	NYR	81	19	34	53	5	141	9	0	3	0	235	8.1
D	3	Tom Poti	NYR	80	11	37	48	–6	60	3	0	2	0	148	7.4
C	11	Mark Messier	NYR	78	18	22	40	–2	30	8	1	5	1	117	15.4
R	36	Matthew Barnaby	NYR	79	14	22	36	9	142	1	0	1	1	104	13.5
C	16	Bobby Holik	NYR	64	16	19	35	–1	50	3	0	2	0	213	7.5
R	9	Pavel Bure	NYR	39	19	11	30	4	16	5	1	3	1	136	14.0
D	2	Brian Leetch	NYR	51	12	18	30	–3	20	5	0	2	1	150	8.0
C	26 *	Jamie Lundmark	NYR	55	8	11	19	–3	16	0	0	0	0	78	10.3
D	23	Vladimir Malakhov	NYR	71	3	14	17	–7	52	1	0	0	0	131	2.3
D	29	Boris Mironov	CHI	20	3	1	4	–1	22	1	0	0	1	14	21.4
			NYR	36	3	9	12	3	34	1	0	0	0	56	5.4
			TOTAL	56	6	10	16	2	56	2	0	0	1	70	8.6
R	10	Sandy McCarthy	NYR	82	6	9	15	–4	81	0	0	1	0	81	7.4
L	38	Ronald Petrovicky	NYR	66	5	9	14	–12	77	2	1	1	0	65	7.7
D	6	Darius Kasparaitis	NYR	80	3	11	14	5	85	0	0	1	0	84	3.6
D	5	Dale Purinton	NYR	58	3	9	12	–2	161	0	0	0	0	50	6.0
L	39	Dan LaCouture	PIT	44	2	2	4	–8	72	0	0	0	0	30	6.7
			NYR	24	1	4	5	4	0	0	0	0	0	17	5.9
			TOTAL	68	3	6	9	–4	72	0	0	0	0	47	6.4
D	18 *	Ales Pisa	EDM	48	1	3	4	11	24	1	0	0	0	34	2.9
			NYR	3	0	0	0	1	0	0	0	0	0	3	0.0
			TOTAL	51	1	3	4	12	24	1	0	0	0	37	2.7
L	8	Ted Donato	NYR	49	2	1	3	–1	6	0	0	0	0	30	6.7
R	42 *	John Tripp	NYR	9	1	2	3	1	2	0	0	0	0	16	6.3
D	33	Dave Karpa	NYR	19	0	2	2	–1	14	0	0	0	0	13	0.0
D	24	Sylvain Lefebvre	NYR	35	0	2	2	–7	10	0	0	0	0	14	0.0
D	22	Mike Wilson	NYR	1	0	0	0	1	0	0	0	0	0	0	0.0
C	28	Roman Lyashenko	NYR	2	0	0	0	–2	0	0	0	0	0	4	0.0
R	12	Dixon Ward	NYR	8	0	0	0	–2	2	0	0	0	0	7	0.0
R	44	Billy Tibbetts	NYR	11	0	0	0	–2	12	0	0	0	0	6	0.0

Goaltending

No.	Goaltender	GPI	Mins	Avg	W	L	T	EN	SO	GA	SA	S%	G	A	PIM
30	Mike Dunham	43	2467	2.29	19	17	5	3	5	94	1229	.924	0	1	0
35	Mike Richter	13	694	2.94	5	6	1	2	0	34	329	.897	0	0	0
40	* Johan Holmqvist	1	39	3.08	0	1	0	0	0	2	18	.889	0	0	0
31	Dan Blackburn	32	1762	3.17	8	16	4	3	1	93	842	.890	0	0	2
	Totals	**82**	**4991**	**2.78**	**32**	**40**	**10**	**8**	**6**	**231**	**2426**	**.905**			

General Managers' History

Lester Patrick, 1926-27 to 1945-46; Frank Boucher, 1946-47 to 1954-55; Muzz Patrick, 1955-56 to 1963-64; Emile Francis, 1964-65 to 1974-75; Emile Francis and John Ferguson, 1975-76; John Ferguson, 1976-77, 1977-78; John Ferguson and Fred Shero, 1978-79; Fred Shero, 1979-80; Fred Shero and Craig Patrick, 1980-81; Craig Patrick, 1981-82 to 1985-86; Phil Esposito, 1986-87 to 1988-89; Neil Smith, 1989-90 to 1999-2000; Glen Sather, 2000-01 to date.

Coaching History

Lester Patrick, 1926-27 to 1938-39; Frank Boucher, 1939-40 to 1947-48; Frank Boucher and Lynn Patrick, 1948-49; Lynn Patrick, 1949-50; Neil Colville, 1950-51; Neil Colville and Bill Cook, 1951-52; Bill Cook, 1952-53; Frank Boucher and Muzz Patrick, 1953-54; Muzz Patrick, 1954-55; Phil Watson, 1955-56 to 1958-59; Phil Watson and Alf Pike, 1959-60; Alf Pike, 1960-61; Doug Harvey, 1961-62; Muzz Patrick and Red Sullivan, 1962-63; Red Sullivan, 1963-64, 1964-65; Red Sullivan and Emile Francis, 1965-66; Emile Francis, 1966-67, 1967-68; Bernie Geoffrion and Emile Francis, 1968-69; Emile Francis, 1969-70 to 1972-73; Larry Popein and Emile Francis, 1973-74; Emile Francis, 1974-75; Ron Stewart and John Ferguson, 1975-76; John Ferguson, 1976-77; Jean-Guy Talbot, 1977-78; Fred Shero, 1978-79, 1979-80; Fred Shero and Craig Patrick, 1980-81; Herb Brooks, 1981-82 to 1983-84; Herb Brooks and Craig Patrick, 1984-85; Ted Sator, 1985-86; Ted Sator, Tom Webster and Phil Esposito, 1986-87; Michel Bergeron, 1987-88; Michel Bergeron and Phil Esposito, 1988-89; Roger Neilson, 1989-90 to 1991-92; Roger Neilson and Ron Smith, 1992-93; Mike Keenan, 1993-94; Colin Campbell, 1994-95 to 1996-97; Colin Campbell and John Muckler, 1997-98; John Muckler, 1998-99; John Muckler and John Tortorella, 1999-2000; Ron Low, 2000-01, 2001-02; Bryan Trottier and Glen Sather, 2002-03; Glen Sather, 2003-04.

Coach and General Manager

SATHER, GLEN
President/Coach/General Manager, New York Rangers
Born in High River, Alta., Sept. 2, 1943.

Glen Sather, who spent parts of four seasons with the New York Rangers as a player from 1970 to 1974, became the franchise's 12 president and tenth general manager on June 2, 2000. On January 30, 2003, during his third season with the team, Sather also took over as coach, becoming the club's 31st head coach after relieving Bryan Trottier of his duties. On July 1, 2003, Sather announced that he would retain the head coaching duties for 2003-04. This marks the third NHL coaching stint of his professional career, following two separate coaching runs with the Edmonton Oilers (1979-80 through 1988-89 and 1993-94).

Sather joined the Rangers following a 24-year career with the Edmonton Oilers, where he was the architect of five Stanley Cup championships between 1984 and 1990. One of the most respected executives in the National Hockey League, Sather was honored for his tremendous achievements in 1997 by becoming the first member of the Oilers organization to be selected to the Hockey Hall of Fame.

Named coach and vice president of hockey operations for the Oilers when the franchise joined the NHL in June of 1979, Sather became general manager and club president in May of 1980. He coached through the 1988-89 season and also returned for 60 games behind the bench in 1993-94. Sather-coached teams won the Stanley Cup four times in the 1980s. As general manager, Sather was instrumental in the Oilers' fifth Cup triumph in 1990.

He played for six different teams during a 10-year NHL career. He scored 80 goals in 658 games.

NHL Coaching Record

			Regular Season				Playoffs	
Season	Team	Games	W	L	T	Games	W	L
1979-80	Edmonton	80	28	39	13	3	0	3
1980-81	Edmonton	62	25	26	11	9	5	4
1981-82	Edmonton	80	48	17	15	5	2	3
1982-83	Edmonton	80	47	21	12	16	11	5
1983-84	Edmonton	80	57	18	5	19	15	4*
1984-85	Edmonton	80	49	20	11	18	15	3*
1985-86	Edmonton	80	56	17	7	10	6	4
1986-87	Edmonton	80	50	24	6	21	16	5*
1987-88	Edmonton	80	44	25	11	18	16	2*
1988-89	Edmonton	80	38	34	8	7	3	4
1993-94	Edmonton	60	22	27	11	....	....	....
2002-03	NY Rangers	28	11	13	4	....	....	....
	NHL Totals	**870**	**475**	**281**	**114**	**126**	**89**	**37**

* Stanley Cup win.

Club Records

Team

(Figures in brackets for season records are games played; records for fewest points, wins, ties, losses, goals, goals against are for 70 or more games)

Most Points **112** 1993-94 (84)
Most Wins **52** 1993-94 (84)
Most Ties **21** 1950-51 (70)
Most Losses **44** 1984-85 (80)
Most Goals **321** 1991-92 (80)
Most Goals Against **345** 1984-85 (80)
Fewest Points **47** 1965-66 (70)
Fewest Wins **17** 1952-53 (70), 1954-55 (70), 1959-60 (70)
Fewest Ties **4** 2001-02 (82)
Fewest Losses **17** 1971-72 (78)
Fewest Goals **150** 1954-55 (70)
Fewest Goals Against **177** 1970-71 (78)
Longest Winning Streak
Overall . . . . **10** Dec. 19/39-Jan. 13/40, Jan. 19-Feb. 10/73
Home . . . . **14** Dec. 19/39-Feb. 25/40
Away . . . . **7** Jan. 12-Feb. 12/35, Oct. 28-Nov. 29/78
Longest Undefeated Streak
Overall . . . . **19** Nov. 23/39-Jan. 13/40 (14 wins, 5 ties)
Home . . . . **26** Mar. 29/70-Jan. 31/71 (19 wins, 7 ties)
Away . . . . **11** Nov. 5/39-Jan. 13/40 (6 wins, 5 ties)
Longest Losing Streak
Overall . . . . **11** Oct. 30-Nov. 27/43
Home . . . . **7** Oct. 20-Nov. 14/76, Mar. 24-Apr. 14/93
Away . . . . **10** Oct. 30-Dec. 23/43, Feb. 2-Mar. 15/61
Longest Winless Streak
Overall . . . . **21** Jan. 23-Mar. 19/44 (17 losses, 4 ties)
Home . . . . **10** Jan. 30-Mar. 19/44 (7 losses, 3 ties)
Away . . . . **16** Oct. 9-Dec. 20/52 (12 losses, 4 ties)
Most Shutouts, Season **13** 1928-29 (44)
Most PIM, Season **2,018** 1989-90 (80)
Most Goals, Game . . . . **12** Nov. 21/71 (Cal. 1 at NYR 12)

Individual

Most Seasons . . . . **18** Rod Gilbert
Most Games . . . . **1,160** Harry Howell
Most Goals, Career . . . . **406** Rod Gilbert
Most Assists, Career . . . . **718** Brian Leetch
Most Points, Career . . . . **1,021** Rod Gilbert (406G, 615A)
Most PIM, Career . . . . **1,226** Ron Greschner
Most Shutouts, Career . . . . **49** Ed Giacomin
Longest Consecutive Games Streak . . . . **560** Andy Hebenton (Oct. 7/55-Mar. 24/63)
Most Goals, Season . . . . **52** Adam Graves (1993-94)
Most Assists, Season . . . . **80** Brian Leetch (1991-92)
Most Points, Season . . . . **109** Jean Ratelle (1971-72; 46G, 63A)
Most PIM, Season . . . . **305** Troy Mallette (1989-90)
Most Points, Defenseman, Season . . . . **102** Brian Leetch (1991-92; 22G, 80A)
Most Points, Center, Season . . . . **109** Jean Ratelle (1971-72; 46G, 63A)
Most Points, Right Wing, Season . . . . **97** Rod Gilbert (1971-72; 43G, 54A), (1974-75; 36G, 61A)
Most Points, Left Wing, Season . . . . **106** Vic Hadfield (1971-72; 50G, 56A)
Most Points, Rookie, Season . . . . **76** Mark Pavelich (1981-82; 33G, 43A)
Most Shutouts, Season . . . . **13** John Ross Roach (1928-29)
Most Goals, Game . . . . **5** Don Murdoch (Oct. 12/76), Mark Pavelich (Feb. 23/83)
Most Assists, Game . . . . **5** Walt Tkaczuk (Feb. 12/72), Rod Gilbert (Mar. 2/75, Mar. 30/75, Oct. 8/76), Don Maloney (Jan. 3/87), Brian Leetch (Apr. 18/95), Wayne Gretzky (Feb. 15/99)
Most Points, Game . . . . **7** Steve Vickers (Feb. 18/76; 3G, 4A)

Retired Numbers

1	Ed Giacomin	1965-1976
7	Rod Gilbert	1960-1978

All-time Record vs. Other Clubs

Regular Season

	At Home								On Road								Total							
	GP	W	L	T	OL	GF	GA	PTS	GP	W	L	T	OL	GF	GA	PTS	GP	W	L	T	OL	GF	GA	PTS
Anaheim	8	3	4	1	0	22	23	7	8	2	6	0	0	25	32	4	16	5	10	1	0	47	55	11
Atlanta	8	3	4	0	1	25	30	7	8	6	2	0	0	30	25	12	16	9	6	0	1	55	55	19
Boston	300	130	115	55	0	916	847	315	296	96	158	42	0	831	1068	234	596	226	273	97	0	1747	1915	549
Buffalo	64	28	21	15	0	210	173	71	66	18	38	10	0	208	275	46	130	46	59	25	0	418	448	117
Calgary	51	24	22	5	0	178	179	53	49	12	27	10	0	148	216	34	100	36	49	15	0	326	395	87
Carolina	43	26	13	3	1	166	112	56	41	16	22	3	0	132	136	35	84	42	35	6	1	298	248	91
Chicago	285	117	113	55	0	841	807	289	285	115	128	42	0	790	868	272	570	232	241	97	0	1631	1675	561
Colorado	33	19	9	4	1	132	96	43	34	13	17	3	1	127	139	30	67	32	26	7	2	259	235	73
Columbus	2	1	0	1	0	7	5	3	3	1	2	0	0	7	11	2	5	2	2	1	0	14	16	5
Dallas	61	35	15	11	0	210	165	81	61	30	19	11	1	221	187	72	122	65	34	22	1	431	352	153
Detroit	283	133	92	58	0	865	737	324	285	76	164	45	0	699	1004	197	568	209	256	103	0	1564	1741	521
Edmonton	29	10	13	6	0	108	108	26	28	13	12	3	0	94	101	29	57	23	25	9	0	202	209	55
Florida	22	10	8	4	0	66	56	24	23	13	9	1	0	64	58	27	45	23	17	5	0	130	114	51
Los Angeles	58	35	17	6	0	233	172	76	59	26	23	10	0	213	197	62	117	61	40	16	0	446	369	138
Minnesota	2	2	0	0	0	7	3	4	3	3	0	0	0	10	6	6	5	5	0	0	0	17	9	10
Montreal	288	118	116	54	0	833	838	290	288	59	190	39	0	662	1122	157	576	177	306	93	0	1495	1960	447
Nashville	5	2	1	1	1	16	11	6	3	2	1	0	0	13	11	4	8	4	2	1	1	29	22	10
New Jersey	81	40	22	19	0	316	242	99	83	33	43	7	0	277	290	73	164	73	65	26	0	593	532	172
NY Islanders	93	52	30	11	0	344	278	115	93	31	54	8	0	293	364	70	186	83	84	19	0	637	642	185
Ottawa	21	10	11	0	0	67	64	20	21	11	6	3	1	63	57	26	42	21	17	3	1	130	121	46
Philadelphia	107	47	37	23	0	349	313	117	106	38	53	14	1	292	345	91	213	85	90	37	1	641	658	208
Phoenix	29	18	9	2	0	128	102	38	30	13	13	4	0	98	105	30	59	31	22	6	0	226	207	68
Pittsburgh	98	50	39	9	0	381	332	109	97	41	40	14	2	354	353	98	195	91	79	23	2	735	685	207
St. Louis	60	44	10	6	0	245	143	94	62	28	24	10	0	198	183	66	122	72	34	16	0	443	326	160
San Jose	10	7	2	1	0	40	29	15	12	9	2	1	0	47	29	19	22	16	4	2	0	87	58	34
Tampa Bay	25	13	10	2	0	84	80	28	23	10	10	3	0	79	81	23	48	23	20	5	0	163	161	51
Toronto	281	120	105	56	0	866	826	296	280	84	156	39	1	736	966	208	561	204	261	95	1	1602	1792	504
Vancouver	53	37	11	5	0	233	136	79	51	33	15	3	0	204	163	69	104	70	26	8	0	437	299	148
Washington	80	37	33	9	1	300	277	84	82	32	41	9	0	267	309	73	162	69	74	18	1	567	586	157
Defunct Clubs	139	87	30	22	0	460	290	196	139	82	34	23	0	441	291	187	278	169	64	45	0	901	581	383
Totals	**2619**	**1258**	**912**	**444**	**5**	**8648**	**7474**	**2965**	**2619**	**946**	**1309**	**357**	**7**	**7623**	**8992**	**2256**	**5238**	**2204**	**2221**	**801**	**12**	**16271**	**16466**	**5221**

Playoffs

	Series	W	L	GP	W	L	T	GF	GA	Last Mtg.	Rnd.	Result
Boston	9	3	6	42	18	22	2	104	114	1973	QF	W 4-1
Buffalo	1	0	1	3	1	2	0	6	11	1978	PRE	L 1-2
Calgary	1	1	0	4	3	1	0	14	8	1980	PRE	W 3-1
Chicago	5	1	4	24	10	14	0	54	66	1973	SF	L 1-4
Colorado	1	1	0	6	4	2	0	25	19	1995	CQF	W 4-2
Detroit	5	1	4	23	10	13	0	49	57	1950	F	L 3-4
Florida	1	1	0	5	4	1	0	13	10	1997	CQF	W 4-1
Los Angeles	2	2	0	6	5	1	0	32	14	1981	PRE	W 3-1
Montreal	14	7	7	61	25	34	2	158	188	1996	CQF	W 4-2
New Jersey	3	3	0	19	12	7	0	56	46	1997	CSF	W 4-1
NY Islanders	8	3	5	39	19	20	0	132	129	1994	CQF	W 4-0
Philadelphia	10	4	6	47	20	27	0	153	157	1997	CF	L 1-4
Pittsburgh	3	0	3	15	3	12	0	45	64	1996	CSF	L 1-4
St. Louis	1	1	0	6	4	2	0	29	22	1981	QF	W 4-2
Toronto	8	5	3	35	19	16	0	86	86	1971	QF	W 4-2
Vancouver	1	1	0	7	4	3	0	21	19	1994	F	W 4-3
Washington	4	2	2	22	11	11	0	71	75	1994	CSF	W 4-1
Defunct Clubs	9	6	3	22	11	7	4	43	29			
Totals	**86**	**42**	**44**	**386**	**183**	**195**	**8**	**1091**	**1114**			

Calgary totals include Atlanta Flames, 1972-73 to 1979-80.
Colorado totals include Quebec, 1979-80 to 1994-95.
Carolina totals include Hartford, 1979-80 to 1996-97.
Dallas totals include Minnesota North Stars, 1967-68 to 1992-93.
New Jersey totals include Kansas City, 1974-75 to 1975-76, and Colorado Rockies, 1976-77 to 1981-82.
Phoenix totals include Winnipeg, 1979-80 to 1995-96.

Playoff Results 2003-1999

(Last playoff appearance: 1997)

Abbreviations: Round: F – Final;
CF – conference final; **CSF** – conference semi-final;
CQF – conference quarter-final; **SF** – semi-final;
QF – quarter-final; **PRE** – preliminary round.

2002-03 Results

Oct.	9	at Carolina	4-1	**Jan.**	4	Washington	2-2
	11	Montreal	1-4		6	Ottawa	2-5
	12	at Pittsburgh	0-6		8	Carolina	5-1
	15	Toronto	5-4		9	at Montreal	2-3
	17	at Buffalo	4-4		11	at Pittsburgh	3-1
	19	Nashville	2-2		13	Toronto	5-1
	21	Tampa Bay	2-4		15	at Washington	2-1*
	23	Washington	1-2		19	Philadelphia	2-4
	25	Los Angeles	2-6		21	at NY Islanders	5-0
	26	at Toronto	4-3		23	at Nashville	4-2
	28	Phoenix	3-2*		25	Atlanta	1-4
	30	at Tampa Bay	0-3		26	at Washington	2-7
Nov.	2	at Boston	2-3		28	at Atlanta	2-5
	3	St. Louis	2-3		30	Colorado	3-4*
	5	Edmonton	5-2	**Feb.**	5	Ottawa	3-5
	7	Calgary	1-0*		6	at St. Louis	4-4
	9	at Columbus	3-6		8	at Philadelphia	1-2
	11	at San Jose	5-4		12	at Florida	3-1
	14	at Calgary	2-1		14	Pittsburgh	1-0
	16	at Vancouver	1-3		15	at Buffalo	4-5
	19	Anaheim	3-2*		17	at Ottawa	2-3
	21	at New Jersey	4-4		19	at Minnesota	4-2
	23	NY Islanders	1-3		21	at Anaheim	6-2
	25	Carolina	3-1		23	at Colorado	1-4
	28	at Atlanta	4-7		25	at New Jersey	3-3
	29	at Dallas	3-3		27	Boston	4-1
Dec.	1	Tampa Bay	4-3	**Mar.**	1	Florida	5-2
	3	Columbus	5-3		3	NY Islanders	1-1
	5	at Philadelphia	2-3*		7	Philadelphia	5-1
	6	Buffalo	1-4		10	Florida	1-2
	8	Boston	1-4		13	at Ottawa	2-3*
	11	Chicago	3-4		15	at New Jersey	1-3
	14	at Toronto	1-4		17	NY Islanders	1-0
	16	San Jose	2-1*		19	Buffalo	3-0
	19	Montreal	1-3		22	at Philadelphia	2-1
	21	at Detroit	2-3		26	Pittsburgh	1-3
	23	New Jersey	2-2		29	at Boston	3-1
	26	Pittsburgh	1-6		31	Atlanta	3-4*
	28	at Florida	2-1*	**Apr.**	1	at NY Islanders	2-2
	29	at Tampa Bay	3-5		4	New Jersey	1-2
	31	at Carolina	2-0		5	at Montreal	4-5

* – Overtime

Entry Draft
Selections 2003-1989

2003
Pick
12	Hugh Jessiman
50	Ivan Baranka
75	Ken Roche
122	Corey Potter
149	Nigel Dawes
176	Ivan Dornic
179	Philippe Furrer
180	Chris Holt
209	Dylan Reese
243	Jan Marek

2002
Pick
33	Lee Falardeau
81	Marcus Jonasen
127	Nate Guenin
143	Mike Walsh
177	Jake Taylor
194	Kim Hirschovits
226	Joey Crabb
240	Petr Prucha
270	Rob Flynn

2001
Pick
10	Dan Blackburn
40	Fedor Tjutin
79	Garth Murray
113	Bryce Lampman
139	Shawn Collymore
176	Marek Zidlicky
206	Petr Precuil
226	Pontus Petterstrom
230	Leonid Zhvachkin
238	Ryan Hollweg
269	Juris Stals

2000
Pick
64	Filip Novak
95	Dominic Moore
112	Premysl Duben
140	Nathan Martz
143	Brandon Snee
175	Sven Helfenstein
205	Henrik Lundqvist
238	Dan Eberly
269	Martin Richter

1999
Pick
4	Pavel Brendl
9	Jamie Lundmark
59	David Inman
79	Johan Asplund
90	Patrick Aufiero
137	Garrett Bembridge
177	Jay Dardis
197	Arto Laatikainen
226	Yevgeny Gusakov
251	Petter Henning
254	Alexei Bulatov

1998
Pick
7	Manny Malhotra
40	Randy Copley
66	Jason Labarbera
114	Boyd Kane
122	Patrick Leahy
131	Tomas Kloucek
180	Stefan Lundqvist
207	Johan Witehall
235	Jan Mertzig

1997
Pick
19	Stefan Cherneski
46	Wes Jarvis
73	Burke Henry
93	Tomi Kallarsson
126	Jason McLean
134	Johan Lindbom
136	Mike York
154	Shawn Degagne
175	Johan Holmqvist
182	Mike Mottau
210	Andrew Proskurnicki
236	Richard Miller

1996
Pick
22	Jeff Brown
48	Daniel Goneau
76	Dmitri Subbotin
131	Colin Pepperall
158	Ola Sandberg
185	Jeff Dessner
211	Ryan McKie
237	Ronnie Sundin

1995
Pick
39	Christian Dube
65	Mike Martin
91	Marc Savard
110	Alexei Vasiliev
117	Dale Purinton
143	Peter Slamiar
169	Jeff Heil
195	Ilja Gorokhov
221	Bob Maudie

1994
Pick
26	Dan Cloutier
52	Rudolf Vercik
78	Adam Smith
100	Alexander Korobolin
104	Sylvain Blouin
130	Martin Ethier
135	Yuri Litvinov
156	David Brosseau
182	Alexei Lazarenko
208	Craig Anderson
209	Vitali Yeremeyev
234	Eric Boulton
260	Radoslav Kropac
267	Jamie Butt
286	Kim Johnsson

1993
Pick
8	Niklas Sundstrom
34	Lee Sorochan
61	Maxim Galanov
86	Sergei Olimpiyev
112	Gary Roach
138	Dave Trofimenkoff
162	Sergei Kondrashkin
164	Todd Marchant
190	Eddy Campbell
216	Ken Shepard
242	Andrei Kudinov
261	Pavel Komarov
268	Maxim Smelnitsky

1992
Pick
24	Peter Ferraro
48	Mattias Norstrom
72	Eric Cairns
85	Chris Ferraro
120	Dmitri Starostenko
144	David Dal Grande
168	Matt Oates
192	Mickey Elick
216	Daniel Brierley
240	Vladimir Vorobiev

1991
Pick
15	Alex Kovalev
37	Darcy Werenka
96	Corey Machanic
125	Fredrik Jax
128	Barry Young
147	John Rushin
169	Corey Hirsch
191	Vyachesl Uvayev
213	Jamie Ram
235	Vitali Chinakhov
257	Brian Wiseman

1990
Pick
13	Michael Stewart
34	Doug Weight
55	John Vary
69	Jeff Nielsen
76	Rick Willis
85	Sergei Zubov
99	Lubos Rob
118	Jason Weinrich
139	Brian Lonsinger
160	Todd Hedlund
181	Andrew Silverman
202	Jon Hillebrandt
223	Brett Lievers
244	Sergei Nemchinov

1989
Pick
20	Steven Rice
40	Jason Prosofsky
45	Rob Zamuner
49	Louie DeBrusk
67	Jim Cummins
88	Aaron Miller
118	Joby Messier
139	Greg Leahy
160	Greg Spenrath
181	Mark Bavis
202	Roman Oksiuta
223	Steve Locke
244	Ken MacDermid

The Rangers re-acquired Alex Kovalev from the Penguins in an eight-player trade on February 10, 2003.

Club Directory

Madison Square Garden

New York Rangers
14th Floor
2 Pennsylvania Plaza
New York, New York 10121
Phone **212/465-6000**
PR FAX 212/465-6494
www.newyorkrangers.com
Capacity: 18,200

Team Executive Management
President and CEO, Cablevision Systems Corporation;
  Chairman, Madison Square Garden . . . . James L. Dolan
President, G.M., Head Coach and Alt. Governor . . . Glen Sather
President, Sports Team Operations, Alt. Governor . . Steve Mills
Senior Vice President, Business Operations . . . . Mark Piazza
Senior Vice President, Legal Affairs, MSG . . . . Marc Schoenfeld
Vice President, Controller . . . . John Cudmore
Vice President, Marketing . . . . Jeanie Baumgartner
Vice President, Public Relations . . . . John Rosasco

Madison Square Garden Executive Management
Executive Vice President, MSG Networks . . . . Mike McCarthy
Executive Vice President, Finance . . . . Robert Pollichino
Senior Vice President, Employee Relations . . . . Alan Gershowitz
Senior Vice President, Sports and
  Facility Event Sales . . . . Joel Fisher
Senior Vice President, Communications . . . . Barry Watkins

Hockey Club Personnel
Vice President, Player Personnel and
  Assistant General Manager . . . . Don Maloney
Vice President, Player Development
  and Assistant Coach . . . . Tom Renney
Vice President, Hockey Administration
  and Scouting . . . . Peter Stephan
Assistant Coaches . . . . Ted Green, Terry O'Reilly
Goaltending Analyst . . . . Sam St. Laurent
Amateur Scouting Staff . . . . Rich Brown, Ray Clearwater, Andre Beaulieu,
                                                             Jan Gajdosik, Ernie Gare, Martin Madden Jr.,
                                                             Christer Rockstom, Bob Crocker, Jamie
                                                             McDonald, Shanon Sather
Head Professional Scout . . . . Dave Brown
Professional Scouting Staff . . . . Gordie Clark, Harry Howell, Gilles Leger,
                                                             Ron Low, Brad Park
Medical Trainer . . . . Jim Ramsay
Equipment Manager . . . . Acacio Marques
Assistant Equipment Manager . . . . James Johnson
Massage Therapist . . . . Bruce Lifrieri
Strength and Conditioning Coordinator . . . . Reg Grant
Video Analyst . . . . Jerry Dineen
Manager, Madison Square Garden Training Center . . Pat Boller

Operations
Director, Business Operations . . . . Barbara Dand
Director, Legal and Business Affairs . . . . Rana Dershowitz
Director, Team Operations . . . . Darren Blake
Executive Assistant to the President and G.M. . . . . . Sara Adamson
Manager, Accounting . . . . Nicole Florit
Operations Coordinator . . . . Victor Saljanin

Public Relations
Director, Public Relations . . . . Jason Vogel
Director, Publicity - MSG Sports Teams . . . . Dan Schoenberg
Manager, Public Relations . . . . Keith Soutar
Public Relations Coordinator . . . . Jennifer Schoenfeld

Marketing
Director, Marketing Partnerships . . . . Rob Scolaro
Manager, Game Presentation . . . . Ryan Halkett
Manager, Marketing . . . . Janet Duch
Manager, Marketing Partnerships . . . . Kelly Jutras
Manager, Website . . . . Jeff Schwartzenberg
Marketing Coordinator . . . . Adam Evert

Community Development
Director, Community Development . . . . Rob Capilli
Director, Special Projects and Community
  Relations Representative . . . . Rod Gilbert
Community Development Assistant . . . . Jan Greenberg

Medical/Training Staff
Team Physician and Orthopedic Surgeon . . . . Dr. Andrew Feldman
Assistant Team Physician . . . . Dr. Anthony Maddalo
Medical Consultant . . . . Dr. Ronald Weissman
Team Dentists . . . . Dr. Don Salomon and Dr. Jeff Shapiro
Sports Psychologist - MSG Sports Teams . . . . Dr. Kimberly Amirault

Additional Information
Television Network . . . . MSG Network
Radio Network . . . . MSG Radio
Practice Facility . . . . Madison Square Garden Training Center

Captains' History

Bill Cook, 1926-27 to 1936-37; Art Coulter, 1937-38 to 1941-42; Ott Heller, 1942-43 to 1944-45; Neil Colville 1945-46 to 1948-49; Buddy O'Connor, 1949-50; Frank Eddolls, 1950-51; Frank Eddolls and Allan Stanley, 1951-52; Allan Stanley, 1952-53; Allan Stanley and Don Raleigh, 1953-54; Don Raleigh, 1954-55; Harry Howell, 1955-56, 1956-57; Red Sullivan, 1957-58 to 1960-61; Andy Bathgate, 1961-62, 1962-63; Andy Bathgate and Camille Henry, 1963-64; Camille Henry and Bob Nevin, 1964-65; Bob Nevin 1965-66 to 1970-71; Vic Hadfield, 1971-72 to 1973-74; Brad Park, 1974-75; Brad Park and Phil Esposito, 1975-76; Phil Esposito, 1976-77, 1977-78; Dave Maloney, 1978-79, 1979-80; Dave Maloney, Walt Tkaczuk and Barry Beck, 1980-81; Barry Beck, 1981-82 to 1985-86; Ron Greschner, 1986-87; Ron Greschner and Kelly Kisio, 1987-88; Kelly Kisio, 1988-89 to 1990-91; Mark Messier, 1991-92 to 1996-97; Brian Leetch, 1997-98 to 1999-2000; Mark Messier, 2000-01 to 2002-03.

Ottawa Senators

2002-03 Results: 52w-21L-8T-1OTL 113PTS.
First, Northeast Division

2003-04 Schedule

Oct.	Thu.	9	Montreal	Sun.	11	at Carolina*
	Sat.	11	Detroit	Tue.	13	at New Jersey
	Wed.	15	at Los Angeles	Thu.	15	NY Islanders
	Fri.	17	at Anaheim	Sat.	17	Boston
	Sat.	18	at San Jose	Mon.	19	at NY Islanders*
	Thu.	23	Washington	Tue.	20	at Carolina
	Sat.	25	at Montreal	Thu.	22	Pittsburgh
	Thu.	30	Florida	Sat.	24	NY Rangers
Nov.	Sat.	1	Buffalo	Wed.	28	at Dallas
	Mon.	3	at NY Islanders	Thu.	29	at Phoenix
	Thu.	6	Edmonton	Sat.	31	at Toronto
	Sat.	8	New Jersey	**Feb.**	Tue. 3	at New Jersey
	Tue.	11	at Atlanta	Thu.	5	Toronto
	Thu.	13	Columbus	Tue.	10	St. Louis
	Sat.	15	Montreal	Thu.	12	Boston
	Mon.	17	Buffalo	Sat.	14	Montreal
	Thu.	20	Carolina	Mon.	16	at NY Rangers*
	Sat.	22	at Pittsburgh	Tue.	17	at Washington
	Sun.	23	at NY Rangers*	Thu.	19	Atlanta
	Tue.	25	at Atlanta	Sat.	21	Calgary*
	Thu.	27	Vancouver	Sun.	22	at Pittsburgh*
	Sat.	29	Toronto	Tue.	24	at Montreal
Dec.	Mon.	1	Philadelphia	Thu.	26	Philadelphia
	Wed.	3	at Florida	Sat.	28	Buffalo
	Thu.	4	at Tampa Bay	**Mar.**	Wed. 3	at Buffalo
	Sat.	6	New Jersey	Fri.	5	at Philadelphia
	Mon.	8	at Boston	Sat.	6	Nashville
	Thu.	11	Tampa Bay	Mon.	8	at Washington
	Sat.	13	Boston	Thu.	11	at Calgary
	Thu.	18	Chicago	Sat.	13	at Vancouver
	Sat.	20	NY Rangers	Sun.	14	at Edmonton
	Mon.	22	Florida	Tue.	16	at Minnesota
	Tue.	23	at Buffalo	Thu.	18	Colorado
	Fri.	26	Pittsburgh	Sat.	20	Carolina
	Sun.	28	Atlanta*	Tue.	23	at Boston
	Tue.	30	at Boston	Thu.	25	at Montreal
Jan.	Thu.	1	NY Islanders	Sat.	27	at Toronto
	Sat.	3	Washington	Mon.	29	at Tampa Bay
	Tue.	6	Tampa Bay	Wed.	31	at Florida
	Thu.	8	at Toronto	**Apr.**	Fri. 2	at Philadelphia
	Fri.	9	at Buffalo	Sat.	3	Toronto

* Denotes afternoon game.

Year-by-Year Record

Season	GP	Home W	L	T	OL	Road W	L	T	OL	Overall W	L	T	OL	GF	GA	Pts.	Finished	Playoff Result
2002-03	82	28	9	3	1	24	12	5	0	52	21	8	1	263	182	113	1st, Northeast Div.	Lost Conf. Championship
2001-02	82	21	13	3	4	18	14	6	3	39	27	9	7	243	208	94	3rd, Northeast Div.	Lost Conf. Semi-Final
2000-01	82	26	7	5	3	22	14	4	1	48	21	9	4	274	205	109	1st, Northeast Div.	Lost Conf. Quarter-Final
1999-2000	82	24	10	5	2	17	18	6	0	41	28	11	2	244	210	95	2nd, Northeast Div.	Lost Conf. Quarter-Final
1998-99	82	22	11	8	...	22	12	7	...	44	23	15	...	239	179	103	1st, Northeast Div.	Lost Conf. Quarter-Final
1997-98	82	18	16	7	...	16	17	8	...	34	33	15	...	193	200	83	5th, Northeast Div.	Lost Conf. Semi-Final
1996-97	82	16	17	8	...	15	19	7	...	31	36	15	...	226	234	77	3rd, Northeast Div.	Lost Conf. Quarter-Final
1995-96	82	8	28	5	...	10	31	0	...	18	59	5	...	191	291	41	6th, Northeast Div.	Out of Playoffs
1994-95	48	5	16	3	...	4	18	2	...	9	34	5	...	117	174	23	7th, Northeast Div.	Out of Playoffs
1993-94	84	8	30	4	...	6	31	5	...	14	61	9	...	201	397	37	7th, Northeast Div.	Out of Playoffs
1992-93	84	9	29	4	...	1	41	0	...	10	70	4	...	202	395	24	6th, Adams Div.	Out of Playoffs

The 2002-03 season saw Marian Hossa establish himself among the game's top snipers. His 45 goals placed him fourth in the NHL and broke Alexei Yashin's club record of 44. The Senators set club records with 52 wins and 113 points.

Franchise date: December 16, 1991

**NORTHEAST
DIVISION**

**12th
NHL
Season**

2003-04 Player Personnel

FORWARDS	HT	WT	S	Place of Birth	Date	2002-03 Club
ALFREDSSON, Daniel	5-11	199	R	Goteborg, Sweden	12/11/72	Ottawa
BONK, Radek	6-3	220	L	Krnov, Czech.	1/9/76	Ottawa
FISHER, Mike	6-1	200	R	Peterborough, Ont.	6/5/80	Ottawa
GIROUX, Alexandre	6-3	190	L	Quebec City, Que.	6/16/81	Binghamton
HAMEL, Denis	6-1	201	L	Lachute, Que.	5/10/77	Buffalo-Rochester
HAVLAT, Martin	6-1	190	L	Mlada Boleslav, Czech.	4/19/81	Ottawa
HOSSA, Marian	6-1	208	L	Stara Lubovna, Czech.	1/12/79	Ottawa
HULL, Jody	6-2	195	R	Petrolia, Ont.	2/2/69	Ottawa
KELLY, Chris	6-0	190	L	Toronto, Ont.	11/11/80	Binghamton
LAICH, Brooks	6-2	199	L	Wawota, Alta.	6/23/83	Seattle
LANGFELD, Josh	6-3	216	R	Fridley, MN	7/17/77	Ottawa-Binghamton
McGRATTAN, Brian	6-5	226	R	Hamilton, Ont.	9/2/81	Binghamton
MURPHY, Joe	6-0	200	R	Didsbury, Alta.	1/21/75	Binghamton
NEIL, Chris	6-0	213	R	Markdale, Ont.	6/18/79	Ottawa
SCHAEFER, Peter	5-11	195	L	Yellow Grass, Sask.	7/12/77	Ottawa
SCHASTLIVY, Petr	6-1	204	L	Angarsk, USSR	4/18/79	Ottawa
SMOLINSKI, Bryan	6-1	208	R	Toledo, OH	12/27/71	Los Angeles-Ottawa
SPEZZA, Jason	6-2	206	R	Mississauga, Ont.	6/13/83	Ottawa-Binghamton
VAN ALLEN, Shaun	6-1	205	L	Calgary, Alta.	8/29/67	Ottawa
VARADA, Vaclav	6-0	208	L	Vsetin, Czech.	4/26/76	Buffalo-Ottawa
VERMETTE, Antoine	6-1	184	L	St-Agapit, Que.	7/20/82	Binghamton
WATSON, Greg	6-2	198	L	Eastend, Sask.	3/2/83	Prince Albert-Brandon
WHITE, Todd	5-10	194	L	Kanata, Ont.	5/21/75	Ottawa
DEFENSEMEN						
BROOKBANK, Wade	6-4	219	L	Lanigan, Sask.	9/29/77	Binghamton
CHARA, Zdeno	6-9	260	L	Trencin, Czech.	3/18/77	Ottawa
HNIDY, Shane	6-2	204	R	Neepawa, Man.	11/8/75	Ottawa
LESCHYSHYN, Curtis	6-1	207	L	Thompson, Man.	9/21/69	Ottawa
PHILLIPS, Chris	6-3	215	L	Calgary, Alta.	3/9/78	Ottawa
PLATIL, Jan	6-2	215	L	Kladno, Czech.	2/9/83	Barrie
POTHIER, Brian	6-0	195	R	New Bedford, MA	4/15/77	Ottawa-Binghamton
RACHUNEK, Karel	6-2	211	R	Gottwaldov, Czech.	8/27/79	Yaroslavl-Ottawa-Binghamton
REDDEN, Wade	6-2	205	L	Lloydminster, Sask.	6/12/77	Ottawa
SCHUBERT, Christoph	6-2	210	L	Munich, West Germany	2/5/82	Binghamton
SMREK, Peter	6-1	215	L	Martin, Czech.	2/16/79	Milwaukee
VAUCLAIR, Julien	6-0	205	L	Delemont, Switz.	10/2/79	Binghamton
VOLCHENKOV, Anton	6-1	227	L	Moscow, USSR	2/25/82	Ottawa

GOALTENDERS	HT	WT	C	Place of Birth	Date	2002-03 Club
EMERY, Ray	6-3	198	L	Cayuga, Ont.	9/28/82	Ottawa-Binghamton
LALIME, Patrick	6-3	185	L	St-Bonaventure, Que.	7/7/74	Ottawa
PRUSEK, Martin	6-1	176	L	Ostrava, Czech.	12/11/75	Ottawa-Binghamton
THOMPSON, Billy	6-2	200	L	Saskatoon, Sask.	9/24/82	Binghamton-Prince George

2002-03 Scoring

* - rookie

Regular Season

Pos	#	Player	Team	GP	G	A	Pts	+/–	PIM	PP	SH	GW	GT	S	%
R	18	Marian Hossa	OTT	80	45	35	80	8	34	14	0	10	1	229	19.7
R	11	Daniel Alfredsson	OTT	78	27	51	78	15	42	9	0	6	0	240	11.3
C	28	Todd White	OTT	80	25	35	60	19	28	8	1	5	0	144	17.4
R	9	Martin Havlat	OTT	67	24	35	59	20	30	9	0	4	0	179	13.4
C	14	Radek Bonk	OTT	70	22	32	54	6	36	11	0	4	2	146	15.1
C	21	Bryan Smolinski	L.A.	58	18	20	38	–1	18	6	1	8	0	150	12.0
			OTT	10	3	5	8	1	2	0	0	0	0	26	11.5
			TOTAL	68	21	25	46	0	20	6	1	8	0	176	11.9
D	6	Wade Redden	OTT	76	10	35	45	23	70	4	0	3	0	154	6.5
D	3	Zdeno Chara	OTT	74	9	30	39	29	116	3	0	2	0	168	5.4
C	12	Mike Fisher	OTT	74	18	20	38	13	54	5	1	3	0	142	12.7
L	20	Magnus Arvedson	OTT	80	16	21	37	13	48	2	0	4	0	138	11.6
C	22	Shaun Van Allen	OTT	78	12	20	32	17	66	2	2	3	0	53	22.6
D	23	Karel Rachunek	OTT	58	4	25	29	23	30	3	0	1	0	110	3.6
L	15	Peter Schaefer	OTT	75	6	17	23	11	32	0	0	1	0	93	6.5
C	39 *	Jason Spezza	OTT	33	7	14	21	–3	8	3	0	0	0	65	10.8
L	19	Petr Schastlivy	OTT	33	9	10	19	3	4	5	0	2	0	68	13.2
L	26	Vaclav Varada	BUF	44	7	4	11	–2	23	1	0	0	0	64	10.9
			OTT	11	2	6	8	3	8	1	0	0	0	17	11.8
			TOTAL	55	9	10	19	1	31	2	0	0	0	81	11.1
D	4	Chris Phillips	OTT	78	3	16	19	7	71	2	0	1	0	97	3.1
D	24 *	Anton Volchenkov	OTT	57	3	13	16	–4	40	0	0	0	0	75	4.0
L	16	Jody Hull	OTT	70	3	8	11	–3	14	0	0	1	0	42	7.1
R	25	Chris Neil	OTT	68	6	4	10	8	147	0	0	0	0	62	9.7
D	34	Shane Hnidy	OTT	67	0	8	8	–1	130	0	0	0	0	58	0.0
D	7	Curtis Leschyshyn	OTT	54	1	6	7	11	18	0	0	0	0	30	3.3
D	2	Brian Pothier	OTT	14	2	4	6	11	6	0	0	1	0	23	8.7
R	38	Brad Smyth	OTT	12	3	1	4	–2	15	2	0	0	0	16	18.8
R	10 *	Toni Dahlman	OTT	12	1	0	1	–1	0	0	0	1	0	5	20.0
R	33 *	Josh Langfeld	OTT	12	0	1	1	2	4	0	0	0	0	16	0.0
R	36	Joey Tetarenko	FLA	2	0	0	0	–1	4	0	0	0	0	2	0.0
			OTT	2	0	0	0	0	5	0	0	0	0	1	0.0
			TOTAL	4	0	0	0	–1	9	0	0	0	0	3	0.0
R	27	Dennis Bonvie	OTT	12	0	0	0	–1	29	0	0	0	0	3	0.0
R	32	Rob Ray	BUF	41	0	0	0	–5	92	0	0	0	0	14	0.0
			OTT	5	0	0	0	0	4	0	0	0	0	0	0.0
			TOTAL	46	0	0	0	–5	96	0	0	0	0	14	0.0

Goaltending

No.	Goaltender	GPI	Mins	Avg	W	L	T	EN	SO	GA	SA	S%	G	A	PIM
1	* Ray Emery	3	85	1.41	1	0	0	0	0	2	26	.923	0	0	0
40	Patrick Lalime	67	3943	2.16	39	20	7	1	8	142	1591	.911	0	1	6
31	Martin Prusek	18	935	2.37	12	2	1	0	0	37	415	.911	0	0	0
	Totals	**82**	**4977**	**2.19**	**52**	**22**	**8**	**1**	**8**	**182**	**2033**	**.910**			

Playoffs

Pos	#	Player	Team	GP	G	A	Pts	+/–	PIM	PP	SH	GW	GT	S	%
R	18	Marian Hossa	OTT	18	5	11	16	–1	6	3	0	1	0	54	9.3
C	14	Radek Bonk	OTT	18	6	5	11	2	10	2	0	0	0	28	21.4
R	9	Martin Havlat	OTT	18	5	6	11	4	14	1	0	2	0	52	9.6
C	21	Bryan Smolinski	OTT	18	2	7	9	4	6	0	0	0	0	32	6.3
D	6	Wade Redden	OTT	18	1	8	9	1	10	0	0	1	1	32	3.1
R	11	Daniel Alfredsson	OTT	18	4	4	8	–3	12	4	0	1	0	41	9.8
D	3	Zdeno Chara	OTT	18	1	6	7	3	14	0	0	0	0	32	3.1
C	28	Todd White	OTT	18	5	1	6	–1	6	1	1	2	1	30	16.7
L	26	Vaclav Varada	OTT	18	2	4	6	4	18	0	0	0	0	23	8.7
D	4	Chris Phillips	OTT	18	2	4	6	3	12	0	0	1	1	22	9.1
L	20	Magnus Arvedson	OTT	18	1	5	6	–4	16	0	0	0	0	17	5.9
L	15	Peter Schaefer	OTT	16	2	3	5	3	6	0	1	0	0	15	13.3
C	12	Mike Fisher	OTT	18	2	2	4	–1	16	0	1	1	0	36	5.6
D	23	Karel Rachunek	OTT	17	1	3	4	–5	14	0	0	0	0	21	4.8
C	39 *	Jason Spezza	OTT	3	1	1	2	1	0	1	0	0	0	3	33.3
D	24 *	Anton Volchenkov	OTT	17	1	1	2	3	4	0	0	1	0	17	5.9
C	22	Shaun Van Allen	OTT	18	1	1	2	–1	12	0	0	1	1	12	8.3
R	25	Chris Neil	OTT	15	1	0	1	1	24	0	0	0	0	16	6.3
D	7	Curtis Leschyshyn	OTT	18	0	1	1	0	10	0	0	0	0	8	0.0
D	34	Shane Hnidy	OTT	1	0	0	0	0	0	0	0	0	0	2	0.0
R	16	Jody Hull	OTT	2	0	0	0	0	0	0	0	0	0	0	0.0

Goaltending

No.	Goaltender	GPI	Mins	Avg	W	L	EN	SO	GA	SA	S%	G	A	PIM
40	Patrick Lalime	18	1122	1.82	11	7	0	1	34	449	.924	0	0	0
	Totals	**18**	**1128**	**1.81**	**11**	**7**	**0**	**1**	**34**	**449**	**.924**			

General Manager

MUCKLER, JOHN
General Manager, Ottawa Senators. Born in Midland, Ont., April 3, 1934.

John Muckler was named the sixth general manager in Senators history on June 12, 2002. Prior to his arrival in Ottawa, Muckler served as coach of the New York Rangers from 1997-98 to 1999-2000. Previously, he was general manager of the Buffalo Sabres from 1993 to 1997, and was named NHL executive of the year by *The Sporting News* for the 1996-97 season. Muckler is the first g.m. hired by the Senators to have previous NHL experience as a general manager.

Working for Glen Sather, Muckler enjoyed Edmonton's great 1980s run. He was an assistant coach with the Stanley Cup winners in 1984 and 1985, and designated co-coach during the 1987 and 1988 championship seasons. When Sather gave up the Oilers' coaching reins in 1989, Muckler stepped in and led the team to its fifth Stanley Cup in seven years. In 1991, he left the Oilers for the Buffalo Sabres.

Muckler has been involved in professional hockey since the 1949-50 season. He was a defenseman in the minor leagues for 13 seasons, playing the bulk of his career in the old Eastern Hockey League. His professional coaching career began while he was still a player in 1959 when he took over the New York Rovers of the EHL. He had great success with the team in the 1960s when they were known as the Long Island Ducks. Muckler joined the Minnesota North Stars after NHL expansion in 1967 and spent six seasons in the organization, mostly as a coach and g.m. in the minor leagues. His first NHL coaching job came with the North Stars midway through the 1968-69 season. He later worked in the Rangers and Canucks organizations before joining the Oilers as coach of their Wichita farm club in 1981.

NHL Coaching Record

		Regular Season				Playoffs		
Season	Team	Games	W	L	T	Games	W	L
1968-69	Minnesota	35	6	23	6	....	....	....
1989-90	Edmonton	80	38	28	14	22	16	6*
1990-91	Edmonton	80	37	37	6	18	9	9
1991-92	Buffalo	52	22	22	8	7	3	4
1992-93	Buffalo	84	38	36	10	8	4	4
1993-94	Buffalo	84	43	32	9	7	3	4
1994-95	Buffalo	48	22	19	7	5	1	4
1997-98	NY Rangers	25	8	15	2	....	....	....
1998-99	NY Rangers	82	33	38	11	....	....	....
1999-2000	NY Rangers	78	29	38	11	....	....	....
	NHL Totals	**648**	**276**	**288**	**84**	**67**	**36**	**31**

* Stanley Cup win.

General Managers' History

Mel Bridgman, 1992-93; Randy Sexton, 1993-94, 1994-95; Randy Sexton and Pierre Gauthier, 1995-96; Pierre Gauthier, 1996-97, 1997-98; Rick Dudley, 1998-99; Marshall Johnston, 1999-2000 to 2001-02; John Muckler, 2002-03 to date.

Club Records

Team

(Figures in brackets for season records are games played; records for fewest points, wins, ties, losses, goals, goals against are for 70 or more games)

Most Points	113	2002-03 (82)
Most Wins	52	2002-03 (82)
Most Ties	15	1996-97 (82), 1997-98 (82), 1998-99 (82)
Most Losses	70	1992-93 (84)
Most Goals	274	2000-01 (82)
Most Goals Against	397	1993-94 (84)
Fewest Points	24	1992-93 (84)
Fewest Wins	10	1992-93 (84)
Fewest Ties	4	1992-93 (84)
Fewest Losses	21	2000-01 (82), 2002-03 (82)
Fewest Goals	191	1995-96 (82)
Fewest Goals Against	179	1998-99 (82)

Longest Winning Streak

Overall	7	Oct. 25-Nov. 13/01
Home	8	Nov. 14-Dec. 14/02
Away	6	Mar. 18-Apr. 5/03

Longest Undefeated Streak

Overall	11	Dec. 28/98-Jan. 16/99 (8 wins, 3 ties), Oct. 25-Nov. 22/01 (9 wins, 2 ties)
Home	8	Four times
Away	7	Twice

** NHL records do not include neutral site games

Longest Losing Streak

Overall	14	Mar. 2-Apr. 7/93
Home	*11	Oct. 27-Dec. 8/93
Away	*38	Oct. 10/92-Apr. 3/93**

Longest Winless Streak

Overall	21	Oct. 10-Nov. 23/92 (20 losses, 1 tie)
Home	*17	Oct. 28/95-Jan. 27/96 (15 losses, 2 ties)
Away	*38	Oct. 10/92-Apr. 3/93 (38 losses)
Most Shutouts, Season	10	2001-02 (82)
Most PIM, Season	1,716	1992-93 (84)
Most Goals, Game	11	Nov. 13/01 (Ott. 11 at Wsh. 5)

Individual

Most Seasons	9	Radek Bonk
Most Games, Career	623	Radek Bonk
Most Goals, Career	218	Alexei Yashin
Most Assists, Career	301	Daniel Alfredsson
Most Points, Career	491	Alexei Yashin (218G, 273A)
Most PIM, Career	625	Dennis Vial
Most Shutouts, Career	25	Patrick Lalime

Longest Consecutive

Games Streak	292	Alexei Yashin (Dec. 31/95-Apr. 17/99)

Most Goals, Season	45	Marian Hossa (2002-03)
Most Assists, Season	51	Daniel Alfredsson (2002-03)
Most Points, Season	94	Alexei Yashin (1998-99; 44G, 50A)
Most PIM, Season	318	Mike Peluso (1992-93)
Most Points, Defenseman, Season	63	Norm Maciver (1992-93; 17G, 46A)
Most Points, Center, Season	94	Alexei Yashin (1998-99; 44G, 50A)
Most Points, Right Wing, Season	80	Marian Hossa (2002-03; 45G, 35A)
Most Points, Left Wing, Season	72	Shawn McEachern (2000-01; 32G, 40A)
Most Points, Rookie, Season	79	Alexei Yashin (1993-94; 30G, 49A)
Most Shutouts, Season	8	Patrick Lalime (2002-03)
Most Goals, Game	4	Marian Hossa (Jan. 2/03)
Most Assists, Game	5	Marian Hossa (Jan. 4/01)
Most Points, Game	6	Dan Quinn (Oct. 15/95; 3G, 3A), Radek Bonk (Jan. 4/01; 3G, 3A)

* NHL Record.

Coaching History

Rick Bowness, 1992-93 to 1994-95; Rick Bowness, Dave Allison and Jacques Martin, 1995-96; Jacques Martin, 1996-97 to 2000-01; Jacques Martin and Roger Neilson, 2001-02; Jacques Martin, 2002-03 to date.

Captains' History

Laurie Boschman, 1992-93; Brad Shaw, Mark Lamb and Gord Dineen, 1993-94; Randy Cunneyworth, 1994-95 to 1997-98; Alexei Yashin, 1998-99; Daniel Alfredsson, 1999-2000 to date.

Retired Numbers

8	Frank Finnigan	1924-1934

All-time Record vs. Other Clubs

Regular Season

	At Home							On Road							Total						
	GP	W	L	T	OL	GF	GA	PTS	GP	W	L	T	OL	GF	GA	PTS	GP	W	L	T	OL	GF	GA	PTS
Anaheim	8	4	3	1	0	24	19	9	8	2	4	0	0	15	21	6	16	6	7	3	0	39	40	15
Atlanta	8	5	1	1	1	40	21	12	8	5	1	1	1	34	25	12	16	10	2	2	2	74	46	24
Boston	28	11	14	3	0	69	88	25	30	8	18	4	0	85	117	20	58	19	32	7	0	154	205	45
Buffalo	30	9	12	6	3	67	82	27	28	7	18	2	1	41	90	17	58	16	30	8	4	108	172	44
Calgary	9	4	3	1	1	25	23	12	10	4	5	1	0	23	34	9	19	8	8	4	1	48	57	21
Carolina	27	11	11	4	1	73	74	27	25	6	16	3	0	60	78	15	52	17	27	7	1	133	152	42
Chicago	8	5	3	0	1	25	29	7	8	2	4	2	0	18	18	6	17	5	9	2	1	43	47	13
Colorado	17	7	7	3	0	51	64	17	15	2	12	1	0	41	70	5	32	9	19	4	0	92	134	22
Columbus	2	1	0	1	0	7	4	3	2	1	0	1	0	9	7	3	4	2	0	2	0	16	11	6
Dallas	9	4	5	0	0	22	24	8	10	4	6	0	0	25	39	8	19	8	11	0	0	47	63	16
Detroit	9	3	5	1	0	26	26	7	9	3	5	0	1	19	33	7	18	6	10	1	1	45	59	14
Edmonton	9	3	5	1	0	16	23	7	10	2	6	2	0	24	36	6	19	5	11	3	0	40	59	13
Florida	20	9	9	2	0	56	55	20	20	10	9	1	0	58	60	21	40	19	18	3	0	114	115	41
Los Angeles	9	4	3	1	1	30	28	10	9	1	7	1	0	18	42	3	18	5	10	2	1	48	70	13
Minnesota	2	1	1	0	0	4	4	2	2	1	0	1	0	6	5	3	4	2	1	1	0	10	9	5
Montreal	28	13	14	1	0	78	80	27	30	10	16	4	0	83	91	24	58	23	30	5	0	161	171	51
Nashville	4	3	1	0	0	11	5	6	4	2	2	0	0	11	8	4	8	5	3	0	0	22	13	10
New Jersey	22	6	12	3	1	46	57	16	21	7	11	2	1	49	64	17	43	13	23	5	2	95	121	33
NY Islanders	21	12	5	4	0	73	58	28	22	13	3	6	0	84	67	32	43	25	8	10	0	157	125	60
NY Rangers	21	7	11	3	0	57	63	17	21	11	10	0	0	64	67	22	42	18	21	3	0	121	130	39
Philadelphia	22	7	10	5	0	60	70	19	21	7	12	2	0	57	67	16	43	14	22	7	0	117	137	35
Phoenix	11	4	6	1	0	29	34	9	9	4	4	1	0	34	33	9	20	8	10	2	0	63	67	18
Pittsburgh	25	7	14	4	0	61	79	18	25	5	16	4	0	57	92	14	50	12	30	8	0	118	171	32
St. Louis	9	3	6	0	0	20	35	6	9	3	4	2	0	25	27	8	18	6	10	2	0	45	62	14
San Jose	9	4	1	4	0	36	26	12	8	3	5	0	0	12	17	6	17	7	6	4	0	48	43	18
Tampa Bay	21	13	8	0	0	80	46	26	21	11	8	2	0	71	65	24	42	24	16	2	0	151	111	50
Toronto	17	12	4	1	0	51	40	25	19	9	9	1	0	50	51	19	36	21	13	2	0	101	91	44
Vancouver	9	5	3	1	0	22	21	11	10	4	5	1	0	24	32	9	19	9	8	2	0	46	53	20
Washington	21	10	9	1	1	74	67	22	22	8	11	3	0	63	74	19	43	18	20	4	1	137	141	41
Totals	436	185	186	55	10	1233	1245	435	436	155	227	50	4	1160	1430	364	872	340	413	105	14	2393	2675	799

Playoffs

	Series	W	L	GP	W	L	T	GF	GA	Last Mtg.	Rnd.	Result
Buffalo	2	0	2	11	3	8	0	19	26	1999	CQF	L 0-4
New Jersey	2	1	1	13	7	6	0	26	29	2003	CF	L 3-4
NY Islanders	1	1	0	5	4	1	0	13	7	2003	CQF	W 4-1
Philadelphia	2	2	0	11	8	3	0	28	12	2003	CSF	W 4-2
Toronto	3	0	3	17	5	12	0	31	43	2002	CSF	L 3-4
Washington	1	0	1	5	1	4	0	7	18	1998	CSF	L 1-4
Totals	11	4	7	62	28	34	0	124	135			

Playoff Results 2003-1999

Year	Round	Opponent	Result	GF	GA
2003	CF	New Jersey	L 3-4	13	17
	CSF	Philadelphia	W 4-2	17	10
	CQF	NY Islanders	W 4-1	13	7
2002	CSF	Toronto	L 3-4	18	16
	CQF	Philadelphia	W 4-1	11	2
2001	CQF	Toronto	L 0-4	3	10
2000	CQF	Toronto	L 2-4	10	17
1999	CQF	Buffalo	L 0-4	6	12

Abbreviations: Round: CF – conference final; **CSF** – conference semi-final; **CQF** – conference quarter-final.

Colorado totals include Quebec, 1992-93 to 1994-95.
Dallas totals include Minnesota North Stars, 1992-93.

Carolina totals include Hartford, 1992-93 to 1996-97.
Phoenix totals include Winnipeg, 1992-93 to 1995-96.

2002-03 Results

Oct.	10	New Jersey	1-2		9	at Calgary	1-0
	12	at Toronto	2-1		11	at Edmonton	2-0
	15	Phoenix	2-1		14	Tampa Bay	7-0
	23	Carolina	4-1		16	Anaheim	3-1
	24	at Boston	2-2		18	Washington	5-2
	26	at Montreal	3-5		20	at Tampa Bay	2-6
	29	at Philadelphia	1-2		22	at Florida	2-1
	30	Pittsburgh	1-4		23	at Atlanta	3-3
Nov.	2	Detroit	5-2		25	Buffalo	4-3*
	6	at Colorado	5-2		27	at Dallas	3-5
	8	Los Angeles	2-3		29	at Anaheim	2-3
	9	at Boston	1-7		30	at Los Angeles	0-3
	12	at NY Islanders	5-3	Feb.	5	at NY Rangers	5-3
	14	Florida	3-2*		6	Philadelphia	3-1
	16	Buffalo	4-1		8	Atlanta	3-1
	19	at Carolina	4-4		12	at Pittsburgh	3-0
	21	Montreal	3-2		13	Edmonton	3-1
	23	Columbus	5-2		15	at Toronto	1-2
	25	Toronto	2-0		17	NY Rangers	3-2
	27	at NY Islanders	2-2		19	at New Jersey	5-3
	29	at Washington	6-2		20	Florida	2-2
	30	NY Islanders	4-2		22	Nashville	4-0
Dec.	4	at Chicago	0-1		25	Minnesota	0-3
	5	at St. Louis	2-2		27	Dallas	3-2*
	7	Carolina	5-2	Mar.	1	Tampa Bay	1-2
	10	at Buffalo	4-2		4	Toronto	4-1
	12	at Boston	5-2		8	at Pittsburgh	5-1
	14	New Jersey	4-3*		9	Pittsburgh	4-2
	16	Montreal	2-3		11	Boston	4-3*
	18	at New Jersey	3-0		13	NY Rangers	3-2*
	19	San Jose	9-3		15	NY Islanders	2-5
	21	at Philadelphia	3-1		16	at Detroit	2-3
	23	Philadelphia	2-2		18	at Carolina	6-5
	26	at Buffalo	3-2		21	at Atlanta	5-1
	27	Montreal	3-2*		22	at Florida	3-1
	30	at Nashville	2-3		25	Colorado	2-2
	31	at Tampa Bay	6-3		28	Washington	2-2
Jan.	2	Atlanta	8-1		29	at Montreal	3-1
	4	Buffalo	1-2*	Apr.	1	Boston	3-2
	6	at NY Rangers	5-2		3	at Washington	5-1
	8	at Vancouver	4-6		5	at Toronto	3-1

* – Overtime

Entry Draft
Selections 2003-1992

2003
Pick
29	Patrick Eaves
67	Igor Mirnov
100	Philippe Seydoux
135	Mattias Karlsson
142	Tim Cook
166	Sergei Gimayev
228	William Colbert
260	Ossi Louhivaara
291	Brian Elliott

2002
Pick
16	Jakub Klepis
47	Alexei Kaigorodov
75	Arttu Luttinen
113	Scott Dobben
125	Johan Bjork
150	Brock Hooton
246	Josef Vavra
276	Vitali Atyushov

2001
Pick
2	Jason Spezza
23	Tim Gleason
81	Neil Komadoski
99	Ray Emery
127	Christoph Schubert
162	Stefan Schauer
193	Brooks Laich
218	Jan Platil
223	Brandon Bochenski
235	Neil Petrucic
256	Gregg Johnson
286	Toni Dahlman

2000
Pick
21	Anton Volchenkov
45	Mathieu Chouinard
55	Antoine Vermette
87	Jan Bohac
122	Derrick Byfuglien
156	Greg Zanon
157	Grant Potulny
158	Sean Connolly
188	Jason Maleyko
283	James Demone

1999
Pick
26	Martin Havlat
48	Simon Lajeunesse
62	Teemu Sainomaa
94	Chris Kelly
154	Andrew Ianiero
164	Martin Prusek
201	Mikko Ruutu
209	Layne Ulmer
213	Alexandre Giroux
269	Konstantin Gorovikov

1998
Pick
15	Mathieu Chouinard
44	Mike Fisher
58	Chris Bala
74	Julien Vauclair
101	Petr Schastlivy
130	Gavin McLeod
161	Chris Neil
188	Michel Periard
223	Sergei Verenikin
246	Rastislav Pavlikovsky

1997
Pick
12	Marian Hossa
58	Jani Hurme
66	Josh Langfeld
119	Magnus Arvedson
146	Jeff Sullivan
173	Robin Bacul
203	Nick Gillis
229	Karel Rachunek

1996
Pick
1	Chris Phillips
81	Antti-Jussi Niemi
136	Andreas Dackell
163	Francois Hardy
212	Erich Goldmann
216	Ivan Ciernik
239	Sami Salo

1995
Pick
1	Bryan Berard
27	Marc Moro
53	Brad Larsen
89	Kevin Bolibruck
103	Kevin Boyd
131	David Hruska
183	Kaj Linna
184	Ray Schultz
231	Erik Kaminski

1994
Pick
3	Radek Bonk
29	Stan Neckar
81	Bryan Masotta
131	Mike Gaffney
133	Daniel Alfredsson
159	Doug Sproule
210	Frederic Cassivi
211	Danny Dupont
237	Stephen MacKinnon
274	Antti Tormanen

1993
Pick
1	Alexandre Daigle
27	Radim Bicanek
53	Patrick Charbonneau
91	Cosmo Dupaul
131	Rick Bodkin
157	Sergei Poleschuk
183	Jason Disher
209	Toby Kvalevog
227	Pavol Demitra
235	Rick Schuwerk

1992
Pick
2	Alexei Yashin
25	Chad Penney
50	Patrick Traverse
73	Radek Hamr
98	Daniel Guerard
121	Al Sinclair
146	Jaroslav Miklenda
169	Jay Kenney
194	Claude Savoie
217	Jake Grimes
242	Tomas Jelinek
264	Petter Ronnqvist

Coach

MARTIN, JACQUES
Coach, Ottawa Senators. Born in St. Pascal, Ont., October 1, 1952.

Jacques Martin led the Ottawa Senators to their best regular season in team history in 2002-03, breaking team records for wins (52) and points (113) the club had established under his leadership two years before. The Senators won the Presidents' Trophy for having the NHL's best overall record and Martin was runner-up in voting for the Jack Adams Award as coach of the year.

When appointed the Senators' third head coach on January 24, 1996, Martin brought 10 years of NHL coaching experience, including five with the Quebec Nordiques, an organization often compared with the Senators, in that both teams were built around young, talented players requiring patience and teaching.

Martin's coaching career began at the collegiate level in 1976. He was appointed head coach of the Guelph Platers (now Storm) in 1985, winning the OHL title, the Memorial Cup and being named the OHL coach of the year. That summer, Martin became head coach of the St. Louis Blues. In his NHL rookie year, he led the Blues to the Norris Division championship and, in two seasons with the Blues, posted a 66-71-23 record. He then spent two seasons as an assistant to Chicago's head coach Mike Keenan, before joining the Nordiques in 1990. With Quebec, he worked four years as assistant coach and one year (1993-94) as both head coach and general manager of the AHL Cornwall Aces.

Coaching Record

Season	Team	Games	Regular Season W	L	T	Playoffs Games	W	L
1983-84	Peterborough (OHL)	70	43	23	4	....	....	....
1984-85	Peterborough (OHL)	66	42	20	4	....	....	....
1985-86	Guelph (OHL)	66	41	23	2	....	....	....
1986-87	**St. Louis (NHL)**	**80**	**32**	**33**	**15**	**6**	**2**	**4**
1987-88	**St. Louis (NHL)**	**80**	**34**	**38**	**8**	**10**	**5**	**5**
1993-94	Cornwall (AHL)	80	33	36	11	13	8	5
1995-96	**Ottawa (NHL)**	**38**	**10**	**24**	**4**	....	....	....
1996-97	**Ottawa (NHL)**	**82**	**31**	**36**	**15**	**7**	**3**	**4**
1997-98	**Ottawa (NHL)**	**82**	**34**	**33**	**15**	**11**	**5**	**6**
1998-99	**Ottawa (NHL)**	**82**	**44**	**23**	**15**	**4**	**0**	**4**
1999-2000	**Ottawa (NHL)**	**82**	**41**	**30**	**11**	**6**	**2**	**4**
2000-01	**Ottawa (NHL)**	**82**	**48**	**25**	**9**	**4**	**0**	**4**
2001-02	**Ottawa (NHL)**	**80**	**38**	**33**	**9**	**12**	**7**	**5**
2002-03	**Ottawa (NHL)**	**82**	**52**	**21**	**8**	**18**	**11**	**7**
	NHL Totals	**770**	**364**	**297**	**109**	**78**	**35**	**43**

Martin stepped aside (with NHL permission) during the final two games of the 2001-02 season in order to allow assistant coach Roger Neilson to reach the 1,000-game plateau, April 11 and 13, 2002.

Club Directory

Corel Centre

Ottawa Senators
Corel Centre
1000 Palladium Drive
Ottawa, Ontario
K2V 1A5
Phone **613/599-0250**
FAX 613/599-0358
www.ottawasenators.com
Capacity: 18,500

Executive
Owner & chairman	Eugene Melnyk
President & CEO	Roy Mlakar
Chief operating officer	Cyril Leeder
Vice-president & executive director, Corel Centre	Tom Conroy
General manager	John Muckler

Hockey operations
Director of legal relations	Peter Chiarelli
Director of player personnel	Anders Hedberg
Assistant to the general manager	Allison Vaughan
Head coach	Jacques Martin
Assistant coaches	Perry Pearn, Don Jackson, Randy Lee
Goaltending coach	Phil Myre
Video coordinator	Pierre Groulx
Mental skills coach	John Phelan
Chief amateur scout	Frank Jay
Scouts	Bob Janecyk, George Fargher, Patrick Savard, Ken Williamson, Lewis Mongelluzzo, Boris Shagas, Nick Polano, Vaclav Burda, Gord Pell
Head athletic therapist	Gerry Townend
Head equipment manager	John Gervais
Massage therapist	Brad Joyal
Assistant equipment manager	Chris Cook
Team doctor	Don Chow, M.D.
Scouting and travel coordinator	Alex Lepore

Communications
Vice-president, communications	Phil Legault
Director, communications	Steve Keogh
Manager, communications	Tim Pattyson

Broadcasting
Vice-president, broadcast	Jim Steel

Computer Services
Director, information technology	Sean Shrubsole

Corporate & Ticket Sales
Senior vice-president, corporate and ticketing sales	Mark Bonneau
Director, corporate sales	Bill Courchaine
Director, business development	Gina Hillcoat
Director, ticketing operations	Ariane Ladouceur
Director, premium seating and customer service	Jody Thorson
Director, sales, premium seats and group sales	Jim Orban

Finance
Vice-president, finance	Erin Crowe
Controller	Geoff Publow

Marketing
Vice-president, marketing	Jeff Kyle
Director, marketing and strategic development	Patti Zebchuk
Director, entertainment and event marketing	Derek Dawley
Director, publications and graphic services	Karen Ruttan
Director, marketing programs	Zoe Thanopoulos
Director, media and Corel Centre marketing	Krista Pogue

Ottawa Senators Foundation
President	Dave Ready

Miscellaneous
Minor league affiliate	Binghamton Senators (AHL)
Team colours	Red, White and Black
Radio	Sports Radio 1200 The Team (English), Radio 1150 CJRC (French)
Television	Rogers Sportsnet, New RO, RDS
Team photographer	Freestyle Photography (Andre Ringuette)
Anthem singer	Lyndon Slewidge
Mascot	Spartacat

Important Numbers
Phil Legault	(613) 599-0327
Steve Keogh	(613) 599-0326
Tim Pattyson	(613) 599-0239
P.R. Fax	(613) 599-5562
Media Information Line	(613) 599-0275
Press Box	(613) 591-5436
Press Box Fax	(613) 591-5435

Still just 22 years old while playing his third season in 2002-03, Martin Havlat established career highs with 24 goals, 35 assists and 59 points. He had five goals and six assists in the playoffs as Ottawa reached the Eastern Conference Final.

Philadelphia Flyers

2002-03 Results: 45w-20l-13t-4otl 107pts.
Second, Atlantic Division

2003-04 Schedule

Oct.	Thu.	9	Buffalo
	Sat.	11	Pittsburgh
	Thu.	16	at San Jose
	Sat.	18	at Phoenix
	Tue.	21	at Los Angeles
	Wed.	22	at Anaheim
	Sat.	25	Carolina
	Mon.	27	Montreal
	Wed.	29	Florida
	Thu.	30	at New Jersey
Nov.	Sat.	1	at Toronto
	Thu.	6	Washington
	Sat.	8	at NY Rangers*
	Tue.	11	NY Islanders
	Thu.	13	Vancouver
	Sat.	15	Atlanta
	Tue.	18	at Carolina
	Thu.	20	Minnesota
	Sat.	22	Boston
	Wed.	26	at Pittsburgh
	Fri.	28	Carolina*
	Sat.	29	at NY Islanders
Dec.	Mon.	1	at Ottawa
	Wed.	3	Pittsburgh
	Fri.	5	Phoenix
	Sat.	6	at Boston
	Mon.	8	at Montreal
	Wed.	10	at Columbus
	Fri.	12	at New Jersey
	Sat.	13	New Jersey
	Tue.	16	Calgary
	Thu.	18	Tampa Bay
	Sat.	20	NY Islanders*
	Sun.	21	at Atlanta
	Tue.	23	at NY Islanders
	Sat.	27	at Colorado
	Mon.	29	at Dallas
	Tue.	30	at St. Louis
Jan.	Fri.	2	at Florida*
	Sat.	3	at Tampa Bay
	Wed.	7	at Buffalo

	Thu.	8	Florida
	Sat.	10	Edmonton
	Mon.	12	Pittsburgh
	Tue.	13	at Buffalo
	Fri.	16	Toronto
	Sat.	17	at Toronto
	Tue.	20	Montreal
	Thu.	22	at NY Rangers
	Sat.	24	Buffalo*
	Sun.	25	at Washington
	Wed.	28	at Florida
	Sat.	31	at Pittsburgh*
Feb.	Mon.	2	Tampa Bay
	Wed.	4	Washington
	Thu.	5	at Atlanta
	Tue.	10	New Jersey
	Thu.	12	at NY Rangers
	Sat.	14	NY Rangers*
	Mon.	16	San Jose
	Tue.	17	at Tampa Bay
	Thu.	19	Boston
	Sat.	21	Atlanta*
	Tue.	24	Chicago
	Thu.	26	at Ottawa
	Sat.	28	at Boston*
	Sun.	29	at Detroit
Mar.	Wed.	3	Nashville
	Fri.	5	Ottawa
	Sat.	6	at Washington
	Tue.	9	at New Jersey
	Thu.	11	Dallas
	Sat.	13	New Jersey*
	Sun.	14	at Pittsburgh*
	Thu.	18	Toronto
	Sat.	20	NY Rangers
	Tue.	23	at Carolina
	Thu.	25	NY Islanders
	Sat.	27	NY Rangers*
Apr.	Thu.	1	at Montreal
	Fri.	2	at Ottawa
	Sun.	4	at NY Islanders*

* Denotes afternoon game.

Franchise date: June 5, 1967

ATLANTIC DIVISION

37th NHL Season

Year-by-Year Record

Season	GP	Home W	L	T	OL	Road W	L	T	OL	Overall W	L	T	OL	GF	GA	Pts.	Finished	Playoff Result
2002-03	82	21	10	8	2	24	10	5	2	45	20	13	4	211	166	107	2nd, Atlantic Div.	Lost Conf. Semi-Final
2001-02	82	20	13	5	3	22	14	5	0	42	27	10	3	234	192	97	1st, Atlantic Div.	Lost Conf. Quarter-Final
2000-01	82	26	11	4	0	17	14	7	3	43	25	11	3	240	207	100	2nd, Atlantic Div.	Lost Conf. Quarter-Final
1999-2000	82	25	6	7	3	20	16	5	0	45	22	12	3	237	179	105	1st, Atlantic Div.	Lost Conf. Championship
1998-99	82	21	9	11	...	16	17	8	...	37	26	19	...	231	196	93	2nd, Atlantic Div.	Lost Conf. Quarter-Final
1997-98	82	24	11	6	...	18	18	5	...	42	29	11	...	242	193	95	1st, Atlantic Div.	Lost Conf. Quarter-Final
1996-97	82	23	12	6	...	22	12	7	...	45	24	13	...	274	217	103	2nd, Atlantic Div.	Lost Final
1995-96	82	27	9	5	...	18	15	8	...	45	24	13	...	282	208	103	1st, Atlantic Div.	Lost Conf. Semi-Final
1994-95	48	16	7	1	...	12	9	3	...	28	16	4	...	150	132	60	1st, Atlantic Div.	Lost Conf. Championship
1993-94	84	19	20	3	...	16	19	7	...	35	39	10	...	294	314	80	6th, Atlantic Div.	Out of Playoffs
1992-93	84	23	14	5	...	13	23	6	...	36	37	11	...	319	319	83	5th, Patrick Div.	Out of Playoffs
1991-92	80	22	11	7	...	10	26	4	...	32	37	11	...	252	273	75	6th, Patrick Div.	Out of Playoffs
1990-91	80	18	16	6	...	15	21	4	...	33	37	10	...	252	267	76	5th, Patrick Div.	Out of Playoffs
1989-90	80	17	19	4	...	13	20	7	...	30	39	11	...	290	297	71	6th, Patrick Div.	Out of Playoffs
1988-89	80	22	15	3	...	14	21	5	...	36	36	8	...	307	285	80	4th, Patrick Div.	Lost Conf. Championship
1987-88	80	20	14	6	...	18	19	3	...	38	33	9	...	292	292	85	3rd, Patrick Div.	Lost Div. Semi-Final
1986-87	80	29	9	2	...	17	17	6	...	46	26	8	...	310	245	100	1st, Patrick Div.	Lost Final
1985-86	80	33	6	1	...	20	17	3	...	53	23	4	...	335	241	110	1st, Patrick Div.	Lost Div. Semi-Final
1984-85	80	32	4	4	...	21	16	3	...	53	20	7	...	348	241	113	1st, Patrick Div.	Lost Final
1983-84	80	25	10	5	...	19	16	5	...	44	26	10	...	350	290	98	3rd, Patrick Div.	Lost Div. Semi-Final
1982-83	80	29	8	3	...	20	15	5	...	49	23	8	...	326	240	106	1st, Patrick Div.	Lost Div. Semi-Final
1981-82	80	25	10	5	...	13	21	6	...	38	31	11	...	325	313	87	3rd, Patrick Div.	Lost Div. Semi-Final
1980-81	80	23	9	8	...	18	15	7	...	41	24	15	...	313	249	97	2nd, Patrick Div.	Lost Quarter-Final
1979-80	80	27	5	8	...	21	7	12	...	48	12	20	...	327	254	116	1st, Patrick Div.	Lost Final
1978-79	80	26	10	4	...	14	15	11	...	40	25	15	...	281	248	95	2nd, Patrick Div.	Lost Quarter-Final
1977-78	80	29	6	5	...	16	14	10	...	45	20	15	...	296	200	105	2nd, Patrick Div.	Lost Semi-Final
1976-77	80	33	6	1	...	15	10	15	...	48	16	16	...	323	213	112	1st, Patrick Div.	Lost Semi-Final
1975-76	80	36	2	2	...	15	11	14	...	51	13	16	...	348	209	118	1st, Patrick Div.	Lost Final
1974-75	**80**	**32**	**6**	**2**	**...**	**19**	**12**	**9**	**...**	**51**	**18**	**11**	**...**	**293**	**181**	**113**	**1st, Patrick Div.**	**Won Stanley Cup**
1973-74	**78**	**28**	**6**	**5**	**...**	**22**	**10**	**7**	**...**	**50**	**16**	**12**	**...**	**273**	**164**	**112**	**1st, West Div.**	**Won Stanley Cup**
1972-73	78	27	8	4	...	10	22	7	...	37	30	11	...	296	256	85	2nd, West Div.	Lost Semi-Final
1971-72	78	19	13	7	...	7	25	7	...	26	38	14	...	200	236	66	5th, West Div.	Out of Playoffs
1970-71	78	20	10	9	...	8	23	8	...	28	33	17	...	207	225	73	3rd, West Div.	Lost Quarter-Final
1969-70	76	11	14	13	...	6	21	11	...	17	35	24	...	197	225	58	5th, West Div.	Out of Playoffs
1968-69	76	14	16	8	...	6	19	13	...	20	35	21	...	174	225	61	3rd, West Div.	Lost Quarter-Final
1967-68	74	17	13	7	...	14	19	4	...	31	32	11	...	173	179	73	1st, West Div.	Lost Quarter-Final

Veteran defenseman Eric Desjardins posted the best plus-minus numbers of his 14-year career in 2002-03. His rating of +30 tied him with Colorado's Adam Foote for the third-best mark among NHL defensemen.

2003-04 Player Personnel

FORWARDS	HT	WT	S	Place of Birth	Date	2002-03 Club
AMONTE, Tony	6-0	200	L	Hingham, MA	8/2/70	Phoenix-Philadelphia
BRASHEAR, Donald	6-2	235	L	Bedford, IN	1/7/72	Philadelphia
CHOUINARD, Eric	6-3	215	L	Atlanta, GA	7/8/80	Utah-Philadelphia
FEDORUK, Todd	6-2	235	L	Redwater, Alta.	2/13/79	Philadelphia
GAGNE, Simon	6-0	190	L	Ste-Foy, Que.	2/29/80	Philadelphia
HANDZUS, Michal	6-5	217	L	Banska Bystrica, Czech.	3/11/77	Philadelphia
KAPANEN, Sami	5-10	185	L	Vantaa, Finland	6/14/73	Carolina-Philadelphia
LAPOINTE, Claude	5-9	188	L	Lachine, Que.	10/11/68	NY Islanders-Philadelphia
LAW, Kirby	6-1	185	R	McCreary, Man.	3/11/77	Phi (AHL)-Phi
LeCLAIR, John	6-3	226	L	St. Albans, VT	7/5/69	Philadelphia
MacNEIL, Ian	6-2	190	L	Halifax, N.S.	4/27/77	Phi-Phi (AHL)
MURPHY, Mark	5-11	200	L	Stoughton, MA	8/6/76	Portland (AHL)
PELUSO, Mike	6-1	208	R	Bismarck, ND	9/2/74	Norfolk
PRIMEAU, Keith	6-5	220	L	Toronto, Ont.	11/24/71	Philadelphia
RECCHI, Mark	5-10	185	L	Kamloops, B.C.	2/1/68	Philadelphia
ROENICK, Jeremy	6-1	196	R	Boston, MA	1/17/70	Philadelphia
SAVAGE, Andre	6-0	195	R	Ottawa, Ont.	5/27/75	Phi-Phi (AHL)
SHARP, Patrick	6-0	197	R	Thunder Bay, Ont.	12/27/81	Phi-Phi (AHL)
SIKLENKA, Mike	6-5	224	R	Meadow Lake, Sask.	12/18/79	Phi-Phi (AHL)
SOMIK, Radovan	6-2	194	R	Martin, Czech.	5/5/77	Philadelphia
WHITE, Peter	5-11	200	L	Montreal, Que.	3/15/69	Chi-Norfolk-Phi (AHL)
WILLIAMS, Justin	6-1	190	R	Cobourg, Ont.	10/4/81	Philadelphia
DEFENSEMEN						
DESJARDINS, Eric	6-1	205	R	Rouyn, Que.	6/14/69	Philadelphia
JOHNSSON, Kim	6-1	205	L	Malmo, Sweden	3/16/76	Philadelphia
PITKANEN, Joni	6-3	200	L	Oulu, Finland	9/19/83	Karpat
RAGNARSSON, Marcus	6-1	215	L	Ostervala, Sweden	8/13/71	San Jose-Philadelphia
SEIDENBERG, Dennis	6-0	200	L	Schwenningen, W. Ger.	7/18/81	Phi-Phi (AHL)
SKOLNEY, Wade	6-0	185	R	Wynyard, Sask.	6/24/81	Philadelphia (AHL)
SLANEY, John	6-0	189	L	St. John's, Nfld.	2/2/72	Philadelphia (AHL)
THERIEN, Chris	6-5	235	L	Ottawa, Ont.	12/14/71	Philadelphia
VANDERMEER, Jim	6-1	218	L	Caroline, Alta.	2/21/80	Phi-Phi (AHL)
WEINRICH, Eric	6-1	207	L	Roanoke, VA	12/19/66	Philadelphia
WOYWITKA, Jeff	6-2	209	L	Vermilion, Alta.	9/1/83	Red Deer

GOALTENDERS	HT	WT	C	Place of Birth	Date	2002-03 Club
ESCHE, Robert	6-1	210	L	Whitesboro, NY	1/22/78	Philadelphia
HACKETT, Jeff	6-1	198	L	London, Ont.	6/1/68	Montreal-Boston
LITTLE, Neil	6-1	193	L	Medicine Hat, Alta.	12/18/71	Philadelphia (AHL)
NIITTYMAKI, Antero	6-0	183	L	Turku, Finland	6/18/80	Philadelphia (AHL)

Coaching History

Keith Allen, 1967-68, 1968-69; Vic Stasiuk, 1969-70, 1970-71; Fred Shero, 1971-72 to 1977-78; Bob McCammon and Pat Quinn, 1978-79; Pat Quinn, 1979-80, 1980-81; Pat Quinn and Bob McCammon, 1981-82; Bob McCammon, 1982-83, 1983-84; Mike Keenan, 1984-85 to 1987-88; Paul Holmgren, 1988-89 to 1990-91; Paul Holmgren and Bill Dineen, 1991-92; Bill Dineen, 1992-93; Terry Simpson, 1993-94; Terry Murray, 1994-95 to 1996-97; Wayne Cashman and Roger Neilson, 1997-98; Roger Neilson, 1998-99, 1999-2000; Craig Ramsay and Bill Barber, 2000-01; Bill Barber, 2001-02; Ken Hitchcock, 2002-03 to date.

Coach

HITCHCOCK, KEN
Coach, Philadelphia Flyers. Born in Edmonton, Alta., December 17, 1951.

The Philadelphia Flyers named Ken Hitchcock as their head coach on May 14, 2002.

Hitchcock is the 15th head coach in Flyers history. Prior to joining the Flyers, he won a gold medal as an associate coach with Team Canada at the 2002 Winter Olympic Games. Hitchcock served as head coach of the Dallas Stars for parts of seven seasons (1995-96 to 2001-02), compiling a 277-166-60 record in 503 regular season games.

Hitchcock served as head coach of Dallas' International Hockey League affiliate, the Kalamazoo Wings/Michigan K-Wings for three seasons, from the 1993-94 season until being named Stars' head coach on January 8, 1996. Prior to joining the Stars' organization, Hitchcock served three seasons as an assistant coach with the Flyers (1990-91 through 1992-93).

Hitchcock joined the Flyers after six seasons as head coach of the Kamloops Blazers of the Western Hockey League from 1984-85 through 1989-90. His .693 winning percentage as head coach at Kamloops is the second highest in the history of the WHL (291-125-15). His international experience also includes serving as an assistant coach for the Team Canada team that captured the gold medal at the 1987 World Junior Championships.

Coaching Record

		Regular Season				Playoffs		
Season	Team	Games	W	L	T	Games	W	L
1984-85	Kamloops (WHL)	71	52	17	2	15	10	5
1985-86	Kamloops (WHL)	72	49	19	4	16	14	2
1986-87	Kamloops (WHL)	72	55	14	3	13	8	5
1987-88	Kamloops (WHL)	72	45	26	1	18	12	6
1988-89	Kamloops (WHL)	72	34	33	5	16	8	8
1989-90	Kamloops (WHL)	72	56	16	0	17	14	3
1993-94	Kalamazoo (IHL)	81	48	26	7	5	1	4
1994-95	Kalamazoo (IHL)	81	43	24	14	16	10	6
1995-96	Michigan (IHL)	40	19	10	11	....	....	....
	Dallas (NHL)	**43**	**15**	**23**	**5**	....	....	....
1996-97	**Dallas (NHL)**	**82**	**48**	**26**	**8**	**7**	**3**	**4**
1997-98	**Dallas (NHL)**	**82**	**49**	**22**	**11**	**17**	**10**	**7**
1998-99	**Dallas (NHL)**	**82**	**51**	**19**	**12**	**23**	**16**	**7***
1999-2000	**Dallas (NHL)**	**82**	**43**	**29**	**10**	**23**	**14**	**9**
2000-01	**Dallas (NHL)**	**82**	**48**	**26**	**8**	**10**	**4**	**6**
2001-02	**Dallas (NHL)**	**50**	**23**	**21**	**6**	....	....	....
2002-03	**Philadelphia (NHL)**	**82**	**45**	**24**	**13**	**13**	**6**	**7**
	NHL Totals	**585**	**322**	**190**	**73**	**93**	**53**	**40**

* Stanley Cup win.

2002-03 Scoring

* - rookie

Regular Season

Pos	#	Player	Team	GP	G	A	Pts	+/–	PIM	PP	SH	GW	GT	S	%
C	97	Jeremy Roenick	PHI	79	27	32	59	20	75	8	1	6	2	197	13.7
R	8	Mark Recchi	PHI	79	20	32	52	0	35	8	1	3	1	171	11.7
R	11	Tony Amonte	PHX	59	13	23	36	–12	26	6	0	3	0	170	7.6
			PHI	13	7	8	15	12	2	1	1	2	1	37	18.9
			TOTAL	72	20	31	51	0	28	7	1	5	1	207	9.7
C	25	Keith Primeau	PHI	80	19	27	46	4	93	6	0	4	1	171	11.1
C	26	Michal Handzus	PHI	82	23	21	44	13	46	1	1	9	0	133	17.3
D	5	Kim Johnsson	PHI	82	10	29	39	11	38	5	0	2	0	159	6.3
D	37	Eric Desjardins	PHI	79	8	24	32	30	35	1	0	2	0	197	4.1
L	24	Sami Kapanen	CAR	43	6	12	18	–17	12	3	0	1	1	108	5.6
			PHI	28	4	9	13	–1	6	2	0	1	0	81	4.9
			TOTAL	71	10	21	31	–18	18	5	0	2	1	189	5.3
L	10	John LeClair	PHI	35	18	10	28	10	16	8	0	4	1	99	18.2
L	12	Simon Gagne	PHI	46	9	18	27	20	16	1	1	3	1	115	7.8
C	39	Marty Murray	PHI	76	11	15	26	–1	13	1	1	0	0	105	10.5
L	87	Donald Brashear	PHI	80	8	17	25	5	161	0	0	1	0	99	8.1
R	14	Justin Williams	PHI	41	8	16	24	15	22	0	0	2	0	105	7.6
D	2	Eric Weinrich	PHI	81	2	18	20	16	40	1	1	0	0	103	1.9
L	20 *	Radovan Somik	PHI	60	8	10	18	9	10	0	1	2	0	95	8.4
C	13	Claude Lapointe	NYI	66	6	6	12	–3	20	0	0	1	0	67	9.0
			PHI	14	2	2	4	5	16	0	0	0	0	20	10.0
			TOTAL	80	8	8	16	2	36	0	0	1	0	87	9.2
D	28	Marcus Ragnarsson	S.J.	25	1	7	8	2	30	0	0	0	0	27	3.7
			PHI	43	2	6	8	5	32	1	0	0	0	52	3.8
			TOTAL	68	3	13	16	7	62	1	0	0	0	79	3.8
D	22	Dmitry Yushkevich	FLA	23	1	6	7	–12	14	0	0	0	0	23	4.3
			L.A.	42	0	3	3	–4	24	0	0	0	0	36	0.0
			PHI	18	2	2	4	7	8	0	0	0	0	16	12.5
			TOTAL	83	3	11	14	–9	46	0	0	0	0	75	4.0
D	36 *	Dennis Seidenberg	PHI	58	4	9	13	8	20	1	0	0	0	123	3.3
L	19 *	Eric Chouinard	PHI	28	4	4	8	2	8	1	0	0	0	45	8.9
D	6	Chris Therien	PHI	67	1	6	7	10	36	0	0	0	0	93	1.1
R	18	Tomi Kallio	ATL	5	0	2	2	–2	4	0	0	0	0	3	0.0
			CBJ	12	1	2	3	–7	8	0	0	0	0	20	5.0
			PHI	7	1	0	1	–1	2	0	0	0	0	5	20.0
			TOTAL	24	2	4	6	–10	14	0	0	0	0	28	7.1
R	15	Joe Sacco	PHI	34	1	5	6	0	20	0	0	1	0	48	2.1
L	29	Todd Fedoruk	PHI	63	1	5	6	1	105	0	0	0	0	33	3.0
L	18	Jamie Wright	CGY	19	2	2	4	1	12	0	0	0	0	16	12.5
			PHI	4	0	0	0	–1	4	0	0	0	0	2	0.0
			TOTAL	23	2	2	4	0	16	0	0	0	0	18	11.1
C	27	Andre Savage	PHI	16	2	1	3	2	4	0	0	1	0	13	15.4
D	23 *	Jim Vandermeer	PHI	24	2	1	3	9	27	0	0	0	0	22	9.1
R	9	Mark Greig	PHI	5	0	1	1	1	2	0	0	0	0	2	0.0
R	21 *	Mike Siklenka	PHI	1	0	0	0	0	0	0	0	0	0	1	0.0
C	34 *	Ian MacNeil	PHI	2	0	0	0	1	0	0	0	0	0	2	0.0
R	47 *	Kirby Law	PHI	2	0	0	0	0	2	0	0	0	0	0	0.0
C	18 *	Patrick Sharp	PHI	3	0	0	0	0	2	0	0	0	0	3	0.0

Goaltending

No.	Goaltender	GPI	Mins	Avg	W	L	T	EN	SO	GA	SA	S%	G	A	PIM
32	Roman Cechmanek	58	3350	1.83	33	15	10	2	6	102	1368	.925	0	0	8
42	Robert Esche	30	1638	2.20	12	9	3	2	2	60	647	.907	0	0	6
	Totals	**82**	**5005**	**1.99**	**45**	**24**	**13**	**4**	**8**	**166**	**2019**	**.918**			

Playoffs

Pos	#	Player	Team	GP	G	A	Pts	+/–	PIM	PP	SH	GW	GT	S	%
R	8	Mark Recchi	PHI	13	7	3	10	4	2	1	0	1	1	29	24.1
C	97	Jeremy Roenick	PHI	13	3	5	8	1	8	0	0	1	0	37	8.1
C	26	Michal Handzus	PHI	13	2	6	8	3	6	0	0	1	0	20	10.0
L	24	Sami Kapanen	PHI	13	4	3	7	2	6	2	0	0	0	25	16.0
R	11	Tony Amonte	PHI	13	1	6	7	2	4	0	0	0	0	37	2.7
R	14	Justin Williams	PHI	12	1	5	6	2	8	0	0	1	0	21	4.8
L	12	Simon Gagne	PHI	13	4	1	5	1	6	0	1	1	0	31	12.9
L	10	John LeClair	PHI	13	2	3	5	5	10	1	0	0	0	31	6.5
C	13	Claude Lapointe	PHI	13	2	3	5	0	14	0	0	0	0	9	22.2
D	2	Eric Weinrich	PHI	13	2	3	5	–2	12	1	0	0	0	16	12.5
D	22	Dmitry Yushkevich	PHI	13	1	4	5	7	2	0	0	1	0	16	6.3
D	37	Eric Desjardins	PHI	5	2	1	3	2	0	0	0	0	0	16	12.5
L	87	Donald Brashear	PHI	13	1	2	3	–1	21	0	0	0	0	15	6.7
D	5	Kim Johnsson	PHI	13	0	3	3	–1	8	0	0	0	0	38	0.0
L	20 *	Radovan Somik	PHI	5	1	1	2	0	6	0	0	0	0	6	16.7
C	25	Keith Primeau	PHI	13	1	1	2	–2	14	0	0	0	0	28	3.6
D	6	Chris Therien	PHI	13	0	2	2	0	2	0	0	0	0	13	0.0
D	23 *	Jim Vandermeer	PHI	8	0	1	1	1	9	0	0	0	0	7	0.0
D	28	Marcus Ragnarsson	PHI	13	0	1	1	4	6	0	0	0	0	10	0.0
L	29	Todd Fedoruk	PHI	1	0	0	0	0	0	0	0	0	0	2	0.0
R	15	Joe Sacco	PHI	4	0	0	0	–2	0	0	0	0	0	4	0.0
C	39	Marty Murray	PHI	4	0	0	0	–2	4	0	0	0	0	5	0.0

Captains' History

Lou Angotti, 1967-68; Ed Van Impe, 1968-69 to 1971-72; Ed Van Impe and Bobby Clarke, 1972-73; Bobby Clarke, 1973-74 to 1978-79; Mel Bridgman, 1979-80, 1980-81; Bill Barber, 1981-82; Bill Barber and Bobby Clarke, 1982-83; Bobby Clarke, 1983-84; Dave Poulin, 1984-85 to 1988-89; Dave Poulin and Ron Sutter, 1989-90; Ron Sutter, 1990-91; Rick Tocchet, 1991-92; no captain, 1992-93; Kevin Dineen, 1993-94; Eric Lindros, 1994-95 to 1998-99; Eric Lindros and Eric Desjardins, 1999-2000; Eric Desjardins, 2000-01; Eric Desjardins and Keith Primeau, 2001-02; Keith Primeau, 2002-03 to date.

Club Records

Team

(Figures in brackets for season records are games played; records for fewest points, wins, ties, losses, goals, goals against are for 70 or more games)

Record		
Most Points	**118**	1975-76 (80)
Most Wins	**53**	1984-85 (80), 1985-86 (80)
Most Ties	***24**	1969-70 (76)
Most Losses	**39**	1989-90 (80), 1993-94 (84)
Most Goals	**350**	1983-84 (80)
Most Goals Against	**319**	1992-93 (84)
Fewest Points	**58**	1969-70 (76)
Fewest Wins	**17**	1969-70 (76)
Fewest Ties	**4**	1985-86 (80)
Fewest Losses	**12**	1979-80 (80)
Fewest Goals	**173**	1967-68 (74)
Fewest Goals Against	**164**	1973-74 (78)
Longest Winning Streak		
Overall	**13**	Oct. 19-Nov. 17/85
Home	***20**	Jan. 4-Apr. 3/76
Away	**8**	Dec. 22/82-Jan. 16/83
Longest Undefeated Streak		
Overall	***35**	Oct. 14/79-Jan. 6/80 (25 wins, 10 ties)
Home	**26**	Oct. 11/79-Feb. 3/80 (19 wins, 7 ties)
Away	**16**	Oct. 20/79-Jan. 6/80 (11 wins, 5 ties)
Longest Losing Streak		
Overall	**6**	Mar. 25-Apr. 4/70, Dec. 5-17/92, Jan. 25-Feb. 5/94
Home	**5**	Jan. 30-Feb. 15/69, Dec. 19/89-Jan. 23/90
Away	**8**	Oct. 25-Nov. 26/72, Mar. 3-29/88
Longest Winless Streak		
Overall	**12**	Feb. 24-Mar. 16/99 (8 losses, 4 ties)
Home	**8**	Dec. 19/68-Jan. 18/69 (4 losses, 4 ties), Nov. 17-Dec. 14/91 (4 losses, 4 ties)
Away	**19**	Oct. 23/71-Jan. 27/72 (15 losses, 4 ties)
Most Shutouts, Season	**13**	1974-75 (80)
Most PIM, Season	**2,621**	1980-81 (80)
Most Goals, Game	**13**	Mar. 22/84 (Pit. 4 at Phi. 13), Oct. 18/84 (Van. 2 at Phi. 13)

Individual

Record		
Most Seasons	**15**	Bobby Clarke
Most Games	**1,144**	Bobby Clarke
Most Goals, Career	**420**	Bill Barber
Most Assists, Career	**852**	Bobby Clarke
Most Points, Career	**1,210**	Bobby Clarke (358G, 852A)
Most PIM, Career	**1,817**	Rick Tocchet
Most Shutouts, Career	**50**	Bernie Parent
Longest Consecutive Game Streak	**484**	Rod Brind'Amour (Feb. 24/93-Apr. 18/99)
Most Goals, Season	**61**	Reggie Leach (1975-76)
Most Assists, Season	**89**	Bobby Clarke (1974-75, 1975-76)
Most Points, Season	**123**	Mark Recchi (1992-93; 53G, 70A)
Most PIM, Season	***472**	Dave Schultz (1974-75)
Most Points, Defenseman, Season	**82**	Mark Howe (1985-86; 24G, 58A)
Most Points, Center, Season	**119**	Bobby Clarke (1975-76; 30G, 89A)
Most Points, Right Wing, Season	**123**	Mark Recchi (1992-93; 53G, 70A)
Most Points, Left Wing, Season	**112**	Bill Barber (1975-76; 50G, 62A)
Most Points, Rookie, Season	**82**	Mikael Renberg (1993-94; 38G, 44A)
Most Shutouts, Season	**12**	Bernie Parent (1973-74, 1974-75)
Most Goals, Game	**4**	Sixteen times
Most Assists, Game	**6**	Eric Lindros (Feb. 26/97)
Most Points, Game	**8**	Tom Bladon (Dec. 11/77; 4G, 4A)

* NHL Record.

Retired Numbers

1	Bernie Parent	1967-1971, 1973-1979
4	Barry Ashbee	1970-1974
7	Bill Barber	1972-1985
16	Bobby Clarke	1969-1984

All-time Record vs. Other Clubs

Regular Season

	At Home								On Road								Total							
	GP	W	L	T	OL	GF	GA	PTS	GP	W	L	T	OL	GF	GA	PTS	GP	W	L	T	OL	GF	GA	PTS
Anaheim	8	3	2	3	0	22	17	9	8	3	3	2	0	25	26	8	16	6	5	5	0	47	43	17
Atlanta	8	5	1	2	0	37	24	12	8	6	1	1	0	28	19	13	16	11	2	3	0	65	43	25
Boston	71	31	29	10	1	235	205	73	74	19	44	10	1	208	279	49	145	50	73	20	2	443	484	122
Buffalo	65	38	15	12	0	224	161	88	61	23	31	7	0	173	202	53	126	61	46	19	0	397	363	141
Calgary	50	33	14	3	0	197	134	69	52	18	25	9	0	172	208	45	102	51	39	12	0	369	342	114
Carolina	41	28	9	4	0	154	101	60	42	21	13	8	0	152	136	50	83	49	22	12	0	306	237	110
Chicago	61	34	16	11	0	201	161	79	60	15	26	19	0	170	205	49	121	49	42	30	0	371	366	128
Colorado	34	22	9	2	1	122	91	47	34	11	11	12	0	120	121	34	68	33	20	14	1	242	212	81
Columbus	2	1	0	1	0	7	3	3	2	1	0	1	0	6	5	3	4	2	0	2	0	13	8	6
Dallas	66	42	9	15	0	253	148	99	65	23	27	15	0	210	214	61	131	65	36	30	0	463	362	160
Detroit	58	34	13	11	0	230	168	79	58	18	30	10	0	180	206	46	116	52	43	21	0	410	374	125
Edmonton	30	20	8	2	0	128	82	42	28	8	14	6	0	83	98	22	58	28	22	8	0	211	180	64
Florida	23	9	8	6	0	57	55	24	22	17	5	0	0	83	53	34	45	26	13	6	0	140	108	58
Los Angeles	63	40	15	7	1	244	156	88	65	37	20	8	0	223	189	82	128	77	35	15	1	467	345	170
Minnesota	3	2	1	0	0	8	2	4	2	0	1	1	0	3	5	1	5	2	2	1	0	11	7	5
Montreal	71	28	26	16	1	217	211	73	72	24	33	14	1	224	252	63	143	52	59	30	2	441	463	136
Nashville	4	1	1	1	1	12	7	4	4	2	0	2	0	7	4	6	8	3	1	3	1	19	11	10
New Jersey	82	49	22	10	1	316	210	109	80	32	41	7	0	277	276	71	162	81	63	17	1	593	486	180
NY Islanders	92	53	26	11	2	333	262	119	95	32	48	14	1	279	348	79	187	85	74	25	3	612	610	198
NY Rangers	106	54	38	14	0	345	292	122	107	37	46	23	1	313	349	98	213	91	84	37	1	658	641	220
Ottawa	21	12	7	2	0	67	57	26	22	10	7	5	0	70	60	25	43	22	14	7	0	137	117	51
Phoenix	30	22	8	0	0	131	81	44	30	15	13	2	0	101	95	32	60	37	21	2	0	232	176	76
Pittsburgh	103	80	16	7	0	437	250	167	103	37	46	20	0	337	366	94	206	117	62	27	0	774	616	261
St. Louis	67	45	12	10	0	264	153	100	67	34	26	7	0	212	192	75	134	79	38	17	0	476	345	175
San Jose	10	6	2	2	0	34	22	14	11	7	3	1	0	31	22	15	21	13	5	3	0	65	44	29
Tampa Bay	23	14	2	7	0	74	39	35	24	16	7	1	0	75	60	33	47	30	9	8	0	149	99	68
Toronto	65	42	15	8	0	248	150	92	65	28	23	14	0	214	209	70	130	70	38	22	0	462	359	162
Vancouver	53	36	16	1	0	230	156	73	51	29	10	12	0	203	144	70	104	65	26	13	0	433	300	143
Washington	81	51	24	6	0	303	216	108	78	33	31	13	1	254	258	80	159	84	55	19	1	557	474	188
Defunct Clubs	34	24	4	6	0	137	67	54	35	13	14	8	0	102	89	34	69	37	18	14	0	239	156	88
Totals	**1425**	**859**	**368**	**190**	**8**	**5267**	**3681**	**1916**	**1425**	**569**	**599**	**252**	**5**	**4535**	**4690**	**1395**	**2850**	**1428**	**967**	**442**	**13**	**9802**	**8371**	**3311**

Playoffs

	Series	W	L	GP	W	L	T	GF	GA	Last Mtg.	Rnd.	Result
Boston	4	2	2	20	9	11	0	57	60	1978	SF	L 1-4
Buffalo	7	5	2	37	23	14	0	110	96	2001	CQF	L 2-4
Calgary	2	1	1	11	7	4	0	43	28	1981	QF	L 3-4
Chicago	1	0	1	4	0	4	0	8	20	1971	QF	L 0-4
Colorado	2	2	0	11	7	4	0	39	29	1985	CF	W 4-2
Dallas	2	2	0	11	8	3	0	41	26	1980	SF	W 4-1
Detroit	1	0	1	4	0	4	0	6	16	1997	F	L 0-4
Edmonton	3	1	2	15	7	8	0	44	49	1987	F	L 3-4
Florida	1	0	1	6	2	4	0	11	15	1996	CSF	L 2-4
Montreal	4	1	3	21	7	14	0	52	72	1989	CF	L 2-4
New Jersey	3	1	2	15	7	8	0	35	41	2000	CF	L 3-4
NY Islanders	4	3	1	25	14	11	0	83	69	1987	DF	W 4-3
NY Rangers	10	6	4	47	27	20	0	157	153	1997	CF	W 4-1
Ottawa	2	0	2	11	3	8	0	12	28	2003	CSF	L 2-4
Pittsburgh	3	3	0	18	12	6	0	66	51	2000	CSF	W 4-2
St. Louis	2	0	2	11	3	8	0	20	34	1969	QF	L 0-4
Tampa Bay	1	1	0	6	4	2	0	26	13	1996	CQF	W 4-2
Toronto	5	4	1	30	18	12	0	102	72	2003	CQF	W 4-3
Vancouver	1	1	0	3	2	1	0	15	9	1979	PRE	W 2-1
Washington	3	1	2	16	7	9	0	55	65	1989	DSF	W 4-2
Totals	**61**	**34**	**27**	**322**	**167**	**155**	**0**	**982**	**946**			

Calgary totals include Atlanta Flames, 1972-73 to 1979-80.
Colorado totals include Quebec, 1979-80 to 1994-95.
New Jersey totals include Kansas City, 1974-75 to 1975-76, and Colorado Rockies, 1976-77 to 1981-82.
Phoenix totals include Winnipeg, 1979-80 to 1995-96.
Carolina totals include Hartford, 1979-80 to 1996-97.
Dallas totals include Minnesota North Stars, 1967-68 to 1992-93.

Playoff Results 2003-1999

Year	Round	Opponent	Result	GF	GA
2003	CSF	Ottawa	L 2-4	10	17
	CQF	Toronto	W 4-3	24	16
2002	CQF	Ottawa	L 1-4	2	11
2001	CQF	Buffalo	L 2-4	13	21
2000	CF	New Jersey	L 3-4	15	18
	CSF	Pittsburgh	W 4-2	15	14
	CQF	Buffalo	W 4-1	14	8
1999	CQF	Toronto	L 2-4	11	9

Abbreviations: Round: F – Final; **CF** – conference final; **CSF** – conference semi-final; **CQF** – conference quarter-final; **DF** – division final; **DSF** – division semi-final; **SF** – semi-final; **QF** – quarter-final; **PRE** – preliminary round.

2002-03 Results

Month	Day	Opponent	Score
Oct.	10	at Edmonton	2-2
	12	at Calgary	5-4
	15	at Montreal	6-2
	17	NY Islanders	3-3
	19	Washington	3-1
	22	at Buffalo	1-2
	24	Montreal	6-2
	26	at NY Islanders	6-2
	29	Ottawa	2-1
	31	Phoenix	6-2
Nov.	2	Washington	2-1
	5	at Carolina	2-1*
	7	New Jersey	0-1
	9	at Washington	1-4
	13	Florida	1-1
	15	at Carolina	1-1
	16	Boston	2-2
	19	at Tampa Bay	3-2
	21	San Jose	2-2
	23	at Toronto	0-6
	27	at Pittsburgh	2-7
	29	Toronto	0-3
	30	at Montreal	2-1*
Dec.	2	New Jersey	0-1*
	5	NY Rangers	3-2*
	7	St. Louis	1-3
	10	at Florida	5-2
	12	Toronto	2-1
	14	Buffalo	2-0
	17	Dallas	2-2
	18	at Atlanta	3-1
	21	Ottawa	1-3
	23	at Ottawa	2-2
	27	at Colorado	2-1*
	28	at Phoenix	0-4
	30	at San Jose	1-2
Jan.	2	at Los Angeles	4-1
	3	at Anaheim	1-0
	5	at Atlanta	5-4
	7	Buffalo	3-2
	9	at NY Islanders	4-0
	11	Detroit	3-2
	13	Atlanta	4-7
	16	Montreal	4-1
	18	Tampa Bay	3-2
	19	at NY Rangers	4-2
	21	at Toronto	3-1
	24	NY Islanders	1-3
	25	at Boston	0-1*
	28	Tampa Bay	0-3
	30	at New Jersey	1-5
Feb.	4	at NY Islanders	2-1
	6	at Ottawa	2-2
	8	NY Rangers	2-1
	10	Minnesota	0-1
	12	at Minnesota	0-2
	13	at St. Louis	4-3*
	15	Carolina	2-2
	18	New Jersey	2-2
	20	Los Angeles	5-0
	22	Florida	2-4
	25	at Chicago	2-0
	27	Chicago	5-2
Mar.	1	at Boston	3-2*
	4	Vancouver	3-0
	7	at NY Rangers	1-5
	8	Colorado	1-2*
	10	at Washington	1-2*
	13	Carolina	5-3
	15	at Pittsburgh	4-1
	17	at New Jersey	4-2
	18	at Buffalo	2-5
	20	Pittsburgh	4-2
	22	NY Rangers	1-2
	24	Atlanta	6-2
	25	at Nashville	1-1
	27	Boston	2-2
	29	Pittsburgh	3-0
	31	at Pittsburgh	6-1
Apr.	1	Columbus	4-0
	4	at Tampa Bay	4-1
	6	at Florida	6-2

* – Overtime

Entry Draft
Selections 2003-1989

2003 Pick		**1999** Pick		**1995** Pick		**1991** Pick	
11	Jeff Carter	22	Maxime Ouellet	22	Brian Boucher	6	Peter Forsberg
24	Mike Richards	119	Jeff Feniak	48	Shane Kenny	50	Yanick Dupre
69	Colin Fraser	160	Konstantin Rudenko	100	Radovan Somik	86	Aris Brimanis
81	Stefan Ruzicka	200	Pavel Kasparik	132	Dmitri Tertyshny	94	Yanick Degrace
85	Alexandre Picard	208	Vaclav Pletka	135	Jamie Sokolsky	116	Clayton Norris
87	Ryan Potulny	224	David Nystrom	152	Martin Spanhel	122	Dmitry Yushkevich
95	Rick Kozak			178	Martin Streit	138	Andrei Lomakin
108	Kevin Romy	**1998** Pick		204	Ruslan Shafikov	182	James Bode
140	David Tremblay	22	Simon Gagne	230	Jeff Lank	204	Josh Bartell
191	Rejean Beauchemin	42	Jason Beckett			226	Neil Little
193	Ville Hostikka	51	Ian Forbes	**1994** Pick		248	John Porco
		109	Jean-Philippe Morin	62	Artem Anisimov		
2002 Pick		124	Francis Belanger	88	Adam Magarrell	**1990** Pick	
4	Joni Pitkanen	139	Garrett Prosofsky	101	Sebastien Vallee	4	Mike Ricci
105	Rosario Ruggeri	168	Antero Niittymaki	140	Alex Selivanov	25	Chris Simon
126	Konstantin Baranov	175	Cam Ondrik	166	Colin Forbes	40	Mikael Renberg
161	Dov Grumet-Morris	195	Tomas Divisek	192	Derek Diener	42	Terran Sandwith
192	Nikita Korovkin	222	Lubomir Pistek	202	Raymond Giroux	44	Kimbi Daniels
193	Joey Mormina	243	Petr Hubacek	218	Johan Hedberg	46	Bill Armstrong
201	Mathieu Brunelle	253	Bruno St. Jacques	244	Andre Payette	47	Chris Therien
		258	Sergei Skrobot	270	Jan Lipiansky	52	Al Kinisky
2001 Pick						88	Dan Kordic
27	Jeff Woywitka	**1997** Pick		**1993** Pick		109	Viacheslav Butsayev
95	Patrick Sharp	30	Jean-Marc Pelletier	36	Janne Niinimaa	151	Patrik Englund
146	Jussi Timonen	50	Pat Kavanagh	71	Vaclav Prospal	172	Toni Porkka
150	Bernd Bruckler	62	Kris Mallette	77	Milos Holan	193	Greg Hanson
158	Roman Malek	103	Mikhail Chernov	114	Vladimir Krechin	214	Tommy Soderstrom
172	Dennis Seidenberg	158	Jordon Flodell	140	Mike Crowley	235	William Lund
177	Andrei Razin	164	Todd Fedoruk	166	Aaron Israel		
208	Thierry Douville	214	Marko Kauppinen	192	Paul Healey	**1989** Pick	
225	David Printz	240	Par Styf	218	Tripp Tracy	33	Greg Johnson
				226	E.J. Bradley	34	Patrik Juhlin
2000 Pick		**1996** Pick		244	Jeff Staples	72	Reid Simpson
28	Justin Williams	15	Dainius Zubrus	270	Ken Hemenway	117	Niklas Eriksson
94	Alexander Drozdetsky	64	Chester Gallant			138	John Callahan Jr.
171	Roman Cechmanek	124	Per-Ragna Bergqvist	**1992** Pick		159	Sverre Sears
195	Colin Shields	133	Jesse Boulerice	7	Ryan Sittler	180	Glen Wisser
210	John Eichelberger	187	Roman Malov	15	Jason Bowen	201	Al Kummu
227	Guillaume Lefebvre	213	Jeff Milleker	31	Denis Metlyuk	222	Matt Brait
259	Regan Kelly			103	Vladislav Buljin	243	James Pollio
287	Milan Kopecky			127	Roman Zolotov		
				151	Kirk Daubenspeck		
				175	Claude Jr. Jutras		
				199	Jonas Hakansson		
				223	Chris Herperger		
				247	Patrice Paquin		

General Managers' History

Bud Poile, 1967-68, 1968-69; Bud Poile and Keith Allen, 1969-70; Keith Allen, 1970-71 to 1982-83; Bob McCammon, 1983-84; Bob Clarke, 1984-85 to 1989-90; Russ Farwell, 1990-91 to 1993-94; Bob Clarke, 1994-95 to date.

President and General Manager

CLARKE, BOB
President/General Manager, Philadelphia Flyers.
Born in Flin Flon, Man., August 13, 1949.

Bob Clarke was named president and general manager of the Philadelphia Flyers on June 15, 1994. Clarke's appointment marked the second time he has served as the Flyers' general manager. The Flin Flon native was the Flyers' vice president and general manager from 1984 to 1990. During his 15 years as the team's general manager, the Flyers have won six divisional titles, three conference championships, reached the Stanley Cup semifinals six times and the finals three times.

Prior to re-joining the Flyers' family in 1994, Clarke served as vice president and general manager of the Florida Panthers. In 1993-94, their first season in the NHL, the Panthers established NHL records for wins (33) and points (83) by an expansion franchise. Clarke also served as the vice president and general manager of the Minnesota North Stars from 1990 to 1992, guiding the team to the Stanley Cup Finals in 1991.

As a player, the former Philadelphia captain led his club to Stanley Cup championships in 1974 and 1975 and captured numerous individual awards, including the Hart Trophy as the league's most valuable player in 1973, 1975 and 1976. The four-time All-Star also received the Bill Masterton Memorial Trophy (perseverance and dedication) in 1972 and the Frank J. Selke Trophy (top defensive forward) in 1983. He appeared in eight All-Star Games and was elected to the Hockey Hall of Fame in 1987. He was awarded the Lester Patrick Trophy in 1979-80 in recognition of his contribution to hockey in the United States. Clarke appeared in 1,144 regular season games, recording 358 goals and 852 assists for 1,210 points. He also added 119 points in 136 playoff games.

Club Directory

Wachovia Center

Philadelphia Flyers
Wachovia Center
3601 South Broad Street
Philadelphia, PA 19148-5290
Phone **215/465-4500**
PR FAX 215/389-9403
www.philadelphiaflyers.com
Capacity: 19,523

Executive Management
Chairman	Ed Snider
Limited Partners	Pat Croce, Jay Snider, Sylvan and Fran Tobin
President	Ron Ryan
General Manager	Bob Clarke
Executive Vice President	Keith Allen
Governor	Ed Snider
Alternate Governors	Bob Clarke, Ron Ryan, Phil Weinberg
Executive Assistants	Lisa D'Aprile, Gina Pelle
President of Comcast-Spectacor Marketing	Dave Coskey
Office Manager	Patty Butler
Senior Vice President, Sales	Joe Croce
Administrative Assistant	Kate Dreyer
Vice President, Marketing and Communications	Shawn Tilger

Hockey Club Personnel
Assistant General Manager	Paul Holmgren
Head Coach	Ken Hitchcock
Assistant Coaches	Wayne Fleming, Craig Hartsburg, Terry Murray
Goaltending Coach	Rejean Lemelin
Director of Pro Hockey Personnel	Ron Hextall
Chief Scout	Dennis Patterson
Scouting Staff	Serge Boudreault, John Chapman, Inge Hammarstrom, Simon Nolet, Chris Pryor, Vaclav Slansky, Evgeny Zimin
Pro Scouts	Al Hill, Dean Lombardi
Assistant to the President	Barry Hanrahan
Video Coordinator	Adam Patterson
Scouting Information Coordinator	Bryan Hardenbergh
Executive Assistant	Dianna Taylor

Medical/Training Staff
Team Physicians	Peter DeLuca, M.D.; Gary Dorshimer, M.D.; Jeff Hartzell, M.D.; Guy Lanzi, D.M.D.
Athletic Trainer	John Worley
Athletic Trainer/Strength and Conditioning Coach	Jim McCrossin
Massage Therapist	Tom D'Ancona
Head Equipment Manager	Jim Evers
Equipment Managers	Anthony Oratorio, Harry Bricker, Luke Clarke
Training Center Maintenance	Mike Craytor

Communications Department
Senior Director of Communications	Zack Hill
Assistant Director of Communications	Jill Lipson
Director of Media Services and Publications	Joe Klueg
Manager of Interactive Media	Kevin Kurz
Communications Assistant	Katie Hammer
Archives and Special Projects	Kerrianne Brady, Katie Lynch

Community Relations Department
Executive Director of Fan Development	Eric Turner
Fan Development Coordinators	Rob Baer, Jason Brinn, Bill Scheier

Customer Service Department
Customer Service Manager	Cindy Stutman
Customer Service Account Managers	Missy Keeler, Maureen McGuckin
Director of Fan Relations	Joe Kadlec

Marketing Department
Advertising and Promotions Manager	Linda Held
Assistants to the VP, Marketing	Scott Bohrer, Debbie Brown

Ticket Sales and Operations
Vice President of Ticket Sales	Jim Van Stone
Vice President, Ticket Operations	Cecilia Baker
Director of Ticket Sales	Tara Ritting
Ticket Office Administration	Joan Kadlec

Finance Department
Director of Finance	Dave Jablonski
Controller	Lisa Cataldo
Payroll Accountant	Susann Schaffer
Accounts Payable	Marilyn Trout

Broadcast Department
Executive Producer/Director of Broadcasting	Bryan Cooper
Associate Producer	Doug Ryan
TV Play-by-Play, Analyst, Color Commentary	Jim Jackson
TV Color Commentary	Steve Coates
TV Analyst	Gary Dornhoefer
Radio Play-by-Play	Tim Saunders
Radio Color Analyst	Brian Propp
TV Rightsholders	Comcast SportsNet, UPN-57 WPSG-TV
Radio Rightsholder	SportsRadio 610 WIP (610 AM)

Advertising Sales Department
Vice President of Advertising Sales	Brian Monihan
National Sales Manager	Lee Stein
Senior Account Executive	Joe Watson
Account Executives	Stephanie Bennett, Dave Gambrill, Mike Garrity, Joe Heyer, Andrew Humphreys, Steve Jeffries, Traci Kloss, Bo Koelle, Ray Lyons, Jon Roche, Rich Rodowicz
Sponsorship Manager	Maura Hood
Manager of Television Services	Shannan Archer
Director of Client Services	Thea Crum-Vogel

Premium Seating Department
Vice President of Premium Seating - Sales & Services	Rick Campbell
Manager of Finance and Inventory	Amanda Keen
Sales Executives	Jimmy Dunk, Chris Genther, Anthony Monaco Pete Seelaus, Dennis Shea
Administrative Assistant	Tarah Walmsley

Comcast-Spectacor Foundation/Flyers Wives Fight for Lives
Executive Director	Fran Tobin
Director	Rita Johanson
Event Coordinators	Robyn McCrossin, Roseanne Uhl

Phoenix Coyotes

2002-03 Results: 31W-35L-11T-5OTL 78PTS.
Fourth, Pacific Division

2003-04 Schedule

Oct.	Fri.	10	St. Louis
	Sun.	12	at Anaheim*
	Wed.	15	at Florida
	Thu.	16	at Tampa Bay
	Sat.	18	Philadelphia
	Thu.	23	Toronto
	Sat.	25	at San Jose
	Sun.	26	at Vancouver
	Tue.	28	Chicago
	Fri.	31	Vancouver
Nov.	Sat.	1	at Los Angeles
	Thu.	6	at Colorado
	Sat.	8	Anaheim
	Sun.	9	at Anaheim*
	Thu.	13	Colorado
	Fri.	14	at Dallas
	Sun.	16	at Columbus*
	Wed.	19	St. Louis
	Fri.	21	San Jose
	Sun.	23	at Atlanta*
	Mon.	24	at Dallas
	Thu.	27	Los Angeles
	Sun.	30	at Boston
Dec.	Tue.	2	at New Jersey
	Thu.	4	at Buffalo
	Fri.	5	at Philadelphia
	Sun.	7	at Chicago
	Wed.	10	Dallas
	Fri.	12	Edmonton
	Mon.	15	Minnesota
	Thu.	18	at Los Angeles
	Sat.	20	at St. Louis
	Mon.	22	at Nashville
	Tue.	23	at Columbus
	Sat.	27	Nashville
	Mon.	29	NY Rangers
	Wed.	31	Los Angeles
Jan.	Fri.	2	at Dallas
	Sun.	4	at Carolina*
	Wed.	7	at Washington
	Fri.	9	at Minnesota

	Sun.	11	Atlanta*
	Tue.	13	Vancouver
	Thu.	15	at Nashville
	Fri.	16	at Detroit
	Wed.	21	San Jose
	Thu.	22	at San Jose
	Sat.	24	Detroit
	Tue.	27	Calgary
	Thu.	29	Ottawa
	Sat.	31	Dallas
Feb.	Mon.	2	Columbus
	Wed.	4	Florida
	Thu.	5	at San Jose
	Wed.	11	at Anaheim
	Fri.	13	NY Islanders
	Sat.	14	Dallas
	Mon.	16	at St. Louis*
	Wed.	18	at Detroit
	Fri.	20	Columbus
	Sat.	21	Nashville
	Mon.	23	Anaheim
	Wed.	25	Pittsburgh
	Fri.	27	Edmonton
	Sun.	29	at Calgary
Mar.	Tue.	2	at Edmonton
	Fri.	5	Montreal
	Sun.	7	Minnesota*
	Tue.	9	at Los Angeles
	Wed.	10	Los Angeles
	Fri.	12	Colorado
	Sun.	14	at Colorado*
	Tue.	16	Anaheim
	Thu.	18	Detroit
	Sun.	21	at Chicago*
	Mon.	22	at Minnesota
	Wed.	24	Calgary
	Fri.	26	San Jose
	Sun.	28	at Edmonton*
	Mon.	29	at Vancouver
	Wed.	31	at Calgary
Apr.	Sat.	3	Chicago*

* Denotes afternoon game.

Year-by-Year Record

		Home				Road				Overall							
Season	GP	W	L	T	OL	W	L	T	OL	W	L	T	OL	GF	GA	Pts.	Finished	Playoff Result
2002-03	82	17	16	6	2	14	19	5	3	31	35	11	5	204	230	78	4th, Pacific Div.	Out of Playoffs
2001-02	82	27	8	3	3	13	19	6	3	40	27	9	6	228	210	95	2nd, Pacific Div.	Lost Conf. Quarter-Final
2000-01	82	21	11	7	2	14	16	10	1	35	27	17	3	214	212	90	4th, Pacific Div.	Out of Playoffs
1999-2000	82	22	16	2	1	17	15	6	3	39	31	8	4	232	228	90	3rd, Pacific Div.	Lost Conf. Quarter-Final
1998-99	82	23	13	5	...	16	18	7	...	39	31	12	...	205	197	90	2nd, Pacific Div.	Lost Conf. Quarter-Final
1997-98	82	19	16	6	...	16	19	6	...	35	35	12	...	224	227	82	4th, Central Div.	Lost Conf. Quarter-Final
1996-97	82	15	19	7	...	23	18	0	...	38	37	7	...	240	243	83	3rd, Central Div.	Lost Conf. Quarter-Final
1995-96*	82	22	16	3	...	14	24	3	...	36	40	6	...	275	291	78	5th, Central Div.	Lost Conf. Quarter-Final
1994-95*	48	10	10	4	...	6	15	3	...	16	25	7	...	157	177	39	6th, Central Div.	Out of Playoffs
1993-94*	84	15	23	4	...	9	28	5	...	24	51	9	...	245	344	57	6th, Central Div.	Out of Playoffs
1992-93*	84	23	16	3	...	17	21	4	...	40	37	7	...	322	320	87	4th, Smythe Div.	Lost Div. Semi-Final
1991-92*	80	20	14	6	...	13	18	9	...	33	32	15	...	251	244	81	4th, Smythe Div.	Lost Div. Semi-Final
1990-91*	80	17	18	5	...	9	25	6	...	26	43	11	...	260	288	63	5th, Smythe Div.	Out of Playoffs
1989-90*	80	22	13	5	...	15	19	6	...	37	32	11	...	298	290	85	3rd, Smythe Div.	Lost Div. Semi-Final
1988-89*	80	17	18	5	...	9	24	7	...	26	42	12	...	300	355	64	5th, Smythe Div.	Out of Playoffs
1987-88*	80	20	14	6	...	13	22	5	...	33	36	11	...	292	310	77	3rd, Smythe Div.	Lost Div. Semi-Final
1986-87*	80	25	12	3	...	15	20	5	...	40	32	8	...	279	271	88	3rd, Smythe Div.	Lost Div. Final
1985-86*	80	18	19	3	...	8	28	4	...	26	47	7	...	295	372	59	3rd, Smythe Div.	Lost Div. Semi-Final
1984-85*	80	21	13	6	...	22	14	4	...	43	27	10	...	358	332	96	2nd, Smythe Div.	Lost Div. Final
1983-84*	80	17	15	8	...	14	23	3	...	31	38	11	...	340	374	73	4th, Smythe Div.	Lost Div. Semi-Final
1982-83*	80	22	16	2	...	11	23	6	...	33	39	8	...	311	333	74	4th, Smythe Div.	Lost Div. Semi-Final
1981-82*	80	18	13	9	...	15	20	5	...	33	33	14	...	319	332	80	2nd, Norris Div.	Lost Div. Semi-Final
1980-81*	80	7	25	8	...	2	32	6	...	9	57	14	...	246	400	32	6th, Smythe Div.	Out of Playoffs
1979-80*	80	13	19	8	...	7	30	3	...	20	49	11	...	214	314	51	5th, Smythe Div.	Out of Playoffs

* Winnipeg Jets

Healthy for a full season in 2002-03, Mike Johnson bounced back with 23 goals and 40 assists to lead the Coyotes in scoring with 63 points. All three numbers were career highs.

Franchise date: June 22, 1979
Transferred from Winnipeg to Phoenix, July 1, 1996

PACIFIC DIVISION

25th NHL Season

2003-04 Player Personnel

FORWARDS	HT	WT	S	Place of Birth	Date	2002-03 Club
BANHAM, Frank	6-0	190	R	Calahoo, Alta.	4/14/75	Jokerit-Phoenix-Springfield
CLEARY, Daniel	6-0	203	L	Carbonear, Nfld.	12/18/78	Edmonton
DOAN, Shane	6-2	216	R	Halkirk, Alta.	10/10/76	Phoenix
FERRARO, Chris	5-9	175	R	Port Jefferson, NY	1/24/73	Portland (AHL)
FERRARO, Peter	5-10	180	R	Port Jefferson, NY	1/24/73	Portland (AHL)
GRATTON, Chris	6-4	225	L	Brantford, Ont.	7/5/75	Buffalo-Phoenix
HRDINA, Jan	6-0	206	R	Hradec Kralove, Czech.	2/5/76	Pittsburgh-Phoenix
JASPERS, Jason	5-11	197	L	Thunder Bay, Ont.	4/8/81	Phoenix-Springfield
JOHNSON, Mike	6-2	201	R	Scarborough, Ont.	10/3/74	Phoenix
KOLANOS, Krystofer	6-3	201	R	Calgary, Alta.	7/27/81	Phoenix
LANGKOW, Daymond	5-11	192	L	Edmonton, Alta.	9/27/76	Phoenix
LUKES, Frantisek	5-9	171	R	Kadan, Czech.	9/25/82	St. Michael's
McLACHLAN, Darren	6-1	230	L	Penticton, B.C.	2/16/83	Seattle
McLEOD, Kiel	6-6	229	R	Ft. Saskatchewan, Alta.	12/30/82	Kelowna
NAGY, Ladislav	5-11	186	L	Saca, Czech.	6/1/79	Kosice-Phoenix
NASH, Tyson	5-11	194	L	Edmonton, Alta.	3/11/75	St. Louis
NAZAROV, Andrei	6-5	241	L	Chelyabinsk, USSR	5/22/74	Phoenix
PODLESAK, Martin	6-6	218	L	Melnik, Czech.	9/26/82	Springfield
RADIVOJEVIC, Branko	6-1	209	R	Piestany, Czech.	11/24/80	Phoenix
SAVAGE, Brian	6-1	200	L	Sudbury, Ont.	2/24/71	Phoenix
SILLINGER, Mike	5-11	196	R	Regina, Sask.	6/29/71	Columbus
SJOSTROM, Fredrik	6-1	214	L	Fargelanda, Sweden	5/6/83	Calgary (WHL)-Springfield
STUTZEL, Mike	6-2	205	L	Victoria, B.C.	2/28/79	Northern Michigan
TAFFE, Jeff	6-3	195	L	Hastings, MN	2/19/81	Phoenix-Springfield
WESTRUM, Erik	6-0	204	L	Minneapolis, MN	7/26/79	Springfield
WILSON, Landon	6-3	226	R	St. Louis, MO	3/13/75	Phoenix
DEFENSEMEN						
BEZINA, Goran	6-2	215	L	Split, Yugoslavia	3/21/80	Springfield
FERENCE, Brad	6-3	210	R	Calgary, Alta.	4/2/79	Florida-Phoenix
HELMER, Bryan	6-1	200	R	Sault Ste. Marie, Ont.	7/15/72	Vancouver-Manitoba
HULSE, Cale	6-3	220	R	Edmonton, Alta.	11/10/73	Nashville
KNYAZEV, Igor	6-0	185	L	Elektrostal, USSR	1/27/83	Lowell
LEROUX, Francois	6-6	247	L	Ste-Adele, Que.	4/18/70	Wilkes-Barre-Springfield
MARA, Paul	6-4	217	L	Ridgewood, NJ	9/7/79	Phoenix
SCHUTTE, Michael	6-2	199	L	Burlington, Ont.	7/28/79	Springfield-Lowell
SIMPSON, Todd	6-3	218	L	North Vancouver, B.C.	5/28/73	Phoenix
SPILLER, Matthew	6-5	225	L	Daysland, Alta.	2/7/83	Seattle
SUCHY, Radoslav	6-2	204	L	Kezmarok, Czech.	4/7/76	Phoenix
TANABE, David	6-1	195	R	White Bear Lake, MN	7/19/80	Carolina
TSELIOS, Nikos	6-5	210	L	Oak Park, IL	1/20/79	Lowell-Springfield
VAANANEN, Ossi	6-4	215	L	Vantaa, Finland	8/18/80	Phoenix
GOALTENDERS	HT	WT	C	Place of Birth	Date	2002-03 Club
BIERK, Zac	6-4	205	L	Peterborough, Ont.	9/17/76	Phoenix-Springfield
BOUCHER, Brian	6-2	190	L	Woonsocket, RI	1/2/77	Phoenix
BURKE, Sean	6-4	211	L	Windsor, Ont.	1/29/67	Phoenix
LENEVEU, David	6-1	170	L	Fernie, B.C.	5/23/83	Cornell
PELLETIER, Jean-Marc	6-3	200	L	Atlanta, GA	3/4/78	Lowell-Phoenix-Springfield

2002-03 Scoring

* - rookie

Regular Season

Pos	#	Player	Team	GP	G	A	Pts	+/-	PIM	PP	SH	GW	GT	S	%
R	12	Mike Johnson	PHX	82	23	40	63	9	47	8	0	3	1	178	12.9
C	19	Shane Doan	PHX	82	21	37	58	3	86	7	0	2	0	225	9.3
L	17	Ladislav Nagy	PHX	80	22	35	57	17	92	8	0	6	0	209	10.5
C	11	Daymond Langkow	PHX	82	20	32	52	20	56	4	2	2	0	196	10.2
C	77	Chris Gratton	BUF	66	15	29	44	-5	86	4	0	1	1	187	8.0
			PHX	14	0	1	1	-11	21	0	0	0	0	28	0.0
			TOTAL	80	15	30	45	-16	107	4	0	2	1	215	7.0
C	24	Jan Hrdina	PIT	57	14	25	39	1	34	11	0	4	0	84	16.7
			PHX	4	0	4	4	3	8	0	0	0	0	2	0.0
			TOTAL	61	14	29	43	4	42	11	0	4	0	86	16.3
D	27	Teppo Numminen	PHX	78	6	24	30	0	30	2	0	1	1	108	5.6
R	29 *	Branko Radivojevic	PHX	79	12	15	27	-2	63	4	0	3	1	109	11.0
D	23	Paul Mara	PHX	73	10	15	25	-7	78	1	0	0	0	95	10.5
D	55	Danny Markov	PHX	64	4	16	20	2	36	2	0	0	1	105	3.8
D	7	Deron Quint	PHX	51	7	10	17	-5	20	2	0	0	0	85	8.2
L	49	Brian Savage	PHX	43	6	10	16	-4	22	1	0	1	1	68	8.8
R	28	Landon Wilson	PHX	31	6	8	14	1	26	0	0	3	0	92	6.5
C	16	Kelly Buchberger	PHX	79	3	9	12	0	109	0	1	0	0	32	9.4
L	18	Paul Ranheim	PHI	28	0	4	4	-4	6	0	0	0	0	37	0.0
			PHX	40	3	4	7	-4	10	0	0	0	0	34	8.8
			TOTAL	68	3	8	11	-8	16	0	0	0	0	71	4.2
D	2	Todd Simpson	PHX	66	2	7	9	7	135	0	0	0	0	67	3.0
D	4	Ossi Vaananen	PHX	67	2	7	9	1	82	0	0	0	0	49	4.1
D	45	Brad Ference	FLA	60	2	6	8	2	118	0	0	0	0	41	4.9
			PHX	15	0	1	1	-5	28	0	0	0	0	8	0.0
			TOTAL	75	2	7	9	-3	146	0	0	0	0	49	4.1
D	15	Radoslav Suchy	PHX	77	1	8	9	2	18	1	0	0	0	48	2.1
L	38	Scott Pellerin	DAL	20	1	3	4	-3	8	1	0	0	0	20	5.0
			PHX	23	0	1	1	-5	8	0	0	0	0	17	0.0
			TOTAL	43	1	4	5	-8	16	1	0	0	0	37	2.7
C	14 *	Jeff Taffe	PHX	20	3	1	4	-4	4	1	0	1	0	18	16.7
L	44	Andrei Nazarov	PHX	59	3	0	3	-9	135	2	0	0	0	35	8.6
D	5	Drake Berehowsky	PHX	7	1	2	3	0	27	0	0	0	0	8	12.5
C	21 *	Jason Jaspers	PHX	2	0	0	0	-1	0	0	0	0	0	8	0.0
C	36	Krystofer Kolanos	PHX	2	0	0	0	-1	0	0	0	0	0	8	0.0
D	52 *	Martin Grenier	PHX	3	0	0	0	-1	0	0	0	0	0	0	0.0
R	34	Frank Banham	PHX	5	0	0	0	-1	2	0	0	0	0	5	0.0

Goaltending

No.	Goaltender	GPI	Mins	Avg	W	L	T	EN	SO	GA	SA	S%	G	A	PIM
1	Sean Burke	22	1248	2.12	12	6	2	2	4	44	632	.930	0	0	4
35	Zac Bierk	16	884	2.17	4	9	1	3	1	32	471	.932	0	0	2
33	Brian Boucher	45	2544	3.02	15	20	8	4	0	128	1210	.894	0	1	0
40 *	Jean-Marc Pelletier	2	119	3.03	0	2	0	0	0	6	48	.875	0	0	0
30 *	Patrick DesRochers	4	175	3.77	0	3	0	0	0	11	88	.875	0	0	0
	Totals	82	5000	2.76	31	40	11	9	3	230	2458	.906			

Coach

FRANCIS, BOB
Coach, Phoenix Coyotes. Born in North Battleford, Sask., December 5, 1958.

The Phoenix Coyotes named Bob Francis as the team's head coach on June 16, 1999. Francis became the 14th head coach in franchise history and the third since moving to Phoenix in 1996. During the 2001-02 season, he led a rebuilding Coyotes club to an impressive 95-point season and was rewarded with the Jack Adams Award as coach of the year.

Francis joined the Coyotes after two successful seasons as an assistant coach with the Boston Bruins. The son of former NHL coaching great Emile Francis joined the Bruins as an assistant on June 27, 1997. He had previously spent two seasons in the Boston organization as head coach of the Bruins' AHL affiliate in Providence.

Francis began his coaching career with the Calgary Flames organization in the 1986-87 season, first as a player/assistant coach with Calgary's IHL affiliate in Salt Lake City. Francis helped guide the Golden Eagles to the IHL championship, winning the Turner Cup that season and successfully defending its title the following year with Francis serving as a full-time assistant coach. In 1989-90, Francis became the Golden Eagles' head coach and held that position for four seasons. The highlight of his coaching career at Salt Lake City was a 50-win season during the 1990-91 campaign. When Calgary moved their development team to Saint John (AHL) in 1993-94, Francis moved as well and served as their head coach before joining Providence.

Before his move to the coaching ranks, Francis played four years of college hockey at the University of New Hampshire (ECAC). Francis spent most of his professional career at the minor-league level though he did play 14 NHL games with Detroit during the 1982-83 season.

Coaching Record

Season	Team	Games	Regular Season W	L	T	Playoffs Games	W	L
1989-90	Salt Lake (IHL)	82	37	36	9	10	5	5
1990-91	Salt Lake (IHL)	83	50	28	5	4	0	4
1991-92	Salt Lake (IHL)	82	33	40	9	5	1	4
1992-93	Salt Lake (IHL)	82	38	39	5	....	....	....
1993-94	Saint John (AHL)	80	37	33	10	7	3	4
1994-95	Saint John (AHL)	80	27	40	13	5	1	4
1995-96	Providence (AHL)	80	30	40	10	4	1	3
1996-97	Providence (AHL)	80	35	40	5	10	4	6
1999-2000	Phoenix (NHL)	82	39	35	8	5	1	4
2000-01	Phoenix (NHL)	82	35	30	17	....	....	....
2001-02	Phoenix (NHL)	82	40	33	9	5	1	4
2002-03	Phoenix (NHL)	82	31	40	11	....	....	....
	NHL Totals	328	145	138	45	10	2	8

The Phoenix Coyotes will play their first game in the new Glendale Arena vs. the Nashville Predators on December 27, 2003.

Coaching History

Tom McVie and Bill Sutherland, 1979-80; Tom McVie, Bill Sutherland and Mike Smith, 1980-81; Tom Watt, 1981-82, 1982-83; Tom Watt and Barry Long, 1983-84; Barry Long, 1984-85; Barry Long and John Ferguson, 1985-86; Dan Maloney, 1986-87, 1987-88; Dan Maloney and Rick Bowness, 1988-89; Bob Murdoch, 1989-90, 1990-91; John Paddock, 1991-92 to 1993-94; John Paddock and Terry Simpson, 1994-95; Terry Simpson, 1995-96; Don Hay, 1996-97; Jim Schoenfeld, 1997-98, 1998-99; Bob Francis, 1999-2000 to date.

Club Records

Team

(Figures in brackets for season records are games played; records for fewest points, wins, ties, losses, goals, goals against are for 70 or more games)

Record		
Most Points	96	1984-85 (80)
Most Wins	43	1984-85 (80)
Most Ties	17	2000-01 (82)
Most Losses	57	1980-81 (80)
Most Goals	358	1984-85 (80)
Most Goals Against	400	1980-81 (80)
Fewest Points	32	1980-81 (80)
Fewest Wins	9	1980-81 (80)
Fewest Ties	6	1995-96 (82)
Fewest Losses	27	1984-85 (80), 2000-01 (82), 2001-02 (82)
Fewest Goals	204	2002-03 (82)
Fewest Goals Against	197	1998-99 (82)
Longest Winning Streak		
Overall	9	Mar. 8-27/85
Home	9	Dec. 27/92-Jan. 23/93
Away	8	Feb. 25-Apr. 6/85
Longest Undefeated Streak		
Overall	14	Oct. 25-Nov. 28/98 (12 wins, 2 ties)
Home	11	Dec. 23/83-Feb. 5/84 (6 wins, 5 ties), Oct. 15-Dec. 20/98 (10 wins, 1 tie)
Away	9	Feb. 25-Apr. 7/85 (8 wins, 1 tie)
Longest Losing Streak		
Overall	10	Nov. 30-Dec. 20/80, Feb. 6-25/94
Home	5	Oct. 29-Nov. 13/93 Mar. 13-23/00
Away	13	Jan. 26-Apr. 14/94
Longest Winless Streak		
Overall	*30	Oct. 19-Dec. 20/80 (23 losses, 7 ties)
Home	14	Oct. 19-Dec. 14/80 (9 losses, 5 ties)
Away	18	Oct. 10-Dec. 20/80 (16 losses, 2 ties)
Most Shutouts, Season	9	1998-99 (82)
Most PIM, Season	2,278	1987-88 (80)
Most Goals, Game	12	Feb. 25/85 (Wpg. 12 at NYR 5)

Individual

Record		
Most Seasons	15	Teppo Numminen
Most Games	1,098	Teppo Numminen
Most Goals, Career	379	Dale Hawerchuk
Most Assists, Career	553	Thomas Steen
Most Points, Career	929	Dale Hawerchuk (379G, 550A)
Most PIM, Career	1,508	Keith Tkachuk
Most Shutouts, Career	21	Nikolai Khabibulin
Longest Consecutive Games Streak	475	Dale Hawerchuk (Dec. 19/82-Dec. 10/88)
Most Goals, Season	76	Teemu Selanne (1992-93)
Most Assists, Season	79	Phil Housley (1992-93)
Most Points, Season	132	Teemu Selanne (1992-93; 76G, 56A)
Most PIM, Season	347	Tie Domi (1993-94)
Most Points, Defenseman, Season	97	Phil Housley (1992-93; 18G, 79A)
Most Points, Center, Season	130	Dale Hawerchuk (1984-85; 53G, 77A)
Most Points, Right Wing, Season	132	Teemu Selanne (1992-93; 76G, 56A)
Most Points, Left Wing, Season	98	Keith Tkachuk (1995-96; 50G, 48A)
Most Points, Rookie, Season	*132	Teemu Selanne (1992-93; 76G, 56A)
Most Shutouts, Season	8	Nikolai Khabibulin (1998-99)
Most Goals, Game	5	Willy Lindstrom (Mar. 2/82), Alexei Zhamnov (Apr. 1/95)
Most Assists, Game	5	Dale Hawerchuk (Mar. 6/84, Mar. 18/89, Mar. 4/90), Phil Housley (Jan. 18/93), Keith Tkachuk (Feb. 23/01)
Most Points, Game	6	Willy Lindstrom (Mar. 2/82; 5G, 1A), Dale Hawerchuk (Dec. 14/83; 3G, 3A, Mar. 5/88; 2G, 4A, Mar. 18/89; 1G, 5A), Thomas Steen (Oct. 24/84; 2G, 4A), Ed Olczyk (Dec. 21/91; 2G, 4A)

* NHL Record.
Records include Winnipeg Jets, 1979-80 through 1995-96.

Captains' History

Lars-Erik Sjoberg, 1979-80; Morris Lukowich, 1980-81; Dave Christian, 1981-82; Dave Christian and Lucien DeBlois, 1982-83; Lucien DeBlois, 1983-84; Dale Hawerchuk, 1984-85 to 1988-89; Randy Carlyle, Dale Hawerchuk and Thomas Steen (tri-captains), 1989-90; Randy Carlyle and Thomas Steen (co-captains), 1990-91; Troy Murray, 1991-92; Troy Murray and Dean Kennedy, 1992-93; Dean Kennedy and Keith Tkachuk, 1993-94; Keith Tkachuk, 1994-95; Kris King, 1995-96; Keith Tkachuk, 1996-97 to 2000-01; Teppo Numminen, 2001-02, 2002-03.

Winnipeg Jets Retired Numbers

9	Bobby Hull	1972-1980
25	Thomas Steen	1981-1995

All-time Record vs. Other Clubs

Regular Season

	At Home								On Road								Total							
	GP	W	L	T	OL	GF	GA	PTS	GP	W	L	T	OL	GF	GA	PTS	GP	W	L	T	OL	GF	GA	PTS
Anaheim	23	10	10	1	2	68	70	23	24	8	12	3	1	61	67	20	47	18	22	4	3	129	137	43
Atlanta	4	4	0	0	0	15	6	8	3	3	0	0	0	12	5	6	7	7	0	0	0	27	11	14
Boston	30	13	14	3	0	101	102	29	29	4	22	3	0	89	133	11	59	17	36	6	0	190	235	40
Buffalo	29	13	14	2	0	87	92	28	30	5	20	5	0	77	125	15	59	18	34	7	0	164	217	43
Calgary	68	34	23	11	0	263	232	79	69	23	37	9	0	225	290	55	137	57	60	20	0	488	522	134
Carolina	31	14	14	2	1	110	112	31	29	9	13	6	1	86	103	25	60	23	27	8	2	196	215	56
Chicago	48	26	18	4	0	160	151	56	46	12	26	8	0	124	180	32	94	38	44	12	0	284	331	88
Colorado	38	15	16	7	0	139	137	37	39	15	17	5	2	131	136	37	77	30	33	12	2	270	273	74
Columbus	6	4	0	2	0	18	10	10	6	2	4	0	0	10	16	4	12	6	4	2	0	28	26	14
Dallas	51	21	26	4	0	161	174	46	52	18	26	8	0	155	191	44	103	39	52	12	0	316	365	90
Detroit	47	16	18	13	0	143	150	45	49	18	24	7	0	165	192	43	96	34	42	20	0	308	342	88
Edmonton	69	29	35	4	1	279	304	63	70	20	43	6	1	228	304	47	139	49	78	10	2	507	608	110
Florida	9	3	3	3	0	21	26	9	7	4	3	0	0	19	22	8	16	7	6	3	0	40	48	17
Los Angeles	73	36	25	11	1	290	243	84	71	32	25	13	1	279	280	78	144	68	50	24	2	569	523	162
Minnesota	6	5	1	0	0	20	10	10	6	2	2	2	0	12	13	6	12	7	3	2	0	32	23	16
Montreal	28	9	12	7	0	91	108	25	29	3	24	2	0	66	142	8	57	12	36	9	0	157	250	33
Nashville	10	7	2	0	1	30	24	15	10	5	2	1	2	28	25	13	20	12	4	1	3	58	49	28
New Jersey	31	21	7	3	0	114	81	45	28	10	12	6	0	84	94	26	59	31	19	9	0	198	175	71
NY Islanders	29	11	14	4	0	94	100	26	30	9	13	8	0	91	113	26	59	20	27	12	0	185	213	52
NY Rangers	30	13	13	4	0	105	98	30	29	9	17	2	1	102	128	21	59	22	30	6	1	207	226	51
Ottawa	9	4	4	1	0	33	34	9	11	6	4	1	0	34	29	13	20	10	8	2	0	67	63	22
Philadelphia	30	13	15	2	0	95	101	28	30	8	22	0	0	81	131	16	60	21	37	2	0	176	232	44
Pittsburgh	30	14	13	3	0	113	103	31	30	10	20	0	0	86	120	20	60	24	33	3	0	199	223	51
St. Louis	49	24	18	7	0	159	151	55	48	13	25	10	0	133	177	36	97	37	43	17	0	292	328	91
San Jose	32	18	9	3	2	106	87	41	29	12	14	3	0	93	100	27	61	30	23	6	2	199	187	68
Tampa Bay	11	6	5	0	0	28	26	12	9	5	4	0	0	32	28	10	20	11	9	0	0	60	54	22
Toronto	38	20	12	6	0	157	137	46	43	21	20	2	0	161	157	44	81	41	32	8	0	318	294	90
Vancouver	67	33	24	10	0	254	237	76	70	19	42	9	0	197	263	47	137	52	66	19	0	451	500	123
Washington	30	15	8	7	0	112	105	37	30	7	17	5	1	82	119	20	60	22	25	12	1	194	224	57
Totals	**956**	**451**	**373**	**124**	**8**	**3366**	**3211**	**1034**	**956**	**312**	**510**	**124**	**10**	**2943**	**3683**	**758**	**1912**	**763**	**883**	**248**	**18**	**6309**	**6894**	**1792**

Playoffs

	Series	W	L	GP	W	L	T	GF	GA	Last Mtg.	Rnd.	Result
Anaheim	1	0	1	7	3	4	0	17	17	1997	CQF	L 3-4
Calgary	3	2	1	13	7	6	0	45	43	1987	DSF	W 4-2
Colorado	1	0	1	5	1	4	0	10	17	2000	CQF	L 1-4
Detroit	2	0	2	12	4	8	0	28	44	1998	CQF	L 2-4
Edmonton	6	0	6	26	4	22	0	75	120	1990	DSF	L 3-4
St. Louis	2	0	2	11	4	7	0	29	39	1999	CQF	L 3-4
San Jose	1	0	1	5	1	4	0	7	13	2002	CQF	L 1-4
Vancouver	2	0	2	13	5	8	0	34	50	1993	DSF	L 2-4
Totals	**18**	**2**	**16**	**92**	**29**	**63**	**0**	**245**	**343**			

Playoff Results 2003-1999

Year	Round	Opponent	Result	GF	GA
2002	CQF	San Jose	L 1-4	7	13
2000	CQF	Colorado	L 1-4	10	17
1999	CQF	St. Louis	L 3-4	16	19

Abbreviations: Round: CQF – conference quarter-final; **DSF** – division semi-final.

Calgary totals include Atlanta Flames, 1979-80.
Colorado totals include Quebec, 1979-80 to 1994-95.
New Jersey totals include Colorado Rockies, 1979-80 to 1981-82.
Carolina totals include Hartford, 1979-80 to 1996-97.
Dallas totals include Minnesota North Stars, 1979-80 to 1992-93.

2002-03 Results

Oct.	9	at Los Angeles	1-4
	12	Dallas	2-5
	14	at Columbus	4-2
	15	at Ottawa	1-2
	17	at Toronto	3-5
	19	at Buffalo	3-2
	22	at Nashville	2-1
	24	Colorado	2-3
	26	Minnesota	1-6
	28	at NY Rangers	2-3*
	29	at NY Islanders	3-2
	31	at Philadelphia	2-6
Nov.	3	Nashville	2-1*
	7	Minnesota	4-1
	9	Vancouver	2-5
	11	at Tampa Bay	2-4
	12	at Carolina	2-3
	15	at Atlanta	5-1
	17	Colorado	4-4
	20	Dallas	2-2
	22	Florida	3-3
	25	at Dallas	1-5
	27	at Anaheim	2-2
	28	Chicago	2-4
	30	at San Jose	3-2
Dec.	3	San Jose	2-3*
	5	Detroit	3-5
	7	Montreal	2-4
	9	Columbus	3-3
	11	Atlanta	4-2
	13	Washington	3-4
	15	Los Angeles	2-1
	17	Pittsburgh	5-2
	20	St. Louis	3-3
	22	at Anaheim	0-4
	26	at Los Angeles	3-4*
	28	Philadelphia	4-0
	30	Edmonton	4-3*
Jan.	1	at Washington	2-1*
	3	at Detroit	4-1
	4	at Columbus	0-2
	8	at Chicago	0-0
	10	at Minnesota	1-2
	11	at Nashville	3-4*
	14	St. Louis	1-4
	18	Buffalo	0-1
	20	San Jose	3-1
	23	at Calgary	7-1
	24	at Edmonton	5-1
	26	at Vancouver	0-1
	28	Calgary	4-3
Feb.	5	at Los Angeles	3-4
	7	at Anaheim	2-3
	8	Dallas	1-3
	12	New Jersey	0-3
	14	at Minnesota	3-2
	15	at St. Louis	5-3
	18	Columbus	5-2
	20	at Chicago	2-1
	21	at Dallas	2-2
	23	Calgary	2-4
	26	Carolina	4-2
	28	Anaheim	3-1
Mar.	2	at Detroit	2-5
	4	at Pittsburgh	4-1
	6	at St. Louis	3-6
	8	San Jose	6-4
	10	at Colorado	2-2
	12	Detroit	2-3
	14	Chicago	0-4
	15	Anaheim	4-2
	18	Boston	2-1
	20	Edmonton	3-2*
	22	Tampa Bay	0-4
	24	at Calgary	0-2
	26	at Edmonton	3-4
	27	at Vancouver	1-5
	29	at Colorado	1-6
	31	Los Angeles	4-5*
Apr.	2	Vancouver	3-3
	4	Nashville	1-0
	6	at San Jose	3-3

* – Overtime

Entry Draft Selections 2003-1989

2003
Pick	
77	Tyler Redenbach
80	Dimitri Pestunov
115	Liam Lindstrom
178	Ryan Gibbons
208	Randall Gelech
242	Eduard Lewandowski
272	Sean Sullivan
290	Loic Burkhalter

2002
Pick	
19	Jakub Koreis
23	Ben Eager
46	David Leneveu
70	Joe Callahan
80	Matt Jones
97	Lance Monych
132	John Zeiler
186	Jeff Pietrasiak
216	Ladislav Kouba
249	Marcus Smith
280	Russell Spence

2001
Pick	
11	Fredrik Sjostrom
31	Matthew Spiller
45	Martin Podlesak
78	Beat Forster
148	David Klema
180	Scott Polaski
210	Steve Belanger
243	Frantisek Lukes
273	Severin Blindenbacher

2000
Pick	
19	Krystofer Kolanos
53	Alexander Tatarinov
85	Ramzi Abid
160	Nate Kiser
186	Brent Gauvreau
217	Igor Samoilov
249	Sami Venalainen
281	Peter Fabus

1999
Pick	
15	Scott Kelman
19	Kirill Safronov
53	Brad Ralph
71	Jason Jaspers
116	Ryan Lauzon
123	Preston Mizzi
168	Erik Lewerstrom
234	Goran Bezina
262	Alexei Litvinenko

1998
Pick	
14	Patrick DesRochers
43	Ossi Vaananen
73	Pat O'Leary
100	Ryan Vanbuskirk
115	Jay Leach
116	Josh Blackburn
129	Robert Schnabel
160	Rickard Wallin
187	Erik Westrum
214	Justin Hansen

1997
Pick	
43	Juha Gustafsson
96	Scott McCallum
123	Curtis Suter
151	Robert Francz
207	Alexander Andreyev
233	Wyatt Smith

1996
Pick	
11	Dan Focht
24	Daniel Briere
62	Per-Anton Lundstrom
119	Richard Lintner
139	Robert Esche
174	Trevor Letowski
200	Nicholas Lent
226	Marc-Etienne Hubert

1995
Pick	
7	Shane Doan
32	Marc Chouinard
34	Jason Doig
67	Brad Isbister
84	Justin Kurtz
121	Brian Elder
136	Sylvain Daigle
162	Paul Traynor
188	Jaroslav Obsut
189	Fredrik Loven
214	Rob Deciantis

1994
Pick	
30	Deron Quint
56	Dorian Anneck
58	Tavis Hansen
82	Steve Cheredaryk
108	Craig Mills
143	Steve Vezina
146	Chris Kibermanis
186	Ramil Saifullin
212	Henrik Smangs
238	Mike Mader
264	Jason Issel

1993
Pick	
15	Mats Lindgren
31	Scott Langkow
43	Alexei Budayev
79	Ruslan Batyrshin
93	Ravil Gusmanov
119	Larry Courville
145	Michal Grosek
171	Martin Woods
197	Adrian Murray
217	Vladimir Potapov
223	Ilja Stashenkov
228	Harijs Vitolinsh
285	Russ Hewson

1992
Pick	
17	Sergei Bautin
27	Boris Mironov
60	Jeremy Stevenson
84	Mark Visheau
132	Alexander Alexeyev
155	Artur Oktyabrev
156	Andrei Raisky
204	Nikolai Khabibulin
228	Yevgeny Garanin
229	Teemu Numminen
252	Andrei Karpovstev
254	Ivan Vologzhaninov

1991
Pick	
5	Aaron Ward
49	Dmitri Filimonov
91	Juha Ylonen
99	Yan Kaminsky
115	Jeff Sebastian
159	Jeff Ricciardi
181	Sean Gauthier
203	Igor Ulanov
225	Jason Jennings
247	Sergei Sorokin

1990
Pick	
19	Keith Tkachuk
35	Mike Muller
74	Roman Meluzin
75	Scott Levins
77	Alexei Zhamnov
98	Craig Martin
119	Daniel Jardemyr
140	John Lilley
161	Henrik Andersson
182	Rauli Raitanen
203	Mika Alatalo
224	Sergei Selyanin
245	Keith Morris

1989
Pick	
4	Stu Barnes
25	Dan Ratushny
46	Jason Cirone
62	Kris Draper
64	Mark Brownschidle
69	Allain Roy
109	Dan Bylsma
130	Pekka Peltola
131	Doug Evans
151	Jim Solly
172	Stephane Gauvin
193	Joe Larson
214	Bradley Podiak
235	Evgeny Davydov
240	Sergei Kharin

General Managers' History

John Ferguson, 1979-80 to 1987-88; John Ferguson and Mike Smith, 1988-89; Mike Smith, 1989-90 to 1992-93; Mike Smith and John Paddock, 1993-94; John Paddock, 1994-95, 1995-96; John Paddock and Bobby Smith, 1996-97; Bobby Smith, 1997-98 to 1999-2000; Bobby Smith and Cliff Fletcher, 2000-01; Cliff Fletcher and Michael Barnett, 2001-02; Michael Barnett, 2002-03 to date.

Vice President and General Manager

BARNETT, MICHAEL
Executive Vice President/General Manager, Phoenix Coyotes.
Born in Olds, Alta., October 9, 1948.

Michael Barnett joined the Coyotes as vice president and general manager on August 28, 2001 after serving as president of International Management Group's (IMG) hockey division since 1990. Barnett is the sixth general manager in franchise history and follows in the footsteps of Brian Burke (Vancouver Canucks), Pierre Lacroix (Colorado Avalanche) and Dean Lombardi (San Jose Sharks) as former player agents who have become NHL general managers.

With over 20 years of experience in the game prior to joining the Coyotes, Barnett left IMG as one of hockey's most distinguished and well-respected player agents. Over the years, Barnett earned acclaim for his integrity, vision and success as a negotiator. He developed a reputation within the NHL as one of the most creative and well-informed agents in the industry. He is reunited in Phoenix with his longtime friend Wayne Gretzky, the Coyotes' managing partner. Barnett served as Gretzky's agent for 20 years. He also represented some of the NHL's most high-profile players including Jaromir Jagr, Brett Hull, Paul Coffey, Alexander Mogilny, Owen Nolan, Mats Sundin and Joe Thornton.

Barnett actually began his career in hockey as a player. He played hockey at St. Lawrence University in Canton, New York and later attended the University of Calgary, where he played both intercollegiate hockey and football for three years. In 1973-74, he turned professional with the Chicago Cougars (WHA) playing left wing for their minor league affiliate, the Long Island Cougars (NAHL). The following season (1974-75), while playing for the Roanoke-Valley Rebels (SHL) — the Houston Aeros' (WHA) minor league affiliate — Barnett suffered a career ending eye injury.

In 1980, Barnett opened a Western Canadian sports management agency and began his long-lasting relationship with Gretzky by signing him on as his top client. In 1990, Barnett merged his company with Mark McCormack's IMG and became president of IMG hockey operations.

Club Directory

America West Arena

Phoenix Coyotes
ALLTEL Ice Den
9375 E. Bell Road
Scottsdale, AZ 85260
Phone **480/473-5600**
FAX 480/473-5699
www.PhoenixCoyotes.com
Capacity: 16,210

Chairman and Governor	Steve Ellman
Co-Owner	Jerry Moyes
Managing Partner & Alternate Governor	Wayne Gretzky
President, COO & Alternate Governor	Douglas Moss
Senior Exec. V.P. of Hockey Operations	Cliff Fletcher
Executive V.P., G.M. & Alternate Governor	Michael Barnett
Executive Vice President, Business Operations	Brian Byrnes
Senior V.P., Corporate Sales & Broadcasting	Dave Groff
Senior Vice President, Finance & Administration	Vaibhav Gupta
Executive Assistant to the President	Sarah Delp

Hockey Operations
V.P. & Assistant General Manager	Laurence Gilman
Head Coach	Bob Francis
Assistant Coach	Rick Bowness
Assistant Coach	Pat Conacher
Goaltending Coach	Benoit Allaire
Special Teams Consultant	Paul Coffey
Vice President, Scouting & Player Personnel	Dave Draper
Director of Amateur Scouting	Vaughn Karpan
Professional Scout	Tom Kurvers
Professional Scout	Warren Rychel
Director of Player Development	Eddie Mio
Coordinator, Hockey Operations	Igor Kuperman
Strength & Conditioning Coordinator	Stieg Theander
Video Coordinator	Steve Peters
Amateur Scouts	Shane Churla, Keith Gretzky, Blair Reid, Evzen Slansky, Boris Yemeljanov
Consultant to the Hockey Department	Charles Henry
Athletic Therapist	Gord Hart
Massage Therapist	Jukka Nieminen
Head Equipment Manager	Stan Wilson
Equipment Manager	Tony Silva
Assistant Equipment Manager	Jason Rudee
Manager of Team Services	Lesa Guth
Executive Assistant, Hockey Operations	Maryjane DeBiasio
Team Physician	Matt Maddox, D.O.
Team Internist	Robert Luberto, D.O.
Team Dentists	Dr. Rick Lawson, Dr. Lawrence Emmott
Springfield Falcons (AHL) Head Coach	Marty McSorley

Communications
Vice President of Communications	Richard Nairn
Director of Media Relations	Rick Braunstein
Manager of Publications & Media Relations	Ryan Lichtenfels

Broadcasting
TV/Radio Play-by-Play	Curt Keilback
TV/Radio Color Analyst	Charlie Simmer
TV/Radio Host	Todd Walsh
Radio Studio Host	Bob Heethuis
Manager of Broadcasting	Graham Taylor

Community Relations
Director of Community Relations/ Managing Director, Coyotes Charities	Heather Bennett
Community Relations Manager	Melissa Doyle
Hockey Programs Manager	Ben Weber
Fan Development Coordinator	Carol McClay

Corporate Sales & Service
Vice President of Corporate Sales	Cullen Maxey
Manager of Corporate Sales	John Allen
Manager of Sponsorship Sales	Nathan Berkowitz
Manager of Corporate Promotions	Jason Levy
Manager of Corporate Sales Services	Ashley Ritt
Manager, Advertising Sales	TBA

Creative Services
Vice President, Strategic Marketing & Creative Services	Becky Thielen
Lead Graphic Designer	A. Brad Hazelton
Web Editorial Director	Damon Markiewicz
Special Projects Coordinator	Kelly Aranowski

Finance & Administration
Vice President and Controller	Joe Leibfried
Assistant Controller	John Gabriel

Marketing
Vice President of Marketing	Brett Rogers
Director of Game Operations	Greg Hanover

Ticket Sales & Service
Vice President, Ticket Sales & Service	Augie Manfredo
Director of Ticket Sales & Service	Nicole Allison
Director of Premium Seating	E. A. McDonough
Director of Ticket Operations	David Drake
Manager of Ticket Operations	Kevin Prebil

Security
Director of Security	Jim O'Neal

Suite Sales
Vice President Luxury Suite Sales	Mike McCoy
Director of Luxury Suite Sales	Mike Briody

Team Information
Training Camp	Scottsdale, Arizona
Broadcast Television Stations	KTVK-3TV, KASW TV-WB61
Cable Television Station	Fox Sports Net
Radio Stations	KDKB 93.3 FM, KDUS 1060 AM

Pittsburgh Penguins

2002-03 Results: 27w-44L-6T-5OTL 65PTS.
Fifth, Atlantic Division

After playing just 13 games due to a leg injury in 2001-02, Martin Straka missed the first 11 games of 2002-03 with a back injury. He had two assists in his first game played and went on to rank second on the team in scoring behind Mario Lemieux.

2003-04 Schedule

Oct.	Fri.	10	Los Angeles		Thu.	8	at Boston
	Sat.	11	at Philadelphia		Sat.	10	Montreal*
	Thu.	16	at Montreal		Mon.	12	at Philadelphia
	Sat.	18	Detroit		Tue.	13	Tampa Bay
	Wed.	22	Carolina		Fri.	16	at Minnesota
	Fri.	24	New Jersey		Sun.	18	at Washington*
	Sat.	25	at NY Islanders		Tue.	20	New Jersey
	Wed.	29	NY Islanders		Thu.	22	at Ottawa
	Thu.	30	at Chicago		Sat.	24	Colorado
Nov.	Sat.	1	Boston*		Tue.	27	Tampa Bay
	Tue.	4	at Toronto		Thu.	29	at Tampa Bay
	Fri.	7	at Florida		Sat.	31	Philadelphia*
	Sat.	8	at Tampa Bay	Feb.	Sun.	1	at Boston*
	Wed.	12	at NY Rangers		Tue.	3	Montreal
	Fri.	14	at Buffalo		Tue.	10	Boston
	Sat.	15	Florida		Thu.	12	at Florida
	Wed.	19	Minnesota		Sat.	14	at St. Louis
	Fri.	21	at New Jersey		Mon.	16	Toronto
	Sat.	22	Ottawa		Wed.	18	at NY Islanders
	Wed.	26	Philadelphia		Fri.	20	Florida
	Fri.	28	NY Rangers		Sun.	22	Ottawa*
	Sat.	29	at Carolina		Wed.	25	at Phoenix
Dec.	Mon.	1	Atlanta		Fri.	27	at San Jose
	Wed.	3	at Philadelphia		Sun.	29	at NY Islanders*
	Sat.	6	at Edmonton	Mar.	Tue.	2	NY Islanders
	Sun.	7	at Calgary		Thu.	4	Nashville
	Tue.	9	at Vancouver		Sat.	6	Anaheim
	Fri.	12	at Atlanta		Sun.	7	at NY Rangers*
	Sat.	13	Columbus		Tue.	9	Dallas
	Tue.	16	Buffalo		Thu.	11	at Toronto
	Thu.	18	at Carolina		Sun.	14	Philadelphia*
	Sat.	20	Atlanta		Tue.	16	Washington
	Mon.	22	at Montreal		Wed.	17	at New Jersey
	Fri.	26	at Ottawa		Fri.	19	Carolina
	Sat.	27	New Jersey		Sun.	21	NY Rangers*
	Mon.	29	Chicago		Tue.	23	at NY Rangers
	Wed.	31	NY Islanders*		Fri.	26	at Buffalo
Jan.	Thu.	1	at Nashville*		Sat.	27	Buffalo
	Sat.	3	NY Rangers*		Tue.	30	at Washington
	Mon.	5	Toronto	Apr.	Fri.	2	at Atlanta
	Wed.	7	at New Jersey		Sun.	4	at Washington*

* Denotes afternoon game.

Franchise date: June 5, 1967

EASTERN CONFERENCE

ATLANTIC DIVISION

37th NHL Season

Year-by-Year Record

Season	GP	Home W	L	T	OL	Road W	L	T	OL	Overall W	L	T	OL	GF	GA	Pts.	Finished	Playoff Result
2002-03	82	15	22	2	2	12	22	4	3	27	44	6	5	189	255	65	5th, Atlantic Div.	Out of Playoffs
2001-02	82	16	20	4	1	12	21	4	4	28	41	8	5	198	249	69	5th, Atlantic Div.	Out of Playoffs
2000-01	82	24	15	2	0	18	13	7	3	42	28	9	3	281	256	96	3rd, Atlantic Div.	Lost Conf. Championship
1999-2000	82	23	11	7	0	14	20	1	6	37	31	8	6	241	236	88	3rd, Atlantic Div.	Lost Conf. Semi-Final
1998-99	82	21	10	10		17	20	4		38	30	14	...	242	225	90	3rd, Atlantic Div.	Lost Conf. Semi-Final
1997-98	82	21	10	10		19	14	8		40	24	18	...	228	188	98	1st, Northeast Div.	Lost Conf. Quarter-Final
1996-97	82	25	11	5		13	25	3		38	36	8	...	285	280	84	2nd, Northeast Div.	Lost Conf. Quarter-Final
1995-96	82	32	9	0		17	20	4		49	29	4	...	362	284	102	1st, Northeast Div.	Lost Conf. Championship
1994-95	48	18	5	1		11	11	2		29	16	3	...	181	158	61	2nd, Northeast Div.	Lost Conf. Semi-Final
1993-94	84	25	9	8		19	18	5		44	27	13	...	299	285	101	1st, Northeast Div.	Lost Conf. Quarter-Final
1992-93	84	32	6	4		24	15	3		56	21	7	...	367	268	119	1st, Patrick Div.	Lost Div. Final
1991-92	**80**	**21**	**13**	**6**		**18**	**19**	**3**		**39**	**32**	**9**	...	**343**	**308**	**87**	**3rd, Patrick Div.**	**Won Stanley Cup**
1990-91	**80**	**25**	**12**	**3**		**16**	**21**	**3**		**41**	**33**	**6**	...	**342**	**305**	**88**	**1st, Patrick Div.**	**Won Stanley Cup**
1989-90	80	22	15	3		10	25	5		32	40	8	...	318	359	72	5th, Patrick Div.	Out of Playoffs
1988-89	80	24	13	3		16	20	4		40	33	7	...	347	349	87	2nd, Patrick Div.	Lost Div. Final
1987-88	80	22	12	6		14	23	3		36	35	9	...	319	316	81	6th, Patrick Div.	Out of Playoffs
1986-87	80	19	15	6		11	23	6		30	38	12	...	297	290	72	5th, Patrick Div.	Out of Playoffs
1985-86	80	20	15	5		14	23	3		34	38	8	...	313	305	76	5th, Patrick Div.	Out of Playoffs
1984-85	80	17	20	3		7	31	2		24	51	5	...	276	385	53	6th, Patrick Div.	Out of Playoffs
1983-84	80	7	29	4		9	29	2		16	58	6	...	254	390	38	6th, Patrick Div.	Out of Playoffs
1982-83	80	14	22	4		4	31	5		18	53	9	...	257	394	45	6th, Patrick Div.	Out of Playoffs
1981-82	80	21	11	8		10	25	5		31	36	13	...	310	337	75	4th, Patrick Div.	Lost Div. Semi-Final
1980-81	80	21	16	3		9	21	10		30	37	13	...	302	345	73	3rd, Norris Div.	Lost Prelim. Round
1979-80	80	20	13	7		10	24	6		30	37	13	...	251	303	73	3rd, Norris Div.	Lost Prelim. Round
1978-79	80	23	12	5		13	19	8		36	31	13	...	281	279	85	2nd, Norris Div.	Lost Quarter-Final
1977-78	80	16	15	9		9	22	9		25	37	18	...	254	321	68	4th, Norris Div.	Out of Playoffs
1976-77	80	22	12	6		12	21	7		34	33	13	...	240	252	81	3rd, Norris Div.	Lost Prelim. Round
1975-76	80	23	11	6		12	22	6		35	33	12	...	339	303	82	3rd, Norris Div.	Lost Prelim. Round
1974-75	80	25	5	10		12	23	5		37	28	15	...	326	289	89	3rd, Norris Div.	Lost Quarter-Final
1973-74	78	15	18	6		13	23	3		28	41	9	...	242	273	65	5th, West Div.	Out of Playoffs
1972-73	78	24	11	4		8	26	5		32	37	9	...	257	265	73	5th, West Div.	Out of Playoffs
1971-72	78	18	15	6		8	23	8		26	38	14	...	220	258	66	4th, West Div.	Lost Quarter-Final
1970-71	78	18	12	9		3	25	11		21	37	20	...	221	240	62	6th, West Div.	Out of Playoffs
1969-70	76	17	13	8		9	25	4		26	38	12	...	182	238	64	2nd, West Div.	Lost Semi-Final
1968-69	76	12	20	6		8	25	5		20	45	11	...	189	252	51	5th, West Div.	Out of Playoffs
1967-68	74	15	12	10		12	22	3		27	34	13	...	195	216	67	5th, West Div.	Out of Playoffs

2003-04 Player Personnel

FORWARDS	HT	WT	S	Place of Birth	Date	2002-03 Club
ABID, Ramzi	6-2	210	L	Montreal, Que.	3/24/80	Phoenix-Springfield-Pittsburgh
ARMSTRONG, Colby	6-2	187	R	Lloydminster, Sask.	11/23/82	Wilkes-Barre
BEECH, Kris	6-2	209	L	Salmon Arm, B.C.	2/5/81	Wilkes-Barre-Pittsburgh
BRADLEY, Matt	6-2	195	R	Stittsville, Ont.	6/13/78	San Jose
BUCHBERGER, Kelly	6-2	210	L	Langenburg, Sask.	12/2/66	Phoenix
CRAMPTON, Steve	6-3	209	R	Winnipeg, Man.	4/12/82	Wheeling
EASTWOOD, Mike	6-3	216	R	Ottawa, Ont.	7/1/67	St. Louis-Chicago
ENDICOTT, Shane	6-4	214	L	Saskatoon, Sask.	12/21/81	Wilkes-Barre
FATA, Rico	6-0	200	L	Sault Ste. Marie, Ont.	2/12/80	NY Rangers-Hartford-Pittsburgh
HOLZINGER, Brian	5-11	186	R	Parma, OH	10/10/72	T.B.-Sprfld-Pit
HUSSEY, Matt	6-2	212	L	New Haven, CT	5/28/79	Wilkes-Barre
KOLTSOV, Konstantin	6-0	201	L	Minsk, USSR	4/17/81	Pittsburgh-Wilkes-Barre
KOSTOPOULOS, Tom	6-0	200	R	Mississauga, Ont.	1/24/79	Pittsburgh-Wilkes-Barre
KRAFT, Milan	6-3	214	L	Plzen, Czech.	1/17/80	Pittsburgh-Wilkes-Barre
LEFEBVRE, Guillaume	6-1	200	L	Amos, Que.	5/7/81	Phi-Phi (AHL)-Pit-Wilkes-Barre
LEMIEUX, Mario	6-4	230	R	Montreal, Que.	10/5/65	Pittsburgh
MALONE, Ryan	6-4	215	L	Pittsburgh, PA	12/1/79	St. Cloud State-Wilkes-Barre
McKENNA, Steve	6-8	252	L	Toronto, Ont.	8/21/73	Pittsburgh
MELOCHE, Eric	5-10	197	R	Montreal, Que.	5/1/76	Pittsburgh-Wilkes-Barre
MOROZOV, Aleksey	6-1	204	L	Moscow, USSR	2/16/77	Pittsburgh
MURLEY, Matt	6-1	204	L	Troy, NY	12/17/79	Wilkes-Barre
OUELLET, Michel	6-0	201	R	Rimouski, Que.	3/5/82	Wheeling-Wilkes-Barre
PETERSEN, Toby	5-9	197	L	Minneapolis, MN	10/27/78	Wilkes-Barre
SIVEK, Michal	6-3	213	L	Nachod, Czech.	1/21/81	Pittsburgh-Wilkes-Barre
STRAKA, Martin	5-9	178	L	Plzen, Czech.	9/3/72	Pittsburgh
SUROVY, Tomas	6-1	203	L	Banska Bystrica, Czech.	9/24/81	Pittsburgh-Wilkes-Barre
DEFENSEMEN						
BERGEVIN, Marc	6-1	209	L	Montreal, Que.	8/11/65	Pittsburgh-Tampa Bay
BUCKLEY, Brendan	6-1	205	R	Needham, MA	2/26/77	Wilkes-Barre
FATA, Drew	6-1	209	L	Sault Ste. Marie, Ont.	7/28/83	St. Michael's-Kingston
FOCHT, Dan	6-6	234	L	Regina, Sask.	12/31/77	Phoenix-Springfield-Pittsburgh
KOCI, David	6-6	228	L	Prague, Czech.	5/12/81	Wilkes-Barre-Wheeling
LUPASCHUK, Ross	6-1	218	R	Edmonton, Alta.	1/19/81	Pittsburgh-Wilkes-Barre
MELICHAR, Josef	6-2	221	L	Ceske Budejovice, Czech.	1/20/79	Pittsburgh
ORPIK, Brooks	6-2	224	L	San Francisco, CA	9/26/80	Pittsburgh-Wilkes-Barre
ROBINSON, Darcy	6-3	235	R	Kamloops, B.C.	5/3/81	Wilkes-Barre-Wheeling
ROULEAU, Alexandre	6-1	190	R	Mont-Laurier, Que.	7/29/83	Val-d'Or-Quebec (QMJHL)
ROZSIVAL, Michal	6-1	212	R	Vlasim, Czech.	9/3/78	Pittsburgh
SCUDERI, Rob	6-0	214	L	Syosset, NY	12/30/78	Wilkes-Barre
TARNSTROM, Dick	6-2	205	L	Sundbyberg, Sweden	1/20/75	Pittsburgh
GOALTENDERS	HT	WT	C	**Place of Birth**	Date	2002-03 Club
AUBIN, Jean-Sebastien	5-11	180	R	Montreal, Que.	7/19/77	Pittsburgh-Wilkes-Barre
BROCHU, Martin	6-0	199	L	Anjou, Que.	3/10/73	Verdun-Cherepovets
CARON, Sebastian	6-1	170	L	Amqui, Que.	6/25/80	Pittsburgh-Wilkes-Barre
CHIODO, Andy	5-11	201	L	Toronto, Ont.	4/25/83	St. Michael's
FLEURY, Marc-Andre	6-1	172	L	Sorel, Que.	11/28/84	Cape Breton

General Managers' History

Jack Riley, 1967-68 to 1969-70; Red Kelly, 1970-71; Red Kelly and Jack Riley, 1971-72; Jack Riley, 1972-73; Jack Riley and Jack Button, 1973-74; Jack Button, 1974-75; Wren Blair, 1975-76; Wren Blair and Baz Bastien, 1976-77; Baz Bastien, 1977-78 to 1982-83; Eddie Johnston, 1983-84 to 1987-88; Tony Esposito, 1988-89; Tony Esposito and Craig Patrick, 1989-90; Craig Patrick, 1990-91 to date.

Coach

OLCZYK, EDDIE
Coach, Pittsburgh Penguins. Born in Chicago, IL, August 16, 1966.

Craig Patrick named former Penguins forward Eddie Olczyk as the successor to Rick Kehoe behind the Pittsburgh bench on June 11, 2003. Olczyk is the 21st head coach in club history and the 18th different person to hold the position. He is also the fifth former Penguins player to guide the team, joining Ken Schinkel, Lou Angotti, Gene Ubriaco and Kehoe.

The Chicago native moved to the bench from the broadcast booth, having spent the three previous seasons as a color commentator for Penguins broadcasts on Fox Sports Net. He also covered the Stanley Cup playoffs for ESPN and NHL Radio. Olczyk moved behind the microphone in 2000 after completing a successful 16-year NHL career. Selected by his hometown Blackhawks third overall in the 1984 draft, "Edzo" went on to record 342 goals and 794 points in 1,031 games with Chicago, Toronto, Winnipeg, the New York Rangers, Los Angeles and Pittsburgh. He topped the 30-goal mark five consecutive seasons (1987 to 1992), netted a single-season high 42 goals with the Maple Leafs in 1987-88 and captured the Stanley Cup as a member of the Rangers in 1994.

Olczyk joined the Penguins at the 1997 trade deadline, coming to Pittsburgh from Los Angeles for Glen Murray. He recorded 33 points (15 goals, 18 assists) in 68 regular season games with the Pens and added three goals in 11 postseason contests. He has no previous coaching experience.

2002-03 Scoring

* - rookie

Regular Season

Pos	#	Player	Team	GP	G	A	Pts	+/−	PIM	PP	SH	GW	GT	S	%
C	66	Mario Lemieux	PIT	67	28	63	91	−25	43	14	0	4	0	235	11.9
L	82	Martin Straka	PIT	60	18	28	46	−18	12	7	0	4	0	136	13.2
D	32	Dick Tarnstrom	PIT	61	7	34	41	−11	50	3	0	0	0	115	6.1
R	95	Aleksey Morozov	PIT	27	9	16	25	−3	16	6	0	2	1	46	19.6
R	37	Mikael Samuelsson	NYR	58	8	14	22	0	32	1	1	2	1	118	6.8
			PIT	22	2	0	2	−21	8	1	0	0	0	36	5.6
			TOTAL	80	10	14	24	−21	40	2	1	2	1	154	6.5
L	10	Ville Nieminen	PIT	75	9	12	21	−25	93	0	2	1	0	86	10.5
R	19	Rico Fata	NYR	36	2	4	6	−1	6	0	0	0	0	30	6.7
			PIT	27	5	8	13	−6	10	0	0	0	0	49	10.2
			TOTAL	63	7	12	19	−7	16	0	0	0	0	79	8.9
L	34 *	Ramzi Abid	PHX	30	10	8	18	1	30	4	0	3	0	52	19.2
			PIT	3	0	0	0	−5	2	0	0	0	0	7	0.0
			TOTAL	33	10	8	18	−4	32	4	0	3	0	59	16.9
C	20	Mathias Johansson	CGY	46	4	5	9	−15	12	1	0	0	0	54	7.4
			PIT	12	1	5	6	1	4	1	0	0	0	16	6.3
			TOTAL	58	5	10	15	−14	16	2	0	0	0	70	7.1
D	39	Joel Bouchard	NYR	27	5	7	12	6	14	1	0	2	0	41	12.2
			PIT	7	0	1	1	−6	0	0	0	0	0	6	0.0
			TOTAL	34	5	8	13	0	14	1	0	2	0	47	10.6
C	14	Milan Kraft	PIT	31	7	5	12	−9	10	1	0	1	0	50	14.0
L	43 *	Tomas Surovy	PIT	26	4	7	11	0	10	1	0	2	0	47	8.5
R	23	Steve McKenna	PIT	79	9	1	10	−18	128	5	0	3	0	59	15.3
D	28	Michal Rozsival	PIT	53	4	6	10	−5	40	1	0	0	0	61	6.6
R	11	Alexandre Daigle	PIT	33	4	3	7	−10	8	1	0	0	0	48	8.3
R	26	Kent Manderville	PIT	82	2	5	7	−22	46	0	0	1	0	72	2.8
R	72	Eric Meloche	PIT	13	5	1	6	−2	4	2	0	1	1	34	14.7
D	6	Richard Lintner	NYR	10	1	0	1	−5	0	1	0	0	0	9	11.1
			PIT	19	3	2	5	−9	10	1	0	0	0	36	8.3
			TOTAL	29	4	2	6	−14	10	2	0	0	0	45	8.9
C	12 *	Michal Sivek	PIT	38	3	3	6	−5	14	1	0	0	0	45	6.7
L	33 *	Guillaume Lefebvre	PHI	14	0	0	0	1	4	0	0	0	0	5	0.0
			PIT	12	2	4	6	1	0	0	0	0	0	14	14.3
			TOTAL	26	2	4	6	2	4	0	0	0	0	19	10.5
D	8	Hans Jonsson	PIT	63	1	4	5	−23	36	0	0	0	0	40	2.5
D	3	Jamie Pushor	PIT	76	3	1	4	−28	76	0	0	0	0	54	5.6
C	15	Brian Holzinger	T.B.	5	0	1	1	1	0	0	0	0	0	3	0.0
			PIT	9	1	2	3	−6	6	0	0	1	0	20	5.0
			TOTAL	14	1	3	4	−5	8	0	0	1	0	23	4.3
D	57	Shawn Heins	S.J.	20	0	1	1	−2	9	0	0	0	0	10	0.0
			PIT	27	1	1	2	−2	33	0	0	1	0	28	3.6
			TOTAL	47	1	2	3	−4	42	0	0	1	0	38	2.6
D	4 *	Dan Focht	PHX	10	0	0	0	−2	10	0	0	0	0	1	0.0
			PIT	12	0	3	3	−7	19	0	0	0	0	11	0.0
			TOTAL	22	0	3	3	−9	29	0	0	0	0	12	0.0
C	19	Vladimir Vujtek	PIT	5	0	1	1	−4	0	0	0	0	0	3	0.0
R	36	Tom Kostopoulos	PIT	8	0	1	1	−4	0	0	0	0	0	6	0.0
C	16	Kris Beech	PIT	12	0	1	1	−3	6	0	0	0	0	6	0.0
L	48 *	Konstantin Koltsov	PIT	2	0	0	0	−2	0	0	0	0	0	4	0.0
L	34 *	Ross Lupaschuk	PIT	3	0	0	0	−3	4	0	0	0	0	0	0.0
D	29 *	Brooks Orpik	PIT	6	0	0	0	−5	2	0	0	0	0	2	0.0
D	2	Josef Melichar	PIT	8	0	0	0	−4	6	0	0	0	0	6	0.0

Goaltending

No.		Goaltender	GPI	Mins	Avg	W	L	T	EN	SO	GA	SA	S%	G	A	PIM
31	*	Sebastien Caron	24	1408	2.64	7	14	2	1	2	62	741	.916	0	0	6
30		Jean-Sebastien Aubin	21	1132	3.13	6	13	0	3	1	59	589	.900	0	1	2
1		Johan Hedberg	41	2410	3.14	14	22	4	4	1	126	1197	.895	0	2	18
		Totals	82	4972	3.08	27	49	6	8	4	255	2535	.899			

Coaching History

Red Sullivan, 1967-68, 1968-69; Red Kelly, 1969-70 to 1971-72; Red Kelly and Ken Schinkel, 1972-73; Ken Schinkel and Marc Boileau, 1973-74; Marc Boileau, 1974-75; Marc Boileau and Ken Schinkel, 1975-76; Ken Schinkel, 1976-77; Johnny Wilson, 1977-78 to 1979-80; Eddie Johnston, 1980-81 to 1982-83; Lou Angotti, 1983-84; Bob Berry, 1984-85 to 1986-87; Pierre Creamer, 1987-88; Gene Ubriaco, 1988-89; Gene Ubriaco and Craig Patrick, 1989-90; Bob Johnson, 1990-91; 1991-92; Scotty Bowman, 1991-92, 1992-93; Eddie Johnston, 1993-94 to 1995-96; Eddie Johnston and Craig Patrick, 1996-97; Kevin Constantine, 1997-98, 1998-99; Kevin Constantine and Herb Brooks, 1999-2000; Ivan Hlinka, 2000-01; Ivan Hlinka and Rick Kehoe, 2001-02; Rick Kehoe, 2002-03; Eddie Olczyk, 2003-04.

Club Records

Team

(Figures in brackets for season records are games played; records for fewest points, wins, ties, losses, goals, goals against are for 70 or more games)

Most Points	**119**	1992-93 (84)
Most Wins	**56**	1992-93 (84)
Most Ties	**20**	1970-71 (78)
Most Losses	**58**	1983-84 (80)
Most Goals	**367**	1992-93 (84)
Most Goals Against	**394**	1982-83 (80)
Fewest Points	**38**	1983-84 (80)
Fewest Wins	**16**	1983-84 (80)
Fewest Ties	**4**	1995-96 (82)
Fewest Losses	**21**	1992-93 (84)
Fewest Goals	**182**	1969-70 (76)
Fewest Goals Against	**188**	1997-98 (82)
Longest Winning Streak		
Overall	***17**	Mar. 9-Apr. 10/93
Home	**11**	Jan. 5-Mar. 7/91
Away	**7**	Mar. 14-Apr. 9/93
Longest Undefeated Streak		
Overall	**18**	Mar. 9-Apr. 14/93 (17 wins, 1 tie)
Home	**20**	Nov. 30/74-Feb. 22/75 (12 wins, 8 ties)
Away	**8**	Mar. 14-Apr. 14/93 (7 wins, 1 tie)
Longest Losing Streak		
Overall	**11**	Jan. 22-Feb. 10/83
Home	**7**	Oct. 8-29/83
Away	**18**	Dec. 23/82-Mar. 4/83
Longest Winless Streak		
Overall	**18**	Jan. 2-Feb. 10/83 (17 losses, 1 tie)
Home	**11**	Oct. 8-Nov. 19/83 (9 losses, 2 ties)
Away	**18**	Oct. 25/70-Jan. 14/71 (11 losses, 7 ties), Dec. 23/82-Mar. 4/83 (18 losses)
Most Shutouts, Season	**9**	1998-99 (82)
Most PIM, Season	**2,670**	1988-89 (80)
Most Goals, Game	**12**	Mar. 15/75 (Wsh. 1 at Pit. 12), Dec. 26/91 (Tor. 1 at Pit. 12)

Individual

Most Seasons	**15**	Mario Lemieux
Most Games	**879**	Mario Lemieux
Most Goals, Career	**682**	Mario Lemieux
Most Assists, Career	**1,010**	Mario Lemieux
Most Points, Career	**1,692**	Mario Lemieux (682G, 1,010A)
Most PIM, Career	**1,023**	Kevin Stevens
Most Shutouts, Career	**22**	Tom Barrasso
Longest Consecutive Games Streak	**320**	Ron Schock (Oct. 24/73-Apr. 3/77)
Most Goals, Season	**85**	Mario Lemieux (1988-89)
Most Assists, Season	**114**	Mario Lemieux (1988-89)
Most Points, Season	**199**	Mario Lemieux (1988-89; 85G, 114A)
Most PIM, Season	**409**	Paul Baxter (1981-82)
Most Points, Defenseman, Season	**113**	Paul Coffey (1988-89; 30G, 83A)
Most Points, Center, Season	**199**	Mario Lemieux (1988-89; 85G, 114A)
Most Points, Right Wing, Season	***149**	Jaromir Jagr (1995-96; 62G, 87A)
Most Points, Left Wing, Season	**123**	Kevin Stevens (1991-92; 54G, 69A)
Most Points, Rookie, Season	**100**	Mario Lemieux (1984-85; 43G, 57A)
Most Shutouts, Season	**7**	Tom Barrasso (1997-98)
Most Goals, Game	**5**	Mario Lemieux (Three times)
Most Assists, Game	**6**	Ron Stackhouse (Mar. 8/75), Greg Malone (Nov. 28/79), Mario Lemieux (Three times)
Most Points, Game	**8**	Mario Lemieux (Oct. 15/88; 2G, 6A, Dec. 31/88; 5G, 3A)

* NHL Record.

Captains' History

Ab McDonald, 1967-68; no captain, 1968-69 to 1972-73; Ron Schock, 1973-74 to 1976-77; Jean Pronovost, 1977-78; Orest Kindrachuk, 1978-79 to 1980-81; Randy Carlyle, 1981-82 to 1983-84; Mike Bullard, 1984-85, 1985-86; Mike Bullard and Terry Ruskowski, 1986-87; Dan Frawley and Mario Lemieux, 1987-88; Mario Lemieux, 1988-89 to 1993-94; Ron Francis, 1994-95; Mario Lemieux, 1995-96, 1996-97; Ron Francis, 1997-98; Jaromir Jagr, 1998-99 to 2000-01; Mario Lemieux, 2001-02 to date.

Retired Numbers

21	Michel Brière	1969-1970

All-time Record vs. Other Clubs

Regular Season

	At Home								On Road								Total							
	GP	W	L	T	OL	GF	GA	PTS	GP	W	L	T	OL	GF	GA	PTS	GP	W	L	T	OL	GF	GA	PTS
Anaheim	8	4	2	2	0	27	26	10	8	3	4	0	1	24	29	7	16	7	6	2	1	51	55	17
Atlanta	8	7	0	0	1	31	15	15	8	8	0	0	0	33	16	16	16	15	0	0	1	64	31	31
Boston	78	31	32	15	0	267	278	77	76	16	54	6	0	216	336	38	154	47	86	21	0	483	614	115
Buffalo	69	35	17	17	0	262	214	87	69	19	33	17	0	187	268	55	138	54	50	34	0	449	482	142
Calgary	44	24	10	10	0	167	133	58	45	11	26	8	0	139	198	30	89	35	36	18	0	306	331	88
Carolina	44	22	17	5	0	180	166	49	46	21	20	5	0	173	172	47	90	43	37	10	0	353	338	96
Chicago	58	28	23	7	0	209	190	63	59	10	39	10	0	156	236	30	117	38	62	17	0	365	426	93
Colorado	36	15	16	5	0	142	147	35	32	13	16	2	1	122	142	29	68	28	32	7	1	264	289	64
Columbus	2	1	1	0	0	7	6	2	3	2	1	0	0	9	10	4	5	3	2	0	0	16	16	6
Dallas	62	37	19	6	0	232	178	80	64	21	36	6	1	213	246	49	126	58	55	12	1	445	424	129
Detroit	64	43	17	4	0	277	192	90	65	13	39	12	1	178	253	39	129	56	56	16	1	455	445	129
Edmonton	30	15	12	3	0	117	127	33	29	7	21	1	0	95	144	15	59	22	33	4	0	212	271	48
Florida	21	12	6	3	0	70	63	27	20	8	9	1	2	46	53	19	41	20	15	4	2	116	116	46
Los Angeles	72	38	24	10	0	265	230	86	69	17	43	8	1	183	265	43	141	55	67	18	1	448	495	129
Minnesota	2	1	1	0	0	4	6	2	2	0	1	1	0	3	5	1	4	1	2	1	0	7	11	3
Montreal	80	28	38	13	1	235	278	70	80	10	58	10	2	201	375	32	160	38	96	23	3	436	653	102
Nashville	4	1	1	2	0	10	8	4	5	2	3	0	0	8	18	4	9	3	4	2	0	18	26	8
New Jersey	76	40	31	4	1	288	262	85	78	28	37	13	0	263	285	69	154	68	68	17	1	551	547	154
NY Islanders	85	40	33	12	0	321	297	92	83	31	44	8	0	277	335	70	168	71	77	20	0	598	632	162
NY Rangers	97	42	41	14	0	353	354	98	98	39	50	9	0	332	381	87	195	81	91	23	0	685	735	185
Ottawa	25	16	5	4	0	92	57	36	25	14	7	4	0	79	61	32	50	30	12	8	0	171	118	68
Philadelphia	103	46	37	20	0	366	337	112	103	16	77	7	3	250	437	42	206	62	114	27	3	616	774	154
Phoenix	30	20	10	0	0	120	86	40	30	13	14	3	0	103	113	29	60	33	24	3	0	223	199	69
St. Louis	64	32	20	12	0	238	190	76	63	15	41	6	1	169	244	37	127	47	61	18	1	407	434	113
San Jose	9	4	4	1	0	41	32	9	12	6	4	2	0	52	30	14	21	10	8	3	0	93	62	23
Tampa Bay	21	15	3	3	0	87	50	33	21	9	9	2	1	59	61	21	42	24	12	5	1	146	111	54
Toronto	67	36	25	6	0	274	215	78	65	23	30	11	1	208	258	58	132	59	55	17	1	482	473	136
Vancouver	50	33	10	7	0	227	171	73	49	23	22	4	0	184	176	50	99	56	32	11	0	411	347	123
Washington	81	45	29	7	0	314	257	97	84	32	42	9	1	307	350	74	165	77	71	16	1	621	607	171
Defunct Clubs	35	22	6	7	0	148	93	51	34	13	10	11	0	108	101	37	69	35	16	18	0	256	194	88
Totals	**1425**	**733**	**490**	**199**	**3**	**5371**	**4658**	**1668**	**1425**	**443**	**790**	**176**	**16**	**4377**	**5598**	**1078**	**2850**	**1176**	**1280**	**375**	**19**	**9748**	**10256**	**2746**

Playoffs

	Series	W	L	GP	W	L	T	GF	GA	Last Mtg.	Rnd.	Result
Boston	4	2	2	19	10	9	0	67	62	1992	CF	W 4-0
Buffalo	2	2	0	10	6	4	0	26	26	2001	CSF	W 4-3
Chicago	2	1	1	8	4	4	0	23	24	1992	F	W 4-0
Dallas	1	1	0	6	4	2	0	28	16	1991	F	W 4-2
Florida	1	0	1	7	3	4	0	15	20	1996	CF	L 3-4
Montreal	1	0	1	6	2	4	0	15	18	1998	CQF	L 2-4
New Jersey	5	3	2	29	14	15	0	80	86	2001	CF	L 1-4
NY Islanders	3	0	3	19	8	11	0	58	67	1993	DF	L 3-4
NY Rangers	3	3	0	15	12	3	0	64	45	1996	CSF	W 4-1
Philadelphia	3	0	3	18	6	12	0	51	66	2000	CSF	L 2-4
St. Louis	3	1	2	13	6	7	0	40	45	1981	PRE	L 2-3
Toronto	3	0	3	12	4	8	0	27	39	1999	CSF	L 2-4
Washington	7	6	1	42	26	16	0	137	121	2001	CQF	W 4-2
Defunct Clubs	1	1	0	4	4	0	0	13	6			
Totals	**39**	**20**	**19**	**208**	**109**	**99**	**0**	**644**	**641**			

Calgary totals include Atlanta Flames, 1972-73 to 1979-80.
Colorado totals include Quebec, 1979-80 to 1994-95.
Carolina totals include Hartford, 1979-80 to 1996-97.
Dallas totals include Minnesota North Stars, 1967-68 to 1992-93.
New Jersey totals include Kansas City, 1974-75 to 1975-76, and Colorado Rockies, 1976-77 to 1981-82.
Phoenix totals include Winnipeg, 1979-80 to 1995-96.

Playoff Results 2003-1999

Year	Round	Opponent	Result	GF	GA
2001	CF	New Jersey	L 1-4	7	17
	CSF	Buffalo	W 4-3	17	17
	CQF	Washington	W 4-2	14	10
2000	CSF	Philadelphia	L 2-4	14	15
	CQF	Washington	W 4-1	17	8
1999	CSF	Toronto	L 2-4	14	18
	CQF	New Jersey	W 4-3	21	18

Abbreviations: Round: F – Final; **CF** – conference final; **CSF** – conference semi-final; **CQF** – conference quarter-final; **DF** – division final; **PRE** – preliminary round.

2002-03 Results

Oct.	10	Toronto	0-6		9	Toronto	2-4
	12	NY Rangers	6-0		11	NY Rangers	1-3
	14	at Toronto	5-4		13	at Boston	2-1
	16	Atlanta	3-2		15	at Carolina	2-0
	19	Tampa Bay	3-3		17	at Tampa Bay	3-2
	22	at Montreal	3-3		18	at Florida	0-3
	25	at Detroit	3-7		21	at Buffalo	0-0
	26	Buffalo	5-2		23	Boston	1-4
	28	Washington	3-2		25	Chicago	5-3
	30	at Ottawa	4-1		28	at NY Islanders	2-5
Nov.	2	Tampa Bay	5-3		30	at Washington	1-2
	6	at Florida	3-4*	**Feb.**	4	Vancouver	2-3
	8	at Tampa Bay	1-4		6	Florida	0-6
	9	at Carolina	2-3		8	at Boston	5-2
	14	at Minnesota	1-1		12	Ottawa	0-3
	16	NY Islanders	2-3		14	at NY Rangers	0-1
	18	at Montreal	4-5*		15	at New Jersey	4-1
	20	Montreal	2-3*		18	Edmonton	4-3*
	22	at Atlanta	3-1		20	Colorado	2-5
	23	San Jose	4-1		22	St. Louis	2-1*
	27	Philadelphia	7-2		23	New Jersey	3-4
	29	at Buffalo	4-1		25	Los Angeles	3-5
	30	Boston	2-3		27	at Nashville	0-6
Dec.	3	Washington	1-4	**Mar.**	1	at Colorado	1-4
	6	at New Jersey	1-3		2	at Dallas	1-3
	7	NY Islanders	3-6		4	Phoenix	1-4
	10	at Toronto	2-4		6	Carolina	0-4
	12	at San Jose	2-5		8	Ottawa	1-5
	14	at Los Angeles	2-3*		9	at Ottawa	2-4
	15	at Anaheim	0-5		12	Nashville	2-2
	17	at Phoenix	2-5		15	Philadelphia	1-4
	19	New Jersey	1-3		16	Florida	2-4
	21	Calgary	2-0		18	Detroit	1-5
	23	Buffalo	5-2		20	at Philadelphia	2-4
	26	at NY Rangers	6-1		21	at New Jersey	1-3
	28	Montreal	3-2		23	at Chicago	1-1
	30	Atlanta	2-3*		26	at NY Rangers	3-1
	31	at Columbus	2-5		29	at Philadelphia	0-3
Jan.	3	at Atlanta	4-1		31	Philadelphia	1-6
	4	NY Islanders	3-2*	**Apr.**	2	Carolina	3-2
	7	at NY Islanders	3-6		5	at Washington	3-5

* – Overtime

Entry Draft
Selections 2003-1989

2003
Pick
1 Marc-Andre Fleury
32 Ryan Stone
70 Jonathan Filewich
73 Daniel Carcillo
121 Paul Bissonnette
161 Evgeni Isakov
169 Lukas Bolf
199 Andy Chiodo
229 Stephen Dixon
232 Joe Jensen
263 Matt Moulson

2002
Pick
5 Ryan Whitney
35 Ondrej Nemec
69 Erik Christensen
101 Daniel Fernholm
136 Andrew Sertich
137 Cam Paddock
171 Robert Goepfert
202 Patrik Bartschi
234 Maxime Talbot
239 Ryan Lannon
265 Dwight Labrosse

2001
Pick
21 Colby Armstrong
54 Noah Welch
86 Drew Fata
96 Alexandre Rouleau
120 Tomas Surovy
131 Ben Eaves
156 Andrew Schneider
217 Tomas Duba
250 Brandon Crawford-West

2000
Pick
18 Brooks Orpik
52 Shane Endicott
84 Peter Hamerlik
124 Michel Ouellet
146 David Koci
185 Patrick Foley
216 Jim Abbott
248 Steve Crampton
273 Roman Simicek
280 Nick Boucher

1999
Pick
18 Konstantin Koltsov
51 Matt Murley
57 Jeremy Van Hoof
86 Sebastian Caron
115 Ryan Malone
144 Tomas Skvaridlo
157 Vladimir Malenkikh
176 Doug Meyer
204 Tom Kostopoulos
233 Darcy Robinson
261 Andrew McPherson

1998
Pick
23 Milan Kraft
54 Alexander Zevakhin
80 David Cameron
110 Scott Myers
134 Rob Scuderi
169 Jan Fadrny
196 Joel Scherban
224 Mika Lehto
244 Toby Petersen
254 Matt Hussey

1997
Pick
17 Robert Dome
44 Brian Gaffaney
71 Josef Melichar
97 Alexandre Mathieu
124 Harlan Pratt
152 Petr Havelka
179 Mark Moore
208 Andrew Ference
234 Eric Lind

1996
Pick
23 Craig Hillier
28 Pavel Skrbek
72 Boyd Kane
77 Boris Protsenko
105 Michal Rozsival
150 Peter Bergman
186 Eric Meloche
238 Timo Seikkula

1995
Pick
24 Aleksey Morozov
76 Jean-Sebastien Aubin
102 Oleg Belov
128 Jan Hrdina
154 Alexei Kolkunov
180 Derrick Pyke
206 Sergei Voronov
232 Frank Ivankovic

1994
Pick
24 Chris Wells
50 Richard Park
57 Sven Butenschon
73 Greg Crozier
76 Alexei Krivchenkov
102 Tom O'Connor
128 Clint Johnson
154 Valentin Morozov
161 Serge Aubin
180 Drew Palmer
206 Boris Zelenko
232 Jason Godbout
258 Mikhail Kazakevich
284 Brian Leitza

1993
Pick
26 Stefan Bergkvist
52 Domenic Pittis
62 Dave Roche
104 Jonas Andersson-Junkka
130 Chris Kelleher
156 Patrick Lalime
182 Sean Selmser
208 Larry McMorran
234 Timothy Harberts
260 Leonid Toropchenko
286 Hans Jonsson

1992
Pick
19 Martin Straka
43 Marc Hussey
67 Travis Thiessen
91 Todd Klassen
115 Philippe DeRouville
139 Artem Kopot
163 Jan Alinc
187 Fran Bussey
211 Brian Bonin
235 Brian Callahan

1991
Pick
16 Markus Naslund
38 Rusty Fitzgerald
60 Shane Peacock
82 Joe Tamminen
104 Robert Melanson
126 Brian Clifford
148 Ed Patterson
170 Peter McLaughlin
192 Jeff Lembke
214 Chris Tok
236 Paul Dyck
258 Pasi Huura

1990
Pick
5 Jaromir Jagr
61 Joe Dziedzic
68 Chris Tamer
89 Brian Farrell
107 Ian Moran
110 Denis Casey
130 Mika Valila
131 Ken Plaquin
145 Pat Neaton
152 Petteri Koskimaki
173 Ladislav Karabin
194 Timothy Fingerhut
215 Michael Thompson
236 Brian Bruininks

1989
Pick
16 Jamie Heward
37 Paul Laus
58 John Brill
79 Todd Nelson
100 Tom Nevers
121 Mike Markovich
126 Mike Needham
142 Patrick Schafhauser
163 Dave Shute
184 Andrew Wolf
205 Greg Hagen
226 Scott Farrell
247 Jason Smart

Vice President and General Manager

PATRICK, CRAIG
Executive Vice President/General Manager, Pittsburgh Penguins.
Born in Detroit, MI, May 20, 1946.

Known for his calm and patient management style, Craig Patrick has led the Penguins to two Stanley Cup championships, one Presidents' Trophy title and five division championships since taking over as general manager on December 5, 1989. In 2000, he and Mario Lemieux were recipients of the Lester Patrick Trophy for their contributions to hockey in the United States. He was elected to the Hockey Hall of Fame in 2001.

A member of one of hockey's most famous families — including grandfather Lester, father Lynn and uncle Muzz — Patrick played collegiate hockey at the University of Denver and captained the Pioneers to the NCAA championship in 1969. He played eight NHL seasons with four different teams, registering 72 goals and 163 points in 401 games before retiring in 1979. He made the transition to management and coaching when he landed the dual role of assistant coach and assistant g.m. of the 1980 U.S. Olympic team that won the gold medal at Lake Placid.

Patrick joined the New York Rangers organization as director of operations in 1980 and became the youngest general manager in club history one year later. He served in that capacity through the 1985-86 season, leading his team to the playoffs every year.

Prior to joining the Penguins, Patrick spent two years as director of athletics and recreation at the University of Denver.

NHL Coaching Record

		Regular Season				Playoffs		
Season	Team	Games	W	L	T	Games	W	L
1980-81	NY Rangers	60	26	23	11	14	7	7
1984-85	NY Rangers	35	11	22	2	3	0	3
1989-90	Pittsburgh	54	22	26	6	....	....	....
1996-97	Pittsburgh	20	7	10	3	5	1	4
	NHL Totals	**169**	**66**	**81**	**22**	**22**	**8**	**14**

Club Directory

Mellon Arena

Pittsburgh Penguins
Mellon Arena
66 Mario Lemieux Place
Pittsburgh, PA 15219
Phone **412/642-1300**
FAX 412/642-1859
Media Relations FAX 412/642-1322
Capacity: 16,958

Ownership . . . . Mario Lemieux and the Lemieux Group LP

Administration
Chairman/CEO . . . . Mario Lemieux
President and Governor. . . . . Ken Sawyer
Executive VP/General Manager . . . . Craig Patrick
Vice President & General Counsel . . . . Ted Black
Vice President & Controller . . . . Kevin Hart
Vice President, Communications/Marketing. . . . . . Tom McMillan
Vice President, Sales . . . . David Soltesz
Executive Assistant . . . . Fay McNamara
Receptionist . . . . Kelly Hart
Mailroom Supervisor . . . . Brett Hart

Hockey Operations
General Manager . . . . Craig Patrick
Assistant General Manager . . . . Ed Johnston
Head Coach . . . . Eddie Olczyk
Assistant Coaches . . . . Randy Hillier, Lorne Molleken, Joe Mullen
Head Scout . . . . Greg Malone
Goaltending Coach/Scout . . . . Gilles Meloche
Scouts . . . . Wayne Daniels, Chuck Grillo, Charlie Hodge, Mark Kelley,
Richard Rose, Neil Shea
Pro Scouts . . . . Rick Kehoe, Glenn Patrick
Head Coach, Wilkes-Barre/Scranton (AHL). . . . . . Michel Therrien
Strength & Conditioning Coach . . . . John Welday
Equipment Manager . . . . Steve Latin
Assistant Equipment Manager . . . . Paul Flati
Equipment Staff . . . . Paul DeFazio
Team Physician . . . . Dr. Charles Burke
Athletic Trainers . . . . Scott Johnson, Mark Mortland
Massage Therapist . . . . Tom Plasko
Executive Assistant . . . . Tracey Botsford
Video Coordinator . . . . Paul Fink
Team Staff . . . . Michael Lang

Communications/Marketing
Vice President, Communications/Marketing . . . . . Tom McMillan
Director of Media Relations . . . . Keith Wehner
Manager of Media Relations . . . . Todd Lepovsky
Director of Marketing . . . . Brian Magness
Director of Public/Alumni Relations . . . . Cindy Himes
Director of Community Relations. . . . . Renee Petrichevich
Director, Video Production Department . . . . . Paul Barto
Director of Operations, Lemieux Hockey Dev. . . . . . Mark Shuttleworth
Director of Alumni Relations . . . . Jack Riley
Manager, Game Presentation . . . . Jason Coe
Manager, Video Production . . . . Joe Hale
Manager, Art and Graphics . . . . Dori Minnis
Director of Publications . . . . Brian Coe
Creative Director . . . . Barb Pilarski
Exec. Producer, Penguins Radio Network . . . . Ray Walker
Multi Media Manager . . . . Chris Devivo
New Media Manager . . . . Brett Robinson

Finance
Vice President & Controller . . . . Kevin Hart
Assistant Controller . . . . Michael McCullough
Accounting Staff . . . . Tawni Love, Troy Ussack, Andrea Winschel

Ticketing
Vice President, Sales . . . . David Soltesz
Senior Director of Ticketing . . . . James Santilli
Director, Premium Seating . . . . Terri Smith
Director, Ticketing . . . . Chad Slencak
Director, Customer Service . . . . Laura Bryer
Manager, Group Sales . . . . Mike Guiffre
Premium Seating Account Representative . . . . Bonnie Golinski, George Murphy
Ticket Sales Representatives . . . . Peter Barakat, George Birman, Jason Florian, Mike McLaughlin, Ross Miller, Chuck Pukansky, Joe Traynor, Craig Wheeler
Box Office Manager . . . . Carol Coulson
Box Office Staff . . . . Kelly Gabany, Jason Onufer, Jenn Tuite
Customer Service Representatives . . . . Kathy Davis, Sherry Huggins, Dana Kirkpatrick, Jill Weisbrod
Data Base Manager . . . . Jill Shaw

Corporates Sales
Vice President, Sales . . . . David Soltesz
Senior Director, Corporate Sales . . . . Kimberly Bogesdorfer
Directors, Corporate Sales . . . . Carl D'Alicandro, Mark DeAndrea
Manager, Sales Service . . . . Marie Mays
Sales Service . . . . Kelly Maza
Corporate Sales Liason . . . . Pierre Larouche

General Information
Team Colors . . . . Black, Gold and White
TV Station . . . . Fox Sports Net Pittsburgh
TV Announcers . . . . Mike Lange, Bob Errey
Radio Announcers . . . . Paul Steigerwald, Phil Bourque
Flagship Radio Station . . . . 3WS (94.5FM), Fox Sports Radio 970AM

St. Louis Blues

2002-03 Results: 41w-24L-11T-6OTL 99PTS.
Second, Central Division

2003-04 Schedule

Oct.	Fri.	10	at Phoenix	Tue.	13	at Montreal
	Sun.	12	at Colorado	Thu.	15	Columbus
	Thu.	16	at Nashville	Sat.	17	Minnesota
	Sat.	18	Washington	Mon.	19	at Florida*
	Tue.	21	at Edmonton	Wed.	21	at Columbus
	Wed.	22	at Vancouver	Fri.	23	at Dallas
	Fri.	24	at Calgary	Sat.	24	Dallas
	Tue.	28	Nashville	Wed.	28	at Atlanta
	Wed.	29	at Detroit	Thu.	29	Vancouver
Nov.	Sat.	1	Chicago	Sat.	31	New Jersey
	Tue.	4	Anaheim	**Feb.** Mon.	2	at Minnesota
	Thu.	6	Vancouver	Wed.	4	at Edmonton
	Sat.	8	Florida	Thu.	5	at Calgary
	Thu.	13	at San Jose	Tue.	10	at Ottawa
	Sat.	15	at Los Angeles*	Thu.	12	Colorado
	Sun.	16	at Anaheim*	Sat.	14	Pittsburgh
	Wed.	19	at Phoenix	Mon.	16	Phoenix*
	Sat.	22	Dallas	Thu.	19	Tampa Bay
	Tue.	25	Boston	Fri.	20	at Detroit
	Fri.	28	at Tampa Bay	Sun.	22	at Chicago*
	Sat.	29	Detroit	Thu.	26	at Colorado
Dec.	Tue.	2	Los Angeles	Sat.	28	at Vancouver
	Thu.	4	Detroit	Sun.	29	at San Jose*
	Sat.	6	Nashville	**Mar.** Tue.	2	Calgary
	Tue.	9	at Toronto	Thu.	4	Edmonton
	Fri.	12	at Columbus	Sat.	6	at NY Islanders
	Sat.	13	Los Angeles	Sun.	7	at Buffalo
	Tue.	16	Columbus	Tue.	9	NY Islanders
	Thu.	18	San Jose	Thu.	11	Nashville
	Sat.	20	Phoenix	Sat.	13	Columbus
	Mon.	22	at Detroit	Sun.	14	Calgary
	Tue.	23	at Chicago	Tue.	16	at Los Angeles
	Fri.	26	Colorado	Wed.	17	at Anaheim
	Mon.	29	at Columbus	Sat.	20	at Dallas*
	Tue.	30	Philadelphia	Thu.	25	Anaheim
Jan.	Thu.	1	NY Rangers	Sat.	27	Chicago*
	Sat.	3	San Jose	Sun.	28	at Chicago*
	Mon.	5	Minnesota	Tue.	30	Edmonton
	Tue.	6	at Carolina	**Apr.** Thu.	1	Detroit
	Sat.	10	at Nashville	Sat.	3	at Nashville*
	Mon.	12	Chicago	Sun.	4	at Minnesota*

Denotes afternoon game.

Three of the Blues' top offensive stars: Pavol Demitra (left) ranked among the NHL leaders with 36 goals and 93 points; Keith Tkachuk was second on the team with 31 goals; and Scott Mellanby scored 26 times for his highest total in six years.

Franchise date: June 5, 1967

CENTRAL DIVISION

37th NHL Season

Year-by-Year Record

Season	GP	Home W	L	T	OL	Road W	L	T	OL	Overall W	L	T	OL	GF	GA	Pts.	Finished	Playoff Result
2002-03	82	23	11	4	3	18	13	7	3	41	24	11	6	253	222	99	2nd, Central Div.	Lost Conf. Quarter-Final
2001-02	82	27	12	1	1	16	15	7	3	43	27	8	4	227	188	98	2nd, Central Div.	Lost Conf. Semi-Final
2000-01	82	28	5	5	3	15	17	7	2	43	22	12	5	249	195	103	2nd, Central Div.	Lost Conf. Championship
1999-2000	82	24	9	7	1	27	10	4	0	51	19	11	1	248	165	114	1st, Central Div.	Lost Conf. Quarter-Final
1998-99	82	18	17	6	...	19	15	7	...	37	32	13	...	237	209	87	2nd, Central Div.	Lost Conf. Semi-Final
1997-98	82	26	10	5	...	19	19	3	...	45	29	8	...	256	204	98	3rd, Central Div.	Lost Conf. Semi-Final
1996-97	82	17	20	4	...	19	15	7	...	36	35	11	...	236	239	83	4th, Central Div.	Lost Conf. Quarter-Final
1995-96	82	15	17	9	...	17	17	7	...	32	34	16	...	219	248	80	4th, Central Div.	Lost Conf. Semi-Final
1994-95	48	16	6	2	...	12	9	3	...	28	15	5	...	178	135	61	2nd, Central Div.	Lost Conf. Quarter-Final
1993-94	84	23	11	8	...	17	22	3	...	40	33	11	...	270	283	91	4th, Central Div.	Lost Conf. Quarter-Final
1992-93	84	22	13	7	...	15	23	4	...	37	36	11	...	282	278	85	4th, Norris Div.	Lost Div. Final
1991-92	80	25	12	3	...	11	21	8	...	36	33	11	...	279	266	83	3rd, Norris Div.	Lost Div. Semi-Final
1990-91	80	24	9	7	...	23	13	4	...	47	22	11	...	310	250	105	2nd, Norris Div.	Lost Div. Final
1989-90	80	20	15	5	...	17	19	4	...	37	34	9	...	295	279	83	2nd, Norris Div.	Lost Div. Final
1988-89	80	22	11	7	...	11	24	5	...	33	35	12	...	275	285	78	2nd, Norris Div.	Lost Div. Final
1987-88	80	18	17	5	...	16	21	3	...	34	38	8	...	278	294	76	2nd, Norris Div.	Lost Div. Final
1986-87	80	21	12	7	...	11	21	8	...	32	33	15	...	281	293	79	1st, Norris Div.	Lost Div. Semi-Final
1985-86	80	23	11	6	...	14	23	3	...	37	34	9	...	302	291	83	3rd, Norris Div.	Lost Conf. Championship
1984-85	80	21	12	7	...	16	19	5	...	37	31	12	...	299	288	86	1st, Norris Div.	Lost Div. Semi-Final
1983-84	80	23	14	3	...	9	27	4	...	32	41	7	...	293	316	71	2nd, Norris Div.	Lost Div. Final
1982-83	80	16	16	8	...	9	24	7	...	25	40	15	...	285	316	65	4th, Norris Div.	Lost Div. Semi-Final
1981-82	80	22	14	4	...	10	26	4	...	32	40	8	...	315	349	72	3rd Norris Div.	Lost Div. Final
1980-81	80	29	7	4	...	16	11	13	...	45	18	17	...	352	281	107	1st, Smythe Div.	Lost Quarter-Final
1979-80	80	20	13	7	...	14	21	5	...	34	34	12	...	266	278	80	2nd, Smythe Div.	Lost Prelim. Round
1978-79	80	14	20	6	...	4	30	6	...	18	50	12	...	249	348	48	3rd, Smythe Div.	Out of Playoffs
1977-78	80	12	20	8	...	8	27	5	...	20	47	13	...	195	304	53	4th, Smythe Div.	Out of Playoffs
1976-77	80	22	13	5	...	10	24	4	...	32	39	9	...	239	276	73	1st, Smythe Div.	Lost Quarter-Final
1975-76	80	20	12	8	...	9	25	6	...	29	37	14	...	249	290	72	2nd, Smythe Div.	Lost Prelim. Round
1974-75	80	23	13	4	...	12	18	10	...	35	31	14	...	269	267	84	2nd, Smythe Div.	Lost Prelim. Round
1973-74	78	16	16	7	...	10	24	5	...	26	40	12	...	206	248	64	6th, West Div.	Out of Playoffs
1972-73	78	21	11	7	...	11	23	5	...	32	34	12	...	233	251	76	4th, West Div.	Lost Quarter-Final
1971-72	78	17	17	5	...	11	22	6	...	28	39	11	...	208	247	67	3rd, West Div.	Lost Semi-Final
1970-71	78	23	7	9	...	11	18	10	...	34	25	19	...	223	208	87	2nd, West Div.	Lost Quarter-Final
1969-70	76	24	9	5	...	13	18	7	...	37	27	12	...	224	179	86	1st, West Div.	Lost Final
1968-69	76	21	8	9	...	16	17	5	...	37	25	14	...	204	157	88	1st, West Div.	Lost Final
1967-68	74	18	12	7	...	9	19	9	...	27	31	16	...	177	191	70	3rd, West Div.	Lost Final

2003-04 Player Personnel

FORWARDS	HT	WT	S	Place of Birth	Date	2002-03 Club
BOGUNIECKI, Eric	5-8	192	R	New Haven, CT	5/6/75	St. Louis
CAJANEK, Petr	5-11	176	L	Gottwaldov, Czech.	8/18/75	St. Louis
DANTON, Mike	5-9	190	R	Brampton, Ont.	10/21/80	New Jersey
DEMITRA, Pavol	6-0	206	L	Dubnica, Czech.	11/29/74	St. Louis
DRAKE, Dallas	6-1	190	L	Trail, B.C.	2/4/69	St. Louis
JOHNSON, Ryan	6-1	200	L	Thunder Bay, Ont.	6/14/76	Florida-St. Louis
LOW, Reed	6-3	222	R	Moose Jaw, Sask.	6/21/76	St. Louis
MARTINS, Steve	5-9	185	L	Gatineau, Que.	4/13/72	Ottawa-Binghamton-St. Louis
MAYERS, Jamal	6-1	217	R	Toronto, Ont.	10/24/74	St. Louis
MELLANBY, Scott	6-1	205	R	Montreal, Que.	6/11/66	St. Louis
POHL, John	6-0	186	R	Rochester, MN	6/29/79	Worcester
RYCROFT, Mark	5-11	192	R	Penticton, B.C.	7/12/78	Worcester
SEJNA, Peter	5-11	198	L	Liptovski Mikulas, Czech.	10/5/79	Colorado College-St. Louis
TKACHUK, Keith	6-2	225	L	Melrose, MA	3/28/72	St. Louis
VARLAMOV, Sergei	5-11	203	L	Kiev, USSR	7/21/78	St. Louis-Worcester
WEIGHT, Doug	5-11	200	L	Warren, MI	1/21/71	St. Louis
DEFENSEMEN						
BACKMAN, Christian	6-4	198	L	Alingsas, Sweden	4/28/80	St. Louis-Worcester
BRIMANIS, Aris	6-3	215	R	Cleveland, OH	3/14/72	Worcester
FINLEY, Jeff	6-2	205	L	Edmonton, Alta.	4/14/67	St. Louis
JACKMAN, Barret	6-1	197	L	Trail, B.C.	3/5/81	St. Louis
KHAVANOV, Alexander	6-2	205	L	Moscow, USSR	1/30/72	St. Louis
KOIVISTO, Tom	5-10	194	R	Turku, Finland	6/4/74	St. Louis-Worcester
LAFLAMME, Christian	6-1	206	R	St-Charles, Que.	11/24/76	St. Louis-Worcester
MacINNIS, Al	6-2	204	R	Inverness, N.S.	7/11/63	St. Louis
PRONGER, Chris	6-6	220	L	Dryden, Ont.	10/10/74	St. Louis
SALVADOR, Bryce	6-2	215	L	Brandon, Man.	2/11/76	St. Louis
WALKER, Matt	6-2	236	R	Beaverlodge, Alta.	4/7/80	St. Louis-Worcester

GOALTENDERS	HT	WT	C	Place of Birth	Date	2002-03 Club
DIVIS, Reinhard	5-11	200	L	Vienna, Austria	7/4/75	St. Louis-Worcester
JOHNSON, Brent	6-2	200	L	Farmington, MI	3/12/77	St. Louis-Worcester
OSGOOD, Chris	5-10	175	L	Peace River, Alta.	11/26/72	NY Islanders-St. Louis
SANFORD, Curtis	5-10	187	R	Owen Sound, Ont.	10/5/79	St. Louis-Worcester

Coaching History

Lynn Patrick and Scotty Bowman, 1967-68; Scotty Bowman, 1968-69, 1969-70; Al Arbour and Scotty Bowman, 1970-71; Sid Abel, Bill McCreary and Al Arbour, 1971-72; Al Arbour and Jean-Guy Talbot, 1972-73; Jean-Guy Talbot and Lou Angotti, 1973-74; Lou Angotti, Lynn Patrick and Garry Young, 1974-75; Garry Young, Lynn Patrick and Leo Boivin, 1975-76; Emile Francis, 1976-77; Leo Boivin and Barclay Plager, 1977-78; Barclay Plager, 1978-79; Barclay Plager and Red Berenson, 1979-80; Red Berenson, 1980-81; Red Berenson and Emile Francis, 1981-82; Emile Francis and Barclay Plager, 1982-83; Jacques Demers, 1983-84 to 1985-86; Jacques Martin, 1986-87, 1987-88; Brian Sutter, 1988-89 to 1991-92; Bob Plager and Bob Berry, 1992-93; Bob Berry, 1993-94; Mike Keenan, 1994-95, 1995-96; Mike Keenan, Jim Roberts and Joel Quenneville, 1996-97; Joel Quenneville, 1997-98 to date.

Coach

QUENNEVILLE, JOEL
Coach, St. Louis Blues. Born in Windsor, Ont., September 15, 1958.

Joel Quenneville was named head coach on January 6, 1997, becoming the 20th head coach in Blues history. His first game in St. Louis was on January 7, 1997. He won the Jack Adams Award as coach of the year in 1999-2000 after leading the Blues to the Presidents' Trophy with a club record 51 wins and 114 points. In 2000-01, he led the team to the Western Conference Finals.

Prior to joining the Blues the former NHL defenseman spent three seasons with the Colorado Avalanche organization as an assistant coach. He was instrumental in the Avalanche's drive for their first Stanley Cup championship during the 1995-96 season.

Prior to joining the Avalanche he was head coach for the Springfield Indians of the American Hockey League during the 1993-94 season. He retired as a player after the 1991-92 season after serving the St. John's Maple Leafs (AHL) as a player/coach. Quenneville played 13 NHL seasons and finished with 803 career games played, 54 goals, 136 assists and 705 penalty minutes. His best years on the ice were spent with Hartford where he earned most valuable defenseman honors in 1984 and 1985. He played an integral part in helping Hartford win a divisional championship in 1986-87.

Coaching Record

		Regular Season				Playoffs		
Season	Team	Games	W	L	T	Games	W	L
1993-94	Springfield (AHL)	80	29	38	13	6	2	4
1996-97	**St. Louis (NHL)**	**40**	**18**	**15**	**7**	**6**	**2**	**4**
1997-98	**St. Louis (NHL)**	**82**	**45**	**29**	**8**	**10**	**6**	**4**
1998-99	**St. Louis (NHL)**	**82**	**37**	**32**	**13**	**13**	**6**	**7**
1999-2000	**St. Louis (NHL)**	**82**	**51**	**20**	**11**	**7**	**3**	**4**
2000-01	**St. Louis (NHL)**	**82**	**43**	**27**	**12**	**15**	**9**	**6**
2001-02	**St. Louis (NHL)**	**82**	**43**	**31**	**8**	**10**	**5**	**5**
2002-03	**St. Louis (NHL)**	**82**	**41**	**30**	**11**	**7**	**3**	**4**
	NHL Totals	**532**	**278**	**154**	**70**	**68**	**34**	**34**

2002-03 Scoring

* - rookie

Regular Season

Pos	#	Player	Team	GP	G	A	Pts	+/–	PIM	PP	SH	GW	GT	S	%
C	38	Pavol Demitra	STL	78	36	57	93	0	32	11	0	4	1	205	17.6
D	2	Al MacInnis	STL	80	16	52	68	22	61	9	1	2	0	299	5.4
L	61	Cory Stillman	STL	79	24	43	67	12	56	6	0	4	0	157	15.3
C	39	Doug Weight	STL	70	15	52	67	–6	52	7	0	3	0	182	8.2
R	19	Scott Mellanby	STL	80	26	31	57	1	176	13	0	4	1	132	19.7
L	7	Keith Tkachuk	STL	56	31	24	55	1	139	14	0	5	0	185	16.8
R	33	Eric Boguniecki	STL	80	22	27	49	22	38	3	1	5	0	117	18.8
C	26	Petr Cajanek	STL	51	9	29	38	16	20	2	2	1	0	90	10.0
D	29	Alexander Khavanov	STL	81	8	25	33	–1	48	2	1	2	0	90	8.9
R	10	Dallas Drake	STL	80	20	10	30	–7	66	4	1	2	1	113	17.7
L	22	Martin Rucinsky	STL	61	16	14	30	–1	38	4	4	3	1	135	11.9
R	13	Valeri Bure	FLA	46	5	21	26	–11	10	3	0	2	0	150	3.3
			STL	5	0	2	2	–2	0	0	0	0	0	11	0.0
			TOTAL	51	5	23	28	–13	10	3	0	2	0	161	3.1
D	5	* Barret Jackman	STL	82	3	16	19	23	190	0	0	0	0	66	4.5
C	12	Steve Martins	OTT	14	2	3	5	3	10	0	0	0	0	13	15.4
			STL	28	3	3	6	–8	18	0	1	0	0	25	12.0
			TOTAL	42	5	6	11	–5	28	0	1	0	0	38	13.2
L	25	Shjon Podein	STL	68	4	6	10	7	28	1	0	0	0	52	7.7
D	27	Bryce Salvador	STL	71	2	8	10	7	95	1	0	0	0	73	2.7
L	9	Tyson Nash	STL	66	6	3	9	0	114	1	0	2	0	77	7.8
D	46	Christian Laflamme	STL	47	0	9	9	1	45	0	0	0	0	44	0.0
R	21	Jamal Mayers	STL	15	2	5	7	1	8	0	0	0	0	26	7.7
C	17	Ryan Johnson	FLA	58	2	5	7	–13	26	0	0	0	0	54	3.7
			STL	17	0	0	0	0	12	0	0	0	0	13	0.0
			TOTAL	75	2	5	7	–13	38	0	0	0	0	67	3.0
D	6	Tom Koivisto	STL	22	2	4	6	1	10	0	0	1	0	26	7.7
R	34	Reed Low	STL	79	2	4	6	3	234	0	0	1	0	48	4.2
C	18	Steve Dubinsky	STL	28	0	6	6	3	4	0	0	0	0	23	0.0
D	44	Chris Pronger	STL	5	1	3	4	–2	10	0	0	0	0	11	9.1
D	37	Jeff Finley	STL	64	1	3	4	–2	46	0	0	1	0	30	3.3
D	43	Mike Van Ryn	STL	20	0	3	3	3	8	0	0	0	0	21	0.0
L	15	* Peter Sejna	STL	1	1	0	1	0	0	1	0	0	0	3	33.3
R	20	Eric Nickulas	STL	8	0	1	1	–2	6	0	0	0	0	3	0.0
D	28	* Matt Walker	STL	16	0	1	1	0	38	0	0	0	0	13	0.0
C	15	Daniel Corso	STL	1	0	0	0	–1	0	0	0	0	0	0	0.0
L	23	Sergei Varlamov	STL	3	0	0	0	1	0	0	0	0	0	5	0.0
D	55	* Christian Backman	STL	4	0	0	0	–3	0	0	0	0	0	4	0.0

Goaltending

No.	Goaltender	GPI	Mins	Avg	W	L	T	EN	SO	GA	SA	S%	G	A	PIM
45	* Cody Rudkowsky	1	30	0.00	1	0	0	0	0	0	10	1.000	0	0	0
50	Reinhard Divis	2	83	0.72	2	0	0	0	0	1	34	.971	0	0	0
1	* Curtis Sanford	8	397	1.96	5	1	0	0	1	13	148	.912	0	0	0
35	Brent Johnson	38	2042	2.47	16	13	5	2	2	84	844	.900	0	1	2
40	Fred Brathwaite	30	1615	2.75	12	9	4	4	2	74	631	.883	0	0	0
30	Chris Osgood	9	532	3.05	4	3	2	1	2	27	241	.888	0	0	0
30	Tom Barrasso	6	293	3.28	1	4	0	0	1	16	132	.879	0	0	0
	Totals	**82**	**5012**	**2.66**	**41**	**30**	**11**	**7**	**8**	**222**	**2047**	**.892**			

Playoffs

Pos	#	Player	Team	GP	G	A	Pts	+/–	PIM	PP	SH	GW	GT	S	%
C	39	Doug Weight	STL	7	5	8	13	0	2	5	0	1	0	18	27.8
L	22	Martin Rucinsky	STL	7	4	2	6	–3	4	0	0	0	0	16	25.0
C	38	Pavol Demitra	STL	7	2	4	6	2	2	1	0	0	0	11	18.2
D	29	Alexander Khavanov	STL	7	2	3	5	0	2	1	0	0	0	13	15.4
R	10	Dallas Drake	STL	7	1	4	5	0	23	0	0	1	0	10	10.0
L	61	Cory Stillman	STL	6	2	2	4	0	2	2	0	1	0	26	7.7
L	7	Keith Tkachuk	STL	7	1	3	4	–1	14	0	0	0	0	19	5.3
D	44	Chris Pronger	STL	7	1	3	4	3	14	0	0	0	0	15	6.7
L	9	Tyson Nash	STL	7	2	1	3	3	6	0	0	0	0	6	33.3
R	33	Eric Boguniecki	STL	7	1	2	3	–2	2	1	0	0	0	9	11.1
R	13	Valeri Bure	STL	6	0	2	2	2	8	0	0	0	0	13	0.0
C	17	Ryan Johnson	STL	6	0	2	2	3	6	0	0	0	0	1	0.0
C	12	Steve Martins	STL	2	0	1	1	1	0	0	0	0	0	2	0.0
D	2	Al MacInnis	STL	3	0	1	1	0	0	0	0	0	0	3	0.0
R	19	Scott Mellanby	STL	6	0	1	1	0	10	0	0	0	0	13	0.0
L	25	Shjon Podein	STL	7	0	1	1	1	6	0	0	0	0	4	0.0
C	26	Petr Cajanek	STL	2	0	0	0	–1	2	0	0	0	0	2	0.0
D	46	Christian Laflamme	STL	5	0	0	0	–1	4	0	0	0	0	4	0.0
D	37	Jeff Finley	STL	6	0	0	0	1	6	0	0	0	0	3	0.0
D	27	Bryce Salvador	STL	7	0	0	0	1	2	0	0	0	0	7	0.0
D	5	* Barret Jackman	STL	7	0	0	0	–2	14	0	0	0	0	3	0.0

Goaltending

No.	Goaltender	GPI	Mins	Avg	W	L	EN	SO	GA	SA	S%	G	A	PIM
30	Chris Osgood	7	417	2.45	3	4	0	1	17	183	.907	0	0	4
	Totals	**7**	**420**	**2.43**	**3**	**4**	**0**	**1**	**17**	**183**	**.907**			

Captains' History

Al Arbour, 1967-68 to 1969-70; Red Berenson and Barclay Plager, 1970-71; Barclay Plager, 1971-72 to 1975-76; no captain, 1976-77; Red Berenson, 1977-78; Barry Gibbs, 1978-79; Brian Sutter, 1979-80 to 1987-88; Bernie Federko, 1988-89; Rick Meagher, 1989-90; Scott Stevens, 1990-91; Garth Butcher, 1991-92; Brett Hull, 1992-93 to 1994-95; Brett Hull, Shayne Corson and Wayne Gretzky, 1995-96; no captain, 1996-97; Chris Pronger, 1997-98 to 2001-02; Al MacInnis, 2002-03; Chris Pronger, 2003-04.

Club Records

Team

(Figures in brackets for season records are games played; records for fewest points, wins, ties, losses, goals, goals against are for 70 or more games)

Most Points	**114**	1999-2000 (82)
Most Wins	**51**	1999-2000 (82)
Most Ties	**19**	1970-71 (78)
Most Losses	**50**	1978-79 (80)
Most Goals	**352**	1980-81 (80)
Most Goals Against	**349**	1981-82 (80)
Fewest Points	**48**	1978-79 (80)
Fewest Wins	**18**	1978-79 (80)
Fewest Ties	**7**	1983-84 (80)
Fewest Losses	**18**	1980-81 (80)
Fewest Goals	**177**	1967-68 (74)
Fewest Goals Against	**157**	1968-69 (76)
Longest Winning Streak		
Overall	**10**	Jan. 3-23/02
Home	**9**	Jan. 26-Feb. 26/91
Away	***10**	Jan. 21-Mar. 2/00
Longest Undefeated Streak		
Overall	**12**	Nov. 10-Dec. 8/68 (5 wins, 7 ties), Nov. 24-Dec. 26/00 (11 wins, 1 tie)
Home	**11**	Four times
Away	**11**	Jan. 21-Mar. 4/00 (10 wins, 1 tie)
Longest Losing Streak		
Overall	**7**	Nov. 12-26/67, Feb. 12-25/89
Home	**6**	Nov. 23-Dec. 19/96
Away	**10**	Jan. 20-Mar. 8/82
Longest Winless Streak		
Overall	**12**	Jan. 17-Feb. 15/78 (10 losses, 2 ties)
Home	**7**	Dec. 28/82-Jan. 25/83 (5 losses, 2 ties)
Away	**17**	Jan. 23-Oct. 9/74 (13 losses, 4 ties)
Most Shutouts, Season	**13**	1968-69 (76)
Most PIM, Season	**2,041**	1990-91 (80)
Most Goals, Game	**11**	Feb. 26/94 (St.L. 11 at Ott. 1)

Individual

Most Seasons	**13**	Bernie Federko
Most Games	**927**	Bernie Federko
Most Goals, Career	**527**	Brett Hull
Most Assists, Career	**721**	Bernie Federko
Most Points, Career	**1,073**	Bernie Federko (352G, 721A)
Most PIM, Career	**1,786**	Brian Sutter
Most Shutouts, Career	**16**	Glenn Hall
Longest Consecutive Games Streak	**662**	Garry Unger (Feb. 7/71-Apr. 8/79)
Most Goals, Season	**86**	Brett Hull (1990-91)
Most Assists, Season	**90**	Adam Oates (1990-91)
Most Points, Season	**131**	Brett Hull (1990-91) (86G, 45A)
Most PIM, Season	**306**	Bob Gassoff (1975-76)
Most Points, Defenseman, Season	**78**	Jeff Brown (1992-93; 25G, 53A)
Most Points, Center, Season	**115**	Adam Oates (1990-91; 25G, 90A)
Most Points, Right Wing, Season	**131**	Brett Hull (1990-91; 86G, 45A)
Most Points, Left Wing, Season	**102**	Brendan Shanahan (1993-94; 52G, 50A)
Most Points, Rookie, Season	**73**	Jorgen Pettersson (1980-81; 37G, 36A)
Most Shutouts, Season	**8**	Glenn Hall (1968-69)
Most Goals, Game	**6**	Red Berenson (Nov. 7/68)
Most Assists, Game	**5**	Brian Sutter (Nov. 22/83), Bernie Federko (Feb. 27/88), Adam Oates (Jan. 26/91)
Most Points, Game	**7**	Red Berenson (Nov. 7/68; 6G, 1A), Garry Unger (Mar. 13/71; 3G, 4A)

* NHL Record.

Retired Numbers

3	Bob Gassoff	1973-1977
8	Barclay Plager	1967-1977
11	Brian Sutter	1976-1988
24	Bernie Federko	1976-1989

All-time Record vs. Other Clubs

Regular Season

	At Home								On Road								Total							
	GP	W	L	T	OL	GF	GA	PTS	GP	W	L	T	OL	GF	GA	PTS	GP	W	L	T	OL	GF	GA	PTS
Anaheim	20	10	7	3	0	62	53	23	20	13	6	1	0	61	49	27	40	23	13	4	0	123	102	50
Atlanta	3	3	0	0	0	11	1	6	3	2	1	0	0	15	13	4	6	5	1	0	0	26	14	10
Boston	58	26	23	9	0	184	195	61	59	15	35	9	0	161	247	39	117	41	58	18	0	345	442	100
Buffalo	50	29	14	7	0	180	125	65	51	16	29	6	0	159	199	38	101	45	43	13	0	339	324	103
Calgary	62	31	22	9	0	227	188	71	60	26	28	5	1	176	199	58	122	57	50	14	1	403	387	129
Carolina	31	19	9	3	0	119	94	41	30	17	11	2	0	97	90	36	61	36	20	5	0	216	184	77
Chicago	112	55	39	17	1	375	346	128	115	34	62	18	1	343	426	87	227	89	101	35	2	718	772	215
Colorado	38	22	13	3	0	145	117	47	39	13	20	6	0	107	135	32	77	35	33	9	0	252	252	79
Columbus	8	6	1	1	0	33	16	13	7	2	2	2	1	19	15	7	15	8	3	3	1	52	31	20
Dallas	115	63	31	21	0	420	326	147	113	40	51	22	0	333	378	102	228	103	82	43	0	753	704	249
Detroit	107	56	32	19	0	368	299	131	107	40	49	17	1	328	392	98	214	96	81	36	1	696	691	229
Edmonton	42	20	16	6	0	155	152	46	42	16	22	4	0	135	152	36	84	36	38	10	0	290	304	82
Florida	8	6	1	1	0	23	12	13	8	4	2	2	0	18	16	10	16	10	3	3	0	41	28	23
Los Angeles	76	48	18	10	0	287	193	106	76	29	35	12	0	220	258	70	152	77	53	22	0	507	451	176
Minnesota	6	3	2	1	0	12	8	7	6	3	1	2	0	13	12	8	12	6	3	3	0	25	20	15
Montreal	57	14	28	15	0	147	195	43	58	11	40	7	0	159	250	29	115	25	68	22	0	306	445	72
Nashville	13	10	3	0	0	47	21	20	14	8	2	3	1	40	27	20	27	18	5	3	1	87	48	40
New Jersey	45	27	10	7	1	191	139	62	46	17	22	7	0	128	146	41	91	44	32	14	1	319	285	103
NY Islanders	46	17	18	9	2	163	151	45	48	12	25	11	0	127	181	35	94	29	43	20	2	290	332	80
NY Rangers	62	24	28	10	0	183	198	58	60	10	44	6	0	143	245	26	122	34	72	16	0	326	443	84
Ottawa	9	4	3	2	0	27	25	10	9	6	3	0	0	35	20	12	18	10	6	2	0	62	45	22
Philadelphia	67	26	32	7	2	192	212	61	67	12	45	10	0	153	264	34	134	38	77	17	2	345	476	95
Phoenix	48	25	13	10	0	177	133	60	49	18	24	7	0	151	159	43	97	43	37	17	0	328	292	103
Pittsburgh	63	42	15	6	0	244	169	90	64	20	31	12	1	190	238	53	127	62	46	18	1	434	407	143
San Jose	26	17	7	1	1	88	60	36	22	18	3	1	0	81	47	37	48	35	10	2	1	169	107	73
Tampa Bay	10	9	1	0	0	40	21	18	12	5	4	2	1	40	36	13	22	14	5	2	1	80	57	31
Toronto	102	58	29	14	1	348	283	131	98	29	58	11	0	289	367	69	200	87	87	25	1	637	650	200
Vancouver	69	40	20	9	0	260	199	89	70	33	27	9	1	228	209	76	139	73	47	18	1	488	408	165
Washington	40	19	13	8	0	161	126	46	39	15	20	4	0	117	136	34	79	34	33	12	0	278	262	80
Defunct Clubs	32	25	4	3	0	131	55	53	33	11	10	12	0	95	100	34	65	36	14	15	0	226	155	87
Totals	**1425**	**754**	**452**	**211**	**8**	**5000**	**4112**	**1727**	**1425**	**495**	**712**	**210**	**8**	**4161**	**5006**	**1208**	**2850**	**1249**	**1164**	**421**	**16**	**9161**	**9118**	**2935**

Playoffs

	Series	W	L	GP	W	L	T	GF	GA	Last Mtg.	Rnd.	Result
Boston	2	0	2	8	0	8	0	15	48	1972	SF	L 0-4
Buffalo	1	0	1	3	1	2	0	8	7	1976	PRE	L 1-2
Calgary	1	0	1	7	3	4	0	22	28	1986	CF	L 3-4
Chicago	10	3	7	50	22	28	0	142	171	2002	CQF	W 4-1
Colorado	1	0	1	5	1	4	0	11	17	2001	CF	L 1-4
Dallas	12	6	6	66	32	34	0	187	197	2001	CSF	W 4-0
Detroit	7	2	5	40	16	24	0	103	125	2002	CSF	L 1-4
Los Angeles	2	2	0	8	8	0	0	32	13	1998	CQF	W 4-0
Montreal	3	0	3	12	0	12	0	14	42	1977	QF	L 0-4
NY Rangers	1	0	1	6	2	4	0	22	29	1981	QF	L 2-4
Philadelphia	2	2	0	11	8	3	0	34	20	1969	QF	W 4-0
Phoenix	2	2	0	11	7	4	0	39	29	1999	CQF	W 4-3
Pittsburgh	3	2	1	13	7	6	0	45	40	1981	PRE	W 3-2
San Jose	2	1	1	13	7	6	0	38	31	2001	CQF	W 4-2
Toronto	5	3	2	31	17	14	0	88	90	1996	CQF	W 4-2
Vancouver	2	0	2	14	6	8	0	48	44	2003	CQF	L 3-4
Totals	**56**	**23**	**33**	**298**	**137**	**161**	**0**	**848**	**931**			

Calgary totals include Atlanta Flames, 1972-73 to 1979-80. Carolina totals include Hartford, 1979-80 to 1996-97.
Colorado totals include Quebec, 1979-80 to 1994-95. Dallas totals include Minnesota North Stars, 1967-68 to 1992-93.
New Jersey totals include Kansas City, 1974-75 to 1975-76, and Colorado Rockies, 1976-77 to 1981-82.
Phoenix totals include Winnipeg, 1979-80 to 1995-96.

Playoff Results 2003-1999

Year	Round	Opponent	Result	GF	GA
2003	CQF	Vancouver	L 3-4	21	17
2002	CSF	Detroit	L 1-4	11	14
	CQF	Chicago	W 4-1	13	5
2001	CF	Colorado	L 1-4	11	17
	CSF	Dallas	W 4-0	13	6
	CQF	San Jose	W 4-2	16	11
2000	CQF	San Jose	L 3-4	22	20
1999	CSF	Dallas	L 2-4	12	17
	CQF	Phoenix	W 4-3	19	16

Abbreviations: Round: CF – conference final; **CSF** – conference semi-final; **CQF** – conference quarter-final; **SF** – semi-final; **QF** – quarter-final; **PRE** – preliminary round.

2002-03 Results

Oct.	10	Anaheim	3-4
	12	Minnesota	2-2
	15	Carolina	2-1*
	17	Columbus	7-1
	19	Dallas	5-3
	24	at Edmonton	2-1
	26	at Calgary	4-3*
	30	Nashville	7-0
Nov.	2	at NY Islanders	6-1
	3	at NY Rangers	3-2
	5	at Montreal	5-2
	7	Columbus	2-5
	9	Toronto	6-3
	12	at Vancouver	3-6
	15	at Edmonton	0-5
	16	at Calgary	1-0
	20	at Columbus	2-3
	21	Los Angeles	3-2*
	23	Colorado	1-3
	25	San Jose	1-4
	27	at Colorado	4-4
	29	Calgary	7-2
	30	New Jersey	4-5*
Dec.	3	at Boston	4-0
	5	Ottawa	2-2
	7	at Philadelphia	3-1
	8	at Detroit	3-4*
	10	at New Jersey	0-2
	12	at Nashville	2-2
	14	Atlanta	4-0
	17	at Los Angeles	2-6
	18	at Anaheim	2-5
	20	at Phoenix	3-3
	23	Los Angeles	5-0
	26	Colorado	3-2
	28	at Columbus	6-1
	29	Columbus	5-2
	31	at Detroit	1-5
Jan.	2	Chicago	1-4
	4	Tampa Bay	5-1
	7	at Nashville	1-2*
	9	at San Jose	4-1
	11	at Los Angeles	2-1
	12	at Anaheim	1-2
	14	at Phoenix	4-1
	16	NY Islanders	2-3*
	18	Chicago	4-2
	20	at Carolina	5-3
	21	at Atlanta	4-8
	23	at Chicago	3-3
	25	Dallas	2-4
	28	at Washington	5-3
	30	Buffalo	2-1*
Feb.	5	at Dallas	2-2
	6	NY Rangers	4-4
	8	San Jose	4-1
	11	at Buffalo	3-2
	13	Philadelphia	3-4*
	15	Phoenix	3-5
	17	Calgary	5-3
	20	Vancouver	2-4
	22	at Pittsburgh	1-2*
	23	at Minnesota	1-3
	27	Edmonton	4-1
Mar.	1	Minnesota	2-0
	4	Nashville	2-1*
	6	Phoenix	6-3
	7	at Detroit	2-7
	11	at San Jose	4-2
	13	at Vancouver	4-4
	15	at Nashville	1-0
	18	Vancouver	6-4
	20	Anaheim	3-2*
	22	Detroit	2-4
	23	at Dallas	1-3
	26	at Minnesota	1-0
	27	Florida	2-1
	29	Detroit	2-6
	31	Edmonton	5-5
Apr.	3	Chicago	4-6
	4	at Chicago	2-2
	6	at Colorado	2-5

* – Overtime

Entry Draft
Selections 2003-1989

2003
Pick
30	Shawn Belle
62	David Backes
84	Konstantin Barulin
88	Zach Fitzgerald
101	Konstantin Zakharov
127	Alexandre Bolduc
148	Lee Stempniak
159	Chris Beckford-Tseu
189	Jonathan Lehun
221	Evgeny Skachkov
253	Andrei Pervyshin
284	Juhamatti Aaltonen

2002
Pick
48	Alexei Shkotov
62	Andrei Mikhnov
89	Tomas Troliga
120	Robin Jonsson
165	Justin Maiser
191	D.J. King
221	Jonas Johnson
253	Tom Koivisto
284	Ryan MacMurchy

2001
Pick
57	Jay McClement
89	Tuomas Nissinen
122	Igor Valeyev
159	Dmitri Semin
190	Brett Scheffelmaier
253	Petr Cajanek
270	Grant Jacobsen
283	Simon Skoog

2000
Pick
30	Jeff Taffe
65	Dave Morisset
75	Justin Papineau
96	Antoine Bergeron
129	Troy Riddle
167	Craig Weller
229	Brett Lutes
261	Reinhard Divis
293	Lauri Kinos

1999
Pick
17	Barret Jackman
85	Peter Smrek
114	Chad Starling
143	Trevor Byrne
180	Tore Vikingstad
203	Phil Osaer
221	Colin Hemingway
232	Alexander Khavanov
260	Brian McMeekin
270	James Desmarais

1998
Pick
24	Christian Backman
41	Maxim Linnik
83	Matt Walker
157	Brad Voth
170	Andrei Troschinsky
197	Brad Twordik
225	Yevgeny Pastukh
255	John Pohl

1997
Pick
40	Tyler Rennette
86	Didier Tremblay
98	Jan Horacek
106	Jame Pollock
149	Nicholas Bilotto
177	Ladislav Nagy
206	Bobby Haglund
232	Dmitri Plekhanov
244	Marek Ivan

1996
Pick
14	Marty Reasoner
67	Gordie Dwyer
95	Jonathan Zukiwsky
97	Andrei Petrakov
159	Stephen Wagner
169	Daniel Corso
177	Reed Low
196	Andrej Podkonicky
203	Tony Hutchins
229	Konstantin Shafranov

1995
Pick
49	Jochen Hecht
75	Scott Roche
101	Michal Handzus
127	Jeff Ambrosio
153	Denis Hamel
179	Jean-Luc Grand-Pierre
205	Derek Bekar
209	Libor Zabransky

1994
Pick
68	Stephane Roy
94	Tyler Harlton
120	Edvin Frylen
172	Roman Vopat
198	Steve Noble
224	Marc Stephan
250	Kevin Harper
276	Scott Fankhouser

1993
Pick
37	Maxim Bets
63	Jamie Rivers
89	Jamal Mayers
141	Todd Kelman
167	Mike Buzak
193	Eric Boguniecki
219	Mike Grier
245	Libor Prochazka
271	Alexander Vasilevski
275	Christer Olsson

1992
Pick
38	Igor Korolev
62	Vitali Karamnov
64	Vitali Prokhorov
86	Lee Leslie
134	Bob Lachance
158	Ian Laperriere
160	Lance Burns
180	Igor Boldin
182	Nick Naumenko
206	Todd Harris
230	Yuri Gunko
259	Wade Salzman

1991
Pick
27	Steve Staios
64	Kyle Reeves
65	Nathan LaFayette
87	Grayden Reid
109	Jeff Callinan
131	Bruce Gardiner
153	Terry Hollinger
175	Chris Kenady
197	Jed Fiebelkorn
219	Chris MacKenzie
241	Kevin Rappana
263	Mike Veisor

1990
Pick
33	Craig Johnson
54	Patrice Tardif
96	Jason Ruff
117	Kurtis Miller
138	Wayne Conlan
180	Parris Duffus
201	Steve Widmeyer
222	Joe Hawley
243	Joe Fleming

1989
Pick
9	Jason Marshall
31	Rick Corriveau
55	Denny Felsner
93	Daniel Laperriere
114	David Roberts
124	Derek Frenette
135	Jeff Batters
156	Kevin Plager
177	John Roderick
198	John Valo
219	Brian Lukowski

Club Directory

Savvis Center

St. Louis Blues
Savvis Center
1401 Clark Avenue
St. Louis, MO 63103
Phone **314/622-2500**
FAX 314/622-2533
www.stlouisblues.com
Capacity: 19,022

Owner and Chairman	Bill Laurie
President and CEO	Mark Sauer
Sr. Vice President and General Manager	Larry Pleau
Head Coach	Joel Quenneville
Assistant Coaches	Mike Kitchen, Don Lever
Goaltending Coach	Keith Allain
Video/Asst. Strength & Conditioning Coach	Jamie Kompon
Athletic Trainer	Ray Barile
Equipment Manager	Bert Godin
Assistant Equipment Manager	Eric Bechtol
Equipment Assistant	Steve Wissman
Massage Therapist	Jeff Wright
Exercise Physiologist	Dr. Howie Wenger
Sr. Vice President of Marketing and Communications	Jim Woodcock
Director of Team Services	Mike Caruso
Director of Communications	Frank Buonomo
Communications Assistants	Scott Bonanni, Rich Jankowski
Team Photographer	Mark Buckner
Radio Station	KTRS 550 AM
Radio Broadcasters	Chris Kerber, Kelly Chase
Television Station	KPLR-TV WB 11
Television Broadcasters	Ken Wilson, Bernie Federko, Dan McLaughlin
Regional Sports Network	Fox Sports Net (Midwest)

With Chris Pronger sidelined for most of the season, rookie Barret Jackman played a key role in helping the Blues post 99 points in 2002-03 and was rewarded with the Calder Trophy.

Vice President and General Manager

PLEAU, LARRY
Senior Vice President/General Manager, St. Louis Blues.
Born in Lynn, MA, June 29, 1947.

Larry Pleau was named general manager on June 9, 1997, becoming the tenth person to hold that position in team history. He has built the Blues into one of the NHL's top teams, winning the President's Trophy in 1999-2000 and reaching the Western Conference Finals in 2000-01.

Pleau joined the Blues after spending eight seasons with the New York Rangers organization, reaching the position of vice president of player personnel. He joined the Rangers in 1989 as assistant general manager of player development. During Pleau's tenure in New York, the Rangers drafted NHL stars Sergei Zubov, Doug Weight, Alex Kovalev and Niklas Sundstrom. Prior to joining the Rangers, Pleau spent 17 seasons with the Hartford Whalers organization as a player, assistant coach, head coach, general manager and minor league general manager and head coach. He was also instrumental in drafting Ray Ferraro, Ron Francis, Kevin Dineen and Ulf Samuelsson while a member of the Whalers organization.

Pleau played three seasons with the Montreal Canadiens (1969-1972) in the National Hockey League before being the first player signed by the Hartford Whalers of the World Hockey Association. He was a center/left wing for the Whalers from 1972 until his retirement in 1979. He played in 468 regular season games for Hartford, accumulating 157 goals and 215 assists for 372 points. He also played for the 1968 United States Olympic team, the 1969 U.S. national team and went to training camp with Team USA for the 1976 Canada Cup tournament.

NHL Coaching Record

			Regular Season				Playoffs	
Season	Team	Games	W	L	T	Games	W	L
1980-81	Hartford	20	6	12	2	....	....	....
1981-82	Hartford	80	21	41	18	....	....	....
1982-83	Hartford	18	4	13	1	....	....	....
1987-88	Hartford	26	13	13	0	6	2	4
1988-89	Hartford	80	37	38	5	4	0	4
	NHL Totals	**224**	**81**	**117**	**26**	**10**	**2**	**8**

General Managers' History

Lynn Patrick, 1967-68; Scotty Bowman, 1968-69 to 1970-71; Lynn Patrick, 1971-72; Sid Abel, 1972-73; Charles Catto, 1973-74; Gerry Ehman, 1974-75; Dennis Ball, 1975-76; Emile Francis, 1976-77 to 1982-83; Ron Caron, 1983-84 to 1993-94; Mike Keenan, 1994-95, 1995-96; Mike Keenan and Ron Caron, 1996-97; Larry Pleau, 1997-98 to date.

San Jose Sharks

2002-03 Results: 28w-37L-9T-8OTL 73PTS.
Fifth, Pacific Division

2003-04 Schedule

Oct.	Thu. 9	at Edmonton
	Sat. 11	at Calgary
	Sun. 12	at Minnesota
	Thu. 16	Philadelphia
	Sat. 18	Ottawa
	Tue. 21	Anaheim
	Thu. 23	Chicago
	Sat. 25	Phoenix
	Tue. 28	at Carolina
	Thu. 30	at Tampa Bay
Nov.	Sat. 1	at Florida
	Sun. 2	at Atlanta
	Wed. 5	at New Jersey
	Thu. 6	at Boston
	Sat. 8	at Washington
	Tue. 11	Colorado
	Thu. 13	St. Louis
	Sat. 15	Toronto
	Tue. 18	NY Rangers
	Fri. 21	at Phoenix
	Sat. 22	Nashville
	Wed. 26	Chicago
	Fri. 28	at Minnesota*
	Sun. 30	at Edmonton
Dec.	Tue. 2	at Calgary
	Thu. 4	Colorado
	Sat. 6	Dallas
	Wed. 10	at Anaheim
	Thu. 11	Edmonton
	Sat. 13	Anaheim
	Wed. 17	at Detroit
	Thu. 18	at St. Louis
	Sun. 21	at Anaheim*
	Mon. 22	Anaheim
	Fri. 26	Los Angeles
	Sat. 27	at Los Angeles
	Mon. 29	Nashville
	Wed. 31	at Columbus
Jan.	Fri. 2	at Chicago
	Sat. 3	at St. Louis
	Mon. 5	at Vancouver
	Thu. 8	Columbus
	Sat. 10	Atlanta*
	Tue. 13	Dallas
	Thu. 15	Vancouver
	Sat. 17	at Colorado
	Mon. 19	Detroit*
	Wed. 21	at Phoenix
	Thu. 22	Phoenix
	Sat. 24	Minnesota
	Wed. 28	Calgary
	Fri. 30	at Dallas
	Sat. 31	at Nashville
Feb.	Tue. 3	Florida
	Thu. 5	Phoenix
	Tue. 10	at Buffalo
	Wed. 11	at Detroit
	Sat. 14	at Columbus
	Mon. 16	at Philadelphia
	Wed. 18	at Nashville
	Thu. 19	at Chicago
	Mon. 23	Columbus
	Thu. 26	at Vancouver
	Fri. 27	Pittsburgh
	Sun. 29	St. Louis
Mar.	Wed. 3	Montreal
	Fri. 5	at Colorado
	Sun. 7	at Dallas*
	Tue. 9	Minnesota
	Thu. 11	NY Islanders
	Sat. 13	Los Angeles*
	Tue. 16	at Dallas
	Thu. 18	at Los Angeles
	Fri. 19	at Anaheim
	Sun. 21	Edmonton*
	Tue. 23	Detroit
	Thu. 25	Calgary
	Fri. 26	at Phoenix
	Sun. 28	Dallas
	Wed. 31	at Los Angeles
Apr.	Fri. 2	Vancouver
	Sun. 4	Los Angeles*

Denotes afternoon game.

Franchise date: May 9, 1990

PACIFIC DIVISION

13th NHL Season

Year-by-Year Record

Season	GP	Home W	L	T	OL	Road W	L	T	OL	Overall W	L	T	OL	GF	GA	Pts.	Finished	Playoff Result
2002-03	82	17	16	5	3	11	21	4	5	28	37	9	8	214	239	73	5th, Pacific Div.	Out of Playoffs
2001-02	82	25	11	3	2	19	16	5	1	44	27	8	3	248	199	99	1st, Pacific Div.	Lost Conf. Semi-Final
2000-01	82	22	14	4	1	18	13	8	2	40	27	12	3	217	192	95	2nd, Pacific Div.	Lost Conf. Semi-Final
1999-2000	82	21	14	3	3	14	16	7	4	35	30	10	7	225	214	87	4th, Pacific Div.	Lost Conf. Semi-Final
1998-99	82	17	15	9	...	14	18	9	...	31	33	18	...	196	191	80	4th, Pacific Div.	Lost Conf. Quarter-Final
1997-98	82	17	19	5	...	17	19	5	...	34	38	10	...	210	216	78	4th, Pacific Div.	Lost Conf. Quarter-Final
1996-97	82	14	23	4	...	13	24	4	...	27	47	8	...	211	278	62	7th, Pacific Div.	Out of Playoffs
1995-96	82	12	26	3	...	8	29	4	...	20	55	7	...	252	357	47	7th, Pacific Div.	Out of Playoffs
1994-95	48	10	13	1	...	9	12	3	...	19	25	4	...	129	161	42	3rd, Pacific Div.	Lost Conf. Semi-Final
1993-94	84	19	13	10	...	14	22	6	...	33	35	16	...	252	265	82	3rd, Pacific Div.	Lost Conf. Semi-Final
1992-93	84	8	33	1	...	3	38	1	...	11	71	2	...	218	414	24	6th, Smythe Div.	Out of Playoffs
1991-92	80	14	23	3	...	3	35	2	...	17	58	5	...	219	359	39	6th, Smythe Div.	Out of Playoffs

Patrick Marleau tied for the team lead in goals last year with a career-high 28. On October 19, 2002, he became the youngest player (23 years, 34 days) to appear in 400 career games since Bobby Carpenter did so at the age of 22 in 1986.

2003-04 Player Personnel

FORWARDS	HT	WT	S	Place of Birth	Date	2002-03 Club
BERNIER, Steve	6-2	230	R	Quebec City, Que.	3/31/85	Moncton
BOYES, Brad	6-0	180	R	Mississauga, Ont.	4/17/82	St. John's-Cleveland
CHEECHOO, Jonathan	6-0	205	R	Moose Factory, Ont.	7/15/80	Cleveland-San Jose
CLOWE, Ryan	6-2	205	R	St. John's, Nfld.	9/30/82	Rimouski-Montreal (QMJHL)
DAMPHOUSSE, Vincent	6-1	200	L	Montreal, Que.	12/17/67	San Jose
DIMITRAKOS, Niko	5-11	190	R	Boston, MA	5/21/79	San Jose-Cleveland
DISALVATORE, Jon	6-1	180	R	Bangor, ME	3/30/81	Providence College
EKMAN, Nils	5-11	185	L	Stockholm, Sweden	3/11/76	Hartford
GOC, Marcel	6-1	190	L	Calw, West Germany	8/24/83	Mannheim
GRAVES, Adam	6-0	205	L	Toronto, Ont.	4/12/68	San Jose
HANSEN, Tavis	6-1	205	R	Prince Albert, Sask.	6/17/75	Cleveland
HARVEY, Todd	6-0	200	R	Hamilton, Ont.	2/17/75	San Jose
KOROLYUK, Alexander	5-9	195	L	Moscow, USSR	1/15/76	Kazan
LEVESQUE, Willie	6-0	195	R	Oak Bluffs, MA	1/22/80	Cleveland
LOYNS, Lynn	5-11	200	L	Naicam, Sask.	2/21/81	San Jose-Cleveland
MARLEAU, Patrick	6-2	210	L	Aneroid, Sask.	9/15/79	San Jose
McCAULEY, Alyn	5-11	190	L	Brockville, Ont.	5/29/77	Toronto-San Jose
MICHALEK, Milan	6-2	207	L	Jindrichuv Hradec, Czech.	12/7/84	Ceske Budejovice-Kladno
MOSCEVSKY, Yuri	6-4	220	L	Yorba Linda, CA	10/20/78	Cleveland
PARKER, Scott	6-5	230	R	Hanford, CA	1/29/78	Colorado
PLIHAL, Tomas	6-1	195	L	Frydlant v Cechach, Czech.	3/28/83	Kootenay
PRIMEAU, Wayne	6-3	220	L	Scarborough, Ont.	6/4/76	Pittsburgh-San Jose
RICCI, Mike	6-0	185	L	Scarborough, Ont.	10/27/71	San Jose
RISSMILLER, Pat	6-3	195	L	Belmont, MA	10/26/78	Cleveland-Cincinnati (ECHL)
SMITH, Mark	5-10	205	L	Edmonton, Alta.	10/24/77	San Jose
STEVENSON, Grant	5-11	170	R	Spruce Grove, Alta.	10/15/81	Minnesota State
STURM, Marco	6-0	195	L	Dingolfing, West Germany	9/8/78	San Jose
THORNTON, Scott	6-3	220	L	London, Ont.	1/9/71	San Jose
VALETTE, Craig	6-0	200	L	Shellbrook, Sask.	10/7/82	Portland (WHL)
ZALESAK, Miroslav	6-0	185	L	Skalica, Czech.	1/2/80	San Jose-Cleveland

DEFENSEMEN						
CARKNER, Matt	6-4	230	R	Winchester, Ont.	11/3/80	Cleveland
CLOUTIER, David	6-1	205	R	Quebec City, Que.	12/17/81	Cleveland
DAVISON, Rob	6-2	225	L	St. Catharines, Ont.	5/1/80	San Jose-Cleveland
EHRHOFF, Christian	6-2	185	L	Moers, West Germany	7/6/82	Krefeld
FAHEY, Jim	6-0	215	R	Boston, MA	5/11/79	San Jose-Cleveland
FIBIGER, Jesse	6-3	210	L	Victoria, B.C.	4/4/78	San Jose-Cleveland
GORGES, Josh	6-1	185	L	Kelowna, B.C.	8/14/84	Kelowna
HANNAN, Scott	6-2	220	L	Richmond, B.C.	1/23/79	San Jose
McLAREN, Kyle	6-4	230	L	Humboldt, Sask.	6/18/77	San Jose
MULICK, Robert	6-2	210	R	Toronto, Ont.	10/23/79	Cleveland
MURRAY, Doug	6-3	245	L	Bromma, Sweden	3/12/80	Cornell
PREISSING, Tom	6-0	205	L	Rosemount, MN	12/3/78	Colorado College
RATHJE, Mike	6-5	245	L	Mannville, Alta.	5/11/74	San Jose
STUART, Brad	6-2	215	L	Rocky Mountain House, Alta.	11/6/79	San Jose

GOALTENDERS	HT	WT	C	Place of Birth	Date	2002-03 Club
KIPRUSOFF, Miikka	6-2	190	L	Turku, Finland	10/26/76	San Jose
KOTYK, Seamus	5-11	180	L	London, Ont.	10/7/80	Cleveland
NABOKOV, Evgeni	6-0	200	L	Ust-Kamenogorsk, USSR	7/25/75	San Jose
PATZOLD, Dimitri	6-0	190	L	Ust-Kamenogorsk, USSR	2/3/83	Mannheim
SCHAEFER, Nolan	6-1	175	L	Yellow Grass, Sask.	1/15/80	Providence College
TOSKALA, Vesa	5-10	190	L	Tampere, Finland	5/20/77	San Jose-Cleveland

Coach

WILSON, RON
Coach, San Jose Sharks. Born in Vikings, Alta., August 19, 1958.

Ron Wilson was hired as the sixth head coach in Sharks history on December 4, 2003. Prior to his arrival in San Jose, Wilson had found both regular season and postseason success in his stops in Washington and Anaheim. Most recently, he spent five seasons (1998 to 2002) behind the Washington Capitals bench where he led his team to the 1998 Stanley Cup Finals and back-to-back Southeast Division titles in 1999-00 and 2000-01. He was a finalist for the Jack Adams Award as the NHL's coach of the year in 1999-00.

After three seasons as an assistant coach with Vancouver from 1990 to 1993, Wilson began his NHL head coaching career when he was named the first head coach for the expansion Mighty Ducks of Anaheim in 1993-94. He spent four seasons with the club, leading the Ducks to their first postseason appearance in 1996-97. A veteran of coaching on the international stage as well, Wilson led Team USA to the gold medal in the 1996 World Cup of Hockey. He also served as Team USA's head coach at the 1994 and 1996 World Championships and at the 1998 Winter Olympic Games in Nagano, Japan.

On the ice, Wilson was originally selected by Toronto in the eighth round (132nd overall) of the 1975 NHL Entry Draft during a standout career at Providence College. In four seasons at Providence from 1973 to 1977, Wilson was an All-America selection twice and a four-time All-ECAC selection. In his sophomore season, the defenseman was named ECAC Player of the Year after leading the nation in scoring.

Wilson began his professional career with the Dallas Blackhawks of the Central Hockey League and later saw his first NHL action in 1977-78 with Toronto. After six seasons in the Swiss Elite League from 1980 to 1986, Wilson signed as a free agent with the Minnesota North Stars where he played for parts of three seasons. He also competed for the U.S. national team in 1975, 1981, 1983 and 1987. Wilson retired from playing in 1988 after posting 93 points (26 goals, 67 assists) in 177 career NHL games with Toronto and Minnesota.

2002-03 Scoring
* - rookie

Regular Season

Pos	#	Player	Team	GP	G	A	Pts	+/-	PIM	PP	SH	GW	GT	S	%
R	8	Teemu Selanne	S.J.	82	28	36	64	-6	30	7	0	5	1	253	11.1
C	25	Vincent Damphousse	S.J.	82	23	38	61	-13	66	15	0	6	0	176	13.1
C	12	Patrick Marleau	S.J.	82	28	29	57	-10	33	8	1	3	1	172	16.3
L	19	Marco Sturm	S.J.	82	28	20	48	9	16	6	0	2	0	208	13.5
C	18	Mike Ricci	S.J.	75	11	23	34	-12	53	5	1	2	0	101	10.9
D	2	Mike Rathje	S.J.	82	7	22	29	-19	48	3	0	1	0	147	4.8
C	10	Alyn McCauley	TOR	64	6	9	15	3	16	0	0	0	0	79	7.6
			S.J.	16	3	7	10	-2	4	3	0	0	0	29	10.3
			TOTAL	80	9	16	25	1	20	3	0	0	0	108	8.3
D	22	Scott Hannan	S.J.	81	3	19	22	0	61	1	0	0	0	103	2.9
L	17	Scott Thornton	S.J.	41	9	12	21	-7	41	4	0	1	0	64	14.1
D	21	Jim Fahey	S.J.	43	1	19	20	-3	33	0	0	0	0	66	1.5
R	13	Todd Harvey	S.J.	76	3	16	19	5	74	0	0	0	0	64	4.7
L	9	Adam Graves	S.J.	82	9	9	18	-14	32	1	0	0	0	118	7.6
C	15	Wayne Primeau	PIT	70	5	11	16	-30	55	1	0	1	0	101	5.0
			S.J.	7	1	1	2	2	0	0	0	0	0	13	7.7
			TOTAL	77	6	12	18	-28	55	1	0	0	0	114	5.3
R	14	* Jonathan Cheechoo	S.J.	66	9	7	16	-5	39	0	0	3	1	94	9.6
C	16	Mark Smith	S.J.	75	4	11	15	1	64	0	0	0	0	68	5.9
D	7	Brad Stuart	S.J.	36	4	10	14	-6	46	2	0	1	0	63	6.3
R	23	* Niko Dimitrakos	S.J.	21	6	7	13	-7	8	3	0	0	1	34	17.6
D	4	Kyle McLaren	S.J.	33	0	8	8	-10	30	0	0	0	0	43	0.0
D	5	Jeff Jillson	S.J.	26	0	6	6	-7	9	0	0	0	0	22	0.0
R	28	Matt Bradley	S.J.	46	2	3	5	-4	37	0	0	0	0	21	9.5
L	26	* Lynn Loyns	S.J.	19	3	0	3	-4	19	0	0	0	0	12	25.0
R	46	* Miroslav Zalesak	S.J.	10	1	2	3	-2	0	0	0	0	0	8	12.5
D	38	* Rob Davison	S.J.	15	1	2	3	4	22	0	0	0	0	15	6.7
C	41	Ryan Kraft	S.J.	7	0	1	1	2	0	0	0	0	0	1	0.0
L	49	* Chad Wiseman	S.J.	4	0	0	0	-2	4	0	0	0	0	1	0.0
D	4	John Jakopin	S.J.	12	0	0	0	0	11	0	0	0	0	3	0.0
D	53	* Jesse Fibiger	S.J.	16	0	0	0	-5	2	0	0	0	0	2	0.0

Goaltending

No.	Goaltender	GPI	Mins	Avg	W	L	T	EN	SO	GA	SA	S%	G	A	PIM
29	* Vesa Toskala	11	537	2.35	4	3	1	1	1	21	287	.927	0	0	0
20	Evgeni Nabokov	55	3227	2.71	19	28	8	5	3	146	1561	.906	0	0	10
37	* Miikka Kiprusoff	22	1199	3.25	5	14	0	1	1	65	537	.879	0	0	0
	Totals	82	4996	2.87	28	45	9	7	5	239	2392	.900			

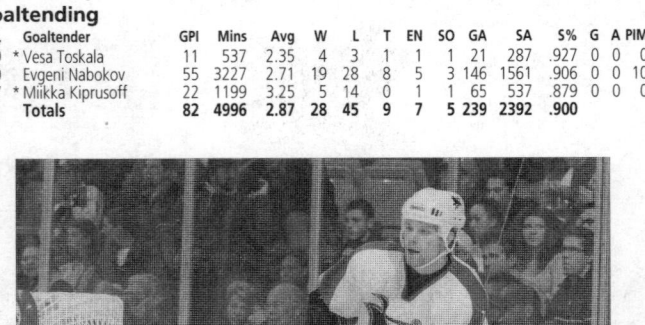

Injuries and extended contract negotiations limited Brad Stuart to just 36 games last season. Still, he ranked fourth on the team in average ice time at 20:53 per game.

Coaching History

George Kingston, 1991-92, 1992-93; Kevin Constantine, 1993-94, 1994-95; Kevin Constantine and Jim Wiley, 1995-96; Al Sims, 1996-97; Darryl Sutter, 1997-98 to 2001-02; Darryl Sutter and Ron Wilson, 2002-03; Ron Wilson, 2003-04.

Coaching Record

			Regular Season				Playoffs		
Season	Team	Games	W	L	T		Games	W	L
1993-94	Anaheim (NHL)	84	33	46	5		....	....	....
1994-95	Anaheim (NHL)	48	16	27	5		....	....	....
1995-96	Anaheim (NHL)	82	35	39	8		....	....	....
1996-97	Anaheim (NHL)	82	36	33	13		11	4	7
1997-98	Washington (NHL)	82	40	30	12		21	12	9
1998-99	Washington (NHL)	82	31	45	6		....	....	....
1999-2000	Washington (NHL)	82	44	26	12		5	1	4
2000-01	Washington (NHL)	82	41	31	10		6	2	4
2001-02	Washington (NHL)	82	36	35	11		....	....	....
2002-03	San Jose (NHL)	57	19	31	7		....	....	....
	NHL Totals	763	331	343	89		43	19	24

Club Records

Team
(Figures in brackets for season records are games played; records for fewest points, wins, ties, losses, goals, goals against are for 70 or more games)

Most Points .... 99 — 2001-02 (82)
Most Wins .... 44 — 2001-02 (82)
Most Ties .... 18 — 1998-99 (82)
Most Losses .... *71 — 1992-93 (84)
Most Goals .... 252 — 1993-94 (84), 1995-96 (82)

Most Goals Against .... 414 — 1992-93 (84)
Fewest Points .... 24 — 1992-93 (84)
Fewest Wins .... 11 — 1992-93 (84)
Fewest Ties .... *2 — 1992-93 (84)
Fewest Losses .... 33 — 1998-99 (82)
Fewest Goals .... 196 — 1998-99 (82)
Fewest Goals Against ...... 191 — 1998-99 (82)

Longest Winning Streak
Overall .... 7 — Mar. 24-Apr. 5/94, Jan. 30-Feb. 28/02
Home .... 5 — Jan. 21-Feb. 15/95, Oct. 11-Nov. 3/01
Away .... 6 — Nov. 30-Dec. 19/01

Longest Undefeated Streak
Overall .... 10 — Nov. 27-Dec. 19/01 (9 wins, 1 tie)
Home .... 7 — Oct. 12-Nov. 22/00 (6 wins, 1 tie)
Away .... 10 — Dec. 26/00-Feb. 16/01 (6 wins, 4 ties)

Longest Losing Streak
Overall .... *17 — Jan. 4-Feb. 12/93
Home .... 9 — Nov. 19-Dec. 19/92
Away .... 19 — Nov. 27/92-Feb. 12/93

Longest Winless Streak
Overall .... 20 — Dec. 29/92-Feb. 12/93 (19 losses, 1 tie)
Home .... 9 — Nov. 19-Dec. 19/92 (9 losses)
Away .... 19 — Nov. 27/92-Feb. 12/93 (19 losses)

Most Shutouts, Season ...... 9 — 2000-01 (82), 2001-02 (82)
Most PIM, Season .... 2,134 — 1992-93 (84)
Most Goals, Game .... 10 — Jan. 13/96 (S.J. 10 at Pit. 8), Mar. 30/02 (CBJ 2 at S.J. 10)

Individual

Most Seasons .... 10 — Mike Rathje
Most Games, Career .... 591 — Mike Rathje
Most Goals, Career .... 206 — Owen Nolan
Most Assists, Career ...... 225 — Owen Nolan
Most Points, Career .... 431 — Owen Nolan (206G, 225A)
Most PIM, Career .... 1,001 — Jeff Odgers
Most Shutouts, Career ..... 17 — Evgeni Nabokov

Longest Consecutive Games Streak .... 228 — Mike Ricci (Nov. 22/97-Oct. 20/00)

Most Goals, Season .... 44 — Owen Nolan (1999-2000)
Most Assists, Season .... 52 — Kelly Kisio (1992-93)
Most Points, Season .... 84 — Owen Nolan (1999-2000; 44G, 40A)

Most PIM, Season .... 326 — Link Gaetz (1991-92)
Most Points, Defenseman, Season .... 64 — Sandis Ozolinsh (1993-94; 26G, 38A)
Most Points, Center, Season .... 78 — Kelly Kisio (1992-93; 26G, 52A)
Most Points, Right Wing, Season .... 84 — Owen Nolan (1999-2000; 44G, 40A)
Most Points, Left Wing, Season .... 66 — Johan Garpenlov (1992-93; 22G, 44A)
Most Points, Rookie, Season .... 59 — Pat Falloon (1991-92; 25G, 34A)
Most Shutouts, Season .... 7 — Evgeni Nabokov (2001-02)
Most Goals, Game .... 4 — Owen Nolan (Dec. 19/95)
Most Assists, Game .... 4 — Seven times
Most Points, Game........... 6 — Owen Nolan (Oct. 4/99; 3G, 3A)

* NHL Record.

Captains' History
Doug Wilson, 1991-92, 1992-93; Bob Errey, 1993-94; Bob Errey and Jeff Odgers, 1994-95; Jeff Odgers, 1995-96; Todd Gill, 1996-97, 1997-98; Owen Nolan, 1998-99 to 2002-03.

All-time Record vs. Other Clubs

Regular Season

	At Home								On Road								Total							
	GP	W	L	T	OL	GF	GA	PTS	GP	W	L	T	OL	GF	GA	PTS	GP	W	L	T	OL	GF	GA	PTS
Anaheim	27	12	12	2	1	80	77	27	27	15	9	2	1	91	72	33	54	27	21	4	2	171	149	60
Atlanta	3	2	0	1	0	11	5	5	3	2	0	0	1	9	5	5	6	4	0	1	1	20	10	10
Boston	11	4	5	2	0	30	38	10	9	0	7	2	0	21	34	2	20	4	12	4	0	51	72	12
Buffalo	10	5	1	4	0	36	33	14	10	0	10	0	0	26	50	0	20	5	11	4	0	62	83	14
Calgary	32	11	17	4	0	93	99	26	30	10	15	4	1	84	110	25	62	21	32	8	1	177	209	51
Carolina	11	7	4	0	0	50	31	14	10	5	5	0	0	23	31	10	21	12	9	0	0	73	62	24
Chicago	24	12	9	2	1	66	65	27	23	9	10	2	2	70	71	22	47	21	19	4	3	136	136	49
Colorado	22	7	15	0	0	60	83	14	21	4	13	4	0	39	76	12	43	11	28	4	0	99	159	26
Columbus	6	6	0	0	0	26	7	12	6	3	3	0	0	17	20	6	12	9	3	0	0	43	27	18
Dallas	27	9	15	1	2	64	80	21	26	10	13	3	0	60	71	23	53	19	28	4	2	124	151	44
Detroit	24	7	13	3	1	76	97	18	23	2	20	1	0	41	97	5	47	9	33	4	1	117	194	23
Edmonton	30	16	10	4	0	108	93	36	31	6	18	7	0	67	106	19	61	22	28	11	0	175	199	55
Florida	8	4	2	2	0	23	17	10	8	1	2	5	0	21	23	7	16	5	4	7	0	44	40	17
Los Angeles	34	19	12	3	0	116	98	41	34	8	21	3	2	76	109	21	68	27	33	6	2	192	207	62
Minnesota	6	3	2	1	0	14	10	7	6	1	3	1	1	12	16	4	12	4	5	2	1	26	26	11
Montreal	10	4	3	2	1	29	25	11	11	2	7	2	0	20	36	6	21	6	10	4	1	49	61	17
Nashville	10	4	5	1	0	22	28	9	10	6	3	1	0	29	19	13	20	10	8	2	0	51	47	22
New Jersey	10	3	5	1	1	24	32	8	11	4	6	1	0	25	41	9	21	7	11	2	1	46	73	17
NY Islanders	11	4	5	1	1	25	36	10	11	4	5	2	0	35	40	10	22	8	10	3	1	60	76	20
NY Rangers	12	2	9	1	0	29	47	5	10	2	6	1	1	29	40	6	22	4	15	2	1	58	87	11
Ottawa	8	5	3	0	0	17	12	10	9	1	4	4	0	26	36	6	17	6	7	4	0	43	48	16
Philadelphia	11	3	7	1	0	22	31	7	10	2	6	2	0	22	34	6	21	5	13	3	0	44	65	13
Phoenix	29	14	11	3	1	100	93	32	32	11	17	3	1	87	106	26	61	25	28	6	2	187	199	58
Pittsburgh	12	4	6	2	0	30	52	10	9	4	4	1	0	32	41	9	21	8	10	3	0	62	93	19
St. Louis	22	3	18	1	0	47	81	7	26	8	16	1	1	60	88	18	48	11	34	2	1	107	169	25
Tampa Bay	10	3	6	1	0	32	36	7	11	4	6	1	0	29	30	9	21	7	12	2	0	61	66	16
Toronto	14	5	7	2	0	30	38	12	18	4	12	2	0	47	69	10	32	9	19	4	0	77	107	22
Vancouver	32	12	15	5	0	94	101	29	30	9	17	4	0	80	111	22	62	21	32	9	0	174	212	51
Washington	10	6	3	1	0	29	26	13	11	6	5	0	0	33	32	12	21	12	8	1	0	62	58	25
Totals	476	196	220	51	9	1383	1471	452	476	143	263	58	12	1208	1614	356	952	339	483	109	21	2591	3085	808

Playoffs

	Series	W	L	GP	W	L	T	GF	GA	Last Mtg.	Rnd.	Result
Calgary	1	1	0	7	4	3	0	26	35	1995	CQF	W 4-3
Colorado	2	0	2	13	5	8	0	38	44	2002	CSF	L 3-4
Dallas	2	0	2	11	3	8	0	19	31	2000	CSF	L 1-4
Detroit	2	1	1	11	4	7	0	27	51	1995	CSF	L 0-4
Phoenix	1	1	0	5	4	1	0	13	7	2002	CQF	W 4-1
St. Louis	2	1	1	13	6	7	0	31	38	2001	CQF	L 3-4
Toronto	1	0	1	7	3	4	0	21	26	1994	CSF	L 3-4
Totals	11	4	7	67	29	38	0	175	232			

Playoff Results 2003-1999

Year	Round	Opponent	Result	GF	GA
2002	CSF	Colorado	L 3-4	21	25
	CQF	Phoenix	W 4-1	13	7
2001	CQF	St. Louis	L 2-4	11	16
2000	CSF	Dallas	L 1-4	7	15
	CQF	St. Louis	W 4-3	20	22
1999	CQF	Colorado	L 2-4	17	19

Abbreviations: Round: CSF – conference semi-final; CQF – conference quarter-final.

2002-03 Results

Date	Opponent	Score		Date	Opponent	Score
Oct. 10	Detroit	3-6		11	Vancouver	3-0
12	at Vancouver	3-5		13	at Los Angeles	2-3*
17	Edmonton	4-3		16	Buffalo	2-2
19	Colorado	1-3		18	Dallas	1-3
21	Vancouver	2-5		20	at Phoenix	1-3
24	at Nashville	2-1		22	New Jersey	4-5*
25	at Columbus	5-4		25	Minnesota	4-1
27	at Chicago	2-3		27	at Los Angeles	3-0
29	at Detroit	2-4		28	Los Angeles	3-1
31	at Minnesota	1-2*		30	Anaheim	3-4
Nov. 3	at Anaheim	4-3	Feb. 5	Carolina	6-2
5	Los Angeles	5-2		7	at Minnesota	3-4
7	Nashville	2-2		8	at St. Louis	3-4
9	Minnesota	2-4		10	at Detroit	4-5
11	NY Rangers	4-5		12	at Columbus	0-1
13	at Atlanta	2-3*		14	at Chicago	4-2
15	at Tampa Bay	2-4		16	at Dallas	1-3
16	at Florida	7-3		17	at Los Angeles	2-3
19	at Washington	3-2		19	NY Islanders	0-3
21	at Philadelphia	2-2		21	Columbus	6-0
23	at Pittsburgh	5-2		24	Calgary	5-2
25	at St. Louis	4-1		27	at Vancouver	3-2
27	at Nashville	2-4	Mar. 1	at Calgary	3-4
30	Phoenix	2-3		4	at Edmonton	1-2
Dec. 3	at Phoenix	3-2*		6	Montreal	4-3*
6	Columbus	3-2		8	at Phoenix	4-6
7	Nashville	2-4		9	at Dallas	0-3
12	Pittsburgh	5-2		11	St. Louis	2-4
14	Washington	2-0		13	at Anaheim	2-3*
16	at NY Rangers	1-2*		15	Calgary	3-2
17	at Montreal	3-1		17	Chicago	2-3*
19	at Ottawa	3-9		20	at Colorado	0-2
21	at Toronto	3-3		21	Boston	3-2
23	at Boston	2-5		22	Anaheim	2-3*
26	Anaheim	4-1		24	Tampa Bay	1-4
28	Chicago	3-3		27	Detroit	3-0
30	Philadelphia	2-1		29	Dallas	3-4
Jan. 2	Dallas	1-3		31	at Colorado	1-3
4	Colorado	1-6	Apr. 2	at Calgary	2-2
6	Edmonton	5-5		3	at Edmonton	3-3
9	St. Louis	1-4		5	Phoenix	3-3

* – Overtime

Carolina totals include Hartford, 1991-92 to 1996-97.
Dallas totals include Minnesota North Stars, 1991-92 to 1992-93.
Colorado totals include Quebec, 1991-92 to 1994-95.
Phoenix totals include Winnipeg, 1991-92 to 1995-96.

Entry Draft Selections 2003-1991

2003

Pick	
6	Milan Michalek
16	Steve Bernier
43	Joshua Hennessy
47	Matthew Carle
139	Patrick Ehelechner
201	Jonathan Tremblay
205	Joe Pavelski
216	Kai Hospelt
236	Alexander Hult
267	Brian O'Hanley
276	Carter Lee

2002

Pick	
27	Mike Morris
52	Dan Spang
86	Jonas Fiedler
139	Kris Newbury
163	Tom Walsh
217	Tim Conboy
288	Michael Hutchins

2001

Pick	
20	Marcel Goc
106	Christian Ehrhoff
107	Dimitri Patzold
140	Tomas Plihal
175	Ryan Clowe
182	Tom Cavanagh

2000

Pick	
41	Tero Maatta
104	Jon Disalvatore
142	Michal Pinc
166	Nolan Schaefer
183	Michal Macho
246	Chad Wiseman
256	Pasi Saarinen

1999

Pick	
14	Jeff Jillson
82	Mark Concannon
111	Willie Levesque
155	Nico Dimitrakos
229	Eric Betournay
241	Doug Murray
257	Hannes Hyvonen

1998

Pick	
3	Brad Stuart
29	Jonathan Cheechoo
65	Eric Laplante
98	Rob Davison
104	Miroslav Zalesak
127	Brandon Coalter
145	Mikael Samuelsson
185	Robert Mulick
212	Jim Fahey

1997

Pick	
2	Patrick Marleau
23	Scott Hannan
82	Adam Colagiacomo
107	Adam Nittel
163	Joe Dusbabek
192	Cam Severson
219	Mark Smith

1996

Pick	
2	Andrei Zyuzin
21	Marco Sturm
55	Terry Friesen
102	Matt Bradley
137	Michel Larocque
164	Jake Deadmarsh
191	Cory Cyrenne
217	David Thibeault

1995

Pick	
12	Teemu Riihijarvi
38	Peter Roed
64	Marko Makinen
90	Vesa Toskala
116	Miikka Kiprusoff
130	Michal Bros
140	Timo Hakanen
142	Jaroslav Kudrna
167	Brad Mehalko
168	Robert Jindrich
194	Ryan Kraft
220	Mikko Markkanen

1994

Pick	
11	Jeff Friesen
37	Angel Nikolov
66	Alexei Yegorov
89	Vaclav Varada
115	Brian Swanson
141	Alexander Korolyuk
167	Sergei Gorbachev
193	Eric Landry
219	Evgeni Nabokov
240	Tomas Pisa
245	Aniket Dhadphale
271	David Beauregard

1993

Pick	
6	Viktor Kozlov
28	Shean Donovan
45	Vlastimil Kroupa
58	Ville Peltonen
80	Alexander Osadchy
106	Andrei Buschan
132	Petri Varis
154	Fredrik Oduya
158	Anatoli Filatov
184	Todd Holt
210	Jonas Forsberg
236	Jeff Salajko
262	Jamie Matthews

1992

Pick	
3	Mike Rathje
10	Andrei Nazarov
51	Alexander Cherbayev
75	Jan Caloun
99	Marcus Ragnarsson
123	Michal Sykora
147	Eric Bellerose
171	Ryan Smith
195	Chris Burns
219	Alexander Kholomeyev
243	Victor Ignatjev

1991

Pick	
2	Pat Falloon
23	Ray Whitney
30	Sandis Ozolinsh
45	Dody Wood
67	Kerry Toporowski
89	Dan Ryder
111	Frank Nilsson
133	Jaroslav Otevrel
155	Dean Grillo
177	Corwin Saurdiff
199	Dale Craigwell
221	Aaron Kriss
243	Mikhail Kravets

General Managers' History

Jack Ferreira, 1991-92; Chuck Grillo (V.P. Director of Player Personnel), 1992-93 to 1995-96; Dean Lombardi, 1996-97 to 2002-03; Doug Wilson, 2003-04.

Vice President and General Manager

WILSON, DOUG
Executive Vice President/General Manager, San Jose Sharks.
Born in Ottawa, Ont., July 5, 1957.

Doug Wilson officially took over as the San Jose Sharks executive vice president and general manager on May 13, 2003. Prior to his appointment, Wilson served as the Sharks director of pro development for five seasons. Working with former g.m. and executive v.p. Dean Lombardi and the entire hockey department, Wilson played a major role in creating a positive atmosphere in the dressing room and on the-ice. He was an integral member of the NHL Players Association for four years before re-joining the Sharks.

Originally acquired by San Jose during training camp before the Sharks inaugural season (1991-92), Wilson brought instant credibility and respect to the young franchise. He played two seasons for the Sharks, serving as the franchise's first captain and was twice named Sharks nominee (1992 and 1993) for the King Clancy Award (for leadership and humanitarian contribution both on-and off-the- ice). Wilson announced his retirement as a player during the Sharks training camp in 1993-94 after playing in 1,024 career games.

A first-round draft choice (sixth overall) of the Blackhawks in 1977 after a stellar junior career with the Ottawa 67s (Ontario Hockey League), Wilson played 14 seasons in Chicago and still ranks as the club's highest scoring defenseman in points (779), goals (225) and assists (554). In addition, he led all Blackhawks defensemen in scoring for 11 consecutive seasons (1980-81 through 1990-91) and captured the 1982 Norris Trophy as the NHL's best defenseman after scoring 39 goals on the season. He played in seven NHL All-Star Games (six with Chicago and one with San Jose) and was named to the NHL First All-Star Team in 1981-82. He was a Second-Team All-Star in 1984-85 and 1989-90. Wilson was inducted into the Chicago Sports Hall of Fame in September 1999. In October 1998, the Ottawa 67s, Wilson's former junior team, honored his stellar career by retiring his number 7 sweater. In addition, during the same weekend of activities in his hometown, he was inducted into the Ottawa Sports Hall of Fame.

Wilson sat on the board of the Canadian Hockey Association and has extensive experience in talent evaluation. He served as management consultant for Canada's entries in the 1994, 1995, 1996 and 1997 World Junior Championship tournaments — resulting in four consecutive gold medal finishes — and served on the management team for Canada's entry in the 1998 Winter Olympic Games in Nagano.

Club Directory

HP Pavilion at San Jose

San Jose Sharks
HP Pavilion at San Jose
525 West Santa Clara Street
San Jose, CA 95113
Phone **408/287-7070**
FAX 408/999-5797
www.sjsharks.com
Capacity: 17,496

San Jose Sports & Entertainment Enterprises
Board Members . . . . Kevin Compton, Greg Reyes, Greg Jamison, Tom McEnery, Brent Jones

Investors in SJSEE include
Blue Line Associates (Kevin Compton, Greg Reyes, Hasso Plattner, Stratton Sclavos, Gary Valenzuela, Harvey Armstrong) William DelBiaggio, George Gund III, Greg Jamison, Floyd Kvamme, Tom McEnery, Gordon Russell, Rudy Staedler

Executive Staff

President & Chief Executive Officer	Greg Jamison
Executive Vice President of Business Operations	Malcolm Bordelon
Executive Vice President & General Manager (HP Pavilion at San Jose)	Jim Goddard
Executive Vice President & General Counsel	Don Gralnek
Executive Vice President & G.M. (Sharks)	Doug Wilson
Executive Vice President & Chief Financial Officer	Gregg Olson
Vice President of Finance	Ken Caveney
Vice President of Corporate Partnerships	Greg Elliott
Vice President of Sales & Marketing	Kent Russell
Vice President of Building Operations	Rich Sotelo
Vice President and Assistant G.M. (Sharks)	Wayne Thomas
Executive Assistants	Tricia Sullivan, Michelle Simmons, Kristen Fuce
Administrative Assistant	Adrienne Sletten

Hockey Operations

Head Coach	Ron Wilson
Assistant Coach	Tim Hunter
Assistant Coach	Rob Zettler
Goaltender Coach	Warren Strelow
Special Consultant to the General Manager	John Ferguson
Professional Scouts	Barry Long, Cap Raeder
Director of Amateur Scouting	Tim Burke
Chief Scout	Ray Payne
Assistant to the General Manager	Joe Will
Scouts	Gilles Cote, Pat Funk, Rob Grillo, Brian Gross, Karel Masopust, Ilkka Sinisalo
Executive Assistant	Brenda Will
Video Scouting Coordinator	Bob Friedlander
Team Services Coordinator	Marshall Dickerson
Head Athletic Trainer	Ray Tufts, A.T.,C
Athletic Trainer	Tom Woodcock, A.T.,C,L
Strength & Conditioning Coordinator	Mac Read
Massage Therapist	Wes Howard
Equipment Manager	Mike Aldrich
Assistant Equipment Manager	Kurt Harvey
Equipment Assistant & Equipment Transportation	Roy Sneesby
Administrative Assistant	Cathy Hancock
Head Coach, Cleveland Barons (AHL)	Roy Sommer
Assistant Coach, Cleveland Barons (AHL)	David Cunniff
Head Trainer, Cleveland Barons (AHL)	Dave Zenobi
Equipment Manager, Cleveland Barons (AHL)	Steve Wissman
Assistant Equip. Manager, Cleveland Barons (AHL)	Phil Simon
Team Physician	Arthur J. Ting, M.D.
Team Dentist	Robert Bonahoom, D.D.S.
Team Vision Specialist	Vincent S. Zuccaro, O.D., F.A.A.O.
Medical Staff	Warren King, M.D., Mark Sontag, M.D., Will Straw, M.D.

Silicon Valley Sports & Entertainment/Business Operations

Senior Director of Media Relations & Publishing	Ken Arnold
Director of Broadcasting	Frank Albin
Director of Marketing	Beth Brigino
Director of Ticket Operations	Mary Enriquez
Director of Ticket Sales	John Castro
Director of Fan Development/The Sharks Foundation	Rob Jaynes
Director of Event Presentation	Steve Maroni
Director of Suite Hospitality	Jay O'Sullivan
Director of Internet Services	Roger Ross
Media Relations Manager	Scott Emmert
Media Relations Coordinator	Ben Stephenson

The Sharks Foundation

Manager, The Sharks Foundation	Jackie Fuce, Julie Vennewitz-Pierce

Finance

Director of Information Technology	James Struckle
Human Resources Manager	Cathy Chandler
Accounting Manager	Tina Park

Building Operations

Director of Ticket Operations	Daniel DeBoer
Director of Booking & Events	Steve Kirsner, Chuck Ryder
Director of Guest Services	Ken Sweezey
Facilities Technical Director	Greg Carrolan
Director of Building Services	Monte Chavez
Chief Engineer	Mark Mullins

Miscellaneous

Television Station	FOX Sports Net
Radio Network Flagship	KFOX 98.5 (KUFX FM)
Television Play-By-Play Broadcaster	Randy Hahn
Television Color Analyst	Drew Remenda
Radio Play-By-Play Broadcaster	Dan Rusanowsky
Radio Color Analyst	Pete Stemkowski
Team Photographers	Don Smith, Rocky Widner
P.A. Announcer	Joe Ike
In Game Host	Danny Miller
Mascot	S.J. Sharkie
Organist	James Day

Tampa Bay Lightning

2002-03 Results: 36w-25L-16T-5OTL 93PTS.
First, Southeast Division

2003-04 Schedule

Oct.	Fri.	10	Boston
	Thu.	16	Phoenix
	Sat.	18	at New Jersey
	Tue.	21	Atlanta
	Thu.	23	at Columbus
	Sat.	25	Minnesota
	Thu.	30	San Jose
Nov.	Sat.	1	Carolina
	Tue.	4	Washington
	Thu.	6	Los Angeles
	Sat.	8	Pittsburgh
	Sun.	9	at Carolina*
	Tue.	11	at Florida
	Fri.	14	at Washington
	Thu.	20	NY Islanders
	Sat.	22	Buffalo
	Sun.	23	at Carolina
	Tue.	25	NY Rangers
	Fri.	28	St. Louis
	Sat.	29	at Atlanta
Dec.	Tue.	2	at Montreal
	Thu.	4	Ottawa
	Sat.	6	at Buffalo
	Sun.	7	at NY Rangers*
	Tue.	9	at NY Islanders
	Thu.	11	at Ottawa
	Sat.	13	Montreal
	Tue.	16	at Toronto
	Thu.	18	at Philadelphia
	Sat.	20	Dallas
	Tue.	23	at Boston
	Fri.	26	at Atlanta
	Sat.	27	Boston
	Mon.	29	Anaheim
	Wed.	31	Florida*
Jan.	Fri.	2	Columbus*
	Sat.	3	Philadelphia
	Tue.	6	at Ottawa
	Thu.	8	at Montreal
	Fri.	9	at New Jersey
	Sun.	11	at NY Rangers*

	Tue.	13	at Pittsburgh
	Thu.	15	Carolina
	Sat.	17	at Florida
	Mon.	19	Colorado
	Wed.	21	at Vancouver
	Thu.	22	at Edmonton
	Sat.	24	at Calgary
	Tue.	27	at Pittsburgh
	Thu.	29	Pittsburgh
	Sat.	31	Atlanta
Feb.	Mon.	2	at Philadelphia
	Tue.	3	at Washington
	Thu.	5	at Nashville
	Tue.	10	Toronto
	Thu.	12	Montreal
	Sat.	14	Florida
	Tue.	17	Philadelphia
	Thu.	19	at St. Louis
	Fri.	20	at Buffalo
	Mon.	23	at Washington
	Wed.	25	at Atlanta
	Thu.	26	Toronto
	Sat.	28	Washington
Mar.	Mon.	1	at Colorado
	Wed.	3	at Chicago
	Fri.	5	New Jersey
	Sat.	6	at Florida
	Mon.	8	at Detroit
	Wed.	10	at Carolina
	Fri.	12	NY Rangers
	Sat.	13	Carolina
	Tue.	16	NY Islanders
	Thu.	18	Buffalo
	Sat.	20	at Boston*
	Sun.	21	at NY Islanders*
	Tue.	23	at Toronto
	Thu.	25	New Jersey
	Sat.	27	Washington
	Mon.	29	Ottawa
Apr.	Thu.	1	Florida
	Sat.	3	Atlanta

* Denotes afternoon game.

Year-by-Year Record

		Home				Road				Overall							
Season	GP	W	L	T	OL	W	L	T	OL	W	L	T	OL	GF	GA	Pts.	Finished	Playoff Result
2002-03	82	22	9	7	3	14	16	9	2	36	25	16	5	219	210	93	1st, Southeast Div.	Lost Conf. Semi-Final
2001-02	82	16	17	5	3	11	23	6	1	27	40	11	4	178	219	69	3rd, Southeast Div.	Out of Playoffs
2000-01	82	17	19	3	2	7	28	3	3	24	47	6	5	201	280	59	5th, Southeast Div.	Out of Playoffs
1999-2000	82	13	20	4	4	6	27	5	3	19	47	9	7	204	310	54	4th, Southeast Div.	Out of Playoffs
1998-99	82	12	25	4	...	7	29	5	...	19	54	9	...	179	292	47	4th, Southeast Div.	Out of Playoffs
1997-98	82	11	23	7	...	6	32	3	...	17	55	10	...	151	269	44	7th, Atlantic Div.	Out of Playoffs
1996-97	82	15	18	8	...	17	22	2	...	32	40	10	...	217	247	74	6th, Atlantic Div.	Out of Playoffs
1995-96	82	22	14	5	...	16	18	7	...	38	32	12	...	238	248	88	5th, Atlantic Div.	Lost Conf. Quarter-Final
1994-95	48	10	14	0	...	7	14	3	...	17	28	3	...	120	144	37	6th, Atlantic Div.	Out of Playoffs
1993-94	84	14	22	6	...	16	21	5	...	30	43	11	...	224	251	71	7th, Atlantic Div.	Out of Playoffs
1992-93	84	12	27	3	...	11	27	4	...	23	54	7	...	245	332	53	6th, Norris Div.	Out of Playoffs

Franchise date: December 16, 1991

SOUTHEAST DIVISION

12th NHL Season

In his first full season with the Lightning, Dan Boyle ranked fifth among the league's top-scoring defensemen with 13 goals and 40 assists, more than double his previous career bests. His seven playoff assists also ranked fifth among defensemen.

2003-04 Player Personnel

FORWARDS

	HT	WT	S	Place of Birth	Date	2002-03 Club
AFANASENKOV, Dmitry	6-2	200	R	Arkhangelsk, USSR	5/12/80	Springfield-Kloten
ALEXEEV, Nikita	6-5	210	L	Murmansk, USSR	12/27/81	Tampa Bay-Springfield
ANDREYCHUK, Dave	6-4	220	R	Hamilton, Ont.	9/29/63	Tampa Bay
CIBAK, Martin	6-1	195	L	Liptovsky Mikulas, Czech.	5/17/80	Springfield
CLYMER, Ben	6-1	199	R	Bloomington, MN	4/11/78	Tampa Bay
DINGMAN, Chris	6-4	225	L	Edmonton, Alta.	7/6/76	Tampa Bay
FEDOTENKO, Ruslan	6-2	195	L	Kiev, Ukraine	1/18/79	Tampa Bay
KEEFE, Sheldon	5-11	185	R	Brampton, Ont.	9/17/80	Tampa Bay-Springfield
LECAVALIER, Vincent	6-4	205	L	Ile Bizard, Que.	4/21/80	Tampa Bay
MODIN, Fredrik	6-4	225	L	Sundsvall, Sweden	10/8/74	Tampa Bay
OLVESTAD, Jimmie	6-1	189	L	Stockholm, Sweden	2/16/80	Tampa Bay-Springfield
PERRIN, Eric	5-9	176	L	Laval, Que.	11/1/75	JYP Jyvaskyla
RICHARDS, Brad	6-1	198	L	Murray Harbour, P.E.I.	5/2/80	Tampa Bay
ROY, Andre	6-4	213	L	Port Chester, NY	2/8/75	Tampa Bay
ST. LOUIS, Martin	5-9	185	L	Laval, Que.	6/18/75	Tampa Bay
SOMERVUORI, Eero	5-10	167	R	Jarvenpaa, Finland	2/7/79	HPK
STILLMAN, Cory	6-0	194	L	Peterborough, Ont.	12/20/73	St. Louis
SVITOV, Alexander	6-3	198	L	Omsk, USSR	11/3/82	Springfield-Tampa Bay
TAYLOR, Tim	6-1	189	L	Stratford, Ont.	2/6/69	Tampa Bay
WILLIS, Shane	6-1	190	R	Edmonton, Alta.	6/13/77	Springfield

DEFENSEMEN

	HT	WT	S	Place of Birth	Date	2002-03 Club
BOYLE, Dan	5-11	190	R	Ottawa, Ont.	7/12/76	Tampa Bay
CULLIMORE, Jassen	6-5	244	L	Simcoe, Ont.	12/4/72	Tampa Bay
HOLMQVIST, Andreas	6-4	190	R	Stockholm, Sweden	7/23/81	Linkopings
KUBINA, Pavel	6-4	230	R	Celadna, Czech.	4/15/77	Tampa Bay
LAUKKANEN, Janne	6-1	196	L	Lahti, Finland	3/19/70	Hartford-Pittsburgh-Tampa Bay
LUKOWICH, Brad	6-1	200	L	Cranbrook, B.C.	8/12/76	Tampa Bay
PRATT, Nolan	6-3	200	L	Fort McMurray, Alta.	8/14/75	Tampa Bay
RUMBLE, Darren	6-1	200	L	Barrie, Ont.	1/23/69	Springfield-Tampa Bay
SARICH, Cory	6-3	204	R	Saskatoon, Sask.	8/16/78	Tampa Bay
TREPANIER, Pascal	6-0	210	R	Gaspe, Que.	9/4/73	Nsh-Milwaukee-San Antonio

GOALTENDERS

	HT	WT	C	Place of Birth	Date	2002-03 Club
GRAHAME, John	6-2	214	L	Denver, CO	8/31/75	Boston-Tampa Bay
KHABIBULIN, Nikolai	6-1	203	L	Sverdlovsk, USSR	1/13/73	Tampa Bay
KONSTANTINOV, Evgeny	6-0	176	L	Kazan, USSR	3/29/81	Tampa Bay-Springfield

Coaching History

Terry Crisp, 1992-93 to 1996-97; Terry Crisp, Rick Paterson and Jacques Demers, 1997-98; Jacques Demers, 1998-99; Steve Ludzik, 1999-2000; Steve Ludzik and John Tortorella, 2000-01; John Tortorella, 2001-02 to date.

Coach

TORTORELLA, JOHN
Coach, Tampa Bay Lightning. Born in Boston, MA, June 24, 1958.

After finishing out the 1999-2000 season as the interim coach of the New York Rangers, John Tortorella joined the Tampa Bay Lightning as an associate coach on July 7, 2000. He took over head coaching duties on January 6, 2001. In 2002-03, he led the team to a club-record 93 points and just the second playoff berth in franchise history. The Lightning's first-round victory marked the team's first playoff series win.

Prior to his season with the Rangers, Tortorella had spent two years as an assistant coach with the Phoenix Coyotes and eight years in the Buffalo Sabres organization. He was an assistant coach in Buffalo from 1989-90 to 1994-95. Tortorella served as the head coach of the Rochester Americans, Buffalo's AHL affiliate, in 1995-96 and 1996-97. He guided Rochester to the Calder Cup championship during his first season behind the bench.

Tortorella starred at the University of Maine for three seasons and was twice named a Conference All-Star. After playing hockey in Sweden, Tortorella played in the Atlantic Coast Hockey League with Virginia, Hampton Roads and Erie. He later spent two seasons (1986-87 and 1987-88) as the coach and general manager of the Virginia Lancers, compiling a record of 87-31 and winning the league championship and coach of the year honors during both campaigns. Following the 1987-88 season, Tortorella joined the Fort Wayne Komets of the IHL for their 1988 playoff run. He was an assistant coach with the New Haven Nighthawks of the AHL in 1988-89.

Coaching Record

Season	Team		Regular Season				Playoffs		
		Games	W	L	T		Games	W	L
1995-96	Rochester (AHL)	80	37	38	5		19	15	4
1996-97	Rochester (AHL)	80	40	30	9		10	6	4
1999-2000	NY Rangers (NHL)	4	0	3	1		....	....	....
2000-01	Tampa Bay (NHL)	43	12	30	1		....	....	....
2001-02	Tampa Bay (NHL)	82	27	44	11		....	....	....
2002-03	Tampa Bay (NHL)	82	36	30	16		11	5	6
	NHL Totals	**211**	**75**	**107**	**29**		**11**	**5**	**6**

2002-03 Scoring
- rookie

Regular Season

Pos	#	Player	Team	GP	G	A	Pts	+/−	PIM	PP	SH	GW	GT	S	%
C	20	Vaclav Prospal	T.B.	80	22	57	79	9	53	9	0	4	0	134	16.4
C	4	Vincent Lecavalier	T.B.	80	33	45	78	0	39	11	2	3	1	274	12.0
C	19	Brad Richards	T.B.	80	17	57	74	3	24	4	0	2	0	277	6.1
R	26	Martin St. Louis	T.B.	82	33	37	70	10	32	12	3	5	3	201	16.4
D	22	Dan Boyle	T.B.	77	13	40	53	9	44	8	0	1	1	136	9.6
L	33	Fredrik Modin	T.B.	76	17	23	40	7	43	2	1	4	1	179	9.5
L	25	Dave Andreychuk	T.B.	72	20	14	34	−12	34	15	0	3	2	170	11.8
R	17	Ruslan Fedotenko	T.B.	76	19	13	32	−7	44	6	0	6	0	114	16.7
D	13	Pavel Kubina	T.B.	75	3	19	22	−7	78	0	0	0	0	139	2.2
R	7	Ben Clymer	T.B.	65	6	12	18	−2	57	1	0	1	0	103	5.8
L	36	Andre Roy	T.B.	62	10	7	17	0	119	0	0	2	0	85	11.8
D	37	Brad Lukowich	T.B.	70	1	14	15	4	46	0	0	0	0	52	1.9
D	21	Cory Sarich	T.B.	82	5	9	14	−3	63	0	0	2	0	79	6.3
C	27	Tim Taylor	T.B.	82	4	8	12	−13	38	0	0	1	0	95	4.2
C	16	* Alexander Svitov	T.B.	63	4	4	8	−4	58	0	0	0	0	69	5.8
D	23	Janne Laukkanen	PIT	17	1	6	7	−3	8	0	0	0	0	10	10.0
			T.B.	2	1	0	1	1	0	0	0	0	0	2	50.0
			TOTAL	19	2	6	8	−2	8	0	0	0	0	12	16.7
D	44	Nolan Pratt	T.B.	67	1	7	8	−6	35	0	0	0	0	38	2.6
R	28	Sheldon Keefe	T.B.	37	2	5	7	−1	24	0	0	1	0	51	3.9
D	3	Marc Bergevin	PIT	69	2	5	7	−9	36	0	0	0	0	27	7.4
			T.B.	1	0	0	0	−2	0	0	0	0	0	0	0.0
			TOTAL	70	2	5	7	−11	36	0	0	0	0	27	7.4
R	15	Nikita Alexeev	T.B.	37	4	2	6	−6	8	1	0	1	1	52	7.7
D	2	Stan Neckar	T.B.	70	1	4	5	−6	43	0	0	0	0	38	2.6
D	5	Jassen Cullimore	T.B.	28	1	3	4	3	31	0	0	0	0	23	4.3
L	11	Chris Dingman	T.B.	51	2	1	3	−11	91	0	0	0	0	41	4.9
R	18	Jimmie Olvestad	T.B.	37	0	3	3	−2	16	0	0	0	0	30	0.0
D	38	Darren Rumble	T.B.	19	0	0	0	−2	6	0	0	0	0	10	0.0

Goaltending

No.	Goaltender	GPI	Mins	Avg	W	L	T	EN	SO	GA	SA	S%	G	A	PIM
47	John Grahame	17	914	2.23	6	5	4	1	2	34	424	.920	0	0	9
35	Nikolai Khabibulin	65	3787	2.47	30	22	11	5	4	156	1760	.911	0	3	8
30	Kevin Hodson	7	283	2.54	0	3	1	1	0	12	101	.881	0	0	2
1	* Evgeny Konstantin	1	20	3.00	0	0	0	0	1	1	6	.833	0	0	2
	Totals	**82**	**5026**	**2.51**	**36**	**30**	**16**	**7**	**6**	**210**	**2298**	**.909**			

Playoffs

Pos	#	Player	Team	GP	G	A	Pts	+/−	PIM	PP	SH	GW	GT	S	%
R	26	Martin St. Louis	T.B.	11	7	5	12	5	0	1	2	3	1	25	28.0
D	22	Dan Boyle	T.B.	11	0	7	7	0	6	0	0	0	0	26	0.0
C	20	Vaclav Prospal	T.B.	11	4	2	6	−3	8	2	0	0	0	23	17.4
L	25	Dave Andreychuk	T.B.	11	3	3	6	−1	10	1	0	1	0	25	12.0
C	4	Vincent Lecavalier	T.B.	11	3	3	6	−2	22	1	0	1	1	32	9.4
C	19	Brad Richards	T.B.	11	0	5	5	−3	12	0	0	0	0	32	0.0
L	33	Fredrik Modin	T.B.	11	2	0	2	−2	18	0	0	0	0	27	7.4
D	5	Jassen Cullimore	T.B.	11	1	1	2	−2	4	0	0	0	0	12	8.3
D	2	Stan Neckar	T.B.	7	1	1	2	0	2	0	0	0	0	4	0.0
D	21	Cory Sarich	T.B.	11	0	2	2	2	6	0	0	0	0	16	0.0
R	7	Ben Clymer	T.B.	11	0	2	2	−2	6	0	0	0	0	11	0.0
L	11	Chris Dingman	T.B.	10	1	1	2	1	18	0	0	0	0	18	5.6
R	15	Nikita Alexeev	T.B.	11	1	0	1	−3	0	0	0	0	0	13	7.7
D	44	Nolan Pratt	T.B.	4	0	1	1	−1	0	0	0	0	0	1	0.0
L	36	Andre Roy	T.B.	5	0	1	1	0	2	0	0	0	0	11	0.0
D	37	Brad Lukowich	T.B.	9	0	1	1	−2	2	0	0	0	0	4	0.0
C	27	Tim Taylor	T.B.	11	0	1	1	1	6	0	0	0	0	14	0.0
R	17	Ruslan Fedotenko	T.B.	11	0	1	1	−6	2	0	0	0	0	17	0.0
D	23	Janne Laukkanen	T.B.	2	0	1	1	0	0	0	0	0	0	1	0.0
C	16	* Alexander Svitov	T.B.	7	0	0	0	−2	6	0	0	0	0	3	0.0
D	13	Pavel Kubina	T.B.	11	0	0	0	−4	12	0	0	0	0	14	0.0

Goaltending

No.	Goaltender	GPI	Mins	Avg	W	L	EN	SO	GA	SA	S%	G	A	PIM
47	John Grahame	1	111	1.08	0	1	0	0	2	48	.958	0	0	0
35	Nikolai Khabibulin	10	644	2.42	5	5	1	0	26	299	.913	0	0	0
	Totals	**11**	**760**	**2.29**	**5**	**6**	**1**	**0**	**29**	**348**	**.917**			

Though he struggled at times, Nikolai Khabibulin set several club records including a 16-game unbeaten streak (12-0-4) and 30 wins.

Club Records

Team

(Figures in brackets for season records are games played; records for fewest points, wins, ties, losses, goals, goals against are for 70 or more games)

Most Points	93	2002-03 (82)
Most Wins	38	1995-96 (82)
Most Ties	16	2002-03 (82)
Most Losses	55	1997-98 (82)
Most Goals	245	1992-93 (84)
Most Goals Against	332	1992-93 (84)
Fewest Points	44	1997-98 (82)
Fewest Wins	17	1997-98 (82)
Fewest Ties	6	2000-01 (82)
Fewest Losses	25	2002-03 (82)
Fewest Goals	151	1997-98 (82)
Fewest Goals Against	210	2002-03 (82)

Longest Winning Streak
Overall	5	Twice
Home	6	Feb. 15-Mar. 10/96, Nov. 17-Dec. 21/01
Away	4	Jan. 6-13/97

Longest Undefeated Streak
Overall	13	Mar. 7-Apr. 2/03 (7 wins, 6 ties)
Home	9	Feb. 25-Apr. 2/03 (5 wins, 4 ties)
Away	6	Twice

Longest Losing Streak
Overall	13	Jan. 3-Feb. 2/98
Home	10	Jan. 3-Feb. 26/98
Away	11	Oct. 24-Dec. 10/97

Longest Winless Streak
Overall	16	Twice
Home	11	Jan. 2-Feb. 26/98 (10 losses, 1 tie)
Away	17	Dec. 2/99-Feb. 19/00 (14 losses, 3 ties)

Most Shutouts, Season	9	2001-02 (82)
Most PIM, Season	1,823	1997-98 (82)
Most Goals, Game	8	Nov. 22/00 (Atl. 2 at T.B. 8)

Individual

Most Seasons	7	Mikael Andersson, Rob Zamuner, Daren Puppa
Most Games, Career	475	Rob Zamuner
Most Goals, Career	114	Vincent Lecavalier
Most Assists, Career	189	Brian Bradley
Most Points, Career	300	Brian Bradley (111G, 189A)
Most PIM, Career	782	Chris Gratton
Most Shutouts, Career	12	Daren Puppa
Longest Consecutive Games Streak	226	Rob Zamuner (Nov. 1/95-Mar. 30/98)
Most Goals, Season	42	Brian Bradley (1992-93)
Most Assists, Season	57	Vaclav Prospal, Brad Richards (2002-03)
Most Points, Season	86	Brian Bradley (1992-93; 42G, 44A)
Most PIM, Season	258	Enrico Ciccone (1995-96)
Most Points, Defenseman, Season	65	Roman Hamrlik (1995-96; 16G, 49A)
Most Points, Center, Season	86	Brian Bradley (1992-93; 42G, 44A)
Most Points, Right Wing, Season	70	Martin St. Louis (2002-03; 33G, 37A)
Most Points, Left Wing, Season	56	Fredrik Modin (2000-01; 32G, 24A)
Most Points, Rookie, Season	62	Brad Richards (2000-01; 21G, 41A)
Most Shutouts, Season	7	Nikolai Khabibulin (2001-02)
Most Goals, Game	4	Chris Kontos (Oct. 7/92)
Most Assists, Game	4	Four times
Most Points, Game	6	Doug Crossman (Nov. 7/92; 3G, 3A)

Captains' History

No captain, 1992-93 to 1994-95; Paul Ysebaert, 1995-96, 1996-97; Paul Ysebaert and Mikael Renberg, 1997-98; Rob Zamuner, 1998-99; Bill Houlder, Chris Gratton and Vincent Lecavalier, 1999-2000; Vincent Lecavalier, 2000-01; no captain, 2001-02; Dave Andreychuk, 2002-03 to date.

All-time Record vs. Other Clubs

Regular Season

	At Home								On Road								Total							
	GP	W	L	T	OL	GF	GA	PTS	GP	W	L	T	OL	GF	GA	PTS	GP	W	L	T	OL	GF	GA	PTS
Anaheim	8	4	4	0	0	17	21	8	8	3	4	1	0	20	24	7	16	7	8	1	0	37	45	15
Atlanta	10	7	1	1	1	40	23	16	10	1	6	3	0	28	41	5	20	8	7	4	1	68	64	21
Boston	21	8	8	3	2	61	63	21	21	1	14	5	1	44	78	8	42	9	22	8	3	105	141	29
Buffalo	21	4	13	3	1	44	68	12	21	7	12	2	0	57	58	16	42	11	25	5	1	101	126	28
Calgary	10	5	4	1	0	31	32	11	9	3	5	0	1	18	30	7	19	8	9	1	1	49	62	18
Carolina	23	12	8	3	0	63	55	27	24	4	14	5	1	60	78	14	47	16	22	8	1	123	133	41
Chicago	11	4	3	3	1	26	28	12	13	3	8	2	0	30	42	8	24	7	11	5	1	56	70	20
Colorado	11	8	2	1	0	35	27	17	12	2	8	2	0	25	50	6	23	10	10	3	0	60	77	23
Columbus	2	2	0	0	0	5	1	4	2	0	1	1	0	3	5	1	4	2	1	1	0	8	6	5
Dallas	12	1	9	2	0	19	35	4	11	3	7	1	0	27	39	7	23	4	16	3	0	46	74	11
Detroit	14	4	8	1	1	43	61	10	11	1	10	0	0	20	46	2	25	5	18	1	1	63	107	12
Edmonton	11	3	5	2	1	31	35	9	9	2	7	0	0	18	24	4	20	5	12	2	1	49	59	13
Florida	25	8	12	5	0	51	70	21	25	7	12	4	2	56	72	20	50	15	24	9	2	107	142	41
Los Angeles	9	5	4	0	0	23	21	10	11	8	1	2	0	36	24	18	20	13	5	2	0	59	45	28
Minnesota	2	0	1	1	0	5	7	1	3	0	3	0	0	8	13	0	5	0	4	1	0	13	20	1
Montreal	21	8	7	5	1	48	53	22	20	9	10	1	0	47	55	19	41	17	17	6	1	95	108	41
Nashville	4	1	1	2	0	11	10	4	5	3	2	0	0	11	16	6	9	4	3	2	0	22	26	10
New Jersey	23	6	12	5	0	54	72	17	24	4	18	2	0	37	90	10	47	10	30	7	0	91	162	27
NY Islanders	24	11	11	2	0	63	75	24	23	11	10	1	1	67	70	24	47	22	21	3	1	130	145	48
NY Rangers	23	10	9	3	1	81	79	24	25	10	12	2	1	80	84	23	48	20	21	5	2	161	163	47
Ottawa	21	8	11	2	0	65	71	18	21	8	13	0	0	46	80	16	42	16	24	2	0	111	151	34
Philadelphia	24	7	15	1	1	60	75	16	23	2	14	7	0	39	74	11	47	9	29	8	1	99	149	27
Phoenix	9	4	5	0	0	28	32	8	11	5	6	0	0	26	28	10	20	9	11	0	0	54	60	18
Pittsburgh	21	10	9	2	0	61	59	22	21	3	14	3	1	50	87	10	42	13	23	5	1	111	146	32
St. Louis	12	5	5	2	0	36	40	12	10	1	9	0	0	21	40	2	22	6	14	2	0	57	80	14
San Jose	11	7	4	0	0	30	29	14	10	6	3	1	1	36	32	13	21	13	7	1	0	66	61	27
Toronto	18	2	15	0	1	34	64	5	19	6	11	1	1	48	71	14	37	8	26	1	2	82	135	19
Vancouver	9	3	5	0	1	31	37	7	8	0	6	2	0	13	35	2	17	3	11	2	1	44	72	9
Washington	26	7	17	2	0	56	85	16	26	5	17	4	0	53	94	14	52	12	34	6	0	109	179	30
Totals	436	164	208	52	12	1152	1328	392	436	118	257	52	9	1024	1474	297	872	282	465	104	21	2176	2802	689

Playoffs

	Series	W	L	GP	W	L	T	GF	GA	Last Mtg.	Rnd.	Result
New Jersey	1	0	1	5	1	4	0	8	14	2003	CSF	L 1-4
Philadelphia	1	0	1	6	2	4	0	13	26	1996	CQF	L 2-4
Washington	1	1	0	6	4	2	0	14	15	2003	CQF	W 4-2
Totals	3	1	2	17	7	10	0	35	55			

Playoff Results 2003-1999

Year	Round	Opponent	Result	GF	GA
2003	CSF	New Jersey	L 1-4	8	14
	CQF	Washington	W 4-2	14	15

Abbreviations: Round: CSF – conference semi-final; **CQF** – conference quarter-final.

Carolina totals include Hartford, 1992-93 to 1996-97.
Dallas totals include Minnesota North Stars, 1992-93.

Colorado totals include Quebec, 1992-93 to 1994-95.
Phoenix totals include Winnipeg, 1992-93 to 1995-96.

2002-03 Results

Date	Opponent	Score	Date	Opponent	Score
Oct. 10	at Florida	4-3*	9	Atlanta	2-3*
12	Carolina	5-1	11	New Jersey	3-3
18	Atlanta	8-5	14	at Ottawa	0-7
19	at Pittsburgh	3-3	17	Pittsburgh	2-3
21	at NY Rangers	4-2	18	at Philadelphia	2-3
23	at Columbus	2-2	20	Ottawa	6-2
25	Washington	3-2	22	Montreal	2-2
26	at New Jersey	1-5	24	at Dallas	4-1
28	at Florida	6-1	25	at Nashville	2-3
30	NY Rangers	3-0	28	at Philadelphia	3-0
Nov. 1	at Washington	2-3	30	Carolina	3-1
2	at Pittsburgh	3-5	Feb. 4	Washington	1-5
5	at Toronto	3-4	6	Toronto	2-3*
8	Pittsburgh	4-1	8	at Florida	4-4
9	Chicago	2-3*	11	at NY Islanders	2-6
11	Phoenix	4-2	14	at Atlanta	2-2
15	San Jose	4-2	15	Boston	5-2
17	at Carolina	2-1*	17	Washington	3-1
19	Philadelphia	2-3	19	Atlanta	2-0
21	NY Islanders	2-7	21	at Carolina	2-2
23	at New Jersey	3-1	23	Buffalo	1-4
27	at Buffalo	1-1	25	Anaheim	2-0
29	Vancouver	3-5	27	Florida	3-1
Dec. 1	at NY Rangers	3-4	Mar. 1	at Ottawa	2-1
3	at Toronto	3-4*	4	at NY Islanders	3-1
5	Edmonton	3-2	5	at Detroit	2-3
7	at Boston	2-3*	7	Colorado	4-3
8	at Chicago	1-3	9	Buffalo	1-1
10	at Minnesota	3-5	12	Los Angeles	4-2
12	at Montreal	3-2	14	at Buffalo	4-2
14	NY Islanders	4-3	15	at Montreal	2-1
18	at Carolina	1-1	17	Minnesota	3-3
19	Toronto	1-2	20	at Los Angeles	2-2
21	Nashville	2-2	22	at Phoenix	4-0
23	at Washington	0-3	24	at San Jose	4-1
27	Boston	5-2	27	New Jersey	2-2
29	NY Rangers	5-3	29	Florida	1-1
31	Ottawa	3-6	31	at Boston	2-2
Jan. 2	at Calgary	1-4	Apr. 2	Montreal	2-1
4	at St. Louis	1-5	4	Philadelphia	1-4
7	Detroit	1-0	6	at Atlanta	2-6

* – Overtime

Entry Draft
Selections 2003-1992

2003 Pick		2000 Pick		1997 Pick		1994 Pick	
34	Mike Egener	8	Nikita Alexeev	7	Paul Mara	8	Jason Wiemer
41	Matt Smaby	34	Ruslan Zainullin	33	Kyle Kos	34	Colin Cloutier
96	Jonathan Boutin	81	Alexander Kharitonov	61	Matt Elich	55	Vadim Epanchintsev
192	Doug O'Brien	126	Johan Hagglund	108	Mark Thompson	86	Dmitri Klevakin
224	Gerald Coleman	161	Pavel Sedov	109	Jan Sulc	137	Daniel Juden
227	Jay Rosehill	191	Aaron Gionet	112	Karel Betik	138	Bryce Salvador
255	Raimonds Danilics	222	Marek Priechodsky	153	Andrei Skopintsev	164	Chris Maillet
256	Brady Greco	226	Brian Eklund	168	Justin Jack	190	Alexei Baranov
273	Albert Vishnyakov	233	Alexander Polukeyev	170	Eero Somervuori	216	Yuri Smirnov
286	Zbynek Hrdel	263	Thomas Ziegler	185	Samuel St-Pierre	242	Shawn Gervais
287	Nick Tarnasky			198	Shawn Skolney	268	Brian White
		1999 Pick		224	Paul Comrie		
2002 Pick		47	Sheldon Keefe			**1993 Pick**	
60	Adam Henrich	67	Evgeny Konstantinov	**1996 Pick**		3	Chris Gratton
100	Dmitri Kazionov	75	Brett Scheffelmaier	16	Mario Larocque	29	Tyler Moss
135	Joseph Pearce	88	Jimmie Olvestad	69	Curtis Tipler	55	Allan Egeland
162	Gerard Dicaire	127	Kaspars Astashenko	125	Jason Robinson	81	Marian Kacir
170	P.J. Atherton	148	Michal Lanicek	152	Nikolai Ignatov	107	Ryan Brown
174	Karri Akkanen	182	Fedor Fedorov	157	Xavier Delisle	133	Kiley Hill
183	Paul Ranger	187	Ivan Rachunek	179	Pavel Kubina	159	Matthieu Raby
213	Fredrik Norrena	216	Erkki Rajamaki			185	Ryan Nauss
233	Vasily Koshechkin	244	Mikko Kuparinen	**1995 Pick**		211	Alexandre Laporte
255	Ryan Craig			5	Daymond Langkow	237	Brett Duncan
256	Darren Reid	**1998 Pick**		30	Mike McBain	263	Mark Szoke
286	Alexei Glukhov	1	Vincent Lecavalier	56	Shane Willis		
287	John Toffey	64	Brad Richards	108	Konstantin Golokhvastov	**1992 Pick**	
		72	Dmitry Afanasenkov	134	Eduard Pershin	1	Roman Hamrlik
2001 Pick		92	Eric Beaudoin	160	Cory Murphy	26	Drew Bannister
3	Alexander Svitov	121	Curtis Rich	186	Joe Cardarelli	49	Brent Gretzky
47	Alexander Polushin	146	Sergei Kuznetsov	212	Zac Bierk	74	Aaron Gavey
61	Andreas Holmqvist	174	Brett Allan			97	Brantt Myhres
94	Evgeni Artukhin	194	Oak Hewer			122	Martin Tanguay
123	Aaron Lobb	221	Daniel Hulak			145	Derek Wilkinson
138	Paul Lynch	229	Chris Lyness			170	Dennis Maxwell
188	Arthur Femenella	252	Martin Cibak			193	Andrew Kemper
219	Dennis Packard					218	Marc Tardif
222	Jeremy Van Hoof					241	Tom MacDonald
252	J.F. Soucy						
259	Dmitri Bezrukov						
261	Vitali Smolyaninov						
281	Ilja Solarev						
289	Henrik Bergfors						

General Managers' History

Phil Esposito, 1992-93 to 1997-98; Jacques Demers, 1998-99; Rick Dudley, 1999-2000 to 2000-01; Rick Dudley and Jay Feaster, 2001-02; Jay Feaster, 2002-03 to date.

Vice President and General Manager

FEASTER, JAY
Executive Vice President/General Manager, Tampa Bay Lightning.
Born in Williamstown, PA, July 30, 1962.

Jay Feaster was named general manager of the Tampa Bay Lightning on February 10, 2002. In his first full season on the job in 2002-03, Tampa Bay qualified for the playoffs for just the second time in franchise history. He had joined the Lightning on October 20, 1998, from the Hershey Bears of the AHL and spent three-plus seasons as Tampa Bay's assistant general manager, overseeing all contractual, collective bargaining and National Hockey League legal issues, as well as the organization's scouting department and its minor league affiliates in Springfield (American Hockey League) and Pensacola (East Coast Hockey League).

Feaster spent nine years with the Hershey Bears, leading the team to a division title (1993-94) and a Calder Cup championship (1997), while establishing three consecutive single-season attendance records (1991-92 to 1993-94) and entering into a five-year affiliation agreement with the NHL's Colorado Avalanche. For his work, Feaster was named the AHL's executive of the year in 1997. In 1996, Feaster negotiated the purchase of an A-League American Professional Soccer League (APSL) Division II franchise by Herco, the Hershey Wildcats, and then served on the A-League committee responsible for finalizing the merger between the APSL and USISL, Inc.

Prior to joining the Hershey Company, Feaster practiced law in Harrisburg, Pennsylvania. He is a Summa Cum Laude graduate of Susquehanna University and a Cum Laude graduate of The Georgetown Law Center in Washington, D.C.

While in Hershey, Feaster spent time on the advisory boards of the Big 33 Scholarship Foundation, the Four Diamonds Fund at the Pennsylvania State University Milton S. Hershey Medical Center, and the Central PA Chapter of the National Multiple Sclerosis Society. He also taught business law and hotel law as a visiting faculty member at the Lebanon Valley College in Annville, PA.

Club Directory

St. Pete Times Forum

Tampa Bay Lightning
St. Pete Times Forum
401 Channelside Drive
Tampa, FL 33602
Phone **813/301-6500**
FAX 813/301-1480
Ticket Info. 813/301-6600
www.tampabaylightning.com
Capacity: 19,758

Executive Staff
Owner: Palace Sports & Entertainment . . . . Bill Davidson
President of Palace Sports & Entertainment/
 Governor . . . . Tom Wilson
President of Tampa Bay Lightning/
 Alternate Governor . . . . Ron Campbell
Executive Vice President, General Manager
 & Alternate Governor . . . . Jay H. Feaster
Executive Vice President & Chief Operating Officer . Sean Henry
Executive Vice President & Chief Marketing Officer . Michael Yormark
Senior Vice President, Communications . . . . Bill Wickett
Vice President & Chief Financial Officer . . . . Joe Fada
Vice President of Legal Affairs, Legal Counsel . . . . Paul Davis
Executive Director, Lightning Foundation . . . . Nancy Crane

Hockey Operations
Executive Vice President, General Manager
 & Alternate Governor . . . . Jay H. Feaster
Director of Player Personnel . . . . Bill Barber
Hockey Operations Assistant . . . . Kathy Paterson
Assistant to the General Manager . . . . Ryan Belec
Head Coach . . . . John Tortorella
Associate Coach . . . . Craig Ramsay
Assistant Coach . . . . Jeff Reese
Strength & Conditioning Coach . . . . Eric Lawson
Video Coach . . . . Nigel Kirwan
Head Scout . . . . Jake Goertzen
Chief Professional Scout . . . . Rick Paterson
Scouting Staff . . . . Mikael Andersson, Stephen Baker,
 Larry Bernard, Dirk Graham, Dave Heitz,
 Karri Kettunen, Yuri Yanchenkov,
 Darrell Young, Glen Zacharias
Director of Team Services . . . . Phil Thibodeau
Head Medical Trainer . . . . Thomas Mulligan
Assistant Medical Trainer . . . . Adam Rambo
Massage Therapist . . . . Mike Griebel
Equipment Manager . . . . Ray Thill
Assistant Equipment Managers . . . . Dana Heinze, Jim Pickard
Team Physician . . . . Dr. Ira Guttentag
Director of Alumni . . . . John Tucker

Executive Suites/Premium Seating
Director of Premium Seating . . . . RJ Martino
Director of Premium Services . . . . Karrie Yager
Premium Seating Manager . . . . Missy Davis
Suite Service Ticket Supervisor . . . . Lakisha Sharpe

Finance
Vice President & Chief Financial Officer . . . . Joe Fada
Finance Manager . . . . Michelle Ekiss
Senior Accountants . . . . Doug Riefler, Dave Weber
Staff Accountants . . . . Jane Sheill, Theresa Thomas

Internal Support Staff
V.P. of IT and Telecommunications . . . . David Everett
Assistant Information Services Managers . . . . Roberto Camejo, Ed Belzer

Box Office
Director of Ticket Operations . . . . Jim Mannino
Box Office Manager . . . . Aaron Corso
Assistant Box Office Manager . . . . Alex Bohne

Sales
Vice President of Sales . . . . Dave Bullock
Director of Corporate Sales . . . . Todd Lambert
Director of Outside Sales . . . . Chad Johnson
Corporate Account Managers . . Derek Beeman, Ross Bley, Ryan Bringger, Patrick Duffy, Alex
 English, Andrew Hammer, Mike Janowicz, Brad Lott, Matt Martin,
 Ryan McCoy, Emily Obletz, Joe Ondrejko, Tim Post, Paul Wallace

Sales & Marketing
Executive Vice President & Chief Marketing Officer . Michael Yormark
Director of Web Services . . . . Martin Quessenberry
Director of Promotions . . . . Mark Gullett
Entertainment Marketing Manager . . . . Jason Franke
Director of Client Services . . . . Alaina Miller
Client Services Managers . . . . Kelly McCoy, Brian Samilian
Director of Corporate Marketing . . . . Chris Hibbs
Corporate Marketing Managers . . . . Aaron Cohn, Scott Morrison, Jarrett Nasca
Director of Event Marketing . . . . Holly Brown
Director of Sports Marketing . . . . Bina Kumar
Director of Broadcasting Prod. & Game Ops . . . . . Jim Ciotoli
Director of Fan Development . . . . David Cole
Web Audio Reporter . . . . Tom Gilbert

Communications
Senior Vice President, Communications . . . . Bill Wickett
Director of Public Relations . . . . Jay Preble
Public Relations Assistant . . . . Mary China
Executive Director, Lightning Foundation . . . . Nancy Crane
Community Relations Manager . . . . Kasey Dowd
Community Relations Assistant . . . . Liz Stowell

Broadcast Information
Director of Broadcasting & Programming . . . . Jason Dixon
Television . . . . Sunshine Network
Television Broadcasters . . . . Rick Peckham, Bobby Taylor, Paul Kennedy
Radio . . . . WDAE 620 AM
Broadcasters . . . . David Mishkin, Phil Esposito

Ed Belfour set a new Leafs record with 37 wins.

Toronto Maple Leafs

2002-03 Results: 44w-28l-7t-3otl 98pts.
Second, Northeast Division

Year-by-Year Record

Season	GP	Home W	L	T	OL	Road W	L	T	OL	Overall W	L	T	OL	GF	GA	Pts.	Finished	Playoff Result
2002-03	82	24	13	4	0	20	15	3	3	44	28	7	3	236	208	98	2nd, Northeast Div.	Lost Conf. Quarter-Final
2001-02	82	24	11	6	0	19	14	4	4	43	25	10	4	249	207	100	2nd, Northeast Div.	Lost Conf. Championship
2000-01	82	19	11	7	4	18	18	4	1	37	29	11	5	232	207	90	3rd, Northeast Div.	Lost Conf. Semi-Final
1999-2000	82	24	12	5	0	21	15	2	3	45	27	7	3	246	222	100	1st, Northeast Div.	Lost Conf. Semi-Final
1998-99	82	23	13	5	...	22	17	2	...	45	30	7	...	268	231	97	2nd, Northeast Div.	Lost Conf. Championship
1997-98	82	16	20	5	...	14	23	4	...	30	43	9	...	194	237	69	6th, Central Div.	Out of Playoffs
1996-97	82	18	20	3	...	12	24	5	...	30	44	8	...	230	273	68	6th, Central Div.	Out of Playoffs
1995-96	82	19	15	7	...	15	21	5	...	34	36	12	...	247	252	80	3rd, Central Div.	Lost Conf. Quarter-Final
1994-95	48	15	7	2	...	6	12	6	...	21	19	8	...	135	146	50	4th, Central Div.	Lost Conf. Quarter-Final
1993-94	84	23	15	4	...	20	14	8	...	43	29	12	...	280	243	98	2nd, Central Div.	Lost Conf. Championship
1992-93	84	25	11	6	...	19	18	5	...	44	29	11	...	288	241	99	3rd, Norris Div.	Lost Conf. Championship
1991-92	80	21	16	3	...	9	27	4	...	30	43	7	...	234	294	67	5th, Norris Div.	Out of Playoffs
1990-91	80	15	21	4	...	8	25	7	...	23	46	11	...	241	318	57	5th, Norris Div.	Out of Playoffs
1989-90	80	24	14	2	...	14	24	2	...	38	38	4	...	337	358	80	3rd, Norris Div.	Lost Div. Semi-Final
1988-89	80	15	20	5	...	13	26	1	...	28	46	6	...	259	342	62	5th, Norris Div.	Out of Playoffs
1987-88	80	14	20	6	...	7	29	4	...	21	49	10	...	273	345	52	4th, Norris Div.	Lost Div. Semi-Final
1986-87	80	22	14	4	...	10	28	2	...	32	42	6	...	286	319	70	4th, Norris Div.	Lost Div. Final
1985-86	80	16	21	3	...	9	27	4	...	25	48	7	...	311	386	57	4th, Norris Div.	Lost Div. Final
1984-85	80	10	28	2	...	10	24	6	...	20	52	8	...	253	358	48	5th, Norris Div.	Out of Playoffs
1983-84	80	17	16	7	...	9	29	2	...	26	45	9	...	303	387	61	5th, Norris Div.	Out of Playoffs
1982-83	80	20	15	5	...	8	25	7	...	28	40	12	...	293	330	68	3rd, Norris Div.	Lost Div. Semi-Final
1981-82	80	12	20	8	...	8	24	8	...	20	44	16	...	298	380	56	5th, Norris Div.	Out of Playoffs
1980-81	80	14	21	5	...	14	16	10	...	28	37	15	...	322	367	71	5th, Adams Div.	Lost Prelim. Round
1979-80	80	17	19	4	...	18	21	1	...	35	40	5	...	304	327	75	4th, Adams Div.	Lost Prelim. Round
1978-79	80	20	12	8	...	14	21	5	...	34	33	13	...	267	252	81	3rd, Adams Div.	Lost Quarter-Final
1977-78	80	21	13	6	...	20	16	4	...	41	29	10	...	271	237	92	3rd, Adams Div.	Lost Semi-Final
1976-77	80	18	13	9	...	15	19	6	...	33	32	15	...	301	285	81	3rd, Adams Div.	Lost Quarter-Final
1975-76	80	23	12	5	...	11	19	10	...	34	31	15	...	294	276	83	3rd, Adams Div.	Lost Quarter-Final
1974-75	80	19	12	9	...	12	21	7	...	31	33	16	...	280	309	78	3rd, Adams Div.	Lost Quarter-Final
1973-74	78	21	11	7	...	14	16	9	...	35	27	16	...	274	230	86	4th, East Div.	Lost Quarter-Final
1972-73	78	20	12	7	...	7	29	3	...	27	41	10	...	247	279	64	6th, East Div.	Out of Playoffs
1971-72	78	21	11	7	...	12	20	7	...	33	31	14	...	209	208	80	4th, East Div.	Lost Quarter-Final
1970-71	78	24	9	6	...	13	24	2	...	37	33	8	...	248	211	82	4th, East Div.	Lost Quarter-Final
1969-70	76	18	13	7	...	11	21	6	...	29	34	13	...	222	242	71	6th, East Div.	Out of Playoffs
1968-69	76	20	8	10	...	15	18	5	...	35	26	15	...	234	217	85	4th, East Div.	Lost Quarter-Final
1967-68	74	24	9	4	...	9	22	6	...	33	31	10	...	209	176	76	5th, East Div.	Out of Playoffs
1966-67	**70**	**21**	**8**	**6**	...	**11**	**19**	**5**	...	**32**	**27**	**11**	...	**204**	**211**	**75**	**3rd,**	**Won Stanley Cup**
1965-66	70	22	9	4	...	12	16	7	...	34	25	11	...	208	187	79	3rd,	Lost Semi-Final
1964-65	70	17	15	3	...	13	11	11	...	30	26	14	...	204	173	74	4th,	Lost Semi-Final
1963-64	**70**	**22**	**7**	**6**	...	**11**	**18**	**6**	...	**33**	**25**	**12**	...	**192**	**172**	**78**	**3rd,**	**Won Stanley Cup**
1962-63	**70**	**21**	**8**	**6**	...	**14**	**15**	**6**	...	**35**	**23**	**12**	...	**221**	**180**	**82**	**1st,**	**Won Stanley Cup**
1961-62	**70**	**25**	**5**	**5**	...	**12**	**17**	**6**	...	**37**	**22**	**11**	...	**232**	**180**	**85**	**2nd,**	**Won Stanley Cup**
1960-61	70	21	6	8	...	18	13	4	...	39	19	12	...	234	176	90	2nd,	Lost Semi-Final
1959-60	70	20	9	6	...	15	17	3	...	35	26	9	...	199	195	79	2nd,	Lost Final
1958-59	70	17	13	5	...	10	19	6	...	27	32	11	...	189	201	65	4th,	Lost Final
1957-58	70	12	16	7	...	9	22	4	...	21	38	11	...	192	226	53	6th,	Out of Playoffs
1956-57	70	12	16	7	...	9	18	8	...	21	34	15	...	174	192	57	5th,	Out of Playoffs
1955-56	70	19	10	6	...	5	23	7	...	24	33	13	...	153	181	61	4th,	Lost Semi-Final
1954-55	70	14	10	11	...	10	14	11	...	24	24	22	...	147	135	70	3rd,	Lost Semi-Final
1953-54	70	22	6	7	...	10	18	7	...	32	24	14	...	152	131	78	3rd,	Lost Semi-Final
1952-53	70	17	12	6	...	10	18	7	...	27	30	13	...	156	167	67	5th,	Out of Playoffs
1951-52	70	17	10	8	...	12	15	8	...	29	25	16	...	168	157	74	3rd,	Lost Semi-Final
1950-51	**70**	**22**	**8**	**5**	...	**19**	**8**	**8**	...	**41**	**16**	**13**	...	**212**	**138**	**95**	**2nd,**	**Won Stanley Cup**
1949-50	70	18	9	8	...	13	18	4	...	31	27	12	...	176	173	74	3rd,	Lost Semi-Final
1948-49	**60**	**12**	**8**	**10**	...	**10**	**17**	**3**	...	**22**	**25**	**13**	...	**147**	**161**	**57**	**4th,**	**Won Stanley Cup**
1947-48	**60**	**22**	**3**	**5**	...	**10**	**12**	**8**	...	**32**	**15**	**13**	...	**182**	**143**	**77**	**1st,**	**Won Stanley Cup**
1946-47	**60**	**20**	**8**	**2**	...	**11**	**11**	**8**	...	**31**	**19**	**10**	...	**209**	**172**	**72**	**2nd,**	**Won Stanley Cup**
1945-46	50	10	13	2	...	9	11	5	...	19	24	7	...	174	185	45	5th,	Out of Playoffs
1944-45	**50**	**13**	**9**	**3**	...	**11**	**13**	**1**	...	**24**	**22**	**4**	...	**183**	**161**	**52**	**3rd,**	**Won Stanley Cup**
1943-44	50	13	11	1	...	10	12	3	...	23	23	4	...	214	174	50	3rd,	Lost Semi-Final
1942-43	50	17	6	2	...	5	13	7	...	22	19	9	...	198	159	53	3rd,	Lost Semi-Final
1941-42	**48**	**18**	**6**	**0**	...	**9**	**12**	**3**	...	**27**	**18**	**3**	...	**158**	**136**	**57**	**2nd,**	**Won Stanley Cup**
1940-41	48	16	5	3	...	12	9	3	...	28	14	6	...	145	99	62	2nd,	Lost Semi-Final
1939-40	48	15	3	6	...	10	14	0	...	25	17	6	...	134	110	56	3rd,	Lost Final
1938-39	48	13	8	3	...	6	12	6	...	19	20	9	...	114	107	47	3rd,	Lost Final
1937-38	48	13	6	5	...	11	9	4	...	24	15	9	...	151	127	57	1st, Cdn. Div.	Lost Final
1936-37	48	14	9	1	...	8	12	4	...	22	21	5	...	119	115	49	3rd, Cdn. Div.	Lost Quarter-Final
1935-36	48	15	4	5	...	8	15	1	...	23	19	6	...	126	106	52	2nd, Cdn. Div.	Lost Final
1934-35	48	16	6	2	...	14	8	2	...	30	14	4	...	157	111	64	1st, Cdn. Div.	Lost Final
1933-34	48	19	2	3	...	7	11	6	...	26	13	9	...	174	119	61	1st, Cdn. Div.	Lost Final
1932-33	48	16	6	2	...	8	12	4	...	24	18	6	...	119	111	54	1st, Cdn. Div.	Lost Final
1931-32	**48**	**17**	**4**	**3**	...	**6**	**14**	**4**	...	**23**	**18**	**7**	...	**155**	**127**	**53**	**2nd, Cdn. Div.**	**Won Stanley Cup**
1930-31	44	15	4	3	...	7	9	6	...	22	13	9	...	118	99	53	2nd, Cdn. Div.	Lost Quarter-Final
1929-30	44	10	8	4	...	7	13	2	...	17	21	6	...	116	124	40	4th, Cdn. Div.	Out of Playoffs
1928-29	44	15	5	2	...	6	13	3	...	21	18	5	...	85	69	47	3rd, Cdn. Div.	Lost Semi-Final
1927-28	44	9	8	5	...	9	10	3	...	18	18	8	...	89	88	44	4th, Cdn. Div.	Out of Playoffs
1926-27*	44	10	10	2	...	5	14	3	...	15	24	5	...	79	94	35	5th, Cdn. Div.	Out of Playoffs
1925-26	36	11	5	2	...	1	16	1	...	12	21	3	...	92	114	27	6th,	Out of Playoffs
1924-25	30	10	5	0	...	9	6	0	...	19	11	0	...	90	84	38	2nd,	Lost NHL S-Final
1923-24	24	7	5	0	...	3	9	0	...	10	14	0	...	59	85	20	3rd,	Out of Playoffs
1922-23	24	8	4	0	...	5	7	0	...	13	10	0	...	82	88	27	3rd,	Out of Playoffs
1921-22	**24**	**8**	**4**	**0**	...	**5**	**6**	**1**	...	**13**	**10**	**1**	...	**98**	**97**	**27**	**2nd,**	**Won Stanley Cup**
1920-21	24	9	3	0	...	6	6	0	...	15	9	0	...	105	100	30	2nd and 1st***	Lost NHL Final
1919-20**	24	8	4	0	...	4	8	0	...	12	12	0	...	119	106	24	3rd and 2nd***	Out of Playoffs
1918-19	18	5	4	0	...	0	9	0	...	5	13	0	...	64	92	10	3rd and 3rd***	Out of Playoffs
1917-18	**22**	**10**	**1**	**0**	...	**3**	**8**	**0**	...	**13**	**9**	**0**	...	**108**	**109**	**26**	**2nd and 1st*****	**Won Stanley Cup**

* Name changed from St. Patricks to Maple Leafs (February, 1927). ** Name changed from Arenas to St. Patricks.
*** Season played in two halves with no combined standing at end.
From 1917-18 through 1925-26, NHL champions played against PCHA/WCHL champions for Stanley Cup.

2003-04 Schedule

Oct.							
Sat.	11	Montreal		Tue.	6	Nashville
Mon.	13	Washington		Thu.	8	Ottawa
Thu.	16	at New Jersey		Sat.	10	New Jersey
Sat.	18	at Montreal		Tue.	13	Calgary
Mon.	20	at NY Islanders		Fri.	16	at Philadelphia
Wed.	22	at Dallas		Sat.	17	Philadelphia
Thu.	23	at Phoenix		Tue.	20	NY Islanders
Sat.	25	Washington		Wed.	21	at Washington
Mon.	27	Atlanta		Sat.	24	at Montreal
Thu.	30	at Buffalo		Tue.	27	Carolina
Nov.						
Sat.	1	Philadelphia		Fri.	30	at Atlanta
Sun.	2	at Carolina*		Sat.	31	Ottawa
Tue.	4	Pittsburgh	**Feb.**	Tue.	3	Chicago
Fri.	7	at New Jersey		Thu.	5	at Ottawa
Sat.	8	Edmonton		Tue.	10	at Tampa Bay
Wed.	12	at Anaheim		Thu.	12	Columbus
Thu.	13	at Los Angeles		Sat.	14	Buffalo
Sat.	15	at San Jose		Mon.	16	at Pittsburgh
Tue.	18	at Calgary		Tue.	17	Boston
Thu.	20	at Edmonton		Thu.	19	at Carolina
Sat.	22	at Vancouver		Sat.	21	Montreal
Mon.	24	Vancouver		Mon.	23	Carolina
Thu.	27	at Atlanta		Wed.	25	at Florida
Sat.	29	at Ottawa		Thu.	26	at Tampa Bay
Sun.	30	at NY Rangers		Sat.	28	New Jersey
Dec.			**Mar.**			
Tue.	2	NY Rangers		Tue.	2	Boston
Thu.	4	at Boston		Thu.	4	NY Islanders
Sat.	6	Detroit		Sat.	6	Buffalo
Tue.	9	St. Louis		Tue.	9	Florida
Thu.	11	at Minnesota		Thu.	11	Pittsburgh
Sat.	13	NY Rangers		Sat.	13	at Montreal
Tue.	16	Tampa Bay		Mon.	15	at Buffalo
Fri.	19	at Washington		Tue.	16	Boston
Sat.	20	Montreal		Thu.	18	at Philadelphia
Tue.	23	Florida		Sat.	20	Colorado
Fri.	26	at NY Rangers		Tue.	23	Tampa Bay
Sat.	27	at NY Islanders		Thu.	25	at Boston
Mon.	29	at Florida		Sat.	27	Ottawa
Jan.				Mon.	29	Atlanta
Thu.	1	at Boston				
Sat.	3	Buffalo	**Apr.**	Fri.	2	at Buffalo
Mon.	5	at Pittsburgh		Sat.	3	at Ottawa

* Denotes afternoon game.

Franchise date: November 22, 1917

NORTHEAST DIVISION

87th NHL Season

2003-04 Player Personnel

FORWARDS	HT	WT	S	Place of Birth	Date	2002-03 Club
ANTROPOV, Nik	6-6	220	L	Vost, USSR	2/18/80	Toronto
DOMI, Tie	5-10	213	R	Windsor, Ont.	11/1/69	Toronto
DRUKEN, Harold	6-0	200	L	St. John's, Nfld.	1/26/79	Van-Car-Tor-St.J's-Car-Lowell (AHL)
FITZGERALD, Tom	6-0	190	R	Billerica, MA	8/28/68	Toronto
GAVEY, Aaron	6-2	189	L	Sudbury, Ont.	2/22/74	Toronto-St. John's
GREEN, Travis	6-2	200	R	Castlegar, B.C.	12/20/70	Toronto
HOLDEN, Josh	6-0	190	L	Calgary, Alta.	1/18/78	Toronto-St. John's
LEEB, Brad	5-11	187	R	Red Deer, Alta.	8/27/79	St. John's
MOGILNY, Alexander	6-0	209	L	Khabarovsk, USSR	2/18/69	Toronto
NOLAN, Owen	6-1	215	R	Belfast, Ireland	2/12/72	San Jose-Toronto
PERROTT, Nathan	6-0	225	R	Owen Sound, Ont.	12/8/76	Nashville-Milwaukee-St. John's
PONIKAROVSKY, Alexei	6-4	220	L	Kiev, USSR	4/9/80	Toronto-St. John's
REICHEL, Robert	5-10	180	L	Litvinov, Czech.	6/25/71	Toronto
RENBERG, Mikael	6-2	235	L	Pitea, Sweden	5/5/72	Toronto
ROBERTS, Gary	6-2	215	L	North York, Ont.	5/23/66	Toronto
STAJAN, Matt	6-1	180	L	Mississauga, Ont.	12/19/83	Belleville-St. John's-Toronto
SUNDIN, Mats	6-5	231	R	Bromma, Sweden	2/13/71	Toronto
TUCKER, Darcy	5-10	178	L	Castor, Alta.	3/15/75	Toronto

DEFENSEMEN	HT	WT	S	Place of Birth	Date	
BELAK, Wade	6-5	221	R	Saskatoon, Sask.	7/3/76	Toronto
BELL, Brendan	6-1	205	L	Ottawa, Ont.	3/31/83	Ottawa (OHL)
BERG, Aki	6-3	213	L	Turku, Finland	7/28/77	Toronto
COLAIACOVO, Carlo	6-1	188	L	Toronto, Ont.	1/27/83	Toronto-Erie (OHL)
HARRISON, Jay	6-4	211	L	Oshawa, Ont.	11/3/82	St. John's
JACKMAN, Ric	6-2	197	R	Toronto, Ont.	6/28/78	Toronto-St. John's
KABERLE, Tomas	6-1	198	L	Rakovnik, Czech.	3/2/78	Toronto
MARCHMENT, Bryan	6-1	200	L	Scarborough, Ont.	5/1/69	San Jose-Colorado
McCABE, Bryan	6-2	220	L	St. Catharines, Ont.	6/8/75	Toronto
MORO, Marc	6-1	218	L	Toronto, Ont.	7/17/77	St. John's
PILAR, Karel	6-3	207	R	Prague, Czech.	12/23/77	Toronto-St. John's
SVEHLA, Robert	6-0	209	R	Martin, Czech.	1/2/69	Toronto
WHITE, Ian	5-10	185	L	Winnipeg, Man.	6/4/84	Swift Current

GOALTENDERS	HT	WT	C	Place of Birth	Date	2002-03 Club
BELFOUR, Ed	5-11	202	L	Carman, Man.	4/21/65	Toronto
HODSON, Jamie	6-2	205	L	Brandon, Man.	4/8/80	St. John's-Greensboro
KIDD, Trevor	6-2	213	L	Dugald, Man.	3/26/72	Toronto
TELLQVIST, Mikael	5-11	194	L	Sundbyberg, Sweden	9/19/79	Toronto-St. John's

Coaching History

Dick Carroll, 1917-18, 1918-19; Frank Heffernan and Harry Sproule, 1919-20; Frank Carroll, 1920-21; George O'Donohue, 1921-22; George O'Donohue and Charles Querrie, 1922-23; Charles Querrie, 1923-24; Eddie Powers, 1924-25, 1925-26; Charles Querrie, Mike Rodden and Alex Romeril, 1926-27; Conn Smythe, 1927-28 to 1929-30; Conn Smythe and Art Duncan, 1930-31; Art Duncan and Dick Irvin, 1931-32; Dick Irvin, 1932-33 to 1939-40; Hap Day, 1940-41 to 1949-50; Joe Primeau, 1950-51 to 1952-53; King Clancy, 1953-54 to 1955-56; Howie Meeker, 1956-57; Billy Reay, 1957-58; Billy Reay and Punch Imlach, 1958-59; Punch Imlach, 1959-60 to 1968-69; John McLellan, 1969-70 to 1972-73; Red Kelly, 1973-74 to 1976-77; Roger Neilson, 1977-78, 1978-79; Floyd Smith, Dick Duff and Punch Imlach, 1979-80; Punch Imlach, Joe Crozier and Mike Nykoluk, 1980-81; Mike Nykoluk, 1981-82 to 1983-84; Dan Maloney, 1984-85, 1985-86; John Brophy, 1986-87, 1987-88; John Brophy and George Armstrong, 1988-89; Doug Carpenter, 1989-90; Doug Carpenter and Tom Watt, 1990-91; Tom Watt, 1991-92; Pat Burns, 1992-93 to 1994-95; Pat Burns and Nick Beverley, 1995-96; Mike Murphy, 1996-97, 1997-98; Pat Quinn, 1998-99 to date.

General Managers' History

Charles Querrie, 1917-18 to 1926-27; Conn Smythe, 1927-28 to 1956-57; Hap Day, 1957-58; Punch Imlach, 1958-59 to 1968-69; Jim Gregory, 1969-70 to 1978-79; Punch Imlach, 1979-80, 1980-81; Punch Imlach and Gerry McNamara, 1981-82; Gerry McNamara, 1982-83 to 1987-88; Gord Stellick, 1988-89; Floyd Smith, 1989-90, 1990-91; Cliff Fletcher, 1991-92 to 1996-97; Ken Dryden, 1997-98, 1998-99; Pat Quinn, 1999-2000 to 2002-03; John Ferguson, 2003-04.

A biography of John Ferguson can be found on page 335.

Captains' History

Hap Day, 1927-28 to 1936-37; Charlie Conacher, 1937-38; Red Horner, 1938-39, 1939-40; Syl Apps, 1940-41 to 1942-43; Bob Davidson, 1943-44, 1944-45; Syl Apps, 1945-46 to 1947-48; Ted Kennedy, 1948-49 to 1954-55; Sid Smith, 1955-56; Jimmy Thomson, Ted Kennedy, 1956-57; George Armstrong, 1957-58 to 1968-69; Dave Keon, 1969-70 to 1974-75; Darryl Sittler, 1975-76 to 1980-81; Rick Vaive, 1981-82 to 1985-86; no captain, 1986-87 to 1988-89; Rob Ramage, 1989-90, 1990-91; Wendel Clark, 1991-92 to 1993-94; Doug Gilmour, 1994-95 to 1996-97; Mats Sundin, 1997-98 to date.

2002-03 Scoring

- rookie

Regular Season

Pos	#	Player	Team	GP	G	A	Pts	+/-	PIM	PP	SH	GW	GT	S	%
R	89	Alexander Mogilny	TOR	73	33	46	79	4	12	5	3	9	0	165	20.0
C	13	Mats Sundin	TOR	75	37	35	72	1	58	16	3	8	1	223	16.6
R	11	Owen Nolan	S.J.	61	22	20	42	-5	91	8	3	4	0	192	11.5
			TOR	14	7	5	12	2	16	5	0	1	0	29	24.1
			TOTAL	75	29	25	54	-3	107	13	3	5	0	221	13.1
D	15	Tomas Kaberle	TOR	82	11	36	47	20	30	4	1	2	1	119	9.2
C	80	Nik Antropov	TOR	72	16	29	45	11	124	2	1	6	0	102	15.7
D	67	Robert Svehla	TOR	82	7	38	45	13	46	2	0	1	0	110	6.4
C	21	Robert Reichel	TOR	81	12	30	42	7	26	1	1	1	0	111	10.8
R	16	Darcy Tucker	TOR	77	10	26	36	-7	119	4	1	1	0	108	9.3
R	19	Mikael Renberg	TOR	67	14	21	35	5	36	7	0	1	0	137	10.2
L	14	Jonas Hoglund	TOR	79	13	19	32	2	12	2	0	3	0	157	8.3
C	93	Doug Gilmour	MTL	61	11	19	30	-6	36	3	0	0	0	85	12.9
			TOR	1	0	0	0	0	0	0	0	0	0	0	0.0
			TOTAL	62	11	19	30	-6	36	3	0	0	0	85	12.9
R	28	Tie Domi	TOR	79	15	14	29	-1	171	4	0	0	0	91	16.5
D	96	Phil Housley	CHI	57	6	23	29	7	24	2	0	2	0	134	4.5
			TOR	1	0	0	0	-1	2	0	0	0	0	3	0.0
			TOTAL	58	6	23	29	6	26	2	0	2	0	137	4.4
C	39	Travis Green	TOR	75	12	12	24	-2	67	2	1	3	0	86	14.0
D	24	Bryan McCabe	TOR	75	6	18	24	9	135	3	0	1	0	149	4.0
D	25	Jyrki Lumme	TOR	73	6	11	17	10	46	1	0	3	0	72	8.3
C	12	Tom Fitzgerald	TOR	66	4	13	17	10	57	0	0	0	0	89	4.5
L	27	Shayne Corson	TOR	46	7	8	15	-5	49	0	0	1	0	69	10.1
D	8	Aki Berg	TOR	78	4	7	11	3	28	0	0	2	0	49	8.2
D	22	Glen Wesley	CAR	63	1	7	8	-5	40	1	0	0	0	72	1.4
			TOR	7	0	3	3	3	4	0	0	0	0	5	0.0
			TOTAL	70	1	10	11	-2	44	1	0	0	0	77	1.3
R	26	Paul Healey	TOR	44	3	7	10	8	16	1	0	0	0	43	7.0
D	2	Wade Belak	TOR	55	3	6	9	-2	196	0	0	0	0	33	9.1
L	7	Gary Roberts	TOR	14	5	3	8	-2	10	3	0	0	0	22	22.7
C	29	* Karel Pilar	TOR	17	3	4	7	-7	12	1	0	1	0	22	13.6
L	23	Alexei Ponikarovsky	TOR	13	0	3	3	4	11	0	0	0	0	13	0.0
D	55	Richard Jackman	TOR	42	0	2	2	-10	41	0	0	0	0	35	0.0
C	41	* Matthew Stajan	TOR	1	1	1	2	1	0	0	0	0	0	1	100.0
C	14	Josh Holden	TOR	5	1	0	1	-2	2	0	0	0	0	6	16.7
D	45	* Carlo Colaiacovo	TOR	2	0	1	1	1	0	0	0	0	0	1	0.0
C	10	Aaron Gavey	TOR	5	0	1	1	1	0	0	0	0	0	8	0.0
D	44	Anders Eriksson	TOR	4	0	0	0	0	0	0	0	0	0	7	0.0

Goaltending

No.	Goaltender	GPI	Mins	Avg	W	L	T	EN	SO	GA	SA	S%	G	A	PIM
20	Ed Belfour	62	3738	2.26	37	20	5	4	7	141	1816	.922	0	2	24
32	* Mikael Tellqvist	3	86	2.79	1	1	0	0	0	4	38	.895	0	0	0
37	Trevor Kidd	19	1143	3.10	6	10	2	0	0	59	565	.896	0	0	0
	Totals	82	4987	2.50	44	31	7	4	7	208	2423	.914			

Playoffs

Pos	#	Player	Team	GP	G	A	Pts	+/-	PIM	PP	SH	GW	GT	S	%
R	89	Alexander Mogilny	TOR	6	5	2	7	2	4	0	1	0	0	13	38.5
C	13	Mats Sundin	TOR	7	1	3	4	-1	6	1	0	0	0	16	6.3
C	39	Travis Green	TOR	7	2	1	3	3	4	0	0	1	1	6	33.3
C	21	Robert Reichel	TOR	7	2	1	3	-4	0	0	0	0	0	16	12.5
D	15	Tomas Kaberle	TOR	7	0	3	3	-6	0	0	0	1	1	11	18.2
R	16	Darcy Tucker	TOR	6	0	3	3	1	6	0	0	0	0	13	0.0
D	67	Robert Svehla	TOR	7	0	3	3	-5	2	0	0	0	0	14	0.0
D	24	Bryan McCabe	TOR	7	0	3	3	-3	10	0	0	0	0	16	0.0
L	7	Gary Roberts	TOR	7	1	1	2	-4	8	1	0	0	0	13	7.7
D	8	Aki Berg	TOR	7	1	1	2	1	2	0	0	0	0	5	20.0
D	25	Jyrki Lumme	TOR	7	0	2	2	4	4	0	0	0	0	8	0.0
R	11	Owen Nolan	TOR	7	0	2	2	-4	2	0	0	0	0	15	0.0
R	28	Tie Domi	TOR	7	1	0	1	0	13	0	0	0	0	11	9.1
R	19	Mikael Renberg	TOR	7	1	0	1	-4	8	1	0	1	0	3	33.3
R	26	Paul Healey	TOR	4	0	1	1	1	2	0	0	0	0	6	0.0
D	22	Glen Wesley	TOR	5	0	1	1	-2	0	0	0	0	0	5	0.0
C	12	Tom Fitzgerald	TOR	7	0	1	1	-2	4	0	0	0	0	12	0.0
L	14	Jonas Hoglund	TOR	7	0	1	1	-1	0	0	0	0	0	4	0.0
L	27	Shayne Corson	TOR	2	0	0	0	-2	2	0	0	0	0	4	0.0
D	2	Wade Belak	TOR	2	0	0	0	-2	4	0	0	0	0	0	0.0
D	96	Phil Housley	TOR	3	0	0	0	-3	0	0	0	0	0	5	0.0
C	80	Nik Antropov	TOR	3	0	0	0	-3	0	0	0	0	0	5	0.0

Goaltending

No.	Goaltender	GPI	Mins	Avg	W	L	EN	SO	GA	SA	S%	G	A	PIM
20	Ed Belfour	7	532	2.71	3	4	0	0	24	282	.915	0	0	4
	Totals	7	532	2.71	3	4	0	0	24	282	.915			

Club Records

Team

(Figures in brackets for season records are games played; records for fewest points, wins, ties, losses, goals, goals against are for 70 or more games)

Most Points **100** 1999-2000 (82), 2001-02 (82)
Most Wins **45** 1998-99 (82), 1999-2000 (82)
Most Ties **22** 1954-55 (70)
Most Losses **52** 1984-85 (80)
Most Goals **337** 1989-90 (80)
Most Goals Against **387** 1983-84 (80)
Fewest Points **48** 1984-85 (80)
Fewest Wins **20** 1981-82 (80), 1984-85 (80)
Fewest Ties **4** 1989-90 (80)
Fewest Losses **16** 1950-51 (70)
Fewest Goals **147** 1954-55 (70)
Fewest Goals Against ***131** 1953-54 (70)
Longest Winning Streak
- **Overall** .... **10** Oct. 7-28/93
- **Home** .... **9** Nov. 11-Dec. 26/53
- **Away** .... **7** Nov. 14-Dec. 15/40, Dec. 4/60-Jan. 5/61

Longest Undefeated Streak
- **Overall** .... **11** Oct. 15-Nov. 8/50 (8 wins, 3 ties), Jan. 6-Feb. 1/94 (7 wins, 4 ties)
- **Home** .... **18** Nov. 28/33-Mar. 10/34 (15 wins, 3 ties), Oct. 31/53-Jan. 23/54 (16 wins, 2 ties)
- **Away** .... **9** Nov. 30/47-Jan. 11/48 (4 wins, 5 ties)

Longest Losing Streak
- **Overall** .... **10** Jan. 15-Feb. 8/67
- **Home** .... **7** Nov. 11-Dec. 5/84
- **Away** .... **11** Feb. 20-Apr. 1/88

Longest Winless Streak
- **Overall** .... **15** Dec. 26/87-Jan. 25/88 (11 losses, 4 ties)
- **Home** .... **11** Dec. 19/87-Jan. 25/88 (7 losses, 4 ties)
- **Away** .... **18** Oct. 6/82-Jan. 5/83 (13 losses, 5 ties)

Most Shutouts, Season **13** 1953-54 (70)
Most PIM, Season **2,419** 1989-90 (80)
Most Goals, Game .... **14** Mar. 16/57 (NYR 1 at Tor. 14)

Individual

Most Seasons .... **21** George Armstrong
Most Games .... **1,187** George Armstrong
Most Goals, Career .... **389** Darryl Sittler
Most Assists, Career .... **620** Borje Salming
Most Points, Career .... **916** Darryl Sittler (389G, 527A)
Most PIM, Career .... **1,777** Tie Domi
Most Shutouts, Career .... **62** Turk Broda
Longest Consecutive Games Streak .... **486** Tim Horton (Feb. 11/61-Feb. 4/68)
Most Goals, Season .... **54** Rick Vaive (1981-82)
Most Assists, Season .... **95** Doug Gilmour (1992-93)
Most Points, Season .... **127** Doug Gilmour (1992-93; 32G, 95A)
Most PIM, Season .... **365** Tie Domi (1997-98)
Most Points, Defenseman, Season .... **79** Ian Turnbull (1976-77; 22G, 57A)
Most Points, Center, Season .... **127** Doug Gilmour (1992-93; 32G, 95A)
Most Points, Right Wing, Season .... **97** Wilf Paiement (1980-81; 40G, 57A)
Most Points, Left Wing, Season .... **99** Dave Andreychuk (1993-94; 53G, 46A)
Most Points, Rookie, Season .... **66** Peter Ihnacak (1982-83; 28G, 38A)
Most Shutouts, Season .... **13** Harry Lumley (1953-54)
Most Goals, Game .... **6** Corb Denneny (Jan. 26/21), Darryl Sittler (Feb. 7/76)
Most Assists, Game .... **6** Babe Pratt (Jan. 8/44), Doug Gilmour (Feb. 13/93)
Most Points, Game .... ***10** Darryl Sittler (Feb. 7/76; 6G, 4A)

* NHL Record.

Retired Numbers

5	Bill Barilko	1946-1951
6	Ace Bailey	1926-1934

Honored Numbers

1	Turk Broda	1936-43, 45-52
	Johnny Bower	1958-1970
7	King Clancy	1930-1937
	Tim Horton	1949-50, 51-70
9	Charlie Conacher	1929-1938
	Ted Kennedy	1942-55, 56-57
10	Syl Apps	1936-43, 45-48
	George Armstrong	1949-50, 51-71
27	Frank Mahovlich	1956-1968
	Darryl Sittler	1970-1982

All-time Record vs. Other Clubs

Regular Season

	At Home								On Road								Total							
	GP	W	L	T	OL	GF	GA	PTS	GP	W	L	T	OL	GF	GA	PTS	GP	W	L	T	OL	GF	GA	PTS
Anaheim	15	9	2	4	0	50	30	22	10	5	4	1	0	27	29	11	25	14	6	5	0	77	59	33
Atlanta	7	4	2	1	0	27	16	9	7	4	3	0	0	24	14	8	14	8	5	1	0	51	30	17
Boston	296	155	90	51	0	999	760	361	295	88	158	47	2	775	964	225	591	243	248	98	2	1774	1724	586
Buffalo	64	28	25	11	0	195	214	67	66	18	42	6	0	173	269	42	130	46	67	17	0	368	483	109
Calgary	52	27	17	7	1	198	188	62	60	22	32	5	1	193	236	50	112	49	49	12	2	391	424	112
Carolina	34	13	16	5	0	119	122	31	35	11	18	6	0	115	142	28	69	24	34	11	0	234	264	59
Chicago	314	164	96	54	0	1070	817	382	318	120	156	42	0	831	968	282	632	284	252	96	0	1901	1785	664
Colorado	34	15	15	4	0	113	131	34	29	7	17	5	0	87	111	19	63	22	32	9	0	200	242	53
Columbus	2	1	0	1	0	6	3	3	1	0	0	0	1	3	4	1	3	1	0	1	1	9	7	4
Dallas	101	49	35	17	0	356	319	115	96	35	50	11	0	303	364	81	197	84	85	28	0	659	683	196
Detroit	315	163	105	47	0	1040	844	373	322	108	168	46	0	792	968	262	637	271	273	93	0	1832	1812	635
Edmonton	36	19	15	2	0	150	153	40	42	14	21	6	1	136	175	35	78	33	36	8	1	286	328	75
Florida	13	7	4	2	0	43	32	16	15	7	4	4	0	47	40	18	28	14	8	6	0	90	72	34
Los Angeles	68	35	22	11	0	266	223	81	64	21	34	9	0	187	230	51	132	56	56	20	0	453	453	132
Minnesota	3	3	0	0	0	11	3	6	0	0	0	0	0	0	0	0	3	3	0	0	0	11	3	6
Montreal	330	170	115	45	0	998	855	385	330	90	197	43	0	819	1157	223	660	260	312	88	0	1817	2012	608
Nashville	5	1	3	1	0	11	17	3	1	0	0	0	1	2	3	1	6	1	3	1	1	13	20	4
New Jersey	46	30	11	5	0	179	137	65	44	14	16	13	1	133	152	42	90	44	27	18	1	312	289	107
NY Islanders	53	26	23	4	0	181	182	56	51	20	28	3	0	152	200	43	104	46	51	7	0	333	382	99
NY Rangers	280	157	84	39	0	966	736	353	281	105	118	56	2	826	866	268	561	262	202	95	2	1792	1602	621
Ottawa	19	9	8	1	1	51	50	20	17	4	11	1	1	40	51	10	36	13	19	2	2	91	101	30
Philadelphia	65	23	27	14	1	209	214	61	65	15	41	8	1	150	248	39	130	38	68	22	2	359	462	100
Phoenix	43	20	21	2	0	157	161	42	38	12	20	6	0	137	157	30	81	32	41	8	0	294	318	72
Pittsburgh	65	31	23	11	0	258	208	73	67	25	36	6	0	215	274	56	132	56	59	17	0	473	482	129
St. Louis	98	58	28	11	1	367	289	128	102	30	58	14	0	283	348	74	200	88	86	25	1	650	637	202
San Jose	18	12	4	2	0	69	47	26	14	7	5	2	0	38	30	16	32	19	9	4	0	107	77	42
Tampa Bay	19	12	6	1	0	71	48	25	18	16	2	0	0	64	34	32	37	28	8	1	0	135	82	57
Vancouver	59	27	21	11	0	217	194	65	63	23	29	11	0	211	222	57	122	50	50	22	0	428	416	122
Washington	46	25	16	5	0	205	160	55	48	17	28	3	0	139	178	37	94	42	44	8	0	344	338	92
Defunct Clubs	232	158	53	21	0	860	515	337	233	84	120	29	0	607	745	197	465	242	173	50	0	1467	1260	534
Totals	**2732**	**1451**	**887**	**390**	**4**	**9442**	**7668**	**3296**	**2732**	**922**	**1416**	**383**	**11**	**7509**	**9179**	**2238**	**5464**	**2373**	**2303**	**773**	**15**	**16951**	**16847**	**5534**

Playoffs

	Series	W	L	GP	W	L	T	GF	GA	Last Mtg.	Rnd.	Result
Boston	13	8	5	62	31	30	1	150	153	1974	QF	L 0-4
Buffalo	1	0	1	5	1	4	0	16	21	1999	CF	L 1-4
Calgary	1	1	0	2	2	0	0	9	5	1979	PRE	W 2-0
Carolina	1	0	1	6	2	4	0	6	10	2002	CF	L 2-4
Chicago	9	6	3	38	22	15	1	111	89	1995	CQF	L 3-4
Dallas	2	0	2	7	1	6	0	26	35	1983	DSF	L 1-3
Detroit	23	12	11	117	58	59	0	311	321	1993	DSF	W 4-3
Los Angeles	3	2	1	12	7	5	0	41	31	1993	CF	L 3-4
Montreal	15	7	8	71	29	42	0	160	215	1979	QF	L 0-4
New Jersey	2	0	2	13	5	8	0	27	37	2001	CSF	L 3-4
NY Islanders	3	2	1	17	8	9	0	42	54	2002	CQF	W 4-3
NY Rangers	8	3	5	35	16	19	0	86	86	1971	QF	L 2-4
Ottawa	3	3	0	17	12	5	0	43	31	2002	CSF	W 4-3
Philadelphia	5	1	4	30	12	18	0	72	102	2003	CQF	L 3-4
Pittsburgh	3	3	0	12	8	4	0	39	27	1999	CSF	W 4-2
St. Louis	5	2	3	31	14	17	0	90	88	1996	CQF	L 2-4
San Jose	1	1	0	7	4	3	0	26	21	1994	CSF	W 4-3
Vancouver	1	0	1	5	1	4	0	9	16	1994	CF	L 1-4
Defunct Clubs	8	6	2	24	12	10	2	59	57			
Totals	**107**	**57**	**50**	**511**	**245**	**262**	**4**	**1323**	**1399**			

Calgary totals include Atlanta Flames, 1972-73 to 1979-80.
Colorado totals include Quebec, 1979-80 to 1994-95.
New Jersey totals include Kansas City, 1974-75 to 1975-76, and Colorado Rockies, 1976-77 to 1981-82.
Phoenix totals include Winnipeg, 1979-80 to 1995-96.
Carolina totals include Hartford, 1979-80 to 1996-97.
Dallas totals include Minnesota North Stars, 1967-68 to 1992-93.

Playoff Results 2003-1999

Year	Round	Opponent	Result	GF	GA
2003	CQF	Philadelphia	L 3-4	16	24
2002	CF	Carolina	L 2-4	6	10
	CSF	Ottawa	W 4-3	16	18
	CQF	NY Islanders	W 4-3	22	21
2001	CSF	New Jersey	L 3-4	18	21
	CQF	Ottawa	W 4-0	10	3
2000	CSF	New Jersey	L 2-4	9	16
	CQF	Ottawa	W 4-2	17	10
1999	CF	Buffalo	L 1-4	16	21
	CSF	Pittsburgh	W 4-2	18	14
	CQF	Philadelphia	W 4-2	9	11

Abbreviations: Round: CF – conference final; **CSF** – conference semi-final; **CQF** – conference quarter-final; **DSF** – division semi-final; **QF** – quarter-final; **PRE** – preliminary round.

2002-03 Results

Oct.	10	at Pittsburgh	6-0		9	at Pittsburgh	4-2
	12	Ottawa	1-2		11	at Boston	2-6
	14	Pittsburgh	4-5		13	at NY Rangers	1-5
	15	at NY Rangers	4-5		14	Calgary	3-2
	17	Phoenix	5-3		17	at Washington	4-1
	19	at Montreal	2-2		18	at Montreal	3-2*
	21	Boston	1-4		21	Philadelphia	1-3
	23	Florida	1-4		24	at Buffalo	0-4
	26	NY Rangers	3-4		25	Colorado	0-3
	28	Anaheim	5-2		29	at Carolina	3-2
	31	Atlanta	3-3		30	at Atlanta	5-2
Nov.	2	Montreal	2-5	**Feb.**	5	at Florida	6-0
	5	Tampa Bay	4-3		6	at Tampa Bay	3-2*
	8	at Dallas	1-2		8	Montreal	3-1
	9	at St. Louis	3-6		11	Edmonton	4-5
	12	Los Angeles	4-3*		12	at Chicago	3-1
	15	at Buffalo	3-2		15	Ottawa	2-1
	16	Detroit	1-2		18	Carolina	4-3
	19	Boston	2-0		20	at Washington	6-2
	23	Philadelphia	6-0		22	at Montreal	5-3
	25	at Ottawa	0-2		23	Nashville	2-5
	26	Washington	5-4		25	NY Islanders	5-2
	29	at Philadelphia	3-0		27	at Detroit	2-7
	30	Buffalo	3-1	**Mar.**	1	Carolina	4-1
Dec.	3	Tampa Bay	4-3*		3	Florida	1-2
	6	at NY Islanders	2-4		4	at Ottawa	1-4
	7	New Jersey	1-0		6	at Buffalo	2-4
	10	Pittsburgh	4-2		8	Vancouver	3-3
	12	at Philadelphia	1-2		10	at Edmonton	3-2
	14	NY Rangers	4-1		13	at Calgary	3-4*
	16	at Atlanta	0-1		15	at Vancouver	1-0
	18	at Florida	2-2		18	NY Islanders	3-3
	19	at Tampa Bay	2-1		20	at Columbus	3-4*
	21	San Jose	3-3		22	Buffalo	3-2*
	23	Atlanta	5-1		24	at Boston	2-3
	27	at Calgary	4-3		25	at Carolina	3-3
	28	at Edmonton	2-3*		28	at NY Islanders	5-2
	31	at Vancouver	5-3		29	Washington	4-3*
Jan.	3	at New Jersey	0-2	**Apr.**	1	at New Jersey	3-2*
	4	New Jersey	2-1		3	Minnesota	2-1
	7	Boston	5-2		5	Ottawa	1-3

* – Overtime

Entry Draft Selections 2003-1989

2003
Pick
57 John Doherty
91 Martin Sagat
125 Konstantin Volkov
158 John Mitchell
220 Jeremy Williams
237 Shaun Landolt

2002
Pick
24 Alexander Steen
57 Matt Stajan
74 Todd Ford
88 Dominic D'Amour
122 David Turon
191 Ian White
222 Scott May
254 Jarkko Immonen
285 Staffan Kronvall

2001
Pick
17 Carlo Colaiacovo
39 Karel Pilar
65 Brendan Bell
82 Jay Harrison
88 Nicolas Corbeil
134 Kyle Wellwood
168 Maxim Kondratjev
183 Jaroslav Sklenar
198 Ivan Kolozvary
213 Jan Chovan
246 Tomas Mojzis
276 Mike Knoepfli

2000
Pick
24 Brad Boyes
51 Kris Vernarsky
70 Mikael Tellqvist
90 Jean-Francois Racine
100 Miguel Delisle
179 Vadim Sozinov
209 Markus Seikola
223 Lubos Velebny
254 Alexander Shinkar
265 Jean-Philippe Cote

1999
Pick
24 Luca Cereda
60 Peter Reynolds
108 Mirko Murovic
110 Jon Zion
151 Vaclav Zavoral
161 Jan Sochor
211 Vladimir Kulikov
239 Pierre Hedin
267 Peter Metcalf

1998
Pick
10 Nik Antropov
35 Petr Svoboda
69 Jamie Hodson
87 Alexei Ponikarovsky
126 Morgan Warren
154 Allan Rourke
181 Jonathan Gagnon
215 Dwight Wolfe
228 Michal Travnicek
236 Sergei Rostov

1997
Pick
57 Jeff Farkas
84 Adam Mair
111 Frantisek Mrazek
138 Eric Gooldy
165 Hugo Marchand
190 Shawn Thornton
194 Russ Bartlett
221 Jonathan Hedstrom

1996
Pick
36 Marek Posmyk
50 Francis Larivee
66 Mike Lankshear
68 Konstantin Kalmikov
86 Jason Sessa
103 Vladimir Antipov
110 Peter Cava
111 Brandon Sugden
140 Dmitri Yakushin
148 Chris Bogas
151 Lucio DeMartinis
178 Reggie Berg
204 Tomas Kaberle
230 Jared Hope

1995
Pick
15 Jeff Ware
54 Ryan Pepperall
139 Doug Bonner
145 Yannick Tremblay
171 Marek Melenovsky
197 Mark Murphy
223 Danny Markov

1994
Pick
16 Eric Fichaud
48 Sean Haggerty
64 Fredrik Modin
126 Mark Deyell
152 Kam White
178 Tommi Rajamaki
204 Rob Butler
256 Sergei Berezin
282 Doug Nolan

1993
Pick
12 Kenny Jonsson
19 Landon Wilson
123 Zdenek Nedved
149 Paul Vincent
175 Jeff Andrews
201 David Brumby
253 Kyle Ferguson
279 Mikhail Lapin

1992
Pick
8 Brandon Convery
23 Grant Marshall
77 Nikolai Borschevsky
95 Mark Raiter
101 Janne Gronvall
106 Chris Deruiter
125 Mikael Hakansson
149 Patrik Augusta
173 Ryan Vandenbussche
197 Wayne Clarke
221 Sergei Simonov
245 Nathan Dempsey

1991
Pick
47 Yanic Perreault
69 Terry Chitaroni
102 Alexei Kudashov
113 Jeff Perry
120 Alexander Kuzminsky
135 Martin Prochazka
160 Dmitri Mironov
164 Robb McIntyre
167 Tomas Kucharcik
179 Guy Lehoux
201 Gary Miller
223 Johnathon Kelley
245 Chris O'Rourke

1990
Pick
10 Drake Berehowsky
31 Felix Potvin
73 Darby Hendrickson
80 Greg Walters
115 Alexander Godynyuk
136 Eric Lacroix
157 Dan Stiver
178 Robert Horyna
199 Rob Chebator
220 Scott Malone
241 Nick Vachon

1989
Pick
3 Scott Thornton
12 Rob Pearson
21 Steve Bancroft
66 Matt Martin
96 Keith Carney
108 David Burke
125 Michael Doers
129 Keith Merkler
150 Derek Langille
171 Jeffrey St. Laurent
192 Justin Tomberlin
213 Mike Jackson
234 Steve Chartrand

Coach

QUINN, PAT
Coach, Toronto Maple Leafs. Born in Hamilton, Ont., January 29, 1943.

Pat Quinn became the 25th head coach of the Toronto Maple Leafs on June 26, 1998. He added the responsibilities of general manager to his coaching duties on July 14, 1999 and held both jobs until the appointment of John Ferguson on August 29, 2003.

Under Quinn's leadership, Toronto advanced to the playoffs for the fifth consecutive season in 2002-03, while Quinn moved into fourth place in all-time NHL coaching wins with (571) and into fifth in all-time games coached with 1,154. He also became only the fourth coach in franchise history to reach the 200-win mark with the club, joining Punch Imlach, Hap Day and Dick Irvin. Previous to his arrival in Toronto he served as coach and/or general manager with Philadelphia, Los Angeles and Vancouver.

In 2001-02, Quinn reached two significant milestones, coaching his 1,000th game on October 25, 2001 and recording his 500th victory on December 6, 2001.

In February 2002, Quinn served as head coach of the Canadian Olympic team and guided Canada to its first hockey gold medal in 50 years of Olympic competition.

Quinn received the Jake Milford Award for dedicated service and contribution to hockey in British Columbia in 1994. In 2002, he was inducted into the British Columbia Hockey Hall of Fame and will also be inducted into the Hamilton Gallery of Distinction. He is active in the community, holding his annual Pat Quinn and Friends golf tournament with the proceeds going to Kids Help Phone, RCMP Drugs and Sport and Hockey Canada.

NHL Coaching Record

		Regular Season				Playoffs		
Season	Team	Games	W	L	T	Games	W	L
1978-79	Philadelphia	30	18	8	4	8	3	5
1979-80	Philadelphia	80	48	12	20	19	13	6
1980-81	Philadelphia	80	41	24	15	12	6	6
1981-82	Philadelphia	72	34	29	9	....	....	....
1984-85	Los Angeles	80	34	32	14	3	0	3
1985-86	Los Angeles	80	23	49	8	....	....	....
1986-87	Los Angeles	42	18	20	4	....	....	....
1990-91	Vancouver	26	9	13	4	6	2	4
1991-92	Vancouver	80	42	26	12	13	6	7
1992-93	Vancouver	84	46	29	9	12	6	6
1993-94	Vancouver	84	41	40	3	24	15	9
1995-96	Vancouver	6	3	3	0	6	2	4
1998-99	Toronto	82	45	30	7	17	9	8
1999-2000	Toronto	82	45	30	7	12	6	6
2000-01	Toronto	82	37	34	11	11	7	4
2001-02	Toronto	82	43	29	10	20	10	10
2002-03	Toronto	82	44	31	7	7	3	4
	NHL Totals	**1154**	**571**	**439**	**144**	**170**	**88**	**82**

Assistant coach Rick Ley posted a 1-1 record as replacement coach when Quinn was sidelined with heart arrythmia, May 21 and 25, 2002. Both games are credited to Quinn's coaching record.

Club Directory

Air Canada Centre

Toronto Maple Leafs
Air Canada Centre
40 Bay St., Suite 400
Toronto, Ontario M5J 2X2
Phone **416/815-5700**
FAX 416/359-9331
www.mapleleafs.com
Capacity: 18,819

Board of Directors
Larry M. Tanenbaum, Robert G. Bertram, James W. Leech, Dean Metcalf, Ivan Fecan, John MacIntyre, Dale H. Lastman, Richard Peddie, Ken Dryden

Maple Leaf Sports & Entertainment Ltd.
Chairman, NHL Governor . . . . . Larry M. Tanenbaum
President, CEO and Alternate NHL Governor . . . . . Richard Peddie
Vice Chairman, Alternate NHL Governor . . . . . Ken Dryden
Alternate NHL Governors . . . . . Dale H. Lastman, Dean Metcalf
Sr. Vice-President, Business, Chief Marketing Officer . . Tom Anselmi
Sr. Vice-President, Chief Financial Officer . . . . . Ian Clarke
Sr. Vice-President and G.M., Air Canada Centre . . . Bob Hunter
Vice-President, Communications & Community Development . . . . . John Lashway
Vice-President, People . . . . . Mardi Walker
Vice-President, General Counsel & Corporate Secretary . . . . . Robin Brudner
Vice-President, Programming, Executive Producer, Leafs TV . . . . . John Shannon

Maple Leafs Management
General Manager . . . . . John Ferguson
Head Coach . . . . . Pat Quinn
Assistant G.M. & Director of Player Personnel . . . . . Mike Penny
Assistant Coaches . . . . . Keith Acton, Rick Ley
Player Development Coach & Scouting Coordinator . . Paul Dennis
Video Coach . . . . . Reid Mitchell
Strength & Conditioning Coach . . . . . Matt Nichol
Community Representatives . . . . . Wendel Clark, Darryl Sittler
Director, Amateur Scouting . . . . . Barry Trapp
Pro Scout . . . . . Murray Oliver
Scouts . . . . . George Armstrong, Bob Johnson, Garth Malarchuk, Mike Palmateer, Mark Yannetti
European Scouts . . . . . Thommie Bergman, Jan Kovac, Nikolai Ladygin
Director, Team Services . . . . . Casey Vanden Heuvel
Travel Coordinator . . . . . Mary Speck
Executive Assistant . . . . . Ann Clark
Executive Assistant to the General Manager . . . . . Maria Tomasevic

Maple Leafs Communications and Community Development
Vice-President, Communications & Community Development . . . . . John Lashway
Director, Media Relations . . . . . Pat Park
Coordinators, Media Relations . . . . . Matthew Frost, Dave Griffiths
Director, Community Relations . . . . . Bev Deeth
Manager, Community Relations . . . . . Dave De Freitas
Coordinators, Community Relations . . . . . Paula Dal Maso, Ryan Janzen
Coordinator, Youth & Amateur Hockey . . . . . Greg Schell
Assistant, Youth & Amateur Hockey Development . . Geoff George
Executive Assistant, Communications . . . . . Laura Leite
Acting Director, Go Kids Go! The Leafs Fund . . . . . Mary Rowe
Coordinators, Go Kids Go! The Leafs Fund . . . . . Ted Warner, Brad Young
Manager, Game Presentation . . . . . Mike Ferriman
Manager, Game Operations . . . . . Nancy Gilks
Assistant, Game Operations . . . . . Stephenie Summerhill
Head Audio Engineer . . . . . Courtney Ross
Alumni Relations . . . . . Susanna Tyson
Team Photographer . . . . . Graig Abel

Maple Leafs Medical and Training Staff
Head Athletic Therapist . . . . . Chris Broadhurst
Athletic Therapist . . . . . Brent Smith
Equipment Manager . . . . . Brian Papineau
Assistant Equipment Managers . . . . . Bobby Hastings, Scott McKay
Team Doctors . . . . . Dr. Michael Clarfield, Dr. Darrell Ogilvie-Harris, Dr. Leith Douglas, Dr. Rob Devenyi, Dr. Simon McGrail
Team Dentist . . . . . Dr. Allan Hawryluk

Broadcast Information
Radio Play-By-Play . . . . . Joe Bowen, Dennis Beyak
Radio Analyst . . . . . Jim Ralph
Television Play-By-Play . . . . . Bob Cole, Joe Bowen
Television Analyst . . . . . Harry Neale

Air Canada Centre
Director, Accounting . . . . . Suzanne Scott
Director, Building Operations . . . . . Diego Roccasalva
Director, Consumer Products . . . . . Jeff Newman
Director, Corporate Sales . . . . . Dave Hopkinson
Director, Event Operations and Production . . . . . Jim Roe
Director, Executive Suite Services . . . . . Kristy Fletcher
Director, Finance & New Media Business . . . . . Kevin Nonomura
Director, Food & Beverage . . . . . Michael Doyle
Director, Food and Beverage Finance . . . . . Alldrick Britto
Director, Guest Services . . . . . Chris Gibbs
Director, Information Technology . . . . . Sasha Puric
Director, Marketing . . . . . Beth Robertson
Director, Marketing Media . . . . . Alon Marcovici
Director, People Relations . . . . . Craig Richardson
Director, Programming and Event Marketing . . . . . Patti-Anne Tarlton
Director, Restaurant Operations, Executive Chef . . . Brad Long
Director, Sales . . . . . Jim Edmonds
Director, Service and Ticketing . . . . . Paul Beirne
Director, Ticket Operations . . . . . Donna Henderson
Legal Counsel . . . . . Peter Miller
Operations Manager, Leafs TV . . . . . Duncan Blair
Coordinating Producer, Leafs TV . . . . . Frank Hayward
Manager, Video and Scoreboard Production . . . . . Curtis Emerson

Vancouver Canucks

2002-03 Results: 45w-23L-13T-1OTL 104PTS.
Second, Northwest Division

Year-by-Year Record

Season	GP	Home				Road				Overall						Pts	Finished	Playoff Result
		W	L	T	OL	W	L	T	OL	W	L	T	OL	GF	GA			
2002-03	82	22	13	6	0	23	10	7	1	45	23	13	1	264	208	104	2nd, Northwest Div.	Lost Conf. Semi-Final
2001-02	82	23	11	5	2	19	19	2	1	42	30	7	3	254	211	94	2nd, Northwest Div.	Lost Conf. Quarter-Final
2000-01	82	21	12	5	3	15	16	6	4	36	28	11	7	239	238	90	3rd, Northwest Div.	Lost Conf. Quarter-Final
1999-2000	82	16	14	5	6	14	15	10	2	30	29	15	8	227	237	83	3rd, Northwest Div.	Out of Playoffs
1998-99	82	14	21	6	...	9	26	6	...	23	47	12	...	192	258	58	4th, Northwest Div.	Out of Playoffs
1997-98	82	15	22	4	...	10	21	10	...	25	43	14	...	224	273	64	7th, Pacific Div.	Out of Playoffs
1996-97	82	20	17	4	...	15	23	3	...	35	40	7	...	257	273	77	4th, Pacific Div.	Out of Playoffs
1995-96	82	15	19	7	...	17	16	8	...	32	35	15	...	278	278	79	3rd, Pacific Div.	Lost Conf. Quarter-Final
1994-95	48	10	8	6	...	8	10	6	...	18	18	12	...	153	148	48	2nd, Pacific Div.	Lost Conf. Semi-Final
1993-94	84	20	19	3	...	21	21	0	...	41	40	3	...	279	276	85	2nd, Pacific Div.	Lost Final
1992-93	84	27	11	4	...	19	18	5	...	46	29	9	...	346	278	101	1st, Smythe Div.	Lost Div. Final
1991-92	80	23	10	7	...	19	16	5	...	42	26	12	...	285	250	96	1st, Smythe Div.	Lost Div. Final
1990-91	80	18	17	5	...	10	26	4	...	28	43	9	...	243	315	65	4th, Smythe Div.	Lost Div. Semi-Final
1989-90	80	13	16	11	...	12	25	3	...	25	41	14	...	245	306	64	5th, Smythe Div.	Out of Playoffs
1988-89	80	19	15	6	...	14	24	2	...	33	39	8	...	251	253	74	4th, Smythe Div.	Lost Div. Semi-Final
1987-88	80	15	20	5	...	10	26	4	...	25	46	9	...	272	320	59	5th, Smythe Div.	Out of Playoffs
1986-87	80	17	19	4	...	12	24	4	...	29	43	8	...	282	314	66	5th, Smythe Div.	Out of Playoffs
1985-86	80	17	18	5	...	6	26	8	...	23	44	13	...	282	333	59	4th, Smythe Div.	Lost Div. Semi-Final
1984-85	80	15	21	4	...	10	25	5	...	25	46	9	...	284	401	59	5th, Smythe Div.	Out of Playoffs
1983-84	80	20	16	4	...	12	23	5	...	32	39	9	...	306	328	73	3rd, Smythe Div.	Lost Div. Semi-Final
1982-83	80	20	12	8	...	10	23	7	...	30	35	15	...	303	309	75	3rd, Smythe Div.	Lost Div. Semi-Final
1981-82	80	20	8	12	...	10	25	5	...	30	33	17	...	290	286	77	2nd, Smythe Div.	Lost Final
1980-81	80	17	12	11	...	11	20	9	...	28	32	20	...	289	301	76	3rd, Smythe Div.	Lost Prelim. Round
1979-80	80	14	17	9	...	13	20	7	...	27	37	16	...	256	281	70	3rd, Smythe Div.	Lost Prelim. Round
1978-79	80	15	18	7	...	10	24	6	...	25	42	13	...	217	291	63	2nd, Smythe Div.	Lost Prelim. Round
1977-78	80	13	15	12	...	7	28	5	...	20	43	17	...	239	320	57	3rd, Smythe Div.	Out of Playoffs
1976-77	80	13	21	6	...	12	21	7	...	25	42	13	...	235	294	63	4th, Smythe Div.	Out of Playoffs
1975-76	80	22	11	7	...	11	21	8	...	33	32	15	...	271	272	81	2nd, Smythe Div.	Lost Prelim. Round
1974-75	80	23	12	5	...	15	20	5	...	38	32	10	...	271	254	86	1st, Smythe Div.	Lost Quarter-Final
1973-74	78	14	18	7	...	10	25	4	...	24	43	11	...	224	296	59	7th, East Div.	Out of Playoffs
1972-73	78	17	18	4	...	5	29	5	...	22	47	9	...	233	339	53	7th, East Div.	Out of Playoffs
1971-72	78	14	20	5	...	6	30	3	...	20	50	8	...	203	297	48	7th, East Div.	Out of Playoffs
1970-71	78	17	18	4	...	7	28	4	...	24	46	8	...	229	296	56	6th, East Div.	Out of Playoffs

2003-04 Schedule

Oct.	Thu.	9	Calgary	Thu.	8	at Los Angeles
	Sat.	11	Edmonton	Fri.	9	at Anaheim
	Mon.	13	at Columbus	Sun.	11	Florida
	Thu.	16	at Detroit	Tue.	13	at Phoenix
	Sat.	18	at Minnesota	Thu.	15	at San Jose
	Mon.	20	Buffalo	Sat.	17	Anaheim
	Wed.	22	St. Louis	Mon.	19	Dallas
	Sun.	26	Phoenix	Wed.	21	Tampa Bay
	Tue.	28	Columbus	Sun.	25	Nashville
	Thu.	30	at Los Angeles	Tue.	27	Chicago
	Fri.	31	at Phoenix	Thu.	29	at St. Louis
Nov.	Mon.	3	Detroit	Sat.	31	at Washington
	Wed.	5	at Nashville	Feb. Mon.	2	at NY Rangers
	Thu.	6	at St. Louis	Tue.	3	at NY Islanders
	Sat.	8	Minnesota	Thu.	5	at New Jersey
	Tue.	11	at Minnesota	Wed.	11	Calgary
	Thu.	13	at Philadelphia	Fri.	13	Atlanta
	Sat.	15	at Boston	Sat.	14	Anaheim
	Tue.	18	Montreal	Mon.	16	at Colorado
	Thu.	20	Chicago	Thu.	19	at Minnesota
	Sat.	22	Toronto	Sat.	21	at Edmonton
	Mon.	24	at Toronto	Tue.	24	Detroit
	Tue.	25	at Montreal	Thu.	26	San Jose
	Thu.	27	at Ottawa	Sat.	28	St. Louis
	Sat.	29	at Calgary	Mar. Wed.	3	at Colorado
Dec.	Thu.	4	Calgary	Fri.	5	at Detroit
	Sat.	6	Minnesota	Sat.	6	at Columbus
	Tue.	9	Pittsburgh	Mon.	8	Colorado
	Thu.	11	Colorado	Wed.	10	Minnesota
	Sun.	14	Carolina	Fri.	12	at Edmonton
	Tue.	16	at Nashville	Sat.	13	Ottawa
	Wed.	17	at Dallas	Tue.	16	Nashville
	Sat.	20	at Edmonton	Thu.	18	at Dallas
	Mon.	22	Los Angeles	Fri.	19	at Chicago
	Fri.	26	at Calgary	Sun.	21	Columbus
	Sat.	27	Edmonton	Wed.	24	Los Angeles
	Mon.	29	at Colorado	Sat.	27	Dallas
	Wed.	31	at Chicago	Mon.	29	Phoenix
Jan.	Fri.	2	Colorado	Wed.	31	at Anaheim
	Sat.	3	at Calgary	Apr. Fri.	2	at San Jose
	Mon.	5	San Jose	Sat.	3	Edmonton

Franchise date: May 22, 1970

NORTHWEST DIVISION

34th NHL Season

With 48 goals last season, Markus Naslund broke his own record for goals by a Canucks captain. His 56 assists and 104 points were both six short of the all-time club records held by André Boudrias (1974-75) and Pavel Bure (1992-93, 1993-94).

2003-04 Player Personnel

FORWARDS	HT	WT	S	Place of Birth	Date	2002-03 Club
BERTUZZI, Todd	6-3	235	L	Sudbury, Ont.	2/2/75	Vancouver
BOUCK, Tyler	6-0	196	L	Camrose, Alta.	1/13/80	Manitoba
CHUBAROV, Artem	6-1	189	L	Gorky, USSR	12/12/79	Vancouver
COOKE, Matt	5-11	205	L	Belleville, Ont.	9/7/78	Vancouver
DAVIDSSON, Johan	6-1	190	R	Jonkoping, Sweden	1/6/76	HV 71
FEDOROV, Fedor	6-3	202	L	Appatity, USSR	6/11/81	Vancouver-Manitoba
HERPERGER, Chris	6-0	190	L	Esterhazy, Sask.	2/24/74	Atlanta-Chicago (AHL)-Manitoba
KESLER, Ryan	6-1	195	R	Detroit, MI	8/31/84	Ohio State
KING, Jason	6-1	195	L	Corner Brook, Nfld.	9/14/81	Vancouver-Manitoba
KOMARNISKI, Zenith	6-0	200	L	Edmonton, Alta.	8/13/78	Vancouver-Manitoba
LANGDON, Darren	6-1	205	L	Deer Lake, Nfld.	1/8/71	Carolina-Vancouver
LINDEN, Trevor	6-4	215	R	Medicine Hat, Alta.	4/11/70	Vancouver
LINDGREN, Mats	6-2	202	L	Skelleftea, Sweden	10/1/74	Vancouver-Manitoba
MAY, Brad	6-1	217	L	Toronto, Ont.	11/29/71	Phoenix-Vancouver
MORRISON, Brendan	5-11	190	L	Pitt Meadows, B.C.	8/15/75	Vancouver
MORRISON, Justin	6-3	205	R	Los Angeles, CA	9/10/79	Manitoba-Columbia
NASLUND, Markus	5-11	195	L	Ornskoldsvik, Sweden	7/30/73	Vancouver
NIELSEN, Chris	6-2	204	R	Moshi, Tanzania	2/16/80	Syr-Chi (AHL)-Manitoba
REID, Brandon	5-8	165	R	Kirkland, Que.	3/9/81	Vancouver-Manitoba
RUUTU, Jarkko	6-2	194	L	Vantaa, Finland	8/23/75	Vancouver
SEDIN, Daniel	6-1	200	L	Ornskoldsvik, Sweden	9/26/80	Vancouver
SEDIN, Henrik	6-2	200	L	Ornskoldsvik, Sweden	9/26/80	Vancouver
SMITH, Tim	5-9	160	L	Whitecourt, Alta.	7/21/81	Manitoba-Columbia

DEFENSEMEN	HT	WT	S	Place of Birth	Date	2002-03 Club
ALLEN, Bryan	6-4	215	L	Kingston, Ont.	8/21/80	Manitoba-Vancouver
BARON, Murray	6-3	215	L	Prince George, B.C.	6/1/67	Vancouver
BAUMGARTNER, Nolan	6-2	205	R	Calgary, Alta.	3/23/76	Vancouver-Manitoba
EAKINS, Dallas	6-2	195	L	Dade City, FL	2/27/67	Chicago (AHL)
GRENIER, Martin	6-5	245	L	Laval, Que.	11/2/80	Phoenix-Springfield
JOKELA, Mikko	6-1	210	R	Lappeenranta, Finland	3/4/80	Albany-Vancouver-Manitoba
JOVANOVSKI, Ed	6-2	210	L	Windsor, Ont.	6/26/76	Vancouver
MALIK, Marek	6-5	215	L	Ostrava, Czech.	6/24/75	Carolina-Vancouver
OBSUT, Jaroslav	6-1	200	L	Presov, Czech.	9/3/76	Manitoba
OHLUND, Mattias	6-2	220	L	Pitea, Sweden	9/9/76	Vancouver
SALO, Sami	6-3	215	R	Turku, Finland	9/2/74	Vancouver
SOPEL, Brent	6-1	205	R	Calgary, Alta.	1/7/77	Vancouver
VYDARENY, Rene	6-1	198	L	Bratislava, Czech.	5/6/81	Manitoba

GOALTENDERS	HT	WT	C	Place of Birth	Date	2002-03 Club
AULD, Alexander	6-4	197	L	Cold Lake, Alta.	1/7/81	Vancouver-Manitoba
CLOUTIER, Dan	6-1	182	L	Mont-Laurier, Que.	4/22/76	Vancouver
HEDBERG, Johan	6-0	184	L	Leksand, Sweden	5/3/73	Pittsburgh
MOSS, Tyler	6-0	185	R	Ottawa, Ont.	6/29/75	Vancouver-Manitoba

Coaching History

Hal Laycoe, 1970-71, 1971-72; Vic Stasiuk, 1972-73; Bill McCreary and Phil Maloney, 1973-74; Phil Maloney, 1974-75, 1975-76; Phil Maloney and Orland Kurtenbach, 1976-77; Orland Kurtenbach, 1977-78; Harry Neale, 1978-79 to 1980-81; Harry Neale and Roger Neilson, 1981-82; Roger Neilson, 1982-83; Roger Neilson and Harry Neale, 1983-84; Bill Laforge and Harry Neale, 1984-85; Tom Watt, 1985-86, 1986-87; Bob McCammon, 1987-88 to 1989-90; Bob McCammon and Pat Quinn, 1990-91; Pat Quinn, 1991-92 to 1993-94; Rick Ley, 1994-95; Rick Ley and Pat Quinn, 1995-96; Tom Renney, 1996-97; Tom Renney and Mike Keenan, 1997-98; Mike Keenan and Marc Crawford, 1998-99; Marc Crawford, 1999-2000 to date.

Coach

CRAWFORD, MARC

Coach, Vancouver Canucks. Born in Belleville, Ont., February 13, 1961.

Marc Crawford became the 15th head coach in Canucks history on January 24, 1999. In four full seasons behind the bench, Vancouver has improved its win and point totals every year. Crawford began his NHL coaching career with the Quebec Nordiques in 1994 and won a Stanley Cup in 1996 when the team moved to Denver to become the Colorado Avalanche. With the win, Crawford became the third-youngest coach in NHL history to win a Stanley Cup. Crawford coached the Avalanche for two seasons after winning the Cup before leaving following the 1997-98 season. He began the 1998-99 season as a colour commentator for CBC's Hockey Night in Canada before joining the Canucks. He led the team to 83 points in his first full season behind the bench in 1999-2000, then guided the Canucks back into the playoffs in 2000-01.

Crawford was the head coach for Team Canada at the 1998 Olympic Winter Games in Nagano, Japan and he was an assistant coach with Canada's silver medal-winning team in the 1996 World Cup of Hockey. He began his coaching career when he was hired by Brian Burke as a playing assistant with Fredericton (AHL) for the 1987-88 season. At the end of the year he moved to Milwaukee where he served as an assistant coach for the Canucks' IHL minor league affiliate for the 1988-89 campaign. He then moved to Cornwall where he served as the Royals' general manager and head coach in 1989-90.

After two seasons with Cornwall, Crawford went on to coach the St. John's Maple Leafs of the AHL before joining the Nordiques in 1994. He received the 1995 Jack Adams Award as the NHL coach of the year, becoming the first rookie coach to win the award since it was inaugurated in 1974.

Crawford played every game of his six-year NHL career with the Vancouver Canucks, recording 19 goals and 31 assists in 176 games. He was a rookie on the Canucks team that made a run to the Stanley Cup finals to face the New York Islanders in 1982.

2002-03 Scoring

* - rookie

Regular Season

Pos	#	Player	Team	GP	G	A	Pts	+/–	PIM	PP	SH	GW	GT	S	%
L	19	Markus Naslund	VAN	82	48	56	104	6	52	24	0	12	1	294	16.3
R	44	Todd Bertuzzi	VAN	82	46	51	97	2	144	25	0	7	1	243	18.9
C	7	Brendan Morrison	VAN	82	25	46	71	18	36	6	2	8	0	167	15.0
D	55	Ed Jovanovski	VAN	67	6	40	46	19	113	2	0	1	1	145	4.1
C	24	Matt Cooke	VAN	82	15	27	42	21	82	1	4	0	0	118	12.7
C	16	Trevor Linden	VAN	71	19	22	41	–1	30	4	1	1	0	116	16.4
C	33	Henrik Sedin	VAN	78	8	31	39	9	38	4	1	1	1	81	9.9
D	3	Brent Sopel	VAN	81	7	30	37	–15	23	6	0	1	0	167	4.2
L	22	Daniel Sedin	VAN	79	14	17	31	8	34	4	0	2	0	134	10.4
D	6	Sami Salo	VAN	79	9	21	30	9	10	4	0	1	1	126	7.1
R	26	Trent Klatt	VAN	82	16	13	29	10	8	3	0	2	0	127	12.6
D	2	Mattias Ohlund	VAN	59	2	27	29	1	42	0	0	0	0	100	2.0
C	10	Trevor Letowski	VAN	78	11	14	25	8	36	1	1	2	0	136	8.1
C	13	Artem Chubarov	VAN	62	7	13	20	4	6	1	0	1	0	78	9.0
D	8	Marek Malik	CAR	10	0	2	2	–3	16	0	0	0	0	9	0.0
			VAN	69	7	11	18	23	52	1	1	2	1	68	10.3
			TOTAL	79	7	13	20	20	68	1	1	2	1	77	9.1
C	25	Mats Lindgren	VAN	54	5	9	14	–2	18	0	2	1	0	51	9.8
D	5	Bryan Allen	VAN	48	5	3	8	8	73	0	0	1	0	43	11.6
L	32	Brad May	PHX	20	3	4	7	3	32	0	0	0	0	24	12.5
			VAN	3	0	0	0	1	10	0	0	0	0	1	0.0
			TOTAL	23	3	4	7	4	42	0	0	0	0	25	12.0
D	23	Murray Baron	VAN	78	2	4	6	13	62	0	0	0	0	34	5.9
C	14	* Brandon Reid	VAN	7	2	3	5	4	0	0	0	0	0	15	13.3
L	37	Jarkko Ruutu	VAN	36	2	2	4	–7	66	0	0	1	0	36	5.6
D	4	Nolan Baumgartner	VAN	8	1	2	3	4	4	1	0	0	0	7	14.3
R	18	* Jason King	VAN	8	0	2	2	0	0	0	0	0	0	12	0.0
R	15	* Pat Kavanagh	VAN	3	1	0	1	2	2	0	0	1	0	4	25.0
L	81	* Fedor Fedorov	VAN	7	0	1	1	0	4	0	0	0	0	2	0.0
L	20	Darren Langdon	CAR	9	0	0	0	0	16	0	0	0	0	4	0.0
			VAN	45	0	1	1	–2	143	0	0	0	0	15	0.0
			TOTAL	54	0	1	1	–2	159	0	0	0	0	19	0.0
D	21	* Zenith Komarniski	VAN	1	0	0	0	0	2	0	0	0	0	0	0.0
D	27	* Mikko Jokela	VAN	1	0	0	0	0	0	0	0	0	0	3	0.0
D	28	Bryan Helmer	VAN	2	0	0	0	1	0	0	0	0	0	2	0.0

Goaltending

No.	Goaltender	GPI	Mins	Avg	W	L	T	EN	SO	GA	SA	S%	G	A	PIM
35	* Alexander Auld	7	382	1.57	3	3	0	0	1	10	165	.939	0	0	0
39	Dan Cloutier	57	3376	2.42	33	16	7	6	2	136	1477	.908	0	3	24
1	Peter Skudra	23	1192	2.72	9	5	6	1	1	54	522	.897	0	1	0
30	Tyler Moss	1	22	2.73	0	0	0	0	0	1	14	.929	0	0	0
	Totals	**82**	**4997**	**2.50**	**45**	**24**	**13**	**7**	**4**	**208**	**2185**	**.905**			

Playoffs

Pos	#	Player	Team	GP	G	A	Pts	+/–	PIM	PP	SH	GW	GT	S	%
L	19	Markus Naslund	VAN	14	5	9	14	–6	18	2	0	1	0	40	12.5
C	7	Brendan Morrison	VAN	14	4	7	11	–4	18	1	0	1	0	27	14.8
D	55	Ed Jovanovski	VAN	14	7	1	8	–5	22	4	1	2	0	37	18.9
D	3	Brent Sopel	VAN	14	2	6	8	–2	4	1	0	1	1	29	6.9
D	2	Mattias Ohlund	VAN	13	3	4	7	1	12	0	0	0	0	23	13.0
R	26	Trent Klatt	VAN	14	2	4	6	1	2	2	0	1	1	31	6.5
R	44	Todd Bertuzzi	VAN	14	2	4	6	–3	60	0	0	0	0	31	6.5
L	22	Daniel Sedin	VAN	14	1	5	6	–2	8	1	0	1	0	22	4.5
C	33	Henrik Sedin	VAN	14	3	2	5	–2	8	1	0	0	0	15	20.0
D	6	Sami Salo	VAN	12	1	3	4	–2	0	0	0	0	0	19	5.3
D	23	Murray Baron	VAN	14	0	4	4	0	10	0	0	0	0	8	0.0
C	24	Matt Cooke	VAN	14	2	1	3	3	12	0	0	0	0	15	13.3
C	16	Trevor Linden	VAN	14	1	2	3	–4	10	0	1	0	0	20	5.0
D	8	Marek Malik	VAN	14	1	1	2	–7	10	1	0	0	0	10	10.0
L	37	Jarkko Ruutu	VAN	13	0	2	2	1	14	0	0	0	0	10	0.0
C	13	Artem Chubarov	VAN	14	0	2	2	–2	4	0	0	0	0	18	0.0
C	10	Trevor Letowski	VAN	6	0	1	1	–1	0	0	0	0	0	6	0.0
C	14	* Brandon Reid	VAN	9	0	1	1	0	0	0	0	0	0	8	0.0
D	5	Bryan Allen	VAN	1	0	0	0	–2	2	0	0	0	0	0	0.0
D	4	Nolan Baumgartner	VAN	2	0	0	0	0	0	0	0	0	0	1	0.0
L	32	Brad May	VAN	14	0	0	0	–5	15	0	0	0	0	10	0.0

Goaltending

No.	Goaltender	GPI	Mins	Avg	W	L	EN	SO	GA	SA	S%	G	A	PIM
35	* Alexander Auld	1	20	3.00	0	0	0	0	1	5	.800	0	0	0
39	Dan Cloutier	14	833	3.24	7	7	1	0	45	341	.868	0	0	8
	Totals	**14**	**860**	**3.28**	**7**	**7**	**1**	**0**	**47**	**347**	**.865**			

Coaching Record

		Regular Season				Playoffs		
Season	Team	Games	W	L	T	Games	W	L
1989-90	Cornwall (OHL)	66	24	38	4	6	2	4
1990-91	Cornwall (OHL)	66	23	42	1	....	....	....
1991-92	St. John's (AHL)	80	39	29	12	16	11	5
1992-93	St. John's (AHL)	80	41	26	13	9	4	5
1993-94	St. John's (AHL)	80	45	23	12	11	6	5
1994-95	**Quebec (NHL)**	**48**	**30**	**13**	**5**	**6**	**2**	**4**
1995-96	**Colorado (NHL)**	**82**	**47**	**25**	**10**	**22**	**16**	**6***
1996-97	**Colorado (NHL)**	**82**	**49**	**24**	**9**	**17**	**10**	**7**
1997-98	**Colorado (NHL)**	**82**	**39**	**26**	**17**	**7**	**3**	**4**
1998-99	**Vancouver (NHL)**	**37**	**8**	**23**	**6**	....	....	....
1999-2000	**Vancouver (NHL)**	**82**	**30**	**37**	**15**	....	....	....
2000-01	**Vancouver (NHL)**	**82**	**36**	**35**	**11**	**4**	**0**	**4**
2001-02	**Vancouver (NHL)**	**82**	**42**	**33**	**7**	**6**	**2**	**4**
2002-03	**Vancouver (NHL)**	**82**	**45**	**24**	**13**	**14**	**7**	**7**
	NHL Totals	**659**	**326**	**240**	**93**	**76**	**40**	**36**

* Stanley Cup win.

Club Records

Team

(Figures in brackets for season records are games played; records for fewest points, wins, ties, losses, goals, goals against are for 70 or more games)

Most Points	**104**	2002-03 (82)
Most Wins	**46**	1992-93 (84)
Most Ties	**20**	1980-81 (80)
Most Losses	**50**	1971-72 (78)
Most Goals	**346**	1992-93 (84)
Most Goals Against	**401**	1984-85 (80)
Fewest Points	**48**	1971-72 (78)
Fewest Wins	**20**	1971-72 (78), 1977-78 (80)
Fewest Ties	**3**	1993-94 (84)
Fewest Losses	**24**	2002-03 (82)
Fewest Goals	**192**	1998-99 (82)
Fewest Goals Against	**208**	2002-03 (82)
Longest Winning Streak		
Overall	**10**	Nov. 9-30/02
Home	**9**	Nov. 6-Dec. 9/92
Away	**5**	Five times
Longest Undefeated Streak		
Overall	**14**	Jan.26-Feb. 25/03 (10 wins, 4 ties)
Home	**18**	Nov. 4/92-Jan. 16/93 (16 wins, 2 ties)
Away	**9**	Feb. 4-Mar. 3/03 (6 wins, 3 ties)
Longest Losing Streak		
Overall	**10**	Oct. 23-Nov. 11/97
Home	**6**	Dec. 18/70-Jan. 20/71
Away	**12**	Nov. 28/81-Feb. 6/82
Longest Winless Streak		
Overall	**13**	Nov. 9-Dec. 7/73 (10 losses, 3 ties)
Home	**11**	Dec. 18/70-Feb. 6/71 (10 losses, 1 tie)
Away	**20**	Jan. 2-Apr. 2/86 (14 losses, 6 ties)
Most Shutouts, Season	**8**	1974-75 (80), 2001-02 (82)
Most PIM, Season	**2,326**	1992-93 (84)
Most Goals, Game	**11**	Mar. 28/71 (Cal. 5 at Van. 11), Nov. 25/86 (L.A. 5 at Van. 11), Mar. 1/92 (Cgy. 0 at Van. 11)

Individual

Most Seasons	**13**	Stan Smyl
Most Games	**896**	Stan Smyl
Most Goals, Career	**278**	Trevor Linden
Most Assists, Career	**411**	Stan Smyl
Most Points, Career	**673**	Stan Smyl (262G, 411A)
Most PIM, Career	**2,127**	Gino Odjick
Most Shutouts, Career	**20**	Kirk McLean
Longest Consecutive Games Streak	**482**	Trevor Linden (Oct. 4/90-Dec. 7/96)
Most Goals, Season	**60**	Pavel Bure (1992-93, 1993-94)
Most Assists, Season	**62**	André Boudrias (1974-75)
Most Points, Season	**110**	Pavel Bure (1992-93; 60G, 50A)
Most PIM, Season	**372**	Donald Brashear (1997-98)
Most Points, Defenseman, Season	**63**	Doug Lidster (1986-87; 12G, 51A)
Most Points, Center, Season	**91**	Patrik Sundstrom (1983-84; 38G, 53A)
Most Points, Right Wing, Season	**110**	Pavel Bure (1992-93; 60G, 50A)
Most Points, Left Wing, Season	**81**	Darcy Rota (1982-83; 42G, 39A)
Most Points, Rookie, Season	**60**	Ivan Hlinka (1981-82; 23G, 37A), Pavel Bure (1991-92; 34G, 26A)
Most Shutouts, Season	**7**	Dan Cloutier (2001-02)
Most Goals, Game	**4**	Nine times
Most Assists, Game	**6**	Patrik Sundstrom (Feb. 29/84)
Most Points, Game	**7**	Patrik Sundstrom (Feb. 29/84; 1G, 6A)

Retired Numbers

12	Stan Smyl	1978-1991

General Managers' History

Bud Poile, 1970-71 to 1972-73; Hal Laycoe, 1973-74; Phil Maloney, 1974-75 to 1976-77; Jake Milford, 1977-78 to 1981-82; Harry Neale, 1982-83 to 1984-85; Jack Gordon, 1985-86, 1986-87; Pat Quinn, 1987-88 to 1997-98; Brian Burke, 1998-99 to date.

Captains' History

Orland Kurtenbach, 1970-71 to 1973-74; no captain, 1974-75; Andre Boudrias, 1975-76; Chris Oddleifson, 1976-77; Don Lever, 1977-78; Don Lever and Kevin McCarthy, 1978-79; Kevin McCarthy, 1979-80 to 1981-82; Stan Smyl, 1982-83 to 1989-90; Dan Quinn, Doug Lidster and Trevor Linden, 1990-91; Trevor Linden, 1991-92 to 1996-97; Mark Messier, 1997-98 to 1999-2000; Markus Naslund, 2000-01 to date.

All-time Record vs. Other Clubs

Regular Season

	At Home								On Road								Total							
	GP	W	L	T	OL	GF	GA	PTS	GP	W	L	T	OL	GF	GA	PTS	GP	W	L	T	OL	GF	GA	PTS
Anaheim	24	16	6	2	0	89	55	34	23	9	7	7	0	67	56	25	47	25	13	9	0	156	111	59
Atlanta	2	1	0	1	0	9	1	3	3	2	1	0	0	12	11	4	5	3	1	1	0	21	12	7
Boston	51	16	26	8	1	166	209	41	51	7	37	7	0	123	215	21	102	23	63	15	1	289	424	62
Buffalo	51	24	16	11	0	187	161	59	52	18	26	8	0	152	186	44	103	42	42	19	0	339	347	103
Calgary	96	35	42	18	1	328	319	89	95	24	57	14	0	274	387	62	191	59	99	32	1	602	706	151
Carolina	29	13	10	6	0	103	80	32	29	12	12	5	0	100	94	29	58	25	22	11	0	203	174	61
Chicago	70	33	22	15	0	212	206	81	69	16	45	7	1	157	260	40	139	49	67	22	1	369	466	121
Colorado	44	17	20	6	1	148	167	41	44	15	21	7	1	124	150	38	88	32	41	13	2	272	317	79
Columbus	6	5	1	0	0	24	15	10	6	3	0	2	1	23	14	9	12	8	1	2	1	47	29	19
Dallas	69	30	28	10	1	247	213	71	69	22	35	12	0	210	253	56	138	52	63	22	1	457	466	127
Detroit	63	27	26	10	0	226	207	64	64	17	38	8	1	185	269	43	127	44	64	18	1	411	476	107
Edmonton	79	30	36	12	1	285	312	73	78	23	47	7	1	246	349	54	157	53	83	19	2	531	661	127
Florida	8	3	1	4	0	23	17	10	8	4	3	1	0	27	21	9	16	7	4	5	0	50	38	19
Los Angeles	95	49	31	15	0	360	296	113	97	30	50	16	1	304	391	77	192	79	81	31	1	664	687	190
Minnesota	7	3	2	1	1	22	21	8	8	4	3	1	0	23	18	9	15	7	5	2	1	45	39	17
Montreal	54	13	33	8	0	141	198	34	52	9	38	5	0	130	242	23	106	22	71	13	0	271	440	57
Nashville	10	8	2	0	0	42	25	16	11	5	5	1	0	34	31	11	21	13	7	1	0	76	56	27
New Jersey	47	27	9	11	0	175	130	65	48	22	20	6	0	155	151	50	95	49	29	17	0	330	281	115
NY Islanders	47	23	21	3	0	155	153	49	46	11	25	10	0	125	169	32	93	34	46	13	0	280	322	81
NY Rangers	51	15	33	3	0	163	204	33	53	11	37	5	0	136	233	27	104	26	70	8	0	299	437	60
Ottawa	10	5	4	1	0	32	24	11	9	3	5	1	0	21	22	7	19	8	9	2	0	53	46	18
Philadelphia	51	10	28	12	1	144	203	33	53	16	36	1	0	156	230	33	104	26	64	13	1	300	433	66
Phoenix	70	42	18	9	1	263	197	94	67	24	32	10	1	237	254	59	137	66	50	19	2	500	451	153
Pittsburgh	49	22	23	4	0	176	184	48	50	10	33	7	0	171	227	27	99	32	56	11	0	347	411	75
St. Louis	70	28	33	9	0	209	228	65	69	20	40	9	0	199	260	49	139	48	73	18	0	408	488	114
San Jose	30	17	9	4	0	111	80	38	32	15	12	5	0	101	94	35	62	32	21	9	0	212	174	73
Tampa Bay	8	6	0	2	0	35	13	14	9	6	3	0	0	37	31	12	17	12	3	2	0	72	44	26
Toronto	63	29	21	11	2	222	211	71	59	21	27	11	0	194	217	53	122	50	48	22	2	416	428	124
Washington	39	18	15	5	1	136	123	42	39	13	21	4	1	114	131	31	78	31	36	9	2	250	254	73
Defunct Clubs	19	14	3	2	0	82	48	30	19	10	8	1	0	71	68	21	38	24	11	3	0	153	116	51
Totals	**1312**	**579**	**519**	**203**	**11**	**4515**	**4300**	**1372**	**1312**	**402**	**724**	**178**	**8**	**3908**	**5034**	**990**	**2624**	**981**	**1243**	**381**	**19**	**8423**	**9334**	**2362**

Playoffs

	Series	W	L	GP	W	L	T	GF	GA	Last Mtg.	Rnd.	Result
Buffalo	2	0	2	7	1	6	0	14	28	1981	PRE	L 0-3
Calgary	5	2	3	25	12	13	0	80	82	1994	CQF	W 4-3
Chicago	2	1	1	9	4	5	0	24	24	1995	CSF	L 0-4
Colorado	2	0	2	10	2	8	0	26	40	2001	CQF	L 0-4
Dallas	1	1	0	5	4	1	0	18	11	1994	CSF	W 4-1
Detroit	1	0	1	6	2	4	0	16	22	2002	CQF	L 2-4
Edmonton	2	0	2	9	2	7	0	20	35	1992	DF	L 2-4
Los Angeles	3	1	2	17	8	9	0	60	66	1993	DF	L 2-4
Minnesota	1	0	1	7	3	4	0	17	26	2003	CSF	L 3-4
Montreal	1	0	1	5	1	4	0	9	20	1975	QF	L 1-4
NY Islanders	2	0	2	6	0	6	0	14	26	1982	F	L 0-4
NY Rangers	1	0	1	7	3	4	0	19	21	1994	F	L 3-4
Philadelphia	1	0	1	3	1	2	0	9	15	1979	PRE	L 1-2
St. Louis	2	2	0	14	8	6	0	44	48	2003	CQF	W 4-3
Toronto	1	1	0	5	4	1	0	16	9	1994	CF	W 4-1
Winnipeg	2	2	0	13	8	5	0	50	34	1993	DSF	W 4-2
Totals	**29**	**10**	**19**	**148**	**63**	**85**	**0**	**436**	**507**			

Calgary totals include Atlanta Flames, 1972-73 to 1979-80.
Carolina totals include Hartford, 1979-80 to 1996-97.
Colorado totals include Quebec, 1979-80 to 1994-95.
Dallas totals include Minnesota North Stars, 1970-71 to 1992-93.
New Jersey totals include Kansas City, 1974-75 to 1975-76, and Colorado Rockies, 1976-77 to 1981-82.
Phoenix totals include Winnipeg, 1979-80 to 1995-96.

Playoff Results 2003-1999

Year	Round	Opponent	Result	GF	GA
2003	CSF	Minnesota	L 3-4	17	26
	CQF	St. Louis	W 4-3	17	21
2002	CQF	Detroit	L 2-4	16	22
2001	CQF	Colorado	L 0-4	9	16

Abbreviations: Round: F – Final; **CF** – conference final; **CSF** – conference semi-final; **CQF** – conference quarter-final; **DF** – division final; **DSF** – division semi-final; **QF** – quarter-final; **PRE** – preliminary round.

2002-03 Results

Oct.	10	at Calgary	3-0
	12	San Jose	5-3
	14	Calgary	2-3
	16	Boston	3-6
	18	at Anaheim	2-2
	19	at Los Angeles	2-2
	21	at San Jose	5-2
	24	Anaheim	2-2
	26	Dallas	1-4
	29	Buffalo	1-1
	31	Colorado	1-5
Nov.	2	at Minnesota	4-2
	4	at Colorado	4-2
	6	at Dallas	0-4
	9	at Phoenix	5-2
	12	St. Louis	6-3
	14	Los Angeles	3-2
	16	NY Rangers	3-1
	20	Chicago	5-3
	22	Detroit	4-1
	25	at Minnesota	2-1
	27	at Carolina	3-2
	29	at Tampa Bay	5-3
	30	at Florida	5-2
Dec.	3	at NY Islanders	1-2
	4	at New Jersey	3-2*
	7	Minnesota	2-4
	9	Calgary	1-2
	11	Colorado	3-1
	14	at Edmonton	6-3
	15	Calgary	3-3
	17	at Chicago	2-3
	19	at Nashville	3-1
	21	Edmonton	4-3*
	23	at Colorado	3-5
	26	at Edmonton	4-2
	28	Anaheim	7-3
	31	Toronto	3-5
Jan.	2	Montreal	3-2
	4	Florida	3-2
	8	Ottawa	6-4
	10	Columbus	2-3
	11	at San Jose	0-3
	14	Nashville	4-3
	16	at Minnesota	2-5
	17	at Chicago	4-2
	19	at Detroit	4-1
	21	at Nashville	2-3
	24	Detroit	2-5
	26	Phoenix	1-0
	28	Minnesota	2-2
	30	Edmonton	3-3
Feb.	4	at Pittsburgh	3-2
	5	at Columbus	4-4
	7	at Buffalo	4-2
	10	Chicago	2-1
	13	Colorado	2-1*
	15	at Calgary	2-2
	18	at Detroit	4-3*
	20	at St. Louis	4-2
	22	at Edmonton	3-2*
	23	Columbus	7-2
	25	Atlanta	8-0
	27	San Jose	2-3
Mar.	1	at Montreal	1-1
	3	at Boston	6-4
	4	at Philadelphia	0-3
	6	at Columbus	4-5*
	8	at Toronto	3-3
	11	NY Islanders	4-3
	13	St. Louis	4-4
	15	Toronto	0-1
	17	at Dallas	4-2
	18	at St. Louis	4-6
	20	Nashville	7-3
	23	Washington	6-0
	25	Dallas	3-4
	27	Phoenix	5-1
	29	at Los Angeles	5-1
	30	at Anaheim	1-3
Apr.	2	at Phoenix	3-3
	6	Los Angeles	0-2

* – Overtime

Entry Draft
Selections 2003-1989

2003
Pick
23	Ryan Kesler
60	Marc-Andre Bernier
111	Brandon Nolan
128	Ty Morris
160	Nicklas Danielsson
190	Chad Brownlee
222	Francois-Pierre Guenette
252	Sergei Topol
254	Nathan Mciver
285	Matthew Hansen

2002
Pick
49	Kirill Koltsov
55	Denis Grot
68	Brett Skinner
83	Lukas Mensator
114	John Laliberte
151	Rob McVicar
214	Marc-Andre Roy
223	Ilja Krikunov
247	Matt Violin
277	Thomas Nussli
278	Matt Gens

2001
Pick
16	R.J. Umberger
66	Fedor Fedorov
114	Evgeny Gladskikh
151	Kevin Bieksa
212	Jason King
245	Konstantin Mikhailov

2000
Pick
23	Nathan Smith
71	Thatcher Bell
93	Tim Branham
144	Pavel Duma
208	Brandon Reid
241	Nathan Barrett
272	Tim Smith

1999
Pick
2	Daniel Sedin
3	Henrik Sedin
69	Rene Vydareny
129	Ryan Thorpe
172	Josh Reed
189	Kevin Swanson
218	Markus Kankaanpera
271	Darrell Hay

1998
Pick
4	Bryan Allen
31	Artem Chubarov
68	Jarkko Ruutu
81	Justin Morrison
90	Regan Darby
136	David Ytfeldt
140	Rick Bertran
149	Paul Cabana
177	Vincent Malts
204	Greg Mischler
219	Curtis Valentine
232	Jason Metcalfe

1997
Pick
10	Brad Ference
34	Ryan Bonni
36	Harold Druken
64	Kyle Freadrich
90	Chris Stanley
114	David Darguzas
117	Matt Cockell
144	Matt Cooke
148	Larry Shapley
171	Rod Leroux
201	Denis Martynyuk
227	Peter Brady

1996
Pick
12	Josh Holden
75	Zenith Komarniski
93	Jonas Soling
121	Tyler Prosofsky
147	Nolan McDonald
175	Clint Cabana
201	Jeff Scissons
227	Lubomir Vaic

1995
Pick
40	Chris McAllister
61	Larry Courville
66	Peter Schaefer
92	Lloyd Shaw
120	Todd Norman
144	Brent Sopel
170	Stewart Bodtker
196	Tyler Willis
222	Jason Cugnet

1994
Pick
13	Mattias Ohlund
39	Robb Gordon
42	Dave Scatchard
65	Chad Allan
92	Mike Dubinsky
117	Yanick Dube
169	Yuri Kuznetsov
195	Rob Trumbley
221	Bill Muckalt
247	Tyson Nash
273	Robert Longpre

1993
Pick
20	Mike Wilson
46	Rick Girard
98	Dieter Kochan
124	Scott Walker
150	Troy Creurer
176	Yevgeni Babariko
202	Sean Tallaire
254	Bert Robertsson
280	Sergei Tkachenko

1992
Pick
21	Libor Polasek
40	Michael Peca
45	Mike Fountain
69	Jeff Connolly
93	Brent Tully
110	Brian Loney
117	Adrian Aucoin
141	Jason Clark
165	Scott Hollis
213	Sonny Mignacca
237	Mark Wotton
261	Aaron Boh

1991
Pick
7	Alek Stojanov
29	Jassen Cullimore
51	Sean Pronger
95	Dan Kesa
117	John Namestnikov
139	Brent Thurston
161	Eric Johnson
183	David Neilson
205	Brad Barton
227	Jason Fitzsimmons
249	Xavier Majic

1990
Pick
2	Petr Nedved
18	Shawn Antoski
23	Jiri Slegr
65	Darin Bader
86	Gino Odjick
128	Daryl Filipek
149	Paul O'Hagan
170	Mark Cipriano
191	Troy Neumier
212	Tyler Ertel
233	Karri Kivi

1989
Pick
8	Jason Herter
29	Robert Woodward
71	Brett Hauer
113	Pavel Bure
134	James Revenberg
155	Rob Sangster
176	Sandy Moger
197	Gus Morschauser
218	Hayden O'Rear
239	Darcy Cahill
248	Jan Bergman

President and General Manager

BURKE, BRIAN
President/General Manager, Vancouver Canucks.
Born in Providence, RI, June 30, 1955.

The Vancouver Canucks announced the appointment of Brian Burke to the position of president and general manager on June 22, 1998. Burke became the eighth general manager in Canucks history after serving as the National Hockey League's senior vice president and director of hockey operations for five years. In his five seasons with the club, Vancouver has improved its win and point totals every year.

Burke's prior experience with the Canucks began when he was named vice president and director of hockey operations on June 2, 1987. Burke worked with former Canucks president and general manager Pat Quinn for five seasons and assisted in rebuilding Vancouver's team through his contract negotiation skills and his overseeing of the club's scouting systems and its minor league affiliates. Burke helped reshape the Canucks from a 59-point team in 1987-88, to a 96-point team in his final season of 1991-92. It was the first time since the 1974-75 regular season that the Canucks finished first in the Smythe Division.

Brian Burke was appointed general manager of the Hartford Whalers on May 26, 1992. In his only season in Hartford, Burke made a number of player moves, changed the team's uniform and completed a major draft-day trade in 1993. After acquiring the second overall selection from San Jose, Burke selected Chris Pronger who has developed into one of the NHL's premier defencemen.

Burke joined the NHL front office in September of 1993. In five years as NHL senior vice president, Burke was most visible in his role as the league's chief disciplinarian. He spent much of his time overseeing the league's on-ice officials and was responsible for many disciplinary decisions handed down by the NHL based on his interpretation of league rules. Brian worked closely with NHL commissioner Gary Bettman on the direction of the league and was a key member of the group that introduced NHL excitement to Japan when the Vancouver Canucks and Mighty Ducks of Anaheim opened the 1997-98 regular season in Tokyo.

Club Directory

Vancouver Canucks
General Motors Place
800 Griffiths Way
Vancouver, B.C. V6B 6G1
Phone **604/899-4600**
FAX 604/899-4640
www.canucks.com
Capacity: 18,630

General Motors Place

Executive Directory
Chairman, OBSE; Governor, NHL	John E. McCaw Jr.
President, Chief Executive Officer, OBSE	Stanley B. McCammon
President & General Manager, Vancouver Canucks, Alternate Governor, NHL	Brian P. Burke
Chief Operating Officer, Alternate Governor, NHL	David Cobb
Corporate Counsel	James Conrad
Vice President, Finance	Victor de Bonis
Vice President, People Development	Susanne Haine
Vice President, Broadcast & New Media	Chris Hebb
Vice President & G.M., Arena Operations	Harvey Jones
Vice-President, Customer Sales & Service	John Rocha
Vice President, Business Development	Ric Thomsen
Executive Assistant	Wendy Bennett

Hockey Operations
President & General Manager	Brian P. Burke
Executive Assistant	Patti Timms
Senior Vice-President & Director Hockey Operations	David M. Nonis
Executive Assistant	Chris Stephens
Vice President, Player Personnel	Steve Tambellini
Head Coach	Marc Crawford
Associate Coaches	Jack McIlhargey, Mike Johnston
General Manager, Manitoba Moose	Craig Heisinger
Head Coach, Manitoba Moose	Stan Smyl
Assistant Coach, Manitoba Moose	Eric Crawford
Assistant Coach, Video	Barry Smith
Goaltending Consultant	Ian Clark
Senior Editor, Alumni Liaison	Norm Jewison
Manager, Media Relations	Chris Brumwell
Coordinator, Media Relations	T.C. Carling
Coordinator, Media & Team Services	Rob Viccars
Media Relations Associate	Ben Brown
Director, Community Relations	Veronica Varhaug
Coordinator, Community Relations	Allanah Mooney
Assistant, Community Relations	Erin McInnis
Accountant, Canucks for Kids Fund	Maria Haycock

Scouting Staff
Chief Scout	Ron Delorme
Professional Scouts	Bob Murray
European Scout	Thomas Gradin
Russian Scout	Sergei Chibisov
Amateur Scouts	Ken Slater, Jack McCartan, Dave Morrison, Barry Dean, Mario Marois, Daryl Stanley, Paul Guay, Tim Lenardon, John McMorrow, Gary Lupul
Coordinator, Scouting & Player Information	Jonathan Wall

Medical & Training Staff
Medical Trainer	Mike Burnstein
Assistant Medical Trainer	Jon Sanderson
Assistant Medical Trainer	Marty Dudgeon
Equipment Manager	Pat O'Neill
Assistant Equipment Manager	Darren Granger
Assistant Equipment Trainer	Jamie Hendricks
Game Dressing Room Attendants	Ron Shute, John Jukitch
Team Doctors	Dr. Bill Regan, Dr. Rui Avelar
Team Dentist	Dr. David Lawson
Team Chiropractor	Dr. Sid Sheard
Team Optometrist	Dr. Alan R. Boyco

Corporate Communications
Manager, Creative Services	Jackie Boucher
Photo Editor/Librarian	Kathy McAdam
Graphic Designers	Kim Sissons, Ken Jones

Broadcast
Director, Facilities and In-house Productions	Paul Brettell
Director, Production Services	Mike Hall
Director, Technical Services	Vic Araujo
Radio Affiliation	CKNW 98 (AM 980)
Television Affiliation	Sportsnet (Channel 22)

Business Development
Directors, Business Development	David Altman, Sharon Butler, Dave Cannon, Tom Mauthe
Sr. Manager, Suite and Sponsorship Services	Darren Moscovitch
Manager, Suite and Sponsorship Services	Deborah Boren
Manager, Hospitality Suite Sales & Service	Lara Aydein

Customer Sales and Service
Director, Customer Sales & Service	Caley Denton
Director, Customer Sales	Jordan Thorsteinson
Senior Manager, Customer Sales	Graham Wall
Managers, Customer Sales	John Bellefeuille, Josh Bender, Mark Lavigne, Andrew Merai, Greg Kettner
Account Managers	Paul Maaker, Andrew Marchand, Martha Vassos

Marketing and Game Presentation
Director, Marketing	Paul Dal Monte

Central Services
Director of Finance	Chris Samis
Assistant Controller	Patricia Bigonzi
Travel Manager	Cathie Moroney
Manager, People Development	Tracey Arnish
Director, Engineering	Jason Hartley
Director, Information Technology	Peter Mills
Manager, Technical Support	William Cheng

Authentix, Fan Apparel and Collectibles
Senior Manager, Retail Operations	Dennis Kim
Merchandise Manager	Karen Saunders-Smith
Arena, Store Manager	Alan Cook

Washington Capitals

2002-03 Results: 39w-29l-8t-6otl 92pts.
Second, Southeast Division

2003-04 Schedule

Oct.	Thu.	9	NY Islanders
	Sat.	11	Atlanta
	Mon.	13	at Toronto
	Tue.	14	at Montreal
	Fri.	17	at Dallas
	Sat.	18	at St. Louis
	Thu.	23	at Ottawa
	Sat.	25	at Toronto
	Wed.	29	Anaheim
	Fri.	31	Atlanta
Nov.	Sat.	1	at Minnesota
	Tue.	4	at Tampa Bay
	Thu.	6	at Philadelphia
	Sat.	8	San Jose
	Mon.	10	Los Angeles
	Wed.	12	Carolina
	Fri.	14	Tampa Bay
	Sat.	15	at Carolina
	Thu.	20	at Boston
	Sat.	22	Florida
	Mon.	24	at Detroit
	Wed.	26	at Buffalo
	Fri.	28	Montreal
	Sat.	29	at Columbus
Dec.	Tue.	2	at NY Islanders
	Thu.	4	at New Jersey
	Sat.	6	at Los Angeles
	Mon.	8	at Colorado
	Thu.	11	Boston
	Sat.	13	Detroit
	Tue.	16	at Atlanta
	Wed.	17	at Florida
	Fri.	19	Toronto
	Sun.	21	NY Islanders
	Tue.	23	Montreal
	Sat.	27	Buffalo
	Mon.	29	Boston
	Wed.	31	at Buffalo
Jan.	Thu.	1	New Jersey
	Sat.	3	at Ottawa
	Sun.	4	at Montreal*

	Wed.	7	Phoenix
	Fri.	9	Carolina
	Sun.	11	Edmonton
	Wed.	14	Calgary
	Sat.	17	at New Jersey*
	Sun.	18	Pittsburgh*
	Wed.	21	Toronto
	Fri.	23	at Florida
	Sun.	25	Philadelphia
	Wed.	28	at NY Rangers
	Thu.	29	at Carolina
	Sat.	31	Vancouver
Feb.	Tue.	3	Tampa Bay
	Wed.	4	at Philadelphia
	Thu.	12	at Carolina
	Fri.	13	at Nashville
	Sun.	15	at Chicago*
	Tue.	17	Ottawa
	Thu.	19	New Jersey
	Sat.	21	Florida
	Mon.	23	Tampa Bay
	Wed.	25	Carolina
	Fri.	27	at Florida
	Sat.	28	at Tampa Bay
Mar.	Tue.	2	Florida
	Fri.	5	at NY Rangers
	Sat.	6	Philadelphia
	Mon.	8	Ottawa
	Wed.	10	Buffalo
	Fri.	12	Chicago
	Sat.	13	at Atlanta
	Tue.	16	at Pittsburgh
	Thu.	18	NY Rangers
	Sat.	20	Atlanta
	Tue.	23	at NY Islanders
	Wed.	24	at Atlanta
	Sat.	27	at Tampa Bay
	Tue.	30	Pittsburgh
Apr.	Thu.	1	at Boston
	Sat.	3	NY Rangers*
	Sun.	4	at Pittsburgh*

* Denotes afternoon game.

Year-by-Year Record

Season	GP	Home W	L	T	OL	Road W	L	T	OL	Overall W	L	T	OL	GF	GA	Pts.	Finished	Playoff Result
2002-03	82	24	13	2	2	15	16	6	4	39	29	8	6	224	220	92	2nd, Southeast Div.	Lost Conf. Quarter-Final
2001-02	82	21	12	6	2	15	21	5	0	36	33	11	2	228	240	85	2nd, Southeast Div.	Out of Playoffs
2000-01	82	24	9	6	2	17	18	4	2	41	27	10	4	233	211	96	1st, Southeast Div.	Lost Conf. Quarter-Final
1999-2000	82	26	5	8	2	18	19	4	0	44	24	12	2	227	194	102	1st, Southeast Div.	Lost Conf. Quarter-Final
1998-99	82	16	23	2	...	15	22	4	...	31	45	6	...	200	218	68	3rd, Southeast Div.	Out of Playoffs
1997-98	82	23	12	6	...	17	18	6	...	40	30	12	...	219	202	92	3rd, Atlantic Div.	Lost Final
1996-97	82	19	17	5	...	14	23	4	...	33	40	9	...	214	231	75	5th, Atlantic Div.	Out of Playoffs
1995-96	82	21	15	5	...	18	17	6	...	39	32	11	...	234	204	89	4th, Atlantic Div.	Lost Conf. Quarter-Final
1994-95	48	15	6	3	...	7	12	5	...	22	18	8	...	136	120	52	3rd, Atlantic Div.	Lost Conf. Quarter-Final
1993-94	84	17	16	9	...	22	19	1	...	39	35	10	...	277	263	88	3rd, Atlantic Div.	Lost Conf. Semi-Final
1992-93	84	21	15	6	...	22	19	1	...	43	34	7	...	325	286	93	2nd, Patrick Div.	Lost Div. Semi-Final
1991-92	80	25	12	3	...	20	15	5	...	45	27	8	...	330	275	98	2nd, Patrick Div.	Lost Div. Semi-Final
1990-91	80	21	14	5	...	16	22	2	...	37	36	7	...	258	258	81	3rd, Patrick Div.	Lost Div. Final
1989-90	80	19	18	3	...	17	20	3	...	36	38	6	...	284	275	78	3rd, Patrick Div.	Lost Conf. Championship
1988-89	80	25	12	3	...	16	17	7	...	41	29	10	...	305	259	92	1st, Patrick Div.	Lost Div. Semi-Final
1987-88	80	22	14	4	...	16	19	5	...	38	33	9	...	281	249	85	2nd, Patrick Div.	Lost Div. Final
1986-87	80	22	15	3	...	16	17	7	...	38	32	10	...	285	278	86	2nd, Patrick Div.	Lost Div. Semi-Final
1985-86	80	30	8	2	...	20	15	5	...	50	23	7	...	315	272	107	2nd, Patrick Div.	Lost Div. Final
1984-85	80	27	11	2	...	19	14	7	...	46	25	9	...	322	240	101	2nd, Patrick Div.	Lost Div. Semi-Final
1983-84	80	26	11	3	...	22	16	2	...	48	27	5	...	308	226	101	2nd, Patrick Div.	Lost Div. Final
1982-83	80	22	12	6	...	17	13	10	...	39	25	16	...	306	283	94	3rd, Patrick Div.	Lost Div. Semi-Final
1981-82	80	16	16	8	...	10	25	5	...	26	41	13	...	319	338	65	5th, Patrick Div.	Out of Playoffs
1980-81	80	16	17	7	...	10	19	11	...	26	36	18	...	286	317	70	5th, Patrick Div.	Out of Playoffs
1979-80	80	20	14	6	...	7	26	7	...	27	40	13	...	261	293	67	5th, Patrick Div.	Out of Playoffs
1978-79	80	15	19	6	...	9	22	9	...	24	41	15	...	273	338	63	4th, Norris Div.	Out of Playoffs
1977-78	80	10	23	7	...	7	26	7	...	17	49	14	...	195	321	48	5th, Norris Div.	Out of Playoffs
1976-77	80	17	15	8	...	7	27	6	...	24	42	14	...	221	307	62	4th, Norris Div.	Out of Playoffs
1975-76	80	6	26	8	...	5	33	2	...	11	59	10	...	224	394	32	5th, Norris Div.	Out of Playoffs
1974-75	80	7	28	5	...	1	39	0	...	8	67	5	...	181	446	21	5th, Norris Div.	Out of Playoffs

A gritty player who leads by example, Steve Konowalchuk has served as captain of the Capitals since 2001. He missed most of the 2001-02 season with a shoulder injury, but bounced back to play 77 games and score 15 goals last year.

Franchise date: June 11, 1974

EASTERN
NHL
CONFERENCE

SOUTHEAST DIVISION

30th NHL Season

2003-04 Player Personnel

FORWARDS	HT	WT	S	Place of Birth	Date	2002-03 Club
BONDRA, Peter	6-0	200	L	Luck, USSR	2/7/68	Washington
FUSSEY, Owen	6-0	185	L	Winnipeg, Man.	4/2/83	Calgary (WHL)-Moose Jaw
GORDON, Boyd	6-0	192	R	Unity, Sask.	10/19/83	Red Deer
GRIER, Mike	6-1	227	R	Detroit, MI	1/5/75	Washington
HALPERN, Jeff	6-0	201	R	Potomac, MD	5/3/76	Washington
HENRY, Alex	6-5	220	L	Elliot Lake, Ont.	10/18/79	Edm-Wsh-Port (AHL)
JAGR, Jaromir	6-2	234	L	Kladno, Czech.	2/15/72	Washington
KONOWALCHUK, Steve	6-2	207	L	Salt Lake City, UT	11/11/72	Washington
LANG, Robert	6-2	216	R	Teplice, Czech.	12/19/70	Washington
METHOT, Francois	6-0	203	R	Montreal, Que.	4/26/78	Rochester
METROPOLIT, Glen	5-10	200	R	Toronto, Ont.	6/25/74	Portland (AHL)-Washington
MILLER, Kip	5-10	190	L	Lansing, MI	6/11/69	Washington
MINK, Graham	6-3	220	R	Stowe, VT	5/12/79	Portland (AHL)
NYLANDER, Michael	6-1	195	L	Stockholm, Sweden	10/3/72	Chicago-Washington
PEAT, Stephen	6-3	210	R	Princeton, B.C.	5/9/80	Washington-Portland (AHL)
PETTINGER, Matt	6-1	205	L	Edmonton, Alta.	10/22/80	Washington-Portland (AHL)
PODKONICKY, Andrej	6-2	202	L	Zvolen, Czech.	5/9/78	Iserlohn
SALOMONSSON, Andreas	6-1	200	L	Ornskoldsvik, Sweden	12/19/73	Washington-Portland (AHL)
SEMIN, Alexander	6-0	174	L	Krasjonarsk, USSR	3/3/84	Togliatti
STROSHEIN, Garret	6-7	245	R	Edmonton, Alta.	4/4/80	Richmond-Portland (WHL)
SUTHERBY, Brian	6-2	180	L	Edmonton, Alta.	3/1/82	Washington-Portland (AHL)
TVRDON, Roman	6-1	189	L	Trencin, Czech.	1/29/81	Portland (AHL)
WHITFIELD, Trent	5-11	204	R	Estevan, Sask.	6/17/77	Washington-Portland (AHL)
ZUBRUS, Dainius	6-4	231	L	Elektrenai, USSR	6/16/78	Washington
DEFENSEMEN						
BERRY, Rick	6-2	210	L	Birtle, Man.	11/4/78	Washington
BOUMEDIENNE, Josef	6-1	200	L	Stockholm, Sweden	1/12/78	Binghamton-Wsh-Port (AHL)
CUTTA, Jakub	6-3	217	L	Jablonec nad Nisou, Czech.	12/29/81	Portland (AHL)
DOIG, Jason	6-3	228	R	Montreal, Que.	1/29/77	Washington-Portland (AHL)
EMINGER, Steve	6-1	196	R	Woodbridge, Ont.	10/31/83	Washington-Kitchener
FORTIN, Jean-Francois	6-2	205	L	Laval, Que.	3/15/79	Washington-Portland (AHL)
GONCHAR, Sergei	6-2	208	L	Chelyabinsk, USSR	4/13/74	Washington
GRUDEN, John	6-0	203	L	Virginia, MN	6/4/70	Eisbaren Berlin
HAJT, Chris	6-3	206	L	Saskatoon, Sask.	7/5/78	Portland (AHL)
RIAZANTSEV, Alexander	6-0	210	R	Moscow, USSR	3/15/80	Hershey-Milwaukee
WITT, Brendan	6-2	229	L	Humboldt, Sask.	2/20/75	Washington
YONKMAN, Nolan	6-6	236	R	Punnichy, Sask.	4/1/81	Portland (AHL)
ZINGER, Dwayne	6-4	225	L	Coronation, Alta.	7/5/76	Portland (AHL)

GOALTENDERS	HT	WT	C	Place of Birth	Date	2002-03 Club
CHARPENTIER, Sebastien	5-9	177	L	Drummondville, Que.	4/18/77	Washington-Portland (AHL)
KOLZIG, Olie	6-3	225	L	Johannesburg, South Africa	4/9/70	Washington
OUELLET, Maxime	6-2	195	L	Beauport, Que.	6/17/81	Portland (AHL)
STANA, Ratislav	6-2	161	L	Kosice, Czech.	1/10/80	Portland (AHL)

2002-03 Scoring

* - rookie

Regular Season

Pos	#	Player	Team	GP	G	A	Pts	+/-	PIM	PP	SH	GW	GT	S	%
R	68	Jaromir Jagr	WSH	75	36	41	77	5	38	13	2	9	0	290	12.4
C	20	Robert Lang	WSH	82	22	47	69	12	22	10	0	2	1	146	15.1
D	55	Sergei Gonchar	WSH	82	18	49	67	13	52	7	0	2	1	224	8.0
C	92	Michael Nylander	CHI	9	0	4	4	0	4	0	0	0	0	20	0.0
			WSH	71	17	39	56	3	36	7	0	2	0	141	12.1
			TOTAL	80	17	43	60	3	40	7	0	2	0	161	10.6
R	12	Peter Bondra	WSH	76	30	26	56	-3	52	9	2	4	0	256	11.7
L	14	Kip Miller	WSH	72	12	38	50	-1	18	3	0	4	0	89	13.5
L	94	Sergei Berezin	CHI	66	18	13	31	-3	8	5	0	0	0	171	10.5
			WSH	9	5	4	9	10	4	0	0	0	0	28	17.9
			TOTAL	75	23	17	40	7	12	5	0	2	0	199	11.6
R	9	Dainius Zubrus	WSH	63	13	22	35	15	43	2	0	0	0	104	12.5
C	11	Jeff Halpern	WSH	82	13	21	34	6	88	1	2	2	0	126	10.3
D	25	Mike Grier	WSH	82	15	17	32	-14	36	2	2	0	0	133	11.3
L	22	Steve Konowalchuk	WSH	77	15	15	30	3	71	2	0	3	0	119	12.6
L	27	Ivan Ciernik	WSH	47	8	10	18	6	24	0	0	2	1	61	13.1
R	25	Ken Klee	WSH	70	1	16	17	22	89	0	0	0	0	67	1.5
D	2	Calle Johansson	WSH	82	3	12	15	9	22	1	0	0	0	77	3.9
D	19	Brendan Witt	WSH	69	2	9	11	12	106	0	0	0	0	80	2.5
C	46 *	Brian Sutherby	WSH	72	2	9	11	7	93	0	0	0	0	38	5.3
D	54	Jason Doig	WSH	55	3	5	8	-3	108	0	0	1	0	41	7.3
C	21	Glen Metropolit	WSH	23	2	3	5	4	6	0	0	1	0	22	9.1
R	16	Andreas Salomonsson	WSH	32	1	4	5	-1	14	0	0	0	1	20	5.0
L	8	Josh Green	EDM	20	0	2	2	-3	12	0	0	0	0	20	0.0
			NYR	4	0	0	0	-1	2	0	0	0	0	3	0.0
			WSH.	21	1	1	2	1	7	0	0	0	0	20	5.0
			TOTAL	45	1	4	5	-3	21	0	0	0	0	43	2.3
D	29 *	Joel Kwiatkowski	OTT	20	0	2	2	2	6	0	0	0	0	28	0.0
			WSH	34	0	3	3	1	12	0	0	0	0	28	0.0
			TOTAL	54	0	5	5	3	18	0	0	0	0	56	0.0
D	4	Rick Berry	WSH	43	2	1	3	-3	87	0	0	1	0	40	5.0
C	23	Trent Whitfield	WSH	14	1	1	2	1	6	0	0	1	0	4	25.0
D	44 *	Steve Eminger	WSH	17	0	2	2	-3	24	0	0	0	0	6	0.0
D	39 *	Josef Boumedienne	WSH	6	1	0	1	-1	0	0	0	1	0	7	14.3
R	51	Stephen Peat	WSH	27	1	0	1	-3	57	0	0	0	0	7	14.3
D	36	Jean-Francois Fortin	WSH	33	0	1	1	-3	22	0	0	0	0	20	0.0
D	3	Sylvain Cote	WSH	1	0	0	0	0	0	0	0	0	0	4	0.0
L	18	Matt Pettinger	WSH	4	0	0	0	-3	0	0	0	0	0	6	0.0
D	41 *	Michael Farrell	WSH	4	0	0	0	1	2	0	0	0	0	0	0.0
C	36	Colin Forbes	EDM	5	0	0	0	-1	0	0	0	0	0	3	0.0
D	45 *	Alex Henry	EDM	3	0	0	0	-1	0	0	0	0	0	0	0.0
			WSH	38	0	0	0	-4	80	0	0	0	0	8	0.0
			TOTAL	41	0	0	0	-5	80	0	0	0	0	8	0.0

Goaltending

No.	Goaltender	GPI	Mins	Avg	W	L	T	EN	SO	GA	SA	S%	G	A	PIM
37	Olaf Kolzig	66	3894	2.40	33	25	6	5	4	156	1925	.919	0	0	0
35 *	Sebastien Charpentier	17	859	2.79	5	7	1	2	0	40	426	.906	0	0	0
1	Craig Billington	5	217	4.70	1	3	1	0	0	17	96	.823	0	0	0
	Totals	**82**	**4995**	**2.64**	**39**	**35**	**8**	**7**	**4**	**220**	**2454**	**.910**			

Playoffs

Pos	#	Player	Team	GP	G	A	Pts	+/-	PIM	PP	SH	GW	GT	S	%
R	68	Jaromir Jagr	WSH	6	2	5	7	2	1	0	0	0	0	22	9.1
R	12	Peter Bondra	WSH	6	4	2	6	2	8	2	0	0	0	29	13.8
C	92	Michael Nylander	WSH	6	3	2	5	0	8	1	0	1	0	15	20.0
C	55	Sergei Gonchar	WSH	6	0	5	5	2	4	0	0	0	0	15	0.0
R	9	Dainius Zubrus	WSH	6	2	2	4	-2	4	1	0	0	0	9	22.2
C	20	Robert Lang	WSH	6	2	1	3	3	2	0	0	0	0	9	22.2
R	25	Mike Grier	WSH	6	1	1	2	0	2	0	0	0	0	10	10.0
L	14	Kip Miller	WSH	5	0	2	2	0	2	0	0	0	0	9	0.0
D	19	Brendan Witt	WSH	6	1	0	1	-1	0	0	0	0	0	9	11.1
C	27	Ivan Ciernik	WSH	2	0	1	1	1	6	0	0	0	0	2	0.0
D	6	Calle Johansson	WSH	6	0	1	1	-4	0	0	0	0	0	5	0.0
L	94	Sergei Berezin	WSH	6	0	1	1	-2	0	0	0	0	0	15	0.0
D	54	Jason Doig	WSH	6	0	1	1	1	6	0	0	0	0	5	0.0
C	11	Jeff Halpern	WSH	6	0	1	1	-2	2	0	0	0	0	9	0.0
C	46 *	Brian Sutherby	WSH	5	0	0	0	0	10	0	0	0	0	5	0.0
D	2	Ken Klee	WSH	6	0	0	0	2	6	0	0	0	0	5	0.0
L	22	Steve Konowalchuk	WSH	6	0	0	0	-3	6	0	0	0	0	5	0.0
C	23	Trent Whitfield	WSH	6	0	0	0	1	10	0	0	0	0	3	0.0
D	29 *	Joel Kwiatkowski	WSH	6	0	0	0	0	2	0	0	0	0	9	0.0

Goaltending

No.	Goaltender	GPI	Mins	Avg	W	L	EN	SO	GA	SA	S%	G	A	PIM
37	Olaf Kolzig	6	404	2.08	2	4	0	1	14	192	.927	0	0	4
	Totals	**6**	**407**	**2.06**	**2**	**4**	**0**	**1**	**14**	**192**	**.927**			

Vice President and General Manager

McPHEE, GEORGE
Vice President/General Manager, Washington Capitals.
Born in Guelph, Ont., July 2, 1958.

On June 9, 1997, George McPhee became the fifth general manager of the Washington Capitals. In his first year on the job, McPhee led the Caps to the Stanley Cup Finals for the first time in franchise history. In the five years since then, the Capitals have finished either first or second in the Southeast Division four times.

A back injury forced McPhee to retire as an active player at the conclusion of the 1988-89 season, after a seven year playing career with the New York Rangers and New Jersey Devils. McPhee originally signed as a free agent with the Rangers in July, 1982, after graduating from Bowling Green State University with a business degree. McPhee did not waste any time in college, tallying 40 goals and 48 assists in his freshman season and easily winning CCHA rookie of the year honors. His outstanding collegiate hockey career was capped off when he was named the recipient of the Hobey Baker Award as the top U.S. collegiate player in his senior season. McPhee also earned All-America honors as a senior and finished his career at Bowling Green as the CCHA's all-time leading scorer with 114-153-267. He was the first player in CCHA history to make the Conference's all-academic team three straight seasons.

General Managers' History

Milt Schmidt, 1974-75; Milt Schmidt and Max McNab, 1975-76; Max McNab, 1976-77 to 1980-81; Max McNab and Roger Crozier, 1981-82; David Poile, 1982-83 to 1996-97; George McPhee, 1997-98 to date.

Club Records

Team

(Figures in brackets for season records are games played; records for fewest points, wins, ties, losses, goals, goals against are for 70 or more games)

Most Points	**107**	1985-86 (80)
Most Wins	**50**	1985-86 (80)
Most Ties	**18**	1980-81 (80)
Most Losses	**67**	1974-75 (80)
Most Goals	**330**	1991-92 (80)
Most Goals Against	***446**	1974-75 (80)
Fewest Points	***21**	1974-75 (80)
Fewest Wins	***8**	1974-75 (80)
Fewest Ties	**5**	1974-75 (80), 1983-84 (80)
Fewest Losses	**23**	1985-86 (80)
Fewest Goals	**181**	1974-75 (80)
Fewest Goals Against	**202**	1997-98 (82)
Longest Winning Streak		
Overall	**10**	Jan. 27-Feb. 18/84
Home	**10**	Jan. 4-Feb. 23/00
Away	**6**	Feb. 26-Apr. 1/84
Longest Undefeated Streak		
Overall	**14**	Nov. 24-Dec. 23/82 (9 wins, 5 ties), Jan. 17-Feb. 18/84 (13 wins, 1 tie)
Home	**13**	Nov. 25/92-Jan. 31/93 (9 wins, 4 ties), Dec. 27/99-Feb. 23/00 (11 wins, 2 ties)
Away	**10**	Nov. 24/82-Jan. 8/83 (6 wins, 4 ties)
Longest Losing Streak		
Overall	***17**	Feb. 18-Mar. 26/75
Home	***11**	Feb. 18-Mar. 30/75
Away	**37**	Oct. 9/74-Mar. 26/75
Longest Winless Streak		
Overall	**25**	Nov. 29/75-Jan. 21/76 (22 losses, 3 ties)
Home	**14**	Dec. 3/75-Jan. 21/76 (11 losses, 3 ties)
Away	**37**	Oct. 9/74-Mar. 26/75 (37 losses)
Most Shutouts, Season	**9**	1995-96 (82)
Most PIM, Season	**2,204**	1989-90 (80)
Most Goals, Game	**12**	Feb. 6/90 (Que. 2 at Wsh. 12)

Individual

Most Seasons	**15**	Calle Johansson
Most Games	**983**	Calle Johansson
Most Goals, Career	**451**	Peter Bondra
Most Assists, Career	**418**	Michal Pivonka
Most Points, Career	**790**	Peter Bondra (451G, 339A)
Most PIM, Career	**2,003**	Dale Hunter
Most Shutouts, Career	**31**	Olaf Kolzig
Longest Consecutive Games Streak	**422**	Bob Carpenter (Oct. 7/81-Nov. 22/86)
Most Goals, Season	**60**	Dennis Maruk (1981-82)
Most Assists, Season	**76**	Dennis Maruk (1981-82)
Most Points, Season	**136**	Dennis Maruk (1981-82; 60G, 76A)
Most PIM, Season	**339**	Alan May (1989-90)
Most Points, Defenseman, Season	**81**	Larry Murphy (1986-87; 23G, 58A)
Most Points, Center, Season	**136**	Dennis Maruk (1981-82; 60G, 76A)
Most Points, Right Wing, Season	**102**	Mike Gartner (1984-85; 50G, 52A)
Most Points, Left Wing, Season	**87**	Ryan Walter (1981-82; 38G, 49A)
Most Points, Rookie, Season	**67**	Bob Carpenter (1981-82; 32G, 35A), Chris Valentine (1981-82; 30G, 37A)
Most Shutouts, Season	**9**	Jim Carey (1995-96)
Most Goals, Game	**5**	Bengt Gustafsson (Jan. 8/84), Peter Bondra (Feb. 5/94)
Most Assists, Game	**6**	Mike Ridley (Jan. 7/89)
Most Points, Game	**7**	Dino Ciccarelli (Mar. 18/89; 4G, 3A)

* NHL Record.

Retired Numbers

5	Rod Langway	1982-1993
7	Yvon Labre	1974-1981
32	Dale Hunter	1987-1999

Coaching History

Jim Anderson, Red Sullivan and Milt Schmidt, 1974-75; Milt Schmidt and Tom McVie, 1975-76; Tom McVie, 1976-77, 1977-78; Danny Belisle, 1978-79; Danny Belisle and Gary Green, 1979-80; Gary Green, 1980-81; Gary Green, Roger Crozier and Bryan Murray, 1981-82; Bryan Murray, 1982-83 to 1988-89; Bryan Murray and Terry Murray, 1989-90; Terry Murray, 1990-91 to 1992-93; Terry Murray and Jim Schoenfeld, 1993-94; Jim Schoenfeld, 1994-95 to 1996-97; Ron Wilson, 1997-98 to 2001-02; Bruce Cassidy, 2002-03 to date.

Captains' History

Doug Mohns, 1974-75; Bill Clement and Yvon Labre, 1975-76; Yvon Labre, 1976-77, 1977-78; Guy Charron, 1978-79; Ryan Walter, 1979-80 to 1981-82; Rod Langway, 1982-83 to 1991-92; Rod Langway and Kevin Hatcher, 1992-93; Kevin Hatcher, 1993-94; Dale Hunter, 1994-95 to 1998-99; Adam Oates, 1999-2000 to 2000-01; Brendan Witt and Steve Konowalchuk, 2001-02; Steve Konowalchuk, 2002-03.

All-time Record vs. Other Clubs

Regular Season

	At Home								On Road								Total							
	GP	W	L	T	OL	GF	GA	PTS	GP	W	L	T	OL	GF	GA	PTS	GP	W	L	T	OL	GF	GA	PTS
Anaheim	8	4	4	0	0	14	18	8	9	2	6	1	0	22	29	5	17	6	10	1	0	36	47	13
Atlanta	10	8	0	2	0	43	22	18	10	4	4	2	0	29	20	10	20	12	4	4	0	72	42	28
Boston	53	16	25	12	0	148	183	44	54	15	30	8	1	146	203	39	107	31	55	20	1	294	386	83
Buffalo	54	15	29	9	1	139	187	40	54	15	33	6	0	143	204	36	108	30	62	15	1	282	391	76
Calgary	40	21	14	5	0	150	136	47	38	7	24	7	0	93	157	21	78	28	38	12	0	243	293	68
Carolina	44	27	13	4	0	151	114	58	46	22	14	9	1	142	121	54	90	49	27	13	1	293	235	112
Chicago	40	21	14	5	0	142	123	47	39	11	22	6	0	116	151	28	79	32	36	11	0	258	274	75
Colorado	33	18	10	4	1	131	105	41	33	14	14	5	0	115	101	33	66	32	24	9	1	246	206	74
Columbus	2	1	0	1	0	8	5	3	3	2	1	0	0	10	8	4	5	3	1	1	0	18	13	7
Dallas	40	15	17	8	0	120	129	38	40	12	20	8	0	108	148	32	80	27	37	16	0	228	277	70
Detroit	45	21	19	5	0	167	142	47	46	14	20	11	1	131	160	40	91	35	39	16	1	298	302	87
Edmonton	28	17	9	2	0	117	93	36	29	10	15	4	0	91	120	24	57	27	24	6	0	208	213	60
Florida	25	15	6	4	0	82	55	34	25	12	10	3	0	64	63	27	50	27	16	7	0	146	118	61
Los Angeles	45	18	20	7	0	183	168	43	46	14	26	6	0	141	180	34	91	32	46	13	0	324	348	77
Minnesota	3	2	1	0	0	7	6	4	2	0	2	0	0	0	4	0	5	2	3	0	0	7	10	4
Montreal	57	25	23	9	0	157	170	59	58	17	33	8	0	125	220	42	115	42	56	17	0	282	390	101
Nashville	4	3	1	0	0	10	8	6	4	1	2	1	0	9	11	3	8	4	3	1	0	19	19	9
New Jersey	77	48	23	5	1	303	220	102	77	33	35	7	2	225	235	75	154	81	58	12	3	528	455	177
NY Islanders	79	39	29	11	0	257	245	89	79	36	41	2	0	251	294	74	158	75	70	13	0	508	539	163
NY Rangers	82	41	30	9	2	309	267	93	80	34	37	9	0	277	300	77	162	75	67	18	2	586	567	170
Ottawa	22	11	8	3	0	74	63	25	21	10	10	1	0	67	74	21	43	21	18	4	0	141	137	46
Philadelphia	78	32	33	13	0	258	254	77	81	24	51	6	0	216	303	54	159	56	84	19	0	474	557	131
Phoenix	30	18	6	5	1	119	82	42	30	8	15	7	0	105	112	23	60	26	21	12	1	224	194	65
Pittsburgh	84	43	31	9	1	350	307	96	81	29	45	7	0	257	314	65	165	72	76	16	1	607	621	161
St. Louis	39	20	15	4	0	136	117	44	40	13	19	8	0	126	161	34	79	33	34	12	0	262	278	78
San Jose	11	5	6	0	0	32	33	10	10	3	6	1	0	26	29	7	21	8	12	1	0	58	62	17
Tampa Bay	26	17	5	4	0	94	53	38	26	17	7	2	0	85	56	36	52	34	12	6	0	179	109	74
Toronto	48	28	16	3	1	178	139	60	46	16	24	5	1	160	205	38	94	44	40	8	2	338	344	98
Vancouver	39	22	13	4	0	131	114	48	39	16	18	5	0	123	136	37	78	38	31	9	0	254	250	85
Defunct Clubs	10	2	8	0	0	28	42	4	10	4	5	1	0	30	39	9	20	6	13	1	0	58	81	13
Totals	**1156**	**573**	**428**	**147**	**8**	**4038**	**3600**	**1301**	**1156**	**415**	**589**	**146**	**6**	**3433**	**4158**	**982**	**2312**	**988**	**1017**	**293**	**14**	**7471**	**7758**	**2283**

Playoffs

	Series	W	L	GP	W	L	T	GF	GA	Last Mtg.	Rnd.	Result
Boston	2	1	1	10	4	6	0	21	28	1998	CQF	W 4-2
Buffalo	1	1	0	6	4	2	0	13	11	1998	CF	W 4-2
Detroit	1	0	1	4	0	4	0	7	13	1998	F	L 0-4
New Jersey	2	1	1	13	7	6	0	44	43	1990	DSF	W 4-2
NY Islanders	6	1	5	30	12	18	0	88	99	1993	DSF	L 2-4
NY Rangers	4	2	2	22	11	11	0	75	71	1994	CSF	L 1-4
Ottawa	1	1	0	5	4	1	0	18	7	1998	CSF	W 4-1
Philadelphia	3	2	1	16	9	7	0	65	55	1989	DSF	L 2-4
Pittsburgh	7	1	6	42	16	26	0	121	137	2001	CQF	L 2-4
Tampa Bay	1	0	1	6	2	4	0	15	14	2003	CQF	L 2-4
Totals	**28**	**10**	**18**	**154**	**69**	**85**	**0**	**467**	**478**			

Calgary totals include Atlanta Flames, 1974-75 to 1979-80. Carolina totals include Hartford, 1979-80 to 1996-97.
Colorado totals include Quebec, 1979-80 to 1994-95. Dallas totals include Minnesota North Stars, 1974-75 to 1992-93.
New Jersey totals include Kansas City, 1974-75 to 1975-76, and Colorado Rockies, 1976-77 to 1981-82.
Phoenix totals include Winnipeg, 1979-80, 1995-96.

Playoff Results 2003-1999

Year	Round	Opponent	Result	GF	GA
2003	CQF	Tampa Bay	L 2-4	15	14
2001	CQF	Pittsburgh	L 2-4	10	14
2000	CQF	Pittsburgh	L 1-4	8	17

Abbreviations: Round: F – Final; **CF** – conference final; **CSF** – conference semi-final; **CQF** – conference quarter-final; **DSF** – division semi-final.

2002-03 Results

Oct.	11	Nashville	5-4		10	at Carolina	4-1
	12	at NY Islanders	2-1		11	Florida	12-2
	17	at Carolina	2-1		13	NY Islanders	4-3*
	19	at Philadelphia	1-3		15	NY Rangers	1-2*
	20	at Dallas	2-5		17	Toronto	1-4
	23	at NY Rangers	2-1		18	at Ottawa	2-5
	25	at Tampa Bay	2-3		20	at Boston	3-3
	26	at Florida	1-1		22	Carolina	5-3
	28	at Pittsburgh	2-3		25	at Montreal	1-1
	30	Boston	2-7		26	NY Rangers	7-2
Nov.	1	Tampa Bay	3-2		28	St. Louis	3-5
	2	at Philadelphia	1-2		30	Pittsburgh	2-1
	5	at Columbus	4-3*	**Feb.**	4	at Tampa Bay	5-1
	7	Florida	2-1*		5	New Jersey	1-4
	9	Philadelphia	4-1		7	NY Islanders	3-0
	13	Dallas	1-6		9	Montreal	0-2
	15	at Chicago	2-2		12	at Atlanta	5-1
	16	at Minnesota	0-1		14	at Carolina	1-3
	19	San Jose	2-3		15	at Florida	2-1
	21	Minnesota	3-4		17	at Tampa Bay	1-3
	23	Atlanta	6-3		20	Toronto	2-6
	26	at Toronto	4-5		22	Detroit	1-5
	27	Calgary	4-2		24	Montreal	4-1
	29	Ottawa	2-6		26	Buffalo	3-2
Dec.	1	at Atlanta	4-5	**Mar.**	1	at New Jersey	1-2*
	3	at Pittsburgh	4-1		2	Carolina	2-0
	6	Atlanta	7-6*		4	at Buffalo	2-1
	7	at Buffalo	3-4		6	Atlanta	4-4
	11	at Anaheim	0-3		8	at Boston	4-5*
	13	at Phoenix	4-3		10	Philadelphia	2-1*
	14	at San Jose	0-2		14	Los Angeles	1-3
	16	at Colorado	2-2		16	Colorado	2-1
	19	Boston	5-3		20	at Calgary	4-1
	21	at NY Islanders	3-1		22	at Edmonton	3-5
	23	Tampa Bay	3-0		23	at Vancouver	0-6
	27	New Jersey	3-2		25	at Montreal	4-3*
	28	at New Jersey	1-2*		28	at Ottawa	3-2
	30	Buffalo	4-3		29	at Toronto	3-4*
Jan.	1	Phoenix	1-2*	**Apr.**	1	Florida	3-0
	3	Columbus	2-2		3	Ottawa	1-5
	4	at NY Rangers	2-2		5	Pittsburgh	5-3

* – Overtime

Entry Draft
Selections 2003-1989

2003 Pick		1999 Pick		1995 Pick		1991 Pick	
18	Eric Fehr	7	Kris Beech	17	Brad Church	14	Pat Peake
83	Stephen Werner	29	Michal Sivek	23	Miika Elomo	21	Trevor Halverson
109	Andreas Valdix	31	Charlie Stephens	43	Dwayne Hay	25	Eric Lavigne
155	Josh Robertson	34	Ross Lupaschuk	93	Sebastien Charpentier	36	Jeff Nelson
249	Andrew Joudrey	37	Nolan Yonkman	95	Joel Theriault	58	Steve Konowalchuk
279	Mark Olafson	132	Roman Tvrdon	105	Benoit Gratton	80	Justin Morrison
		175	Kyle Clark	124	Joel Cort	146	Dave Morissette
2002		192	David Bornhammar	147	Frederick Jobin	168	Rick Corriveau
Pick		219	Maxim Orlov	199	Vasili Turkovsky	190	Trevor Duhaime
12	Steve Eminger	249	Igor Schadilov	225	Scott Swanson	209	Rob Leask
13	Alexander Semin					212	Carl Leblanc
17	Boyd Gordon	**1998**		**1994**		234	Rob Puchniak
59	Maxime Daigneault	**Pick**		**Pick**		256	Bill Kovacs
77	Patrick Wellar	49	Jomar Cruz	10	Nolan Baumgartner		
92	Derek Krestanovich	59	Todd Hornung	15	Alexander Kharlamov	**1990**	
109	Jevon Desautels	106	Krys Barch	41	Scott Cherrey	**Pick**	
118	Petr Dvorak	107	Chris Corrinet	93	Matt Herr	9	John Slaney
145	Rob Gherson	118	Mike Siklenka	119	Yanick Jean	30	Rod Pasma
179	Marian Havel	125	Erik Wendell	145	Dmitri Mekeshkin	51	Chris Longo
209	Joni Lindlof	179	Nate Forster	171	Daniel Reja	72	Randy Pearce
242	Igor Ignatushkin	193	Ratislav Stana	197	Chris Patrick	93	Brian Sakic
272	Patric Blomdahl	220	Mike Farrell	223	John Tuohy	94	Mark Ouimet
		251	Blake Evans	249	Richard Zednik	114	Andrei Kovalev
2001				275	Sergei Tertyshny	135	Roman Kontsek
Pick		**1997**				156	Peter Bondra
58	Nathan Paetsch	**Pick**		**1993**		159	Steve Martell
90	Owen Fussey	9	Nick Boynton	**Pick**		177	Ken Klee
125	Jeff Lucky	35	Jean-Francois Fortin	11	Brendan Witt	198	Michael Boback
160	Artem Ternavsky	89	Curtis Cruickshank	17	Jason Allison	219	Alan Brown
191	Zbynek Novak	116	Kevin Caulfield	69	Patrick Boileau	240	Todd Hlushko
221	John Oduya	143	Henrik Petre	147	Frank Banham		
249	Matt Maglione	200	Pierre-Luc Therrien	173	Daniel Hendrickson	**1989**	
254	Peter Polcik	226	Matt Oikawa	174	Andrew Brunette	**Pick**	
275	Robert Muller			199	Joel Poirier	19	Olaf Kolzig
284	Viktor Hubl	**1996**		225	Jason Gladney	35	Byron Dafoe
		Pick		251	Mark Seliger	59	Jim Mathieson
2000		4	Alexandre Volchkov	277	Dany Bousquet	61	Jason Woolley
Pick		17	Jaroslav Svejkovsky			82	Trent Klatt
26	Brian Sutherby	43	Jan Bulis	**1992**		145	Dave Lorentz
43	Matt Pettinger	58	Sergei Zimakov	**Pick**		166	Dean Holoien
61	Jakub Cutta	74	Dave Weninger	14	Sergei Gonchar	187	Victor Gervais
121	Ryan Vanbuskirk	78	Shawn McNeil	32	Jim Carey	208	Jiri Vykoukal
163	Ivan Nepryayev	85	Justin Davis	53	Stefan Ustorf	229	Sidorov Sidorov
289	Bjorn Nord	126	Matthew Lahey	71	Martin Gendron	250	Ken House
		153	Andrew Van Bruggen	119	John Varga		
		180	Michael Anderson	167	Mark Matier		
		206	Oleg Orekhovsky	191	Mike Mathers		
		232	Chad Cavanagh	215	Brian Stagg		
				239	Gregory Callahan		
				263	Billy Jo MacPherson		

Coach

CASSIDY, BRUCE
Coach, Washington Capitals. Born in Ottawa, Ont., May 20, 1965.

A former first-round draft pick (18th overall) by the Chicago Black Hawks in 1983, Bruce Cassidy became the 12th head coach of the Washington Capitals on June 25, 2002. The hiring came shortly after Cassidy was named American Hockey League coach of the year for the 2001-02 season. In his first year with the Capitals in 2002-03, he led the team to within one point of first place in the Southeast Division.

Cassidy played just 36 games over parts of six NHL seasons following a severe knee injury suffered while he was still a teenager. His pro career spanned 14 seasons, several leagues and four countries before another knee injury a decade later essentially ended his playing career. He played on championship clubs (including the 1984 Memorial Cup and the 1990 Turner Cup), made all-star teams and developed a reputation as a guy with a good head for the game. His coaching career began early in the 1996-97 season when he decided to give up playing at the age of 31. Cassidy stepped directly from the ice to the back of the bench as the head man of one of the worst teams in hockey, the Jacksonville Lizard Kings of the East Coast Hockey League. He spent six seasons as a minor league coach while also doubling as the director of hockey operations for Indianapolis of the IHL in 1998-99 and Trenton of the ECHL in 1999-2000. He guided Grand Rapids to the best record in the IHL in 2000-01 and had another successful season when the Griffins moved into the AHL for the 2001-02 season.

Known as "Butch" since he was 10 years old, Cassidy cites Darryl Sutter and Mike Keenan among those who have had an impact on his career to date.

Coaching Record

Season	Team	Games	Regular Season			Playoffs		
			W	L	T	Games	W	L
1996-97	Jacksonville (ECHL)	50	15	25	10	....	....	....
1997-98	Jacksonville (ECHL)	70	35	29	6	....	....	....
1998-99	Indianapolis (IHL)	82	33	37	12	7	3	4
1999-00	Trenton (ECHL)	70	37	29	4	14	8	6
2000-01	Grand Rapids (IHL)	82	53	22	7	10	6	4
2001-02	Grand Rapids (AHL)	82	42	27	11	5	2	3
2002-03	**Washington (NHL)**	**82**	**39**	**35**	**8**	**6**	**2**	**4**
	NHL Totals	82	39	35	8	6	2	4

Club Directory

MCI Center

Washington Capitals
401 Ninth Street, NW, Suite 750
Washington, DC 20004
Phone **202/226-2200**
PR FAX 202/266-2360
www.washingtoncaps.com
Capacity: 18,277

Executive Management
Majority Owner and Chairman	Ted Leonsis
Owner and President	Richard M. Patrick
Owners	Raul Fernandez, Jack Davies, Richard Kay, George Stamas, Richard Fairbank, Jeong Kim
Executive Assistant	Michelle Trostle

Hockey Operations
Vice President and General Manager	George McPhee
Director of Hockey Operations	Shawn Simpson
Assistant General Manager	Frank Provenzano
Head Coach	Bruce Cassidy
Assistant Coaches	Glen Hanlon, Randy Carlyle
Goaltending Coach	Dave Prior
Strength/Conditioning Coach	Jim Fox
Director of Team Services	Todd Warren
Scouting Coordinator	Kristian T. Wagner
Video Coordinator	Ted Dent
Piney Orchard Staff	Alex Walker
Security Representative	James Wiseman
Executive Assistant	Katy Headman

Scouting Staff
Director of Amateur Scouting	Ross Mahoney
Pro Scouts	Archie Henderson, Brian MacLellan
Ontario Scout	Steve Bowman
Western Scout	Dale Derkatch
Quebec Scout	Martin Pouliot
U.S. Scout	Steve Richmond
European Scouts	Gleb Chistyakov, Calle Johansson
Pro Scout	Mike Backman
European Scout	Vojtech Kucera
Eastern U.S. Scout	Ed McColgan

Medical Staff
Head Athletic Trainer	Greg Smith
Assistant Athletic Trainer	Tim Clark
Massage Therapist	Curt Millar
Team Physician	Ben Shaffer, MD
Team Internist	Richard Feldman, MD
Team Ophthalmologist	Michael Herr, MD
Team Dentist	Howard Salob, DDS

Equipment Staff
Head Equipment Manager	Doug Shearer
Assistant Equipment Manager	Craig Leydig
Equipment Assistant	Brian Metzger

Business Operations
Senior Vice President of Business Oper.	Declan J. Bolger
Director of Operations	George Parr
Director of Sponsorship Partnerships	Chris Hudgins
IT Manager	Kevin McDermott
Executive Assistant	Korrynn Lancaster
Receptionist	Shayla Miller
Mailroom Clerk	Jennifer Whittington

Communications
Senior Director of Communications	Kurt Kehl
Manager of Media Relations	Brian Potter
Manager of Information	Matt Charbonneau
Manager of Community Development	Stephanie Boyer

New Media
Manager of New Media	Sean Parker
Senior Sports Media Producer	Mike Vogel
Website and Publications Coordinator	Ben Solomon

Finance
Controller	Keith Burrows
Senior Accountant	Michael Mercer
Accounts Payable Manager	Jennifer Simpson
Staff Accountant	Jill Ruehle

Marketing
Senior Director of Marketing	John Vidalin
Director of Game Operations	Mark Tamar
Advertising and Promotions Manager	Missy Rentz
Manager of Fan Dev./Alum. Relations	Chris Lewis
Fan Development Coordinator	Ryan Ahern
Mascot Coordinator	Desi Deceder
Game Operations Coordinator	Katie Evereth
Promotions Coordinator	Erin Young
Marketing Coordinator	Jennifer Hudnell

Sales
Vice President, Sales	Kevin M. Morgan
Director of Group Sales	Brian Simpson
Senior Regional Sales Managers	Darren Bruening, Tim Bronaugh
Regional Sales Managers	Letitia Petrillo, Brad Vaughn, Doug Pristach, John Blackburn, Darren Montgomery, David Boettinger, Ryan Smith, J.P. Gibbons III, Anthony Aspaas, Josh Havey, Deanne Andringa, Audrius Zubrus
Executive Assistant	Carolyn Weaver

Ticket Operations & Guest Services
Director of Ticket Oper. & Guest Services	Laini Delawter
Assistant Director of Guest Services	Greg Monares
Assistant Manager of Guest Services	Jenny Carter
Manager, Ticket Operations	Kelly Shultz
Assistant Manager of Ticket Operations, Finance	Jennifer Casswell
Coordinator of Ticket Operations, Internet	Jeff Keeney
Coordinator of Ticket Operations, Plans	Lori Murphy
Assistant Ticket Manager of Oper. and Groups	Eric Spat
Coordinators of Guest Services	Megan Donohoo, Eric Garvey

2002-2003 Final Statistics

Standings

Abbreviations: **GP** – games played; **W** – wins; **L** – losses; **T** – ties; **OTL** – overtime losses; **GF** – goals for; **GA** – goals against; **PTS** – points.

EASTERN CONFERENCE

Northeast Division

	GP	W	L	T	OTL	GF	GA	PTS
Ottawa	82	52	21	8	1	263	182	113
Toronto	82	44	28	7	3	236	208	98
Boston	82	36	31	11	4	245	237	87
Montreal	82	30	35	8	9	206	234	77
Buffalo	82	27	37	10	8	190	219	72

Atlantic Division

	GP	W	L	T	OTL	GF	GA	PTS
New Jersey	82	46	20	10	6	216	166	108
Philadelphia	82	45	20	13	4	211	166	107
NY Islanders	82	35	34	11	2	224	231	83
NY Rangers	82	32	36	10	4	210	231	78
Pittsburgh	82	27	44	6	5	189	255	65

Southeast Division

	GP	W	L	T	OTL	GF	GA	PTS
Tampa Bay	82	36	25	16	5	219	210	93
Washington	82	39	29	8	6	224	220	92
Atlanta	82	31	39	7	5	226	284	74
Florida	82	24	36	13	9	176	237	70
Carolina	82	22	43	11	6	171	240	61

WESTERN CONFERENCE

Central Division

	GP	W	L	T	OTL	GF	GA	PTS
Detroit	82	48	20	10	4	269	203	110
St. Louis	82	41	24	11	6	253	222	99
Chicago	82	30	33	13	6	207	226	79
Nashville	82	27	35	13	7	183	206	74
Columbus	82	29	42	8	3	213	263	69

Pacific Division

	GP	W	L	T	OTL	GF	GA	PTS
Dallas	82	46	17	15	4	245	169	111
Anaheim	82	40	27	9	6	203	193	95
Los Angeles	82	33	37	6	6	203	221	78
Phoenix	82	31	35	11	5	204	230	78
San Jose	82	28	37	9	8	214	239	73

Northwest Division

	GP	W	L	T	OTL	GF	GA	PTS
Colorado	82	42	19	13	8	251	194	105
Vancouver	82	45	23	13	1	264	208	104
Minnesota	82	42	29	10	1	198	178	95
Edmonton	82	36	26	11	9	231	230	92
Calgary	82	29	36	13	4	186	228	75

With seven goals in his last five games, including two in Colorado's final game of the regular season, Milan Hejduk wound up as the NHL's top goal scorer with an even 50.

INDIVIDUAL LEADERS

Goal Scoring

Player	Team	GP	G
Milan Hejduk	Colorado	82	50
Markus Naslund	Vancouver	82	48
Todd Bertuzzi	Vancouver	82	46
Marian Hossa	Ottawa	80	45
Glen Murray	Boston	82	44
Dany Heatley	Atlanta	77	41
Ilya Kovalchuk	Atlanta	81	38
Mats Sundin	Toronto	75	37
Ziggy Palffy	Los Angeles	76	37
Alex Kovalev	Pit., NYR	78	37
Brett Hull	Detroit	82	37

Assists

Player	Team	GP	A
Peter Forsberg	Colorado	75	77
Joe Thornton	Boston	77	65
Mario Lemieux	Pittsburgh	67	63
Pavol Demitra	St. Louis	78	57
Mike Modano	Dallas	79	57
Vaclav Prospal	Tampa Bay	80	57
Brad Richards	Tampa Bay	80	57
Markus Naslund	Vancouver	82	56
Paul Kariya	Anaheim	82	56

Power-play Goals

Player	Team	GP	PP
Todd Bertuzzi	Vancouver	82	25
Markus Naslund	Vancouver	82	24
Dany Heatley	Atlanta	77	19
Milan Hejduk	Colorado	82	18
Mats Sundin	Toronto	75	16

Short-handed Goals

Player	Team	GP	SH
Shawn Bates	NY Islanders	74	6
Brian Rolston	Boston	81	5
Martin Rucinsky	St. Louis	61	4
Curtis Brown	Buffalo	74	4
Kirk Maltby	Detroit	82	4
Matt Cooke	Vancouver	82	4

Game-winning Goals

Player	Team	GP	GW
Markus Naslund	Vancouver	82	12
Sergei Fedorov	Detroit	80	11
Marian Hossa	Ottawa	80	10
Alexander Mogilny	Toronto	73	9
Jaromir Jagr	Washington	75	9
Michal Handzus	Philadelphia	82	9

Game-tying Goals

Player	Team	GP	GT
Kristian Huselius	Florida	78	3
Andrew Brunette	Minnesota	82	3
Martin St. Louis	Tampa Bay	82	3

Shots

Player	Team	GP	S
Glen Murray	Boston	82	331
Jarome Iginla	Calgary	75	316
Jeff O'Neill	Carolina	82	316
Al MacInnis	St. Louis	80	299
Petr Sykora	Anaheim	82	299

Shooting Percentage

(minimum 82 shots)

Player	Team	GP	G	S	%
Milan Hejduk	Colorado	82	50	244	20.5
Alexander Mogilny	Toronto	73	33	165	20.0
Brenden Morrow	Dallas	71	21	105	20.0
Marian Hossa	Ottawa	80	45	229	19.7
Scott Mellanby	St. Louis	80	26	132	19.7

Penalty Minutes

Player	Team	GP	PIM
Jody Shelley	Columbus	68	249
Reed Low	St. Louis	79	234
Matt Johnson	Minnesota	60	201
Wade Belak	Toronto	55	196
Peter Worrell	Florida	63	193

Plus/Minus

Player	Team	GP	+/–
Peter Forsberg	Colorado	75	52
Milan Hejduk	Colorado	82	52
Nicklas Lidstrom	Detroit	82	40
Jere Lehtinen	Dallas	80	39
Derian Hatcher	Dallas	82	37

Individual Leaders

Abbreviations: GP – games played; **G** – goals; **A** – assists; **Pts** – points; **+/–** – difference between Goals For (**GF**) scored when a player is on the ice with his team at even strength or short-handed and Goals Against (**GA**) scored when the same player is on the ice with his team at even strength or on a power play; **PIM** – penalties in minutes; **PP** – power play goals; **SH** – short-handed goals; **GW** – game-winning goals; **GT** – game-tying goals; **S** – shots on goal; **%** – percentage of shots on goal resulting in goals.

Individual Scoring Leaders for Art Ross Trophy

Player	Team	GP	G	A	Pts	+/–	PIM	PP	SH	GW	GT	S	%
Peter Forsberg	Colorado	75	29	77	106	52	70	8	0	2	0	166	17.5
Markus Naslund	Vancouver	82	48	56	104	6	52	24	0	12	1	294	16.3
Joe Thornton	Boston	77	36	65	101	12	109	12	2	4	1	196	18.4
Milan Hejduk	Colorado	82	50	48	98	52	18	0	4	1	0	244	20.5
Todd Bertuzzi	Vancouver	82	46	51	97	2	144	25	0	7	1	243	18.9
Pavol Demitra	St. Louis	78	36	57	93	0	32	11	0	4	1	205	17.6
Glen Murray	Boston	82	44	48	92	9	64	12	0	5	2	331	13.3
Mario Lemieux	Pittsburgh	67	28	63	91	–25	43	14	0	4	0	235	11.9
Dany Heatley	Atlanta	77	41	48	89	–8	58	19	1	6	0	252	16.3
Ziggy Palffy	Los Angeles	76	37	48	85	22	47	10	2	6	0	277	13.4
Mike Modano	Dallas	79	28	57	85	34	30	5	2	6	0	193	14.5
Sergei Fedorov	Detroit	80	36	47	83	15	52	10	2	11	0	281	12.8
Paul Kariya	Anaheim	82	25	56	81	–3	48	11	1	2	1	257	9.7
Marian Hossa	Ottawa	80	45	35	80	8	34	14	0	10	1	229	19.7
Alexander Mogilny	Toronto	73	33	46	79	4	12	5	3	9	0	165	20.0
Vaclav Prospal	Tampa Bay	80	22	57	79	9	53	9	0	4	0	134	16.4
Vincent Lecavalier	Tampa Bay	80	33	45	78	0	39	11	2	3	1	274	12.0
Daniel Alfredsson	Ottawa	78	27	51	78	15	42	9	0	6	0	240	11.3
Alex Kovalev	Pit., NYR	78	37	40	77	–9	70	11	0	3	1	271	13.7
Jaromir Jagr	Washington	75	36	41	77	5	38	13	2	9	0	290	12.4
Brett Hull	Detroit	82	37	39	76	11	22	12	1	4	1	262	14.1
Ray Whitney	Columbus	81	24	52	76	–26	22	8	2	2	1	235	10.2
Miroslav Satan	Buffalo	79	26	49	75	–3	20	11	1	3	1	240	10.8
Brad Richards	Tampa Bay	80	17	57	74	3	24	4	0	2	0	277	6.1
Mats Sundin	Toronto	75	37	35	72	1	58	16	3	8	1	223	16.6

Defencemen Scoring Leaders

Player	Team	GP	G	A	Pts	+/–	PIM	PP	SH	GW	GT	S	%
Al MacInnis	St. Louis	80	16	52	68	22	61	9	1	2	0	299	5.4
Sergei Gonchar	Washington	82	18	49	67	13	52	7	0	2	1	224	8.0
Nicklas Lidstrom	Detroit	82	18	44	62	40	38	8	1	4	0	175	10.3
Sergei Zubov	Dallas	82	11	44	55	21	26	8	0	2	0	158	7.0
Dan Boyle	Tampa Bay	77	13	40	53	9	44	8	0	1	1	136	9.6
Mathieu Schneider	L.A. Det.	78	16	34	50	2	73	11	0	1	0	199	8.0
Derek Morris	Colorado	75	11	37	48	16	68	9	0	7	0	191	5.8
Tom Poti	NY Rangers	80	11	37	48	–6	60	3	0	1	0	148	7.4
Tomas Kaberle	Toronto	82	11	36	47	20	30	4	1	2	1	119	9.2
Ed Jovanovski	Vancouver	67	6	40	46	19	113	2	0	1	1	145	4.1

CONSECUTIVE SCORING STREAKS

Goals

Games	Player	Team	G
7	Geoff Sanderson	Columbus	8
7	Milan Hejduk	Colorado	8
6	Owen Nolan	San Jose	8
6	Keith Tkachuk	St. Louis	8
6	Markus Naslund	Vancouver	8
6	Patrick Marleau	San Jose	7
5	Alex Kovalev	Pittsburgh	7
5	Milan Hejduk	Colorado	7
5	Mike York	Edmonton	7
5	Martin St. Louis	Tampa Bay	6
5	Jere Lehtinen	Dallas	5
5	Jarome Iginla	Calgary	5

Assists

Games	Player	Team	A
11	Mario Lemieux	Pittsburgh	21
8	Doug Weight	St. Louis	11
8	Alex Tanguay	Colorado	11
8	Igor Larionov	Detroit	9
8	Sergei Fedorov	Dallas	9
7	Pavel Datsyuk	Detroit	13
7	Doug Weight	St. Louis	12
7	Doug Weight	St. Louis	11
7	Dick Tarnstrom	Pittsburgh	11
7	Martin Gelinas	Calgary	8
7	Trevor Linden	Vancouver	8
7	Kimmo Timonen	Nashville	8
7	Jeff O'Neill	Carolina	7
6	Vyacheslav Kozlov	Atlanta	10
6	Paul Kariya	Anaheim	10
6	Dany Heatley	Atlanta	9
6	Saku Koivu	Montreal	8
6	Brendan Morrison	Vancouver	8
6	Scott Hartnell	Nashville	8
6	Al MacInnis	St. Louis	7
6	Joe Sakic	Colorado	7
6	Keith Tkachuk	St. Louis	7
6	Ray Whitney	Columbus	7
6	Pavol Demitra	St. Louis	7
6	Ed Jovanovski	Vancouver	7
6	Brad Richards	Tampa Bay	7
6	Sergei Zholtok	Minnesota	6
6	Brad Richards	Tampa Bay	6

Points

Games	Player	Team	G	A	PTS
16	Alex Tanguay	Colorado	10	16	26
13	Marian Hossa	Ottawa	12	10	22
13	Milan Hejduk	Colorado	8	13	21
13	Milan Hejduk	Colorado	12	9	21
12	Keith Tkachuk	St. Louis	11	9	20
12	Todd Bertuzzi	Vancouver	6	8	14
12	Jeff Friesen	New Jersey	8	5	13
11	Mario Lemieux	Pittsburgh	8	21	29
11	Alex Kovalev	Pittsburgh	10	9	19

Peter Forsberg became the first Swedish-born player to lead the NHL in scoring, passing Markus Naslund, a fellow native of Ornskoldsvik, on the final day of the season.

One year after setting a career high with 26 goals, Washington's Sergei Gonchar established career bests with 49 assists and 67 points.

The Blue Jackets' Rick Nash was the youngest player in the NHL in 2002-03. He finished third among rookie scorers and placed third in voting for the Calder Trophy.

Individual Rookie Scoring Leaders

Rookie	Team	GP	G	A	Pts	+/−	PIM	PP	SH	GW	GT	S	%
Henrik Zetterberg	Detroit	79	22	22	44	6	8	5	1	4	0	135	16.3
Tyler Arnason	Chicago	82	19	20	39	7	20	3	0	6	0	178	10.7
Rick Nash	Columbus	74	17	22	39	−27	78	6	0	2	0	154	11.0
Ales Kotalik	Buffalo	68	21	14	35	−2	30	4	0	2	2	138	15.2
Niko Kapanen	Dallas	82	5	29	34	25	44	0	1	1	0	80	6.3
Alexander Frolov	Los Angeles	79	14	17	31	12	34	1	0	3	0	141	9.9
Stanislav Chistov	Anaheim	79	12	18	30	4	54	3	0	2	0	114	10.5
Ales Hemsky	Edmonton	59	6	24	30	5	14	0	0	1	0	50	12.0
Adam Hall	Nashville	79	16	12	28	−8	31	8	0	2	0	146	11.0
Branko Radivojevic	Phoenix	79	12	15	27	−2	63	1	0	3	1	109	11.0
Jaroslav Bednar	L.A., Fla.	67	5	22	27	1	18	2	0	1	2	95	5.3

Goal Scoring

Name	Team	GP	G
Henrik Zetterberg	Detroit	79	22
Ales Kotalik	Buffalo	68	21
Tyler Arnason	Chicago	82	19
Rick Nash	Columbus	74	17
Adam Hall	Nashville	79	16
Jason Chimera	Edmonton	66	14
Alexander Frolov	Los Angeles	79	14
Branko Radivojevic	Phoenix	79	12
Stanislav Chistov	Anaheim	79	12
Ramzi Abid	Phx., Pit.	33	10
Dan Snyder	Atlanta	36	10

Assists

Name	Team	GP	A
Niko Kapanen	Dallas	82	29
Ales Hemsky	Edmonton	59	24
Jaroslav Bednar	L.A., Fla.	67	22
Rick Nash	Columbus	74	22
Henrik Zetterberg	Detroit	79	22
Tyler Arnason	Chicago	82	20
Jim Fahey	San Jose	43	19
Stanislav Chistov	Anaheim	79	18
Mattias Weinhandl	NY Islanders	47	17
Alexander Frolov	Los Angeles	79	17
Barret Jackman	St. Louis	82	16

Power-play Goals

Name	Team	GP	PP
Adam Hall	Nashville	79	8
Rick Nash	Columbus	74	6
Pierre-Marc Bouchard	Minnesota	50	5
Henrik Zetterberg	Detroit	79	5
Ramzi Abid	Phx., Pit.	33	4
Ales Kotalik	Buffalo	68	4

Short-handed Goals

Name	Team	GP	SH
Mike Zigomanis	Carolina	19	1
Fernando Pisani	Edmonton	35	1
Dan Snyder	Atlanta	36	1
Radovan Somik	Philadelphia	60	1
Jason Chimera	Edmonton	66	1
Henrik Zetterberg	Detroit	79	1
Niko Kapanen	Dallas	82	1

Game-winning Goals

Name	Team	GP	GW
Tyler Arnason	Chicago	82	6
Jason Chimera	Edmonton	66	4
Henrik Zetterberg	Detroit	79	4
Mike Rupp	New Jersey	26	3
Ramzi Abid	Phx., Pit.	33	3
Jonathan Cheechoo	San Jose	66	3
Branko Radivojevic	Phoenix	79	3
Alexander Frolov	Los Angeles	79	3

Game-tying Goals

Name	Team	GP	GT
Jaroslav Bednar	L.A., Fla.	67	2
Ales Kotalik	Buffalo	68	2
Jay Bouwmeester	Florida	82	2
Scottie Upshall	Nashville	8	1
Blair Betts	Calgary	9	1
Jason Williams	Detroit	16	1
Niko Dimitrakos	San Jose	21	1
Dan Snyder	Atlanta	36	1
Jesse Boulerice	Carolina	48	1
Jason Chimera	Edmonton	66	1
Jonathan Cheechoo	San Jose	66	1
Branko Radivojevic	Phoenix	79	1

Shots

Name	Team	GP	S
Tyler Arnason	Chicago	82	178
Rick Nash	Columbus	74	154
Adam Hall	Nashville	79	146
Alexander Frolov	Los Angeles	79	141
Ales Kotalik	Buffalo	68	138

Shooting Percentage
(minimum 82 shots)

Name	Team	GP	G	S	%
Henrik Zetterberg	Detroit	79	22	135	16.3
Jason Chimera	Edmonton	66	14	90	15.6
Ales Kotalik	Buffalo	68	21	138	15.2
Rick Nash	Columbus	74	17	154	11.0
Adam Hall	Nashville	79	16	146	11.0
Branko Radivojevic	Phoenix	79	12	109	11.0

Penalty Minutes

Name	Team	GP	PIM
Barret Jackman	St. Louis	82	190
Steve Montador	Calgary	50	114
Jesse Boulerice	Carolina	48	108
Brian Sutherby	Washington	72	93
Alex Henry	Washington	41	80

Plus/Minus

Name	Team	GP	+/−
Niko Kapanen	Dallas	82	25
Barret Jackman	St. Louis	82	23
Ales Pisa	Edm., NYR	51	12
Alexander Frolov	Los Angeles	79	12

Three-or-More-Goal Games

Player	Team	Date	Final Score	G	Player	Team	Date	Final Score	G	Player	Team	Date	Final Score	G
*Tyler Arnason	Chicago	Dec. 28	Chi. 3 S.J. 3	3	Marian Hossa	Ottawa	Jan. 02	Atl. 1 Ott. 8	4	Petr Nedved	NY Rangers	Jan. 13	Tor. 1 NYR 5	3
Jason Arnott	Dallas	Dec. 04	Mtl. 1 Dal. 5	3	Brett Hull	Detroit	Mar. 16	Ott. 2 Det. 6	3	Mark Parrish	NY Islanders	Jan. 03	Bos. 4 NYI 8	3
Eric Belanger	Los Angeles	Dec. 17	St.L. 2 L.A. 6	3	Brett Hull	Detroit	Mar. 29	Det. 6 St.L. 2	3	*Kamil Piros	Atlanta	Apr. 06	T.B. 2 Atl. 5	3
Todd Bertuzzi	Vancouver	Mar. 17	Van. 4 Dal. 2	3	Jarome Iginla	Calgary	Feb. 07	Cgy. 4 Edm. 3	3	*Fernando Pisani	Edmonton	Mar. 22	Wsh. 3 Edm. 5	3
Jason Blake	NY Islanders	Jan. 11	Atl. 3 NYI 7	3	Jarome Iginla	Calgary	Feb. 23	Cgy. 4 Phx. 2	3	Taylor Pyatt	Buffalo	Mar. 28	Mtl. 1 Buf. 4	3
Curtis Brown	Buffalo	Dec. 04	Ana. 0 Buf. 4	3	Jaromir Jagr	Washington	Jan. 11	Fla. 2 Wsh.12	3	Mark Recchi	Philadelphia	Oct. 12	Phi. 5 Cgy. 4	3
Pavel Bure	NY Rangers	Dec. 03	CBJ 3 NYR 5	3	Jaromir Jagr	Washington	Feb. 04	Wsh. 5 T.B. 1	3	Steve Reinprecht	Colorado	Jan. 04	Col. 6 S.J. 1	3
Erik Cole	Carolina	Nov. 23	Car. 7 Mtl. 3	3	Andreas Johansson	Nashville	Nov. 27	S.J. 2 Nsh. 4	3	Joe Sakic	Colorado	Mar. 13	Col. 5 CBJ 1	3
Eric Daze	Chicago	Dec. 11	Chi. 4 NYR 3	3	Paul Kariya	Anaheim	Oct. 31	Ana. 4 Bos. 1	3	Geoff Sanderson	Columbus	Mar. 29	CBJ 6 Cgy. 4	4
Eric Daze	Chicago	Mar. 09	Bos. 5 Chi. 8	3	Saku Koivu	Montreal	Nov. 18	Pit. 4 Mtl. 5	3	Miroslav Satan	Buffalo	Dec. 06	Buf. 4 NYR 1	3
Adam Deadmarsh	Los Angeles	Oct. 25	L.A. 6 NYR 2	3	Ilya Kovalchuk	Atlanta	Dec. 06	Atl. 6 Wsh. 7	3	Dave Scatchard	NY Islanders	Jan. 07	Pit. 3 NYI 6	3
Pavol Demitra	St. Louis	Nov. 29	Cgy. 2 St.L. 7	3	Alex Kovalev	Pittsburgh	Jan. 25	Chi. 3 Pit. 5	3	Dave Scatchard	NY Islanders	Feb. 11	T.B. 2 NYI 6	3
Patrik Elias	New Jersey	Mar. 30	NYI 0 N.J. 6	4	Daymond Langkow	Phoenix	Jan. 24	Phx. 5 Edm. 1	3	Brendan Shanahan	Detroit	Feb. 20	Edm. 2 Det. 6	3
Sergei Fedorov	Detroit	Oct. 25	Pit. 3 Det. 7	3	Martin Lapointe	Boston	Mar. 13	N.J. 3 Bos. 4	3	Bryan Smolinski	Los Angeles	Feb. 07	Car. 2 L.A. 8	3
Sergei Fedorov	Detroit	Mar. 07	St.L. 2 Det. 7	3	Vincent Lecavalier	Tampa Bay	Nov. 08	Pit. 1 T.B. 4	3	Martin St. Louis	Tampa Bay	Jan. 30	Car. 1 T.B. 3	3
Peter Forsberg	Colorado	Dec. 29	L.A. 1 Col. 6	3	Vincent Lecavalier	Tampa Bay	Mar. 22	T.B. 4 Phx. 0	3	Steve Sullivan	Chicago	Mar. 09	Bos. 5 Chi. 8	3
Peter Forsberg	Colorado	Feb. 09	Cgy. 2 Col. 4	3	John LeClair	Philadelphia	Oct. 15	Phi. 6 Mtl. 2	4	Alex Tanguay	Colorado	Mar. 22	Chi. 1 Col. 8	3
Marian Gaborik	Minnesota	Nov. 04	Min. 5 L.A. 2	3	Jere Lehtinen	Dallas	Jan. 07	L.A. 4 Dal. 7	3	Ray Whitney	Columbus	Mar. 01	L.A. 1 CBJ 3	3
Marian Gaborik	Minnesota	Nov. 23	Nsh. 2 Min. 4	3	John Madden	New Jersey	Feb. 05	N.J. 4 Wsh. 1	3	Tyler Wright	Columbus	Oct. 27	L.A. 1 CBJ 5	3
Marian Gaborik	Minnesota	Dec. 07	Min. 4 Van. 2	3	Shawn McEachern	Atlanta	Oct. 12	Fla. 5 Atl. 4	3	Tyler Wright	Columbus	Mar. 20	Tor. 3 CBJ 5	3
Martin Havlat	Ottawa	Jan. 27	Ott. 3 Dal. 5	3	Marty McInnis	Boston	Mar. 06	NYI 1 Bos. 4	3	Alexei Yashin	NY Islanders	Mar. 25	NYI 9 Chi. 2	4
Dany Heatley	Atlanta	Jan. 13	Atl. 7 Phi. 4	3	Scott Mellanby	St. Louis	Mar. 06	Phx. 3 St.L. 6	4					
Dany Heatley	Atlanta	Jan. 25	Atl. 4 NYR 1	3	Alexander Mogilny	Toronto	Nov. 05	T.B. 3 Tor. 4	3					
Milan Hejduk	Colorado	Feb. 08	Det. 3 Col. 5	3	Alexander Mogilny	Toronto	Dec. 23	Atl. 1 Tor. 5	3					
Jan Hlavac	Carolina	Nov. 29	Det. 4 Car. 6	3	Glen Murray	Boston	Nov. 26	Cgy. 2 Bos. 7	3					
Marian Hossa	Ottawa	Nov. 06	Ott. 5 Col. 2	3	Markus Naslund	Vancouver	Oct. 21	Van. 5 S.J. 2	3					
Marian Hossa	Ottawa	Nov. 23	CBJ 2 Ott. 5	3	Markus Naslund	Vancouver	Dec. 14	Van. 6 Edm. 3	4					

* indicates rookie

2002-03 Penalty Shots

Scored

Pavel Bure (NY Rangers) scored against Tomas Vokoun (Nashville), October 19. Final score: Nashville 2 at NY Rangers 2.

Brenden Morrow (Dallas) scored against Dan Cloutier (Vancouver), November 6. Final score: Vancouver 0 at Dallas 4.

Patrick Marleau (San Jose) scored against Dan Blackburn (NY Rangers), November 11. Final score: NY Rangers 5 at San Jose 4.

Michal Handzus (Philadelphia) scored against Dan Blackburn (NY Rangers) December 5. Final score: NY Rangers 2 at Philadelphia 3.

Alexei Zhamnov (Chicago) scored against Martin Biron (Buffalo), December 13. Final score: Chicago 1 at Buffalo 1.

Miroslav Satan (Buffalo) scored against Mike Dunham (NY Rangers), February 15. Final score: NY Rangers 4 at Buffalo 5.

Mike Knuble (Boston) scored against Jocelyn Thibault (Chicago), March 9. Final score: Boston 5 at Chicago 8.

Pavel Bure (NY Rangers) scored against Patrick Lalime (Ottawa), Mach 13. Final score: NY Rangers 2 at Ottawa 3.

Steve Thomas (Anaheim) scored against Tomas Vokoun (Nashville), Apr 1. Final score: Anaheim 2 at Nashville 1.

Stopped

Tomas Vokoun (Nashville) stopped Brad Isbister (NY Islanders), October 15. Final score: Nashville 3 at NY Islanders 4.

Mike Dunham (Nashville) stopped Cory Stillman (St. Louis), October 30. Final score: Nashville 0 at St. Louis 7.

Martin Prusek (Ottawa) stopped Glen Murray (Boston), November 9. Final score: Ottawa 1 at Boston 7.

Martin Prusek (Ottawa) stopped Dave Scatchard (NY Islanders), November 12. Final score: Ottawa 5 at NY Islanders 3.

Olaf Kolzig (Washington) stopped Steve Sullivan (Chicago), November 15. Final score: Washington 2 at Chicago 2.

Marty Turco (Dallas) stopped Mathieu Dandenault (Detroit), December 6. Final score: Detroit 3 at Dallas 3.

Rick DiPietro (NY Islanders) stopped Michael Nylander (Washington), December 21. Final score: Washington 3 at NY Islanders 1.

Ed Belfour (Toronto) stopped Mike Comrie (Edmonton), December 28. Final score: Toronto 2 at Edmonton 3.

Roman Turek (Calgary) stopped Petr Sykora (Anaheim), December 29. Final score: Anaheim 2 at Calgary 4.

Dan Cloutier (Vancouver) stopped Tomas Holmstrom (Detroit), January 19. Final score: Vancouver 4 at Detroit 1.

Nikolai Khabibulin (Tampa Bay) stopped Saku Koivu (Montreal), January 22. Final score: Montreal 2 at Tampa Bay 2.

Jani Hurme (Florida) stopped Magnus Arvedson (Ottawa), January 22. Final score: Ottawa 2 at Florida 1.

Mike Dunham (NY Rangers) stopped Rem Murray (Nashville), January 23. Final score: NY Rangers 4 at Nashville 2.

Marc Denis (Columbus) stopped Dean McAmmond (Colorado), January 23. Final score: Columbus 0 at Colorado 5.

Jocelyn Thibault (Chicago) stopped Marian Gaborik (Minnesota), February 5. Final score: Chicago 1 at Minnesota 2.

Steve Shields (Boston) stopped Adam Hall (Nashville), February 17. Final score: Boston 1 at Nashville 5.

Evgeni Nabokov (San Jose) stopped Ziggy Palffy (Los Angeles), February 17. Final score: San Jose 2 at Los Angeles 3.

Milan Hnilicka (Atlanta) stopped Vincent Lecavalier (Tampa Bay), February 19. Final score: Atlanta 0 at Tampa Bay 2.

Tomas Vokoun (Nashville) stopped Robert Reichel (Toronto), February 23. Final score: Nashville 5 at Toronto 2.

Garth Snow (NY Islanders) stopped Mats Sundin (Toronto), February 25. Final score: NY Islanders 2 at Toronto 5.

Roman Cechmanek (Philadelphia) stopped Steve Sullivan (Chicago), February 25. Final score: Philadelphia 2 at Chicago 0.

Jocelyn Thibault (Chicago) stopped Mike Johnson (Phoenix), March 14. Final score: Chicago 4 at Phoenix 0.

Vesa Toskala (San Jose) stopped Jarome Iginla (Calgary), March 15. Final score: Calgary 2 at San Jose 3.

Jamie McLennan (Calgary) stopped Paul Kariya (Anaheim), March 16. Final score: Calgary 2 at Anaheim 2.

Steve Shields (Boston) stopped Patrick Marleau (San Jose), March 21. Final score: Boston 2 at San Jose 3.

Evgeni Nabokov (San Jose) stopped Martin St. Louis (Tampa Bay), Mar 24. Final score: Tampa Bay 4 at San Jose 1.

Olaf Kolzig (Washington) stopped Andrei Markov (Montreal), March 25. Final score: Washington 4 at Montreal 3.

Cristobal Huet (Los Angeles) stopped Andrej Nedorost (Columbus), March 25. Final score: Columbus 2 at Los Angeles 1.

Tomas Vokoun (Nashville) stopped Dany Heatley (Atlanta), March 29. Final score: Atlanta 3 at Nashville 2.

Vesa Toskala (San Jose) stopped Mike Comrie (Edmonton), Apr 3. Final score: San Jose 3 at Edmonton 3.

Summary

39 penalty shots resulted in 9 goals

Goaltending Leaders

Minimum 25 games

Goals-Against Average

Goaltender	Team	GPI	MINS	GA	Avg
Marty Turco	Dallas	55	3203	92	1.72
Roman Cechmanek	Philadelphia	58	3350	102	1.83
Dwayne Roloson	Minnesota	50	2945	98	2.00
Martin Brodeur	New Jersey	73	4374	147	2.02
Patrick Lalime	Ottawa	67	3943	142	2.16

Save Percentage

Goaltender	Team	GPI	MINS	GA	SA	S%	W	L	T
Marty Turco	Dallas	55	3203	92	1359	.932	31	10	10
Dwayne Roloson	Minnesota	50	2945	98	1334	.927	23	16	8
Roman Cechmanek	Philadelphia	58	3350	102	1368	.925	33	15	10
Manny Legace	Detroit	25	1406	51	681	.925	14	5	4
Manny Fernandez	Minnesota	35	1979	74	972	.924	19	13	2

Wins

Goaltender	Team	GPI	MINS	W	L	T
Martin Brodeur	New Jersey	73	4374	41	23	9
Patrick Lalime	Ottawa	67	3943	39	20	7
Ed Belfour	Toronto	62	3738	37	20	5
Patrick Roy	Colorado	63	3769	35	15	13
Curtis Joseph	Detroit	61	3566	34	19	6
J-S Giguere	Anaheim	65	3775	34	22	6

Shutouts

Goaltender	Team	GPI	MINS	SO	W	L	T
Martin Brodeur	New Jersey	73	4374	9	41	23	9
Jocelyn Thibault	Chicago	62	3650	8	26	28	7
J-S Giguere	Anaheim	65	3775	8	34	22	6
Patrick Lalime	Ottawa	67	3943	8	39	20	7
Marty Turco	Dallas	55	3203	7	31	10	10
Ed Belfour	Toronto	62	3738	7	37	20	5

Team-by-Team Point Totals

1998-99 to 2002-03

(Ranked by five-year point %)

	02-03	01-02	00-01	99-00	98-99	Pts%
Detroit	110	116	111	108	93	.656
Dallas	111	90	106	102	114	.638
New Jersey	108	95	111	103	105	.637
Colorado	105	99	118	96	98	.629
Ottawa	113	94	109	95	103	.627
Philadelphia	107	97	100	105	93	.612
St. Louis	99	98	103	114	87	.611
Toronto	98	100	90	100	97	.591
Phoenix	78	95	90	90	90	.540
Washington	92	85	96	102	68	.540
Edmonton	92	92	93	88	78	.540
Boston	87	101	88	73	91	.537
San Jose	73	99	95	87	80	.529
Vancouver	104	94	90	83	58	.523
Buffalo	72	82	98	85	91	.522
Los Angeles	78	95	92	94	69	.522
Carolina	61	91	88	84	86	.500
Pittsburgh	65	69	96	88	90	.498
Anaheim	95	69	66	83	83	.483
Chicago	79	96	71	78	70	.480
Minnesota	95	73	68	—	—	.480
Montreal	77	87	70	83	75	.478
NY Rangers	78	80	72	73	77	.463
Calgary	75	79	73	77	72	.459
Florida	70	60	66	98	78	.454
Nashville	74	69	80	70	63	.434
NY Islanders	83	96	52	58	58	.423
Columbus	69	57	71	—	—	.400
Tampa Bay	93	69	59	54	47	.393
Atlanta	74	54	60	39	—	.346

Team Record When Scoring First Goal of a Game

Team	FG	W	L	T
Anaheim	42	28	11	3
Atlanta	40	20	17	3
Boston	40	27	10	3
Buffalo	38	18	17	3
Calgary	36	20	9	7
Carolina	30	13	15	2
Chicago	44	23	15	6
Colorado	49	30	13	6
Columbus	34	17	13	4
Dallas	44	31	7	6
Detroit	51	35	10	6
Edmonton	43	26	11	6
Florida	34	17	12	5
Los Angeles	42	22	16	4
Minnesota	36	31	4	1
Montreal	41	21	16	4
Nashville	40	22	10	8
New Jersey	48	34	7	7
NY Islanders	37	21	9	7
NY Rangers	42	20	16	6
Ottawa	51	37	8	6
Philadelphia	39	29	3	7
Phoenix	33	21	7	5
Pittsburgh	40	19	18	3
San Jose	40	16	19	5
St. Louis	36	19	12	5
Tampa Bay	40	24	10	6
Toronto	51	33	12	6
Vancouver	43	26	7	10
Washington	43	28	11	4

Team Plus/Minus Differential

Team	GF	PPGF	Net GF	GA	PPGA	Net GA	Goal Differential
Dallas	245	62	183	169	50	119	+64
Colorado	251	68	183	194	63	131	+52
Ottawa	263	83	180	182	50	132	+48
Philadelphia	211	47	164	166	50	116	+48
New Jersey	216	36	180	166	32	134	+46
Detroit	269	76	193	203	55	148	+45
Vancouver	264	87	177	208	62	146	+31
St. Louis	253	80	173	222	71	151	+22
Toronto	236	63	173	208	56	152	+21
Washington	224	57	167	220	72	148	+19
Boston	245	59	186	237	65	172	+14
Minnesota	198	52	146	178	43	135	+11
Edmonton	231	56	175	230	61	169	+6
NY Islanders	224	58	166	231	67	164	+2
Chicago	207	39	168	226	56	170	-2
NY Rangers	210	55	155	231	73	158	-3
Phoenix	204	55	149	230	77	153	-4
Anaheim	203	56	147	193	42	151	-5
Tampa Bay	219	70	149	210	55	155	-6
Los Angeles	203	52	151	221	62	159	-8
Montreal	206	44	162	234	58	176	-14
Nashville	183	58	125	206	61	145	-20
Calgary	186	47	139	228	65	163	-24
San Jose	214	68	146	239	68	171	-25
Buffalo	190	51	139	219	53	166	-27
Florida	176	49	127	237	66	171	-44
Carolina	171	58	113	240	71	169	-56
Atlanta	226	64	162	284	65	219	-57
Columbus	213	71	142	263	60	203	-61
Pittsburgh	189	66	123	255	58	197	-74

Team Record When Leading, Trailing, Tied

Team	Leading after 1 period W	L	T	Leading after 2 periods W	L	T	Trailing after 1 period W	L	T	Trailing after 2 periods W	L	T	Tied after 1 period W	L	T	Tied after 2 periods W	L	T
Anaheim	18	6	2	26	6	2	5	15	3	5	22	2	17	12	4	9	5	5
Atlanta	15	11	2	20	6	1	6	21	2	2	31	1	10	12	3	9	7	5
Boston	18	4	2	26	2	3	6	19	5	2	27	5	12	12	4	8	6	3
Buffalo	13	11	0	16	9	2	3	20	3	2	30	3	11	14	7	9	6	5
Calgary	14	5	3	15	5	4	4	20	1	2	29	2	11	15	7	12	6	7
Carolina	9	5	1	14	5	3	7	25	4	2	35	2	6	19	6	6	9	6
Chicago	17	3	2	24	2	7	5	17	3	2	26	4	8	19	8	4	11	2
Colorado	25	8	5	31	4	6	2	11	5	4	16	3	15	3	7	7	4	5
Columbus	14	8	3	23	4	5	4	28	2	2	32	2	11	9	3	4	9	1
Dallas	28	3	3	37	1	4	8	11	4	8	12	5	10	7	8	1	8	6
Detroit	28	5	1	38	3	4	4	12	2	2	15	2	16	7	7	8	6	4
Edmonton	20	5	4	20	5	5	6	21	2	2	24	4	10	9	5	14	6	2
Florida	12	2	4	19	3	2	1	24	3	3	32	7	11	19	6	2	10	4
Los Angeles	14	3	2	25	5	1	6	20	0	3	33	1	13	20	4	5	5	4
Minnesota	21	0	1	30	0	1	5	21	3	4	25	5	16	9	6	8	5	4
Montreal	16	10	4	25	8	5	5	19	1	0	28	0	9	15	3	5	8	3
Nashville	18	6	4	18	2	2	3	21	4	3	27	3	6	15	5	6	13	8
New Jersey	23	2	3	33	1	5	5	16	2	6	16	2	18	8	5	5	7	3
NY Islanders	17	4	5	28	1	5	6	24	3	4	26	4	12	8	2	2	9	2
NY Rangers	15	6	4	20	2	1	4	19	1	1	29	6	13	15	5	11	9	3
Ottawa	30	2	3	36	2	4	6	7	1	3	18	0	16	13	4	13	12	6
Philadelphia	19	1	2	30	1	3	8	12	3	2	15	6	18	11	8	13	8	4
Phoenix	16	3	2	19	1	3	6	25	3	2	30	5	9	12	6	10	9	3
Pittsburgh	15	9	1	20	2	1	3	23	2	2	38	2	9	17	3	5	7	6
San Jose	16	9	2	20	5	3	6	21	3	3	28	4	6	15	4	5	12	2
St. Louis	14	6	3	25	5	2	13	15	1	6	22	4	14	7	7	8	8	4
Tampa Bay	17	5	2	24	5	4	3	18	6	5	21	7	16	7	8	7	4	5
Toronto	20	6	5	28	2	3	5	12	1	9	21	2	19	13	1	7	9	5
Vancouver	25	5	4	35	1	6	6	23	2	4	19	3	10	9	1	4	10	2
Washington	21	4	3	27	3	3	6	18	4	6	25	2	12	13	1	7	7	3

With stellar goaltending from Dwayne Roloson (and Manny Fernandez), Minnesota did not lose a regular-season game in which they led after the first or second period.

Team Statistics

TEAMS' HOME AND ROAD RECORD

Eastern Conference

	Home								Road							
	GP	W	L	T	OTL	GF	GA	PTS	GP	W	L	T	OTL	GF	GA	PTS
OTT	41	28	9	3	1	134	82	60	41	24	12	5	0	129	100	53
NJ	41	25	11	3	2	121	85	55	41	21	9	7	4	95	81	53
PHI	41	21	10	8	2	103	76	52	41	24	10	5	2	108	90	55
TOR	41	24	13	4	0	123	101	52	41	20	15	3	3	113	107	46
T.B.	41	22	9	7	3	119	98	54	41	14	16	9	2	100	112	39
WSH	41	24	13	2	2	128	116	52	41	15	16	4	6	96	104	40
BOS	41	23	11	5	2	139	107	53	41	13	20	6	2	106	130	34
NYI	41	18	18	5	0	114	116	41	41	17	16	6	2	110	115	42
NYR	41	17	18	4	2	100	107	40	41	15	18	6	2	110	124	38
MTL	41	16	16	5	4	110	122	41	41	14	19	3	5	96	112	36
ATL	41	15	19	4	3	109	131	37	41	16	20	3	2	117	153	37
BUF	41	18	16	5	2	112	106	43	41	9	21	5	6	78	113	29
FLA	41	8	21	7	5	78	125	28	41	16	15	4	6	98	112	42
PIT	41	15	22	2	2	99	132	34	41	12	22	4	3	90	123	31
CAR	41	12	17	9	3	84	102	36	41	10	26	2	3	87	138	25
Total	615	286	223	73	33	1673	1606	678	615	240	255	76	44	1533	1714	600

Western Conference

	GP	W	L	T	OTL	GF	GA	PTS	GP	W	L	T	OTL	GF	GA	PTS
DAL	41	28	5	6	2	131	75	64	41	18	12	9	2	114	94	47
DET	41	28	6	5	2	150	96	63	41	20	14	5	2	119	107	47
COL	41	21	9	8	3	129	94	53	41	21	10	5	5	122	100	52
VAN	41	22	13	6	0	135	104	50	41	23	10	7	1	129	104	54
ST.L	41	23	11	4	3	144	110	53	41	18	13	7	3	109	112	46
MIN	41	25	13	3	0	108	79	53	41	17	16	7	1	90	99	42
ANA	41	22	10	7	2	105	84	53	41	18	17	2	4	98	109	42
EDM	41	20	12	5	4	111	105	49	41	16	14	6	5	120	125	43
CHI	41	17	15	7	2	101	103	43	41	13	18	6	4	106	123	36
L.A.	41	19	19	2	1	109	108	41	41	14	18	4	5	94	113	37
PHX	41	17	16	6	2	107	116	42	41	14	19	5	3	97	114	36
CGY	41	14	16	10	1	95	111	39	41	15	20	3	3	91	117	36
NSH	41	18	17	5	1	98	90	42	41	9	18	4	6	85	116	32
S.J.	41	17	16	5	3	117	115	42	41	11	21	4	5	97	124	31
CBJ	41	20	14	5	2	116	105	47	41	9	28	3	1	97	158	22
Total	615	311	192	84	28	1756	1495	734	615	236	248	81	50	1568	1715	603
	1230	597	415	157	61	3429	3101	1412	1230	476	503	157	94	3101	3429	1203

TEAMS' DIVISIONAL RECORD

Northeast Division

	Against Own Division								Against Other Divisions							
	GP	W	L	T	OTL	GF	GA	PTS	GP	W	L	T	OTL	GF	GA	PTS
OTT	20	14	4	1	1	57	44	30	62	38	17	7	0	206	138	83
TOR	20	9	10	1	0	43	53	19	62	35	18	6	3	193	155	79
BOS	20	9	9	1	1	66	60	20	62	27	22	10	3	179	177	67
MTL	20	7	9	1	3	53	61	18	62	23	26	7	6	153	173	59
BUF	20	9	9	0	2	57	58	20	62	18	28	10	6	133	161	52
Total	100	48	41	4	7	276	276	107	310	141	111	40	18	864	804	340

Atlantic Division

	GP	W	L	T	OTL	GF	GA	PTS	GP	W	L	T	OTL	GF	GA	PTS
N.J.	20	13	2	5	0	61	35	31	62	33	18	5	6	155	131	77
PHI	20	11	6	2	1	53	43	25	62	34	14	11	3	158	153	82
NYI	20	6	9	4	1	44	61	17	62	29	25	7	1	180	170	66
NYR	20	6	8	5	1	39	47	18	62	26	28	5	3	171	184	60
PIT	20	6	14	0	0	50	61	12	62	21	30	6	5	139	194	53
Total	100	42	39	16	3	247	247	103	310	143	115	34	18	803	802	338

Southeast Division

	GP	W	L	T	OTL	GF	GA	PTS	GP	W	L	T	OTL	GF	GA	PTS
T.B.	20	10	4	5	1	56	46	26	62	26	21	11	4	163	164	67
WSH	20	14	4	2	0	74	41	30	62	25	25	6	6	150	179	62
ATL	20	7	7	3	3	67	71	20	62	24	32	4	2	159	213	54
FLA	20	7	7	3	3	43	60	20	62	17	29	10	6	133	177	50
CAR	20	4	11	3	2	37	59	13	62	18	32	8	4	134	181	48
Total	100	42	33	16	9	277	277	109	310	110	139	39	22	739	914	281

Central Division

	GP	W	L	T	OTL	GF	GA	PTS	GP	W	L	T	OTL	GF	GA	PTS
DET	20	14	3	2	1	75	51	31	62	34	17	8	3	194	152	79
ST.L	20	7	8	3	2	59	60	19	62	34	16	8	4	194	162	80
CHI	20	11	3	3	3	66	49	28	62	19	30	10	3	141	177	51
NSH	20	6	9	4	1	42	53	17	62	21	26	9	6	141	153	57
CBJ	20	5	13	2	0	42	71	12	62	24	29	6	3	171	192	57
Total	100	43	36	14	7	284	284	107	310	132	118	41	19	841	836	324

Pacific Division

	GP	W	L	T	OTL	GF	GA	PTS	GP	W	L	T	OTL	GF	GA	PTS
DAL	20	14	3	3	0	59	34	31	62	32	14	4	4	186	135	80
ANA	20	8	9	3	0	50	56	19	62	32	18	6	6	153	137	76
L.A.	20	10	9	1	0	56	57	21	62	23	28	5	6	147	164	57
PHX	20	6	7	4	3	49	60	19	62	25	28	7	2	155	170	59
S.J.	20	6	10	1	3	49	56	16	62	22	27	8	5	165	183	57
Total	100	44	38	12	6	263	263	106	310	134	115	38	23	806	789	329

Northwest Division

	GP	W	L	T	OTL	GF	GA	PTS	GP	W	L	T	OTL	GF	GA	PTS
COL	20	8	5	4	3	54	49	23	62	34	14	9	5	197	145	82
VAN	20	10	6	4	0	56	51	24	62	35	17	9	1	208	157	80
MIN	20	7	8	4	1	48	50	19	62	35	21	6	0	150	128	76
EDM	20	7	7	2	4	53	57	20	62	29	19	9	5	178	173	72
CGY	20	9	6	4	1	48	52	23	62	20	30	9	3	138	176	52
Total	100	41	32	18	9	259	259	109	310	153	101	42	14	871	779	362

TEAM STREAKS

Consecutive Wins

Games	Team	From	To
10	Vancouver	Nov. 9	Nov. 30
9	St. Louis	Oct. 15	Nov. 5
8	Detroit	Feb. 20	Mar. 7
6	Philadelphia	Oct. 24	Nov. 5
6	Philadelphia	Jan. 2	Jan. 11
6	New Jersey	Jan. 13	Jan. 24
6	Colorado	Jan. 30	Feb. 11
6	Detroit	Mar. 10	Mar. 22

Consecutive Home Wins

Games	Team	From	To
11	Detroit	Feb. 20	Apr. 3
8	Boston	Nov. 2	Nov. 29
8	Ottawa	Nov. 14	Dec. 14
8	Toronto	Nov. 19	Dec. 14
8	New Jersey	Jan. 3	Feb. 4
7	Colorado	Jan. 23	Feb. 25
7	Nashville	Feb. 13	Mar. 1
6	Dallas	Nov. 6	Nov. 27
6	Anaheim	Dec. 1	Dec. 22
6	St. Louis	Feb. 27	Mar. 20
6	Colorado	Mar. 20	Apr. 6

Consecutive Road Wins

Games	Team	From	To
7	Toronto	Jan. 29	Feb. 22
6	Philadelphia	Jan. 2	Jan. 21
6	Ottawa	Mar. 18	Apr. 5
5	St. Louis	Oct. 24	Nov. 5
5	Vancouver	Nov. 9	Nov. 30
5	Ottawa	Dec. 10	Dec. 26

Consecutive Undefeated

Games	Team	W	T	From	To
14	Vancouver	10	4	Jan. 26	Feb. 25
13	Tampa Bay	7	6	Mar. 7	Apr. 2
12	Dallas	9	3	Dec. 27	Jan. 22
10	St. Louis	9	1	Oct. 12	Nov. 5
10	Vancouver	10	0	Nov. 9	Nov. 30
10	Ottawa	8	2	Nov. 12	Nov. 30
10	Colorado	8	2	Jan. 20	Feb. 11
9	Detroit	6	3	Dec. 14	Dec. 31
9	New Jersey	8	1	Jan. 7	Jan. 24

Consecutive Home Undefeated

Games	Team	W	T	From	To
13	Toronto	12	1	Nov. 19	Jan. 14
11	Detroit	11	0	Feb. 20	Apr. 3
9	Dallas	7	2	Nov. 6	Dec. 6
9	Anaheim	6	3	Nov. 24	Dec. 22
9	Tampa Bay	5	4	Feb. 25	Apr. 2
8	Boston	8	0	Nov. 2	Nov. 29
8	Ottawa	8	0	Nov. 14	Dec. 14
8	New Jersey	8	0	Jan. 3	Feb. 4
8	Ottawa	7	1	Jan. 14	Feb. 17
8	Colorado	7	1	Jan. 20	Feb. 25
8	Nashville	7	1	Feb. 13	Mar. 6
8	Colorado	7	1	Mar. 1	Apr. 6

Consecutive Road Undefeated

Games	Team	W	T	From	To
10	Dallas	7	3	Dec. 27	Feb. 25
9	Vancouver	6	3	Feb. 4	Mar. 3
7	Detroit	4	3	Dec. 5	Jan. 5
7	Chicago	4	3	Dec. 10	Jan. 4
7	Toronto	7	0	Jan. 29	Feb. 22
7	New Jersey	4	3	Mar. 18	Apr. 6

TEAM PENALTIES

Abbreviations: GP – games played; **PEN** – total penalty minutes including bench minutes; **BMI** – total bench minor minutes; **AVG** – average penalty minutes/game calculated by dividing total penalty minutes by games played.

Team	GP	PEN	BMI	AVG
MTL	82	900	22	11.0
N.J.	82	938	18	11.4
ANA	82	954	20	11.6
NSH	82	969	20	11.8
PHI	82	1003	30	12.2
MIN	82	1063	28	13.0
COL	82	1084	24	13.2
T.B.	82	1079	30	13.2
S.J.	82	1112	30	13.6
FLA	82	1127	26	13.7
PIT	82	1125	32	13.7
OTT	82	1135	22	13.8
L.A.	82	1146	50	14.0
DAL	82	1166	28	14.2
VAN	82	1178	36	14.4
CHI	82	1189	30	14.5

Team	GP	PEN	BMI	AVG
CAR	82	1208	16	14.7
EDM	82	1203	16	14.7
DET	82	1214	26	14.8
NYI	82	1244	30	15.2
ATL	82	1253	26	15.3
WSH	82	1268	22	15.5
BUF	82	1276	30	15.6
NYR	82	1308	14	16.0
BOS	82	1370	24	16.7
CGY	82	1391	22	17.0
TOR	82	1390	22	17.0
PHX	82	1433	24	17.5
CBJ	82	1505	28	18.4
ST.L.	82	1618	16	19.7
Total	**1230**	**35849**	**762**	
Two-Team Avg. PIM/GP				**29.1**

Vincent Damphousse scored 15 of his 23 goals last season while the Sharks had a man advantage, giving San Jose one of the league's best power-play records.

TEAMS' POWER-PLAY RECORD

Abbreviations: ADV – total advantages; **PPGF** – power-play goals for; **%** – calculated by dividing number of power-play goals by total advantages.

	Home					Road					Overall				
	Team	GP	ADV	PPGF	%	Team	GP	ADV	PPGF	%	Team	GP	ADV	PPGF	%
1	DET	41	174	44	25.3	DET	41	145	32	22.1	DET	82	319	76	23.8
2	VAN	41	236	51	21.6	OTT	41	183	39	21.3	OTT	82	391	83	21.2
3	OTT	41	208	44	21.2	DAL	41	152	31	20.4	VAN	82	419	87	20.8
4	ST.L.	41	213	45	21.1	PIT	41	168	34	20.2	ST.L.	82	391	80	20.5
5	BOS	41	170	35	20.6	VAN	41	183	36	19.7	DAL	82	327	62	19.0
6	S.J.	41	190	37	19.5	ST.L.	41	178	35	19.7	COL	82	363	68	18.7
7	CBJ	41	216	41	19.0	ANA	41	160	31	19.4	PIT	82	360	66	18.3
8	WSH	41	185	35	18.9	COL	41	181	35	19.3	BOS	82	325	59	18.2
9	NYR	41	164	30	18.3	ATL	41	170	32	18.8	S.J.	82	375	68	18.1
10	T.B.	41	218	40	18.3	TOR	41	175	31	17.7	T.B.	82	391	70	17.9
11	COL	41	182	33	18.1	EDM	41	183	32	17.5	TOR	82	359	63	17.5
12	DAL	41	175	31	17.7	T.B.	41	173	30	17.3	CBJ	82	410	71	17.3
13	TOR	41	184	32	17.4	S.J.	41	185	31	16.8	ATL	82	371	64	17.3
14	L.A.	41	197	33	16.8	BOS	41	155	24	15.5	WSH	82	331	57	17.2
15	PIT	41	192	32	16.7	CBJ	41	194	30	15.5	NYR	82	339	55	16.2
16	ATL	41	201	32	15.9	BUF	41	169	26	15.4	ANA	82	348	56	16.1
17	PHX	41	203	31	15.3	NYI	41	183	28	15.3	NYI	82	384	58	15.1
18	NYI	41	201	30	14.9	PHI	41	145	22	15.2	L.A.	82	354	52	14.7
19	FLA	41	179	26	14.5	WSH	41	146	22	15.1	EDM	82	386	56	14.5
20	MTL	41	180	26	14.4	NSH	41	214	32	15.0	BUF	82	354	51	14.4
21	N.J.	41	167	24	14.4	CAR	41	207	31	15.0	PHX	82	385	55	14.3
22	MIN	41	194	27	13.9	MIN	41	172	25	14.5	PHI	82	328	47	14.3
23	PHI	41	183	25	13.7	NYR	41	175	25	14.3	MIN	82	366	52	14.2
24	BUF	41	185	25	13.5	FLA	41	168	23	13.7	FLA	82	347	49	14.1
25	ANA	41	188	25	13.3	MTL	41	135	18	13.3	MTL	82	315	44	14.0
26	CAR	41	213	27	12.7	PHX	41	182	24	13.2	NSH	82	418	58	13.9
27	CGY	41	197	25	12.7	CHI	41	142	18	12.7	CAR	82	420	58	13.8
28	NSH	41	204	26	12.7	L.A.	41	157	19	12.1	CHI	82	308	39	12.7
29	CHI	41	166	21	12.7	CGY	41	192	22	11.5	CGY	82	389	47	12.1
30	EDM	41	203	24	11.8	N.J.	41	136	12	8.8	N.J.	82	303	36	11.9
TOTAL		**1230**	**5768**	**957**	**16.6**		**1230**	**5108**	**830**	**16.2**		**1230**	**10876**	**1787**	**16.4**

TEAMS' PENALTY KILLING RECORD

Abbreviations: TSH – total times short-handed; **PPGA** – power-play goals against; **%** – calculated by dividing times short minus power-play goals against by times short.

	Home					Road					Overall				
	Team	GP	TSH	PPGA	%	Team	GP	TSH	PPGA	%	Team	GP	TSH	PPGA	%
1	N.J.	41	128	13	89.8	TOR	41	224	25	88.8	N.J.	82	264	32	87.9
2	DAL	41	176	21	88.1	ANA	41	179	21	88.3	ANA	82	333	42	87.4
3	BUF	41	174	22	87.4	DET	41	201	24	88.1	TOR	82	426	56	86.9
4	CBJ	41	193	26	86.5	N.J.	41	136	19	86.0	MIN	82	308	43	86.0
5	NSH	41	163	22	86.5	MIN	41	163	23	85.9	DAL	82	346	50	85.5
6	ANA	41	154	21	86.4	L.A.	41	199	28	85.9	BUF	82	363	53	85.4
7	MIN	41	145	20	86.2	OTT	41	190	27	85.8	DET	82	377	55	85.4
8	CHI	41	177	25	85.9	PHI	41	196	28	85.7	CBJ	82	409	60	85.3
9	TOR	41	202	31	84.7	CBJ	41	216	34	84.3	PHI	82	338	50	85.2
10	CGY	41	188	29	84.6	BOS	41	208	33	84.1	OTT	82	332	50	84.9
11	VAN	41	187	29	84.5	CHI	41	192	31	83.9	CHI	82	369	56	84.8
12	PHI	41	142	22	84.5	PIT	41	180	29	83.9	VAN	82	389	62	84.1
13	NYI	41	192	30	84.4	VAN	41	202	33	83.7	NYI	82	405	67	83.5
14	ST.L.	41	194	31	84.0	BUF	41	189	31	83.6	PIT	82	352	58	83.5
15	OTT	41	142	23	83.8	NYR	41	199	33	83.4	L.A.	82	371	62	83.3
16	T.B.	41	153	25	83.7	MTL	41	142	24	83.1	CGY	82	389	65	83.3
17	CAR	41	164	27	83.5	COL	41	194	33	83.0	NSH	82	353	61	82.7
18	EDM	41	167	28	83.2	DAL	41	170	29	82.9	BOS	82	375	65	82.7
19	WSH	41	167	28	83.2	NYI	41	213	37	82.6	T.B.	82	316	55	82.6
20	PIT	41	172	29	83.1	EDM	41	184	33	82.1	EDM	82	351	61	82.6
21	FLA	41	165	29	82.4	CGY	41	201	36	82.1	COL	82	359	63	82.5
22	DET	41	176	31	82.4	S.J.	41	189	34	82.0	CAR	82	392	71	81.9
23	ATL	41	168	30	82.1	T.B.	41	163	30	81.6	ST.L.	82	389	71	81.7
24	COL	41	165	30	81.8	PHX	41	230	43	81.3	MTL	82	317	58	81.7
25	PHX	41	182	34	81.3	ATL	41	187	35	81.3	ATL	82	355	65	81.7
26	BOS	41	167	32	80.8	CAR	41	228	44	80.7	FLA	82	356	66	81.5
27	MTL	41	175	34	80.6	FLA	41	191	37	80.6	PHX	82	412	77	81.3
28	L.A.	41	172	34	80.2	WSH	41	217	44	79.7	WSH	82	384	72	81.3
29	S.J.	41	169	34	79.9	NSH	41	190	39	79.5	NYR	82	388	73	81.2
30	NYR	41	189	40	78.8	ST.L.	41	195	40	79.5	S.J.	82	358	68	81.0
TOTAL		**1230**	**5108**	**830**	**83.8**		**1230**	**5768**	**957**	**83.4**		**1230**	**10876**	**1787**	**83.6**

SHORT-HANDED GOALS FOR

	Home			Road			Overall		
	Team	GP	SHGF	Team	GP	SHGF	Team	GP	SHGF
1	EDM	41	9	VAN	41	8	EDM	82	13
2	MIN	41	8	DET	41	8	NYI	82	12
3	ST.L.	41	7	CBJ	41	8	CBJ	82	12
4	DAL	41	6	TOR	41	7	VAN	82	12
5	NYI	41	6	NYI	41	6	TOR	82	11
6	BOS	41	6	PHI	41	6	ST.L.	82	11
7	NYR	41	5	FLA	41	6	DET	82	11
8	CHI	41	5	ANA	41	5	BOS	82	10
9	BUF	41	4	ATL	41	5	DAL	82	9
10	CBJ	41	4	L.A.	41	5	MIN	82	9
11	WSH	41	4	T.B.	41	4	NYR	82	8
12	TOR	41	4	BOS	41	4	L.A.	82	8
13	N.J.	41	4	BUF	41	4	BUF	82	8
14	VAN	41	4	WSH	41	4	CHI	82	8
15	CAR	41	3	EDM	41	4	ANA	82	8
16	L.A.	41	3	CGY	41	4	PHI	82	8
17	ATL	41	3	ST.L.	41	4	ATL	82	8
18	ANA	41	3	NYR	41	3	WSH	82	8
19	DET	41	3	DAL	41	3	N.J.	82	7
20	COL	41	2	PHX	41	3	FLA	82	7
21	OTT	41	2	N.J.	41	3	CAR	82	6
22	S.J.	41	2	CHI	41	3	T.B.	82	6
23	MTL	41	2	CAR	41	3	COL	82	5
24	T.B.	41	2	S.J.	41	3	CGY	82	5
25	PHI	41	2	COL	41	3	S.J.	82	5
26	PIT	41	1	NSH	41	2	PHX	82	4
27	FLA	41	1	OTT	41	2	OTT	82	4
28	CGY	41	1	PIT	41	2	PIT	82	3
29	PHX	41	1	MIN	41	1	MTL	82	2
30	NSH	41	0	MTL	41	0	NSH	82	2
TOTAL		**1230**	**107**		**1230**	**123**		**1230**	**230**

SHORT-HANDED GOALS AGAINST

	Home			Road			Overall		
	Team	GP	SHGA	Team	GP	SHGA	Team	GP	SHGA
1	CAR	41	1	NYI	41	1	L.A.	82	4
2	NYR	41	1	N.J.	41	1	N.J.	82	4
3	T.B.	41	1	MIN	41	1	DET	82	4
4	WSH	41	2	L.A.	41	1	WSH	82	4
5	DAL	41	2	TOR	41	2	NYI	82	5
6	DET	41	2	ANA	41	2	T.B.	82	5
7	COL	41	3	DET	41	2	ANA	82	5
8	L.A.	41	3	WSH	41	2	MIN	82	5
9	CBJ	41	3	EDM	41	2	COL	82	6
10	MTL	41	3	S.J.	41	2	DAL	82	6
11	N.J.	41	3	PIT	41	2	MTL	82	6
12	ANA	41	3	PHX	41	3	TOR	82	7
13	PHI	41	3	VAN	41	3	ST.L.	82	7
14	OTT	41	4	MTL	41	3	NYR	82	8
15	FLA	41	4	COL	41	3	OTT	82	8
16	ST.L.	41	4	ST.L.	41	3	CHI	82	8
17	MIN	41	4	DAL	41	4	EDM	82	8
18	NYI	41	4	CHI	41	4	PHI	82	8
19	NSH	41	4	T.B.	41	4	NSH	82	8
20	CHI	41	4	NSH	41	4	CAR	82	9
21	BOS	41	4	OTT	41	4	CBJ	82	9
22	TOR	41	5	BUF	41	4	FLA	82	9
23	CGY	41	6	CGY	41	4	PIT	82	10
24	EDM	41	6	PHI	41	5	CGY	82	10
25	ATL	41	6	FLA	41	5	VAN	82	10
26	BUF	41	7	CBJ	41	6	S.J.	82	10
27	VAN	41	7	NYR	41	7	PHX	82	11
28	PIT	41	8	BOS	41	7	BUF	82	11
29	S.J.	41	8	ATL	41	8	BOS	82	11
30	PHX	41	8	CAR	41	8	ATL	82	14
TOTAL		**1230**	**123**		**1230**	**107**		**1230**	**230**

Regular-Season Overtime Results

1983-84 to 2002-03

	2002-03				2001-02				2000-01				1999-2000				1998-99			
Team	**GP**	**W**	**L**	**T**	**GP**	**W**	**L**	**T**	**GP**	**W**	**L**	**T**	**GP**	**W**	**L**	**T**	**GP**	**W**	**L**	**T**
ANA	21	6	6	9	14	3	3	8	20	4	5	11	18	3	3	12	17	1	3	13
ATL	19	7	5	7	19	3	5	11	16	2	2	12	11	0	4	7	...	...	...	...
BOS	21	6	4	11	24	9	9	6	20	4	8	8	26	1	6	19	17	2	2	13
BUF	21	3	8	10	16	4	1	11	10	4	1	5	20	5	4	11	23	3	3	17
CGY	23	6	4	13	17	2	3	12	22	3	4	15	26	11	5	10	16	3	1	12
CAR/HFD	19	2	6	11	27	6	5	16	18	6	3	9	14	4	0	10	24	1	5	18
CHI	23	4	6	13	17	3	1	13	15	2	5	8	17	5	2	10	15	1	2	12
COL/QUE	28	7	8	13	13	4	1	8	20	6	4	10	17	5	1	11	12	2	0	10
CBJ	15	4	3	8	15	2	5	8	18	3	6	9	...	...	...	...	...	...	...	...
DAL/MIN	24	5	4	15	21	3	5	13	16	6	2	8	19	3	6	10	16	3	1	12
DET	21	7	4	10	24	10	4	10	23	10	4	9	16	4	2	10	10	2	1	7
EDM	27	7	9	11	19	3	4	12	20	5	3	12	27	3	8	16	20	3	5	12
FLA	26	4	9	13	16	0	6	10	24	2	9	13	15	3	6	6	21	1	2	18
L.A.	19	6	7	6	18	3	4	11	19	3	3	13	21	5	4	12	12	5	2	5
MIN	19	8	1	10	21	0	9	12	22	4	5	13	...	...	...	...	...	...	...	...
MTL	19	2	9	8	17	2	3	12	16	2	6	8	17	4	4	9	15	0	4	11
NSH	25	5	7	13	18	5	0	13	17	5	3	9	18	4	7	7	10	1	2	7
N.J.	24	8	6	10	19	6	4	9	20	5	3	12	16	3	5	8	15	3	1	11
NYI	18	5	2	11	18	6	4	8	12	2	3	7	15	5	1	9	17	1	6	10
NYR	20	6	4	10	13	5	4	4	11	5	1	5	21	6	3	12	19	5	3	11
OTT	16	7	1	8	19	3	7	9	16	3	4	9	15	2	2	11	18	1	2	15
PHI	23	6	4	13	16	3	3	10	19	5	3	11	21	6	3	12	24	2	3	19
PHX/WPG	20	4	5	11	19	4	6	9	23	3	3	17	16	4	4	8	15	2	1	12
PIT	14	3	5	6	20	7	5	8	15	3	3	9	17	3	6	8	22	7	1	14
ST.L.	23	6	6	11	18	6	4	8	23	6	5	12	17	5	1	11	15	1	1	13
S.J.	19	2	8	9	13	2	3	8	22	7	3	12	21	4	7	10	21	1	2	18
T.B.	23	2	5	16	19	4	4	11	13	2	5	6	16	0	7	9	12	1	2	9
TOR	17	7	3	7	17	3	4	10	19	3	5	11	17	7	3	7	14	6	1	7
VAN	19	5	1	13	14	4	3	7	23	5	7	11	27	4	8	15	13	0	1	12
WSH	20	6	6	8	19	6	2	11	16	2	4	10	19	5	2	12	11	2	3	6
Totals	**313**	**156**		**157**	**270**	**121**		**149**	**274**	**122**		**152**	**260**	**114**		**146**	**222**	**60**		**162**

	1997-98				1996-97				1995-96				1994-95				1993-94			
Team	**GP**	**W**	**L**	**T**	**GP**	**W**	**L**	**T**	**GP**	**W**	**L**	**T**	**GP**	**W**	**L**	**T**	**GP**	**W**	**L**	**T**
ANA	20	3	4	13	16	3	0	13	16	6	2	8	7	2	0	5	12	2	5	5
ATL	...	...	...	...	...	...	...	...	...	...	...	...	...	...	...	...	...	...	...	...
BOS	17	3	1	13	15	3	3	9	19	2	6	11	8	2	3	3	17	2	2	13
BUF	21	3	1	17	21	5	4	12	15	2	6	7	9	1	1	7	13	0	4	9
CGY	22	4	3	15	16	3	4	9	16	2	3	11	9	1	1	7	18	3	2	13
CAR/HFD	12	2	2	8	18	3	4	11	14	2	3	9	9	1	1	7	14	4	1	9
CHI	18	1	4	13	19	1	5	13	19	1	4	14	7	2	0	5	16	2	5	9
COL/QUE	22	2	3	17	15	2	3	10	6	1	0	5	8	0	0	8	15	3	3	9
CBJ	...	...	...	...	...	...	...	...	...	...	...	...	...	...	...	...	...	...	...	...
DAL/MIN	17	5	1	11	15	4	3	8	15	1	0	14	9	0	1	8	22	6	3	13
DET	15	0	0	15	27	7	2	18	11	3	1	7	4	0	0	4	15	5	2	8
EDM	15	3	2	10	16	1	6	9	14	4	2	8	7	1	2	4	21	1	6	14
FLA	20	3	2	15	26	3	4	19	13	0	3	10	9	0	3	6	24	2	5	17
L.A.	16	3	2	11	14	0	3	11	23	3	2	18	9	0	0	9	18	3	3	12
MIN	...	...	...	...	...	...	...	...	...	...	...	...	...	...	...	...	...	...	...	...
MTL	20	3	4	13	21	2	4	15	15	2	3	10	10	1	2	7	19	3	2	14
NSH	...	...	...	...	...	...	...	...	...	...	...	...	...	...	...	...	...	...	...	...
N.J.	16	2	3	11	17	1	2	14	19	7	0	12	11	1	2	8	14	1	1	12
NYI	13	0	2	11	17	3	2	12	17	2	5	10	7	1	1	5	19	5	2	12
NYR	24	2	4	18	13	3	0	10	17	2	1	14	3	0	0	3	12	3	1	8
OTT	17	2	0	15	17	0	2	15	8	0	3	5	7	1	1	5	17	4	4	9
PHI	15	3	1	11	18	3	2	13	20	4	3	13	8	3	1	4	18	3	5	10
PHX/WPG	14	0	2	12	16	5	4	7	8	2	0	6	9	0	2	7	15	1	5	9
PIT	23	3	2	18	13	1	4	8	9	3	2	4	5	1	1	3	19	4	2	13
ST.L.	12	2	2	8	13	1	1	11	18	1	1	16	7	1	1	5	17	4	2	11
S.J.	12	0	2	10	12	3	1	8	9	1	1	7	5	1	0	4	19	2	1	16
T.B.	13	0	3	10	16	4	2	10	18	3	3	12	7	2	2	3	18	3	4	11
TOR	10	1	0	9	10	1	1	8	18	4	2	12	8	0	0	8	17	4	1	12
VAN	17	0	3	14	14	5	2	7	20	1	4	15	13	0	1	12	12	5	4	3
WSH	17	4	1	12	13	2	2	9	16	4	1	11	9	0	1	8	14	2	2	10
Totals	**219**	**54**		**165**	**214**	**70**		**144**	**201**	**64**		**137**	**101**	**26**		**75**	**214**	**74**		**140**

2002-03
Home Team Wins: 94
Visiting Team Wins: 62

	1992-93				1991-92				1990-91				1989-90				1988-89			
Team	**GP**	**W**	**L**	**T**	**GP**	**W**	**L**	**T**	**GP**	**W**	**L**	**T**	**GP**	**W**	**L**	**T**	**GP**	**W**	**L**	**T**
ANA	...	...	...	...	...	...	...	...	...	...	...	...	...	...	...	...	...	...	...	...
ATL	...	...	...	...	...	...	...	...	...	...	...	...	...	...	...	...	...	...	...	...
BOS	15	5	3	7	20	6	2	12	17	5	0	12	14	3	2	9	19	3	2	14
BUF	18	4	4	10	16	2	2	12	24	3	2	19	15	4	3	8	13	2	4	7
CGY	19	4	4	11	19	2	5	12	15	3	4	8	21	3	3	15	17	5	3	9
CAR/HFD	18	3	9	6	18	2	3	13	9	1	1	7	9	0	0	9	10	1	4	5
CHI	16	1	3	12	19	2	2	15	12	3	1	8	10	2	2	6	17	2	3	12
COL/QUE	15	4	1	10	17	0	5	12	18	1	3	14	8	0	1	7	10	2	1	7
CBJ	...	...	...	...	...	...	...	...	...	...	...	...	...	...	...	...	...	...	...	...
DAL/MIN	10	0	0	10	8	0	2	6	17	0	3	14	11	3	4	4	17	0	1	16
DET	11	2	0	9	16	3	1	12	14	2	4	8	17	2	1	14	16	3	1	12
EDM	17	5	4	8	12	0	2	10	15	4	5	6	20	5	1	14	15	4	3	8
FLA	...	...	...	...	...	...	...	...	...	...	...	...	...	...	...	...	...	...	...	...
L.A.	13	2	1	10	16	1	1	14	16	4	2	10	12	3	2	7	14	6	1	7
MIN	...	...	...	...	...	...	...	...	...	...	...	...	...	...	...	...	...	...	...	...
MTL	14	5	3	6	20	6	3	11	17	3	3	11	17	4	2	11	11	2	0	9
NSH	...	...	...	...	...	...	...	...	...	...	...	...	...	...	...	...	...	...	...	...
N.J.	11	4	0	7	17	2	4	11	17	1	1	15	16	3	4	9	17	1	4	12
NYI	13	3	3	7	16	3	2	11	15	2	3	10	16	3	2	11	11	3	3	5
NYR	17	2	4	11	11	5	1	5	16	1	2	13	17	2	2	13	10	1	1	8
OTT	10	0	6	4	...	...	...	...	...	...	...	...	...	...	...	...	...	...	...	...
PHI	17	4	2	11	17	2	4	11	11	1	0	10	18	2	5	11	14	1	5	8
PHX/WPG	11	2	2	7	20	1	4	15	14	1	2	11	19	4	4	11	20	6	2	12
PIT	10	3	0	7	12	2	1	9	12	4	2	6	14	3	3	8	10	2	1	7
ST.L.	17	2	4	11	15	2	2	11	18	3	4	11	15	2	4	9	16	3	1	12
S.J.	10	3	5	2	9	1	3	5	...	...	...	...	...	...	...	...	...	...	...	...
T.B.	14	3	4	7	...	...	...	...	...	...	...	...	...	...	...	...	...	...	...	...
TOR	13	1	1	11	11	4	0	7	17	4	2	11	11	3	4	4	11	1	4	6
VAN	10	1	0	9	17	4	1	12	15	3	3	9	21	2	5	14	14	2	4	8
WSH	11	2	2	7	12	2	2	8	14	4	3	7	9	2	1	6	16	2	4	10
Totals	**165**	**65**		**100**	**169**	**52**		**117**	**166**	**54**		**112**	**155**	**55**		**100**	**149**	**52**		**97**

	1987-88				1986-87				1985-86				1984-85				1983-84			
Team	**GP**	**W**	**L**	**T**	**GP**	**W**	**L**	**T**	**GP**	**W**	**L**	**T**	**GP**	**W**	**L**	**T**	**GP**	**W**	**L**	**T**
ANA	...	...	...	...	...	...	...	...	...	...	...	...	...	...	...	...	...	...	...	...
ATL	...	...	...	...	...	...	...	...	...	...	...	...	...	...	...	...	...	...	...	...
BOS	14	4	4	6	12	2	3	7	17	2	3	12	18	4	4	10	7	1	0	6
BUF	12	0	1	11	13	1	4	8	9	1	2	6	17	0	3	14	13	5	1	7
CGY	15	2	4	9	4	1	0	3	12	1	2	9	14	1	1	12	18	4	0	14
CAR/HFD	12	3	2	7	9	2	0	7	7	1	2	4	17	4	4	9	15	2	3	10
CHI	15	4	2	9	15	1	0	14	12	3	1	8	12	2	3	7	9	0	1	8
COL/QUE	9	2	2	5	14	0	4	10	11	4	1	6	14	3	2	9	15	0	5	10
CBJ	...	...	...	...	...	...	...	...	...	...	...	...	...	...	...	...	...	...	...	...
DAL/MIN	16	1	2	13	14	2	2	10	15	4	2	9	15	1	2	12	18	5	3	10
DET	16	2	3	11	17	2	5	10	13	2	5	6	14	0	2	12	11	3	1	7
EDM	16	3	2	11	14	5	3	6	14	5	2	7	12	0	1	11	9	4	0	5
FLA	...	...	...	...	...	...	...	...	...	...	...	...	...	...	...	...	...	...	...	...
L.A.	12	1	3	8	12	2	2	8	14	3	3	8	19	3	2	14	17	1	3	13
MIN	...	...	...	...	...	...	...	...	...	...	...	...	...	...	...	...	...	...	...	...
MTL	16	1	2	13	16	2	4	10	14	1	6	7	18	3	3	12	7	1	1	5
NSH	...	...	...	...	...	...	...	...	...	...	...	...	...	...	...	...	...	...	...	...
N.J.	12	4	2	6	13	3	4	6	10	4	3	3	12	0	2	10	15	1	7	7
NYI	13	3	0	10	19	4	3	12	17	4	1	12	15	1	8	6	10	3	3	4
NYR	11	0	1	10	19	5	6	8	13	0	7	6	17	2	5	10	17	5	3	9
OTT	...	...	...	...	...	...	...	...	...	...	...	...	...	...	...	...	...	...	...	...
PHI	13	1	3	9	10	1	1	8	9	4	1	4	9	1	1	7	14	3	1	10
PHX/WPG	21	8	2	11	11	2	1	8	8	0	1	7	14	3	1	10	24	7	6	11
PIT	16	5	2	9	21	5	4	12	14	3	3	8	8	3	0	5	12	1	5	6
ST.L.	14	2	4	8	21	4	2	15	17	5	3	9	15	2	1	12	11	3	1	7
S.J.	...	...	...	...	...	...	...	...	...	...	...	...	...	...	...	...	...	...	...	...
T.B.	...	...	...	...	...	...	...	...	...	...	...	...	...	...	...	...	...	...	...	...
TOR	13	1	2	10	13	3	4	6	17	4	6	7	15	5	2	8	13	1	3	9
VAN	11	0	2	9	10	2	0	8	16	1	2	13	17	7	1	9	16	3	4	9
WSH	15	2	4	9	17	5	2	10	11	4	0	7	12	3	0	9	9	1	3	5
Totals	**146**	**49**		**97**	**147**	**54**		**93**	**135**	**56**		**79**	**152**	**48**		**104**	**140**	**54**		**86**

NHL Record Book

Year-By-Year Final Standings & Leading Scorers

*Stanley Cup winner

1917-18

First Half

Team	GP	W	L	T	GF	GA	PTS
Montreal	14	10	4	0	81	47	20
Toronto	14	8	6	0	71	75	16
Ottawa	14	5	9	0	67	79	10
**Mtl. Wanderers	6	1	5	0	17	35	2

**Montreal Arena burned down and Wanderers forced to withdraw from League. Montreal Canadiens and Toronto each counted a win for defaulted games with Wanderers.

Second Half

Team							
*Toronto	8	5	3	0	37	34	10
Ottawa	8	4	4	0	35	35	8
Montreal	8	3	5	0	34	37	6

Leading Scorers

Player	Club	GP	G	A	PTS	PIM
Malone, Joe	Montreal	20	44	4	48	30
Denneny, Cy	Ottawa	20	36	10	46	80
Noble, Reg	Toronto	20	30	10	40	35
Lalonde, Newsy	Montreal	14	23	7	30	51
Denneny, Corb	Toronto	21	20	9	29	14
Cameron, Harry	Toronto	21	17	10	27	28
Pitre, Didier	Montreal	20	17	6	23	29
Gerard, Eddie	Ottawa	20	13	7	20	26
Darragh, Jack	Ottawa	18	14	5	19	26
Nighbor, Frank	Ottawa	10	11	8	19	6
Meeking, Harry	Toronto	21	10	9	19	28

1918-19

First Half

Team	GP	W	L	T	GF	GA	PTS
• Montreal	10	7	3	0	57	50	14
Ottawa	10	5	5	0	39	39	10
Toronto	10	3	7	0	42	49	6

Second Half

Team							
Ottawa	8	7	1	0	32	14	14
Montreal	8	3	5	0	31	28	6
Toronto	8	2	6	0	22	43	4

• NHL Champion. Stanley Cup not awarded due to influenza epidemic.

Leading Scorers

Player	Club	GP	G	A	PTS	PIM
Lalonde, Newsy	Montreal	17	22	10	32	40
Cleghorn, Odie	Montreal	17	22	6	28	22
Nighbor, Frank	Ottawa	18	19	9	28	27
Denneny, Cy	Ottawa	18	18	4	22	58
Pitre, Didier	Montreal	17	14	5	19	12
Skinner, Alf	Toronto	17	12	4	16	26
Cameron, Harry	Tor., Ott.	14	11	3	14	35
Darragh, Jack	Ottawa	14	11	3	14	33
Randall, Ken	Toronto	15	8	6	14	27
Cleghorn, Sprague	Ottawa	18	7	6	13	27

All-Time Standings of NHL Teams

(ranked by percentage)

Active Clubs

Team	Games	Wins	Losses	Ties	OT Losses	Goals For	Goals Against	Points	Pts %	First Season
Montreal	5464	2808	1804	830	22	18077	14594	6468	.591	1917-18
Philadelphia	2850	1428	967	442	13	9802	8371	3311	.578	1967-68
Boston	5304	2523	1978	776	27	17244	15701	5849	.549	1924-25
Buffalo	2624	1220	988	402	14	8856	8031	2856	.541	1970-71
Edmonton	1912	904	734	250	24	7166	6583	2082	.539	1979-80
Calgary	2468	1100	980	372	16	8591	8135	2588	.520	1972-73
Detroit	5238	2311	2109	804	14	16281	15785	5440	.517	1926-27
Colorado	1912	857	793	248	14	6664	6494	1976	.512	1979-80
St. Louis	2850	1249	1164	421	16	9161	9118	2935	.511	1967-68
Toronto	5464	2373	2303	773	15	16951	16847	5534	.505	1917-18
NY Islanders	2468	1074	1048	336	10	8352	7967	2494	.502	1972-73
NY Rangers	5238	2204	2221	801	12	16271	16466	5221	.497	1926-27
Washington	2312	988	1017	293	14	7471	7758	2283	.490	1974-75
Chicago	5238	2156	2265	803	14	15655	15877	5129	.488	1926-27
Dallas	2850	1164	1223	446	17	8981	9339	2791	.487	1967-68
Pittsburgh	2850	1176	1280	375	19	9748	10256	2746	.479	1967-68
Los Angeles	2850	1133	1291	408	18	9533	10150	2692	.469	1967-68
Phoenix	1912	763	883	248	18	6309	6894	1792	.464	1979-80
Florida	788	294	337	127	30	2036	2221	745	.463	1993-94
Anaheim	788	309	365	97	17	2036	2225	732	.454	1993-94
Minnesota	246	93	103	35	15	561	626	236	.453	2000-01
New Jersey	2312	891	1087	316	18	7186	7981	2116	.453	1974-75
Ottawa	872	340	413	105	14	2393	2675	799	.450	1992-93
Carolina	1912	733	916	249	14	5931	6664	1729	.448	1979-80
Vancouver	2624	981	1243	381	19	8423	9334	2362	.447	1970-71
San Jose	952	339	483	109	21	2591	3085	808	.415	1991-92
Nashville	410	145	199	49	17	954	1137	356	.412	1998-99
Tampa Bay	872	282	465	104	21	2176	2802	689	.388	1992-93
Columbus	246	79	128	25	14	567	751	197	.379	2000-01
Atlanta	328	87	188	37	16	794	1174	227	.326	1999-2000

Defunct Clubs

Team	Games	Wins	Losses	Ties	Goals For	Goals Against	Points	Pts %	First Season	Last Season
Ottawa Senators	542	258	221	63	1458	1333	579	.534	1917-18	1933-34
Montreal Maroons	622	271	260	91	1474	1405	633	.509	1924-25	1937-38
NY/Brooklyn Americans	784	255	402	127	1643	2182	637	.406	1925-26	1941-42
Hamilton Tigers	126	47	78	1	414	475	95	.377	1920-21	1924-25
Cleveland Barons	160	47	87	26	470	617	120	.375	1976-77	1977-78
Pittsburgh Pirates	212	67	122	23	376	519	157	.370	1925-26	1929-30
Calif./Oakland Seals	698	182	401	115	1826	2580	479	.343	1967-68	1975-76
St. Louis Eagles	48	11	31	6	86	144	28	.292	1934-35	1934-35
Quebec Bulldogs	24	4	20	0	91	177	8	.167	1919-20	1919-20
Montreal Wanderers	6	1	5	0	17	35	2	.167	1917-18	1917-18
Philadelphia Quakers	44	4	36	4	76	184	12	.136	1930-31	1930-31

Calgary totals include Atlanta Flames, 1972-73 to 1979-80.
Carolina totals include Hartford, 1979-80 to 1996-97.
Colorado totals include Quebec, 1979-80 to 1994-95.
Dallas totals include Minnesota North Stars, 1967-68 to 1992-93.
Detroit totals include Cougars, 1926-27 to 1929-30, and Falcons, 1930-31 to 1931-32.
New Jersey totals include Kansas City, 1974-75 to 1975-76, and Colorado Rockies, 1976-77 to 1981-82.
Phoenix totals include Winnipeg, 1979-80 to 1995-96.
Toronto totals include Arenas, 1917-18 to 1918-19, and St. Patricks, 1919-20 to 1925-56.

1919-20

First Half

Team	GP	W	L	T	GF	GA	PTS
Ottawa	12	9	3	0	59	23	18
Montreal	12	8	4	0	62	51	16
Toronto	12	5	7	0	52	62	10
Quebec	12	2	10	0	44	81	4

Second Half

Team							
*Ottawa	12	10	2	0	62	41	20
Toronto	12	7	5	0	67	44	14
Montreal	12	5	7	0	67	62	10
Quebec	12	2	10	0	47	96	4

Leading Scorers

Player	Club	GP	G	A	PTS	PIM
Malone, Joe	Quebec	24	39	10	49	12
Lalonde, Newsy	Montreal	23	37	9	46	34
Nighbor, Frank	Ottawa	23	26	15	41	18
Denneny, Corb	Toronto	24	24	12	36	20
Darragh, Jack	Ottawa	23	22	14	36	22
Noble, Reg	Toronto	24	24	9	33	52
Arbour, Amos	Montreal	22	21	5	26	13
Wilson, Cully	Toronto	23	20	6	26	86
Pitre, Didier	Montreal	22	14	12	26	6
Broadbent, Punch	Ottawa	21	19	6	25	40

1920-21

First Half

Team	GP	W	L	T	GF	GA	PTS
*Ottawa	10	8	2	0	49	23	16
Toronto	10	5	5	0	39	47	10
Montreal	10	4	6	0	37	51	8
Hamilton	10	3	7	0	34	38	6

Second Half

Team							
Toronto	14	10	4	0	66	53	20
Montreal	14	9	5	0	75	48	18
Ottawa	14	6	8	0	48	52	12
Hamilton	14	3	11	0	58	94	6

Leading Scorers

Player	Club	GP	G	A	PTS	PIM
Lalonde, Newsy	Montreal	24	33	10	43	36
Dye, Babe	Ham., Tor.	24	35	5	40	32
Denneny, Cy	Ottawa	24	34	5	39	10
Malone, Joe	Hamilton	20	28	9	37	6
Nighbor, Frank	Ottawa	24	19	10	29	10
Noble, Reg	Toronto	24	19	8	27	54
Cameron, Harry	Toronto	24	18	9	27	35
Prodgers, Goldie	Hamilton	24	18	9	27	8
Denneny, Corb	Toronto	20	19	7	26	29
Darragh, Jack	Ottawa	24	11	15	26	20

1921-22

Team	GP	W	L	T	GF	GA	PTS
Ottawa	24	14	8	2	106	84	30
*Toronto	24	13	10	1	98	97	27
Montreal	24	12	11	1	88	94	25
Hamilton	24	7	17	0	88	105	14

Leading Scorers

Player	Club	GP	G	A	PTS	PIM
Broadbent, Punch	Ottawa	24	32	14	46	28
Denneny, Cy	Ottawa	22	27	12	39	20
Dye, Babe	Toronto	24	31	7	38	39
Cameron, Harry	Toronto	24	18	17	35	22
Malone, Joe	Hamilton	24	24	7	31	4
Denneny, Corb	Toronto	24	19	9	28	28
Noble, Reg	Toronto	24	17	11	28	19
Cleghorn, Sprague	Montreal	24	17	9	26	80
Boucher, Georges	Ottawa	23	13	12	25	12
Cleghorn, Odie	Montreal	23	21	3	24	26

1922-23

Team	GP	W	L	T	GF	GA	PTS
*Ottawa	24	14	9	1	77	54	29
Montreal	24	13	9	2	73	61	28
Toronto	24	13	10	1	82	88	27
Hamilton	24	6	18	0	81	110	12

Leading Scorers

Player	Club	GP	G	A	PTS	PIM
Dye, Babe	Toronto	22	26	11	37	19
Denneny, Cy	Ottawa	24	23	11	34	28
Boucher, Billy	Montreal	24	24	7	31	55
Adams, Jack	Toronto	23	19	9	28	42
Roach, Mickey	Hamilton	24	17	10	27	8
Cleghorn, Odie	Montreal	24	19	6	25	18
Boucher, Georges	Ottawa	24	14	9	23	58
Noble, Reg	Toronto	24	12	11	23	47
Wilson, Cully	Hamilton	23	16	5	21	46
Joliat, Aurel	Montreal	24	12	9	21	37

1923-24

Team	GP	W	L	T	GF	GA	PTS
Ottawa	24	16	8	0	74	54	32
*Montreal	24	13	11	0	59	48	26
Toronto	24	10	14	0	59	85	20
Hamilton	24	9	15	0	63	68	18

Leading Scorers

Player	Club	GP	G	A	PTS	PIM
Denneny, Cy	Ottawa	22	22	2	24	10
Boucher, Georges	Ottawa	21	13	10	23	38
Boucher, Billy	Montreal	23	16	6	22	48
Burch, Billy	Hamilton	24	16	6	22	6
Joliat, Aurel	Montreal	24	15	5	20	27
Dye, Babe	Toronto	19	16	3	19	23
Adams, Jack	Toronto	22	14	4	18	51
Noble, Reg	Toronto	23	12	5	17	79
Morenz, Howie	Montreal	24	13	3	16	20
Clancy, King	Ottawa	24	8	8	16	26

1924-25

Team	GP	W	L	T	GF	GA	PTS
Hamilton	30	19	10	1	90	60	39
Toronto	30	19	11	0	90	84	38
• Montreal	30	17	11	2	93	56	36
Ottawa	30	17	12	1	83	66	35
Mtl. Maroons	30	9	19	2	45	65	20
Boston	30	6	24	0	49	119	12

• NHL Champion (Stanley Cup won by Victoria Cougars, WCHL)

Leading Scorers

Player	Club	GP	G	A	PTS	PIM
Dye, Babe	Toronto	29	38	8	46	41
Denneny, Cy	Ottawa	29	27	15	42	16
Joliat, Aurel	Montreal	25	30	11	41	85
Morenz, Howie	Montreal	30	28	11	39	46
Green, Red	Hamilton	30	19	15	34	81
Adams, Jack	Toronto	27	21	10	31	67
Boucher, Billy	Montreal	30	17	13	30	92
Burch, Billy	Hamilton	27	20	7	27	10
Herberts, Jimmy	Boston	30	17	7	24	55
Smith, Hooley	Ottawa	30	10	13	23	81

1925-26

Team	GP	W	L	T	GF	GA	PTS
Ottawa	36	24	8	4	77	42	52
*Mtl. Maroons	36	20	11	5	91	73	45
Pittsburgh	36	19	16	1	82	70	39
Boston	36	17	15	4	92	85	38
NY Americans	36	12	20	4	68	89	28
Toronto	36	12	21	3	92	114	27
Montreal	36	11	24	1	79	108	23

Leading Scorers

Player	Club	GP	G	A	PTS	PIM
Stewart, Nels	Mtl. Maroons	36	34	8	42	119
Denneny, Cy	Ottawa	36	24	12	36	18
Cooper, Carson	Boston	36	28	3	31	10
Herberts, Jimmy	Boston	36	26	5	31	47
Morenz, Howie	Montreal	31	23	3	26	39
Adams, Jack	Toronto	36	21	5	26	52
Joliat, Aurel	Montreal	35	17	9	26	52
Burch, Billy	NY Americans	36	22	3	25	33
Smith, Hooley	Ottawa	28	16	9	25	53
Nighbor, Frank	Ottawa	35	12	13	25	40

1926-27

Canadian Division

Team	GP	W	L	T	GF	GA	PTS
*Ottawa	44	30	10	4	86	69	64
Montreal	44	28	14	2	99	67	58
Mtl. Maroons	44	20	20	4	71	68	44
NY Americans	44	17	25	2	82	91	36
Toronto	44	15	24	5	79	94	35

American Division

NY Rangers	44	25	13	6	95	72	56
Boston	44	21	20	3	97	89	45
Chicago	44	19	22	3	115	116	41
Pittsburgh	44	15	26	3	79	108	33
Detroit	44	12	28	4	76	105	28

Leading Scorers

Player	Club	GP	G	A	PTS	PIM
Cook, Bill	NY Rangers	44	33	4	37	58
Irvin, Dick	Chicago	43	18	18	36	34
Morenz, Howie	Montreal	44	25	7	32	49
Fredrickson, Frank	Det., Bos.	41	18	13	31	46
Dye, Babe	Chicago	41	25	5	30	14
Bailey, Ace	Toronto	42	15	13	28	82
Boucher, Frank	NY Rangers	44	13	15	28	17
Burch, Billy	NY Americans	43	19	8	27	40
Oliver, Harry	Boston	42	18	6	24	17
Keats, Duke	Bos., Det.	42	16	8	24	52

1927-28

Canadian Division

Team	GP	W	L	T	GF	GA	PTS
Montreal	44	26	11	7	116	48	59
Mtl. Maroons	44	24	14	6	96	77	54
Ottawa	44	20	14	10	78	57	50
Toronto	44	18	18	8	89	88	44
NY Americans	44	11	27	6	63	128	28

American Division

Boston	44	20	13	11	77	70	51
*NY Rangers	44	19	16	9	94	79	47
Pittsburgh	44	19	17	8	67	76	46
Detroit	44	19	19	6	88	79	44
Chicago	44	7	34	3	68	134	17

Leading Scorers

Player	Club	GP	G	A	PTS	PIM
Morenz, Howie	Montreal	43	33	18	51	66
Joliat, Aurel	Montreal	44	28	11	39	105
Boucher, Frank	NY Rangers	44	23	12	35	15
Hay, George	Detroit	42	22	13	35	20
Stewart, Nels	Mtl. Maroons	41	27	7	34	104
Gagne, Art	Montreal	44	20	10	30	75
Cook, Bun	NY Rangers	44	14	14	28	45
Carson, Bill	Toronto	32	20	6	26	36
Finnigan, Frank	Ottawa	38	20	5	25	34
Cook, Bill	NY Rangers	43	18	6	24	42
Keats, Duke	Det., Chi.	38	14	10	24	60

1928-29

Canadian Division

Team	GP	W	L	T	GF	GA	PTS
Montreal	44	22	7	15	71	43	59
NY Americans	44	19	13	12	53	53	50
Toronto	44	21	18	5	85	69	47
Ottawa	44	14	17	13	54	67	41
Mtl. Maroons	44	15	20	9	67	65	39

American Division

*Boston	44	26	13	5	89	52	57
NY Rangers	44	21	13	10	72	65	52
Detroit	44	19	16	9	72	63	47
Pittsburgh	44	9	27	8	46	80	26
Chicago	44	7	29	8	33	85	22

Leading Scorers

Player	Club	GP	G	A	PTS	PIM
Bailey, Ace	Toronto	44	22	10	32	78
Stewart, Nels	Mtl. Maroons	44	21	8	29	74
Cooper, Carson	Detroit	43	18	9	27	14
Morenz, Howie	Montreal	42	17	10	27	47
Blair, Andy	Toronto	44	12	15	27	41
Boucher, Frank	NY Rangers	44	10	16	26	8
Oliver, Harry	Boston	43	17	6	23	24
Cook, Bill	NY Rangers	43	15	8	23	41
Ward, Jimmy	Mtl. Maroons	43	14	8	22	46

Seven players tied with 19 points

1929-30

Canadian Division

Team	GP	W	L	T	GF	GA	PTS
Mtl. Maroons	44	23	16	5	141	114	51
*Montreal	44	21	14	9	142	114	51
Ottawa	44	21	15	8	138	118	50
Toronto	44	17	21	6	116	124	40
NY Americans	44	14	25	5	113	161	33

American Division

Boston	44	38	5	1	179	98	77
Chicago	44	21	18	5	117	111	47
NY Rangers	44	17	17	10	136	143	44
Detroit	44	14	24	6	117	133	34
Pittsburgh	44	5	36	3	102	185	13

Leading Scorers

Player	Club	GP	G	A	PTS	PIM
Weiland, Cooney	Boston	44	43	30	73	27
Boucher, Frank	NY Rangers	42	26	36	62	16
Clapper, Dit	Boston	44	41	20	61	48
Cook, Bill	NY Rangers	44	29	30	59	56
Kilrea, Hec	Ottawa	44	36	22	58	72
Stewart, Nels	Mtl. Maroons	44	39	16	55	81
Morenz, Howie	Montreal	44	40	10	50	72
Himes, Normie	NY Americans	44	28	22	50	15
Lamb, Joe	Ottawa	44	29	20	49	119
Gainor, Dutch	Boston	42	18	31	49	39

1930-31

Canadian Division

Team	GP	W	L	T	GF	GA	PTS
*Montreal	44	26	10	8	129	89	60
Toronto	44	22	13	9	118	99	53
Mtl. Maroons	44	20	18	6	105	106	46
NY Americans	44	18	16	10	76	74	46
Ottawa	44	10	30	4	91	142	24

American Division

Boston	44	28	10	6	143	90	62
Chicago	44	24	17	3	108	78	51
NY Rangers	44	19	16	9	106	87	47
Detroit	44	16	21	7	102	105	39
Philadelphia	44	4	36	4	76	184	12

Leading Scorers

Player	Club	GP	G	A	PTS	PIM
Morenz, Howie	Montreal	39	28	23	51	49
Goodfellow, Ebbie	Detroit	44	25	23	48	32
Conacher, Charlie	Toronto	37	31	12	43	78
Cook, Bill	NY Rangers	43	30	12	42	39
Bailey, Ace	Toronto	40	23	19	42	46
Primeau, Joe	Toronto	38	9	32	41	18
Stewart, Nels	Mtl. Maroons	42	25	14	39	75
Boucher, Frank	NY Rangers	44	12	27	39	20
Weiland, Cooney	Boston	44	25	13	38	14
Cook, Bun	NY Rangers	44	18	17	35	72
Joliat, Aurel	Montreal	43	13	22	35	73

1931-32

Canadian Division

Team	GP	W	L	T	GF	GA	PTS
Montreal	48	25	16	7	128	111	57
*Toronto	48	23	18	7	155	127	53
Mtl. Maroons	48	19	22	7	142	139	45
NY Americans	48	16	24	8	95	142	40

American Division

Team	GP	W	L	T	GF	GA	PTS
NY Rangers	48	23	17	8	134	112	54
Chicago	48	18	19	11	86	101	47
Detroit	48	18	20	10	95	108	46
Boston	48	15	21	12	122	117	42

Leading Scorers

Player	Club	GP	G	A	PTS	PIM
Jackson, Busher	Toronto	48	28	25	53	63
Primeau, Joe	Toronto	46	13	37	50	25
Morenz, Howie	Montreal	48	24	25	49	46
Conacher, Charlie	Toronto	44	34	14	48	66
Cook, Bill	NY Rangers	48	34	14	48	33
Trottier, Dave	Mtl. Maroons	48	26	18	44	94
Smith, Hooley	Mtl. Maroons	43	11	33	44	49
Siebert, Babe	Mtl. Maroons	48	21	18	39	64
Clapper, Dit	Boston	48	17	22	39	21
Joliat, Aurel	Montreal	48	15	24	39	46

1932-33

Canadian Division

Team	GP	W	L	T	GF	GA	PTS
Toronto	48	24	18	6	119	111	54
Mtl. Maroons	48	22	20	6	135	119	50
Montreal	48	18	25	5	92	115	41
NY Americans	48	15	22	11	91	118	41
Ottawa	48	11	27	10	88	131	32

American Division

Team	GP	W	L	T	GF	GA	PTS
Boston	48	25	15	8	124	88	58
Detroit	48	25	15	8	111	93	58
*NY Rangers	48	23	17	8	135	107	54
Chicago	48	16	20	12	88	101	44

Leading Scorers

Player	Club	GP	G	A	PTS	PIM
Cook, Bill	NY Rangers	48	28	22	50	51
Jackson, Busher	Toronto	48	27	17	44	43
Northcott, Baldy	Mtl. Maroons	48	22	21	43	30
Smith, Hooley	Mtl. Maroons	48	20	21	41	66
Haynes, Paul	Mtl. Maroons	48	16	25	41	18
Joliat, Aurel	Montreal	48	18	21	39	53
Barry, Marty	Boston	48	24	13	37	40
Cook, Bun	NY Rangers	48	22	15	37	35
Stewart, Nels	Boston	47	18	18	36	62
Morenz, Howie	Montreal	46	14	21	35	32
Gagnon, Johnny	Montreal	48	12	23	35	64
Shore, Eddie	Boston	48	8	27	35	102
Boucher, Frank	NY Rangers	46	7	28	35	4

1933-34

Canadian Division

Team	GP	W	L	T	GF	GA	PTS
Toronto	48	26	13	9	174	119	61
Montreal	48	22	20	6	99	101	50
Mtl. Maroons	48	19	18	11	117	122	49
NY Americans	48	15	23	10	104	132	40
Ottawa	48	13	29	6	115	143	32

American Division

Team	GP	W	L	T	GF	GA	PTS
Detroit	48	24	14	10	113	98	58
*Chicago	48	20	17	11	88	83	51
NY Rangers	48	21	19	8	120	113	50
Boston	48	18	25	5	111	130	41

Leading Scorers

Player	Club	GP	G	A	PTS	PIM
Conacher, Charlie	Toronto	42	32	20	52	38
Primeau, Joe	Toronto	45	14	32	46	8
Boucher, Frank	NY Rangers	48	14	30	44	4
Barry, Marty	Boston	48	27	12	39	12
Dillon, Cecil	NY Rangers	48	13	26	39	10
Stewart, Nels	Boston	48	21	17	38	68
Jackson, Busher	Toronto	38	20	18	38	38
Joliat, Aurel	Montreal	48	22	15	37	27
Smith, Hooley	Mtl. Maroons	47	18	19	37	58
Thompson, Paul	Chicago	48	20	16	36	17

1934-35

Canadian Division

Team	GP	W	L	T	GF	GA	PTS
Toronto	48	30	14	4	157	111	64
*Mtl. Maroons	48	24	19	5	123	92	53
Montreal	48	19	23	6	110	145	44
NY Americans	48	12	27	9	100	142	33
St. Louis	48	11	31	6	86	144	28

American Division

Team	GP	W	L	T	GF	GA	PTS
Boston	48	26	16	6	129	112	58
Chicago	48	26	17	5	118	88	57
NY Rangers	48	22	20	6	137	139	50
Detroit	48	19	22	7	127	114	45

Leading Scorers

Player	Club	GP	G	A	PTS	PIM
Conacher, Charlie	Toronto	47	36	21	57	24
Howe, Syd	St.L., Det.	50	22	25	47	34
Aurie, Larry	Detroit	48	17	29	46	24
Boucher, Frank	NY Rangers	48	13	32	45	2
Jackson, Busher	Toronto	42	22	22	44	27
Lewis, Herbie	Detroit	47	16	27	43	26
Chapman, Art	NY Americans	47	9	34	43	4
Barry, Marty	Boston	48	20	20	40	33
Schriner, Sweeney	NY Americans	48	18	22	40	6
Stewart, Nels	Boston	47	21	18	39	45
Thompson, Paul	Chicago	48	16	23	39	20

1935-36

Canadian Division

Team	GP	W	L	T	GF	GA	PTS
Mtl. Maroons	48	22	16	10	114	106	54
Toronto	48	23	19	6	126	106	52
NY Americans	48	16	25	7	109	122	39
Montreal	48	11	26	11	82	123	33

American Division

Team	GP	W	L	T	GF	GA	PTS
*Detroit	48	24	16	8	124	103	56
Boston	48	22	20	6	92	83	50
Chicago	48	21	19	8	93	92	50
NY Rangers	48	19	17	12	91	96	50

Leading Scorers

Player	Club	GP	G	A	PTS	PIM
Schriner, Sweeney	NY Americans	48	19	26	45	8
Barry, Marty	Detroit	48	21	19	40	16
Thompson, Paul	Chicago	45	17	23	40	19
Thoms, Bill	Toronto	48	23	15	38	29
Conacher, Charlie	Toronto	44	23	15	38	74
Smith, Hooley	Mtl. Maroons	47	19	19	38	75
Romnes, Doc	Chicago	48	13	25	38	6
Chapman, Art	NY Americans	47	10	28	38	14
Lewis, Herbie	Detroit	45	14	23	37	25
Northcott, Baldy	Mtl. Maroons	48	15	21	36	41

1936-37

Canadian Division

Team	GP	W	L	T	GF	GA	PTS
Montreal	48	24	18	6	115	111	54
Mtl. Maroons	48	22	17	9	126	110	53
Toronto	48	22	21	5	119	115	49
NY Americans	48	15	29	4	122	161	34

American Division

Team	GP	W	L	T	GF	GA	PTS
*Detroit	48	25	14	9	128	102	59
Boston	48	23	18	7	120	110	53
NY Rangers	48	19	20	9	117	106	47
Chicago	48	14	27	7	99	131	35

Leading Scorers

Player	Club	GP	G	A	PTS	PIM
Schriner, Sweeney	NY Americans	48	21	25	46	17
Apps, Syl	Toronto	48	16	29	45	10
Barry, Marty	Detroit	48	17	27	44	6
Aurie, Larry	Detroit	45	23	20	43	20
Jackson, Busher	Toronto	46	21	19	40	12
Gagnon, Johnny	Montreal	48	20	16	36	38
Gracie, Bob	Mtl. Maroons	47	11	25	36	18
Stewart, Nels	Bos., NYA	43	23	12	35	37
Thompson, Paul	Chicago	47	17	18	35	28
Cowley, Bill	Boston	46	13	22	35	4

1937-38

Canadian Division

Team	GP	W	L	T	GF	GA	PTS
Toronto	48	24	15	9	151	127	57
NY Americans	48	19	18	11	110	111	49
Montreal	48	18	17	13	123	128	49
Mtl. Maroons	48	12	30	6	101	149	30

American Division

Team	GP	W	L	T	GF	GA	PTS
Boston	48	30	11	7	142	89	67
NY Rangers	48	27	15	6	149	96	60
*Chicago	48	14	25	9	97	139	37
Detroit	48	12	25	11	99	133	35

Leading Scorers

Player	Club	GP	G	A	PTS	PIM
Drillon, Gordie	Toronto	48	26	26	52	4
Apps, Syl	Toronto	47	21	29	50	9
Thompson, Paul	Chicago	48	22	22	44	14
Mantha, Georges	Montreal	47	23	19	42	12
Dillon, Cecil	NY Rangers	48	21	18	39	6
Cowley, Bill	Boston	48	17	22	39	8
Schriner, Sweeney	NY Americans	49	21	17	38	22
Thoms, Bill	Toronto	48	14	24	38	14
Smith, Clint	NY Rangers	48	14	23	37	0
Stewart, Nels	NY Americans	48	19	17	36	29
Colville, Neil	NY Rangers	45	17	19	36	11

1938-39

Team	GP	W	L	T	GF	GA	PTS
*Boston	48	36	10	2	156	76	74
NY Rangers	48	26	16	6	149	105	58
Toronto	48	19	20	9	114	107	47
NY Americans	48	17	21	10	119	157	44
Detroit	48	18	24	6	107	128	42
Montreal	48	15	24	9	115	146	39
Chicago	48	12	28	8	91	132	32

Leading Scorers

Player	Club	GP	G	A	PTS	PIM
Blake, Toe	Montreal	48	24	23	47	10
Schriner, Sweeney	NY Americans	48	13	31	44	20
Cowley, Bill	Boston	34	8	34	42	2
Smith, Clint	NY Rangers	48	21	20	41	2
Barry, Marty	Detroit	48	13	28	41	4
Apps, Syl	Toronto	44	15	25	40	4
Anderson, Tom	NY Americans	48	13	27	40	14
Gottselig, Johnny	Chicago	48	16	23	39	15
Haynes, Paul	Montreal	47	5	33	38	27
Conacher, Roy	Boston	47	26	11	37	12
Carr, Lorne	NY Americans	46	19	18	37	16
Colville, Neil	NY Rangers	48	18	19	37	12
Watson, Phil	NY Rangers	48	15	22	37	42

1939-40

Team	GP	W	L	T	GF	GA	PTS
Boston	48	31	12	5	170	98	67
*NY Rangers	48	27	11	10	136	77	64
Toronto	48	25	17	6	134	110	56
Chicago	48	23	19	6	112	120	52
Detroit	48	16	26	6	90	126	38
NY Americans	48	15	29	4	106	140	34
Montreal	48	10	33	5	90	168	25

Leading Scorers

Player	Club	GP	G	A	PTS	PIM
Schmidt, Milt	Boston	48	22	30	52	37
Dumart, Woody	Boston	48	22	21	43	16
Bauer, Bobby	Boston	48	17	26	43	2
Drillon, Gordie	Toronto	43	21	19	40	13
Cowley, Bill	Boston	48	13	27	40	24
Hextall, Bryan	NY Rangers	48	24	15	39	52
Colville, Neil	NY Rangers	48	19	19	38	22
Howe, Syd	Detroit	46	14	23	37	17
Blake, Toe	Montreal	48	17	19	36	48
Armstrong, Murray	NY Americans	48	16	20	36	12

The center on Boston's famed Kraut Line, Milt Schmidt led the NHL in scoring in 1940. He helped the Bruins win the Stanley Cup in 1939 and 1941.

1940-41

Team	GP	W	L	T	GF	GA	PTS
*Boston	48	27	8	13	168	102	67
Toronto	48	28	14	6	145	99	62
Detroit	48	21	16	11	112	102	53
NY Rangers	48	21	19	8	143	125	50
Chicago	48	16	25	7	112	139	39
Montreal	48	16	26	6	121	147	38
NY Americans	48	8	29	11	99	186	27

Leading Scorers

Player	Club	GP	G	A	PTS	PIM
Cowley, Bill	Boston	46	17	45	62	16
Hextall, Bryan	NY Rangers	48	26	18	44	16
Drillon, Gordie	Toronto	42	23	21	44	2
Apps, Syl	Toronto	41	20	24	44	6
Patrick, Lynn	NY Rangers	48	20	24	44	12
Howe, Syd	Detroit	48	20	24	44	8
Colville, Neil	NY Rangers	48	14	28	42	28
Wiseman, Eddie	Boston	48	16	24	40	10
Bauer, Bobby	Boston	48	17	22	39	2
Schriner, Sweeney	Toronto	48	24	14	38	6
Conacher, Roy	Boston	40	24	14	38	7
Schmidt, Milt	Boston	44	13	25	38	23

1941-42

Team	GP	W	L	T	GF	GA	PTS
NY Rangers	48	29	17	2	177	143	60
*Toronto	48	27	18	3	158	136	57
Boston	48	25	17	6	160	118	56
Chicago	48	22	23	3	145	155	47
Detroit	48	19	25	4	140	147	42
Montreal	48	18	27	3	134	173	39
Brooklyn	48	16	29	3	133	175	35

Leading Scorers

Player	Club	GP	G	A	PTS	PIM
Hextall, Bryan	NY Rangers	48	24	32	56	30
Patrick, Lynn	NY Rangers	47	32	22	54	18
Grosso, Don	Detroit	48	23	30	53	13
Watson, Phil	NY Rangers	48	15	37	52	48
Abel, Sid	Detroit	48	18	31	49	45
Blake, Toe	Montreal	47	17	28	45	19
Thoms, Bill	Chicago	47	15	30	45	8
Drillon, Gordie	Toronto	48	23	18	41	6
Apps, Syl	Toronto	38	18	23	41	0
Anderson, Tom	Brooklyn	48	12	29	41	54

1942-43

Team	GP	W	L	T	GF	GA	PTS
*Detroit	50	25	14	11	169	124	61
Boston	50	24	17	9	195	176	57
Toronto	50	22	19	9	198	159	53
Montreal	50	19	19	12	181	191	50
Chicago	50	17	18	15	179	180	49
NY Rangers	50	11	31	8	161	253	30

Leading Scorers

Player	Club	GP	G	A	PTS	PIM
Bentley, Doug	Chicago	50	33	40	73	18
Cowley, Bill	Boston	48	27	45	72	10
Bentley, Max	Chicago	47	26	44	70	2
Patrick, Lynn	NY Rangers	50	22	39	61	28
Carr, Lorne	Toronto	50	27	33	60	15
Taylor, Billy	Toronto	50	18	42	60	2
Hextall, Bryan	NY Rangers	50	27	32	59	28
Blake, Toe	Montreal	48	23	36	59	28
Lach, Elmer	Montreal	45	18	40	58	14
O'Connor, Buddy	Montreal	50	15	43	58	2

1943-44

Team	GP	W	L	T	GF	GA	PTS
*Montreal	50	38	5	7	234	109	83
Detroit	50	26	18	6	214	177	58
Toronto	50	23	23	4	214	174	50
Chicago	50	22	23	5	178	187	49
Boston	50	19	26	5	223	268	43
NY Rangers	50	6	39	5	162	310	17

Leading Scorers

Player	Club	GP	G	A	PTS	PIM
Cain, Herb	Boston	48	36	46	82	4
Bentley, Doug	Chicago	50	38	39	77	22
Carr, Lorne	Toronto	50	36	38	74	9
Liscombe, Carl	Detroit	50	36	37	73	17
Lach, Elmer	Montreal	48	24	48	72	23
Smith, Clint	Chicago	50	23	49	72	4
Cowley, Bill	Boston	36	30	41	71	12
Mosienko, Bill	Chicago	50	32	38	70	10
Jackson, Art	Boston	49	28	41	69	8
Bodnar, Gus	Toronto	50	22	40	62	18

1944-45

Team	GP	W	L	T	GF	GA	PTS
Montreal	50	38	8	4	228	121	80
Detroit	50	31	14	5	218	161	67
*Toronto	50	24	22	4	183	161	52
Boston	50	16	30	4	179	219	36
Chicago	50	13	30	7	141	194	33
NY Rangers	50	11	29	10	154	247	32

Leading Scorers

Player	Club	GP	G	A	PTS	PIM
Lach, Elmer	Montreal	50	26	54	80	37
Richard, Maurice	Montreal	50	50	23	73	36
Blake, Toe	Montreal	49	29	38	67	15
Cowley, Bill	Boston	49	25	40	65	2
Kennedy, Ted	Toronto	49	29	25	54	14
Mosienko, Bill	Chicago	50	28	26	54	0
Carveth, Joe	Detroit	50	26	28	54	6
DeMarco, Ab	NY Rangers	50	24	30	54	10
Smith, Clint	Chicago	50	23	31	54	0
Howe, Syd	Detroit	46	17	36	53	6

1945-46

Team	GP	W	L	T	GF	GA	PTS
*Montreal	50	28	17	5	172	134	61
Boston	50	24	18	8	167	156	56
Chicago	50	23	20	7	200	178	53
Detroit	50	20	20	10	146	159	50
Toronto	50	19	24	7	174	185	45
NY Rangers	50	13	28	9	144	191	35

Leading Scorers

Player	Club	GP	G	A	PTS	PIM
Bentley, Max	Chicago	47	31	30	61	6
Stewart, Gaye	Toronto	50	37	15	52	8
Blake, Toe	Montreal	50	29	21	50	2
Smith, Clint	Chicago	50	26	24	50	2
Richard, Maurice	Montreal	50	27	21	48	50
Mosienko, Bill	Chicago	40	18	30	48	12
DeMarco, Ab	NY Rangers	50	20	27	47	20
Lach, Elmer	Montreal	50	13	34	47	34
Kaleta, Alex	Chicago	49	19	27	46	17
Taylor, Billy	Toronto	48	23	18	41	14
Horeck, Pete	Chicago	50	20	21	41	34

1946-47

Team	GP	W	L	T	GF	GA	PTS
Montreal	60	34	16	10	189	138	78
*Toronto	60	31	19	10	209	172	72
Boston	60	26	23	11	190	175	63
Detroit	60	22	27	11	190	193	55
NY Rangers	60	22	32	6	167	186	50
Chicago	60	19	37	4	193	274	42

Leading Scorers

Player	Club	GP	G	A	PTS	PIM
Bentley, Max	Chicago	60	29	43	72	12
Richard, Maurice	Montreal	60	45	26	71	69
Taylor, Billy	Detroit	60	17	46	63	35
Schmidt, Milt	Boston	59	27	35	62	40
Kennedy, Ted	Toronto	60	28	32	60	27
Bentley, Doug	Chicago	52	21	34	55	18
Bauer, Bobby	Boston	58	30	24	54	4
Conacher, Roy	Detroit	60	30	24	54	6
Mosienko, Bill	Chicago	59	25	27	52	2
Dumart, Woody	Boston	60	24	28	52	12

1947-48

Team	GP	W	L	T	GF	GA	PTS
*Toronto	60	32	15	13	182	143	77
Detroit	60	30	18	12	187	148	72
Boston	60	23	24	13	167	168	59
NY Rangers	60	21	26	13	176	201	55
Montreal	60	20	29	11	147	169	51
Chicago	60	20	34	6	195	225	46

Leading Scorers

Player	Club	GP	G	A	PTS	PIM
Lach, Elmer	Montreal	60	30	31	61	72
O'Connor, Buddy	NY Rangers	60	24	36	60	8
Bentley, Doug	Chicago	60	20	37	57	16
Stewart, Gaye	Tor., Chi.	61	27	29	56	83
Bentley, Max	Chi., Tor.	59	26	28	54	14
Poile, Bud	Tor., Chi.	58	25	29	54	17
Richard, Maurice	Montreal	53	28	25	53	89
Apps, Syl	Toronto	55	26	27	53	12
Lindsay, Ted	Detroit	60	33	19	52	95
Conacher, Roy	Chicago	52	22	27	49	4

1948-49

Team	GP	W	L	T	GF	GA	PTS
Detroit	60	34	19	7	195	145	75
Boston	60	29	23	8	178	163	66
Montreal	60	28	23	9	152	126	65
*Toronto	60	22	25	13	147	161	57
Chicago	60	21	31	8	173	211	50
NY Rangers	60	18	31	11	133	172	47

Leading Scorers

Player	Club	GP	G	A	PTS	PIM
Conacher, Roy	Chicago	60	26	42	68	8
Bentley, Doug	Chicago	58	23	43	66	38
Abel, Sid	Detroit	60	28	26	54	49
Lindsay, Ted	Detroit	50	26	28	54	97
Conacher, Jim	Det., Chi.	59	26	23	49	43
Ronty, Paul	Boston	60	20	29	49	11
Watson, Harry	Toronto	60	26	19	45	0
Reay, Billy	Montreal	60	22	23	45	33
Bodnar, Gus	Chicago	59	19	26	45	14
Peirson, Johnny	Boston	59	22	21	43	45

1949-50

Team	GP	W	L	T	GF	GA	PTS
*Detroit	70	37	19	14	229	164	88
Montreal	70	29	22	19	172	150	77
Toronto	70	31	27	12	176	173	74
NY Rangers	70	28	31	11	170	189	67
Boston	70	22	32	16	198	228	60
Chicago	70	22	38	10	203	244	54

Leading Scorers

Player	Club	GP	G	A	PTS	PIM
Lindsay, Ted	Detroit	69	23	55	78	141
Abel, Sid	Detroit	69	34	35	69	46
Howe, Gordie	Detroit	70	35	33	68	69
Richard, Maurice	Montreal	70	43	22	65	114
Ronty, Paul	Boston	70	23	36	59	8
Conacher, Roy	Chicago	70	25	31	56	16
Bentley, Doug	Chicago	64	20	33	53	28
Peirson, Johnny	Boston	57	27	25	52	49
Prystai, Metro	Chicago	65	29	22	51	31
Guidolin, Bep	Chicago	70	17	34	51	42

1950-51

Team	GP	W	L	T	GF	GA	PTS
Detroit	70	44	13	13	236	139	101
*Toronto	70	41	16	13	212	138	95
Montreal	70	25	30	15	173	184	65
Boston	70	22	30	18	178	197	62
NY Rangers	70	20	29	21	169	201	61
Chicago	70	13	47	10	171	280	36

Leading Scorers

Player	Club	GP	G	A	PTS	PIM
Howe, Gordie	Detroit	70	43	43	86	74
Richard, Maurice	Montreal	65	42	24	66	97
Bentley, Max	Toronto	67	21	41	62	34
Abel, Sid	Detroit	69	23	38	61	30
Schmidt, Milt	Boston	62	22	39	61	33
Kennedy, Ted	Toronto	63	18	43	61	32
Lindsay, Ted	Detroit	67	24	35	59	110
Sloan, Tod	Toronto	70	31	25	56	105
Kelly, Red	Detroit	70	17	37	54	24
Smith, Sid	Toronto	70	30	21	51	10
Gardner, Cal	Toronto	66	23	28	51	42

1951-52

Team	GP	W	L	T	GF	GA	PTS
*Detroit	70	44	14	12	215	133	100
Montreal	70	34	26	10	195	164	78
Toronto	70	29	25	16	168	157	74
Boston	70	25	29	16	162	176	66
NY Rangers	70	23	34	13	192	219	59
Chicago	70	17	44	9	158	241	43

Leading Scorers

Player	Club	GP	G	A	PTS	PIM
Howe, Gordie	Detroit	70	47	39	86	78
Lindsay, Ted	Detroit	70	30	39	69	123
Lach, Elmer	Montreal	70	15	50	65	36
Raleigh, Don	NY Rangers	70	19	42	61	14
Smith, Sid	Toronto	70	27	30	57	6
Geoffrion, Bernie	Montreal	67	30	24	54	66
Mosienko, Bill	Chicago	70	31	22	53	10
Abel, Sid	Detroit	62	17	36	53	32
Kennedy, Ted	Toronto	70	19	33	52	33
Schmidt, Milt	Boston	69	21	29	50	57
Peirson, Johnny	Boston	68	20	30	50	30

1952-53

Team	GP	W	L	T	GF	GA	PTS
Detroit	70	36	16	18	222	133	90
*Montreal	70	28	23	19	155	148	75
Boston	70	28	29	13	152	172	69
Chicago	70	27	28	15	169	175	69
Toronto	70	27	30	13	156	167	67
NY Rangers	70	17	37	16	152	211	50

Leading Scorers

Player	Club	GP	G	A	PTS	PIM
Howe, Gordie	Detroit	70	49	46	95	57
Lindsay, Ted	Detroit	70	32	39	71	111
Richard, Maurice	Montreal	70	28	33	61	112
Hergesheimer, Wally	NY Rangers	70	30	29	59	10
Delvecchio, Alex	Detroit	70	16	43	59	28
Ronty, Paul	NY Rangers	70	16	38	54	20
Prystai, Metro	Detroit	70	16	34	50	12
Kelly, Red	Detroit	70	19	27	46	8
Olmstead, Bert	Montreal	69	17	28	45	83
Mackell, Fleming	Boston	65	27	17	44	63
McFadden, Jim	Chicago	70	23	21	44	29

1953-54

Team	GP	W	L	T	GF	GA	PTS
*Detroit	70	37	19	14	191	132	88
Montreal	70	35	24	11	195	141	81
Toronto	70	32	24	14	152	131	78
Boston	70	32	28	10	177	181	74
NY Rangers	70	29	31	10	161	182	68
Chicago	70	12	51	7	133	242	31

Leading Scorers

Player	Club	GP	G	A	PTS	PIM
Howe, Gordie	Detroit	70	33	48	81	109
Richard, Maurice	Montreal	70	37	30	67	112
Lindsay, Ted	Detroit	70	26	36	62	110
Geoffrion, Bernie	Montreal	54	29	25	54	87
Olmstead, Bert	Montreal	70	15	37	52	85
Kelly, Red	Detroit	62	16	33	49	18
Reibel, Dutch	Detroit	69	15	33	48	18
Sandford, Ed	Boston	70	16	31	47	42
Mackell, Fleming	Boston	67	15	32	47	60
Mosdell, Ken	Montreal	67	22	24	46	64
Ronty, Paul	NY Rangers	70	13	33	46	18

1954-55

Team	GP	W	L	T	GF	GA	PTS
*Detroit	70	42	17	11	204	134	95
Montreal	70	41	18	11	228	157	93
Toronto	70	24	24	22	147	135	70
Boston	70	23	26	21	169	188	67
NY Rangers	70	17	35	18	150	210	52
Chicago	70	13	40	17	161	235	43

Leading Scorers

Player	Club	GP	G	A	PTS	PIM
Geoffrion, Bernie	Montreal	70	38	37	75	57
Richard, Maurice	Montreal	67	38	36	74	125
Béliveau, Jean	Montreal	70	37	36	73	58
Reibel, Dutch	Detroit	70	25	41	66	15
Howe, Gordie	Detroit	64	29	33	62	68
Sullivan, Red	Chicago	69	19	42	61	51
Olmstead, Bert	Montreal	70	10	48	58	103
Smith, Sid	Toronto	70	33	21	54	14
Mosdell, Ken	Montreal	70	22	32	54	82
Lewicki, Danny	NY Rangers	70	29	24	53	8

1955-56

Team	GP	W	L	T	GF	GA	PTS
*Montreal	70	45	15	10	222	131	100
Detroit	70	30	24	16	183	148	76
NY Rangers	70	32	28	10	204	203	74
Toronto	70	24	33	13	153	181	61
Boston	70	23	34	13	147	185	59
Chicago	70	19	39	12	155	216	50

Leading Scorers

Player	Club	GP	G	A	PTS	PIM
Béliveau, Jean	Montreal	70	47	41	88	143
Howe, Gordie	Detroit	70	38	41	79	100
Richard, Maurice	Montreal	70	38	33	71	89
Olmstead, Bert	Montreal	70	14	56	70	94
Sloan, Tod	Toronto	70	37	29	66	100
Bathgate, Andy	NY Rangers	70	19	47	66	59
Geoffrion, Bernie	Montreal	59	29	33	62	66
Reibel, Dutch	Detroit	68	17	39	56	10
Delvecchio, Alex	Detroit	70	25	26	51	24
Creighton, Dave	NY Rangers	70	20	31	51	43
Gadsby, Bill	NY Rangers	70	9	42	51	84

1956-57

Team	GP	W	L	T	GF	GA	PTS
Detroit	70	38	20	12	198	157	88
*Montreal	70	35	23	12	210	155	82
Boston	70	34	24	12	195	174	80
NY Rangers	70	26	30	14	184	227	66
Toronto	70	21	34	15	174	192	57
Chicago	70	16	39	15	169	225	47

Leading Scorers

Player	Club	GP	G	A	PTS	PIM
Howe, Gordie	Detroit	70	44	45	89	72
Lindsay, Ted	Detroit	70	30	55	85	103
Béliveau, Jean	Montreal	69	33	51	84	105
Bathgate, Andy	NY Rangers	70	27	50	77	60
Litzenberger, Ed	Chicago	70	32	32	64	48
Richard, Maurice	Montreal	63	33	29	62	74
McKenney, Don	Boston	69	21	39	60	31
Moore, Dickie	Montreal	70	29	29	58	56
Richard, Henri	Montreal	63	18	36	54	71
Ullman, Norm	Detroit	64	16	36	52	47

1957-58

Team	GP	W	L	T	GF	GA	PTS
*Montreal	70	43	17	10	250	158	96
NY Rangers	70	32	25	13	195	188	77
Detroit	70	29	29	12	176	207	70
Boston	70	27	28	15	199	194	69
Chicago	70	24	39	7	163	202	55
Toronto	70	21	38	11	192	226	53

Leading Scorers

Player	Club	GP	G	A	PTS	PIM
Moore, Dickie	Montreal	70	36	48	84	65
Richard, Henri	Montreal	67	28	52	80	56
Bathgate, Andy	NY Rangers	65	30	48	78	42
Howe, Gordie	Detroit	64	33	44	77	40
Horvath, Bronco	Boston	67	30	36	66	71
Litzenberger, Ed	Chicago	70	32	30	62	63
Mackell, Fleming	Boston	70	20	40	60	72
Béliveau, Jean	Montreal	55	27	32	59	93
Delvecchio, Alex	Detroit	70	21	38	59	22
McKenney, Don	Boston	70	28	30	58	22

1958-59

Team	GP	W	L	T	GF	GA	PTS
*Montreal	70	39	18	13	258	158	91
Boston	70	32	29	9	205	215	73
Chicago	70	28	29	13	197	208	69
Toronto	70	27	32	11	189	201	65
NY Rangers	70	26	32	12	201	217	64
Detroit	70	25	37	8	167	218	58

Leading Scorers

Player	Club	GP	G	A	PTS	PIM
Moore, Dickie	Montreal	70	41	55	96	61
Béliveau, Jean	Montreal	64	45	46	91	67
Bathgate, Andy	NY Rangers	70	40	48	88	48
Howe, Gordie	Detroit	70	32	46	78	57
Litzenberger, Ed	Chicago	70	33	44	77	37
Geoffrion, Bernie	Montreal	59	22	44	66	30
Sullivan, Red	NY Rangers	70	21	42	63	56
Hebenton, Andy	NY Rangers	70	33	29	62	8
McKenney, Don	Boston	70	32	30	62	20
Sloan, Tod	Chicago	59	27	35	62	79

1959-60

Team	GP	W	L	T	GF	GA	PTS
*Montreal	70	40	18	12	255	178	92
Toronto	70	35	26	9	199	195	79
Chicago	70	28	29	13	191	180	69
Detroit	70	26	29	15	186	197	67
Boston	70	28	34	8	220	241	64
NY Rangers	70	17	38	15	187	247	49

Leading Scorers

Player	Club	GP	G	A	PTS	PIM
Hull, Bobby	Chicago	70	39	42	81	68
Horvath, Bronco	Boston	68	39	41	80	60
Béliveau, Jean	Montreal	60	34	40	74	57
Bathgate, Andy	NY Rangers	70	26	48	74	28
Richard, Henri	Montreal	70	30	43	73	66
Howe, Gordie	Detroit	70	28	45	73	46
Geoffrion, Bernie	Montreal	59	30	41	71	36
McKenney, Don	Boston	70	20	49	69	28
Stasiuk, Vic	Boston	69	29	39	68	121
Prentice, Dean	NY Rangers	70	32	34	66	43

1960-61

Team	GP	W	L	T	GF	GA	PTS
Montreal	70	41	19	10	254	188	92
Toronto	70	39	19	12	234	176	90
*Chicago	70	29	24	17	198	180	75
Detroit	70	25	29	16	195	215	66
NY Rangers	70	22	38	10	204	248	54
Boston	70	15	42	13	176	254	43

Leading Scorers

Player	Club	GP	G	A	PTS	PIM
Geoffrion, Bernie	Montreal	64	50	45	95	29
Béliveau, Jean	Montreal	69	32	58	90	57
Mahovlich, Frank	Toronto	70	48	36	84	131
Bathgate, Andy	NY Rangers	70	29	48	77	22
Howe, Gordie	Detroit	64	23	49	72	30
Ullman, Norm	Detroit	70	28	42	70	34
Kelly, Red	Toronto	64	20	50	70	12
Moore, Dickie	Montreal	57	35	34	69	62
Richard, Henri	Montreal	70	24	44	68	91
Delvecchio, Alex	Detroit	70	27	35	62	26

1961-62

Team	GP	W	L	T	GF	GA	PTS
Montreal	70	42	14	14	259	166	98
*Toronto	70	37	22	11	232	180	85
Chicago	70	31	26	13	217	186	75
NY Rangers	70	26	32	12	195	207	64
Detroit	70	23	33	14	184	219	60
Boston	70	15	47	8	177	306	38

Leading Scorers

Player	Club	GP	G	A	PTS	PIM
Hull, Bobby	Chicago	70	50	34	84	35
Bathgate, Andy	NY Rangers	70	28	56	84	44
Howe, Gordie	Detroit	70	33	44	77	54
Mikita, Stan	Chicago	70	25	52	77	97
Mahovlich, Frank	Toronto	70	33	38	71	87
Delvecchio, Alex	Detroit	70	26	43	69	18
Backstrom, Ralph	Montreal	66	27	38	65	29
Ullman, Norm	Detroit	70	26	38	64	54
Hay, Bill	Chicago	60	11	52	63	34
Provost, Claude	Montreal	70	33	29	62	22

1962-63

Team	GP	W	L	T	GF	GA	PTS
*Toronto	70	35	23	12	221	180	82
Chicago	70	32	21	17	194	178	81
Montreal	70	28	19	23	225	183	79
Detroit	70	32	25	13	200	194	77
NY Rangers	70	22	36	12	211	233	56
Boston	70	14	39	17	198	281	45

Leading Scorers

Player	Club	GP	G	A	PTS	PIM
Howe, Gordie	Detroit	70	38	48	86	100
Bathgate, Andy	NY Rangers	70	35	46	81	54
Mikita, Stan	Chicago	65	31	45	76	69
Mahovlich, Frank	Toronto	67	36	37	73	56
Richard, Henri	Montreal	67	23	50	73	57
Béliveau, Jean	Montreal	69	18	49	67	68
Bucyk, John	Boston	69	27	39	66	36
Delvecchio, Alex	Detroit	70	20	44	64	8
Hull, Bobby	Chicago	65	31	31	62	27
Oliver, Murray	Boston	65	22	40	62	38

1963-64

Team	GP	W	L	T	GF	GA	PTS
Montreal	70	36	21	13	209	167	85
Chicago	70	36	22	12	218	169	84
*Toronto	70	33	25	12	192	172	78
Detroit	70	30	29	11	191	204	71
NY Rangers	70	22	38	10	186	242	54
Boston	70	18	40	12	170	212	48

Leading Scorers

Player	Club	GP	G	A	PTS	PIM
Mikita, Stan	Chicago	70	39	50	89	146
Hull, Bobby	Chicago	70	43	44	87	50
Béliveau, Jean	Montreal	68	28	50	78	42
Bathgate, Andy	NYR, Tor.	71	19	58	77	34
Howe, Gordie	Detroit	69	26	47	73	70
Wharram, Kenny	Chicago	70	39	32	71	18
Oliver, Murray	Boston	70	24	44	68	41
Goyette, Phil	NY Rangers	67	24	41	65	15
Gilbert, Rod	NY Rangers	70	24	40	64	62
Keon, Dave	Toronto	70	23	37	60	6

1964-65

Team	GP	W	L	T	GF	GA	PTS
Detroit	70	40	23	7	224	175	87
*Montreal	70	36	23	11	211	185	83
Chicago	70	34	28	8	224	176	76
Toronto	70	30	26	14	204	173	74
NY Rangers	70	20	38	12	179	246	52
Boston	70	21	43	6	166	253	48

Leading Scorers

Player	Club	GP	G	A	PTS	PIM
Mikita, Stan	Chicago	70	28	59	87	154
Ullman, Norm	Detroit	70	42	41	83	70
Howe, Gordie	Detroit	70	29	47	76	104
Hull, Bobby	Chicago	61	39	32	71	32
Delvecchio, Alex	Detroit	68	25	42	67	16
Provost, Claude	Montreal	70	27	37	64	28
Gilbert, Rod	NY Rangers	70	25	36	61	52
Pilote, Pierre	Chicago	68	14	45	59	162
Bucyk, John	Boston	68	26	29	55	24
Backstrom, Ralph	Montreal	70	25	30	55	41
Esposito, Phil	Chicago	70	23	32	55	44

1965-66

Team	GP	W	L	T	GF	GA	PTS
*Montreal	70	41	21	8	239	173	90
Chicago	70	37	25	8	240	187	82
Toronto	70	34	25	11	208	187	79
Detroit	70	31	27	12	221	194	74
Boston	70	21	43	6	174	275	48
NY Rangers	70	18	41	11	195	261	47

Leading Scorers

Player	Club	GP	G	A	PTS	PIM
Hull, Bobby	Chicago	65	54	43	97	70
Mikita, Stan	Chicago	68	30	48	78	58
Rousseau, Bobby	Montreal	70	30	48	78	20
Béliveau, Jean	Montreal	67	29	48	77	50
Howe, Gordie	Detroit	70	29	46	75	83
Ullman, Norm	Detroit	70	31	41	72	35
Delvecchio, Alex	Detroit	70	31	38	69	16
Nevin, Bob	NY Rangers	69	29	33	62	10
Richard, Henri	Montreal	62	22	39	61	47
Oliver, Murray	Boston	70	18	42	60	30

1966-67

Team	GP	W	L	T	GF	GA	PTS
Chicago	70	41	17	12	264	170	94
Montreal	70	32	25	13	202	188	77
*Toronto	70	32	27	11	204	211	75
NY Rangers	70	30	28	12	188	189	72
Detroit	70	27	39	4	212	241	58
Boston	70	17	43	10	182	253	44

Leading Scorers

Player	Club	GP	G	A	PTS	PIM
Mikita, Stan	Chicago	70	35	62	97	12
Hull, Bobby	Chicago	66	52	28	80	52
Ullman, Norm	Detroit	68	26	44	70	26
Wharram, Kenny	Chicago	70	31	34	65	21
Howe, Gordie	Detroit	69	25	40	65	53
Rousseau, Bobby	Montreal	68	19	44	63	58
Esposito, Phil	Chicago	69	21	40	61	40
Goyette, Phil	NY Rangers	70	12	49	61	6
Mohns, Doug	Chicago	61	25	35	60	58
Richard, Henri	Montreal	65	21	34	55	28
Delvecchio, Alex	Detroit	70	17	38	55	10

1967-68

East Division

Team	GP	W	L	T	GF	GA	PTS
*Montreal	74	42	22	10	236	167	94
NY Rangers	74	39	23	12	226	183	90
Boston	74	37	27	10	259	216	84
Chicago	74	32	26	16	212	222	80
Toronto	74	33	31	10	209	176	76
Detroit	74	27	35	12	245	257	66

West Division

Team	GP	W	L	T	GF	GA	PTS
Philadelphia	74	31	32	11	173	179	73
Los Angeles	74	31	33	10	200	224	72
St. Louis	74	27	31	16	177	191	70
Minnesota	74	27	32	15	191	226	69
Pittsburgh	74	27	34	13	195	216	67
Oakland	74	15	42	17	153	219	47

Leading Scorers

Player	Club	GP	G	A	PTS	PIM
Mikita, Stan	Chicago	72	40	47	87	14
Esposito, Phil	Boston	74	35	49	84	21
Howe, Gordie	Detroit	74	39	43	82	53
Ratelle, Jean	NY Rangers	74	32	46	78	18
Gilbert, Rod	NY Rangers	73	29	48	77	12
Hull, Bobby	Chicago	71	44	31	75	39
Ullman, Norm	Det., Tor.	71	35	37	72	28
Delvecchio, Alex	Detroit	74	22	48	70	14
Bucyk, John	Boston	72	30	39	69	8
Wharram, Kenny	Chicago	74	27	42	69	18

1968-69

East Division

Team	GP	W	L	T	GF	GA	PTS
*Montreal	76	46	19	11	271	202	103
Boston	76	42	18	16	303	221	100
NY Rangers	76	41	26	9	231	196	91
Toronto	76	35	26	15	234	217	85
Detroit	76	33	31	12	239	221	78
Chicago	76	34	33	9	280	246	77

West Division

Team	GP	W	L	T	GF	GA	PTS
St. Louis	76	37	25	14	204	157	88
Oakland	76	29	36	11	219	251	69
Philadelphia	76	20	35	21	174	225	61
Los Angeles	76	24	42	10	185	260	58
Pittsburgh	76	20	45	11	189	252	51
Minnesota	76	18	43	15	189	270	51

Leading Scorers

Player	Club	GP	G	A	PTS	PIM
Esposito, Phil	Boston	74	49	77	126	79
Hull, Bobby	Chicago	74	58	49	107	48
Howe, Gordie	Detroit	76	44	59	103	58
Mikita, Stan	Chicago	74	30	67	97	52
Hodge, Ken	Boston	75	45	45	90	75
Cournoyer, Yvan	Montreal	76	43	44	87	31
Delvecchio, Alex	Detroit	72	25	58	83	8
Berenson, Red	St. Louis	76	35	47	82	43
Béliveau, Jean	Montreal	69	33	49	82	55
Mahovlich, Frank	Detroit	76	49	29	78	38
Ratelle, Jean	NY Rangers	75	32	46	78	26

1969-70

East Division

Team	GP	W	L	T	GF	GA	PTS
Chicago	76	45	22	9	250	170	99
*Boston	76	40	17	19	277	216	99
Detroit	76	40	21	15	246	199	95
NY Rangers	76	38	22	16	246	189	92
Montreal	76	38	22	16	244	201	92
Toronto	76	29	34	13	222	242	71

West Division

Team	GP	W	L	T	GF	GA	PTS
St. Louis	76	37	27	12	224	179	86
Pittsburgh	76	26	38	12	182	238	64
Minnesota	76	19	35	22	224	257	60
Oakland	76	22	40	14	169	243	58
Philadelphia	76	17	35	24	197	225	58
Los Angeles	76	14	52	10	168	290	38

Leading Scorers

Player	Club	GP	G	A	PTS	PIM
Orr, Bobby	Boston	76	33	87	120	125
Esposito, Phil	Boston	76	43	56	99	50
Mikita, Stan	Chicago	76	39	47	86	50
Goyette, Phil	St. Louis	72	29	49	78	16
Tkaczuk, Walt	NY Rangers	76	27	50	77	38
Ratelle, Jean	NY Rangers	75	32	42	74	28
Berenson, Red	St. Louis	67	33	39	72	38
Parise, Jean-Paul	Minnesota	74	24	48	72	72
Howe, Gordie	Detroit	76	31	40	71	58
Mahovlich, Frank	Detroit	74	38	32	70	59
Balon, Dave	NY Rangers	76	33	37	70	100
McKenzie, John	Boston	72	29	41	70	114

1970-71

East Division

Team	GP	W	L	T	GF	GA	PTS
Boston	78	57	14	7	399	207	121
NY Rangers	78	49	18	11	259	177	109
*Montreal	78	42	23	13	291	216	97
Toronto	78	37	33	8	248	211	82
Buffalo	78	24	39	15	217	291	63
Vancouver	78	24	46	8	229	296	56
Detroit	78	22	45	11	209	308	55

West Division

Team	GP	W	L	T	GF	GA	PTS
Chicago	78	49	20	9	277	184	107
St. Louis	78	34	25	19	223	208	87
Philadelphia	78	28	33	17	207	225	73
Minnesota	78	28	34	16	191	223	72
Los Angeles	78	25	40	13	239	303	63
Pittsburgh	78	21	37	20	221	240	62
California	78	20	53	5	199	320	45

Leading Scorers

Player	Club	GP	G	A	PTS	PIM
Esposito, Phil	Boston	78	76	76	152	71
Orr, Bobby	Boston	78	37	102	139	91
Bucyk, John	Boston	78	51	65	116	8
Hodge, Ken	Boston	78	43	62	105	113
Hull, Bobby	Chicago	78	44	52	96	32
Ullman, Norm	Toronto	73	34	51	85	24
Cashman, Wayne	Boston	77	21	58	79	100
McKenzie, John	Boston	65	31	46	77	120
Keon, Dave	Toronto	76	38	38	76	4
Béliveau, Jean	Montreal	70	25	51	76	40
Stanfield, Fred	Boston	75	24	52	76	12

1971-72

East Division

Team	GP	W	L	T	GF	GA	PTS
*Boston	78	54	13	11	330	204	119
NY Rangers	78	48	17	13	317	192	109
Montreal	78	46	16	16	307	205	108
Toronto	78	33	31	14	209	208	80
Detroit	78	33	35	10	261	262	76
Buffalo	78	16	43	19	203	289	51
Vancouver	78	20	50	8	203	297	48

West Division

Team	GP	W	L	T	GF	GA	PTS
Chicago	78	46	17	15	256	166	107
Minnesota	78	37	29	12	212	191	86
St. Louis	78	28	39	11	208	247	67
Pittsburgh	78	26	38	14	220	258	66
Philadelphia	78	26	38	14	200	236	66
California	78	21	39	18	216	288	60
Los Angeles	78	20	49	9	206	305	49

Leading Scorers

Player	Club	GP	G	A	PTS	PIM
Esposito, Phil	Boston	76	66	67	133	76
Orr, Bobby	Boston	76	37	80	117	106
Ratelle, Jean	NY Rangers	63	46	63	109	4
Hadfield, Vic	NY Rangers	78	50	56	106	142
Gilbert, Rod	NY Rangers	73	43	54	97	64
Mahovlich, Frank	Montreal	76	43	53	96	36
Hull, Bobby	Chicago	78	50	43	93	24
Cournoyer, Yvan	Montreal	73	47	36	83	15
Bucyk, John	Boston	78	32	51	83	4
Clarke, Bobby	Philadelphia	78	35	46	81	87
Lemaire, Jacques	Montreal	77	32	49	81	26

1972-73

East Division

Team	GP	W	L	T	GF	GA	PTS
*Montreal	78	52	10	16	329	184	120
Boston	78	51	22	5	330	235	107
NY Rangers	78	47	23	8	297	208	102
Buffalo	78	37	27	14	257	219	88
Detroit	78	37	29	12	265	243	86
Toronto	78	27	41	10	247	279	64
Vancouver	78	22	47	9	233	339	53
NY Islanders	78	12	60	6	170	347	30

West Division

Team	GP	W	L	T	GF	GA	PTS
Chicago	78	42	27	9	284	225	93
Philadelphia	78	37	30	11	296	256	85
Minnesota	78	37	30	11	254	230	85
St. Louis	78	32	34	12	233	251	76
Pittsburgh	78	32	37	9	257	265	73
Los Angeles	78	31	36	11	232	245	73
Atlanta	78	25	38	15	191	239	65
California	78	16	46	16	213	323	48

Leading Scorers

Player	Club	GP	G	A	PTS	PIM
Esposito, Phil	Boston	78	55	75	130	87
Clarke, Bobby	Philadelphia	78	37	67	104	80
Orr, Bobby	Boston	63	29	72	101	99
MacLeish, Rick	Philadelphia	78	50	50	100	69
Lemaire, Jacques	Montreal	77	44	51	95	16
Ratelle, Jean	NY Rangers	78	41	53	94	12
Redmond, Mickey	Detroit	76	52	41	93	24
Bucyk, John	Boston	78	40	53	93	12
Mahovlich, Frank	Montreal	78	38	55	93	51
Pappin, Jim	Chicago	76	41	51	92	82

Chicago's Pierre Pilote won the Norris Trophy as best defenseman for the third straight season in 1964-65. He also finished eighth in the NHL in scoring that year.

1973-74
East Division

Team	GP	W	L	T	GF	GA	PTS
Boston	78	52	17	9	349	221	113
Montreal	78	45	24	9	293	240	99
NY Rangers	78	40	24	14	300	251	94
Toronto	78	35	27	16	274	230	86
Buffalo	78	32	34	12	242	250	76
Detroit	78	29	39	10	255	319	68
Vancouver	78	24	43	11	224	296	59
NY Islanders	78	19	41	18	182	247	56

West Division

Team	GP	W	L	T	GF	GA	PTS
*Philadelphia	78	50	16	12	273	164	112
Chicago	78	41	14	23	272	164	105
Los Angeles	78	33	33	12	233	231	78
Atlanta	78	30	34	14	214	238	74
Pittsburgh	78	28	41	9	242	273	65
St. Louis	78	26	40	12	206	248	64
Minnesota	78	23	38	17	235	275	63
California	78	13	55	10	195	342	36

Leading Scorers

Player	Club	GP	G	A	PTS	PIM
Esposito, Phil	Boston	78	68	77	145	58
Orr, Bobby	Boston	74	32	90	122	82
Hodge, Ken	Boston	76	50	55	105	43
Cashman, Wayne	Boston	78	30	59	89	111
Clarke, Bobby	Philadelphia	77	35	52	87	113
Martin, Rick	Buffalo	78	52	34	86	38
Apps Jr., Syl	Pittsburgh	75	24	61	85	37
Sittler, Darryl	Toronto	78	38	46	84	55
MacDonald, Lowell	Pittsburgh	78	43	39	82	14
Park, Brad	NY Rangers	78	25	57	82	148
Hextall, Dennis	Minnesota	78	20	62	82	138

1974-75
PRINCE OF WALES CONFERENCE
Norris Division

Team	GP	W	L	T	GF	GA	PTS
Montreal	80	47	14	19	374	225	113
Los Angeles	80	42	17	21	269	185	105
Pittsburgh	80	37	28	15	326	289	89
Detroit	80	23	45	12	259	335	58
Washington	80	8	67	5	181	446	21

Adams Division

Team	GP	W	L	T	GF	GA	PTS
Buffalo	80	49	16	15	354	240	113
Boston	80	40	26	14	345	245	94
Toronto	80	31	33	16	280	309	78
California	80	19	48	13	212	316	51

CLARENCE CAMPBELL CONFERENCE
Patrick Division

Team	GP	W	L	T	GF	GA	PTS
*Philadelphia	80	51	18	11	293	181	113
NY Rangers	80	37	29	14	319	276	88
NY Islanders	80	33	25	22	264	221	88
Atlanta	80	34	31	15	243	233	83

Smythe Division

Team	GP	W	L	T	GF	GA	PTS
Vancouver	80	38	32	10	271	254	86
St. Louis	80	35	31	14	269	267	84
Chicago	80	37	35	8	268	241	82
Minnesota	80	23	50	7	221	341	53
Kansas City	80	15	54	11	184	328	41

Leading Scorers

Player	Club	GP	G	A	PTS	PIM
Orr, Bobby	Boston	80	46	89	135	101
Esposito, Phil	Boston	79	61	66	127	62
Dionne, Marcel	Detroit	80	47	74	121	14
Lafleur, Guy	Montreal	70	53	66	119	37
Mahovlich, Pete	Montreal	80	35	82	117	64
Clarke, Bobby	Philadelphia	80	27	89	116	125
Robert, Rene	Buffalo	74	40	60	100	75
Gilbert, Rod	NY Rangers	76	36	61	97	22
Perreault, Gilbert	Buffalo	68	39	57	96	36
Martin, Rick	Buffalo	68	52	43	95	72

1975-76
PRINCE OF WALES CONFERENCE
Norris Division

Team	GP	W	L	T	GF	GA	PTS
*Montreal	80	58	11	11	337	174	127
Los Angeles	80	38	33	9	263	265	85
Pittsburgh	80	35	33	12	339	303	82
Detroit	80	26	44	10	226	300	62
Washington	80	11	59	10	224	394	32

Adams Division

Team	GP	W	L	T	GF	GA	PTS
Boston	80	48	15	17	313	237	113
Buffalo	80	46	21	13	339	240	105
Toronto	80	34	31	15	294	276	83
California	80	27	42	11	250	278	65

CLARENCE CAMPBELL CONFERENCE
Patrick Division

Team	GP	W	L	T	GF	GA	PTS
Philadelphia	80	51	13	16	348	209	118
NY Islanders	80	42	21	17	297	190	101
Atlanta	80	35	33	12	262	237	82
NY Rangers	80	29	42	9	262	333	67

Smythe Division

Team	GP	W	L	T	GF	GA	PTS
Chicago	80	32	30	18	254	261	82
Vancouver	80	33	32	15	271	272	81
St. Louis	80	29	37	14	249	290	72
Minnesota	80	20	53	7	195	303	47
Kansas City	80	12	56	12	190	351	36

Leading Scorers

Player	Club	GP	G	A	PTS	PIM
Lafleur, Guy	Montreal	80	56	69	125	36
Clarke, Bobby	Philadelphia	76	30	89	119	13
Perreault, Gilbert	Buffalo	80	44	69	113	36
Barber, Bill	Philadelphia	80	50	62	112	104
Larouche, Pierre	Pittsburgh	76	53	58	111	33
Ratelle, Jean	Bos., NYR	80	36	69	105	18
Mahovlich, Pete	Montreal	80	34	71	105	76
Pronovost, Jean	Pittsburgh	80	52	52	104	24
Sittler, Darryl	Toronto	79	41	59	100	90
Apps Jr., Syl	Pittsburgh	80	32	67	99	24

1976-77
PRINCE OF WALES CONFERENCE
Norris Division

Team	GP	W	L	T	GF	GA	PTS
*Montreal	80	60	8	12	387	171	132
Los Angeles	80	34	31	15	271	241	83
Pittsburgh	80	34	33	13	240	252	81
Washington	80	24	42	14	221	307	62
Detroit	80	16	55	9	183	309	41

Adams Division

Team	GP	W	L	T	GF	GA	PTS
Boston	80	49	23	8	312	240	106
Buffalo	80	48	24	8	301	220	104
Toronto	80	33	32	15	301	285	81
Cleveland	80	25	42	13	240	292	63

CLARENCE CAMPBELL CONFERENCE
Patrick Division

Team	GP	W	L	T	GF	GA	PTS
Philadelphia	80	48	16	16	323	213	112
NY Islanders	80	47	21	12	288	193	106
Atlanta	80	34	34	12	264	265	80
NY Rangers	80	29	37	14	272	310	72

Smythe Division

Team	GP	W	L	T	GF	GA	PTS
St. Louis	80	32	39	9	239	276	73
Minnesota	80	23	39	18	240	310	64
Chicago	80	26	43	11	240	298	63
Vancouver	80	25	42	13	235	294	63
Colorado	80	20	46	14	226	307	54

Leading Scorers

Player	Club	GP	G	A	PTS	PIM
Lafleur, Guy	Montreal	80	56	80	136	20
Dionne, Marcel	Los Angeles	80	53	69	122	12
Shutt, Steve	Montreal	80	60	45	105	28
MacLeish, Rick	Philadelphia	79	49	48	97	42
Perreault, Gilbert	Buffalo	80	39	56	95	30
Young, Tim	Minnesota	80	29	66	95	58
Ratelle, Jean	Boston	78	33	61	94	22
McDonald, Lanny	Toronto	80	46	44	90	77
Sittler, Darryl	Toronto	73	38	52	90	89
Clarke, Bobby	Philadelphia	80	27	63	90	71

1977-78
PRINCE OF WALES CONFERENCE
Norris Division

Team	GP	W	L	T	GF	GA	PTS
*Montreal	80	59	10	11	359	183	129
Detroit	80	32	34	14	252	266	78
Los Angeles	80	31	34	15	243	245	77
Pittsburgh	80	25	37	18	254	321	68
Washington	80	17	49	14	195	321	48

Adams Division

Team	GP	W	L	T	GF	GA	PTS
Boston	80	51	18	11	333	218	113
Buffalo	80	44	19	17	288	215	105
Toronto	80	41	29	10	271	237	92
Cleveland	80	22	45	13	230	325	57

CLARENCE CAMPBELL CONFERENCE
Patrick Division

Team	GP	W	L	T	GF	GA	PTS
NY Islanders	80	48	17	15	334	210	111
Philadelphia	80	45	20	15	296	200	105
Atlanta	80	34	27	19	274	252	87
NY Rangers	80	30	37	13	279	280	73

Smythe Division

Team	GP	W	L	T	GF	GA	PTS
Chicago	80	32	29	19	230	220	83
Colorado	80	19	40	21	257	305	59
Vancouver	80	20	43	17	239	320	57
St. Louis	80	20	47	13	195	304	53
Minnesota	80	18	53	9	218	325	45

Leading Scorers

Player	Club	GP	G	A	PTS	PIM
Lafleur, Guy	Montreal	78	60	72	132	26
Trottier, Bryan	NY Islanders	77	46	77	123	46
Sittler, Darryl	Toronto	80	45	72	117	100
Lemaire, Jacques	Montreal	76	36	61	97	14
Potvin, Denis	NY Islanders	80	30	64	94	81
Bossy, Mike	NY Islanders	73	53	38	91	6
O'Reilly, Terry	Boston	77	29	61	90	211
Perreault, Gilbert	Buffalo	79	41	48	89	20
Clarke, Bobby	Philadelphia	71	21	68	89	83
McDonald, Lanny	Toronto	74	47	40	87	54
Paiement, Wilf	Colorado	80	31	56	87	114

1978-79
PRINCE OF WALES CONFERENCE
Norris Division

Team	GP	W	L	T	GF	GA	PTS
*Montreal	80	52	17	11	337	204	115
Pittsburgh	80	36	31	13	281	279	85
Los Angeles	80	34	34	12	292	286	80
Washington	80	24	41	15	273	338	63
Detroit	80	23	41	16	252	295	62

Adams Division

Team	GP	W	L	T	GF	GA	PTS
Boston	80	43	23	14	316	270	100
Buffalo	80	36	28	16	280	263	88
Toronto	80	34	33	13	267	252	81
Minnesota	80	28	40	12	257	289	68

CLARENCE CAMPBELL CONFERENCE
Patrick Division

Team	GP	W	L	T	GF	GA	PTS
NY Islanders	80	51	15	14	358	214	116
Philadelphia	80	40	25	15	281	248	95
NY Rangers	80	40	29	11	316	292	91
Atlanta	80	41	31	8	327	280	90

Smythe Division

Team	GP	W	L	T	GF	GA	PTS
Chicago	80	29	36	15	244	277	73
Vancouver	80	25	42	13	217	291	63
St. Louis	80	18	50	12	249	348	48
Colorado	80	15	53	12	210	331	42

Leading Scorers

Player	Club	GP	G	A	PTS	PIM
Trottier, Bryan	NY Islanders	76	47	87	134	50
Dionne, Marcel	Los Angeles	80	59	71	130	30
Lafleur, Guy	Montreal	80	52	77	129	28
Bossy, Mike	NY Islanders	80	69	57	126	25
MacMillan, Bob	Atlanta	79	37	71	108	14
Chouinard, Guy	Atlanta	80	50	57	107	14
Potvin, Denis	NY Islanders	73	31	70	101	58
Federko, Bernie	St. Louis	74	31	64	95	14
Taylor, Dave	Los Angeles	78	43	48	91	124
Gillies, Clark	NY Islanders	75	35	56	91	68

1979-80

PRINCE OF WALES CONFERENCE

Norris Division

Team	GP	W	L	T	GF	GA	PTS
Montreal	80	47	20	13	328	240	107
Los Angeles	80	30	36	14	290	313	74
Pittsburgh	80	30	37	13	251	303	73
Hartford	80	27	34	19	303	312	73
Detroit	80	26	43	11	268	306	63

Adams Division

Team	GP	W	L	T	GF	GA	PTS
Buffalo	80	47	17	16	318	201	110
Boston	80	46	21	13	310	234	105
Minnesota	80	36	28	16	311	253	88
Toronto	80	35	40	5	304	327	75
Quebec	80	25	44	11	248	313	61

CLARENCE CAMPBELL CONFERENCE

Patrick Division

Team	GP	W	L	T	GF	GA	PTS
Philadelphia	80	48	12	20	327	254	116
*NY Islanders	80	39	28	13	281	247	91
NY Rangers	80	38	32	10	308	284	86
Atlanta	80	35	32	13	282	269	83
Washington	80	27	40	13	261	293	67

Smythe Division

Team	GP	W	L	T	GF	GA	PTS
Chicago	80	34	27	19	241	250	87
St. Louis	80	34	34	12	266	278	80
Vancouver	80	27	37	16	256	281	70
Edmonton	80	28	39	13	301	322	69
Winnipeg	80	20	49	11	214	314	51
Colorado	80	19	48	13	234	308	51

Leading Scorers

Player	Club	GP	G	A	PTS	PIM
Dionne, Marcel	Los Angeles	80	53	84	137	32
Gretzky, Wayne	Edmonton	79	51	86	137	21
Lafleur, Guy	Montreal	74	50	75	125	12
Perreault, Gilbert	Buffalo	80	40	66	106	57
Rogers, Mike	Hartford	80	44	61	105	10
Trottier, Bryan	NY Islanders	78	42	62	104	68
Simmer, Charlie	Los Angeles	64	56	45	101	65
Stoughton, Blaine	Hartford	80	56	44	100	16
Sittler, Darryl	Toronto	73	40	57	97	62
MacDonald, Blair	Edmonton	80	46	48	94	6
Federko, Bernie	St. Louis	79	38	56	94	24

1980-81

PRINCE OF WALES CONFERENCE

Norris Division

Team	GP	W	L	T	GF	GA	PTS
Montreal	80	45	22	13	332	232	103
Los Angeles	80	43	24	13	337	290	99
Pittsburgh	80	30	37	13	302	345	73
Hartford	80	21	41	18	292	372	60
Detroit	80	19	43	18	252	339	56

Adams Division

Team	GP	W	L	T	GF	GA	PTS
Buffalo	80	39	20	21	327	250	99
Boston	80	37	30	13	316	272	87
Minnesota	80	35	28	17	291	263	87
Quebec	80	30	32	18	314	318	78
Toronto	80	28	37	15	322	367	71

CLARENCE CAMPBELL CONFERENCE

Patrick Division

Team	GP	W	L	T	GF	GA	PTS
*NY Islanders	80	48	18	14	355	260	110
Philadelphia	80	41	24	15	313	249	97
Calgary	80	39	27	14	329	298	92
NY Rangers	80	30	36	14	312	317	74
Washington	80	26	36	18	286	317	70

Smythe Division

Team	GP	W	L	T	GF	GA	PTS
St. Louis	80	45	18	17	352	281	107
Chicago	80	31	33	16	304	315	78
Vancouver	80	28	32	20	289	301	76
Edmonton	80	29	35	16	328	327	74
Colorado	80	22	45	13	258	344	57
Winnipeg	80	9	57	14	246	400	32

Leading Scorers

Player	Club	GP	G	A	PTS	PIM
Gretzky, Wayne	Edmonton	80	55	109	164	28
Dionne, Marcel	Los Angeles	80	58	77	135	70
Nilsson, Kent	Calgary	80	49	82	131	26
Bossy, Mike	NY Islanders	79	68	51	119	32
Taylor, Dave	Los Angeles	72	47	65	112	130
Stastny, Peter	Quebec	77	39	70	109	37
Simmer, Charlie	Los Angeles	65	56	49	105	62
Rogers, Mike	Hartford	80	40	65	105	32
Federko, Bernie	St. Louis	78	31	73	104	47
Richard, Jacques	Quebec	78	52	51	103	39
Middleton, Rick	Boston	80	44	59	103	16
Trottier, Bryan	NY Islanders	73	31	72	103	74

1981-82

CLARENCE CAMPBELL CONFERENCE

Norris Division

Team	GP	W	L	T	GF	GA	PTS
Minnesota	80	37	23	20	346	288	94
Winnipeg	80	33	33	14	319	332	80
St. Louis	80	32	40	8	315	349	72
Chicago	80	30	38	12	332	363	72
Toronto	80	20	44	16	298	380	56
Detroit	80	21	47	12	270	351	54

Smythe Division

Team	GP	W	L	T	GF	GA	PTS
Edmonton	80	48	17	15	417	295	111
Vancouver	80	30	33	17	290	286	77
Calgary	80	29	34	17	334	345	75
Los Angeles	80	24	41	15	314	369	63
Colorado	80	18	49	13	241	362	49

PRINCE OF WALES CONFERENCE

Adams Division

Team	GP	W	L	T	GF	GA	PTS
Montreal	80	46	17	17	360	223	109
Boston	80	43	27	10	323	285	96
Buffalo	80	39	26	15	307	273	93
Quebec	80	33	31	16	356	345	82
Hartford	80	21	41	18	264	351	60

Patrick Division

Team	GP	W	L	T	GF	GA	PTS
*NY Islanders	80	54	16	10	385	250	118
NY Rangers	80	39	27	14	316	306	92
Philadelphia	80	38	31	11	325	313	87
Pittsburgh	80	31	36	13	310	337	75
Washington	80	26	41	13	319	338	65

Leading Scorers

Player	Club	GP	G	A	PTS	PIM
Gretzky, Wayne	Edmonton	80	92	120	212	26
Bossy, Mike	NY Islanders	80	64	83	147	22
Stastny, Peter	Quebec	80	46	93	139	91
Maruk, Dennis	Washington	80	60	76	136	128
Trottier, Bryan	NY Islanders	80	50	79	129	88
Savard, Denis	Chicago	80	32	87	119	82
Dionne, Marcel	Los Angeles	78	50	67	117	50
Smith, Bobby	Minnesota	80	43	71	114	82
Ciccarelli, Dino	Minnesota	76	55	51	106	138
Taylor, Dave	Los Angeles	78	39	67	106	130

1982-83

CLARENCE CAMPBELL CONFERENCE

Norris Division

Team	GP	W	L	T	GF	GA	PTS
Chicago	80	47	23	10	338	268	104
Minnesota	80	40	24	16	321	290	96
Toronto	80	28	40	12	293	330	68
St. Louis	80	25	40	15	285	316	65
Detroit	80	21	44	15	263	344	57

Smythe Division

Team	GP	W	L	T	GF	GA	PTS
Edmonton	80	47	21	12	424	315	106
Calgary	80	32	34	14	321	317	78
Vancouver	80	30	35	15	303	309	75
Winnipeg	80	33	39	8	311	333	74
Los Angeles	80	27	41	12	308	365	66

PRINCE OF WALES CONFERENCE

Adams Division

Team	GP	W	L	T	GF	GA	PTS
Boston	80	50	20	10	327	228	110
Montreal	80	42	24	14	350	286	98
Buffalo	80	38	29	13	318	285	89
Quebec	80	34	34	12	343	336	80
Hartford	80	19	54	7	261	403	45

Patrick Division

Team	GP	W	L	T	GF	GA	PTS
Philadelphia	80	49	23	8	326	240	106
*NY Islanders	80	42	26	12	302	226	96
Washington	80	39	25	16	306	283	94
NY Rangers	80	35	35	10	306	287	80
New Jersey	80	17	49	14	230	338	48
Pittsburgh	80	18	53	9	257	394	45

Leading Scorers

Player	Club	GP	G	A	PTS	PIM
Gretzky, Wayne	Edmonton	80	71	125	196	59
Stastny, Peter	Quebec	75	47	77	124	78
Savard, Denis	Chicago	78	35	86	121	99
Bossy, Mike	NY Islanders	79	60	58	118	20
Dionne, Marcel	Los Angeles	80	56	51	107	22
Pederson, Barry	Boston	77	46	61	107	47
Messier, Mark	Edmonton	77	48	58	106	72
Goulet, Michel	Quebec	80	57	48	105	51
Anderson, Glenn	Edmonton	72	48	56	104	70
Nilsson, Kent	Calgary	80	46	58	104	10
Kurri, Jari	Edmonton	80	45	59	104	22

1983-84

CLARENCE CAMPBELL CONFERENCE

Norris Division

Team	GP	W	L	T	GF	GA	PTS
Minnesota	80	39	31	10	345	344	88
St. Louis	80	32	41	7	293	316	71
Detroit	80	31	42	7	298	323	69
Chicago	80	30	42	8	277	311	68
Toronto	80	26	45	9	303	387	61

Smythe Division

Team	GP	W	L	T	GF	GA	PTS
*Edmonton	80	57	18	5	446	314	119
Calgary	80	34	32	14	311	314	82
Vancouver	80	32	39	9	306	328	73
Winnipeg	80	31	38	11	340	374	73
Los Angeles	80	23	44	13	309	376	59

PRINCE OF WALES CONFERENCE

Adams Division

Team	GP	W	L	T	GF	GA	PTS
Boston	80	49	25	6	336	261	104
Buffalo	80	48	25	7	315	257	103
Quebec	80	42	28	10	360	278	94
Montreal	80	35	40	5	286	295	75
Hartford	80	28	42	10	288	320	66

Patrick Division

Team	GP	W	L	T	GF	GA	PTS
NY Islanders	80	50	26	4	357	269	104
Washington	80	48	27	5	308	226	101
Philadelphia	80	44	26	10	350	290	98
NY Rangers	80	42	29	9	314	304	93
New Jersey	80	17	56	7	231	350	41
Pittsburgh	80	16	58	6	254	390	38

Leading Scorers

Player	Club	GP	G	A	PTS	PIM
Gretzky, Wayne	Edmonton	74	87	118	205	39
Coffey, Paul	Edmonton	80	40	86	126	104
Goulet, Michel	Quebec	75	56	65	121	76
Stastny, Peter	Quebec	80	46	73	119	73
Bossy, Mike	NY Islanders	67	51	67	118	8
Pederson, Barry	Boston	80	39	77	116	64
Kurri, Jari	Edmonton	64	52	61	113	14
Trottier, Bryan	NY Islanders	68	40	71	111	59
Federko, Bernie	St. Louis	79	41	66	107	43
Middleton, Rick	Boston	80	47	58	105	14

1984-85

CLARENCE CAMPBELL CONFERENCE

Norris Division

Team	GP	W	L	T	GF	GA	PTS
St. Louis	80	37	31	12	299	288	86
Chicago	80	38	35	7	309	299	83
Detroit	80	27	41	12	313	357	66
Minnesota	80	25	43	12	268	321	62
Toronto	80	20	52	8	253	358	48

Smythe Division

Team	GP	W	L	T	GF	GA	PTS
*Edmonton	80	49	20	11	401	298	109
Winnipeg	80	43	27	10	358	332	96
Calgary	80	41	27	12	363	302	94
Los Angeles	80	34	32	14	339	326	82
Vancouver	80	25	46	9	284	401	59

PRINCE OF WALES CONFERENCE

Adams Division

Team	GP	W	L	T	GF	GA	PTS
Montreal	80	41	27	12	309	262	94
Quebec	80	41	30	9	323	275	91
Buffalo	80	38	28	14	290	237	90
Boston	80	36	34	10	303	287	82
Hartford	80	30	41	9	268	318	69

Patrick Division

Team	GP	W	L	T	GF	GA	PTS
Philadelphia	80	53	20	7	348	241	113
Washington	80	46	25	9	322	240	101
NY Islanders	80	40	34	6	345	312	86
NY Rangers	80	26	44	10	295	345	62
New Jersey	80	22	48	10	264	346	54
Pittsburgh	80	24	51	5	276	385	53

Leading Scorers

Player	Club	GP	G	A	PTS	PIM
Gretzky, Wayne	Edmonton	80	73	135	208	52
Kurri, Jari	Edmonton	73	71	64	135	30
Hawerchuk, Dale	Winnipeg	80	53	77	130	74
Dionne, Marcel	Los Angeles	80	46	80	126	46
Coffey, Paul	Edmonton	80	37	84	121	97
Bossy, Mike	NY Islanders	76	58	59	117	38
Ogrodnick, John	Detroit	79	55	50	105	30
Savard, Denis	Chicago	79	38	67	105	56
Federko, Bernie	St. Louis	76	30	73	103	27
Gartner, Mike	Washington	80	50	52	102	71

1985-86
CLARENCE CAMPBELL CONFERENCE
Norris Division

Team	GP	W	L	T	GF	GA	PTS
Chicago	80	39	33	8	351	349	86
Minnesota	80	38	33	9	327	305	85
St. Louis	80	37	34	9	302	291	83
Toronto	80	25	48	7	311	386	57
Detroit	80	17	57	6	266	415	40

Smythe Division

Team	GP	W	L	T	GF	GA	PTS
Edmonton	80	56	17	7	426	310	119
Calgary	80	40	31	9	354	315	89
Winnipeg	80	26	47	7	295	372	59
Vancouver	80	23	44	13	282	333	59
Los Angeles	80	23	49	8	284	389	54

PRINCE OF WALES CONFERENCE
Adams Division

Team	GP	W	L	T	GF	GA	PTS
Quebec	80	43	31	6	330	289	92
*Montreal	80	40	33	7	330	280	87
Boston	80	37	31	12	311	288	86
Hartford	80	40	36	4	332	302	84
Buffalo	80	37	37	6	296	291	80

Patrick Division

Team	GP	W	L	T	GF	GA	PTS
Philadelphia	80	53	23	4	335	241	110
Washington	80	50	23	7	315	272	107
NY Islanders	80	39	29	12	327	284	90
NY Rangers	80	36	38	6	280	276	78
Pittsburgh	80	34	38	8	313	305	76
New Jersey	80	28	49	3	300	374	59

Leading Scorers

Player	Club	GP	G	A	PTS	PIM
Gretzky, Wayne	Edmonton	80	52	163	215	52
Lemieux, Mario	Pittsburgh	79	48	93	141	43
Coffey, Paul	Edmonton	79	48	90	138	120
Kurri, Jari	Edmonton	78	68	63	131	22
Bossy, Mike	NY Islanders	80	61	62	123	14
Stastny, Peter	Quebec	76	41	81	122	60
Savard, Denis	Chicago	80	47	69	116	111
Naslund, Mats	Montreal	80	43	67	110	16
Hawerchuk, Dale	Winnipeg	80	46	59	105	44
Broten, Neal	Minnesota	80	29	76	105	47

1986-87
CLARENCE CAMPBELL CONFERENCE
Norris Division

Team	GP	W	L	T	GF	GA	PTS
St. Louis	80	32	33	15	281	293	79
Detroit	80	34	36	10	260	274	78
Chicago	80	29	37	14	290	310	72
Toronto	80	32	42	6	286	319	70
Minnesota	80	30	40	10	296	314	70

Smythe Division

Team	GP	W	L	T	GF	GA	PTS
*Edmonton	80	50	24	6	372	284	106
Calgary	80	46	31	3	318	289	95
Winnipeg	80	40	32	8	279	271	88
Los Angeles	80	31	41	8	318	341	70
Vancouver	80	29	43	8	282	314	66

PRINCE OF WALES CONFERENCE
Adams Division

Team	GP	W	L	T	GF	GA	PTS
Hartford	80	43	30	7	287	270	93
Montreal	80	41	29	10	277	241	92
Boston	80	39	34	7	301	276	85
Quebec	80	31	39	10	267	276	72
Buffalo	80	28	44	8	280	308	64

Patrick Division

Team	GP	W	L	T	GF	GA	PTS
Philadelphia	80	46	26	8	310	245	100
Washington	80	38	32	10	285	278	86
NY Islanders	80	35	33	12	279	281	82
NY Rangers	80	34	38	8	307	323	76
Pittsburgh	80	30	38	12	297	290	72
New Jersey	80	29	45	6	293	368	64

Leading Scorers

Player	Club	GP	G	A	PTS	PIM
Gretzky, Wayne	Edmonton	79	62	121	183	28
Kurri, Jari	Edmonton	79	54	54	108	41
Lemieux, Mario	Pittsburgh	63	54	53	107	57
Messier, Mark	Edmonton	77	37	70	107	73
Gilmour, Doug	St. Louis	80	42	63	105	58
Ciccarelli, Dino	Minnesota	80	52	51	103	92
Hawerchuk, Dale	Winnipeg	80	47	53	100	54
Goulet, Michel	Quebec	75	49	47	96	61
Kerr, Tim	Philadelphia	75	58	37	95	57
Bourque, Raymond	Boston	78	23	72	95	36

1987-88
CLARENCE CAMPBELL CONFERENCE
Norris Division

Team	GP	W	L	T	GF	GA	PTS
Detroit	80	41	28	11	322	269	93
St. Louis	80	34	38	8	278	294	76
Chicago	80	30	41	9	284	328	69
Toronto	80	21	49	10	273	345	52
Minnesota	80	19	48	13	242	349	51

Smythe Division

Team	GP	W	L	T	GF	GA	PTS
Calgary	80	48	23	9	397	305	105
*Edmonton	80	44	25	11	363	288	99
Winnipeg	80	33	36	11	292	310	77
Los Angeles	80	30	42	8	318	359	68
Vancouver	80	25	46	9	272	320	59

PRINCE OF WALES CONFERENCE
Adams Division

Team	GP	W	L	T	GF	GA	PTS
Montreal	80	45	22	13	298	238	103
Boston	80	44	30	6	300	251	94
Buffalo	80	37	32	11	283	305	85
Hartford	80	35	38	7	249	267	77
Quebec	80	32	43	5	271	306	69

Patrick Division

Team	GP	W	L	T	GF	GA	PTS
NY Islanders	80	39	31	10	308	267	88
Washington	80	38	33	9	281	249	85
Philadelphia	80	38	33	9	292	292	85
New Jersey	80	38	36	6	295	296	82
NY Rangers	80	36	34	10	300	283	82
Pittsburgh	80	36	35	9	319	316	81

Leading Scorers

Player	Club	GP	G	A	PTS	PIM
Lemieux, Mario	Pittsburgh	77	70	98	168	92
Gretzky, Wayne	Edmonton	64	40	109	149	24
Savard, Denis	Chicago	80	44	87	131	95
Hawerchuk, Dale	Winnipeg	80	44	77	121	59
Robitaille, Luc	Los Angeles	80	53	58	111	82
Stastny, Peter	Quebec	76	46	65	111	69
Messier, Mark	Edmonton	77	37	74	111	103
Carson, Jimmy	Los Angeles	80	55	52	107	45
Loob, Hakan	Calgary	80	50	56	106	47
Goulet, Michel	Quebec	80	48	58	106	56

1988-89
CLARENCE CAMPBELL CONFERENCE
Norris Division

Team	GP	W	L	T	GF	GA	PTS
Detroit	80	34	34	12	313	316	80
St. Louis	80	33	35	12	275	285	78
Minnesota	80	27	37	16	258	278	70
Chicago	80	27	41	12	297	335	66
Toronto	80	28	46	6	259	342	62

Smythe Division

Team	GP	W	L	T	GF	GA	PTS
*Calgary	80	54	17	9	354	226	117
Los Angeles	80	42	31	7	376	335	91
Edmonton	80	38	34	8	325	306	84
Vancouver	80	33	39	8	251	253	74
Winnipeg	80	26	42	12	300	355	64

PRINCE OF WALES CONFERENCE
Adams Division

Team	GP	W	L	T	GF	GA	PTS
Montreal	80	53	18	9	315	218	115
Boston	80	37	29	14	289	256	88
Buffalo	80	38	35	7	291	299	83
Hartford	80	37	38	5	299	290	79
Quebec	80	27	46	7	269	342	61

Patrick Division

Team	GP	W	L	T	GF	GA	PTS
Washington	80	41	29	10	305	259	92
Pittsburgh	80	40	33	7	347	349	87
NY Rangers	80	37	35	8	310	307	82
Philadelphia	80	36	36	8	307	285	80
New Jersey	80	27	41	12	281	325	66
NY Islanders	80	28	47	5	265	325	61

Leading Scorers

Player	Club	GP	G	A	PTS	PIM
Lemieux, Mario	Pittsburgh	76	85	114	199	100
Gretzky, Wayne	Los Angeles	78	54	114	168	26
Yzerman, Steve	Detroit	80	65	90	155	61
Nicholls, Bernie	Los Angeles	79	70	80	150	96
Brown, Rob	Pittsburgh	68	49	66	115	118
Coffey, Paul	Pittsburgh	75	30	83	113	193
Mullen, Joe	Calgary	79	51	59	110	16
Kurri, Jari	Edmonton	76	44	58	102	69
Carson, Jimmy	Edmonton	80	49	51	100	36
Robitaille, Luc	Los Angeles	78	46	52	98	65

1989-90
CLARENCE CAMPBELL CONFERENCE
Norris Division

Team	GP	W	L	T	GF	GA	PTS
Chicago	80	41	33	6	316	294	88
St. Louis	80	37	34	9	295	279	83
Toronto	80	38	38	4	337	358	80
Minnesota	80	36	40	4	284	291	76
Detroit	80	28	38	14	288	323	70

Smythe Division

Team	GP	W	L	T	GF	GA	PTS
Calgary	80	42	23	15	348	265	99
*Edmonton	80	38	28	14	315	283	90
Winnipeg	80	37	32	11	298	290	85
Los Angeles	80	34	39	7	338	337	75
Vancouver	80	25	41	14	245	306	64

PRINCE OF WALES CONFERENCE
Adams Division

Team	GP	W	L	T	GF	GA	PTS
Boston	80	46	25	9	289	232	101
Buffalo	80	45	27	8	286	248	98
Montreal	80	41	28	11	288	234	93
Hartford	80	38	33	9	275	268	85
Quebec	80	12	61	7	240	407	31

Patrick Division

Team	GP	W	L	T	GF	GA	PTS
NY Rangers	80	36	31	13	279	267	85
New Jersey	80	37	34	9	295	288	83
Washington	80	36	38	6	284	275	78
NY Islanders	80	31	38	11	281	288	73
Pittsburgh	80	32	40	8	318	359	72
Philadelphia	80	30	39	11	290	297	71

Leading Scorers

Player	Club	GP	G	A	PTS	PIM
Gretzky, Wayne	Los Angeles	73	40	102	142	42
Messier, Mark	Edmonton	79	45	84	129	79
Yzerman, Steve	Detroit	79	62	65	127	79
Lemieux, Mario	Pittsburgh	59	45	78	123	78
Hull, Brett	St. Louis	80	72	41	113	24
Nicholls, Bernie	L.A., NYR	79	39	73	112	86
Turgeon, Pierre	Buffalo	80	40	66	106	29
LaFontaine, Pat	NY Islanders	74	54	51	105	38
Coffey, Paul	Pittsburgh	80	29	74	103	95
Sakic, Joe	Quebec	80	39	63	102	27
Oates, Adam	St. Louis	80	23	79	102	30

1990-91
CLARENCE CAMPBELL CONFERENCE
Norris Division

Team	GP	W	L	T	GF	GA	PTS
Chicago	80	49	23	8	284	211	106
St. Louis	80	47	22	11	310	250	105
Detroit	80	34	38	8	273	298	76
Minnesota	80	27	39	14	256	266	68
Toronto	80	23	46	11	241	318	57

Smythe Division

Team	GP	W	L	T	GF	GA	PTS
Los Angeles	80	46	24	10	340	254	102
Calgary	80	46	26	8	344	263	100
Edmonton	80	37	37	6	272	272	80
Vancouver	80	28	43	9	243	315	65
Winnipeg	80	26	43	11	260	288	63

PRINCE OF WALES CONFERENCE
Adams Division

Team	GP	W	L	T	GF	GA	PTS
Boston	80	44	24	12	299	264	100
Montreal	80	39	30	11	273	249	89
Buffalo	80	31	30	19	292	278	81
Hartford	80	31	38	11	238	276	73
Quebec	80	16	50	14	236	354	46

Patrick Division

Team	GP	W	L	T	GF	GA	PTS
*Pittsburgh	80	41	33	6	342	305	88
NY Rangers	80	36	31	13	297	265	85
Washington	80	37	36	7	258	258	81
New Jersey	80	32	33	15	272	264	79
Philadelphia	80	33	37	10	252	267	76
NY Islanders	80	25	45	10	223	290	60

Leading Scorers

Player	Club	GP	G	A	PTS	PIM
Gretzky, Wayne	Los Angeles	78	41	122	163	16
Hull, Brett	St. Louis	78	86	45	131	22
Oates, Adam	St. Louis	61	25	90	115	29
Recchi, Mark	Pittsburgh	78	40	73	113	48
Cullen, John	Pit., Hfd.	78	39	71	110	101
Sakic, Joe	Quebec	80	48	61	109	24
Yzerman, Steve	Detroit	80	51	57	108	34
Fleury, Theoren	Calgary	79	51	53	104	136
MacInnis, Al	Calgary	78	28	75	103	90
Larmer, Steve	Chicago	80	44	57	101	79

1991-92
CLARENCE CAMPBELL CONFERENCE
Norris Division

Team	GP	W	L	T	GF	GA	PTS
Detroit	80	43	25	12	320	256	98
Chicago	80	36	29	15	257	236	87
St. Louis	80	36	33	11	279	266	83
Minnesota	80	32	42	6	246	278	70
Toronto	80	30	43	7	234	294	67

Smythe Division

Team	GP	W	L	T	GF	GA	PTS
Vancouver	80	42	26	12	285	250	96
Los Angeles	80	35	31	14	287	296	84
Edmonton	80	36	34	10	295	297	82
Winnipeg	80	33	32	15	251	244	81
Calgary	80	31	37	12	296	305	74
San Jose	80	17	58	5	219	359	39

PRINCE OF WALES CONFERENCE
Adams Division

Team	GP	W	L	T	GF	GA	PTS
Montreal	80	41	28	11	267	207	93
Boston	80	36	32	12	270	275	84
Buffalo	80	31	37	12	289	299	74
Hartford	80	26	41	13	247	283	65
Quebec	80	20	48	12	255	318	52

Patrick Division

Team	GP	W	L	T	GF	GA	PTS
NY Rangers	80	50	25	5	321	246	105
Washington	80	45	27	8	330	275	98
*Pittsburgh	80	39	32	9	343	308	87
New Jersey	80	38	31	11	289	259	87
NY Islanders	80	34	35	11	291	299	79
Philadelphia	80	32	37	11	252	273	75

Leading Scorers

Player	Club	GP	G	A	PTS	PIM
Lemieux, Mario	Pittsburgh	64	44	87	131	94
Stevens, Kevin	Pittsburgh	80	54	69	123	254
Gretzky, Wayne	Los Angeles	74	31	90	121	34
Hull, Brett	St. Louis	73	70	39	109	48
Robitaille, Luc	Los Angeles	80	44	63	107	95
Messier, Mark	NY Rangers	79	35	72	107	76
Roenick, Jeremy	Chicago	80	53	50	103	23
Yzerman, Steve	Detroit	79	45	58	103	64
Leetch, Brian	NY Rangers	80	22	80	102	26
Oates, Adam	St.L., Bos.	80	20	79	99	22

1992-93
CLARENCE CAMPBELL CONFERENCE
Norris Division

Team	GP	W	L	T	GF	GA	PTS
Chicago	84	47	25	12	279	230	106
Detroit	84	47	28	9	369	280	103
Toronto	84	44	29	11	288	241	99
St. Louis	84	37	36	11	282	278	85
Minnesota	84	36	38	10	272	293	82
Tampa Bay	84	23	54	7	245	332	53

Smythe Division

Team	GP	W	L	T	GF	GA	PTS
Vancouver	84	46	29	9	346	278	101
Calgary	84	43	30	11	322	282	97
Los Angeles	84	39	35	10	338	340	88
Winnipeg	84	40	37	7	322	320	87
Edmonton	84	26	50	8	242	337	60
San Jose	84	11	71	2	218	414	24

PRINCE OF WALES CONFERENCE
Adams Division

Team	GP	W	L	T	GF	GA	PTS
Boston	84	51	26	7	332	268	109
Quebec	84	47	27	10	351	300	104
*Montreal	84	48	30	6	326	280	102
Buffalo	84	38	36	10	335	297	86
Hartford	84	26	52	6	284	369	58
Ottawa	84	10	70	4	202	395	24

Patrick Division

Team	GP	W	L	T	GF	GA	PTS
Pittsburgh	84	56	21	7	367	268	119
Washington	84	43	34	7	325	286	93
NY Islanders	84	40	37	7	335	297	87
New Jersey	84	40	37	7	308	299	87
Philadelphia	84	36	37	11	319	319	83
NY Rangers	84	34	39	11	304	308	79

Leading Scorers

Player	Club	GP	G	A	PTS	PIM
Lemieux, Mario	Pittsburgh	60	69	91	160	38
LaFontaine, Pat	Buffalo	84	53	95	148	63
Oates, Adam	Boston	84	45	97	142	32
Yzerman, Steve	Detroit	84	58	79	137	44
Selanne, Teemu	Winnipeg	84	76	56	132	45
Turgeon, Pierre	NY Islanders	83	58	74	132	26
Mogilny, Alexander	Buffalo	77	76	51	127	40
Gilmour, Doug	Toronto	83	32	95	127	100
Robitaille, Luc	Los Angeles	84	63	62	125	100
Recchi, Mark	Philadelphia	84	53	70	123	95

1993-94
EASTERN CONFERENCE
Northeast Division

Team	GP	W	L	T	GF	GA	PTS
Pittsburgh	84	44	27	13	299	285	101
Boston	84	42	29	13	289	252	97
Montreal	84	41	29	14	283	248	96
Buffalo	84	43	32	9	282	218	95
Quebec	84	34	42	8	277	292	76
Hartford	84	27	48	9	227	288	63
Ottawa	84	14	61	9	201	397	37

Atlantic Division

Team	GP	W	L	T	GF	GA	PTS
*NY Rangers	84	52	24	8	299	231	112
New Jersey	84	47	25	12	306	220	106
Washington	84	39	35	10	277	263	88
NY Islanders	84	36	36	12	282	264	84
Florida	84	33	34	17	233	233	83
Philadelphia	84	35	39	10	294	314	80
Tampa Bay	84	30	43	11	224	251	71

WESTERN CONFERENCE
Central Division

Team	GP	W	L	T	GF	GA	PTS
Detroit	84	46	30	8	356	275	100
Toronto	84	43	29	12	280	243	98
Dallas	84	42	29	13	286	265	97
St. Louis	84	40	33	11	270	283	91
Chicago	84	39	36	9	254	240	87
Winnipeg	84	24	51	9	245	344	57

Pacific Division

Team	GP	W	L	T	GF	GA	PTS
Calgary	84	42	29	13	302	256	97
Vancouver	84	41	40	3	279	276	85
San Jose	84	33	35	16	252	265	82
Anaheim	84	33	46	5	229	251	71
Los Angeles	84	27	45	12	294	322	66
Edmonton	84	25	45	14	261	305	64

Leading Scorers

Player	Club	GP	G	A	PTS	PIM
Gretzky, Wayne	Los Angeles	81	38	92	130	20
Fedorov, Sergei	Detroit	82	56	64	120	34
Oates, Adam	Boston	77	32	80	112	45
Gilmour, Doug	Toronto	83	27	84	111	105
Bure, Pavel	Vancouver	76	60	47	107	86
Roenick, Jeremy	Chicago	84	46	61	107	125
Recchi, Mark	Philadelphia	84	40	67	107	46
Shanahan, Brendan	St. Louis	81	52	50	102	211
Andreychuk, Dave	Toronto	83	53	46	99	98
Jagr, Jaromir	Pittsburgh	80	32	67	99	61

Brett Hull had at least 70 goals for three straight seasons from 1989-90 to 1991-92, including an 86-goal performance in 1990-91. He enters the 2003-04 season with a chance to move into third all-time in NHL goal scoring.

1994-95

EASTERN CONFERENCE
Northeast Division

Team	GP	W	L	T	GF	GA	PTS
Quebec	48	30	13	5	185	134	65
Pittsburgh	48	29	16	3	181	158	61
Boston	48	27	18	3	150	127	57
Buffalo	48	22	19	7	130	119	51
Hartford	48	19	24	5	127	141	43
Montreal	48	18	23	7	125	148	43
Ottawa	48	9	34	5	117	174	23

Atlantic Division

Team	GP	W	L	T	GF	GA	PTS
Philadelphia	48	28	16	4	150	132	60
*New Jersey	48	22	18	8	136	121	52
Washington	48	22	18	8	136	120	52
NY Rangers	48	22	23	3	139	134	47
Florida	48	20	22	6	115	127	46
Tampa Bay	48	17	28	3	120	144	37
NY Islanders	48	15	28	5	126	158	35

WESTERN CONFERENCE
Central Division

Team	GP	W	L	T	GF	GA	PTS
Detroit	48	33	11	4	180	117	70
St. Louis	48	28	15	5	178	135	61
Chicago	48	24	19	5	156	115	53
Toronto	48	21	19	8	135	146	50
Dallas	48	17	23	8	136	135	42
Winnipeg	48	16	25	7	157	177	39

Pacific Division

Team	GP	W	L	T	GF	GA	PTS
Calgary	48	24	17	7	163	135	55
Vancouver	48	18	18	12	153	148	48
San Jose	48	19	25	4	129	161	42
Los Angeles	48	16	23	9	142	174	41
Edmonton	48	17	27	4	136	183	38
Anaheim	48	16	27	5	125	164	37

Leading Scorers

Player	Club	GP	G	A	PTS	PIM
Jagr, Jaromir	Pittsburgh	48	32	38	70	37
Lindros, Eric	Philadelphia	46	29	41	70	60
Zhamnov, Alexei	Winnipeg	48	30	35	65	20
Sakic, Joe	Quebec	47	19	43	62	30
Francis, Ron	Pittsburgh	44	11	48	59	18
Fleury, Theoren	Calgary	47	29	29	58	112
Coffey, Paul	Detroit	45	14	44	58	72
Renberg, Mikael	Philadelphia	47	26	31	57	20
LeClair, John	Mtl., Phi.	46	26	28	54	30
Messier, Mark	NY Rangers	46	14	39	53	40
Oates, Adam	Boston	48	12	41	53	8

1995-96

EASTERN CONFERENCE
Northeast Division

Team	GP	W	L	T	GF	GA	PTS
Pittsburgh	82	49	29	4	362	284	102
Boston	82	40	31	11	282	269	91
Montreal	82	40	32	10	265	248	90
Hartford	82	34	39	9	237	259	77
Buffalo	82	33	42	7	247	262	73
Ottawa	82	18	59	5	191	291	41

Atlantic Division

Team	GP	W	L	T	GF	GA	PTS
Philadelphia	82	45	24	13	282	208	103
NY Rangers	82	41	27	14	272	237	96
Florida	82	41	31	10	254	234	92
Washington	82	39	32	11	234	204	89
Tampa Bay	82	38	32	12	238	248	88
New Jersey	82	37	33	12	215	202	86
NY Islanders	82	22	50	10	229	315	54

WESTERN CONFERENCE
Central Division

Team	GP	W	L	T	GF	GA	PTS
Detroit	82	62	13	7	325	181	131
Chicago	82	40	28	14	273	220	94
Toronto	82	34	36	12	247	252	80
St. Louis	82	32	34	16	219	248	80
Winnipeg	82	36	40	6	275	291	78
Dallas	82	26	42	14	227	280	66

Pacific Division

Team	GP	W	L	T	GF	GA	PTS
*Colorado	82	47	25	10	326	240	104
Calgary	82	34	37	11	241	240	79
Vancouver	82	32	35	15	278	278	79
Anaheim	82	35	39	8	234	247	78
Edmonton	82	30	44	8	240	304	68
Los Angeles	82	24	40	18	256	302	66
San Jose	82	20	55	7	252	357	47

Leading Scorers

Player	Club	GP	G	A	PTS	PIM
Lemieux, Mario	Pittsburgh	70	69	92	161	54
Jagr, Jaromir	Pittsburgh	82	62	87	149	96
Sakic, Joe	Colorado	82	51	69	120	44
Francis, Ron	Pittsburgh	77	27	92	119	56
Forsberg, Peter	Colorado	82	30	86	116	47
Lindros, Eric	Philadelphia	73	47	68	115	163
Kariya, Paul	Anaheim	82	50	58	108	20
Selanne, Teemu	Wpg., Ana.	79	40	68	108	22
Mogilny, Alexander	Vancouver	79	55	52	107	16
Fedorov, Sergei	Detroit	78	39	68	107	48

1996-97

EASTERN CONFERENCE
Northeast Division

Team	GP	W	L	T	GF	GA	PTS
Buffalo	82	40	30	12	237	208	92
Pittsburgh	82	38	36	8	285	280	84
Ottawa	82	31	36	15	226	234	77
Montreal	82	31	36	15	249	276	77
Hartford	82	32	39	11	226	256	75
Boston	82	26	47	9	234	300	61

Atlantic Division

Team	GP	W	L	T	GF	GA	PTS
New Jersey	82	45	23	14	231	182	104
Philadelphia	82	45	24	13	274	217	103
Florida	82	35	28	19	221	201	89
NY Rangers	82	38	34	10	258	231	86
Washington	82	33	40	9	214	231	75
Tampa Bay	82	32	40	10	217	247	74
NY Islanders	82	29	41	12	240	250	70

WESTERN CONFERENCE
Central Division

Team	GP	W	L	T	GF	GA	PTS
Dallas	82	48	26	8	252	198	104
*Detroit	82	38	26	18	253	197	94
Phoenix	82	38	37	7	240	243	83
St. Louis	82	36	35	11	236	239	83
Chicago	82	34	35	13	223	210	81
Toronto	82	30	44	8	230	273	68

Pacific Division

Team	GP	W	L	T	GF	GA	PTS
Colorado	82	49	24	9	277	205	107
Anaheim	82	36	33	13	245	233	85
Edmonton	82	36	37	9	252	247	81
Vancouver	82	35	40	7	257	273	77
Calgary	82	32	41	9	214	239	73
Los Angeles	82	28	43	11	214	268	67
San Jose	82	27	47	8	211	278	62

Leading Scorers

Player	Club	GP	G	A	PTS	PIM
Lemieux, Mario	Pittsburgh	76	50	72	122	65
Selanne, Teemu	Anaheim	78	51	58	109	34
Kariya, Paul	Anaheim	69	44	55	99	6
LeClair, John	Philadelphia	82	50	47	97	58
Gretzky, Wayne	NY Rangers	82	25	72	97	28
Jagr, Jaromir	Pittsburgh	63	47	48	95	40
Sundin, Mats	Toronto	82	41	53	94	59
Palffy, Ziggy	NY Islanders	80	48	42	90	43
Francis, Ron	Pittsburgh	81	27	63	90	20
Shanahan, Brendan	Hfd., Det.	81	47	41	88	131

Wayne Gretzky won the Art Ross Trophy for the tenth and final time in 1993-94.

Ziggy Palfy made his first appearance among the NHL's top 10 scorers in 1996-97.

Paul Kariya was a top-10 scorer four times in his nine seasons with the Mighty Ducks.

1997-98
EASTERN CONFERENCE
Northeast Division

Team	GP	W	L	T	GF	GA	PTS
Pittsburgh	82	40	24	18	228	188	98
Boston	82	39	30	13	221	194	91
Buffalo	82	36	29	17	211	187	89
Montreal	82	37	32	13	235	208	87
Ottawa	82	34	33	15	193	200	83
Carolina	82	33	41	8	200	219	74

Atlantic Division

Team	GP	W	L	T	GF	GA	PTS
New Jersey	82	48	23	11	225	166	107
Philadelphia	82	42	29	11	242	193	95
Washington	82	40	30	12	219	202	92
NY Islanders	82	30	41	11	212	225	71
NY Rangers	82	25	39	18	197	231	68
Florida	82	24	43	15	203	256	63
Tampa Bay	82	17	55	10	151	269	44

WESTERN CONFERENCE
Central Division

Team	GP	W	L	T	GF	GA	PTS
Dallas	82	49	22	11	242	167	109
*Detroit	82	44	23	15	250	196	103
St. Louis	82	45	29	8	256	204	98
Phoenix	82	35	35	12	224	227	82
Chicago	82	30	39	13	192	199	73
Toronto	82	30	43	9	194	237	69

Pacific Division

Team	GP	W	L	T	GF	GA	PTS
Colorado	82	39	26	17	231	205	95
Los Angeles	82	38	33	11	227	225	87
Edmonton	82	35	37	10	215	224	80
San Jose	82	34	38	10	210	216	78
Calgary	82	26	41	15	217	252	67
Anaheim	82	26	43	13	205	261	65
Vancouver	82	25	43	14	224	273	64

Leading Scorers

Player	Club	GP	G	A	PTS	PIM
Jagr, Jaromir	Pittsburgh	77	35	67	102	64
Forsberg, Peter	Colorado	72	25	66	91	94
Bure, Pavel	Vancouver	82	51	39	90	48
Gretzky, Wayne	NY Rangers	82	23	67	90	28
LeClair, John	Philadelphia	82	51	36	87	32
Palffy, Ziggy	NY Islanders	82	45	42	87	34
Francis, Ron	Pittsburgh	81	25	62	87	20
Selanne, Teemu	Anaheim	73	52	34	86	30
Allison, Jason	Boston	81	33	50	83	60
Stumpel, Jozef	Los Angeles	77	21	58	79	53

1998-99
EASTERN CONFERENCE
Northeast Division

Team	GP	W	L	T	GF	GA	PTS
Ottawa	82	44	23	15	239	179	103
Toronto	82	45	30	7	268	231	97
Boston	82	39	30	13	214	181	91
Buffalo	82	37	28	17	207	175	91
Montreal	82	32	39	11	184	209	75

Atlantic Division

Team	GP	W	L	T	GF	GA	PTS
New Jersey	82	47	24	11	248	196	105
Philadelphia	82	37	26	19	231	196	93
Pittsburgh	82	38	30	14	242	225	90
NY Rangers	82	33	38	11	217	227	77
NY Islanders	82	24	48	10	194	244	58

Southeast Division

Team	GP	W	L	T	GF	GA	PTS
Carolina	82	34	30	18	210	202	86
Florida	82	30	34	18	210	228	78
Washington	82	31	45	6	200	218	68
Tampa Bay	82	19	54	9	179	292	47

WESTERN CONFERENCE
Central Division

Team	GP	W	L	T	GF	GA	PTS
Detroit	82	43	32	7	245	202	93
St Louis	82	37	32	13	237	209	87
Chicago	82	29	41	12	202	248	70
Nashville	82	28	47	7	190	261	63

Pacific Division

Team	GP	W	L	T	GF	GA	PTS
*Dallas	82	51	19	12	236	168	114
Phoenix	82	39	31	12	205	197	90
Anaheim	82	35	34	13	215	206	83
San Jose	82	31	33	18	196	191	80
Los Angeles	82	32	45	5	189	222	69

Northwest Division

Team	GP	W	L	T	GF	GA	PTS
Colorado	82	44	28	10	239	205	98
Edmonton	82	33	37	12	230	226	78
Calgary	82	30	40	12	211	234	72
Vancouver	82	23	47	12	192	258	58

Leading Scorers

Player	Club	GP	G	A	PTS	PIM
Jagr, Jaromir	Pittsburgh	81	44	83	127	66
Selanne, Teemu	Anaheim	75	47	60	107	30
Kariya, Paul	Anaheim	82	39	62	101	40
Forsberg, Peter	Colorado	78	30	67	97	108
Sakic, Joe	Colorado	73	41	55	96	29
Yashin, Alexei	Ottawa	82	44	50	94	54
Lindros, Eric	Philadelphia	71	40	53	93	120
Fleury, Theoren	Cgy., Col.	75	40	53	93	86
LeClair, John	Philadelphia	76	43	47	90	30
Demitra, Pavol	St Louis	82	37	52	89	16

1999-2000
EASTERN CONFERENCE
Northeast Division

Team	GP	W	L	T	OTL	GF	GA	PTS
Toronto	82	45	27	7	3	246	222	100
Ottawa	82	41	28	11	2	244	210	95
Buffalo	82	35	32	11	4	213	204	85
Montreal	82	35	34	9	4	196	194	83
Boston	82	24	33	19	6	210	248	73

Atlantic Division

Team	GP	W	L	T	OTL	GF	GA	PTS
Philadelphia	82	45	22	12	3	237	179	105
*New Jersey	82	45	24	8	5	251	203	103
Pittsburgh	82	37	31	8	6	241	236	88
NY Rangers	82	29	38	12	3	218	246	73
NY Islanders	82	24	48	9	1	194	275	58

Southeast Division

Team	GP	W	L	T	OTL	GF	GA	PTS
Washington	82	44	24	12	2	227	194	102
Florida	82	43	27	6	6	244	209	98
Carolina	82	37	35	10	0	217	216	84
Tampa Bay	82	19	47	9	7	204	310	54
Atlanta	82	14	57	7	4	170	313	39

WESTERN CONFERENCE
Central Division

Team	GP	W	L	T	OTL	GF	GA	PTS
St. Louis	82	51	19	11	1	248	165	114
Detroit	82	48	22	10	2	278	210	108
Chicago	82	33	37	10	2	242	245	78
Nashville	82	28	40	7	7	199	240	70

Pacific Division

Team	GP	W	L	T	OTL	GF	GA	PTS
Dallas	82	43	23	10	6	211	184	102
Los Angeles	82	39	27	12	4	245	228	94
Phoenix	82	39	31	8	4	232	228	90
San Jose	82	35	30	10	7	225	214	87
Anaheim	82	34	33	12	3	217	227	83

Northwest Division

Team	GP	W	L	T	OTL	GF	GA	PTS
Colorado	82	42	28	11	1	233	201	96
Edmonton	82	32	26	16	8	226	212	88
Vancouver	82	30	29	15	8	227	237	83
Calgary	82	31	36	10	5	211	256	77

Leading Scorers

Player	Club	GP	G	A	PTS	PIM
Jagr, Jaromir	Pittsburgh	63	42	54	96	50
Bure, Pavel	Florida	74	58	36	94	16
Recchi, Mark	Philadelphia	82	28	63	91	50
Kariya, Paul	Anaheim	74	42	44	86	24
Selanne, Teemu	Anaheim	79	33	52	85	12
Nolan, Owen	San Jose	78	44	40	84	110
Amonte, Tony	Chicago	82	43	41	84	48
Modano, Mike	Dallas	77	38	43	81	48
Sakic, Joe	Colorado	60	28	53	81	28
Yzerman, Steve	Detroit	78	35	44	79	34

Mike Modano cracked the top 10 in scoring for the second straight season in 2002-03. His 57 assists last season were the most he's had since reaching 60 back in 1992-93.

The NHL's scoring leader in 2001-02, Jarome Iginla battled injuries during the 2002-03 campaign but still ranked among the league's top snipers with 35 goals.

2000-2001

EASTERN CONFERENCE
Northeast Division

Team	GP	W	L	T	OTL	GF	GA	PTS
Ottawa	82	48	21	9	4	274	205	109
Buffalo	82	46	30	5	1	218	184	98
Toronto	82	37	29	11	5	232	207	90
Boston	82	36	30	8	8	227	249	88
Montreal	82	28	40	8	6	206	232	70

Atlantic Division

Team	GP	W	L	T	OTL	GF	GA	PTS
New Jersey	82	48	19	12	3	295	195	111
Philadelphia	82	43	25	11	3	240	207	100
Pittsburgh	82	42	28	9	3	281	256	96
NY Rangers	82	33	43	5	1	250	290	72
NY Islanders	82	21	51	7	3	185	268	52

Southeast Division

Team	GP	W	L	T	OTL	GF	GA	PTS
Washington	82	41	27	10	4	233	211	96
Carolina	82	38	32	9	3	212	225	88
Florida	82	22	38	13	9	200	246	66
Atlanta	82	23	45	12	2	211	289	60
Tampa Bay	82	24	47	6	5	201	280	59

WESTERN CONFERENCE
Central Division

Team	GP	W	L	T	OTL	GF	GA	PTS
Detroit	82	49	20	9	4	253	202	111
St. Louis	82	43	22	12	5	249	195	103
Nashville	82	34	36	9	3	186	200	80
Chicago	82	29	40	8	5	210	246	71
Columbus	82	28	39	9	6	190	233	71

Pacific Division

Team	GP	W	L	T	OTL	GF	GA	PTS
Dallas	82	48	24	8	2	241	187	106
San Jose	82	40	27	12	3	217	192	95
Los Angeles	82	38	28	13	3	252	228	92
Phoenix	82	35	27	17	3	214	212	90
Anaheim	82	25	41	11	5	188	245	66

Northwest Division

Team	GP	W	L	T	OTL	GF	GA	PTS
*Colorado	82	52	16	10	4	270	192	118
Edmonton	82	39	28	12	3	243	222	93
Vancouver	82	36	28	11	7	239	238	90
Calgary	82	27	36	15	4	197	236	73
Minnesota	82	25	39	13	5	168	210	68

Leading Scorers

Player	Club	GP	G	A	PTS	PIM
Jagr, Jaromir	Pittsburgh	81	52	69	121	42
Sakic, Joe	Colorado	82	54	64	118	30
Elias, Patrik	New Jersey	82	40	56	96	51
Kovalev, Alexei	Pittsburgh	79	44	51	95	96
Allison, Jason	Boston	82	36	59	95	85
Straka, Martin	Pittsburgh	82	27	68	95	38
Bure, Pavel	Florida	82	59	33	92	58
Weight, Doug	Edmonton	82	25	65	90	91
Palffy, Ziggy	Los Angeles	73	38	51	89	20
Forsberg, Peter	Colorado	73	27	62	89	54

2001-2002

EASTERN CONFERENCE
Northeast Division

Team	GP	W	L	T	OTL	GF	GA	PTS
Boston	82	43	24	6	9	236	201	101
Toronto	82	43	25	10	4	249	207	100
Ottawa	82	39	27	9	7	243	208	94
Montreal	82	36	31	12	3	207	209	87
Buffalo	82	35	35	11	1	213	200	82

Atlantic Division

Team	GP	W	L	T	OTL	GF	GA	PTS
Philadelphia	82	42	27	10	3	234	192	97
NY Islanders	82	42	28	8	4	239	220	96
New Jersey	82	41	28	9	4	205	187	95
NY Rangers	82	36	38	4	4	227	258	80
Pittsburgh	82	28	41	8	5	198	249	69

Southeast Division

Team	GP	W	L	T	OTL	GF	GA	PTS
Carolina	82	35	26	16	5	217	217	91
Washington	82	36	33	11	2	228	240	85
Tampa Bay	82	27	40	11	4	178	219	69
Florida	82	22	44	10	6	180	250	60
Atlanta	82	19	47	11	5	187	288	54

WESTERN CONFERENCE
Central Division

Team	GP	W	L	T	OTL	GF	GA	PTS
*Detroit	82	51	17	10	4	251	187	116
St. Louis	82	43	27	8	4	227	188	98
Chicago	82	41	27	13	1	216	207	96
Nashville	82	28	41	13	0	196	230	69
Columbus	82	22	47	8	5	164	255	57

Pacific Division

Team	GP	W	L	T	OTL	GF	GA	PTS
San Jose	82	44	27	8	3	248	199	99
Phoenix	82	40	27	9	6	228	210	95
Los Angeles	82	40	27	11	4	214	190	95
Dallas	82	36	28	13	5	215	213	90
Anaheim	82	29	42	8	3	175	198	69

Northwest Division

Team	GP	W	L	T	OTL	GF	GA	PTS
Colorado	82	45	28	8	1	212	169	99
Vancouver	82	42	30	7	3	254	211	94
Edmonton	82	38	28	12	4	205	182	92
Calgary	82	32	35	12	3	201	220	79
Minnesota	82	26	35	12	9	195	238	73

Leading Scorers

Player	Club	GP	G	A	PTS	PIM
Iginla, Jarome	Calgary	82	52	44	96	77
Naslund, Markus	Vancouver	81	40	50	90	50
Bertuzzi, Todd	Vancouver	72	36	49	85	110
Sundin, Mats	Toronto	82	41	39	80	94
Jagr, Jaromir	Washington	69	31	48	79	30
Sakic, Joe	Colorado	82	26	53	79	18
Demitra, Pavol	St. Louis	82	35	43	78	46
Oates, Adam	Wsh., Phi.	80	14	64	78	28
Modano, Mike	Dallas	78	34	43	77	38
Francis, Ron	Carolina	80	27	50	77	18

2002-2003

EASTERN CONFERENCE
Northeast Division

Team	GP	W	L	T	OTL	GF	GA	PTS
Ottawa	82	52	21	8	1	263	182	113
Toronto	82	44	28	7	3	236	208	98
Boston	82	36	31	11	4	245	237	87
Montreal	82	30	35	8	9	206	234	77
Buffalo	82	27	37	10	8	190	219	72

Atlantic Division

Team	GP	W	L	T	OTL	GF	GA	PTS
*New Jersey	82	46	20	10	6	216	166	108
Philadelphia	82	45	20	13	4	211	166	107
NY Islanders	82	35	34	11	2	224	231	83
NY Rangers	82	32	36	10	4	210	231	78
Pittsburgh	82	27	44	6	5	189	255	65

Southeast Division

Team	GP	W	L	T	OTL	GF	GA	PTS
Tampa Bay	82	36	25	16	5	219	210	93
Washington	82	39	29	8	6	224	220	92
Atlanta	82	31	39	7	5	226	284	74
Florida	82	24	36	13	9	176	237	70
Carolina	82	22	43	11	6	171	240	61

WESTERN CONFERENCE
Central Division

Team	GP	W	L	T	OTL	GF	GA	PTS
Detroit	82	48	20	10	4	269	203	110
St. Louis	82	41	24	11	6	253	222	99
Chicago	82	30	33	13	6	207	226	79
Nashville	82	27	35	13	7	183	206	74
Columbus	82	29	42	8	3	213	263	69

Pacific Division

Team	GP	W	L	T	OTL	GF	GA	PTS
Dallas	82	46	17	15	4	245	169	111
Anaheim	82	40	27	9	6	203	193	95
Los Angeles	82	33	37	6	6	203	221	78
Phoenix	82	31	35	11	5	204	230	78
San Jose	82	28	37	9	8	214	239	73

Northwest Division

Team	GP	W	L	T	OTL	GF	GA	PTS
Colorado	82	42	19	13	8	251	194	105
Vancouver	82	45	23	13	1	264	208	104
Minnesota	82	42	29	10	1	198	178	95
Edmonton	82	36	26	11	9	231	230	92
Calgary	82	29	36	13	4	186	228	75

Leading Scorers

Player	Club	GP	G	A	PTS	PIM
Forsberg, Peter	Colorado	75	29	77	106	70
Naslund, Markus	Vancouver	82	48	56	104	52
Thornton, Joe	Boston	77	36	65	101	109
Hejduk, Milan	Colorado	82	50	48	98	52
Bertuzzi, Todd	Vancouver	82	46	51	97	144
Demitra, Pavol	St. Louis	78	36	57	93	32
Murray, Glen	Boston	82	44	48	92	64
Lemieux, Mario	Pittsburgh	67	28	63	92	43
Heatley, Dany	Atlanta	77	41	48	89	58
Palffy, Ziggy	Los Angeles	76	37	48	85	47
Modano, Mike	Dallas	79	28	57	85	30

Note: Detailed statistics for 2002-2003 are listed in the Final Statistics, 2002-2003 section of the *NHL Guide & Record Book*. **See page 133.**

The first pick in the 1997 Entry Draft, Joe Thornton was named captain of the Bruins in 2002-03. His 101 points last season marked a 30-point improvement over his previous career high and placed him third in the NHL.

Team Records

Regular Season

FINAL STANDINGS

MOST POINTS, ONE SEASON:
- **132 – Montreal Canadiens**, 1976-77. 60w-8L-12T. 80GP
- 131 – Detroit Red Wings, 1995-96. 62w-13L-7T. 82GP
- 129 – Montreal Canadiens, 1977-78. 59w-10L-11T. 80GP

BEST POINTS PERCENTAGE, ONE SEASON:
- **.875 – Boston Bruins**, 1929-30. 38w-5L-1T. 77PTS in 44GP
- .830 – Montreal Canadiens, 1943-44. 38w-5L-7T. 83PTS in 50GP
- .825 – Montreal Canadiens, 1976-77. 60w-8L-12T. 132PTS in 80GP
- .806 – Montreal Canadiens, 1977-78. 59w-10L-11T. 129PTS in 80GP
- .800 – Montreal Canadiens, 1944-45. 38w-8L-4T. 80PTS in 50GP

FEWEST POINTS, ONE SEASON:
- **8 – Quebec Bulldogs**, 1919-20. 4w-20L-0T. 24GP
- 10 – Toronto Arenas, 1918-19. 5w-13L-0T. 18GP
- 12 – Hamilton Tigers, 1920-21. 6w-18L-0T. 24GP
- – Hamilton Tigers, 1922-23. 6w-18L-0T. 24GP
- – Boston Bruins, 1924-25. 6w-24L-0T. 30GP
- – Philadelphia Quakers, 1930-31. 4w-36L-4T. 44GP

FEWEST POINTS, ONE SEASON (MINIMUM 70-GAME SCHEDULE):
- **21 – Washington Capitals**, 1974-75. 8w-67L-5T. 80GP
- 24 – Ottawa Senators, 1992-93. 10w-70L-4T. 84GP
- – San Jose Sharks, 1992-93. 11w-71L-2T. 84GP
- 30 – NY Islanders, 1972-73. 12w-60L-6T. 78GP

WORST POINTS PERCENTAGE, ONE SEASON:
- **.131 – Washington Capitals**, 1974-75. 8w-67L-5T. 21PTS in 80GP
- .136 – Philadelphia Quakers, 1930-31. 4w-36L-4T. 12PTS in 44GP
- .143 – Ottawa Senators, 1992-93. 10w-70L-4T. 24PTS in 84GP
- .143 – San Jose Sharks, 1992-93. 11w-71L-2T. 24PTS in 84GP
- .148 – Pittsburgh Pirates, 1929-30. 5w-36L-3T. 13PTS in 44GP

TEAM WINS

Most Wins

MOST WINS, ONE SEASON:
- **62 – Detroit Red Wings**. 1995-96. 82GP
- 60 – Montreal Canadiens, 1976-77. 80GP
- 59 – Montreal Canadiens, 1977-78. 80GP

MOST HOME WINS, ONE SEASON:
- **36 – Philadelphia Flyers**, 1975-76. 40GP
- – **Detroit Red Wings**, 1995-96. 41GP
- 33 – Boston Bruins, 1970-71. 39GP
- – Boston Bruins, 1973-74. 39GP
- – Montreal Canadiens, 1976-77. 40GP
- – Philadelphia Flyers, 1976-77. 40GP
- – NY Islanders, 1981-82. 40GP
- – Philadelphia Flyers, 1985-86. 40GP

MOST ROAD WINS, ONE SEASON:
- **28 – New Jersey Devils**, 1998-99. 41GP
- 27 – Montreal Canadiens, 1976-77. 40GP
- – Montreal Canadiens, 1977-78. 40GP
- – St. Louis Blues, 1999-2000. 41GP
- 26 – Boston Bruins, 1971-72. 39GP
- – Montreal Canadiens, 1975-76. 40GP
- – Edmonton Oilers, 1983-84. 40GP
- – Detroit Red Wings, 1995-96. 41GP

Fewest Wins

FEWEST WINS, ONE SEASON:
- **4 – Quebec Bulldogs**, 1919-20. 24GP
- – **Philadelphia Quakers**, 1930-31. 44GP
- 5 – Toronto Arenas, 1918-19. 18GP
- Pittsburgh Pirates, 1929-30. 44GP

FEWEST WINS, ONE SEASON (MINIMUM 70-GAME SCHEDULE):
- **8 – Washington Capitals**, 1974-75. 80GP
- 9 – Winnipeg Jets, 1980-81. 80GP
- 10 – Ottawa Senators, 1992-93. 84GP

FEWEST HOME WINS, ONE SEASON:
- **2 – Chicago Blackhawks**, 1927-28. 22GP
- 3 – Boston Bruins, 1924-25. 15GP
- – Chicago Blackhawks, 1928-29. 22GP
- – Philadelphia Quakers, 1930-31. 22GP

FEWEST HOME WINS, ONE SEASON (MINIMUM 70-GAME SCHEDULE):
- **6 – Chicago Blackhawks**, 1954-55. 35GP
- – **Washington Capitals**, 1975-76. 40GP
- 7 – Boston Bruins, 1962-63. 35GP
- – Washington Capitals, 1974-75. 40GP
- – Winnipeg Jets, 1980-81. 40GP
- – Pittsburgh Penguins, 1983-84. 40GP

FEWEST ROAD WINS, ONE SEASON:
- **0 – Toronto Arenas**, 1918-19. 9GP
- – **Quebec Bulldogs**, 1919-20. 12GP
- – **Pittsburgh Pirates**, 1929-30. 22GP
- 1 – Hamilton Tigers, 1921-22. 12GP
- – Toronto St. Patricks, 1925-26. 18GP
- – Philadelphia Quakers, 1930-31. 22GP
- – NY Americans, 1940-41. 24GP
- – Washington Capitals, 1974-75. 40GP
- * – Ottawa Senators, 1992-93. 41GP

FEWEST ROAD WINS, ONE SEASON (MINIMUM 70-GAME SCHEDULE):
- **1 – Washington Capitals**, 1974-75. 40GP
- * – **Ottawa Senators**, 1992-93. 41GP
- 2 – Boston Bruins, 1960-61. 35GP
- – Los Angeles Kings, 1969-70. 38GP
- – NY Islanders, 1972-73. 39GP
- – California Golden Seals, 1973-74. 39GP
- – Colorado Rockies, 1977-78. 40GP
- – Winnipeg Jets, 1980-81. 40GP
- – Quebec Nordiques, 1991-92. 40GP

TEAM LOSSES

Fewest Losses

FEWEST LOSSES, ONE SEASON:
- **5 – Ottawa Senators**, 1919-20. 24GP
- – **Boston Bruins**, 1929-30. 44GP
- – **Montreal Canadiens**, 1943-44. 50GP

FEWEST HOME LOSSES, ONE SEASON:
- **0 – Ottawa Senators**, 1922-23. 12GP
- – **Montreal Canadiens**, 1943-44. 25GP
- 1 – Toronto Arenas, 1917-18. 11GP
- – Ottawa Senators, 1918-19. 9GP
- – Ottawa Senators, 1919-20. 12GP
- – Toronto St. Patricks, 1922-23. 12GP
- – Boston Bruins, 1929-30. 22GP
- – Boston Bruins, 1930-31. 22GP
- – Montreal Canadiens, 1976-77. 40GP
- – Quebec Nordiques, 1994-95. 24GP

FEWEST ROAD LOSSES, ONE SEASON:
- **3 – Montreal Canadiens**, 1928-29. 22GP
- 4 – Ottawa Senators, 1919-20. 12GP
- – Montreal Canadiens, 1927-28. 22GP
- – Boston Bruins, 1929-30. 20GP
- – Boston Bruins, 1940-41. 24GP

FEWEST LOSSES, ONE SEASON (MINIMUM 70-GAME SCHEDULE):
- **8 – Montreal Canadiens**, 1976-77. 80GP
- 10 – Montreal Canadiens, 1972-73. 78GP
- – Montreal Canadiens, 1977-78. 80GP
- 11 – Montreal Canadiens, 1975-76. 80GP

FEWEST HOME LOSSES, ONE SEASON (MINIMUM 70-GAME SCHEDULE):
- **1 – Montreal Canadiens**, 1976-77. 40GP
- 2 – Montreal Canadiens, 1961-62. 35GP
- – NY Rangers, 1970-71. 39GP
- – Philadelphia Flyers, 1975-76. 40GP

FEWEST ROAD LOSSES, ONE SEASON (MINIMUM 70-GAME SCHEDULE):
- **6 – Montreal Canadiens**, 1972-73. 39GP
- – **Montreal Canadiens**, 1974-75. 40GP
- – **Montreal Canadiens**, 1977-78. 40GP
- 7 – Detroit Red Wings, 1951-52. 35GP
- – Montreal Canadiens, 1976-77. 40GP
- – Philadelphia Flyers, 1979-80. 40GP

Most Losses

MOST LOSSES, ONE SEASON:
- **71 – San Jose Sharks**, 1992-93. 84GP
- 70 – Ottawa Senators, 1992-93. 84GP
- 67 – Washington Capitals, 1974-75. 80GP
- 61 – Quebec Nordiques, 1989-90. 80GP
- – Ottawa Senators, 1993-94. 84GP

MOST HOME LOSSES, ONE SEASON:
- ***32 – San Jose Sharks**, 1992-93. 41GP
- 29 – Pittsburgh Penguins, 1983-84. 40GP
- * – Ottawa Senators, 1993-94. 41GP

MOST ROAD LOSSES, ONE SEASON:
- ***40 – Ottawa Senators**, 1992-93. 41GP
- 39 – Washington Capitals, 1974-75. 40GP
- 37 – California Golden Seals, 1973-74. 39GP
- * – San Jose Sharks, 1992-93. 41GP

* – Does not include neutral site games

TEAM TIES

Most Ties

MOST TIES, ONE SEASON:
24 – Philadelphia Flyers, 1969-70. 76GP
23 – Montreal Canadiens, 1962-63. 70GP
– Chicago Blackhawks, 1973-74. 78GP

MOST HOME TIES, ONE SEASON:
13 – NY Rangers, 1954-55. 35GP
– **Philadelphia Flyers**, 1969-70. 38GP
– **California Golden Seals**, 1971-72. 39GP
– **California Golden Seals**, 1972-73. 39GP
– **Chicago Blackhawks**, 1973-74. 39GP

MOST ROAD TIES, ONE SEASON:
15 – Philadelphia Flyers, 1976-77. 40GP
14 – Montreal Canadiens, 1952-53. 35GP
– Montreal Canadiens, 1974-75. 40GP
– Philadelphia Flyers, 1975-76. 40GP

Fewest Ties

FEWEST TIES, ONE SEASON (Since 1926-27):
1 – Boston Bruins, 1929-30. 44GP
2 – Montreal Canadiens, 1926-27. 44GP
– NY Americans, 1926-27. 44GP
– Boston Bruins, 1938-39. 48GP
– NY Rangers, 1941-42. 48GP
– San Jose Sharks, 1992-93. 84GP

FEWEST TIES, ONE SEASON (MINIMUM 70-GAME SCHEDULE):
2 – San Jose Sharks, 1992-93. 84GP
3 – New Jersey Devils, 1985-86. 80GP
– Calgary Flames, 1986-87. 80GP
– Vancouver Canucks, 1993-94. 84GP

WINNING STREAKS

LONGEST WINNING STREAK, ONE SEASON:
17 Games – Pittsburgh Penguins, Mar. 9 – Apr. 10, 1993.
15 Games – NY Islanders, Jan. 21 – Feb. 20, 1982.
14 Games – Boston Bruins, Dec. 3, 1929 – Jan. 9, 1930.

LONGEST HOME WINNING STREAK, ONE SEASON:
20 Games – Boston Bruins, Dec. 3, 1929 – Mar. 18, 1930.
– **Philadelphia Flyers**, Jan. 4 – Apr. 3, 1976.

LONGEST ROAD WINNING STREAK, ONE SEASON:
10 Games – Buffalo Sabres, Dec. 10, 1983 – Jan. 23, 1984.
– **St. Louis Blues**, Jan. 21 – Mar. 2, 2000.
– **New Jersey Devils**, Feb. 27 – Apr. 7, 2001.
8 Games – Boston Bruins, Feb. 17 – Mar. 8, 1972.
Los Angeles Kings, Dec. 18, 1974 – Jan. 16, 1975.
Montreal Canadiens, Dec. 18, 1977 – Jan. 18, 1978.
NY Islanders, Feb. 27 – Mar. 29, 1981.
Montreal Canadiens, Jan. 21 – Feb. 21, 1982.
Philadelphia Flyers, Dec. 22, 1982 – Jan. 16, 1983.
Winnipeg Jets, Feb. 25 – Apr. 6, 1985.
Edmonton Oilers, Dec. 9, 1986 – Jan. 17, 1987.
Boston Bruins, Mar. 15 – Apr. 14, 1993.
Detroit Red Wings, Feb. 4 – Mar. 9, 2002.

LONGEST WINNING STREAK FROM START OF SEASON:
10 Games – Toronto Maple Leafs, 1993-94.
8 Games – Toronto Maple Leafs, 1934-35.
– Buffalo Sabres, 1975-76.
7 Games – Edmonton Oilers, 1983-84.
– Quebec Nordiques, 1985-86.
– Pittsburgh Penguins, 1986-87.
– Pittsburgh Penguins, 1994-95.

LONGEST HOME WINNING STREAK FROM START OF SEASON:
11 Games – Chicago Blackhawks, 1963-64.
10 Games – Ottawa Senators, 1925-26.
9 Games – Montreal Canadiens, 1953-54.
– Chicago Blackhawks, 1971-72.

LONGEST ROAD WINNING STREAK FROM START OF SEASON:
7 Games – Toronto Maple Leafs, Nov. 14 – Dec. 15, 1940.
– **Philadelphia Flyers**, Oct. 12 – Nov. 16, 1985.

LONGEST WINNING STREAK, INCLUDING PLAYOFFS:
15 Games – Detroit Red Wings, Feb. 27 – Apr. 5, 1955.
(9 regular-season games, 6 playoff games)

LONGEST HOME WINNING STREAK, INCLUDING PLAYOFFS:
24 Games – Philadelphia Flyers, Jan. 4 – Apr. 25, 1976.
(20 regular-season games, 4 playoff games)

LONGEST ROAD WINNING STREAK, INCLUDING PLAYOFFS:
11 Games – New Jersey Devils, Feb. 27 – Apr. 17, 2001.
(10 regular-season games, 1 playoff game)

UNDEFEATED STREAKS

LONGEST UNDEFEATED STREAK, ONE SEASON:
35 Games – Philadelphia Flyers, Oct. 14, 1979 – Jan. 6, 1980. 25w-10T
28 Games – Montreal Canadiens, Dec. 18, 1977 – Feb. 23, 1978. 23w-5T

LONGEST HOME UNDEFEATED STREAK, ONE SEASON:
34 Games – Montreal Canadiens, Nov. 1, 1976 – Apr. 2, 1977. 28w-6T
27 Games – Boston Bruins, Nov. 22, 1970 – Mar. 20, 1971. 26w-1T

LONGEST ROAD UNDEFEATED STREAK, ONE SEASON:
23 Games – Montreal Canadiens, Nov. 27, 1974 – Mar. 12, 1975. 14w-9T
17 Games – Montreal Canadiens, Dec. 18, 1977 – Mar. 1, 1978. 14w-3T

LONGEST UNDEFEATED STREAK FROM START OF SEASON:
15 Games – Edmonton Oilers, 1984-85. 12w-3T
14 Games – Montreal Canadiens, 1943-44. 11w-3T

LONGEST HOME UNDEFEATED STREAK FROM START OF SEASON:
25 Games – Montreal Canadiens, Oct. 30, 1943 – Mar. 18, 1944. 22w-3T

LONGEST ROAD UNDEFEATED STREAK FROM START OF SEASON:
15 Games – Detroit Red Wings, Oct. 18 – Dec. 20, 1951. 10w-5T

LONGEST UNDEFEATED STREAK, INCLUDING PLAYOFFS:
21 Games – Pittsburgh Penguins, Mar. 9 – Apr. 22, 1993.
17w-1T in regular season and 3w in playoffs.

LONGEST HOME UNDEFEATED STREAK, INCLUDING PLAYOFFS:
38 Games – Montreal Canadiens, Nov. 1, 1976 – Apr. 26, 1977.
28w-6T in regular season and 4w in playoffs.

LONGEST ROAD UNDEFEATED STREAK, INCLUDING PLAYOFFS:
13 Games – Philadelphia Flyers, Feb. 26 – Apr. 21, 1977. 6w-4T in
regular season and 3w in playoffs.
– **Montreal Canadiens**, Feb. 26 – Apr. 20, 1980. 6w-4T in
regular season and 3w in playoffs.
– **NY Islanders**, Mar. 16 – May 1, 1980. 3w-3T in regular season
and 7w in playoffs.

LOSING STREAKS

LONGEST LOSING STREAK, ONE SEASON:
17 Games – Washington Capitals, Feb. 18 – Mar. 26, 1975.
– **San Jose Sharks**, Jan. 4 – Feb. 12, 1993.
15 Games – Philadelphia Quakers, Nov. 29, 1930 – Jan. 8, 1931.

LONGEST HOME LOSING STREAK, ONE SEASON:
11 Games – Boston Bruins, Dec. 8, 1924 – Feb. 17, 1925.
– **Washington Capitals**, Feb. 18 – Mar. 30, 1975.
– **Ottawa Senators**, Oct. 27 – Dec. 8, 1993.
– **Atlanta Thrashers**, Jan. 24 – Mar. 16, 2000.

LONGEST ROAD LOSING STREAK, ONE SEASON:
*38 Games – Ottawa Senators, Oct. 10, 1992 – Apr. 3, 1993.
37 Games – Washington Capitals, Oct. 9, 1974 – Mar. 26, 1975.

LONGEST LOSING STREAK FROM START OF SEASON:
11 Games – NY Rangers, 1943-44.
7 Games – Montreal Canadiens, 1938-39.
– Chicago Blackhawks, 1947-48.
– Washington Capitals, 1983-84.
– Chicago Blackhawks, 1997-98.

LONGEST HOME LOSING STREAK FROM START OF SEASON:
8 Games – Los Angeles Kings, Oct. 13 – Nov. 6, 1971.

LONGEST ROAD LOSING STREAK FROM START OF SEASON:
*38 Games – Ottawa Senators, Oct. 10, 1992 – Apr. 3, 1993.

WINLESS STREAKS

LONGEST WINLESS STREAK, ONE SEASON:
30 Games – Winnipeg Jets, Oct. 19 – Dec. 20, 1980. 23L-7T
27 Games – Kansas City Scouts, Feb. 12 – Apr. 4, 1976. 21L-6T
25 Games – Washington Capitals, Nov. 29, 1975 – Jan. 21, 1976. 22L-3T

LONGEST HOME WINLESS STREAK, ONE SEASON:
17 Games – Ottawa Senators, Oct. 28, 1995 – Jan. 27, 1996. 15L-2T
– **Atlanta Thrashers**, Jan. 19 – Mar. 29, 2000. 15L-2T
15 Games – Chicago Blackhawks, Dec. 16, 1928 – Feb. 28, 1929. 11L-4T
– Montreal Canadiens, Dec. 16, 1939 – Mar. 7, 1940. 12L-3T

LONGEST ROAD WINLESS STREAK, ONE SEASON:
*38 Games – Ottawa Senators, Oct. 10, 1992 – Apr. 3, 1993. 38L
37 Games – Washington Capitals, Oct. 9, 1974 – Mar. 26, 1975. 37L

LONGEST WINLESS STREAK FROM START OF SEASON:
15 Games – NY Rangers, 1943-44. 14L-1T
11 Games – Pittsburgh Pirates, 1927-28. 8L-3T
– Minnesota North Stars, 1973-74. 5L-6T
– San Jose Sharks, 1995-96. 7L-4T

LONGEST HOME WINLESS STREAK FROM START OF SEASON:
11 Games – Pittsburgh Penguins, Oct. 8 – Nov. 19, 1983. 9L-2T

LONGEST ROAD WINLESS STREAK FROM START OF SEASON:
*38 Games – Ottawa Senators, Oct. 10, 1992 – Apr. 3, 1993. 38L

NON-SHUTOUT STREAKS

LONGEST NON-SHUTOUT STREAK:
264 Games – Calgary Flames, Nov. 12, 1981 – Jan. 9, 1985.
261 Games – Los Angeles Kings, Mar. 15, 1986 – Oct. 22, 1989.
244 Games – Washington Capitals, Oct. 31, 1989 – Nov. 11, 1993.
236 Games – NY Rangers, Dec. 20, 1989 – Dec. 13, 1992.
230 Games – Quebec Nordiques, Feb. 10, 1980 – Jan. 12, 1983.

LONGEST NON-SHUTOUT STREAK, INCLUDING PLAYOFFS:
264 Games – Los Angeles Kings, Mar. 15, 1986 – Apr. 6, 1989.
(5 playoff games in 1987; 5 in 1988; 2 in 1989).
262 Games – Chicago Blackhawks, Mar. 14, 1970 – Feb. 21, 1973.
(8 playoff games in 1971; 8 in 1972).
251 Games – Quebec Nordiques, Feb. 10, 1980 – Jan. 12, 1983.
(5 playoff games in 1981; 16 in 1982).
246 Games – Pittsburgh Penguins, Jan. 7, 1989 – Oct. 26, 1991.
(11 playoff games in 1989; 24 in 1991).

TEAM GOALS

Most Goals

MOST GOALS, ONE SEASON:
446 – Edmonton Oilers, 1983-84. 80GP
426 – Edmonton Oilers, 1985-86. 80GP
424 – Edmonton Oilers, 1982-83. 80GP
417 – Edmonton Oilers, 1981-82. 80GP
401 – Edmonton Oilers, 1984-85. 80GP

MOST GOALS, ONE TEAM, ONE GAME:
16 – Montreal Canadiens, Mar. 3, 1920, at Quebec. Montreal won 16-3.

MOST GOALS, BOTH TEAMS, ONE GAME:
21 – Montreal Canadiens (14), Toronto St. Patricks (7), Jan. 10, 1920, at Montreal.
– **Edmonton Oilers (12), Chicago Blackhawks (9)**, Dec. 11, 1985, at Chicago.
20 – Edmonton Oilers (12), Minnesota North Stars (8), Jan. 4, 1984, at Edmonton.
– Toronto Maple Leafs (11), Edmonton Oilers (9), Jan. 8, 1986, at Toronto.
19 – Montreal Wanderers (10), Toronto Arenas (9), Dec. 19, 1917, at Montreal.
– Montreal Canadiens (16), Quebec Bulldogs (3), Mar. 3, 1920, at Quebec.
– Montreal Canadiens (13), Hamilton Tigers (6), Feb. 26, 1921, at Montreal.
– Boston Bruins (10), NY Rangers (9), Mar. 4, 1944, at Boston.
– Detroit Red Wings (10), Boston Bruins (9), Mar. 16, 1944, at Detroit.
– Vancouver Canucks (10), Minnesota North Stars (9), Oct. 7, 1983, at Vancouver.

MOST GOALS, ONE TEAM, ONE PERIOD:
9 – Buffalo Sabres, Mar. 19, 1981, at Buffalo, second period during 14-4 win over Toronto.
8 – Detroit Red Wings, Jan. 23, 1944, at Detroit, third period during 15-0 win over NY Rangers.
– Boston Bruins, Mar. 16, 1969, at Boston, second period during 11-3 win over Toronto.
– NY Rangers, Nov. 21, 1971, at NY Rangers, third period during 12-1 win over California.
– Philadelphia Flyers, Mar. 31, 1973, at Philadelphia, second period during 10-2 win over NY Islanders.
– Buffalo Sabres, Dec. 21, 1975, at Buffalo, third period during 14-2 win over Washington.
– Minnesota North Stars, Nov. 11, 1981, at Minnesota, second period during 15-2 win over Winnipeg.
– Pittsburgh Penguins, Dec. 17, 1991, at Pittsburgh, second period during 10-2 win over San Jose.
– Washington Capitals, Feb. 3, 1999, at Washington, second period during 10-1 win over Tampa Bay.

MOST GOALS, BOTH TEAMS, ONE PERIOD:
12 – Buffalo Sabres (9), Toronto Maple Leafs (3), Mar. 19, 1981, at Buffalo, second period. Buffalo won 14-4.
– **Edmonton Oilers (6), Chicago Blackhawks (6),** Dec. 11, 1985, at Chicago, second period. Edmonton won 12-9.
10 – NY Rangers (7), NY Americans (3), Mar. 16, 1939, at NY Americans, third period. NY Rangers won 11-5.
– Toronto Maple Leafs (6), Detroit Red Wings (4), Mar. 17, 1946, at Detroit, third period. Toronto won 11-7.
– Buffalo Sabres (6), Vancouver Canucks (4), Jan. 8, 1976, at Buffalo, third period. Buffalo won 8-5.
– Buffalo Sabres (5), Montreal Canadiens (5), Oct. 26, 1982, at Montreal, first period. Teams tied 7-7.
– Quebec Nordiques (6), Boston Bruins (4), Dec. 7, 1982, at Quebec, second period. Quebec won 10-5.
– Vancouver Canucks (6), Calgary Flames (4), Jan. 16, 1987, at Vancouver, first period. Vancouver won 9-5.
– Detroit Red Wings (7), Winnipeg Jets (3), Nov. 25, 1987, at Detroit, third period. Detroit won 10-8.
– Chicago Blackhawks (5), St. Louis Blues (5), Mar. 15, 1988, at St. Louis, third period. Teams tied 7-7.

MOST CONSECUTIVE GOALS, ONE TEAM, ONE GAME:
15 – Detroit Red Wings, Jan. 23, 1944, at Detroit during 15-0 win over NY Rangers.

Fewest Goals

FEWEST GOALS, ONE SEASON:
33 – Chicago Blackhawks, 1928-29. 44GP
45 – Montreal Maroons, 1924-25. 30GP
46 – Pittsburgh Pirates, 1928-29. 44GP

FEWEST GOALS, ONE SEASON (MINIMUM 70-GAME SCHEDULE):
133 – Chicago Blackhawks, 1953-54. 70GP
147 – Toronto Maple Leafs, 1954-55. 70GP
– Boston Bruins, 1955-56. 70GP
150 – NY Rangers, 1954-55. 70GP

TEAM POWER-PLAY GOALS

MOST POWER-PLAY GOALS, ONE SEASON:
119 – Pittsburgh Penguins, 1988-89. 80GP
113 – Detroit Red Wings, 1992-93. 84GP
111 – NY Rangers, 1987-88. 80GP
110 – Pittsburgh Penguins, 1987-88. 80GP
– Winnipeg Jets, 1987-88, 80GP

TEAM SHORTHAND GOALS

MOST SHORTHAND GOALS, ONE SEASON:
36 – Edmonton Oilers, 1983-84. 80GP
28 – Edmonton Oilers, 1986-87. 80GP
27 – Edmonton Oilers, 1985-86. 80GP
– Edmonton Oilers, 1988-89. 80GP

TEAM GOALS-PER-GAME

HIGHEST GOALS-PER-GAME AVERAGE, ONE SEASON:
5.58 – Edmonton Oilers, 1983-84. 446G in 80GP.
5.38 – Montreal Canadiens, 1919-20. 129G in 24GP.
5.33 – Edmonton Oilers, 1985-86. 426G in 80GP.
5.30 – Edmonton Oilers, 1982-83. 424G in 80GP.
5.23 – Montreal Canadiens, 1917-18. 115G in 22GP.

LOWEST GOALS-PER-GAME AVERAGE, ONE SEASON:
0.75 – Chicago Blackhawks, 1928-29. 33G in 44GP.
1.05 – Pittsburgh Pirates, 1928-29. 46G in 44GP.
1.20 – NY Americans, 1928-29. 53G in 44GP.

TEAM ASSISTS

MOST ASSISTS, ONE SEASON:
737 – Edmonton Oilers, 1985-86. 80GP
736 – Edmonton Oilers, 1983-84. 80GP
706 – Edmonton Oilers, 1981-82. 80GP

FEWEST ASSISTS, ONE SEASON (Since 1926-27):
45 – NY Rangers, 1926-27. 44GP

FEWEST ASSISTS, ONE SEASON (MINIMUM 70-GAME SCHEDULE):
206 – Chicago Blackhawks, 1953-54. 70GP

TEAM TOTAL POINTS

MOST SCORING POINTS, ONE SEASON:
1,182 – Edmonton Oilers, 1983-84. 80GP
1,163 – Edmonton Oilers, 1985-86. 80GP
1,123 – Edmonton Oilers, 1981-82. 80GP

MOST SCORING POINTS, ONE TEAM, ONE GAME:
40 – Buffalo Sabres, Dec. 21, 1975, at Buffalo. Buffalo defeated Washington 14-2, and had 26A.
39 – Minnesota North Stars, Nov. 11, 1981, at Minnesota. Minnesota defeated Winnipeg 15-2, and had 24A.
37 – Detroit Red Wings, Jan. 23, 1944, at Detroit. Detroit defeated NY Rangers 15-0, and had 22A.
– Toronto Maple Leafs, Mar. 16, 1957, at Toronto. Toronto defeated NY Rangers 14-1, and had 23A.
– Buffalo Sabres, Feb. 25, 1978, at Cleveland. Buffalo defeated Cleveland 13-3, and had 24A.
– Calgary Flames, Feb. 10, 1993, at Calgary. Calgary defeated San Jose 13-1, and had 24A.

MOST SCORING POINTS, BOTH TEAMS, ONE GAME:
62 – Edmonton Oilers, Chicago Blackhawks, Dec. 11, 1985, at Chicago. Edmonton won 12-9. Edmonton had 24A, Chicago, 17A.
53 – Quebec Nordiques, Washington Capitals, Feb. 22, 1981, at Washington. Quebec won 11-7. Quebec had 22A, Washington, 13A.
– Edmonton Oilers, Minnesota North Stars, Jan. 4, 1984, at Edmonton. Edmonton won 12-8. Edmonton had 20A, Minnesota, 13A.
– Minnesota North Stars, St. Louis Blues, Jan. 27, 1984, at St. Louis. Minnesota won 10-8. Minnesota had 19A, St. Louis, 16A.
– Toronto Maple Leafs, Edmonton Oilers, Jan. 8, 1986, at Toronto. Toronto won 11-9. Toronto had 17A, Edmonton, 16A.
52 – Montreal Maroons, NY Americans, Feb. 18, 1936, at NY Americans. Teams tied 8-8. NY Americans had 20A, Montreal, 16A. (3A allowed for each goal.)
– Vancouver Canucks, Minnesota North Stars, Oct. 7, 1983, at Vancouver. Vancouver won 10-9. Vancouver had 16A, Minnesota, 17A.

MOST SCORING POINTS, ONE TEAM, ONE PERIOD:
23 – **NY Rangers**, Nov. 21, 1971, at NY Rangers, third period during
   12-1 win over California. NY Rangers had 8G, 15A.
   – **Buffalo Sabres**, Dec. 21, 1975, at Buffalo, third period during
   14-2 win over Washington. Buffalo had 8G, 15A.
   – **Buffalo Sabres**, Mar. 19, 1981, at Buffalo, second period
   during 14-4 win over Toronto. Buffalo had 9G, 14A.
22 – Detroit Red Wings, Jan. 23, 1944, at Detroit, third period during
   15-0 win over NY Rangers. Detroit had 8G, 14A.
   – Boston Bruins, Mar. 16, 1969, at Boston, second period during
   11-3 win over Toronto. Boston had 8G, 14A.
   – Minnesota North Stars, Nov. 11, 1981, at Minnesota, second period
   during 15-2 win over Winnipeg. Minnesota had 8G, 14A.
   – Pittsburgh Penguins, Dec. 17, 1991, at Pittsburgh, second period
   during 10-2 win over San Jose. Pittsburgh had 8G, 14A.
   – Washington Capitals, Feb. 3, 1999, at Washington, second period
   during 10-1 win over Tampa Bay. Washington had 8G, 14A.

MOST SCORING POINTS, BOTH TEAMS, ONE PERIOD:
35 – **Edmonton, Oilers, Chicago Blackhawks**, Dec. 11, 1985, at Chicago,
   second period. Edmonton won 12-9. Edmonton had 6G, 12A; Chicago,
   6G, 11A.
31 – Buffalo Sabres, Toronto Maple Leafs, Mar. 19, 1981, at Buffalo,
   second period. Buffalo won 14-4. Buffalo had 9G, 14A; Toronto, 3G, 5A.
29 – Winnipeg Jets, Detroit Red Wings, Nov. 25, 1987, at Detroit,
   third period. Detroit won 10-8. Detroit had 7G, 13A; Winnipeg, 3G, 6A.
   – Chicago Blackhawks, St. Louis Blues, Mar. 15, 1988, at St. Louis,
   third period. Teams tied 7-7. St. Louis had 5G, 10A; Chicago, 5G, 9A.

FASTEST GOALS

FASTEST SIX GOALS, BOTH TEAMS:
3:00 – **Quebec Nordiques, Washington Capitals**, Feb. 22, 1981, at
   Washington. Scorers: Peter Stastny, Quebec, 18:51; Pierre Lacroix, Quebec,
   19:57 (first period); Anton Stastny, Quebec, 0:34; Jacques Richard, Quebec,
   1:07 and 1:37; Rick Green, Washington, 1:51 (second period). Quebec won
   11-7.
3:15 – Montreal Canadiens, Toronto Maple Leafs, Jan. 4, 1944, at Montreal, first
   period. Scorers: Maurice Richard, Montreal, 14:10; Don Webster, Toronto,
   15:13; Fern Majeau, Montreal, 15:41; Phil Watson, Montreal, 15:52; Lorne
   Carr, Toronto, 16:55; Butch Bouchard, Montreal, 17:25. Montreal won 6-3.

FASTEST FIVE GOALS, BOTH TEAMS:
1:24 – **Chicago Blackhawks, Toronto Maple Leafs**, Oct. 15, 1983, at Toronto,
   second period. Scorers: Gaston Gingras, Toronto, 16:49; Denis Savard,
   Chicago, 17:12; Steve Larmer, Chicago, 17:27; Denis Savard, Chicago,
   17:42; John Anderson, Toronto, 18:13. Toronto won 10-8.
1:39 – Detroit Red Wings, Toronto Maple Leafs, Nov. 15, 1944, at Toronto, third
   period. Scorers: Ted Kennedy, Toronto, 10:36 and 10:55; Harold Jackson,
   Detroit, 11:48; Steve Wojciechowski, Detroit, 12:02; Don Grosso, Detroit,
   12:15. Detroit won 8-4.

FASTEST FIVE GOALS, ONE TEAM:
2:07 – **Pittsburgh Penguins**, Nov. 22, 1972, at Pittsburgh, third period. Scorers:
   Bryan Hextall, Jr., 12:00; Jean Pronovost, 12:18; Al McDonough, 13:40;
   Ken Schinkel, 13:49; Ron Schock, 14:07. Pittsburgh defeated St. Louis 10-
   4.
2:37 – NY Islanders, Jan. 26, 1982, at NY Islanders, first period. Scorers: Duane
   Sutter, 1:31; John Tonelli, 2:30; Bryan Trottier, 2:46 and 3:31; Duane Sutter,
   4:08. NY Islanders defeated Pittsburgh 9-2.
2:55 – Boston Bruins, Dec. 19, 1974, at Boston. Scorers: Bobby Schmautz, 19:13
   (first period); Ken Hodge, 0:18; Phil Esposito, 0:43; Don Marcotte, 0:58;
   John Bucyk, 2:08 (second period). Boston defeated NY Rangers 11-3.

FASTEST FOUR GOALS, BOTH TEAMS:
0:53 – **Chicago Blackhawks, Toronto Maple Leafs**, Oct. 15, 1983, at Toronto,
   second period. Scorers: Gaston Gingras, Toronto, 16:49; Denis Savard,
   Chicago, 17:12; Steve Larmer, Chicago, 17:27; Denis Savard, Chicago,
   17:42. Toronto won 10-8.
0:57 – Quebec Nordiques, Detroit Red Wings, Jan. 27, 1990, at Quebec, first
   period. Scorers: Paul Gillis, Quebec, 18:01; Claude Loiselle, Quebec, 18:12;
   Joe Sakic, Quebec, 18:27; Jimmy Carson, Detroit, 18:58. Detroit won 8-6.
1:01 – Colorado Rockies, NY Rangers, Jan. 15, 1980, at NY Rangers, first period.
   Scorers: Doug Sulliman, NY Rangers, 7:52; Eddie Johnstone, NY Rangers,
   7:57; Warren Miller, NY Rangers, 8:20; Rob Ramage, Colorado, 8:53.
   Teams tied 6-6.
   – Chicago Blackhawks, Toronto Maple Leafs, Oct. 15, 1983, at Toronto,
   second period. Scorers: Denis Savard, Chicago, 17:12; Steve Larmer,
   Chicago, 17:27; Denis Savard, Chicago, 17:42; John Anderson, Toronto,
   18:13. Toronto won 10-8.

FASTEST FOUR GOALS, ONE TEAM:
1:20 – **Boston Bruins**, Jan. 21, 1945, at Boston, second period. Scorers: Bill
   Thoms, 6:34; Frank Mario, 7:08 and 7:27; Ken Smith, 7:54. Boston
   defeated NY Rangers 14-3.

FASTEST THREE GOALS, BOTH TEAMS:
0:15 – **Minnesota North Stars, NY Rangers**, Feb. 10, 1983, at Minnesota,
   second period. Scorers: Mark Pavelich, NY Rangers, 19:18; Ron Greschner,
   NY Rangers, 19:27; Willi Plett, Minnesota, 19:33. Minnesota won 7-5.
0:18 – Montreal Canadiens, NY Rangers, Dec. 12, 1963, at Montreal, first period.
   Scorers: Dave Balon, Montreal, 0:58; Gilles Tremblay, Montreal, 1:04;
   Camille Henry, NY Rangers, 1:16. Montreal won 6-4.
   – California Golden Seals, Buffalo Sabres, Feb. 1, 1976, at California, third
   period. Scorers: Jim Moxey, California, 19:38; Wayne Merrick, California,
   19:45; Danny Gare, Buffalo, 19:56. Buffalo won 9-5.

FASTEST THREE GOALS, ONE TEAM:
0:20 – **Boston Bruins**, Feb. 25, 1971, at Boston, third period. Scorers: John
   Bucyk, 4:50; Ed Westfall, 5:02; Ted Green, 5:10. Boston defeated
   Vancouver 8-3.
0:21 – Chicago Blackhawks, Mar. 23, 1952, at NY Rangers, third period. Bill
   Mosienko scored all three goals, at 6:09, 6:20 and 6:30. Chicago defeated
   NY Rangers 7-6.
   – Washington Capitals, Nov. 23, 1990, at Washington, first period. Scorers:
   Michal Pivonka, 16:18; Stephen Leach, 16:29 and 16:39. Washington
   defeated Pittsburgh 7-3.

FASTEST THREE GOALS FROM START OF PERIOD, BOTH TEAMS:
1:05 – **Hartford Whalers, Montreal Canadiens**, Mar. 11, 1989, at Montreal,
   second period. Scorers: Kevin Dineen, Hartford, 0:11; Guy Carbonneau,
   Montreal, 0:36; Petr Svoboda, Montreal, 1:05. Montreal won 5-3.

FASTEST THREE GOALS FROM START OF PERIOD, ONE TEAM:
0:53 – **Calgary Flames**, Feb. 10, 1993, at Calgary, third period. Scorers: Gary
   Suter, 0:17; Chris Lindberg, 0:40; Ron Stern, 0:53. Calgary defeated San
   Jose 13-1.

FASTEST TWO GOALS, BOTH TEAMS:
0:02 – **St. Louis Blues, Boston Bruins**, Dec. 19, 1987, at Boston, third period.
   Scorers: Ken Linseman, Boston, 19:50; Doug Gilmour, St. Louis, 19:52. St.
   Louis won 7-5.
0:03 – Chicago Blackhawks, Minnesota North Stars, Nov. 5, 1988, at Minnesota,
   third period. Scorers: Steve Thomas, Chicago, 6:03; Dave Gagner,
   Minnesota, 6:06. Teams tied 5-5.

FASTEST TWO GOALS, ONE TEAM:
0:04 – **Montreal Maroons**, Jan. 3, 1931, at Montreal, third period. Nels Stewart
   scored both goals, at 8:24 and 8:28. Mtl. Maroons defeated Boston 5-3.
   – **Buffalo Sabres**, Oct. 17, 1974, at Buffalo, third period. Scorers: Lee
   Fogolin, Jr., 14:55; Don Luce, 14:59. Buffalo defeated California 6-1.
   – **Toronto Maple Leafs**, Dec. 29, 1988, at Quebec, third period. Scorers: Ed
   Olczyk, 5:24; Gary Leeman, 5:28. Toronto defeated Quebec 6-5.
   – **Calgary Flames**, Oct. 17, 1989, at Quebec, third period. Scorers: Doug
   Gilmour, 19:45; Paul Ranheim, 19:49. Teams tied 8-8.
   – **Winnipeg Jets**, Dec. 15, 1995, at Winnipeg, second period. Deron Quint
   scored both goals, at 7:51 and 7:55. Winnipeg defeated Edmonton 9-4.

FASTEST TWO GOALS FROM START OF GAME, ONE TEAM:
0:24 – **Edmonton Oilers**, Mar. 28, 1982, at Los Angeles. Scorers: Mark Messier,
   0:14; Dave Lumley, 0:24. Edmonton defeated Los Angeles 6-2.
0:27 – Boston Bruins, Feb. 14, 2003, at Florida. Scorer: Mike Knuble scored both
   goals, at 0:10 and 0:27. Calgary defeated Hartford 6-1.
0:29 – Pittsburgh Penguins, Dec. 6, 1980, at Pittsburgh. Scorers: George
   Ferguson, 0:17; Greg Malone, 0:29. Pittsburgh defeated Chicago 6-4.

FASTEST TWO GOALS FROM START OF PERIOD, BOTH TEAMS:
0:14 – **NY Rangers, Quebec Nordiques**, Nov. 5, 1983, at Quebec, third
   period. Scorers: Andre Savard, Quebec, 0:08; Pierre Larouche, NY Rangers,
   0:14. Teams tied 4-4.
0:26 – Buffalo Sabres, St. Louis Blues, Jan. 3, 1993, at Buffalo, third period.
   Scorers: Alexander Mogilny, Buffalo, 0:08; Philippe Bozon, St. Louis, 0:26.
   Buffalo won 6-5.
0:28 – Boston Bruins, Montreal Canadiens, Oct. 11, 1989, at Montreal, third
   period. Scorers: Jim Wiemer, Boston 0:10; Tom Chorske, Montreal, 0:28.
   Montreal won 4-2.

FASTEST TWO GOALS FROM START OF PERIOD, ONE TEAM:
0:21 – **Chicago Blackhawks**, Nov. 5, 1983, at Minnesota, second period. Scorers:
   Ken Yaremchuk, 0:12; Darryl Sutter, 0:21. Minnesota defeated Chicago
   10-5.
0:24 – Edmonton Oilers, Mar. 28, 1982, at Los Angeles, first period. Scorers: Mark
   Messier, 0:14; Dave Lumley, 0:24. Edmonton defeated Los Angeles 6-2.
0:29 – Pittsburgh Penguins, Dec. 6, 1980, at Pittsburgh, first period. Scorers: George
   Ferguson, 0:17; Greg Malone, 0:29. Pittsburgh defeated Chicago 6-4.

Winnipeg's Dale Hawerchuk, checked here by Kirk Muller of the New Jersey Devils, scored a career-high 20 power-play goals in 1987-88. That season, the Jets, Penguins and Rangers all surpassed the existing single-season League record of 99 power-play goals.

50, 40, 30, 20-GOAL SCORERS

MOST 50-OR-MORE GOAL SCORERS, ONE SEASON:

3 – **Edmonton Oilers**, 1983-84. 80GP. Wayne Gretzky, 87; Glenn Anderson, 54; Jari Kurri, 52.
– **Edmonton Oilers**, 1985-86. 80GP. Jari Kurri, 68; Glenn Anderson, 54; Wayne Gretzky, 52.
2 – Boston Bruins, 1970-71. 78GP. Phil Esposito, 76; John Bucyk, 51.
– Boston Bruins, 1973-74. 78GP. Phil Esposito, 68; Ken Hodge, 50.
– Philadelphia Flyers, 1975-76. 80GP. Reggie Leach, 61; Bill Barber, 50.
– Pittsburgh Penguins, 1975-76. 80GP. Pierre Larouche, 53; Jean Pronovost, 52.
– Montreal Canadiens, 1976-77. 80GP. Steve Shutt, 60; Guy Lafleur, 56.
– Los Angeles Kings, 1979-80. 80GP. Charlie Simmer, 56; Marcel Dionne, 53.
– Montreal Canadiens, 1979-80. 80GP. Pierre Larouche, 50; Guy Lafleur, 50.
– Los Angeles Kings, 1980-81. 80GP. Marcel Dionne, 58; Charlie Simmer, 56.
– Edmonton Oilers, 1981-82. 80GP. Wayne Gretzky, 92; Mark Messier, 50.
– NY Islanders, 1981-82. 80GP. Mike Bossy, 64; Bryan Trottier, 50.
– Edmonton Oilers, 1984-85. 80GP. Wayne Gretzky, 73; Jari Kurri, 71.
– Washington Capitals, 1984-85. 80GP. Bob Carpenter, 53; Mike Gartner, 50.
– Edmonton Oilers, 1986-87. 80GP. Wayne Gretzky, 62; Jari Kurri, 54.
– Calgary Flames, 1987-88. 80GP. Joe Nieuwendyk, 51; Hakan Loob, 50.
– Los Angeles Kings, 1987-88. 80GP. Jimmy Carson, 55; Luc Robitaille, 53.
– Los Angeles Kings, 1988-89. 80GP. Bernie Nicholls, 70; Wayne Gretzky, 54.
– Calgary Flames, 1988-89. 80GP. Joe Nieuwendyk, 51; Joe Mullen, 51.
– Buffalo Sabres, 1992-93. 84GP. Alexander Mogilny, 76; Pat LaFontaine, 53.
– Pittsburgh Penguins, 1992-93. 84GP. Mario Lemieux, 69; Kevin Stevens, 55.
– St. Louis Blues, 1992-93. 84GP. Brett Hull, 54; Brendan Shanahan, 51.
– St. Louis Blues, 1993-94. 84GP. Brett Hull, 57; Brendan Shanahan, 52.
– Detroit Red Wings, 1993-94. 84GP. Sergei Fedorov, 56; Ray Sheppard, 52.
– Pittsburgh Penguins, 1995-96. 82GP. Mario Lemieux, 69; Jaromir Jagr, 62.

MOST 40-OR-MORE GOAL SCORERS, ONE SEASON:

4 – **Edmonton Oilers**, 1982-83. 80GP. Wayne Gretzky, 71; Glenn Anderson, 48; Mark Messier, 48; Jari Kurri, 45.
– **Edmonton Oilers**, 1983-84. 80GP. Wayne Gretzky, 87; Glenn Anderson, 54; Jari Kurri, 52; Paul Coffey, 40.
– **Edmonton Oilers**, 1984-85. 80GP. Wayne Gretzky, 73; Jari Kurri, 71; Mike Krushelnyski, 43; Glenn Anderson, 42.
– **Edmonton Oilers**, 1985-86. 80GP. Jari Kurri, 68; Glenn Anderson, 54; Wayne Gretzky, 52; Paul Coffey, 48.
– **Calgary Flames**, 1987-88. 80GP. Joe Nieuwendyk, 51; Hakan Loob, 50; Mike Bullard, 48; Joe Mullen, 40.
3 – Boston Bruins, 1970-71. 78GP. Phil Esposito, 76; John Bucyk, 51; Ken Hodge, 43.
– NY Rangers, 1971-72. 78GP. Vic Hadfield, 50; Jean Ratelle, 46; Rod Gilbert, 43.
– Buffalo Sabres, 1975-76. 80GP. Danny Gare, 50; Rick Martin, 49; Gilbert Perreault, 44.
– Montreal Canadiens, 1979-80. 80GP. Guy Lafleur, 50; Pierre Larouche, 50; Steve Shutt, 47.
– Buffalo Sabres, 1979-80. 80GP. Danny Gare, 56; Rick Martin, 45; Gilbert Perreault, 40.
– Los Angeles Kings, 1980-81. 80GP. Marcel Dionne, 58; Charlie Simmer, 56; Dave Taylor, 47.
– Los Angeles Kings, 1984-85. 80GP. Marcel Dionne, 46; Bernie Nicholls, 46; Dave Taylor, 41.
– NY Islanders, 1984-85. 80GP. Mike Bossy, 58; Brent Sutter, 42; John Tonelli; 42.
– Chicago Blackhawks, 1985-86. 80GP. Denis Savard, 47; Troy Murray, 45; Al Secord, 40.
– Chicago Blackhawks, 1987-88. 80GP. Denis Savard, 44; Rick Vaive, 43; Steve Larmer, 41.
– Edmonton Oilers, 1987-88. 80GP. Craig Simpson, 43; Jari Kurri, 43; Wayne Gretzky, 40.
– Los Angeles Kings, 1988-89. 80GP. Bernie Nicholls, 70; Wayne Gretzky, 54; Luc Robitaille, 46.
– Los Angeles Kings, 1990-91. 80GP. Luc Robitaille, 45; Tomas Sandstrom, 45; Wayne Gretzky, 41.
– Pittsburgh Penguins, 1991-92. 80GP. Kevin Stevens, 54; Mario Lemieux, 44; Joe Mullen, 42.
– Pittsburgh Penguins, 1992-93. 84GP. Mario Lemieux, 69; Kevin Stevens, 55; Rick Tocchet, 48.
– Calgary Flames, 1993-94. 84GP. Gary Roberts, 41; Robert Reichel, 40; Theoren Fleury, 40.
– Pittsburgh Penguins, 1995-96. 82GP. Mario Lemieux, 69; Jaromir Jagr, 62; Petr Nedved, 45.

MOST 30-OR-MORE GOAL SCORERS, ONE SEASON:

6 – **Buffalo Sabres**, 1974-75. 80GP. Rick Martin, 52; Rene Robert, 40; Gilbert Perreault, 39; Don Luce, 33; Rick Dudley, 31; Danny Gare, 31.
– **NY Islanders**, 1977-78. 80GP. Mike Bossy, 53; Bryan Trottier, 46; Clark Gillies, 35; Denis Potvin, 30; Bob Nystrom, 30; Bob Bourne, 30.
– **Winnipeg Jets**, 1984-85. 80GP. Dale Hawerchuk, 53; Paul MacLean, 41; Laurie Boschman, 32; Brian Mullen, 32; Doug Smail, 31; Thomas Steen, 30.
5 – Chicago Blackhawks, 1968-69. 76GP
– Boston Bruins, 1970-71. 78GP
– Montreal Canadiens, 1971-72. 78GP
– Philadelphia Flyers, 1972-73. 78GP
– Boston Bruins, 1973-74. 78GP
– Montreal Canadiens, 1974-75. 80GP
– Montreal Canadiens, 1975-76. 80GP
– Pittsburgh Penguins, 1975-76. 80GP
– NY Islanders, 1978-79. 80GP
– Detroit Red Wings, 1979-80. 80GP
– Philadelphia Flyers, 1979-80. 80GP
– NY Islanders, 1980-81. 80GP
– St. Louis Blues, 1980-81. 80GP
– Chicago Blackhawks, 1981-82. 80GP
– Edmonton Oilers, 1981-82. 80GP
– Montreal Canadiens, 1981-82. 80GP
– Quebec Nordiques, 1981-82. 80GP
– Washington Capitals, 1981-82. 80GP
– Edmonton Oilers, 1982-83. 80GP
– Edmonton Oilers, 1983-84. 80GP
– Edmonton Oilers, 1984-85. 80GP
– Los Angeles Kings, 1984-85. 80GP
– Edmonton Oilers, 1985-86. 80GP
– Edmonton Oilers, 1986-87. 80GP
– Edmonton Oilers, 1987-88. 80GP
– Edmonton Oilers, 1988-89. 80GP
– Detroit Red Wings, 1991-92. 80GP
– NY Rangers, 1991-92. 80GP
– Pittsburgh Penguins, 1991-92. 80GP
– Detroit Red Wings, 1992-93. 84GP
– Pittsburgh Penguins, 1992-93. 84GP

MOST 20-OR-MORE GOAL SCORERS, ONE SEASON:

11 – **Boston Bruins**, 1977-78. 80GP. Peter McNab, 41; Terry O'Reilly, 29; Bobby Schmautz, 27; Stan Jonathan, 27; Jean Ratelle, 25; Rick Middleton, 25; Wayne Cashman, 24; Gregg Sheppard, 23; Brad Park, 22; Don Marcotte, 20; Bob Miller, 20.
10 – Boston Bruins, 1970-71. 78GP
– Montreal Canadiens, 1974-75. 80GP
– St. Louis Blues, 1980-81. 80GP

A charter member of the United States Hockey Hall of Fame, Sam LoPresti is best remembered for facing 83 shots against Boston on March 4, 1941. LoPresti made 80 saves in a 3-2 Chicago loss.

100-POINT SCORERS

MOST 100 OR-MORE-POINT SCORERS, ONE SEASON:
4 – **Boston Bruins**, 1970-71. 78GP. Phil Esposito, 76G-76A-152PTS;
Bobby Orr, 37G-102A-139PTS; John Bucyk, 51G-65A-116PTS;
Ken Hodge, 43G-62A-105PTS.
  – **Edmonton Oilers**, 1982-83. 80GP. Wayne Gretzky, 71G-125A-196PTS;
Mark Messier, 48G-58A-106PTS; Glenn Anderson, 48G-56A-104PTS;
Jari Kurri, 45G-59A-104PTS.
  – **Edmonton Oilers**, 1983-84. 80GP. Wayne Gretzky, 87G-118A-205PTS;
Paul Coffey, 40G-86A-126PTS; Jari Kurri, 52G-61A-113PTS;
Mark Messier, 37G-64A-101PTS.
  – **Edmonton Oilers**, 1985-86. 80GP. Wayne Gretzky, 52G-163A-215PTS;
Paul Coffey, 48G-90A-138PTS; Jari Kurri, 68G-63A-131PTS;
Glenn Anderson, 54G-48A-102PTS.
  – **Pittsburgh Penguins**, 1992-93. 84GP. Mario Lemieux, 69G-91A-160PTS;
Kevin Stevens, 55G-56A-111PTS; Rick Tocchet, 48G-61A-109PTS;
Ron Francis, 24G-76A-100PTS.
3 – **Boston Bruins**, 1973-74. 78GP. Phil Esposito, 68G-77A-145PTS;
Bobby Orr, 32G-90A-122PTS; Ken Hodge, 50G-55A-105PTS.
  – **NY Islanders**, 1978-79. 80GP. Bryan Trottier, 47G-87A-134PTS;
Mike Bossy, 69G-57A-126PTS; Denis Potvin, 31G-70A-101PTS.
  – **Los Angeles Kings**, 1980-81. 80GP. Marcel Dionne, 58G-77A-135PTS;
Dave Taylor, 47G-65A-112PTS; Charlie Simmer, 56G-49A-105PTS.
  – **Edmonton Oilers**, 1984-85. 80GP. Wayne Gretzky, 73G-135A-208PTS;
Jari Kurri, 71G-64A-135PTS; Paul Coffey, 37G-84A-121PTS.
  – **NY Islanders**, 1984-85. 80GP. Mike Bossy, 58G-59A-117PTS;
Brent Sutter, 42G-60A-102PTS; John Tonelli, 42G-58A-100PTS.
  – **Edmonton Oilers**, 1986-87. 80GP. Wayne Gretzky, 62G-121A-183PTS;
Jari Kurri, 54G-54A-108PTS; Mark Messier, 37G-70A-107PTS.
  – **Pittsburgh Penguins**, 1988-89. 80GP. Mario Lemieux, 85G-114A-199PTS;
Rob Brown, 49G-66A-115PTS; Paul Coffey, 30G-83A-113PTS.
  – **Pittsburgh Penguins**, 1995-96. 82GP. Mario Lemieux, 69G-92A-161PTS;
Jaromir Jagr, 62G-87A-149PTS; Ron Francis, 27G-92A-119PTS.

SHOTS ON GOAL

MOST SHOTS, BOTH TEAMS, ONE GAME:
141 – **NY Americans, Pittsburgh Pirates**, Dec. 26, 1925, at NY Americans.
NY Americans won 3-1 with 73 shots; Pittsburgh had 68 shots.

MOST SHOTS, ONE TEAM, ONE GAME:
83 – **Boston Bruins**, Mar. 4, 1941, at Boston. Boston defeated Chicago 3-2.
73 – NY Americans, Dec. 26, 1925, at NY Americans. NY Americans defeated
Pittsburgh 3-1.
  – Boston Bruins, Mar. 21, 1991, at Boston. Boston tied Quebec 3-3.
72 – Boston Bruins, Dec. 10, 1970, at Boston. Boston defeated Buffalo 8-2.

MOST SHOTS, ONE TEAM, ONE PERIOD:
33 – **Boston Bruins**, Mar. 4, 1941, at Boston, second period.
Boston defeated Chicago 3-2.

TEAM GOALS AGAINST

Fewest Goals Against

FEWEST GOALS AGAINST, ONE SEASON:
42 – **Ottawa Senators**, 1925-26. 36GP.
43 – Montreal Canadiens, 1928-29. 44GP.
48 – Montreal Canadiens, 1923-24. 24GP.
  – Montreal Canadiens, 1927-28. 44GP.

**FEWEST GOALS AGAINST, ONE SEASON
(MINIMUM 70-GAME SCHEDULE):**
131 – **Toronto Maple Leafs**, 1953-54. 70GP.
  – **Montreal Canadiens**, 1955-56. 70GP.
132 – Detroit Red Wings, 1953-54. 70GP.
133 – Detroit Red Wings, 1951-52. 70GP.
  – Detroit Red Wings, 1952-53. 70GP.

LOWEST GOALS-AGAINST-PER-GAME AVERAGE, ONE SEASON:
0.98 – **Montreal Canadiens**, 1928-29. 43GA in 44GP.
1.09 – Montreal Canadiens, 1927-28. 48GA in 44GP.
1.17 – Ottawa Senators, 1925-26. 42GA in 36GP.

Most Goals Against

MOST GOALS AGAINST, ONE SEASON:
446 – **Washington Capitals**, 1974-75. 80GP.
415 – Detroit Red Wings, 1985-86. 80GP.
414 – San Jose Sharks, 1992-93. 84GP.
407 – Quebec Nordiques, 1989-90. 80GP.
403 – Hartford Whalers, 1982-83. 80GP.

HIGHEST GOALS-AGAINST-PER-GAME AVERAGE, ONE SEASON:
7.38 – **Quebec Bulldogs**, 1919-20. 177GA in 24GP.
6.20 – NY Rangers, 1943-44. 310GA in 50GP.
5.58 – Washington Capitals, 1974-75. 446GA in 80GP.

MOST POWER-PLAY GOALS AGAINST, ONE SEASON:
122 – **Chicago Blackhawks**, 1988-89. 80GP.
120 – Pittsburgh Penguins, 1987-88. 80GP.
115 – New Jersey Devils, 1988-89. 80GP.
  – Ottawa Senators, 1992-93. 84GP.
114 – Los Angeles Kings, 1992-93. 84GP.

MOST SHORTHAND GOALS AGAINST, ONE SEASON:
22 – **Pittsburgh Penguins**, 1984-85. 80GP.
  – **Minnesota North Stars**, 1991-92. 80GP.
  – **Colorado Avalanche**, 1995-96. 82GP.
21 – Calgary Flames, 1984-85. 80GP.
  – Pittsburgh Penguins, 1989-90. 80GP.

SHUTOUTS

MOST SHUTOUTS, ONE SEASON:
22 – **Montreal Canadiens**, 1928-29. All by George Hainsworth. 44GP.
16 – NY Americans, 1928-29. Roy Worters 13; Flat Walsh 3. 44GP.
15 – Ottawa Senators, 1925-26. All by Alex Connell. 36GP.
  – Ottawa Senators, 1927-28. All by Alex Connell. 44GP.
  – Boston Bruins, 1927-28. All by Hal Winkler. 44GP.
  – Chicago Blackhawks, 1969-70. All by Tony Esposito. 76GP.

MOST CONSECUTIVE SHUTOUTS, ONE SEASON:
6 – **Ottawa Senators**, Jan. 31 – Feb. 18, 1928. All by Alex Connell.

MOST CONSECUTIVE SHUTOUTS TO START SEASON:
5 – **Toronto Maple Leafs**, Nov. 13 – 22, 1930. Lorne Chabot 3,
Benny Grant 2.

MOST GAMES SHUTOUT, ONE SEASON:
20 – **Chicago Blackhawks**, 1928-29. 44GP.

MOST CONSECUTIVE GAMES SHUTOUT:
8 – **Chicago Blackhawks**, Feb. 7 – 28, 1929.

MOST CONSECUTIVE GAMES SHUTOUT TO START SEASON:
3 – **Montreal Maroons**, Nov. 11 – 18, 1930.

TEAM PENALTIES

MOST PENALTY MINUTES, ONE SEASON:
2,713 – **Buffalo Sabres**, 1991-92. 80GP.
2,670 – Pittsburgh Penguins, 1988-89. 80GP.
2,663 – Chicago Blackhawks, 1991-92. 80GP.
2,643 – Calgary Flames, 1991-92. 80GP.
2,621 – Philadelphia Flyers, 1980-81. 80GP.

MOST PENALTIES, BOTH TEAMS, ONE GAME:
85 – **Edmonton Oilers (44), Los Angeles Kings (41)**, Feb. 28, 1990, at
Los Angeles. Edmonton received 26 minors, 7 majors, 6 10-minute
misconducts, 4 game misconducts and 1 match penalty; Los Angeles
received 26 minors, 9 majors, 3 10-minute misconducts and 3 game
misconducts.

MOST PENALTY MINUTES, BOTH TEAMS, ONE GAME:
406 – **Minnesota North Stars (211), Boston Bruins (195)**, Feb. 26, 1981, at
Boston. Minnesota received 18 minors, 13 majors, 4 10-minute
misconducts and 7 game misconducts. Boston received 20 minors, 13
majors, 3 10-minute misconducts and six game misconducts.

MOST PENALTIES, ONE TEAM, ONE GAME:
44 – **Edmonton Oilers**, Feb. 28, 1990, at Los Angeles. Edmonton received
26 minors, 7 majors, 6 10-minute misconducts, 4 game misconducts
and 1 match penalty.
42 – Minnesota North Stars, Feb. 26, 1981, at Boston. Minnesota received
18 minors, 13 majors, 4 10-minute misconducts and 7 game misconducts.
  – Boston Bruins, Feb. 26, 1981, at Boston vs. Minnesota. Boston received
20 minors, 13 majors, 3 10-minute misconducts and 6 game misconducts.

MOST PENALTY MINUTES, ONE TEAM, ONE GAME:
211 – **Minnesota North Stars**, Feb. 26, 1981, at Boston. Minnesota received
18 minors, 13 majors, 4 10-minute misconducts and 7 game misconducts.

MOST PENALTIES, BOTH TEAMS, ONE PERIOD:
67 – **Minnesota North Stars (34), Boston Bruins (33)**, Feb. 26, 1981, at
Boston, first period. Minnesota received 15 minors, 8 majors, 4 10-minute
misconducts and 7 game misconducts. Boston had 16 minors, 8 majors,
3 10-minute misconducts and 6 game misconducts.

MOST PENALTY MINUTES, BOTH TEAMS, ONE PERIOD:
372 – **Los Angeles Kings (184), Philadelphia Flyers (188)**, Mar. 11, 1979, at
Philadelphia, first period. Los Angeles received 2 minors, 8 majors,
6 10-minute misconducts and 8 game misconducts. Philadelphia received
4 minors, 8 majors, 6 10-minute misconducts and 8 game misconducts.

MOST PENALTIES, ONE TEAM, ONE PERIOD:
34 – **Minnesota North Stars**, Feb. 26, 1981, at Boston, first period.
Minnesota received 15 minors, 8 majors, 4 10-minute misconducts and
7 game misconducts.

MOST PENALTY MINUTES, ONE TEAM, ONE PERIOD:
190 – **Calgary Flames**, Dec. 8, 2001, at Calgary vs. Anaheim, third
period. Calgary received 10 minors, 10 majors, 8 10-minute
misconducts and 4 game misconducts.
188 – Philadelphia Flyers, Mar. 11, 1979, at Philadelphia vs. Los Angeles,
first period. Philadelphia received 4 minors, 8 majors, 6 10-minute
misconducts and 8 game misconducts.

NHL Individual Scoring Records - History

Six individual scoring records stand as benchmarks in the history of the game: most goals, single-season and career; most assists, single-season and career; and most points, single-season and career. The evolution of these six records is traced here, beginning with 1917-18, the NHL's first season. New research has resulted in changes to scoring records in the NHL's first nine seasons.

MOST GOALS, ONE SEASON

44 —Joe Malone, Montreal, 1917-18.
      Scored goal #44 against Toronto's Harry Holmes on March 2, 1918 and finished season with 44 goals.
50 —Maurice Richard, Montreal, 1944-45.
      Scored goal #45 against Toronto's Frank McCool on February 25, 1945 and finished the season with 50 goals.
50 —Bernie Geoffrion, Montreal, 1960-61.
      Scored goal #50 against Toronto's Cesare Maniago on March 16, 1961 and finished the season with 50 goals.
50 —Bobby Hull, Chicago, 1961-62.
      Scored goal #50 against NY Rangers' Gump Worsley on March 25, 1962 and finished the season with 50 goals.
54 —Bobby Hull, Chicago, 1965-66.
      Scored goal #51 against NY Rangers' Cesare Maniago on March 12, 1966 and finished the season with 54 goals.
58 —Bobby Hull, Chicago, 1968-69.
      Scored goal #55 against Boston's Gerry Cheevers on March 20, 1969 and finished the season with 58 goals.
76 —Phil Esposito, Boston, 1970-71.
      Scored goal #59 against Los Angeles' Denis DeJordy on March 11, 1971 and finished the season with 76 goals.
92 —Wayne Gretzky, Edmonton, 1981-82.
      Scored goal #77 against Buffalo's Don Edwards on February 24, 1982 and finished the season with 92 goals.

MOST ASSISTS, ONE SEASON

10 —Cy Denneny, Ottawa, 1917-18.
      —Reg Noble, Toronto, 1917-18.
      —Harry Cameron, Toronto, 1917-18.
      —Newsy Lalonde, Montreal, 1918-19.
15 —Frank Nighbor, Ottawa, 1919-20.
      —Jack Darragh, Ottawa, 1920-21.
17 —Harry Cameron, Toronto, 1921-22.
18 —Dick Irvin, Chicago, 1926-27.
18 —Howie Morenz, Montreal, 1927-28.
36 —Frank Boucher, NY Rangers, 1929-30.
37 —Joe Primeau, Toronto, 1931-32.
45 —Bill Cowley, Boston, 1940-41.
45 —Bill Cowley, Boston, 1942-43.
49 —Clint Smith, Chicago, 1943-44.
54 —Elmer Lach, Montreal, 1944-45.
55 —Ted Lindsay, Detroit, 1949-50.
56 —Bert Olmstead, Montreal, 1955-56.
58 —Jean Beliveau, Montreal, 1960-61.
58 —Andy Bathgate, NY Rangers/Toronto, 1963-64.
59 —Stan Mikita, Chicago, 1964-65.
62 —Stan Mikita, Chicago, 1966-67.
77 —Phil Esposito, Boston, 1968-69.
87 —Bobby Orr, Boston, 1969-70.
102 —Bobby Orr, Boston, 1970-71.
109 —Wayne Gretzky, Edmonton, 1980-81.
120 —Wayne Gretzky, Edmonton, 1981-82.
125 —Wayne Gretzky, Edmonton, 1982-83.
135 —Wayne Gretzky, Edmonton, 1984-85.
163 —Wayne Gretzky, Edmonton, 1985-86.

MOST POINTS, ONE SEASON

48 —Joe Malone, Montreal, 1917-18.
49 —Joe Malone, Montreal, 1919-20.
51 —Howie Morenz, Montreal, 1927-28.
73 —Cooney Weiland, Boston, 1929-30.
73 —Doug Bentley, Chicago, 1942-43.
82 —Herb Cain, Boston, 1943-44.
86 —Gordie Howe, Detroit, 1950-51.
95 —Gordie Howe, Detroit, 1952-53.
96 —Dickie Moore, Montreal, 1958-59.
97 —Bobby Hull, Chicago, 1965-66.
97 —Stan Mikita, Chicago, 1966-67.
126 —Phil Esposito, Boston, 1968-69.
152 —Phil Esposito, Boston, 1970-71.
164 —Wayne Gretzky, Edmonton, 1980-81.
212 —Wayne Gretzky, Edmonton, 1981-82.
215 —Wayne Gretzky, Edmonton, 1985-86.

MOST REGULAR-SEASON GOALS, CAREER

44 —Joe Malone, 1917-18, Montreal.
      Malone led the NHL in goals in the league's first season and finished with 44 goals in 22 games in 1917-18.
54 —Cy Denneny, 1918-19, Ottawa.
      Denneny passed Malone during the 1918-19 season, finishing the year with a two-year total of 54 goals. He held the career goal- scoring mark until 1919-20.
143 —Joe Malone, Montreal, Quebec Bulldogs, Hamilton.
      Malone passed Denneny in 1919-20 and remained the NHL's career goal-scoring leader until 1922-23.
248 —Cy Denneny, Ottawa, Boston.
      Denneny passed Malone with goal #144 in 1922-23 and remained the NHL's career goal-scoring leader until his retirement. He finished with a career total of 248 goals.
271 —Howie Morenz, Montreal, Chicago, NY Rangers.
      Morenz passed Denneny with goal #249 in 1933-34 and finished his career with 271 goals.
324 —Nels Stewart, Montreal Maroons, Boston, NY Americans.
      Stewart passed Morenz with goal #272 in 1936-37 and remained the NHL's career goal-scoring leader until his retirement. He finished his career with 324 goals.
544 —Maurice Richard, Montreal.
      Richard passed Nels Stewart with goal #325 on Nov. 8, 1952 and remained the NHL's career goal-scoring leader until his retirement. He finished his career with 544 goals.
801 —Gordie Howe, Detroit, Hartford.
      Howe passed Richard with goal #545 on Nov. 10, 1963 and remained the NHL's career goal-scoring leader until his retirement. He finished his career with 801 goals.
894 —Wayne Gretzky, Edmonton, Los Angeles, St. Louis, NY Rangers.
      Gretzky passed Gordie Howe with goal #802 on March 23, 1994. He retired as the NHL's current goal-scoring leader with 894.

MOST REGULAR-SEASON ASSISTS, CAREER

(minimum 100 assists)

100 —Frank Boucher, Ottawa, NY Rangers.
In 1930-31, Boucher became the first NHL player to reach the
100-assist milestone.

263 —Frank Boucher, Ottawa, NY Rangers.
Boucher retired as the NHL's career assist leader in 1938 with 253. He
returned to the NHL in 1943-44 and remained the NHL's career assist leader
until he was overtaken by Bill Cowley in 1943-44. He finished his career
with 263 assists.

353 —Bill Cowley, St. Louis Eagles, Boston.
Cowley passed Boucher with assist #264 in 1943-44. He retired as the
NHL's career assist leader in 1947 with 353.

408 —Elmer Lach, Montreal.
Lach passed Cowley with assist #354 in 1951-52. He retired as the
NHL's career assist leader in 1954 with 408.

1,049 —Gordie Howe, Detroit, Hartford.
Howe passed Lach with assist #409 in 1957-58. He retired as the
NHL's career assist leader in 1980 with 1,049.

1,963 —Wayne Gretzky, Edmonton, Los Angeles, St. Louis, NY Rangers.
Gretzky passed Howe with assist #1,050 in 1988-89. He retired as the
NHL's current career assist leader with 1,963.

MOST REGULAR-SEASON POINTS, CAREER

(minimum 100 points)

100 —Joe Malone, Montreal, Quebec Bulldogs, Hamilton.
In 1919-20, Malone became the first player in NHL history to
record 100 points.

200 —Cy Denneny, Ottawa.
In 1923-24, Denneny became the first player in NHL history to
record 200 points.

300 —Cy Denneny, Ottawa.
In 1926-27, Denneny became the first player in NHL history to
record 300 points.

333 —Cy Denneny, Ottawa, Boston.
Denneny retired as the NHL's career point-scoring leader
in 1929 with 333 points.

472 —Howie Morenz, Montreal, Chicago, NY Rangers.
Morenz passed Cy Denneny with point #334 in 1931-32. At the time his
career ended in 1937, he was the NHL's career point- scoring leader with
472 points.

515 —Nels Stewart, Montreal Maroons, Boston, NY Americans.
Stewart passed Morenz with point #473 in 1938-39. He retired as the NHL's
career point-scoring leader in 1940 with 515 points.

528 —Syd Howe, Ottawa, Philadelphia Quakers,
Toronto, St. Louis Eagles, Detroit.
Howe passed Nels Stewart with point #516 on March 8, 1945.
He retired as the NHL's career point-scoring leader in 1946 with 528 points.

548 —Bill Cowley, St. Louis Eagles, Boston.
Cowley passed Syd Howe with point #529 on Feb. 12, 1947.
He retired as the NHL's career point-scoring leader in 1947
with 548 points.

610 —Elmer Lach, Montreal.
Lach passed Bill Cowley with point #549 on Feb. 23, 1952. He remained the
NHL's career point-scoring leader until he was overtaken by Maurice Richard
in 1953-54. He finished his career with 623 points.

946 —Maurice Richard, Montreal.
Richard passed teammate Elmer Lach with point #611 on
Dec. 12, 1953. He remained the NHL's career point-scoring leader until he
was overtaken by Gordie Howe in 1959-60. He finished his career with
965 points.

1,850 —Gordie Howe, Detroit, Hartford.
Howe passed Richard with point #947 on Jan. 16, 1960. He retired as the
NHL's career point-scoring leader in 1980 with 1,850 points.

2,857 —Wayne Gretzky, Edmonton, Los Angeles, St. Louis, NY Rangers.
Gretzky passed Howe with point #1,851 on Oct. 15, 1989. He retired as the
NHL's current career points leader with 2,857.

*At the time Gerry Cheevers (above) surrendered Bobby Hull's record-breaking 55th goal of the 1968-69 season, the Golden Jet was still one of only three NHL players to have
reached the 50-goal plateau. (Of course, Hull himself had accomplished the feat four times.) Back in 1960-61, Frank Mahovlich (facing page, parked in front of Terry
Sawchuk) nearly became the second player in NHL history to score 50 in a season. Mahovlich of the Toronto Maple Leafs was scoring at a record rate, but he slumped down
the stretch just as Montreal's Bernie Geoffrion got red hot. Season's end found Mahovlich with 48 goals, but Geoffrion reached the magic 50 and added 45 assists to win
the Art Ross Trophy. Still, Mahovlich's 48 goals stood as a Maple Leafs record until Rick Vaive scored 54 goals in 1981-82.*

Individual Records

Regular Season

SEASONS

MOST SEASONS:
26 – Gordie Howe, Detroit, 1946-47 – 1970-71; Hartford, 1979-80.
24 – Alex Delvecchio, Detroit, 1950-51 – 1973-74.
– Tim Horton, Toronto, NY Rangers, Pittsburgh, Buffalo, 1949-50, 1951-52 – 1973-74.
– Mark Messier, Edmonton, NY Rangers, Vancouver, 1979-80 – 2002-03.
23 – John Bucyk, Detroit, Boston, 1955-56 – 1977-78.
22 – Dean Prentice, NY Rangers, Boston, Detroit, Pittsburgh, Minnesota, 1952-53 – 1973-74.
– Doug Mohns, Boston, Chicago, Minnesota, Atlanta, Washington, 1953-54 – 1974-75.
– Stan Mikita, Chicago, 1958-59 – 1979-80.
– Raymond Bourque, Boston, Colorado, 1979-80 – 2000-01.
– Ron Francis, Hartford, Pittsburgh, Carolina, 1981-82 – 2002-03.
– Al MacInnis, Calgary, St. Louis, 1981-82 – 2002-03.

GAMES

MOST GAMES:
1,767 – Gordie Howe, Detroit, 1946-47 – 1970-71; Hartford, 1979-80.
1,680 – Mark Messier, Edmonton, NY Rangers, Vancouver, 1979-80 – 2002-03.
1,651 – Ron Francis, Hartford, Pittsburgh, Carolina, 1981-82 – 2002-03.
1,615 – Larry Murphy, Los Angeles, Washington, Minnesota North Stars, Pittsburgh, Toronto, Detroit, 1980-81 – 2000-01.
1,612 – Raymond Bourque, Boston, Colorado, 1979-80 – 2000-01.

MOST GAMES, INCLUDING PLAYOFFS:
1,924 – Gordie Howe, Detroit, Hartford, 1,767 regular-season games, 157 playoff games.
1,916 – Mark Messier, Edmonton, NY Rangers, Vancouver, 1,680 regular-season games, 236 playoff games.
1,830 – Larry Murphy, Los Angeles, Washington, Minnesota North Stars, Pittsburgh, Toronto, Detroit, 1,615 regular-season games, 215 playoff games.
1,826 – Raymond Bourque, Boston, Colorado, 1,612 regular-season games, 214 playoff games.
1,810 – Ron Francis, Hartford, Pittsburgh, Carolina, 1,651 regular-season games, 159 playoff games.

MOST CONSECUTIVE GAMES:
964 – Doug Jarvis, Montreal, Washington, Hartford, Oct. 8, 1975 – Oct. 10, 1987.
914 – Garry Unger, Toronto, Detroit, St. Louis, Atlanta, Feb. 24, 1968 – Dec. 21, 1979.
884 – Steve Larmer, Chicago, Oct. 6, 1982 – Apr. 15, 1993.
776 – Craig Ramsay, Buffalo, Mar. 27, 1973 – Feb. 10, 1983.
630 – Andy Hebenton, NY Rangers, Boston, Oct. 7, 1955 – Mar. 22, 1964.

GOALS

MOST GOALS:
894 – Wayne Gretzky, Edmonton, Los Angeles, St. Louis, NY Rangers, in 20 seasons. 1,487GP
801 – Gordie Howe, Detroit, Hartford, in 26 seasons. 1,767GP
731 – Marcel Dionne, Detroit, Los Angeles, NY Rangers, in 18 seasons. 1,348GP
717 – Phil Esposito, Chicago, Boston, NY Rangers, in 18 seasons. 1,282GP
716 – Brett Hull, Calgary, St. Louis, Dallas, Detroit, in 17 seasons. 1,183GP

MOST GOALS, INCLUDING PLAYOFFS:
1,016 – Wayne Gretzky, Edmonton, Los Angeles, St. Louis, NY Rangers, 894G in 1,487 regular-season games, 122G in 208 playoff games.
869 – Gordie Howe, Detroit, Hartford, 801G in 1,767 regular-season games, 68G in 157 playoff games.
816 – Brett Hull, Calgary, St. Louis, Dallas, Detroit, 716G in 1,183 regular-season games, 100G in 190 playoff games.
785 – Mark Messier, Edmonton, NY Rangers, Vancouver, 676G in 1,680 regular-season games, 109G in 236 playoff games.
778 – Phil Esposito, Chicago, Boston, NY Rangers, 717G in 1,282 regular-season games, 61G in 130 playoff games.

MOST GOALS, ONE SEASON:
92 – Wayne Gretzky, Edmonton, 1981-82. 80GP – 80 game schedule.
87 – Wayne Gretzky, Edmonton, 1983-84. 74GP – 80 game schedule.
86 – Brett Hull, St. Louis, 1990-91. 78GP – 80 game schedule.
85 – Mario Lemieux, Pittsburgh, 1988-89. 76GP – 80 game schedule.
76 – Phil Esposito, Boston, 1970-71. 78GP – 78 game schedule.
– Alexander Mogilny, Buffalo, 1992-93. 77GP – 84 game schedule.
– Teemu Selanne, Winnipeg, 1992-93. 84GP – 84 game schedule.
73 – Wayne Gretzky, Edmonton, 1984-85. 80GP – 80 game schedule.
72 – Brett Hull, St. Louis, 1989-90. 80GP – 80 game schedule.
71 – Wayne Gretzky, Edmonton, 1982-83. 80GP – 80 game schedule.
– Jari Kurri, Edmonton, 1984-85. 73GP – 80 game schedule.
70 – Mario Lemieux, Pittsburgh, 1987-88. 77GP – 80 game schedule.
– Bernie Nicholls, Los Angeles, 1988-89. 79GP – 80 game schedule.
– Brett Hull, St. Louis, 1991-92. 73GP – 80 game schedule.

MOST GOALS, ONE SEASON, INCLUDING PLAYOFFS:
100 – Wayne Gretzky, Edmonton, 1983-84.
87G in 74 regular-season games, 13G in 19 playoff games.
97 – Wayne Gretzky, Edmonton, 1981-82.
92G in 80 regular-season games, 5G in 5 playoff games.
– Mario Lemieux, Pittsburgh, 1988-89.
85G in 76 regular-season games, 12G in 11 playoff games.
– Brett Hull, St. Louis, 1990-91,
86G in 78 regular-season games, 11G in 13 playoff games.
90 – Wayne Gretzky, Edmonton, 1984-85,
73G in 80 regular-season games, 17G in 18 playoff games.
– Jari Kurri, Edmonton, 1984-85,
71G in 80 regular-season games, 19G in 18 playoff games.
85 – Mike Bossy, NY Islanders, 1980-81,
68G in 79 regular-season games, 17G in 18 playoff games.
– Brett Hull, St. Louis, 1989-90,
72G in 80 regular-season games, 13G in 12 playoff games.
83 – Wayne Gretzky, Edmonton, 1982-83,
71G in 73 regular-season games, 12G in 16 playoff games.
– Alexander Mogilny, Buffalo, 1992-93,
76G in 77 regular-season games, 7G in 7 playoff games.

MOST GOALS, 50 GAMES FROM START OF SEASON:
61 – Wayne Gretzky, Edmonton, 1981-82.
Oct. 7, 1981 – Jan. 22, 1982. (80-game schedule)
– **Wayne Gretzky**, Edmonton, 1983-84.
Oct. 5, 1983 – Jan. 25, 1984. (80-game schedule)
54 – Mario Lemieux, Pittsburgh, 1988-89.
Oct. 7, 1988 – Jan. 31, 1989. (80-game schedule)
53 – Wayne Gretzky, Edmonton, 1984-85.
Oct. 11, 1984 – Jan. 28, 1985. (80-game schedule)
52 – Brett Hull, St. Louis, 1990-91.
Oct. 4, 1990 – Jan. 26, 1991. (80-game schedule)
50 – Maurice Richard, Montreal, 1944-45.
Oct. 28, 1944 – Mar. 18, 1945. (50-game schedule)
– Mike Bossy, NY Islanders, 1980-81.
Oct. 11, 1980 – Jan. 24, 1981. (80-game schedule)
– Brett Hull, St. Louis, 1991-92.
Oct. 5, 1991 – Jan. 28, 1992. (80-game schedule)

MOST GOALS, ONE GAME:
7 – Joe Malone, Quebec, Jan. 31, 1920, at Quebec.
Quebec 10, Toronto 6.
6 – Newsy Lalonde, Montreal, Jan. 10, 1920, at Montreal.
Montreal 14, Toronto 7.
– Joe Malone, Quebec, Mar. 10, 1920, at Quebec.
Quebec 10, Ottawa 4.
– Corb Denneny, Toronto, Jan. 26, 1921, at Toronto.
Toronto 10, Hamilton 3.
– Cy Denneny, Ottawa, Mar. 7, 1921, at Ottawa.
Ottawa 12, Hamilton 5.
– Syd Howe, Detroit, Feb. 3, 1944, at Detroit.
Detroit 12, NY Rangers 2.
– Red Berenson, St. Louis, Nov. 7, 1968, at Philadelphia.
St. Louis 8, Philadelphia 0.
– Darryl Sittler, Toronto, Feb. 7, 1976, at Toronto.
Toronto 11, Boston 4.

Both Mark Messier and Wayne Gretzky entered the NHL as 18-year-olds in 1979-80. Today, their names are sprinkled liberally throughout the pages of the record section of the NHL Official Guide and Record Book.

Cy Denneny of the Ottawa Senators (top left) is one of only seven players to score six goals in an NHL game. Cy recorded his double hat trick a mere six weeks after his brother Corb scored six in one game.

MOST GOALS, ONE ROAD GAME:
6 – **Red Berenson**, St. Louis, Nov. 7, 1968, at Philadelphia. St. Louis 8, Philadelphia 0.
5 – Joe Malone, Montreal, Dec. 19, 1917, at Ottawa. Montreal 7, Ottawa 4.
  – Red Green, Hamilton, Dec. 5, 1924, at Toronto. Hamilton 10, Toronto 3.
  – Babe Dye, Toronto, Dec. 22, 1924, at Boston. Toronto 10, Boston 1.
  – Punch Broadbent, Mtl. Maroons, Jan. 7, 1925, at Hamilton. Mtl. Maroons 6, Hamilton 2.
  – Don Murdoch, NY Rangers, Oct. 12, 1976, at Minnesota. NY Rangers 10, Minnesota 4.
  – Tim Young, Minnesota, Jan. 15, 1979, at NY Rangers. Minnesota 8, NY Rangers 1.
  – Willy Lindstrom, Winnipeg, Mar. 2, 1982, at Philadelphia. Winnipeg 7, Philadelphia 6.
  – Bengt Gustafsson, Washington, Jan. 8, 1984, at Philadelphia. Washington 7, Philadelphia 1.
  – Wayne Gretzky, Edmonton, Dec. 15, 1984, at St. Louis. Edmonton 8, St. Louis 2.
  – Dave Andreychuk, Buffalo, Feb. 6, 1986, at Boston. Buffalo 8, Boston 6.
  – Mats Sundin, Quebec, Mar. 5, 1992, at Hartford. Quebec 10, Hartford 4.
  – Mario Lemieux, Pittsburgh, Apr. 9, 1993, at NY Rangers. Pittsburgh 10, NY Rangers 4.
  – Mike Ricci, Quebec, Feb. 17, 1994, at San Jose. Quebec 8, San Jose 2.
  – Alexei Zhamnov, Winnipeg, Apr. 1, 1995, at Los Angeles. Winnipeg 7, Los Angeles 7.

MOST GOALS, ONE PERIOD:
4 – **Busher Jackson**, Toronto, Nov. 20, 1934, at St. Louis, third period. Toronto 5, St. Louis 2.
  – **Max Bentley**, Chicago, Jan. 28, 1943, at Chicago, third period. Chicago 10, NY Rangers 1.
  – **Clint Smith**, Chicago, Mar. 4, 1945, at Chicago, third period. Chicago 6, Montreal 4.
  – **Red Berenson**, St. Louis, Nov. 7, 1968, at Philadelphia, second period. St. Louis 8, Philadelphia 0.
  – **Wayne Gretzky**, Edmonton, Feb. 18, 1981, at Edmonton, third period. Edmonton 9, St. Louis 2.
  – **Grant Mulvey**, Chicago, Feb. 3, 1982, at Chicago, first period. Chicago 9, St. Louis 5.
  – **Bryan Trottier**, NY Islanders, Feb. 13, 1982, at NY Islanders, second period. NY Islanders 8, Philadelphia 2.
  – **Al Secord**, Chicago, Jan. 7, 1987, at Chicago, second period. Chicago 6, Toronto 4.
  – **Joe Nieuwendyk**, Calgary, Jan. 11, 1989, at Calgary, second period. Calgary 8, Winnipeg 3.
  – **Peter Bondra**, Washington, Feb. 5, 1994, at Washington, first period. Washington 6, Tampa Bay 3.
  – **Mario Lemieux**, Pittsburgh, Jan. 26, 1997, at Montreal, third period. Pittsburgh 5, Montreal 2.

ASSISTS

MOST ASSISTS:
1,963 – **Wayne Gretzky**, Edmonton, Los Angeles, St. Louis, NY Rangers, in 20 seasons. 1,487GP.
1,222 – Ron Francis, Hartford, Pittsburgh, Carolina, in 22 seasons. 1,651GP.
1,169 – Raymond Bourque, Boston, Colorado, in 22 seasons. 1,612GP.
1,168 – Mark Messier, Edmonton, NY Rangers, Vancouver, in 24 seasons. 1,680GP.
1,135 – Paul Coffey, Edmonton, Pittsburgh, Los Angeles, Detroit, Hartford, Philadelphia, Chicago, Carolina, Boston, in 21 seasons. 1,409GP.

MOST ASSISTS, INCLUDING PLAYOFFS:
2,223 – **Wayne Gretzky**, Edmonton, Los Angeles, St. Louis, NY Rangers, 1,963A in 1,487 regular-season games, 260A in 208 playoff games.
1,354 – Mark Messier, Edmonton, NY Rangers, Vancouver, 1,168A in 1,680 regular-season games, 186A in 236 playoff games.
1,315 – Ron Francis, Hartford, Pittsburgh, Carolina, 1,222A in 1,651 regular-season games, 93A in 159 playoff games.
1,308 – Raymond Bourque, Boston, Colorado, 1,169A in 1,612 regular-season games, 139A in 214 playoff games.
1,272 – Paul Coffey, Edmonton, Pittsburgh, Los Angeles, Detroit, Hartford, Philadelphia, Chicago, Carolina, Boston, 1,135A in 1,409 regular-season games, 137A in 194 playoff games.

MOST ASSISTS, ONE SEASON:
163 – **Wayne Gretzky**, Edmonton, 1985-86. 80GP – 80 game schedule.
135 – Wayne Gretzky, Edmonton, 1984-85. 80GP – 80 game schedule.
125 – Wayne Gretzky, Edmonton, 1982-83. 80GP – 80 game schedule.
122 – Wayne Gretzky, Los Angeles, 1990-91. 78GP – 80 game schedule.
121 – Wayne Gretzky, Edmonton, 1986-87. 79GP – 80 game schedule.
120 – Wayne Gretzky, Edmonton, 1981-82. 80GP – 80 game schedule.
118 – Wayne Gretzky, Edmonton, 1983-84. 74GP – 80 game schedule.
114 – Wayne Gretzky, Los Angeles, 1988-89. 78GP – 80 game schedule.
  – Mario Lemieux, Pittsburgh, 1988-89. 76GP – 80 game schedule.
109 – Wayne Gretzky, Edmonton, 1980-81. 80GP – 80 game schedule.
  – Wayne Gretzky, Edmonton, 1987-88. 64GP – 80 game schedule.
102 – Bobby Orr, Boston, 1970-71. 78GP – 78 game schedule.
  – Wayne Gretzky, Los Angeles, 1989-90. 73GP – 80 game schedule.

MOST ASSISTS, ONE SEASON, INCLUDING PLAYOFFS:
174 – **Wayne Gretzky**, Edmonton, 1985-86,
163A in 80 regular-season games, 11A in 10 playoff games.
165 – Wayne Gretzky, Edmonton, 1984-85,
135A in 80 regular-season games, 30A in 18 playoff games.
151 – Wayne Gretzky, Edmonton, 1982-83,
125A in 80 regular-season games, 26A in 16 playoff games.
150 – Wayne Gretzky, Edmonton, 1986-87,
121A in 79 regular-season games, 29A in 21 playoff games.
140 – Wayne Gretzky, Edmonton, 1983-84,
118A in 74 regular-season games, 22A in 19 playoff games.
– Wayne Gretzky, Edmonton, 1987-88,
109A in 64 regular-season games, 31A in 19 playoff games.
133 – Wayne Gretzky, Los Angeles, 1990-91,
122A in 78 regular-season games, 11A in 12 playoff games.
131 – Wayne Gretzky, Los Angeles, 1988-89,
114A in 78 regular-season games, 17A in 11 playoff games.
127 – Wayne Gretzky, Edmonton, 1981-82,
120A in 80 regular-season games, 7A in 5 playoff games.
123 – Wayne Gretzky, Edmonton, 1980-81,
109A in 80 regular-season games, 14A in 9 playoff games.
121 – Mario Lemieux, Pittsburgh, 1988-89,
114A in 76 regular-season games, 7A in 11 playoff games.

MOST ASSISTS, ONE GAME:
7 – **Billy Taylor**, Detroit, Mar. 16, 1947, at Chicago. Detroit 10, Chicago 6.
– **Wayne Gretzky**, Edmonton, Feb. 15, 1980, at Edmonton.
Edmonton 8, Washington 2.
– **Wayne Gretzky**, Edmonton, Dec. 11, 1985, at Chicago.
Edmonton 12, Chicago 9.
– **Wayne Gretzky**, Edmonton, Feb. 14, 1986, at Edmonton.
Edmonton 8, Quebec 2.
6 – Six assists have been recorded in one game on 24 occasions since
Elmer Lach of Montreal first accomplished the feat vs. Boston on
Feb. 6, 1943. The most recent player is Eric Lindros of Philadelphia
on Feb. 26, 1997 at Ottawa.

MOST ASSISTS, ONE ROAD GAME:
7 – **Billy Taylor**, Detroit, Mar. 16, 1947, at Chicago. Detroit 10, Chicago 6.
– Wayne Gretzky, Edmonton, Dec. 11, 1985, at Chicago.
Edmonton 12, Chicago 9.
6 – Bobby Orr, Boston, Jan. 1, 1973, at Vancouver. Boston 8, Vancouver 2.
– Patrik Sundstrom, Vancouver, Feb. 29, 1984, at Pittsburgh.
Vancouver 9, Pittsburgh 5.
– Mario Lemieux, Pittsburgh, Dec. 5, 1992, at San Jose.
Pittsburgh 9, San Jose 4.
– Eric Lindros, Philadelphia, Feb. 26, 1997, at Ottawa.
Philadelphia 8, Ottawa 5.

MOST ASSISTS, ONE PERIOD:
5 – **Dale Hawerchuk**, Winnipeg, Mar. 6, 1984, at Los Angeles,
second period. Winnipeg 7, Los Angeles 3.
4 – Four assists have been recorded in one period on 63 occasions since
Mickey Roach of Hamilton first accomplished the feat vs. Toronto
on Feb. 23, 1921. The most recent player is Paul Kariya of Anaheim
on Dec. 16, 1998 vs. Nashville.

POINTS

MOST POINTS:
2,857 – **Wayne Gretzky**, Edmonton, Los Angeles, St. Louis, NY Rangers,
in 20 seasons. 1,487GP (894G–1,963A).
1,850 – Gordie Howe, Detroit, Hartford, in 26 seasons. 1,767GP (801G–1,049A)
1,844 – Mark Messier, Edmonton, NY Rangers, Vancouver,
in 24 seasons. 1,680GP (676G–1,168A)
1,771 – Marcel Dionne, Detroit, Los Angeles, NY Rangers,
in 18 seasons. 1,348GP (731G–1,040A)
1,758 – Ron Francis, Hartford, Pittsburgh, Carolina,
in 22 seasons. 1,651GP (536G–1,222A)

MOST POINTS, INCLUDING PLAYOFFS:
3,239 – **Wayne Gretzky**, Edmonton, Los Angeles, St. Louis, NY Rangers,
2,857PTS in 1,487 regular-season games, 382PTS in 208 playoff games.
2,139 – Mark Messier, Edmonton, NY Rangers, Vancouver,
1,844PTS in 1,680 regular-season games, 295PTS in 236 playoff games.
2,010 – Gordie Howe, Detroit, Hartford,
1,850PTS in 1,767 regular-season games, 160PTS in 157 playoff games.
1,897 – Ron Francis, Hartford, Pittsburgh, Carolina,
1,758PTS in 1,651 regular-season games, 139PTS in 159 playoff games
1,864 – Mario Lemieux, Pittsburgh,
1,692PTS in 879 regular-season games, 172PTS in 107 playoff games.

MOST POINTS, ONE SEASON:
215 – **Wayne Gretzky**, Edmonton, 1985-86. 80GP – 80 game schedule.
212 – Wayne Gretzky, Edmonton, 1981-82. 80GP – 80 game schedule.
208 – Wayne Gretzky, Edmonton, 1984-85. 80GP – 80 game schedule.
205 – Wayne Gretzky, Edmonton, 1983-84. 74GP – 80 game schedule.
199 – Mario Lemieux, Pittsburgh, 1988-89. 76GP – 80 game schedule.
196 – Wayne Gretzky, Edmonton, 1982-83. 80GP – 80 game schedule.
183 – Wayne Gretzky, Edmonton, 1986-87. 79GP – 80 game schedule.
168 – Mario Lemieux, Pittsburgh, 1987-88. 77GP – 80 game schedule.
– Wayne Gretzky, Los Angeles, 1988-89. 78GP – 80 game schedule.
164 – Wayne Gretzky, Edmonton, 1980-81. 80GP – 80 game schedule.
163 – Wayne Gretzky, Los Angeles, 1990-91. 78GP – 80 game schedule.
161 – Mario Lemieux, Pittsburgh, 1995-96. 70GP – 82 game schedule.
160 – Mario Lemieux, Pittsburgh, 1992-93. 60GP – 84 game schedule.

MOST POINTS, ONE SEASON, INCLUDING PLAYOFFS:
255 – **Wayne Gretzky**, Edmonton, 1984-85,
208PTS in 80 regular-season games, 47PTS in 18 playoff games.
240 – Wayne Gretzky, Edmonton, 1983-84,
205PTS in 74 regular-season games, 35PTS in 19 playoff games.
234 – Wayne Gretzky, Edmonton, 1982-83,
196PTS in 80 regular-season games, 38PTS in 16 playoff games.
– Wayne Gretzky, Edmonton, 1985-86,
215PTS in 80 regular-season games, 19PTS in 10 playoff games.
224 – Wayne Gretzky, Edmonton, 1981-82,
212PTS in 80 regular-season games, 12PTS in 5 playoff games.
218 – Mario Lemieux, Pittsburgh, 1988-89,
199PTS in 76 regular-season games, 19PTS in 11 playoff games.
217 – Wayne Gretzky, Edmonton, 1986-87,
183PTS in 79 regular-season games, 34PTS in 21 playoff games.
192 – Wayne Gretzky, Edmonton, 1987-88,
149PTS in 64 regular-season games, 43PTS in 19 playoff games.
190 – Wayne Gretzky, Los Angeles, 1988-89,
168PTS in 78 regular-season games, 22PTS in 11 playoff games.
188 – Mario Lemieux, Pittsburgh, 1995-96,
161PTS in 70 regular-season games, 27PTS in 18 playoff games.
185 – Wayne Gretzky, Edmonton, 1980-81,
164PTS in 80 regular-season games, 21PTS in 9 playoff games.

*Ron Francis recorded the 1,200th assist of his career on December 22, 2003.
Wayne Gretzky is the only other player to reach that milestone.
Francis enters the 2003-04 season needing just 13 points to
move into fourth place on the NHL's career scoring list.*

MOST POINTS, ONE GAME:

10 – Darryl Sittler, Toronto, Feb. 7, 1976, at Toronto, 6G-4A. Toronto 11, Boston 4.

8 – Maurice Richard, Montreal, Dec. 28, 1944, at Montreal, 5G-3A. Montreal 9, Detroit 1.

– Bert Olmstead, Montreal, Jan. 9, 1954, at Montreal, 4G-4A. Montreal 12, Chicago 1.

– Tom Bladon, Philadelphia, Dec. 11, 1977, at Philadelphia, 4G-4A. Philadelphia 11, Cleveland 1.

– Bryan Trottier, NY Islanders, Dec. 23, 1978, at NY Islanders, 5G-3A. NY Islanders 9, NY Rangers 4.

– Peter Stastny, Quebec, Feb. 22, 1981, at Washington, 4G-4A. Quebec 11, Washington 7.

– Anton Stastny, Quebec, Feb. 22, 1981, at Washington, 3G-5A. Quebec 11, Washington 7.

– Wayne Gretzky, Edmonton, Nov. 19, 1983, at Edmonton, 3G-5A. Edmonton 13, New Jersey 4.

– Wayne Gretzky, Edmonton, Jan. 4, 1984, at Edmonton, 4G-4A. Edmonton 12, Minnesota 8.

– Paul Coffey, Edmonton, Mar. 14, 1986, at Edmonton, 2G-6A. Edmonton 12, Detroit 3.

– Mario Lemieux, Pittsburgh, Oct. 15, 1988, at Pittsburgh, 2G-6A. Pittsburgh 9, St. Louis 2.

– Bernie Nicholls, Los Angeles, Dec. 1, 1988, at Los Angeles, 2G-6A. Los Angeles 9, Toronto 3.

– Mario Lemieux, Pittsburgh, Dec. 31, 1988, at Pittsburgh, 5G-3A. Pittsburgh 8, New Jersey 6.

MOST POINTS, ONE ROAD GAME:

8 – Peter Stastny, Quebec, Feb. 22, 1981, at Washington. 4G-4A. Quebec 11, Washington 7.

– **Anton Stastny**, Quebec, Feb. 22, 1981, at Washington. 3G-5A. Quebec 11, Washington 7.

7 – Red Green, Hamilton, Dec. 5, 1924, at Toronto. 5G-2A. Hamilton 10, Toronto 3.

– Billy Taylor, Detroit, Mar. 16, 1947, at Chicago. 7A. Detroit 10, Chicago 6.

– Red Berenson, St. Louis, Nov. 7, 1968, at Philadelphia. 6G-1A. St. Louis 8, Philadelphia 0.

– Gilbert Perreault, Buffalo, Feb. 1, 1976, at California. 2G-5A. Buffalo 9, California 5.

– Peter Stastny, Quebec, Apr. 1, 1982, at Boston. 3G-4A. Quebec 8, Boston 5.

– Wayne Gretzky, Edmonton, Nov. 6, 1983, at Winnipeg. 4G-3A. Edmonton 8, Winnipeg 5.

– Patrik Sundstrom, Vancouver, Feb. 29, 1984, at Pittsburgh. 1G-6A. Vancouver 9, Pittsburgh 5.

– Wayne Gretzky, Edmonton, Dec. 11, 1985, at Chicago. 7A. Edmonton 12, Chicago 9.

– Cam Neely, Boston, Oct. 16, 1988, at Chicago. 3G-4A. Boston 10, Chicago 3.

– Mario Lemieux, Pittsburgh, Jan. 21, 1989, at Edmonton. 2G-5A. Pittsburgh 7, Edmonton 4.

– Dino Ciccarelli, Washington, Mar. 18, 1989, at Hartford. 4G-3A. Washington 8, Hartford 2.

– Mats Sundin, Quebec, Mar. 5, 1992, at Hartford. 5G-2A. Quebec 10, Hartford 4.

– Mario Lemieux, Pittsburgh, Dec. 5, 1992, at San Jose. 1G-6A. Pittsburgh 9, San Jose 4.

– Eric Lindros, Philadelphia, Feb. 26, 1997, at Ottawa. 1G-6A. Philadelphia 8, Ottawa 5.

MOST POINTS, ONE PERIOD:

6 – Bryan Trottier, NY Islanders, Dec. 23, 1978, at NY Islanders, second period. 3G-3A. NY Islanders 9, NY Rangers 4.

5 – Bill Cook, NY Rangers, Mar. 12, 1933, at NY Americans third period. 3G-2A. NY Rangers 8, NY Americans 2.

– Les Cunningham, Chicago, Jan. 28, 1940, at Chicago, third period. 2G-3A. Chicago 8, Montreal 1.

– Max Bentley, Chicago, Jan. 28, 1943, at Chicago, third period. 4G-1A. Chicago 10, NY Rangers 1.

– Leo Labine, Boston, Nov. 28, 1954, at Boston, second period. 3G-2A. Boston 6, Detroit 2.

– Darryl Sittler, Toronto, Feb. 7, 1976, at Toronto, second period. 3G-2A. Toronto 11, Boston 4.

– Grant Mulvey, Chicago, Feb. 3, 1982, at Chicago, first period. 4G-1A. Chicago 9, St. Louis 5.

– Dale Hawerchuk, Winnipeg, Mar. 6, 1984, at Los Angeles, second period. 5A. Winnipeg 7, Los Angeles 3.

– Jari Kurri, Edmonton, Oct. 26, 1984, at Edmonton, second period. 2G-3A. Edmonton 8, Los Angeles 2.

– Pat Elynuik, Winnipeg, Jan. 20, 1989, at Winnipeg, second period. 2G-3A. Winnipeg 7, Pittsburgh 3.

– Ray Ferraro, Hartford, Dec. 9, 1989, at Hartford, first period. 3G-2A. Hartford 7, New Jersey 3.

– Stephane Richer, Montreal, Feb. 14, 1990, at Montreal, first period. 2G-3A. Montreal 10, Vancouver 1.

– Cliff Ronning, Vancouver, Apr. 15, 1993, at Los Angeles, third period. 3G-2A. Vancouver 8, Los Angeles 6.

– Peter Forsberg, Colorado, Mar. 3, 1999, at Florida, third period. 2G-3A. Colorado 7, Florida 5.

POWER-PLAY AND SHORTHAND GOALS

MOST POWER-PLAY GOALS, CAREER:

260 – Dave Andreychuk, Buffalo, Toronto, New Jersey, Boston, Colorado, Tampa Bay, in 21 seasons. 1,515GP

255 – Brett Hull, Calgary, St. Louis, Dallas, Detroit, in 17 seasons. 1,183GP

249 – Phil Esposito, Chicago, Boston, NY Rangers, in 18 seasons. 1,282GP

MOST POWER-PLAY GOALS, ONE SEASON:

34 – Tim Kerr, Philadelphia, 1985-86. 76GP – 80 game schedule.

32 – Dave Andreychuk, Buffalo, Toronto, 1992-93. 83GP – 84 game schedule.

31 – Joe Nieuwendyk, Calgary, 1987-88. 75GP – 80 game schedule.

– Mario Lemieux, Pittsburgh, 1988-89. 76GP – 80 game schedule.

– Mario Lemieux, Pittsburgh, 1995-96. 70GP – 82 game schedule.

29 – Michel Goulet, Quebec, 1987-88. 80GP – 80 game schedule.

– Brett Hull, St. Louis, 1990-91. 78GP – 80 game schedule.

– Brett Hull, St. Louis, 1992-93. 80GP – 84 game schedule.

MOST SHORTHAND GOALS, ONE SEASON:

13 – Mario Lemieux, Pittsburgh, 1988-89. 76GP – 80 game schedule.

12 – Wayne Gretzky, Edmonton, 1983-84. 74GP – 80 game schedule.

11 – Wayne Gretzky, Edmonton, 1984-85. 80GP – 80 game schedule.

10 – Marcel Dionne, Detroit, 1974-75. 80GP – 80 game schedule.

– Mario Lemieux, Pittsburgh, 1987-88. 77GP – 80 game schedule.

– Dirk Graham, Chicago, 1988-89. 80GP – 80 game schedule.

MOST SHORTHAND GOALS, ONE GAME:

3 – Theoren Fleury, Calgary, Mar. 9, 1991, at St. Louis. Calgary 8, St. Louis 4.

OVERTIME SCORING

MOST OVERTIME GOALS, CAREER:

13 – Steve Thomas, Toronto, Chicago, NY Islanders, New Jersey, Anaheim.

12 – Sergei Fedorov, Detroit.

– Jaromir Jagr, Pittsburgh, Washington.

– Mats Sundin, Quebec, Toronto.

11 – Mario Lemieux, Pittsburgh.

– Theoren Fleury, Calgary, Colorado, NY Rangers, Chicago.

– Pierre Turgeon, Buffalo, NY Islanders, Montreal, St. Louis, Dallas.

MOST OVERTIME ASSISTS, CAREER:

17 – Adam Oates, Detroit, St. Louis, Boston, Washington, Philadelphia, Anaheim.

– **Mark Messier**, Edmonton, NY Rangers, Vancouver.

15 – Wayne Gretzky, Edmonton, Los Angeles, St. Louis, NY Rangers.

– Doug Gilmour, St. Louis, Calgary, Toronto, New Jersey, Chicago, Buffalo, Montreal.

13 – Raymond Bourque, Boston, Colorado.

– Nicklas Lidstrom, Detroit.

– Scott Stevens, Washington, St. Louis, New Jersey.

MOST OVERTIME POINTS, CAREER:

25 – Mark Messier, Edmonton, NY Rangers, Vancouver. 8G-17A

23 – Steve Thomas, Toronto, Chicago, NY Islanders, New Jersey, Chicago, Anaheim. 13G-10A

22 – Mario Lemieux, Pittsburgh. 11G-11A

– Adam Oates, Detroit, St. Louis, Boston, Washington, Philadelphia, Anaheim. 5G-17A

21 – Sergei Fedorov, Detroit. 12G-9A

Doug Gilmour, who starred with Toronto in the early 1990s, rejoined the Maple Leafs at last year's trade deadline. A great playmaker and a clutch performer, Gilmour ranks among the NHL leaders in overtime assists.

SCORING BY A CENTER

MOST GOALS BY A CENTER, CAREER
894 – Wayne Gretzky, Edmonton, Los Angeles, St. Louis, NY Rangers, in 20 seasons. 1,487GP
731 – Marcel Dionne, Detroit, Los Angeles, NY Rangers, in 18 seasons. 1,348GP
717 – Phil Esposito, Chicago, Boston, NY Rangers, in 18 seasons. 1,282GP
682 – Mario Lemieux, Pittsburgh, in 15 seasons. 879GP
676 – Mark Messier, Edmonton, NY Rangers, Vancouver, in 24 seasons. 1,680GP

MOST GOALS BY A CENTER, ONE SEASON:
92 – Wayne Gretzky, Edmonton, 1981-82. 80GP – 80 game schedule.
87 – Wayne Gretzky, Edmonton, 1983-84. 74GP – 80 game schedule.
85 – Mario Lemieux, Pittsburgh, 1988-89. 76GP – 80 game schedule.
76 – Phil Esposito, Boston, 1970-71. 78GP – 78 game schedule.
73 – Wayne Gretzky, Edmonton, 1984-85. 80GP – 80 game schedule.

MOST ASSISTS BY A CENTER, CAREER:
1,963 – Wayne Gretzky, Edmonton, Los Angeles, St. Louis, NY Rangers, in 20 seasons. 1,487GP
1,222 – Ron Francis, Hartford, Pittsburgh, Carolina, in 22 seasons. 1,651GP
1,168 – Mark Messier, Edmonton, NY Rangers, Vancouver, in 24 seasons. 1,680GP
1,063 – Adam Oates, Detroit, St. Louis, Boston, Washington, Philadelphia, Anaheim, in 18 seasons. 1,277GP
1,040 – Marcel Dionne, Detroit, Los Angeles, NY Rangers, in 18 seasons. 1,348GP

MOST ASSISTS BY A CENTER, ONE SEASON:
163 – Wayne Gretzky, Edmonton, 1985-86. 80GP – 80 game schedule.
135 – Wayne Gretzky, Edmonton, 1984-85. 80GP – 80 game schedule.
125 – Wayne Gretzky, Edmonton, 1982-83. 80GP – 80 game schedule.
122 – Wayne Gretzky, Los Angeles, 1990-91. 78GP – 80 game schedule.
121 – Wayne Gretzky, Edmonton, 1986-87. 79GP – 80 game schedule.

MOST POINTS BY A CENTER, CAREER:
2,857 – Wayne Gretzky, Edmonton, Los Angeles, St. Louis, NY Rangers, in 20 seasons. 1,487GP
1,844 – Mark Messier, Edmonton, NY Rangers, Vancouver, in 24 seasons. 1,680GP
1,771 – Marcel Dionne, Detroit, Los Angeles, NY Rangers, in 18 seasons. 1,348GP
1,758 – Ron Francis, Hartford, Pittsburgh, Carolina, in 22 seasons. 1,651GP
1,692 – Mario Lemieux, Pittsburgh, in 15 seasons. 879GP

MOST POINTS BY A CENTER, ONE SEASON:
215 – Wayne Gretzky, Edmonton, 1985-86. 80GP – 80 game schedule.
212 – Wayne Gretzky, Edmonton, 1981-82. 80GP – 80 game schedule.
208 – Wayne Gretzky, Edmonton, 1984-85. 80GP – 80 game schedule.
205 – Wayne Gretzky, Edmonton, 1983-84. 74GP – 80 game schedule.
199 – Mario Lemieux, Pittsburgh, 1988-89. 76GP – 80 game schedule.

SCORING BY A LEFT WING

MOST GOALS BY A LEFT WING, CAREER:
631 – Luc Robitaille, Los Angeles, Pittsburgh, NY Rangers, Detroit, in 17 seasons. 1,286GP
613 – Dave Andreychuk, Buffalo, Toronto, New Jersey, Boston, Colorado, Tampa Bay, in 21 seasons. 1,515GP
610 – Bobby Hull, Chicago, Winnipeg, Hartford, in 16 seasons. 1,063GP
556 – John Bucyk, Detroit, Boston, in 23 seasons. 1,540GP
548 – Michel Goulet, Quebec, Chicago, in 15 seasons. 1,089GP

MOST GOALS BY A LEFT WING, ONE SEASON:
63 – Luc Robitaille, Los Angeles, 1992-93. 84GP – 84 game schedule.
60 – Steve Shutt, Montreal, 1976-77. 80GP – 80 game schedule.
58 – Bobby Hull, Chicago, 1968-69. 74GP – 76 game schedule.
57 – Michel Goulet, Quebec, 1982-83. 80GP – 80 game schedule.
56 – Charlie Simmer, Los Angeles, 1979-80. 64GP – 80 game schedule.
– Charlie Simmer, Los Angeles, 1980-81. 65GP – 80 game schedule.
– Michel Goulet, Quebec, 1983-84. 75GP – 80 game schedule.

MOST ASSISTS BY A LEFT WING, CAREER:
813 – John Bucyk, Detroit, Boston, in 23 seasons. 1,540GP
688 – Luc Robitaille, Los Angeles, Pittsburgh, NY Rangers, Detroit, in 17 seasons. 1,286GP
668 – Dave Andreychuk, Buffalo, Toronto, New Jersey, Boston, Colorado, Tampa Bay, in 21 seasons. 1,515GP
604 – Michel Goulet, Quebec, Chicago, in 15 seasons. 1,089GP
579 – Brian Propp, Philadelphia, Boston, Minnesota, Hartford, in 15 seasons. 1,016GP

MOST ASSISTS BY A LEFT WING, ONE SEASON:
70 – Joe Juneau, Boston, 1992-93. 84GP – 84 game schedule.
69 – Kevin Stevens, Pittsburgh, 1991-92. 80GP – 80 game schedule.
67 – Mats Naslund, Montreal, 1985-86. 80GP – 80 game schedule.
65 – John Bucyk, Boston, 1970-71. 78GP – 78 game schedule.
– Michel Goulet, Quebec, 1983-84. 75GP – 80 game schedule.
64 – Mark Messier, Edmonton, 1983-84. 73GP – 80 game schedule.

MOST POINTS BY A LEFT WING, CAREER:
1,369 – John Bucyk, Detroit, Boston, in 23 seasons. 1,540GP
1,319 – Luc Robitaille, Los Angeles, Pittsburgh, NY Rangers, Detroit, in 17 seasons. 1,286GP
1,281 – Dave Andreychuk, Buffalo, Toronto, New Jersey, Boston, Colorado, Tampa Bay, in 21 seasons. 1,515GP
1,170 – Bobby Hull, Chicago, Winnipeg, Hartford, in 16 seasons. 1,063GP
1,152 – Michel Goulet, Quebec, Chicago, in 15 seasons. 1,089GP

MOST POINTS BY A LEFT WING, ONE SEASON:
125 – Luc Robitaille, Los Angeles, 1992-93. 84GP – 84 game schedule.
123 – Kevin Stevens, Pittsburgh, 1991-92. 80GP – 80 game schedule.
121 – Michel Goulet, Quebec, 1983-84. 75GP – 80 game schedule.
116 – John Bucyk, Boston, 1970-71. 78GP – 78 game schedule.
112 – Bill Barber, Philadelphia, 1975-76. 80GP – 80 game schedule.

SCORING BY A RIGHT WING

MOST GOALS BY A RIGHT WING, CAREER:
801 – Gordie Howe, Detroit, Hartford, in 26 seasons. 1,767GP
716 – Brett Hull, Calgary, St. Louis, Dallas, Detroit, in 17 seasons. 1,183GP
708 – Mike Gartner, Washington, Minnesota, NY Rangers, Toronto, Phoenix, in 19 seasons. 1,432GP
608 – Dino Ciccarelli, Minnesota, Washington, Detroit, Tampa Bay, Florida, in 19 seasons. 1,232GP
601 – Jari Kurri, Edmonton, Los Angeles, NY Rangers, Anaheim, Colorado, in 17 seasons. 1,251GP

MOST GOALS BY A RIGHT WING, ONE SEASON:
86 – Brett Hull, St. Louis, 1990-91. 78GP – 80 game schedule.
76 – Alexander Mogilny, Buffalo, 1992-93. 77GP – 84 game schedule.
– Teemu Selanne, Winnipeg, 1992-93. 84GP – 84 game schedule.
72 – Brett Hull, St. Louis, 1989-90. 80GP – 80 game schedule.
71 – Jari Kurri, Edmonton, 1984-85. 73GP – 80 game schedule.
70 – Brett Hull, St. Louis, 1991-92. 73GP – 80 game schedule.

MOST ASSISTS BY A RIGHT WING, CAREER:
1,049 – Gordie Howe, Detroit, Hartford, in 26 seasons. 1,767GP
797 – Jari Kurri, Edmonton, Los Angeles, NY Rangers, Anaheim, Colorado, in 17 seasons. 1,251GP
793 – Guy Lafleur, Montreal, NY Rangers, Quebec, in 17 seasons. 1,126GP
729 – Jaromir Jagr, Pittsburgh, Washington, in 13 seasons. 950GP
696 – Mark Recchi, Pittsburgh, Philadelphia, Montreal, in 15 seasons. 1,091GP

MOST ASSISTS BY A RIGHT WING, ONE SEASON:
87 – Jaromir Jagr, Pittsburgh, 1995-96. 82GP – 82 game schedule.
83 – Mike Bossy, NY Islanders, 1981-82. 80GP – 80 game schedule.
– Jaromir Jagr, Pittsburgh, 1998-99. 81GP – 82 game schedule.
80 – Guy Lafleur, Montreal, 1976-77. 80GP – 80 game schedule.
77 – Guy Lafleur, Montreal, 1978-79. 80GP – 80 game schedule.

Luc Robitaille returns to the Los Angeles Kings for the 2003-04 season. Robitaille holds the NHL's single-season and career goal-scoring records for left wingers. He needs 51 points to overtake John Bucyk and become the League's all-time point-scoring leader at his position.

MOST POINTS BY A RIGHT WING, CAREER:
  1,850 – **Gordie Howe**, Detroit, Hartford, in 26 seasons. 1,767GP
  1,398 – Jari Kurri, Edmonton, Los Angeles, NY Rangers, Anaheim, Colorado, in 17 seasons. 1,251GP
  1,353 – Guy Lafleur, Montreal, NY Rangers, Quebec, in 17 seasons. 1,126GP
  1,335 – Mike Gartner, Washington, Minnesota, NY Rangers, Toronto, Phoenix, in 19 seasons. 1,432GP
  1,322 – Brett Hull, Calgary, St. Louis, Dallas, Detroit, in 17 seasons. 1,183GP

MOST POINTS BY A RIGHT WING, ONE SEASON:
  149 – **Jaromir Jagr**, Pittsburgh, 1995-96. 82GP – 82 game schedule.
  147 – Mike Bossy, NY Islanders, 1981-82. 80GP – 80 game schedule.
  136 – Guy Lafleur, Montreal, 1976-77. 80GP – 80 game schedule.
  135 – Jari Kurri, Edmonton, 1984-85. 73GP – 80 game schedule.
  132 – Guy Lafleur, Montreal, 1977-78. 78GP – 80 game schedule.
    – Teemu Selanne, Winnipeg, 1992-93. 84GP – 84 game schedule.

SCORING BY A DEFENSEMAN

MOST GOALS BY A DEFENSEMAN, CAREER:
  410 – **Raymond Bourque**, Boston, Colorado, in 22 seasons. 1,612GP
  396 – Paul Coffey, Edmonton, Pittsburgh, Los Angeles, Detroit, Hartford, Philadelphia, Chicago, Carolina, Boston, in 21 seasons. 1,409GP
  340 – Al MacInnis, Calgary, St. Louis, in 22 seasons. 1,413GP
  338 – Phil Housley, Buffalo, Winnipeg, St. Louis, Calgary, New Jersey, Washington, Chicago, Toronto, in 21 seasons. 1,495GP
  310 – Denis Potvin, NY Islanders, in 15 seasons. 1,060GP

MOST GOALS BY A DEFENSEMAN, ONE SEASON:
  48 – **Paul Coffey**, Edmonton, 1985-86. 79GP – 80 game schedule.
  46 – Bobby Orr, Boston, 1974-75. 80GP – 80 game schedule.
  40 – Paul Coffey, Edmonton, 1983-84. 80GP – 80 game schedule.
  39 – Doug Wilson, Chicago, 1981-82. 76GP – 80 game schedule.
  37 – Bobby Orr, Boston, 1970-71. 78GP – 78 game schedule.
    – Bobby Orr, Boston, 1971-72. 76GP – 78 game schedule.
    – Paul Coffey, Edmonton, 1984-85. 80GP – 80 game schedule.

MOST GOALS BY A DEFENSEMAN, ONE GAME:
  5 – **Ian Turnbull**, Toronto, Feb. 2, 1977, at Toronto. Toronto 9, Detroit 1.
  4 – Harry Cameron, Toronto, Dec. 26, 1917, at Toronto. Toronto 7, Montreal 5.
    – Harry Cameron, Montreal, Mar. 3, 1920, at Quebec. Montreal 16, Quebec 3.
    – Sprague Cleghorn, Montreal, Jan. 14, 1922, at Montreal. Montreal 10, Hamilton 6.
    – John McKinnon, Pittsburgh, Nov. 19, 1929, at Pittsburgh. Pittsburgh 10, Toronto 5.
    – Hap Day, Toronto, Nov. 19, 1929, at Pittsburgh. Pittsburgh 10, Toronto 5.
    – Tom Bladon, Philadelphia, Dec. 11, 1977, at Philadelphia. Philadelphia 11, Cleveland 1.
    – Ian Turnbull, Los Angeles, Dec. 12, 1981, at Los Angeles. Los Angeles 7, Vancouver 5.
    – Paul Coffey, Edmonton, Oct. 26, 1984, at Calgary. Edmonton 6, Calgary 5.

MOST ASSISTS BY A DEFENSEMAN, CAREER:
  1,169 – **Raymond Bourque**, Boston, Colorado, in 22 seasons. 1,612GP
  1,135 – Paul Coffey, Edmonton, Pittsburgh, Los Angeles, Detroit, Hartford, Philadelphia, Chicago, Carolina, Boston, in 21 seasons. 1,409GP
  932 – Al MacInnis, Calgary, St. Louis, in 22 seasons. 1,413GP
  929 – Larry Murphy, Los Angeles, Washington, Minnesota North Stars, Pittsburgh, Toronto, Detroit, in 21 seasons. 1,615GP
  894 – Phil Housley, Buffalo, Winnipeg, St. Louis, Calgary, New Jersey, Washington, Chicago, Toronto, in 21 seasons. 1,495GP

MOST ASSISTS BY A DEFENSEMAN, ONE SEASON:
  102 – **Bobby Orr**, Boston, 1970-71. 78GP – 78 game schedule.
  90 – Bobby Orr, Boston, 1973-74. 74GP – 78 game schedule.
    – Paul Coffey, Edmonton, 1985-86. 79GP – 80 game schedule.
  89 – Bobby Orr, Boston, 1974-75. 80GP – 80 game schedule.
  87 – Bobby Orr, Boston, 1969-70. 76GP – 78 game schedule.

MOST ASSISTS BY A DEFENSEMAN, ONE GAME:
  6 – **Babe Pratt**, Toronto, Jan. 8, 1944, at Toronto. Toronto 12, Boston 3.
    – **Pat Stapleton**, Chicago, Mar. 30, 1969, at Chicago. Chicago 9, Detroit 5.
    – **Bobby Orr**, Boston, Jan. 1, 1973, at Vancouver. Boston 8, Vancouver 2.
    – **Ron Stackhouse**, Pittsburgh, Mar. 8, 1975, at Pittsburgh. Pittsburgh 8, Philadelphia 2.
    – **Paul Coffey**, Edmonton, Mar. 14, 1986, at Edmonton. Edmonton 12, Detroit 3.
    – **Gary Suter**, Calgary, Apr. 4, 1986, at Calgary. Calgary 9, Edmonton 3.

MOST POINTS BY A DEFENSEMAN, CAREER:
  1,579 – **Raymond Bourque**, Boston, Colorado, in 22 seasons. 1,612GP
  1,531 – Paul Coffey, Edmonton, Pittsburgh, Los Angeles, Detroit, Hartford, Philadelphia, Chicago, Carolina, Boston, in 21 seasons. 1,409GP
  1,272 – Al MacInnis, Calgary, St. Louis, in 22 seasons. 1,413GP
  1,232 – Phil Housley, Buffalo, Winnipeg, St. Louis, Calgary, New Jersey, Washington, Chicago, Toronto, in 21 seasons. 1,495GP
  1,216 – Larry Murphy, Los Angeles, Washington, Minnesota North Stars, Pittsburgh, Toronto, Detroit, in 21 seasons. 1,615GP

MOST POINTS BY A DEFENSEMAN, ONE SEASON:
  139 – **Bobby Orr**, Boston, 1970-71. 78GP – 78 game schedule.
  138 – Paul Coffey, Edmonton, 1985-86. 79GP – 80 game schedule.
  135 – Bobby Orr, Boston, 1974-75. 80GP – 80 game schedule.
  126 – Paul Coffey, Edmonton, 1983-84. 80GP – 80 game schedule.
  122 – Bobby Orr, Boston, 1973-74. 74GP – 78 game schedule.

MOST POINTS BY A DEFENSEMAN, ONE GAME:
  8 – **Tom Bladon**, Philadelphia, Dec. 11, 1977, at Philadelphia. 4G-4A. Philadelphia 11, Cleveland 1.
    – **Paul Coffey**, Edmonton, Mar. 14, 1986, at Edmonton. 2G-6A. Edmonton 12, Detroit 3.
  7 – Bobby Orr, Boston, Nov. 15, 1973, at Boston. 3G-4A. Boston 10, NY Rangers 2.

SCORING BY A GOALTENDER

MOST POINTS BY A GOALTENDER, CAREER:
  48 – **Tom Barrasso**, Buffalo, Pittsburgh, Ottawa, Carolina, Toronto, St. Louis, in 19 seasons. 777GP
  46 – Grant Fuhr, Edmonton, Toronto, Buffalo, Los Angeles, St. Louis, Calgary, in 19 seasons. 868GP

MOST POINTS BY A GOALTENDER, ONE SEASON:
  14 – **Grant Fuhr**, Edmonton, 1983-84. 45GP – 80 game schedule.
  9 – Curtis Joseph, St. Louis, 1991-92. 60GP – 80 game schedule.
  8 – Mike Palmateer, Washington, 1980-81. 49GP – 80 game schedule.
    – Grant Fuhr, Edmonton, 1987-88. 75GP – 80 game schedule.
    – Ron Hextall, Philadelphia, 1988-89. 64GP – 80 game schedule.
    – Tom Barrasso, Pittsburgh, 1992-93. 63GP – 84 game schedule.

MOST POINTS BY A GOALTENDER, ONE GAME:
  3 – **Jeff Reese**, Calgary, Feb. 10, 1993, at Calgary. Calgary 13, San Jose 1.

Not only did Raymond Bourque cap his career and the 2000-01 season with a Stanley Cup victory, he also passed Paul Coffey to become the NHL's career leader in assists and points by a defenseman.

SCORING BY A ROOKIE

MOST GOALS BY A ROOKIE, ONE SEASON:
76 – Teemu Selanne, Winnipeg, 1992-93. 84GP – 84 game schedule.
 53 – Mike Bossy, NY Islanders, 1977-78. 73GP – 80 game schedule.
 51 – Joe Nieuwendyk, Calgary, 1987-88. 75GP – 80 game schedule.
 45 – Dale Hawerchuk, Winnipeg, 1981-82. 80GP – 80 game schedule.
  – Luc Robitaille, Los Angeles, 1986-87. 79GP – 80 game schedule.

MOST GOALS BY A PLAYER IN HIS FIRST NHL SEASON, ONE GAME:
5 – Howie Meeker, Toronto, Jan. 8, 1947, at Toronto. Toronto 10, Chicago 4.
  – Don Murdoch, NY Rangers, Oct. 12, 1976, at Minnesota.
  NY Rangers 10, Minnesota 4.

MOST GOALS BY A PLAYER IN HIS FIRST NHL GAME:
3 – Alex Smart, Montreal, Jan. 14, 1943, at Montreal. Montreal 5, Chicago 1.
  – Real Cloutier, Quebec, Oct. 10, 1979, at Quebec. Atlanta 5, Quebec 3.

MOST ASSISTS BY A ROOKIE, ONE SEASON:
70 – Peter Stastny, Quebec, 1980-81. 77GP – 80 game schedule.
  – Joe Juneau, Boston, 1992-93. 84GP – 84 game schedule.
 63 – Bryan Trottier, NY Islanders, 1975-76. 80GP – 80 game schedule.
 62 – Sergei Makarov, Calgary, 1989-90. 80GP – 80 game schedule.
 60 – Larry Murphy, Los Angeles, 1980-81. 80GP – 80 game schedule.

MOST ASSISTS BY A PLAYER IN HIS FIRST NHL SEASON, ONE GAME:
7 – Wayne Gretzky, Edmonton, Feb. 15, 1980, at Edmonton.
  Edmonton 8, Washington 2.
 6 – Gary Suter, Calgary, Apr. 4, 1986, at Calgary. Calgary 9, Edmonton 3.

MOST ASSISTS BY A PLAYER IN HIS FIRST NHL GAME:
4 – Dutch Reibel, Detroit, Oct. 8, 1953, at Detroit. Detroit 4, NY Rangers 1.
  – Roland Eriksson, Minnesota, Oct. 6, 1976, at NY Rangers.
  NY Rangers 6, Minnesota 5.
 3 – Al Hill, Philadelphia, Feb. 14, 1977, at Philadelphia. Philadelphia 6,
  St. Louis 4.
  – Jarno Kultanen, Boston, Oct. 5, 2000, at Boston. Boston 4, Ottawa 4.
  – Stanislav Chistov, Anaheim, Oct. 10, 2002, at St. Louis. Anaheim 4,
  St. Louis 3.

MOST POINTS BY A ROOKIE, ONE SEASON:
132 – Teemu Selanne, Winnipeg, 1992-93. 84GP – 84 game schedule.
 109 – Peter Stastny, Quebec, 1980-81. 77GP – 80 game schedule.
 103 – Dale Hawerchuk, Winnipeg, 1981-82. 80GP – 80 game schedule.
 102 – Joe Juneau, Boston, 1992-93. 84GP – 84 game schedule.
 100 – Mario Lemieux, Pittsburgh, 1984-85. 73GP – 80 game schedule.

MOST POINTS BY A PLAYER IN HIS FIRST NHL SEASON, ONE GAME:
8 – Peter Stastny, Quebec, Feb. 22, 1981, at Washington. 4G-4A.
  Quebec 11, Washington 7.
  – Anton Stastny, Quebec, Feb. 22, 1981, at Washington. 3G-5A.
  Quebec 11, Washington 7.
 7 – Wayne Gretzky, Edmonton, Feb. 15, 1980, at Edmonton. 7A.
  Edmonton 8, Washington 2.
  – Sergei Makarov, Calgary, Feb. 25, 1990, at Calgary. 2G-5A.
  Calgary 10, Edmonton 4.
 6 – Wayne Gretzky, Edmonton, Mar. 29, 1980, at Toronto. 2G-4A.
  Edmonton 8, Toronto 5.
  – Gary Suter, Calgary, Apr. 4, 1986, at Calgary. 6A.
  Calgary 9, Edmonton 3.

MOST POINTS BY A PLAYER IN HIS FIRST NHL GAME:
5 – Al Hill, Philadelphia, Feb. 14, 1977, at Philadelphia. 2G-3A.
  Philadelphia 6, St. Louis 4.
 4 – Alex Smart, Montreal, Jan. 14, 1943, at Montreal. 3G-1A.
  Montreal 5, Chicago 1.
  – Dutch Reibel, Detroit, Oct. 8, 1953, at Detroit. 4A.
  Detroit 4, NY Rangers 1.
  – Roland Eriksson, Minnesota, Oct. 6, 1976, at NY Rangers. 4A.
  NY Rangers 6, Minnesota 5.
  – Stanislav Chistov, Anaheim, Oct. 10, 2002, at St. Louis. 1G-3A.
  Anaheim 4, St. Louis 3.

SCORING BY A ROOKIE DEFENSEMAN

MOST GOALS BY A ROOKIE DEFENSEMAN, ONE SEASON:
23 – Brian Leetch, NY Rangers, 1988-89. 68GP – 80 game schedule.
 22 – Barry Beck, Colorado, 1977-78. 75GP – 80 game schedule.
 19 – Reed Larson, Detroit, 1977-78. 75GP – 80 game schedule.
  – Phil Housley, Buffalo, 1982-83. 77GP – 80 game schedule.

MOST ASSISTS BY A ROOKIE DEFENSEMAN, ONE SEASON:
60 – Larry Murphy, Los Angeles, 1980-81. 80GP – 80 game schedule.
 55 – Chris Chelios, Montreal, 1984-85. 74GP – 80 game schedule.
 50 – Stefan Persson, NY Islanders, 1977-78. 66GP – 80 game schedule.
  – Gary Suter, Calgary, 1985-86. 80GP – 80 game schedule.
 49 – Nicklas Lidstrom, Detroit, 1991-92. 80GP – 80 game schedule.

MOST POINTS BY A ROOKIE DEFENSEMAN, ONE SEASON:
76 – Larry Murphy, Los Angeles, 1980-81. 80GP – 80 game schedule.
 71 – Brian Leetch, NY Rangers, 1988-89. 68GP – 80 game schedule.
 68 – Gary Suter, Calgary, 1985-86. 80GP – 80 game schedule.
 66 – Phil Housley, Buffalo, 1982-83. 77GP – 80 game schedule.
 65 – Raymond Bourque, Boston, 1979-80. 80GP – 80 game schedule.

Mike Bossy set a rookie scoring record with 53 goals in 1977-78 and went on to top 50 for a record nine consecutive seasons.
He fell short only in his final season of 1986–87 when injuries limited him to 38 goals in 63 games.

PER-GAME SCORING AVERAGES

HIGHEST GOALS-PER-GAME AVERAGE, CAREER
(AMONG PLAYERS WITH 200-OR-MORE GOALS):
.776 – **Mario Lemieux**, Pittsburgh, 1984-85 – 1996-97,
2000-01 – 2002-03, with 682G in 879GP.
.762 – Mike Bossy, NY Islanders, 1977-78 – 1986-87, with 573G in 752GP.
.756 – Cy Denneny, Ottawa, Boston, 1917-18 – 1928-29, with 248G in 328GP.
.742 – Babe Dye, Toronto, Hamilton, Chicago, NY Americans,
1919-20 – 1930-31, with 201G in 271GP.
.623 – Pavel Bure, Vancouver, Florida, NY Rangers, 1991-92 – 2002-03,
with 437G in 702GP.

HIGHEST GOALS-PER-GAME AVERAGE, ONE SEASON
(AMONG PLAYERS WITH 20-OR-MORE GOALS):
2.20 – **Joe Malone**, Montreal, 1917-18, with 44G in 20GP.
1.80 – Cy Denneny, Ottawa, 1917-18, with 36G in 20GP.
1.64 – Newsy Lalonde, Montreal, 1917-18, with 23G in 14GP.
1.63 – Joe Malone, Quebec, 1919-20, with 39G in 24GP.
1.61 – Newsy Lalonde, Montreal, 1919-20, with 37G in 23GP.

HIGHEST GOALS-PER-GAME AVERAGE, ONE SEASON
(AMONG PLAYERS WITH 50-OR-MORE GOALS):
1.18 – **Wayne Gretzky**, Edmonton, 1983-84, with 87G in 74GP.
1.15 – Wayne Gretzky, Edmonton, 1981-82, with 92G in 80GP.
     – Mario Lemieux, Pittsburgh, 1992-93, with 69G in 60GP.
1.12 – Mario Lemieux, Pittsburgh, 1988-89, with 85G in 76GP.
1.10 – Brett Hull, St. Louis, 1990-91, with 86G in 78GP.
1.02 – Cam Neely, Boston, 1993-94, with 50G in 49GP.
1.00 – Maurice Richard, Montreal, 1944-45, with 50G in 50GP.

HIGHEST ASSISTS-PER-GAME AVERAGE, CAREER
(AMONG PLAYERS WITH 300-OR-MORE ASSISTS):
1.320 – **Wayne Gretzky**, Edmonton, Los Angeles, St. Louis, NY Rangers,
1979-80 – 1998-99, with 1,963A in 1,487GP.
1.149 – Mario Lemieux, Pittsburgh, 1984-85 – 1996-97,
2000-01 – 2002-03, with 1,010A in 879GP.
.982 – Bobby Orr, Boston, Chicago, 1966-67 – 1978-79, with 645A in 657GP.
.902 – Peter Forsberg, Quebec, Colorado, 1994-95 – 2000-01, 2002-03,
with 488A in 541GP.
.832 – Adam Oates, Detroit, St. Louis, Boston, Washington, Philadelphia,
Anaheim, 1984-85 – 2002-03, with 1,063A in 1,277GP.

HIGHEST ASSISTS-PER-GAME AVERAGE, ONE SEASON
(AMONG PLAYERS WITH 35-OR-MORE ASSISTS):
2.04 – **Wayne Gretzky, Edmonton**, 1985-86, with 163A in 80GP.
1.70 – Wayne Gretzky, Edmonton, 1987-88, with 109A in 64GP.
1.69 – Wayne Gretzky, Edmonton, 1984-85, with 135A in 80GP.
1.59 – Wayne Gretzky, Edmonton, 1983-84, with 118A in 74GP.
1.56 – Wayne Gretzky, Edmonton, 1982-83, with 125A in 80GP.
1.56 – Wayne Gretzky, Los Angeles, 1990-91, with 122A in 78GP.
1.53 – Wayne Gretzky, Edmonton, 1986-87, with 121A in 79GP.
1.52 – Mario Lemieux, Pittsburgh, 1992-93, with 91A in 60GP.
1.50 – Wayne Gretzky, Edmonton, 1981-82, with 120A in 80GP.
1.50 – Mario Lemieux, Pittsburgh, 1988-89, with 114A in 76GP.

HIGHEST POINTS-PER-GAME AVERAGE, CAREER:
(AMONG PLAYERS WITH 500-OR-MORE POINTS):
1.925 – **Mario Lemieux**, Pittsburgh, 1984-85 – 1996-97,
2000-01 – 2002-03, with 1,692PTS (682G-1,010A) in 879GP.
1.921 – Wayne Gretzky, Edmonton, Los Angeles, St. Louis, NY Rangers,
1979-80 – 1998-99, with 2,857PTS (894G-1,963A) in 1,487GP.
1.497 – Mike Bossy, NY Islanders, 1977-78 – 1986-87, with 1,126PTS (573G-553A)
in 752GP.
1.393 – Bobby Orr, Boston, Chicago, 1966-67 – 1978-79, with 915PTS
(270G-645A) in 657GP.
1.314 – Marcel Dionne, Detroit, Los Angeles, NY Rangers, 1971-72 – 1988-89, with
1,771PTS (731G-1,040A) in 1,348GP.

HIGHEST POINTS-PER-GAME AVERAGE, ONE SEASON
(AMONG PLAYERS WITH 50-OR-MORE POINTS):
2.77 – **Wayne Gretzky**, Edmonton, 1983-84, with 205PTS in 74GP.
2.69 – Wayne Gretzky, Edmonton, 1985-86, with 215PTS in 80GP.
2.67 – Mario Lemieux, Pittsburgh, 1992-93, with 160PTS in 60GP.
2.65 – Wayne Gretzky, Edmonton, 1981-82, with 212PTS in 80GP.
2.62 – Mario Lemieux, Pittsburgh, 1988-89, with 199PTS in 76GP.
2.60 – Wayne Gretzky, Edmonton, 1984-85, with 208PTS in 80GP.
2.45 – Wayne Gretzky, Edmonton, 1982-83, with 196PTS in 80GP.
2.33 – Wayne Gretzky, Edmonton, 1987-88, with 149PTS in 64GP.
2.32 – Wayne Gretzky, Edmonton, 1986-87, with 183PTS in 79GP.
2.30 – Mario Lemieux, Pittsburgh, 1995-96, with 161PTS in 70GP.
2.18 – Mario Lemieux, Pittsburgh, 1987-88, with 168PTS in 77GP.
2.15 – Wayne Gretzky, Los Angeles, 1988-89, with 168PTS in 78GP.
2.09 – Wayne Gretzky, Los Angeles, 1990-91, with 163PTS in 78GP.
2.08 – Mario Lemieux, Pittsburgh, 1989-90, with 123PTS in 59GP.

*Dave Andreychuk scored his 600th goal
on November 23, 2002 and went on to
reach the 20-goal plateau for the 18th time
in his career. Andreychuk also broke
Phil Esposito's record of 249 career
power-play goals in 2002-03.*

SCORING PLATEAUS

MOST 20-OR-MORE GOAL SEASONS:
22 – **Gordie Howe**, Detroit, Hartford, in 26 seasons.
20 – Ron Francis, Hartford, Pittsburgh, Carolina, in 22 seasons.
18 – Dave Andreychuk, Buffalo, Toronto, New Jersey, Boston, Colorado,
Tampa Bay, in 21 seasons.
17 – Marcel Dionne, Detroit, Los Angeles, NY Rangers, in 18 seasons.
   – Mike Gartner, Washington, Minnesota, NY Rangers, Toronto,
Phoenix, in 19 seasons.
   – Wayne Gretzky, Edmonton, Los Angeles, St. Louis, NY Rangers,
in 20 seasons.
   – Mark Messier, Edmonton, NY Rangers, Vancouver, in 24 seasons.

MOST CONSECUTIVE 20-OR-MORE GOAL SEASONS:
22 – **Gordie Howe**, Detroit, 1949-50 – 1970-71.
17 – Marcel Dionne, Detroit, Los Angeles, NY Rangers, 1971-72 – 1987-88.
16 – Phil Esposito, Chicago, Boston, NY Rangers, 1964-65 – 1979-80.
   – Brett Hull, Calgary, St. Louis, Dallas, Detroit, 1987-88 – 2002-03.
15 – Mike Gartner, Washington, Minnesota, NY Rangers, Toronto,
1979-80 – 1993-94.
   – Brendan Shanahan, New Jersey, St. Louis, Hartford, Detroit,
1988-89 – 2002-03.

MOST 30-OR-MORE GOAL SEASONS:
   17 – Mike Gartner, Washington, Minnesota, NY Rangers, Toronto, Phoenix, in 19 seasons.
   14 – Gordie Howe, Detroit, Hartford, in 26 seasons.
     – Marcel Dionne, Detroit, Los Angeles, NY Rangers, in 18 seasons.
     – Wayne Gretzky, Edmonton, Los Angeles, St. Louis, NY Rangers, in 20 seasons.
   13 – Bobby Hull, Chicago, Winnipeg, Hartford, in 16 seasons.
     – Phil Esposito, Chicago, Boston, NY Rangers, in 18 seasons.

MOST CONSECUTIVE 30-OR-MORE GOAL SEASONS:
   15 – Mike Gartner, Washington, Minnesota, NY Rangers, Toronto, 1979-80 – 1993-94.
   13 – Bobby Hull, Chicago, 1959-60 – 1971-72.
     – Phil Esposito, Boston, NY Rangers, 1967-68 – 1979-80.
     – Wayne Gretzky, Edmonton, Los Angeles, 1979-80 – 1991-92.
   12 – Marcel Dionne, Detroit, Los Angeles,1974-75 – 1985-86.
     – Jaromir Jagr, Pittsburgh, Washington, 1991-92 – 2002-03.

MOST 40-OR-MORE GOAL SEASONS:
   12 – Wayne Gretzky, Edmonton, Los Angeles, St. Louis, NY Rangers, in 20 seasons.
   10 – Marcel Dionne, Detroit, Los Angeles, NY Rangers, in 18 seasons.
     – Mario Lemieux, Pittsburgh, in 15 seasons.
    9 – Mike Bossy, NY Islanders, in 10 seasons.
     – Mike Gartner, Washington, Minnesota, NY Rangers, Toronto, Phoenix, in 19 seasons.

MOST CONSECUTIVE 40-OR-MORE GOAL SEASONS:
   12 – Wayne Gretzky, Edmonton, Los Angeles, 1979-80 – 1990-91.
    9 – Mike Bossy, NY Islanders, 1977-78 – 1985-86.
    8 – Luc Robitaille, Los Angeles, 1986-87 – 1993-94.
    7 – Phil Esposito, Boston, 1968-69 – 1974-75.
     – Michel Goulet, Quebec, 1981-82 – 1987-88.
     – Jari Kurri, Edmonton, 1982-83 – 1988-89.

MOST 50-OR-MORE GOAL SEASONS:
    9 – Mike Bossy, NY Islanders, in 10 seasons.
     – Wayne Gretzky, Edmonton, Los Angeles, St. Louis, NY Rangers, in 20 seasons.
    6 – Guy Lafleur, Montreal, NY Rangers, Quebec, in 17 seasons.
     – Marcel Dionne, Detroit, Los Angeles, NY Rangers, in 18 seasons.
     – Mario Lemieux, Pittsburgh, in 15 seasons.
    5 – Bobby Hull, Chicago, Winnipeg, Hartford, in 16 seasons.
     – Phil Esposito, Chicago, Boston, NY Rangers, in 18 seasons.
     – Brett Hull, Calgary, St. Louis, Dallas, Detroit, in 17 seasons.
     – Steve Yzerman, Detroit, in 20 seasons.
     – Pavel Bure, Vancouver, Florida, NY Rangers, in 12 seasons.

MOST CONSECUTIVE 50-OR-MORE GOAL SEASONS:
    9 – Mike Bossy, NY Islanders, 1977-78 – 1985-86.
    8 – Wayne Gretzky, Edmonton, 1979-80 – 1986-87.
    6 – Guy Lafleur, Montreal, 1974-75 – 1979-80.
    5 – Phil Esposito, Boston, 1970-71 – 1974-75.
     – Marcel Dionne, Los Angeles, 1978-79 – 1982-83.
     – Brett Hull, St. Louis, 1989-90 – 1993-94.

MOST 60-OR-MORE GOAL SEASONS:
    5 – Mike Bossy, NY Islanders, in 10 seasons.
     – Wayne Gretzky, Edmonton, Los Angeles, St. Louis, NY Rangers, in 20 seasons.
    4 – Phil Esposito, Chicago, Boston, NY Rangers, in 18 seasons.
     – Mario Lemieux, Pittsburgh, in 15 seasons.

MOST CONSECUTIVE 60-OR-MORE GOAL SEASONS:
    4 – Wayne Gretzky, Edmonton, 1981-82 – 1984-85.
    3 – Mike Bossy, NY Islanders, 1980-81 – 1982-83.
     – Brett Hull, St. Louis, 1989-90 – 1991-92.
    2 – Phil Esposito, Boston, 1970-71 – 1971-72, 1973-74 – 1974-75.
     – Jari Kurri, Edmonton, 1984-85 – 1985-86.
     – Mario Lemieux, Pittsburgh, 1987-88 – 1988-89.
     – Steve Yzerman, Detroit, 1988-89 – 1989-90.
     – Pavel Bure, Vancouver, 1992-93 – 1993-94.

MOST 100-OR-MORE POINT SEASONS:
   15 – Wayne Gretzky, Edmonton, Los Angeles, St. Louis, NY Rangers, in 20 seasons.
   10 – Mario Lemieux, Pittsburgh, in 15 seasons.
    8 – Marcel Dionne, Detroit, Los Angeles, NY Rangers, in 18 seasons.
    7 – Mike Bossy, NY Islanders, in 10 seasons.
     – Peter Stastny, Quebec, New Jersey, St. Louis, in 15 seasons.

MOST CONSECUTIVE 100-OR-MORE POINT SEASONS:
   13 – Wayne Gretzky, Edmonton, Los Angeles, 1979-80 – 1991-92.
    6 – Bobby Orr, Boston, 1969-70 – 1974-75.
     – Guy Lafleur, Montreal, 1974-75 – 1979-80.
     – Mike Bossy, NY Islanders,1980-81 – 1985-86.
     – Peter Stastny, Quebec, 1980-81 – 1985-86.
     – Mario Lemieux, Pittsburgh, 1984-85 – 1989-90.
     – Steve Yzerman, Detroit, 1987-88 – 1992-93.

THREE-OR-MORE-GOAL GAMES

MOST THREE-OR-MORE GOAL GAMES, CAREER:
   50 – Wayne Gretzky, Edmonton, Los Angeles, St. Louis, NY Rangers, in 20 seasons, 37 three-goal games, 9 four-goal games, 4 five-goal games.
   40 – Mario Lemieux, Pittsburgh, in 15 seasons, 27 three-goal games, 10 four-goal games, 3 five-goal games.
   39 – Mike Bossy, NY Islanders, in 10 seasons, 30 three-goal games, 9 four-goal games.
   33 – Brett Hull, Calgary, St. Louis, Dallas, Detroit, in 18 seasons, 30 three-goal games, 3 four-goal games.
   32 – Phil Esposito, Chicago, Boston, NY Rangers, in 18 seasons, 27 three-goal games, 5 four-goal games.

MOST THREE-OR-MORE GOAL GAMES, ONE SEASON:
   10 – Wayne Gretzky, Edmonton, 1981-82. 6 three-goal games, 3 four-goal games, 1 five-goal game.
     – Wayne Gretzky, Edmonton, 1983-84. 6 three-goal games, 4 four-goal games.
    9 – Mike Bossy, NY Islanders, 1980-81. 6 three-goal games, 3 four-goal games.
     – Mario Lemieux, Pittsburgh, 1988-89. 7 three-goal games, 1 four-goal game, 1 five-goal game.
    8 – Brett Hull, St. Louis, 1991-92. 8 three-goal games.
    7 – Joe Malone, Montreal, 1917-18. 2 three-goal games, 2 four-goal games, 3 five-goal games.
     – Phil Esposito, Boston, 1970-71. 7 three-goal games.
     – Rick Martin, Buffalo, 1975-76. 6 three-goal games, 1 four-goal game.
     – Alexander Mogilny, Buffalo, 1992-93. 5 three-goal games, 2 four-goal games.

With 30 goals in 2002-03, the Bruins' Mike Knuble doubled his previous best single-season goal-scoring output. On February 14, 2003, he scored two goals in the first 27 seconds of Boston's 6-5 victory over Florida.

SCORING STREAKS

LONGEST CONSECUTIVE GOAL-SCORING STREAK:
16 Games – Punch Broadbent, Ottawa, 1921-22. 27G
14 Games – Joe Malone, Montreal, 1917-18. 35G
13 Games – Newsy Lalonde, Montreal, 1920-21. 24G
– Charlie Simmer, Los Angeles, 1979-80. 17G
12 Games – Cy Denneny, Ottawa, 1917-18. 23G
– Dave Lumley, Edmonton, 1981-82. 15G
– Mario Lemieux, Pittsburgh, 1992-93. 18G

LONGEST CONSECUTIVE ASSIST-SCORING STREAK:
23 Games – Wayne Gretzky, Los Angeles, 1990-91. 48A
18 Games – Adam Oates, Boston, 1992-93. 28A
17 Games – Wayne Gretzky, Edmonton, 1983-84. 38A
– Paul Coffey, Edmonton, 1985-86. 27A
– Wayne Gretzky, Los Angeles, 1989-90. 35A
16 Games – Jaromir Jagr, Pittsburgh, 2000-01. 24A

LONGEST CONSECUTIVE POINT-SCORING STREAK:
51 Games – Wayne Gretzky, Edmonton, 1983-84. 61G-92A-153PTS
46 Games – Mario Lemieux, Pittsburgh, 1989-90. 39G-64A-103PTS
39 Games – Wayne Gretzky, Edmonton, 1985-86. 33G-75A-108PTS
30 Games – Wayne Gretzky, Edmonton, 1982-83. 24G-52A-76PTS
– Mats Sundin, Quebec, 1992-93. 21G-25A-46PTS
28 Games – Guy Lafleur, Montreal, 1976-77. 19G-42A-61PTS
– Wayne Gretzky, Edmonton, 1984-85. 20G-43A-63PTS
– Mario Lemieux, Pittsburgh, 1985-86. 21G-38A-59PTS
– Paul Coffey, Edmonton, 1985-86. 16G-39A-55PTS
– Steve Yzerman, Detroit, 1988-89. 29G-36A-65PTS

LONGEST CONSECUTIVE POINT-SCORING STREAK FROM START OF SEASON:
51 Games – Wayne Gretzky, Edmonton, 1983-84. 61G-92A-153PTS. Streak ended by goaltender Markus Mattsson and Los Angeles on Jan. 28, 1984.

LONGEST CONSECUTIVE POINT-SCORING STREAK BY A DEFENSEMAN:
28 Games – Paul Coffey, Edmonton, 1985-86. 16G-39A-55PTS
19 Games – Raymond Bourque, Boston, 1987-88. 6G-21A-27PTS
17 Games – Raymond Bourque, Boston, 1984-85. 4G-24A-28PTS
– Brian Leetch, NY Rangers, 1991-92. 5G-24A-29PTS
16 Games – Gary Suter, Calgary, 1987-88. 8G-17A-25PTS
15 Games – Bobby Orr, Boston, 1970-71. 10G-23A-33PTS
– Bobby Orr, Boston, 1973-74. 8G-15A-23PTS
– Steve Duchesne, Quebec, 1992-93. 4G-17A-21PTS
– Chris Chelios, Chicago, 1995-96. 4G-16A-20PTS

FASTEST GOALS AND ASSISTS

FASTEST GOAL FROM START OF A GAME:
0:05 – Doug Smail, Winnipeg, Dec. 20, 1981, at Winnipeg. Winnipeg 5, St. Louis 4.
– **Bryan Trottier**, NY Islanders, Mar. 22, 1984, at Boston. NY Islanders 3, Boston 3.
– **Alexander Mogilny**, Buffalo, Dec. 21, 1991, at Toronto. Buffalo 4, Toronto 1.
0:06 – Henry Boucha, Detroit, Jan. 28, 1973, at Montreal. Detroit 4, Montreal 2.
– Jean Pronovost, Pittsburgh, Mar. 25, 1976, at St. Louis. St. Louis 5, Pittsburgh 2.
0:07 – Charlie Conacher, Toronto, Feb. 6, 1932, at Toronto. Toronto 6, Boston 0.
– Danny Gare, Buffalo, Dec. 17, 1978, at Buffalo. Buffalo 6, Vancouver 3.
– Tiger Williams, Los Angeles, Feb. 14, 1987, at Los Angeles. Los Angeles 5, Harford 2.
0:08 – Ron Martin, NY Americans, Dec. 4, 1932, at NY Americans. NY Americans 4, Montreal 2.
– Chuck Arnason, Colorado, Jan. 28, 1977, at Atlanta. Colorado 3, Atlanta 3.
– Wayne Gretzky, Edmonton, Dec. 14, 1983, at NY Rangers. Edmonton 9, NY Rangers 4.
– Gaetan Duchesne, Washington, Mar. 14, 1987, at St. Louis. Washington 3, St. Louis 3.
– Tim Kerr, Philadelphia, Mar. 7, 1989, at Philadelphia. Philadelphia 4, Edmonton 4.
– Grant Ledyard, Buffalo, Dec. 4, 1991, at Winnipeg. Buffalo 4, Winnipeg 4.
– Brent Sutter, Chicago, Feb. 5, 1995, at Vancouver. Chicago 9, Vancouver 4.
– Paul Kariya, Anaheim, Mar. 9, 1997, at Colorado. Anaheim 2, Colorado 2.
– Tony Hrkac, Dallas, Nov. 7, 1998, at Los Angeles. Dallas 4, Los Angeles 3.
– Sergei Fedorov, Detroit, Nov. 21, 1998, at Vancouver. Detroit 4, Vancouver 2.

FASTEST GOAL FROM START OF A PERIOD:
0:04 – Claude Provost, Montreal, Nov. 9, 1957, at Montreal, second period. Montreal 4, Boston 2.
– **Denis Savard**, Chicago, Jan. 12, 1986, at Chicago, third period. Chicago 4, Hartford 2.

FASTEST GOAL BY A PLAYER IN HIS FIRST NHL GAME:
0:15 – Gus Bodnar, Toronto, Oct. 30, 1943, at Toronto. Toronto 5, NY Rangers 2.
0:18 – Danny Gare, Buffalo, Oct. 10, 1974, at Buffalo. Buffalo 9, Boston 5.
0:20 – Alexander Mogilny, Buffalo, Oct. 5, 1989, at Buffalo. Buffalo 4, Quebec 3.

FASTEST TWO GOALS FROM START OF A GAME:
0:27 – Mike Knuble, Boston, Feb. 14, 2003, at Florida at 0:10 and 0:27. Boston 6, Florida 5.

FASTEST TWO GOALS:
0:04 – Nels Stewart, Mtl. Maroons, Jan. 3, 1931, at Montreal at 8:24 and 8:28, third period. Mtl. Maroons 5, Boston 3.
– **Deron Quint**, Winnipeg, Dec. 15, 1995, at Winnipeg at 7:51 and 7:55, second period. Winnipeg 9, Edmonton 4.
0:05 – Pete Mahovlich, Montreal, Feb. 20, 1971, at Montreal at 12:16 and 12:21, third period. Montreal 7, Chicago 1.
0:06 – Jim Pappin, Chicago, Feb. 16, 1972, at Chicago at 2:57 and 3:03, third period. Chicago 3, Philadelphia 3.
– Ralph Backstrom, Los Angeles, Nov. 2, 1972, at Los Angeles at 8:30 and 8:36, third period. Los Angeles 5, Boston 2.
– Lanny McDonald, Calgary, Mar. 22, 1984, at Calgary at 16:23 and 16:29, first period. Detroit 6, Calgary 4.
– Sylvain Turgeon, Hartford, Mar. 28, 1987, at Hartford at 13:59 and 14:05, second period. Hartford 5, Pittsburgh 4.

FASTEST THREE GOALS:
0:21 – Bill Mosienko, Chicago, Mar. 23, 1952, at NY Rangers, against goaltender Lorne Anderson. Mosienko scored at 6:09, 6:20 and 6:30 of third period, all with both teams at full strength. Chicago 7, NY Rangers 6.
0:44 – Jean Béliveau, Montreal, Nov. 5, 1955, at Montreal, against goaltender Terry Sawchuk. Béliveau scored at 0:42, 1:08 and 1:26 of second period, all with Montreal holding a 6-4 man advantage. Montreal 4, Boston 2.

FASTEST THREE ASSISTS:
0:21 – Gus Bodnar, Chicago, Mar. 23, 1952, at NY Rangers, Bodnar assisted on Bill Mosienko's three goals at 6:09, 6:20 and 6:30 of third period. Chicago 7, NY Rangers 6.
0:44 – Bert Olmstead, Montreal, Nov. 5, 1955, at Montreal, Olmstead assisted on Jean Béliveau's three goals at 0:42, 1:08 and 1:26 of second period. Montreal 4, Boston 2.

SHOTS ON GOAL

MOST SHOTS ON GOAL, ONE SEASON:
550 – Phil Esposito, Boston, 1970-71. 78GP – 78 game schedule.
429 – Paul Kariya, Anaheim, 1998-99. 82GP – 82 game schedule.
426 – Phil Esposito, Boston, 1971-72. 76GP – 78 game schedule.
414 – Bobby Hull, Chicago, 1968-69. 74GP – 76 game schedule.

PENALTIES

MOST PENALTY MINUTES, CAREER:
3,966 – Tiger Williams, Toronto, Vancouver, Detroit, Los Angeles, Hartford, in 14 seasons. 962GP
3,565 – Dale Hunter, Quebec, Washington, Colorado, in 19 seasons. 1,407GP
3,381 – Marty McSorley, Pittsburgh, Edmonton, Los Angeles, NY Rangers, San Jose, Boston, in 17 seasons. 961GP
3,300 – Bob Probert, Detroit, Chicago, in 17 seasons. 935GP
3,198 – Tie Domi, Toronto, NY Rangers, Winnipeg, in 14 seasons. 863GP

MOST PENALTY MINUTES, CAREER, INCLUDING PLAYOFFS:
4,421 – Tiger Williams, Toronto, Vancouver, Detroit, Los Angeles, Hartford, 3,966 in 962 regular-season games; 455 in 83 playoff games.
4,294 – Dale Hunter, Quebec, Washington, Colorado, 3,565 in 1,407 regular-season games; 729 in 186 playoff games.
3,755 – Marty McSorley, Pittsburgh, Edmonton, Los Angeles, NY Rangers, San Jose, Boston, 3,381 in 961 regular-season games; 374 in 115 playoff games.
3,584 – Chris Nilan, Montreal, NY Rangers, Boston, 3,043 in 688 regular-season games; 541 in 111 playoff games.
3,574 – Bob Probert, Detroit, Chicago, 3,300 in 935 regular season games; 274 in 81 playoff games.

MOST PENALTY MINUTES, ONE SEASON:
472 – Dave Schultz, Philadelphia, 1974-75.
409 – Paul Baxter, Pittsburgh, 1981-82.
408 – Mike Peluso, Chicago, 1991-92.
405 – Dave Schultz, Los Angeles, Pittsburgh, 1977-78.

MOST PENALTIES, ONE GAME:
10 – Chris Nilan, Boston, Mar. 31, 1991, at Boston vs. Hartford. 6 minors, 2 majors, 1 10-minute misconduct, 1 game misconduct.
9 – Jim Dorey, Toronto, Oct. 16, 1968, at Toronto vs. Pittsburgh. 4 minors, 2 majors, 2 10-minute misconducts, 1 game misconduct.
– Dave Schultz, Pittsburgh, Apr. 6, 1978, at Detroit. 5 minors, 2 majors, 2 10-minute misconducts.
– Randy Holt, Los Angeles, Mar. 11, 1979, at Philadelphia. 1 minor, 3 majors, 2 10-minute misconducts, 3 game misconducts.
– Russ Anderson, Pittsburgh, Jan. 19, 1980, at Pittsburgh. 3 minors, 3 majors, 3 game misconducts.
– Kim Clackson, Quebec, Mar. 8, 1981, at Quebec. 4 minors, 3 majors, 2 game misconducts.
– Terry O'Reilly, Boston, Dec. 19, 1984, at Hartford. 5 minors, 3 majors, 1 game misconduct.
– Larry Playfair, Los Angeles, Dec. 9, 1986, at NY Islanders. 6 minors, 2 majors, 1 10-minute misconduct.
– Marty McSorley, Los Angeles, Apr. 14, 1992, at Vancouver. 5 minors, 2 majors, 1 10-minute misconduct, 1 game misconduct.
– Reed Low, St. Louis, Dec. 31, 2002, at St. Louis. 4 minors, 1 major, 1 10-minute misconduct, 3 game misconduct.

MOST PENALTY MINUTES, ONE GAME:
67 – Randy Holt, Los Angeles, Mar. 11, 1979, at Philadelphia. 1 minor, 3 majors, 2 10-minute misconducts, 3 game misconducts.
57 – Brad Smith, Toronto, Nov. 15, 1986, at Toronto vs. Detroit. 1 minor, 3 majors, 1 10-minute misconducts, 2 game misconducts.
– Reed Low, St. Louis, Feb. 28, 2002, at St. Louis vs. Calgary. 1 minor, 3 majors, 1 10-minute misconduct, 3 game misconducts.

MOST PENALTIES, ONE PERIOD:
  9 – **Randy Holt**, Los Angeles, Mar. 11, 1979, at Philadelphia, first period.
      1 minor, 3 majors, 2 10-minute misconducts, 3 game misconducts.

MOST PENALTY MINUTES, ONE PERIOD:
  67 – **Randy Holt**, Los Angeles, Mar. 11, 1979, at Philadelphia, first period.
      1 minor, 3 majors, 2 10-minute misconducts, 3 game misconducts.

GOALTENDING

MOST GAMES APPEARED IN BY A GOALTENDER, CAREER:
  1,029 – Patrick Roy, Montreal, Colorado,1984-85 – 2002-03.
    971 – Terry Sawchuk, Detroit, Boston, Toronto, Los Angeles, NY Rangers,
        1949-50 – 1969-70.
    906 – Glenn Hall, Detroit, Chicago, St. Louis, 1952-53 – 1970-71.
    886 – Tony Esposito, Montreal, Chicago, 1968-69 – 1983-84.
    882 – John Vanbiesbrouck, NY Rangers, Florida, Philadelphia, NY Islanders,
        New Jersey, 1981-82 – 2001-02.

MOST CONSECUTIVE COMPLETE GAMES BY A GOALTENDER:
  502 – Glenn Hall, Detroit, Chicago. Played 502 games from beginning of
      1955-56 season through first 12 games of 1962-63 season. In his 503rd
      straight game, Nov. 7, 1962, at Chicago, Hall was removed from the
      game against Boston with a back injury in the first period.

MOST GAMES APPEARED IN BY A GOALTENDER, ONE SEASON:
  79 – Grant Fuhr, St. Louis, 1995-96.
    77 – Martin Brodeur, New Jersey, 1995-96.
      – Bill Ranford, Edmonton, Boston, 1995-96.
      – Arturs Irbe, Carolina, 2000-01.
      – Marc Denis, Columbus, 2002-03.

MOST MINUTES PLAYED BY A GOALTENDER, CAREER:
  60,235 – Patrick Roy, Montreal, Colorado, 1984-85 – 2002-03.
  57,194 – Terry Sawchuk, Detroit, Boston, Toronto, Los Angeles, NY Rangers,
        1949-50 – 1969-70.

MOST MINUTES PLAYED BY A GOALTENDER, ONE SEASON:
  4,511 – Marc Denis, Columbus, 2002-03.

MOST SHUTOUTS, CAREER:
  103 – Terry Sawchuk, Detroit, Boston, Toronto, Los Angeles, NY Rangers,
      in 21 seasons.
    94 – George Hainsworth, Montreal, Toronto, in 11 seasons.
    84 – Glenn Hall, Detroit, Chicago, St. Louis, in 18 seasons.

MOST SHUTOUTS, ONE SEASON:
  22 – George Hainsworth, Montreal, 1928-29. 44GP
    15 – Alex Connell, Ottawa, 1925-26. 36GP
      – Alex Connell, Ottawa, 1927-28. 44GP
      – Hal Winkler, Boston, 1927-28. 44GP
      – Tony Esposito, Chicago, 1969-70. 63GP
    14 – George Hainsworth, Montreal, 1926-27. 44GP

LONGEST SHUTOUT SEQUENCE BY A GOALTENDER:
  461:29 – Alex Connell, Ottawa, 1927-28, six consecutive shutouts.
      (Forward passing not permitted in attacking zones in 1927-28.)
    343:05 – George Hainsworth, Montreal, 1928-29, four consecutive shutouts.
      (Forward passing not permitted in attacking zones in 1928-29.)
    324:40 – Roy Worters, NY Americans, 1930-31, four consecutive shutouts.
    309:21 – Bill Durnan, Montreal, 1948-49, four consecutive shutouts.

MOST WINS BY A GOALTENDER, CAREER:
  551 – Patrick Roy, Montreal, Colorado, in 19 seasons. 1,029GP
    447 – Terry Sawchuk, Detroit, Boston, Toronto, Los Angeles, NY Rangers,
        in 21 seasons. 971GP
    435 – Jacques Plante, Montreal, NY Rangers, St. Louis, Toronto, Boston,
        in 18 seasons. 837GP
    423 – Tony Esposito, Montreal, Chicago, in 16 seasons. 886GP

MOST WINS BY A GOALTENDER, ONE SEASON:
  47 – Bernie Parent, Philadelphia, 1973-74. 73GP
    44 – Bernie Parent, Philadelphia, 1974-75. 68GP
      – Terry Sawchuk, Detroit, 1950-51. 70GP
      – Terry Sawchuk, Detroit, 1951-52. 70GP

LONGEST WINNING STREAK BY A GOALTENDER, ONE SEASON:
  17 – Gilles Gilbert, Boston, 1975-76.
    14 – Tiny Thompson, Boston, 1929-30.
      – Ross Brooks, Boston, 1973-74.
      – Tom Barrasso, Pittsburgh, 1992-93.

LONGEST UNDEFEATED STREAK BY A GOALTENDER, ONE SEASON:
  32 Games – **Gerry Cheevers**, Boston, 1971-72. 24w-8T
  31 Games – Pete Peeters, Boston, 1982-83. 26w-5T
  27 Games – Pete Peeters, Philadelphia, 1979-80. 22w-5T

LONGEST UNDEFEATED STREAK BY A GOALTENDER IN HIS FIRST NHL SEASON:
  23 Games – **Grant Fuhr**, Edmonton, 1981-82. 15w-8T

LONGEST UNDEFEATED STREAK BY A GOALTENDER FROM START OF CAREER:
  16 Games – **Patrick Lalime**, Pittsburgh, 1996-97. 14w-2T

MOST 40-OR-MORE WIN SEASONS BY A GOALTENDER:
  4 – Martin Brodeur, New Jersey, in 11 seasons.
    3 – Terry Sawchuk, Detroit, Boston, Toronto, Los Angeles, NY Rangers,
        in 21 seasons.
      – Jacques Plante, Montreal, NY Rangers, St. Louis, Toronto, Boston,
        in 18 seasons.
    2 – Bernie Parent, Boston, Philadelphia, Toronto, in 13 seasons.
      – Ken Dryden, Montreal, in 8 seasons.
      – Ed Belfour, Chicago, San Jose, Dallas, Toronto, in 14 seasons.

MOST CONSECUTIVE 40-OR-MORE WIN SEASONS BY A GOALTENDER:
  2 – Terry Sawchuk, Detroit, 1950-51 – 1951-52.
    – **Bernie Parent**, Philadelphia, 1973-74 – 1974-75.
    – **Ken Dryden**, Montreal, 1975-76 – 1976-77.
    – **Martin Brodeur**, New Jersey, 1999-2000 – 2000-01.

MOST 30-OR-MORE WIN SEASONS BY A GOALTENDER:
  13 – Patrick Roy, Montreal, Colorado, in 19 seasons.
    8 – Tony Esposito, Montreal, Chicago, in 16 seasons.
      – Ed Belfour, Chicago, San Jose, Dallas, Toronto, in 14 seasons.
      – Martin Brodeur, New Jersey, in 11 seasons.
    7 – Jacques Plante, Montreal, NY Rangers, St. Louis, Toronto, Boston,
        in 18 seasons.
      – Ken Dryden, Montreal, in 8 seasons.

MOST CONSECUTIVE 30-OR-MORE WIN SEASONS BY A GOALTENDER:
  8 – Patrick Roy, Montreal, Colorado, 1995-96 – 2002-03.
    – **Martin Brodeur**, New Jersey, 1995-96 – 2002-03.
    7 – Tony Esposito, Chicago, 1969-70 – 1975-76.
    6 – Jacques Plante, Montreal, 1954-55 – 1959-60.
    5 – Terry Sawchuk, Detroit, 1950-51 – 1954-55.
      – Ken Dryden, Montreal, 1974-75 – 1978-79.

MOST LOSSES BY A GOALTENDER, CAREER:
  352 – Gump Worsley, NY Rangers, Montreal, Minnesota, in 21 seasons. 861GP
    351 – Gilles Meloche, Chicago, California, Cleveland, Minnesota, Pittsburgh,
        in 18 seasons. 788GP
    346 – John Vanbiesbrouck, NY Rangers, Florida, Philadelphia, NY Islanders,
        New Jersey, in 20 seasons. 882GP
    332 – Terry Sawchuk, Detroit, Boston, Toronto, Los Angeles, NY Rangers,
        in 21 seasons. 971GP

MOST LOSSES BY A GOALTENDER, ONE SEASON:
  48 – Gary Smith, California, 1970-71. 71GP
    47 – Al Rollins, Chicago, 1953-54. 66GP
    46 – Peter Sidorkiewicz, Ottawa, 1992-93. 64GP
    44 – Harry Lumley, Chicago, 1951-52. 70GP

*A talented goaltender rarely lucky enough to play with a contending team,
Gilles Meloche missed the playoffs in each of his first full eight seasons.
His 351 regular-season losses are second-most in NHL history. Only
Gump Worsley, who lost 352 games, has more.*

Active NHL Players' Three-or-More-Goal Games

Regular Season

Teams named are the ones the players were with at the time of their multiple-scoring games. Players listed alphabetically.

Three-time Selke Trophy winner Jere Lehtinen scored a career-high 31 goals last season. He netted his second career hat trick in a 7-4 Dallas win over Los Angeles on January 7, 2003.

Player	Team	3-Goals	4-Goals	5-Goals
Alfredsson, Daniel	Ottawa	4	—	—
Allison, Jason	Boston	4	—	—
Amonte, Tony	NYR, Chi.	7	—	—
Andersson, Niklas	NY Islanders	1	—	—
Andreychuk, Dave	Buf., Tor., Bos.	7	3	1
Antropov, Nik	Toronto	1	—	—
Arnason, Tyler	Chicago	1	—	—
Arnott, Jason	Edm., N.J., Dal.	4	—	—
Arvedson, Magnus	Ottawa	1	—	—
Audette, Donald	Buf., Atl.	4	—	—
Barnes, Stu	Wpg., Pit.	3	—	—
Battaglia, Bates	Carolina	1	—	—
Belanger, Eric	Los Angeles	1	—	—
Berezin, Sergei	Toronto	2	—	—
Bertuzzi, Todd	Vancouver	3	—	—
Blake, Jason	NY Islanders	1	—	—
Blake, Rob	Los Angeles	1	—	—
Bondra, Peter	Washington	12	5	1
Bonk, Radek	Ottawa	1	—	—
Brind'Amour, Rod	Phi., Car.	2	—	—
Brown, Curtis	Buffalo	1	—	—
Buchberger, Kelly	Edmonton	1	—	—
Bure, Pavel	Van., Fla., NYR	17	3	—
Bure, Valeri	Calgary	1	—	—
Butsayev, Viacheslav	Philadelphia	1	—	—
Carter, Anson	Boston	1	—	—
Cassels, Andrew	Vancouver	1	—	—
Cole, Erik	Carolina	2	—	—
Conroy, Craig	St. Louis	1	—	—
Corson, Shayne	Mtl., Edm.	3	—	—
Czerkawski, Mariusz	Edm., NYI	4	—	—
Dackell, Andreas	Ottawa	1	—	—
Dahlen, Ulf	NYR, Min., S.J.	4	—	—
Damphousse, Vincent	Tor., Edm., Mtl., S.J.	11	1	—
Dawe, Jason	Buffalo	2	—	—
Daze, Eric	Chicago	5	1	—
Deadmarsh, Adam	Col., L.A.	2	—	—
Demitra, Pavol	St. Louis	3	—	—
Devereaux, Boyd	Edmonton	1	—	—
Donovan, Shean	Atlanta	1	—	—
Dopita, Jiri	Philadelphia	—	1	—
Druken, Harold	Vancouver	1	—	—
Dumont, Jean-Pierre	Chi., Buf.	3	—	—
Dvorak, Radek	NY Rangers	1	1	—
Eastwood, Mike	St. Louis	1	—	—
Elias, Patrik	New Jersey	5	1	—
Fedorov, Sergei	Detroit	4	1	1
Fleury, Theoren	Cgy., Col., NYR	15	—	—
Forsberg, Peter	Colorado	6	—	—
Francis, Ron	Hfd., Pit.	10	1	—
Friesen, Jeff	San Jose	2	—	—
Gaborik, Marian	Minnesota	5	—	—
Gagne, Simon	Philadelphia	1	—	—
Gelinas, Martin	Edm., Van.	2	1	—
Gilchrist, Brent	Montreal	1	—	—
Gilmour, Doug	St.L., Tor.	3	—	—
Gomez, Scott	New Jersey	1	—	—
Gonchar, Sergei	Washington	1	—	—
Gratton, Chris	Tampa Bay	1	—	—
Graves, Adam	Edm., NYR	6	—	—
Green, Travis	NY Islanders	1	—	—
Grier, Mike	Edmonton	1	—	—
Grosek, Michal	Buffalo	1	—	—
Guerin, Bill	N.J., Bos.	3	—	—
Handzus, Michal	St. Louis	1	—	—
Harvey, Todd	Dal., S.J.	2	—	—
Havlat, Martin	Ottawa	3	—	—
Heatley, Dany	Atlanta	1	—	—
Heinze, Steve	Bos., Buf.	5	—	—
Hejduk, Milan	Colorado	1	—	—
Hlavac, Jan	NYR, Car.	3	—	—
Hoglund, Jonas	Toronto	1	—	—
Hogue, Benoit	NY Islanders	1	—	—
Holik, Bobby	New Jersey	3	—	—
Holmstrom, Tomas	Detroit	1	—	—
Hossa, Marian	Ottawa	3	1	—
Housley, Phil	Buffalo	2	—	—
Hull, Brett	Cgy., St.L., Dal., Det.	30	3	—
Hull, Jody	Hartford	1	—	—
Iginla, Jarome	Calgary	2	1	—
Jagr, Jaromir	Pittsburgh	10	1	—
Johansson, Andreas	Nashville	1	—	—
Juneau, Joe	Bos., Wsh.	2	—	—
Kallio, Tomi	Atlanta	1	—	—
Kapanen, Sami	Carolina	3	—	—
Kariya, Paul	Anaheim	8	—	—
Klatt, Trent	Philadelphia	1	—	—
Knutsen, Espen	Columbus	1	—	—
Koivu, Saku	Montreal	1	—	—
Konowalchuk, Steve	Washington	3	—	—
Korolev, Igor	Winnipeg	1	—	—
Kovalchuk, Ilya	Atlanta	1	—	—
Kovalev, Alex	NYR, Pit.	10	—	—
Kozlov, Viktor	Florida	1	—	—
Kozlov, Vyacheslav	Detroit	2	1	—
Laaksonen, Antti	Minnesota	1	—	—
Langkow, Daymond	Phoenix	2	—	—
Laperriere, Ian	Los Angeles	1	—	—
Lapointe, Martin	Det., Bos.	2	—	—
Laraque, Georges	Edmonton	1	—	—
Larionov, Igor	Van., S.J.	4	—	—
Lecavalier, Vincent	Tampa Bay	2	—	—
LeClair, John	Philadelphia	8	3	—
Lehtinen, Jere	Dallas	2	—	—
Lemieux, Claude	Mtl., N.J., Col.	1	—	—
Lemieux, Mario	Pittsburgh	27	10	3
Linden, Trevor	Van., Mtl.	5	—	—
Lindros, Eric	Phi., NYR	12	1	—
MacInnis, Al	Cgy., St.L.	3	—	—
Madden, John	New Jersey	1	1	—
Malakhov, Vladimir	Montreal	1	—	—
Maltby, Kirk	Detroit	1	—	—
Manderville, Kent	Hartford	1	—	—
Marleau, Patrick	San Jose	2	—	—
McEachern, Shawn	Ott., Atl.	2	—	—
McInnis, Marty	Cgy., Ana., Bos.	3	—	—
McKay, Randy	New Jersey	1	1	—
McKenzie, Jim	Phoenix	1	—	—
Mellanby, Scott	St. Louis	—	1	—
Messier, Mark	Edm., NYR	15	4	—
Miller, Kevin	Det., St.L., S.J.	4	—	—
Modano, Mike	Min., Dal.	6	1	—
Modin, Fredrik	Tampa Bay	1	—	—
Mogilny, Alexander	Buf., Van., N.J., Tor.	15	2	—
Morozov, Aleksey	Pittsburgh	2	—	—
Muller, Kirk	N.J., Mtl., Tor.	7	—	—
Murray, Glen	L.A., Bos.	4	—	—
Murray, Rem	Edmonton	1	—	—
Naslund, Markus	Pit., Van.	8	1	—
Nedved, Petr	Pit., NYR	6	1	—
Nemchinov, Sergei	NY Rangers	1	—	—
Nieuwendyk, Joe	Cgy., Dal.	9	3	1
Nolan, Owen	Que., S.J.	9	1	—
Nylander, Michael	Hfd., Chi.	1	1	—
Oates, Adam	Bos., Wsh.	6	1	—
Odelein, Lyle	Montreal	1	—	—
Oliver, David	Edmonton	1	—	—
O'Neill, Jeff	Hartford	2	—	—
Ozolinsh, Sandis	Col., Car.	1	—	—
Palffy, Ziggy	NYI, L.A.	8	—	—
Parrish, Mark	Fla., NYI	3	1	—
Peca, Michael	Buffalo	1	—	—
Perreault, Yanic	L.A., Tor., Mtl.	3	1	—
Petersen, Toby	Pittsburgh	1	—	—
Petrov, Oleg	Montreal	1	—	—
Piros, Kamil	Atlanta	1	—	—
Pisani, Fernando	Edmonton	1	—	—
Podein, Shjon	Colorado	1	—	—
Primeau, Keith	Philadelphia	1	—	—
Pyatt, Taylor	Buffalo	1	—	—
Quint, Deron	Columbus	1	—	—
Ranheim, Paul	Calgary	1	—	—
Recchi, Mark	Pit., Mtl., Phi.	5	—	—
Reichel, Robert	Cgy., NYI	5	—	—
Reinprecht, Steve	Colorado	2	—	—
Renberg, Mikael	Phi., T.B.	2	—	—
Rheaume, Pascal	Atlanta	—	1	—
Ricci, Mike	Que., S.J.	1	—	1
Roberts, Gary	Cgy., Car., Tor.	12	1	—
Robitaille, Luc	L.A., Pit.	11	3	—
Roenick, Jeremy	Chi., Phx.	7	2	—
Rolston, Brian	New Jersey	1	—	—
Ronning, Cliff	St.L., Van.	3	—	—
Rucinsky, Martin	Montreal	2	—	—
Sakic, Joe	Que., Col.	11	1	—
Salo, Sami	Ottawa	1	—	—
Samsonov, Sergei	Boston	1	—	—
Sanderson, Geoff	Har., Buf., CBJ	7	1	—
Satan, Miroslav	Buffalo	4	—	—
Savage, Brian	Montreal	6	1	—
Savard, Marc	Calgary	1	1	—
Scatchard, Dave	NY Islanders	2	—	—
Selanne, Teemu	Wpg., Ana., S.J.	16	2	—
Shanahan, Brendan	N.J., St.L., Hfd., Det.	14	1	—
Smolinski, Bryan	Bos., L.A.	3	—	—
Smyth, Ryan	Edmonton	4	—	—
St. Louis, Martin	Tampa Bay	1	—	—
Stillman, Cory	Cgy., St.L.	3	—	—
Straka, Martin	Pittsburgh	4	—	—
Stumpel, Jozef	Bos., L.A.	2	—	—
Sturm, Marco	San Jose	1	—	—
Sullivan, Steve	Tor., Chi.	2	1	—
Sundin, Mats	Que., Tor.	5	—	1
Sydor, Darryl	Dallas	1	—	—
Tanguay, Alex	Colorado	1	—	—
Tenkrat, Petr	Nashville	1	—	—
Thomas, Steve	Chi., NYI	4	2	—
Thornton, Joe	Boston	2	—	—
Thornton, Scott	San Jose	1	—	—
Tkachuk, Keith	Phoenix	7	2	—
Toms, Jeff	NY Rangers	1	—	—
Turgeon, Pierre	Buf., NYI, Mtl., St.L.	15	—	—
Valicevic, Robert	Nashville	1	—	—
Valk, Garry	Anaheim	1	—	—
Vrbata, Radim	Colorado	1	—	—
Walker, Scott	Nashville	1	—	—
Ward, Dixon	Buffalo	1	—	—
Weight, Doug	Edmonton	1	—	—
Wesley, Glen	Boston	1	—	—
Whitney, Ray	Columbus	1	—	—
Wiemer, Jason	Tampa Bay	1	—	—
Willis, Shane	Carolina	1	—	—
Wright, Tyler	Columbus	3	—	—
Yachmenev, Vitali	Los Angeles	1	—	—
Yashin, Alexei	Ott., NYI	8	—	—
Young, Scott	Que., Col.	4	—	—
Yzerman, Steve	Detroit	17	1	—
Zamuner, Rob	Tampa Bay	1	—	—
Zednik, Richard	Washington	1	—	—
Zhamnov, Alexei	Wpg., Chi.	5	—	1
Zubrus, Dainus	Montreal	1	—	—

Top 100 All-Time Goal-Scoring Leaders

* active player

	Player	Seasons	Games	Goals	Goals per game
1.	Wayne Gretzky, Edm., L.A., St.L., NYR .	20	1487	**894**	.601
2.	Gordie Howe, Det., Hfd.	26	1767	**801**	.453
3.	Marcel Dionne, Det., L.A., NYR	18	1348	**731**	.542
4.	Phil Esposito, Chi., Bos., NYR	18	1282	**717**	.559
* 5.	Brett Hull, Cgy., St.L., Dal., Det.	18	1183	**716**	.605
6.	Mike Gartner, Wsh., Min., NYR, Tor., Phx.	19	1432	**708**	.494
* 7.	Mario Lemieux, Pit.	16	879	**682**	.776
* 8.	Mark Messier, Edm., NYR, Van.	24	1680	**676**	.402
* 9.	Steve Yzerman, Det.	20	1378	**660**	.479
* 10.	Luc Robitaille, L.A., Pit., NYR, Det.	17	1286	**631**	.491
* 11.	Dave Andreychuk, Buf., Tor., N.J., Bos., Col., T.B.	21	1515	**613**	.405
12.	Bobby Hull, Chi., Wpg., Hfd.	16	1063	**610**	.574
13.	Dino Ciccarelli, Min., Wsh., Det., T.B., Fla.	19	1232	**608**	.494
14.	Jari Kurri, Edm., L.A., NYR, Ana., Col.	17	1251	**601**	.480
15.	Mike Bossy, NYI	10	752	**573**	.762
16.	Guy Lafleur, Mtl., NYR, Que.	17	1126	**560**	.497
17.	John Bucyk, Det., Bos.	23	1540	**556**	.361
18.	Michel Goulet, Que., Chi.	15	1089	**548**	.503
19.	Maurice Richard, Mtl.	18	978	**544**	.556
20.	Stan Mikita, Chi.	22	1394	**541**	.388
* 21.	Ron Francis, Hfd., Pit., Car.	22	1651	**536**	.325
22.	Frank Mahovlich, Tor., Det., Mtl.	18	1181	**533**	.451
* 23.	Brendan Shanahan, N.J., St.L., Hfd., Det.	16	1186	**533**	.449
24.	Bryan Trottier, NYI, Pit.	18	1279	**524**	.410
25.	Pat Verbeek, N.J., Hfd., NYR, Dal., Det.	20	1424	**522**	.367
26.	Dale Hawerchuk, Wpg., Buf., St.L., Phi.	16	1188	**518**	.436
27.	Gilbert Perreault, Buf.	17	1191	**512**	.430
* 28.	Joe Nieuwendyk, Cgy., Dal., N.J.	17	1113	**511**	.459
* 29.	Joe Sakic, Que., Col.	15	1074	**509**	.474
30.	Jean Beliveau, Mtl.	20	1125	**507**	.451
* 31.	Jaromir Jagr, Pit., Wsh.	13	950	**506**	.533
32.	Joe Mullen, St.L., Cgy., Pit., Bos.	17	1062	**502**	.473
33.	Lanny McDonald, Tor., Col., Cgy.	16	1111	**500**	.450
34.	Glenn Anderson, Edm., Tor., NYR, St.L.	16	1129	**498**	.441
35.	Jean Ratelle, NYR, Bos.	21	1281	**491**	.383
36.	Norm Ullman, Det., Tor.	20	1410	**490**	.348
37.	Brian Bellows, Min., Mtl., T.B., Ana., Wsh.	17	1188	**485**	.408
38.	Darryl Sittler, Tor., Phi., Det.	15	1096	**484**	.442
* 39.	Pierre Turgeon, Buf., NYI, Mtl., St.L., Dal.	16	1139	**480**	.421
40.	Bernie Nicholls, L.A., NYR, Edm., N.J., Chi., S.J.	18	1127	**475**	.421
41.	Denis Savard, Chi., Mtl., T.B.	17	1196	**473**	.395
42.	Pat LaFontaine, NYI, Buf., NYR.	15	865	**468**	.541
43.	Alex Delvecchio, Det.	24	1549	**456**	.294
* 44.	Jeremy Roenick, Chi., Phx., Phi.	15	1062	**456**	.429
* 45.	Theoren Fleury, Cgy., Col., NYR, Chi.	15	1084	**455**	.420
* 46.	Alexander Mogilny, Buf., Van., N.J., Tor.	14	919	**453**	.493
* 47.	Peter Bondra, Wsh.	13	907	**451**	.497
* 48.	Doug Gilmour, St.L., Cgy., Tor., N.J., Chi., Buf., Mtl.	20	1474	**450**	.305
49.	Peter Stastny, Que., N.J., St.L.	15	977	**450**	.461
50.	Rick Middleton, NYR, Bos.	14	1005	**448**	.446
* 51.	Mike Modano, Min., Dal.	15	1025	**444**	.433
52.	Rick Vaive, Van., Tor., Chi., Buf.	13	876	**441**	.503
53.	Steve Larmer, Chi., NYR	15	1006	**441**	.438
54.	Rick Tocchet, Phi., Pit., L.A., Bos., Wsh., Phx.	18	1144	**440**	.385
* 55.	Pavel Bure, Van., Fla., NYR	12	702	**437**	.623
56.	Teemu Selanne, Wpg., Ana., S.J.	11	801	**436**	.544
* 57.	Mats Sundin, Que., Tor.	13	1005	**434**	.432
58.	Dave Taylor, L.A.	17	1111	**431**	.388
* 59.	Mark Recchi, Pit., Phi., Mtl.	15	1091	**430**	.394
60.	Yvan Cournoyer, Mtl.	16	968	**428**	.442
61.	Brian Propp, Phi., Bos., Min., Hfd.	15	1016	**425**	.418
62.	Steve Shutt, Mtl., L.A.	13	930	**424**	.456
63.	Stephane Richer, Mtl., N.J., T.B., St.L., Pit.	17	1054	**421**	.399
* 64.	Vincent Damphousse, Tor., Edm., Mtl., S.J.	17	1296	**420**	.324
65.	Bill Barber, Phi.	14	903	**420**	.465
66.	Garry Unger, Tor., Det., St.L., Atl., L.A., Edm.	16	1105	**413**	.374
67.	John MacLean, N.J., S.J., NYR, Dal.	18	1194	**413**	.346
* 68.	Steve Thomas, Tor., Chi., NYI, N.J., Ana.	19	1191	**411**	.345
69.	Raymond Bourque, Bos., Col.	22	1612	**410**	.254
70.	Ray Ferraro, Hfd., NYI, NYR, L.A., Atl., St.L.	18	1258	**408**	.324
71.	Rod Gilbert, NYR	18	1065	**406**	.381
72.	John Ogrodnick, Det., Que., NYR	14	928	**402**	.433
* 73.	Sergei Fedorov, Det.	13	908	**400**	.441
* 74.	Keith Tkachuk, Wpg., Phx., St.L.	12	781	**398**	.510
75.	Dave Keon, Tor., Hfd.	18	1296	**396**	.306

Though he finished eighth in the NHL with 91 points (28 goals, 63 assists) in just 67 games last season, there were those who doubted that Mario Lemieux would play again in 2003-04. He enters the season just 18 goals shy of 700 for his career.

	Player	Seasons	Games	Goals	Goals per game
76.	Paul Coffey, Edm., Pit., L.A., Det., Hfd., Phi., Chi., Car., Bos.	21	1409	**396**	.281
77.	Cam Neely, Van., Bos.	13	726	**395**	.544
78.	Pierre Larouche, Pit., Mtl., Hfd., NYR	14	812	**395**	.486
79.	Tomas Sandstrom, NYR, L.A., Pit., Det., Ana.	15	983	**394**	.401
80.	Bernie Geoffrion, Mtl., NYR	16	883	**393**	.445
81.	Dean Prentice, NYR, Bos., Det., Pit., Min.	22	1378	**391**	.284
82.	Jean Pronovost, Pit., Atl., Wsh.	14	998	**391**	.392
83.	Rick Martin, Buf., L.A.	11	685	**384**	.561
84.	Reggie Leach, Bos., Cal., Phi., Det.	13	934	**381**	.408
85.	Ted Lindsay, Det., Chi.	17	1068	**379**	.355
* 86.	Claude Lemieux, Mtl., N.J., Col., Phx., Dal.	20	1197	**379**	.317
87.	Butch Goring, L.A., NYI, Bos.	16	1107	**375**	.339
* 88.	Tony Amonte, NYR, Chi., Phx., Phi.	13	933	**372**	.399
89.	Rick Kehoe, Tor., Pit.	14	906	**371**	.409
90.	Tim Kerr, Phi., NYR, Hfd.	13	655	**370**	.565
* 91.	Gary Roberts, Cgy., Car., Tor.	17	957	**369**	.386
92.	Bernie Federko, St.L., Det.	14	1000	**369**	.369
93.	Geoff Courtnall, Bos., Edm., Wsh., St.L., Van.	17	1048	**367**	.350
94.	Jacques Lemaire, Mtl.	12	853	**366**	.429
95.	Brent Sutter, NYI, Chi.	18	1111	**363**	.327
96.	Peter McNab, Buf., Bos., Van., N.J.	14	954	**363**	.381
97.	Ivan Boldirev, Bos., Cal., Chi., Atl., Van., Det.	15	1052	**361**	.343
* 98.	John LeClair, Mtl., Phi.	13	798	**359**	.450
99.	Henri Richard, Mtl.	20	1256	**358**	.285
100.	Bobby Clarke, Phi.	15	1144	**358**	.313

Top 100 Active Goal-Scoring Leaders

	Player	Seasons	Games	Goals	Goals per game
1.	Brett Hull, Cgy., St.L., Dal., Det.	18	1183	716	.605
2.	Mario Lemieux, Pit.	16	879	682	.776
3.	Mark Messier, Edm., NYR, Van.	24	1680	676	.402
4.	Steve Yzerman, Det.	20	1378	660	.479
5.	Luc Robitaille, L.A., Pit., NYR, Det.	17	1286	631	.491
6.	Dave Andreychuk, Buf., Tor., N.J., Bos., Col., T.B.	21	1515	613	.405
7.	Ron Francis, Hfd., Pit., Car.	22	1651	536	.325
8.	Brendan Shanahan, N.J., St.L., Hfd., Det.	16	1186	533	.449
9.	Joe Nieuwendyk, Cgy., Dal., N.J.	17	1113	511	.459
10.	Joe Sakic, Que., Col.	15	1074	509	.474
11.	Jaromir Jagr, Pit., Wsh.	13	950	506	.533
12.	Pierre Turgeon, Buf., NYI, Mtl., St.L., Dal.	16	1139	480	.421
13.	Jeremy Roenick, Chi., Phx., Phi.	15	1062	456	.429
14.	Theoren Fleury, Cgy., Col., NYR, Chi.	15	1084	455	.420
15.	Alexander Mogilny, Buf., Van., N.J., Tor.	14	919	453	.493
16.	Peter Bondra, Wsh.	13	907	451	.497
17.	Doug Gilmour, St.L., Cgy., Tor., N.J., Chi., Buf., Mtl.	20	1474	450	.305
18.	Mike Modano, Min., Dal.	15	1025	444	.433
19.	Pavel Bure, Van., Fla., NYR	12	702	437	.623
20.	Teemu Selanne, Wpg., Ana., S.J.	11	801	436	.544
21.	Mats Sundin, Que., Tor.	13	1005	434	.432
22.	Mark Recchi, Pit., Phi., Mtl.	15	1091	430	.394
23.	Vincent Damphousse, Tor., Edm., Mtl., S.J.	17	1296	420	.324
24.	Steve Thomas, Tor., Chi., NYI, N.J., Ana.	19	1191	411	.345
25.	Sergei Fedorov, Det.	13	908	400	.441
26.	Keith Tkachuk, Wpg., Phx., St.L.	12	781	398	.510
27.	Claude Lemieux, Mtl., N.J., Col., Phx., Dal.	20	1197	379	.317
28.	Tony Amonte, NYR, Chi., Phx., Phi.	13	933	372	.399
29.	Gary Roberts, Cgy., Car., Tor.	17	957	369	.386
30.	John LeClair, Mtl., Phi.	13	798	359	.450
31.	Kirk Muller, N.J., Mtl., NYI, Tor., Fla., Dal.	19	1349	357	.265
32.	Eric Lindros, Phi., NYR	10	639	346	.541
33.	Al MacInnis, Cgy., St.L.	22	1413	340	.241
34.	Adam Oates, Det., St.L., Bos., Wsh., Phi., Ana.	18	1277	339	.265
35.	Rod Brind'Amour, St.L., Phi., Car.	15	1031	339	.329
36.	Phil Housley, Buf., Wpg., St.L., Cgy., N.J., Wsh., Chi., Tor.	21	1495	338	.226
37.	Trevor Linden, Van., NYI, Mtl., Wsh.	15	1079	335	.310
38.	Owen Nolan, Que., Col., S.J., Tor.	13	850	330	.388
39.	Adam Graves, Det., Edm., NYR, S.J.	16	1152	329	.286
40.	Scott Mellanby, Phi., Edm., Fla., St.L.	18	1223	326	.267
41.	Scott Young, Hfd., Pit., Que., Col., Ana., St.L., Dal.	15	1049	316	.301
42.	Ziggy Palffy, NYI, L.A.	10	607	302	.498
43.	Ulf Dahlen, NYR, Min., Dal., S.J., Chi., Wsh.	14	966	301	.312
44.	Paul Kariya, Ana.	9	606	300	.495
45.	Geoff Sanderson, Hfd., Car., Van., Buf., CBJ	13	848	300	.354
46.	Cliff Ronning, St.L., Van., Phx., Nsh., L.A., Min.	17	1097	297	.271
47.	Petr Nedved, Van., St.L., NYR, Pit.	12	808	282	.349
48.	Bill Guerin, N.J., Edm., Bos., Dal.	12	797	281	.353
49.	Alex Kovalev, NYR, Pit.	11	771	278	.361
50.	Alexei Yashin, Ott., NYI	9	663	276	.416
51.	Shayne Corson, Mtl., Edm., St.L., Tor.	18	1139	268	.235
52.	Derek King, NYI, Hfd., Tor., St.L.	14	830	261	.314
53.	Dmitri Khristich, Wsh., L.A., Bos., Tor.	12	811	259	.319
54.	Keith Primeau, Det., Hfd., Car., Phi.	13	846	258	.305
55.	Bobby Holik, Hfd., N.J., NYR	13	942	256	.272
56.	Markus Naslund, Pit., Van.	10	712	255	.358
57.	Martin Gelinas, Edm., Que., Van., Car., Cgy.	15	976	252	.258
58.	Donald Audette, Buf., L.A., Atl., Dal., Mtl.	14	684	251	.367
59.	Robert Reichel, Cgy., NYI, Phx., Tor.	10	761	241	.317
60.	Alexei Zhamnov, Wpg., Chi.	11	740	237	.320
61.	Shawn McEachern, Pit., L.A., Bos., Ott., Atl.	12	801	237	.296
62.	Glen Murray, Bos., Pit., L.A.	12	742	236	.318
63.	Vyacheslav Kozlov, Det., Buf., Atl.	12	724	232	.320
64.	Miroslav Satan, Edm., Buf.	8	622	230	.370
65.	Brian Leetch, NYR	16	1072	227	.212
66.	Mike Ricci, Phi., Que., Col., S.J.	13	943	226	.240
67.	Jason Arnott, Edm., N.J., Dal.	10	670	223	.333
68.	Eric Daze, Chi.	9	581	222	.382

Petr Nedved of the Rangers scored 27 goals last season, giving him 282 in his career, ranking him 47th among active goal scorers. Nedved has scored at least 20 goals for seven straight seasons, dating back to 1995-96 when he scored a career-high 45 goals.

	Player	Seasons	Games	Goals	Goals per game
69.	Bryan Smolinski, Bos., Pit., NYI, L.A., Ott.	11	749	212	.283
70.	Stu Barnes, Wpg., Fla., Pit., Buf., Dal.	12	820	210	.256
71.	Doug Weight, NYR, Edm., St.L.	13	837	210	.251
72.	Jarome Iginla, Cgy.	8	545	209	.383
73.	Peter Forsberg, Que., Col.	9	541	198	.366
74.	Martin Rucinsky, Edm., Que., Col., Mtl., Dal., NYR, St.L.	12	735	194	.264
75.	Andrew Cassels, Mtl., Hfd., Cgy., Van., CBJ	14	926	194	.210
76.	Scott Stevens, Wsh., St.L., N.J.	21	1597	193	.121
77.	Pavol Demitra, Ott., St.L.	10	485	193	.398
78.	Ray Whitney, S.J., Edm., Fla., CBJ	12	633	191	.302
79.	Jeff Friesen, S.J., Ana., N.J.	9	689	191	.277
80.	Daniel Alfredsson, Ott.	8	552	187	.339
81.	Adam Deadmarsh, Que., Col., L.A.	9	567	184	.325
82.	Jeff O'Neill, Hfd., Car.	8	606	184	.304
83.	Mariusz Czerkawski, Bos., Edm., NYI, Mtl.	10	629	182	.289
84.	Martin Straka, Pit., Ott., NYI, Fla.	11	676	182	.269
85.	Todd Bertuzzi, NYI, Van.	8	559	181	.324
86.	Yanic Perreault, Tor., L.A., Mtl.	10	602	179	.297
87.	Steve Heinze, Bos., CBJ, Buf., L.A.	12	694	178	.256
88.	Mikael Renberg, Phi., T.B., Phx., Tor.	9	602	178	.296
89.	Chris Chelios, Mtl., Chi., Det.	20	1326	176	.133
90.	Ryan Smyth, Edm.	9	560	175	.313
91.	Rob Blake, L.A., Col.	14	829	173	.209
92.	Brian Rolston, N.J., Col., Bos.	9	654	171	.261
93.	Travis Green, NYI, Ana., Phx., Tor.	11	793	171	.216
94.	Marty McInnis, NYI, Cgy., Ana., Bos.	12	796	170	.214
95.	Patrik Elias, N.J.	8	476	169	.355
96.	Igor Larionov, Van., S.J., Det., Fla.	13	872	168	.193
97.	Brian Savage, Mtl., Phx.	10	534	167	.313
98.	Dave Lowry, Van., St.L., Fla., S.J., Cgy.	18	1066	163	.153
99.	Nicklas Lidstrom, Det.	12	935	163	.174
100.	Randy McKay, Det., N.J., Dal., Mtl.	15	932	162	.174

Top 100 All-Time Assist Leaders

* active player

	Player	Seasons	Games	Assists	Assists per game
1.	Wayne Gretzky, Edm., L.A., St.L., NYR.	20	1487	1963	1.320
* 2.	Ron Francis, Hfd., Pit., Car.	22	1651	1222	.740
3.	Raymond Bourque, Bos., Col.	22	1612	1169	.725
* 4.	Mark Messier, Edm., NYR, Van.	24	1680	1168	.695
5.	Paul Coffey, Edm., Pit., L.A., Det., Hfd., Phi., Chi., Car., Bos.	21	1409	1135	.806
* 6.	Adam Oates, Det., St.L., Bos., Wsh., Phi., Ana.	18	1277	1063	.832
7.	Gordie Howe, Det., Hfd.	26	1767	1049	.594
8.	Marcel Dionne, Det., L.A., NYR.	18	1348	1040	.772
* 9.	Mario Lemieux, Pit.	16	879	1010	1.149
* 10.	Steve Yzerman, Det.	20	1378	1010	.733
* 11.	Doug Gilmour, St.L., Cgy., Tor., N.J., Chi., Buf., Mtl.	20	1474	964	.654
* 12.	Al MacInnis, Cgy., St.L.	22	1413	932	.660
13.	Larry Murphy, L.A., Wsh., Min., Pit., Tor., Det.	21	1615	929	.575
14.	Stan Mikita, Chi.	22	1394	926	.664
15.	Bryan Trottier, NYI, Pit.	18	1279	901	.704
* 16.	Phil Housley, Buf., Wpg., St.L., Cgy., N.J., Wsh., Chi., Tor.	21	1495	894	.598
17.	Dale Hawerchuk, Wpg., Buf., St.L., Phi.	16	1188	891	.750
18.	Phil Esposito, Chi., Bos., NYR	18	1282	873	.681
19.	Denis Savard, Chi., Mtl., T.B.	17	1196	865	.723
20.	Bobby Clarke, Phi.	15	1144	852	.745
21.	Alex Delvecchio, Det.	24	1549	825	.533
22.	Gilbert Perreault, Buf.	17	1191	814	.683
23.	John Bucyk, Det., Bos.	23	1540	813	.528
* 24.	Joe Sakic, Que., Col.	15	1074	806	.750
25.	Jari Kurri, Edm., L.A., NYR, Ana., Col.	17	1251	797	.637
26.	Guy Lafleur, Mtl., NYR, Que.	17	1126	793	.704
27.	Peter Stastny, Que., N.J., St.L.	15	977	789	.808
28.	Jean Ratelle, NYR, Bos.	21	1281	776	.606
29.	Bernie Federko, St.L., Det.	14	1000	761	.761
* 30.	Pierre Turgeon, Buf., NYI, Mtl., St.L., Dal.	16	1139	754	.662
31.	Larry Robinson, Mtl., L.A.	20	1384	750	.542
* 32.	Vincent Damphousse, Tor., Edm., Mtl., S.J.	17	1296	744	.574
33.	Denis Potvin, NYI.	15	1060	742	.700
34.	Norm Ullman, Det., Tor.	20	1410	739	.524
35.	Bernie Nicholls, L.A., NYR, Edm., N.J., Chi., S.J.	18	1127	734	.651
* 36.	Jaromir Jagr, Pit., Wsh.	13	950	729	.767
* 37.	Brian Leetch, NYR.	16	1072	718	.670
* 38.	Chris Chelios, Mtl., Chi., Det.	20	1326	717	.541
39.	Jean Beliveau, Mtl.	20	1125	712	.633
* 40.	Scott Stevens, Wsh., St.L., N.J.	21	1597	703	.440
41.	Dale Hunter, Que., Wsh., Col.	19	1407	697	.495
* 42.	Mark Recchi, Pit., Phi., Mtl.	15	1091	696	.638
43.	Henri Richard, Mtl.	20	1256	688	.548
* 44.	Luc Robitaille, L.A., Pit., NYR, Det.	17	1286	688	.535
45.	Brad Park, NYR, Bos., Det.	17	1113	683	.614
46.	Bobby Smith, Min., Mtl.	15	1077	679	.630
* 47.	Dave Andreychuk, Buf., Tor., N.J., Bos., Col., T.B.	21	1515	668	.441
48.	Bobby Orr, Bos., Chi.	12	657	645	.982
49.	Gary Suter, Cgy., Chi., S.J.	17	1145	641	.560
50.	Dave Taylor, L.A.	17	1111	638	.574
51.	Darryl Sittler, Tor., Phi., Det.	15	1096	637	.581
52.	Borje Salming, Tor., Det.	17	1148	637	.555
53.	Neal Broten, Min., Dal., N.J., L.A.	17	1099	634	.577
* 54.	Theoren Fleury, Cgy., Col., NYR, Chi.	15	1084	633	.584
55.	Mike Gartner, Wsh., Min., NYR, Tor., Phx.	19	1432	627	.438
56.	Andy Bathgate, NYR, Tor., Det., Pit.	17	1069	624	.584
* 57.	Mike Modano, Min., Dal.	15	1025	618	.603
* 58.	Jeremy Roenick, Chi., Phx., Phi.	15	1062	617	.581
59.	Rod Gilbert, NYR	18	1065	615	.577
* 60.	Brett Hull, Cgy., St.L., Dal., Det.	18	1183	606	.512
61.	Michel Goulet, Que., Chi.	15	1089	604	.555
* 62.	Kirk Muller, N.J., Mtl., NYI, Tor., Fla., Dal.	19	1349	602	.446
63.	Glenn Anderson, Edm., Tor., NYR, St.L.	16	1129	601	.532
64.	Dino Ciccarelli, Min., Wsh., Det., T.B., Fla.	19	1232	592	.481
65.	Dave Keon, Tor., Hfd.	18	1296	590	.455
66.	Doug Wilson, Chi., S.J.	16	1024	590	.576
67.	Dave Babych, Wpg., Hfd., Van., L.A.	19	1195	581	.486
* 68.	Mats Sundin, Que., Tor.	13	1005	580	.577
69.	Brian Propp, Phi., Bos., Min., Hfd.	15	1016	579	.570
70.	Steve Larmer, Chi., NYR	15	1006	571	.568
71.	Frank Mahovlich, Tor., Det., Mtl.	18	1181	570	.483

Wayne Gretzky's ability to see patterns in the play made him such a brilliant playmaker. Gretzky set a new record for assists five times in his career, reaching a high of 163 in 1985-86. He led or shared the league lead in assists 16 times in 20 years.

	Player	Seasons	Games	Assists	Assist per game
* 72.	Brendan Shanahan, N.J., St.L., Hfd., Det.	16	1186	565	.476
73.	Craig Janney, Bos., St.L., S.J., Wpg., Phx., T.B., NYI.	12	760	563	.741
74.	Joe Mullen, St.L., Cgy., Pit., Bos.	17	1062	561	.528
75.	Bobby Hull, Chi., Wpg., Hfd.	16	1063	560	.527
* 76.	Sergei Fedorov, Det.	13	908	554	.610
77.	Mike Bossy, NYI	10	752	553	.735
* 78.	Doug Weight, NYR, Edm., St.L.	13	837	553	.661
79.	Thomas Steen, Wpg.	14	950	553	.582
80.	Ken Linseman, Phi., Edm., Bos., Tor.	14	860	551	.641
81.	Tom Lysiak, Atl., Chi.	13	919	551	.600
* 82.	Cliff Ronning, St.L., Van., Phx., Nsh., L.A., Min.	17	1097	548	.500
83.	Pat LaFontaine, NYI, Buf., NYR.	15	865	545	.630
84.	Mark Howe, Hfd., Phi., Det.	16	929	545	.587
85.	Red Kelly, Det., Tor.	20	1316	542	.412
86.	Pat Verbeek, N.J., Hfd., NYR, Dal., Det.	20	1424	541	.380
87.	Rick Middleton, NYR, Bos.	14	1005	540	.537
88.	Brian Bellows, Min., Mtl., T.B., Ana., Wsh.	17	1188	537	.452
* 89.	Rod Brind'Amour, St.L., Phi., Car.	15	1031	534	.518
90.	Steve Duchesne, L.A., Phi., Que., St.L., Ott., Det.	16	1113	525	.472
* 91.	Nicklas Lidstrom, Det.	12	935	525	.561
* 92.	Alexander Mogilny, Buf., Van., N.J., Tor.	14	919	524	.570
93.	Dennis Maruk, Cal., Cle., Min., Wsh.	14	888	522	.588
94.	Wayne Cashman, Bos.	17	1027	516	.502
95.	Butch Goring, L.A., NYI, Bos.	16	1107	513	.463
96.	Rick Tocchet, Phi., Pit., L.A., Bos., Wsh., Phx.	18	1144	512	.448
97.	John Tonelli, NYI, Cgy., L.A., Chi., Que.	14	1028	511	.497
98.	Lanny McDonald, Tor., Col., Cgy.	16	1111	506	.455
99.	Ivan Boldirev, Bos., Cal., Chi., Atl., Van., Det.	15	1052	505	.480
*100.	Joe Nieuwendyk, Cgy., Dal., N.J.	17	1113	501	.450

Top 100 Active Assist Leaders

Player	Seasons	Games	Assists	Assists per game
1. **Ron Francis**, Hfd., Pit., Car.	22	1651	**1222**	.740
2. **Mark Messier**, Edm., NYR, Van.	24	1680	**1168**	.695
3. **Adam Oates**, Det., St.L., Bos., Wsh., Phi., Ana.	18	1277	**1063**	.832
4. **Mario Lemieux**, Pit.	16	879	**1010**	1.149
5. **Steve Yzerman**, Det.	20	1378	**1010**	.733
6. **Doug Gilmour**, St.L., Cgy., Tor., N.J., Buf., Mtl.	20	1474	**964**	.654
7. **Al MacInnis**, Cgy., St.L.	22	1413	**932**	.660
8. **Phil Housley**, Buf., Wpg., St.L., Cgy., N.J., Wsh., Chi., Tor.	21	1495	**894**	.598
9. **Joe Sakic**, Que., Col.	15	1074	**806**	.750
10. **Pierre Turgeon**, Buf., NYI, Mtl., St.L., Dal.	16	1139	**754**	.662
11. **Vincent Damphousse**, Tor., Edm., Mtl., S.J.	17	1296	**744**	.574
12. **Jaromir Jagr**, Pit., Wsh.	13	950	**729**	.767
13. **Brian Leetch**, NYR.	16	1072	**718**	.670
14. **Chris Chelios**, Mtl., Chi., Det.	20	1326	**717**	.541
15. **Scott Stevens**, Wsh., St.L., N.J.	21	1597	**703**	.440
16. **Mark Recchi**, Pit., Phi., Mtl.	15	1091	**696**	.638
17. **Luc Robitaille**, L.A., Pit., NYR, Det.	17	1286	**688**	.535
18. **Dave Andreychuk**, Buf., Tor., N.J., Bos., Col., T.B.	21	1515	**668**	.441
19. **Theoren Fleury**, Cgy., Col., NYR, Chi.	15	1084	**633**	.584
20. **Mike Modano**, Min., Dal.	15	1025	**618**	.603
21. **Jeremy Roenick**, Chi., Phx., Phi.	15	1062	**617**	.581
22. **Brett Hull**, Cgy., St.L., Dal., Det.	18	1183	**606**	.512
23. **Kirk Muller**, N.J., Mtl., NYI, Tor., Fla., Dal.	19	1349	**602**	.446
24. **Mats Sundin**, Que., Tor.	13	1005	**580**	.577
25. **Brendan Shanahan**, N.J., St.L., Hfd., Det.	16	1186	**565**	.476
26. **Sergei Fedorov**, Det.	13	908	**554**	.610
27. **Doug Weight**, NYR, Edm., St.L.	13	837	**553**	.661
28. **Cliff Ronning**, St.L., Van., Phx., Nsh., L.A., Min.	17	1097	**548**	.500
29. **Rod Brind'Amour**, St.L., Phi., Car.	15	1031	**534**	.518
30. **Nicklas Lidstrom**, Det.	12	935	**525**	.561
31. **Alexander Mogilny**, Buf., Van., N.J., Tor.	14	919	**524**	.570
32. **Joe Nieuwendyk**, Cgy., Dal., N.J.	17	1113	**501**	.450
33. **Steve Thomas**, Tor., Chi., NYI, N.J., Ana.	19	1191	**500**	.420
34. **Andrew Cassels**, Mtl., Hfd., Cgy., Van., CBJ.	14	926	**500**	.540
35. **Peter Forsberg**, Que., Col.	9	541	**488**	.902
36. **James Patrick**, NYR, Hfd., Cgy., Buf.	20	1225	**483**	.394
37. **Teemu Selanne**, Wpg., Ana., S.J.	11	801	**483**	.603
38. **Igor Larionov**, Van., S.J., Det., Fla.	13	872	**465**	.533
39. **Sergei Zubov**, NYR, Pit., Dal.	11	779	**449**	.576
40. **Trevor Linden**, Van., NYI, Mtl., Wsh.	15	1079	**443**	.411
41. **Eric Lindros**, Phi., NYR.	10	639	**439**	.687
42. **Alexei Zhamnov**, Wpg., Chi.	11	740	**436**	.589
43. **Fredrik Olausson**, Wpg., Edm., Ana., Pit., Det.	16	1022	**434**	.425
44. **Teppo Numminen**, Wpg., Phx.	15	1098	**426**	.388
45. **Shayne Corson**, Mtl., Edm., St.L., Tor.	18	1139	**415**	.364
46. **Scott Mellanby**, Phi., Edm., Fla., St.L.	18	1223	**413**	.338
47. **Calle Johansson**, Buf., Wsh.	16	1101	**410**	.372
48. **Eric Desjardins**, Mtl., Phi.	15	1050	**408**	.389
49. **Joe Juneau**, Bos., Wsh., Buf., Ott., Phx., Mtl.	12	758	**406**	.536
50. **Claude Lemieux**, Mtl., N.J., Col., Phx., Dal.	20	1197	**406**	.339
51. **Tony Amonte**, NYR, Chi., Phx., Phi.	13	933	**403**	.432
52. **Gary Roberts**, Cgy., Car., Tor.	17	957	**389**	.406
53. **Scott Young**, Hfd., Pit., Que., Col., Ana., St.L., Dal.	15	1049	**376**	.358
54. **Glen Wesley**, Bos., Hfd., Car., Tor.	16	1173	**376**	.321
55. **Paul Kariya**, Ana.	9	606	**369**	.609
56. **Jozef Stumpel**, Bos., L.A.	12	694	**368**	.530
57. **Rob Blake**, L.A., Col.	14	829	**367**	.443
58. **Keith Tkachuk**, Wpg., Phx., St.L.	12	781	**363**	.465
59. **Robert Reichel**, Cgy., NYI, Phx., Tor.	10	761	**359**	.472
60. **Owen Nolan**, Que., Col., S.J., Tor.	13	850	**357**	.420
61. **Alex Kovalev**, NYR, Pit.	11	771	**357**	.463
62. **Sandis Ozolinsh**, S.J., Col., Car., Fla., Ana.	11	743	**356**	.479
63. **Alexei Yashin**, Ott., NYI.	9	663	**355**	.535
64. **Ulf Dahlen**, NYR, Min., Dal., S.J., Chi., Wsh.	14	966	**354**	.366
65. **Jyrki Lumme**, Mtl., Van., Phx., Dal., Tor.	15	985	**354**	.359
66. **Mathieu Schneider**, Mtl., NYI, Tor., NYR, L.A., Det.	15	914	**352**	.385

Colorado's Joe Sakic collected both his 500th goal and his 800th assist during the 2002-03 season. Sakic, Luc Robitaille and Brett Hull all reached the 1,300-point plateau last season.

Player	Games	Assists	Assists per game
67. **Petr Nedved**, Van., St.L., NYR, Pit.	808	**352**	.436
68. **Derek King**, NYI, Hfd., Tor., St.L.	830	**351**	.423
69. **John LeClair**, Mtl., Phi.	798	**347**	.435
70. **Pavel Bure**, Van., Fla., NYR	702	**342**	.487
71. **Peter Bondra**, Wsh.	907	**339**	.374
72. **Dmitri Khristich**, Wsh., L.A., Bos., Tor.	811	**337**	.416
73. **Mike Ricci**, Phi., Que., Col., S.J.	943	**336**	.356
74. **Keith Primeau**, Det., Hfd., Car., Phi.	846	**332**	.392
75. **Jeff Norton**, NYI, S.J., St.L., Edm., T.B., Fla., Pit., Bos.	799	**332**	.416
76. **Bobby Holik**, Hfd., N.J., NYR	942	**330**	.350
77. **Ziggy Palffy**, NYI, L.A.	607	**328**	.540
78. **Scott Niedermayer**, N.J.	811	**324**	.400
79. **Darryl Sydor**, L.A., Dal.	863	**323**	.374
80. **Martin Straka**, Pit., Ott., NYI, Fla.	676	**322**	.476
81. **Roman Hamrlik**, T.B., Edm., NYI	792	**302**	.381
82. **Daniel Alfredsson**, Ott.	552	**301**	.545
83. **Ray Whitney**, S.J., Edm., Fla., CBJ.	633	**301**	.476
84. **Michael Nylander**, Hfd., Cgy., T.B., Chi., Wsh.	630	**294**	.467
85. **Mike Keane**, Mtl., Col., NYR, Dal., St.L.	1097	**293**	.267
86. **Alexei Zhitnik**, L.A., Buf.	814	**291**	.357
87. **Markus Naslund**, Pit., Van.	712	**290**	.407
88. **Jason Arnott**, Edm., N.J., Dal.	670	**288**	.430
89. **Jason Allison**, Wsh., Bos., L.A.	486	**288**	.593
90. **Eric Weinrich**, N.J., Hfd., Chi., Mtl., Bos., Phi.	1002	**287**	.286
91. **Adam Graves**, Det., Edm., NYR, S.J.	1152	**287**	.249
92. **Shawn McEachern**, Pit., L.A., Bos., Ott., Atl.	801	**279**	.348
93. **Chris Gratton**, T.B., Phi., Buf., Phx.	770	**277**	.360
94. **Geoff Sanderson**, Hfd., Car., Van., Buf., CBJ	848	**276**	.325
95. **Bryan Smolinski**, Bos., Pit., NYI, L.A., Ott.	749	**276**	.368
96. **Vyacheslav Kozlov**, Det., Buf., Atl.	724	**275**	.380
97. **Stu Barnes**, Wpg., Fla., Pit., Buf., Dal.	820	**274**	.334
98. **Bill Guerin**, N.J., Edm., Bos., Dal.	797	**273**	.343
99. **Todd Gill**, Tor., S.J., St.L., Det., Phx., Col., Chi.	1007	**272**	.270
100. **Martin Rucinsky**, Edm., Que., Col., Mtl., Dal., NYR, St.L.	735	**269**	.366

Top 100 All-Time Point Leaders

* active player

Elected to the Hockey Hall of Fame in 2003, Pat LaFontaine had 468 goals and 545 assists in his career for a total of 1,013 points in just 865 games. He enjoyed his best season in 1992-93 when he had 53 goals and 95 assists for 148 points.

Player	Seasons	Games	Goals	Assists	Points	Points per game
1. **Wayne Gretzky**, Edm., L.A., St.L., NYR	20	1487	894	1963	**2857**	1.921
2. **Gordie Howe**, Det., Hfd.	26	1767	801	1049	**1850**	1.047
* 3. **Mark Messier**, Edm., NYR, Van.	24	1680	676	1168	**1844**	1.098
4. **Marcel Dionne**, Det., L.A., NYR	18	1348	731	1040	**1771**	1.314
* 5. **Ron Francis**, Hfd., Pit., Car.	22	1651	536	1222	**1758**	1.065
* 6. **Mario Lemieux**, Pit.	16	879	682	1010	**1692**	1.925
* 7. **Steve Yzerman**, Det.	20	1378	660	1010	**1670**	1.212
8. **Phil Esposito**, Chi., Bos., NYR	18	1282	717	873	**1590**	1.240
9. **Raymond Bourque**, Bos., Col.	22	1612	410	1169	**1579**	.980
10. **Paul Coffey**, Edm., Pit., L.A., Det., Hfd., Phi., Chi., Car., Bos.	21	1409	396	1135	**1531**	1.087
11. **Stan Mikita**, Chi.	22	1394	541	926	**1467**	1.052
12. **Bryan Trottier**, NYI, Pit.	18	1279	524	901	**1425**	1.114
* 13. **Doug Gilmour**, St.L., Cgy., Tor., N.J., Chi., Buf., Mtl.	20	1474	450	964	**1414**	.959
14. **Dale Hawerchuk**, Wpg., Buf., St.L., Phi.	16	1188	518	891	**1409**	1.186
* 15. **Adam Oates**, Det., St.L., Bos., Wsh., Phi., Ana.	18	1277	339	1063	**1402**	1.098
16. **Jari Kurri**, Edm., L.A., NYR, Ana., Col.	17	1251	601	797	**1398**	1.118
17. **John Bucyk**, Det., Bos.	23	1540	556	813	**1369**	.889
18. **Guy Lafleur**, Mtl., NYR, Que.	17	1126	560	793	**1353**	1.202
19. **Denis Savard**, Chi., Mtl., T.B.	17	1196	473	865	**1338**	1.119
20. **Mike Gartner**, Wsh., Min., NYR, Tor., Phx.	19	1432	708	627	**1335**	.932
21. **Gilbert Perreault**, Buf.	17	1191	512	814	**1326**	1.113
* 22. **Brett Hull**, Cgy., St.L., Dal., Det.	18	1183	716	606	**1322**	1.117
* 23. **Luc Robitaille**, L.A., Pit., NYR, Det.	17	1286	631	688	**1319**	1.026
* 24. **Joe Sakic**, Que., Col.	15	1074	509	806	**1315**	1.224
* 25. **Dave Andreychuk**, Buf., Tor., N.J., Bos., Col., T.B.	21	1515	613	668	**1281**	.846
26. **Alex Delvecchio**, Det.	24	1549	456	825	**1281**	.827
* 27. **Al MacInnis**, Cgy., St.L.	22	1413	340	932	**1272**	.900
28. **Jean Ratelle**, NYR, Bos.	21	1281	491	776	**1267**	.989
29. **Peter Stastny**, Que., N.J., St.L.	15	977	450	789	**1239**	1.268
* 30. **Jaromir Jagr**, Pit., Wsh.	13	950	506	729	**1235**	1.300
* 31. **Pierre Turgeon**, Buf., NYI, Mtl., St.L., Dal.	16	1139	480	754	**1234**	1.083
* 32. **Phil Housley**, Buf., Wpg., St.L., Cgy., N.J., Wsh., Chi., Tor.	21	1495	338	894	**1232**	.824
33. **Norm Ullman**, Det., Tor.	20	1410	490	739	**1229**	.872
34. **Jean Beliveau**, Mtl.	20	1125	507	712	**1219**	1.084
35. **Larry Murphy**, L.A., Wsh., Min., Pit., Tor., Det.	21	1615	287	929	**1216**	.753
36. **Bobby Clarke**, Phi.	15	1144	358	852	**1210**	1.058
37. **Bernie Nicholls**, L.A., NYR, Edm., N.J., Chi., S.J.	18	1127	475	734	**1209**	1.073
38. **Dino Ciccarelli**, Min., Wsh., Det., T.B., Fla.	19	1232	608	592	**1200**	.974
39. **Bobby Hull**, Chi., Wpg., Hfd.	16	1063	610	560	**1170**	1.101
* 40. **Vincent Damphousse**, Tor., Edm., Mtl., S.J.	17	1296	420	744	**1164**	.898
41. **Michel Goulet**, Que., Chi.	15	1089	548	604	**1152**	1.058
42. **Bernie Federko**, St.L., Det.	14	1000	369	761	**1130**	1.130
* 43. **Mark Recchi**, Pit., Phi., Mtl.	15	1091	430	696	**1126**	1.032
44. **Mike Bossy**, NYI	10	752	573	553	**1126**	1.497
45. **Darryl Sittler**, Tor., Phi., Det.	15	1096	484	637	**1121**	1.023
46. **Frank Mahovlich**, Tor., Det., Mtl.	18	1181	533	570	**1103**	.934
47. **Glenn Anderson**, Edm., Tor., NYR, St.L.	16	1129	498	601	**1099**	.973
* 48. **Brendan Shanahan**, N.J., St.L., Hfd., Det.	16	1186	533	565	**1098**	.926
* 49. **Theoren Fleury**, Cgy., Col., NYR, Chi.	15	1084	455	633	**1088**	1.004
* 50. **Jeremy Roenick**, Chi., Phx., Phi.	15	1062	456	617	**1073**	1.010
51. **Dave Taylor**, L.A.	17	1111	431	638	**1069**	.962
52. **Pat Verbeek**, N.J., Hfd., NYR, Dal., Det.	20	1424	522	541	**1063**	.746
53. **Joe Mullen**, St.L., Cgy., Pit., Bos.	17	1062	502	561	**1063**	1.001
* 54. **Mike Modano**, Min., Dal.	15	1025	444	618	**1062**	1.036
55. **Denis Potvin**, NYI	15	1060	310	742	**1052**	.992
56. **Henri Richard**, Mtl.	20	1256	358	688	**1046**	.833
57. **Bobby Smith**, Min., Mtl.	15	1077	357	679	**1036**	.962
58. **Brian Bellows**, Min., Mtl., T.B., Ana., Wsh.	17	1188	485	537	**1022**	.860
59. **Rod Gilbert**, NYR	18	1065	406	615	**1021**	.959
60. **Dale Hunter**, Que., Wsh., Col.	19	1407	323	697	**1020**	.725
* 61. **Mats Sundin**, Que., Tor.	13	1005	434	580	**1014**	1.009
62. **Pat LaFontaine**, NYI, Buf., NYR	15	865	468	545	**1013**	1.171
63. **Steve Larmer**, Chi., NYR	15	1006	441	571	**1012**	1.006
* 64. **Joe Nieuwendyk**, Cgy., Dal., N.J.	17	1113	511	501	**1012**	.909
65. **Lanny McDonald**, Tor., Col., Cgy.	16	1111	500	506	**1006**	.905
66. **Brian Propp**, Phi., Bos., Min., Hfd.	15	1016	425	579	**1004**	.988
67. **Rick Middleton**, NYR, Bos.	14	1005	448	540	**988**	.983
68. **Dave Keon**, Tor., Hfd.	18	1296	396	590	**986**	.761
* 69. **Alexander Mogilny**, Buf., Van., N.J., Tor.	14	919	453	524	**977**	1.063
70. **Andy Bathgate**, NYR, Tor., Det., Pit.	17	1069	349	624	**973**	.910
71. **Maurice Richard**, Mtl.	18	978	544	421	**965**	.987
* 72. **Kirk Muller**, N.J., Mtl., NYI, Tor., Fla., Dal.	19	1349	357	602	**959**	.711
73. **Larry Robinson**, Mtl., L.A.	20	1384	208	750	**958**	.692
* 74. **Sergei Fedorov**, Det.	13	908	400	554	**954**	1.051
75. **Rick Tocchet**, Phi., Pit., L.A., Bos., Wsh., Phx.	18	1144	440	512	**952**	.832
* 76. **Brian Leetch**, NYR	16	1072	227	718	**945**	.882
77. **Neal Broten**, Min., Dal., N.J., L.A.	17	1099	289	634	**923**	.840
* 78. **Teemu Selanne**, Wpg., Ana., S.J.	11	801	436	483	**919**	1.147
79. **Bobby Orr**, Bos., Chi.	12	657	270	645	**915**	1.393
* 80. **Steve Thomas**, Tor., Chi., NYI, N.J., Ana.	19	1191	411	500	**911**	.765
81. **Ray Ferraro**, Hfd., NYI, NYR, L.A., Atl., St.L.	18	1258	408	490	**898**	.714
* 82. **Scott Stevens**, Wsh., St.L., N.J.	21	1597	193	703	**896**	.561
83. **Brad Park**, NYR, Bos., Det.	17	1113	213	683	**896**	.805
* 84. **Chris Chelios**, Mtl., Chi., Det.	20	1326	176	717	**893**	.673
85. **Butch Goring**, L.A., NYI, Bos.	16	1107	375	513	**888**	.802
86. **Bill Barber**, Phi.	14	903	420	463	**883**	.978
87. **Dennis Maruk**, Cal., Cle., Min., Wsh.	14	888	356	522	**878**	.989
* 88. **Rod Brind'Amour**, St.L., Phi., Car.	15	1031	339	534	**873**	.847
89. **Ivan Boldirev**, Bos., Cal., Chi., Atl., Van., Det.	15	1052	361	505	**866**	.823
90. **Yvan Cournoyer**, Mtl.	16	968	428	435	**863**	.892
91. **Dean Prentice**, NYR, Bos., Det., Pit., Min.	22	1378	391	469	**860**	.624
92. **Tomas Sandstrom**, NYR, L.A., Pit., Det., Ana.	15	983	394	462	**856**	.871
93. **Ted Lindsay**, Det., Chi.	17	1068	379	472	**851**	.797
* 94. **Cliff Ronning**, St.L., Van., Phx., Nsh., L.A., Min.	17	1097	297	548	**845**	.770
95. **Gary Suter**, Cgy., Chi., S.J.	17	1145	203	641	**844**	.737
96. **Tom Lysiak**, Atl., Chi.	13	919	292	551	**843**	.917
97. **John MacLean**, N.J., S.J., NYR, Dal.	18	1194	413	429	**842**	.705
98. **John Tonelli**, NYI, Cgy., L.A., Chi., Que.	14	1028	325	511	**836**	.813
99. **Jacques Lemaire**, Mtl.	12	853	366	469	**835**	.979
100. **Brent Sutter**, NYI, Chi.	18	1111	363	466	**829**	.746

Top 100 Active Points Leaders

With two goals in the final game of the season, Peter Bondra reached 30 for the year and pushed his career points total to 790, one more than Mike Gartner's previous franchise record in Washington.

Player	Seasons	Games	Goals	Assists	Points	Points per game
1. Mark Messier, Edm., NYR, Van.	24	1680	676	1168	**1844**	1.098
2. Ron Francis, Hfd., Pit., Car.	22	1651	536	1222	**1758**	1.065
3. Mario Lemieux, Pit.	16	879	682	1010	**1692**	1.925
4. Steve Yzerman, Det.	20	1378	660	1010	**1670**	1.212
5. Doug Gilmour, St.L., Cgy., Tor., N.J., Chi., Buf., Mtl.	20	1474	450	964	**1414**	.959
6. Adam Oates, Det., St.L., Bos., Wsh., Phi., Ana.	18	1277	339	1063	**1402**	1.098
7. Brett Hull, Cgy., St.L., Dal., Det.	18	1183	716	606	**1322**	1.117
8. Luc Robitaille, L.A., Pit., NYR, Det.	17	1286	631	688	**1319**	1.026
9. Joe Sakic, Que., Col.	15	1074	509	806	**1315**	1.224
10. Dave Andreychuk, Buf., Tor., N.J., Bos., Col., T.B.	21	1515	613	668	**1281**	.846
11. Al MacInnis, Cgy., St.L.	22	1413	340	932	**1272**	.900
12. Jaromir Jagr, Pit., Wsh.	13	950	506	729	**1235**	1.300
13. Pierre Turgeon, Buf., NYI, Mtl., St.L., Dal.	16	1139	480	754	**1234**	1.083
14. Phil Housley, Buf., Wpg., St.L., Cgy., N.J., Wsh., Chi., Tor.	21	1495	338	894	**1232**	.824
15. Vincent Damphousse, Tor., Edm., Mtl., S.J.	17	1296	420	744	**1164**	.898
16. Mark Recchi, Pit., Phi., Mtl.	15	1091	430	696	**1126**	1.032
17. Brendan Shanahan, N.J., St.L., Hfd., Det.	16	1186	533	565	**1098**	.926
18. Theoren Fleury, Cgy., Col., NYR, Chi.	15	1084	455	633	**1088**	1.004
19. Jeremy Roenick, Chi., Phx.	15	1062	456	617	**1073**	1.010
20. Mike Modano, Min., Dal.	15	1025	444	618	**1062**	1.036
21. Mats Sundin, Que., Tor.	13	1005	434	580	**1014**	1.009
22. Joe Nieuwendyk, Cgy., Dal., N.J.	17	1113	511	501	**1012**	.909
23. Alexander Mogilny, Buf., Van., N.J., Tor.	14	919	453	524	**977**	1.063
24. Kirk Muller, N.J., Mtl., NYI, Tor., Fla., Dal.	19	1349	357	602	**959**	.711
25. Sergei Fedorov, Det.	13	908	400	554	**954**	1.051
26. Brian Leetch, NYR	16	1072	227	718	**945**	.882
27. Teemu Selanne, Wpg., Ana., S.J.	11	801	436	483	**919**	1.147
28. Steve Thomas, Tor., Chi., NYI, N.J., Ana.	19	1191	411	500	**911**	.765
29. Scott Stevens, Wsh., St.L., N.J.	21	1597	193	703	**896**	.561
30. Chris Chelios, Mtl., Chi., Det.	20	1326	176	717	**893**	.673
31. Rod Brind'Amour, St.L., Phi., Car.	15	1031	339	534	**873**	.847
32. Cliff Ronning, St.L., Van., Phx., Nsh., L.A., Min.	17	1097	297	548	**845**	.770
33. Peter Bondra, Wsh.	13	907	451	339	**790**	.871
34. Eric Lindros, Phi., NYR	10	639	346	439	**785**	1.228
35. Claude Lemieux, Mtl., N.J., Col., Phx., Dal.	20	1197	379	406	**785**	.656
36. Pavel Bure, Van., Fla., NYR	12	702	437	342	**779**	1.110
37. Trevor Linden, Van., NYI, Mtl., Wsh.	15	1079	335	443	**778**	.721
38. Tony Amonte, NYR, Chi., Phx., Phi.	13	933	372	403	**775**	.831
39. Doug Weight, NYR, Edm., St.L.	13	837	210	553	**763**	.912
40. Keith Tkachuk, Wpg., Phx., St.L.	12	781	398	363	**761**	.974
41. Gary Roberts, Cgy., Car., Tor.	17	957	369	389	**758**	.792
42. Scott Mellanby, Phi., Edm., Fla., St.L.	18	1223	326	413	**739**	.604
43. John LeClair, Mtl., Phi.	13	798	359	347	**706**	.885
44. Andrew Cassels, Mtl., Hfd., Cgy., Van., CBJ	14	926	194	500	**694**	.749
45. Scott Young, Hfd., Pit., Que., Col., Ana., St.L., Dal.	15	1049	316	376	**692**	.660
46. Nicklas Lidstrom, Det.	12	935	163	525	**688**	.736
47. Owen Nolan, Que., Col., S.J., Tor.	13	850	330	357	**687**	.808
48. Peter Forsberg, Que., Col.	9	541	198	488	**686**	1.268
49. Shayne Corson, Mtl., Edm., St.L., Tor.	18	1139	268	415	**683**	.600
50. Alexei Zhamnov, Wpg., Chi.	11	740	237	436	**673**	.909
51. Paul Kariya, Ana.	9	606	300	369	**669**	1.104
52. Ulf Dahlen, NYR, Min., Dal., S.J., Chi., Wsh.	14	966	301	354	**655**	.678
53. Alex Kovalev, NYR, Pit.	11	771	278	357	**635**	.824
54. Petr Nedved, Van., St.L., NYR, Pit.	12	808	282	352	**634**	.785
55. Igor Larionov, Van., S.J., Det., Fla.	13	872	168	465	**633**	.726
56. Alexei Yashin, Ott., NYI	9	663	276	355	**631**	.952
57. Ziggy Palffy, NYI, L.A.	10	607	302	328	**630**	1.038
58. James Patrick, NYR, Hfd., Cgy., Buf.	20	1225	145	483	**628**	.513
59. Adam Graves, Det., Edm., NYR, S.J.	16	1152	329	287	**616**	.535
60. Derek King, NYI, Hfd., Tor., St.L.	14	830	261	351	**612**	.737
61. Robert Reichel, Cgy., NYI, Phx., Tor.	10	761	241	359	**600**	.788
62. Dmitri Khristich, Wsh., L.A., Bos., Tor.	12	811	259	337	**596**	.735
63. Keith Primeau, Det., Hfd., Car., Phi.	13	846	258	332	**590**	.697
64. Bobby Holik, Hfd., N.J., NYR	13	942	256	330	**586**	.622
65. Fredrik Olausson, Wpg., Edm., Ana., Pit., Det.	16	1022	147	434	**581**	.568
66. Geoff Sanderson, Hfd., Car., Van., Buf., CBJ	13	848	300	276	**576**	.679
67. Sergei Zubov, NYR, Pit., Dal.	11	779	116	449	**565**	.725
68. Mike Ricci, Phi., Que., Col., S.J.	13	943	226	336	**562**	.596
69. Joe Juneau, Bos., Wsh., Buf., Ott., Phx., Mtl.	12	758	151	406	**557**	.735
70. Bill Guerin, N.J., Edm., Bos., Dal.	12	797	281	273	**554**	.695
71. Markus Naslund, Pit., Van.	10	712	255	290	**545**	.765
72. Benoit Hogue, Buf., NYI, Tor., Dal., T.B., Phx., Bos., Wsh.	15	863	222	321	**543**	.629
73. Rob Blake, L.A., Col.	14	829	173	367	**540**	.651
74. Eric Desjardins, Mtl., Phi.	15	1050	131	408	**539**	.513
75. Teppo Numminen, Wpg., Phx.	15	1098	108	426	**534**	.486
76. Calle Johansson, Buf., Wsh.	16	1101	119	410	**529**	.480
77. Martin Gelinas, Edm., Que., Van., Car., Cgy.	15	976	252	268	**520**	.533
78. Shawn McEachern, Pit., L.A., Bos., Ott., Atl.	12	801	237	279	**516**	.644
79. Jason Arnott, Edm., N.J., Dal.	10	670	223	288	**511**	.763
80. Jozef Stumpel, Bos., L.A.	12	694	143	368	**511**	.736
81. Sandis Ozolinsh, S.J., Col., Car., Fla., Ana.	11	743	153	356	**509**	.685
82. Vyacheslav Kozlov, Det., Buf., Atl.	12	724	232	275	**507**	.700
83. Mathieu Schneider, Mtl., NYI, Tor., NYR, L.A., Det.	15	914	154	352	**506**	.554
84. Martin Straka, Pit., Ott., NYI, Fla.	11	676	182	322	**504**	.746
85. Glen Wesley, Bos., Hfd., Car., Tor.	16	1173	124	376	**500**	.426
86. Ray Whitney, S.J., Edm., Fla., CBJ	12	633	191	301	**492**	.777
87. Bryan Smolinski, Bos., Pit., NYI, L.A., Ott.	11	749	212	276	**488**	.652
88. Daniel Alfredsson, Ott.	8	552	187	301	**488**	.884
89. Donald Audette, Buf., L.A., Atl., Dal.	14	684	251	237	**488**	.713
90. Stu Barnes, Wpg., Fla., Pit., Buf., Dal.	12	820	210	274	**484**	.590
91. Jyrki Lumme, Mtl., Van., Phx., Dal., Tor.	15	985	114	354	**468**	.475
92. Glen Murray, Bos., Pit., L.A.	12	742	236	227	**463**	.624
93. Martin Rucinsky, Edm., Que., Col., Mtl., Dal., NYR, St.L.	12	735	194	269	**463**	.630
94. Miroslav Satan, Edm., Buf.	8	622	230	232	**462**	.743
95. Pavol Demitra, Ott., St.L.	10	485	193	268	**461**	.951
96. Jeff Friesen, S.J., Ana., N.J.	9	689	191	265	**456**	.662
97. Mike Keane, Mtl., Col., NYR, Dal., St.L.	15	1097	160	293	**453**	.413
98. Mikael Renberg, Phi., T.B., Phx., Tor.	9	602	178	261	**439**	.729
99. Chris Gratton, T.B., Phi., Buf., Phx.	10	770	161	277	**438**	.569
100. Michael Nylander, Hfd., Cgy., T.B., Chi., Wsh.	10	630	139	294	**433**	.687

All-Time Games Played Leaders

Regular Season

* active player

		Player	Team	Seasons	GP
	1.	**Gordie Howe**	Detroit	25	1687
			Hartford	1	80
			Total	**26**	**1,767**
*	2.	**Mark Messier**	Edmonton	12	851
			NY Rangers	9	622
			Vancouver	3	207
			Total	**24**	**1,680**
*	3.	**Ron Francis**	Hartford	9¾	714
			Pittsburgh	7¼	533
			Carolina	5	404
			Total	**22**	**1,651**
	4.	**Larry Murphy**	Los Angeles	3¼	242
			Washington	5½	453
			Minnesota	1¾	121
			Pittsburgh	4½	336
			Toronto	1¾	151
			Detroit	4¼	312
			Total	**21**	**1,615**
	5.	**Raymond Bourque**	Boston	20¾	1,518
			Colorado	1¼	94
			Total	**22**	**1,612**
*	6.	**Scott Stevens**	Washington	8	601
			St. Louis	1	78
			New Jersey	12	918
			Total	**21**	**1,597**
	7.	**Alex Delvecchio**	**Detroit**	**24**	**1,549**
	8.	**John Bucyk**	Detroit	2	104
			Boston	21	1,436
			Total	**23**	**1,540**
*	9.	**Dave Andreychuk**	Buffalo	11½	837
			Toronto	3¼	223
			New Jersey	3¼	224
			Boston	¾	63
			Colorado	¼	14
			Tampa Bay	2	154
			Total	**21**	**1,515**
*	10.	**Phil Housley**	Buffalo	8	608
			Winnipeg	3	232
			St. Louis	1	26
			Calgary	4¾	328
			New Jersey	¼	22
			Washington	2	141
			Chicago	1¾	137
			Toronto	¼	1
			Total	**21**	**1,495**
	11.	**Wayne Gretzky**	Edmonton	9	696
			Los Angeles	7¾	539
			St. Louis	¼	18
			NY Rangers	3	234
			Total	**20**	**1,487**
*	12.	**Doug Gilmour**	St. Louis	5	384
			Calgary	3½	266
			Toronto	5½	393
			New Jersey	1¼	83
			Chicago	1¾	135
			Buffalo	1¼	82
			Montreal	1¾	131
			Total	**20**	**1,474**
	13.	**Tim Horton**	Toronto	19¾	1,185
			NY Rangers	1¼	93
			Pittsburgh	1	44
			Buffalo	2	124
			Total	**24**	**1,446**
	14.	**Mike Gartner**	Washington	9¾	758
			Minnesota	1	80
			NY Rangers	4	322
			Toronto	2¼	130
			Phoenix	2	142
			Total	**19**	**1,432**
	15.	**Pat Verbeek**	New Jersey	7	463
			Hartford	5¾	433
			NY Rangers	1¼	88
			Dallas	4	305
			Detroit	2	135
			Total	**20**	**1,424**
*	16.	**Al MacInnis**	Calgary	13	803
			St. Louis	9	610
			Total	**22**	**1,413**
	17.	**Harry Howell**	NY Rangers	17	1,160
			Oakland	1	55
			California	½	28
			Los Angeles	2½	168
			Total	**21**	**1,411**
	18.	**Norm Ullman**	Detroit	12½	875
			Toronto	7½	535
			Total	**20**	**1,410**
	19.	**Paul Coffey**	Edmonton	7	532
			Pittsburgh	4¾	331
			Los Angeles	¾	60
			Detroit	3½	231
			Hartford	¼	20
			Philadelphia	1¾	94
			Chicago	¼	10
			Carolina	1¾	113
			Boston	1	18
			Total	**21**	**1,409**
	20.	**Dale Hunter**	Quebec	7	523
			Washington	11¾	872
			Colorado	¼	12
			Total	**19**	**1,407**
	21.	**Stan Mikita**	**Chicago**	**22**	**1,394**
	22.	**Doug Mohns**	Boston	11	710
			Chicago	6½	415
			Minnesota	2½	162
			Atlanta	1	28
			Washington	1	75
			Total	**22**	**1,390**
	23.	**Larry Robinson**	Montreal	17	1,202
			Los Angeles	3	182
			Total	**20**	**1,384**
	24.	**Dean Prentice**	NY Rangers	10½	666
			Boston	3	170
			Detroit	3½	230
			Pittsburgh	2	144
			Minnesota	3	168
			Total	**22**	**1,378**
*	25.	**Steve Yzerman**	**Detroit**	**20**	**1,378**
	26.	**Ron Stewart**	Toronto	13	838
			Boston	2	126
			St. Louis	½	19
			NY Rangers	4	306
			Vancouver	1	42
			NY Islanders	½	22
			Total	**21**	**1,353**
*	27.	**Kirk Muller**	New Jersey	7	556
			Montreal	3¾	267
			NY Islanders	¾	27
			Toronto	1¼	102
			Florida	2¼	162
			Dallas	4	235
			Total	**19**	**1,349**
	28.	**Marcel Dionne**	Detroit	4	309
			Los Angeles	11¾	921
			NY Rangers	2¼	118
			Total	**18**	**1,348**
*	29.	**Chris Chelios**	Montreal	7	402
			Chicago	8¾	664
			Detroit	4¼	260
			Total	**20**	**1,326**
	30.	**Guy Carbonneau**	Montreal	13	912
			St. Louis	1	42
			Dallas	5	364
			Total	**19**	**1,318**
	31.	**Red Kelly**	Detroit	12½	846
			Toronto	7½	470
			Total	**20**	**1,316**
	32.	**Dave Keon**	Toronto	15	1,062
			Hartford	3	234
			Total	**18**	**1,296**
*	33.	**Vincent Damphousse**	Toronto	5	394
			Edmonton	1	80
			Montreal	6¾	519
			San Jose	4¼	303
			Total	**17**	**1,296**
*	34.	**Luc Robitaille**	Los Angeles	12	932
			Pittsburgh	1	46
			NY Rangers	2	146
			Detroit	2	162
			Total	**17**	**1,286**
	35.	**Ken Daneyko**	**New Jersey**	**19**	**1,283**
	36.	**Phil Esposito**	Chicago	4	235
			Boston	8¼	625
			NY Rangers	5¾	422
			Total	**18**	**1,282**
	37.	**Jean Ratelle**	NY Rangers	15¼	862
			Boston	5¾	419
			Total	**21**	**1,281**
	38.	**Bryan Trottier**	NY Islanders	15	1,123
			Pittsburgh	3	156
			Total	**18**	**1,279**
*	39.	**Adam Oates**	Detroit	4	246
			St. Louis	2¾	195
			Boston	5	368
			Washington	5	387
			Philadelphia	¼	14
			Anaheim	1	67
			Total	**18**	**1,277**
	40.	**Ray Ferraro**	Hartford	6¼	442
			NY Islanders	4¾	316
			NY Rangers	¾	65
			Los Angeles	3¼	197
			Atlanta	2¾	223
			St. Louis	¼	15
			Total	**18**	**1,258**
	41.	**Henri Richard**	**Montreal**	**20**	**1,256**
	42.	**Craig Ludwig**	Montreal	8	597
			NY Islanders	1	75
			Minnesota	2	151
			Dallas	6	433
			Total	**17**	**1,256**
	43.	**Kevin Lowe**	Edmonton	15	1,037
			NY Rangers	4	217
			Total	**19**	**1,254**
	44.	**Jari Kurri**	Edmonton	10	754
			Los Angeles	4¾	331
			NY Rangers	¼	14
			Anaheim	1	82
			Colorado	1	70
			Total	**17**	**1,251**
	45.	**Bill Gadsby**	Chicago	8½	468
			NY Rangers	6½	457
			Detroit	5	323
			Total	**20**	**1,248**
	46.	**Allan Stanley**	NY Rangers	6¼	307
			Chicago	1¾	111
			Boston	2	129
			Toronto	10	633
			Philadelphia	1	64
			Total	**21**	**1,244**
	47.	**Dino Ciccarelli**	Minnesota	8¾	602
			Washington	3¼	223
			Detroit	4	254
			Tampa Bay	1½	111
			Florida	1½	42
			Total	**19**	**1,232**
	48.	**Ed Westfall**	Boston	11	734
			NY Islanders	7	493
			Total	**18**	**1,227**
*	49.	**James Patrick**	NY Rangers	10¼	671
			Hartford	½	47
			Calgary	4¼	217
			Buffalo	5	290
			Total	**20**	**1,225**
*	50.	**Scott Mellanby**	Philadelphia	6	355
			Edmonton	2	149
			Florida	7¾	552
			St. Louis	2¼	167
			Total	**18**	**1,223**
	51.	**Brad McCrimmon**	Boston	3	228
			Philadelphia	5	367
			Calgary	3	231
			Detroit	3	203
			Hartford	3	156
			Phoenix	1	37
			Total	**18**	**1,222**
	52.	**Eric Nesterenko**	Toronto	5	206
			Chicago	16	1,013
			Total	**21**	**1,219**
	53.	**Marcel Pronovost**	Detroit	16	983
			Toronto	5	223
			Total	**21**	**1,206**
*	54.	**Claude Lemieux**	Montreal	7	281
			New Jersey	5¾	423
			Colorado	4¼	297
			Phoenix	2½	164
			Dallas	½	32
			Total	**20**	**1,197**
	55.	**Denis Savard**	Chicago	12¼	881
			Montreal	3	210
			Tampa Bay	1¾	105
			Total	**17**	**1,196**
	56.	**Dave Babych**	Winnipeg	5¼	390
			Hartford	5¾	349
			Vancouver	6¾	409
			Philadelphia	1	39
			Los Angeles	¼	8
			Total	**19**	**1,195**
	57.	**John MacLean**	New Jersey	13¼	934
			San Jose	¾	51
			NY Rangers	2¼	161
			Dallas	1½	48
			Total	**18**	**1,194**
	58.	**Gilbert Perrault**	**Buffalo**	**17**	**1,191**
*	59.	**Steve Thomas**	Toronto	6	377
			Chicago	6	334
			NY Islanders	3¾	275
			New Jersey	3	193
			Anaheim	¼	12
			Total	**19**	**1,191**
	60.	**Dale Hawerchuk**	Winnipeg	9	713
			Buffalo	5	342
			St. Louis	¾	66
			Philadelphia	1¼	67
			Total	**16**	**1,188**
	61.	**Brian Bellows**	Minnesota	10	753
			Montreal	3	200
			Tampa Bay	1¼	86
			Anaheim	¾	62

	Player	Team	Seasons	GP
		Washington	2	87
		Total	**17**	**1,188**
62.	**George Armstrong**	**Toronto**	**21**	**1,187**
* 63.	**Brendan Shanahan**	New Jersey	4	281
		St. Louis	4	277
		Hartford	1¼	76
		Detroit	6¾	552
		Total	**16**	**1,186**
64.	**Kevin Dineen**	Hartford	8¾	587
		Philadelphia	4¼	284
		Carolina	2	121
		Ottawa	1	67
		Columbus	2	125
		Total	**18**	**1,184**
* 65.	**Luke Richardson**	Toronto	4	278
		Edmonton	6	436
		Philadelphia	5	387
		Columbus	1	82
		Total	**16**	**1,183**
* 66.	**Brett Hull**	Calgary	1¾	57
		St. Louis	10¼	744
		Dallas	3	218
		Detroit	2	164
		Total	**17**	**1,183**
67.	**Frank Mahovlich**	Toronto	11¾	720
		Detroit	2¾	198
		Montreal	3½	263
		Total	**18**	**1,181**
68.	**Bob Carpenter**	Washington	6¼	490
		NY Rangers	½	28
		Los Angeles	1¾	120
		Boston	3½	187
		New Jersey	6	353
		Total	**18**	**1,178**
69.	**Don Marshall**	Montreal	10	585
		NY Rangers	7	479
		Buffalo	1	62
		Toronto	1	50
		Total	**19**	**1,176**
* 70.	**Glen Wesley**	Boston	7	537
		Hartford	3	184
		Carolina	5¾	445
		Toronto	¼	7
		Total	**16**	**1,173**
71.	**Sylvain Cote**	Hartford	7	382
		Washington	9¾	622
		Toronto	1½	94
		Chicago	½	45
		Dallas	¼	28
		Total	**19**	**1,171**
72.	**Bob Gainey**	**Montreal**	**16**	**1,160**
73.	**Kevin Hatcher**	Washington	10	685
		Dallas	2	121
		Pittsburgh	3	220
		NY Rangers	1	74
		Carolina	1	57
		Total	**17**	**1,157**
* 74.	**Adam Graves**	Detroit	2¼	78
		Edmonton	1¾	139
		NY Rangers	10	772
		San Jose	2	163
		Total	**16**	**1,152**
75.	**Leo Boivin**	Toronto	3¼	137
		Boston	11½	717
		Detroit	1¼	85
		Pittsburgh	1½	114
		Minnesota	1½	97
		Total	**19**	**1,150**
76.	**Garry Galley**	Los Angeles	5½	361
		Washington	1½	76
		Boston	3½	257
		Philadelphia	3¼	236
		Buffalo	2¼	163
		NY Islanders	1	56
		Total	**17**	**1,149**
77.	**Borje Salming**	Toronto	16	1,099
		Detroit	1	49
		Total	**17**	**1,148**
78.	**Gary Suter**	Calgary	8½	617
		Chicago	4½	301
		San Jose	4	227
		Total	**17**	**1,145**
79.	**Bobby Clarke**	**Philadelphia**	**15**	**1,144**
80.	**Rick Tocchet**	Philadelphia	10	621
		Pittsburgh	2¼	150
		Los Angeles	1½	80
		Boston	1¼	67
		Washington	¼	13
		Phoenix	2¾	213
		Total	**18**	**1,144**
* 81.	**Shayne Corson**	Montreal	10¾	662
		Edmonton	3	192
		St. Louis	1¼	88
		Toronto	3	197
		Total	**18**	**1,139**
* 82.	**Pierre Turgeon**	Buffalo	4¼	322
		NY Islanders	3½	255
		Montreal	1½	104
		St. Louis	4¾	327
		Dallas	2	131
		Total	**16**	**1,139**
* 83.	**Marc Bergevin**	Chicago	4¼	266
		NY Islanders	1¾	76
		Hartford	2	79
		Tampa Bay	3¼	206
		Detroit	1	70
		St. Louis	5	326
		Pittsburgh	1¾	107
		Total	**19**	**1,130**
84.	**Glenn Anderson**	Edmonton	11½	845
		Toronto	2¾	221
		NY Rangers	¼	12
		St. Louis	1½	51
		Total	**16**	**1,129**
85.	**Dave Ellett**	Winnipeg	6¼	475
		Toronto	6½	446
		New Jersey	¼	20
		Boston	2	136
		St. Louis	1	52
		Total	**16**	**1,129**
86.	**Bob Nevin**	Toronto	5¾	250
		NY Rangers	7¼	505
		Minnesota	2	138
		Los Angeles	3	235
		Total	**18**	**1,128**
87.	**Jamie Macoun**	Calgary	8½	586
		Toronto	6¼	466
		Detroit	1¼	76
		Total	**16**	**1,128**
88.	**Murray Oliver**	Detroit	2½	101
		Boston	6½	429
		Toronto	3	226
		Minnesota	5	371
		Total	**17**	**1,127**
89.	**Bernie Nicholls**	Los Angeles	8½	602
		NY Rangers	1¾	104
		Edmonton	1¼	95
		New Jersey	1½	84
		Chicago	2	107
		San Jose	3	135
		Total	**18**	**1,127**
90.	**Guy Lafleur**	Montreal	14	961
		NY Rangers	1	67
		Quebec	2	98
		Total	**17**	**1,126**
91.	**Jean Beliveau**	**Montreal**	**20**	**1,125**
92.	**Doug Harvey**	Montreal	14	890
		NY Rangers	3	151
		Detroit	1	2
		St. Louis	1	70
		Total	**19**	**1,113**
93.	**Brad Park**	NY Rangers	7½	465
		Boston	7½	501
		Detroit	2	147
		Total	**17**	**1,113**
94.	**Steve Duchesne**	Los Angeles	5¾	442
		Philadelphia	1¼	89
		Quebec	1	82
		St. Louis	3	163
		Ottawa	2	140
		Detroit	3	197
		Total	**16**	**1,113**
* 95.	**Joe Nieuwendyk**	Calgary	9	577
		Dallas	6¾	442
		New Jersey	1¼	94
		Total	**17**	**1,113**
96.	**Lanny McDonald**	Toronto	6½	477
		Colorado	1¾	142
		Calgary	7¾	441
		Total	**16**	**1,111**
97.	**Dave Taylor**	**Los Angeles**	**17**	**1,111**
98.	**Brent Sutter**	NY Islanders	11¼	694
		Chicago	6¾	417
		Total	**18**	**1,111**
* 99.	**Kelly Buchberger**	Edmonton	13	795
		Atlanta	¾	68
		Los Angeles	2¼	169
		Phoenix	1	79
		Total	**17**	**1,111**
100.	**Butch Goring**	Los Angeles	10¾	736
		NY Islanders	4¾	332
		Boston	½	39
		Total	**16**	**1,107**
101.	**Garry Unger**	Toronto	½	15
		Detroit	3	216
		St. Louis	8½	662
		Atlanta	1	79
		Los Angeles	¾	58
		Edmonton	2¼	75
		Total	**16**	**1,105**
102.	**Dave Manson**	Chicago	6¼	431
		Edmonton	2¾	219
		Winnipeg	2¼	139
		Phoenix	¾	66
		Montreal	1½	101
		Dallas	1¼	60
		Toronto	1¼	87
		Total	**16**	**1,103**
103.	**Pit Martin**	Detroit	3¼	119
		Boston	1¾	111
		Chicago	10¼	740
		Vancouver	1¾	131
		Total	**17**	**1,101**
104.	**Calle Johansson**	Buffalo	1¾	118
		Washington	14¼	983
		Total	**16**	**1,101**
105.	**Neal Broten**	Minnesota	13	876
		Dallas	2	116
		New Jersey	1¾	88
		Los Angeles	¼	19
		Total	**17**	**1,099**
106.	**Jay Wells**	Los Angeles	9	604
		Philadelphia	1¾	126
		Buffalo	2	85
		NY Rangers	3¼	186
		St. Louis	1	76
		Tampa Bay	1	21
		Total	**18**	**1,098**
* 107.	**Teppo Numinen**	Winnipeg	8	547
		Phoenix	7	551
		Total	**15**	**1,098**
108.	**Gordie Roberts**	Hartford	1½	107
		Minnesota	7	555
		Philadelphia	¼	11
		St. Louis	2½	166
		Pittsburgh	1¾	134
		Boston	2	124
		Total	**15**	**1,097**
* 109.	**Mike Keane**	Montreal	7¼	506
		Colorado	3	223
		NY Rangers	¾	70
		Dallas	3¼	242
		St. Louis	¾	56
		Total	**15**	**1,097**
* 110.	**Cliff Ronning**	St. Louis	3¾	180
		Vancouver	5¼	366
		Phoenix	2¼	156
		Nashville	3½	301
		Los Angeles	¼	14
		Minnesota	1	80
		Total	**16**	**1,097**
111.	**Darryl Sittler**	Toronto	11½	844
		Philadelphia	2½	191
		Detroit	1	61
		Total	**15**	**1,096**
112.	**Craig MacTavish**	Boston	5	217
		Edmonton	8¾	701
		NY Rangers	¼	12
		Philadelphia	1¾	100
		St. Louis	1¼	63
		Total	**17**	**1,093**
113.	**Ron Sutter**	Philadelphia	9	555
		St. Louis	2½	163
		Quebec	½	37
		NY Islanders	1	27
		Boston	1	18
		San Jose	4	272
		Calgary	1	21
		Total	**19**	**1,093**
* 114.	**Mark Recchi**	Pittsburgh	3¾	225
		Philadelphia	7	520
		Montreal	4¼	346
		Total	**15**	**1,091**
115.	**Michel Goulet**	Quebec	10¾	813
		Chicago	4¼	276
		Total	**15**	**1,089**
116.	**Carol Vadnais**	Montreal	2	42
		Oakland	2	152
		California	1¾	94
		Boston	3½	263
		NY Rangers	6¾	485
		New Jersey	1	51
		Total	**17**	**1,087**
117.	**Brad Marsh**	Atlanta	2	160
		Calgary	1¼	97
		Philadelphia	6¾	514
		Toronto	2¾	181
		Detroit	1¼	75
		Ottawa	1	59
		Total	**15**	**1,086**
* 118.	**Theoren Fleury**	Calgary	10¾	791
		Colorado	¼	15
		NY Rangers	3	224
		Chicago	1	54
		Total	**15**	**1,084**
119.	**Ulf Samuelsson**	Hartford	6¾	463
		Pittsburgh	4¼	277
		NY Rangers	3¾	287
		Detroit	¼	4
		Philadelphia	1	49
		Total	**16**	**1,080**
120.	**Bob Pulford**	Toronto	14	947
		Los Angeles	2	132
		Total	**16**	**1,079**
* 121.	**Trevor Linden**	Vancouver	11½	837
		NY Islanders	1¼	107
		Montreal	1¾	107
		Washington	½	28
		Total	**15**	**1,079**
122.	**Bobby Smith**	Minnesota	8¼	572
		Montreal	6¾	505
		Total	**15**	**1,077**
* 123.	**Joe Sakic**	Quebec	7	508
		Colorado	8	566
		Total	**15**	**1,074**
* 124.	**Brian Leetch**	**NY Rangers**	**16**	**1,072**
125.	**Doug Bodger**	Pittsburgh	4¼	299
		Buffalo	7	479
		San Jose	2¼	166
		New Jersey	½	49
		Los Angeles	1	65
		Vancouver	1	13
		Total	**16**	**1,071**
126.	**Murray Craven**	Detroit	2	46
		Philadelphia	7¼	523
		Hartford	1½	128
		Vancouver	1¼	88
		Chicago	3	157
		San Jose	3	129
		Total	**18**	**1,071**
127.	**Craig Ramsay**	**Buffalo**	**14**	**1,070**

	Player	Team	Seasons	GP
128.	Mike Ramsey	Buffalo	13¾	911
		Pittsburgh	1¼	77
		Detroit	3	82
		Total	**18**	**1,070**
129.	Andy Bathgate	NY Rangers	11¾	719
		Toronto	1¼	70
		Detroit	2	130
		Pittsburgh	2	150
		Total	**17**	**1,069**
130.	Ted Lindsay	Detroit	14	862
		Chicago	3	206
		Total	**17**	**1,068**
131.	Terry Harper	Montreal	10	554
		Los Angeles	3	234
		Detroit	4	252
		St. Louis	1	11
		Colorado	1	15
		Total	**19**	**1,066**
* 132.	Dave Lowry	Vancouver	3	165
		St. Louis	5	311
		Florida	4¼	272
		San Jose	2¾	143
		Calgary	3	175
		Total	**18**	**1,066**
133.	Rod Gilbert	**NY Rangers**	**18**	**1,065**
134.	Bobby Hull	Chicago	15	1,036
		Winnipeg	⅔	18
		Hartford	⅓	9
		Total	**16**	**1,063**
135.	Joe Mullen	St. Louis	4½	301
		Calgary	4½	345
		Pittsburgh	6	379
		Boston	1	37
		Total	**16**	**1,062**
* 136.	Jeremy Roenick	Chicago	8	524
		Phoenix	5	384
		Philadelphia	2	154
		Total	**15**	**1,062**
137.	Bob Rouse	Minnesota	5¾	351
		Washington	2	130
		Toronto	3¼	237
		Detroit	4	247
		San Jose	2	96
		Total	**17**	**1,061**
138.	Denis Potvin	**NY Islanders**	**15**	**1,060**
139.	Kelly Miller	NY Rangers	2½	117
		Washington	12½	940
		Total	**15**	**1,057**
140.	Jean Guy Talbot	Montreal	13	791
		Minnesota	¼	4
		Detroit	½	32
		St. Louis	2½	172
		Buffalo	¾	57
		Total	**17**	**1,056**
141.	Greg Adams	New Jersey	3	186
		Vancouver	7¾	489
		Dallas	3¼	177
		Phoenix	2	144
		Florida	1	60
		Total	**17**	**1,056**
142.	Randy Carlyle	Toronto	2	94
		Pittsburgh	5¾	397
		Winnipeg	9¼	564
		Total	**17**	**1,055**
143.	Stephane Richer	Montreal	8½	490
		New Jersey	5¼	360
		Tampa Bay	2	110
		St. Louis	½	36
		Pittsburgh	¾	58
		Total	**17**	**1,054**
* 144.	Craig Berube	Philadelphia	6¼	323
		Toronto	½	40
		Calgary	3½	234
		Washington	6¼	419
		NY Islanders	½	38
		Total	**17**	**1,054**
145.	Ivan Boldirev	Boston	1¼	13
		California	2¾	191
		Chicago	4¾	384
		Atlanta	1	65
		Vancouver	2¾	216
		Detroit	2½	183
		Total	**15**	**1,052**
* 146.	Don Sweeney	**Boston**	**15**	**1,052**
* 147.	Eric Desjardins	Montreal	6½	405
		Philadelphia	8½	645
		Total	**15**	**1,050**
* 148.	Scott Young	Hartford	3½	197
		Pittsburgh	½	43
		Quebec	3	206
		Colorado	2	153
		Anaheim	1	73
		St. Louis	4	298
		Dallas	1	79
		Total	**15**	**1,049**
149.	Geoff Courtnall	Boston	4¾	259
		Edmonton	¼	12
		Washington	2	159
		St. Louis	5¾	326
		Washington	4½	292
		Total	**17**	**1,048**
150.	Eddie Shack	NY Rangers	2¼	141
		Toronto	8¾	504
		Boston	2	120
		Los Angeles	1¼	84
		Buffalo	1½	111
		Pittsburgh	1¼	87
		Total	**17**	**1,047**
151.	Rob Ramage	Colorado	3	234
		St. Louis	5¾	441
		Calgary	1¼	80
		Toronto	2	160
		Minnesota	1	34
		Tampa Bay	¾	66
		Montreal	½	14
		Philadelphia	½	15
		Total	**15**	**1,044**
152.	Serge Savard	Montreal	15	917
		Winnipeg	2	123
		Total	**17**	**1,040**
153.	Ron Ellis	**Toronto**	**16**	**1,034**
154.	Harold Snepsts	Vancouver	11¾	781
		Minnesota	1	71
		Detroit	3	120
		St. Louis	1¼	61
		Total	**17**	**1,033**
155.	Ralph Backstrom	Montreal	14½	844
		Los Angeles	2¼	172
		Chicago	¼	16
		Total	**17**	**1,032**
156.	Ed Olczyk	Chicago	5	322
		Toronto	3¼	257
		Winnipeg	3½	214
		NY Rangers	2¼	103
		Los Angeles	¾	67
		Pittsburgh	1¼	68
		Total	**16**	**1,031**
* 157.	Rod Brind'Amour	St. Louis	2	157
		Philadelphia	8½	633
		Carolina	3½	241
		Total	**14**	**1,031**
158.	Dick Duff	Toronto	9¾	582
		NY Rangers	¾	43
		Montreal	5	305
		Los Angeles	¾	39
		Buffalo	1¾	61
		Total	**18**	**1,030**
159.	Russ Courtnall	Toronto	5¼	309
		Montreal	3¾	250
		Minnesota	1	84
		Dallas	1½	116
		Vancouver	2½	141
		NY Rangers	¼	14
		Los Angeles	2	115
		Total	**16**	**1,029**
160.	John Tonelli	NY Islanders	7¾	584
		Calgary	2¼	161
		Los Angeles	3	231
		Chicago	¾	33
		Quebec	¼	19
		Total	**14**	**1,028**
161.	Gaetan Duchesne	Washington	6	451
		Quebec	2	150
		Minnesota	4	297
		San Jose	1¾	117
		Florida	¼	13
		Total	**14**	**1,028**
162.	Petr Svoboda	Montreal	7¾	534
		Buffalo	3	139
		Philadelphia	3¾	232
		Tampa Bay	2½	123
		Total	**17**	**1,028**
163.	Grant Ledyard	NY Rangers	1¼	69
		Los Angeles	2½	142
		Washington	1	82
		Buffalo	4¼	240
		Dallas	4¼	270
		Vancouver	¾	49
		Boston	1¼	69
		Ottawa	1	40
		Tampa Bay	1¾	67
		Total	**18**	**1,028**
164.	Wayne Cashman	**Boston**	**17**	**1,027**
* 165.	Mike Modano	Minnesota	4	317
		Dallas	10	708
		Total	**14**	**1,025**
166.	Doug Wilson	Chicago	14	938
		San Jose	2	86
		Total	**16**	**1,024**
167.	Jim Neilson	NY Rangers	12	810
		California	2	98
		Cleveland	2	115
		Total	**16**	**1,023**
168.	Keith Acton	Montreal	4¼	228
		Minnesota	4¼	343
		Edmonton	1	72
		Philadelphia	4½	303
		Washington	¼	6
		NY Islanders	¾	71
		Total	**15**	**1,023**
* 169.	Fredrik Olausson	Winnipeg	7¼	496
		Edmonton	2¼	108
		Anaheim	3¾	244
		Pittsburgh	1¾	127
		Detroit	1	47
		Total	**16**	**1,022**
170.	Don Lever	Vancouver	7⅔	593
		Atlanta	⅓	28
		Calgary	1¼	85
		Colorado	¾	59
		New Jersey	3	216
		Buffalo	2	39
		Total	**15**	**1,020**
171.	Mike Foligno	Detroit	2½	186
		Buffalo	9	664
		Toronto	2¾	129
		Florida	¾	39
		Total	**15**	**1,018**
172.	Charlie Huddy	Edmonton	11	694
		Los Angeles	3¼	226
		Buffalo	2½	85
		St. Louis	¼	12
		Total	**17**	**1,017**
173.	Phil Russell	Chicago	6¾	504
		Atlanta	1¼	93
		Calgary	3	229
		New Jersey	2¾	172
		Buffalo	1¼	18
		Total	**15**	**1,016**
174.	Brian Propp	Philadelphia	10¾	790
		Boston	¼	14
		Minnesota	3	147
		Hartford	1	65
		Total	**15**	**1,016**
* 175.	Paul Ranheim	Calgary	5¾	354
		Hartford	3¼	202
		Carolina	3	230
		Philadelphia	2½	187
		Phoenix	½	40
		Total	**15**	**1,013**
176.	Laurie Boschman	Toronto	2¾	187
		Edmonton	1	73
		Winnipeg	7¼	526
		New Jersey	2	153
		Ottawa	1	70
		Total	**14**	**1,009**
177.	Dave Christian	Winnipeg	4	230
		Washington	6½	504
		Boston	1½	128
		St. Louis	1	78
		Chicago	2	69
		Total	**15**	**1,009**
178.	Dave Lewis	NY Islanders	6¾	514
		Los Angeles	3¼	221
		New Jersey	3	209
		Detroit	2	64
		Total	**15**	**1,008**
179.	Bob Murray	**Chicago**	**15**	**1,008**
* 180.	Todd Gill	Toronto	12	639
		Pittsburgh	1¾	143
		St. Louis	¾	39
		Detroit	1¾	104
		Phoenix	¾	41
		Colorado	1	36
		Chicago	1	5
		Total	**19**	**1,007**
181.	Jimmy Roberts	Montreal	9⅔	611
		St. Louis	5⅓	395
		Total	**15**	**1,006**
182.	Steve Larmer	Chicago	13	891
		NY Rangers	2	115
		Total	**15**	**1,006**
183.	Claude Provost	**Montreal**	**15**	**1,005**
184.	Rick Middleton	NY Rangers	2	124
		Boston	12	881
		Total	**14**	**1,005**
* 185.	Mats Sundin	Quebec	4	324
		Toronto	9	681
		Total	**13**	**1,005**
186.	Ryan Walter	Washington	4	307
		Montreal	9	604
		Vancouver	2	92
		Total	**15**	**1,003**
187.	Vic Hadfield	NY Rangers	13	839
		Pittsburgh	3	163
		Total	**16**	**1,002**
* 188.	Eric Weinrich	New Jersey	4	173
		Hartford	1½	87
		Chicago	5	356
		Montreal	2½	203
		Boston	¼	22
		Philadelphia	2	161
		Total	**15**	**1,002**
189.	Bernie Federko	St. Louis	14	927
		Detroit	1	73
		Total	**15**	**1,000**

Goaltending Records

All-Time Shutout Leaders (Minimum 40 Shutouts)

Goaltender	Team	Seasons	Games	Shutouts
Terry Sawchuk (1949-1970)	Detroit	14	734	85
	Boston	2	102	11
	Toronto	3	91	4
	Los Angeles	1	36	2
	NY Rangers	1	8	1
	Total	21	971	**103**
George Hainsworth (1926-1937)	Montreal	7½	318	75
	Toronto	3½	147	19
	Total	11	465	**94**
Glenn Hall (1952-1971)	Detroit	4	148	17
	Chicago	10	618	51
	St. Louis	4	140	16
	Total	18	906	**84**
Jacques Plante (1952-1973)	Montreal	11	556	58
	NY Rangers	2	98	5
	St. Louis	2	69	10
	Toronto	2¾	106	7
	Boston	¼	8	2
	Total	18	837	**82**
Tiny Thompson (1928-1940)	Boston	10¼	468	74
	Detroit	1¾	85	7
	Total	12	553	**81**
Alex Connell (1924-1937)	Ottawa	8	293	64
	Detroit	1	48	6
	NY Americans	1	1	0
	Mtl. Maroons	2	75	11
	Total	12	417	**81**
Tony Esposito (1968-1984)	Montreal	1	13	2
	Chicago	15	873	74
	Total	16	886	**76**
Lorne Chabot (1926-1937)	NY Rangers	2	80	21
	Toronto	5	214	33
	Montreal	1	47	8
	Chicago	1	48	8
	Mtl. Maroons	1	16	2
	NY Americans	1	6	1
	Total	11	411	**73**
Harry Lumley (1943-1960)	Detroit	6½	324	26
	NY Rangers	½	1	0
	Chicago	2	134	5
	Toronto	4	267	34
	Boston	3	78	6
	Total	16	804	**71**
Roy Worters (1925-1937)	Pittsburgh Pirates	3	123	22
	NY Americans	9	360	45
	* Montreal		1	0
	Total	12	484	**67**
Patrick Roy (1984-2003)	Montreal	11½	551	29
	Colorado	7½	478	37
	Total	19	1,029	**66**
Ed Belfour (1988-2003)	Chicago	7⅔	415	30
	San Jose	⅓	13	1
	Dallas	5	307	27
	Toronto	1	62	7
	Total	14	797	**65**
Martin Brodeur (1991-2003)	New Jersey	11	665	**64**
Turk Broda (1936-1952)	Toronto	14	629	**62**
Dominik Hasek (1990-2002)	Chicago	2	25	1
	Buffalo	9	491	55
	Detroit	1	65	5
	Total	12	581	**61**
Clint Benedict (1917-1930)	Ottawa	7	158	19
	Mtl. Maroons	6	204	39
	Total	13	362	**58**
John Ross Roach (1921-1935)	Toronto	7	222	13
	NY Rangers	4	89	30
	Detroit	3	180	15
	Total	14	491	**58**
Bernie Parent (1965-1979)	Boston	2	57	1
	Philadelphia	9½	486	50
	Toronto	1½	65	3
	Total	13	608	**54**
Ed Giacomin (1965-1978)	NY Rangers	10¼	539	49
	Detroit	2¾	71	5
	Total	13	610	**54**
Dave Kerr (1930-1941)	Mtl. Maroons	3	101	11
	NY Americans	1	1	0
	NY Rangers	7	324	40
	Total	11	426	**51**
Rogie Vachon (1966-1982)	Montreal	5¼	206	13
	Los Angeles	6¾	389	32
	Detroit	2	109	4
	Boston	2	91	2
	Total	16	795	**51**
Ken Dryden (1970-1979)	Montreal	8	397	**46**
Gump Worsley (1952-1974)	NY Rangers	10	582	24
	Montreal	6½	172	16
	Minnesota	4½	107	3
	Total	21	861	**43**
Charlie Gardiner (1927-1934)	Chicago	7	316	**42**
Curtis Joseph (1989-2003)	St. Louis	6	280	5
	Edmonton	3	177	14
	Toronto	4	249	17
	Detroit	1	61	5
	Total	14	767	**41**
Frank Brimsek (1938-1950)	Boston	9	444	35
	Chicago	1	70	5
	Total	10	514	**40**
John Vanbiesbrouck (1981-2002)	NY Rangers	11	449	16
	Florida	5	268	13
	Philadelphia	2	112	9
	NY Islanders	¾	44	1
	New Jersey	1¼	9	1
	Total	20	882	**40**

*Played 1 game for Montreal in 1929-30.

Ten or More Shutouts, One Season

Number of Shutouts	Goaltender	Team	Season	Length of Schedule
22	George Hainsworth	Montreal	1928-29	44
15	Alex Connell	Ottawa	1925-26	36
	Alex Connell	Ottawa	1927-28	44
	Hal Winkler	Boston	1927-28	44
	Tony Esposito	Chicago	1969-70	76
14	George Hainsworth	Montreal	1926-27	44
13	Clint Benedict	Mtl. Maroons	1926-27	44
	Alex Connell	Ottawa	1926-27	44
	George Hainsworth	Montreal	1927-28	44
	John Ross Roach	NY Rangers	1928-29	44
	Roy Worters	NY Americans	1928-29	44
	Harry Lumley	Toronto	1953-54	70
	Dominik Hasek	Buffalo	1997-98	82
12	Lorne Chabot	Toronto	1928-29	44
	Tiny Thompson	Boston	1928-29	44
	Charlie Gardiner	Chicago	1930-31	44
	Terry Sawchuk	Detroit	1951-52	70
	Terry Sawchuk	Detroit	1953-54	70
	Terry Sawchuk	Detroit	1954-55	70
	Glenn Hall	Detroit	1955-56	70
	Bernie Parent	Philadelphia	1973-74	78
	Bernie Parent	Philadelphia	1974-75	80
11	Lorne Chabot	NY Rangers	1927-28	44
	Hap Holmes	Detroit	1927-28	44
	Roy Worters	Pittsburgh Pirates	1927-28	44
	Clint Benedict	Mtl. Maroons	1928-29	44
	Joe Miller	Pittsburgh Pirates	1928-29	44
	Tiny Thompson	Boston	1932-33	48
	Terry Sawchuk	Detroit	1950-51	70
	Dominik Hasek	Buffalo	2000-01	82
10	Lorne Chabot	NY Rangers	1926-27	44
	Dolly Dolson	Detroit	1928-29	44
	John Ross Roach	Detroit	1932-33	48
	Charlie Gardiner	Chicago	1933-34	48
	Tiny Thompson	Boston	1935-36	48
	Frank Brimsek	Boston	1938-39	48
	Bill Durnan	Montreal	1948-49	60
	Harry Lumley	Toronto	1952-53	70
	Gerry McNeil	Montreal	1952-53	70
	Tony Esposito	Chicago	1973-74	78
	Ken Dryden	Montreal	1976-77	80
	Martin Brodeur	New Jersey	1996-97	82
	Martin Brodeur	New Jersey	1997-98	82
	Byron Dafoe	Boston	1998-99	82
	Roman Cechmanek	Philadelphia	2000-01	82

All-Time Win Leaders

(Minimum 225 Wins)

Wins	Goaltender	GP	Dec.	Losses	Ties
551	Patrick Roy	1029	997	315	131
447	Terry Sawchuk	971	949	330	172
435	Jacques Plante	837	827	247	145
423	Tony Esposito	886	880	306	151
407	Glenn Hall	906	896	326	163
403	Grant Fuhr	868	812	295	114
401	* Ed Belfour	797	768	262	105
385	Mike Vernon	781	750	273	92
380	* Curtis Joseph	706	767	279	87
374	John Vanbiesbrouck	882	839	346	119
372	Andy Moog	713	669	209	88
369	Tom Barrasso	777	732	277	86
365	* Martin Brodeur	592	665	191	94
355	Rogie Vachon	795	773	291	127
335	Gump Worsley	861	837	352	150
330	Harry Lumley	803	801	329	142
305	Billy Smith	680	643	233	105
302	Turk Broda	629	627	224	101
301	* Mike Richter	666	632	258	73
296	Ron Hextall	608	579	214	69
294	Mike Liut	663	639	271	74
289	Ed Giacomin	610	594	208	97
288	* Dominik Hasek	581	557	189	80
288	* Sean Burke	715	683	301	94
286	Dan Bouchard	655	631	232	113
284	Tiny Thompson	553	553	194	75
274	* Chris Osgood	501	484	152	58
271	Bernie Parent	608	590	198	121
271	Kelly Hrudey	677	624	265	88
270	Gilles Meloche	788	752	351	131
268	Don Beaupre	667	620	277	75
258	Ken Dryden	397	389	57	74
254	* Felix Potvin	607	585	252	79
252	Frank Brimsek	514	514	182	80
250	Johnny Bower	552	535	195	90
246	Pete Peeters	489	452	155	51
246	George Hainsworth	465	465	145	74
245	Kirk McLean	612	579	262	72
240	Bill Ranford	647	595	279	76
236	Reggie Lemelin	507	461	162	63
234	Eddie Johnston	592	571	257	80
231	Glenn Resch	571	537	224	82
230	Gerry Cheevers	418	406	102	74
225	Ken Wregget	575	526	248	53

* active player

Active Shutout Leaders

(Minimum 25 Shutouts)

Goaltender	Teams	Seasons	Games	Shutouts
Ed Belfour	Chi., S.J., Dal., Tor.	14	797	65
Martin Brodeur	New Jersey	11	665	64
Dominik Hasek	Chi., Buf., Det.	12	581	61
Curtis Joseph	St.L., Edm., Tor., Det.	14	767	41
Chris Osgood	Det., NYI, St.L.	10	501	38
Jocelyn Thibault	Que., Col., Mtl., Chi.	10	522	35
Tommy Salo	NY Islanders, Edmonton	9	477	34
Arturs Irbe	S.J., Dal., Van., Car.	12	558	33
Sean Burke	N.J., Hfd., Car., Van., Phi., Fla., Phx.	15	715	33
Nikolai Khabibulin	Wpg., Phx., T.B.	8	421	32
Olaf Kolzig	Washington	12	481	31
Patrick Lalime	Pittsburgh, Ottawa	5	265	28
Felix Potvin	Tor., NYI, Van., L.A.	12	607	28
Byron Dafoe	Wsh., L.A., Bos., Atl.	11	397	26
Ron Tugnutt	Que., Edm., Ana., Mtl., Ott., Pit., CBJ, Dal.	15	526	25

All-Time Penalty-Minute Leaders

* active player

(Regular season. Minimum 2,000 minutes)

	Player	Seasons	Games	Penalty Minutes	Mins. per game
1.	**Tiger Williams**, Tor., Van., Det., L.A., Hfd.	14	962	**3966**	4.12
2.	**Dale Hunter**, Que., Wsh., Col.	19	1407	**3565**	2.53
3.	**Marty McSorley**, Pit., Edm., L.A., NYR, S.J., Bos.	17	961	**3381**	3.52
4.	**Bob Probert**, Det., Chi.	16	935	**3300**	3.53
* 5.	**Tie Domi**, Tor., NYR, Wpg.	14	863	**3198**	3.71
* 6.	**Rob Ray**, Buf., Ott.	14	894	**3193**	3.57
* 7.	**Craig Berube**, Phi., Tor., Cgy., Wsh., NYI	17	1054	**3149**	2.99
8.	**Tim Hunter**, Cgy., Que., Van., S.J.	16	815	**3146**	3.86
9.	**Chris Nilan**, Mtl., NYR, Bos.	13	688	**3043**	4.42
10.	**Rick Tocchet**, Phi., Pit., L.A., Bos., Wsh., Phx.	18	1144	**2972**	2.60

Goals Against Average Leaders (Minimum 25 games played)

(Exceptions: Minimum 13 games played, 1994-95; minimum 26 games played, 1992-93 to 1993-94; minimum 15 games played, 1917-18 to 1925-26)

Season	Goaltender and Club	GP	Mins.	GA	SO	AVG.
2002-03	Marty Turco, Dallas	55	3,203	92	7	1.72
2001-02	Patrick Roy, Colorado	63	3,773	122	9	1.94
2000-01	Marty Turco, Dallas	26	1,266	40	3	1.90
99-2000	Brian Boucher, Philadelphia	35	2,038	65	4	1.91
1998-99	Ron Tugnutt, Ottawa	43	2,508	75	3	1.79
1997-98	Ed Belfour, Dallas	61	3,581	112	9	1.88
1996-97	Martin Brodeur, New Jersey	67	3,838	120	10	1.88
1995-96	Ron Hextall, Philadelphia	53	3,102	112	4	2.17
1994-95	Dominik Hasek, Buffalo	41	2,416	85	5	2.11
1993-94	Dominik Hasek, Buffalo	58	3,358	109	7	1.95
1992-93	Felix Potvin, Toronto	48	2,781	116	2	2.50
1991-92	Patrick Roy, Montreal	67	3,935	155	5	2.36
1990-91	Ed Belfour, Chicago	74	4,127	170	4	2.47
1989-90	Mike Liut, Hartford, Washington	37	2,161	91	4	2.53
1988-89	Patrick Roy, Montreal	48	2,744	113	4	2.47
1987-88	Pete Peeters, Washington	35	1,896	88	2	2.78
1986-87	Brian Hayward, Montreal	37	2,178	102	1	2.81
1985-86	Bob Froese, Philadelphia	51	2,728	116	5	2.55
1984-85	Tom Barrasso, Buffalo	54	3,248	144	5	2.66
1983-84	Pat Riggin, Washington	41	2,299	102	4	2.66
1982-83	Pete Peeters, Boston	62	3,611	142	8	2.36
1981-82	Denis Herron, Montreal	27	1,547	68	3	2.64
1980-81	Richard Sevigny, Montreal	33	1,777	71	2	2.40
1979-80	Bob Sauve, Buffalo	32	1,880	74	4	2.36
1978-79	Ken Dryden, Montreal	47	2,814	108	5	2.30
1977-78	Ken Dryden, Montreal	52	3,071	105	5	2.05
1976-77	Michel Larocque, Montreal	26	1,525	53	4	2.09
1975-76	Ken Dryden, Montreal	62	3,580	121	8	2.03
1974-75	Bernie Parent, Philadelphia	68	4,041	137	12	2.03
1973-74	Bernie Parent, Philadelphia	73	4,314	136	12	1.89
1972-73	Ken Dryden, Montreal	54	3,165	119	6	2.26
1971-72	Tony Esposito, Chicago	48	2,780	82	9	1.77
1970-71	Jacques Plante, Toronto	40	2,329	73	4	1.88
1969-70	Ernie Wakely, St. Louis	30	1,651	58	4	2.11
1968-69	Jacques Plante, St. Louis	37	2,139	70	5	1.96
1967-68	Gump Worsley, Montreal	40	2,213	73	6	1.98
1966-67	Glenn Hall, Chicago	32	1,664	66	2	2.38
1965-66	Johnny Bower, Toronto	35	1,998	75	3	2.25
1964-65	Johnny Bower, Toronto	34	2,040	81	3	2.38
1963-64	Johnny Bower, Toronto	51	3,009	106	5	2.11
1962-63	Don Simmons, Toronto	28	1,680	69	1	2.46
1961-62	Jacques Plante, Montreal	70	4,200	166	4	2.37
1960-61	Charlie Hodge, Montreal	30	1,800	74	4	2.47
1959-60	Jacques Plante, Montreal	69	4,140	175	3	2.54
1958-59	Jacques Plante, Montreal	67	4,000	144	9	2.16
1957-58	Jacques Plante, Montreal	57	3,386	119	9	2.11
1956-57	Jacques Plante, Montreal	61	3,660	122	9	2.00
1955-56	Jacques Plante, Montreal	64	3,840	119	7	1.86
1954-55	Harry Lumley, Toronto	69	4,140	134	8	1.94
1953-54	Harry Lumley, Toronto	69	4,140	128	13	1.86
1952-53	Terry Sawchuk, Detroit	63	3,780	120	9	1.90
1951-52	Terry Sawchuk, Detroit	70	4,200	133	12	1.90
1950-51	Al Rollins, Toronto	40	2,367	70	5	1.77
1949-50	Bill Durnan, Montreal	64	3,840	141	8	2.20
1948-49	Bill Durnan, Montreal	60	3,600	126	10	2.10
1947-48	Turk Broda, Toronto	60	3,600	143	5	2.38
1946-47	Bill Durnan, Montreal	60	3,600	138	4	2.30
1945-46	Bill Durnan, Montreal	40	2,400	104	4	2.60
1944-45	Bill Durnan, Montreal	50	3,000	121	1	2.42
1943-44	Bill Durnan, Montreal	50	3,000	109	2	2.18
1942-43	Johnny Mowers, Detroit	50	3,010	124	6	2.47
1941-42	Frank Brimsek, Boston	47	2,930	115	3	2.35
1940-41	Turk Broda, Toronto	48	2,970	99	5	2.00
1939-40	Dave Kerr, NY Rangers	48	3,000	77	8	1.54
1938-39	Frank Brimsek, Boston	43	2,610	68	10	1.56
1937-38	Tiny Thompson, Boston	48	2,970	89	7	1.80
1936-37	Normie Smith, Detroit	48	2,980	102	6	2.05
1935-36	Tiny Thompson, Boston	48	2,930	82	10	1.68
1934-35	Lorne Chabot, Chicago	48	2,940	88	8	1.80
1933-34	Wilf Cude, Detroit, Montreal	30	1,920	47	5	1.47
1932-33	Tiny Thompson, Boston	48	3,000	88	11	1.76
1931-32	Charlie Gardiner, Chicago	48	2,989	92	4	1.85
1930-31	Roy Worters, NY Americans	44	2,760	74	8	1.61
1929-30	Tiny Thompson, Boston	44	2,680	98	3	2.19
1928-29	George Hainsworth, Montreal	44	2,800	43	22	0.92
1927-28	George Hainsworth, Montreal	44	2,730	48	13	1.05
1926-27	Clint Benedict, Mtl. Maroons	43	2,748	65	13	1.42
1925-26	Alex Connell, Ottawa	36	2,251	42	15	1.12
1924-25	Georges Vezina, Montreal	30	1,860	56	5	1.81
1923-24	Georges Vezina, Montreal	24	1,459	48	3	1.97
1922-23	Clint Benedict, Ottawa	24	1,478	54	4	2.18
1921-22	Clint Benedict, Ottawa	24	1,508	84	2	3.34
1920-21	Clint Benedict, Ottawa	24	1,462	75	2	3.08
1919-20	Clint Benedict, Ottawa	24	1,444	64	5	2.66
1918-19	Clint Benedict, Ottawa	18	1,152	53	2	2.76
1917-18	Georges Vezina, Montreal	21	1,282	84	1	3.93

All-Time Regular Season NHL Coaching Register

Regular Season, 1917-2003

Coach	Team	Games Coached	Wins	Losses	Ties	Years	Cup Wins	Career
Abel, Sid	Chicago	140	39	79	22	2		
	Detroit	811	340	339	132	12		
	St. Louis	10	3	6	1	1		
	Kansas City	3	0	3	0	1		
	Total	964	382	427	155	16		1952-76
Adams, Jack	Detroit	964	413	390	161	20	3	1927-47
Allen, Keith	Philadelphia	150	51	67	32	2		1967-69
Allison, Dave	Ottawa	25	2	22	1	1		1995-96
Anderson, Jim	Washington	54	4	45	5	1		1974-75
Angotti, Lou	St. Louis	32	6	20	6	2		
	Pittsburgh	80	16	58	6	1		
	Total	112	22	78	12	3		1973-84
Arbour, Al	St. Louis	107	42	40	25	3		
	NY Islanders	1499	739	537	223	19	4	
	Total	1606	781	577	248	22	4	1970-94
Armstrong, George	Toronto	47	17	26	4	1		1988-89
Babcock, Mike	Anaheim	82	40	33	9	1		2002-03
Barber, Bill	Philadelphia	136	73	46	17	2		2000-02
Barkley, Doug	Detroit	77	20	46	11	3		1970-76
Beaulieu, Andre	Minnesota	32	6	23	3	1		1977-78
Belisle, Danny	Washington	96	28	51	17	2		1978-80
Berenson, Red	St. Louis	204	100	72	32	3		1979-82
Bergeron, Michel	Quebec	634	265	283	86	8		
	NY Rangers	158	73	67	18	2		
	Total	792	338	350	104	10		1980-90
Berry, Bob	Los Angeles	240	107	94	39	3		
	Montreal	223	116	71	36	3		
	Pittsburgh	240	88	127	25	3		
	St. Louis	157	73	63	21	2		
	Total	860	384	355	121	11		1978-94
Beverley, Nick	Toronto	17	9	6	2	1		1995-96
Blackburn, Don	Hartford	140	42	63	35	2		1979-81
Blair, Wren	Minnesota	147	48	65	34	3		1967-70
Blake, Toe	Montreal	914	500	255	159	13	8	1955-68
Boileau, Marc	Pittsburgh	151	66	61	24	3		1973-76
Boivin, Leo	St. Louis	97	28	53	16	2		1975-78
Boucher, Frank	NY Rangers	527	181	263	83	11	1	1939-54
Boucher, Georges	Mtl. Maroons	12	6	5	1	1		
	Ottawa	48	13	29	6	1		
	St. Louis	35	9	20	6	1		
	Boston	70	22	32	16	1		
	Total	165	50	86	29	4		1930-50
Bowman, Scotty	St. Louis	238	110	83	45	4		
	Montreal	634	419	110	105	8	5	
	Buffalo	404	210	134	60	7		
	Pittsburgh	164	95	53	16	2	1	
	Detroit	701	410	204	87	9	3	
	Total	2141	1244	584	313	30	9	1967-02
Bowness, Rick	Winnipeg	28	8	17	3	1		
	Boston	80	36	32	12	1		
	Ottawa	235	39	178	18	4		
	NY Islanders	100	38	50	12	2		
	Total	443	121	277	45	8		1988-98
Brooks, Herb	NY Rangers	285	131	113	41	4		
	Minnesota	80	19	48	13	1		
	New Jersey	84	40	37	7	1		
	Pittsburgh	58	29	24	5	1		
	Total	507	219	222	66	7		1981-00
Brophy, John	Toronto	193	64	111	18	3		1986-89
Burnett, George	Edmonton	35	12	20	3	1		1994-95
Burns, Charlie	Minnesota	86	22	50	14	2		1969-75
Burns, Pat	Montreal	320	174	104	42	4		
	Toronto	281	133	107	41	4		
	Boston	254	105	103	46	4		
	New Jersey	82	46	26	10	1	1	
	Total	937	458	340	139	13	1	1988-03
Bush, Eddie	Kansas City	32	1	23	8	1		1975-76
Campbell, Colin	NY Rangers	269	118	108	43	4		1994-98
Carpenter, Doug	New Jersey	290	100	166	24	4		
	Toronto	91	39	47	5	2		
	Total	381	139	213	29	6		1984-91
Carroll, Dick	Toronto	40	18	22	0	2	1	1917-19
Carroll, Frank	Toronto	24	15	9	0	1		1920-21
Cashman, Wayne	Philadelphia	61	32	20	9	1		1997-98
Cassidy, Bruce	Washington	82	39	35	8	1		2002-03
Chambers, Dave	Quebec	98	19	64	15	2		1990-92
Charron, Guy	Calgary	16	6	7	3	1		
	Anaheim	49	14	28	7	1		
	Total	65	20	35	10	2		1991-01
Cheevers, Gerry	Boston	376	204	126	46	5		1980-85
Cherry, Don	Boston	400	231	105	64	5		
	Colorado	80	19	48	13	1		
	Total	480	250	153	77	6		1974-80
Clancy, King	Mtl. Maroons	18	6	11	1	1		
	Toronto	210	80	81	49	3		
	Total	228	86	92	50	4		1937-56
Clapper, Dit	Boston	230	102	88	40	4		1945-49
Cleghorn, Odie	Pittsburgh	168	62	86	20	4		1925-29
Cleghorn, Sprague	Mtl. Maroons	48	19	22	7	1		1931-32
Colville, Neil	NY Rangers	93	26	41	26	2		1950-52
Conacher, Charlie	Chicago	162	56	84	22	3		1947-50
Constantine, Kevin	San Jose	157	55	78	24	3		
	Pittsburgh	188	86	67	35	3		
	New Jersey	31	20	9	2	1		
	Total	376	161	154	61	7		1993-02
Cook, Bill	NY Rangers	117	34	59	24	2		1951-53
Crawford, Marc	Quebec	48	30	13	5	1		
	Colorado	246	135	75	36	3	1	
	Vancouver	365	161	152	52	5		
	Total	659	326	240	93	9	1	1994-03
Creamer, Pierre	Pittsburgh	80	36	35	9	1		1987-88
Creighton, Fred	Atlanta	348	156	136	56	5		
	Boston	73	40	20	13	1		
	Total	421	196	156	69	6		1974-80
Crisp, Terry	Calgary	240	144	63	33	3	1	
	Tampa Bay	391	142	204	45	6		
	Total	631	286	267	78	9	1	1987-98
Crozier, Joe	Buffalo	192	77	80	35	3		
	Toronto	40	13	22	5	1		
	Total	232	90	102	40	4		1971-81
Crozier, Roger	Washington	1	0	1	0	1		1981-82
Cunniff, John	Hartford	13	3	9	1	1		
	New Jersey	133	59	56	18	2		
	Total	146	62	65	19	3		1982-91
Curry, Alex	Ottawa	36	24	8	4	1		1925-26
Dandurand, Leo	Montreal	163	78	76	9	6		1921-35
Day, Hap	Toronto	546	259	206	81	10	5	1940-50
Dea, Billy	Detroit	11	3	8	0	1		1981-82
Delvecchio, Alex	Detroit	245	82	131	32	4		1973-77
Demers, Jacques	Quebec	80	25	44	11	1		
	St. Louis	240	106	106	28	3		
	Detroit	320	137	136	47	4		
	Montreal	221	107	87	27	4	1	
	Tampa Bay	145	34	94	17	2		
	Total	1006	409	467	130	14	1	1979-99
Denneny, Cy	Boston	44	26	13	5	1	1	
	Ottawa	48	11	27	10	1		
	Total	92	37	40	15	2	1	1928-33
Dineen, Bill	Philadelphia	140	60	60	20	2		1991-93
Dudley, Rick	Buffalo	188	85	72	31	3		1989-92
Duff, Dick	Toronto	2	0	2	0	1		1979-80
Dugal, Jules	Montreal	18	9	6	3	1		1938-39
Duncan, Art	Detroit	33	10	21	2	1		
	Toronto	47	21	16	10	2	1	
	Total	80	31	37	12	3	1	1926-32
Dutton, Red	NY Americans	288	90	151	47	6		
	Brooklyn	48	16	29	3	1		
	Total	336	106	180	50	7		1935-42
Eddolls, Frank	Chicago	70	13	40	17	1		1954-55
Esposito, Phil	NY Rangers	45	24	21	0	2		1986-89
Evans, Jack	California	80	27	42	11	1		
	Cleveland	160	47	87	26	2		
	Hartford	374	163	174	37	5		
	Total	614	237	303	74	8		1975-88
Fashoway, Gordie	Oakland	10	4	5	1	1		1967-68
Ferguson, John	NY Rangers	121	43	59	19	2		
	Winnipeg	14	7	6	1	1		
	Total	135	50	65	20	3		1975-86
Filion, Maurice	Quebec	6	1	3	2	1		1980-81
Francis, Bob	Phoenix	328	145	138	45	4		1999-03
Francis, Emile	NY Rangers	654	342	209	103	10		
	St. Louis	124	46	64	14	3		
	Total	778	388	273	117	13		1965-83
Fraser, Curt	Atlanta	279	64	184	31	4		1999-03
Fredrickson, Frank	Pittsburgh	44	5	36	3	1		1929-30
Ftorek, Robbie	Los Angeles	132	65	56	11	2		
	New Jersey	156	88	49	19	2		
	Boston	155	76	65	14	2		
	Total	443	229	170	44	6		1987-03
Gadsby, Bill	Detroit	78	35	31	12	2		1968-70
Gainey, Bob	Minnesota	244	95	119	30	3		
	Dallas	171	70	71	30	3		
	Total	415	165	190	60	6		1990-96
Gardiner, Herb	Chicago	32	5	23	4	1		1929-30
Gardner, Jimmy	Hamilton	30	19	10	1	1		1924-25
Garvin, Ted	Detroit	11	2	8	1	1		1973-74
Geoffrion, Bernie	NY Rangers	43	22	18	3	1		
	Atlanta	208	77	92	39	3		
	Montreal	30	15	9	6	1		
	Total	281	114	119	48	5		1968-80
Gerard, Eddie	Ottawa	22	9	13	0	1		
	Mtl. Maroons	294	129	122	43	7	1	
	NY Americans	92	34	40	18	2		
	St. Louis	13	2	11	0	1		
	Total	421	174	186	61	11	1	1917-35
Gilbert, Greg	Calgary	121	42	62	17	3		2000-03
Gill, David	Ottawa	132	64	41	27	3	1	1926-29
Glover, Fred	Oakland	152	51	76	25	2		
	California	204	45	131	28	4		
	Los Angeles	68	18	42	8	1		
	Total	424	114	249	61	7		1968-74
Goodfellow, Ebbie	Chicago	140	30	91	19	2		1950-52
Gordon, Jackie	Minnesota	289	116	123	50	5		1970-75
Goring, Butch	Boston	93	42	38	13	2		
	NY Islanders	147	41	92	14	2		
	Total	240	83	130	27	4		1985-01
Gorman, Tommy	NY Americans	80	31	33	16	2		
	Chicago	73	28	28	17	2	1	
	Mtl. Maroons	174	74	71	29	4	1	
	Total	327	133	132	62	8	2	1925-38

Coach	Team	Games Coached	Wins	Losses	Ties	Years	Cup Wins	Career
Gottselig, Johnny	Chicago	187	62	105	20	4		1944-48
Goyette, Phil	NY Islanders	48	6	38	4	1		1972-73
Graham, Dirk	Chicago	59	16	35	8	1		1998-99
Granato, Tony	Colorado	51	32	15	4	1		2002-03
Green, Gary	Washington	157	50	78	29	3		1979-82
Green, Pete	Ottawa	150	94	52	4	6	3	1919-25
Green, Shorty	NY Americans	44	11	27	6	1		1927-28
Green, Ted	Edmonton	188	65	102	21	3		1991-94
Guidolin, Aldo	Colorado	59	12	39	8	1		1978-79
Guidolin, Bep	Boston	104	72	23	9	2		
	Kansas City	125	26	84	15	2		
	Total	229	98	107	24	4		1972-76
Harkness, Ned	Detroit	38	12	22	4	1		1970-71
Harris, Ted	Minnesota	179	48	104	27	3		1975-78
Hart, Cecil	Montreal	394	196	125	73	9	2	1926-39
Hartley, Bob	Colorado	359	193	118	48	5	1	
	Atlanta	39	19	15	5	1		
	Total	398	212	133	53	5	1	1998-03
Hartsburg, Craig	Chicago	246	104	102	40	3		
	Anaheim	197	80	88	29	3		
	Total	443	184	190	69	6		1995-01
Harvey, Doug	NY Rangers	70	26	32	12	1		1961-62
Hay, Don	Phoenix	82	38	37	7	1		
	Calgary	68	23	32	13	1		
	Total	150	61	69	20	2		1996-01
Heffernan, Frank	Toronto	12	5	7	0	1		1919-20
Henning, Lorne	Minnesota	158	68	72	18	2		
	NY Islanders	65	19	39	7	2		
	Total	223	87	111	25	4		1985-01
Hitchcock, Ken	Dallas	503	277	166	60	7	1	
	Philadelphia	82	45	24	13	1		
	Total	585	322	190	73	8	1	1995-03
Hlinka, Ivan	Pittsburgh	86	42	35	9	2		2000-02
Holmgren, Paul	Philadelphia	264	107	126	31	4		
	Hartford	161	54	93	14	4		
	Total	425	161	219	45	8		1988-96
Howell, Harry	Minnesota	11	3	6	2	1		1978-79
Imlach, Punch	Toronto	770	370	275	125	12	4	
	Buffalo	119	32	62	25	2		
	Total	889	402	337	150	14	4	1958-80
Ingarfield, Earl	NY Islanders	30	6	22	2	1		1972-73
Inglis, Bill	Buffalo	56	28	18	10	1		1978-79
Irvin, Dick	Chicago	126	45	62	19	3		
	Toronto	427	216	152	59	9	1	
	Montreal	896	431	313	152	15	3	
	Total	1449	692	527	230	27	4	1928-56
Ivan, Tommy	Detroit	470	262	118	90	7	3	
	Chicago	103	26	56	21	2		
	Total	573	288	174	111	9	3	1947-58
Iverson, Emil	Chicago	21	8	7	6	1		1932-33
Johnson, Bob	Calgary	400	193	155	52	5		
	Pittsburgh	80	41	33	6	1	1	
	Total	480	234	188	58	6	1	1982-91
Johnson, Tom	Boston	208	142	43	23	3	1	1970-73
Johnston, Eddie	Chicago	80	34	27	19	1		
	Pittsburgh	516	232	224	60	7		
	Total	596	266	251	79	8		1979-97
Johnston, Marshall	California	69	13	45	11	2		
	Colorado	56	15	32	9	1		
	Total	125	28	77	20	3		1973-82
Julien, Claude	Montreal	36	12	21	3	1		2002-03
Kasper, Steve	Boston	164	66	78	20	2		1995-97
Keats, Duke	Detroit	11	2	7	2	1		1926-27
Keenan, Mike	Philadelphia	320	190	102	28	4		
	Chicago	320	153	126	41	4		
	NY Rangers	84	52	24	8	1	1	
	St. Louis	163	75	66	22	3		
	Vancouver	108	36	54	18	2		
	Boston	74	33	34	7	1		
	Florida	138	40	77	21	2		
	Total	1207	579	483	145	17	1	1984-03
Kehoe, Rick	Pittsburgh	160	55	91	14	2		2001-03
Kelly, Pat	Colorado	101	22	54	25	2		1977-79
Kelly, Red	Los Angeles	150	55	75	20	2		
	Pittsburgh	274	90	132	52	4		
	Toronto	318	133	123	62	4		
	Total	742	278	330	134	10		1967-77
King, Dave	Calgary	216	109	76	31	3		
	Columbus	204	64	119	21	3		
	Total	420	173	195	52	6		1992-03
Kingston, George	San Jose	164	28	129	7	2		1991-93
Kish, Larry	Hartford	49	12	32	5	1		1982-83
Kromm, Bobby	Detroit	231	79	111	41	3		1977-80
Kurtenbach, Orland	Vancouver	125	36	62	27	2		1976-78
LaForge, Bill	Vancouver	20	4	14	2	1		1984-85
Lalonde, Newsy	Montreal	207	96	97	14	8		
	NY Americans	44	17	25	2	1		
	Ottawa	88	31	45	12	2		
	Total	339	144	167	28	11		1917-35
Lapointe, Ron	Quebec	89	33	50	6	2		1987-89
Laviolette, Peter	NY Islanders	164	77	68	19	2		2001-03
Laycoe, Hal	Los Angeles	24	5	18	1	1		
	Vancouver	156	44	96	16	2		
	Total	180	49	114	17	3		1969-72
Lehman, Hugh	Chicago	21	3	17	1	1		1927-28
Lemaire, Jacques	Montreal	97	48	37	12	2		
	New Jersey	378	199	122	57	5	1	
	Minnesota	246	93	118	35	3		
	Total	721	340	277	104	10	1	1983-03
Lepine, Pit	Montreal	48	10	33	5	1		1939-40
LeSueur, Percy	Hamilton	10	3	7	0	1		1923-24
Lewis, Dave*	Detroit	87	52	25	10	2		1998-03

*Shared a record of 4-1-0 with co-coach Barry Smith in 1998-99

Coach	Team	Games Coached	Wins	Losses	Ties	Years	Cup Wins	Career
Ley, Rick	Hartford	160	69	71	20	2		
	Vancouver	124	47	50	27	2		
	Total	284	116	121	47	4		1989-96
Lindsay, Ted	Detroit	29	5	21	3	2		1979-81
Long, Barry	Winnipeg	205	87	93	25	3		1983-86
Loughlin, Clem	Chicago	144	61	63	20	3		1934-37
Lowe, Ron	Edmonton	341	139	162	40	5		
	NY Rangers	164	69	86	9	2		
	Total	505	208	248	49	7		1994-02
Lowe, Kevin	Edmonton	82	32	34	16	1		1999-00
Ludzik, Steve	Tampa Bay	121	31	76	14	2		1999-01
MacDonald, Parker	Minnesota	61	20	30	11	1		
	Los Angeles	42	13	24	5	1		
	Total	103	33	54	16	2		1973-82
MacLean, Doug	Florida	187	83	71	33	3		
	Columbus	42	15	23	4	1		
	Total	229	98	94	37	4		1995-03
MacMillan, Bill	Colorado	80	22	45	13	1		
	New Jersey	100	19	67	14	2		
	Total	180	41	112	27	3		1980-84
MacNeil, Al	Montreal	55	31	15	9	1	1	
	Atlanta	80	35	32	13	1		
	Calgary	171	72	66	33	3		
	Total	306	138	113	55	5		1970-03
MacTavish, Craig	Edmonton	246	113	98	35	3		2000-03
Magnuson, Keith	Chicago	132	49	57	26	2		1980-82
Mahoney, Bill	Minnesota	93	42	39	12	2		1983-85
Maloney, Dan	Toronto	160	45	100	15	2		
	Winnipeg	212	91	93	28	3		
	Total	372	136	193	43	5		1984-89
Maloney, Phil	Vancouver	232	95	105	32	4		1973-77
Mantha, Sylvio	Montreal	48	11	26	11	1		1935-36
Marshall, Bert	Colorado	24	3	17	4	1		1981-82
Martin, Jacques	St. Louis	160	66	71	23	2		
	Ottawa	610	298	226	86	8		
	Total	770	364	297	109	10		1986-03
Matheson, Godfrey	Chicago	2	0	2	0	1		1932-33
Maurice, Paul	Hartford	152	61	72	19	2		
	Carolina	492	199	221	72	6		
	Total	644	260	293	91	8		1995-03
Maxner, Wayne	Detroit	129	34	68	27	2		1980-82
McCammon, Bob	Philadelphia	218	119	68	31	4		
	Vancouver	294	102	156	36	4		
	Total	512	221	224	67	8		1978-91
McCreary, Bill	St. Louis	24	6	14	4	1		
	Vancouver	41	9	25	7	1		
	California	32	8	20	4	1		
	Total	97	23	59	15	3		1971-75
McGuire, Pierre	Hartford	67	23	37	7	1		1993-94
McLellan, John	Toronto	310	126	139	45	4		1969-73
McVie, Tom	Washington	204	49	122	33	3		
	Winnipeg	105	20	67	18	2		
	New Jersey	153	57	74	22	3		
	Total	462	126	263	73	8		1975-92
Meeker, Howie	Toronto	70	21	34	15	1		1956-57
Melrose, Barry	Los Angeles	209	79	101	29	3		1992-95
Milbury, Mike	Boston	160	90	49	21	2		
	NY Islanders	191	56	111	24	4		
	Total	351	146	160	45	6		1989-99
Molleken, Lorne	Chicago	47	18	21	8	2		1998-00
Muckler, John	Minnesota	35	6	23	6	1		
	Edmonton	160	75	65	20	2	1	
	Buffalo	268	125	109	34	4		
	NY Rangers	185	70	91	24	3		
	Total	648	276	288	84	10	1	1968-00
Muldoon, Pete	Chicago	44	19	22	3	1		1926-27
Munro, Dunc	Mtl. Maroons	76	37	29	10	2		1929-31
Murdoch, Bob	Chicago	80	30	41	9	1		
	Winnipeg	160	63	75	22	2		
	Total	240	93	116	31	3		1987-91
Murphy, Mike	Los Angeles	65	20	37	8	2		
	Toronto	164	60	87	17	2		
	Total	229	80	124	25	4		1986-98
Murray, Andy	Los Angeles	328	150	136	42	4		1999-03
Murray, Bryan	Washington	672	343	246	83	9		
	Detroit	244	124	91	29	3		
	Florida	59	17	31	11	1		
	Anaheim	82	29	45	8	1		
	Total	1057	513	413	131	14		1981-02
Murray, Terry	Washington	325	163	134	28	5		
	Philadelphia	212	118	64	30	3		
	Florida	200	79	90	31	3		
	Total	737	360	288	89	11		1989-01
Nanne, Lou	Minnesota	29	7	18	4	1		1977-78
Neale, Harry	Vancouver	407	142	189	76	6		
	Detroit	35	8	23	4	1		
	Total	442	150	212	80	7		1978-86
Neilson, Roger	Toronto	160	75	62	23	2		
	Buffalo	80	39	20	21	1		
	Vancouver	133	51	61	21	3		
	Los Angeles	28	8	17	3	1		
	NY Rangers	280	141	104	35	4		
	Florida	132	53	56	23	2		
	Philadelphia	185	92	60	33	3		
	Ottawa	2	1	1	0	1		
	Total	1000	460	381	159	17		1977-02

Coach	Team	Games Coached	Wins	Losses	Ties	Years	Cup Wins	Career
Nolan, Ted	Buffalo	164	73	72	19	2		1995-97
Nykoluk, Mike	Toronto	280	89	144	47	4		1980-84
O'Connell, Mike	Boston	9	3	3	3	1		2002-03
O'Donoghue, George	Toronto	29	15	13	1	2	1	1921-23
O'Reilly, Terry	Boston	227	115	86	26	3		1986-89
Oliver, Murray	Minnesota	41	21	12	8	2		1981-83
Olmstead, Bert	Oakland	64	11	37	16	1		1967-68
Paddock, John	Winnipeg	281	106	138	37	4		1991-95
Page, Pierre	Minnesota	160	63	77	20	2		
	Quebec	230	98	103	29	3		
	Calgary	164	66	78	20	2		
	Anaheim	82	26	43	13	1		
	Total	636	253	301	82	8		1988-98
Park, Brad	Detroit	45	9	34	2	1		1985-86
Paterson, Rick	Tampa Bay	8	0	8	0	1		1997-98
Patrick, Craig	NY Rangers	95	37	45	13	2		
	Pittsburgh	74	29	36	9	2		
	Total	169	66	81	22	4		1980-97
Patrick, Frank	Boston	96	48	36	12	2		1934-36
Patrick, Lester	NY Rangers	604	281	216	107	13	2	1926-39
Patrick, Lynn	NY Rangers	107	40	51	16	2		
	Boston	310	117	130	63	5		
	St. Louis	26	8	15	3	3		
	Total	443	165	196	82	10		1948-76
Patrick, Muzz	NY Rangers	136	43	66	27	4		1953-63
Perron, Jean	Montreal	240	126	84	30	3	1	
	Quebec	47	16	26	5	1		
	Total	287	142	110	35	4	1	1985-89
Perry, Don	Los Angeles	168	52	85	31	3		1981-84
Pike, Alf	NY Rangers	123	36	66	21	2		1959-61
Pilous, Rudy	Chicago	387	162	151	74	6	1	1957-63
Plager, Barclay	St. Louis	178	49	96	33	4		1977-83
Plager, Bob	St. Louis	11	4	6	1	1		1992-93
Pleau, Larry	Hartford	224	81	117	26	5		1980-89
Polano, Nick	Detroit	240	79	127	34	3		1982-85
Popein, Larry	NY Rangers	41	18	14	9	1		1973-74
Powers, Eddie	Toronto	66	31	32	3	2		1924-26
Primeau, Joe	Toronto	210	97	71	42	3	1	1950-53
Pronovost, Marcel	Buffalo	104	52	29	23	2		1977-79
Pulford, Bob	Los Angeles	396	178	150	68	5		
	Chicago	433	185	180	68	7		
	Total	829	363	330	136	12		1972-00
Quenneville, Joel	St. Louis	532	278	184	70	7		1996-03
Querrie, Charles	Toronto	72	29	38	5	3		1922-27
Quinn, Mike	Quebec	24	4	20	0	1		1919-20
Quinn, Pat	Philadelphia	262	141	73	48	4		
	Los Angeles	202	75	101	26	3		
	Vancouver	280	141	111	28	5		
	Toronto	410	214	154	42	5		
	Total	1154	571	439	144	16		1978-03
Raeder, Cap	San Jose	1	1	0	0	1		2002-03
Ramsay, Craig	Buffalo	21	4	15	2	1		
	Philadelphia	28	12	12	4	1		
	Total	49	16	27	6	2		1986-01
Randall, Ken	Hamilton	14	6	8	0	1		1923-24
Reay, Billy	Toronto	90	26	50	14	2		
	Chicago	1012	516	335	161	14		
	Total	1102	542	385	175	16		1957-77
Regan, Larry	Los Angeles	88	27	47	14	2		1970-72
Renney, Tom	Vancouver	101	39	53	9	2		1996-98
Risebrough, Doug	Calgary	144	71	56	17	2		1990-92
Roberts, Jim	Buffalo	45	21	16	8	1		
	Hartford	80	26	41	13	1		
	St. Louis	9	3	3	3	1		
	Total	134	50	60	24	3		1981-97
Robinson, Larry	Los Angeles	328	122	161	45	4		
	New Jersey	141	73	49	19	3	1	
	Total	469	195	210	64	7	1	1995-02
Rodden, Mike	Toronto	2	0	2	0	1		1926-27
Romeril, Alex	Toronto	13	7	5	1	1		1926-27
Ross, Art	Mtl. Wanderers	6	1	5	0	1		
	Hamilton	24	6	18	0	1		
	Boston	728	361	277	90	16	1	
	Total	758	368	300	90	18	1	1917-45
Ruel, Claude	Montreal	305	172	82	51	5	2	1968-81
Ruff, Lindy	Buffalo	492	216	205	71	6		1997-03
Sather, Glen	Edmonton	842	464	268	110	11	4	
	NY Rangers	28	11	13	4	1		
	Total	870	475	281	114	12	4	1979-03
Sator, Ted	NY Rangers	99	41	48	10	2		
	Buffalo	207	96	89	22	3		
	Total	306	137	137	32	5		1985-89
Savard, Andre	Quebec	24	10	13	1	1		1987-88
Schinkel, Ken	Pittsburgh	203	83	92	28	4		1972-77
Schmidt, Milt	Boston	726	245	360	121	11		
	Washington	44	5	34	5	2		
	Total	770	250	394	126	13		1954-76
Schoenfeld, Jim	Buffalo	43	19	19	5	1		
	New Jersey	124	50	59	15	3		
	Washington	249	113	102	34	4		
	Phoenix	164	74	66	24	2		
	Total	580	256	248	78	10		1985-99
Shaughnessy, Tom	Chicago	21	10	8	3	1		1929-30
Shero, Fred	Philadelphia	554	308	151	95	7	2	
	NY Rangers	180	82	74	24	3		
	Total	734	390	225	119	10	2	1971-81
Simpson, Joe	NY Americans	144	42	72	30	3		1932-35
Simpson, Terry	NY Islanders	187	81	82	24	3		
	Philadelphia	84	35	39	10	1		
	Winnipeg	97	43	47	7	2		
	Total	368	159	168	41	6		1986-96
Sims, Al	San Jose	82	27	47	8	1		1996-97
Sinden, Harry	Boston	327	153	116	58	6	1	1966-85
Skinner, Jimmy	Detroit	247	123	78	46	4	1	1954-58
Smeaton, Cooper	Philadelphia	44	4	36	4	1		1930-31
Smith, Alf	Ottawa	18	12	6	0	1		1918-19
Smith, Barry*	Detroit	5	4	1	0	1		1998-99
*Results shared with co-coach Dave Lewis								
Smith, Floyd	Buffalo	241	143	62	36	4		
	Toronto	68	30	33	5	1		
	Total	309	173	95	41	5		1971-80
Smith, Mike	Winnipeg	23	2	17	4	1		1980-81
Smith, Ron	NY Rangers	44	15	22	7	1		1992-93
Smythe, Conn	Toronto	134	57	57	20	4		1927-31
Sonmor, Glen	Minnesota	417	174	161	82	7		1978-87
Sproule, Harvey	Toronto	12	7	5	0	1		1919-20
Stanley, Barney	Chicago	23	4	17	2	1		1927-31
Stasiuk, Vic	Philadelphia	154	45	68	41	2		
	California	75	21	38	16	1		
	Vancouver	78	22	47	9	1		
	Total	307	88	153	66	4		1969-73
Stewart, Bill	Chicago	69	22	35	12	2	1	1937-39
Stewart, Bill	NY Islanders	37	11	19	7	1		1998-99
Stewart, Ron	NY Rangers	39	15	20	4	1		
	Los Angeles	80	31	34	15	1		
	Total	119	46	54	19	2		1975-78
Suhonen, Alpo	Chicago	82	29	45	8	1		2000-01
Sullivan, Red	NY Rangers	196	58	103	35	4		
	Pittsburgh	150	47	79	24	2		
	Washington	18	2	16	0	1		
	Total	364	107	198	59	7		1962-75
Sutherland, Bill	Winnipeg	32	7	22	3	2		1979-81
Sutter, Brian	St. Louis	320	153	124	43	4		
	Boston	216	120	73	23	3		
	Calgary	246	87	122	37	3		
	Chicago	164	71	67	26	2		
	Total	946	431	386	129	12		1988-03
Sutter, Darryl	Chicago	216	110	80	26	3		
	San Jose	434	192	182	60	6		
	Calgary	46	19	19	8	1		
	Total	696	321	281	94	9		1992-03
Sutter, Duane	Florida	72	22	42	8	2		2000-02
Talbot, Jean-Guy	St. Louis	120	52	53	15	2		
	NY Rangers	80	30	37	13	1		
	Total	200	82	90	28	3		1972-78
Tessier, Orval	Chicago	213	99	93	21	3		1982-85
Therrien, Michel	Montreal	190	77	90	23	3		2000-03
Thompson, Paul	Chicago	272	104	127	41	7		1938-45
Thompson, Percy	Hamilton	48	13	35	0	2		1920-22
Tippett, Dave	Dallas	82	46	21	15	1		2002-03
Tobin, Bill	Chicago	71	29	29	13	2		1929-32
Tortorella, John	NY Rangers	4	0	3	1	1		
	Tampa Bay	207	75	104	28	3		
	Total	211	75	107	29	4		1999-03
Tremblay, Mario	Montreal	159	71	63	25	2		1995-97
Trottier, Bryan	NY Rangers	54	21	27	6	1		2002-03
Trotz, Barry	Nashville	410	145	216	49	5		1998-03
Ubriaco, Gene	Pittsburgh	106	50	47	9	2		1988-90
Vachon, Rogie	Los Angeles	10	4	3	3	3		1983-95
Vigneault, Alain	Montreal	266	109	122	35	4		1997-01
Waddell, Don	Atlanta	10	4	5	1	1		2002-03
Watson, Bryan	Edmonton	18	4	9	5	1		1980-81
Watson, Phil	NY Rangers	295	119	124	52	5		
	Boston	84	16	55	13	2		
	Total	379	135	179	65	7		1955-63
Watt, Tom	Winnipeg	181	72	85	24	3		
	Vancouver	160	52	87	21	2		
	Toronto	149	52	80	17	2		
	Total	490	176	252	62	7		1981-92
Webster, Tom	NY Rangers	18	5	9	4	1		
	Los Angeles	240	115	94	31	3		
	Total	258	120	103	35	4		1986-92
Weiland, Cooney	Boston	96	58	20	18	2	1	1939-41
White, Bill	Chicago	46	16	24	6	1		1976-77
Wiley, Jim	San Jose	57	17	37	3	1		1995-96
Wilson, Johnny	Los Angeles	52	9	34	9	1		
	Detroit	145	67	56	22	2		
	Colorado	80	20	46	14	1		
	Pittsburgh	240	91	105	44	3		
	Total	517	187	241	89	7		1969-80
Wilson, Larry	Detroit	36	3	29	4	1		1976-77
Wilson, Rick	Dallas	32	13	12	7	1		2001-02
Wilson, Ron	Anaheim	296	120	145	31	4		
	Washington	410	192	167	51	6		
	San Jose	57	19	31	7	1		
	Total	763	331	343	89	10		1993-03
Young, Garry	California	12	2	7	3	1		
	St. Louis	98	41	41	16	2		
	Total	110	43	48	19	3		1972-76

Year-by-Year Individual Regular-Season Leaders

Season	Goals	G	Assists	A	Points	Pts.	Penalty Minutes	PIM
1917-18	Joe Malone	44	Cy Denneny Reg Noble Harry Cameron	10 10 10	Joe Malone	48	Joe Hall	100
1918-19	Newsy Lalonde	22	Newsy Lalonde Eddie Gerard	10 10	Newsy Lalonde	32	Joe Hall	135
1919-20	Joe Malone	39	Frank Nighbor	15	Joe Malone	49	Cully Wilson	86
1920-21	Babe Dye	35	Jack Darragh	15	Newsy Lalonde	43	Bert Corbeau	86
1921-22	Punch Broadbent	32	Harry Cameron	17	Punch Broadbent	46	Sprague Cleghorn	63
1922-23	Babe Dye	26	Edmond Bouchard	12	Babe Dye	37	Georges Boucher	58
1923-24	Cy Denneny	22	Georges Boucher	10	Cy Denneny	24	Bert Corbeau	55
1924-25	Babe Dye	38	Cy Denneny Red Green	15 15	Babe Dye	46	Georges Boucher	95
1925-26	Nels Stewart	34	Frank Nighbor	13	Nels Stewart	42	Bert Corbeau	121
1926-27	Bill Cook	33	Dick Irvin	18	Bill Cook	37	Nels Stewart	133
1927-28	Howie Morenz	33	Howie Morenz	18	Howie Morenz	51	Eddie Shore	165
1928-29	Ace Bailey	22	Frank Boucher	16	Ace Bailey	32	Red Dutton	139
1929-30	Cooney Weiland	43	Frank Boucher	36	Cooney Weiland	73	Joe Lamb	119
1930-31	Charlie Conacher	31	Joe Primeau	32	Howie Morenz	51	Harvey Rockburn	118
1931-32	Charlie Conacher Bill Cook	34 34	Joe Primeau	37	Busher Jackson	53	Red Dutton	107
1932-33	Bill Cook	28	Frank Boucher	28	Bill Cook	50	Red Horner	144
1933-34	Charlie Conacher	32	Joe Primeau	32	Charlie Conacher	52	Red Horner	126 *
1934-35	Charlie Conacher	36	Art Chapman	34	Charlie Conacher	57	Red Horner	125
1935-36	Charlie Conacher Bill Thoms	23 23	Art Chapman	28	Sweeney Schriner	45	Red Horner	167
1936-37	Larry Aurie Nels Stewart	23 23	Syl Apps	29	Sweeney Schriner	46	Red Horner	124
1937-38	Gordie Drillon	26	Syl Apps	29	Gordie Drillon	52	Red Horner	82 *
1938-39	Roy Conacher	26	Bill Cowley	34	Toe Blake	47	Red Horner	85
1939-40	Bryan Hextall	24	Milt Schmidt	30	Milt Schmidt	52	Red Horner	87
1940-41	Bryan Hextall	26	Bill Cowley	45	Bill Cowley	62	Jimmy Orlando	99
1941-42	Lynn Patrick	32	Phil Watson	37	Bryan Hextall	56	Pat Egan	124
1942-43	Doug Bentley	33	Bill Cowley	45	Doug Bentley	73	Jimmy Orlando	89 *
1943-44	Doug Bentley	38	Clint Smith	49	Herb Cain	82	Mike McMahon	98
1944-45	Maurice Richard	50	Elmer Lach	54	Elmer Lach	80	Pat Egan	86
1945-46	Gaye Stewart	37	Elmer Lach	34	Max Bentley	61	Jack Stewart	73
1946-47	Maurice Richard	45	Billy Taylor	46	Max Bentley	72	Gus Mortson	133
1947-48	Ted Lindsay	33	Doug Bentley	37	Elmer Lach	61	Bill Barilko	147
1948-49	Sid Abel	28	Doug Bentley	43	Roy Conacher	68	Bill Ezinicki	145
1949-50	Maurice Richard	43	Ted Lindsay	55	Ted Lindsay	78	Bill Ezinicki	144
1950-51	Gordie Howe	43	Gordie Howe Ted Kennedy	43 43	Gordie Howe	86	Gus Mortson	142
1951-52	Gordie Howe	47	Elmer Lach	50	Gordie Howe	86	Gus Kyle	127
1952-53	Gordie Howe	49	Gordie Howe	46	Gordie Howe	95	Maurice Richard	112
1953-54	Maurice Richard	37	Gordie Howe	48	Gordie Howe	81	Gus Mortson	132
1954-55	Maurice Richard Bernie Geoffrion	38 38	Bert Olmstead	48	Bernie Geoffrion	75	Fern Flaman	150
1955-56	Jean Beliveau	47	Bert Olmstead	56	Jean Beliveau	88	Lou Fontinato	202
1956-57	Gordie Howe	44	Ted Lindsay	55	Gordie Howe	89	Gus Mortson	147
1957-58	Dickie Moore	36	Henri Richard	52	Dickie Moore	84	Lou Fontinato	152
1958-59	Jean Beliveau	45	Dickie Moore	55	Dickie Moore	96	Ted Lindsay	184
1959-60	Bobby Hull Bronco Horvath	39 39	Don McKenney	49	Bobby Hull	81	Carl Brewer	150
1960-61	Bernie Geoffrion	50	Jean Beliveau	58	Bernie Geoffrion	95	Pierre Pilote	165
1961-62	Bobby Hull	50	Andy Bathgate	56	Bobby Hull Andy Bathgate	84 84	Lou Fontinato	167
1962-63	Gordie Howe	38	Henri Richard	50	Gordie Howe	86	Howie Young	273
1963-64	Bobby Hull	43	Andy Bathgate	58	Stan Mikita	89	Vic Hadfield	151
1964-65	Norm Ullman	42	Stan Mikita	59	Stan Mikita	87	Carl Brewer	177
1965-66	Bobby Hull	54	Stan Mikita Bobby Rousseau Jean Beliveau	48 48 48	Bobby Hull	97	Reggie Fleming	166
1966-67	Bobby Hull	52	Stan Mikita	62	Stan Mikita	97	John Ferguson	177
1967-68	Bobby Hull	44	Phil Esposito	49	Stan Mikita	87	Barclay Plager	153
1968-69	Bobby Hull	58	Phil Esposito	77	Phil Esposito	126	Forbes Kennedy	219
1969-70	Phil Esposito	43	Bobby Orr	87	Bobby Orr	120	Keith Magnuson	213
1970-71	Phil Esposito	76	Bobby Orr	102	Phil Esposito	152	Keith Magnuson	291
1971-72	Phil Esposito	66	Bobby Orr	80	Phil Esposito	133	Bryan Watson	212
1972-73	Phil Esposito	55	Phil Esposito	75	Phil Esposito	130	Dave Schultz	259
1973-74	Phil Esposito	68	Bobby Orr	90	Phil Esposito	145	Dave Schultz	348
1974-75	Phil Esposito	61	Bobby Orr Bobby Clarke	89 89	Bobby Orr	135	Dave Schultz	472
1975-76	Reggie Leach	61	Bobby Clarke	89	Guy Lafleur	125	Steve Durbano	370
1976-77	Steve Shutt	60	Guy Lafleur	80	Guy Lafleur	136	Tiger Williams	338
1977-78	Guy Lafleur	60	Bryan Trottier	77	Guy Lafleur	132	Dave Schultz	405
1978-79	Mike Bossy	69	Bryan Trottier	87	Bryan Trottier	134	Tiger Williams	298
1979-80	Charlie Simmer Danny Gare Blaine Stoughton	56 56 56	Wayne Gretzky	86	Marcel Dionne Wayne Gretzky	137 137	Jimmy Mann	287
1980-81	Mike Bossy	68	Wayne Gretzky	109	Wayne Gretzky	164	Tiger Williams	343
1981-82	Wayne Gretzky	92	Wayne Gretzky	120	Wayne Gretzky	212	Paul Baxter	409
1982-83	Wayne Gretzky	71	Wayne Gretzky	125	Wayne Gretzky	196	Randy Holt	275
1983-84	Wayne Gretzky	87	Wayne Gretzky	118	Wayne Gretzky	205	Chris Nilan	338
1984-85	Wayne Gretzky	73	Wayne Gretzky	135	Wayne Gretzky	208	Chris Nilan	358
1985-86	Jari Kurri	68	Wayne Gretzky	163	Wayne Gretzky	215	Joe Kocur	377
1986-87	Wayne Gretzky	62	Wayne Gretzky	121	Wayne Gretzky	183	Tim Hunter	361
1987-88	Mario Lemieux	70	Wayne Gretzky	109	Mario Lemieux	168	Bob Probert	398
1988-89	Mario Lemieux	85	Mario Lemieux Wayne Gretzky	114 114	Mario Lemieux	199	Tim Hunter	375
1989-90	Brett Hull	72	Wayne Gretzky	102	Wayne Gretzky	142	Basil McRae	351
1990-91	Brett Hull	86	Wayne Gretzky	122	Wayne Gretzky	163	Rob Ray	350
1991-92	Brett Hull	70	Wayne Gretzky	90	Mario Lemieux	131	Mike Peluso	408
1992-93	Teemu Selanne Alexander Mogilny	76 76	Adam Oates	97	Mario Lemieux	160	Marty McSorley	399
1993-94	Pavel Bure	60	Wayne Gretzky	92	Wayne Gretzky	130	Tie Domi	347
1994-95	Peter Bondra	34	Ron Francis	48	Jaromir Jagr Eric Lindros	70 70	Enrico Ciccone	225
1995-96	Mario Lemieux	69	Mario Lemieux Ron Francis	92 92	Mario Lemieux	161	Matthew Barnaby	335
1996-97	Keith Tkachuk	52	Mario Lemieux Wayne Gretzky	72 72	Mario Lemieux	122	Gino Odjick	371
1997-98	Teemu Selanne Peter Bondra	52 52	Jaromir Jagr Wayne Gretzky	67 67	Jaromir Jagr	102	Donald Brashear	372
1998-99	Teemu Selanne	47	Jaromir Jagr	83	Jaromir Jagr	127	Rob Ray	261
99-2000	Pavel Bure	58	Mark Recchi	63	Jaromir Jagr	96	Denny Lambert	219
2000-01	Pavel Bure	59	Jaromir Jagr Adam Oates	69 69	Jaromir Jagr	121	Matthew Barnaby	265
2001-02	Jarome Iginla	52	Adam Oates	64	Jarome Iginla	96	Peter Worrell	354
2002-03	Milan Hejduk	50	Peter Forsberg	77	Peter Forsberg	106	Jody Shelley	249

* Match Misconduct penalty not included in total penalty minutes.
1946-47 was the first season that a Match penalty was automatically written into the player's total penalty minutes as 20 minutes.
Beginning in 1947-48 all penalties, Match, Game Misconduct, and Misconduct, are written as 10 minutes.

One Season Scoring Records

Goals-Per-Game Leaders, One Season

(Among players with 20 goals or more in one season)

Player	Team	Season	Games	Goals	Average
Joe Malone	Montreal	1917-18	20	44	2.20
Cy Denneny	Ottawa	1917-18	20	36	1.80
Newsy Lalonde	Montreal	1917-18	14	23	1.64
Joe Malone	Quebec	1919-20	24	39	1.63
Newsy Lalonde	Montreal	1919-20	23	37	1.61
Reg Noble	Toronto	1917-18	20	30	1.50
Babe Dye	Ham., Tor.	1920-21	24	35	1.46
Cy Denneny	Ottawa	1920-21	24	34	1.42
Joe Malone	Hamilton	1920-21	20	28	1.40
Newsy Lalonde	Montreal	1920-21	24	33	1.38
Punch Broadbent	Ottawa	1921-22	24	32	1.33
Babe Dye	Toronto	1924-25	29	38	1.31
Babe Dye	Toronto	1921-22	24	31	1.29
Newsy Lalonde	Montreal	1918-19	17	22	1.29
Odie Cleghorn	Montreal	1918-19	17	22	1.29
Cy Denneny	Ottawa	1921-22	22	27	1.23
Aurel Joliat	Montreal	1924-25	25	30	1.20
Wayne Gretzky	Edmonton	1983-84	74	87	1.18
Babe Dye	Toronto	1922-23	22	26	1.18
Wayne Gretzky	Edmonton	1981-82	80	92	1.15
Mario Lemieux	Pittsburgh	1992-93	60	69	1.15
Frank Nighbor	Ottawa	1919-20	23	26	1.13
Mario Lemieux	Pittsburgh	1988-89	76	85	1.12
Brett Hull	St. Louis	1990-91	78	86	1.10
Cam Neely	Boston	1993-94	49	50	1.02
Maurice Richard	Montreal	1944-45	50	50	1.00
Reg Noble	Toronto	1919-20	24	24	1.00
Corb Denneny	Toronto	1919-20	24	24	1.00
Joe Malone	Hamilton	1921-22	24	24	1.00
Billy Boucher	Montreal	1922-23	24	24	1.00
Cy Denneny	Ottawa	1923-24	22	22	1.00
Alexander Mogilny	Buffalo	1992-93	77	76	0.99
Mario Lemieux	Pittsburgh	1995-96	70	69	0.99
Cooney Weiland	Boston	1929-30	44	43	0.98
Phil Esposito	Boston	1970-71	78	76	0.97
Jari Kurri	Edmonton	1984-85	73	71	0.97

Alexander Mogilny had 76 goals in 77 games for the Buffalo Sabres back in 1992-93. Last year, he became the first Toronto player other than Mats Sundin to lead the Leafs in scoring since 1993-94.

Assists-Per-Game Leaders, One Season

(Among players with 35 assists or more in one season)

Player	Team	Season	Games	Assists	Average
Wayne Gretzky	Edmonton	1985-86	80	163	2.04
Wayne Gretzky	Edmonton	1987-88	64	109	1.70
Wayne Gretzky	Edmonton	1984-85	80	135	1.69
Wayne Gretzky	Edmonton	1983-84	74	118	1.59
Wayne Gretzky	Edmonton	1982-83	80	125	1.56
Wayne Gretzky	Los Angeles	1990-91	78	122	1.56
Wayne Gretzky	Edmonton	1986-87	79	121	1.53
Mario Lemieux	Pittsburgh	1992-93	60	91	1.52
Wayne Gretzky	Edmonton	1981-82	80	120	1.50
Mario Lemieux	Pittsburgh	1988-89	76	114	1.50
Adam Oates	St. Louis	1990-91	61	90	1.48
Wayne Gretzky	Los Angeles	1988-89	78	114	1.46
Wayne Gretzky	Los Angeles	1989-90	73	102	1.40
Wayne Gretzky	Edmonton	1980-81	80	109	1.36
Mario Lemieux	Pittsburgh	1991-92	64	87	1.36
Mario Lemieux	Pittsburgh	1989-90	59	78	1.32
Bobby Orr	Boston	1970-71	78	102	1.31
Mario Lemieux	Pittsburgh	1995-96	70	92	1.31
Mario Lemieux	Pittsburgh	1987-88	77	98	1.27
Bobby Orr	Boston	1973-74	74	90	1.22
Wayne Gretzky	Los Angeles	1991-92	74	90	1.22
Ron Francis	Pittsburgh	1995-96	77	92	1.19
Mario Lemieux	Pittsburgh	1985-86	79	93	1.18
Bobby Clarke	Philadelphia	1975-76	76	89	1.17
Peter Stastny	Quebec	1981-82	80	93	1.16
Adam Oates	Boston	1992-93	84	97	1.15
Doug Gilmour	Toronto	1992-93	83	95	1.14
Wayne Gretzky	Los Angeles	1993-94	81	92	1.14
Paul Coffey	Edmonton	1985-86	79	90	1.14
Bobby Orr	Boston	1969-70	76	87	1.14
Bryan Trottier	NY Islanders	1978-79	76	87	1.14
Bobby Orr	Boston	1972-73	63	72	1.14
Bill Cowley	Boston	1943-44	36	41	1.14
Pat LaFontaine	Buffalo	1992-93	84	95	1.13
Steve Yzerman	Detroit	1988-89	80	90	1.13
Paul Coffey	Pittsburgh	1987-88	46	52	1.13
Bobby Orr	Boston	1974-75	80	89	1.11
Bobby Clarke	Philadelphia	1974-75	80	89	1.11

Player	Team	Season	Games	Assists	Average
Paul Coffey	Pittsburgh	1988-89	75	83	1.11
Wayne Gretzky	Los Angeles	1992-93	45	49	1.11
Denis Savard	Chicago	1982-83	78	86	1.10
Denis Savard	Chicago	1981-82	80	87	1.09
Denis Savard	Chicago	1987-88	80	87	1.09
Wayne Gretzky	Edmonton	1979-80	79	86	1.09
Ron Francis	Pittsburgh	1994-95	44	48	1.09
Paul Coffey	Edmonton	1983-84	80	86	1.08
Elmer Lach	Montreal	1944-45	50	54	1.08
Peter Stastny	Quebec	1985-86	76	81	1.07
Jaromir Jagr	Pittsburgh	1995-96	82	87	1.06
Mark Messier	Edmonton	1989-90	79	84	1.06
Peter Forsberg	Colorado	1995-96	82	86	1.05
Paul Coffey	Edmonton	1984-85	80	84	1.05
Marcel Dionne	Los Angeles	1979-80	80	84	1.05
Bobby Orr	Boston	1971-72	76	80	1.05
Mike Bossy	NY Islanders	1981-82	80	83	1.04
Adam Oates	Boston	1993-94	77	80	1.04
Phil Esposito	Boston	1968-69	74	77	1.04
Bryan Trottier	NY Islanders	1983-84	68	71	1.04
Pete Mahovlich	Montreal	1974-75	80	82	1.03
Kent Nilsson	Calgary	1980-81	80	82	1.03
Peter Stastny	Quebec	1982-83	75	77	1.03
Denis Savard	Chicago	1988-89	58	59	1.02
Jaromir Jagr	Pittsburgh	1998-99	81	83	1.02
Doug Gilmour	Toronto	1993-94	83	84	1.01
Bernie Nicholls	Los Angeles	1988-89	79	80	1.01
Guy Lafleur	Montreal	1979-80	74	75	1.01
Guy Lafleur	Montreal	1976-77	80	80	1.00
Marcel Dionne	Los Angeles	1984-85	80	80	1.00
Brian Leetch	NY Rangers	1991-92	80	80	1.00
Bryan Trottier	NY Islanders	1977-78	77	77	1.00
Mike Bossy	NY Islanders	1983-84	67	67	1.00
Jean Ratelle	NY Rangers	1971-72	63	63	1.00
Steve Yzerman	Detroit	1993-94	58	58	1.00
Ron Francis	Hartford	1985-86	53	53	1.00
Guy Chouinard	Calgary	1980-81	52	52	1.00
Elmer Lach	Montreal	1943-44	48	48	1.00

Points-Per-Game Leaders, One Season

(Among players with 50 points or more in one season)

Player	Team	Season	Games	Points	Average
Wayne Gretzky	Edmonton	1983-84	74	205	2.77
Wayne Gretzky	Edmonton	1985-86	80	215	2.69
Mario Lemieux	Pittsburgh	1992-93	60	160	2.67
Wayne Gretzky	Edmonton	1981-82	80	212	2.65
Mario Lemieux	Pittsburgh	1988-89	76	199	2.62
Wayne Gretzky	Edmonton	1984-85	80	208	2.60
Wayne Gretzky	Edmonton	1982-83	80	196	2.45
Wayne Gretzky	Edmonton	1987-88	64	149	2.33
Wayne Gretzky	Edmonton	1986-87	79	183	2.32
Mario Lemieux	Pittsburgh	1995-96	70	161	2.30
Mario Lemieux	Pittsburgh	1987-88	77	168	2.18
Wayne Gretzky	Los Angeles	1988-89	78	168	2.15
Wayne Gretzky	Los Angeles	1990-91	78	163	2.09
Mario Lemieux	Pittsburgh	1989-90	59	123	2.08
Wayne Gretzky	Edmonton	1980-81	80	164	2.05
Mario Lemieux	Pittsburgh	1991-92	64	131	2.05
Bill Cowley	Boston	1943-44	36	71	1.97
Phil Esposito	Boston	1970-71	78	152	1.95
Wayne Gretzky	Los Angeles	1989-90	73	142	1.95
Steve Yzerman	Detroit	1988-89	80	155	1.94
Bernie Nicholls	Los Angeles	1988-89	79	150	1.90
Adam Oates	St. Louis	1990-91	61	115	1.89
Phil Esposito	Boston	1973-74	78	145	1.86
Jari Kurri	Edmonton	1984-85	73	135	1.85
Mike Bossy	NY Islanders	1981-82	80	147	1.84
Jaromir Jagr	Pittsburgh	1995-96	82	149	1.82
Mario Lemieux	Pittsburgh	1985-86	79	141	1.78
Bobby Orr	Boston	1970-71	78	139	1.78
Jari Kurri	Edmonton	1983-84	64	113	1.77
Mario Lemieux	Pittsburgh	2000-01	43	76	1.77
Pat LaFontaine	Buffalo	1992-93	84	148	1.76
Bryan Trottier	NY Islanders	1978-79	76	134	1.76
Mike Bossy	NY Islanders	1983-84	67	118	1.76
Paul Coffey	Edmonton	1985-86	79	138	1.75
Phil Esposito	Boston	1971-72	76	133	1.75
Peter Stastny	Quebec	1981-82	80	139	1.74
Wayne Gretzky	Edmonton	1979-80	79	137	1.73
Jean Ratelle	NY Rangers	1971-72	63	109	1.73
Marcel Dionne	Los Angeles	1979-80	80	137	1.71
Herb Cain	Boston	1943-44	48	82	1.71
Guy Lafleur	Montreal	1976-77	80	136	1.70
Dennis Maruk	Washington	1981-82	80	136	1.70
Phil Esposito	Boston	1968-69	74	126	1.70
Guy Lafleur	Montreal	1974-75	70	119	1.70
Mario Lemieux	Pittsburgh	1986-87	63	107	1.70
Adam Oates	Boston	1992-93	84	142	1.69
Bobby Orr	Boston	1974-75	80	135	1.69
Marcel Dionne	Los Angeles	1980-81	80	135	1.69
Guy Lafleur	Montreal	1977-78	78	132	1.69
Guy Lafleur	Montreal	1979-80	74	125	1.69
Rob Brown	Pittsburgh	1988-89	68	115	1.69
Jari Kurri	Edmonton	1985-86	78	131	1.68
Brett Hull	St. Louis	1990-91	78	131	1.68
Phil Esposito	Boston	1972-73	78	130	1.67
Cooney Weiland	Boston	1929-30	44	73	1.66
Alexander Mogilny	Buffalo	1992-93	77	127	1.65
Peter Stastny	Quebec	1982-83	75	124	1.65
Bobby Orr	Boston	1973-74	74	122	1.65
Kent Nilsson	Calgary	1980-81	80	131	1.64
Denis Savard	Chicago	1987-88	80	131	1.64
Wayne Gretzky	Los Angeles	1991-92	74	121	1.64
Steve Yzerman	Detroit	1992-93	84	137	1.63
Marcel Dionne	Los Angeles	1978-79	80	130	1.63
Dale Hawerchuk	Winnipeg	1984-85	80	130	1.63
Mark Messier	Edmonton	1989-90	79	129	1.63
Bryan Trottier	NY Islanders	1983-84	68	111	1.63
Pat LaFontaine	Buffalo	1991-92	57	93	1.63
Charlie Simmer	Los Angeles	1980-81	65	105	1.62
Guy Lafleur	Montreal	1978-79	80	129	1.61
Bryan Trottier	NY Islanders	1981-82	80	129	1.61
Phil Esposito	Boston	1974-75	79	127	1.61
Steve Yzerman	Detroit	1989-90	79	127	1.61
Peter Stastny	Quebec	1985-86	76	122	1.61
Mario Lemieux	Pittsburgh	1996-97	76	122	1.61
Michel Goulet	Quebec	1983-84	75	121	1.61
Wayne Gretzky	Los Angeles	1993-94	81	130	1.60
Bryan Trottier	NY Islanders	1977-78	77	123	1.60
Bobby Orr	Boston	1972-73	63	101	1.60
Guy Chouinard	Calgary	1980-81	52	83	1.60
Elmer Lach	Montreal	1944-45	50	80	1.60
Pierre Turgeon	NY Islanders	1992-93	83	132	1.59
Steve Yzerman	Detroit	1987-88	64	102	1.59
Mike Bossy	NY Islanders	1978-79	80	126	1.58
Paul Coffey	Edmonton	1983-84	80	126	1.58
Marcel Dionne	Los Angeles	1984-85	80	126	1.58
Bobby Orr	Boston	1969-70	76	120	1.58
Eric Lindros	Philadelphia	1995-96	73	115	1.58
Charlie Simmer	Los Angeles	1979-80	64	101	1.58
Teemu Selanne	Winnipeg	1992-93	84	132	1.57
Jaromir Jagr	Pittsburgh	1998-99	81	127	1.57
Bobby Clarke	Philadelphia	1975-76	76	119	1.57
Guy Lafleur	Montreal	1975-76	80	125	1.56
Dave Taylor	Los Angeles	1980-81	72	112	1.56
Denis Savard	Chicago	1982-83	78	121	1.55
Ron Francis	Pittsburgh	1995-96	77	119	1.55
Mike Bossy	NY Islanders	1985-86	80	123	1.54
Kevin Stevens	Pittsburgh	1991-92	80	123	1.54
Bobby Orr	Boston	1971-72	76	117	1.54
Mike Bossy	NY Islanders	1984-85	76	117	1.54
Kevin Stevens	Pittsburgh	1992-93	72	111	1.54
Doug Bentley	Chicago	1943-44	50	77	1.54
Doug Gilmour	Toronto	1992-93	83	127	1.53
Marcel Dionne	Los Angeles	1976-77	80	122	1.53
Jaromir Jagr	Pittsburgh	99-2000	63	96	1.52
Eric Lindros	Philadelphia	1996-97	52	79	1.52
Eric Lindros	Philadelphia	1994-95	46	70	1.52
Marcel Dionne	Detroit	1974-75	80	121	1.51
Mike Bossy	NY Islanders	1980-81	79	119	1.51
Paul Coffey	Edmonton	1984-85	80	121	1.51
Dale Hawerchuk	Winnipeg	1987-88	80	121	1.51
Paul Coffey	Pittsburgh	1988-89	75	113	1.51
Jaromir Jagr	Pittsburgh	1996-97	63	95	1.51
Cam Neely	Boston	1993-94	49	74	1.51

The only defenseman to win the Art Ross Trophy (he did it twice), Bobby Orr is one of only two defensemen to average more than one-and-a-half points per game in a season. Orr did it six times. Paul Coffey did it four times.

The rules for what constitutes a rookie changed after Soviet veteran Sergei Makarov (left) posted 86 points in 1989-90. Ron Francis (right) came right out of junior hockey as an 18-year-old early in the 1981-82 season and had 68 points.

Rookie Scoring Records

All-Time Top 50 Goal-Scoring Rookies

	Rookie	Team	Position	Season	GP	G	A	PTS
1.	* Teemu Selanne	Winnipeg	Right wing	1992-93	84	**76**	56	132
2.	* Mike Bossy	NY Islanders	Right wing	1977-78	73	**53**	38	91
3.	* Joe Nieuwendyk	Calgary	Center	1987-88	75	**51**	41	92
4.	* Dale Hawerchuk	Winnipeg	Center	1981-82	80	**45**	58	103
	* Luc Robitaille	Los Angeles	Left wing	1986-87	79	**45**	39	84
6.	Rick Martin	Buffalo	Left wing	1971-72	73	**44**	30	74
	Barry Pederson	Boston	Center	1981-82	80	**44**	48	92
8.	* Steve Larmer	Chicago	Right wing	1982-83	80	**43**	47	90
	* Mario Lemieux	Pittsburgh	Center	1984-85	73	**43**	57	100
10.	Eric Lindros	Philadelphia	Center	1992-93	61	**41**	34	75
11.	Darryl Sutter	Chicago	Left wing	1980-81	76	**40**	22	62
	Sylvain Turgeon	Hartford	Left wing	1983-84	76	**40**	32	72
	Warren Young	Pittsburgh	Left wing	1984-85	80	**40**	32	72
14.	* Eric Vail	Atlanta	Left wing	1974-75	72	**39**	21	60
	Anton Stastny	Quebec	Left wing	1980-81	80	**39**	46	85
	* Peter Stastny	Quebec	Center	1980-81	77	**39**	70	109
	Steve Yzerman	Detroit	Center	1983-84	80	**39**	48	87
18.	* Gilbert Perreault	Buffalo	Center	1970-71	78	**38**	34	72
	Neal Broten	Minnesota	Center	1981-82	73	**38**	60	98
	Ray Sheppard	Buffalo	Right wing	1987-88	74	**38**	27	65
	Mikael Renberg	Philadelphia	Left wing	1993-94	83	**38**	44	82
22.	Jorgen Pettersson	St. Louis	Left wing	1980-81	62	**37**	36	73
	Jimmy Carson	Los Angeles	Center	1986-87	80	**37**	42	79
24.	Mike Foligno	Detroit	Right wing	1979-80	80	**36**	35	71
	Mike Bullard	Pittsburgh	Center	1981-82	75	**36**	27	63
	Paul MacLean	Winnipeg	Right wing	1981-82	74	**36**	25	61
	Tony Granato	NY Rangers	Right wing	1988-89	78	**36**	27	63
28.	Marian Stastny	Quebec	Center	1981-82	74	**35**	54	89
	Brian Bellows	Minnesota	Right wing	1982-83	78	**35**	30	65
	Tony Amonte	NY Rangers	Right wing	1991-92	79	**35**	34	69
31.	Nels Stewart	Mtl. Maroons	Center	1925-26	36	**34**	8	42
	* Danny Grant	Minnesota	Left wing	1968-69	75	**34**	31	65
	Norm Ferguson	Oakland	Right wing	1968-69	76	**34**	20	54
	Brian Propp	Philadelphia	Left wing	1979-80	80	**34**	41	75
	Wendel Clark	Toronto	Left wing	1985-86	66	**34**	11	45
	* Pavel Bure	Vancouver	Right wing	1991-92	65	**34**	26	60
37.	* Willi Plett	Atlanta	Right wing	1976-77	64	**33**	23	56
	Dale McCourt	Detroit	Center	1977-78	76	**33**	39	72
	Mark Pavelich	NY Rangers	Center	1981-82	79	**33**	43	76
	Ron Flockhart	Philadelphia	Center	1981-82	72	**33**	39	72
	Steve Bozek	Los Angeles	Center	1981-82	71	**33**	23	56
	Jason Arnott	Edmonton	Center	1993-94	78	**33**	35	68
43.	Bill Mosienko	Chicago	Right wing	1943-44	50	**32**	38	70
	Michel Bergeron	Detroit	Right wing	1975-76	72	**32**	27	59
	* Bryan Trottier	NY Islanders	Center	1975-76	80	**32**	63	95
	Don Murdoch	NY Rangers	Right wing	1976-77	59	**32**	24	56
	Jari Kurri	Edmonton	Left wing	1980-81	75	**32**	43	75
	Bobby Carpenter	Washington	Center	1981-82	80	**32**	35	67
	Kjell Dahlin	Montreal	Right wing	1985-86	77	**32**	39	71
	Petr Klima	Detroit	Left wing	1985-86	74	**32**	24	56
	Darren Turcotte	NY Rangers	Right wing	1989-90	76	**32**	34	66
	Joe Juneau	Boston	Center	1992-93	84	**32**	70	102

All-Time Top 50 Point-Scoring Rookies

	Rookie	Team	Position	Season	GP	G	A	PTS
1.	* Teemu Selanne	Winnipeg	Right wing	1992-93	84	76	56	**132**
2.	* Peter Stastny	Quebec	Center	1980-81	77	39	70	**109**
3.	* Dale Hawerchuk	Winnipeg	Center	1981-82	80	45	58	**103**
4.	Joe Juneau	Boston	Center	1992-93	84	32	70	**102**
5.	* Mario Lemieux	Pittsburgh	Center	1984-85	73	43	57	**100**
6.	Neal Broten	Minnesota	Center	1981-82	73	38	60	**98**
7.	* Bryan Trottier	NY Islanders	Center	1975-76	80	32	63	**95**
8.	Barry Pederson	Boston	Center	1981-82	80	44	48	**92**
	* Joe Nieuwendyk	Calgary	Center	1987-88	75	51	41	**92**
10.	* Mike Bossy	NY Islanders	Right wing	1977-78	73	53	38	**91**
11.	* Steve Larmer	Chicago	Right wing	1982-83	80	43	47	**90**
12.	Marian Stastny	Quebec	Center	1981-82	74	35	54	**89**
13.	Steve Yzerman	Detroit	Center	1983-84	80	39	48	**87**
14.	* Sergei Makarov	Calgary	Right wing	1989-90	80	24	62	**86**
15.	Anton Stastny	Quebec	Left wing	1980-81	80	39	46	**85**
16.	* Luc Robitaille	Los Angeles	Left wing	1986-87	79	45	39	**84**
17.	Mikael Renberg	Philadelphia	Left wing	1993-94	83	38	44	**82**
18.	Jimmy Carson	Los Angeles	Center	1986-87	80	37	42	**79**
	Sergei Fedorov	Detroit	Center	1990-91	77	31	48	**79**
	Alexei Yashin	Ottawa	Center	1993-94	83	30	49	**79**
21.	Marcel Dionne	Detroit	Center	1971-72	78	28	49	**77**
22.	Larry Murphy	Los Angeles	Defense	1980-81	80	16	60	**76**
	Mark Pavelich	NY Rangers	Center	1981-82	79	33	43	**76**
	Dave Poulin	Philadelphia	Center	1983-84	73	31	45	**76**
25.	Brian Propp	Philadelphia	Left wing	1979-80	80	34	41	**75**
	Jari Kurri	Edmonton	Left wing	1980-81	75	32	43	**75**
	Denis Savard	Chicago	Center	1980-81	76	28	47	**75**
	Mike Modano	Minnesota	Center	1989-90	80	29	46	**75**
	Eric Lindros	Philadelphia	Center	1992-93	61	41	34	**75**
30.	Rick Martin	Buffalo	Left wing	1971-72	73	44	30	**74**
	* Bobby Smith	Minnesota	Center	1978-79	80	30	44	**74**
32.	Jorgen Pettersson	St. Louis	Left wing	1980-81	62	37	36	**73**
33.	* Gilbert Perreault	Buffalo	Center	1970-71	78	38	34	**72**
	Dale McCourt	Detroit	Center	1977-78	76	33	39	**72**
	Ron Flockhart	Philadelphia	Center	1981-82	72	33	39	**72**
	Sylvain Turgeon	Hartford	Left wing	1983-84	76	40	32	**72**
	Warren Young	Pittsburgh	Left wing	1984-85	80	40	32	**72**
	Carey Wilson	Calgary	Center	1984-85	74	24	48	**72**
	Alexei Zhamnov	Winnipeg	Center	1992-93	68	25	47	**72**
40.	Mike Foligno	Detroit	Right wing	1979-80	80	36	35	**71**
	Dave Christian	Winnipeg	Center	1980-81	80	28	43	**71**
	Mats Naslund	Montreal	Left wing	1982-83	74	26	45	**71**
	Kjell Dahlin	Montreal	Right wing	1985-86	77	32	39	**71**
	* Brian Leetch	NY Rangers	Defense	1988-89	68	23	48	**71**
45.	Bill Mosienko	Chicago	Right wing	1943-44	50	32	38	**70**
	* Scott Gomez	New Jersey	Center	99-2000	82	19	51	**70**
47.	Roland Eriksson	Minnesota	Center	1976-77	80	25	44	**69**
	Tony Amonte	NY Rangers	Right wing	1991-92	79	35	34	**69**
49.	Jude Drouin	Minnesota	Center	1970-71	75	16	52	**68**
	Pierre Larouche	Pittsburgh	Center	1974-75	79	31	37	**68**
	Ron Francis	Hartford	Center	1981-82	59	25	43	**68**
	* Gary Suter	Calgary	Defense	1985-86	80	18	50	**68**
	Jason Arnott	Edmonton	Center	1993-94	84	33	35	**68**

* Calder Trophy Winner

50-Goal Seasons

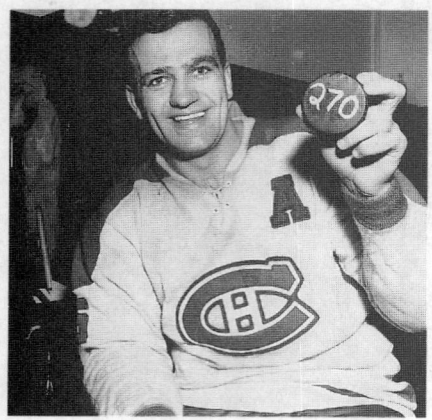

Bernie Geoffrion

Blaine Stoughton

Wayne Gretzky

Player	Team	Date of 50th Goal	Score			Goaltender	Player's Game No.	Team Game No.	Total Goals	Total Games	Age When First 50th Scored (Yrs. & Mos.)
Maurice Richard	Mtl.	18-3-45	Mtl. 4	at	Bos. 2	Harvey Bennett	50	50	50	50	23.7
Bernie Geoffrion	Mtl.	16-3-61	Tor. 2	at	Mtl. 5	Cesare Maniago	62	68	50	64	30.1
Bobby Hull	Chi.	25-3-62	Chi. 1	at	NYR 4	Gump Worsley	70	70	50	70	23.2
Bobby Hull	Chi.	2-3-66	Det. 4	at	Chi. 5	Hank Bassen	52	57	54	65	
Bobby Hull	Chi.	18-3-67	Chi. 5	at	Tor. 9	Bruce Gamble	63	66	52	66	
Bobby Hull	Chi.	5-3-69	NYR 4	at	Chi. 4	Ed Giacomin	64	66	58	74	
Phil Esposito	Bos.	20-2-71	Bos. 4	at	L.A. 5	Denis DeJordy	58	58	76	78	29.0
John Bucyk	Bos.	16-3-71	Bos. 11	at	Det. 4	Roy Edwards	69	69	51	78	35.10
Phil Esposito	Bos.	20-2-72	Bos. 3	at	Chi. 1	Tony Esposito	60	60	66	76	
Bobby Hull	Chi.	2-4-72	Det. 1	at	Chi. 5	Andy Brown	78	78	50	78	
Vic Hadfield	NYR	2-4-72	Mtl. 6	at	NYR 5	Denis DeJordy	78	78	50	78	31.6
Phil Esposito	Bos.	25-3-73	Buf. 1	at	Bos. 6	Roger Crozier	75	75	55	78	
Mickey Redmond	Det.	27-3-73	Det. 8	at	Tor. 1	Ron Low	73	75	52	76	25.3
Rick MacLeish	Phi.	1-4-73	Phi. 4	at	Pit. 5	Cam Newton	78	78	50	78	23.2
Phil Esposito	Bos.	20-2-74	Bos. 5	at	Min. 5	Cesare Maniago	56	56	68	78	
Mickey Redmond	Det.	23-3-74	NYR 3	at	Det. 5	Ed Giacomin	69	71	51	76	
Ken Hodge	Bos.	6-4-74	Bos. 2	at	Mtl. 6	Michel Larocque	75	77	50	78	29.10
Rick Martin	Buf.	7-4-74	St.L. 2	at	Buf. 5	Wayne Stephenson	78	78	52	78	22.9
Phil Esposito	Bos.	8-2-75	Bos. 8	at	Det. 5	Jim Rutherford	54	54	61	79	
Guy Lafleur	Mtl.	29-3-75	K.C. 1	at	Mtl. 4	Denis Herron	66	76	53	70	23.6
Danny Grant	Det.	2-4-75	Wsh. 3	at	Det. 8	John Adams	78	78	50	80	29.2
Rick Martin	Buf.	3-4-75	Bos. 2	at	Buf. 4	Ken Broderick	67	79	52	68	
Reggie Leach	Phi.	14-3-76	Atl. 1	at	Phi. 6	Dan Bouchard	69	69	61	80	25.11
Jean Pronovost	Pit.	24-3-76	Pit. 5	at	Pit. 5	Gilles Gilbert	74	74	52	80	30.3
Guy Lafleur	Mtl.	27-3-76	K.C. 2	at	Mtl. 8	Denis Herron	76	76	56	80	
Bill Barber	Phi.	3-4-76	Buf. 2	at	Phi. 5	Al Smith	79	79	50	80	23.9
Pierre Larouche	Pit.	3-4-76	Wsh. 5	at	Pit. 4	Ron Low	75	79	53	76	20.5
Danny Gare	Buf.	4-4-76	Tor. 2	at	Buf. 5	Gord McRae	79	80	50	79	21.11
Steve Shutt	Mtl.	1-3-77	Mtl. 5	at	NYI 4	Glenn Resch	65	65	60	80	24.8
Guy Lafleur	Mtl.	6-3-77	Mtl. 1	at	Buf. 4	Don Edwards	68	68	56	80	
Marcel Dionne	L.A.	2-4-77	Min. 2	at	L.A. 7	Pete LoPresti	79	79	53	80	25.8
Guy Lafleur	Mtl.	8-3-78	Wsh. 3	at	Mtl. 4	Jim Bedard	63	65	60	78	
Mike Bossy	NYI	1-4-78	Wsh. 2	at	NYI 3	Bernie Wolfe	69	76	53	73	21.2
Mike Bossy	NYI	24-2-79	Det. 1	at	NYI 3	Rogie Vachon	58	58	69	80	
Marcel Dionne	L.A.	11-3-79	L.A. 3	at	Phi. 6	Wayne Stephenson	68	68	59	80	
Guy Lafleur	Mtl.	31-3-79	Pit. 3	at	Mtl. 5	Denis Herron	76	76	52	80	
Guy Chouinard	Atl.	6-4-79	NYR 2	at	Atl. 9	John Davidson	79	79	50	80	22.5
Marcel Dionne	L.A.	12-3-80	L.A. 4	at	Pit. 4	Nick Ricci	70	70	53	80	
Mike Bossy	NYI	16-3-80	NYI 6	at	Chi. 1	Tony Esposito	68	71	51	75	
Charlie Simmer	L.A.	19-3-80	Det. 3	at	L.A. 4	Jim Rutherford	57	73	56	64	26.0
Pierre Larouche	Mtl.	25-3-80	Chi. 4	at	Mtl. 8	Tony Esposito	72	75	50	73	
Danny Gare	Buf.	27-3-80	Det. 1	at	Buf. 10	Jim Rutherford	71	75	56	76	
Blaine Stoughton	Hfd.	28-3-80	Hfd. 4	at	Van. 4	Glen Hanlon	75	75	56	80	27.0
Guy Lafleur	Mtl.	2-4-80	Mtl. 7	at	Det. 2	Rogie Vachon	72	78	50	74	
Wayne Gretzky	Edm.	2-4-80	Min. 1	at	Edm. 1	Gary Edwards	78	79	51	79	19.2
Reggie Leach	Phi.	3-4-80	Wsh. 2	at	Phi. 4	empty net	75	79	50	76	
Mike Bossy	NYI	24-1-81	Que. 3	at	NYI 7	Ron Grahame	50	50	68	79	
Charlie Simmer	L.A.	26-1-81	L.A. 7	at	Que. 5	Michel Dion	51	51	56	65	
Marcel Dionne	L.A.	8-3-81	L.A. 4	at	Wpg. 1	Markus Mattsson	68	68	58	80	
Wayne Babych	St.L.	12-3-81	St.L. 3	at	Mtl. 4	Richard Sevigny	70	68	54	78	22.9
Wayne Gretzky	Edm.	15-3-81	Edm. 3	at	Cgy. 3	Pat Riggin	69	69	55	80	
Rick Kehoe	Pit.	16-3-81	Pit. 7	at	Edm. 6	Eddie Mio	70	70	55	80	29.7
Jacques Richard	Que.	29-3-81	Mtl. 0	at	Que. 4	Richard Sevigny	75	76	52	78	28.6
Dennis Maruk	Wsh.	5-4-81	Det. 2	at	Wsh. 7	Larry Lozinski	80	80	50	80	25.3
Wayne Gretzky	Edm.	30-12-81	Phi. 5	at	Edm. 7	empty net	39	39	92	80	
Dennis Maruk	Wsh.	21-2-82	Wpg. 3	at	Wsh. 6	Doug Soetaert	61	61	60	80	
Mike Bossy	NYI	4-3-82	Tor. 1	at	NYI 10	Michel Larocque	66	66	64	80	
Dino Ciccarelli	Min.	8-3-82	St.L. 1	at	Min. 8	Mike Liut	67	68	55	76	22.1
Rick Vaive	Tor.	24-3-82	St.L. 3	at	Tor. 4	Mike Liut	72	75	54	77	22.10
Blaine Stoughton	Hfd.	28-3-82	Min. 5	at	Hfd. 2	Gilles Meloche	76	76	52	80	
Rick Middleton	Bos.	28-3-82	Bos. 5	at	Buf. 9	Paul Harrison	72	77	51	75	28.11
Marcel Dionne	L.A.	30-3-82	Cgy. 2	at	L.A. 5	Pat Riggin	75	77	50	78	
Mark Messier	Edm.	31-3-82	L.A. 3	at	Edm. 7	Mario Lessard	78	79	50	78	21.3
Bryan Trottier	NYI	3-4-82	Phi. 3	at	NYI 6	Pete Peeters	79	79	50	80	25.9
Lanny McDonald	Cgy.	18-2-83	Cgy. 1	at	Buf. 6	Bob Sauve	60	60	66	80	30.0
Wayne Gretzky	Edm.	19-2-83	Edm. 10	at	Pit. 7	Nick Ricci	60	60	71	80	
Michel Goulet	Que.	5-3-83	Hfd. 3	at	Que. 10	Mike Veisor	67	67	57	80	22.11
Mike Bossy	NYI	12-3-83	Wsh. 2	at	NYI 6	Al Jensen	70	71	60	79	
Marcel Dionne	L.A.	17-3-83	Que. 3	at	L.A. 4	Dan Bouchard	71	71	56	80	
Al Secord	Chi.	20-3-83	Tor. 3	at	Chi. 7	Mike Palmateer	73	73	54	80	25.0
Rick Vaive	Tor.	30-3-83	Tor. 4	at	Det. 2	Gilles Gilbert	76	78	51	78	
Wayne Gretzky	Edm.	7-1-84	Hfd. 3	at	Edm. 5	Greg Millen	42	42	87	74	
Michel Goulet	Que.	8-3-84	Que. 8	at	Pit. 6	Denis Herron	63	69	56	75	
Rick Vaive	Tor.	14-3-84	Min. 3	at	Tor. 3	Gilles Meloche	69	72	52	76	
Mike Bullard	Pit.	14-3-84	Pit. 6	at	L.A. 7	Markus Mattsson	71	72	51	76	23.0
Jari Kurri	Edm.	15-3-84	Edm. 2	at	Mtl. 3	Rick Wamsley	57	73	52	64	23.10
Glenn Anderson	Edm.	21-3-84	Hfd. 3	at	Edm. 5	Greg Millen	76	76	54	80	23.6
Tim Kerr	Phi.	22-3-84	Pit. 4	at	Phi. 13	Denis Herron	74	75	54	79	24.3
Mike Bossy	NYI	31-3-84	NYI 3	at	Wsh. 1	Pat Riggin	67	79	51	67	
Wayne Gretzky	Edm.	26-1-85	Pit. 3	at	Edm. 6	Denis Herron	49	49	73	80	
Jari Kurri	Edm.	3-2-85	Hfd. 3	at	Edm. 6	Greg Millen	50	53	71	73	
Mike Bossy	NYI	5-3-85	Phi. 5	at	NYI 4	Bob Froese	61	65	58	76	
Michel Goulet	Que.	6-3-85	Buf. 3	at	Que. 4	Tom Barrasso	62	73	55	69	
Tim Kerr	Phi.	7-3-85	Wsh. 6	at	Phi. 9	Pat Riggin	63	65	54	74	
John Ogrodnick	Det.	13-3-85	Det. 6	at	Edm. 7	Grant Fuhr	69	69	55	79	25.9
Bob Carpenter	Wsh.	21-3-85	Wsh. 2	at	Mtl. 3	Steve Penney	72	72	53	80	21.9

Player	Team	Date of 50th Goal	Score		Goaltender	Player's Game No.	Team Game No.	Total Goals	Total Games	Age When First 50th Scored (Yrs. & Mos.)
Dale Hawerchuk	Wpg.	29-3-85	Chi. 5	at Wpg. 5	W. Skorodenski	77	77	53	80	21.11
Mike Gartner	Wsh.	7-4-85	Pit. 3	at Wsh. 7	Brian Ford	80	80	50	80	25.5
Jari Kurri	Edm.	4-3-86	Edm. 6	at Van. 2	Richard Brodeur	63	65	68	78	
Mike Bossy	NYI	11-3-86	Cgy. 4	at NYI 8	Reggie Lemelin	67	67	61	80	
Glenn Anderson	Edm.	14-3-86	Det. 3	at Edm. 12	Greg Stefan	63	71	54	72	
Michel Goulet	Que.	17-3-86	Que. 8	at Mtl. 6	Patrick Roy	67	72	53	75	
Wayne Gretzky	Edm.	18-3-86	Wpg. 2	at Edm. 6	Brian Hayward	72	72	52	80	
Tim Kerr	Phi.	20-3-86	Pit. 1	at Phi. 5	Roberto Romano	68	72	58	76	
Wayne Gretzky	Edm.	4-2-87	Edm. 6	at Min. 5	Don Beaupre	55	55	62	79	
Dino Ciccarelli	Min.	7-3-87	Pit. 7	at Min. 3	Gilles Meloche	66	66	52	80	
Mario Lemieux	Pit.	12-3-87	Que. 3	at Pit. 6	Mario Gosselin	53	70	54	63	21.5
Tim Kerr	Phi.	17-3-87	NYR 1	at Phi. 4	J. Vanbiesbrouck	67	71	58	75	
Jari Kurri	Edm.	17-3-87	N.J. 4	at Edm. 7	Craig Billington	69	70	54	79	
Mario Lemieux	Pit.	2-2-88	Wsh. 2	at Pit. 3	Pete Peeters	51	54	70	77	
Steve Yzerman	Det.	1-3-88	Buf. 0	at Det. 4	Tom Barrasso	64	64	50	64	22.10
Joe Nieuwendyk	Cgy.	12-3-88	Buf. 4	at Cgy. 10	Tom Barrasso	66	70	51	75	21.5
Craig Simpson	Edm.	15-3-88	Buf. 4	at Edm. 6	Jacques Cloutier	71	71	56	80	21.1
Jimmy Carson	L.A.	26-3-88	Chi. 5	at L.A. 9	Darren Pang	77	77	55	88	19.8
Luc Robitaille	L.A.	1-4-88	L.A. 6	at Cgy. 3	Mike Vernon	79	79	53	80	21.10
Hakan Loob	Cgy.	3-4-88	Min. 1	at Cgy. 4	Don Beaupre	80	80	50	80	27.9
Stephane Richer	Mtl.	3-4-88	Mtl. 4	at Buf. 4	Tom Barrasso	72	80	50	72	21.10
Mario Lemieux	Pit.	20-1-89	Pit. 3	at Wpg. 7	Pokey Reddick	44	46	85	76	
Bernie Nicholls	L.A.	28-1-89	Edm. 7	at L.A. 6	Grant Fuhr	51	51	70	79	27.7
Steve Yzerman	Det.	5-2-89	Det. 6	at Wpg. 2	Pokey Reddick	55	55	65	80	
Wayne Gretzky	L.A.	4-3-89	Phi. 2	at L.A. 6	Ron Hextall	66	67	54	78	
Joe Nieuwendyk	Cgy.	21-3-89	NYI 1	at Cgy. 4	Mark Fitzpatrick	72	74	51	77	
Joe Mullen	Cgy.	31-3-89	Wpg. 1	at Cgy. 4	Bob Essensa	78	79	51	79	32.1
Brett Hull	St.L.	6-2-90	Tor. 4	at St.L. 6	Jeff Reese	54	54	72	80	25.6
Steve Yzerman	Det.	24-2-90	Det. 3	at NYI 3	Glenn Healy	63	63	62	79	
Cam Neely	Bos.	10-3-90	Bos. 3	at NYI 3	Mark Fitzpatrick	69	71	55	76	24.9
Luc Robitaille	L.A.	31-3-90	L.A. 3	at Van. 6	Kirk McLean	79	79	52	80	
Brian Bellows	Min.	22-3-90	Min. 5	at Det. 1	Tim Cheveldae	75	75	55	80	25.6
Pat LaFontaine	NYI	24-3-90	NYI 5	at Edm. 5	Bill Ranford	71	77	54	74	25.1
Stephane Richer	Mtl.	24-3-90	Mtl. 4	at Hfd. 7	Peter Sidorkiewicz	75	77	51	75	
Gary Leeman	Tor.	28-3-90	NYI 6	at Tor. 3	Mark Fitzpatrick	78	78	51	80	26.1
Brett Hull	St.L.	25-1-91	St.L. 9	at Det. 4	David Gagnon	49	49	86	78	
Cam Neely	Bos.	26-3-91	Bos. 7	at Que. 4	empty net	67	78	51	69	
Theoren Fleury	Cgy.	26-3-91	Van. 2	at Cgy. 7	Bob Mason	77	77	51	79	22.9
Steve Yzerman	Det.	30-3-91	NYR 5	at Det. 6	Mike Richter	79	79	51	80	
Brett Hull	St.L.	28-1-92	St.L. 3	at L.A. 3	Kelly Hrudey	50	50	70	73	
Jeremy Roenick	Chi.	7-3-92	Chi. 2	at Bos. 1	Daniel Berthiaume	67	67	53	80	22.2
Kevin Stevens	Pit.	24-3-92	Pit. 3	at Det. 4	Tim Cheveldae	74	74	54	80	26.11
Gary Roberts	Cgy.	31-3-92	Edm. 2	at Cgy. 5	Bill Ranford	73	77	53	76	25.10
Alexander Mogilny	Buf.	3-2-93	Hfd. 2	at Buf. 3	Sean Burke	46	53	76	77	23.11
Teemu Selanne	Wpg.	28-2-93	Min. 6	at Wpg. 7	Darcy Wakaluk	63	63	76	84	22.6
Pavel Bure	Van.	1-3-93	Van. 5	at Buf. 2*	Grant Fuhr	63	63	60	83	21.11
Steve Yzerman	Det.	10-3-93	Det. 6	at Edm. 3	Bill Ranford	70	70	58	84	
Luc Robitaille	L.A.	15-3-93	L.A. 4	at Buf. 2	Grant Fuhr	69	69	63	84	
Brett Hull	St.L.	20-3-93	St.L. 2	at L.A. 3	Robb Stauber	73	73	54	80	
Mario Lemieux	Pit.	21-3-93	Pit. 6	at Edm. 4**	Ron Tugnutt	48	72	69	60	
Kevin Stevens	Pit.	21-3-93	Pit. 6	at Edm. 4**	Ron Tugnutt	62	72	55	72	
Dave Andreychuk	Tor.	23-3-93	Tor. 5	at Wpg. 4	Bob Essensa	72	73	54	83	29.6
Pat LaFontaine	Buf.	28-3-93	Ott. 1	at Buf. 3	Peter Sidorkiewicz	75	75	53	84	
Pierre Turgeon	NYI	2-4-93	NYI 3	at NYR 2	Mike Richter	75	76	58	83	23.8
Mark Recchi	Phi.	3-4-93	T.B. 2	at Phi. 6	J-C Bergeron	77	77	53	84	25.2
Jeremy Roenick	Chi.	15-4-93	Tor. 2	at Chi. 3	Felix Potvin	84	84	50	84	
Brendan Shanahan	St.L.	15-4-93	T.B. 5	at St.L. 6	Pat Jablonski	71	84	51	71	24.3
Cam Neely	Bos.	7-3-94	Wsh. 3	at Bos. 6	Don Beaupre	44	66	50	49	
Sergei Fedorov	Det.	15-3-94	Van. 2	at Det. 5	Kirk McLean	67	69	56	82	24.3
Pavel Bure	Van.	23-3-94	Van. 6	at L.A. 3	empty net	65	73	60	76	
Adam Graves	NYR	23-3-94	NYR 5	at Edm. 3	Bill Ranford	74	74	52	84	25.11
Dave Andreychuk	Tor.	24-3-94	S.J. 2	at Tor. 1	Arturs Irbe	73	74	53	83	
Brett Hull	St.L.	25-3-94	Dal. 3	at St.L. 5	Andy Moog	71	74	52	81	
Ray Sheppard	Det.	29-3-94	Hfd. 2	at Det. 6	Sean Burke	74	76	52	82	27.10
Brendan Shanahan	St.L.	12-4-94	St.L. 5	at Dal. 9	Andy Moog	80	83	52	81	
Mike Modano	Dal.	12-4-94	St.L. 5	at Dal. 9	Curtis Joseph	75	83	50	76	23.11
Mario Lemieux	Pit.	23-2-96	Hfd. 4	at Pit. 5	Sean Burke	50	59	69	70	
Jaromir Jagr	Pit.	23-2-96	Hfd. 4	at Pit. 5	Sean Burke	59	59	62	82	24.0
Alexander Mogilny	Van.	29-2-96	St.L. 2	at Van. 2	Grant Fuhr	60	63	55	79	
Peter Bondra	Wsh.	3-4-96	Wsh. 5	at Buf. 1	Andrei Trefilov	62	77	52	67	28.1
Joe Sakic	Col.	7-4-96	Col. 4	at Dal. 1	empty net	79	79	51	82	26.7
John LeClair	Phi.	10-4-96	Phi. 5	at N.J. 1	Corey Schwab	80	80	51	82	26.7
Keith Tkachuk	Wpg.	12-4-96	L.A. 3	at Wpg. 5	empty net	75	81	50	76	24.0
Paul Kariya	Ana.	14-4-96	Wpg. 2	at Ana. 5	N. Khabibulin	82	82	50	82	21.5
Keith Tkachuk	Phx.	6-4-97	Phx. 1	at Col. 2	Patrick Roy	78	79	52	81	
Teemu Selanne	Ana.	9-4-97	L.A. 1	at Ana. 4	empty net	77	81	51	78	
Mario Lemieux	Pit.	11-4-97	Pit. 2	at Fla. 4	J. Vanbiesbrouck	75	81	50	76	
John LeClair	Phi.	13-4-97	N.J. 4	at Phi. 5	Mike Dunham	82	82	50	82	
Teemu Selanne	Ana.	25-3-98	Ana. 3	at Chi. 2	Jeff Hackett	66	71	52	73	
John LeClair	Phi.	13-4-98	Phi. 1	at Buf. 2	Dominik Hasek	79	79	51	82	
Pavel Bure	Van.	17-4-98	Cgy. 4	at Van. 2	Dwayne Roloson	81	81	51	82	
Peter Bondra	Wsh.	18-4-98	Wsh. 4	at Car. 3	Mike Fountain	75	80	52	76	
Pavel Bure	Fla.	18-3-00	Fla. 4	at NYI 2	empty net	63	71	58	74	
Pavel Bure	Fla.	16-3-01	Pit. 6	at Fla. 3	Johan Hedberg	72	72	59	82	
Joe Sakic	Col.	4-4-01	Ana. 1	at Col. 1	J-S Giguere	80	80	54	82	
Jaromir Jagr	Pit.	4-4-01	T.B. 2	at Pit. 4	Kevin Weekes	80	80	52	81	
Jarome Iginla	Cgy.	7-4-02	Cgy. 2	at Chi. 3	Jocelyn Thibault	79	79	52	82	24.9
Milan Hejduk	Col.	6-4-03	St.L. 2	at Col. 5	Brent Johnson	82	82	50	82	27.1

* neutral site game played at Hamilton; ** neutral site game played at Cleveland

Dino Ciccarelli

Mario Lemieux

Milan Hejduk

100-Point Seasons

Guy Lafleur

Denis Potvin

Bobby Smith

Player	Team	Date of 100th Point	G or A	Score		Player's Game No.	Team Game No.	G - A PTS	Total Games	Age when first 100th point scored (Yrs. & Mos.)
Phil Esposito	Bos.	2-3-69	(G)	Pit. 0	at Bos. 4	60	62	49-77 — 126	74	27.1
Bobby Hull	Chi.	20-3-69	(G)	Chi. 5	at Bos. 5	71	71	58-49 — 107	76	30.2
Gordie Howe	Det.	30-3-69	(G)	Det. 5	at Chi. 9	76	76	44-59 — 103	76	41.0
Bobby Orr	Bos.	15-3-70	(G)	Det. 5	at Bos. 5	67	67	33-87 — 120	76	22.11
Phil Esposito	Bos.	6-2-71	(A)	Buf. 3	at Bos. 4	51	51	76-76 — 152	78	
Bobby Orr	Bos.	20-2-71	(A)	Bos. 4	at L.A. 5	58	58	37-102 — 139	78	
John Bucyk	Bos.	13-3-71	(G)	Bos. 6	at Van. 3	68	68	51-65 — 116	78	35.10
Ken Hodge	Bos.	21-3-71	(A)	Buf. 7	at Bos. 5	72	72	43-62 — 105	78	26.9
Jean Ratelle	NYR	18-2-72	(A)	NYR 2	at Cal. 2	58	58	46-63 — 109	63	31.4
Phil Esposito	Bos.	19-2-72	(A)	Bos. 6	at Min. 4	59	59	66-67 — 133	76	
Bobby Orr	Bos.	2-3-72	(A)	Van. 3	at Bos. 7	64	64	37-80 — 117	76	
Vic Hadfield	NYR	25-3-72	(A)	NYR 3	at Mtl. 3	74	74	50-56 — 106	78	31.5
Phil Esposito	Bos.	3-3-73	(A)	Bos. 1	at Mtl. 5	64	64	55-75 — 130	78	
Bobby Clarke	Phi.	29-3-73	(G)	Atl. 2	at Phi. 4	76	76	37-67 — 104	78	23.7
Bobby Orr	Bos.	31-3-73	(A)	Bos. 3	at Tor. 7	62	77	29-72 — 101	63	
Rick MacLeish	Phi.	1-4-73	(G)	Phi. 4	at Pit. 5	78	78	50-50 — 100	78	23.3
Phil Esposito	Bos.	13-2-74	(A)	Bos. 9	at Cal. 6	53	53	68-77 — 145	78	
Bobby Orr	Bos.	12-3-74	(A)	Buf. 0	at Bos. 4	62	66	32-90 — 122	74	
Ken Hodge	Bos.	24-3-74	(A)	Mtl. 3	at Bos. 6	72	72	50-55 — 105	76	
Phil Esposito	Bos.	8-2-75	(A)	Bos. 8	at Det. 5	54	54	61-66 — 127	79	
Bobby Orr	Bos.	13-2-75	(A)	Bos. 1	at Buf. 3	57	57	46-89 — 135	80	
Guy Lafleur	Mtl.	7-3-75	(G)	Wsh. 4	at Mtl. 8	56	66	53-66 — 119	70	24.6
Pete Mahovlich	Mtl.	9-3-75	(A)	Mtl. 5	at NYR 3	67	67	35-82 — 117	80	29.5
Marcel Dionne	Det.	9-3-75	(A)	Det. 5	at Phi. 8	67	67	47-74 — 121	80	23.7
Bobby Clarke	Phi.	22-3-75	(A)	Min. 0	at Phi. 4	72	72	27-89 — 116	80	
Rene Robert	Buf.	5-4-75	(A)	Buf. 4	at Tor. 2	74	80	40-60 — 100	74	26.4
Guy Lafleur	Mtl.	10-3-76	(G)	Mtl. 5	at Chi. 1	69	69	56-69 — 125	80	
Bobby Clarke	Phi.	11-3-76	(A)	Buf. 1	at Phi. 6	64	68	30-89 — 119	76	
Bill Barber	Phi.	18-3-76	(A)	Van. 2	at Phi. 3	71	71	50-62 — 112	80	23.8
Gilbert Perreault	Buf.	21-3-76	(A)	K.C. 1	at Buf. 3	73	73	44-69 — 113	80	25.4
Pierre Larouche	Pit.	24-3-76	(G)	Bos. 5	at Pit. 5	70	74	53-58 — 111	76	20.4
Pete Mahovlich	Mtl.	28-3-76	(A)	Mtl. 2	at Bos. 2	77	77	34-71 — 105	80	
Jean Ratelle	Bos.	30-3-76	(G)	Buf. 4	at Bos. 4	77	77	36-69 — 105	80	
Jean Pronovost	Pit.	3-4-76	(A)	Wsh. 5	at Pit. 4	79	79	52-52 — 104	80	30.4
Darryl Sittler	Tor.	3-4-76	(A)	Bos. 4	at Tor. 2	78	79	41-59 — 100	79	25.7
Guy Lafleur	Mtl.	26-2-77	(A)	Cle. 3	at Mtl. 5	63	63	56-80 — 136	80	
Marcel Dionne	L.A.	5-3-77	(G)	Pit. 3	at L.A. 3	67	67	53-69 — 122	80	
Steve Shutt	Mtl.	27-3-77	(A)	Mtl. 6	at Det. 0	77	77	60-45 — 105	80	24.9
Bryan Trottier	NYI	25-2-78	(A)	Chi. 1	at NYI 7	59	60	46-77 — 123	77	21.7
Guy Lafleur	Mtl.	28-2-78	(A)	Det. 3	at Mtl. 9	59	61	60-72 — 132	78	
Darryl Sittler	Tor.	12-3-78	(A)	Tor. 7	at Pit. 1	67	67	45-72 — 117	80	
Guy Lafleur	Mtl.	27-2-79	(A)	Mtl. 3	at NYI 7	61	61	52-77 — 129	80	
Bryan Trottier	NYI	6-3-79	(A)	Buf. 3	at NYI 2	59	63	47-87 — 134	76	
Marcel Dionne	L.A.	8-3-79	(G)	L.A. 4	at Buf. 6	66	66	59-71 — 130	80	
Mike Bossy	NYI	11-3-79	(G)	NYI 4	at Bos. 4	66	66	69-57 — 126	80	22.2
Bob MacMillan	Atl.	15-3-79	(A)	Atl. 4	at Phi. 5	68	69	37-71 — 108	79	26.6
Guy Chouinard	Atl.	30-3-79	(G)	L.A. 3	at Atl. 5	75	75	50-57 — 107	80	22.5
Denis Potvin	NYI	8-4-79	(A)	NYI 5	at NYR 2	73	80	31-70 — 101	73	25.5
Marcel Dionne	L.A.	6-2-80	(A)	L.A. 3	at Hfd. 7	53	53	53-84 — 137	80	
Guy Lafleur	Mtl.	10-2-80	(A)	Mtl. 3	at Bos. 2	55	55	50-75 — 125	74	
Wayne Gretzky	Edm.	24-2-80	(A)	Bos. 4	at Edm. 2	61	62	51-86 — 137	79	19.2
Bryan Trottier	NYI	30-3-80	(A)	NYI 9	at Que. 6	75	77	42-62 — 104	78	
Gilbert Perreault	Buf.	1-4-80	(A)	Buf. 5	at Atl. 2	77	77	40-66 — 106	80	
Mike Rogers	Hfd.	4-4-80	(A)	Que. 2	at Hfd. 9	79	79	44-61 — 105	80	25.5
Charlie Simmer	L.A.	5-4-80	(A)	Van. 5	at L.A. 3	64	80	56-45 — 101	64	26.0
Blaine Stoughton	Hfd.	6-4-80	(A)	Det. 3	at Hfd. 5	80	80	56-44 — 100	80	27.0
Wayne Gretzky	Edm.	6-2-81	(G)	Wpg. 4	at Edm. 10	53	53	55-109 — 164	80	
Marcel Dionne	L.A.	12-2-81	(A)	L.A. 5	at Chi. 5	58	58	58-77 — 135	80	
Charlie Simmer	L.A.	14-2-81	(A)	Bos. 5	at L.A. 4	59	59	56-49 — 105	65	
Kent Nilsson	Cgy.	27-2-81	(G)	Hfd. 1	at Cgy. 5	64	64	49-82 — 131	80	24.6
Mike Bossy	NYI	3-3-81	(G)	Edm. 8	at NYI 8	65	66	68-51 — 119	79	
Dave Taylor	L.A.	14-3-81	(G)	Min. 4	at L.A. 10	63	70	47-65 — 112	72	25.3
Mike Rogers	Hfd.	22-3-81	(G)	Tor. 3	at Hfd. 3	74	74	40-65 — 105	80	
Bernie Federko	St.L.	28-3-81	(A)	Buf. 4	at St.L. 7	74	76	31-73 — 104	78	24.10
Rick Middleton	Bos.	28-3-81	(A)	Chi. 2	at Bos. 5	76	76	44-59 — 103	80	27.4
Jacques Richard	Que.	29-3-81	(G)	Mtl. 0	at Que. 4	75	76	52-51 — 103	78	28.6
Bryan Trottier	NYI	29-3-81	(G)	NYI 5	at Wsh. 4	69	76	31-72 — 103	73	
Peter Stastny	Que.	29-3-81	(A)	Mtl. 0	at Que. 4	73	76	39-70 — 109	77	24.6
Wayne Gretzky	Edm.	27-12-81	(G)	L.A. 3	at Edm. 10	38	38	92-120 — 212	80	
Mike Bossy	NYI	13-2-82	(A)	Phi. 2	at NYI 8	55	55	64-83 — 147	80	
Peter Stastny	Que.	16-2-82	(A)	Wpg. 3	at Que. 7	60	60	46-93 — 139	80	
Dennis Maruk	Wsh.	20-2-82	(G)	Wsh. 3	at Min. 7	60	60	60-76 — 136	80	26.3
Bryan Trottier	NYI	23-2-82	(G)	Chi. 1	at NYI 5	61	61	50-79 — 129	80	
Denis Savard	Chi.	27-2-82	(G)	Chi. 5	at L.A. 3	64	64	32-87 — 119	80	21.1
Bobby Smith	Min.	3-3-82	(A)	Det. 4	at Min. 6	66	66	43-71 — 114	80	24.1
Marcel Dionne	L.A.	6-3-82	(A)	L.A. 6	at Hfd. 7	64	66	50-67 — 117	78	
Dave Taylor	L.A.	20-3-82	(G)	Pit. 5	at L.A. 7	71	72	39-67 — 106	78	
Dale Hawerchuk	Wpg.	24-3-82	(G)	L.A. 3	at Wpg. 5	74	74	45-58 — 103	80	18.11
Dino Ciccarelli	Min.	27-3-82	(A)	Min. 6	at Bos. 5	72	76	55-52 — 107	76	21.8
Glenn Anderson	Edm.	28-3-82	(G)	Edm. 6	at L.A. 2	78	78	38-67 — 105	80	21.7
Mike Rogers	NYR	2-4-82	(G)	Pit. 7	at NYR 5	79	79	38-65 — 103	80	

Player	Team	Date of 100th Point	G or A	Score	Player's Game No.	Team Game No.	G - A — PTS	Total Games	Age when first 100th point scored (Yrs. & Mos.)
Wayne Gretzky	Edm.	5-1-83	(A)	Edm. 8 at Wpg. 3	42	42	71-125 — 196	80	
Mike Bossy	NYI	3-3-83	(A)	Tor. 1 at NYI. 5	66	67	60-58 — 118	79	
Peter Stastny	Que.	5-3-83	(A)	Hfd. 3 at Que. 10	62	67	47-77 — 124	75	
Denis Savard	Chi.	6-3-83	(G)	Mtl. 4 at Chi. 5	65	67	35-86 — 121	78	
Mark Messier	Edm.	23-3-83	(G)	Edm. 4 at Wpg. 3	73	76	48-58 — 106	77	22.2
Barry Pederson	Bos.	26-3-83	(A)	Hfd. 4 at Bos. 7	73	76	46-61 — 107	77	22.0
Marcel Dionne	L.A.	26-3-83	(A)	Edm. 9 at L.A. 3	75	75	56-51 — 107	80	
Michel Goulet	Que.	27-3-83	(A)	Que. 6 at Buf. 6	77	77	57-48 — 105	80	22.11
Glenn Anderson	Edm.	29-3-83	(A)	Edm. 7 at Van. 4	70	78	48-56 — 104	72	
Jari Kurri	Edm.	29-3-83	(A)	Edm. 7 at Van. 4	78	78	45-59 — 104	80	22.10
Kent Nilsson	Cgy.	29-3-83	(G)	L.A. 3 at Cgy. 5	78	78	46-58 — 104	80	
Wayne Gretzky	Edm.	18-12-83	(G)	Edm. 7 at Wpg. 5	34	34	87-118 — 205	74	
Paul Coffey	Edm.	4-3-84	(A)	Mtl. 1 at Edm. 6	68	68	40-86 — 126	80	22.9
Michel Goulet	Que.	4-3-84	(A)	Que. 1 at Buf. 1	62	67	56-65 — 121	75	
Jari Kurri	Edm.	7-3-84	(G)	Chi. 4 at Edm. 7	53	69	52-61 — 113	64	
Peter Stastny	Que.	8-3-84	(A)	Que. 8 at Pit. 6	69	69	46-73 — 119	80	
Mike Bossy	NYI	8-3-84	(G)	Tor. 5 at NYI 9	56	68	51-67 — 118	67	
Barry Pederson	Bos.	14-3-84	(A)	Bos. 4 at Det. 2	71	71	39-77 — 116	80	
Bryan Trottier	NYI	18-3-84	(G)	NYI 4 at Hfd. 5	62	73	40-71 — 111	68	
Bernie Federko	St.L.	20-3-84	(A)	Wpg. 3 at St.L. 9	75	76	41-66 — 107	79	
Rick Middleton	Bos.	27-3-84	(A)	Bos. 6 at Que. 4	77	77	47-58 — 105	80	
Dale Hawerchuk	Wpg.	27-3-84	(G)	Wpg. 3 at L.A. 3	77	77	37-65 — 102	80	
Mark Messier	Edm.	27-3-84	(G)	Edm. 9 at Cgy. 2	72	79	37-64 — 101	73	
Wayne Gretzky	Edm.	29-12-84	(A)	Det. 3 at Edm. 6	35	35	73-135 — 208	80	
Jari Kurri	Edm.	29-1-85	(G)	Edm. 4 at Cgy. 2	48	51	71-64 — 135	73	
Mike Bossy	NYI	23-2-85	(G)	Bos. 1 at NYI 5	56	60	58-59 — 117	76	
Dale Hawerchuk	Wpg.	25-2-85	(A)	Wpg. 12 at NYR 5	64	64	53-77 — 130	80	
Marcel Dionne	L.A.	5-3-85	(A)	Pit. 0 at L.A. 6	66	66	46-80 — 126	80	
Brent Sutter	NYI	12-3-85	(A)	NYI 6 at St.L. 5	68	68	42-60 — 102	72	22.10
John Ogrodnick	Det.	22-3-85	(A)	NYR 3 at Det. 5	73	73	55-50 — 105	79	25.9
Paul Coffey	Edm.	26-3-85	(A)	Edm. 7 at NYI 5	74	74	37-84 — 121	80	
Denis Savard	Chi.	29-3-85	(A)	Chi. 5 at Wpg. 5	75	76	38-67 — 105	79	
Peter Stastny	Que.	2-4-85	(A)	Bos. 4 at Que. 6	74	77	32-68 — 100	75	
Bernie Federko	St.L.	4-4-85	(A)	NYR 5 at St.L. 4	74	78	30-73 — 103	76	
John Tonelli	NYI	6-4-85	(G)	N.J. 5 at NYI 5	80	80	42-58 — 100	80	28.1
Paul MacLean	Wpg.	6-4-85	(A)	Wpg. 6 at Edm. 5	78	79	41-60 — 101	79	27.1
Bernie Nicholls	L.A.	6-4-85	(A)	Van. 4 at L.A. 4	80	80	46-54 — 100	80	22.9
Mike Gartner	Wsh.	7-4-85	(G)	Pit. 3 at Wsh. 7	80	80	50-52 — 102	80	25.6
Mario Lemieux	Pit.	7-4-85	(G)	Pit. 3 at Wsh. 7	73	80	43-57 — 100	73	19.6
Wayne Gretzky	Edm.	4-1-86	(A)	Hfd. 3 at Edm. 4	39	39	52-163 — 215	80	
Mario Lemieux	Pit.	15-2-86	(G)	Van. 4 at Pit. 9	55	56	48-93 — 141	79	
Paul Coffey	Edm.	19-2-86	(A)	Tor. 5 at Edm. 9	59	60	48-90 — 138	79	
Peter Stastny	Que.	1-3-86	(A)	Buf. 8 at Que. 4	66	68	41-81 — 122	76	
Jari Kurri	Edm.	2-3-86	(A)	Phi. 1 at Edm. 2	62	64	68-63 — 131	78	
Mike Bossy	NYI	8-3-86	(G)	Wsh. 6 at NYI 2	65	65	61-62 — 123	80	
Denis Savard	Chi.	12-3-86	(A)	Buf. 7 at Chi. 6	69	69	47-69 — 116	80	
Mats Naslund	Mtl.	13-3-86	(A)	Mtl. 2 at Bos. 3	70	70	43-67 — 110	80	26.4
Michel Goulet	Que.	24-3-86	(A)	Que. 1 at Min. 0	70	75	53-50 — 103	75	
Glenn Anderson	Edm.	25-3-86	(G)	Edm. 7 at Det. 2	66	74	54-48 — 102	72	
Neal Broten	Min.	26-3-86	(A)	Min. 6 at Tor. 1	76	76	29-76 — 105	80	26.4
Dale Hawerchuk	Wpg.	31-3-86	(A)	Wpg. 5 at L.A. 2	78	78	46-59 — 105	80	
Bernie Federko	St.L.	5-4-86	(G)	Chi. 5 at St.L. 7	79	79	34-68 — 102	80	
Wayne Gretzky	Edm.	11-1-87	(A)	Cgy. 3 at Edm. 5	42	42	62-121 — 183	79	
Jari Kurri	Edm.	14-3-87	(A)	Buf. 3 at Edm. 5	67	68	54-54 — 108	79	
Mario Lemieux	Pit.	18-3-87	(A)	St.L. 4 at Pit. 5	55	72	54-53 — 107	63	
Mark Messier	Edm.	19-3-87	(A)	Edm. 4 at Cgy. 5	71	71	37-70 — 107	77	
Dino Ciccarelli	Min.	30-3-87	(A)	NYR 4 at Min. 5	78	78	52-51 — 103	80	
Doug Gilmour	St.L.	2-4-87	(A)	Buf. 3 at St.L. 5	78	78	42-63 — 105	80	23.10
Dale Hawerchuk	Wpg.	5-4-87	(A)	Wpg. 3 at Cgy. 1	80	80	47-53 — 100	80	
Mario Lemieux	Pit.	20-1-88	(G)	Pit. 8 at Chi. 3	45	48	70-98 — 168	77	
Wayne Gretzky	Edm.	11-2-88	(A)	Edm. 7 at Van. 2	43	56	40-109 — 149	64	
Denis Savard	Chi.	12-2-88	(A)	St.L. 3 at Chi. 4	57	57	44-87 — 131	80	
Dale Hawerchuk	Wpg.	23-2-88	(G)	Wpg. 4 at Pit. 3	61	61	44-77 — 121	80	
Steve Yzerman	Det.	27-2-88	(A)	Det. 4 at Que. 5	63	63	50-52 — 102	64	22.10
Peter Stastny	Que.	8-3-88	(A)	Hfd. 4 at Que. 6	63	67	46-65 — 111	76	
Mark Messier	Edm.	15-3-88	(A)	Buf. 4 at Edm. 6	68	71	37-74 — 111	77	
Jimmy Carson	L.A.	26-3-88	(A)	Chi. 5 at L.A. 9	77	77	55-52 — 107	80	19.8
Hakan Loob	Cgy.	26-3-88	(A)	Van. 1 at Cgy. 6	76	76	50-56 — 106	80	27.9
Mike Bullard	Cgy.	26-3-88	(A)	Van. 1 at Cgy. 6	76	76	48-55 — 103	79	27.1
Michel Goulet	Que.	27-3-88	(A)	Pit. 6 at Que. 3	76	76	48-58 — 106	80	
Luc Robitaille	L.A.	30-3-88	(G)	Cgy. 7 at L.A. 9	78	78	53-58 — 111	80	22.1
Mario Lemieux	Pit.	31-12-88	(A)	N.J. 6 at Pit. 8	36	38	85-114 — 199	76	
Wayne Gretzky	L.A.	21-1-89	(A)	L.A. 4 at Hfd. 5	47	48	54-114 — 168	78	
Bernie Nicholls	L.A.	21-1-89	(A)	L.A. 4 at Hfd. 5	48	48	70-80 — 150	79	
Steve Yzerman	Det.	27-1-89	(A)	Tor. 1 at Det. 8	50	50	65-90 — 155	80	
Rob Brown	Pit.	16-3-89	(A)	Pit. 2 at N.J. 1	60	72	49-66 — 115	68	20.11
Paul Coffey	Pit.	20-3-89	(A)	Pit. 2 at Min. 7	69	74	30-83 — 113	75	
Joe Mullen	Cgy.	23-3-89	(A)	Cgy. 4 at Cgy. 4	74	75	51-59 — 110	79	32.1
Jari Kurri	Edm.	29-3-89	(A)	Edm. 5 at Van. 2	75	79	44-58 — 102	76	
Jimmy Carson	Edm.	2-4-89	(A)	Edm. 2 at Cgy. 4	80	80	49-51 — 100	80	
Mario Lemieux	Pit.	28-1-90	(G)	Pit. 2 at Buf. 7	50	50	45-78 — 123	59	
Wayne Gretzky	L.A.	30-1-90	(A)	N.J. 2 at L.A. 5	51	51	40-102 — 142	73	
Steve Yzerman	Det.	19-2-90	(A)	Mtl. 5 at Det. 5	61	61	62-65 — 127	79	
Mark Messier	Edm.	20-2-90	(A)	Edm. 4 at Van. 2	62	62	45-84 — 129	79	
Brett Hull	St.L.	3-3-90	(A)	NYI 4 at St.L. 5	67	67	72-41 — 113	80	25.7
Bernie Nicholls	NYR	12-3-90	(A)	L.A. 6 at NYR 5	70	71	39-73 — 112	79	
Pierre Turgeon	Buf.	25-3-90	(G)	N.J. 4 at Buf. 3	76	76	40-66 — 106	80	20.7
Paul Coffey	Pit.	25-3-90	(A)	Pit. 2 at Hfd. 4	77	77	29-74 — 103	80	
Pat LaFontaine	NYI	27-3-90	(A)	Cgy. 4 at NYI 2	72	78	54-51 — 105	74	25.1
Adam Oates	St.L.	29-3-90	(G)	Pit. 4 at St.L. 5	79	79	23-79 — 102	80	27.7

Paul Coffey

John Ogrodnick

Rob Brown

Peter Forsberg

Markus Naslund

Joe Thornton

Player	Team	Date of 100th Point	G or A	Score			Player's Game No.	Team Game No.	G - A PTS	Total Games	Age when first 100th point scored (Yrs. & Mos.)
Joe Sakic	Que.	31-3-90	(G)	Hfd. 3	at	Que. 2	79	79	39-63 — 102	80	20.8
Ron Francis	Hfd.	31-3-90	(G)	Hfd. 3	at	Que. 2	79	79	32-69 — 101	80	27.0
Luc Robitaille	L.A.	1-4-90	(A)	L.A. 4	at	Cgy. 8	80	80	52-49 — 101	80	
Wayne Gretzky	L.A.	30-1-91	(A)	N.J. 4	at	L.A. 2	50	51	41-122 — 163	78	
Brett Hull	St.L.	23-2-91	(G)	Bos. 2	at	St.L. 9	60	62	86-45 — 131	78	
Mark Recchi	Pit.	5-3-91	(G)	Van. 1	at	Pit. 4	66	67	40-73 — 113	78	23.1
Steve Yzerman	Det.	10-3-91	(G)	Det. 4	at	St.L. 1	72	72	51-57 — 108	80	
John Cullen	Hfd.	16-3-91	(G)	N.J. 2	at	Hfd. 6	71	71	39-71 — 110	78	26.7
Adam Oates	St.L.	17-3-91	(A)	St.L. 4	at	Chi. 6	54	73	25-90 — 115	61	
Joe Sakic	Que.	19-3-91	(G)	Edm. 7	at	Que. 6	74	74	48-61 — 109	80	
Steve Larmer	Chi.	24-3-91	(A)	Min. 4	at	Chi. 5	76	76	44-57 — 101	80	29.9
Theoren Fleury	Cgy.	26-3-91	(G)	Van. 2	at	Cgy. 7	77	77	51-53 — 104	79	22.9
Al MacInnis	Cgy.	28-3-91	(A)	Edm. 4	at	Cgy. 4	78	78	28-75 — 103	78	27.8
Brett Hull	St.L.	2-3-92	(G)	St.L. 5	at	Van. 3	66	66	70-39 — 109	73	
Wayne Gretzky	L.A.	3-3-92	(A)	Phi. 1	at	L.A. 4	66	66	31-90 — 121	74	
Kevin Stevens	Pit.	7-3-92	(A)	Pit. 3	at	L.A. 5	66	66	54-69 — 123	80	26.11
Mario Lemieux	Pit.	10-3-92	(A)	Cgy. 2	at	Pit. 5	53	67	44-87 — 131	64	
Luc Robitaille	L.A.	17-3-92	(A)	Wpg. 4	at	L.A. 5	73	73	44-63 — 107	80	
Mark Messier	NYR	22-3-92	(G)	N.J. 3	at	NYR 6	74	75	35-72 — 107	79	
Jeremy Roenick	Chi.	29-3-92	(G)	Tor. 1	at	Chi. 5	77	77	53-50 — 103	80	22.2
Steve Yzerman	Det.	14-4-92	(G)	Det. 7	at	Min. 4	79	80	45-58 — 103	79	
Brian Leetch	NYR	16-4-92	(G)	Pit. 1	at	NYR 7	80	80	22-80 — 102	80	24.1
Mario Lemieux	Pit.	31-12-92	(G)	Tor. 3	at	Pit. 3	38	39	69-91 — 160	60	
Pat LaFontaine	Buf.	10-2-93	(A)	Buf. 6	at	Wpg. 2	55	55	53-95 — 148	84	
Adam Oates	Bos.	14-2-93	(A)	Bos. 3	at	T.B. 3	58	58	45-97 — 142	84	
Steve Yzerman	Det.	24-2-93	(A)	Det. 7	at	Buf. 10	64	64	58-79 — 137	84	
Pierre Turgeon	NYI	28-2-93	(G)	NYI 7	at	Hfd. 6	62	63	58-74 — 132	83	
Doug Gilmour	Tor.	3-3-93	(A)	Min. 1	at	Tor. 3	64	64	32-95 — 127	83	
Alexander Mogilny	Buf.	5-3-93	(A)	Hfd. 4	at	Buf. 2	58	65	76-51 — 127	77	24.1
Mark Recchi	Phi.	7-3-93	(A)	Phi. 3	at	N.J. 7	66	66	53-70 — 123	84	
Teemu Selanne	Wpg.	9-3-93	(G)	Wpg. 4	at	T.B. 2	68	68	76-56 — 132	84	22.7
Luc Robitaille	L.A.	15-3-93	(A)	L.A. 4	at	Buf. 2	69	69	63-62 — 125	84	
Kevin Stevens	Pit.	23-3-93	(A)	S.J. 2	at	Pit. 7	63	73	55-56 — 111	72	
Mats Sundin	Que.	27-3-93	(G)	Phi. 3	at	Que. 8	71	75	47-67 — 114	80	22.1
Pavel Bure	Van.	1-4-93	(G)	Van. 5	at	T.B. 3	77	77	60-50 — 110	83	22.0
Jeremy Roenick	Chi.	4-4-93	(G)	St.L. 4	at	Chi. 5	79	79	50-57 — 107	84	
Craig Janney	St.L.	4-4-93	(A)	St.L. 4	at	Chi. 5	79	79	24-82 — 106	84	25.7
Rick Tocchet	Pit.	7-4-93	(G)	Mtl. 3	at	Pit. 4	77	81	48-61 — 109	80	28.11
Joe Sakic	Que.	8-4-93	(A)	Que. 2	at	Bos. 6	75	81	48-57 — 105	78	
Ron Francis	Pit.	9-4-93	(A)	Pit. 10	at	NYR 4	82	82	24-76 — 100	84	
Brett Hull	St.L.	11-4-93	(G)	Min. 1	at	St.L. 5	78	82	54-47 — 101	80	
Theoren Fleury	Cgy.	11-4-93	(G)	Cgy. 3	at	Van. 6	82	82	34-66 — 100	83	
Joe Juneau	Bos.	14-4-93	(A)	Bos. 4	at	Ott. 2	84	84	32-70 — 102	84	25.3
Wayne Gretzky	L.A.	14-2-94	(A)	Bos. 3	at	L.A. 2	56	56	38-92 — 130	81	
Sergei Fedorov	Det.	1-3-94	(A)	Cgy. 2	at	Det. 5	63	63	56-64 — 120	82	24.2
Doug Gilmour	Tor.	23-3-94	(G)	Tor. 1	at	Fla. 1	74	74	27-84 — 111	83	
Adam Oates	Bos.	26-3-94	(A)	Mtl. 3	at	Bos. 6	68	75	32-80 — 112	77	
Mark Recchi	Phi.	27-3-94	(A)	Ana. 3	at	Phi. 2	76	76	40-67 — 107	84	
Pavel Bure	Van.	28-3-94	(A)	Tor. 2	at	Van. 3	68	76	60-47 — 107	76	
Jeremy Roenick	Chi.	31-3-94	(G)	Chi. 3	at	Wsh. 6	78	78	46-61 — 107	84	
Brendan Shanahan	St.L.	12-4-94	(G)	St.L. 5	at	Dal. 9	80	83	52-50 — 102	81	25.2
Mario Lemieux	Pit.	16-1-96	(G)	Col. 5	at	Pit. 2	38	44	69-92 — 161	70	
Jaromir Jagr	Pit.	6-2-96	(G)	Bos. 5	at	Pit. 6	52	52	62-87 — 149	82	23.12
Ron Francis	Pit.	9-3-96	(A)	N.J. 4	at	Pit. 3	61	66	27-92 — 119	77	
Peter Forsberg	Col.	9-3-96	(A)	Col. 7	at	Van. 5	68	68	30-86 — 116	82	22.7
Joe Sakic	Col.	17-3-96	(A)	Edm. 1	at	Col. 8	70	70	51-69 — 120	82	
Teemu Selanne	Ana.	25-3-96	(A)	Ana. 1	at	Det. 5	70	73	40-68 — 108	79	
Alexander Mogilny	Van.	25-3-96	(A)	L.A. 1	at	Van. 4	72	75	55-52 — 107	79	
Eric Lindros	Phi.	25-3-96	(A)	Hfd. 0	at	Phi. 3	65	73	47-68 — 115	73	23.0
Wayne Gretzky	St.L.	28-3-96	(A)	N.J. 4	at	St.L. 4	76	75	23-79 — 102	80	
Doug Weight	Edm.	30-3-96	(G)	Tor. 4	at	Edm. 3	76	76	25-79 — 104	82	25.3
Sergei Fedorov	Det.	2-4-96	(A)	Det. 3	at	S.J. 6	72	76	39-68 — 107	78	
Paul Kariya	Ana.	7-4-96	(G)	Ana. 5	at	S.J. 3	78	78	50-58 — 108	82	21.5
Mario Lemieux	Pit.	8-3-97	(A)	Phi. 2	at	Pit. 3	61	65	50-72 — 122	76	
Teemu Selanne	Ana.	1-4-97	(A)	Chi. 3	at	Ana. 3	74	78	51-58 — 109	78	
Jaromir Jagr	Pit.	15-4-98	(G)	T.B. 1	at	Pit. 5	76	80	35-67 — 102	77	
Jaromir Jagr	Pit.	13-3-99	(G)	Phi. 0	at	Pit. 4	65	65	44-83 — 127	81	
Teemu Selanne	Ana.	5-4-99	(A)	Ana. 2	at	Det. 3	69	76	47-60 — 107	75	
Paul Kariya	Ana.	17-4-99	(G)	Ana. 3	at	S.J. 3	82	82	39-62 — 101	82	
Jaromir Jagr	Pit.	10-3-01	(G)	Cgy. 3	at	Pit. 6	68	68	52-69 — 121	81	
Joe Sakic	Col.	18-3-01	(G)	Min. 3	at	Col. 4	72	72	54-64 — 118	82	
Markus Naslund	Van.	27-3-03	(A)	Phx. 1	at	Van. 5	78	78	48-56 — 104	82	
Peter Forsberg	Col.	31-3-03	(A)	S.J. 1	at	Col. 3	72	79	29-77 — 106	79	
Joe Thornton	Bos.	5-4-03	(A)	Buf. 5	at	Bos. 8	77	82	36-65 — 101	77	

Five-or-more-Goal Games

Player	Team	Date	Score			Opposing Goaltender
SEVEN GOALS						
Joe Malone	Quebec Bulldogs	Jan. 31/20	Tor. 6	at	Que. 10	Ivan Mitchell
SIX GOALS						
Newsy Lalonde	Montreal	Jan. 10/20	Tor. 7	at	Mtl. 14	Ivan Mitchell
Joe Malone	Quebec Bulldogs	Mar. 10/20	Ott. 4	at	Que. 10	Clint Benedict
Corb Denneny	Toronto St. Pats	Jan. 26/21	Ham. 3	at	Tor. 10	Howard Lockhart
Cy Denneny	Ottawa Senators	Mar. 7/21	Ham. 5	at	Ott. 12	Howard Lockhart
Syd Howe	Detroit	Feb. 3/44	NYR 2	at	Det. 12	Ken McAuley
Red Berenson	St. Louis	Nov. 7/68	St.L. 8	at	Phi. 0	Doug Favell
Darryl Sittler	Toronto	Feb. 7/76	Bos. 4	at	Tor. 11	Dave Reece
FIVE GOALS						
Joe Malone	Montreal	Dec. 19/17	Mtl. 7	at	Ott. 4	Clint Benedict
Harry Hyland	Mtl. Wanderers	Dec. 19/17	Tor. 9	at	Mtl. W. 10	Art Brooks
Joe Malone	Montreal	Jan. 12/18	Ott. 4	at	Mtl. 9	Clint Benedict
Joe Malone	Montreal	Feb. 2/18	Tor. 2	at	Mtl. 11	Hap Holmes
Mickey Roach	Toronto St. Pats	Mar. 6/20	Que. 2	at	Tor. 11	Frank Brophy
Newsy Lalonde	Montreal	Feb. 16/21	Ham. 5	at	Mtl. 10	Howard Lockhart
Babe Dye	Toronto St. Pats	Dec. 16/22	Mtl. 2	at	Tor. 7	Georges Vezina
Red Green	Hamilton Tigers	Dec. 5/24	Ham. 10	at	Tor. 3	John Ross Roach
Babe Dye	Toronto St. Pats	Dec. 22/24	Tor. 10	at	Bos. 1	Charles Stewart
Punch Broadbent	Mtl. Maroons	Jan. 7/25	Mtl. 6	at	Ham. 2	Jake Forbes
Pit Lepine	Montreal	Dec. 14/29	Ott. 4	at	Mtl. 6	Alex Connell
Howie Morenz	Montreal	Mar. 18/30	NYA 3	at	Mtl. 8	Roy Worters
Charlie Conacher	Toronto	Jan. 19/32	NYA 3	at	Tor. 11	Roy Worters
Ray Getliffe	Montreal	Feb. 6/43	Bos. 3	at	Mtl. 8	Frank Brimsek
Maurice Richard	Montreal	Dec. 28/44	Det. 1	at	Mtl. 9	Harry Lumley
Howie Meeker	Toronto	Jan. 8/47	Chi. 4	at	Tor. 10	Paul Bibeault
Bernie Geoffrion	Montreal	Feb. 19/55	NYR 2	at	Mtl. 10	Gump Worsley
Bobby Rousseau	Montreal	Feb. 1/64	Det. 3	at	Mtl. 9	Roger Crozier
Yvan Cournoyer	Montreal	Feb. 15/75	Chi. 3	at	Mtl. 12	Mike Veisor
Don Murdoch	NY Rangers	Oct. 12/76	NYR 10	at	Min. 4	Gary Smith
Ian Turnbull	Toronto	Feb. 2/77	Det. 1	at	Tor. 9	Ed Giacomin (2) / Jim Rutherford (3)
Bryan Trottier	NY Islanders	Dec. 23/78	NYR 4	at	NYI 9	Wayne Thomas (4) / John Davidson (1)
Tim Young	Minnesota	Jan. 15/79	Min. 8	at	NYR 1	Doug Soetaert (3) / Wayne Thomas (2)
John Tonelli	NY Islanders	Jan. 6/81	Tor. 3	at	NYI 6	Jiri Crha (4) / empty net (1)
Wayne Gretzky	Edmonton	Feb. 18/81	St.L. 2	at	Edm. 9	Mike Liut (3) / Ed Staniowski (2)
Wayne Gretzky	Edmonton	Dec. 30/81	Phi. 5	at	Edm. 7	Pete Peeters (4) / empty net (1)
Grant Mulvey	Chicago	Feb. 3/82	St.L. 5	at	Chi. 9	Mike Liut (4) / Gary Edwards (1)
Bryan Trottier	NY Islanders	Feb. 13/82	Phi. 2	at	NYI 8	Pete Peeters
Willy Lindstrom	Winnipeg	Mar. 2/82	Wpg. 7	at	Phi. 6	Pete Peeters
Mark Pavelich	NY Rangers	Feb. 23/83	Hfd. 3	at	NYR 11	Greg Millen
Jari Kurri	Edmonton	Nov. 19/83	N.J. 4	at	Edm. 13	Glenn Resch (3) / Ron Low (2)
Bengt Gustafsson	Washington	Jan. 8/84	Wsh. 7	at	Phi. 1	Pelle Lindbergh
Pat Hughes	Edmonton	Feb. 3/84	Cgy. 5	at	Edm. 10	Don Edwards (3) / Reggie Lemelin (2)
Wayne Gretzky	Edmonton	Dec. 15/84	Edm. 8	at	St.L. 2	Rick Wamsley (4) / Mike Liut (1)
Dave Andreychuk	Buffalo	Feb. 6/86	Buf. 8	at	Bos. 6	Pat Riggin (1) / Doug Keans (4)
Wayne Gretzky	Edmonton	Dec. 6/87	Min. 4	at	Edm. 10	Don Beaupre (4) / Kari Takko (1)
Mario Lemieux	Pittsburgh	Dec. 31/88	N.J. 6	at	Pit. 8	Bob Sauve (3) / Chris Terreri (2)
Joe Nieuwendyk	Calgary	Jan. 11/89	Wpg. 3	at	Cgy. 8	Daniel Berthiaume
Mats Sundin	Quebec	Mar. 5/92	Que. 10	at	Hfd. 4	Peter Sidorkiewicz (3) / Kay Whitmore (2)
Mario Lemieux	Pittsburgh	Apr. 9/93	Pit. 10	at	NYR 4	Corey Hirsch (3) / Mike Richter (2)
Peter Bondra	Washington	Feb. 5/94	T.B. 3	at	Wsh. 6	Daren Puppa (4) / Pat Jablonski (1)
Mike Ricci	Quebec	Feb. 17/94	Que. 8	at	S.J. 2	Arturs Irbe (3) / Jimmy Waite (2)
Alexei Zhamnov	Winnipeg	Apr. 1/95	Wpg. 7	at	L.A. 7	Kelly Hrudey (3) / Grant Fuhr (2)
Mario Lemieux	Pittsburgh	Mar. 26/96	St.L. 4	at	Pit. 8	Grant Fuhr (1) / Jon Casey (4)
Sergei Fedorov	Detroit	Dec. 26/96	Wsh. 4	at	Det. 5	Jim Carey

Players' 500th Goals

Regular Season

Player	Team	Date	Game No.	Score			Opposing Goaltender	Total Goals	Total Games
Maurice Richard	Montreal	Oct. 19/57	863	Chi. 1	at	Mtl. 3	Glenn Hall	544	978
Gordie Howe	Detroit	Mar. 14/62	1,045	Det. 2	at	NYR 3	Gump Worsley	801	1,767
Bobby Hull	Chicago	Feb. 21/70	861	NYR 2	at	Chi. 4	Ed Giacomin	610	1,063
Jean Béliveau	Montreal	Feb. 11/71	1,101	Min. 2	at	Mtl. 6	Gilles Gilbert	507	1,125
Frank Mahovlich	Montreal	Mar. 21/73	1,105	Van. 2	at	Mtl. 3	Dunc Wilson	533	1,181
Phil Esposito	Boston	Dec. 22/74	803	Det. 4	at	Bos. 5	Jim Rutherford	717	1,282
John Bucyk	Boston	Oct. 30/75	1,370	St.L. 2	at	Bos. 3	Yves Bélanger	556	1,540
Stan Mikita	Chicago	Feb. 27/77	1,221	Van. 4	at	Chi. 3	Cesare Maniago	541	1,394
Marcel Dionne	Los Angeles	Dec. 14/82	887	L.A. 2	at	Wsh. 7	Al Jensen	731	1,348
Guy Lafleur	Montreal	Dec. 20/83	918	Mtl. 6	at	N.J. 0	Glenn Resch	560	1,126
Mike Bossy	NY Islanders	Jan. 2/86	647	Bos. 5	at	NYI 7	empty net	573	752
Gilbert Perreault	Buffalo	Mar. 9/86	1,159	N.J. 3	at	Buf. 4	Alain Chevrier	512	1,191
Wayne Gretzky	Edmonton	Nov. 22/86	575	Van. 2	at	Edm. 5	empty net	894	1,487
Lanny McDonald	Calgary	Mar. 21/89	1,107	NYI 1	at	Cgy. 4	Mark Fitzpatrick	500	1,111
Bryan Trottier	NY Islanders	Feb. 13/90	1,104	Cgy. 4	at	NYI 2	Rick Wamsley	524	1,279
Mike Gartner	NY Rangers	Oct. 14/91	936	Wsh. 5	at	NYR 3	Mike Liut	708	1,432
Michel Goulet	Chicago	Feb. 16/92	951	Cgy. 5	at	Chi. 5	Jeff Reese	548	1,089
Jari Kurri	Los Angeles	Oct. 17/92	833	Bos. 6	at	L.A. 8	empty net	601	1,251
Dino Ciccarelli	Detroit	Jan. 8/94	946	Det. 6	at	L.A. 3	Kelly Hrudey	608	1,232
*Mario Lemieux	Pittsburgh	Oct. 26/95	605	Pit. 7	at	NYI 5	Tommy Soderstrom	682	879
*Mark Messier	NY Rangers	Nov. 6/95	1,141	Cgy. 2	at	NYR 4	Rick Tabaracci	676	1,680
*Steve Yzerman	Detroit	Jan. 17/96	906	Col. 2	at	Det. 3	Patrick Roy	660	1,378
Dale Hawerchuk	St. Louis	Jan. 31/96	1,103	St.L. 4	at	Tor. 0	Felix Potvin	518	1,188
*Brett Hull	St. Louis	Dec. 22/96	693	L.A. 4	at	St.L. 7	Stephane Fiset	716	1,183
Joe Mullen	Pittsburgh	Mar. 14/97	1,052	Pit. 3	at	Col. 6	Patrick Roy	502	1,062
*Dave Andreychuk	New Jersey	Mar. 15/97	1,070	Wsh. 2	at	N.J. 3	Bill Ranford	613	1,515
*Luc Robitaille	Los Angeles	Jan. 7/99	928	Buf. 2	at	L.A. 4	Dwayne Roloson	631	1,286
Pat Verbeek	Detroit	Mar. 22/00	1,285	Cgy. 2	at	Det. 2	Fred Brathwaite	522	1,424
*Ron Francis	Carolina	Jan. 2/02	1,533	Bos. 6	at	Car. 3	Byron Dafoe	536	1,651
*Brendan Shanahan	Detroit	Mar. 23/02	1,100	Det. 2	at	Col. 0	Patrick Roy	533	1,186
*Joe Sakic	Colorado	Dec. 11/02	1,044	Col. 1	at	Van. 3	Dan Cloutier	509	1,074
*Joe Nieuwendyk	New Jersey	Jan. 17/03	1,094	N.J. 2	at	Car. 1	Kevin Weekes	511	1,113
*Jaromir Jagr	Washington	Feb. 4/03	928	Wsh. 5	at	T.B. 1	John Grahame	506	950

*Active

A five-time NHL scoring champion, Jaromir Jagr has continued to rank among the NHL leaders during his first two seasons with Washington. Jagr had 36 goals last season and joined Joe Sakic and Joe Nieuwendyk in reaching 500 for their careers.

Players' 1,000th Points

Regular Season

Player	Team	Date	Game No.	G or A	Score	Total Points G	A	PTS	Total Games
Gordie Howe	Detroit	Nov. 27/60	938	(A)	Tor. 0 at Det. 2	801	1,049	1,850	1,767
Jean Béliveau	Montreal	Mar. 3/68	911	(G)	Mtl. 2 at Det. 5	507	712	1,219	1,125
Alex Delvecchio	Detroit	Feb. 16/69	1,143	(A)	L.A. 3 at Det. 6	456	825	1,281	1,549
Bobby Hull	Chicago	Dec. 13/70	909	(A)	Min. 2 at Chi. 5	610	560	1,170	1,063
Norm Ullman	Toronto	Oct. 16/71	1,113	(A)	NYR 5 at Tor. 3	490	739	1,229	1,410
Stan Mikita	Chicago	Oct. 15/72	924	(A)	St.L. 3 at Chi. 1	541	926	1,467	1,394
John Bucyk	Boston	Nov. 9/72	1,144	(A)	Det. 3 at Bos. 8	556	813	1,369	1,540
Frank Mahovlich	Montreal	Feb. 17/73	1,090	(A)	Phi. 7 at Mtl. 6	533	570	1,103	1,181
Henri Richard	Montreal	Dec. 20/73	1,194	(A)	Mtl. 2 at Buf. 2	358	688	1,046	1,256
Phil Esposito	Boston	Feb. 15/74	745	(A)	Bos. 4 at Van. 2	717	873	1,590	1,282
Rod Gilbert	NY Rangers	Feb. 19/77	1,027	(G)	NYR 2 at NYI 5	406	615	1,021	1,065
Jean Ratelle	Boston	Apr. 3/77	1,007	(A)	Tor. 4 at Bos. 7	491	776	1,267	1,281
Marcel Dionne	Los Angeles	Jan. 7/81	740	(A)	L.A. 5 at Hfd. 3	731	1,040	1,771	1,348
Guy Lafleur	Montreal	Mar. 4/81	720	(G)	Mtl. 9 at Wpg. 3	560	793	1,353	1,126
Bobby Clarke	Philadelphia	Mar. 19/81	922	(G)	Bos. 3 at Phi. 5	358	852	1,210	1,144
Gilbert Perreault	Buffalo	Apr. 3/82	871	(A)	Buf. 5 at Mtl. 4	512	814	1,326	1,191
Darryl Sittler	Philadelphia	Jan. 20/83	927	(A)	Cgy. 2 at Phi. 5	484	637	1,121	1,096
Wayne Gretzky	Edmonton	Dec. 19/84	424	(A)	L.A. 3 at Edm. 7	894	1,963	2,875	1,487
Bryan Trottier	NY Islanders	Jan. 29/85	726	(G)	Min. 4 at NYI 4	524	901	1,425	1,279
Mike Bossy	NY Islanders	Jan. 24/86	656	(G)	NYI 7 at Wsh. 5	573	553	1,126	752
Denis Potvin	NY Islanders	Apr. 4/87	987	(G)	Buf. 6 at NYI 6	310	742	1,052	1,060
Bernie Federko	St. Louis	Mar. 19/88	855	(A)	Hfd. 5 at St.L. 3	369	761	1,130	1,000
Lanny McDonald	Calgary	Mar. 7/89	1,101	(G)	Wpg. 5 at Cgy. 9	500	506	1,006	1,111
Peter Stastny	Quebec	Oct. 19/89	682	(G)	Que. 5 at Chi. 3	450	789	1,239	977
Jari Kurri	Edmonton	Jan. 2/90	716	(G)	Edm. 6 at St.L. 4	601	797	1,398	1,251
Denis Savard	Chicago	Mar. 11/90	727	(A)	St.L. 6 at Chi. 4	473	865	1,338	1,196
Paul Coffey	Pittsburgh	Dec. 22/90	770	(A)	Pit. 4 at NYI 3	396	1,135	1,531	1,409
*Mark Messier	Edmonton	Jan. 13/91	822	(A)	Edm. 5 at Phi. 3	676	1,168	1,844	1,680
Dave Taylor	Los Angeles	Feb. 5/91	930	(A)	L.A. 3 at Phi. 2	431	638	1,069	1,111
Michel Goulet	Chicago	Feb. 23/91	878	(A)	Chi. 3 at Min. 3	548	604	1,152	1,089
Dale Hawerchuk	Buffalo	Mar. 8/91	781	(G)	Chi. 5 at Buf. 3	518	891	1,409	1,188
Bobby Smith	Minnesota	Nov. 30/91	986	(A)	Min. 4 at Tor. 3	357	679	1,036	1,077
Mike Gartner	NY Rangers	Jan. 4/92	971	(A)	NYR 4 at N.J. 6	708	627	1,335	1,432
Raymond Bourque	Boston	Feb. 29/92	933	(A)	Wsh. 5 at Bos. 5	410	1,169	1,579	1,612
*Mario Lemieux	Pittsburgh	Mar. 24/92	513	(A)	Pit. 3 at Det. 4	682	1,010	1,692	879
Glenn Anderson	Toronto	Feb. 22/93	954	(G)	Tor. 8 at Van. 1	498	601	1,099	1,129
*Steve Yzerman	Detroit	Feb. 24/93	737	(A)	Det. 7 at Buf. 10	660	1,010	1,670	1,378
*Ron Francis	Pittsburgh	Oct. 28/93	893	(A)	Que. 7 at Pit. 3	536	1,222	1,758	1,651
Bernie Nicholls	New Jersey	Feb. 13/94	858	(G)	N.J. 3 at T.B. 3	475	734	1,209	1,127
Dino Ciccarelli	Detroit	Mar. 9/94	957	(G)	Det. 5 at Cgy. 1	608	592	1,200	1,232
Brian Propp	Hartford	Mar. 19/94	1,008	(G)	Hfd. 5 at Phi. 3	425	579	1,004	1,016
Joe Mullen	Pittsburgh	Feb. 7/95	935	(A)	Fla. 3 at Pit. 7	502	561	1,063	1,062
Steve Larmer	NY Rangers	Mar. 8/95	983	(A)	N.J. 4 at NYR 6	441	571	1,012	1,006
*Doug Gilmour	Toronto	Dec. 23/95	935	(G)	Edm. 1 at Tor. 6	450	964	1,414	1,474
Larry Murphy	Toronto	Mar. 27/96	1,228	(A)	Tor. 6 at Van. 2	287	929	1,216	1,615
*Dave Andreychuk	New Jersey	Apr. 7/96	998	(G)	NYR 2 at N.J. 4	613	668	1,281	1,515
*Adam Oates	Washington	Oct. 8/97	830	(A)	Wsh. 6 at NYI 3	339	1,063	1,402	1,277
*Phil Housley	Washington	Nov. 8/97	1,081	(A)	Edm. 1 at Wsh. 2	338	894	1,232	1,495
Dale Hunter	Washington	Jan. 9/98	1,308	(A)	Phi. 1 at Wsh. 4	323	697	1,020	1,407
Pat LaFontaine	NY Rangers	Jan. 22/98	847	(A)	Phi. 4 at NYR 3	468	545	1,013	865
*Luc Robitaille	Los Angeles	Jan. 29/98	882	(A)	Cgy. 3 at L.A. 5	631	688	1,319	1,286
*Al MacInnis	St. Louis	Apr. 7/98	1,056	(A)	St.L. 3 at Det. 5	340	932	1,272	1,413
*Brett Hull	Dallas	Nov. 14/98	815	(A)	Dal. 3 at Bos. 1	716	606	1,322	1,183
Brian Bellows	Washington	Jan. 2/99	1,147	(A)	Tor. 2 at Wsh. 5	485	537	1,022	1,188
*Pierre Turgeon	St. Louis	Oct. 9/99	881	(G)	St.L. 4 at Edm. 3	480	754	1,234	1,139
*Joe Sakic	Colorado	Dec. 27/99	810	(A)	St.L. 1 at Col. 5	509	806	1,315	1,074
Pat Verbeek	Detroit	Feb. 27/00	1,275	(A)	T.B. 1 at Det. 3	522	541	1,063	1,424
*V. Damphousse	San Jose	Oct. 14/00	1,090	(A)	Bos. 2 at S.J. 5	420	744	1,164	1,296
*Jaromir Jagr	Pittsburgh	Dec. 30/00	763	(A)	Ott. 3 at Pit. 5	506	729	1,235	950
*Mark Recchi	Philadelphia	Mar. 13/01	920	(A)	St.L. 2 at Phi. 5	430	696	1,126	1,091
*Theoren Fleury	NY Rangers	Oct. 29/01	960	(A)	Dal. 2 at NYR 4	455	633	1,088	1,084
*B. Shanahan	Detroit	Jan. 12/02	1,073	(A)	Dal. 2 at Det. 5	533	565	1,098	1,186
*Jeremy Roenick	Philadelphia	Jan. 30/02	961	(G)	Phi. 1 at Ott. 3	456	617	1,073	1,062
*Mike Modano	Dallas	Nov. 15/02	965	(G)	Col. 3 at Dal. 4	444	618	1,062	1,025
*Joe Nieuwendyk	New Jersey	Feb. 23/03	1,094	(G)	N.J. 4 at Pit. 3	511	501	1,012	1,113
*Mats Sundin	Toronto	Mar. 10/03	994	(G)	Tor. 3 at Edm. 2	434	580	1,014	1,005

*Active

Mike Modano (top), Joe Nieuwendyk (center) and Mats Sundin (above) each reached the 1,000-point plateau during the 2002-03 season. Modano and Sundin also reached 1,000 games played.

Individual Awards

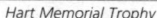

Hart Memorial Trophy

Art Ross Trophy

Calder Memorial Trophy

James Norris Memorial Trophy

HART MEMORIAL TROPHY

An annual award "to the player adjudged to be the most valuable to his team." Winner selected in a poll by the Professional Hockey Writers' Association in the 30 NHL cities at the end of the regular schedule. The winner receives $10,000 and the runners-up $6,000 and $4,000.

History: The Hart Memorial Trophy was presented by the National Hockey League in 1960 after the original Hart Trophy was retired to the Hockey Hall of Fame. The original Hart Trophy was donated to the NHL in 1923 by Dr. David A. Hart, father of Cecil Hart, former manager-coach of the Montreal Canadiens.

2002-03 Winner: **Peter Forsberg, Colorado Avalanche**
Runners-up: Markus Naslund, Vancouver Canucks
Martin Brodeur, New Jersey Devils

Center Peter Forsberg of the Colorado Avalanche captured the Hart Memorial Trophy ahead of fellow Ornskoldsvik, Sweden native Markus Naslund of the Vancouver Canucks. In winning the trophy for the first time, Forsberg becomes the first native of Sweden to be named the NHL's most valuable player. He was named on 60 of 62 ballots and received 38 first-place votes for 508 points. Naslund received votes on 59 ballots and earned five first-place votes for 342 points. Martin Brodeur of the New Jersey Devils received 14 first-place votes, but had just 311 points overall.

Forsberg captured the Art Ross Trophy as the NHL's points leader with 29 goals and 77 assists for 106 points in 75 games. He also led the league in assists and shared the plus-minus lead with teammate Milan Hejduk (+52). The line of Forsberg, right winger Hejduk and left winger Alex Tanguay averaged four points per game following the hiring of new head coach Tony Granato on December 19, helping Colorado capture its NHL-record ninth consecutive division title.

ART ROSS TROPHY

An annual award "to the player who leads the league in scoring points at the end of the regular season." The winner receives $10,000 and the runners-up $6,000 and $4,000.

History: Arthur Howie Ross, former manager-coach of the Boston Bruins, presented the trophy to the National Hockey League in 1947. If two players finish the schedule with the same number of points, the trophy is awarded in the following manner: 1. Player with most goals. 2. Player with fewer games played. 3. Player scoring first goal of the season.

2002-03 Winner: **Peter Forsberg, Colorado Avalanche**
Runners-up: Markus Naslund, Vancouver Canucks
Joe Thornton, Boston Bruins

Center Peter Forsberg of the Colorado Avalanche received the Art Ross Trophy for the first time, becoming the first Swedish-born player to lead the NHL in scoring after tallying 106 points (29 goals, 77 assists) in 75 games. Forsberg passed fellow Swede Markus Naslund of Vancouver (48 goals, 56 assists, 104 points) to claim the scoring title on the last day of the NHL season. He also led Colorado past the Canucks for top spot in the Northwest Division (105 points to 104) to claim their record ninth straight divisional title. Boston's Joe Thornton finished third in scoring with 101 points (36 goals, 65 assists). With a rare combination of grace and power, Forsberg has scored at least 80 points six times in his career, including more than 100 twice.

CALDER MEMORIAL TROPHY

An annual award "to the player selected as the most proficient in his first year of competition in the National Hockey League." Winner selected in a poll by the Professional Hockey Writers' Association at the end of the regular schedule. The winner receives $10,000 and the runners-up $6,000 and $4,000.

History: From 1936-37 until his death in 1943, Frank Calder, NHL President, bought a trophy each year to be given permanently to the outstanding rookie. After Calder's death, the NHL presented the Calder Memorial Trophy in his memory. To be eligible for the award, a player cannot have played more than 25 games in any single preceding season nor in six or more games in each of any two preceding seasons in any major professional league. Beginning in 1990-91, to be eligible for this award a player must not have attained his twenty-sixth birthday by September 15th of the season in which he is eligible.

2002-03 Winner: **Barret Jackman, St. Louis Blues**
Runners-up: Henrik Zetterberg, Detroit Red Wings
Rick Nash, Columbus Blue Jackets

Defenseman Barret Jackman of the St. Louis Blues was elected winner of the Calder Memorial Trophy. Jackman received 39 of 62 first-place votes and was the second choice on 15 other ballots for 506 points. Henrik Zetterberg of Detroit, named on each of the 62 ballots, had 18 first-place votes and ranked second with 462 points. Rick Nash received two first-place votes and finished third in balloting with 190 points.

With Norris Trophy and Hart Trophy-winning defenseman Chris Pronger sidelined for most of the season, Jackman played a key role in helping the Blues post 99 points on the season. Jackman was the only Blues player to skate in all 82 games and played an average of 20:04 per game. He also led the Blues, and finished second among all rookies, in plus-minus (+23).

Jackman is the first Calder Trophy winner in the Blues' 36-year history and the first defenseman since the New York Islanders' Bryan Berard in 1997. He is just the sixth defenseman since 1968 (Jackman, Berard, the New York Rangers' Brian Leetch in 1989, Calgary's Gary Suter in 1986, Boston's Raymond Bourque in 1980 and the Islanders' Denis Potvin in 1974) to be named the NHL's rookie of the year.

JAMES NORRIS MEMORIAL TROPHY

An annual award "to the defense player who demonstrates throughout the season the greatest all-round ability in the position." Winner selected in a poll by the Professional Hockey Writers' Association at the end of the regular schedule. The winner receives $10,000 and the runners-up $6,000 and $4,000.

History: The James Norris Memorial Trophy was presented in 1953 by the four children of the late James Norris in memory of the former owner-president of the Detroit Red Wings.

2002-03 Winner: **Nicklas Lidstrom, Detroit Red Wings**
Runners-up: Al MacInnis, St. Louis Blues
Derian Hatcher, Dallas Stars

Nicklas Lidstrom of the Detroit Red Wings won his third consecutive James Norris Memorial Trophy after having finished as the runner-up for three straight years prior to his first win in 2001. Lidstrom was named on all 62 ballots and received 42 first-place votes for 560 points, ahead of second-place Al MacInnis of the St. Louis Blues (20 first-place votes, 486 points) and Dallas Stars captain Derian Hatcher (142 points). MacInnis also was named on all 62 ballots. Lidstrom is the first defenseman to win the Norris Trophy in three consecutive seasons since Boston's Bobby Orr captured the award a record eight consecutive times, from 1968 through 1975.

Lidstrom finished third in scoring among defensemen with 62 points (18 goals, 44 assists) in 82 games, led all players in ice time per game (29:20) and ranked third in plus-minus (+40).

Vezina Trophy

Lady Byng Memorial Trophy

Frank J. Selke Trophy

Conn Smythe Trophy

VEZINA TROPHY

An annual award "to the goalkeeper adjudged to be the best at his position" as voted by the general managers of each of the 30 clubs. The winner receives $10,000, and the runners-up $6,000 and $4,000.

History: Leo Dandurand, Louis Letourneau and Joe Cattarinich, former owners of the Montreal Canadiens, presented the trophy to the National Hockey League in 1926-27 in memory of Georges Vezina, outstanding goalkeeper of the Canadiens who collapsed during an NHL game on November 28, 1925, and died of tuberculosis a few months later. Until the 1981-82 season, the goalkeeper(s) of the team allowing the fewest number of goals during the regular season were awarded the Vezina Trophy.

2002-03 Winner: Martin Brodeur, New Jersey Devils
Runners-up: Marty Turco, Dallas Stars
Ed Belfour, Toronto Maple Leafs

Martin Brodeur of the New Jersey Devils captured the Vezina Trophy for the first time in his career in his fourth year as a finalist. He had finished second in 1997 and 1998 and third in 2001. Brodeur received votes on 29 of 30 ballots, including 24 first-place votes, to post 131 points. The Dallas Stars' Marty Turco, in his first year as a finalist, was named on 23 of 30 ballots, including three first-place votes, to finish second with 59 points. Toronto's Ed Belfour had two first-place votes and finished third in the balloting with 28 points.

Brodeur posted a 41-23-9 record with a 2.02 goals-against average in 73 games, leading all goaltenders in victories and shutouts (nine) and capturing the William M. Jennings Trophy as the goaltender on the club allowing the fewest goals in the regular season for the third time in his career.

CONN SMYTHE TROPHY

An annual award "to the most valuable player for his team in the playoffs." Winner selected by the Professional Hockey Writers' Association at the conclusion of the final game in the Stanley Cup Finals. The winner receives $10,000.

History: Presented by Maple Leaf Gardens Limited in 1964 to honor Conn Smythe, the former coach, manager, president and owner-governor of the Toronto Maple Leafs.

2002-03 Winner: Jean-Sebastien Giguere, Mighty Ducks of Anaheim

Mighty Ducks of Anaheim goaltender Jean-Sebastien Giguere won the Conn Smythe Trophy after posting a 15-6 record in 21 games with a 1.62 goals-against average, .945 save percentage and five shutouts during his first appearance in the playoffs. Giguere is the fifth player to win the Conn Smythe Trophy as a member of the losing team in the Stanley Cup Finals, joining fellow goaltenders Roger Crozier (Detroit Red Wings, 1966), Glenn Hall (St. Louis Blues, 1968), and Ron Hextall (Philadelphia Flyers, 1987), plus right winger Reggie Leach (Philadelphia, 1976). During the playoffs, Giguere mounted a shutout streak of 217:54, the fifth longest in NHL history, and went 7-0 in overtime, becoming the first goaltender to win each of his first seven overtime playoff decisions. His current playoff overtime shutout streak of 168:27 is the longest in NHL history.

LADY BYNG MEMORIAL TROPHY

An annual award "to the player adjudged to have exhibited the best type of sportsmanship and gentlemanly conduct combined with a high standard of playing ability." Winner selected in a poll by the Professional Hockey Writers' Association at the end of the regular schedule. The winner receives $10,000 and the runners-up $6,000 and $4,000.

History: Lady Byng, wife of Canada's Governor-General at the time, presented the Lady Byng Trophy in the 1924-25 season. After Frank Boucher of the New York Rangers won the award seven times in eight seasons, he was given the trophy to keep and Lady Byng donated another trophy in 1936. After Lady Byng's death in 1949, the National Hockey League presented a new trophy, changing the name to Lady Byng Memorial Trophy.

2002-03 Winner: Alexander Mogilny, Toronto Maple Leafs
Runners-up: Nicklas Lidstrom, Detroit Red Wings
Mike Modano, Dallas Stars

Toronto Maple Leafs right winger Alexander Mogilny earned the Lady Byng Memorial Trophy in the closest NHL trophy race of the year. Mogilny edged Detroit's Nicklas Lidstrom by a count of 200 points to 172. Both players received 10 first-place votes, but Lidstrom finished second in overall voting for the fourth time in the past five seasons. Mike Modano of Dallas was third with six first-place votes and 130 points.

FRANK J. SELKE TROPHY

An annual award "to the forward who best excels in the defensive aspects of the game." Winner selected in a poll by the Professional Hockey Writers' Association at the end of the regular schedule. The winner receives $10,000 and the runners-up $6,000 and $4,000.

History: Presented to the National Hockey League in 1977 by the Board of Governors of the NHL in honor of Frank J. Selke, one of the great architects of NHL championship teams.

2002-03 Winner: Jere Lehtinen, Dallas Stars
Runners-up: John Madden, New Jersey Devils
Wes Walz, Minnesota Wild

Dallas Stars right winger Jere Lehtinen captured the Frank J. Selke Trophy for the third time in his career. Lehtinen outdistanced the field by receiving 39 first-place votes and was named on 57 of 62 ballots for 476 points. New Jersey Devils center John Madden, the 2001 Selke winner, was second with 241 points. He had seven first-place votes. Wes Walz of Minnesota received two first-place votes and finished third in balloting with 130 points.

Lehtinen led the Stars, and was fourth in the NHL overall, with a +39 rating – the best of his eight-year career. He also led the team with a career-high 31 goals and was second among Stars forwards in ice time per game (18:47). He joins Bob Gainey (four) and Guy Carbonneau (three) as the only players with three or more Selke Trophy wins.

WILLIAM M. JENNINGS TROPHY

An annual award "to the goalkeeper(s) having played a minimum of 25 games for the team with the fewest goals scored against it." Winners selected on regular-season play. The winner receives $10,000, and the runners-up $6,000 and $4,000.

History: The Jennings Trophy was presented in 1981-82 by the National Hockey League's Board of Governors to honor the late William M. Jennings, longtime governor and president of the New York Rangers and one of the great builders of hockey in the United States.

2002-03 Winners: Martin Brodeur, New Jersey Devils
Roman Cechmanek and Robert Esche, Philadelphia Flyers
Runners-up: Marty Turco and Ron Tugnutt, Dallas Stars
Dwayne Roloson and Manny Fernandez, Minnesota Wild

The New Jersey Devils' Martin Brodeur and the Philadelphia Flyers' goaltending tandem of Roman Cechmanek and Robert Esche were presented with the William M. Jennings Trophy. Brodeur played in 73 of the Devils' 82 games, led all goaltenders in victories (41) and shutouts (nine) and was fourth in goals-against average (2.02). The Devils allowed 166 goals, tied with the Philadelphia Flyers for the fewest in the NHL. It is the third time Brodeur has won the Jennings Trophy.

Cechmanek, later acquired by the Los Angeles Kings in a trade on May 28, earned his first career Jennings Trophy. Cechmanek appeared in 58 games and posted a 33-15-10 record, 1.83 goals-against average and .925 save percentage. He finished among goaltending leaders in goals-against average (second) and save percentage (third). Esche is also a first-time winner. He appeared in 30 games, posting a 12-9-3 record, 2.20 goals-against average and .907 save percentage.

William M. Jennings Trophy

Jack Adams Award

Bill Masterton Trophy

Lester Patrick Trophy

Lester B. Pearson Award

JACK ADAMS AWARD

An annual award presented by the National Hockey League Broadcasters' Association to "the NHL coach adjudged to have contributed the most to his team's success." Winner selected by a poll among members of the NHL Broadcasters' Association at the end of the regular season. The winner receives $1,000 from the NHLBA.

History: The award was presented by the NHL Broadcasters' Association in 1974 to commemorate the late Jack Adams, coach and general manager of the Detroit Red Wings, whose lifetime dedication to hockey serves as an inspiration to all who aspire to further the game.

2002-03 Winner: **Jacques Lemaire, Minnesota Wild**
        Runners-up: **John Tortorella, Tampa Bay Lightning**
                        Jacques Martin, Ottawa Senators

Minnesota Wild head coach Jacques Lemaire captured the Jack Adams Award for the second time in his career, having won it previously with New Jersey in 1994. Lemaire received 41 first-place votes and 242 points, easily outdistancing Tampa Bay's John Tortorella (eight first-place votes, 107 points) and Ottawa's Jacques Martin (six and 79). Lemaire guided the Minnesota Wild to a 42-29-10-1 record for 95 points, a 22-point improvement over 2001-02 and the second-best mark by a third-year club since 1967. The Wild became the third expansion team since 1990 to earn a Stanley Cup playoff berth in its third NHL season and the team's goals-against average of 2.14 ranked fourth in the league.

BILL MASTERTON MEMORIAL TROPHY

An annual award under the trusteeship of the Professional Hockey Writers' Association to "the National Hockey League player who best exemplifies the qualities of perseverance, sportsmanship and dedication to hockey." Winner selected by a poll among the 30 chapters of the PHWA at the end of the regular season. A $2,500 grant from the PHWA is awarded annually to the Bill Masterton Scholarship Fund, based in Bloomington, MN, in the name of the Masterton Trophy winner.

History: The trophy was presented by the NHL Writers' Association in 1968 to commemorate the late Bill Masterton, a player with the Minnesota North Stars, who exhibited to a high degree the qualities of perseverance, sportsmanship and dedication to hockey, and who died January 15, 1968.

2002-03 Winner: **Steve Yzerman, Detroit Red Wings**
        Runners-up: **Bryan Berard, Boston Bruins**
                        Steve Rucchin, Mighty Ducks of Anaheim

Detroit Red Wings captain Steve Yzerman made a triumphant and emotional return from off-season knee surgery on February 24 in a 5-4 victory against the Los Angeles Kings, eight months after completing a dream season highlighted by an Olympic gold medal and Stanley Cup championship. In order to return for his 20th NHL season, Yzerman underwent an osteotomy, a realignment procedure, followed by months of arduous rehabilitation. Inspired by the return of their leader, the longest serving captain in NHL history, the Red Wings were 14-1-0-1 with Yzerman in the lineup and earned the Western Conference's second seed. Yzerman has battled through several knee injuries during his great career.

LESTER PATRICK TROPHY

An annual award "for outstanding service to hockey in the United States." Eligible recipients are players, officials, coaches, executives and referees. Winners are selected by an award committee consisting of the commissioner of the NHL, an NHL governor, a representative of the New York Rangers, a member of the Hockey Hall of Fame builder's section, a member of the Hockey Hall of Fame player's section, a member of the U.S. Hockey Hall of Fame, a member of the NHL Broadcasters' Association and a member of the Professional Hockey Writers' Association. Each except the League Commissioner is rotated annually. The winner receives a miniature of the trophy.

History: Presented by the New York Rangers in 1966 to honor the late Lester Patrick, longtime general manager and coach of the New York Rangers, whose teams finished out of the playoffs only once in his first 16 years with the club.

2002-03 Winners: **Raymond Bourque**
                         Ron DeGregorio
                         Willie O'Ree

Raymond Bourque, who retired following the 2000–01 season, spent 22 years in the NHL, 21 of them with the Boston Bruins (he was traded to Colorado late in his 21st season). With 1,612 games played, he ranks fifth on the all-time list, trailing only Gordie Howe, Mark Messier, Ron Francis and Larry Murphy. His number, 77, is one of nine to have been retired by the Bruins, and his distinguished career on the ice is mirrored by tireless off-ice contributions to a variety of youth hockey programs. Bourque won the Calder Memorial Trophy as NHL rookie of the year in 1980, won the Norris Trophy as the league's top defenseman five times, was a first-team NHL All-Star a record 13 times, and won the Stanley Cup as a member of the Colorado Avalanche in 2001.

Ron DeGregorio, a current USA Hockey vice president and chairperson of the organization's International Council, has been a player, coach and administrator for more than 40 years. He was instrumental in the development of amateur hockey in New England and is a member of the Board of Directors of USA Hockey.

The first player of African-American descent to play in the NHL, Willie O'Ree has contributed greatly to the growth of the game in his current position as director of youth development for the NHL and NHL Diversity. O'Ree travels throughout North America to promote hockey and annually hosts the Willie O'Ree All-Star Weekend, an event that brings together young hockey players (boys and girls) from diverse ethnic and economic backgrounds. O'Ree played two games for the Boston Bruins in 1957–58 and 43 more in 1960–61. He also played 13 seasons in the Western Hockey League, six with the Los Angeles Blades and seven with the San Diego Gulls.

LESTER B. PEARSON AWARD

An annual award presented to the NHL's outstanding player as selected by the members of the National Hockey League Players' Association. The winner receives $20,000, and the two finalists receive $10,000 each to donate to the grassroots hockey program of their choice, through the NHLPA's Goals & Dreams Fund.

History: The award was first presented in 1970-71 by the NHLPA in honor of the late Lester B. Pearson, former Prime Minister of Canada.

2002-03 Winner: **Markus Naslund, Vancouver Canucks**
        Runners-up: **Peter Forsberg, Colorado Avalanche**
                        Joe Thornton, Boston Bruins

Markus Naslund, a 10-year veteran and team captain of the Vancouver Canucks, became the first Swedish-born player, and the first Vancouver Canucks player, to win the Lester B. Pearson Award. Naslund finished second for the scoring title with 48 goals and 56 assists for 104 points. He led the league in game-winning goals (12) and power-play points (54). Naslund designated the Garth Brooks Teammates for Kids Foundation as the beneficiary of the $20,000 that accompanies the award. Garth Brooks' charity will triple the donation and distribute the funds to grassroots hockey and community-based programs in Naslund's home country of Sweden. As finalists, Peter Forsberg allocated $10,000 to a grassroots hockey program, while Thornton designated his $10,000 to the St. Thomas Minor Hockey Association.

King Clancy Memorial Trophy

Bud Light Plus-Minus Award

Presidents' Trophy

Maurice "Rocket" Richard Trophy

KING CLANCY MEMORIAL TROPHY

An annual award "to the player who best exemplifies leadership qualities on and off the ice and has made a noteworthy humanitarian contribution in his community."

History: The King Clancy Memorial Trophy was presented to the National Hockey League by the Board of Governors in 1988 to honor the late Frank "King" Clancy.

2002-03 Winner: Brendan Shanahan, Detroit Red Wings

Detroit Red Wings left winger Brendan Shanahan's generous spirit and kind heart continue to touch the lives of those less fortunate. Concerned about the number of unnecessary house fire-related deaths, and in honor of his late father, a fire fighter, Shanahan started a program with the City of Detroit and Detroit Fire Department to assist low-income families with the purchase and installation of smoke detectors. Shanahan produced a public service announcement encouraging donations and joined the Fire Department in installing the devices in residents' homes. In recognition of his outstanding service, which has resulted in the installation of thousands of smoke detectors, the Detroit Fire Department named Shanahan its 2001 Outstanding Citizen.

Quietly and without fanfare, Shanahan often visits and hosts terminally ill children and adults through his involvement with the Make-A-Wish Foundation. As numerous families will attest, Shanahan is aware of his responsibility as a role model and that a few minutes of his time can leave a lasting impression. A long-standing friendship with a young cancer patient, also named Brendan, is indicative. Over years of visits and Christmas card exchanges, the bond between the two grew and extended to their entire families. When the younger Brendan lost his battle in 2003, Shanahan scored a hat trick against Edmonton on February 20 in honor of his late friend and served as a pallbearer at his funeral the following day.

PRESIDENTS' TROPHY

An annual award to the club finishing the regular-season with the best overall record. The winner receives $350,000, to be split between the team and its players.

History: Presented to the National Hockey League in 1985-86 by the NHL Board of Governors to recognize the team compiling the top regular-season record.

2002-03 Winner: Ottawa Senators
Runners-up: Dallas Stars
Detroit Red Wings

The Ottawa Senators finished the 2002-03 regular season with a 52-21-8-1 record, collecting a franchise-high 52 wins and 113 points. They won the Presidents' Trophy and were the Eastern Conference leaders for the first time in team history while picking up their third Northeast Division title. The Senators were the NHL's third-best team at home (28-9-3-1) as well as the third best on the road (24-12-5-0) and were the only team in the NHL to finish in the top five in both goals for (263) and goals against (182). They are the first Canadian-based team to top the NHL in points since the 1989 Calgary Flames. Following Ottawa in the overall standings were a pair of Western Conference teams. The Dallas Stars finished with a record of 46-17-15-4 and 111 points, edging out Detroit for the best record in the west by a single point on the final day of the season. The Red Wings were 48-20-10-4 with 110 points.

MAURICE "ROCKET" RICHARD TROPHY

An annual award "presented to the player finishing the regular season as the League's goal-scoring leader." The winner receives $10,000.

History: A gift to the NHL from the Montreal Canadiens in 1999, the Maurice "Rocket" Richard Trophy honors one of the game's greatest stars. During his 18-year career with the Canadiens from 1942-43 through 1959-60, Richard was the first player in NHL history to score 50 goals in a season and 500 in his career. He played on eight Stanley Cup champions and led the League in goal scoring five times.

2002-03 Winner: Milan Hejduk, Colorado Avalanche
Runners-up: Markus Naslund, Vancouver Canucks
Todd Bertuzzi, Vancouver Canucks

Right winger Milan Hejduk of the Colorado Avalanche is the recipient of the Maurice "Rocket" Richard Trophy. Hejduk staged a dramatic late-season flourish to claim his first career goal-scoring title with 50 goals. Hejduk finished the season with goals in each of his last five games, scoring seven times, and provided the overtime game-winner with 10 seconds remaining at Anaheim on April 4 that enabled the Avalanche to win their NHL-record ninth consecutive division title two days later. Hejduk also had a seven-game goal streak from February 11 to 23, the longest in the NHL since 1998-99. Finishing behind Hejduk were Vancouver Canucks teammates Markus Naslund and Todd Bertuzzi. Naslund, who had a career-high 48 goals, also finished as the runner-up to Peter Forsberg for the Art Ross Trophy (106 points to 104). Bertuzzi's 46 goals were also a career high.

BUD LIGHT PLUS-MINUS AWARD

An annual award "to the player, having played a minimum of 60 games, who leads the League in plus-minus statistics" at the end of the regular season.

Bud Light will contribute $5,000 on behalf of the winner to the charity of his choice.

History: This award was first presented to the NHL in 1997-98 by Anheuser-Busch Inc. to recognize the League leader in plus-minus statistics. Plus-minus statistics are calculated by giving a player a "plus" when on-ice for an even-strength or short-handed goal scored by his team. He receives a "minus" when on-ice for an even-strength or short-handed goal scored by the opposing team. A plus-minus award has been presented since the 1982-83 season.

2002-03 Winners: Peter Forsberg, Colorado Avalanche
Milan Hejduk, Colorado Avalanche
Runners-up: Nicklas Lidstrom, Detroit Red Wings
Jere Lehtinen, Dallas Stars

Teammates Peter Forsberg and Milan Hejduk of the Colorado Avalanche, whose +52 rating led all National Hockey League players, were co-winners of the Bud Light Plus-Minus Award. Forsberg and Hejduk were followed by Detroit Red Wings defenseman Nicklas Lidstrom (+40), and three members of the Dallas Stars, Jere Lehtinen (+39), Derian Hatcher (+37) and Mike Modano (+34). Alex Tanguay (+34) and Adam Foote (+30) gave the Avalanche four players in the top 10.

MBNA Roger Crozier Saving Grace Award

Bud Light NHL All-Star Game
MVP Award

MBNA ROGER CROZIER SAVING GRACE AWARD

An award "presented to the goaltender having played a minimum of 25 games with the NHL's best save percentage during the regular season." The winner receives $25,000 to be donated to the youth hockey or educational program of his choice.

History: This award was first presented to the league in 1999-2000 by MBNA Corporation. It is named for Roger Crozier, one of the NHL's top goaltenders during his career. Crozier joined MBNA America Bank in 1983. He passed away on Jan. 11, 1996. Save percentage is calculated by dividing total saves by total shots faced.

2002-03 Winner: **Marty Turco, Dallas Stars**
**Runners-up: Dwayne Roloson, Minnesota Wild
Roman Cechmanek, Philadelphia Flyers**

Dallas Stars goaltender Marty Turco finished the regular season with a .932 save percentage (1,451 shots, 1,359 saves) in 55 games. He earned the Roger Crozier Saving Grace Award for a second time, winning previously in the 2000-01 season. Turco also led the league with a 1.72 goals-against average last season, the lowest goals-against average since 1939-40 (Dave Kerr, New York Rangers, 1.54), and helped lead Dallas to a first-place finish in the Western Conference. A check for $25,000 was donated to charity in his name. Trailing Turco were Dwayne Roloson of the Minnesota Wild (.927), Roman Cechmanek of the Philadelphia Flyers (.925), Manny Legace of the Detroit Red Wings (.925) and Manny Fernandez of the Minnesota Wild (.924).

BUD LIGHT NHL ALL-STAR GAME MVP AWARD

1962	Eddie Shack, Tor.	1983	Wayne Gretzky, Edm.
1963	Frank Mahovlich, Tor.	1984	Don Maloney, NYR
1964	Jean Beliveau, Mtl.	1985	Mario Lemieux, Pit.
1965	Gordie Howe, Det.	1986	Grant Fuhr, Edm.
1967	Henri Richard, Mtl.	1988	Mario Lemieux, Pit.
1968	Bruce Gamble, Tor.	1989	Wayne Gretzky, L.A.
1969	Frank Mahovlich, Det.	1990	Mario Lemieux, Pit.
1970	Bobby Hull, Chi.	1991	Vincent Damphousse, Tor.
1971	Bobby Hull, Chi.	1992	Brett Hull, St.L.
1972	Bobby Orr, Bos.	1993	Mike Gartner, NYR
1973	Greg Polis, Pit.	1994	Mike Richter, NYR
1974	Garry Unger, St.L.	1996	Raymond Bourque, Bos.
1975	Syl Apps Jr., Pit.	1997	Mark Recchi, Mtl.
1976	Pete Mahovlich, Mtl.	1998	Teemu Selanne, Ana.
1977	Rick Martin, Buf.	1999	Wayne Gretzky, NYR
1978	Billy Smith, NYI	2000	Pavel Bure, Fla.
1980	Reggie Leach, Phi.	2001	Bill Guerin, Bos.
1981	Mike Liut, St.L.	2002	Eric Daze, Chi.
1982	Mike Bossy, NYI	2003	Dany Heatley, Atl.

NHL AWARD MONEY BREAKDOWN — 2002-03

(Players on each club determine how team award money is divided.)

TEAM AWARDS

Stanley Cup Playoffs	Number of Clubs	Share Per Club	Total
Conference Quarter-Final Losers	8	$ 263,350	$2,106,800
Conference Semi-Final Losers	4	458,525	1,834,100
Conference Championship Losers	2	1,003,175	2,006,350
Stanley Cup Losers	1	1,631,250	1,631,250
Stanley Cup Winners	1	2,381,500	2,381,500
TOTAL PLAYOFF AWARD MONEY			$9,960,000

Final Standings, Regular Season	Number of Clubs	Share Per Club	Total
Presidents' Trophy			
Club's Share	1	$ 100,000	$ 100,000
Players' Share	1	250,000	250,000
Conference First Place*	2	500,000	1,000,000
Conference Second Place*	2	375,000	750,000
Conference Third Place*	2	250,000	500,000
Conference Fourth Place*	2	125,000	250,000
*based on points.			
TOTAL REGULAR-SEASON AWARD MONEY			$2,850,000

INDIVIDUAL AWARDS	Winner	First Runner-up	Second Runner-up
Hart, Calder, Norris, Ross, Vezina, Byng, Selke, Jennings, Masterton Trophies	$10,000	$6,000	$4,000
King Clancy Trophy	$ 3,000	$1,000	
Conn Smythe and Maurice Richard Trophies	$10,000		
TOTAL INDIVIDUAL AWARD MONEY			$204,000

ALL-STARS	Number of winners	Per Player	Total
First Team All-Stars	6	$10,000	$ 60,000
Second Team All-Stars	6	5,000	$ 30,000
TOTAL ALL-STAR AWARD MONEY			$ 90,000
TOTAL AWARD MONEY			**$13,104,000**

2002-03
NHL Player of the Week/Month Award Winners

Player of the Week

Week Ending	Player
Oct. 13	**Bill Guerin,** Dallas
Oct. 20	**Mario Lemieux,** Pittsburgh
Oct. 27	**Marian Gaborik,** Minnesota
Nov. 3	**Joe Sakic,** Colorado
Nov. 10	**Jocelyn Thibault,** Chicago
Nov. 17	**Nikolai Khabibulin,** Tampa Bay
Nov. 24	**Ed Belfour,** Toronto
Dec. 1	**Joe Thornton,** Boston
Dec. 8	**Miroslav Satan,** Buffalo
Dec. 15	**Jean-Sebastien Giguere,** Anaheim
Dec. 22	**Paul Kariya,** Anaheim
Dec. 29	**Brent Johnson,** St. Louis
Jan. 5	**Sean Burke,** Phoenix
Jan. 12	**Mike Modano,** Dallas
Jan. 19	**Martin Brodeur,** New Jersey
Jan. 26	**Patrick Roy,** Colorado
Feb. 9	**Patrick Roy,** Colorado
Feb. 16	**Dan Cloutier,** Vancouver
Feb. 23	**Brendan Morrison,** Vancouver
Mar. 2	**Nikolai Khabibulin,** Tampa Bay
Mar. 9	**Tommy Salo,** Edmonton
Mar. 16	**Vaclav Prospal,** Tampa Bay
Mar. 23	**Todd Bertuzzi,** Vancouver
Mar. 30	**Dany Heatley,** Atlanta
Apr. 6	**Milan Hejduk,** Colorado
	Mary Turco, Dallas (co-winners)

Player of the Month

Month	Player
October	**Mario Lemieux,** Pittsburgh
November	**Dan Cloutier,** Vancouver
December	**Todd White,** Ottawa
January	**Marty Turco,** Dallas
February	**Peter Forsberg,** Colorado
March	**Nikolai Khabibulin,** Tampa Bay

Rookie of the Month

Month	Player
October	**Tyler Arnason,** Chicago
November	**Rick Nash,** Columbus
December	**Tyler Arnason,** Chicago
January	**Ales Kotalik,** Buffalo
February	**Henrik Zetterberg,** Detroit
March	**Ales Hemsky,** Edmonton

NATIONAL HOCKEY LEAGUE INDIVIDUAL AWARD WINNERS

ART ROSS TROPHY

	Winner	Runner-up
2003	Peter Forsberg, Col.	Markus Naslund, Van.
2002	Jarome Iginla, Cgy.	Markus Naslund, Van.
2001	Jaromir Jagr, Pit.	Joe Sakic, Col.
2000	Jaromir Jagr, Pit.	Pavel Bure, Fla.
1999	Jaromir Jagr, Pit.	Teemu Selanne, Ana.
1998	Jaromir Jagr, Pit.	Peter Forsberg, Col.
1997	Mario Lemieux, Pit.	Teemu Selanne, Ana.
1996	Mario Lemieux, Pit.	Jaromir Jagr, Pit.
1995	Jaromir Jagr, Pit.	Eric Lindros, Phi.
1994	Wayne Gretzky, L.A.	Sergei Fedorov, Det.
1993	Mario Lemieux, Pit.	Pat LaFontaine, Buf.
1992	Mario Lemieux, Pit.	Kevin Stevens, Pit.
1991	Wayne Gretzky, L.A.	Brett Hull, St.L.
1990	Wayne Gretzky, L.A.	Mark Messier, Edm.
1989	Mario Lemieux, Pit.	Wayne Gretzky, L.A.
1988	Mario Lemieux, Pit.	Wayne Gretzky, Edm.
1987	Wayne Gretzky, Edm.	Jari Kurri, Edm.
1986	Wayne Gretzky, Edm.	Mario Lemieux, Pit.
1985	Wayne Gretzky, Edm.	Jari Kurri, Edm.
1984	Wayne Gretzky, Edm.	Paul Coffey, Edm.
1983	Wayne Gretzky, Edm.	Peter Stastny, Que.
1982	Wayne Gretzky, Edm.	Mike Bossy, NYI
1981	Wayne Gretzky, Edm.	Marcel Dionne, L.A.
1980	Marcel Dionne, L.A.	Wayne Gretzky, Edm.
1979	Bryan Trottier, NYI	Marcel Dionne, L.A.
1978	Guy Lafleur, Mtl.	Bryan Trottier, NYI
1977	Guy Lafleur, Mtl.	Marcel Dionne, L.A.
1976	Guy Lafleur, Mtl.	Bobby Clarke, Phi.
1975	Bobby Orr, Bos.	Phil Esposito, Bos.
1974	Phil Esposito, Bos.	Bobby Orr, Bos.
1973	Phil Esposito, Bos.	Bobby Clarke, Phi.
1972	Phil Esposito, Bos.	Bobby Orr, Bos.
1971	Phil Esposito, Bos.	Bobby Orr, Bos.
1970	Bobby Orr, Bos.	Phil Esposito, Bos.
1969	Phil Esposito, Bos.	Bobby Hull, Chi.
1968	Stan Mikita, Chi.	Phil Esposito, Bos.
1967	Stan Mikita, Chi.	Bobby Hull, Chi.
1966	Bobby Hull, Chi.	Stan Mikita, Chi.
1965	Stan Mikita, Chi.	Norm Ullman, Det.
1964	Stan Mikita, Chi.	Bobby Hull, Chi.
1963	Gordie Howe, Det.	Andy Bathgate, NYR
1962	Bobby Hull, Chi.	Andy Bathgate, NYR
1961	Bernie Geoffrion, Mtl.	Jean Beliveau, Mtl.
1960	Bobby Hull, Chi.	Bronco Horvath, Bos.
1959	Dickie Moore, Mtl.	Jean Beliveau, Mtl.
1958	Dickie Moore, Mtl.	Henri Richard, Mtl.
1957	Gordie Howe, Det.	Ted Lindsay, Det.
1956	Jean Beliveau, Mtl.	Gordie Howe, Det.
1955	Bernie Geoffrion, Mtl.	Maurice Richard, Mtl.
1954	Gordie Howe, Det.	Maurice Richard, Mtl.
1953	Gordie Howe, Det.	Ted Lindsay, Det.
1952	Gordie Howe, Det.	Ted Lindsay, Det.
1951	Gordie Howe, Det.	Maurice Richard, Mtl.
1950	Ted Lindsay, Det.	Sid Abel, Det.
1949	Roy Conacher, Chi.	Doug Bentley, Chi.
1948*	Elmer Lach, Mtl.	Buddy O'Connor, NYR
1947	Max Bentley, Chi.	Maurice Richard, Mtl.
1946	Max Bentley, Chi.	Gaye Stewart, Tor.
1945	Elmer Lach, Mtl.	Maurice Richard, Mtl.
1944	Herb Cain, Bos.	Doug Bentley, Chi.
1943	Doug Bentley, Chi.	Bill Cowley, Bos.
1942	Bryan Hextall, NYR	Lynn Patrick, NYR
1941	Bill Cowley, Bos.	Bryan Hextall, NYR
1940	Milt Schmidt, Bos.	Woody Dumart, Bos.
1939	Toe Blake, Mtl.	Sweeney Schriner, NYA
1938	Gordie Drillon, Tor.	Syl Apps, Tor.
1937	Sweeney Schriner, NYA	Syl Apps, Tor.
1936	Sweeney Schriner, NYA	Marty Barry, Det.
1935	Charlie Conacher, Tor.	Syd Howe, St.L., Det.
1934	Charlie Conacher, Tor.	Joe Primeau, Tor
1933	Bill Cook, NYR	Busher Jackson, Tor.
1932	Busher Jackson, Tor.	Joe Primeau, Tor.
1931	Howie Morenz, Mtl.	Ebbie Goodfellow, Det.
1930	Cooney Weiland, Bos.	Frank Boucher, NYR
1929	Ace Bailey, Tor.	Nels Stewart, Mtl.M
1928	Howie Morenz, Mtl.	Aurel Joliat, Mtl.
1927	Bill Cook, NYR	Dick Irvin, Chi.
1926	Nels Stewart, Mtl.M.	Cy Denneny, Ott.
1925	Babe Dye, Tor.	Cy Denneny, Ott.
1924	Cy Denneny, Ott.	Billy Boucher, Mtl.
1923	Babe Dye, Tor.	Cy Denneny, Ott.
1922	Punch Broadbent, Ott.	Cy Denneny, Ott.
1921	Newsy Lalonde, Mtl.	Babe Dye, Ham., Tor.
1920	Joe Malone, Que.	Newsy Lalonde, Mtl.
1919	Newsy Lalonde, Mtl.	Odie Cleghorn, Mtl.
1918	Joe Malone, Mtl.	Cy Denneny, Ott.

* Trophy first awarded in 1948.
  Scoring leaders listed from 1918 to 1947.

HART MEMORIAL TROPHY

	Winner	Runner-up
2003	Peter Forsberg, Col.	Markus Naslund, Van.
2002	Jose Theodore, Mtl.	Jarome Iginla, Cgy.
2001	Joe Sakic, Col.	Mario Lemieux, Pit.
2000	Chris Pronger, St.L.	Jaromir Jagr, Pit.
1999	Jaromir Jagr, Pit.	Alexei Yashin, Ott.
1998	Dominik Hasek, Buf.	Jaromir Jagr, Pit.
1997	Dominik Hasek, Buf.	Paul Kariya, Ana.
1996	Mario Lemieux, Pit.	Mark Messier, NYR
1995	Eric Lindros, Phi.	Jaromir Jagr, Pit.
1994	Sergei Fedorov, Det.	Dominik Hasek, Buf.
1993	Mario Lemieux, Pit.	Doug Gilmour, Tor.
1992	Mark Messier, NYR	Patrick Roy, Mtl.
1991	Brett Hull, St.L.	Wayne Gretzky, L.A.
1990	Mark Messier, Edm.	Raymond Bourque, Bos.
1989	Wayne Gretzky, L.A.	Mario Lemieux, Pit.
1988	Mario Lemieux, Pit.	Grant Fuhr, Edm.
1987	Wayne Gretzky, Edm.	Raymond Bourque, Bos.
1986	Wayne Gretzky, Edm.	Mario Lemieux, Pit.
1985	Wayne Gretzky, Edm.	Dale Hawerchuk, Wpg.
1984	Wayne Gretzky, Edm.	Rod Langway, Wsh.
1983	Wayne Gretzky, Edm.	Pete Peeters, Bos.
1982	Wayne Gretzky, Edm.	Bryan Trottier, NYI
1981	Wayne Gretzky, Edm.	Mike Liut, St.L.
1980	Wayne Gretzky, Edm.	Marcel Dionne, L.A.
1979	Bryan Trottier, NYI	Guy Lafleur, Mtl
1978	Guy Lafleur, Mtl.	Bryan Trottier, NYI
1977	Guy Lafleur, Mtl.	Bobby Clarke, Phi.
1976	Bobby Clarke, Phi.	Denis Potvin, NYI
1975	Bobby Clarke, Phi.	Rogie Vachon, L.A.
1974	Phil Esposito, Bos.	Bernie Parent, Phi.
1973	Bobby Clarke, Phi.	Phil Esposito, Bos.
1972	Bobby Orr, Bos.	Ken Dryden, Mtl.
1971	Bobby Orr, Bos.	Phil Esposito, Bos.
1970	Bobby Orr, Bos.	Tony Esposito, Chi.
1969	Phil Esposito, Bos.	Jean Beliveau, Mtl.
1968	Stan Mikita, Chi.	Jean Beliveau, Mtl.
1967	Stan Mikita, Chi.	Ed Giacomin, NYR
1966	Bobby Hull, Chi.	Jean Beliveau, Mtl.
1965	Bobby Hull, Chi.	Norm Ullman, Det.
1964	Jean Beliveau, Mtl.	Bobby Hull, Chi.
1963	Gordie Howe, Det.	Stan Mikita, Chi.
1962	Jacques Plante, Mtl.	Doug Harvey, NYR
1961	Bernie Geoffrion, Mtl.	Johnny Bower, Tor.
1960	Gordie Howe, Det.	Bobby Hull, Chi.
1959	Andy Bathgate, NYR	Gordie Howe, Det.
1958	Gordie Howe, Det.	Andy Bathgate, NYR
1957	Gordie Howe, Det.	Jean Beliveau, Mtl.
1956	Jean Beliveau, Mtl.	Tod Sloan, Tor.
1955	Ted Kennedy, Tor.	Harry Lumley, Tor.
1954	Al Rollins, Chi.	Red Kelly, Det.
1953	Gordie Howe, Det.	Al Rollins, Chi.
1952	Gordie Howe, Det.	Elmer Lach, Mtl.
1951	Milt Schmidt, Bos.	Maurice Richard, Mtl.
1950	Chuck Rayner, NYR	Ted Kennedy, Tor.
1949	Sid Abel, Det.	Bill Durnan, Mtl.
1948	Buddy O'Connor, NYR	Frank Brimsek, Bos.
1947	Maurice Richard, Mtl.	Milt Schmidt, Bos.
1946	Max Bentley, Chi.	Gaye Stewart, Tor.
1945	Elmer Lach, Mtl.	Maurice Richard, Mtl.
1944	Babe Pratt, Tor.	Bill Cowley, Bos.
1943	Bill Cowley, Bos.	Doug Bentley, Chi.
1942	Tom Anderson, Bro.	Syl Apps, Tor.
1941	Bill Cowley, Bos.	Dit Clapper, Bos.
1940	Ebbie Goodfellow, Det.	Syl Apps, Tor.
1939	Toe Blake, Mtl.	Syl Apps, Tor.
1938	Eddie Shore, Bos.	Paul Thompson, Chi.
1937	Babe Siebert, Mtl.	Lionel Conacher, Mtl.M
1936	Eddie Shore, Bos.	Hooley Smith, Mtl.M
1935	Eddie Shore, Bos.	Charlie Conacher, Tor.
1934	Aurel Joliat, Mtl.	Lionel Conacher, Chi.
1933	Eddie Shore, Bos.	Bill Cook, NYR
1932	Howie Morenz, Mtl.	Ching Johnson, NYR
1931	Howie Morenz, Mtl.	Eddie Shore, Bos.
1930	Nels Stewart, Mtl.M.	Lionel Hitchman, Bos.
1929	Roy Worters, NYA	Ace Bailey, Tor.
1928	Howie Morenz, Mtl.	Roy Worters, Pit.
1927	Herb Gardiner, Mtl.	Bill Cook, NYR
1926	Nels Stewart, Mtl.M.	Sprague Cleghorn, Bos.
1925	Billy Burch, Ham.	Howie Morenz, Mtl.
1924	Frank Nighbor, Ott.	Sprague Cleghorn, Mtl.

BUD LIGHT PLUS-MINUS AWARD

2003	Peter Forsberg	Colorado
	Milan Hejduk	Colorado
2002	Chris Chelios	Detroit
2001	Patrik Elias	New Jersey
	Joe Sakic	Colorado
2000	Chris Pronger	St. Louis
1999	John LeClair	Philadelphia
1998	Chris Pronger	St. Louis
1997	John LeClair	Philadelphia

WILLIAM M. JENNINGS TROPHY

	Winner	Runner-up
2003	Martin Brodeur, N.J. (tie)	Marty Turco, Dal.
	Roman Cechmanek, Phi. (tie)	Ron Tugnutt, Dal.
	Robert Esche, Phi.	
2002	Patrick Roy, Col.	Tommy Salo, Edm.
2001	Dominik Hasek, Buf.	Ed Belfour, Dal.
		Marty Turco, Dal.
2000	Roman Turek, St.L.	John Vanbiesbrouck, Phi.
		Brian Boucher, Phi.
1999	Ed Belfour, Dal.	Dominik Hasek, Buf.
	Roman Turek, Dal.	
1998	Martin Brodeur, N.J.	Ed Belfour, Dal.
1997	Martin Brodeur, N.J.	Chris Osgood, Det.
	Mike Dunham, N.J.	Mike Vernon, Det.
1996	Chris Osgood, Det.	Martin Brodeur, N.J.
	Mike Vernon, Det.	
1995	Ed Belfour, Chi.	Mike Vernon, Det.
		Chris Osgood, Det.
1994	Dominik Hasek, Buf.	Martin Brodeur, N.J.
	Grant Fuhr, Buf.	Chris Terreri, N.J.
1993	Ed Belfour, Chi.	Felix Potvin, Tor.
		Grant Fuhr, Tor.
1992	Patrick Roy, Mtl.	Ed Belfour, Chi.
1991	Ed Belfour, Chi.	Patrick Roy, Mtl.
1990	Andy Moog, Bos.	Patrick Roy, Mtl.
	Reggie Lemelin, Bos.	Brian Hayward, Mtl.
1989	Patrick Roy, Mtl.	Mike Vernon, Cgy.
	Brian Hayward, Mtl.	Rick Wamsley, Cgy.
1988	Patrick Roy, Mtl.	Clint Malarchuk, Wsh.
	Brian Hayward, Mtl.	Pete Peeters, Wsh.
1987	Patrick Roy, Mtl.	Ron Hextall, Phi.
	Brian Hayward, Mtl.	
1986	Bob Froese, Phi.	Al Jensen, Wsh.
	Darren Jensen, Phi.	Pete Peeters, Wsh.
1985	Tom Barrasso, Buf.	Pat Riggin, Wsh.
	Bob Sauve, Buf.	
1984	Al Jensen, Wsh.	Tom Barrasso, Buf.
	Pat Riggin, Wsh.	Bob Sauve, Buf.
1983	Roland Melanson, NYI	Pete Peeters, Bos.
	Billy Smith, NYI	
1982	Rick Wamsley, Mtl.	Billy Smith, NYI
	Denis Herron, Mtl.	Roland Melanson, NYI

BILL MASTERTON MEMORIAL TROPHY

2003	Steve Yzerman	Detroit
2002	Saku Koivu	Montreal
2001	Adam Graves	NY Rangers
2000	Ken Daneyko	New Jersey
1999	John Cullen	Tampa Bay
1998	Jamie McLennan	St. Louis
1997	Tony Granato	San Jose
1996	Gary Roberts	Calgary
1995	Pat LaFontaine	Buffalo
1994	Cam Neely	Boston
1993	Mario Lemieux	Pittsburgh
1992	Mark Fitzpatrick	NY Islanders
1991	Dave Taylor	Los Angeles
1990	Gord Kluzak	Boston
1989	Tim Kerr	Philadelphia
1988	Bob Bourne	Los Angeles
1987	Doug Jarvis	Hartford
1986	Charlie Simmer	Boston
1985	Anders Hedberg	NY Rangers
1984	Brad Park	Detroit
1983	Lanny McDonald	Calgary
1982	Glenn Resch	Colorado
1981	Blake Dunlop	St. Louis
1980	Al MacAdam	Minnesota
1979	Serge Savard	Montreal
1978	Butch Goring	Los Angeles
1977	Ed Westfall	NY Islanders
1976	Rod Gilbert	NY Rangers
1975	Don Luce	Buffalo
1974	Henri Richard	Montreal
1973	Lowell MacDonald	Pittsburgh
1972	Bobby Clarke	Philadelphia
1971	Jean Ratelle	NY Rangers
1970	Pit Martin	Chicago
1969	Ted Hampson	Oakland
1968	Claude Provost	Montreal

LADY BYNG MEMORIAL TROPHY

	Winner	Runner-up
2003	Alexander Mogilny, Tor.	Nicklas Lidstrom, Det.
2002	Ron Francis, Car.	Joe Sakic, Col.
2001	Joe Sakic, Col.	Nicklas Lidstrom, Det.
2000	Pavol Demitra, St.L.	Nicklas Lidstrom, Det.
1999	Wayne Gretzky, NYR.	Nicklas Lidstrom, Det.
1998	Ron Francis, Pit.	Teemu Selanne, Ana.
1997	Paul Kariya, Ana.	Teemu Selanne, Ana.
1996	Paul Kariya, Ana.	Adam Oates, Bos.
1995	Ron Francis, Pit.	Adam Oates, Bos.
1994	Wayne Gretzky, L.A.	Adam Oates, Bos.
1993	Pierre Turgeon, NYI	Adam Oates, Bos.
1992	Wayne Gretzky, L.A.	Joe Sakic, Que.
1991	Wayne Gretzky, L.A.	Brett Hull, St.L.
1990	Brett Hull, St.L.	Wayne Gretzky, L.A.
1989	Joe Mullen, Cgy.	Wayne Gretzky, L.A.
1988	Mats Naslund, Mtl.	Wayne Gretzky, Edm.
1987	Joe Mullen, Cgy.	Wayne Gretzky, Edm.
1986	Mike Bossy, NYI	Jari Kurri, Edm.
1985	Jari Kurri, Edm.	Joe Mullen, St.L.
1984	Mike Bossy, NYI	Rick Middleton, Bos.
1983	Mike Bossy, NYI	Rick Middleton, Bos.
1982	Rick Middleton, Bos.	Mike Bossy, NYI
1981	Rick Kehoe, Pit.	Wayne Gretzky, Edm.
1980	Wayne Gretzky, Edm.	Marcel Dionne, L.A.
1979	Bob MacMillan, Atl.	Marcel Dionne, L.A.
1978	Butch Goring, L.A.	Peter McNab, Bos.
1977	Marcel Dionne, L.A.	Jean Ratelle, Bos.
1976	Jean Ratelle, NYR, Bos.	Jean Pronovost, Pit.
1975	Marcel Dionne, Det.	John Bucyk, Bos.
1974	John Bucyk, Bos.	Lowell MacDonald, Pit.
1973	Gilbert Perreault, Buf.	Jean Ratelle, NYR
1972	Jean Ratelle, NYR	John Bucyk, Bos.
1971	John Bucyk, Bos.	Dave Keon, Tor.
1970	Phil Goyette, St.L.	John Bucyk, Bos.
1969	Alex Delvecchio, Det.	Ted Hampson, Oak.
1968	Stan Mikita, Chi.	John Bucyk, Bos.
1967	Stan Mikita, Chi.	Dave Keon, Tor.
1966	Alex Delvecchio, Det.	Bobby Rousseau, Mtl.
1965	Bobby Hull, Chi.	Alex Delvecchio, Det.
1964	Kenny Wharram, Chi.	Dave Keon, Tor.
1963	Dave Keon, Tor.	Camille Henry, NYR
1962	Dave Keon, Tor.	Claude Provost, Mtl.
1961	Red Kelly, Tor.	Norm Ullman, Det.
1960	Don McKenney, Bos.	Andy Hebenton, NYR
1959	Alex Delvecchio, Det.	Andy Hebenton, NYR
1958	Camille Henry, NYR	Don Marshall, Mtl.
1957	Andy Hebenton, NYR	Dutch Reibel, Det.
1956	Dutch Reibel, Det.	Floyd Curry, Mtl.
1955	Sid Smith, Tor.	Danny Lewicki, NYR
1954	Red Kelly, Det.	Don Raleigh, NYR
1953	Red Kelly, Det.	Wally Hergesheimer, NYR
1952	Sid Smith, Tor.	Red Kelly, Det.
1951	Red Kelly, Det.	Woody Dumart, Bos.
1950	Edgar Laprade, NYR	Red Kelly, Det.
1949	Bill Quackenbush, Det.	Harry Watson, Tor.
1948	Buddy O'Connor, NYR	Syl Apps, Tor.
1947	Bobby Bauer, Bos.	Syl Apps, Tor.
1946	Toe Blake, Mtl.	Clint Smith, Chi.
1945	Bill Mosienko, Chi.	Syd Howe, Det.
1944	Clint Smith, Chi.	Herb Cain, Bos.
1943	Max Bentley, Chi.	Buddy O'Connor, Mtl.
1942	Syl Apps, Tor.	Gordie Drillon, Tor.
1941	Bobby Bauer, Bos.	Gordie Drillon, Tor.
1940	Bobby Bauer, Bos.	Clint Smith, NYR
1939	Clint Smith, NYR	Marty Barry, Det.
1938	Gordie Drillon, Tor.	Clint Smith, NYR
1937	Marty Barry, Det.	Gordie Drillon, Tor.
1936	Doc Romnes, Chi.	Sweeney Schriner, NYA
1935	Frank Boucher, NYR	Russ Blinco, Mtl.M
1934	Frank Boucher, NYR	Joe Primeau, Tor.
1933	Frank Boucher, NYR	Joe Primeau, Tor.
1932	Joe Primeau, Tor.	Frank Boucher, NYR
1931	Frank Boucher, NYR	Normie Himes, NYA
1930	Frank Boucher, NYR	Normie Himes, NYA
1929	Frank Boucher, NYR	Harold Darragh, Pit.
1928	Frank Boucher, NYR	George Hay, Det.
1927	Billy Burch, NYA	Dick Irvin, Chi.
1926	Frank Nighbor, Ott.	Billy Burch, NYA
1925	Frank Nighbor, Ott.	none

KING CLANCY MEMORIAL TROPHY

2003	Brendan Shanahan	Detroit
2002	Ron Francis	Carolina
2001	Shjon Podein	Colorado
2000	Curtis Joseph	Toronto
1999	Rob Ray	Buffalo
1998	Kelly Chase	St. Louis
1997	Trevor Linden	Vancouver
1996	Kris King	Winnipeg
1995	Joe Nieuwendyk	Calgary
1994	Adam Graves	NY Rangers
1993	Dave Poulin	Boston
1992	Raymond Bourque	Boston
1991	Dave Taylor	Los Angeles
1990	Kevin Lowe	Edmonton
1989	Bryan Trottier	NY Islanders
1988	Lanny McDonald	Calgary

VEZINA TROPHY

	Winner	Runner-up
2003	Martin Brodeur, N.J.	Marty Turco, Dal.
2002	Jose Theodore, Mtl.	Patrick Roy, Col.
2001	Dominik Hasek, Buf.	Roman Cechmanek, Phi.
2000	Olaf Kolzig, Wsh.	Roman Turek, St.L.
1999	Dominik Hasek, Buf.	Curtis Joseph, Tor.
1998	Dominik Hasek, Buf.	Martin Brodeur, N.J.
1997	Dominik Hasek, Buf.	Martin Brodeur, N.J.
1996	Jim Carey, Wsh.	Chris Osgood, Det.
1995	Dominik Hasek, Buf.	Ed Belfour, Chi.
1994	Dominik Hasek, Buf.	John Vanbiesbrouck, Fla.
1993	Ed Belfour, Chi.	Tom Barrasso, Pit.
1992	Patrick Roy, Mtl.	Kirk McLean, Van.
1991	Ed Belfour, Chi.	Patrick Roy, Mtl.
1990	Patrick Roy, Mtl.	Daren Puppa, Buf.
1989	Patrick Roy, Mtl.	Mike Vernon, Cgy.
1988	Grant Fuhr, Edm.	Tom Barrasso, Buf.
1987	Ron Hextall, Phi.	Mike Liut, Hfd.
1986	John Vanbiesbrouck, NYR	Bob Froese, Phi.
1985	Pelle Lindbergh, Phi.	Tom Barrasso, Buf.
1984	Tom Barrasso, Buf.	Reggie Lemelin, Cgy.
1983	Pete Peeters, Bos.	Roland Melanson, NYI
1982	Billy Smith, NYI	Grant Fuhr, Edm.
1981	Richard Sevigny, Mtl.	Pete Peeters, Phi.
	Denis Herron, Mtl.	Rick St. Croix, Phi.
	Michel Larocque, Mtl.	
1980	Bob Sauve, Buf.	Gerry Cheevers, Bos.
	Don Edwards, Buf.	Gilles Gilbert, Bos.
1979	Ken Dryden, Mtl.	Glenn Resch, NYI
	Michel Larocque, Mtl.	Billy Smith, NYI
1978	Ken Dryden, Mtl.	Bernie Parent, Phi.
	Michel Larocque, Mtl.	Wayne Stephenson, Phi.
1977	Ken Dryden, Mtl.	Glenn Resch, NYI
	Michel Larocque, Mtl.	Billy Smith, NYI
1976	Ken Dryden, Mtl.	Glenn Resch, NYI
		Billy Smith, NYI
1975	Bernie Parent, Phi.	Rogie Vachon, L.A.
		Gary Edwards, L.A.
1974	Bernie Parent, Phi. (tie)	Gilles Gilbert, Bos.
	Tony Esposito, Chi. (tie)	
1973	Ken Dryden, Mtl.	Ed Giacomin, NYR
		Gilles Villemure, NYR
1972	Tony Esposito, Chi.	Cesare Maniago, Min.
	Gary Smith, Chi.	Gump Worsley, Min.
1971	Ed Giacomin, NYR	Tony Esposito, Chi.
	Gilles Villemure, NYR	
1970	Tony Esposito, Chi.	Jacques Plante, St.L.
		Ernie Wakely, St.L.
1969	Jacques Plante, St.L.	Ed Giacomin, NYR
	Glenn Hall, St.L.	
1968	Gump Worsley, Mtl.	Johnny Bower, Tor.
	Rogie Vachon, Mtl.	Bruce Gamble, Tor.
1967	Glenn Hall, Chi.	Charlie Hodge, Mtl.
	Denis DeJordy, Chi.	
1966	Gump Worsley, Mtl.	Glenn Hall, Chi.
	Charlie Hodge, Mtl.	
1965	Terry Sawchuk, Tor.	Roger Crozier, Det.
	Johnny Bower, Tor.	
1964	Charlie Hodge, Mtl.	Glenn Hall, Chi.
1963	Glenn Hall, Chi.	Johnny Bower, Tor.
		Don Simmons, Tor.
1962	Jacques Plante, Mtl.	Johnny Bower, Tor.
1961	Johnny Bower, Tor.	Glenn Hall, Chi.
1960	Jacques Plante, Mtl.	Glenn Hall, Chi.
1959	Jacques Plante, Mtl.	Johnny Bower, Tor.
		Ed Chadwick, Tor.
1958	Jacques Plante, Mtl.	Gump Worsley, NYR
		Marcel Paille, NYR
1957	Jacques Plante, Mtl.	Glenn Hall, Det.
1956	Jacques Plante, Mtl.	Glenn Hall, Det.
1955	Terry Sawchuk, Det.	Harry Lumley, Tor.
1954	Harry Lumley, Tor.	Terry Sawchuk, Det.
1953	Terry Sawchuk, Det.	Gerry McNeil, Mtl.
1952	Terry Sawchuk, Det.	Al Rollins, Tor.
1951	Al Rollins, Tor.	Terry Sawchuk, Det.
1950	Bill Durnan, Mtl.	Harry Lumley, Det.
1949	Bill Durnan, Mtl.	Harry Lumley, Det.
1948	Turk Broda, Tor.	Harry Lumley, Det.
1947	Bill Durnan, Mtl.	Turk Broda, Tor.
1946	Bill Durnan, Mtl.	Frank Brimsek, Bos.
1945	Bill Durnan, Mtl.	Frank McCool, Tor. (tie)
		Harry Lumley, Det. (tie)
1944	Bill Durnan, Mtl.	Paul Bibeault, Tor.
1943	Johnny Mowers, Det.	Turk Broda, Tor.
1942	Frank Brimsek, Bos.	Turk Broda, Tor.
1941	Turk Broda, Tor.	Frank Brimsek, Bos. (tie)
		Johnny Mowers, Det. (tie)
1940	Dave Kerr, NYR	Frank Brimsek, Bos.
1939	Frank Brimsek, Bos.	Dave Kerr, NYR
1938	Tiny Thompson, Bos.	Dave Kerr, NYR
1937	Normie Smith, Det.	Dave Kerr, NYR
1936	Tiny Thompson, Bos.	Mike Karakas, Chi.
1935	Lorne Chabot, Chi.	Alex Connell, Mtl.M.
1934	Charlie Gardiner, Chi.	Wilf Cude, Det.
1933	Tiny Thompson, Bos.	John Ross Roach, Det.
1932	Charlie Gardiner, Chi.	Alex Connell, Det.
1931	Roy Worters, NYA	Charlie Gardiner, Chi.
1930	Tiny Thompson, Bos.	Charlie Gardiner, Chi.
1929	George Hainsworth, Mtl.	Tiny Thompson, Bos.
1928	George Hainsworth, Mtl.	Alex Connell, Ott.
1927	George Hainsworth, Mtl.	Clint Benedict, Mtl.M.

CALDER MEMORIAL TROPHY

	Winner	Runner-up
2003	Barret Jackman, St.L.	Henrik Zetterberg, Det.
2002	Dany Heatley, Atl.	Ilya Kovalchuk, Atl.
2001	Evgeni Nabokov, S.J.	Brad Richards, T.B.
2000	Scott Gomez, N.J.	Brad Stuart, S.J.
1999	Chris Drury, Col.	Marian Hossa, Ott.
1998	Sergei Samsonov, Bos.	Mattias Ohlund, Van.
1997	Bryan Berard, NYI	Jarome Iginla, Cgy.
1996	Daniel Alfredsson, Ott.	Eric Daze, Chi.
1995	Peter Forsberg, Que.	Jim Carey, Wsh.
1994	Martin Brodeur, N.J.	Jason Arnott, Edm.
1993	Teemu Selanne, Wpg.	Joe Juneau, Bos.
1992	Pavel Bure, Van.	Nicklas Lidstrom, Det
1991	Ed Belfour, Chi.	Sergei Fedorov, Det.
1990	Sergei Makarov, Cgy.	Mike Modano, Min.
1989	Brian Leetch, NYR	Trevor Linden, Van.
1988	Joe Nieuwendyk, Cgy.	Ray Sheppard, Buf.
1987	Luc Robitaille, L.A.	Ron Hextall, Phi.
1986	Gary Suter, Cgy.	Wendel Clark, Tor.
1985	Mario Lemieux, Pit.	Chris Chelios, Mtl.
1984	Tom Barrasso, Buf.	Steve Yzerman, Det.
1983	Steve Larmer, Chi.	Phil Housley, Buf.
1982	Dale Hawerchuk, Wpg.	Barry Pederson, Bos.
1981	Peter Stastny, Que.	Larry Murphy, L.A.
1980	Raymond Bourque, Bos.	Mike Foligno, Det.
1979	Bobby Smith, Min	Ryan Walter, Wsh.
1978	Mike Bossy, NYI	Barry Beck, Col.
1977	Willi Plett, Atl.	Don Murdoch, NYR
1976	Bryan Trottier, NYI	Glenn Resch, NYI
1975	Eric Vail, Atl.	Pierre Larouche, Pit.
1974	Denis Potvin, NYI	Tom Lysiak, Atl.
1973	Steve Vickers, NYR	Bill Barber, Phi.
1972	Ken Dryden, Mtl.	Rick Martin, Buf.
1971	Gilbert Perreault, Buf.	Jude Drouin, Min.
1970	Tony Esposito, Chi.	Bill Fairbairn, NYR
1969	Danny Grant, Min.	Norm Ferguson, Oak.
1968	Derek Sanderson, Bos.	Jacques Lemaire, Mtl.
1967	Bobby Orr, Bos.	Ed Van Impe, Chi.
1966	Brit Selby, Tor.	Bert Marshall, Det.
1965	Roger Crozier, Det.	Ron Ellis, Tor.
1964	Jacques Laperriere, Mtl.	John Ferguson, Mtl.
1963	Kent Douglas, Tor.	Doug Barkley, Det.
1962	Bobby Rousseau, Mtl.	Cliff Pennington, Bos.
1961	Dave Keon, Tor.	Bob Nevin, Tor.
1960	Bill Hay, Chi.	Murray Oliver, Det.
1959	Ralph Backstrom, Mtl.	Carl Brewer, Tor.
1958	Frank Mahovlich, Tor.	Bobby Hull, Chi.
1957	Larry Regan, Bos.	Ed Chadwick, Tor.
1956	Glenn Hall, Det.	Andy Hebenton, NYR
1955	Ed Litzenberger, Chi.	Don McKenney, Bos.
1954	Camille Henry, NYR	Dutch Reibel, Det.
1953	Gump Worsley, NYR	Gord Hannigan, Tor.
1952	Bernie Geoffrion, Mtl.	Hy Buller, NYR
1951	Terry Sawchuk, Det.	Al Rollins, Tor.
1950	Jack Gelineau, Bos.	Phil Maloney, Bos.
1949	Pentti Lund, NYR	Allan Stanley, NYR
1948	Jim McFadden, Det.	Pete Babando, Bos.
1947	Howie Meeker, Tor.	Jim Conacher, Det.
1946	Edgar Laprade, NYR	George Gee, Chi.
1945	Frank McCool, Tor.	Ken Smith, Bos.
1944	Gus Bodnar, Tor.	Bill Durnan, Mtl.
1943	Gaye Stewart, Tor.	Glen Harmon, Mtl.
1942	Grant Warwick, NYR	Buddy O'Connor, Mtl.
1941	John Quilty, Mtl.	Johnny Mowers, Det.
1940	Kilby MacDonald, NYR	Wally Stanowski, Tor.
1939	Frank Brimsek, Bos.	Roy Conacher, Bos.
1938	Cully Dahlstrom, Chi.	Murph Chamberlain, Tor.
1937	Syl Apps, Tor.	Gordie Drillon, Tor.
1936	Mike Karakas, Chi.	Bucko McDonald, Det.
1935	Sweeney Schriner, NYA	Bert Connelly, NYR
1934	Russ Blinco, Mtl.M.	none
1933	Carl Voss, Det.	none

FRANK J. SELKE TROPHY

	Winner	Runner-up
2003	Jere Lehtinen, Dal.	John Madden, N.J.
2002	Michael Peca, NYI	Craig Conroy, Cgy.
2001	John Madden, N.J.	Joe Sakic, Col.
2000	Steve Yzerman, Det.	Michal Handzus, St.L.
1999	Jere Lehtinen, Dal.	Magnus Arvedson, Ott.
1998	Jere Lehtinen, Dal.	Michael Peca, Buf.
1997	Michael Peca, Buf.	Peter Forsberg, Col.
1996	Sergei Fedorov, Det.	Ron Francis, Pit.
1995	Ron Francis, Pit.	Esa Tikkanen, St.L.
1994	Sergei Fedorov, Det.	Doug Gilmour, Tor.
1993	Doug Gilmour, Tor.	Dave Poulin, Bos.
1992	Guy Carbonneau, Mtl.	Sergei Fedorov, Det.
1991	Dirk Graham, Chi.	Esa Tikkanen, Edm.
1990	Rick Meagher, St.L.	Guy Carbonneau, Mtl.
1989	Guy Carbonneau, Mtl.	Esa Tikkanen, Edm.
1988	Guy Carbonneau, Mtl.	Steve Kasper, Bos.
1987	Dave Poulin, Phi.	Guy Carbonneau, Mtl.
1986	Troy Murray, Chi.	Ron Sutter, Phi.
1985	Craig Ramsay, Buf.	Doug Jarvis, Wsh.
1984	Doug Jarvis, Wsh.	Bryan Trottier, NYI
1983	Bobby Clarke, Phi.	Jari Kurri, Edm.
1982	Steve Kasper, Bos.	Bob Gainey, Mtl.
1981	Bob Gainey, Mtl.	Craig Ramsay, Buf.
1980	Bob Gainey, Mtl.	Craig Ramsay, Buf.
1979	Bob Gainey, Mtl.	Don Marcotte, Bos.
1978	Bob Gainey, Mtl.	Craig Ramsay, Buf.

CONN SMYTHE TROPHY

2003	Jean-Sebastien Giguere	Anaheim
2002	Nicklas Lidstrom	Detroit
2001	Patrick Roy	Colorado
2000	Scott Stevens	New Jersey
1999	Joe Nieuwendyk	Dallas
1998	Steve Yzerman	Detroit
1997	Mike Vernon	Detroit
1996	Joe Sakic	Colorado
1995	Claude Lemieux	New Jersey
1994	Brian Leetch	NY Rangers
1993	Patrick Roy	Montreal
1992	Mario Lemieux	Pittsburgh
1991	Mario Lemieux	Pittsburgh
1990	Bill Ranford	Edmonton
1989	Al MacInnis	Calgary
1988	Wayne Gretzky	Edmonton
1987	Ron Hextall	Philadelphia
1986	Patrick Roy	Montreal
1985	Wayne Gretzky	Edmonton
1984	Mark Messier	Edmonton
1983	Billy Smith	NY Islanders
1982	Mike Bossy	NY Islanders
1981	Butch Goring	NY Islanders
1980	Bryan Trottier	NY Islanders
1979	Bob Gainey	Montreal
1978	Larry Robinson	Montreal
1977	Guy Lafleur	Montreal
1976	Reggie Leach	Philadelphia
1975	Bernie Parent	Philadelphia
1974	Bernie Parent	Philadelphia
1973	Yvan Cournoyer	Montreal
1972	Bobby Orr	Boston
1971	Ken Dryden	Montreal
1970	Bobby Orr	Boston
1969	Serge Savard	Montreal
1968	Glenn Hall	St. Louis
1967	Dave Keon	Toronto
1966	Roger Crozier	Detroit
1965	Jean Beliveau	Montreal

JAMES NORRIS MEMORIAL TROPHY

	Winner	Runner-up
2003	Nicklas Lidstrom, Det.	Al MacInnis, St.L.
2002	Nicklas Lidstrom, Det.	Chris Chelios, Det.
2001	Nicklas Lidstrom, Det.	Raymond Bourque, Col.
2000	Chris Pronger, St.L.	Nicklas Lidstrom, Det.
1999	Al MacInnis, St.L.	Nicklas Lidstrom, Det.
1998	Rob Blake, L.A.	Nicklas Lidstrom, Det.
1997	Brian Leetch, NYR	V. Konstantinov, Det.
1996	Chris Chelios, Chi.	Raymond Bourque, Bos.
1995	Paul Coffey, Det.	Chris Chelios, Chi.
1994	Raymond Bourque, Bos.	Scott Stevens, N.J.
1993	Chris Chelios, Chi.	Raymond Bourque, Bos.
1992	Brian Leetch, NYR	Raymond Bourque, Bos.
1991	Raymond Bourque, Bos.	Al MacInnis, Cgy.
1990	Raymond Bourque, Bos.	Al MacInnis, Cgy.
1989	Chris Chelios, Mtl	Paul Coffey, Pit.
1988	Raymond Bourque, Bos.	Scott Stevens, Wsh.
1987	Raymond Bourque, Bos.	Mark Howe, Phi.
1986	Paul Coffey, Edm.	Mark Howe, Phi.
1985	Paul Coffey, Edm.	Raymond Bourque, Bos.
1984	Rod Langway, Wsh.	Paul Coffey, Edm.
1983	Rod Langway, Wsh.	Mark Howe, Phi.
1982	Doug Wilson, Chi.	Raymond Bourque, Bos.
1981	Randy Carlyle, Pit.	Denis Potvin, NYI
1980	Larry Robinson, Mtl.	Borje Salming, Tor.
1979	Denis Potvin, NYI	Larry Robinson, Mtl.
1978	Denis Potvin, NYI	Brad Park, Bos.
1977	Larry Robinson, Mtl.	Borje Salming, Tor.
1976	Denis Potvin, NYI	Brad Park, NYR, Bos.
1975	Bobby Orr, Bos.	Denis Potvin, NYI
1974	Bobby Orr, Bos.	Brad Park, NYR
1973	Bobby Orr, Bos.	Guy Lapointe, Mtl.
1972	Bobby Orr, Bos.	Brad Park, NYR
1971	Bobby Orr, Bos.	Brad Park, NYR
1970	Bobby Orr, Bos.	Brad Park, NYR
1969	Bobby Orr, Bos.	Tim Horton, Tor.
1968	Bobby Orr, Bos.	J.C. Tremblay, Mtl.
1967	Harry Howell, NYR	Pierre Pilote, Chi.
1966	Jacques Laperriere, Mtl.	Pierre Pilote, Chi.
1965	Pierre Pilote, Chi.	Jacques Laperriere, Mtl.
1964	Pierre Pilote, Chi.	Tim Horton, Tor.
1963	Pierre Pilote, Chi.	Carl Brewer, Tor.
1962	Doug Harvey, NYR	Pierre Pilote, Chi.
1961	Doug Harvey, Mtl.	Marcel Pronovost, Det.
1960	Doug Harvey, Mtl.	Allan Stanley, Tor.
1959	Tom Johnson, Mtl.	Bill Gadsby, NYR
1958	Doug Harvey, Mtl.	Bill Gadsby, NYR
1957	Doug Harvey, Mtl.	Red Kelly, Det.
1956	Doug Harvey, Mtl.	Bill Gadsby, NYR
1955	Doug Harvey, Mtl.	Red Kelly, Det.
1954	Red Kelly, Det.	Doug Harvey, Mtl.

MAURICE "ROCKET" RICHARD TROPHY

2003	Milan Hejduk	Colorado
2002	Jarome Iginla	Calgary
2001	Pavel Bure	Florida
2000	Pavel Bure	Florida
1999	Teemu Selanne	Anaheim

LESTER PATRICK TROPHY

2003	Raymond Bourque
	Ron DeGregorio
	Willie O'Ree
2002	1960 U.S. Olympic Team
	Herb Brooks
	Larry Pleau
2001	Scotty Bowman
	David Poile
	Gary Bettman
2000	Mario Lemieux
	Craig Patrick
	Lou Vairo
1999	Harry Sinden
	1998 U.S. Olympic Women's Team
1998	Peter Karmanos
	Neal Broten
	John Mayasich
	Max McNab
1997	Seymour H. Knox III
	Bill Cleary
	Pat LaFontaine
1996	George Gund
	Ken Morrow
	Milt Schmidt
1995	Joe Mullen
	Brian Mullen
	Bob Fleming
1994	Wayne Gretzky
	Robert Ridder
1993	*Frank Boucher
	*Mervyn "Red" Dutton
	Bruce McNall
	Gil Stein
1992	Al Arbour
	Art Berglund
	Lou Lamoriello
1991	Rod Gilbert
	Mike Ilitch
1990	Len Ceglarski
1989	Dan Kelly
	Lou Nanne
	*Lynn Patrick
	Bud Poile
1988	Keith Allen
	Fred Cusick
	Bob Johnson
1987	*Hobey Baker
	Frank Mathers
1986	John MacInnes
	Jack Riley
1985	Jack Butterfield
	Arthur M. Wirtz
1984	John A. Ziegler, Jr.
	*Arthur Howie Ross
1983	Bill Torrey
1982	Emile P. Francis
1981	Charles M. Schulz
1980	Bobby Clarke
	Edward M. Snider
	Frederick A. Shero
	1980 U.S. Olympic Team
1979	Bobby Orr
1978	Phil Esposito
	Tom Fitzgerald
	William T. Tutt
	William W. Wirtz
1977	John P. Bucyk
	Murray A. Armstrong
	John Mariucci
1976	Stanley Mikita
	George A. Leader
	Bruce A. Norris
1975	Donald M. Clark
	William L. Chadwick
	Thomas N. Ivan
1974	Alex Delvecchio
	Murray Murdoch
	*Weston W. Adams, Sr.
	*Charles L. Crovat
1973	Walter L. Bush, Jr.
1972	Clarence S. Campbell
	John A. "Snooks" Kelly
	Ralph "Cooney" Weiland
	*James D. Norris
1971	William M. Jennings
	*John B. Sollenberger
	*Terrance G. Sawchuk
1970	Edward W. Shore
	*James C. V. Hendy
1969	Robert M. Hull
	*Edward J. Jeremiah
1968	Thomas F. Lockhart
	*Walter A. Brown
	*Gen. John R. Kilpatrick
1967	Gordon Howe
	*Charles F. Adams
	*James Norris, Sr.
1966	J.J. "Jack" Adams

* awarded posthumously

PRESIDENTS' TROPHY

	Winner	Runner-up
2003	Ottawa Senators	Dallas Stars
2002	Detroit Red Wings	Boston Bruins
2001	Colorado Avalanche	Detroit Red Wings
2000	St. Louis Blues	Detroit Red Wings
1999	Dallas Stars	New Jersey Devils
1998	Dallas Stars	New Jersey Devils
1997	Colorado Avalanche	Dallas Stars
1996	Detroit Red Wings	Colorado Avalanche
1995	Detroit Red Wings	Quebec Nordiques
1994	New York Rangers	New Jersey Devils
1993	Pittsburgh Penguins	Boston Bruins
1992	New York Rangers	Washington Capitals
1991	Chicago Blackhawks	St. Louis Blues
1990	Boston Bruins	Calgary Flames
1989	Calgary Flames	Montreal Canadiens
1988	Calgary Flames	Montreal Canadiens
1987	Edmonton Oilers	Philadelphia Flyers
1986	Edmonton Oilers	Philadelphia Flyers

LESTER B. PEARSON AWARD

2003	Markus Naslund	Vancouver
2002	Jarome Iginla	Calgary
2001	Joe Sakic	Colorado
2000	Jaromir Jagr	Pittsburgh
1999	Jaromir Jagr	Pittsburgh
1998	Dominik Hasek	Buffalo
1997	Dominik Hasek	Buffalo
1996	Mario Lemieux	Pittsburgh
1995	Eric Lindros	Philadelphia
1994	Sergei Fedorov	Detroit
1993	Mario Lemieux	Pittsburgh
1992	Mark Messier	NY Rangers
1991	Brett Hull	St. Louis
1990	Mark Messier	Edmonton
1989	Steve Yzerman	Detroit
1988	Mario Lemieux	Pittsburgh
1987	Wayne Gretzky	Edmonton
1986	Mario Lemieux	Pittsburgh
1985	Wayne Gretzky	Edmonton
1984	Wayne Gretzky	Edmonton
1983	Wayne Gretzky	Edmonton
1982	Wayne Gretzky	Edmonton
1981	Mike Liut	St. Louis
1980	Marcel Dionne	Los Angeles
1979	Marcel Dionne	Los Angeles
1978	Guy Lafleur	Montreal
1977	Guy Lafleur	Montreal
1976	Guy Lafleur	Montreal
1975	Bobby Orr	Boston
1974	Phil Esposito	Boston
1973	Bobby Clarke	Philadelphia
1972	Jean Ratelle	NY Rangers
1971	Phil Esposito	Boston

JACK ADAMS AWARD

	Winner	Runner-up
2003	Jacques Lemaire, Min.	John Tortorella, T.B.
2002	Bob Francis, Phx.	Brian Sutter, Chi.
2001	Bill Barber, Phi.	Scotty Bowman, Det.
2000	Joel Quenneville, St.L.	Alain Vigneault, Mtl.
1999	Jacques Martin, Ott.	Pat Quinn, Tor.
1998	Pat Burns, Bos.	Larry Robinson, L.A.
1997	Ted Nolan, Buf.	Ken Hitchcock, Dal.
1996	Scotty Bowman, Det.	Doug MacLean, Fla.
1995	Marc Crawford, Que.	Scotty Bowman, Det.
1994	Jacques Lemaire, N.J.	Kevin Constantine, S.J.
1993	Pat Burns, Tor.	Brian Sutter, Bos.
1992	Pat Quinn, Van.	Roger Neilson, NYR
1991	Brian Sutter, St.L.	Tom Webster, L.A.
1990	Bob Murdoch, Wpg.	Mike Milbury, Bos.
1989	Pat Burns, Mtl.	Bob McCammon, Van.
1988	Jacques Demers, Det.	Terry Crisp, Cgy.
1987	Jacques Demers, Det.	Jack Evans, Hfd.
1986	Glen Sather, Edm.	Jacques Demers, St.L.
1985	Mike Keenan, Phi.	Barry Long, Wpg.
1984	Bryan Murray, Wsh.	Scotty Bowman, Buf.
1983	Orval Tessier, Chi.	
1982	Tom Watt, Wpg.	
1981	Red Berenson, St.L.	Bob Berry, L.A.
1980	Pat Quinn, Phi.	
1979	Al Arbour, NYI	Fred Shero, NYR
1978	Bobby Kromm, Det.	Don Cherry, Bos.
1977	Scotty Bowman, Mtl.	Tom McVie, Wsh.
1976	Don Cherry, Bos.	
1975	Bob Pulford, L.A.	
1974	Fred Shero, Phi.	

MBNA ROGER CROZIER SAVING GRACE AWARD

	Winner	Runner-up
2003	Marty Turco, Dal.	Dwayne Roloson, Min.
2002	Jose Theodore, Mtl.	Patrick Roy, Col.
2001	Marty Turco, Dal.	Mike Dunham, N.J.
2000	Ed Belfour, Dal.	Jose Theodore, Mtl.

NHL Entry Draft
History

Year	Location	Date	Players Drafted
1963	Queen Elizabeth Hotel, Montreal	June 5	21
1964	Queen Elizabeth Hotel, Montreal	June 11	24
1965	Queen Elizabeth Hotel, Montreal	April 27	11
1966	Mount Royal Hotel, Montreal	April 25	24
1967	Queen Elizabeth Hotel, Montreal	June 7	18
1968	Queen Elizabeth Hotel, Montreal	June 13	24
1969	Queen Elizabeth Hotel, Montreal	June 12	84
1970	Queen Elizabeth Hotel, Montreal	June 11	115
1971	Queen Elizabeth Hotel, Montreal	June 10	117
1972	Queen Elizabeth Hotel, Montreal	June 8	152
1973	Mount Royal Hotel, Montreal	May 15	168
1974	NHL Montreal Office	May 28	247
1975	NHL Montreal Office	June 3	217
1976	NHL Montreal Office	June 1	135
1977	NHL Montreal Office	June 14	185
1978	Queen Elizabeth Hotel, Montreal	June 15	234
1979	Queen Elizabeth Hotel, Montreal	August 9	126
1980	Montreal Forum	June 11	210
1981	Montreal Forum	June 10	211
1982	Montreal Forum	June 9	252
1983	Montreal Forum	June 8	242
1984	Montreal Forum	June 9	250
1985	Toronto Convention Centre	June 15	252
1986	Montreal Forum	June 21	252
1987	Joe Louis Arena, Detroit	June 13	252
1988	Montreal Forum	June 11	252
1989	Met Sports Center, Bloomington	June 17	252
1990	B.C. Place, Vancouver	June 16	250
1991	Memorial Auditorium, Buffalo	June 22	264
1992	Montreal Forum	June 20	264
1993	Le Colisee, Quebec	June 26	286
1994	Hartford Civic Center	June 28-29	286
1995	Edmonton Coliseum	July 8	234
1996	Kiel Center, St. Louis	June 22	241
1997	Civic Arena, Pittsburgh	June 21	246
1998	Marine Midland Arena, Buffalo	June 27	258
1999	FleetCenter, Boston	June 26	272
2000	Saddledome, Calgary	June 24-25	293
2001	National Car Rental Center, Florida	June 23-24	289
2002	Air Canada Centre, Toronto	June 22-23	290
2003	Gaylord Entertainment Center, Nashville	June 21-22	292

First Selections

Year	Player	Pos	Team	Drafted From	Age
1963	Garry Monahan	LW	Montreal	St. Michael's Juveniles	16.7
1964	Claude Gauthier		Detroit	Comite des jeunes (Rosemont)	
1965	Andre Veilleux	RW	NY Rangers	Montreal Ranger Jr. B	
1966	Barry Gibbs	D	Boston	Estevan Bruins	17.7
1967	Rick Pagnutti	D	Los Angeles	Garson Native Sons	20.6
1968	Michel Plasse	G	Montreal	Drummondville Rangers	20.0
1969	Rejean Houle	LW	Montreal	Montreal Jr. Canadiens	19.8
1970	Gilbert Perreault	C	Buffalo	Montreal Jr. Canadiens	19.7
1971	Guy Lafleur	RW	Montreal	Quebec Remparts	19.9
1972	Billy Harris	RW	NY Islanders	Toronto Marlboros	20.4
1973	Denis Potvin	D	NY Islanders	Ottawa 67s	19.7
1974	Greg Joly	D	Washington	Regina Pats	20.0
1975	Mel Bridgman	C	Philadelphia	Victoria Cougars	20.1
1976	Rick Green	D	Washington	London Knights	20.3
1977	Dale McCourt	C	Detroit	St. Catharines Fincups	20.4
1978	Bobby Smith	C	Minnesota	Ottawa 67's	20.4
1979	Rob Ramage	D	Colorado	London Knights	20.5
1980	Doug Wickenheiser	C	Montreal	Regina Pats	19.2
1981	Dale Hawerchuk	C	Winnipeg	Cornwall Royals	18.2
1982	Gord Kluzak	D	Boston	Nanaimo Islanders	18.3
1983	Brian Lawton	C	Minnesota	Mount St. Charles HS	18.11
1984	Mario Lemieux	C	Pittsburgh	Laval Voisins	18.8
1985	Wendel Clark	LW/D	Toronto	Saskatoon Blades	18.7
1986	Joe Murphy	C	Detroit	Michigan State	18.8
1987	Pierre Turgeon	C	Buffalo	Granby Bisons	17.10
1988	Mike Modano	C	Minnesota	Prince Albert Raiders	18.0
1989	Mats Sundin	RW	Quebec	Nacka (Sweden)	18.4
1990	Owen Nolan	RW	Quebec	Cornwall Royals	18.4
1991	Eric Lindros	C	Quebec	Oshawa Generals	18.3
1992	Roman Hamrlik	D	Tampa Bay	ZPS Zlin (Czech.)	18.2
1993	Alexandre Daigle	C	Ottawa	Victoriaville Tigres	18.5
1994	Ed Jovanovski	D	Florida	Windsor Spitfires	18.0
1995	Bryan Berard	D	Ottawa	Detroit Jr. Red Wings	18.4
1996	Chris Phillips	D	Ottawa	Prince Albert Raiders	18.3
1997	Joe Thornton	C	Boston	Sault Ste. Marie	17.11
1998	Vincent Lecavalier	C	Tampa Bay	Rimouski Oceanic	18.2
1999	Patrik Stefan	C	Atlanta	Long Beach Ice Dogs (IHL)	18.9
2000	Rick DiPietro	G	NY Islanders	Boston University	18.9
2001	Ilya Kovalchuk	RW	Atlanta	Spartak (Russia)	18.2
2002	Rick Nash	LW	Columbus	London Knights	18.0
2003	Marc-Andre Fleury	G	Pittsburgh	Cape Breton Screaming Eagles	18.0

Draft Summary

Following is a summary of the players drafted from the Ontario Hockey League (OHL), Quebec Major Junior Hockey League (QMJHL), Western Hockey League (WHL), United States colleges, United States high schools, European leagues and other North American leagues since 1969. "Other" may include Canadian and U.S. Jr. A and Jr. B, minor professional leagues (AHL, IHL), midget and other teams playing in leagues not listed above.

Year	Total Picks	OHL Picks	%	QMJHL Picks	%	WHL Picks	%	College Picks	%	Hi School Picks	%	Int'l Picks	%	Other Picks	%
1969	84	36	42.9	11	13.1	20	23.8	7	8.3	-	-	1	1.2	9	10.7
1970	115	51	44.3	13	11.3	22	19.1	16	13.9	-	-	-	-	13	11.3
1971	117	41	35.0	13	11.1	28	23.9	22	18.8	-	-	-	-	13	11.1
1972	152	46	30.3	30	19.7	44	28.9	21	13.8	-	-	-	-	11	7.2
1973	168	56	33.3	24	14.3	49	29.2	25	14.9	-	-	-	-	14	8.3
1974	247	69	27.9	40	16.2	66	26.7	41	16.6	-	-	6	2.4	25	10.1
1975	217	55	25.3	28	12.9	57	26.3	59	27.2	-	-	6	2.8	12	5.5
1976	135	47	34.8	18	13.3	33	24.4	26	19.3	-	-	8	5.9	3	2.2
1977	185	42	22.7	40	21.6	44	23.8	49	26.5	-	-	5	2.7	5	2.7
1978	234	59	25.2	22	9.4	48	20.5	73	31.2	-	-	16	6.8	16	6.8
1979	126	48	38.1	19	15.1	37	29.4	15	11.9	-	-	6	4.8	1	0.8
1980	210	73	34.8	24	11.4	41	19.5	42	20.0	7	3.3	13	6.2	10	4.8
1981	211	59	28.0	28	13.3	37	17.5	21	10.0	17	8.1	32	15.2	17	8.1
1982	252	60	23.8	17	6.7	55	21.8	20	7.9	47	18.7	35	13.9	18	7.1
1983	242	57	23.6	24	9.9	41	16.9	14	5.8	35	14.5	34	14.0	37	15.3
1984	250	55	22.0	16	6.4	37	14.8	22	8.8	44	17.6	40	16.0	36	14.4
1985	252	59	23.4	15	6.0	48	19.0	20	7.9	48	19.0	31	12.3	31	12.3
1986	252	66	26.2	22	8.7	32	12.7	22	8.7	40	15.9	28	11.1	42	16.7
1987	252	32	12.7	17	6.7	36	14.3	40	15.9	69	27.4	38	15.1	20	7.9
1988	252	32	12.7	22	8.7	30	11.9	48	19.0	56	22.2	39	15.5	25	9.9
1989	252	39	15.5	16	6.3	44	17.5	48	19.0	47	18.7	38	15.1	20	7.9
1990	250	39	15.6	14	5.6	33	13.2	38	15.2	57	22.8	53	21.2	16	6.4
1991	264	43	16.3	25	9.5	40	15.2	43	16.3	37	14.0	55	20.8	21	8.0
1992	264	57	21.6	22	8.3	45	17.0	9	3.4	25	9.5	84	31.8	22	8.3
1993	286	60	21.0	23	8.0	44	15.4	17	5.9	33	11.5	78	27.3	31	10.8
1994	286	45	15.7	28	9.8	66	23.1	6	2.1	28	9.8	80	28.0	33	11.5
1995	234	54	23.1	35	15.0	55	23.5	5	2.1	2	0.9	69	29.5	14	6.0
1996	241	51	21.2	31	12.9	54	22.4	25	10.4	6	2.5	58	24.1	16	6.6
1997	246	52	21.1	19	7.7	63	25.6	26	10.6	4	1.6	63	25.6	19	7.7
1998	258	50	19.4	41	15.9	44	17.1	27	10.5	7	2.7	75	29.1	14	5.4
1999	272	52	19.1	20	7.4	40	14.7	36	13.2	9	3.3	94	34.6	21	7.7
2000	293	39	13.3	21	7.2	41	14.0	35	11.9	7	2.4	123	42.0	27	9.2
2001	289	41	14.2	26	9.0	45	15.6	24	8.3	8	2.8	119	41.2	26	9.0
2002	290	35	12.1	23	7.9	43	14.8	41	14.1	6	2.1	110	37.9	32	11.0
2003	292	44	15.1	38	13.0	41	14.0	23	7.9	10	3.4	93	31.8	43	14.7
Total	7970	1744	21.9	825	10.4	1503	18.9	1006	12.6	649	8.1	1530	19.2	713	8.9

Total Players Drafted (1969-2003): 7,970

Top prospects for the 2003 Entry Draft, wearing the jerseys of their 2002-03 teams, pose for a picture on stage in between concerts at the Gaylord Entertainment Center in Nashville: Left to right, front row, Milan Michalek (Budejovice, RW, selected 6th overall by San Jose); Zach Parise (University of North Dakota, C, 17th by New Jersey); Ryan Suter (U.S. national team, D, 7th by Nashville); Thomas Vanek (University of Minnesota, LW, 5th by Buffalo) and Dustin Brown (Guelph Storm, RW, 13th by Los Angeles). Back row, Nathan Horton (Oshawa Generals, C, 3rd by Florida); Eric Staal (Peterborough Petes, C, 2nd by Carolina); Andrei Kastsitsyn (Belarus World Junior team, W, 10th by Montreal) and Marc-Andre Fleury (Canada World Junior team, G, 1st by Pittsburgh).

Ontario Hockey League

Club	'69	'70	'71	'72	'73	'74	'75	'76	'77	'78	'79	'80	'81	'82	'83	'84	'85	'86	'87	'88	'89	'90	'91	'92	'93	'94	'95	'96	'97	'98	'99	'00	'01	'02	'03	Total
Peterborough	5	5	4	5	9	4	8	1	4	6	9	10	3	5	7	3	9	2	5	2	2	4	3	4	4	2	5	4	5	1	4	1	2	1	5	153
Oshawa	5	4	3	5	5	7	6	6	1	3	3	2	9	5	5	6	6	6	3	2	4	2	4	4	4	1	10	1	3	4	3	2	1	3	3	141
Kitchener	1	6	2	8	4	13	3	1	3	4	4	4	5	5	8	4	6	3	2	1	7	5	3	1	4	2	4	2	3	5	–	1	1	4	1	130
London	4	9	1	5	6	6	3	5	4	3	6	2	5	5	3	7	1	3	2	6	3	3	1	3	4	1	1	4	1	8	4	1	2	2	4	128
Ottawa	2	4	3	4	6	5	6	5	5	5	3	8	4	9	2	2	3	3	2	1	–	5	5	6	4	1	1	2	5	2	6	2	3	–	2	126
Sudbury	–	–	–	–	6	6	4	5	4	4	3	7	2	4	–	2	5	3	1	–	1	2	8	2	10	2	2	1	3	5	5	–	2	1	1	101
S.S. Marie	–	–	–	–	4	5	2	5	1	5	3	3	8	1	6	4	5	7	1	2	3	1	2	7	3	4	3	4	1	4	1	1	1	2	1	100
Kingston	–	–	–	–	–	4	4	6	4	9	2	8	5	2	1	3	3	4	1	1	–	2	2	3	5	2	3	4	4	1	4	–	2	1	1	91
Windsor	–	–	–	–	–	–	–	2	1	4	2	3	5	3	2	2	3	7	–	5	2	1	–	3	–	3	4	1	5	1	2	2	2	2	2	69
Guelph	–	–	–	–	–	–	–	–	–	–	–	–	–	–	1	5	3	8	2	–	4	–	–	2	2	7	5	6	1	5	3	1	4	2	1	62
North Bay	–	–	–	–	–	–	–	–	–	–	–	–	–	–	4	4	3	3	3	3	1	4	2	5	2	7	2	1	1	2	2	2	3	2	–	56
Belleville	–	–	–	–	–	–	–	–	–	–	–	–	–	–	3	4	4	5	2	–	4	2	1	4	–	3	3	–	5	2	5	1	3	2	–	53
Plymouth	–	–	–	–	–	–	–	–	–	–	–	–	–	–	–	–	–	–	–	–	–	–	2	2	7	2	6	3	4	2	2	6	3	3	3	45
Sarnia	–	–	–	–	–	–	–	–	–	–	–	–	–	–	–	–	–	–	–	–	–	–	–	–	–	–	1	7	2	3	1	3	1	2	5	25
Owen Sound	–	–	–	–	–	–	–	–	–	–	–	–	–	–	–	–	–	–	–	–	–	1	1	2	4	3	2	3	2	1	–	1	–	1	1	22
Barrie	–	–	–	–	–	–	–	–	–	–	–	–	–	–	–	–	–	–	–	–	–	–	–	–	–	–	–	2	4	3	6	3	1	1	1	21
Brampton	–	–	–	–	–	–	–	–	–	–	–	–	–	–	–	–	–	–	–	–	–	–	–	–	–	–	–	–	–	–	2	6	3	3	4	18
Erie	–	–	–	–	–	–	–	–	–	–	–	–	–	–	–	–	–	–	–	–	–	–	–	–	–	–	–	–	3	1	2	3	2	2	–	13
St. Michael's	–	–	–	–	–	–	–	–	–	–	–	–	–	–	–	–	–	–	–	–	–	–	–	–	–	–	–	–	–	–	–	1	5	1	5	12
Mississauga	–	–	–	–	–	–	–	–	–	–	–	–	–	–	–	–	–	–	–	–	–	–	–	–	–	–	–	–	–	–	–	2	–	–	2	4
Saginaw	–	–	–	–	–	–	–	–	–	–	–	–	–	–	–	–	–	–	–	–	–	–	–	–	–	–	–	–	–	–	–	–	–	–	2	1
Teams no longer operating																																				
Toronto	3	7	6	5	6	8	4	4	7	5	4	10	2	6	4	4	3	4	1	2	2	–	–	–	–	–	–	–	–	–	–	–	–	–	–	97
Niagara Falls	4	2	1	4	–	–	–	–	2	3	5	8	6	6	–	–	–	–	–	–	4	4	4	4	4	3	2	6	–	–	–	–	–	–	–	72
Hamilton	2	3	5	4	6	4	7	3	–	8	1	–	–	–	–	–	3	6	4	4	–	–	2	–	–	–	–	–	–	–	–	–	–	–	–	62
St. Catharines	5	5	8	5	4	7	8	4	6	–	–	–	–	–	–	–	–	–	–	–	–	–	–	–	–	–	–	–	–	–	–	–	–	–	–	52
Cornwall	–	–	–	–	–	–	–	–	–	–	–	–	–	7	4	3	2	2	3	3	2	3	3	5	–	–	–	–	–	–	–	–	–	–	–	37
Brantford	–	–	–	–	–	–	–	–	–	–	3	8	5	2	7	2	–	–	–	–	–	–	–	–	–	–	–	–	–	–	–	–	–	–	–	27
Montreal	5	6	8	1	–	–	–	–	–	–	–	–	–	–	–	–	–	–	–	–	–	–	–	–	–	–	–	–	–	–	–	–	–	–	–	20
Newmarket	–	–	–	–	–	–	–	–	–	–	–	–	–	–	–	–	–	–	–	–	–	–	–	–	3	2	–	–	–	–	–	–	–	–	–	5

Quebec Major Junior Hockey League

Club	'69	'70	'71	'72	'73	'74	'75	'76	'77	'78	'79	'80	'81	'82	'83	'84	'85	'86	'87	'88	'89	'90	'91	'92	'93	'94	'95	'96	'97	'98	'99	'00	'01	'02	'03	Total
Shawinigan	3	2	1	6	1	5	3	–	3	–	–	2	2	5	5	2	–	2	1	–	2	–	2	3	1	1	2	4	1	3	1	1	1	2	2	69
Hull	–	–	–	–	–	–	3	2	2	3	–	3	1	–	3	1	–	4	3	2	2	3	3	3	3	1	3	3	–	3	4	–	2	5	4	66
Sherbrooke	–	–	2	2	4	3	7	5	6	3	4	1	5	2	–	–	–	–	–	–	–	–	–	–	3	2	4	–	1	5	–	–	3	–	1	63
Drummondville	2	4	1	4	2	1	–	–	–	–	–	–	–	–	–	1	2	2	2	4	1	–	4	2	2	1	4	3	2	2	–	1	1	–	1	49
Chicoutimi	–	–	–	–	–	1	–	–	5	1	1	3	6	1	3	–	3	1	2	2	1	1	–	1	1	3	2	–	2	1	–	1	1	3	1	47
Victoriaville	–	–	–	–	–	–	–	–	–	–	–	–	–	–	–	–	–	–	–	4	–	1	–	2	6	1	1	3	2	1	2	3	1	3	–	30
Halifax	–	–	–	–	–	–	–	–	–	–	–	–	–	–	–	–	–	–	–	–	–	–	–	–	–	–	3	1	3	3	–	2	3	–	6	21
Val-d'Or	–	–	–	–	–	–	–	–	–	–	–	–	–	–	–	–	–	–	–	–	–	–	–	–	–	1	2	4	2	–	3	2	2	1	1	18
Rimouski	–	–	–	–	–	–	–	–	–	–	–	–	–	–	–	–	–	–	–	–	–	–	–	–	–	–	–	–	–	5	2	2	4	–	4	17
St. Hyacinthe	–	–	–	–	–	–	–	–	–	–	–	–	–	–	–	–	–	–	–	–	–	3	1	2	1	4	–	4	–	–	–	–	–	–	–	15
Quebec	–	–	–	–	–	–	–	–	–	–	–	–	–	–	–	–	–	–	–	–	–	–	–	–	–	–	–	–	–	4	3	–	3	1	3	14
Baie-Comeau	–	–	–	–	–	–	–	–	–	–	–	–	–	–	–	–	–	–	–	–	–	–	–	–	–	–	–	–	–	3	–	2	3	1	2	11
Moncton	–	–	–	–	–	–	–	–	–	–	–	–	–	–	–	–	–	–	–	–	–	–	–	–	–	–	–	1	1	2	2	–	–	2	3	11
Rouyn-Noranda	–	–	–	–	–	–	–	–	–	–	–	–	–	–	–	–	–	–	–	–	–	–	–	–	–	–	–	–	–	3	1	4	–	–	2	10
Cape Breton	–	–	–	–	–	–	–	–	–	–	–	–	–	–	–	–	–	–	–	–	–	–	–	–	–	–	–	–	–	3	–	1	1	2	2	9
Acadie-Bathurst	–	–	–	–	–	–	–	–	–	–	–	–	–	–	–	–	–	–	–	–	–	–	–	–	–	–	–	–	–	–	2	–	–	2	3	7
Montreal Rocket	–	–	–	–	–	–	–	–	–	–	–	–	–	–	–	–	–	–	–	–	–	–	–	–	–	–	–	–	–	–	–	2	1	1	3	7
Teams no longer operating																																				
Laval	–	–	–	1	–	2	1	1	4	2	1	–	–	2	1	2	–	5	3	1	3	3	4	1	2	5	4	2	1	3	–	–	–	–	–	54
Quebec	1	1	2	4	6	6	1	3	7	1	3	2	2	1	2	2	3	–	–	–	–	–	–	–	–	–	–	–	–	–	–	–	–	–	–	47
Trois Rivieres	–	1	2	2	2	2	3	2	6	3	2	2	2	1	3	–	3	–	1	3	3	1	2	1	–	–	–	–	–	–	–	–	–	–	–	47
Cornwall	2	1	2	6	4	8	1	3	1	6	1	5	5	–	–	–	–	–	–	–	–	–	–	–	–	–	–	–	–	–	–	–	–	–	–	45
Montreal	–	–	–	–	4	4	8	1	3	2	4	3	–	3	–	–	–	–	–	–	–	–	–	–	–	–	–	–	–	–	–	–	–	–	–	32
Granby	–	–	–	–	–	–	–	–	–	–	–	–	–	2	1	3	2	2	4	–	2	–	2	–	1	5	2	3	1	–	–	–	–	–	–	30
Sorel	2	3	1	3	1	8	1	1	3	–	–	–	5	–	–	–	–	–	–	–	–	–	–	–	–	–	–	–	–	–	–	–	–	–	–	28
Verdun	–	1	1	2	–	–	–	–	–	1	3	3	–	–	3	3	–	3	0	3	1	–	–	3	–	–	–	–	–	–	–	–	–	–	–	27
Beauport	–	–	–	–	–	–	–	–	–	–	–	–	–	–	–	–	–	–	–	–	–	–	1	3	1	3	7	3	3	–	–	–	–	–	–	21
St. Jean	–	–	–	–	–	–	–	–	–	–	–	–	–	–	2	–	1	1	0	3	1	–	3	1	2	1	1	–	–	–	–	–	–	–	–	16
Longueuil	–	–	–	–	–	–	–	–	–	–	–	–	–	–	1	2	1	2	1	–	–	2	3	–	–	–	–	–	–	–	–	–	–	–	–	12
St. Jerome	1	–	1	–	–	–	–	–	–	–	–	–	–	–	–	–	–	–	–	–	–	–	–	–	–	–	–	–	–	–	–	–	–	–	–	2

Western Hockey League

Club	'69	'70	'71	'72	'73	'74	'75	'76	'77	'78	'79	'80	'81	'82	'83	'84	'85	'86	'87	'88	'89	'90	'91	'92	'93	'94	'95	'96	'97	'98	'99	'00	'01	'02	'03	Total
Regina	–	–	5	5	1	8	5	3	1	4	1	3	5	6	8	4	4	3	2	–	5	1	–	4	–	3	2	4	3	2	4	2	2	1	2	103
Portland	–	–	–	–	–	–	–	–	4	8	7	8	6	7	7	5	2	4	3	1	4	1	1	4	4	3	2	1	3	3	1	6	–	2	1	98
Kamloops	–	–	–	–	–	4	4	4	4	–	–	–	–	2	4	4	4	4	3	1	5	4	6	3	2	9	5	4	3	1	4	4	2	5	2	97
Saskatoon	1	–	1	3	8	4	5	3	4	1	2	2	3	5	5	3	1	5	4	4	3	2	2	3	2	4	2	2	2	2	4	1	4	–	–	97
Medicine Hat	–	–	–	4	6	4	5	3	5	4	–	4	2	1	2	1	6	2	5	1	4	1	3	3	1	6	2	7	2	3	1	–	2	3	3	96
Brandon	–	3	1	5	2	7	4	–	3	1	10	5	2	2	1	3	2	1	3	3	–	1	1	1	2	5	6	2	5	4	–	–	2	4	3	94
Seattle	–	–	–	–	–	–	–	–	–	4	2	3	–	6	–	1	3	1	2	4	2	6	3	2	4	5	5	1	8	2	6	4	5	1	5	85
Lethbridge	–	–	–	–	–	–	3	2	3	5	4	1	4	7	2	1	5	1	–	3	3	4	7	3	4	3	3	1	5	1	–	3	1	2	2	83
Prince Albert	–	–	–	–	–	–	–	–	–	–	–	–	–	4	2	2	6	6	1	3	3	4	6	2	5	3	4	3	5	3	3	2	4	1	2	74
Swift Current	1	–	1	–	3	6	–	–	–	–	–	–	–	–	–	–	–	–	5	2	2	2	1	1	5	4	4	1	2	2	1	3	1	4	2	53
Moose Jaw	–	–	–	–	–	–	–	–	–	–	–	–	–	–	–	–	4	1	3	–	3	1	2	3	2	3	4	4	4	2	1	5	3	3	3	51
Spokane	–	–	–	–	–	–	–	–	–	–	–	–	1	–	–	–	–	–	1	3	2	1	5	7	4	4	4	5	4	1	1	2	3	3	–	51
Tri-City	–	–	–	–	–	–	–	–	–	–	–	–	–	–	–	–	–	–	–	–	4	3	3	5	2	2	6	6	1	4	1	2	2	3	1	45
Red Deer	–	–	–	–	–	–	–	–	–	–	–	–	–	–	–	–	–	–	–	–	–	–	–	–	3	5	2	4	3	5	1	1	6	4	4	38
Calgary	–	–	–	–	–	–	–	–	–	–	–	–	–	–	–	–	–	–	–	–	–	–	–	–	–	–	–	3	–	3	6	4	1	2	3	22
Kelowna	–	–	–	–	–	–	–	–	–	–	–	–	–	–	–	–	–	–	–	–	–	–	–	–	–	–	–	4	7	2	2	1	1	1	4	22
Prince George	–	–	–	–	–	–	–	–	–	–	–	–	–	–	–	–	–	–	–	–	–	–	–	–	–	–	2	2	2	4	2	–	4	–	2	18
Kootenay	–	–	–	–	–	–	–	–	–	–	–	–	–	–	–	–	–	–	–	–	–	–	–	–	–	–	–	–	–	–	2	1	2	3	1	9
Vancouver	–	–	–	–	–	–	–	–	–	–	–	–	–	–	–	–	–	–	–	–	–	–	–	–	–	–	–	–	–	–	–	–	–	1	1	2
Teams no longer operating																																				
Victoria	–	–	–	2	2	5	7	4	3	3	1	8	6	2	3	4	2	1	2	4	4	2	–	1	2	2	–	–	–	–	–	–	–	–	–	70
Calgary	3	5	2	7	4	8	4	4	4	3	–	2	5	4	3	3	3	2	–	–	–	–	–	–	–	–	–	–	–	–	–	–	–	–	–	66
New Westm'r	–	–	–	6	8	7	9	5	8	6	5	1	–	–	–	2	1	1	2	1	–	–	–	–	–	–	–	–	–	–	–	–	–	–	–	62
Flin Flon	4	4	5	2	4	7	4	3	1	5	–	–	–	–	–	–	–	–	–	–	–	–	–	–	–	–	–	–	–	–	–	–	–	–	–	39
Edmonton	4	4	5	6	6	2	3	2	–	–	2	–	–	–	–	–	–	–	–	–	–	–	–	–	–	–	–	–	4	–	–	–	–	–	–	38
Winnipeg	3	2	4	2	5	4	4	–	4	–	–	–	1	4	1	–	–	–	–	–	–	–	–	–	–	–	–	–	–	–	–	–	–	–	–	34
Billings	–	–	–	–	–	–	–	–	–	4	3	4	2	–	–	–	–	–	–	–	–	–	–	–	–	–	–	–	–	–	–	–	–	–	–	13
Estevan	4	4	4	–	–	–	–	–	–	–	–	–	–	–	–	–	–	–	–	–	–	–	–	–	–	–	–	–	–	–	–	–	–	–	–	12

Sabres goalie Martin Biron (top) was one of seven players selected from Beauport of the QMJHL in 1995. Shane Doan of Phoenix (above) was selected seventh overall that year from the Kamloops Blazers of the Western Hockey League.

Western Hockey League *continued*

School	'69	'70	'71	'72	'73	'74	'75	'76	'77	'78	'79	'80	'81	'82	'83	'84	'85	'86	'87	'88	'89	'90	'91	'92	'93	'94	'95	'96	'97	'98	'99	'00	'01	'02	'03	Total
Tacoma	–	–	–	–	–	–	–	–	–	–	–	–	–	–	–	–	–	–	–	–	–	–	–	3	2	5	2	–	–	–	–	–	–	–	–	12
Kelowna	–	–	–	–	–	–	–	–	–	–	–	–	–	–	2	4	5	–	–	–	–	–	–	–	–	–	–	–	–	–	–	–	–	–	–	11
Nanaimo	–	–	–	–	–	–	–	–	–	–	–	–	–	5	1	–	–	–	–	–	–	–	–	–	–	–	–	–	–	–	–	–	–	–	–	6
Vancouver	–	–	–	2	–	–	–	–	–	–	–	–	–	–	–	–	–	–	–	–	–	–	–	–	–	–	–	–	–	–	–	–	–	–	–	2

U.S. College Hockey

School	'69	'70	'71	'72	'73	'74	'75	'76	'77	'78	'79	'80	'81	'82	'83	'84	'85	'86	'87	'88	'89	'90	'91	'92	'93	'94	'95	'96	'97	'98	'99	'00	'01	'02	'03	Total
Minnesota	1	3	2	–	–	9	4	4	5	5	2	3	1	1	1	–	–	2	1	1	1	–	–	–	–	–	2	3	2	1	3	3	–	3	2	65
Michigan	1	–	–	–	2	2	3	3	1	6	–	4	–	–	–	1	1	–	1	2	3	5	4	2	1	1	–	3	1	3	2	1	2	3	2	60
Boston U.	–	4	–	–	1	1	1	1	4	5	1	–	1	–	–	1	1	2	2	3	1	2	2	1	1	–	1	1	1	2	3	1	2	3	–	49
Michigan Tech	–	–	3	1	2	5	4	4	1	2	1	4	–	1	–	2	2	2	1	1	2	1	2	–	1	2	–	1	–	–	–	–	1	–	–	46
Michigan State	–	–	1	–	1	1	1	1	–	–	–	2	–	2	–	2	–	1	1	4	4	5	4	1	1	1	–	1	1	1	2	2	–	4	1	45
Wisconsin	–	1	2	4	5	4	4	2	3	–	1	–	3	2	–	1	1	–	1	–	1	–	1	–	–	–	–	–	–	–	2	3	–	–	–	41
Denver	1	3	2	4	2	3	1	2	2	2	2	1	–	1	–	–	1	2	4	1	1	–	–	–	–	–	–	–	3	–	1	–	–	1	–	40
North Dakota	2	3	3	1	4	2	1	–	1	2	3	3	1	–	–	1	–	–	–	–	2	1	1	–	–	–	–	–	2	–	1	1	–	1	1	37
Boston College	–	1	–	–	–	–	1	1	–	5	–	2	1	1	–	–	–	1	2	–	2	–	–	–	–	–	–	2	3	3	–	3	2	3	1	34
Providence	–	–	–	–	–	–	3	2	3	4	–	5	4	1	2	–	1	1	–	–	–	1	–	–	–	–	–	–	1	2	–	2	–	1	1	34
Harvard	–	–	2	–	–	–	2	–	2	2	–	–	–	1	1	–	2	–	1	1	2	–	–	–	2	1	–	3	1	2	1	2	2	3	–	33
Clarkson	–	–	2	2	1	–	2	–	2	2	1	1	1	1	1	1	–	–	1	1	1	3	2	1	1	–	–	–	–	3	1	1	–	–	–	32
Colorado	2	1	–	–	–	1	3	1	2	2	–	1	–	–	–	3	–	1	–	1	–	2	–	–	–	–	1	–	–	3	1	2	1	1	2	31
Cornell	–	–	–	2	1	1	–	1	1	1	–	1	1	1	–	1	2	–	1	2	5	2	–	–	–	–	–	–	1	–	2	2	–	1	2	31
New Hampshire	–	–	–	1	1	3	6	–	4	1	1	2	1	1	1	2	–	–	–	1	–	–	–	–	–	–	–	–	1	–	1	2	–	1	–	30
Notre Dame	–	–	2	3	–	–	7	2	–	3	1	1	–	–	–	–	–	–	–	–	–	–	–	–	–	–	–	1	2	–	2	1	1	2	–	28
Bowling Green	–	–	–	–	–	1	3	2	1	1	1	1	–	–	1	–	–	–	–	3	2	1	3	1	–	–	–	–	1	1	1	–	1	1	–	26
RPI	–	–	–	–	1	–	–	–	1	3	–	1	2	1	1	–	1	–	2	2	–	–	3	1	–	–	–	–	1	–	2	2	1	–	–	25
Lake Superior	–	–	–	–	1	1	1	–	–	3	–	–	–	–	–	1	–	3	–	3	2	3	1	–	1	–	–	1	1	–	1	–	–	1	–	24
St. Lawrence	–	–	–	–	–	–	1	–	1	4	–	–	–	3	–	1	1	1	1	1	1	1	2	–	1	–	–	1	1	–	1	–	–	1	–	23
W. Michigan	–	–	–	–	–	–	–	–	2	–	–	2	–	–	2	2	–	2	1	1	1	1	4	–	2	–	–	–	1	1	–	–	–	1	–	23
Maine	–	–	–	–	–	–	–	–	–	–	–	–	–	1	1	–	–	1	–	3	2	1	–	–	1	–	–	1	1	1	4	1	–	–	2	20
Northern Mich.	–	–	–	–	–	–	–	–	–	4	–	1	2	1	–	–	–	–	4	1	2	–	1	–	–	–	–	1	–	–	–	1	–	–	2	20
Ohio State	–	–	–	–	–	–	–	–	2	1	–	–	–	–	–	1	–	–	2	2	–	1	1	1	1	–	–	1	1	–	1	–	2	2	1	20
Vermont	–	–	–	–	1	–	4	–	1	1	–	1	1	–	1	1	2	–	–	1	–	–	1	–	–	1	–	1	–	–	–	–	2	–	–	19
Miami of Ohio	–	–	–	–	–	–	–	–	–	–	–	–	–	–	–	–	1	–	2	4	2	–	2	1	1	–	–	–	–	1	–	–	1	1	–	16
Minn.-Duluth	–	–	2	1	–	–	–	–	1	1	–	–	1	–	–	–	–	–	–	2	1	2	1	–	–	–	–	–	–	1	–	–	–	–	–	13
Yale	–	–	–	1	–	–	1	–	–	2	–	1	–	–	–	–	–	1	2	–	1	–	–	–	1	–	–	–	–	–	–	–	–	3	–	13
Brown	–	–	–	–	1	2	1	–	3	2	–	–	–	1	–	–	–	–	–	–	–	–	1	–	–	–	–	–	–	–	–	1	–	–	–	12
Colgate	–	–	–	–	–	1	–	–	–	2	1	–	–	–	–	–	–	–	–	1	1	2	2	–	–	–	–	–	–	–	–	–	–	1	–	11
Northeastern	–	–	–	–	–	1	–	–	–	1	–	1	–	–	1	–	1	1	–	–	1	1	–	–	–	–	–	–	–	1	1	–	–	–	–	10
Princeton	–	–	–	–	–	–	1	–	–	1	–	1	1	–	1	–	–	–	1	–	1	–	–	–	1	–	–	–	–	1	–	–	1	–	–	10

Colleges with fewer than 10 players drafted: 8 - Dartmouth, Ferris State, Merrimack; 6 - Lowell, Illinois-Chicago, St.Cloud State, St. Louis; 5 - Pennsylvania, Union College; 4 - Alaska-Anchorage; 3 - Babson College, Mass.-Amherst, Nebraska-Omaha; 2 - Alaska-Fairbanks; 1 - Air Force, American International College, Army, Bemidji State, Greenway, Hamilton, Minnesota State (Mankato), St. Anselem College, St. Thomas, Salem State, San Diego U., Wisconsin-River Falls.

U.S. High Schools and Prep Schools (10 or more players drafted)

School	'80	'81	'82	'83	'84	'85	'86	'87	'88	'89	'90	'91	'92	'93	'94	'95	'96	'97	'98	'99	'00	'01	'02	'03	Total
Northwood Prep (NY)	–	–	2	1	–	2	2	4	1	1	3	1	–	1	1	–	–	–	–	–	1	–	–	–	20
Cushing Acad. (MA)	–	–	–	–	1	–	–	–	3	2	3	1	–	2	2	–	1	1	–	–	–	1	–	–	17
Belmont Hill (MA)	–	–	–	1	–	2	1	2	1	3	2	1	2	–	1	–	–	–	–	–	–	–	–	–	16
Edina (MN)	–	1	4	2	2	–	–	1	2	2	1	–	1	–	–	–	–	–	–	–	–	–	–	–	16
Hill-Murray (MN)	–	–	–	–	3	–	3	3	–	2	3	–	–	–	1	–	–	–	–	–	–	–	–	–	15
Mount St. Charles (RI)	–	1	–	3	1	–	2	1	2	1	1	–	–	–	–	–	–	–	–	–	–	–	–	–	12
Culver Mil. Acad. (IN)	–	–	–	–	–	–	–	2	1	2	2	1	2	2	–	–	–	–	–	–	–	–	–	–	12
Catholic Memorial (MA)	–	–	–	–	–	2	–	1	1	2	–	–	2	1	2	–	–	–	1	–	–	–	–	–	12
Deerfield (IL)	–	–	–	–	1	1	–	1	1	2	–	1	–	–	–	–	–	–	–	1	2	–	1	1	12
St. Sebastien's (MA)	–	–	–	–	–	–	–	–	–	–	–	–	2	2	1	–	–	–	1	–	–	1	1	4	12
Canterbury (CT)	–	–	–	–	–	–	2	–	3	–	2	–	2	1	–	–	–	–	–	–	–	–	–	1	11
Matignon (MA)	1	1	1	–	3	–	–	3	–	–	–	1	–	–	–	–	–	–	–	–	–	–	–	–	10
Roseau (MN)	1	–	1	1	1	–	1	–	–	1	3	1	–	–	–	–	–	–	–	–	–	–	–	–	10
Choate (CT)	–	–	–	–	–	1	–	2	3	–	1	1	1	–	–	–	–	–	–	–	1	–	–	–	10
Hotchkiss (CT)	–	–	–	–	–	1	–	–	1	–	1	–	–	–	3	1	2	–	–	–	–	1	–	–	10

U.S. College and High School Firsts

1967 – First U.S. College Player Drafted
Michigan Tech center Al Karlander was selected 17th overall by the Detroit Red Wings.

1979 – First U.S. College First-Round Selection
Minnesota-born defenseman Mike Ramsey (currently an assistant coach with the Minnesota Wild) was selected 11th overall by the Buffalo Sabres.

1980 – First U.S. High School Player Drafted
Center Jay North of Bloomington-Jefferson H.S. was taken 62nd overall by the Buffalo Sabres in 1980.

1981 – First U.S. High School First- Round Selection
Center Bob Carpenter of St. John's prep school was selected third overall by Washington in 1981.

1983 – First U.S. High School Player Drafted First Overall
Minnesota North Stars selected left winger Brian Lawton from Mount St. Charles H.S. first overall in 1983.

1986 – First U.S. College Player Drafted First Overall
Detroit selected right winger Joe Murphy from Michigan State first overall in 1986.

2003 – Most U.S. College Players Selected in the First Round
The 2003 draft saw seven U.S. college players selected in the first round, the most in Entry Draft history. Six were selected in the first round in 2000, five in 2002, four in 2001 and three in each of the 1986 and 1999 Entry Drafts.

Draft Evolution and Eligibility

The NHL Entry Draft celebrated its 40th anniversary on June 21-22, 2003 at Nashville's Gaylord Entertainment Center. Since 1963, the event has grown from a small gathering of hockey executives to a spectacle seen by hundreds of thousands of hockey fans throughout the world.

Inception of the Amateur Draft

In an effort to eliminate the sponsorship of amateur teams and players by its member clubs, the National Hockey League began developing a drafting system that would provide each team with an equal opportunity to acquire amateur players.

"I'm trying to work out a system whereby all amateur players who will attain their 17th birthdays before August of each year will be available for drafting by NHL teams in the reverse order of the standing," said NHL President Clarence Campbell during the 1962-63 season. "We're ultimately hopeful it will produce a uniform opportunity for each team to acquire a star player."

The end result was the establishment of the NHL's Amateur Draft.

The first NHL Amateur Draft was held at the Queen Elizabeth Hotel in Montreal on June 5, 1963. All amateur players, 17 years of age and older who were not already sponsored by an NHL club, were eligible to be drafted. Garry Monahan, a 17-year-old center from the St. Michael's Juveniles of Toronto, was selected first overall by the Montreal Canadiens.

The 1969 Draft marked the first year that the effects of NHL amateur sponsorship would not be seen, as every junior of qualifying age (20 years) was available for selection. Eighty-four players were selected that year, more than four times the average number of players chosen in the first six years of the Draft.

Entry Draft Replaces the Amateur Draft

In 1979, the name of the Draft was changed from "Amateur" to "Entry" to reflect the inclusion of young players eligible for selection who had played professionally in the now-defunct World Hockey Association.

Draft Eligibility

Beginning with the 1980 Entry Draft and continuing today, all 18, 19 and 20-year old North American and non-North American-born players have been eligible to be drafted. In addition, non-North American players aged 21-years or older are eligible for claim. From 1987 to 1991, the selection of 18 and 19-year-old players was restricted to the first three rounds of the draft, unless the player met qualifying criteria that dealt with hockey experience in major junior, U.S. college and high school or European hockey. Starting with the 1992 Draft, those players were available in all rounds.

International

Country	'69	'70	'71	'72	'73	'74	'75	'76	'77	'78	'79	'80	'81	'82	'83	'84	'85	'86	'87	'88	'89	'90	'91	'92	'93	'94	'95	'96	'97	'98	'99	'00	'01	'02	'03	Total
USSR/CIS/Russia	–	–	–	–	–	–	1	–	–	2	–	–	–	3	5	1	2	11	18	14	25	45	31	35	27	17	16	22	29	44	36	33	32	452
Sweden	–	–	–	–	5	2	5	2	8	5	9	14	14	10	14	16	9	15	14	9	7	11	11	18	11	18	21	14	17	20	20	28	28	21	20	377
Czech Republic and Slovakia	–	–	–	–	–	–	2	1	–	4	13	9	13	8	6	11	5	8	21	9	17	15	18	21	14	17	20	20	28	28	21	20	349
Finland	1	–	–	–	1	3	2	3	2	–	4	12	5	9	10	4	10	6	7	3	9	6	8	9	8	12	7	11	12	17	19	29	26	12	267
Germany	–	–	–	–	–	–	–	–	2	–	–	2	–	1	2	1	–	1	2	–	1	1	3	1	1	3	1	–	1	7	1	4	35
Switzerland	–	–	–	–	–	1	–	–	–	–	–	–	–	–	–	–	–	–	1	–	2	1	1	3	2	3	7	5	4	5	35
Norway	–	–	–	–	–	–	–	–	–	–	–	–	–	–	2	–	2	1	–	1	–	7
Denmark	–	–	–	–	–	–	–	–	–	–	–	–	1	1	–	–	–	–	2
Poland	–	–	–	–	–	–	–	1	–	1	2
Scotland	–	–	–	–	–	–	–	1	1
Japan	–	–	–	–	–	–	1	1
Hungary	–	–	–	–	1	1

Czech Republic and Slovakia

Club	'74	'75	'76	'77	'78	'79	'80	'81	'82	'83	'84	'85	'86	'87	'88	'89	'90	'91	'92	'93	'94	'95	'96	'97	'98	'99	'00	'01	'02	'03	Total
Chemopetrol Litvinov[1]	–	–	–	–	–	–	–	3	1	2	–	–	2	2	1	3	2	4	2	2	1	1	–	1	–	2	31
Dukla Jihlava	–	–	–	–	–	–	2	4	3	1	–	3	1	1	3	2	1	1	1	1	–	28
HC Ceske Budejovice[2]	–	–	–	–	–	2	1	1	–	1	–	1	2	–	1	2	3	1	2	1	1	3	2	–	2	26
Slavia Praha	–	–	–	–	–	1	–	–	–	–	–	1	–	4	5	2	3	5	2	2	25
Dukla Trencin	–	–	–	–	1	–	–	1	1	–	2	2	–	1	2	1	–	2	3	–	3	23
Slovan Bratislava	–	–	1	1	–	2	–	1	1	1	–	1	–	3	–	1	1	1	2	–	1	3	22
Sparta Praha	–	–	–	–	2	1	1	1	2	1	2	1	–	1	1	1	1	2	1	1	21
HC Kladno[3]	–	–	2	1	–	1	–	–	–	–	1	2	–	1	2	–	2	1	1	–	1	18
ZPS Zlin[4]	–	–	–	–	1	–	1	1	–	–	–	2	2	1	–	2	1	2	2	–	18
HC Vitkovice[5]	–	–	–	1	–	1	–	–	–	1	1	3	1	1	1	1	1	–	2	15
HC Kosice[6]	–	–	–	1	2	–	1	–	–	–	1	1	1	–	3	–	13
HC Pardubice[7]	–	–	–	–	2	–	2	1	–	1	–	–	2	1	–	1	1	–	1	3	–	13
Interconex Plzen[8]	–	–	–	–	–	–	1	–	–	3	1	–	1	1	1	1	1	2	–	11
HC Vsetin	–	–	–	–	–	–	–	–	–	–	2	1	–	2	2	3	1	8
Zetor Brno	–	–	–	–	–	1	–	3	–	2	–	1	–	1	–	1	–	7
AC Nitra	–	–	–	–	–	–	2	–	1	2	1	2	–	7
HC Olomouc[9]	–	–	–	–	–	–	1	–	2	1	2	–	1	–	7
ZTK Zvolen	–	–	–	–	–	–	–	1	1	–	2	2	–	7
Zelezarny Trinec	–	–	–	–	–	1	–	–	2	–	–	1	1	5
ZTS Martin	–	–	–	–	–	1	–	2	–	1	1	1	1	6
HC Karlovy Vary	–	–	–	–	–	–	1	1	1	1	4
Havirov	–	–	–	–	–	2	2	–	3
HC Liberec	–	–	–	–	–	1	2	–	2
Ingstav Brno	–	–	–	–	–	1	1	–	2
IS Banska Bystrica	–	–	–	–	2	–	2
Michalovce	–	–	–	1	1	–	2
Partizan Liptovsky Mikulas	–	–	–	1	–	1	–	2
VTJ Pisek	–	–	–	1	–	1	–	2
ZPA Presov	–	–	–	1	–	1	2

Former club names: [1]–CHZ Litvinov, [2]–Motor Ceske Budejovice, [3]–Poldi Kladno, [4]–TJ Gottwaldov, TJ Zlin, [5]–TJ Vitkovice, [6]–VSZ Kosice, [7]–Tesla Pardubice, [8]–Skoda Plzen, [9]–DS Olomouc.

Teams with one player selected: Banik Sokolov, Dubnica, Havlickuv Brod, KLH Chomutov, KC SKP Poprad, KC Skalica, HK Trnava, KHM Zvolen, Ostrava, Spisska Nova Ves.

Finland

Club	'69	'70	'71	'72	'73	'74	'75	'76	'77	'78	'79	'80	'81	'82	'83	'84	'85	'86	'87	'88	'89	'90	'91	'92	'93	'94	'95	'96	'97	'98	'99	'00	'01	'02	'03	Total
TPS Turku	–	–	–	–	–	–	–	–	–	1	6	–	–	1	1	–	–	–	–	–	3	2	3	1	3	3	1	3	3	1	1	33
Jokerit	–	–	–	–	–	–	–	–	2	1	–	1	–	1	–	1	1	–	2	–	3	–	1	1	1	3	3	4	6	2	33
HIFK Helsinki	1	–	–	–	–	–	–	1	1	2	1	2	1	–	2	1	–	2	–	1	–	1	2	4	2	2	5	–	32
Ilves	–	–	–	1	2	–	1	–	2	–	2	2	–	1	–	1	–	–	1	–	2	1	3	4	2	–	27
Karpat	–	–	–	–	–	–	1	–	1	–	1	–	1	–	1	–	–	–	1	–	1	–	3	3	3	20
Tappara	–	–	–	–	1	–	–	–	2	–	–	4	1	–	1	1	1	–	1	2	1	–	2	19
Lukko	–	–	–	2	1	–	–	–	2	–	1	–	1	–	1	–	2	1	3	1	1	17
Assat	–	–	–	2	–	–	1	–	1	2	2	–	1	–	1	–	1	–	1	14
Blues Espoo	–	–	–	–	–	–	1	–	1	1	–	2	1	–	1	–	2	2	1	14
HPK Hameenlinna	–	–	–	–	–	–	1	–	1	–	1	1	1	3	1	1	–	11
JyP Jyvaskyla	–	–	–	–	–	–	–	1	–	2	1	–	3	–	1	2	–	10
KalPa Kuopio	–	–	–	–	–	–	1	–	2	–	1	–	–	1	–	1	2	–	9
Reipas Lahti	–	–	–	1	1	1	–	1	–	1	–	–	2	1	–	1	7
SaiPa Lappeenranta	–	–	–	–	–	2	–	–	1	–	1	1	–	5
Kiekoo-67 Turku	–	–	–	–	–	–	3	–	–	3
Sapko Savonlinna	–	–	–	1	1	–	2
Sport Vaasa	–	–	–	1	1	–	2
KooKoo Kouvola	–	–	1	–	–	1	2

Teams with one player selected: Ahmat Hyvinkaa, GrIFK Kauniainen, S-Kiekko Seinajoki, Junkkarit Kalajoki, Hermes Kokkola, TuTo.

Center Marco Sturm (top) of the San Jose Sharks was drafted 21st overall in the 1996 Entry Draft. Sturm previously palyed for EV Landshut in the Deutsche Eishockey Liga. Defenseman Zdeno Chara was also drafted in 1996. Selected 56th overall by the New York Islanders, he played one season of junior with Prince George before turning pro. He was traded to Ottawa June 23, 2001.

Opting-In and Re-Entering the Draft

Opting-in to the Entry Draft

Beginning with the 1995 Entry Draft, all players 18 years of age are required to opt-in to be eligible for selection. For 2003, any player born between Sept. 16, 1984 and Sept. 15, 1985 is considered to be 18 years of age and, therefore, must opt-in to the Entry Draft.

Any player born prior to Sept. 16, 1984 is automatically eligible for selection and is _not_ required to opt-in.

A player has until the later of May 1, 2003 or up until seven days of his team's last game to opt-in to be considered eligible for selection.

Re-Entering the Draft

In 1978, the NHL saw the first players re-enter the Entry Draft after being selected in 1977.

Any player 20 years of age or younger who has not signed a contract within two years of being drafted or has not received a bona fide offer from the NHL club that drafted him within one year of being drafted is subject to re-enter the Entry Draft.

European players who have not signed a contract or whose rights have been released by the NHL club that drafted them, without playing in North America as an 18, 19 or 20-year-old, are subject to re-entry.

If a player is drafted twice and remains without a contract, he is not subject to re-entry.

Draft Becomes an Event for Fans

Prior to 1980, the Entry Draft was closed to the public. The 1980 Draft was held in the Montreal Forum in front of 2,500 fans.

The Canadian Broadcasting Corporation (CBC) and Radio-Canada provided the first live network television coverage in both English and French in 1984. Coverage in the U.S. was first provided by SportsChannel America in 1989.

The 2003 NHL Entry Draft was seen in Canada on The Sports Network (TSN) and in the United States on ESPN2. French-language television coverage was provided by Reseau Des Sports (RDS).

In recent years the NHL has staged a Top Prospects Preview, introducing the top-rated players of the current year to fans and members of the media.

USSR/CIS/Russia

Club	'74	'75	'76	'77	'78	'79	'80	'81	'82	'83	'84	'85	'86	'87	'88	'89	'90	'91	'92	'93	'94	'95	'96	'97	'98	'99	'00	'01	'02	'03	Total
CSKA Moscow	–	–	–	–	1	–	–	–	1	4	–	1	1	1	5	8	3	4	7	3	5	2	3	–	1	3	–	–	–	3	56
Dynamo Moscow	–	–	–	–	–	–	–	–	–	–	–	–	–	–	2	3	4	7	10	2	1	7	1	1	1	2	2	–	–	1	44
Krylja Sovetov Moscow	–	–	–	–	–	–	–	–	–	–	–	–	–	–	1	1	2	4	3	1	5	3	2	1	1	2	1	1	1	–	29
Lokomotiv-2 Yaroslavl[1]	–	–	–	–	–	–	–	–	–	–	–	–	–	–	–	–	–	–	–	–	–	1	2	2	4	–	9	1	1	3	23
Lokomotiv Yaroslavl[1]	–	–	–	–	–	–	–	–	–	–	–	–	–	–	–	–	1	2	–	–	1	5	1	1	3	1	1	–	2	4	22
Spartak Moscow	–	–	–	–	–	–	–	–	1	–	–	1	–	1	–	–	–	1	4	–	6	1	–	–	–	1	–	6	–	–	22
Dynamo-2 Moscow	–	–	–	–	–	–	–	–	–	–	–	–	–	–	–	–	–	–	2	1	2	–	–	3	3	–	4	–	–	1	16
Elemash Elektrostal	–	–	–	–	–	–	–	–	–	–	–	–	–	–	–	–	–	–	3	–	–	–	–	1	–	–	–	1	9	2	16
Traktor Chelyabinsk	–	–	–	–	–	–	–	–	–	–	–	–	–	–	–	2	–	–	2	7	1	1	–	1	1	–	–	–	1	–	16
Khimik Voskresensk	–	–	–	–	–	–	–	–	–	1	–	–	–	–	–	1	3	1	2	–	1	–	–	–	2	–	1	1	–	1	14
Lada Togliatti	–	–	–	–	–	–	–	–	–	–	–	–	–	–	–	–	–	–	1	2	–	–	1	3	1	2	2	–	2	–	14
Severstal Cherepovets[2]	–	–	–	–	–	–	–	–	–	–	–	–	–	–	–	–	–	–	1	1	–	1	1	–	–	5	1	–	–	2	12
HC CSKA Moscow	–	–	–	–	–	–	–	–	–	–	–	–	–	–	–	–	–	–	–	–	–	–	–	–	–	2	5	–	4	–	11
SKA St. Peterburg[3]	–	–	–	–	1	–	–	–	1	–	–	–	–	–	–	–	–	2	1	–	1	–	–	–	–	2	1	2	–	–	11
Sokol Kiev	–	–	–	–	–	–	–	–	–	–	1	–	–	–	1	–	1	2	3	1	–	2	–	–	–	–	–	–	–	–	11
Pardaugava Riga[4]	–	1	–	–	–	–	–	–	–	–	–	–	–	–	1	2	–	1	4	1	–	–	–	–	–	–	–	–	–	–	10
Avangard Omsk	–	–	–	–	–	–	–	–	–	–	–	–	–	–	–	–	–	–	–	–	3	–	1	–	–	–	1	3	1	–	9
Salavat Yulayev Ufa	–	–	–	–	–	–	–	–	–	–	–	–	–	–	–	–	–	–	–	2	2	1	1	1	–	–	1	–	–	1	9
Torpedo Ust-Kamenogorsk	–	–	–	–	–	–	–	–	–	–	–	–	–	–	–	–	–	–	1	1	2	1	–	–	2	1	–	–	–	1	9
CSKA-2 Moscow	–	–	–	–	–	–	–	–	–	–	–	–	–	–	–	–	–	–	–	–	1	–	2	2	–	–	–	–	–	2	7
Metallurg Novokuznetsk	–	–	–	–	–	–	–	–	–	–	–	–	–	–	–	–	–	–	–	–	–	–	–	–	–	2	2	1	–	1	6
AK Bars Kazan	–	–	–	–	–	–	–	–	–	–	–	–	–	–	–	–	–	–	–	–	1	–	–	–	1	–	1	1	–	1	5
Lada-2 Togliatti	–	–	–	–	–	–	–	–	–	–	–	–	–	–	–	–	–	–	–	–	–	–	–	–	–	1	2	2	–	–	5
Metallurg Magnitogorsk	–	–	–	–	–	–	–	–	–	–	–	–	–	–	–	–	–	–	–	–	–	–	–	–	–	–	–	3	1	1	5
Molot-Prikamje Perm	–	–	–	–	–	–	–	–	–	–	–	–	–	–	–	–	–	–	–	–	1	1	–	–	–	–	1	1	1	–	5
Neftekhimik Nizhnekamsk	–	–	–	–	–	–	–	–	–	–	–	–	–	–	–	–	–	–	–	–	–	–	–	1	–	–	2	2	–	–	5
Avangard-2 Omsk	–	–	–	–	–	–	–	–	–	–	–	–	–	–	–	–	–	–	–	–	–	–	–	–	–	–	–	3	–	1	4
Dynamo-Energiya Yekaterinburg[5]	–	–	–	–	–	–	–	–	–	–	–	–	–	–	–	–	–	–	–	–	–	–	1	–	1	1	–	–	–	1	4
CSK VVS Samara	–	–	–	–	–	–	–	–	–	–	–	–	–	–	–	–	–	–	–	–	–	1	–	–	–	1	–	1	–	1	4
Krylja Sovetov Moscow 2	–	–	–	–	–	–	–	–	–	–	–	–	–	–	–	–	–	–	–	1	–	–	–	–	–	–	–	–	3	–	4
Tivali Minsk[6]	–	–	–	–	–	–	–	–	–	–	–	–	–	–	1	–	–	–	–	2	1	–	–	–	–	–	–	–	–	–	4
Torpedo Nizhny Novgorod[7]	–	–	–	–	–	–	–	–	–	–	–	–	–	–	–	–	1	–	2	–	–	–	–	–	–	–	1	–	–	–	4
Ak-Bars-2 Kazan	–	–	–	–	–	–	–	–	–	–	–	–	–	–	–	–	–	–	–	–	–	–	–	–	–	1	–	1	–	1	3
Severstal-2 Cherepovets	–	–	–	–	–	–	–	–	–	–	–	–	–	–	–	–	–	–	–	–	–	–	–	–	–	1	1	–	1	–	3
Dizelist Penza	–	–	–	–	–	–	–	–	–	–	–	–	–	–	–	–	–	–	1	–	–	–	–	–	–	–	1	–	–	–	2
Kristall Saratov	–	–	–	–	–	–	–	–	–	–	–	–	–	–	–	–	–	–	–	1	–	–	–	–	–	–	–	1	–	–	2
Metallurg-2 Novokuznetsk	–	–	–	–	–	–	–	–	–	–	–	–	–	–	–	–	–	–	–	–	–	–	–	–	–	–	2	–	–	–	2
Torpedo Nizhny Novgorod 2	–	–	–	–	–	–	–	–	–	–	–	–	–	–	–	–	–	–	–	–	–	–	–	–	–	–	–	–	2	–	2

Former club names: [1]–Torpedo Yaroslavl, [2]–Metallurg Cherepovets, [3]–SKA Leningrad, [4]–Dynamo Riga, HC Riga, [5]–Avtomobilist Yekaterinburg, [6]–Dynamo Minsk, [7]–Torpedo Gorky,

Teams with one player selected: Amur Khabarovsk, Argus Moscow, Dynamo Khazov, Dynamo-81 Riga, Gazovik Tyumen, Izohets St. Petersburg, Kapitan Stupino, Khimik Novopolotsk, Mechel Chelyabinsk, Neftekhimik Nizhnekamsk, Salavat Novoil Ufa, SKA-2 St. Petersburg, Sibir-2 Novosibirsk-1, Stalkers-Juniors, THC Tver, Vityaz Podolsk, Vityaz-2 Podolsk, HC CSKA Moscow 2, Khimik Voskresensk 2, Metalurgs Liepaja, Mostovik Kurgan, Torpedo Nizhny Novgorod 2, Yunost Minsk.

Sweden

Club	'74	'75	'76	'77	'78	'79	'80	'81	'82	'83	'84	'85	'86	'87	'88	'89	'90	'91	'92	'93	'94	'95	'96	'97	'98	'99	'00	'01	'02	'03	Total
Djurgarden Stockholm	1	1	1	–	–	1	2	–	1	2	1	–	1	2	–	1	1	2	1	1	–	3	2	2	–	1	4	1	2	–	34
MoDo Ornskoldsvik	–	–	1	–	–	1	–	–	1	–	2	–	–	1	–	–	–	2	2	5	–	–	3	3	–	7	3	–	3	–	34
Farjestad Karlstad	–	–	–	2	2	–	1	2	1	1	1	2	–	–	–	1	–	1	2	1	–	2	–	3	6	1	–	1	2	–	32
Leksand	1	–	–	–	–	1	–	–	1	–	2	2	1	1	2	1	–	2	–	2	2	–	1	–	2	–	5	–	–	2	28
Vastra Frolunda Goteborg	–	–	–	–	–	–	–	–	–	–	2	1	–	1	1	1	–	–	1	–	3	1	1	–	1	2	4	3	3	2	27
AIK Solna	–	–	1	–	1	1	–	2	3	1	–	4	–	–	–	–	1	1	1	–	1	–	–	1	1	3	–	1	1	–	24
Brynas Gavle	1	–	–	–	1	1	1	1	–	1	2	–	–	4	–	–	–	–	–	1	–	–	1	1	2	1	1	2	–	2	23
HV 71 Jonkoping	–	–	–	–	–	–	–	1	–	–	–	–	–	1	1	–	1	–	–	–	2	–	2	1	4	3	1	–	1	1	19
Sodertalje	–	–	–	–	1	–	–	1	1	1	2	2	2	–	–	2	–	–	–	1	–	–	–	–	1	–	1	1	–	2	18
Malmo	–	–	–	–	–	–	–	–	–	–	–	–	–	–	1	–	–	–	1	1	1	–	2	–	–	1	1	–	4	1	13
Skelleftea	–	1	1	–	–	–	–	1	1	2	1	–	–	–	1	–	–	–	–	1	–	–	–	1	–	–	–	–	–	–	10
Lulea	–	–	–	–	–	–	1	1	–	–	–	–	1	1	1	–	–	–	1	–	–	–	–	1	1	–	2	–	–	–	10
Vasteras	–	–	–	–	–	–	–	–	–	–	–	–	–	–	2	2	1	1	–	1	1	–	–	–	–	–	1	–	1	–	10
Rogle Angelholm	–	–	–	–	–	–	–	–	–	–	–	–	–	1	2	–	–	–	–	2	2	1	–	–	–	1	–	–	–	–	9
Hammarby Stockholm	–	–	–	–	–	–	1	1	–	–	–	–	–	–	–	–	–	–	–	1	1	–	–	–	1	–	–	1	–	3	9
Timra1	–	–	–	–	–	–	1	2	–	–	–	1	1	–	–	–	–	–	–	–	1	–	–	–	–	1	–	–	1	–	8
Huddinge	–	–	–	–	–	–	–	–	–	–	–	–	–	–	–	–	–	1	–	–	–	–	2	–	–	1	–	1	1	–	6
Mora	–	–	–	–	–	–	–	–	–	1	–	–	1	–	–	–	–	–	–	–	–	–	1	1	–	–	–	1	–	1	6
Bjorkloven Umea	–	–	–	–	–	–	2	1	–	–	–	1	–	–	1	–	–	–	–	–	–	–	–	–	–	–	–	–	–	–	5
Orebro	–	–	1	–	1	–	–	–	–	1	–	1	–	1	–	–	–	–	–	–	–	–	–	–	–	–	–	–	–	–	5
Nacka	–	–	–	–	–	–	–	–	–	–	–	–	1	–	–	1	–	–	2	–	–	–	–	–	–	–	–	–	–	–	4
Troja/Ljungby	–	–	–	–	–	–	–	–	–	–	–	1	–	–	1	–	–	–	–	–	–	–	–	–	–	1	–	–	–	1	4
Falun	–	–	–	–	–	–	–	1	–	–	–	–	–	–	1	–	–	1	–	–	–	–	–	–	–	–	–	–	–	–	3
Team Kiruna	–	–	–	–	1	–	–	–	1	–	–	–	–	–	–	–	–	–	–	1	–	–	–	–	–	–	–	–	–	–	3
Boden	1	–	–	–	–	–	–	–	–	–	–	–	1	–	–	–	–	–	–	–	1	–	–	–	–	–	–	–	–	–	3
Pitea	–	–	–	–	–	–	–	–	1	–	–	–	–	–	–	–	1	–	–	–	1	–	–	–	–	–	–	–	–	–	3
Grums	–	–	–	–	–	–	–	–	–	–	–	–	–	–	–	–	–	–	–	–	1	–	–	–	–	1	1	–	–	–	3
Morrum	–	–	–	–	–	–	–	–	–	–	–	–	–	–	–	–	–	–	–	–	–	–	–	–	–	–	–	1	2	–	3
Ostersund	–	–	–	–	–	–	–	–	–	–	–	1	–	1	–	–	–	–	–	–	–	–	–	–	–	–	–	–	–	–	2
Hasten	–	–	–	–	–	–	–	–	–	–	–	–	–	–	–	–	–	–	–	–	–	–	1	–	–	–	–	–	1	–	2

Teams with one player selected: Almtuna, Arboga, Arvika, Danderyd Hockey, Fagersta, Karskoga, Linkoping, Stocksund, S/G Hockey 83 Gavle, Talje, Tingsryd, Tunabro, Uppsala, Vallentuna, Bofors, Sunne.

2003 Entry Draft Analysis

Country of Origin

Country	Players Drafted
Canada	129
USA	59
Russia	28
Czech Republic	18
Sweden	16
Finland	13
Slovakia	10
Switzerland	5
Germany	4
Kazakhstan	3
Latvia	2
Belarus	2
Poland	1
Austria	1
Ukraine	1

Birth Year

Year	Players Drafted
1985	142
1984	109
1983	30
1982	1
1981	2
1980	3
1979	1
1978	1
1977	2
1976	1

Position

Position	Players Drafted
Defense	87
Center	74
Right Wing	56
Left Wing	46
Goaltender	29

Note: Players drafted in the international category played outside North America in their draft year. European-born players drafted from the OHL, QMJHL, WHL, U.S. colleges or other North American leagues are not counted as International players. See Country of Origin above

European Draft Firsts

1969 – First European (and Finn) Selected The first European-trained player selected was left winger Tommi Salmelainen taken 66th overall by the St. Louis Blues in 1969.

1974 – First Swede Selected Center Per Alexandersson was selected by the Toronto Maple Leafs 49th overall in 1974. Four other Swedish-born players were selected that year, including defenseman Stefan Persson (214th overall, NY Islanders) who became the first European to play on a Stanley Cup winner. (four times, 1980-83).

1975 – First Russian Selected The Philadelphia Flyers selected center Viktor Khatulev 160th overall in 1975.

1976 – First European Taken in the First Round The California Seals selected Swedish defenseman Bjorn Johansson with their first pick, fifth overall, in the 1976 Amateur Draft.

1976 – First Swiss Player Selected The St. Louis Blues selected center Jacques Soguel 121st overall in 1976.

1978 – First Czechoslovak Selected The Detroit Red Wings selected left winger Ladislav Svozil 194th overall in 1978

1978 – First German Selected The first German players were also drafted in 1978. The Atlanta Flames selected goaltender Bernard Englbrecht 196th overall and St. Louis selected forward Gerd Truntschka 200th overall.

1989 – First European Taken First Overall The Quebec Nordiques selected Swedish center Mats Sundin first overall in 1989.

Notes on 2003 First-Round Selections

1. PITTSBURGH • **MARC-ANDRE FLEURY** • G • With a quick glove hand and very good foot and pad quickness, Marc-Andre Fleury's net coverage is exceptional. He is a very strong skater with excellent flexibility, agility and lateral movement. Fleury stays upright and square to the shooter while employing a strong, well-balanced butterfly stance. He led team Canada to a silver medal at the 2003 World Junior Championships and was named best goaltender. He is the type of goalie who can elevate the emotions of his team.

2. CAROLINA • **ERIC STAAL** • C • The top-rated prospect entering the draft, Eric Staal is an excellent skater with a long, fluid stride. He handles the puck well in traffic, makes quick, accurate passes and has a hard, accurate shot with a quick release. Staal has the talent to dominate games. His vision of the ice and ability to anticipate make him a dangerous playmaker who is difficult to defend against. His cousin, Jeff Heerema, was Carolina's top pick in 1998.

3. FLORIDA • **NATHAN HORTON** • C • A powerful skater with excellent speed and acceleration, Nathan Horton's combination of size and speed makes him a difficult player to defend against. He has good passing and puckhandling skills, plus his quick hands and physical strength enable him to be very effective on face-offs. He also has a good touch around the net. Horton has the size (6'2", 201 lbs.) to be effective along the boards and does not shy away from physical play.

4. COLUMBUS • **NIKOLAI ZHERDEV** • W • Central Scouting's top-ranked European prospect, Nikolai Zherdev is an explosive, excellent skater with a great skill level. He is an excellent stickhandler with great agility. He has good hands and good puck control with a good, quick wrist shot. Zherdev is also good in traffic and in front of the net. He starred with the Russian team at the 2002 Under-18 Championships and won a gold medal at the 2003 World Junior Championships.

5. BUFFALO • **THOMAS VANEK** • LW • A native of Austria, Thomas Vanek is a natural goal scorer with exceptional offensive instincts. He has excellent hands and reach and possesses an accurate, heavy wrist shot. He has a long stride, good acceleration and deceptive speed. Vanek is the first European to play at the University of Minnesota and was the first freshman in 48 years to be named team MVP. He helped the Gophers win their second straight NCAA title in 2003.

6. SAN JOSE • **MILAN MICHALEK** • RW • A good, fast skater with excellent balance and fine acceleration, Milan Michalek has an extremely high overall skill level. He is a talented player with great moves and good hands. He has a good, quick shot and is a creative playmaker At 6'2" and 205 lbs., Michalek has size and strength and the ability to score big goals, but he needs to work on his defensive game.

7. NASHVILLE • **RYAN SUTER** • D • The son of 1980 U.S. Olympian Bob Suter and the nephew of former NHLer Gary Suter, Ryan Suter is a very good skater with a smooth, powerful stride. He has excellent lateral movement and is difficult to beat one-on-one. He also has excellent vision and is a good passer with a hard shot from the point. Suter is a graduate of the U.S. National Team Development Program.

8. ATLANTA • **BRAYDON COBURN** • D • The top-rated defenseman in Central Scouting's final rankings, Braydon Coburn uses his size (6'5") to his advantage. He is an excellent skater with a long, powerful stride and good lateral movement. He is also a good passer with a strong, accurate shot. Coburn was the 2002 WHL rookie of the year. He played for Canada's gold medal-winning 2003 Under-18 team.

9. CALGARY • **DION PHANEUF** • D • A tough competitor who is very effective at clearing the front of his net, Dion Phaneuf is a strong player who uses his strength effectively. He is a solid skater with excellent balance, mobility and agility. Phaneuf has a knack for catching opponents with their head down in open ice and is effective pinching in in the offensive zone. He is a good passer with a hard slap shot.

10. MONTREAL • **ANDREI KASTITSYN** • W • An above average skater with fast acceleration, Andrei Kastsitsyn sees the whole ice and is a good stick and puck handler. He plays well in open ice and can also take a hit. Kastsitsyn has a heavy shot, both wrist and slap, and a quick release. He starred for Belarus at the 2003 World Junior Championships and was second in scoring (6-9-15) at the World Under-18s.

11. PHILADELPHIA • **JEFF CARTER** • C • A very good skater with a long, powerful stride, Jeff Carter can beat a defenseman with a burst of speed. He is a good playmaker who passes the puck well and is effective in heavy traffic, using his long reach to protect the puck. Carter has a good shot with a quick release and is effective at deflecting shots in front of the net. He was a member of Canada's gold-medal winning team at the 2003 Under-18 World Championships.

12. NY RANGERS • **HUGH JESSIMAN** • RW • A very good skater with a long, smooth stride, Hugh Jessiman has a good jump to his skating. He possesses very quick hands and is a good stickhandler with a hard, accurate shot he gets away quickly from any angle. Jessiman is also a very good playmaker who sees the ice well and has very good hockey sense. At 6'4" and 200 lbs., finishes checks with authority. He was the 2002-03 ECAC Rookie of the Year with Dartmouth.

13. LOS ANGELES • **DUSTIN BROWN** • RW • A fierce player who is fearless and tough to knock down, Dustin Brown is a strong skater who's strong along the boards and in the corners. He anticipates the play well and has good passing and puck skills. Brown has an excellent wrist shot which he can release quickly at full speed. He is the first player in OHL history to win the Bobby Smith Award as Scholastic Player of the Year three years in a row.

14. CHICAGO • **BRENT SEABROOK** • D • The blueline anchor on Canada's gold medal-winning Under-18 team in 2003, Brent Seabrook is a big defenseman (6'2", 220 lbs.) who's strong on his skates. He's good at passing the puck up the ice and has a powerful shot which he releases quickly and accurately. Seabrook makes smart decisions with the puck and though he does not play an overly physical game, he will stand up for his teammates and for himself.

15. NY ISLANDERS • **ROBERT NILSSON** • C • The son of former NHL star Kent Nilsson, Robert Nilsson is also an offensive-minded player. His 21 points for Leksands in 2002-03 broke Markus Naslund's Swedish Elite League record for the most points by a 17-year-old. Nilsson has excellent puck skills and great moves and dekes. He is a smooth skater and very good playmaker with a quick wrist shot and a powerful, accurate slap shot. Nilsson has excellent hockey sense.

16. SAN JOSE • **STEVE BERNIER** • RW • The second-leading scorer (4-4-8) on Canada's gold medal-winning team at the Under-18 World Championships, Steve Bernier has very good hands and good hockey sense. He is very solid on his skates and hard to knock down. Bernier can set up players with his precise passing skills and has a quick, accurate wrist shot. At 6'2" and 233 lbs., he is also a punishing checker.

17. NEW JERSEY • **ZACH PARISE** • C • The son of former NHL player J.P. Parise, Zach Parise is a talented playmaker and confident player with excellent balance and a quick wrist shot. He is a tenacious two-way player who was a high school scoring star and a Hobey Baker finalist as a freshman at North Dakota in 2003. He was a member of the U.S. team that won the 2002 Under-18 World Championships and the top scorer (4-4-8) on the 2003 U.S. World Junior team.

18. WASHINGTON • **ERIC FEHR** • RW • An effective passer with very soft hands, Eric Fehr is a strong skater once in stride. He has good agility and balance and is a good puckhandler who can stickhandle through traffic. He has a hard wrist shot with a very quick release. Although not overly aggressive, Fehr finishes checks and drives hard to the net. He will roll off defenders, making him hard to contain.

19. ANAHEIM • **RYAN GETZLAF** • C • An intelligent player who plays both a finesse and a physical game, Ryan Getzlaf competes hard for the puck and will pay the price to score or set up a goal. He has good balance and agility and possesses very good hands and playmaking abilities. Getzlaf has a quick, accurate wrist shot and slap shot. He played for Canada's gold medal-winning 2003 World Under-18 team.

20. MINNESOTA • **BRENT BURNS** • RW • With good hockey sense in all areas of the game, Brent Burns has a combination of size (6'4"), speed and toughness that make him difficult to defend. He has a very good power move to the outside and is hard to handle in front of the net. Burns is a strong skater with very good speed and agility. He has good passing and puck skills as well as a good wrist shot.

21. BOSTON • **MARK STUART** • D • A very strong and powerful skater with a long stride and excellent balance and agility, Mark Stuart is a defenseman who carries the puck with confidence. He is a poised and confident player who can skate the puck out of trouble and has a hard, low wrist shot from the point. A member of the U.S. National Team Development program he captained the 2002 U.S. team to a gold medal at the Under-18 World championships.

22. EDMONTON • **MARC-ANTOINE POULIOT** • C • A strong skater with a good stride, Marc-Antoine Pouliot is a finesse player who pays attention in his own end of the ice. He sees the ice and reads the play very well. Pouliot carries the puck with confidence and has an accurate wrist shot and a hard slap shot. He is also creative with the puck. Pouliot was the top scorer (2-7-9) on Canada's 2003 gold medal-winning World Under-18 Championships team.

23. VANCOUVER • **RYAN KESLER** • C • A powerful skater who's strong on his feet, Ryan Kesler is aggressive around the net. He is a good puckhandler and smart passer who has a quick release on his wrist shot. Kesler goes hard to the net for rebounds and is very effective in the face-off circle. He won a gold medal with the 2002 U.S. Under-18 team and was second in U.S. scoring (3-4-7) at the 2003 World Juniors.

24. PHILADELPHIA • **MIKE RICHARDS** • C • A skilled center with very good hands and playmaking abilities, Mike Richards is smart and creative with the puck. He sees the ice well and carries the puck with confidence. Richards has an accurate wrist shot and a hard slap shot, and is effective along the boards. He was the top-scorer (37-50-87) on the 2003 Memorial Cup-winning Kitchener Rangers.

25. FLORIDA • **ANTHONY STEWART** • C • An excellent skater with a powerful stride, Anthony Stewart won the full lap contest at the 2003 Top Prospects skills competition. He handles the puck well at top speed and has a hard shot he uses off the rush. Stewart uses his size (6'1", 239 lbs.) to protect the puck. His six goals led Canada's gold medal-winning team at the 2003 Under-18 World Championships.

26. LOS ANGELES • **BRIAN BOYLE** • C • Standing 6'6" and weighing 222 lbs., Brian Boyle is a strong skater with very good agility and quickness. He is very strong on the puck and passes with authority. Boyle also has an excellent shot, both slap and wrist, which he gets on goal quickly and accurately. He is a very good goal-scorer and is strong on face-offs. Boyle was named to the 2003 all-New England prep school first all-star team and will attend Boston College. in 2003-04.

27. LOS ANGELES • **JEFF TAMBELLINI** • LW • The son of former player and current NHL executive Steve Tambellini, Jeff Tambellini is an excellent skater, possessing outstanding speed, balance and lateral movement. He is a natural goal scorer with a great touch around the net. Tambellini has very good passing and puckhandling skills, and has an excellent wrist shot with a quick release. He led the University of Michigan in scoring as a rookie in 2002-03 (26-19-45).

28. ANAHEIM • **COREY PERRY** • RW • A creative playmaker who is patient and elusive when handling the puck, Corey Perry sees the ice very well and is effective at sending teammates on breakaways. He has good hands and passes the puck well. Perry uses his size (6'2") and long reach well to protect the puck. He has a hard, accurate shot and steadily improved his intensity over the course of the 2002-03 season. He led London (OHL) in scoring (25-53-78).

29. OTTAWA • **PATRICK EAVES** • RW • The son of former NHL player Mike Eaves, Patrick Eaves overcame serious injuries with Boston College in 2002-03. He is a quick and agile skater who has the ability to change directions at full speed while carrying the puck. He is a talented scorer and playmaker who controls the puck well in traffic. Eaves is a graduate of the U.S. National Team Development Program.

30. ST. LOUIS • **SHAWN BELLE** • D • An exceptional skater with a smooth, effortless stride, Shawn Belle won both the 60' and 150' dash at the 2003 Top Prospects skills competition. His skating allows him to carry the puck out of trouble or join in the offensive rush. Belle has a good, hard slap and wrist shot from the point and delivers firm, accurate passes to his forwards. He was a member of Canada's gold medal-winning team at the 2003 World Under-18 tourney.

Players selected first through tenth in the 2003 NHL Entry Draft (All rows left to right): Top row: 1. Marc-Andre Fleury, G, Pittsburgh; 2. Eric Staal, C, Carolina. Second row: 3. Nathan Horton, C, Florida. 4. Nikolai Zherdev, W, Columbus. Third row: 5. Thomas Vanek, LW, Buffalo; 6. Milan Michalek, RW, San Jose. Fourth row: 7. Ryan Suter, D, Nashville; 8. Braydon Coburn, D, Atlanta. Bottom row: 9. Dion Phaneuf, D, Calgary; 10. Andrei Kastsitsyn, RW, Montreal.

2003 NHL Entry Draft

Pick	Claimed by	Amateur Club	Position

FIRST ROUND

Pick	Claimed by		Amateur Club	Position
1	Pit.	Marc-Andre Fleury	Cape Breton	G
2	Car.	Eric Staal	Peterborough	C
3	Fla.	Nathan Horton	Oshawa	C
4	CBJ	Nikolai Zherdev	CSKA Moscow	W
5	Buf.	Thomas Vanek	U. of Minnesota	LW
6	S.J.	Milan Michalek	Budejovice	RW
7	Nsh.	Ryan Suter	U.S. National U-18	D
8	Atl.	Braydon Coburn	Portland	D
9	Cgy.	Dion Phaneuf	Red Deer	D
10	Mtl.	Andrei Kastsitsyn	CSKA Moscow 2	RW
11	Phi.	Jeff Carter	Sault Ste. Marie	C
12	NYR	Hugh Jessiman	Dartmouth	RW
13	L.A.	Dustin Brown	Guelph	RW
14	Chi.	Brent Seabrook	Lethbridge	D
15	NYI	Robert Nilsson	Leksand	RW
16	S.J.	Steve Bernier	Moncton	RW
17	N.J.	Zach Parise	North Dakota	C
18	Wsh.	Eric Fehr	Brandon	RW
19	Ana.	Ryan Getzlaf	Calgary	C
20	Min.	Brent Burns	Brampton	RW
21	Bos.	Mark Stuart	Colorado College	D
22	Edm.	Marc-Antoine Pouliot	Rimouski	C
23	Van.	Ryan Kesler	Ohio State	C
24	Phi.	Mike Richards	Kitchener	C
25	Fla.	Anthony Stewart	Kingston	C
26	L.A.	Brian Boyle	St. Sebastian's H.S.	C
27	L.A.	Jeff Tambellini	U. of Michigan	LW
28	Ana.	Corey Perry	London	RW
29	Ott.	Patrick Eaves	Boston College	RW
30	St.L.	Shawn Belle	Tri-City	D

SECOND ROUND

Pick	Claimed by		Amateur Club	Position
31	Car.	Danny Richmond	U. of Michigan	D
32	Pit.	Ryan Stone	Brandon	C
33	Dal.	Loui Eriksson	Vastra Frolunda Jr.	LW
34	T.B.	Mike Egener	Calgary	D
35	Nsh.	Konstantin Glazachev	Yaroslavl	LW
36	Dal.	Vojtech Polak	Karlovy Vary	LW
37	Nsh.	Kevin Klein	St. Michael's	D
38	Fla.	Kamil Kreps	Brampton	C
39	Cgy.	Tim Ramholt	Zurich	D
40	Mtl.	Cory Urquhart	Montreal	C
41	T.B.	Matt Smaby	Shattuck St. Mary's H.S.	D
42	N.J.	Petr Vrana	Halifax	LW
43	S.J.	Joshua Hennessy	Quebec	C
44	L.A.	Konstantin Pushkarev	Ust-Kamenogorsk	RW
45	Bos.	Patrice Bergeron-Cleary	Acadie-Bathurst	C
46	CBJ	Dan Fritsche	Sarnia	C
47	S.J.	Matthew Carle	River City	D
48	NYI	Dmitri Chernykh	Khimik Voskresensk	RW
49	Nsh.	Shea Weber	Kelowna	D
50	NYR	Ivan Baranka	Dubnica Jr.	D
51	Edm.	Colin McDonald	New England	RW
52	Chi.	Corey Crawford	Moncton	G
53	NYI	Yevgeni Tunik	Elektrostal	C
54	Dal.	Brandon Crombeen	Barrie	RW
55	Fla.	Stefan Meyer	Medicine Hat	LW
56	Min.	Patrick O'Sullivan	Mississauga	C
57	Tor.	John Doherty	Phillips-Andover	D
58	NYI	Jeremy Colliton	Prince Albert	C
59	Chi.	Michal Barinka	Budejovice	D
60	Van.	Marc-Andre Bernier	Halifax	RW
61	Mtl.	Maxim Lapierre	Montreal	C
62	St.L.	David Backes	Lincoln	C
63	Col.	David Liffiton	Plymouth	D
64	Det.	James Howard	U. of Maine	G
65	Buf.	Branislav Fabry	Bratislava Jr.	LW
66	Bos.	Masi Marjamaki	Red Deer	LW
67	Ott.	Igor Mirnov	Dynamo	LW
68	Edm.	Jean-Francois Jacques	Baie-Comeau	LW

THIRD ROUND

Pick	Claimed by		Amateur Club	Position
69	Phi.	Colin Fraser	Red Deer	C
70	Pit.	Jonathan Filewich	Prince George	RW
71	CBJ	Dmitri Kosmachev	CSKA Moscow	D
72	Edm.	Mishail Joukov	Arboga	LW
73	Pit.	Daniel Carcillo	Sarnia	LW
74	Buf.	Clarke MacArthur	Medicine Hat	LW
75	NYR	Ken Roche	St. Sebastian's H.S.	C
76	Nsh.	Richard Stehlik	Sherbrooke	D
77	Phx.	Tyler Redenbach	Swift Current	C
78	Min.	Danny Irmen	Lincoln	C
79	Mtl.	Ryan O'Byrne	Nanaimo	D
80	Phx.	Dmitri Pestunov	Magnitogorsk	C
81	Phi.	Stefan Ruzicka	Nitra	LW
82	L.A.	Ryan Munce	Sarnia	G
83	Wsh.	Stephen Werner	Mass-Amherst	RW
84	St.L.	Konstantin Barulin	Tjumen	G
85	Phi.	Alexandre Picard	Halifax	D
86	Ana.	Shane Hynes	Cornell	RW
87	Phi.	Ryan Potulny	Lincoln	C
88	St.L.	Zach Fitzgerald	Seattle	D

[continued]

Pick	Claimed by		Amateur Club	Position
89	Nsh.	Paul Brown	Kamloops	RW
90	Ana.	Juha Alen	Northern Michigan	D
91	Tor.	Martin Sagat	Dukla Trencin	LW
92	Nsh.	Alexander Sulzer	Hamburg	D
93	N.J.	Ivan Khomutov	Elektrostal	RW
94	Edm.	Zachery Stortini	Sudbury	RW
95	Phi.	Rick Kozak	Brandon	RW
96	T.B.	Jonathan Boutin	Halifax	G
97	Cgy.	Ryan Donally	Windsor	LW
98	Nsh.	Grigory Shafigulin	Yaroslavl	C
99	Dal.	Matt Nickerson	Texas	D
100	Ott.	Philippe Seydoux	Kloten	D
101	St.L.	Konstantin Zakharov	Yunost	LW

FOURTH ROUND

Pick	Claimed by		Amateur Club	Position
102	Car.	Aaron Dawson	Peterborough	D
103	CBJ	Kevin Jarman	Stouffville	LW
104	CBJ	Philippe Dupuis	Hull	C
105	Fla.	Martin Lojek	Brampton	D
106	Buf.	Jan Hejda	Slavia Praha	D
107	Bos.	Byron Bitz	Nanaimo	RW
108	Phi.	Kevin Romy	Geneve	C
109	Wsh.	Andreas Valdix	Malmo	LW
110	Atl.	James Sharrow	Halifax	D
111	Van.	Brandon Nolan	Oshawa	C
112	Cgy.	Jamie Tardif	Peterborough	RW
113	Mtl.	Corey Locke	Ottawa	C
114	Buf.	Denis Ezhov	Samara	D
115	Phx.	Liam Lindstrom	Mora	C
116	Atl.	Guillaume Desbiens	Rouyn Noranda	RW
117	Nsh.	Teemu Lassila	TPS Turku	G
118	Bos.	Frank Rediker	Windsor	D
119	Ana.	Nathan Saunders	Moncton	D
120	NYI	Stefan Blaho	Dukla Trencin Jr.	RW
121	Pit.	Paul Bissonnette	Saginaw	D
122	NYR	Corey Potter	Michigan State	D
123	Mtl.	Danny Stewart	Rimouski	LW
124	Fla.	James Pemberton	Providence College	D
125	Tor.	Konstantin Volkov	Dynamo 2	RW
126	Car.	Kevin Nastiuk	Medicine Hat	G
127	St.L.	Alexandre Bolduc	Rouyn Noranda	C
128	Van.	Ty Morris	St. Albert Jr. A.	LW
129	Bos.	Patrik Valcak	Ostrava Jr.	C
130	Car.	Matej Trojovsky	Regina	D
131	Col.	David Svagrovsky	Seattle	RW
132	Det.	Kyle Quincey	London	D
133	Nsh.	Rustam Sidikov	CSKA Moscow 2.	G
134	Dal.	Alexander Naurov	Yaroslavl 2	RW
135	Ott.	Mattias Karlsson	Brynas Jr.	D
136	Atl.	Michael Vannelli	Sioux Falls	D

FIFTH ROUND

Pick	Claimed by		Amateur Club	Position
137	Car.	Tyson Strachan	Vernon Jr. A	D
138	CBJ	Arsi Piispanen	Jokerit Jr.	RW
139	S.J.	Patrick Ehelechner	Hannover	G
140	Phi.	David Tremblay	Hull	G
141	Fla.	Dan Travis	Deerfield Academy	RW
142	Ott.	Tim Cook	River City	D
143	Cgy.	Greg Moore	U. of Maine	RW
144	Dal.	Eero Kilpelainen	Kalpa Jr.	G
145	Atl.	Brett Sterling	Colorado College	LW
146	Col.	Mark McCutcheon	New England	C
147	Edm.	Kalle Olsson	Frolunda Jr.	RW
148	St.L.	Lee Stempniak	Dartmouth	RW
149	NYR	Nigel Dawes	Kootenay	LW
150	Buf.	Thomas Morrow	Des Moines	D
151	Chi.	Lasse Kukkonen	Karpat	D
152	L.A.	Brady Murray	Salmon Arm	C
153	Bos.	Mike Brown	Saginaw	C
154	Edm.	David Rohlfs	Compuware	RW
155	Wsh.	Josh Robertson	Proctor	C
156	Chi.	Alexei Ivanov	Yaroslavl 2	C
157	Min.	Marcin Kolusz	Nowy Targ	RW
158	Tor.	John Mitchell	Plymouth	C
159	St.L.	Chris Beckford-Tseu	Oshawa	G
160	Van.	Nicklas Danielsson	Brynas Gavle	RW
161	Pit.	Yevgeny Isakov	Cherepovets	RW
162	Fla.	Martin Tuma	Litvinov Jr.	D
163	Col.	Brad Richardson	Owen Sound	C
164	Det.	Ryan Oulahen	Brampton	C
165	Dal.	Gino Guyer	U. of Minnesota	C
166	Ott.	Sergei Gimayev	Cherepovets	D
167	N.J.	Zach Tarkir	Chilliwack	D

SIXTH ROUND

Pick	Claimed by		Amateur Club	Position
168	CBJ	Marc Methot	London	D
169	Pit.	Lukas Bolf	Sparta Praha Jr.	D
170	Det.	Andreas Sundin	Linkoping	LW
171	Fla.	Denis Stasyuk	Novokuznetsk	RW
172	Buf.	Pavel Voroshnin	Mississauga	D
173	Cgy.	Tyler Johnson	Moose Jaw	C
174	L.A.	Esa Pirnes	Tappara Tampere	C
175	Atl.	Mike Hamilton	Merritt	F
176	NYR	Ivan Dornic	Bratislava Jr.	C
177	Mtl.	Chris Heino-Lindberg	Hammarby Jr.	G
178	Phx.	Ryan Gibbons	Seattle	RW
179	NYR	Philippe Furrer	Bern	D

Pick	Claimed by		Amateur Club	Position
180	NYR	Chris Holt	U.S. National U-18	G
181	Chi.	Johan Andersson	Troja/Ljunby	C
182	NYI	Bruno Gervais	Acadie-Bathurst	D
183	Bos.	Nate Thompson	Seattle	C
184	Edm.	Dragan Umicevic	Sodertalje	LW
185	Dal.	Francis Wathier	Hull	LW
186	Ana.	Andrew Miller	River City	LW
187	Min.	Miroslav Kopriva	Kladno Jr.	G
188	Mtl.	Mark Flood	Peterborough	D
189	St.L.	Jonathan Lehun	St. Cloud State	C
190	Van.	Chad Brownlee	Vernon Jr. A	D
191	Phi.	Rejean Beauchemin	Prince Albert	G
192	T.B.	Doug O'Brien	Hull	D
193	Phi.	Ville Hostikka	Saipa	G
194	Det.	Stefan Blom	Hammarby Jr.	D
195	Dal.	Drew Bagnall	Battlefords	D
196	Dal.	Elias Granath	Leksand Jr.	D
197	N.J.	Jason Smith	Lennoxville	G

SEVENTH ROUND

Pick	Claimed by		Amateur Club	Position
198	Car.	Shay Stephenson	Red Deer	LW
199	Pit.	Andy Chiodo	St. Michael's	G
200	CBJ	Alexander Gusjkov	Yaroslavl	D
201	S.J.	Jonathan Tremblay	Acadie-Bathurst	RW
202	Buf.	Nathan Paetsch	Moose Jaw	D
203	Atl.	Denis Loginov	Kazan 2	C
204	Col.	Linus Videll	Sodertalje Jr.	LW
205	S.J.	Joe Pavelski	Waterloo Jr. A	C
206	Cgy.	Thomas Bellemare	Drummondville	D
207	Min.	Grigory Misharin	Yekaterinburg	D
208	Phx.	Randall Gelech	Kelowna	C
209	NYR	Dylan Reese	Pittsburgh	D
210	Nsh.	Andrei Mukhachev	CSKA Moscow	D
211	Chi.	Mike Brodeur	Camrose	G
212	NYI	Denis Rehak	Dukla Trencin Jr.	D
213	Nsh.	Miroslav Hanuljak	Litvinov Jr.	G
214	Edm.	Kyle Brodziak	Moose Jaw	C
215	Edm.	Mathieu Roy	Val-d'Or	D
216	S.J.	Kai Hospelt	Koln	C
217	Mtl.	Oskari Korpikari	Karpat	D
218	Ana.	Dirk Southern	Northern Michigan	C
219	Min.	Adam Courchaine	Vancouver	C
220	Tor.	Jeremy Williams	Swift Current	C
221	St.L.	Yevgeny Skachkov	Kapitan	LW
222	Van.	Francois-Pierre Guenette	Halifax	C
223	Fla.	Dany Roussin	Rimouski	C
224	T.B.	Gerald Coleman	London	G
225	Col.	Brett Hemingway	Coquitlam	W
226	Det.	Tomas Kollar	Hammarby	LW
227	T.B.	Jay Rosehill	Olds	D
228	Ott.	William Colbert	Ottawa	D
229	Pit.	Stephen Dixon	Cape Breton	C

EIGHTH ROUND

Pick	Claimed by		Amateur Club	Position
230	Car.	Jamie Hoffmann	Des Moines	C
231	L.A.	Matt Zaba	Vernon Jr. A	G
232	Pit.	Joe Jensen	St. Cloud State	C
233	CBJ	Mathieu Gravel	Shawinigan	LW
234	Fla.	Petr Kadlec	Slavia Praha	D
235	Buf.	Jeff Weber	Plymouth	G
236	S.J.	Alexander Hult	HV 71 Jonkoping Jr.	C
237	Tor.	Shaun Landolt	Calgary	RW
238	NYI	Cody Blanshan	U. Nebraska-Omaha	D
239	Atl.	Tobias Enstrom	MoDo Ornskoldsvik	D
240	Cgy.	Cam Cunning	Kamloops	LW
241	Mtl.	Jimmy Bonneau	Montreal	LW
242	Phx.	Eduard Lewandowski	Koln	LW
243	NYR	Jan Marek	Trinec	F
244	L.A.	Mike Sullivan	Stouffville	C
245	Chi.	Dustin Byfuglien	Prince George	D
246	NYI	Igor Volkov	Ufa	LW
247	Bos.	Benoit Mondou	Shawinigan	C
248	Edm.	Josef Hrabal	Vsetin Jr.	D
249	Wsh.	Andrew Joudrey	Notre Dame	C
250	Ana.	Shane O'Brien	St. Michael's	D
251	Min.	Mathieu Melanson	Chicoutimi	LW
252	Van.	Sergei Topol	Omsk 2	RW
253	St.L.	Andrei Pervyshin	Yaroslavl	D
254	Van.	Nathan Mciver	St. Michael's	D
255	T.B.	Raimonds Danilics	Stalkers-Juniors	C
256	T.B.	Brady Greco	Chicago	D
257	Col.	Darryl Yacboski	Regina	D
258	Det.	Vladimir Kutny	Quebec	LW
259	Dal.	Niko Vainio	Jokerit Jr.	D
260	Ott.	Ossi Louhivaara	KooKoo Kouvola	RW
261	N.J.	Joey Tenute	Sarnia	C

NINTH ROUND

Pick	Claimed by		Amateur Club	Position
262	Car.	Ryan Rorabeck	St. Michael's	C
263	Pit.	Matt Moulson	Cornell	LW
264	Fla.	John Hecimovic	Sarnia	RW
265	Fla.	Tanner Glass	Nanaimo	LW
266	Buf.	Louis Philippe Martin	Baie-Comeau	RW
267	S.J.	Brian O'Hanley	Boston College H.S.	D
268	Nsh.	Lauris Darzins	Lukko Jr.	RW
269	Atl.	Rylan Kaip	Notre Dame	C
270	Cgy.	Kevin Harvey	Georgetown	LW
271	Mtl.	Jaroslav Halak	Bratislava Jr.	G
272	Phx.	Sean Sullivan	St. Sebastian's H.S.	D
273	T.B.	Albert Vishnyakov	Kazan	LW
274	L.A.	Martin Guerin	Des Moines	RW
275	Chi.	Michael Grenzy	Chicago	D
276	S.J.	Carter Lee	Canterbury	F
277	Bos.	Kevin Regan	St. Sebastian's H.S.	G
278	Edm.	Troy Bodie	Kelowna	RW
279	Wsh.	Mark Olafson	Kelowna	RW
280	Ana.	Ville Mantymaa	Tappara Tampere	D
281	Min.	Jean-Michel Bolduc	Quebec	D
282	Chi.	Chris Porter	Lincoln	C
283	CBJ	Trevor Hendrikx	Peterborough	D
284	St.L.	Juhamatti Tapi Aaltonen	Karpat Jr.	RW
285	Van.	Matthew Hansen	Seattle	D
286	T.B.	Zbynek Hrdel	Rimouski	C
287	T.B.	Nick Tarnasky	Lethbridge	C
288	Col.	David Jones	Coquitlam	RW
289	Det.	Mikael Johansson	Arvika	C
290	Phx.	Loic Burkhalter	Ambri	C
291	Ott.	Brian Elliott	Ajax	G
292	N.J.	Arseny Bondarev	Yaroslavl 2	LW

Florida selected Jay Bouwmeester with the third pick in the 2002 Entry Draft. He played in all 82 games with the Panthers as a rookie in 2002-03 and averaged 20:08 of ice time.

First Two Rounds 2002–2000

2002

FIRST ROUND

Pick	Claimed by		Amateur Club	Position
1	CBJ	Rick Nash	London	LW
2	Atl.	Kari Lehtonen	Jokerit	G
3	Fla.	Jay Bouwmeester	Medicine Hat	D
4	Phi.	Joni Pitkanen	Karpat	D
5	Pit.	Ryan Whitney	Boston U.	D
6	Nsh.	Scottie Upshall	Kamloops	RW
7	Ana.	Joffrey Lupul	Medicine Hat	C
8	Min.	Pierre-Marc Bouchard	Chicoutimi	C
9	Fla.	Petr Taticek	Sault Ste. Marie	C
10	Cgy.	Eric Nystrom	U. of Michigan	LW
11	Buf.	Keith Ballard	U. of Minnesota	D
12	Wsh.	Steve Eminger	Kitchener	D
13	Wsh.	Alexander Semin	Chelyabinsk	LW
14	Mtl.	Christopher Higgins	Yale	C
15	Edm.	Jesse Niinimaki	Ilves Tampere	C
16	Ott.	Jakub Klepis	Portland	C
17	Wsh.	Boyd Gordon	Red Deer	RW
18	L.A.	Denis Grebeshkov	Yaroslavl	D
19	Phx.	Jakub Koreis	Plzen	C
20	Buf.	Dan Paille	Guelph	LW
21	Chi.	Anton Babchuk	Elektrostal	D
22	NYI	Sean Bergenheim	Jokerit	C
23	Phx.	Ben Eager	Oshawa	LW
24	Tor.	Alexander Steen	Vastra Frolunda	C
25	Car.	Cam Ward	Red Deer	G
26	Dal.	Martin Vagner	Hull	D
27	S.J.	Mike Morris	St. Sebastian's H.S.	RW
28	Col.	Jonas Johansson	HV 71 Jonkoping Jr.	RW
29	Bos.	Hannu Toivonen	HPK Jr.	G
30	Atl.	Jim Slater	Michigan State	C

SECOND ROUND

Pick	Claimed by		Amateur Club	Position
31	Edm.	Jeff Deslauriers	Chicoutimi	G
32	Dal.	Janos Vas	Malmo Jr.	LW
33	NYR	Lee Falardeau	Michigan State	C
34	Dal.	Tobias Stephan	Chur	G
35	Pit.	Ondrej Nemec	Vsetin	D
36	Edm.	Jarret Stoll	Kootenay	C
37	Ana.	Tim Brent	St. Michaell's	C
38	Min.	Josh Harding	Regina	G
39	Cgy.	Brian McConnell	Boston U.	C
40	Fla.	Rob Globke	Notre Dame	C
41	CBJ	Joakim Lindstrom	MoDo Ornskoldsvik	C
42	Dal.	Marius Holtet	Farjestad Jr.	C
43	Dal.	Trevor Daley	Sault Ste. Marie	D
44	Edm.	Matt Greene	Green Bay	D
45	Mtl.	Tomas Linhart	Pardubice Jr.	D
46	Phx.	David Leneveu	Cornell	G
47	Ott.	Alexei Kaigorodov	Magnitogorsk	C
48	St.L.	Alexei Shkotov	Elektrostal Jr.	RW
49	Van.	Kirill Koltsov	Omsk	D
50	L.A.	Sergei Anshakov	CSKA Moscow	LW
51	N.J.	Anton Kadeikin	Elektrostal	D
52	S.J.	Dan Spang	Winchester H.S.	D
53	N.J.	Barry Tallackson	U. of Minnesota	RW
54	Chi.	Duncan Keith	Michigan State	D
55	Van.	Denis Grot	Elektrostal	D
56	Bos.	Vladislav Yevseyev	CSKA Moscow	LW
57	Tor.	Matt Stajan	Belleville	C
58	Det.	Jiri Hudler	Vsetin	C
59	Wsh.	Maxime Daigneault	Val-d'Or	G
60	T.B.	Adam Henrich	Brampton	LW
61	Col.	Johnny Boychuk	Calgary	D
62	St.L.	Andrei Mikhnov	Sudbury	C
63	Det.	Tomas Fleischmann	Vitkovice Jr.	LW

2001

FIRST ROUND

Pick	Claimed by		Amateur Club	Position
1	Atl.	Ilya Kovalchuk	Krylja Sovetov	LW
2	Ott.	Jason Spezza	Windsor	C
3	T.B.	Alexander Svitov	Avangard Omsk	C
4	Fla.	Stephen Weiss	Plymouth	C
5	Ana.	Stanislav Chistov	Avangard Omsk	LW
6	Min.	Mikko Koivu	TPS Turku	C
7	Mtl.	Mike Komisarek	U. of Michigan	D
8	CBJ	Pascal Leclaire	Halifax	G
9	Chi.	Tuomo Ruutu	Jokerit	C/LW
10	NYR	Dan Blackburn	Kootenay	G
11	Phx.	Fredrik Sjostrom	Vastra Frolunda	RW
12	Nsh.	Dan Hamhuis	Prince George	D
13	Edm.	Ales Hemsky	Hull	RW
14	Cgy.	Chuck Kobasew	Boston College	C
15	Car.	Igor Knyazev	Spartak	D
16	Van.	R.J. Umberger	Ohio State	C
17	Tor.	Carlo Colaiacovo	Erie	D
18	L.A.	Jens Karlsson	Vastra Frolunda	RW
19	Bos.	Shaone Morrisonn	Kamloops	D
20	S.J.	Marcel Goc	Schwenningen	C
21	Pit.	Colby Armstrong	Red Deer	RW
22	Buf.	Jiri Novotny	Budejovice	C
23	Ott.	Tim Gleason	Windsor	D
24	Fla.	Lukas Krajicek	Peterborough	D
25	Mtl.	Alexander Perezhogin	Avangard Omsk	C
26	Dal.	Jason Bacashihua	Chicago (NAHL)	G
27	Phi.	Jeff Woywitka	Red Deer	D
28	N.J.	Adrian Foster	Saskatoon	C
29	Chi.	Adam Munro	Erie	G
30	L.A.	Dave Steckel	Ohio State	C

SECOND ROUND

Pick	Claimed by		Amateur Club	Position
31	Phx.	Matthew Spiller	Seattle	D
32	Buf.	Derek Roy	Kitchener	C
33	Nsh.	Timofei Shishkanov	Spartak	LW
34	Fla.	Greg Watson	Prince Albert	C
35	Ana.	Mark Popovic	St. Michael's	D
36	Min.	Kyle Wanvig	Red Deer	RW
37	Mtl.	Duncan Milroy	Swift Current	RW
38	CBJ	Tim Jackman	Minnesota State	RW
39	Tor.	Karel Pilar	Litvinov	D
40	NYR	Fedor Tutin	St. Petersburg	D
41	Cgy.	Andrei Taratukhin	Omsk	C
42	Nsh.	Tomas Slovak	Kosice	D
43	Edm.	Doug Lynch	Red Deer	D
44	N.J.	Igor Pohanka	Prince Albert	C
45	Phx.	Martin Podlesak	Lethbridge	C
46	Car.	Mike Zigomanis	Kingston	C
47	T.B.	Alexander Polushin	Tver	C
48	N.J.	Thomas Pihlman	JYP Jyvaskyla	LW
49	L.A.	Mike Cammalleri	U. of Michigan	C
50	Buf.	Chris Thorburn	North Bay	C
51	L.A.	Jaroslav Bednar	HIFK Helsinki	RW
52	Edm.	Ed Caron	Phillips-Exeter	C
53	CBJ	Kiel McLeod	Kelowna	C
54	Pit.	Noah Welch	St. Sebastian's H.S.	D
55	Buf.	Jason Pominville	Shawinigan	RW
56	Cgy.	Andrei Medvedev	Spartak	G
57	St.L.	Jay McClement	Brampton	C
58	Wsh.	Nathan Paetsch	Moose Jaw	D

Pick	Claimed by	Amateur Club	Position
59 Chi.	Matt Keith	Spokane	RW
60 N.J.	Victor Uchevatov	Yaroslavl	D
61 T.B.	Andreas Holmqvist	Hammarby	D
62 Det.	Igor Grigorenko	Lada Togliatti	RW
63 Col.	Peter Budaj	St. Michael's	G

A native of the Czech Republic who played two seasons of junior hockey with the Hull Olympiques, Ales Hemsky was Edmonton's first choice (13th overall) in the 2001 Entry Draft.

2000

FIRST ROUND

Pick	Claimed by	Amateur Club	Position
1 NYI	Rick DiPietro	Boston U.	G
2 Atl.	Dany Heatley	U. of Wisconsin	RW
3 Min.	Marian Gaborik	Dukla Trencin	RW
4 CBJ	Rostislav Klesla	Brampton	D
5 NYI	Raffi Torres	Brampton	LW
6 Nsh.	Scott Hartnell	Prince Albert	LW
7 Bos.	Lars Jonsson	Leksand	D
8 T.B.	Nikita Alexeev	Erie	RW
9 Cgy.	Brent Krahn	Calgary	G
10 Chi.	Mikhail Yakubov	Lada Togliatti	C
11 Chi.	Pavel Vorobiev	Yaroslavl	RW
12 Ana.	Alexei Smirnov	Tver	LW
13 Mtl.	Ron Hainsey	U. of Mass-Lowell	D
14 Col.	Vaclav Nedorost	Budejovice	C
15 Buf.	Artem Kryukov	Yaroslavl	C
16 Mtl.	Marcel Hossa	Portland	LW
17 Edm.	Alexei Mikhnov	Yaroslavl	LW
18 Pit.	Brooks Orpik	Boston College	D
19 Phx.	Krys Kolanos	Boston College	C
20 L.A.	Alexander Frolov	Yaroslavl 2	LW
21 Ott.	Anton Volchenkov	HC Moscow	D
22 N.J.	David Hale	Sioux City	D
23 Van.	Nathan Smith	Swift Current	C
24 Tor.	Brad Boyes	Erie	C
25 Dal.	Steve Ott	Windsor	C
26 Wsh.	Brian Sutherby	Moose Jaw	C
27 Bos.	Martin Samuelsson	MoDo Ornskoldsvik	RW
28 Phi.	Justin Williams	Plymouth	RW
29 Det.	Niklas Kronwall	Djurgarden	D
30 St.L.	Jeff Taffe	U. of Minnesota	C

SECOND ROUND

Pick	Claimed by	Amateur Club	Position
31 Atl.	Ilja Nikulin	Tver	D
32 Car.	Tomas Kurka	Plymouth	LW
33 Min.	Nick Schultz	Prince Albert	D
34 T.B.	Ruslan Zainullin	Ak Bars Kazan	RW
35 Edm.	Brad Winchester	U. of Wisconsin	LW
36 Nsh.	Daniel Widing	Leksand	RW
37 Bos.	Andy Hilbert	U. of Michigan	C/LW
38 Det.	Tomas Kopecky	Dukla Trencin	C
39 N.J.	Teemu Laine	Jokerit	RW
40 Cgy.	Kurtis Foster	Peterborough	D
41 S.J.	Tero Maatta	Jokerit	D
42 Atl.	Libor Ustrnul	Plymouth	D
43 Wsh.	Matt Pettinger	Calgary	LW
44 Ana.	Ilja Bryzgalov	Lada Togliatti	G
45 Chi.	Mathieu Chouinard	Shawinigan	G
46 Cgy.	Jarret Stoll	Kootenay	C
47 Col.	Jared Aulin	Kamloops	C/RW
48 Buf.	Gerard Dicaire	Seattle	D
49 Chi.	Jonas Nordqvist	Leksand	C
50 Col.	Sergei Soin	Krylja Sovetov	C/LW
51 Tor.	Kris Vernarsky	Plymouth	C

Pick	Claimed by	Amateur Club	Position
52 Pit.	Shane Endicott	Seattle	C
53 Phx.	Alexander Tatarinov	Yaroslavl	RW
54 L.A.	Andreas Lilja	Malmo	D
55 Ott.	Antoine Vermette	Victoriaville	C
56 N.J.	Alexander Suglobov	Yaroslavl	RW
57 N.J.	Matt DeMarchi	U. of Minnesota	D
58 Fla.	Vladimir Sapozhnikov	Novokuznetsk	D
59 Bos.	Ivan Huml	Langley	LW
60 Dal.	Dan Ellis	Omaha	G
61 Wsh.	Jakub Cutta	Swift Current	D
62 N.J.	Paul Martin	Elk River H.S.	D
63 Col.	Agris Saviels	Owen Sound	D
64 NYR	Filip Novak	Regina	D
65 St.L.	Dave Morisset	Seattle	RW

First Round and Other Notable Selections
1999–1969

1999

FIRST ROUND

Pick	Claimed by	Amateur Club	Position
1 Atl.	Patrik Stefan	Long Beach	C
2 Van.	Daniel Sedin	MoDo Ornskoldsvik	LW
3 Van.	Henrik Sedin	MoDo Ornskoldsvik	C
4 NYR	Pavel Brendl	Calgary	RW
5 NYI	Tim Connolly	Erie	C
6 Nsh.	Brian Finley	Barrie	G
7 Wsh.	Kris Beech	Calgary	C
8 NYI	Taylor Pyatt	Sudbury	LW
9 NYR	Jamie Lundmark	Moose Jaw	C
10 NYI	Branislav Mezei	Belleville	D
11 Cgy.	Oleg Saprykin	Seattle	LW
12 Fla.	Denis Shvidki	Barrie	RW
13 Edm.	Jani Rita	Jokerit	LW
14 S.J.	Jeff Jillson	U. of Michigan	D
15 Phx.	Scott Kelman	Seattle	C
16 Car.	David Tanabe	U. of Wisconsin	D
17 St.L.	Barret Jackman	Regina	D
18 Pit.	Konstantin Koltsov	Cherepovets	RW
19 Phx.	Kirill Safronov	St. Petersburg	D
20 Buf.	Barrett Heisten	U. of Maine	LW
21 Bos.	Nick Boynton	Ottawa	D
22 Phi.	Maxime Ouellet	Quebec	G
23 Chi.	Steve McCarthy	Kootenay	D
24 Tor.	Luca Cereda	Ambri	C
25 Col.	Mikhail Kuleshov	Cherepovets	LW
26 Ott.	Martin Havlat	Trinec	LW
27 N.J.	Ari Ahonen	JyP HT Jr.	G
28 NYI	Kristian Kudroc	Michalovce	D

OTHER NOTABLE SELECTIONS

Pick	Claimed by	Amateur Club	Position
47 T.B.	Sheldon Keefe	Barrie	RW
70 Fla.	Niklas Hagman	HIFK	LW
76 L.A.	Frantisek Kaberle	MoDo Ornskoldsvik	D
83 Ana.	Niclas Havelid	Malmo	D
88 T.B.	Jimmie Olvestad	Djurgarden	LW
91 Edm.	Mike Comrie	U. of Michigan	C
191 Nsh.	Martin Erat	ZPS Zlin Jr.	LW
212 Col.	Radim Vrbata	Hull	RW
230 Ana.	Petr Tenkrat	Kladno	RW
232 St.L.	Alexander Khavanov	Dynamo	D
247 Bos.	Mikko Eloranta	TPS Turku	LW

1998

FIRST ROUND

Pick	Claimed by	Amateur Club	Position
1 T.B.	Vincent Lecavalier	Rimouski	C
2 Nsh.	David Legwand	Plymouth	C
3 S.J.	Brad Stuart	Regina	D
4 Van.	Bryan Allen	Oshawa	D
5 Ana.	Vitaly Vishnevski	Yaroslavl 2	D
6 Cgy.	Rico Fata	London	RW
7 NYR	Manny Malhotra	Guelph	C
8 Chi.	Mark Bell	Ottawa	C
9 NYI	Mike Rupp	Erie	RW
10 Tor.	Nik Antropov	Ust-Kamenogorsk	C
11 Car.	Jeff Heerema	Sarnia	RW
12 Col.	Alex Tanguay	Halifax	LW
13 Edm.	Michael Henrich	Barrie	RW
14 Phx.	Patrick DesRochers	Sarnia	G
15 Ott.	Mathieu Chouinard	Shawinigan	G
16 Mtl.	Eric Chouinard	Quebec	LW
17 Col.	Martin Skoula	Barrie	D
18 Buf.	Dmitri Kalinin	Chelyabinsk	D
19 Col.	Robyn Regehr	Kamloops	D
20 Col.	Scott Parker	Kelowna	RW
21 L.A.	Mathieu Biron	Shawinigan	D
22 Phi.	Simon Gagne	Quebec	LW
23 Pit.	Milan Kraft	Keramika Plzen Jr.	C
24 St.L.	Christian Backman	Vastra Frolunda Jr.	D
25 Det.	Jiri Fischer	Hull	D
26 N.J.	Mike Van Ryn	U. of Michigan	D
27 N.J.	Scott Gomez	Tri-City	C

OTHER NOTABLE SELECTIONS

Pick	Claimed by	Amateur Club	Position
31 Van.	Artem Chubarov	Dynamo	C
43 Phx.	Ossi Vaananen	Jokerit Jr.	D
44 Ott.	Mike Fisher	Sudbury	C
48 Bos.	Jonathan Girard	Laval	D
60 Nsh.	Denis Arkhipov	Ak Bars Kazan	C
64 T.B.	Brad Richards	Rimouski	C
91 Car.	Josef Vasicek	Slavia Praha Jr.	C
93 Car.	Tommy Westlund	Brynas Gavle	RW
99 Edm.	Shawn Horcoff	Michigan State	C
117 Fla.	Jaroslav Spacek	Farjestad Karlstad	D
162 Mtl.	Andrei Markov	Khimik Voskresensk	D
230 Nsh.	Karlis Skrastins	TPS Turku	D

Selected first overall by Tampa Bay in 1998, Vincent Lecavalier enjoyed his best season in 2002-03, collecting 33 goals and 45 assists while helping the Lightning win the Southeast Division.

1997

FIRST ROUND

Pick	Claimed by	Amateur Club	Position
1 Bos.	Joe Thornton	Sault Ste. Marie	C
2 S.J.	Patrick Marleau	Seattle	C
3 L.A.	Olli Jokinen	HIFK Helsinki	C
4 NYI	Roberto Luongo	Val-d'Or	G
5 NYI	Eric Brewer	Prince George	D
6 Cgy.	Daniel Tkaczuk	Barrie	C
7 T.B.	Paul Mara	Sudbury	D
8 Bos.	Sergei Samsonov	Detroit	LW
9 Wsh.	Nick Boynton	Ottawa	D
10 Van.	Brad Ference	Spokane	D
11 Mtl.	Jason Ward	Erie	RW
12 Ott.	Marian Hossa	Dukla Trencin	RW
13 Chi.	Daniel Cleary	Belleville	RW
14 Edm.	Michel Riesen	Biel-Bienne	RW
15 L.A.	Matt Zultek	Ottawa	LW
16 Chi.	Ty Jones	Spokane	RW
17 Pit.	Robert Dome	Las Vegas (IHL)	RW
18 Ana.	Mikael Holmqvist	Djurgarden	C
19 NYR	Stefan Cherneski	Brandon	RW
20 Fla.	Mike Brown	Red Deer	LW
21 Buf.	Mika Noronen	Tappara Tampere	G
22 Car.	Nikos Tselios	Belleville	D
23 S.J.	Scott Hannan	Kelowna	D
24 N.J.	J-F Damphousse	Moncton	G
25 Dal.	Brenden Morrow	Portland	LW
26 Col.	Kevin Grimes	Kingston	D

OTHER NOTABLE SELECTIONS

Pick	Claimed by	Amateur Club	Position
27 Bos.	Ben Clymer	Minnesota-Duluth	LW
70 Cgy.	Erik Andersson	U. of Denver	C
95 Fla.	Ivan Novoseltsev	Krylja Sovetov	RW
119 Ott.	Magnus Arvedson	Farjestad Karlstad	LW
130 Chi.	Kyle Calder	Regina	LW
136 NYR	Mike York	Michigan State	LW
144 Van.	Matt Cooke	Windsor	C
177 St.L.	Ladislav Nagy	Dragon Presov	LW
191 Bos.	Antti Laaksonen	U. of Denver	LW

1996

FIRST ROUND

Pick	Claimed by	Player	Amateur Club	Position
1	Ott.	Chris Phillips	Prince Albert	D
2	S.J.	Andrei Zyuzin	Salavat Yulayev Ufa	D
3	NYI	J.P. Dumont	Val-d'Or	RW
4	Wsh.	Alexandre Volchkov	Barrie	C
5	Dal.	Richard Jackman	Sault Ste. Marie	D
6	Edm.	Boyd Devereaux	Kitchener	C
7	Buf.	Erik Rasmussen	Minnesota-Duluth	LW/C
8	Bos.	Johnathan Aitken	Medicine Hat	D
9	Ana.	Ruslan Salei	Las Vegas (IHL)	D
10	N.J.	Lance Ward	Red Deer	D
11	Phx.	Dan Focht	Tri-City	D
12	Van.	Josh Holden	Regina	C
13	Cgy.	Derek Morris	Regina	D
14	St.L.	Marty Reasoner	Boston College	C
15	Phi.	Dainius Zubrus	Pembroke Jr. A	RW
16	T.B.	Mario Larocque	Hull	D
17	Wsh.	Jaroslav Svejkovsky	Tri-City	RW
18	Mtl.	Matt Higgins	Moose Jaw	C
19	Edm.	Matthieu Descoteaux	Shawinigan	D
20	Fla.	Marcus Nilson	Djurgarden	LW
21	S.J.	Marco Sturm	Landshut	LW
22	NYR	Jeff Brown	Sarnia	D
23	Pit.	Craig Hillier	Ottawa	G
24	Phx.	Daniel Briere	Drummondville	C
25	Col.	Peter Ratchuk	Shattuck St. Mary's H.S.	D
26	Det.	Jesse Wallin	Red Deer	D

OTHER NOTABLE SELECTIONS

Pick	Claimed by	Player	Amateur Club	Position
35	Ana.	Matt Cullen	St. Cloud State	C
49	N.J.	Colin White	Hull	D
56	NYI	Zdeno Chara	Dukla Trencin	D
59	Edm.	Tom Poti	Cushing Academy	D
65	Fla.	Oleg Kvasha	CSKA Moscow	LW/C
79	Col.	Mark Parrish	St. Cloud State	RW
136	Ott.	Andreas Dackell	Brynas Gavle	RW
139	Phx.	Robert Esche	Detroit	G
174	Phx.	Trevor Letowski	Sarnia	RW
179	T.B.	Pavel Kubina	Vitkovice	D
204	Tor.	Tomas Kaberle	Kladno	D

1995

FIRST ROUND

Pick	Claimed by	Player	Amateur Club	Position
1	Ott.	Bryan Berard	Detroit	D
2	NYI	Wade Redden	Brandon	D
3	L.A.	Aki Berg	Kiekko-67 Turku	D
4	Ana.	Chad Kilger	Kingston	C
5	T.B.	Daymond Langkow	Tri-City	C
6	Edm.	Steve Kelly	Prince Albert	C
7	Wpg.	Shane Doan	Kamloops	RW
8	Mtl.	Terry Ryan	Tri-City	LW
9	Bos.	Kyle McLaren	Tacoma	D
10	Fla.	Radek Dvorak	HC Ceske Budejovice	RW
11	Dal.	Jarome Iginla	Kamloops	RW
12	S.J.	Teemu Riihijarvi	Kiekko-Espoo	LW
13	Hfd.	Jean-Sebastien Giguere	Halifax	G
14	Buf.	Jay McKee	Niagara Falls	D
15	Tor.	Jeff Ware	Oshawa	D
16	Buf.	Martin Biron	Beauport	G
17	Wsh.	Brad Church	Prince Albert	LW
18	N.J.	Petr Sykora	Detroit	RW
19	Chi.	Dmitri Nabokov	Krylja Sovetov	C/LW
20	Cgy.	Denis Gauthier	Drummondville	D
21	Bos.	Sean Brown	Belleville	D
22	Phi.	Brian Boucher	Tri-City	G
23	Wsh.	Miika Elomo	Kiekko-67 Turku	LW
24	Pit.	Aleksey Morozov	Krylja Sovetov	RW
25	Col.	Marc Denis	Chicoutimi	G
26	Det.	Maxim Kuznetsov	Dynamo	D

OTHER NOTABLE SELECTIONS

Pick	Claimed by	Player	Amateur Club	Position
31	Edm.	Georges Laraque	St-Jean	RW
45	Chi.	Christian Laflamme	Beauport	D
59	L.A.	Vladimir Tsyplakov	Fort Wayne IHL	LW
67	Wpg.	Brad Isbister	Portland	LW
79	N.J.	Alyn McCauley	Ottawa	C
87	Hfd.	Sami Kapanen	HIFK Helsinki	RW
91	NYR	Marc Savard	Oshawa	C
101	St.L.	Michal Handzus	IS Banska Bystrica	C
128	Pit.	Jan Hrdina	Seattle	C
145	Tor.	Yannick Tremblay	Beauport	D
150	Cgy.	Clarke Wilm	Saskatoon	C
166	Fla.	Peter Worrell	Hull	LW
177	Bos.	P.J. Axelsson	Vastra Frolunda	LW
223	Tor.	Danny Markov	Spartak	D

1994

FIRST ROUND

Pick	Claimed by	Player	Amateur Club	Position
1	Fla.	Ed Jovanovski	Windsor	D
2	Ana.	Oleg Tverdovsky	Krylja Sovetov	D
3	Ott.	Radek Bonk	Las Vegas (IHL)	C
4	Edm.	Jason Bonsignore	Niagara Falls	C
5	Hfd.	Jeff O'Neill	Guelph	RW
6	Edm.	Ryan Smyth	Moose Jaw	LW
7	L.A.	Jamie Storr	Owen Sound	G
8	T.B.	Jason Wiemer	Portland	C
9	NYI	Brett Lindros	Kingston	RW
10	Wsh.	Nolan Baumgartner	Kamloops	D
11	S.J.	Jeff Friesen	Regina	LW
12	Que.	Wade Belak	Saskatoon	D/RW
13	Van.	Mattias Ohlund	Pitea	D
14	Chi.	Ethan Moreau	Niagara Falls	LW
15	Wsh.	Alexander Kharlamov	CSKA Moscow	C
16	Tor.	Eric Fichaud	Chictoutimi	G
17	Buf.	Wayne Primeau	Owen Sound	C
18	Mtl.	Brad Brown	North Bay	D
19	Cgy.	Chris Dingman	Brandon	LW
20	Dal.	Jason Botterill	U. of Michigan	LW
21	Bos.	Evgeni Ryabchikov	Molot Perm	G
22	Que.	Jeffrey Kealty	Catholic Memorial H.S.	D
23	Det.	Yan Golubovsky	Dynamo 2	D
24	Pit.	Chris Wells	Seattle	C
25	N.J.	Vadim Sharifijanov	Salavat Yulayev Ufa	LW
26	NYR	Dan Cloutier	Sault Ste. Marie	G

OTHER NOTABLE SELECTIONS

Pick	Claimed by	Player	Amateur Club	Position
27	Fla.	Rhett Warrener	Saskatoon	D
29	Ott.	Stan Neckar	HC Ceske Budejovice	D
43	Buf.	Curtis Brown	Moose Jaw	C/LW
49	Det.	Mathieu Dandenault	Sherbrooke	RW/D
51	N.J.	Patrik Elias	Kladno	C
59	L.A.	Vitali Yachmenev	North Bay	LW
64	Tor.	Fredrik Modin	Timra	LW
132	Ana.	Bates Battaglia	Caledon Jr. A	LW
133	Ott.	Daniel Alfredsson	Vastra Frolunda	RW
140	Phi.	Alex Selivanov	Spartak	RW

1993

FIRST ROUND

Pick	Claimed by	Player	Amateur Club	Position
1	Ott.	Alexandre Daigle	Victoriaville	C
2	Hfd.	Chris Pronger	Peterborough	D
3	T.B.	Chris Gratton	Kingston	C
4	Ana.	Paul Kariya	U. of Maine	LW
5	Fla.	Rob Niedermayer	Medicine Hat	C
5	Det.	Benoit Larose	Laval	D
6	S.J.	Viktor Kozlov	Dynamo	C
7	Edm.	Jason Arnott	Oshawa	C
8	NYR	Niklas Sundstrom	MoDo Ornskoldsvik	RW
9	Dal.	Todd Harvey	Detroit	RW/C
10	Que.	Jocelyn Thibault	Sherbrooke	G
11	Wsh.	Brendan Witt	Seattle	D
12	Tor.	Kenny Jonsson	Rogle Angelholm	D
13	N.J.	Denis Pederson	Prince Albert	C/RW
14	Que.	Adam Deadmarsh	Portland	RW
15	Wpg.	Mats Lindgren	Skelleftea	C/LW
16	Edm.	Nick Stajduhar	London	D
17	Wsh.	Jason Allison	London	C
18	Cgy.	Jesper Mattsson	Malmo	C
19	Tor.	Landon Wilson	Dubuque Jr. A	RW
20	Van.	Mike Wilson	Sudbury	D
21	Mtl.	Saku Koivu	TPS Turku	C
22	Det.	Anders Eriksson	MoDo Ornskoldsvik	D
23	NYI	Todd Bertuzzi	Guelph	RW
24	Chi.	Eric Lecompte	Hull	LW
25	Bos.	Kevyn Adams	Miami of Ohio	C
26	Pit.	Stefan Bergkvist	Leksand	D

OTHER NOTABLE SELECTIONS

Pick	Claimed by	Player	Amateur Club	Position
28	S.J.	Shean Donovan	Ottawa	RW
71	Phi.	Vaclav Prospal	Motor Ceske Budejovice	C
72	Hfd.	Marek Malik	Vitkovice	D
90	Chi.	Eric Daze	Beauport	RW
111	Edm.	Miroslav Satan	Dukla Trencin	LW
118	NYI	Tommy Salo	Vasteras	G
124	Van.	Scott Walker	Owen Sound	RW
151	Mtl.	Darcy Tucker	Kamloops	RW
164	NYR	Todd Marchant	Clarkson	C
207	Bos.	Hal Gill	Nashoba H.S.	D
219	St.L.	Mike Grier	St. Sebastian's H.S.	RW
227	Ott.	Pavol Demitra	Dukla Trencin	LW
252	Cgy.	German Titov	TPS Turku	LW

1992

FIRST ROUND

Pick	Claimed by	Player	Amateur Club	Position
1	T.B.	Roman Hamrlik	ZPS Zlin	D
2	Ott.	Alexei Yashin	Dynamo	C
3	S.J.	Mike Rathje	Medicine Hat	D
4	Que.	Todd Warriner	Windsor	LW
5	NYI	Darius Kasparaitis	Dynamo	D
6	Cgy.	Cory Stillman	Windsor	LW
7	Phi.	Ryan Sittler	Nichols H.S.	LW
8	Tor.	Brandon Convery	Sudbury	C
9	Hfd.	Robert Petrovicky	Dukla Trencin	C
10	S.J.	Andrei Nazarov	Dynamo	LW
11	Buf.	David Cooper	Medicine Hat	D
12	Chi.	Sergei Krivokrasov	CSKA Moscow	RW
13	Edm.	Joe Hulbig	St. Sebastian's H.S.	LW
14	Wsh.	Sergei Gonchar	Chelyabinsk	D
15	Phi.	Jason Bowen	Tri-City	D
16	Bos.	Dmitri Kvartalnov	San Diego (IHL)	LW
17	Wpg.	Sergei Bautin	Dynamo	D
18	N.J.	Jason Smith	Regina	D
19	Pit.	Martin Straka	HC Skoda Plzen	C
20	Mtl.	David Wilkie	Kamloops	D
21	Van.	Libor Polasek	Vitkovice	C
22	Det.	Curtis Bowen	Ottawa	LW
23	Tor.	Grant Marshall	Ottawa	RW
24	NYR	Peter Ferraro	Waterloo Jr. A	LW

OTHER NOTABLE SELECTIONS

Pick	Claimed by	Player	Amateur Club	Position
27	Wpg.	Boris Mironov	CSKA Moscow	D
33	Mtl.	Valeri Bure	Spokane	RW
36	Chi.	Jeff Shantz	Regina	C
38	St.L.	Igor Korolev	Dynamo	C
40	Van.	Michael Peca	Ottawa	C
42	N.J.	Sergei Brylin	CSKA Moscow	C
46	Det.	Darren McCarty	Bellevile	RW
48	NYR	Mattias Norstrom	AIK Solna	D
65	Edm.	Kirk Maltby	Owen Sound	RW
78	Cgy.	Robert Svehla	Dukla Trencin	D
83	Buf.	Matthew Barnaby	Beauport	RW
158	St.L.	Ian Laperriere	Drummondville	C/RW
186	N.J.	Stephane Yelle	Oshawa	C
204	Wpg.	Nikolai Khabibulin	CSKA Moscow	G

1991

FIRST ROUND

Pick	Claimed by	Player	Amateur Club	Position
1	Que.	Eric Lindros	Oshawa	C
2	S.J.	Pat Falloon	Spokane	RW
3	N.J.	Scott Niedermayer	Kamloops	D
4	NYI	Scott Lachance	Boston U.	D
5	Wpg.	Aaron Ward	U. of Michigan	D
6	Phi.	Peter Forsberg	MoDo Ornskoldsvik	C
7	Van.	Alek Stojanov	Hamilton	RW
8	Min.	Richard Matvichuk	Saskatoon	D
9	Hfd.	Patrick Poulin	St-Hyacinthe	C
10	Det.	Martin Lapointe	Laval	RW
11	N.J.	Brian Rolston	Detroit Compuware Jr. A	C/RW
12	Edm.	Tyler Wright	Swift Current	C
13	Buf.	Philippe Boucher	Granby	D
14	Wsh.	Pat Peake	Detroit	C
15	NYR	Alexei Kovalev	Dynamo	RW
16	Pit.	Markus Naslund	MoDo Ornskoldsvik	LW
17	Mtl.	Brent Bilodeau	Seattle	D
18	Bos.	Glen Murray	Sudbury	RW
19	Cgy.	Niklas Sundblad	AIK Solna	RW
20	Edm.	Martin Rucinsky	CHZ Litvinov	LW
21	Wsh.	Trevor Halverson	North Bay	LW
22	Chi.	Dean McAmmond	Prince Albert	LW

OTHER NOTABLE SELECTIONS

Pick	Claimed by	Player	Amateur Club	Position
23	S.J.	Ray Whitney	Spokane	LW
26	NYI	Ziggy Palffy	AC Nitra	RW
30	S.J.	Sandis Ozolinsh	Dynamo Riga	D
40	Bos.	Jozef Stumpel	AC Nitra	C
52	Cgy.	Sandy McCarthy	Laval	RW
58	Wsh.	Steve Konowalchuk	Portland	LW
59	Hfd.	Michael Nylander	Huddinge	C
71	Chi.	Igor Kravchuk	CSKA Moscow	D
81	L.A.	Alexei Zhitnik	Sokol Kiev	D
103	Que.	Bill Lindsay	Tri-City	RW
106	Bos.	Mariusz Czerkawski	GKS Tychy	RW
122	Phi.	Dmitry Yushkevich	Yaroslavl	D
203	Wpg.	Igor Ulanov	Khimik Voskresensk	D

1990

FIRST ROUND

Pick	Claimed by	Player	Amateur Club	Position
1	Que.	Owen Nolan	Cornwall	RW
2	Van.	Petr Nedved	Seattle	C
3	Det.	Keith Primeau	Niagara Falls	C
4	Phi.	Mike Ricci	Peterborough	C
5	Pit.	Jaromir Jagr	Kladno	RW
6	NYI	Scott Scissons	Saskatoon	C
7	L.A.	Darryl Sydor	Kamloops	D
8	Min.	Derian Hatcher	North Bay	D
9	Wsh.	John Slaney	Cornwall	D
10	Tor.	Drake Berehowsky	Kingston	D
11	Cgy.	Trevor Kidd	Brandon	G
12	Mtl.	Turner Stevenson	Seattle	RW
13	NYR	Michael Stewart	Michigan State	D
14	Buf.	Brad May	Niagara Falls	LW
15	Hfd.	Mark Greig	Lethbridge	RW
16	Chi.	Karl Dykhuis	Hull	D
17	Edm.	Scott Allison	Prince Albert	C
18	Van.	Shawn Antoski	North Bay	LW
19	Wpg.	Keith Tkachuk	Malden Catholic H.S.	LW
20	N.J.	Martin Brodeur	St-Hyacinthe	G
21	Bos.	Bryan Smolinski	Michigan State	C

OTHER NOTABLE SELECTIONS

Pick	Claimed by	Player	Amateur Club	Position
23	Van.	Jiri Slegr	CHZ Litvinov	D
31	Tor.	Felix Potvin	Chicoutimi	G
34	NYR	Doug Weight	Lake Superior State	C
36	Hfd.	Geoff Sanderson	Swift Current	LW
40	Phi.	Mikael Renberg	Pitea	RW
45	Det.	Vyacheslav Kozlov	Khimik Voskresensk	RW
85	NYR	Sergei Zubov	CSKA Moscow	D
86	Van.	Gino Odjick	Laval	RW
97	Buf.	Richard Smehlik	Vitkovice	D
156	Wsh.	Peter Bondra	Kosice	RW

Pick	Claimed by		Amateur Club	Position
177	Wsh.	Ken Klee	Bowling Green	D
244	NYR	Sergei Nemchinov	Krylja Sovetov	LW

1989

FIRST ROUND

Pick	Claimed by		Amateur Club	Position
1	Que.	Mats Sundin	Nacka	C
2	NYI	Dave Chyzowski	Kamloops	LW
3	Tor.	Scott Thornton	Belleville	LW
4	Wpg.	Stu Barnes	Tri-City	C
5	N.J.	Bill Guerin	Springfield Jr. B	RW
6	Chi.	Adam Bennett	Sudbury	D
7	Min.	Doug Zmolek	John Marshall H.S.	D
8	Van.	Jason Herter	North Dakota	D
9	St.L.	Jason Marshall	Vernon Jr. A	D
10	Hfd.	Bobby Holik	Dukla Jihlava	C
11	Det.	Mike Sillinger	Regina	C
12	Tor.	Rob Pearson	Belleville	RW
13	Mtl.	Lindsay Vallis	Seattle	D
14	Buf.	Kevin Haller	Regina	D
15	Edm.	Jason Soules	Niagara Falls	D
16	Pit.	Jamie Heward	Regina	D
17	Bos.	Shayne Stevenson	Kitchener	RW
18	N.J.	Jason Miller	Medicine Hat	LW
19	Wsh.	Olaf Kolzig	Tri-City	G
20	NYR	Steven Rice	Kitchener	RW
21	Tor.	Steve Bancroft	Belleville	D

OTHER NOTABLE SELECTIONS

Pick	Claimed by		Amateur Club	Position
22	Que.	Adam Foote	Sault Ste. Marie	D
23	NYI	Travis Green	Spokane	C
53	Det.	Nicklas Lidstrom	Vasteras	D
62	Wpg.	Kris Draper	Canadian National	C
73	Hfd.	Jim McKenzie	Victoria	LW
74	Det.	Sergei Fedorov	CSKA Moscow	C
82	Wsh.	Trent Klatt	Osseo H.S.	RW
113	Van.	Pavel Bure	CSKA Moscow	RW
116	Det.	Dallas Drake	Northern Michigan	RW
183	Buf.	Donald Audette	Laval	RW
196	Min.	Arturs Irbe	Dynamo Riga	G
221	Det.	Vladimir Konstantinov	CSKA Moscow	D

1988

FIRST ROUND

Pick	Claimed by		Amateur Club	Position
1	Min.	Mike Modano	Prince Albert	C
2	Van.	Trevor Linden	Medicine Hat	RW
3	Que.	Curtis Leschyshyn	Saskatoon	D
4	Pit.	Darrin Shannon	Windsor	LW
5	Que.	Daniel Dore	Drummondville	RW
6	Tor.	Scott Pearson	Kingston	LW
7	L.A.	Martin Gelinas	Hull	LW
8	Chi.	Jeremy Roenick	Thayer Academy	C
9	St.L.	Rod Brind'Amour	Notre Dame Jr. A	C
10	Wpg.	Teemu Selanne	Jokerit	RW
11	Hfd.	Chris Govedaris	Toronto	LW
12	N.J.	Corey Foster	Peterborough	D
13	Buf.	Joel Savage	Victoria	RW
14	Phi.	Claude Boivin	Drummondville	LW
15	Wsh.	Reggie Savage	Victoriaville	C
16	NYI	Kevin Cheveldayoff	Brandon	D
17	Det.	Kory Kocur	Saskatoon	RW
18	Bos.	Rob Cimetta	Toronto	W
19	Edm.	Francois Leroux	St-Jean	D
20	Mtl.	Eric Charron	Trois-Rivieres	D
21	Cgy.	Jason Muzzatti	Michigan State	G

OTHER NOTABLE SELECTIONS

Pick	Claimed by		Amateur Club	Position
27	Tor.	Tie Domi	Peterborough	RW
60	Bos.	Steve Heinze	Lawrence Academy	RW
67	Pit.	Mark Recchi	Kamloops	RW
68	NYR	Tony Amonte	Thayer Academy	RW
89	Buf.	Alexander Mogilny	CSKA Moscow	RW
97	Buf.	Rob Ray	Cornwall	RW
120	Wsh.	Dmitri Khristich	Sokol Kiev	LW/C
163	NYI	Marty McInnis	Milton Academy	RW
198	St.L.	Bret Hedican	North St. Paul H.S.	D
234	Que.	Claude Lapointe	Laval	LW/C

1987

FIRST ROUND

Pick	Claimed by		Amateur Club	Position
1	Buf.	Pierre Turgeon	Granby	C
2	N.J.	Brendan Shanahan	London	LW
3	Bos.	Glen Wesley	Portland	D
4	L.A.	Wayne McBean	Medicine Hat	D
5	Pit.	Chris Joseph	Seattle	D
6	Min.	Dave Archibald	Portland	C/LW
7	Tor.	Luke Richardson	Peterborough	D
8	Chi.	Jimmy Waite	Chicoutimi	G
9	Que.	Bryan Fogarty	Kingston	D
10	NYR	Jay More	New Westminster	D
11	Det.	Yves Racine	Longueuil	D
12	St.L.	Keith Osborne	North Bay	RW
13	NYI	Dean Chynoweth	Medicine Hat	D
14	Bos.	Stephane Quintal	Granby	D
15	Que.	Joe Sakic	Swift Current	C
16	Wpg.	Bryan Marchment	Belleville	D
17	Mtl.	Andrew Cassels	Ottawa	C
18	Hfd.	Jody Hull	Peterborough	RW
19	Cgy.	Bryan Deasley	U. of Michigan	LW
20	Phi.	Darren Rumble	Kitchener	D
21	Edm.	Peter Soberlak	Swift Current	LW

OTHER NOTABLE SELECTIONS

Pick	Claimed by		Amateur Club	Position
25	Cgy.	Stephane Matteau	Hull	LW
33	Mtl.	John LeClair	Bellows Academy	LW
38	Mtl.	Eric Desjardins	Granby	D
44	Mtl.	Mathieu Schneider	Cornwall	D
71	Tor.	Joe Sacco	Medford H.S.	RW
108	Van.	Garry Valk	Sherwood Park Jr. A	RW
110	Pit.	Shawn McEachern	Matignon H.S.	RW
159	St.L.	Guy Hebert	Hamilton College	G
166	Cgy.	Theoren Fleury	Moose Jaw	RW

1986

FIRST ROUND

Pick	Claimed by		Amateur Club	Position
1	Det.	Joe Murphy	Michigan State	RW
2	L.A.	Jimmy Carson	Verdun	C
3	N.J.	Neil Brady	Medicine Hat	C
4	Pit.	Zarley Zalapski	Canadian National	D
5	Buf.	Shawn Anderson	Canadian National	D
6	Tor.	Vincent Damphousse	Laval	C
7	Van.	Dan Woodley	Portland	RW
8	Wpg.	Pat Elynuik	Prince Albert	RW
9	NYR	Brian Leetch	Avon Old Farms H.S.	D
10	St.L.	Jocelyn Lemieux	Laval	RW
11	Hfd.	Scott Young	Boston U.	RW
12	Min.	Warren Babe	Lethbridge	LW
13	Bos.	Craig Janney	Boston College	C
14	Chi.	Everett Sanipass	Verdun	LW
15	Mtl.	Mark Pederson	Medicine Hat	LW
16	Cgy.	George Pelawa	Bemidji H.S.	RW
17	NYI	Tom Fitzgerald	Austin Prep	RW
18	Que.	Ken McRae	Sudbury	C
19	Wsh.	Jeff Greenlaw	Canadian National	LW
20	Phi.	Kerry Huffman	Guelph	D
21	Edm.	Kim Issel	Prince Albert	RW

OTHER NOTABLE SELECTIONS

Pick	Claimed by		Amateur Club	Position
22	Det.	Adam Graves	Windsor	LW
27	Mtl.	Benoit Brunet	Hull	LW
29	Wpg.	Teppo Numminen	Tappara Tampere	D
47	Buf.	Bob Corkum	U. of Maine	C
57	Mtl.	Jyrki Lumme	Ilves Tampere	D
67	Pit.	Rob Brown	Kamloops	RW
72	NYR	Mark Janssens	Regina	C
85	Det.	Johan Garpenlov	Nacka	LW
114	NYR	Darren Turcotte	North Bay	C
141	Mtl.	Lyle Odelein	Moose Jaw	D
143	NYI	Rich Pilon	Prince Albert AAA	D
167	Phi.	Murray Baron	Vernon Jr. A	D

1985

FIRST ROUND

Pick	Claimed by		Amateur Club	Position
1	Tor.	Wendel Clark	Saskatoon	LW/D
2	Pit.	Craig Simpson	Michigan State	LW
3	N.J.	Craig Wolanin	Kitchener	D
4	Van.	Jim Sandlak	London	RW
5	Hfd.	Dana Murzyn	Calgary	D
6	NYI	Brad Dalgarno	Hamilton	RW
7	NYR	Ulf Dahlen	Ostersund	LW
8	Det.	Brent Fedyk	Regina	LW
9	L.A.	Craig Duncanson	Sudbury	LW
10	L.A.	Dan Gratton	Oshawa	C
11	Chi.	Dave Manson	Prince Albert	D
12	Mtl.	Jose Charbonneau	Drummondville	RW
13	NYI	Derek King	Sault Ste. Marie	LW
14	Buf.	Calle Johansson	Vastra Frolunda	D
15	Que.	David Latta	Kitchener	LW
16	Mtl.	Tom Chorske	Minneapolis SW H.S.	LW
17	Cgy.	Chris Biotti	Belmont Hill H.S.	D
18	Wpg.	Ryan Stewart	Kamloops	C
19	Wsh.	Yvon Corriveau	Toronto	LW
20	Edm.	Scott Metcalfe	Kingston	LW
21	Phi.	Glen Seabrooke	Peterborough	C

OTHER NOTABLE SELECTIONS

Pick	Claimed by		Amateur Club	Position
24	N.J.	Sean Burke	Toronto	G
27	Cgy.	Joe Nieuwendyk	Cornell	C
28	NYR	Mike Richter	Northwood Prep	G
32	N.J.	Eric Weinrich	North Yarmouth Academy	D
35	Buf.	Benoit Hogue	St-Jean	C
52	Bos.	Bill Ranford	New Westminster	G
81	Wpg.	Fredrik Olausson	Farjestad Karlstad	D
113	Det.	Randy McKay	Michigan Tech	RW
119	Buf.	Joe Reekie	Cornwall	D
142	Mtl.	Ed Cristofoli	Penticton Jr. A	RW
188	Edm.	Kelly Buchberger	Moose Jaw	RW
214	Van.	Igor Larionov	CSKA Moscow	C

1984

FIRST ROUND

Pick	Claimed by		Amateur Club	Position
1	Pit.	Mario Lemieux	Laval	C
2	N.J.	Kirk Muller	Guelph	LW
3	Chi.	Eddie Olczyk	Team USA	C
4	Tor.	Al Iafrate	Belleville	D
5	Mtl.	Petr Svoboda	CHZ Litvinov	D
6	L.A.	Craig Redmond	U. of Denver	D
7	Det.	Shawn Burr	Kitchener	LW/C
8	Mtl.	Shayne Corson	Brantford	LW
9	Pit.	Doug Bodger	Kamloops	D
10	Van.	J.J. Daigneault	Longueuil	D
11	Hfd.	Sylvain Cote	Quebec	D
12	Cgy.	Gary Roberts	Ottawa	LW
13	Min.	David Quinn	Kent H.S.	D
14	NYR	Terry Carkner	Peterborough	D
15	Que.	Trevor Stienburg	Guelph	RW
16	Pit.	Roger Belanger	Kingston	C
17	Wsh.	Kevin Hatcher	North Bay	D
18	Buf.	Mikael Andersson	Vastra Frolunda	LW
19	Bos.	Dave Pasin	Prince Albert	RW
20	NYI	Duncan MacPherson	Saskatoon	D
21	Edm.	Selmar Odelein	Regina	D

OTHER NOTABLE SELECTIONS

Pick	Claimed by		Amateur Club	Position
25	Tor.	Todd Gill	Windsor	D
27	Phi.	Scott Mellanby	Henry Carr Jr. B	RW
29	Mtl.	Stephane Richer	Granby	RW
38	Cgy.	Paul Ranheim	Edina H.S.	LW
51	Mtl.	Patrick Roy	Granby	G
59	Wsh.	Michal Pivonka	Kladno	C
60	Buf.	Ray Sheppard	Cornwall	RW
117	Cgy.	Brett Hull	Penticton Jr. A	RW
119	NYR	Kjell Samuelsson	Leksand	D
134	St.L.	Cliff Ronning	New Westminster	C
166	Bos.	Don Sweeney	St. Paul's H.S.	D
171	L.A.	Luc Robitaille	Hull	LW
180	Cgy.	Gary Suter	U. of Wisconsin	D

1983

FIRST ROUND

Pick	Claimed by		Amateur Club	Position
1	Min.	Brian Lawton	Mount St. Charles H.S.	LW
2	Hfd.	Sylvain Turgeon	Hull	LW
3	NYI	Pat LaFontaine	Verdun	C
4	Det.	Steve Yzerman	Peterborough	C
5	Buf.	Tom Barrasso	Acton-Boxborough	G
6	N.J.	John MacLean	Oshawa	RW
7	Tor.	Russ Courtnall	Victoria	RW
8	Wpg.	Andrew McBain	North Bay	RW
9	Van.	Cam Neely	Portland	RW
10	Buf.	Normand Lacombe	New Hampshire	RW
11	Buf.	Adam Creighton	Ottawa	C
12	NYR	Dave Gagner	Brantford	C
13	Cgy.	Dan Quinn	Belleville	C
14	Wpg.	Bobby Dollas	Laval	D
15	Pit.	Bob Errey	Peterborough	LW
16	NYI	Gerald Diduck	Lethbridge	D
17	Mtl.	Alfie Turcotte	Portland	C
18	Chi.	Bruce Cassidy	Ottawa	D
19	Edm.	Jeff Beukeboom	Sault Ste. Marie	D
20	Hfd.	David Jensen	Lawrence Academy	C
21	Bos.	Nevin Markwart	Regina	LW

OTHER NOTABLE SELECTIONS

Pick	Claimed by		Amateur Club	Position
26	Mtl.	Claude Lemieux	Trois-Rivieres	RW
46	Det.	Bob Probert	Brantford	LW
60	Chi.	Marc Bergevin	Chicoutimi	D
82	Edm.	Esa Tikkanen	HIFK Helsinki	LW
88	Det.	Petr Klima	Dukla Jihlava	W
91	Det.	Joe Kocur	Saskatoon	RW
103	L.A.	Garry Galley	Bowling Green	D
114	Van.	Dave Lowry	London	LW
125	Phi.	Rick Tocchet	Sault Ste. Marie	RW
207	Chi.	Dominik Hasek	Pardubice	G
223	Buf.	Uwe Krupp	Koln	D
241	Cgy.	Sergei Makarov	CSKA Moscow	RW

1982

FIRST ROUND

Pick	Claimed by		Amateur Club	Position
1	Bos.	Gord Kluzak	Billings	D
2	Min.	Brian Bellows	Kitchener	LW
3	Tor.	Gary Nylund	Portland	D
4	Phi.	Ron Sutter	Lethbridge	C
5	Wsh.	Scott Stevens	Kitchener	D
6	Buf.	Phil Housley	South St. Paul H.S.	D
7	Chi.	Ken Yaremchuk	Portland	C
8	N.J.	Rocky Trottier	Nanaimo	RW
9	Buf.	Paul Cyr	Victoria	LW
10	Pit.	Rich Sutter	Lethbridge	RW
11	Van.	Michel Petit	Sherbrooke	D
12	Wpg.	Jim Kyte	Cornwall	D
13	Que.	David Shaw	Kitchener	D
14	Hfd.	Paul Lawless	Windsor	LW
15	NYR	Chris Kontos	Toronto	LW/C
16	Buf.	Dave Andreychuk	Oshawa	LW
17	Det.	Murray Craven	Medicine Hat	LW
18	N.J.	Ken Daneyko	Seattle	D
19	Mtl.	Alain Heroux	Chicoutimi	LW
20	Edm.	Jim Playfair	Portland	D
21	NYI	Pat Flatley	U. of Wisconsin	RW

OTHER NOTABLE SELECTIONS

Pick	Claimed by		Amateur Club	Position
36	NYR	Tomas Sandstrom	Farjestad Karlstad	RW

Pick	Claimed by		Amateur Club	Position
43	N.J.	Pat Verbeek	Sudbury	RW
45	Tor.	Ken Wregget	Lethbridge	G
56	Hfd.	Kevin Dineen	U. of Denver	RW
60	Bos.	Dave Reid	Peterborough	LW
67	Hfd.	Ulf Samuelsson	Leksand	D
75	Wpg.	Dave Ellett	Ottawa Jr. A	D
80	Min.	Bob Rouse	Nanaimo	D
88	Hfd.	Ray Ferraro	Penticton Jr. A	C
119	Phi.	Ron Hextall	Brandon	G
120	NYR	Tony Granato	Northwood Prep	RW
134	St.L.	Doug Gilmour	Cornwall	C
140	Phi.	Dave Brown	Saskatoon	RW
181	Que.	Mike Hough	Kitchener	LW
183	NYR	Kelly Miller	Michigan State	LW

1981
FIRST ROUND

Pick	Claimed by		Amateur Club	Position
1	Wpg.	Dale Hawerchuk	Cornwall	C
2	L.A.	Doug Smith	Ottawa	C
3	Wsh.	Bob Carpenter	St. John's Prep	C
4	Hfd.	Ron Francis	Sault Ste. Marie	C
5	Col.	Joe Cirella	Oshawa	D
6	Tor.	Jim Benning	Portland	D
7	Mtl.	Mark Hunter	Brantford	RW
8	Edm.	Grant Fuhr	Victoria	G
9	NYR	James Patrick	Prince Albert	D
10	Van.	Garth Butcher	Regina	D
11	Que.	Randy Moller	Lethbridge	D
12	Chi.	Tony Tanti	Oshawa	RW
13	Min.	Ron Meighan	Niagara Falls	D
14	Bos.	Normand Leveille	Chicoutimi	LW
15	Cgy.	Al MacInnis	Kitchener	D
16	Phi.	Steve Smith	Sault Ste. Marie	D
17	Buf.	Jiri Dudacek	Kladno	RW
18	Mtl.	Gilbert Delorme	Chicoutimi	D
19	Mtl.	Jan Ingman	Farjestad Karlstad	LW
20	St.L.	Marty Ruff	Lethbridge	D
21	NYI	Paul Boutilier	Sherbrooke	D

OTHER NOTABLE SELECTIONS

Pick	Claimed by		Amateur Club	Position
40	Mtl.	Chris Chelios	Moose Jaw	D
56	Cgy.	Mike Vernon	Calgary	G
72	NYR	John Vanbiesbrouck	Sault Ste. Marie	G
108	Col.	Bruce Driver	U. of Wisconsin	D
111	Edm.	Steve Smith	London	D
116	Que.	Mike Eagles	Kitchener	C/LW
145	Mtl.	Tom Kurvers	Minnesota-Duluth	D
152	Wsh.	Gaetan Duchesne	Quebec	LW

1980
FIRST ROUND

Pick	Claimed by		Amateur Club	Position
1	Mtl.	Doug Wickenheiser	Regina	C
2	Wpg.	Dave Babych	Portland	D
3	Chi.	Denis Savard	Montreal	C
4	L.A.	Larry Murphy	Peterborough	D
5	Wsh.	Darren Veitch	Regina	D
6	Edm.	Paul Coffey	Kitchener	D
7	Van.	Rick Lanz	Oshawa	D
8	Hfd.	Fred Arthur	Cornwall	C
9	Pit.	Mike Bullard	Brantford	C
10	L.A.	Jim Fox	Ottawa	RW
11	Det.	Mike Blaisdell	Regina	RW

Barry Pederson scored 65 goals in his last season of junior hockey. Selected 18th overall by the Bruins in 1980, he would go on to record 45, 49 and 39-goal seasons in Boston. He was traded to Vancouver for Cam Neely and a first-round choice in 1987. The Bruins used this pick to select Glen Wesley.

Pick	Claimed by		Amateur Club	Position
12	St.L.	Rik Wilson	Kingston	D
13	Cgy.	Denis Cyr	Montreal	RW
14	NYR	Jim Malone	Toronto	C
15	Chi.	Jerome Dupont	Toronto	D
16	Min.	Brad Palmer	Victoria	LW
17	NYI	Brent Sutter	Red Deer Jr. A	C
18	Bos.	Barry Pederson	Victoria	C
19	Col.	Paul Gagne	Windsor	LW
20	Buf.	Steve Patrick	Brandon	RW
21	Phi.	Mike Stothers	Kingston	D

OTHER NOTABLE SELECTIONS

Pick	Claimed by		Amateur Club	Position
37	Min.	Don Beaupre	Sudbury	G
38	NYI	Kelly Hrudey	Medicine Hat	G
39	Cgy.	Steve Konroyd	Oshawa	D
46	Det.	Mark Osborne	Niagara Falls	LW
61	Mtl.	Craig Ludwig	North Dakota	D
69	Edm.	Jari Kurri	Jokerit	RW
73	L.A.	Bernie Nicholls	Kingston	C
80	NYI	Greg Gilbert	Toronto	LW
81	Bos.	Steve Kasper	Verdun	C
106	Col.	Aaron Broten	Minnesota-Duluth	LW/C
120	Chi.	Steve Larmer	Niagara Falls	RW
124	Mtl.	Mike McPhee	RPI	LW
128	Wpg.	Brian Mullen	U.S. Jr. National	RW
132	Edm.	Andy Moog	Billings	G
133	Van.	Doug Lidster	Colorado College	D
167	Buf.	Randy Cunneyworth	Ottawa	LW

1979
FIRST ROUND

Pick	Claimed by		Amateur Club	Position
1	Col.	Rob Ramage	London	D
2	St.L.	Perry Turnbull	Portland	C
3	Det.	Mike Foligno	Sudbury	RW
4	Wsh.	Mike Gartner	Niagara Falls	RW
5	Van.	Rick Vaive	Sherbrooke	RW
6	Min.	Craig Hartsburg	Sault Ste. Marie	D
7	Chi.	Keith Brown	Portland	D
8	Bos.	Raymond Bourque	Verdun	D
9	Tor.	Laurie Boschman	Brandon	C
10	Min.	Tom McCarthy	Oshawa	LW
11	Buf.	Mike Ramsey	Minnesota-Duluth	D
12	Atl.	Paul Reinhart	Kitchener	D
13	NYR	Doug Sulliman	Kitchener	RW
14	Phi.	Brian Propp	Brandon	LW
15	Bos.	Brad McCrimmon	Brandon	D
16	L.A.	Jay Wells	Kingston	D
17	NYI	Duane Sutter	Lethbridge	RW
18	Hfd.	Ray Allison	Brandon	RW
19	Wpg.	Jimmy Mann	Sherbrooke	RW
20	Que.	Michel Goulet	Quebec	LW
21	Edm.	Kevin Lowe	Quebec	D

OTHER NOTABLE SELECTIONS

Pick	Claimed by		Amateur Club	Position
26	Van.	Brent Ashton	Saskatoon	LW
30	L.A.	Mark Hardy	Montreal	D
32	Buf.	Lindy Ruff	Lethbridge	D/LW
37	Mtl.	Mats Naslund	Brynas Gavle	LW
40	Wpg.	Dave Christian	North Dakota	RW
41	Que.	Dale Hunter	Sudbury	C
42	Min.	Neal Broten	Minnesota-Duluth	C
44	Mtl.	Guy Carbonneau	Chicoutimi	C
48	Edm.	Mark Messier	St. Albert Jr. A	C
54	Atl.	Tim Hunter	Seattle	RW
66	Det.	John Ogrodnick	New Westminster	LW
69	Edm.	Glenn Anderson	U. of Denver	RW
75	Atl.	Jim Peplinski	Toronto	RW
83	Que.	Anton Stastny	Slovan Bratislava	LW
89	Van.	Dirk Graham	Regina	RW/LW
103	Wpg.	Thomas Steen	Leksand	C
120	Bos.	Mike Krushelnyski	Montreal	LW/C

1978
FIRST ROUND

Pick	Claimed by		Amateur Club	Position
1	Min.	Bobby Smith	Ottawa	C
2	Wsh.	Ryan Walter	Seattle	C/LW
3	St.L.	Wayne Babych	Portland	RW
4	Van.	Bill Derlago	Brandon	C
5	Col.	Mike Gillis	Kingston	LW
6	Phi.	Behn Wilson	Kingston	D
7	Phi.	Ken Linseman	Kingston	C
8	Mtl.	Danny Geoffrion	Cornwall	RW
9	Det.	Willie Huber	Hamilton	D
10	Chi.	Tim Higgins	Ottawa	RW
11	Atl.	Brad Marsh	London	D
12	Det.	Brent Peterson	Portland	C
13	Buf.	Larry Playfair	Portland	D
14	Phi.	Danny Lucas	Sault Ste. Marie	RW
15	NYI	Steve Tambellini	Lethbridge	C
16	Bos.	Al Secord	Hamilton	LW
17	Atl.	Dave Hunter	Sudbury	LW
18	Wsh.	Tim Coulis	Hamilton	LW

OTHER NOTABLE SELECTIONS

Pick	Claimed by		Amateur Club	Position
19	Min.	Steve Payne	Ottawa	LW
21	Tor.	Joel Quenneville	Windsor	D
26	NYR	Don Maloney	Kitchener	LW
32	Buf.	Tony McKegney	Kingston	LW
40	Van.	Stan Smyl	New Westminster	RW
54	Min.	Curt Giles	Minnesota-Duluth	D
55	Wsh.	Bengt-Ake Gustafsson	Farjestad Karlstad	RW
93	NYR	Tom Laidlaw	Northern Michigan	D
103	Mtl.	Keith Acton	Peterborough	C
109	St.L.	Paul MacLean	Hull	RW
153	Bos.	Craig MacTavish	University of Lowell	C
173	Atl.	Risto Siltanen	Ilves Tampere	D
179	Chi.	Darryl Sutter	Lethbridge	LW
231	Mtl.	Chris Nilan	Northeastern	RW

1977
FIRST ROUND

Pick	Claimed by		Amateur Club	Position
1	Det.	Dale McCourt	St. Catharines	C
2	Col.	Barry Beck	New Westminster	D
3	Wsh.	Robert Picard	Montreal	D
4	Van.	Jere Gillis	Sherbrooke	LW
5	Cle.	Mike Crombeen	Kingston	RW
6	Chi.	Doug Wilson	Ottawa	D
7	Min.	Brad Maxwell	New Westminster	D
8	NYR	Lucien DeBlois	Sorel	C
9	St.L.	Scott Campbell	London	D
10	Mtl.	Mark Napier	Toronto	RW
11	Tor.	John Anderson	Toronto	RW
12	Tor.	Trevor Johansen	Toronto	D
13	NYR	Ron Duguay	Sudbury	C/RW
14	Buf.	Ric Seiling	St. Catharines	RW/C
15	NYI	Mike Bossy	Laval	RW
16	Bos.	Dwight Foster	Kitchener	RW
17	Phi.	Kevin McCarthy	Winnipeg	D
18	Mtl.	Norm Dupont	Montreal	LW

OTHER NOTABLE SELECTIONS

Pick	Claimed by		Amateur Club	Position
25	Min.	Dave Semenko	Brandon	LW
33	NYI	John Tonelli	Toronto	LW
36	Mtl.	Rod Langway	New Hampshire	D
43	Atl.	Alain Cote	Chicoutimi	LW
54	Mtl.	Gordie Roberts	Victoria	D
62	NYR	Mario Marois	Quebec	D
66	Pit.	Mark Johnson	U. of Wisconsin	C
102	Pit.	Greg Millen	Peterborough	G
118	Atl.	Bobby Gould	New Hampshire	RW
135	Phi.	Pete Peeters	Medicine Hat	G
162	Mtl.	Craig Laughlin	Clarkson	RW

1976
FIRST ROUND

Pick	Claimed by		Amateur Club	Position
1	Wsh.	Rick Green	London	D
2	Pit.	Blair Chapman	Saskatoon	RW
3	Min.	Glen Sharpley	Hull	C
4	Det.	Fred Williams	Saskatoon	C
5	Cal.	Bjorn Johansson	Orebro	D
6	NYR	Don Murdoch	Medicine Hat	RW
7	St.L.	Bernie Federko	Saskatoon	C
8	Atl.	Dave Shand	Peterborough	D
9	Chi.	Real Cloutier	Quebec	RW
10	Atl.	Harold Phillipoff	New Westminster	LW
11	K.C.	Paul Gardner	Oshawa	C
12	Mtl.	Peter Lee	Ottawa	RW
13	Mtl.	Rod Schutt	Sudbury	LW
14	NYI	Alex McKendry	Sudbury	W
15	Wsh.	Greg Carroll	Medicine Hat	C
16	Bos.	Clayton Pachal	New Westminster	C/LW
17	Phi.	Mark Suzor	Kingston	D
18	Mtl.	Bruce Baker	Ottawa	RW

OTHER NOTABLE SELECTIONS

Pick	Claimed by		Amateur Club	Position
20	St.L.	Brian Sutter	Lethbridge	LW
22	Det.	Reed Larson	Minnesota-Duluth	D
30	Tor.	Randy Carlyle	Sudbury	D
42	NYR	Mike McEwen	Toronto	D
45	Chi.	Thomas Gradin	MoDo Ornskoldsvik	C
47	Pit.	Morris Lukowich	Medicine Hat	LW
56	St.L.	Mike Liut	Bowling Green	G
64	Atl.	Kent Nilsson	Djurgarden	C
68	Mtl.	Ken Morrow	Bowling Green	D
133	Mtl.	Ron Wilson	St. Catharines	C

1975
FIRST ROUND

Pick	Claimed by		Amateur Club	Position
1	Phi.	Mel Bridgman	Victoria	C
2	K.C.	Barry Dean	Medicine Hat	LW
3	Cal.	Ralph Klassen	Saskatoon	C
4	Min.	Bryan Maxwell	Medicine Hat	D
5	Det.	Rick Lapointe	Victoria	D
6	Tor.	Don Ashby	Calgary	C
7	Chi.	Greg Vaydik	Medicine Hat	C
8	Atl.	Richard Mulhern	Sherbrooke	D
9	Mtl.	Robin Sadler	Edmonton	D
10	Van.	Rick Blight	Brandon	RW
11	NYI	Pat Price	Saskatoon	D
12	NYR	Wayne Dillon	Toronto	C
13	Pit.	Gord Laxton	New Westminster	G
14	Bos.	Doug Halward	Peterborough	D
15	Mtl.	Pierre Mondou	Montreal	C
16	L.A.	Tim Young	Ottawa	C

Pick	Claimed by	Amateur Club	Position

Defenseman Pat Price had a 95-point season for the junior Saskatoon Blades in 1973-74, earning an all-star berth. Drafted 11th overall in 1975, he would play for six NHL clubs in 13 seasons.

OTHER NOTABLE SELECTIONS

17	Buf.	Bob Sauve	Laval	G
21	Cal.	Dennis Maruk	London	C
24	Tor.	Doug Jarvis	Peterborough	C
43	Chi.	Mike O'Connell	Kingston	D
57	Cal.	Greg Smith	Colorado College	D
80	Atl.	Willi Plett	St. Catharines	RW
108	Phi.	Paul Holmgren	U. of Minnesota	RW
210	L.A.	Dave Taylor	Clarkson	RW

1974
FIRST ROUND

1	Wsh.	Greg Joly	Regina	D
2	K.C.	Wilf Paiement	St. Catharines	RW
3	Cal.	Rick Hampton	St. Catharines	LW/D
4	NYI	Clark Gillies	Regina	LW
5	Mtl.	Cam Connor	Flin Flon	RW
6	Min.	Doug Hicks	Flin Flon	D
7	Mtl.	Doug Risebrough	Kitchener	C
8	Pit.	Pierre Larouche	Sorel	C
9	Det.	Bill Lochead	Oshawa	LW
10	Mtl.	Rick Chartraw	Kitchener	D/RW
11	Buf.	Lee Fogolin Jr.	Oshawa	D
12	Mtl.	Mario Tremblay	Montreal	RW
13	Tor.	Jack Valiquette	Sault Ste. Marie	C
14	NYR	Dave Maloney	Kitchener	D
15	Mtl.	Gord McTavish	Sudbury	C
16	Chi.	Grant Mulvey	Calgary	RW
17	Cal.	Ron Chipperfield	Brandon	C
18	Bos.	Don Larway	Swift Current	RW

Stefan Persson was selected 214th overall by the New York Islanders in 1974. He didn't come to North America until 1977 when he was 22 and fit right into the Islanders' improving defense corps. He played nine NHL seasons and won the Stanley Cup from 1980 to 1983.

OTHER NOTABLE SELECTIONS

22	NYI	Bryan Trottier	Swift Current	C
25	Bos.	Mark Howe	Toronto	D
29	Buf.	Danny Gare	Calgary	RW
31	Tor.	Tiger Williams	Swift Current	LW
32	NYR	Ron Greschner	New Westminster	D
38	K.C.	Bob Bourne	Saskatoon	C
39	Cal.	Charlie Simmer	Sault Ste. Marie	LW
52	Chi.	Bob Murray	Cornwall	D
59	Van.	Harold Snepsts	Edmonton	D
70	Chi.	Terry Ruskowski	Swift Current	C
125	Phi.	Reggie Lemelin	Sherbrooke	G
199	Mtl.	Dave Lumley	New Hampshire	RW
214	NYI	Stefan Persson	Brynas Gavle	D

1973
FIRST ROUND

1	NYI	Denis Potvin	Ottawa	D
2	Atl.	Tom Lysiak	Medicine Hat	C
3	Van.	Dennis Ververgaert	London	RW
4	Tor.	Lanny McDonald	Medicine Hat	RW
5	St.L.	John Davidson	Calgary	G
6	Bos.	Andre Savard	Quebec	C
7	Pit.	Blaine Stoughton	Flin Flon	RW
8	Mtl.	Bob Gainey	Peterborough	LW
9	Van.	Bob Dailey	Toronto	D
10	Tor.	Bob Neely	Peterborough	LW
11	Det.	Terry Richardson	New Westminster	G
12	Buf.	Morris Titanic	Sudbury	LW
13	Chi.	Darcy Rota	Edmonton	LW
14	NYR	Rick Middleton	Oshawa	RW
15	Tor.	Ian Turnbull	Ottawa	D
16	Atl.	Vic Mercredi	New Westminster	C

OTHER NOTABLE SELECTIONS

21	Atl.	Eric Vail	Sudbury	LW
27	Pit.	Colin Campbell	Peterborough	D
30	NYR	Pat Hickey	Hamilton	LW
33	NYI	Dave Lewis	Saskatoon	D
49	NYI	Andre St. Laurent	Montreal	C
85	Atl.	Ken Houston	Chatham Jr. B	RW
130	Cal.	Larry Patey	Braintree H.S.	C
134	Pit.	Gord Lane	New Westminster	D
162	Atl.	Greg Fox	U. of Michigan	D

1972
FIRST ROUND

1	NYI	Billy Harris	Toronto	RW
2	Atl.	Jacques Richard	Quebec	LW
3	Van.	Don Lever	Niagara Falls	LW
4	Mtl.	Steve Shutt	Toronto	LW
5	Buf.	Jim Schoenfeld	Niagara Falls	D
6	Mtl.	Michel Larocque	Ottawa	G
7	Phi.	Bill Barber	Kitchener	LW
8	Mtl.	Dave Gardner	Toronto	C
9	St.L.	Wayne Merrick	Ottawa	C
10	NYR	Al Blanchard	Kitchener	LW
11	Tor.	George Ferguson	Toronto	C
12	Min.	Jerry Byers	Kitchener	LW
13	Chi.	Phil Russell	Edmonton	D
14	Mtl.	John Van Boxmeer	Guelph	D
15	NYR	Bob MacMillan	St. Catharines	RW
16	Bos.	Mike Bloom	St. Catharines	LW

OTHER NOTABLE SELECTIONS

17	NYI	Lorne Henning	New Westminster	C
23	Phi.	Tom Bladon	Edmonton	D
33	NYI	Bob Nystrom	Calgary	RW
39	Phi.	Jimmy Watson	Calgary	D
55	Phi.	Al MacAdam	University of PEI	RW
85	Buf.	Peter McNab	U. of Denver	C
97	NYI	Richard Brodeur	Cornwall	G
139	Tor.	Pat Boutette	Minnesota-Duluth	C/RW
144	NYI	Garry Howatt	Flin Flon	LW

1971
FIRST ROUND

1	Mtl.	Guy Lafleur	Quebec	RW
2	Det.	Marcel Dionne	St. Catharines	C
3	Van.	Jocelyn Guevremont	Montreal	D
4	St.L.	Gene Carr	Flin Flon	C
5	Buf.	Rick Martin	Montreal	LW
6	Bos.	Ron Jones	Edmonton	D
7	Mtl.	Chuck Arnason	Flin Flon	RW
8	Phi.	Larry Wright	Regina	C
9	Phi.	Pierre Plante	Drummondville	RW
10	NYR	Steve Vickers	Toronto	LW
11	Mtl.	Murray Wilson	Ottawa	LW
12	Chi.	Dan Spring	Edmonton	C
13	NYR	Steve Durbano	Toronto	D
14	Bos.	Terry O'Reilly	Oshawa	RW

OTHER NOTABLE SELECTIONS

17	Van.	Bobby Lalonde	Montreal	C
19	Buf.	Craig Ramsay	Peterborough	LW
20	Mtl.	Larry Robinson	Kitchener	D
22	Tor.	Rick Kehoe	Hamilton	RW

33	Buf.	Bill Hajt	Saskatoon	D
48	L.A.	Neil Komadoski	Winnipeg	D
55	NYR	Jerry Butler	Hamilton	RW

1970
FIRST ROUND

1	Buf.	Gilbert Perreault	Montreal	C
2	Van.	Dale Tallon	Toronto	D
3	Bos.	Reggie Leach	Flin Flon	RW
4	Bos.	Rick MacLeish	Peterborough	C
5	Mtl.	Ray Martyniuk	Flin Flon	G
6	Mtl.	Chuck Lefley	Canadian National	LW
7	Pit.	Greg Polis	Estevan	LW
8	Tor.	Darryl Sittler	London	C
9	Bos.	Ron Plumb	Peterborough	D
10	Cal.	Chris Oddleifson	Winnipeg	C
11	NYR	Norm Gratton	Montreal	LW
12	Det.	Serge Lajeunesse	Montreal	D/RW
13	Bos.	Bob Stewart	Oshawa	D
14	Chi.	Dan Maloney	London	LW

OTHER NOTABLE SELECTIONS

18	Phi.	Bill Clement	Ottawa	C
22	Tor.	Errol Thompson	Charlottetown Sr.	LW
25	NYR	Mike Murphy	Toronto	RW
27	Bos.	Dan Bouchard	London	G
32	Phi.	Bob Kelly	Oshawa	LW
40	Det.	Yvon Lambert	Drummondville	LW
59	L.A.	Billy Smith	Cornwall	G
70	Chi.	Gilles Meloche	Verdun	G
88	Oak.	Terry Murray	Ottawa	D
103	Tor.	Ron Low	Dauphin Jr. A	G

Dick Redmond was selected fifth overall by the Minnesota North Stars in the first universal Amateur Draft in 1969. A defenseman, he played with six teams over a 13-year career. His brother Mickey was a two-time 50-goal scorer.

1969
FIRST ROUND

1	Mtl.	Rejean Houle	Montreal	W
2	Mtl.	Marc Tardif	Montreal	LW
3	Bos.	Don Tannahill	Niagara Falls	LW
4	Bos.	Frank Spring	Edmonton	RW
5	Min.	Dick Redmond	St. Catharines	D
6	Phi.	Bob Currier	Cornwall	C
7	Oak.	Tony Featherstone	Peterborough	RW
8	NYR	Andre Dupont	Montreal	D
9	Tor.	Ernie Moser	Estevan	RW
10	Det.	Jim Rutherford	Hamilton	G
11	Bos.	Ivan Boldirev	Oshawa	C
12	NYR	Pierre Jarry	Ottawa	LW

OTHER NOTABLE SELECTIONS

17	Phi.	Bobby Clarke	Flin Flon	C
18	Oak.	Ron Stackhouse	Peterborough	D
25	Min.	Gilles Gilbert	London	G
26	Pit.	Michel Briere	Shawinigan	C
51	L.A.	Butch Goring	Dauphin Jr. A	C
52	Phi.	Dave Schultz	Sorel	LW
55	Tor.	Brian Spencer	Swift Current	LW
64	Phi.	Don Saleski	Regina	RW

NHL Clubs' Minor-League Affiliations, 2003-04

NHL CLUB	MINOR-LEAGUE AFFILIATES
Anaheim	Cincinnati Mighty Ducks (AHL)
Atlanta	Chicago Wolves (AHL)
	Greenville Grrrowl (ECHL)
Boston	Providence Bruins (AHL)
Buffalo	Rochester Americans (AHL)
Calgary	Lowell Lock Monsters (AHL)
	Las Vegas Wranglers (ECHL)
Carolina	Lowell Lock Monsters (AHL)
	Florida Everblades (ECHL)
Chicago	Norfolk Admirals (AHL)
	Roanoke Express (ECHL)
Colorado	Hershey Bears (AHL)
Columbus	Syracuse Crunch (AHL)
	Dayton Bombers (ECHL)
	Elmira Jackals (UHL)
Dallas	Utah Grizzlies (AHL)
	Fort Worth Brahmas (CHL)
Detroit	Grand Rapids Griffins (AHL)
	Toledo Storm (ECHL)
Edmonton	Toronto Roadrunners (AHL)
	Columbus Cottonmouths (ECHL)
	Odessa Jackalopes (CHL)
Florida	San Antonio Rampage (AHL)
Los Angeles	Manchester Monarchs (AHL)
	Reading Royals (ECHL)
Minnesota	Houston Aeros (AHL)
	Louisiana IceGators (ECHL)

NHL CLUB	MINOR-LEAGUE AFFILIATES
Montreal	Hamilton Bulldogs (AHL)
Nashville	Milwaukee Admirals (AHL)
	Toledo Storm (ECHL)
New Jersey	Albany River Rats (AHL)
NY Islanders	Bridgeport Sound Tigers (AHL)
NY Rangers	Hartford Wolf Pack (AHL)
Ottawa	Binghamton Senators (AHL)
Philadelphia	Philadelphia Phantoms (AHL)
	Trenton Titans (ECHL)
Phoenix	Springfield Falcons (AHL)
Pittsburgh	Wilkes-Barre/Scranton Penguins (AHL)
	Wheeling Nailers (ECHL)
St. Louis	Worcester IceCats (AHL)
	Peoria Rivermen (ECHL)
San Jose	Cleveland Barons (AHL)
	Fresno Falcons (ECHL)
	Johnstown Chiefs (ECHL)
Tampa Bay	Hershey Bears (AHL)
	Hamilton Bulldogs (AHL)
	Pensacola Ice Pilots (ECHL)
Toronto	St. John's Maple Leafs (AHL)
	Memphis RiverKings (CHL)
Vancouver	Manitoba Moose (AHL)
	Columbia Inferno (ECHL)
Washington	Portland Pirates (AHL)
	Quad City Mallards (UHL)

NHL All-Stars

Active Players' All-Star Selection Records

	First Team Selections	Second Team Selections	Total
GOALTENDERS			
Dominik Hasek	(6) 1993-94; 1994-95; 1996-97; 1997-98; 1998-99; 2000-01	(0)	6
Ed Belfour	(2) 1990-91; 1992-93.	(1) 1994-95	3
Martin Brodeur	(1) 2002-03.	(2) 1996-97; 1997-98.	3
Olaf Kolzig	(1) 99-2000.	(0)	1
Chris Osgood	(0)	(1) 1995-96.	1
Byron Dafoe	(0)	(1) 1998-99.	1
Roman Turek	(0)	(1) 99-2000.	1
Roman Cechmanek	(0)	(1) 2000-01.	1
Jose Theodore	(0)	(1) 2001-02.	1
Marty Turco	(0)	(1) 2002-03.	1
DEFENSEMEN			
Chris Chelios	(5) 1988-89; 1992-93; 1994-95; 1995-96; 2001-02.	(2) 1990-91; 1996-97.	7
Al MacInnis	(4) 1989-90; 1990-91; 1998-99; 2002-03.	(3) 1986-87; 1988-89; 1993-94.	7
Nicklas Lidstrom	(6) 1997-98; 1998-99; 99-2000; 2000-01; 2001-02; 2002-03.	(0)	6
Brian Leetch	(2) 1991-92; 1996-97.	(3) 1990-91; 1993-94; 1995-96.	5
Scott Stevens	(2) 1987-88; 1993-94.	(3) 1991-92; 1996-97; 2000-01.	5
Rob Blake	(1) 1997-98.	(3) 99-2000; 2000-01; 2001-02.	4
Chris Pronger	(1) 99-2000.	(1) 1997-98.	2
Eric Desjardins	(0)	(2) 1998-99; 99-2000.	2
Sergei Gonchar	(0)	(2) 2001-02; 2002-03.	2
Sandis Ozolinsh	(1) 1996-97.	(0)	1
Phil Housley	(0)	(1) 1991-92.	1
Scott Niedermayer	(0)	(1) 1997-98.	1
Derian Hatcher	(0)	(1) 2002-03.	1
CENTERS			
Mario Lemieux	(5) 1987-88; 1988-89; 1992-93; 1995-96; 1996-97.	(4) 1985-86; 1986-87; 1991-92; 2000-01.	9
Peter Forsberg	(3) 1997-98; 1998-99; 2002-03.	(0)	3
Mark Messier	(2) 1989-90; 1991-92.	(0)	2
Joe Sakic	(2) 2000-01; 2001-02.	(0)	2
Eric Lindros	(1) 1994-95.	(1) 1995-96.	2
Sergei Fedorov	(1) 1993-94.	(0)	1
Steve Yzerman	(1) 99-2000.	(0)	1
Adam Oates	(0)	(1) 1990-91.	1
Alexei Zhamnov	(0)	(1) 1994-95.	1
Alexei Yashin	(0)	(1) 1998-99.	1
Mike Modano	(0)	(1) 99-2000.	1
Mats Sundin	(0)	(1) 2001-02.	1
Joe Thornton	(0)	(1) 2002-03.	1
RIGHT WINGERS			
Jaromir Jagr	(6) 1994-95; 1995-96; 1997-98; 1998-99; 99-2000; 2000-01.	(1) 1996-97.	7
Teemu Selanne	(2) 1992-93; 1996-97.	(2) 1997-98; 1998-99.	4
Brett Hull	(3) 1989-90; 1990-91; 1991-92.	(0)	3
Pavel Bure	(1) 1993-94.	(2) 99-2000; 2000-01.	3
Alexander Mogilny	(0)	(2) 1992-93; 1995-96.	2
Jarome Iginla	(1) 2001-02.	(0)	1
Todd Bertuzzi	(1) 2002-03.	(0)	1
Mark Recchi	(0)	(1) 1991-92.	1
Theoren Fleury	(0)	(1) 1994-95.	1
Bill Guerin	(0)	(1) 2001-02.	1
Milan Hejduk	(0)	(1) 2002-03.	1
LEFT WINGERS			
Luc Robitaille	(5) 1987-88; 1988-89; 1989-90; 1990-91; 1992-93.	(3) 1986-87; 1991-92; 2000-01.	8
Paul Kariya	(3) 1995-96; 1996-97; 1998-99.	(2) 99-2000; 2002-03.	5
John LeClair	(2) 1994-95; 1997-98.	(3) 1995-96; 1996-97; 1998-99.	5
Mark Messier	(2) 1981-82; 1982-83.	(1) 1983-84.	3
Brendan Shanahan	(2) 1993-94; 99-2000.	(1) 2001-02.	3
Markus Naslund	(2) 2001-02; 2002-03.	(0)	2
Keith Tkachuk	(0)	(2) 1994-95; 1997-98.	2
Patrik Elias	(1) 2000-01.	(0)	1
Adam Graves	(0)	(1) 1993-94.	1

Leading NHL All-Stars 1930-31 to 2002-03

Player	Pos	Team	NHL Seasons	First Team Selections	Second Team Selections	Total Selections
Howe, Gordie	RW	Detroit	26	12	9	21
Bourque, Raymond	D	Bos., Col.	22	13	6	19
Gretzky, Wayne	C	Edm., L.A., NYR	20	8	7	15
Richard, Maurice	RW	Montreal	18	8	6	14
Hull, Bobby	LW	Chicago	16	10	2	12
Harvey, Doug	D	Mtl., NYR	19	10	1	11
Hall, Glenn	G	Det., Chi., St.L.	18	7	4	11
Beliveau, Jean	C	Montreal	20	6	4	10
Seibert, Earl	D	NYR, Chi.	15	4	6	10
Orr, Bobby	D	Boston	12	8	1	9
Lindsay, Ted	LW	Detroit	17	8	1	9
* Lemieux, Mario	C	Pittsburgh	15	5	4	9
Mahovlich, Frank	LW	Tor., Det., Mtl.	18	3	6	9
Shore, Eddie	D	Boston	14	7	1	8
Esposito, Phil	C	Boston	18	6	2	8
Kelly, Red	D	Detroit	20	6	2	8
Mikita, Stan	C	Chicago	22	6	2	8
Bossy, Mike	RW	NY Islanders	10	5	3	8
Pilote, Pierre	D	Chicago	14	5	3	8
* Robitaille, Luc	LW	Los Angeles	17	5	3	8
Coffey, Paul	D	Edm., Pit., Det.	21	4	4	8
Brimsek, Frank	G	Boston	10	2	6	8
* Jagr, Jaromir	RW	Pittsburgh	13	6	1	7
Potvin, Denis	D	NY Islanders	15	5	2	7
Park, Brad	D	NYR, Bos.	17	5	2	7
* Chelios, Chris	D	Mtl., Chi.	20	5	2	7
* MacInnis, Al	D	Cgy., St.L.	22	4	3	7
Plante, Jacques	G	Mtl., Tor.	18	3	4	7
Gadsby, Bill	D	Chi., NYR, Det.	20	3	4	7
Sawchuk, Terry	G	Detroit	21	3	4	7
Durnan, Bill	G	Montreal	7	6	0	6
Hasek, Dominik	G	Buffalo	12	6	0	6
* Lidstrom, Nicklas	D	Detroit	12	6	0	6
Lafleur, Guy	RW	Montreal	17	6	0	6
Dryden, Ken	G	Montreal	8	5	1	6
Roy, Patrick	G	Montreal	19	4	2	6
Clapper, Dit	RW/D	Boston	20	3	3	6
Robinson, Larry	D	Montreal	20	3	3	6
Horton, Tim	D	Toronto	24	3	3	6
Salming, Borje	D	Toronto	17	1	5	6
Cowley, Bill	C	Boston	13	4	1	5
Jackson, Busher	LW	Toronto	15	4	1	5
* Messier, Mark	LW/C	Edm., NYR	24	4	1	5
* Kariya, Paul	LW	Anaheim	9	3	2	5
Conacher, Charlie	RW	Toronto	12	3	2	5
Stewart, Jack	D	Detroit	12	3	2	5
Blake, Toe	LW	Montreal	14	3	2	5
Lach, Elmer	C	Montreal	14	3	2	5
Quackenbush, Bill	D	Det., Bos.	14	3	2	5
Goulet, Michel	LW	Quebec	15	3	2	5
Esposito, Tony	G	Chicago	16	3	2	5
Reardon, Ken	D	Montreal	7	2	3	5
Apps, Syl	C	Toronto	10	2	3	5
* LeClair, John	LW	Mtl., Phi.	13	2	3	5
Giacomin, Ed	G	NY Rangers	13	2	3	5
* Leetch, Brian	D	NY Rangers	15	2	3	5
Kurri, Jari	RW	Edmonton	17	2	3	5
* Stevens, Scott	D	Wsh., N.J.	20	2	3	5

Position Leaders in All-Star Selections

Position	Player	First Team	Second Team	Total
GOAL	Glenn Hall	7	4	11
	Frank Brimsek	2	6	8
	Jacques Plante	3	4	7
	Terry Sawchuk	3	4	7
	Bill Durnan	6	0	6
	* Dominik Hasek	6	0	6
	Ken Dryden	5	1	6
	Patrick Roy	4	2	6
DEFENSE	Raymond Bourque	13	6	19
	Doug Harvey	10	1	11
	Earl Seibert	4	6	10
	Bobby Orr	8	1	9
	Eddie Shore	7	1	8
	Red Kelly	6	2	8
	Pierre Pilote	5	3	8
	Paul Coffey	4	4	8

Position	Player	First Team	Second Team	Total
LEFT WING	Bobby Hull	10	2	12
	Ted Lindsay	8	1	9
	Frank Mahovlich	3	6	9
	* Luc Robitaille	5	3	8
RIGHT WING	Gordie Howe	12	9	21
	Maurice Richard	8	6	14
	Mike Bossy	5	3	8
	* Jaromir Jagr	6	1	7
	Guy Lafleur	6	0	6
CENTER	Wayne Gretzky	8	7	15
	Jean Beliveau	6	4	10
	* Mario Lemieux	5	4	9
	Phil Esposito	6	2	8
	Stan Mikita	6	2	8

* active player

The 2004 NHL All-Star Weekend will be hosted by the Minnesota Wild, February 7th and 8th, 2004.

All-Star Teams

1930-2003

Voting for the NHL All-Star Team is conducted among the representatives of the Professional Hockey Writers' Association at the end of the season.

Following is a list of the First and Second All-Star Teams since their inception in 1930-31.

2002-03

First Team		Second Team
Brodeur, Martin, N.J.	G	Turco, Marty, Dal.
MacInnis, Al, St.L.	D	Gonchar, Sergei, Wsh.
Lidstrom, Nicklas, Det.	D	Hatcher, Derian, Dal.
Forsberg, Peter, Col.	C	Thornton, Joe, Bos.
Bertuzzi, Todd, Van.	RW	Hejduk, Milan, Col.
Naslund, Markus, Van.	LW	Kariya, Paul, Ana.

2001-02

First Team		Second Team
Roy, Patrick, Col.	G	Theodore, Jose, Mtl.
Lidstrom, Nicklas, Det.	D	Blake, Rob, L.A., Col.
Chelios, Chris, Det.	D	Gonchar, Sergei, Wsh.
Sakic, Joe, Col.	C	Sundin, Mats, Tor.
Iginla, Jarome, Cgy.	RW	Guerin, Bill, Bos.
Naslund, Markus, Van.	LW	Shanahan, Brendan, Det.

2000-01

First Team		Second Team
Hasek, Dominik, Buf.	G	Cechmanek, Roman, Phi.
Lidstrom, Nicklas, Det.	D	Blake, Rob, L.A., Col.
Bourque, Raymond, Col.	D	Stevens, Scott, N.J.
Sakic, Joe, Col.	C	Lemieux, Mario, Pit.
Jagr, Jaromir, Pit.	RW	Bure, Pavel, Fla.
Elias, Patrik, N.J.	LW	Robitaille, Luc, L.A.

1999-2000

First Team		Second Team
Kolzig, Olaf, Wsh.	G	Turek, Roman, St.L.
Pronger, Chris, St.L.	D	Blake, Rob, L.A.
Lidstrom, Nicklas, Det.	D	Desjardins, Eric, Phi.
Yzerman, Steve, Det.	C	Modano, Mike, Dal.
Jagr, Jaromir, Pit.	RW	Bure, Pavel, Fla.
Shanahan, Brendan, Det.	LW	Kariya, Paul, Ana.

1998-99

First Team		Second Team
Hasek, Dominik, Buf.	G	Dafoe, Byron, Bos.
MacInnis, Al, St.L.	D	Bourque, Raymond, Bos.
Lidstrom, Nicklas, Det.	D	Desjardins, Eric, Phi.
Forsberg, Peter, Col.	C	Yashin, Alexei, Ott.
Jagr, Jaromir, Pit.	RW	Selanne, Teemu, Ana.
Kariya, Paul, Ana.	LW	LeClair, John, Phi.

1997-98

First Team		Second Team
Hasek, Dominik, Buf.	G	Brodeur, Martin, N.J.
Lidstrom, Nicklas, Det.	D	Pronger, Chris, St.L.
Blake, Rob, L.A.	D	Niedermayer, Scott, N.J.
Forsberg, Peter, Col.	C	Gretzky, Wayne, NYR
Jagr, Jaromir, Pit.	RW	Selanne, Teemu, Ana.
LeClair, John, Phi.	LW	Tkachuk, Keith, Phx.

1996-97

First Team		Second Team
Hasek, Dominik, Buf.	G	Brodeur, Martin, N.J.
Leetch, Brian, NYR	D	Chelios, Chris, Chi.
Ozolinsh, Sandis, Col.	D	Stevens, Scott, N.J.
Lemieux, Mario, Pit.	C	Gretzky, Wayne, NYR
Selanne, Teemu, Ana.	RW	Jagr, Jaromir, Pit.
Kariya, Paul, Ana.	LW	LeClair, John, Phi.

1995-96

First Team		Second Team
Carey, Jim, Wsh.	G	Osgood, Chris, Det.
Chelios, Chris, Chi.	D	Konstantinov, V., Det.
Bourque, Raymond, Bos.	D	Leetch, Brian, NYR
Lemieux, Mario, Pit.	C	Lindros, Eric, Phi.
Jagr, Jaromir, Pit.	RW	Mogilny, Alexander, Van.
Kariya, Paul, Ana.	LW	LeClair, John, Phi.

1994-95

First Team		Second Team
Hasek, Dominik, Buf.	G	Belfour, Ed, Chi.
Coffey, Paul, Det.	D	Bourque, Raymond, Bos.
Chelios, Chris, Chi.	D	Murphy, Larry, Pit.
Lindros, Eric, Phi.	C	Zhamnov, Alexei, Wpg.
Jagr, Jaromir, Pit.	RW	Fleury, Theoren, Cgy.
LeClair, John, Mtl., Phi.	LW	Tkachuk, Keith, Wpg.

1993-94

First Team		Second Team
Hasek, Dominik, Buf.	G	Vanbiesbrouck, John, Fla.
Bourque, Raymond, Bos.	D	MacInnis, Al, Cgy.
Stevens, Scott, N.J.	D	Leetch, Brian, NYR
Fedorov, Sergei, Det.	C	Gretzky, Wayne, L.A.
Bure, Pavel, Van.	RW	Neely, Cam, Bos.
Shanahan, Brendan, St.L.	LW	Graves, Adam, NYR

1992-93

First Team		Second Team
Belfour, Ed, Chi.	G	Barrasso, Tom, Pit.
Chelios, Chris, Chi.	D	Murphy, Larry, Pit.
Bourque, Raymond, Bos.	D	Iafrate, Al, Wsh.
Lemieux, Mario, Pit.	C	LaFontaine, Pat, Buf.
Selanne, Teemu, Wpg.	RW	Mogilny, Alexander, Buf.
Robitaille, Luc, L.A.	LW	Stevens, Kevin, Pit.

1991-92

First Team		Second Team
Roy, Patrick, Mtl.	G	McLean, Kirk, Van.
Leetch, Brian, NYR	D	Housley, Phil, Wpg.
Bourque, Raymond, Bos.	D	Stevens, Scott, N.J.
Messier, Mark, NYR	C	Lemieux, Mario, Pit.
Hull, Brett, St.L.	RW	Recchi, Mark, Pit., Phi.
Stevens, Kevin, Pit.	LW	Robitaille, Luc, L.A.

1990-91

First Team		Second Team
Belfour, Ed, Chi.	G	Roy, Patrick, Mtl.
Bourque, Raymond, Bos.	D	Chelios, Chris, Chi.
MacInnis, Al, Cgy.	D	Leetch, Brian, NYR
Gretzky, Wayne, L.A.	C	Oates, Adam, St.L.
Hull, Brett, St.L.	RW	Neely, Cam, Bos.
Robitaille, Luc, L.A.	LW	Stevens, Kevin, Pit.

1989-90

First Team		Second Team
Roy, Patrick, Mtl.	G	Puppa, Daren, Buf.
Bourque, Raymond, Bos.	D	Coffey, Paul, Pit.
MacInnis, Al, Cgy.	D	Wilson, Doug, Chi.
Messier, Mark, Edm.	C	Gretzky, Wayne, L.A.
Hull, Brett, St.L.	RW	Neely, Cam, Bos.
Robitaille, Luc, L.A.	LW	Bellows, Brian, Min.

1988-89

First Team		Second Team
Roy, Patrick, Mtl.	G	Vernon, Mike, Cgy.
Chelios, Chris, Mtl.	D	MacInnis, Al, Cgy.
Coffey, Paul, Pit.	D	Bourque, Raymond, Bos.
Lemieux, Mario, Pit.	C	Gretzky, Wayne, L.A.
Mullen, Joe, Cgy.	RW	Kurri, Jari, Edm.
Robitaille, Luc, L.A.	LW	Gallant, Gerard, Det.

1987-88

First Team		Second Team
Fuhr, Grant, Edm.	G	Roy, Patrick, Mtl.
Bourque, Raymond, Bos.	D	Suter, Gary, Cgy.
Stevens, Scott, Wsh.	D	McCrimmon, Brad, Cgy.
Lemieux, Mario, Pit.	C	Gretzky, Wayne, Edm.
Loob, Hakan, Cgy.	RW	Neely, Cam, Bos.
Robitaille, Luc, L.A.	LW	Goulet, Michel, Que.

1986-87

First Team		Second Team
Hextall, Ron, Phi.	G	Liut, Mike, Hfd.
Bourque, Raymond, Bos.	D	Murphy, Larry, Wsh.
Howe, Mark, Phi.	D	MacInnis, Al, Cgy.
Gretzky, Wayne, Edm.	C	Lemieux, Mario, Pit.
Kurri, Jari, Edm.	RW	Kerr, Tim, Phi.
Goulet, Michel, Que.	LW	Robitaille, Luc, L.A.

1985-86

First Team		Second Team
Vanbiesbrouck, John, NYR	G	Froese, Bob, Phi.
Coffey, Paul, Edm.	D	Robinson, Larry, Mtl.
Howe, Mark, Phi.	D	Bourque, Raymond, Bos.
Gretzky, Wayne, Edm.	C	Lemieux, Mario, Pit.
Bossy, Mike, NYI	RW	Kurri, Jari, Edm.
Goulet, Michel, Que.	LW	Naslund, Mats, Mtl.

1984-85

First Team		Second Team
Lindbergh, Pelle, Phi.	G	Barrasso, Tom, Buf.
Coffey, Paul, Edm.	D	Langway, Rod, Wsh.
Bourque, Raymond, Bos.	D	Wilson, Doug, Chi.
Gretzky, Wayne, Edm.	C	Hawerchuk, Dale, Wpg.
Kurri, Jari, Edm.	RW	Bossy, Mike, NYI
Ogrodnick, John, Det.	LW	Tonelli, John, NYI

1983-84

First Team		Second Team
Barrasso, Tom, Buf.	G	Riggin, Pat, Wsh.
Langway, Rod, Wsh.	D	Coffey, Paul, Edm.
Bourque, Raymond, Bos.	D	Potvin, Denis, NYI
Gretzky, Wayne, Edm.	C	Trottier, Bryan, NYI
Bossy, Mike, NYI	RW	Kurri, Jari, Edm.
Goulet, Michel, Que.	LW	Messier, Mark, Edm.

1982-83

First Team		Second Team
Peeters, Pete, Bos.	G	Melanson, Roland, NYI
Howe, Mark, Phi.	D	Bourque, Raymond, Bos.
Langway, Rod, Wsh.	D	Coffey, Paul, Edm.
Gretzky, Wayne, Edm.	C	Savard, Denis, Chi.
Bossy, Mike, NYI	RW	McDonald, Lanny, Cgy.
Messier, Mark, Edm.	LW	Goulet, Michel, Que.

1981-82

First Team		Second Team
Smith, Billy, NYI	G	Fuhr, Grant, Edm.
Wilson, Doug, Chi.	D	Coffey, Paul, Edm.
Bourque, Raymond, Bos.	D	Engblom, Brian, Mtl.
Gretzky, Wayne, Edm.	C	Trottier, Bryan, NYI
Bossy, Mike, NYI	RW	Middleton, Rick, Bos.
Messier, Mark, Edm.	LW	Tonelli, John, NYI

Canucks linemates Todd Bertuzzi (left) and Markus Naslund were both named First-Team All-Stars last season.

1980-81

First Team		Second Team
Liut, Mike, St.L.	G	Lessard, Mario, L.A.
Potvin, Denis, NYI	D	Robinson, Larry, Mtl.
Carlyle, Randy, Pit.	D	Bourque, Raymond, Bos.
Gretzky, Wayne, Edm.	C	Dionne, Marcel, L.A.
Bossy, Mike, NYI	RW	Taylor, Dave, L.A.
Simmer, Charlie, L.A.	LW	Barber, Bill, Phi.

1979-80

First Team		Second Team
Esposito, Tony, Chi.	G	Edwards, Don, Buf.
Robinson, Larry, Mtl.	D	Salming, Borje, Tor.
Bourque, Raymond, Bos.	D	Schoenfeld, Jim, Buf.
Dionne, Marcel, L.A.	C	Gretzky, Wayne, Edm.
Lafleur, Guy, Mtl.	RW	Gare, Danny, Buf.
Simmer, Charlie, L.A.	LW	Shutt, Steve, Mtl.

1978-79

First Team		Second Team
Dryden, Ken, Mtl.	G	Resch, Glenn, NYI
Potvin, Denis, NYI	D	Salming, Borje, Tor.
Robinson, Larry, Mtl.	D	Savard, Serge, Mtl.
Trottier, Bryan, NYI	C	Dionne, Marcel, L.A.
Lafleur, Guy, Mtl.	RW	Bossy, Mike, NYI
Gillies, Clark, NYI	LW	Barber, Bill, Phi.

1977-78

First Team		Second Team
Dryden, Ken, Mtl.	G	Edwards, Don, Buf.
Potvin, Denis, NYI	D	Robinson, Larry, Mtl.
Park, Brad, Bos.	D	Salming, Borje, Tor.
Trottier, Bryan, NYI	C	Sittler, Darryl, Tor.
Lafleur, Guy, Mtl.	RW	Bossy, Mike, NYI
Gillies, Clark, NYI	LW	Shutt, Steve, Mtl.

1976-77

First Team		Second Team
Dryden, Ken, Mtl.	G	Vachon, Rogie, L.A.
Robinson, Larry, Mtl.	D	Potvin, Denis, NYI
Salming, Borje, Tor.	D	Lapointe, Guy, Mtl.
Dionne, Marcel, L.A.	C	Perreault, Gilbert, Buf.
Lafleur, Guy, Mtl.	RW	McDonald, Lanny, Tor.
Shutt, Steve, Mtl.	LW	Martin, Rick, Buf.

1975-76

First Team		Second Team
Dryden, Ken, Mtl.	G	Resch, Glenn, NYI
Potvin, Denis, NYI	D	Salming, Borje, Tor.
Park, Brad, Bos.	D	Lapointe, Guy, Mtl.
Clarke, Bobby, Phi.	C	Perreault, Gilbert, Buf.
Lafleur, Guy, Mtl.	RW	Leach, Reggie, Phi.
Barber, Bill, Phi.	LW	Martin, Rick, Buf.

1974-75

First Team		Second Team
Parent, Bernie, Phi.	G	Vachon, Rogie, L.A.
Orr, Bobby, Bos.	D	Lapointe, Guy, Mtl.
Potvin, Denis, NYI	D	Salming, Borje, Tor.
Clarke, Bobby, Phi.	C	Esposito, Phil, Bos.
Lafleur, Guy, Mtl.	RW	Robert, René, Buf.
Martin, Rick, Buf.	LW	Vickers, Steve, NYR

1973-74

First Team		Second Team
Parent, Bernie, Phi.	G	Esposito, Tony, Chi.
Orr, Bobby, Bos.	D	White, Bill, Chi.
Park, Brad, NYR	D	Ashbee, Barry, Phi.
Esposito, Phil, Bos.	C	Clarke, Bobby, Phi.
Hodge, Ken, Bos.	RW	Redmond, Mickey, Det.
Martin, Rick, Buf.	LW	Cashman, Wayne, Bos.

1972-73

First Team		Second Team
Dryden, Ken, Mtl.	G	Esposito, Tony, Chi.
Orr, Bobby, Bos.	D	Park, Brad, NYR
Lapointe, Guy, Mtl.	D	White, Bill, Chi.
Esposito, Phil, Bos.	C	Clarke, Bobby, Phi.
Redmond, Mickey, Det.	RW	Cournoyer, Yvan, Mtl.
Mahovlich, Frank, Mtl.	LW	Hull, Dennis, Chi.

1971-72

First Team		Second Team
Esposito, Tony, Chi.	G	Dryden, Ken, Mtl.
Orr, Bobby, Bos.	D	White, Bill, Chi.
Park, Brad, NYR	D	Stapleton, Pat, Chi.
Esposito, Phil, Bos.	C	Ratelle, Jean, NYR
Gilbert, Rod, NYR	RW	Cournoyer, Yvan, Mtl.
Hull, Bobby, Chi.	LW	Hadfield, Vic, NYR

1970-71

First Team		Second Team
Giacomin, Ed, NYR	G	Plante, Jacques, Tor.
Orr, Bobby, Bos.	D	Park, Brad, NYR
Tremblay, J.C., Mtl.	D	Stapleton, Pat, Chi.
Esposito, Phil, Bos.	C	Keon, Dave, Tor.
Hodge, Ken, Bos.	RW	Cournoyer, Yvan, Mtl.
Bucyk, John, Bos.	LW	Hull, Bobby, Chi.

1969-70

First Team		Second Team
Esposito, Tony, Chi.	G	Giacomin, Ed, NYR
Orr, Bobby, Bos.	D	Brewer, Carl, Det.
Park, Brad, NYR	D	Laperriere, Jacques, Mtl.
Esposito, Phil, Bos.	C	Mikita, Stan, Chi.
Howe, Gordie, Det.	RW	McKenzie, John, Bos.
Hull, Bobby, Chi.	LW	Mahovlich, Frank, Det.

1968-69

First Team		Second Team
Hall, Glenn, St.L.	G	Giacomin, Ed, NYR
Orr, Bobby, Bos.	D	Green, Ted, Bos.
Horton, Tim, Tor.	D	Harris, Ted, Mtl.
Esposito, Phil, Bos.	C	Béliveau, Jean, Mtl.
Howe, Gordie, Det.	RW	Cournoyer, Yvan, Mtl.
Hull, Bobby, Chi.	LW	Mahovlich, Frank, Det.

1967-68

First Team		Second Team
Worsley, Gump, Mtl.	G	Giacomin, Ed, NYR
Orr, Bobby, Bos.	D	Tremblay, J.C., Mtl.
Horton, Tim, Tor.	D	Neilson, Jim, NYR
Mikita, Stan, Chi.	C	Esposito, Phil, Bos.
Howe, Gordie, Det.	RW	Gilbert, Rod, NYR
Hull, Bobby, Chi.	LW	Bucyk, John, Bos.

1966-67

First Team		Second Team
Giacomin, Ed, NYR	G	Hall, Glenn, Chi.
Pilote, Pierre, Chi.	D	Horton, Tim, Tor.
Howell, Harry, NYR	D	Orr, Bobby, Bos.
Mikita, Stan, Chi.	C	Ullman, Norm, Det.
Wharram, Kenny, Chi.	RW	Howe, Gordie, Det.
Hull, Bobby, Chi.	LW	Marshall, Don, NYR

1965-66

First Team		Second Team
Hall, Glenn, Chi.	G	Worsley, Gump, Mtl.
Laperriere, Jacques, Mtl.	D	Stanley, Allan, Tor.
Pilote, Pierre, Chi.	D	Stapleton, Pat, Chi.
Mikita, Stan, Chi.	C	Béliveau, Jean, Mtl.
Howe, Gordie, Det.	RW	Rousseau, Bobby, Mtl.
Hull, Bobby, Chi.	LW	Mahovlich, Frank, Tor.

1964-65

First Team		Second Team
Crozier, Roger, Det.	G	Hodge, Charlie, Mtl.
Pilote, Pierre, Chi.	D	Gadsby, Bill, Det.
Laperriere, Jacques, Mtl.	D	Brewer, Carl, Tor.
Ullman, Norm, Det.	C	Mikita, Stan, Chi.
Provost, Claude, Mtl.	RW	Howe, Gordie, Det.
Hull, Bobby, Chi.	LW	Mahovlich, Frank, Tor.

1963-64

First Team		Second Team
Hall, Glenn, Chi.	G	Hodge, Charlie, Mtl.
Pilote, Pierre, Chi.	D	Vasko, Moose, Chi.
Horton, Tim, Tor.	D	Laperriere, Jacques, Mtl.
Mikita, Stan, Chi.	C	Béliveau, Jean, Mtl.
Wharram, Kenny, Chi.	RW	Howe, Gordie, Det.
Hull, Bobby, Chi.	LW	Mahovlich, Frank, Tor.

1962-63

First Team		Second Team
Hall, Glenn, Chi.	G	Sawchuk, Terry, Det.
Pilote, Pierre, Chi.	D	Horton, Tim, Tor.
Brewer, Carl, Tor.	D	Vasko, Moose, Chi.
Mikita, Stan, Chi.	C	Richard, Henri, Mtl.
Howe, Gordie, Det.	RW	Bathgate, Andy, NYR
Mahovlich, Frank, Tor.	LW	Hull, Bobby, Chi.

1961-62

First Team		Second Team
Plante, Jacques, Mtl.	G	Hall, Glenn, Chi.
Harvey, Doug, NYR	D	Brewer, Carl, Tor.
Talbot, Jean-Guy, Mtl.	D	Pilote, Pierre, Chi.
Mikita, Stan, Chi.	C	Keon, Dave, Tor.
Bathgate, Andy, NYR	RW	Howe, Gordie, Det.
Hull, Bobby, Chi.	LW	Mahovlich, Frank, Tor.

1960-61

First Team		Second Team
Bower, Johnny, Tor.	G	Hall, Glenn, Chi.
Harvey, Doug, Mtl.	D	Stanley, Allan, Tor.
Pronovost, Marcel, Det.	D	Pilote, Pierre, Chi.
Béliveau, Jean, Mtl.	C	Richard, Henri, Mtl.
Geoffrion, Bernie, Mtl.	RW	Howe, Gordie, Det.
Mahovlich, Frank, Tor.	LW	Moore, Dickie, Mtl.

1959-60

First Team		Second Team
Hall, Glenn, Chi.	G	Plante, Jacques, Mtl.
Harvey, Doug, Mtl.	D	Stanley, Allan, Tor.
Pronovost, Marcel, Det.	D	Pilote, Pierre, Chi.
Béliveau, Jean, Mtl.	C	Horvath, Bronco, Bos.
Howe, Gordie, Det.	RW	Geoffrion, Bernie, Mtl.
Hull, Bobby, Chi.	LW	Prentice, Dean, NYR

1958-59

First Team		Second Team
Plante, Jacques, Mtl.	G	Sawchuk, Terry, Det.
Johnson, Tom, Mtl.	D	Pronovost, Marcel, Det.
Gadsby, Bill, NYR	D	Harvey, Doug, Mtl.
Béliveau, Jean, Mtl.	C	Richard, Henri, Mtl.
Bathgate, Andy, NYR	RW	Howe, Gordie, Det.
Moore, Dickie, Mtl.	LW	Delvecchio, Alex, Det.

1957-58

First Team		Second Team
Hall, Glenn, Chi.	G	Plante, Jacques, Mtl.
Harvey, Doug, Mtl.	D	Flaman, Fern, Bos.
Gadsby, Bill, NYR	D	Pronovost, Marcel, Det.
Richard, Henri, Mtl.	C	Béliveau, Jean, Mtl.
Howe, Gordie, Det.	RW	Bathgate, Andy, NYR
Moore, Dickie, Mtl.	LW	Henry, Camille, NYR

1956-57

First Team		Second Team
Hall, Glenn, Det.	G	Plante, Jacques, Mtl.
Harvey, Doug, Mtl.	D	Flaman, Fern, Bos.
Kelly, Red, Det.	D	Gadsby, Bill, NYR
Béliveau, Jean, Mtl.	C	Litzenberger, Ed, Chi.
Howe, Gordie, Det.	RW	Richard, Maurice, Mtl.
Lindsay, Ted, Det.	LW	Chevrefils, Real, Bos.

1955-56

First Team		Second Team
Plante, Jacques, Mtl.	G	Hall, Glenn, Det.
Harvey, Doug, Mtl.	D	Kelly, Red, Det.
Gadsby, Bill, NYR	D	Johnson, Tom, Mtl.
Béliveau, Jean, Mtl.	C	Sloan, Tod, Tor.
Richard, Maurice, Mtl.	RW	Howe, Gordie, Det.
Lindsay, Ted, Det.	LW	Olmstead, Bert, Mtl.

1954-55

First Team		Second Team
Lumley, Harry, Tor.	G	Sawchuk, Terry, Det.
Harvey, Doug, Mtl.	D	Goldham, Bob, Det.
Kelly, Red, Det.	D	Flaman, Fern, Bos.
Béliveau, Jean, Mtl.	C	Mosdell, Ken, Mtl.
Richard, Maurice, Mtl.	RW	Geoffrion, Bernie, Mtl.
Smith, Sid, Tor.	LW	Lewicki, Danny, NYR

First Team		Second Team

1953-54

First Team		Second Team
Lumley, Harry, Tor.	G	Sawchuk, Terry, Det.
Kelly, Red, Det.	D	Gadsby, Bill, Chi.
Harvey, Doug, Mtl.	D	Horton, Tim, Tor.
Mosdell, Ken, Mtl.	C	Kennedy, Ted, Tor.
Howe, Gordie, Det.	RW	Richard, Maurice, Mtl.
Lindsay, Ted, Det.	LW	Sandford, Ed, Bos.

1952-53

First Team		Second Team
Sawchuk, Terry, Det.	G	McNeil, Gerry, Mtl.
Kelly, Red, Det.	D	Quackenbush, Bill, Bos.
Harvey, Doug, Mtl.	D	Gadsby, Bill, Chi.
Mackell, Fleming, Bos.	C	Delvecchio, Alex, Det.
Howe, Gordie, Det.	RW	Richard, Maurice, Mtl.
Lindsay, Ted, Det.	LW	Olmstead, Bert, Mtl.

1951-52

First Team		Second Team
Sawchuk, Terry, Det.	G	Henry, Jim, Bos.
Kelly, Red, Det.	D	Buller, Hy, NYR
Harvey, Doug, Mtl.	D	Thomson, Jimmy, Tor.
Lach, Elmer, Mtl.	C	Schmidt, Milt, Bos.
Howe, Gordie, Det.	RW	Richard, Maurice, Mtl.
Lindsay, Ted, Det.	LW	Smith, Sid, Tor.

1950-51

First Team		Second Team
Sawchuk, Terry, Det.	G	Rayner, Chuck, NYR
Kelly, Red, Det.	D	Thomson, Jimmy, Tor.
Quackenbush, Bill, Bos.	D	Reise Jr., Leo, Det.
Schmidt, Milt, Bos.	C	Abel, Sid, Det.
	(tied)	Kennedy, Ted, Tor.
Howe, Gordie, Det.	RW	Richard, Maurice, Mtl.
Lindsay, Ted, Det.	LW	Smith, Sid, Tor.

1949-50

First Team		Second Team
Durnan, Bill, Mtl.	G	Rayner, Chuck, NYR
Mortson, Gus, Tor.	D	Reise Jr., Leo, Det.
Reardon, Ken, Mtl.	D	Kelly, Red, Det.
Abel, Sid, Det.	C	Kennedy, Ted, Tor.
Richard, Maurice, Mtl.	RW	Howe, Gordie, Det.
Lindsay, Ted, Det.	LW	Leswick, Tony, NYR

1948-49

First Team		Second Team
Durnan, Bill, Mtl.	G	Rayner, Chuck, NYR
Quackenbush, Bill, Det.	D	Harmon, Glen, Mtl.
Stewart, Jack, Det.	D	Reardon, Ken, Mtl.
Abel, Sid, Det.	C	Bentley, Doug, Chi.
Richard, Maurice, Mtl.	RW	Howe, Gordie, Det.
Conacher, Roy, Chi.	LW	Lindsay, Ted, Det.

1947-48

First Team		Second Team
Broda, Turk, Tor.	G	Brimsek, Frank, Bos.
Quackenbush, Bill, Det.	D	Reardon, Ken, Mtl.
Stewart, Jack, Det.	D	Colville, Neil, NYR
Lach, Elmer, Mtl.	C	O'Connor, Buddy, NYR
Richard, Maurice, Mtl.	RW	Poile, Bud, Tor.
Lindsay, Ted, Det.	LW	Stewart, Gaye, Chi.

1946-47

First Team		Second Team
Durnan, Bill, Mtl.	G	Brimsek, Frank, Bos.
Reardon, Ken, Mtl.	D	Stewart, Jack, Det.
Bouchard, Butch, Mtl.	D	Quackenbush, Bill, Det.
Schmidt, Milt, Bos.	C	Bentley, Max, Chi.
Richard, Maurice, Mtl.	RW	Bauer, Bobby, Bos.
Bentley, Doug, Chi.	LW	Dumart, Woody, Bos.

1945-46

First Team		Second Team
Durnan, Bill, Mtl.	G	Brimsek, Frank, Bos.
Crawford, Jack, Bos.	D	Reardon, Ken, Mtl.
Bouchard, Butch, Mtl.	D	Stewart, Jack, Det.
Bentley, Max, Chi.	C	Lach, Elmer, Mtl.
Richard, Maurice, Mtl.	RW	Mosienko, Bill, Chi.
Stewart, Gaye, Tor.	LW	Blake, Toe, Mtl.
Irvin, Dick, Mtl.	Coach	Gottselig, Johnny, Chi.

1944-45

First Team		Second Team
Durnan, Bill, Mtl.	G	Karakas, Mike, Chi.
Bouchard, Butch, Mtl.	D	Harmon, Glen, Mtl.
Hollett, Flash, Det.	D	Pratt, Babe, Tor.
Lach, Elmer, Mtl.	C	Cowley, Bill, Bos.
Richard, Maurice, Mtl.	RW	Mosienko, Bill, Chi.
Blake, Toe, Mtl.	LW	Howe, Syd, Det.
Irvin, Dick, Mtl.	Coach	Adams, Jack, Det.

1943-44

First Team		Second Team
Durnan, Bill, Mtl.	G	Bibeault, Paul, Tor.
Seibert, Earl, Chi.	D	Bouchard, Butch, Mtl.
Pratt, Babe, Tor.	D	Clapper, Dit, Bos.
Cowley, Bill, Bos.	C	Lach, Elmer, Mtl.
Carr, Lorne, Tor.	RW	Richard, Maurice, Mtl.
Bentley, Doug, Chi.	LW	Cain, Herb, Bos.
Irvin, Dick, Mtl.	Coach	Day, Hap, Tor.

1942-43

First Team		Second Team
Mowers, Johnny, Det.	G	Brimsek, Frank, Bos.
Seibert, Earl, Chi.	D	Crawford, Jack, Bos.
Stewart, Jack, Det.	D	Hollett, Flash, Bos.
Cowley, Bill, Bos.	C	Apps, Syl, Tor.
Carr, Lorne, Tor.	RW	Hextall, Bryan, NYR
Bentley, Doug, Chi.	LW	Patrick, Lynn, NYR
Adams, Jack, Det.	Coach	Ross, Art, Bos.

1941-42

First Team		Second Team
Brimsek, Frank, Bos.	G	Broda, Turk, Tor.
Seibert, Earl, Chi.	D	Egan, Pat, Bro.
Anderson, Tom, Bro.	D	McDonald, Bucko, Tor.
Apps, Syl, Tor.	C	Watson, Phil, NYR
Hextall, Bryan, NYR	RW	Drillon, Gordie, Tor.
Patrick, Lynn, NYR	LW	Abel, Sid, Det.
Boucher, Frank, NYR	Coach	Thompson, Paul, Chi.

1940-41

First Team		Second Team
Broda, Turk, Tor.	G	Brimsek, Frank, Bos.
Clapper, Dit, Bos.	D	Seibert, Earl, Chi.
Stanowski, Wally, Tor.	D	Heller, Ott, NYR
Cowley, Bill, Bos.	C	Apps, Syl, Tor.
Hextall, Bryan, NYR	RW	Bauer, Bobby, Bos.
Schriner, Sweeney, Tor.	LW	Dumart, Woody, Bos.
Weiland, Cooney, Bos.	Coach	Irvin, Dick, Mtl.

1939-40

First Team		Second Team
Kerr, Dave, NYR	G	Brimsek, Frank, Bos.
Clapper, Dit, Bos.	D	Coulter, Art, NYR
Goodfellow, Ebbie, Det.	D	Seibert, Earl, Chi.
Schmidt, Milt, Bos.	C	Colville, Neil, NYR
Hextall, Bryan, NYR	RW	Bauer, Bobby, Bos.
Blake, Toe, Mtl.	LW	Dumart, Woody, Bos.
Thompson, Paul, Chi.	Coach	Boucher, Frank, NYR

1938-39

First Team		Second Team
Brimsek, Frank, Bos.	G	Robertson, Earl, NYA
Shore, Eddie, Bos.	D	Seibert, Earl, Chi.
Clapper, Dit, Bos.	D	Coulter, Art, NYR
Apps, Syl, Tor.	C	Colville, Neil, NYR
Drillon, Gordie, Tor.	RW	Bauer, Bobby, Bos.
Blake, Toe, Mtl.	LW	Gottselig, Johnny, Chi.
Ross, Art, Bos.	Coach	Dutton, Red, NYA

1937-38

First Team		Second Team
Thompson, Tiny, Bos.	G	Kerr, Dave, NYR
Shore, Eddie, Bos.	D	Coulter, Art, NYR
Siebert, Babe, Mtl.	D	Seibert, Earl, Chi.
Cowley, Bill, Bos.	C	Apps, Syl, Tor.
Dillon, Cecil, NYR	RW	
Drillon, Gordie, Tor.	(tied)	
Thompson, Paul, Chi.	LW	Blake, Toe, Mtl.
Patrick, Lester, NYR	Coach	Ross, Art, Bos.

1936-37

First Team		Second Team
Smith, Normie, Det.	G	Cude, Wilf, Mtl.
Siebert, Babe, Mtl.	D	Seibert, Earl, Chi.
Goodfellow, Ebbie, Det.	D	Conacher, Lionel, Mtl. M.
Barry, Marty, Det.	C	Chapman, Art, NYA
Aurie, Larry, Det.	RW	Dillon, Cecil, NYR
Jackson, Busher, Tor.	LW	Schriner, Sweeney, NYA
Adams, Jack, Det.	Coach	Hart, Cecil, Mtl.

1935-36

First Team		Second Team
Thompson, Tiny, Bos.	G	Cude, Wilf, Mtl.
Shore, Eddie, Bos.	D	Seibert, Earl, Chi.
Siebert, Babe, Bos.	D	Goodfellow, Ebbie, Det.
Smith, Hooley, Mtl. M.	C	Thoms, Bill, Tor.
Conacher, Charlie, Tor.	RW	Dillon, Cecil, NYR
Schriner, Sweeney, NYA	LW	Thompson, Paul, Chi.
Patrick, Lester, NYR	Coach	Gorman, Tommy, Mtl. M.

1934-35

First Team		Second Team
Chabot, Lorne, Chi.	G	Thompson, Tiny, Bos.
Shore, Eddie, Bos.	D	Wentworth, Cy, Mtl. M.
Seibert, Earl, NYR	D	Coulter, Art, Chi.
Boucher, Frank, NYR	C	Weiland, Cooney, Det.
Conacher, Charlie, Tor.	RW	Clapper, Dit, Bos.
Jackson, Busher, Tor.	LW	Joliat, Aurel, Mtl.
Patrick, Lester, NYR	Coach	Irvin, Dick, Tor.

1933-34

First Team		Second Team
Gardiner, Charlie, Chi.	G	Worters, Roy, NYA
Clancy, King, Tor.	D	Shore, Eddie, Bos.
Conacher, Lionel, Chi.	D	Johnson, Ching, NYR
Boucher, Frank, NYR	C	Primeau, Joe, Tor.
Conacher, Charlie, Tor.	RW	Cook, Bill, NYR
Jackson, Busher, Tor.	LW	Joliat, Aurel, Mtl.
Patrick, Lester, NYR	Coach	Irvin, Dick, Tor.

1932-33

First Team		Second Team
Roach, John Ross, Det.	G	Gardiner, Charlie, Chi.
Shore, Eddie, Bos.	D	Clancy, King, Tor.
Johnson, Ching, NYR	D	Conacher, Lionel, Mtl. M.
Boucher, Frank, NYR	C	Morenz, Howie, Mtl.
Cook, Bill, NYR	RW	Conacher, Charlie, Tor.
Northcott, Baldy, Mtl M.	LW	Jackson, Busher, Tor.
Patrick, Lester, NYR	Coach	Irvin, Dick, Tor.

1931-32

First Team		Second Team
Gardiner, Charlie, Chi.	G	Worters, Roy, NYA
Shore, Eddie, Bos.	D	Mantha, Sylvio, Mtl.
Johnson, Ching, NYR	D	Clancy, King, Tor.
Morenz, Howie, Mtl.	C	Smith, Hooley, Mtl. M.
Cook, Bill, NYR	RW	Conacher, Charlie, Tor.
Jackson, Busher, Tor.	LW	Joliat, Aurel, Mtl.
Patrick, Lester, NYR	Coach	Irvin, Dick, Tor.

1930-31

First Team		Second Team
Gardiner, Charlie, Chi.	G	Thompson, Tiny, Bos.
Shore, Eddie, Bos.	D	Mantha, Sylvio, Mtl.
Clancy, King, Tor.	D	Johnson, Ching, NYR
Morenz, Howie, Mtl.	C	Boucher, Frank, NYR
Cook, Bill, NYR	RW	Clapper, Dit, Bos.
Joliat, Aurel, Mtl.	LW	Cook, Bun, NYR
Patrick, Lester, NYR	Coach	Irvin, Dick, Chi.

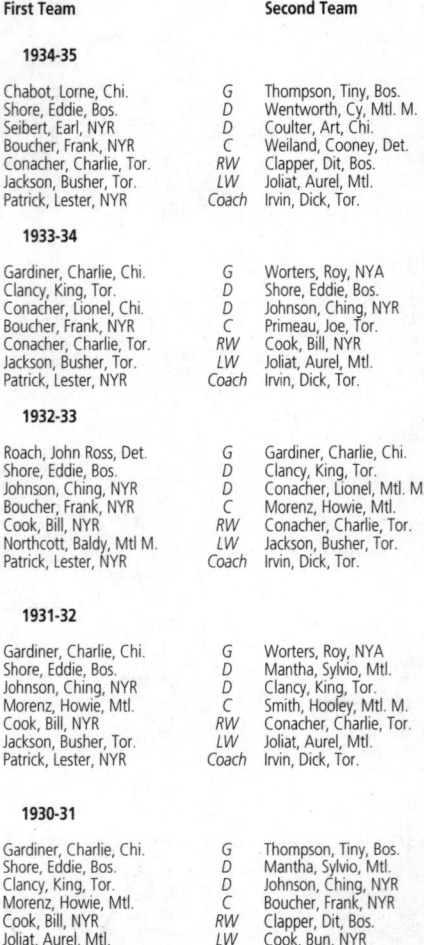

Between 1931 and 1941, Dit Clapper was named a Second-Team All-Star twice at right wing twice and was a First-Team All-Star three times as a defenseman. Clapper and Neil Colville are the only players in NHL history named to an All-Star Team at both forward and defence.

All-Star Game Results

Year	Venue	Score	Coaches	Attendance
2003	Florida	West 6, East 5	Marc Crawford, Jacques Martin	19,250
2002	Los Angeles	World 8, North America 5	Scotty Bowman, Pat Quinn	18,118
2001	Colorado	North America 14, World 12	Joel Quenneville, Jacques Martin	18,646
2000	Toronto	World 9, North America 4	Scotty Bowman, Pat Quinn	19,300
1999	Tampa Bay	North America 8, World 6	Lindy Ruff, Ken Hitchcock	19,758
1998	Vancouver	North America 8, World 7	Jacques Lemaire, Ken Hitchcock	18,422
1997	San Jose	East 11, West 7	Doug MacLean, Ken Hitchcock	17,422
1996	Boston	East 5, West 4	Doug MacLean, Scotty Bowman	17,565
1994	NY Rangers	East 9, West 8	Jacques Demers, Barry Melrose	18,200
1993	Montreal	Wales 16, Campbell 6	Scotty Bowman, Mike Keenan	17,137
1992	Philadelphia	Campbell 10, Wales 6	Bob Gainey, Scotty Bowman	17,380
1991	Chicago	Campbell 11, Wales 5	John Muckler, Mike Milbury	18,472
1990	Pittsburgh	Wales 12, Campbell 7	Pat Burns, Terry Crisp	16,236
1989	Edmonton	Campbell 9, Wales 5	Glen Sather, Terry O'Reilly	17,503
1988	St. Louis	Wales 6, Campbell 5 OT	Mike Keenan, Glen Sather	17,878
1986	Hartford	Wales 4, Campbell 3 OT	Mike Keenan, Glen Sather	15,100
1985	Calgary	Wales 6, Campbell 4	Al Arbour, Glen Sather	16,825
1984	New Jersey	Wales 7, Campbell 6	Al Arbour, Glen Sather	18,939
1983	NY Islanders	Campbell 9, Wales 3	Roger Neilson, Al Arbour	15,230
1982	Washington	Wales 4, Campbell 2	Al Arbour, Glen Sonmor	18,130
1981	Los Angeles	Campbell 4, Wales 1	Pat Quinn, Scotty Bowman	15,761
1980	Detroit	Wales 6, Campbell 3	Scotty Bowman, Al Arbour	21,002
1978	Buffalo	Wales 3, Campbell 2 OT	Scotty Bowman, Fred Shero	16,433
1977	Vancouver	Wales 4, Campbell 3	Scotty Bowman, Fred Shero	15,607
1976	Philadelphia	Wales 7, Campbell 5	Floyd Smith, Fred Shero	16,436
1975	Montreal	Wales 7, Campbell 1	Bep Guidolin, Fred Shero	16,080
1974	Chicago	West 6, East 4	Billy Reay, Scotty Bowman	16,426
1973	NY Rangers	East 5, West 4	Tom Johnson, Billy Reay	16,986
1972	Minnesota	East 3, West 2	Al MacNeil, Billy Reay	15,423
1971	Boston	West 2, East 1	Scotty Bowman, Harry Sinden	14,790
1970	St. Louis	East 4, West 1	Claude Ruel, Scotty Bowman	16,587
1969	Montreal	East 3, West 3	Toe Blake, Scotty Bowman	16,260
1968	Toronto	Toronto 4, All-Stars 3	Punch Imlach, Toe Blake	15,753
1967	Montreal	Montreal 3, All-Stars 0	Toe Blake, Sid Abel	14,284
1965	Montreal	All-Stars 5, Montreal 2	Billy Reay, Toe Blake	13,529
1964	Toronto	All-Stars 3, Toronto 2	Sid Abel, Punch Imlach	14,232
1963	Toronto	All-Stars 3, Toronto 3	Sid Abel, Punch Imlach	14,034
1962	Toronto	Toronto 4, All-Stars 1	Punch Imlach, Rudy Pilous	14,236
1961	Chicago	All-Stars 3, Chicago 1	Sid Abel, Rudy Pilous	14,534
1960	Montreal	All-Stars 2, Montreal 1	Punch Imlach, Toe Blake	13,949
1959	Montreal	Montreal 6, All-Stars 1	Toe Blake, Punch Imlach	13,818
1958	Montreal	Montreal 6, All-Stars 3	Toe Blake, Milt Schmidt	13,989
1957	Montreal	All-Stars 5, Montreal 3	Milt Schmidt, Toe Blake	13,003
1956	Montreal	All-Stars 1, Montreal 1	Jim Skinner, Toe Blake	13,095
1955	Detroit	Detroit 3, All-Stars 1	Jim Skinner, Dick Irvin	10,111
1954	Detroit	All-Stars 2, Detroit 2	King Clancy, Jim Skinner	10,689
1953	Montreal	All-Stars 3, Montreal 1	Lynn Patrick, Dick Irvin	14,153
1952	Detroit	1st Team 1, 2nd Team 1	Tommy Ivan, Dick Irvin	10,680
1951	Toronto	1st Team 2, 2nd Team 2	Joe Primeau, Dick Irvin	11,469
1950	Detroit	Detroit 7, All-Stars 1	Tommy Ivan, Lynn Patrick	9,166
1949	Toronto	All-Stars 3, Toronto 1	Tommy Ivan, Hap Day	13,541
1948	Chicago	All-Stars 3, Toronto 1	Tommy Ivan, Hap Day	12,794
1947	Toronto	All-Stars 4, Toronto 3	Dick Irvin, Hap Day	14,169

There was no All-Star contest during the calendar year of 1966 because the game was moved from the start of season to mid-season. In 1979, the Challenge Cup series between the Soviet Union and Team NHL replaced the All-Star Game. In 1987, Rendez-Vous '87, two games between the Soviet Union and Team NHL replaced the All-Star Game. Rendez-Vous '87 scores: game one, NHL All-Stars 4, Soviet Union 3; game two, Soviet Union 5, NHL All-Stars 3. There was no All-Star Game in 1995 due to a labor disruption.

NHL All★Star Game
SOUTH FLORIDA 03

2002-03 All-Star Game Summary

February 2, 2003 at Sunrise, FL   West 6, East 5

PLAYERS ON ICE: **East** — Khabibulin, Brodeur, Lalime, Poti, Ozolinsh, Chara, Gonchar, Hamrlik, S. Stevens, Jagr, Kovalev, Lecavalier, Heatley, Hossa, Jokinen, G. Murray, O'Neill, Roenick, Satan, St. Louis, Thornton

West — Roy, Thibault, Turco, R. Blake, Lidstrom, Brewer, Jovanovski, MacInnis, Schneider, Guerin, Modano, Selanne, Bertuzzi, S. Fedorov, Forsberg, Gaborik, Iginla, P. Kariya, Naslund, Weight, Whitney

SUMMARY

First Period

1. East	Heatley (1)	(Hamrlik)	5:39
2. West	Forsberg (1)	(Naslund, Lidstrom)	7:14
3. West	Modano (1)	(Whitney, Schneider)	8:58
4. East	Heatley (2)	(Jagr, Jokinen)	10:26
5. West	Gaborik (1)	(Schneider, Fedorov)	15:55

PENALTIES: None

Second Period

6. East	Heatley (3)	(Jokinen)	2:47
7. West	Jovanovski (1)	(Iginla, Gaborik)	12:12
8. East	Heatley (4)	(Jagr, Jokinen)	13:58

PENALTIES: None

Third Period

9. West	MacInnis (1)	(Fedorov, Gaborik)	1:26
10. East	Jokinen (1)	(Jagr, Heatley)	9:38

PENALTIES: None

Overtime

No scoring
PENALTIES: None

Shootout

East — Kovalev (missed), Heatley (scored), Satan (missed), Jokinen (missed).
West — Fedorov (missed), Naslund (scored), Guerin (scored), Kariya (scored).

SHOTS ON GOAL BY:

East	11	12	8	3	**34**
West	14	9	14	5	**42**

	Goaltenders:	Time	SA	GA	ENG	Dec
East	Khabibulin	20:00	14	3	0	
East	Brodeur	20:00	9	1	0	
East	Lalime	25:00	19	1	0	L
West	Roy	20:00	11	2	0	
West	Thibault	20:00	12	2	0	
West	Turco	25:00	11	1	0	W

PP Conversions: East 0/0; West 0/0.
Referees: Dennis LaRue, Dan O'Halloran
Linesmen: Jean Morin, Tim Nowak
Attendance: 19,250.

NHL ALL-ROOKIE TEAM

Voting for the NHL All-Rookie Team is conducted among the representatives of the Professional Hockey Writers' Association at the end of the season. The rookie all-star team was first selected for the 1982-83 season.

2002-03
Goal Sebastian Caron, Pittsburgh
Defense Jay Bouwmeester, Florida
Defense Barret Jackman, St. Louis
Forward Tyler Arnason, Chicago
Forward Rick Nash, Columbus
Forward Henrik Zetterberg, Detroit

2001-02
Goal Dan Blackburn, NY Rangers
Defense Nick Boynton, Boston
Defense Rostislav Klesla, Columbus
Forward Dany Heatley, Atlanta
Forward Ilya Kovalchuk, Atlanta
Forward Kristian Huselius, Florida

2000-01
Goal Evgeni Nabokov, San Jose
Defense Lubomir Visnovsky, Los Angeles
Defense Colin White, New Jersey
Forward Martin Havlat, Ottawa
Forward Brad Richards, Tampa Bay
Forward Shane Willis, Carolina

1999-2000
Goal Brian Boucher, Philadelphia
Defense Brian Rafalski, New Jersey
Defense Brad Stuart, San Jose
Forward Simon Gagne, Philadelphia
Forward Scott Gomez, New Jersey
Forward Mike York, NY Rangers

1998-99
Goal Jamie Storr, Los Angeles
Defense Tom Poti, Edmonton
Defense Sami Salo, Ottawa
Forward Chris Drury, Colorado
Forward Milan Hejduk, Colorado
Forward Marian Hossa, Ottawa

1997-98
Jamie Storr, Los Angeles
Mattias Ohlund, Vancouver
Derek Morris, Calgary
Sergei Samsonov, Boston
Patrick Elias, New Jersey
Mike Johnson, Toronto

1996-97
Patrick Lalime, Pittsburgh
Bryan Berard, NY Islanders
Janne Niinimaa, Philadelphia
Jarome Iginla, Calgary
Jim Campbell, St. Louis
Sergei Berezin, Toronto

1995-96
Corey Hirsch, Vancouver
Ed Jovanovski, Florida
Kyle McLaren, Boston
Daniel Alfredsson, Ottawa
Eric Daze, Chicago
Petr Sykora, New Jersey

1994-95
Jim Carey, Washington
Chris Therien, Philadelphia
Kenny Jonsson, Toronto
Peter Forsberg, Quebec
Jeff Friesen, San Jose
Paul Kariya, Anaheim

1993-94
Martin Brodeur, New Jersey
Chris Pronger, Hartford
Boris Mironov, Wpg./Edm.
Jason Arnott, Edmonton
Mikael Renberg, Philadelphia
Oleg Petrov, Montreal

1992-93
Felix Potvin, Toronto
Vladimir Malakhov, NY Islanders
Scott Niedermayer, New Jersey
Eric Lindros, Philadelphia
Teemu Selanne, Winnipeg
Joe Juneau, Boston

1991-92
Dominik Hasek, Chicago
Nicklas Lidstrom, Detroit
Vladimir Konstantinov, Detroit
Kevin Todd, New Jersey
Tony Amonte, NY Rangers
Gilbert Dionne, Montreal

1990-91
Ed Belfour, Chicago
Eric Weinrich, New Jersey
Rob Blake, Los Angeles
Sergei Fedorov, Detroit
Ken Hodge, Boston
Jaromir Jagr, Pittsburgh

1989-90
Bob Essensa, Winnipeg
Brad Shaw, Hartford
Geoff Smith, Edmonton
Mike Modano, Minnesota
Sergei Makarov, Calgary
Rod Brind'Amour, St. Louis

1988-89
Peter Sidorkiewicz, Hartford
Brian Leetch, NY Rangers
Zarley Zalapski, Pittsburgh
Trevor Linden, Vancouver
Tony Granato, NY Rangers
David Volek, NY Islanders

1987-88
Darren Pang, Chicago
Glen Wesley, Boston
Calle Johansson, Buffalo
Joe Nieuwendyk, Calgary
Ray Sheppard, Buffalo
Iain Duncan, Winnipeg

1986-87
Ron Hextall, Philadelphia
Steve Duchesne, Los Angeles
Brian Benning, St. Louis
Jimmy Carson, Los Angeles
Jim Sandlak, Vancouver
Luc Robitaille, Los Angeles

1985-86
Patrick Roy, Montreal
Gary Suter, Calgary
Dana Murzyn, Hartford
Mike Ridley, NY Rangers
Kjell Dahlin, Montreal
Wendel Clark, Toronto

1984-85
Steve Penney, Montreal
Chris Chelios, Montreal
Bruce Bell, Quebec
Mario Lemieux, Pittsburgh
Tomas Sandstrom, NY Rangers
Warren Young, Pittsburgh

1983-84
Tom Barrasso, Buffalo
Thomas Eriksson, Philadelphia
Jamie Macoun, Calgary
Steve Yzerman, Detroit
Hakan Loob, Calgary
Sylvain Turgeon, Hartford

1982-83
Pelle Lindbergh, Philadelphia
Scott Stevens, Washington
Phil Housley, Buffalo
Dan Daoust, Mtl./Tor.
Steve Larmer, Chicago
Mats Naslund, Montreal

All-Star Game Records 1947 through 2003

TEAM RECORDS

MOST GOALS, BOTH TEAMS, ONE GAME:
26 — North America 14, World 12, 2001 at Colorado
22 — Wales 16, Campbell 6, 1993 at Montreal
19 — Wales 12, Campbell 7, 1990 at Pittsburgh
18 — East 11, West 7, 1997 at San Jose
17 — East 9, West 8, 1994 at NY Rangers
16 — Campbell 11, Wales 5, 1991 at Chicago
— Campbell 10, Wales 6, 1992 at Philadelphia
15 — North America 8, World 7, 1998 at Vancouver

FEWEST GOALS, BOTH TEAMS, ONE GAME:
2 — NHL All-Stars 1, Montreal Canadiens 1, 1956 at Montreal
— First Team All-Stars 1, Second Team All-Stars 1, 1952 at Detroit
3 — West 2, East 1, 1971 at Boston
— Montreal Canadiens 3, NHL All-Stars 0, 1967 at Montreal
— NHL All-Stars 2, Montreal Canadiens 1, 1960 at Montreal

MOST GOALS, ONE TEAM, ONE GAME:
16 — Wales 16, Campbell 6, 1993 at Montreal
14 — North America 14, World 12, 2001 at Colorado
12 — Wales 12, Campbell 7, 1990 at Pittsburgh
— World 12, North America 14, 2001 at Colorado
11 — Campbell 11, Wales 5, 1991 at Chicago
— East 11, West 7, 1997 at San Jose

FEWEST GOALS, ONE TEAM, ONE GAME:
0 — NHL All-Stars 0, Montreal Canadiens 3, 1967 at Montreal
1 — 17 times (1981, 1975, 1971, 1970, 1962, 1961, 1960, 1959, both teams 1956, 1955, 1953, both teams 1952, 1950, 1949, 1948)

MOST SHOTS, BOTH TEAMS, ONE GAME (SINCE 1955):
102 — 1994 at NY Rangers — East 9 (56 shots),
West 8 (46 shots)
98 — 2001 at Colorado — North America 14 (53 shots),
World 12 (45 shots)
90 — 1993 at Montreal — Wales 16 (49 shots),
Campbell 6 (41 shots)
89 — 2002 at Los Angeles — World 8 (39 shots),
North America 5 (50 shots)

FEWEST SHOTS, BOTH TEAMS, ONE GAME (SINCE 1955):
52 — 1978 at Buffalo — Campbell 2 (12 shots)
Wales 3 (40 shots)
53 — 1960 at Montreal — NHL All-Stars 2 (27 shots)
Montreal Canadiens 1 (26 shots)
55 — 1956 at Montreal — NHL All-Stars 1 (28 shots)
Montreal Canadiens 1 (27 shots)
— 1971 at Boston — West 2 (28 shots)
East 1 (27 shots)

MOST SHOTS, ONE TEAM, ONE GAME (SINCE 1955):
56 — 1994 at NY Rangers — East (9-8 vs. West)
53 — 2001 at Colorado — North America (14-12 vs. World)
50 — 2002 at Los Angeles — North America (5-8 vs. World)
49 — 1993 at Montreal — Wales (16-6 vs. Campbell)
— 1999 at Tampa Bay — North America (8-6 vs. World)

FEWEST SHOTS, ONE TEAM, ONE GAME (SINCE 1955):
12 — 1978 at Buffalo — Campbell (2-3 vs. Wales)
17 — 1970 at St. Louis — West (1-4 vs. East)
23 — 1961 at Chicago — Chicago Black Hawks (1-3 vs. NHL All-Stars)
24 — 1976 at Philadelphia — Campbell (5-7 vs. Wales)

MOST POWER-PLAY GOALS, BOTH TEAMS, ONE GAME (SINCE 1950):
3 — 1953 at Montreal — NHL All-Stars 3 (2 power-play goals),
Montreal Canadiens 1 (1 power-play goal)
— 1954 at Detroit — NHL All-Stars 2 (1 power-play goal)
Detroit Red Wings 2 (2 power-play goals)
— 1958 at Montreal — NHL All-Stars 3 (1 power-play goal)
Montreal Canadiens 6 (2 power-play goals)

FEWEST POWER-PLAY GOALS, BOTH TEAMS, ONE GAME (SINCE 1950):
0 — 21 times (1952, 1959, 1960, 1967, 1968, 1969, 1972, 1973, 1976, 1980, 1981, 1984, 1985, 1992, 1994, 1996, 1999, 2000, 2001, 2002, 2003)

FASTEST TWO GOALS, BOTH TEAMS, FROM START OF GAME:
0:37 — 1970 at St. Louis — Jacques Laperriere scored at 0:20 for East and Dean Prentice scored at 0:37 for West. Final score: East 4, West 1.
2:15 — 1998 at Vancouver — Teemu Selanee scored at 0:53 and Jaromir Jagr scored at 2:15 for World. Final score: North America 8, World 7.
3:37 — 1993 at Montreal — Mike Gartner scored at 3:15 and at 3:37 for Wales. Final score: Wales 16, Campbell 6.

FASTEST TWO GOALS, BOTH TEAMS:
0:08 — 1997 at San Jose — Owen Nolan scored at 18:54 and 19:02 of second period for West. Final Score: East 11, West 7.
0:10 — 1976 at Philadelphia — Dennis Ververgaert scored at 4:33 and at 4:43 of third period for Campbell. Final score: Wales 7, Campbell 5.
0:13 — 1998 at Vancouver — Teemu Selanne scored at 4:00 of first period for World and John LeClair scored at 4:13 for North America. Final score: North America 8, World 7.

FASTEST THREE GOALS, BOTH TEAMS:
1:08 — 1993 at Montreal — all by Wales — Mike Gartner scored at 3:15 and at 3:37 of first period; Peter Bondra scored at 4:23. Final score: Wales 16, Campbell 6.
1:14 — 1994 at NY Rangers — Bob Kudelski scored at 9:46 of first period for East; Sergei Fedorov scored at 10:20 for West; Eric Lindros scored at 11:00 for East. Final score: East 9, West 8.
1:23 — 1999 at Tampa Bay — Mats Sundin scored at 2:57 of third period for World; Darryl Sydor scored at 4:02 for North America; Sergei Zubov scored at 4:20 for World. Final score: North America 8, World 6.

FASTEST FOUR GOALS, BOTH TEAMS:
2:24 — 1997 at San Jose — Brendan Shanahan scored at 16:38 of second period for West; Dale Hawerchuk scored at 17:28 for East; Owen Nolan scored at 18:54 and 19:02 for West. Final score: East 11, West 7.
2:57 — 2002 at Los Angeles — all by World — Sergei Fedorov scored at 16:59 of third period; Markus Naslund scored at 18:17; Alexei Zhamnov scored at 19:12; Sami Kapanen scored at 19:56. Final score: World 8, North America 5.
3:04 — 1997 at San Jose — Mark Recchi scored at 15:32 of first period for East; Dale Hawerchuk scored at 16:19 for East; Pavel Bure scored at 17:36 for West; Paul Kariya scored at 18:36 for West. Final score: East 11, West 7.

FASTEST TWO GOALS, ONE TEAM, FROM START OF GAME:
2:15 — 1998 at Vancouver — World — Teemu Selanee scored at 0:53 and Jaromir Jagr scored at 2:15. Final score: North America 8, World 7.
3:37 — 1993 at Montreal — Wales — Mike Gartner scored at 3:15 and at 3:37. Final score: Wales 16, Campbell 6.
4:19 — 1980 at Detroit — Wales — Larry Robinson scored at 3:58 and Steve Payne scored at 4:19. Final score: Wales 6, Campbell 3.

FASTEST TWO GOALS, ONE TEAM:
0:08 — 1997 at San Jose — West — Owen Nolan scored at 18:54 and at 19:02 of second period. Final score: East 11, West 7.
0:10 — 1976 at Philadelphia — Campbell — Dennis Ververgaert scored at 4:33 and at 4:43 of third period. Final score: Wales 7, Campbell 5.
0:14 — 1989 at Edmonton — Campbell — Steve Yzerman and Gary Leeman scored at 17:21 and 17:35 of second period. Final score: Campbell 9, Wales 5.

FASTEST THREE GOALS, ONE TEAM:
1:08 — 1993 at Montreal — Wales — Mike Gartner scored at 3:15 and 3:37 of first period; Peter Bondra scored at 4:23. Final score: Wales 16, Campbell 6.
1:32 — 1980 at Detroit — Wales — Ron Stackhouse scored at 11:40 of third period; Craig Hartsburg scored at 12:40; Reed Larson scored at 13:12. Final score: Wales 6, Campbell 3.
1:39 — 2002 at Los Angeles — World — Markus Naslund scored at 18:17 of third period; Alexei Zhamnov scored at 19:12; Sami Kapanen scored at 19:56. Final score: World 8, North America 5.

FASTEST FOUR GOALS, ONE TEAM:
2:57 — 2002 at Los Angeles — World — Sergei Fedorov scored at 16:59 of third period; Markus Naslund scored at 18:17; Alexei Zhamnov scored at 19:12; Sami Kapanen scored at 19:56. Final score: World 8, North America 5.
4:19 — 1992 at Philadelphia — Campbell — Brian Bellows scored at 7:40 of second period; Jeremy Roenick scored at 8:13; Theoren Fleury scored at 11:06, Brett Hull scored at 11:59. Final score: Campbell 10, Wales 6.
4:26 — 1980 at Detroit — Wales — Ron Stackhouse scored at 11:40 of third period; Craig Hartsburg scored at 12:40; Reed Larson scored at 13:12; Real Cloutier scored at 16:06. Final score: Wales 6, Campbell 3.

MOST GOALS, BOTH TEAMS, ONE PERIOD:
10 — 1997 at San Jose — Second period — East (6), West (4). Final score: East 11, West 7.
— 2001 at Colorado — Second period — North America (6), World (4). Final score: North America 14, World 12.
— 2001 at Colorado — Third period — North America (5), World (5). Final score: North America 14, World 12.
9 — 1990 at Pittsburgh — First period — Wales (7), Campbell (2). Final score: Wales 12, Campbell 7.

MOST GOALS, ONE TEAM, ONE PERIOD:
7 — 1990 at Pittsburgh — First period — Wales.
Final score: Wales 12, Campbell 7.
6 — 1983 at NY Islanders — Third period — Campbell.
Final score: Campbell 9, Wales 3.
— 1992 at Philadelphia — Second Period — Campbell.
Final score: Campbell 10, Wales 6.
— 1993 at Montreal — First period — Wales.
Final score: Wales 16, Campbell 6.
— 1993 at Montreal — Second period — Wales.
Final score: Wales 16, Campbell 6.
— 1997 at San Jose — Second period — East.
Final score: East 11, West 7.
— 2001 at Colorado — Second period — North America.
Final score: North America 14, World 12.

MOST SHOTS, BOTH TEAMS, ONE PERIOD:
39 — 1994 at NY Rangers — Second period — West (21), East (18).
Final score: East 9, West 8.
— 2001 at Colorado — Third period — World (23), North America (16).
Final score: North America 14, World 12.
36 — 1990 at Pittsburgh — Third period — Campbell (22), Wales (14).
Final score: Wales 12, Campbell 7.
— 1994 at NY Rangers — First period — East (19), West (17).
Final score: East 9, West 8.
— 2002 at Los Angeles — Third period — North America (20), World (16).
Final score: World 8, North America 5.

MOST SHOTS, ONE TEAM, ONE PERIOD:
23 — 2001 at Colorado — Third period — World.
Final score: North America 14, World 12.
22 — 1990 at Pittsburgh — Third period — Campbell.
Final score: Wales 12, Campbell 7.
— 1991 at Chicago — Third Period — Wales.
Final score: Campbell 11, Wales 5.
— 1993 at Montreal — First period — Wales.
Final score: Wales 16, Campbell 6.

FEWEST SHOTS, BOTH TEAMS, ONE PERIOD:
9 — 1971 at Boston — Third period — East (2), West (7).
Final score: West 2, East 1.
— 1980 at Detroit — Second period — Campbell (4), Wales (5).
Final score: Wales 6, Campbell 3.
13 — 1982 at Washington — Third period — Campbell (6), Wales (7).
Final score: Campbell 4, Wales 2.
14 — 1978 at Buffalo — First period — Campbell (7), Wales (7).
Final score: Wales 3, Campbell 2.
— 1986 at Hartford — First period — Campbell (6), Wales (8).
Final score: Wales 4, Campbell 3.

FEWEST SHOTS, ONE TEAM, ONE PERIOD:
2 — 1971 at Boston — Third period — East.
Final score: West 2, East 1.
— 1978 at Buffalo — Second period — Campbell.
Final score: Wales 3, Campbell 2.
3 — 1978 at Buffalo — Third period — Campbell.
Final score: Wales 3, Campbell 2.
4 — 1955 at Detroit — First period — NHL All-Stars.
Final score: Detroit Red Wings 3, NHL All-Stars 1.
— 1980 at Detroit — Second period — Campbell.
Final score: Wales 6, Campbell 3.

INDIVIDUAL RECORDS

Games

MOST GAMES PLAYED:
23 — Gordie Howe from 1948 through 1980
19 — Raymond Bourque from 1981 through 2001
18 — Wayne Gretzky from 1980 through 1999
15 — Frank Mahovlich from 1959 through 1974
14 — Paul Coffey from 1982 through 1997
— Mark Messier from 1982 through 2000

Goals

MOST GOALS (CAREER):
13 — Wayne Gretzky in 18GP
— Mario Lemieux in 10GP
10 — Gordie Howe in 23GP
8 — Frank Mahovlich in 15GP
— Luc Robitaille in 8GP
— Teemu Selanne in 8GP

MOST GOALS, ONE GAME:
4 — Wayne Gretzky, Campbell, 1983
— Mario Lemieux, Wales, 1990
— Vince Damphousse, Campbell, 1991
— Mike Gartner, Wales, 1993
— Dany Heatley, East, 2003
3 — Ted Lindsay, Detroit, 1950
— Mario Lemieux, Wales, 1988
— Pierre Turgeon, Wales, 1993
— Mark Recchi, East, 1997
— Owen Nolan, West, 1997
— Teemu Selanne, World, 1998
— Pavel Bure, World, 2000
— Bill Guerin, North America, 2001

MOST GOALS, ONE PERIOD:
4 — Wayne Gretzky, Campbell, Third period, 1983
3 — Mario Lemieux, Wales, First period, 1990
— Vince Damphousse, Campbell, Third period, 1991
— Mike Gartner, Wales, First period, 1993

Assists

MOST ASSISTS (CAREER):
13 — Mark Messier in 14GP
— Raymond Bourque in 19GP
12 — Adam Oates in 5GP
— Joe Sakic in 8GP
— Wayne Gretzky in 18GP

MOST ASSISTS, ONE GAME:
5 — Mats Naslund, Wales, 1988
4 — Raymond Bourque, Wales, 1985
— Adam Oates, Campbell, 1991
— Adam Oates, Wales, 1993
— Mark Recchi, Wales, 1993
— Pierre Turgeon, East, 1994
— Fredrik Modin, World, 2001

MOST ASSISTS, ONE PERIOD:
4 — Adam Oates, Wales, First period, 1993
3 — Mark Messier, Campbell, Third period, 1983

Thrashers sensation Dany Heatley (far left) is welcomed back to the bench by Jeremy Roenick, Olli Jokinen, Jaromir Jagr, Martin St. Louis and Joe Thornton during his record-tying four-goal performance in the 2003 All-Star Game.

Points

MOST POINTS, CAREER:
25 — Wayne Gretzky (13G-12A in 18GP)
23 — Mario Lemieux (13G-10A in 10GP)
19 — Gordie Howe (10G-9A in 23GP)
18 — Mark Messier (5G-13A in 14GP)
17 — Raymond Bourque (4G-13A in 19GP)

MOST POINTS, ONE GAME:
6 — Mario Lemieux, Wales, 1988 (3G-3A)
5 — Mats Naslund, Wales, 1988 (5A)
— Adam Oates, Campbell, 1991 (1G-4A)
— Mike Gartner, Wales, 1993 (4G-1A)
— Mark Recchi, Wales, 1993 (1G-4A)
— Pierre Turgeon, Wales, 1993 (3G-2A)
— Bill Guerin, North America, 2001 (3G-2A)
— Dany Heatley, East, 2003 (4G-1A)

MOST POINTS, ONE PERIOD:
4 — Wayne Gretzky, Campbell, Third period, 1983 (4G)
— **Mike Gartner,** Wales, First period, 1993 (3G-1A)
— **Adam Oates,** Wales, First period, 1993 (4A)
3 — Gordie Howe, NHL All-Stars, Second period, 1965 (1G-2A)
— Pete Mahovlich, Wales, First period, 1976 (1G-2A)
— Mark Messier, Campbell, Third period, 1983 (3A)
— Mario Lemieux, Wales, Second period, 1988 (1G-2A)
— Mario Lemieux, Wales, First period, 1990 (3G)
— Vincent Damphousse, Campbell, Third period, 1991 (3G)
— Mark Recchi, Wales, Second period, 1993 (1G-2A)
— Tony Amonte, North America, Second period, 2001 (2G-1A)

Power-Play Goals

MOST POWER-PLAY GOALS, CAREER:
6 — Gordie Howe in 23GP
3 — Bobby Hull in 12GP
— Maurice Richard in 13GP

Fastest Goals

FASTEST GOAL FROM START OF GAME:
0:19 — Ted Lindsay, Detroit, 1950
0:20 — Jacques Laperriere, East, 1970
0:21 — Mario Lemieux, Wales, 1990
0:35 — Vincent Damphousse, North America, 2002
0:36 — Chico Maki, West, 1971

FASTEST GOAL FROM START OF A PERIOD:
0:17 — Raymond Bourque, North America, 1999 (second period)
0:19 — Ted Lindsay, Detroit, 1950 (first period)
— Rick Tocchet, Wales, 1993 (second period)
0:20 — Jacques Laperriere, East, 1970 (first period)
0:21 — Mario Lemieux, Wales, 1990 (first period)
0:26 — Wayne Gretzky, Campbell, 1982 (second period)

FASTEST TWO GOALS (ONE PLAYER) FROM START OF GAME:
3:37 — Mike Gartner, Wales, 1993, at 3:15 and 3:37.
4:00 — Teemu Selanne, World, 1998, at 0:53 and 4:00
5:25 — Wally Hergesheimer, NHL All-Stars, 1953, at 4:06 and 5:25.

FASTEST TWO GOALS (ONE PLAYER) FROM START OF A PERIOD:
3:37 — Mike Gartner, Wales, 1993, at 3:15 and 3:37 of first period.
4:00 — Teemu Selanne, World, 1998, at 0:53 and 4:00 of first period.
4:43 — Dennis Ververgaert, Campbell, 1976, at 4:33 and 4:43 of third period.

FASTEST TWO GOALS (ONE PLAYER):
0:08 — Owen Nolan, West, 1997. Scored at 18:54 and 19:02 of second period.
0:10 — Dennis Ververgaert, Campbell, 1976. Scored at 4:33 and 4:43 of third period.
0:22 — Mike Gartner, Wales, 1993. Scored at 3:15 and 3:37 of first period.

Penalties

MOST PENALTY MINUTES:
25 — Gordie Howe in 23GP
21 — Gus Mortson in 9GP
16 — Harry Howell in 7GP

Goaltenders

MOST GAMES PLAYED:
13 — Glenn Hall from 1955 through 1969
11 — Terry Sawchuk from 1950 through 1968
— Patrick Roy from 1988 through 2003
8 — Jacques Plante from 1956 through 1970

MOST MINUTES PLAYED:
540 — Glenn Hall in 13GP
467 — Terry Sawchuk in 11GP
370 — Jacques Plante in 8GP
250 — Patrick Roy in 11GP
209 — Turk Broda in 4GP

MOST GOALS AGAINST:
31 — Patrick Roy in 11GP
22 — Glenn Hall in 13GP
21 — Mike Vernon in 5GP
19 — Terry Sawchuk in 11GP
18 — Jacques Plante in 8GP
— Andy Moog in 4GP

BEST GOALS-AGAINST-AVERAGE AMONG THOSE WITH AT LEAST TWO GAMES PLAYED:
0.68 — Gilles Villemure in 3GP
1.49 — Gerry McNeil in 3GP
1.50 — Johnny Bower in 4GP
1.51 — Frank Brimsek in 3GP
1.64 — Gump Worsley in 4GP

Boston's Frank Brimsek played in a 1939 All-Star Game to benefit the family of Babe Siebert. He later played in the first official NHL All-Star Game in 1947 and the second game a year later. He allowed just three goals in 119 minutes of play.

Hockey Hall of Fame

(Year of induction is listed after each Honoured Members name)

Grant Fuhr was a perfect fit with Edmonton's high-powered offense, earning a reputation as a goalie who would not surrender the big goal. He won 403 games and enters the Hall of Fame with Pat LaFontaine, Michael Ilitch and Brian Kilrea.

Location: BCE Place, at the corner of Front and Yonge Streets in the heart of downtown Toronto. Easy access from all major highways running into Toronto. Close to TTC and Union Station.

Telephone: administration (416) 360-7735; information (416) 360-7765.

Public Hours of Operation: Open every day except Christmas Day, New Year's Day and Induction Day (November 3, 2003). Please call our information number (above) or visit our website (below) for times.

The Hockey Hall of Fame can be booked for private functions after hours.

Website address: www.hhof.com

History: The Hockey Hall of Fame was established in 1943. Members were first honoured in 1945. On August 26, 1961, the Hockey Hall of Fame opened its doors to the public in a building located on the grounds of the Canadian National Exhibition in Toronto. The Hockey Hall of Fame relocated to its new site at BCE Place and welcomed the hockey world on June 18, 1993.

Honour Roll: There are 332 Honoured Members in the Hockey Hall of Fame. 227 have been inducted as players, 91 as builders and 14 as Referees/Linesmen. In addition, there are 70 media honourees.

Founding/Premiere Sponsors: Special thanks to Blockbuster Video, IBM Canada, Imperial Oil, Kodak Canada, London Life Insurance Company, Molson Canada, National Hockey League Players' Association, Panasonic Canada, Pepsi-Cola Canada, Sun Media (Toronto)/The Toronto Sun, The Sports Network (TSN/RDS), WorldCom Canada.

PLAYERS

* Abel, Sidney Gerald 1969
* Adams, John James "Jack" 1959
* Apps, Charles Joseph Sylvanus "Syl" 1961
  Armstrong, George Edward 1975
* Bailey, Irvine Wallace "Ace" 1975
* Bain, Donald H. "Dan" 1945
* Baker, Hobart "Hobey" 1945
  Barber, William Charles "Bill" 1990
* Barry, Martin J. "Marty" 1965
  Bathgate, Andrew James "Andy" 1978
* Bauer, Robert Theodore "Bobby" 1996
  Béliveau, Jean Arthur 1972
* Benedict, Clinton S. 1965
* Bentley, Douglas Wagner 1964
* Bentley, Maxwell H. L. 1966
* Blake, Hector "Toe" 1966
  Boivin, Leo Joseph 1986
* Boon, Richard R. "Dickie" 1952
  Bossy, Michael 1991
  Bouchard, Emile Joseph "Butch" 1966
* Boucher, Frank 1958
* Boucher, Georges "Buck" 1960
  Bower, John William 1976
* Bowie, Russell 1945
* Brimsek, Francis Charles 1966
* Broadbent, Harry L. "Punch" 1962
* Broda, Walter Edward "Turk" 1967
  Bucyk, John Paul 1981
* Burch, Billy 1974
* Cameron, Harold Hugh "Harry" 1962
  Cheevers, Gerald Michael "Gerry" 1985
* Clancy, Francis Michael "King" 1958
* Clapper, Aubrey "Dit" 1947
  Clarke, Robert "Bobby" 1987
* Cleghorn, Sprague 1958
* Colville, Neil MacNeil 1967
* Conacher, Charles W. 1961
* Conacher, Lionel Pretoria 1994
* Conacher, Roy Gordon 1998
* Connell, Alex 1958
* Cook, Fred "Bun" 1995
* Cook, William Osser 1952
* Coulter, Arthur Edmund 1974
  Cournoyer, Yvan Serge 1982
* Cowley, William Mailes 1968
* Crawford, Samuel Russell "Rusty" 1962
* Darragh, John Proctor "Jack" 1962
* Davidson, Allan M. "Scotty" 1950
* Day, Clarence Henry "Hap" 1961
  Delvecchio, Alex 1977
* Denneny, Cyril "Cy" 1959
  Dionne, Marcel 1992
* Drillon, Gordon Arthur 1975

* Drinkwater, Charles Graham 1950
  Dryden, Kenneth Wayne 1983
* Dumart, Woodrow "Woody" 1992
* Dunderdale, Thomas 1974
* Durnan, William Ronald 1964
* Dutton, Mervyn A. "Red" 1958
* Dye, Cecil Henry "Babe" 1970
  Esposito, Anthony James "Tony" 1988
  Esposito, Philip Anthony 1984
* Farrell, Arthur F. 1965
  Federko, Bernie 2002
  Fetisov, Viacheslav 2001
  Flaman, Ferdinand Charles "Fern" 1990
* Foyston, Frank 1958
* Fredrickson, Frank 1958
  Fuhr, Grant S. 2003
  Gadsby, William Alexander 1970
  Gainey, Bob 1992
* Gardiner, Charles Robert "Chuck" 1945
* Gardiner, Herbert Martin "Herb" 1958
* Gardner, James Henry "Jimmy" 1962
  Gartner, Michael Alfred 2001
  Geoffrion, Jos. A. Bernard "Boom Boom" 1972
* Gerard, Eddie 1945
  Giacomin, Edward "Eddie" 1987
  Gilbert, Rodrigue Gabriel "Rod" 1982
  Gillies, Clark 2002
* Gilmour, Hamilton Livingstone "Billy" 1962
* Goheen, Frank Xavier "Moose" 1952
* Goodfellow, Ebenezer R. "Ebbie" 1963
  Goulet, Michel 1998
* Grant, Michael "Mike" 1950
* Green, Wilfred "Shorty" 1962
  Gretzky, Wayne Douglas 1999
* Griffis, Silas Seth "Si" 1950
* Hainsworth, George 1961
  Hall, Glenn Henry 1975
* Hall, Joseph Henry 1961
* Harvey, Douglas Norman 1973
  Hawerchuk, Dale Martin 2001
* Hay, George 1958
* Hern, William Milton "Riley" 1962
* Hextall, Bryan Aldwyn 1969
* Holmes, Harry "Hap" 1972
  Hooper, Charles Thomas "Tom" 1962
  Horner, George Reginald "Red" 1965
* Horton, Miles Gilbert "Tim" 1977
  Howe, Gordon 1972
* Howe, Sydney Harris 1965
  Howell, Henry Vernon "Harry" 1979
  Hull, Robert Marvin 1983
* Hutton, John Bower "Bouse" 1962
* Hyland, Harry M. 1962

* Irvin, James Dickenson "Dick" 1958
* Jackson, Harvey "Busher" 1971
* Johnson, Ernest "Moose" 1952
* Johnson, Ivan "Ching" 1958
  Johnson, Thomas Christian 1970
* Joliat, Aurel 1947
* Keats, Gordon "Duke" 1958
  Kelly, Leonard Patrick "Red" 1969
  Kennedy, Theodore Samuel "Teeder" 1966
  Keon, David Michael 1986
  Kurri, Jari 2001
  Lach, Elmer James 1966
  Lafleur, Guy Damien 1988
  LaFontaine, Pat 2003
* Lalonde, Edouard Charles "Newsy" 1950
  Langway, Rod Corry 2002
  Laperriere, Jacques 1987
  Lapointe, Guy 1993
  Laprade, Edgar 1993
* Laviolette, Jean Baptiste "Jack" 1962
* Lehman, Hugh 1958
  Lemaire, Jacques Gerard 1984
  Lemieux, Mario 1997
* LeSueur, Percy 1961
* Lewis, Herbert A. 1989
  Lindsay, Robert Blake Theodore "Ted" 1966
  Lumley, Harry 1980
* MacKay, Duncan "Mickey" 1952
  Mahovlich, Frank William 1981
* Malone, Joseph "Joe" 1950
  Mantha, Sylvio 1960
* Marshall, John "Jack" 1965
* Maxwell, Fred G. "Steamer" 1962
  McDonald, Lanny 1992
* McGee, Frank 1945
* McGimsie, William George "Billy" 1962
* McNamara, George 1958
  Mikita, Stanley 1983
  Moore, Richard Winston "Dickie" 1974
* Moran, Patrick Joseph "Paddy" 1958
  Morenz, Howie 1945
* Mosienko, William "Billy" 1965
  Mullen, Joseph P. 2000
* Nighbor, Frank 1947
* Noble, Edward Reginald "Reg" 1962
* O'Connor, Herbert William "Buddy" 1988
* Oliver, Harry 1967
  Olmstead, Murray Albert "Bert" 1985
  Orr, Robert Gordon 1979
  Parent, Bernard Marcel 1984
  Park, Douglas Bradford "Brad" 1988
* Patrick, Joseph Lynn 1980
* Patrick, Lester 1947

Perreault, Gilbert 1990
* Phillips, Tommy 1945
  Pilote, Joseph Albert Pierre Paul 1975
* Pitre, Didier "Pit" 1962
* Plante, Joseph Jacques Omer 1978
  Potvin, Denis 1991
* Pratt, Walter "Babe" 1966
* Primeau, A. Joseph 1963
  Pronovost, Joseph René Marcel 1978
  Pulford, Bob 1991
* Pulford, Harvey 1945
* Quackenbush, Hubert George "Bill" 1976
* Rankin, Frank 1961
  Ratelle, Joseph Gilbert Yvan Jean "Jean" 1985
* Rayner, Claude Earl "Chuck" 1973
  Reardon, Kenneth Joseph 1966
  Richard, Joseph Henri 1979
* Richard, Joseph Henri Maurice "Rocket" 1961
* Richardson, George Taylor 1950
* Roberts, Gordon 1971
  Robinson, Larry 1995
* Ross, Arthur Howie 1945
* Russel, Blair 1965
* Russell, Ernest 1965
* Ruttan, J.D. "Jack" 1962
  Salming, Borje Anders 1996
  Savard, Denis Joseph 2000
  Savard, Serge A. 1986
* Sawchuk, Terrance Gordon "Terry" 1971
* Scanlan, Fred 1965
  Schmidt, Milton Conrad "Milt" 1961
* Schriner, David "Sweeney" 1962
* Seibert, Earl Walter 1963
* Seibert, Oliver Levi 1961
* Shore, Edward W. "Eddie" 1947
  Shutt, Stephen 1993
* Siebert, Albert C. "Babe" 1964
* Simpson, Harold Edward "Bullet Joe" 1962
  Sittler, Darryl Glen 1989
* Smith, Alfred E. 1962
  Smith, Clint 1991
* Smith, Reginald "Hooley" 1972
* Smith, Thomas James 1973
  Smith, William John "Billy" 1993
  Stanley, Allan Herbert 1981
* Stanley, Russell "Barney" 1962
  Stastny, Peter 1998
* Stewart, John Sherratt "Black Jack" 1964
* Stewart, Nelson "Nels" 1962
* Stuart, Bruce 1961
* Stuart, Hod 1945
* Taylor, Frederick "Cyclone" (O.B.E.) 1947
* Thompson, Cecil R. "Tiny" 1959
  Tretiak, Vladislav 1989
* Trihey, Col. Harry J. 1950
  Trottier, Bryan 1997
  Ullman, Norman V. Alexander "Norm" 1982
* Vezina, Georges 1945
* Walker, John Phillip "Jack" 1960
* Walsh, Martin "Marty" 1962
* Watson, Harry E. 1962
* Watson, Harry 1994
* Weiland, Ralph "Cooney" 1971
* Westwick, Harry 1962
* Whitcroft, Fred 1962
* Wilson, Gordon Allan "Phat" 1962
  Worsley, Lorne John "Gump" 1980
* Worters, Roy 1969

BUILDERS

* Adams, Charles 1960
* Adams, Weston W. 1972
* Ahearn, Thomas Franklin "Frank" 1962
* Ahearne, John Francis "Bunny" 1977
* Allan, Sir Montagu (C.V.O.) 1945
  Allen, Keith 1992
  Arbour, Alger Joseph "Al" 1996
* Ballard, Harold Edwin 1977
* Bauer, Father David 1989
* Bickell, John Paris 1978
  Bowman, Scotty 1991
* Brown, George V. 1961
* Brown, Walter A. 1962
* Buckland, Frank 1975
  Bush, Walter Sr. 2000
  Butterfield, Jack Arlington 1980
* Calder, Frank 1947
* Campbell, Angus D. 1964
* Campbell, Clarence Sutherland 1966

* Cattarinich, Joseph 1977
* Dandurand, Joseph Viateur "Leo" 1963
* Dilio, Francis Paul 1964
* Dudley, George S. 1958
* Dunn, James A. 1968
  Francis, Emile 1982
* Gibson, Dr. John L. "Jack" 1976
* Gorman, Thomas Patrick "Tommy" 1963
* Griffiths, Frank A. 1993
* Hanley, William 1986
* Hay, Charles 1974
* Hendy, James C. 1968
* Hewitt, Foster 1965
* Hewitt, William Abraham 1947
* Hume, Fred J. 1962
  Ilitch, Mike 2003
* Imlach, George "Punch" 1984
* Ivan, Thomas N. 1974
* Jennings, William M. 1975
* Johnson, Bob 1992
* Juckes, Gordon W. 1979
* Kilpatrick, Gen. John Reed 1960
  Kilrea, Brian Blair 2003
* Knox, Seymour H. III 1993
* Leader, George Alfred 1969
* LeBel, Robert 1970
* Lockhart, Thomas F. 1965
* Loicq, Paul 1961
* Mariucci, John 1985
  Mathers, Frank 1992
* McLaughlin, Major Frederic 1963
* Milford, John "Jake" 1984
* Molson, Hon. Hartland de Montarville 1973
  Morrison, Ian "Scotty" 1999
* Murray, Monsignor Athol 1998
* Neilson, Roger 2002
* Nelson, Francis 1947
* Norris, Bruce A. 1969
* Norris, Sr., James 1958
* Norris, James Dougan 1962
* Northey, William M. 1947
* O'Brien, John Ambrose 1962
  O'Neill, Brian 1994
* Page, Fred 1993
  Patrick, Craig 2001
* Patrick, Frank 1958
* Pickard, Allan W. 1958
* Pilous, Rudy 1985
  Poile, Norman "Bud" 1990
  Pollock, Samuel Patterson Smyth 1978
* Raymond, Sen. Donat 1958
* Robertson, John Ross 1947
* Robinson, Claude C. 1947
* Ross, Philip D. 1976
* Sabetzki, Dr. Gunther 1995
  Sather, Glen 1997
* Selke, Frank J. 1960
  Sinden, Harry James 1983
* Smith, Frank D. 1962
  Smythe, Conn 1958
  Snider, Edward M. 1988
* Stanley of Preston, Lord (G.C.B.) 1945
* Sutherland, Cap. James T. 1947
* Tarasov, Anatoli V. 1974
  Torrey, Bill 1995
* Turner, Lloyd 1958
* Tutt, William Thayer 1978
* Voss, Carl Potter 1974
* Waghorn, Fred C. 1961
* Wirtz, Arthur Michael 1971
  Wirtz, William W. "Bill" 1976
  Ziegler, John A. Jr. 1987

REFEREES/LINESMEN

  Armstrong, Neil 1991
  Ashley, John George 1981
  Chadwick, William L. 1964
  D'Amico, John 1993
* Elliott, Chaucer 1961
* Hayes, George William 1988
* Hewitson, Robert W. 1963
* Ion, Fred J. "Mickey" 1961
  Pavelich, Matt 1987
* Rodden, Michael J. "Mike" 1962
* Smeaton, J. Cooper 1961
  Storey, Roy Alvin "Red" 1967
  Udvari, Frank Joseph 1973
  Van Hellemond, Andy 1999

Elmer Ferguson Memorial Award Winners

In recognition of distinguished members of the newspaper profession whose words have brought honor to journalism and to hockey. Selected by the Professional Hockey Writers' Association.

* Barton, Charlie, Buffalo-Courier Express 1985
* Beauchamp, Jacques, Montreal Matin/Journal de Montréal 1984
* Brennan, Bill, Detroit News 1987
* Burchard, Jim, New York World Telegram 1984
* Burnett, Red, Toronto Star 1984
* Carroll, Dink, Montreal Gazette 1984
* Coleman, Jim, Southam Newspapers 1984
  Conway, Russ, Eagle-Tribune 1999
* Damata, Ted, Chicago Tribune 1984
  Delano, Hugh, New York Post 1991
  Desjardins, Marcel, Montréal La Presse 1984
  Duhatschek, Eric, Calgary Herald/Globe and Mail 2001
* Dulmage, Jack, Windsor Star 1984
  Dunnell, Milt, Toronto Star 1984
  Dupont, Kevin Paul, Boston Globe 2002
  Farber, Michael, Montreal Gazette/Sports Illustrated 2003
* Ferguson, Elmer, Montreal Herald/Star 1984
* Fitzgerald, Tom, Boston Globe 1984
  Frayne, Trent, Toronto Telegram/Globe and Mail/Sun 1984
  Gatecliff, Jack, St. Catherines Standard 1995
  Gross, George, Toronto Telegram/Sun 1985
  Johnston, Dick, Buffalo News 1986
* Laney, Al, New York Herald-Tribune 1984
* Larochelle, Claude, Le Soleil 1989
  L'Esperance, Zotique, Journal de Montréal/le Petit Journal 1985
* MacLeod, Rex, Toronto Globe and Mail/Star 1987
  Matheson, Jim, Edmonton Journal 2000
* Mayer, Charles, Journal de Montréal/la Patrie 1985
* McKenzie, Ken, The Hockey News 1997
  Monahan, Leo, Boston Daily Record/Record-American/Herald American 1986
  Moriarty, Tim, UPI/Newsday 1986
* Nichols, Joe, New York Times 1984
* O'Brien, Andy, Weekend Magazine 1985
  Orr, Frank, Toronto Star 1989
  Olan, Ben, New York Associated Press 1987
* O'Meara, Basil, Montreal Star 1984
  Pedneault, Yvon, La Presse/Journal de Montréal 1998
* Proudfoot, Jim, Toronto Star 1988
  Raymond, Bertrand, Journal de Montréal 1990
  Rosa, Fran, Boston Globe 1987
  Strachan, Al, Globe and Mail/Toronto Sun 1993
* Vipond, Jim, Toronto Globe and Mail 1984
  Walter, Lewis, Detroit Times 1984
  Young, Scott, Toronto Globe and Mail/Telegram 1988

Foster Hewitt Memorial Award Winners

In recognition of members of the radio and television industry who made outstanding contributions to their profession and the game during their career in hockey broadcasting. Selected by the NHL Broadcasters' Association.

  Cole, Bob, Hockey Night in Canada 1996
  Cusick, Fred, Boston 1984
* Darling, Ted, Buffalo 1994
* Gallivan, Danny, Montreal 1984
  Garneau, Richard, Montreal 1999
* Hart, Gene, Philadelphia 1997
* Hewitt, Foster, Toronto 1984
  Irvin, Dick, Montreal 1988
* Kelly, Dan, St. Louis 1989
  Lange, Mike, Pittsburgh 2001
* Lecavelier, René, Montreal 1984
  Lynch, Budd, Detroit 1985
  Martyn, Bruce, Detroit 1991
  McDonald, Jiggs, Los Angeles, Atlanta, NY Islanders 1990
  McFarlane, Brian, Hockey Night in Canada 1995
* McKnight, Wes, Toronto 1986
  Meeker, Howie, Hockey Night in Canada 1998
  Miller, Bob, Los Angeles 2000
  Pettit, Lloyd, Chicago 1986
  Phillips, Rod, Edmonton 2003
  Robson, Jim, Vancouver 1992
  Shaver, Al, Minnesota 1993
* Smith, Doug, Montreal 1985
  Tremblay, Gilles, La Soirée du Hockey 2002
  Wilson, Bob, Boston 1987

* Deceased

United States
Hockey Hall of Fame

The United States Hockey Hall of Fame was opened on June 21, 1973 as the national shrine of American Hockey. It is dedicated to honoring the sport of ice hockey in the United States by preserving those precious memories and legends of the game. It is located in Eveleth, Minnesota, 60 miles north of Duluth on Highway 53. The facility is open Monday to Saturday, 9 a.m. to 5 p.m. and Sundays from 10 a.m. to 3 p.m. Admission is $8.00 for adults, $7.00 for seniors and youths (13-17) and $6.00 for children (6-12). Call for any further information: 1-800-443-7825 or 218-744-5167. Web site address: www.ushockeyhall.com

There are now 119 enshrined members consisting of 72 players, 24 coaches, 19 administrators, one player/administrator, one referee and two teams. New members are inducted annually in the fall and must have made a significant contribution towards hockey in the United States during the course of their career. A special Wayne Gretzky Award pays tribute to international individuals who have made major contributions to hockey in the USA. Support for the Hall of Fame comes from sponsorships, admissions, gift store sales, special events and grants from the hockey community and government agencies.

EVELETH, MN

PLAYERS

* Abel, Clarence "Taffy" 1973
* Baker, Hobart "Hobey" 1973
* Bartholome, Earl 1977
* Bessone, Peter 1978
  Blake, Robert 1985
  Boucha, Henry 1995
* Brimsek, Frank 1973
  Broten, Neal 2000
  Cavanagh, Joe 1994
* Chaisson, Ray 1974
* Chase, John P. 1973
  Christian, Dave 2001
  Christian, Roger 1989
  Christian, William "Bill" 1984
  Cleary, Robert 1981
  Cleary, William 1976
* Conroy, Anthony 1975
  Curran, Mike 1998
* Dahlstrom, Carl "Cully" 1973
* Desjardins, Victor 1974
* Desmond, Richard 1988
* Dill, Robert 1979
  Dougherty, Richard "Dick" 2003
* Everett, Doug 1974
  Ftorek, Robbie 1991
  Fusco, Mark 2002
  Fusco, Scott 2002
* Garrison, John B. 1973
  Garrity, Jack 1986
* Goheen, Frank "Moose" 1973
  Grant, Wally 1994
* Harding, Austin "Austie" 1975
  Howe, Mark 2003
* Iglehart, Stewart 1975
  Johnson, Paul 2001
* Johnson, Virgil 1974
* Karakas, Mike 1973
  Kirrane, Jack 1987
  LaFontaine, Pat 2003
* Lane, Myles J. 1973
  Langevin, David R. 1993
  Langway, Rod 1999
  Larson, Reed 1996
* Linder, Joseph 1975
* LoPresti, Sam L. 1973
* Mariucci, John 1973
  Matchefts, John 1991
* Mather, Bruce 1998
  Mayasich, John 1976
  McCartan, Jack 1983
* Moe, William 1974
  Morrow, Ken 1995
* Moseley, Fred 1975
  Mullen, Joe 1998
* Murray, Sr., Hugh "Muzz" 1987
* Nelson, Hubert "Hub" 1978
* Nyrop, William D. 1997
* Olson , Eddie 1977
* Owen, Jr., George 1973
* Palmer, Winthrop 1973
  Paradise, Robert 1989
* Purpur, Clifford "Fido" 1974
  Ramsey, Mike 2001
* Riley, Joe 2002
  Riley, William 1977
  Roberts, Gordie 1999
* Romnes, Elwin "Doc" 1973
* Rondeau, Richard 1985
  Sheehy, Timothy K. 1997
* Williams, Thomas 1981
* Winters, Frank "Coddy" 1973
* Yackel, Ken 1986

COACHES

* Almquist, Oscar 1983
  Bessone, Amo 1992
* Brooks, Herbert 1990
  Ceglarski, Len 1992
* Cuniff, John 2003
* Fullerton, James 1992
  Gambucci, Sergio 1996
* Gordon, Malcolm K. 1973
  Harkness, Nevin D. "Ned" 1994
  Heyliger, Victor 1974
* Holt, Jr. Charles E. 1997
  Ikola, Willard 1990
* Jeremiah, Edward J. 1973
* Johnson, Bob 1991
* Kelley, John "Snooks" 1974
  Kelley, John H. "Jack" 1993
  Patrick, Craig 1996
* Pleban, Jon "Connie" 1990
  Riley, Jack 1979
* Ross, Larry 1988
* Thompson, Clifford, R. 1973
* Stewart, William 1982
* Winsor, Alfred "Ralph" 1973
  Woog, Doug 2002

ADMINISTRATORS

* Brown, George V. 1973
* Brown, Walter A. 1973
  Bush, Walter 1980
* Clark, Donald 1978
  Claypool, James 1995
* Gibson, J.C. "Doc" 1973
* Jennings, William M. 1981
* Kahler, Nick 1980
* Lockhart, Thomas F. 1973
* Marvin, Cal 1982
  Palazzari, Doug 2000
  Pleau, Larry 2000
* Ridder, Robert 1976
* Schulz, Charles M. 1993
  Trumble, Harold 1985
* Tutt, William Thayer 1973
  Watson, Sid 1999
  Wirtz, William W. "Bill" 1984
* Wright, Lyle Z.1973

PLAYER/ADMINISTRATOR

Nanne, Lou 1998

REFEREE

Chadwick, William 1974

TEAM

1960 U.S. Olympic Team, 2000
1980 Olympic Team, 2003

WAYNE GRETZKY INTERNATIONAL AWARD

Wayne Gretzky 1999
The Howe family 2000
Scotty Morrison 2001
Scotty Bowman 2002
Bobby Hull 2003

*Deceased

Before turning pro, Mark Howe won a silver medal with the U.S. team at the 1972 Winter Olympics. A forward before he reached the NHL, he became an All-Star defenseman. He had a lengthy career, like his father Gordie, playing 22 pro seasons.

NHL League and Team Websites

National Hockey League . . . . . . www.nhl.com
NHL Games on Radio. . . . . www.nhl.com/intheslot/listen/radio/index.html
NHL Site for Kids . . . . www.nhl.com/kids
NHL Merchandise Shop . . . . www.shop.nhl.com
NHL Trivia . . . . nhltrivia.buzztime.com
NHL Job Postings . . . . hockeyjobs.nhl.com
Hockey Fights Cancer . . . . www.nhl.com/nhlhq/hockeyfightscancer/index.html

Official NHL Team Websites:

Anaheim . . . . www.mightyducks.com
Atlanta. . . . . www.atlantathrashers.com
Boston . . . . www.bostonbruins.com
Buffalo . . . . www.sabres.com
Calgary . . . . www.calgaryflames.com
Carolina . . . . www.caneshockey.com
Chicago . . . . www.chicagoblackhawks.com
Colorado . . . . www.coloradoavalanche.com
Columbus . . . . www.bluejackets.com
Dallas. . . . . www.dallasstars.com
Detroit . . . . www.detroitredwings.com
Edmonton . . . . www.edmontonoilers.com
Florida . . . . www.floridapanthers.com
Los Angeles . . . . www.lakings.com
Minnesota . . . . www.wild.com
Montreal . . . . www.canadiens.com
Nashville. . . . . www.nashvillepredators.com
New Jersey. . . . . www.newjerseydevils.com
NY Islanders . . . . www.newyorkislanders.com
NY Rangers . . . . www.newyorkrangers.com
Ottawa. . . . . www.ottawasenators.com
Philadelphia . . . . www.philadelphiaflyers.com
Phoenix . . . . www.phoenixcoyotes.com
Pittsburgh . . . . www.pittsburghpenguins.com
St. Louis. . . . . www.stlouisblues.com
San Jose. . . . . www.sjsharks.com
Tampa Bay . . . . www.tampabaylightning.com
Toronto . . . . www.torontomapleleafs.com
Vancouver . . . . www.canucks.com
Washington . . . . www.washingtoncaps.com

To order the *NHL Official Guide & Record Book* and other books:
www.nhlofficialguide.com

Results

2003 Stanley Cup Playoffs

CONFERENCE QUARTER-FINALS
(Best-of-seven series)

Eastern Conference

Series 'A'

Wed. Apr. 9	NY Islanders 3	at	Ottawa 0
Sat. Apr. 12	NY Islanders 0	at	Ottawa 3
Mon. Apr. 14	Ottawa 3	at	NY Islanders 2*
Wed. Apr. 16	Ottawa 3	at	NY Islanders 1
Thu. Apr. 17	NY Islanders 1	at	Ottawa 4

*Todd White Scored at 22:25 of Overtime
(Ottawa Won Series 4-1)

Series 'B'

Wed. Apr. 9	Boston 1	at	New Jersey 2
Fri. Apr. 11	Boston 2	at	New Jersey 4
Sun. Apr. 13	New Jersey 3	at	Boston 0
Tue. Apr. 15	New Jersey 1	at	Boston 5
Thu. Apr. 17	Boston 0	at	New Jersey 3

(New Jersey Won Series 4-1)

Series 'C'

Thu. Apr. 10	Washington 3	at	Tampa Bay 0
Sat. Apr. 12	Washington 6	at	Tampa Bay 3
Tue. Apr. 15	Tampa Bay 4	at	Washington 3*
Wed. Apr. 16	Tampa Bay 3	at	Washington 1
Fri. Apr. 18	Washington 1	at	Tampa Bay 2
Sun. Apr. 20	Tampa Bay 2	at	Washington 1**

*Vincent Lecavalier Scored at 2:29 of Overtime
**Martin St. Louis Scored at 44:03 of Overtime
(Tampa Bay Won Series 4-2)

Series 'D'

Wed. Apr. 9	Toronto 5	at	Philadelphia 3
Fri. Apr. 11	Toronto 1	at	Philadelphia 4
Mon. Apr. 14	Philadelphia 3	at	Toronto 4*
Wed. Apr. 16	Philadelphia 3	at	Toronto 2**
Sat. Apr. 19	Toronto 1	at	Philadelphia 4
Mon. Apr. 21	Philadelphia 1	at	Toronto 2***
Tue. Apr. 22	Toronto 1	at	Philadelphia 6

*Tomas Kaberle Scored at 27:20 of Overtime
**Mark Recchi Scored at 53:54 of Overtime
***Travis Green Scored at 30:51 of Overtime
(Philadelphia Won Series 4-3)

Western Conference

Series 'E'

Wed. Apr. 9	Edmonton 2	at	Dallas 1
Fri. Apr. 11	Edmonton 1	at	Dallas 6
Sun. Apr. 13	Dallas 2	at	Edmonton 3
Tue. Apr. 15	Dallas 3	at	Edmonton 1
Thu. Apr. 17	Dallas 3	at	Dallas 5
Sat. Apr. 19	Dallas 3	at	Edmonton 2

(Dallas Won Series 4-2)

Series 'F'

Thu. Apr. 10	Anaheim 2	at	Detroit 1*
Sat. Apr. 12	Anaheim 3	at	Detroit 2
Mon. Apr. 14	Detroit 1	at	Anaheim 2
Wed. Apr. 16	Detroit 2	at	Anaheim 3**

*Paul Kariya Scored at 43:18 of Overtime
**Steve Rucchin Scored at 6:53 of Overtime
(Anaheim Won Series 4-0)

Series 'G'

Thu. Apr. 10	Minnesota 4	at	Colorado 2
Sat. Apr. 12	Minnesota 2	at	Colorado 3
Mon. Apr. 14	Colorado 3	at	Minnesota 0
Wed. Apr. 16	Colorado 3	at	Minnesota 1
Sat. Apr. 19	Minnesota 3	at	Colorado 2
Mon. Apr. 21	Colorado 3	at	Minnesota 3*
Tue. Apr. 22	Minnesota 3	at	Colorado 2**

*Richard Park Scored at 4:22 of Overtime
**Andrew Brunette Scored at 3:25 of Overtime
(Minnesota Won Series 4-3)

Series 'H'

Thu. Apr. 10	St. Louis 6	at	Vancouver 0
Sat. Apr. 12	St. Louis 1	at	Vancouver 2
Mon. Apr. 14	Vancouver 1	at	St. Louis 3
Wed. Apr. 16	Vancouver 1	at	St. Louis 4
Fri. Apr. 18	St. Louis 3	at	Vancouver 5
Sun. Apr. 20	Vancouver 4	at	St. Louis 3
Tue. Apr. 22	St. Louis 1	at	Vancouver 4

(Vancouver Won Series 4-3)

CONFERENCE SEMI-FINALS
(Best-of-seven series)

Eastern Conference

Series 'I'

Fri. Apr. 25	Philadelphia 2	at	Ottawa 4
Sun. Apr. 27	Philadelphia 2	at	Ottawa 0
Tue. Apr. 29	Ottawa 3	at	Philadelphia 2*
Thu. May 1	Ottawa 0	at	Philadelphia 1
Sat. May 3	Philadelphia 2	at	Ottawa 5
Mon. May 5	Ottawa 5	at	Philadelphia 1

*Wade Redden Scored at 6:43 of Overtime
(Ottawa Won Series 4-2)

Series 'J'

Thu. Apr. 24	Tampa Bay 0	at	New Jersey 3
Sat. Apr. 26	Tampa Bay 2	at	New Jersey 3*
Mon. Apr. 28	New Jersey 3	at	Tampa Bay 4
Wed. Apr. 30	New Jersey 3	at	Tampa Bay 1
Fri. May 2	Tampa Bay 1	at	New Jersey 2**

*Jamie Langenbrunner Scored at 2:09 of Overtime
**Grant Marshall Scored at 51:12 of Overtime
(New Jersey Won Series 4-1)

Western Conference

Series 'K'

Thu. Apr. 24	Anaheim 4	at	Dallas 3*
Sat. Apr. 26	Anaheim 3	at	Dallas 2**
Mon. Apr. 28	Dallas 2	at	Anaheim 1
Wed. Apr. 30	Dallas 0	at	Anaheim 1
Sat. May 3	Anaheim 1	at	Dallas 4
Mon. May 5	Dallas 3	at	Anaheim 4

*Petr Sykora Scored at 80:48 of Overtime
**Mike Leclerc Scored at 1:44 of Overtime
(Anaheim Won Series 4-2)

Series 'L'

Fri. Apr. 25	Minnesota 3	at	Vancouver 4*
Sun. Apr. 27	Minnesota 3	at	Vancouver 2
Tue. Apr. 29	Vancouver 3	at	Minnesota 2
Fri. May 2	Vancouver 3	at	Minnesota 2**
Mon. May 5	Minnesota 7	at	Vancouver 2
Wed. May 7	Vancouver 1	at	Minnesota 5
Thu. May 8	Minnesota 4	at	Vancouver 2

*Trent Klatt Scored at 3:42 of Overtime
**Brent Sopel Scored at 15:52 of Overtime
(Minnesota Won Series 4-3)

CONFERENCE FINALS
(Best-of-seven series)

Eastern Conference

Series 'M'

Sat. May 10	New Jersey 2	at	Ottawa 3*
Tue. May 13	New Jersey 4	at	Ottawa 1
Thu. May 15	Ottawa 0	at	New Jersey 1
Sat. May 17	Ottawa 2	at	New Jersey 5
Mon. May 19	New Jersey 1	at	Ottawa 3
Wed. May 21	Ottawa 2	at	New Jersey 1**
Fri. May 23	New Jersey 3	at	Ottawa 2

*Shaun Van Allen Scored at 3:08 of Overtime
**Chris Phillips Scored at 15:51 of Overtime
(New Jersey Won Series 4-3)

Western Conference

Series 'N'

Sat. May 10	Anaheim 1	at	Minnesota 0*
Mon. May 12	Anaheim 2	at	Minnesota 0
Wed. May 14	Minnesota 0	at	Anaheim 4
Fri. May 16	Minnesota 1	at	Anaheim 2

*Petr Sykora Scored at 28:06 of Overtime
(Anaheim Won Series 4-0)

STANLEY CUP CHAMPIONSHIP
(Best-of-seven series)

Series 'O'

Tue. May 27	Anaheim 0	at	New Jersey 3
Thu. May 29	Anaheim 0	at	New Jersey 3
Sat. May 31	New Jersey 2	at	Anaheim 3*
Mon. June 2	New Jersey 0	at	Anaheim 1**
Thu. June 5	Anaheim 3	at	New Jersey 6
Sat. June 7	New Jersey 2	at	Anaheim 5
Mon. June 9	Anaheim 0	at	New Jersey 3

*Ruslan Salei Scored at 6:59 of Overtime
**Steve Thomas Scored at 0:39 of Overtime
(New Jersey Won Series 4-3)

Team Playoff Records

	GP	W	L	GF	GA	%
New Jersey	24	16	8	63	41	.667
Anaheim	21	15	6	45	40	.714
Ottawa	18	11	7	43	34	.611
Minnesota	18	8	10	43	43	.444
Vancouver	14	7	7	34	47	.500
Dallas	12	6	6	34	25	.500
Philadelphia	13	6	7	34	33	.462
Tampa Bay	11	5	6	22	29	.455
St. Louis	7	3	4	21	17	.429
Colorado	7	3	4	17	16	.429
Toronto	7	3	4	16	24	.429
Washington	6	2	4	15	14	.333
Edmonton	6	2	4	11	20	.333
Boston	5	1	4	8	13	.200
NY Islanders	5	1	4	7	13	.200
Detroit	4	0	4	6	10	.000

Individual Leaders

Abbreviations: GP – games played; **G** – goals; **A** – assists; **Pts** – points; **+/–** – difference between Goals For (**GF**) scored when a player is on the ice with his team at even strength or short-handed and Goals Against (**GA**) scored when the same player is on the ice with his team at even strength or on a power play; **PIM** – penalties in minutes; **PP** – power play goals; **SH** – short-handed goals; **GW** – game-winning goals; **OT** – overtime goals; **S** – shots on goal; **%** – percentage of shots on goal resulting in goals.

Playoff Scoring Leaders

Player	Team	GP	G	A	Pts	+/–	PIM	PP	SH	GW	OT	S	%
Jamie Langenbrunner	New Jersey	24	11	7	18	11	16	1	0	4	1	53	20.8
Scott Niedermayer	New Jersey	24	2	16	18	11	16	1	0	0	0	40	5.0
Marian Gaborik	Minnesota	18	9	8	17	2	6	4	0	0	0	52	17.3
John Madden	New Jersey	24	6	10	16	10	2	2	1	1	0	77	7.8
Marian Hossa	Ottawa	18	5	11	16	-1	6	3	0	1	0	54	9.3
Mike Modano	Dallas	12	5	10	15	2	4	1	0	2	0	30	16.7
Jeff Friesen	New Jersey	24	10	4	14	10	6	1	0	4	0	46	21.7
Markus Naslund	Vancouver	14	5	9	14	-6	18	2	0	1	0	40	12.5
Sergei Zubov	Dallas	12	4	10	14	2	4	2	0	0	0	27	14.8
Wes Walz	Minnesota	18	7	6	13	5	14	0	2	2	1	29	24.1
Andrew Brunette	Minnesota	18	7	6	13	-3	4	4	0	1	1	33	21.2
Doug Weight	St. Louis	7	5	8	13	0	2	5	0	1	0	18	27.8
Patrik Elias	New Jersey	24	5	8	13	5	26	2	0	2	0	59	8.5
Adam Oates	Anaheim	21	4	9	13	2	6	3	0	1	0	18	22.2
Petr Sykora	Anaheim	21	4	9	13	3	12	1	0	2	2	58	6.9
Sergei Zholtok	Minnesota	18	2	11	13	-7	0	1	0	0	0	34	5.9
Martin St. Louis	Tampa Bay	11	7	5	12	5	0	1	2	3	1	25	28.0
Paul Kariya	Anaheim	21	6	6	12	6	6	0	0	1	1	53	11.3
Jay Pandolfo	New Jersey	24	6	6	12	9	2	0	0	1	0	38	15.8
Scott Gomez	New Jersey	24	3	9	12	3	2	0	0	0	0	56	5.4
Radek Bonk	Ottawa	18	6	5	11	2	10	2	0	0	0	28	21.4
Martin Havlat	Ottawa	18	5	6	11	4	14	1	0	2	0	52	9.6
Brendan Morrison	Vancouver	14	4	7	11	-4	18	1	0	1	0	27	14.8
Mike Leclerc	Anaheim	21	2	9	11	3	12	1	0	0	1	55	3.6
Brian Rafalski	New Jersey	23	2	9	11	7	8	2	0	0	0	36	5.6

Playoff Defencemen Scoring Leaders

Player	Team	GP	G	A	Pts	+/–	PIM	PP	SH	GW	OT	S	%
Scott Niedermayer	New Jersey	24	2	16	18	11	16	1	0	0	0	40	5.0
Sergei Zubov	Dallas	12	4	10	14	2	4	2	0	0	0	27	14.8
Brian Rafalski	New Jersey	23	2	9	11	7	8	2	0	0	0	36	5.6
Scott Stevens	New Jersey	24	3	6	9	14	14	1	0	1	0	33	9.1
Wade Redden	Ottawa	18	1	8	9	1	10	0	0	1	1	32	3.1
Ed Jovanovski	Vancouver	14	7	1	8	-5	22	4	1	2	0	37	18.9
Filip Kuba	Minnesota	18	3	5	8	-8	24	3	0	0	0	21	14.3
Brent Sopel	Vancouver	14	2	6	8	-2	4	1	0	1	1	29	6.9
Sandis Ozolinsh	Anaheim	21	2	6	8	8	10	0	0	1	0	39	5.1
Mattias Ohlund	Vancouver	13	3	4	7	1	12	0	0	0	0	23	13.0
Zdeno Chara	Ottawa	18	1	6	7	3	14	0	0	0	0	32	3.1
Dan Boyle	Tampa Bay	11	0	7	7	0	6	0	0	0	0	26	.0

GOALTENDING LEADERS

Goals-Against Average

Goaltender	Team	GP	Mins	GA	Avg.
J-S Giguere	Anaheim	21	1407	38	1.62
Martin Brodeur	New Jersey	24	1491	41	1.65
Patrick Lalime	Ottawa	18	1122	34	1.82
Marty Turco	Dallas	12	798	25	1.88
Manny Fernandez	Minnesota	9	552	18	1.96

Wins

Goaltender	Team	GP	Mins	W	L
Martin Brodeur	New Jersey	24	1491	16	8
J-S Giguere	Anaheim	21	1407	15	6
Patrick Lalime	Ottawa	18	1122	11	7
Dan Cloutier	Vancouver	14	833	7	7
Marty Turco	Dallas	12	798	6	6
Roman Cechmanek	Philadelphia	13	867	6	7

Save Percentage

Goaltender	Team	GP	Mins	GA	SA	S%	W	L
J-S Giguere	Anaheim	21	1407	38	697	.945	15	6
Martin Brodeur	New Jersey	24	1491	41	622	.934	16	8
Manny Fernandez	Minnesota	9	552	18	253	.929	3	4
Patrick Lalime	Ottawa	18	1122	34	449	.924	11	7
Marty Turco	Dallas	12	798	25	310	.919	6	6

Shutouts

Goaltender	Team	GP	Mins	SO
Martin Brodeur	New Jersey	24	1491	7
J-S Giguere	Anaheim	21	1407	5
Roman Cechmanek	Philadelphia	13	867	2
Garth Snow	NY Islanders	5	305	1
Olaf Kolzig	Washington	6	404	1
Chris Osgood	St. Louis	7	417	1
Patrick Roy	Colorado	7	423	1
Patrick Lalime	Ottawa	18	1122	1

Goal Scoring

Name	Team	GP	G
Jamie Langenbrunner	New Jersey	24	11
Jeff Friesen	New Jersey	24	10
Marian Gaborik	Minnesota	18	9
Martin St. Louis	Tampa Bay	11	7
Mark Recchi	Philadelphia	13	7
Ed Jovanovski	Vancouver	14	7
Wes Walz	Minnesota	18	7
Andrew Brunette	Minnesota	18	7
Steve Rucchin	Anaheim	21	7
Joe Sakic	Colorado	7	6
Radek Bonk	Ottawa	18	6
Paul Kariya	Anaheim	21	6
Grant Marshall	New Jersey	24	6
Jay Pandolfo	New Jersey	24	6
John Madden	New Jersey	24	6

Assists

Name	Team	GP	A
Scott Niedermayer	New Jersey	24	16
Sergei Zholtok	Minnesota	18	11
Marian Hossa	Ottawa	18	11
Mike Modano	Dallas	12	10
Sergei Zubov	Dallas	12	10
John Madden	New Jersey	24	10
Markus Naslund	Vancouver	14	9
Adam Oates	Anaheim	21	9
Petr Sykora	Anaheim	21	9
Mike Leclerc	Anaheim	21	9
Brian Rafalski	New Jersey	23	9
Scott Gomez	New Jersey	24	9

Power-play Goals

Name	Team	GP	PP
Doug Weight	St. Louis	7	5
Ed Jovanovski	Vancouver	14	4
Andrew Brunette	Minnesota	18	4
Daniel Alfredsson	Ottawa	18	4
Marian Gaborik	Minnesota	18	4
Filip Kuba	Minnesota	18	3
Marian Hossa	Ottawa	18	3
Adam Oates	Anaheim	21	3

Game-winning Goals

Name	Team	GP	GW
Jamie Langenbrunner	New Jersey	24	4
Jeff Friesen	New Jersey	24	4
Martin St. Louis	Tampa Bay	11	3
Steve Thomas	Anaheim	21	3
10 players with two			

Short-handed Goals

Name	Team	GP	SH
Martin St. Louis	Tampa Bay	11	2
Wes Walz	Minnesota	18	2
Rob Niedermayer	Anaheim	21	2

Overtime Goals

Name	Team	GP	OT
Petr Sykora	Anaheim	21	2
20 players with one			

Shots

Name	Team	GP	S
John Madden	New Jersey	24	77
Patrik Elias	New Jersey	24	59
Brian Gionta	New Jersey	24	59
Petr Sykora	Anaheim	21	58
Scott Gomez	New Jersey	24	56

Plus/Minus

Name	Team	GP	+/–
Scott Stevens	New Jersey	24	14
Scott Niedermayer	New Jersey	24	11
Jamie Langenbrunner	New Jersey	24	11
Jeff Friesen	New Jersey	24	10
John Madden	New Jersey	24	10

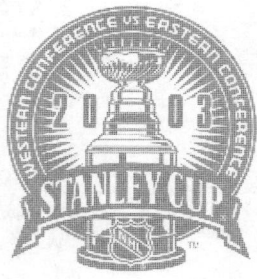

TEAMS' PLAYOFF HOME/ROAD RECORD
89 games played.

	HOME						ROAD					
	GP	W	L	GF	GA	%	GP	W	L	GF	GA	%
N.J.	13	12	1	39	13	.923	11	4	7	24	28	.364
ANA	10	9	1	26	13	.900	11	6	5	19	27	.545
OTT	10	6	4	25	20	.600	8	5	3	18	14	.625
MIN	8	2	6	13	18	.250	10	6	4	30	25	.600
VAN	8	4	4	21	28	.500	6	3	3	13	19	.500
DAL	6	3	3	21	13	.500	6	3	3	13	12	.500
PHI	7	4	3	21	16	.571	6	2	4	13	17	.333
T.B.	5	2	3	10	16	.400	6	3	3	12	13	.500
ST.L.	3	2	1	10	6	.667	4	1	3	11	11	.250
COL	4	1	3	9	12	.250	3	2	1	8	4	.667
TOR	3	2	1	8	7	.667	4	1	3	8	17	.250
WSH	3	0	3	5	9	.000	3	2	1	10	5	.667
EDM	3	1	2	6	8	.333	3	1	2	5	12	.333
BOS	2	1	1	5	4	.500	3	0	3	3	9	.000
NYI	2	0	2	3	6	.000	3	1	2	4	7	.333
DET	2	0	2	3	5	.000	2	0	2	3	5	.000

TEAMS' POWER-PLAY RECORD
Abbreviations: ADV-total advantages; **PPGF**-power play goals for; **%** arrived by dividing number of power-play goals by total advantages. 89 games played.

		HOME					ROAD					OVERALL		
	Team	GP	ADV	PPGF	%	Team	GP	ADV	PPGF	%	Team	GP	ADV	PPGF	%
1	ST.L.	3	20	5	25.0	MIN	10	38	10	26.3	MIN	18	73	16	21.9
2	N.J.	13	49	10	20.4	COL	3	8	2	25.0	ST.L.	7	48	10	20.8
3	BOS	2	10	2	20.0	WSH	3	13	3	23.1	WSH	6	27	5	18.5
4	TOR	3	10	2	20.0	VAN	6	36	8	22.2	VAN	14	73	13	17.8
5	DAL	6	36	7	19.4	OTT	8	28	6	21.4	DAL	12	58	10	17.2
6	ANA	10	37	7	18.9	ST.L.	4	28	5	17.9	BOS	5	18	3	16.7
7	PHI	7	28	5	17.9	T.B.	6	21	3	14.3	N.J.	24	84	13	15.5
8	MIN	8	35	6	17.1	DAL	6	22	3	13.6	COL	7	26	4	15.4
9	DET	2	6	1	16.7	DET	2	8	1	12.5	OTT	18	81	12	14.8
10	WSH	3	14	2	14.3	NYI	3	16	2	12.5	DET	4	14	2	14.3
11	VAN	8	37	5	13.5	BOS	3	8	1	12.5	T.B.	11	37	5	13.5
12	T.B.	5	16	2	12.5	N.J.	11	35	3	8.6	TOR	7	25	3	12.0
13	OTT	10	53	6	11.3	EDM	3	14	1	7.1	ANA	21	70	8	11.4
14	COL	4	18	2	11.1	TOR	4	15	1	6.7	PHI	13	50	5	10.0
15	NYI	2	15	1	6.7	ANA	11	33	1	3.0	NYI	5	31	3	9.7
16	EDM	3	9	0	0.0	PHI	6	22	0	0.0	EDM	6	23	1	4.3
	Total		**393**	**63**	**16.0**			**345**	**50**	**14.5**			**738**	**113**	**15.3**

TEAMS' PENALTY KILLING RECORD
Abbreviations: TSH – Total times short-handed; **PPGA** – power-play goals against; **%** arrived by dividing times short-handed minus power-play goals against by times short. 89 games played.

		HOME					ROAD					OVERALL		
	Team	GP	TSH	PPGA	%	Team	GP	TSH	PPGA	%	Team	GP	TSH	PPGA	%
1	BOS	2	7	0	100.0	DET	2	7	0	100.0	DET	4	14	0	100.0
2	DET	2	7	0	100.0	WSH	3	11	1	90.9	OTT	18	73	6	91.8
3	TOR	3	13	0	100.0	COL	3	11	1	90.9	DAL	12	50	5	90.0
4	OTT	10	37	2	94.6	OTT	8	36	4	88.9	N.J.	24	74	8	89.2
5	N.J.	13	30	2	93.3	NYI	3	17	2	88.2	ANA	21	70	9	87.1
6	DAL	6	29	2	93.1	ANA	11	32	4	87.5	BOS	5	22	3	86.4
7	EDM	3	10	1	90.0	N.J.	11	44	6	86.4	NYI	5	28	4	85.7
8	ANA	10	38	5	86.8	DAL	6	21	3	85.7	WSH	6	27	4	85.2
9	ST.L.	3	20	3	85.0	MIN	10	35	5	85.7	ST.L.	7	47	7	85.1
10	NYI	2	11	2	81.8	ST.L.	4	27	4	85.2	TOR	7	33	5	84.8
11	PHI	7	22	4	81.8	T.B.	6	24	4	83.3	EDM	6	39	7	82.1
12	WSH	3	16	3	81.3	PHI	6	28	5	82.1	PHI	13	50	9	82.0
13	VAN	8	40	8	80.0	BOS	3	15	3	80.0	MIN	18	63	12	81.0
14	MIN	8	28	7	75.0	EDM	3	29	6	79.3	T.B.	11	43	9	79.1
15	T.B.	5	19	5	73.7	TOR	4	20	5	75.0	VAN	14	76	18	76.3
16	COL	4	18	6	66.7	VAN	6	36	10	72.2	COL	7	29	7	75.9
	Total		**345**	**50**	**85.5**			**393**	**63**	**84.0**			**738**	**113**	**84.7**

SHORT HAND GOALS
89 games played.

GOALS FOR				GOALS AGAINST		
Team	GP	GF		Team	GP	GA
OTT	18	3		T.B.	11	0
ANA	21	3		EDM	6	0
TOR	7	2		NYI	5	0
T.B.	11	2		BOS	5	0
VAN	14	2		DET	4	0
MIN	18	2		ANA	21	1
EDM	6	1		OTT	18	1
DAL	12	1		VAN	14	1
PHI	13	1		TOR	7	1
N.J.	24	1		COL	7	1
DET	4	0		ST.L.	7	1
NYI	5	0		WSH	6	1
BOS	5	0		N.J.	24	2
WSH	6	0		DAL	12	2
COL	7	0		MIN	18	3
ST.L.	7	0		PHI	13	4
Total		**18**		**Total**		**18**

TEAM PENALTIES
Abbreviations: GP – games played; **PEN** – total penalty minutes, including bench penalties; **BMI** – total bench minor minutes; **AVG** – average penalty minutes per game. 89 games played.

Team	GP	PEN	BMI	AVG
ANA	21	166	8	7.9
N.J.	24	214	2	8.9
DET	4	36	2	9.0
COL	7	68	2	9.7
MIN	18	193	2	10.7
PHI	13	152	4	11.7
OTT	18	214	2	11.9
T.B.	11	134	4	12.2
TOR	7	89	2	12.7
BOS	5	70	0	14.0
DAL	12	176	8	14.7
WSH	6	88	4	14.7
VAN	14	239	2	17.1
ST.L.	7	137	4	19.6
NYI	5	108	0	21.6
EDM	6	131	2	21.8
Total		**2215**	**48**	
Two-Team average. PIM/GP				**24.9**

Scott Niedermayer was part of the first brother combination to oppose each other in the Stanley Cup Finals since Ken and Terry Reardon in 1946. Scott's playoff-leading 16 assists helped New Jersey down Rob Niedermayer and the Mighty Ducks.

Stanley Cup Record Book

Stanley Cup Winners

Year	W-L-T in Finals	Winner	Coach	Finalist	Coach
2003	4-3	New Jersey	Pat Burns	Anaheim	Mike Babcock
2002	4-1	Detroit	Scotty Bowman	Carolina	Paul Maurice
2001	4-3	Colorado	Bob Hartley	New Jersey	Larry Robinson
2000	4-2	New Jersey	Larry Robinson	Dallas	Ken Hitchcock
1999	4-2	Dallas	Ken Hitchcock	Buffalo	Lindy Ruff
1998	4-0	Detroit	Scotty Bowman	Washington	Ron Wilson
1997	4-0	Detroit	Scotty Bowman	Philadelphia	Terry Murray
1996	4-0	Colorado	Marc Crawford	Florida	Doug MacLean
1995	4-0	New Jersey	Jacques Lemaire	Detroit	Scotty Bowman
1994	4-3	NY Rangers	Mike Keenan	Vancouver	Pat Quinn
1993	4-1	Montreal	Jacques Demers	Los Angeles	Barry Melrose
1992	4-0	Pittsburgh	Scotty Bowman	Chicago	Mike Keenan
1991	4-2	Pittsburgh	Bob Johnson	Minnesota	Bob Gainey
1990	4-1	Edmonton	John Muckler	Boston	Mike Milbury
1989	4-2	Calgary	Terry Crisp	Montreal	Pat Burns
1988	4-0	Edmonton	Glen Sather	Boston	Terry O'Reilly
1987	4-3	Edmonton	Glen Sather	Philadelphia	Mike Keenan
1986	4-1	Montreal	Jean Perron	Calgary	Bob Johnson
1985	4-1	Edmonton	Glen Sather	Philadelphia	Mike Keenan
1984	4-1	Edmonton	Glen Sather	NY Islanders	Al Arbour
1983	4-0	NY Islanders	Al Arbour	Edmonton	Glen Sather
1982	4-0	NY Islanders	Al Arbour	Vancouver	Roger Neilson
1981	4-1	NY Islanders	Al Arbour	Minnesota	Glen Sonmor
1980	4-2	NY Islanders	Al Arbour	Philadelphia	Pat Quinn
1979	4-1	Montreal	Scotty Bowman	NY Rangers	Fred Shero
1978	4-2	Montreal	Scotty Bowman	Boston	Don Cherry
1977	4-0	Montreal	Scotty Bowman	Boston	Don Cherry
1976	4-0	Montreal	Scotty Bowman	Philadelphia	Fred Shero
1975	4-2	Philadelphia	Fred Shero	Buffalo	Floyd Smith
1974	4-2	Philadelphia	Fred Shero	Boston	Bep Guidolin
1973	4-2	Montreal	Scotty Bowman	Chicago	Billy Reay
1972	4-2	Boston	Tom Johnson	NY Rangers	Emile Francis
1971	4-3	Montreal	Al MacNeil	Chicago	Billy Reay
1970	4-0	Boston	Harry Sinden	St. Louis	Scotty Bowman
1969	4-0	Montreal	Claude Ruel	St. Louis	Scotty Bowman
1968	4-0	Montreal	Toe Blake	St. Louis	Scotty Bowman
1967	4-2	Toronto	Punch Imlach	Montreal	Toe Blake
1966	4-2	Montreal	Toe Blake	Detroit	Sid Abel
1965	4-3	Montreal	Toe Blake	Chicago	Billy Reay
1964	4-3	Toronto	Punch Imlach	Detroit	Sid Abel
1963	4-1	Toronto	Punch Imlach	Detroit	Sid Abel
1962	4-2	Toronto	Punch Imlach	Chicago	Rudy Pilous
1961	4-2	Chicago	Rudy Pilous	Detroit	Sid Abel
1960	4-0	Montreal	Toe Blake	Toronto	Punch Imlach
1959	4-1	Montreal	Toe Blake	Toronto	Punch Imlach
1958	4-2	Montreal	Toe Blake	Boston	Milt Schmidt
1957	4-1	Montreal	Toe Blake	Boston	Milt Schmidt
1956	4-1	Montreal	Toe Blake	Detroit	Jimmy Skinner
1955	4-3	Detroit	Jimmy Skinner	Montreal	Dick Irvin
1954	4-3	Detroit	Tommy Ivan	Montreal	Dick Irvin
1953	4-1	Montreal	Dick Irvin	Boston	Lynn Patrick
1952	4-0	Detroit	Tommy Ivan	Montreal	Dick Irvin
1951	4-1	Toronto	Joe Primeau	Montreal	Dick Irvin
1950	4-3	Detroit	Tommy Ivan	NY Rangers	Lynn Patrick
1949	4-0	Toronto	Hap Day	Detroit	Tommy Ivan
1948	4-0	Toronto	Hap Day	Detroit	Tommy Ivan
1947	4-2	Toronto	Hap Day	Montreal	Dick Irvin
1946	4-1	Montreal	Dick Irvin	Boston	Dit Clapper
1945	4-3	Toronto	Hap Day	Detroit	Jack Adams
1944	4-0	Montreal	Dick Irvin	Chicago	Paul Thompson
1943	4-0	Detroit	Jack Adams	Boston	Art Ross
1942	4-3	Toronto	Hap Day	Detroit	Jack Adams
1941	4-0	Boston	Cooney Weiland	Detroit	Ebbie Goodfellow
1940	4-2	NY Rangers	Frank Boucher	Toronto	Dick Irvin
1939	4-1	Boston	Art Ross	Toronto	Dick Irvin
1938	3-1	Chicago	Bill Stewart	Toronto	Dick Irvin
1937	3-2	Detroit	Jack Adams	NY Rangers	Lester Patrick
1936	3-1	Detroit	Jack Adams	Toronto	Dick Irvin
1935	3-0	Mtl. Maroons	Tommy Gorman	Toronto	Dick Irvin
1934	3-1	Chicago	Tommy Gorman	Detroit	Herbie Lewis
1933	3-1	NY Rangers	Lester Patrick	Toronto	Dick Irvin
1932	3-0	Toronto	Dick Irvin	NY Rangers	Lester Patrick
1931	3-2	Montreal	Cecil Hart	Chicago	Dick Irvin
1930	2-0	Montreal	Cecil Hart	Boston	Art Ross
1929	2-0	Boston	Cy Denneny	NY Rangers	Lester Patrick
1928	3-2	NY Rangers	Lester Patrick	Mtl. Maroons	Eddie Gerard
1927	2-0-2	Ottawa	Dave Gill	Boston	Art Ross

The National Hockey League assumed control of Stanley Cup competition after 1926

1926	3-1	Mtl. Maroons	Eddie Gerard	Victoria	Lester Patrick
1925	3-1	Victoria	Lester Patrick	Montreal	Leo Dandurand
1924	2-0	Montreal	Leo Dandurand	Cgy. Tigers	Eddie Oatman
	2-0			Van. Maroons	Art Duncan/Frank Patrick
1923	2-0	Ottawa	Pete Green	Edm. Eskimos	Ken McKenzie
	3-1			Van. Maroons	Lloyd Cook/Frank Patrick
1922	3-2	Tor. St. Pats	George O'Donoghue	Van. Millionaires	Lloyd Cook/Frank Patrick
1921	3-2	Ottawa	Pete Green	Van. Millionaires	Lloyd Cook/Frank Patrick
1920	3-2	Ottawa	Pete Green	Seattle	Pete Muldoon
1919	2-2-1	No decision - series between Montreal and Seattle cancelled due to influenza epidemic			
1918	3-2	Tor. Arenas	Dick Carroll	Van. Millionaires	Frank Patrick

History: The Stanley Cup, the oldest trophy competed for by professional athletes in North America, was donated by Frederick Arthur, Lord Stanley of Preston and son of the Earl of Derby, in 1893. Lord Stanley purchased the trophy for 10 guineas ($50 at that time) for presentation to the amateur hockey champions of Canada. Since 1910, when the National Hockey Association took possession of the Stanley Cup, the trophy has been the symbol of professional hockey supremacy. It has been competed for only by NHL teams since 1926-27 and has been under the exclusive control of the NHL since 1947.

Stanley Cup Standings

1918-2003
(ranked by Cup wins)

Teams	Cup Wins	Yrs.	Series	Wins	Losses	Games	Wins	Losses	Ties	Goals For	Goals Against	Winning %
Montreal	23 [1]	73	135 [2]	85	49	650	387	255	8	2009	1630	.602
Toronto	13	63	107	57	50	511	245	262	4	1323	1399	.483
Detroit	10	52	97	55	42	482	251	230	1	1361	1258	.522
Boston	5	61	103	47	56	505	239	260	6	1474	1497	.479
Edmonton	5	19	45	31	14	227	137	90	0	868	702	.604
NY Rangers	4	48	86	42	44	386	183	195	8	1091	1114	.484
NY Islanders	4	19	45	30	15	230	132	98	0	776	685	.574
Chicago	3	53	90	40	50	411	188	218	5	1176	1311	.464
New Jersey [3]	3	15	32	20	12	188	106	82	0	527	449	.564
Philadelphia	2	29	61	34	27	322	167	155	0	982	946	.519
Pittsburgh	2	21	39	20	19	208	109	99	0	644	641	.524
Colorado [4]	2	17	37	22	15	213	116	97	0	641	596	.545
Dallas [5]	1	25	50	26	24	272	139	133	0	815	819	.511
Calgary [6]	1	21	32	12	20	156	69	87	0	529	573	.442
St. Louis	0	33	56	23	33	298	137	161	0	848	931	.460
Buffalo	0	25	42	17	25	209	99	110	0	626	639	.474
Los Angeles	0	23	34	11	23	170	65	105	0	511	649	.382
Vancouver	0	19	29	10	19	148	63	85	0	436	507	.426
Washington	0	18	28	10	18	154	69	85	0	467	478	.448
Phoenix [7]	0	16	18	2	16	92	29	63	0	245	343	.315
Carolina [8]	0	11	15	4	11	84	35	49	0	208	256	.417
San Jose	0	7	11	4	7	67	29	38	0	175	232	.433
Ottawa [9]	0	7	11	4	7	62	28	34	0	124	135	.452
Anaheim	0	3	7	4	3	36	19	17	0	76	87	.528
Florida	0	3	6	3	3	31	13	18	0	77	82	.419
Tampa Bay	0	2	3	1	2	17	7	10	0	35	55	.412
Minnesota	0	1	3	2	1	18	8	10	0	43	43	.444

[1] Montreal also won the Stanley Cup in 1916.
[2] 1919 final incomplete due to influenza epidemic.
[3] Includes totals of Colorado Rockies 1976-82.
[4] Includes totals of Quebec 1979-95.
[5] Includes totals of Minnesota North Stars 1967-93.
[6] Includes totals of Atlanta Flames 1972-80.
[7] Includes totals of Winnipeg 1979-96.
[8] Includes totals of Hartford 1979-97.
[9] Modern Ottawa franchise only 1992 to date.

Stanley Cup Winners Prior to Formation of NHL in 1917

Season	Champions	Manager	Coach
1916-17	Seattle Metropolitans	Pete Muldoon	Pete Muldoon
1915-16	Montreal Canadiens	George Kennedy	George Kennedy
1914-15	Vancouver Millionaires	Frank Patrick	Frank Patrick
1913-14	Toronto Blueshirts	Jack Marshall	Scotty Davidson*
1912-13**	Quebec Bulldogs	M.J. Quinn	Joe Malone*
1911-12	Quebec Bulldogs	M.J. Quinn	C. Nolan
1910-11	Ottawa Senators		Bruce Stuart*
1909-10	Montreal Wanderers (Mar. 1910)	Dickie Boon	Pud Glass*
1909-10	Ottawa Senators (Jan. 1910)		Bruce Stuart*
1908-09	Ottawa Senators		Bruce Stuart*
1907-08	Montreal Wanderers	Dickie Boon	Cecil Blachford
1906-07	Montreal Wanderers (Mar. 1907)	Dickie Boon	Cecil Blachford
1906-07	Kenora Thistles (Jan./Mar. 1907)	F.A. Hudson	Tom Phillips*
1905-06	Montreal Wanderers (Mar. 1906)	Cecil Blachford*	
1905-06	Ottawa Silver Seven (Feb. 1906)		Alf Smith
1904-05	Ottawa Silver Seven		Alf Smith
1903-04	Ottawa Silver Seven		Alf Smith
1902-03	Ottawa Silver Seven (Mar. 1903)		Alf Smith
1902-03	Montreal A.A.A. (Feb. 1903)		Clare McKerrow
1901-02	Montreal A.A.A. (Mar. 1902)		Clare McKerrow
1901-02	Winnipeg Victorias (Jan. 1902)		
1900-01	Winnipeg Victorias	Dan Bain*	
1899-1900	Montreal Shamrocks	Harry Trihey*	
1898-99	Montreal Shamrocks (Mar. 1899)	Harry Trihey*	
1898-99	Montreal Victorias (Feb. 1899)	Mike Grant*	
1897-98	Montreal Victorias	Frank Richardson	
1896-97	Montreal Victorias	Mike Grant*	
1895-96	Montreal Victorias (Dec. 1896)	Mike Grant*	
1895-96	Winnipeg Victorias (Feb. 1896)	Jack Armitage	
1894-95	Montreal Victorias	Mike Grant*	
1893-94	Montreal A.A.A.		
1892-93	Montreal A.A.A.		

* In the early years the teams were frequently run by the Captain. *Indicates Captain
** Victoria defeated Quebec in challenge series. No official recognition.

Championship Trophies

PRINCE OF WALES TROPHY

Beginning with the 1993-94 season, the club which advances to the Stanley Cup Finals as the winner of the Eastern Conference Championship is presented with the Prince of Wales Trophy.

History: His Royal Highness, the Prince of Wales, donated the trophy to the National Hockey League in 1924. From 1927-28 through 1937-38, the award was presented to the team finishing first in the American Division of the NHL. (The team finishing first in the Canadian Division received the O'Brien Trophy during these years.) From 1938-39, when the NHL reverted to one section, to 1966-67, it was presented to the team winning the NHL regular-season championship. With expansion in 1967-68, it again became a divisional trophy, awarded to the regular-season champions of the East Division through to the end of the 1973-74 season. Beginning in 1974-75, it was awarded to the regular-season winner of the conference bearing the name of the trophy. From 1981-82 to 1992-93 the trophy was presented to the playoff champion in the Wales Conference. Since 1993-94, the trophy has been presented to the playoff champion in the Eastern Conference.

2002-03 Winner: New Jersey Devils

The New Jersey Devils won their third Prince of Wales Trophy in the last four years on May 23, 2003 after defeating the Ottawa Senators 3-2 in game seven of the Eastern Conference Championship series. Before defeating the Senators, the Devils had series wins over the Boston Bruins and Tampa Bay Lightning.

PRINCE OF WALES TROPHY WINNERS

2002-03	New Jersey Devils	1962-63	Toronto Maple Leafs
2001-02	Carolina Hurricanes	1961-62	Montreal Canadiens
2000-01	New Jersey Devils	1960-61	Montreal Canadiens
99-2000	New Jersey Devils	1959-60	Montreal Canadiens
1998-99	Buffalo Sabres	1958-59	Montreal Canadiens
1997-98	Washington Capitals	1957-58	Montreal Canadiens
1996-97	Philadelphia Flyers	1956-57	Detroit Red Wings
1995-96	Florida Panthers	1955-56	Montreal Canadiens
1994-95	New Jersey Devils	1954-55	Detroit Red Wings
1993-94	New York Rangers	1953-54	Detroit Red Wings
1992-93	Montreal Canadiens	1952-53	Detroit Red Wings
1991-92	Pittsburgh Penguins	1951-52	Detroit Red Wings
1990-91	Pittsburgh Penguins	1950-51	Detroit Red Wings
1989-90	Boston Bruins	1949-50	Detroit Red Wings
1988-89	Montreal Canadiens	1948-49	Detroit Red Wings
1987-88	Boston Bruins	1947-48	Toronto Maple Leafs
1986-87	Philadelphia Flyers	1946-47	Montreal Canadiens
1985-86	Montreal Canadiens	1945-46	Montreal Canadiens
1984-85	Philadelphia Flyers	1944-45	Montreal Canadiens
1983-84	New York Islanders	1943-44	Montreal Canadiens
1982-83	New York Islanders	1942-43	Detroit Red Wings
1981-82	New York Islanders	1941-42	New York Rangers
1980-81	Montreal Canadiens	1940-41	Boston Bruins
1979-80	Buffalo Sabres	1939-40	Boston Bruins
1978-79	Montreal Canadiens	1938-39	Boston Bruins
1977-78	Montreal Canadiens	1937-38	Boston Bruins
1976-77	Montreal Canadiens	1936-37	Detroit Red Wings
1975-76	Montreal Canadiens	1935-36	Detroit Red Wings
1974-75	Buffalo Sabres	1934-35	Boston Bruins
1973-74	Boston Bruins	1933-34	Detroit Red Wings
1972-73	Montreal Canadiens	1932-33	Boston Bruins
1971-72	Boston Bruins	1931-32	New York Rangers
1970-71	Boston Bruins	1930-31	Boston Bruins
1969-70	Chicago Blackhawks	1929-30	Boston Bruins
1968-69	Montreal Canadiens	1928-29	Boston Bruins
1967-68	Montreal Canadiens	1927-28	Boston Bruins
1966-67	Chicago Blackhawks	1926-27	Ottawa Senators
1965-66	Montreal Canadiens	1925-26	Montreal Maroons
1964-65	Detroit Red Wings	1924-25	Montreal Canadiens
1963-64	Montreal Canadiens	1923-24	Montreal Canadiens

CLARENCE S. CAMPBELL BOWL

Beginning with the 1993-94 season, the club which advances to the Stanley Cup Finals as the winner of the Western Conference Championship is presented with the Clarence S. Campbell Bowl.

History: Presented by the member clubs in 1968 for perpetual competition by the National Hockey League in recognition of the services of Clarence S. Campbell, President of the NHL from 1946 to 1977. From 1967-68 through 1973-74, the trophy was awarded to the regular-season champions of the West Division. Beginning in 1974-75, it was awarded to the regular-season winner of the conference bearing the name of the trophy. From 1981-82 to 1992-93 the trophy was presented to the playoff champion in the Campbell Conference. Since 1993-94, the trophy has been presented to the playoff champion in the Western Conference. The trophy itself is a hallmark piece made of sterling silver and was crafted by a British silversmith in 1878.

2002-03 Winner: Anaheim Mighty Ducks

The Anaheim Mighty Ducks won their first Clarence Campbell Bowl on May 16, 2003 after defeating the Minnesota Wild 2-1 in game four of the Western Conference Championship series. Before defeating the Wild, the Ducks had series wins over the Detroit Red Wings and Dallas Stars.

CLARENCE S. CAMPBELL BOWL WINNERS

2002-03	Anaheim Mighty Ducks	1984-85	Edmonton Oilers
2001-02	Detroit Red Wings	1983-84	Edmonton Oilers
2000-01	Colorado Avalanche	1982-83	Edmonton Oilers
99-2000	Dallas Stars	1981-82	Vancouver Canucks
1998-99	Dallas Stars	1980-81	New York Islanders
1997-98	Detroit Red Wings	1979-80	Philadelphia Flyers
1996-97	Detroit Red Wings	1978-79	New York Islanders
1995-96	Colorado Avalanche	1977-78	New York Islanders
1994-95	Detroit Red Wings	1976-77	Philadelphia Flyers
1993-94	Vancouver Canucks	1975-76	Philadelphia Flyers
1992-93	Los Angeles Kings	1974-75	Philadelphia Flyers
1991-92	Chicago Blackhawks	1973-74	Philadelphia Flyers
1990-91	Minnesota North Stars	1972-73	Chicago Blackhawks
1989-90	Edmonton Oilers	1971-72	Chicago Blackhawks
1988-89	Calgary Flames	1970-71	Chicago Blackhawks
1987-88	Edmonton Oilers	1969-70	St. Louis Blues
1986-87	Edmonton Oilers	1968-69	St. Louis Blues
1985-86	Calgary Flames	1967-68	Philadelphia Flyers

Prince of Wales Trophy

Clarence S. Campbell Bowl

Stanley Cup

Stanley Cup Winners

Rosters and Final Series Scores

2002-03* — New Jersey Devils — Scott Stevens (Captain), Tommy Albelin, Jiri Bicek, Martin Brodeur, Sergei Brylin, Ken Daneyko, Patrik Elias, Jeff Friesen, Brian Gionta, Scott Gomez, Jamie Langenbrunner, John Madden, Grant Marshall, Jim McKenzie, Scott Niedermayer, Joe Nieuwendyk, Jay Pandolfo, Brian Rafalski, Pascal Rheaume, Mike Rupp, Corey Schwab, Richard Smehlik, Turner Stevenson, Oleg Tverdovsky, Colin White, Lou Lamoriello (CEO/President/General Manager), Pat Burns (Head Coach), Bob Carpenter (Assistant Coach), John MacLean (Assistant Coach), Jacques Caron (Goaltending Coach), Larry Robinson (Special Assignment Coach), David Conte (Director, Scouting), Claude Carrier (Assistant Director, Scouting), Chris Lamoriello (Scout/Albany GM), Milt Fisher (Scout), Dan Labraaten (Scout), Marcel Pronovost (Scout), Bob Hoffmeyer (Pro Scout), Jan Ludvig (Pro Scout), Dr. Barry Fisher (Orthopedist), Vladimir Bure (Fitness Consultant), Taran Singleton (Hockey Operations), Bill Murray (Medical Trainer), Michael Vasalani (Strength/Conditioning Coordinator), Rich Matthews (Equipment Mnagaer), Juergen Merz (Massage Therapist), Alex Abasto (Assistant Equipment Manager).

Scores: May 27, at New Jersey - New Jersey 3, Anaheim 0; May 29, at New Jersey - New Jersey 3, Anaheim 0; May 31, at Anaheim - Anaheim 3, New Jersey 2; June 2, at Anaheim - Anaheim 1, New Jersey 0; June 5, at New Jersey - New Jersey 6, Anaheim 3; June 7, at Anaheim - Anaheim 5, New Jersey 2; June 9, at New Jersey - New Jersey 3, Anaheim 0.

* List of names for 2003 not finalized at press time.

2001-02 — Detroit Red Wings — Steve Yzerman (Captain), Chris Chelios, Mathieu Dandenault, Pavel Datsyuk, Boyd Devereaux, Kris Draper, Steve Duchesne, Sergei Fedorov, Jiri Fischer, Dominik Hasek, Tomas Holmstrom, Brett Hull, Igor Larionov, Manny Legace, Nicklas Lidstrom, Kirk Maltby, Darren McCarty, Fredrik Olausson, Luc Robitaille, Brendan Shanahan, Jiri Slegr, Jason Williams, Michael Ilitch (Owner/Governor), Marian Ilitch (Owner/Secretary Treasurer), Ronald Ilitch, Michael Ilitch Jr., Lisa Ilitch Murray, Atanas Ilitch, Carole Ilitch Trepeck, Jim Devallano (Senior Vice President), Christopher Ilitch (Vice President), Denise Ilitch (Alternate Governor), Ken Holland (General Manager), Jim Nill (Assistant General Manager), Scotty Bowman (Head Coach), Dave Lewis (Associate Coach), Barry Smith (Associate Coach), Jim Berard (Goaltending Consultant), Joe Kocur (Video Coordinator), John Wharton (Athletic Trainer), Paul Boyer (Equipment Manager), Piet Van Zant (Assistant Athletic Trainer), Tim Abbott (Assistant Equipment Manager), Sergei Tchekmarev (Masseur), Dan Belisle (Pro Scout), Mark Howe (Pro Scout), Bob McCammon (Pro Scout), Hakan Andersson (Director of European Scouting), Mark Leach (Scout), Bruce Haralson (Scout), Joe McDonnell (Scout), Glenn Merkosky (Scout).

Scores: June 4, at Detroit - Carolina 3, Detroit 2; June 6, at Detroit - Detroit 3, Carolina 1; June 8, at Carolina - Detroit 3, Carolina 2; June 10, at Carolina - Detroit 3, Carolina 0; June 13, at Detroit - Detroit 3, Carolina 1.

2000-01 — Colorado Avalanche — Joe Sakic (Captain), David Aebischer, Rob Blake, Raymond Bourque, Greg de Vries, Chris Dingman, Chris Drury, Adam Foote, Peter Forsberg, Milan Hejduk, Dan Hinote, Jon Klemm, Eric Messier, Bryan Muir, Ville Nieminen, Scott Parker, Shjon Podein, Nolan Pratt, Dave Reid, Steve Reinprecht, Patrick Roy, Martin Skoula, Alex Tanguay, Stephane Yelle, E. Stanley Kroenke (Owner/Governor), Pierre Lacroix (President and General Manager), Bob Hartley (Head Coach), Jacques Cloutier (Assistant Coach), Bryan Trottier (Assistant Coach), Paul Fixter (Video Coach), Francois Giguere (Vice President of Hockey Operations), Brian MacDonald (Assistant General Manager), Michel Goulet (Vice President of Player Personnel), Jean Martineau (Vice President of Communications/Team Services), Pat Karns (Head Athletic Trainer), Matthew Sokolowski (Assistant Athletic Trainer), Wayne Flemming (Equipment Manager), Mark Miller (Equipment Manager), Dave Randolph (Assistant Equipment Manager), Paul Goldberg (Strength and Conditioning Coach), Gregorio Pradera (Massage Therapist), Brad Smith (Pro Scout), Jim Hammett (Chief Scout), Garth Joy, Steve Lyons, Joni Lehto, Orval Tessier (Scouts), Charlotte Grahame (Director of Hockey Operations).
Scores: May 26, at Colorado - Colorado 5, New Jersey 0; May 29, at Colorado - New Jersey 2, Colorado 1; May 31, at New Jersey - Colorado 3, New Jersey 1; June 2, at New Jersey - New Jersey 3, Colorado 2; June 4, at Colorado - New Jersey 4, Colorado 1; June 7, at New Jersey - Colorado 4, New Jersey 0; June 9, at Colorado - Colorado 3, New Jersey 1.

1999-2000 — New Jersey Devils — Scott Stevens (Captain), Jason Arnott, Brad Bombardir, Martin Brodeur, Steve Brule, Sergei Brylin, Ken Daneyko, Patrik Elias, Scott Gomez, Bobby Holik, Steve Kelly, Claude Lemieux, John Madden, Vladimir Malakhov, Randy McKay, Alexander Mogilny, Sergei Nemchinov, Scott Niedermayer, Krzysztof Oliwa, Jay Pandolfo, Brian Rafalski, Ken Sutton, Petr Sykora, Chris Terreri, Colin White, Dr. John J. McMullen (Owner/Chairman), Peter S. McMullen (Owner), Lou Lamoriello (President/General Manager), Larry Robinson (Head Coach), Viacheslav Fetisov (Assistant Coach), Bob Carpenter (Assistant Coach), Jacques Caron (Goaltending Coach), John Cunniff (AHL Coach), David Conte (Director of Scouting), Milt Fisher (Scout), Claude Carrier (Assistant Director of Scouting), Dan Labraaten (Scout), Marcel Pronovost (Scout), Bob Hoffmeyer (Pro Scout), Dr. Barry Fisher (Orthopedist), Dennis Gendron (AHL Assistant Coach), Robbie Ftorek (Coach), Vladimir Bure (Consultant), Taran Singleton (Hockey Operations), Marie Carnevale (Hockey Operations), Callie Smith (Hockey Operations), Bill Murray (Medical Trainer), Michael Vasalani (Strength/Conditioning Coordinator), Dana McGuane (Equipment Manager), Juergen Merz (Massage Therapist), Harry Bricker (Assistant Equipment Manager), Lou Centanni (Assistant Equipment Manager).
Scores: May 30, at New Jersey - New Jersey 7, Dallas 3; June 1, at New Jersey - Dallas 2, New Jersey 1; June 3, at Dallas - New Jersey 2, Dallas 1; June 5, at Dallas - New Jersey 3, Dallas 1; June 8, at New Jersey - Dallas 1 - New Jersey 0; at Dallas, New Jersey 2 - Dallas 1.

1998-99 — Dallas Stars — Derian Hatcher (Captain), Ed Belfour, Guy Carbonneau, Shawn Chambers, Benoit Hogue, Tony Hrkac, Brett Hull, Mike Keane, Jamie Langenbrunner, Jere Lehtinen, Craig Ludwig, Grant Marshall, Richard Matvichuk, Mike Modano, Joe Nieuwendyk, Derek Plante, Dave Reid, Jon Sim, Brian Skrudland, Blake Sloan, Darryl Sydor, Roman Turek, Pat Verbeek, Sergei Zubov, Thomas Hicks (Chairman of the Board and Owner), Jim Lites (President), Bob Gainey (Vice President, Hockey Operations and General Manager), Doug Armstrong (Assistant General Manager), Craig Button (Director of Player Personnel), Ken Hitchcock (Head Coach), Doug Jarvis (Assistant Coach), Rick Wilson (Assistant Coach), Rick McLaughlin (Vice President and Chief Financial Officer), Jeff Cogen (Vice President, Marketing and Promotion), Bill Strong (Vice President, Marketing and Broadcasting), Tim Bernhardt (Director of Amateur Scouting), Doug Overton (Director of Pro Scouting), Bob Gernander (Chief Scout), Stu MacGregor (Western Scout), Dave Suprenant (Medical Trainer), Dave Smith (Equipment Manager), Rich Matthews (Equipment Manager), J.J. McQueen (Strength and Conditioning Coach), Rick St. Croix (Goaltending Consultant), Dan Stuchal (Director of Team Services), Larry Kelly (Director of Public Relations).

Scores: June 8, at Dallas - Buffalo 3, Dallas 2; June 10, at Dallas - Dallas 4, Buffalo 2; June 12, at Buffalo - Dallas 2, Buffalo 1; June 15, at Buffalo - Buffalo 2, Dallas 1; June 17, at Dallas - Dallas 2, Buffalo 0; June 19, at Buffalo - Dallas 2, Buffalo 1.

1997-98 — Detroit Red Wings — Steve Yzerman (Captain), Doug Brown, Mathieu Dandenault, Kris Draper, Anders Eriksson, Sergei Fedorov, Viacheslav Fetisov, Brent Gilchrist, Kevin Hodson, Tomas Holmstrom, Mike Knuble, Joe Kocur, Vladimir Konstantinov, Vyacheslav Kozlov, Martin Lapointe, Igor Larionov, Nicklas Lidstrom, Jamie Macoun, Kirk Maltby, Darren McCarty, Dmitri Mironov, Larry Murphy, Chris Osgood, Bob Rouse, Brendan Shanahan, Aaron Ward, Mike Ilitch, (Owner/Chairman), Marian Ilitch (Owner), Atanas Ilitch (Vice President), Christopher Ilitch (Vice President), Denise Ilitch, Ronald Ilitch, Michael Ilitch Jr., Lisa Ilitch Murray, Carole Ilitch Trepeck, Jim Devellano (Senior Vice President), Scotty Bowman (Head Coach), Ken Holland (General Manager), Don Waddell (Assistant General Manager), Barry Smith (Associate Coach), Dave Lewis (Associate Coach), Jim Bedard (Goaltending Consultant), Jim Nill (Director of Player Development), Dan Belisle (Pro Scout), Mark Howe (Pro Scout), Hakan Andersson (Director of European Scouting), Mark Leach (USA Scout), Moe McDonnell (Eastern Scout), Bruce Haralson (Western Scout), John Wharton (Athletic Trainer), Paul Boyer (Equipment Manager) Tim Abbott (Assistant Equipment Manager), Bob Huddleston (Masseur), Sergei Mnatsakanov (Masseur), Wally Crossman (Dressing Room Assistant).
Scores: June 9, at Detroit — Detroit 2, Washington 1; June 11, at Detroit — Detroit 5, Washington 4; June 13, at Washington — Detroit 2, Washington 1; June 16, at Washington — Detroit 4, Washington 1.

1996-97 — Detroit Red Wings — Steve Yzerman (Captain), Doug Brown, Mathieu Dandenault, Kris Draper, Sergei Fedorov, Viacheslav Fetisov, Kevin Hodson, Tomas Holmstrom, Joe Kocur, Vladimir Konstantinov, Vyacheslav Kozlov, Martin Lapointe, Igor Larionov, Nicklas Lidstrom, Kirk Maltby, Darren McCarty, Larry Murphy, Chris Osgood, Jamie Pushor, Bob Rouse, Tomas Sandstrom, Brendan Shanahan, Tim Taylor, Mike Vernon, Aaron Ward, Mike Ilitch (Owner/Chairman), Marian Ilitch (Owner), Atanas Ilitch (Vice President), Christopher Ilitch (Vice President), Denise Ilitch Lites, Ronald Ilitch, Michael Ilitch, Jr., Lisa Ilitch Murray, Carole Ilitch Trepeck, Jim Devellano (Senior Vice President), Scotty Bowman (Head Coach/Director of Player Personnel), Ken Holland (Assistant General Manager), Barry Smith (Associate Coach), Dave Lewis (Associate Coach), Mike Krushelnyski (Assistant Coach). Jim Nill (Director of Player Development), Dan Belisle (Pro Scout), Mark Howe (Pro Scout), Hakan Andersson (Director of European Scouting), John Wharton (Athletic Trainer), Paul Boyer (Equipment Manager) Tim Abbott (Assistant Equipment Manager), Sergei Mnatsakanov (Masseur).
Scores: May 31, at Philadelphia — Detroit 4, Philadelphia 2; June 3, at Philadelphia — Detroit 4, Philadelphia 2; June 5, at Detroit — Detroit 6, Philadelphia 1; June 7, at Detroit — Detroit 2, Philadelphia 1.

1995-96 — Colorado Avalanche — Joe Sakic (Captain), Rene Corbet, Adam Deadmarsh, Stephane Fiset, Adam Foote, Peter Forsberg, Alexei Gusarov, Dave Hannan, Valeri Kamensky, Mike Keane, Jon Klemm, Uwe Krupp, Sylvain Lefebvre, Claude Lemieux, Curtis Leschyshyn, Troy Murray, Sandis Ozolinsh, Mike Ricci, Patrick Roy, Warren Rychel, Chris Simon, Craig Wolanin, Stephane Yelle, Scott Young, Charlie Lyons (Chairman, CEO), Pierre Lacroix (Exec. V.P., G.M.), Marc Crawford (Head Coach), Joel Quenneville (Assistant Coach), Jacques Cloutier (Assistant Coach), Francois Giguere (Assistant General Manager), Michel Goulet (Director of Player Personnel), Dave Draper (Chief Scout), Jean Martineau (Director of Public Relations), Pat Karns (Trainer), Matthew Sokolowski (Assistant Trainer), Rob McLean (Equipment Manager), Mike Kramer (Assistant Equipment Manager), Brock Gibbins (Assistant Equipment Manager), Skip Allen (Strength and Conditioning Coach), Paul Fixter (Video Coordinator), Leo Vyssokov (Massage Therapist).
Scores: June 4, at Colorado — Colorado 3, Florida 1; June 6, at Colorado — Colorado 8, Florida 1; June 8, at Florida — Colorado 3, Florida 2; June 10, at Florida — Colorado 1, Florida 0.

1994-95 — New Jersey Devils — Scott Stevens (Captain), Tommy Albelin, Martin Brodeur, Neal Broten, Sergei Brylin, Bob Carpenter, Shawn Chambers, Tom Chorske, Danton Cole, Ken Daneyko, Kevin Dean, Jim Dowd, Bruce Driver (Alternate Captain), Bill Guerin, Bobby Holik, Claude Lemieux, John MacLean (Alternate Captain), Chris McAlpine, Randy McKay, Scott Niedermayer, Mike Peluso, Stephane Richer, Brian Rolston, Chris Terreri, Valeri Zelepukin, Dr. John J. McMullen (Owner/Chairman), Peter S. McMullen (Owner), Lou Lamoriello (President/General Manager), Jacques Lemaire (Head Coach), Jacques Caron (Goaltender Coach), Dennis Gendron (Assistant Coach), Larry Robinson (Assistant Coach), Robbie Ftorek (AHL Coach), Alex Abasto (Assistant Equipment Manager), Bob Huddleston (Massage Therapist), David Nichols (Equipment Manager), Ted Schuch (Medical Trainer), Mike Vasalani (Strength Coach), David Conte (Director of Scouting) Claude Carrier (Scout), Milt Fisher (Scout), Dan Labraaten (Scout), Marcel Pronovost (Scout).
Scores: June 17, at Detroit — New Jersey 2, Detroit 1; June 20, at Detroit — New Jersey 4, Detroit 2; June 22, at New Jersey — New Jersey 5, Detroit 2; June 24, at New Jersey — New Jersey 5, Detroit 2.

1993-94 — New York Rangers — Mark Messier (Captain), Brian Leetch, Kevin Lowe, Adam Graves, Steve Larmer, Glenn Anderson, Jeff Beukeboom, Greg Gilbert, Mike Hartman, Glenn Healy, Mike Hudson, Alexander Karpovtsev, Joe Kocur, Alexei Kovalev, Nick Kypreos, Doug Lidster, Stephane Matteau, Craig MacTavish, Sergei Nemchinov, Brian Noonan, Ed Olczyk, Mike Richter, Esa Tikkanen, Jay Wells, Sergei Zubov, Neil Smith (President, General Manager and Governor), Robert Gutkowski, Stanley Jaffe, Kenneth Munoz (Governors), Larry Pleau (Assistant General Manager), Mike Keenan (Head Coach), Colin Campbell (Associate Coach), Dick Todd (Assistant Coach), Matthew Loughren (Manager, Team Operations), Barry Watkins (Director, Communications), Christer Rockstrom, Tony Feltrin, Martin Madden, Herb Hammond, Darwin Bennett (Scouts), Dave Smith, Joe Murphy, Mike Folga, Bruce Lifrieri (Trainers).
Scores: May 31, at New York — Vancouver 3, NY Rangers 2; June 2, at New York — NY Rangers 3, Vancouver 1; June 4, at Vancouver — NY Rangers 5, Vancouver 1; June 7, at Vancouver — NY Rangers 4, Vancouver 2; June 9, at New York — Vancouver 6, at NY Rangers 3; June 11, at Vancouver — Vancouver 4, NY Rangers 1; June 14, at New York — NY Rangers 3, Vancouver 2.

1992-93 — Montreal Canadiens — Guy Carbonneau (Captain), Patrick Roy, Mike Keane, Eric Desjardins, Stephan Lebeau, Mathieu Schneider, J.J. Daigneault, Denis Savard, Lyle Odelein, Todd Ewen, Kirk Muller, John LeClair, Gilbert Dionne, Benoit Brunet, Patrice Brisebois, Paul Di Pietro, Andre Racicot, Donald Dufresne, Mario Roberge, Sean Hill, Ed Ronan, Kevin Haller, Vincent Damphousse, Brian Bellows, Gary Leeman, Rob Ramage, Ronald Corey (President), Serge Savard (Managing Director & Vice-President Hockey), Jacques Demers (Head Coach), Jacques Laperriere (Assistant Coach), Charles Thiffault (Assistant Coach), Francois Allaire (Goaltending Instructor), Jean Béliveau (Senior Vice-President, Corporate Affairs), Fred Steer (Vice-President, Finance & Adminstration), Aldo Giampaolo (Vice-President, Operations), Bernard Brisset (Vice-President, Marketing & Communications), André Boudrias (Assistant to the Managing Director & Director of Scouting), Jacques Lemaire (Assistant to the Managing Director), Gaeten Lefebvre (Athletic Trainer), John Shipman (Assistant to the Athletic Trainer), Eddy Palchak (Equipment Manager), Pierre Gervais (Assistant to the Equipment Manager), Robert Boulanger (Assistant to the Equipment Manager), Pierre Ouellete (Assistant to the Equipment Manager).
Scores: June 1, at Montreal — Los Angeles 4, Montreal 1; June 2, at Montreal — Montreal 3, Los Angeles 2; June 5, at Los Angeles — Montreal 4, Los Angeles 3; June 7, at Los Angeles — Montreal 3, Los Angeles 2; June 9, at Montreal — Montreal 4, Los Angeles 1.

1991-92 — Pittsburgh Penguins — Mario Lemieux (Captain), Ron Francis, Bryan Trottier, Kevin Stevens, Bob Errey, Phil Bourque, Troy Loney, Rick Tocchet, Joe Mullen, Jaromir Jagr, Jiri Hrdina, Shawn McEachern, Ulf Samuelsson, Kjell Samuelsson, Larry Murphy, Gordie Roberts, Jim Paek, Paul Stanton, Tom Barrasso, Ken Wregget, Jay Caufield, Jamie Leach, Wendell Young, Grant Jennings, Peter Taglianetti, Jock Callander, Dave Michayluk, Mike Needham, Jeff Chychrun, Ken Priestlay, Jeff Daniels, Howard Baldwin (Owner and President), Morris Belzberg (Owner), Thomas Ruta (Owner), Donn Patton (Executive Vice President and Chief Financial Officer), Paul Martha (Executive Vice President and General Counsel), Craig Patrick (Executive Vice President and General Manager), Bob Johnson (Coach), Scotty Bowman (Director of Player Development and Coach), Barry Smith, Rick Kehoe, Pierre McGuire, Gilles Meloche, Rick Paterson (Assistant Coaches), Steve Latin (Equipment Manager), Skip Thayer (Trainer), John Welday (Strength and Conditioning Coach), Greg Malone, Les Binkley, Charlie Hodge, John Gill, Ralph Cox (Scouts).
Scores: May 26, at Pittsburgh — Pittsburgh 5, Chicago 4; May 28, at Pittsburgh — Pittsburgh 3, Chicago 1; May 30, at Chicago — Pittsburgh 1, Chicago 0; June 1, at Chicago — Pittsburgh 6, Chicago 5.

1990-91 — Pittsburgh Penguins — Mario Lemieux (Captain), Paul Coffey, Randy Hillier, Bob Errey, Tom Barrasso, Phil Bourque, Jay Caufield, Ron Francis, Randy Gilhen, Jiri Hrdina, Jaromir Jagr, Grant Jennings, Troy Loney, Joe Mullen, Larry Murphy, Jim Paek, Frank Pietrangelo, Barry Pederson, Mark Recchi, Gordie Roberts, Ulf Samuelsson, Paul Stanton, Kevin Stevens, Peter Taglianetti, Bryan Trottier, Scott Young, Wendell Young, Edward J. DeBartolo, Sr. (Owner), Marie D. DeBartolo York (President), Paul Martha (Vice-President & General Counsel), Craig Patrick (General Manager), Scotty Bowman (Director of Player Development & Recruitment), Bob Johnson (Coach), Rick Kehoe (Assistant Coach), Gilles Meloche (Goaltending Coach & Scout), Rick Paterson (Assistant Coach), Barry Smith (Assistant Coach), Steve Latin (Equipment Manager), Skip Thayer (Trainer), John Welday (Strength & Conditioning Coach), Greg Malone (Scout).
Scores: May 15, at Pittsburgh — Minnesota 5, Pittsburgh 4; May 17, at Pittsburgh — Pittsburgh 4, Minnesota 1; May 19, at Minnesota — Minnesota 3, Pittsburgh 1; May 21, at Minnesota — Pittsburgh 5, Minnesota 3; May 23, at Pittsburgh — Pittsburgh 6, Minnesota 4; May 25, at Minnesota — Pittsburgh 8, Minnesota 0.

1989-90 — Edmonton Oilers — Kevin Lowe, Steve Smith, Jeff Beukeboom, Mark Lamb, Joe Murphy, Glenn Anderson, Mark Messier (Captain), Adam Graves, Craig MacTavish, Kelly Buchberger, Jari Kurri, Craig Simpson, Martin Gelinas, Randy Gregg, Charlie Huddy, Geoff Smith, Reijo Ruotsalainen, Craig Muni, Bill Ranford, Dave Brown, Pokey Reddick, Petr Klima, Esa Tikkanen, Grant Fuhr, Peter Pocklington (Owner), Glen Sather (President/General Manager), John Muckler (Coach), Ted Green (Co-Coach), Ron Low (Ass't Coach), Bruce MacGregor (Ass't General Manager), Barry Fraser (Director of Player Personnel), John Blackwell (Director of Operations, AHL), Ace Bailey, Ed Chadwick, Lorne Davis, Harry Howell, Matti Vaisanen and Albert Reeves (Scouts), Bill Tuele (Director of Public Relations), Werner Baum (Controller), Dr. Gordon Cameron (Medical Chief of Staff), Dr. David Reid (Team Physician), Barrie Stafford (Athletic Trainer), Ken Lowe (Athletic Therapist), Stuart Poirier (Massage Therapist), Lyle Kulchisky (Ass't Trainer).
Scores: May 15, at Boston — Edmonton 3, Boston 2; May 18, at Boston — Edmonton 7, Boston 2; May 20, at Edmonton — Boston 2, Edmonton 1; May 22, at Edmonton — Edmonton 5, Boston 1; May 24, at Boston — Edmonton 4, Boston 1.

1988-89 — Calgary Flames — Mike Vernon, Rick Wamsley, Al MacInnis, Brad McCrimmon, Dana Murzyn, Ric Nattress, Joe Mullen, Lanny McDonald (Co-captain), Gary Roberts, Colin Patterson, Hakan Loob, Theoren Fleury, Jiri Hrdina, Tim Hunter (Ass't. captain), Gary Suter, Mark Hunter, Jim Peplinski (Co-captain), Joe Nieuwendyk, Brian MacLellan, Joel Otto, Jamie Macoun, Doug Gilmour, Rob Ramage. Norman Green, Harley Hotchkiss, Norman Kwong, Sonia Scurfield, B.J. Seaman, D.K. Seaman (Owners), Cliff Fletcher (President and General Manager), Al MacNeil (Ass't. General Manager), Al Coates (Ass't. to the President), Terry Crisp (Head Coach), Doug Risebrough, Tom Watt (Ass't. Coaches), Glenn Hall (Goaltending Consultant), Jim Murray (Trainer), Bob Stewart (Equipment Manager), Al Murray (Ass't. Trainer).
Scores: May 14, at Calgary — Calgary 3, Montreal 2; May 17, at Calgary— Montreal 4, Calgary 2; May 19, at Montreal — Montreal 4, Calgary 3; May 21, at Montreal — Calgary 4, Montreal 2; May 23, at Calgary — Calgary 3, Montreal 2; May 25, at Montreal — Calgary 4, Montreal 2.

1987-88 — Edmonton Oilers — Keith Acton, Glenn Anderson, Jeff Beukeboom, Geoff Courtnall, Grant Fuhr, Randy Gregg, Wayne Gretzky (Captain), Dave Hannan, Charlie Huddy, Mike Krushelnyski, Jari Kurri, Normand Lacombe, Kevin Lowe, Craig MacTavish, Kevin McClelland, Marty McSorley, Mark Messier, Craig Muni, Bill Ranford, Craig Simpson, Steve Smith, Esa Tikkanen, Peter Pocklington (Owner), Glen Sather (General Manager/Coach), John Muckler (Co-Coach), Ted Green (Ass't. Coach), Bruce MacGregor (Ass't. General Manager), Barry Fraser (Director of Player Personnel), Bill Tuele (Director of Public Relations), Dr. Gordon Cameron (Team Physician), Peter Millar (Athletic Therapist), Barrie Stafford (Trainer), Juergen Mers (Massage Therapist), Lyle Kulchisky (Ass't. Trainer).
Scores: May 18, at Edmonton — Edmonton 2, Boston 1; May 20, at Edmonton — Edmonton 4, Boston 2; May 22, at Boston — Edmonton 6, Boston 3; May 24, at Boston — Boston 3, Edmonton 3 (suspended due to power failure); May 26, at Edmonton — Edmonton 6, Boston 3.

1986-87 — Edmonton Oilers — Glenn Anderson, Jeff Beukeboom, Kelly Buchberger, Paul Coffey, Grant Fuhr, Randy Gregg, Wayne Gretzky (Captain), Charlie Huddy, Dave Hunter, Mike Krushelnyski, Jari Kurri, Moe Lemay, Kevin Lowe, Craig MacTavish, Kevin McClelland, Marty McSorley, Mark Messier, Andy Moog, Craig Muni, Kent Nilsson, Jaroslav Pouzar, Reijo Ruotsalainen, Steve Smith, Esa Tikkanen, Peter Pocklington (Owner), Glen Sather (General Manager/Coach), John Muckler (Co-Coach), Ted Green (Ass't. Coach), Ron Low (Ass't. Coach), Bruce MacGregor (Ass't. General Manager), Barry Fraser (Director of Player Personnel), Peter Millar (Athletic Therapist), Barrie Stafford (Trainer), Lyle Kulchisky (Ass't. Trainer).
Scores: May 17, at Edmonton — Edmonton 4, Philadelphia 2; May 20, at Edmonton — Edmonton 3, Philadelphia 2; May 22, at Philadelphia — Philadelphia 5, Edmonton 3; May 24, at Philadelphia — Edmonton 4, Philadelphia 1; May 26, at Edmonton — Philadelphia 4, Edmonton 3; May 28, at Philadelphia — Philadelphia 3, Edmonton 2; May 31, at Edmonton — Edmonton 3, Philadelphia 1.

1985-86 — Montreal Canadiens — Bob Gainey (Captain), Doug Soetaert, Patrick Roy, Rick Green, David Maley, Ryan Walter, Serge Boisvert, Mario Tremblay, Bobby Smith, Craig Ludwig, Tom Kurvers, Kjell Dahlin, Larry Robinson, Guy Carbonneau, Chris Chelios, Petr Svoboda, Mats Naslund, Lucien DeBlois, Steve Rooney, Gaston Gingras, Mike Lalor, Chris Nilan, John Kordic, Claude Lemieux, Mike McPhee, Brian Skrudland, Stephane Richer, Ronald Corey (President), Serge Savard (General Manager), Jean Perron (Coach), Jacques Laperrière (Ass't. Coach), Jean Béliveau (Vice President), Francois-Xavier Seigneur (Vice President), Fred Steer (Vice President), Jacques Lemaire (Ass't. General Manager), André Boudrias (Ass't. General Manager), Claude Ruel (Scouting), Yves Belanger (Athletic Therapist), Gaetan Lefebvre (Ass't. Athletic Therapist), Eddy Palchak (Trainer), Sylvain Toupin (Ass't. Trainer).
Scores: May 16, at Calgary — Calgary 5, Montreal 2; May 18, at Calgary — Montreal 3, Calgary 2; May 20, at Montreal — Montreal 5, Calgary 3; May 22, at Montreal — Montreal 1, Calgary 0; May 24, at Calgary — Montreal 4, Calgary 3.

1984-85 — Edmonton Oilers — Glenn Anderson, Billy Carroll, Paul Coffey, Lee Fogolin, Grant Fuhr, Randy Gregg, Wayne Gretzky (Captain), Charlie Huddy, Pat Hughes, Dave Hunter, Don Jackson, Mike Krushelnyski, Jari Kurri, Willy Lindstrom, Kevin Lowe, Dave Lumley, Kevin McClelland, Larry Melnyk, Mark Messier, Andy Moog, Mark Napier, Jaroslav Pouzar, Dave Semenko, Esa Tikkanen, Peter Pocklington (Owner), Glen Sather (General Manager/Coach), John Muckler (Ass't. Coach), Ted Green (Ass't. Coach), Bruce MacGregor (Ass't. General Manager), Barry Fraser (Director of Player Personnel/Chief Scout), Peter Millar (Athletic Therapist), Barrie Stafford, Lyle Kulchisky (Trainers)
Scores: May 21, at Philadelphia — Philadelphia 4, Edmonton 1; May 23, at Philadelphia — Edmonton 3, Philadelphia 1; May 25, at Edmonton — Edmonton 4, Philadelphia 3; May 28, at Edmonton — Edmonton 5, Philadelphia 3; May 30, at Edmonton — Edmonton 8, Philadelphia 3.

1983-84 — Edmonton Oilers — Glenn Anderson, Paul Coffey, Pat Conacher, Lee Fogolin, Grant Fuhr, Randy Gregg, Wayne Gretzky (Captain), Charlie Huddy, Pat Hughes, Dave Hunter, Don Jackson, Jari Kurri, Willy Lindstrom, Ken Linseman, Kevin Lowe, Dave Lumley, Kevin McClelland, Mark Messier, Andy Moog, Jaroslav Pouzar, Dave Semenko, Peter Pocklington (Owner), Glen Sather (General Manager/Coach), John Muckler (Ass't. Coach), Ted Green (Ass't. Coach), Bruce MacGregor (Ass't. General Manager), Barry Fraser (Director of Player Personnel/Chief Scout), Peter Millar (Athletic Therapist), Barrie Stafford (Trainer)
Scores: May 10, at New York — Edmonton 1, NY Islanders 0; May 12, at New York — NY Islanders 6, Edmonton 1; May 15, at Edmonton — Edmonton 7, NY Islanders 2; May 17, at Edmonton — Edmonton 7, NY Islanders 2; May 19, at Edmonton — Edmonton 5, NY Islanders 2.

1982-83 — New York Islanders — Mike Bossy, Bob Bourne, Paul Boutilier, Billy Carroll, Greg Gilbert, Clark Gillies, Butch Goring, Mats Hallin, Tomas Jonsson, Anders Kallur, Gord Lane, Dave Langevin, Mike McEwen, Roland Melanson, Wayne Merrick, Ken Morrow, Bob Nystrom, Stefan Persson, Denis Potvin (Captain), Billy Smith, Brent Sutter, Duane Sutter, John Tonelli, Bryan Trottier, Al Arbour (Coach), Lorne Henning (Ass't. Coach), Bill Torrey (General Manager), Ron Waske, Jim Pickard (Trainers)
Scores: May 10, at Edmonton — NY Islanders 2, Edmonton 0; May 12, at Edmonton — NY Islanders 6, Edmonton 3; May 14, at New York — NY Islanders 5, Edmonton 1; May 17, at New York — NY Islanders 4, Edmonton 2

1981-82 — New York Islanders — Mike Bossy, Bob Bourne, Billy Carroll, Butch Goring, Greg Gilbert, Clark Gillies, Tomas Jonsson, Anders Kallur, Gord Lane, Dave Langevin, Hector Marini, Mike McEwen, Roland Melanson, Wayne Merrick, Ken Morrow, Bob Nystrom, Stefan Persson, Denis Potvin (Captain), Billy Smith, Brent Sutter, Duane Sutter, John Tonelli, Bryan Trottier, Al Arbour (Coach), Lorne Henning (Ass't. Coach), Bill Torrey (General Manager), Jim Devellano (ass't. general manager/dir. of scouting), Ron Waske, Jim Pickard (Trainers)
Scores: May 8, at New York — NY Islanders 6, Vancouver 5; May 11, at New York — NY Islanders 6, Vancouver 4; May 13, at Vancouver — NY Islanders 3, Vancouver 0; May 16, at Vancouver — NY Islanders 3, Vancouver 1

1980-81 — New York Islanders — Denis Potvin (Captain), Mike McEwen, Ken Morrow, Gord Lane, Bob Lorimer, Stefan Persson, Dave Langevin, Mike Bossy, Bryan Trottier, Butch Goring, Wayne Merrick, Clark Gillies, John Tonelli, Bob Nystrom, Billy Carroll, Bob Bourne, Hector Marini, Anders Kallur, Duane Sutter, Garry Howatt, Lorne Henning, Billy Smith, Roland Melanson, Al Arbour (Coach), Bill Torrey (General Manager), Jim Devellano (Chief Scout), Ron Waske, Jim Pickard (Trainers).
Scores: May 12, at New York — NY Islanders 6, Minnesota 3; May 14, at New York — NY Islanders 6, Minnesota 3; May 17, at Minnesota — NY Islanders 7, Minnesota 5; May 19, at Minnesota— Minnesota 4, NY Islanders 2; May 21, at New York — NY Islanders 5, Minnesota 1.

1979-80 — New York Islanders — Gord Lane, Jean Potvin, Bob Lorimer, Denis Potvin (Captain), Stefan Persson, Ken Morrow, Dave Langevin, Duane Sutter, Garry Howatt, Clark Gillies, Lorne Henning, Wayne Merrick, Bob Bourne, Steve Tambellini, Bryan Trottier, Mike Bossy, Bob Nystrom, John Tonelli, Anders Kallur, Butch Goring, Alex McKendry, Glenn Resch, Billy Smith, Al Arbour (Coach), Bill Torrey (General Manager), Jim Devellano (Chief Scout), Ron Waske, Jim Pickard (Trainers).
Scores: May 13, at Philadelphia — NY Islanders 4, Philadelphia 3; May 15, at Philadelphia — Philadelphia 8, NY Islanders 3; May 17, at New York — NY Islanders 6, Philadelphia 2; May 19, at New York — NY Islanders 5, Philadelphia 2; May 22 at Philadelphia — Philadelphia 6, NY Islanders 3; May 24, at New York — NY Islanders 5, Philadelphia 4.

1978-79 — Montreal Canadiens — Ken Dryden, Larry Robinson, Serge Savard, Guy Lapointe, Brian Engblom, Gilles Lupien, Rick Chartraw, Guy Lafleur, Steve Shutt, Jacques Lemaire, Yvan Cournoyer (Captain), Réjean Houle, Pierre Mondou, Bob Gainey, Doug Jarvis, Yvon Lambert, Doug Risebrough, Pierre Larouche, Mario Tremblay, Cam Connor, Pat Hughes, Rod Langway, Mark Napier, Michel Larocque, Richard Sévigny, Scotty Bowman (Coach), Irving Grundman (Managing Director), Eddy Palchak, Pierre Meilleur (Trainers).
Scores: May 13, at Montreal — NY Rangers 4, Montreal 1; May 15, at Montreal — Montreal 6, NY Rangers 2; May 17, at New York — Montreal 4, NY Rangers 1; May 19, at New York — Montreal 4, NY Rangers 3; May 21, at Montreal — Montreal 4, NY Rangers 1.

1977-78 — Montreal Canadiens — Ken Dryden, Larry Robinson, Serge Savard, Guy Lapointe, Bill Nyrop, Pierre Bouchard, Brian Engblom, Gilles Lupien, Rick Chartraw, Guy Lafleur, Steve Shutt, Jacques Lemaire, Yvan Cournoyer (Captain), Réjean Houle, Pierre Mondou, Bob Gainey, Doug Jarvis, Yvon Lambert, Doug Risebrough, Pierre Larouche, Mario Tremblay, Michel Larocque, Murray Wilson, Scotty Bowman (Coach), Sam Pollock (General Manager), Eddy Palchak, Pierre Meilleur (Trainers).
Scores: May 13, at Montreal — Montreal 4, Boston 1; May 16, at Montreal — Montreal 3, Boston 2; May 18, at Boston — Boston 4, Montreal 0; May 21, at Boston — Boston 4, Montreal 3; May 23, at Montreal — Montreal 4, Boston 1; May 25, at Boston — Montreal 4, Boston 1.

1976-77 — Montreal Canadiens — Ken Dryden, Guy Lapointe, Larry Robinson, Serge Savard, Jimmy Roberts, Rick Chartraw, Bill Nyrop, Pierre Bouchard, Brian Engblom, Yvan Cournoyer (Captain), Guy Lafleur, Jacques Lemaire, Steve Shutt, Pete Mahovlich, Murray Wilson, Doug Jarvis, Yvon Lambert, Bob Gainey, Doug Risebrough, Mario Tremblay, Rejean Houle, Pierre Mondou, Mike Polich, Michel Larocque, Scotty Bowman (Coach), Sam Pollock (General Manager), Eddy Palchak, Pierre Meilleur (Trainers).
Scores: May 7, at Montreal — Montreal 7, Boston 3; May 10, at Montreal — Montreal 3, Boston 0; May 12, at Boston — Montreal 4, Boston 2; May 14, at Boston — Montreal 2, Boston 1.

1975-76 — Montreal Canadiens — Ken Dryden, Serge Savard, Guy Lapointe, Larry Robinson, Bill Nyrop, Pierre Bouchard, Jimmy Roberts, Guy Lafleur, Steve Shutt, Pete Mahovlich, Yvan Cournoyer (Captain), Jacques Lemaire, Yvon Lambert, Bob Gainey, Doug Jarvis, Doug Risebrough, Murray Wilson, Mario Tremblay, Rick Chartraw, Michel Larocque, Scotty Bowman (Coach), Sam Pollock (General Manager), Eddy Palchak, Pierre Meilleur (Trainers).
Scores: May 9, at Montreal — Montreal 4, Philadelphia 3; May 11, at Montreal — Montreal 2, Philadelphia 1; May 13, at Philadelphia — Montreal 3, Philadelphia 2; May 16, at Philadelphia — Montreal 5, Philadelphia 3.

1974-75 — Philadelphia Flyers — Bernie Parent, Wayne Stephenson, Ed Van Impe, Tom Bladon, André Dupont, Joe Watson, Jimmy Watson, Ted Harris, Larry Goodenough, Rick MacLeish, Bobby Clarke (Captain), Bill Barber, Reggie Leach, Gary Dornhoefer, Ross Lonsberry, Bob Kelly, Terry Crisp, Don Saleski, Dave Schultz, Orest Kindrachuk, Bill Clement, Fred Shero (Coach), Keith Allen (general manager), Frank Lewis, Jim McKenzie (Trainers).
Scores: May 15, at Philadelphia — Philadelphia 4, Buffalo 1; May 18, at Philadelphia — Philadelphia 2, Buffalo 1; May 20, at Buffalo — Buffalo 5, Philadelphia 4; May 22, at Buffalo — Buffalo 4, Philadelphia 2; May 25, at Philadelphia — Philadelphia 5, Buffalo 1; May 27, at Buffalo — Philadelphia 2, Buffalo 0.

1973-74 — Philadelphia Flyers — Bernie Parent, Ed Van Impe, Tom Bladon, André Dupont, Joe Watson, Jimmy Watson, Barry Ashbee, Bill Barber, Dave Schultz, Don Saleski, Gary Dornhoefer, Terry Crisp, Bobby Clarke (Captain), Simon Nolet, Ross Lonsberry, Rick MacLeish, Bill Flett, Orest Kindrachuk, Bill Clement, Bob Kelly, Bruce Cowick, Al MacAdam, Bobby Taylor, Fred Shero (Coach), Keith Allen (General Manager), Frank Lewis, Jim McKenzie (Trainers).
Scores: May 7, at Boston — Boston 3, Philadelphia 2; May 9, at Boston — Philadelphia 3, Boston 2; May 12, at Philadelphia — Philadelphia 4, Boston 1; May 14, at Philadelphia — Philadelphia 4, Boston 2; May 16, at Boston — Boston 5, Philadelphia 1; May 19, at Philadelphia — Philadelphia 1, Boston 0.

1972-73 — Montreal Canadiens — Ken Dryden, Guy Lapointe, Serge Savard, Larry Robinson, Jacques Laperrière, Bob Murdoch, Pierre Bouchard, Jimmy Roberts, Yvan Cournoyer, Frank Mahovlich, Jacques Lemaire, Pete Mahovlich, Marc Tardif, Henri Richard (Captain), Réjean Houle, Guy Lafleur, Chuck Lefley, Claude Larose, Murray Wilson, Steve Shutt, Michel Plasse, Scotty Bowman (Coach), Sam Pollock (General Manager), Eddy Palchak, Bob Williams (Trainers).
Scores: April 29, at Montreal — Montreal 8, Chicago 3; May 1, at Montreal — Montreal 4, Chicago 1; May 3, at Chicago — Chicago 7, Montreal 4; May 6, at Chicago — Montreal 4, Chicago 0; May 8, at Montreal — Chicago 8, Montreal 7; May 10, at Chicago — Montreal 6, Chicago 4.

1971-72 — Boston Bruins — Gerry Cheevers, Eddie Johnston, Bobby Orr, Ted Green, Carol Vadnais, Dallas Smith, Don Awrey, Phil Esposito, Ken Hodge, John Bucyk, Mike Walton, Wayne Cashman, Garnet Bailey, Derek Sanderson, Fred Stanfield, Ed Westfall, John McKenzie, Don Marcotte, Garry Peters, Chris Hayes, Tom Johnson (Coach), Milt Schmidt (General Manager), Dan Canney, John Forristall (Trainers).
Scores: April 30, at Boston — Boston 6, NY Rangers 5; May 2, at Boston — Boston 2, NY Rangers 1; May 4, at New York — NY Rangers 5, Boston 2; May 7, at New York — Boston 3, NY Rangers 2; May 9, at Boston — NY Rangers 3, Boston 2; May 11, at New York — Boston 3, NY Rangers 0.

1970-71 — Montreal Canadiens — Ken Dryden, Rogie Vachon, Jacques Laperrière, J.C. Tremblay, Guy Lapointe, Terry Harper, Pierre Bouchard, Jean Béliveau (Captain), Marc Tardif, Yvan Cournoyer, Réjean Houle, Claude Larose, Henri Richard, Phil Roberto, Pete Mahovlich, Leon Rochefort, John Ferguson, Bobby Sheehan, Jacques Lemaire, Frank Mahovlich, Bob Murdoch, Chuck Lefley, Al MacNeil (Coach), Sam Pollock (General Manager), Yvon Belanger, Eddy Palchak (Trainers).
Scores: May 4, at Chicago — Chicago 2, Montreal 1; May 6, at Chicago — Chicago 5, Montreal 3; May 9, at Montreal — Montreal 4, Chicago 2; May 11, at Montreal — Montreal 5, Chicago 2; May 13, at Chicago — Chicago 2, Montreal 0; May 16, at Montreal — Montreal 4, Chicago 3; May 18, at Chicago — Montreal 3, Chicago 2.

1969-70 — Boston Bruins — Gerry Cheevers, Eddie Johnston, Bobby Orr, Rick Smith, Dallas Smith, Bill Speer, Gary Doak, Don Awrey, Phil Esposito, Ken Hodge, John Bucyk, Wayne Carleton, Wayne Cashman, Derek Sanderson, Fred Stanfield, Ed Westfall, John McKenzie, Jim Lorentz, Don Marcotte, Bill Lesuk, Danny Schock, Harry Sinden (Coach), Milt Schmidt (General Manager), Dan Canney, John Forristall (Trainers).
Scores: May 3, at St. Louis — Boston 6, St. Louis 1; May 5, at St. Louis — Boston 6, St. Louis 2; May 7, at Boston — Boston 4, St. Louis 1; May 10, at Boston — Boston 4, St. Louis 3.

1968-69 — Montreal Canadiens — Gump Worsley, Rogie Vachon, Jacques Laperrière, J.C. Tremblay, Ted Harris, Serge Savard, Jean Béliveau (Captain), Ralph Backstrom, Dick Duff, Yvan Cournoyer, Claude Provost, Bobby Rousseau, Henri Richard, John Ferguson, Christian Bordeleau, Mickey Redmond, Jacques Lemaire, Lucien Grenier, Tony Esposito, Claude Ruel (Coach), Sam Pollock (General Manager), Larry Aubut, Eddy Palchak (Trainers).
Scores: April 27, at Montreal — Montreal 3, St. Louis 1; April 29, at Montreal — Montreal 3, St. Louis 1; May 1 at St. Louis — Montreal 4, St. Louis 0; May 4, at St. Louis — Montreal 2, St. Louis 1.

1967-68 — Montreal Canadiens — Gump Worsley, Rogie Vachon, Jacques Laperrière, J.C. Tremblay, Ted Harris, Serge Savard, Terry Harper, Carol Vadnais, Jean Béliveau (Captain), Gilles Tremblay, Ralph Backstrom, Dick Duff, Claude Larose, Yvan Cournoyer, Claude Provost, Bobby Rousseau, Henri Richard, John Ferguson, Danny Grant, Jacques Lemaire, Mickey Redmond, Toe Blake (Coach), Sam Pollock (General Manager), Larry Aubut, Eddy Palchak (Trainers).
Scores: May 5, at St. Louis — Montreal 3, St. Louis 2; May 7, at St. Louis — Montreal 1, St. Louis 0; May 9, at Montreal — Montreal 4, St. Louis 3; May 11, at Montreal — Montreal 3, St. Louis 2.

1966-67 — Toronto Maple Leafs — Johnny Bower, Terry Sawchuk, Larry Hillman, Marcel Pronovost, Tim Horton, Bob Baun, Aut Erickson, Allan Stanley, Red Kelly, Ron Ellis, George Armstrong (Captain), Pete Stemkowski, Dave Keon, Mike Walton, Jim Pappin, Bob Pulford, Brian Conacher, Eddie Shack, Frank Mahovlich, Milan Marcetta, Larry Jeffrey, Bruce Gamble, Punch Imlach (Manager-Coach), Bob Haggart (Trainer).
Scores: April 20, at Montreal — Toronto 2, Montreal 6; April 22, at Montreal — Toronto 3, Montreal 0; April 25, at Toronto — Toronto 3, Montreal 2; April 27, at Toronto — Toronto 2, Montreal 6; April 29, at Montreal — Toronto 4, Montreal 1; May 2, at Toronto — Toronto 3, Montreal 1.

1965-66 — Montreal Canadiens — Gump Worsley, Charlie Hodge, J.C. Tremblay, Ted Harris, Jean-Guy Talbot, Terry Harper, Jacques Laperrière, Noel Price, Jean Béliveau (Captain), Ralph Backstrom, Dick Duff, Gilles Tremblay, Claude Larose, Yvan Cournoyer, Claude Provost, Bobby Rousseau, Henri Richard, John Ferguson, Leon Rochefort, Jimmy Roberts, Toe Blake (Coach), Sam Pollock (general manager), Larry Aubut, Andy Galley (Trainers).
Scores: April 24, at Montreal — Detroit 3, Montreal 2; April 26, at Montreal — Detroit 5, Montreal 2; April 28, at Detroit — Montreal 4, Detroit 2; May 1, at Detroit — Montreal 2, Detroit 1; May 3, at Montreal — Montreal 5, Detroit 1; May 5, at Detroit — Montreal 3, Detroit 2.

1964-65 — Montreal Canadiens — Gump Worsley, Charlie Hodge, J.C. Tremblay, Ted Harris, Jean-Guy Talbot, Terry Harper, Jacques Laperrière, Jean Gauthier, Noel Picard, Jean Béliveau (Captain), Ralph Backstrom, Dick Duff, Claude Larose, Yvan Cournoyer, Claude Provost, Bobby Rousseau, Henri Richard, Dave Balon, John Ferguson, Red Berenson, Jimmy Roberts, Toe Blake (Coach), Sam Pollock (general manager), Larry Aubut, Andy Galley (Trainers).
Scores: April 17, at Montreal — Montreal 3, Chicago 2; April 20, at Montreal — Montreal 2, Chicago 0; April 22, at Chicago — Montreal 1, Chicago 3; April 25, at Chicago — Montreal 1, Chicago 5; April 7, at Montreal — Montreal 6, Chicago 0; April 29, at Chicago — Montreal 1, Chicago 2; May 1, at Montreal — Montreal 4, Chicago 0.

1963-64 — Toronto Maple Leafs — Johnny Bower, Don Simmons, Carl Brewer, Tim Horton, Bob Baun, Allan Stanley, Larry Hillman, Al Arbour, Red Kelly, Gerry Ehman, Andy Bathgate, George Armstrong (Captain), Ron Stewart, Dave Keon, Billy Harris, Don McKenney, Jim Pappin, Bob Pulford, Eddie Shack, Frank Mahovlich, Ed Litzenberger, Punch Imlach (Manager-Coach), Bob Haggart (Trainer).
Scores April 11, at Toronto — Toronto 3, Detroit 2; April 14, at Toronto — Toronto 3, Detroit 4; April 16, at Detroit — Toronto 3, Detroit 4; April 18, at Detroit — Toronto 4, Detroit 2; April 21, at Toronto — Toronto 1, Detroit 4; April 23, at Detroit — Toronto 4, Detroit 3; April 25, at Toronto — Toronto 4, Detroit 0.

1962-63 — Toronto Maple Leafs — Johnny Bower, Don Simmons, Carl Brewer, Tim Horton, Kent Douglas, Allan Stanley, Bob Baun, Larry Hillman, Red Kelly, Dick Duff, George Armstrong (Captain), Bob Nevin, Ron Stewart, Dave Keon, Billy Harris, Bob Pulford, Eddie Shack, Ed Litzenberger, Frank Mahovlich, John MacMillan, Punch Imlach (Manager-Coach), Bob Haggart (Trainer).
Scores: April 9, at Toronto — Toronto 4, Detroit 2; April 11, at Toronto — Toronto 4, Detroit 2; April 14, at Detroit — Toronto 2, Detroit 3; April 16 at Detroit — Toronto 4, Detroit 2; April 18, at Toronto — Toronto 3, Detroit 1.

1961-62 — Toronto Maple Leafs — Johnny Bower, Don Simmons, Carl Brewer, Tim Horton, Bob Baun, Allan Stanley, Al Arbour, Larry Hillman, Red Kelly, Dick Duff, George Armstrong (Captain), Frank Mahovlich, Bob Nevin, Ron Stewart, Billy Harris, Bert Olmstead, Bob Pulford, Eddie Shack, Dave Keon, Ed Litzenberger, John MacMillan, Punch Imlach (Manager-Coach), Bob Haggart (Trainer).
Scores: April 10, at Toronto — Toronto 4, Chicago 1; April 12, at Toronto — Toronto 3, Chicago 2; April 15, at Chicago — Toronto 0, Chicago 3; April 17, at Chicago — Toronto 1, Chicago 4; April 19, at Toronto —Toronto 8, Chicago 4; April 22, at Chicago — Toronto 2, Chicago 1.

1960-61 — Chicago Black Hawks — Glenn Hall, Al Arbour, Pierre Pilote, Moose Vasko, Jack Evans, Dollard St. Laurent, Reggie Fleming, Tod Sloan, Ron Murphy, Ed Litzenberger (Captain), Bill Hay, Wayne Hillman, Bobby Hull, Ab McDonald, Eric Nesterenko, Kenny Wharram, Earl Balfour, Stan Mikita, Murray Balfour, Chico Maki, Wayne Hicks, Tommy Ivan (Manager), Rudy Pilous (Coach), Nick Garen (Trainer).
Scores: April 6, at Chicago — Chicago 3, Detroit 2; April 8, at Detroit — Detroit 3, Chicago 1; April 10, at Chicago — Chicago 3, Detroit 1; April 12, at Detroit — Detroit 2, Chicago 1; April 14, at Chicago — Chicago 6, Detroit 3; April 16, at Detroit — Chicago 5, Detroit 1.

1959-60 — Montreal Canadiens — Jacques Plante, Charlie Hodge, Doug Harvey, Tom Johnson, Bob Turner, Jean-Guy Talbot, Albert Langlois, Ralph Backstrom, Jean Béliveau, Marcel Bonin, Bernie Geoffrion, Phil Goyette, Bill Hicke, Don Marshall, Ab McDonald, Dickie Moore, André Pronovost, Claude Provost, Henri Richard, Maurice Richard (Captain), Frank Selke (Manager), Toe Blake (Coach), Hector Dubois, Larry Aubut (Trainers).
Scores: April 7, at Montreal — Montreal 4, Toronto 2; April 9, at Montreal — Montreal 2, Toronto 1; April 12, at Toronto — Montreal 5, Toronto 2; April 14, at Toronto — Montreal 4, Toronto 0.

Bernie Parent was a big reason why the Philadelphia Flyers won back-to-back Stanley Cup championships in 1974 and 1975. Parent won the Conn Smythe Trophy both years.

1958-59 — Montreal Canadiens — Jacques Plante, Charlie Hodge, Doug Harvey, Tom Johnson, Bob Turner, Jean-Guy Talbot, Albert Langlois, Bernie Geoffrion, Ralph Backstrom, Bill Hicke, Maurice Richard (Captain), Dickie Moore, Claude Provost, Ab McDonald, Henri Richard, Marcel Bonin, Phil Goyette, Don Marshall, André Pronovost, Jean Béliveau, Frank Selke (Manager), Toe Blake (Coach), Hector Dubois, Larry Aubut (Trainers).
Scores: April 9, at Montreal — Montreal 5, Toronto 3; April 11, at Montreal — Montreal 3, Toronto 1; April 14, at Toronto — Toronto 3, Montreal 2; April 16, at Toronto — Montreal 3, Toronto 2; April 18, at Montreal — Montreal 5, Toronto 3.

1957-58 — Montreal Canadiens — Jacques Plante, Gerry McNeil, Doug Harvey, Tom Johnson, Bob Turner, Dollard St. Laurent, Jean-Guy Talbot, Albert Langlois, Jean Béliveau, Bernie Geoffrion, Maurice Richard (Captain), Dickie Moore, Claude Provost, Floyd Curry, Bert Olmstead, Henri Richard, Marcel Bonin, Phil Goyette, Don Marshall, André Pronovost, Connie Broden, Ab McDonald, Frank Selke (Manager), Toe Blake (Coach), Hector Dubois, Larry Aubut (Trainers).
Scores: April 8, at Montreal — Montreal 2, Boston 1; April 10, at Montreal — Boston 5, Montreal 2; April 13, at Boston — Montreal 3, Boston 0; April 15, at Boston — Boston 3, Montreal 1; April 17, at Montreal — Montreal 3, Boston 2; April 20, at Boston — Montreal 5, Boston 3.

1956-57 — Montreal Canadiens — Jacques Plante, Gerry McNeil, Doug Harvey, Tom Johnson, Bob Turner, Dollard St. Laurent, Jean-Guy Talbot, Jean Béliveau, Bernie Geoffrion, Floyd Curry, Dickie Moore, Maurice Richard (Captain), Claude Provost, Bert Olmstead, Henri Richard, Phil Goyette, Don Marshall, André Pronovost, Connie Broden, Frank Selke (Manager), Toe Blake (Coach), Hector Dubois, Larry Aubut (Trainers).
Scores: April 6, at Montreal — Montreal 5, Boston 1; April 9, at Montreal — Montreal 1, Boston 0; April 11, at Boston — Montreal 4, Boston 2; April 14, at Boston — Boston 2, Montreal 0; April 16, at Montreal — Montreal 5, Boston 1.

1955-56 — Montreal Canadiens — Jacques Plante, Doug Harvey, Butch Bouchard (Captain), Bob Turner, Tom Johnson, Jean-Guy Talbot, Dollard St. Laurent, Jean Béliveau, Bernie Geoffrion, Bert Olmstead, Floyd Curry, Jack Leclair, Maurice Richard, Dickie Moore, Henri Richard, Ken Mosdell, Don Marshall, Claude Provost, Frank Selke (Manager), Toe Blake (Coach), Hector Dubois (Trainer).
Scores: March 31, at Montreal — Montreal 6, Detroit 4; April 3, at Montreal — Montreal 5, Detroit 1; April 5, at Detroit — Detroit 3, Montreal 1; April 8, at Detroit — Montreal 3, Detroit 0; April 10, at Montreal — Montreal 3, Detroit 1.

1954-55 — Detroit Red Wings — Terry Sawchuk, Red Kelly, Bob Goldham, Marcel Pronovost, Benny Woit, Jim Hay, Larry Hillman, Ted Lindsay (Captain), Tony Leswick, Gordie Howe, Alex Delvecchio, Marty Pavelich, Glen Skov, Earl Reibel, Johnny Wilson, Bill Dineen, Vic Stasiuk, Marcel Bonin, Jack Adams (Manager), Jimmy Skinner (Coach), Carl Mattson (Trainer).
Scores: April 3, at Detroit — Detroit 4, Montreal 2; April 5, at Detroit — Detroit 7, Montreal 1, April 7, at Montreal — Montreal 4, Detroit 2; April 9, at Montreal — Montreal 5, Detroit 3; April 10, at Detroit — Detroit 5, Montreal 1; April 12, at Montreal — Montreal 6, Detroit 3; April 14, at Detroit — Detroit 3, Montreal 1.

1953-54 — Detroit Red Wings — Terry Sawchuk, Red Kelly, Bob Goldham, Benny Woit, Marcel Pronovost, Al Arbour, Keith Allen, Ted Lindsay (Captain), Tony Leswick, Gordie Howe, Marty Pavelich, Alex Delvecchio, Gilles Dube, Glen Skov, Johnny Wilson, Bill Dineen, Jimmy Peters, Earl Reibel, Vic Stasiuk, Jack Adams (Manager), Tommy Ivan (Coach), Carl Mattson (Trainer).
Scores: April 4, at Detroit — Detroit 3, Montreal 1; April 6, at Detroit — Montreal 3, Detroit 1; April 8, at Montreal — Detroit 5, Montreal 2; April 10, at Montreal — Detroit 2, Montreal 0; April 11, at Detroit — Montreal 1, Detroit 0; April 13, at Montreal — Montreal 4, Detroit 1; April 16, at Detroit — Detroit 2, Montreal 1.

1952-53 — Montreal Canadiens — Gerry McNeil, Jacques Plante, Doug Harvey, Butch Bouchard (Captain), Tom Johnson, Dollard St. Laurent, Bud MacPherson, Maurice Richard, Elmer Lach, Paul Meger, Bert Olmstead, Floyd Curry, Paul Masnick, Billy Reay, Dickie Moore, Ken Mosdell, Dick Gamble, John McCormack, Lorne Davis, Calum MacKay, Eddie Mazur, Frank Selke (Manager), Dick Irvin (Coach), Hector Dubois (Trainer).
Scores: April 9, at Montreal — Montreal 4, Boston 2; April 11, at Montreal — Boston 4, Montreal 1; April 12, at Boston — Montreal 3, Boston 0; April 14, at Boston — Montreal 7, Boston 3; April 16, at Montreal — Montreal 1, Boston 0.

1951-52 — Detroit Red Wings — Terry Sawchuk, Bob Goldham, Benny Woit, Red Kelly, Leo Reise Jr., Marcel Pronovost, Ted Lindsay, Tony Leswick, Gordie Howe, Metro Prystai, Marty Pavelich, Sid Abel (Captain), Glen Skov, Alex Delvecchio, John Wilson, Vic Stasiuk, Larry Zeidel, Jack Adams (Manager) Tommy Ivan (Coach), Carl Mattson (Trainer).
Scores: April 10, at Montreal — Detroit 3, Montreal 1; April 12, at Montreal — Detroit 2, Montreal 1; April 13, at Detroit — Detroit 3, Montreal 0; April 15, at Detroit — Detroit 3, Montreal 0.

1950-51 — Toronto Maple Leafs — Turk Broda, Al Rollins, Jimmy Thomson, Gus Mortson, Bill Barilko, Bill Juzda, Fern Flaman, Hugh Bolton, Ted Kennedy (Captain), Sid Smith, Tod Sloan, Cal Gardner, Howie Meeker, Harry Watson, Max Bentley, Joe Klukay, Danny Lewicki, Ray Timgren, Fleming Mackell, John McCormack, Bob Hassard, Conn Smythe (Manager), Joe Primeau (Coach), Tim Daly (Trainer).
Scores: April 11, at Toronto — Toronto 3, Montreal 2; April 14, at Toronto — Montreal 3, Toronto 2; April 17, at Montreal — Toronto 2, Montreal 1; April 19, at Montreal — Toronto 3, Montreal 2; April 21, at Toronto — Toronto 3, Montreal 2.

1949-50 — Detroit Red Wings — Harry Lumley, Jack Stewart, Leo Reise Jr., Clare Martin, Doug McKay, Al Dewsbury, Lee Fogolin, Marcel Pronovost, Red Kelly, Ted Lindsay, Sid Abel (Captain), Gordie Howe, George Gee, Jimmy Peters, Marty Pavelich, Jim McFadden, Pete Babando, Max McNab, Gerry Couture, Joe Carveth, Steve Black, Johnny Wilson, Larry Wilson, Jack Adams (Manager), Tommy Ivan (Coach), Carl Mattson (Trainer).
Scores: April 11, at Detroit — NY Rangers 1; April 13, at Toronto* — NY Rangers 3, Detroit 1; April 15, at Toronto — Detroit 4, NY Rangers 3; April 18, at Detroit — NY Rangers 4, Detroit 3; April 20, at Detroit — NY Rangers 2, Detroit 1; April 22, at Detroit — Detroit 5, NY Rangers 4; April 23, at Detroit — Detroit 4, NY Rangers 3.

* Ice was unavailable in Madison Square Garden and Rangers elected to play second and third games on Toronto ice.

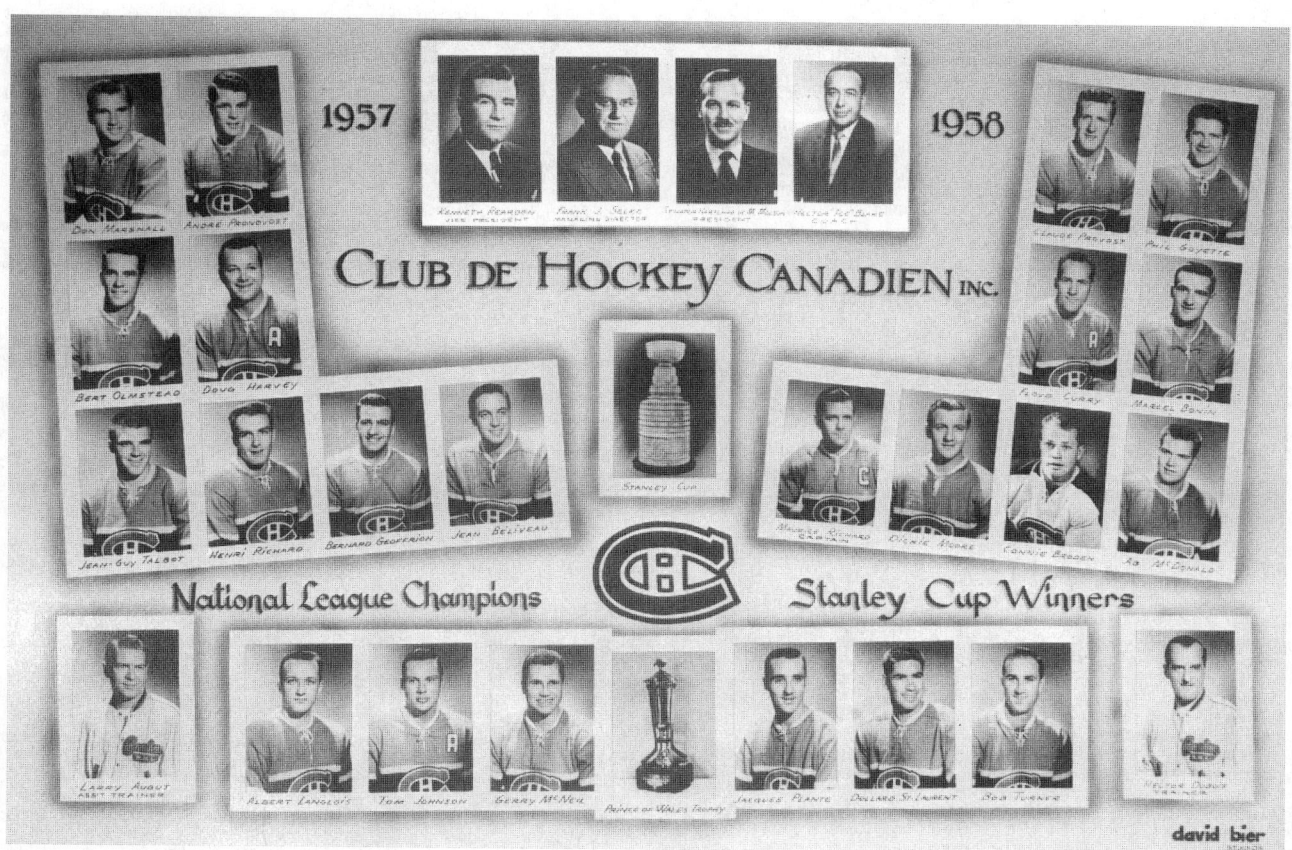

Montreal's third straight Stanley Cup championship in 1958 equaled the NHL record set by the Toronto Maple Leafs between 1947 and 1949. The Canadiens would go on to make it five in a row with wins again in 1959 and 1960.

1948-49 — Toronto Maple Leafs — Turk Broda, Jimmy Thomson, Gus Mortson, Bill Barilko, Garth Boesch, Bill Juzda, Ted Kennedy (Captain), Howie Meeker, Vic Lynn, Harry Watson, Bill Ezinicki, Cal Gardner, Max Bentley, Joe Klukay, Sid Smith, Don Metz, Ray Timgren, Fleming MacKell, Harry Taylor, Bob Dawes, Tod Sloan, Conn Smythe (Manager), Hap Day (Coach), Tim Daly (Trainer).
Scores: April 8, at Detroit — Toronto 3, Detroit 2; April 10, at Detroit — Toronto 3, Detroit 1; April 13, at Toronto — Toronto 3, Detroit 1; April 16, at Toronto — Toronto 3, Detroit 1.

1947-48 — Toronto Maple Leafs — Turk Broda, Jimmy Thomson, Wally Stanowski, Garth Boesch, Bill Barilko, Gus Mortson, Phil Samis, Syl Apps (Captain), Bill Ezinicki, Harry Watson, Ted Kennedy, Howie Meeker, Vic Lynn, Nick Metz, Max Bentley, Joe Klukay, Les Costello, Don Metz, Sid Smith, Conn Smythe (Manager), Hap Day (Coach), Tim Daly (Trainer).
Scores: April 7, at Toronto — Toronto 5, Detroit 3; April 10, at Toronto — Toronto 4, Detroit 2; April 11, at Detroit — Toronto 2, Detroit 0; April 14, at Detroit — Toronto 7, Detroit 2.

1946-47 — Toronto Maple Leafs — Turk Broda, Garth Boesch, Gus Mortson, Jimmy Thomson, Wally Stanowski, Bill Barilko, Harry Watson, Bud Poile, Ted Kennedy, Syl Apps (Captain), Don Metz, Nick Metz, Bill Ezinicki, Vic Lynn, Howie Meeker, Gaye Stewart, Joe Klukay, Gus Bodnar, Bob Goldham, Conn Smythe (Manager), Hap Day (Coach), Tim Daly (Trainer).
Scores: April 8, at Montreal — Montreal 6, Toronto 0; April 10, at Montreal — Toronto 4, Montreal 0; April 12, at Toronto — Toronto 4, Montreal 2; April 15, at Toronto — Toronto 2, Montreal 1; April 17, at Montreal — Montreal 3, Toronto 1; April 19, at Toronto — Toronto 2, Montreal 1.

1945-46 — Montreal Canadiens — Elmer Lach, Toe Blake (Captain), Maurice Richard, Bob Fillion, Dutch Hiller, Murph Chamberlain, Ken Mosdell, Buddy O'Connor, Glen Harmon, Jimmy Peters, Butch Bouchard, Billy Reay, Ken Reardon, Leo Lamoureux, Frank Eddolls, Gerry Plamondon, Bill Durnan, Tommy Gorman (Manager), Dick Irvin (Coach), Ernie Cook (Trainer).
Scores: March 30, at Montreal — Montreal 4, Boston 3; April 2, at Montreal — Montreal 3, Boston 2; April 4, at Boston — Montreal 4, Boston 2; April 7, at Boston — Boston 3, Montreal 2; April 9, at Montreal — Montreal 6, Boston 3.

1944-45 — Toronto Maple Leafs — Don Metz, Frank McCool, Wally Stanowski, Reg Hamilton, Moe Morris, John McCreedy, Tom O'Neill, Ted Kennedy, Babe Pratt, Gus Bodnar, Art Jackson, Jack McLean, Mel Hill, Nick Metz, Bob Davidson (Captain), Sweeney Schriner, Lorne Carr, Conn Smythe (Manager), Frank Selke (Business Manager), Hap Day (Coach), Tim Daly (Trainer).
Scores: April 6, at Detroit — Toronto 1, Detroit 0; April 8, at Detroit — Toronto 2, Detroit 0; April 12, at Toronto — Toronto 1, Detroit 0; April 14, at Toronto — Detroit 5, Toronto 3; April 19, at Detroit — Detroit 2, Toronto 0; April 21, at Toronto — Detroit 1, Toronto 0; April 22, at Detroit — Toronto 2, Detroit 1.

1943-44 — Montreal Canadiens — Toe Blake (Captain), Maurice Richard, Elmer Lach, Ray Getliffe, Murph Chamberlain, Phil Watson, Butch Bouchard, Glen Harmon, Buddy O'Connor, Gerry Heffernan, Mike McMahon, Leo Lamoureux, Fern Majeau, Bob Fillion, Bill Durnan, Tommy Gorman (Manager), Dick Irvin (Coach), Ernie Cook (Trainer).
Scores: April 4, at Montreal — Montreal 5, Chicago 1; April 6, at Chicago — Montreal 3, Chicago 1; April 9, at Chicago — Montreal 3, Chicago 2; April 13, at Montreal — Montreal 5, Chicago 4.

1942-43 — Detroit Red Wings — Jack Stewart, Jimmy Orlando, Sid Abel (Captain), Alex Motter, Harry Watson, Joe Carveth, Mud Bruneteau, Eddie Wares, Johnny Mowers, Cully Simon, Don Grosso, Carl Liscombe, Connie Brown, Syd Howe, Les Douglas, Harold Jackson, Joe Fisher, Jack Adams (Manager), Ebbie Goodfellow (Playing Coach), Honey Walker (Trainer).
Scores: April 1, at Detroit — Detroit 6, Boston 2; April 4, at Detroit — Detroit 4, Boston 3; April 7, at Boston — Detroit 4, Boston 0; April 8, at Boston — Detroit 2, Boston 0.

1941-42 — Toronto Maple Leafs — Wally Stanowski, Syl Apps (Captain), Bob Goldham, Gordie Drillon, Hank Goldup, Ernie Dickens, Sweeney Schriner, Bucko McDonald, Bob Davidson, Nick Metz, Bingo Kampman, Don Metz, Gaye Stewart, Turk Broda, John McCreedy, Lorne Carr, Pete Langelle, Billy Taylor, Conn Smythe (Manager), Hap Day (Coach), Frank Selke (Business Manager), Tim Daly (Trainer).
Scores: April 4, at Toronto — Detroit 3, Toronto 2; April 7, at Toronto — Detroit 4, Toronto 2; April 9, at Detroit — Detroit 5, Toronto 2; April 12, at Detroit — Toronto 4, Detroit 3; April 14, at Toronto — Toronto 9, Detroit 3; April 16, at Detroit — Toronto 3, Detroit 0; April 18, at Toronto — Toronto 3, Detroit 1.

1940-41 — Boston Bruins — Bill Cowley, Des Smith, Dit Clapper (Captain), Frank Brimsek, Flash Hollett, Jack Crawford, Bobby Bauer, Pat McReavy, Herb Cain, Mel Hill, Milt Schmidt, Woody Dumart, Roy Conacher, Terry Reardon, Art Jackson, Eddie Wiseman, Art Ross (Manager), Cooney Weiland (Coach), Win Green (Trainer).
Scores: April 6, at Boston — Detroit 2, Boston 3; April 8, at Boston — Detroit 1, Boston 2; April 10, at Detroit — Boston 4, Detroit 2; April 12, at Detroit — Boston 3, Detroit 1.

1939-40 — New York Rangers — Dave Kerr, Art Coulter (Captain), Ott Heller, Alex Shibicky, Mac Colville, Neil Colville, Phil Watson, Lynn Patrick, Clint Smith, Muzz Patrick, Babe Pratt, Bryan Hextall, Kilby MacDonald, Dutch Hiller, Alf Pike, Stan Smith, Lester Patrick (Manager), Frank Boucher (Coach), Harry Westerby (Trainer).
Scores: April 2, at New York — NY Rangers 2, Toronto 1; April 3, at New York — NY Rangers 6, Toronto 2; April 6, at Toronto — NY Rangers 1, Toronto 2; April 9, at Toronto — NY Rangers 0, Toronto 3; April 11, at Toronto — NY Rangers 2, Toronto 1; April 13, at Toronto — NY Rangers 3, Toronto 2.

1938-39 — Boston Bruins — Bobby Bauer, Mel Hill, Flash Hollett, Roy Conacher, Gord Pettinger, Charlie Sands, Milt Schmidt, Woody Dumart, Jack Crawford, Ray Getliffe, Frank Brimsek, Eddie Shore, Dit Clapper, Bill Cowley, Jack Portland, Red Hamill, Cooney Weiland (Captain), Art Ross (Manager-Coach), Win Green (Trainer).
Scores: April 6, at Boston — Toronto 1, Boston 2; April 9, at Boston — Toronto 3, Boston 2; April 11, at Toronto — Toronto 1, Boston 3; April 13, at Toronto — Toronto 0, Boston 2; April 16, at Boston — Toronto 1, Boston 3.

1937-38 — Chicago Black Hawks — Art Wiebe, Carl Voss, Harold Jackson, Mike Karakas, Mush March, Jack Shill, Earl Seibert, Cully Dahlstrom, Alex Levinsky, Johnny Gottselig (Captain), Lou Trudel, Pete Palangio, Bill MacKenzie, Doc Romnes, Paul Thompson, Roger Jenkins, Alfie Moore, Bert Connelly, Virgil Johnson, Paul Goodman, Bill Stewart (Manager-Coach), Eddie Froelich (Trainer).
Scores: April 5, at Toronto — Chicago 3, Toronto 1; April 7, at Toronto — Chicago 1, Toronto 5; April 10, at Chicago — Chicago 2, Toronto 1; April 12, at Chicago — Chicago 4, Toronto 1.

1936-37 — Detroit Red Wings — Normie Smith, Pete Kelly, Larry Aurie, Herbie Lewis, Hec Kilrea, Mud Bruneteau, Syd Howe, Wally Kilrea, Jimmy Franks, Bucko McDonald, Gord Pettinger, Ebbie Goodfellow, John Gallagher, Ralph Bowman, John Sorrell, Marty Barry, Earl Robertson, John Sherf, Howie Mackie, Rolly Roulston, Doug Young (Captain), Jack Adams (Manager-Coach), Honey Walker (Trainer).
Scores: April 6, at New York — Detroit 1, NY Rangers 5; April 8, at Detroit — Detroit 4, NY Rangers 2; April 11, at Detroit — Detroit 0, NY Rangers 1; April 13, at Detroit — Detroit 1, NY Rangers 0; April 15, at Detroit — Detroit 3, NY Rangers 0.

1935-36 — Detroit Red Wings — John Sorrell, Syd Howe, Marty Barry, Herbie Lewis, Mud Bruneteau, Wally Kilrea, Hec Kilrea, Gord Pettinger, Bucko McDonald, Ralph Bowman, Pete Kelly, Doug Young (Captain), Ebbie Goodfellow, Normie Smith, Larry Aurie, Jack Adams (Manager-Coach), Honey Walker (Trainer).
Scores: April 5, at Detroit — Detroit 3, Toronto 1; April 7, at Detroit — Detroit 9, Toronto 4; April 9, at Toronto — Detroit 3, Toronto 4; April 11, at Toronto — Detroit 3, Toronto 2.

1934-35 — Montreal Maroons — Lionel Conacher, Cy Wentworth, Alex Connell, Toe Blake, Stewart Evans, Earl Robinson, Bill Miller, Dave Trottier, Jimmy Ward, Baldy Northcott, Hooley Smith, Russ Blinco, Al Shields, Sammy McManus, Gus Marker, Bob Gracie, Herb Cain, Tommy Gorman (Manager-Coach), Bill O'Brien (Trainer).
Scores: April 4, at Toronto — Mtl. Maroons 3, Toronto 2; April 6, at Toronto — Mtl. Maroons 3, Toronto 1; April 9, at Montreal — Mtl. Maroons 4, Toronto 1.

1933-34 — Chicago Black Hawks — Clarence Abel, Rosie Couture, Lou Trudel, Lionel Conacher, Paul Thompson, Leroy Goldsworthy, Art Coulter, Roger Jenkins, Don McFadyen, Tom Cook, Doc Romnes, Johnny Gottselig, Mush March, Johnny Sheppard, Charlie Gardiner (Captain), Bill Kendall, Tommy Gorman (Manager-Coach), Eddie Froelich (Trainer).
Scores: April 3, at Detroit — Chicago 2, Detroit 1; April 5, at Detroit — Chicago 4, Detroit 1; April 8, at Chicago — Detroit 5, Chicago 2; April 10, at Chicago — Chicago 1, Detroit 0.

1932-33 — New York Rangers — Ching Johnson, Butch Keeling, Frank Boucher, Art Somers, Babe Siebert, Bun Cook, Andy Aitkenhead, Ott Heller, Oscar Asmundson, Gord Pettinger, Doug Brennan, Cecil Dillon, Bill Cook (Captain), Murray Murdoch, Earl Seibert, Lester Patrick (Manager-Coach), Harry Westerby (Trainer).
Scores: April 4, at New York — NY Rangers 5, Toronto 1; April 8, at Toronto — NY Rangers 3, Toronto 1; April 11, at Toronto — Toronto 3, NY Rangers 2; April 13, at Toronto — NY Rangers 1, Toronto 0.

1931-32 — Toronto Maple Leafs — Charlie Conacher, Busher Jackson, King Clancy, Andy Blair, Red Horner, Lorne Chabot, Alex Levinsky, Joe Primeau, Harold Darragh, Baldy Cotton, Frank Finnigan, Hap Day (Captain), Ace Bailey, Bob Gracie, Fred Robertson, Earl Miller, Conn Smythe (Manager), Dick Irvin (Coach), Tim Daly (Trainer).
Scores: April 5, at New York — Toronto 6, NY Rangers 4; April 7, at Boston* — Toronto 6, NY Rangers 2; April 9, at Toronto — Toronto 6, NY Rangers 4.

* Ice was unavailable in Madison Square Garden and Rangers elected to play the second game on neutral ice.

1930-31 — Montreal Canadiens — George Hainsworth, Wildor Larochelle, Marty Burke, Sylvio Mantha (Captain), Howie Morenz, Johnny Gagnon, Aurel Joliat, Armand Mondou, Pit Lepine, Albert Leduc, Georges Mantha, Art Lesieur, Nick Wasnie, Bert McCaffrey, Gus Rivers, Jean Pusie, Léo Dandurand (Manager), Cecil Hart (Coach), Ed Dufour (Trainer).
Scores: April 3, at Chicago — Montreal 2, Chicago 1; April 5, at Chicago — Chicago 2, Montreal 1; April 9, at Montreal — Chicago 3, Montreal 2; April 11, at Montreal — Montreal 4, Chicago 2; April 14, at Montreal — Montreal 2, Chicago 0.

1929-30 — Montreal Canadiens — George Hainsworth, Marty Burke, Sylvio Mantha (Captain), Howie Morenz, Bert McCaffrey, Aurel Joliat, Albert Leduc, Pit Lepine, Wildor Larochelle, Nick Wasnie, Gerry Carson, Armand Mondou, Georges Mantha, Gus Rivers, Léo Dandurand (Manager), Cecil Hart (Coach), Ed Dufour (Trainer).
Scores: April 1, at Boston — Montreal 3, Boston 0; April 3, at Montreal — Montreal 4, Boston 3.

1928-29 — Boston Bruins — Tiny Thompson, Eddie Shore, Lionel Hitchman (Captain), Percy Galbraith, Eric Pettinger, Frank Fredrickson, Mickey Mackay, Red Green, Dutch Gainor, Harry Oliver, Eddie Rodden, Dit Clapper, Cooney Weiland, Lloyd Klein, Cy Denneny, Bill Carson, George Owen, Myles Lane, Art Ross (Manager-Coach), Win Green (Trainer).
Scores: March 28, at Boston — Boston 2, NY Rangers 0; March 29, at New York — Boston 2, NY Rangers 1.

1927-28 — New York Rangers — Lorne Chabot, Clarence Abel, Leo Bourgeault, Ching Johnson, Bill Cook (Captain), Bun Cook, Frank Boucher, Bill Boyd, Murray Murdoch, Paul Thompson, Alex Gray, Joe Miller, Patsy Callighen, Lester Patrick (Manager-Coach), Harry Westerby (Trainer).
Scores: April 5, at Montreal — Mtl. Maroons 2, NY Rangers 0; April 7, at Montreal — NY Rangers 2, Mtl. Maroons 1; April 10, at Montreal — Mtl. Maroons 2, NY Rangers 0; April 12, at Montreal — NY Rangers 1, Mtl. Maroons 0; April 14, at Montreal — NY Rangers 2, Mtl. Maroons 1.

1926-27 — Ottawa Senators — Alex Connell, King Clancy, Georges Boucher, Ed Gorman, Frank Finnigan, Alex Smith, Hec Kilrea, Hooley Smith, Cy Denneny, Frank Nighbor, Jack Adams, Milt Halliday, Dave Gill (Manager-Coach).
Scores: April 7, at Boston — Ottawa 0, Boston 0; April 9, at Boston — Ottawa 3, Boston 1; April 11, at Ottawa — Boston 1, Ottawa 1; April 13, at Ottawa — Ottawa 3, Boston 1.

1925-26 — Montreal Maroons — Clint Benedict, Reg Noble, Frank Carson, Dunc Munro, Nels Stewart, Punch Broadbent, Babe Siebert, Chuck Dinsmore, Merlyn Phillips, Hobie Kitchen, Sam Rothschild, Albert Holway, George Horne, Bernie Brophy, Eddie Gerard (Manager-Coach), Bill O'Brien (Trainer).
Scores: March 30, at Montreal — Mtl. Maroons 3, Victoria 0; April 1, at Montreal — Mtl. Maroons 3, Victoria 0; April 3, at Montreal — Victoria 3, Mtl. Maroons 2; April 6, at Montreal — Mtl. Maroons 2, Victoria 0.

The series in the spring of 1926 ended the annual playoffs between the champions of the East and the champions of the West. Since 1926-27 the annual playoffs in the National Hockey League have decided the Stanley Cup champions.

1924-25 — Victoria Cougars — Hap Holmes, Clem Loughlin, Gord Fraser, Frank Fredrickson, Jack Walker, Gizzy Hart, Harold Halderson, Frank Foyston, Wally Elmer, Harry Meeking, Jocko Anderson, Lester Patrick (Manager-Coach).
Scores: March 21, at Victoria — Victoria 5, Montreal 2; March 23, at Vancouver — Victoria 3, Montreal 1; March 27, at Victoria — Montreal 4, Victoria 2; March 30, at Victoria — Victoria 6, Montreal 1.

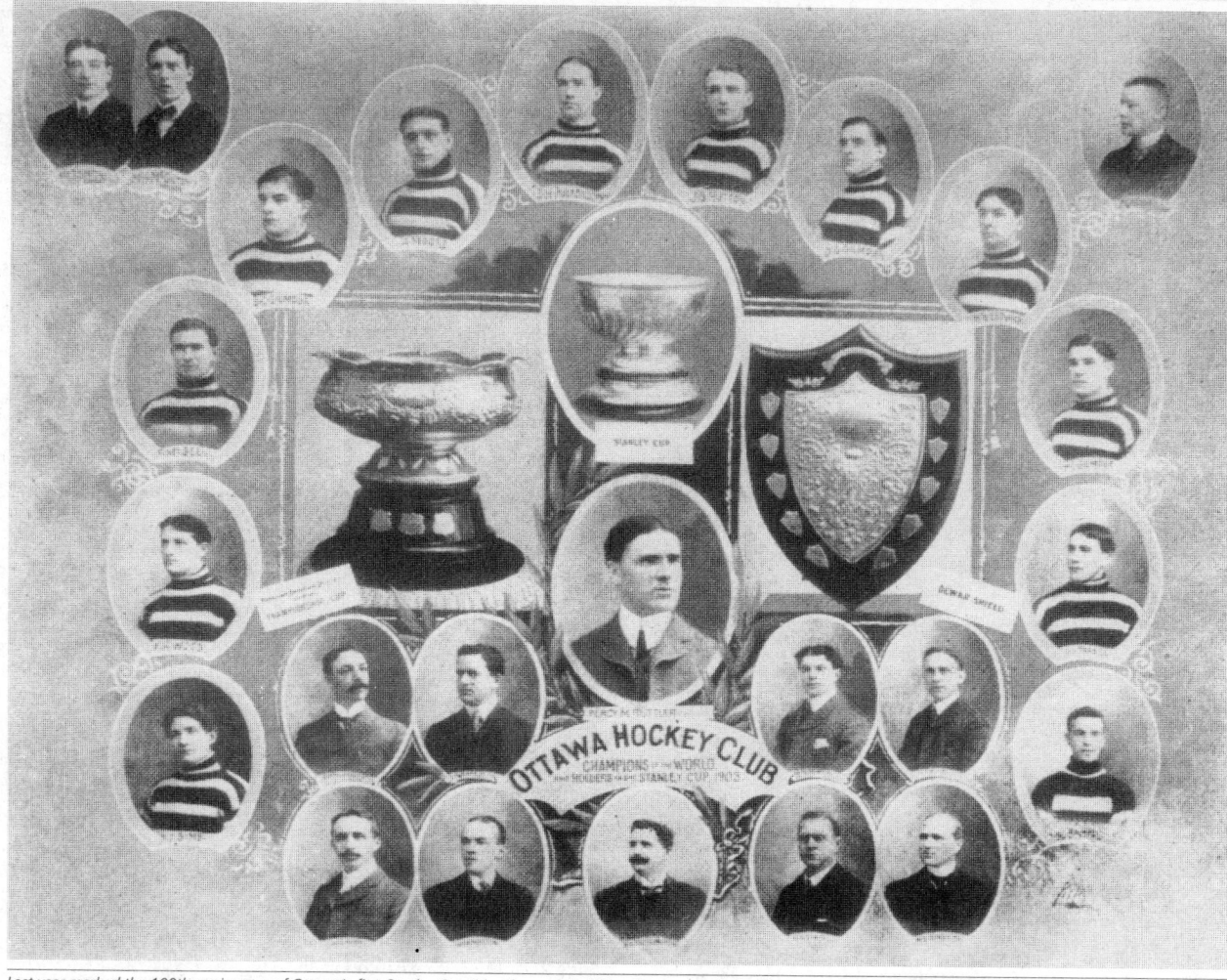

Last year marked the 100th anniversary of Ottawa's first Stanley Cup title. The so-called Silver Seven won the Stanley Cup in 1903, 1904 and 1905. They defeated two more challengers during the 1906 season but were beaten at year's end.

1923-24 — Montreal Canadiens — Georges Vezina, Sprague Cleghorn (Captain), Billy Coutu, Howie Morenz, Aurel Joliat, Billy Boucher, Odie Cleghorn, Sylvio Mantha, Bobby Boucher, Billy Bell, Billy Cameron, Joe Malone, Charles Fortier, Leo Dandurand (Manager-Coach).
Scores: March 18, at Montreal — Montreal 3, Van. Maroons 2; March 20, at Montreal — Montreal 2, Van. Maroons 1. March 22, at Montreal — Montreal 6, Cgy. Tigers 1; March 25, at Ottawa* — Montreal 3, Cgy. Tigers 0.
* Game transferred to Ottawa to benefit from artificial ice surface.

1922-23 — Ottawa Senators — Georges Boucher, Lionel Hitchman, Frank Nighbor, King Clancy, Harry Helman, Clint Benedict, Jack Darragh, Eddie Gerard, Cy Denneny, Punch Broadbent, Tommy Gorman (Manager), Pete Green (Coach), F. Dolan (Trainer).
Scores: March 16, at Vancouver — Ottawa 1, Van. Maroons 0; March 19, at Vancouver — Van. Maroons 4, Ottawa 1; March 23, at Vancouver — Ottawa 3, Van. Maroons 2; March 26, at Vancouver — Ottawa 5, Van. Maroons 1; March 29, at Vancouver — Ottawa 2, Edm. Eskimos 1; March 31, at Vancouver — Ottawa 1, Edm. Eskimos 0.

1921-22 — Toronto St. Pats — Ted Stackhouse, Corb Denneny, Rod Smylie, Lloyd Andrews, John Ross Roach, Harry Cameron, Billy Stuart, Babe Dye, Ken Randall, Reg Noble, Eddie Gerard (borrowed for one game from Ottawa), Stan Jackson, Ivan Mitchell, Charlie Querrie (Manager), George O'Donoghue (Coach).
Scores: March 17, at Toronto — Van. Millionaires 4, Toronto 3; March 20, at Toronto — Toronto 2, Van. Millionaires 1; March 23, at Toronto — Van. Millionaires 3, Toronto 0; March 25, at Toronto — Toronto 6, Van. Millionaires 0; March 28, at Toronto — Toronto 5, Van. Millionaires 1.

1920-21 — Ottawa Senators — Jack MacKell, Jack Darragh, Morley Bruce, Georges Boucher, Eddie Gerard, Clint Benedict, Sprague Cleghorn, Frank Nighbor, Punch Broadbent, Cy Denneny, Leth Graham, Tommy Gorman (Manager), Pete Green (Coach), F. Dolan (Trainer).
Scores: March 21, at Vancouver — Van. Millionaires 2, Ottawa 1; March 24, at Vancouver — Ottawa 4, Van. Millionaires 3; March 28, at Vancouver — Ottawa 3, Van. Millionaires 2; March 31, at Vancouver — Van. Millionaires 3, Ottawa 2; April 4, at Vancouver — Ottawa 2, Van. Millionaires 1

1919-20 — Ottawa Senators — Jack MacKell, Jack Darragh, Morley Bruce, Horrace Merrill, Georges Boucher, Eddie Gerard, Clint Benedict, Sprague Cleghorn, Frank Nighbor, Punch Broadbent, Cy Denneny, Tommy Gorman (Manager), Pete Green (Coach).
Scores: March 22, at Ottawa — Ottawa 3, Seattle 2; March 24, at Ottawa — Ottawa 3, Seattle 0; March 27, at Ottawa — Seattle 3, Ottawa 1; March 30, at Toronto* — Seattle 5, Ottawa 2; April 1, at Toronto* — Ottawa 6, Seattle 1.
* Games transferred to Toronto to benefit from artificial ice surface.

1918-19 — No decision, Series halted by Spanish influenza epidemic, illness of several players and death of Joe Hall of Montreal Canadiens from flu. Five games had been played when the series was halted, each team having won two and tied one. The results are shown:
Scores: March 19, at Seattle — Seattle 7, Montreal 0; March 22, at Seattle — Montreal 4, Seattle 2; March 24, at Seattle — Seattle 7, Montreal 2, at Seattle — Montreal 0, Seattle 0; March 30, at Seattle — Montreal 4, Seattle 3.

1917-18 — Toronto Arenas — Rusty Crawford, Harry Meeking, Ken Randall, Corb Denneny, Harry Cameron, Jack Adams, Alf Skinner, Harry Mummery, Hap Holmes, Reg Noble, Sammy Hebert, Jack Marks, Jack Coughlin, Charlie Querrie (Manager), Dick Carroll (Coach), Frank Carroll (Trainer).
Scores: March 20, at Toronto — Toronto 5, Van. Millionaires 3; March 23, at Toronto — Van. Millionaires 6, Toronto 4; March 26, at Toronto — Toronto 6, Van. Millionaires 3; March 28, at Toronto — Van. Millionaires 8, Toronto 1; March 30, at Toronto — Toronto 2, Van. Millionaires 1.

1916-17 — Seattle Metropolitans — Hap Holmes, Ed Carpenter, Cully Wilson, Jack Walker, Bernie Morris, Frank Foyston, Roy Rickey, Jim Riley, Bobby Rowe (Captain), Peter Muldoon (Manager).
Scores: March 17, at Seattle — Montreal 8, Seattle 4; March 20, at Seattle — Seattle 6, Montreal 1; March 23, at Seattle — Seattle 4, Montreal 1; March 25, at Seattle — Seattle 9, Montreal 1.

1915-16 — Montreal Canadiens — Georges Vezina, Bert Corbeau, Jack Laviolette, Newsy Lalonde, Louis Berlinquette, Goldie Prodgers, Howard McNamara (Captain), Didier Pitre, Skene Ronan, Amos Arbour, Skinner Poulin, Jack Fournier, George Kennedy (Manager).
Scores: March 20, at Montreal — Portland 2, Montreal 0; March 22, at Montreal — Montreal 2, Portland 1; March 25, at Montreal — Montreal 6, Portland 3; March 28, at Montreal — Portland 6, Montreal 5; March 30, at Montreal — Montreal 2, Portland 1.

1914-15 — Vancouver Millionaires — Ken Mallen, Frank Nighbor, Cyclone Taylor, Hugh Lehman, Lloyd Cook, Mickey MacKay, Barney Stanley, Jim Seaborn, Si Griffis (Captain), Johnny Matz, Frank Patrick (Playing Manager).
Scores: March 22, at Vancouver — Van. Millionaires 6, Ottawa 2; March 24, at Vancouver — Van. Millionaires 8, Ottawa 3; March 26, at Vancouver — Van. Millionaires 12, Ottawa 3.

1913-14 — Toronto Blueshirts — Con Corbeau, Roy McGiffen, Jack Walker, George McNamara, Cully Wilson, Frank Foyston, Harry Cameron, Hap Holmes, Scotty Davidson (Captain), Harriston, Jack Marshall (Playing Manager), Frank and Dick Carroll (Trainers).
Scores: March 14, at Toronto — Toronto 5, Victoria 2; March 17, at Toronto — Toronto 6, Victoria 5; March 19, at Toronto — Toronto 2, Victoria 1.

1912-13 — Quebec Bulldogs — Joe Malone, Joe Hall, Paddy Moran, Harry Mummery, Tommy Smith, Jack Marks, Rusty Crawford, Billy Creighton, Jeff Malone, Rocket Power, M.J. Quinn (Manager), D. Beland (Trainer).
Scores: March 8, at Quebec — Que. Bulldogs 14, Sydney 3; March 10, at Quebec — Que. Bulldogs 6, Sydney 2.

Victoria challenged Quebec but the Bulldogs refused to put the Stanley Cup in competition so the two teams played an exhibition series with Victoria winning two games to one by scores of 7-5, 3-6, 6-1. It was the first meeting between the Eastern champions and the Western champions. The following year, and until the Western Hockey League disbanded after the 1926 playoffs, the Cup went to the winner of the series between East and West.

1911-12 — Quebec Bulldogs — Goldie Prodgers, Joe Hall, Walter Rooney, Paddy Moran, Jack Marks, Jack McDonald, Eddie Oatman, George Leonard, Joe Malone (Captain), C. Nolan (Coach), M.J. Quinn (Manager), D. Beland (Trainer).
Scores: March 11, at Quebec — Que. Bulldogs 9, Moncton 3; March 13, at Quebec — Que. Bulldogs 8, Moncton 0.

Prior to 1912, teams could challenge the Stanley Cup champions for the title, thus there was more than one Championship Series played in most of the seasons between 1894 and 1911.

1910-11 — Ottawa Senators — Hamby Shore, Percy LeSueur, Jack Darragh, Bruce Stuart, Marty Walsh, Bruce Ridpath, Fred Lake, Dubbie Kerr, Alex Currie, Horace Gaul.
Scores: March 13, at Ottawa — Ottawa 7, Galt 4; March 16, at Ottawa — Ottawa 13, Port Arthur 4.

1909-10 (March) **— Montreal Wanderers** — Cecil Blachford, Moose Johnson, Ernie Russell, Riley Hern, Harry Hyland, Jack Marshall, Pud Glass (Captain), Jimmy Gardner, Dickie Boon (Manager).
Scores: March 12, at Montreal — Mtl. Wanderers 7, Berlin (Kitchener) 3.

1909-10 (January) **— Ottawa Senators** — Dubbie Kerr, Fred Lake, Percy LeSueur, Ken Mallen, Bruce Ridpath, Gord Roberts, Hamby Shore, Bruce Stuart, Marty Walsh.
Scores: January 5, at Ottawa — Ottawa 12, Galt 3; January 7, at Ottawa — Ottawa 3, Galt 1; January 18, at Ottawa — Ottawa 8, Edmonton 4; January 20, at Ottawa — Ottawa 13, Edmonton 7.

1908-09 — Ottawa Senators — Fred Lake, Percy LeSueur, Cyclone Taylor, Billy Gilmour, Dubbie Kerr, Edgar Dey, Marty Walsh, Bruce Stuart (Captain).
Scores: Ottawa, as champions of the Eastern Canada Hockey Association took over the Stanley Cup in 1909 and, although a challenge was accepted by the Cup trustees from Winnipeg Shamrocks, games could not be arranged because of the lateness of the season. No other challenges were made in 1909. The following season — 1909-10 — however, the Senators accepted two challenges as defending Cup Champions. The first was against Galt in a two-game, total-goals series, and the second against Edmonton, also a two-game, total-goals series. Results: January 5, at Ottawa —Ottawa 12, Galt 3; January 7, at Ottawa — Ottawa 3, Galt 1. January 18, at Ottawa — Ottawa 8, Edm. Eskimos 4; January 20, at Ottawa — Ottawa 13, Edm. Eskimos 7.

1907-08 — Montreal Wanderers — Riley Hern, Art Ross, Walter Smaill, Pud Glass, Bruce Stuart, Ernie Russell, Moose Johnson, Cecil Blachford (Captain), Tom Hooper, Larry Gilmour, Ernie Liffiton, Dickie Boon (Manager).
Scores: Wanderers accepted four challenges for the Cup: January 9, at Montreal — Mtl. Wanderers 9, Ott. Victorias 3; January 13, at Montreal — Mtl. Wanderers 13, Ott. Victorias 1; March 10, at Montreal — Mtl. Wanderers 11, Wpg. Maple Leafs 5; March 12, at Montreal — Mtl. Wanderers 9, Wpg. Maple Leafs 3; March 14, at Montreal — Mtl. Wanderers 6, Toronto (OPHL) 4. At start of following season, 1908-09, Wanderers were challenged by Edmonton. Results: December 28, at Montreal — Mtl. Wanderers 7, Edm. Eskimos 3; December 30, at Montreal — Edm. Eskimos 7, Mtl. Wanderers 6. Total goals: Mtl. Wanderers 13, Edm. Eskimos 10.

1906-07 — (March 25) **— Montreal Wanderers** — Billy Strachan, Riley Hern, Lester Patrick, Hod Stuart, Pud Glass, Ernie Russell, Cecil Blachford (Captain), Moose Johnson, Rod Kennedy, Jack Marshall, Dickie Boon (Manager).

1906-07 — (March 18) **— Kenora Thistles** — Eddie Giroux, Si Griffis, Tom Hooper, Fred Whitcroft, Alf Smith, Harry Westwick, Roxy Beaudro, Tommy Phillips (Captain), Russell Phillips.
Scores: March 16, at Winnipeg — Kenora 8, Brandon 6; March 18, at Winnipeg — Kenora 4, Brandon 1; March 23, at Winnipeg — Mtl. Wanderers 7, Kenora 2; March 25, at Winnipeg — Kenora 6, Mtl. Wanderers 5. Total goals: Mtl. Wanderers 12, Kenora 8.

1906-07 — (January) **— Kenora Thistles** — Eddie Giroux, Art Ross, Si Griffis, Tom Hooper, Billy McGimsie, Roxy Beaudro, Tommy Phillips (Captain), Joe Hall, Russell Phillips.
Scores: January 17, at Montreal — Kenora 4, Mtl. Wanderers 2; Jan. 21, at Montreal — Kenora 8, Mtl. Wanderers 6.

1905-06 — (March) **— Montreal Wanderers** — Henri Menard, Billy Strachan, Rod Kennedy, Lester Patrick, Pud Glass, Ernie Russell, Moose Johnson, Cecil Blachford (Captain), Josh Arnold, Dickie Boon (Manager).
Scores: March 14, at Montreal — Mtl. Wanderers 9, Ottawa 1; March 17, at Ottawa — Ottawa 9, Mtl. Wanderers 3. Total goals: Mtl. Wanderers 12, Ottawa 10. Wanderers accepted a challenge from New Glasgow, N.S., prior to the start of the 1906-07 season. Results: December 27, at Montreal — Mtl. Wanderers 10, New Glasgow 3; December 29, at Montreal — Mtl. Wanderers 7, New Glasgow 2.

1905-06 — (February) **— Ottawa Silver Seven** — Harvey Pulford (Captain), Arthur Moore, Harry Westwick, Frank McGee, Alf Smith (Playing Coach), Billy Gilmour, Billy Hague, Percy LeSueur, Harry Smith, Tommy Smith, Dion, Ebbs.
Scores: February 27, at Ottawa — Ottawa 16, Queen's University 7; February 28, at Ottawa — Ottawa 12, Queen's University 7; March 6, at Ottawa — Ottawa 6, Smiths Falls 5; March 8, at Ottawa — Ottawa 8, Smiths Falls 2.

1904-05 — Ottawa Silver Seven — Dave Finnie, Harvey Pulford (Captain), Arthur Moore, Harry Westwick, Frank McGee, Alf Smith (Playing Coach), Billy Gilmour, Frank White, Horace Gaul, Hamby Shore, Bones Allen.
Scores: January 13, at Ottawa — Ottawa 9, Dawson City 2; January 16, at Ottawa — Ottawa 23, Dawson City 2; March 7, at Ottawa — Rat Portage 9, Ottawa 3; March 9, at Ottawa — Ottawa 4, Rat Portage 2; March 11, at Ottawa — Ottawa 5, Rat Portage 4.

1903-04 — Ottawa Silver Seven — Suddy Gilmour, Arthur Moore, Frank McGee, Bouse Hutton, Billy Gilmour, Jim McGee, Harry Westwick, Harvey Pulford (Captain), Scott, Alf Smith (Playing Coach).
Scores: December 30, at Ottawa — Ottawa 9, Wpg. Rowing Club 1; January 1, at Ottawa — Wpg. Rowing Club 6, Ottawa 2; January 4, at Ottawa — Ottawa 2, Wpg. Rowing Club 0. February 23, at Ottawa — Ottawa 6, Tor. Marlboros 3; February 25, at Ottawa — Ottawa 11, Tor. Marlboros 2; March 2, at Montreal — Ottawa 5, Mtl. Wanderers 5. Following the tie game, a new two-game series was ordered to be played in Ottawa but the Wanderers refused unless the tie game was replayed in Montreal. When no settlement could be reached, the series was abandoned and Ottawa retained the Cup and accepted a two-game challenge from Brandon. Results: (both games at Ottawa), March 9, Ottawa 6, Brandon 3; March 11, Ottawa 9, Brandon 3.

1902-03 — (March) **— Ottawa Silver Seven** — Suddy Gilmour, Percy Sims, Bouse Hutton, Dave Gilmour, Billy Gilmour, Harry Westwick, Frank McGee, F.H. Wood, A.A. Fraser, Charles Spittal, Harvey Pulford (Captain), Arthur Moore, Alf Smith (coach.)
Scores: March 7, at Montreal — Ottawa 1, Mtl. Victorias 1; March 10, at Ottawa — Ottawa 8, Mtl. Victorias 0. Total goals: Ottawa 9, Mtl. Victorias 1; March 12, at Ottawa — Ottawa 6, Rat Portage 2; March 14, at Ottawa — Ottawa 4, Rat Portage 2.

1902-03 — (February) **— Montreal AAA** — Tom Hodge, Dickie Boon, Billy Nicholson, Tommy Phillips, Art Hooper, Billy Bellingham, Charles Liffiton, Jack Marshall, Jimmy Gardner, Cecil Blachford, George Smith.
Scores: January 29, at Montreal — Mtl. AAA 8, Wpg. Victorias 1; January 31, at Montreal — Wpg. Victorias 2, Mtl. AAA 2; February 2, at Montreal — Wpg. Victorias 4, Mtl. AAA 2; February 4, at Montreal — Mtl. AAA 5, Wpg. Victorias 1.

1901-02 — (March) **— Montreal AAA** — Tom Hodge, Dickie Boon, Billy Nicholson, Archie Hooper, Billy Bellingham, Charles Liffiton, Jack Marshall, Roland Elliott, Jimmy Gardner.
Scores: March 13, at Winnipeg — Wpg. Victorias 1, Mtl. AAA 0; March 15, at Winnipeg — Mtl. AAA 5, Wpg. Victorias 0; March 17, at Winnipeg — Mtl. AAA 2, Wpg. Victorias 1.

1901-02 — (January) **— Winnipeg Victorias** — Burke Wood, Tony Gingras, Charles Johnstone, Rod Flett, Magnus Flett, Dan Bain (Captain), Fred Scanlon, F. Cadham, G. Brown.
Scores: January 21, at Winnipeg — Wpg. Victorias 5, Tor Wellingtons 3; January 23, at Winnipeg — Wpg. Victorias 5, Tor. Wellingtons 3.

1900-01 — Winnipeg Victorias — Burke Wood, Jack Marshall, Tony Gingras, Charles Johnstone, Rod Flett, Magnus Flett, Dan Bain (Captain), Art Brown.
Scores: January 29, at Montreal — Wpg. Victorias 4, Mtl. Shamrocks 3; January 31, at Montreal — Wpg. Victorias 2, Mtl. Shamrocks 1.

1899-1900 — Montreal Shamrocks — Joe McKenna, Frank Tansey, Frank Wall, Art Farrell, Fred Scanlon, Harry Trihey (Captain), Jack Brannen.
Scores: February 12, at Montreal — Mtl. Shamrocks 4, Wpg. Victorias 3; February 14, at Montreal — Wpg. Victorias 3, Mtl. Shamrocks 2; February 16, at Montreal — Mtl. Shamrocks 5, Wpg. Victorias 4; March 5, at Montreal — Mtl. Shamrocks 10, Halifax 2; March 7, at Montreal — Mtl. Shamrocks 11, Halifax 0.

1898-99 — (March) **— Montreal Shamrocks** — Joe McKenna, Frank Tansey, Frank Wall, Harry Trihey (Captain), Art Farrell, Fred Scanlon, Jack Brannen, John Dobby, Charles Hoerner.
Scores: March 14, at Montreal — Mtl. Shamrocks 6, Queen's University 2.

1898-99 — (February) **— Montreal Victorias** — Gordon Lewis, Mike Grant, Graham Drinkwater, Cam Davidson, Bob McDougall, Ernie McLea, Frank Richardson, Jack Ewing, Russell Bowie, Douglas Acer, Fred McRobie.
Scores: February 15, at Montreal — Mtl. Victorias 2, Wpg. Victorias 1; February 18, at Montreal — Mtl. Victorias 3, Wpg. Victorias 2.

1897-98 — Montreal Victorias — Gordon Lewis, Hartland McDougall, Mike Grant, Graham Drinkwater, Cam Davidson, Bob McDougall, Ernie McLea, Frank Richardson (Captain), Jack Ewing. The Victorias as champions of the Amateur Hockey Association, retained the Cup and were not called upon to defend it.

1896-97 — Montreal Victorias — Gordon Lewis, Harold Henderson, Mike Grant (Captain), Cam Davidson, Graham Drinkwater, Bob McDougall, Ernie McLea, Shirley Davidson, Hartland McDougall, Jack Ewing, Percy Molson, David Gillilan, McLellan.
Scores: December 27, at Montreal — Mtl. Victorias 15, Ott. Capitals 2.

1895-96 — (December) **— Montreal Victorias** — Harold Henderson, Mike Grant (Captain), Bob McDougall, Graham Drinkwater, Shirley Davidson, Ernie McLea, W. Wallace, Robert Jones, Cam Davidson, David Gillilan, Stanley Willett.
Scores: December 30, at Winnipeg — Mtl. Victorias 6, Wpg. Victorias 5.

1895-96 — (February) **— Winnipeg Victorias** — Whitey Merritt, Rod Flett, Fred Higginbotham, Jack Armitage (Captain), Tote Campbell, Dan Bain, Bobby Benson, Attie Howard.
Scores: February 14, at Montreal — Wpg. Victorias 2, Mtl. Victorias 0.

1894-95 — Montreal Victorias — Robert Jones, Harold Henderson, Mike Grant (Captain), Shirley Davidson, Bob McDougall, Norman Rankin, Graham Drinkwater, Roland Elliot, William Pullan, Hartland McDougall, Art Fenwick, A. McDougall. Montreal Victorias, as champions of the Amateur Hockey Association, were prepared to defend the Stanley Cup. However, the Stanley Cup trustees had already accepted a challenge match between the 1894 champion Montreal AAA and Queen's University. It was declared that if Montreal AAA defeated Queen's University, Montreal Victorias would be declared Stanley Cup champions. If Queen's University won, the Cup would go to the university club. In a game played March 9, 1895, Montreal AAA defeated Queen's University 5-1. As a result, Montreal Victorias were awarded the Stanley Cup.

1893-94 — Montreal AAA — Herb Collins, Allan Cameron, George James, Billy Barlow, Clare Mussen, Archie Hodgson, Haviland Routh, Alex Irving, James Stewart, E. O'Brien, A.C. (Toad) Wand, A.B. Kingan.
Scores: March 17, at Mtl. Victorias — Mtl. AAA 3, Mtl. Victorias 2; March 22, at Montreal — Mtl. AAA 3, Ott. Capitals 1.

1892-93 — Montreal AAA — Tom Paton, James Stewart, Allan Cameron, Haviland Routh, Archie Hodgson, Billy Barlow, A.B. Kingan, G.S. Lowe.
In accordance with the terms governing the presentation of the Stanley Cup, it was awarded for the first time to the Montreal AAA as champions of the Amateur Hockey Association in 1893. Once Montreal AAA had been declared holders of the Stanley Cup, any Canadian hockey team could challenge for the trophy.

All-Time NHL Playoff Formats

1917-18 — The regular-season was split into two halves. The winners of both halves faced each other in a two-game, total-goals series for the NHL championship and the right to meet the PCHA champion in the best-of-five Stanley Cup Finals.

1918-19 — Same as 1917-18, except that the Stanley Cup Finals was extended to a best-of-seven series.

1919-20 — Same as 1917-1918, except that Ottawa won both halves of the split regular-season schedule to earn an automatic berth into the best-of-five Stanley Cup Finals against the PCHA champions.

1921-22 — The top two teams at the conclusion of the regular-season faced each other in a two-game, total-goals series for the NHL championship. The NHL champion then moved on to play the winner of the PCHA-WCHL playoff series in the best-of-five Stanley Cup Finals.

1922-23 — The top two teams at the conclusion of the regular-season faced each other in a two-game, total-goals series for the NHL championship. The NHL champion then moved on to play the PCHA champion in the best-of-three Stanley Cup Semi-Finals, and the winner of the Semi-Finals played the WCHL champion, which had been given a bye, in the best-of-three Stanley Cup Finals.

1923-24 — The top two teams at the conclusion of the regular-season faced each other in a two-game, total-goals series for the NHL championship. The NHL champion then moved on to play the loser of the PCHA-WCHL playoff (the winner of the PCHA-WCHL playoff earned a bye into the Stanley Cup Finals) in the best-of-three Stanley Cup Semi-Finals. The winner of this series met the PCHA-WCHL playoff winner in the best-of-three Stanley Cup Finals.

1924-25 — The first place team (Hamilton) at the conclusion of the regular-season was supposed to play the winner of a two-game, total-goals series between the second (Toronto) and third (Montreal) place clubs. However, Hamilton refused to abide by this new format, demanding greater compensation than offered by the League. Thus, Toronto and Montreal played their two-game, total-goals series, and the winner (Montreal) earned the NHL title and then played the WCHL champion (Victoria) in the best-of-five Stanley Cup Finals.

1925-26 — The format which was intended for 1924-25 went into effect. The winner of the two-game, total-goals series between the second and third place teams squared off against the first place team in the two-game, total-goals NHL championship series. The NHL champion then moved on to play the WHL champion in the best-of-five Stanley Cup Finals.

After the 1925-26 season, the NHL was the only major professional hockey league still in existence and consequently took over sole control of the Stanley Cup competition.

1926-27 — The 10-team league was divided into two divisions — Canadian and American — of five teams apiece. In each division, the winner of the two-game, total-goals series between the second and third place teams faced the first place team in another two-game, total-goals series for the division title. The two division title winners then met in the best-of-five Stanley Cup Finals.

1928-29 — Both first place teams in the two divisions played each other in a best-of-five series. Both second place teams in the two divisions played each other in a two-game, total-goals series as did the two third place teams. The winners of these latter two series then played each other in a best-of-three series for the right to meet the winner of the series between the two first place clubs. This Stanley Cup Final was a best-of-three.

Series A: First in Canadian Division vs. first in American (best-of-five)
Series B: Second in Canadian Division vs. second in American (two-game, total-goals)
Series C: Third in Canadian Division vs. third in American (two-game, total-goals)
Series D: Winner of Series B vs. winner of Series C (best-of-three)
Series E: Winner of Series A vs. winner of Series D (best-of-three) for Stanley Cup

1931-32 — Same as 1928-29, except that Series D was changed to a two-game, total-goals format and Series E was changed to best-of-five.

1936-37 — Same as 1931-32, except that Series B, C, and D were each best-of-three.

1938-39 — With the NHL reduced to seven teams, the two-division system was replaced by one seven-team league. Based on final regular-season standings, the following playoff format was adopted:

Series A: First vs. Second (best-of-seven)
Series B: Third vs. Fourth (best-of-three)
Series C: Fifth vs. Sixth (best-of-three)
Series D: Winner of Series B vs. winner of Series C (best-of-three)
Series E: Winner of Series A vs. winner of Series D (best-of-seven)

1942-43 — With the NHL reduced to six teams (the "original six"), only the top four finishers qualified for playoff action. The best-of-seven Semi-Finals pitted Team #1 vs. Team #3 and Team #2 vs. Team #4. The winners of each Semi-Final series met in the best-of-seven Stanley Cup Finals.

1967-68 — When it doubled in size from 6 to 12 teams, the NHL once again was divided into two divisions — East and West — of six teams apiece. The top four clubs in each division qualified for the playoffs (all series were best-of-seven):

Series A: Team #1 (East) vs. Team #3 (East)
Series B: Team #2 (East) vs. Team #4 (East)
Series C: Team #1 (West) vs. Team #3 (West)
Series D: Team #2 (West) vs. Team #4 (West)
Series E: Winner of Series A vs. winner of Series B
Series F: Winner of Series C vs. winner of Series D
Series G: Winner of Series E vs. Winner of Series F

1970-71 — Same as 1967-68 except that Series E matched the winners of Series A and D, and Series F matched the winners of Series B and C.

1971-72 — Same as 1970-71, except that Series A and C matched Team #1 vs. Team #4, and Series B and D matched Team #2 vs. Team #3.

1974-75 — With the League now expanded to 18 teams in four divisions, a completely new playoff format was introduced. First, the #2 and #3 teams in each of the four divisions were pooled together in the Preliminary round. These eight (#2 and #3) clubs were ranked #1 to #8 based on regular-season record:

Series A: Team #1 vs. Team #8 (best-of-three)
Series B: Team #2 vs. Team #7 (best-of-three)
Series C: Team #3 vs. Team #6 (best-of-three)
Series D: Team #4 vs. Team #5 (best-of-three)
The winners of this Preliminary round then pooled together with the four division winners, which had received byes into this Quarter-Final round. These eight teams were again ranked #1 to #8 based on regular-season record:
Series E: Team #1 vs. Team #8 (best-of-seven)
Series F: Team #2 vs. Team #7 (best-of-seven)
Series G: Team #3 vs. Team #6 (best-of-seven)
Series H: Team #4 vs. Team #5 (best-of-seven)
The four Quarter-Finals winners, which moved on to the Semi-Finals, were then ranked #1 to #4 based on regular season record:
Series I: Team #1 vs. Team #4 (best-of-seven)
Series J: Team #2 vs. Team #3 (best-of-seven)
Series K: Winner of Series I vs. winner of Series J (best-of-seven)

1977-78 — Same as 1974-75, except that the Preliminary round consisted of the #2 teams in the four divisions and the next four teams based on regular-season record (not their standings within their divisions).

1979-80 — With the addition of four WHA franchises, the League expanded its playoff structure to include 16 of its 21 teams. The four first place teams in the four divisions automatically earned playoff berths. Among the 17 other clubs, the top 12, according to regular-season record, also earned berths. All 16 teams were then pooled together and ranked #1 to #16 based on regular-season record:

Series A: Team #1 vs. Team #16 (best-of-five)
Series B: Team #2 vs. Team #15 (best-of-five)
Series C: Team #3 vs. Team #14 (best-of-five)
Series D: Team #4 vs. Team #13 (best-of-five)
Series E: Team #5 vs. Team #12 (best-of-five)
Series F: Team #6 vs. Team #11 (best-of-five)
Series G: Team #7 vs. Team #10 (best-of-five)
Series H: Team #8 vs. Team # 9 (best-of-five)

The eight Preliminary round winners, ranked #1 to #8 based on regular-season record, moved on to the Quarter-Finals:
Series I: Team #1 vs. Team #8 (best-of-seven)
Series J: Team #2 vs. Team #7 (best-of-seven)
Series K: Team #3 vs. Team #6 (best-of-seven)
Series L: Team #4 vs. Team #5 (best-of-seven)
The four Quarter-Finals winners, ranked #1 to #4 based on regular-season record, moved on to the semi-finals:
Series M: Team #1 vs. Team #4 (best-of-seven)
Series N: Team #2 vs. Team #3 (best-of-seven)
Series O: Winner of Series M vs. winner of Series N (best-of-seven)

1981-82 — The first four teams in each division earned playoff berths. In each division, the first-place team opposed the fourth-place team and the second-place team opposed the third-place team in a best-of-five Division Semi-Final series (DSF). In each division, the two winners of the DSF met in a best-of-seven Division Final series (DF). The two DF winners in each conference met in a best-of-seven Conference Final series (CF). In the Prince of Wales Conference, the Adams Division winner opposed the Patrick Division winner; in the Clarence Campbell Conference, the Smythe Division winner opposed the Norris Division winner. The two CF winners met in a best-of-seven Stanley Cup Final (F) series.

1986-87 — Division Semi-Final series changed from best-of-five to best-of-seven.

1993-94 — The NHL's playoff draw is conference-based rather than division-based. At the conclusion of the regular season, the top eight teams in each of the Eastern and Western Conferences qualify for the playoffs. The teams that finish in first place in each of the League's divisions are seeded first and second in each conference's playoff draw and are assured of home ice advantage in the first two playoff rounds. The remaining teams are seeded based on their regular-season point totals. In each conference, the team seeded #1 plays #8; #2 vs. #7; #3 vs. #6; and #4 vs. #5. All series are best-of-seven with home ice rotating on a 2-2-1-1-1 basis, with the exception of matchups between Central and Pacific Division teams. These matchups will be played on a 2-3-2 basis to reduce travel. In a 2-3-2 series, the team with the most points will have its choice to start the series at home or on the road. The Eastern Conference champion will face the Western Conference champion in the Stanley Cup Final.

1994-95 — Same as 1993-94, except that in first, second or third-round playoff series involving Central and Pacific Division teams, the team with the better record has the choice of using either a 2-3-2 or a 2-2-1-1-1 format. When a 2-3-2 format is selected, the higher-ranked team also has the choice of playing games 1, 2, 6 and 7 at home or playing games 3, 4 and 5 at home. The format for the Stanley Cup Final remains 2-2-1-1-1.

1998-99 — The NHL's clubs are re-aligned into two conferences each consisting of three divisions. The number of teams qualifying for the Stanley Cup Playoffs remains unchanged at 16.

First-round playoff berths will be awarded to the first-place team in each division as well as to the next five best teams based on regular-season point totals in each conference. The three division winners in each conference will be seeded first through third, in order of points, for the playoffs and the next five best teams, in order of points, will be seeded fourth through eighth. In each conference, the team seeded #1 will play #8; #2 vs. #7; #3 vs. #6; and #4 vs. #5 in the quarterfinal round. Home-ice in the Conference Quarter-Finals is granted to those teams seeded first through fourth in each conference.

In the Conference Semi-Finals and Conference Finals, teams will be re-seeded according to the same criteria as the Conference Quarter-Finals. Higher seeded teams will have home-ice advantage.

Home-ice advantage for the Stanley Cup Finals will be determined by points.

All series remain best-of-seven.

Minnesota's Brian Bellows tries to cut in front of Pittsburgh goalie Tom Barrasso during the 1991 Stanley Cup Finals. The Penguins won 11 straight games en route to their second championship in 1992 and pushed their win streak to 14 in 1993.

Team Records

1918-2003

GAMES PLAYED

MOST GAMES PLAYED BY ALL TEAMS, ONE PLAYOFF YEAR:
92 — **1991.** There were 51 DSF, 24 DF, 11 CF and 6 F games.
90 — 1994. There were 48 CQF, 23 CSF, 12 CF and 7 F games.
— 2002. There were 47 CQF, 25 CSF, 13 CF and 5 F games.

MOST GAMES PLAYED, ONE TEAM, ONE PLAYOFF YEAR:
26 — **Philadelphia Flyers,** 1987. Won DSF 4-2 vs. NY Rangers, DF 4-3 vs. NY Islanders, CF 4-2 vs. Montreal, and lost F 4-3 vs. Edmonton.
25 — New Jersey Devils, 2001. Won CQF 4-2 vs. Carolina, CSF 4-3 vs. Toronto, CF 4-1 vs. Pittsburgh, and lost F 4-3 vs. Colorado.
24 — Pittsburgh Penguins,1991. Won DSF 4-3 vs. New Jersey, DF 4-1 vs. Washington, CF 4-2 vs. Boston, and F 4-2 vs. Minnesota.
— Los Angeles Kings, 1993. Won DSF 4-2 vs. Calgary, DF 4-2 vs. Vancouver, CF 4-3 vs. Toronto, and lost F 4-1 vs. Montreal.
— Vancouver Canucks, 1994. Won CQF 4-3 vs. Calgary, CSF 4-1 vs. Dallas, CF 4-1 vs. Toronto, and lost F 4-3 vs. NY Rangers.
— New Jersey Devils, 2003. Won CQF 4-1 vs. Boston, CSF 4-1 vs. Tampa Bay, CF 4-3 vs. Ottawa, and F 4-3 vs. Anaheim.

PLAYOFF APPEARANCES

MOST STANLEY CUP CHAMPIONSHIPS:
23 — **Montreal Canadiens** (1924-30-31-44-46-53-56-57-58-59-60-65-66-68-69-71-73-76-77-78-79-86-93)
13 — Toronto Maple Leafs (1918-22-32-42-45-47-48-49-51-62-63-64-67)
10 — Detroit Red Wings (1936-37-43-50-52-54-55-97-98-02)

MOST CONSECUTIVE STANLEY CUP CHAMPIONSHIPS:
5 — **Montreal Canadiens** (1956-57-58-59-60)
4 — Montreal Canadiens (1976-77-78-79)
— New York Islanders (1980-81-82-83)

MOST FINAL SERIES APPEARANCES:
32 — **Montreal Canadiens** in 86-year history.
22 — Detroit Red Wings in 77-year history.
21 — Toronto Maple Leafs in 86-year history.

MOST CONSECUTIVE FINAL SERIES APPEARANCES:
10 — **Montreal Canadiens,** (1951-60, inclusive)
5 — Montreal Canadiens, (1965-69, inclusive)
— New York Islanders, (1980-84, inclusive)

MOST YEARS IN PLAYOFFS:
73 — **Montreal Canadiens** in 86-year history.
63 — Toronto Maple Leafs in 86-year history.
61 — Boston Bruins in 79-year history.

MOST CONSECUTIVE PLAYOFF APPEARANCES:
29 — **Boston Bruins** (1968-96, inclusive)
28 — Chicago Blackhawks (1970-97, inclusive)
24 — Montreal Canadiens (1971-94, inclusive)
— St. Louis Blues (1980-2003, inclusive)
21 — Montreal Canadiens (1949-69, inclusive)

TEAM WINS

MOST HOME WINS, ONE TEAM, ONE PLAYOFF YEAR:
12 — **New Jersey Devils,** 2003 in 13 home games.
11 — Edmonton Oilers, 1988 in 11 home games.
10 — Edmonton Oilers, 1985 in 10 home games.
— Montreal Canadiens, 1986 in 11 home games.
— Montreal Canadiens, 1993 in 11 home games.

MOST ROAD WINS, ONE TEAM, ONE PLAYOFF YEAR:
10 — **New Jersey Devils,** 1995. Won three at Boston in CQF; two at Pittsburgh in CSF; three at Philadelphia in CF; two at Detroit in F.
— **New Jersey Devils,** 2000. Won two at Florida in CQF; two at Toronto in CSF; three at Philadelphia in CF; three at Dallas in F.
8 — New York Islanders, 1980. Won two at Los Angeles in PRE; three at Boston in QF; two at Buffalo in SF; one at Philadelphia in F.
— Philadelphia Flyers, 1987. Won two at NY Rangers in DSF; two at NY Islanders in DF; three at Montreal in CF; one at Edmonton in F.
— Edmonton Oilers, 1990. Won one at Winnipeg in DSF; two at Los Angeles in DF; two at Chicago in CF; three at Boston in F.
— Pittsburgh Penguins, 1992. Won two at Washington in DSF; two at NY Rangers in DF; two at Boston in CF; two at Chicago in F.
— Vancouver Canucks, 1994. Won three at Calgary in CQF; two at Dallas in CSF; one at Toronto in CF; two at NY Rangers in F.
— Colorado Avalanche, 1996. Won two at Vancouver in CQF; two at Chicago in CSF; two at Detroit in CF; two at Florida in F.
— Detroit Red Wings, 1998. Won two at Phoenix in CQF; three at St. Louis in CSF; one at Dallas in CF; two at Washington in F.
— Colorado Avalanche, 1999. Won three at San Jose in CQF; three at Detroit in CSF; two at Dallas in CF.
— New Jersey Devils, 2001. Won two at Carolina in CQF; two at Toronto in CSF; two at Pittsburgh in CF; two at Colorado in F.
— Detroit Red Wings, 2002. Won three at Vancouver in CQF; one at St. Louis in CSF; two at Colorado in CF; two at Carolina in F.

MOST ROAD WINS, ALL TEAMS, ONE PLAYOFF YEAR:
46 — **1987.** Of 87 games played, road teams won 46 (22 DSF, 14 DF, 8 CF, 2 F).

MOST OVERTIME WINS, ONE TEAM, ONE PLAYOFF YEAR:
10 — **Montreal Canadiens, 1993.** Won two vs. Quebec in DSF; three vs. Buffalo in DF; two vs. NY Islanders in CF; three vs. Los Angeles in F.
7 — Carolina Hurricanes, 2002. Won two vs. New Jersey in CQF; one vs. Montreal in CSF; three vs. Toronto in CF; one vs. Detroit in F.
— Mighty Ducks of Anaheim, 2003. Won two vs. Detroit in CQF; two vs. Dallas in CSF; one vs. Minnestoa in CF; two vs. New Jersey in F.

MOST OVERTIME WINS AT HOME, ONE TEAM, ONE PLAYOFF YEAR:
4 — **St. Louis Blues, 1968.** Won one vs. Philadelphia in QF; three vs. Minnesota in SF.
— **Montreal Canadiens, 1993.** Won one vs. Quebec in DSF; one vs. Buffalo in DF; one vs. NY Islanders in CF; one vs. Los Angeles in F.

MOST OVERTIME WINS ON THE ROAD, ONE TEAM, ONE PLAYOFF YEAR:
6 — **Montreal Canadiens, 1993.** Won one vs. Quebec in DSF; two vs. Buffalo in DF; one vs. NY Islanders in CF; two vs. Los Angeles in F.

TEAM LOSSES

MOST LOSSES, ONE TEAM, ONE PLAYOFF YEAR:
11 — **Philadelphia Flyers, 1987.** Lost two vs. NY Rangers in DSF; three vs. NY Islanders in DF; two vs. Montreal in CF; four vs. Edmonton in F.

MOST HOME LOSSES, ONE TEAM, ONE PLAYOFF YEAR:
6 — **Philadelphia Flyers, 1987.** Lost one vs. NY Rangers in DSF; two vs. NY Islanders in DF; two vs. Montreal in CF; one vs. Edmonton in F.
— **Washington Capitals, 1998.** Lost two vs. Boston in CQF; two vs. Buffalo in CF; two vs. Detroit in F.
— **Colorado Avalanche, 1999.** Lost two vs. San Jose in CQF; two vs. Detroit in CSF; two vs. Dallas in CF.
— **New Jersey Devils, 2001.** Lost one vs. Carolina in CQF; two vs. Toronto in CSF; one vs. Pittsburgh in CF; two vs Colorado in F.
— **Minnesota Wild, 2003.** Lost two vs. Colorado in CQF; two vs. Vancouver in CSF; two vs. Anaheim in CF.

MOST ROAD LOSSES, ONE TEAM, ONE PLAYOFF YEAR:
7 — **New Jersey Devils, 2003.** Lost one at Boston in CQF; one at Tampa Bay in CSF; two at Ottawa in CF; three at Anaheim in F.

MOST OVERTIME LOSSES, ONE TEAM, ONE PLAYOFF YEAR:
4 — **Montreal Canadiens, 1951.** Lost four vs. Toronto in F.
— **St. Louis Blues, 1968.** Lost one vs. Philadelphia in QF; one vs. Minnesota in SF; two vs. Montreal in F.
— **New York Rangers, 1979.** Lost one vs. Philadelphia in QF; two vs. NY Islanders in SF; one vs. Montreal in F.
— **Los Angeles Kings, 1991.** Lost one vs. Vancouver in DSF; three vs. Edmonton in DF.
— **Los Angeles Kings, 1993.** Lost one vs. Toronto in CF; three vs. Montreal in F.
— **New Jersey Devils, 1994.** Lost one vs. Buffalo in CQF; one vs. Boston in CSF; two vs. NY Rangers in CF.
— **Chicago Blackhawks, 1995.** Lost one vs. Toronto in CQF; three vs. Detroit in CF.
— **Philadelphia Flyers, 1996.** Lost two vs. Tampa Bay in CQF; two vs. Florida in CSF.
— **Dallas Stars, 1999.** Lost two vs. St. Louis in CSF; one vs. Colorado in CF; one vs. Buffalo in F.
— **Detroit Red Wings, 2002.** Lost one vs. Vancouver in CQF; two vs. Colorado in CF; one vs. Carolina in F.
— **New Jersey Devils, 2003.** Lost two vs. Ottawa in CF; two vs. Anaheim in F.

MOST OVERTIME LOSSES AT HOME, ONE TEAM, ONE PLAYOFF YEAR:
4 — **Detroit Red Wings, 2002.** Lost one vs. Vancouver in CQF; two vs. Colorado in CF; one vs. Carolina in F.

MOST OVERTIME LOSSES ON THE ROAD, ONE TEAM, ONE PLAYOFF YEAR:
3 — **Los Angeles Kings, 1991.** Lost one at Vancouver in DSF; two at Edmonton in DF.
— **Chicago Blackhawks, 1995.** Lost one at Toronto in CQF; two at Detroit in CF.
— **St. Louis Blues, 1996.** Lost two at Toronto in CQF; one at Detroit in CSF.
— **Dallas Stars, 1999.** Lost two at St. Louis in CSF; one at Colorado in CF.
— **New Jersey Devils, 2003.** Lost one at Ottawa in CF; two at Anaheim in F.

PLAYOFF WINNING STREAKS

LONGEST PLAYOFF WINNING STREAK:
14 — **Pittsburgh Penguins.** Streak started on May 9, 1992 as Pittsburgh won the first of three straight games in DF vs. NY Rangers. Continued with four wins vs. Boston in 1992 CF and four wins vs. Chicago in 1992 F. Pittsburgh then won the first three games of 1993 DSF vs. New Jersey. New Jersey ended the streak April 25, 1993, at New Jersey with a 4-1 win vs. Pittsburgh in the fourth game of 1993 DSF.
12 — **Edmonton Oilers.** Streak started on May 15, 1984 as Edmonton won the first of three straight games in F vs. NY Islanders. Continued with three wins vs. Los Angeles in 1985 DSF and four wins vs. Winnipeg in 1985 DF. Edmonton then won the first two games of 1985 CF vs. Chicago. Chicago ended the streak May 9, 1985, at Chicago with a 5-2 win vs. Edmonton in the third game of 1985 CF.

MOST CONSECUTIVE WINS, ONE TEAM, ONE PLAYOFF YEAR:
11 — **Chicago Blackhawks** in 1992. Chicago won last three games of DSF vs. St. Louis to win series 4-2, defeated Detroit 4-0 in DF and Edmonton 4-0 in CF.
— **Pittsburgh Penguins** in 1992. Pittsburgh won last three games of DF vs. NY Rangers to win series 4-2, defeated Boston 4-0 in CF and Chicago 4-0 in F.
— **Montreal Canadiens** in 1993. Montreal won last four games of DSF vs. Quebec to win series 4-2, defeated Buffalo 4-0 in DF and won first three games of CF vs. NY Islanders.

PLAYOFF LOSING STREAKS

LONGEST PLAYOFF LOSING STREAK:
16 — **Chicago Black Hawks.** Streak started April 20, 1975 at Chicago with a 6-2 loss in fourth game of QF vs. Buffalo won by Buffalo 4-1. Continued with four consecutive losses vs. Montreal in 1976 QF and two straight losses vs. NY Islanders in 1977 best-of-three PRE. Chicago then lost four games vs. Boston in 1978 QF and four games vs. NY Islanders in 1979 QF. Chicago ended the streak April 8, 1980, at Chicago with a 3-2 win vs. St. Louis in the opening game of 1980 PRE.
14 — **Los Angeles Kings.** Streak started June 3, 1993 at Montreal with a 3-2 loss in second game of F vs. Montreal, won by Montreal 4-1. Los Angeles failed to qualify for the playoffs for the next four years. Then Los Angeles lost four games vs. St. Louis in 1998 CQF; missed the 1999 playoffs and lost four games vs. Detroit in 2000 CQF. Los Angeles then lost the first two games of 2001 CQF vs. Detroit. Los Angeles ended the streak April 15, 2001, at Los Angeles with a 2-1 win.

Defenseman Ken Morrow joined the New York Islanders straight from the 1980 "Miracle on Ice" U.S. Olympic team. He helped the Islanders win the Cup that spring and was a key part of the dynasty that won four consecutive championships.

MOST GOALS IN A SERIES, ONE TEAM

MOST GOALS, ONE TEAM, ONE PLAYOFF SERIES:
  44 — **Edmonton Oilers** in 1985 CF. Edmonton won best-of-seven series 4-2, outscoring Chicago 44-25.
  35 — Edmonton Oilers in 1983 DF. Edmonton won best-of-seven series 4-1, outscoring Calgary 35-13.
   — Calgary Flames in 1995 CQF. Calgary lost best-of-seven series 4-3, outscoring San Jose 35-26.

MOST GOALS, ONE TEAM, TWO-GAME SERIES:
  11 — **Buffalo Sabres** in 1977 PRE. Buffalo won best-of-three series 2-0, outscoring Minnesota 11-3.
   — **Toronto Maple Leafs** in 1978 PRE. Toronto won best-of-three series 2-0, outscoring Los Angeles 11-3.

MOST GOALS, ONE TEAM, THREE-GAME SERIES:
  23 — **Chicago Black Hawks** in 1985 DSF. Chicago won best-of-five series 3-0, outscoring Detroit 23-8.
  20 — Minnesota North Stars in 1981 PRE. Minnesota won best-of-five series 3-0, outscoring Boston 20-13.
   — New York Islanders in 1981 PRE. NY Islanders won best-of-five series 3-0, outscoring Toronto 20-4.

MOST GOALS, ONE TEAM, FOUR-GAME SERIES:
  28 — **Boston Bruins** in 1972 SF. Boston won best-of-seven series 4-0, outscoring St. Louis 28-8.

MOST GOALS, ONE TEAM, FIVE-GAME SERIES:
  35 — **Edmonton Oilers** in 1983 DF. Edmonton won best-of-seven series 4-1, outscoring Calgary 35-13.
  32 — Edmonton Oilers in 1987 DSF. Edmonton won best-of-seven series 4-1, outscoring Los Angeles 32-20.
  30 — Calgary Flames in 1988 DSF. Calgary won best-of-seven series 4-1, outscoring Los Angeles 30-18.

MOST GOALS, ONE TEAM, SIX-GAME SERIES:
  44 — **Edmonton Oilers** in 1985 CF. Edmonton won best-of-seven series 4-2, outscoring Chicago 44-25.
  33 — Montreal Canadiens in 1973 F. Montreal won best-of-seven series 4-2, outscoring Chicago 33-23.
   — Chicago Black Hawks in 1985 DF. Chicago won best-of-seven series 4-2, outscoring Minnesota 33-29.
   — Los Angeles Kings in 1993 DSF. Los Angeles won best-of-seven series 4-2, outscoring Calgary 33-28.

MOST GOALS, ONE TEAM, SEVEN-GAME SERIES:
  35 — **Calgary Flames** in 1995 CQF. Calgary lost best-of-seven series 4-3, outscoring San Jose 35-26.
  33 — Philadelphia Flyers in 1976 QF. Philadelphia won best-of-seven series 4-3, outscoring Toronto 33-23.
   — Boston Bruins in 1983 DF. Boston won best-of-seven series 4-3, outscoring Buffalo 33-23.
   — Edmonton Oilers in 1984 DF. Edmonton won best-of-seven series 4-3, outscoring Calgary 33-27.

FEWEST GOALS IN A SERIES, ONE TEAM

FEWEST GOALS, ONE TEAM, TWO-GAME SERIES:
  0 — **New York Americans** in 1929 SF. NY Americans lost two-game, total-goals series 1-0 vs. NY Rangers.
   — **Chicago Black Hawks** in 1935 SF. Chicago lost two-game, total-goals series 1-0 vs. Mtl. Maroons.
   — **Montreal Maroons** in 1937 SF. Mtl. Maroons lost best-of-three series 2-0, outscored by NY Rangers 5-0.
   — **New York Americans** in 1939 QF. NY Americans lost best-of-three series 2-0, outscored by Toronto 5-0.

FEWEST GOALS, ONE TEAM, THREE-GAME SERIES:
  1 — **Montreal Maroons** in 1936 SF. Mtl. Maroons lost best-of-five series 3-0, outscored by Detroit 6-1.

FEWEST GOALS, ONE TEAM, FOUR-GAME SERIES:
  1 — **Minnesota Wild** in 2003 CF. Minnesota lost best-of-seven series 4-0, outscored by Anaheim 9-1.

FEWEST GOALS, ONE TEAM, FIVE-GAME SERIES:
  2 — **Philadelphia Flyers** in 2002 CQF. Philadelphia lost best-of-seven series 4-1, outscored by Ottawa 11-2.

FEWEST GOALS, ONE TEAM, SIX-GAME SERIES:
  5 — **Boston Bruins** in 1951 SF. Boston lost best-of-seven series 4-1 with 1 tie, outscored by Toronto 17-5.

FEWEST GOALS, ONE TEAM, SEVEN-GAME SERIES:
  9 — **Toronto Maple Leafs**, in 1945 F. Toronto won best-of- seven series 4-3; teams tied in scoring 9-9.
   — **Detroit Red Wings**, in 1945 F. Detroit lost best-of-seven series 4-3; teams tied in scoring 9-9.

Frank McCool joined the Maple Leafs while many players (like Syl Apps, left) were in the military. McCool had shutouts in the first three games of the 1945 Finals as Toronto beat Detroit in the lowest-scoring seven-game series in NHL history.

MOST GOALS IN A SERIES, BOTH TEAMS

MOST GOALS, BOTH TEAMS, ONE PLAYOFF SERIES:
  69 — **Edmonton Oilers (44), Chicago Black Hawks (25)** in 1985 CF. Edmonton won best-of-seven series 4-2.
  62 — Chicago Black Hawks (33), Minnesota North Stars (29) in 1985 DF. Chicago won best-of-seven series 4-2.
  61 — Los Angeles Kings (33), Calgary Flames (28) in 1993 DSF. Los Angeles won best-of-seven series 4-2.
   — Calgary Flames (35), San Jose Sharks (26) in 1995 CQF. San Jose won best-of-seven series 4-3.

MOST GOALS, BOTH TEAMS, TWO-GAME SERIES:
  17 — **Toronto St. Patricks (10), Montreal Canadiens (7)** in 1918 NHL F. Toronto won two-game total-goals series.
  15 — Boston Bruins (10), Chicago Black Hawks (5) in 1927 QF. Boston won two-game total-goals series.
   — Pittsburgh Penguins (9), St. Louis Blues (6) in 1975 PRE. Pittsburgh won best-of-three series 2-0.

MOST GOALS, BOTH TEAMS, THREE-GAME SERIES:
  33 — **Minnesota North Stars (20), Boston Bruins (13)** in 1981 PRE. Minnesota won best-of-five series 3-0.
  31 — Chicago Black Hawks (23), Detroit Red Wings (8) in 1985 DSF. Chicago won best-of-five series 3-0.
  28 — Toronto Maple Leafs (18), New York Rangers (10) in 1932 F. Toronto won best-of-five series 3-0.

MOST GOALS, BOTH TEAMS, FOUR-GAME SERIES:
  36 — **Boston Bruins (28), St. Louis Blues (8)** in 1972 SF. Boston won best-of-seven series 4-0.
   — **Minnesota North Stars (18), Toronto Maple Leafs (18)** in 1983 DSF. Minnesota won best-of-five series 3-1.
   — **Edmonton Oilers (25), Chicago Black Hawks (11)** in 1983 CF. Edmonton won best-of-seven series 4-0.
  35 — New York Rangers (23), Los Angeles Kings (12) in 1981 PRE. NY Rangers won best-of-five series 3-1.

MOST GOALS, BOTH TEAMS, FIVE-GAME SERIES:
- **52 — Edmonton Oilers (32), Los Angeles Kings (20)** in 1987 DSF. Edmonton won best-of-seven series 4-1.
- 50 — Los Angeles Kings (27), Edmonton Oilers (23) in 1982 DSF. Los Angeles won best-of-five series 3-2.
- 48 — Edmonton Oilers (35), Calgary Flames (13) in 1983 DF. Edmonton won best-of-seven series 4-1.
- — Calgary Flames (30), Los Angeles Kings (18) in 1988 DSF. Calgary won best-of-seven series 4-1.

MOST GOALS, BOTH TEAMS, SIX-GAME SERIES:
- **69 — Edmonton Oilers (44), Chicago Black Hawks (25)** in 1985 CF. Edmonton won best-of-seven series 4-2.
- 62 — Chicago Black Hawks (33), Minnesota North Stars (29) in 1985 DF. Chicago won best-of-seven series 4-2.
- 61 — Los Angeles Kings (33), Calgary Flames (28) in 1993 DSF. Los Angeles won best-of-seven series 4-2.

MOST GOALS, BOTH TEAMS, SEVEN-GAME SERIES:
- **61 — Calgary Flames (35), San Jose Sharks (26)** in 1995 CQF. San Jose won best-of-seven series 4-3.
- 60 — Edmonton Oilers (33), Calgary Flames (27) in 1984 DF. Edmonton won best-of-seven series 4-3.

FEWEST GOALS IN A SERIES, BOTH TEAMS

FEWEST GOALS, BOTH TEAMS, TWO-GAME SERIES:
- **1 — New York Rangers (1), New York Americans (0)** in 1929 SF. NY Rangers won two-game total-goals series.
- — Montreal Maroons (1), Chicago Black Hawks (0) in 1935 SF. Mtl. Maroons won two-game total-goals series.

FEWEST GOALS, BOTH TEAMS, THREE-GAME SERIES:
- **7 — Boston Bruins (5), Montreal Canadiens (2)** in 1929 SF. Boston won best-of-five series 3-0.
- — Detroit Red Wings (6), Montreal Maroons (1) in 1936 SF. Detroit won best-of-five series 3-0.

FEWEST GOALS, BOTH TEAMS, FOUR-GAME SERIES:
- **9 — Toronto Maple Leafs (7), Boston Bruins (2)** in 1935 SF. Toronto won best-of-five series 3-1.

FEWEST GOALS, BOTH TEAMS, FIVE-GAME SERIES:
- **11 — Montreal Maroons (6), New York Rangers (5)** in 1928 F. NY Rangers won best-of-five series 3-2.

FEWEST GOALS, BOTH TEAMS, SIX-GAME SERIES:
- **16 — Carolina Hurricanes (10), Toronto Maple Leafs (6)** in 2002 CF. Carolina won best-of-seven series 4-2.

FEWEST GOALS, BOTH TEAMS, SEVEN-GAME SERIES:
- **18 — Toronto Maple Leafs (9), Detroit Red Wings (9)** in 1945 F. Toronto won best-of-seven series 4-3.

MOST GOALS IN A GAME OR PERIOD

MOST GOALS, ONE TEAM, ONE GAME:
- **13 — Edmonton Oilers** April 9, 1987, vs. Los Angeles at Edmonton. Edmonton won 13-3.
- 12 — Los Angeles Kings, April 10, 1990, vs. Calgary at Los Angeles. Los Angeles won 12-4.
- 11 — Montreal Canadiens, March 30, 1944, vs. Toronto at Montreal. Montreal won 11-0.
- — Edmonton Oilers, May 4, 1985, vs. Chicago at Edmonton. Edmonton won 11-2.

MOST GOALS, ONE TEAM, ONE PERIOD:
- **7 — Montreal Canadiens,** March 30, 1944, vs. Toronto at Montreal, third period. Montreal won 11-0.

MOST GOALS, BOTH TEAMS, ONE GAME:
- **18 — Los Angeles Kings (10), Edmonton Oilers (8),** April 7, 1982, at Edmonton. Los Angeles won best-of-five DSF 3-2.
- 17 — Pittsburgh Penguins (10), Philadelphia Flyers (7), April 25, 1989, at Pittsburgh. Pittsburgh won best-of-seven DF 4-3.
- 16 — Edmonton Oilers (13), Los Angeles Kings (3), April 9, 1987, at Edmonton. Edmonton won best-of-seven DSF 4-1.
- — Los Angeles Kings (12), Calgary Flames (4), April 10, 1990, at Los Angeles. Los Angeles won best-of-seven DF 4-2.

MOST GOALS, BOTH TEAMS, ONE PERIOD:
- **9 — New York Rangers (6), Philadelphia Flyers (3),** April 24, 1979, third period, at Philadelphia. NY Rangers won 8-3.
- — **Los Angeles Kings (8), Calgary Flames (4),** April 10, 1990, second period, at Los Angeles. Los Angeles won 12-4.
- 8 — Chicago Black Hawks (5), Montreal Canadiens (3), May 8, 1973, second period, at Montreal. Chicago won 8-7.
- — Chicago Black Hawks (5), Edmonton Oilers (3), May 12, 1985, first period, at Chicago. Chicago won 8-6.
- — Edmonton Oilers (6), Winnipeg Jets (2), April 6, 1988, third period, at Edmonton. Edmonton won 7-4.
- — Hartford Whalers (5), Montreal Canadiens (3), April 10, 1988, third period, at Montreal. Hartford won 7-5.
- — Vancouver Canucks (5), New York Rangers (3), June 9, 1994, third period, at NY Rangers. Vancouver won 6-3.

TEAM POWER-PLAY GOALS

MOST POWER-PLAY GOALS BY ALL TEAMS, ONE PLAYOFF YEAR:
- **199 — 1988** in 83 games.

MOST POWER-PLAY GOALS, ONE TEAM, ONE PLAYOFF YEAR:
- **35 — Minnesota North Stars,** 1991, in 23 games.
- 32 — Edmonton Oilers, 1988, in 18 games.
- 31 — New York Islanders, 1981, in 18 games.

MOST POWER-PLAY GOALS, ONE TEAM, ONE SERIES:
- **15 — New York Islanders** in 1980 F vs. Philadelphia. NY Islanders won series 4-2.
- — **Minnesota North Stars** in 1991 DSF vs. Chicago. Minnesota won series 4-2.
- 13 — New York Islanders in 1981 QF vs. Edmonton. NY Islanders won series 4-2.
- — Calgary Flames in 1986 CF vs. St. Louis. Calgary won series 4-3.
- 12 — Toronto Maple Leafs in 1976 QF vs. Philadelphia. Philadelphia won series 4-3.

MOST POWER-PLAY GOALS, BOTH TEAMS, ONE SERIES:
- **21 — New York Islanders (15), Philadelphia Flyers (6)** in 1980 best-of-seven F won by NY Islanders 4-2.
- — **New York Islanders (13), Edmonton Oilers (8)** in 1981 best-of-seven QF won by NY Islanders 4-2.
- — **Philadelphia Flyers (11), Pittsburgh Penguins (10)** in 1989 best-of-seven DF won by Philadelphia 4-3.
- — **Minnesota North Stars (15), Chicago Black Hawks (6)** in 1991 best-of-seven DSF won by Minnesota 4-2.
- 20 — Toronto Maple Leafs (12), Philadelphia Flyers (8) in 1976 best-of-seven QF won by Philadelphia 4-3.

MOST POWER-PLAY GOALS, ONE TEAM, ONE GAME:
- **6 — Boston Bruins,** April 2, 1969, at Boston vs. Toronto. Boston won 10-0.

MOST POWER-PLAY GOALS, BOTH TEAMS, ONE GAME:
- **8 — Minnesota North Stars (4), St. Louis Blues (4),** April 24, 1991, at Minnesota. Minnesota won 8-4.
- 7 — Minnesota North Stars (4), Edmonton Oilers (3), April 28, 1984, at Minnesota. Edmonton won 8-5.
- — Philadelphia Flyers (4), New York Rangers (3), April 13, 1985, at NY Rangers. Philadelphia won 6-5.
- — Chicago Black Hawks (5), Edmonton Oilers (2), April 28, 1984, at Minnesota. Edmonton won 8-5.
- — Edmonton Oilers (5), Los Angeles Kings (2), April 9, 1987, at Edmonton. Edmonton won 13-3.
- — Vancouver Canucks (4), Calgary Flames (3), April 9, 1989, at Vancouver. Vancouver won 5-3.

MOST POWER-PLAY GOALS, ONE TEAM, ONE PERIOD:
- **4 — Toronto Maple Leafs,** March 26, 1936, second period vs. Boston at Toronto. Toronto won 8-3.
- — **Minnesota North Stars,** April 28, 1984, second period vs. Edmonton at Minnesota. Edmonton won 8-5.
- — **Boston Bruins,** April 11, 1991, third period vs. Hartford at Boston. Boston won 6-1.
- — **Minnesota North Stars,** April 24, 1991, second period vs. St. Louis at Minnesota. Minnesota won 8-4.
- — **St. Louis Blues,** April 27, 1998, third period at Los Angeles. St. Louis won 4-3.

MOST POWER-PLAY GOALS, BOTH TEAMS, ONE PERIOD:
- **5 — Minnesota North Stars (4), Edmonton Oilers (1),** April 28, 1984, at Minnesota. Edmonton won 8-5.
- — **Vancouver Canucks (3), Calgary Flames (2),** April 9, 1989, at Vancouver. Vancouver won 5-3.
- — **Minnesota North Stars (4), St. Louis Blues (1),** April 24, 1991, at Minnesota. Minnesota won 8-4.

TEAM SHORTHAND GOALS

MOST SHORTHAND GOALS BY ALL TEAMS, ONE PLAYOFF YEAR:
- **33 — 1988,** in 83 games.

MOST SHORTHAND GOALS, ONE TEAM, ONE PLAYOFF YEAR:
- **10 — Edmonton Oilers,** 1983, in 16 games.
- 9 — New York Islanders, 1981, in 19 games.
- 8 — Philadelphia Flyers, 1989, in 19 games.

MOST SHORTHAND GOALS, ONE TEAM, ONE SERIES:
6 — **Calgary Flames** in 1995 vs. San Jose in best-of-seven CQF won by San Jose 4-3.
— **Vancouver Canucks** in 1995 vs. St. Louis in best-of-seven CQF won by Vancouver 4-3.
5 — New York Rangers in 1979 vs. Philadelphia in best-of-seven QF won by New York Rangers 4-1.
— Edmonton Oilers in 1983 vs. Calgary in best-of-seven DF won by Edmonton 4-1.

MOST SHORTHAND GOALS, BOTH TEAMS, ONE SERIES:
7 — **Boston Bruins (4), New York Rangers (3),** in 1958 SF won by Boston 4-2.
— **Edmonton Oilers (5), Calgary Flames (2),** in 1983 DF won by Edmonton 4-1.
— **Vancouver Canucks (6), St. Louis Blues (1),** in 1995 CQF won by Vancouver 4-3.

MOST SHORTHAND GOALS, ONE TEAM, ONE GAME:
3 — **Boston Bruins,** April 11, 1981, at Minnesota North Stars. Minnesota won 6-3.
— **New York Islanders,** April 17, 1983, at NY Rangers. NY Rangers won 7-6.
— **Toronto Maple Leafs,** May 8, 1994, at San Jose Sharks. Toronto won 8-3.

MOST SHORTHAND GOALS, BOTH TEAMS, ONE GAME:
4 — **Boston Bruins (3), Minnesota North Stars (1),** April 11, 1981, at Minnesota. Minnesota won 6-3.
— **New York Islanders (3), New York Rangers (1),** April 17, 1983, at NY Rangers. NY Rangers won 7-6.
— **Toronto Maple Leafs (3), San Jose Sharks (1),** May 8, 1994, at San Jose. Toronto won 8-3.
3 — Toronto Maple Leafs (2), Detroit Red Wings (1), April 5, 1947, at Toronto. Toronto won 6-1.
— New York Rangers (2), Boston Bruins (1), April 1, 1958, at Boston. NY Rangers won 5-2.
— Minnesota North Stars (2), Philadelphia Flyers (1), May 4, 1980, at Minnesota. Philadelphia won 5-3.
— Winnipeg Jets (2), Edmonton Oilers (1), April 9, 1988, at Winnipeg. Winnipeg won 6-4.
— New York Islanders (2), New Jersey Devils (1), April 14, 1988, at New Jersey. New Jersey won 6-5.
— Montreal Canadiens (2), New Jersey Devils (1), April 17, 1997, at New Jersey. New Jersey won 5-2.
— Dallas Stars (2), San Jose Sharks (1), May 5, 2000, at San Jose. Dallas won 5-4.

MOST SHORTHAND GOALS, ONE TEAM, ONE PERIOD:
2 — **Toronto Maple Leafs,** April 5, 1947, first period vs. Detroit at Toronto. Toronto won 6-1.
— **Toronto Maple Leafs,** April 13, 1965, first period vs. Montreal at Toronto. Montreal won 4-3.
— **Boston Bruins,** April 20, 1969, first period vs. Montreal at Boston. Boston won 3-2.
— **Boston Bruins,** April 8, 1970, second period vs. NY Rangers at Boston. Boston won 8-2.
— **Boston Bruins,** April 30, 1972, first period vs. NY Rangers at Boston. Boston won 6-5.
— **Chicago Black Hawks,** May 3, 1973, first period vs. Montreal at Chicago. Chicago won 7-4.
— **Montreal Canadiens,** April 23, 1978, first period at Detroit. Montreal won 8-0.
— **New York Islanders,** April 8, 1980, second period vs. Los Angeles at NY Islanders. NY Islanders won 8-1.
— **Los Angeles Kings,** April 9, 1980, first period at NY Islanders. Los Angeles won 6-3.
— **Boston Bruins,** April 13, 1980, second period at Pittsburgh. Boston won 8-3.
— **Minnesota North Stars,** May 4, 1980, second period vs. Philadelphia at Minnesota. Philadelphia won 5-3.
— **Boston Bruins,** April 11, 1981, third period at Minnesota. Minnesota won 6-3.
— **New York Islanders,** May 12, 1981, first period vs. Minnesota at NY Islanders. NY Islanders won 6-3.
— **Montreal Canadiens,** April 7, 1982, third period vs. Quebec at Montreal. Montreal won 5-1.
— **Edmonton Oilers,** April 24, 1983, third period vs. Chicago at Edmonton. Edmonton won 8-4.
— **Winnipeg Jets,** April 14, 1985, second period at Calgary. Winnipeg won 5-3.
— **Boston Bruins,** April 6, 1988, first period vs. Buffalo at Boston. Boston won 7-3.
— **New York Islanders,** April 14, 1988, third period at New Jersey. New Jersey won 6-5.
— **Detroit Red Wings,** April 29, 1993, second period at Toronto. Detroit won 7-3.
— **Toronto Maple Leafs,** May 8, 1994, third period at San Jose. Toronto won 8-3.
— **Calgary Flames,** May 11, 1995, first period at San Jose. Calgary won 9-2.
— **Vancouver Canucks,** May 15, 1995, second period at St. Louis. Vancouver won 6-5.
— **Montreal Canadiens,** April 17, 1997, second period at New Jersey. New Jersey won 5-2.
— **Philadelphia Flyers,** April 26, 1997, first period vs. Pittsburgh at Philadelphia. Philadelphia won 6-3.
— **Phoenix Coyotes,** April 24, 1998, second period at Detroit. Phoenix won 7-4.
— **Buffalo Sabres,** April 27, 1998, second period vs. Philadelphia at Buffalo. Buffalo won 6-1.
— **San Jose Sharks,** April 30, 1999, third period at Colorado. San Jose won 7-3.
— **Detroit Red Wings,** April 27, 2002, second period at Vancouver. Detroit won 6-4.

MOST SHORTHAND GOALS, BOTH TEAMS, ONE PERIOD:
3 — **Toronto Maple Leafs (2), Detroit Red Wings (1),** April 5, 1947, first period at Toronto. Toronto won 6-1.
— **Toronto Maple Leafs (2), San Jose Sharks (1),** May 8, 1994, third period at San Jose. Toronto won 8-3.

FASTEST GOALS

FASTEST FIVE GOALS, BOTH TEAMS:
3:06 — **Minnesota North Stars, Chicago Black Hawks,** April 21, 1985, at Chicago. Keith Brown scored for Chicago at 1:12 of the second period; Ken Yaremchuk, Chicago, 1:27; Dino Ciccarelli, Minnesota, 2:48; Tony McKegney, Minnesota, 4:07; and Curt Fraser, Chicago, 4:18. Chicago won 6-2 and won best-of-seven DF 4-2.
3:20 — Minnesota North Stars, Philadelphia Flyers, April 29, 1980, at Philadelphia. Paul Shmyr scored for Minnesota at 13:20 of the first period; Steve Christoff, Minnesota, 13:59; Ken Linseman, Philadelphia, 14:54; Tom Gorence, Philadelphia, 15:36; and Ken Linseman, Philadelphia, 16:40. Minnesota won 6-5. Philadelphia won best-of-seven SF 4-1.
4:00 — Los Angeles Kings, Detroit Red Wings, April 15, 2000, at Detroit. Brendan Shanahan scored for Detroit at 0:55 of the first period; Martin Lapointe, Detroit, 1:33; Luc Robitaille, Los Angeles, 2:04; Kris Draper, Detroit, 3:32; and Ziggy Palffy, Los Angeles, 4:55. Detroit won 8-5 and best-of-seven CQF 4-0.

FASTEST FIVE GOALS, ONE TEAM:
3:36 — **Montreal Canadiens,** March 30, 1944, at Montreal vs. Toronto. Toe Blake scored at 7:58 and 8:37 of the third period; Maurice Richard, 9:17; Ray Getliffe, 10:33; and Buddy O'Connor, 11:34. Canadiens won 11-0 and best-of-seven SF 4-1.

FASTEST FOUR GOALS, BOTH TEAMS:
1:33 — **Toronto Maple Leafs, Philadelphia Flyers,** April 20, 1976, at Philadelphia. Don Saleski scored for Philadelphia at 10:04 of the second period; Bob Neely, Toronto, 10:42; Gary Dornhoefer, Philadelphia, 11:24; and Don Saleski, Philadelphia, 11:37. Philadelphia won 7-1 and best-of-seven SF 4-3.
1:34 — Calgary Flames, Montreal Canadiens, May 20, 1986, at Montreal. Joel Otto scored for Calgary at 17:59 of the first period; Bobby Smith, Montreal, 18:25; Mats Naslund, Montreal, 19:17; and Bob Gainey, Montreal, 19:33. Montreal won 5-3 and best-of-seven F 4-1.
1:38 — Boston Bruins, Philadelphia Flyers, April 26, 1977, at Philadelphia. Gregg Sheppard scored for Boston at 14:01 of the second period; Mike Milbury, Boston, 15:01; Gary Dornhoefer, Philadelphia, 15:16; and Jean Ratelle, Boston, 15:39. Boston won 5-4 and best-of-seven SF 4-0.

FASTEST FOUR GOALS, ONE TEAM:
2:35 — **Montreal Canadiens,** March 30, 1944, at Montreal. Toe Blake scored at 7:58 and 8:37 of the third period; Maurice Richard, 9:17; and Ray Getliffe, 10:33. Montreal won 11-0 and best-of-seven SF 4-1.

FASTEST THREE GOALS, BOTH TEAMS:
0:21 — **Chicago Black Hawks, Edmonton Oilers,** May 7, 1985, at Edmonton. Behn Wilson scored for Chicago at 19:22 of the third period; Jari Kurri, Edmonton, 19:36; and Glenn Anderson, Edmonton, 19:43. Edmonton won 7-3 and best-of-seven CF 4-2.
0:27 — Phoenix Coyotes, Detroit Red Wings, April 24, 1998, at Detroit. Jeremy Roenick scored for Phoenix at 13:24 of the second period; Mathieu Dandenault, Detroit, 13:32; and Keith Tkachuk, Phoenix, 13:51. Phoenix won 7-4. Detroit won best-of-seven CQF 4-2.
0:30 — Pittsburgh Penguins, Chicago Blackhawks, June 1, 1992, at Chicago. Dirk Graham scored for Chicago at 6:21 of the first period; Kevin Stevens, Pittsburgh, 6:33; and Dirk Graham, Chicago, 6:51. Pittsburgh won 6-5 and best-of-seven F 4-0.

FASTEST THREE GOALS, ONE TEAM:
0:23 — **Toronto Maple Leafs,** April 12, 1979, at Toronto vs. Atlanta. Darryl Sittler scored at 4:04 and 4:16 of the first period; and Ron Ellis, 4:27. Toronto won 7-4 and best-of-three PRE 2-0.
0:38 — New York Rangers, April 12, 1986, at NY Rangers vs. Philadelphia. Jim Weimer scored at 12:29 of the third period; Bob Brooke, 12:43; and Ron Greschner, 13:07. NY Rangers won 5-2 and best-of-five DSF 3-2.
— Colorado Avalanche, April 18, 2001, at Vancouver. Peter Forsberg scored at 9:11 of the third period; Joe Sakic, 9:28; and Eric Messier, 9:49. Colorado won 5-1 and best-of-seven CQF 4-0.

FASTEST TWO GOALS, BOTH TEAMS:
0:05 — **Pittsburgh Penguins, Buffalo Sabres,** April 14, 1979, at Buffalo. Gilbert Perreault scored for Buffalo at 12:59 of the first period; and Jim Hamilton, Pittsburgh, 13:04. Pittsburgh won 4-3 and best-of-three PRE 2-1.
0:08 — St. Louis Blues, Minnesota North Stars, April 9, 1989, at Minnesota. Bernie Federko scored for St. Louis at 2:28 of the third period; and Perry Berezan, Minnesota, 2:36. Minnesota won 5-4. St. Louis won best-of-seven DSF 4-1.
— Phoenix Coyotes, Detroit Red Wings, April 24, 1998, at Detroit. Jeremy Roenick scored for Phoenix at 13:24 of the second period; and Mathieu Dandenault, Detroit, 13:32. Phoenix won 7-4. Detroit won best-of-seven CQF 4-2.

FASTEST TWO GOALS, ONE TEAM:
0:05 — **Detroit Red Wings,** April 11, 1965, at Detroit vs. Chicago. Norm Ullman scored at 17:35 and 17:40 of the second period. Detroit won 4-2. Chicago won best-of-seven SF 4-3.

Martin Brodeur (top) set a new playoff record with seven shutouts in 2003. His Devils won the Stanley Cup. Anaheim's Jean-Sebastien Giguere (bottom) had a scoreless streak of 217:44 (fifth longest in history) and won the Conn Smythe Trophy.

SHUTOUTS

MOST SHUTOUTS, ONE PLAYOFF YEAR, ALL TEAMS:
- 25 — **2002.** Of 90 games played, Detroit had 6; Ottawa had 4; Carolina, Colorado, St. Louis and Toronto had 3 each; while Los Angeles, New Jersey and Philadelphia had 1 each.
- 19 — 2001. Of 86 games played, Colorado and New Jersey had 4 each, Toronto had 3, Pittsburgh and Los Angeles had 2 each, while Buffalo, Washington, Detroit and San Jose had 1 each.
- 18 — 2003. Of 89 games played, New Jersey had 7; Anaheim had 5; Philadelphia had 2; Colorado, NY Islanders, Ottawa, St. Louis and Washington had 1 each.

FEWEST SHUTOUTS, ONE PLAYOFF YEAR, ALL TEAMS:
- 0 — **1959.** 18 games played.

MOST SHUTOUTS, BOTH TEAMS, ONE SERIES:
- 5 — **Toronto Maple Leafs (3), Detroit Red Wings (2),** in 1945. Toronto won best-of-seven series F 4-3.
- — **Toronto Maple Leafs (3), Detroit Red Wings (2),** in 1950. Toronto won best-of-seven SF 4-3.

TEAM PENALTIES

FEWEST PENALTIES, BOTH TEAMS, BEST-OF-SEVEN SERIES:
- 19 — **Detroit Red Wings, Toronto Maple Leafs** in 1945 F. Detroit received 10 minors, Toronto received 9 minors. Toronto won best-of-seven series 4-3.

FEWEST PENALTIES, ONE TEAM, BEST-OF-SEVEN SERIES:
- 9 — **Toronto Maple Leafs** in 1945 F vs. Detroit. Toronto received 9 minors. Toronto won best-of-seven series 4-3.

MOST PENALTIES, BOTH TEAMS, ONE SERIES:
- 218 — **New Jersey Devils, Washington Capitals** in 1988 DF. New Jersey received 97 minors, 11 majors, 9 misconducts and 1 match penalty. Washington received 80 minors, 11 majors, 8 misconducts and 1 match penalty. New Jersey won best-of-seven series 4-3.

MOST PENALTY MINUTES, BOTH TEAMS, ONE SERIES:
- 654 — **New Jersey Devils (349), Washington Capitals (305)** in 1988 DF. New Jersey won best-of-seven series 4-3.

MOST PENALTIES, ONE TEAM, ONE SERIES:
- 118 — **New Jersey Devils** in 1988 DF vs. Washington. New Jersey received 97 minors, 11 majors, 9 misconducts and 1 match penalty. New Jersey won best-of-seven series 4-3.

MOST PENALTY MINUTES, ONE TEAM, ONE SERIES:
- 349 — **New Jersey Devils** in 1988 DF vs. Washington. New Jersey won best-of-seven series 4-3.

MOST PENALTIES, BOTH TEAMS, ONE GAME:
- 66 — **Detroit Red Wings (33), St. Louis Blues (33),** April 12, 1991, at St. Louis. St. Louis won 6-1.
- 63 — Minnesota North Stars (34), Chicago Black Hawks (29), April 6, 1990, at Chicago. Chicago won 5-3.
- 62 — New Jersey Devils (32), Washington Capitals (30), April 22, 1988, at New Jersey. New Jersey won 10-4.

MOST PENALTY MINUTES, BOTH TEAMS, ONE GAME:
- 298 — **Detroit Red Wings (152), St. Louis Blues (146),** April 12, 1991, at St. Louis. Detroit received 33 penalties; St. Louis received 33 penalties. St. Louis won 6-1.
- 267 — New York Rangers (142), Los Angeles Kings (125), April 9, 1981, at Los Angeles. NY Rangers received 31 penalties; Los Angeles received 28 penalties. Los Angeles won 5-4.

MOST PENALTIES, ONE TEAM, ONE GAME:
- 34 — **Minnesota North Stars,** April 6, 1990, at Chicago. Chicago won 5-3.
- 33 — Detroit Red Wings, April 12, 1991, at St. Louis. St. Louis won 6-1.
- — St. Louis Blues, April 12, 1991, at St. Louis vs. Detroit. St. Louis won 6-1.

MOST PENALTY MINUTES, ONE TEAM, ONE GAME:
- 152 — **Detroit Red Wings,** April 12, 1991, at St. Louis. St. Louis won 6-1.
- 146 — St. Louis Blues, April 12, 1991, at St. Louis vs. Detroit. St. Louis won 6-1.
- 142 — New York Rangers, April 9, 1981, at Los Angeles. Los Angeles won 5-4.

MOST PENALTIES, BOTH TEAMS, ONE PERIOD:
- 43 — **New York Rangers (24), Los Angeles Kings (19),** April 9, 1981, first period at Los Angeles. Los Angeles won 5-4.

MOST PENALTY MINUTES, BOTH TEAMS, ONE PERIOD:
- 248 — **New York Islanders (124), Boston Bruins (124),** April 17, 1980, first period at Boston. NY Islanders won 5-4.

MOST PENALTIES, ONE TEAM, ONE PERIOD:
- 24 — **New York Rangers,** April 9, 1981, first period at Los Angeles. Los Angeles won 5-4.

MOST PENALTY MINUTES, ONE TEAM, ONE PERIOD:
- 125 — **New York Rangers,** April 9, 1981, first period at Los Angeles. Los Angeles won 5-4.

OVERTIME

SHORTEST OVERTIME:
- 0:09 — **Montreal Canadiens, Calgary Flames,** May 18, 1986, at Calgary. Montreal won 3-2 on Brian Skrudland's goal at 0:09 of the first overtime period. Montreal won best-of-seven F 4-1.
- 0:11 — New York Islanders, New York Rangers, April 11, 1975, at NY Rangers. NY Islanders won 4-3 on J.P. Parise's goal at 0:11 of the first overtime period. NY Islanders won best-of-three PRE 2-1.

LONGEST OVERTIME:
- 116:30 — **Detroit Red Wings, Montreal Maroons,** March 24, 1936, at Montreal. Mtl. Maroons won 1-0 on Mud Bruneteau's goal at 16:30 of the sixth overtime period. Detroit won best-of-five SF 3-0.

MOST OVERTIME GAMES, ONE PLAYOFF YEAR:
- 28 — **1993.** Of 85 games played, 28 went into overtime.
- 26 — 2001. Of 86 games played, 26 went into overtime.
- 22 — 2003. Of 89 games played, 22 went into overtime.
- 21 — 1999. Of 86 games played, 21 went into overtime.

FEWEST OVERTIME GAMES, ONE PLAYOFF YEAR:
- 0 — **1963.** None of the 16 games went into overtime, the only year since 1926 that no overtime was required in any playoff series.

MOST OVERTIME GAMES, ONE SERIES:
- 5 — **Toronto Maple Leafs, Montreal Canadiens** in 1951. Toronto won best-of-seven F 4-1.
- 4 — Toronto Maple Leafs, Boston Bruins in 1933. Toronto won best-of-five SF 3-2.
- — Boston Bruins, NY Rangers in 1939. Boston won best-of-seven SF 4-3.
- — St. Louis Blues, Minnesota North Stars in 1968. St. Louis won best-of-seven SF 4-3.
- — Dallas Stars, St. Louis Blues in 1999. Dallas won best-of-seven CSF 4-2.
- — Dallas Stars, Edmonton Oilers in 2001. Dallas won best-of-seven CQF 4-2.

THREE-OR-MORE GOAL GAMES

MOST THREE-OR-MORE GOAL GAMES BY ALL TEAMS, ONE PLAYOFF YEAR:
- 12 — **1983** in 66 games.
- — **1988** in 83 games.
- 11 — 1985 in 70 games.
- — 1992 in 86 games.

MOST THREE-OR-MORE GOAL GAMES, ONE TEAM, ONE PLAYOFF YEAR:
- 6 — **Edmonton Oilers,** 1983, in 16 games.
- — **Edmonton Oilers,** 1985, in 18 games.

Individual Records

GAMES PLAYED

MOST YEARS IN PLAYOFFS:
21 — Raymond Bourque, Boston, Colorado (1980-96 inclusive; 98-2001 inclusive)
20 — Gordie Howe, Detroit, Hartford
— Larry Robinson, Montreal, Los Angeles
— Larry Murphy, Los Angeles, Washington, Minnesota, Pittsburgh, Toronto, Detroit
— Scott Stevens, Washington, St. Louis, New Jersey

MOST CONSECUTIVE YEARS IN PLAYOFFS:
20 — Larry Robinson, Montreal, Los Angeles (1973-92, inclusive).
18 — Larry Murphy, Los Angeles, Washington, Minnesota, Pittsburgh, Toronto, Detroit (1984-2001, inclusive).
— Brett Hull, Calgary, St. Louis, Dallas, Detroit (1986-2003, inclusive).
17 — Brad Park, NY Rangers, Boston, Detroit (1969-85, inclusive).
— Raymond Bourque, Boston (1980-96, inclusive).

MOST PLAYOFF GAMES:
247 — Patrick Roy, Montreal, Colorado
236 — Mark Messier, Edmonton, NY Rangers
233 — Claude Lemieux, Montreal, New Jersey, Colorado, Phoenix, Dallas
— Scott Stevens, Washington, St. Louis, New Jersey
231 — Guy Carbonneau, Montreal, St. Louis, Dallas

GOALS

MOST GOALS IN PLAYOFFS (CAREER):
122 — Wayne Gretzky, Edmonton, Los Angeles, St. Louis, NY Rangers
109 — Mark Messier, Edmonton, NY Rangers
106 — Jari Kurri, Edmonton, Los Angeles, NY Rangers, Anaheim
100 — Brett Hull, Calgary, St. Louis, Dallas, Detroit
93 — Glenn Anderson, Edmonton, Toronto, NY Rangers, St. Louis

MOST GOALS, ONE PLAYOFF YEAR:
19 — Reggie Leach, Philadelphia, 1976. 16 games.
— **Jari Kurri, Edmonton,** 1985. 18 games.
18 — Joe Sakic, Colorado, 1996. 22 games.
17 — Newsy Lalonde, Montreal, 1919. 10 games.
— Mike Bossy, NY Islanders, 1981. 18 games.
— Steve Payne, Minnesota, 1981. 19 games.
— Mike Bossy, NY Islanders, 1982. 19 games.
— Mike Bossy, NY Islanders, 1983. 19 games
— Wayne Gretzky, Edmonton, 1985. 18 games.
— Kevin Stevens, Pittsburgh, 1991. 24 games.

MOST GOALS IN ONE SERIES (OTHER THAN FINAL):
12 — Jari Kurri, Edmonton, in 1985 CF, 6 games vs. Chicago.
11 — Newsy Lalonde, Montreal, in 1919 NHL F, 5 games vs. Ottawa.
10 — Tim Kerr, Philadelphia, in 1989 DF, 7 games vs. Pittsburgh.
9 — Reggie Leach, Philadelphia, in 1976 SF, 5 games vs. Boston.
— Bill Barber, Philadelphia, in 1980 SF, 5 games vs. Minnesota.
— Mike Bossy, NY Islanders, in 1983 CF, 6 games vs. Boston.
— Mario Lemieux, Pittsburgh, in 1989 DF, 7 games vs. Philadelphia.

MOST GOALS IN FINAL SERIES (NHL PLAYERS ONLY):
9 — Babe Dye, Toronto, in 1922, 5 games vs. Van. Millionaires.
8 — Alf Skinner, Toronto, in 1918, 5 games vs. Van. Millionaires.
7 — Jean Beliveau, Montreal, in 1956, 5 games vs. Detroit.
— Mike Bossy, NY Islanders, in 1982, 4 games vs. Vancouver.
— Wayne Gretzky, Edmonton, in 1985, 5 games vs. Philadelphia.

MOST GOALS, ONE GAME:
5 — Newsy Lalonde, Montreal, March 1, 1919, at Montreal. Final score: Montreal 6, Ottawa 3.
— **Maurice Richard, Montreal,** March 23, 1944, at Montreal. Final score: Montreal 5, Toronto 1.
— **Darryl Sittler, Toronto,** April 22, 1976, at Toronto. Final score: Toronto 8, Philadelphia 5.
— **Reggie Leach, Philadelphia,** May 6, 1976, at Philadelphia. Final score: Philadelphia 6, Boston 3.
— **Mario Lemieux, Pittsburgh,** April 25, 1989, at Pittsburgh. Final score: Pittsburgh 10, Philadelphia 7.

MOST GOALS, ONE PERIOD:
4 — Tim Kerr, Philadelphia, April 13, 1985, at NY Rangers, second period. Final score: Philadelphia 6, NY Rangers 5.
— **Mario Lemieux, Pittsburgh,** April 25, 1989, at Pittsburgh vs. Philadelphia, first period. Final score: Pittsburgh 10, Philadelphia 7.

ASSISTS

MOST ASSISTS IN PLAYOFFS (CAREER):
260 — Wayne Gretzky, Edmonton, Los Angeles, St. Louis, NY Rangers
186 — Mark Messier, Edmonton, NY Rangers
139 — Raymond Bourque, Boston, Colorado
137 — Paul Coffey, Edmonton, Pittsburgh, Los Angeles, Detroit, Philadelphia, Carolina
128 — Doug Gilmour, St. Louis, Calgary, Toronto, New Jersey, Buffalo, Montreal

MOST ASSISTS, ONE PLAYOFF YEAR:
31 — Wayne Gretzky, Edmonton, 1988. 19 games.
30 — Wayne Gretzky, Edmonton, 1985. 18 games.
29 — Wayne Gretzky, Edmonton, 1987. 21 games.
28 — Mario Lemieux, Pittsburgh, 1991. 23 games.
26 — Wayne Gretzky, Edmonton, 1983. 16 games.

MOST ASSISTS IN ONE SERIES (OTHER THAN FINAL):
14 — Rick Middleton, Boston, in 1983 DF, 7 games vs. Buffalo.
— **Wayne Gretzky, Edmonton,** in 1985 CF, 6 games vs. Chicago.
13 — Wayne Gretzky, Edmonton, in 1987 DSF, 5 games vs. Los Angeles.
— Doug Gilmour, Toronto, in 1994 CSF, 7 games vs. San Jose.
11 — Al MacInnis, Calgary, in 1984 DF, 7 games vs. Edmonton.
— Mark Messier, Edmonton, in 1989 DSF, 7 games vs. Los Angeles.
— Mike Ridley, Washington, in 1992 DSF, 7 games vs. Pittsburgh.
— Ron Francis, Pittsburgh, in 1995 CQF, 7 games vs. Washington.
10 — Fleming Mackell, Boston, in 1958 SF, 6 games vs. NY Rangers.
— Stan Mikita, Chicago, in 1962 SF, 6 games vs. Montreal.
— Bob Bourne, NY Islanders, in 1983 DF, 6 games vs. NY Rangers.
— Wayne Gretzky, Edmonton, in 1988 DSF, 5 games vs. Winnipeg.
— Mario Lemieux, Pittsburgh, in 1992 DSF, 6 games vs. Washington.

MOST ASSISTS IN FINAL SERIES:
10 — Wayne Gretzky, Edmonton, in 1988, 4 games plus suspended game vs. Boston.
9 — Jacques Lemaire, Montreal, in 1973, 6 games vs. Chicago.
— Wayne Gretzky, Edmonton, in 1987, 7 games vs. Philadelphia.
— Larry Murphy, Pittsburgh, in 1991, 6 games vs. Minnesota.

MOST ASSISTS, ONE GAME:
6 — Mikko Leinonen, NY Rangers, April 8, 1982, at NY Rangers. Final score: NY Rangers 7, Philadelphia 3.
— **Wayne Gretzky, Edmonton,** April 9, 1987, at Edmonton. Final score: Edmonton 13, Los Angeles 3.
5 — Toe Blake, Montreal, March 23, 1944, at Montreal. Final score: Montreal 5, Toronto 1.
— Maurice Richard, Montreal, March 27, 1956, at Montreal. Final score: Montreal 7, NY Rangers 0.
— Bert Olmstead, Montreal, March 30, 1957, at Montreal. Final score: Montreal 8, NY Rangers 3.
— Don McKenney, Boston, April 5, 1958, at Boston. Final score: Boston 8, NY Rangers 2.
— Stan Mikita, Chicago, April 4, 1973, at Chicago. Final score: Chicago 7, St. Louis 1.
— Wayne Gretzky, Edmonton, April 8, 1981, at Montreal. Final score: Edmonton 6, Montreal 3.
— Paul Coffey, Edmonton, May 14, 1985, at Edmonton. Final score: Edmonton 10, Chicago 5.
— Doug Gilmour, St. Louis, April 15, 1986, at Minnesota. Final score: St. Louis 6, Minnesota 3.
— Risto Siltanen, Quebec, April 14, 1987, at Hartford. Final score: Quebec 7, Hartford 5.
— Patrik Sundstrom, New Jersey, April 22, 1988, at New Jersey. Final score: New Jersey 10, Washington 4.
— Geoff Courtnall, St. Louis, April 23, 1998, at St. Louis. Final score: St. Louis 8, Los Angeles 3.

MOST ASSISTS, ONE PERIOD:
3 — Three assists by one player in one period of a playoff game has been recorded on 75 occasions. Cliff Ronning of the Minnesota Wild is the most recent to equal this mark with 3 assists in the third period at Vancouver, May 7, 2003. Final score: Minnesota 5, Vancouver 1.
— Wayne Gretzky has had 3 assists in one period 5 times; Raymond Bourque, 3 times; Toe Blake, Jean Beliveau, Doug Harvey and Bobby Orr, twice each. Joe Primeau of Toronto was the first player to be credited with 3 assists in one period of a playoff game; third period at Boston vs. NY Rangers, April 7, 1932. Final score: Toronto 6, NY Rangers 2.

POINTS

MOST POINTS IN PLAYOFFS (CAREER):
382 — Wayne Gretzky, Edmonton, Los Angeles, St. Louis, NY Rangers, 122G, 260A
295 — Mark Messier, Edmonton, NY Rangers, 109G, 186A
233 — Jari Kurri, Edmonton, Los Angeles, NY Rangers, Anaheim, 106G, 127A
214 — Glenn Anderson, Edmonton, Toronto, NY Rangers, St. Louis, 93G, 121A
196 — Paul Coffey, Edmonton, Pittsburgh, Los Angeles, Detroit, Philadelphia, Carolina, 59G, 137A

MOST POINTS, ONE PLAYOFF YEAR:
47 — Wayne Gretzky, Edmonton, in 1985. 17 goals, 30 assists in 18 games.
44 — Mario Lemieux, Pittsburgh, in 1991. 16 goals, 28 assists in 23 games.
43 — Wayne Gretzky, Edmonton, in 1988. 12 goals, 31 assists in 19 games.
40 — Wayne Gretzky, Los Angeles, in 1993. 15 goals, 25 assists in 24 games.
38 — Wayne Gretzky, Edmonton, in 1983. 12 goals, 26 assists in 16 games.

MOST POINTS IN ONE SERIES (OTHER THAN FINAL):
19 — Rick Middleton, Boston, in 1983 DF, 7 games vs. Buffalo. 5 goals, 14 assists.
18 — Wayne Gretzky, Edmonton, in 1985 CF, 6 games vs. Chicago. 4 goals, 14 assists.
17 — Mario Lemieux, Pittsburgh, in 1992 DSF, 6 games vs. Washington. 7 goals, 10 assists.
16 — Barry Pederson, Boston, in 1983 DF, 7 games vs. Buffalo. 7 goals, 9 assists.
— Doug Gilmour, Toronto, in 1994 CSF, 7 games vs. San Jose. 3 goals, 13 assists.
15 — Jari Kurri, Edmonton, in 1985 CF, 6 games vs. Chicago. 12 goals, 3 assists.
— Wayne Gretzky, Edmonton, in 1987 DSF, 5 games vs. Los Angeles. 2 goals, 13 assists.
— Tim Kerr, Philadelphia, in 1989 DF, 7 games vs. Pittsburgh. 10 goals, 5 assists.
— Mario Lemieux, Pittsburgh, in 1991 CF, 6 games vs. Boston. 6 goals, 9 assists.

MOST POINTS IN FINAL SERIES:
13 — Wayne Gretzky, Edmonton, in 1988, 4 games plus suspended game vs. Boston. 3 goals, 10 assists.
12 — Gordie Howe, Detroit, in 1955, 7 games vs. Montreal. 5 goals, 7 assists.
— Yvan Cournoyer, Montreal, in 1973, 6 games vs. Chicago. 6 goals, 6 assists.
— Jacques Lemaire, Montreal, in 1973, 6 games vs. Chicago. 3 goals, 9 assists.
— Mario Lemieux, Pittsburgh, in 1991, 5 games vs. Minnesota. 5 goals, 7 assists.

MOST POINTS, ONE GAME:
8 — Patrik Sundstrom, New Jersey, April 22, 1988, at New Jersey in 10-4 win vs. Washington. Sundstrom had 3 goals, 5 assists.
— **Mario Lemieux, Pittsburgh,** April 25, 1989, at Pittsburgh in 10-7 win vs. Philadelphia. Lemieux had 5 goals, 3 assists.
7 — Wayne Gretzky, Edmonton, April 17, 1983, at Calgary in 10-2 win. Gretzky had 4 goals, 3 assists.
— Wayne Gretzky, Edmonton, April 25,1985, at Winnipeg in 8-3 win. Gretzky had 3 goals, 4 assists.
— Wayne Gretzky, Edmonton, April 9, 1987, at Edmonton in 13-3 win vs. Los Angeles. Gretzky had 1 goal, 6 assists.
6 — Dickie Moore, Montreal, March 25, 1954, at Montreal in 8-1 win vs. Boston. Moore had 2 goals, 4 assists.
— Phil Esposito, Boston, April 2, 1969, at Boston in 10-0 win vs. Toronto. Esposito had 4 goals, 2 assists.
— Darryl Sittler, Toronto, April 22, 1976, at Toronto in 8-5 win vs. Philadelphia. Sittler had 5 goals, 1 assist.
— Guy Lafleur, Montreal, April 11, 1977, at Montreal in 7-2 win vs. St. Louis. Lafleur had 3 goals, 3 assists.
— Mikko Leinonen, NY Rangers, April 8, 1982, at NY Rangers in 7-3 win vs. Philadelphia. Leinonen had 6 assists.
— Paul Coffey, Edmonton, May 14, 1985, at Edmonton in 10-5 win vs. Chicago. Coffey had 1 goal, 5 assists.
— John Anderson, Hartford, April 12, 1986, at Hartford in 9-4 win vs. Quebec. Anderson had 2 goals, 4 assists.
— Mario Lemieux, Pittsburgh, April 23, 1992, at Pittsburgh in 6-4 win vs. Washington. Lemieux had 3 goals, 3 assists.
— Geoff Courtnall, St. Louis, April 23, 1998, at St. Louis in 8-3 win vs. Los Angeles. Courtnall had 1 goal, 5 assists.

MOST POINTS, ONE PERIOD:
4 — Maurice Richard, Montreal, March 29, 1945; at Montreal, third period, in 10-3 win vs. Toronto. 3 goals, 1 assist.
— **Dickie Moore,** Montreal, March 25, 1954, at Montreal, first period, in 8-1 win vs. Boston. 2 goals, 2 assists.
— **Barry Pederson,** Boston, April 8, 1982, at Boston, second period, in 7-3 win vs. Buffalo. 3 goals, 1 assist.
— **Peter McNab,** Boston, April 11, 1982, at Buffalo, second period, in 5-2 win vs. Buffalo. 1 goal, 3 assists.
— **Tim Kerr,** Philadelphia, April 13, 1985, at NY Rangers, second period, in 6-5 win vs. NY Rangers. 4 goals.
— **Ken Linseman,** Boston, April 14, 1985, at Boston, second period, in 7-6 win vs. Montreal. 2 goals, 2 assists.
— **Wayne Gretzky,** Edmonton, April 12, 1987, at Los Angeles, third period, in 6-3 win vs. Los Angeles. 1 goal, 3 assists.
— **Glenn Anderson,** Edmonton, April 6, 1988, at Edmonton, third period, in 7-4 win vs. Winnipeg. 3 goals, 1 assist.
— **Mario Lemieux,** Pittsburgh, April 25, 1989, at Pittsburgh, first period, in 10-7 win vs. Philadelphia. 4 goals.
— **Dave Gagner,** Minnesota, April 8, 1991, at Minnesota, first period, in 6-5 loss vs. Chicago. 2 goals, 2 assists.
— **Mario Lemieux,** Pittsburgh, April 23, 1992, at Pittsburgh, second period, in 6-4 win vs. Washington. 2 goals, 2 assists.
— **Alexander Mogilny,** New Jersey, April 28, 2001, at New Jersey, second period, in 6-5 win vs. Toronto. 1 goal, 3 assists.

POWER-PLAY GOALS

MOST POWER-PLAY GOALS IN PLAYOFFS (CAREER):
37 — Brett Hull, St. Louis, Dallas, Detroit
35 — Mike Bossy, NY Islanders
34 — Dino Ciccarelli, Minnesota, Washington, Detroit
— Wayne Gretzky, Edmonton, Los Angeles, St. Louis, NY Rangers
29 — Mario Lemieux, Pittsburgh

MOST POWER-PLAY GOALS, ONE PLAYOFF YEAR:
9 — Mike Bossy, NY Islanders, 1981. 18 games vs. Toronto, Edmonton, NY Rangers and Minnesota.
— **Cam Neely, Boston,** 1991. 19 games vs. Hartford, Montreal and Pittsburgh.
8 — Tim Kerr, Philadelphia, 1989. 19 games.
— John Druce, Washington, 1990. 15 games.
— Brian Propp, Minnesota, 1991. 23 games.
— Mario Lemieux, Pittsburgh, 1992. 15 games.

MOST POWER-PLAY GOALS, ONE PLAYOFF SERIES:
, **6 — Chris Kontos, Los Angeles,** 1989 DSF vs. Edmonton, won by Los Angeles 4-3.
5 — Andy Bathgate, Detroit, 1966 SF vs. Chicago, won by Detroit 4-2.
— Denis Potvin, NY Islanders, 1981 QF vs. Edmonton, won by NY Islanders 4-2.
— Ken Houston, Calgary, 1981 QF vs. Philadelphia, won by Calgary 4-3.
— Rick Vaive, Chicago, 1988 DSF vs. St. Louis, won by St. Louis 4-1.
— Tim Kerr, Philadelphia, 1989 DF vs. Pittsburgh, won by Philadelphia 4-3.
— Mario Lemieux, Pittsburgh, 1989 DF vs. Philadelphia, won by Philadelphia 4-3.
— John Druce, Washington, 1990 DF vs. NY Rangers, won by Washington 4-1.
— Pat LaFontaine, Buffalo, 1992 DSF vs. Boston, won by Boston 4-3.
— Adam Graves, NY Rangers, 1996 CQF vs Montreal, won by NY Rangers 4-2.
— Doug Weight, St. Louis, 2003 CQF vs. Vancouver, won by Vancouver 4-3.

MOST POWER-PLAY GOALS, ONE GAME:
3 — Syd Howe, Detroit, March 23, 1939, at Detroit vs. Montreal. Detroit won 7-3.
— **Sid Smith, Toronto,** April 10, 1949, at Detroit vs. Detroit. Toronto won 3-1.
— **Phil Esposito, Boston,** April 2, 1969, at Boston vs. Toronto. Boston won 10-0.
— **John Bucyk, Boston,** April 21, 1974, at Boston vs. Chicago. Boston won 8-6.
— **Denis Potvin, NY Islanders,** April 17, 1981, at NY Islanders vs. Edmonton. NY Islanders won 6-3.
— **Tim Kerr, Philadelphia,** April 13, 1985, at NY Rangers. Philadelphia won 6-5.
— **Jari Kurri, Edmonton,** April 9, 1987, at Edmonton vs. Los Angeles. Edmonton won 13-3.
— **Mark Johnson, New Jersey,** April 22, 1988, at New Jersey vs. Washington. New Jersey won 10-4.
— **Dino Ciccarelli, Detroit,** April 29, 1993, at Toronto. Detroit won 7-3.
— **Dino Ciccarelli, Detroit,** May 11, 1995, at Dallas. Detroit won 5-1.
— **Valeri Kamensky, Colorado,** April 24, 1997, at Colorado vs. Chicago. Colorado won 7-0.

MOST POWER-PLAY GOALS, ONE PERIOD:
3 — Tim Kerr, Philadelphia, April 13, 1985, at NY Rangers, second period in 6-5 win.
2 — Two power-play goals have been scored by one player in one period on 53 occasions. Charlie Conacher of Toronto was the first to score two power-play goals in one period, setting the mark with two power-play goals in the second period at Toronto vs. Boston, March 26, 1936. Final score: Toronto 8, Boston 3. Brendan Shanahan of the Detroit Red Wings is the most recent to equal this mark with two power-play goals in the first period at Phoenix, May 3, 1988. Final score: Detroit 5, Phoenix 2.

SHORTHAND GOALS

MOST SHORTHAND GOALS IN PLAYOFFS (CAREER):
14 — Mark Messier, Edmonton, NY Rangers
11 — Wayne Gretzky, Edmonton, Los Angeles, St. Louis
10 — Jari Kurri, Edmonton, Los Angeles, NY Rangers
8 — Ed Westfall, Boston, NY Islanders
— Hakan Loob, Calgary

MOST SHORTHAND GOALS, ONE PLAYOFF YEAR:
3 — Derek Sanderson, Boston, 1969. 1 vs. Toronto in QF, won by Boston 4-0; 2 vs. Montreal in SF, won by Montreal, 4-2.
— **Bill Barber, Philadelphia,** 1980. All vs. Minnesota in SF, won by Philadelphia 4-1.
— **Lorne Henning, NY Islanders,** 1980. 1 vs. Boston in QF, won by NY Islanders 4-1; 1 vs. Buffalo in SF, won by NY Islanders 4-2; 1 vs. Philadelphia in F, won by NY Islanders 4-2.
— **Wayne Gretzky, Edmonton,** 1983. 2 vs. Winnipeg in DSF, won by Edmonton 3-0; 1 vs. Calgary in DF, won by Edmonton 4-1.
— **Wayne Presley, Chicago,** 1989. All vs. Detroit in DSF, won by Chicago 4-2.
— **Todd Marchant, Edmonton,** 1997. 1 vs. Dallas in CQF, won by Edmonton 4-3; 2 vs. Colorado in CSF, won by Colorado 4-1.

A four-time 40-goal scorer who reached 51 in 1981-82, Rick Middleton set a playoff record with 19 points (five goals, 14 assists) when Boston defeated Buffalo in a seven-game Division Final series in 1983.

MOST SHORTHAND GOALS, ONE PLAYOFF SERIES:
3 — **Bill Barber, Philadelphia,** 1980 SF vs. Minnesota, won by Philadelphia 4-1.
 — **Wayne Presley, Chicago,** 1989 DSF vs. Detroit, won by Chicago 4-2.
2 — Mac Colville, NY Rangers, 1940 SF vs. Boston, won by NY Rangers 4-2.
 — Jerry Toppazzini, Boston, 1958 SF vs. NY Rangers, won by Boston 4-2.
 — Dave Keon, Toronto, 1963 F vs. Detroit, won by Toronto 4-1.
 — Bob Pulford, Toronto, 1964 F vs. Detroit, won by Toronto 4-3.
 — Serge Savard, Montreal, 1968 F vs. St. Louis, won by Montreal 4-0.
 — Derek Sanderson, Boston, 1969 SF vs. Montreal, won by Montreal 4-2.
 — Bryan Trottier, NY Islanders, 1980 PRE vs. Los Angeles, won by NY Islanders 3-1.
 — Bobby Lalonde, Boston, 1981 PRE vs. Minnesota, won by Minnesota 3-0.
 — Butch Goring, NY Islanders, 1981 SF vs. NY Rangers, won by NY Islanders 4-0.
 — Wayne Gretzky, Edmonton, 1983 DSF vs. Winnipeg, won by Edmonton 3-0.
 — Mark Messier, Edmonton, 1983 DF vs. Calgary, won by Edmonton 4-1.
 — Jari Kurri, Edmonton, 1983 CF vs. Chicago, won by Edmonton 4-0.
 — Wayne Gretzky, Edmonton, 1985 DF vs. Winnipeg, won by Edmonton 4-0.
 — Kevin Lowe, Edmonton, 1987 F vs. Philadelphia, won by Edmonton 4-3.
 — Bob Gould, Washington, 1988 DSF vs. Philadelphia, won by Washington 4-3.
 — Dave Poulin, Philadelphia, 1989 DF vs. Pittsburgh, won by Philadelphia 4-3.
 — Russ Courtnall, Montreal, 1991 DF vs. Boston, won by Boston 4-3.
 — Sergei Fedorov, Detroit, 1992 DSF vs. Minnesota, won by Detroit 4-3.
 — Mark Messier, NY Rangers, 1992 DSF vs. New Jersey, won by NY Rangers 4-3.
 — Tom Fitzgerald, NY Islanders, 1993 DF vs. Pittsburgh, won by NY Islanders 4-3.
 — Mark Osborne, Toronto, 1994 CSF vs. San Jose, won by Toronto 4-3.
 — Tony Amonte, Chicago, 1997 CQF vs. Colorado, won by Colorado 4-2.
 — Brian Rolston, New Jersey, 1997 CQF vs. Montreal, won by New Jersey 4-1.
 — Rod Brind'Amour, Philadelphia, 1997 CQF vs. Pittsburgh, won by Philadelphia 4-1.
 — Todd Marchant, Edmonton, 1997 CSF vs. Colorado, won by Colorado 4-1.
 — Jeremy Roenick, Phoenix, 1998 CQF vs. Detroit, won by Detroit 4-2.
 — Vincent Damphousse, San Jose, 1999 CQF vs. Colorado, won by Colorado 4-2.
 — Dixon Ward, Buffalo, 1999 CF vs. Toronto, won by Buffalo 4-1.
 — Curtis Brown, Buffalo, 2001 CSF vs. Pittsburgh, won by Pittsburgh 4-3.

MOST SHORTHAND GOALS, ONE GAME:
2 — **Dave Keon, Toronto,** April 18, 1963, at Toronto, in 3-1 win vs. Detroit.
 — **Bryan Trottier, NY Islanders,** April 8, 1980, at NY Islanders, in 8-1 win vs. Los Angeles.
 — **Bobby Lalonde, Boston,** April 11, 1981, at Minnesota, in 6-3 loss vs. Minnesota.
 — **Wayne Gretzky, Edmonton,** April 6, 1983, at Edmonton, in 6-3 win vs. Winnipeg.
 — **Jari Kurri, Edmonton,** April 24, 1983, at Edmonton, in 8-3 win vs. Chicago.
 — **Mark Messier, NY Rangers,** April 21, 1992, at NY Rangers, in 7-3 loss vs. New Jersey.
 — **Tom Fitzgerald, NY Islanders,** May 8, 1993, at NY Islanders, in 6-5 win vs. Pittsburgh.
 — **Rod Brind'Amour, Philadelphia,** April 26, 1997, at Philadelphia, in 6-3 win vs. Pittsburgh.
 — **Jeremy Roenick, Phoenix,** April 24, 1998, at Detroit, in 7-4 win vs. Detroit.
 — **Vincent Damphousse, San Jose,** April 30, 1999, at Colorado, in 7-3 win vs. Colorado.

MOST SHORTHAND GOALS, ONE PERIOD:
2 — **Bryan Trottier, NY Islanders,** April 8, 1980, second period, at NY Islanders, in 8-1 win vs. Los Angeles.
 — **Bobby Lalonde, Boston,** April 11, 1981, third period, at Minnesota, in 6-3 loss vs. Minnesota.
 — **Jari Kurri, Edmonton,** April 24, 1983, third period, at Edmonton, in 8-4 win vs. Chicago.
 — **Rod Brind'Amour, Philadelphia,** April 26, 1997, first period, at Philadelphia, in 6-3 win vs. Pittsburgh.
 — **Jeremy Roenick, Phoenix,** April 24, 1998, second period, at Detroit, in 7-4 win vs. Detroit.
 — **Vincent Damphousse, San Jose,** April 30, 1999, third period, at Colorado, in 7-3 win vs. Colorado.

GAME-WINNING GOALS

MOST GAME-WINNING GOALS IN PLAYOFFS, CAREER:
24 — **Wayne Gretzky, Edmonton, Los Angeles, St. Louis, NY Rangers**
23 — Brett Hull, St. Louis, Dallas, Detroit
19 — Claude Lemieux, Montreal, New Jersey, Colorado
18 — Maurice Richard, Montreal
17 — Mike Bossy, NY Islanders
 — Glenn Anderson, Edmonton, Toronto, NY Rangers, St. Louis

MOST GAME-WINNING GOALS, ONE PLAYOFF YEAR:
6 — **Joe Sakic, Colorado,** 1996. 22 games.
 — **Joe Nieuwendyk, Dallas,** 1999. 23 games.
5 — Mike Bossy, NY Islanders, 1983. 19 games.
 — Jari Kurri, Edmonton, 1987. 21 games.
 — Bobby Smith, Minnesota, 1991. 23 games.
 — Mario Lemieux, Pittsburgh, 1992. 15 games.

MOST GAME-WINNING GOALS, ONE PLAYOFF SERIES:
4 — **Mike Bossy, NY Islanders,** 1983 CF vs. Boston, won by NY Islanders 4-2.

OVERTIME GOALS

MOST OVERTIME GOALS IN PLAYOFFS, CAREER:
6 — **Maurice Richard, Montreal** (1 in 1946; 3 in 1951; 1 in 1957; 1 in 1958.)
5 — Glenn Anderson, Edmonton, Toronto, St. Louis
4 — Bob Nystrom, NY Islanders
 — Dale Hunter, Quebec, Washington
 — Wayne Gretzky, Edmonton, Los Angeles
 — Stephane Richer, Montreal, New Jersey
 — Joe Murphy, Edmonton, Chicago
 — Esa Tikkanen, Edmonton, NY Rangers
 — Jaromir Jagr, Pittsburgh
 — Kirk Muller, Montreal, Dallas
 — Joe Sakic, Colorado

MOST OVERTIME GOALS, ONE PLAYOFF YEAR:
3 — **Mel Hill, Boston,** 1939. All vs. NY Rangers in best-of-seven SF, won by Boston 4-3.
 — **Maurice Richard, Montreal,** 1951. Two vs. Detroit in best-of-seven SF, won by Montreal 4-2; one vs. Toronto in best-of-seven F, won by Toronto 4-1.

MOST OVERTIME GOALS, ONE PLAYOFF SERIES:
3 — **Mel Hill, Boston,** 1939, SF vs. NY Rangers, won by Boston 4-3. Hill scored at 59:25 of overtime March 21 for a 2-1 win; at 8:24 of overtime, March 23 for a 3-2 win; and at 48:00 of overtime, April 2 for a 2-1 win.

Tampa Bay's Martin St. Louis exploded for 33 goals and 37 assists in 2002-03. He added seven more goals in 11 playoff games, including two shorthand goals and three game winners. He also scored an overtime power-play goal to beat Washington.

SCORING BY A DEFENSEMAN

MOST GOALS BY A DEFENSEMAN, ONE PLAYOFF YEAR:
12 — Paul Coffey, Edmonton, 1985. 18 games.
11 — Brian Leetch, NY Rangers, 1994. 23 games.
9 — Bobby Orr, Boston, 1970. 14 games.
— Brad Park, Boston, 1978. 15 games.
8 — Denis Potvin, NY Islanders, 1981. 18 games.
— Raymond Bourque, Boston, 1983. 17 games.
— Denis Potvin, NY Islanders, 1983. 20 games.
— Paul Coffey, Edmonton, 1984. 19 games.

MOST GOALS BY A DEFENSEMAN, ONE GAME:
3 — Bobby Orr, Boston, April 11, 1971, at Montreal. Final score: Boston 5, Montreal 2.
— **Dick Redmond, Chicago,** April 4, 1973, at Chicago. Final score: Chicago 7, St. Louis 1.
— **Denis Potvin, NY Islanders,** April 17, 1981, at NY Islanders. Final score: NY Islanders 6, Edmonton 3.
— **Paul Reinhart, Calgary,** April 14, 1983, at Edmonton. Final score: Edmonton 6, Calgary 3.
— **Doug Halward, Vancouver,** April 7, 1984, at Vancouver. Final score: Vancouver 7, Calgary 0.
— **Paul Reinhart, Calgary,** April 8, 1984, at Vancouver. Final score: Calgary 5, Vancouver 1.
— **Al Iafrate, Washington,** April 26, 1993, at Washington. Final score: Washington 6, NY Islanders 4.
— **Eric Desjardins, Montreal,** June 3, 1993, at Montreal. Final score: Montreal 3, Los Angeles 2.
— **Gary Suter, Chicago,** April 24, 1994, at Chicago. Final score: Chicago 4, Toronto 3.
— **Brian Leetch, NY Rangers,** May 22, 1995, at Philadelphia. Final score: Philadelphia 4, NY Rangers 3.
— **Andy Delmore, Philadelphia,** May 7, 2000, at Philadelphia. Final score: Philadelphia 6, Pittsburgh 3.

MOST ASSISTS BY A DEFENSEMAN, ONE PLAYOFF YEAR:
25 — Paul Coffey, Edmonton, 1985. 18 games.
24 — Al MacInnis, Calgary, 1989. 22 games.
23 — Brian Leetch, NY Rangers, 1994. 23 games.
19 — Bobby Orr, Boston, 1972. 15 games.
18 — Raymond Bourque, Boston, 1988. 23 games.
— Raymond Bourque, Boston, 1991. 19 games.
— Larry Murphy, Pittsburgh, 1991. 23 games.

MOST ASSISTS BY A DEFENSEMAN, ONE GAME:
5 — Paul Coffey, Edmonton, May 14, 1985 at Edmonton vs. Chicago. Edmonton won 10-5.
— **Risto Siltanen, Quebec,** April 14, 1987 at Hartford. Quebec won 7-5.

MOST POINTS BY A DEFENSEMAN, ONE PLAYOFF YEAR:
37 — Paul Coffey, Edmonton, 1985. 12 goals, 25 assists in 18 games.
34 — Brian Leetch, NY Rangers, 1994. 11 goals, 23 assists in 23 games.
31 — Al MacInnis, Calgary, 1989. 7 goals, 24 assists in 22 games.
25 — Denis Potvin, NY Islanders, 1981. 8 goals, 17 assists in 18 games.
— Raymond Bourque, Boston, 1991. 7 goals, 18 assists in 19 games.

MOST POINTS BY A DEFENSEMAN, ONE GAME:
6 — Paul Coffey, Edmonton, May 14, 1985, at Edmonton vs. Chicago. 1 goal, 5 assists. Edmonton won 10-5.
5 — Eddie Bush, Detroit, April 9, 1942, at Detroit vs. Toronto. 1 goal, 4 assists. Detroit won 5-2.
— Bob Dailey, Philadelphia, May 1, 1980, at Philadelphia vs. Minnesota. 1 goal, 4 assists. Philadelphia won 7-0.
— Denis Potvin, NY Islanders, April 17, 1981, at NY Islanders vs. Edmonton. 3 goals, 2 assists. NY Islanders won 6-3.
— Risto Siltanen, Quebec, April 14, 1987, at Hartford. 5 assists. Quebec won 7-5.

SCORING BY A ROOKIE

MOST GOALS BY A ROOKIE, ONE PLAYOFF YEAR:
14 — Dino Ciccarelli, Minnesota, 1981. 19 games.
11 — Jeremy Roenick, Chicago, 1990. 20 games.
10 — Claude Lemieux, Montreal, 1986. 20 games.
9 — Pat Flatley, NY Islanders, 1984. 21 games.
8 — Steve Christoff, Minnesota, 1980. 14 games.
— Brad Palmer, Minnesota, 1981. 19 games.
— Mike Krushelnyski, Boston, 1983. 17 games.
— Bob Joyce, Boston, 1988. 23 games.

MOST POINTS BY A ROOKIE, ONE PLAYOFF YEAR:
21 — Dino Ciccarelli, Minnesota, 1981. 14 goals, 7 assists in 19 games.
20 — Don Maloney, NY Rangers, 1979. 7 goals, 13 assists in 18 games.

THREE-OR-MORE-GOAL GAMES

MOST THREE-OR-MORE-GOAL GAMES IN PLAYOFFS, CAREER:
10 — Wayne Gretzky, Edmonton, Los Angeles, NY Rangers. Eight three-goal games; two four-goal games.
7 — Maurice Richard, Montreal. Four three-goal games; two four-goal games; one five-goal game.
— Jari Kurri, Edmonton. Six three-goal games; one four-goal game.
6 — Dino Ciccarelli, Minnesota, Washington, Detroit. Five three-goal games; one four-goal game.
5 — Mike Bossy, NY Islanders. Four three-goal games; one four-goal game.

MOST THREE-OR-MORE-GOAL GAMES, ONE PLAYOFF YEAR:
4 — Jari Kurri, Edmonton, 1985. 1 four-goal game; 3 three-goal games.
3 — Mark Messier, Edmonton, 1983. 3 three-goal games.
— Mike Bossy, NY Islanders, 1983. 1 four-goal game; 2 three-goal games
2 — Newsy Lalonde, Montreal, 1919. 1 five-goal game; 1 four-goal game.
— Maurice Richard, Montreal, 1944. 1 five-goal game; 1 four-goal game.
— Doug Bentley, Chicago, 1944. 2 three-goal games.
— Norm Ullman, Detroit, 1964. 2 three-goal games.
— Phil Esposito, Boston, 1970. 2 three-goal games.
— Pit Martin, Chicago, 1973. 2 three-goal games.
— Rick MacLeish, Philadelphia, 1975. 2 three-goal games.
— Lanny McDonald, Toronto, 1977. 1 four-goal game; 1 three-goal game.
— Wayne Gretzky, Edmonton, 1981. 2 three-goal games.
— Wayne Gretzky, Edmonton, 1983. 2 four-goal games.
— Wayne Gretzky, Edmonton, 1985. 2 three-goal games.
— Petr Klima, Detroit, 1988. 2 three-goal games.
— Cam Neely, Boston, 1991. 2 three-goal games.
— Wayne Gretzky, NY Rangers, 1997. 2 three-goal games.
— Daniel Alfredsson, Ottawa, 1998. 2 three-goal games.

MOST THREE-OR-MORE-GOAL GAMES, ONE PLAYOFF SERIES:
3 — Jari Kurri, Edmonton, 1985 CF vs. Chicago, won by Edmonton 4-2. Kurri scored 3 goals May 7 at Edmonton in 7-3 win, 3 goals May 14 at Edmonton in 10-5 win and 4 goals May 16 at Chicago in 8-2 win.
2 — Doug Bentley, Chicago, 1944 SF vs. Detroit, won by Chicago 4-1. Bentley scored 3 goals Mar. 28 at Chicago in 7-1 win and 3 goals Mar. 30 at Detroit in 5-2 win.
— Norm Ullman, Detroit, 1964 SF vs. Chicago, won by Detroit 4-3. Ullman scored 3 goals Mar. 29 at Chicago in 5-4 win and 3 goals April 7 at Detroit in 7-2 win.
— Mark Messier, Edmonton, 1983 DF vs. Calgary, won by Edmonton 4-1. Messier scored 4 goals April 14 at Edmonton in 6-3 win and 3 goals April 17 at Calgary in 10-2 win.
— Mike Bossy, NY Islanders, 1983 CF vs. Boston, won by NY Islanders 4-2. Bossy scored 3 goals May 3 at NY Islanders in 8-3 win and 4 goals May 7 at NY Islanders in 8-4 win.

SCORING STREAKS

LONGEST CONSECUTIVE GOAL-SCORING STREAK, ONE PLAYOFF YEAR:
10 Games — Reggie Leach, Philadelphia, 1976. Streak started April 17 at Toronto and ended May 9 at Montreal. He scored one goal in each of eight games; two in one game; and five in another; a total of 15 goals.

LONGEST CONSECUTIVE POINT-SCORING STREAK, ONE PLAYOFF YEAR:
18 games — Bryan Trottier, NY Islanders, 1981. 11 goals, 18 assists, 29 points.
17 games — Wayne Gretzky, Edmonton, 1988. 12 goals, 29 assists, 41 points.
— Al MacInnis, Calgary, 1989. 7 goals, 19 assists, 26 points.

LONGEST CONSECUTIVE POINT-SCORING STREAK, MORE THAN ONE PLAYOFF YEAR:
27 games — Bryan Trottier, NY Islanders, 1980, 1981 and 1982. Seven games in 1980 (3 goals, 5 assists, 8 points), 18 games in 1981 (11 goals, 18 assists, 29 points), and two games in 1982 (2 goals, 3 assists, 5 points). Total points, 42.
19 games — Wayne Gretzky, Edmonton, Los Angeles, 1988 and 1989. 17 games in 1988 (12 goals, 29 assists, 41 points with Edmonton), and two games in 1989 (1 goal, 2 assists, 3 points with Los Angeles). Total points, 44.
— Al MacInnis, Calgary, 1989 and 1990. 17 games in 1989 (7 goals, 19 assists, 26 points), and two games in 1990 (2 goals, 1 assist, 3 points). Total points, 29.

FASTEST GOALS

FASTEST GOAL FROM START OF GAME:
0:06 — Don Kozak, Los Angeles, April 17, 1977, at Los Angeles vs. Boston and goaltender Gerry Cheevers. Los Angeles won 7-4.
0:07 — Bob Gainey, Montreal, May 5, 1977, at NY Islanders vs. goaltender Glenn Resch. Montreal won 2-1.
— Terry Murray, Philadelphia, April 12, 1981, at Quebec vs. goaltender Dan Bouchard. Quebec won 4-3 in overtime.

FASTEST GOAL FROM START OF PERIOD (OTHER THAN FIRST):
0:06 — Pelle Eklund, Philadelphia, April 25, 1989, at Pittsburgh vs. goaltender Tom Barrasso, second period. Pittsburgh won 10-7.
0:09 — Bill Collins, Minnesota, April 9, 1968, at Minnesota vs. Los Angeles and goaltender Wayne Rutledge, third period. Minnesota won 7-5.
— Dave Balon, Minnesota, April 25, 1968, at St. Louis vs. goaltender Glenn Hall, third period. Minnesota won 5-1.
— Murray Oliver, Minnesota, April 8, 1971, at St. Louis vs. goaltender Ernie Wakely, third period. St. Louis won 4-2.
— Clark Gillies, NY Islanders, April 15, 1977, at Buffalo vs. goaltender Don Edwards, third period. NY Islanders won 4-3.
— Eric Vail, Atlanta, April 11, 1978, at Atlanta vs. Detroit and goaltender Ron Low, third period. Detroit won 5-3.
— Stan Smyl, Vancouver, April 10, 1979, at Philadelphia vs. goaltender Wayne Stephenson, third period. Vancouver won 3-2.
— Wayne Gretzky, Edmonton, April 6, 1983, at Edmonton vs. Winnipeg and goaltender Brian Hayward, second period. Edmonton won 6-3.
— Mark Messier, Edmonton, April 16, 1984, at Calgary vs. goaltender Don Edwards, third period. Edmonton won 5-3.
— Brian Skrudland, Montreal, May 18, 1986, at Calgary vs. goaltender Mike Vernon, first overtime period. Montreal won 3-2.

FASTEST TWO GOALS:
0:05 — Norm Ullman, Detroit, April 11, 1965, at Detroit vs. Chicago and goaltender Glenn Hall. Ullman scored at 17:35 and 17:40 of second period. Detroit won 4-2.

FASTEST TWO GOALS FROM START OF A GAME:
  1:08 — Dick Duff, Toronto, April 9, 1963, at Toronto vs. Detroit and goaltender Terry Sawchuk. Duff scored at 0:49 and 1:08. Toronto won 4-2.

FASTEST TWO GOALS FROM START OF A PERIOD:
  0:35 — Pat LaFontaine, NY Islanders, May 19, 1984, at Edmonton vs. goaltender Andy Moog. LaFontaine scored at 0:13 and 0:35 of third period. Edmonton won 5-2.

PENALTIES

MOST PENALTY MINUTES IN PLAYOFFS, CAREER:
729 — Dale Hunter, Quebec, Washington, Colorado
 541 — Chris Nilan, Montreal, NY Rangers, Boston
 529 — Claude Lemieux, Montreal, New Jersey, Colorado, Phoenix, Dallas
 471 — Rick Tocchet, Philadelphia, Pittsburgh, Boston, Phoenix
 466 — Willi Plett, Atlanta, Calgary, Minnesota, Boston

MOST PENALTIES, ONE GAME:
  8 — Forbes Kennedy, Toronto, April 2, 1969, at Boston. Kennedy was assessed 4 minors, 2 majors, 1 10-minute misconduct, 1 game misconduct. Boston won 10-0.
  — **Kim Clackson, Pittsburgh,** April 14, 1980, at Boston. Clackson was assessed 5 minors, 2 majors, 1 10-minute misconduct. Boston won 6-2.

MOST PENALTY MINUTES, ONE GAME:
 42 — Dave Schultz, Philadelphia, April 22, 1976, at Toronto. Schultz was assessed 1 minor, 2 majors, 1 10-minute misconduct and 2 game-misconducts. Toronto won 8-5.

MOST PENALTIES, ONE PERIOD AND MOST PENALTY MINUTES, ONE PERIOD:
6 Penalties; 39 Minutes — Ed Hospodar, NY Rangers, April 9, 1981, at Los Angeles, first period. Hospodar was assessed 2 minors, 1 major, 1 10-minute misconduct, 2 game misconducts. Los Angeles won 5-4.

GOALTENDING

MOST PLAYOFF GAMES APPEARED IN BY A GOALTENDER, CAREER:
247 — Patrick Roy, Montreal, Colorado
 150 — Grant Fuhr, Edmonton, Buffalo, St. Louis
 148 — Ed Belfour, Chicago, Dallas, Toronto
 139 — Martin Brodeur, New Jersey
 138 — Mike Vernon, Calgary, Detroit, San Jose, Florida

MOST MINUTES PLAYED BY A GOALTENDER, CAREER:
15,209 — Patrick Roy, Montreal, Colorado
 9,171 — Ed Belfour, Chicago, Dallas, Toronto
 8,834 — Grant Fuhr, Edmonton, Buffalo, St. Louis
 8,702 — Martin Brodeur, New Jersey
 8,214 — Mike Vernon, Calgary, Detroit, San Jose, Florida

MOST MINUTES PLAYED BY A GOALTENDER, ONE PLAYOFF YEAR:
1,544 — Kirk McLean, Vancouver, 1994. 24 games.
  — **Ed Belfour, Dallas,** 1999. 23 games.
 1,540 — Ron Hextall, Philadelphia, 1987. 26 games.
 1,505 — Martin Brodeur, New Jersey, 2001. 25 games.

MOST SHUTOUTS IN PLAYOFFS (CAREER):
23 — Patrick Roy, Montreal, Colorado
 20 — Martin Brodeur, New Jersey
 15 — Curtis Joseph, St. Louis, Edmonton, Toronto
 14 — Clint Benedict, Ottawa, Mtl. Maroons
  — Jacques Plante, Montreal, St. Louis

MOST SHUTOUTS, ONE PLAYOFF YEAR:
 7 — Martin Brodeur, New Jersey, 2003. 24 games.
 6 — Dominik Hasek, Detroit, 2002. 23 games.
 5 — Jean-Sebastien Giguere, Anaheim, 2003. 21 games.

MOST SHUTOUTS, ONE PLAYOFF SERIES:
 3 — Clint Benedict, Mtl. Maroons, 1926 F vs. Victoria. 4 games.
  — **Dave Kerr, NY Rangers,** 1940 SF vs. Boston. 6 games.
  — **Frank McCool, Toronto,** 1945 F vs. Detroit. 7 games.
  — **Turk Broda, Toronto,** 1950 SF vs. Detroit. 7 games.
  — **Felix Potvin, Toronto,** 1994 CQF vs. Chicago. 6 games.
  — **Martin Brodeur, New Jersey,** 1995 CQF vs. Boston. 7 games.
  — **Brent Johnson, St. Louis,** 2002 CQF vs. Chicago. 5 games.
  — **Patrick Lalime, Ottawa,** 2002 CQF vs. Philadelphia. 5 games.
  — **Jean-Sebastien Giguere, Anaheim,** 2003 CF vs. Minnesota. 4 games.
  — **Martin Brodeur, New Jersey,** 2003 F vs. Anaheim. 7 games.

MOST WINS BY A GOALTENDER, (CAREER):
151 — Patrick Roy, Montreal, Colorado
 92 — Grant Fuhr, Edmonton, Buffalo, St. Louis
 88 — Billy Smith, NY Islanders
 83 — Martin Brodeur, New Jersey
 82 — Ed Belfour, Chicago, Dallas, Toronto

MOST WINS BY A GOALTENDER, ONE PLAYOFF YEAR:
 16 — Sixteen wins by a goaltender in one playoff year has been recorded on 15 occasions. Martin Brodeur of the New Jersey Devils is the most recent to equal this mark, posting a record of 16 wins and 8 losses in 24 games in 2003. It was first accomplished by Grant Fuhr in 1988.

MOST CONSECUTIVE WINS BY A GOALTENDER, MORE THAN ONE PLAYOFF YEAR:
 14 — Tom Barrasso, Pittsburgh, 1992, 1993; 3 wins vs. NY Rangers in 1992 DF, won by Pittsburgh 4-2; 4 wins vs. Boston in 1992 CF, won by Pittsburgh 4-0; 4 wins vs. Chicago in 1992 F, won by Pittsburgh 4-0; and 3 wins vs. New Jersey in 1993 DSF, won by Pittsburgh 4-1.

MOST CONSECUTIVE WINS BY A GOALTENDER, ONE PLAYOFF YEAR:
 11 — Ed Belfour, Chicago, 1992. 3 wins vs. St. Louis in DSF, won by Chicago 4-2; 4 wins vs. Detroit in DF, won by Chicago 4-0; and 4 wins vs. Edmonton in CF, won by Chicago 4-0.
  — **Tom Barrasso, Pittsburgh,** 1992. 3 wins vs. NY Rangers in DF, won by Pittsburgh 4-2; 4 wins vs. Boston in CF, won by Pittsburgh 4-0; and 4 wins vs. Chicago in F, won by Pittsburgh 4-0.
  — **Patrick Roy, Montreal,** 1993. 4 wins vs. Quebec in DSF, won by Montreal 4-2; 4 wins vs. Buffalo in DF, won by Montreal 4-0; and 3 wins vs. NY Islanders in CF, won by Montreal 4-1.

LONGEST SHUTOUT SEQUENCE:
270:08 — George Hainsworth, Montreal, 1930. Hainsworth's shutout streak began after Murray Murdoch scored a goal for the NY Rangers at 15:34 of the first period in the first game of a SF series on March 28, 1930. Hainsworth did not allow another goal in the final 113:18 of that game, won by Montreal 2-1 at 8:52 of the 4th overtime period. Hainsworth then shutout the NY Rangers in the next and final game of the series on March 30, 1930, won by Montreal 2-0. The streak continued with a 3-0 win over Boston in the opening game of the F series on April 1, 1930. His streak ended on April 3, 1930 when Boston's Eddie Shore scored at 16:50 of the second period in the second game of the F series.

MOST CONSECUTIVE SHUTOUTS:
 3 — Clint Benedict, Mtl. Maroons, 1926. Benedict shut out Ottawa 1-0, Mar. 27; he then shut out Victoria twice, 3-0, Mar. 30; 3-0, Apr. 1. Mtl. Maroons won NHL F vs. Ottawa 2 goals to 1 and won the best-of-five F vs. Victoria 3-1.
  — **John Ross Roach, NY Rangers,** 1929. Roach shut out NY Americans twice, 0-0, Mar. 19; 1-0, Mar. 21; he then shut out Toronto 1-0, Mar. 24. NY Rangers won QF vs. NY Americans 1 goal to 0 and won the best-of-three SF vs. Toronto 2-0.
  — **Frank McCool, Toronto,** 1945. McCool shut out Detroit 1-0, April 6; 2-0, April 8; 1-0, April 12. Toronto won the best-of-seven F 4-3.
  — **Brent Johnson, St. Louis,** 2002. Johnson shut out Chicago three times; 2-0, April 20; 4-0, April 21; 1-0, April 23. St. Louis won the best-of-seven CQF 4-1.
  — **Patrick Lalime, Ottawa,** 2002. Lalime shut out Philadelphia three times; 2-0, April 20; 3-0, April 22; 3-0, April 24. Ottawa won the best-of-seven CQF 4-1.
  — **Jean-Sebastien Giguere, Anaheim,** 2003. Giguere shut out Minnesota 1-0, May 10; 2-0, May 12; 4-0, May 14. Anaheim won the best-of-seven CF 4-0.

Early Playoff Records

1893-1918
Team Records

MOST GOALS, BOTH TEAMS, ONE GAME:
 25 — Ottawa Silver Seven, Dawson City at Ottawa, Jan. 16, 1905. Ottawa 23, Dawson City 2. Ottawa won best-of-three series 2-0.

MOST GOALS, ONE TEAM, ONE GAME:
 23 — Ottawa Silver Seven at Ottawa, Jan. 16, 1905. Ottawa defeated Dawson City 23-2.

MOST GOALS, BOTH TEAMS, BEST-OF-THREE SERIES:
 42 — Ottawa Silver Seven, Queen's University at Ottawa, 1906. Ottawa defeated Queen's 16-7, Feb. 27, and 12-7, Feb. 28.

MOST GOALS, ONE TEAM, BEST-OF-THREE SERIES:
 32 — Ottawa Silver Seven in 1905 at Ottawa. Defeated Dawson City 9-2, Jan. 13, and 23-2, Jan. 16.

MOST GOALS, BOTH TEAMS, BEST-OF-FIVE SERIES:
 39 — Toronto Arenas, Vancouver Millionaires at Toronto, 1918. Toronto won 5-3, Mar. 20; 6-3, Mar. 26; 2-1, Mar. 30. Vancouver won 6-4, Mar. 23, and 8-1, Mar. 28. Toronto scored 18 goals; Vancouver 21.

MOST GOALS, ONE TEAM, BEST-OF-FIVE SERIES:
 26 — Vancouver Millionaires in 1915 at Vancouver. Defeated Ottawa Senators 6-2, Mar. 22; 8-3, Mar. 24; and 12-3, Mar. 26.

Individual Records

MOST GOALS IN PLAYOFFS:
 63 — Frank McGee, Ottawa Silver Seven, in 22 playoff games. Seven goals in four games, 1903; 21 goals in eight games, 1904; 18 goals in four games, 1905; 17 goals in six games, 1906.

MOST GOALS, ONE PLAYOFF SERIES:
 15 — Frank McGee, Ottawa Silver Seven, in two games in 1905 at Ottawa. Scored one goal, Jan. 13, in 9-2 victory over Dawson City and 14 goals, Jan. 16, in 23-2 victory.

MOST GOALS, ONE PLAYOFF GAME:
 14 — Frank McGee, Ottawa Silver Seven, at Ottawa, Jan. 16, 1905, in 23-2 victory over Dawson City.

FASTEST THREE GOALS:
 40 Seconds — Marty Walsh, Ottawa Senators, at Ottawa, March 16, 1911, at 3:00, 3:10, and 3:40 of third period. Ottawa defeated Port Arthur 13-4.

All-Time Playoff Goal Leaders since 1918

(40 or more goals)

Player	Teams	Yrs.	GP	G
Wayne Gretzky	Edm., L.A., St.L., NYR	16	208	122
*Mark Messier	Edm., NYR, Van.	18	236	109
Jari Kurri	Edm., L.A., NYR, Ana., Col.	15	200	106
*Brett Hull	Cgy., St.L., Dal., Det.	18	190	100
Glenn Anderson	Edm., Tor., NYR, St.L.	15	225	93
Mike Bossy	NYI	10	129	85
Maurice Richard	Mtl.	15	133	82
*Claude Lemieux	Mtl., N.J., Col., Phx., Dal.	18	233	80
Jean Beliveau	Mtl.	17	162	79
*Mario Lemieux	Pit.	9	107	76
Dino Ciccarelli	Min., Wsh., Det., T.B., Fla.	14	141	73
Esa Tikkanen	Edm., NYR, St.L., N.J., Van., Fla., Wsh.	13	186	72
*Joe Sakic	Que., Col.	10	142	71
Bryan Trottier	NYI, Pit.	17	221	71
Gordie Howe	Det., Hfd.	20	157	68
*Jaromir Jagr	Pit., Wsh.	12	146	67
*Steve Yzerman	Det.	18	181	67
Denis Savard	Chi., Mtl., T.B.	16	169	66
Yvan Cournoyer	Mtl.	12	147	64
Brian Propp	Phi., Bos., Min., Hfd.	13	160	64
Bobby Smith	Min., Mtl.	13	184	64
Bobby Hull	Chi., Wpg., Hfd.	14	119	62
Phil Esposito	Chi., Bos., NYR	15	130	61
Jacques Lemaire	Mtl.	11	145	61
Joe Mullen	St.L., Cgy., Pit., Bos.	15	143	60
*Joe Nieuwendyk	Cgy., Dal., N.J.	15	149	60
*Doug Gilmour	St.L., Cgy., Tor., N.J., Chi., Buf., Mtl.	19	182	60
Stan Mikita	Chi.	18	155	59
Paul Coffey	Edm., Pit., L.A., Det., Hfd., Phi., Chi., Car., Bos.	16	194	59
Guy Lafleur	Mtl., NYR, Que.	14	128	58
Bernie Geoffrion	Mtl., NYR	16	132	58
*Luc Robitaille	L.A., Pit., NYR, Det.	15	159	58
Cam Neely	Van., Bos.	9	93	57
Steve Larmer	Chi., NYR	13	140	56
Denis Potvin	NYI	14	185	56
Rick MacLeish	Phi., Hfd., Pit., Det.	11	114	54
*Steve Thomas	Tor., Chi., NYI, N.J., Ana.	16	168	54
*Peter Forsberg	Que., Col.	9	122	53
Bill Barber	Phi.	11	129	53
Stephane Richer	Mtl., N.J., T.B., St.L., Pit.	13	134	53
Rick Tocchet	Phi., Pit., L.A., Bos., Wsh., Phx.	13	145	52
Frank Mahovlich	Tor., Det., Mtl.	14	137	51
*Brendan Shanahan	N.J., St.L., Hfd., Det.	14	139	51
Brian Bellows	Min., Mtl., T.B., Ana., Wsh.	13	143	51
Steve Shutt	Mtl., L.A.	12	99	50
*Mike Modano	Min., Dal.	11	139	50
*Sergei Fedorov	Det.	13	162	50
Henri Richard	Mtl.	18	180	49
Reggie Leach	Bos., Cal., Phi., Det.	8	94	47
*Jeremy Roenick	Chi., Phx., Phi.	14	118	47
Ted Lindsay	Det., Chi.	16	133	47
Clark Gillies	NYI, Buf.	13	164	47
Kevin Stevens	Pit., Bos., L.A., NYR, Phi.	7	103	46
Dickie Moore	Mtl., Tor., St.L.	14	135	46
*Ron Francis	Hfd., Pit., Car.	17	159	46
Rick Middleton	NYR, Bos.	12	114	45
Lanny McDonald	Tor., Col., Cgy.	13	117	44
Ken Linseman	Phi., Edm., Bos., Tor.	11	113	43
Mike Gartner	Wsh., Min., NYR, Tor., Phx.	15	122	43
*Scott Young	Hfd., Pit., Que., Col., Ana., St.L., Dal.	13	137	43
*Vyacheslav Kozlov	Det., Buf., Atl.	10	114	42
Bernie Nicholls	L.A., NYR, Edm., N.J., Chi., S.J.	13	118	42
Bobby Clarke	Phi.	13	136	42
*Dave Andreychuk	Buf., Tor., N.J., Bos., Col., T.B.	17	139	42
*Adam Oates	Det., St.L., Bos., Wsh., Phi., Ana.	15	163	42
Dale Hunter	Que., Wsh., Col.	18	186	42
John Bucyk	Det., Bos.	14	124	41
Raymond Bourque	Bos., Col.	21	214	41
Tim Kerr	Phi., NYR, Hfd.	10	81	40
Peter McNab	Buf., Bos., Van., N.J.	10	107	40
*John LeClair	Mtl., Phi.	13	136	40
Bob Bourne	NYI, L.A.	13	139	40
John Tonelli	NYI, Cgy., L.A., Chi., Que.	13	172	40

*Active

All-Time Playoff Assist Leaders since 1918

(60 or more assists)

Player	Teams	Yrs.	GP	A
Wayne Gretzky	Edm., L.A., St.L., NYR	16	208	260
*Mark Messier	Edm., NYR, Van.	18	236	186
Raymond Bourque	Bos., Col.	21	214	139
Paul Coffey	Edm., Pit., L.A., Det., Hfd., Phi., Chi., Car., Bos.	16	194	137
*Doug Gilmour	St.L., Cgy., Tor., N.J., Chi., Buf., Mtl.	19	182	128
Jari Kurri	Edm., L.A., NYR, Ana., Col.	15	200	127
*Al MacInnis	Cgy., St.L.	19	177	121
Glenn Anderson	Edm., Tor., NYR, St.L.	15	225	121
Larry Robinson	Mtl., L.A.	20	227	116
Larry Murphy	L.A., Wsh., Min., Pit., Tor., Det.	20	215	115
*Adam Oates	Det., St.L., Bos., Wsh., Phi., Ana.	15	163	114
*Sergei Fedorov	Det.	13	162	113
Bryan Trottier	NYI, Pit.	17	221	113
Denis Savard	Chi., Mtl., T.B.	16	169	109
*Steve Yzerman	Det.	18	181	109
Denis Potvin	NYI	14	185	108
*Chris Chelios	Mtl., Chi., Det.	19	214	106
Jean Beliveau	Mtl.	17	162	97
*Mario Lemieux	Pit.	9	107	96
Bobby Smith	Min., Mtl.	13	184	96
*Ron Francis	Hfd., Pit., Car.	17	159	93
Gordie Howe	Det., Hfd.	20	157	92
*Scott Stevens	Wsh., St.L., N.J.	20	233	92
Stan Mikita	Chi.	18	155	91
*Peter Forsberg	Que., Col.	9	122	90
Brad Park	NYR, Bos., Det.	17	161	90
*Jaromir Jagr	Pit., Wsh.	12	146	87
Craig Janney	Bos., St.L., S.J., Wpg., Phx., T.B., NYI	11	120	86
*Joe Sakic	Que., Col.	10	142	86
*Brett Hull	Cgy., St.L., Dal., Det.	18	190	85
Brian Propp	Phi., Bos., Min., Hfd.	13	160	84
Henri Richard	Mtl.	18	180	80
*Sergei Zubov	NYR, Pit., Dal.	9	137	78
Jacques Lemaire	Mtl.	11	145	78
*Claude Lemieux	Mtl., N.J., Col., Phx., Dal.	18	233	78
Ken Linseman	Phi., Edm., Bos., Tor.	11	113	77
Bobby Clarke	Phi.	13	136	77
*Nicklas Lidstrom	Det.	12	156	77
Guy Lafleur	Mtl., NYR, Que.	14	128	76
Phil Esposito	Chi., Bos., NYR	15	130	76
Dale Hunter	Que., Wsh., Col.	18	186	76
Mike Bossy	NYI	10	129	75
Steve Larmer	Chi., NYR	13	140	75
John Tonelli	NYI, Cgy., L.A., Chi., Que.	13	172	75
*Mike Modano	Min., Dal.	11	139	74
Peter Stastny	Que., N.J., St.L.	12	93	72
Bernie Nicholls	L.A., NYR, Edm., N.J., Chi., S.J.	13	118	72
Brian Bellows	Min., Mtl., T.B., Ana., Wsh.	13	143	71
Gilbert Perreault	Buf.	11	90	70
Geoff Courtnall	Bos., Edm., Wsh., St.L., Van.	15	156	70
Dale Hawerchuk	Wpg., Buf., St.L., Phi.	15	97	69
Alex Delvecchio	Det.	14	121	69
*Luc Robitaille	L.A., Pit., NYR, Det.	15	159	69
Bobby Hull	Chi., Wpg., Hfd.	14	119	67
*Sandis Ozolinsh	S.J., Col., Car., Fla., Ana.	10	134	67
Frank Mahovlich	Tor., Det., Mtl.	14	137	67
*Igor Larionov	Van., S.J., Det., Fla.	12	149	67
Bobby Orr	Bos., Chi.	8	74	66
Bernie Federko	St.L., Det.	11	91	66
Jean Ratelle	NYR, Bos.	15	123	66
Charlie Huddy	Edm., L.A., Buf., St.L.	14	183	66
Dickie Moore	Mtl., Tor., St.L.	14	135	64
Doug Harvey	Mtl., NYR, Det., St.L.	15	137	64
Neal Broten	Min., Dal., N.J., L.A.	13	135	63
Yvan Cournoyer	Mtl.	12	147	63
John Bucyk	Det., Bos.	14	124	62
*Brian Leetch	NYR	8	82	61
Doug Wilson	Chi., S.J.	12	95	61
Steve Duchesne	L.A., Phi., Que., St.L., Ott., Det.	14	121	61
Kevin Stevens	Pit., Bos., L.A., NYR, Phi.	7	103	60
*Trevor Linden	Van., NYI, Mtl., Wsh.	10	105	60
Bernie Geoffrion	Mtl., NYR	16	132	60
*Brendan Shanahan	N.J., St.L., Hfd., Det.	14	139	60
Rick Tocchet	Phi., Pit., L.A., Bos., Wsh., Phx.	13	145	60
Esa Tikkanen	Edm., NYR, St.L., N.J., Van., Fla., Wsh.	13	186	60

All-Time Playoff Point Leaders since 1918

(100 or more points)

Player	Teams	Yrs.	GP	G	A	Pts.
Wayne Gretzky	Edm., L.A., St.L., NYR	16	208	122	260	382
*Mark Messier	Edm., NYR, Van.	18	236	109	186	295
Jari Kurri	Edm., L.A., NYR, Ana., Col.	15	200	106	127	233
Glenn Anderson	Edm., Tor., NYR, St.L.	15	225	93	121	214
Paul Coffey	Edm., Pit., L.A., Det., Hfd., Phi., Chi., Car., Bos.	16	194	59	137	196
*Doug Gilmour	St.L., Cgy., Tor., N.J., Chi., Buf., Mtl.	19	182	60	128	188
*Brett Hull	Cgy., St.L., Dal., Det.	18	190	100	85	185
Bryan Trottier	NYI, Pit.	17	221	71	113	184
Raymond Bourque	Bos., Col.	21	214	41	139	180
Jean Beliveau	Mtl.	17	162	79	97	176
*Steve Yzerman	Det.	18	181	67	109	176
Denis Savard	Chi., Mtl., T.B.	16	169	66	109	175
*Mario Lemieux	Pit.	9	107	76	96	172
Denis Potvin	NYI	14	185	56	108	164
*Sergei Fedorov	Det.	13	162	50	113	163
Mike Bossy	NYI	10	129	85	75	160
Gordie Howe	Det., Hfd.	20	157	68	92	160
*Al MacInnis	Cgy., St.L.	19	177	39	121	160
Bobby Smith	Min., Mtl.	13	184	64	96	160
*Claude Lemieux	Mtl., N.J., Col., Phx., Dal.	18	233	80	78	158
*Joe Sakic	Que., Col.	10	142	71	86	157
*Adam Oates	Det., St.L., Bos., Wsh., Phi., Ana.	15	163	42	114	156
*Jaromir Jagr	Pit., Wsh.	12	146	67	87	154
Larry Murphy	L.A., Wsh., Min., Pit., Tor., Det.	20	215	37	115	152
Stan Mikita	Chi.	18	155	59	91	150
Brian Propp	Phi., Bos., Min., Hfd.	13	160	64	84	148
Larry Robinson	Mtl., L.A.	20	227	28	116	144
*Peter Forsberg	Que., Col.	9	122	53	90	143
Jacques Lemaire	Mtl.	11	145	61	78	139
*Ron Francis	Hfd., Pit., Car.	17	159	46	93	139
Phil Esposito	Chi., Bos., NYR	15	130	61	76	137
*Chris Chelios	Mtl., Chi., Det.	19	214	30	106	136
Guy Lafleur	Mtl., NYR, Que.	14	128	58	76	134
Esa Tikkanen	Edm., NYR, St.L., N.J., Van., Fla., Wsh.	13	186	72	60	132
Steve Larmer	Chi., NYR	13	140	56	75	131
Bobby Hull	Chi., Wpg., Hfd.	14	119	62	67	129
Henri Richard	Mtl.	18	180	49	80	129
Yvan Cournoyer	Mtl.	12	147	64	63	127
*Luc Robitaille	L.A., Pit., NYR, Det.	15	159	58	69	127
Maurice Richard	Mtl.	15	133	82	44	126
Brad Park	NYR, Bos., Det.	17	161	35	90	125
*Mike Modano	Min., Dal.	11	139	50	74	124
Brian Bellows	Min., Mtl., T.B., Ana., Wsh.	13	143	51	71	122
Ken Linseman	Phi., Edm., Bos., Tor.	11	113	43	77	120
Bobby Clarke	Phi.	13	136	42	77	119
Bernie Geoffrion	Mtl., NYR	16	132	58	60	118
Frank Mahovlich	Tor., Det., Mtl.	14	137	51	67	118
Dino Ciccarelli	Min., Wsh., Det., T.B., Fla.	14	141	73	45	118
Dale Hunter	Que., Wsh., Col.	18	186	42	76	118
*Scott Stevens	Wsh., St.L., N.J.	20	233	26	92	118
John Tonelli	NYI, Cgy., L.A., Chi., Que.	13	172	40	75	115
Bernie Nicholls	L.A., NYR, Edm., N.J., Chi., S.J.	13	118	42	72	114
Rick Tocchet	Phi., Pit., L.A., Bos., Wsh., Phx.	13	145	52	60	112
*Brendan Shanahan	N.J., St.L., Hfd., Det.	14	139	51	60	111
Craig Janney	Bos., St.L., S.J., Wpg., Phx., T.B., NYI	11	120	24	86	110
Dickie Moore	Mtl., Tor., St.L.	14	135	46	64	110
*Joe Nieuwendyk	Cgy., Dal., N.J.	15	149	60	50	110
Geoff Courtnall	Bos., Edm., Wsh., St.L., Van.	15	156	39	70	109
*Nicklas Lidstrom	Det.	12	156	32	77	109
Bill Barber	Phi.	11	129	53	55	108
Rick MacLeish	Phi., Hfd., Pit., Det.	11	114	54	53	107
Kevin Stevens	Pit., Bos., L.A., NYR, Phi.	7	103	46	60	106
Joe Mullen	St.L., Cgy., Pit., Bos.	15	143	60	46	106
*Steve Thomas	Tor., Chi., NYI, N.J., Ana.	16	168	54	52	106
Peter Stastny	Que., N.J., St.L.	12	93	33	72	105
Alex Delvecchio	Det.	14	121	35	69	104
Gilbert Perreault	Buf.	11	90	33	70	103
*Jeremy Roenick	Chi., Phx., Phi.	14	118	47	56	103
John Bucyk	Det., Bos.	14	124	41	62	103
Bernie Federko	St.L., Det.	11	91	35	66	101
Rick Middleton	NYR, Bos.	12	114	45	55	100

Three-or-more-Goal Games, Playoffs 1918–2003

Player	Team	Date	City	Total Goals	Opposing Goaltender	Score	
Wayne Gretzky (10)	Edm.	Apr. 11/81	Edm.	3	Richard Sevigny	Edm. 6	Mtl. 2
		Apr. 19/81	Edm.	3	Billy Smith	Edm. 5	NYI 2
		Apr. 6/83	Edm.	4	Brian Hayward	Edm. 6	Wpg. 3
		Apr. 17/83	Cgy.	4	Reggie Lemelin	Edm. 10	Cgy. 2
		Apr. 25/85	Wpg.	3	Brian Hayward (2)		
					Marc Behrend (1)	Edm. 8	Wpg. 3
		May 25/85	Edm.	3	Pelle Lindbergh	Edm. 4	Phi. 3
		Apr. 24/86	Cgy.	3	Mike Vernon	Edm. 7	Cgy. 4
	L.A.	May 29/93	Tor.	3	Felix Potvin	L.A. 5	Tor. 4
	NYR	Apr. 23/97	NYR	3	John Vanbiesbrouck	NYR 3	Fla. 2
		May 18/97	Phi.	3	Garth Snow	NYR 5	Phi. 4
Maurice Richard (7)	Mtl.	Mar. 23/44	Mtl.	5	Paul Bibeault	Mtl. 5	Tor. 1
		Apr. 7/44	Chi.	3	Mike Karakas	Mtl. 3	Chi. 1
		Mar. 29/45	Mtl.	4	Frank McCool	Mtl. 10	Tor. 3
		Apr. 14/53	Bos.	3	Gord Henry	Mtl. 7	Bos. 3
		Mar. 20/56	Mtl.	3	Gump Worsley	Mtl. 7	NYR 1
		Apr. 6/57	Mtl.	4	Don Simmons	Mtl. 5	Bos. 1
		Apr. 1/58	Det.	3	Terry Sawchuk	Mtl. 4	Det. 3
Jari Kurri (7)	Edm.	Apr. 4/84	Edm.	3	Doug Soetaert (1)		
					Mike Veisor (2)	Edm. 9	Wpg. 2
		Apr. 25/85	Wpg.	3	Brian Hayward (2)		
					Marc Behrend (1)	Edm. 8	Wpg. 3
		May 7/85	Edm.	3	Murray Bannerman	Edm. 7	Chi. 3
		May 14/85	Edm.	3	Murray Bannerman	Edm. 10	Chi. 5
		May 16/85	Chi.	4	Murray Bannerman	Edm. 8	Chi. 2
		Apr. 9/87	Edm.	4	Roland Melanson (2)		
					Darren Eliot (2)	Edm. 13	L.A. 3
		May 18/90	Bos.	3	Andy Moog (2)		
					Reggie Lemelin (1)	Edm. 7	Bos. 2
Dino Ciccarelli (6)	Min.	May 5/81	Min.	3	Pat Riggin	Min. 7	Cgy. 4
		Apr. 10/82	Min.	3	Murray Bannerman	Min. 7	Chi. 1
	Wsh.	Apr. 5/90	N.J.	3	Sean Burke	Wsh. 5	N.J. 4
		Apr. 25/92	Pit.	4	Tom Barrasso (1)		
					Ken Wregget (3)	Wsh. 7	Pit. 2
	Det.	Apr. 29/93	Tor.	3	Felix Potvin (2)		
					Daren Puppa (1)	Det. 7	Tor. 3
		May 11/95	Dal.	3	Andy Moog (2)		
					Darcy Wakaluk (1)	Det. 5	Dal. 1
Mike Bossy (5)	NYI	Apr. 16/79	NYI	3	Tony Esposito	NYI 6	Chi. 2
		May 8/82	NYI	3	Richard Brodeur	NYI 6	Van. 5
		Apr. 10/83	Wsh.	3	Al Jensen	NYI 6	Wsh. 3
		May 3/83	NYI	3	Pete Peeters	NYI 8	Bos. 3
		May 7/83	NYI	4	Pete Peeters	NYI 8	Bos. 4
Phil Esposito (4)	Bos.	Apr. 2/69	Bos.	4	Bruce Gamble	Bos. 10	Tor. 0
		Apr. 8/70	Bos.	3	Ed Giacomin	Bos. 8	NYR 2
		Apr. 19/70	Chi.	3	Tony Esposito	Bos. 6	Chi. 3
		Apr. 8/75	Bos.	3	Tony Esposito (2)		
					Michel Dumas (1)	Bos. 8	Chi. 2
Mark Messier (4)	Edm.	Apr. 14/83	Edm.	4	Reggie Lemelin	Edm. 6	Cgy. 3
		Apr. 17/83	Cgy.	3	Reggie Lemelin (1)	Edm. 10	Cgy. 2
					Don Edwards (2)		
		Apr. 26/83	Edm.	3	Murray Bannerman	Edm. 8	Chi. 2
	NYR	May 25/94	N.J.	3	Martin Brodeur (2)	NYR 4	N.J. 2
					ENG (1)		
Steve Yzerman (4)	Det.	Apr. 6/89	Det.	3	Alain Chevrier	Chi. 5	Det. 4
		Apr. 4/91	St.L.	3	Vincent Riendeau (2)	Det. 6	St.L. 3
					Pat Jablonski (1)		
		May 8/96	St.L.	3	Jon Casey	St.L. 5	Det. 4
		Apr. 21/99	Det.	3	Guy Hebert (2)	Det. 5	Ana. 3
					Pat Jablonski (1)		
Bernie Geoffrion (3)	Mtl.	Mar. 27/52	Mtl.	3	Jim Henry	Mtl. 4	Bos. 0
		Apr. 7/55	Mtl.	3	Terry Sawchuk	Mtl. 4	Det. 2
		Mar. 30/57	Mtl.	3	Gump Worsley	Mtl. 8	NYR 3
Norm Ullman (3)	Det.	Mar. 29/64	Chi.	3	Glenn Hall	Det. 5	Chi. 4
		Apr. 7/64	Det.	3	Glenn Hall (2)		
					Denis DeJordy (1)	Det. 7	Chi. 2
		Apr. 11/65	Det.	3	Glenn Hall	Det. 4	Chi. 2
John Bucyk (3)	Bos.	May 3/70	St.L.	3	Jacques Plante (1)		
					Ernie Wakely (2)	Bos. 6	St.L. 1
		Apr. 20/72	Bos.	3	Jacques Caron (1)		
					Ernie Wakely (2)	Bos. 10	St.L. 2
		Apr. 21/74	Bos.	3	Tony Esposito	Bos. 8	Chi. 6
Rick MacLeish (3)	Phi.	Apr. 11/74	Phi.	3	Phil Myre	Phi. 5	Atl. 1
		Apr. 13/75	Phi.	3	Gord McRae	Phi. 6	Tor. 3
		May 13/75	Phi.	3	Glenn Resch	Phi. 4	NYI 1
Denis Savard (3)	Chi.	Apr. 19/82	Chi.	3	Mike Liut	Chi. 7	StL. 4
		Apr. 10/86	Chi.	4	Ken Wregget	Tor. 6	Chi. 4
		Apr. 9/88	St.L.	3	Greg Millen	Chi. 6	St.L. 3
Tim Kerr (3)	Phi.	Apr. 13/85	NYR	4	Glen Hanlon	Phi. 6	NYR 5
		Apr. 20/87	Phi.	3	Kelly Hrudey	Phi. 4	NYI 2
		Apr. 19/89	Pit.	3	Tom Barrasso	Phi. 4	Pit. 2
Cam Neely (3)	Bos.	Apr. 9/87	Mtl.	3	Patrick Roy	Mtl. 4	Bos. 3
		Apr. 5/91	Bos.	3	Peter Sidorkiewicz	Bos. 4	Hfd. 3
		Apr. 25/91	Bos.	3	Patrick Roy	Bos. 4	Mtl. 1
Petr Klima (3)	Det.	Apr. 7/88	Tor.	3	Alan Bester (2)		
					Ken Wregett (1)	Det. 6	Tor. 2
		Apr. 21/88	St.L.	3	Greg Millen	Det. 6	St.L. 0
	Edm.	May 4/91	Edm.	3	Jon Casey	Edm. 7	Min. 2
Esa Tikkanen (3)	Edm.	May 22/88	Edm.	3	Reggie Lemelin	Edm. 6	Bos. 3
		Apr. 16/91	Cgy.	3	Mike Vernon	Edm. 5	Cgy. 4
		Apr. 26/92	L.A.	3	Kelly Hrudey (2)	Edm. 5	L.A. 2
					Tom Askey (1)		
Mike Gartner (3)	NYR	Apr. 13/90	NYR	3	Mark Fitzpatrick (2)		
					Glenn Healy (1)	NYR 6	NYI 5
		Apr. 27/92	NYR	3	Chris Terreri	NYR 8	N.J. 5
	Tor.	Apr. 25/96	Tor.	3	Jon Casey	Tor. 5	St.L. 4
Mario Lemieux (3)	Pit.	Apr. 25/89	Pit.	5	Ron Hextall	Pit. 10	Phi. 7
		Apr. 23/92	Pit.	3	Don Beaupre	Pit. 6	Wsh. 4
		May 11/96	Pit.	3	Mike Richter	Pit. 7	NYR 3

Player	Team	Date	City	Total Goals	Opposing Goaltender	Score	
Newsy Lalonde (2)	Mtl.	Mar. 1/19	Mtl.	5	Clint Benedict	Mtl. 6	Ott. 3
		Mar. 22/19	Sea.	4	Hap Holmes	Mtl. 4	Sea. 2
Howie Morenz (2)	Mtl.	Mar. 22/24	Mtl.	3	Charles Reid	Mtl. 6	Cgy.T. 1
		Mar. 27/25	Mtl.	3	Hap Holmes	Mtl. 4	Vic. 2
Doug Bentley (2)	Chi.	Mar. 28/44	Chi.	3	Connie Dion	Chi. 7	Det. 1
		Mar. 30/44	Det.	3	Connie Dion	Chi. 5	Det. 2
Toe Blake (2)	Mtl.	Mar. 22/38	Mtl.	3	Mike Karakas	Mtl. 6	Chi. 4
		Mar. 26/46	Chi.	3	Mike Karakas	Mtl. 7	Chi. 2
Ted Kennedy (2)	Tor.	Apr. 14/45	Tor.	3	Harry Lumley	Det. 5	Tor. 3
		Mar. 27/48	Tor.	4	Frank Brimsek	Tor. 5	Bos. 3
F. St. Marseille (2)	St.L.	Apr. 28/70	St.L.	3	Al Smith	St.L. 5	Pit. 0
		Apr. 6/72	Min.	3	Cesare Maniago	Min. 6	St.L. 5
Bobby Hull (2)	Chi.	Apr. 7/63	Det.	3	Terry Sawchuk	Det. 7	Chi. 4
		Apr. 9/72	Pit.	3	Jim Rutherford	Chi. 6	Pit. 5
Pit Martin (2)	Chi.	Apr. 4/73	Chi.	3	Wayne Stephenson	Chi. 7	St.L. 1
		May 10/73	Chi.	3	Ken Dryden	Mtl. 6	Chi. 4
Yvan Cournoyer (2)	Mtl.	Apr. 5/73	Mtl.	3	Dave Dryden	Mtl. 7	Buf. 3
		Apr. 11/74	Mtl.	3	Ed Giacomin	Mtl. 4	NYR 1
Guy Lafleur (2)	Mtl.	May 1/75	Mtl.	3	Roger Crozier (1)		
					Gerry Desjardins (2)	Mtl. 7	Buf. 0
		Apr. 11/77	Mtl.	3	Ed Staniowski	Mtl. 7	St.L. 2
Lanny McDonald (2)	Tor.	Apr. 9/77	Pit.	3	Denis Herron	Tor. 5	Pit. 2
		Apr. 17/77	Tor.	4	Wayne Stephenson	Phi. 6	Tor. 5
Bill Barber (2)	Phi.	May 4/80	Min.	4	Gilles Meloche	Phi. 5	Min. 3
		Apr. 9/81	Phi.	3	Dan Bouchard	Phi. 8	Que. 5
Bryan Trottier (2)	NYI	Apr. 8/80	NYI	3	Doug Keans	NYI 8	L.A. 1
		Apr. 9/81	NYI	3	Michel Larocque	NYI 5	Tor. 1
Butch Goring (2)	L.A.	Apr. 9/77	L.A.	3	Phil Myre	L.A. 4	Atl. 2
	NYI	May 17/81	Min.	3	Gilles Meloche	NYI 7	Min. 5
Paul Reinhart (2)	Cgy.	Apr. 14/83	Edm.	3	Andy Moog	Edm. 6	Cgy. 3
		Apr. 8/84	Van	3	Richard Brodeur	Cgy. 5	Van. 1
Brian Propp (2)	Phi.	Apr. 22/81	Phi.	3	Pat Riggin	Phi. 9	Cgy. 4
		Apr. 21/85	Phi.	3	Billy Smith	Phi. 5	NYI 2
Peter Stastny (2)	Que.	Apr. 5/83	Bos.	3	Pete Peeters	Bos. 4	Que. 3
		Apr. 11/87	Que.	3	Mike Liut (2)		
					Steve Weeks (1)	Que. 5	Hfd. 1
Michel Goulet (2)	Que.	Apr. 23/85	Que.	3	Steve Penney	Que. 7	Mtl. 6
		Apr. 12/87	Que.	3	Mike Liut	Que. 4	Hfd. 1
Glenn Anderson (2)	Edm.	Apr. 26/83	Edm.	4	Murray Bannerman	Edm. 8	Chi. 2
		Apr. 6/88	Wpg.	3	Daniel Berthiaume	Edm. 7	Wpg. 4
Peter Zezel (2)	Phi.	Apr. 13/86	NYR	3	John Vanbiesbrouck	Phi. 7	NYR 1
	St.L.	Apr. 11/89	St.L.	3	Jon Casey (2)		
					Kari Takko (1)	St.L. 6	Min. 1
Geoff Courtnall (2)	Van.	Apr. 4/91	L.A.	3	Kelly Hrudey	Van. 6	L.A. 5
		Apr. 30/92	Van.	3	Rick Tabaracci	Van. 5	Win. 0
Joe Sakic (2)	Que.	May 6/95	Que.	3	Mike Richter	Que. 5	NYR 4
	Col.	Apr. 25/96	Col.	3	Corey Hirsch	Col. 5	Van. 4
Daniel Alfredsson (2)	Ott.	Apr. 28/98	Ott.	3	Martin Brodeur	Ott. 4	N.J. 3
		May 11/98	Ott.	3	Olaf Kolzig	Ott. 4	Wsh. 3
Harry Meeking	Tor.	Mar. 11/18	Tor.	3	Georges Vezina	Tor. 7	Mtl. 3
Alf Skinner	Tor.	Mar. 23/18	Tor.	3	Hugh Lehman	Van.M. 6	Tor. 4
Joe Malone	Mtl.	Feb. 23/19	Mtl.	3	Clint Benedict	Mtl. 8	Ott. 4
Odie Cleghorn	Mtl.	Feb. 27/19	Ott.	3	Clint Benedict	Mtl. 5	Ott. 3
Jack Darragh	Ott.	Apr. 1/20	Tor.	3	Hap Holmes	Ott. 6	Sea. 1
George Boucher	Ott.	Mar. 10/21	Ott.	3	Jake Forbes	Ott. 5	Tor. 0
Babe Dye	Tor.	Mar. 28/22	Tor.	4	Hugh Lehman	Tor. 5	Van.M. 1
Percy Galbraith	Bos.	Mar. 31/27	Bos.	3	Hugh Lehman	Bos. 4	Chi. 4
Busher Jackson	Tor.	Apr. 5/32	NYR	3	John Ross Roach	Tor. 6	NYR 4
Frank Boucher	NYR	Apr. 9/32	Tor.	3	Lorne Chabot	Tor. 6	NYR 4
Charlie Conacher	Tor.	Mar. 26/36	Tor.	3	Tiny Thompson	Tor. 8	Bos. 3
Syd Howe	Det.	Mar. 23/39	Det.	3	Claude Bourque	Det. 7	Mtl. 3
Bryan Hextall	NYR	Apr. 3/40	NYR	3	Turk Broda	NYR 6	Tor. 2
Joe Benoit	Mtl.	Mar. 22/41	Mtl.	3	Sam LoPresti	Mtl. 4	Chi. 3
Syl Apps	Tor.	Mar. 25/41	Tor.	3	Frank Brimsek	Tor. 7	Bos. 2
Jack McGill	Bos.	Mar. 29/42	Bos.	3	Johnny Mowers	Det. 6	Bos. 4
Don Metz	Tor.	Apr. 14/42	Tor.	3	Johnny Mowers	Tor. 9	Det. 3
Mud Bruneteau	Det.	Apr. 1/43	Det.	3	Frank Brimsek	Det. 6	Bos. 2
Don Grosso	Det.	Apr. 7/43	Bos.	3	Frank Brimsek	Det. 4	Bos. 0
Carl Liscombe	Det.	Apr. 3/45	Bos.	4	Paul Bibeault	Det. 5	Bos. 3
Billy Reay	Mtl.	Apr. 1/47	Bos.	4	Frank Brimsek	Mtl. 5	Bos. 1
Gerry Plamondon	Mtl.	Mar. 24/49	Det.	3	Harry Lumley	Mtl. 4	Det. 3
Sid Smith	Tor.	Apr. 10/49	Det.	3	Harry Lumley	Tor. 3	Det. 1
Pentti Lund	NYR	Apr. 2/50	NYR	3	Bill Durnan	NYR 4	Mtl. 1
Ted Lindsay	Det.	Apr. 5/55	Det.	4	Charlie Hodge (1)		
					Jacques Plante (3)	Det. 7	Mtl. 1
Gordie Howe	Det.	Apr. 10/55	Det.	3	Jacques Plante	Det. 5	Mtl. 1
Phil Goyette	Mtl.	Mar. 25/58	Mtl.	3	Terry Sawchuk	Mtl. 8	Det. 1
Jerry Toppazzini	Bos.	Apr. 5/58	Bos.	3	Gump Worsley	Bos. 8	NYR 2
Bob Pulford	Tor.	Apr. 19/62	Tor.	3	Glenn Hall	Tor. 8	Chi. 4
Dave Keon	Tor.	Apr. 9/64	Mtl.	3	Charlie Hodge (2)	Tor. 3	Mtl. 1
					ENG (1)		
Henri Richard	Mtl.	Apr. 20/67	Mtl.	3	Terry Sawchuk (2)		
					Johnny Bower (1)	Mtl. 6	Tor. 2
Rosaire Paiement	Phi.	Apr. 13/68	Phi.	3	Glenn Hall (1)		
					Seth Martin (2)	Phi. 6	St.L. 1
Jean Beliveau	Mtl.	Apr. 20/68	Mtl.	3	Denis DeJordy	Mtl. 4	Chi. 1
Red Berenson	St.L.	Apr. 15/69	St.L.	3	Gerry Desjardins	St.L. 4	L.A. 0
Ken Schinkel	Pit.	Apr. 11/70	Oak.	3	Gary Smith	Pit. 5	Oak. 2
Jim Pappin	Chi.	Apr. 11/71	Phi.	3	Bruce Gamble	Chi. 6	Phi. 2
Bobby Orr	Bos.	Apr. 11/71	Mtl.	3	Ken Dryden	Bos. 5	Mtl. 2
Jacques Lemaire	Mtl.	Apr. 20/71	Mtl.	3	Gump Worsley	Mtl. 7	Min. 2
Vic Hadfield	NYR	Apr. 22/71	NYR	3	Tony Esposito	NYR 4	Chi. 1
Fred Stanfield	Bos.	Apr. 18/72	Bos.	3	Jacques Caron	Bos. 6	St.L. 1
Ken Hodge	Bos.	Apr. 30/72	Bos.	3	Ed Giacomin	Bos. 6	NYR 5
Dick Redmond	Chi.	Apr. 4/73	Chi.	3	Wayne Stephenson	Chi. 7	St.L. 1
Steve Vickers	NYR	Apr. 10/73	Bos.	3	Ross Brooks (2)		
					Eddie Johnston (1)	NYR 6	Bos. 3
Tom Williams	L.A.	Apr. 14/74	L.A.	3	Mike Veisor	L.A. 5	Chi. 1
Marcel Dionne	L.A.	Apr. 15/76	L.A.	3	Gilles Gilbert	L.A. 6	Bos. 4

Player	Team	Date	City	Total Goals	Opposing Goaltender	Score	
Don Saleski	Phi.	Apr. 20/76	Phi.	3	Wayne Thomas	Phi. 7	Tor. 1
Darryl Sittler	Tor.	Apr. 22/76	Tor.	5	Bernie Parent	Tor. 8	Phi. 5
Reggie Leach	Phi.	May 6/76	Phi.	5	Gilles Gilbert	Phi. 6	Bos. 3
Jim Lorentz	Buf.	Apr. 7/77	Min.	3	Pete LoPresti (2) Gary Smith (1)	Buf. 7	Min. 1
Bobby Schmautz	Bos.	Apr. 11/77	Bos.	3	Rogie Vachon	Bos. 8	L.A. 3
Billy Harris	NYI	Apr. 23/77	Mtl.	3	Ken Dryden	Mtl. 4	NYI 3
George Ferguson	Tor.	Apr. 11/78	Tor.	3	Rogie Vachon	Tor. 7	L.A. 3
Jean Ratelle	Bos.	May 3/79	Bos.	3	Ken Dryden	Bos. 4	Mtl. 3
Stan Jonathan	Bos.	May 8/79	Bos.	3	Ken Dryden	Bos. 5	Mtl. 2
Ron Duguay	NYR	Apr. 20/80	NYR	3	Pete Peeters	NYR 4	Phi. 2
Steve Shutt	Mtl.	Apr. 22/80	Mtl.	3	Gilles Meloche	Mtl. 6	Min. 2
Gilbert Perreault	Buf.	May 6/80	NYI	3	Billy Smith (2) ENG (1)	Buf. 7	NYI 4
Paul Holmgren	Phi.	May 15/80	Phi.	3	Billy Smith	Phi. 8	NYI 3
Steve Payne	Min.	Apr. 8/81	Bos.	3	Rogie Vachon	Min. 5	Bos. 4
Denis Potvin	NYI	Apr. 17/81	NYI	3	Andy Moog	NYI 6	Edm. 3
Barry Pederson	Bos.	Apr. 8/82	Bos.	3	Don Edwards	Bos. 7	Buf. 3
Duane Sutter	NYI	Apr. 15/83	NYI	3	Glen Hanlon	NYI 5	NYR 0
Doug Halward	Van.	Apr. 7/84	Van.	3	Reggie Lemelin (2) Don Edwards (1)	Van. 7	Cgy. 0
Jorgen Pettersson	St.L.	Apr. 8/84	Det.	3	Eddie Mio	St.L. 3	Det. 2
Clark Gillies	NYI	May 12/84	NYI	3	Grant Fuhr	NYI 6	Edm. 1
Ken Linseman	Bos.	Apr. 14/85	Bos.	3	Steve Penney	Bos. 7	Mtl. 6
Dave Andreychuk	Buf.	Apr. 14/85	Buf.	3	Dan Bouchard	Buf. 7	Que. 4
Greg Paslawski	St.L.	Apr. 15/86	Min.	3	Don Beaupre	St.L. 6	Min. 3
Doug Risebrough	Cgy.	May 4/86	Cgy.	3	Rick Wamsley	Cgy. 8	St.L. 2
Mike McPhee	Mtl.	Apr. 11/87	Bos.	3	Doug Keans	Mtl. 5	Bos. 4
John Ogrodnick	Que.	Apr. 14/87	Hfd.	3	Mike Liut	Que. 7	Hfd. 5
Pelle Eklund	Phi.	May 10/87	Mtl.	3	Patrick Roy (1) Brian Hayward (2)	Phi. 6	Mtl. 3
John Tucker	Buf.	Apr. 9/88	Bos.	4	Andy Moog	Buf. 6	Bos. 2
Tony Hrkac	St.L.	Apr. 10/88	St.L.	4	Darren Pang	St.L. 6	Chi. 5
Hakan Loob	Cgy.	Apr. 10/88	Cgy.	3	Glenn Healy	Cgy. 7	L.A. 3
Ed Olczyk	Tor.	Apr. 12/88	Tor.	3	Greg Stefan (2) Glen Hanlon (1)	Tor. 6	Det. 5
Aaron Broten	N.J.	Apr. 20/88	N.J.	3	Pete Peeters	N.J. 5	Wsh. 2
Mark Johnson	N.J.	Apr. 22/88	Wsh.	4	Pete Peeters	N.J. 10	Wsh. 4
Patrik Sundstrom	N.J.	Apr. 22/88	Wsh.	3	Pete Peeters (2) Clint Malarchuk (1)	N.J. 10	Wsh. 4
Bob Brooke	Min.	Apr. 5/89	St.L.	3	Greg Millen	St.L. 4	Min. 3
Chris Kontos	L.A.	Apr. 6/89	L.A.	3	Grant Fuhr	L.A. 5	Edm. 2
Wayne Presley	Chi.	Apr. 13/89	Chi.	3	Greg Stefan (1) Glen Hanlon (2)	Chi. 7	Det. 1
Tony Granato	L.A.	Apr. 10/90	L.A.	3	Mike Vernon (1) Rick Wamsley (2)	L.A. 12	Cgy. 4
Tomas Sandstrom	L.A.	Apr. 10/90	L.A.	3	Mike Vernon (1) Rick Wamsley (2)	L.A. 12	Cgy. 4
Dave Taylor	L.A.	Apr. 10/90	L.A.	3	Mike Vernon (1) Rick Wamsley (2)	L.A. 12	Cgy. 4
Bernie Nicholls	NYR	Apr. 19/90	NYR	3	Mike Liut	NYR 7	Wsh. 3
John Druce	Wsh.	Apr. 21/90	NYR	3	John Vanbiesbrouck	Wsh. 6	NYR 3
Adam Oates	St.L.	Apr. 12/91	St.L.	3	Tim Chevaldae	St.L. 6	Det. 1
Luc Robitaille	L.A.	Apr. 26/91	L.A.	3	Grant Fuhr	L.A. 5	Edm. 2
Ray Sheppard	Det.	Apr. 24/92	Min.	3	Jon Casey	Min. 5	Det. 2
Pavel Bure	Van.	Apr. 28/92	Wpg.	3	Rick Tabaracci	Van. 8	Wpg. 3
Joe Murphy	Edm.	May 6/92	Edm.	3	Kirk McLean	Edm. 5	Van. 2
Ron Francis	Pit.	May 9/92	Pit.	3	Mike Richter (2) John V'brouck (1)	Pit. 5	NYR. 4
Kevin Stevens	Pit.	May 21/92	Bos.	4	Andy Moog	Pit. 5	Bos. 2
Dirk Graham	Chi.	Jun. 1/92	Chi.	3	Tom Barrasso	Pit. 5	Chi. 2
Brian Noonan	Chi.	Apr. 18/93	Chi.	3	Curtis Joseph	St.L. 4	Chi. 3
Dale Hunter	Wsh.	Apr. 20/93	Wsh.	3	Glenn Healy	NYI 5	Wsh. 4
Teemu Selanne	Wpg.	Apr. 23/93	Wpg.	3	Kirk McLean	Wpg. 5	Van. 4
Ray Ferraro	NYI	Apr. 26/93	Wsh.	4	Don Beaupre	Wsh. 6	NYI 4
Al Iafrate	Wsh.	Apr. 26/93	Wsh.	3	Glenn Healy (2) Mark Fitzpatrick (1)	Wsh. 6	NYI 4
Paul Di Pietro	Mtl.	Apr. 28/93	Mtl.	3	Ron Hextall	Mtl. 6	Que. 2
Wendel Clark	Tor.	May 27/93	L.A.	3	Kelly Hrudey	L.A. 5	Tor. 4
Eric Desjardins	Mtl.	Jun. 3/93	Mtl.	3	Kelly Hrudey	Mtl. 3	L.A. 2
Tony Amonte	Chi.	Apr. 23/94	Chi.	4	Felix Potvin	Chi. 5	Tor. 4
Gary Suter	Chi.	Apr. 24/94	Chi.	3	Felix Potvin	Chi. 4	Tor. 3
Ulf Dahlen	S.J.	May 6/94	S.J.	3	Felix Potvin	S.J. 5	Tor. 2
Mike Sullivan	Cgy.	May 11/95	S.J.	3	Arturs Irbe (2) Wade Flaherty (1)	Cgy. 9	S.J. 2
Theoren Fleury	Cgy.	May 13/95	S.J.	4	Arturs Irbe (3) ENG (1)	Cgy. 6	S.J. 4
Brendan Shanahan	St.L.	May 13/95	Van.	3	Kirk McLean	St.L. 5	Van. 2
John LeClair	Phi.	May 21/95	Phi.	3	Mike Richter	Phi. 5	NYR 4
Brian Leetch	NYR	May 22/95	Phi.	3	Ron Hextall	Phi. 4	NYR 3
Trevor Linden	Van.	Apr. 25/96	Col.	3	Patrick Roy	Col. 5	Van. 4
Jaromir Jagr	Pit.	May 11/96	Pit.	3	Mike Richter	Pit. 7	NYR 3
Peter Forsberg	Col.	Jun. 6/96	Col.	3	John Vanbiesbrouck	Col. 8	Fla. 1
Valeri Zelepukin	N.J.	Apr. 22/97	Mtl.	3	Jocelyn Thibault	N.J. 6	Mtl. 4
Valeri Kamensky	Col.	Apr. 24/97	Col.	3	Jeff Hackett (2) Chris Terreri (1)	Col. 7	Chi. 0
Eric Lindros	Phi.	May 20/97	NYR	3	Mike Richter	Phi. 6	NYR 3
Matthew Barnaby	Buf.	May 10/98	Buf.	3	Andy Moog (2) ENG (1)	Buf. 6	Mtl. 3
Martin Straka	Pit.	Apr. 25/99	Pit.	3	Martin Brodeur	Pit. 4	N.J. 2
Martin Lapointe	Det.	Apr. 15/00	Det.	3	Stephane Fiset (2) Jamie Storr (1)	Det. 8	L.A. 5
Doug Weight	Edm.	Apr. 16/00	Edm.	3	Ed Belfour	Edm. 5	Dal. 2
Bill Guerin	Edm.	Apr. 18/00	Edm.	3	Ed Belfour	Dal. 4	Edm. 3
Scott Young	St.L.	Apr. 23/00	S.J.	3	Steve Shields	St.L. 6	S.J. 2
Andy Delmore	Phi.	May 7/00	Phi.	3	Ron Tugnutt (2) Peter Skudra (1)	Phi. 6	Pit. 3
Brett Hull	Det.	Apr. 27/02	Van.	3	Peter Skudra	Det. 6	Van. 4
Keith Tkachuk	St.L.	May 7/02	St.L.	3	Dominik Hasek	St.L. 6	Det. 1
Darren McCarty	Det.	May 18/02	Det.	3	Patrick Roy	Det. 5	Col. 3
Alexander Mogilny	Tor.	Apr. 9/03	Phi.	3	Roman Cechmanek (2) ENG (1)	Tor. 5	Phi. 3

Leading Playoff Scorers, 1918–2003

Season	Player and Club	Games Played	Goals	Assists	Points
2002-03	Jamie Langenbrunner, New Jersey	24	11	7	18
	Scott Niedermayer, New Jersey	24	2	16	18
2001-02	Peter Forsberg, Colorado	20	9	18	27
2000-01	Joe Sakic, Colorado	21	13	13	26
99-2000	Brett Hull, Dallas	23	11	13	24
1998-99	Peter Forsberg, Colorado	19	8	16	24
1997-98	Steve Yzerman, Detroit	22	6	18	24
1996-97	Eric Lindros, Philadelphia	19	12	14	26
1995-96	Joe Sakic, Colorado	22	18	16	34
1994-95	Sergei Fedorov, Detroit	17	7	17	24
1993-94	Brian Leetch, NY Rangers	23	11	23	34
1992-93	Wayne Gretzky, Los Angeles	24	15	25	40
1991-92	Mario Lemieux, Pittsburgh	15	16	18	34
1990-91	Mario Lemieux, Pittsburgh	23	16	28	44
1989-90	Craig Simpson, Edmonton	22	16	15	31
	Mark Messier, Edmonton	22	9	22	31
1988-89	Al MacInnis, Calgary	22	7	24	31
1987-88	Wayne Gretzky, Edmonton	19	12	31	43
1986-87	Wayne Gretzky, Edmonton	21	5	29	34
1985-86	Doug Gilmour, St. Louis	19	9	12	21
	Bernie Federko, St. Louis	19	7	14	21
1984-85	Wayne Gretzky, Edmonton	18	17	30	47
1983-84	Wayne Gretzky, Edmonton	19	13	22	35
1982-83	Wayne Gretzky, Edmonton	16	12	26	38
1981-82	Bryan Trottier, NY Islanders	19	6	23	29
1980-81	Mike Bossy, NY Islanders	18	17	18	35
1979-80	Bryan Trottier, NY Islanders	21	12	17	29
1978-79	Jacques Lemaire, Montreal	16	11	12	23
	Guy Lafleur, Montreal	16	10	13	23
1977-78	Guy Lafleur, Montreal	15	10	11	21
	Larry Robinson, Montreal	15	4	17	21
1976-77	Guy Lafleur, Montreal	14	9	17	26
1975-76	Reggie Leach, Philadelphia	16	19	5	24
1974-75	Rick MacLeish, Philadelphia	17	11	9	20
1973-74	Rick MacLeish, Philadelphia	17	13	9	22
1972-73	Yvan Cournoyer, Montreal	17	15	10	25
1971-72	Phil Esposito, Boston	15	9	15	24
	Bobby Orr, Boston	15	5	19	24
1970-71	Frank Mahovlich, Montreal	20	14	13	27
1969-70	Phil Esposito, Boston	14	13	14	27
1968-69	Phil Esposito, Boston	10	8	10	18
1967-68	Bill Goldsworthy, Minnesota	14	8	7	15
1966-67	Jim Pappin, Toronto	12	7	8	15
1965-66	Norm Ullman, Detroit	12	6	9	15
1964-65	Bobby Hull, Chicago	14	10	7	17
1963-64	Gordie Howe, Detroit	14	9	10	19
1962-63	Gordie Howe, Detroit	11	7	9	16
	Norm Ullman, Detroit	11	4	12	16
1961-62	Stan Mikita, Chicago	12	6	15	21
1960-61	Gordie Howe, Detroit	11	4	11	15
	Pierre Pilote, Chicago	12	3	12	15
1959-60	Henri Richard, Montreal	8	3	9	12
	Bernie Geoffrion, Montreal	8	2	10	12
1958-59	Dickie Moore, Montreal	11	5	12	17
1957-58	Fleming MacKell, Boston	12	5	14	19
1956-57	Bernie Geoffrion, Montreal	11	11	7	18
1955-56	Jean Béliveau, Montreal	10	12	7	19
1954-55	Gordie Howe, Detroit	11	9	11	20
1953-54	Dickie Moore, Montreal	11	5	8	13
1952-53	Ed Sandford, Boston	11	8	3	11
1951-52	Ted Lindsay, Detroit	8	5	2	7
	Floyd Curry, Montreal	11	4	3	7
	Metro Prystai, Detroit	8	2	5	7
	Gordie Howe, Detroit	8	2	5	7
1950-51	Maurice Richard, Montreal	11	9	4	13
	Max Bentley, Toronto	11	2	11	13
1949-50	Pentti Lund, NY Rangers	12	6	5	11
1948-49	Gordie Howe, Detroit	11	8	3	11
1947-48	Ted Kennedy, Toronto	9	8	6	14
1946-47	Maurice Richard, Montreal	10	6	5	11
1945-46	Elmer Lach, Montreal	9	5	12	17
1944-45	Joe Carveth, Detroit	14	5	6	11
1943-44	Toe Blake, Montreal	9	7	11	18
1942-43	Carl Liscombe, Detroit	10	6	8	14
1941-42	Don Grosso, Detroit	12	8	6	14
	Syl Apps, Toronto	13	5	9	14
1940-41	Milt Schmidt, Boston	11	5	6	11
1939-40	Phil Watson, NY Rangers	12	3	6	9
	Neil Colville, NY Rangers	12	2	7	9
1938-39	Bill Cowley, Boston	12	3	11	14
1937-38	Johnny Gottselig, Chicago	10	5	3	8
	Gordie Drillon, Toronto	7	7	1	8
1936-37	Marty Barry, Detroit	10	4	7	11
1935-36	Frank Boll, Toronto	9	7	3	10
1934-35	Baldy Northcott, Mtl. Maroons	7	4	1	5
	Busher Jackson, Toronto	7	3	2	5
	Cy Wentworth, Mtl. Maroons	7	3	2	5
	Charlie Conacher, Toronto	7	1	4	5
1933-34	Larry Aurie, Detroit	9	3	7	10
1932-33	Cecil Dillon, NY Rangers	8	8	2	10
1931-32	Frank Boucher, NY Rangers	7	3	6	9
1930-31	Cooney Weiland, Boston	5	6	3	9
1929-30	Marty Barry, Boston	6	3	3	6
	Cooney Weiland, Boston	6	1	5	6
1928-29	Andy Blair, Toronto	4	3	0	3
	Butch Keeling, NY Rangers	6	3	0	3
	Ace Bailey, Toronto	4	1	2	3
1927-28	Frank Boucher, NY Rangers	9	7	3	10
1926-27	Harry Oliver, Boston	8	4	2	6
	Percy Galbraith, Boston	8	3	3	6
1925-26	Nels Stewart, Mtl. Maroons	8	6	3	9
1924-25	Howie Morenz, Montreal	6	7	0	7
1923-24	Howie Morenz, Montreal	6	7	3	10
1922-23	Punch Broadbent, Ottawa	8	6	1	7
1921-22	Babe Dye, Toronto	7	11	1	12
1920-21	Cy Denneny, Ottawa	7	4	2	6
1919-20	Frank Nighbor, Ottawa	5	6	1	7
	Jack Darragh, Ottawa	5	5	2	7
1918-19	Newsy Lalonde, Montreal	10	17	2	19
1917-18	Alf Skinner, Toronto	7	8	3	11

Overtime Games since 1918

Abbreviations: Teams/Cities: — **Ana.** - Anaheim; **Atl.** - Atlanta; **Bos.** - Boston; **Buf.** - Buffalo; **Cgy.** - Calgary; **Cgy. T.** - Calgary Tigers (Western Canada Hockey League); **Chi.** - Chicago; **Col.** - Colorado; **Dal.** - Dallas; **Det.** - Detroit; **Edm.** - Edmonton; **Edm. E.** - Edmonton Eskimos (WCHL); **Fla.** - Florida; **Hfd.** - Hartford; **K.C.** - Kansas City; **L.A.** - Los Angeles; **Min.** - Minnesota; **Mtl.** - Montreal; **Mtl. M.** - Montreal Maroons; **N.J.** - New Jersey; **NYA** - NY Americans; **NYI** - New York Islanders; **NYR** - New York Rangers; **Oak.** - Oakland; **Ott.** - Ottawa; **Phi.** - Philadelphia; **Phx.** - Phoenix; **Pit.** - Pittsburgh; **Que.** - Quebec; **St.L.** - St. Louis; **Sea.** - Seattle Metropolitans (Pacific Coast Hockey Association); **S.J.** - San Jose; **T.B.** - Tampa Bay; **Tor.** - Toronto; **Van.** - Vancouver; **Van. M.** - Vancouver Millionaires (PCHA); **Vic.** - Victoria Cougars (WCHL); **Wpg.** - Winnipeg; **Wsh.** - Washington.

SERIES — **CF** - conference final; **CSF** - conference semi-final; **CQF** - conference quarter-final; **DF** - division final; **DSF** - division semi-final; **F** - final; **PRE** - preliminary round; **QF** - quarter final; **SF** - semi-final.

Date	City	Series	Score		Scorer	Overtime	Series Winner
Mar. 26/19	Sea.	F	Mtl. 0	Sea. 0	no scorer	20:00	....
Mar. 30/19	Sea.	F	Mtl. 4	Sea. 3	Odie Cleghorn	15:57	....
Mar. 20/22	Tor.	F	Tor. 2	Van. M. 1	Babe Dye	4:50	Tor.
Mar. 29/23	Van.	F	Ott. 2	Edm. E. 1	Cy Denneny	2:08	Ott.
Mar. 31/27	Mtl.	QF	Mtl. 1	Mtl. M. 0	Howie Morenz	12:05	Mtl.
Apr. 7/27	Bos.	F	Ott. 0	Bos. 0	no scorer	20:00	Ott.
Apr. 11/27	Ott.	F	Bos. 1	Ott. 1	no scorer	20:00	Ott.
Apr. 3/28	Mtl.	QF	Mtl. M. 1	Mtl. 0	Russell Oatman	8:20	Mtl. M.
Apr. 7/28	Mtl.	F	NYR 2	Mtl. M. 1	Frank Boucher	7:05	NYR
Mar. 21/29	NYR	QF	NYR 1	NYA 0	Butch Keeling	29:50	NYR
Mar. 26/29	Tor.	SF	NYR 2	Tor. 1	Frank Boucher	2:03	NYR
Mar. 20/30	Mtl.	SF	Bos. 2	Mtl. M. 1	Harry Oliver	45:35	Bos.
Mar. 25/30	Bos.	SF	Mtl. M. 1	Bos. 0	Archie Wilcox	26:27	Bos.
Mar. 26/30	Mtl.	QF	Chi. 2	Mtl. 2	Howie Morenz (Mtl.)	51:43	Mtl.
Mar. 28/30	Mtl.	SF	Mtl. 2	NYR 1	Gus Rivers	68:52	Mtl.
Mar. 24/31	Bos.	SF	Bos. 5	Mtl. 4	Cooney Weiland	18:56	Mtl.
Mar. 26/31	Chi.	QF	Chi. 2	Tor. 1	Stew Adams	19:20	Chi.
Mar. 28/31	Mtl.	SF	Mtl. 4	Bos. 3	Georges Mantha	5:10	Mtl.
Apr. 1/31	Mtl.	SF	Mtl. 3	Bos. 2	Wildor Larochelle	19:00	Mtl.
Apr. 5/31	Chi.	F	Chi. 2	Mtl. 1	Johnny Gottselig	24:50	Mtl.
Apr. 9/31	Mtl.	F	Chi. 3	Mtl. 2	Cy Wentworth	53:50	Mtl.
Mar. 26/32	Mtl.	SF	NYR 4	Mtl. 3	Fred Cook	59:32	NYR
Apr. 2/32	Tor.	SF	Tor. 3	Mtl. M. 2	Bob Gracie	17:59	Tor.
Mar. 25/33	Bos.	SF	Bos. 2	Tor. 1	Marty Barry	14:14	Tor.
Mar. 28/33	Bos.	SF	Tor. 1	Bos. 0	Busher Jackson	15:03	Tor.
Mar. 30/33	Tor.	SF	Bos. 2	Tor. 1	Eddie Shore	4:23	Tor.
Apr. 3/33	Tor.	SF	Tor. 1	Bos. 0	Ken Doraty	104:46	Tor.
Apr. 13/33	Tor.	F	NYR 1	Tor. 0	Bill Cook	7:33	NYR
Mar. 22/34	Tor.	SF	Det. 2	Tor. 1	Herbie Lewis	1:33	Det.
Mar. 25/34	Chi.	QF	Chi. 1	Mtl. 1	Mush March (Chi)	11:05	Chi.
Apr. 3/34	Det.	F	Chi. 2	Det. 1	Paul Thompson	21:10	Chi.
Apr. 10/34	Chi.	F	Chi. 1	Det. 0	Mush March	30:05	Chi.
Mar. 23/35	Bos.	SF	Bos. 1	Tor. 0	Dit Clapper	33:26	Tor.
Mar. 26/35	Chi.	QF	Mtl. M. 1	Chi. 0	Baldy Northcott	4:02	Mtl. M.
Mar. 30/35	Tor.	SF	Tor. 2	Bos. 1	Pep Kelly	1:36	Tor.
Apr. 4/35	Tor.	F	Mtl. M. 3	Tor. 2	Dave Trottier	5:28	Mtl. M.
Mar. 24/36	Mtl.	SF	Det. 1	Mtl. M. 0	Mud Bruneteau	116:30	Det.
Apr. 9/36	Tor.	F	Tor. 4	Det. 3	Buzz Boll	0:31	Det.
Mar. 25/37	NYR	QF	NYR 2	Tor. 1	Babe Pratt	13:05	NYR
Apr. 1/37	Mtl.	SF	Det. 2	Mtl. 1	Hec Kilrea	51:49	Det.
Mar. 22/38	NYR	QF	NYA 2	NYR 1	John Sorrell	21:25	NYA
Mar. 24/38	Tor.	SF	Tor. 1	Bos. 0	George Parsons	21:31	Tor.
Mar. 26/38	Mtl.	QF	Chi. 3	Mtl. 2	Paul Thompson	11:49	Chi.
Mar. 27/38	NYR	QF	NYA 3	NYR 2	Lorne Carr	60:40	NYA
Mar. 29/38	Bos.	SF	Tor. 3	Bos. 2	Gordie Drillon	10:04	Tor.
Mar. 31/38	Chi.	SF	Chi. 1	NYA 0	Cully Dahlstrom	33:01	Chi.
Mar. 21/39	NYR	SF	Bos. 2	NYR 1	Mel Hill	59:25	Bos.
Mar. 23/39	Bos.	SF	Bos. 3	NYR 2	Mel Hill	8:24	Bos.
Mar. 26/39	Det.	QF	Det. 1	Mtl. 0	Marty Barry	7:47	Det.
Mar. 30/39	Bos.	SF	NYR 2	Bos. 1	Clint Smith	17:19	Bos.
Apr. 1/39	Tor.	SF	Tor. 5	Det. 4	Gordie Drillon	5:42	Tor.
Apr. 2/39	Bos.	SF	Bos. 2	NYR 1	Mel Hill	48:00	Bos.
Apr. 9/39	Bos.	F	Tor. 3	Bos. 2	Doc Romnes	10:38	Bos.
Mar. 19/40	Det.	QF	Det. 2	NYA 1	Syd Howe	0:25	Det.
Mar. 19/40	Tor.	QF	Tor. 3	Chi. 2	Syl Apps	6:35	Tor.
Apr. 2/40	NYR	F	NYR 2	Tor. 1	Alf Pike	15:30	NYR
Apr. 11/40	Tor.	F	NYR 2	Tor. 1	Muzz Patrick	31:43	NYR
Apr. 13/40	Tor.	F	NYR 3	Tor. 2	Bryan Hextall	2:07	NYR
Mar. 20/41	Det.	QF	Det. 2	NYR 1	Gus Giesebrecht	12:01	Det.
Mar. 22/41	Mtl.	QF	Mtl. 4	Chi. 3	Charlie Sands	34:04	Chi.
Mar. 29/41	Bos.	SF	Tor. 2	Bos. 1	Pete Langelle	17:31	Bos.
Mar. 30/41	Chi.	SF	Det. 2	Chi. 1	Gus Giesebrecht	9:15	Det.
Mar. 22/42	Chi.	QF	Bos. 2	Chi. 1	Des Smith	6:51	Bos.
Mar. 21/43	Bos.	SF	Bos. 5	Mtl. 4	Don Gallinger	12:30	Bos.
Mar. 23/43	Det.	SF	Tor. 3	Det. 2	Jack McLean	70:18	Det.
Mar. 25/43	Mtl.	SF	Bos. 3	Mtl. 2	Busher Jackson	3:20	Bos.
Mar. 30/43	Tor.	SF	Det. 3	Tor. 2	Adam Brown	9:21	Det.
Mar. 30/43	Bos.	SF	Bos. 5	Mtl. 4	Ab DeMarco	3:41	Bos.
Apr. 13/44	Mtl.	F	Mtl. 5	Chi. 4	Toe Blake	9:12	Mtl.
Mar. 27/45	Tor.	SF	Tor. 4	Mtl. 3	Gus Bodnar	12:36	Tor.
Mar. 29/45	Det.	SF	Det. 3	Bos. 2	Mud Bruneteau	17:12	Det.
Apr. 21/45	Tor.	F	Det. 1	Tor. 0	Eddie Bruneteau	14:16	Tor.
Mar. 28/46	Bos.	SF	Bos. 4	Det. 3	Don Gallinger	9:51	Bos.
Mar. 30/46	Mtl.	F	Mtl. 4	Bos. 3	Maurice Richard	9:08	Mtl.
Apr. 2/46	Mtl.	F	Mtl. 3	Bos. 2	Jimmy Peters	16:55	Mtl.
Apr. 7/46	Bos.	F	Bos. 3	Mtl. 2	Terry Reardon	15:13	Mtl.
Mar. 26/47	Tor.	SF	Tor. 3	Det. 2	Howie Meeker	3:05	Tor.
Mar. 27/47	Mtl.	SF	Mtl. 2	Bos. 1	Ken Mosdell	5:38	Mtl.
Apr. 3/47	Mtl.	SF	Mtl. 4	Bos. 3	John Quilty	36:40	Mtl.
Apr. 15/47	Tor.	F	Tor. 2	Mtl. 1	Syl Apps	16:36	Tor.
Mar. 24/48	Tor.	SF	Tor. 5	Bos. 4	Nick Metz	17:03	Tor.
Mar. 22/49	Det.	SF	Det. 2	Mtl. 1	Max McNab	44:52	Det.
Mar. 24/49	Det.	SF	Mtl. 4	Det. 3	Gerry Plamondon	2:59	Det.
Mar. 26/49	Tor.	SF	Bos. 5	Tor. 4	Woody Dumart	16:14	Tor.
Apr. 8/49	Det.	F	Tor. 3	Det. 2	Joe Klukay	17:31	Tor.
Apr. 4/50	Tor.	SF	Det. 2	Tor. 1	Leo Reise Jr.	20:38	Det.
Apr. 4/50	Mtl.	SF	Mtl. 3	NYR 2	Elmer Lach	15:19	NYR
Apr. 9/50	Det.	SF	Det. 1	Tor. 0	Leo Reise Jr.	8:39	Det.
Apr. 18/50	Det.	F	NYR 4	Det. 3	Don Raleigh	8:34	Det.
Apr. 20/50	Det.	F	NYR 2	Det. 1	Don Raleigh	1:38	Det.
Apr. 23/50	Det.	F	Det. 4	NYR 3	Pete Babando	28:31	Det.
Mar. 27/51	Det.	SF	Mtl. 3	Det. 2	Maurice Richard	61:09	Mtl.
Mar. 29/51	Det.	SF	Mtl. 1	Det. 0	Maurice Richard	42:20	Mtl.
Mar. 31/51	Tor.	SF	Bos. 1	Tor. 1	no scorer	20:00	Tor.
Apr. 11/51	Tor.	F	Tor. 3	Mtl. 2	Sid Smith	5:51	Tor.
Apr. 14/51	Tor.	F	Mtl. 3	Tor. 2	Maurice Richard	2:55	Tor.
Apr. 17/51	Mtl.	F	Tor. 2	Mtl. 1	Ted Kennedy	4:47	Tor.
Apr. 19/51	Mtl.	F	Tor. 3	Mtl. 2	Harry Watson	5:15	Tor.
Apr. 21/51	Tor.	F	Tor. 3	Mtl. 2	Bill Barilko	2:53	Tor.
Apr. 6/52	Bos.	SF	Mtl. 3	Bos. 2	Paul Masnick	27:49	Mtl.
Mar. 29/53	Bos.	SF	Bos. 2	Det. 1	Jack McIntyre	12:29	Bos.
Mar. 29/53	Chi.	SF	Chi. 2	Mtl. 1	Al Dewsbury	5:18	Mtl.
Apr. 16/53	Mtl.	F	Mtl. 1	Bos. 0	Elmer Lach	1:22	Mtl.
Apr. 1/54	Det.	SF	Det. 4	Tor. 3	Ted Lindsay	21:01	Det.
Apr. 11/54	Det.	F	Mtl. 1	Det. 0	Ken Mosdell	5:45	Det.
Apr. 16/54	Det.	F	Det. 2	Mtl. 1	Tony Leswick	4:29	Det.
Mar. 29/55	Bos.	SF	Mtl. 4	Bos. 3	Don Marshall	3:05	Mtl.
Mar. 24/56	Tor.	SF	Det. 5	Tor. 4	Ted Lindsay	4:22	Det.
Mar. 28/57	NYR	SF	NYR 4	Mtl. 3	Andy Hebenton	13:38	Mtl.
Apr. 4/57	Mtl.	SF	Mtl. 4	NYR 3	Maurice Richard	1:11	Mtl.
Mar. 27/58	NYR	SF	Bos. 4	NYR 3	Jerry Toppazzini	4:46	Bos.
Mar. 30/58	Det.	SF	Mtl. 2	Det. 1	André Pronovost	11:52	Mtl.
Apr. 17/58	Mtl.	F	Mtl. 3	Bos. 2	Maurice Richard	5:45	Mtl.
Mar. 28/59	Tor.	SF	Tor. 3	Bos. 2	Gerry Ehman	5:02	Tor.
Mar. 31/59	Tor.	SF	Tor. 3	Bos. 2	Frank Mahovlich	11:21	Tor.
Apr. 14/59	Tor.	F	Tor. 3	Mtl. 2	Dick Duff	10:06	Mtl.
Mar. 26/60	Mtl.	SF	Mtl. 4	Chi. 3	Doug Harvey	8:38	Mtl.
Mar. 27/60	Det.	SF	Tor. 5	Det. 4	Frank Mahovlich	43:00	Tor.
Mar. 29/60	Det.	SF	Det. 2	Tor. 1	Gerry Melnyk	1:54	Tor.
Mar. 22/61	Tor.	SF	Tor. 3	Det. 2	George Armstrong	24:51	Det.
Mar. 26/61	Chi.	SF	Chi. 2	Mtl. 1	Murray Balfour	52:12	Chi.
Apr. 5/62	Tor.	SF	Tor. 3	NYR 2	Red Kelly	24:23	Tor.
Apr. 2/64	Det.	SF	Chi. 3	Det. 2	Murray Balfour	8:21	Det.
Apr. 14/64	Tor.	F	Det. 4	Tor. 3	Larry Jeffrey	7:52	Tor.
Apr. 23/64	Det.	F	Tor. 4	Det. 3	Bob Baun	1:43	Tor.
Apr. 6/65	Tor.	SF	Tor. 3	Mtl. 2	Dave Keon	4:17	Mtl.
Apr. 13/65	Tor.	SF	Mtl. 4	Tor. 3	Claude Provost	16:33	Mtl.
May 5/66	Det.	F	Mtl. 3	Det. 2	Henri Richard	2:20	Mtl.
Apr. 13/67	NYR	SF	Mtl. 2	NYR 1	John Ferguson	6:28	Mtl.
Apr. 25/67	Tor.	F	Tor. 3	Mtl. 2	Bob Pulford	28:26	Tor.
Apr. 10/68	St.L.	QF	St.L. 3	Phi. 2	Larry Keenan	24:10	St.L.
Apr. 16/68	St.L.	QF	Phi. 2	St.L. 1	Don Blackburn	31:18	St.L.
Apr. 16/68	Min.	QF	Min. 4	L.A. 3	Milan Marcetta	9:11	Min.
Apr. 22/68	Min.	SF	Min. 3	St.L. 2	Parker MacDonald	3:41	St.L.
Apr. 27/68	St.L.	SF	St.L. 4	Min. 3	Gary Sabourin	1:32	St.L.
Apr. 28/68	Mtl.	SF	Mtl. 4	Chi. 3	Jacques Lemaire	2:14	Mtl.
Apr. 29/68	St.L.	SF	St.L. 3	Min. 2	Bill McCreary	17:27	St.L.
May 3/68	St.L.	SF	St.L. 2	Min. 1	Ron Schock	22:50	St.L.
May 5/68	St.L.	F	Mtl. 3	St.L. 2	Jacques Lemaire	1:41	Mtl.
May 9/68	Mtl.	F	Mtl. 4	St.L. 3	Bobby Rousseau	1:13	Mtl.
Apr. 2/69	Oak.	QF	L.A. 5	Oak. 4	Ted Irvine	0:19	L.A.
Apr. 10/69	Mtl.	SF	Mtl. 3	Bos. 2	Ralph Backstrom	0:42	Mtl.
Apr. 13/69	Mtl.	SF	Mtl. 4	Bos. 3	Mickey Redmond	4:55	Mtl.
Apr. 24/69	Bos.	SF	Mtl. 2	Bos. 1	Jean Béliveau	31:28	Mtl.
Apr. 12/70	Oak.	QF	Pit. 3	Oak. 2	Michel Briere	8:28	Pit.
May 10/70	Bos.	F	Bos. 4	St.L. 3	Bobby Orr	0:40	Bos.
Apr. 15/71	Tor.	QF	NYR 2	Tor. 1	Bob Nevin	9:07	NYR
Apr. 18/71	Chi.	SF	NYR 2	Chi. 1	Pete Stemkowski	1:37	Chi.
Apr. 27/71	Chi.	SF	Chi. 3	NYR 2	Bobby Hull	6:35	Chi.
Apr. 29/71	NYR	SF	NYR 3	Chi. 2	Pete Stemkowski	41:29	Chi.
May 4/71	Chi.	F	Chi. 2	Mtl. 1	Jim Pappin	21:11	Mtl.
Apr. 6/72	Bos.	QF	Tor. 4	Bos. 3	Jim Harrison	2:58	Bos.
Apr. 6/72	Min.	QF	Min. 6	St.L. 5	Bill Goldsworthy	1:36	St.L.
Apr. 9/72	Pit.	QF	Chi. 6	Pit. 5	Pit Martin	0:12	Chi.
Apr. 16/72	Min.	QF	St.L. 2	Min. 1	Kevin O'Shea	10:07	St.L.
Apr. 1/73	Mtl.	QF	Buf. 3	Mtl. 2	René Robert	9:18	Mtl.
Apr. 10/73	Phi.	QF	Phi. 3	Min. 2	Gary Dornhoefer	8:35	Phi.
Apr. 14/73	Mtl.	SF	Phi. 5	Mtl. 4	Rick MacLeish	2:56	Mtl.
Apr. 17/73	Mtl.	SF	Mtl. 4	Phi. 3	Larry Robinson	6:45	Mtl.
Apr. 14/74	Tor.	QF	Bos. 4	Tor. 3	Ken Hodge	1:27	Bos.
Apr. 14/74	Atl.	QF	Phi. 4	Atl. 3	Dave Schultz	5:40	Phi.
Apr. 16/74	Mtl.	QF	NYR 3	Mtl. 2	Ron Harris	4:07	NYR
Apr. 23/74	Chi.	SF	Chi. 4	Bos. 3	Jim Pappin	3:48	Bos.
Apr. 28/74	NYR	SF	NYR 2	Phi. 1	Rod Gilbert	4:20	Phi.
May 9/74	Bos.	F	Phi. 3	Bos. 2	Bobby Clarke	12:01	Phi.
Apr. 8/75	L.A.	PRE	L.A. 3	Tor. 2	Mike Murphy	8:53	Tor.
Apr. 10/75	Tor.	PRE	Tor. 3	L.A. 2	Blaine Stoughton	10:19	Tor.
Apr. 10/75	Chi.	PRE	Chi. 4	Bos. 3	Ivan Boldirev	7:33	Chi.
Apr. 11/75	NYR	PRE	NYI 4	NYR 3	J.P. Parise	0:11	NYI
Apr. 17/75	Chi.	QF	Chi. 5	Buf. 4	Stan Mikita	2:31	Buf.
Apr. 19/75	Tor.	QF	Phi. 4	Tor. 3	André Dupont	1:45	Phi.
Apr. 22/75	Mtl.	QF	Mtl. 5	Van. 4	Guy Lafleur	17:06	Mtl.
Apr. 27/75	Buf.	SF	Buf. 6	Mtl. 5	Danny Gare	4:42	Buf.
May 1/75	Phi.	SF	Phi. 5	NYI 4	Bobby Clarke	2:56	Phi.
May 6/75	Buf.	SF	Buf. 5	Mtl. 4	René Robert	5:56	Buf.
May 7/75	NYI	SF	NYI 4	Phi. 3	Jude Drouin	1:53	Phi.
May 20/75	Buf.	F	Buf. 5	Phi. 4	René Robert	18:29	Phi.
Apr. 8/76	Buf.	PRE	Buf. 3	St.L. 2	Danny Gare	11:43	Buf.
Apr. 9/76	Buf.	PRE	Buf. 2	St.L. 1	Don Luce	14:27	Buf.
Apr. 13/76	Bos.	QF	L.A. 3	Bos. 2	Butch Goring	0:27	Bos.
Apr. 13/76	Buf.	QF	Buf. 3	NYI 2	Danny Gare	14:04	NYI
Apr. 22/76	L.A.	QF	L.A. 4	Bos. 3	Butch Goring	18:28	Bos.
Apr. 29/76	Phi.	SF	Phi. 2	Bos. 1	Reggie Leach	13:38	Phi.
Apr. 15/77	Tor.	QF	Phi. 4	Tor. 3	Rick MacLeish	2:55	Phi.
Apr. 17/77	Tor.	QF	Phi. 6	Tor. 5	Reggie Leach	19:10	Phi.
Apr. 24/77	Phi.	SF	Bos. 4	Phi. 3	Rick Middleton	2:57	Bos.
Apr. 26/77	Phi.	SF	Bos. 5	Phi. 4	Terry O'Reilly	30:07	Bos.
May 3/77	Mtl.	SF	NYI 4	Mtl. 3	Billy Harris	3:58	Mtl.

Date	City	Series	Score		Scorer	Overtime	Series Winner
May 14/77	Bos.	F	Mtl. 2	Bos. 1	Jacques Lemaire	4:32	Mtl.
Apr. 11/78	Phi.	PRE	Phi. 3	Col. 2	Mel Bridgman	0:23	Phi.
Apr. 13/78	NYR	PRE	NYR 4	Buf. 3	Don Murdoch	1:37	Buf.
Apr. 19/78	Bos.	QF	Bos. 4	Chi. 3	Terry O'Reilly	1:50	Bos.
Apr. 19/78	NYI	QF	NYI 3	Tor. 2	Mike Bossy	2:50	Tor.
Apr. 21/78	Chi.	QF	Bos. 4	Chi. 3	Peter McNab	10:17	Bos.
Apr. 25/78	NYI	QF	NYI 2	Tor. 1	Bob Nystrom	8:02	Tor.
Apr. 29/78	NYI	QF	Tor. 2	NYI 1	Lanny McDonald	4:13	Tor.
May 2/78	Bos.	SF	Bos. 3	Phi. 2	Rick Middleton	1:43	Bos.
May 16/78	Mtl.	F	Mtl. 3	Bos. 2	Guy Lafleur	13:09	Mtl.
May 21/78	Bos.	F	Bos. 4	Mtl. 3	Bobby Schmautz	6:22	Mtl.
Apr. 12/79	L.A.	PRE	NYR 2	L.A. 1	Phil Esposito	6:11	NYR
Apr. 14/79	Buf.	PRE	Pit. 4	Buf. 3	George Ferguson	0:47	Pit.
Apr. 16/79	Phi.	QF	Phi. 3	NYR 2	Ken Linseman	0:44	NYR
Apr. 18/79	NYI	QF	NYI 1	Chi. 0	Mike Bossy	2:31	NYI
Apr. 21/79	Tor.	QF	Mtl. 4	Tor. 3	Cam Connor	25:25	Mtl.
Apr. 22/79	Tor.	QF	Mtl. 5	Tor. 4	Larry Robinson	4:14	Mtl.
Apr. 28/79	NYI	SF	NYI 4	NYR 3	Denis Potvin	8:02	NYR
May 3/79	NYR	SF	NYI 3	NYR 2	Bob Nystrom	3:40	NYR
May 3/79	Bos.	SF	Bos. 4	Mtl. 3	Jean Ratelle	3:46	Mtl.
May 10/79	Mtl.	SF	Mtl. 5	Bos. 4	Yvon Lambert	9:33	Mtl.
May 19/79	NYR	F	Mtl. 4	NYR 3	Serge Savard	7:25	Mtl.
Apr. 8/80	NYR	PRE	NYR 2	Atl. 1	Steve Vickers	0:33	NYR
Apr. 8/80	Phi.	PRE	Phi. 4	Edm. 3	Bobby Clarke	8:06	Phi.
Apr. 8/80	Chi.	PRE	Chi. 3	St.L. 2	Doug Lecuyer	12:34	Chi.
Apr. 11/80	Hfd.	PRE	Mtl. 4	Hfd. 3	Yvon Lambert	0:29	Mtl.
Apr. 11/80	Tor.	PRE	Min. 4	Tor. 3	Al MacAdam	0:32	Min.
Apr. 11/80	L.A.	PRE	NYI 4	L.A. 3	Ken Morrow	6:55	NYI
Apr. 11/80	Edm.	PRE	Phi. 3	Edm. 2	Ken Linseman	23:56	Phi.
Apr. 16/80	Bos.	QF	NYI 2	Bos. 1	Clark Gillies	1:02	NYI
Apr. 17/80	Bos.	QF	NYI 5	Bos. 4	Bob Bourne	1:24	NYI
Apr. 21/80	NYI	QF	Bos. 4	NYI 3	Terry O'Reilly	17:13	NYI
May 1/80	Buf.	SF	NYI 2	Buf. 1	Bob Nystrom	21:20	NYI
May 13/80	Phi.	F	NYI 4	Phi. 3	Denis Potvin	4:07	NYI
May 24/80	NYI	F	NYI 5	Phi. 4	Bob Nystrom	7:11	NYI
Apr. 8/81	Buf.	PRE	Buf. 3	Van. 2	Alan Haworth	5:00	Buf.
Apr. 8/81	Bos.	PRE	Min. 5	Bos. 4	Steve Payne	3:34	Min.
Apr. 11/81	Chi.	PRE	Cgy. 5	Chi. 4	Willi Plett	35:17	Cgy.
Apr. 12/81	Que.	PRE	Que. 4	Phi. 3	Dale Hunter	0:37	Phi.
Apr. 14/81	St.L.	PRE	St.L. 4	Pit. 3	Mike Crombeen	25:16	St.L.
Apr. 16/81	Buf.	QF	Min. 4	Buf. 3	Steve Payne	0:22	Min.
Apr. 20/81	Min.	QF	Buf. 5	Min. 4	Craig Ramsay	16:32	Min.
Apr. 20/81	Edm.	QF	NYI 5	Edm. 4	Ken Morrow	5:41	NYI
Apr. 7/82	Min.	DSF	Chi. 3	Min. 2	Greg Fox	3:34	Chi.
Apr. 8/82	Edm.	DSF	Edm. 3	L.A. 2	Wayne Gretzky	6:20	L.A.
Apr. 8/82	Van.	DSF	Van. 2	Cgy. 1	Tiger Williams	14:20	Van.
Apr. 10/82	Pit.	DSF	Pit. 2	NYI 1	Rick Kehoe	4:14	NYI
Apr. 10/82	L.A.	DSF	L.A. 6	Edm. 5	Daryl Evans	2:35	L.A.
Apr. 13/82	Mtl.	DSF	Que. 3	Mtl. 2	Dale Hunter	0:22	Que.
Apr. 13/82	NYI	DSF	NYI 4	Pit. 3	John Tonelli	6:19	NYI
Apr. 16/82	Van.	DF	L.A. 3	Van. 2	Steve Bozek	4:33	Van.
Apr. 18/82	Que.	DF	Que. 3	Bos. 2	Wilf Paiement	11:44	Que.
Apr. 18/82	NYR	DF	NYI 4	NYR 3	Bryan Trottier	3:00	NYI
Apr. 18/82	L.A.	DF	Van. 4	L.A. 3	Colin Campbell	1:23	Van.
Apr. 21/82	St.L.	DF	St.L. 3	Chi. 2	Bernie Federko	3:28	Chi.
Apr. 23/82	Que.	DF	Bos. 6	Que. 5	Peter McNab	10:54	Que.
Apr. 27/82	Chi.	CF	Van. 2	Chi. 1	Jim Nill	28:58	Van.
May 1/82	Que.	CF	NYI 5	Que. 4	Wayne Merrick	16:52	NYI
May 8/82	NYI	F	NYI 6	Van. 5	Mike Bossy	19:58	NYI
Apr. 5/83	Bos.	DSF	Bos. 4	Que. 3	Barry Pederson	1:46	Bos.
Apr. 6/83	Cgy.	DSF	Cgy. 4	Van. 3	Eddy Beers	12:27	Cgy.
Apr. 7/83	Min.	DSF	Min. 5	Tor. 4	Bobby Smith	5:03	Min.
Apr. 10/83	Tor.	DSF	Min. 5	Tor. 4	Dino Ciccarelli	8:05	Min.
Apr. 10/83	Van.	DSF	Cgy. 4	Van. 3	Greg Meredith	1:06	Cgy.
Apr. 18/83	Min.	DF	Chi. 4	Min. 3	Rich Preston	10:34	Chi.
Apr. 24/83	Bos.	DF	Bos. 3	Buf. 2	Brad Park	1:52	Bos.
Apr. 5/84	Edm.	DSF	Edm. 5	Wpg. 4	Randy Gregg	0:21	Edm.
Apr. 7/84	Det.	DSF	St.L. 4	Det. 3	Mark Reeds	37:07	St.L.
Apr. 8/84	Det.	DSF	St.L. 3	Det. 2	Jorgen Pettersson	2:42	St.L.
Apr. 10/84	NYI	DSF	NYI 3	NYR 2	Ken Morrow	8:56	NYI
Apr. 13/84	Min.	DF	St.L. 4	Min. 3	Doug Gilmour	16:16	Min.
Apr. 13/84	Edm.	DF	Cgy. 6	Edm. 5	Carey Wilson	3:42	Edm.
Apr. 13/84	NYI	DF	NYI 5	Wsh. 4	Anders Kallur	7:35	NYI
Apr. 16/84	Mtl.	DF	Que. 4	Mtl. 3	Bo Berglund	3:00	Mtl.
Apr. 20/84	Cgy.	DF	Cgy. 5	Edm. 4	Lanny McDonald	1:04	Edm.
Apr. 22/84	Min.	DF	Min. 4	St.L. 3	Steve Payne	6:00	Min.
Apr. 10/85	Phi.	DSF	Phi. 5	NYR 4	Mark Howe	8:01	Phi.
Apr. 10/85	Wsh.	DSF	Wsh. 4	NYI 3	Alan Haworth	2:28	NYI
Apr. 10/85	Edm.	DSF	Edm. 3	L.A. 2	Lee Fogolin	3:01	Edm.
Apr. 10/85	Wpg.	DSF	Wpg. 5	Cgy. 4	Brian Mullen	7:56	Wpg.
Apr. 11/85	Wsh.	DSF	Wsh. 2	NYI 1	Mike Gartner	21:23	NYI
Apr. 13/85	L.A.	DSF	Edm. 4	L.A. 3	Glenn Anderson	0:46	Edm.
Apr. 18/85	Mtl.	DF	Que. 2	Mtl. 1	Mark Kumpel	12:23	Que.
Apr. 23/85	Que.	DF	Que. 7	Mtl. 6	Dale Hunter	18:36	Que.
Apr. 25/85	Min.	DF	Chi. 7	Min. 6	Darryl Sutter	21:57	Chi.
Apr. 28/85	Chi.	DF	Min. 5	Chi. 4	Dennis Maruk	1:14	Chi.
Apr. 30/85	Min.	DF	Chi. 6	Min. 5	Darryl Sutter	15:41	Chi.
May 2/85	Mtl.	DF	Que. 3	Mtl. 2	Peter Stastny	2:22	Que.
May 5/85	Que.	CF	Que. 2	Phi. 1	Peter Stastny	6:20	Phi.
Apr. 9/86	Que.	DSF	Hfd. 3	Que. 2	Sylvain Turgeon	2:36	Hfd.
Apr. 12/86	Wpg.	DSF	Cgy. 4	Wpg. 3	Lanny McDonald	8:25	Cgy.
Apr. 17/86	Wsh.	DF	NYR 4	Wsh. 3	Brian MacLellan	1:16	NYR
Apr. 20/86	Edm.	DF	Edm. 6	Cgy. 5	Glenn Anderson	1:04	Cgy.
Apr. 23/86	Hfd.	DF	Hfd. 2	Mtl. 1	Kevin Dineen	1:07	Mtl.
Apr. 23/86	NYR	DF	NYR 6	Wsh. 5	Bob Brooke	2:40	NYR
Apr. 26/86	St L.	DF	St L. 4	Tor. 3	Mark Reeds	7:11	St L.
Apr. 29/86	Mtl.	DF	Mtl. 2	Hfd. 1	Claude Lemieux	5:55	Mtl.
May 5/86	NYR	CF	Mtl. 4	NYR 3	Claude Lemieux	9:41	Mtl.
May 12/86	St L.	CF	St L. 6	Cgy. 5	Doug Wickenheiser	7:30	Cgy.
May 18/86	Cgy.	F	Mtl. 3	Cgy. 2	Brian Skrudland	0:09	Mtl.
Apr. 8/87	Hfd.	DSF	Hfd. 3	Que. 2	Paul MacDermid	2:20	Que.
Apr. 9/87	Mtl.	DSF	Mtl. 4	Bos. 3	Mats Naslund	2:38	Mtl.
Apr. 9/87	St.L.	DSF	Tor. 3	St.L. 2	Rick Lanz	10:17	Tor.
Apr. 11/87	Wpg.	DSF	Cgy. 3	Wpg. 2	Mike Bullard	3:53	Wpg.
Apr. 11/87	Chi.	DSF	Det. 4	Chi. 3	Shawn Burr	4:51	Det.
Apr. 16/87	Que.	DSF	Que. 5	Hfd. 4	Peter Stastny	6:05	Que.
Apr. 18/87	Wsh.	DSF	NYI 3	Wsh. 2	Pat LaFontaine	68:47	NYI
Apr. 21/87	Edm.	DF	Edm. 3	Wpg. 2	Glenn Anderson	0:36	Edm.
Apr. 26/87	Que.	DF	Mtl. 3	Que. 2	Mats Naslund	5:30	Mtl.
Apr. 27/87	Tor.	DF	Tor. 3	Det. 2	Mike Allison	9:31	Det.
May 4/87	Phi.	CF	Phi. 4	Mtl. 3	Ilkka Sinislao	9:11	Phi.
May 20/87	Edm.	F	Edm. 3	Phi. 2	Jari Kurri	6:50	Edm.
Apr. 6/88	NYI	DSF	NYI 4	N.J. 3	Pat LaFontaine	6:11	N.J.
Apr. 10/88	Phi.	DSF	Phi. 5	Wsh. 4	Murray Craven	1:18	Wsh.
Apr. 10/88	N.J.	DSF	NYI 5	N.J. 4	Brent Sutter	15:07	N.J.
Apr. 10/88	Buf.	DSF	Buf. 6	Bos. 5	John Tucker	5:32	Bos.
Apr. 12/88	Det.	DSF	Tor. 6	Det. 5	Ed Olczyk	0:34	Det.
Apr. 16/88	Wsh.	DSF	Wsh. 5	Phi. 4	Dale Hunter	5:57	Wsh.
Apr. 21/88	Cgy.	DF	Edm. 5	Cgy. 4	Wayne Gretzky	7:54	Edm.
May 4/88	Bos.	CF	N.J. 3	Bos. 2	Doug Brown	17:46	Bos.
May 9/88	Det.	CF	Edm. 4	Det. 3	Jari Kurri	11:02	Edm.
Apr. 5/89	St.L.	DSF	St.L. 4	Min. 3	Brett Hull	11:55	St.L.
Apr. 5/89	Cgy.	DSF	Van. 4	Cgy. 3	Paul Reinhart	2:47	Cgy.
Apr. 6/89	St.L.	DSF	St.L. 4	Min. 3	Rick Meagher	5:30	St.L.
Apr. 6/89	Det.	DSF	Chi. 5	Det. 4	Duane Sutter	14:36	Chi.
Apr. 8/89	Hfd.	DSF	Mtl. 5	Hfd. 4	Stephane Richer	5:01	Mtl.
Apr. 8/89	Phi.	DSF	Wsh. 4	Phi. 3	Kelly Miller	0:51	Phi.
Apr. 9/89	Hfd.	DSF	Mtl. 4	Hfd. 3	Russ Courtnall	15:12	Mtl.
Apr. 15/89	Cgy.	DSF	Cgy. 4	Van. 3	Joel Otto	19:21	Cgy.
Apr. 18/89	Cgy.	DF	Cgy. 4	L.A. 3	Doug Gilmour	7:47	Cgy.
Apr. 19/89	Mtl.	DF	Mtl. 3	Bos. 2	Bobby Smith	12:24	Mtl.
Apr. 20/89	St.L.	DF	St.L. 5	Chi. 4	Tony Hrkac	33:49	Chi.
Apr. 21/89	Phi.	DF	Pit. 4	Phi. 3	Phil Bourque	12:08	Phi.
May 8/89	Chi.	CF	Cgy. 2	Chi. 1	Al MacInnis	15:05	Cgy.
May 9/89	Mtl.	CF	Phi. 2	Mtl. 1	Dave Poulin	5:02	Mtl.
May 19/89	Mtl.	F	Mtl. 4	Cgy. 3	Ryan Walter	38:08	Cgy.
Apr. 5/90	N.J.	DSF	Wsh. 5	N.J. 4	Dino Ciccarelli	5:34	Wsh.
Apr. 6/90	Edm.	DSF	Edm. 3	Wpg. 2	Mark Lamb	4:21	Edm.
Apr. 8/90	Tor.	DSF	St.L. 6	Tor. 5	Sergio Momesso	6:04	St.L.
Apr. 8/90	L.A.	DSF	L.A. 2	Cgy. 1	Tony Granato	8:37	L.A.
Apr. 9/90	Mtl.	DSF	Mtl. 2	Buf. 1	Brian Skrudland	12:35	Mtl.
Apr. 9/90	NYI	DSF	NYI 4	NYR 3	Brent Sutter	20:59	NYR
Apr. 10/90	Wpg.	DSF	Wpg. 4	Edm. 3	Dave Ellett	21:08	Edm.
Apr. 14/90	L.A.	DSF	L.A. 4	Cgy. 3	Mike Krushelnyski	23:14	L.A.
Apr. 15/90	Hfd.	DSF	Hfd. 3	Bos. 2	Kevin Dineen	12:30	Bos.
Apr. 21/90	Bos.	DF	Bos. 5	Mtl. 4	Garry Galley	3:42	Bos.
Apr. 24/90	L.A.	DF	Edm. 6	L.A. 5	Joe Murphy	4:42	Edm.
Apr. 25/90	Wsh.	DF	Wsh. 4	NYR 3	Rod Langway	0:34	Wsh.
Apr. 27/90	NYR	DF	Wsh. 2	NYR 1	John Druce	6:48	Wsh.
May 15/90	Bos.	F	Edm. 3	Bos. 2	Petr Klima	55:13	Edm.
Apr. 4/91	Chi.	DSF	Min. 4	Chi. 3	Brian Propp	4:14	Min.
Apr. 5/91	Pit.	DSF	Pit. 5	N.J. 4	Jaromir Jagr	8:52	Pit.
Apr. 6/91	L.A.	DSF	L.A. 3	Van. 2	Wayne Gretzky	11:08	L.A.
Apr. 8/91	Van.	DSF	Van. 2	L.A. 1	Cliff Ronning	3:12	L.A.
Apr. 11/91	NYR	DSF	Wsh. 5	NYR 4	Dino Ciccarelli	6:44	Wsh.
Apr. 11/91	Mtl.	DSF	Mtl. 4	Buf. 3	Russ Courtnall	5:56	Mtl.
Apr. 14/91	Edm.	DSF	Cgy. 2	Edm. 1	Theoren Fleury	4:40	Edm.
Apr. 16/91	Cgy.	DSF	Edm. 5	Cgy. 4	Esa Tikkanen	6:58	Edm.
Apr. 18/91	L.A.	DF	L.A. 4	Edm. 3	Luc Robitaille	2:13	Edm.
Apr. 19/91	Bos.	DF	Mtl. 4	Bos. 3	Stephane Richer	0:27	Bos.
Apr. 19/91	Pit.	DF	Pit. 7	Wsh. 6	Kevin Stevens	8:10	Pit.
Apr. 20/91	L.A.	DF	Edm. 4	L.A. 3	Petr Klima	24:48	Edm.
Apr. 22/91	Edm.	DF	Edm. 4	L.A. 3	Esa Tikkanen	20:48	Edm.
Apr. 27/91	Mtl.	DF	Mtl. 3	Bos. 2	Shayne Corson	17:47	Bos.
Apr. 28/91	Edm.	DF	Edm. 4	L.A. 3	Craig MacTavish	16:57	Edm.
May 3/91	Bos.	CF	Bos. 5	Pit. 4	Vladimir Ruzicka	8:14	Pit.
Apr. 21/92	Bos.	DSF	Bos. 3	Buf. 2	Adam Oates	11:14	Bos.
Apr. 22/92	Min.	DSF	Det. 5	Min. 4	Yves Racine	1:15	Det.
Apr. 22/92	St.L.	DSF	St.L. 5	Chi. 4	Brett Hull	23:33	Chi.
Apr. 25/92	Buf.	DSF	Bos. 5	Buf. 4	Ted Donato	2:08	Bos.
Apr. 28/92	Min.	DSF	Det. 1	Min. 0	Sergei Fedorov	16:13	Det.
Apr. 29/92	Hfd.	DSF	Hfd. 2	Mtl. 1	Yvon Corriveau	0:24	Mtl.
May 1/92	Mtl.	DSF	Mtl. 3	Hfd. 2	Russ Courtnall	25:26	Mtl.
May 3/92	Van.	DF	Edm. 4	Van. 3	Joe Murphy	8:36	Edm.
May 5/92	Mtl.	DF	Bos. 3	Mtl. 2	Peter Douris	3:12	Bos.
May 7/92	Pit.	DF	NYR 6	Pit. 5	Kris King	1:29	Pit.
May 9/92	Pit.	DF	Pit. 5	NYR 4	Ron Francis	2:47	Pit.
May 17/92	Pit.	CF	Pit. 4	Bos. 3	Jaromir Jagr	9:44	Pit.
May 20/92	Edm.	CF	Chi. 4	Edm. 3	Jeremy Roenick	2:45	Chi.
Apr. 18/93	Bos.	DSF	Buf. 5	Bos. 4	Bob Sweeney	11:03	Buf.
Apr. 18/93	Que.	DSF	Que. 3	Mtl. 2	Scott Young	16:49	Mtl.
Apr. 20/93	Wsh.	DSF	NYI 5	Wsh. 4	Brian Mullen	34:50	NYI
Apr. 22/93	Mtl.	DSF	Mtl. 2	Que. 1	Vincent Damphousse	10:30	Mtl.
Apr. 22/93	Buf.	DSF	Buf. 4	Bos. 3	Yuri Khmylev	1:05	Buf.
Apr. 22/93	NYI	DSF	NYI 4	Wsh. 3	Ray Ferraro	4:46	NYI
Apr. 24/93	Buf.	DSF	Buf. 6	Bos. 5	Brad May	4:48	Buf.
Apr. 24/93	NYI	DSF	NYI 4	Wsh. 3	Ray Ferraro	25:40	NYI
Apr. 25/93	St.L.	DSF	St.L. 4	Chi. 3	Craig Janney	10:43	St.L.
Apr. 26/93	Que.	DSF	Mtl. 5	Que. 4	Kirk Muller	8:17	Mtl.
Apr. 27/93	Det.	DSF	Tor. 5	Det. 4	Mike Foligno	2:05	Tor.
Apr. 27/93	Van.	DSF	Wpg. 4	Van. 3	Teemu Selanne	6:18	Van.
Apr. 29/93	Wpg.	DSF	Van. 4	Wpg. 3	Greg Adams	4:30	Van.
May 1/93	Det.	DSF	Tor. 4	Det. 3	Nikolai Borschevsky	2:35	Tor.
May 3/93	Tor.	DF	Tor. 2	St.L. 1	Doug Gilmour	23:16	Tor.
May 4/93	Mtl.	DF	Mtl. 4	Buf. 3	Guy Carbonneau	2:50	Mtl.
May 5/93	Tor.	DF	St.L. 2	Tor. 1	Jeff Brown	23:03	Tor.
May 6/93	Buf.	DF	Mtl. 4	Buf. 3	Gilbert Dionne	8:28	Mtl.
May 8/93	Buf.	DF	Mtl. 4	Buf. 3	Kirk Muller	11:37	Mtl.
May 11/93	Van.	DF	L.A. 4	Van. 3	Gary Shuchuk	26:31	L.A.
May 14/93	Pit.	DF	NYI 4	Pit. 3	Dave Volek	5:16	NYI
May 18/93	Mtl.	CF	Mtl. 4	NYI 3	Stephan Lebeau	26:21	Mtl.
May 20/93	NYI	CF	Mtl. 2	NYI 1	Guy Carbonneau	12:34	Mtl.
May 25/93	Tor.	CF	Tor. 3	L.A. 2	Glenn Anderson	19:20	L.A.
May 27/93	L.A.	CF	L.A. 5	Tor. 4	Wayne Gretzky	1:41	L.A.

Date	City	Series	Score		Scorer	Overtime	Series Winner
Jun. 3/93	Mtl.	F	Mtl. 3	L.A. 2	Eric Desjardins	0:51	Mtl.
Jun. 5/93	L.A.	F	Mtl. 4	L.A. 3	John LeClair	0:34	Mtl.
Jun. 7/93	L.A.	F	Mtl. 3	L.A. 2	John LeClair	14:37	Mtl.
Apr. 20/94	Tor.	CQF	Tor. 1	Chi. 0	Todd Gill	2:15	Tor.
Apr. 22/94	St.L.	CQF	Dal. 5	St.L. 4	Paul Cavallini	8:34	Dal.
Apr. 24/94	Chi.	CQF	Chi. 4	Tor. 3	Jeremy Roenick	1:23	Tor.
Apr. 25/94	Bos.	CQF	Mtl. 2	Bos. 1	Kirk Muller	17:18	Bos.
Apr. 26/94	Cgy.	CQF	Van. 2	Cgy. 1	Geoff Courtnall	7:15	Van.
Apr. 27/94	Buf.	CQF	Buf. 1	N.J. 0	Dave Hannan	65:43	N.J.
Apr. 28/94	Van.	CQF	Van. 3	Cgy. 2	Trevor Linden	16:43	Van.
Apr. 30/94	Cgy.	CQF	Van. 4	Cgy. 3	Pavel Bure	22:20	Van.
May 3/94	N.J.	CSF	Bos. 6	N.J. 5	Don Sweeney	9:08	N.J.
May 7/94	Bos.	CSF	N.J. 5	Bos. 4	Stephane Richer	14:19	N.J.
May 8/94	Van.	CSF	Van. 2	Dal. 1	Sergio Momesso	11:01	Van.
May 12/94	Tor.	CSF	Tor. 3	S.J. 2	Mike Gartner	8:53	Tor.
May 15/94	NYR	CF	N.J. 4	NYR 3	Stephane Richer	35:23	NYR
May 16/94	Tor.	CF	Tor. 3	Van. 2	Peter Zezel	16:55	Van.
May 19/94	N.J.	CF	NYR 3	N.J. 2	Stephane Matteau	26:13	NYR
May 24/94	Van.	CF	Van. 4	Tor. 3	Greg Adams	20:14	Van.
May 27/94	NYR	CF	NYR 2	N.J. 1	Stephane Matteau	24:24	NYR
May 31/94	NYR	F	Van. 3	NYR 2	Greg Adams	19:26	NYR
May 7/95	Phi.	CQF	Phi. 4	Buf. 3	Karl Dykhuis	10:06	Phi.
May 9/95	Cgy.	CQF	S.J. 5	Cgy. 4	Ulf Dahlen	12:21	S.J.
May 12/95	NYR	CQF	NYR 3	Que. 2	Steve Larmer	8:09	NYR
May 12/95	N.J.	CQF	N.J. 1	Bos. 0	Randy McKay	8:51	N.J.
May 14/95	Pit.	CQF	Pit. 6	Wsh. 5	Luc Robitaille	4:30	Pit.
May 15/95	St.L.	CQF	Van. 6	St.L. 5	Cliff Ronning	1:48	Van.
May 17/95	Tor.	CQF	Tor. 5	Chi. 4	Randy Wood	10:00	Chi.
May 19/95	Cgy.	CQF	S.J. 5	Cgy. 4	Ray Whitney	21:54	S.J.
May 21/95	Phi.	CSF	Phi. 5	NYR 4	Eric Desjardins	7:03	Phi.
May 21/95	Chi.	CSF	Chi. 2	Van. 1	Joe Murphy	9:04	Chi.
May 22/95	Phi.	CSF	Phi. 4	NYR 3	Kevin Haller	0:25	Phi.
May 25/95	Van.	CSF	Chi. 3	Van. 2	Chris Chelios	6:22	Chi.
May 26/95	N.J.	CSF	N.J. 2	Pit. 1	Neal Broten	18:36	N.J.
May 27/95	Van.	CSF	Chi. 4	Van. 3	Chris Chelios	5:35	Chi.
Jun. 1/95	Det.	CF	Det. 2	Chi. 1	Nicklas Lidstrom	1:01	Det.
Jun. 6/95	Chi.	CF	Det. 4	Chi. 3	Vladimir Konstantinov	29:25	Det.
Jun. 7/95	N.J.	CF	Phi. 3	N.J. 2	Eric Lindros	4:19	N.J.
Jun. 11/95	Det.	CF	Det. 2	Chi. 1	Vyacheslav Kozlov	22:25	Det.
Apr. 16/96	NYR	CQF	Mtl. 3	NYR 2	Vincent Damphousse	5:04	NYR
Apr. 18/96	Tor.	CQF	Tor. 5	St.L. 4	Mats Sundin	4:02	St.L.
Apr. 18/96	Phi.	CQF	T.B. 2	Phi. 1	Brian Bellows	9:05	Phi.
Apr. 21/96	St.L.	CQF	St.L. 3	Tor. 2	Glenn Anderson	1:24	St.L.
Apr. 21/96	T.B.	CQF	T.B. 5	Phi. 4	Alex Selivanov	2:04	Phi.
Apr. 23/96	Cgy.	CQF	Chi. 2	Cgy. 1	Joe Murphy	50:02	Chi.
Apr. 24/96	Wsh.	CQF	Pit. 3	Wsh. 2	Petr Nedved	79:15	Pit.
Apr. 25/96	Col.	CQF	Col. 5	Van. 4	Joe Sakic	0:51	Col.
Apr. 25/96	Tor.	CQF	Tor. 5	St.L. 4	Mike Gartner	7:31	St.L.
May 2/96	Col.	CSF	Chi. 3	Col. 2	Jeremy Roenick	6:29	Col.
May 6/96	Chi.	CSF	Chi. 4	Col. 3	Sergei Krivokrasov	0:46	Col.
May 8/96	St.L.	CSF	St.L. 5	Det. 4	Igor Kravchuk	3:23	Det.
May 8/96	Chi.	CSF	Col. 3	Chi. 2	Joe Sakic	44:33	Col.
May 9/96	Fla.	CSF	Fla. 4	Phi. 3	Dave Lowry	4:06	Fla.
May 12/96	Phi.	CSF	Fla. 2	Phi. 1	Mike Hough	28:05	Fla.
May 13/96	Chi.	CSF	Col. 4	Chi. 3	Sandis Ozolinsh	25:18	Col.
May 16/96	Det.	CSF	Det. 1	St.L. 0	Steve Yzerman	21:15	Det.
May 19/96	Det.	CF	Col. 3	Det. 2	Mike Keane	17:31	Col.
Jun. 10/96	Fla.	F	Col. 1	Fla. 0	Uwe Krupp	44:31	Col.
Apr. 20/97	Chi.	CQF	Chi. 4	Col. 3	Sergei Krivokrasov	31:03	Col.
Apr. 20/97	Edm.	CQF	Edm. 4	Dal. 3	Kelly Buchberger	9:15	Edm.
Apr. 22/97	NYR	CQF	NYR 4	Fla. 3	Esa Tikkanen	16:29	NYR
Apr. 23/97	Ott.	CQF	Ott. 1	Buf. 0	Daniel Alfredsson	2:34	Buf.
Apr. 24/97	Mtl.	CQF	Mtl. 4	N.J. 3	Patrice Brisebois	47:37	N.J.
Apr. 25/97	Fla.	CQF	NYR 3	Fla. 2	Esa Tikkanen	12:02	NYR
Apr. 25/97	Dal.	CQF	Edm. 1	Dal. 0	Ryan Smyth	20:22	Edm.
Apr. 27/97	Phx.	CQF	Ana. 3	Phx. 2	Paul Kariya	7:29	Ana.
Apr. 29/97	Buf.	CQF	Buf. 3	Ott. 2	Derek Plante	5:24	Buf.
Apr. 29/97	Dal.	CQF	Edm. 4	Dal. 3	Todd Marchant	12:26	Edm.
May 2/97	Det.	CSF	Det. 2	Ana. 1	Martin Lapointe	0:59	Det.
May 4/97	Det.	CSF	Det. 3	Ana. 2	Vyacheslav Kozlov	41:31	Det.
May 8/97	Ana.	CSF	Det. 3	Ana. 2	Brendan Shanahan	37:03	Det.
May 9/97	Phi.	CSF	Buf. 5	Phi. 4	Ed Ronan	6:24	Phi.
May 9/97	Edm.	CSF	Col. 3	Edm. 2	Claude Lemieux	8:35	Col.
May 11/97	N.J.	CSF	NYR 2	N.J. 1	Adam Graves	14:08	NYR
Apr. 22/98	N.J.	CQF	Ott. 2	N.J. 1	Bruce Gardiner	5:58	Ott.
Apr. 23/98	Pit.	CQF	Mtl. 3	Pit. 2	Benoit Brunet	18:43	Mtl.
Apr. 24/98	Wsh.	CQF	Bos. 4	Wsh. 3	Darren Van Impe	20:54	Wsh.
Apr. 26/98	Ott.	CQF	Ott. 2	N.J. 1	Alexei Yashin	2:47	Ott.
Apr. 26/98	Bos.	CQF	Wsh. 3	Bos. 2	Joe Juneau	26:31	Wsh.
Apr. 26/98	Edm.	CQF	Col. 5	Edm. 4	Joe Sakic	15:25	Edm.
Apr. 28/98	S.J.	CQF	S.J. 1	Dal. 0	Andrei Zyuzin	6:31	Dal.
May 1/98	Phi.	CQF	Buf. 3	Phi. 2	Michal Grosek	5:40	Buf.
May 2/98	S.J.	CQF	Dal. 3	S.J. 2	Mike Keane	3:43	Dal.
May 3/98	Bos.	CQF	Wsh. 3	Bos. 2	Brian Bellows	15:24	Wsh.
May 3/98	Buf.	CSF	Buf. 3	Mtl. 2	Geoff Sanderson	2:37	Buf.
May 11/98	Edm.	CSF	Dal. 1	Edm. 0	Benoit Hogue	13:07	Dal.
May 12/98	Mtl.	CSF	Buf. 5	Mtl. 4	Michael Peca	21:24	Buf.
May 12/98	St.L.	CSF	Det. 3	St.L. 2	Brendan Shanahan	31:12	Det.
May 25/98	Wsh.	CF	Wsh. 3	Buf. 2	Todd Krygier	3:01	Wsh.
May 28/98	Buf.	CF	Wsh. 4	Buf. 3	Peter Bondra	9:37	Wsh.
Jun. 3/98	Dal.	CF	Dal. 3	Det. 2	Jamie Langenbrunner	0:46	Det.
Jun. 4/98	Buf.	CF	Wsh. 3	Buf. 2	Joe Juneau	6:24	Wsh.
Jun. 11/98	Det.	F	Det. 5	Wsh. 4	Kris Draper	15:24	Det.
Apr. 23/99	Ott.	CQF	Buf. 3	Ott. 2	Miroslav Satan	30:35	Buf.
Apr. 24/99	Car.	CQF	Car. 3	Bos. 2	Ray Sheppard	17:05	Bos.
Apr. 24/99	Phx.	CQF	Phx. 4	St.L. 3	Shane Doan	8:58	St.L.
Apr. 26/99	S.J.	CQF	Col. 2	S.J. 1	Milan Hejduk	7:53	Col.
Apr. 27/99	Edm.	CQF	Dal. 3	Edm. 2	Joe Nieuwendyk	57:34	Dal.
Apr. 30/99	Tor.	CQF	Tor. 2	Phi. 1	Yanic Perreault	11:51	Tor.
Apr. 30/99	Car.	CQF	Bos. 4	Car. 3	Anson Carter	34:45	Bos.
Apr. 30/99	Phx..	CQF	St.L. 2	Phx. 1	Scott Young	5:43	St.L.
May 2/99	Pit.	CQF	Pit. 3	N.J. 2	Jaromir Jagr	8:59	Pit.
May 3/99	S.J.	CQF	Col. 3	S.J. 2	Milan Hejduk	13:12	Col.
May 4/99	Phx.	CQF	St.L. 1	Phx. 0	Pierre Turgeon	17:59	St.L.
May 7/99	Col.	CSF	Det. 3	Col. 2	Kirk Maltby	4:18	Col.
May 8/99	Dal.	CSF	Dal. 5	St.L. 4	Joe Nieuwendyk	8:22	Dal.
May 10/99	St.L.	CSF	St.L. 3	Dal. 2	Pavol Demitra	2:43	Dal.
May 12/99	St.L.	CSF	St.L. 3	Dal. 2	Pierre Turgeon	5:52	Dal.
May 13/99	Pit.	CSF	Tor. 3	Pit. 2	Sergei Berezin	2:18	Tor.
May 17/99	Pit.	CSF	Tor. 4	Pit. 3	Garry Valk	1:57	Tor.
May 17/99	St.L.	CSF	Dal. 2	St.L. 1	Mike Modano	2:21	Dal.
May 28/99	Col.	CF	Col. 3	Dal. 2	Chris Drury	19:29	Dal.
Jun. 8/99	Dal.	F	Buf. 3	Dal. 2	Jason Woolley	15:30	Dal.
Jun. 19/99	Buf.	F	Dal. 2	Buf. 1	Brett Hull	54:51	Dal.
Apr. 15/00	Pit.	CQF	Pit. 2	Wsh. 1	Jaromir Jagr	5:49	Pit.
Apr. 18/00	Buf.	CQF	Buf. 3	Phi. 2	Stu Barnes	4:42	Phi.
Apr. 22/00	Tor.	CQF	Tor. 2	Ott. 1	Steve Thomas	14:47	Tor.
May 2/00	Pit.	CSF	Phi. 4	Pit. 3	Andy Delmore	11:01	Phi.
May 3/00	Det.	CSF	Col. 3	Det. 2	Chris Drury	10:21	Col.
May 4/00	Pit.	CSF	Phi. 2	Pit. 1	Keith Primeau	92:01	Phi.
May 23/00	Dal.	CF	Dal. 3	Col. 2	Joe Nieuwendyk	12:10	Dal.
Jun. 8/00	N.J.	F	Dal. 1	N.J. 0	Mike Modano	46:21	N.J.
Jun. 10/00	Dal.	F	N.J. 2	Dal. 1	Jason Arnott	28:20	N.J.
Apr. 11/01	Dal.	CQF	Dal. 2	Edm. 1	Jamie Langenbrunner	2:08	Dal.
Apr. 13/01	Ott.	CQF	Tor. 1	Ott. 0	Mats Sundin	10:49	Tor.
Apr. 14/01	Phi.	CQF	Buf. 4	Phi. 3	Jay McKee	18:02	Buf.
Apr. 15/01	Edm.	CQF	Dal. 3	Edm. 2	Benoit Hogue	19:48	Dal.
Apr. 16/01	Tor.	CQF	Tor. 3	Ott. 2	Cory Cross	2:16	Tor.
Apr. 16/01	Van.	CQF	Col. 4	Van. 3	Peter Forsberg	2:50	Col.
Apr. 17/01	Buf.	CQF	Buf. 4	Phi. 3	Curtis Brown	6:13	Buf.
Apr. 17/01	Edm.	CQF	Edm. 2	Dal. 1	Mike Comrie	17:19	Dal.
Apr. 18/01	Car.	CQF	Car. 3	N.J. 2	Rod Brind'Amour	:46	N.J.
Apr. 18/01	Pit.	CQF	Wsh. 4	Pit. 3	Jeff Halpern	4:01	Pit.
Apr. 18/01	L.A.	CQF	L.A. 4	Det. 3	Eric Belanger	2:36	L.A.
Apr. 19/01	Dal.	CQF	Dal. 4	Edm. 3	Kirk Muller	8:01	Dal.
Apr. 19/01	St.L.	CQF	St.L. 3	S.J. 2	Bryce Salvador	9:54	St.L.
Apr. 23/01	Pit.	CQF	Pit. 4	Wsh. 3	Martin Straka	13:04	Pit.
Apr. 23/01	L.A.	CQF	L.A. 3	Det. 2	Adam Deadmarsh	4:48	L.A.
Apr. 26/01	Col.	CSF	L.A. 4	Col. 3	Jaroslav Modry	14:23	Col.
Apr. 28/01	N.J.	CSF	N.J. 6	Tor. 5	Randy McKay	5:31	N.J.
May 1/01	Tor.	CSF	N.J. 3	Tor. 2	Brian Rafalski	7:00	N.J.
May 1/01	St.L.	CSF	St.L. 3	Dal. 2	Cory Stillman	29:26	St.L.
May 5/01	Buf.	CSF	Buf. 3	Pit. 2	Stu Barnes	8:34	Pit.
May 6/01	L.A.	CSF	L.A. 1	Col. 0	Glen Murray	22:41	Col.
May 8/01	Pit.	CSF	Pit. 3	Buf. 2	Martin Straka	11:29	Pit.
May 10/01	Buf.	CSF	Pit. 3	Buf. 2	Darius Kasparaitis	13:01	Pit.
May 16/01	St.L.	CF	St.L. 4	Col. 3	Scott Young	30:27	Col.
May 18/01	St.L.	CF	Col. 4	St.L. 3	Stephane Yelle	4:23	Col.
May 21/01	Col.	CF	Col. 2	St.L. 1	Joe Sakic	:24	Col.
Apr. 17/02	Phi.	CQF	Phi. 1	Ott. 0	Ruslan Fedotenko	7:47	Ott.
Apr. 17/02	Det.	CQF	Van. 4	Det. 3	Henrik Sedin	13:59	Det.
Apr. 19/02	Car.	CQF	Car. 2	N.J. 1	Bates Battaglia	15:26	Car.
Apr. 24/02	Car.	CQF	Car. 3	N.J. 2	Josef Vasicek	8:16	Car.
Apr. 25/02	Col.	CQF	L.A. 1	Col. 0	Craig Johnson	2:19	Col.
Apr. 26/02	Phi.	CQF	Ott. 2	Phi. 1	Martin Havlat	7:33	Ott.
May 4/02	Tor.	CSF	Tor. 3	Ott. 2	Gary Roberts	44:30	Tor.
May 7/02	Mtl.	CSF	Mtl. 2	Car. 1	Donald Audette	2:26	Car.
May 9/02	Mtl.	CSF	Car. 4	Mtl. 3	Niclas Wallin	3:14	Car.
May 13/02	S.J.	CSF	Col. 2	S.J. 1	Peter Forsberg	2:47	Col.
May 19/02	Car.	CF	Car. 2	Tor. 1	Niclas Wallin	13:42	Car.
May 20/02	Det.	CF	Col. 4	Det. 3	Chris Drury	2:17	Det.
May 21/02	Tor.	CF	Car. 2	Tor. 1	Jeff O'Neill	6:01	Car.
May 22/02	Col.	CF	Det. 2	Col. 1	Fredrik Olausson	12:44	Det.
May 27/02	Det.	CF	Col. 2	Det. 1	Peter Forsberg	6:24	Det.
May 28/02	Tor.	CF	Car. 2	Tor. 1	Martin Gelinas	8:05	Car.
Jun. 4/02	Det.	F	Car. 3	Det. 2	Ron Francis	:58	Det.
Jun. 8/02	Car.	F	Det. 3	Car. 2	Igor Larionov	54:47	Det.
Apr. 10/03	Det.	CQF	Ana. 2	Det. 1	Paul Kariya	43:18	Ana.
Apr. 14/03	NYI	CQF	Ott. 3	NYI 2	Todd White	22:25	Ott.
Apr. 14/03	Tor.	CQF	Tor. 4	Phi. 3	Tomas Kaberle	27:20	Phi.
Apr. 15/03	Wsh.	CQF	T.B. 4	Wsh. 3	Vincent Lecavalier	2:29	T.B.
Apr. 16/03	Tor.	CQF	Phi. 3	Tor. 2	Mark Recchi	53:54	Phi.
Apr. 16/03	Ana.	CQF	Ana. 3	Det. 2	Steve Rucchin	6:53	Ana.
Apr. 20/03	Wsh.	CQF	T.B. 2	Wsh. 1	Martin St. Louis	44:03	T.B.
Apr. 21/03	Tor.	CQF	Tor. 2	Phi. 1	Travis Green	30:51	Phi.
Apr. 21/03	Min.	CQF	Min. 3	Col. 2	Richard Park	4:22	Min.
Apr. 22/03	Col.	CQF	Min. 3	Col. 2	Andrew Brunette	3:25	Min.
Apr. 24/03	Dal.	CSF	Ana. 4	Dal. 3	Petr Sykora	80:48	Ana.
Apr. 25/03	Van.	CSF	Van. 4	Min. 3	Trent Klatt	3:42	Min.
Apr. 26/03	N.J.	CSF	N.J. 3	T.B. 2	Jamie Langenbrunner	2:09	N.J.
Apr. 26/03	Dal.	CSF	Ana. 3	Dal. 2	Mike Leclerc	1:44	Ana.
Apr. 29/03	Phi.	CSF	Ott. 3	Phi. 2	Wade Redden	6:43	Ott.
May 2/03	Min.	CSF	Van. 3	Min. 2	Brent Sopel	15:52	Min.
May 2/03	N.J.	CSF	N.J. 2	T.B. 1	Grant Marshall	51:12	N.J.
May 10/03	Min.	CF	Ana. 1	Min. 0	Petr Sykora	28:06	Ana.
May 10/03	Ott.	CF	Ott. 3	N.J. 2	Shaun Van Allen	3:08	N.J.
May 21/03	N.J.	CF	Ott. 2	N.J. 1	Chris Phillips	15:51	N.J.
May 31/03	Ana.	F	Ana. 3	N.J. 2	Ruslan Salei	6:59	N.J.
Jun. 2/03	Ana.	F	Ana. 1	N.J. 0	Steve Thomas	0:39	N.J.

NHL Playoff Coaching Records

Coach	Team	Games Coached	Wins	Losses	Ties	Playoff Years	Cup Wins	Career
Abel, Sid	Chicago	7	3	4	0	1		
	Detroit	69	29	40	0	8		
	Total	76	32	44	0	9		1952-76
Adams, Jack	Detroit	105	52	52	1	15	3	1927-47
Allen, Keith	Philadelphia	11	3	8	0	2		1967-69
Arbour, Al	St. Louis	11	4	7	0	1		
	NY Islanders	198	119	79	0	15	4	
	Total	209	123	86	0	16	4	1970-94
Babcock, Mike	Anaheim	21	15	6	0	1		2002-03
Barber, Bill	Philadelphia	11	3	8	0	2		2000-02
Berenson, Red	St. Louis	14	5	9	0	2		1979-82
Bergeron, Michel	Quebec	68	31	37	0	7		1980-90
Berry, Bob	Los Angeles	10	2	8	0	3		
	Montreal	8	2	6	0	1		
	St. Louis	15	7	8	0	2		
	Total	33	11	22	0	7		1978-94
Beverley, Nick	Toronto	6	2	4	0	1		1995-96
Blackburn, Don	Hartford	3	0	3	0	1		1979-81
Blair, Wren	Minnesota	14	7	7	0	1		1967-70
Blake, Toe	Montreal	119	82	37	0	13	8	1955-68
Boileau, Marc	Pittsburgh	9	5	4	0	1		1973-76
Boivin, Leo	St. Louis	3	1	2	0	1		1975-78
Boucher, Frank	NY Rangers	27	13	14	0	4	1	1939-54
Boucher, Georges	Mtl. Maroons	2	0	2	0	1		1930-50
Bowman, Scotty	St. Louis	52	26	26	0	4		
	Montreal	98	70	28	0	8	5	
	Buffalo	36	18	18	0	5		
	Pittsburgh	33	23	10	0	2	1	
	Detroit	134	86	48	0	9	3	
	Total	353	223	130	0	28	9	1967-02
Bowness, Rick	Boston	15	8	7	0	1		1988-98
Brooks, Herb	NY Rangers	24	12	12	0	3		
	New Jersey	5	1	4	0	1		
	Pittsburgh	11	6	5	0	1		
	Total	40	19	21	0	5		1981-00
Brophy, John	Toronto	19	9	10	0	2		1986-89
Burns, Charlie	Minnesota	6	2	4	0	1		1969-75
Burns, Pat	Montreal	56	30	26	0	4		
	Toronto	46	23	23	0	3		
	Boston	18	8	10	0	2		
	New Jersey	24	16	8	0	1	1	
	Total	144	77	67	0	10	1	1988-03
Campbell, Colin	NY Rangers	36	18	18	0	3		1994-98
Carpenter, Doug	Toronto	5	1	4	0	1		1984-91
Carroll, Dick	Toronto	9	4	5	0	2	1	1917-19
Cassidy, Bruce	Washington	6	2	4	0	1		2002-03
Cheevers, Gerry	Boston	34	15	19	0	4		1980-85
Cherry, Don	Boston	55	31	24	0	5		1974-80
Clancy, King	Toronto	14	2	12	0	3		1937-56
Clapper, Dit	Boston	25	8	17	0	4		1945-49
Cleghorn, Odie	Pittsburgh	4	1	2	1	1		1925-29
Cleghorn, Sprague	Mtl. Maroons	4	1	1	2	1		1931-32
Constantine, Kevin	San Jose	25	11	14	0	2		
	Pittsburgh	19	8	11	0	2		
	New Jersey	6	2	4	0	1		
	Total	50	21	29	0	5		1993-02
Crawford, Marc	Quebec	6	2	4	0	1		
	Colorado	46	29	17	0	3	1	
	Vancouver	24	9	15	0	3		
	Total	76	40	36	0	7	1	1994-03
Creighton, Fred	Atlanta	9	2	7	0	4		1974-80
Crisp, Terry	Calgary	37	22	15	0	3	1	
	Tampa Bay	6	2	4	0	1		
	Total	43	24	19	0	4	1	1987-98
Crozier, Joe	Buffalo	6	2	4	0	1		1971-81
Cunniff, John	New Jersey	6	2	4	0	1		1982-91
Curry, Alex	Ottawa	2	0	1	1	1		1925-26
Dandurand, Leo	Montreal	16	10	6	0	4	1	1921-35
Day, Hap	Toronto	80	49	31	0	9	5	1940-50
Demers, Jacques	St. Louis	33	16	17	0	3		
	Detroit	38	20	18	0	3		
	Montreal	27	19	8	0	1	1	
	Total	98	55	43	0	8	1	1979-99
Denneny, Cy	Boston	5	5	0	0	1	1	1928-33
Dudley, Rick	Buffalo	12	4	8	0	2		1989-92
Dugal, Jules	Montreal	3	1	2	0	1		1938-39
Duncan, Art	Toronto	2	0	1	1	1		1926-32
Dutton, Red	NY Americans	16	6	10	0	4		1935-42
Esposito, Phil	NY Rangers	10	2	8	0	2		1986-89
Evans, Jack	Hartford	16	8	8	0	2		1975-88
Ferguson, John	Winnipeg	3	0	3	0	1		1975-86
Francis, Bob	Phoenix	10	2	8	0	2		1999-02
Francis, Emile	NY Rangers	75	34	41	0	9		
	St. Louis	14	5	9	0	2		
	Total	89	39	50	0	11		1965-83
Ftorek, Robbie	Los Angeles	16	5	11	0	2		
	New Jersey	7	3	4	0	1		
	Boston	6	2	4	0	1		
	Total	29	10	19	0	4		1987-02
Gainey, Bob	Minnesota	30	17	13	0	2		
	Dallas	14	6	8	0	2		
	Total	44	23	21	0	4		1990-96
Geoffrion, Bernie	Atlanta	4	0	4	0	1		1968-80
Gerard, Eddie	Mtl. Maroons	25	11	9	5	5	1	1917-35
Gill, David	Ottawa	8	3	2	3	2	1	1926-29
Glover, Fred	Oakland	11	3	8	0	2		1968-74
Gordon, Jackie	Minnesota	25	11	14	0	3		1970-75
Goring, Butch	Boston	3	0	3	0	1		1985-01
Gorman, Tommy	NY Americans	2	0	1	1	1		
	Chicago	8	6	1	1	1	1	
	Mtl. Maroons	15	7	6	2	3	1	
	Total	25	13	8	4	5	2	1925-38
Gottselig, Johnny	Chicago	4	0	4	0	1		1944-48
Granato, Tony	Colorado	7	3	4	0	1		2002-03
Green, Pete	Ottawa	26	14	9	3	6	3	1919-25
Green, Ted	Edmonton	16	8	8	0	1		1991-94
Guidolin, Bep	Boston	21	11	10	0	2		1972-76
Harris, Ted	Minnesota	2	0	2	0	1		1975-78
Hart, Cecil	Montreal	37	16	17	4	8	2	1926-39
Hartley, Bob	Colorado	80	49	31	0	4	1	1998-02
Hartsburg, Craig	Chicago	16	8	8	0	2		
	Anaheim	4	0	4	0	1		
	Total	20	8	12	0	3		1995-01
Harvey, Doug	NY Rangers	6	2	4	0	1		1961-62
Hay, Don	Phoenix	7	3	4	0	1		1996-01
Henning, Lorne	Minnesota	5	2	3	0	1		1985-01
Hitchcock, Ken	Dallas	80	47	33	0	5	1	
	Philadelphia	13	6	7	0	1		
	Total	93	53	40	0	6	1	1995-03
Hlinka, Ivan	Pittsburgh	18	9	9	0	1		2000-02
Holmgren, Paul	Philadelphia	19	10	9	0	1		1988-96
Imlach, Punch	Toronto	92	44	48	0	11	4	1958-80
Inglis, Billy	Buffalo	3	1	2	0	1		1978-79
Irvin, Dick	Chicago	9	5	3	1	1		
	Toronto	66	33	32	1	9	1	
	Montreal	115	62	53	0	14	3	
	Total	190	100	88	2	24	4	1928-56
Ivan, Tommy	Detroit	67	36	31	0	7	3	1947-58
Johnson, Bob	Calgary	52	25	27	0	5		
	Pittsburgh	24	16	8	0	1	1	
	Total	76	41	35	0	6	1	1982-91
Johnson, Tom	Boston	22	15	7	0	2	1	1970-73
Johnston, Eddie	Chicago	7	3	4	0	1		
	Pittsburgh	46	22	24	0	5		
	Total	53	25	28	0	6		1979-97
Kasper, Steve	Boston	5	1	4	0	1		1995-97
Keenan, Mike	Philadelphia	57	32	25	0	4		
	Chicago	60	33	27	0	4		
	NY Rangers	23	16	7	0	1	1	
	St. Louis	20	10	10	0	2		
	Total	160	91	69	0	11	1	1984-02
Kelly, Pat	Colorado	2	0	2	0	1		1977-79
Kelly, Red	Los Angeles	18	7	11	0	2		
	Pittsburgh	14	6	8	0	2		
	Toronto	30	11	19	0	4		
	Total	62	24	38	0	8		1967-77
King, Dave	Calgary	20	8	12	0	3		1992-02
Kromm, Bobby	Detroit	7	3	4	0	1		1977-80
Lalonde, Newsy	Montreal	16	7	6	3	4		
	Ottawa	2	0	1	1	1		
	Total	18	7	7	4	5		1917-35
Laviolette, Peter	NY Islanders	12	4	8	0	2		2001-03
Lemaire, Jacques	Montreal	27	15	12	0	2		
	New Jersey	56	34	22	0	4	1	
	Minnesota	18	8	10	0	1		
	Total	101	57	44	0	7	1	1983-03
Lewis, Dave	Detroit	4	0	4	0	1		1998-03
Ley, Rick	Hartford	13	5	8	0	2		
	Vancouver	11	4	7	0	1		
	Total	24	9	15	0	3		1989-96
Long, Barry	Winnipeg	11	3	8	0	2		1983-86
Loughlin, Clem	Chicago	4	1	2	1	2		1934-37
Low, Ron	Edmonton	28	10	18	0	3		1994-00
Lowe, Kevin	Edmonton	5	1	4	0	1		1999-00
MacLean, Doug	Florida	27	13	14	0	1		1995-98
MacNeil, Al	Montreal	20	12	8	0	1	1	
	Atlanta	4	1	3	0	1		
	Calgary	19	9	10	0	2		
	Total	43	22	21	0	4	1	1970-82
MacTavish, Craig	Edmonton	12	4	8	0	2		2000-03
Magnuson, Keith	Chicago	3	0	3	0	1		1980-82
Mahoney, Bill	Minnesota	16	7	9	0	1		1983-85
Maloney, Dan	Toronto	10	6	4	0	1		
	Winnipeg	15	5	10	0	2		
	Total	25	11	14	0	3		1984-89
Maloney, Phil	Vancouver	7	1	6	0	2		1973-77
Martin, Jacques	St. Louis	16	7	9	0	2		
	Ottawa	62	28	34	0	7		
	Total	78	35	43	0	9		1986-03
Maurice, Paul	Carolina	35	17	18	0	3		1995-02
McCammon, Bob	Philadelphia	10	1	9	0	3		
	Vancouver	7	3	4	0	1		
	Total	17	4	13	0	4		1978-91
McLellan, John	Toronto	11	3	8	0	2		1969-73
McVie, Tom	New Jersey	14	6	8	0	2		1975-92
Melrose, Barry	Los Angeles	24	13	11	0	1		1992-95
Milbury, Mike	Boston	40	23	17	0	2		1989-98
Muckler, John	Edmonton	40	25	15	0	2	1	
	Buffalo	27	11	16	0	4		
	Total	67	36	31	0	6	1	1968-00

Coach	Team	Games Coached	Wins	Losses	Ties	Playoff Years	Cup Wins	Career
Muldoon, Pete	Chicago	2	0	1	1	1		1926-27
Munro, Dunc	Mtl. Maroons	4	1	3	0	1		1929-31
Murdoch, Bob	Chicago	5	1	4	0	1		
	Winnipeg	7	3	4	0	1		
	Total	12	4	8	0	2		1987-91
Murphy, Mike	Los Angeles	5	1	4	0	1		1986-98
Murray, Andy	Los Angeles	24	10	14	0	3		1999-02
Murray, Bryan	Washington	53	24	29	0	7		
	Detroit	25	10	15	0	3		
	Total	78	34	44	0	10		1981-02
Murray, Terry	Washington	39	18	21	0	4		
	Philadelphia	46	28	18	0	3		
	Florida	4	0	4	0	1		
	Total	89	46	43	0	8		1989-01
Neale, Harry	Vancouver	14	3	11	0	4		1978-86
Neilson, Roger	Toronto	19	8	11	0	2		
	Buffalo	8	4	4	0	1		
	Vancouver	21	12	9	0	2		
	NY Rangers	29	13	16	0	3		
	Philadelphia	29	14	15	0	3		
	Total	106	51	55	0	11		1977-02
Nolan, Ted	Buffalo	12	5	7	0	1		1995-97
Nykoluk, Mike	Toronto	7	1	6	0	2		1980-84
O'Connell, Mike	Boston	5	1	4	0	1		2002-03
O'Donoghue, George	Toronto	7	4	2	1	1		1921-23
O'Reilly, Terry	Boston	37	17	19	1	3		1986-89
Oliver, Murray	Minnesota	13	5	8	0	2		1981-83
Paddock, John	Winnipeg	13	5	8	0	2		1991-95
Page, Pierre	Minnesota	12	4	8	0	2		
	Quebec	6	2	4	0	1		
	Calgary	4	0	4	0	1		
	Total	22	6	16	0	4		1988-98
Patrick, Craig	NY Rangers	17	7	10	0	2		
	Pittsburgh	5	1	4	0	1		
	Total	22	8	14	0	3		1980-97
Patrick, Frank	Boston	6	2	4	0	2		1934-36
Patrick, Lester	NY Rangers	65	32	26	7	12	2	1926-39
Patrick, Lynn	NY Rangers	12	7	5	0	1		
	Boston	28	9	18	1	4		
	Total	40	16	23	1	5		1948-76
Perron, Jean	Montreal	48	30	18	0	3	1	1985-89
Perry, Don	Los Angeles	10	4	6	0	1		1981-84
Pilous, Rudy	Chicago	41	19	22	0	5	1	1957-63
Plager, Barclay	St. Louis	4	1	3	0	2		1977-83
Pleau, Larry	Hartford	10	2	8	0	2		1980-89
Polano, Nick	Detroit	7	1	6	0	2		1982-85
Powers, Eddie	Toronto	2	0	2	0	1		1924-26
Primeau, Joe	Toronto	15	8	6	1	2	1	1950-53
Pronovost, Marcel	Buffalo	8	3	5	0	1		1977-79
Pulford, Bob	Los Angeles	26	10	16	0	4		
	Chicago	45	17	28	0	6		
	Total	71	27	44	0	10		1972-00
Quenneville, Joel	St. Louis	68	34	34	0	7		1996-03
Quinn, Pat	Philadelphia	39	22	17	0	3		
	Los Angeles	3	0	3	0	1		
	Vancouver	61	31	30	0	5		
	Toronto	67	35	32	0	5		
	Total	170	88	82	0	14		1978-03
Reay, Billy	Chicago	116	56	60	0	12		1957-77
Risebrough, Doug	Calgary	7	3	4	0	1		1990-92
Roberts, Jim	Hartford	7	3	4	0	1		1981-97
Robinson, Larry	Los Angeles	4	0	4	0	1		
	New Jersey	48	31	17	0	2	1	
	Total	52	31	21	0	3	1	1995-02
Ross, Art	Boston	65	27	33	5	11	1	1917-45
Ruel, Claude	Montreal	27	18	9	0	3	2	1968-81
Ruff, Lindy	Buffalo	54	32	22	0	4		1997-02
Sather, Glen	Edmonton	127	89	37	1	10	4	1979-94
Sator, Ted	NY Rangers	16	8	8	0	1		
	Buffalo	11	3	8	0	2		
	Total	27	11	16	0	3		1985-89
Schinkel, Ken	Pittsburgh	6	2	4	0	2		1972-77
Schmidt, Milt	Boston	34	15	19	0	4		1954-76
Schoenfeld, Jim	New Jersey	20	11	9	0	1		
	Washington	24	10	14	0	3		
	Phoenix	13	5	8	0	2		
	Total	57	26	31	0	6		1985-99
Shero, Fred	Philadelphia	83	48	35	0	6	2	
	NY Rangers	27	15	12	0	2		
	Total	110	63	47	0	8	2	1971-81
Simpson, Terry	NY Islanders	20	9	11	0	2		
	Winnipeg	6	2	4	0	1		
	Total	26	11	15	0	3		1986-96
Sinden, Harry	Boston	43	24	19	0	5	1	1966-85
Skinner, Jimmy	Detroit	26	14	12	0	3	1	1954-58
Smith, Alf	Ottawa	5	1	4	0	1		1918-19
Smith, Floyd	Buffalo	32	16	16	0	3		1971-80
Smythe, Conn	Toronto	4	2	2	0	1		1927-31
Sonmor, Glen	Minnesota	43	25	18	0	3		1978-87
Stasiuk, Vic	Philadelphia	4	0	4	0	1		1969-73
Stewart, Bill	Chicago	10	7	3	0	1	1	1937-39
Stewart, Ron	Los Angeles	2	0	2	0	1		1975-78
Sutter, Brian	St. Louis	41	20	21	0	4		
	Boston	22	7	15	0	3		
	Chicago	5	1	4	0	1		
	Total	68	28	40	0	8		1988-02
Sutter, Darryl	Chicago	26	11	15	0	3		
	San Jose	42	18	24	0	5		
	Total	68	29	39	0	8		1992-02
Talbot, Jean-Guy	St. Louis	5	1	4	0	1		
	NY Rangers	3	1	2	0	1		
	Total	8	2	6	0	2		1972-78
Tessier, Orval	Chicago	18	9	9	0	2		1982-85
Therrien, Michel	Montreal	12	6	6	0	1		2000-02
Thompson, Paul	Chicago	19	7	12	0	4		1938-45
Tippett, Dave	Dallas	12	6	6	0	1		2002-03
Tobin, Bill	Chicago	4	1	2	1	2		1929-32
Tortorella, John	Tampa Bay	11	5	6	0	1		1999-03
Tremblay, Mario	Montreal	11	3	8	0	1		1995-97
Ubriaco, Gene	Pittsburgh	11	7	4	0	1		1988-90
Vigneault, Alain	Montreal	10	4	6	0	1		1997-01
Watson, Phil	NY Rangers	16	4	12	0	3		1955-63
Watt, Tom	Winnipeg	7	1	6	0	2		
	Vancouver	3	0	3	0	1		
	Total	10	1	9	0	3		1981-92
Webster, Tom	Los Angeles	28	12	16	0	2		1986-92
Weiland, Cooney	Boston	17	10	7	0	2	1	1939-41
White, Bill	Chicago	2	0	2	0	1		1976-77
Wilson, Johnny	Pittsburgh	12	4	8	0	2		1969-80
Wilson, Ron	Anaheim	11	4	7	0	1		
	Washington	32	15	17	0	3		
	Total	43	19	24	0	4		1993-02
Young, Garry	St. Louis	2	0	2	0	1		1972-76

Goaltender Gerry McNeil surrendered four overtime goals, including Bill Barilko's famed series winner, during the 1951 Stanley Cup Finals. All five games of the series between Toronto and Montreal required overtime.

Penalty Shots in Stanley Cup Playoff Games

Date	Player	Goaltender	Scored	Final Score			Series
Mar. 25/37	Lionel Conacher, Mtl. Maroons	Tiny Thompson, Boston	No	Mtl. M.	0	at Bos.	4	QF
Apr. 15/37	Alex Shibicky, NY Rangers	Earl Robertson, Detroit	No	NYR	0	at Det.	3	F
Apr. 13/44	Virgil Johnson, Chicago	Bill Durnan, Montreal	No	Chi.	4	at Mtl.	5*	F
Apr. 9/68	Wayne Connelly, Minnesota	Terry Sawchuk, Los Angeles	Yes	L.A.	5	at Min.	7	QF
Apr. 27/68	Jimmy Roberts, St. Louis	Cesare Maniago, Minnesota	No	St.L.	4	at Min.	3	SF
May 16/71	Frank Mahovlich, Montreal	Tony Esposito, Chicago	No	Chi.	3	at Mtl.	4	F
May 7/75	Bill Barber, Philadelphia	Glenn Resch, NY Islanders	No	Phi.	3	at NYI	4*	SF
Apr. 20/79	Mike Walton, Chicago	Glenn Resch, NY Islanders	No	NYI	3	at Chi.	0	QF
Apr. 9/81	Peter McNab, Boston	Don Beaupre, Minnesota	No	Min.	5	at Bos.	4*	PR
Apr. 17/81	Anders Hedberg, NY Rangers	Mike Liut, St. Louis	Yes	NYR	6	at St.L.	4	QF
Apr. 9/83	Denis Potvin, NY Islanders	Pat Riggin, Washington	No	NYI	6	at Wsh.	2	DSF
Apr. 28/84	Wayne Gretzky, Edmonton	Don Beaupre, Minnesota	Yes	Edm.	8	at Min.	5	CF
May 1/84	Mats Naslund, Montreal	Billy Smith, NY Islanders	No	Mtl.	1	at NYI	3	CF
Apr. 14/85	Bob Carpenter, Washington	Billy Smith, NY Islanders	No	Wsh.	4	at NYI.	6	DF
May 28/85	Ron Sutter, Philadelphia	Grant Fuhr, Edmonton	No	Phi.	3	at Edm.	4	F
May 30/85	Dave Poulin, Philadelphia	Grant Fuhr, Edmonton	No	Phi.	3	at Edm.	8	F
Apr. 9/88	John Tucker, Buffalo	Andy Moog, Boston	Yes	Bos.	2	at Buf.	6	DSF
Apr. 9/88	Petr Klima, Detroit	Allan Bester, Toronto	Yes	Det.	6	at Tor.	4	DSF
Apr. 8/89	Neal Broten, Minnesota	Greg Millen, St. Louis	Yes	St.L.	5	at Min.	3	DSF
Apr. 4/90	Al MacInnis, Calgary	Kelly Hrudey, Los Angeles	Yes	L.A.	5	at Cgy.	3	DSF
Apr. 5/90	Randy Wood, NY Islanders	Mike Richter, NY Rangers	No	NYI	1	at NYR	2	DSF
May 3/90	Kelly Miller, Washington	Andy Moog, Boston	No	Wsh.	3	at Bos.	5	CF
May 18/90	Petr Klima, Edmonton	Reggie Lemelin, Boston	No	Edm.	7	at Bos.	2	F
Apr. 6/91	Basil McRae, Minnesota	Ed Belfour, Chicago	Yes	Min.	2	at Chi.	5	DSF
Apr. 10/91	Steve Duchesne, Los Angeles	Kirk McLean, Vancouver	Yes	L.A.	6	at Van.	5	DSF
May 11/92	Jaromir Jagr, Pittsburgh	John Vanbiesbrouck, NYR	Yes	Pit.	3	at NYR	2	DF
May 13/92	Shawn McEachern, Pittsburgh	John Vanbiesbrouck, NYR	No	NYR	1	at Pit.	5	DF
Jun. 7/94	Pavel Bure, Vancouver	Mike Richter, NYR	No	NYR	4	at Van.	2	F
May 9/95	Patrick Poulin, Chicago	Felix Potvin, Toronto	No	Tor.	3	at Chi.	0	CQF
May 10/95	Michal Pivonka, Washington	Tom Barrasso, Pittsburgh	No	Pit.	2	at Wsh.	6	CQF
Apr. 24/96	Joe Juneau, Washington	Ken Wregget, Pittsburgh	No	Pit.	3	at Wsh.	2**	CQF
May 11/97	Eric Lindros, Philadelphia	Steve Shields, Buffalo	Yes	Phi.	6	at Buf.	3	CSF
Apr. 23/98	Aleksey Morozov, Pittsburgh	Andy Moog, Montreal	No	Mtl.	3	at Pit.	2**	CQF
Apr. 22/99	Mats Sundin, Toronto	John Vanbiesbrouck, Phi.	No	Phi.	1	at Tor.	3	CQF
May 29/99	Mats Sundin, Toronto	Dominik Hasek, Buffalo	Yes	Tor.	2	at Buf.	5	CF
Apr. 16/00	Eric Desjardins, Philadelphia	Dominik Hasek, Buffalo	No	Phi.	2	at Buf.	0	CQF
Apr. 11/01	Mark Recchi, Philadelphia	Dominik Hasek, Buffalo	No	Buf.	2	at Phi.	1	CQF
May 2/01	Martin Straka, Pittsburgh	Dominik Hasek, Buffalo	No	Buf.	5	at Pit.	2	CSF
May 12/01	Joe Sakic, Colorado	Roman Turek, St. Louis	Yes	St.L.	1	at Col.	4	CF
Apr. 21/02	Todd Bertuzzi, Vancouver	Dominik Hasek, Detroit	No	Det.	3	at Van.	1	CQF
Apr. 24/02	Shawn Bates, NY Islanders	Curtis Joseph, Toronto	Yes	Tor.	3	at NYI	4	CQF
Apr. 26/02	Mike Johnson, Phoenix	Evgeni Nabokov, San Jose	Yes	Phx.	1	at S.J.	4	CQF
Apr. 15/03	Dainius Zubrus, Washington	Nikolai Khabibulin, Tampa Bay	No	T.B.	4	at Wsh.	3	CQF
Apr. 21/03	Robert Reichel, Toronto	Roman Cechmanek, Philadelphia	No	Phi.	1	at Tor.	2	CQF

* Game was decided in overtime, but shot taken during regulation time.
** Shot taken in overtime.

Petr Sykora scored 48 seconds into the fifth overtime period to give Anaheim a 4-3 win over Dallas in the first game of their Western Conference Semifinal. It was the fourth-longest game in NHL history.

Overtime Record of Current Teams

(Listed by number of OT games played)

Team	Overall				Home				Last OT Game	Road				Last OT Game
	GP	W	L	T	GP	W	L	T		GP	W	L	T	
Montreal	122	70	50	2	57	37	19	1	May 9/02	65	33	31	1	May 8/98
Toronto	104	54	49	1	67	36	30	1	Apr. 21/03	37	18	19	0	May 19/02
Boston	98	38	57	3	45	20	24	1	May 3/98	53	18	33	2	Apr. 30/99
Detroit	74	33	41	0	44	16	28	0	Apr. 10/03	30	17	13	0	Apr. 16/03
NY Rangers	63	30	33	0	27	12	15	0	Apr. 22/97	36	18	18	0	May 11/97
Chicago	62	30	30	2	30	16	13	1	Apr. 20/97	32	14	17	1	May 2/96
Philadelphia	56	26	30	0	25	13	13	0	Apr. 29/03	31	14	17	0	Apr. 21/03
Dallas[1]	52	23	29	0	25	10	15	0	Apr. 26/03	27	13	14	0	May 1/01
St. Louis	49	27	22	0	26	20	6	0	May 18/01	23	7	16	0	May 21/01
Colorado[2]	47	27	20	0	19	9	10	0	Apr. 22/03	28	18	10	0	Apr. 21/03
Buffalo	46	25	21	0	26	16	10	0	May 10/01	20	9	11	0	May 8/01
NY Islanders	39	29	10	0	18	14	4	0	Apr. 14/03	21	15	6	0	May 18/93
Edmonton	38	21	17	0	21	11	10	0	Apr. 17/01	17	10	7	0	Apr. 19/01
Los Angeles	35	17	18	0	19	11	8	0	May 6/01	16	6	10	0	Apr. 25/02
Vancouver	33	16	17	0	14	6	8	0	Apr. 25/03	19	10	9	0	May 2/03
New Jersey[4]	33	10	23	0	14	5	9	0	May 21/03	19	5	14	0	Jun. 2/03
Washington	31	14	17	0	12	5	7	0	Apr. 20/03	19	9	10	0	Apr. 23/01
Calgary[3]	30	11	19	0	14	4	10	0	Apr. 23/96	16	7	9	0	Apr. 28/94
Pittsburgh	28	15	13	0	18	10	8	0	May 8/01	10	5	5	0	May 10/01
Carolina[5]	23	14	9	0	14	9	5	0	Jun. 8/02	9	5	4	0	Jun. 4/02
Ottawa	15	8	7	0	5	3	2	0	May 10/03	10	5	5	0	May 21/03
Phoenix[6]	12	5	7	0	8	3	5	0	May 4/99	4	2	2	0	Apr. 27/93
Anaheim	11	8	3	0	4	3	1	0	Jun. 2/03	7	5	2	0	May 10/03
San Jose	9	3	6	0	5	1	4	0	May 13/02	4	2	2	0	Apr. 19/01
Tampa Bay	6	4	2	0	1	1	0	0	Apr. 21/96	5	3	2	0	May 2/03
Florida	5	2	3	0	3	1	2	0	Apr. 25/97	2	1	1	0	Apr. 22/97
Minnesota	5	2	3	0	3	1	2	0	May 10/03	2	1	1	0	Apr. 25/03

[1] Totals include those of Minnesota North Stars 1967-93.
[2] Totals include those of Quebec 1979-95.
[3] Totals include those of Atlanta Flames 1972-80.
[4] Totals include those of Kansas City and Colorado Rockies 1974-82.
[5] Totals include those of Hartford 1979-97.
[6] Totals include those of Winnipeg 1979-96.

The Mighty Ducks had a perfect 7-0 overtime record during their Cinderella playoff run of 2003. Steve Thomas ended the season's shortest overtime session when he scored after just 39 seconds in game four of the Stanley Cup Finals.

Ten Longest Overtime Games

Date	City	Series	Score				Scorer	Overtime	Series Winner
Mar. 24/36	Mtl.	SF	Det. 1		Mtl. M.	0	Mud Bruneteau	116:30	Det.
Apr. 3/33	Tor.	SF	Tor. 1		Bos.	0	Ken Doraty	104:46	Tor.
May 4/00	Pit.	CSF	Phi. 2		Pit.	1	Keith Primeau	92:01	Phi.
Apr. 24/03	**Dal.**	**CSF**	**Ana. 4**		**Dal.**	**3**	**Petr Sykora**	**80:48**	**Ana.**
Apr. 24/96	Wsh.	CQF	Pit. 3		Wsh.	2	Petr Nedved	79:15	Pit.
Mar. 23/43	Det.	SF	Det. 2		Tor.	1	Jack McLean	70:18	Det.
Mar. 28/30	Mtl.	SF	Mtl. 2		NYR	1	Gus Rivers	68:52	Mtl.
Apr. 18/87	Wsh.	DSF	NYI 3		Wsh.	2	Pat LaFontaine	68:47	NYI
Apr. 27/94	Buf.	CQF	Buf. 1		N.J.	0	Dave Hannan	65:43	N.J.
Mar. 27/51	Det.	SF	Mtl. 3		Det.	2	Maurice Richard	61:09	Mtl.

Key to Prospect, NHL Player and Goaltender Registers

Demographics: Position, shooting side (catching hand for goaltenders), height, weight, place and date of birth as well as draft information, if any, is located on this line.

Major Junior, NCAA, minor pro, senior European and NHL clubs form a permanent part of each player's data panel. If a player sees action with more than one club in any of the above categories, a separate line is included for each one.

Olympic Team statistics are also listed.

Player's NHL organization as of August 25, 2003. This includes players under contract, unsigned draft choices and other players on reserve lists. Free agents as of August 25, 2003 show a blank here.

The complete career data panels of players with NHL experience who announced their retirement before the start of the 2002-03 season are included in the 2002-03 Player Register. These newly-retired players also show a blank here.

Each NHL club's minor-pro affiliates are listed on page 220.

						Regular Season													Playoffs							
Season	Club	League	GP	G	A	Pts	PIM	PP	SH	GW	S	%	+/–	TF	F%	Min	GP	G	A	Pts	PIM	PP	SH	G	Min

LANGENBRUNNER, Jamie (lan-gehn-BRUH-nuhr, JAY-mee)   **N.J.**

Right wing. Shoots right. 6'1", 200 lbs.   Born, Duluth, MN, July 24, 1975. Dallas' 2nd choice, 35th overall, in 1993 Entry Draft.

Season	Club	League	GP	G	A	Pts	PIM	PP	SH	GW	S	%	+/–	TF	F%	Min	GP	G	A	Pts	PIM	PP	SH	G	Min
1990-91	Cloquet High	Hi-School	20	6	16	22	8																		
1991-92	Cloquet High	Hi-School	23	16	23	39	24																		
1992-93	Cloquet High	Hi-School	27	27	62	89	18																		
1993-94	Peterborough	OHL	62	33	58	91	53										7	4	6	10	2				
1994-95	Peterborough	OHL	62	42	57	99	84										11	8	14	22	12				
	Dallas	**NHL**	2	0	0	0	2	0	0	0	1	0.0	0				11	1	3	4	2				
	Kalamazoo Wings	IHL																							
1995-96	**Dallas**	**NHL**	12	2	2	4	6	1	0	0	15	13.3	–2				10	3	10	13				1	
	Michigan	IHL	59	25	40	65	129										5	1	1	2	14	0	0	1	
1996-97	**Dallas**	**NHL**	76	13	26	39	51	3	0	3	112	11.6	–2				16	1	4	5	14	0	0	1	
1997-98	**Dallas**	**NHL**	81	23	29	52	61	8	0	6	159	14.5	9												
	United States	Olympics	3	0	0	0	4																		
1998-99◆	**Dallas**	**NHL**	75	12	33	45	62	4	0	1	145	8.3	10	217	46.1	15:51	23	10	7	17	16	4	0	3	17:43
99-00	**Dallas**	**NHL**	65	18	21	39	68	4	2	6	153	11.8	16	40	50.0	17:33	15	1	7	8	18	1	0	0	15:28
2000-01	**Dallas**	**NHL**	53	12	18	30	57	3	2	4	104	11.5	4	316	45.3	16:30	1	2	2	4	6	0	0	1	19:26
2001-02	**Dallas**	**NHL**	68	10	16	26	54	0	1	2	132	7.6	–11	120	45.0	15:45									
	New Jersey	**NHL**	14	3	3	6	23	0	0	2	31	9.7	2	2	50.0	15:27	5	0	1	1	8	0	0	0	14:57
2002-03◆	**New Jersey**	**NHL**	78	22	33	55	65	5	1	5	197	11.2	17	72	47.2	17:48	24	*11	7	*18	16	0	0	4	17:34
	NHL Totals		524	115	181	296	449	28	6	29	1049	11.0		767	45.9	16:39	98	26	29	55	92	6	0	10	17:16

Traded to **New Jersey** by **Dallas** with Joe Nieuwendyk for Jason Arnott, Randy McKay and New Jersey's 1st round choice (later traded to Columbus – later traded to Buffalo – Buffalo selected Dan Paille) in 2002 Entry Draft, March 19, 2002.

Diamond (◆) indicates member of Stanley Cup-winning team.

Asterisk (*) indicates league leader in this statistical category.

Trade and free agent signing dates are based on when the player's contract is filed with NHL Central Registry. This date often differs from the date when the club announces that it has made a trade or come to terms with a free agent.

All-Star Team selections and awards are listed below player's year-by-year data.

NHL All-Star Game appearances are listed above trade notes.

All trades, free agent signings and other transactions involving NHL clubs are listed in chronological order. First draft selection for players who re-enter the NHL Entry Draft is noted here. Other special notes are also listed here. These are highlighted with a bullet (•).

THIS 72ND EDITION OF THE *NHL Official Guide & Record Book* is the fifth to include additional statistical categories for forwards and defensemen in the National Hockey League. These categories are, from left to right in the sample panel above, power-play goals (PP), shorthand goals (SH), game-winning goals (GW), shots on goal (S), percentage of shots that score (%), plus-minus rating (+/–), total faceoffs taken (TF), faceoff winning percentage (F%), and average time-on-ice per game played (Min).

To integrate this data, the Player Register has been is split into two sections. The Prospect Register presents data on players who have yet to play in the NHL. The NHL Player Register, containing more information and a photo of each player, lists all active players who have appeared in an NHL regular-season or playoff game at any time.

Goaltenders, whether prospects or active NHLers, are included in one register.

Registers (with their starting page) are presented in the following order: Prospects (267), NHL Players (336), Goaltenders (574), Retired Players (598) and Retired Goaltenders (632).

Late additions to the Registers and a list of league abbreviations are found on page 335.

Pronunciation of Player Names

United Press International phonetic style.

AY	long A as in mate
A	short A as in cat
AI	nasal A as on air
AH	short A as in father
AW	broad A as in talk
EE	long E as in meat
EH	short E as in get
UH	hollow E as in the
AY	French long E with acute accent as in Pathe
IH	middle E as in pretty
EW	EW dipthong as in few
IGH	long I as in time
EE	French long I as in machine
IH	short I as in pity
OH	long O as in note
AH	short O as in hot
AW	broad O as in fought
OI	OI dipthong as in noise
OO	long double OO as in fool
U	short double O as in foot
OW	OW dipthong as in how
EW	long U as in mule
OO	long U as in rule
U	middle U as in put
UH	short U as in shut or hurt
K	hard C as in cat
S	soft C as in cease
SH	soft CH as in machine
CH	hard CH or TCH as in catch
Z	hard S as in bells
S	soft S as in sun
G	hard G as in gang
J	soft G as in general
ZH	soft J as in French version of Joliet
KH	gutteral CH as in Scottish version of Loch

Some information is unavailable at press time. Readers are encouraged to contribute. See page 5 for contact names and addresses.

2003-04 Prospect Register

Note: The 2003-04 Prospect Register lists forwards and defensemen only. Goaltenders are listed separately. The Prospect Register lists every player drafted in the first five rounds of the 2003 Entry Draft, players on NHL Reserve Lists and other players who have not yet played in the NHL. Trades and roster changes are current as of August 25, 2003.

Abbreviations: A – assists; **G** – goals; **GP** – games played; **PIM** – penalties in minutes; **TP** – total points; ***** – league-leading total.

NHL Player Register begins on page 336.
Goaltender Register begins on page 574.
League Abbreviations are listed on page 335.

ABBOTT, Jim (A-buht, JIHM) **PIT.**

Left wing. Shoots left. 6'1", 190 lbs. Born, New York, NY, May 3, 1980.
(Pittsburgh's 7th choice, 216th overall, in 2000 Entry Draft).

			Regular Season					Playoffs				
Season	Club	League	GP	G	A	TP	PIM	GP	G	A	TP	PIM
1997-98	Pittsburgh	MTJHL	50	30	23	53	128	5	5	3	8	0
1998-99	St. Louis Sting	NAJHL	56	*45	33	78	35	9	7	2	9	12
99-2000	New Hampshire	H-East	28	7	6	13	22	....	....	....	....	....
2000-01	New Hampshire	H-East	33	10	12	22	52	....	....	....	....	....
2001-02	New Hampshire	H-East	38	9	20	29	48	....	....	....	....	....
2002-03	New Hampshire	H-East	42	12	18	30	34	....	....	....	....	....

MTJHL Rookie of the Year (1998) • NAJHL First All-Star Team (1999)

ADAMS, John (A-duhms, JAWN) **BUF.**

Defense. Shoots left. 6'2", 188 lbs. Born, Orono, ME, December 21, 1982.
(Buffalo's 4th choice, 82nd overall, in 2002 Entry Draft).

			Regular Season					Playoffs				
Season	Club	League	GP	G	A	TP	PIM	GP	G	A	TP	PIM
99-2000	Breck Mustangs	Hi-School	25	6	30	36	....	....	....	....	....	....
2000-01	Breck Mustangs	Hi-School	25	13	29	42	....	....	....	....	....	....
2001-02	Boston College	H-East	25	0	5	5	20	....	....	....	....	....
2002-03	Boston College	H-East	34	2	5	7	22	....	....	....	....	....

All-Metro Second All-Star Team (2000) • All-Metro First All-Star Team (2001)

ADDUONO, Jeremy (uh-DOO-noh, JAIR-eh-mee)

Right wing. Shoots right. 6', 182 lbs. Born, Thunder Bay, Ont., August 4, 1978.
(Buffalo's 8th choice, 184th overall, in 1997 Entry Draft).

			Regular Season					Playoffs				
Season	Club	League	GP	G	A	TP	PIM	GP	G	A	TP	PIM
1994-95	Thunder Bay Flyers	USHL	40	11	10	21	8	....	....	....	....	....
1995-96	Sudbury Wolves	OHL	66	15	22	37	14	....	....	....	....	....
1996-97	Sudbury Wolves	OHL	66	29	40	69	24	....	....	....	....	....
1997-98	Sudbury Wolves	OHL	66	37	69	106	40	10	5	5	10	10
1998-99	Team Canada	Nat-Tm	44	10	18	28	10	....	....	....	....	....
99-2000	Rochester	AHL	51	23	22	45	20	21	6	11	17	2
2000-01	Rochester	AHL	76	24	30	54	53	4	1	0	1	4
2001-02	Rochester	AHL	79	15	20	35	38	1	1	0	1	0
2002-03	Bridgeport	AHL	54	13	13	26	14	9	2	5	7	2

AHOSILTA, Marko (ah-hoh-SIHL-tuh, mahr-KOH) **N.J.**

Center. Shoots left. 5'8", 165 lbs. Born, Kuopio, Finland, January 24, 1980.
(New Jersey's 11th choice, 227th overall, in 1998 Entry Draft).

			Regular Season					Playoffs				
Season	Club	League	GP	G	A	TP	PIM	GP	G	A	TP	PIM
1994-95	KalPa Kuopio-C	Finn-Jr.	13	4	6	10	10	....	....	....	....	....
1995-96	KalPa Kuopio Jr.	Finn-Jr.	12	4	8	12	10	....	....	....	....	....
1996-97	KalPa Kuopio Jr.	Finn-Jr.	35	15	21	36	36	5	2	0	2	2
1997-98	KalPa Kuopio Jr.	Finn-Jr.	14	14	13	27	10	....	....	....	....	....
	KalPa Kuopio	Finland	2	0	0	0	0	....	....	....	....	....
1998-99	KalPa Kuopio Jr.	Finn-Jr.	24	7	7	14	10	....	....	....	....	....
	KalPa Kuopio	Finland	1	0	0	0	0	....	....	....	....	....
99-2000	KalPa Kuopio Jr.	Finn-Jr.	10	6	4	10	8	....	....	....	....	....
	KJT Jarvenpaa	Finland-2	30	19	5	24	14	....	....	....	....	....
2000-01			DID NOT PLAY									
2001-02	KalPa Kuopio	Finland-2	44	17	20	37	24	3	0	1	1	2
2002-03	KalPa Kuopio	Finland-2	39	23	22	45	32	4	0	1	1	2

AIKINS, Justin (AY-kihns, JUHS-tihn) **CBJ**

Center. Shoots left. 6', 176 lbs. Born, Surrey, B.C., January 12, 1982.
(Columbus' 7th choice, 173rd overall, in 2001 Entry Draft).

			Regular Season					Playoffs				
Season	Club	League	GP	G	A	TP	PIM	GP	G	A	TP	PIM
1998-99	Langley Hornets	BCHL	52	6	21	27	16	....	....	....	....	....
99-2000	Langley Hornets	BCHL	59	29	38	67	46	....	....	....	....	....
2000-01	Langley Hornets	BCHL	59	30	61	91	47	....	....	....	....	....
2001-02	New Hampshire	H-East	29	4	4	8	6	....	....	....	....	....
2002-03	New Hampshire	H-East	42	4	18	22	20	....	....	....	....	....

AKKANEN, Karri (ah-KAHN-uhn, KAH-ree) **T.B.**

Center. Shoots right. 6'6", 202 lbs. Born, Tampere, Finland, January 29, 1984.
(Tampa Bay's 6th choice, 174th overall, in 2002 Entry Draft).

			Regular Season					Playoffs				
Season	Club	League	GP	G	A	TP	PIM	GP	G	A	TP	PIM
2000-01	Ilves Tampere-B	Finn-Jr.	32	5	10	15	20	....	....	....	....	....
2001-02	Ilves Tampere-B	Finn-Jr.	15	6	6	12	30	4	0	1	1	4
	Ilves Tampere Jr.	Finn-Jr.	5	0	1	1	4	....	....	....	....	....
2002-03	Ilves Tampere	Finland	21	0	1	1	0	....	....	....	....	....
	Ilves Tampere-B	Finn-Jr.	11	1	6	7	65	....	....	....	....	....
	Ilves Tampere Jr.	Finn-Jr.	13	6	14	20	16	....	....	....	....	....

ALBERTS, Andrew (AL-buhrts, AN-droo) **BOS.**

Defense. Shoots left. 6'4", 218 lbs. Born, Minneapolis, MN, June 30, 1981.
(Boston's 5th choice, 179th overall, in 2001 Entry Draft).

			Regular Season					Playoffs				
Season	Club	League	GP	G	A	TP	PIM	GP	G	A	TP	PIM
1998-99	Benilde High	Hi-School	26	10	25	35	....	....	....	....	....	....
99-2000	Waterloo	USHL	49	2	2	4	55	4	0	0	0	12
2000-01	Waterloo	USHL	54	4	10	14	128	....	....	....	....	....
2001-02	Boston College	H-East	38	2	10	12	52	....	....	....	....	....
2002-03	Boston College	H-East	39	6	16	22	60	....	....	....	....	....

ALEN, Juha (AL-ehn, YOO-haw) **ANA.**

Defense. Shoots left. 6'3", 210 lbs. Born, Tampere, Finland, October 25, 1981.
(Anaheim's 4th choice, 90th overall, in 2003 Entry Draft).

			Regular Season					Playoffs				
Season	Club	League	GP	G	A	TP	PIM	GP	G	A	TP	PIM
1998-99	KooVee Jr.	Finn-Jr.	36	6	7	13	42	....	....	....	....	....
99-2000	KooVee Jr.	Finn-Jr.	22	2	4	6	28	....	....	....	....	....
2000-01	Ilves Tampere Jr.	Finn-Jr.	42	2	12	14	62	....	....	....	....	....
2001-02	Soo Indians	NAHL	54	10	10	20	46	2	0	1	1	0
2002-03	Northern Michigan	CCHA	40	4	19	23	64	....	....	....	....	....

ALMTORP, Jonas (AHLM-tohrp, YOH-nuhs) **EDM.**

Center. Shoots left. 6'1", 190 lbs. Born, Uppsala, Sweden, November 17, 1983.
(Edmonton's 7th choice, 111th overall, in 2002 Entry Draft).

			Regular Season					Playoffs				
Season	Club	League	GP	G	A	TP	PIM	GP	G	A	TP	PIM
99-2000	MoDo-18	Swede-Jr.	22	*19	12	31	*55	....	....	....	....	....
	MoDo Jr.	Swede-Jr.	7	1	0	1	0	....	....	....	....	....
2000-01	MoDo-18	Swede-Jr.	12	11	1	12	30	....	....	....	....	....
	MoDo Jr.	Swede-Jr.	27	19	7	26	38	7	6	1	7	10
2001-02	MoDo	Sweden	3	0	0	0	0	....	....	....	....	....
	MoDo Jr.	Swede-Jr.	37	26	18	44	102	2	1	1	2	4
2002-03	MoDo	Sweden	28	1	1	2	22	....	....	....	....	....
	MoDo	Swede-2	12	5	4	9	49	....	....	....	....	....
	MoDo Jr.	Swede-Jr.	5	2	2	4	0	....	....	....	....	....

ALTAREV, Dmitri (al-ta-REHV, dih-MEE-tree) **NYI**

Left wing. Shoots left. 6'3", 191 lbs. Born, Penza, USSR, August 12, 1980.
(NY Islanders' 8th choice, 264th overall, in 2000 Entry Draft).

			Regular Season					Playoffs				
Season	Club	League	GP	G	A	TP	PIM	GP	G	A	TP	PIM
1997-98	Dizelist Penza 2	Russia-3	57	15	8	23	83	....	....	....	....	....
1998-99	Dizelist Penza 2	Russia-4	35	4	3	7	30	....	....	....	....	....
	Dizelist Penza	Russia-3	6	2	0	2	8	....	....	....	....	....
99-2000	Dizelist Penza 2	Russia-3	44	10	8	18	25	....	....	....	....	....
2000-01	Nizhny Novgorod	Russia	36	1	2	3	26	....	....	....	....	....
2001-02	Niz. Novgorod 2	Russia-3	10	5	6	11	12	....	....	....	....	....
	Nizhny Novgorod	Russia	32	2	3	5	42	....	....	....	....	....
2002-03	Dizelist Penza	Russia-3	47	22	26	48	106	....	....	....	....	....

ANDERSON, Erik (AN-duhr-suhn, AIR-ihk)

Center. Shoots left. 5'9", 190 lbs. Born, Plymouth, MI, March 6, 1978.

			Regular Season					Playoffs				
Season	Club	League	GP	G	A	TP	PIM	GP	G	A	TP	PIM
1995-96	Stratford Cullitons	OJHL-B	38	29	43	72	10					
1996-97	Stratford Cullitons	OJHL-B	48	54	*91	*145	40					
1997-98	St. Lawrence	ECAC	33	5	13	18	12					
1998-99	St. Lawrence	ECAC	39	10	30	40	18					
99-2000	St. Lawrence	ECAC	36	14	25	39	20					
2000-01	St. Lawrence	ECAC	32	17	34	51	4					
2001-02	Milwaukee	AHL	49	4	6	10	10					
	Cincinnati	ECHL	17	6	13	19	19					
2002-03	Milwaukee	AHL	34	4	8	12	10					
	Toledo Storm	ECHL	36	9	15	24	10	7	3	4	7	6

ECAC First All-Star Team (2001) • ECAC Player of the Year (2001) • NCAA East First All-American Team (2001)

Signed as a free agent by **Nashville**, July 5, 2001.

ANDRESEN, Joel (AN-druh-suhn, JOHL) L.A.

Defense. Shoots left. 6'3", 200 lbs. Born, St. Albert, Alta., April 11, 1983.
(Los Angeles' 7th choice, 157th overall, in 2002 Entry Draft).

			Regular Season					Playoffs				
Season	Club	League	GP	G	A	TP	PIM	GP	G	A	TP	PIM
1998-99	Spruce Grove	AMBHL	36	6	14	20	32					
99-2000	St. Albert Raiders	AMHL	35	10	15	25	49					
	St. Albert Saints	AJHL	5	0	0	0	6					
2000-01	St. Albert Saints	AJHL	45	2	9	11	47	7	1	1	2	6
2001-02	St. Albert Saints	AJHL	53	9	19	28	62	6	0	2	2	12
2002-03	Nebraska-Omaha	CCHA	37	2	7	9	22					

AJHL Top Defenseman (2002)

ANDREWS, Bobby (AN-drooz, BAW-bee) NYR

Center. Shoots left. 6'1", 200 lbs. Born, Birtle, Man., January 5, 1978.

			Regular Season					Playoffs				
Season	Club	League	GP	G	A	TP	PIM	GP	G	A	TP	PIM
1996-97	Cleveland	NAJHL	45	21	22	43	259					
1997-98	Langley Thunder	BCHL	59	26	48	74	143					
1998-99	Alaska-Fairbanks	CCHA	31	5	11	16	38					
99-2000	Alaska-Fairbanks	CCHA	34	13	12	25	72					
2000-01	Alaska-Fairbanks	CCHA	36	9	16	25	46					
2001-02	Alaska-Fairbanks	CCHA	37	14	23	37	46					
	Hartford Wolf Pack	AHL	1	0	0	0	0	7	0	0	0	2
2002-03	Hartford Wolf Pack	AHL	58	6	7	13	33	2	0	0	0	0

BCHL Central First All-Star Team (1998) • CCHA Second All-Star Team (2002)

Signed as a free agent by **NY Rangers**, March 19, 2002.

ANDREWS, Daryl (AN-drews, DAI-rihl)

Defense. Shoots left. 6'3", 215 lbs. Born, Campbell River, B.C., April 27, 1977.
(New Jersey's 11th choice, 173rd overall, in 1996 Entry Draft).

			Regular Season					Playoffs				
Season	Club	League	GP	G	A	TP	PIM	GP	G	A	TP	PIM
1995-96	Melfort Mustangs	SJHL	55	2	12	14	51					
1996-97	West-Michigan	CCHA	37	6	20	26	86					
1997-98	West-Michigan	CCHA	36	3	0	3	81					
1998-99	West-Michigan	CCHA	33	3	11	14	42					
99-2000	West-Michigan	CCHA	36	3	16	19	52					
	Albany River Rats	AHL	9	0	2	2	9	5	0	0	0	0
2000-01	Albany River Rats	AHL	80	2	8	10	49					
2001-02	Albany River Rats	AHL	69	3	10	13	60					
2002-03	Albany River Rats	AHL	75	3	6	9	52					

CCHA Rookie of the Year (1997)

ANGELSTAD, Mel (AN-gehl-stahd, MEHL)

Left wing. Shoots left. 6'2", 214 lbs. Born, Saskatoon, Sask., October 31, 1972.

			Regular Season					Playoffs				
Season	Club	League	GP	G	A	TP	PIM	GP	G	A	TP	PIM
1988-89	Allan Legionnaires	MAHA	35	15	23	38	256					
1989-90	Warman Valley	MJHL	38	1	5	6	411					
1990-91	Flin Flon Bombers	MJHL	62	6	11	17	463					
1991-92	Dauphin Kings	MJHL	44	8	29	37	*296					
1992-93	Thunder Bay	ColHL	45	2	5	7	256	5	0	0	0	10
	Nashville Knights	ECHL	1	0	0	0	14					
1993-94	Thunder Bay	ColHL	58	1	20	21	374	9	1	2	3	65
	P.E.I. Senators	AHL	1	0	0	0	5					
1994-95	Thunder Bay	ColHL	46	0	8	8	317	7	0	3	3	62
	P.E.I. Senators	AHL	3	0	0	0	16					
1995-96	Thunder Bay	ColHL	51	3	3	6	335	16	0	6	6	94
	Phoenix	IHL	5	0	0	0	43					
1996-97	Thunder Bay	ColHL	66	10	21	31	422	7	0	1	1	21
1997-98	Fort Worth	WPHL	19	1	6	7	102					
	Las Vegas Thunder	IHL	3	0	0	0	5					
	Orlando	IHL	63	1	3	4	321	8	0	0	0	29
1998-99	Michigan K-Wings	IHL	78	3	5	8	421	5	1	0	1	16
99-2000	Michigan K-Wings	IHL	33	3	4	7	144					
2000-01	Manitoba Moose	IHL	67	1	5	6	232	8	0	0	0	26
2001-02	Portland Pirates	AHL	53	1	7	8	212					
2002-03	Portland Pirates	AHL	57	5	2	7	139	3	0	0	0	6

Signed as a free agent by **Dallas**, July 29, 1998.

ANGER, Niklas (AN-guhr, NIHK-lahs) MTL.

Right wing. Shoots left. 6'1", 185 lbs. Born, Gavle, Sweden, July 31, 1977.
(Montreal's 5th choice, 112th overall, in 1995 Entry Draft).

			Regular Season					Playoffs				
Season	Club	League	GP	G	A	TP	PIM	GP	G	A	TP	PIM
1994-95	Djurgarden Jr.	Swede-Jr.	30	14	12	26	26					
	Djurgarden	Sweden	1	0	0	0	0					
1995-96	Djurgarden Jr.	Swede-Jr.	24	13	16	29	26					
	Djurgarden	Sweden	10	0	0	0	2					
1996-97	Djurgarden Jr.	Swede-Jr.	2	1	2	3	0					
	Arlanda Mastra	Swede-2	16	5	9	14	6					
	Linkopings HC	Swede-2	10	2	2	4	10	14	3	7	10	2
	Djurgarden	Sweden	4	0	0	0	0					
1997-98	Djurgarden	Sweden	45	2	5	7	37	12	0	1	1	2
1998-99	AIK Solna Jr.	Swede-Jr.	1	0	0	0	0					
	AIK Solna	Sweden	47	6	6	12	16					
99-2000	AIK Solna	Sweden	50	11	13	24	14					
2000-01	AIK Solna	Sweden	50	5	10	15	22	5	0	1	1	2
2001-02	AIK Solna	Sweden	50	12	20	32	16					
2002-03	Brynas IF Gavle	Sweden	48	20	12	32	28					

ANSHAKOV, Sergei (an-sha-KAHV, SAIR-gay) L.A.

Left wing. Shoots left. 6'3", 179 lbs. Born, Moscow, USSR, January 13, 1984.
(Los Angeles' 2nd choice, 50th overall, in 2002 Entry Draft).

			Regular Season					Playoffs				
Season	Club	League	GP	G	A	TP	PIM	GP	G	A	TP	PIM
2000-01	Dyn. Moscow-18	Exhib.	6	7	1	8	2					
2001-02	HC CSKA 2	Russia-3	3	3	1	4	0					
	HC CSKA Moscow	Russia-2	46	20	12	22	10					
2002-03	CSKA Moscow	Russia	25	1	2	3	4					

AQUINO, Anthony (a-KEE-noh, AN-thuh-nee) ATL.

Right wing. Shoots right. 5'10", 175 lbs. Born, Mississauga, Ont., August 1, 1982.
(Dallas' 3rd choice, 92nd overall, in 2001 Entry Draft).

			Regular Season					Playoffs				
Season	Club	League	GP	G	A	TP	PIM	GP	G	A	TP	PIM
1997-98	Mississauga	OPJHL	50	10	13	23	14					
1998-99	Bramalea Blues	OPJHL	47	31	44	75	31					
99-2000	Merrimack College	H-East	36	15	14	29	12					
2000-01	Merrimack College	H-East	38	17	25	42	22					
2001-02	Merrimack College	H-East	36	24	20	44	20					
2002-03	Oshawa Generals	OHL	14	10	9	19	6					
	Chicago Wolves	AHL	5	0	0	0	4					

Hockey East All-Rookie Team (2000) • Hockey East Second All-Star Team (2001)

• Left Merrimack (H-East) and signed as a free agent by **Oshawa** (OHL), September 25, 2002. • Ruled ineligible to play remainder of 2002-03 OHL season because of OHL overage restrictions, November 7, 2002. Rights traded to **Atlanta** by **Dallas** for Dallas' 6th round choice (previously acquired, Dallas selected Drew Bagnall) in 2003 Entry Draft and future considerations, March 11, 2003.

ARCHER, Andrew (AHR-chuhr, AN-droo) MTL.

Defense. Shoots right. 6'4", 212 lbs. Born, Calgary, Alta., May 15, 1983.
(Montreal's 7th choice, 203rd overall, in 2001 Entry Draft).

			Regular Season					Playoffs				
Season	Club	League	GP	G	A	TP	PIM	GP	G	A	TP	PIM
1998-99	Richmond Hill	OMHA		STATISTICS NOT AVAILABLE								
99-2000	Oshawa Generals	OHL	47	0	1	1	24	3	0	1	1	2
2000-01	Oshawa Generals	OHL	2	0	0	0	4					
	Guelph Storm	OHL	50	0	2	2	59	4	0	0	0	4
2001-02	Guelph Storm	OHL	58	3	10	13	76	9	0	2	2	16
2002-03	Guelph Storm	OHL	65	2	16	18	138	11	2	2	4	18

ARMSTRONG, Colby (AHRM-stawng, KOHL-bee) PIT.

Right wing. Shoots right. 6'2", 187 lbs. Born, Lloydminster, Sask., November 23, 1982.
(Pittsburgh's 1st choice, 21st overall, in 2001 Entry Draft).

			Regular Season					Playoffs				
Season	Club	League	GP	G	A	TP	PIM	GP	G	A	TP	PIM
1998-99	Sask. Contacts	SMHL	33	21	19	40	103					
	Red Deer Rebels	WHL	1	0	1	1	0					
99-2000	Red Deer Rebels	WHL	68	13	25	38	122	2	0	1	1	11
2000-01	Red Deer Rebels	WHL	72	36	42	78	156	21	6	6	12	29
2001-02	Red Deer Rebels	WHL	64	27	41	68	115	23	6	10	16	32
2002-03	Wilkes-Barre	AHL	73	7	11	18	76	3	0	0	0	4

ARTEMENKOV, Yuri (ahr-TUH-mehn-kahv, YOO-ree) CGY.

Right wing. Shoots left. 6'1", 174 lbs. Born, Moscow, USSR, February 3, 1984.
(Calgary's 4th choice, 112th overall, in 2002 Entry Draft).

			Regular Season					Playoffs				
Season	Club	League	GP	G	A	TP	PIM	GP	G	A	TP	PIM
99-2000	Team Russia	Nat-Tm	5	1	1	2	0					
2000-01	Krylja Sovetov 2	Russia-3	2	0	0	0	4					
2001-02	Krylja Sovetov 2	Russia-3	32	24	15	42	10					
2002-03	Krylja Sovetov	Russia	3	0	0	0	0					
	Krylja Sovetov 2	Russia-3	7	2	2	4	12					
	Kirovo-Chepetsk	Russia-2	1	0	0	0	0					

ARTUKHIN, Evgeni (ahr-TYEW-khin, yehv-GEH-nee) T.B.

Right wing. Shoots left. 6'4", 215 lbs. Born, Moscow, USSR, April 4, 1983.
(Tampa Bay's 4th choice, 94th overall, in 2001 Entry Draft).

			Regular Season					Playoffs				
Season	Club	League	GP	G	A	TP	PIM	GP	G	A	TP	PIM
99-2000	Vityaz Podolsk 2	Russia-3	26	9	8	17	46					
	Vityaz Podolsk	Russia-2	3	0	0	0	2					
2000-01	Vityaz Podolsk	Russia	24	0	1	1	14					
2001-02	Vityaz Podolsk 2	Russia-3	4	3	1	4	6					
	Vityaz Podolsk	Russia-2	49	15	7	22	94	12	0	1	1	18
2002-03	Moncton Wildcats	QMJHL	53	13	27	40	204	6	1	2	3	29

ASLUND, Calle (AZ-luhnd, KAL-ee) BUF.

Defense. Shoots left. 6'2", 198 lbs. Born, Haninge, Sweden, March 29, 1983.
(Buffalo's 6th choice, 234th overall, in 2001 Entry Draft).

			Regular Season					Playoffs				
Season	Club	League	GP	G	A	TP	PIM	GP	G	A	TP	PIM
99-2000	Huddinge IK-18	Swede-Jr.	17	1	5	6	48					
2000-01	Huddinge IK-18	Swede-Jr.	8	1	3	4	30					
	Huddinge IK Jr.	Swede-Jr.	7	0	1	1	14					
2001-02	Huddinge IK Jr.	Swede-Jr.	27	1	6	7	66					
	Huddinge IK	Swede-2	26	0	0	0	47					
2002-03	Huddinge IK Jr.	Swede-Jr.	5	0	2	2	16	3	0	0	0	25
	Huddinge IK	Swede-2	37	3	3	6	66	2	0	0	0	6

ATHERTON, P.J. (A-thur-tuhn, PEE-JAY) T.B.

Defense. Shoots right. 6'2", 208 lbs. Born, Edina, MN, August 16, 1982.
(Tampa Bay's 5th choice, 170th overall, in 2002 Entry Draft).

			Regular Season					Playoffs				
Season	Club	League	GP	G	A	TP	PIM	GP	G	A	TP	PIM
99-2000	Edina Hornets	Hi-School	38	7	15	22	....					
	Cedar Rapids	USHL	5	0	1	1	4					
2000-01	Cedar Rapids	USHL	43	4	9	13	99	4	2	0	2	10
2001-02	Cedar Rapids	USHL	51	7	22	29	101	8	0	0	0	14
2002-03	U. of Minnesota	WCHA	20	2	2	4	20					

ATYUSHOV, Vitali (a-tew-SHAWF, vih-TAL-ee) OTT.

Defense. Shoots left. 6'1", 205 lbs. Born, Penza, USSR, July 4, 1979.
(Ottawa's 8th choice, 276th overall, in 2002 Entry Draft).

			Regular Season					Playoffs				
Season	Club	League	GP	G	A	TP	PIM	GP	G	A	TP	PIM
1997-98	Krylja Sovetov	Russia	4	0	0	0	2	....	....	....	....	....
1998-99	Dizelist Penza 2	Russia-4	2	1	1	2	2	....	....	....	....	....
	Dizelist Penza	Russia-2	22	0	0	0	22	....	....	....	....	....
	Krylja Sovetov	Russia	17	1	0	1	20	....	....	....	....	....
	Krylja Sovetov	Russia-Q	21	0	5	5	50	....	....	....	....	....
99-2000	Perm	Russia	38	4	0	4	50	3	0	0	0	12
2000-01	Perm	Russia	44	3	9	12	32	....	....	....	....	....
2001-02	Perm	Russia	51	4	8	12	66	....	....	....	....	....
2002-03	Ak Bars Kazan	Russia	33	0	9	9	12	2	0	0	0	0

AUFIERO, Patrick (ow-fee-AIR-oh, PAT-rihk) NYR

Defense. Shoots right. 6'2", 186 lbs. Born, Winchester, MA, July 1, 1980.
(NY Rangers' 5th choice, 90th overall, in 1999 Entry Draft).

			Regular Season					Playoffs				
Season	Club	League	GP	G	A	TP	PIM	GP	G	A	TP	PIM
1995-96	Winchester High	Hi-School	25	13	18	31	....	....	....	....	....	....
1996-97	Winchester High	Hi-School	27	27	21	48	....	....	....	....	....	....
1997-98	U.S. National U-18	USDP	56	10	11	21	111	....	....	....	....	....
1998-99	Boston University	H-East	22	3	4	7	14	....	....	....	....	....
99-2000	Boston University	H-East	38	3	20	23	37	....	....	....	....	....
2000-01	Boston University	H-East	34	5	8	13	30	....	....	....	....	....
2001-02	Boston University	H-East	26	2	10	12	16	....	....	....	....	....
2002-03	Hartford Wolf Pack	AHL	32	1	6	7	29	....	....	....	....	....
	Charlotte	ECHL	8	2	4	6	6	....	....	....	....	....

Hockey East Second All-Star Team (2000)

BABCHUK, Anton (bab-CHUHK, an-TAWN) CHI.

Defense. Shoots right. 6'5", 202 lbs. Born, Kiev, USSR, May 6, 1984.
(Chicago's 1st choice, 21st overall, in 2002 Entry Draft).

			Regular Season					Playoffs				
Season	Club	League	GP	G	A	TP	PIM	GP	G	A	TP	PIM
99-2000	Elektrostal-18	Russia-Jr.	5	0	0	0	18	....	....	....	....	....
	Elektrostal Jr.	Russia-Jr.	6	0	0	0	8	....	....	....	....	....
	Elektrostal 2	Russia-3	18	0	1	1	18	....	....	....	....	....
2000-01	Elektrostal	Russia-2	7	0	0	0	12	....	....	....	....	....
2001-02	Elektrostal	Russia-2	40	7	8	15	90	....	....	....	....	....
	Elektrostal 2	Russia-3	3	0	0	0	8	....	....	....	....	....
2002-03	Ak Bars Kazan	Russia	10	0	0	0	4	....	....	....	....	....
	SKA St. Petersburg	Russia	20	3	0	3	10	....	....	....	....	....

BABY, Stephen (BAY-bee, STEE-vehn) ATL.

Right wing. Shoots right. 6'5", 235 lbs. Born, Chicago, IL, January 31, 1980.
(Atlanta's 8th choice, 188th overall, in 1999 Entry Draft).

			Regular Season					Playoffs				
Season	Club	League	GP	G	A	TP	PIM	GP	G	A	TP	PIM
1997-98	Green Bay	USHL	56	17	17	34	85	4	1	3	4	8
1998-99	Green Bay	USHL	55	23	24	47	83	6	1	1	2	4
99-2000	Cornell Big Red	ECAC	31	4	10	14	52	....	....	....	....	....
2000-01	Cornell Big Red	ECAC	32	8	20	28	47	....	....	....	....	....
2001-02	Cornell Big Red	ECAC	35	9	23	32	42	....	....	....	....	....
2002-03	Cornell Big Red	ECAC	36	8	*33	41	60	....	....	....	....	....

ECAC Second All-Star Team (2002) • NCAA East Second All-American Team (2003)

BACKER, Per (BAK-uhr, PAIR) DET.

Right wing. Shoots left. 6'1", 161 lbs. Born, Grums, Sweden, January 4, 1982.
(Detroit's 7th choice, 187th overall, in 2000 Entry Draft).

			Regular Season					Playoffs				
Season	Club	League	GP	G	A	TP	PIM	GP	G	A	TP	PIM
1998-99	Grums IK	Swede-2	17	1	1	2	4	....	....	....	....	....
99-2000	Grums IK	Swede-2	46	12	10	22	24	....	....	....	....	....
2000-01	Bofors IK	Swede-2	27	9	10	19	10	....	....	....	....	....
	Bofors IK	Swede-Q	14	11	5	16	6	....	....	....	....	....
2001-02	Farjestad	Sweden	47	4	8	12	12	10	5	1	6	10
2002-03	Farjestad	Sweden	49	11	16	27	46	12	1	1	2	12

BACKES, David (BA-kuhs, DAY-vihd) ST.L.

Center. Shoots right. 6'2", 200 lbs. Born, Blaine, MN, May 1, 1984.
(St. Louis' 2nd choice, 62nd overall, in 2003 Entry Draft).

			Regular Season					Playoffs				
Season	Club	League	GP	G	A	TP	PIM	GP	G	A	TP	PIM
99-2000	Spring Lake Park	Hi-School	24	35	40	75	....	....	....	....	....	....
2000-01	Spring Lake Park	Hi-School	26	36	33	69	....	....	....	....	....	....
2001-02	Chicago Steel	USHL	30	11	10	21	54	3	0	0	0	2
2002-03	Lincoln Stars	USHL	57	28	41	69	126	7	4	1	5	17

USHL First All-Star Team (2003)

Signed Letter of Intent to attend **Minnesota State** (WCHA), October 1, 2001.

BAHEN, Chris (BAY-hehn, KRIHS) COL.

Defense. Shoots left. 6', 180 lbs. Born, Montreal, Que., November 16, 1980.
(Colorado's 10th choice, 189th overall, in 2000 Entry Draft).

			Regular Season					Playoffs				
Season	Club	League	GP	G	A	TP	PIM	GP	G	A	TP	PIM
1994-95	Thornhill	OMHA	40	12	38	50	82	....	....	....	....	....
1995-96	Thornhill	OMHA	40	18	51	69	96	....	....	....	....	....
1996-97	Thornhill	OMHA	40	23	42	65	108	....	....	....	....	....
1997-98	Thornhill Rattlers	MTJHL	45	5	9	14	131	....	....	....	....	....
1998-99	Milton Merchants	OPJHL	32	3	14	17	20	....	....	....	....	....
99-2000	Clarkson Knights	ECAC	34	8	10	18	54	....	....	....	....	....
2000-01	Clarkson Knights	ECAC	34	3	7	10	45	....	....	....	....	....
2001-02	Clarkson Knights	ECAC	37	2	6	8	36	....	....	....	....	....
2002-03	Clarkson Knights	ECAC	34	3	14	17	45	....	....	....	....	....

ECAC All-Academic Team (2002)

BAINES, Ajay (BAYNZ, AY-JAY) CHI.

Center. Shoots left. 5'10", 178 lbs. Born, Kamloops, B.C., March 25, 1978.

			Regular Season					Playoffs				
Season	Club	League	GP	G	A	TP	PIM	GP	G	A	TP	PIM
1994-95	Kamloops	BCAHA	52	45	79	124	139	....	....	....	....	....
1995-96	Kamloops Blazers	WHL	68	14	29	43	43	....	....	....	....	....
1996-97	Kamloops Blazers	WHL	70	32	43	75	106	5	4	1	5	6
1997-98	Kamloops Blazers	WHL	72	34	25	59	88	....	....	....	....	....
1998-99	Kamloops Blazers	WHL	72	33	32	65	145	15	7	6	13	20
99-2000	Greenville Grrrowl	ECHL	67	24	31	55	102	15	2	5	7	13
2000-01	Norfolk Admirals	AHL	73	18	18	36	92	9	0	1	1	2
2001-02	Norfolk Admirals	AHL	80	16	28	44	70	4	0	1	1	0
2002-03	Norfolk Admirals	AHL	74	8	14	22	108	9	2	1	3	18

Signed as a free agent by **Chicago**, August 1, 2001.

BALAN, Scott (BAY-luhn, SKAWT) CHI.

Defense. Shoots right. 6'3", 195 lbs. Born, Medicine Hat, Alta., May 29, 1982.
(Chicago's 5th choice, 106th overall, in 2000 Entry Draft).

			Regular Season					Playoffs				
Season	Club	League	GP	G	A	TP	PIM	GP	G	A	TP	PIM
1997-98	Regina Chiefs	SMHL	56	6	25	31	139	....	....	....	....	....
	Regina Pats	WHL	1	0	1	1	0	....	....	....	....	....
1998-99	Regina Pats	WHL	63	1	8	9	42	....	....	....	....	....
99-2000	Regina Pats	WHL	67	3	11	14	157	7	0	1	1	17
2000-01	Regina Pats	WHL	42	2	5	7	69	....	....	....	....	....
	Saskatoon Blades	WHL	28	0	5	5	49	....	....	....	....	....
2001-02	Saskatoon Blades	WHL	27	1	10	11	40	....	....	....	....	....
2002-03	Roanoke Express	ECHL	44	1	9	10	63	4	0	0	0	2
	Norfolk Admirals	AHL	15	0	0	0	27	....	....	....	....	....

• Missed majority of 2001-02 season recovering from knee injury suffered in game vs. Saskatoon (WHL), December 18, 2001.

BALASTIK, Jaroslav (ba-LASH-tihk, YAHR-roh-slav) CBJ

Right wing. Shoots left. 6', 198 lbs. Born, Gottwaldov, Czech., November 28, 1979.
(Columbus' 9th choice, 184th overall, in 2002 Entry Draft).

			Regular Season					Playoffs				
Season	Club	League	GP	G	A	TP	PIM	GP	G	A	TP	PIM
2000-01	Zlin	Czech	52	8	17	25	32	6	1	1	2	6
2001-02	Zlin	Czech	50	25	19	44	32	11	3	5	8	14
2002-03	HPK Hameenlinna	Finland	13	5	7	12	2	13	4	3	7	6
	HC Hame Zlin	Czech	31	14	8	22	26	....	....	....	....	....

BALEJ, Josef (BAH-lay, YOH-zehf) MTL.

Right wing. Shoots right. 6'1", 187 lbs. Born, Myjava, Czech., February 22, 1982.
(Montreal's 3rd choice, 78th overall, in 2000 Entry Draft).

			Regular Season					Playoffs				
Season	Club	League	GP	G	A	TP	PIM	GP	G	A	TP	PIM
1997-98	Dukla Trencin Jr.	Slovak-Jr.	52	57	40	97	60	....	....	....	....	....
1998-99	Thunder Bay Flyers	USHL	38	8	7	15	9	....	....	....	....	....
	Rochester	USHL	17	0	1	1	2	....	....	....	....	....
99-2000	Portland	WHL	65	22	23	45	33	....	....	....	....	....
2000-01	Portland	WHL	46	32	21	53	18	16	9	6	15	6
2001-02	Portland	WHL	65	51	41	92	52	7	0	2	2	6
2002-03	Hamilton Bulldogs	AHL	56	5	15	20	29	....	....	....	....	....

WHL West First All-Star Team (2002)

BALLANTYNE, Paul (BAL-uhn-tughn, PAWL) DET.

Defense. Shoots right. 6'3", 200 lbs. Born, Waterloo, Ont., July 16, 1982.
(Detroit's 8th choice, 196th overall, in 2000 Entry Draft).

			Regular Season					Playoffs				
Season	Club	League	GP	G	A	TP	PIM	GP	G	A	TP	PIM
1997-98	Waterloo Lions	OMHA	30	4	16	20	55	....	....	....	....	....
	Waterloo Siskins	OJHL-B	1	0	0	0	0	....	....	....	....	....
1998-99	Sault Ste. Marie	OHL	53	0	6	6	33	5	1	0	1	4
99-2000	Sault Ste. Marie	OHL	58	4	15	19	60	17	2	3	5	17
2000-01	Sault Ste. Marie	OHL	63	12	28	40	60	....	....	....	....	....
2001-02	Sault Ste. Marie	OHL	68	4	24	28	40	6	1	1	2	8
2002-03	Toledo Storm	ECHL	56	10	16	26	41	7	0	1	1	2
	Grand Rapids	AHL	7	0	0	0	8	....	....	....	....	....

BALLARD, Keith (BAL-uhrd, KEETH) COL.

Defense. Shoots left. 5'11", 202 lbs. Born, Baudette, MN, November 26, 1982.
(Buffalo's 1st choice, 11th overall, in 2002 Entry Draft).

			Regular Season					Playoffs				
Season	Club	League	GP	G	A	TP	PIM	GP	G	A	TP	PIM
99-2000	U.S. National U-18	USDP	58	12	21	33	....	....	....	....	....	....
2000-01	Omaha Lancers	USHL	56	22	29	51	168	10	1	6	7	8
2001-02	U. of Minnesota	WCHA	41	10	13	23	42	....	....	....	....	....
2002-03	U. of Minnesota	WCHA	41	12	29	41	78	....	....	....	....	....

USHL First All-Star Team (2000) • WCHA All-Rookie Team (2002) • WCHA First All-Star Team (2003)

Traded to **Colorado** by **Buffalo** for Steve Reinprecht, July 3, 2003.

BARANKA, Ivan (ba-RAN-kuh, IGH-vuhn) NYR

Defense. Shoots left. 6'2", 180 lbs. Born, Ilava, Czech., May 19, 1985.
(NY Rangers' 2nd choice, 50th overall, in 2003 Entry Draft).

			Regular Season					Playoffs				
Season	Club	League	GP	G	A	TP	PIM	GP	G	A	TP	PIM
2002-03	Dubnica Jr.	Slovak-Jr.	27	1	7	8	44	....	....	....	....	....
	Dubnica	Slovak-2	2	0	0	0	0	....	....	....	....	....

BARANOV, Konstantin (buh-RA-nawf, kawn-stuhn-TEEN) PHI.

Right wing. Shoots left. 6'2", 185 lbs. Born, Omsk, USSR, January 11, 1982.
(Philadelphia's 3rd choice, 126th overall, in 2002 Entry Draft).

			Regular Season					Playoffs				
Season	Club	League	GP	G	A	TP	PIM	GP	G	A	TP	PIM
1998-99	Omsk 2	Russia-4	23	18	8	26	40	....	....	....	....	....
	Avangard Omsk	Russia	1	0	0	0	0	2	0	0	0	0
99-2000	Omsk 2	Russia-3	33	15	8	23	46	....	....	....	....	....
	Avangard Omsk	Russia	1	0	0	0	2	....	....	....	....	....
2000-01	Kristall Saratov	Russia-2	26	6	9	15	26	....	....	....	....	....
	Ufa	Russia	8	1	0	1	4	....	....	....	....	....
2001-02	Avangard Omsk	Russia	5	0	0	0	6	....	....	....	....	....
	Mechel	Russia	6	1	2	3	2	....	....	....	....	....
	Lada Togliatti	Russia	20	2	4	6	18	3	0	2	2	0
2002-03	Avangard Omsk	Russia	6	0	1	1	2	....	....	....	....	....
	Ufa	Russia	11	2	2	4	0	....	....	....	....	....
	CSKA Moscow	Russia	14	4	1	5	10	....	....	....	....	....

BARARUK, David (BAIR-a-ruhk, DAY-vihd) DAL.

Center. Shoots left. 6', 175 lbs. Born, Moose Jaw, Sask., May 26, 1983.
(Dallas' 8th choice, 147th overall, in 2002 Entry Draft).

			Regular Season					Playoffs				
Season	Club	League	GP	G	A	TP	PIM	GP	G	A	TP	PIM
99-2000	Moose Jaw	WHL	21	0	2	2	0	2	0	0	0	0
2000-01	Moose Jaw	WHL	53	6	9	15	9	3	0	0	0	0
2001-02	Moose Jaw	WHL	72	33	29	62	31	12	3	2	5	0
2002-03	Moose Jaw	WHL	66	29	64	93	44	13	5	9	14	4

WHL East Second All-Star Team (2003)

BARBER, Greg (BAHR-buhr, GREHG) BOS.

Right wing. Shoots right. 6', 185 lbs. Born, Dawson Creek, B.C., May 26, 1980.
(Boston's 7th choice, 207th overall, in 1999 Entry Draft).

			Regular Season					Playoffs				
Season	Club	League	GP	G	A	TP	PIM	GP	G	A	TP	PIM
1996-97	Kelowna Spartans	BCAHA	54	36	48	84	90	....	....	....	....	....
1997-98	Victoria Salsa	BCHL	60	15	22	37	24	7	2	2	4	4
1998-99	Victoria Salsa	BCHL	60	41	41	82	95	....	....	....	....	....
99-2000	U. of Denver	WCHA	40	7	8	15	24	....	....	....	....	....
2000-01	U. of Denver	WCHA	35	7	8	15	22	....	....	....	....	....
2001-02	U. of Denver	WCHA	38	18	17	35	28	....	....	....	....	....
2002-03	U. of Denver	WCHA	32	10	17	27	22	....	....	....	....	....

BARINKA, Michal (ba-RIHN-kuh, MIGH-kuhl) CHI.

Defense. Shoots left. 6'3", 200 lbs. Born, Vyskov, Czech., June 12, 1984.
(Chicago's 3rd choice, 59th overall, in 2003 Entry Draft).

			Regular Season					Playoffs				
Season	Club	League	GP	G	A	TP	PIM	GP	G	A	TP	PIM
99-2000	HC Budejovice Jr.	Czech-Jr.	48	1	12	13	26	6	0	2	2	4
2000-01	HC Budejovice Jr.	Czech-Jr.	33	1	9	10	20	3	0	0	0	0
2001-02	HC Budejovice Jr.	Czech-Jr.	31	3	13	16	60	7	3	4	7	35
	Ceske Budejovice	Czech	3	0	0	0	0	....	....	....	....	....
2002-03	Ceske Budejovice	Czech	31	0	1	1	14	4	0	0	0	2
	HC Budejovice Jr.	Czech-Jr.	14	1	5	6	34	....	....	....	....	....

BARKUNOV, Alexander (bahr-koo-NAHF, al-ehx-AN-duhr) CHI.

Defense. Shoots right. 6'1", 199 lbs. Born, Novosibirsk, USSR, May 13, 1981.
(Chicago's 7th choice, 151st overall, in 2000 Entry Draft).

			Regular Season					Playoffs				
Season	Club	League	GP	G	A	TP	PIM	GP	G	A	TP	PIM
1996-97	Yaroslavl 2	Russia-3	1	0	0	0	0	....	....	....	....	....
1997-98	Torpedo Yaroslavl	Russia	20	1	1	2	6	....	....	....	....	....
1998-99	Yaroslavl 2	Russia-3	19	0	3	3	8	....	....	....	....	....
99-2000	Torpedo Yaroslavl	Russia	38	5	9	14	16	8	2	1	3	0
2000-01	Yaroslavl	Russia	34	5	1	6	10	2	0	0	0	2
2001-02	Yaroslavl 2	Russia-3	10	1	4	5	2	....	....	....	....	....
	Yaroslavl	Russia	15	0	0	0	2	....	....	....	....	....
	Amur Khabarovsk	Russia	7	0	0	0	0	....	....	....	....	....
2002-03	Perm	Russia	28	0	1	1	16	....	....	....	....	....

BARNES, Ryan (BAHR-nz, RIGH-uhn) DET.

Left wing. Shoots left. 6'1", 201 lbs. Born, Dunnville, Ont., January 30, 1980.
(Detroit's 2nd choice, 55th overall, in 1998 Entry Draft).

			Regular Season					Playoffs				
Season	Club	League	GP	G	A	TP	PIM	GP	G	A	TP	PIM
1996-97	Quinte Hawks	MTJHL	46	15	19	34	245	....	....	....	....	....
1997-98	Sudbury Wolves	OHL	46	13	18	31	111	10	0	2	2	24
1998-99	Sudbury Wolves	OHL	8	2	0	2	23	....	....	....	....	....
	St. Michael's	OHL	31	11	14	25	*215	....	....	....	....	....
	Barrie Colts	OHL	24	16	14	30	*161	12	2	4	6	40
99-2000	Barrie Colts	OHL	31	17	12	29	98	25	7	7	14	49
2000-01	Cincinnati	AHL	1	0	0	0	7	....	....	....	....	....
	Toledo Storm	ECHL	16	2	4	6	31	....	....	....	....	....
2001-02	Toledo Storm	ECHL	1	1	0	1	0	....	....	....	....	....
	Cincinnati	AHL	46	2	3	5	152	....	....	....	....	....
2002-03	Grand Rapids	AHL	73	5	6	11	151	15	1	1	2	17

• Suspended for 25 games for stick-swinging incident in game vs. Oshawa (OHL), October 3, 1999. • Missed majority of 2000-01 season recovering from head injury suffered in training camp, September, 2000.

BARRETT, Nathan (BAIR-uht, NAY-thun) TOR.

Center. Shoots left. 6', 189 lbs. Born, Vancouver, B.C., August 3, 1981.
(Vancouver's 6th choice, 241st overall, in 2000 Entry Draft).

			Regular Season					Playoffs				
Season	Club	League	GP	G	A	TP	PIM	GP	G	A	TP	PIM
1996-97	Langley Bantams	BCAHA	90	107	109	216	96	....	....	....	....	....
1997-98	Tri-City Americans	WHL	47	1	1	2	23	....	....	....	....	....
1998-99	Tri-City Americans	WHL	33	9	9	18	19	....	....	....	....	....
	Lethbridge	WHL	22	12	9	21	19	4	1	0	1	0
99-2000	Lethbridge	WHL	72	44	38	82	38	....	....	....	....	....
2000-01	Lethbridge	WHL	70	46	53	99	66	5	1	1	2	6
2001-02	Lethbridge	WHL	72	45	*62	*107	100	4	0	1	1	6
2002-03	St. John's	AHL	69	9	22	31	35	....	....	....	....	....

WHL East Second All-Star Team (2001) • WHL East First All-Star Team (2002)

Signed as a free agent by **Toronto**, July 31, 2002.

BARTSCHI, Patrik (BAIRT-chee, PAT-rihk) PIT.

Center/Right wing. Shoots right. 6', 199 lbs. Born, Bulach, Switz., August 20, 1984.
(Pittsburgh's 8th choice, 202nd overall, in 2002 Entry Draft).

			Regular Season					Playoffs				
Season	Club	League	GP	G	A	TP	PIM	GP	G	A	TP	PIM
99-2000	Kloten Flyers Jr.	Swiss-Jr.	26	12	14	26	14	....	....	....	....	....
2000-01	Kloten Flyers Jr.	Swiss-Jr.	36	38	30	68	14	6	11	3	14	6
	EHC Kloten	Swiss	2	0	0	0	0	....	....	....	....	....
	HC Thurgau	Swiss-2	1	1	0	1	0	....	....	....	....	....
2001-02	Kloten Flyers Jr.	Swiss-Jr.	9	10	7	17	4	2	3	2	5	2
	Kloten Flyers	Swiss	24	4	4	8	8	11	2	2	4	2
2002-03	Kloten Flyers	Swiss	44	21	16	37	39	5	1	3	4	4

BATEMAN, Jeff (BAYT-mahn, JEHF) DAL.

Center. Shoots left. 5'11", 184 lbs. Born, Belleville, Ont., August 29, 1981.
(Dallas' 4th choice, 126th overall, in 1999 Entry Draft).

			Regular Season					Playoffs				
Season	Club	League	GP	G	A	TP	PIM	GP	G	A	TP	PIM
1996-97	Belleville	OMHA	51	102	64	166	....	....	....	....	....	....
1997-98	Wellington Dukes	MTJHL	50	26	35	61	68	....	....	....	....	....
1998-99	Brampton	OHL	68	23	35	58	27	....	....	....	....	....
99-2000	Brampton	OHL	64	23	41	64	62	6	2	1	3	4
2000-01	Brampton	OHL	53	15	44	59	81	9	5	7	12	18
2001-02	Fort Worth	CHL	27	7	11	18	32	1	1	0	1	0
	Utah Grizzlies	AHL	35	1	6	7	26	4	0	2	2	2
2002-03	Utah Grizzlies	AHL	60	8	8	16	60	2	0	0	0	0
	Lexington	ECHL	2	1	1	2	8	....	....	....	....	....

BAUM, Dan (BAWM, DAN) EDM.

Center. Shoots left. 6'1", 189 lbs. Born, Biggar, Sask., June 4, 1983.
(Edmonton's 8th choice, 215th overall, in 2001 Entry Draft).

			Regular Season					Playoffs				
Season	Club	League	GP	G	A	TP	PIM	GP	G	A	TP	PIM
99-2000	Prince George	WHL	55	6	10	16	82	12	1	0	1	19
2000-01	Prince George	WHL	59	9	14	23	169	6	1	2	3	27
2001-02	Prince George	WHL	72	32	35	67	197	6	5	3	8	25
2002-03	Prince George	WHL	72	32	41	73	218	5	2	0	2	9

BEAULIEU, Pierre-Olivier (BOI-loh, pee-AIR-oh-LIH-vee-ay) DET.

Defense. Shoots left. 6'4", 184 lbs. Born, St-Pierre Becquets, Que., February 24, 1984.
(Detroit's 8th choice, 260th overall, in 2002 Entry Draft).

			Regular Season					Playoffs				
Season	Club	League	GP	G	A	TP	PIM	GP	G	A	TP	PIM
99-2000	Cap-de-Madelaine	QAAA	38	3	5	8	28	....	....	....	....	....
2000-01	Montreal Rocket	QMJHL	61	3	8	11	31	....	....	....	....	....
2001-02	Montreal Rocket	QMJHL	31	4	3	7	21	....	....	....	....	....
	Quebec Remparts	QMJHL	31	0	4	4	44	9	0	0	0	6
2002-03	Quebec Remparts	QMJHL	20	3	2	5	29	....	....	....	....	....
	Victoriaville Tigres	QMJHL	22	0	5	5	12	3	0	0	0	6

BECKETT, Jason (Beh-keht, JAY-suhn) MIN.

Defense. Shoots right. 6'3", 218 lbs. Born, Lethbridge, Alta., July 23, 1980.
(Philadelphia's 2nd choice, 42nd overall, in 1998 Entry Draft).

			Regular Season					Playoffs				
Season	Club	League	GP	G	A	TP	PIM	GP	G	A	TP	PIM
1996-97	Lethbridge	AMHL	34	7	10	17	118	....	....	....	....	....
1997-98	Seattle	WHL	71	1	11	12	241	5	0	0	0	16
1998-99	Seattle	WHL	70	4	26	30	195	11	0	1	1	40
99-2000	Seattle	WHL	70	3	15	18	183	7	1	1	2	12
2000-01	Trenton Titans	ECHL	17	2	2	4	24	15	0	1	1	26
	Philadelphia	AHL	56	2	10	12	107	....	....	....	....	....
2001-02	Philadelphia	AHL	9	0	0	0	11	....	....	....	....	....
	Milwaukee	AHL	28	2	4	6	56	....	....	....	....	....
	Trenton Titans	ECHL	14	1	1	2	49	3	0	0	0	4
2002-03	Milwaukee	AHL	64	2	10	12	130	6	0	1	1	12

Traded to **Nashville** by **Philadelphia** with Petr Hubacek for Yves Sarault, January 11, 2002.
Signed as a free agent by **Minnesota**, August 6, 2003.

BELAK, Graham (BEE-lak, GRAY-ham) NYI

Defense. Shoots left. 6'5", 230 lbs. Born, Saskatoon, Sask., August 1, 1979.
(Colorado's 2nd choice, 53rd overall, in 1997 Entry Draft).

			Regular Season					Playoffs				
Season	Club	League	GP	G	A	TP	PIM	GP	G	A	TP	PIM
1993-94	North Battleford	SMBHL	50	3	14	17	110	5	0	3	3	30
1994-95	North Battleford	SMBHL	48	10	20	30	152	....	....	....	....	....
1995-96	North Battleford	SJHL	55	3	14	17	110	....	....	....	....	....
1996-97	Edmonton Ice	WHL	61	3	5	8	251	....	....	....	....	....
1997-98	Edmonton Ice	WHL	47	5	5	10	168	....	....	....	....	....
	Hershey Bears	AHL	1	0	0	0	15	....	....	....	....	....
1998-99	Kootenay Ice	WHL	45	3	1	4	201	7	0	0	0	38
99-2000	Kootenay Ice	WHL	49	4	9	13	197	21	2	3	5	*61
2000-01	U. of Alberta	CWUAA	1	0	0	0	0	....	....	....	....	....
2001-02	Bridgeport	AHL	7	0	0	0	5	....	....	....	....	....
	Trenton Titans	ECHL	60	6	6	12	305	....	....	....	....	....
	Trenton Titans	ECHL	60	6	6	12	305	....	....	....	....	....
2002-03	Trenton Titans	ECHL	2	0	0	0	15	....	....	....	....	....
	Bridgeport	AHL	30	0	1	1	60	2	0	0	0	0
	Cincinnati	ECHL	40	1	0	1	157	....	....	....	....	....

BELL, Brendan (BEHL, BREHN-duhn) TOR.

Defense. Shoots left. 6'1", 205 lbs. Born, Ottawa, Ont., March 31, 1983.
(Toronto's 3rd choice, 65th overall, in 2001 Entry Draft).

			Regular Season					Playoffs				
Season	Club	League	GP	G	A	TP	PIM	GP	G	A	TP	PIM
1998-99	Ottawa Jr. Sens	OCJHL	54	7	20	27	46	....	....	....	....	....
99-2000	Ottawa 67's	OHL	48	1	32	33	34	5	0	1	1	4
2000-01	Ottawa 67's	OHL	68	7	32	39	59	20	1	11	12	22
2001-02	Ottawa 67's	OHL	67	10	36	46	56	13	2	5	7	25
2002-03	Ottawa 67's	OHL	55	14	39	53	46	23	8	19	27	25

OCJHL All-Rookie Team (1999) • OCJHL Rookie of the Year (1999) • OHL First All-Star Team (2003) • Canadian Major Junior First All-Star Team (2003) • Canadian Major Junior Defenseman of the Year (2003)

BELLE, Shawn (BEHL, SHAWN) ST.L.

Defense. Shoots left. 6'1", 220 lbs. Born, Edmonton, Alta., January 3, 1985.
(St. Louis' 1st choice, 30th overall, in 2003 Entry Draft).

			Regular Season					Playoffs				
Season	Club	League	GP	G	A	TP	PIM	GP	G	A	TP	PIM
99-2000	K of C Squires	AMBHL	34	7	20	27	36	....	....	....	....	....
2000-01	K of C Squires	AMBHL	39	18	30	48	69	....	....	....	....	....
	Regina Pats	WHL	4	0	3	3	0	....	....	....	....	....
	Tri City Americans	WHL	2	0	1	1	0	....	....	....	....	....
2001-02	Tri City Americans	WHL	64	1	17	18	51	5	2	1	3	2
2002-03	Tri-City Americans	WHL	66	7	14	21	79	....	....	....	....	....

BELLISSIMO, Vince (behl-IHS-ih-moh, VIHNTS) **FLA.**

Center. Shoots right. 6', 199 lbs. Born, Toronto, Ont., December 14, 1982.
(Florida's 6th choice, 158th overall, in 2002 Entry Draft).

			Regular Season					Playoffs				
Season	Club	League	GP	G	A	TP	PIM	GP	G	A	TP	PIM
99-2000	St. Michael's B	OPJHL	47	30	29	59	31	....	....	....	....	....
2000-01	St. Michael's B	OPJHL	47	32	64	96	28	6	6	8	14	....
2001-02	Topeka	USHL	61	37	39	76	33	....	....	....	....	....
2002-03	Western Michigan	CCHA	37	19	17	36	18	....	....	....	....	....

USHL First All-Star Team (2002) • USHL Top Forward (2002) • CCHA All-Rookie Team (2003)

BEMBRIDGE, Garrett (bem-BRIHDJ, GAHR-reht) **CGY.**

Right wing. Shoots right. 6', 180 lbs. Born, Melfort, Sask., July 6, 1981.
(Calgary's 8th choice, 207th overall, in 2001 Entry Draft).

			Regular Season					Playoffs				
Season	Club	League	GP	G	A	TP	PIM	GP	G	A	TP	PIM
1997-98	Saskatoon Blazers	SMHL	44	29	45	74	74	....	....	....	....	....
	Saskatoon Blades	WHL	6	1	1	2	0	1	0	0	0	0
1998-99	Saskatoon Blades	WHL	68	23	27	50	30	....	....	....	....	....
99-2000	Saskatoon Blades	WHL	72	27	31	58	41	11	5	5	10	2
2000-01	Saskatoon Blades	WHL	72	38	40	78	40	....	....	....	....	....
2001-02	Saint John Flames	AHL	66	9	12	21	22	....	....	....	....	....
2002-03	Saint John Flames	AHL	64	9	10	19	33	....	....	....	....	....

• Re-entered NHL Entry Draft. Originally NY Rangers' 6th choice, 137th overall, in 1999 Entry Draft.

BERGENHEIM, Sean (BUHR-gehn-highm, SHAWN) **NYI**

Center. Shoots left. 5'11", 194 lbs. Born, Helsinki, Finland, February 8, 1984.
(NY Islanders' 1st choice, 22nd overall, in 2002 Entry Draft).

			Regular Season					Playoffs				
Season	Club	League	GP	G	A	TP	PIM	GP	G	A	TP	PIM
99-2000	Jokerit Helsinki Jr.	Finn-Jr.	30	22	11	33	34	3	1	0	1	0
	Jokerit Jr.-B	Finn-Jr.	17	10	8	18	14	3	1	0	1	2
	Jokerit Jr.-C	Finn-Jr.	5	7	4	11	49	5	9	2	11	2
2000-01	Jokerit Helsinki Jr.	Finn-Jr.	19	7	4	11	30	8	9	5	14	12
	Jokerit Jr.-B	Finn-Jr.	1	1	0	1	4	2	0	0	0	2
2001-02	Jokerit Helsinki	Finland	28	2	2	4	4	....	....	....	....	....
	Jokerit Helsinki Jr.	Finn-Jr.	23	11	19	30	36	6	6	2	8	20
	Kiekko Vantaa	Finland-2	4	0	0	0	52	....	....	....	....	....
	Jokerit Jr.-B	Finn-Jr.	....	....	....	....	....	5	6	2	8	18
2002-03	Jokerit Helsinki	Finland	38	3	3	6	4	2	0	0	0	0

BERGERON, Patrice (BAIR-zhuhr-uhn, pa-TREEZ) **BOS.**

Center. Shoots right. 6', 178 lbs. Born, Ancienne-Lorette, Que., July 24, 1985.
(Boston's 2nd choice, 45th overall, in 2003 Entry Draft).

			Regular Season					Playoffs				
Season	Club	League	GP	G	A	TP	PIM	GP	G	A	TP	PIM
2001-02	St. Francois	QAAA	38	25	37	62	18	....	....	....	....	....
	Acadie-Bathurst	QMJHL	4	0	1	1	0	....	....	....	....	....
2002-03	Acadie-Bathurst	QMJHL	70	23	50	73	62	11	6	9	15	6

QAAA Second All-Star Team (2002)

BERGFORS, Henrik (BAIRG-fohrz, HEHN-rihk) **T.B.**

Defense. Shoots right. 6' 4", 227 lbs. Born, Stockholm, Sweden, May 15, 1982.
(Tampa Bay's 14th choice, 289th overall, in 2001 Entry Draft).

			Regular Season					Playoffs				
Season	Club	League	GP	G	A	TP	PIM	GP	G	A	TP	PIM
99-2000	AIK Solna-18	Swede-Jr.	19	1	1	2	55	....	....	....	....	....
	AIK Solna Jr.	Swede-Jr.	12	0	1	1	6	....	....	....	....	....
2000-01	Sodertalje SK Jr.	Swede-Jr.	14	1	0	1	16	....	....	....	....	....
2001-02	Sodertalje SK Jr.	Swede-Jr.	40	4	4	8	62	2	1	0	1	2
2002-03	Sodertalje SK	Sweden	8	0	0	0	0	....	....	....	....	....
	HC Orebro	Swede-2	18	0	0	0	60	....	....	....	....	....
	Sodertalje SK Jr.	Swede-Jr.	7	0	2	2	29	....	....	....	....	....

BERGGREN, Johan (BUHR-gruhn, YOH-han) **DET.**

Defense. Shoots left. 6'3", 176 lbs. Born, Vastra Amtevik, Sweden, May 18, 1984.
(Detroit's 4th choice, 131st overall, in 2002 Entry Draft).

			Regular Season					Playoffs				
Season	Club	League	GP	G	A	TP	PIM	GP	G	A	TP	PIM
2001-02	HC Sunne	Swede-3	25	1	7	8	22	....	....	....	....	....
2002-03	HC Sunne Jr.	Swede-Jr.	12	4	0	4	20	....	....	....	....	....
	HC Sunne	Swede-3	36	1	10	11	40	....	....	....	....	....

BERNIER, Marc-Andre (BAIRN-yay, MAHRK-AWN-dray) **VAN.**

Right wing. Shoots right. 6'4", 198 lbs. Born, Laval, Que., February 5, 1985.
(Vancouver's 2nd choice, 60th overall, in 2003 Entry Draft).

			Regular Season					Playoffs				
Season	Club	League	GP	G	A	TP	PIM	GP	G	A	TP	PIM
99-2000	Laval Laurentides	QAAA	15	2	3	5	10	9	1	0	1	2
2000-01	Laval Laurentides	QAAA	STATISTICS NOT AVAILABLE									
2001-02	Halifax	QMJHL	49	0	6	6	20	2	0	0	0	0
2002-03	Halifax	QMJHL	67	29	29	58	43	21	9	8	17	8

BERNIER, Steve (BAIRN-yay, STEEV) **S.J.**

Right wing. Shoots right. 6'2", 230 lbs. Born, Quebec City, Que., March 31, 1985.
(San Jose's 2nd choice, 16th overall, in 2003 Entry Draft).

			Regular Season					Playoffs				
Season	Club	League	GP	G	A	TP	PIM	GP	G	A	TP	PIM
1998-99	Quebec AA Aces	QAHA	28	33	23	56	24	....	....	....	....	....
99-2000	Quebec AA Aces	QAHA	26	12	23	35	42	....	....	....	....	....
2000-01	Ste-Foy	QAAA	39	17	35	52	48	16	9	17	26	8
2001-02	Moncton Wildcats	QMJHL	66	31	28	59	51	....	....	....	....	....
2002-03	Moncton Wildcats	QMJHL	71	49	52	101	90	2	1	0	1	2

QMJHL All-Rookie Team (2002) • QMJHL Second All-Star Team (2003)

BERNIKOV, Ruslan (BAIR-nih-kahf, roos-LAHN) **DAL.**

Right wing. Shoots left. 6'3", 198 lbs. Born, Vidnoye, USSR, December 4, 1977.
(Dallas' 6th choice, 139th overall, in 2000 Entry Draft).

			Regular Season					Playoffs				
Season	Club	League	GP	G	A	TP	PIM	GP	G	A	TP	PIM
1996-97	DynamoMoscow2	Russia-3	32	11	4	15	20	....	....	....	....	....
	Dynamo Moscow	Russia	2	0	0	0	0	....	....	....	....	....
1997-98	Yekaterinburg 2	Russia-3	2	1	1	2	0	....	....	....	....	....
	Yekaterinburg	Russia	43	7	7	14	55	....	....	....	....	....
1998-99	Dynamo Moscow	Russia	6	0	1	1	2	....	....	....	....	....
	Krylja Sovetov	Russia	20	3	1	4	24	....	....	....	....	....
	CSKA Moscow	Russia	1	0	0	0	0	....	....	....	....	....
	Cherepovets	Russia	5	0	0	0	0	1	0	0	0	0
99-2000	Dynamo Moscow	Russia	6	2	1	3	2	....	....	....	....	....
	Amur Khabarovsk	Russia	14	3	6	9	10	5	3	1	4	2
2000-01	Amur Khabarovsk	Russia	33	1	4	5	40	....	....	....	....	....
2001-02	Amur Khabarovsk	Russia	38	7	10	17	20	....	....	....	....	....
2002-03	Krylja Sovetov	Russia	50	15	10	25	40	....	....	....	....	....

BERZINS, Armands (BUHR-zihnsh, AHR-muhnds) **MIN.**

Center. Shoots left. 6'3", 218 lbs. Born, Riga, Latvia, December 27, 1983.
(Minnesota's 5th choice, 155th overall, in 2002 Entry Draft).

			Regular Season					Playoffs				
Season	Club	League	GP	G	A	TP	PIM	GP	G	A	TP	PIM
99-2000	HC Essamika-B	EEHL	9	2	1	3	0	....	....	....	....	....
	Prizma Riga-18	Latvia-Jr.	STATISTICS NOT AVAILABLE									
2000-01	Prizma Riga-18	Latvia-Jr.	21	9	11	20	....	....	....	....	....	....
	HC Riga	EEHL	12	1	2	3	....	....	....	....	....	....
	HC Riga	Latvia	4	0	0	0	....	....	....	....	....	....
2001-02	Shawinigan	QMJHL	63	17	18	35	59	12	2	2	4	6
2002-03	Shawinigan	QMJHL	59	24	19	43	22	9	4	1	5	2

BETTS, Kaleb (BEHTZ, KAHL-uhb) **NSH.**

Center. Shoots left. 5'10", 185 lbs. Born, Maple Ridge, B.C., January 10, 1983.
(Nashville's 6th choice, 235th overall, in 2002 Entry Draft).

			Regular Season					Playoffs				
Season	Club	League	GP	G	A	TP	PIM	GP	G	A	TP	PIM
2000-01	Chilliwack Chiefs	BCHL	58	17	20	37	79	....	....	....	....	....
2001-02	Chilliwack Chiefs	BCHL	54	35	37	72	92	....	....	....	....	....
2002-03	Nebraska-Omaha	CCHA	DID NOT PLAY – ACADEMICALLY INELIGIBLE									

BEZINA, Goran (BEH-zee-nuh, GOH-ran) **PHX.**

Defense. Shoots left. 6'2", 215 lbs. Born, Split, Yugoslavia, March 21, 1980.
(Phoenix's 8th choice, 234th overall, in 1999 Entry Draft).

			Regular Season					Playoffs				
Season	Club	League	GP	G	A	TP	PIM	GP	G	A	TP	PIM
1998-99	Fribourg	EuroHL	6	0	0	0	0	....	....	....	....	....
	Fribourg Jr.	Swiss-Jr.	22	11	6	17	64	....	....	....	....	....
	Fribourg	Swiss	38	0	0	0	14	4	0	0	0	2
99-2000	Fribourg Jr.	Swiss-Jr.	2	0	1	1	16	2	1	1	2	8
	Fribourg	Swiss	44	3	6	9	10	4	0	0	0	6
	EHC Visp	Swiss-2	2	0	0	0	2	....	....	....	....	....
2000-01	Fribourg	Swiss	44	10	10	20	44	5	1	1	2	12
2001-02	Springfield Falcons	AHL	66	2	11	13	50	....	....	....	....	....
2002-03	Springfield Falcons	AHL	64	3	4	7	27	6	0	1	1	0

BEZRUKOV, Dmitri (behz-ROO-kahv, dih-MEE-tree) **T.B.**

Left wing. Shoots left. 6'3", 187 lbs. Born, Kazan, USSR, November 9, 1977.
(Tampa Bay's 11th choice, 259th overall, in 2001 Entry Draft).

			Regular Season					Playoffs				
Season	Club	League	GP	G	A	TP	PIM	GP	G	A	TP	PIM
1997-98	Nizhnekamsk 2	Russia-3	8	0	1	1	6	....	....	....	....	....
	Nizhnekamsk	Russia	14	5	3	8	4	....	....	....	....	....
1998-99	Nizhnekamsk 2	Russia-4	1	3	0	3	0	....	....	....	....	....
	Nizhnekamsk	Russia	39	4	6	10	18	3	1	0	1	2
99-2000	Nizhnekamsk 2	Russia-3	4	0	0	0	6	....	....	....	....	....
	Leninogorsk	Russia-2	8	2	1	3	8	....	....	....	....	....
	Nizhnekamsk	Russia	28	5	6	11	45	3	0	1	1	2
2000-01	Nizhnekamsk	Russia	35	7	10	17	54	4	0	2	2	2
2001-02	Nizhnekamsk	Russia	38	5	6	11	45	....	....	....	....	....
2002-03	Spartak Moscow	Russia	51	10	12	22	24	....	....	....	....	....

BIEKSA, Kevin (BEEKS-ah, KEH-vihn) **VAN.**

Defense. Shoots right. 6'1", 180 lbs. Born, Grimsby, Ont., June 16, 1981.
(Vancouver's 4th choice, 151st overall, in 2001 Entry Draft).

			Regular Season					Playoffs				
Season	Club	League	GP	G	A	TP	PIM	GP	G	A	TP	PIM
1997-98	Burlington	OPJHL	27	0	3	3	10	....	....	....	....	....
1998-99	Burlington	OPJHL	49	8	29	37	83	....	....	....	....	....
99-2000	Burlington	OPJHL	49	6	27	33	139	....	....	....	....	....
2000-01	Bowling Green	CCHA	35	4	9	13	90	....	....	....	....	....
2001-02	Bowling Green	CCHA	40	5	10	15	68	....	....	....	....	....
2002-03	Bowling Green	CCHA	34	8	17	25	92	....	....	....	....	....

BIRBRAER, Max (beer-BRIEGH-uhr, max) **FLA.**

Right wing. Shoots left. 6'2", 200 lbs. Born, Ust-Kamenogorsk, USSR, December 15, 1980.
(New Jersey's 6th choice, 67th overall, in 2000 Entry Draft).

			Regular Season					Playoffs				
Season	Club	League	GP	G	A	TP	PIM	GP	G	A	TP	PIM
1997-98	Shelburne Wolves	MTJHL	12	7	11	18	8	....	....	....	....	....
1998-99	Shelburne Wolves	OPJHL	35	20	22	42	25	....	....	....	....	....
99-2000	Newmarket	OPJHL	47	50	32	82	52	....	....	....	....	....
2000-01	Albany River Rats	AHL	50	7	6	13	24	....	....	....	....	....
2001-02	Albany River Rats	AHL	40	6	7	13	22	....	....	....	....	....
2002-03	Albany River Rats	AHL	57	6	6	12	42	....	....	....	....	....

Signed as a free agent by **Florida**, July 11, 2003.

BISHAI, Mike (BIHSH-igh, MIGHK) **EDM.**

Center. Shoots left. 5'11", 185 lbs. Born, Edmonton, Alta., May 30, 1979.

			Regular Season					Playoffs				
Season	**Club**	**League**	**GP**	**G**	**A**	**TP**	**PIM**	**GP**	**G**	**A**	**TP**	**PIM**
1996-97	South Surrey	BCHL	38	6	13	19	10	....	....	....	....	....
1997-98	South Surrey	BCHL	47	48	52	100	36	....	....	....	....	....
1998-99	West-Michigan	CCHA	26	0	3	3	20	....	....	....	....	....
99-2000	West-Michigan	CCHA	35	18	19	37	52	....	....	....	....	....
2000-01	West-Michigan	CCHA	37	23	*45	*68	37	....	....	....	....	....
2001-02	West-Michigan	CCHA	34	10	27	37	28	....	....	....	....	....
	Hamilton Bulldogs	AHL	3	0	0	0	0	....	....	....	....	....
2002-03	Hamilton Bulldogs	AHL	27	7	5	12	11	6	2	1	3	2
	Columbus	ECHL	25	12	17	29	24	....	....	....	....	....

CCHA Second All-Star Team (2001) • NCAA West Second All-American Team (2001)

Signed as a free agent by **Edmonton**, April 4, 2002.

BISSONNETTE, Paul (bih-sawn-EHT, PAWL) **PIT.**

Defense. Shoots left. 6'3", 211 lbs. Born, Welland, Ont., March 11, 1985.
(Pittsburgh's 5th choice, 121st overall, in 2003 Entry Draft).

			Regular Season					Playoffs				
Season	**Club**	**League**	**GP**	**G**	**A**	**TP**	**PIM**	**GP**	**G**	**A**	**TP**	**PIM**
2001-02	North Bay	OHL	57	3	3	6	21	5	0	0	0	2
2002-03	Saginaw Spirit	OHL	67	7	16	23	57	....	....	....	....	....

BITZ, Byron (BIHTZ, BRIGH-uhn) **BOS.**

Right wing. Shoots right. 6'3", 200 lbs. Born, Saskatoon, Sask., July 21, 1984.
(Boston's 4th choice, 107th overall, in 2003 Entry Draft).

			Regular Season					Playoffs				
Season	**Club**	**League**	**GP**	**G**	**A**	**TP**	**PIM**	**GP**	**G**	**A**	**TP**	**PIM**
2000/02	Saskatoon	SMHL	STATISTICS NOT AVAILABLE									
2002-03	Nanaimo Clippers	BCHL	58	27	46	73	59	....	....	....	....	....

BJORK, Johan (b'YAWRK, YOH-han) **OTT.**

Defense. Shoots left. 6'1", 176 lbs. Born, Malmo, Sweden, August 28, 1984.
(Ottawa's 5th choice, 125th overall, in 2002 Entry Draft).

			Regular Season					Playoffs				
Season	**Club**	**League**	**GP**	**G**	**A**	**TP**	**PIM**	**GP**	**G**	**A**	**TP**	**PIM**
99-2000	Malmo IF-18 Jr.	Swede-Jr.	8	0	1	1	8	....	....	....	....	....
2000-01	Malmo IF Jr.	Swede-Jr.	22	0	2	2	12	....	....	....	....	....
	Malmo IF-18 Jr.	Swede-Jr.	3	0	0	0	8	....	....	....	....	....
2001-02	Malmo IF Jr.	Swede-Jr.	36	1	4	5	72	3	0	0	0	2
2002-03	Malmo	Sweden	21	0	0	0	6	....	....	....	....	....
	Malmo IF Jr.	Swede-Jr.	22	7	12	19	36	6	0	2	2	6

BLACK, Greg (BLAK, GREHG) **ST.L.**

Center. Shoots right. 6', 203 lbs. Born, Surrey, B.C., May 13, 1982.

			Regular Season					Playoffs				
Season	**Club**	**League**	**GP**	**G**	**A**	**TP**	**PIM**	**GP**	**G**	**A**	**TP**	**PIM**
1998-99	South Surrey	BCHL	STATISTICS NOT AVAILABLE									
	Seattle	WHL	2	0	0	0	0	....	....	....	....	....
99-2000	Seattle	WHL	63	8	7	15	114	7	0	1	1	14
2000-01	Seattle	WHL	59	9	11	20	178	....	....	....	....	....
2001-02	Seattle	WHL	63	27	18	45	205	11	5	2	7	37
2002-03	Seattle	WHL	71	36	27	63	203	8	5	5	10	14

Signed as a free agent by **St. Louis**, March 20, 2003.

BLAHO, Stefan (BLA-hoh, STEH-fan) **NYI**

Right wing. Shoots left. 6'1", 198 lbs. Born, Trencin, Czech., June 22, 1985.
(NY Islanders' 5th choice, 120th overall, in 2003 Entry Draft).

			Regular Season					Playoffs				
Season	**Club**	**League**	**GP**	**G**	**A**	**TP**	**PIM**	**GP**	**G**	**A**	**TP**	**PIM**
2002-03	Dukla Trencin Jr.	Slovak-Jr.	17	6	5	11	50	16	4	7	11	30

BLANAR, Jan (BLAH-nuhr, YAN) **FLA.**

Defense. Shoots left. 6'3", 185 lbs. Born, Trencin, Czech., June 6, 1983.
(Florida's 11th choice, 263rd overall, in 2001 Entry Draft).

			Regular Season					Playoffs				
Season	**Club**	**League**	**GP**	**G**	**A**	**TP**	**PIM**	**GP**	**G**	**A**	**TP**	**PIM**
2000-01	Dukla Trencin Jr.	Slovak-Jr.	35	3	6	9	16	....	....	....	....	....
2001-02	Dukla Trencin Jr.	Slovak-Jr.	42	3	12	15	....	....	....	....	....	....
	Dukla Trencin	Slovakia	11	0	0	0	2	....	....	....	....	....
2002-03	Dukla Trencin Jr.	Slovak-Jr.	42	3	11	14	40	3	0	1	1	10
	Dukla Trencin	Slovakia	2	0	0	0	0	2	0	0	0	0

BLATAK, Miroslav (BLAT-ak, MEER-oh-slahv) **DET.**

Defense. Shoots left. 5'11", 172 lbs. Born, Gottwaldov, Czech., May 25, 1982.
(Detroit's 3rd choice, 129th overall, in 2001 Entry Draft).

			Regular Season					Playoffs				
Season	**Club**	**League**	**GP**	**G**	**A**	**TP**	**PIM**	**GP**	**G**	**A**	**TP**	**PIM**
99-2000	Vsetin-18	Czech-Jr.	30	0	0	0	12	....	....	....	....	....
	Vsetin Jr.	Czech-Jr.	12	0	2	2	10	....	....	....	....	....
2000-01	Vsetin-18	Czech-Jr.	33	7	8	15	56	....	....	....	....	....
	Vsetin Jr.	Czech-Jr.	12	2	4	6	54	7	0	6	6	6
	Zlin	Czech	8	0	2	2	0	6	0	0	0	0
2001-02	Dukla Jihlava Jr.	Czech-Jr.	3	0	0	0	0	....	....	....	....	....
	Zlin Jr.	Czech-Jr.	3	0	0	0	8	....	....	....	....	....
	HC Dukla Jihlava	Czech-2	1	0	0	0	0	2	0	0	0	0
	Zlin	Czech	39	4	7	11	18	11	1	2	3	8
2002-03	HC Hame Zlin	Czech	49	4	12	16	34	....	....	....	....	....

BLAZEK, Michal (BLA-zhehk, MEE-kuhl) **DAL.**

Defense. Shoots left. 6'2", 187 lbs. Born, Vsetin, Czech., April 2, 1982.
(Dallas' 6th choice, 167th overall, in 2001 Entry Draft).

			Regular Season					Playoffs				
Season	**Club**	**League**	**GP**	**G**	**A**	**TP**	**PIM**	**GP**	**G**	**A**	**TP**	**PIM**
99-2000	Vsetin Jr.	Czech-Jr.	49	0	3	3	67	....	....	....	....	....
2000-01	Vsetin Jr.	Czech-Jr.	52	9	18	27	116	....	....	....	....	....
2001-02	Vsetin Jr.	Czech-Jr.	40	6	12	18	160	11	0	3	3	22
2002-03	Vsetin Jr.	Czech-Jr.	36	10	10	20	108	8	0	3	3	6
	Vsetin	Czech	1	0	0	0	2	....	....	....	....	....

BLINDENBACHER, Severin (blihn-duhn-BAH-khur, SEH-vuhr-ihn) **PHX.**

Defense. Shoots right. 5'11", 189 lbs. Born, Bulach, Switz., March 15, 1983.
(Phoenix's 9th choice, 273rd overall, in 2001 Entry Draft).

			Regular Season					Playoffs				
Season	**Club**	**League**	**GP**	**G**	**A**	**TP**	**PIM**	**GP**	**G**	**A**	**TP**	**PIM**
1998-99	Kloten Flyers Jr.	Swiss-Jr.	5	0	2	2	4	....	....	....	....	....
99-2000	Kloten Flyers Jr.	Swiss-Jr.	30	8	10	18	18	4	1	1	2	8
2000-01	EHC Kloten	Swiss	27	0	2	2	17	9	0	0	0	10
2001-02	Kloten Flyers	Swiss	38	1	3	4	22	10	0	2	2	10
	Kloten Flyers	Swiss-Jr.	....	....	....	....	....	1	0	1	1	2
2002-03	Kloten Flyers	Swiss	43	4	19	23	52	5	1	0	1	4

BLOMDAHL, Patric (BLAWM-dahl, PAT-rihk) **WSH.**

Right wing. Shoots left. 6'1", 202 lbs. Born, Stockholm, Sweden, January 30, 1984.
(Washington's 13th choice, 272nd overall, in 2002 Entry Draft).

			Regular Season					Playoffs				
Season	**Club**	**League**	**GP**	**G**	**A**	**TP**	**PIM**	**GP**	**G**	**A**	**TP**	**PIM**
2000-01	AIK Solna-18	Swede-Jr.	9	5	1	6	35	....	....	....	....	....
2001-02	AIK Solna Jr.	Swede-Jr.	20	7	6	13	18	....	....	....	....	....
	AIK Solna-18	Swede-Jr.	3	0	0	0	2	....	....	....	....	....
2002-03	AIK Solna Jr.	Swede-Jr.	19	6	5	11	107	....	....	....	....	....
	AIK Solna	Swede-2	12	1	0	1	10	....	....	....	....	....
	AIK Solna	Swede-Q	9	0	1	1	4	7	1	0	1	4

BOBROV, Viktor (bawb-RAWV, VIHK-tohr) **CGY.**

Center. Shoots left. 6'1", 176 lbs. Born, Novocheboksarsk, USSR, January 1, 1984.
(Calgary's 7th choice, 146th overall, in 2002 Entry Draft).

			Regular Season					Playoffs				
Season	**Club**	**League**	**GP**	**G**	**A**	**TP**	**PIM**	**GP**	**G**	**A**	**TP**	**PIM**
2000-01	CSKA Moscow	Russia-Jr.	31	30	17	47	32	4	4	3	7	4
2001-02	HC CSKA 2	Russia-3	36	11	16	27	20	....	....	....	....	....
2002-03	Elemash Elektrosal	Russia-2	48	7	7	14	16	....	....	....	....	....

BOCHENSKI, Brandon (boh-CHEHN-skee, BRAHN-duhn) **OTT.**

Right wing. Shoots right. 6', 180 lbs. Born, Blaine, MN, April 4, 1982.
(Ottawa's 9th choice, 223rd overall, in 2001 Entry Draft).

			Regular Season					Playoffs				
Season	**Club**	**League**	**GP**	**G**	**A**	**TP**	**PIM**	**GP**	**G**	**A**	**TP**	**PIM**
99-2000	Blaine Bengals	Hi-School	28	32	30	62	....	....	....	....	....	....
2000-01	Lincoln Stars	USHL	55	*47	33	80	22	11	5	7	12	4
2001-02	North Dakota	WCHA	36	17	15	32	34	....	....	....	....	....
2002-03	North Dakota	WCHA	43	35	27	62	42	....	....	....	....	....

USHL First All-Star Team (2001) • USHL Rookie of the Year (2001) • WCHA All-Rookie Team (2002) • WCHA Rookie of the Year (2002) • WCHA Second All-Star Team (2003)

BOHAC, Jan (BOH-hach, YAHN) **OTT.**

Center. Shoots left. 6'4", 201 lbs. Born, Tabor, Czech., February 3, 1982.
(Ottawa's 4th choice, 87th overall, in 2000 Entry Draft).

			Regular Season					Playoffs				
Season	**Club**	**League**	**GP**	**G**	**A**	**TP**	**PIM**	**GP**	**G**	**A**	**TP**	**PIM**
1997-98	HC Slavia Praha Jr.	Czech-Jr.	39	8	12	20	12	....	....	....	....	....
1998-99	HC Slavia Praha Jr.	Czech-Jr.	35	6	6	12	10	....	....	....	....	....
	HC Slavia Praha	Czech	2	0	0	0	0	....	....	....	....	....
99-2000	HC Slavia Praha Jr.	Czech-Jr.	22	7	8	15	6	7	0	1	1	4
	HC Slavia Praha	Czech	25	1	2	3	4	....	....	....	....	....
2000-01	HC Slavia Praha	Czech	19	2	0	2	0	2	0	0	0	0
	HC Banik Most	Czech-2	5	0	2	2	0	....	....	....	....	....
2001-02	Trinec Jr.	Czech-Jr.	2	0	1	1	0	....	....	....	....	....
	HC Ocelari Trinec	Czech	16	0	1	1	4	....	....	....	....	....
	HC Banik Most	Czech-3	5	0	2	2	0	....	....	....	....	....
	Liberec	Czech-2	10	0	2	2	0	2	0	0	0	0
2002-03	Usti nad Labem	Czech-2	8	0	1	1	2	....	....	....	....	....

BOISVERT, Hugo (bwuh-VAIR, HEW-goh)

Center. Shoots left. 6', 200 lbs. Born, St-Eustache, Que., February 11, 1976.

			Regular Season					Playoffs				
Season	**Club**	**League**	**GP**	**G**	**A**	**TP**	**PIM**	**GP**	**G**	**A**	**TP**	**PIM**
1994-95	Cornwall Colts	OCJHL	27	13	19	32	26	....	....	....	....	....
1995-96	Cornwall Colts	OCJHL	54	40	90	130	102	15	15	20	35	44
1996-97	Ohio State	CCHA	38	11	27	38	44	....	....	....	....	....
1997-98	Ohio State	CCHA	42	23	*35	58	70	....	....	....	....	....
1998-99	Ohio State	CCHA	41	24	27	51	54	....	....	....	....	....
99-2000	Team Canada	Nat-Tm	39	10	14	24	12	....	....	....	....	....
2000-01	Orlando	IHL	68	6	12	18	41	16	4	5	9	23
2001-02	Grand Rapids	AHL	74	11	18	29	48	5	1	3	4	4
2002-03	Grand Rapids	AHL	78	18	13	31	68	15	5	1	6	10

CCHA First All-Star Team (1998, 1999) • NCAA West First All-American Team (1998) • NCAA West Second All-American Team (1999)

Signed as a free agent by **Atlanta**, June 25, 1999.

BOLDT, Tyler (BOHLT, TIGH-luhr) **ATL.**

Defense. Shoots left. 6'1", 200 lbs. Born, Thunder Bay, Ont., January 3, 1984.
(Atlanta's 9th choice, 236th overall, in 2002 Entry Draft).

			Regular Season					Playoffs				
Season	**Club**	**League**	**GP**	**G**	**A**	**TP**	**PIM**	**GP**	**G**	**A**	**TP**	**PIM**
99-2000	Wpg. Monarchs	MMHL	35	15	25	40	175	....	....	....	....	....
	Kamloops Blazers	WHL	6	0	0	0	2	....	....	....	....	....
2000-01	Kamloops Blazers	WHL	58	3	6	9	58	4	0	1	1	6
2001-02	Kamloops Blazers	WHL	62	5	14	19	76	4	1	0	1	0
2002-03	Kamloops Blazers	WHL	67	8	20	28	102	6	0	3	3	16

BOLDUC, Alexandre (bohl-DUHK, ahl-ehx-AHN-druh) **ST.L.**

Center. Shoots left. 6'1", 178 lbs. Born, Montreal, Que., June 26, 1985.
(St. Louis' 6th choice, 127th overall, in 2003 Entry Draft).

			Regular Season					Playoffs				
Season	**Club**	**League**	**GP**	**G**	**A**	**TP**	**PIM**	**GP**	**G**	**A**	**TP**	**PIM**
2001-02	Rouyn-Noranda	QMJHL	64	6	14	20	69	4	1	1	2	4
2002-03	Rouyn-Noranda	QMJHL	66	14	29	43	131	4	0	2	2	2

BOLIBRUCK, Kevin (BOH-lee-bruhk, KEH-vihn)

Defense. Shoots left. 6'1", 200 lbs. Born, Peterborough, Ont., February 8, 1977.
(Edmonton's 7th choice, 176th overall, in 1997 Entry Draft).

			Regular Season					Playoffs				
Season	Club	League	GP	G	A	TP	PIM	GP	G	A	TP	PIM
1993-94	Thorold	OJHL-B	38	6	18	24	78	....	....	....	....	....
1994-95	Peterborough	OHL	66	2	16	18	88	11	1	1	2	14
1995-96	Peterborough	OHL	57	6	21	27	105	24	3	6	9	46
1996-97	Peterborough	OHL	46	4	26	30	63	11	3	3	6	14
1997-98	Team Canada	Nat-Tm	49	2	5	7	65	....	....	....	....	....
1998-99	Hamilton Bulldogs	AHL	64	1	6	7	42	11	0	1	1	4
99-2000	Hamilton Bulldogs	AHL	54	1	4	5	67	10	0	1	1	4
2000-01	Rochester	AHL	76	2	5	7	52	3	0	0	0	0
2001-02	Houston Aeros	AHL	60	3	15	18	59	11	1	2	3	10
2002-03	Bridgeport	AHL	20	0	0	0	22	....	....	....	....	....
	Rochester	AHL	43	3	11	14	31	3	0	0	0	10

• Re-entered NHL Entry Draft. Originally Ottawa's 4th choice, 89th overall, in 1995 Entry Draft.

OHL First All-Star Team (1996)

Rights traded to **Chicago** by **Ottawa** with Denis Chasse and Ottawa's 6th round choice (later traded back to Ottawa – Ottawa selected Chris Neil) in 1998 Entry Draft for Mike Prokopec, March 18, 1997. Signed as a free agent by **Rochester** (AHL), September 20, 2000.

BOOGAARD, Derek (BOO-gard, DAIR-ihk) **MIN.**

Left wing. Shoots right. 6'7", 250 lbs. Born, Saskatoon, Sask., June 23, 1982.
(Minnesota's 6th choice, 202nd overall, in 2001 Entry Draft).

			Regular Season					Playoffs				
Season	Club	League	GP	G	A	TP	PIM	GP	G	A	TP	PIM
1998-99	Regina Caps	SJHL	35	2	3	5	166	....	....	....	....	....
99-2000	Regina Pats	WHL	5	0	0	0	17	....	....	....	....	....
	Prince George	WHL	33	0	0	0	149	....	....	....	....	....
2000-01	Prince George	WHL	61	1	8	9	245	6	1	0	1	31
2001-02	Prince George	WHL	2	0	0	0	16	....	....	....	....	....
	Medicine Hat	WHL	46	1	8	9	178	....	....	....	....	....
2002-03	Medicine Hat	WHL	27	1	2	3	65	....	....	....	....	....
	Louisiana	ECHL	33	1	2	3	240	2	0	0	0	0

• Released by **Medicine Hat** (WHL) and signed as a free agent by **Louisiana** (ECHL), December 13, 2002.

BOOTLAND, Darryl (BOOT-land, DAIR-ihl) **DET.**

Right wing. Shoots right. 6'1", 194 lbs. Born, Toronto, Ont., November 2, 1981.
(Colorado's 12th choice, 252nd overall, in 2000 Entry Draft).

			Regular Season					Playoffs				
Season	Club	League	GP	G	A	TP	PIM	GP	G	A	TP	PIM
1997-98	Orangeville	OJHL-B	44	22	26	48	177	....	....	....	....	....
1998-99	Barrie Colts	OHL	38	18	11	29	89	....	....	....	....	....
	St. Michael's	OHL	28	12	6	18	80	....	....	....	....	....
99-2000	St. Michael's	OHL	65	24	30	54	166	....	....	....	....	....
2000-01	St. Michael's	OHL	56	32	33	65	136	11	3	1	4	20
2001-02	St. Michael's	OHL	61	41	56	97	137	15	8	10	18	50
2002-03	Grand Rapids	AHL	16	1	4	5	41	15	3	2	5	46
	Toledo Storm	ECHL	54	17	19	36	322	....	....	....	....	....

Signed as a free agent by **Detroit**, August 20, 2003.

BORNHAMMAR, David (BOHRN-ham-uhr, DAY-vihd) **WSH.**

Defense. Shoots left. 6', 176 lbs. Born, Lidingo, Sweden, June 15, 1981.
(Washington's 8th choice, 192nd overall, in 1999 Entry Draft).

			Regular Season					Playoffs				
Season	Club	League	GP	G	A	TP	PIM	GP	G	A	TP	PIM
1997-98	AIK Solna Jr.	Swede-Jr.	13	0	1	1	10	....	....	....	....	....
1998-99	AIK Solna Jr.	Swede-Jr.	33	5	5	10	30	....	....	....	....	....
99-2000	Kelowna Rockets	WHL	62	3	24	27	36	2	0	0	0	0
2000-01	AIK Solna Jr.	Swede-Jr.	10	0	3	3	37	....	....	....	....	....
	AIK Solna	Sweden	37	4	2	6	57	4	0	1	1	0
2001-02	AIK Solna	Sweden	48	1	6	7	34	....	....	....	....	....
	AIK Solna	Swede-Q	8	0	1	1	4	....	....	....	....	....
2002-03	AIK Solna	Swede-2	50	8	9	17	32	4	1	0	1	8

• Name when drafted was David Johannson.

BOYCHUK, Johnny (BOY-chuhk, JAW-nee) **COL.**

Defense. Shoots right. 6'2", 205 lbs. Born, Edmonton, Alta., January 19, 1984.
(Colorado's 2nd choice, 61st overall, in 2002 Entry Draft).

			Regular Season					Playoffs				
Season	Club	League	GP	G	A	TP	PIM	GP	G	A	TP	PIM
1998-99	Edm. Cycle	AMBHL	36	8	20	28	59	....	....	....	....	....
99-2000	Edm. Cycle	AMHL	35	6	17	23	59	....	....	....	....	....
2000-01	Calgary Hitmen	WHL	66	4	8	12	61	12	1	1	2	17
2001-02	Calgary Hitmen	WHL	70	8	32	40	85	7	1	1	2	6
2002-03	Calgary Hitmen	WHL	40	8	18	26	58	....	....	....	....	....
	Moose Jaw	WHL	27	5	17	22	32	13	2	6	8	29

BOYES, Brad (BOIZ, BRAD) **S.J.**

Center. Shoots right. 6', 180 lbs. Born, Mississauga, Ont., April 17, 1982.
(Toronto's 1st choice, 24th overall, in 2000 Entry Draft).

			Regular Season					Playoffs				
Season	Club	League	GP	G	A	TP	PIM	GP	G	A	TP	PIM
1997-98	Mississauga Reps	MTHL	44	27	50	77	....	....	....	....	....	....
1998-99	Erie Otters	OHL	59	24	36	60	30	5	1	2	3	10
99-2000	Erie Otters	OHL	68	36	46	82	38	13	6	8	14	10
2000-01	Erie Otters	OHL	59	45	45	90	42	15	10	13	23	8
2001-02	Erie Otters	OHL	47	36	41	77	42	21	22	*19	41	27
2002-03	St. John's	AHL	65	23	28	51	45	....	....	....	....	....
	Cleveland Barons	AHL	15	7	6	13	21	....	....	....	....	....

Canadian Major Junior Scholastic Player of the Year (2000) • OHL Second All-Star Team (2001) • OHL First All-Star Team (2002) • AHL All-Rookie Team (2003)

Traded to **San Jose** by **Toronto** with Alyn McCauley and Toronto's 1st round choice (later traded to Boston – Boston selected Mark Stuart) in 2003 Entry Draft for Owen Nolan, March 5, 2003.

BOYLE, Brian (BOIL, BRIGH-uhn) **L.A.**

Center. Shoots left. 6'6", 222 lbs. Born, Dorchester, MA, December 18, 1984.
(Los Angeles' 2nd choice, 26th overall, in 2003 Entry Draft).

			Regular Season					Playoffs				
Season	Club	League	GP	G	A	TP	PIM	GP	G	A	TP	PIM
2000-01	St. Sebastian's	Hi-School	25	20	19	39	....	....	....	....	....	....
2001-02	St. Sebastian's	Hi-School	28	21	26	47	22	....	....	....	....	....
2002-03	St. Sebastian's	Hi-School	31	32	31	62	46	....	....	....	....	....

Prep School Player of the Year (2003)

Signed Letter of Intent to attend **Boston College** (H-East), November 20, 2002.

BRANDNER, Christoph (BRAND-nuhr, KRIH-stahf) **MIN.**

Left wing. Shoots left. 6'4", 224 lbs. Born, Bruck an der Mur, Austria, July 5, 1975.
(Minnesota's 8th choice, 237th overall, in 2002 Entry Draft).

			Regular Season					Playoffs				
Season	Club	League	GP	G	A	TP	PIM	GP	G	A	TP	PIM
99-2000	Klagenfurter AC	IEL	34	29	19	48	30	....	....	....	....	....
	Klagenfurter AC	Austria	16	8	3	11	20	....	....	....	....	....
2000-01	Klagenfurter AC	Austria	6	6	2	8	4	....	....	....	....	....
	Krefeld Pinguine	Germany	59	24	24	48	34	....	....	....	....	....
2001-02	Krefeld Pinguine	Germany	50	30	25	55	20	3	1	0	1	4
	Austria	Olympics	4	0	1	1	2	....	....	....	....	....
2002-03	Krefeld Pinguine	Germany	49	*28	17	45	26	14	9	9	18	8

BRAXENHOLM, Per (BRAX-ehn-hohlm, PAIR) **NYI**

Defense. Shoots left. 6'3", 215 lbs. Born, Karlskrona, Sweden, October 31, 1983.
(NY Islanders' 7th choice, 283rd overall, in 2002 Entry Draft).

			Regular Season					Playoffs				
Season	Club	League	GP	G	A	TP	PIM	GP	G	A	TP	PIM
2001-02	Morrum GoIS IK	Swede-2	25	0	2	2	2	....	....	....	....	....
	Kallinge/Ronneby	Swede-2	1	1	0	1	4	....	....	....	....	....
2002-03	Morrum GoIS IK	Swede-2	37	1	1	2	8	2	0	0	0	0

BRENK, Jake (BREHNK, JAYK) **EDM.**

Center. Shoots right. 6'2", 187 lbs. Born, Detroit Lakes, MN, April 16, 1982.
(Edmonton's 6th choice, 154th overall, in 2001 Entry Draft).

			Regular Season					Playoffs				
Season	Club	League	GP	G	A	TP	PIM	GP	G	A	TP	PIM
99-2000	Breck Mustangs	Hi-School	28	18	23	41	....	....	....	....	....	....
2000-01	Breck Mustangs	Hi-School	22	28	30	58	22	....	....	....	....	....
2001-02	Minnesota State	WCHA	21	3	3	6	6	....	....	....	....	....
2002-03	Minnesota State	WCHA	36	3	9	12	38	....	....	....	....	....

BRENT, Tim (BREHNT, TIHM) **ANA.**

Center. Shoots right. 6', 175 lbs. Born, Cambridge, Ont., March 10, 1984.
(Anaheim's 2nd choice, 37th overall, in 2002 Entry Draft).

			Regular Season					Playoffs				
Season	Club	League	GP	G	A	TP	PIM	GP	G	A	TP	PIM
99-2000	Cambridge	OJHL-B	40	19	16	35	42	....	....	....	....	....
2000-01	St. Michael's	OHL	64	9	19	28	31	18	2	8	10	6
2001-02	St. Michael's	OHL	61	19	40	59	52	14	7	12	19	20
2002-03	St. Michael's	OHL	60	24	42	66	74	19	7	17	24	14

BROOKBANK, Sheldon (BRUK-bank, SHEHL-duhn) **ANA.**

Defense. Shoots right. 6'2", 200 lbs. Born, Lanigan, Sask., October 3, 1980.

			Regular Season					Playoffs				
Season	Club	League	GP	G	A	TP	PIM	GP	G	A	TP	PIM
2000-01	Humboldt Broncos	SJHL	59	14	35	49	281	....	....	....	....	....
2001-02	Mississippi	ECHL	62	8	21	29	137	10	1	4	5	27
	Grand Rapids	AHL	6	0	1	1	24	....	....	....	....	....
2002-03	Grand Rapids	AHL	69	2	11	13	136	15	1	3	4	28

Signed as a free agent by **Anaheim**, July 21, 2003.

BROOKBANK, Wade (BRUK-bank, WAYD) **OTT.**

Defense. Shoots left. 6'4", 219 lbs. Born, Lanigan, Sask., September 29, 1977.

			Regular Season					Playoffs				
Season	Club	League	GP	G	A	TP	PIM	GP	G	A	TP	PIM
1997-98	Melville	SJHL	58	8	21	29	330	....	....	....	....	....
	Anchorage Aces	WCHL	7	0	0	0	46	4	0	0	0	20
1998-99	Anchorage Aces	WCHL	56	0	4	4	337	....	....	....	....	....
99-2000	Oklahoma City	CHL	68	3	9	12	354	7	1	1	2	29
2000-01	Orlando	IHL	29	0	1	1	122	4	0	0	0	6
	Oklahoma City	CHL	46	1	13	14	267	5	0	0	0	24
2001-02	Grand Rapids	AHL	73	1	6	7	337	3	0	1	1	14
2002-03	Binghamton	AHL	8	0	0	0	28	....	....	....	....	....

Signed as a free agent by **Orlando** (IHL), September 1, 2000. Signed as a free agent by **Ottawa**, July 27, 2001. • Missed majority of 2002-03 season recovering from knee injury suffered in game vs. Wilkes-Barre (AHL), November 2, 2002.

BROOKS, Alex (BROOKS, AL-ehx) **N.J.**

Defense. Shoots right. 6'1", 195 lbs. Born, Madison, WI, August 21, 1976.

			Regular Season					Playoffs				
Season	Club	League	GP	G	A	TP	PIM	GP	G	A	TP	PIM
1993-94	Madison Capitols	USHL	13	3	11	14	....	....	....	....	....	....
1994-95	Madison West	Hi-School	24	13	28	41	....	....	....	....	....	....
1995-96	Green Bay	USHL	46	3	22	25	....	....	....	....	....	....
1996-97	U. of Wisconsin	WCHA	DID NOT PLAY – INJURED									
1997-98	U. of Wisconsin	WCHA	40	1	4	5	72	....	....	....	....	....
1998-99	U. of Wisconsin	WCHA	37	0	3	3	73	....	....	....	....	....
99-2000	U. of Wisconsin	WCHA	41	4	10	14	78	....	....	....	....	....
2000-01	U. of Wisconsin	WCHA	41	3	16	19	76	....	....	....	....	....
2001-02	Jokerit Helsinki	Finland	53	1	3	4	109	12	0	0	0	11
2002-03	Albany River Rats	AHL	66	0	7	7	56	....	....	....	....	....

• Missed entire 1996-97 season recovering from back injury suffered during off-season training, August, 1996. • Signed as a free agent by **New Jersey**, July 12, 2002.

BROS, Michal (BROHSH, MEE-khahl) **MIN.**

Center. Shoots right. 6'1", 195 lbs. Born, Olomouc, Czech., January 25, 1976.
(San Jose's 6th choice, 130th overall, in 1995 Entry Draft).

			Regular Season					Playoffs				
Season	Club	League	GP	G	A	TP	PIM	GP	G	A	TP	PIM
1994-95	HC Olomouc Jr.	Czech-Jr.	34	29	32	61	....	....	....	....	....	....
1995-96	HC Olomouc	Czech	35	8	11	19	....	4	2	0	2	....
1996-97	HC Olomouc	Czech	50	13	14	27	28	....	....	....	....	....
1997-98	HC Petra Vsetin	Czech	47	14	18	32	28	10	3	1	4	2
	HC Petra Vsetin	EuroHL	9	3	0	3	2	....	....	....	....	....
1998-99	HC Slovnaft Vsetin	Czech	42	10	18	28	18	12	1	3	4	....
99-2000	HC Sparta Praha	Czech	49	6	30	36	49	9	1	3	4	4
2000-01	HC Sparta Praha	Czech	27	3	13	16	22	13	4	6	10	8
2001-02	HC Sparta Praha	Czech	48	19	29	48	71	13	7	*11	*18	8
2002-03	HC Sparta Praha	Czech	40	13	17	30	90	10	2	4	6	8

Selected by **Minnesota** from **San Jose** in Expansion Draft, June 23, 2000.

BROWN, Dustin (BROWN, DUHS-tihn) L.A.

Right wing. Shoots right. 6', 195 lbs. Born, Ithaca, NY, November 4, 1984.
(Los Angeles' 1st choice, 13th overall, in 2003 Entry Draft).

			Regular Season					Playoffs				
Season	Club	League	GP	G	A	TP	PIM	GP	G	A	TP	PIM
1998-99	Ithaca High	Hi-School	18	4	13	17	....	....	....	....	....	....
99-2000	Ithaca High	Hi-School	24	33	21	53	....	....	....	....	....	....
	Syracuse Stars	MYHA	STATISTICS NOT AVAILABLE									
2000-01	Guelph Storm	OHL	53	23	22	45	45	4	0	0	0	10
2001-02	Guelph Storm	OHL	63	41	32	73	56	9	8	5	13	14
2002-03	Guelph Storm	OHL	58	34	42	76	89	11	7	8	15	6

OHL All-Rookie Team (2001) • Canadian Major Junior Scholastic Player of the Year (2003)

BROWN, Marc (BROWN, MAHRK) ST.L.

Left wing. Shoots left. 6'1", 196 lbs. Born, White Rock, B.C., March 10, 1979.

			Regular Season					Playoffs				
Season	Club	League	GP	G	A	TP	PIM	GP	G	A	TP	PIM
1995-96	Abbotsford Pilots	PIJHL	35	20	15	35	15	....	....	....	....	....
1996-97	Spokane Chiefs	WHL	52	4	8	12	37	2	0	0	0	0
1997-98	Spokane Chiefs	WHL	41	10	15	25	35	....	....	....	....	....
	Prince Albert	WHL	23	6	8	14	21	....	....	....	....	....
1998-99	Prince Albert	WHL	72	35	45	80	47	14	12	6	18	6
99-2000	Worcester IceCats	AHL	72	13	11	24	24	17	3	1	4	0
2000-01	Worcester IceCats	AHL	34	9	10	19	27	10	0	1	1	6
2001-02	Worcester IceCats	AHL	74	30	25	55	42	3	2	2	4	0
2002-03	Worcester IceCats	AHL	58	13	15	28	24	....	....	....	....	....

Signed as a free agent by **St. Louis**, September 24, 1999. • Missed majority of 2000-01 season recovering from abdominal injury suffered in training camp, September 27, 2000.

BROWN, Paul (BROWN, PAWL) NSH.

Right wing. Shoots right. 6'2", 177 lbs. Born, Edmonton, Alta., July 21, 1984.
(Nashville's 6th choice, 89th overall, in 2003 Entry Draft).

			Regular Season					Playoffs				
Season	Club	League	GP	G	A	TP	PIM	GP	G	A	TP	PIM
99-2000	Prince George	BCAHA	65	84	120	204	260	....	....	....	....	....
	Regina Pats	WHL	3	0	0	0	0	....	....	....	....	....
2000-01	Regina Pats	WHL	33	3	1	4	83	....	....	....	....	....
	Kamloops Blazers	WHL	30	6	11	17	118	2	0	0	0	4
2001-02	Kamloops Blazers	WHL	37	7	12	19	130	1	0	0	0	0
2002-03	Kamloops Blazers	WHL	67	21	36	57	231	6	3	0	3	20

• Missed majority of 2001-02 season recovering from off-season ankle injury, August 20, 2001.

BRUNELLE, Mathieu (broo-nehl, MA-tyew) PHI.

Left wing. Shoots left. 5'11", 180 lbs. Born, Warwick, Que., April 6, 1983.
(Philadelphia's 7th choice, 201st overall, in 2002 Entry Draft).

			Regular Season					Playoffs				
Season	Club	League	GP	G	A	TP	PIM	GP	G	A	TP	PIM
99-2000	Magog	QAAA	42	26	31	57	64	19	8	7	15	20
2000-01	Victoriaville Tigers	QMJHL	65	7	11	18	39	13	1	1	2	0
2001-02	Victoriaville Tigres	QMJHL	72	43	64	107	105	14	7	6	13	35
2002-03	Victoriaville Tigres	QMJHL	39	21	29	50	75	....	....	....	....	....
	Hull Olympiques	QMJHL	31	17	19	36	42	20	*22	16	38	20

BUCKLEY, Brendan (BUHK-lee, BREHN-duhn) PIT.

Defense. Shoots right. 6'1", 205 lbs. Born, Needham, MA, February 26, 1977.
(Anaheim's 3rd choice, 117th overall, in 1996 Entry Draft).

			Regular Season					Playoffs				
Season	Club	League	GP	G	A	TP	PIM	GP	G	A	TP	PIM
1994-95	Boston Jr. Bruins	Exhib.	48	22	43	65	164	....	....	....	....	....
1995-96	Boston College	H-East	34	0	4	4	72	....	....	....	....	....
1996-97	Boston College	H-East	38	2	6	8	90	....	....	....	....	....
1997-98	Boston College	H-East	41	1	12	13	69	....	....	....	....	....
1998-99	Boston College	H-East	43	1	13	14	75	....	....	....	....	....
99-2000	Cincinnati	AHL	4	0	0	0	6	....	....	....	....	....
	Quad City	UHL	61	1	10	11	73	9	1	0	1	10
2000-01	Wilkes-Barre	AHL	63	2	8	10	62	21	0	2	2	33
2001-02	Wilkes-Barre	AHL	80	1	19	20	116	....	....	....	....	....
2002-03	Wilkes-Barre	AHL	80	2	6	8	99	6	0	0	0	2

Signed as a free agent by **Pittsburgh**, September 28, 2000.

BULATOV, Alexei (boo-LA-tahf, al-EHX-ay) NYR

Right wing. Shoots left. 6'1", 185 lbs. Born, Sverdlovsk, USSR, January 24, 1978.
(NY Rangers' 11th choice, 254th overall, in 1999 Entry Draft).

			Regular Season					Playoffs				
Season	Club	League	GP	G	A	TP	PIM	GP	G	A	TP	PIM
1996-97	Yekaterinburg	Russia	20	2	4	6	2	....	....	....	....	....
	Yekaterinburg	Russia-Q	22	6	6	12	10	....	....	....	....	....
1997-98	Yekaterinburg	Russia	15	5	3	8	10	....	....	....	....	....
	Yekaterinburg	Russia-Q	22	7	6	13	14	....	....	....	....	....
1998-99	Yekaterinburg	Russia-2	47	21	16	37	24	....	....	....	....	....
99-2000	Cherepovets	Russia	9	1	0	1	0	....	....	....	....	....
	Ufa	Russia	6	0	3	3	2	....	....	....	....	....
	CSK VVS Samara	Russia	6	0	0	0	2	....	....	....	....	....
2000-01	Magnitogorsk	Russia	32	2	3	5	4	....	....	....	....	....
2001-02	Novokuznetsk	Russia	25	2	6	8	6	....	....	....	....	....
2002-03	Moskovik Kurgan	Russia-2	25	8	8	16	12	....	....	....	....	....

BUMAGIN, Yevgeny (boo-MA-gihn, yehv-GEH-nee) DET.

Center. Shoots left. 6', 170 lbs. Born, Belgorod, USSR, April 7, 1982.
(Detroit's 11th choice, 260th overall, in 2000 Entry Draft).

			Regular Season					Playoffs				
Season	Club	League	GP	G	A	TP	PIM	GP	G	A	TP	PIM
1997-98	Lada Togliatti 2	Russia-3	7	0	0	0	2	....	....	....	....	....
1998-99	Lada Togliatti 2	Russia-4	40	7	8	15	22	....	....	....	....	....
99-2000	Lada Togliatti 2	Russia-3	36	23	8	31	....	....	....	....	....	....
2000-01	CSK VVS Samara	Russia-2	13	1	0	1	10	....	....	....	....	....
2001-02	Dizelist Penza	Russia-2	40	2	0	2	0	....	....	....	....	....
2002-03	Motor Barnaul	Russia-2	41	4	3	7	14	....	....	....	....	....

BURISH, Adam (BUHR-ish, A-duhm) CHI.

Right wing. Shoots right. 6'1", 175 lbs. Born, Madison, WI, January 6, 1983.
(Chicago's 9th choice, 282nd overall, in 2002 Entry Draft).

			Regular Season					Playoffs				
Season	Club	League	GP	G	A	TP	PIM	GP	G	A	TP	PIM
2000-01	Edgewood High	Hi-School	22	25	30	55	22	....	....	....	....	....
2001-02	Green Bay	USHL	61	24	33	57	122	1	0	0	0	0
2002-03	U. of Wisconsin	WCHA	19	0	6	6	32	....	....	....	....	....

BURKHALTER, Loic (buhrk-HAHL-tuhr, LOIK) PHX.

Center. Shoots left. 6', 202 lbs. Born, La Chaux-de-Fonds, Switz., February 11, 1980.
(Phoenix's 8th choice, 290th overall, in 2003 Entry Draft).

			Regular Season					Playoffs				
Season	Club	League	GP	G	A	TP	PIM	GP	G	A	TP	PIM
1996-97	La Chaux-de-Fonds	Swiss	24	1	0	1	0	....	....	....	....	....
1997-98	La Chaux-de-Fonds	Swiss	36	3	4	7	8	12	1	0	1	2
1998-99	La Chaux-de-Fonds	Swiss-2	38	19	29	48	28	12	4	8	12	10
99-2000	Rapperswil	Swiss	44	7	5	12	16	11	2	9	11	0
2000-01	Rapperswil	Swiss	31	7	5	12	20	4	1	1	2	0
2001-02	HC Ambri-Piotta	Switz.	44	9	12	21	28	6	2	2	4	6
2002-03	HC Ambri-Piotta	Switz.	44	12	22	34	42	4	1	0	1	2

BURNETT, Garrett (buhr-NEHT, GAIR-eht) ANA.

Left wing. Shoots left. 6'3", 230 lbs. Born, Coquitlam, B.C., September 23, 1975.

			Regular Season					Playoffs				
Season	Club	League	GP	G	A	TP	PIM	GP	G	A	TP	PIM
1993-94	Trail Smoke Eaters	RIJHL	26	2	1	3	248	....	....	....	....	....
1994-95	Sault Ste. Marie	OHL	14	0	1	1	78	....	....	....	....	....
	Kitchener Rangers	OHL	22	0	1	1	74	3	0	1	1	23
1995-96	Utica Blizzard	ColHL	15	0	1	1	78	....	....	....	....	....
	Oklahoma City	CHL	3	0	0	0	20	....	....	....	....	....
	Tulsa Oilers	CHL	6	1	0	1	94	....	....	....	....	....
	Nashville Knights	ECHL	3	0	0	0	22	....	....	....	....	....
	Jacksonville	ECHL	8	0	1	1	38	1	0	0	0	0
1996-97	Knoxville	ECHL	50	5	11	16	321	....	....	....	....	....
1997-98	Johnstown Chiefs	ECHL	34	1	1	2	331	....	....	....	....	....
	Philadelphia	AHL	14	1	2	3	129	....	....	....	....	....
1998-99	Kentucky	AHL	31	1	0	1	186	....	....	....	....	....
99-2000	Kentucky	AHL	58	3	3	6	*506	4	0	0	0	31
2000-01	Cleveland	IHL	54	2	4	6	250	....	....	....	....	....
2001-02	New Haven	UHL	4	1	0	1	40	....	....	....	....	....
	Cincinnati	AHL	32	1	0	1	175	....	....	....	....	....
2002-03	Hartford Wolf Pack	AHL	62	6	1	7	*346	1	0	0	0	2

Signed as a free agent by **San Jose**, July 2, 1998. • Misseed majority of 2001-02 season recovering from knee injury suffered in game vs. New Haven (AHL), January 15, 2002. Signed as a free agent by **Hartford** (AHL), August 22, 2002. Signed as a free agent by **Anaheim**, July 25, 2003.

BURNS, Brent (BUHRNZ, BREHNT) MIN.

Right wing. Shoots right. 6'4", 200 lbs. Born, Ajax, Ont., March 9, 1985.
(Minnesota's 1st choice, 20th overall, in 2003 Entry Draft).

			Regular Season					Playoffs				
Season	Club	League	GP	G	A	TP	PIM	GP	G	A	TP	PIM
2000-01	North York	MTHL	46	4	7	11	16	....	....	....	....	....
2001-02	Couchiching	OPJHL	68	15	25	40	14	....	....	....	....	....
2002-03	Brampton	OHL	68	15	25	40	14	11	5	6	11	6

BUT, Anton (BOOT, AN-tawn) T.B.

Left wing. Shoots left. 6'1", 190 lbs. Born, Kharkov, USSR, July 3, 1980.
(New Jersey's 7th choice, 119th overall, in 1998 Entry Draft).

			Regular Season					Playoffs				
Season	Club	League	GP	G	A	TP	PIM	GP	G	A	TP	PIM
1995-96	Yaroslavl 2	CIS-2	60	30	12	42	10	....	....	....	....	....
1996-97	Yaroslavl 2	Russia-3	70	30	20	50	20	....	....	....	....	....
1997-98	Yaroslavl 2	Russia-2	48	12	5	17	28	....	....	....	....	....
1998-99	Yaroslavl 2	Russia-3	22	12	8	20	59	....	....	....	....	....
	Torpedo Yaroslavl	Russia	5	0	0	0	0	....	....	....	....	....
99-2000	Yaroslavl 2	Russia-3	1	0	0	0	2	....	....	....	....	....
	Torpedo Yaroslavl	Russia	26	2	5	7	16	8	2	1	3	0
2000-01	Yaroslavl	Russia	42	14	6	20	14	11	1	3	4	8
2001-02	Yaroslavl	Russia	48	14	11	25	14	6	0	1	1	2
2002-03	Yaroslavl	Russia	44	16	13	29	16	9	1	2	3	6

Rights traded to **Tampa Bay** by **New Jersey** with Josef Boumedienne and Sascha Goc for Andrei Zyuzin, November 9, 2001.

BUTURLIN, Alexander (boo-tuhr-LIHN, AL-ehx-an-DEHR) MTL.

Right wing. Shoots left. 5'11", 182 lbs. Born, Moscow, USSR, September 3, 1981.
(Montreal's 1st choice, 39th overall, in 1999 Entry Draft).

			Regular Season					Playoffs				
Season	Club	League	GP	G	A	TP	PIM	GP	G	A	TP	PIM
1997-98	CSKA Moscow 2	Russia-3	50	12	15	27	46	....	....	....	....	....
	CSKA Moscow	Russia	2	0	0	0	0	....	....	....	....	....
1998-99	CSKA Moscow	Russia	16	1	0	1	6	3	1	0	1	2
99-2000	Sarnia Sting	OHL	57	20	27	47	46	7	4	2	6	12
2000-01	Sarnia Sting	OHL	57	28	37	65	27	4	3	1	4	0
2001-02	Ufa	Russia	32	3	3	6	42	....	....	....	....	....
2002-03	Lada Togliatti	Russia	49	6	14	20	71	10	3	0	3	4

BYRNE, Trevor (BUHR-ne, TREH-vohr) ST.L.

Defense. Shoots left. 6'3", 205 lbs. Born, Hingham, MA, May 7, 1980.
(St. Louis' 4th choice, 143rd overall, in 1999 Entry Draft).

			Regular Season					Playoffs				
Season	Club	League	GP	G	A	TP	PIM	GP	G	A	TP	PIM
1997-98	Deerfield Academy	Hi-School	25	5	14	19	16	....	....	....	....	....
1998-99	Deerfield Academy	Hi-School	25	9	19	28	22	....	....	....	....	....
99-2000	Dartmouth	ECAC	30	3	9	12	40	....	....	....	....	....
2000-01	Dartmouth	ECAC	34	5	21	26	52	....	....	....	....	....
2001-02	Dartmouth	ECAC	32	5	16	21	38	....	....	....	....	....
2002-03	Dartmouth	ECAC	34	8	16	24	28	....	....	....	....	....

ECAC Second All-Star Team (2001, 2002)

CALDWELL, Ryan (KAWLD-wehl, RIGH-uhn) NYI

Defense. Shoots left. 6'2", 174 lbs. Born, Deloraine, Man., June 15, 1981.
(NY Islanders' 7th choice, 202nd overall, in 2000 Entry Draft).

			Regular Season					Playoffs				
Season	Club	League	GP	G	A	TP	PIM	GP	G	A	TP	PIM
1998-99	Shat.-St. Mary's	Hi-School	29	24	55	79	22	....	....	....	....	....
99-2000	Thunder Bay Flyers	USHL	46	3	20	23	152	....	....	....	....	....
2000-01	U. of Denver	WCHA	36	3	20	23	76	....	....	....	....	....
2001-02	U. of Denver	WCHA	40	3	16	19	76	....	....	....	....	....
2002-03	U. of Denver	WCHA	38	5	14	19	58	....	....	....	....	....

WCHA All-Rookie Team (2001)

CALLAHAN, Joe (kal-AH-han, JOH) **PHX.**

Defense. Shoots right. 6'3", 219 lbs. Born, Brockton, MA, December 20, 1982.
(Phoenix's 4th choice, 70th overall, in 2002 Entry Draft).

			Regular Season					Playoffs				
Season	**Club**	**League**	**GP**	**G**	**A**	**TP**	**PIM**	**GP**	**G**	**A**	**TP**	**PIM**
2000-01	B.C. High Irish	Hi-School	STATISTICS NOT AVAILABLE									
2001-02	Yale University	ECAC	31	3	8	11	20	....	....	....	....	....
2002-03	Yale University	ECAC	32	2	11	13	38	....	....	....	....	....

CAMERON, Scott (KAM-erh-RAWN, SCAWT) **N.J.**

Center. Shoots left. 6', 195 lbs. Born, Sudbury, Ont., April 11, 1981.
(New Jersey's 6th choice, 185th overall, in 1999 Entry Draft).

			Regular Season					Playoffs				
Season	**Club**	**League**	**GP**	**G**	**A**	**TP**	**PIM**	**GP**	**G**	**A**	**TP**	**PIM**
1997-98	Port Colborne	OJHL-B	40	16	35	51	73	....	....	....	....	....
1998-99	Barrie Colts	OHL	66	10	32	42	14	12	2	2	4	2
99-2000	Barrie Colts	OHL	21	2	4	6	19	....	....	....	....	....
	North Bay	OHL	49	26	28	54	13	6	3	0	3	4
	Albany River Rats	AHL	3	1	0	1	0	1	0	0	0	0
2000-01	North Bay	OHL	68	37	43	80	45	4	0	1	1	2
2001-02	Albany River Rats	AHL	54	3	6	9	12	....	....	....	....	....
2002-03	Albany River Rats	AHL	80	9	19	28	17	....	....	....	....	....

OJHL-B Rookie of the Year (1998)

CAMPBELL, Ed (KAM-behl, EHD) **BOS.**

Defense. Shoots left. 6'2", 204 lbs. Born, Worcester, MA, November 26, 1974.
(NY Rangers' 9th choice, 190th overall, in 1993 Entry Draft).

			Regular Season					Playoffs				
Season	**Club**	**League**	**GP**	**G**	**A**	**TP**	**PIM**	**GP**	**G**	**A**	**TP**	**PIM**
1992-93	Omaha Lancers	USHL	42	9	19	28	160	....	....	....	....	....
1993-94	U. Mass-Lowell	H-East	40	8	16	24	114	....	....	....	....	....
1994-95	U. Mass-Lowell	H-East	34	6	24	30	105	....	....	....	....	....
1995-96	U. Mass-Lowell	H-East	39	6	33	39	*107	....	....	....	....	....
1996-97	Binghamton	AHL	74	5	17	22	108	4	0	0	0	2
1997-98	Hartford Wolf Pack	AHL	9	0	1	1	9	14	0	2	2	33
	Fort Wayne	IHL	50	10	5	15	147	....	....	....	....	....
1998-99	Hartford Wolf Pack	AHL	18	0	3	3	24	7	0	3	3	14
	Fort Wayne	IHL	46	1	16	17	137	....	....	....	....	....
99-2000	Orlando	IHL	81	2	7	9	217	3	0	0	0	6
2000-01	Worcester IceCats	AHL	78	5	27	32	207	10	1	0	1	10
2001-02	Worcester IceCats	AHL	70	3	15	18	172	3	0	0	0	5
2002-03	Grand Rapids	AHL	80	0	12	12	140	15	0	1	1	22

Signed as a free agent by **St. Louis**, July 1, 2001. Signed as a free agent by **Detroit**, August 5, 2002. Signed as a free agent by **Boston**, July 31, 2003.

CAMPBELL, Gregory (KAM-behl, GREH-goh-ree) **FLA.**

Left wing. Shoots left. 6', 191 lbs. Born, London, Ont., December 17, 1983.
(Florida's 4th choice, 67th overall, in 2002 Entry Draft).

			Regular Season					Playoffs				
Season	**Club**	**League**	**GP**	**G**	**A**	**TP**	**PIM**	**GP**	**G**	**A**	**TP**	**PIM**
1998-99	Aylmer Aces	OJHL-B	49	5	9	14	44	....	....	....	....	....
99-2000	St. Thomas Stars	OJHL-B	51	12	8	20	51	....	....	....	....	....
2000-01	Plymouth Whalers	OHL	65	2	12	14	40	10	0	0	0	7
2001-02	Plymouth Whalers	OHL	65	17	36	53	105	6	0	2	2	13
2002-03	Kitchener Rangers	OHL	55	23	33	56	116	21	15	4	19	34

Memorial Cup All-Star Team (2003) • Ed Chynoweth Trophy (Memorial Cup Tournament Leading Scorer) (2003)

CAMPBELL, Joe (KAM-behl, JOH) **CGY.**

Defense. Shoots left. 6'4", 172 lbs. Born, Duluth, MN, June 26, 1982.
(Calgary's 10th choice, 233rd overall, in 2001 Entry Draft).

			Regular Season					Playoffs				
Season	**Club**	**League**	**GP**	**G**	**A**	**TP**	**PIM**	**GP**	**G**	**A**	**TP**	**PIM**
2000-01	Des Moines	USHL	56	7	11	18	53	3	0	1	1	4
2001-02	U. of Wisconsin	WCHA	7	0	0	0	0	....	....	....	....	....
2002-03	U. of Wisconsin	WCHA	1	0	0	0	0	....	....	....	....	....
	Des Moines	USHL	34	3	15	18	60	....	....	....	....	....

• Left **U. of Wisconsin** (WCHA) and signed as a free agent with **Des Moines** (USHL), December 27, 2002.

CARCILLO, Daniel (KAR-sihl-oh, DAN-yuhl) **PIT.**

Left wing. Shoots left. 5'11", 183 lbs. Born, King City, Ont., January 28, 1985.
(Pittsburgh's 4th choice, 73rd overall, in 2003 Entry Draft).

			Regular Season					Playoffs				
Season	**Club**	**League**	**GP**	**G**	**A**	**TP**	**PIM**	**GP**	**G**	**A**	**TP**	**PIM**
2000-01	North York	GTHL	STATISTICS NOT AVAILABLE									
2001-02	Milton Merchants	OJHL-B	47	15	16	31	162	....	....	....	....	....
2002-03	Sarnia Sting	OHL	68	29	37	66	157	6	0	4	4	14

CARKNER, Matt (KARK-nehr, MAT) **S.J.**

Defense. Shoots right. 6'4", 230 lbs. Born, Winchester, Ont., November 3, 1980.
(Montreal's 2nd choice, 58th overall, in 1999 Entry Draft).

			Regular Season					Playoffs				
Season	**Club**	**League**	**GP**	**G**	**A**	**TP**	**PIM**	**GP**	**G**	**A**	**TP**	**PIM**
1996-97	Winchester Hawks	OJHL-B	29	1	18	19	....	....	....	....	....	....
1997-98	Peterborough	OHL	57	0	6	6	121	4	0	0	0	2
1998-99	Peterborough	OHL	60	2	16	18	173	5	0	0	0	20
99-2000	Peterborough	OHL	62	3	13	16	177	5	0	1	1	6
2000-01	Peterborough	OHL	53	8	8	16	128	7	0	3	3	25
2001-02	Cleveland Barons	AHL	74	0	3	3	335	....	....	....	....	....
2002-03	Cleveland Barons	AHL	39	1	4	5	104	....	....	....	....	....

Signed as a free agent by **San Jose**, June 6, 2001.

CARLE, Matthew (KARL, MA-thew) **S.J.**

Defense. Shoots left. 6', 182 lbs. Born, Anchorage, AK, September 25, 1984.
(San Jose's 4th choice, 47th overall, in 2003 Entry Draft).

			Regular Season					Playoffs				
Season	**Club**	**League**	**GP**	**G**	**A**	**TP**	**PIM**	**GP**	**G**	**A**	**TP**	**PIM**
99-2000	Alaska All-Stars	AASHA	42	14	28	42	....	....	....	....	....	....
2000-01	U.S. National U-17	USDP	68	1	5	6	31	....	....	....	....	....
2001-02	U.S. National U-18	USDP	64	4	15	19	51	....	....	....	....	....
2002-03	River City Lancers	USHL	59	12	30	42	98	11	2	2	4	20

USHL First All-Star Team ((2003) • USHL Defenseman of the Year (2003)

• Signed Letter of Intent to attend **U. of Denver** (WCHA), October 17, 2002.

CARON, Ed (kahr-OHN, EHD) **EDM.**

Center. Shoots left. 6'2", 228 lbs. Born, Nashua, NH, April 30, 1982.
(Edmonton's 3rd choice, 52nd overall, in 2001 Entry Draft).

			Regular Season					Playoffs				
Season	**Club**	**League**	**GP**	**G**	**A**	**TP**	**PIM**	**GP**	**G**	**A**	**TP**	**PIM**
1998-99	Phillips Exeter	Hi-School	31	39	30	69	28	....	....	....	....	....
99-2000	Phillips Exeter	Hi-School	26	22	26	48	24	....	....	....	....	....
2000-01	Phillips Exeter	Hi-School	17	30	20	50	42	....	....	....	....	....
2001-02	New Hampshire	H-East	34	6	7	13	51	....	....	....	....	....
2002-03	Yale University	ECAC	DID NOT PLAY – TRANSFERRED COLLEGES									

• Left **New Hampshire** (H-East) and signed Letter of Intent to attend **Yale** (ECAC), April 26, 2002. • Left **Yale** (ECAC) and returned to **New Hampshire** (H-East), January 16, 2003.

CARON, Francois (ka-RAW, fran-SWUH) **ANA.**

Defense. Shoots left. 6'3", 182 lbs. Born, Montreal, Que., March 15, 1984.
(Anaheim's 7th choice, 261st overall, in 2002 Entry Draft).

			Regular Season					Playoffs				
Season	**Club**	**League**	**GP**	**G**	**A**	**TP**	**PIM**	**GP**	**G**	**A**	**TP**	**PIM**
99-2000	Montreal Bourassa	QAAA	42	2	9	11	48	3	1	0	1	2
2000-01	Chicoutimi	QMJHL	24	1	3	4	6	....	....	....	....	....
	Moncton Wildcats	QMJHL	24	0	9	9	24	....	....	....	....	....
2001-02	Moncton Wildcats	QMJHL	68	3	17	20	99	....	....	....	....	....
2002-03	Moncton Wildcats	QMJHL	70	4	14	18	77	6	0	1	1	2

CARTELLI, Mario (car-TEHL-lee, MAHR-ee-oh) **ATL.**

Defense. Shoots right. 6'1", 196 lbs. Born, Karvina, Czech., November 16, 1979.
(Atlanta's 9th choice, 262nd overall, in 2001 Entry Draft).

			Regular Season					Playoffs				
Season	**Club**	**League**	**GP**	**G**	**A**	**TP**	**PIM**	**GP**	**G**	**A**	**TP**	**PIM**
1998-99	Trinec	Czech	34	1	1	2	14	8	2	1	3	4
99-2000	Trinec Jr.	Czech-Jr.	5	3	0	3	0	....	....	....	....	....
	HC Ocelari Trinec	Czech	42	7	4	11	14	4	0	0	0	0
2000-01	HC Ocelari Trinec	Czech	46	11	16	27	24	....	....	....	....	....
2001-02	HC Ocelari Trinec	Czech	20	0	1	1	12	....	....	....	....	....
	Kladno	Czech	24	3	8	11	14	....	....	....	....	....
	HC Prostejov	Czech-2	3	0	2	2	2	....	....	....	....	....
	Kladno	Czech-Q	5	0	1	1	16	....	....	....	....	....
2002-03	HC Ocelari Trinec	Czech	29	1	9	10	16	....	....	....	....	....
	Havirov	Czech	13	1	4	5	20	....	....	....	....	....

CARTER, Jeff (KAR-tuhr, JEHF) **PHI.**

Center. Shoots right. 6'3", 182 lbs. Born, London, Ont., January 1, 1985.
(Philadelphia's 1st choice, 11th overall, in 2003 Entry Draft).

			Regular Season					Playoffs				
Season	**Club**	**League**	**GP**	**G**	**A**	**TP**	**PIM**	**GP**	**G**	**A**	**TP**	**PIM**
2000-01	Strathroy Rockets	OJHL-B	49	27	20	47	10	....	....	....	....	....
2001-02	Sault Ste. Marie	OHL	63	18	17	35	12	4	0	0	0	2
2002-03	Sault Ste. Marie	OHL	61	35	36	71	55	4	0	2	2	2

CASS, Bill (KAS, BIHL) **ANA.**

Defense. Shoots left. 6', 208 lbs. Born, Hingham, MA, September 30, 1980.
(Anaheim's 5th choice, 153rd overall, in 2000 Entry Draft).

			Regular Season					Playoffs				
Season	**Club**	**League**	**GP**	**G**	**A**	**TP**	**PIM**	**GP**	**G**	**A**	**TP**	**PIM**
1997-98	U.S. National U-18	USDP	38	4	9	13	75	2	0	0	0	0
1998-99	U.S. National U-18	USDP	41	0	6	6	22	....	....	....	....	....
99-2000	Boston College	H-East	41	1	8	9	26	....	....	....	....	....
2000-01	Boston College	H-East	40	0	6	6	52	....	....	....	....	....
2001-02	Boston College	H-East	36	3	5	8	40	....	....	....	....	....
2002-03	Boston College	H-East	32	0	1	1	39	....	....	....	....	....
	Cincinnati	AHL	2	0	2	2	0	....	....	....	....	....

CAVANAGH, Tom (KAV-a-NAW, TAWM) **S.J.**

Left wing. Shoots left. 5'10", 178 lbs. Born, Warwick, RI, March 24, 1982.
(San Jose's 6th choice, 182nd overall, in 2001 Entry Draft).

			Regular Season					Playoffs				
Season	**Club**	**League**	**GP**	**G**	**A**	**TP**	**PIM**	**GP**	**G**	**A**	**TP**	**PIM**
1997-98	Toll Gate Titans	Hi-School	15	5	17	22	6	4	2	8	10	4
1998-99	Toll Gate Titans	Hi-School	15	9	20	29	26	5	5	4	9	6
99-2000	Toll Gate Titans	Hi-School	18	25	29	*54	28	5	0	12	12	9
2000-01	Phillips Exeter	Hi-School	31	*42	40	82	34	....	....	....	....	....
2001-02	Harvard Crimson	ECAC	34	8	17	25	4	....	....	....	....	....
2002-03	Harvard Crimson	ECAC	34	14	13	27	31	....	....	....	....	....

CAVANAUGH, Dan (KAV-a-naw, DAN) **MIN.**

Center. Shoots right. 6'1", 190 lbs. Born, Springfield, MA, March 3, 1980.
(Calgary's 2nd choice, 38th overall, in 1999 Entry Draft).

			Regular Season					Playoffs				
Season	**Club**	**League**	**GP**	**G**	**A**	**TP**	**PIM**	**GP**	**G**	**A**	**TP**	**PIM**
1995-96	New England	EJHL	43	8	7	15	....	....	....	....	....	....
1996-97	New England	EJHL	56	23	46	69	....	....	....	....	....	....
1997-98	New England	EJHL	38	31	*47	*78	58	13	8	12	30	....
1998-99	Boston University	H-East	36	6	8	14	60	....	....	....	....	....
99-2000	Boston University	H-East	40	9	25	34	62	....	....	....	....	....
2000-01	Boston University	H-East	35	7	21	28	43	....	....	....	....	....
2001-02	Houston Aeros	AHL	70	3	16	19	41	5	0	0	0	0
2002-03	Houston Aeros	AHL	77	13	13	26	126	23	2	2	4	20

EJHL Most Valuable Player (1998)

Rights traded to **Minnesota** by **Calgary** with Calgary's 8th round choice (Jake Riddle) in 2001 Entry Draft for Mike Vernon, June 23, 2000.

CAVOSIE, Marc (kuh-VOI-see, MAHRK) **MIN.**

Center. Shoots left. 6', 173 lbs. Born, Albany, NY, August 6, 1981.
(Minnesota's 3rd choice, 99th overall, in 2000 Entry Draft).

			Regular Season					Playoffs				
Season	**Club**	**League**	**GP**	**G**	**A**	**TP**	**PIM**	**GP**	**G**	**A**	**TP**	**PIM**
1995-96	Albany	Hi-School	22	8	27	31	....	....	....	....	....	....
1996-97	Albany	Hi-School	28	26	45	71	....	....	....	....	....	....
1997-98	Albany	Hi-School	28	38	33	71	....	....	....	....	....	....
1998-99	Albany	Hi-School	28	23	20	43	32	....	....	....	....	....
99-2000	RPI Engineers	ECAC	29	11	17	28	10	....	....	....	....	....
2000-01	RPI Engineers	ECAC	28	13	16	29	47	....	....	....	....	....
2001-02	RPI Engineers	ECAC	36	23	*27	*50	44	....	....	....	....	....
2002-03	Houston Aeros	AHL	54	5	14	19	24	19	3	5	8	12

ECAC First All-Star Team (2002) • ECAC Player of the Year (2002)

CEREDA, Luca (suh-REH-duh, LOO-ka) TOR.

Center. Shoots left. 6'2", 212 lbs. Born, Lugano, Switz., September 7, 1981.
(Toronto's 1st choice, 24th overall, in 1999 Entry Draft).

			Regular Season					Playoffs				
Season	Club	League	GP	G	A	TP	PIM	GP	G	A	TP	PIM
1996-97	HC Ambri-Piotta	Swiss	35	13	8	21	....	....	....	....	....	....
1997-98	HC Ambri-Piotta	Swiss	28	17	27	44	24	....	....	....	....	....
1998-99	Ambri Jr.	Swiss-Jr.	3	4	3	7	20	....	....	....	....	....
	HC Ambri-Piotta	Swiss	38	6	10	16	8	15	0	6	6	4
99-2000	HC Ambri-Piotta	Swiss	44	1	5	6	14	9	0	1	1	2
2000-01	Ottawa 67's	OHL	DID NOT PLAY									
2001-02	St. John's	AHL	71	5	8	13	23	11	2	1	3	10
2002-03	St. John's	AHL	68	7	18	25	26	....	....	....	....	....

• Missed entire 2000-01 season recovering from heart surgery, September, 2000.

CETKOVSKY, Jiri (tseht-KAWF-skee, YIH-ree) CGY.

Center. Shoots left. 6'4", 209 lbs. Born, Prostejov, Czech., November 4, 1983.
(Calgary's 5th choice, 141st overall, in 2002 Entry Draft).

			Regular Season					Playoffs				
Season	Club	League	GP	G	A	TP	PIM	GP	G	A	TP	PIM
99-2000	MHK Prostejov Jr.	Czech-Jr.	5	3	2	5	0	....	....	....	....	....
	HC Olomouc-18	Czech-Jr.	25	7	3	10	18	....	....	....	....	....
2000-01	MHK Prostejov Jr.	Czech-Jr.	28	7	7	14	75	....	....	....	....	....
2001-02	Zlin Jr.	Czech-Jr.	30	9	6	15	44	....	....	....	....	....
2002-03	Calgary Hitmen	WHL	57	5	2	7	126	5	0	0	0	15

CHABADA, Martin (KHA-ba-da, MAHR-tehn) NYI

Left wing. Shoots right. 6'1", 203 lbs. Born, Prague, Czech., June 14, 1977.
(NY Islanders' 6th choice, 252nd overall, in 2002 Entry Draft).

			Regular Season					Playoffs				
Season	Club	League	GP	G	A	TP	PIM	GP	G	A	TP	PIM
1996-97	HC Sparta Praha	EuroHL	1	0	0	0	0	4	0	0	0	2
	HC Sparta Praha	Czech	16	1	2	3	4	4	0	1	1	2
1997-98	HC Sparta Praha	EuroHL	4	0	1	1	4	....	....	....	....	....
	HC Sparta Praha	Czech	40	7	12	19	57	11	1	0	1	4
1998-99	HC Sparta Praha	EuroHL	6	1	1	2	10	2	2	1	3	6
	HC Sparta Praha	Czech	39	3	9	12	14	1	0	0	0	0
99-2000	HC Sparta Praha	Czech	35	7	12	19	12	9	2	2	4	4
2000-01	HC Sparta Praha	Czech	43	9	10	19	36	12	0	0	0	8
2001-02	HC Sparta Praha	Czech	51	19	21	40	113	13	4	7	11	4
2002-03	Bridgeport	AHL	66	17	13	30	50	9	3	4	7	4

CHARTIER, Christian (SHAR-tee-yay, KRIHS-t'yehn) TOR.

Defense. Shoots left. 6', 216 lbs. Born, Russell, Man., December 29, 1980.
(Edmonton's 8th choice, 199th overall, in 1999 Entry Draft).

			Regular Season					Playoffs				
Season	Club	League	GP	G	A	TP	PIM	GP	G	A	TP	PIM
1995-96	Yellowhead Chiefs	MMHL	36	8	23	31	68	....	....	....	....	....
1996-97	Saskatoon Blades	WHL	64	2	23	25	32	....	....	....	....	....
1997-98	Saskatoon Blades	WHL	68	8	33	41	43	6	0	3	3	12
1998-99	Saskatoon Blades	WHL	62	2	14	16	71	....	....	....	....	....
99-2000	Saskatoon Blades	WHL	11	2	2	4	4	....	....	....	....	....
	Prince George	WHL	57	16	36	52	60	13	4	9	13	12
2000-01	Prince George	WHL	63	12	56	68	99	6	1	4	5	6
2001-02	St. John's	AHL	65	5	10	15	18	11	0	4	4	4
2002-03	St. John's	AHL	67	4	22	26	48	....	....	....	....	....

WHL West Second All-Star Team (2000) • WHL West First All-Star Team (2001)

Signed as a free agent by **Toronto**, June 25, 2001.

CHERNOV, Artem (chair-NAHF, AR-tehm) DAL.

Center. Shoots left. 5'10", 176 lbs. Born, Novokuznetsk, USSR, April 28, 1982.
(Dallas' 7th choice, 162nd overall, in 2000 Entry Draft).

			Regular Season					Playoffs				
Season	Club	League	GP	G	A	TP	PIM	GP	G	A	TP	PIM
1997-98	Novokuznetsk 2	Russia-3	4	0	0	0	0	....	....	....	....	....
1998-99	Novokuznetsk 2	Russia-4	32	9	7	16	14	....	....	....	....	....
99-2000	Magnitogorsk	Russia	10	2	3	5	0	5	0	0	0	0
2000-01	Magnitogorsk	Russia	44	15	17	32	30	....	....	....	....	....
2001-02	Avangard Omsk	Russia	43	6	5	11	4	....	....	....	....	....
2002-03	Avangard Omsk	Russia	48	9	10	19	6	12	1	1	2	4

CHERNYKH, Dmitri (TCHAIR-nihk, dih-MEE-tree) NYI

Right wing. Shoots left. 6', 180 lbs. Born, Voskresensk, USSR, February 27, 1985.
(NY Islanders' 2nd choice, 48th overall, in 2003 Entry Draft).

			Regular Season					Playoffs				
Season	Club	League	GP	G	A	TP	PIM	GP	G	A	TP	PIM
2001-02	Voskresensk 2	Russia-3	28	9	6	15	32	....	....	....	....	....
	Voskresensk	Russia-2	7	0	0	0	2	....	....	....	....	....
2002-03	Voskresensk	Russia-2	29	5	4	9	29	....	....	....	....	....
	Voskresensk 2	Russia-3	1	0	0	0	18	....	....	....	....	....

CHRISTEEN, Mats (KRIHS-teen, MATS) NSH.

Defense. Shoots left. 6'1", 181 lbs. Born, Sodertalje, Sweden, February 13, 1982.
(Nashville's 11th choice, 236th overall, in 2000 Entry Draft).

			Regular Season					Playoffs				
Season	Club	League	GP	G	A	TP	PIM	GP	G	A	TP	PIM
99-2000	Sodertalje SK-18	Swede-Jr.	5	0	1	1	8	....	....	....	....	....
	Sodertalje SK Jr.	Swede-Jr.	30	1	0	1	30	4	1	0	1	6
2000-01	Sodertalje SK Jr.	Swede-Jr.	19	2	8	10	16	....	....	....	....	....
	Sodertalje SK	Swede-2	15	0	3	3	4	....	....	....	....	....
2001-02	Sodertalje SK Jr.	Swede-Jr.	19	3	7	10	47	2	0	0	0	4
	Tierps HK	Swede-2	15	3	1	4	14	....	....	....	....	....
	Sodertalje SK	Sweden	6	0	0	0	0	....	....	....	....	....
2002-03	Sodertalje SK Jr.	Swede-Jr.	13	3	3	6	62	....	....	....	....	....
	Sodertalje SK	Sweden	10	0	0	0	0	....	....	....	....	....
	HC Orebro 90	Swede-2	9	2	0	2	10	....	....	....	....	....

CHRISTENSEN, Erik (KRIHS-tehn-suhn, AIR-ihk) PIT.

Center. Shoots left. 6'1", 185 lbs. Born, Edmonton, Alta., December 17, 1983.
(Pittsburgh's 3rd choice, 69th overall, in 2002 Entry Draft).

			Regular Season					Playoffs				
Season	Club	League	GP	G	A	TP	PIM	GP	G	A	TP	PIM
1998-99	Leduc Oil Kings	AMBHL	36	34	42	76	70	....	....	....	....	....
99-2000	Kamloops Blazers	WHL	66	9	5	14	41	4	0	0	0	2
2000-01	Kamloops Blazers	WHL	72	21	23	44	36	4	1	1	2	0
2001-02	Kamloops Blazers	WHL	70	22	36	58	68	4	0	0	0	4
2002-03	Kamloops Blazers	WHL	67	*54	54	*108	60	6	1	7	8	14

WHL West First All-Star Team (2003)

CHVATAL, Marek (KHVA-tuhl, MAIR-ehk) N.J.

Defense. Shoots left. 6'1", 180 lbs. Born, Pardubice, Czech., January 27, 1984.
(New Jersey's 4th choice, 84th overall, in 2002 Entry Draft).

			Regular Season					Playoffs				
Season	Club	League	GP	G	A	TP	PIM	GP	G	A	TP	PIM
99-2000	Dukla Jihlava-18	Czech-Jr.	36	7	8	15	110	....	....	....	....	....
	Dukla Jihlava Jr.	Czech-Jr.	1	0	0	0	2	....	....	....	....	....
2000-01	Trinec-18	Czech-Jr.	9	3	4	7	10	....	....	....	....	....
	Trinec Jr.	Czech-Jr.	44	2	2	4	22	....	....	....	....	....
2001-02	Trinec Jr.	Czech-Jr.	40	10	13	23	91	....	....	....	....	....
	HC Ocelari Trinec	Czech	3	0	0	0	2	1	0	0	0	0
2002-03	Sarnia Sting	OHL	65	4	19	23	32	6	0	0	0	2

CIZEK, Martin (CHEE-zhehk, MAHR-tehn) BUF.

Defense. Shoots left. 6'1", 188 lbs. Born, Beroun, Czech., May 17, 1984.
(Buffalo's 10th choice, 271st overall, in 2002 Entry Draft).

			Regular Season					Playoffs				
Season	Club	League	GP	G	A	TP	PIM	GP	G	A	TP	PIM
99-2000	HC Slavia Praha Jr.	Czech-Jr.	46	1	11	12	24	....	....	....	....	....
2000-01	HC Slavia Praha Jr.	Czech-Jr.	53	14	10	24	26	....	....	....	....	....
2001-02	HC Slavia Praha Jr.	Czech-Jr.	42	2	6	8	30	....	....	....	....	....
2002-03	Plymouth Whalers	OHL	58	2	7	9	40	18	1	1	2	6

CLARKE, Noah (KLAHRK, NOH-uh) L.A.

Left wing. Shoots left. 5'9", 175 lbs. Born, LaVerne, CA, June 11, 1979.
(Los Angeles' 10th choice, 250th overall, in 1999 Entry Draft).

			Regular Season					Playoffs				
Season	Club	League	GP	G	A	TP	PIM	GP	G	A	TP	PIM
1996-97	Shat.-St. Mary's	Hi-School	30	33	44	77	....	....	....	....	....	....
1997-98	Des Moines	USHL	54	19	30	49	29	12	2	9	11	23
1998-99	Des Moines	USHL	52	31	32	63	47	13	8	2	10	16
99-2000	Colorado College	WCHA	39	17	20	37	30	....	....	....	....	....
2000-01	Colorado College	WCHA	41	12	20	32	22	....	....	....	....	....
2001-02	Colorado College	WCHA	42	13	24	37	32	....	....	....	....	....
2002-03	Colorado College	WCHA	42	21	*49	70	15	....	....	....	....	....
	Manchester	AHL	3	1	1	2	0	....	....	....	....	....

USHL All-Rookie Team (1998) • USHL First All-Star Team (1999) • Curt Hammer Award (Most Gentlemanly Player – USHL) (1999) • WCHA All-Rookie Team (2000) • WCHA Second All-Star Team (2003) • NCAA West First All-American Team (2003)

CLOUTHIER, Brett (KLOO-tyay, BREHT) N.J.

Left wing. Shoots left. 6'5", 225 lbs. Born, Ottawa, Ont., June 9, 1981.
(New Jersey's 3rd choice, 50th overall, in 1999 Entry Draft).

			Regular Season					Playoffs				
Season	Club	League	GP	G	A	TP	PIM	GP	G	A	TP	PIM
1997-98	Kanata Valley	OCJHL	50	12	10	22	135	....	....	....	....	....
1998-99	Kingston	OHL	64	8	14	22	227	5	1	1	2	4
99-2000	Kingston	OHL	65	13	26	39	*266	5	2	0	2	17
2000-01	Kingston	OHL	68	28	29	57	165	4	1	0	1	10
2001-02	Albany River Rats	AHL	62	4	0	4	109	....	....	....	....	....
2002-03	Albany River Rats	AHL	74	6	7	13	220	....	....	....	....	....

CLOUTIER, David (KLOO-tyay, DAY-vihd) S.J.

Defense. Shoots right. 6'1", 205 lbs. Born, Quebec City, Que., December 17, 1981.

			Regular Season					Playoffs				
Season	Club	League	GP	G	A	TP	PIM	GP	G	A	TP	PIM
1997-98	Levis	QAAA	42	5	17	22	....	4	1	0	1	0
1998-99	Sherbrooke	QMJHL	46	2	2	4	39	4	0	0	0	2
99-2000	Montreal Rocket	QMJHL	33	2	7	9	36	....	....	....	....	....
	Val-d'Or Foreurs	QMJHL	30	5	8	13	24	....	....	....	....	....
2000-01	Val-d'Or Foreurs	QMJHL	72	14	20	34	200	21	3	9	12	36
2001-02	Val-d'Or Foreurs	QMJHL	38	16	16	32	123	....	....	....	....	....
	Cape Breton	QMJHL	22	9	17	26	60	16	7	15	22	24
2002-03	Cleveland Barons	AHL	80	10	17	27	90	....	....	....	....	....

Signed as a free agent by **San Jose**, July 10, 2002.

CLOWE, Ryan (KLOH, RIGH-uhn) S.J.

Right wing. Shoots right. 6'2", 205 lbs. Born, St. John's, Nfld., September 30, 1982.
(San Jose's 5th choice, 175th overall, in 2001 Entry Draft).

			Regular Season					Playoffs				
Season	Club	League	GP	G	A	TP	PIM	GP	G	A	TP	PIM
99-2000	St. John's	NFAHA	STATISTICS NOT AVAILABLE									
2000-01	Rimouski Oceanic	QMJHL	32	15	10	25	43	11	8	1	9	12
2001-02	Rimouski Oceanic	QMJHL	53	28	45	73	120	7	1	6	7	2
2002-03	Rimouski Oceanic	QMJHL	17	8	19	27	44	....	....	....	....	....
	Montreal Rocket	QMJHL	43	18	30	48	60	7	3	7	10	6

COBURN, Braydon (KOH-buhrn, BRAY-duhn) ATL.

Defense. Shoots left. 6'5", 205 lbs. Born, Calgary, Alta., February 27, 1985.
(Atlanta's 1st choice, 8th overall, in 2003 Entry Draft).

			Regular Season					Playoffs				
Season	Club	League	GP	G	A	TP	PIM	GP	G	A	TP	PIM
2000-01	Notre Dame	SMHL	32	3	19	22	70	....	....	....	....	....
	Portland	WHL	2	0	1	1	0	14	0	4	4	2
2001-02	Portland	WHL	68	4	33	37	100	7	1	1	2	9
2002-03	Portland	WHL	53	3	16	19	147	7	0	1	1	8

WHL Rookie of the Year (2002)

COLE, Phil (KOHL, FIHL) N.J.

Defense. Shoots left. 6'4", 205 lbs. Born, Winnipeg, Man., September 6, 1982.
(New Jersey's 8th choice, 125th overall, in 2000 Entry Draft).

			Regular Season					Playoffs				
Season	Club	League	GP	G	A	TP	PIM	GP	G	A	TP	PIM
1997-98	Winnipeg Sharks	MMHL	45	0	18	18	68	5	0	4	4	2
1998-99	Lethbridge	WHL	45	2	1	3	64	4	0	0	0	0
99-2000	Lethbridge	WHL	51	1	6	7	112					
2000-01	Lethbridge	WHL	63	6	15	21	129	1	0	0	0	2
2001-02	Lethbridge	WHL	33	3	13	16	87					
	Vancouver Giants	WHL	6	0	1	1	18					
	Medicine Hat	WHL	15	1	5	6	49					
2002-03	Albany River Rats	AHL	4	0	0	0	6					
	Columbus	ECHL	51	4	5	9	135					

COLLINS, Brian (KAW-lihns, BRIGH-uhn) NYI

Center. Shoots left. 6'1", 190 lbs. Born, Worcester, MA, September 13, 1980.
(NY Islanders' 6th choice, 87th overall, in 1999 Entry Draft).

			Regular Season					Playoffs				
Season	Club	League	GP	G	A	TP	PIM	GP	G	A	TP	PIM
1998-99	St. John's Pioneers	Hi-School	28	38	35	73	20	....	....	....	....	....
99-2000	Boston University	Hi-East	42	13	11	24	61	....	....	....	....	....
2000-01	Boston University	H-East	37	14	16	30	16	....	....	....	....	....
2001-02	Boston University	H-East	38	12	8	20	22	....	....	....	....	....
2002-03	Boston University	H-East	42	11	14	25	16	....	....	....	....	....

COLLINS, Rob (KAW-lihns, RAWB) NYI

Center. Shoots right. 5'10", 174 lbs. Born, Kitchener, Ont., March 15, 1974.

			Regular Season					Playoffs				
Season	Club	League	GP	G	A	TP	PIM	GP	G	A	TP	PIM
1998-99	Ferris State	CCHA	36	3	9	12	14	....	....	....	....	....
99-2000	Ferris State	CCHA	38	11	20	31	39	....	....	....	....	....
2000-01	Ferris State	CCHA	35	15	17	32	23	....	....	....	....	....
2001-02	Ferris State	CCHA	36	15	33	48	30	....	....	....	....	....
	Grand Rapids	AHL	5	0	2	2	0	....	....	....	....	....
2002-03	Grand Rapids	AHL	73	11	20	31	16	15	3	8	11	10

CCHA First All-Star Team (2002) • NCAA West Second All-American Team (2002)

Signed as a free agent by **NY Islanders**, July, 2003.

COLLINS, Sean (KAW-lihns, SHAWN) COL.

Left wing. Shoots left. 5'9", 180 lbs. Born, Boston, MA, February 9, 1983.
(Colorado's 10th choice, 289th overall, in 2002 Entry Draft).

			Regular Season					Playoffs				
Season	Club	League	GP	G	A	TP	PIM	GP	G	A	TP	PIM
1997-98	Reading High	Hi-School	22	32	26	58	....	....	....	....	....	....
1998-99	Reading High	Hi-School	25	32	35	67	....	....	....	....	....	....
99-2000	Reading High	Hi-School	22	37	42	79	....	....	....	....	....	....
2000-01	Reading High	Hi-School	24	28	36	64	....	....	....	....	....	....
2001-02	New Hampshire	H-East	40	20	25	45	4	....	....	....	....	....
2002-03	New Hampshire	H-East	41	22	8	30	12	....	....	....	....	....

COLLITON, Jeremy (KAW-lih-tuhn, JAIR-eh-mee) NYI

Center. Shoots right. 6'2", 195 lbs. Born, Blackie, Alta., January 13, 1985.
(NY Islanders' 4th choice, 58th overall, in 2003 Entry Draft).

			Regular Season					Playoffs				
Season	Club	League	GP	G	A	TP	PIM	GP	G	A	TP	PIM
99-2000	Airdrie Express	AMHL	33	16	25	41	28	....	....	....	....	....
2000-01	Crows Nest Pass	AJHL	63	18	30	48	98	....	....	....	....	....
2001-02	Prince Albert	WHL	68	11	21	32	53	....	....	....	....	....
2002-03	Prince Albert	WHL	58	20	28	48	76	....	....	....	....	....

AJHL South Second All-Star Team (2001)

COLLYMORE, Shawn (KAW-lee-mohr, SHAWN) NYR

Right wing. Shoots right. 5'11", 180 lbs. Born, Ville de LaSalle, Que., May 2, 1983.
(NY Rangers' 5th choice, 139th overall, in 2001 Entry Draft).

			Regular Season					Playoffs				
Season	Club	League	GP	G	A	TP	PIM	GP	G	A	TP	PIM
1998-99	Lac St-Louis Lions	QAAA	41	12	20	32	36	....	....	....	....	....
99-2000	Quebec Remparts	QMJHL	64	8	16	24	22	11	0	2	2	0
2000-01	Quebec Remparts	QMJHL	71	24	43	67	32	4	0	3	3	0
2001-02	Quebec Remparts	QMJHL	52	23	34	57	37	9	2	4	6	0
2002-03	Quebec Remparts	QMJHL	35	15	16	31	11	....	....	....	....	....
	Val-d'Or Foreurs	QMJHL	34	18	16	34	34	9	2	3	5	0

CONBOY, Tim (KAWN-boy, TIHM) S.J.

Defense. Shoots right. 6'1", 205 lbs. Born, Farmington, MN, March 22, 1982.
(San Jose's 6th choice, 217th overall, in 2002 Entry Draft).

			Regular Season					Playoffs				
Season	Club	League	GP	G	A	TP	PIM	GP	G	A	TP	PIM
99-2000	Brainerd High	Hi-School	22	20	26	46	....	....	....	....	....	....
2000-01	Rochester	USHL	51	5	9	14	256	....	....	....	....	....
2001-02	Rochester	USHL	14	1	6	7	65	....	....	....	....	....
	Topeka	USHL	29	4	15	19	128	....	....	....	....	....
2002-03	St. Cloud State	WCHA	31	3	12	15	48	....	....	....	....	....

CONCANNON, Mark (KAHN-kan-nuhn, MAHRK) S.J.

Left wing. Shoots left. 6', 200 lbs. Born, Boston, MA, June 12, 1980.
(San Jose's 2nd choice, 82nd overall, in 1999 Entry Draft).

			Regular Season					Playoffs				
Season	Club	League	GP	G	A	TP	PIM	GP	G	A	TP	PIM
1997-98	Hull High	Hi-School	20	38	35	73	....	....	....	....	....	....
1998-99	Winchendon High	Hi-School	26	23	38	61	11	....	....	....	....	....
99-2000	U. Mass-Lowell	H-East	23	4	3	7	8	....	....	....	....	....
2000-01	U. Mass-Lowell	H-East	19	2	7	9	6	....	....	....	....	....
2001-02	U. Mass-Lowell	H-East	38	8	13	21	14	....	....	....	....	....
2002-03	U. Mass-Lowell	H-East	36	10	11	21	28	....	....	....	....	....
	Cleveland Barons	AHL	3	0	0	0	0	....	....	....	....	....

CONNE, Flavien (KAW-neh, FLA-vee-ehn) L.A.

Center. Shoots left. 5'9", 176 lbs. Born, Geneva, Switz., April 1, 1980.
(Los Angeles' 10th choice, 250th overall, in 2000 Entry Draft).

			Regular Season					Playoffs				
Season	Club	League	GP	G	A	TP	PIM	GP	G	A	TP	PIM
1995-96	Geneva Jr.	Swiss-Jr.	22	39	27	56	32	....	....	....	....	....
1996-97	Geneva	Swiss-2	30	9	8	17	8	5	1	1	2	4
1997-98	Geneva Jr.	Swiss-Jr.	37	15	12	27	57	3	0	2	2	2
	Geneva	Swiss-2	9	11	6	17	12	....	....	....	....	....
	HC Ambri-Piotta	Swiss	1	0	0	0	0	....	....	....	....	....
1998-99	Fribourg Jr.	Swiss-Jr.	1	1	1	2	2	....	....	....	....	....
	Fribourg	Swiss	37	14	14	28	59	4	4	1	5	6
	Fribourg	EuroHL	3	0	0	0	0	....	....	....	....	....
99-2000	Fribourg	Swiss	44	19	22	41	38	4	0	1	1	0
2000-01	HC Lugano	Swiss	42	9	14	23	8	15	2	6	8	37
2001-02	HC Lugano	Swiss	44	12	13	25	20	5	1	1	2	0
	Switzerland	Olympics	1	0	0	0	0	....	....	....	....	....
2002-03	HC Lugano	Swiss	42	15	23	38	32	16	4	4	8	10

COOK, Tim (KUK, TIHM) OTT.

Defense. Shoots right. 6'4", 190 lbs. Born, Montclair, NJ, March 13, 1984.
(Ottawa's 5th choice, 142nd overall, in 2003 Entry Draft).

			Regular Season					Playoffs				
Season	Club	League	GP	G	A	TP	PIM	GP	G	A	TP	PIM
2000-01	Hotchkiss High	Hi-School	22	2	10	12	22	....	....	....	....	....
2001-02	Omaha Lancers	USHL	42	2	4	6	39	5	0	1	1	2
2002-03	River City Lancers	USHL	59	3	12	15	62	10	0	2	2	18

• Signed Letter of Intent to attend **U. of Michigan** (CCHA), November 20, 2002.

CORAZZINI, Carl (koh-ra-ZEE-nee, KAHRL) BOS.

Center. Shoots right. 5'10", 182 lbs. Born, Framingham, MA, April 21, 1979.

			Regular Season					Playoffs				
Season	Club	League	GP	G	A	TP	PIM	GP	G	A	TP	PIM
1996-97	St. Sebastian's	Hi-School	25	29	31	60	....	....	....	....	....	....
1997-98	Boston University	H-East	36	9	6	15	4	....	....	....	....	....
1998-99	Boston University	H-East	37	15	9	24	12	....	....	....	....	....
99-2000	Boston University	H-East	42	22	20	42	44	....	....	....	....	....
2000-01	Boston University	H-East	35	16	20	36	48	....	....	....	....	....
2001-02	Providence Bruins	AHL	61	7	8	15	10	....	....	....	....	....
2002-03	Providence Bruins	AHL	33	7	6	13	4	4	0	0	0	0
	Atlantic City	ECHL	27	13	8	21	14	....	....	....	....	....

Hockey East All-Rookie Team (1998) • Hockey East First All-Star Team (2001) • NCAA East Second All-American Team (2001)

Signed as a free agent by **Boston**, August 8, 2001.

COX, Justin (KAWKS, JUH-stihn) DAL.

Right wing. Shoots right. 6', 173 lbs. Born, Merritt, B.C., March 13, 1981.
(Dallas' 6th choice, 184th overall, in 1999 Entry Draft).

			Regular Season					Playoffs				
Season	Club	League	GP	G	A	TP	PIM	GP	G	A	TP	PIM
1996-97	Spruce Grove	AMHL	78	57	92	149	86	....	....	....	....	....
1997-98	Prince George	WHL	40	1	4	5	15	2	0	0	0	0
1998-99	Prince George	WHL	72	9	13	22	51	7	1	0	1	13
99-2000	Prince George	WHL	71	33	38	71	74	13	2	4	6	16
2000-01	Prince George	WHL	71	30	38	68	91	6	3	4	7	20
2001-02	Utah Grizzlies	AHL	74	10	7	17	53	5	0	1	1	0
	Fort Worth	CHL	2	2	0	2	0	....	....	....	....	....
2002-03	Utah Grizzlies	AHL	53	3	12	15	22	2	0	0	0	2

CRABB, Joey (KRAB, JOE-ee) NYR

Right wing. Shoots right. 6'1", 179 lbs. Born, Anchorage, AK, April 3, 1983.
(NY Rangers' 7th choice, 226th overall, in 2002 Entry Draft).

			Regular Season					Playoffs				
Season	Club	League	GP	G	A	TP	PIM	GP	G	A	TP	PIM
1998-99	Diamond Lynx	Hi-School		Statistics not available								
99-2000	U.S. National U-17	USDP	55	13	10	23	69	....	....	....	....	....
2000-01	U.S. National U-18	USDP	60	12	13	25	40	....	....	....	....	....
2001-02	Green Bay	USHL	61	15	27	42	94	7	4	8	12	21
2002-03	Colorado College	WCHA	35	4	4	8	40	....	....	....	....	....

CRAIG, Ryan (KRAIG, RIGH-uhn) T.B.

Center. Shoots left. 6'1", 208 lbs. Born, Abbotsford, B.C., January 6, 1982.
(Tampa Bay's 10th choice, 255th overall, in 2002 Entry Draft).

			Regular Season					Playoffs				
Season	Club	League	GP	G	A	TP	PIM	GP	G	A	TP	PIM
1997-98	Abbotsford	BCAHA	80	118	120	238	110	....	....	....	....	....
	Brandon	WHL	1	0	0	0	0	....	....	....	....	....
1998-99	Brandon	WHL	54	11	12	23	46	5	0	0	0	4
99-2000	Brandon	WHL	65	17	19	36	40	....	....	....	....	....
2000-01	Brandon	WHL	70	38	33	71	49	6	3	0	3	7
2001-02	Brandon	WHL	52	29	35	64	52	19	11	10	21	13
2002-03	Brandon	WHL	60	42	32	74	69	17	5	8	13	29

WHL East First All-Star Team (2003) • Canadian Major Junior Humanitarian Player of the Year (2003)

CRAMPTON, Steve (KRAMP-tuhn, STEE-vehn) PIT.

Right wing. Shoots right. 6'3", 209 lbs. Born, Winnipeg, Man., April 12, 1982.
(Pittsburgh's 8th choice, 248th overall, in 2000 Entry Draft).

			Regular Season					Playoffs				
Season	Club	League	GP	G	A	TP	PIM	GP	G	A	TP	PIM
1997-98	Winnipeg Sharks	MMHL	29	33	38	71	76	....	....	....	....	....
1998-99	Moose Jaw	WHL	52	7	5	12	31	9	1	1	2	4
99-2000	Moose Jaw	WHL	69	22	20	42	91	4	0	3	3	9
2000-01	Moose Jaw	WHL	72	26	33	59	153	4	1	2	3	6
2001-02	Moose Jaw	WHL	37	19	24	43	71	12	4	10	14	20
2002-03	Wheeling Nailers	ECHL	69	13	26	39	79	....	....	....	....	....

CROMBEEN, Brandon (KRAWM-been, BRAN-duhn) DAL.

Right wing. Shoots right. 6'2", 200 lbs. Born, Denver, CO, July 10, 1985.
(Dallas' 3rd choice, 54th overall, in 2003 Entry Draft).

			Regular Season					Playoffs				
Season	Club	League	GP	G	A	TP	PIM	GP	G	A	TP	PIM
2000-01	Newmarket	OPJHL	35	14	14	28	63	....	....	....	....	....
2001-02	Barrie Colts	OHL	60	12	13	25	118	20	1	1	2	31
2002-03	Barrie Colts	OHL	63	22	24	46	133	6	1	0	1	8

CUDDIHY, James (KUH-dih-hee, JAYMZ) DET.

Center. Shoots left. 6'3", 194 lbs. Born, Ottawa, Ont., April 22, 1984.
(Detroit's 6th choice, 197th overall, in 2002 Entry Draft).

			Regular Season					Playoffs				
Season	Club	League	GP	G	A	TP	PIM	GP	G	A	TP	PIM
99-2000	Gatineau	QAAA	41	14	13	27	24	....	....	....	....	....
2000-01	Shawinigan	QMJHL	61	5	11	16	46	10	0	0	0	0
2001-02	Shawinigan	QMJHL	56	9	18	27	69	10	0	1	1	8
2002-03	Shawinigan	QMJHL	66	14	40	54	96	9	1	13	14	10

CULL, Trent (KUHL, TREHNT)

Defense. Shoots left. 6'2", 215 lbs. Born, Brampton, Ont., September 27, 1973.

			Regular Season					Playoffs				
Season	Club	League	GP	G	A	TP	PIM	GP	G	A	TP	PIM
1988-89	Georgetown	OJHL-B	36	1	5	6	51	....	....	....	....	....
1989-90	Owen Sound	OHL	57	0	5	5	53	12	0	2	2	11
1990-91	Owen Sound	OHL	24	1	2	3	19	....	....	....	....	....
	Windsor Spitfires	OHL	33	1	6	7	34	11	0	0	0	8
1991-92	Windsor Spitfires	OHL	32	0	6	6	66	....	....	....	....	....
	Kingston	OHL	18	0	0	0	31	....	....	....	....	....
1992-93	Kingston	OHL	60	11	28	39	144	16	2	8	10	37
1993-94	Kingston	OHL	50	2	30	32	147	6	0	1	1	6
1994-95	St. John's	AHL	43	0	1	1	53	....	....	....	....	....
	Brantford Smoke	ColHL	4	0	0	0	14	....	....	....	....	....
1995-96	St. John's	AHL	46	2	1	3	118	4	0	0	0	6
1996-97	St. John's	AHL	75	4	5	9	219	8	0	1	1	18
1997-98	Houston Aeros	IHL	72	4	8	12	201	4	0	0	0	4
1998-99	Houston Aeros	IHL	72	2	14	16	232	19	0	2	2	34
99-2000	Springfield Falcons	AHL	28	0	2	2	74	....	....	....	....	....
	Houston Aeros	IHL	35	2	7	9	133	5	0	0	0	24
2000-01	Wilkes-Barre	AHL	71	11	15	26	166	21	3	2	5	28
2001-02	Houston Aeros	AHL	74	1	11	12	158	12	0	2	2	8
2002-03	Syracuse Crunch	AHL	40	0	8	8	115	....	....	....	....	....

Signed as a free agent by **Toronto**, June 4, 1994. Signed as a free agent by **Phoenix**, August 26, 1999. Signed as a free agent by **Pittsburgh**, August 28, 2000. Signed as a free agent by **Minnesota**, July 13, 2001.

CULLEN, Joe (KUH-lehn, JOH) EDM.

Center. Shoots left. 6'1", 210 lbs. Born, Virginia, MN, February 14, 1981.
(Edmonton's 7th choice, 211th overall, in 2000 Entry Draft).

			Regular Season					Playoffs				
Season	Club	League	GP	G	A	TP	PIM	GP	G	A	TP	PIM
1997-98	Moorhead Spuds	Hi-School	23	18	18	36	....	....	....	....	....	....
1998-99	U.S. National U-17	USDP	52	11	15	26	33	....	....	....	....	....
99-2000	Colorado College	WCHA	29	4	6	10	30	....	....	....	....	....
2000-01	Colorado College	WCHA	34	8	12	20	38	....	....	....	....	....
2001-02	Colorado College	WCHA	43	9	12	21	42	....	....	....	....	....
2002-03	Colorado College	WCHA	42	20	15	35	56	....	....	....	....	....

CULLEN, Mark (KUH-lehn, MAHRK) MIN.

Center. Shoots left. 5'11", 175 lbs. Born, Moorhead, MN, October 28, 1978.

			Regular Season					Playoffs				
Season	Club	League	GP	G	A	TP	PIM	GP	G	A	TP	PIM
1998-99	Colorado College	WCHA	42	8	25	33	22	....	....	....	....	....
99-2000	Colorado College	WCHA	37	11	20	31	22	....	....	....	....	....
2000-01	Colorado College	WCHA	31	20	33	53	26	....	....	....	....	....
2001-02	Colorado College	WCHA	43	14	36	50	14	....	....	....	....	....
2002-03	Houston Aeros	AHL	72	22	25	47	20	15	3	7	10	4

WCHA First All-Star Team (2001) • NCAA West Second All-American Team (2001)

Signed as a free agent by **Minnesota**, April 8, 2002.

CURRY, Sean (KUH-ree, SHAWN) CAR.

Defense. Shoots right. 6'4", 230 lbs. Born, Burnsville, MN, April 29, 1982.
(Carolina's 6th choice, 211th overall, in 2001 Entry Draft).

			Regular Season					Playoffs				
Season	Club	League	GP	G	A	TP	PIM	GP	G	A	TP	PIM
99-2000	Burnsville	Hi-School	23	8	18	26	....	....	....	....	....	....
2000-01	Tri-City Americans	WHL	72	5	12	17	113	....	....	....	....	....
2001-02	Tri-City Americans	WHL	36	6	6	12	84	....	....	....	....	....
	Medicine Hat	WHL	24	4	13	17	43	....	....	....	....	....
2002-03	Lowell	AHL	35	0	2	2	62	....	....	....	....	....
	Florida Everblades	ECHL	32	1	6	7	77	1	0	0	0	0

DALEY, Trevor (DAY-lee, TREH-vuhr) DAL.

Defense. Shoots left. 5'9", 197 lbs. Born, Toronto, Ont., October 9, 1983.
(Dallas' 5th choice, 43rd overall, in 2002 Entry Draft).

			Regular Season					Playoffs				
Season	Club	League	GP	G	A	TP	PIM	GP	G	A	TP	PIM
1998-99	Vaughan Vipers	OPJHL	44	10	36	46	79	....	....	....	....	....
99-2000	Sault Ste. Marie	OHL	54	16	30	46	77	15	3	7	10	12
2000-01	Sault Ste. Marie	OHL	58	14	27	41	105	....	....	....	....	....
2001-02	Sault Ste. Marie	OHL	47	9	39	48	38	6	2	2	4	4
2002-03	Sault Ste. Marie	OHL	57	20	33	53	128	1	0	0	0	2

DALLMAN, Kevin (DAL-mahn, KEH-vihn) BOS.

Defense. Shoots right. 5'11", 195 lbs. Born, Niagara Falls, Ont., February 26, 1981.

			Regular Season					Playoffs				
Season	Club	League	GP	G	A	TP	PIM	GP	G	A	TP	PIM
1996-97	Niagrara Falls	OJHL-B	3	0	1	1	2	....	....	....	....	....
1997-98	Niagrara Falls	OJHL-B	47	13	25	38	42	....	....	....	....	....
1998-99	Guelph Storm	OHL	68	8	30	38	52	11	1	4	5	2
99-2000	Guelph Storm	OHL	67	13	46	59	38	6	0	2	2	11
2000-01	Guelph Storm	OHL	66	25	52	77	88	1	0	0	0	0
2001-02	Guelph Storm	OHL	67	23	63	86	68	9	8	8	16	22
2002-03	Providence Bruins	AHL	72	2	19	21	53	....	....	....	....	....

Signed as a free agent by **Boston**, July 18, 2002.

D'AMOUR, Dominic (dah-MOHR, DOHM-ihn-ihk) TOR.

Defense. Shoots left. 6'3", 202 lbs. Born, La Salle, Que., January 28, 1984.
(Toronto's 4th choice, 88th overall, in 2002 Entry Draft).

			Regular Season					Playoffs				
Season	Club	League	GP	G	A	TP	PIM	GP	G	A	TP	PIM
99-2000	Charles-Lemoyne	QAAA	35	3	8	11	47	16	1	1	2	14
2000-01	Charles-Lemoyne	QAAA	11	1	4	5	36	....	....	....	....	....
	Rouyn-Noranda	QMJHL	18	0	0	0	10	....	....	....	....	....
2001-02	Hull Olympiques	QMJHL	68	5	5	10	225	12	0	3	3	32
2002-03	Hull Olympiques	QMJHL	65	5	25	30	211	17	2	3	5	51

DANIELSSON, Nicklas (DAN-yehl-suhn, NIHK-las) VAN.

Right wing. Shoots right. 6'1", 169 lbs. Born, Uppsala, Sweden, December 7, 1984.
(Vancouver's 5th choice, 160th overall, in 2003 Entry Draft).

			Regular Season					Playoffs				
Season	Club	League	GP	G	A	TP	PIM	GP	G	A	TP	PIM
2000-01	Vasteras Jr.	Swede-Jr.	9	6	8	14	12	....	....	....	....	....
	Vasteras IK	Sweden-4	13	3	5	8	2	....	....	....	....	....
2001-02	Brynas IF Gavle Jr.	Swede-Jr.	42	15	14	29	74	....	....	....	....	....
2002-03	Brynas IF Gavle Jr.	Swede-Jr.	21	21	12	33	24	2	1	0	1	2
	Brynas IF Gavle	Sweden	26	0	4	4	10	....	....	....	....	....
	Brynas IF Gavle	Sweden-Q	6	0	0	0	4	....	....	....	....	....

DARBY, Regan (DAHR-bee, REE-gan) VAN.

Defense. Shoots left. 6'2", 200 lbs. Born, Estevan, Sask., July 17, 1980.
(Vancouver's 5th choice, 90th overall, in 1998 Entry Draft).

			Regular Season					Playoffs				
Season	Club	League	GP	G	A	TP	PIM	GP	G	A	TP	PIM
1996-97	Swift Current	SMHL	36	10	20	30	210	....	....	....	....	....
1997-98	Spokane Chiefs	WHL	7	0	1	1	28	....	....	....	....	....
	Tri-City Americans	WHL	32	1	2	3	125	....	....	....	....	....
1998-99	Tri-City Americans	WHL	38	2	4	6	152	....	....	....	....	....
	Red Deer Rebels	WHL	19	1	6	7	90	9	0	1	1	18
99-2000	Red Deer Rebels	WHL	18	3	6	9	79	....	....	....	....	....
	Prince Albert	WHL	44	1	9	10	143	6	0	1	1	23
2000-01	Kansas City Blades	IHL	55	1	5	6	164	....	....	....	....	....
2001-02	Manitoba Moose	AHL	39	0	1	1	196	....	....	....	....	....
	Columbia Inferno	ECHL	7	0	2	2	14	3	0	0	0	0
2002-03	Manitoba Moose	AHL	10	0	0	0	30	....	....	....	....	....
	Columbia Inferno	ECHL	48	1	7	8	170	17	0	1	1	20

DAVIS, George (DAY-vihs, JOHRJ) ANA.

Right wing. Shoots right. 6'2", 225 lbs. Born, North Sydney, N.S., July 28, 1983.
(Anaheim's 5th choice, 140th overall, in 2002 Entry Draft).

			Regular Season					Playoffs				
Season	Club	League	GP	G	A	TP	PIM	GP	G	A	TP	PIM
2000-01	Cape Breton	QMJHL	44	0	1	1	196	5	0	0	0	14
2001-02	Cape Breton	QMJHL	46	4	1	5	274	16	1	2	3	18
2002-03	Cape Breton	QMJHL	43	5	8	13	182	....	....	....	....	....
	Halifax	QMJHL	25	0	2	2	89	25	1	3	4	32

DAVIS, Greg (DAY-vihs, GREHG) ST.L.

Right wing. Shoots right. 6'4", 195 lbs. Born, Calgary, Alta., July 26, 1979.

			Regular Season					Playoffs				
Season	Club	League	GP	G	A	TP	PIM	GP	G	A	TP	PIM
1997-98	Olds Grizzlies	AJHL	56	12	21	33	37	8	0	2	2	10
1998-99	Olds Grizzlies	AJHL	61	19	28	47	97	....	....	....	....	....
99-2000	McGill Redmen	OUAA	38	23	16	39	22	....	....	....	....	....
2000-01	McGill Redmen	OUAA	33	30	35	65	38	....	....	....	....	....
2001-02	Worcester IceCats	AHL	57	12	6	18	10	....	....	....	....	....
	Peoria Rivermen	ECHL	3	0	1	1	0	....	....	....	....	....
2002-03	Worcester IceCats	AHL	54	8	10	18	18	1	0	0	0	0
	Peoria Rivermen	ECHL	10	5	5	10	4	4	1	1	2	2

Signed as a free agent by **St. Louis**, May 5, 2001.

DAWES, Nigel (DAWZ, NIGH-juhl) NYR

Left wing. Shoots left. 5'8", 170 lbs. Born, Winnipeg, Man., February 9, 1985.
(NY Rangers' 5th choice, 149th overall, in 2003 Entry Draft).

			Regular Season					Playoffs				
Season	Club	League	GP	G	A	TP	PIM	GP	G	A	TP	PIM
2000-01	Winnipeg Warriors	MMHL	36	55	41	96	74	....	....	....	....	....
2001-02	Kootenay Ice	WHL	54	15	19	34	14	22	9	6	15	8
2002-03	Kootenay Ice	WHL	72	47	45	92	54	11	4	8	12	6

DAWSON, Aaron (DAW-suhn, AIR-ruhn) CAR.

Defense. Shoots left. 6'5", 220 lbs. Born, Terre Haute, IN, March 11, 1985.
(Carolina's 3rd choice, 102nd overall, in 2003 Entry Draft).

			Regular Season					Playoffs				
Season	Club	League	GP	G	A	TP	PIM	GP	G	A	TP	PIM
2000-01	Peoria Mustangs	CSJHL	STATISTICS NOT AVAILABLE									
2001-02	Peterborough	OPJHL	41	9	20	29	79	....	....	....	....	....
	Peterborough	OHL	5	0	0	0	2	....	....	....	....	....
2002-03	Peterborough	OHL	65	1	8	9	76	7	0	0	0	8

DeMARCHI, Matt (dih-MAHR-shee, MAT) N.J.

Defense. Shoots left. 6'3", 180 lbs. Born, Bemidji, MN, May 4, 1981.
(New Jersey's 4th choice, 57th overall, in 2000 Entry Draft).

			Regular Season					Playoffs				
Season	Club	League	GP	G	A	TP	PIM	GP	G	A	TP	PIM
1997-98	North Iowa	USHL	34	1	2	3	66	10	0	1	1	19
1998-99	North Iowa	USHL	53	4	14	18	131	....	....	....	....	....
99-2000	U. of Minnesota	WCHA	39	1	6	7	82	....	....	....	....	....
2000-01	U. of Minnesota	WCHA	39	4	9	13	*149	....	....	....	....	....
2001-02	U. of Minnesota	WCHA	36	3	8	11	112	....	....	....	....	....
2002-03	U. of Minnesota	WCHA	44	8	9	17	130	....	....	....	....	....

NCAA Championship All-Tournament Team (2003)

DENISOV, Denis (den-NEES-ahf, deh-NEES) BUF.

Left wing. Shoots left. 6', 183 lbs. Born, Kalinin, USSR, December 31, 1981.
(Buffalo's 4th choice, 149th overall, in 2000 Entry Draft).

			Regular Season					Playoffs				
Season	Club	League	GP	G	A	TP	PIM	GP	G	A	TP	PIM
1997-98	HC CSKA Moscow	Russia	7	0	0	0	4	....	....	....	....	....
1998-99	HC CSKA Moscow	Russia-2	42	1	6	7	16	....	....	....	....	....
99-2000	HC CSKA Moscow	Russia-2	39	1	8	9	16	....	....	....	....	....
2000-01	HC CSKA Moscow	Russia-2	41	0	3	3	6	....	....	....	....	....
2001-02	Krylja Sovetov	Russia	47	3	4	7	37	....	....	....	....	....
	Krylja Sovetov 2	Russia-3	3	0	1	1	18	....	....	....	....	....
2002-03	Ufa	Russia	50	2	8	10	12	3	0	1	1	0

DESAUTELS, Jevon (DEH-soh-tehl, jeh-VAWN) WSH.

Left wing. Shoots left. 6'3", 215 lbs. Born, Redvers, Sask., March 15, 1984.
(Washington's 7th choice, 109th overall, in 2002 Entry Draft).

			Regular Season					Playoffs				
Season	Club	League	GP	G	A	TP	PIM	GP	G	A	TP	PIM
2000-01	Spokane Chiefs	WHL	49	1	2	3	77	....	....	....	....	....
2001-02	Spokane Chiefs	WHL	60	6	11	17	162	11	1	0	1	20
2002-03	Spokane Chiefs	WHL	70	7	12	19	184	11	2	3	5	32

DESBIENS, Guillaume (deh-BYEHN, gwee-AHM) ATL.

Right wing. Shoots left. 6'2", 190 lbs. Born, Alma, Que., April 20, 1985.
(Atlanta's 3rd choice, 116th overall, in 2003 Entry Draft).

			Regular Season					Playoffs				
Season	Club	League	GP	G	A	TP	PIM	GP	G	A	TP	PIM
2001-02	Rouyn-Noranda	QMJHL	65	14	10	24	115	4	1	1	2	9
2002-03	Rouyn-Noranda	QMJHL	64	15	18	33	233	4	0	0	0	4

DESCHENES, Nick (duh-SHAYN, NIHK) PHI.

Left wing. Shoots left. 6'3", 223 lbs. Born, Morinville, Alta., December 6, 1978.

			Regular Season					Playoffs				
Season	Club	League	GP	G	A	TP	PIM	GP	G	A	TP	PIM
1998-99	Fort Saskatchewan	AJHL	STATISTICS NOT AVAILABLE									
99-2000	Yale University	ECAC	29	6	9	15	15	....	....	....	....	....
2000-01	Yale University	ECAC	31	17	20	37	22	....	....	....	....	....
2001-02	Yale University	ECAC	23	5	11	16	4	....	....	....	....	....
2002-03	Yale University	ECAC	31	8	11	19	37	....	....	....	....	....

Signed as a free agent by **Philadelphia**, May 21, 2003.

DEVEAUX, Andre (de-VOH, AWN-dray) MTL.

Center. Shoots right. 6'3", 220 lbs. Born, Freeport, Bahamas, February 23, 1984.
(Montreal's 4th choice, 182nd overall, in 2002 Entry Draft).

			Regular Season					Playoffs				
Season	Club	League	GP	G	A	TP	PIM	GP	G	A	TP	PIM
2000-01	Belleville Bulls	OHL	58	3	6	9	65	10	3	6	9	6
2001-02	Belleville Bulls	OHL	64	8	13	21	89	11	1	2	3	30
2002-03	Belleville Bulls	OHL	34	6	12	18	93	....	....	....	....	....
	Owen Sound	OHL	29	9	10	19	33	4	2	2	4	6

DeWOLF, Josh (duh-WOOLF, JAWSH)

Defense. Shoots left. 6'2", 203 lbs. Born, Bloomington, MN, July 25, 1977.
(New Jersey's 3rd choice, 41st overall, in 1996 Entry Draft).

			Regular Season					Playoffs				
Season	Club	League	GP	G	A	TP	PIM	GP	G	A	TP	PIM
1993-94	Bloomington-Jeff.	Hi-School	25	1	14	15	32	....	....	....	....	....
1994-95	Bloomington-Jeff.	Hi-School	28	6	22	28	52	....	....	....	....	....
1995-96	Twin Cities	USHL	40	11	15	26	38	....	....	....	....	....
1996-97	St. Cloud State	WCHA	31	3	11	14	62	....	....	....	....	....
1997-98	St. Cloud State	WCHA	37	9	9	18	78	....	....	....	....	....
	Albany River Rats	AHL	2	0	0	0	0	....	....	....	....	....
1998-99	Albany River Rats	AHL	75	1	17	18	111	5	0	0	0	2
99-2000	Albany River Rats	AHL	58	3	11	14	38	....	....	....	....	....
	Quebec Citadelles	AHL	15	1	0	1	17	3	0	1	1	0
2000-01	Quebec Citadelles	AHL	58	3	8	11	65	7	0	1	1	16
2001-02	Cincinnati	AHL	76	4	11	15	88	3	0	0	0	2
2002-03	Cincinnati	AHL	67	1	17	18	105	....	....	....	....	....

Traded to **Montreal** by **New Jersey** with Sheldon Souray and New Jersey's 2nd round choice (later traded to Washington – later traded to Tampa Bay – Tampa Bay selected Andreas Holmqvist) in 2001 Entry Draft for Vladimir Malakhov, March 1, 2000. Signed as a free agent by **Anaheim**, August 22, 2002.

DICAIRE, Gerard (dih-KAIR, zhehr-AHR) T.B.

Defense. Shoots left. 6'2", 198 lbs. Born, Faro, Yukon, September 14, 1982.
(Tampa Bay's 4th choice, 162nd overall, in 2002 Entry Draft).

			Regular Season					Playoffs				
Season	Club	League	GP	G	A	TP	PIM	GP	G	A	TP	PIM
1997-98	Tumber Ridge	NWJHL	35	15	28	43	63	....	....	....	....	....
1998-99	Prince George	BCHL	51	6	22	28	28	....	....	....	....	....
99-2000	Seattle	WHL	68	11	25	36	38	7	0	1	1	6
2000-01	Seattle	WHL	69	15	36	51	33	9	0	2	2	2
2001-02	Seattle	WHL	41	4	25	29	25	....	....	....	....	....
	Kootenay Ice	WHL	25	2	21	23	9	22	1	14	15	24
2002-03	Kootenay Ice	WHL	72	15	44	59	79	11	2	6	8	12

• Re-entered NHL Entry Draft. Originally Buffalo's 2nd choice, 48th overall, in 2000 Entry Draft.

WHL West Second All-Star Team (2001, 2003)

DiCASMIRRO, Nate (dee-CAZ-MIHR-oh, NAYT) EDM.

Left wing. Shoots left. 5'11", 205 lbs. Born, Burnsville, MN, September 27, 1978.

			Regular Season					Playoffs				
Season	Club	League	GP	G	A	TP	PIM	GP	G	A	TP	PIM
1996-97	North Iowa	USHL	51	18	22	40	86	12	0	6	6	22
1997-98	North Iowa	USHL	52	29	45	74	118	11	5	5	10	34
1998-99	St. Cloud State	WCHA	34	6	8	14	46	....	....	....	....	....
99-2000	St. Cloud State	WCHA	40	19	24	43	26	....	....	....	....	....
2000-01	St. Cloud State	WCHA	32	9	20	29	26	....	....	....	....	....
2001-02	St. Cloud State	WCHA	41	17	33	50	58	....	....	....	....	....
	Hamilton Bulldogs	AHL	1	0	0	0	0	10	0	5	5	6
2002-03	Hamilton Bulldogs	AHL	49	5	12	17	22	16	2	1	3	8

USHL First All-Star Team (1998) • USHL MVP (1998)

Signed as a free agent by **Edmonton**, April 8, 2002.

DISALVATORE, Jon (dih-sal-vuh-TOH-ray, JAWN) S.J.

Right wing. Shoots right. 6'1", 180 lbs. Born, Bangor, ME, March 30, 1981.
(San Jose's 2nd choice, 104th overall, in 2000 Entry Draft).

			Regular Season					Playoffs				
Season	Club	League	GP	G	A	TP	PIM	GP	G	A	TP	PIM
1997-98	New England	EJHL	38	24	41	65	....	....	....	....	....	....
1998-99	New England	EJHL	48	44	76	*120	38	....	....	....	....	....
99-2000	Providence College	H-East	38	15	12	27	12	....	....	....	....	....
2000-01	Providence College	H-East	36	9	16	25	29	....	....	....	....	....
2001-02	Providence College	H-East	38	16	26	42	6	....	....	....	....	....
2002-03	Providence College	H-East	36	19	29	48	12	....	....	....	....	....

EJHL First All-Star Team (1999) • EJHL MVP (1999)

DOBBEN, Scott (DAW-behn, SKAWT) OTT.

Center/Left wing. Shoots left. 6'1", 193 lbs. Born, Palmerston, Ont., April 10, 1983.
(Ottawa's 4th choice, 113th overall, in 2002 Entry Draft).

			Regular Season					Playoffs				
Season	Club	League	GP	G	A	TP	PIM	GP	G	A	TP	PIM
99-2000	Elmira Sugar Kings	OJHL-B	48	6	15	21	24	....	....	....	....	....
2000-01	Erie Otters	OHL	57	8	9	17	18	15	0	1	1	10
2001-02	Erie Otters	OHL	68	31	32	63	72	21	4	11	15	24
2002-03	Erie Otters	OHL	18	3	5	8	27	....	....	....	....	....
	Sault Ste. Marie	OHL	45	14	20	34	42	4	1	0	1	4

DOBRYSHKIN, Yuri (doh-BRIHSH-kihn, yew-REE) ATL.

Left wing. Shoots right. 6', 190 lbs. Born, Penza, USSR, July 19, 1979.
(Atlanta's 7th choice, 159th overall, in 1999 Entry Draft).

			Regular Season					Playoffs				
Season	Club	League	GP	G	A	TP	PIM	GP	G	A	TP	PIM
1996-97	Krylja Sovetov 2	Russia-3	35	13	5	18	42	....	....	....	....	....
	Krylja Sovetov	Russia	2	0	0	0	0	2	0	0	0	0
1997-98	Krylja Sovetov 2	Russia-3	26	12	5	17	68	....	....	....	....	....
	Krylja Sovetov	Russia	22	4	0	4	12	....	....	....	....	....
1998-99	Krylja Sovetov	Russia	50	11	5	16	86	....	....	....	....	....
99-2000	Ak Bars Kazan	Russia	27	6	9	15	24	17	2	0	2	10
2000-01	Ak Bars Kazan	Russia	40	10	5	15	32	4	2	0	2	2
2001-02	Ak Bars Kazan	Russia	38	9	8	17	22	11	0	2	2	6
2002-03	Cherepovets	Russia	49	19	7	26	82	12	5	2	7	12

DOHERTY, John (DOH-her-tee, JAWN) TOR.

Defense. Shoots right. 6'4", 213 lbs. Born, Malden, MA, March 25, 1984.
(Toronto's 1st choice, 57th overall, in 2003 Entry Draft).

			Regular Season					Playoffs				
Season	Club	League	GP	G	A	TP	PIM	GP	G	A	TP	PIM
2001-02	Phillips Andover	Hi-School	24	5	18	23	....	....	....	....	....	....
2002-03	Phillips Andover	Hi-School	24	12	12	24	40	....	....	....	....	....
	NH Jr. Monarchs	EJHL	11	1	4	5	36	....	....	....	....	....

Signed Letter of Intent to attend **New Hampshire** (H-East), November 2, 2002.

DONALLY, Ryan (DAWN-ah-lee, RIGH-uhn) CGY.

Left wing. Shoots left. 6'4", 210 lbs. Born, Tecumseh, Ont., February 4, 1985.
(Calgary's 3rd choice, 97th overall, in 2003 Entry Draft).

			Regular Season					Playoffs				
Season	Club	League	GP	G	A	TP	PIM	GP	G	A	TP	PIM
2001-02	Windsor Spitfires	OHL	53	6	7	13	77	16	0	2	2	6
2002-03	Windsor Spitfires	OHL	65	11	15	26	108	7	0	1	1	8

DONIKA, Mikhail (DAW-nih-ka, mihk-high-EHL) DAL.

Defense. Shoots left. 6', 185 lbs. Born, Yaroslavl, USSR, May 15, 1979.
(Dallas' 11th choice, 272nd overall, in 1999 Entry Draft).

			Regular Season					Playoffs				
Season	Club	League	GP	G	A	TP	PIM	GP	G	A	TP	PIM
1996-97	Yaroslavl 2	Russia-3	15	3	5	8	6	....	....	....	....	....
	Torpedo Yaroslavl	Russia	22	1	0	1	6	2	0	0	0	0
1997-98	Yaroslavl 2	Russia-2	19	1	2	3	32	....	....	....	....	....
	Torpedo Yaroslavl	Russia	30	0	2	2	14	....	....	....	....	....
1998-99	Yaroslavl 2	Russia-3	6	2	1	3	4	....	....	....	....	....
	Torpedo Yaroslavl	Russia	37	0	1	1	10	....	....	....	....	....
99-2000	Torpedo Yaroslavl	Russia	35	0	1	1	22	10	0	0	0	4
2000-01	Dynamo Moscow	Russia	43	1	3	4	12	....	....	....	....	....
2001-02	Amur Khabarovsk	Russia	51	1	3	4	66	....	....	....	....	....
2002-03	Spartak Moscow	Russia	51	4	7	11	16	....	....	....	....	....

DOULL, Doug (DOOL, DUHG) BOS.

Left wing. Shoots left. 6'2", 216 lbs. Born, Green Bay, N.S., May 31, 1974.

			Regular Season					Playoffs				
Season	Club	League	GP	G	A	TP	PIM	GP	G	A	TP	PIM
1990-91	Wexford Raiders	MTHL	39	22	36	58	141	....	....	....	....	....
1991-92	Belleville Bulls	OHL	62	6	11	17	123	....	....	....	....	....
1992-93	Belleville Bulls	OHL	65	19	37	56	143	....	....	....	....	....
1993-94	Belleville Bulls	OHL	62	13	24	37	143	....	....	....	....	....
1994-95	Belleville Bulls	OHL	29	7	12	19	71	16	2	13	15	39
1995-96	St. Mary's Huskies	AUAA	11	4	4	8	54	....	....	....	....	....
1996-97	St. Mary's Huskies	AUAA	18	3	10	13	138	....	....	....	....	....
1997-98	St. Mary's Huskies	AUAA	25	4	11	15	227	....	....	....	....	....
1998-99	Michigan K-Wings	IHL	55	4	11	15	227	3	1	1	2	4
99-2000	Detroit Vipers	IHL	17	0	2	2	69	....	....	....	....	....
	Manitoba Moose	IHL	45	4	4	8	184	2	0	0	0	2
2000-01	Manchester Storm	Britain	15	1	6	7	51	....	....	....	....	....
	Saint John Flames	AHL	49	3	10	13	167	16	0	1	1	32
2001-02	St. John's	AHL	36	5	8	13	166	9	0	1	1	17
2002-03	St. John's	AHL	70	15	10	25	257	....	....	....	....	....

Signed as a free agent by **Manchester** (Britain), August 15, 2000. Signed to a 25-game tryout contract by **Saint John** (AHL) after securing release from **Manchester** (Britain), December 19, 2000. Signed as a free agent by **Saint John** (AHL), February 18, 2001. Signed as a free agent by **Toronto**, July 25, 2001. • Missed majority of 2001-02 season recovering from ankle injury suffered in game vs. Manitoba (AHL), October 19, 2001. Signed as a free agent by **Boston**, July 28, 2003.

DOWN, Blaine (DOWN, BLAYN) NYI

Left wing. Shoots left. 5'11", 170 lbs. Born, Whitby, Ont., July 16, 1982.

			Regular Season					Playoffs				
Season	Club	League	GP	G	A	TP	PIM	GP	G	A	TP	PIM
1998-99	Oshawa	OPJHL	36	18	22	40	75	....	....	....	....	....
99-2000	Barrie Colts	OHL	43	17	22	39	49	22	10	6	16	18
2000-01	Barrie Colts	OHL	62	35	38	73	80	5	2	0	2	10
2001-02	Barrie Colts	OHL	63	25	36	61	92	20	15	10	25	34
2002-03	Bridgeport	AHL	54	8	13	21	30	9	0	0	0	21

Signed as a free agent by **NY Islanders**, August 13, 2002.

DRANEY, Brett (DRAY-nee, BREHT) DAL.

Left wing. Shoots left. 6'1", 195 lbs. Born, Merritt, B.C., March 12, 1981.
(Dallas' 7th choice, 186th overall, in 1999 Entry Draft).

			Regular Season					Playoffs				
Season	Club	League	GP	G	A	TP	PIM	GP	G	A	TP	PIM
1996-97	Kamloops	BCAHA	43	69	73	132	54	....	....	....	....	....
1997-98	Kamloops Blazers	WHL	42	2	2	4	16	7	0	0	0	0
1998-99	Kamloops Blazers	WHL	58	7	10	17	48	15	1	1	2	8
99-2000	Kamloops Blazers	WHL	62	18	27	45	63	4	1	1	2	11
2000-01	Medicine Hat	WHL	57	20	28	48	84	....	....	....	....	....
2001-02	Medicine Hat	WHL	51	18	37	55	78	....	....	....	....	....
	Fort Worth	CHL	....	....	....	....	....	4	0	1	1	4
	Utah Grizzlies	AHL	6	1	2	3	6	5	0	0	0	4
2002-03	Utah Grizzlies	AHL	11	1	1	2	7	....	....	....	....	....
	Lexington	ECHL	50	13	19	32	64	3	1	0	1	10

DROZDETSKY, Alexander (drawz-DEHT-skee, al-ehx-AN-duhr) PHI.

Right wing. Shoots left. 6', 180 lbs. Born, Moscow, USSR, November 10, 1981.
(Philadelphia's 2nd choice, 94th overall, in 2000 Entry Draft).

			Regular Season					Playoffs				
Season	Club	League	GP	G	A	TP	PIM	GP	G	A	TP	PIM
1997-98	St. Petersburg 2	Russia-3	19	0	1	1	0	....	....	....	....	....
1998-99	St. Petersburg 2	Russia-4	24	5	3	8	12	....	....	....	....	....
99-2000	St. Petersburg 2	Russia-3	4	4	1	5	2	....	....	....	....	....
	SKA St. Petersburg	Russia	32	2	0	2	10	4	0	0	0	0
2000-01	SKA St. Petersburg	Russia	42	6	7	13	74	....	....	....	....	....
2001-02	CSKA Moscow	Russia	49	11	6	17	26	....	....	....	....	....
2002-03	CSKA Moscow	Russia	46	14	13	27	30	....	....	....	....	....

DUBEC, Marek (DOO-behts, MAIR-ehk) BUF.

Left wing. Shoots left. 6', 179 lbs. Born, Bratislava, Czech., February 26, 1982.
(Buffalo's 7th choice, 247th overall, in 2001 Entry Draft).

			Regular Season					Playoffs				
Season	Club	League	GP	G	A	TP	PIM	GP	G	A	TP	PIM
2000-01	Vsetin Jr.	Czech-Jr.	45	27	15	42	52	8	7	2	9	20
2001-02	Vsetin Jr.	Czech-Jr.	18	12	9	21	32	....	....	....	....	....
	Vsetin	Czech	5	1	0	1	0	4	2	0	2	4
2002-03	Vsetin	Czech	22	2	4	6	24	4	0	0	0	2
	Vsetin Jr.	Czech-Jr.	8	6	6	12	24	5	1	0	1	12
	Slavia Trebec	Czech-2	16	3	2	5	24	....	....	....	....	....

DUBEN, Premysl (DUH-behn, PREHM-uh-suhl) NYR

Defense. Shoots left. 6'3", 220 lbs. Born, Jihlava, Czech., October 5, 1981.
(NY Rangers' 3rd choice, 112th overall, in 2000 Entry Draft).

			Regular Season					Playoffs				
Season	Club	League	GP	G	A	TP	PIM	GP	G	A	TP	PIM
1997-98	Dukla Jihlava Jr.	Czech-Jr.	25	1	6	7	34	....	....	....	....	....
1998-99	Dukla Jihlava Jr.	Czech-Jr.	41	1	5	6	18	....	....	....	....	....
99-2000	Dukla Jihlava Jr.	Czech-Jr.	27	4	2	6	36	....	....	....	....	....
	HC Dukla Jihlava	Czech-2	19	0	1	1	10	14	0	1	1	4
2000-01	HC Dukla Jihlava	Czech-2	5	0	0	0	10	....	....	....	....	....
	Baie-Comeau	QMJHL	32	0	8	8	36	9	1	0	1	12
2001-02	Dukla Jihlava Jr.	Czech-Jr.	13	0	5	5	20	....	....	....	....	....
	HC Dukla Jihlava	Czech-2	33	0	1	1	36	6	0	0	0	2
2002-03	HC Dukla Jihlava	Czech-2	24	0	1	1	20	12	0	0	0	10

DUDA, Radek (DOO-duh, RA-dehk) CGY.

Right wing. Shoots left. 6'1", 193 lbs. Born, Skolov, Czech., January 28, 1979.
(Calgary's 7th choice, 192nd overall, in 1998 Entry Draft).

			Regular Season					Playoffs				
Season	Club	League	GP	G	A	TP	PIM	GP	G	A	TP	PIM
1994-95	Sokolov Jr.	Czech-Jr.	36	67	37	104	....	....	....	....	....	....
1995-96	Sparta Praha Jr.	Czech-Jr.	39	15	10	25	....	....	....	....	....	....
1996-97	Sparta Praha Jr.	Czech-Jr.	21	9	14	23	....	....	....	....	....	....
	Sokolov Jr.	Czech-Jr.	1	0	0	0	....	....	....	....	....	....
	HC Sparta Praha	Czech	....	....	....	....	....	1	0	0	0	0
1997-98	HC Sparta Praha	Czech	39	3	3	6	41	10	0	2	2	6
1998-99	Regina Pats	WHL	65	24	31	55	139	....	....	....	....	....
99-2000	Lethbridge	WHL	69	42	64	106	193	....	....	....	....	....
2000-01	HC Keramika Plzen	Czech	24	5	6	11	49	....	....	....	....	....
	HC Sparta Praha	Czech	18	2	1	3	66	....	....	....	....	....
2001-02	HC Keramika Plzen	Czech	49	17	18	35	156	6	1	5	6	18
2002-03	HC Keramika Plzen	Czech	13	5	8	13	47	....	....	....	....	....
	HC Slavia Praha	Czech	31	12	15	27	105	17	7	3	10	40

DUFORT, J.F. (doo-FOHR, JAY-EHF) EDM.

Left wing. Shoots left. 6'2", 200 lbs. Born, Drummondville, Que., March 9, 1982.
(Edmonton's 10th choice, 205th overall, in 2002 Entry Draft).

			Regular Season					Playoffs				
Season	Club	League	GP	G	A	TP	PIM	GP	G	A	TP	PIM
1997-98	Antoine-Girouard	QAAA	38	13	16	29	....	....	....	....	....	....
1998-99	Magog	QAAA	40	23	30	53	102	....	....	....	....	....
	Shawinigan	QMJHL	3	0	0	0	0	....	....	....	....	....
99-2000	Shawinigan	QMJHL	70	14	34	48	218	6	2	4	6	2
2000-01	Shawinigan	QMJHL	46	21	32	53	194	10	3	3	6	18
2001-02	Shawinigan	QMJHL	42	11	32	43	147	....	....	....	....	....
	Cape Breton	QMJHL	26	11	9	20	120	16	4	9	13	24
2002-03	Cape Breton	QMJHL	51	14	22	36	287	....	....	....	....	....

DUPUIS, Philippe (doo-PWEE, fihl-EEP) CBJ

Center. Shoots right. 6', 192 lbs. Born, Laval, Que., April 24, 1985.
(Columbus' 5th choice, 104th overall, in 2003 Entry Draft).

			Regular Season					Playoffs				
Season	Club	League	GP	G	A	TP	PIM	GP	G	A	TP	PIM
2000-01	Laval-Laurentides	QAAA	46	16	27	43	74	8	1	5	6	30
2001-02	Hull Olympiques	QMJHL	67	7	14	21	59	12	6	5	11	14
2002-03	Hull Olympiques	QMJHL	68	22	34	56	89	20	2	4	6	22

DUSABLON, Benoit (doo-sah=BLAW, BEHN-wah) NYR

Center. Shoots left. 6'1", 207 lbs. Born, Ste Anne de la Perad, Que., August 1, 1979.

			Regular Season					Playoffs				
Season	Club	League	GP	G	A	TP	PIM	GP	G	A	TP	PIM
1996-97	Halifax	QMJHL	61	7	7	14	181	....	....	....	....	....
1997-98	Halifax	QMJHL	7	1	0	1	7	....	....	....	....	....
	Val d'Or Foreurs	QMJHL	57	14	11	25	56	19	2	9	11	33
1998-99	Val d'Or Foreurs	QMJHL	67	42	74	116	63	6	2	6	8	4
99-2000	Val d'Or Foreurs	QMJHL	41	29	53	82	45	....	....	....	....	....
	Halifax	QMJHL	31	18	35	53	18	10	6	7	13	12
2000-01	Johnstown Chiefs	ECHL	11	2	3	5	4	....	....	....	....	....
	Tallahassee	ECHL	49	21	29	50	33	....	....	....	....	....
2001-02	Charlotte	ECHL	19	12	13	25	2	....	....	....	....	....
	Hartford Wolf Pack	AHL	38	8	15	23	16	9	1	2	3	4
2002-03	Hartford Wolf Pack	AHL	50	8	16	24	41	1	0	0	0	0

Signed as a free agent by **NY Rangers**, October 1, 2001.

DVORAK, Petr (duv-VOHR-ak, PEE-tuhr) WSH.

Center. Shoots right. 6', 194 lbs. Born, Roznov, Czech., October 11, 1983.
(Washington's 8th choice, 118th overall, in 2002 Entry Draft).

			Regular Season					Playoffs				
Season	Club	League	GP	G	A	TP	PIM	GP	G	A	TP	PIM
99-2000	Havirov Jr.	Czech-Jr.	47	28	28	56	79	....	....	....	....	....
2000-01	Havirov Jr.	Czech-Jr.	36	12	15	27	18	....	....	....	....	....
	HC Femax Havirov	Czech	1	0	0	0	0	....	....	....	....	....
2001-02	Havirov Jr.	Czech-Jr.	40	24	25	49	90	....	....	....	....	....
	Sumperk	Czech-2	1	0	1	1	0	....	....	....	....	....
	HC Femax Havirov	Czech	7	0	0	0	0	....	....	....	....	....
2002-03	Regina Pats	WHL	64	16	23	39	30	5	2	1	3	2

DWYER, Jeff (DWIGH-uhr, JEHF) ATL.

Defense. Shoots left. 6'2", 205 lbs. Born, Greenwich, CT, November 22, 1980.
(Atlanta's 8th choice, 178th overall, in 2000 Entry Draft).

			Regular Season					Playoffs				
Season	Club	League	GP	G	A	TP	PIM	GP	G	A	TP	PIM
1996-97	Choate-Rosemary	Hi-School	28	5	11	16	....	....	....	....	....	....
1997-98	Choate-Rosemary	Hi-School	28	9	14	23	....	....	....	....	....	....
1998-99	Choate-Rosemary	Hi-School	27	8	22	30	....	....	....	....	....	....
99-2000	Choate-Rosemary	Hi-School	25	11	30	41	25	....	....	....	....	....
2000-01	Yale University	ECAC	31	3	18	21	16	....	....	....	....	....
2001-02	Yale University	ECAC	31	6	9	15	16	....	....	....	....	....
2002-03	Yale University	ECAC	32	1	17	18	26	....	....	....	....	....

DWYER, Patrick (DWIGH-uhr, PAT-rihk) ATL.

Right wing. Shoots right. 5'10", 170 lbs. Born, Great Falls, MT, June 22, 1983.
(Atlanta's 3rd choice, 116th overall, in 2002 Entry Draft).

			Regular Season					Playoffs				
Season	Club	League	GP	G	A	TP	PIM	GP	G	A	TP	PIM
2000-01	Great Falls	NWJHL	40	33	57	90	106	12	10	12	22	....
2001-02	West-Michigan	CCHA	38	17	17	34	26	....	....	....	....	....
2002-03	West-Michigan	CCHA	33	9	10	19	20	....	....	....	....	....

NWJHL First All-Star Team (2001) • NWJHL MVP (2001) • CCHA All-Rookie Team (2002) • CCHA Rookie of the Year (2002)

DYMENT, Chris (DIGH-mehnt, KRIHS) MIN.

Defense. Shoots right. 6'3", 207 lbs. Born, Reading, MA, October 24, 1979.
(Montreal's 3rd choice, 97th overall, in 1999 Entry Draft).

			Regular Season					Playoffs				
Season	Club	League	GP	G	A	TP	PIM	GP	G	A	TP	PIM
1997-98	Reading High	Hi-School	22	22	22	44	15	....	....	....	....	....
1998-99	Boston University	H-East	25	1	5	6	16	....	....	....	....	....
99-2000	Boston University	H-East	42	11	20	31	42	....	....	....	....	....
2000-01	Boston University	H-East	37	1	10	11	38	....	....	....	....	....
2001-02	Boston University	H-East	38	7	18	25	24	....	....	....	....	....
2002-03	Houston Aeros	AHL	40	2	3	5	64	17	0	1	1	8

Hockey East First All-Star Team (2000) • NCAA East Second All-American Team (2000) • Hockey East Second All-Star Team (2002)

Traded to **Minnesota** by **Montreal** for Minnesota's 5th round choice (later traded to Calgary – Calgary selected Jiri Cetkovsky) in 2002 Entry Draft, May 25, 2002.

EAGER, Ben (EE-guhr, BEHN) PHX.

Left wing. Shoots left. 6'3", 215 lbs. Born, Ottawa, Ont., January 22, 1984.
(Phoenix's 2nd choice, 23rd overall, in 2002 Entry Draft).

			Regular Season					Playoffs				
Season	Club	League	GP	G	A	TP	PIM	GP	G	A	TP	PIM
99-2000	Ottawa Jr. Sens	OCJHL	50	8	11	19	119	....	....	....	....	....
2000-01	Oshawa Generals	OHL	61	4	6	10	120	....	....	....	....	....
2001-02	Oshawa Generals	OHL	63	14	23	37	255	5	0	1	1	13
2002-03	Oshawa Generals	OHL	58	16	24	40	216	8	0	4	4	8

EAVES, Ben (EEVZ, BEHN) PIT.

Center. Shoots right. 5'8", 180 lbs. Born, Minneapolis, MN, March 27, 1982.
(Pittsburgh's 6th choice, 131st overall, in 2001 Entry Draft).

			Regular Season					Playoffs				
Season	Club	League	GP	G	A	TP	PIM	GP	G	A	TP	PIM
1998-99	Minnesota Selects	USAHA	71	68	88	156	12	....	....	....	....	....
99-2000	Shat.-St. Mary's	Hi-School	57	47	71	118	16	....	....	....	....	....
2000-01	Boston College	H-East	40	13	26	39	12	....	....	....	....	....
2001-02	Boston College	H-East	23	13	26	39	12	....	....	....	....	....
2002-03	Boston College	H-East	36	18	*39	*57	18	....	....	....	....	....

Hockey East Second All-Star Team (2002) • Hockey East First All-Star Team (2003) • Hockey East Player of the Year (2003) (co-winner - Michael Ayers) • NCAA East First All-American Team (2003)

EAVES, Patrick (EEVZ, PAT-rihk) OTT.

Right wing. Shoots right. 5'11", 174 lbs. Born, Calgary, Alta., May 1, 1984.
(Ottawa's 1st choice, 29th overall, in 2003 Entry Draft).

			Regular Season					Playoffs				
Season	Club	League	GP	G	A	TP	PIM	GP	G	A	TP	PIM
99-2000	Shat.-St. Mary's	Hi-School	50	23	24	47	....	....	....	....	....	....
2000-01	U.S. National U-17	USDP	47	19	19	38	78	....	....	....	....	....
	United States	Nt-Team	12	8	8	16	18	....	....	....	....	....
2001-02	U.S. National U-18	USDP	49	25	28	53	142	....	....	....	....	....
	United States	Nt-Team	11	6	12	18	47	....	....	....	....	....
2002-03	Boston College	H-East	14	10	8	18	61	....	....	....	....	....

• Missed majority of 2002-03 season recovering from neck injury suffered in game vs. Maine (H-East), December 7, 2002.

EBERLY, Dan (EH-bur-lee, DAN) NYR

Defense. Shoots left. 6', 180 lbs. Born, Newton, MA, October 28, 1980.
(NY Rangers' 8th choice, 238th overall, in 2000 Entry Draft).

			Regular Season					Playoffs				
Season	Club	League	GP	G	A	TP	PIM	GP	G	A	TP	PIM
1998-99	Catholic Memorial	Hi-School		STATISTICS NOT AVAILABLE								
99-2000	RPI Engineers	ECAC	21	2	5	7	8	....	....	....	....	....
2000-01	RPI Engineers	ECAC	28	3	8	11	20	....	....	....	....	....
2001-02	RPI Engineers	ECAC	35	3	14	17	26	....	....	....	....	....
2002-03	RPI Engineers	ECAC	32	6	10	16	40	....	....	....	....	....

ECKERBLOM, Niklas (EK-kuhr-blawm, NIHK-las) MIN.

Center. Shoots left. 6'1", 196 lbs. Born, Vasterhaninge, Sweden, January 4, 1984.
(Minnesota's 7th choice, 204th overall, in 2002 Entry Draft).

			Regular Season					Playoffs				
Season	Club	League	GP	G	A	TP	PIM	GP	G	A	TP	PIM
99-2000	Djurgarden-18	Swede-Jr.	13	5	3	8	37	....	....	....	....	....
2000-01					DID NOT PLAY							
2001-02	Djurgarden-18	Swede-Jr.	5	9	2	11	8	....	....	....	....	....
	Djurgarden Jr.	Swede-Jr.	1	0	0	0	0	....	....	....	....	....
2002-03	Djurgarden Jr.	Swede-Jr.	6	0	2	2	4	....	....	....	....	....
	Djurgarden	Sweden	10	0	1	1	0	5	0	0	0	0
	Trangsunds IF	Swede-3	19	0	3	3	12	....	....	....	....	....

EGENER, Mike (EHG-eh-nuhr, MIGHK) T.B.

Defense. Shoots left. 6'4", 195 lbs. Born, Lahr, West Germany, September 26, 1984.
(Tampa Bay's 1st choice, 34th overall, in 2003 Entry Draft).

			Regular Season					Playoffs				
Season	Club	League	GP	G	A	TP	PIM	GP	G	A	TP	PIM
99-2000	Calgary Bruins	CMHA	27	4	9	13	88	....	....	....	....	....
2000-01	Calgary Hitmen	WHL	52	1	0	1	91	6	0	0	0	5
2001-02	Calgary Hitmen	WHL	68	2	7	9	175	6	0	0	0	23
2002-03	Calgary Hitmen	WHL	40	2	8	10	210	3	1	0	1	8

EHRHOFF, Christian (AIR-hawf, KRIHS-tyan) S.J.

Defense. Shoots left. 6'2", 185 lbs. Born, Moers, West Germany, July 6, 1982.
(San Jose's 2nd choice, 106th overall, in 2001 Entry Draft).

			Regular Season					Playoffs				
Season	Club	League	GP	G	A	TP	PIM	GP	G	A	TP	PIM
1998-99	Krefeld Jr.	Ger.-Jr.	22	10	14	24	46	....	....	....	....	....
99-2000	Duisburger SC	German-3	41	3	12	15	50	....	....	....	....	....
	Krefeld Pinguine	Germany	9	1	0	1	6	3	0	0	0	0
2000-01	Duisburger SC	German-3	6	1	2	3	12	....	....	....	....	....
	Krefeld Pinguine	Germany	58	3	11	14	73	....	....	....	....	....
2001-02	Krefeld Pinguine	Germany	46	7	17	24	81	3	0	0	0	2
	Germany	Olympics	7	0	0	0	8	....	....	....	....	....
2002-03	Krefeld Pinguine	Germany	48	10	17	27	54	14	3	6	9	24

EICHELBERGER, John (IGH-kehl-buhr-guhr, JAWN) PHI.

Center. Shoots left. 6'2", 185 lbs. Born, Atlanta, GA, February 23, 1981.
(Philadelphia's 5th choice, 210th overall, in 2000 Entry Draft).

			Regular Season					Playoffs				
Season	Club	League	GP	G	A	TP	PIM	GP	G	A	TP	PIM
1997-98	U.S. National U-18	USDP	65	11	28	39	54	....	....	....	....	....
1998-99	U.S. National U-18	USDP	31	5	11	16	24	....	....	....	....	....
99-2000	Green Bay	USHL	49	19	50	69	58	....	....	....	....	....
2000-01	U. of Wisconsin	WCHA	25	0	5	5	2	....	....	....	....	....
2001-02	U. of Wisconsin	WCHA	36	2	7	9	29	....	....	....	....	....
2002-03	U. of Wisconsin	WCHA	37	2	9	11	14	....	....	....	....	....

ELLIOTT, Paul (EHL-lee-awt, PAWL) FLA.

Defense. Shoots left. 6'2", 210 lbs. Born, White Rock, B.C., June 2, 1980.
(Edmonton's 5th choice, 128th overall, in 1998 Entry Draft).

			Regular Season					Playoffs				
Season	Club	League	GP	G	A	TP	PIM	GP	G	A	TP	PIM
1995-96	Surrey Eagles	BCAHA	45	23	60	83	77	....	....	....	....	....
	Lethbridge	WHL	2	0	0	0	0	....	....	....	....	....
1996-97	Lethbridge	WHL	46	0	8	8	17	1	0	0	0	0
1997-98	Lethbridge	WHL	48	4	18	22	35	....	....	....	....	....
	Medicine Hat	WHL	24	7	9	16	12	....	....	....	....	....
1998-99	Medicine Hat	WHL	71	11	36	47	80	....	....	....	....	....
99-2000	Medicine Hat	WHL	66	15	28	43	91	....	....	....	....	....
2000-01	Kamloops Blazers	WHL	40	10	33	43	37	....	....	....	....	....
	Regina Pats	WHL	27	8	17	25	51	6	0	4	4	2
2001-02	Utah Grizzlies	AHL	35	2	2	4	14	....	....	....	....	....
	Florida Everblades	ECHL	5	2	2	4	0	6	2	3	5	10
2002-03	San Antonio	AHL	63	4	11	15	44	2	0	0	0	0

Memorial Cup All-Star Team (2001)

Signed as a free agent by **Florida**, July 3, 2001.

ELLISON, Matt (EHL-ih-suhn, MAT) CHI.

Right wing. Shoots right. 6', 192 lbs. Born, Duncan, B.C., December 8, 1983.
(Chicago's 4th choice, 128th overall, in 2002 Entry Draft).

			Regular Season					Playoffs				
Season	Club	League	GP	G	A	TP	PIM	GP	G	A	TP	PIM
1997-98	Cowichan Valley	BCAHA	24	27	31	58	10	....	....	....	....	....
1998-99	Kerry Park	VIJHL	38	40	47	87	110	....	....	....	....	....
99-2000	Cowichan	BCHL	60	11	23	34	95	....	....	....	....	....
2000-01	Cowichan	BCHL	60	22	44	66	102	....	....	....	....	....
2001-02	Cowichan	BCHL	60	42	*75	*117	76	10	5	6	11	8
2002-03	Red Deer Rebels	WHL	72	40	56	96	80	22	7	13	20	28

BCHL Coastal Division First All-Star Team (2002) • BCHL Coastal Division MVP (2002) • WHL East Second All-Star Team (2003) • Canadian Major Junior Rookie of the Year (2003)

ELOFSSON, Jonas (EHL-uhf-suhn, YOH-nuhs) CHI.

Defense. Shoots left. 6'1", 180 lbs. Born, Ulricehamn, Sweden, January 31, 1979.
(Edmonton's 4th choice, 94th overall, in 1997 Entry Draft).

			Regular Season					Playoffs				
Season	Club	League	GP	G	A	TP	PIM	GP	G	A	TP	PIM
1995-96	Farjestad Jr.	Swede-Jr.	26	6	11	17	18	....	....	....	....	....
1996-97	Farjestad	Sweden	3	0	0	0	0	5	0	1	1	0
	Farjestad	EuroHL	2	1	1	2	0	....	....	....	....	....
1997-98	Farjestad	Sweden	29	3	2	5	14	12	0	1	1	6
	Farjestad	EuroHL	7	1	1	2	4	....	....	....	....	....
1998-99	Farjestad	Sweden	40	2	7	9	18	4	0	0	0	0
	Farjestad	EuroHL	5	1	0	1	4	....	....	....	....	....
99-2000	Farjestad	Sweden	47	3	6	9	44	4	0	0	0	6
2000-01	HV 71 Jonkoping	Sweden	30	1	3	4	12	....	....	....	....	....
	TPS Turku	Finland	10	0	0	0	0	....	....	....	....	....
2001-02	Leksands IF	Sweden	30	8	20	28	12	....	....	....	....	....
	Leksands IF	Swede-Q	10	1	4	5	4	10	1	1	2	10
2002-03	Leksands IF	Sweden	46	6	3	9	26	5	0	0	0	8

Traded to **Chicago** by **Edmonton** with Boris Mironov and Dean McAmmond for Chad Kilger, Daniel Cleary, Ethan Moreau and Christian Laflamme, March 20, 1999.

ELOMO, Teemu (eh-LOH-moh, TEE-moo) DAL.

Left wing. Shoots left. 5'11", 176 lbs. Born, Turku, Finland, January 13, 1979.
(Dallas' 5th choice, 132nd overall, in 1997 Entry Draft).

			Regular Season					Playoffs				
Season	Club	League	GP	G	A	TP	PIM	GP	G	A	TP	PIM
1993-94	TPS Turku-C	Finn-Jr.	34	7	25	32	56	....	....	....	....	....
1994-95	TPS Turku-C	Finn-Jr.	24	19	22	41	82	....	....	....	....	....
	TPS Turku-B	Finn-Jr.	8	5	2	7	12	2	1	0	1	0
1995-96	TPS Turku-B	Finn-Jr.	17	9	8	17	28	....	....	....	....	....
	TPS Turku Jr.	Finn-Jr.	2	0	0	0	0	....	....	....	....	....
	Kiekko-67 Turku	Finland-2	11	1	0	1	14	6	2	0	2	8
1996-97	TPS Turku Jr.	Finn-Jr.	9	6	2	8	16	....	....	....	....	....
	Kiekko-67 Turku	Finland-2	15	4	3	7	24	....	....	....	....	....
	TPS Turku	Finland	6	0	1	1	0	3	0	0	0	2
1997-98	TPS Turku	Finland	26	3	3	6	14	3	1	0	1	2
	TPS Turku	EuroHL	3	0	0	0	2	....	....	....	....	....
1998-99	TPS Turku	Finland	34	4	8	12	16	5	0	0	0	2
99-2000	TPS Turku	Finland	52	9	7	16	28	11	3	2	5	0
2000-01	TPS Turku	Finland	56	2	10	12	44	10	1	3	4	0
2001-02	Blues Espoo	Finland	49	12	14	26	66	3	0	0	0	14
2002-03	Blues Espoo	Finland	54	13	29	42	60	7	1	1	2	4

EMOND, Pierre-Luc (ee-MOHN, pee-AIR-LOOK) COL.

Center. Shoots left. 6', 195 lbs. Born, Valleyfield, Que., October 10, 1982.
(Colorado's 7th choice, 165th overall, in 2001 Entry Draft).

			Regular Season					Playoffs				
Season	Club	League	GP	G	A	TP	PIM	GP	G	A	TP	PIM
1998-99	Gatineau Intrepide	QAAA	42	7	17	24	24	....	....	....	....	....
99-2000	Drummondville	QMJHL	58	8	11	19	74	16	6	3	9	10
2000-01	Drummondville	QMJHL	62	10	36	46	110	6	2	0	2	10
2001-02	Cape Breton	QMJHL	72	19	29	48	63	16	3	2	5	4
2002-03	Hershey Bears	AHL	4	1	0	1	2	....	....	....	....	....
	Cape Breton	QMJHL	48	11	30	41	95	4	1	1	2	4

ENEQVIST, Johan (EHN-uh-kvist, YOH-han) MTL.

Left wing. Shoots left. 6', 183 lbs. Born, Nacka, Sweden, January 21, 1982.
(Montreal's 5th choice, 109th overall, in 2000 Entry Draft).

			Regular Season					Playoffs				
Season	Club	League	GP	G	A	TP	PIM	GP	G	A	TP	PIM
99-2000	Leksands IF-18	Swede-Jr.	5	1	1	2	28	....	....	....	....	....
	Leksands IF Jr.	Swede-Jr.	36	10	13	23	36	2	0	0	0	0
2000-01	Leksands IF Jr.	Swede-Jr.	21	19	15	34	2	2	1	1	2	4
	Leksands IF	Sweden	2	0	0	0	0	....	....	....	....	....
2001-02	Leksands IF Jr.	Swede-Jr.	7	3	6	9	18	....	....	....	....	....
	Leksands IF	Sweden	45	3	7	10	24	....	....	....	....	....
2002-03	Leksands IF	Sweden	42	2	6	8	77	5	0	0	0	6

ERICKSON, Mike (AIR-ihk-suhn, MIGHK) MIN.

Right wing. Shoots right. 6'2", 201 lbs. Born, Minneapolis, MN, April 12, 1983.
(Minnesota's 3rd choice, 72nd overall, in 2002 Entry Draft).

			Regular Season					Playoffs				
Season	Club	League	GP	G	A	TP	PIM	GP	G	A	TP	PIM
1998-99	Eden Prairie Eagles	Hi-School	23	24	18	42	....	....	....	....	....	....
99-2000	Eden Prairie Eagles	Hi-School	25	38	25	63	....	....	....	....	....	....
2000-01	Eden Prairie Eagles	Hi-School	22	24	26	50	....	....	....	....	....	....
	Des Moines	USHL	4	0	0	0	0	3	0	0	0	0
2001-02	U. of Minnesota	WCHA	9	1	2	3	2	....	....	....	....	....
2002-03	U. of Minnesota	WCHA	16	0	2	2	4	....	....	....	....	....
	Des Moines	USHL	28	12	18	30	10	4	1	3	4	0

All-Conference All-Star Team (1999, 2000, 2001)

• Missed majority of 2001-02 season recovering from foot injury suffered in game vs. U. of Minnesota-Duluth (WCHA), November 17, 2001. • Granted leave of absence by U. of Minnesota (WCHA), January 14, 2003. • Signed as a free agent by **Des Moines** (USHL), January 14, 2003.

ERIKSSON, Loui (AIR-ohk-suhn, LOO-ee) DAL.

Left wing. Shoots left. 6'1", 183 lbs. Born, Goteborg, Sweden, July 17, 1985.
(Dallas' 1st choice, 33rd overall, in 2003 Entry Draft).

			Regular Season					Playoffs				
Season	Club	League	GP	G	A	TP	PIM	GP	G	A	TP	PIM
2000-01	Vasteras IK-18	Swede-Jr.	9	5	3	8	4	....	....	....	....	....
	V. Frolunda Jr.	Swede-Jr.	1	0	0	0	0	....	....	....	....	....
2001-02	Vasteras IK-18	Swede-Jr.	1	1	0	1	0	....	....	....	....	....
	V. Frolunda Jr.	Swede-Jr.	35	7	15	22	2	8	2	3	5	2
2002-03	V. Frolunda Jr.	Swede-Jr.	30	16	15	31	10	8	4	6	10	4

ERIKSSON, Tim (AIR-ihk-suhn, TIHM) L.A.

Center. Shoots left. 5'9", 161 lbs. Born, Sodertalje, Sweden, February 5, 1982.
(Los Angeles' 7th choice, 206th overall, in 2000 Entry Draft).

			Regular Season					Playoffs				
Season	Club	League	GP	G	A	TP	PIM	GP	G	A	TP	PIM
1997-98	Sodertalje SK Jr.	Swede-Jr.	11	7	12	19	10	....	....	....	....	....
1998-99	V. Frolunda Jr.	Swede-Jr.	29	7	8	15	6	....	....	....	....	....
99-2000	V. Frolunda Jr.	Swede-Jr.	36	16	25	41	82	....	....	....	....	....
2000-01	Hammarby	Swede-2	1	2	1	3	0	....	....	....	....	....
	Hammarby	Swede-2	38	9	22	31	10	14	2	4	6	8
2001-02	Hammarby	Swede-2	44	10	30	40	34	2	0	1	1	0
2002-03	Linkopings HC	Sweden	49	2	8	10	8	....	....	....	....	....
	Linkopings HC	Swede-Q	10	1	4	5	16	....	....	....	....	....

ESTRADA, Kevin (eh-STRA-duh, KEH-vihn) CAR.

Right wing. Shoots left. 5'11", 185 lbs. Born, Surrey, B.C., May 28, 1982.
(Carolina's 3rd choice, 91st overall, in 2001 Entry Draft).

			Regular Season					Playoffs				
Season	Club	League	GP	G	A	TP	PIM	GP	G	A	TP	PIM
1997-98	Chilliwack Chiefs	BCHL	35	1	5	6	17	....	....	....	....	....
1998-99	Chilliwack Chiefs	BCHL	58	13	29	42	58	....	....	....	....	....
99-2000	Chilliwack Chiefs	BCHL	45	9	20	29	29	30	6	27	33	14
2000-01	Chilliwack Chiefs	BCHL	59	34	*84	*118	65	....	....	....	....	....
2001-02	Michigan State	CCHA	40	4	7	11	24	....	....	....	....	....
2002-03	Michigan State	CCHA	35	7	4	11	16	....	....	....	....	....

BCHL Coastal Conference First All-Star Team (2001)

EVANS, Blake (EH-vans, BLAYK) **ST.L.**

Center. Shoots right. 6'1", 210 lbs. Born, Smiley, Sask., July 2, 1980.
(Washington's 10th choice, 251st overall, in 1998 Entry Draft).

			Regular Season					Playoffs				
Season	**Club**	**League**	**GP**	**G**	**A**	**TP**	**PIM**	**GP**	**G**	**A**	**TP**	**PIM**
1995-96	Sask. Contacts	SMHL	41	15	23	38	84	....	....	....	....	....
1996-97	Spokane Chiefs	WHL	53	4	7	11	19	7	0	0	0	0
1997-98	Spokane Chiefs	WHL	16	6	5	11	29	....	....	....	....	....
	Tri-City Americans	WHL	57	13	29	42	102	....	....	....	....	....
1998-99	Tri-City Americans	WHL	72	18	29	47	131	12	0	4	4	16
99-2000	Tri-City Americans	WHL	72	27	43	70	110	4	1	0	1	6
2000-01	Tri-City Americans	WHL	40	28	31	59	70	....	....	....	....	....
	Regina Pats	WHL	27	24	19	43	50	6	6	2	8	8
2001-02	Worcester IceCats	AHL	28	4	5	9	18	3	0	0	0	2
	Peoria Rivermen	ECHL	43	17	20	37	26	....	....	....	....	....
2002-03	Worcester IceCats	AHL	78	13	21	34	79	3	0	0	0	0

WHL East Second All-Star Team (2001)

Signed as a free agent by **St. Louis**, April 11, 2001.

EVSEEV, Vladislav (yehv-SAY-ehv, VLAD-ih-slav) **BOS.**

Left wing. Shoots left. 6'2", 200 lbs. Born, Moscow, USSR, September 10, 1984.
(Boston's 2nd choice, 56th overall, in 2002 Entry Draft).

			Regular Season					Playoffs				
Season	**Club**	**League**	**GP**	**G**	**A**	**TP**	**PIM**	**GP**	**G**	**A**	**TP**	**PIM**
2000-01	Dyno. Moscow Jr.	Russia-Jr.	6	5	2	7	2	....	....	....	....	....
2001-02	CSKA Moscow 2	Russia-3	8	2	1	3	2	....	....	....	....	....
	HC CSKA	Russia-2	15	2	5	7	10	....	....	....	....	....
2002-03	Dynamo Moscow	Russia	22	1	1	2	2	1	0	0	0	0

EZHOV, Denis (YEHZH-awf, DEH-nihs) **BUF.**

Defense. Shoots left. 5'11", 200 lbs. Born, Togliatti, USSR, February 28, 1985.
(Buffalo's 5th choice, 114th overall, in 2003 Entry Draft).

			Regular Season					Playoffs				
Season	**Club**	**League**	**GP**	**G**	**A**	**TP**	**PIM**	**GP**	**G**	**A**	**TP**	**PIM**
99-2000	Lada Togliatti 2	Russia-3	4	0	0	0	4	....	....	....	....	....
2000-01	Lada Togliatti 2	Russia-3	....	....	....	....	....	....	....	....	....	....
2001-02	Lada Togliatti 2	Russia-3	....	....	....	....	....	....	....	....	....	....
	Lada Togliatti	Russia	15	0	0	0	6	....	....	....	....	....
2002-03	Lada Togliatti 2	Russia-3	15	2	7	9	4	....	....	....	....	....
	CSK VVS Samara	Russia-2	9	0	1	1	8	....	....	....	....	....

FABRY, Branislav (FA-bree, BRAN-ih-slav) **BUF.**

Left wing. Shoots left. 6', 185 lbs. Born, Bratislava, Czech., January 15, 1985.
(Buffalo's 2nd choice, 65th overall, in 2003 Entry Draft).

			Regular Season					Playoffs				
Season	**Club**	**League**	**GP**	**G**	**A**	**TP**	**PIM**	**GP**	**G**	**A**	**TP**	**PIM**
2000-01	Slov. Bratislava Jr.	Slovak-Jr.	47	22	25	47	....	....	....	....	....	....
2001-02	Slov. Bratislava Jr.	Slovak-Jr.	48	29	37	66	....	....	....	....	....	....
2002-03	Slov. Bratislava Jr.	Slovak-Jr.	32	12	15	27	84	....	....	....	....	....
	Slov. Bratislava	Slovakia	8	0	0	0	0	....	....	....	....	....

FALARDEAU, Lee (FAL-ahr-doh, LEE) **NYR**

Center. Shoots left. 6'4", 203 lbs. Born, Midland, MI, July 22, 1983.
(NY Rangers' 1st choice, 33rd overall, in 2002 Entry Draft).

			Regular Season					Playoffs				
Season	**Club**	**League**	**GP**	**G**	**A**	**TP**	**PIM**	**GP**	**G**	**A**	**TP**	**PIM**
1998-99	Det. Honeybaked	MMHL		STATISTICS NOT AVAILABLE								
99-2000	U.S. National U-17	USDP	61	9	14	23	....	....	....	....	....	....
2000-01	U.S. National U-18	USDP	61	10	21	31	26	....	....	....	....	....
2001-02	Michigan State	CCHA	34	4	10	14	24	....	....	....	....	....
2002-03	Michigan State	CCHA	39	9	6	15	39	....	....	....	....	....

FAST, Brad (FAST, BRAD) **CAR.**

Defense. Shoots left. 6', 185 lbs. Born, Fort St. John, B.C., February 21, 1980.
(Carolina's 2nd choice, 84th overall, in 1999 Entry Draft).

			Regular Season					Playoffs				
Season	**Club**	**League**	**GP**	**G**	**A**	**TP**	**PIM**	**GP**	**G**	**A**	**TP**	**PIM**
1994-95	Fort St. John	BCAHA	40	9	26	35	40	....	....	....	....	....
1995-96	Fort St. John	BCAHA	60	53	52	105	70	....	....	....	....	....
1996-97	Prince George	BCHL	49	3	7	10	19	....	....	....	....	....
1997-98	Prince George	BCHL	59	10	33	43	22	....	....	....	....	....
1998-99	Prince George	BCHL	59	27	46	73	....	....	....	....	....	....
99-2000	Michigan State	CCHA	42	5	9	14	20	....	....	....	....	....
2000-01	Michigan State	CCHA	42	4	24	28	16	....	....	....	....	....
2001-02	Michigan State	CCHA	41	10	16	26	26	....	....	....	....	....
2002-03	Michigan State	CCHA	39	11	35	46	28	....	....	....	....	....
	Lowell	AHL	7	0	1	1	12	....	....	....	....	....

CCHA First All-Star Team (2003) • NCAA West Second All-American Team (2003)

FATA, Drew (FA-tuh, DROO) **PIT.**

Defense. Shoots left. 6'1", 209 lbs. Born, Sault Ste. Marie, Ont., July 28, 1983.
(Pittsburgh's 3rd choice, 86th overall, in 2001 Entry Draft).

			Regular Season					Playoffs				
Season	**Club**	**League**	**GP**	**G**	**A**	**TP**	**PIM**	**GP**	**G**	**A**	**TP**	**PIM**
99-2000	St. Michael's B	OPJHL	49	9	18	27	144	....	....	....	....	....
2000-01	St. Michael's	OHL	58	5	15	20	134	18	1	3	4	26
2001-02	St. Michael's	OHL	67	7	21	28	175	15	1	9	10	38
2002-03	St. Michael's	OHL	35	6	13	19	66	....	....	....	....	....
	Kingston	OHL	34	2	17	19	64	....	....	....	....	....

FEDOROV, Yevgeny (FEH-duh-rahf, yehv-GEH-nee) **L.A.**

Center. Shoots left. 5'10", 187 lbs. Born, Sverdlovsk, USSR, November 11, 1980.
(Los Angeles' 6th choice, 201st overall, in 2000 Entry Draft).

			Regular Season					Playoffs				
Season	**Club**	**League**	**GP**	**G**	**A**	**TP**	**PIM**	**GP**	**G**	**A**	**TP**	**PIM**
1997-98	Krylja Sovetov 2	Russia-3	20	1	6	7	48	....	....	....	....	....
	Krylja Sovetov	Russia	32	1	0	1	12	....	....	....	....	....
1998-99	Krylja Sovetov	Russia	52	5	3	8	61	....	....	....	....	....
99-2000	Perm	Russia	37	5	5	10	20	3	0	1	1	4
2000-01	Perm	Russia	43	9	9	18	18	....	....	....	....	....
2001-02	Ak Bars Kazan	Russia	45	10	12	22	12	11	0	0	0	2
2002-03	Ak Bars Kazan	Russia	46	4	11	15	26	5	1	0	1	2

FEHR, Eric (FAIR, AIR-ihk) **WSH.**

Right wing. Shoots right. 6'3", 187 lbs. Born, Winkler, Man., September 7, 1985.
(Washington's 1st choice, 18th overall, in 2003 Entry Draft).

			Regular Season					Playoffs				
Season	**Club**	**League**	**GP**	**G**	**A**	**TP**	**PIM**	**GP**	**G**	**A**	**TP**	**PIM**
2000-01	Pembina	MMHL	36	45	13	58	30	....	....	....	....	....
	Brandon	WHL	4	0	0	0	0	....	....	....	....	....
2001-02	Brandon	WHL	63	11	16	27	29	12	1	1	2	0
2002-03	Brandon	WHL	70	26	29	55	76	17	4	8	12	26

FEMENELLA, Arthur (feh-meh-NEHL-uh, AHR-thuhr) **T.B.**

Defense. Shoots right. 6'7", 235 lbs. Born, Annandale, NJ, June 6, 1982.
(Tampa Bay's 7th choice, 188th overall, in 2001 Entry Draft).

			Regular Season					Playoffs				
Season	**Club**	**League**	**GP**	**G**	**A**	**TP**	**PIM**	**GP**	**G**	**A**	**TP**	**PIM**
1998-99	U.S. National U-17	USDP	51	0	2	2	135	....	....	....	....	....
99-2000	U.S. National U-17	USDP	54	0	8	8	156	....	....	....	....	....
	Sioux City	USHL	3	0	0	0	7	....	....	....	....	....
2000-01	Sioux City	USHL	52	1	1	2	*252	3	0	0	0	2
2001-02	Sioux City	USHL	56	1	10	11	215	12	0	1	1	32
2002-03	Sioux City	USHL	48	1	6	7	197	....	....	....	....	....

• Signed Letter of Intent to attend **U. of Vermont**, April 8, 2003.

FERGUSON, Troy (fuhr-GUH-suhn, TROI) **CAR.**

Right wing. Shoots right. 5'10", 170 lbs. Born, Calgary, Alta., September 30, 1980.
(Carolina's 7th choice, 276th overall, in 2000 Entry Draft).

			Regular Season					Playoffs				
Season	**Club**	**League**	**GP**	**G**	**A**	**TP**	**PIM**	**GP**	**G**	**A**	**TP**	**PIM**
1996-97	Kitchener	OJHL-B	47	14	15	29	16	....	....	....	....	....
1997-98	U.S. National U-18	USDP	54	11	9	20	14	....	....	....	....	....
1998-99	U.S. National U-17	USDP	24	3	10	13	14	....	....	....	....	....
	U.S. National U-18	USDP	29	4	4	8	20	....	....	....	....	....
99-2000	Michigan State	CCHA	42	5	7	12	10	....	....	....	....	....
2000-01	Michigan State	CCHA	41	4	10	14	12	....	....	....	....	....
2001-02	Michigan State	CCHA	39	1	5	6	14	....	....	....	....	....
2002-03	Michigan State	CCHA	39	2	7	9	4	....	....	....	....	....
	Lowell	AHL	6	1	0	1	2	....	....	....	....	....

FERLAND, Jonathan (fair-LAWN, JAWN-ah-thun) **MTL.**

Right wing. Shoots right. 6'2", 208 lbs. Born, Quebec City, Que., February 9, 1983.
(Montreal's 5th choice, 212th overall, in 2002 Entry Draft).

			Regular Season					Playoffs				
Season	**Club**	**League**	**GP**	**G**	**A**	**TP**	**PIM**	**GP**	**G**	**A**	**TP**	**PIM**
1998-99	Levi	QAAA	42	18	17	35	50	....	....	....	....	....
99-2000	Moncton Wildcats	QMJHL	52	3	6	9	21	11	0	1	1	0
2000-01	Acadie-Bathurst	QMJHL	70	17	11	28	135	13	0	4	4	47
2001-02	Acadie-Bathurst	QMJHL	55	28	46	74	104	10	2	10	12	8
2002-03	Acadie-Bathurst	QMJHL	68	45	44	89	94	11	4	5	9	16

FERNHOLM, Daniel (FUHRN-hohlm, DAN-yehl) **PIT.**

Defense. Shoots left. 6'4", 218 lbs. Born, Stockholm, Sweden, December 20, 1983.
(Pittsburgh's 4th choice, 101st overall, in 2002 Entry Draft).

			Regular Season					Playoffs				
Season	**Club**	**League**	**GP**	**G**	**A**	**TP**	**PIM**	**GP**	**G**	**A**	**TP**	**PIM**
99-2000	Mora IK Jr.	Swede-Jr.	33	3	3	6	8	1	0	0	0	0
	Mora IK Jr.	Swede-Jr.	2	1	1	2	4	....	....	....	....	....
2000-01	Mora IK Jr.	Swede-Jr.	3	0	1	1	2	....	....	....	....	....
	Mora IK	Swede-2	2	0	0	0	0	....	....	....	....	....
2001-02	Djurgarden Jr.	Swede-Jr.	8	6	13	19	12	3	0	0	0	0
2002-03	Huddinge IK	Swede-2	39	6	10	16	20	2	1	0	1	0
	Huddinge IK Jr.	Swede-Jr.	1	0	0	0	2	....	....	....	....	....

FIEDLER, Jonas (FIHD-luhr, YOH-nahsh) **S.J.**

Right wing. Shoots right. 6'2", 180 lbs. Born, Jihlava, Czech., May 29, 1984.
(San Jose's 3rd choice, 86th overall, in 2002 Entry Draft).

			Regular Season					Playoffs				
Season	**Club**	**League**	**GP**	**G**	**A**	**TP**	**PIM**	**GP**	**G**	**A**	**TP**	**PIM**
99-2000	Dukla Jihlava Jr.	Czech-Jr.	48	11	11	22	48	....	....	....	....	....
2000-01	Dukla Jihlava Jr.	Czech-Jr.	44	29	33	62	167	....	....	....	....	....
2001-02	Plymouth Whalers	OHL	68	8	12	20	27	6	0	1	1	4
2002-03	Plymouth Whalers	OHL	63	7	21	28	59	18	5	9	14	10

FILEWICH, Jonathan (FIGHL-uh-which, JAWN-ah-thun) **PIT.**

Right wing. Shoots right. 6'2", 208 lbs. Born, Kelowna, B.C., October 2, 1984.
(Pittsburgh's 3rd choice, 70th overall, in 2003 Entry Draft).

			Regular Season					Playoffs				
Season	**Club**	**League**	**GP**	**G**	**A**	**TP**	**PIM**	**GP**	**G**	**A**	**TP**	**PIM**
1998-99	Sherwood Park	AMBHL	36	29	43	72	90	....	....	....	....	....
99-2000	Sherwood Park	AMHL	33	28	20	48	59	....	....	....	....	....
	Prince George	WHL	3	0	0	0	0	....	....	....	....	....
2000-01	Prince George	WHL	61	9	16	25	32	....	....	....	....	....
2001-02	Prince George	WHL	66	13	19	32	23	7	2	0	2	2
2002-03	Prince George	WHL	51	27	27	54	45	5	1	1	2	2

FILIPOWICZ, Jayme (fihl-ih-POW-its, JAY-mee)

Defense. Shoots left. 6'2", 215 lbs. Born, Arlington Heights, IL, June 15, 1976.

			Regular Season					Playoffs				
Season	**Club**	**League**	**GP**	**G**	**A**	**TP**	**PIM**	**GP**	**G**	**A**	**TP**	**PIM**
1994/96	Dubuque	USHL	127	18	55	73	....	....	....	....	....	....
1996-97	New Hampshire	H-East	35	3	16	19	43	....	....	....	....	....
1997-98	New Hampshire	H-East	38	3	28	31	47	....	....	....	....	....
1998-99	New Hampshire	H-East	41	8	30	38	56	....	....	....	....	....
99-2000	Milwaukee	IHL	76	9	23	32	118	3	0	1	1	0
2000-01	Milwaukee	IHL	68	0	13	13	101	2	0	0	0	2
2001-02	Quebec Citadelles	AHL	63	0	7	7	107	1	0	0	0	2
2002-03	Saint John Flames	AHL	63	2	13	15	106	....	....	....	....	....
	Richmond	ECHL	20	1	8	9	36	....	....	....	....	....

• Statistics for **Dubuque** (USHL) are career totals for 1994-1996 seasons. • Hockey East First All-Star Team (1999) • NCAA East Second All-American Team (1999) • NCAA Championship All-Tournament Team (1999)

Signed as a free agent by **Nashville**, June 17, 1999.

FILPPULA, Valtteri (FIHL-poo-luh, VAL-tuhr-ee) DET.

Center. Shoots left. 5'11", 172 lbs. Born, Vantaa, Finland, March 20, 1984.
(Detroit's 3rd choice, 95th overall, in 2002 Entry Draft).

			Regular Season					Playoffs				
Season	Club	League	GP	G	A	TP	PIM	GP	G	A	TP	PIM
2000-01	Jokerit Helsinki-B	Finn-Jr.	31	18	29	47	4	....	....	....	....	....
	Jokerit Helsinki Jr.	Finn-Jr.	1	0	1	1	0	....	....	....	....	....
2001-02	Jokerit Helsinki-B	Finn-Jr.	1	0	1	1	0	....	....	....	....	....
	Jokerit Helsinki Jr.	Finn-Jr.	40	8	15	23	14	9	4	9	13	2
2002-03	Jokerit Helsinki Jr.	Finn-Jr.	35	16	37	53	39	11	4	10	14	4

FINGER, Jeff (FIHN-guhr, JEHF) COL.

Defense. Shoots left. 6'1", 195 lbs. Born, Hancock, MI, December 18, 1979.
(Colorado's 11th choice, 240th overall, in 1999 Entry Draft).

			Regular Season					Playoffs				
Season	Club	League	GP	G	A	TP	PIM	GP	G	A	TP	PIM
1997-98	Green Bay	USHL	51	5	9	14	208	4	0	0	0	18
1998-99	Green Bay	USHL	54	11	28	39	199	6	0	3	3	14
99-2000	Green Bay	USHL	55	13	35	48	15	14	3	11	14	40
2000-01	St. Cloud State	WCHA	41	4	5	9	84	....	....	....	....	....
2001-02	St. Cloud State	WCHA	42	6	20	26	105	....	....	....	....	....
2002-03	St. Cloud State	WCHA	24	5	8	13	46	....	....	....	....	....

FITZGERALD, Zach (FIHTZ-jair-uhld, ZAK) ST.L.

Defense. Shoots left. 6'2", 205 lbs. Born, Two Harbors, MN, June 16, 1985.
(St. Louis' 4th choice, 88th overall, in 2003 Entry Draft).

			Regular Season					Playoffs				
Season	Club	League	GP	G	A	TP	PIM	GP	G	A	TP	PIM
2001-02	Seattle	WHL	61	3	7	10	214	10	0	2	2	19
2002-03	Seattle	WHL	64	8	14	22	232	15	0	4	4	33

FITZRANDOLPH, Colin (fihts-RAN-dawlf, KAW-lihn) ATL.

Center. Shoots left. 6'3", 220 lbs. Born, Canton, NY, April 23, 1982.
(Atlanta's 8th choice, 201st overall, in 2001 Entry Draft).

			Regular Season					Playoffs				
Season	Club	League	GP	G	A	TP	PIM	GP	G	A	TP	PIM
2000-01	Phillips Exeter	Hi-School	23	7	33	40	....	....	....	....	....	....
2001-02	St. Lawrence	ECAC	13	0	3	3	21	....	....	....	....	....
2002-03	St. Lawrence	ECAC	31	2	4	6	16	....	....	....	....	....

FLACHE, Paul (FLAK, PAWL) ATL.

Defense. Shoots right. 6'5", 215 lbs. Born, Toronto, Ont., March 4, 1982.
(Atlanta's 5th choice, 144th overall, in 2002 Entry Draft).

			Regular Season					Playoffs				
Season	Club	League	GP	G	A	TP	PIM	GP	G	A	TP	PIM
1998-99	Cobourg Cougars	OPJHL	41	1	6	7	50	....	....	....	....	....
99-2000	Brampton	OHL	54	1	0	1	59	6	0	0	0	8
2000-01	Brampton	OHL	68	8	16	24	100	9	1	1	2	18
2001-02	Brampton	OHL	68	9	35	44	148	....	....	....	....	....
2002-03	Greenville Grrrowl	ECHL	46	1	9	10	64	4	0	4	4	6

• Re-entered NHL Entry Draft. Originally Edmonton's 5th choice, 152nd overall, in 2000 Entry Draft.

FLEISCHMANN, Tomas (FLIGHSH-muhn, TAW-mash) DET.

Left wing. Shoots left. 6', 165 lbs. Born, Koprivnice, Czech., May 16, 1984.
(Detroit's 2nd choice, 63rd overall, in 2002 Entry Draft).

			Regular Season					Playoffs				
Season	Club	League	GP	G	A	TP	PIM	GP	G	A	TP	PIM
99-2000	HC Vitkovice Jr.	Czech-Jr.	46	9	13	22	6	....	....	....	....	....
2000-01	HC Vitkovice-18	Czech-Jr.	30	28	34	62	8	....	....	....	....	....
	HC Vitkovice Jr.	Czech-Jr.	21	4	9	13	8	....	....	....	....	....
2001-02	HC Vitkovice Jr.	Czech-Jr.	46	26	35	51	16	....	....	....	....	....
	TJ Novy Jicin	Czech-3	8	3	2	5	8	7	3	4	7	35
2002-03	Moose Jaw	WHL	65	21	50	71	36	12	4	11	15	6

FLYNN, Rob (FLIHN, RAWB) NYR

Right wing. Shoots right. 6'2", 210 lbs. Born, Boston, MA, January 8, 1983.
(NY Rangers' 9th choice, 270th overall, in 2002 Entry Draft).

			Regular Season					Playoffs				
Season	Club	League	GP	G	A	TP	PIM	GP	G	A	TP	PIM
99-2000	Milton Academy	Hi-School	30	27	29	56	....	....	....	....	....	....
2000-01	U.S. National U-18	USDP	65	8	17	25	50	....	....	....	....	....
2001-02	Harvard University	ECAC	30	1	3	4	6	....	....	....	....	....
2002-03	Harvard University	ECAC	19	4	1	5	14	....	....	....	....	....

FOLEY, Patrick (FOH-lee, PAT-rihk) PIT.

Left wing. Shoots left. 6'1", 220 lbs. Born, Boston, MA, January 24, 1981.
(Pittsburgh's 6th choice, 185th overall, in 2000 Entry Draft).

			Regular Season					Playoffs				
Season	Club	League	GP	G	A	TP	PIM	GP	G	A	TP	PIM
1996-97	St. Sebastian's	Hi-School	23	11	12	23	....	....	....	....	....	....
1997-98	St. Sebastian's	Hi-School	25	17	24	41	....	....	....	....	....	....
	U.S. National U-18	USDP	8	3	3	6	8	....	....	....	....	....
1998-99	U.S. National U-17	USDP	52	7	9	16	146	....	....	....	....	....
99-2000	New Hampshire	H-East	30	3	7	10	61	....	....	....	....	....
2000-01	New Hampshire	H-East	DID NOT PLAY – INJURED									
2001-02	New Hampshire	H-East	35	8	4	12	58	....	....	....	....	....
2002-03	New Hampshire	H-East	39	8	10	18	38	....	....	....	....	....

• Missed entire 2000-01 season recovering from head injury suffered in game vs. U. Mass-Lowell (H-East), February 4, 2000.

FORBES, Ian (FOHRBZ, EE-an)

Defense. Shoots left. 6'6", 215 lbs. Born, Brampton, Ont., August 2, 1980.
(Philadelphia's 3rd choice, 51st overall, in 1998 Entry Draft).

			Regular Season					Playoffs				
Season	Club	League	GP	G	A	TP	PIM	GP	G	A	TP	PIM
1996-97	Mississauga Reps	MTHL	39	10	32	42	178	....	....	....	....	....
1997-98	Guelph Fire	OJHL-B	3	0	1	1	19	....	....	....	....	....
	Guelph Storm	OHL	61	2	3	5	164	12	0	0	0	16
1998-99	Guelph Storm	OHL	60	1	8	9	182	5	0	1	1	8
99-2000	Guelph Storm	OHL	62	2	7	9	143	6	0	0	0	11
2000-01	Trenton Titans	ECHL	33	0	2	2	133	....	....	....	....	....
2001-02	Trenton Titans	ECHL	42	0	5	5	204	....	....	....	....	....
	Philadelphia	AHL	18	1	0	1	50	2	0	0	0	0
2002-03	Philadelphia	AHL	20	1	1	2	38	....	....	....	....	....
	Trenton Titans	ECHL	32	0	2	2	122	3	0	0	0	2

FORREST, J.D. (FOH-rehst, JAY-DEE) CAR.

Defense. Shoots left. 5'9", 170 lbs. Born, Auburn, NY, April 15, 1981.
(Carolina's 5th choice, 181st overall, in 2000 Entry Draft).

			Regular Season					Playoffs				
Season	Club	League	GP	G	A	TP	PIM	GP	G	A	TP	PIM
1997-98	U.S. National U-18	USDP	74	7	26	33	41	....	....	....	....	....
1998-99	U.S. National U-17	USDP	2	1	0	1	4	....	....	....	....	....
	U.S. National U-18	USDP	48	5	21	26	34	....	....	....	....	....
99-2000	U.S. National U-17	USDP	49	6	28	34	36	....	....	....	....	....
	U.S. National U-18	USDP	8	0	0	0	2	....	....	....	....	....
2000-01	Boston College	H-East	38	6	17	23	40	....	....	....	....	....
2001-02	Boston College	H-East	35	8	19	27	28	....	....	....	....	....
2002-03	Boston College	H-East	34	6	25	31	28	....	....	....	....	....

NAJHL All-League First All-Star Team (2000) • Hockey East Second All-Star Team (2003) • NCAA East Second All-American Team (2003)

FORSANDER, Johan (fohr-SAHN-duhr, YOH-hahn) DET.

Left wing. Shoots left. 6'1", 174 lbs. Born, Jonkoping, Sweden, April 28, 1978.
(Detroit's 3rd choice, 108th overall, in 1996 Entry Draft).

			Regular Season					Playoffs				
Season	Club	League	GP	G	A	TP	PIM	GP	G	A	TP	PIM
1994-95	HV 71 Jr.	Swede-Jr.	25	2	2	4	6	....	....	....	....	....
1995-96	HV 71 Jr.	Swede-Jr.	27	15	8	23	12	....	....	....	....	....
	HV 71 Jonkoping	Sweden	6	0	0	0	0	3	0	0	0	2
1996-97	HV 71 Jr.	Swede-Jr.	6	7	3	10	6	....	....	....	....	....
	HV 71 Jonkoping	Sweden	44	3	2	5	6	5	0	0	0	0
1997-98	HV 71 Jr.	Swede-Jr.	5	1	1	2	6	....	....	....	....	....
	HV 71 Jonkoping	Sweden	46	3	2	5	12	5	0	0	0	0
1998-99	HV 71 Jonkoping	Sweden	48	5	4	9	6	....	....	....	....	....
99-2000	HV 71 Jonkoping	Sweden	48	9	9	18	6	6	0	0	0	4
2000-01	HV 71 Jonkoping	Sweden	DID NOT PLAY – INJURED									
2001-02	Djurgarden	Sweden	48	5	6	11	16	5	0	0	0	4
2002-03	Djurgarden	Sweden	41	1	2	3	49	10	2	2	4	4

• Missed entire 2000-01 season recovering from foot injury suffered in training camp, September 2, 2000.

FORSTER, Beat (FOHRS-tuhr, BEE-at) PHX.

Defense. Shoots left. 6'1", 209 lbs. Born, Herisau, Switz., February 2, 1983.
(Phoenix's 4th choice, 78th overall, in 2001 Entry Draft).

			Regular Season					Playoffs				
Season	Club	League	GP	G	A	TP	PIM	GP	G	A	TP	PIM
99-2000	HC Davos Jr.	Swiss-Jr.	34	4	15	19	40	6	1	0	1	6
2000-01	HC Davos Jr.	Swiss-Jr.	27	6	7	13	44	....	....	....	....	....
	SC Hersiau	Swiss-2	3	0	0	0	16	....	....	....	....	....
	HC Davos	Swiss	7	0	0	0	6	3	0	0	0	2
2001-02	HC Davos	Swiss-Jr.	4	2	2	4	12	....	....	....	....	....
	HC Davos	Swiss	33	1	3	4	51	16	0	1	1	2
2002-03	HC Davos	Swiss	30	1	4	5	24	17	0	1	1	16

FOSTER, Adrian (FAW-stuhr, AY-dree-uhn) N.J.

Center. Shoots left. 6'1", 205 lbs. Born, Lethbridge, Alta., January 15, 1982.
(New Jersey's 1st choice, 28th overall, in 2001 Entry Draft).

			Regular Season					Playoffs				
Season	Club	League	GP	G	A	TP	PIM	GP	G	A	TP	PIM
1997-98	Calgary Buffaloes	AMHL	36	26	54	80	50	9	3	14	17	18
1998-99	Calgary Canucks	AJHL	18	15	17	32	18	....	....	....	....	....
99-2000	Saskatoon Blades	WHL	7	1	2	3	6	....	....	....	....	....
2000-01	Saskatoon Blades	WHL	5	0	5	5	4	....	....	....	....	....
2001-02	Saskatoon Blades	WHL	13	9	3	12	18	....	....	....	....	....
	Brandon	WHL	14	5	10	15	23	15	4	11	15	14
2002-03	Albany River Rats	AHL	9	3	0	3	4	....	....	....	....	....

• Missed majority of 1998-99 season recovering from ankle injury. • Missed majority of 1999-2000, 2000-01, 2001-02 and 2002-03 seasons recovering from abdominal injury, October, 1999.

FOY, Matt (FOI, MAT) MIN.

Right wing. Shoots right. 6'2", 219 lbs. Born, Oakville, Ont., May 18, 1983.
(Minnesota's 6th choice, 175th overall, in 2002 Entry Draft).

			Regular Season					Playoffs				
Season	Club	League	GP	G	A	TP	PIM	GP	G	A	TP	PIM
2000-01	Wexford Raiders	OPJHL	47	43	49	92	30	....	....	....	....	....
2001-02	Merrimack College	H-East	31	7	17	24	48	....	....	....	....	....
2002-03	Ottawa 67's	OHL	68	61	71	132	112	21	11	20	31	47

OHL First All-Star Team (2003)

• Officially announced intention to withdraw from **Merrimack** (H-East) for academic reasons, May 30, 2002.

FRASER, Colin (FRAY-zuhr, KAW-lihn) PHI.

Center. Shoots left. 6', 175 lbs. Born, Sicamous, B.C., January 28, 1985.
(Philadelphia's 3rd choice, 69th overall, in 2003 Entry Draft).

			Regular Season					Playoffs				
Season	Club	League	GP	G	A	TP	PIM	GP	G	A	TP	PIM
2000-01	Port Coquitlam	PIJHL	38	16	24	40	90	8	2	2	4	21
2001-02	Red Deer Rebels	WHL	67	11	31	42	126	23	2	1	3	39
2002-03	Red Deer Rebels	WHL	69	15	37	52	192	22	7	6	13	40

FRETTER, Colton (FREH-tuhr, KOHL-tuhn) ATL.

Center. Shoots right. 5'10", 187 lbs. Born, Harrow, Ont., March 12, 1982.
(Atlanta's 8th choice, 230th overall, in 2002 Entry Draft).

			Regular Season					Playoffs				
Season	Club	League	GP	G	A	TP	PIM	GP	G	A	TP	PIM
2000-01	Chatham Maroons	OJHL-B	54	33	39	72	....	15	7	6	13	....
2001-02	Chatham Maroons	OJHL-B	52	51	53	104	62	15	5	3	8	2
2002-03	Michigan State	CCHA	35	7	15	22	36	....	....	....	....	....

FRIED, Robert (FREED, RAW-buhrt) FLA.

Right wing. Shoots right. 6'2", 210 lbs. Born, Philadelphia, PA, March 8, 1981.
(Florida's 2nd choice, 77th overall, in 2000 Entry Draft).

			Regular Season					Playoffs				
Season	Club	League	GP	G	A	TP	PIM	GP	G	A	TP	PIM
1998-99	Deerfield Academy	Hi-School	24	13	20	33	28	....	....	....	....	....
99-2000	Deerfield Academy	Hi-School	26	25	20	45	35	....	....	....	....	....
2000-01	Harvard University	ECAC	30	4	1	5	22	....	....	....	....	....
2001-02	Harvard University	ECAC	31	7	5	12	16	....	....	....	....	....
2002-03	Harvard University	ECAC	33	3	10	13	26	....	....	....	....	....

FRITSCHE, Dan (FRIHCH, DAN) **CBJ**

Center. Shoots right. 6'1", 198 lbs. Born, Cleveland, OH, July 13, 1985.
(Columbus' 2nd choice, 46th overall, in 2003 Entry Draft).

			Regular Season					Playoffs				
Season	Club	League	GP	G	A	TP	PIM	GP	G	A	TP	PIM
2000-01	Cleveland Barons	NAJHL	49	23	29	52	47	1	1	1	2	0
2001-02	Sarnia Sting	OHL	17	5	13	18	20	....	....	....	....	....
2002-03	Sarnia Sting	OHL	61	32	39	71	79	5	2	2	4	4

• Missed majority of 2001-02 season recovering from shoulder surgery, December 12, 2001.

FROGREN, Jonas (FREW-grehn, YOH-nuhs) **CGY.**

Defense. Shoots left. 6'1", 190 lbs. Born, Falun, Sweden, August 28, 1980.
(Calgary's 8th choice, 206th overall, in 1998 Entry Draft).

			Regular Season					Playoffs				
Season	Club	League	GP	G	A	TP	PIM	GP	G	A	TP	PIM
1996-97	Farjestad Jr.	Swede-Jr.	20	2	7	9	4	....	....	....	....	....
1997-98	Farjestad Jr.	Swede-Jr.	28	5	6	11	12	2	1	0	1	0
1998-99	Farjestad Jr.	Swede-Jr.	28	10	8	18	16	6	0	2	2	10
	Farjestad	Sweden	22	0	0	0	2	....	....	....	....	....
99-2000	Bofors IK	Swede-2	43	2	7	9	40	....	....	....	....	....
2000-01	Farjestad	Sweden	49	3	0	3	10	16	0	0	0	4
2001-02	Farjestad	Sweden	50	3	6	9	18	10	0	0	0	4
2002-03	Farjestad	Sweden	50	1	7	8	48	14	0	0	0	16

FUSSEY, Owen (FOO-see, OH-when) **WSH.**

Right wing. Shoots left. 6', 185 lbs. Born, Winnipeg, Man., April 2, 1983.
(Washington's 2nd choice, 90th overall, in 2001 Entry Draft).

			Regular Season					Playoffs				
Season	Club	League	GP	G	A	TP	PIM	GP	G	A	TP	PIM
1998-99	Winnipeg Warriors	MMHL	40	38	33	71	24	....	....	....	....	....
99-2000	Calgary Hitmen	WHL	51	7	6	13	35	12	3	4	7	2
2000-01	Calgary Hitmen	WHL	48	15	10	25	33	12	2	1	3	6
2001-02	Calgary Hitmen	WHL	72	43	27	70	61	7	3	1	4	4
2002-03	Calgary Hitmen	WHL	39	17	18	35	31	....	....	....	....	....
	Moose Jaw	WHL	27	24	12	36	20	13	6	6	12	10

GABINET, Mike (GA-bihn-AY, MIGHK) **L.A.**

Defense. Shoots left. 6'3", 180 lbs. Born, Edmonton, Alta., September 26, 1981.
(Los Angeles' 10th choice, 237th overall, in 2001 Entry Draft).

			Regular Season					Playoffs				
Season	Club	League	GP	G	A	TP	PIM	GP	G	A	TP	PIM
1998-99	Edmonton Leafs	AMHL	33	1	15	16	34	....	....	....	....	....
99-2000	Lloydminster	AJHL	56	4	25	29	30	9	2	4	6	4
2000-01	Nebraska-Omaha	CCHA	30	2	13	15	14	....	....	....	....	....
2001-02	Nebraska-Omaha	CCHA	21	0	4	4	8	....	....	....	....	....
2002-03	Nebraska-Omaha	CCHA	40	0	4	4	46	....	....	....	....	....

AJHL North First All-Star Team (2000)

GAJIC, Milan (GAY-jihk, MEE-lan) **ATL.**

Center. Shoots right. 5'11", 182 lbs. Born, Vancouver, B.C., January 6, 1981.
(Atlanta's 4th choice, 112th overall, in 2001 Entry Draft).

			Regular Season					Playoffs				
Season	Club	League	GP	G	A	TP	PIM	GP	G	A	TP	PIM
1997-98	Merritt	BCHL	51	6	14	20	....	....	....	....	....	....
1998-99	Burnaby Bulldogs	BCHL	56	29	30	59	41	....	....	....	....	....
99-2000	Burnaby Bulldogs	BCHL	56	34	47	81	42	....	....	....	....	....
2000-01	Burnaby Bulldogs	BCHL	50	46	52	98	84	....	....	....	....	....
2001-02	U. of Michigan	CCHA	39	9	13	22	22	....	....	....	....	....
2002-03	U. of Michigan	CCHA	38	11	10	21	38	....	....	....	....	....

GELLARD, Mike (GEHL-ahrd, MIGHK) **BOS.**

Left wing. Shoots left. 6'1", 193 lbs. Born, Markham, Ont., October 10, 1978.

			Regular Season					Playoffs				
Season	Club	League	GP	G	A	TP	PIM	GP	G	A	TP	PIM
1995-96	Thornhill Islanders	MTJHL	49	15	24	39	2	16	6	9	15	0
1996-97	Thornhill Islanders	MTJHL	43	29	37	66	4	9	3	10	13	0
1997-98	St. Lawrence	ECAC	31	4	6	10	18	....	....	....	....	....
1998-99	St. Lawrence	ECAC	39	10	11	21	22	....	....	....	....	....
99-2000	St. Lawrence	ECAC	36	14	22	36	36	....	....	....	....	....
2000-01	St. Lawrence	ECAC	37	19	*38	*57	14	....	....	....	....	....
2001-02			DID NOT PLAY									
2002-03	Providence Bruins	AHL	63	5	11	16	24	4	0	0	0	2

MTJHL Metro All-Star Team (1997) • MTJHL Central Sportsmanlike Player of the Year (1997) • ECAC First All-Star Team (2001)

Signed as a free agent by **Boston**, August 2, 2001. • Missed entire 2001-02 season recovering from viral infection diagnosed during training camp, September 20, 2001.

GENOVY, Jeff (jeh-NOH-vee, JEHF) **CBJ**

Left wing. Shoots left. 6'3", 191 lbs. Born, Kalamazoo, MI, December 4, 1982.
(Columbus' 4th choice, 96th overall, in 2002 Entry Draft).

			Regular Season					Playoffs				
Season	Club	League	GP	G	A	TP	PIM	GP	G	A	TP	PIM
1998-99	Soo Hawks	GLHL	43	10	10	20	39	....	....	....	....	....
99-2000	West-Michigan	MMHL		STATISTICS NOT AVAILABLE								
	Det. Compuware	NAJHL	9	0	3	3	2	2	0	0	0	0
2000-01	Sault Ste. Marie	NAJHL	54	12	14	26	26	8	0	1	1	4
2001-02	Des Moines	USHL	52	23	23	46	86	3	1	4	5	2
2002-03	Clarkson Knights	ECAC	34	5	8	13	45	....	....	....	....	....

GENS, Matt (GEHZ, MAT) **VAN.**

Defense. Shoots right. 6', 180 lbs. Born, Detroit Lakes, MN, March 31, 1983.
(Vancouver's 11th choice, 278th overall, in 2002 Entry Draft).

			Regular Season					Playoffs				
Season	Club	League	GP	G	A	TP	PIM	GP	G	A	TP	PIM
99-2000	U.S. National U-17	USDP	54	4	9	13	46	....	....	....	....	....
2000-01	U.S. National U-18	USDP	57	14	13	27	50	....	....	....	....	....
2001-02	St. Cloud State	WCHA	40	6	17	23	28	....	....	....	....	....
2002-03	St. Cloud State	WCHA	36	4	10	14	30	....	....	....	....	....

GETZLAF, Ryan (GEHTZ-laf, RIGH-uhn) **ANA.**

Center. Shoots right. 6'2", 195 lbs. Born, Regina, Sask., May 10, 1985.
(Anaheim's 1st choice, 19th overall, in 2003 Entry Draft).

			Regular Season					Playoffs				
Season	Club	League	GP	G	A	TP	PIM	GP	G	A	TP	PIM
2000-01	Regina Rangers	SBHL	41	33	41	74	189	....	....	....	....	....
	Regina P.C.	SMHL	8	4	3	7	8	....	....	....	....	....
2001-02	Calgary Hitmen	WHL	63	9	9	18	34	7	2	1	3	4
2002-03	Calgary Hitmen	WHL	70	29	39	68	121	5	1	1	2	6

GIBBONS, Ryan (GIH-buhnz, RIGH-uhn) **PHX.**

Right wing. Shoots right. 6'4", 210 lbs. Born, N. Vancouver, B.C., January 1, 1985.
(Phoenix's 4th choice, 178th overall, in 2003 Entry Draft).

			Regular Season					Playoffs				
Season	Club	League	GP	G	A	TP	PIM	GP	G	A	TP	PIM
2001-02	Seattle	WHL	49	2	2	4	41	10	0	0	0	2
2002-03	Seattle	WHL	67	9	6	15	91	15	3	1	4	22

GILBERT, Tom (GIHL-buhrt, TAWM) **COL.**

Defense. Shoots right. 6'2", 190 lbs. Born, Minneapolis, MN, January 10, 1983.
(Colorado's 5th choice, 129th overall, in 2002 Entry Draft).

			Regular Season					Playoffs				
Season	Club	League	GP	G	A	TP	PIM	GP	G	A	TP	PIM
99-2000	Bloomington-Jeff.	Hi-School	18	7	18	25	....	....	....	....	....	....
2000-01	Bloomington-Jeff.	Hi-School	23	20	18	38	....	....	....	....	....	....
	Chicago Steel	USHL	1	0	0	0	0	....	....	....	....	....
2001-02	Chicago Steel	USHL	57	13	15	28	62	4	0	0	0	4
2002-03	U. of Wisconsin	WCHA	39	7	13	20	36	....	....	....	....	....

GIMAYEV, Sergei (gih-MIGH-ehv, SAIR-gay) **OTT.**

Defense. Shoots left. 6'1", 183 lbs. Born, Moscow, USSR, February 16, 1984.
(Ottawa's 6th choice, 166th overall, in 2003 Entry Draft).

			Regular Season					Playoffs				
Season	Club	League	GP	G	A	TP	PIM	GP	G	A	TP	PIM
2001-02	CSKA Moscow 2	Russia-3	36	0	10	10	50	....	....	....	....	....
2002-03	Cherepovets	Russia	11	0	0	0	4	....	....	....	....	....

GIROUX, Alexandre (ZHIH-roo, al-ehx-AN-dreh) **OTT.**

Center/Left wing. Shoots left. 6'3", 190 lbs. Born, Quebec City, Que., June 16, 1981.
(Ottawa's 9th choice, 213th overall, in 1999 Entry Draft).

			Regular Season					Playoffs				
Season	Club	League	GP	G	A	TP	PIM	GP	G	A	TP	PIM
1997-98	Ste-Foy	QAAA	42	28	30	58	96	....	....	....	....	....
1998-99	Hull Olympiques	QMJHL	67	15	22	37	124	22	2	2	4	8
99-2000	Hull Olympiques	QMJHL	72	52	47	99	117	15	12	6	18	30
2000-01	Hull Olympiques	QMJHL	38	31	32	63	62	....	....	....	....	....
	Rouyn-Noranda	QMJHL	25	13	14	27	56	9	2	6	8	22
2001-02	Grand Rapids	AHL	70	11	16	27	74	....	....	....	....	....
2002-03	Binghamton	AHL	67	19	16	35	101	10	1	0	1	10

GLADSKIKH, Evgeny (glad-SKEEKH, ehv-GEH-nee) **VAN.**

Right wing. Shoots left. 6', 176 lbs. Born, Magnitogorsk, USSR, April 24, 1982.
(Vancouver's 3rd choice, 114th overall, in 2001 Entry Draft).

			Regular Season					Playoffs				
Season	Club	League	GP	G	A	TP	PIM	GP	G	A	TP	PIM
1998-99	Magnitogorsk 2	Russia-4	16	3	3	6	6	....	....	....	....	....
99-2000	Magnitogorsk 2	Russia-3	39	17	2	19	24	....	....	....	....	....
	Magnitogorsk	Russia	1	0	0	0	0	....	....	....	....	....
2000-01	Magnitogorsk 2	Russia-3	11	10	7	17	6	....	....	....	....	....
	Magnitogorsk	Russia	31	3	5	8	10	12	0	2	2	2
2001-02	Magnitogorsk	Russia	32	5	6	11	6	4	0	0	0	4
2002-03	Magnitogorsk	Russia	42	4	7	11	18	3	0	0	0	2

GLAZACHEV, Konstantin (GLAH-zuh-chehv, kawn-stuhn-TIHN) **NSH.**

Left wing. Shoots right. 6', 165 lbs. Born, Arkhangelsk, USSR, February 18, 1985.
(Nashville's 2nd choice, 35th overall, in 2003 Entry Draft).

			Regular Season					Playoffs				
Season	Club	League	GP	G	A	TP	PIM	GP	G	A	TP	PIM
2001-02	Yaroslavl-18	Russia-Jr.	30	22	21	43	38	....	....	....	....	....
	Yaroslavl-2	Russia-3	7	5	6	11	6	....	....	....	....	....
2002-03	Yaroslavl-2	Russia-3		STATISTICS NOT AVAILABLE								
	Yaroslavl	Russia	13	3	4	7	4	4	0	0	0	0

GLEASON, Tim (GLEE-suhn, TIHM) **L.A.**

Defense. Shoots left. 6'1", 202 lbs. Born, Southfield, MI, January 29, 1983.
(Ottawa's 2nd choice, 23rd overall, in 2001 Entry Draft).

			Regular Season					Playoffs				
Season	Club	League	GP	G	A	TP	PIM	GP	G	A	TP	PIM
1998-99	Leamington Flyers	OJHL-B	52	5	26	31	76	....	....	....	....	....
99-2000	Windsor Spitfires	OHL	55	5	13	18	101	12	2	4	6	14
2000-01	Windsor Spitfires	OHL	47	8	28	36	124	9	1	2	3	23
2001-02	Windsor Spitfires	OHL	67	17	42	59	109	16	7	13	20	40
2002-03	Windsor Spitfires	OHL	45	7	31	38	75	7	5	2	7	17

Rights traded to **Los Angeles** by **Ottawa** with future considerations for Bryan Smolinski, March 11, 2003.

GLENN, Ryan (GLEHN, RIGH-unh) **MTL.**

Defense. Shoots left. 6'3", 210 lbs. Born, New Westminster, B.C., June 7, 1980.
(Montreal's 7th choice, 145th overall, in 2000 Entry Draft).

			Regular Season					Playoffs				
Season	Club	League	GP	G	A	TP	PIM	GP	G	A	TP	PIM
99-2000	Walpole Jr. Stars	EJHL	42	19	40	59	54	8	4	13	17	....
2000-01	St. Lawrence	ECAC	37	3	1	4	34	....	....	....	....	....
2001-02	St. Lawrence	ECAC	32	3	6	9	27	....	....	....	....	....
2002-03	St. Lawrence	ECAC	36	5	9	14	42	....	....	....	....	....

EJHL First All-Star Team (2000) • EJHL Defencemen of the Year (2000)

GLOBKE, Rob (GLAWB-kee, RAWB) **FLA.**

Center. Shoots right. 6'2", 200 lbs. Born, Farmington, MI, October 24, 1982.
(Florida's 3rd choice, 40th overall, in 2002 Entry Draft).

			Regular Season					Playoffs				
Season	Club	League	GP	G	A	TP	PIM	GP	G	A	TP	PIM
1998-99	Det. Compuware	NAJHL	55	8	14	22	111	7	1	2	3	2
99-2000	U.S. National U-18	USDP	54	15	21	36	68	....	....	....	....	....
2000-01	U. of Notre Dame	CCHA	33	17	9	26	74	....	....	....	....	....
2001-02	U. of Notre Dame	CCHA	33	11	11	22	79	....	....	....	....	....
2002-03	U. of Notre Dame	CCHA	40	21	15	36	44	....	....	....	....	....

GLOVER, Dan (GLUH-vuhr, DAN) **N.J.**

Defense. Shoots left. 6'2", 175 lbs. Born, Delburne, Alta., May 4, 1983.
(New Jersey's 10th choice, 250th overall, in 2002 Entry Draft).

			Regular Season					Playoffs				
Season	Club	League	GP	G	A	TP	PIM	GP	G	A	TP	PIM
2000-01	Red Deer Chiefs	AMHL	35	1	5	6	40	....	....	....	....	....
2001-02	Camrose Kodiacs	AJHL	55	1	10	11	110	....	....	....	....	....
2002-03	Camrose Kodiacs	AJHL	61	5	14	19	118	27	0	6	6	32

GOC, Marcel (GAWCH, mahr-SEHL) S.J.

Center. Shoots left. 6'1", 190 lbs. Born, Calw, West Germany, August 24, 1983.
(San Jose's 1st choice, 20th overall, in 2001 Entry Draft).

			Regular Season					Playoffs				
Season	Club	League	GP	G	A	TP	PIM	GP	G	A	TP	PIM
1998-99	Schwenningen Jr.	Ger.-Jr.	12	23	10	33	12	....	....	....	....	....
99-2000	Schwenningen	Germany	51	0	3	3	4	11	1	1	2	2
2000-01	Schwenningen	Germany	58	13	28	41	12	....	....	....	....	....
2001-02	Schwenningen	Germany	45	8	9	17	24	....	....	....	....	....
	Adler Mannheim	Germany	8	0	2	2	0	....	....	....	....	....
2002-03	Adler Mannheim	Germany	36	6	14	20	16	8	1	2	3	0

GOERTZEN, Steve (GUHRT-sehn, STEEV) CBJ

Right wing. Shoots right. 6'1", 190 lbs. Born, Stony Plain, Alta., May 26, 1984.
(Columbus' 11th choice, 225th overall, in 2002 Entry Draft).

			Regular Season					Playoffs				
Season	Club	League	GP	G	A	TP	PIM	GP	G	A	TP	PIM
99-2000	Spruce Grove	AMBHL	36	16	17	33	30	....	....	....	....	....
2000-01	St. Albert Raiders	AMHL	34	11	19	30	70	....	....	....	....	....
	St. Albert Saints	AJHL	1	0	0	0	0	....	....	....	....	....
2001-02	Seattle	WHL	66	6	9	15	45	11	2	0	2	4
2002-03	Seattle	WHL	71	12	19	31	95	14	4	3	7	9

GOLOVIN, Alexander (goh-loh-VEEN, al-ehx-AN-duhr) CHI.

Left wing. Shoots right. 5'11", 194 lbs. Born, Moscow, USSR, March 26, 1983.
(Chicago's 9th choice, 174th overall, in 2001 Entry Draft).

			Regular Season					Playoffs				
Season	Club	League	GP	G	A	TP	PIM	GP	G	A	TP	PIM
1998-99	Omsk 2	Russia-4	6	2	4	6	4	....	....	....	....	....
99-2000	Omsk 2	Russia-3	24	12	14	26	10	....	....	....	....	....
2000-01	Omsk 2	Russia-3	40	22	34	56	12	....	....	....	....	....
2001-02	Mostovik Kurgan	Russia-2	56	16	23	39	20	....	....	....	....	....
2002-03	Avangard Omsk	Russia	8	2	0	2	0	....	....	....	....	....
	Omsk 2	Russia-3	13	14	8	22	16	....	....	....	....	....
	Sibir Novosibirsk	Russia	20	4	3	7	4	....	....	....	....	....

GORBUNOV, Vladimir (gohr-buh-NAHF, vla-DIH-meer) NYI

Right wing. Shoots left. 6', 174 lbs. Born, Moscow, USSR, April 22, 1982.
(NY Islanders' 4th choice, 105th overall, in 2000 Entry Draft).

			Regular Season					Playoffs				
Season	Club	League	GP	G	A	TP	PIM	GP	G	A	TP	PIM
99-2000	HC CSKA	Russia-2	22	11	7	18	32	....	....	....	....	....
2000-01	HC CSKA	Russia-2	43	10	14	24	63	....	....	....	....	....
2001-02	HC CSKA	Russia-2	46	16	18	34	22	....	....	....	....	....
	CSKA Moscow 2	Russia-3	3	1	1	2	0	....	....	....	....	....
2002-03	CSKA Moscow	Russia	35	5	5	10	46	....	....	....	....	....
	CSKA Moscow 2	Russia-3	STATISTICS NOT AVAILABLE									

GORDON, Boyd (GOHR-duhn, BOYD) WSH.

Right wing. Shoots right. 6', 192 lbs. Born, Unity, Sask., October 19, 1983.
(Washington's 3rd choice, 17th overall, in 2002 Entry Draft).

			Regular Season					Playoffs				
Season	Club	League	GP	G	A	TP	PIM	GP	G	A	TP	PIM
1998-99	Regina Rangers	SMBHL	60	70	102	172	53	....	....	....	....	....
99-2000	Red Deer Rebels	WHL	66	10	26	36	24	4	0	1	1	16
2000-01	Red Deer Rebels	WHL	72	12	27	39	39	22	3	6	9	2
2001-02	Red Deer Rebels	WHL	66	22	29	51	19	23	10	12	22	8
2002-03	Red Deer Rebels	WHL	56	33	48	81	28	23	8	12	20	14

WHL East First All-Star Team (2003)

GORGES, Josh (GOHR-juhz, JAWSH) S.J.

Defense. Shoots left. 6'1", 185 lbs. Born, Kelowna, B.C., August 14, 1984.

			Regular Season					Playoffs				
Season	Club	League	GP	G	A	TP	PIM	GP	G	A	TP	PIM
2000-01	Kelowna Rockets	WHL	57	4	6	10	24	6	1	1	2	4
2001-02	Kelowna Rockets	WHL	72	7	34	41	74	15	1	7	8	8
2002-03	Kelowna Rockets	WHL	54	11	48	59	76	19	3	17	20	16

Signed as a free agent by **San Jose**, September 20, 2002.

GORNICK, Brian (GOHR-nihk, BRIGH-uhn) ANA.

Center. Shoots left. 6'5", 210 lbs. Born, St. Paul, MN, March 17, 1980.
(Anaheim's 7th choice, 258th overall, in 1999 Entry Draft).

			Regular Season					Playoffs				
Season	Club	League	GP	G	A	TP	PIM	GP	G	A	TP	PIM
1998-99	Air Force Falcons	CHA	34	10	11	21	20	....	....	....	....	....
99-2000	Air Force Falcons	CHA	39	13	25	38	26	....	....	....	....	....
2000-01	Air Force Falcons	CHA	36	16	17	33	18	....	....	....	....	....
2001-02	Air Force Falcons	CHA	21	6	5	11	14	....	....	....	....	....
2002-03	Cincinnati	AHL	54	2	4	6	14	....	....	....	....	....

CHA Second All-Star Team (2000) • CHA First All-Star Team (2001)

GOROVIKOV, Konstantin (goh-roh-vih-KAHF, kawn-stehn-TEEN) OTT.

Left wing. Shoots left. 5'11", 172 lbs. Born, Novosibirsk, USSR, August 31, 1977.
(Ottawa's 10th choice, 269th overall, in 1999 Entry Draft).

			Regular Season					Playoffs				
Season	Club	League	GP	G	A	TP	PIM	GP	G	A	TP	PIM
1994-95	St. Petersburg 2	CIS-2	38	6	5	11	22	....	....	....	....	....
	SKA St. Petersburg	CIS	13	1	0	1	4	2	0	0	0	0
1995-96	St. Petersburg 2	CIS-2	3	2	0	2	0	....	....	....	....	....
	SKA St. Petersburg	CIS	45	2	4	6	18	2	0	0	0	0
1996-97	SKA St. Petersburg	Russia	37	4	2	6	20	....	....	....	....	....
1997-98	SKA St. Petersburg	Russia	44	6	12	18	22	....	....	....	....	....
1998-99	SKA St. Petersburg	Russia	42	12	7	19	14	....	....	....	....	....
99-2000	Grand Rapids	IHL	57	9	14	23	30	8	1	0	1	4
2000-01	Grand Rapids	IHL	68	7	19	26	48	....	....	....	....	....
2001-02	Ufa	Russia	51	13	18	31	32	....	....	....	....	....
2002-03	Ufa	Russia	48	10	5	15	44	3	0	1	1	0

GRASBERG, Gustav (GRAHS-buhrg, GOO-stahv) NSH.

Center. Shoots left. 6', 193 lbs. Born, Furudal, Sweden, April 6, 1983.
(Nashville's 8th choice, 240th overall, in 2001 Entry Draft).

			Regular Season					Playoffs				
Season	Club	League	GP	G	A	TP	PIM	GP	G	A	TP	PIM
99-2000	Mora IK-18	Swede-Jr.	1	0	0	0	6	....	....	....	....	....
	Mora IK Jr.	Swede-Jr.	37	10	15	25	44	....	....	....	....	....
2000-01	Mora IK Jr.	Swede-Jr.	15	6	4	10	40	2	1	2	3	4
	Mora IK	Swede-2	12	1	0	1	4	....	....	....	....	....
	Mora IK-18	Swede-Jr.	7	3	4	7	12	7	1	2	3	10
2001-02	Mora IK Jr.	Swede-Jr.	1	0	0	0	8	....	....	....	....	....
	Mora IK	Swede-2	46	13	7	20	72	3	0	0	0	2
2002-03	Hammarby	Swede-2	28	5	7	12	62	....	....	....	....	....
	Hammarby Jr.	Swede-Jr.	8	4	4	8	14	....	....	....	....	....
	Hammarby	Swede-Q	10	0	0	0	25	4	0	0	0	2

GREBESHKOV, Denis (greh-behsh-KAHV, DEH-nihs) L.A.

Defense. Shoots left. 6', 190 lbs. Born, Yaroslavl, USSR, October 11, 1983.
(Los Angeles' 1st choice, 18th overall, in 2002 Entry Draft).

			Regular Season					Playoffs				
Season	Club	League	GP	G	A	TP	PIM	GP	G	A	TP	PIM
99-2000	Yaroslavl 2	Russia-3	42	2	1	3	12	....	....	....	....	....
2000-01	Yaroslavl 2	Russia-3	34	7	2	9	20	....	....	....	....	....
2001-02	Yaroslavl 2	Russia-3	7	1	1	2	2	....	....	....	....	....
	Yaroslavl	Russia	27	1	2	3	10	....	....	....	....	....
2002-03	Yaroslavl	Russia	48	0	7	7	26	10	0	1	1	2

GREEN, Mike (GREEN, MIGHK) FLA.

Center. Shoots right. 5'11", 192 lbs. Born, Calgary, Alta., August 23, 1979.

			Regular Season					Playoffs				
Season	Club	League	GP	G	A	TP	PIM	GP	G	A	TP	PIM
1996-97	Cgy. North Stars	AMHL	35	34	27	61	78	....	....	....	....	....
	Edmonton Ice	WHL	7	0	2	2	0	....	....	....	....	....
1997-98	Edmonton Ice	WHL	71	15	26	41	16	....	....	....	....	....
1998-99	Kootenay Ice	WHL	71	35	45	80	37	7	2	2	4	4
99-2000	Kootenay Ice	WHL	69	43	49	92	63	21	9	16	25	20
2000-01	Port Huron	UHL	11	1	5	6	6	....	....	....	....	....
	Louisville Panthers	AHL	24	2	1	3	4	....	....	....	....	....
	Knoxville Speed	UHL	48	18	24	42	35	1	0	0	0	0
2001-02	Macon Whoopee	ECHL	54	27	35	62	18	....	....	....	....	....
	Cincinnati	AHL	22	2	9	11	4	3	0	0	0	0
2002-03	San Antonio	AHL	80	26	34	60	25	3	0	2	2	0

WHL East Second All-Star Team (2000)

Signed as a free agent by **Florida**, April 7, 2000.

GREENE, Matt (GREEN, MAT) EDM.

Defense. Shoots right. 6'3", 223 lbs. Born, Grand Ledge, MI, May 13, 1983.
(Edmonton's 4th choice, 44th overall, in 2002 Entry Draft).

			Regular Season					Playoffs				
Season	Club	League	GP	G	A	TP	PIM	GP	G	A	TP	PIM
2000-01	U.S. National U-18	USDP	54	0	10	10	59	....	....	....	....	....
2001-02	Green Bay	USHL	55	4	20	24	150	7	0	1	1	31
2002-03	North Dakota	WCHA	39	0	4	4	*135	....	....	....	....	....

USHL Second All-Star Team (2002)

GRIGORENKO, Igor (grih-goh-REHN-koh, EE-gohr) DET.

Right wing. Shoots right. 5'10", 178 lbs. Born, Togliatti, USSR, April 9, 1983.
(Detroit's 1st choice, 62nd overall, in 2001 Entry Draft).

			Regular Season					Playoffs				
Season	Club	League	GP	G	A	TP	PIM	GP	G	A	TP	PIM
1998-99	Lada Togliatti 2	Russia-4	19	3	3	6	2	....	....	....	....	....
99-2000	Lada Togliatti 2	Russia-3	38	17	18	35	36	....	....	....	....	....
2000-01	Lada Togliatti 2	Russia-3	6	5	4	9	....	....	....	....	....	....
	CSK VVS Samara	Russia-2	39	10	10	20	....	....	....	....	....	....
	Lada Togliatti	Russia	....	....	....	....	....	5	1	0	1	4
2001-02	Lada Togliatti	Russia	41	8	9	17	58	4	1	0	1	2
2002-03	Lada Togliatti	Russia	47	19	11	30	82	10	1	*6	7	10

GROT, Denis (GROHT, DEH-nihs) VAN.

Defense. Shoots left. 6', 185 lbs. Born, Minsk, USSR, June 1, 1984.
(Vancouver's 2nd choice, 55th overall, in 2002 Entry Draft).

			Regular Season					Playoffs				
Season	Club	League	GP	G	A	TP	PIM	GP	G	A	TP	PIM
2000-01	Yaroslavl 2	Russia-3	34	5	1	6	10	....	....	....	....	....
	Team Russia	Nat-Tm	5	0	2	2	8	....	....	....	....	....
2001-02	Yaroslavl 2	Russia-3	14	1	0	1	10	....	....	....	....	....
	Elektrostal 2	Russia-3	3	0	1	1	2	....	....	....	....	....
	Elektrostal	Russia-2	33	1	1	2	42	....	....	....	....	....
2002-03	HC Lipetsk	Russia-2	27	4	4	8	28	....	....	....	....	....

GROULX, Danny (GROO, DA-nee) DET.

Defense. Shoots left. 6', 205 lbs. Born, LaSalle, Que., June 23, 1981.

			Regular Season					Playoffs				
Season	Club	League	GP	G	A	TP	PIM	GP	G	A	TP	PIM
1996-97	Charles-Lemoyne	QAAA	40	2	26	28	....	15	3	15	18	....
1997-98	Val-d'Or Foreurs	QMJHL	63	4	16	20	61	19	1	4	5	18
1998-99	Val-d'Or Foreurs	QMJHL	36	3	26	29	55	....	....	....	....	....
	Acadie-Bathurst	QMJHL	36	2	15	17	51	18	0	2	2	6
99-2000	Victoriaville Tigres	QMJHL	66	12	55	67	131	6	0	4	4	14
2000-01	Victoriaville Tigres	QMJHL	72	16	71	87	164	13	2	19	21	46
2001-02	Victoriaville Tigres	QMJHL	68	29	83	112	165	22	9	*30	39	68
2002-03	Grand Rapids	AHL	71	3	7	10	52	7	0	1	1	7

QMJHL First All-Star Team (2001, 2002) • Canadian Major Junior First All-Star Team (2002) • Memorial Cup All-Star Team (2002) • Memorial Cup MVP (2002)

Signed as a free agent by **Detroit**, August 12, 2002.

GUENIN, Nate (GEH-nihn, NAYT) NYR

Defense. Shoots right. 6'2", 191 lbs. Born, Sewickley, PA, December 10, 1982.
(NY Rangers' 3rd choice, 127th overall, in 2002 Entry Draft).

			Regular Season					Playoffs				
Season	Club	League	GP	G	A	TP	PIM	GP	G	A	TP	PIM
99-2000	Pittsburgh Hornets	AAHA	40	3	10	13	122	....	....	....	....	....
2000-01	Green Bay	USHL	54	2	11	13	70	4	1	1	2	6
2001-02	Green Bay	USHL	56	4	11	15	150	7	3	3	6	10
2002-03	Ohio State	CCHA	42	2	9	11	85	....	....	....	....	....

USHL All-Rookie Team (2001)

GUITE, Ben (GEE-tay, BEHN)

Right wing. Shoots right. 6'1", 205 lbs. Born, Montreal, Que., July 17, 1978.
(Montreal's 8th choice, 172nd overall, in 1997 Entry Draft).

			Regular Season					Playoffs				
Season	Club	League	GP	G	A	TP	PIM	GP	G	A	TP	PIM
1994-95	Lac St-Louis Lions	QAAA	40	9	12	21	....	4	0	0	0	0
1995-96	Capital District	Exhib.	STATISTICS NOT AVAILABLE									
1996-97	U. of Maine	H-East	34	7	7	14	21	....	....	....	....	....
1997-98	U. of Maine	H-East	32	6	12	18	20	....	....	....	....	....
1998-99	U. of Maine	H-East	40	12	16	28	30	....	....	....	....	....
99-2000	U. of Maine	H-East	40	22	14	36	36	....	....	....	....	....
2000-01	Tallahassee	ECHL	68	11	18	29	34	....	....	....	....	....
2001-02	Bridgeport	AHL	68	12	18	30	39	....	....	....	....	....
	Cincinnati	AHL	10	2	5	7	4	3	0	0	0	2
2002-03	Cincinnati	AHL	80	13	16	29	44	....	....	....	....	....

Signed as a free agent by **NY Islanders**, August, 2001. Traded to **Anaheim** by **NY Islanders** with the rights to Bjorn Mellin for Dave Roche, March 19, 2002.

GUSEV, Vladimir (GOO-sehv, vla-DIH-meer) CHI.

Defense. Shoots left. 6'2", 205 lbs. Born, Novosibirsk, USSR, November 24, 1982.
(Chicago's 6th choice, 115th overall, in 2001 Entry Draft).

			Regular Season					Playoffs				
Season	Club	League	GP	G	A	TP	PIM	GP	G	A	TP	PIM
99-2000	Novokuznetsk 2	Russia-3	21	1	0	1	52	....	....	....	....	....
	Magnitogorsk	Russia	....	....	....	....	....	3	0	0	0	0
2000-01	Amur Khabarovsk	Russia	1	0	0	0	0	....	....	....	....	....
	Sibir Novosibirsk 2	Russia-3	3	0	0	0	8	....	....	....	....	....
	Sibir Novosibirsk	Russia-2	1	0	0	0	0	....	....	....	....	....
	Omsk 2	Russia-3	4	1	0	1	4	....	....	....	....	....
2001-02	Sibir Novosibirsk	Russia-2	42	1	3	4	82	....	....	....	....	....
2002-03	Sibir Novosibirsk 2	Russia-3	28	6	12	18	42	....	....	....	....	....

GUSKOV, Alexander (goos-KAWF, ahl-ehx-AN-duhr) CBJ

Defense. Shoots left. 6'2", 202 lbs. Born, Gorky, USSR, November 26, 1976.
(Columbus' 8th choice, 200th overall, in 2003 Entry Draft).

			Regular Season					Playoffs				
Season	Club	League	GP	G	A	TP	PIM	GP	G	A	TP	PIM
1996-97	Motor Zavolzhje	Russia-2	32	3	3	6	20	....	....	....	....	....
1997-98	Motor Zavolzhje	Russia-2	24	2	4	6	26	....	....	....	....	....
	Lada Togliatti	Russia	10	0	1	1	8	....	....	....	....	....
1998-99	Chelyabinsk	Russia	11	2	0	2	4	....	....	....	....	....
	Lada Togliatti	Russia	30	1	3	4	10	5	0	0	0	4
99-2000	Nizhnekamsk	Russia	36	4	17	21	40	4	0	0	0	4
2000-01	Nizhnekamsk	Russia	43	4	9	13	24	4	0	0	0	0
2001-02	Yaroslavl	Russia	51	9	9	18	28	9	1	2	3	2
2002-03	Yaroslavl	Russia	48	10	17	27	32	10	1	1	2	6

GUYER, Gino (GIGH-uhr, JEE-noh) DAL.

Center. Shoots left. 5'10", 184 lbs. Born, Grand Rapids, MN, October 14, 1983.
(Dallas' 7th choice, 165th overall, in 2003 Entry Draft).

			Regular Season					Playoffs				
Season	Club	League	GP	G	A	TP	PIM	GP	G	A	TP	PIM
2000-01	Lincoln Stars	USHL	5	2	2	4	2	10	3	5	8	0
2001-02	Greenway High	Hi-School	26	35	50	85	....	....	....	....	....	....
	Lincoln Stars	USHL	15	7	10	17	0	4	0	1	1	0
2002-03	U. of Minnesota	WCHA	41	13	16	29	10	....	....	....	....	....

HAFNER, Peter (HAF-nuhr, PEE-tuhr) FLA.

Defense. Shoots right. 6'5", 195 lbs. Born, Summit, NJ, July 26, 1983.
(Florida's 10th choice, 232nd overall, in 2002 Entry Draft).

			Regular Season					Playoffs				
Season	Club	League	GP	G	A	TP	PIM	GP	G	A	TP	PIM
2000-01	Taft High School	Hi-School	24	1	9	10	12	....	....	....	....	....
2001-02	Taft High School	Hi-School	26	2	19	21	20	....	....	....	....	....
2002-03	Harvard Crimson	ECAC	25	0	2	2	14	....	....	....	....	....

HAGGLUND, Johan (HAG-luhnd, YOH-hahn) T.B.

Center. Shoots left. 6'2", 212 lbs. Born, Ornskoldsvik, Sweden, June 9, 1982.
(Tampa Bay's 4th choice, 126th overall, in 2000 Entry Draft).

			Regular Season					Playoffs				
Season	Club	League	GP	G	A	TP	PIM	GP	G	A	TP	PIM
1998-99	MoDo Jr.	Swede-Jr.	28	16	22	38	52	....	....	....	....	....
99-2000	MoDo-18	Swede-Jr.	7	1	2	3	8	....	....	....	....	....
	MoDo Jr.	Swede-Jr.	35	7	10	17	75	2	1	0	1	0
2000-01	MoDo Jr.	Swede-Jr.	21	9	9	18	66	....	....	....	....	....
2001-02	Orebro IK	Swede-2	36	6	4	10	50	....	....	....	....	....
2002-03	Orebro IK	Swede-2	19	8	6	14	26	....	....	....	....	....
	Hammarby	Swede-2	21	2	5	7	8	9	1	1	2	6

HAGOS, Yared (HA-gohs, YAIR-ehd) DAL.

Center. Shoots left. 6'1", 202 lbs. Born, Stockholm, Sweden, March 27, 1983.
(Dallas' 2nd choice, 70th overall, in 2001 Entry Draft).

			Regular Season					Playoffs				
Season	Club	League	GP	G	A	TP	PIM	GP	G	A	TP	PIM
1998-99	AIK Solna Jr.	Swede-Jr.	32	8	12	20	22	....	....	....	....	....
99-2000	AIK Solna-18	Swede-Jr.	13	4	6	10	6	....	....	....	....	....
	AIK Solna Jr.	Swede-Jr.	17	6	4	10	10	....	....	....	....	....
2000-01	AIK Solna Jr.	Swede-Jr.	24	8	13	21	46	2	2	1	3	2
	AIK Solna	Sweden	....	....	....	....	....	5	0	0	0	0
2001-02	AIK Solna Jr.	Swede-Jr.	1	0	3	3	2	1	0	2	2	0
	AIK Solna	Sweden	45	4	6	10	36	....	....	....	....	....
	AIK Solna	Swede-Q	9	0	0	0	12	....	....	....	....	....
2002-03	AIK Solna	Swede-2	49	10	22	32	67	4	0	1	1	2
	AIK Solna Jr.	Swede-Jr.	1	0	1	1	0	....	....	....	....	....

HAJEK, David (HIGH-ehk, DAV-vihd) CGY.

Defense. Shoots left. 5'11", 165 lbs. Born, Chomutov, Czech., June 13, 1980.
(Calgary's 8th choice, 239th overall, in 2000 Entry Draft).

			Regular Season					Playoffs				
Season	Club	League	GP	G	A	TP	PIM	GP	G	A	TP	PIM
1996-97	KLH Chomutov Jr.	Czech-Jr.	36	8	14	22	30	4	0	0	0	2
1997-98	KLH Chomutov Jr.	Czech-Jr.	36	3	9	12	18	....	....	....	....	....
1998-99	Melville	SJHL	25	10	19	29	....	....	....	....	....	....
	Spokane Chiefs	WHL	27	0	3	3	10	....	....	....	....	....
99-2000	KLH Chomutov Jr.	Czech-Jr.	7	1	5	6	14	....	....	....	....	....
	KLH Chomutov	Czech-2	28	1	5	6	14	12	1	3	4	10
2000-01	Kladno	Czech	40	1	1	2	66	....	....	....	....	....
2001-02	Kladno	Czech	48	0	7	7	16	5	0	1	1	4
2002-03	Kladno	Czech-2	4	0	0	0	0	....	....	....	....	....
	Hradec Kralove	Czech-2	4	0	1	1	4	....	....	....	....	....
	Hradec Kralove	Czech-Q	6	0	1	1	2	....	....	....	....	....

HAKEWILL, James (HAYK-wihl, JAYMZ) CGY.

Defense. Shoots left. 6'3", 205 lbs. Born, Wilmette, IL, June 7, 1982.
(Calgary's 6th choice, 145th overall, in 2001 Entry Draft).

			Regular Season					Playoffs				
Season	Club	League	GP	G	A	TP	PIM	GP	G	A	TP	PIM
99-2000	Westminster High	Hi-School	23	3	13	16	22	....	....	....	....	....
2000-01	Westminster High	Hi-School	23	4	15	19	30	....	....	....	....	....
2001-02	St. Lawrence	ECAC	30	2	2	4	18	....	....	....	....	....
2002-03	St. Lawrence	ECAC	34	1	3	4	61	....	....	....	....	....

HALE, David (HAYL, DAY-vihd) N.J.

Defense. Shoots left. 6'2", 210 lbs. Born, Colorado Springs, CO, June 18, 1981.
(New Jersey's 1st choice, 22nd overall, in 2000 Entry Draft).

			Regular Season					Playoffs				
Season	Club	League	GP	G	A	TP	PIM	GP	G	A	TP	PIM
1997-98	Colorado North	Hi-School	25	11	33	44	154	....	....	....	....	....
1998-99	Sioux City	USHL	56	3	15	18	127	5	0	0	0	18
99-2000	Sioux City	USHL	54	6	18	24	187	5	0	2	2	6
2000-01	North Dakota	WCHA	44	4	5	9	79	....	....	....	....	....
2001-02	North Dakota	WCHA	34	4	5	9	63	....	....	....	....	....
2002-03	North Dakota	WCHA	26	2	6	8	49	....	....	....	....	....

USHL First All-Star Team (2000)

HALVARDSSON, Johan (HAL-vahrds-sohn, YOH-hahn) NYI

Defense. Shoots left. 6'3", 198 lbs. Born, Jonkoping, Sweden, December 26, 1979.
(NY Islanders' 8th choice, 102nd overall, in 1999 Entry Draft).

			Regular Season					Playoffs				
Season	Club	League	GP	G	A	TP	PIM	GP	G	A	TP	PIM
1997-98	HV 71 Jr.	Swede-Jr.	28	5	5	10	65	....	....	....	....	....
1998-99	HV 71 Jonkoping	Sweden	17	1	2	3	33	....	....	....	....	....
99-2000	HV 71 Jonkoping	Sweden	46	0	3	3	75	5	0	0	0	8
2000-01	HV 71 Jonkoping	Sweden	33	0	0	0	24	....	....	....	....	....
2001-02	HV 71 Jonkoping	Sweden	3	0	0	0	0	....	....	....	....	....
2002-03	HV 71 Jonkoping	Sweden	39	0	1	1	14	7	0	0	0	0

• Missed majority of 2001-02 season recovering from knee injury suffered in game vs. Sodertalje (Sweden), September 23, 2001.

HAMALAINEN, Ville (ha-muh-LAY-nuhn, VIHL-ee) CGY.

Left wing. Shoots left. 5'11", 178 lbs. Born, Lappeenranta, Finland, July 6, 1981.
(Calgary's 11th choice, 251st overall, in 2001 Entry Draft).

			Regular Season					Playoffs				
Season	Club	League	GP	G	A	TP	PIM	GP	G	A	TP	PIM
1997-98	SaiPa Jr.	Finn-Jr.	31	8	27	35	24	....	....	....	....	....
1998-99	SaiPa Jr.	Finn-Jr.	12	6	26	32	26	14	10	12	22	22
	SaiPa	Finland	12	1	0	1	8	....	....	....	....	....
99-2000	SaiPa	Finland	47	6	4	10	20	....	....	....	....	....
	KooKoo Kouvola	Finland-2	3	0	1	1	2	....	....	....	....	....
	SaiPa Jr.	Finn-Jr.	1	2	2	4	2	2	1	1	2	2
2000-01	SaiPa	Finland	42	0	4	4	10	....	....	....	....	....
	SaiPa Jr.	Finn-Jr.	1	1	1	2	0	....	....	....	....	....
2001-02	SaiPa	Finland	51	4	9	13	24	....	....	....	....	....
	SaiPa Jr.	Finn-Jr.	5	4	4	8	2	9	5	6	11	18
2002-03	FPS Forssa	Finn-2	13	4	8	12	6	....	....	....	....	....
	Tappara Tampere	Finland	35	1	2	3	6	6	0	0	0	2

HAMHUIS, Dan (HAM-yoos, DAN) NSH.

Defense. Shoots left. 6', 205 lbs. Born, Smithers, B.C., December 13, 1982.
(Nashville's 1st choice, 12th overall, in 2001 Entry Draft).

			Regular Season					Playoffs				
Season	Club	League	GP	G	A	TP	PIM	GP	G	A	TP	PIM
1997-98	Smithers A's	BCAHA	59	59	72	131	59	....	....	....	....	....
1998-99	Prince George	WHL	56	1	3	4	45	7	1	2	3	8
99-2000	Prince George	WHL	70	10	23	33	140	13	2	3	5	35
2000-01	Prince George	WHL	62	13	47	60	125	6	2	3	5	15
2001-02	Prince George	WHL	59	10	50	60	135	7	0	5	5	16
2002-03	Milwaukee	AHL	68	6	21	27	81	6	0	3	3	2

WHL West First All-Star Team (2001, 2002) • WHL Player of the Year (2002) • Canadian Major Junior First All-Star Team (2002) • Canadian Major Junior Defenseman of the Year (2002)

HAMILTON, Jeff (HAM-ihl-tuhn, JEHF) NYI

Center. Shoots right. 5'10", 180 lbs. Born, Englewood, OH, September 4, 1977.

			Regular Season					Playoffs				
Season	Club	League	GP	G	A	TP	PIM	GP	G	A	TP	PIM
1995-96	Avon Old Farms	Hi-School	24	29	23	52	....	....	....	....	....	....
1996-97	Yale University	ECAC	31	10	13	23	26	....	....	....	....	....
1997-98	Yale University	ECAC	33	27	20	47	28	....	....	....	....	....
1998-99	Yale University	ECAC	30	20	28	48	51	....	....	....	....	....
99-2000	Yale University	ECAC	2	0	1	1	0	....	....	....	....	....
2000-01	Yale University	ECAC	31	23	32	55	39	....	....	....	....	....
2001-02	Karpat Oulu	Finland	39	18	15	33	16	3	0	0	0	0
2002-03	Bridgeport	AHL	67	22	16	38	35	9	3	3	6	0

ECAC All-Rookie Team (1997) • ECAC First All-Star Team (1998, 1999, 2001) • Ivy League First All-Star Team (1998, 1999, 2001) • NCAA East Second All-American Team (1998, 1999) • NCAA East First All-American Team (2001) • Ivy League Player of the Year (2001)

• Missed majority of 1999-2000 season recovering from abdominal injury originally suffered in game vs. U. of Michigan (CCHA), October 30, 1999. • Announced official withdrawl from **Yale** (ECAC) for 1999-2000 semester, December 3, 1999. Signed as a free agent by **Karpat** (Finland), October 4, 2001. Signed as a free agent by **NY Islanders**, August 6, 2002.

HANNULA, Mika (HAH-noo-lah, MEE-kah) MIN.

Right wing. Shoots left. 5'11", 180 lbs. Born, Huddinge, Sweden, April 2, 1979.
(Minnesota's 10th choice, 269th overall, in 2002 Entry Draft).

			Regular Season					Playoffs				
Season	Club	League	GP	G	A	TP	PIM	GP	G	A	TP	PIM
1997-98	Djurgarden Jr.	Swede-Jr.	14	10	6	16	22	2	1	1	2	0
	Lukko Rauma	Finn-Jr.	6	2	0	2	36	....	....	....	....	....
1998-99	Lidingo HC	Sweden-2	32	10	0	10	47	....	....	....	....	....
99-2000	Hammarby	Sweden-2	43	10	10	20	53	2	0	0	0	2
2000-01	Malmo IF	Sweden	45	2	9	11	26	8	3	2	5	14
	Malmo IF Jr.	Swede-Jr.	1	1	1	2	0	....	....	....	....	....
2001-02	Malmo IF	Sweden	41	10	7	17	14	5	2	1	3	0
2002-03	Malmo IF	Sweden	49	15	15	30	72	....	....	....	....	....

HANNUS, Tommi (HA-nuhs, TAW-mee) L.A.

Left wing. Shoots right. 6', 180 lbs. Born, Vantaa, Finland, June 27, 1980.
(Los Angeles' 7th choice, 190th overall, in 1998 Entry Draft).

			Regular Season					Playoffs				
Season	Club	League	GP	G	A	TP	PIM	GP	G	A	TP	PIM
1994-95	TPS Turku-C	Finn-Jr.	27	24	13	37	43	....	....	....	....	....
1995-96	TPS Turku-C	Finn-Jr.	29	34	22	56	67	....	....	....	....	....
	TPS Turku-B	Finn-Jr.	1	1	0	1	2	....	....	....	....	....
1996-97	TPS Turku Jr.	Finn-Jr.	27	7	7	14	6	....	....	....	....	....
	TPS Turku-B	Finn-Jr.	18	7	7	14	6	6	4	2	6	10
1997-98	TPS Turku Jr.	Finn-Jr.	19	6	3	9	4	....	....	....	....	....
	TPS Turku-B	Finn-Jr.	9	5	4	9	8	....	....	....	....	....
1998-99	TPS Turku Jr.	Finn-Jr.	8	5	4	9	22	....	....	....	....	....
	TuTo Turku	Finland-2	18	6	4	10	16	8	0	2	2	8
99-2000	TPS Turku Jr.	Finn-Jr.	3	4	3	7	6	....	....	....	....	....
	TuTo Turku	Finland-2	27	11	6	17	20	....	....	....	....	....
	Assat Pori	Finland	13	1	0	1	4	....	....	....	....	....
2000-01	TuTo Turku	Finland-2	29	9	8	17	16	11	*7	7	14	*24
2001-02	TPS Turku	Finland	47	4	2	6	6	3	1	0	1	0
2002-03	Jokerit Helsinki	Finland	31	1	0	1	25	....	....	....	....	....
	Kiekko-Vantaa	Finland-2	14	7	7	14	4	12	3	5	8	8

HARANT, Tomas (HAH-rant, TAW-mahsh) NSH.

Defense. Shoots left. 6'3", 201 lbs. Born, Zilina, Czech., April 28, 1980.
(Nashville's 8th choice, 173rd overall, in 2000 Entry Draft).

			Regular Season					Playoffs				
Season	Club	League	GP	G	A	TP	PIM	GP	G	A	TP	PIM
1997-98	HK SKP Zilina Jr.	Slovak-Jr.	41	5	7	12	72	....	....	....	....	....
	HK SKP Zilina	Slovak-2	5	0	0	0	0	....	....	....	....	....
1998-99	HK SKP Zilina Jr.	Slovak-Jr.	33	1	6	7	108	....	....	....	....	....
99-2000	HK SKP Zilina	Slovak-2	26	0	3	3	34	....	....	....	....	....
2000-01	Trinec Jr.	Czech-Jr.	5	1	2	3	8	1	0	0	0	4
	HC Ocelari Trinec	Czech	15	1	2	3	14	....	....	....	....	....
2001-02	MsHK SKP Zilina	Slovakia	51	2	3	5	46	4	0	0	0	4
2002-03	MsHK SKP Zilina	Slovakia	28	2	3	5	86	4	1	0	1	24
	Havirov	Czech	19	0	1	1	40	....	....	....	....	....

HARIKKALA, Jaakko (HAHR-ee-kuh-lah, YAH-koh) BOS.

Defense. Shoots left. 6'2", 215 lbs. Born, Kalanti, Finland, March 30, 1981.
(Boston's 4th choice, 118th overall, in 1999 Entry Draft).

			Regular Season					Playoffs				
Season	Club	League	GP	G	A	TP	PIM	GP	G	A	TP	PIM
1997-98	Jaa-Kotkat	Finland-3	5	0	2	2	8	....	....	....	....	....
	Jaa-Kotkat	Finland-2	45	2	6	8	65	....	....	....	....	....
1998-99	Lukko Rauma Jr.	Finn-Jr.	11	1	3	4	22	....	....	....	....	....
	Lukko Rauma	Finland	35	0	0	0	10	....	....	....	....	....
99-2000	Lukko Rauma	Finland	24	0	0	0	2	....	....	....	....	....
2000-01	Lukko Rauma Jr.	Finn-Jr.	2	2	0	2	2	....	....	....	....	....
	Jaa-Kotkat	Finland-2	10	0	2	2	16	....	....	....	....	....
	Lukko Rauma	Finland	10	0	0	0	0	....	....	....	....	....
2001-02	Lukko Rauma	Finland	47	4	8	12	40	....	....	....	....	....
	Lukko Rauma Jr.	Finn-Jr.	3	0	1	1	0	....	....	....	....	....
2002-03	Lukko Rauma	Finland	54	7	6	13	48	....	....	....	....	....

HARRISON, Jay (HAIR-ih-suhn, JAY) TOR.

Defense. Shoots left. 6'4", 211 lbs. Born, Oshawa, Ont., November 3, 1982.
(Toronto's 4th choice, 82nd overall, in 2001 Entry Draft).

			Regular Season					Playoffs				
Season	Club	League	GP	G	A	TP	PIM	GP	G	A	TP	PIM
1997-98	Oshawa	OJHL-B	42	1	11	12	143	....	....	....	....	....
1998-99	Brampton	OHL	63	1	14	15	108	....	....	....	....	....
99-2000	Brampton	OHL	68	2	18	20	139	6	0	2	2	15
2000-01	Brampton	OHL	53	4	15	19	112	9	1	1	2	17
2001-02	Brampton	OHL	61	12	31	43	116	....	....	....	....	....
	Memphis	CHL	....	....	....	....	....	1	0	0	0	2
	St. John's	AHL	7	0	1	1	2	10	0	0	0	4
2002-03	St. John's	AHL	72	2	8	10	72	....	....	....	....	....

OHL All-Rookie Team (1999)

HARTSBURG, Chris (HAHRTZ-buhrg, KRIHS) N.J.

Right wing. Shoots right. 6', 200 lbs. Born, Edina, MN, May 30, 1980.
(New Jersey's 7th choice, 214th overall, in 1999 Entry Draft).

			Regular Season					Playoffs				
Season	Club	League	GP	G	A	TP	PIM	GP	G	A	TP	PIM
1995-96	Cambridge	OJHL-B	46	12	15	27	10	....	....	....	....	....
1996-97	Cambridge	OJHL-B	47	14	19	33	29	....	....	....	....	....
1997-98	Omaha Lancers	USHL	54	16	19	35	58	12	2	2	4	20
1998-99	Colorado College	WCHA	34	6	4	10	60	....	....	....	....	....
99-2000	Colorado College	WCHA	33	3	2	5	50	....	....	....	....	....
2000-01	Colorado College	WCHA	41	8	7	15	38	....	....	....	....	....
2001-02	Colorado College	WCHA	40	14	8	22	50	....	....	....	....	....
2002-03	Albany River Rats	AHL	40	7	3	10	22	....	....	....	....	....

HAVEL, Marian (HAH-vuhl, MAHR-ee-uhn) WSH.

Center/Left wing. Shoots left. 6', 176 lbs. Born, Jihlava, Czech., January 26, 1984.
(Washington's 10th choice, 179th overall, in 2002 Entry Draft).

			Regular Season					Playoffs				
Season	Club	League	GP	G	A	TP	PIM	GP	G	A	TP	PIM
99-2000	Dukla Jihlava Jr.	Czech-Jr.	50	35	22	57	70	....	....	....	....	....
	Sioux City	USHL	4	0	1	1	0	....	....	....	....	....
2000-01	Dukla Jihlava-18	Czech-Jr.	7	11	18	29	36	....	....	....	....	....
	Dukla Jihlava Jr.	Czech-Jr.	14	9	10	19	64	....	....	....	....	....
	HC Dukla Jihlava	Czech-2	26	2	2	4	14	....	....	....	....	....
2001-02	Vancouver Giants	WHL	67	17	16	33	83	....	....	....	....	....
2002-03	Vancouver Giants	WHL	5	1	2	3	12	....	....	....	....	....
	Swift Current	WHL	56	8	19	27	46	4	0	0	0	2

HAVELKA, Petr (huh-VEHL-kah, PEE-tuhr) PIT.

Left wing. Shoots left. 6'2", 187 lbs. Born, Most, Czech., March 4, 1979.
(Pittsburgh's 6th choice, 152nd overall, in 1997 Entry Draft).

			Regular Season					Playoffs				
Season	Club	League	GP	G	A	TP	PIM	GP	G	A	TP	PIM
1995-96	Sparta Praha Jr.	Czech-Jr.	40	15	10	25	....	....	....	....	....	....
1996-97	Sparta Praha Jr.	Czech-Jr.	22	14	13	27	....	....	....	....	....	....
	HC Sparta Praha	Czech	....	....	....	....	....	1	0	0	0	0
1997-98	Sparta Praha Jr.	Czech-Jr.	DID NOT PLAY – INJURED									
1998-99	Sparta Praha Jr.	Czech-Jr.	5	7	3	10	....	4	1	1	2	....
	HC Velvana Kladno	Czech	5	0	0	0	0	....	....	....	....	....
99-2000	Sparta Praha Jr.	Czech-Jr.	2	1	0	1	0	....	....	....	....	....
	Beroun	Czech-2	5	2	4	6	29	....	....	....	....	....
	HC Velvana Kladno	Czech	6	1	2	3	2	....	....	....	....	....
	HC Sparta Praha	Czech	10	0	1	1	0	3	0	0	0	0
2000-01	Beroun	Czech-2	3	0	0	0	0	....	....	....	....	....
	HC Sparta Praha	Czech	....	....	....	....	....	7	1	0	1	2
2001-02	Sparta Praha Jr.	Czech-Jr.	2	1	0	1	0	....	....	....	....	....
	Usti nad Labem	Czech-3	2	0	0	0	2	....	....	....	....	....
	HC Sparta Praha	Czech	35	3	4	7	12	6	0	0	0	2
2002-03	HC Sparta Praha	Czech	47	10	6	16	38	8	1	3	4	0

HAVERN, Ned (HA-vuhrn, NEHD) DAL.

Left wing. Shoots left. 6'1", 190 lbs. Born, Boston, MA, October 1, 1982.
(Dallas' 12th choice, 273rd overall, in 2002 Entry Draft).

			Regular Season					Playoffs				
Season	Club	League	GP	G	A	TP	PIM	GP	G	A	TP	PIM
2001-02	Boston College	H-East	38	6	6	12	10	....	....	....	....	....
2002-03	Boston College	H-East	36	4	8	12	10	....	....	....	....	....

HAY, Darrell (HAY, DAIR-ehl) VAN.

Defense. Shoots right. 6', 190 lbs. Born, Kamloops, B.C, April 2, 1980.
(Vancouver's 8th choice, 271st overall, in 1999 Entry Draft).

			Regular Season					Playoffs				
Season	Club	League	GP	G	A	TP	PIM	GP	G	A	TP	PIM
1995-96	Kamloops Lions	BCAHA	65	34	57	91	155	....	....	....	....	....
1996-97	Tri-City Americans	WHL	61	0	10	10	41	....	....	....	....	....
1997-98	Tri-City Americans	WHL	71	5	33	38	90	....	....	....	....	....
1998-99	Tri-City Americans	WHL	72	13	49	62	87	12	2	10	12	22
99-2000	Tri-City Americans	WHL	64	15	36	51	85	4	0	1	1	8
2000-01	Florida Everblades	ECHL	40	5	4	9	26	5	2	1	3	0
	Kansas City Blades	IHL	9	0	0	0	19	....	....	....	....	....
2001-02	Columbia Inferno	ECHL	15	0	13	13	15	....	....	....	....	....
	Manitoba Moose	AHL	53	5	8	13	29	7	1	1	2	2
2002-03	Manitoba Moose	AHL	43	3	10	13	29	....	....	....	....	....
	Columbia Inferno	ECHL	12	2	3	5	13	17	2	9	11	23

WHL West Second All-Star Team (2000)

HEALEY, Eric (HEE-lee, AIR-ihk) ATL.

Left wing. Shoots left. 5'11", 200 lbs. Born, Hull, MA, January 20, 1975.

			Regular Season					Playoffs				
Season	Club	League	GP	G	A	TP	PIM	GP	G	A	TP	PIM
1993-94	New England	NEJHL	37	61	76	137	....	....	....	....	....	....
1994-95	RPI Engineers	ECAC	37	13	11	24	35	....	....	....	....	....
1995-96	RPI Engineers	ECAC	35	18	22	40	57	....	....	....	....	....
1996-97	RPI Engineers	ECAC	36	30	26	56	63	....	....	....	....	....
1997-98	RPI Engineers	ECAC	35	21	27	48	42	....	....	....	....	....
1998-99	Saint John Flames	AHL	64	14	24	38	77	....	....	....	....	....
	Orlando	IHL	13	5	4	9	13	8	1	0	1	12
99-2000	Springfield Falcons	AHL	32	14	15	29	51	1	0	0	0	2
2000-01	Springfield Falcons	AHL	66	16	17	33	53	....	....	....	....	....
2001-02	Jackson Bandits	ECHL	2	1	1	2	0	....	....	....	....	....
	Manchester	AHL	65	24	34	58	45	5	2	2	4	8
2002-03	Manchester	AHL	75	*42	31	73	47	3	1	0	1	2

ECAC Second All-Star Team (1997) • NCAA East Second All-American Team (1997, 1998) • ECAC First All-Star Team (1998) • Fred Hunt Memorial Trophy (Sportsmanship – AHL) (2003) (co-winner - Chris Ferraro)

Signed as a free agent by **Calgary**, September 22, 1998. Signed as a free agent by **Phoenix**, July 26, 1999. Signed to try-out contract by **Manchester** (AHL), September 30, 2001. Signed as a free agent by **Atlanta**, August 12, 2003.

HEDIN, Pierre (heh-DEEN, PEE-air) TOR.

Defense. Shoots left. 6'1", 198 lbs. Born, Ornskoldsvik, Sweden, February 19, 1978.
(Toronto's 8th choice, 239th overall, in 1999 Entry Draft).

			Regular Season					Playoffs				
Season	Club	League	GP	G	A	TP	PIM	GP	G	A	TP	PIM
1994-95	MoDo Jr.	Swede-Jr.	21	0	3	3	20	....	....	....	....	....
1995-96	MoDo Jr.	Swede-Jr.	29	6	8	14	34	....	....	....	....	....
1996-97	MoDo	Sweden	19	1	2	3	6	....	....	....	....	....
1997-98	MoDo Jr.	Swede-Jr.	7	1	6	7	10	....	....	....	....	....
	MoDo	Sweden	29	2	1	3	26	9	1	1	2	4
1998-99	MoDo	Sweden	41	6	5	11	28	13	1	1	2	12
99-2000	MoDo	Sweden	48	9	5	14	36	13	0	2	2	8
2000-01	MoDo	Sweden	46	5	8	13	59	7	3	0	3	4
2001-02	MoDo	Sweden	39	7	9	16	20	14	*8	2	10	10
2002-03	MoDo	Sweden	46	8	14	22	32	6	0	1	1	4

HEFFERNAN, Scott (HEH-fuhr-nuhn, SKAWT) CBJ

Defense. Shoots left. 6'5", 200 lbs. Born, Montreal, Que., March 9, 1982.
(Columbus' 4th choice, 138th overall, in 2000 Entry Draft).

			Regular Season					Playoffs				
Season	Club	League	GP	G	A	TP	PIM	GP	G	A	TP	PIM
1998-99	Pembroke	OCJHL	44	3	5	8	51	....	....	....	....	....
99-2000	Sarnia Sting	OHL	55	5	10	15	24	7	0	1	1	4
2000-01	Sarnia Sting	OHL	51	2	20	22	30	4	0	1	1	0
2001-02	Sarnia Sting	OHL	10	0	9	9	16	....	....	....	....	....
	St. Michael's	OHL	58	4	17	21	77	9	1	2	3	4
2002-03	Dayton Bombers	ECHL	6	1	0	1	7	....	....	....	....	....

HEID, Chris (HIGHD, KRIHS) MIN.

Defense. Shoots left. 6'2", 205 lbs. Born, Langley, B.C., March 14, 1983.
(Minnesota's 3rd choice, 74th overall, in 2001 Entry Draft).

			Regular Season					Playoffs				
Season	Club	League	GP	G	A	TP	PIM	GP	G	A	TP	PIM
1998-99	Kamloops	BCAHA	58	26	34	60	65	....	....	....	....	....
	Spokane Chiefs	WHL	1	0	0	0	0	....	....	....	....	....
99-2000	Spokane Chiefs	WHL	44	1	7	8	25	6	0	0	0	4
2000-01	Spokane Chiefs	WHL	51	2	15	17	76	12	0	4	4	12
2001-02	Spokane Chiefs	WHL	69	7	28	35	56	11	1	4	5	8
2002-03	Spokane Chiefs	WHL	60	9	36	45	66	11	2	11	13	10

HEJDA, Jan (HAY-dah, YAHN) BUF.

Defense. Shoots left. 6'3", 209 lbs. Born, Prague, Czech., June 18, 1978.
(Buffalo's 4th choice, 106th overall, in 2003 Entry Draft).

			Regular Season					Playoffs				
Season	Club	League	GP	G	A	TP	PIM	GP	G	A	TP	PIM
1997-98	HC Slavia Praha	Czech	44	2	5	7	51	5	0	0	0	6
1998-99	HC Slavia Praha	Czech	34	1	2	3	38	....	....	....	....	....
99-2000	HC Slavia Praha	Czech	26	1	2	3	14	....	....	....	....	....
	HC Femax Havirov	Czech	7	0	2	2	6	....	....	....	....	....
	HC Stadion Liberec	Czech-2	1	0	0	0	4	....	....	....	....	....
2000-01	HC Slavia Praha	Czech	38	2	6	8	70	11	3	0	3	12
	SK Kadan	Czech-2	8	1	0	1	6	....	....	....	....	....
2001-02	HC Slavia Praha	Czech	42	9	8	17	52	9	1	1	2	14
2002-03	HC Slavia Praha	Czech	52	6	11	17	44	17	5	8	13	12

HELBLING, Timo (HEHL-blihng, TEE-moh) NSH.

Defense. Shoots right. 6'3", 209 lbs. Born, Basel, Switz., July 21, 1981.
(Nashville's 11th choice, 162nd overall, in 1999 Entry Draft).

			Regular Season					Playoffs				
Season	Club	League	GP	G	A	TP	PIM	GP	G	A	TP	PIM
1997-98	HC Davos Jr.	Swiss-Jr.	34	6	6	12	38	....	....	....	....	....
1998-99	HC Davos Jr.	Swiss-Jr.	28	5	10	15	116	2	1	3	4	35
	HC Davos	Swiss	44	0	0	0	8	4	0	0	0	0
99-2000	HC Davos	Swiss	44	0	0	0	49	5	0	0	0	0
2000-01	Windsor Spitfires	OHL	54	7	14	21	90	7	0	2	2	11
	Milwaukee	IHL	....	....	....	....	....	1	0	0	0	0
2001-02	Milwaukee	AHL	67	2	6	8	59	....	....	....	....	....
2002-03	Milwaukee	AHL	23	0	1	1	37	....	....	....	....	....
	Toledo Storm	ECHL	35	3	8	11	75	7	0	1	1	2

HELFENSTEIN, Sven (hehl-fehn-SHTIGHN, SVEHN) NYR

Left wing. Shoots right. 5'10", 176 lbs. Born, Winterthur, Switz., July 30, 1982.
(NY Rangers' 6th choice, 175th overall, in 2000 Entry Draft).

			Regular Season					Playoffs				
Season	Club	League	GP	G	A	TP	PIM	GP	G	A	TP	PIM
1997-98	Kloten Flyers Jr.	Swiss-Jr.	31	6	8	14	14	....	....	....	....	....
1998-99	Kloten Flyers Jr.	Swiss-Jr.	33	25	18	43	14	7	5	3	8	2
	EHC Kloten	Swiss	2	0	0	0	0	....	....	....	....	....
99-2000	EHC Kloten	Swiss	40	6	3	9	28	6	0	1	1	0
2000-01	Kloten Flyers Jr.	Swiss-Jr.	2	3	3	6	0	....	....	....	....	....
	EHC Kloten	Swiss	8	1	1	2	0	....	....	....	....	....
	La Chaux-de-Fonds	Swiss	23	2	8	10	6	12	1	3	4	6
	HC Thurgau	Swiss-2	4	2	1	3	8	....	....	....	....	....
2001-02	SC Bern	Swiss	35	2	10	12	39	6	0	0	0	4
	SC Bern Jr.	Swiss-Jr.	....	....	....	....	....	4	4	2	6	2
2002-03	SC Bern	Swiss	32	2	3	5	14	11	0	0	0	4
	EHC Biel	Swiss-2	11	3	4	7	12	....	....	....	....	....

HELMINEN, Dwight (HEHL-mih-nehn, DWIGHT) EDM.

Center. Shoots left. 5'9", 185 lbs. Born, Hancock, MI, June 22, 1983.
(Edmonton's 12th choice, 244th overall, in 2002 Entry Draft).

			Regular Season					Playoffs				
Season	Club	League	GP	G	A	TP	PIM	GP	G	A	TP	PIM
2000-01	U.S. National-18	USDP-18	67	21	44	65	30	....	....	....	....	....
2001-02	U. of Michigan	CCHA	39	10	8	18	10	....	....	....	....	....
2002-03	U. of Michigan	CCHA	39	17	16	33	34	....	....	....	....	....

HEMINGWAY, Colin (HEH-mihng-way, CAW-lihn) ST.L.

Right wing. Shoots right. 6', 170 lbs. Born, Surrey, B.C., August 12, 1980.
(St. Louis' 7th choice, 221st overall, in 1999 Entry Draft).

			Regular Season					Playoffs				
Season	Club	League	GP	G	A	TP	PIM	GP	G	A	TP	PIM
1996-97	Port Coquitlam	PIJHL	34	23	24	47	52	....	....	....	....	....
1997-98	South Surrey	BCHL	58	12	16	28	46	....	....	....	....	....
1998-99	South Surrey	BCHL	59	40	64	104	52	....	....	....	....	....
99-2000	New Hampshire	H-East	22	3	5	8	6	....	....	....	....	....
2000-01	New Hampshire	H-East	37	9	18	27	16	....	....	....	....	....
2001-02	New Hampshire	H-East	40	*33	33	66	30	....	....	....	....	....
2002-03	New Hampshire	H-East	40	22	25	47	51	....	....	....	....	....

Hockey East First All-Star Team (2002) • Hockey East Second All-Star Team (2003) • NCAA East Second All-American Team (2003)

HENDRICKS, Matt (HEHN-drihks, MAT) NSH.

Center. Shoots left. 6', 215 lbs. Born, Blaine, MN, June 17, 1981.
(Nashville's 5th choice, 131st overall, in 2000 Entry Draft).

			Regular Season					Playoffs				
Season	Club	League	GP	G	A	TP	PIM	GP	G	A	TP	PIM
1998-99	Blaine Bengals	Hi-School	22	23	34	57	42	....	....	....	....	....
99-2000	Blaine Bengals	Hi-School	21	23	30	53	28	....	....	....	....	....
2000-01	St. Cloud State	WCHA	37	3	9	12	23	....	....	....	....	....
2001-02	St. Cloud State	WCHA	42	19	20	39	74	....	....	....	....	....
2002-03	St. Cloud State	WCHA	37	18	18	36	64	....	....	....	....	....

HENNESSY, Joshua (HEHN-eh-see, JAW-shoo-wuh) S.J.

Center. Shoots left. 6', 180 lbs. Born, Brockton, MA, February 7, 1985.
(San Jose's 3rd choice, 43rd overall, in 2003 Entry Draft).

			Regular Season					Playoffs				
Season	Club	League	GP	G	A	TP	PIM	GP	G	A	TP	PIM
2000-01	Milton Academy	Hi-School	STATISTICS NOT AVAILABLE									
2001-02	Quebec Remparts	QMJHL	70	20	20	40	24	9	3	9	12	8
2002-03	Quebec Remparts	QMJHL	72	33	51	84	44	11	6	9	15	10

HENNING, Petter (HEH-nihng, PEH-tehr) NYR

Right wing. Shoots left. 6', 209 lbs. Born, Ornskoldsvik, Sweden, September 15, 1980.
(NY Rangers' 10th choice, 251st overall, in 1999 Entry Draft).

			Regular Season					Playoffs				
Season	Club	League	GP	G	A	TP	PIM	GP	G	A	TP	PIM
1997-98	MoDo Jr.	Swede-Jr.	27	7	6	13	12	....	....	....	....	....
1998-99	MoDo Jr.	Swede-Jr.	38	10	10	20	74	....	....	....	....	....
	MoDo	Sweden	1	0	0	0	0	....	....	....	....	....
99-2000	Sodertalje SK Jr.	Swede-Jr.	3	1	0	1	0	....	....	....	....	....
	Skelleftea AIK	Swede-2	8	0	0	0	2	....	....	....	....	....
2000-01	Tingsryds AIF	Swede-2	40	3	5	8	18	3	0	0	0	6
2001-02	Tingsryds AIF	Swede-2	32	9	4	13	18	....	....	....	....	....
	Tingsryds AIF	Swede-Q	13	2	0	2	12	2	0	0	0	0
2002-03	Tingsryds AIF	Swede-3	40	13	19	32	....					

HENRICH, Adam (HEHN-rihch, A-duhm) T.B.

Left wing. Shoots left. 6'4", 219 lbs. Born, Toronto, Ont., January 19, 1984.
(Tampa Bay's 1st choice, 60th overall, in 2002 Entry Draft).

			Regular Season					Playoffs				
Season	Club	League	GP	G	A	TP	PIM	GP	G	A	TP	PIM
99-2000	Don Mills Flyers	GTHL	54	30	52	82	86	....	....	....	....	....
2000-01	Brampton	OHL	48	5	4	9	27	9	0	0	0	6
2001-02	Brampton	OHL	66	33	30	63	92	....	....	....	....	....
2002-03	Brampton	OHL	63	31	33	64	84	11	4	1	5	25

HENRICH, Michael (HEHN-rihch, MIGH-kuhl) EDM.

Right wing. Shoots right. 6'2", 206 lbs. Born, Thornhill, Ont., March 3, 1980.
(Edmonton's 1st choice, 13th overall, in 1998 Entry Draft).

			Regular Season					Playoffs				
Season	Club	League	GP	G	A	TP	PIM	GP	G	A	TP	PIM
1995-96	Wexford Raiders	MTJHL	4	1	0	1	0	....	....	....	....	....
1996-97	Barrie Colts	OHL	52	9	15	24	19	9	0	5	5	0
1997-98	Barrie Colts	OHL	66	41	22	63	75	5	1	3	4	0
1998-99	Barrie Colts	OHL	62	38	33	71	42	12	0	2	2	4
99-2000	Barrie Colts	OHL	66	38	48	86	69	25	10	18	28	30
2000-01	Tallahassee	ECHL	6	1	1	2	0	....	....	....	....	....
	Hamilton Bulldogs	AHL	73	5	10	15	36	....	....	....	....	....
2001-02	Hamilton Bulldogs	AHL	67	14	24	38	24	9	2	2	4	2
2002-03	Hamilton Bulldogs	AHL	12	0	0	0	2	....	....	....	....	....
	Mora IK	Swede-2	12	3	1	4	16	....	....	....	....	....
	Hershey Bears	AHL	9	0	1	1	4	1	0	0	0	0

HIGGINS, Christopher (HIH-gihns, KRIHS-toh-fuhr) MTL.

Center. Shoots left. 5'11", 192 lbs. Born, Smithtown, NY, June 2, 1983.
(Montreal's 1st choice, 14th overall, in 2002 Entry Draft).

			Regular Season					Playoffs				
Season	Club	League	GP	G	A	TP	PIM	GP	G	A	TP	PIM
99-2000	Avon Old Farms	Hi-School	27	19	20	39	10	....	....	....	....	....
2000-01	Avon Old Farms	Hi-School	24	22	14	36	29	....	....	....	....	....
2001-02	Yale University	ECAC	27	14	17	31	32	....	....	....	....	....
2002-03	Yale University	ECAC	28	20	21	41	41	....	....	....	....	....

ECAC All-Rookie Team (2002) • ECAC Second All-Star Team (2002) • ECAC Rookie of the Year (2002) • ECAC First All-Star Team (2003) • ECAC Player of the Year (2003) (co-winner - David LeNeveu) • NCAA East First All-American Team (2003)

HILL, Ed (HIHL, EHD) CAR.

Defense. Shoots left. 6'3", 215 lbs. Born, Newburyport, MA, October 24, 1980.
(Nashville's 5th choice, 61st overall, in 1999 Entry Draft).

			Regular Season					Playoffs				
Season	Club	League	GP	G	A	TP	PIM	GP	G	A	TP	PIM
1996-97	Green Bay	USHL	61	4	11	15	36	17	0	1	1	14
1997-98	Green Bay	USHL	51	1	16	17	76	3	0	0	0	0
1998-99	Barrie Colts	OHL	53	7	17	24	42	12	0	2	2	8
99-2000	Barrie Colts	OHL	66	1	18	19	63	25	1	3	4	14
2000-01	Barrie Colts	OHL	60	3	19	22	104	5	0	1	1	2
2001-02	Florida Everblades	ECHL	34	2	12	14	22	....	....	....	....	....
	Lowell	AHL	37	0	0	0	37	5	0	1	1	12
2002-03	Lowell	AHL	29	1	3	4	30	....	....	....	....	....
	Florida Everblades	ECHL	16	1	5	6	10	1	0	0	0	0

Signed as a free agent by **Carolina**, July 16, 2002.

HINZ, Chad (HIHNZ, CHAD) EDM.

Center. Shoots right. 5'10", 190 lbs. Born, Saskatoon, Sask., March 21, 1979.
(Edmonton's 8th choice, 187th overall, in 1997 Entry Draft).

			Regular Season					Playoffs				
Season	Club	League	GP	G	A	TP	PIM	GP	G	A	TP	PIM
1994-95	Sask. Contacts	SMHL	29	25	21	46	41	....	....	....	....	....
1995-96	Moose Jaw	WHL	70	22	32	54	65	....	....	....	....	....
1996-97	Moose Jaw	WHL	72	37	47	84	47	12	4	1	5	11
1997-98	Moose Jaw	WHL	72	20	57	77	45	4	1	2	3	2
1998-99	Moose Jaw	WHL	71	42	*75	117	40	11	4	12	16	12
	Hamilton Bulldogs	AHL	3	0	0	0	2	....	....	....	....	....
99-2000	Hamilton Bulldogs	AHL	18	1	4	5	2	5	1	0	1	0
	Tallahassee	ECHL	49	15	25	40	35	....	....	....	....	....
2000-01	Hamilton Bulldogs	AHL	78	13	22	35	30	....	....	....	....	....
2001-02	Hamilton Bulldogs	AHL	71	6	13	19	27	15	2	8	10	8
2002-03	Hamilton Bulldogs	AHL	65	12	12	24	36	22	1	5	6	17

WHL East First All-Star Team (1999)

HIRSCHOVITS, Kim (HUHR-shoh-vihts, KIHM) NYR

Center. Shoots left. 6'1", 180 lbs. Born, Helsinki, Finland, May 9, 1982.
(NY Rangers' 6th choice, 194th overall, in 2002 Entry Draft).

			Regular Season					Playoffs				
Season	Club	League	GP	G	A	TP	PIM	GP	G	A	TP	PIM
2000-01	HIFK Helsinki Jr.	Finn-Jr.	35	24	20	44	41	9	6	6	12	4
	HIFK Helsinki	Finland	2	0	0	0	0	....	....	....	....	....
2001-02	Chicago Steel	USHL	6	2	2	4	6	....	....	....	....	....
	HIFK Helsinki	Finland	45	6	10	16	24	....	....	....	....	....
	HIFK Helsinki Jr.	Finn-Jr.	5	4	7	11	8	4	3	6	9	0
2002-03	HIFK Helsinki	Finland	55	4	11	15	26	4	0	0	0	0
	KJT Jarvenpaa	Finland-2	3	1	2	3	6	....	....	....	....	....

HOGEBOOM, Greg (HOH-guh-BOOM, GREHG) L.A.

Right wing. Shoots right. 6', 190 lbs. Born, Toronto, Ont., September 26, 1982.
(Los Angeles' 6th choice, 152nd overall, in 2002 Entry Draft).

			Regular Season					Playoffs				
Season	Club	League	GP	G	A	TP	PIM	GP	G	A	TP	PIM
1998-99	North York	GTHL	STATISTICS NOT AVAILABLE									
99-2000	Wexford Raiders	OPJHL	48	32	47	79	44	....	....	....	....	....
2000-01	Miami RedHawks	CCHA	38	8	5	13	20	....	....	....	....	....
2001-02	Miami RedHawks	CCHA	36	14	9	23	22	....	....	....	....	....
2002-03	Miami RedHawks	CCHA	41	24	18	42	16	....	....	....	....	....

HOGGAN, Jeff (HOH-guhn, JEHF) MIN.

Right wing. Shoots right. 6', 200 lbs. Born, Hope, B.C., February 1, 1978.

			Regular Season					Playoffs				
Season	Club	League	GP	G	A	TP	PIM	GP	G	A	TP	PIM
99-2000	Nebraska-Omaha	CCHA	34	16	9	25	82	....	....	....	....	....
2000-01	Nebraska-Omaha	CCHA	42	12	17	29	78	....	....	....	....	....
2001-02	Nebraska-Omaha	CCHA	41	24	21	45	92	....	....	....	....	....
	Houston Aeros	AHL	....	....	....	....	....	4	0	0	0	2
2002-03	Houston Aeros	AHL	65	6	5	11	45	14	1	2	3	23

CCHA First All-Star Team (2002) • NCAA West Second All-American Team (2002)

Signed to a try-out contract by **Houston** (AHL), April 4, 2002. Signed as a free agent by **Minnesota**, August 20, 2002.

HOHENER, Martin (HOH-ehn-uhr, MAHR-tihn) NSH.

Defense. Shoots left. 6'1", 192 lbs. Born, Zurich, Switz., June 23, 1980.
(Nashville's 12th choice, 284th overall, in 2000 Entry Draft).

			Regular Season					Playoffs				
Season	Club	League	GP	G	A	TP	PIM	GP	G	A	TP	PIM
1996-97	Kloten Flyers Jr.	Swiss-Jr.	37	4	7	11	....	....	....	....	....	....
1997-98	Kloten Flyers Jr.	Swiss-Jr.	25	2	9	11	31	....	....	....	....	....
	EHC Bulach	Swiss-2	4	0	0	0	0	....	....	....	....	....
1998-99	Kloten Flyers Jr.	Swiss-Jr.	21	5	8	13	22	2	1	0	1	2
	EHC Kloten	Swiss	20	0	1	1	2	9	0	1	1	0
99-2000	EHC Kloten	Swiss	44	4	2	6	20	5	0	1	1	2
2000-01	EHC Kloten	Swiss	35	4	5	9	32	9	0	1	1	6
2001-02	Kloten Flyers	Swiss	44	4	12	16	12	9	0	1	1	2
	Switzerland	Olympics	4	0	0	0	0	....	....	....	....	....
2002-03	Kloten Flyers	Swiss	30	0	2	2	8	3	0	0	0	4

HOLMQVIST, Andreas (HOHLM-kvihst, ahn-DRAY-uhs) T.B.

Defense. Shoots right. 6'4", 190 lbs. Born, Stockholm, Sweden, July 23, 1981.
(Tampa Bay's 3rd choice, 61st overall, in 2001 Entry Draft).

			Regular Season					Playoffs				
Season	Club	League	GP	G	A	TP	PIM	GP	G	A	TP	PIM
99-2000	Hammarby Jr.	Swede-Jr.	33	8	12	20	16	6	1	2	3	4
2000-01	Hammarby Jr.	Swede-Jr.	47	6	15	21	40	....	....	....	....	....
2001-02	Hammarby	Swede-2	42	11	13	24	97	....	....	....	....	....
2002-03	Linkopings HC	Sweden	43	4	9	13	28	....	....	....	....	....

HOLMQVIST, Mikael (HOHLM-kvihst, MIHK-al) ANA.

Center. Shoots left. 6'3", 189 lbs. Born, Stockholm, Sweden, June 8, 1979.
(Anaheim's 1st choice, 18th overall, in 1997 Entry Draft).

			Regular Season					Playoffs				
Season	Club	League	GP	G	A	TP	PIM	GP	G	A	TP	PIM
1995-96	Djurgarden Jr.	Swede-Jr.	24	7	2	9	4	....	....	....	....	....
1996-97	Djurgarden Jr.	Swede-Jr.	39	29	35	64	110	....	....	....	....	....
	Djurgarden	Sweden	9	0	0	0	0	....	....	....	....	....
1997-98	Farjestad	Sweden	41	2	3	5	6	7	0	0	0	0
	Farjestad	EuroHL	5	2	2	4	2	....	....	....	....	....
1998-99	Farjestad Jr.	Swede-Jr.	2	2	2	4	2	....	....	....	....	....
	Farjestad	EuroHL	3	0	0	0	0	1	0	0	0	0
	Farjestad	Sweden	15	0	0	0	6	....	....	....	....	....
	Hammarby	Swede-2	3	2	0	2	0	....	....	....	....	....
99-2000	TPS Turku	Finland	54	12	3	15	14	11	2	3	5	4
2000-01	TPS Turku	Finland	46	4	5	9	8	10	1	3	4	2
2001-02	TPS Turku	Finland	56	9	13	22	16	8	1	0	1	12
2002-03	TPS Turku	Finland	56	15	25	40	36	7	0	0	0	4

HOLTET, Marius (HOHL-teht, MAIR-ee-uhs) DAL.

Center. Shoots right. 6', 183 lbs. Born, Hamar, Norway, August 31, 1984.
(Dallas' 4th choice, 42nd overall, in 2002 Entry Draft).

			Regular Season					Playoffs				
Season	Club	League	GP	G	A	TP	PIM	GP	G	A	TP	PIM
2000-01	Farjestad Jr.	Swede-Jr.	26	5	4	9	34	....	....	....	....	....
2001-02	Farjestad Jr.	Swede-Jr.	37	12	7	19	70	....	....	....	....	....
2002-03	Skare BK	Swede-3	STATISTICS NOT AVAILABLE									
	Bofors IK	Swede-2	14	1	1	2	8	2	0	0	0	2

HOLUB, Jan (HOH-luhb, YAN) NYI

Defense. Shoots left. 6'3", 185 lbs. Born, Liberec, Czech., May 3, 1983.
(NY Islanders' 4th choice, 197th overall, in 2001 Entry Draft).

			Regular Season					Playoffs				
Season	Club	League	GP	G	A	TP	PIM	GP	G	A	TP	PIM
99-2000	HC Liberec Jr.	Czech-Jr.	2	0	0	0	0	....	....	....	....	....
	HC Liberec-18	Czech-Jr.	33	2	5	7	65	....	....	....	....	....
2000-01	HC Liberec Jr.	Czech-Jr.	43	0	6	6	42	....	....	....	....	....
2001-02	HC Liberec Jr.	Czech-Jr.	11	2	0	2	24	....	....	....	....	....
	Jablonec nad Nisou	Czech-3	3	0	0	0	2	....	....	....	....	....
	HC Tygri Liberec	Czech-3	30	1	3	4	22	12	0	0	0	2
2002-03	Liberec	Czech	21	2	2	4	4	....	....	....	....	....
	Liberec Jr.	Czech-Jr.	13	0	6	6	63	8	0	1	1	8

HOOTON, Brock (HOO-tuhn, BRAWK) OTT.

Right wing. Shoots right. 6'1", 185 lbs. Born, Smithers, B.C., March 20, 1983.
(Ottawa's 6th choice, 150th overall, in 2002 Entry Draft).

			Regular Season					Playoffs				
Season	Club	League	GP	G	A	TP	PIM	GP	G	A	TP	PIM
1998-99	Smithers Selects	BCAHA	40	30	55	85	30	....	....	....	....	....
99-2000	Campbell River	VIJHL	40	8	17	25	8	....	....	....	....	....
2000-01	Quesnel	BCHL	60	11	26	37	....	....	....	....	....	....
2001-02	Quesnel	BCHL	60	34	50	84	33	....	....	....	....	....
2002-03	St. Cloud State	WCHA	26	1	6	7	14	....	....	....	....	....

BCHL Interior First All-Star Team (2002)

HOPE, Joey (HOHP, JOE-ee) PHI.

Defense. Shoots right. 6', 180 lbs. Born, Anchorage, AK, January 1, 1982.

			Regular Season					Playoffs				
Season	Club	League	GP	G	A	TP	PIM	GP	G	A	TP	PIM
2000-01	Prince George	WHL	13	1	3	4	6	....	....	....	....	....
	Portland	WHL	56	6	24	30	103	13	1	7	8	10
2001-02	Portland	WHL	64	9	27	36	124	3	0	2	2	8
2002-03	Portland	WHL	54	12	27	39	142	....	....	....	....	....

Signed as a free agent by **Philadelphia**, July 14, 2003.

HORACEK, Jan (HOHR-uh-chehk, YAN) EDM.

Defense. Shoots right. 6'4", 221 lbs. Born, Benesov, Czech., May 22, 1979.
(St. Louis' 3rd choice, 98th overall, in 1997 Entry Draft).

			Regular Season					Playoffs				
Season	Club	League	GP	G	A	TP	PIM	GP	G	A	TP	PIM
1995-96	HC Slavia Praha Jr.	Czech-Jr.	18	1	5	6	0	....	....	....	....	....
	Karlovy Vary	Czech-2	11	0	0	0	0	....	....	....	....	....
	HC Slavia Praha	Czech	8	0	1	1	4	....	....	....	....	....
1996-97	HC Slavia Praha Jr.	Czech-Jr.	25	4	14	18	....	....	....	....	....	....
	H+S Beroun	Czech-2	2	0	0	0	....	....	....	....	....	....
	HC Slavia Praha	Czech	9	0	0	0	6	3	0	0	0	0
1997-98	Moncton Wildcats	QMJHL	54	3	18	21	146	10	1	5	6	20
1998-99	HC Slavia Praha	Czech	1	0	0	0	2	....	....	....	....	....
	Worcester IceCats	AHL	53	1	13	14	119	4	0	0	0	6
99-2000	Worcester IceCats	AHL	68	1	8	9	145	9	0	0	0	2
2000-01	Peoria Rivermen	ECHL	6	0	3	3	8	....	....	....	....	....
	Worcester IceCats	AHL	11	0	1	1	20	2	0	0	0	2
2001-02	Hamilton Bulldogs	AHL	44	0	5	5	99	13	0	1	1	10
2002-03	Liberec	Czech	4	0	0	0	2	....	....	....	....	....
	Vsetin	Czech	19	1	2	3	86	....	....	....	....	....
	HC Slavia Praha	Czech	4	0	0	0	4	....	....	....	....	....
	Havirov	Czech	12	0	3	3	22	....	....	....	....	....

• Missed majority of 2000-01 season recovering from wrist surgery, October 23, 2000. Traded to **Edmonton** by **St. Louis** with Marty Reasoner and Jochen Hecht for Doug Weight and Michel Riesen, July 1, 2001.

HORTON, Nathan (HOHR-tohn, NAY-thun) FLA.

Center. Shoots right. 6'2", 201 lbs. Born, Welland, Ont., May 29, 1985.
(Florida's 1st choice, 3rd overall, in 2003 Entry Draft).

			Regular Season					Playoffs				
Season	Club	League	GP	G	A	TP	PIM	GP	G	A	TP	PIM
2000-01	Thorold	OJHL-B	41	16	31	47	75	....	....	....	....	....
2001-02	Oshawa Generals	OHL	64	31	36	67	84	5	1	2	3	10
2002-03	Oshawa Generals	OHL	54	33	35	68	111	13	9	6	15	10

OHL All-Rookie Team (2002)

HRUSKA, David (huhr-OOSH-kah, dah-VEED) OTT.

Right wing. Shoots right. 5'10", 206 lbs. Born, Sokolov, Czech., January 8, 1977.
(Ottawa's 6th choice, 131st overall, in 1995 Entry Draft).

			Regular Season					Playoffs				
Season	Club	League	GP	G	A	TP	PIM	GP	G	A	TP	PIM
1994-95	Sokolov	Czech-2	5	2	4	6	4	....	....	....	....	....
1995-96	Red Deer Rebels	WHL	28	14	14	28	6	....	....	....	....	....
	HC Petra Vsetin	Czech	5	1	0	1	....	1	0	0	0	....
1996-97	HC Petra Vsetin	Czech	20	4	2	6	4	6	2	4	6	0
	Sokolov	Czech-2	4	3	0	3	....	....	....	....	....	....
1997-98	HC Petra Vsetin	Czech	14	5	1	6	0	....	....	....	....	....
	HC Petra Vsetin	EuroHL	5	0	0	0	0	....	....	....	....	....
1998-99	HC Opava	Czech	4	1	0	1	0	....	....	....	....	....
99-2000	HC Karlovy Vary	Czech	43	17	10	27	8	....	....	....	....	....
2000-01	HC Karlovy Vary	Czech	50	14	5	19	12	....	....	....	....	....
2001-02	Litvinov	Czech	19	*14	3	17	0	....	....	....	....	....
	HC Femax Havirov	Czech	23	*17	12	29	2	....	....	....	....	....
	Kloten Flyers	Swiss	....	....	....	....	....	1	0	0	0	0
2002-03	HC Slavia Praha	Czech	37	13	13	26	10	15	2	2	4	0

HUBL, Viktor (HEW-buhl, VIHK-tohr) WSH.

Left wing. Shoots left. 6', 183 lbs. Born, Chomutov, Czech., August 13, 1978.
(Washington's 10th choice, 284th overall, in 2001 Entry Draft).

			Regular Season					Playoffs				
Season	Club	League	GP	G	A	TP	PIM	GP	G	A	TP	PIM
1997-98	KLH Chomutov	Czech-2	50	18	17	35	....	....	....	....	....	....
1998-99	KLH Chomutov	Czech-2	5	2	1	3	....	....	....	....	....	....
	Litvinov	Czech	27	2	6	8	10	....	....	....	....	....
99-2000	KLH Chomutov	Czech-2	8	2	4	6	4	....	....	....	....	....
	Litvinov	Czech	36	6	9	15	16	....	....	....	....	....
2000-01	HC Slavia Praha	Czech	50	16	24	40	24	11	0	2	2	6
2001-02	HC Slavia Praha	Czech	48	11	14	25	34	8	0	1	1	6
2002-03	Litvinov	Czech	39	8	13	21	30	....	....	....	....	....

HUDLER, Jiri (HUHD-luhr, YIH-ree) DET.

Center. Shoots left. 5'9", 178 lbs. Born, Olomouc, Czech., January 4, 1984.
(Detroit's 1st choice, 58th overall, in 2002 Entry Draft).

			Regular Season					Playoffs				
Season	Club	League	GP	G	A	TP	PIM	GP	G	A	TP	PIM
99-2000	Vsetin Jr.	Czech-Jr.	53	29	31	60	75	....	....	....	....	....
	Vsetin	Czech	2	0	1	1	0	....	....	....	....	....
2000-01	Vsetin Jr.	Czech-Jr.	16	8	14	22	16	....	....	....	....	....
	HC Slovnaft Vsetin	Czech	22	1	4	5	10	....	....	....	....	....
	HC Femax Havirov	Czech	15	5	1	6	12	....	....	....	....	....
2001-02	Vsetin	Czech	46	15	31	46	54	....	....	....	....	....
	Liberec	Czech-2	13	9	7	16	10	....	....	....	....	....
	HC Olomouc	Czech-3	1	0	2	2	4	....	....	....	....	....
2002-03	Vsetin	Czech	30	19	27	46	22	....	....	....	....	....
	Ak Bars Kazan	Russia	11	1	5	6	12	1	0	0	0	0

HULVA, Jakub (HUHL-vuh, YA-kuhb) BUF.

Right wing. Shoots left. 6', 172 lbs. Born, Opava, Czech., May 6, 1984.
(Buffalo's 5th choice, 108th overall, in 2002 Entry Draft).

			Regular Season					Playoffs				
Season	Club	League	GP	G	A	TP	PIM	GP	G	A	TP	PIM
99-2000	HC Vitkovice Jr.	Czech-Jr.	49	20	34	54	38	....	....	....	....	....
2000-01	HC Vitkovice-18	Czech-Jr.	30	28	40	68	22	....	....	....	....	....
	HC Vitkovice Jr.	Czech-Jr.	20	5	6	11	6	....	....	....	....	....
	HC Vitkovice	Czech	1	0	0	0	0	....	....	....	....	....
2001-02	HC Vitkovice Jr.	Czech-Jr.	45	25	24	49	36	....	....	....	....	....
	HC Opava	Czech-2	4	0	0	0	2	....	....	....	....	....
	HC Vitkovice	Czech	1	0	0	0	0	2	0	0	0	0
2002-03	HC Vitkovice Jr.	Czech-Jr.	28	13	16	29	28	1	0	3	3	2
	HC Opava	Czech-2	6	0	0	0	0	....	....	....	....	....
	HC Vitkovice	Czech	5	0	1	1	0	3	0	0	0	0

HUNTER, J.J. (HUHN-tuhr, JAY-JAY) **EDM.**

Right wing. Shoots left. 6'1", 185 lbs. Born, Shaunavon, Sask., July 6, 1980.

			Regular Season					Playoffs				
Season	**Club**	**League**	**GP**	**G**	**A**	**TP**	**PIM**	**GP**	**G**	**A**	**TP**	**PIM**
1998-99	Kelowna Rockets	WHL	66	18	32	50	61	6	1	2	3	2
99-2000	Kelowna Rockets	WHL	66	22	26	48	61	5	1	0	1	2
2000-01	Kelowna Rockets	WHL	12	1	5	6	4	....	....	....	....	....
	Prince Albert	WHL	58	28	17	45	40	....	....	....	....	....
2001-02	Columbus	ECHL	60	23	22	45	59	....	....	....	....	....
	Hamilton Bulldogs	AHL	1	0	0	0	0	1	0	0	0	0
2002-03	Hamilton Bulldogs	AHL	2	0	0	0	2	....	....	....	....	....
	Columbus	ECHL	70	17	36	53	82	....	....	....	....	....

Signed as a free agent by **Edmonton**, August 19, 2002.

HUSKINS, Kent (HUHS-kihns, KEHNT) **FLA.**

Defense. Shoots left. 6'3", 215 lbs. Born, Ottawa, Ont., May 4, 1979.
(Chicago's 3rd choice, 156th overall, in 1998 Entry Draft).

			Regular Season					Playoffs				
Season	**Club**	**League**	**GP**	**G**	**A**	**TP**	**PIM**	**GP**	**G**	**A**	**TP**	**PIM**
1995-96	Kanata Valley	OCJHL	49	6	21	27	18	....	....	....	....	....
1996-97	Kanata Valley	OCJHL	53	11	36	47	89	....	....	....	....	....
1997-98	Clarkson Knights	ECAC	35	2	8	10	46	....	....	....	....	....
1998-99	Clarkson Knights	ECAC	37	5	11	16	28	....	....	....	....	....
99-2000	Clarkson Knights	ECAC	28	2	16	18	30	....	....	....	....	....
2000-01	Clarkson Knights	ECAC	35	6	28	34	22	....	....	....	....	....
2001-02	Norfolk Admirals	AHL	65	4	11	15	44	4	0	1	1	0
2002-03	Norfolk Admirals	AHL	80	5	22	27	48	9	2	2	4	4

ECAC First All-Star Team (2000, 2001) • NCAA East First All-American Team (2001)

Signed as a free agent by **Florida**, August 14, 2003.

HUSSEY, Matt (HUH-see, MAT) **PIT.**

Center. Shoots left. 6'2", 212 lbs. Born, New Haven, CT, May 28, 1979.
(Pittsburgh's 10th choice, 254th overall, in 1998 Entry Draft).

			Regular Season					Playoffs				
Season	**Club**	**League**	**GP**	**G**	**A**	**TP**	**PIM**	**GP**	**G**	**A**	**TP**	**PIM**
1996-97	Wayzata High	Hi-School	48	34	31	65	....	....	....	....	....	....
1997-98	Avon Old Farms	Hi-School	26	26	23	49	20	....	....	....	....	....
1998-99	U. of Wisconsin	WCHA	37	10	5	15	18	....	....	....	....	....
99-2000	U. of Wisconsin	WCHA	35	5	11	16	8	....	....	....	....	....
2000-01	U. of Wisconsin	WCHA	40	9	11	20	24	....	....	....	....	....
2001-02	U. of Wisconsin	WCHA	39	18	15	33	16	....	....	....	....	....
2002-03	Wilkes-Barre	AHL	69	12	11	23	28	2	0	0	0	0

HUTCHINS, Michael (HUHCH-ihns, MIGH-kuhl) **S.J.**

Defense. Shoots left. 6', 185 lbs. Born, Wolfeboro, NH, October 27, 1982.
(San Jose's 7th choice, 288th overall, in 2002 Entry Draft).

			Regular Season					Playoffs				
Season	**Club**	**League**	**GP**	**G**	**A**	**TP**	**PIM**	**GP**	**G**	**A**	**TP**	**PIM**
99-2000	St. Paul's Prep	Hi-School	30	5	12	17	....	....	....	....	....	....
2000-01	St. Paul's Prep	Hi-School	27	8	27	35	36	....	....	....	....	....
2001-02	Des Moines	USHL	60	7	30	37	133	3	0	1	1	2
2002-03	New Hampshire	H-East		DID NOT PLAY – FRESHMAN								

HUTCHINSON, Andrew (HUHT-chihn-suhn, AN-droo) **NSH.**

Defense. Shoots right. 6'2", 204 lbs. Born, Evanston, IL, March 24, 1980.
(Nashville's 4th choice, 54th overall, in 1999 Entry Draft).

			Regular Season					Playoffs				
Season	**Club**	**League**	**GP**	**G**	**A**	**TP**	**PIM**	**GP**	**G**	**A**	**TP**	**PIM**
1996-97	Det. Caesars	MNHL	82	15	41	56	....	....	....	....	....	....
1997-98	U.S. National U-18	USDP	59	7	21	28	53	....	....	....	....	....
1998-99	Michigan State	CCHA	37	3	12	15	26	....	....	....	....	....
99-2000	Michigan State	CCHA	42	5	12	17	64	....	....	....	....	....
2000-01	Michigan State	CCHA	42	5	19	24	46	....	....	....	....	....
2001-02	Michigan State	CCHA	39	6	16	22	24	....	....	....	....	....
	Milwaukee	AHL	5	0	1	1	0	....	....	....	....	....
2002-03	Toledo Storm	ECHL	10	2	5	7	4	....	....	....	....	....
	Milwaukee	AHL	63	9	17	26	40	3	1	0	1	0

CCHA Second All-Star Team (2001, 2002) • NCAA West Second All-American Team (2002)

HYMOVITZ, David (HIH-moh-vihtz, DAY-vihd)

Left wing. Shoots left. 5'11", 170 lbs. Born, Randolph, MA, May 30, 1974.
(Chicago's 9th choice, 209th overall, in 1992 Entry Draft).

			Regular Season					Playoffs				
Season	**Club**	**League**	**GP**	**G**	**A**	**TP**	**PIM**	**GP**	**G**	**A**	**TP**	**PIM**
1991-92	Thayer Academy	Hi-School	26	28	21	49	22	....	....	....	....	....
1992-93	Boston College	H-East	37	7	6	13	6	....	....	....	....	....
1993-94	Boston College	H-East	36	18	14	32	18	....	....	....	....	....
1994-95	Boston College	H-East	35	21	19	40	22	....	....	....	....	....
1995-96	Boston College	H-East	36	26	18	44	32	....	....	....	....	....
1996-97	Columbus Chill	ECHL	58	39	32	71	29	5	4	1	5	2
	Indianapolis Ice	IHL	6	0	1	1	0	1	0	0	0	0
1997-98	Indianapolis Ice	IHL	63	11	15	26	20	5	1	1	2	6
1998-99	Indianapolis Ice	IHL	78	46	30	76	42	5	2	3	5	2
99-2000	Lowell	AHL	67	19	17	36	30	....	....	....	....	....
	Houston Aeros	IHL	18	10	3	13	16	11	3	4	7	8
2000-01	Lowell	AHL	60	14	15	29	52	4	2	1	3	17
2001-02	Grand Rapids	AHL	80	15	33	48	22	5	1	2	3	0
2002-03	Binghamton	AHL	76	15	19	34	46	14	1	0	1	11

IHL Second All-Star Team (1999)

Signed as a free agent by **Los Angeles**, June 10, 1999. Traded to **Houston** (IHL) by **Lowell** (AHL) with Los Angeles retaining NHL rights for Jeff Daw, March 17, 2000. Signed as a free agent by **Ottawa**, July 13, 2001.

HYNES, Shane (HIGHNZ, SHAYN) **ANA.**

Right wing. Shoots right. 6'3", 210 lbs. Born, Montreal, Que., November 7, 1983.
(Anaheim's 3rd choice, 86th overall, in 2003 Entry Draft).

			Regular Season					Playoffs				
Season	**Club**	**League**	**GP**	**G**	**A**	**TP**	**PIM**	**GP**	**G**	**A**	**TP**	**PIM**
99-2000	Calgary Flames	AMHL	30	8	12	20	20	....	....	....	....	....
2000-01	Calgary Flames	AMHL	28	18	21	38	76	....	....	....	....	....
2001-02	Nanaimo Clippers	BCHL	50	38	36	74	183	....	....	....	....	....
2002-03	Cornell Big Red	ECAC	32	11	9	20	36	....	....	....	....	....

BCHL All-Rookie Team (2002)

IGNATUSHKIN, Igor (ihg-nah-TOOSH-kihn, EE-gohr) **WSH.**

Center. Shoots left. 5'11", 161 lbs. Born, Elektrostal, USSR, April 7, 1984.
(Washington's 12th choice, 242nd overall, in 2002 Entry Draft).

			Regular Season					Playoffs				
Season	**Club**	**League**	**GP**	**G**	**A**	**TP**	**PIM**	**GP**	**G**	**A**	**TP**	**PIM**
2001-02	Elektrostal 2	Russia-3	6	2	3	5	6	....	....	....	....	....
	Elektrostal	Russia-2	46	1	4	5	20	....	....	....	....	....
2002-03	Elektrostal	Russia-2	36	9	10	19	8	....	....	....	....	....

IMMONEN, Jarkko (IH-moh-nihn, YAHR-koh) **TOR.**

Center. Shoots right. 6', 202 lbs. Born, Rantasalmi, Finland, April 19, 1982.
(Toronto's 8th choice, 254th overall, in 2002 Entry Draft).

			Regular Season					Playoffs				
Season	**Club**	**League**	**GP**	**G**	**A**	**TP**	**PIM**	**GP**	**G**	**A**	**TP**	**PIM**
1997-98	SaPKo Jr.	Finn-Jr.	14	8	12	20	0	....	....	....	....	....
1998-99	SaPKo Savonlinna	Finland-2	36	2	2	4	6	....	....	....	....	....
	SaPKo Jr.	Finn-Jr.	12	6	10	16	34	....	....	....	....	....
99-2000	SaPKo Savonlinna	Finland-2	42	18	16	34	34	....	....	....	....	....
	SaPKo Jr.	Finn-Jr.	2	1	1	2	2	....	....	....	....	....
2000-01	TuTo Turku	Finland-2	41	20	20	40	22	11	5	7	12	10
	TuTo Turku Jr.	Finn-Jr.	....	....	....	....	....	....	....	....	....	....
2001-02	Assat Pori	Finland	44	0	2	2	6	....	....	....	....	....
	Assat Pori Jr.	Finn-Jr.	3	1	1	2	4	8	5	1	6	10
2002-03	JYP Jyvaskyla	Finland	56	10	23	33	34	7	1	1	2	8

IRGL, Zbynek (UHR-guhl, ZBIH-nehk) **NSH.**

Center. Shoots right. 5'11", 183 lbs. Born, Vitkovice, Czech., November 29, 1980.
(Nashville's 9th choice, 197th overall, in 2000 Entry Draft).

			Regular Season					Playoffs				
Season	**Club**	**League**	**GP**	**G**	**A**	**TP**	**PIM**	**GP**	**G**	**A**	**TP**	**PIM**
1996-97	HC Vitkovice Jr.	Czech-Jr.	43	44	22	66	....	....	....	....	....	....
1997-98	HC Vitkovice Jr.	Czech-Jr.	37	17	10	27	....	....	....	....	....	....
1998-99	HC Vitkovice Jr.	Czech-Jr.	18	9	8	17	....	....	....	....	....	....
	HC Vitkovice	Czech	33	2	2	4	6	4	0	0	0	....
99-2000	HC Dukla Jihlava	Czech-2	1	0	0	0	0	....	....	....	....	....
	HC Vitkovice	Czech	47	7	5	12	10	....	....	....	....	....
2000-01	HC Vitkovice	Czech	37	0	1	1	8	4	0	0	0	0
	HC Slean Opava	Czech-2	9	3	2	5	2	....	....	....	....	....
	HC Vitkovice Jr.	Czech-Jr.	4	6	3	9	2	....	....	....	....	....
2001-02	HC Vitkovice	Czech	39	2	8	10	8	13	4	0	4	6
2002-03	HC Vitkovice	Czech	51	6	7	13	14	5	0	1	1	0

IRMEN, Danny (UHR-mehn, DA-nee) **MIN.**

Center. Shoots right. 5'11", 185 lbs. Born, Fargo, ND, September 6, 1984.
(Minnesota's 3rd choice, 78th overall, in 2003 Entry Draft).

			Regular Season					Playoffs				
Season	**Club**	**League**	**GP**	**G**	**A**	**TP**	**PIM**	**GP**	**G**	**A**	**TP**	**PIM**
2001-02	Lincoln Stars	USHL	61	17	36	53	....	....	....	....	....	....
2002-03	Lincoln Stars	USHL	45	21	34	55	78	10	8	6	14	17

• Signed Letter of Intent to attend **University of Minnesota**, November 15, 2002.

ISAKOV , Yevgeny (ih-SA-kawf, yehv-GEH-nee) **PIT.**

Right wing. Shoots left. 6', 196 lbs. Born, Krasnoyarsk, USSR, October 13, 1984.
(Pittsburgh's 6th choice, 161st overall, in 2003 Entry Draft).

			Regular Season					Playoffs				
Season	**Club**	**League**	**GP**	**G**	**A**	**TP**	**PIM**	**GP**	**G**	**A**	**TP**	**PIM**
99-2000	Rubin Tyumen 2	Russia-3	7	0	2	2	16	....	....	....	....	....
2000-01	Rubin Tyumen 2	Russia-3	....	....	....	....	....	....	....	....	....	....
	Gazovik Tyumen	Russia-3	11	1	1	2	12	....	....	....	....	....
2001-02	Gazovik Tyumen	Russia-2	19	2	2	4	2	....	....	....	....	....
	Elektrostal	Russia-2	29	3	2	5	24	....	....	....	....	....
	Elektrostal 2	Russia-3	11	3	3	6	43	....	....	....	....	....
2002-03	Cherepovets	Russia	36	0	3	3	12	1	0	0	0	0

ISOSALO, Samu (ee-soh-SA-low, SA-moo) **ATL.**

Right wing. Shoots left. 6'3", 205 lbs. Born, Rauma, Finland, October 10, 1981.
(Atlanta's 10th choice, 230th overall, in 2000 Entry Draft).

			Regular Season					Playoffs				
Season	**Club**	**League**	**GP**	**G**	**A**	**TP**	**PIM**	**GP**	**G**	**A**	**TP**	**PIM**
1996-97	Lukko Rauma-B	Finn-Jr.	21	5	6	11	45	....	....	....	....	....
	Lukko Rauma Jr.	Finn-Jr.	1	0	0	0	0	....	....	....	....	....
1997-98	Lukko Rauma Jr.	Finn-Jr.	34	21	19	40	48	....	....	....	....	....
1998-99	North Bay	OHL	59	13	12	25	19	4	0	0	0	4
99-2000	North Bay	OHL	48	17	25	42	26	3	0	0	0	0
2000-01	Lukko Rauma Jr.	Finn-Jr.	14	11	9	20	42	3	1	2	3	0
	Jaa-Kotkat	Finland-2	3	2	1	3	2	....	....	....	....	....
	Lukko Rauma	Finland	31	1	1	2	33	1	0	0	0	0
2001-02	Lukko Rauma Jr.	Finn-Jr.	2	0	3	3	2	....	....	....	....	....
	Lukko Rauma	Finland	4	0	0	0	2	....	....	....	....	....
2002-03	Lukko Rauma	Finland	52	5	5	10	6	....	....	....	....	....

IVANOV, Alexei (ih-van-AWF, al-EHX-ay) **CHI.**

Center. Shoots left. 5'8", 174 lbs. Born, Tynda, USSR, January 5, 1985.
(Chicago's 5th choice, 156th overall, in 2003 Entry Draft).

			Regular Season					Playoffs				
Season	**Club**	**League**	**GP**	**G**	**A**	**TP**	**PIM**	**GP**	**G**	**A**	**TP**	**PIM**
2001-02	Yaroslavl 2	Russia-3	26	9	10	19	16	....	....	....	....	....
2002-03	Yaroslavl 2	Russia-3		STATISTICS NOT AVAILABLE								
	Yaroslavl Jr.	Russia-Jr.	6	5	3	8	0	....	....	....	....	....

JAAKOLA, Topi (YAH-koh-luh, TOH-pee) **FLA.**

Defense. Shoots left. 6'1", 185 lbs. Born, Oulu, Finland, November 15, 1983.
(Florida's 5th choice, 134th overall, in 2002 Entry Draft).

			Regular Season					Playoffs				
Season	**Club**	**League**	**GP**	**G**	**A**	**TP**	**PIM**	**GP**	**G**	**A**	**TP**	**PIM**
99-2000	Karpat Oulu Jr.	Finn-Jr.	36	5	12	17	71	5	1	1	2	4
2000-01	Karpat Oulu Jr.	Finn-Jr.	35	4	10	14	47	6	0	2	2	6
	Karpat Oulu	Finland	4	0	0	0	2	....	....	....	....	....
2001-02	Karpat Oulu Jr.	Finn-Jr.	3	0	0	0	2	2	1	0	1	4
	Karpat Oulu	Finland	44	0	4	4	18	4	0	0	0	4
2002-03	Karpat Oulu	Finland	52	2	2	4	18	15	0	0	0	8

JAASKELAINEN, Teemu (yas-keh-LIGH-nuhn, TEE-moo) CHI.

Defense. Shoots left. 6'1", 207 lbs. Born, Tampere, Finland, June 6, 1983.
(Chicago's 11th choice, 205th overall, in 2001 Entry Draft).

			Regular Season					Playoffs				
Season	Club	League	GP	G	A	TP	PIM	GP	G	A	TP	PIM
1998-99	Ilves Tampere-C	Finn-Jr.	22	1	4	5	8	3	0	0	0	2
99-2000	Ilves Tampere-B	Finn-Jr.	36	5	1	6	20	....	....	....	....	....
2000-01	Ilves Tampere-B	Finn-Jr.	5	1	1	2	16	....	....	....	....	....
	Ilves Tampere Jr.	Finn-Jr.	41	4	1	5	30	....	....	....	....	....
2001-02	Ilves Tampere Jr.	Finn-Jr.	13	1	6	7	8	....	....	....	....	....
	Ilves Tampere	Finland	38	0	0	0	24	3	0	0	0	0
2002-03	Ilves Tampere	Finland	48	1	4	5	16	....	....	....	....	....
	Ilves Tampere Jr.	Finn-Jr.	7	3	4	7	4	....	....	....	....	....

JACKMAN, Tim (JAK-man, TIHM) CBJ

Right wing. Shoots right. 6'3", 190 lbs. Born, Minot, ND, November 14, 1981.
(Columbus' 2nd choice, 38th overall, in 2001 Entry Draft).

			Regular Season					Playoffs				
Season	Club	League	GP	G	A	TP	PIM	GP	G	A	TP	PIM
1998-99	Park Center High	Hi-School	22	22	22	44	....	....	....	....	....	....
99-2000	Park Center High	Hi-School	19	34	22	56	....	....	....	....	....	....
	Twin Cities	USHL	25	11	9	20	58	13	8	5	13	12
2000-01	Minnesota State	WCHA	37	11	14	25	92	....	....	....	....	....
2001-02	Minnesota State	WCHA	36	14	14	28	86	....	....	....	....	....
2002-03	Syracuse Crunch	AHL	77	9	7	16	48	....	....	....	....	....

Minnesota High School All-Conference Team (1999, 2000) • Minnesota All-State Team (2000)

JACKSON, Todd (JAK-suhn, TAWD) DET.

Right wing. Shoots right. 5'11", 170 lbs. Born, Syracuse, NY, April 10, 1981.
(Detroit's 10th choice, 251st overall, in 2000 Entry Draft).

			Regular Season					Playoffs				
Season	Club	League	GP	G	A	TP	PIM	GP	G	A	TP	PIM
1998-99	U.S. National U-17	USDP	53	11	9	20	56	....	....	....	....	....
99-2000	U.S. National U-17	USDP	29	8	10	18	25	....	....	....	....	....
	U.S. National U-18	USDP	23	8	6	14	12	....	....	....	....	....
2000-01	U. of Maine	H-East	39	4	8	12	8	....	....	....	....	....
2001-02	U. of Maine	H-East	39	7	21	28	10	....	....	....	....	....
2002-03	U. of Maine	H-East	39	13	13	26	22	....	....	....	....	....

JACQUES, Jean-Francois (ZHAWK, ZHAWN-fran-SWUH) EDM.

Left wing. Shoots left. 6'4", 217 lbs. Born, Terrebonne, Que., April 29, 1985.
(Edmonton's 3rd choice, 68th overall, in 2003 Entry Draft).

			Regular Season					Playoffs				
Season	Club	League	GP	G	A	TP	PIM	GP	G	A	TP	PIM
2000-01	Cap-d-Madeleine	QAAA	39	22	13	35	28	10	5	8	13	14
2001-02	Baie-Comeau	QMJHL	66	10	14	24	136	5	1	0	1	2
2002-03	Baie-Comeau	QMJHL	67	12	21	33	123	12	4	2	6	13

JAMES, Connor (JAYMZ, KAW-nuhr) L.A.

Right wing. Shoots right. 5'10", 168 lbs. Born, Calgary, Alta., August 25, 1982.
(Los Angeles' 11th choice, 279th overall, in 2002 Entry Draft).

			Regular Season					Playoffs				
Season	Club	League	GP	G	A	TP	PIM	GP	G	A	TP	PIM
1998-99	Calgary Buffaloes	AMHL	36	33	53	86	20	....	....	....	....	....
99-2000	Calgary Royals	AJHL	64	36	57	93	41	....	....	....	....	....
2000-01	U. of Denver	WCHA	38	8	19	27	14	....	....	....	....	....
2001-02	U. of Denver	WCHA	41	16	26	42	18	....	....	....	....	....
2002-03	U. of Denver	WCHA	41	20	23	43	12	....	....	....	....	....

AJHL All-Rookie Team (2000) • AJHL First All-Star Team (2000) • AJHL Rookie of the Year (2000)

JAMINKI, Tommi (yah-MIHN-kee,TAW-mee) CHI.

Left wing. Shoots right. 6'2", 196 lbs. Born, Turku, Finland, February 11, 1983.
(Chicago's 8th choice, 142nd overall, in 2001 Entry Draft).

			Regular Season					Playoffs				
Season	Club	League	GP	G	A	TP	PIM	GP	G	A	TP	PIM
99-2000	KJT Kerawa Jr.	Finn-Jr.	35	9	10	19	106	....	....	....	....	....
2000-01	Blues Espoo Jr.	Finn-Jr.	36	6	6	12	16	....	....	....	....	....
2001-02	Blues Espoo Jr.	Finn-Jr.	31	9	7	16	66	2	0	0	0	2
	Blues Espoo	Finland	4	0	0	0	0	....	....	....	....	....
2002-03	Ilves Tampere	Finland	45	2	0	2	0	....	....	....	....	....
	Ilves Tampere Jr.	Finn-Jr.	20	15	7	22	27	....	....	....	....	....

JAMTIN, Andreas (yahm-TEEN, ahn-DRAY-uhs) DET.

Right wing. Shoots left. 5'11", 185 lbs. Born, Stockholm, Sweden, May 4, 1983.
(Detroit's 4th choice, 157th overall, in 2001 Entry Draft).

			Regular Season					Playoffs				
Season	Club	League	GP	G	A	TP	PIM	GP	G	A	TP	PIM
1998-99	AIK Solna Jr.	Swede-Jr.	44	33	29	62	105	....	....	....	....	....
99-2000	Farjestad Jr.	Swede-Jr.	28	6	6	12	36	....	....	....	....	....
2000-01	Farjestad-18	Swede-Jr.	1	1	0	1	2	....	....	....	....	....
	Farjestad Jr.	Swede-Jr.	13	5	8	13	83	....	....	....	....	....
	Farjestad	Sweden	1	0	0	0	0	....	....	....	....	....
2001-02	AIK Solna	Sweden	42	2	3	5	55	....	....	....	....	....
	AIK Stockholm	Swede-2	12	12	15	27	61	1	2	2	4	2
	AIK Stockholm	Swede-Q	10	1	2	3	4	....	....	....	....	....
2002-03	AIK Stockholm	Swede-2	52	23	20	43	139	4	2	1	3	6

JANCEVSKI, Dan (jan-SEHV-skee, DAN) DAL.

Defense. Shoots left. 6'3", 212 lbs. Born, Windsor, Ont., June 15, 1981.
(Dallas' 2nd choice, 66th overall, in 1999 Entry Draft).

			Regular Season					Playoffs				
Season	Club	League	GP	G	A	TP	PIM	GP	G	A	TP	PIM
1995-96	Riverside Selects	OMHA	59	9	22	31	67	....	....	....	....	....
1996-97	Windsor Lions	OMHA	47	6	20	26	99	....	....	....	....	....
1997-98	Tecumseh	OJHL-B	49	3	11	14	145	....	....	....	....	....
1998-99	London Knights	OHL	68	2	12	14	115	25	1	7	8	24
99-2000	London Knights	OHL	59	8	15	23	138	....	....	....	....	....
2000-01	London Knights	OHL	39	4	23	27	95	....	....	....	....	....
	Sudbury Wolves	OHL	31	3	14	17	42	12	0	9	9	17
2001-02	Utah Grizzlies	AHL	77	0	13	13	147	5	0	0	0	4
2002-03	Utah Grizzlies	AHL	76	1	10	11	172	2	0	1	1	12

JANSSEN, Cam (JAN-suhn, KAM) N.J.

Right wing. Shoots right. 5'11", 210 lbs. Born, St. Louis, MO, April 15, 1984.
(New Jersey's 6th choice, 117th overall, in 2002 Entry Draft).

			Regular Season					Playoffs				
Season	Club	League	GP	G	A	TP	PIM	GP	G	A	TP	PIM
2000-01	St. Louis Jr. Blues	NAJHL	45	1	2	3	244	....	....	....	....	....
2001-02	Windsor Spitfires	OHL	64	5	17	22	*268	10	0	0	0	13
2002-03	Windsor Spitfires	OHL	50	1	12	13	211	7	0	1	1	22

JARMAN, Kevin (JAR-muhn, KEH-vihn) CBJ

Left wing. Shoots left. 6', 184 lbs. Born, Toronto, Ont., March 12, 1985.
(Columbus' 4th choice, 103rd overall, in 2003 Entry Draft).

			Regular Season					Playoffs				
Season	Club	League	GP	G	A	TP	PIM	GP	G	A	TP	PIM
2000-01	Tor. Young Nats	GTHL	STATISTICS NOT AVAILABLE									
2001-02	Stouffville Spirit	OPJHL	44	20	13	33	53	....	....	....	....	....
2002-03	Stouffville Spirit	OPJHL	46	41	39	80	49	11	5	3	8	6

• Signed Letter of Intent to attend **U. of Massachusetts-Amherst** (H-East), November 20, 2002.

JARRETT, Patrick (JEHR-eht, PAT-rihk) NSH.

Center. Shoots left. 5'11", 181 lbs. Born, Sault Ste. Marie, Ont., February 6, 1984.
(Nashville's 3rd choice, 138th overall, in 2002 Entry Draft).

			Regular Season					Playoffs				
Season	Club	League	GP	G	A	TP	PIM	GP	G	A	TP	PIM
1998-99	Soo Thunder	NOHA	35	32	39	*71	....	....	....	....	....	....
99-2000	Soo Thunder	NOBHL	39	22	32	54	57	....	....	....	....	....
2000-01	Mississauga	OHL	60	15	38	53	22	....	....	....	....	....
2001-02	Mississauga	OHL	20	3	10	13	14	....	....	....	....	....
	Owen Sound	OHL	27	3	14	17	10	....	....	....	....	....
2002-03	Owen Sound	OHL	63	16	39	55	49	4	1	4	5	2

NOHA Rookie of the Year (1999)

JENSEN, Erik (JEHN-sehn, AIR-ihk) N.J.

Right wing. Shoots right. 6'1", 195 lbs. Born, Madison, WI, September 4, 1979.
(New Jersey's 10th choice, 199th overall, in 1998 Entry Draft).

			Regular Season					Playoffs				
Season	Club	League	GP	G	A	TP	PIM	GP	G	A	TP	PIM
1997-98	Des Moines	USHL	41	12	14	26	90	....	....	....	....	....
1998-99	Des Moines	USHL	26	5	11	16	62	14	4	3	7	35
99-2000	U. of Wisconsin	WCHA	22	3	3	6	30	....	....	....	....	....
2000-01	U. of Wisconsin	WCHA	39	6	7	13	57	....	....	....	....	....
2001-02	U. of Wisconsin	WCHA	36	1	5	6	94	....	....	....	....	....
2002-03	U. of Wisconsin	WCHA	35	5	4	9	73	....	....	....	....	....

JESSIMAN, Hugh (JEHS-ih-muhn, HEW) NYR

Right wing. Shoots right. 6'5", 218 lbs. Born, New York, NY, March 28, 1984.
(NY Rangers' 1st choice, 12th overall, in 2003 Entry Draft).

			Regular Season					Playoffs				
Season	Club	League	GP	G	A	TP	PIM	GP	G	A	TP	PIM
2001-02	Brunswick Bruins	Hi-School	18	25	27	52	40	....	....	....	....	....
2002-03	Dartmouth	ECAC	34	23	24	47	48	....	....	....	....	....

ECAC All-Rookie Team (2003) • ECAC Rookie of the Year (2003)

JOHANSSON, Daniel (yoh-HAN-suhn, DAN-yehl) L.A.

Center. Shoots left. 5'11", 176 lbs. Born, Ornskoldsvik, Sweden, July 5, 1981.
(Los Angeles' 6th choice, 125th overall, in 1999 Entry Draft).

			Regular Season					Playoffs				
Season	Club	League	GP	G	A	TP	PIM	GP	G	A	TP	PIM
1997-98	MoDo Jr.	Swede-Jr.	6	0	0	0	0	....	....	....	....	....
1998-99	MoDo Jr.	Swede-Jr.	43	10	19	29	....	....	....	....	....	....
99-2000	MoDo Jr.	Swede-Jr.	35	11	21	32	34	....	....	....	....	....
	MoDo	EuroHL	2	0	0	0	0	....	....	....	....	....
2000-01	Bodens IK	Swede-2	36	4	3	7	10	4	0	0	0	0
2001-02	Bodens IK	Swede-2	37	2	3	5	10	....	....	....	....	....
	Vaxjo HC	Swede-3	8	2	5	7	6	....	....	....	....	....
2002-03	Vaxjo HC	Swede-3	44	6	18	24	....	....	....	....	....	....

JOHANSSON, Eric (joh-HAHN-suhn, AIR-ihk) N.J.

Center. Shoots left. 6', 195 lbs. Born, Edmonton, Alta., January 7, 1982.
(New Jersey's 8th choice, 187th overall, in 2002 Entry Draft).

			Regular Season					Playoffs				
Season	Club	League	GP	G	A	TP	PIM	GP	G	A	TP	PIM
1997-98	Edmonton CAC	AMHA	22	13	10	23	19	....	....	....	....	....
1998-99	Tri-City Americans	WHL	48	8	14	22	20	6	1	1	2	2
99-2000	Tri-City Americans	WHL	72	24	36	60	38	4	0	0	0	2
2000-01	Tri-City Americans	WHL	72	36	44	80	72	....	....	....	....	....
2001-02	Tri-City Americans	WHL	69	44	59	103	73	5	1	2	3	5
2002-03	Albany River Rats	AHL	66	7	9	16	24	....	....	....	....	....

• Re-entered NHL Entry Draft. Originally Minnesota's 9th choice, 255th overall, in 2000 Entry Draft.

WHL West Second All-Star Team (2002)

JOHANSSON, Fredrik (yoh-HAHN-suhn, FREHD-rihk) EDM.

Center. Shoots left. 5'11", 180 lbs. Born, Munkedal, Sweden, February 27, 1984.
(Edmonton's 14th choice, 274th overall, in 2002 Entry Draft).

			Regular Season					Playoffs				
Season	Club	League	GP	G	A	TP	PIM	GP	G	A	TP	PIM
2000-01	V. Frolunda Jr.	Swede-Jr.	22	3	4	7	8	3	0	1	1	4
	V. Frolunda-18	Swede-Jr.	6	5	1	6	4	....	....	....	....	....
2001-02	V. Frolunda Jr.	Swede-Jr.	42	13	23	36	39	....	....	....	....	....
	V. Frolunda-18	Swede-Jr.	1	0	1	1	0	....	....	....	....	....
2002-03	V. Frolunda Jr.	Swede-Jr.	30	13	34	47	24	3	0	2	2	2
	Vastra Frolunda	Sweden	9	0	0	0	2	5	0	0	0	0

JOHANSSON, Jonas (yoh-HAHN-suhn, YOH-nuhs) COL.

Right wing. Shoots right. 6'1", 180 lbs. Born, Jonkoping, Sweden, March 18, 1984.
(Colorado's 1st choice, 28th overall, in 2002 Entry Draft).

			Regular Season					Playoffs				
Season	Club	League	GP	G	A	TP	PIM	GP	G	A	TP	PIM
99-2000	HV 71 Jr.	Swede-Jr.	9	6	3	9	2	2	0	0	0	4
2000-01	HV 71 Jr.	Swede-Jr.	27	13	8	21	14	2	1	0	1	0
2001-02	HV 71 Jr.	Swede-Jr.	26	15	19	34	20	....	....	....	....	....
	HV 71 Jonkoping	Sweden	5	0	0	0	0	2	0	0	0	0
2002-03	Kamloops Blazers	WHL	26	10	25	35	8	6	1	2	3	4

JOHNSON, Aaron (JAWN-suhn, AIR-ruhn) CBJ

Defense. Shoots left. 6', 186 lbs. Born, Port Hawkesbury, N.S., April 30, 1983.
(Columbus' 4th choice, 85th overall, in 2001 Entry Draft).

			Regular Season					Playoffs				
Season	Club	League	GP	G	A	TP	PIM	GP	G	A	TP	PIM
99-2000	Rimouski Oceanic	QMJHL	63	1	14	15	57	8	0	0	0	0
2000-01	Rimouski Oceanic	QMJHL	64	12	41	53	128	11	2	4	6	35
2001-02	Rimouski Oceanic	QMJHL	68	17	49	66	172	7	1	2	3	12
2002-03	Rimouski Oceanic	QMJHL	25	4	20	24	41	....	....	....	....	....
	Quebec Remparts	QMJHL	32	6	31	37	41	11	4	4	8	25

JOHNSON, Gregg (JAWN-suhn, GREHG) OTT.

Center. Shoots left. 5'11", 183 lbs. Born, Windsor, CT, June 18, 1982.
(Ottawa's 11th choice, 256th overall, in 2001 Entry Draft).

			Regular Season					Playoffs				
Season	Club	League	GP	G	A	TP	PIM	GP	G	A	TP	PIM
1997-98	New England	EJHL	40	13	24	37	....	....	....	....	....	....
1998-99	New England	EJHL	40	29	27	56	....	....	....	....	....	....
99-2000	New England	EJHL	40	40	69	109	....	....	....	....	....	....
2000-01	Boston University	H-East	35	5	5	10	20	....	....	....	....	....
2001-02	Boston University	H-East	33	5	18	23	34	....	....	....	....	....
2002-03	Boston University	H-East	24	1	4	5	18	....	....	....	....	....

EJHL Rookie of the Year (1998) • EJHL MVP (2000)

JOHNSON, Jonas (YAWN-suhn, YEW-nuhs) ST.L.

Center. Shoots left. 6'2", 185 lbs. Born, Gavle, Sweden, March 23, 1970.
(St. Louis' 7th choice, 221st overall, in 2002 Entry Draft).

			Regular Season					Playoffs				
Season	Club	League	GP	G	A	TP	PIM	GP	G	A	TP	PIM
1987-88	Stromsboro	Swede-2	13	4	3	7	0	....	....	....	....	....
1988-89	Stromsboro	Swede-2	27	5	3	8	10	....	....	....	....	....
1989-90	Stromsboro	Swede-2	24	13	6	19	8	2	1	1	2	0
1990-91	Bjorkloven	Swede-2	36	10	15	25	32	2	0	0	0	0
1991-92	Brynas IF Gavle	Sweden	36	6	9	15	8	5	3	0	3	0
1992-93	Brynas IF Gavle	Sweden	39	8	16	24	24	10	6	4	10	6
1993-94	Brynas IF Gavle	Sweden	39	11	16	27	14	7	2	1	3	8
1994-95	Brynas IF Gavle	Sweden	39	9	15	24	26	14	4	6	10	14
1995-96	Brynas IF Gavle	Sweden	22	11	6	17	12	....	....	....	....	....
	Brynas IF Gavle	Swede-Q	18	6	25	31	4	10	1	9	10	8
1996-97	Landshut	Germany	48	7	19	26	6	7	2	0	2	4
1997-98	Landshut	Germany	48	8	6	14	26	6	0	1	1	8
1998-99	Vastra Frolunda	Sweden	46	13	21	34	44	4	1	1	2	6
99-2000	Vastra Frolunda	Sweden	50	17	18	35	73	5	0	2	2	6
2000-01	Vastra Frolunda	Sweden	50	15	29	44	75	5	4	3	7	12
2001-02	Vastra Frolunda	Sweden	50	14	31	45	24	10	3	3	6	4
2002-03	Vastra Frolunda	Sweden	49	12	23	35	24	16	3	3	6	27

JOKILA, Janne (YOHK-ih-luh, YAHN-ee) CBJ

Left wing. Shoots left. 5'9", 174 lbs. Born, Turku, Finland, April 22, 1982.
(Columbus' 7th choice, 200th overall, in 2000 Entry Draft).

			Regular Season					Playoffs				
Season	Club	League	GP	G	A	TP	PIM	GP	G	A	TP	PIM
1996-97	TPS Turku-C	Finn-Jr.	30	25	17	42	24	6	*5	*5	*10	2
1997-98	TPS Turku-B	Finn-Jr.	30	11	10	21	28	6	3	1	4	2
1998-99	TPS Turku Jr.	Finn-Jr.	36	17	15	32	77	....	....	....	....	....
99-2000	TPS Turku Jr.	Finn-Jr.	35	10	7	17	32	13	3	3	6	4
2000-01	TPS Turku Jr.	Finn-Jr.	22	15	15	30	30	2	0	1	1	4
	TPS Turku	Finland	2	0	0	0	0	....	....	....	....	....
	SaiPa	Finland	8	1	1	2	0	....	....	....	....	....
2001-02	TPS Turku	Finland	14	1	1	2	4	....	....	....	....	....
	SaiPa	Finland	12	0	0	0	2	....	....	....	....	....
	Lukko Rauma	Finland	14	0	1	1	18	....	....	....	....	....
2002-03	River City	USHL	45	15	17	32	57	7	1	5	6	4

JOKINEN, Jussi (YOH-kih-nihn, YOO-see) DAL.

Center. Shoots left. 5'11", 183 lbs. Born, Kalajoki, Finland, April 1, 1983.
(Dallas' 7th choice, 192nd overall, in 2001 Entry Draft).

			Regular Season					Playoffs				
Season	Club	League	GP	G	A	TP	PIM	GP	G	A	TP	PIM
1998-99	Karpat Oulu-C	Finn-Jr.	27	29	34	63	12	....	....	....	....	....
99-2000	Karpat Oulu Jr.	Finn-Jr.	28	4	6	10	14	....	....	....	....	....
	Karpat Oulu-B	Finn-Jr.	15	6	25	31	14	6	2	3	5	0
2000-01	Karpat Oulu-B	Finn-Jr.	1	2	1	3	0	....	....	....	....	....
	Karpat Oulu Jr.	Finn-Jr.	41	18	31	49	69	6	2	2	4	0
2001-02	Karpat Oulu	Finland	54	10	6	16	34	4	1	0	1	0
	Karpat Oulu Jr.	Finn-Jr.	2	4	1	5	2	1	1	1	2	0
2002-03	Karpat Oulu	Finland	51	14	23	37	10	15	2	1	3	33

JONASEN, Marcus (YOH-nuh-suhn, MAHR-kuhs) NYR

Left wing. Shoots right. 6'4", 220 lbs. Born, Vasteras, Sweden, January 12, 1984.
(NY Rangers' 2nd choice, 81st overall, in 2002 Entry Draft).

			Regular Season					Playoffs				
Season	Club	League	GP	G	A	TP	PIM	GP	G	A	TP	PIM
2000-01	Vasteras IK Jr.	Swede-Jr.	3	2	1	3	0	....	....	....	....	....
	Vasteras IK	Sweden	13	3	5	8	6	....	....	....	....	....
2001-02	Vasteras IK Jr.	Swede-Jr.	3	0	0	0	4	....	....	....	....	....
	Vasteras IK	Swede-2	16	2	1	3	6	....	....	....	....	....
	Vasteras IK	Swede-Q	2	0	0	0	0	....	....	....	....	....
2002-03	Hammarby Jr.	Swede-Jr.	27	16	9	25	28	2	1	0	1	2

JONES, Matt (JOHNZ, MAT) PHX.

Defense. Shoots left. 6', 214 lbs. Born, Downers Grove, IL, August 8, 1983.
(Phoenix's 5th choice, 80th overall, in 2002 Entry Draft).

			Regular Season					Playoffs				
Season	Club	League	GP	G	A	TP	PIM	GP	G	A	TP	PIM
99-2000	Green Bay	USHL	54	1	4	5	59	13	0	0	0	2
2000-01	Green Bay	USHL	52	3	10	13	58	4	0	0	0	2
2001-02	North Dakota	WCHA	37	2	5	7	20	....	....	....	....	....
2002-03	North Dakota	WCHA	39	1	6	7	26	....	....	....	....	....

JONES, Randy (JOHNZ, RAN-dee) PHI.

Defense. Shoots left. 6'2", 200 lbs. Born, Quispamsis, N.B., July 23, 1981.

			Regular Season					Playoffs				
Season	Club	League	GP	G	A	TP	PIM	GP	G	A	TP	PIM
2000-01	Cobourg Cougars	OPJHL	28	15	21	36	46	....	....	....	....	....
2001-02	Clarkson University	ECAC	34	9	11	20	32	....	....	....	....	....
2002-03	Clarkson University	ECAC	33	13	20	33	65	....	....	....	....	....

ECAC First All-Star Team (2003)

Signed as a free agent by **Philadelphia**, July 24, 2003.

JONSSON, Lars (YAWN-suhn, LARZ) BOS.

Defense. Shoots left. 6'1", 198 lbs. Born, Borlange, Sweden, January 2, 1982.
(Boston's 1st choice, 7th overall, in 2000 Entry Draft).

			Regular Season					Playoffs				
Season	Club	League	GP	G	A	TP	PIM	GP	G	A	TP	PIM
1998-99	Leksands IF Jr.	Swede-Jr.	40	4	8	12	42	....	....	....	....	....
99-2000	Leksands IF Jr.	Swede-Jr.	34	16	22	38	50	2	0	0	0	0
	Leksands IF	Sweden	5	0	0	0	4	....	....	....	....	....
2000-01	Leksands IF Jr.	Swede-Jr.	7	1	3	4	6	....	....	....	....	....
	Leksands IF	Sweden	31	2	1	3	12	....	....	....	....	....
2001-02	Leksands IF Jr.	Swede-Jr.	3	2	1	3	4	1	0	0	0	0
	Leksands IF	Swede-2	28	1	7	8	59	....	....	....	....	....
	Leksands IF	Swede-Q	12	1	7	8	35	8	0	2	2	6
2002-03	Leksands IF	Sweden	21	0	0	0	12	5	0	0	0	2
	IF Bjorkloven Umea	Swede-2	9	3	4	7	10	....	....	....	....	....
	IFK Arboga IK	Swede-2	4	0	0	0	4	....	....	....	....	....

JONSSON, Robin (YAWN-suhn, RAW-bihn) ST.L.

Defense. Shoots right. 6'2", 194 lbs. Born, Upplands Vasby, Sweden, December 10, 1983.
(St. Louis' 4th choice, 120th overall, in 2002 Entry Draft).

			Regular Season					Playoffs				
Season	Club	League	GP	G	A	TP	PIM	GP	G	A	TP	PIM
99-2000	Farjestad-18	Swede-Jr.	8	0	0	0	24	....	....	....	....	....
	Farjestad Jr.	Swede-Jr.	18	2	2	4	12	....	....	....	....	....
2000-01	Farjestad Jr.	Swede-Jr.	24	3	8	11	34	....	....	....	....	....
	Farjestad	Sweden	....	....	....	....	....	1	0	0	0	0
2001-02	Bofors IK	Swede-2	55	3	4	7	36	....	....	....	....	....
	Farjestad	Sweden	1	0	0	0	0	....	....	....	....	....
2002-03	Bofors IK	Swede-2	7	0	2	2	6	....	....	....	....	....

• Missed majority of 2002-03 season recovering from cancer surgery, October 30, 2002.

JORDE, Ryan (JOHR-dee, RIGH-uhn) BUF.

Defense. Shoots right. 6'3", 223 lbs. Born, Kelowna, B.C., March 23, 1982.
(Buffalo's 8th choice, 279th overall, in 2001 Entry Draft).

			Regular Season					Playoffs				
Season	Club	League	GP	G	A	TP	PIM	GP	G	A	TP	PIM
1997-98	Tri-City Americans	WHL	3	0	1	1	2	....	....	....	....	....
1998-99	Tri-City Americans	WHL	19	0	1	1	7	....	....	....	....	....
	Lethbridge	WHL	21	2	5	7	22	4	0	0	0	0
99-2000	Lethbridge	WHL	54	1	6	7	112	....	....	....	....	....
2000-01	Lethbridge	WHL	11	0	0	0	49	....	....	....	....	....
	Tri-City Americans	WHL	56	1	6	7	170	....	....	....	....	....
2001-02	Tri-City Americans	WHL	29	0	6	6	68	....	....	....	....	....
	Moose Jaw	WHL	23	0	4	4	62	8	0	1	1	2
2002-03	Rochester	AHL	70	0	2	2	136	....	....	....	....	....

JOUKOV, Mishail (ZHOO-kawv, mee-shigh-EHL) EDM.

Left wing. Shoots left. 6'3", 187 lbs. Born, Leningrad, USSR, January 3, 1985.
(Edmonton's 4th choice, 72nd overall, in 2003 Entry Draft).

			Regular Season					Playoffs				
Season	Club	League	GP	G	A	TP	PIM	GP	G	A	TP	PIM
2000-01	Mora IK Jr.	Swede-Jr.	28	9	14	23	6	9	2	4	6	0
2001-02	IFK Arboga IK	Swede-2	37	4	9	13	12	3	1	0	1	2
2002-03	IFK Arboga IK	Swede-2	41	9	14	23	30	3	3	1	4	0

JUNTUNEN, Henrik (YUN-tuh-nehn, HEHN-rihk) L.A.

Right wing. Shoots right. 6'2", 185 lbs. Born, Goteborg, Sweden, April 24, 1983.
(Los Angeles' 5th choice, 83rd overall, in 2001 Entry Draft).

			Regular Season					Playoffs				
Season	Club	League	GP	G	A	TP	PIM	GP	G	A	TP	PIM
99-2000	Karpat Oulu Jr.	Finn-Jr.	34	16	7	23	18	5	0	0	0	2
2000-01	Karpat Oulu Jr.	Finn-Jr.	17	4	4	8	12	....	....	....	....	....
	Karpat Oulu	Finland	....	....	....	....	....	2	0	0	0	0
2001-02	Karpat Oulu Jr.	Finn-Jr.	34	19	11	30	42	3	1	1	2	0
	Karpat Oulu	Finland	13	0	0	0	2	....	....	....	....	....
2002-03	Karpat Oulu	Finland	50	5	4	9	30	15	2	0	2	4
	Karpat Oulu Jr.	Finn-Jr.	2	0	0	0	0	....	....	....	....	....

JURCINA, Milan (YEWR-chee-nah, MEE-lan) BOS.

Defense. Shoots right. 6' 4", 198 lbs. Born, Liptovsky Mikulas, Czech., June 7, 1983.
(Boston's 7th choice, 241st overall, in 2001 Entry Draft).

			Regular Season					Playoffs				
Season	Club	League	GP	G	A	TP	PIM	GP	G	A	TP	PIM
99-2000	L. Mikulas Jr.	Slovak-Jr.	STATISTICS NOT AVAILABLE									
2000-01	Halifax	QMJHL	68	0	5	5	56	6	0	2	2	12
2001-02	Halifax	QMJHL	61	4	16	20	58	13	5	3	8	10
2002-03	Halifax	QMJHL	51	15	13	28	102	25	6	6	12	40

KACZOWKA, David (kuh-ZOW-kuh, DAY-vihd) ATL.

Left wing. Shoots left. 6'3", 235 lbs. Born, Regina, Sask., July 5, 1981.
(Atlanta's 4th choice, 98th overall, in 1999 Entry Draft).

			Regular Season					Playoffs				
Season	Club	League	GP	G	A	TP	PIM	GP	G	A	TP	PIM
1997-98	Prince Albert	SMHL	56	5	13	18	334	....	....	....	....	....
1998-99	Seattle	WHL	60	3	2	5	247	9	0	0	0	24
99-2000	Seattle	WHL	63	3	3	6	211	1	0	0	0	0
2000-01	Regina Pats	WHL	63	4	6	10	*414	6	0	0	0	6
2001-02	Greenville Grrrowl	ECHL	32	1	1	2	182	....	....	....	....	....
	Chicago Wolves	AHL	1	0	0	0	0	....	....	....	....	....
2002-03	Greenville Grrrowl	ECHL	59	3	7	10	242	4	0	0	0	18

• Missed majority of 2001-02 season recovering from head injury suffered in game vs. Florida (ECHL), February 12, 2002.

KADEYKIN, Anton (ka-DAY-kihn, an-TAWN) N.J.

Defense. Shoots left. 6'3", 200 lbs. Born, Elektrostal, USSR, May 17, 1984.
(New Jersey's 1st choice, 51st overall, in 2002 Entry Draft).

			Regular Season					Playoffs				
Season	Club	League	GP	G	A	TP	PIM	GP	G	A	TP	PIM
99-2000	Elektrostal 2	Russia-3	5	0	0	0	0	....	....	....	....	....
2000-01	Elektrostal 2	Russia-3	3	0	1	1	2	....	....	....	....	....
2001-02	Elektrostal 2	Russia-3	21	2	2	4	46	....	....	....	....	....
	Elektrostal	Russia-2	20	0	0	0	16	....	....	....	....	....
2002-03	Sarnia Sting	OHL	55	2	8	10	34	6	0	1	1	0

KAHNBERG, Magnus (KAHN-buhrg, MAHG-nus) CAR.

Left wing. Shoots left. 6'1", 185 lbs. Born, Kullered, Sweden, February 25, 1980.
(Carolina's 6th choice, 212th overall, in 2000 Entry Draft).

			Regular Season					Playoffs				
Season	Club	League	GP	G	A	TP	PIM	GP	G	A	TP	PIM
1997-98	V. Frolunda-18	Swede-Jr.	11	15	6	21	6	8	5	8	13	6
	V. Frolunda Jr.	Swede-Jr.	28	6	7	13	8	2	0	0	0	0
1998-99	V. Frolunda Jr.	Swede-Jr.	34	23	18	41	4	4	1	1	2	0
99-2000	V. Frolunda Jr.	Swede-Jr.	35	45	21	66	30	6	7	4	11	4
	Vastra Frolunda	Sweden	4	0	0	0	0	....	....	....	....	....
2000-01	V. Frolunda-18	Swede-Jr.	1	8	1	9	0	....	....	....	....	....
	V. Frolunda Jr.	Swede-Jr.	2	*2	1	3	2	....	....	....	....	....
	Vastra Frolunda	Sweden	50	8	6	14	6	5	0	0	0	2
2001-02	Vastra Frolunda	Sweden	50	14	11	25	24	10	5	0	5	2
2002-03	Vastra Frolunda	Sweden	50	14	20	34	22	15	2	6	8	12

KAIGORODOV, Alexei (kay-goh-ROH-dahv, al-EHX-ay) OTT.

Center. Shoots left. 6'1", 183 lbs. Born, Chelyabinsk, USSR, July 29, 1983.
(Ottawa's 2nd choice, 47th overall, in 2002 Entry Draft).

			Regular Season					Playoffs				
Season	Club	League	GP	G	A	TP	PIM	GP	G	A	TP	PIM
1998-99	Magnitogorsk 2	Russia-4	10	6	4	10	2	....	....	....	....	....
99-2000	Magnitogorsk 2	Russia-3	19	2	3	5	8	....	....	....	....	....
2000-01	Magnitogorsk 2	Russia-3	45	12	30	42	26	....	....	....	....	....
2001-02	Magnitogorsk	Russia	46	4	12	16	20	9	0	3	3	2
2002-03	Magnitogorsk	Russia	46	8	14	22	20	3	0	1	1	0

KALTEVA, Mikko (KAL-tuh-vah, MEE-koh) COL.

Defense. Shoots left. 6'3", 190 lbs. Born, Hyvinkaa, Finland, May 25, 1984.
(Colorado's 4th choice, 107th overall, in 2002 Entry Draft).

			Regular Season					Playoffs				
Season	Club	League	GP	G	A	TP	PIM	GP	G	A	TP	PIM
2000-01	Jokerit-B Jr.	Finn-Jr.	11	1	4	5	6	6	3	1	4	2
	Jokerit Helsinki Jr.	Finn-Jr.	34	0	3	3	12	....	....	....	....	....
2001-02	Jokerit Helsinki Jr.	Finn-Jr.	29	5	3	8	10	1	0	0	0	0
	Jokerit-B Jr.	Finn-Jr.	....	....	....	....	....	8	2	2	4	0
2002-03	Jokerit-B Jr.	Finn-Jr.	34	7	8	15	30	10	2	4	6	4

KANE, Boyd (KAYN, BOIYD) PHI.

Left wing. Shoots left. 6'2", 218 lbs. Born, Swift Current, Sask., April 18, 1978.
(NY Rangers' 4th choice, 114th overall, in 1998 Entry Draft).

			Regular Season					Playoffs				
Season	Club	League	GP	G	A	TP	PIM	GP	G	A	TP	PIM
1994-95	Regina Pats	WHL	25	6	5	11	6	4	0	0	0	0
1995-96	Regina Pats	WHL	72	21	42	63	155	11	5	7	12	12
1996-97	Regina Pats	WHL	66	25	50	75	154	5	1	1	2	15
1997-98	Regina Pats	WHL	68	48	45	93	133	9	5	7	12	29
1998-99	Hartford Wolf Pack	AHL	56	3	5	8	23	....	....	....	....	....
	Charlotte	ECHL	12	5	6	11	14	....	....	....	....	....
99-2000	Charlotte	ECHL	47	10	19	29	110	....	....	....	....	....
	Hartford Wolf Pack	AHL	8	0	0	0	9	....	....	....	....	....
	Binghamton	UHL	3	0	2	2	4	1	0	0	0	0
2000-01	Charlotte	ECHL	12	9	8	17	6	....	....	....	....	....
	Hartford Wolf Pack	AHL	56	11	17	28	81	5	2	0	2	2
2001-02	Hartford Wolf Pack	AHL	78	17	22	39	193	10	1	2	3	50
2002-03	Springfield Falcons	AHL	72	15	22	37	121	6	3	1	4	8

• Re-entered NHL Entry Draft. Originally Pittsburgh's 3rd choice, 72nd overall, in 1996 Entry Draft.
Traded to **Tampa Bay** by **NY Rangers** for Gordie Dwyer, October 10, 2002.Signed as a free agent by **Philadelphia**, July 14, 2003.

KANKAANPERA, Markus (kan-kahn-PEHR-a, MAHR-kus) VAN.

Defense. Shoots left. 6'1", 191 lbs. Born, Skelleftea, Sweden, April 27, 1980.
(Vancouver's 7th choice, 218th overall, in 1999 Entry Draft).

			Regular Season					Playoffs				
Season	Club	League	GP	G	A	TP	PIM	GP	G	A	TP	PIM
1995-96	JYP HT Jyvaskyla-B	Finn-Jr.	9	1	1	2	4	....	....	....	....	....
1996-97	JYP Jyvaskyla Jr.	Finn-Jr.	33	3	5	8	83	....	....	....	....	....
1997-98	JYP Jyvaskyla-B	Finn-Jr.	13	4	10	14	18	5	3	2	5	6
	JYP Jyvaskyla Jr.	Finn-Jr.	32	0	0	0	2	....	....	....	....	....
1998-99	JYP Jyvaskyla Jr.	Finn-Jr.	1	0	0	0	4	....	....	....	....	....
	JYP Jyvaskyla	Finland	50	0	2	2	85	3	0	0	0	0
99-2000	JYP Jyvaskyla Jr.	Finn-Jr.	3	1	1	2	2	3	0	1	1	6
	JYP Jyvaskyla	Finland	47	0	5	5	87	....	....	....	....	....
2000-01	JYP Jyvaskyla	Finland	53	5	4	9	60	....	....	....	....	....
2001-02	HPK Hameenlinna	Finland	51	4	3	7	80	8	0	0	0	10
2002-03	Jokerit Helsinki	Finland	52	1	4	5	94	10	1	2	3	6

KANKO, Petr (KAN-koh, PEE-tuhr) L.A.

Right wing. Shoots left. 5'9", 195 lbs. Born, Pribram, Czech., February 7, 1984.
(Los Angeles' 3rd choice, 66th overall, in 2002 Entry Draft).

			Regular Season					Playoffs				
Season	Club	League	GP	G	A	TP	PIM	GP	G	A	TP	PIM
2000-01	Sparta Praha Jr.	Czech-Jr.	43	27	10	37	80	....	....	....	....	....
	HC Sparta Praha	Czech	6	1	0	1	0	....	....	....	....	....
2001-02	Kitchener Rangers	OHL	61	28	32	60	54	4	0	2	2	0
2002-03	Kitchener Rangers	OHL	60	33	34	67	123	20	11	16	27	17

KANTEE, Kevin (KAN-tee, KEH-vihn) CHI.

Defense. Shoots left. 6'2", 189 lbs. Born, Idaho Falls, ID, January 29, 1984.
(Chicago's 6th choice, 188th overall, in 2002 Entry Draft).

			Regular Season					Playoffs				
Season	Club	League	GP	G	A	TP	PIM	GP	G	A	TP	PIM
99-2000	Jokerit Helsinki Jr.	Finn-Jr.	13	0	2	2	6	....	....	....	....	....
	Jokerit Helsinki-C	Finn-Jr.	9	2	8	10	8	6	2	1	3	44
2000-01	Jokerit Helsinki Jr.	Finn-Jr.	34	10	8	18	16	6	0	2	2	4
2001-02	Jokerit Helsinki Jr.	Finn-Jr.	34	2	7	9	16	1	0	0	0	0
	Jokerit Helsinki-B	Finn-Jr.	1	2	0	2	12	5	2	1	3	....
2002-03	Jokerit Helsinki Jr.	Finn-Jr.	34	5	17	22	34	11	3	4	7	16

KARLSSON, Gabriel (KARLS-suhn, ga-BREE-ehl) DAL.

Center. Shoots left. 6'1", 189 lbs. Born, Borlange, Sweden, January 22, 1980.
(Dallas' 3rd choice, 86th overall, in 1998 Entry Draft).

			Regular Season					Playoffs				
Season	Club	League	GP	G	A	TP	PIM	GP	G	A	TP	PIM
1996-97	HV 71 Jr.	Swede-Jr.	25	7	9	16	....	....	....	....	....	....
1997-98	HV 71 Jr.	Swede-Jr.	27	11	15	26	32	....	....	....	....	....
	HV 71 Jonkoping	Sweden	1	0	0	0	0	....	....	....	....	....
1998-99	HV 71 Jr.	Swede-Jr.	12	4	9	13	4	....	....	....	....	....
	HV 71 Jonkoping	Sweden	33	2	1	3	2	....	....	....	....	....
99-2000	HV 71 Jonkoping	Sweden	50	5	3	8	12	6	0	0	0	2
2000-01	Assat Pori	Finland	17	2	2	4	6	....	....	....	....	....
	Leksands IF	Sweden	35	9	8	17	10	....	....	....	....	....
2001-02	Sodertalje SK	Sweden	47	8	7	15	18	....	....	....	....	....
2002-03	Sodertalje SK	Sweden	39	4	3	7	12	....	....	....	....	....

KARLSSON, Jens (KARLS-suhn, YEHNZ) L.A.

Right wing. Shoots right. 6'3", 205 lbs. Born, Goteborg, Sweden, November 7, 1982.
(Los Angeles' 1st choice, 18th overall, in 2001 Entry Draft).

			Regular Season					Playoffs				
Season	Club	League	GP	G	A	TP	PIM	GP	G	A	TP	PIM
1997-98	V. Frolunda-16	Swede-Jr.	8	9	3	12	32	....	....	....	....	....
	V. Frolunda Jr.	Swede-Jr.	17	2	3	5	4	....	....	....	....	....
1998-99	V. Frolunda-18	Swede-Jr.	32	27	17	44	110	4	2	2	4	0
99-2000	V. Frolunda-18	Swede-Jr.	3	6	3	9	6	....	....	....	....	....
	V. Frolunda Jr.	Swede-Jr.	32	24	13	37	82	6	3	0	3	42
2000-01	V. Frolunda Jr.	Swede-Jr.	25	20	15	35	154	1	0	1	1	2
	Molndals IF	Swede-2	5	1	1	2	35	....	....	....	....	....
	Vastra Frolunda	Sweden	19	2	0	2	4	5	1	3	4	50
2001-02	Vastra Frolunda	Sweden	46	6	9	15	44	10	1	0	1	18
	V. Frolunda Jr.	Swede-Jr.	....	....	....	....	....	2	0	1	1	12
2002-03	Vastra Frolunda	Sweden	45	5	6	11	101	11	3	2	5	41

KARLSSON, Mattias (KARL-suhn, MA-tee-uhs) OTT.

Defense. Shoots left. 6'2", 191 lbs. Born, Stora, Sweden, April 15, 1985.
(Ottawa's 4th choice, 135th overall, in 2003 Entry Draft).

			Regular Season					Playoffs				
Season	Club	League	GP	G	A	TP	PIM	GP	G	A	TP	PIM
2000-01	Guldsmedshytte SK	Sweden-4	....	2	0	2	....	....	....	....	....	....
2001-02	Brynas IF Gavle Jr.	Swede-Jr.	18	2	2	4	18	....	....	....	....	....
2002-03	Brynas IF Gavle Jr.	Swede-Jr.	27	11	6	17	93	2	0	0	0	4
	Brynas IF Gavle	Sweden	3	0	0	0	0	....	....	....	....	....
	Brynas IF Gavle	Sweden-Q	3	0	0	0	0	....	....	....	....	....

KASPARIK, Pavel (kas-PAHR-ihk, PAH-vehl) PHI.

Center. Shoots left. 6'2", 198 lbs. Born, Pisek, Czech., November 11, 1979.
(Philadelphia's 4th choice, 200th overall, in 1999 Entry Draft).

			Regular Season					Playoffs				
Season	Club	League	GP	G	A	TP	PIM	GP	G	A	TP	PIM
1996-97	IHC Pisek Jr.	Czech-Jr.	36	12	5	17	....	....	....	....	....	....
1997-98	IHC Pisek Jr.	Czech-Jr.	39	21	19	40	....	....	....	....	....	....
	IHC Pisek	Czech-2	15	3	3	6	....	....	....	....	....	....
1998-99	IHC Pisek Jr.	Czech-Jr.	7	2	3	5	....	....	....	....	....	....
	IHC Pisek	Czech-2	51	20	23	43	....	....	....	....	....	....
99-2000	IHC Pisek	Czech-2	24	6	9	15	....	....	....	....	....	....
	HC Femax Havirov	Czech	1	0	0	0	0	....	....	....	....	....
	HC Sparta Praha	Czech	22	1	1	2	0	....	....	....	....	....
2000-01	HC Karlovy Vary	Czech	29	1	2	3	20	....	....	....	....	....
	HC Sparta Praha	Czech	19	5	1	6	18	13	2	0	2	12
2001-02	HC Sparta Praha	Czech	50	14	11	25	10	13	2	0	2	4
2002-03	HC Sparta Praha	Czech	21	0	4	4	4	....	....	....	....	....
	Liberec	Czech	30	8	9	17	26	....	....	....	....	....

KASTITSYN, Andrei (kaws-TIHT-sihn, AWN-dray) MTL.

Wing. Shoots right. 6', 189 lbs. Born, Novopolotsk, USSR, February 3, 1985.
(Montreal's 1st choice, 10th overall, in 2003 Entry Draft).

			Regular Season					Playoffs				
Season	Club	League	GP	G	A	TP	PIM	GP	G	A	TP	PIM
2000-01	Novopolotsk	Belarus	1	2	1	3	2	....	....	....	....	....
	Novopolotsk	EEHL	5	1	0	1	0	....	....	....	....	....
	Yunost Minsk	Belarus	3	1	4	5	8	....	....	....	....	....
	HC Vitebsk	Belarus	17	17	6	23	42	....	....	....	....	....
2001-02	Novopolotsk	Belarus	17	9	6	15	28	....	....	....	....	....
	Novopolotsk	EEHL	29	9	8	17	16	....	....	....	....	....
	Yunost Minsk	Belarus	6	2	0	2	8	....	....	....	....	....
2002-03	CSKA Moscow	Russia	6	0	0	0	2	....	....	....	....	....
	Voskresensk	Russia-2	2	1	1	2	0	....	....	....	....	....
	Yunost Minsk	Belarus	4	6	4	10	43	....	....	....	....	....
	CSKA Moscow 2	Russia-3	3	2	2	4	25	....	....	....	....	....

KAUPPINEN, Marko (KOW-pih-nehn, MAHR-koh) PHI.

Defense. Shoots left. 6', 178 lbs. Born, Mikkeli, Finland, March 23, 1979.
(Philadelphia's 7th choice, 214th overall, in 1997 Entry Draft).

			Regular Season					Playoffs				
Season	Club	League	GP	G	A	TP	PIM	GP	G	A	TP	PIM
1994-95	Jukurit Mikkeli-C	Finn-Jr.	31	12	11	23	48	....	....	....	....	....
1995-96	Jukurit Mikkeli	Finland-3	19	1	5	6	10	3	0	0	0	0
1996-97	JYP Jyvaskyla Jr.	Finn-Jr.	29	2	3	5	14	7	0	0	0	29
1997-98	JYP Jyvaskyla Jr.	Finn-Jr.	16	2	4	6	16	....	....	....	....	....
	Diskos Jyvaskyla	Finland-2	2	2	1	3	0	....	....	....	....	....
	JYP Jyvaskyla	Finland	33	2	6	8	26	....	....	....	....	....
1998-99	JYP Jyvaskyla Jr.	Finn-Jr.	3	2	1	3	6	....	....	....	....	....
	JYP Jyvaskyla	Finland	49	5	7	12	56	3	0	0	0	6
99-2000	Jokerit Helsinki Jr.	Finn-Jr.	5	0	3	3	8	1	1	0	1	4
	Jokerit Helsinki	Finland	47	4	9	13	16	10	1	3	4	2
2000-01	AIK Solna	Sweden	4	0	0	0	4	....	....	....	....	....
	Jokerit Helsinki	Finland	48	5	7	12	41	5	0	0	0	8
2001-02	TPS Turku	Finland	55	4	9	13	55	5	1	0	1	2
2002-03	TPS Turku	Finland	53	3	10	13	52	7	0	0	0	27

KAZIONOV, Dmitri (ka-zee-OH-nahv, dih-MEE-tree) T.B.

Center. Shoots left. 6'3", 185 lbs. Born, Moscow, USSR, May 13, 1984.
(Tampa Bay's 2nd choice, 100th overall, in 2002 Entry Draft).

			Regular Season					Playoffs				
Season	Club	League	GP	G	A	TP	PIM	GP	G	A	TP	PIM
99-2000	DynamoMoscow2	Russia-3	2	1	0	1	0	....	....	....	....	....
2000-01	THC Tver	Russia-2	33	1	1	2	6	....	....	....	....	....
2001-02	HC CSKA	Russia-2	2	0	1	1	0	....	....	....	....	....
	HC CSKA 2	Russia-3	10	1	0	1	4	....	....	....	....	....
	Lada Togliatti	Russia	3	0	0	0	0	....	....	....	....	....
2002-03	Lada Togliatti	Russia	5	0	1	1	4	....	....	....	....	....
	Lada Togliatti 2	Russia-3	34	14	13	27	26	....	....	....	....	....

KEITH, Duncan (KEETH, DUHN-kuhn) CHI.

Defense. Shoots left. 6', 168 lbs. Born, Winnipeg, Man., July 16, 1983.
(Chicago's 2nd choice, 54th overall, in 2002 Entry Draft).

			Regular Season					Playoffs				
Season	Club	League	GP	G	A	TP	PIM	GP	G	A	TP	PIM
1998-99	Penticton	BCAHA	44	51	57	108	45	....	....	....	....	....
99-2000	Penticton Panthers	BCHL	59	9	27	36	37	....	....	....	....	....
2000-01	Penticton Panthers	BCHL	60	18	64	82	61	9	4	6	10	18
2001-02	Michigan State	CCHA	41	3	12	15	18	....	....	....	....	....
2002-03	Michigan State	CCHA	15	3	6	9	8	....	....	....	....	....
	Kelowna Rockets	WHL	37	11	35	46	60	19	3	11	14	12

BCHL First All-Star Team (2001) • BCHL Top Defenseman (2001)

• Left Michigan State (CCHA) and signed as a free agent by **Kelowna** (WHL), December 27, 2002.

KEITH, Matt (KEETH, MAT) CHI.

Right wing. Shoots right. 6'2", 194 lbs. Born, Edmonton, Alta., April 11, 1983.
(Chicago's 3rd choice, 59th overall, in 2001 Entry Draft).

			Regular Season					Playoffs				
Season	Club	League	GP	G	A	TP	PIM	GP	G	A	TP	PIM
1998-99	Banff Icemen	HJHL	STATISTICS NOT AVAILABLE									
	Spokane Chiefs	WHL	7	1	0	1	4	....	....	....	....	....
99-2000	Spokane Chiefs	WHL	39	1	3	4	37	15	1	2	3	11
2000-01	Spokane Chiefs	WHL	33	13	14	27	63	12	1	3	4	14
2001-02	Spokane Chiefs	WHL	68	34	33	67	71	11	5	5	10	16
2002-03	Spokane Chiefs	WHL	7	2	2	4	11	....	....	....	....	....
	Red Deer Rebels	WHL	49	25	26	51	32	23	6	7	13	30

• Missed majority of 2000-01 season recovering from shoulder injury suffered in game vs. Tri-City (WHL), September 22, 2000.

KELLY, Chris (KEHL-lee, KRIHS) OTT.

Center/Left wing. Shoots left. 6', 190 lbs. Born, Toronto, Ont., November 11, 1980.
(Ottawa's 4th choice, 94th overall, in 1999 Entry Draft).

			Regular Season					Playoffs				
Season	Club	League	GP	G	A	TP	PIM	GP	G	A	TP	PIM
1995-96	Toronto Marlies	MTHL	42	25	45	70	25	....	....	....	....	....
1996-97	Aurora Tigers	OPJHL	49	14	20	34	11	....	....	....	....	....
1997-98	London Knights	OHL	54	15	14	29	4	16	4	5	9	12
1998-99	London Knights	OHL	68	36	41	77	60	25	9	17	26	22
99-2000	London Knights	OHL	63	29	43	72	57	....	....	....	....	....
2000-01	London Knights	OHL	31	21	34	55	46	....	....	....	....	....
	Sudbury Wolves	OHL	19	5	16	21	17	12	11	5	16	14
2001-02	Muskegon Fury	UHL	4	1	2	3	0	....	....	....	....	....
	Grand Rapids	AHL	31	3	3	6	20	5	1	1	2	5
2002-03	Binghamton	AHL	77	17	14	31	73	14	2	3	5	8

KELLY, Regan (KEHL-lee, REE-guhn) TOR.

Defense. Shoots left. 6'2", 200 lbs. Born, Watrous, Sask., March 9, 1981.
(Philadelphia's 7th choice, 259th overall, in 2000 Entry Draft).

			Regular Season					Playoffs				
Season	Club	League	GP	G	A	TP	PIM	GP	G	A	TP	PIM
1997-98	Tisdale Trojans	SMHL	41	2	13	15	24	....	....	....	....	....
1998-99	Nipawin Hawks	SJHL	52	4	14	18	30	....	....	....	....	....
99-2000	Nipawin Hawks	SJHL	46	8	21	29	20	....	....	....	....	....
2000-01	Providence College	H-East	36	4	21	25	58	....	....	....	....	....
2001-02	Providence College	H-East	38	6	10	16	48	....	....	....	....	....
2002-03	St. John's	AHL	71	3	15	18	36	....	....	....	....	....

SJHL All-Rookie Team (1999) • Hockey East All-Rookie Team (2001) • Hockey East All-Tournament Team (2001)

Rights traded to **Toronto** by **Philadelphia** for Chris McAllister, September 26, 2000.

KESA, Teemu (KEH-sah, TEE-moo) N.J.

Defense. Shoots right. 6', 185 lbs. Born, Helsinki, Finland, June 7, 1981.
(New Jersey's 5th choice, 100th overall, in 1999 Entry Draft).

			Regular Season					Playoffs				
Season	Club	League	GP	G	A	TP	PIM	GP	G	A	TP	PIM
1996-97	Tappara Jr.	Finn-Jr.	32	1	5	6	58	4	1	0	4	29
1997-98	Ilves Tampere-B	Finn-Jr.	33	8	1	9	78	....	....	....	....	....
1998-99	Ilves Tampere-B	Finn-Jr.	24	4	5	9	146	....	....	....	....	....
	Ilves Tampere Jr.	Finn-Jr.	6	0	1	1	10	....	....	....	....	....
99-2000	Ilves Tampere Jr.	Finn-Jr.	31	1	7	8	92	....	....	....	....	....
	Ilves Tampere	Finland	5	0	0	0	8	....	....	....	....	....
2000-01	Ilves Tampere Jr.	Finn-Jr.	4	1	0	1	4	....	....	....	....	....
	Sport Vassa	Finland-2	1	0	1	1	0	....	....	....	....	....
2001-02	Lukko Rauma	Finland	34	2	0	2	32	....	....	....	....	....
	Lukko Rauma Jr.	Finn-Jr.	3	0	4	4	4	....	....	....	....	....
2002-03	Lukko Rauma	Finland	37	1	0	1	22	....	....	....	....	....

KESLER, Ryan (KEHZ-luhr, RIGH-uhn) VAN.

Center. Shoots right. 6'1", 195 lbs. Born, Detroit, MI, August 31, 1984.
(Vancouver's 1st choice, 23rd overall, in 2003 Entry Draft).

			Regular Season					Playoffs				
Season	Club	League	GP	G	A	TP	PIM	GP	G	A	TP	PIM
99-2000	Det. Honey Baked	MWEHL	72	44	73	117	....	....	....	....	....	....
2000-01	U.S. National U-18	USDP	82	15	41	56	64	....	....	....	....	....
2001-02	U.S. National U-18	USDP	69	21	44	65	37	....	....	....	....	....
2002-03	Ohio State	CCHA	40	11	20	31	44	....	....	....	....	....

KHOMITSKY, Vadim (khoh-MIHT-skee, va-DEEM) DAL.

Defense. Shoots left. 6'1", 185 lbs. Born, Voskresensk, USSR, July 21, 1982.
(Dallas' 5th choice, 123rd overall, in 2000 Entry Draft).

			Regular Season					Playoffs				
Season	Club	League	GP	G	A	TP	PIM	GP	G	A	TP	PIM
1998-99	Voskresensk	Russia	9	0	0	0	10	....	....	....	....	....
99-2000	Voskresensk	Russia-2	17	0	0	0	31	....	....	....	....	....
	HC CSKA	Russia-2	11	0	1	1	10	....	....	....	....	....
2000-01	HC CSKA	Russia-2	44	2	7	9	89	....	....	....	....	....
2001-02	HC CSKA	Russia-2	68	2	18	20	63	....	....	....	....	....
2002-03	CSKA Moscow	Russia	51	3	2	5	58	....	....	....	....	....

KHOMUTOV, Ivan (khoh-moo-TAWF, ih-VAHN) N.J.

Right wing. Shoots left. 6'2", 200 lbs. Born, Saratov, USSR, March 11, 1985.
(New Jersey's 3rd choice, 93rd overall, in 2003 Entry Draft).

			Regular Season					Playoffs				
Season	Club	League	GP	G	A	TP	PIM	GP	G	A	TP	PIM
2001-02	HC CSKA 2	Russia 3	30	11	8	19	14	....	....	....	....	....
2002-03	Elektrostal	Russia 2	20	1	1	2	8	....	....	....	....	....

KINCH, Matt (KIHNCH, MATT) NYR

Defense. Shoots left. 6', 195 lbs. Born, Red Deer, Alta., February 17, 1980.
(Buffalo's 8th choice, 146th overall, in 1999 Entry Draft).

			Regular Season					Playoffs				
Season	Club	League	GP	G	A	TP	PIM	GP	G	A	TP	PIM
1995-96	Red Deer	AMHL	35	6	17	23	31	....	....	....	....	....
	Calgary Hitmen	WHL	1	0	1	1	2	....	....	....	....	....
1996-97	Calgary Hitmen	WHL	64	10	22	32	31	....	....	....	....	....
1997-98	Calgary Hitmen	WHL	55	7	24	31	13	18	3	2	5	4
1998-99	Calgary Hitmen	WHL	68	14	69	83	16	21	8	15	23	59
99-2000	Calgary Hitmen	WHL	62	14	61	75	24	13	2	12	14	8
2000-01	Calgary Hitmen	WHL	70	18	66	84	52	12	3	6	9	6
2001-02	Hartford Wolf Pack	AHL	40	1	7	8	4	....	....	....	....	....
	Charlotte	ECHL	26	3	12	15	13	5	3	2	5	0
2002-03	Hartford Wolf Pack	AHL	66	7	22	29	28	2	0	0	0	0

WHL East First All-Star Team (1999, 2001) • Memorial Cup All-Star Team (1999) • WHL East Second All-Star Team (2000) • Canadian Major Junior First All-Star Team (2001)

Signed as a free agent by **NY Rangers**, June 26, 2001.

KINKEL, Bill (KIHN-kuhl, BIHL) N.J.

Left wing. Shoots left. 6'5", 225 lbs. Born, Buffalo, NY, February 27, 1984.
(New Jersey's 11th choice, 281st overall, in 2002 Entry Draft).

			Regular Season					Playoffs				
Season	Club	League	GP	G	A	TP	PIM	GP	G	A	TP	PIM
2000-01	Nichols School	Hi-School	35	15	20	35	0	....	....	....	....	....
2001-02	Kitchener Rangers	OHL	53	1	2	3	75	1	0	0	0	0
2002-03	Kitchener Rangers	OHL	41	5	7	12	76	....	....	....	....	....
	Kingston	OHL	28	5	8	13	65	....	....	....	....	....

KINOS, Lauri (KEE-nohs, LOH-ree) ST.L.

Defense. Shoots left. 6'2", 195 lbs. Born, Jyvaskyla, Finland, June 29, 1980.
(St. Louis' 9th choice, 293rd overall, in 2000 Entry Draft).

			Regular Season					Playoffs				
Season	Club	League	GP	G	A	TP	PIM	GP	G	A	TP	PIM
1996-97	Diskos Jr.	Finn-Jr.	24	2	0	2	32	....	....	....	....	....
1997-98	JYP Jyvaskyla Jr.	Finn-Jr.	29	8	6	14	30	2	0	0	0	0
1998-99	JYP Jyvaskyla Jr.	Finn-Jr.	27	3	1	4	30	....	....	....	....	....
99-2000	Montreal Rocket	QMJHL	69	12	17	29	80	5	1	1	2	6
2000-01	Worcester IceCats	AHL	11	0	0	0	8	....	....	....	....	....
	Peoria Rivermen	ECHL	55	4	12	16	56	9	0	1	1	6
2001-02	Peoria Rivermen	ECHL	46	2	9	11	30	5	0	1	1	4
	Worcester IceCats	AHL	10	0	1	1	8	....	....	....	....	....
2002-03	Peoria Rivermen	ECHL	33	2	9	11	34	4	1	1	2	2

KLEIN, Kevin (KLIGHN, KEH-vihn) NSH.

Defense. Shoots right. 6'1", 187 lbs. Born, Kitchener, Ont., December 13, 1984.
(Nashville's 3rd choice, 37th overall, in 2003 Entry Draft).

			Regular Season					Playoffs				
Season	Club	League	GP	G	A	TP	PIM	GP	G	A	TP	PIM
99-2000	Kitchener	OMHA	STATISTICS NOT AVAILABLE									
2000-01	St. Michael's	OHL	58	3	16	19	21	18	0	5	5	17
2001-02	St. Michael's	OHL	68	5	22	27	35	15	2	7	9	12
2002-03	St. Michael's	OHL	67	11	33	44	88	17	1	9	10	8

KLEMA, David (KLEE-mah, DAY-vihd) PHX.

Center. Shoots left. 6', 178 lbs. Born, Roseau, MN, April 3, 1982.
(Phoenix's 5th choice, 148th overall, in 2001 Entry Draft).

			Regular Season					Playoffs				
Season	Club	League	GP	G	A	TP	PIM	GP	G	A	TP	PIM
1998-99	Roseau Rams	Hi-School	28	25	35	63	....	....	....	....	....	....
99-2000	Roseau Rams	Hi-School	28	16	31	47	8	....	....	....	....	....
	Fargo-Moorhead	USHL	6	0	2	2	4	....	....	....	....	....
	Des Moines	USHL	4	1	1	2	0	6	1	1	2	0
2000-01	Des Moines	USHL	56	13	40	53	58	3	1	0	1	0
2001-02	Boston University	H-East	38	6	11	17	4	....	....	....	....	....
2002-03	Boston University	H-East	28	5	8	13	14	....	....	....	....	....

KLEPIS, Jakub (KLEH-pihsh, YA-kuhb) BUF.

Center. Shoots right. 6', 200 lbs. Born, Prague, Czech., June 5, 1984.
(Ottawa's 1st choice, 16th overall, in 2002 Entry Draft).

			Regular Season					Playoffs				
Season	Club	League	GP	G	A	TP	PIM	GP	G	A	TP	PIM
99-2000	HC Slavia Praha Jr.	Czech-Jr.	48	14	26	40	30	....	....	....	....	....
2000-01	HC Slavia Praha Jr.	Czech-Jr.	52	21	25	46	82	....	....	....	....	....
2001-02	Portland	WHL	70	14	50	64	111	7	0	3	3	22
2002-03	HC Slavia Praha	Czech	38	2	6	8	22	4	0	0	0	6
	HC Slavia Praha Jr.	Czech-Jr.	11	4	5	9	59	3	0	3	3	4

Traded to **Buffalo** by **Ottawa** for Vaclav Varada and Buffalo's 5th round choice (Tim Cook) in 2003 Entry Draft, February 25, 2003.

KLYAZMIN, Sergei (klee-YAZ-mihn, SAIR-gay) COL.

Left wing. Shoots left. 6'3", 190 lbs. Born, Moscow, USSR, March 1, 1982.
(Colorado's 6th choice, 92nd overall, in 2000 Entry Draft).

			Regular Season					Playoffs				
Season	Club	League	GP	G	A	TP	PIM	GP	G	A	TP	PIM
1998-99	Krylja Sovetov 2	Russia-4	21	1	4	5	14	....	....	....	....	....
99-2000	DynamoMoscow2	Russia-3	16	3	2	5	18	....	....	....	....	....
2000-01	Halifax	QMJHL	65	33	28	61	76	6	1	2	3	16
2001-02	Halifax	QMJHL	46	24	37	61	34	....	....	....	....	....
2002-03	Hershey Bears	AHL	8	0	0	0	2	....	....	....	....	....

KNOEPFLI, Mike (NAWF-lee, MIGHK) TOR.

Left wing. Shoots left. 6' 1", 185 lbs. Born, Georgetown, Ont., April 9, 1982.
(Toronto's 12th choice, 276th overall, in 2001 Entry Draft).

			Regular Season					Playoffs				
Season	Club	League	GP	G	A	TP	PIM	GP	G	A	TP	PIM
99-2000	Georgetown	OPJHL	48	37	47	84	75	....	....	....	....	....
2000-01	Georgetown	OPJHL	47	45	38	83	....	....	....	....	....	....
2001-02	Cornell Big Red	ECAC	34	4	11	15	14	....	....	....	....	....
2002-03	Cornell Big Red	ECAC	36	8	16	24	8	....	....	....	....	....

KNOPP, Ben (KUH-nawp, BEHN) CBJ

Right wing. Shoots right. 6'1", 190 lbs. Born, Calgary, Alta., April 8, 1982.
(Columbus' 2nd choice, 69th overall, in 2000 Entry Draft).

			Regular Season					Playoffs				
Season	**Club**	**League**	**GP**	**G**	**A**	**TP**	**PIM**	**GP**	**G**	**A**	**TP**	**PIM**
1997-98	Calgary Buffaloes	AMHL	35	28	48	76	34	10	10	6	16	30
1998-99	Calgary Canucks	AJHL	55	37	45	82	161	6	6	6	12	6
99-2000	Moose Jaw	WHL	72	30	30	60	101	4	2	2	4	4
2000-01	Moose Jaw	WHL	58	22	34	56	105	4	0	0	0	11
2001-02	Moose Jaw	WHL	37	18	14	32	56	....	....	....	....	....
	Kamloops Blazers	WHL	41	26	25	51	63	4	0	1	1	4
2002-03	Syracuse Crunch	AHL	12	1	1	2	2	....	....	....	....	....
	Dayton Bombers	ECHL	53	7	13	20	83	....	....	....	....	....

KNYAZEV, Igor (kuh-NYA-zhev, EE-gohr) PHX.

Defense. Shoots left. 6', 185 lbs. Born, Elektrostal, USSR, January 27, 1983.
(Carolina's 1st choice, 15th overall, in 2001 Entry Draft).

			Regular Season					Playoffs				
Season	**Club**	**League**	**GP**	**G**	**A**	**TP**	**PIM**	**GP**	**G**	**A**	**TP**	**PIM**
99-2000	Spartak Moscow 2	Russia-3	13	2	4	6	74	....	....	....	....	....
	Spartak Moscow	Russia-2	26	1	1	2	6	....	....	....	....	....
2000-01	Spartak Moscow	Russia-2	53	6	5	11	101	....	....	....	....	....
2001-02	Spartak Moscow	Russia	3	0	0	0	8	....	....	....	....	....
	Spartak Moscow 2	Russia-3	2	0	1	1	0	....	....	....	....	....
	Ak Bars Kazan	Russia	14	0	1	1	4	3	0	0	0	0
2002-03	Lowell	AHL	68	2	5	7	68	....	....	....	....	....

Traded to **Phoenix** by **Carolina** with David Tanabe for Danny Markov and future considerations, June 21, 2003.

KOALSKA, Matt (KOHL-skuh, MAT) NSH.

Center. Shoots left. 6'1", 196 lbs. Born, St. Paul, MN, May 16, 1980.
(Nashville's 7th choice, 154th overall, in 2000 Entry Draft).

			Regular Season					Playoffs				
Season	**Club**	**League**	**GP**	**G**	**A**	**TP**	**PIM**	**GP**	**G**	**A**	**TP**	**PIM**
1998-99	Hill-Murray	Hi-School	26	20	50	70	18	....	....	....	....	....
99-2000	Twin Cities	USHL	57	24	34	58	19	13	5	5	10	4
2000-01	U. of Minnesota	WCHA	42	10	24	34	36	....	....	....	....	....
2001-02	U. of Minnesota	WCHA	44	10	23	33	34	....	....	....	....	....
2002-03	U. of Minnesota	WCHA	41	9	31	40	26	....	....	....	....	....

First All-Conference Schoolboy Team (1999) • First All-State Schoolboy Team (1999)

KOCI, David (KOH-chee, DAY-vihd) PIT.

Defense. Shoots left. 6'6", 228 lbs. Born, Prague, Czech., May 12, 1981.
(Pittsburgh's 5th choice, 146th overall, in 2000 Entry Draft).

			Regular Season					Playoffs				
Season	**Club**	**League**	**GP**	**G**	**A**	**TP**	**PIM**	**GP**	**G**	**A**	**TP**	**PIM**
1997-98	Sparta Praha Jr.	Czech-Jr.	41	2	9	11	105	....	....	....	....	....
1998-99	Hvezda Praha Jr.	Czech-Jr.	22	1	3	4	36	....	....	....	....	....
	Sparta Praha Jr.	Czech-Jr.	7	0	0	0	4	....	....	....	....	....
99-2000	Sparta Praha Jr.	Czech-Jr.	47	0	6	6	124	....	....	....	....	....
2000-01	Prince George	WHL	70	2	7	9	155	6	0	0	0	20
2001-02	Wheeling Nailers	ECHL	33	2	4	6	105	....	....	....	....	....
	Wilkes-Barre	AHL	26	1	3	4	98	....	....	....	....	....
2002-03	Wilkes-Barre	AHL	9	0	0	0	4	....	....	....	....	....
	Wheeling Nailers	ECHL	48	0	1	1	103	....	....	....	....	....

KOIVISTO, Toni (KOI-vihs-toh, TOH-nee) FLA.

Left wing. Shoots left. 6', 180 lbs. Born, Ylitornio, Finland, November 5, 1982.
(Florida's 9th choice, 200th overall, in 2001 Entry Draft).

			Regular Season					Playoffs				
Season	**Club**	**League**	**GP**	**G**	**A**	**TP**	**PIM**	**GP**	**G**	**A**	**TP**	**PIM**
1997-98	Lukko Rauma-B	Finn-Jr.	10	10	4	14	0	....	....	....	....	....
1998-99	Lukko Rauma-B	Finn-Jr.	8	6	5	11	2	....	....	....	....	....
	Lukko Rauma Jr.	Finn-Jr.	24	5	2	7	8	....	....	....	....	....
99-2000	Lukko Rauma Jr.	Finn-Jr.	32	21	12	33	8	8	2	1	3	0
	Lukko Rauma	Finland	11	1	0	1	2	....	....	....	....	....
2000-01	Lukko Rauma	Finland	47	5	1	6	6	2	0	0	0	0
	Lukko Rauma Jr.	Finn-Jr.	16	9	15	24	6	1	0	0	0	0
	Jaa-Kotkat	Finland-2	2	0	0	0	0	....	....	....	....	....
2001-02	Lukko Rauma Jr.	Finn-Jr.	6	7	3	10	2	....	....	....	....	....
	Lukko Rauma	Finland	52	4	10	14	8	....	....	....	....	....
2002-03	Lukko Rauma	Finland	56	7	6	13	16	....	....	....	....	....

KOIVU, Mikko (KOI-voo, MEE-koh) MIN.

Center. Shoots left. 6'2", 205 lbs. Born, Turku, Finland, March 12, 1983.
(Minnesota's 1st choice, 6th overall, in 2001 Entry Draft).

			Regular Season					Playoffs				
Season	**Club**	**League**	**GP**	**G**	**A**	**TP**	**PIM**	**GP**	**G**	**A**	**TP**	**PIM**
1997-98	TPS Turku-C	Finn-Jr.	32	6	12	18	34	....	....	....	....	....
1998-99	TPS Turku-C	Finn-Jr.	30	17	42	59	26	5	2	*9	*11	25
99-2000	TPS Turku Jr.	Finn-Jr.	41	8	17	25	40	13	1	4	5	8
2000-01	TPS Turku Jr.	Finn-Jr.	26	9	36	45	26	4	2	2	4	8
	TPS Turku	Finland	21	0	1	1	2	....	....	....	....	....
2001-02	TPS Turku	Finland	48	4	3	7	34	8	0	3	3	4
	TPS Turku Jr.	Finn-Jr.	2	0	1	1	12	....	....	....	....	....
2002-03	TPS Turku	Finland	37	7	13	20	20	7	2	2	4	6

KOJEVNIKOV, Alexander (kuh-ZHEHV-nih-kahv, al-ehx-AN-duhr) CHI.

Left wing. Shoots left. 6', 185 lbs. Born, Moscow, USSR, April 12, 1984.
(Chicago's 3rd choice, 93rd overall, in 2002 Entry Draft).

			Regular Season					Playoffs				
Season	**Club**	**League**	**GP**	**G**	**A**	**TP**	**PIM**	**GP**	**G**	**A**	**TP**	**PIM**
2001-02	Krylja Sovetov 2	Russia-3	32	12	15	27	59	....	....	....	....	....
	Krylja Sovetov-18	Russia-Jr.	31	30	17	47	140	....	....	....	....	....
2002-03	Krylja Sovetov	Russia	5	0	0	0	4	....	....	....	....	....

KOKOREV, Dimitri (KOH-koh-rehf, DEH-mee-tree) CGY.

Defense. Shoots left. 6'3", 198 lbs. Born, Moscow, USSR, January 9, 1979.
(Calgary's 4th choice, 51st overall, in 1997 Entry Draft).

			Regular Season					Playoffs				
Season	**Club**	**League**	**GP**	**G**	**A**	**TP**	**PIM**	**GP**	**G**	**A**	**TP**	**PIM**
1996-97	DynamoMoscow2	Russia-3	27	2	4	6	24	....	....	....	....	....
	Dynamo Moscow	Russia	1	0	0	0	0	....	....	....	....	....
1997-98	Dynamo Moscow	Russia	24	1	2	3	20	....	....	....	....	....
1998-99	Dynamo Moscow	Russia	26	0	1	1	20	8	1	0	1	0
	DynamoMoscow2	Russia-3	14	0	2	2	20	....	....	....	....	....
99-2000	THC Tver	Russia-2	20	6	3	9	32	....	....	....	....	....
	Dynamo Moscow	Russia	22	0	1	1	14	1	0	0	0	0
2000-01	Dynamo Moscow	Russia	5	0	1	1	4	....	....	....	....	....
2001-02	CSKA Moscow 2	Russia-3	11	2	2	4	22	....	....	....	....	....
	CSKA Moscow	Russia	32	1	3	4	32	....	....	....	....	....
2002-03	Sibir Novosibirsk	Russia	26	0	1	1	59	....	....	....	....	....

KOLARIK, Tyler (koh-LAHR-ihk, TIGH-luhr) CBJ

Center. Shoots right. 5'10", 185 lbs. Born, Philadelphia, PA, January 26, 1981.
(Columbus' 5th choice, 150th overall, in 2000 Entry Draft).

			Regular Season					Playoffs				
Season	**Club**	**League**	**GP**	**G**	**A**	**TP**	**PIM**	**GP**	**G**	**A**	**TP**	**PIM**
99-2000	Deerfield Academy	Hi-School	26	31	22	53	8	....	....	....	....	....
	NY/Mid-Atlantic	MBHL	3	4	3	7	0	....	....	....	....	....
2000-01	Harvard Crimson	ECAC	32	13	15	28	36	....	....	....	....	....
2001-02	Harvard Crimson	ECAC	32	9	21	30	32	....	....	....	....	....
2002-03	Harvard Crimson	ECAC	30	15	13	28	20	....	....	....	....	....

KOLOZVARY, Ivan (KOH-lohzh-vah-ree, EE-vahn) TOR.

Center. Shoots left. 6', 169 lbs. Born, Ilava, Czech., February 16, 1983.
(Toronto's 9th choice, 198th overall, in 2001 Entry Draft).

			Regular Season					Playoffs				
Season	**Club**	**League**	**GP**	**G**	**A**	**TP**	**PIM**	**GP**	**G**	**A**	**TP**	**PIM**
1998-99	Dukla Trencin Jr.	Slovak-Jr.	46	13	24	37	12	....	....	....	....	....
99-2000	Dukla Trencin Jr.	Slovak-Jr.	51	10	27	37	14	....	....	....	....	....
2000-01	Dukla Trencin Jr.	Slovak-Jr.	39	13	10	23	14	....	....	....	....	....
	Dukla Trencin	Slovakia	14	0	0	0	2	7	0	2	2	2
2001-02	Dukla Trencin	Slovakia	31	1	5	6	2	5	1	1	2	0
2002-03	Dukla Trencin	Slovakia	48	6	11	17	28	12	2	2	4	4

KOLTSOV, Ivan (kohlt-SAHV, ee-VAHN) EDM.

Defense. Shoots left. 6'2", 182 lbs. Born, Cherepovets, USSR, March 7, 1984.
(Edmonton's 6th choice, 106th overall, in 2002 Entry Draft).

			Regular Season					Playoffs				
Season	**Club**	**League**	**GP**	**G**	**A**	**TP**	**PIM**	**GP**	**G**	**A**	**TP**	**PIM**
2000-01	Cherepovets 2	Russia-3	5	0	1	1	2	....	....	....	....	....
	Team Russia-18	Nat-Tm	5	1	1	2	2	....	....	....	....	....
2001-02	Cherepovets 2	Russia-3	27	2	2	4	24	....	....	....	....	....
2002-03	Leninogorsk	Russia-2	1	0	1	1	2	....	....	....	....	....

KOLTSOV, Kirill (kohlt-SAHV, kih-RIHL) VAN.

Defense. Shoots left. 5'11", 183 lbs. Born, Chelyabinsk, USSR, February 1, 1983.
(Vancouver's 1st choice, 49th overall, in 2002 Entry Draft).

			Regular Season					Playoffs				
Season	**Club**	**League**	**GP**	**G**	**A**	**TP**	**PIM**	**GP**	**G**	**A**	**TP**	**PIM**
1997-98	California	CBHL	STATISTICS NOT AVAILABLE									
1998-99	Streetsville Derbys	OPJHL	20	5	7	12	4	....	....	....	....	....
99-2000	Omsk 2	Russia-3	27	0	7	7	30	....	....	....	....	....
	Avangard Omsk	Russia	2	0	0	0	0	....	....	....	....	....
2000-01	Avangard Omsk	Russia	39	0	1	1	20	16	1	3	4	12
2001-02	Avangard Omsk	Russia	41	1	5	6	34	11	1	0	1	8
2002-03	Avangard Omsk	Russia	45	4	8	12	54	12	1	3	4	8

KOLUSZ, Marcin (KOH-loosh, MART-sihn) MIN.

Right wing. Shoots left. 6'1", 180 lbs. Born, Limanowa, Poland, January 18, 1985.
(Minnesota's 4th choice, 157th overall, in 2003 Entry Draft).

			Regular Season					Playoffs				
Season	**Club**	**League**	**GP**	**G**	**A**	**TP**	**PIM**	**GP**	**G**	**A**	**TP**	**PIM**
2000-01	Nowy Targ	Poland	5	0	0	0	2	....	....	....	....	....
2001-02	Nowy Targ Jr.	Poland-Jr.	11	13	5	18	22	....	....	....	....	....
2002-03	Nowy Targ	Poland	30	2	4	6	10	2	0	0	0	0

KOMADOSKI, Neil (koh-mah-DAW-skee, NEEL) OTT.

Defense. Shoots left. 6'2", 215 lbs. Born, Chesterfield, MO, February 10, 1982.
(Ottawa's 3rd choice, 81st overall, in 2001 Entry Draft).

			Regular Season					Playoffs				
Season	**Club**	**League**	**GP**	**G**	**A**	**TP**	**PIM**	**GP**	**G**	**A**	**TP**	**PIM**
1997-98	Aurora Tigers	OPJHL	1	0	0	0	0	....	....	....	....	....
1998-99	USA National U-17	USDP	1	1	0	1	0	....	....	....	....	....
	USA National U-18	USDP	50	8	7	15	202	....	....	....	....	....
99-2000	USA National U-18	USDP	49	3	11	14	222	....	....	....	....	....
2000-01	U. of Notre Dame	CCHA	30	2	5	7	106	....	....	....	....	....
2001-02	U. of Notre Dame	CCHA	37	2	9	11	100	....	....	....	....	....
2002-03	U. of Notre Dame	CCHA	40	1	23	24	46	....	....	....	....	....

KOMAROV, Alexei (KOH-muh-rahf, al-EHX-ay) DAL.

Defense. Shoots left. 6'4", 194 lbs. Born, Moscow, USSR, June 11, 1978.
(Dallas' 8th choice, 216th overall, in 1997 Entry Draft).

			Regular Season					Playoffs				
Season	**Club**	**League**	**GP**	**G**	**A**	**TP**	**PIM**	**GP**	**G**	**A**	**TP**	**PIM**
1996-97	DynamoMoscow2	Russia-3	32	2	3	5	12	....	....	....	....	....
1997-98	Yekaterinburg	Russia	19	0	0	0	6	....	....	....	....	....
	Yekaterinburg	Russia-Q	22	0	1	1	14	....	....	....	....	....
1998-99	Spartak Moscow	Russia	21	1	0	1	6	....	....	....	....	....
99-2000	Spartak Moscow	Russia-2	32	0	5	5	22	....	....	....	....	....
2000-01	Spartak Moscow	Russia-2	33	2	5	7	28	12	0	3	3	8
2001-02	Spartak Moscow 2	Russia-3	2	1	2	3	0	....	....	....	....	....
	Spartak Moscow	Russia	36	3	5	8	43	....	....	....	....	....
2002-03	Utah Grizzlies	AHL	55	5	12	17	44	1	0	0	0	2

KONDRATIEV, Maxim (kohn-DRAT-yehv, mahx-EEM) TOR.

Defense. Shoots left. 6'1", 176 lbs. Born, Togliatti, USSR, January 20, 1983.
(Toronto's 7th choice, 168th overall, in 2001 Entry Draft).

			Regular Season					Playoffs				
Season	**Club**	**League**	**GP**	**G**	**A**	**TP**	**PIM**	**GP**	**G**	**A**	**TP**	**PIM**
99-2000	Lada Togliatti 2	Russia-3	16	0	2	2	6	....	....	....	....	....
	Lada Togliatti	Russia-2	20	1	1	2		....	....	....	....	....
2000-01	Lada Togliatti 2	Russia-3	STATISTICS NOT AVAILABLE									
	CSK VVS Samara	Russia-2	18	2	1	3	24	....	....	....	....	....
2001-02	Lada Togliatti	Russia	43	3	3	6	32	4	0	0	0	0
2002-03	Lada Togliatti	Russia	47	2	3	5	56	10	0	0	0	6

KONSORADA, Tim (kawn-sohr-A-duh, TIHM) CBJ

Right wing. Shoots right. 6', 201 lbs. Born, Ft. Saskatchewan, Alta., March 21, 1984.
(Columbus' 8th choice, 168th overall, in 2002 Entry Draft).

					Regular Season					Playoffs		
Season	Club	League	GP	G	A	TP	PIM	GP	G	A	TP	PIM
1998-99	Fort Saskatchewan	ABHL	36	26	45	71	8	....	....	....	....	....
99-2000	Brandon	AMHL	34	11	23	34	6	....	....	....	....	....
	Brandon	WHL	5	1	2	3	0	....	....	....	....	....
2000-01	Brandon	WHL	67	9	14	23	33	5	2	3	5	11
2001-02	Brandon	WHL	71	17	28	45	36	19	2	11	13	8
2002-03	Brandon	WHL	72	22	48	70	74	17	4	10	14	19

KOPECKY, Milan (koh-PEHTS-kee, MEE-lan) PHI.

Left wing. Shoots left. 6', 180 lbs. Born, Kolin, Czech., May 11, 1981.
(Philadelphia's 8th choice, 287th overall, in 2000 Entry Draft).

					Regular Season					Playoffs		
Season	Club	League	GP	G	A	TP	PIM	GP	G	A	TP	PIM
1998-99	Sparta Praha Jr.	Czech-Jr.	49	14	21	35	....	....	....	....	....	....
99-2000	HC Slavia Praha Jr.	Czech-Jr.	36	17	7	24	24	7	5	3	8	0
	HC Slavia Praha	Czech	2	0	0	0	0	....	....	....	....	....
2000-01	HC Slavia Praha Jr.	Czech-Jr.	38	19	17	36	36	....	....	....	....	....
	SC Kalin	Czech-2	8	2	4	6	2	....	....	....	....	....
2001-02	HC Slavia Praha Jr.	Czech-Jr.	3	2	0	2	4	....	....	....	....	....
	Beroun	Czech-2	36	10	9	19	16	....	....	....	....	....
	HC Slavia Praha	Czech	....	....	....	....	....	1	0	0	0	0
2002-03	HC Slavia Praha	Czech	33	4	6	10	20	17	2	1	3	8
	Beroun	Czech-2	7	2	4	6	6	....	....	....	....	....

KOPECKY, Tomas (koh-PEHTS-kee, TAW-mahsh) DET.

Center. Shoots left. 6'3", 187 lbs. Born, Ilava, Czech., February 5, 1982.
(Detroit's 2nd choice, 38th overall, in 2000 Entry Draft).

					Regular Season					Playoffs		
Season	Club	League	GP	G	A	TP	PIM	GP	G	A	TP	PIM
1997-98	Dukla Trencin Jr.	Slovak-Jr.	41	19	22	41	....	....	....	....	....	....
1998-99	Dukla Trencin Jr.	Slovak-Jr.	44	13	16	29	18	....	....	....	....	....
99-2000	Dukla Trencin Jr.	Slovak-Jr.	14	8	9	17	36	....	....	....	....	....
	Dukla Trencin	Slovakia	52	3	4	7	24	5	0	0	0	0
2000-01	Lethbridge	WHL	49	22	28	50	52	5	1	1	2	6
	Cincinnati	AHL	1	0	0	0	0	....	....	....	....	....
2001-02	Lethbridge	WHL	60	34	42	76	94	4	2	1	3	15
	Cincinnati	AHL	2	1	1	2	6	2	0	0	0	0
2002-03	Grand Rapids	AHL	70	17	21	38	32	14	0	0	0	6

KOREIS, Jakub (KOHR-ays, YA-kuhb) PHX.

Center. Shoots left. 6'2", 212 lbs. Born, Plzen, Czech, June 26, 1984.
(Phoenix's 1st choice, 19th overall, in 2002 Entry Draft).

					Regular Season					Playoffs		
Season	Club	League	GP	G	A	TP	PIM	GP	G	A	TP	PIM
99-2000	Plzen 18	Czech-Jr.	41	21	22	43	44	....	....	....	....	....
	Plzen Jr.	Czech-Jr.	3	2	1	3	2	....	....	....	....	....
2000-01	Plzen 18	Czech-Jr.	9	7	10	17	28	....	....	....	....	....
	Plzen Jr.	Czech-Jr.	43	14	15	29	83	....	....	....	....	....
2001-02	Plzen Jr.	Czech-Jr.	23	14	14	28	38	....	....	....	....	....
	HC Keramika Plzen	Czech	20	3	0	3	10	....	....	....	....	....
2002-03	HC Keramika Plzen	Czech	23	1	6	7	8	....	....	....	....	....
	Plzen Jr.	Czech-Jr.	10	3	5	8	28	....	....	....	....	....

KORNEEV, Konstantin (kor-NEE-ehv, kawn-stuhn-TIHN) MTL.

Defense. Shoots left. 5'11", 176 lbs. Born, Moscow, USSR, June 5, 1984.
(Montreal's 6th choice, 275th overall, in 2002 Entry Draft).

					Regular Season					Playoffs		
Season	Club	League	GP	G	A	TP	PIM	GP	G	A	TP	PIM
2001-02	Krylja Sovetov 2	Russia-3	26	9	19	28	44	....	....	....	....	....
	Krylja Sovetov	Russia	4	0	2	2	0	2	0	0	0	2
2002-03	Krylja Sovetov	Russia	49	2	8	10	28	....	....	....	....	....

KOROVKIN, Nikita (koh-RAWV-kihn, nih-KEE-tah) PHI.

Defense. Shoots right. 6'2", 198 lbs. Born, Zlatoust, USSR, December 3, 1983.
(Philadelphia's 5th choice, 192nd overall, in 2002 Entry Draft).

					Regular Season					Playoffs		
Season	Club	League	GP	G	A	TP	PIM	GP	G	A	TP	PIM
1998-99	Chelyabinsk Jr.	Russia-Jr.	50	18	33	51	39	....	....	....	....	....
99-2000	Chelyabinsk Jr.	Russia-Jr.	50	24	30	54	58	....	....	....	....	....
	Chelyabinsk 2	Russia-3	17	0	1	1	10	....	....	....	....	....
2000-01	Kamloops Blazers	WHL	46	3	1	4	58	1	0	0	0	0
2001-02	Kamloops Blazers	WHL	72	4	23	27	103	1	0	0	0	2
2002-03	Kamloops Blazers	WHL	63	12	17	29	60	2	0	0	0	0

KORSUNOV, Vladimir (KOHR-suhn-ahv, vla-DIH-meer) ANA.

Defense. Shoots left. 6'2", 202 lbs. Born, Moscow, USSR, March 16, 1983.
(Anaheim's 5th choice, 105th overall, in 2001 Entry Draft).

					Regular Season					Playoffs		
Season	Club	League	GP	G	A	TP	PIM	GP	G	A	TP	PIM
99-2000	Spartak Moscow 2	Russia-3	22	1	11	12	60	....	....	....	....	....
2000-01	Spartak Moscow	Russia-2	10	0	0	0	2	....	....	....	....	....
2001-02	Spartak Moscow 2	Russia-3	2	1	0	1	8	....	....	....	....	....
	Spartak Moscow	Russia	40	0	3	3	28	....	....	....	....	....
2002-03	Spartak Moscow	Russia	42	1	4	5	50	....	....	....	....	....

KOSMACHEV, Dmitri (kaws-ma-CHEHV, dih-MEE-tree) CBJ

Defense. Shoots right. 6'3", 209 lbs. Born, Gorky, USSR, June 7, 1985.
(Columbus' 3rd choice, 71st overall, in 2003 Entry Draft).

					Regular Season					Playoffs		
Season	Club	League	GP	G	A	TP	PIM	GP	G	A	TP	PIM
2001-02	HC CSKA 2	Russia-3	6	1	0	1	2	....	....	....	....	....
	HC CSKA Moscow	Russia-2	49	0	1	1	12	....	....	....	....	....
2002-03	CSKA Moscow	Russia	27	0	0	0	2	....	....	....	....	....

KOSTADINE, Jason (KAWZ-tuh-dighn, JAY-suhn) CHI.

Right wing. Shoots right. 6'1", 211 lbs. Born, Silver Spring, MD, October 22, 1983.
(Chicago's 8th choice, 251st overall, in 2002 Entry Draft).

					Regular Season					Playoffs		
Season	Club	League	GP	G	A	TP	PIM	GP	G	A	TP	PIM
2000-01	Hull Olympiques	QMJHL	53	1	9	10	103	4	0	1	1	0
2001-02	Hull Olympiques	QMJHL	70	8	5	13	295	12	1	0	1	37
2002-03	Quebec Remparts	QMJHL	72	9	22	31	207	11	0	1	1	43

KOTARY, Sean (koh-TAH-ree, SHAWN) COL.

Center. Shoots right. 6', 180 lbs. Born, New Hartford, NY, April 28, 1981.
(Colorado's 13th choice, 266th overall, in 2000 Entry Draft).

					Regular Season					Playoffs		
Season	Club	League	GP	G	A	TP	PIM	GP	G	A	TP	PIM
1995/98	New Hartford High	Hi-School	74	54	55	109	....	....	....	....	....	....
1998-99	Loomis-Chaffee	Hi-School	25	32	26	58	....	....	....	....	....	....
99-2000	Northfield Prep	Hi-School	41	49	57	106	21	....	....	....	....	....
2000-01	Bowling Green	CCHA	5	0	0	0	4	....	....	....	....	....
2001-02	Des Moines	USHL	46	12	14	26	39	3	0	0	0	0
2002-03	U. of Findlay	CHA	34	4	7	11	34	....	....	....	....	....

• Statistics for **New Hartford** (Hi-School) are career totals from the 1995-1998 seasons

KOUBA, Ladislav (KOH-bah, LA-dih-slahf) PHX.

Left wing. Shoots left. 6'2", 210 lbs. Born, Vimperk, Czech., September 10, 1983.
(Phoenix's 9th choice, 216th overall, in 2002 Entry Draft).

					Regular Season					Playoffs		
Season	Club	League	GP	G	A	TP	PIM	GP	G	A	TP	PIM
99-2000	Plzen Jr.	Czech-Jr.	34	28	20	48	....	....	....	....	....	....
2000-01	Red Deer Rebels	WHL	62	5	7	12	29	3	0	0	0	2
2001-02	Red Deer Rebels	WHL	62	16	14	30	33	23	5	3	8	6
2002-03	Red Deer Rebels	WHL	68	12	28	40	48	23	5	6	11	4

KOVAC, Kristian (KOH-vach, KRIHST-yan) COL.

Right wing. Shoots right. 6'2", 205 lbs. Born, Kosice, Czech., January 1, 1981.
(Colorado's 5th choice, 122nd overall, in 1999 Entry Draft).

					Regular Season					Playoffs		
Season	Club	League	GP	G	A	TP	PIM	GP	G	A	TP	PIM
1997-98	HC Kosice Jr.	Slovak-Jr.	47	22	11	33	103	....	....	....	....	....
1998-99	HC Kosice Jr.	Slovak-Jr.	39	30	20	50	73	2	1	0	1	2
	HC Kosice	Slovakia	6	0	0	0	2	....	....	....	....	....
99-2000	Victoriaville Tigres	QMJHL	65	11	18	29	50	5	0	0	0	4
2000-01	Victoriaville Tigres	QMJHL	51	10	20	30	38	13	2	3	5	4
2001-02	HC Kosice	Slovakia	26	5	9	14	10	11	0	0	0	4
2002-03	HC Kosice	Slovakia	48	6	8	14	54	7	1	0	1	2

KOZAK, Rick (KOH-zak, RIHK) PHI.

Right wing. Shoots right. 6'2", 187 lbs. Born, Winnipeg, Man., August 19, 1985.
(Philadelphia's 7th choice, 95th overall, in 2003 Entry Draft).

					Regular Season					Playoffs		
Season	Club	League	GP	G	A	TP	PIM	GP	G	A	TP	PIM
2000-01	Norman	MMHL	31	17	27	44	166	....	....	....	....	....
2001-02	Swan Valley	MJHL		STATISTICS NOT AVAILABLE								
	Prince George	WHL	4	0	0	0	11	....	....	....	....	....
2002-03	Swan Valley	MJHL	25	17	20	37	99	....	....	....	....	....
	Brandon	WHL	38	9	6	15	87	16	6	5	11	51

KRACIK, Jaroslav (KRAH-chihk, YAHR-roh-slav) CBJ

Right wing. Shoots left. 6', 178 lbs. Born, Plzen, Czech., January 18, 1983.
(Columbus' 12th choice, 231st overall, in 2002 Entry Draft).

					Regular Season					Playoffs		
Season	Club	League	GP	G	A	TP	PIM	GP	G	A	TP	PIM
99-2000	Plzen 18	Czech-Jr.	45	31	36	67	28	....	....	....	....	....
	Plzen Jr.	Czech-Jr.	6	1	0	1	2	....	....	....	....	....
2000-01	Plzen Jr.	Czech-Jr.	47	20	28	48	16	....	....	....	....	....
2001-02	Plzen Jr.	Czech-Jr.	39	14	35	49	46	....	....	....	....	....
	HC Klatovy	Czech-3	6	5	3	8	0	....	....	....	....	....
	HC Keramika Plzen	Czech	4	0	1	1	0	2	0	0	0	0
2002-03	Plzen Jr.	Czech-Jr.	33	11	17	28	40	1	0	1	1	0
	HC Keramika Plzen	Czech	4	0	0	0	0	....	....	....	....	....
	Usti nad Labem	Czech-2	9	1	1	2	4	4	0	0	0	0

KREPS, Kamil (KREHPS, KA-mihl) FLA.

Center. Shoots right. 6'1", 190 lbs. Born, Litomerice, Czech., November 18, 1984.
(Florida's 3rd choice, 38th overall, in 2003 Entry Draft).

					Regular Season					Playoffs		
Season	Club	League	GP	G	A	TP	PIM	GP	G	A	TP	PIM
99-2000	Litvinov Jr.	Czech-Jr.	48	18	16	34	10	....	....	....	....	....
2000-01	Litvinov Jr.	Czech-Jr.	47	16	23	39	6	6	2	6	8	10
2001-02	Brampton	OHL	68	19	24	43	14	....	....	....	....	....
2002-03	Brampton	OHL	53	19	42	61	12	11	3	5	8	4

KRESTANOVICH, Derek (krehs-TAN-oh-vihch, DAIR-ihk) WSH.

Center. Shoots left. 6'1", 175 lbs. Born, Surrey, B.C., April 29, 1983.
(Washington's 6th choice, 92nd overall, in 2002 Entry Draft).

					Regular Season					Playoffs		
Season	Club	League	GP	G	A	TP	PIM	GP	G	A	TP	PIM
2000-01	Kamloops Blazers	WHL	67	4	13	17	72	3	0	0	0	6
2001-02	Kamloops Blazers	WHL	30	6	13	19	41	....	....	....	....	....
	Moose Jaw	WHL	33	9	20	29	52	12	7	4	11	16
2002-03	Moose Jaw	WHL	55	24	21	45	129	13	1	2	3	29

KRIKUNOV, Ilja (krih-koo-NAWF, IHL-yah) VAN.

Left wing. Shoots left. 5'11", 169 lbs. Born, Elektrostal, USSR, February 27, 1984.
(Vancouver's 8th choice, 223rd overall, in 2002 Entry Draft).

					Regular Season					Playoffs		
Season	Club	League	GP	G	A	TP	PIM	GP	G	A	TP	PIM
2001-02	Elektrostal 2	Russia-3	5	3	6	9	4	....	....	....	....	....
	Elektrostal	Russia-2	48	12	10	22	28	....	....	....	....	....
2002-03	Elektrostal	Russia-2	48	19	9	28	34	....	....	....	....	....

KRISTOFFERSSON, Marcus (KRIHST-aw-fuhr-SOHN, MAHRK) DAL.

Left wing. Shoots left. 6'3", 217 lbs. Born, Ostersund, Sweden, January 22, 1979.
(Dallas' 4th choice, 105th overall, in 1997 Entry Draft).

					Regular Season					Playoffs		
Season	Club	League	GP	G	A	TP	PIM	GP	G	A	TP	PIM
1995-96	Mora IK Jr.	Swede-Jr.	16	2	2	4	28	....	....	....	....	....
	Mora IK	Swede-2	26	1	0	1	20	5	0	0	0	2
1996-97	Mora IK	Swede-2	33	1	5	6	26	....	....	....	....	....
1997-98	Mora IK	Swede-2	27	7	6	13	40	....	....	....	....	....
1998-99	HV 71 Jr.	Swede-Jr.	3	0	1	1	27	....	....	....	....	....
	HV 71 Jonkoping	Sweden	34	0	1	1	65	....	....	....	....	....
99-2000	HV 71 Jr.	Swede-Jr.	7	5	9	14	41	....	....	....	....	....
	HV 71 Jonkoping	Sweden	10	0	0	0	0	....	....	....	....	....
	Blues Espoo	Finland	29	7	4	11	42	1	1	0	1	0
2000-01	Assat Pori	Finland	9	1	0	1	16	....	....	....	....	....
	Djurgarden	Sweden	29	4	2	6	72	12	2	2	4	45
2001-02	Utah Grizzlies	AHL	50	6	10	16	42	....	....	....	....	....
2002-03	Utah Grizzlies	AHL	62	10	9	19	58	2	1	0	1	2

KRONVALL, Staffan (KRAWN-wahl, STAH-fuhn) **TOR.**

Defense. Shoots left. 6'3", 209 lbs. Born, Jarfalla, Sweden, September 10, 1982.
(Toronto's 9th choice, 285th overall, in 2002 Entry Draft).

			Regular Season					Playoffs				
Season	Club	League	GP	G	A	TP	PIM	GP	G	A	TP	PIM
99-2000	Huddinge IK Jr.	Swede-Jr.	34	2	0	2	38	....	....	....	....	....
	Huddinge IK 18	Swede-Jr.	7	0	3	3	0	....	....	....	....	....
2000-01	Huddinge IK Jr.	Swede-Jr.	23	6	1	7	16	....	....	....	....	....
	Huddinge IK	Swede-2	1	0	0	0	0	....	....	....	....	....
2001-02	Huddinge IK	Swede-2	42	4	7	11	30	....	....	....	....	....
	Huddinge IK Jr.	Swede-Jr.	1	0	0	0	0	4	2	1	3	27
2002-03	Djurgarden	Sweden	50	5	13	18	46	12	3	2	5	18

KRONWALL, Niklas (KRAHN-wuhl, NIHK-las) **DET.**

Defense. Shoots left. 5'11", 165 lbs. Born, Stockholm, Sweden, January 12, 1981.
(Detroit's 1st choice, 29th overall, in 2000 Entry Draft).

			Regular Season					Playoffs				
Season	Club	League	GP	G	A	TP	PIM	GP	G	A	TP	PIM
1996-97	Djurgarden Jr.	Swede-Jr.	1	0	0	0	0	....	....	....	....	....
1997-98	Djurgarden Jr.	Swede-Jr.	27	4	3	7	71	2	0	0	0	2
1998-99	Huddinge IK	Swede-2	14	0	1	1	10	....	....	....	....	....
	Huddinge IK	Swede-Q	10	1	0	1	14	....	....	....	....	....
	Huddinge IK Jr.	Swede-Jr.	2	0	0	0	6	....	....	....	....	....
99-2000	Djurgarden	Sweden	37	1	4	5	16	8	0	0	0	8
2000-01	Djurgarden	Sweden	31	1	9	10	32	15	0	1	1	8
2001-02	Djurgarden	Sweden	48	5	7	12	34	5	0	0	0	0
2002-03	Djurgarden	Sweden	50	5	13	18	46	12	3	2	5	18

KRUCHININ, Andrei (kroo-CHIHN-ihn, AWN-dray) **MTL.**

Defense. Shoots left. 5'11", 187 lbs. Born, Karaganda, USSR, May 18, 1978.
(Montreal's 7th choice, 189th overall, in 1998 Entry Draft).

			Regular Season					Playoffs				
Season	Club	League	GP	G	A	TP	PIM	GP	G	A	TP	PIM
1996-97	Lada Togliatti	Russia	19	0	1	1	8	11	0	0	0	0
1997-98	Lada Togliatti	Russia	43	0	4	4	73	....	....	....	....	....
1998-99	Lada Togliatti	Russia	41	1	4	5	56	6	0	1	1	2
99-2000	CSK VVS Samara	Russia	6	1	0	1	0	....	....	....	....	....
	Lada Togliatti	Russia	25	1	2	3	24	6	1	0	1	4
2000-01	Perm	Russia	14	1	3	4	10	....	....	....	....	....
	Lada Togliatti	Russia	14	0	2	2	12	3	0	0	0	0
2001-02	Avangard Omsk	Russia	21	0	0	0	6	....	....	....	....	....
	Nizhnekamsk	Russia	17	1	3	4	8	....	....	....	....	....
2002-03	Nizhnekamsk	Russia	30	1	6	7	16	....	....	....	....	....

KRYUKOV, Artem (KREE-oo-kahf, AHR-tehm) **BUF.**

Center. Shoots left. 6'3", 180 lbs. Born, Novosibirsk, USSR, March 5, 1982.
(Buffalo's 1st choice, 15th overall, in 2000 Entry Draft).

			Regular Season					Playoffs				
Season	Club	League	GP	G	A	TP	PIM	GP	G	A	TP	PIM
1997-98	Torpedo Yaroslavl	Russia	7	0	0	0	2	....	....	....	....	....
1998-99	Yaroslavl 2	Russia-3	20	2	2	4	6	....	....	....	....	....
99-2000	Yaroslavl 2	Russia-3	14	1	1	2	12	....	....	....	....	....
	Torpedo Yaroslavl	Russia	3	0	0	0	4	....	....	....	....	....
2000-01	Yaroslavl 2	Russia-3	6	0	0	0	2	11	0	0	0	8
	SKA St. Petersburg	Russia	14	0	2	2	14	....	....	....	....	....
2001-02	Yaroslavl	Russia	15	1	3	4	10	6	1	0	1	8
2002-03	Sibir Novosibirsk	Russia	9	0	0	0	27	....	....	....	....	....

KUBISTA, Jan (KOO-bihsh-tuh, YAHN) **BOS.**

Right wing. Shoots left. 6', 189 lbs. Born, Kolin, Czech., April 12, 1984.
(Boston's 3rd choice, 130th overall, in 2002 Entry Draft).

			Regular Season					Playoffs				
Season	Club	League	GP	G	A	TP	PIM	GP	G	A	TP	PIM
99-2000	Pardubice-18	Czech-Jr.	44	16	18	34	10	....	....	....	....	....
	SC Kolin Jr.	Czech-Jr.	5	4	2	6	0	....	....	....	....	....
2000-01	Pardubice-18	Czech-Jr.	53	33	24	57	61	8	6	7	13	16
	Pardubice Jr.	Czech-Jr.	1	0	1	1	0	....	....	....	....	....
2001-02	Pardubice Jr.	Czech-Jr.	48	12	12	24	36	....	....	....	....	....
2002-03	Pardubice Jr.	Czech-Jr.	32	16	11	27	40	....	....	....	....	....
	Pardubice	Czech	9	1	1	2	0	....	....	....	....	....
	Hradec Kralove	Czech-2	2	0	0	0	0	....	....	....	....	....

KUHTINOV, Roman (kukh-TEEN-nawv, ROH-muhn) **NYI**

Defense. Shoots right. 6'1", 207 lbs. Born, Belgorod, USSR, December 1, 1975.
(NY Islanders' 7th choice, 280th overall, in 2001 Entry Draft).

			Regular Season					Playoffs				
Season	Club	League	GP	G	A	TP	PIM	GP	G	A	TP	PIM
1993-94	Krylja Sovetov	CIS	4	0	0	0	0	....	....	....	....	....
1994-95	DynamoMoscow2	CIS-2		STATISTICS NOT AVAILABLE								
	SKA St. Petersburg	CIS	5	1	0	1	2	....	....	....	....	....
1995-96	Raichikhinsk	CIS-2		STATISTICS NOT AVAILABLE								
	Nizhnekamsk	CIS	7	0	0	0	0	....	....	....	....	....
1996-97	Raichikhinsk	Russia-3		STATISTICS NOT AVAILABLE								
1997-98	Raichikhinsk	Russia-3	36	18	8	26	46	....	....	....	....	....
1998-99	Novokuznetsk	Russia	42	2	9	11	26	6	0	0	0	2
99-2000	Novokuznetsk	Russia	37	2	6	8	28	14	1	1	2	8
2000-01	Novokuznetsk	Russia	44	7	10	17	36	....	....	....	....	....
2001-02	Ufa	Russia	51	11	10	21	74	....	....	....	....	....
2002-03	Ufa	Russia	50	4	7	11	72	3	2	0	2	4

KUKKONEN, Lasse (koo-KOH-nuhn, LA-she) **CHI.**

Defense. Shoots left. 6', 187 lbs. Born, Oulu, Finland, September 18, 1981.
(Chicago's 4th choice, 151st overall, in 2003 Entry Draft).

			Regular Season					Playoffs				
Season	Club	League	GP	G	A	TP	PIM	GP	G	A	TP	PIM
1997-98	Karpat Oulu Jr.	Finn-Jr.	36	5	16	21	46	....	....	....	....	....
1998-99	Karpat Oulu Jr.	Finn-Jr.	34	2	13	15	24	....	....	....	....	....
99-2000	Karpat Oulu Jr.	Finn-Jr.	27	9	11	20	26	....	....	....	....	....
	Karpat Oulu	Finland-2	22	0	4	4	14	....	....	....	....	....
2000-01	Karpat Oulu	Finland	47	1	5	6	46	9	0	2	2	4
2001-02	Karpat Oulu	Finland	55	2	6	8	42	4	0	3	3	4
	Karpat Oulu Jr.	Finn-Jr.	....	....	....	....	....	1	1	0	1	0
2002-03	Karpat Oulu	Finland	56	6	12	18	67	15	1	4	5	16

KULESHOV, Mikhail (koo-leh-SHAWV, mihk-AIL) **COL.**

Left wing. Shoots right. 6'2", 205 lbs. Born, Perm, USSR, January 7, 1981.
(Colorado's 1st choice, 25th overall, in 1999 Entry Draft).

			Regular Season					Playoffs				
Season	Club	League	GP	G	A	TP	PIM	GP	G	A	TP	PIM
1997-98	Omsk 2	Russia-3	12	12	3	15	12	....	....	....	....	....
	Avangard Omsk	Russia	4	1	0	1	4	....	....	....	....	....
1998-99	Cherepovets 3	Russia-4	3	2	1	3	32	....	....	....	....	....
	Cherepovets 2	Russia-3	25	7	5	12	12	....	....	....	....	....
	Cherepovets	Russia	15	2	0	2	8	3	0	0	0	4
99-2000	Cherepovets	Russia	8	0	0	0	4	3	0	0	0	2
2000-01	SKA St. Petersburg	Russia	7	0	0	0	8	....	....	....	....	....
	Hershey Bears	AHL	3	0	0	0	4	11	1	0	1	0
2001-02	Hershey Bears	AHL	60	8	11	19	43	7	0	1	1	4
2002-03	Hershey Bears	AHL	77	7	13	20	76	5	0	0	0	6

KUNITZ, Chris (KOO-hihtz, KRIHS) **ANA.**

Left wing. Shoots left. 6', 186 lbs. Born, Regina, Sask., September 26, 1979.

			Regular Season					Playoffs				
Season	Club	League	GP	G	A	TP	PIM	GP	G	A	TP	PIM
99-2000	Ferris State	CCHA	38	20	9	29	70	....	....	....	....	....
2000-01	Ferris State	CCHA	37	16	13	29	81	....	....	....	....	....
2001-02	Ferris State	CCHA	35	*28	10	38	68	....	....	....	....	....
2002-03	Ferris State	CCHA	42	*35	*44	*79	56	....	....	....	....	....

CCHA First All-Star Team (2002, 2003) • CCHA Player of the Year (2003) • NCAA West First All-American Team (2003

Signed as a free agent by **Anaheim**, April 1, 2003.

LAATIKAINEN, Arto (lah-tee-KIGH-nuhn, AHR-toh) **NYR**

Defense. Shoots left. 6', 187 lbs. Born, Espoo, Finland, May 24, 1980.
(NY Rangers' 8th choice, 197th overall, in 1999 Entry Draft).

			Regular Season					Playoffs				
Season	Club	League	GP	G	A	TP	PIM	GP	G	A	TP	PIM
1996-97	Kiekko Espoo Jr.	Finn-Jr.	34	2	9	11	34	....	....	....	....	....
	Kiekko Espoo B	Finn-Jr.	11	2	5	7	2	....	....	....	....	....
1997-98	Kiekko Espoo B	Finn-Jr.	7	2	1	3	6	....	....	....	....	....
	Kiekko Espoo Jr.	Finn-Jr.	35	7	9	16	24	5	2	0	2	2
1998-99	Blues Espoo Jr.	Finn-Jr.	3	0	1	1	4	1	1	1	2	0
	Blues Espoo	Finland	48	0	6	6	14	4	0	2	2	2
99-2000	Blues Espoo Jr.	Finn-Jr.	1	0	0	0	2	....	....	....	....	....
	Blues Espoo	Finland	51	6	5	11	12	4	1	0	1	4
2000-01	Blues Espoo	Finland	54	5	9	14	38	....	....	....	....	....
	KJT Jarvenpaa	Finland-2	1	1	1	2	0	....	....	....	....	....
2001-02	Blues Espoo	Finland	56	5	6	11	32	3	0	0	0	0
2002-03	Blues Espoo	Finland	51	1	8	9	24	7	0	3	3	4

LAICH, Brooks (LAYCH, BROOKS) **OTT.**

Center. Shoots left. 6'2", 199 lbs. Born, Wawota, Alta., June 23, 1983.
(Ottawa's 7th choice, 193rd overall, in 2001 Entry Draft).

			Regular Season					Playoffs				
Season	Club	League	GP	G	A	TP	PIM	GP	G	A	TP	PIM
99-2000	Tisdale Trojans	SMHL	57	51	52	103	....	....	....	....	....	....
2000-01	Moose Jaw	WHL	71	9	21	30	28	4	0	0	0	5
2001-02	Moose Jaw	WHL	28	6	14	20	12	....	....	....	....	....
	Seattle	WHL	47	22	36	58	42	11	5	3	8	11
2002-03	Seattle	WHL	60	41	53	94	65	15	5	14	19	24

WHL West First All-Star Team (2003)

LAINE, Teemu (LIGH-neh, TEE-moo) **N.J.**

Right wing. Shoots left. 6'1", 200 lbs. Born, Helsinki, Finland, August 9, 1982.
(New Jersey's 2nd choice, 39th overall, in 2000 Entry Draft).

			Regular Season					Playoffs				
Season	Club	League	GP	G	A	TP	PIM	GP	G	A	TP	PIM
1997-98	Jokerit Helsinki-B	Finn-Jr.	20	20	24	44	54	5	1	3	4	4
1998-99	Jokerit Helsinki Jr.	Finn-Jr.	29	20	17	37	83	6	0	2	2	6
99-2000	Jokerit Helsinki Jr.	Finn-Jr.	23	5	9	14	42	....	....	....	....	....
	Jokerit Helsinki	Finland	14	1	1	2	8	....	....	....	....	....
2000-01	Jokerit Helsinki Jr.	Finn-Jr.	4	1	2	3	18	1	0	0	0	0
	Kiekko Vantaa	Finland-2	18	2	4	6	30	....	....	....	....	....
	Jokerit Helsinki	Finland	25	3	2	5	10	5	1	0	1	2
2001-02	Jokerit Helsinki Jr.	Finn-Jr.	8	9	5	14	50	1	0	0	0	2
	Kiekko Vantaa	Finland-2	9	6	4	10	4	....	....	....	....	....
	Jokerit Helsinki	Finland	38	0	1	1	45	7	0	0	0	2
2002-03	Jokerit Helsinki	Finland	53	7	5	12	52	9	1	1	2	2

LALIBERTE, John (lal-IH-buhr-tee, JAWN) **VAN.**

Right wing. Shoots left. 6'1", 185 lbs. Born, Portland, ME, August 5, 1983.
(Vancouver's 5th choice, 114th overall, in 2002 Entry Draft).

			Regular Season					Playoffs				
Season	Club	League	GP	G	A	TP	PIM	GP	G	A	TP	PIM
99-2000	Exeter Eagles	Hi-School	32	37	40	77	60	....	....	....	....	....
2000-01	N.H. Jr. Monarchs	EJHL	53	33	42	75	42	....	....	....	....	....
2001-02	N.H. Jr. Monarchs	EJHL	35	39	44	*83	60	....	....	....	....	....
2002-03	Boston University	H-East	26	5	6	11	12	....	....	....	....	....

EJHL First All-Star Team (2002) • EJHL MVP (2002)

LAMBERT, Michael (lam-BAIR, MIGH-kuhl) **MTL.**

Left wing. Shoots left. 6'2", 180 lbs. Born, Trois-Rivieres, Que., March 10, 1984.
(Montreal's 3rd choice, 99th overall, in 2002 Entry Draft).

			Regular Season					Playoffs				
Season	Club	League	GP	G	A	TP	PIM	GP	G	A	TP	PIM
1998-99	Cap-d-Madeleine	QAAA	3	0	0	0	0	....	....	....	....	....
99-2000	Cap-d-Madeleine	QAAA	42	20	16	36	38	1	0	2	2	0
2000-01	Acadie-Bathurst	QMJHL	23	2	5	7	15	....	....	....	....	....
	Montreal Rocket	QMJHL	33	6	12	18	14	....	....	....	....	....
2001-02	Montreal Rocket	QMJHL	71	29	24	53	111	7	1	6	7	15
2002-03	Montreal Rocket	QMJHL	71	28	32	60	53	7	2	2	4	10

LAMPMAN, Bryce (LAMP-man, BRIGHS) NYR

Defense. Shoots left. 6'1", 193 lbs. Born, Rochester, MN, August 31, 1982.
(NY Rangers' 4th choice, 113th overall, in 2001 Entry Draft).

			Regular Season					Playoffs				
Season	Club	League	GP	G	A	TP	PIM	GP	G	A	TP	PIM
1998-99	Rochester	USHL	53	3	8	11	33	....	....	....	....	....
99-2000	Rochester	USHL	10	0	0	0	14	....	....	....	....	....
	Omaha Lancers	USHL	11	1	2	3	38	4	0	0	0	0
2000-01	Omaha Lancers	USHL	55	10	11	21	77	12	1	4	5	12
2001-02	Nebraska-Omaha	CCHA	26	0	4	4	28	....	....	....	....	....
2002-03	Kamloops Blazers	WHL	29	1	17	18	32	....	....	....	....	....
	Hartford Wolf Pack	AHL	45	0	6	6	32	2	0	1	1	0

• Left **Nebraska-Omaha** (CCHA) and signed as a free agent by **Kamloops** (WHL), August 1, 2002.

LANE, Jesse (LAYN, JEH-see) CAR.

Defense. Shoots left. 6'1", 210 lbs. Born, Boston, MA, March 2, 1983.
(Carolina's 2nd choice, 91st overall, in 2002 Entry Draft).

			Regular Season					Playoffs				
Season	Club	League	GP	G	A	TP	PIM	GP	G	A	TP	PIM
1998-99	Walpole Jr. Stars	EJHL		STATISTICS NOT AVAILABLE								
99-2000	Des Moines	USHL	54	3	15	18	89	9	1	1	2	6
2000-01	U.S. National U-18	USDP	62	7	20	27	84	....	....	....	....	....
2001-02	Harvard Crimson	ECAC	3	0	1	1	....	....	....	....	....	....
	Hull Olympiques	QMJHL	48	16	24	40	83	11	1	9	10	18
2002-03	Hull Olympiques	QMJHL	39	6	33	39	86	....	....	....	....	....
	Victoriaville Tigres	QMJHL	31	8	28	36	68	4	0	3	3	23

QMJHL First All-Star Team (2003)

• Left **Harvard** (ECAC) and signed as a free agent by **Hull** (QMJHL), November 10, 2001.

LANNON, Ryan (LA-nuhn, RIGH-uhn) PIT.

Defense. Shoots left. 6'2", 220 lbs. Born, Worcester, MA, December 14, 1982.
(Pittsburgh's 10th choice, 239th overall, in 2002 Entry Draft).

			Regular Season					Playoffs				
Season	Club	League	GP	G	A	TP	PIM	GP	G	A	TP	PIM
2000-01	Cushing Academy	Hi-School		STATISTICS NOT AVAILABLE								
2001-02	Harvard University	ECAC	34	0	2	2	38	....	....	....	....	....
2002-03	Harvard University	ECAC	34	3	11	14	39	....	....	....	....	....

LAPIERRE, Maxim (la-PEE-air, MAX-ihm) MTL.

Center. Shoots right. 6'2", 174 lbs. Born, St. Leonard, Que., March 29, 1985.
(Montreal's 3rd choice, 61st overall, in 2003 Entry Draft).

			Regular Season					Playoffs				
Season	Club	League	GP	G	A	TP	PIM	GP	G	A	TP	PIM
2001-02	Cap-de-la-M'laine	Midget	35	16	26	42	....	....	....	....	....	....
	Montreal Rocket	QMJHL	9	2	0	2	2	....	....	....	....	....
2002-03	Montreal Rocket	QMJHL	72	22	21	43	55	7	1	3	4	6

LAPLANTE, Eric (LA-plawnt, AIR-ihk)

Left wing. Shoots left. 6', 185 lbs. Born, St. Maurice, Que., December 1, 1979.
(San Jose's 3rd choice, 65th overall, in 1998 Entry Draft).

			Regular Season					Playoffs				
Season	Club	League	GP	G	A	TP	PIM	GP	G	A	TP	PIM
1995-96	Cap-d-Madeleine	QAAA	41	13	18	31	138	....	....	....	....	....
1996-97	Halifax	QMJHL	68	20	30	50	245	18	3	11	14	28
1997-98	Halifax	QMJHL	40	19	22	41	193	....	....	....	....	....
1998-99	Drummondville	QMJHL	42	14	25	39	258	....	....	....	....	....
	Quebec Remparts	QMJHL	23	4	17	21	58	13	8	7	15	45
99-2000	Quebec Remparts	QMJHL	47	24	35	59	234	10	3	5	8	*83
2000-01	Kentucky	AHL	62	5	8	13	181	3	0	0	0	6
2001-02	Cleveland Barons	AHL	78	7	14	21	326	....	....	....	....	....
2002-03	Cleveland Barons	AHL	76	8	10	18	240	....	....	....	....	....

LaROSE, Chad (lah-ROHZ, CHAD) CAR.

Right wing. Shoots right. 5'10", 173 lbs. Born, Fraser, MI, March 27, 1982.

			Regular Season					Playoffs				
Season	Club	League	GP	G	A	TP	PIM	GP	G	A	TP	PIM
99-2000	Sioux-Falls	USHL	54	29	26	55	28	3	0	1	1	0
2000-01	Sioux-Falls	USHL	24	11	22	33	50	....	....	....	....	....
	Plymouth Whalers	OHL	32	18	7	25	24	19	10	10	20	22
2001-02	PlymouthWhalers	OHL	53	32	27	59	40	6	3	4	7	16
2002-03	Plymouth Whalers	OHL	67	61	56	117	52	15	9	8	17	25

OHL Second All-Star Team (2003)

Signed as a free agent by **Carolina**, August 6, 2003.

LAROSE, Cory (la-ROHZ, KOH-ree) NYR

Center. Shoots left. 6', 188 lbs. Born, Campbellton, N.B., May 14, 1975.

			Regular Season					Playoffs				
Season	Club	League	GP	G	A	TP	PIM	GP	G	A	TP	PIM
1993-94	Kimball Union	Hi-School	21	18	11	29	14	....	....	....	....	....
1994-95	Langley Thunder	BCJHL		STATISTICS NOT AVAILABLE								
1995-96	Langley Thunder	BCJHL	54	28	46	74	61	....	....	....	....	....
1996-97	U. of Maine	H-East	35	10	27	37	32	....	....	....	....	....
1997-98	U. of Maine	H-East	34	15	25	40	22	....	....	....	....	....
1998-99	U. of Maine	H-East	38	21	31	52	34	....	....	....	....	....
99-2000	U. of Maine	H-East	39	15	*36	51	45	....	....	....	....	....
2000-01	Cleveland	IHL	4	1	1	2	6	....	....	....	....	....
	Jackson Bandits	ECHL	63	21	32	53	73	5	2	2	4	12
2001-02	Houston Aeros	AHL	78	32	32	64	73	14	6	8	14	15
2002-03	Houston Aeros	AHL	58	18	38	56	57	....	....	....	....	....
	Hartford Wolf Pack	AHL	24	9	10	19	20	2	0	1	1	0

BCJHL Playoff MVP (1996) • Hockey East First All-Star Team (2000) • NCAA East Second All-American Team (2000) • AHL All-Rookie Team (2002)

Signed as a free agent by **Minnesota**, May 10, 2000. Traded to **NY Rangers** by **Minnesota** for Jay Henderson, February 20, 2003.

LARRIVEE, Christian (la-ree-VAY, krihs-TYEH) MTL.

Center. Shoots left. 6'3", 192 lbs. Born, Gaspe, Que., August 25, 1982.
(Montreal's 6th choice, 114th overall, in 2000 Entry Draft).

			Regular Season					Playoffs				
Season	Club	League	GP	G	A	TP	PIM	GP	G	A	TP	PIM
1998-99	Jonquiere Elites	QAAA	42	26	36	62	10	....	....	....	....	....
99-2000	Chicoutimi	QMJHL	69	8	15	23	18	....	....	....	....	....
2000-01	Chicoutimi	QMJHL	72	32	48	80	46	7	3	1	4	4
2001-02	Chicoutimi	QMJHL	72	48	52	100	60	4	2	5	7	0
2002-03	Chicoutimi	QMJHL	50	18	40	58	49	....	....	....	....	....

LAVRENTIEV, Anton (lahv-REHN-tee-yehv, an-TAWN) NSH.

Defense. Shoots right. 6'4", 196 lbs. Born, Kazan, USSR, August 25, 1983.
(Nashville's 7th choice, 178th overall, in 2001 Entry Draft).

			Regular Season					Playoffs				
Season	Club	League	GP	G	A	TP	PIM	GP	G	A	TP	PIM
2000-01	Ak Bars Kazan 2	Russia-3		STATISTICS NOT AVAILABLE								
2001-02	Sudbury Wolves	OHL	10	0	0	0	17	....	....	....	....	....
	Ak Bars Kazan 2	Russia-3		STATISTICS NOT AVAILABLE								
2002-03	Yuzhny Ural Orsk	Russia-3	13	0	1	1	14	....	....	....	....	....

LAWSON, Lucas (LAW-suhn, LOO-kuhs) NYR

Center. Shoots left. 6'1", 195 lbs. Born, Braeside, Ont., August 10, 1979.

			Regular Season					Playoffs				
Season	Club	League	GP	G	A	TP	PIM	GP	G	A	TP	PIM
99-2000	U. of Maine	H-East	23	2	3	5	12	....	....	....	....	....
2000-01	U. of Maine	H-East	39	9	11	20	16	....	....	....	....	....
2001-02	U. of Maine	H-East	44	18	13	31	37	....	....	....	....	....
2002-03	U. of Maine	H-East	39	21	16	37	18	....	....	....	....	....
	Hartford Wolf Pack	AHL	....	....	....	....	....	2	0	0	0	0

Hockey East Second All-Star Team (2003)

Signed as a free agent by **NY Rangers**, April 4, 2003.

LEAHY, Patrick (LEH-hey, PAT-rihk) BOS.

Right wing. Shoots right. 6'3", 190 lbs. Born, Brighton, MA, June 9, 1979.
(NY Rangers' 5th choice, 122nd overall, in 1998 Entry Draft).

			Regular Season					Playoffs				
Season	Club	League	GP	G	A	TP	PIM	GP	G	A	TP	PIM
1996-97	B.C. High Irish	Hi-School	25	24	24	48	....	....	....	....	....	....
1997-98	Miami-Ohio	CCHA	28	0	1	1	24	....	....	....	....	....
1998-99	Miami-Ohio	CCHA	34	10	20	30	40	....	....	....	....	....
99-2000	Miami-Ohio	CCHA	36	16	22	38	89	....	....	....	....	....
2000-01	Miami-Ohio	CCHA	37	13	19	32	14	....	....	....	....	....
2001-02	Trenton Titans	ECHL	41	20	21	41	64	....	....	....	....	....
	Hershey Bears	AHL	9	1	2	3	8	....	....	....	....	....
	Portland Pirates	AHL	9	1	1	2	8	....	....	....	....	....
	Bridgeport	AHL	14	2	2	4	2	20	3	4	7	4
2002-03	Providence Bruins	AHL	66	20	23	43	63	4	1	0	1	18

Signed as a free agent by **Boston**, July 28, 2003.

LEE, Brian (LEE, BRIGH-uhn) ANA.

Defense. Shoots left. 6'2", 187 lbs. Born, Berrien Springs, MI, July 5, 1984.
(Anaheim's 3rd choice, 71st overall, in 2002 Entry Draft).

			Regular Season					Playoffs				
Season	Club	League	GP	G	A	TP	PIM	GP	G	A	TP	PIM
99-2000	Det. Honeybaked	MMHL	65	15	35	50	....	....	....	....	....	....
2000-01	Erie Otters	OHL	50	0	3	3	35	9	0	0	0	4
2001-02	Erie Otters	OHL	66	5	14	19	115	21	1	6	7	41
2002-03	Erie Otters	OHL	68	4	7	11	148	....	....	....	....	....
	Cincinnati	AHL	9	1	0	1	4	....	....	....	....	....

LEGG, Chris (LEHG, KRIHS) EDM.

Center. Shoots left. 6', 194 lbs. Born, London, Ont., February 19, 1980.
(Edmonton's 7th choice, 171st overall, in 1999 Entry Draft).

			Regular Season					Playoffs				
Season	Club	League	GP	G	A	TP	PIM	GP	G	A	TP	PIM
1996-97	London Nationals	OJHL-B	43	6	16	22	31	....	....	....	....	....
1997-98	London Nationals	OJHL-B	50	36	32	68	45	....	....	....	....	....
1998-99	London Nationals	OJHL-B	52	38	40	78	28	....	....	....	....	....
99-2000	Brown U.	ECAC	23	2	3	5	4	....	....	....	....	....
2000-01	Brown U.	ECAC	26	3	5	8	6	....	....	....	....	....
2001-02	Brown U.	ECAC	29	4	6	10	4	....	....	....	....	....
2002-03	Brown U.	ECAC	34	4	7	11	26	....	....	....	....	....

LEHOUX, Jason (luh-HOO, JAY-suhn)

Left wing. Shoots left. 6'2", 220 lbs. Born, Ste-Marie-Beauce, Que., July 21, 1979.

			Regular Season					Playoffs				
Season	Club	League	GP	G	A	TP	PIM	GP	G	A	TP	PIM
1995-96	Cap-d-Madeleine	QAAA	42	22	23	45	....	5	2	1	3	16
1996-97	Rimouski Oceanic	QMJHL	16	1	2	3	111	....	....	....	....	....
1997-98	Rouyn-Noranda	QMJHL	28	6	1	7	95	6	3	1	4	6
1998-99	Rouyn-Noranda	QMJHL	64	13	20	33	288	6	1	2	3	49
99-2000	Rouyn-Noranda	QMJHL	14	4	7	11	54	....	....	....	....	....
	Hull Olympiques	QMJHL	29	11	7	18	109	15	6	4	10	14
2000-01	Albany River Rats	AHL	52	8	7	15	101	....	....	....	....	....
2001-02	Albany River Rats	AHL	67	4	6	10	135	....	....	....	....	....
2002-03	Albany River Rats	AHL	64	10	11	21	175	....	....	....	....	....

Signed as a free agent by **New Jersey**, June 27, 2000.

LEHOUX, Yanick (luh-HOO, YAH-nihk) L.A.

Center. Shoots right. 6'1", 200 lbs. Born, Montreal, Que., April 8, 1982.
(Los Angeles' 3rd choice, 86th overall, in 2000 Entry Draft).

			Regular Season					Playoffs				
Season	Club	League	GP	G	A	TP	PIM	GP	G	A	TP	PIM
1997-98	Cap-d-Madeleine	QAAA	42	29	50	79	26	....	....	....	....	....
1998-99	Baie-Comeau	QMJHL	63	10	20	30	31	....	....	....	....	....
99-2000	Baie-Comeau	QMJHL	67	31	61	92	14	6	1	2	3	2
2000-01	Baie-Comeau	QMJHL	70	67	68	135	62	11	8	16	24	0
2001-02	Baie-Comeau	QMJHL	66	56	69	125	63	5	5	4	9	0
	Manchester	AHL	....	....	....	....	....	1	0	0	0	0
2002-03	Manchester	AHL	78	16	21	37	26	1	0	0	0	0

QMJHL Second All-Star Team (2002)

LEHTONEN, Mikko (LEHT-oh-nehn, MEE-koh) NSH.

Defense. Shoots left. 6'1", 194 lbs. Born, Oulu, Finland, June 12, 1979.
(Nashville's 9th choice, 271st overall, in 2001 Entry Draft).

			Regular Season					Playoffs				
Season	Club	League	GP	G	A	TP	PIM	GP	G	A	TP	PIM
1995-96	Karpat Oulu-B	Finn-Jr.	15	4	5	9	30	....	....	....	....	....
1996-97	Karpat Oulu Jr.	Finn-Jr.	35	6	19	25	82	....	....	....	....	....
1997-98	Karpat Oulu Jr.	Finn-Jr.	20	3	4	7	40	....	....	....	....	....
	Karpat Oulu-B	Finn-Jr.	11	5	7	12	31	....	....	....	....	....
1998-99	Karpat Oulu Jr.	Finn-Jr.	22	7	8	15	51	....	....	....	....	....
	Karpat Oulu	Finland-2	2	0	0	0	0	....	....	....	....	....
	Karpat Oulu-B	Finn-Jr.	13	6	14	20	14	....	....	....	....	....
99-2000	Karpat Oulu	Finland-2	45	5	10	15	26	6	0	0	0	4
2000-01	Karpat Oulu	Finland	54	6	9	15	58	9	0	3	3	4
2001-02	Karpat Oulu	Finland	55	8	11	19	32	4	1	1	2	4
2002-03	Karpat Oulu	Finland	55	5	12	17	50	15	3	1	4	22

LEPHART, Mike (LEHP-huhrt, MIGHK)

Left wing. Shoots right. 5'11", 194 lbs. Born, Niskayuna, NY, April 3, 1977.

			Regular Season					Playoffs				
Season	Club	League	GP	G	A	TP	PIM	GP	G	A	TP	PIM
1994-95	Springfield	NEJHL	45	20	30	50	....	....	....	....	....	....
1995-96	Omaha Lancers	USHL	45	12	12	24	40	....	....	....	....	....
1996-97	Omaha Lancers	USHL	54	40	50	*90	76	10	4	5	9	16
1997-98	Boston College	H-East	40	15	12	27	24	....	....	....	....	....
1998-99	Boston College	H-East	36	11	16	27	28	....	....	....	....	....
99-2000	Boston College	H-East	42	14	19	33	66	....	....	....	....	....
2000-01	Boston College	H-East	43	15	19	34	46	....	....	....	....	....
2001-02	Philadelphia	AHL	43	10	8	18	18	5	0	1	1	0
2002-03	Philadelphia	AHL	75	6	8	14	23	....	....	....	....	....

USHL First All-Star Team (1997) • Hockey East All-Academic Team (2000, 2001) • Hockey East Defensive Player of the Year (2001)

Signed as a free agent by **Philadelphia**, June 11, 2001.

LEVESQUE, Willie (luh-VEHK, WIHL-lee) S.J.

Right wing. Shoots right. 6', 195 lbs. Born, Oak Bluffs, MA, January 22, 1980.
(San Jose's 3rd choice, 111th overall, in 1999 Entry Draft).

			Regular Season					Playoffs				
Season	Club	League	GP	G	A	TP	PIM	GP	G	A	TP	PIM
1997-98	U.S. National U-18	USDP	60	12	24	36	118	....	....	....	....	....
1998-99	Northeastern	H-East	34	12	10	22	38	....	....	....	....	....
99-2000	Northeastern	H-East	33	9	13	22	45	....	....	....	....	....
2000-01	Northeastern	H-East	35	13	16	29	62	....	....	....	....	....
2001-02	Northeastern	H-East	30	6	10	16	42	....	....	....	....	....
2002-03	Cleveland Barons	AHL	64	4	5	9	32	....	....	....	....	....

Hockey East All-Rookie Team (1999)

LEVINSKI, Dimitri (leh-VIHN-skee, DEH-mih-TREE) CHI.

Left wing. Shoots left. 6'1", 183 lbs. Born, Ust-Kamenogorsk, USSR, June 23, 1981.
(Chicago's 2nd choice, 46th overall, in 1999 Entry Draft).

			Regular Season					Playoffs				
Season	Club	League	GP	G	A	TP	PIM	GP	G	A	TP	PIM
1996-97	Avangard Omsk 2	Russia-3	15	6	2	8	8	....	....	....	....	....
1997-98	Avangard Omsk 2	Russia-3	18	5	2	7	8	....	....	....	....	....
1998-99	Cherepovets 3	Russia-4	3	2	0	2	2	....	....	....	....	....
	Cherepovets 2	Russia-3	26	4	2	6	39	....	....	....	....	....
	Cherepovets	Russia	1	0	0	0	0	....	....	....	....	....
99-2000	SKA St. Petersburg	Russia	25	0	2	2	4	4	0	0	0	0
2000-01	Khabarovsk 2	Russia-3	22	0	2	2	2	....	....	....	....	....
	Amur Khabarovsk	Russia	19	0	2	2	2	....	....	....	....	....
2001-02	HC CSKA	Russia-2	49	6	2	8	28	....	....	....	....	....
2002-03	SKA St. Petersburg	Russia	21	0	1	1	4	....	....	....	....	....
	St. Petersburg 2	Russia-3	10	10	5	15	0	....	....	....	....	....

LEVOKARI, Pauli (leh-voh-KAHR-ee, PAWL-ee) CBJ

Defense. Shoots left. 6'7", 260 lbs. Born, Luvia, Finland, April 7, 1979.
(Atlanta's 10th choice, 257th overall, in 2002 Entry Draft).

			Regular Season					Playoffs				
Season	Club	League	GP	G	A	TP	PIM	GP	G	A	TP	PIM
1993-94	Assat Pori-C	Finn-Jr.	32	1	2	3	50	....	....	....	....	....
1994-95	Assat Pori-C	Finn-Jr.		STATISTICS NOT AVAILABLE								
1995-96	Assat Pori-B	Finn-Jr.	28	5	6	11	42	....	....	....	....	....
	Assat Pori Jr.	Finn-Jr.	10	0	1	1	22	....	....	....	....	....
1996-97	Assat Pori Jr.	Finn-Jr.	35	3	8	11	78	4	0	0	0	10
	Assat Pori	Finland	1	0	0	0	0	....	....	....	....	....
1997-98	Assat Pori Jr.	Finn-Jr.	27	2	5	7	79	....	....	....	....	....
	Assat Pori	Finland	16	0	0	0	0	1	0	0	0	0
1998-99	Assat Pori Jr.	Finn-Jr.	19	4	3	7	68	....	....	....	....	....
	Assat Pori	Finland	27	0	2	2	8	....	....	....	....	....
99-2000	Assat Pori	Finland	51	3	2	5	80	....	....	....	....	....
2000-01	Assat Pori	Finland	12	1	0	1	12	....	....	....	....	....
	Jokerit Helsinki	Finland	10	0	0	0	6	....	....	....	....	....
	Kiekko-Vantaa	Finland-2	22	3	6	9	68	3	0	1	1	6
2001-02	HIFK Helsinki	Finland	29	3	5	8	86	....	....	....	....	....
2002-03	Chicago Wolves	AHL	6	0	1	1	12	....	....	....	....	....
	Greenville Grrrowl	ECHL	4	0	0	0	8	....	....	....	....	....
	Syracuse Crunch	AHL	45	4	6	10	88	....	....	....	....	....

Traded to **Columbus** by **Atlanta** with Tomi Kallio for Chris Nielsen and Petteri Nummelin, December 2, 2002.

LEWANDOWSKI, Eduard (luh-wan-DOW-skee, EHD-wahrd) PHX.

Left wing. Shoots left. 6'1", 205 lbs. Born, Krasnoturjinsk, USSR, May 3, 1980.
(Phoenix's 6th choice, 242nd overall, in 2003 Entry Draft).

			Regular Season					Playoffs				
Season	Club	League	GP	G	A	TP	PIM	GP	G	A	TP	PIM
1997-98	EC Wilhelmshaven	German-3	48	19	12	31	46	....	....	....	....	....
1998-99	EC Wilhelmshaven	German-3	49	35	21	56	96	....	....	....	....	....
99-2000	EC Wilhelmshaven	German-2	48	15	26	41	104	....	....	....	....	....
2000-01	EC Wilhelmshaven	German-2	42	21	28	49	8	....	....	....	....	....
2001-02	Eisbaren Berlin	Germany	59	7	15	22	57	4	0	0	0	2
2002-03	Kolner Haie	Germany	46	6	14	20	46	13	3	3	6	43

LIFFITON, David (LIH-fih-tuhn, DAY-vihd) COL.

Defense. Shoots left. 6'2", 201 lbs. Born, Windsor, Ont., October 18, 1984.
(Colorado's 1st choice, 63rd overall, in 2003 Entry Draft).

			Regular Season					Playoffs				
Season	Club	League	GP	G	A	TP	PIM	GP	G	A	TP	PIM
2000-01	Aylmer Aces	OJHL-B	51	1	9	10	51	....	....	....	....	....
2001-02	Plymouth Whalers	OHL	62	3	9	12	65	6	0	0	0	0
2002-03	Plymouth Whalers	OHL	64	5	11	16	139	18	1	3	4	29

LILES, John-Michael (LIGH-uhls, JAWN-MIGHK-uhl) COL.

Defense. Shoots left. 5'10", 185 lbs. Born, Zionsville, IN, November 25, 1980.
(Colorado's 8th choice, 159th overall, in 2000 Entry Draft).

			Regular Season					Playoffs				
Season	Club	League	GP	G	A	TP	PIM	GP	G	A	TP	PIM
1997-98	U.S. National U-17	USDP	67	6	14	20	44	....	....	....	....	....
1998-99	U.S. National U-17	USDP	13	2	5	7	6	....	....	....	....	....
	U.S. National U-18	USDP	46	4	14	18	47	....	....	....	....	....
99-2000	Michigan State	CCHA	40	8	20	28	26	....	....	....	....	....
2000-01	Michigan State	CCHA	42	7	18	25	28	....	....	....	....	....
2001-02	Michigan State	CCHA	41	13	22	35	18	....	....	....	....	....
2002-03	Hershey Bears	AHL	5	0	1	1	4	5	0	0	0	2
	Michigan State	CCHA	39	16	34	50	46	....	....	....	....	....

CCHA Second All-Star Team (2001) • CCHA First All-Star Team (2002, 2003) • NCAA West Second All-American Team (2002) • NCAA West First All-American Team (2003)

LINDLOF, Joni (LIHND-lawf, YOH-nee) WSH.

Left wing. Shoots left. 6'1", 172 lbs. Born, Tampere, Finland, May 17, 1984.
(Washington's 11th choice, 209th overall, in 2002 Entry Draft).

			Regular Season					Playoffs				
Season	Club	League	GP	G	A	TP	PIM	GP	G	A	TP	PIM
2000-01	Tappara B	Finn-Jr.	33	10	6	16	42	2	0	0	0	2
	Tappara Jr.	Finn-Jr.	2	0	0	0	0	....	....	....	....	....
2001-02	Tappara Jr.	Finn-Jr.	33	17	8	25	14	....	....	....	....	....
	Tappara B	Finn-Jr.	2	3	1	4	2	....	....	....	....	....
2002-03	Kelowna Rockets	WHL	70	11	20	31	53	19	3	8	11	8

LINDSTROM, Andreas (LIHND-struhm, an-DRAY-uhs) BOS.

Right wing. Shoots left. 6'5", 210 lbs. Born, Lulea, Sweden, September 1, 1982.
(Boston's 12th choice, 279th overall, in 2000 Entry Draft).

			Regular Season					Playoffs				
Season	Club	League	GP	G	A	TP	PIM	GP	G	A	TP	PIM
99-2000	Lulea HF Jr.	Swede-Jr.	9	2	2	4	14	....	....	....	....	....
2000-01	Lulea HF Jr.	Swede-Jr.	21	8	6	14	18	....	....	....	....	....
	Lulea HF	Sweden	3	0	0	0	0	8	1	0	1	0
2001-02	Lulea HF Jr.	Swede-Jr.	17	5	4	9	40	2	1	0	1	6
	Lulea HF	Sweden	....	....	....	....	....	1	0	0	0	4
2002-03	Bodens IK	Swede-2	35	0	2	2	24	....	....	....	....	....

LINDSTROM, Joakim (LIHND-struhm, YOH-ah-kihm) CBJ

Center. Shoots left. 6', 187 lbs. Born, Skelleftea, Sweden, December 5, 1983.
(Columbus' 2nd choice, 41st overall, in 2002 Entry Draft).

			Regular Season					Playoffs				
Season	Club	League	GP	G	A	TP	PIM	GP	G	A	TP	PIM
99-2000	MoDo-18	Swede-Jr.	17	6	*14	20	32	....	....	....	....	....
	MoDo Jr.	Swede-Jr.	10	4	4	8	2	....	....	....	....	....
2000-01	MoDo Jr.	Swede-Jr.	12	7	14	21	46	4	2	3	5	24
	MoDo	Sweden	10	2	3	5	2	7	0	1	1	0
2001-02	MoDo Jr.	Swede-Jr.	10	9	6	15	67	....	....	....	....	....
	IF Troja-Ljungby	Swede-2	3	0	0	0	12	....	....	....	....	....
	MoDo	Sweden	42	4	3	7	20	14	3	5	8	8
2002-03	MoDo	Sweden	29	4	2	6	14	6	1	1	2	2
	MoDo Jr.	Swede-Jr.	2	5	1	6	8	....	....	....	....	....
	Ornskoldsvik SK	Swede-2	2	1	1	2	4	....	....	....	....	....

LINDSTROM, Liam (LIHND-struhm, LEE-uhm) PHX.

Center. Shoots left. 6', 189 lbs. Born, Edmonton, Alta., January 12, 1985.
(Phoenix's 3rd choice, 115th overall, in 2003 Entry Draft).

			Regular Season					Playoffs				
Season	Club	League	GP	G	A	TP	PIM	GP	G	A	TP	PIM
2000-01	Mora IK Jr.	Swede-Jr.	15	3	4	7	16	1	0	0	0	0
2001-02	Mora IK Jr.	Swede-Jr.	28	7	8	15	16	1	1	0	1	0
	Mora IK	Sweden-2	1	1	0	1	0	....	....	....	....	....
2002-03	Mora IK Jr.	Swede-Jr.	27	6	8	14	69	....	....	....	....	....
	Mora IK	Sweden-2	14	0	0	0	0	....	....	....	....	....

LINDSTROM, Sanny (LIHND-struhm, SAN-nee) COL.

Defense. Shoots left. 6'2", 205 lbs. Born, Stockholm, Sweden, December 24, 1979.
(Colorado's 4th choice, 112th overall, in 1999 Entry Draft).

			Regular Season					Playoffs				
Season	Club	League	GP	G	A	TP	PIM	GP	G	A	TP	PIM
1997-98	Huddinge IK	Swede-2	32	6	6	12	46	....	....	....	....	....
1998-99	Huddinge IK	Swede-2	37	4	4	8	65	....	....	....	....	....
99-2000	Hershey Bears	AHL	42	1	2	3	57	....	....	....	....	....
	Baton Rouge	ECHL	11	1	2	3	16	....	....	....	....	....
2000-01	Hershey Bears	AHL	24	0	0	0	61	....	....	....	....	....
	Quad City	UHL	5	1	1	2	10	....	....	....	....	....
2001-02	Quad City	UHL	38	4	23	27	71	12	0	3	3	20
	Hershey Bears	AHL	2	0	0	0	0	....	....	....	....	....
2002-03	Timra IK	Sweden	39	1	1	2	81	9	0	1	1	0

• Missed majority of 2000-01 season recovering from knee injury suffered in practice, March 5, 2000.

LINHART, Tomas (LIHN-hart, TAW-mash) MTL.

Defense. Shoots left. 6'2", 209 lbs. Born, Pardubice, Czech., February 16, 1984.
(Montreal's 2nd choice, 45th overall, in 2002 Entry Draft).

			Regular Season					Playoffs				
Season	Club	League	GP	G	A	TP	PIM	GP	G	A	TP	PIM
99-2000	Pardubice-18	Czech-Jr.	45	2	8	10	83	....	....	....	....	....
2000-01	Pardubice-18	Czech-Jr.	23	5	7	12	82	....	....	....	....	....
	Pardubice Jr.	Czech-Jr.	29	1	6	7	12	4	0	0	0	0
2001-02	Pardubice Jr.	Czech-Jr.	38	2	4	6	28	....	....	....	....	....
	Sumperk	Czech-2	1	0	0	0	2	....	....	....	....	....
2002-03	Mississauga	OHL	27	0	2	2	12	....	....	....	....	....
	London Knights	OHL	28	0	2	2	18	1	0	0	0	0

LITVINENKO, Alexei (liht-vihn-EHN-koh, al-EHX-ay) PHX.

Defense. Shoots left. 6'4", 180 lbs. Born, Ust-Kamenogorsk, USSR, March 7, 1980.
(Phoenix's 9th choice, 262nd overall, in 1999 Entry Draft).

			Regular Season					Playoffs				
Season	Club	League	GP	G	A	TP	PIM	GP	G	A	TP	PIM
1997-98	Ust-Kamenog. 2	Russia-3	12	0	0	0	8	....	....	....	....	....
	Ust-Kamenogorsk	Russia-2	2	0	0	0	0	....	....	....	....	....
1998-99	Ust-Kamenog. 2	Russia-4	31	3	4	7	52	....	....	....	....	....
	Ust-Kamenog. 2	Russia-3	16	0	4	4	14	....	....	....	....	....
99-2000	Dynamo Moscow	Russia	7	0	0	0	4	....	....	....	....	....
2000-01	Dynamo Moscow	Russia	6	0	0	0	0	....	....	....	....	....
	Yekaterinburg	Russia	26	0	0	0	42	....	....	....	....	....
2001-02	Magnitogorsk	Russia	20	0	3	3	29	9	1	1	2	20
2002-03	Magnitogorsk	Russia	21	0	2	2	28	....	....	....	....	....

LOCKE, Corey (LAWK, KOHR-ee) MTL.

Center. Shoots left. 5'9", 175 lbs. Born, Toronto, Ont., May 8, 1984.
(Montreal's 5th choice, 113th overall, in 2003 Entry Draft).

			Regular Season					Playoffs				
Season	Club	League	GP	G	A	TP	PIM	GP	G	A	TP	PIM
2000-01	Newmarket	OPJHL	49	34	51	85	16	16	10	12	22	14
2001-02	Ottawa 67's	OHL	55	18	25	43	18	13	6	7	13	10
2002-03	Ottawa 67's	OHL	66	*63	*88	*151	83	23	*19	19	*38	30

OHL First All-Star Team (2003) • Canadian Major Junior First All-Star Team (2003) • OHL Player of the Year (2003) • Canadian Major Junior Player of the Year (2003)

LOJEK, Martin (LOI-yehk, MAHR-tehn) FLA.

Defense. Shoots right. 6'5", 220 lbs. Born, Brno, Czech., August 19, 1985.
(Florida's 5th choice, 105th overall, in 2003 Entry Draft).

			Regular Season					Playoffs				
Season	Club	League	GP	G	A	TP	PIM	GP	G	A	TP	PIM
2000-01	Pardubice Jr.	Czech-Jr.	48	2	2	4	42	7	0	0	0	6
2001-02	Pardubice Jr.	Czech-Jr.	40	2	4	6	24	7	1	0	1	2
2002-03	Brampton	OHL	65	1	13	14	47	11	0	1	1	6

LOMBARDI, Matthew (lawm-BAHR-dee, MA-thew) CGY.

Center. Shoots left. 5'11", 191 lbs. Born, Montreal, Que., March 18, 1982.
(Calgary's 3rd choice, 90th overall, in 2002 Entry Draft).

			Regular Season					Playoffs				
Season	Club	League	GP	G	A	TP	PIM	GP	G	A	TP	PIM
1997-98	Gatineau Intrepide	QAAA	42	10	13	23	....	13	4	7	11	....
1998-99	Victoriaville Tigres	QMJHL	47	6	10	16	8	5	0	0	0	0
99-2000	Victoriaville Tigres	QMJHL	65	18	26	44	28	6	0	0	0	6
2000-01	Victoriaville Tigres	QMJHL	72	28	39	67	66	13	12	6	18	10
2001-02	Victoriaville Tigres	QMJHL	66	57	73	130	70	22	*17	18	35	18
2002-03	Saint John Flames	AHL	76	25	21	46	41	....	....	....	....	....

• Re-entered NHL Entry Draft. Originally Edmonton's 7th choice, 215th overall, in 2000 Entry Draft.

Memorial Cup All-Star Team (2002)

LUCHKIN, Vladislav (LOOCH-kihn, VLA-dihs-lav) CHI.

Center. Shoots left. 6'1", 185 lbs. Born, Cherepovets, USSR, February 3, 1982.
(Chicago's 11th choice, 225th overall, in 2000 Entry Draft).

			Regular Season					Playoffs				
Season	Club	League	GP	G	A	TP	PIM	GP	G	A	TP	PIM
1997-98	Cherepovets 2	Russia-3	23	2	5	7	12	....	....	....	....	....
1998-99	Cherepovets 2	Russia-3	25	6	4	10	8	....	....	....	....	....
	Cherepovets 3	Russia-4	8	1	3	4	10	....	....	....	....	....
99-2000	Cherepovets 2	Russia-3	30	23	10	33	36	....	....	....	....	....
2000-01	Cherepovets	Russia	28	2	3	5	10	6	2	0	2	4
2001-02	Cherepovets 2	Russia-3	6	5	6	11	0	....	....	....	....	....
	Cherepovets	Russia	27	4	6	10	12	....	....	....	....	....
2002-03	Cherepovets	Russia	2	0	0	0	2	....	....	....	....	....
	SKA St. Petersburg	Russia	4	0	0	0	0	....	....	....	....	....
	Cherepovets 2	Russia-3	12	3	9	12	88	....	....	....	....	....

LUKES, Frantisek (LOO-kehsh, FRAHN-tih-sehk) PHX.

Left wing. Shoots right. 5'9", 171 lbs. Born, Kadan, Czech., September 25, 1982.
(Phoenix's 8th choice, 243rd overall, in 2001 Entry Draft).

			Regular Season					Playoffs				
Season	Club	League	GP	G	A	TP	PIM	GP	G	A	TP	PIM
99-2000	Litvinov Jr.	Czech-Jr.	36	15	13	28	....	....	....	....	....	....
2000-01	St. Michael's	OHL	61	23	33	56	37	18	4	9	13	12
2001-02	St. Michael's	OHL	63	27	37	64	50	15	7	11	18	16
2002-03	St. Michael's	OHL	62	27	46	73	55	19	8	15	23	28

LUNDBERG, Eric (LUHND-buhrg, AIR-ihk) COL.

Defense. Shoots right. 6'3", 200 lbs. Born, Vernon, CT, April 13, 1983.
(Colorado's 3rd choice, 94th overall, in 2002 Entry Draft).

			Regular Season					Playoffs				
Season	Club	League	GP	G	A	TP	PIM	GP	G	A	TP	PIM
99-2000	New England	EJHL	36	8	36	42	106	....	....	....	....	....
2000-01	New England	EJHL	36	6	28	34	92	10	2	10	12	14
2001-02	Providence College	H-East	36	0	9	9	28	....	....	....	....	....
2002-03	Providence College	H-East	33	0	6	6	30	....	....	....	....	....

LUNDBOHM, Bryan (LUHND-bawm, BRIGH-uhn)

Right wing. Shoots left. 5'10", 184 lbs. Born, Roseau, MN, August 24, 1977.

			Regular Season					Playoffs				
Season	Club	League	GP	G	A	TP	PIM	GP	G	A	TP	PIM
1996-97	Lincoln Stars	USHL	52	13	33	45	33	14	8	4	12	33
1997-98	Lincoln Stars	USHL	55	26	38	64	10	9	2	7	9	0
1998-99	North Dakota	WCHA	32	2	9	11	4	....	....	....	....	....
99-2000	North Dakota	WCHA	44	22	22	44	14	....	....	....	....	....
2000-01	North Dakota	WCHA	46	*32	27	69	38	....	....	....	....	....
2001-02	Milwaukee	AHL	79	11	23	34	63	....	....	....	....	....
2002-03	Milwaukee	AHL	80	9	17	26	63	6	1	5	6	0

USHL First All-Star Team (1998) • WCHA First All-Star Team (2001) • NCAA West Second All-American Team (2001) • NCAA Championship All-Tournament Team (2001)

Signed as a free agent by **Nashville**, May 1, 2001.

LUNDQVIST, Joel (LOOND-kvihst, JOHL) DAL.

Center. Shoots left. 6', 185 lbs. Born, Are, Sweden, March 2, 1982.
(Dallas' 3rd choice, 68th overall, in 2000 Entry Draft).

			Regular Season					Playoffs				
Season	Club	League	GP	G	A	TP	PIM	GP	G	A	TP	PIM
1997-98	Rogle Jr.	Swede-Jr.	59	36	40	76	....	....	....	....	....	....
1998-99	V. Frolunda-18	Swede-Jr.	32	26	38	64	37	4	3	1	4	2
99-2000	V. Frolunda-18	Swede-Jr.	4	2	4	6	4	....	....	....	....	....
	V. Frolunda Jr.	Swede-Jr.	25	7	12	19	2	6	2	3	5	2
2000-01	V. Frolunda Jr.	Swede-Jr.	18	14	27	41	12	....	....	....	....	....
	Molndals HS	Swede-2	26	18	13	31	22	....	....	....	....	....
	Vastra Frolunda	Sweden	9	0	0	0	0	....	....	....	....	....
2001-02	Vastra Frolunda	Sweden	46	12	14	26	28	10	1	3	4	8
	V. Frolunda Jr.	Swede-Jr.	....	....	....	....	....	1	0	0	0	0
2002-03	Vastra Frolunda	Sweden	50	17	20	37	113	16	6	3	9	12

LUNDQVIST, Stefan (LUHND-kvihst, STEH-fan) NYR

Right wing. Shoots left. 6'3", 209 lbs. Born, Gavle, Sweden, February 18, 1978.
(NY Rangers' 7th choice, 180th overall, in 1998 Entry Draft).

			Regular Season					Playoffs				
Season	Club	League	GP	G	A	TP	PIM	GP	G	A	TP	PIM
1994-95	Avesta BK	Swede-2	3	0	1	1	0	....	....	....	....	....
1995-96	Avesta BK	Swede-3	27	24	13	37	10	....	....	....	....	....
1996-97	Avesta BK	Swede-3	31	37	29	66	....	....	....	....	....	....
1997-98	Brynas IF Gavle jr.	Swede-Jr.	21	23	15	38	2	....	....	....	....	....
	Brynas IF Gavle	Sweden	27	2	2	4	0	1	0	0	0	0
1998-99	Brynas IF Gavle	Sweden	13	0	0	0	0	....	....	....	....	....
	Uppsala	Swede-2	15	7	8	15	0	....	....	....	....	....
	Mora IK	Swede-2	23	10	7	17	22	4	2	2	4	2
99-2000	Brynas IF Gavle	Sweden	48	6	4	10	12	11	1	0	1	0
	Brynas IF Gavle	EuroHL	6	1	1	2	2	....	....	....	....	....
2000-01	Skelleftea AIK	Swede-2	35	21	11	32	14	1	0	0	0	0
2001-02	Skelleftea AIK	Swede-2	40	28	14	42	20	5	1	0	1	4
2002-03	Vasteras	Swede-2	40	23	14	37	12	....	....	....	....	....

LUOMA, Mikko (loo-OH-mah, MEE-koh) EDM.

Defense. Shoots left. 6'3", 207 lbs. Born, Jyvaskyla, Finland, June 22, 1976.
(Edmonton's 9th choice, 181st overall, in 2002 Entry Draft).

			Regular Season					Playoffs				
Season	Club	League	GP	G	A	TP	PIM	GP	G	A	TP	PIM
1998-99	JYP Jyvaskyla	Finland	53	2	8	10	60	3	0	0	0	4
99-2000	JYP Jyvaskyla	Finland	51	2	6	8	58	....	....	....	....	....
2000-01	Tappara Tampere	Finland	56	10	11	21	72	10	0	2	2	10
2001-02	Tappara Tampere	Finland	56	11	18	29	74	10	1	2	3	10
2002-03	Tappara Tampere	Finland	55	4	13	17	52	14	2	1	3	12

LUPUL, Joffrey (LOO-puhl, JAWF-ree) ANA.

Center. Shoots right. 6'1", 194 lbs. Born, Edmonton, Alta., September 23, 1983.
(Anaheim's 1st choice, 7th overall, in 2002 Entry Draft).

			Regular Season					Playoffs				
Season	Club	League	GP	G	A	TP	PIM	GP	G	A	TP	PIM
1998-99	Ft. Saskatchewan	ABHL	36	40	50	90	40	....	....	....	....	....
99-2000	Ft. Saskatchewan	AMHL	34	43	30	*73	47	4	0	1	1	2
2000-01	Medicine Hat	WHL	69	30	26	56	39	22	3	6	9	2
2001-02	Medicine Hat	WHL	72	*56	50	106	95	....	....	....	....	....
2002-03	Medicine Hat	WHL	50	41	37	78	82	11	4	11	15	20

WHL East First All-Star Team (2002) • Canadian Major Junior First All-Star Team (2002)

LUTTINEN, Arttu (LOO-tuh-nehn, AHR-too) OTT.

Left wing. Shoots left. 5'10", 205 lbs. Born, Helsinki, Finland, September 9, 1983.
(Ottawa's 3rd choice, 75th overall, in 2002 Entry Draft).

			Regular Season					Playoffs				
Season	Club	League	GP	G	A	TP	PIM	GP	G	A	TP	PIM
99-2000	HIFK Helsinki Jr.	Finn-Jr.	17	5	9	14	10	2	0	0	0	2
2000-01	HIFK Helsinki-B	Finn-Jr.	20	14	20	34	141	....	....	....	....	....
	HIFK Helsinki Jr.	Finn-Jr.	8	4	2	6	4	8	0	1	1	2
2001-02	HIFK Helsinki Jr.	Finn-Jr.	24	16	17	23	60	1	0	0	0	0
2002-03	HIFK Helsinki	Finland	41	4	4	8	10	1	0	0	0	0
	HIFK Helsinki Jr.	Finn-Jr.	10	8	9	17	52	8	4	6	10	20

LYNCH, Darren (LIHNCH, DAIR-uhn) CGY.

Right wing. Shoots right. 5'11", 175 lbs. Born, Regina, Sask., July 7, 1983.

			Regular Season					Playoffs				
Season	Club	League	GP	G	A	TP	PIM	GP	G	A	TP	PIM
2001-02	Vancouver Giants	WHL	72	30	31	61	51	....	....	....	....	....
2002-03	Vancouver Giants	WHL	70	29	53	82	44	4	0	0	0	6

Signed as a free agent by **Calgary**, September 27, 2002.

LYNCH, Doug (LIHNCH, DUHG) EDM.

Defense. Shoots left. 6'3", 214 lbs. Born, North Vancouver, B.C., April 4, 1983.
(Edmonton's 2nd choice, 43rd overall, in 2001 Entry Draft).

			Regular Season					Playoffs				
Season	Club	League	GP	G	A	TP	PIM	GP	G	A	TP	PIM
1998-99	Port Coquitlam	BCAHA	45	47	48	95	120	....	....	....	....	....
	Red Deer Rebels	WHL	2	0	1	1	2	....	....	....	....	....
99-2000	Red Deer Rebels	WHL	65	9	5	14	57	4	0	0	0	5
2000-01	Red Deer Rebels	WHL	72	12	37	49	181	21	1	9	10	30
2001-02	Red Deer Rebels	WHL	71	21	27	48	202	22	5	4	9	12
2002-03	Red Deer Rebels	WHL	13	7	5	12	27	....	....	....	....	....
	Spokane Chiefs	WHL	42	6	12	18	129	4	1	0	1	16

LYNCH, Paul (LIHNCH, PAWL) T.B.

Defense. Shoots left. 6'4", 195 lbs. Born, Salem, MA, April 23, 1982.
(Tampa Bay's 6th choice, 138th overall, in 2001 Entry Draft).

			Regular Season					Playoffs				
Season	Club	League	GP	G	A	TP	PIM	GP	G	A	TP	PIM
99-2000	Brooks High	Hi-School	23	21	25	46	34	....	....	....	....	....
2000-01	Valley Juniors	EJHL	21	3	4	7	143	....	....	....	....	....
2001-02	U. of Maine	H-East	22	2	4	6	24	....	....	....	....	....
2002-03	U. of Maine	H-East	10	0	3	3	6	....	....	....	....	....

LYSAK, Brett (LIGH-sak, BREHT) CAR.

Center. Shoots left. 6', 190 lbs. Born, Edmonton, Alta., December 30, 1980.
(Carolina's 2nd choice, 49th overall, in 1999 Entry Draft).

			Regular Season					Playoffs				
Season	Club	League	GP	G	A	TP	PIM	GP	G	A	TP	PIM
1995-96	St. Albert Saints	AJHL	35	20	23	43	68	....	....	....	....	....
1996-97	Regina Pats	WHL	66	11	14	25	41	5	0	1	1	5
1997-98	Regina Pats	WHL	70	22	38	60	82	9	6	2	8	8
1998-99	Regina Pats	WHL	61	39	49	88	84	....	....	....	....	....
99-2000	Regina Pats	WHL	70	38	40	78	24	7	5	4	9	2
2000-01	Regina Pats	WHL	64	35	48	83	44	6	5	1	6	4
2001-02	Lowell	AHL	53	6	8	14	26	3	0	0	0	0
	Florida Everblades	ECHL	16	2	7	9	14	6	3	1	4	6
2002-03	Lowell	AHL	49	6	9	15	59	....	....	....	....	....

WHL East Second All-Star Team (1999) • Memorial Cup All-Star Team (2001)

LYUBUSHIN, Mikhail (l'yoo-BOOSH-ihn, mee-kigh-EHL) L.A.

Defense. Shoots left. 6'1", 183 lbs. Born, Moscow, USSR, July 24, 1983.
(Los Angeles' 9th choice, 215th overall, in 2002 Entry Draft).

			Regular Season					Playoffs				
Season	Club	League	GP	G	A	TP	PIM	GP	G	A	TP	PIM
2001-02	Krylja Sovetov 2	Russia-3	20	3	6	9	24	....	....	....	....	....
	THC Tver	Russia-2	22	1	0	1	18	....	....	....	....	....
	Krylja Sovetov	Russia	13	0	1	1	14	3	0	0	0	0
2002-03	Krylja Sovetov	Russia	49	0	6	6	26	....	....	....	....	....

MAATTA, Tero (MAH-tuh, TEH-roh) S.J.

Defense. Shoots left. 6'1", 220 lbs. Born, Vantaa, Finland, January 2, 1982.
(San Jose's 1st choice, 41st overall, in 2000 Entry Draft).

			Regular Season					Playoffs				
Season	Club	League	GP	G	A	TP	PIM	GP	G	A	TP	PIM
1996-97	Kiekko Vantaa-C	Finn-Jr.	20	2	6	8	6	....	....	....	....	....
	Haukat-C	Finn-Jr.	8	3	1	4	10	....	....	....	....	....
1997-98	Jokerit Helsinki-B	Finn-Jr.	28	4	7	11	10	2	0	0	0	2
1998-99	Jokerit Helsinki Jr.	Finn-Jr.	38	4	8	12	75	8	1	3	4	6
99-2000	Jokerit Helsinki-B	Finn-Jr.	13	4	10	14	24	1	0	0	0	25
	Jokerit Helsinki Jr.	Finn-Jr.	31	4	4	8	53	....	....	....	....	....
2000-01	Blues Espoo Jr.	Finn-Jr.	6	0	1	1	6	....	....	....	....	....
	KJT Jarvenpaa	Finland-2	6	0	3	3	31	....	....	....	....	....
	Blues Espoo	Finland	44	4	4	8	24	....	....	....	....	....
2001-02	Blues Espoo Jr.	Finn-Jr.	8	2	6	8	2	....	....	....	....	....
	Blues Espoo	Finland	51	4	6	10	65	3	0	0	0	0
2002-03	Assat Pori	Finland	7	0	0	0	29	....	....	....	....	....
	Blues Espoo	Finland	43	0	3	3	56	7	0	1	1	4

MacARTHUR, Clarke (muh-KAR-thuhr, KLAHRK) BUF.

Left wing. Shoots left. 6', 180 lbs. Born, Lloydminster, Alta., April 6, 1985.
(Buffalo's 3rd choice, 74th overall, in 2003 Entry Draft).

			Regular Season					Playoffs				
Season	Club	League	GP	G	A	TP	PIM	GP	G	A	TP	PIM
99-2000	Lloydminster	CABHL	24	19	45	64	51	5	9	6	15	4
2000-01	Strathcona	AMBHL	38	36	63	99	44	8	6	2	8	10
2001-02	Drayton Valley	AJHL	61	22	40	62	33	16	5	8	13	34
2002-03	Medicine Hat	WHL	70	23	52	75	104	11	3	6	9	8

MacDONALD, Jason (MAK-DAWN-uhld, JAY-suhn)

Right wing. Shoots right. 5'11", 205 lbs. Born, Charlottetown, P.E.I., April 1, 1974.
(Detroit's 5th choice, 142nd overall, in 1992 Entry Draft).

			Regular Season					Playoffs				
Season	Club	League	GP	G	A	TP	PIM	GP	G	A	TP	PIM
1989-90	Charlottetown	MJrHL	29	11	29	40	206	....	....	....	....	....
1990-91	North Bay	OHL	57	12	15	27	126	10	3	3	6	15
1991-92	North Bay	OHL	17	5	8	13	50	....	....	....	....	....
	Owen Sound	OHL	42	17	19	36	129	5	0	3	3	16
1992-93	Owen Sound	OHL	56	46	43	89	197	8	6	5	11	28
1993-94	Owen Sound	OHL	66	55	61	116	177	9	7	11	18	36
	Adirondack	AHL	....	....	....	....	....	1	0	0	0	0
1994-95	Adirondack	AHL	68	14	21	35	238	4	0	0	0	2
1995-96	Adirondack	AHL	43	9	13	22	99	....	....	....	....	....
	Toledo Storm	ECHL	9	5	5	10	26	9	3	1	4	39
1996-97	Adirondack	AHL	1	0	0	0	2	....	....	....	....	....
	Fredericton	AHL	63	22	25	47	189	....	....	....	....	....
1997-98	Team Canada	Nat-Tm	51	15	20	35	133	....	....	....	....	....
	Saint John Flames	AHL	6	2	0	2	27	11	1	3	4	17
1998-99	Manitoba Moose	IHL	82	25	27	52	283	5	2	2	4	13
99-2000	Manitoba Moose	IHL	30	5	10	15	77	....	....	....	....	....
	Orlando	IHL	29	7	7	14	113	4	0	0	0	19
2000-01	Wilkes-Barre	AHL	74	17	16	33	290	17	1	3	4	*66
2001-02	Wilkes-Barre	AHL	57	8	13	21	330	....	....	....	....	....
2002-03	Wilkes-Barre	AHL	56	4	7	11	137	1	0	0	0	0

OHL Second All-Star Team (1994)

Traded to **Montreal** by **Detroit** for cash, November 8, 1996. Signed as a free agent by **Pittsburgh**, July 18, 2001.

MACHO, Michal (MA-khoh, MEE-khuhl) S.J.

Center. Shoots right. 6'1", 170 lbs. Born, Martin, Czech., January 17, 1982.
(San Jose's 5th choice, 183rd overall, in 2000 Entry Draft).

			Regular Season					Playoffs				
Season	Club	League	GP	G	A	TP	PIM	GP	G	A	TP	PIM
1997-98	MHC Martin Jr.	Slovak-Jr.	55	44	58	102	....	....	....	....	....	....
1998-99	King's Edge Hill	Hi-School	50	45	55	100	....	....	....	....	....	....
99-2000	MHC Martin Jr.	Slovak-Jr.	30	38	44	82	....	....	....	....	....	....
	MHC Martin	Slovak-2	8	1	5	6	4	....	....	....	....	....
2000-01	MHC Martin	Slovakia	37	5	10	15	12	3	1	1	2	2
2001-02	MHC Martin	Slovakia	40	12	8	20	20	....	....	....	....	....
2002-03	Slov. Bratislava	Slovakia	51	5	4	9	26	12	1	0	1	0

MacLEAN, Cail (mihk-LAYN, KAYL) NYI

Right wing. Shoots right. 6', 205 lbs. Born, Middleton, N.S., September 30, 1976.

			Regular Season					Playoffs				
Season	Club	League	GP	G	A	TP	PIM	GP	G	A	TP	PIM
1993-94	Kingston	OHL	53	7	7	14	15	1	0	0	0	0
1994-95	Kingston	OHL	65	11	17	28	17	6	0	0	0	0
1995-96	Kingston	OHL	66	15	37	52	53	6	2	2	4	2
1996-97	Kingston	OHL	60	34	42	76	47	5	1	1	2	2
1997-98	Jacksonville	ECHL	66	30	35	65	44	....	....	....	....	....
	Cleveland	IHL	1	0	0	0	0	....	....	....	....	....
	Cincinnati	AHL	7	0	1	1	4	....	....	....	....	....
1998-99	Jacksonville	ECHL	40	29	28	57	14	....	....	....	....	....
	Indianapolis Ice	IHL	35	13	7	20	20	7	2	2	4	0
99-2000	Trenton Titans	ECHL	50	34	25	59	24	14	10	5	15	6
	Michigan K-Wings	IHL	14	0	3	3	6	....	....	....	....	....
	Lowell	AHL	5	0	1	1	0	....	....	....	....	....
	Philadelphia	AHL	3	0	0	0	0	....	....	....	....	....
2000-01	Trenton Titans	ECHL	49	28	17	45	26	19	13	4	17	10
	Grand Rapids	IHL	16	2	0	2	0	....	....	....	....	....
	Philadelphia	AHL	9	0	1	1	4	....	....	....	....	....
2001-02	Providence Bruins	AHL	9	1	0	1	0	....	....	....	....	....
	Hartford Wolf Pack	AHL	1	0	0	0	0	....	....	....	....	....
	Trenton Titans	ECHL	41	17	17	34	18	....	....	....	....	....
	Lowell	AHL	3	0	1	1	0	....	....	....	....	....
	Hershey Bears	AHL	21	4	6	10	4	6	0	0	0	0
2002-03	Hershey Bears	AHL	74	16	13	29	14	5	0	0	0	0

Signed as a free agent by **NY Islanders**, July 22, 2003.

MacMILLAN, Jeff (muhk-MIHL-uhn, JEHF) DAL.

Defense. Shoots left. 6'3", 206 lbs. Born, Durham, Ont., March 30, 1979.
(Dallas' 8th choice, 215th overall, in 1999 Entry Draft).

			Regular Season					Playoffs				
Season	Club	League	GP	G	A	TP	PIM	GP	G	A	TP	PIM
1995-96	Hanover Barons	OJHL-C	29	7	13	20	26	....	....	....	....	....
1996-97	Oshawa Generals	OHL	39	0	4	4	15	15	0	0	0	4
1997-98	Oshawa Generals	OHL	64	3	12	15	72	7	0	3	3	11
1998-99	Oshawa Generals	OHL	65	3	18	21	109	15	3	6	9	28
99-2000	Michigan K-Wings	IHL	53	0	3	3	54	....	....	....	....	....
	Fort Wayne	UHL	7	1	1	2	25	9	0	2	2	10
2000-01	Utah Grizzlies	IHL	81	5	15	20	105	....	....	....	....	....
2001-02	Utah Grizzlies	AHL	77	6	9	15	146	5	1	0	1	17
2002-03	Utah Grizzlies	AHL	78	8	7	15	132	2	0	0	0	6

MacMURCHY, Ryan (mak-MUHR-chee, RIGH-uhn) ST.L.

Right wing. Shoots right. 5'11", 190 lbs. Born, Regina, Sask., April 27, 1983.
(St. Louis' 9th choice, 284th overall, in 2002 Entry Draft).

			Regular Season					Playoffs				
Season	Club	League	GP	G	A	TP	PIM	GP	G	A	TP	PIM
99-2000	Regina Capitals	SMHL	38	23	44	67	....	....	....	....	....	....
2000-01	Vernon Vipers	BCHL	30	4	6	10	....	....	....	....	....	....
2001-02	Notre Dame	AJHL	61	32	52	84	63	11	2	5	7	13
2002-03	U. of Wisconsin	WCHA	39	10	14	24	69	....	....	....	....	....

MAGLIONE, Matt (US, MAT) WSH.

Defense. Shoots left. 6'1", 185 lbs. Born, Syracuse, NY, April 20, 1982.
(Washington's 7th choice, 249th overall, in 2001 Entry Draft).

			Regular Season					Playoffs				
Season	Club	League	GP	G	A	TP	PIM	GP	G	A	TP	PIM
1996-97	Syracuse	MTJHL	40	0	4	4	20	....	....	....	....	....
1997-98	Syracuse	MTJHL	40	3	13	16	86	....	....	....	....	....
1998-99	Auburn Jr. Crunch	OPJHL	44	12	24	36	44	....	....	....	....	....
99-2000	U.S. National U-18	USDP	48	4	6	10	23	....	....	....	....	....
2000-01	Princeton	ECAC	30	4	5	9	12	....	....	....	....	....
2001-02	Princeton	ECAC	27	2	6	8	12	....	....	....	....	....
2002-03	Princeton	ECAC	29	5	9	14	22	....	....	....	....	....

MAGOWAN, Ken (muh-GOW-uhn, KEHN) N.J.

Left wing. Shoots left. 6'2", 207 lbs. Born, Kelowna, B.C., July 22, 1981.
(New Jersey's 11th choice, 198th overall, in 2000 Entry Draft).

			Regular Season					Playoffs				
Season	Club	League	GP	G	A	TP	PIM	GP	G	A	TP	PIM
1996-97	Kelowna Rockets	BCAHA	57	68	66	134	78	....	....	....	....	....
1997-98	Kelowna Vikings	BCAHA	47	45	45	90	80	....	....	....	....	....
1998-99	Vernon Vipers	BCHL	60	15	25	40	40	....	....	....	....	....
99-2000	Vernon Vipers	BCHL	58	31	36	68	....	....	....	....	....	....
2000-01	Boston University	H-East	34	5	1	6	22	....	....	....	....	....
2001-02	Boston University	H-East	37	6	15	21	28	....	....	....	....	....
2002-03	Boston University	H-East	38	11	13	24	20	....	....	....	....	....

BCHL Interior First All-Star Team (1999)

MAISER, Justin (MAY-zuhr, JUHS-tihn) ST.L.

Center. Shoots left. 6'1", 191 lbs. Born, Milwaukee, WI, June 29, 1983.
(St. Louis' 5th choice, 165th overall, in 2002 Entry Draft).

			Regular Season					Playoffs				
Season	Club	League	GP	G	A	TP	PIM	GP	G	A	TP	PIM
99-2000	U.S. National U-17	USDP	48	11	20	31	114	....	....	....	....	....
2000-01	U.S. National U-18	USDP	58	20	18	38	127	....	....	....	....	....
2001-02	Boston University	H-East	36	8	14	22	65	....	....	....	....	....
2002-03	Boston University	H-East	40	12	11	23	66	....	....	....	....	....

MAKELA, Tuukka (MA-kuh-luh TUH-kuh) BOS.

Defense. Shoots left. 6'3", 202 lbs. Born, Helsinki, Finland, May 24, 1982.
(Boston's 5th choice, 66th overall, in 2000 Entry Draft).

			Regular Season					Playoffs				
Season	Club	League	GP	G	A	TP	PIM	GP	G	A	TP	PIM
1997-98	HIFK Helsinki Jr.	Finn-Jr.	5	0	0	0	4	....	....	....	....	....
1998-99	HIFK Helsinki Jr.	Finn-Jr.	32	1	1	2	20	3	0	1	1	0
99-2000	HIFK Helsinki Jr.	Finn-Jr.	36	2	5	7	22	2	0	0	0	0
2000-01	Montreal Rocket	QMJHL	9	2	1	3	14	....	....	....	....	....
2001-02	HPK-Jr.	Finn-Jr.	12	3	0	3	26	7	2	2	4	18
	HPK Hameenlinna	Finland	49	2	3	5	44	8	0	0	0	10
2002-03	HPK Hameenlinna	Finland	52	1	5	6	86	13	0	0	0	14

• Missed majority of 2000-01 season recovering from head injury suffered in game vs. Rouyn-Noranda (QMJHL), September 20, 2000.

MAKI, Tomi (MA-kee, TAW-mee) CGY.

Right wing. Shoots left. 5'11", 172 lbs. Born, Helsinki, Finland, August 19, 1983.
(Calgary's 4th choice, 108th overall, in 2001 Entry Draft).

			Regular Season					Playoffs				
Season	Club	League	GP	G	A	TP	PIM	GP	G	A	TP	PIM
1997-98	Jokerit Helsinki-C	Finn-Jr.	4	0	1	1	0	2	0	0	0	0
1998-99	Jokerit Helsinki-C	Finn-Jr.	32	20	22	42	40	....	....	....	....	....
99-2000	Jokerit Helsinki Jr.	Finn-Jr.	33	6	1	7	12	3	0	0	0	0
2000-01	Jokerit Helsinki-B	Finn-Jr.	10	4	9	13	4	6	4	3	7	0
	Jokerit Helsinki Jr.	Finn-Jr.	39	7	8	15	10	2	0	0	0	2
2001-02	Jokerit Helsinki Jr.	Finn-Jr.	29	12	13	25	12	1	0	0	0	2
	Kiekko Vantaa	Finland-2	5	0	0	0	0	....	....	....	....	....
	Jokerit Helsinki	Finland	8	0	1	1	2	....	....	....	....	....
2002-03	Jokerit Helsinki	Finland	18	2	2	4	4	1	0	0	0	0
	Kiekko-Vantaa	Finland-2	5	0	0	0	0	....	....	....	....	....
	Jokerit Helsinki Jr.	Finn-Jr.	14	4	4	8	12	11	3	3	6	4

MALENKYKH, Vladimir (MAH-lihn-keh, vla-DIH-meer) PIT.

Defense. Shoots left. 6'1", 187 lbs. Born, Togliatti, USSR, October 1, 1980.
(Pittsburgh's 7th choice, 157th overall, in 1999 Entry Draft).

			Regular Season					Playoffs				
Season	Club	League	GP	G	A	TP	PIM	GP	G	A	TP	PIM
1997-98	Lada Togliatti 2	Russia-3	39	6	4	10	112	....	....	....	....	....
1998-99	Lada Togliatti 2	Russia-4	38	6	3	9	68	....	....	....	....	....
	Lada Togliatti	Russia	9	0	0	0	2	....	....	....	....	....
99-2000	Lada Togliatti 2	Russia-3	34	7	9	16	98	....	....	....	....	....
	CSK VVS Samara	Russia	7	0	1	1	14	....	....	....	....	....
	Lada Togliatti	Russia	1	0	0	0	0	....	....	....	....	....
	CSK VVS Samara 2	Russia-3	1	0	1	1	2	....	....	....	....	....
2000-01	Lada Togliatti	Russia	25	1	1	2	14	5	0	0	0	26
2001-02	Lada Togliatti	Russia	47	5	4	9	88	4	0	0	0	2
2002-03	Lada Togliatti	Russia	30	3	1	4	36	10	0	0	0	6

MALMIVAARA, Olli (mal-MIH-vah-ruh, OH-lee) CHI.

Defense. Shoots left. 6'7", 220 lbs. Born, Kajaani, Finland, March 13, 1982.
(Chicago's 6th choice, 117th overall, in 2000 Entry Draft).

			Regular Season					Playoffs				
Season	Club	League	GP	G	A	TP	PIM	GP	G	A	TP	PIM
1998-99	Jokerit Helsinki-B	Finn-Jr.	35	1	8	9	10	7	0	0	0	2
99-2000	Jokerit Helsinki-B	Finn-Jr.	8	3	4	7	8	1	0	0	0	2
	Jokerit Helsinki Jr.	Finn-Jr.	27	3	3	6	12	12	0	2	2	2
2000-01	Jokerit Helsinki Jr.	Finn-Jr.	33	10	13	23	24	2	0	0	0	0
	Kiekko Vantaa	Finland-2	4	1	0	1	2	....	....	....	....	....
	Jokerit Helsinki	Finland	5	0	0	0	2	....	....	....	....	....
2001-02	Jokerit Helsinki Jr.	Finn-Jr.	2	0	1	1	0	....	....	....	....	....
	Jokerit Helsinki	Finland	53	0	6	6	16	11	0	0	0	2
2002-03	Jokerit Helsinki	Finland	42	1	0	1	22	5	0	0	0	0
	Kiekko Vantaa	Finland-2	2	1	1	2	2	....	....	....	....	....

MALONE, Ryan (MA-lohn, RIGH-yan) **PIT.**

Left wing. Shoots left. 6'4", 215 lbs. Born, Pittsburgh, PA, December 1, 1979.
(Pittsburgh's 5th choice, 115th overall, in 1999 Entry Draft).

			Regular Season					Playoffs				
Season	Club	League	GP	G	A	TP	PIM	GP	G	A	TP	PIM
1997-98	Shat.-St. Mary's	Hi-School	50	41	44	85	69	....	....	....	....	....
1998-99	Omaha Lancers	USHL	51	14	22	36	81	12	2	4	6	23
99-2000	St. Cloud State	WCHA	38	9	21	30	68	....	....	....	....	....
2000-01	St. Cloud State	WCHA	36	7	18	25	52	....	....	....	....	....
2001-02	St. Cloud State	WCHA	41	24	25	49	76	....	....	....	....	....
2002-03	St. Cloud State	WCHA	27	16	20	36	85	....	....	....	....	....
	Wilkes-Barre	AHL	3	0	1	1	2	....	....	....	....	....

MALONEY, Brian (muh-LOH-nee, BRIGH-uhn) **ATL.**

Left wing. Shoots left. 6'1", 205 lbs. Born, Bassano, Alta., September 27, 1978.

			Regular Season					Playoffs				
Season	Club	League	GP	G	A	TP	PIM	GP	G	A	TP	PIM
99-2000	Michigan State	CCHA	42	12	19	31	87	....	....	....	....	....
2000-01	Michigan State	CCHA	41	15	22	37	86	....	....	....	....	....
2001-02	Michigan State	CCHA	37	17	16	33	71	....	....	....	....	....
2002-03	Chicago Wolves	AHL	4	0	1	1	11	....	....	....	....	....
	Michigan State	CCHA	39	19	16	35	48	....	....	....	....	....

Signed as a free agent by **Atlanta**, April 2, 2003.

MANSON, Lane (MAN-suhn, LAYN) **ATL.**

Defense. Shoots left. 6'8", 245 lbs. Born, Watrous, Sask., February 14, 1984.
(Atlanta's 4th choice, 124th overall, in 2002 Entry Draft).

			Regular Season					Playoffs				
Season	Club	League	GP	G	A	TP	PIM	GP	G	A	TP	PIM
99-2000	North Battleford	SMBHL	41	7	12	19	110	....	....	....	....	....
2000-01	North Battleford	MMHL	40	14	12	26	180	....	....	....	....	....
2001-02	Moose Jaw	WHL	67	4	3	7	88	12	0	1	1	6
2002-03	Moose Jaw	WHL	66	0	5	5	192	13	0	0	0	12

MANTYLA, Tuukka (man-TYEW-la, TOO-OO-kuh) **L.A.**

Defense. Shoots left. 5'9", 172 lbs. Born, Tampere, Finland, May 25, 1981.
(Los Angeles' 8th choice, 153rd overall, in 2001 Entry Draft).

			Regular Season					Playoffs				
Season	Club	League	GP	G	A	TP	PIM	GP	G	A	TP	PIM
1995-96	Tappara-C	Finn-Jr.	32	2	2	4	28	....	....	....	....	....
1996-97	Tappara-C	Finn-Jr.	32	12	25	37	52	4	1	2	3	4
	Tappara-B	Finn-Jr.	2	0	0	0	2	....	....	....	....	....
1997-98	Tappara-B	Finn-Jr.	31	2	23	25	49	....	....	....	....	....
	Tappara Jr.	Finn-Jr.	2	0	0	0	0	6	0	0	0	4
1998-99	Tappara-B	Finn-Jr.	10	4	4	8	42	....	....	....	....	....
	Tappara Jr.	Finn-Jr.	34	5	13	18	42	....	....	....	....	....
99-2000	Tappara Jr.	Finn-Jr.	7	2	5	7	22	5	2	5	7	4
	Tappara Tampere	Finland	43	2	8	10	16	4	0	0	0	0
2000-01	Tappara Tampere	Finland	53	6	14	20	32	10	2	2	4	10
2001-02	Tappara Tampere	Finland	56	5	10	15	70	10	2	4	6	8
2002-03	Tappara Tampere	Finland	54	3	19	22	58	15	0	2	2	6

MARJAMAKI, Masi (mahr-juh-MA-kee, MAH-see) **BOS.**

Left wing. Shoots left. 6'2", 184 lbs. Born, Pori, Finland, January 16, 1985.
(Boston's 3rd choice, 66th overall, in 2003 Entry Draft).

			Regular Season					Playoffs				
Season	Club	League	GP	G	A	TP	PIM	GP	G	A	TP	PIM
2001-02	Assat Pori Jr.	Finn-Jr.	25	6	16	22	93	6	3	3	6	4
2002-03	Red Deer Rebels	WHL	65	15	20	35	56	23	1	2	3	20

MAROIS, Jerome (MAIR-wuh, jair-OHM) **MTL.**

Left wing. Shoots left. 6'1", 199 lbs. Born, Quebec City, Que., January 27, 1981.
(Montreal's 11th choice, 253rd overall, in 1999 Entry Draft).

			Regular Season					Playoffs				
Season	Club	League	GP	G	A	TP	PIM	GP	G	A	TP	PIM
1996-97	Ste-Foy	QAAA	44	29	24	53	....	10	8	8	16	....
1997-98	Quebec Remparts	QMJHL	55	5	12	17	12	12	2	0	2	2
1998-99	Quebec Remparts	QMJHL	52	8	15	23	48	12	0	4	4	13
99-2000	Cape Breton	QMJHL	66	28	34	62	95	4	2	1	3	14
2000-01	Rouyn-Noranda	QMJHL	68	36	47	83	119	6	1	0	1	17
2001-02	Quebec Citadelles	AHL	10	0	0	0	2	....	....	....	....	....
	Mississippi	ECHL	44	12	10	22	47	10	5	2	7	4
2002-03	Columbus	ECHL	20	0	6	6	6	....	....	....	....	....
	Odessa	CHL	29	3	5	8	11	....	....	....	....	....

MARS, Per (MAHRZ, PAIR) **CBJ**

Center. Shoots left. 6'3", 210 lbs. Born, Ostersund, Sweden, October 23, 1982.
(Columbus' 5th choice, 87th overall, in 2001 Entry Draft).

			Regular Season					Playoffs				
Season	Club	League	GP	G	A	TP	PIM	GP	G	A	TP	PIM
2000-01	Brynas IF Gavle jr.	Swede-Jr.	23	7	7	14	62	....	....	....	....	....
	Brynas IF Gavle	Sweden	6	0	0	0	0	2	0	0	0	0
2001-02	Brynas IF Gavle	Sweden	12	0	0	0	14	....	....	....	....	....
	Tierp HK	Swede-2	29	1	4	5	22	11	1	0	1	35
2002-03	Brynas IF Gavle	Sweden	7	0	0	0	2	....	....	....	....	....
	Lincoln Stars	USHL	42	9	9	18	60	9	1	2	3	14

MARSH, Tyson (MAHRSH, TIGH-suhn) **TOR.**

Defense. Shoots left. 6'1", 190 lbs. Born, Quesnel, B.C, June 20, 1984.

			Regular Season					Playoffs				
Season	Club	League	GP	G	A	TP	PIM	GP	G	A	TP	PIM
2000-01	Quesnel	BCHL	52	4	2	6	25	....	....	....	....	....
2001-02	Vancouver Giants	WHL	69	2	14	16	85	....	....	....	....	....
2002-03	Vancouver Giants	WHL	68	3	15	18	143	3	0	1	1	4

Signed as a free agent by **Toronto**, September 18, 2002.

MARTENSSON, Tony (MOHR-tehn-suhn, TOH-nee) **ANA.**

Center. Shoots left. 6', 189 lbs. Born, Upplands Vasby, Sweden, June 23, 1980.
(Anaheim's 9th choice, 224th overall, in 2001 Entry Draft).

			Regular Season					Playoffs				
Season	Club	League	GP	G	A	TP	PIM	GP	G	A	TP	PIM
1997-98	Arlanda Mastra	Swede-2	12	2	4	6	0	2	0	0	0	0
1998-99	Arlanda Mastra	Swede-2	37	8	22	30	8	2	0	0	0	0
99-2000	Arlanda Mastra	Swede-2	44	21	28	49	14	....	....	....	....	....
2000-01	Brynas IF Gavle	Sweden	50	15	11	26	20	4	0	1	1	2
	Brynas IF Gavle Jr.	Swede-Jr.	1	1	0	1	0	....	....	....	....	....
2001-02	Brynas IF Gavle	Sweden	50	9	17	26	14	4	1	3	4	0
2002-03	Cincinnati	AHL	79	17	36	53	20	....	....	....	....	....

MARTIN, Joey (MAHR-tihn, JOH-ee) **CHI.**

Defense. Shoots left. 6'4", 212 lbs. Born, Fridley, MN, July 17, 1981.
(Chicago's 9th choice, 193rd overall, in 2000 Entry Draft).

			Regular Season					Playoffs				
Season	Club	League	GP	G	A	TP	PIM	GP	G	A	TP	PIM
1998-99	Buffalo MN High	Hi-School	23	10	9	19	19	....	....	....	....	....
99-2000	Omaha Lancers	USHL	56	1	4	5	41	4	0	0	0	0
2000-01	U. of Minnesota	WCHA	18	0	2	2	2	....	....	....	....	....
2001-02	U. of Minnesota	WCHA	11	0	4	4	14	....	....	....	....	....
2002-03	U. of Minnesota	WCHA	24	3	4	7	16	....	....	....	....	....

MARTIN, Mike (MAHR-tihn, MIGHK)

Defense. Shoots right. 6'2", 205 lbs. Born, Stratford, Ont., October 27, 1976.
(NY Rangers' 2nd choice, 65th overall, in 1995 Entry Draft).

			Regular Season					Playoffs				
Season	Club	League	GP	G	A	TP	PIM	GP	G	A	TP	PIM
1991-92	Stratford Cullitons	OJHL-B	16	2	3	5	14	....	....	....	....	....
1992-93	Windsor Spitfires	OHL	61	2	7	9	80	....	....	....	....	....
1993-94	Windsor Spitfires	OHL	64	2	29	31	94	4	1	2	3	4
1994-95	Windsor Spitfires	OHL	53	9	28	37	79	10	1	3	4	21
1995-96	Windsor Spitfires	OHL	65	19	48	67	128	7	0	6	6	14
1996-97	Binghamton	AHL	62	2	7	9	45	3	0	1	1	2
1997-98	Hartford Wolf Pack	AHL	60	4	11	15	70	4	0	0	0	2
1998-99	Fort Wayne	IHL	75	6	20	26	89	2	0	0	0	4
99-2000	Michigan K-Wings	IHL	74	8	15	23	99	....	....	....	....	....
2000-01	Saint John Flames	AHL	60	7	16	23	69	16	1	2	3	14
2001-02	Saint John Flames	AHL	13	1	8	9	14	....	....	....	....	....
2002-03	Saint John Flames	AHL	71	2	18	20	73	....	....	....	....	....

US Airways/PHPA Man of the Year Award (2002)

Signed as a free agent by **Calgary**, August 18, 2000. • Missed majority of 2001-02 season recovering from knee injury suffered on November 9, 2001.

MARTIN, Paul (MAHR-tihn, PAWL) **N.J.**

Defense. Shoots left. 6'2", 195 lbs. Born, Minneapolis, MN, March 5, 1981.
(New Jersey's 5th choice, 62nd overall, in 2000 Entry Draft).

			Regular Season					Playoffs				
Season	Club	League	GP	G	A	TP	PIM	GP	G	A	TP	PIM
1998-99	Elk River Elks	Hi-School	24	9	11	20	....	....	....	....	....	....
99-2000	Elk River Elks	Hi-School	24	15	35	50	26	....	....	....	....	....
2000-01	U. of Minnesota	WCHA	38	3	17	20	8	....	....	....	....	....
2001-02	U. of Minnesota	WCHA	44	8	30	38	22	....	....	....	....	....
2002-03	U. of Minnesota	WCHA	45	9	30	39	32	....	....	....	....	....

Minnesota High School Player of the Year (1999) • WCHA All-Rookie Team (2001) • WCHA Second All-Star Team (2002, 2003) • NCAA West Second All-American Team (2003) • NCAA Championship All-Tournament Team (2003)

MARTTINEN, Jyri (MAHR-tih-nehn, YUHR-ee) **CGY.**

Defense. Shoots left. 5'11", 190 lbs. Born, Tikkakoski, Finland, September 1, 1982.
(Calgary's 12th choice, 238th overall, in 2002 Entry Draft).

			Regular Season					Playoffs				
Season	Club	League	GP	G	A	TP	PIM	GP	G	A	TP	PIM
2000-01	JYP Jyvaskyla Jr.	Finn-Jr.	40	2	8	10	73	6	1	1	2	6
	JYP Jyvaskyla	Finland	8	1	0	1	6	....	....	....	....	....
2001-02	JYP Jyvaskyla	Finland	50	1	4	5	67	....	....	....	....	....
	JYP Jyvaskyla Jr.	Finn-Jr.	5	0	2	2	2	1	0	0	0	0
2002-03	JYP Jyvaskyla	Finland	29	3	2	5	32	....	....	....	....	....

MARTYNYUK, Denis (mahr-tih-nyook, DEH-nihs) **VAN.**

Left wing. Shoots left. 6'3", 190 lbs. Born, Kapfenberg, Austria, July 26, 1979.
(Vancouver's 11th choice, 201st overall, in 1997 Entry Draft).

			Regular Season					Playoffs				
Season	Club	League	GP	G	A	TP	PIM	GP	G	A	TP	PIM
1994-95	CSKA Moscow Jr.	CIS-Jr.	34	25	25	50	20	....	....	....	....	....
1995-96	CSKA Moscow Jr.	CIS-Jr.	36	10	15	25	20	....	....	....	....	....
	HC CSKA	Russia-2	25	2	5	7	20	....	....	....	....	....
1996-97	CSKA Moscow 2	Russia-3	41	7	4	11	12	....	....	....	....	....
	HC CSKA	Russia	3	1	0	1	0	....	....	....	....	....
1997-98	Spartak Moscow 2	Russia-3	45	9	5	14	34	....	....	....	....	....
1998-99	Spartak Moscow	Russia	17	0	0	0	8	....	....	....	....	....
99-2000	Spartak Moscow	Russia-2	STATISTICS NOT AVAILABLE									
2000-01	Spartak Moscow 2	Russia-3	6	1	3	4	0	....	....	....	....	....
	Amur Khabarovsk	Russia	1	0	0	0	0	....	....	....	....	....
2001-02	Columbia Inferno	ECHL	52	14	8	22	42	....	....	....	....	....
	Manitoba Moose	AHL	15	1	2	3	0	5	0	0	0	0
2002-03	Columbia Inferno	ECHL	56	10	10	20	84	12	2	0	2	8
	Manitoba Moose	AHL	8	0	0	0	4	....	....	....	....	....

MARTZ, Nathan (MAHRTZ, NAY-thun) **NYR**

Center. Shoots left. 6'3", 169 lbs. Born, Chilliwack, B.C., March 4, 1981.
(NY Rangers' 4th choice, 140th overall, in 2000 Entry Draft).

			Regular Season					Playoffs				
Season	Club	League	GP	G	A	TP	PIM	GP	G	A	TP	PIM
1997-98	Chilliwack Chiefs	BCHL	59	8	13	21	86	....	....	....	....	....
1998-99	Chilliwack Chiefs	BCHL	59	20	38	58	....	....	....	....	....	....
99-2000	Chilliwack Chiefs	BCHL	59	35	75	110	97	....	....	....	....	....
2000-01	New Hampshire	H-East	37	5	14	19	20	....	....	....	....	....
2001-02	New Hampshire	H-East	28	3	7	10	12	....	....	....	....	....
2002-03	New Hampshire	H-East	42	12	15	27	20	....	....	....	....	....

NCAA Championship All-Tournament Team (2003)

MASSEN, James (MA-suhn, JAYMS) **N.J.**

Right wing. Shoots right. 6'1", 228 lbs. Born, Bismarck, ND, January 13, 1982.
(New Jersey's 9th choice, 194th overall, in 2001 Entry Draft).

			Regular Season					Playoffs				
Season	Club	League	GP	G	A	TP	PIM	GP	G	A	TP	PIM
99-2000	Sioux Falls	USHL	53	16	17	33	25	3	0	0	0	2
2000-01	Sioux Falls	USHL	56	37	38	75	56	8	6	2	8	4
2001-02	North Dakota	WCHA	34	5	8	13	18	....	....	....	....	....
2002-03	North Dakota	WCHA	42	15	20	35	12	....	....	....	....	....

USHL First All-Star Team (2001)

MATEJOVSKY, Radek (ma-teh-YAHV-skee, ra-DEHK) NYI

Right wing. Shoots right. 6'1", 187 lbs. Born, Praha, Czech., November 17, 1977.
(NY Islanders' 9th choice, 250th overall, in 1998 Entry Draft).

			Regular Season					Playoffs				
Season	Club	League	GP	G	A	TP	PIM	GP	G	A	TP	PIM
1992-93	C. Budejovice Jr.	Czech-Jr.	25	38	24	62	....	....	....	....	....	....
1993-94	Slavia IPS Praha Jr.	Czech-Jr.	45	30	26	56	....	....	....	....	....	....
1994-95	HC Slavia Praha Jr.	Czech-Jr.	28	7	8	15	12	....	....	....	....	....
1995-96	HC Slavia Praha Jr.	Czech-Jr.	47	37	21	58	24	....	....	....	....	....
1996-97	HC Slavia Praha Jr.	Czech-Jr.	4	1	1	2	....	....	....	....	....	....
	H+S Beroun	Czech-2	12	3	1	4	18	....	....	....	....	....
	HC Slavia Praha	Czech	41	3	4	7	10	3	0	0	0	0
1997-98	HC Slavia Praha	Czech	52	9	4	13	24	3	0	0	0	0
1998-99	HC Dukla Jihlava	Czech	52	12	10	22	57	....	....	....	....	....
99-2000	HC Slavia Praha	Czech	25	4	3	7	22	....	....	....	....	....
	Pardubice	Czech	25	2	4	6	18	3	0	0	0	0
2000-01	HC Slavia Praha	Czech	39	6	8	14	63	11	1	2	3	18
2001-02	HC Slavia Praha	Czech	35	3	1	4	42	9	0	0	0	6
2002-03	HC Keramika Plzen	Czech	42	7	11	18	126	....	....	....	....	....

MAULDIN, Greg (MAWL-dihn, GREHG) CBJ

Center. Shoots right. 5'11", 180 lbs. Born, Boston, MA, June 10, 1982.
(Columbus' 10th choice, 199th overall, in 2002 Entry Draft).

			Regular Season					Playoffs				
Season	Club	League	GP	G	A	TP	PIM	GP	G	A	TP	PIM
99-2000	Boston Jr. Bruins	EJHL	58	45	42	87	14	....	....	....	....	....
2000-01	Boston Jr. Bruins	EJHL	53	48	58	106	73	....	....	....	....	....
2001-02	Massachusetts	H-East	33	12	12	24	10	....	....	....	....	....
2002-03	Massachusetts	H-East	36	21	20	41	26	....	....	....	....	....

EJHL First All-Star Team (2000, 2001) • EJHL MVP (2000)

MAXIMENKO, Andrei (max-EE-mehn-koh, AWN-dray) DET.

Left wing. Shoots right. 5'11", 172 lbs. Born, Moscow, USSR, January 10, 1981.
(Detroit's 2nd choice, 149th overall, in 1999 Entry Draft).

			Regular Season					Playoffs				
Season	Club	League	GP	G	A	TP	PIM	GP	G	A	TP	PIM
1997-98	Krylja Sovetov 2	Russia-3	42	2	4	6	12	....	....	....	....	....
1998-99	Krylja Sovetov	Russia	28	1	2	3	24	....	....	....	....	....
99-2000	Krylja Sovetov 2	Russia-3	6	4	2	6	26	....	....	....	....	....
	Krylja Sovetov	Russia-2	39	6	7	13	41	....	....	....	....	....
2000-01	Krylja Sovetov	Russia-2	28	2	5	7	8	....	....	....	....	....
2001-02	THC Tver	Russia-2	20	3	7	10	6	....	....	....	....	....
	Krylja Sovetov 2	Russia-3	7	3	5	8	2	....	....	....	....	....
	Perm	Russia	9	0	1	1	2	....	....	....	....	....
2002-03	Kristall Saratov	Russia-2	47	12	12	24	36	....	....	....	....	....

MAY, Scott (MAY, SKAWT) TOR.

Right wing. Shoots right. 5'9", 185 lbs. Born, Calgary, Alta., January 8, 1982.
(Toronto's 7th choice, 222nd overall, in 2002 Entry Draft).

			Regular Season					Playoffs				
Season	Club	League	GP	G	A	TP	PIM	GP	G	A	TP	PIM
99-2000	South Surrey	BCHL	54	42	42	84	....	....	....	....	....	....
2000-01	Ohio State	CCHA	37	9	9	18	26	....	....	....	....	....
2001-02	Ohio State	CCHA	40	12	18	30	42	*....	....	....	....	....
2002-03	Ohio State	CCHA	43	10	25	35	56	....	....	....	....	....

McASLAN, Sean (mihk-AZ-luhn, SHAWN) EDM.

Left wing. Shoots right. 6'1", 190 lbs. Born, Okotoks, Alta., January 12, 1980.

			Regular Season					Playoffs				
Season	Club	League	GP	G	A	TP	PIM	GP	G	A	TP	PIM
1996-97	Calgary Hitmen	WHL	26	2	3	5	22	....	....	....	....	....
1997-98	Calgary Hitmen	WHL	69	8	16	24	83	....	....	....	....	....
1998-99	Calgary Hitmen	WHL	71	7	16	23	110	21	2	1	3	18
99-2000	Calgary Hitmen	WHL	72	18	16	34	117	13	4	2	6	49
2000-01	Calgary Hitmen	WHL	51	21	32	53	137	12	3	5	8	29
2001-02	Columbus	ECHL	72	16	21	37	139	....	....	....	....	....
2002-03	Columbus	ECHL	53	15	17	32	132	....	....	....	....	....
	Hamilton Bulldogs	AHL	1	0	0	0	0	....	....	....	....	....

Signed as a free agent by **Edmonton**, March 14, 2001.

McCAMBRIDGE, Keith (muh-KAYM-brihdj, KEETH)

Defense. Shoots left. 6'2", 205 lbs. Born, Thompson, Man., February 1, 1974.
(Calgary's 10th choice, 201st overall, in 1994 Entry Draft).

			Regular Season					Playoffs				
Season	Club	League	GP	G	A	TP	PIM	GP	G	A	TP	PIM
1991-92	Swift Current	WHL	72	1	4	5	84	8	0	0	0	2
1992-93	Swift Current	WHL	70	0	6	6	87	17	0	1	1	27
1993-94	Swift Current	WHL	71	0	10	10	179	7	0	0	0	4
1994-95	Swift Current	WHL	48	5	7	12	120	....	....	....	....	....
	Kamloops Blazers	WHL	21	0	6	6	90	21	0	5	5	49
1995-96	Saint John Flames	AHL	48	1	3	4	89	16	0	0	0	6
1996-97	Saint John Flames	AHL	56	2	1	3	109	....	....	....	....	....
1997-98	Saint John Flames	AHL	56	4	4	8	118	....	....	....	....	....
	Las Vegas Thunder	IHL	10	0	1	1	16	4	0	0	0	9
1998-99	Las Vegas Thunder	IHL	18	1	2	3	56	....	....	....	....	....
	Long Beach	IHL	52	2	5	7	200	8	0	0	0	20
99-2000	Providence Bruins	AHL	47	0	2	2	135	....	....	....	....	....
	Manitoba Moose	IHL	3	0	1	1	4	....	....	....	....	....
2000-01	Providence Bruins	AHL	63	1	5	6	215	10	0	0	0	18
2001-02	Providence Bruins	AHL	59	1	3	4	263	2	0	0	0	5
2002-03	Houston Aeros	AHL	11	0	0	0	22	....	....	....	....	....
	Cleveland Barons	AHL	38	0	3	3	106	....	....	....	....	....

Signed as free agent by **Boston**, August 20, 1999.

McCARTHY, Jeremiah (mih-KAHR-thee, jeh-rih-MIGH-uh)

Defense. Shoots left. 6', 210 lbs. Born, Boston, MA, March 1, 1976.

			Regular Season					Playoffs				
Season	Club	League	GP	G	A	TP	PIM	GP	G	A	TP	PIM
1994-95	Harvard Crimson	ECAC	25	3	5	8	4	....	....	....	....	....
1995-96	Harvard Crimson	ECAC	32	4	12	16	20	....	....	....	....	....
1996-97	Harvard Crimson	ECAC	32	4	9	13	22	....	....	....	....	....
1997-98	Harvard Crimson	ECAC	28	11	10	21	38	....	....	....	....	....
1998-99	Peoria Rivermen	ECHL	6	1	2	3	6	....	....	....	....	....
	Worcester IceCats	AHL	59	5	10	15	37	4	0	2	2	0
99-2000	Missouri	UHL	33	10	25	35	45	....	....	....	....	....
	Springfield Falcons	AHL	43	5	9	14	16	5	1	1	2	0
2000-01	Cincinnati	IHL	69	6	12	18	34	3	0	0	0	0
2001-02	Lowell	AHL	74	7	28	35	43	5	0	2	2	0
2002-03	Amur Khabarovsk	Russia	4	0	0	0	2	....	....	....	....	....
	Lowell	AHL	44	1	16	17	44	....	....	....	....	....
	Grand Rapids	AHL	11	0	1	1	2	12	0	1	1	6

Signed as a free agent by **Carolina**, August 21, 2000. Signed as a free agent by **Amur** (Russia), July 19, 2002.

McCLEMENT, Jay (muh-KLEHM-ehnt, JAY) ST.L.

Center. Shoots left. 6'1", 193 lbs. Born, Kingston, Ont., March 2, 1983.
(St. Louis' 1st choice, 57th overall, in 2001 Entry Draft).

			Regular Season					Playoffs				
Season	Club	League	GP	G	A	TP	PIM	GP	G	A	TP	PIM
1997-98	Kingston	OPJHL	48	3	8	11	15	....	....	....	....	....
1998-99	Kingston	OPJHL	51	25	28	53	34	....	....	....	....	....
99-2000	Brampton	OHL	63	13	16	29	34	6	0	4	4	8
2000-01	Brampton	OHL	66	30	19	49	61	9	4	2	6	10
2001-02	Brampton	OHL	61	26	29	55	43	....	....	....	....	....
2002-03	Brampton	OHL	45	22	27	49	37	11	3	4	7	11
	Worcester IceCats	AHL	....	....	....	....	....	1	0	0	0	0

McCONNELL, Brian (mih-CAW-nuhl, BRIGH-uhn) CGY.

Center. Shoots left. 6'2", 190 lbs. Born, Boston, MA, February 1, 1983.
(Calgary's 2nd choice, 39th overall, in 2002 Entry Draft).

			Regular Season					Playoffs				
Season	Club	League	GP	G	A	TP	PIM	GP	G	A	TP	PIM
1998-99	Thayer Academy	Hi-School	23	12	27	39	....	....	....	....	....	....
99-2000	U.S. National U-17	USDP	48	8	11	19	76	....	....	....	....	....
2000-01	U.S. National U-18	USDP	62	19	25	44	143	....	....	....	....	....
2001-02	Boston University	H-East	38	11	15	26	68	....	....	....	....	....
2002-03	Boston University	H-East	34	11	14	25	70	....	....	....	....	....

McCORMICK, Cody (muh-KOHR-mihk, KOH-dee) COL.

Center/Right wing. Shoots right. 6'2", 200 lbs. Born, London, Ont., April 18, 1983.
(Colorado's 5th choice, 144th overall, in 2001 Entry Draft).

			Regular Season					Playoffs				
Season	Club	League	GP	G	A	TP	PIM	GP	G	A	TP	PIM
1998-99	Elgin-Middlesex	MHAO	58	22	40	62	81	....	....	....	....	....
99-2000	Belleville Bulls	OHL	45	3	4	7	42	9	1	0	1	10
2000-01	Belleville Bulls	OHL	66	7	16	23	135	10	1	1	2	23
2001-02	Belleville Bulls	OHL	63	10	17	27	118	11	2	4	6	24
2002-03	Belleville Bulls	OHL	61	36	33	69	166	7	4	7	11	11

OHL First All-Star Team (2003)

McCUTCHEON, Mark (mih-KUH-chuhn, MAHRK) COL.

Center. Shoots right. 6', 177 lbs. Born, Ithaca, NY, May 21, 1984.
(Colorado's 3rd choice, 146th overall, in 2003 Entry Draft).

			Regular Season					Playoffs				
Season	Club	League	GP	G	A	TP	PIM	GP	G	A	TP	PIM
2001-02	New England	EJHL	36	24	26	50	84	....	....	....	....	....
2002-03	New England	EJHL	35	27	22	49	76	10	8	5	13	24

• Signed Letter of Intent to attend **Cornell** (ECAC), July 15, 2002.

McDONALD, Brent (muhk-DAW-nuhld, BREHNT) CAR.

Center. Shoots right. 5'11", 180 lbs. Born, Olds, Alta., October 7, 1979.
(Carolina's 10th choice, 239th overall, in 1998 Entry Draft).

			Regular Season					Playoffs				
Season	Club	League	GP	G	A	TP	PIM	GP	G	A	TP	PIM
1994-95	Red Deer Vipers	AMHL	26	16	24	40	55	....	....	....	....	....
1995-96	Red Deer Rebels	WHL	68	1	7	8	55	6	0	1	1	2
1996-97	Red Deer Rebels	WHL	69	11	17	28	94	16	4	3	7	38
1997-98	Red Deer Rebels	WHL	69	18	27	45	93	5	0	2	2	4
1998-99	Red Deer Rebels	WHL	38	17	18	35	64	....	....	....	....	....
	Prince George	WHL	34	13	13	26	40	7	1	1	2	18
99-2000	Prince George	WHL	7	1	3	4	6	....	....	....	....	....
	Spokane Chiefs	WHL	61	28	30	58	77	15	5	8	13	42
2000-01	Florida Everblades	ECHL	67	11	11	22	55	5	1	0	1	4
2001-02	Florida Everblades	ECHL	69	12	20	32	92	6	2	2	4	4
	Lowell	AHL	2	0	0	0	0	2	0	0	0	0
2002-03	Lowell	AHL	52	7	8	15	29	....	....	....	....	....
	Florida Everblades	ECHL	18	10	4	14	14	1	1	0	1	2

McDONALD, Colin (mihk-DAW-nuhld, KAW-lihn) EDM.

Right wing. Shoots right. 6'2", 190 lbs. Born, New Haven, CT, September 30, 1984.
(Edmonton's 2nd choice, 51st overall, in 2003 Entry Draft).

			Regular Season					Playoffs				
Season	Club	League	GP	G	A	TP	PIM	GP	G	A	TP	PIM
2001-02	New England	EJHL	39	16	20	36	50	....	....	....	....	....
2002-03	New England	EJHL	44	28	40	*68	59	....	....	....	....	....

EJHL MVP (2003)

Signed Letter of Intent to attend **Providence College** (H-East), November 27, 2002.

McGRATTAN, Brian (muhk-GRA-tuhn, BRIGH-uhn) OTT.

Right wing. Shoots right. 6'5", 226 lbs. Born, Hamilton, Ont., September 2, 1981.
(Los Angeles' 5th choice, 104th overall, in 1999 Entry Draft).

			Regular Season					Playoffs				
Season	Club	League	GP	G	A	TP	PIM	GP	G	A	TP	PIM
1997-98	Guelph Royals	OJHL-B	15	4	3	7	94	....	....	....	....	....
	Guelph Storm	OHL	25	3	2	5	11	....	....	....	....	....
1998-99	Guelph Storm	OHL	6	1	3	4	15	....	....	....	....	....
	Sudbury Wolves	OHL	53	7	10	17	153	4	0	0	0	8
99-2000	Sudbury Wolves	OHL	25	2	8	10	79	....	....	....	....	....
	Mississauga	OHL	42	9	13	22	166	....	....	....	....	....
2000-01	Mississauga	OHL	31	20	9	29	83	....	....	....	....	....
2001-02	Mississauga	OHL	7	2	3	5	16	....	....	....	....	....
	Owen Sound	OHL	2	0	0	0	0	....	....	....	....	....
	Oshawa Generals	OHL	25	10	5	15	72	....	....	....	....	....
	Sault Ste. Marie	OHL	26	8	7	15	71	6	2	0	2	20
2002-03	Binghamton	AHL	59	9	10	19	173	1	0	0	0	0

Signed as a free agent by **Ottawa**, June 2, 2002.

McLACHLAN, Darren (muhk-LAWK-luhn, DAIR-rehn) PHX.

Left wing. Shoots left. 6'1", 230 lbs. Born, Penticton, B.C., February 16, 1983.
(Boston's 2nd choice, 77th overall, in 2001 Entry Draft).

			Regular Season					Playoffs				
Season	Club	League	GP	G	A	TP	PIM	GP	G	A	TP	PIM
1998-99	Campbell River	VIJHL	31	15	25	40	212	....	....	....	....	....
	Seattle	WHL	2	0	1	1	7	....	....	....	....	....
99-2000	Seattle	WHL	54	5	1	6	175	7	0	0	0	9
2000-01	Seattle	WHL	42	10	9	19	161	9	1	3	4	18
2001-02	Seattle	WHL	51	15	16	31	153	10	1	0	1	20
2002-03	Seattle	WHL	66	17	43	60	195	5	1	0	1	11

Traded to **Phoenix** by **Boston** for Phoenix's 5th round choice in 2004 Entry Draft, May 30, 2003.

McLAREN, Steve (muh-KLAIR-uhn, STEEV) ST.L.

Defense. Shoots left. 6', 210 lbs. Born, Owen Sound, Ont., February 3, 1975.
(Chicago's 3rd choice, 85th overall, in 1994 Entry Draft).

			Regular Season					Playoffs				
Season	Club	League	GP	G	A	TP	PIM	GP	G	A	TP	PIM
1992-93	N. Bay Trappers	NOJHA	30	15	18	33	110	....	....	....	....	....
1993-94	North Bay	OHL	55	2	15	17	130	18	0	3	3	50
1994-95	North Bay	OHL	27	3	10	13	119	6	2	1	3	23
1995-96	Indianapolis Ice	IHL	54	1	2	3	170	3	0	0	0	2
1996-97	Indianapolis Ice	IHL	63	2	5	7	309	4	0	0	0	10
1997-98	Indianapolis Ice	IHL	61	3	5	8	208	5	0	0	0	24
1998-99	Philadelphia	AHL	52	4	3	7	216	7	0	0	0	2
99-2000	Philadelphia	AHL	64	1	2	3	247	....	....	....	....	....
2000-01	Philadelphia	AHL	48	3	1	4	177	8	0	0	0	38
2001-02	Worcester IceCats	AHL	58	0	4	4	251	1	0	0	0	2
2002-03	Worcester IceCats	AHL	40	0	0	0	80	3	0	0	0	4

Signed as a free agent by **Philadelphia**, August 24, 1998. Signed as a free agent by **St. Louis**, July 16, 2001.

McLEOD, Kiel (muk-KLOWD, KIGHL) PHX.

Center. Shoots right. 6'6", 229 lbs. Born, Ft. Saskatchewan, Alta., December 30, 1982.
(Columbus' 3rd choice, 53rd overall, in 2001 Entry Draft).

			Regular Season					Playoffs				
Season	Club	League	GP	G	A	TP	PIM	GP	G	A	TP	PIM
1997-98	North Delta	BCAHA	55	57	55	112	202	....	....	....	....	....
1998-99	Kelowna Rockets	WHL	55	12	15	27	48	6	0	1	1	2
99-2000	Kelowna Rockets	WHL	59	17	13	30	100	5	2	1	3	2
2000-01	Kelowna Rockets	WHL	65	38	28	66	94	4	4	1	5	8
2001-02	Kelowna Rockets	WHL	41	17	31	48	62	15	3	10	13	14
2002-03	Kelowna Rockets	WHL	68	39	51	90	163	8	5	5	10	4

WHL West Second All-Star Team (2003)

Signed as a free agent by **Phoenix**, June 9, 2003.

McNEILL, Grant (muhk-NEEL, GRANT) FLA.

Defense. Shoots left. 6'2", 210 lbs. Born, Vermillion, Alta., June 8, 1983.
(Florida's 5th choice, 68th overall, in 2001 Entry Draft).

			Regular Season					Playoffs				
Season	Club	League	GP	G	A	TP	PIM	GP	G	A	TP	PIM
99-2000	Prince Albert	WHL	58	1	1	2	43	6	0	1	1	0
2000-01	Prince Albert	WHL	61	2	6	8	280	....	....	....	....	....
2001-02	Prince Albert	WHL	70	7	6	13	326	....	....	....	....	....
2002-03	Prince Albert	WHL	71	1	8	9	280	....	....	....	....	....

MEECH, Derek (MEECH, DAIR-ihk) DET.

Defense. Shoots left. 5'11", 182 lbs. Born, Winnipeg, Man., April 21, 1984.
(Detroit's 7th choice, 229th overall, in 2002 Entry Draft).

			Regular Season					Playoffs				
Season	Club	League	GP	G	A	TP	PIM	GP	G	A	TP	PIM
99-2000	Winnipeg Warriors	MMMHL	36	15	40	55	24	....	....	....	....	....
	Red Deer Rebels	WHL	5	1	0	1	2	....	....	....	....	....
2000-01	Red Deer Rebels	WHL	60	2	7	9	40	22	0	0	0	9
	Red Deer Rebels	M-Cup	4	1	0	1	0	....	....	....	....	....
2001-02	Red Deer Rebels	WHL	71	8	19	27	33	13	1	1	2	6
2002-03	Red Deer Rebels	WHL	65	6	16	22	53	12	1	1	2	12

MELIN, Bjorn (MEH-lihn, b-YUHRN) ANA.

Right wing. Shoots right. 6'1", 178 lbs. Born, Jonkoping, Sweden, July 4, 1981.
(NY Islanders' 11th choice, 163rd overall, in 1999 Entry Draft).

			Regular Season					Playoffs				
Season	Club	League	GP	G	A	TP	PIM	GP	G	A	TP	PIM
1997-98	HV 71 Jr.	Swede-Jr.	8	0	3	3	2	....	....	....	....	....
1998-99	HV 71 Jr.	Swede-Jr.	30	12	7	19	50	....	....	....	....	....
99-2000	HV 71 Jr.	Swede-Jr.	24	19	16	35	70	....	....	....	....	....
	HV 71 Jonkoping	Sweden	23	3	0	3	2	5	0	0	0	0
2000-01	HV 71 Jr.	Swede-Jr.	10	6	5	11	66	....	....	....	....	....
	HV 71 Jonkoping	Sweden	43	2	1	3	26	....	....	....	....	....
2001-02	HV 71 Jonkoping	Sweden	50	7	9	16	40	8	0	0	0	6
2002-03	HV 71 Jonkoping	Sweden	48	7	9	16	44	7	0	2	2	6

Rights traded to **Anaheim** by **NY Islanders** with Ben Guite for Dave Roche, March 19, 2002.

METCALF, Peter (MEHT-kaf, PEE-tuhr) BOS.

Defense. Shoots left. 6', 200 lbs. Born, Steamboat Springs, CO, February 25, 1979.
(Toronto's 9th choice, 267th overall, in 1999 Entry Draft).

			Regular Season					Playoffs				
Season	Club	League	GP	G	A	TP	PIM	GP	G	A	TP	PIM
1997-98	Cushing Academy	Hi-School	25	18	48	66	....	....	....	....	....	....
1998-99	U. of Maine	H-East	33	6	17	23	34	....	....	....	....	....
99-2000	U. of Maine	H-East	40	4	17	21	56	....	....	....	....	....
2000-01	U. of Maine	H-East	31	5	9	14	44	....	....	....	....	....
2001-02	U. of Maine	H-East	44	9	41	50	66	....	....	....	....	....
2002-03	Providence Bruins	AHL	40	0	6	6	24	....	....	....	....	....
	Atlantic City	ECHL	18	2	11	13	48	19	4	6	10	25

Hockey East First All-Star Team (2002) • NCAA Championship All-Tournament Team (2002)

Signed as a free agent by **Boston**, August 8, 2002.

METHOT, Francois (meh-THOH, FRAN-swaw) WSH.

Center. Shoots right. 6', 203 lbs. Born, Montreal, Que., April 26, 1978.
(Buffalo's 4th choice, 54th overall, in 1996 Entry Draft).

			Regular Season					Playoffs				
Season	Club	League	GP	G	A	TP	PIM	GP	G	A	TP	PIM
1993-94	Montreal-Bourassa	QAAA	44	17	38	55	....	4	3	1	4	4
1994-95	St-Hyacinthe Laser	QMJHL	60	14	38	52	22	5	0	1	1	0
1995-96	St-Hyacinthe Laser	QMJHL	68	32	62	94	22	12	6	6	12	4
1996-97	Rouyn-Noranda	QMJHL	47	21	30	51	22	....	....	....	....	....
	Shawinigan	QMJHL	18	8	17	25	2	7	2	6	8	2
1997-98	Shawinigan	QMJHL	36	23	42	65	10	6	1	3	4	5
1998-99	Rochester	AHL	58	5	8	13	8	9	0	1	1	0
99-2000	Rochester	AHL	80	14	18	32	20	21	2	4	6	16
2000-01	Rochester	AHL	79	22	33	55	35	4	1	3	4	0
2001-02	Rochester	AHL	59	17	17	34	28	2	1	0	1	0
2002-03	Rochester	AHL	58	19	34	53	22	3	0	4	4	0

Signed as a free agent by **Washington**, August 19, 2003.

MEYER, Freddy (MAY-uhr, FREHD) PHI.

Defense. Shoots left. 5'10", 192 lbs. Born, Sanbornville, NH, January 4, 1981.

			Regular Season					Playoffs				
Season	Club	League	GP	G	A	TP	PIM	GP	G	A	TP	PIM
99-2000	U.S. National U-18	USDP	28	3	8	11	60	....	....	....	....	....
	Boston University	H-East	25	1	11	12	52	....	....	....	....	....
2000-01	Boston University	H-East	28	6	13	19	82	....	....	....	....	....
2001-02	Boston University	H-East	37	5	15	20	78	....	....	....	....	....
2002-03	Boston University	H-East	36	5	16	21	76	....	....	....	....	....

Hockey East First All-Star Team (2003) • NCAA East First All-American Team (2003)

Signed as a free agent by **Philadelphia**, May 21, 2003.

MEYER, Stefan (MAY-uhr, steh-FAN) FLA.

Left wing. Shoots left. 6'1", 194 lbs. Born, Medicine Hat, Alta., July 20, 1985.
(Florida's 4th choice, 55th overall, in 2003 Entry Draft).

			Regular Season					Playoffs				
Season	Club	League	GP	G	A	TP	PIM	GP	G	A	TP	PIM
2000-01	Notre Dame	SBHL	50	36	52	88	71	....	....	....	....	....
2001-02	Medicine Hat	WHL	67	18	22	40	48	....	....	....	....	....
2002-03	Medicine Hat	WHL	70	36	16	52	90	11	3	3	6	14

MICHALEK, Milan (mih-KHAL-ihk, MEE-lahn) S.J.

Right wing. Shoots left. 6'2", 207 lbs. Born, Jindrichuv Hradec, Czech., December 7, 1984.
(San Jose's 1st choice, 6th overall, in 2003 Entry Draft).

			Regular Season					Playoffs				
Season	Club	League	GP	G	A	TP	PIM	GP	G	A	TP	PIM
99-2000	C. Budejovice Jr.	Czech-Jr.	48	16	26	42	42	6	3	1	4	4
2000-01	C. Budejovice Jr.	Czech-Jr.	30	10	13	23	30	4	1	3	4	2
	Ceske Budejovice	Czech	5	0	0	0	0	....	....	....	....	....
2001-02	Ceske Budejovice	Czech	47	6	11	17	12	....	....	....	....	....
	C. Budejovice Jr.	Czech-Jr.	5	3	2	5	4	7	5	4	9	14
2002-03	Ceske Budejovice	Czech	46	3	5	8	14	4	1	0	1	2
	Kladno	Czech-2	....	....	....	....	....	6	2	2	4	16

MICHALEK, Zbynek (mih-KHAL-ihk, ZBIGH-nehk) MIN.

Defense. Shoots right. 6'1", 199 lbs. Born, Jindrichuv Hradec, Czech., December 23, 1982.

			Regular Season					Playoffs				
Season	Club	League	GP	G	A	TP	PIM	GP	G	A	TP	PIM
2000-01	Shawinigan	QMJHL	69	10	29	39	52	3	0	0	0	0
2001-02	Shawinigan	QMJHL	68	16	35	51	54	10	8	7	15	10
2002-03	Houston Aeros	AHL	62	4	10	14	26	23	1	1	2	6

Signed as a free agent by **Minnesota**, September 29, 2001.

MICKA, Tomas (MIHTSKA, TAW-mas) EDM.

Left wing. Shoots left. 6'2", 180 lbs. Born, Jihlava, Czech., June 7, 1983.
(Edmonton's 13th choice, 245th overall, in 2002 Entry Draft).

			Regular Season					Playoffs				
Season	Club	League	GP	G	A	TP	PIM	GP	G	A	TP	PIM
99-2000	HC Slavia Praha Jr.	Czech-Jr.	42	17	18	35	24	....	....	....	....	....
2000-01	HC Slavia Praha Jr.	Czech-Jr.	45	2	8	10	65	3	0	1	1	0
2001-02	HC Slavia Praha Jr.	Czech-Jr.	46	12	16	28	79	....	....	....	....	....
	HC Slavia Praha	Czech	1	0	0	0	0	....	....	....	....	....
2002-03	Havirov	Czech	23	1	0	1	12	....	....	....	....	....
	Havirov Jr.	Czech-Jr.	11	4	3	7	12	....	....	....	....	....
	Zdar nad Sazavou	Czech-2	4	1	0	1	2	....	....	....	....	....

MIETTINEN, Antti (mih-EHT-tih-nehn, AN-tee) DAL.

Center. Shoots right. 5'11", 180 lbs. Born, Hameenlinna, Finland, July 3, 1980.
(Dallas' 10th choice, 224th overall, in 2000 Entry Draft).

			Regular Season					Playoffs				
Season	Club	League	GP	G	A	TP	PIM	GP	G	A	TP	PIM
1996-97	HPK-B	Finn-Jr.	36	24	29	53	34	....	....	....	....	....
1997-98	HPK-B	Finn-Jr.	34	13	28	41	63	8	1	0	1	2
	HPK Jr.	Finn-Jr.	8	1	0	1	2	....	....	....	....	....
1998-99	HPK Jr.	Finn-Jr.	35	17	22	39	28	....	....	....	....	....
	FoPS Forssa	Finland-2	4	3	1	4	6	....	....	....	....	....
	HPK Hameenlinna	Finland	13	0	0	0	2	4	0	0	0	0
99-2000	HPK Jr.	Finn-Jr.	16	11	13	24	16	....	....	....	....	....
	HPK Hameenlinna	Finland	39	2	1	3	8	7	1	0	1	0
2000-01	HPK Jr.	Finn-Jr.	4	3	10	13	2	....	....	....	....	....
	HPK Hameenlinna	Finland	55	13	11	24	20	....	....	....	....	....
2001-02	HPK Hameenlinna	Finland	56	19	37	56	50	8	2	4	6	8
2002-03	HPK Hameenlinna	Finland	53	25	25	50	54	10	1	7	8	29

MIETTINEN, Tommi (mih-EHT-tih-nehn,TAW-mee) ANA.

Center. Shoots left. 5'10", 165 lbs. Born, Kuopio, Finland, December 3, 1975.
(Anaheim's 9th choice, 236th overall, in 1994 Entry Draft).

			Regular Season					Playoffs				
Season	Club	League	GP	G	A	TP	PIM	GP	G	A	TP	PIM
1991-92	KalPa Kuopio Jr.	Finn-Jr.	37	9	16	25	12					
1992-93	KalPa Kuopio-B	Finn-Jr.	7	3	8	11	2					
	KalPa Kuopio Jr.	Finn-Jr.	26	16	27	43	14					
	KalPa Kuopio	Finland	14	0	0	0	0					
1993-94	KalPa Kuopio Jr.	Finn-Jr.	9	5	9	14	10					
	KalPa Kuopio	Finland	47	5	7	12	14					
1994-95	KalPa Kuopio Jr.	Finn-Jr.	2	1	3	4	2					
	KalPa Kuopio	Finland	48	13	16	29	26	3	1	1	2	2
1995-96	TPS Turku	Finland	36	3	10	13	10	10	2	1	3	29
1996-97	TPS Turku	Finland	41	6	15	21	6	12	3	4	7	8
1997-98	TPS Turku	Finland	42	8	6	14	26	4	0	0	0	0
	TPS Turku	EuroHL	3	0	0	0	2					
1998-99	TPS Turku	Finland	54	10	17	27	26	10	4	4	8	0
99-2000	Ilves Tampere	Finland	54	13	20	33	24					
2000-01	Ilves Tampere	Finland	55	10	20	30	38	9	0	1	1	4
2001-02	Ilves Tampere	Finland	55	11	31	42	36	3	0	0	0	2
2002-03	Brynas IF Gavle	Sweden	50	9	17	26	76					

MIKHAILOV, Konstantin (mih-KHIGH-lawv, kawn-stuhn-TEEN) VAN.

Center. Shoots left. 5'11", 174 lbs. Born, Moscow, USSR, February 12, 1983.
(Vancouver's 6th choice, 245th overall, in 2001 Entry Draft).

			Regular Season					Playoffs				
Season	Club	League	GP	G	A	TP	PIM	GP	G	A	TP	PIM
99-2000	DynamoMoscow2	Russia-3	14	3	2	5	14					
2000-01	Nizhnekamsk	Russia	24	0	2	2	12					
2001-02	Nizhnekamsk	Russia	38	3	6	9	10					
2002-03	Dynamo Moscow	Russia	14	0	1	1	31					
	Nizhnekamsk	Russia	15	1	1	2	6					

MIKHNOV, Alexei (MIHKH-nahf, al-EHX-ay) EDM.

Left wing. Shoots left. 6'5", 200 lbs. Born, Kiev, USSR, August 31, 1982.
(Edmonton's 1st choice, 17th overall, in 2000 Entry Draft).

			Regular Season					Playoffs				
Season	Club	League	GP	G	A	TP	PIM	GP	G	A	TP	PIM
1997-98	Torpedo Yaroslavl	Russia	6	0	0	0	0					
1998-99	Yaroslavl 2	Russia-3	14	2	2	4	4					
99-2000	Yaroslavl 2	Russia-3	53	24	17	41	10					
2000-01	HC CSKA	Russia-2	4	0	0	0	2					
	THC Tver	Russia-2	22	5	11	16	6					
2001-02	DynamoMoscow2	Russia-3	8	8	6	14	0					
	Dynamo Moscow	Russia	35	2	1	3	4	3	0	0	0	2
	Salavat Yulayev	Russia	1	0	0	0	0					
2002-03	Sibir Novosibirsk	Russia	51	7	9	16	10					

MIKHNOV, Andrei (mihkh-NAWV, AWN-dray) ST.L.

Center. Shoots left. 6'5", 192 lbs. Born, Kiev, USSR, November 26, 1983.
(St. Louis' 2nd choice, 62nd overall, in 2002 Entry Draft).

			Regular Season					Playoffs				
Season	Club	League	GP	G	A	TP	PIM	GP	G	A	TP	PIM
2001-02	Sudbury Wolves	OHL	67	14	18	32	43					
2002-03	Kingston	OHL	39	7	11	18	24					
	St. Michael's	OHL	26	1	6	7	23	12	0	2	2	4

MIKKOLA, Ilkka (mih-KOHLA, IHL-ka) MTL.

Defense. Shoots left. 6', 189 lbs. Born, Oulu, Finland, January 18, 1979.
(Montreal's 3rd choice, 65th overall, in 1997 Entry Draft).

			Regular Season					Playoffs				
Season	Club	League	GP	G	A	TP	PIM	GP	G	A	TP	PIM
1993-94	Karpat Oulu-C	Finn-Jr.	22	3	6	9	4	4	0	1	1	4
1994-95	Karpat Oulu-C	Finn-Jr.	31	17	27	44	24	3	0	0	0	8
1995-96	Karpat Oulu-B	Finn-Jr.	4	2	0	2	0					
	Karpat Oulu Jr.	Finn-Jr.	21	2	3	5	20					
	Karpat Oulu	Finland-2	10	0	4	4	29	2	0	0	0	2
1996-97	Karpat Oulu Jr.	Finn-Jr.	40	7	12	19	32	6	0	0	0	4
1997-98	Karpat Oulu Jr.	Finn-Jr.	8	4	2	6	10					
	Karpat Oulu	Finland-2	27	7	2	9	34					
1998-99	TPS Turku	Finland	42	1	3	4	41	10	1	0	1	6
99-2000	TPS Turku	Finland	54	2	6	8	48	11	0	0	0	6
2000-01	TPS Turku	Finland	37	3	6	9	22	10	0	1	1	4
2001-02	Jokerit Helsinki	Finland	55	3	2	5	14	12	1	3	4	6
2002-03	Jokerit Helsinki	Finland	38	4	10	14	8	10	0	1	1	10

MIKKONEN, Tuomas (mih-KOH-nehn, TWOH-muhs) DAL.

Left wing. Shoots left. 6'1", 183 lbs. Born, Jyvaskyla, Finland, March 25, 1983.
(Dallas' 11th choice, 243rd overall, in 2002 Entry Draft).

			Regular Season					Playoffs				
Season	Club	League	GP	G	A	TP	PIM	GP	G	A	TP	PIM
99-2000	JYP Jyvaskyla Jr.	Finn-Jr.	36	7	2	9	100					
2000-01	JYP Jyvaskyla Jr.	Finn-Jr.	27	7	8	15	16					
2001-02	JYP Jyvaskyla	Finland	12	1	2	3	12					
	JYP Jyvaskyla Jr.	Finn-Jr.	17	5	9	14	47	4	0	2	2	0
2002-03	JYP Jyvaskyla	Finland	48	5	3	8	41	2	0	1	1	25

MILES, Jeff (MIGHLZ, JEHF) CHI.

Center. Shoots right. 6', 191 lbs. Born, Pickering, Ont., July 12, 1981.
(Chicago's 13th choice, 268th overall, in 2001 Entry Draft).

			Regular Season					Playoffs				
Season	Club	League	GP	G	A	TP	PIM	GP	G	A	TP	PIM
1998-99	Thunder Bay Flyers	USHL	56	11	19	30	57	3	2	0	2	2
99-2000	Thornhill Rattlers	OPJHL	31	40	38	78	32	20	17	16	33	38
2000-01	U. of Vermont	ECAC	34	8	23	31	14					
2001-02	U. of Vermont	ECAC	30	5	18	23	18					
2002-03	U. of Vermont	ECAC	35	19	17	36	32					

MILROY, Duncan (MIHL-roi, DUHN-can) MTL.

Right wing. Shoots right. 6', 197 lbs. Born, Edmonton, Alta., February 8, 1983.
(Montreal's 3rd choice, 37th overall, in 2001 Entry Draft).

			Regular Season					Playoffs				
Season	Club	League	GP	G	A	TP	PIM	GP	G	A	TP	PIM
1998-99	Edm. Leafs	AMHL	34	34	36	70	73					
	Swift Current	WHL	3	0	0	0	0					
99-2000	Swift Current	WHL	68	15	15	30	20	12	3	5	8	12
2000-01	Swift Current	WHL	68	38	54	92	51	19	9	12	21	6
2001-02	Swift Current	WHL	26	20	11	31	20					
	Kootenay Ice	WHL	38	25	31	56	24	22	*17	*20	*37	26
2002-03	Kootenay Ice	WHL	61	34	44	78	40	11	5	3	8	8

MINAKOV, Oleg (mih-nah-KAHV, OH-lehg) CHI.

Right wing. Shoots left. 6'2", 183 lbs. Born, Elektrostal, USSR, February 18, 1983.
(Chicago's 12th choice, 216th overall, in 2001 Entry Draft).

			Regular Season					Playoffs				
Season	Club	League	GP	G	A	TP	PIM	GP	G	A	TP	PIM
99-2000	Elektrostal 2	Russia-3	19	10	2	12	16					
	Kristall Elektrostal	Russia	4	0	0	0	0					
2000-01	Elektrostal	Russia-2	25	0	3	3	6					
2001-02	Elektrostal 2	Russia-3	26	9	7	16	14					
	Elektrostal	Russia-2	16	0	1	1	14					
2002-03	Amur Khabarovsk	Russia	47	5	0	5	12					
	Khabarovsk 2	Russia-3	3	2	1	3	0					

MINK, Graham (MIHNK, GRAY-uhm) WSH.

Center. Shoots right. 6'3", 220 lbs. Born, Stowe, VT, May 12, 1979.

			Regular Season					Playoffs				
Season	Club	League	GP	G	A	TP	PIM	GP	G	A	TP	PIM
1997-98	Mount Hermon	Hi-School	25	17	25	42						
1998-99	U. of Vermont	ECAC	27	4	2	6	34					
99-2000	U. of Vermont	ECAC	17	7	4	11	14					
2000-01	U. of Vermont	ECAC	32	17	12	29	52					
2001-02	Richmond	ECHL	29	8	9	17	78					
	Portland Pirates	AHL	56	17	17	34	50					
2002-03	Portland Pirates	AHL	71	22	15	37	115					

Signed as a free agent by **Portland** (AHL), September 30, 2001. Signed as a free agent by **Washington**, April 9, 2002.

MIRNOV, Igor (mihr-NAWF, EE-gohr) OTT.

Left wing. Shoots left. 5'11", 191 lbs. Born, Chita, USSR, September 19, 1984.
(Ottawa's 2nd choice, 67th overall, in 2003 Entry Draft).

			Regular Season					Playoffs				
Season	Club	League	GP	G	A	TP	PIM	GP	G	A	TP	PIM
2001-02	Dynamo Moscow 2	Russia-3	30	33	17	50	34					
	Dynamo Moscow	Russia	6	0	0	0	0					
2002-03	Dynamo Moscow	Russia	50	3	7	10	49	5	0	0	0	2

MISCHLER, Greg (MIH-schluhr, GREHG)

Center. Shoots left. 6'3", 174 lbs. Born, Holbrook, NY, September 15, 1978.
(Vancouver's 10th choice, 204th overall, in 1998 Entry Draft).

			Regular Season					Playoffs				
Season	Club	League	GP	G	A	TP	PIM	GP	G	A	TP	PIM
1997-98	Northeastern	H-East	39	7	13	20	22					
1998-99	Northeastern	H-East	33	8	15	23	36					
99-2000	Northeastern	H-East	34	9	14	23	22					
2000-01	Northeastern	H-East	36	10	*32	42	34					
2001-02	Cleveland Barons	AHL	65	10	14	24	71					
2002-03	Cleveland Barons	AHL	67	12	12	24	64					

Signed as a free agent by **San Jose**, June 13, 2001.

MITCHELL, John (MIH-chuhl, JAWN) TOR.

Center. Shoots left. 6'1", 182 lbs. Born, Oakville, Ont., January 22, 1985.
(Toronto's 4th choice, 158th overall, in 2003 Entry Draft).

			Regular Season					Playoffs				
Season	Club	League	GP	G	A	TP	PIM	GP	G	A	TP	PIM
2000-01	Waterloo Siskens	OPJHL	47	15	29	44	33					
2001-02	Plymouth Whalers	OHL	62	9	9	18	23	6	1	0	1	4
2002-03	Plymouth Whalers	OHL	68	18	37	55	31	18	2	10	12	8

MOEN, Travis (MOH-ehn, TRA-vihs) CHI.

Left wing. Shoots left. 6'2", 210 lbs. Born, Stewart Valley, Sask., April 6, 1982.
(Calgary's 6th choice, 155th overall, in 2000 Entry Draft).

			Regular Season					Playoffs				
Season	Club	League	GP	G	A	TP	PIM	GP	G	A	TP	PIM
1998-99	Swift Current	SMHL	STATISTICS NOT AVAILABLE									
	Kelowna Rockets	WHL	4	0	0	0	0					
99-2000	Kelowna Rockets	WHL	66	9	6	15	96	5	1	1	2	2
2000-01	Kelowna Rockets	WHL	40	8	8	16	106					
2001-02	Kelowna Rockets	WHL	71	10	17	27	197	13	1	0	1	28
2002-03	Norfolk Admirals	AHL	42	1	2	3	62	9	0	0	0	20

Signed as a free agent by **Chicago**, October 21, 2002.

MOJZIS, Tomas (MOI-shihsh, TAW-mash) VAN.

Defense. Shoots left. 6'1", 186 lbs. Born, Kolin, Czech., May 2, 1982.
(Toronto's 11th choice, 246th overall, in 2001 Entry Draft).

			Regular Season					Playoffs				
Season	Club	League	GP	G	A	TP	PIM	GP	G	A	TP	PIM
99-2000	Pardubice Jr.	Czech-Jr.	40	7	1	8						
2000-01	Moose Jaw	WHL	72	11	25	36	115	4	0	1	1	8
2001-02	Moose Jaw	WHL	28	2	11	13	43					
	Seattle	WHL	36	8	15	23	66	11	1	3	4	20
2002-03	Seattle	WHL	62	21	49	70	126	15	1	6	7	36

WHL West First All-Star Team (2003) • Canadian Major Junior First All-Star Team (2003)

Traded to **Vancouver** by **Toronto** for Brad Leeb, September 4, 2002.

MOKHOV, Stepan (MOH-khohv, STEH-pan) CHI.

Defense. Shoots left. 6'2", 190 lbs. Born, Ust-Kamenogorsk, USSR, January 22, 1981.
(Chicago's 3rd choice, 63rd overall, in 1999 Entry Draft).

			Regular Season					Playoffs				
Season	Club	League	GP	G	A	TP	PIM	GP	G	A	TP	PIM
1997-98	Omsk 2	Russia-3	18	0	1	1	8					
1998-99	Cherepovets 2	Russia-3	25	2	0	2	34					
	Cherepovets 3	Russia-4	3	0	0	0	6					
	Cherepovets	Russia	1	0	0	0	0					
99-2000	Magnitogorsk	Russia	18	0	1	1	6	14	1	0	1	4
2000-01	Krylja Sovetov	Russia-2	30	0	5	5	4					
2001-02	Spartak Moscow 2	Russia-3	16	2	9	11	16					
	Spartak Moscow	Russia	11	1	0	1	2					
2002-03	THC Tver	Russia-2	39	5	6	11	46					

MONYCH, Lance (MOH-nihch, LANTS) PHX.

Right wing. Shoots right. 6'3", 204 lbs. Born, Red Deer, Alta., July 25, 1984.
(Phoenix's 6th choice, 97th overall, in 2002 Entry Draft).

			Regular Season					Playoffs				
Season	Club	League	GP	G	A	TP	PIM	GP	G	A	TP	PIM
99-2000	Brandon Hawks	MBHL	30	32	34	66	98					
	Brandon	WHL	3	0	0	0	0					
2000-01	Brandon	WHL	53	14	8	22	34	6	1	0	1	0
2001-02	Brandon	WHL	71	18	30	48	96	19	4	3	7	20
2002-03	Brandon	WHL	70	19	26	45	111	17	7	3	10	20

MOORE, Dominic (MOOR, DOHM-ih-nihk) NYR

Center. Shoots left. 6', 180 lbs. Born, Thornhill, Ont., August 3, 1980.
(NY Rangers' 2nd choice, 95th overall, in 2000 Entry Draft).

			Regular Season					Playoffs				
Season	Club	League	GP	G	A	TP	PIM	GP	G	A	TP	PIM
1996-97	Thornhill Islanders	MTJHL	29	4	6	10	48	1	0	1	1	0
1997-98	Aurora Tigers	OPJHL	51	10	15	25	16	....	....	....	....	....
1998-99	Aurora Tigers	OPJHL	51	34	53	87	70	....	....	....	....	....
99-2000	Harvard Crimson	ECAC	30	12	24	28	16	....	....	....	....	....
2000-01	Harvard Crimson	ECAC	32	15	28	43	40	....	....	....	....	....
2001-02	Harvard Crimson	ECAC	32	13	16	29	37	....	....	....	....	....
2002-03	Harvard Crimson	ECAC	34	*24	27	*51	30	....	....	....	....	....

ECAC All-Rookie Team (2000) • ECAC Second All-Star Team (2001) • ECAC First All-Star Team (2003) • NCAA East First All-American Team (2003)

MOORE, Greg (MOOR, GREHG) CGY.

Right wing. Shoots right. 6'1", 206 lbs. Born, Lisbon, ME, March 26, 1984.
(Calgary's 5th choice, 143rd overall, in 2003 Entry Draft).

			Regular Season					Playoffs				
Season	Club	League	GP	G	A	TP	PIM	GP	G	A	TP	PIM
99-2000	St. Dominic High	Hi-School	31	32	40	72	....	....	....	....	....	....
2000-01	U.S. National U-17	USDP	69	12	18	30	23	....	....	....	....	....
2001-02	U.S. National U-18	USDP	53	13	24	37	20	....	....	....	....	....
2002-03	U. of Maine	H-East	33	9	7	16	10	....	....	....	....	....

MORGAN, Gavin (MOHR-guhn, GA-vign) DAL.

Center. Shoots right. 5'11", 191 lbs. Born, Scarborough, Ont., July 9, 1976.

			Regular Season					Playoffs				
Season	Club	League	GP	G	A	TP	PIM	GP	G	A	TP	PIM
1992-93	Wexford Raiders	MTJHL	3	0	1	1	0	....	....	....	....	....
1993-94	Wexford Raiders	MTJHL	49	18	32	50	91	....	....	....	....	....
1994-95	Wexford Raiders	MTJHL	49	26	39	65	170	....	....	....	....	....
1995-96	U. of Denver	WCHA	28	2	9	11	47	....	....	....	....	....
1996-97	U. of Denver	WCHA	41	8	15	23	46	....	....	....	....	....
1997-98	U. of Denver	WCHA	37	9	8	17	42	....	....	....	....	....
1998-99	U. of Denver	WCHA	40	13	16	29	85	....	....	....	....	....
99-2000	Idaho Steelheads	WCHL	54	17	33	50	150	3	0	3	3	4
	Long Beach	IHL	7	0	1	1	10	....	....	....	....	....
	Utah Grizzlies	IHL	10	0	2	2	4	2	1	0	1	2
2000-01	Utah Grizzlies	IHL	79	7	14	21	187	....	....	....	....	....
2001-02	Utah Grizzlies	AHL	76	8	24	32	249	5	0	1	1	2
2002-03	Utah Grizzlies	AHL	73	15	24	39	244	2	0	1	1	17

Signed as a free agent by **Idaho** (WCHL), August 25, 1999. Signed as a free agent by **Utah** (IHL), June 26, 2000. Signed as a free agent by **Dallas**, July 17, 2001.

MORRIS, Mike (MOHR-his, MIGHK) S.J.

Right wing. Shoots right. 6', 182 lbs. Born, Dorchester, MA, July 14, 1983.
(San Jose's 1st choice, 27th overall, in 2002 Entry Draft).

			Regular Season					Playoffs				
Season	Club	League	GP	G	A	TP	PIM	GP	G	A	TP	PIM
2000-01	St. Sebastian's	Hi-School	28	20	28	48	18	....	....	....	....	....
2001-02	St. Sebastian's	Hi-School	31	29	29	58	26	....	....	....	....	....
2002-03	Northeastern	H-East	26	9	12	21	16	....	....	....	....	....

Massachusetts Independent League MVP (2002)

MORRIS, Ty (MOH-rihs, TIGH) VAN.

Left wing. Shoots left. 6'1", 200 lbs. Born, Millet, Alta., February 2, 1984.
(Vancouver's 4th choice, 128th overall, in 2003 Entry Draft).

			Regular Season					Playoffs				
Season	Club	League	GP	G	A	TP	PIM	GP	G	A	TP	PIM
2000-01	Leduc Oil Kings	AMHL	32	24	24	48	107	....	....	....	....	....
	St. Albert Saints	AJHL	4	0	0	0	2	....	....	....	....	....
2001-02	St. Albert Saints	AJHL	60	23	24	47	137	6	1	1	2	36
2002-03	St. Albert Saints	AJHL	58	28	54	82	226	20	18	14	32	46

MORRISON, Justin (MOHR-rihs-OHN, JUHS-tihn) VAN.

Right wing. Shoots right. 6'3", 205 lbs. Born, Los Angeles, CA, September 10, 1979.
(Vancouver's 4th choice, 81st overall, in 1998 Entry Draft).

			Regular Season					Playoffs				
Season	Club	League	GP	G	A	TP	PIM	GP	G	A	TP	PIM
1996-97	Omaha Lancers	USHL	62	12	24	36	44	10	2	4	6	8
1997-98	Colorado College	WCHA	42	4	9	13	8	....	....	....	....	....
1998-99	Colorado College	WCHA	38	23	15	38	33	....	....	....	....	....
99-2000	Colorado College	WCHA	38	7	19	26	28	....	....	....	....	....
2000-01	Colorado College	WCHA	41	21	14	35	42	....	....	....	....	....
2001-02	Manitoba Moose	AHL	64	10	9	19	37	7	1	0	1	4
2002-03	Manitoba Moose	AHL	30	10	6	16	13	14	2	3	5	4
	Columbia Inferno	ECHL	40	20	35	55	39	2	0	0	0	4

MORROW, Josh (MOHR-oh, JAWSH) NSH.

Defense. Shoots left. 6'1", 210 lbs. Born, Edmonton, Alta., June 12, 1983.
(Nashville's 5th choice, 203rd overall, in 2002 Entry Draft).

			Regular Season					Playoffs				
Season	Club	League	GP	G	A	TP	PIM	GP	G	A	TP	PIM
1998-99	Ft-Saskatchewan	AJHL	Statistics Not Available									
	Medicine Hat	WHL	10	0	1	1	2	....	....	....	....	....
99-2000	Medicine Hat	WHL	49	1	8	9	57	....	....	....	....	....
2000-01	Medicine Hat	WHL	46	0	7	7	111	....	....	....	....	....
2001-02	Medicine Hat	WHL	46	4	15	19	137	....	....	....	....	....
	Tri-City Americans	WHL	30	6	12	18	62	....	....	....	....	....
2002-03	Tri-City Americans	WHL	17	4	4	8	35	....	....	....	....	....
	Kamloops Blazers	WHL	23	3	11	14	63	....	....	....	....	....

MORROW, Thomas (MOHR-roh, TAW-muhs) BUF.

Defense. Shoots left. 6'6", 198 lbs. Born, St. Paul, MN, October 21, 1983.
(Buffalo's 6th choice, 150th overall, in 2003 Entry Draft).

			Regular Season					Playoffs				
Season	Club	League	GP	G	A	TP	PIM	GP	G	A	TP	PIM
2001-02	Hill-Murray	Hi-School	31	3	27	39	....	....	....	....	....	....
2002-03	Tri-City Storm	USHL	23	1	3	4	64	....	....	....	....	....
	Des Moines	USHL	34	1	6	7	40	....	....	....	....	....

• Signed Letter of Intent to attend **Boston University** (H-East), February 16, 2003.

MOSCEVSKY, Yuri (mawz-CHEHV-skee, YUH-ree) S.J.

Left wing. Shoots left. 6'4", 220 lbs. Born, Yorba Linda, CA, October 20, 1978.

			Regular Season					Playoffs				
Season	Club	League	GP	G	A	TP	PIM	GP	G	A	TP	PIM
1997-98	St. Louis Sting	NAHL	22	0	2	2	41	....	....	....	....	....
1998-99			Did Not Play									
99-2000	Topeka	CHL	4	1	0	1	7	....	....	....	....	....
	Bakersfield	WCHL	6	1	0	1	26	....	....	....	....	....
	San Diego Gulls	WCHL	9	0	1	1	59	....	....	....	....	....
2000-01			Statistics Not Available									
2001-02	Toledo Storm	ECHL	14	0	0	0	50	....	....	....	....	....
	Mississippi	ECHL	29	3	3	6	130	10	1	0	1	20
2002-03	Cleveland Barons	AHL	65	1	2	3	172	....	....	....	....	....

Signed as a free agent by **Cleveland** (AHL), August 19, 2002. Signed as a free agent by **San Jose**, June 30, 2003.

MOSOVSKY, Karel (moh-SAWV-skee, KA-rehl) BUF.

Left wing. Shoots right. 6'2", 198 lbs. Born, Piesk, Czech., August 22, 1981.
(Buffalo's 6th choice, 117th overall, in 1999 Entry Draft).

			Regular Season					Playoffs				
Season	Club	League	GP	G	A	TP	PIM	GP	G	A	TP	PIM
1997-98	C. Budejovice Jr.	Czech-Jr.	36	15	17	32	52	....	....	....	....	....
1998-99	Regina Pats	WHL	68	26	25	51	58	....	....	....	....	....
99-2000	Regina Pats	WHL	56	24	34	58	80	7	3	1	4	12
2000-01	Regina Pats	WHL	61	25	26	51	59	6	1	3	4	8
2001-02	Rochester	AHL	5	1	1	2	0	....	....	....	....	....
2002-03	Rochester	AHL	62	5	4	9	75	....	....	....	....	....

• Missed majority of 2001-02 season recovering from shoulder injury suffered in training camp, September 9, 2001.

MOSS, David (MAWS, DAY-vihd) CGY.

Left wing. Shoots left. 6'3", 185 lbs. Born, Dearborn, MI, December 28, 1981.
(Calgary's 9th choice, 220th overall, in 2001 Entry Draft).

			Regular Season					Playoffs				
Season	Club	League	GP	G	A	TP	PIM	GP	G	A	TP	PIM
99-2000	Catholic Central	Hi-School	28	18	20	28	20	....	....	....	....	....
2000-01	St. Louis Sting	NAJHL	9	2	2	4	2	....	....	....	....	....
	Cedar Rapids	USHL	51	20	18	38	14	4	0	1	1	2
2001-02	U. of Michigan	CCHA	43	4	9	13	10	....	....	....	....	....
2002-03	U. of Michigan	CCHA	43	14	17	31	37	....	....	....	....	....

MOTZKO, Joe (MAWTS-koh, JOH) CBJ

Right wing. Shoots right. 6', 180 lbs. Born, Bemidji, MN, March 14, 1980.

			Regular Season					Playoffs				
Season	Club	League	GP	G	A	TP	PIM	GP	G	A	TP	PIM
1998-99	Omaha Lancers	USHL	51	15	21	36	60	12	7	3	10	12
99-2000	St. Cloud State	WCHA	36	9	15	24	52	....	....	....	....	....
2000-01	St. Cloud State	WCHA	41	17	20	37	54	....	....	....	....	....
2001-02	St. Cloud State	WCHA	39	9	30	39	34	....	....	....	....	....
2002-03	St. Cloud State	WCHA	38	17	25	42	59	....	....	....	....	....
	Syracuse Crunch	AHL	2	0	0	0	0	....	....	....	....	....

Signed as a free agent by **Columbus**, May 15, 2003.

MOZYAKIN, Sergei (mohz-YA-kihn, SAIR-gay) CBJ

Left wing. Shoots right. 5'10", 165 lbs. Born, Yaroslavl, USSR, March 30, 1981.
(Columbus' 13th choice, 263rd overall, in 2002 Entry Draft).

			Regular Season					Playoffs				
Season	Club	League	GP	G	A	TP	PIM	GP	G	A	TP	PIM
99-2000	CSKA Moscow 2	Russia-3	6	9	3	12	6	....	....	....	....	....
	HC CSKA Moscow	Russia-2	44	23	25	48	10	....	....	....	....	....
2000-01	HC CSKA Moscow	Russia-2	37	22	28	50	18	....	....	....	....	....
	CSKA Moscow	Russia	9	0	2	2	0	....	....	....	....	....
2001-02	HC CSKA Moscow	Russia-2	66	43	42	85	14	....	....	....	....	....
2002-03	CSKA Moscow	Russia	33	12	15	27	18	....	....	....	....	....

MULICK, Robert (muhl-LIHK, RAW-buhrt) S.J.

Defense. Shoots right. 6'2", 210 lbs. Born, Toronto, Ont., October 23, 1979.
(San Jose's 8th choice, 185th overall, in 1998 Entry Draft).

			Regular Season					Playoffs				
Season	Club	League	GP	G	A	TP	PIM	GP	G	A	TP	PIM
1994-95	Mississauga Reps	MTHL	52	8	23	31	80	....	....	....	....	....
1995-96	Sault Ste. Marie	OHL	54	0	3	3	58	3	0	0	0	0
1996-97	Sault Ste. Marie	OHL	60	2	8	10	49	11	0	1	1	12
1997-98	Sault Ste. Marie	OHL	61	0	10	10	109	....	....	....	....	....
1998-99	Sault Ste. Marie	OHL	66	1	12	13	83	5	0	1	1	10
99-2000	Kentucky	AHL	52	0	0	0	52	9	0	0	0	10
2000-01	Kentucky	AHL	71	0	6	6	55	2	0	0	0	0
2001-02	Cleveland Barons	AHL	60	0	2	2	77	....	....	....	....	....
2002-03	Cleveland Barons	AHL	24	0	0	0	14	....	....	....	....	....

MURATOV, Yevgeny (muhr-A-tahf, ehv-GEH-nee) EDM.

Left wing. Shoots right. 5'10", 178 lbs. Born, Nizhny Tagil, USSR, January 28, 1981.
(Edmonton's 10th choice, 274th overall, in 2000 Entry Draft).

			Regular Season					Playoffs				
Season	Club	League	GP	G	A	TP	PIM	GP	G	A	TP	PIM
1997-98	Nizhnekamsk 2	Russia-3	39	7	7	14	2	....	....	....	....	....
1998-99	Nizhnekamsk 2	Russia-4	37	26	9	35	32	....	....	....	....	....
	Nizhnekamsk	Russia	4	0	0	0	0	3	1	0	1	2
99-2000	Nizhnekamsk	Russia	29	9	7	16	2	....	....	....	....	....
	Ak Bars Kazan	Russia	8	2	2	4	2	9	0	0	0	2
2000-01	Nizhnekamsk	Russia	42	9	8	17	14	4	0	0	0	0
2001-02	Nizhnekamsk	Russia	45	5	13	18	4	....	....	....	....	....
2002-03	Nizhnekamsk	Russia	51	10	11	21	41	....	....	....	....	....

MURLEY, Matt (MUHR-lee, MAT) PIT.

Left wing. Shoots left. 6'1", 204 lbs. Born, Troy, NY, December 17, 1979.
(Pittsburgh's 2nd choice, 51st overall, in 1999 Entry Draft).

			Regular Season					Playoffs				
Season	Club	League	GP	G	A	TP	PIM	GP	G	A	TP	PIM
1996-97	Syracuse	MTJHL	48	52	58	110	111	....	....	....	....	....
1997-98	Syracuse	MTJHL	49	56	70	126	103	....	....	....	....	....
1998-99	RPI Engineers	ECAC	36	17	32	49	32	....	....	....	....	....
99-2000	RPI Engineers	ECAC	35	9	29	38	42	....	....	....	....	....
2000-01	RPI Engineers	ECAC	34	*24	18	42	34	....	....	....	....	....
2001-02	RPI Engineers	ECAC	32	*24	22	46	26	....	....	....	....	....
2002-03	Wilkes-Barre	AHL	73	21	37	58	45	6	0	2	2	15

ECAC First All-Star Team (2002)

MURPHY, Joe (MUHR-fee, JOH) **OTT.**

Right wing. Shoots right. 6', 200 lbs. Born, Didsbury, Alta., January 21, 1975.

			Regular Season					Playoffs				
Season	Club	League	GP	G	A	TP	PIM	GP	G	A	TP	PIM
1993-94	Olds Grizzlies	AJHL	52	34	38	72	121	....	....	....	....	....
1994-95	Olds Grizzlies	AJHL	52	30	29	59	65	....	....	....	....	....
1995-96	U. of Denver	WCHA	29	1	6	7	16	....	....	....	....	....
1996-97	U. of Denver	WCHA	36	8	14	22	40	....	....	....	....	....
1997-98	U. of Denver	WCHA	38	7	14	21	60	....	....	....	....	....
1998-99	U. of Denver	WCHA	33	3	13	16	25	....	....	....	....	....
	Huntsville Tornado	CHL	....	....	....	....	....	13	1	5	6	20
99-2000	Roanoke Express	ECHL	34	12	19	31	34	....	....	....	....	....
	Rochester	AHL	32	0	6	6	8	21	4	2	6	27
2000-01	Rochester	AHL	74	20	15	35	43	4	0	1	1	4
2001-02	Grand Rapids	AHL	57	8	14	22	24	5	1	0	1	0
2002-03	Binghamton	AHL	73	22	24	46	27	14	5	5	10	2

Signed as a free agent by **Buffalo**, July 28, 1998. Signed as a free agent by **Ottawa**, August 1, 2001.

MURPHY, Mark (MUHR-fee, MAHRK) **PHI.**

Left wing. Shoots left. 5'11", 200 lbs. Born, Stoughton, MA, August 6, 1976.
(Toronto's 6th choice, 197th overall, in 1995 Entry Draft).

			Regular Season					Playoffs				
Season	Club	League	GP	G	A	TP	PIM	GP	G	A	TP	PIM
1994-95	Stratford Cullitons	OJHL-B	47	52	56	108	64	....	....	....	....	....
1995-96	Stratford Cullitons	OJHL-B	1	0	0	0	0	....	....	....	....	....
	RPI Engineers	ECAC	32	1	1	2	50	....	....	....	....	....
1996-97	RPI Engineers	ECAC	34	9	18	27	56	....	....	....	....	....
1997-98	RPI Engineers	ECAC	35	8	27	35	63	....	....	....	....	....
1998-99	RPI Engineers	ECAC	37	11	30	41	76	....	....	....	....	....
99-2000	Wilkes-Barre	AHL	38	11	22	33	35	....	....	....	....	....
	Trenton Titans	ECHL	37	21	18	39	60	12	2	8	10	17
	Philadelphia	AHL	....	....	....	....	....	2	0	0	0	0
2000-01	Portland Pirates	AHL	76	29	41	70	92	3	2	0	2	2
2001-02	Portland Pirates	AHL	77	20	37	57	56	....	....	....	....	....
2002-03	Portland Pirates	AHL	55	18	24	42	84	3	0	1	1	2

Signed as a free agent by **Washington**, July 13, 2000. Signed as a free agent by **Philadelphia**, July 24, 2003.

MURPHY, Patrick (MUHR-fee, PAT-rihk) **EDM.**

Left wing. Shoots left. 6'1", 195 lbs. Born, Van Nuys, CA, July 24, 1983.
(Edmonton's 11th choice, 211th overall, in 2002 Entry Draft).

			Regular Season					Playoffs				
Season	Club	League	GP	G	A	TP	PIM	GP	G	A	TP	PIM
2000-01	Newmarket	OPJHL	40	13	18	31	95	....	....	....	....	....
2001-02	Newmarket	OPJHL	48	11	21	32	99	....	....	....	....	....
2002-03	Northern Michigan	CCHA	22	1	2	3	26	....	....	....	....	....

MURPHY, Ryan (MUHR-fee, RIGH-yan) **N.J.**

Left wing. Shoots left. 6'1", 195 lbs. Born, Van Nuys, CA, March 21, 1979.
(Carolina's 4th choice, 113th overall, in 1999 Entry Draft).

			Regular Season					Playoffs				
Season	Club	League	GP	G	A	TP	PIM	GP	G	A	TP	PIM
1995-96	Thornhill Islanders	MTJHL	32	13	16	29	49	1	0	0	0	0
1996-97	Thornhill Islanders	MTJHL	41	22	32	54	36	12	7	8	15	....
1997-98	Bowling Green	CCHA	36	3	9	12	27	....	....	....	....	....
1998-99	Bowling Green	CCHA	34	10	23	33	38	....	....	....	....	....
99-2000	Bowling Green	CCHA	36	9	10	19	63	....	....	....	....	....
2000-01	Bowling Green	CCHA	38	23	15	38	22	....	....	....	....	....
2001-02	Florida Everblades	ECHL	66	13	18	31	38	6	1	2	3	4
2002-03	Florida Everblades	ECHL	58	28	17	45	47	1	0	0	0	0
	Lowell	AHL	12	1	2	3	4	....	....	....	....	....

Signed as a free agent by **New Jersey**, July 30, 2003.

MURRAY, Andrew (MUHR-ree, AN-droo) **CBJ**

Center. Shoots left. 6'2", 210 lbs. Born, Selkirk, Man., November 6, 1981.
(Columbus' 11th choice, 242nd overall, in 2001 Entry Draft).

			Regular Season					Playoffs				
Season	Club	League	GP	G	A	TP	PIM	GP	G	A	TP	PIM
2000-01	Selkirk Steelers	MJHL	64	46	56	102	72	5	3	0	3	6
2001-02	Bemidji State	CHA	35	15	15	30	22	....	....	....	....	....
2002-03	Bemidji State	CHA	36	9	18	27	38	....	....	....	....	....

MJHL First All-Star Team (2001) • CHA All-Rookie Team (2002)

MURRAY, Brady (MUHR-ree, BRAY-dee) **L.A.**

Center. Shoots left. 5'9", 165 lbs. Born, Brandon, Man., August 17, 1984.
(Los Angeles' 6th choice, 152nd overall, in 2003 Entry Draft).

			Regular Season					Playoffs				
Season	Club	League	GP	G	A	TP	PIM	GP	G	A	TP	PIM
2001-02	Shat.-St. Mary's	Hi-School	60	58	92	150	50	....	....	....	....	....
2002-03	Salmon Arm	BCHL	59	42	59	101	30	....	....	....	....	....

• Signed Letter of Intent to attend **North Dakota** (WCHA), December 2, 2002.

MURRAY, Doug (MUHR-ree, DUHG) **S.J.**

Defense. Shoots left. 6'3", 245 lbs. Born, Bromma, Sweden, March 12, 1980.
(San Jose's 6th choice, 241st overall, in 1999 Entry Draft).

			Regular Season					Playoffs				
Season	Club	League	GP	G	A	TP	PIM	GP	G	A	TP	PIM
1998-99	NY Apple Core	MJBHL	60	17	47	64	62	....	....	....	....	....
99-2000	Cornell Big Red	ECAC	32	3	6	9	38	....	....	....	....	....
2000-01	Cornell Big Red	ECAC	25	5	13	18	39	....	....	....	....	....
2001-02	Cornell Big Red	ECAC	35	11	21	32	67	....	....	....	....	....
2002-03	Cornell Big Red	ECAC	35	5	20	25	30	....	....	....	....	....

ECAC First All-Star Team (2002, 2003) • NCAA East First All-American Team (2003)

MURRAY, Garth (MUHR-ree, GARTH) **NYR**

Center. Shoots left. 6'1", 205 lbs. Born, Regina, Sask., September 17, 1982.
(NY Rangers' 3rd choice, 79th overall, in 2001 Entry Draft).

			Regular Season					Playoffs				
Season	Club	League	GP	G	A	TP	PIM	GP	G	A	TP	PIM
1997-98	Calgary Buffaloes	AMHL	56	26	34	60	110	....	....	....	....	....
	Regina Pats	WHL	4	0	0	0	2	2	0	0	0	0
1998-99	Regina Pats	WHL	60	3	5	8	101	....	....	....	....	....
99-2000	Regina Pats	WHL	68	14	26	40	155	7	1	1	2	7
2000-01	Regina Pats	WHL	72	28	16	44	183	6	1	1	2	10
2001-02	Regina Pats	WHL	62	33	30	63	154	6	2	3	5	9
	Hartford Wolf Pack	AHL	4	0	0	0	0	9	1	3	4	6
2002-03	Hartford Wolf Pack	AHL	64	10	14	24	121	2	0	0	0	6

NAUROV, Alexander (naw-OO-rawf, ahl-ehx-AN-duhr) **DAL.**

Right wing. Shoots left. 5'11", 191 lbs. Born, Saratov, USSR, March 4, 1985.
(Dallas' 5th choice, 134th overall, in 2003 Entry Draft).

			Regular Season					Playoffs				
Season	Club	League	GP	G	A	TP	PIM	GP	G	A	TP	PIM
2001-02	Yaroslavl Jr.	Russia-Jr.	36	15	18	33	42	....	....	....	....	....
	Yaroslavl 2	Russia-3	12	0	0	0	16	....	....	....	....	....
2002-03	Yaroslavl 2	Russia-3		STATISTICS NOT AVAILABLE								

NEMEC, Ondrej (NEH-mehts, AWN-dray) **PIT.**

Defense. Shoots right. 6'1", 196 lbs. Born, Trebic, Czech., April 18, 1984.
(Pittsburgh's 2nd choice, 35th overall, in 2002 Entry Draft).

			Regular Season					Playoffs				
Season	Club	League	GP	G	A	TP	PIM	GP	G	A	TP	PIM
99-2000	Vsetin Jr.	Czech-Jr.	5	0	2	2	4	....	....	....	....	....
	Vsetin-18	Czech-Jr.	48	6	18	24	62	....	....	....	....	....
2000-01	Vsetin Jr.	Czech-Jr.	42	10	12	22	77	....	....	....	....	....
	Vsetin-18	Czech-Jr.	8	3	7	10	20	....	....	....	....	....
2001-02	Vsetin Jr.	Czech-Jr.	8	4	7	11	47	....	....	....	....	....
	Trebic	Czech-2	9	1	0	1	18	....	....	....	....	....
	Vsetin	Czech	44	5	3	8	79	....	....	....	....	....
2002-03	Vsetin	Czech	39	2	7	9	40	4	0	0	0	2
	SK Trebic	Czech-2	2	0	0	0	6	....	....	....	....	....

NEPRYAYEV, Ivan (neh-pree-YIGH-ehv, IGH-van) **WSH.**

Center. Shoots left. 6'1", 178 lbs. Born, Yaroslavl, USSR, February 4, 1982.
(Washington's 5th choice, 163rd overall, in 2000 Entry Draft).

			Regular Season					Playoffs				
Season	Club	League	GP	G	A	TP	PIM	GP	G	A	TP	PIM
1997-98	Torpedo Yaroslavl	Russia	6	0	0	0	0	....	....	....	....	....
1998-99	Yaroslavl 2	Russia-3	15	1	0	1	0	....	....	....	....	....
99-2000	Yaroslavl 2	Russia-3	40	8	14	22	....	....	....	....	....	....
2000-01	Yaroslavl	Russia	10	0	0	0	2	....	....	....	....	....
2001-02	Yaroslavl 2	Russia-3	2	1	0	1	18	....	....	....	....	....
	Yaroslavl	Russia	36	3	8	11	28	....	....	....	....	....
2002-03	Yaroslavl	Russia	26	3	6	9	12	6	1	0	1	0

NEWBURY, Kris (new-BUHR-ee, KRIHS) **S.J.**

Center. Shoots left. 5'10", 200 lbs. Born, Brampton, Ont., February 19, 1982.
(San Jose's 4th choice, 139th overall, in 2002 Entry Draft).

			Regular Season					Playoffs				
Season	Club	League	GP	G	A	TP	PIM	GP	G	A	TP	PIM
1996-97	Brampton Capitals	OPJHL	28	9	4	13	36	....	....	....	....	....
1997-98	Brampton Capitals	OPJHL	46	11	21	32	161	....	....	....	....	....
1998-99	Belleville Bulls	OHL	51	6	8	14	89	....	....	....	....	....
99-2000	Belleville Bulls	OHL	34	6	18	24	72	....	....	....	....	....
	Sarnia Sting	OHL	27	6	8	14	44	7	0	3	3	16
2000-01	Sarnia Sting	OHL	64	28	30	58	126	4	1	3	4	20
2001-02	Sarnia Sting	OHL	66	42	62	104	141	5	1	3	4	15
2002-03	Sarnia Sting	OHL	64	34	58	92	149	6	4	4	8	16

NEWMAN, Jared (NOO-muhn, JAH-rehd) **CAR.**

Defense. Shoots right. 6'2", 201 lbs. Born, Detroit, MI, March 7, 1982.
(Carolina's 4th choice, 110th overall, in 2000 Entry Draft).

			Regular Season					Playoffs				
Season	Club	League	GP	G	A	TP	PIM	GP	G	A	TP	PIM
1997-98	Det. Compuware	NAJHL	49	1	4	5	69	....	....	....	....	....
1998-99	Plymouth Whalers	OHL	66	2	15	17	57	11	1	2	3	9
99-2000	Plymouth Whalers	OHL	50	1	15	16	123	23	0	5	5	34
2000-01	Plymouth Whalers	OHL	34	0	4	4	114	6	0	3	3	26
2001-02	Plymouth Whalers	OHL	60	2	14	16	106	6	0	1	1	8
2002-03	Florida Everblades	ECHL	29	1	1	2	82	....	....	....	....	....

NICKERSON, Matt (NIH-kuhr-suhn, MAT) **DAL.**

Defense. Shoots right. 6'4", 230 lbs. Born, New Haven, CT, January 11, 1985.
(Dallas' 4th choice, 99th overall, in 2003 Entry Draft).

			Regular Season					Playoffs				
Season	Club	League	GP	G	A	TP	PIM	GP	G	A	TP	PIM
2001-02	Texas Tornado	NAHL	47	1	12	13	97	6	0	0	0	6
2002-03	Texas Tornado	NAHL	47	6	23	29	277	6	0	1	1	*18

• Signed Letter of Intent to attend **U. of Michigan** (CCHA), January 19, 2003.

NIELSEN, Evan (NEEL-suhn, EH-vuhn) **ATL.**

Defense. Shoots right. 6'2", 195 lbs. Born, Evanston, IL, May 28, 1981.
(Atlanta's 11th choice, 242nd overall, in 2000 Entry Draft).

			Regular Season					Playoffs				
Season	Club	League	GP	G	A	TP	PIM	GP	G	A	TP	PIM
1996-97	Evanston High	Hi-School	23	14	17	31	....	....	....	....	....	....
1997-98	Taft Eagles	Hi-School	20	5	12	17	....	....	....	....	....	....
1998-99	Taft Eagles	Hi-School	20	7	5	12	12	....	....	....	....	....
99-2000	U. of Notre Dame	CCHA	48	4	10	14	63	....	....	....	....	....
2000-01	U. of Notre Dame	CCHA	37	2	10	12	54	....	....	....	....	....
2001-02	U. of Notre Dame	CCHA	38	7	13	20	44	....	....	....	....	....
2002-03	U. of Notre Dame	CCHA	40	3	18	21	32	....	....	....	....	....
	Chicago Wolves	AHL	5	1	0	1	4	....	....	....	....	....

NIELSEN, Frans (NEEL-sehn, FRAHNS) **NYI**

Center. Shoots left. 5'11", 172 lbs. Born, Herning, Denmark, April 24, 1984.
(NY Islanders' 2nd choice, 87th overall, in 2002 Entry Draft).

			Regular Season					Playoffs				
Season	Club	League	GP	G	A	TP	PIM	GP	G	A	TP	PIM
99-2000	Herning IK Jr.	Denmark	36	18	16	34	6	....	....	....	....	....
2000-01	Herning IK	Denmark	38	18	19	37	6	....	....	....	....	....
2001-02	Malmo IF	Sweden	20	0	1	1	0	....	....	....	....	....
	Malmo IF Jr.	Swede-Jr.	29	15	27	42	8	7	3	7	10	2
2002-03	Malmo	Sweden	47	3	6	9	10	....	....	....	....	....
	Malmo IF Jr.	Swede-Jr.	2	1	3	4	0	....	....	....	....	....

NIINIMAKI, Jesse (NIH-nee-ma-kee, JEH-see) EDM.

Center. Shoots left. 6'2", 183 lbs. Born, Tampere, Finland, August 19, 1983.
(Edmonton's 1st choice, 15th overall, in 2002 Entry Draft).

			Regular Season					Playoffs				
Season	Club	League	GP	G	A	TP	PIM	GP	G	A	TP	PIM
1998-99	Tappara-C	Finn-Jr.	22	7	22	29	18	4	0	2	2	2
99-2000	Ilves Tampere Jr.	Finn-Jr.	14	0	5	5	6	....	....	....	....	....
2000-01	Ilves Tampere-18	Finn-Jr.	16	3	5	8	40	....	....	....	....	....
	Ilves Tampere Jr.	Finn-Jr.	18	2	4	6	6	....	....	....	....	....
2001-02	Ilves Tampere Jr.	Finn-Jr.	27	9	23	32	54	....	....	....	....	....
	Ilves Tampere	Finland	16	2	4	6	4	3	0	0	0	0
2002-03	Ilves Tampere	Finland	41	4	13	17	12	....	....	....	....	....
	Ilves Tampere Jr.	Finn-Jr.	9	2	7	9	4	....	....	....	....	....
	Sport Vaasa	Finland-2	2	0	1	1	10	....	....	....	....	....

NIKOLOV, Angel (NIH-koh-lohv, AYN-jehl) S.J.

Defense. Shoots left. 6'2", 205 lbs. Born, Most, Czech., November 18, 1975.
(San Jose's 2nd choice, 37th overall, in 1994 Entry Draft).

			Regular Season					Playoffs				
Season	Club	League	GP	G	A	TP	PIM	GP	G	A	TP	PIM
1993-94	Litvinov	Czech	10	2	2	4	....	3	0	0	0	....
1994-95	Litvinov	Czech	41	1	4	5	18	4	0	0	0	27
1995-96	Litvinov	Czech	40	1	7	8	....	10	0	1	1	....
1996-97	Litvinov	Czech	47	0	9	9	44	....	....	....	....	....
1997-98	Litvinov	Czech	51	1	4	5	53	4	0	3	3	27
1998-99	Litvinov	Czech	51	5	12	17	54	....	....	....	....	....
99-2000	Litvinov	Czech	51	6	15	21	32	7	1	2	3	2
2000-01	Litvinov	Czech	48	5	11	16	85	6	0	1	1	6
2001-02	JYP Jyvaskyla	Finland	53	4	16	20	56	....	....	....	....	....
2002-03	JYP Jyvaskyla	Finland	46	2	11	13	54	7	0	3	3	6

NIKULIN, Ilja (nij-KOO-lihn, ihl-YUH) ATL.

Defense. Shoots left. 6'3", 210 lbs. Born, Moscow, USSR, March 12, 1982.
(Atlanta's 2nd choice, 31st overall, in 2000 Entry Draft).

			Regular Season					Playoffs				
Season	Club	League	GP	G	A	TP	PIM	GP	G	A	TP	PIM
1998-99	DynamoMoscow2	Russia-3	23	0	2	2	18	....	....	....	....	....
99-2000	DynamoMoscow2	Russia-3	4	2	1	3	10	....	....	....	....	....
	THC Tver	Russia-2	39	3	6	9	84	....	....	....	....	....
2000-01	Dynamo Moscow	Russia	44	0	4	4	61	....	....	....	....	....
2001-02	DynamoMoscow2	Russia-3	2	0	1	1	2	....	....	....	....	....
	Dynamo Moscow	Russia	47	2	1	3	44	3	0	0	0	0
2002-03	Dynamo Moscow	Russia	40	1	4	5	46	5	0	1	1	4

NILSSON, Magnus (NIHL-suhn, MAG-nuhs) DET.

Right wing. Shoots left. 6'1", 187 lbs. Born, Finspang, Sweden, February 1, 1978.
(Detroit's 5th choice, 144th overall, in 1996 Entry Draft).

			Regular Season					Playoffs				
Season	Club	League	GP	G	A	TP	PIM	GP	G	A	TP	PIM
1995-96	Vita Hasten	Swede-2	28	3	3	6	16	....	....	....	....	....
1996-97	Malmo IF Jr.	Swede-Jr.	14	10	9	19	45	....	....	....	....	....
	Malmo IF	Sweden	12	0	0	0	0	....	....	....	....	....
1997-98	Malmo IF	Sweden	45	6	1	7	6	....	....	....	....	....
1998-99	Malmo IF	Sweden	42	0	0	0	10	4	0	0	0	0
99-2000	Malmo IF	Sweden	44	5	5	10	63	6	0	0	0	25
2000-01	Louisiana	ECHL	68	13	11	24	66	11	3	2	5	8
2001-02	Toledo Storm	ECHL	57	15	20	35	63	....	....	....	....	....
2002-03	Lulea HF	Sweden	47	9	5	14	72	4	0	2	2	2

NILSSON, Mattias (NIHL-suhn, MA-tee-uhs) NSH.

Defense. Shoots left. 6'3", 195 lbs. Born, Ornskoldsvik, Sweden, February 16, 1982.
(Nashville's 3rd choice, 72nd overall, in 2000 Entry Draft).

			Regular Season					Playoffs				
Season	Club	League	GP	G	A	TP	PIM	GP	G	A	TP	PIM
1997-98	MoDo Jr.	Swede-Jr.	40	20	14	34	34	....	....	....	....	....
1998-99	MoDo Jr.	Swede-Jr.	30	7	7	14	26	....	....	....	....	....
99-2000	MoDo Jr.	Swede-Jr.	33	5	5	10	56	2	0	0	0	0
	MoDo-18	Swede-Jr.	7	0	2	2	10	....	....	....	....	....
2000-01	MoDo Jr.	Swede-Jr.	18	2	3	5	62	....	....	....	....	....
2001-02	Hammarby Jr.	Swede-Jr.	25	3	8	11	40	....	....	....	....	....
	Hammarby	Swede-2	20	0	1	1	18	2	1	0	1	0
2002-03	Hammarby	Swede-2	28	2	2	4	41	....	....	....	....	....
	Hammarby Jr.	Swede-Jr.	2	1	0	1	2	....	....	....	....	....

NILSSON, Robert (NIHL-suhn, RAW-buhrt) NYI

Center. Shoots left. 5'11", 176 lbs. Born, Calgary, Alta., January 10, 1985.
(NY Islanders' 1st choice, 15th overall, in 2003 Entry Draft).

			Regular Season					Playoffs				
Season	Club	League	GP	G	A	TP	PIM	GP	G	A	TP	PIM
2000-01	Leksands IF Jr.	Swede-Jr.	23	14	28	42	26	....	....	....	....	....
	Leksands IF-18	Swede-Jr.	4	6	3	9	6	2	0	2	2	2
2001-02	Leksands IF Jr.	Swede-Jr.	21	13	18	31	24	5	0	5	5	8
	Leksands IF	Swede-2	14	1	4	5	8	....	....	....	....	....
2002-03	Leksands IF	Sweden	41	8	13	21	10	5	0	1	1	2
	Leksands IF Jr.	Swede-Jr.	....	....	....	....	....	2	1	1	2	2

NITTEL, Ahren (NIH-tuhl, AH-rehn) N.J.

Left wing. Shoots left. 6'3", 225 lbs. Born, Waterloo, Ont., December 6, 1983.
(New Jersey's 5th choice, 85th overall, in 2002 Entry Draft).

			Regular Season					Playoffs				
Season	Club	League	GP	G	A	TP	PIM	GP	G	A	TP	PIM
99-2000	Streetsville Derbys	OPJHL	11	1	5	6	10	....	....	....	....	....
2000-01	Windsor Spitfires	OHL	46	6	4	10	56	7	3	1	4	16
2001-02	Windsor Spitfires	OHL	52	19	11	30	100	9	4	1	5	23
2002-03	Windsor Spitfires	OHL	22	5	4	9	30	....	....	....	....	....
	Oshawa Generals	OHL	20	15	7	22	25	13	5	2	7	10

NOLAN, Brandon (NOH-lan, BRAN-duhn) VAN.

Center. Shoots left. 6', 180 lbs. Born, Sault Ste. Marie, Ont., July 18, 1983.
(Vancouver's 3rd choice, 111th overall, in 2003 Entry Draft).

			Regular Season					Playoffs				
Season	Club	League	GP	G	A	TP	PIM	GP	G	A	TP	PIM
99-2000	St. Catharines	OJHL-B	47	18	13	31	10	....	....	....	....	....
2000-01	Oshawa Generals	OHL	52	15	23	38	21	....	....	....	....	....
2001-02	Oshawa Generals	OHL	57	30	28	58	78	5	2	4	6	4
2002-03	Oshawa Generals	OHL	68	36	52	88	57	13	10	7	17	4

• Re-entered NHL Entry Draft. Originally New Jersey's 6th choice, 72nd overall, in 2001 Entry Draft.

OHL Second All-Star Team (2003)

NORDGREN, Niklas (NORHD-grehn, NIHK-lahs) CAR.

Left wing. Shoots right. 5'11", 185 lbs. Born, Ornskoldsvik, Sweden, June 28, 1979.
(Carolina's 7th choice, 195th overall, in 1997 Entry Draft).

			Regular Season					Playoffs				
Season	Club	League	GP	G	A	TP	PIM	GP	G	A	TP	PIM
1995-96	MoDo-18	Swede-Jr.	30	37	27	64	....	....	....	....	....	....
1996-97	MoDo Jr.	Swede-Jr.	22	14	6	20	....	....	....	....	....	....
	MoDo	Sweden	5	0	0	0	0	....	....	....	....	....
1997-98	MoDo Jr.	Swede-Jr.	28	15	15	30	52	....	....	....	....	....
1998-99	MoDo	Sweden	7	0	0	0	2	....	....	....	....	....
	MoDo Jr.	Swede-Jr.	22	7	4	11	22	3	2	1	3	0
99-2000	IF Sundsvall	Swede-2	27	21	11	32	58	....	....	....	....	....
	MoDo	EuroHL	1	0	0	0	0	1	0	0	0	0
2000-01	IF Sundsvall	Swede-2	35	22	19	41	45	....	....	....	....	....
2001-02	Timra IK Jr.	Swede-Jr.	1	1	1	2	0	....	....	....	....	....
	Timra IK	Sweden	49	8	6	14	16	....	....	....	....	....
	Timra IK	Swede-Q	10	3	3	5	4	....	....	....	....	....
2002-03	Timra IK	Sweden	47	20	23	43	40	10	1	4	5	4

NORDQVIST, Jonas (NAWRD-kvihst, YOH-nuhs) CHI.

Center. Shoots left. 6'3", 202 lbs. Born, Leksand, Sweden, April 26, 1982.
(Chicago's 3rd choice, 49th overall, in 2000 Entry Draft).

			Regular Season					Playoffs				
Season	Club	League	GP	G	A	TP	PIM	GP	G	A	TP	PIM
1997-98	Leksands IF Jr.	Swede-Jr.	42	26	35	61	....	....	....	....	....	....
1998-99	Leksands IF Jr.	Swede-Jr.	32	14	25	39	....	....	....	....	....	....
99-2000	Leksands IF Jr.	Swede-Jr.	34	15	24	39	32	2	0	0	0	2
	Leksands IF	Sweden	3	0	0	0	0	....	....	....	....	....
	Leksands IF-18	Swede-Jr.	2	0	2	2	0	4	3	5	8	0
2000-01	Leksands IF Jr.	Swede-Jr.	10	6	13	19	6	5	1	6	7	2
	Leksands IF	Sweden	42	3	4	7	4	....	....	....	....	....
2001-02	Leksands IF Jr.	Swede-Jr.	8	14	7	21	6	1	0	1	1	0
	Leksands IF	Swede-2	40	8	7	15	16	....	....	....	....	....
2002-03	Rogle	Swede-2	27	12	19	32	4	....	....	....	....	....
	Rogle	Swede-Q	14	4	2	6	4	10	2	1	3	4

NOVAK, Filip (NOH-vak, FIH-lihp) FLA.

Defense. Shoots left. 6'1", 185 lbs. Born, Ceske Budejovice, Czech., May 7, 1982.
(NY Rangers' 1st choice, 64th overall, in 2000 Entry Draft).

			Regular Season					Playoffs				
Season	Club	League	GP	G	A	TP	PIM	GP	G	A	TP	PIM
1998-99	C. Budejovice Jr.	Czech-Jr.	68	8	10	18	34	....	....	....	....	....
99-2000	Regina Pats	WHL	47	7	32	39	70	7	1	4	5	5
2000-01	Regina Pats	WHL	64	17	50	67	75	6	1	4	5	6
2001-02	Regina Pats	WHL	60	12	46	58	125	6	2	2	4	19
2002-03	San Antonio	AHL	57	10	17	27	79	1	0	0	0	0

WHL East Second All-Star Team (2001) • WHL East First All-Star Team (2002) • AHL All-Rookie Team (2003)

Traded to **Florida** by **NY Rangers** with Igor Ulanov, NY Rangers' 1st (later traded to Calgary – Calgary selected Eric Nystrom) and 2nd (Rob Globke) round choices in 2002 Entry Draft and NY Rangers' 4th round choice (later traded to Atlanta – Atlanta selected Guillaume Desbiens) in 2003 Entry Draft for Pavel Bure and Florida's 2nd round choice (Lee Falardeau) in 2002 Entry Draft, March 18, 2002.

NOVAK, Zbynek (NOH-vahk, z'BIHN-nehk) WSH.

Left wing. Shoots left. 6'2", 194 lbs. Born, Kutna Hora, Czech., July 23, 1983.
(Washington's 5th choice, 191st overall, in 2001 Entry Draft).

			Regular Season					Playoffs				
Season	Club	League	GP	G	A	TP	PIM	GP	G	A	TP	PIM
99-2000	HC Slavia Praha Jr.	Czech-Jr.	15	1	2	3	8	2	1	0	1	0
	HC Slavia Praha-18	Czech-Jr.	31	14	12	26	12	....	....	....	....	....
2000-01	HC Slavia Praha Jr.	Czech-Jr.	44	10	8	18	24	3	1	0	1	2
2001-02	HC Slavia Praha-18	Czech-Jr.	3	1	0	1	2	....	....	....	....	....
	HC Slavia Praha Jr.	Czech-Jr.	23	11	12	23	8	....	....	....	....	....
	HC Slavia Praha	Czech	27	0	1	1	2	....	....	....	....	....
	HC Brod	Czech-3	5	0	2	2	0	2	1	0	1	2
2002-03	Beroun	Czech-2	30	4	7	11	14	....	....	....	....	....
	HC Slavia Praha	Czech	10	1	0	1	0	6	0	0	0	0
	HC Slavia Praha Jr.	Czech-Jr.	3	1	1	2	2	2	1	0	1	4

NOVOTNY, Jiri (NOH-vaht-nee, YOO-ree) BUF.

Center. Shoots right. 6'2", 194 lbs. Born, Pelhrimov, Czech., August 12, 1983.
(Buffalo's 1st choice, 22nd overall, in 2001 Entry Draft).

			Regular Season					Playoffs				
Season	Club	League	GP	G	A	TP	PIM	GP	G	A	TP	PIM
99-2000	C. Budejovice Jr.	Czech-Jr.	36	11	10	21	6	....	....	....	....	....
	C. Budejovice-18	Czech-Jr.	11	5	7	12	4	....	....	....	....	....
	HC Slezan Opava	Czech-2	17	2	2	4	6	....	....	....	....	....
2000-01	C. Budejovice Jr.	Czech-Jr.	33	10	10	20	....	....	....	....	....	....
	SHC Hradec	Czech-3	1	0	0	0	0	....	....	....	....	....
2001-02	C. Budejovice Jr.	Czech-Jr.	7	4	4	8	4	....	....	....	....	....
	Jindrichuv Hradec	Czech-3	3	1	3	4	0	....	....	....	....	....
	Ceske Budejovice	Czech	41	8	6	14	6	....	....	....	....	....
2002-03	Rochester	AHL	43	2	9	11	14	3	0	1	1	10

NOWAK, Brett (NOH-wak, BREHT) BOS.

Center. Shoots left. 6'2", 192 lbs. Born, New Haven, CT, May 20, 1981.
(Boston's 7th choice, 102nd overall, in 2000 Entry Draft).

			Regular Season					Playoffs				
Season	Club	League	GP	G	A	TP	PIM	GP	G	A	TP	PIM
1997-98	Hotchkiss High	Hi-School	21	24	42	66	42	....	....	....	....	....
1998-99	Hotchkiss High	Hi-School	20	21	36	57	6	....	....	....	....	....
99-2000	Harvard Crimson	ECAC	26	6	11	17	20	....	....	....	....	....
2000-01	Harvard Crimson	ECAC	24	7	9	16	26	....	....	....	....	....
2001-02	Harvard Crimson	ECAC	33	14	17	31	50	....	....	....	....	....
2002-03	Harvard Crimson	ECAC	33	12	29	41	57	....	....	....	....	....

ECAC Second All-Star Team (2002)

NUSSLI, Thomas (NEWS-lee, TAW-muhs) VAN.

Right wing. Shoots left. 6'2", 207 lbs. Born, Nesskin, Switz., March 12, 1982.
(Vancouver's 10th choice, 277th overall, in 2002 Entry Draft).

			Regular Season					Playoffs				
Season	Club	League	GP	G	A	TP	PIM	GP	G	A	TP	PIM
1998-99	HC Herisau Jr.	Swiss-Jr.	33	30	15	45	24	....	....	....	....	....
	SC Herisau	Swiss-2	5	1	0	1	0	3	1	0	1	0
99-2000	EV Zug	Swiss	2	0	0	0	0	....	....	....	....	....
	EV Zug Jr.	Swiss-Jr.	33	14	18	32	99	2	1	1	2	8
	EV Zug	Swiss	2	0	0	0	0	....	....	....	....	....
2000-01	EHC Basel	Swiss-2	6	1	2	3	6	....	....	....	....	....
	EV Zug Jr.	Swiss-Jr.	9	7	7	14	30	....	....	....	....	....
	EV Zug	Swiss	34	6	2	8	10	4	0	0	0	2
2001-02	EV Zug Jr.	Swiss-Jr.	1	0	1	1	0	....	....	....	....	....
	EV Zug	Swiss	19	2	2	4	8	....	....	....	....	....
	EHC Basel	Swiss-2	15	3	1	4	70	....	....	....	....	....
	Rapperswil	Swiss-2	....	....	....	....	....	5	1	1	2	2
2002-03	Rapperswil	Swiss	40	6	5	11	43	6	0	0	0	4

NYCHOLAT, Lawrence (NIH-coh-lat, LAW-rehnts) NYR

Defense. Shoots left. 6', 192 lbs. Born, Calgary, Alta., May 7, 1979.

			Regular Season					Playoffs				
Season	Club	League	GP	G	A	TP	PIM	GP	G	A	TP	PIM
1995-96	Notre Dame Argos	SMHL	42	10	36	46	66	....	....	....	....	....
1996-97	Swift Current	WHL	67	8	13	21	82	10	0	0	0	24
1997-98	Swift Current	WHL	71	13	35	48	108	1	0	0	0	0
1998-99	Swift Current	WHL	72	16	44	60	125	6	2	2	4	12
99-2000	Swift Current	WHL	70	22	58	80	92	2	0	0	0	0
2000-01	Jackson Bandits	ECHL	5	1	2	3	5	....	....	....	....	....
	Cleveland	IHL	42	3	7	10	69	4	0	0	0	2
2001-02	Houston Aeros	AHL	72	3	11	14	92	14	1	0	1	23
2002-03	Houston Aeros	AHL	66	11	28	39	155	....	....	....	....	....
	Hartford Wolf Pack	AHL	15	2	9	11	6	2	2	0	2	0

Signed as a free agent by **Minnesota**, August 31, 2000. Traded to **NY Rangers** by **Minnesota** for Johan Holmqvist, March 11, 2003.

NYSTROM, David (NEW-strawm, DAY-vihd) PHI.

Left wing. Shoots right. 6', 174 lbs. Born, Hagersten, Sweden, February 21, 1980.
(Philadelphia's 6th choice, 224th overall, in 1999 Entry Draft).

			Regular Season					Playoffs				
Season	Club	League	GP	G	A	TP	PIM	GP	G	A	TP	PIM
1996-97	V. Frolunda Jr.	Swede-Jr.	23	6	2	8	....	....	....	....	....	....
1997-98	V. Frolunda Jr.	Swede-Jr.	29	17	18	35	26	2	0	0	0	0
1998-99	V. Frolunda Jr.	Swede-Jr.	28	15	16	31	20	....	....	....	....	....
99-2000	IF Troja-Ljungby	Swede-2	45	20	15	35	34	2	0	0	0	0
2000-01	IF Troja-Ljungby	Swede-2	38	20	11	31	30	4	0	0	0	0
2001-02	Skelleftea AIK	Swede-2	45	4	5	9	16	6	0	0	0	4
2002-03	Halmstad	Swede-2	39	13	12	25	47	....	....	....	....	....

NYSTROM, Eric (NIGH-stuhm, AIR-ihk) CGY.

Left wing. Shoots left. 6'1", 195 lbs. Born, Syosset, NY, February 14, 1983.
(Calgary's 1st choice, 10th overall, in 2002 Entry Draft).

			Regular Season					Playoffs				
Season	Club	League	GP	G	A	TP	PIM	GP	G	A	TP	PIM
1998-99	Nassau Lions	NYAHA	STATISTICS NOT AVAILABLE									
99-2000	U.S. National U-17	USDP	55	7	16	23	57	....	....	....	....	....
2000-01	U.S. National U-18	USDP	66	15	17	32	102	....	....	....	....	....
2001-02	U. of Michigan	CCHA	40	18	13	31	42	....	....	....	....	....
2002-03	U. of Michigan	CCHA	39	15	11	26	24	....	....	....	....	....

CCHA All-Rookie Team (2002)

O'BRIEN, Doug (oh-BRIGH-uhn, DUHG) T.B.

Defense. Shoots left. 6'1", 200 lbs. Born, St. John'S, Nfld., February 16, 1984.
(Tampa Bay's 4th choice, 192nd overall, in 2003 Entry Draft).

			Regular Season					Playoffs				
Season	Club	League	GP	G	A	TP	PIM	GP	G	A	TP	PIM
2001-02	Hull Olympiques	QMJHL	46	1	5	6	36	12	0	0	0	14
2002-03	Hull Olympiques	QMJHL	71	10	34	44	102	19	3	12	15	18

O'BYRNE, Ryan (oh-BUHRN, RIGH-uhn) MTL.

Defense. Shoots right. 6'5", 210 lbs. Born, Victoria, B.C., July 19, 1984.
(Montreal's 4th choice, 79th overall, in 2003 Entry Draft).

			Regular Season					Playoffs				
Season	Club	League	GP	G	A	TP	PIM	GP	G	A	TP	PIM
2001-02	Victoria Salsa	BCHL	52	2	9	11	91	....	....	....	....	....
2002-03	Victoria Salsa	BCHL	32	3	6	9	94	....	....	....	....	....
	Nanaimo Clippers	BCHL	9	2	4	6	24	....	....	....	....	....

• Signed Letter of Intent to attend **Cornell** (ECAC), February 19, 2003.

O'CONNOR, Sean (oh-KAW-nuhr, SHAWN) FLA.

Right wing. Shoots right. 6'3", 220 lbs. Born, Victoria, B.C., October 19, 1981.
(Florida's 3rd choice, 82nd overall, in 2000 Entry Draft).

			Regular Season					Playoffs				
Season	Club	League	GP	G	A	TP	PIM	GP	G	A	TP	PIM
1995-96	Victoria Racquet	BCAHA	60	23	45	68	70	....	....	....	....	....
1996-97	Victoria Racquet	BCAHA	50	59	73	132	190	....	....	....	....	....
1997-98	Victoria Salsa	BCHL	50	9	17	26	145	....	....	....	....	....
1998-99	Victoria Salsa	BCHL	53	17	18	35	197	....	....	....	....	....
99-2000	Moose Jaw	WHL	51	5	8	13	166	2	0	0	0	2
2000-01	Moose Jaw	WHL	71	34	15	49	192	4	0	1	1	15
2001-02	Moose Jaw	WHL	62	15	19	34	135	12	0	3	3	4
2002-03	San Antonio	AHL	8	0	0	0	4	1	0	0	0	0
	Jackson Bandits	ECHL	49	12	11	23	149	1	0	0	0	0

ODUYA, John (oh-DOO-yuh, JAWN) WSH.

Defense. Shoots left. 6', 200 lbs. Born, Stockholm, Sweden, October 1, 1981.
(Washington's 6th choice, 221st overall, in 2001 Entry Draft).

			Regular Season					Playoffs				
Season	Club	League	GP	G	A	TP	PIM	GP	G	A	TP	PIM
1997-98	Hammarby Jr.	Swede-Jr.	26	3	11	14	70	....	....	....	....	....
1998-99	Hammarby Jr.	Swede-Jr.	38	14	31	45	45	....	....	....	....	....
99-2000	Hammarby Jr.	Swede-Jr.	32	3	18	21	48	6	1	2	3	4
	Hammarby	Swede-2	1	0	0	0	0	1	0	0	0	0
2000-01	Moncton Wildcats	QMJHL	44	11	38	49	147	....	....	....	....	....
	Victoriaville Tigres	QMJHL	24	3	16	19	112	13	4	9	13	10
2001-02	Hammarby	Swede-2	46	11	14	25	66	2	1	0	1	4
2002-03	Hammarby	Swede-2	48	15	25	40	200	....	....	....	....	....

OLSON, Josh (OHL-suhn, JAWSH) FLA.

Left wing. Shoots left. 6'5", 225 lbs. Born, Grand Forks, ND, July 13, 1981.
(Florida's 6th choice, 190th overall, in 2000 Entry Draft).

			Regular Season					Playoffs				
Season	Club	League	GP	G	A	TP	PIM	GP	G	A	TP	PIM
1998-99	Fargo-Moorhead	USHL	11	2	2	4	8	....	....	....	....	....
99-2000	Fargo-Moorhead	USHL	18	2	5	7	37	....	....	....	....	....
	Omaha Lancers	USHL	43	6	7	13	44	4	0	0	0	4
2000-01	Portland	WHL	72	22	38	60	86	16	5	4	9	17
2001-02	Utah Grizzlies	AHL	1	0	0	0	0	1	0	0	0	0
	Portland	WHL	72	40	48	88	85	7	4	3	7	8
2002-03	San Antonio	AHL	23	0	1	1	14	....	....	....	....	....
	Jackson Bandits	ECHL	39	10	17	27	13	1	0	1	1	0

OLSSON, Kalle (OHL-suhn, KAL-ay) EDM.

Right wing. Shoots left. 6', 183 lbs. Born, Munkedal, Sweden, January 31, 1985.
(Edmonton's 6th choice, 147th overall, in 2003 Entry Draft).

			Regular Season					Playoffs				
Season	Club	League	GP	G	A	TP	PIM	GP	G	A	TP	PIM
2000-01	Lysekils HK Viking	Sweden-4	30	5	5	10	12	....	....	....	....	....
2001-02	V. Frolunda Jr.	Swede-Jr.	35	10	10	20	10	8	1	5	6	4
2002-03	V. Frolunda Jr.	Swede-Jr.	30	22	13	35	18	6	4	3	7	4

OREKHOVSKY, Oleg (oh-reh-KHOHV-skee, OH-lehg) MIN.

Defense. Shoots right. 6', 180 lbs. Born, Krasnoyarsk, USSR, November 3, 1977.
(Washington's 11th choice, 206th overall, in 1996 Entry Draft).

			Regular Season					Playoffs				
Season	Club	League	GP	G	A	TP	PIM	GP	G	A	TP	PIM
1994-95	Dynamo Moscow	CIS	30	0	1	1	18	....	....	....	....	....
1995-96	Dynamo Moscow	CIS	22	1	2	3	14	8	0	0	0	6
1996-97	Dynamo Moscow	Russia	32	4	2	6	16	4	2	1	3	2
1997-98	Dynamo Moscow	EuroHL	7	2	1	3	12	....	....	....	....	....
	Dynamo Moscow	Russia	40	4	5	9	34	....	....	....	....	....
1998-99	Dynamo Moscow	EuroHL	3	1	1	2	2	6	0	0	0	6
	Dynamo Moscow	Russia	42	1	1	2	22	16	1	2	3	6
99-2000	Dynamo Moscow	EuroHL	6	1	0	1	2	....	....	....	....	....
	Dynamo Moscow	Russia	37	3	6	9	38	15	1	0	1	4
2000-01	Dynamo Moscow	Russia	40	2	4	6	44	....	....	....	....	....
2001-02	Dynamo Moscow	Russia	50	2	15	17	50	3	1	0	1	2
2002-03	Dynamo Moscow	Russia	38	1	4	5	20	5	0	1	1	4

Selected by **Minnesota** from **Washington** in Expansion Draft, June 23, 2000.

ORLOV, Maxim (ohr-LAHF, max-EEM) WSH.

Center. Shoots left. 6', 176 lbs. Born, Moscow, USSR, March 31, 1981.
(Washington's 9th choice, 219th overall, in 1999 Entry Draft).

			Regular Season					Playoffs				
Season	Club	League	GP	G	A	TP	PIM	GP	G	A	TP	PIM
1998-99	CSKA Moscow	Russia	2	0	0	0	2	1	0	0	0	0
99-2000	CSKA Moscow	Russia	25	0	0	0	2	2	0	0	0	2
2000-01	CSKA Moscow	Russia	41	5	4	9	14	....	....	....	....	....
2001-02	CSKA Moscow 2	Russia-3	7	7	4	11	4	....	....	....	....	....
	CSKA Moscow	Russia	35	3	5	8	14	....	....	....	....	....
2002-03	MGU-Pingviny	Russia-3	2	0	0	0	0	....	....	....	....	....
	Leninogorsk	Russia-2	25	3	8	11	24	....	....	....	....	....

ORR, Colton (OHR, KOHL-tuhn) BOS.

Right wing. Shoots right. 6'3", 210 lbs. Born, Winnipeg, Man., March 3, 1982.

			Regular Season					Playoffs				
Season	Club	League	GP	G	A	TP	PIM	GP	G	A	TP	PIM
1998-99	Swift Current	WHL	2	0	0	0	0	....	....	....	....	....
99-2000	Swift Current	WHL	61	3	2	5	130	12	1	0	1	25
2000-01	Swift Current	WHL	19	0	4	4	67	....	....	....	....	....
	Kamloops Blazers	WHL	41	8	1	9	179	3	0	0	0	20
2001-02	Kamloops Blazers	WHL	1	0	0	0	7	2	0	0	0	2
2002-03	Kamloops Blazers	WHL	3	2	0	2	17	....	....	....	....	....
	Regina Pats	WHL	37	6	2	8	170	3	0	0	0	19
	Providence Bruins	AHL	1	0	0	0	7	....	....	....	....	....

Signed as a free agent by **Boston**, September 19, 2001. • Missed majority of 2001-02 season recovering from wrist injury suffered in game vs. Red Deer (WHL), October 20, 2001.

ORTMEYER, Jed (OHRT-migh-uhr, JEHD) NYR

Center. Shoots right. 6'1", 186 lbs. Born, Omaha, NE, September 3, 1978.

			Regular Season					Playoffs				
Season	Club	League	GP	G	A	TP	PIM	GP	G	A	TP	PIM
1997-98	Omaha Lancers	USHL	54	23	25	48	52	14	3	4	7	31
1998-99	Omaha Lancers	USHL	52	23	36	59	81	12	5	6	11	16
99-2000	U. of Michigan	CCHA	41	8	16	24	40	....	....	....	....	....
2000-01	U. of Michigan	CCHA	27	10	11	21	52	....	....	....	....	....
2001-02	U. of Michigan	CCHA	41	15	23	38	40	....	....	....	....	....
2002-03	U. of Michigan	CCHA	36	18	16	34	48	....	....	....	....	....

Signed as a free agent by **NY Rangers**, May 10, 2003.

O'SULLIVAN, Patrick (oh-SUHL-ih-van, PAT-rihk) MIN.

Center. Shoots left. 5'11", 190 lbs. Born, Winston Salem, NC, February 1, 1985.
(Minnesota's 2nd choice, 56th overall, in 2003 Entry Draft).

			Regular Season					Playoffs				
Season	Club	League	GP	G	A	TP	PIM	GP	G	A	TP	PIM
99-2000	Strathroy Rockets	OJHL-B	STATISTICS NOT AVAILABLE									
2000-01	U.S. National U-17	USDP	64	30	45	75	69	....	....	....	....	....
2001-02	Mississauga	OHL	68	34	58	92	61	....	....	....	....	....
	U.S. National U-18	USDP	1	1	0	1	2	....	....	....	....	....
2002-03	Mississauga	OHL	56	40	41	81	57	5	2	9	11	18

OTTOSSON, Kristofer (AW-toh-suhn, KRIHS-tuh-fuhr) NYI

Right wing. Shoots left. 5'10", 187 lbs. Born, Stockholm, Sweden, January 9, 1976.
(NY Islanders' 6th choice, 148th overall, in 2000 Entry Draft).

			Regular Season					Playoffs				
Season	Club	League	GP	G	A	TP	PIM	GP	G	A	TP	PIM
1993-94	Djurgarden Jr.	Swede-Jr.	13	3	6	9	4	....	....	....	....	....
1994-95	Djurgarden Jr.	Swede-Jr.	15	8	23	31	2	....	....	....	....	....
	Djurgarden	Sweden	30	0	0	0	2	3	0	0	0	0
1995-96	Djurgarden Jr.	Swede-Jr.	15	5	12	17	4	....	....	....	....	....
	Djurgarden	Sweden	32	1	0	1	2	2	0	0	0	0
1996-97	Djurgarden Jr.	Swede-Jr.	2	1	1	2	0	....	....	....	....	....
	Arlanda Mastra	Swede-2	6	6	0	6	0	....	....	....	....	....
	Djurgarden	Sweden	20	0	0	0	2	....	....	....	....	....
	Huddinge IK	Swede-2	13	1	3	4	2	2	0	1	1	0
1997-98	Huddinge IK	Swede-2	16	10	13	23	6	14	7	7	14	8
1998-99	Huddinge IK	Swede-2	27	12	17	29	14	14	3	2	5	2
	Djurgarden	EuroHL	1	0	0	0	0	....	....	....	....	....
99-2000	Djurgarden	Sweden	47	25	15	40	12	13	7	2	9	2
2000-01	Djurgarden	Sweden	46	17	24	41	14	14	*7	4	11	4
2001-02	Djurgarden	Sweden	41	13	8	21	12	4	0	0	0	0
2002-03	Djurgarden	Sweden	46	19	19	38	30	12	1	4	5	0

OUELLET, Michel (oo-LEHT, mih-SHEHL) PIT.

Right wing. Shoots right. 6', 201 lbs. Born, Rimouski, Que., March 5, 1982.
(Pittsburgh's 4th choice, 124th overall, in 2000 Entry Draft).

			Regular Season					Playoffs				
Season	Club	League	GP	G	A	TP	PIM	GP	G	A	TP	PIM
1997-98	Jonquiere Elites	QAAA	33	20	32	52	52	....	....	....	....	....
1998-99	Rimouski Oceanic	QMJHL	28	7	13	20	10	11	0	1	1	6
99-2000	Rimouski Oceanic	QMJHL	72	36	53	89	38	14	4	5	9	14
2000-01	Rimouski Oceanic	QMJHL	63	42	50	92	50	11	6	7	13	8
2001-02	Rimouski Oceanic	QMJHL	61	40	58	98	66	7	3	6	9	4
2002-03	Wheeling Nailers	ECHL	55	20	26	46	40	....	....	....	....	....
	Wilkes-Barre	AHL	4	0	2	2	0	....	....	....	....	....

OULAHEN, Ryan (OO-la-hehn, RIGH-uhn) DET.

Center. Shoots left. 6'1", 180 lbs. Born, Newmarket, Ont., March 26, 1985.
(Detroit's 3rd choice, 164th overall, in 2003 Entry Draft).

			Regular Season					Playoffs				
Season	Club	League	GP	G	A	TP	PIM	GP	G	A	TP	PIM
2000-01	Wexford Raiders	OMHA	66	38	58	96	18	....	....	....	....	....
2001-02	Newmarket	OPJHL	48	18	17	35	4	....	....	....	....	....
2002-03	Brampton	OHL	61	21	22	43	6	11	2	1	3	2

OYSTRICK, Nathan (OI-strihk, NAY-thun) ATL.

Defense. Shoots left. 5'11", 195 lbs. Born, Regina, Sask., December 17, 1982.
(Atlanta's 7th choice, 198th overall, in 2002 Entry Draft).

			Regular Season					Playoffs				
Season	Club	League	GP	G	A	TP	PIM	GP	G	A	TP	PIM
99-2000	Reg. Pat Canadiens	SMHL	43	6	22	28	214	....	....	....	....	....
2000-01	South Surrey	BCHL	STATISTICS NOT AVAILABLE									
2001-02	South Surrey	BCHL	50	15	42	57	142	....	....	....	....	....
2002-03	Northern Michigan	CCHA	34	2	10	12	26	....	....	....	....	....

PACKARD, Dennis (PA-kuhrd, DEH-nihs) T.B.

Left wing. Shoots left. 6'4", 195 lbs. Born, St. Catherines, Ont., February 9, 1982.
(Tampa Bay's 8th choice, 219th overall, in 2001 Entry Draft).

			Regular Season					Playoffs				
Season	Club	League	GP	G	A	TP	PIM	GP	G	A	TP	PIM
99-2000	U.S. National U-18	USDP	55	11	14	25	85	....	....	....	....	....
2000-01	Harvard Crimson	ECAC	33	4	4	8	28	....	....	....	....	....
2001-02	Harvard Crimson	ECAC	32	9	10	19	34	....	....	....	....	....
2002-03	Harvard Crimson	ECAC	30	8	8	16	32	....	....	....	....	....

PADDOCK, Cam (PA-dawk, KAM) PIT.

Center. Shoots right. 6'1", 185 lbs. Born, Vancouver, B.C., March 22, 1983.
(Pittsburgh's 6th choice, 137th overall, in 2002 Entry Draft).

			Regular Season					Playoffs				
Season	Club	League	GP	G	A	TP	PIM	GP	G	A	TP	PIM
99-2000	Kelowna Rockets	WHL	46	5	5	10	42	5	0	0	0	0
2000-01	Kelowna Rockets	WHL	72	14	10	24	110	6	0	0	0	4
2001-02	Kelowna Rockets	WHL	72	38	35	73	122	15	8	6	14	35
2002-03	Kelowna Rockets	WHL	71	33	26	59	107	19	11	8	19	18

PAETSCH, Nathan (PASH, NAY-thuhn) BUF.

Defense. Shoots left. 6', 195 lbs. Born, Humboldt, Sask., March 30, 1983.
(Buffalo's 8th choice, 202nd overall, in 2003 Entry Draft).

			Regular Season					Playoffs				
Season	Club	League	GP	G	A	TP	PIM	GP	G	A	TP	PIM
1998-99	Tisdale Trojans	SMHL	74	20	55	75	120	....	....	....	....	....
	Moose Jaw	WHL	2	0	0	0	0	....	....	....	....	....
99-2000	Moose Jaw	WHL	68	9	35	44	49	4	0	1	1	0
2000-01	Moose Jaw	WHL	70	8	54	62	118	4	1	2	3	6
2001-02	Moose Jaw	WHL	59	16	36	52	86	12	0	4	4	16
2002-03	Moose Jaw	WHL	59	15	39	54	81	13	3	10	13	6

• Re-entered NHL Entry Draft. Originally Washington's 1st choice, 58th overall, in 2001 Entry Draft.

WHL East Second All-Star Team (2003)

PAILLE, Dan (PIGH-yay, DAN) BUF.

Left wing. Shoots left. 6', 200 lbs. Born, Welland, Ont., April 15, 1984.
(Buffalo's 2nd choice, 20th overall, in 2002 Entry Draft).

			Regular Season					Playoffs				
Season	Club	League	GP	G	A	TP	PIM	GP	G	A	TP	PIM
99-2000	Welland Cougars	OJHL-B	42	14	17	31	19	16	16	16	32	....
2000-01	Guelph Storm	OHL	64	22	31	53	57	4	2	0	2	2
2001-02	Guelph Storm	OHL	62	27	30	57	54	9	5	2	7	9
2002-03	Guelph Storm	OHL	54	30	27	57	28	11	8	6	14	6

PANDOLFO, Mike (pan-DAHL-foh, MIGHK) CBJ

Left wing. Shoots left. 6'3", 221 lbs. Born, Winchester, MA, September 15, 1979.
(Buffalo's 5th choice, 77th overall, in 1998 Entry Draft).

			Regular Season					Playoffs				
Season	Club	League	GP	G	A	TP	PIM	GP	G	A	TP	PIM
1996-97	St. Sebastian's	Hi-School	32	27	28	55	30	....	....	....	....	....
1997-98	St. Sebastian's	Hi-School	28	29	23	52	18	....	....	....	....	....
1998-99	Boston University	H-East	34	13	4	17	26	....	....	....	....	....
99-2000	Boston University	H-East	41	13	10	23	37	....	....	....	....	....
2000-01	Boston University	H-East	37	16	13	29	30	....	....	....	....	....
2001-02	Boston University	H-East	38	22	18	40	22	....	....	....	....	....
2002-03	Syracuse Crunch	AHL	74	9	9	18	31	....	....	....	....	....

Rights traded to **Columbus** by **Buffalo** with Detroit's 1st round choice (previously acquired, later traded to Atlanta – Atlanta selected Jim Slater) in 2002 Entry Draft for New Jersey's 1st round choice (previously acquired, Buffalo selected Dan Paille) in 2002 Entry Draft, June 22, 2002.

PANOV, Konstantin (PAN-ahv, KAWN-stan-tihn) NSH.

Left wing. Shoots left. 6', 195 lbs. Born, Chelyabinsk, USSR, June 29, 1980.
(Nashville's 10th choice, 131st overall, in 1999 Entry Draft).

			Regular Season					Playoffs				
Season	Club	League	GP	G	A	TP	PIM	GP	G	A	TP	PIM
1996-97	Chelyabinsk 2	Russia-3	25	18	30	48	22	....	....	....	....	....
1997-98	Yunior-T Kurgan	Russia-3	20	7	3	10	6	....	....	....	....	....
	Chelyabinsk	Russia	6	2	0	2	4	2	0	0	0	0
1998-99	Kamloops Blazers	WHL	62	33	30	63	62	13	5	3	8	10
99-2000	Kamloops Blazers	WHL	64	43	30	73	47	....	....	....	....	....
2000-01	Kamloops Blazers	WHL	69	44	56	100	54	4	1	0	1	2
2001-02	Milwaukee	AHL	15	1	5	6	2	....	....	....	....	....
2002-03	Milwaukee	AHL	67	11	20	31	30	2	0	0	0	0
	Toledo Storm	ECHL	2	1	0	1	0	....	....	....	....	....

WHL West Second All-Star Team (2000) • WHL West First All-Star Team (2001)

PANZER, Jeff (PAN-zuhr, JEHF) ST.L.

Center. Shoots left. 5'7", 160 lbs. Born, Grand Forks, ND, April 7, 1978.

			Regular Season					Playoffs				
Season	Club	League	GP	G	A	TP	PIM	GP	G	A	TP	PIM
1996-97	Fargo-Moorhead	USHL	49	30	40	70	52	6	3	7	10	0
1997-98	North Dakota	WCHA	37	14	23	37	18	....	....	....	....	....
1998-99	North Dakota	WCHA	37	21	26	47	14	....	....	....	....	....
99-2000	North Dakota	WCHA	44	19	*44	63	16	....	....	....	....	....
2000-01	North Dakota	WCHA	46	26	*55	*81	28	....	....	....	....	....
2001-02	Worcester IceCats	AHL	70	26	27	53	29	3	0	2	2	0
2002-03	Worcester IceCats	AHL	80	22	32	54	36	3	1	1	2	0

WCHA Second All-Star Team (1999) • WCHA First All-Star Team (2000, 2001) • NCAA West First All-American Team (2000, 2001)

Signed as a free agent by **St. Louis**, April 30, 2001.

PARADISE, Chris (PAIR-a-dighz, KRIHS) BOS.

Center. Shoots right. 6'2", 200 lbs. Born, St. Paul, MN, August 6, 1977.

			Regular Season					Playoffs				
Season	Club	League	GP	G	A	TP	PIM	GP	G	A	TP	PIM
1996-97	Twin Cities	USHL	53	16	21	37	92	5	1	0	1	28
1997-98	Omaha Lancers	USHL	55	23	22	45	65	14	*11	5	16	6
1998-99	U. of Denver	WCHA	32	5	4	9	31	....	....	....	....	....
99-2000	U. of Denver	WCHA	40	4	19	23	46	....	....	....	....	....
2000-01	U. of Denver	WCHA	38	17	16	33	50	....	....	....	....	....
2001-02	U. of Denver	WCHA	40	22	19	41	40	....	....	....	....	....
2002-03	Atlantic City	ECHL	14	5	2	7	12	....	....	....	....	....
	Providence Bruins	AHL	46	4	7	11	53	....	....	....	....	....

Signed as a free agent by **Boston**, August 6, 2002.

PARENTEAU, Pierre (pair-ehn-TOH, PEE-air) ANA.

Center. Shoots right. 5'11", 156 lbs. Born, Hull, Que., March 24, 1983.
(Anaheim's 11th choice, 264th overall, in 2001 Entry Draft).

			Regular Season					Playoffs				
Season	Club	League	GP	G	A	TP	PIM	GP	G	A	TP	PIM
99-2000	Charles-Lemoyne	QAAA	40	25	40	65	18	16	4	9	13	8
2000-01	Moncton Wildcats	QMJHL	45	10	19	29	38	....	....	....	....	....
	Chicoutimi	QMJHL	28	10	13	23	14	7	4	7	11	2
2001-02	Chicoutimi	QMJHL	68	51	67	118	120	4	3	1	4	10
2002-03	Chicoutimi	QMJHL	31	20	35	55	56	....	....	....	....	....
	Sherbrooke	QMJHL	28	13	35	48	84	12	8	11	19	6

PARISE, Zach (pah-REE-say, ZAK) N.J.

Center. Shoots left. 5'11", 186 lbs. Born, Minneapolis, MN, July 28, 1984.
(New Jersey's 1st choice, 17th overall, in 2003 Entry Draft).

			Regular Season					Playoffs				
Season	Club	League	GP	G	A	TP	PIM	GP	G	A	TP	PIM
2000-01	Shat.-St. Mary's	Hi-School	58	69	93	162	....	....	....	....	....	....
2001-02	Shat.-St. Mary's	Hi-School	67	77	101	178	58	....	....	....	....	....
	U.S. National U-18	USDP	12	7	7	14	6	....	....	....	....	....
2002-03	North Dakota	WCHA	39	26	35	61	34	....	....	....	....	....

WCHA All-Rookie Team (2003)

PAROULEK, Martin (PAHR-oh-lehk, MAHR-tihn) CBJ

Right wing. Shoots right. 6', 193 lbs. Born, Uherske Hradiste, Czech., November 4, 1979.
(Columbus' 9th choice, 278th overall, in 2000 Entry Draft).

			Regular Season					Playoffs				
Season	Club	League	GP	G	A	TP	PIM	GP	G	A	TP	PIM
1998-99	Vsetin Jr.	Czech-Jr.	45	25	19	44	....	....	....	....	....	....
	HC Slovnaft Vsetin	Czech	11	1	1	2	....	7	0	1	1	0
99-2000	HC Slovnaft Vsetin	Czech	48	11	14	25	24	8	1	1	2	4
2000-01	Sumperk	Czech-2	14	0	1	1	27	....	....	....	....	....
	HC Slovnaft Vsetin	Czech	28	10	4	14	16	14	3	3	6	10
2001-02	Syracuse Crunch	AHL	59	11	14	25	31	9	1	1	2	4
2002-03	Syracuse Crunch	AHL	9	0	1	1	6	....	....	....	....	....
	HC Sparta Praha	Czech	16	1	4	5	16	9	1	1	2	8

• Released by **Syracuse** (AHL) and signed as a free agent by **Sparta Praha** (Czech) with Columbus retaining NHL rights, January 13, 2003.

PARROS, George (PAIR-ohs, JOHRJ) L.A.

Right wing. Shoots right. 6'4", 210 lbs. Born, Washington, PA, December 29, 1979.
(Los Angeles' 9th choice, 222nd overall, in 1999 Entry Draft).

			Regular Season					Playoffs				
Season	Club	League	GP	G	A	TP	PIM	GP	G	A	TP	PIM
1997-98	Delbarton Wave	Hi-School	STATISTICS NOT AVAILABLE									
1998-99	Chicago Freeze	NAJHL	54	30	20	50	126	....	....	....	....	....
99-2000	Princeton	ECAC	27	4	2	6	14	....	....	....	....	....
2000-01	Princeton	ECAC	31	7	10	17	38	....	....	....	....	....
2001-02	Princeton	ECAC	31	9	13	22	36	....	....	....	....	....
2002-03	Manchester	AHL	9	0	1	1	7	....	....	....	....	....
	Princeton	ECAC	22	0	7	7	29	....	....	....	....	....

NAJHL All-Rookie Team (1999) • NAJHL Rookie of the Year (1999)

PAULSSON, Marcus (POWL-suhn, MAHR-kuhs) NYI

Center. Shoots left. 6'1", 185 lbs. Born, Karlskrona, Sweden, January 10, 1984.
(NY Islanders' 3rd choice, 149th overall, in 2002 Entry Draft).

			Regular Season					Playoffs				
Season	Club	League	GP	G	A	TP	PIM	GP	G	A	TP	PIM
2000-01	Morrums GoIS IK	Swede-2	12	0	1	1	4	....	....	....	....	....
2001-02	Morrums GoIS IK	Swede-2	41	0	1	1	4	....	....	....	....	....
2002-03	Saskatoon Blades	WHL	56	13	18	31	20	6	1	3	4	2

PAVLIKOVSKY, Rastislav (pahv-lih-KAWV-skee, RA-this-LAHV)

Left wing. Shoots left. 6'1", 180 lbs. Born, Dubnica, Czech., March 22, 1977.
(Ottawa's 10th choice, 246th overall, in 1998 Entry Draft).

			Regular Season					Playoffs				
Season	Club	League	GP	G	A	TP	PIM	GP	G	A	TP	PIM
1993-94	Dukla Trencin	Slovakia	3	0	1	1	0	....	....	....	....	....
1994-95	Dukla Trencin	Slovakia	14	0	7	7	4	6	1	1	2	0
1995-96	Sault Ste. Marie	OHL	13	0	3	3	6	....	....	....	....	....
	Dukla Trencin	Slovakia	10	1	1	2	6	12	4	1	5	....
1996-97	Dukla Trencin	Slovakia	35	9	11	20	....	7	1	2	3	....
1997-98	Dukla Trencin	Slovakia	3	2	1	3	0	....	....	....	....	....
	Las Vegas Thunder	IHL	1	0	0	0	0	....	....	....	....	....
	Utah Grizzlies	IHL	74	17	29	46	54	2	0	0	0	6
1998-99	Cincinnati	IHL	31	4	12	16	28	....	....	....	....	....
	Cincinnati	AHL	36	12	23	35	59	2	0	1	1	4
99-2000	Grand Rapids	IHL	15	0	5	5	24	....	....	....	....	....
	Philadelphia	AHL	12	4	7	11	8	....	....	....	....	....
	Cincinnati	AHL	17	3	5	8	10	....	....	....	....	....
2000-01	Grand Rapids	IHL	1	0	0	0	0	....	....	....	....	....
	Jokerit Helsinki	Finland	7	0	1	1	0	....	....	....	....	....
	HV 71 Jonkoping	Sweden	23	6	8	14	93	....	....	....	....	....
2001-02	HV 71 Jonkoping	Sweden	46	14	16	30	102	8	2	2	4	6
	Slovakia	Olympics	4	2	3	5	6	....	....	....	....	....
2002-03	Houston Aeros	AHL	44	14	13	27	47	23	3	10	13	18

Signed as a free agent by **Minnesota**, May 31, 2002.

PECKER, Cory (PEH-kuhr, KOH-ree) ANA.

Center. Shoots right. 6', 195 lbs. Born, Montreal, Que., March 20, 1981.
(Calgary's 7th choice, 166th overall, in 1999 Entry Draft).

			Regular Season					Playoffs				
Season	Club	League	GP	G	A	TP	PIM	GP	G	A	TP	PIM
1995-96	Lac St-Louis Lions	QAAA	5	0	0	0	0	....	....	....	....	....
1996-97	Lac St-Louis Lions	QAAA	40	30	40	70	....	7	4	2	6	....
1997-98	Sault Ste. Marie	OHL	29	3	4	7	15	....	....	....	....	....
1998-99	Sault Ste. Marie	OHL	68	25	34	59	24	5	1	2	3	2
99-2000	Sault Ste. Marie	OHL	65	33	36	69	38	12	6	8	14	8
2000-01	Sault Ste. Marie	OHL	31	24	16	40	37	....	....	....	....	....
	Erie Otters	OHL	30	17	22	39	32	15	14	9	23	16
2001-02	Erie Otters	OHL	56	*53	46	99	108	21	*25	17	*42	36
2002-03	Cincinnati	AHL	77	20	13	33	66	....	....	....	....	....

OHL Second All-Star Team (2001) • OHL First All-Star Team (2002) • Memorial Cup All-Star Team (2002)

• Missed majority of 1997-98 season after being diagnosed with Chron's Disease. Signed as a free agent by **Anaheim**, July 8, 2002.

PEMBERTON, James (PEHM-buhr-tuhn, JAYMZ) FLA.

Defense. Shoots right. 6'4", 215 lbs. Born, Providence, RI, October 2, 1983.
(Florida's 6th choice, 124th overall, in 2003 Entry Draft).

			Regular Season					Playoffs				
Season	Club	League	GP	G	A	TP	PIM	GP	G	A	TP	PIM
2000-01	Mount St. Charles	Hi-School	18	5	14	19	8	5	1	8	9	6
2001-02	New England	EJHL	32	9	13	22	59	13	8	5	13	10
2002-03	Providence College	H-East	33	2	9	11	18	....	....	....	....	....

PEREZ, Bryan (PAIR-ehz, BRIGH-uhn) NYI

Center. Shoots left. 6'1", 198 lbs. Born, Blaine, MN, February 5, 1982.
(NY Islanders' 6th choice, 260th overall, in 2001 Entry Draft).

			Regular Season					Playoffs				
Season	Club	League	GP	G	A	TP	PIM	GP	G	A	TP	PIM
1998-99	U.S. National U-18	USDP	51	5	7	12	103	....	....	....	....	....
99-2000	U.S. National U-18	USDP	51	7	14	21	119	....	....	....	....	....
2000-01	Michigan Tech	WCHA	DID NOT PLAY – FRESHMAN									
2001-02	Michigan Tech	WCHA	32	6	10	16	20	....	....	....	....	....
2002-03	Michigan Tech	WCHA	38	9	19	28	62	....	....	....	....	....

PEREZHOGIN, Alexander (pehr-eh-ZHO-ghin, al-ehx-AN-duhr) MTL.

Left wing. Shoots left. 6', 185 lbs. Born, Ust-Kamenogorsk, USSR, August 10, 1983.
(Montreal's 2nd choice, 25th overall, in 2001 Entry Draft).

			Regular Season					Playoffs				
Season	Club	League	GP	G	A	TP	PIM	GP	G	A	TP	PIM
1998-99	Avangard Omsk 2	Russia-4	4	0	1	1	0	....	....	....	....	....
	Avangard Omsk	Russia	22	12	11	23	12	....	....	....	....	....
99-2000	Avangard Omsk 2	Russia-3	22	12	11	23	12	....	....	....	....	....
	Avangard Omsk	Russia	1	0	0	0	0	....	....	....	....	....
2000-01	Omsk Jr.	Russia-Jr.	6	1	5	6	4	....	....	....	....	....
	Avangard Omsk 2	Russia-3	41	47	24	71	40	....	....	....	....	....
	Avangard Omsk	Russia	....	....	....	....	....	1	0	0	0	0
2001-02	Avangard Omsk	Russia	4	1	0	1	4	....	....	....	....	....
	Mostovik Kurgan	Russia-2	19	14	10	24	10	....	....	....	....	....
2002-03	Avangard Omsk	Russia	48	15	6	21	28	8	0	2	2	4

PERIARD, Michel (pair-EE-ahr, mee-SHEHL) FLA.

Defense. Shoots left. 5'11", 183 lbs. Born, Montreal, Que., November 10, 1979.
(Ottawa's 8th choice, 188th overall, in 1998 Entry Draft).

			Regular Season					Playoffs				
Season	Club	League	GP	G	A	TP	PIM	GP	G	A	TP	PIM
1996-97	Charles-Lemoyne	QAAA	40	8	15	23	64	15	7	20	27	....
1997-98	Shawinigan	QMJHL	68	14	30	44	64	5	0	0	0	18
1998-99	Shawinigan	QMJHL	64	14	40	54	90	6	1	2	3	4
99-2000	Rimouski Oceanic	QMJHL	70	25	75	100	58	14	5	17	22	16
2000-01	Port Huron	UHL	23	1	8	9	30	....	....	....	....	....
	Rockford IceHogs	UHL	31	3	14	17	20	....	....	....	....	....
	Louisville Panthers	AHL	7	0	1	1	0	....	....	....	....	....
2001-02	Macon Whoopee	ECHL	72	4	19	23	26	....	....	....	....	....
2002-03	San Antonio	AHL	10	3	5	8	6	....	....	....	....	....
	Laredo Bucks	CHL	50	18	35	53	26	9	3	5	8	4

QMJHL First All-Star Team (2000) • Canadian Major Junior First All-Star Team (2000) • Memorial Cup All-Star Team (2000)

Signed as a free agent by **Florida**, August 1, 2000.

PERREAULT, Joel (PAIR-oh, JOHL) ANA.

Right wing. Shoots right. 6'1", 163 lbs. Born, Montreal, Que., April 6, 1983.
(Anaheim's 7th choice, 137th overall, in 2001 Entry Draft).

			Regular Season					Playoffs				
Season	Club	League	GP	G	A	TP	PIM	GP	G	A	TP	PIM
99-2000	Antoine-Girouard	QAAA	19	4	7	11	6	....	....	....	....	....
2000-01	Baie-Comeau	QMJHL	68	10	14	24	46	11	1	1	2	10
2001-02	Baie-Comeau	QMJHL	57	18	44	62	96	5	2	0	2	6
2002-03	Baie-Comeau	QMJHL	70	51	65	*116	93	12	3	7	10	14

QMJHL First All-Star Team (2003) • Canadian Major Junior First All-Star Team (2003)

PERRIN, Eric (peh-REHN, AIR-ihk) T.B.

Center. Shoots left. 5'9", 176 lbs. Born, Laval, Que., November 1, 1975.

			Regular Season					Playoffs				
Season	Club	League	GP	G	A	TP	PIM	GP	G	A	TP	PIM
1993-94	U. of Vermont	ECAC	32	24	21	45	34	....	....	....	....	....
1994-95	U. of Vermont	ECAC	35	28	39	67	38	....	....	....	....	....
1995-96	U. of Vermont	ECAC	38	29	56	85	38	....	....	....	....	....
1996-97	U. of Vermont	ECAC	36	26	33	59	40	....	....	....	....	....
1997-98	Cleveland	IHL	69	12	31	43	34	....	....	....	....	....
	Quebec Rafales	IHL	13	2	12	14	4	....	....	....	....	....
1998-99	Kansas City Blades	IHL	82	24	37	61	71	3	0	0	0	0
99-2000	Kansas City Blades	IHL	21	3	15	18	16	....	....	....	....	....
2000-01	Jokerit Helsinki	Finland	6	1	1	2	4	....	....	....	....	....
	Assat Pori	Finland	43	15	23	38	70	....	....	....	....	....
2001-02	Assat Pori	Finland	45	13	13	26	16	....	....	....	....	....
	HPK Hameenlinna	Finland	12	5	10	15	4	8	2	4	6	6
2002-03	JYP Jyvaskyla	Finland	56	18	28	46	36	7	4	6	10	8

ECAC First All-Star Team (1995, 1996) • NCAA East First All-American Team (2003)

Signed as a free agent by **Tampa Bay**, June 19, 2003.

PERRY, Corey (PAIR-ee, KOHR-ee) ANA.

Right wing. Shoots right. 6'2", 184 lbs. Born, Peterborough, Ont., May 16, 1985.
(Anaheim's 2nd choice, 28th overall, in 2003 Entry Draft).

			Regular Season					Playoffs				
Season	Club	League	GP	G	A	TP	PIM	GP	G	A	TP	PIM
2000-01	Peterborough	OMHA	64	69	46	115	20	3	3	0	3	0
2001-02	London Knights	OHL	67	28	31	59	56	12	2	3	5	30
2002-03	London Knights	OHL	67	25	53	78	145	14	7	16	23	27

PERSSON, Kristofer (PAIR-suhn, KRIHS-toh-fuhr) CGY.

Right wing. Shoots left. 6'3", 194 lbs. Born, Umea, Sweden, January 14, 1984.
(Calgary's 8th choice, 159th overall, in 2002 Entry Draft).

			Regular Season					Playoffs				
Season	Club	League	GP	G	A	TP	PIM	GP	G	A	TP	PIM
99-2000	Bjorkloven Jr.	Swede-Jr.	8	4	1	5	2	....	....	....	....	....
	Team Sweden-16	Nat-Tm	3	1	0	1	0	....	....	....	....	....
2000-01	MoDo Jr.	Swede-Jr.	16	8	3	11	4	6	1	0	1	2
2001-02	MoDo Jr.	Swede-Jr.	26	9	7	16	2	3	2	0	2	0
2002-03	MoDo Jr.	Swede-Jr.	24	16	12	28	10	....	....	....	....	....
	Ornskoldsviks SK	Swede-2	20	4	5	9	8	....	....	....	....	....

PESTUNOV, Dmitri (pehs-too-NAWF, dih-MEE-tree) PHX.

Center. Shoots left. 5'9", 196 lbs. Born, Ust-Kamenogorsk, USSR, January 22, 1985.
(Phoenix's 2nd choice, 80th overall, in 2003 Entry Draft).

			Regular Season					Playoffs				
Season	Club	League	GP	G	A	TP	PIM	GP	G	A	TP	PIM
2001-02	Magnitogorsk 2	Russia-3	STATISTICS NOT AVAILABLE									
2002-03	Magnitogorsk	Russia	32	4	0	4	0	....	....	....	....	....

PETER, Emanuel (PEE-tuhr, ih-MAN-yew-ehl) CGY.

Center. Shoots left. 6', 198 lbs. Born, Nieder Uzwil, Switz., June 9, 1984.
(Calgary's 6th choice, 142nd overall, in 2002 Entry Draft).

			Regular Season					Playoffs				
Season	Club	League	GP	G	A	TP	PIM	GP	G	A	TP	PIM
99-2000	SC Herisau-Jr.	Swiss-Jr.	18	2	12	14	....	....	....	....	....	....
2000-01	Uzwil Jr.	Swiss-Jr.	26	6	20	26	14	1	0	0	0	0
	EHC Uzwil Hawks	Swiss-3	18	2	10	12	....	....	....	....	....	....
2001-02	Kloten Flyers	Swiss	39	1	7	8	14	3	0	0	0	0
	Kloten Flyers Jr.	Swiss-Jr.	4	1	2	3	4	3	1	0	1	4
2002-03	Kloten Flyers	Swiss	43	0	10	10	42	5	0	0	0	4

PETERS, Andrew (PEE-tuhrs, AN-droo) BUF.

Left wing. Shoots left. 6'4", 223 lbs. Born, St. Catharines, Ont., May 5, 1980.
(Buffalo's 2nd choice, 34th overall, in 1998 Entry Draft).

			Regular Season					Playoffs				
Season	Club	League	GP	G	A	TP	PIM	GP	G	A	TP	PIM
1996-97	Georgetown	OPJHL	46	11	16	27	65	....	....	....	....	....
1997-98	Oshawa Generals	OHL	60	11	7	18	220	7	2	0	2	19
1998-99	Oshawa Generals	OHL	54	14	10	24	137	15	2	7	9	36
99-2000	Kitchener Rangers	OHL	42	6	13	19	95	4	0	1	1	14
2000-01	Rochester	AHL	49	0	4	4	118	....	....	....	....	....
2001-02	Rochester	AHL	67	4	1	5	*388	....	....	....	....	....
2002-03	Rochester	AHL	57	3	0	3	223	3	0	0	0	24

PETERS, Dan (PEE-tuhrs, DAN)

Defense. Shoots left. 5'10", 183 lbs. Born, Cottage Grove, MN, November 24, 1977.

			Regular Season					Playoffs				
Season	Club	League	GP	G	A	TP	PIM	GP	G	A	TP	PIM
1995-96	Omaha Lancers	USHL	54	11	36	47	....	....	....	....	....	....
1996-97	Colorado College	WCHA	36	4	12	16	62	....	....	....	....	....
1997-98	Colorado College	WCHA	37	5	16	21	108	....	....	....	....	....
1998-99	Colorado College	WCHA	36	8	21	29	82	....	....	....	....	....
99-2000	Colorado College	WCHA	27	2	8	10	58	....	....	....	....	....
2000-01	Philadelphia	AHL	73	2	14	16	71	6	1	4	5	8
2001-02	Philadelphia	AHL	66	6	12	18	91	5	0	1	1	2
2002-03	Philadelphia	AHL	41	1	4	5	48	....	....	....	....	....

WCHA Second All-Star Team (1999)

Signed as a free agent by **Philadelphia**, May 5, 2000.

PETIOT, Richard (PEH-tee-awt, RIH-chuhrd) L.A.

Defense. Shoots left. 6'2", 190 lbs. Born, Daysland, Alta., August 20, 1982.
(Los Angeles' 6th choice, 116th overall, in 2001 Entry Draft).

			Regular Season					Playoffs				
Season	Club	League	GP	G	A	TP	PIM	GP	G	A	TP	PIM
99-2000	Camrose Nordics	AAHA	STATISTICS NOT AVAILABLE									
2000-01	Camrose Kodiacs	AJHL	55	8	16	24	81	8	2	1	3	8
2001-02	Colorado College	WCHA	39	4	6	10	35	....	....	....	....	....
2002-03	Colorado College	WCHA	38	1	6	7	86	....	....	....	....	....

AJHL All-Rookie Team (2001) • AJHL South Second All-Star Team (2001)

PETRASEK, David (PEH-truh-sehk, DAY-vihd) DET.

Defense. Shoots right. 6', 187 lbs. Born, Jonkoping, Sweden, February 1, 1976.
(Detroit's 10th choice, 226th overall, in 1998 Entry Draft).

			Regular Season					Playoffs				
Season	Club	League	GP	G	A	TP	PIM	GP	G	A	TP	PIM
1993-94	HV 71 Jr.	Swede-Jr.	14	3	3	6	26	....	....	....	....	....
1994-95	HV 71 Jr.	Swede-Jr.	19	8	9	17	55	....	....	....	....	....
	HV 71 Jonkoping	Sweden	30	0	1	1	6	11	0	0	0	0
1995-96	HV 71 Jr.	Swede-Jr.	12	1	5	6	16	....	....	....	....	....
	HV 71 Jonkoping	Sweden	36	0	1	1	14	1	0	0	0	0
1996-97	HV 71 Jr.	Swede-Jr.	3	0	0	0	....	....	....	....	....	....
	HV 71 Jonkoping	Sweden	49	2	4	6	14	5	0	0	0	4
1997-98	HV 71 Jonkoping	Sweden	43	6	7	13	80	5	2	2	4	14
1998-99	HV 71 Jonkoping	Sweden	45	3	4	7	48	....	....	....	....	....
99-2000	HV 71 Jonkoping	Sweden	46	4	6	10	54	5	1	1	2	41
2000-01	Malmo IF	Sweden	47	7	7	14	74	9	1	1	2	8
2001-02	Malmo IF	Sweden	47	2	9	11	48	2	1	0	1	2
2002-03	Malmo IF	Sweden	50	7	6	13	72	....	....	....	....	....

PETRE, Henrik (PEH-truh, HEHN-rihk) WSH.

Defense. Shoots left. 6'1", 187 lbs. Born, Stockholm, Sweden, April 9, 1979.
(Washington's 5th choice, 143rd overall, in 1997 Entry Draft).

			Regular Season					Playoffs				
Season	Club	League	GP	G	A	TP	PIM	GP	G	A	TP	PIM
1995-96	Djurgarden Jr.	Swede-Jr.	21	6	4	10	8	....	....	....	....	....
1996-97	Djurgarden Jr.	Swede-Jr.	20	7	6	13	....	....	....	....	....	....
1997-98	Huddinge IK	Swede-2	30	4	4	8	30	....	....	....	....	....
	Djurgarden	Sweden	3	0	0	0	0	....	....	....	....	....
1998-99	Huddinge IK	Swede-2	14	0	1	1	20	....	....	....	....	....
	Djurgarden	Sweden	9	0	0	0	10	....	....	....	....	....
99-2000	Brynas IF Gavle	Sweden	47	3	3	6	73	11	1	0	1	12
	Brynas IF Gavle	EuroHL	5	0	2	2	4	....	....	....	....	....
2000-01	Brynas IF Gavle	Sweden	27	2	3	5	20	4	0	1	1	27
2001-02	Brynas IF Gavle	Sweden	24	2	1	3	49	4	0	0	0	4
2002-03	Brynas IF Gavle	Sweden	47	1	5	6	32	....	....	....	....	....
	Brynas IF Gavle	Swede-Q	10	1	1	2	10	....	....	....	....	....

PETROCHININ, Evgeny (peht-roh-CHIH-nihn, ehv-GEH-nee) CBJ

Defense. Shoots left. 6'2", 190 lbs. Born, Murmansk, USSR, February 7, 1976.
(Dallas' 5th choice, 150th overall, in 1994 Entry Draft).

			Regular Season					Playoffs				
Season	Club	League	GP	G	A	TP	PIM	GP	G	A	TP	PIM
1993-94	Spartak Moscow	CIS	2	0	0	0	0	....	....	....	....	....
1994-95	Spartak Moscow	CIS	45	0	2	2	14	....	....	....	....	....
1995-96	Spartak Moscow	CIS	50	5	17	22	18	5	3	0	3	0
1996-97	Spartak Moscow	Russia	32	5	6	11	52	....	....	....	....	....
1997-98	Spartak Moscow	Russia	46	12	6	18	100	....	....	....	....	....
1998-99	Spartak Moscow	Russia	21	4	6	10	14	....	....	....	....	....
	Ak Bars Kazan	Russia	6	0	2	2	2	9	1	1	2	24
99-2000	Magnitogorsk	Russia	33	7	10	17	38	14	2	1	3	26
2000-01	Cherepovets	Russia	40	8	7	15	38	9	2	0	2	40
2001-02	Cherepovets	Russia	35	35	2	8	10	1	0	0	0	0
2002-03	Cherepovets	Russia	29	3	6	9	14	10	1	0	1	0

Rights traded to **Columbus** by **Dallas** for Kirk Muller, September 28, 2001.

PETROW, Chris (PEH-troh, KRIHS) ANA.

Defense. Shoots right. 6'3", 188 lbs. Born, Haliburton, Ont., June 5, 1984.
(Anaheim's 8th choice, 267th overall, in 2002 Entry Draft).

			Regular Season					Playoffs				
Season	Club	League	GP	G	A	TP	PIM	GP	G	A	TP	PIM
2000-01	Cobourg Cougars	OPJHL	36	3	13	16	68	....	....	....	....	....
2001-02	Oshawa Generals	OHL	29	1	5	6	19	5	0	2	2	0
2002-03	Oshawa Generals	OHL	46	0	7	7	38	....	....	....	....	....

PETRUIC, Neil (peh-TROO-ihk, NEEL) OTT.

Defense. Shoots left. 6'1", 183 lbs. Born, Regina, Sask., July 30, 1982.
(Ottawa's 10th choice, 235th overall, in 2001 Entry Draft).

			Regular Season					Playoffs				
Season	Club	League	GP	G	A	TP	PIM	GP	G	A	TP	PIM
99-2000	Kindersley Klippers	SJHL	68	5	25	30	....	....	....	....	....	....
2000-01	Kindersley Klippers	SJHL	68	18	24	42	123	....	....	....	....	....
2001-02	U. Minn-Duluth	WCHA	40	3	6	9	54	....	....	....	....	....
2002-03	U. Minn-Duluth	WCHA	40	6	8	14	78	....	....	....	....	....

SJHL First All-Star Team (2001)

PETTERSTROM, Pontus (PEH-tuhr-stawm, PAWN-tuhs) NYR

Left wing. Shoots left. 6', 174 lbs. Born, Nybro, Sweden, April 21, 1982.
(NY Rangers' 8th choice, 226th overall, in 2001 Entry Draft).

			Regular Season					Playoffs				
Season	Club	League	GP	G	A	TP	PIM	GP	G	A	TP	PIM
99-2000	Leksands IF-18	Swede-Jr.	7	1	2	3	4	....	....	....	....	....
	Leksands IF Jr.	Swede-Jr.	37	13	10	23	26	2	0	0	0	4
2000-01	Tingsryds AIF	Swede-2	24	6	5	11	24	....	....	....	....	....
	Tingsryds AIF	Swede-Q	14	2	0	2	0	3	0	2	2	2
2001-02	Tingsryds AIF	Swede-2	41	8	7	15	0	....	....	....	....	....
2002-03	Skelleftea	Swede-2	26	9	5	14	12	....	....	....	....	....
	Skelleftea	Swede-Q	12	6	0	6	6	8	2	1	3	4

PHANEUF, Dion (fah-NOOF, DEE-awn) CGY.

Defense. Shoots left. 6'2", 205 lbs. Born, Edmonton, Alta., April 10, 1985.
(Calgary's 1st choice, 9th overall, in 2003 Entry Draft).

			Regular Season					Playoffs				
Season	Club	League	GP	G	A	TP	PIM	GP	G	A	TP	PIM
2000-01	Southgate Lions	AMBHL	35	15	50	65	208	4	3	4	7	15
2001-02	Red Deer Rebels	WHL	67	5	12	17	170	21	0	2	2	14
2002-03	Red Deer Rebels	WHL	71	16	14	30	185	23	7	7	14	34

PICARD, Alexandre (pee-KAR, ahl-ehx-AHN-druh) PHI.

Defense. Shoots left. 6'2", 214 lbs. Born, Gatineau, Que., July 5, 1985.
(Philadelphia's 5th choice, 85th overall, in 2003 Entry Draft).

			Regular Season					Playoffs				
Season	Club	League	GP	G	A	TP	PIM	GP	G	A	TP	PIM
2000-01	Gatineau Intrepide	QAAA	42	6	15	21	38	11	0	1	1	8
2001-02	Halifax	QMJHL	59	2	12	14	28	13	2	3	5	6
2002-03	Halifax	QMJHL	71	4	30	34	64	25	1	5	6	14

PIHLMAN, Thomas (PIHL-mahn, TAWH-muhs) N.J.

Left wing. Shoots left. 6'2", 205 lbs. Born, Espoo, Finland, November 13, 1982.
(New Jersey's 3rd choice, 48th overall, in 2001 Entry Draft).

			Regular Season					Playoffs				
Season	Club	League	GP	G	A	TP	PIM	GP	G	A	TP	PIM
1996-97	JYP Jyvaskyla-C	Finn-Jr.	25	9	10	19	28	....	....	....	....	....
1997-98	JYP Jyvaskyla-C	Finn-Jr.	1	0	1	1	0	....	....	....	....	....
	JYP Jyvaskyla-B	Finn-Jr.	30	2	5	7	18	4	1	3	4	6
1998-99	JYP Jyvaskyla-B	Finn-Jr.	35	21	20	41	64	6	1	1	2	12
99-2000	JYP Jyvaskyla Jr.	Finn-Jr.	20	4	4	8	54	4	0	0	0	8
	JYP Jyvaskyla	Finland	17	0	0	0	18	....	....	....	....	....
2000-01	JYP Jyvaskyla Jr.	Finn-Jr.	1	0	1	1	0	....	....	....	....	....
	JYP Jyvaskyla	Finland	47	3	6	9	59	....	....	....	....	....
2001-02	JYP Jyvaskyla Jr.	Finn-Jr.	3	1	1	2	4	....	....	....	....	....
	JYP Jyvaskyla	Finland	44	9	2	11	93	....	....	....	....	....
2002-03	JYP Jyvaskyla	Finland	53	19	15	34	58	1	0	0	0	0

PIISPANEN, Arsi (pihz-PAH-nehn, AHR-see) CBJ

Right wing. Shoots right. 6'3", 163 lbs. Born, Jyvaskyla, Finland, July 23, 1985.
(Columbus' 6th choice, 138th overall, in 2003 Entry Draft).

			Regular Season					Playoffs				
Season	Club	League	GP	G	A	TP	PIM	GP	G	A	TP	PIM
2001-02	Jokerit Helsinki Jr.	Finn-Jr.	27	7	19	26	8	8	4	3	7	12
2002-03	Jokerit Helsinki Jr.	Finn-Jr.	41	20	15	35	10	13	3	5	8	2

PIKKARAINEN, Ilkka (pih-kar-AY-nihn, IHL-kah) N.J.

Right wing. Shoots right. 6'2", 190 lbs. Born, Sonkajarvi, Finland, April 19, 1981.
(New Jersey's 9th choice, 218th overall, in 2002 Entry Draft).

			Regular Season					Playoffs				
Season	Club	League	GP	G	A	TP	PIM	GP	G	A	TP	PIM
1998-99	HIFK Helsinki Jr.	Finn-Jr.	37	12	13	25	38	2	1	0	1	27
99-2000	HIFK Helsinki Jr.	Finn-Jr.	STATISTICS NOT AVAILABLE									
2000-01	HIFK Helsinki Jr.	Finn-Jr.	38	27	31	58	186	9	2	5	7	26
	HIFK Helsinki	Finland	4	0	0	0	8	2	0	0	0	0
2001-02	HIFK Helsinki	Finland	54	9	9	18	111	....	....	....	....	....
2002-03	HIFK Helsinki	Finland	47	11	12	23	40	....	....	....	....	....

PIRNES, Esa (PEER-nehz, EH-sah) L.A.

Center. Shoots left. 6', 189 lbs. Born, Oulu, Finland, April 1, 1977.
(Los Angeles' 7th choice, 174th overall, in 2003 Entry Draft).

			Regular Season					Playoffs				
Season	Club	League	GP	G	A	TP	PIM	GP	G	A	TP	PIM
1994-95	Karpat Oulu Jr.	Finn-Jr.	32	8	9	17	16	....	....	....	....	....
1995-96	Karpat Oulu Jr.	Finn-Jr.	24	19	13	32	8	....	....	....	....	....
	Karpat Oulu	Finland-2	20	8	4	12	12	3	0	0	0	0
1996-97	Karpat Oulu	Finland-2	36	17	16	33	20	3	0	0	0	12
	Karpat Oulu Jr.	Finn-Jr.	9	5	5	10	6	....	....	....	....	....
1997-98	Karpat Oulu	Finland-2	32	6	15	21	12	....	....	....	....	....
	Karpat Oulu Jr.	Finn-Jr.	15	9	23	32	4	....	....	....	....	....
1998-99	Karpat Oulu	Finland-2	47	26	26	52	16	5	0	3	3	2
99-2000	Blues Espoo	Finland	51	15	24	39	12	4	0	1	1	2
2000-01	Blues Espoo	Finland	54	10	8	18	51	....	....	....	....	....
2001-02	Tappara Tampere	Finland	49	8	16	24	30	10	0	1	1	2
2002-03	Tappara Tampere	Finland	56	23	14	37	6	15	5	*9	*14	2

PITKANEN, Joni (PIHT-ka-nuhn, YOH-nee) PHI.

Defense. Shoots left. 6'3", 200 lbs. Born, Oulu, Finland, September 19, 1983.
(Philadelphia's 1st choice, 4th overall, in 2002 Entry Draft).

			Regular Season					Playoffs				
Season	Club	League	GP	G	A	TP	PIM	GP	G	A	TP	PIM
1998-99	Karpat Oulu Jr.	Finn-Jr.	30	1	5	6	12	....	....	....	....	....
99-2000	Karpat Oulu Jr.	Finn-Jr.	38	12	14	26	26	6	1	4	5	2
2000-01	Karpat Oulu Jr.	Finn-Jr.	24	6	11	17	77	....	....	....	....	....
	Karpat Oulu	Finland	21	0	0	0	10	2	0	0	0	2
2001-02	Karpat Oulu	Finland	49	4	15	19	65	4	0	0	0	12
	Karpat Oulu Jr.	Finn-Jr.	....	....	....	....	....	1	0	0	0	0
2002-03	Karpat Oulu	Finland	35	5	15	20	38	....	....	....	....	....

PIVKO, Libor (PIHV-koh, LEE-bohr) NSH.

Left wing. Shoots left. 6'2", 195 lbs. Born, Novy Vicin, Czech., March 29, 1980.
(Nashville's 4th choice, 89th overall, in 2000 Entry Draft).

			Regular Season					Playoffs				
Season	Club	League	GP	G	A	TP	PIM	GP	G	A	TP	PIM
1995-96	Slezan Opava Jr.	Czech-Jr.	37	19	14	33	30	....	....	....	....	....
1996-97	Slezan Opava Jr.	Czech-Jr.	16	12	9	21	22	....	....	....	....	....
1997-98	HC Opava Jr.	Czech-Jr.	37	15	11	26	36	....	....	....	....	....
1998-99	HC Opava Jr.	Czech-Jr.	38	21	14	35	....	....	....	....	....	....
	HC Opava	Czech	5	0	1	1	0	....	....	....	....	....
99-2000	Havirov Jr.	Czech-Jr.	5	1	3	4	4	....	....	....	....	....
	HC Femax Havirov	Czech	40	11	11	22	41	....	....	....	....	....
	HC Ytong Brno	Czech-3	....	....	....	....	....	4	3	4	7	0
2000-01	HC Femax Havirov	Czech	45	7	12	19	58	....	....	....	....	....
2001-02	Zlin	Czech	46	8	20	28	36	9	5	3	8	8
2002-03	HC Hame Zlin	Czech	52	13	12	25	60	....	....	....	....	....

PLATIL, Jan (PLA-tihl, YAN) OTT.

Defense. Shoots left. 6'2", 215 lbs. Born, Kladno, Czech., February 9, 1983.
(Ottawa's 8th choice, 218th overall, in 2001 Entry Draft).

			Regular Season					Playoffs				
Season	Club	League	GP	G	A	TP	PIM	GP	G	A	TP	PIM
99-2000	Kladno Jr.	Czech-Jr.	39	5	6	11	....	....	....	....	....	....
2000-01	Barrie Colts	OHL	60	6	18	24	114	5	0	0	0	12
2001-02	Barrie Colts	OHL	68	13	34	47	136	20	1	5	6	51
2002-03	Barrie Colts	OHL	61	15	36	51	163	6	1	5	6	8

PLATONOV, Denis (PLAH-tah-nahv, DIHN-ihs) NSH.

Right wing. Shoots left. 6'3", 202 lbs. Born, Saratov, USSR, November 6, 1981.
(Nashville's 4th choice, 75th overall, in 2001 Entry Draft).

			Regular Season					Playoffs				
Season	Club	League	GP	G	A	TP	PIM	GP	G	A	TP	PIM
1997-98	Kristall Saratov 2	Russia-3	20	4	2	6	34	....	....	....	....	....
1998-99	Kristall Saratov	Russia-2	14	1	0	1	61	....	....	....	....	....
99-2000	Kristall Saratov 2	Russia-3	5	0	0	0	37	....	....	....	....	....
	Kristall Saratov	Russia-2	32	9	4	13	60	....	....	....	....	....
2000-01	Kristall Saratov	Russia-2	51	14	6	20	75	....	....	....	....	....
2001-02	Kristall Saratov	Russia-2	50	18	14	32	96	....	....	....	....	....
2002-03	Ak Bars Kazan	Russia	47	8	9	17	49	5	0	0	0	2

PLATT, Jason (PLAT, JAY-suhn) EDM.

Defense. Shoots left. 6'1", 210 lbs. Born, San Francisco, CA, April 29, 1981.
(Edmonton's 9th choice, 247th overall, in 2000 Entry Draft).

			Regular Season					Playoffs				
Season	Club	League	GP	G	A	TP	PIM	GP	G	A	TP	PIM
1998-99	Omaha Lancers	USHL	56	2	9	11	65	11	0	0	0	8
99-2000	Omaha Lancers	USHL	49	1	6	7	65	4	0	0	0	9
2000-01	Providence College	H-East	26	0	2	2	12	....	....	....	....	....
2001-02	Providence College	H-East	36	2	5	7	60	....	....	....	....	....
2002-03	Providence College	H-East	30	1	7	8	41	....	....	....	....	....

PLEKANEC, Tomas (pleh-KA-nyehts, TAW-mahsh) MTL.

Left wing. Shoots left. 5'10", 189 lbs. Born, Kladno, Czech., October 31, 1982.
(Montreal's 4th choice, 71st overall, in 2001 Entry Draft).

			Regular Season					Playoffs				
Season	Club	League	GP	G	A	TP	PIM	GP	G	A	TP	PIM
99-2000	Kladno Jr.	Czech-Jr.	43	14	16	30	....	....	....	....	....	....
2000-01	Kladno	Czech	47	9	9	18	24	....	....	....	....	....
2001-02	Kladno	Czech	48	7	16	23	28	....	....	....	....	....
	Kladno	Czech-Q	5	0	1	1	0	....	....	....	....	....
2002-03	Hamilton Bulldogs	AHL	77	19	27	46	74	13	3	2	5	8

PLIHAL, Tomas (PLEE-hahl, TAW-mahsh) S.J.

Center. Shoots left. 6'1", 195 lbs. Born, Frydlant v Cechach, Czech., March 28, 1983.
(San Jose's 4th choice, 140th overall, in 2001 Entry Draft).

			Regular Season					Playoffs				
Season	Club	League	GP	G	A	TP	PIM	GP	G	A	TP	PIM
2000-01	HC Liberec Jr.	Czech-Jr.	33	16	12	28	....	....	....	....	....	....
2001-02	Kootenay Ice	WHL	72	32	54	86	28	22	4	10	14	14
2002-03	Kootenay Ice	WHL	67	35	42	77	113	11	2	4	6	18

PODHRADSKY, Peter (pohd-RAD-skee, PEE-tuhr)

Defense. Shoots right. 6'2", 204 lbs. Born, Bratislava, Czech., December 10, 1979.
(Anaheim's 4th choice, 134th overall, in 2000 Entry Draft).

			Regular Season					Playoffs				
Season	Club	League	GP	G	A	TP	PIM	GP	G	A	TP	PIM
1995-96	S. Bratislava Jr.	Slovak-Jr.	50	14	17	31	....	....	....	....	....	....
1996-97	S. Bratislava Jr.	Slovak-Jr.	41	2	6	8	28	....	....	....	....	....
1997-98	S. Bratislava Jr.	Slovak-Jr.	48	11	13	24	58	....	....	....	....	....
1998-99	S. Bratislava Jr.	Slovak-Jr.	25	9	14	23	57	2	0	1	1	0
	Slov. Bratislava	Slovakia	23	1	4	5	37	4	0	0	0	0
99-2000	HK Kabat Trnava	Slovak-2	1	0	0	0	0	....	....	....	....	....
	Slov. Bratislava	Slovakia	40	4	11	15	63	8	1	0	1	2
2000-01	Cincinnati	AHL	59	4	5	9	27	2	0	0	0	0
2001-02	Cincinnati	AHL	49	0	8	8	19	....	....	....	....	....
2002-03	Cincinnati	AHL	78	9	8	17	85	....	....	....	....	....

PODLESAK, Martin (PAWD-leh-shahk, MAHR-tihn) PHX.

Center. Shoots left. 6'6", 218 lbs. Born, Melnik, Czech., September 26, 1982.
(Phoenix's 3rd choice, 45th overall, in 2001 Entry Draft).

			Regular Season					Playoffs				
Season	Club	League	GP	G	A	TP	PIM	GP	G	A	TP	PIM
99-2000	Sparta Praha Jr.	Czech-Jr.	24	6	5	11	....	11	6	2	8	....
2000-01	Tri-City Americans	WHL	39	13	13	26	36	....	....	....	....	....
	Lethbridge	WHL	21	8	6	14	23	3	1	1	2	2
2001-02	Lethbridge	WHL	34	14	20	34	33	....	....	....	....	....
2002-03	Springfield Falcons	AHL	3	0	0	0	4	....	....	....	....	....

• Missed majority of 2002-03 season recovering from head injury suffered in game vs. Manchester (AHL), October 23, 2002.

POHANKA, Igor (poh-HAHN-kah, EE-gohr) ANA.

Center. Shoots left. 6'3", 185 lbs. Born, Piestany, Czech., July 5, 1983.
(New Jersey's 2nd choice, 44th overall, in 2001 Entry Draft).

			Regular Season					Playoffs				
Season	Club	League	GP	G	A	TP	PIM	GP	G	A	TP	PIM
99-2000	S. Bratislava Jr.	Slovak-Jr.	57	36	41	77	62	....	....	....	....	....
2000-01	Prince Albert	WHL	70	16	33	49	24	....	....	....	....	....
2001-02	Prince Albert	WHL	58	25	43	68	18	....	....	....	....	....
2002-03	Prince Albert	WHL	56	25	31	56	28	....	....	....	....	....

Traded to **Anaheim** by **New Jersey** with Petr Sykora, Mike Commodore and Jean-Francois Damphousse for Jeff Friesen, Oleg Tverdovsky and Maxim Balmochnykh, July 6, 2002.

POHL, John (PAWL, JAWN) ST.L.

Center. Shoots right. 6', 186 lbs. Born, Rochester, MN, June 29, 1979.
(St. Louis' 8th choice, 255th overall, in 1998 Entry Draft).

			Regular Season					Playoffs				
Season	Club	League	GP	G	A	TP	PIM	GP	G	A	TP	PIM
1997-98	Red Wing Wingers	Hi-School	28	30	77	107	18	....	....	....	....	....
	Twin Cities	USHL	10	5	3	8	10	....	....	....	....	....
1998-99	U. of Minnesota	WCHA	42	7	10	17	18	....	....	....	....	....
99-2000	U. of Minnesota	WCHA	41	18	41	59	26	....	....	....	....	....
2000-01	U. of Minnesota	WCHA	38	19	26	45	24	....	....	....	....	....
2001-02	U. of Minnesota	WCHA	44	27	*52	*79	26	....	....	....	....	....
2002-03	Worcester IceCats	AHL	58	26	32	58	34	3	0	1	1	6

Minnesota High School Player of the Year (1998) • WCHA Second All-Star Team (2000) • WCHA First All-Star Team (2002) • NCAA Championship All-Tournament Team (2002)

POLAK, Vojtech (POH-lahk, VOI-tehk) DAL.

Left wing. Shoots left. 5'11", 180 lbs. Born, Ostrov nad Ohri, Czech., June 27, 1985.
(Dallas' 2nd choice, 36th overall, in 2003 Entry Draft).

			Regular Season					Playoffs				
Season	Club	League	GP	G	A	TP	PIM	GP	G	A	TP	PIM
99-2000	Karlovy Vary Jr.	Czech-Jr.	49	17	23	40	48	....	....	....	....	....
2000-01	Karlovy Vary Jr.	Czech-Jr.	47	36	33	69	38	....	....	....	....	....
	Karlovy Vary	Czech	2	0	0	0	0	....	....	....	....	....
2001-02	Karlovy Vary Jr.	Czech-Jr.	37	11	14	25	26	....	....	....	....	....
	Karlovy Vary	Czech	9	1	1	2	2	....	....	....	....	....
2002-03	Karlovy Vary	Czech	41	7	9	16	51	....	....	....	....	....
	Karlovy Vary Jr.	Czech-Jr.	6	3	7	10	18	....	....	....	....	....

POLASKI, Scott (poh-LAHZ-kee, SKAWT) PHX.

Right wing. Shoots right. 6'2", 182 lbs. Born, Colorado Springs, CO, August 4, 1982.
(Phoenix's 6th choice, 180th overall, in 2001 Entry Draft).

			Regular Season					Playoffs				
Season	Club	League	GP	G	A	TP	PIM	GP	G	A	TP	PIM
1998-99	Pikes Point Selects	AAHA	60	40	46	86	....	....	....	....	....	....
99-2000	Sioux City	USHL	58	15	22	37	46	5	3	6	9	0
2000-01	Sioux City	USHL	51	18	26	44	65	3	0	1	1	0
2001-02	Colorado College	WCHA	38	4	12	16	28	....	....	....	....	....
2002-03	Colorado College	WCHA	42	4	6	10	24	....	....	....	....	....

POLCIK, Peter (POHL-chihk, PEE-tuhr) WSH.

Right wing. Shoots left. 6'4", 187 lbs. Born, Nitra, Czech., July 23, 1983.
(Washington's 8th choice, 254th overall, in 2001 Entry Draft).

			Regular Season					Playoffs				
Season	Club	League	GP	G	A	TP	PIM	GP	G	A	TP	PIM
1998-99	MHC Nitra Jr.	Slovak-Jr.	35	13	16	29	14	....	....	....	....	....
99-2000	MHC Nitra Jr.	Slovak-Jr.	40	26	20	46	82	....	....	....	....	....
2000-01	MHC Nitra Jr.	Slovak-Jr.	42	8	10	18	32	....	....	....	....	....
2001-02	Montreal Rocket	QMJHL	70	9	12	21	35	2	0	0	0	0
2002-03	MHC Nitra Jr.	Slovak-Jr.	45	20	21	41	53	2	1	0	1	2
	HKM Nitra	Slovak-2	18	3	1	4	2	....	....	....	....	....

POLLOCK, Jame (PAWL-lawk, JAYM)

Right wing. Shoots right. 6'1", 210 lbs. Born, Quebec City, Que., June 16, 1979.
(St. Louis' 4th choice, 106th overall, in 1997 Entry Draft).

			Regular Season					Playoffs				
Season	Club	League	GP	G	A	TP	PIM	GP	G	A	TP	PIM
1994-95	Victoria Legion	BCAHA	43	22	56	78	96	....	....	....	....	....
1995-96	Seattle	WHL	32	0	1	1	15	....	....	....	....	....
1996-97	Seattle	WHL	66	15	19	34	94	15	3	5	8	16
1997-98	Seattle	WHL	66	11	36	47	78	5	0	1	1	17
1998-99	Seattle	WHL	59	10	32	42	78	11	3	4	7	8
99-2000	Worcester IceCats	AHL	56	12	12	24	50	9	5	3	8	6
2000-01	Worcester IceCats	AHL	55	15	8	23	36	11	1	7	8	10
2001-02	Worcester IceCats	AHL	71	23	43	66	89	3	1	0	1	2
2002-03	Worcester IceCats	AHL	44	5	17	22	50	3	1	0	1	2

POLUSHIN, Alexander (puh-LOOSH-ihn, al-ehx-AN-duhr) T.B.

Center. Shoots left. 6'3", 200 lbs. Born, Kirovo-Chepetsk, USSR, May 8, 1983.
(Tampa Bay's 2nd choice, 47th overall, in 2001 Entry Draft).

			Regular Season					Playoffs				
Season	Club	League	GP	G	A	TP	PIM	GP	G	A	TP	PIM
99-2000	DynamoMoscow2	Russia-3	18	4	3	7	14	....	....	....	....	....
	Spartak Moscow	Russia-2	14	1	0	1	2	....	....	....	....	....
2000-01	THC Tver	Russia-2	38	10	5	15	10	....	....	....	....	....
2001-02	HC CSKA	Russia-2	55	28	21	49	18	....	....	....	....	....
2002-03	CSKA Moscow	Russia	47	5	6	11	22	....	....	....	....	....

POMINVILLE, Jason (paw-MIHN-vihl, JAY-suhn) BUF.

Right wing. Shoots right. 6', 178 lbs. Born, Repentigny, Que., November 30, 1982.
(Buffalo's 4th choice, 55th overall, in 2001 Entry Draft).

			Regular Season					Playoffs				
Season	Club	League	GP	G	A	TP	PIM	GP	G	A	TP	PIM
1998-99	Rive-Nord Elites	QAHA	STATISTICS NOT AVAILABLE									
	Shawinigan	QMJHL	2	0	0	0	0	....	....	....	....	....
99-2000	Shawinigan	QMJHL	60	4	17	21	12	13	2	3	5	0
2000-01	Shawinigan	QMJHL	71	46	67	113	24	10	6	6	12	0
2001-02	Shawinigan	QMJHL	66	57	64	121	32	2	0	0	0	0
2002-03	Rochester	AHL	73	13	21	34	16	3	1	1	2	0

QMJHL First All-Star Team (2002)

POPOVIC, Mark (poh-PUH-vihk, MAHRK) **ANA.**

Defense. Shoots left. 6'1", 191 lbs. Born, Stoney Creek, Ont., October 11, 1982.
(Anaheim's 2nd choice, 35th overall, in 2001 Entry Draft).

			Regular Season					Playoffs				
Season	Club	League	GP	G	A	TP	PIM	GP	G	A	TP	PIM
1997-98	Mississauga	OPJHL	51	10	16	26	32	....	....	....	....	....
1998-99	St. Michael's	OHL	60	6	26	32	46	....	....	....	....	....
99-2000	St. Michael's	OHL	68	11	29	40	68	....	....	....	....	....
2000-01	St. Michael's	OHL	61	7	35	42	54	18	3	5	8	22
2001-02	St. Michael's	OHL	58	12	29	41	42	15	1	11	12	10
2002-03	Cincinnati	AHL	73	3	21	24	46	....	....	....	....	....

OHL First All-Star Team (2002)

POTTER, Corey (PAW-tuhr, KOHR-ee) **NYR**

Defense. Shoots right. 6'2", 183 lbs. Born, Lansing, MI, January 5, 1984.
(NY Rangers' 4th choice, 122nd overall, in 2003 Entry Draft).

			Regular Season					Playoffs				
Season	Club	League	GP	G	A	TP	PIM	GP	G	A	TP	PIM
2000-01	U.S. National U-17	USDP	66	4	4	8	26	....	....	....	....	....
2001-02	U.S. National U-18	USDP	61	6	11	17	65	....	....	....	....	....
2002-03	Michigan State	CCHA	35	4	4	8	30	....	....	....	....	....

POTULNY, Grant (puh-TUHL-nee, GRANT) **OTT.**

Center. Shoots left. 6'2", 198 lbs. Born, Grand Forks, ND, March 4, 1980.
(Ottawa's 7th choice, 157th overall, in 2000 Entry Draft).

			Regular Season					Playoffs				
Season	Club	League	GP	G	A	TP	PIM	GP	G	A	TP	PIM
1998-99	Lincoln Stars	USHL	46	7	11	18	76	10	2	1	3	7
99-2000	Lincoln Stars	USHL	56	25	30	55	85	10	3	4	7	4
2000-01	U. of Minnesota	WCHA	42	22	11	33	38	....	....	....	....	....
2001-02	U. of Minnesota	WCHA	43	15	19	34	38	....	....	....	....	....
2002-03	U. of Minnesota	WCHA	23	15	8	23	12	....	....	....	....	....

NCAA Championship All-Tournament Team (2002) • NCAA Championship Tournament MVP (2002)

POTULNY, Ryan (poh-TOOL-nee, RIGH-uhn) **PHI.**

Center. Shoots left. 6', 190 lbs. Born, Grand Forks, ND, September 5, 1984.
(Philadelphia's 6th choice, 87th overall, in 2003 Entry Draft).

			Regular Season					Playoffs				
Season	Club	League	GP	G	A	TP	PIM	GP	G	A	TP	PIM
2001-02	Lincoln Stars	USHL	60	23	34	57	65	4	0	1	1	2
2002-03	Lincoln Stars	USHL	54	35	*43	*78	18	10	6	*11	*17	8

USHL First All-Star Team (2003) • USHL Player of the Year (2003) • USA Junior Player of the Year (2003)

• Signed Letter of Intent to attend **U. of Minnesota** (WCHA), April 9, 2003.

POULIOT, Marc-Antoine (poo-YOH, MAHRK-AN-twahn) **EDM.**

Center. Shoots right. 6'1", 195 lbs. Born, Quebec City, Que., May 22, 1985.
(Edmonton's 1st choice, 22nd overall, in 2003 Entry Draft).

			Regular Season					Playoffs				
Season	Club	League	GP	G	A	TP	PIM	GP	G	A	TP	PIM
2001-02	Rimouski Oceanic	QMJHL	28	9	14	23	32	5	0	0	0	4
2002-03	Rimouski Oceanic	QMJHL	65	32	41	73	100	....	....	....	....	....

PRATT, Harlan (PRAT, HAR-lahn)

Defense. Shoots left. 6'1", 195 lbs. Born, Fort McMurray, Alta., December 10, 1978.
(Pittsburgh's 5th choice, 124th overall, in 1997 Entry Draft).

			Regular Season					Playoffs				
Season	Club	League	GP	G	A	TP	PIM	GP	G	A	TP	PIM
1994-95	Seattle	WHL	33	1	0	1	17	1	0	0	0	0
1995-96	Red Deer Rebels	WHL	60	2	3	5	22	10	0	0	0	4
1996-97	Red Deer Rebels	WHL	2	0	0	0	2	....	....	....	....	....
	Prince Albert	WHL	65	7	26	33	49	4	1	1	2	4
1997-98	Prince Albert	WHL	37	6	14	20	12	....	....	....	....	....
	Regina Pats	WHL	24	2	6	8	23	9	2	2	4	2
1998-99	Portland	WHL	10	1	3	4	10	....	....	....	....	....
	Toledo Storm	ECHL	61	4	35	39	32	3	0	0	0	0
99-2000	Florida Everblades	ECHL	68	4	29	33	38	5	0	1	1	2
2000-01	Cincinnati	IHL	73	6	23	29	45	2	0	1	1	2
2001-02	Lowell	AHL	17	1	6	7	6	....	....	....	....	....
	Florida Everblades	ECHL	13	0	7	7	4	....	....	....	....	....
	Springfield Falcons	AHL	19	0	4	4	17	....	....	....	....	....
	Pensacola	ECHL	17	2	8	10	14	3	0	4	4	2
2002-03	Springfield Falcons	AHL	13	1	0	1	2	....	....	....	....	....
	Pensacola	ECHL	2	0	1	1	2	....	....	....	....	....
	Cincinnati	AHL	43	4	6	10	34	....	....	....	....	....

Signed as a free agent by **Carolina**, August 21, 2000. Traded to **Tampa Bay** by **Carolina** for Kaspars Astashenko, December 28, 2001.

PREISSING, Tom (PREH-sihng, TAWM) **S.J.**

Defense. Shoots . 6', 205 lbs. Born, Rosemount, MN, December 3, 1978.

			Regular Season					Playoffs				
Season	Club	League	GP	G	A	TP	PIM	GP	G	A	TP	PIM
1998-99	Green Bay	USHL	53	18	37	55	40	6	3	6	9	2
99-2000	Colorado College	WCHA	36	4	14	18	20	....	....	....	....	....
2000-01	Colorado College	WCHA	33	6	18	24	26	....	....	....	....	....
2001-02	Colorado College	WCHA	43	6	26	32	42	....	....	....	....	....
2002-03	Colorado College	WCHA	42	23	29	52	16	....	....	....	....	....

WCHA First All-Star Team (2003) • NCAA West First All-American Team (2003)

Signed as a free agent by **San Jose**, April 4, 2003.

PRESTBERG, Pelle (PREHST-buhrg, PEHL-lee) **ANA.**

Left wing. Shoots left. 5'10", 170 lbs. Born, Jonkoping, Sweden, February 5, 1975.
(Anaheim's 7th choice, 233rd overall, in 1998 Entry Draft).

			Regular Season					Playoffs				
Season	Club	League	GP	G	A	TP	PIM	GP	G	A	TP	PIM
1990-91	IFK Munkfors	Swede-3	3	0	3	3	....	....	....	....	....	....
1991-92	IFK Munkfors	Swede-3	26	6	10	16	18	....	....	....	....	....
1992-93	IFK Munkfors	Swede-3	36	8	8	16	20	....	....	....	....	....
1993-94	Sunne IK	Swede-2	32	8	6	14	16	....	....	....	....	....
1994-95	IFK Munkfors	Swede-3	27	13	9	22	44	....	....	....	....	....
1995-96	IFK Munkfors	Swede-3	30	20	11	31	32	....	....	....	....	....
1996-97	IFK Munkfors	Swede-3	32	28	10	38	50	....	....	....	....	....
1997-98	Farjestad	Sweden	45	29	15	44	22	12	*9	2	11	8
1998-99	Farjestad	Sweden	48	18	15	33	28	4	0	1	1	4
99-2000	Farjestad	Sweden	48	13	9	22	26	7	1	1	2	18
2000-01	Vastra Frolunda	Sweden	50	14	9	23	18	5	0	0	0	8
2001-02	Vastra Frolunda	Sweden	50	14	11	25	28	10	5	0	5	12
2002-03	Farjestad	Sweden	45	12	6	18	26	14	5	1	6	8

PREUCIL, Petr (PREE-oo-chihl, PEE-tuhr) **NYR**

Center. Shoots left. 6'1", 168 lbs. Born, Most, Czech., January 21, 1983.
(NY Rangers' 7th choice, 206th overall, in 2001 Entry Draft).

			Regular Season					Playoffs				
Season	Club	League	GP	G	A	TP	PIM	GP	G	A	TP	PIM
99-2000	Litvinov Jr.	Czech-Jr.	23	7	4	11	....	....	....	....	....	....
2000-01	Quebec Remparts	QMJHL	70	12	35	47	121	4	1	0	1	11
2001-02	Quebec Remparts	QMJHL	57	14	20	34	116	9	2	3	5	24
2002-03	Drummondville	QMJHL	32	14	19	33	46	....	....	....	....	....
	Baie-Comeau	QMJHL	26	3	9	12	55	12	7	4	11	35

PRINTZ, David (PRIHNTS, DAY-vihd) **PHI.**

Defense. Shoots left. 6'5", 220 lbs. Born, Stockholm, Sweden, July 24, 1980.
(Philadelphia's 9th choice, 225th overall, in 2001 Entry Draft).

			Regular Season					Playoffs				
Season	Club	League	GP	G	A	TP	PIM	GP	G	A	TP	PIM
1996-97	AIK Solna Jr.	Swede-Jr.	1	0	0	0	0	....	....	....	....	....
1997-98	AIK Solna Jr.	Swede-Jr.	8	0	0	0	6	....	....	....	....	....
1998-99	AIK Solna Jr.	Swede-Jr.	23	1	0	1	14	....	....	....	....	....
99-2000	AIK Solna Jr.	Swede-Jr.	36	8	4	12	53	....	....	....	....	....
2000-01	Great Falls	AWHL	54	13	23	36	93	13	3	5	8	16
2001-02	AIK Solna Jr.	Swede-Jr.	8	2	3	5	20	....	....	....	....	....
	AIK Solna	Sweden	37	3	2	5	59	....	....	....	....	....
	AIK Solna	Swede-Q	10	0	0	0	12	....	....	....	....	....
2002-03	HPK Hameenlinna	Finland	17	1	0	1	10	....	....	....	....	....
	Ilves Tampere	Finland	25	1	2	3	10	....	....	....	....	....

PRUCHA, Petr (PROO-khah, PEE-tuhr) **NYR**

Right wing. Shoots right. 5'10", 161 lbs. Born, Chrudim, Czech., September 14, 1982.
(NY Rangers' 8th choice, 240th overall, in 2002 Entry Draft).

			Regular Season					Playoffs				
Season	Club	League	GP	G	A	TP	PIM	GP	G	A	TP	PIM
99-2000	HC Chrudim Jr.	Czech-Jr.	43	35	27	62	62	....	....	....	....	....
2000-01	Pardubice Jr.	Czech	54	39	22	61	18	....	....	....	....	....
2001-02	Pardubice Jr.	Czech	28	38	28	66	18	3	2	6	8	0
	Sumperk	Czech-2	8	6	4	10	0	....	....	....	....	....
	Sumperk	Czech-Q	5	5	3	8	0	....	....	....	....	....
	Pardubice	Czech	20	1	1	2	2	5	0	0	0	0
2002-03	Pardubice	Czech	49	7	9	16	12	17	2	6	8	8
	Pardubice Jr.	Czech	4	5	4	9	25	....	....	....	....	....
	HC Kralove	Czech-2	11	3	5	8	35	....	....	....	....	....

PUDLICK, Michael (PUHD-lihk, MIGHK-uhl)

Defense. Shoots left. 6'3", 190 lbs. Born, Blaine, MN, February 24, 1978.

			Regular Season					Playoffs				
Season	Club	League	GP	G	A	TP	PIM	GP	G	A	TP	PIM
1995-96	Blaine Bengals	Hi-School	25	9	30	39	....	....	....	....	....	....
1996-97	Twin Cities	USHL	49	10	19	29	93	5	0	2	2	4
1997-98	Twin Cities	USHL	50	3	14	17	138	....	....	....	....	....
1998-99	St. Cloud State	WCHA	37	13	12	25	74	....	....	....	....	....
99-2000	St. Cloud State	WCHA	40	8	22	30	65	....	....	....	....	....
2000-01	Lowell	AHL	57	7	13	20	39	4	0	1	1	2
2001-02	Manchester	AHL	64	9	6	15	42	3	0	0	0	6
2002-03	Manchester	AHL	68	7	17	24	52	1	0	0	0	0

WCHA First All-Star Team (2000) • NCAA West Second All-American Team (2000)

Signed as a free agent by **Los Angeles**, April 5, 2000.

PULLIAINEN, Tuukka (poo-le-AY-nehn, TOO-kuh) **L.A.**

Right wing. Shoots left. 5'11", 176 lbs. Born, Turku, Finland, August 25, 1984.
(Los Angeles' 10th choice, 248th overall, in 2002 Entry Draft).

			Regular Season					Playoffs				
Season	Club	League	GP	G	A	TP	PIM	GP	G	A	TP	PIM
2000-01	TuTu Turku Jr.	Finn-Jr.	37	3	11	14	8	1	1	1	2	0
2001-02	TuTu Turku	Finland-2	41	11	8	19	8	2	0	1	1	25
	TuTu Turku Jr.	Finn-Jr.	3	0	2	2	0	1	0	0	0	2
2002-03	TuTu Turku	Finland-2	42	15	17	32	12	....	....	....	....	....

PUNCOCHAR, Petr (POON-choh-hahr, PEE-tuhr) **CHI.**

Defense. Shoots right. 6'1", 215 lbs. Born, Tabor, Czech., June 8, 1983.
(Chicago's 10th choice, 186th overall, in 2001 Entry Draft).

			Regular Season					Playoffs				
Season	Club	League	GP	G	A	TP	PIM	GP	G	A	TP	PIM
1998-99	C. Budejovice Jr.	Czech-Jr.	45	6	12	18	20	....	....	....	....	....
99-2000	C. Budejovice Jr.	Czech-Jr.	18	1	3	4	4	....	....	....	....	....
	Karlovy Vary Jr.	Czech-Jr.	23	1	1	2	4	2	0	0	0	2
	HC Karlovy Vary	Czech	1	0	0	0	0	....	....	....	....	....
2000-01	Karlovy Vary Jr.	Czech-Jr.	35	8	5	13	14	....	....	....	....	....
	HC Karlovy Vary	Czech	8	1	0	1	4	....	....	....	....	....
	HC Banik Most	Czech-3	1	0	0	0	0	....	....	....	....	....
2001-02	Karlovy Vary Jr.	Czech-Jr.	5	0	0	0	6	....	....	....	....	....
	HC Banik	Czech-3	7	2	1	3	0	....	....	....	....	....
	HC Karlovy Vary	Czech	32	0	2	2	36	....	....	....	....	....
2002-03	Karlovy Vary	Czech	17	0	3	3	16	....	....	....	....	....
	Karlovy Vary Jr.	Czech-Jr.	15	5	4	9	8	....	....	....	....	....
	KLH Chomutov	Czech-2	5	0	1	1	2	....	....	....	....	....
	Havirov	Czech	9	0	0	0	2	....	....	....	....	....
	Havirov	Czech-Q	....	....	....	....	....	4	0	0	0	2

PUSHKAREV, Konstantin (puhsh-kar-EHV, kawn-stuhn-TIHN) **L.A.**

Right wing. Shoots left. 6', 169 lbs. Born, Ust-Kamenogorsk, USSR, February 12, 1985.
(Los Angeles' 4th choice, 44th overall, in 2003 Entry Draft).

			Regular Season					Playoffs				
Season	Club	League	GP	G	A	TP	PIM	GP	G	A	TP	PIM
2001-02	Kamenogorsk 2	Russia 3		STATISTICS NOT AVAILABLE								
2002-03	Kamenogorsk 2	Russia 3		STATISTICS NOT AVAILABLE								
	Ust-Kamenogorsk	Russia 2	4	0	0	0	4	....	....	....	....	....

QUINCEY, Kyle (KWIHN-see, KIGHL) **DET.**

Defense. Shoots left. 6'1", 194 lbs. Born, Kitchener, Ont., August 12, 1985.
(Detroit's 2nd choice, 132nd overall, in 2003 Entry Draft).

			Regular Season					Playoffs				
Season	Club	League	GP	G	A	TP	PIM	GP	G	A	TP	PIM
2001-02	Mississauga	OPJHL	27	5	14	19	31	....	....	....	....	....
2002-03	London Knights	OHL	66	6	12	18	77	14	3	4	7	11

RACHUNEK, Ivan (ra-KHOO-nuhk, EE-vahn) **T.B.**

Left wing. Shoots left. 5'9", 180 lbs. Born, Gottwaldov, Czech., July 6, 1981.
(Tampa Bay's 8th choice, 187th overall, in 1999 Entry Draft).

			Regular Season					Playoffs				
Season	Club	League	GP	G	A	TP	PIM	GP	G	A	TP	PIM
1997-98	Zlin Jr.	Czech-Jr.	48	15	25	40	172	....	....	....	....	....
1998-99	Zlin Jr.	Czech-Jr.	40	37	22	59	70	....	....	....	....	....
	HC ZPS-Barum Zlin	Czech	5	0	0	0	0	....	....	....	....	....
99-2000	Zlin	Czech	5	0	1	1	2	....	....	....	....	....
	Zlin Jr.	Czech-Jr.	3	0	7	7	4	....	....	....	....	....
	Windsor Spitfires	OHL	15	2	2	4	21	....	....	....	....	....
2000-01	Zlin	Czech	50	8	9	17	95	6	1	0	1	8
2001-02	Zlin	Czech	48	9	11	20	143	11	3	4	7	6
2002-03	HC Hame Zlin	Czech	48	9	16	25	52	....	....	....	....	....

RADUNSKE, Brock (ra-DOON-skee, BRAWK) **EDM.**

Left wing. Shoots left. 6'4", 196 lbs. Born, Kitchener, Ont., April 5, 1983.
(Edmonton's 5th choice, 79th overall, in 2002 Entry Draft).

			Regular Season					Playoffs				
Season	Club	League	GP	G	A	TP	PIM	GP	G	A	TP	PIM
99-2000	Aurora Tigers	OPJHL	42	6	14	20	23	4	4	8	12	2
2000-01	Newmarket	OPJHL	48	30	39	69	65	....	....	....	....	....
2001-02	Michigan State	CCHA	41	4	9	13	28	....	....	....	....	....
2002-03	Michigan State	CCHA	36	11	18	29	30	....	....	....	....	....

RAJAMAKI, Erkki (righ-ya-MA-kee, UHR-kee) **T.B.**

Left wing. Shoots left. 6'2", 205 lbs. Born, Vantaa, Finland, October 30, 1978.
(Tampa Bay's 9th choice, 216th overall, in 1999 Entry Draft).

			Regular Season					Playoffs				
Season	Club	League	GP	G	A	TP	PIM	GP	G	A	TP	PIM
1993-94	Vantaa HT-C	Finn-Jr.	10	0	1	1	0	....	....	....	....	....
1994-95	Kiekko Vantaa Jr.	Finn-Jr.	2	0	0	0	0	....	....	....	....	....
1995-96	Kiekko Vantaa Jr.	Finn-Jr.	DID NOT PLAY – INJURED									
1996-97	Kiekko Vantaa-B	Finn-Jr.	33	14	19	33	32	....	....	....	....	....
1997-98	HIFK Helsinki Jr.	Finn-Jr.	14	1	2	3	2	....	....	....	....	....
	Kiekko Vantaa-B	Finn-Jr.	....	....	....	....	....	10	3	0	3	2
1998-99	HIFK Helsinki-B	Finn-Jr.	14	2	2	4	8	....	....	....	....	....
	HIFK Helsinki	Finland	14	0	0	0	2	....	....	....	....	....
	HIFK Helsinki Jr.	Finn-Jr.	....	....	....	....	....	13	7	3	10	45
99-2000	Colgate	ECAC	31	1	6	7	20	....	....	....	....	....
2000-01	Newcastle Jesters	Britain	11	1	0	1	0	....	....	....	....	....
	FoPS Forssa	Finland-2	4	1	3	4	0	....	....	....	....	....
	HIFK Helsinki	Finland	50	1	2	3	10	5	0	0	0	2
2001-02	HPK Hameenlinna	Finland	56	12	7	19	75	8	1	2	3	2
2002-03	HPK Hameenlinna	Finland	40	4	3	7	100	10	1	0	1	36

RAKHMATULLIN, Ashkat (rahkh-ma-TOO-lihn, ahs-KHAHT) **MIN.**

Left wing. Shoots left. 5'11", 165 lbs. Born, Ufa, USSR, May 31, 1978.
(Hartford's 10th choice, 231st overall, in 1996 Entry Draft).

			Regular Season					Playoffs				
Season	Club	League	GP	G	A	TP	PIM	GP	G	A	TP	PIM
1996-97	Ufa	Russia	28	1	3	4	8	3	0	0	0	0
1997-98	Ufa	Russia	14	0	1	1	6	....	....	....	....	....
1998-99	Asheville Smoke	UHL	31	6	10	16	23	4	1	0	1	0
	Fayetteville Force	CHL	4	0	0	0	4	....	....	....	....	....
	Florida Everblades	ECHL	6	0	1	1	2	....	....	....	....	....
99-2000	Ufa	Russia	34	5	8	13	14	....	....	....	....	....
2000-01	Ufa	Russia	44	7	15	22	22	....	....	....	....	....
2001-02	SKA St. Petersburg	Russia	30	7	7	14	14	....	....	....	....	....
2002-03	Sibir Novosibirsk	Russia	11	1	1	2	4	....	....	....	....	....
	Krylja Sovetov	Russia	19	2	1	3	16	....	....	....	....	....

Rights transferred to **Carolina** after **Hartford** franchise relocated, June 25, 1997. Traded to **Minnesota** by **Carolina** with Carolina's 3rd round choice (later traded to NY Rangers – NY Rangers selected Garth Murray) in 2001 Entry Draft and Carolina's compensatory 5th round choice (Armands Berzins) in 2002 Entry Draft for Scott Pellerin, March 1, 2001.

RAMHOLT, Tim (RAM-hohlt, TIHM) **CGY.**

Defense. Shoots left. 6'1", 194 lbs. Born, Zurich, Switz., November 2, 1984.
(Calgary's 2nd choice, 39th overall, in 2003 Entry Draft).

			Regular Season					Playoffs				
Season	Club	League	GP	G	A	TP	PIM	GP	G	A	TP	PIM
99-2000	Grasshopper Jr.	Swiss-Jr.	35	2	9	11	26	4	0	2	2	4
	Grasshopper	Swiss-2	2	0	0	0	0	....	....	....	....	....
2000-01	GC SCK Lions	Swiss-2	37	0	2	2	38	3	0	0	0	4
	GC SCK Lions Jr.	Swiss-Jr.	17	3	6	9	10	....	....	....	....	....
2001-02	ZSC Lions Zurich	Swiss	37	3	0	3	14	17	0	3	3	2
	GCK Zurich Jr.	Swiss-Jr.	5	2	2	4	4	....	....	....	....	....
	GCK Zurich	Swiss-2	3	0	0	0	0	....	....	....	....	....
2002-03	ZSC Lions Zurich	Swiss	30	2	0	2	12	9	0	1	1	0
	GCK Lions Zurich	Swiss-2	12	0	4	4	6	....	....	....	....	....

RANGER, Paul (RAIN-juhr, PAWL) **T.B.**

Defense. Shoots left. 6'3", 198 lbs. Born, North York, Ont., September 12, 1984.
(Tampa Bay's choice, 183rd overall, in 2002 Entry Draft).

			Regular Season					Playoffs				
Season	Club	League	GP	G	A	TP	PIM	GP	G	A	TP	PIM
2001-02	Oshawa Generals	OHL	62	0	9	9	49	5	0	0	0	4
2002-03	Oshawa Generals	OHL	68	10	28	38	70	13	0	3	3	10

RAWLYK, Rory (RAW-lihk, ROHR-ee) **NYR**

Defense. Shoots right. 6'3", 175 lbs. Born, Edmonton, Alta., September 9, 1983.

			Regular Season					Playoffs				
Season	Club	League	GP	G	A	TP	PIM	GP	G	A	TP	PIM
1998-99	Edm. Maple Leafs	AMBHL	36	6	18	24	58	....	....	....	....	....
99-2000	Edm. United Cycle	AMHL	28	3	14	17	34	....	....	....	....	....
2000-01	Camrose Kodiaks	AJHL	24	3	6	9	16	16	1	5	6	32
	Medicine Hat	WHL	17	0	1	1	6	....	....	....	....	....
2001-02	Medicine Hat	WHL	40	2	9	11	59	....	....	....	....	....
	Vancouver Giants	WHL	28	3	7	10	21	....	....	....	....	....
2002-03	Vancouver Giants	WHL	4	1	1	2	8	....	....	....	....	....
	Prince Albert	WHL	28	6	9	15	16	....	....	....	....	....
	Red Deer Rebels	WHL	20	4	5	9	16	23	2	9	11	30

Signed as a free agent by **NY Rangers**, September 15, 2001.

RAZIN, Andrei (RAH-zihn, AN-dray) **PHI.**

Center. Shoots left. 5'11", 180 lbs. Born, Togliatti, Russia, October 23, 1973.
(Philadelphia's 7th choice, 177th overall, in 2001 Entry Draft).

			Regular Season					Playoffs				
Season	Club	League	GP	G	A	TP	PIM	GP	G	A	TP	PIM
1990-91	Mayak Samara	USSR-3	2	0	0	0	2	....	....	....	....	....
1991-92	Mayak Samara	CIS-3	41	15	16	31	26	....	....	....	....	....
	Lada Togliatti	CIS	7	0	0	0	2	....	....	....	....	....
1992-93	Mayak Samara	CIS-2	29	8	7	15	12	....	....	....	....	....
	Lada Togliatti	CIS	12	1	2	3	0	1	0	0	0	0
1993-94	Lada Togliatti 2	CIS-3	4	4	0	4	0	....	....	....	....	....
	Lada Togliatti	CIS	15	1	1	2	0	....	....	....	....	....
1994-95	Magnitogorsk	CIS	49	11	14	25	12	7	3	2	5	16
1995-96	Magnitogorsk	CIS	40	6	11	17	28	4	0	0	0	2
	Magnitogorsk 2	CIS-2	5	3	0	3	0	....	....	....	....	....
1996-97	Magnitogorsk 2	Russia-3	4	5	3	8	4	....	....	....	....	....
	CSK VVS Samara	Russia	32	7	8	15	12	2	0	1	1	2
1997-98	Magnitogorsk 2	Russia-3	1	1	2	3	0	....	....	....	....	....
	Magnitogorsk	Russia	46	6	32	38	12	....	....	....	....	....
1998-99	Magnitogorsk	EuroHL	6	2	4	6	2	6	2	5	7	4
	Magnitogorsk 2	Russia-4	1	2	2	4	0	....	....	....	....	....
	Magnitogorsk	Russia	39	7	25	32	14	16	4	3	7	6
99-2000	Magnitogorsk	EuroHL	2	0	2	2	4	5	2	0	2	20
	Magnitogorsk 2	Russia-3	4	3	5	8	0	....	....	....	....	....
	Magnitogorsk	Russia	29	11	10	21	8	12	3	2	5	4
2000-01	Magnitogorsk	Russia	44	16	*31	*47	78	12	7	6	13	20
2001-02	Dynamo Moscow	Russia	51	11	*32	43	96	3	2	2	4	0
2002-03	Dynamo Moscow	Russia	40	9	28	37	55	5	1	3	4	24

READY, Ryan (REH-dee, RIGH-yan) **VAN.**

Left wing. Shoots left. 6'2", 195 lbs. Born, Peterborough, Ont., November 7, 1978.
(Calgary's 8th choice, 100th overall, in 1997 Entry Draft).

			Regular Season					Playoffs				
Season	Club	League	GP	G	A	TP	PIM	GP	G	A	TP	PIM
1994-95	Peterborough	OPJHL	48	20	33	53	65	....	....	....	....	....
1995-96	Belleville Bulls	OHL	63	5	13	18	54	10	0	2	2	2
1996-97	Belleville Bulls	OHL	66	23	24	47	102	6	1	3	4	4
1997-98	Belleville Bulls	OHL	66	33	39	72	80	10	5	2	7	12
1998-99	Belleville Bulls	OHL	63	33	59	92	73	21	10	28	38	22
99-2000	Syracuse Crunch	AHL	70	4	12	16	59	2	0	0	0	0
2000-01	Kansas City Blades	IHL	67	10	15	25	75	....	....	....	....	....
2001-02	Manitoba Moose	AHL	72	23	32	55	73	7	5	1	6	4
2002-03	Manitoba Moose	AHL	68	24	26	50	52	14	2	5	7	2

OHL First All-Star Team (1999)

Signed as a free agent by **Vancouver**, June 16, 1999.

REDENBACH, Tyler (REH-dehn-bak, TIGH-luhr) **PHX.**

Center. Shoots left. 5'11", 184 lbs. Born, Regina, Sask., September 25, 1984.
(Phoenix's 1st choice, 77th overall, in 2003 Entry Draft).

			Regular Season					Playoffs				
Season	Club	League	GP	G	A	TP	PIM	GP	G	A	TP	PIM
2000-01	North Kamloops	BCAHA	49	60	66	126	22	....	....	....	....	....
2001-02	Prince George	WHL	65	3	18	21	30	7	0	1	1	2
2002-03	Prince George	WHL	36	8	34	42	29	....	....	....	....	....
	Swift Current	WHL	24	9	17	26	6	4	0	4	4	4

REDIKER, Frank (REH-dih-kuhr, FRANK) **BOS.**

Defense. Shoots left. 6'1", 200 lbs. Born, Sterling Heights, MI, March 15, 1985.
(Boston's 5th choice, 118th overall, in 2003 Entry Draft).

			Regular Season					Playoffs				
Season	Club	League	GP	G	A	TP	PIM	GP	G	A	TP	PIM
2000-01	Det. Compuware	NAJHL	39	3	7	10	131	3	0	0	0	8
2001-02	Windsor Spitfires	OHL	59	9	13	22	170	8	0	0	0	22
2002-03	Windsor Spitfires	OHL	51	8	8	16	120	7	0	2	2	10

REDLIHS, Jekabs (REHD-lihs, YEH-kabs) **CBJ**

Defense. Shoots left. 6'2", 185 lbs. Born, Riga, Latvia, March 29, 1982.
(Columbus' 6th choice, 119th overall, in 2002 Entry Draft).

			Regular Season					Playoffs				
Season	Club	League	GP	G	A	TP	PIM	GP	G	A	TP	PIM
1998-99	Dynamo Riga-18	Latvia-Jr.	STATISTICS NOT AVAILABLE									
99-2000	HC Essamika-Jr.	EEHL	16	1	4	5	6	....	....	....	....	....
	Metalurgs Liepaja	Latvia	1	0	0	0	0	....	....	....	....	....
	Metalurgs Liepaja	EEHL	11	0	0	0	2	....	....	....	....	....
2000-01	Metalurgs Liepaja	EEHL	31	1	3	4	....	....	....	....	....	....
	Metalurgs Liepaja	Latvia	23	4	5	9	....	....	....	....	....	....
2001-02	NY Apple Core	EJHL	38	3	16	19	24	....	....	....	....	....
2002-03	Boston University	H-East	40	4	12	16	12	....	....	....	....	....

EJHL First All-Star Team (2002) • EJHL Defensive Player of the Year (2002) • Hockey East All-Rookie Team (2003)

REDLIHS, Krisjanis (REHD-lihs, krihs-JA-nihs) **N.J.**

Defense. Shoots left. 6'2", 190 lbs. Born, Riga, Latvia, January 15, 1981.
(New Jersey's 7th choice, 154th overall, in 2002 Entry Draft).

			Regular Season					Playoffs				
Season	Club	League	GP	G	A	TP	PIM	GP	G	A	TP	PIM
1998-99	Dynamo Riga-18	Latvia-Jr.	STATISTICS NOT AVAILABLE									
99-2000	Metalurgs Liepaja	EEHL	12	1	3	4	0	....	....	....	....	....
2000-01	Metalurgs Liepaja	EEHL	27	2	2	4	....	....	....	....	....	....
	Metalurgs Liepaja	Latvia	22	1	6	7	....	....	....	....	....	....
2001-02	Metalurgs Liepaja	EEHL	32	0	2	2	....	11	1	1	2	....
	Metalurgs Liepaja	Latvia	13	0	6	6	4	3	2	2	4	0
2002-03	Albany River Rats	AHL	61	1	9	10	20	....	....	....	....	....

REED, Josh (REED, JAWSH) **VAN.**

Defense. Shoots right. 6'2", 204 lbs. Born, Vernon, B.C., May 21, 1979.
(Vancouver's 5th choice, 172nd overall, in 1999 Entry Draft).

			Regular Season					Playoffs				
Season	Club	League	GP	G	A	TP	PIM	GP	G	A	TP	PIM
1994-95	Vernon M.L.	BCAHA	56	13	41	54	136	....	....	....	....	....
1995-96	Vernon Vikings	BCAHA	50	9	43	52	150	....	....	....	....	....
1996-97	Cowichan	BCHL	42	3	3	6	61	....	....	....	....	....
1997-98	Cowichan	BCHL	50	5	20	25	115	....	....	....	....	....
1998-99	Vernon Vipers	BCHL	54	16	38	54	110	....	....	....	....	....
99-2000	U. Mass-Lowell	H-East	30	2	10	12	24	....	....	....	....	....
2000-01	U. Mass-Lowell	H-East	17	1	6	7	22	....	....	....	....	....
2001-02	U. Mass-Lowell	H-East	37	4	9	13	38	....	....	....	....	....
2002-03	U. Mass-Lowell	H-East	23	2	5	7	10	....	....	....	....	....

REICH, Jeremy (REECH, JAIR-eh-MEE) CBJ

Left wing. Shoots left. 6'1", 204 lbs. Born, Craik, Sask., February 11, 1979.
(Chicago's 3rd choice, 39th overall, in 1997 Entry Draft).

			Regular Season					Playoffs				
Season	Club	League	GP	G	A	TP	PIM	GP	G	A	TP	PIM
1993-94	Pilote Butte	SAHA	80	70	65	135	120	....	....	....	....	....
1994-95	Sask. Contacts	SMHL	35	13	20	33	81	....	....	....	....	....
1995-96	Seattle	WHL	65	11	11	22	88	5	0	1	1	10
1996-97	Seattle	WHL	62	19	31	50	134	15	2	5	7	36
1997-98	Seattle	WHL	43	24	23	47	121	....	....	....	....	....
	Swift Current	WHL	22	8	8	16	47	12	5	6	11	37
1998-99	Swift Current	WHL	67	21	28	49	220	6	0	3	3	26
99-2000	Swift Current	WHL	72	33	58	91	167	12	2	10	12	19
2000-01	Syracuse Crunch	AHL	56	6	9	15	108	5	0	0	0	6
2001-02	Syracuse Crunch	AHL	59	9	7	16	178	10	4	0	4	16
2002-03	Syracuse Crunch	AHL	78	14	13	27	195	....	....	....	....	....

REID, Darren (REED, DAIR-uhn) T.B.

Right wing. Shoots right. 6'2", 185 lbs. Born, Lac La Biche, Alta., May 8, 1983.
(Tampa Bay's 11th choice, 256th overall, in 2002 Entry Draft).

			Regular Season					Playoffs				
Season	Club	League	GP	G	A	TP	PIM	GP	G	A	TP	PIM
2000-01	Drayton Valley	AJHL		STATISTICS NOT AVAILABLE								
2001-02	Drayton Valley	AJHL	31	9	12	21	195	....	....	....	....	....
	Medicine Hat	WHL	37	8	9	17	70	....	....	....	....	....
2002-03	Medicine Hat	WHL	63	14	30	44	163	11	5	0	5	19

REITZ, Erik (RIGHTZ, AIR-ihk) MIN.

Defense. Shoots right. 6'1", 210 lbs. Born, Detroit, MI, July 29, 1982.
(Minnesota's 5th choice, 170th overall, in 2000 Entry Draft).

			Regular Season					Playoffs				
Season	Club	League	GP	G	A	TP	PIM	GP	G	A	TP	PIM
1998-99	Leamington Flyers	OJHL-B	50	5	10	15	80	....	....	....	....	....
99-2000	Barrie Colts	OHL	63	2	10	12	85	25	0	5	5	44
2000-01	Barrie Colts	OHL	68	5	21	26	178	5	1	0	1	21
2001-02	Barrie Colts	OHL	61	13	27	40	153	20	4	16	20	40
2002-03	Houston Aeros	AHL	62	6	13	19	112	11	0	3	3	31

Memorial Cup All-Star Team (2000) • OHL First All-Star Team (2002)

RENNETTE, Tyler (REHN-neht, TIGH-luhr) ST.L.

Center. Shoots right. 6'1", 179 lbs. Born, North Bay, Ont., April 16, 1979.
(St. Louis' 1st choice, 40th overall, in 1997 Entry Draft).

			Regular Season					Playoffs				
Season	Club	League	GP	G	A	TP	PIM	GP	G	A	TP	PIM
1994-95	N. Bay Athletics	NOHA	52	24	42	66	72	....	....	....	....	....
1995-96	Waterloo	OJHL-B	45	27	47	74	64	....	....	....	....	....
1996-97	North Bay	OHL	63	24	34	58	42	....	....	....	....	....
1997-98	North Bay	OHL	31	17	14	31	37	....	....	....	....	....
	Erie Otters	OHL	24	16	17	33	20	6	3	3	6	2
1998-99	Erie Otters	OHL	61	30	37	67	40	5	6	1	7	8
99-2000	Worcester IceCats	AHL	55	8	17	25	16	7	2	3	5	4
2000-01	Worcester IceCats	AHL	29	3	8	11	24	....	....	....	....	....
	Peoria Rivermen	ECHL	7	5	1	6	6	14	9	2	11	14
2001-02	Worcester IceCats	AHL	4	0	1	1	8	....	....	....	....	....
	Peoria Rivermen	ECHL	62	23	22	45	24	5	1	0	1	8
2002-03	Hamilton Bulldogs	AHL	4	0	2	2	4	....	....	....	....	....
	Peoria Rivermen	ECHL	65	42	32	74	98	4	1	2	3	6
	Bridgeport	AHL	....	....	....	....	....	2	0	0	0	0

REYNOLDS, Peter (REH-nolds, PEE-tuhr) CAR.

Defense. Shoots right. 6'3", 200 lbs. Born, Waterloo, Ont., April 27, 1981.
(Carolina's 8th choice, 274th overall, in 2001 Entry Draft).

			Regular Season					Playoffs				
Season	Club	League	GP	G	A	TP	PIM	GP	G	A	TP	PIM
1996-97	Caledon	MTJHL	45	1	10	11	69	....	....	....	....	....
1997-98	London Knights	OHL	55	0	8	8	30	16	0	0	0	10
1998-99	London Knights	OHL	59	2	25	27	55	23	2	3	5	24
99-2000	North Bay	OHL	61	3	29	32	53	6	1	3	4	10
2000-01	North Bay	OHL	58	2	27	29	85	4	0	1	1	7
	St. John's	AHL	2	0	0	0	0	1	0	0	0	0
2001-02	Lowell	AHL	45	1	2	3	38	....	....	....	....	....
	Florida Everblades	ECHL	7	0	0	0	10	....	....	....	....	....
2002-03	Florida Everblades	ECHL	66	1	9	10	111	1	0	0	0	0

• Re-entered NHL Entry Draft. Originally Toronto's 2nd choice, 60th overall, in 1999 Entry Draft.

RIAZANTSEV, Alexander (ree-ZAHNT-sehv, al-ehx-AN-duhr) WSH.

Defense. Shoots right. 6', 210 lbs. Born, Moscow, USSR, March 15, 1980.
(Colorado's 10th choice, 167th overall, in 1998 Entry Draft).

			Regular Season					Playoffs				
Season	Club	League	GP	G	A	TP	PIM	GP	G	A	TP	PIM
1996-97	Spartak Moscow 2	Russia-3	18	0	0	0	8	....	....	....	....	....
	Spartak Moscow	Russia	20	1	2	3	4	....	....	....	....	....
1997-98	Spartak Moscow 2	Russia-3	31	3	8	11	26	....	....	....	....	....
	Victoriaville Tigres	QMJHL	22	6	9	15	14	4	0	0	0	0
1998-99	Victoriaville Tigres	QMJHL	64	17	40	57	57	6	0	3	3	10
	Hershey Bears	AHL	2	0	0	0	0	....	....	....	....	....
99-2000	Victoriaville Tigres	QMJHL	48	17	45	62	45	6	2	5	7	20
	Hershey Bears	AHL	2	0	1	1	2	6	1	1	2	0
2000-01	Hershey Bears	AHL	66	5	18	23	26	11	0	0	0	2
2001-02	Hershey Bears	AHL	76	5	19	24	28	5	0	1	1	4
2002-03	Hershey Bears	AHL	57	5	10	15	65	....	....	....	....	....
	Milwaukee	AHL	14	3	4	7	9	5	0	4	4	2

Traded to **Nashville** by **Colorado** for Nashville's 7th round choice (Linus Videll) in 2003 Entry Draft, March 11, 2003. Traded to **Washington** by **Nashville** for Mike Farrell, July 14, 2003.

RICHARDS, Mike (RIH-chahrds, MIGHK) PHI.

Center. Shoots left. 5'11", 185 lbs. Born, Kenora, Ont., February 11, 1985.
(Philadelphia's 2nd choice, 24th overall, in 2003 Entry Draft).

			Regular Season					Playoffs				
Season	Club	League	GP	G	A	TP	PIM	GP	G	A	TP	PIM
2000-01	Kenora Stars	NOHA	85	76	73	149	20	....	....	....	....	....
2001-02	Kitchener Rangers	OHL	65	20	38	58	52	4	0	1	1	6
2002-03	Kitchener Rangers	OHL	67	37	50	87	99	21	9	18	27	24

RICHARDSON, Brad (RIH-chard-suhn, BRAD) COL.

Center. Shoots left. 5'11", 178 lbs. Born, Belleville, Ont., February 4, 1985.
(Colorado's 4th choice, 163rd overall, in 2003 Entry Draft).

			Regular Season					Playoffs				
Season	Club	League	GP	G	A	TP	PIM	GP	G	A	TP	PIM
2001-02	Owen Sound	OHL	58	12	21	33	20	....	....	....	....	....
2002-03	Owen Sound	OHL	67	27	40	67	54	4	1	1	2	10

RICHMOND, Danny (RIHCH-muhnd, DA-nee) CAR.

Defense. Shoots left. 6', 175 lbs. Born, Chicago, IL, August 1, 1984.
(Carolina's 2nd choice, 31st overall, in 2003 Entry Draft).

			Regular Season					Playoffs				
Season	Club	League	GP	G	A	TP	PIM	GP	G	A	TP	PIM
2000-01	Team Illinois	MWEHL	79	25	40	65	....	....	....	....	....	....
2001-02	Chicago Steel	USHL	56	8	45	53	129	4	0	4	4	20
2002-03	U. of Michigan	CCHA	43	3	19	22	48	....	....	....	....	....

USHL All-Rookie Team (2002) • USHL First All-Star Team (2002) • USHL Rookie of the Year (2002) • CCHA All-Rookie Team (2003)

RICHTER, Martin (RIHKH-tuhr, MAHR-tihn) NYR

Defense. Shoots right. 6'1", 196 lbs. Born, Prostejov, Czech., June 2, 1977.
(NY Rangers' 9th choice, 269th overall, in 2000 Entry Draft).

			Regular Season					Playoffs				
Season	Club	League	GP	G	A	TP	PIM	GP	G	A	TP	PIM
1995-96	HC Olomouc	Czech	3	0	0	0	0	1	0	0	0	0
1996-97	HC Olomouc	Czech	27	1	0	1	26	....	....	....	....	....
1997-98	HC Karlovy Vary	Czech	42	1	2	3	32	....	....	....	....	....
1998-99	HC Karlovy Vary	Czech	51	3	6	9	44	....	....	....	....	....
99-2000	HC Karlovy Vary	Czech	24	0	5	5	18	....	....	....	....	....
	SaiPa	Finland	26	1	3	4	54	....	....	....	....	....
2000-01	SaiPa	Finland	41	4	5	9	80	....	....	....	....	....
	Hartford Wolf Pack	AHL	1	0	0	0	0	....	....	....	....	....
2001-02	Hartford Wolf Pack	AHL	29	1	1	2	36	....	....	....	....	....
	HC Sparta Praha	Czech	8	0	0	0	14	13	0	0	0	10
2002-03	HC Sparta Praha	Czech	34	2	7	9	77	8	0	0	0	10

RIDDLE, Jake (RIH-duhl, JAYK)

Left wing. Shoots left. 6'1", 205 lbs. Born, Fridley, MN, April 22, 1983.
(Minnesota's 7th choice, 239th overall, in 2001 Entry Draft).

			Regular Season					Playoffs				
Season	Club	League	GP	G	A	TP	PIM	GP	G	A	TP	PIM
1998-99	St. Margaret's	Hi-School		STATISTICS NOT AVAILABLE								
99-2000	U.S. National U-17	USDP	33	7	6	13	93	....	....	....	....	....
2000-01	Seattle	WHL	67	13	20	33	109	6	0	2	2	2
2001-02	Seattle	WHL	70	16	15	31	109	11	1	2	3	18
2002-03	Seattle	WHL	14	2	2	4	19	....	....	....	....	....
	Tri-City Americans	WHL	58	30	28	58	171	....	....	....	....	....

RIDDLE, Troy (RIH-duhl, TROI) ST.L.

Center. Shoots right. 6', 172 lbs. Born, Minneapolis, MN, August 24, 1981.
(St. Louis' 5th choice, 129th overall, in 2000 Entry Draft).

			Regular Season					Playoffs				
Season	Club	League	GP	G	A	TP	PIM	GP	G	A	TP	PIM
1997-98	St. Margaret's	Hi-School	29	33	35	68	....	....	....	....	....	....
1998-99	St. Margaret's	Hi-School	29	54	45	99	....	....	....	....	....	....
99-2000	Des Moines	USHL	53	36	30	66	95	8	2	2	4	31
2000-01	U. of Minnesota	WCHA	38	16	14	30	49	....	....	....	....	....
2001-02	U. of Minnesota	WCHA	44	16	31	47	46	....	....	....	....	....
2002-03	U. of Minnesota	WCHA	45	26	26	52	50	....	....	....	....	....

USHL Second All-Star Team (2000) • USHL Rookie of the Year (2000)

RISSMILLER, Pat (RIGHZ-mih-luhr, PAT) S.J.

Left wing. Shoots left. 6'3", 195 lbs. Born, Belmont, MA, October 26, 1978.

			Regular Season					Playoffs				
Season	Club	League	GP	G	A	TP	PIM	GP	G	A	TP	PIM
1998-99	Holy Cross	MAAC	34	13	28	41	23	....	....	....	....	....
99-2000	Holy Cross	MAAC	35	10	17	27	22	....	....	....	....	....
2000-01	Holy Cross	MAAC	29	14	15	29	40	....	....	....	....	....
2001-02	Holy Cross	MAAC	33	16	*30	*46	31	....	....	....	....	....
2002-03	Cleveland Barons	AHL	72	14	26	40	24	....	....	....	....	....
	Cincinnati	ECHL	2	2	2	4	0	....	....	....	....	....

MAAC First All-Star Team (2002)

Signed as a free agent by **Cleveland** (AHL), September 23, 2002. Signed as a free agent by **San Jose**, June 30, 2003.

RIVA, Danny (REE-vuh, DA-nee)

Center. Shoots right. 6', 190 lbs. Born, Framingham, MA, September 17, 1975.

			Regular Season					Playoffs				
Season	Club	League	GP	G	A	TP	PIM	GP	G	A	TP	PIM
1995-96	RPI Engineers	ECAC	35	3	7	10	30	....	....	....	....	....
1996-97	RPI Engineers	ECAC	36	12	14	26	30	....	....	....	....	....
1997-98	RPI Engineers	ECAC	35	10	18	28	16	....	....	....	....	....
1998-99	RPI Engineers	ECAC	36	*22	*35	*57	35	....	....	....	....	....
	Milwaukee	IHL	8	0	2	2	4	1	0	1	1	0
99-2000	Milwaukee	IHL	67	8	12	20	18	3	0	0	0	2
2000-01	Milwaukee	IHL	75	12	9	21	23	5	0	1	1	2
2001-02	Reading Royals	ECHL	37	10	17	27	38	....	....	....	....	....
	Manchester	AHL	29	4	1	5	8	3	0	0	0	12
2002-03	Reading Royals	ECHL	14	8	8	16	8	....	....	....	....	....
	Manchester	AHL	19	2	1	3	10	....	....	....	....	....
	Cincinnati	AHL	33	2	6	8	11	....	....	....	....	....

ECAC First All-Star Team (1999)

Signed as a free agent by **Nashville**, May 4, 1999.

ROBERTSON, Josh (RAW-buhrt-suhn, JAWSH) WSH.

Center. Shoots right. 5'11", 186 lbs. Born, Whitman, MA, August 25, 1984.
(Washington's 4th choice, 155th overall, in 2003 Entry Draft).

			Regular Season					Playoffs				
Season	Club	League	GP	G	A	TP	PIM	GP	G	A	TP	PIM
2000-01	Whitman-Hanson	Hi-School	28	30	28	58	....	....	....	....	....	....
2001-02	Whitman-Hanson	Hi-School	30	50	55	105	....	....	....	....	....	....
2002-03	Proctor Academy	Hi-School	34	37	44	81	....	....	....	....	....	....

• Signed Letter of Intent to attend **Northeastern** (ECAC), April 1, 2003.

ROBINSON, Darcy (RAW-bihn-suhn, DAHR-see) PIT.

Defense. Shoots right. 6'3", 235 lbs. Born, Kamloops, B.C., May 3, 1981.
(Pittsburgh's 10th choice, 233rd overall, in 1999 Entry Draft).

			Regular Season					Playoffs				
Season	Club	League	GP	G	A	TP	PIM	GP	G	A	TP	PIM
1996-97	Kamloops	BCAHA	59	18	42	60	188	....	....	....	....	....
1997-98	Saskatoon Blades	WHL	62	1	2	3	84	4	0	0	0	2
1998-99	Saskatoon Blades	WHL	48	3	6	9	86	....	....	....	....	....
99-2000	Saskatoon Blades	WHL	59	5	9	14	91	10	1	3	4	13
2000-01	Saskatoon Blades	WHL	41	2	6	8	80	....	....	....	....	....
	Red Deer Rebels	WHL	30	1	5	6	70	20	1	1	2	20
2001-02	Wheeling Nailers	ECHL	10	2	3	5	43	....	....	....	....	....
	Wilkes-Barre	AHL	40	0	5	5	35	....	....	....	....	....
2002-03	Wilkes-Barre	AHL	48	1	7	8	89	6	1	0	1	5
	Wheeling Nailers	ECHL	1	0	1	1	0	....	....	....	....	....

ROCHE, Ken (ROHCH, KEHN) NYR

Center. Shoots left. 5'11", 185 lbs. Born, Boston, MA, January 2, 1984.
(NY Rangers' 3rd choice, 75th overall, in 2003 Entry Draft).

			Regular Season					Playoffs				
Season	Club	League	GP	G	A	TP	PIM	GP	G	A	TP	PIM
2002-03	St. Sebastian's	Hi-School	29	25	28	53	16	....	....	....	....	....

• Signed Letter of Intent to attend **Boston University** (H-East), March 28, 2002.

RODMAN, Marcel (RAWD-muhn, mahr-SEHL) BOS.

Right wing. Shoots right. 6'1", 183 lbs. Born, Jesenice, Yugoslavia, September 25, 1981.
(Boston's 8th choice, 282nd overall, in 2001 Entry Draft).

			Regular Season					Playoffs				
Season	Club	League	GP	G	A	TP	PIM	GP	G	A	TP	PIM
1997-98	Acroni Jesenice Jr.	Sloven.-Jr.	44	29	44	73	14	....	....	....	....	....
1998-99	Pickering Panthers	OPJHL	37	30	21	51	8	....	....	....	....	....
99-2000	Peterborough	OHL	61	17	20	37	16	5	1	2	3	0
2000-01	Peterborough	OHL	61	36	35	71	14	7	4	2	6	2
2001-02	Acroni Jesenice	EEHL	7	4	2	6	4	....	....	....	....	....
	Acroni Jesenice	Slovenia	9	12	6	18	4	....	....	....	....	....
2002-03	EHC Graz	Austria	44	22	25	47	22	....	....	....	....	....

Signed as a free agent by **EHC Graz** (Austria) with Boston retaining NHL rights, July 20, 2002.

ROGERS, Brandon (RAW-juhrs, BRAN-duhn) ANA.

Defense. Shoots right. 6'1", 190 lbs. Born, Rochester, NH, February 27, 1982.
(Anaheim's 6th choice, 118th overall, in 2001 Entry Draft).

			Regular Season					Playoffs				
Season	Club	League	GP	G	A	TP	PIM	GP	G	A	TP	PIM
99-2000	Hotchkiss High	Hi-School	25	9	12	21	35	....	....	....	....	....
2000-01	Hotchkiss High	Hi-School	22	10	13	23	45	....	....	....	....	....
2001-02	U. of Michigan	CCHA	32	2	1	3	30	....	....	....	....	....
2002-03	U. of Michigan	CCHA	43	4	21	25	65	....	....	....	....	....

ROHLFS, David (ROHLFS, DAY-vihd) EDM.

Right wing. Shoots right. 6'3", 219 lbs. Born, Ann Arbor, MI, June 4, 1984.
(Edmonton's 7th choice, 154th overall, in 2003 Entry Draft).

			Regular Season					Playoffs				
Season	Club	League	GP	G	A	TP	PIM	GP	G	A	TP	PIM
2001-02	Det. Compuware	NAJHL	60	13	10	23	36	....	....	....	....	....
2002-03	Det. Compuware	NAHL	53	30	14	44	36	5	2	1	3	8

• Signed Letter of Intent to attend **U. of Michigan** (WCHA), January 19, 2003.

ROME, Aaron (ROHM, AIR-uhn) L.A.

Defense. Shoots left. 6'1", 203 lbs. Born, Nesbitt, Man., September 27, 1983.
(Los Angeles' 4th choice, 104th overall, in 2002 Entry Draft).

			Regular Season					Playoffs				
Season	Club	League	GP	G	A	TP	PIM	GP	G	A	TP	PIM
1998-99	Sask. Contacts	SMHL		STATISTICS NOT AVAILABLE								
	Saskatoon Blades	WHL	1	0	0	0	0	....	....	....	....	....
99-2000	Saskatoon Blades	WHL	47	0	6	6	22	1	0	0	0	0
2000-01	Saskatoon Blades	WHL	3	0	0	0	2	....	....	....	....	....
	Kootenay Ice	WHL	53	2	8	10	43	11	1	3	4	6
2001-02	Kootenay Ice	WHL	33	4	13	17	55	....	....	....	....	....
	Swift Current	WHL	37	3	11	14	113	10	1	4	5	23
2002-03	Swift Current	WHL	61	12	44	56	201	4	1	0	1	20

ROMY, Kevin (ROH-mee, KEH-vihn) PHI.

Center. Shoots left. 5'11", 180 lbs. Born, La Chaux-de-Fonds, Switz., January 31, 1985.
(Philadelphia's 8th choice, 108th overall, in 2003 Entry Draft).

			Regular Season					Playoffs				
Season	Club	League	GP	G	A	TP	PIM	GP	G	A	TP	PIM
2000-01	Chaux-de-Fonds Jr.	Swiss-Jr.	24	28	16	44	42	....	....	....	....	....
	La Chaux-de-Fonds	Swiss	17	0	0	0	0	2	0	0	0	0
2001-02	La Chaux-de-Fonds	Swiss-2	35	10	13	23	16	10	5	5	10	6
	Chaux-de-Fonds Jr.	Swiss-Jr.	1	0	0	0	0	....	....	....	....	....
2002-03	Geneve	Swiss	35	2	2	4	18	6	0	0	0	2
	La Chaux-de-Fonds	Swiss-2	1	0	0	0	0	....	....	....	....	....

ROONEEM, Mark (ROO-neem, MAHRK) L.A.

Left wing. Shoots left. 6'2", 185 lbs. Born, Hinton, Alta., January 9, 1983.
(Los Angeles' 5th choice, 115th overall, in 2002 Entry Draft).

			Regular Season					Playoffs				
Season	Club	League	GP	G	A	TP	PIM	GP	G	A	TP	PIM
1998-99	Spruce Grove	AMBHL	36	32	30	62	183	....	....	....	....	....
99-2000	Kamloops Blazers	WHL	50	3	8	11	39	4	0	0	0	4
2000-01	Kamloops Blazers	WHL	62	8	9	17	77	4	1	0	1	8
2001-02	Kamloops Blazers	WHL	69	18	23	41	77	4	0	0	0	10
2002-03	Kamloops Blazers	WHL	40	9	6	15	60	....	....	....	....	....
	Calgary Hitmen	WHL	31	2	8	10	43	5	0	2	2	0

ROSA, Marco (ROH-zuh, MAHR-koh) DAL.

Center. Shoots left. 6', 170 lbs. Born, Scarborough, Ont., January 15, 1982.
(Dallas' 8th choice, 255th overall, in 2001 Entry Draft).

			Regular Season					Playoffs				
Season	Club	League	GP	G	A	TP	PIM	GP	G	A	TP	PIM
1998-99	Wexford Raiders	OPJHL	42	12	13	25	35	....	....	....	....	....
99-2000	Wexford Raiders	OPJHL	49	29	52	81	23	6	1	7	9	0
2000-01	Merrimack College	H-East	33	6	18	24	22	....	....	....	....	....
2001-02	Merrimack College	H-East	36	5	21	26	22	....	....	....	....	....
2002-03	Merrimack College	H-East	30	10	12	22	26	....	....	....	....	....

ROULEAU, Alexandre (ROO-loh, al-ehx-AHN-druh) PIT.

Defense. Shoots left. 6'1", 190 lbs. Born, Mont-Laurier, Que., July 29, 1983.
(Pittsburgh's 4th choice, 96th overall, in 2001 Entry Draft).

			Regular Season					Playoffs				
Season	Club	League	GP	G	A	TP	PIM	GP	G	A	TP	PIM
1998-99	Amos Forestiers	QAAA	41	7	6	13	144	....	....	....	....	....
99-2000	Val-d'Or Foreurs	QMJHL	41	3	3	6	39	....	....	....	....	....
1999-001	Amos Forestiers	QAAA	25	5	10	15	114	....	....	....	....	....
2000-01	Val-d'Or Foreurs	QMJHL	70	8	17	25	124	21	1	0	1	46
2001-02	Val-d'Or Foreurs	QMJHL	69	14	25	39	174	7	0	2	2	16
2002-03	Val-d'Or Foreurs	QMJHL	31	7	12	19	92	....	....	....	....	....
	Quebec Remparts	QMJHL	24	9	17	26	74	11	2	4	6	23

QMJHL Second All-Star Team (2003)

ROURKE, Allan (RAWRK, AL-lan) CAR.

Defense. Shoots left. 6'1", 214 lbs. Born, Mississauga, Ont., March 6, 1980.
(Toronto's 6th choice, 154th overall, in 1998 Entry Draft).

			Regular Season					Playoffs				
Season	Club	League	GP	G	A	TP	PIM	GP	G	A	TP	PIM
1995-96	Mississauga Reps	MTHL	38	15	25	40	173	....	....	....	....	....
1996-97	Kitchener Rangers	OHL	25	1	1	2	12	6	0	0	0	0
1997-98	Kitchener Rangers	OHL	48	5	17	22	59	6	1	1	2	6
1998-99	Kitchener Rangers	OHL	66	11	28	39	79	1	0	0	0	2
99-2000	Kitchener Rangers	OHL	67	31	43	74	57	5	0	6	6	13
2000-01	St. John's	AHL	64	9	19	28	36	....	....	....	....	....
2001-02	St. John's	AHL	62	2	9	11	48	10	0	2	2	6
2002-03	St. John's	AHL	65	12	19	31	49	....	....	....	....	....

OHL Second All-Star Team (2000)

Traded to **Carolina** by **Toronto** for Harold Druken, May 29, 2003.

ROUSSIN, Dany (roo-SEH, DA-nee) FLA.

Center. Shoots left. 6'1", 190 lbs. Born, Quebec City, Que., January 9, 1985.
(Florida's 10th choice, 223rd overall, in 2003 Entry Draft).

			Regular Season					Playoffs				
Season	Club	League	GP	G	A	TP	PIM	GP	G	A	TP	PIM
2001-02	Sherbrooke	QMJHL	66	10	14	24	38	....	....	....	....	....
2002-03	Sherbrooke	QMJHL	33	8	8	16	18	....	....	....	....	....
	Rimouski Oceanic	QMJHL	38	12	26	38	69	....	....	....	....	....

ROY, Derek (ROI, DEHR-ihk) BUF.

Center. Shoots left. 5'9", 186 lbs. Born, Ottawa, Ont., May 4, 1983.
(Buffalo's 2nd choice, 32nd overall, in 2001 Entry Draft).

			Regular Season					Playoffs				
Season	Club	League	GP	G	A	TP	PIM	GP	G	A	TP	PIM
1998-99	Ontario East	OMHA	34	61	31	92	42	....	....	....	....	....
99-2000	Kitchener Rangers	OHL	66	34	53	87	44	5	4	1	5	6
2000-01	Kitchener Rangers	OHL	65	42	39	81	114	....	....	....	....	....
2001-02	Kitchener Rangers	OHL	62	43	46	89	92	4	1	2	3	2
2002-03	Kitchener Rangers	OHL	49	28	50	78	73	21	9	*23	32	14

OHL All-Rookie Team (2000) • OHL Rookie of the Year (2000) • CHL All-Rookie Team (2000) • CHL Plus/Minus Award (2000) • CHL Most Sportsmanlike Playerr (2000) • Memorial Cup All-Star Team (2003) • Stafford Smythe Memorial Trophy (Memorial Cup MVP) (2003)

ROY, Jimmy (ROI, JIHM-mee)

Center. Shoots right. 5'11", 170 lbs. Born, Sioux Lookout, Ont., September 22, 1975.
(Dallas' 7th choice, 254th overall, in 1994 Entry Draft).

			Regular Season					Playoffs				
Season	Club	League	GP	G	A	TP	PIM	GP	G	A	TP	PIM
1993-94	Thunder Bay Flyers	USHL	46	21	33	54	101	....	....	....	....	....
1994-95	Michigan Tech	WCHA	38	5	11	16	62	....	....	....	....	....
1995-96	Michigan Tech	WCHA	42	17	17	34	84	....	....	....	....	....
1996-97	Team Canada	Nat-Tm	55	10	17	27	82	....	....	....	....	....
1997-98	Manitoba Moose	IHL	61	8	10	18	133	3	0	0	0	6
1998-99	Manitoba Moose	IHL	78	10	16	26	185	5	0	1	1	6
99-2000	Manitoba Moose	IHL	74	12	9	21	187	1	0	0	0	16
2000-01	Manitoba Moose	IHL	77	18	13	31	150	12	1	1	2	22
2001-02	Manitoba Moose	AHL	73	16	22	38	167	7	2	0	2	28
2002-03	Manitoba Moose	AHL	50	5	10	15	95	14	4	4	8	27

ROY, Marc-Andre (WAH, MAHRK-AWN-dray) VAN.

Left wing. Shoots left. 6'2", 205 lbs. Born, Montreal, Que., October 27, 1983.
(Vancouver's 7th choice, 214th overall, in 2002 Entry Draft).

			Regular Season					Playoffs				
Season	Club	League	GP	G	A	TP	PIM	GP	G	A	TP	PIM
99-2000	Magog	QAAA	2	0	0	0	0	....	....	....	....	....
2000-01	Magog	QAAA	39	5	19	24	40	17	1	5	6	20
	Baie-Comeau	QMJHL	5	0	0	0	5	....	....	....	....	....
2001-02	Baie-Comeau	QMJHL	58	0	1	1	432	5	0	0	0	0
2002-03	Baie-Comeau	QMJHL	68	2	3	5	*653	6	0	0	0	25

ROZAKOV, Roman (roh-zah-KAWF, ROH-muhn) CGY.

Defense. Shoots left. 6'1", 198 lbs. Born, Murmansk, USSR, March 29, 1981.
(Calgary's 4th choice, 106th overall, in 1999 Entry Draft).

			Regular Season					Playoffs				
Season	Club	League	GP	G	A	TP	PIM	GP	G	A	TP	PIM
1997-98	Lada Togliatti 2	Russia-3	36	0	2	2	43	....	....	....	....	....
1998-99	Lada Togliatti 2	Russia-4	30	0	0	0	14	....	....	....	....	....
99-2000	Krylja Sovetov	Russia-2	23	0	1	1	41	....	....	....	....	....
2000-01	Magnitogorsk	Russia	21	0	1	1	10	....	....	....	....	....
2001-02	CSK VVS Samara	Russia-2	5	0	0	0	0	....	....	....	....	....
	CSKA Moscow	Russia	16	1	1	2	8	....	....	....	....	....
2002-03	Lada Togliatti	Russia	4	0	0	0	0	....	....	....	....	....
	Cherepovets	Russia	17	1	0	1	18	2	0	0	0	0

RUDENKO, Konstantin (roo-DEHN-koh, KOHN-stan-tihn) PHI.

Left wing. Shoots right. 5'11", 180 lbs. Born, Ust-Kamenogorsk, USSR, July 23, 1981.
(Philadelphia's 3rd choice, 160th overall, in 1999 Entry Draft).

			Regular Season					Playoffs				
Season	Club	League	GP	G	A	TP	PIM	GP	G	A	TP	PIM
1997-98	Omsk 2	Russia-3	22	7	8	15	4	....	....	....	....	....
1998-99	Cherepovets	Russia	28	15	9	24	67	....	....	....	....	....
	Cherepovets 2	Russia-3	3	0	1	1	4	....	....	....	....	....
99-2000	St. Petersburg-2	Russia-2	7	2	4	6	2	....	....	....	....	....
	St. Petersburg	Russia	19	1	1	2	10	1	0	0	0	0
2000-01	Yaroslavl	Russia	18	2	3	5	28	9	2	1	3	8
2001-02	Yaroslavl 2	Russia-3	2	1	1	2	2	....	....	....	....	....
	Yaroslavl	Russia	8	0	2	2	12	1	0	0	0	0
2002-03	Yaroslavl	Russia	20	3	4	7	20	2	0	0	0	0

RUGGERI, Rosario (ROO-gee-AIR-ee, roh-ZAHR-ee-oh) PHI.

Defense. Shoots left. 6'1", 202 lbs. Born, Montreal, Que., June 8, 1984.
(Philadelphia's 2nd choice, 105th overall, in 2002 Entry Draft).

			Regular Season					Playoffs				
Season	Club	League	GP	G	A	TP	PIM	GP	G	A	TP	PIM
99-2000	Lac St-Louis Lions	QAAA	40	0	7	7	70	....	....	....	....	....
2000-01	Lac St-Louis Lions	QAAA	24	6	11	17	117	5	1	3	4	4
	Montreal Rocket	QMJHL	9	0	0	0	8	....	....	....	....	....
2001-02	Chicoutimi	QMJHL	60	2	15	17	131	4	1	1	2	10
2002-03	Chicoutimi	QMJHL	70	10	37	47	64	3	0	0	0	21

RULLIER, Joe (ROO-yay, JOH) L.A.

Defense. Shoots right. 6'3", 211 lbs. Born, Montreal, Que., January 28, 1980.
(Los Angeles' 5th choice, 133rd overall, in 1998 Entry Draft).

			Regular Season					Playoffs				
Season	Club	League	GP	G	A	TP	PIM	GP	G	A	TP	PIM
1996-97	Montreal-Bourassa	QAAA	24	5	10	15	....	....	....	....	....	....
	Rimouski Oceanic	QMJHL	23	0	3	3	87	4	0	0	0	11
1997-98	Rimouski Oceanic	QMJHL	55	1	10	11	176	16	1	4	5	34
1998-99	Rimouski Oceanic	QMJHL	54	7	32	39	202	11	2	3	5	26
99-2000	Rimouski Oceanic	QMJHL	49	3	32	35	161	14	1	8	9	34
2000-01	Lowell	AHL	63	1	1	2	162	4	0	1	1	2
2001-02	Manchester	AHL	62	2	2	4	133	3	0	0	0	5
2002-03	Manchester	AHL	62	3	6	9	166	3	0	0	0	2

RUUTU, Mikko (ROO-too, MIH-koh) OTT.

Left wing. Shoots left. 6'4", 190 lbs. Born, Vantaa, Finland, September 10, 1978.
(Ottawa's 7th choice, 201st overall, in 1999 Entry Draft).

			Regular Season					Playoffs				
Season	Club	League	GP	G	A	TP	PIM	GP	G	A	TP	PIM
1997-98	HIFK Helsinki Jr.	Finn-Jr.	24	4	2	6	37	....	....	....	....	....
1998-99	HIFK Helsinki Jr.	Finn-Jr.	23	13	8	21	30	....	....	....	....	....
	HIFK Helsinki	Finland	31	3	1	4	12	4	0	0	0	2
	HIFK Helsinki	EuroHL	1	0	0	0	0	....	....	....	....	....
99-2000	Clarkson Knights	ECAC	33	5	6	11	26	....	....	....	....	....
2000-01	Jokerit Helsinki	Finland	56	5	6	11	38	5	0	1	1	2
2001-02	Jokerit Helsinki	Finland	47	3	3	6	65	5	1	0	1	27
2002-03	Jokerit Helsinki	Finland	23	2	4	6	4	10	0	1	1	4

RUUTU, Tuomo (ROO-too, TOO-oh-moh) CHI.

Center/Left wing. Shoots left. 6', 201 lbs. Born, Vantaa, Finland, February 16, 1983.
(Chicago's 1st choice, 9th overall, in 2001 Entry Draft).

			Regular Season					Playoffs				
Season	Club	League	GP	G	A	TP	PIM	GP	G	A	TP	PIM
1997-98	HIFK Helsinki-C	Finn-Jr.	22	4	11	15	10	3	0	1	1	4
1998-99	HIFK Helsinki-C	Finn-Jr.	3	6	3	9	25	5	*4	2	6	8
	HIFK Helsinki-B	Finn-Jr.	25	9	11	20	88	2	1	1	2	2
99-2000	HIFK Helsinki Jr.	Finn-Jr.	35	11	16	27	32	3	0	1	1	4
	HIFK Helsinki	Finland	1	0	0	0	2	....	....	....	....	....
2000-01	HIFK Helsinki Jr.	Finn-Jr.	2	1	0	1	0	....	....	....	....	....
	Jokerit Helsinki	Finland	47	11	11	22	86	5	0	0	0	4
2001-02	Jokerit Helsinki	Finland	51	7	16	23	69	10	0	6	6	29
2002-03	HIFK Helsinki	Finland	30	12	15	27	24	....	....	....	....	....

RUZICKA, Stefan (roo-ZHEECH-kuh, STEH-fan) PHI.

Left wing. Shoots right. 5'11", 189 lbs. Born, Nitra, Czech., February 17, 1985.
(Philadelphia's 4th choice, 81st overall, in 2003 Entry Draft).

			Regular Season					Playoffs				
Season	Club	League	GP	G	A	TP	PIM	GP	G	A	TP	PIM
2000-01	MHC Nitra Jr.	Slovak-Jr.	38	30	15	45	....	....	....	....	....	....
2001-02	MHC Nitra Jr.	Slovak-Jr.	29	27	25	52	....	....	....	....	....	....
	MHC Nitra	Slovak	19	0	5	5	29	....	....	....	....	....
2002-03	HKm Nitra Jr.	Slovak-Jr.	30	18	22	40	64	....	....	....	....	....
	HKm Nitra	Slovak-2	17	5	7	12	4	....	....	....	....	....

RYABYKIN, Dmitri (ryah-BEE-kihn, dih-MEE-tree) CGY.

Defense. Shoots right. 6'1", 203 lbs. Born, Chirchik, USSR, March 24, 1976.
(Calgary's 2nd choice, 45th overall, in 1994 Entry Draft).

			Regular Season					Playoffs				
Season	Club	League	GP	G	A	TP	PIM	GP	G	A	TP	PIM
1994-95	Dynamo Moscow	CIS	48	0	0	0	12	11	0	2	2	0
1995-96	Dynamo Moscow	CIS	47	3	1	4	49	13	1	1	2	6
1996-97	Dynamo Moscow	Russia	34	1	10	11	12	4	0	0	0	8
1997-98	Dynamo Moscow	EuroHL	7	1	1	2	6	....	....	....	....	....
	Dynamo Moscow	Russia	34	1	4	5	16	....	....	....	....	....
1998-99	Avangard Omsk	Russia	40	3	10	13	42	5	0	0	0	42
99-2000	Avangard Omsk	Russia	36	5	10	15	42	8	3	2	5	2
2000-01	Avangard Omsk	Russia	43	3	8	11	101	16	3	4	7	16
2001-02	Avangard Omsk	Russia	17	4	7	11	60	11	4	3	7	6
2002-03	Avangard Omsk	Russia	51	7	18	25	113	12	1	2	3	33

RYAN, Michael (RIGH-yan, MIGHK-uhl)) BUF.

Center. Shoots left. 6'1", 180 lbs. Born, Boston, MA, May 16, 1980.
(Dallas' 1st choice, 32nd overall, in 1999 Entry Draft).

			Regular Season					Playoffs				
Season	Club	League	GP	G	A	TP	PIM	GP	G	A	TP	PIM
1997-98	B.C. High Irish	Hi-School	23	22	14	36	28	....	....	....	....	....
1998-99	B.C. High Irish	Hi-School	21	20	24	44	22	....	....	....	....	....
99-2000	Northeastern	H-East	32	4	9	13	47	....	....	....	....	....
2000-01	Northeastern	H-East	33	17	12	29	52	....	....	....	....	....
2001-02	Northeastern	H-East	36	24	15	39	54	....	....	....	....	....
2002-03	Northeastern	H-East	34	18	14	32	30	....	....	....	....	....

Traded to **Buffalo** by **Dallas** with Dallas's 2nd round choice (Branislav Fabry) in 2003 Entry Draft for Stu Barnes, March 10, 2003.

RYBIN, Maxim (ray-bihn, max-EEM) ANA.

Left wing. Shoots right. 5'8", 182 lbs. Born, Zhukovsky, USSR, June 15, 1981.
(Anaheim's 4th choice, 141st overall, in 1999 Entry Draft).

			Regular Season					Playoffs				
Season	Club	League	GP	G	A	TP	PIM	GP	G	A	TP	PIM
1996-97	Spartak Moscow 2	Russia-3	5	0	0	0	4	....	....	....	....	....
	Spartak Moscow	Russia	6	0	0	0	0	....	....	....	....	....
1997-98	Spartak Moscow 2	Russia-3	25	13	5	18	26	....	....	....	....	....
	Spartak Moscow	Russia	5	0	0	0	0	....	....	....	....	....
1998-99	Spartak Moscow	Russia	53	15	12	27	83	....	....	....	....	....
99-2000	Sarnia Sting	OHL	66	29	27	56	47	7	4	1	5	2
2000-01	Sarnia Sting	OHL	67	34	36	70	60	4	0	3	3	2
2001-02	Ufa	Russia	41	6	4	10	30	....	....	....	....	....
2002-03	Cherepovets	Russia	3	0	1	1	2	....	....	....	....	....
	Spartak Moscow	Russia	29	9	4	13	65	....	....	....	....	....

RYDER, Michael (RIGH-duhr, MIGH-kuhl) MTL.

Right wing. Shoots right. 6'1", 195 lbs. Born, St. John's, Nfld., March 31, 1980.
(Montreal's 9th choice, 216th overall, in 1998 Entry Draft).

			Regular Season					Playoffs				
Season	Club	League	GP	G	A	TP	PIM	GP	G	A	TP	PIM
1996-97	Bonavista Saints	NFAHA	23	31	17	48	....	....	....	....	....	....
1997-98	Hull Olympiques	QMJHL	69	34	28	62	41	10	4	2	6	4
1998-99	Hull Olympiques	QMJHL	69	44	43	87	65	23	*20	16	36	39
99-2000	Hull Olympiques	QMJHL	63	50	58	108	50	15	11	17	28	28
2000-01	Tallahassee	ECHL	5	4	5	9	6	....	....	....	....	....
	Quebec Citadelles	AHL	61	6	9	15	14	....	....	....	....	....
2001-02	Mississippi	ECHL	20	14	13	27	2	....	....	....	....	....
	Quebec Citadelles	AHL	50	11	17	28	9	3	0	1	1	2
2002-03	Hamilton Bulldogs	AHL	69	34	33	67	43	23	11	6	17	8

RYZNAR, Jason (RIHZ-nuhr, JAY-suhn) N.J.

Left wing. Shoots left. 6'3", 205 lbs. Born, Anchorage, AK, February 19, 1983.
(New Jersey's 3rd choice, 64th overall, in 2002 Entry Draft).

			Regular Season					Playoffs				
Season	Club	League	GP	G	A	TP	PIM	GP	G	A	TP	PIM
1998-99	Alaska All-Stars	AAHA		STATISTICS NOT AVAILABLE								
99-2000	U.S. National U-17	USDP	52	5	10	15	22	....	....	....	....	....
2000-01	U.S. National U-18	USDP	66	15	17	32	102	....	....	....	....	....
2001-02	U. of Michigan	CCHA	40	9	7	16	22	....	....	....	....	....
2002-03	U. of Michigan	CCHA	34	7	9	16	24	....	....	....	....	....

SAARINEN, Pasi (SAH-rih-nehn, PAH-see) S.J.

Defense. Shoots right. 5'11", 194 lbs. Born, Hyvinkaa, Finland, April 17, 1977.
(San Jose's 7th choice, 256th overall, in 2000 Entry Draft).

			Regular Season					Playoffs				
Season	Club	League	GP	G	A	TP	PIM	GP	G	A	TP	PIM
1993-94	Ilves Tampere Jr.	Finn-Jr.	34	5	4	9	24	6	1	2	3	4
1994-95	Ilves Tampere Jr.	Finn-Jr.	24	4	5	9	55	....	....	....	....	....
	Ilves Tampere	Finland	1	0	0	0	0	....	....	....	....	....
1995-96	Ilves Tampere	Finn-Jr.	8	2	2	4	24	....	....	....	....	....
	KooVee Tampere	Finland-2	7	1	1	2	22	....	....	....	....	....
	Ilves Tampere	Finland	7	0	1	1	10	....	....	....	....	....
1996-97	Ilves Tampere Jr.	Finn-Jr.	9	3	3	6	22	....	....	....	....	....
	Ilves Tampere	Finland	44	4	3	7	83	6	1	0	1	10
1997-98	Ilves Tampere	Finland	36	11	8	19	73	....	....	....	....	....
1998-99	Ilves Tampere	Finland	45	2	8	10	56	4	1	0	1	8
	Ilves Tampere	EuroHL	....	....	....	....	....	6	2	0	2	6
99-2000	Ilves Tampere	Finland	50	9	19	28	79	3	0	0	0	26
2000-01	Jokerit Helsinki	Finland	52	6	9	15	79	5	2	0	2	4
2001-02	Jokerit Helsinki	Finland	32	0	0	0	48	10	0	2	2	0
2002-03	HIFK Helsinki	Finland	53	2	3	5	53	2	0	0	0	2

SAGAT, Martin (SHA-gat, MAHR-tehn) TOR.

Left wing. Shoots right. 6'3", 191 lbs. Born, Handlova, Czech., November 11, 1984.
(Toronto's 2nd choice, 91st overall, in 2003 Entry Draft).

			Regular Season					Playoffs				
Season	Club	League	GP	G	A	TP	PIM	GP	G	A	TP	PIM
2001-02	Dukla Trencin Jr.	Slovak-Jr.		STATISTICS NOT AVAILABLE								
2002-03	Dukla Trencin Jr.	Slovak-Jr.	37	18	20	38	49	3	1	3	4	4
	Dukla Trencin	Slovakia	17	0	0	0	0	2	0	0	0	0

SAINOMAA, Teemu (SIGH-noh-muh, TEE-moo) OTT.

Left wing. Shoots left. 6'3", 202 lbs. Born, Helsinki, Finland, May 15, 1981.
(Ottawa's 3rd choice, 62nd overall, in 1999 Entry Draft).

			Regular Season					Playoffs				
Season	Club	League	GP	G	A	TP	PIM	GP	G	A	TP	PIM
1997-98	Jokerit Helsinki-B	Finn-Jr.	12	3	5	8	8	3	1	1	2	6
1998-99	Jokerit Helsinki Jr.	Finn-Jr.	11	4	5	9	0	....	....	....	....	....
99-2000	Jokerit Helsinki Jr.	Finn-Jr.	30	6	7	13	59	11	6	2	8	20
	Jokerit Helsinki	Finland	6	0	0	0	0	....	....	....	....	....
2000-01	Jokerit Helsinki Jr.	Finn-Jr.	24	17	8	25	37	1	0	1	1	0
	Jokerit Helsinki	Finland	28	1	3	4	2	4	0	1	1	0
2001-02	Jokerit Helsinki Jr.	Finn-Jr.	6	2	2	4	27	....	....	....	....	....
	Kiekko Vantaa	Finland-2	1	0	0	0	0	....	....	....	....	....
	Jokerit Helsinki	Finland	44	1	4	5	4	1	0	0	0	0
2002-03	Pelicans Lahti	Finland	51	2	3	5	10	....	....	....	....	....

SALMELAINEN, Tony (sal-meh-LIGH-nehn, TOH-nee) EDM.

Left wing. Shoots right. 5'9", 185 lbs. Born, Espoo, Finland, August 8, 1981.
(Edmonton's 3rd choice, 41st overall, in 1999 Entry Draft).

			Regular Season					Playoffs				
Season	Club	League	GP	G	A	TP	PIM	GP	G	A	TP	PIM
1996-97	Kiekko Espoo Jr.	Finn-Jr.	30	8	5	13	38	....	....	....	....	....
1997-98	Kiekko Espoo-B	Finn-Jr.	5	2	2	4	10	....	....	....	....	....
	HIFK Helsinki-B	Finn-Jr.	28	23	16	39	30	....	....	....	....	....
	HIFK Helsinki Jr.	Finn-Jr.	5	0	0	0	0	....	....	....	....	....
1998-99	HIFK Helsinki-B	Finn-Jr.	21	13	10	23	45	....	....	....	....	....
	HIFK Helsinki Jr.	Finn-Jr.	....	....	....	....	....	10	10	8	18	10
99-2000	HIFK Helsinki Jr.	Finn-Jr.	1	0	1	1	0	....	....	....	....	....
	HIFK Helsinki	Finland	1	1	0	1	0	....	....	....	....	....
	HIFK Helsinki	EuroHL	1	0	0	0	0	....	....	....	....	....
2000-01	HIFK Helsinki Jr.	Finn-Jr.	3	3	3	6	0	....	....	....	....	....
	HIFK Helsinki	Finland	19	1	0	1	6	....	....	....	....	....
	Ilves Tampere Jr.	Finn-Jr.	3	1	2	3	2	....	....	....	....	....
	Ilves Tampere	Finland	26	3	10	13	4	3	0	0	0	0
2001-02	Ilves Tampere Jr.	Finn-Jr.	6	2	2	4	27	....	....	....	....	....
	Ilves Tampere	Finland	49	10	9	19	30	3	0	0	0	2
2002-03	Hamilton Bulldogs	AHL	67	14	19	33	14	17	6	8	14	0

SAMOILOV, Igor (sam-OI-lawf, EE-gohr) PHX.

Defense. Shoots left. 5'11", 195 lbs. Born, Moscow, USSR, January 23, 1982.
(Phoenix's 6th choice, 217th overall, in 2000 Entry Draft).

			Regular Season					Playoffs				
Season	Club	League	GP	G	A	TP	PIM	GP	G	A	TP	PIM
1998-99	Yaroslavl 2	Russia-3	16	0	1	1	6	....	....	....	....	....
99-2000	Yaroslavl 2	Russia-3	40	1	3	4	50	....	....	....	....	....
2000-01	SKA St. Petersburg	Russia	10	0	2	2	22	....	....	....	....	....
2001-02	Cherepovets	Russia	35	1	2	3	14	4	0	0	0	2
2002-03	Cherepovets	Russia	5	0	0	0	14	....	....	....	....	....

SANDSTROM, Jan (SAND-struhm, YAN) ANA.

Defense. Shoots left. 6', 190 lbs. Born, Pitea, Sweden, January 24, 1978.
(Anaheim's 5th choice, 173rd overall, in 1999 Entry Draft).

			Regular Season					Playoffs				
Season	Club	League	GP	G	A	TP	PIM	GP	G	A	TP	PIM
1994-95	Pitea HC	Swede-2	12	1	0	1	4	....	....	....	....	....
1995-96	Pitea HC	Swede-2	29	1	11	12	18	....	....	....	....	....
1996-97	Pitea HC	Swede-2	28	3	4	7	28	....	....	....	....	....
1997-98	AIK Solna	Sweden	38	0	2	2	16	....	....	....	....	....
1998-99	AIK Solna	Sweden	47	2	7	9	18	....	....	....	....	....
99-2000	AIK Solna	Sweden	49	2	6	8	22	....	....	....	....	....
2000-01	Skelleftea AIK	Swede-2	22	0	5	5	14	....	....	....	....	....
	AIK Solna	Sweden	18	1	3	4	10	....	....	....	....	....
2001-02	Lulea HF	Sweden	41	2	4	6	12	5	0	2	2	2
2002-03	Lulea HF	Sweden	48	3	5	8	36	4	1	0	1	6

SANNITZ, Raffaele (ZAH-nihts, ra-FIGH-ehl-lay) CBJ

Center. Shoots left. 6'1", 187 lbs. Born, Mendrisio, Switz., May 18, 1983.
(Columbus' 9th choice, 204th overall, in 2001 Entry Draft).

			Regular Season					Playoffs				
Season	Club	League	GP	G	A	TP	PIM	GP	G	A	TP	PIM
1997-98	HC Lugano Jr.	Swiss-Jr.	33	7	12	19	54	....	....	....	....	....
1998-99	HC Lugano Jr.	Swiss-Jr.	38	5	12	17	62	....	....	....	....	....
	HC Lugano	Swiss	8	0	1	1	0	....	....	....	....	....
99-2000	HC Lugano Jr.	Swiss-Jr.	33	13	16	29	47	....	....	....	....	....
	HC Lugano	Swiss	1	0	0	0	2	....	....	....	....	....
2000-01	HC Sierre	Swiss-2	2	0	0	0	0	....	....	....	....	....
	HC Lugano Jr.	Swiss-Jr.	35	22	30	52	152	2	0	0	0	0
	HC Lugano	Swiss	13	1	0	1	0	2	0	0	0	0
2001-02	HC Lugano Jr.	Swiss-Jr.	14	14	13	27	18	3	3	2	5	4
	HC Lugano	Swiss	38	3	4	7	37	12	1	1	2	2
2002-03	HC Lugano	Swiss	14	1	1	2	37	....	....	....	....	....
	HC Lugano Jr.	Swiss-Jr.	STATISTICS NOT AVAILABLE									

SANTALA, Tommi (SAHN-tah-luh, TAW-mee) ATL.

Center. Shoots right. 6'2", 205 lbs. Born, Helsinki, Finland, June 27, 1979.
(Atlanta's 10th choice, 245th overall, in 1999 Entry Draft).

			Regular Season					Playoffs				
Season	Club	League	GP	G	A	TP	PIM	GP	G	A	TP	PIM
1994-95	Jokerit Helsinki-C	Finn-Jr.	27	8	13	21	40	6	0	0	0	0
1995-96	Jokerit Helsinki-B	Finn-Jr.	25	8	4	12	12	6	1	2	3	4
1996-97	Jokerit Helsinki-B	Finn-Jr.	30	13	19	32	64	....	....	....	....	....
	Jokerit Helsinki Jr.	Finn-Jr.	20	0	2	2	10	5	0	0	0	0
1997-98	Jokerit Helsinki Jr.	Finn-Jr.	36	10	28	38	48	8	0	1	1	4
1998-99	Jokerit Helsinki Jr.	Finn-Jr.	30	20	24	44	20	8	1	3	4	22
	Jokerit Helsinki	Finland	30	0	0	0	14	3	0	0	0	0
	Jokerit Helsinki	EuroHL	1	0	2	2	9	....	....	....	....	....
99-2000	Jokerit Helsinki Jr.	Finn-Jr.	5	6	4	10	4	....	....	....	....	....
	Jokerit Helsinki	Finland	14	0	1	1	0	....	....	....	....	....
	HPK Jr.	Finn-Jr.	5	6	4	10	4	....	....	....	....	....
	HPK Hameenlinna	Finland	38	8	19	27	65	8	3	4	7	10
2000-01	HPK Hameenlinna	Finland	56	16	24	40	90	....	....	....	....	....
2001-02	HPK Hameenlinna	Finland	17	6	16	22	14	....	....	....	....	....
2002-03	HPK Hameenlinna	Finland	50	13	*38	51	92	13	6	6	12	18

SAPOZHNIKOV, Vladimir (suh-POHZH-nih-kahf, vla-DIH-meer) FLA.

Defense. Shoots left. 6'3", 205 lbs. Born, Seversk, USSR, August 2, 1982.
(Florida's 1st choice, 58th overall, in 2000 Entry Draft).

			Regular Season					Playoffs				
Season	Club	League	GP	G	A	TP	PIM	GP	G	A	TP	PIM
1997-98	Sibir Novosibirsk 2	Russia-3	15	0	0	0	2	....	....	....	....	....
1998-99	Novokuznetsk Jr.	Russia-Jr.	STATISTICS NOT AVAILABLE									
99-2000	Novokuznetsk 2	Russia-3	STATISTICS NOT AVAILABLE									
	Kristall Saratov Jr.	Russia-Jr.	4	0	0	0	6	....	....	....	....	....
2000-01	North Bay	OHL	53	0	6	6	70	4	0	0	0	2
2001-02	North Bay	OHL	29	0	4	4	28	5	0	0	0	0
	Utah Grizzlies	AHL	4	0	0	0	4	....	....	....	....	....
2002-03	San Antonio	AHL	4	0	0	0	4	....	....	....	....	....

SARNO, Peter (SAHR-noh, PEE-tuhr) EDM.

Center. Shoots left. 5'11", 185 lbs. Born, Toronto, Ont., July 26, 1979.
(Edmonton's 6th choice, 141st overall, in 1997 Entry Draft).

			Regular Season					Playoffs				
Season	Club	League	GP	G	A	TP	PIM	GP	G	A	TP	PIM
1995-96	North York	MTJHL	52	39	57	96	27	....	....	....	....	....
1996-97	Windsor Spitfires	OHL	66	20	63	83	59	5	0	3	3	6
1997-98	Windsor Spitfires	OHL	64	33	*88	*121	18	....	....	....	....	....
	Hamilton Bulldogs	AHL	8	1	1	2	2	....	....	....	....	....
1998-99	Sarnia Sting	OHL	68	37	*93	*130	49	6	1	7	8	2
99-2000	Hamilton Bulldogs	AHL	67	10	36	46	31	....	....	....	....	....
2000-01	Hamilton Bulldogs	AHL	79	19	46	65	64	....	....	....	....	....
2001-02	Hamilton Bulldogs	AHL	76	12	40	52	38	15	6	7	13	4
2002-03	Blues Espoo	Finland	45	17	23	40	34	7	2	1	3	2

OHL All-Rookie Team (1997) • OHL Rookie of the Year (1997)

SAUNDERS, Nathan (SAWN-duhrs, NAY-thun) ANA.

Defense. Shoots right. 6'4", 210 lbs. Born, Charlottetown, PEI, April 25, 1985.
(Anaheim's 5th choice, 119th overall, in 2003 Entry Draft).

			Regular Season					Playoffs				
Season	Club	League	GP	G	A	TP	PIM	GP	G	A	TP	PIM
2001-02	Moncton Wildcats	QMJHL	54	4	11	15	88	....	....	....	....	....
2002-03	Moncton Wildcats	QMJHL	69	1	13	14	241	6	2	3	5	12

SAVIELS, Agris (sah-VEE-ehls, AG-rihs) COL.

Defense. Shoots left. 6'2", 200 lbs. Born, Riga, Latvia, January 15, 1982.
(Colorado's 4th choice, 63rd overall, in 2000 Entry Draft).

			Regular Season					Playoffs				
Season	Club	League	GP	G	A	TP	PIM	GP	G	A	TP	PIM
1996-97	Dynamo Riga	Lat.-Jr.	15	1	2	3	4	....	....	....	....	....
	HK Lido-Nafta	Latvia	40	4	15	19	40	....	....	....	....	....
1997-98	Dynamo Riga	Lat.-Jr.	15	1	2	3	4	....	....	....	....	....
	HK Lido-Nafta	Latvia	40	7	21	28	30	....	....	....	....	....
1998-99	Notre Dame	SMBHL	18	6	9	15	25	....	....	....	....	....
	Notre Dame	SJHL	30	6	13	19	....	....	....	....	....	....
99-2000	Owen Sound	OHL	65	7	25	32	56	....	....	....	....	....
2000-01	Owen Sound	OHL	68	14	37	51	46	5	0	1	1	2
2001-02	Owen Sound	OHL	60	5	27	32	37	....	....	....	....	....
2002-03	Hershey Bears	AHL	43	0	3	3	33	3	0	0	0	0
	Reading Royals	ECHL	8	1	0	1	4	....	....	....	....	....

SCHADILOV, Igor (sha-DEE-lahf, EE-gor) WSH.

Defense. Shoots left. 6'2", 189 lbs. Born, Moscow, USSR, June 7, 1980.
(Washington's 10th choice, 249th overall, in 1999 Entry Draft).

			Regular Season					Playoffs				
Season	Club	League	GP	G	A	TP	PIM	GP	G	A	TP	PIM
1996-97	Dyno. Moscow Jr.	Russia-Jr.	30	3	7	10	30	....	....	....	....	....
1997-98	Dynamo Moscow	Russia	38	1	0	1	6	....	....	....	....	....
1998-99	Dynamo Moscow	Russia	28	2	9	11	15	....	....	....	....	....
	Dynamo Moscow	Russia	2	0	0	0	0	....	....	....	....	....
	Krylja Sovetov	Russia	9	0	0	0	0	....	....	....	....	....
99-2000	THC Tver	Russia-2	14	0	3	3	6	....	....	....	....	....
	Dynamo Moscow	Russia	26	0	2	2	8	16	0	0	0	2
2000-01	Dynamo Moscow	Russia	34	1	5	6	12	....	....	....	....	....
2001-02	Cherepovets	Russia	33	7	3	10	10	4	0	0	0	2
2002-03	Cherepovets	Russia	32	3	3	6	28	12	1	3	4	4

SCHAUER, Stefan (SHOW-uhr, SHTEH-fuhn) OTT.

Defense. Shoots left. 6'1", 180 lbs. Born, Schongau, West Germany, January 12, 1983.
(Ottawa's 6th choice, 162nd overall, in 2001 Entry Draft).

			Regular Season					Playoffs				
Season	Club	League	GP	G	A	TP	PIM	GP	G	A	TP	PIM
99-2000	Riessersee-16	Ger.-Jr.	14	4	8	12	85	....	....	....	....	....
	Riessersee Jr.	Ger.-Jr.	30	7	14	21	82	....	....	....	....	....
	Riessersee	German-3	3	0	0	0	0	....	....	....	....	....
2000-01	Riessersee Jr.	Ger.-Jr.	11	1	7	8	24	....	....	....	....	....
	Riessersee	German-3	39	1	2	3	12	5	0	1	1	0
2001-02	Riessersee	German-2	46	2	18	20	46	8	0	2	2	18
2002-03	Kolner Haie	Germany	28	0	1	1	12	15	1	0	1	2
	EV Duisburg	German-2	23	1	4	5	10	....	....	....	....	....

SCHEFFELMAIER, Brett (sch-EHFEHL-mai-uhr, BREHT) ST.L.

Defense. Shoots right. 6'5", 214 lbs. Born, Coronation, Alta., March 31, 1981.
(St. Louis' 5th choice, 190th overall, in 2001 Entry Draft).

			Regular Season					Playoffs				
Season	Club	League	GP	G	A	TP	PIM	GP	G	A	TP	PIM
1997-98	Red Deer	AMHL	13	0	4	4	36	....	....	....	....	....
	Medicine Hat	WHL	25	0	1	1	69	....	....	....	....	....
1998-99	Medicine Hat	WHL	69	3	10	13	252	....	....	....	....	....
99-2000	Medicine Hat	WHL	71	1	9	10	281	....	....	....	....	....
2000-01	Medicine Hat	WHL	62	3	10	13	279	....	....	....	....	....
2001-02	Medicine Hat	WHL	45	4	6	10	180	....	....	....	....	....
2002-03	Worcester IceCats	AHL	54	0	2	2	143	3	0	0	0	7

• Re-entered NHL Entry Draft. Originally Tampa Bay's 3rd choice, 75th overall, in 1999 Entry Draft.

SCHELL, Brad (SHEHL, BRAD) ATL.

Center. Shoots left. 6', 180 lbs. Born, Scott, Sask., August 5, 1984.
(Atlanta's 6th choice, 167th overall, in 2002 Entry Draft).

			Regular Season					Playoffs				
Season	Club	League	GP	G	A	TP	PIM	GP	G	A	TP	PIM
99-2000	North Battleford	SMHL	62	38	42	80	28	....	....	....	....	....
	Spokane Chiefs	WHL	1	0	0	0	0	....	....	....	....	....
2000-01	Spokane Chiefs	WHL	60	7	6	13	10	12	0	2	2	2
2001-02	Spokane Chiefs	WHL	70	20	36	56	16	11	0	8	8	6
2002-03	Spokane Chiefs	WHL	37	8	13	21	26	10	0	5	5	2

Missed majority of 2002-03 season recovering from off-season back surgery.

SCHEVJEV, Maxim (shehv-YAWF-yehv, MAX-ihm) BUF.

Center. Shoots left. 6', 178 lbs. Born, Noginsk, USSR, July 5, 1984.
(Buffalo's 7th choice, 178th overall, in 2002 Entry Draft).

			Regular Season					Playoffs				
Season	Club	League	GP	G	A	TP	PIM	GP	G	A	TP	PIM
2001-02	Elektrostal 2	Russia-3	6	1	2	3	2	....	....	....	....	....
	Elektrostal	Russia-2	49	6	9	15	34	....	....	....	....	....
2002-03	Amur Khabarovsk	Russia	21	0	0	0	10	....	....	....	....	....

SCHNEIDER, Andrew (SHNIGH-duhr, AN-droo) PIT.

Defense. Shoots left. 6'1", 215 lbs. Born, Grand Forks, ND, July 31, 1981.
(Pittsburgh's 7th choice, 156th overall, in 2001 Entry Draft).

			Regular Season					Playoffs				
Season	Club	League	GP	G	A	TP	PIM	GP	G	A	TP	PIM
1998-99	Lincoln Stars	USHL	9	0	4	4	8	4	0	0	0	2
99-2000	Lincoln Stars	USHL	46	7	10	17	102	10	6	4	10	27
2000-01	Lincoln Stars	USHL	54	12	24	36	134	....	....	....	....	....
2001-02	North Dakota	WCHA	35	3	11	14	65	....	....	....	....	....
2002-03	North Dakota	WCHA	43	11	30	41	52	....	....	....	....	....

SCHUBERT, Christoph (SHOO-buhrt, KRIHS-tawf) OTT.

Defense. Shoots left. 6'2", 210 lbs. Born, Munich, West Germany, February 5, 1982.
(Ottawa's 5th choice, 127th overall, in 2001 Entry Draft).

			Regular Season					Playoffs				
Season	Club	League	GP	G	A	TP	PIM	GP	G	A	TP	PIM
1998-99	EV Landshut Jr.	Ger.-Jr.	28	15	20	35	77	....	....	....	....	....
99-2000	EV Landshut Jr.	Ger.-Jr.	11	14	11	25	51	....	....	....	....	....
	EV Landshut	German-3	55	7	5	12	68	....	....	....	....	....
2000-01	Munchen Barons	Germany	55	6	3	9	80	10	0	2	2	27
2001-02	Munchen Barons	Germany	50	5	11	16	125	9	3	4	7	32
2002-03	Binghamton	AHL	70	2	8	10	102	8	0	1	1	2

SCHUTTE, Michael (SHOOT, MIGH-kuhl) PHX.

Defense. Shoots left. 6'2", 199 lbs. Born, Burlington, Ont., July 28, 1979.

			Regular Season					Playoffs				
Season	Club	League	GP	G	A	TP	PIM	GP	G	A	TP	PIM
1998-99	Burlington	OPJHL	47	26	44	70	....	....	....	....	....	....
99-2000	U. of Maine	H-East	23	2	7	9	14	....	....	....	....	....
2000-01	U. of Maine	H-East	38	15	10	25	20	....	....	....	....	....
2001-02	U. of Maine	H-East	39	13	18	31	31	....	....	....	....	....
2002-03	Springfield Falcons	AHL	48	5	11	16	27	....	....	....	....	....
	Lowell	AHL	13	2	5	7	8	....	....	....	....	....

OPJHL Defenseman of the Year (1999) • NCAA Championship All-Tournament Team (2002)

Signed as a free agent by **Phoenix**, May 30, 2002.

SCUDERI, Rob (SKUD-uhree, RAWB) PIT.

Defense. Shoots left. 6', 214 lbs. Born, Syosset, NY, December 30, 1978.
(Pittsburgh's 5th choice, 134th overall, in 1998 Entry Draft).

			Regular Season					Playoffs				
Season	Club	League	GP	G	A	TP	PIM	GP	G	A	TP	PIM
1995-96	NY Apple Core	MJBHL	76	18	60	78	....	....	....	....	....	....
1996-97	NY Apple Core	MJBHL	82	42	70	112	64	....	....	....	....	....
1997-98	Boston College	H-East	42	0	24	24	12	....	....	....	....	....
1998-99	Boston College	H-East	41	2	8	10	20	....	....	....	....	....
99-2000	Boston College	H-East	42	1	12	13	22	....	....	....	....	....
2000-01	Boston College	H-East	43	4	19	23	42	....	....	....	....	....
2001-02	Wilkes-Barre	AHL	75	1	22	23	66	....	....	....	....	....
2002-03	Wilkes-Barre	AHL	74	4	17	21	44	6	0	1	1	4

NCAA Championship All-Tournament Team (2001)

SEABROOK, Brent (SEE-bruk, BREHNT) CHI.

Defense. Shoots right. 6'3", 220 lbs. Born, Richmond, B.C., April 20, 1985.
(Chicago's 1st choice, 14th overall, in 2003 Entry Draft).

			Regular Season					Playoffs				
Season	Club	League	GP	G	A	TP	PIM	GP	G	A	TP	PIM
2000-01	Delta Ice Hawks	PIJHL	54	16	26	42	55	....	....	....	....	....
	Lethbridge	WHL	4	0	0	0	0	....	....	....	....	....
2001-02	Lethbridge	WHL	67	6	33	39	70	4	1	1	2	2
2002-03	Lethbridge	WHL	69	9	33	42	113	....	....	....	....	....

PIJHL Rookie of the Year (2001)

SEDOV, Pavel (se-DAHF, PAH-vehl) T.B.

Right wing. Shoots left. 6'3", 200 lbs. Born, Voskresensk, USSR, January 12, 1982.
(Tampa Bay's 5th choice, 161st overall, in 2000 Entry Draft).

			Regular Season					Playoffs				
Season	Club	League	GP	G	A	TP	PIM	GP	G	A	TP	PIM
99-2000	Voskresensk	Russia-2	10	0	0	0	2	....	....	....	....	....
2000-01	Voskresensk	Russia-2	38	2	1	3	10	....	....	....	....	....
2001-02	Voskresensk 2	Russia-3	12	4	1	5	0	....	....	....	....	....
	Voskresensk	Russia-2	18	3	1	4	0	....	....	....	....	....
2002-03	Voskresensk	Russia-2	25	1	5	6	6	....	....	....	....	....

SEELEY, Richard (SEE-lee, RIH-chahrd) L.A.

Defense. Shoots left. 6'2", 205 lbs. Born, Powell River, B.C., April 30, 1979.
(Los Angeles' 6th choice, 137th overall, in 1997 Entry Draft).

			Regular Season					Playoffs				
Season	Club	League	GP	G	A	TP	PIM	GP	G	A	TP	PIM
1995-96	Powell River	BCJHL	44	1	8	9	42	....	....	....	....	....
1996-97	Lethbridge	WHL	3	0	0	0	11	....	....	....	....	....
	Prince Albert	WHL	18	0	1	1	9	4	0	0	0	2
1997-98	Prince Albert	WHL	65	8	21	29	114	....	....	....	....	....
1998-99	Prince Albert	WHL	61	10	48	58	110	14	1	11	12	14
99-2000	Lowell	AHL	36	5	1	6	37	....	....	....	....	....
2000-01	Lowell	AHL	55	2	8	10	102	....	....	....	....	....
	Trenton Titans	ECHL	9	0	2	2	18	....	....	....	....	....
2001-02	Manchester	AHL	61	2	10	12	78	5	0	0	0	6
2002-03	Manchester	AHL	69	4	14	18	127	3	0	1	1	0

SEGAL, Brandon (SEE-guhl, BRAN-duhn) NSH.

Right wing. Shoots right. 6'3", 214 lbs. Born, Richmond, B.C., July 12, 1983.
(Nashville's 2nd choice, 102nd overall, in 2002 Entry Draft).

			Regular Season					Playoffs				
Season	Club	League	GP	G	A	TP	PIM	GP	G	A	TP	PIM
99-2000	Calgary Hitmen	WHL	44	2	6	8	76	13	1	1	2	13
	Delta Ice Hawks	PIJHL	....	....	....	....	....	3	0	1	1	2
2000-01	Calgary Hitmen	WHL	72	16	11	27	103	12	1	1	2	17
2001-02	Calgary Hitmen	WHL	71	43	40	83	122	7	1	4	5	16
2002-03	Calgary Hitmen	WHL	71	31	27	58	104	5	2	2	4	4

SEIKOLA, Markus (SAY-koh-la, MAHR-kuhs) TOR.

Defense. Shoots right. 6'1", 194 lbs. Born, Laitila, Finland, June 5, 1982.
(Toronto's 7th choice, 209th overall, in 2000 Entry Draft).

			Regular Season					Playoffs				
Season	Club	League	GP	G	A	TP	PIM	GP	G	A	TP	PIM
1996-97	TPS Turku-C	Finn-Jr.	4	1	0	1	4	1	0	0	0	0
1997-98	TPS Turku Jr.	Finn-Jr.	2	0	0	0	0	1	0	0	0	2
1998-99	TPS Turku Jr.	Finn-Jr.	36	2	10	12	24	....	....	....	....	....
99-2000	TPS Turku-B	Finn-Jr.	9	2	1	3	6	....	....	....	....	....
2000-01	TPS Turku Jr.	Finn-Jr.	26	13	7	20	6	3	1	0	1	0
	TPS Turku	Finland	23	1	0	1	16	....	....	....	....	....
2001-02	TPS Turku	Finland	51	4	4	8	20	7	1	1	2	12
	TPS Turku Jr.	Finn-Jr.	1	0	1	1	2	2	1	0	1	2
2002-03	TPS Turku	Finland	56	5	4	9	36	7	1	0	1	2

SELIG, Scott (SEH-lihg, SKAWT) MTL.

Right wing. Shoots right. 6'3", 178 lbs. Born, Philadelphia, PA, March 2, 1981.
(Montreal's 8th choice, 172nd overall, in 2000 Entry Draft).

			Regular Season					Playoffs				
Season	Club	League	GP	G	A	TP	PIM	GP	G	A	TP	PIM
99-2000	Thayer Academy	Hi-School	28	32	25	57	25	....	....	....	....	....
2000-01	Northeastern	H-East	35	7	8	15	34	....	....	....	....	....
2001-02	Northeastern	H-East	26	3	1	4	28	....	....	....	....	....
2002-03	Northeastern	H-East	33	3	7	10	22	....	....	....	....	....

SELUYANOV, Alexander (sehl-oo-YA-nahf, al-ehx-AN-duhr) DET.

Defense. Shoots right. 5'11", 172 lbs. Born, Ufa, USSR, March 24, 1982.
(Detroit's 5th choice, 128th overall, in 2000 Entry Draft).

			Regular Season					Playoffs				
Season	Club	League	GP	G	A	TP	PIM	GP	G	A	TP	PIM
1997-98	Novoil Ufa	Russia-3	19	0	1	1	8	....	....	....	....	....
1998-99	Novoil Ufa	Russia-4	20	3	3	6	8	....	....	....	....	....
99-2000	Ufa 2	Russia-3	18	3	4	7	10	....	....	....	....	....
	Ufa	Russia	13	1	2	3	4	....	....	....	....	....
2000-01	Ufa	Russia	30	0	3	3	10	....	....	....	....	....
2001-02	CSK VVS Samara	Russia-2	30	2	7	9	58	....	....	....	....	....
	Lada Togliatti	Russia	6	0	0	0	0	....	....	....	....	....
2002-03	Lada Togliatti	Russia	26	2	4	6	12	4	0	0	0	4
	CSK VVS Samara	Russia-2	16	4	4	8	34	....	....	....	....	....

SEMENOV, Dmitri (seh-MEH-nahv, dih-MEE-tree) DET.

Right wing. Shoots left. 5'10", 178 lbs. Born, Moscow, USSR, April 19, 1982.
(Detroit's 4th choice, 127th overall, in 2000 Entry Draft).

			Regular Season					Playoffs				
Season	Club	League	GP	G	A	TP	PIM	GP	G	A	TP	PIM
1997-98	Dynamo Moscow	Russia	13	2	1	3	2	....	....	....	....	....
1998-99	DynamoMoscow2	Russia-3	26	14	4	18	16	....	....	....	....	....
99-2000	THC Tver	Russia-2	16	4	2	6	63	....	....	....	....	....
2000-01	Dynamo Moscow	Russia	12	0	0	0	8	....	....	....	....	....
	Yekaterinburg	Russia	24	0	0	0	18	....	....	....	....	....
2001-02	DynamoMoscow2	Russia-3	6	5	2	7	6	....	....	....	....	....
	Yekaterinburg	Russia-2	6	1	2	3	2	....	....	....	....	....
	Dynamo Moscow	Russia	25	2	1	3	8	....	....	....	....	....
2002-03	Spartak Moscow	Russia	6	0	0	0	4	....	....	....	....	....

SEMIN, Alexander (SEH-min, al-ehx-AN-duhr) WSH.

Left wing. Shoots left. 6', 174 lbs. Born, Krasjonarsk, USSR, March 3, 1984.
(Washington's 2nd choice, 13th overall, in 2002 Entry Draft).

			Regular Season					Playoffs				
Season	Club	League	GP	G	A	TP	PIM	GP	G	A	TP	PIM
99-2000	Chelyabinsk-18	Russia-Jr.	6	2	2	4	14	....	....	....	....	....
2000-01	Team Russia	Nat-Tm	9	4	1	5	30	....	....	....	....	....
2001-02	Chelyabinsk-18	Russia-Jr.	4	6	0	6	24	....	....	....	....	....
	Chelyabinsk	Russia-2	48	15	8	23	52	....	....	....	....	....
2002-03	Lada Togliatti	Russia	47	10	7	17	36	10	*5	3	8	10

SEMIN, Dmitri (SEH-min, dih-MEE-tree) ST.L.

Center. Shoots left. 5'10", 185 lbs. Born, Moscow, USSR, August 14, 1983.
(St. Louis' 4th choice, 159th overall, in 2001 Entry Draft).

			Regular Season					Playoffs				
Season	Club	League	GP	G	A	TP	PIM	GP	G	A	TP	PIM
99-2000	Spartak Moscow 2	Russia-3	27	9	10	19	10	....	....	....	....	....
	Spartak Moscow	Russia-2	1	0	0	0	0	....	....	....	....	....
2000-01	Spartak Moscow	Russia-2	32	8	6	14	8	....	....	....	....	....
2001-02	Spartak Moscow 2	Russia-3	4	5	0	5	4	....	....	....	....	....
	Spartak Moscow	Russia	44	2	6	8	14	....	....	....	....	....
2002-03	Spartak Moscow	Russia	51	9	13	22	30	....	....	....	....	....

SERTICH, Andrew (SUHR-tihch, AN-droo) PIT.

Left wing. Shoots left. 6', 171 lbs. Born, Coleraine, MN, May 6, 1983.
(Pittsburgh's 5th choice, 136th overall, in 2002 Entry Draft).

			Regular Season					Playoffs				
Season	Club	League	GP	G	A	TP	PIM	GP	G	A	TP	PIM
2000-01	Greenway Raiders	Hi-School	31	35	45	80	14	....	....	....	....	....
2001-02	Greenway Raiders	Hi-School	26	24	48	72	35	....	....	....	....	....
	Sioux Falls	USHL	13	2	4	6	0	2	0	0	0	2
2002-03	U. of Minnesota	WCHA	44	5	9	14	12	....	....	....	....	....

All-State First All-Star Team (2002)

SETZINGER, Oliver (SEHT-zihn-guhr, AW-lih-vuhr) NSH.

Center. Shoots left. 6', 189 lbs. Born, Horn, Austria, July 11, 1983.
(Nashville's 5th choice, 76th overall, in 2001 Entry Draft).

			Regular Season					Playoffs				
Season	Club	League	GP	G	A	TP	PIM	GP	G	A	TP	PIM
1998-99	Wiener EV Jr.	Austria-Jr.	30	25	27	52	30	....	....	....	....	....
99-2000	Ilves Tampere Jr.	Finn-Jr.	35	6	4	10	65	....	....	....	....	....
	Ilves Tampere-B	Finn-Jr.	18	16	9	25	38	....	....	....	....	....
	Ilves Tampere	Finland	1	0	0	0	2	....	....	....	....	....
	Ilves Tampere	Finland-2	18	16	9	25	38	....	....	....	....	....
2000-01	Ilves Tampere Jr.	Finn-Jr.	31	8	12	20	74	....	....	....	....	....
	Ilves Tampere	Finland	14	0	1	1	10	....	....	....	....	....
2001-02	Ilves Tampere Jr.	Finn-Jr.	1	0	0	0	2	....	....	....	....	....
	Ilves Tampere	Finland	10	1	0	1	4	....	....	....	....	....
	Sport Vaasa	Finland-2	8	5	2	7	6	....	....	....	....	....
	Austria	Olympics	4	1	0	1	2	....	....	....	....	....
	EHC Linz	Austria	8	6	7	13	4	13	4	14	18	14
2002-03	Pelicans Lahti	Finland	56	7	14	21	54	....	....	....	....	....

SEYDOUX, Philippe (SAY-doo, fihl-EEP) OTT.

Defense. Shoots left. 6'2", 185 lbs. Born, Bern, Switz., February 23, 1985.
(Ottawa's 3rd choice, 100th overall, in 2003 Entry Draft).

			Regular Season					Playoffs				
Season	Club	League	GP	G	A	TP	PIM	GP	G	A	TP	PIM
2000-01	SC Bern Jr.	Swiss-Jr.	30	1	3	4	8	4	1	2	0	6
2001-02	SC Bern Jr.	Swiss-Jr.	35	8	17	25	94	7	3	5	0	24
	SC Bern	Swiss	7	0	0	0	0	2	0	0	0	0
2002-03	Kloten Flyers Jr.	Swiss-Jr.	14	2	10	12	50	....	....	....	....	....
	Kloten Flyers	Swiss	14	0	1	1	4	5	0	0	0	6

SHAFIGULIN, Grigory (sha-fih-GOO-lihn, grih-GOH-ree) NSH.

Center. Shoots left. 6'2", 185 lbs. Born, Chelyabinsk, USSR, January 13, 1985.
(Nashville's 8th choice, 98th overall, in 2003 Entry Draft).

			Regular Season					Playoffs				
Season	Club	League	GP	G	A	TP	PIM	GP	G	A	TP	PIM
2001-02	Yaroslavl 2	Russia-3	19	2	2	4	12	....	....	....	....	....
2002-03	Yaroslavl 2	Russia-3	19	2	2	4	12	....	....	....	....	....
	Yaroslavl	Russia	11	0	1	1	4	8	0	0	0	4

SHARROW, James (SHA-row, JAYMZ) ATL.

Defense. Shoots right. 6'2", 175 lbs. Born, Framingham, MA, January 31, 1985.
(Atlanta's 2nd choice, 110th overall, in 2003 Entry Draft).

			Regular Season					Playoffs				
Season	Club	League	GP	G	A	TP	PIM	GP	G	A	TP	PIM
2001-02	U.S. National U-17	USDP	61	5	16	21	30	....	....	....	....	....
2002-03	Halifax	QMJHL	70	2	14	16	54	25	2	4	6	24

QMJHL All-Rookie Team (2003)

SHASBY, Matt (SHAS-bee, MAT) MTL.

Defense. Shoots left. 6'3", 188 lbs. Born, Sioux Falls, SD, July 2, 1980.
(Montreal's 7th choice, 150th overall, in 1999 Entry Draft).

			Regular Season					Playoffs				
Season	Club	League	GP	G	A	TP	PIM	GP	G	A	TP	PIM
1997-98	Lincoln Stars	USHL	43	1	15	16	30	8	0	0	0	2
1998-99	Des Moines	USHL	49	4	22	26	34	11	0	1	1	12
99-2000	Alaska-Anchorage	WCHA	32	1	8	9	36	....	....	....	....	....
2000-01	Alaska-Anchorage	WCHA	35	4	14	18	32	....	....	....	....	....
2001-02	Alaska-Anchorage	WCHA	35	7	20	27	72	....	....	....	....	....
2002-03	Alaska-Anchorage	WCHA	25	0	11	11	18	....	....	....	....	....

WCHA Second All-Star Team (2002)

SHASTIN, Yegor (SHAS-tihn, yeh-GOHR) CGY.

Left wing. Shoots left. 5'9", 172 lbs. Born, Kiev, USSR, September 10, 1982.
(Calgary's 5th choice, 124th overall, in 2001 Entry Draft).

			Regular Season					Playoffs				
Season	Club	League	GP	G	A	TP	PIM	GP	G	A	TP	PIM
1997-98	Omsk 2	Russia-3	4	0	1	1	0					
1998-99	Omsk 2	Russia-4	19	11	17	28	30					
	Avangard Omsk	Russia	4	0	0	0	0	4	0	1	1	0
99-2000	Omsk 2	Russia-3	11	6	5	11	20					
	Avangard Omsk	Russia	26	2	4	6	20	7	3	1	4	16
2000-01	Omsk 2	Russia-3	14	13	9	22	62					
	Avangard Omsk	Russia	35	3	11	14	59	9	1	0	1	18
2001-02	Avangard Omsk	Russia	26	2	5	7	10	11	1	0	1	8
2002-03	HC Ambri-Piotta	Swiss	44	2	3	5	18	3	1	0	1	2
	HC Sierre	Swiss-2	2	1	0	1	0					

SHEFER, Andrei (SHEH-fuhr, AN-dray) L.A.

Left wing. Shoots left. 6'1", 194 lbs. Born, Yekaterinburg, USSR, July 26, 1981.
(Los Angeles' 1st choice, 43rd overall, in 1999 Entry Draft).

			Regular Season					Playoffs				
Season	Club	League	GP	G	A	TP	PIM	GP	G	A	TP	PIM
1997-98	Yekaterinburg 2	Russia-3	16	3	3	6	18					
1998-99	Cherepovets 3	Russia-4	6	2	2	4	18					
	Cherepovets 2	Russia-3	21	6	5	11	20					
	Cherepovets	Russia	8	1	0	1	4					
99-2000	Halifax	QMJHL	72	34	42	76	30	10	0	5	5	4
2000-01	SKA St. Petersburg	Russia	11	6	1	7	4					
	Cherepovets	Russia	20	1	1	2	10	6	1	0	1	0
2001-02	Cherepovets 2	Russia-3	3	1	2	3	2					
	Cherepovets	Russia	8	0	0	0	6					
	SKA St. Petersburg	Russia	28	4	4	8	10					
2002-03	Cherepovets	Russia	37	2	4	6	10	10	0	0	0	0

SHEMETOV, Sergei (shuh-MEH-tawf, SAIR-gay) COL.

Left wing. Shoots left. 6'1", 185 lbs. Born, Yaroslavl, USSR, September 3, 1984.
(Colorado's 9th choice, 258th overall, in 2002 Entry Draft).

			Regular Season					Playoffs				
Season	Club	League	GP	G	A	TP	PIM	GP	G	A	TP	PIM
2000-01	Yaroslavl 2	Russia-3	30	7	0	7	24					
2001-02	Yaroslavl 2	Russia-3	17	3	4	7	42					
	Elektrostal 2	Russia-3	3	0	0	0	8					
	Elektrostal	Russia-2	15	1	1	2	26					
2002-03	HC Voronezh	Russia-2	13	0	1	1	35					

SHIELDS, Colin (SHEELDZ, KAW-lihn) PHI.

Right wing. Shoots right. 6', 175 lbs. Born, Glasgow, Scotland, January 27, 1980.
(Philadelphia's 4th choice, 195th overall, in 2000 Entry Draft).

			Regular Season					Playoffs				
Season	Club	League	GP	G	A	TP	PIM	GP	G	A	TP	PIM
1998-99	Cleveland Barons	NAJHL	55	30	30	60	131					
99-2000	Cleveland Barons	NAJHL	55	46	*49	*95	40	3	1	3	4	2
2000-01	U. of Maine	H-East	DID NOT PLAY – ACADEMICALLY INELIGIBLE									
2001-02	U. of Maine	H-East	42	29	17	46	39					
2002-03	U. of Maine	H-East	34	14	13	27	18					

NAJHL First All-Star Team (2000) • Hockey East All-Rookie Team (2002)

• Ruled ineligible to play 2000-01 season by Hockey East officials due to academic violations while playing U.S. junior hockey, October 10, 2000.

SHIKHANOV, Sergei (shih-KHAHN-ohf, SAIR-gay) CHI.

Right wing. Shoots left. 6'2", 190 lbs. Born, Togliatti, USSR, April 8, 1978.
(Chicago's 10th choice, 204th overall, in 1997 Entry Draft).

			Regular Season					Playoffs				
Season	Club	League	GP	G	A	TP	PIM	GP	G	A	TP	PIM
1996-97	Lada Togliatti	Russia	19	4	4	8	20	8	1	0	1	10
	Nizhnekamsk	Russia	5	1	1	2	2					
1997-98	Nizhnekamsk 2	Russia-3	32	9	7	16	14					
	Lada Togliatti	Russia	19	3	0	3	4					
1998-99	Lada Togliatti	Russia	29	4	5	9	65	3	0	0	0	2
	CSK VVS Samara	Russia	11	3	4	7	10	3	1	0	1	2
99-2000	Torpedo Yaroslavl	Russia	31	2	3	5	24	7	0	2	2	4
2000-01	Magnitogorsk	Russia	24	4	4	8	39	10	1	0	1	4
2001-02	Ufa	Russia	37	5	5	10	57					
2002-03	Perm	Russia	43	3	18	21	64					

SHINKAR, Alexander (shihn-KAHR, al-ehx-AN-duhr) TOR.

Right wing. Shoots left. 6', 176 lbs. Born, Ufa, USSR, July 3, 1981.
(Toronto's 9th choice, 254th overall, in 2000 Entry Draft).

			Regular Season					Playoffs				
Season	Club	League	GP	G	A	TP	PIM	GP	G	A	TP	PIM
1997-98	Novoil Ufa	Russia-3	22	6	2	8	4					
1998-99	Cherepovets 2	Russia-3	25	7	2	9	8					
	Cherepovets 3	Russia-4	8	0	4	4	4					
99-2000	Cherepovets	Russia	18	1	1	2	2	8	0	0	0	0
2000-01	SKA St. Petersburg	Russia	43	7	4	11	50					
2001-02	Ufa	Russia	27	3	3	6	8					
	SKA St. Petersburg	Russia	18	3	4	7	10					
2002-03	Cherepovets	Russia	32	3	1	4	12	11	0	1	1	6

SHISHKANOV, Timofei (SHIHSH-kuh-nahv, tee-moh-FAY) NSH.

Left wing. Shoots right. 6'1", 213 lbs. Born, Moscow, USSR, June 10, 1983.
(Nashville's 2nd choice, 33rd overall, in 2001 Entry Draft).

			Regular Season					Playoffs				
Season	Club	League	GP	G	A	TP	PIM	GP	G	A	TP	PIM
99-2000	Spartak Moscow 2	Russia-3	14	6	5	11	10					
	Spartak Moscow	Russia-2	14	1	0	1	2					
2000-01	Spartak Moscow 2	Russia-3	STATISTICS NOT AVAILABLE									
	Spartak Moscow	Russia-2	12	0	0	0	2					
2001-02	HC CSKA Moscow	Russia-2	23	7	6	13	8					
	HC CSKA 2	Russia-3	13	7	9	16	14					
2002-03	Quebec Remparts	QMJHL	51	36	46	82	60	11	5	12	17	14

QMJHL First All-Star Team (2003)

SHKOTOV, Alexei (SHKOH-tahv, al-EHX-ay) ST.L.

Right wing. Shoots left. 5'11", 161 lbs. Born, Elektrostal, USSR, June 22, 1984.
(St. Louis' 1st choice, 48th overall, in 2002 Entry Draft).

			Regular Season					Playoffs				
Season	Club	League	GP	G	A	TP	PIM	GP	G	A	TP	PIM
99-2000	Elektrostal 2	Russia-3	2	0	0	0	0					
2000-01	Elektrostal 2	Russia-3	STATISTICS NOT AVAILABLE									
2001-02	Elektrostal 2	Russia-3	4	4	5	9	2					
	Elektrostal	Russia-2	52	17	9	26	40					
2002-03	CSKA Moscow	Russia	33	5	1	6	20					

SIDORENKO, Kirill (sih-dohr-EHN-koh, KIH-rihl) DAL.

Center. Shoots left. 6'3", 187 lbs. Born, Omsk, USSR, March 30, 1983.
(Dallas' 9th choice, 180th overall, in 2002 Entry Draft).

			Regular Season					Playoffs				
Season	Club	League	GP	G	A	TP	PIM	GP	G	A	TP	PIM
1998-99	Omsk 2	Russia-4	2	0	0	0	2					
99-2000	Omsk 2	Russia-3	26	2	11	13	14					
2000-01	Omsk 2	Russia-3	30	8	7	15	44					
2001-02	Mostovik Kurgan	Russia-2	50	11	6	17	64					
2002-03	Sibir Novosibirsk	Russia	30	1	1	2	2					

SIDYAKIN, Andrei (sihd-YA-kihn, AN-dray) MTL.

Right wing. Shoots left. 5'11", 169 lbs. Born, Ufa, USSR, January 20, 1979.
(Montreal's 10th choice, 202nd overall, in 1997 Entry Draft).

			Regular Season					Playoffs				
Season	Club	League	GP	G	A	TP	PIM	GP	G	A	TP	PIM
1994-95	Ufa	CIS	7	0	1	1	0					
1995-96	Ufa	CIS	25	1	0	1	4	3	0	0	0	2
1996-97	Ufa	Russia	29	3	5	8	4					
1997-98	Ufa	Russia	42	5	4	9	32					
1998-99	Ufa	Russia	36	6	4	10	14	2	0	0	0	2
99-2000	Ufa	Russia	38	7	2	9	32					
2000-01	Ufa	Russia	44	10	13	23	42					
2001-02	Ufa	Russia	43	9	7	16	20					
2002-03	Cherepovets	Russia	38	8	8	16	20	2	0	0	0	4

SIPOTZ, Brian (SIHP-awtz, BRIGH-uhn) ATL.

Defense. Shoots right. 6'7", 245 lbs. Born, South Bend, IN, September 16, 1981.
(Atlanta's 3rd choice, 100th overall, in 2001 Entry Draft).

			Regular Season					Playoffs				
Season	Club	League	GP	G	A	TP	PIM	GP	G	A	TP	PIM
99-2000	Culver Academy	Hi-School	45	14	22	36	56					
2000-01	Miami RedHawks	CCHA	32	0	1	1	48					
2001-02	Miami RedHawks	CCHA	25	0	1	1	28					
2002-03	Miami RedHawks	CCHA	26	0	0	0	24					

SJOSTROM, Fredrik (SHAW-strahm, FREHD-rihk) PHX.

Right wing. Shoots left. 6'1", 214 lbs. Born, Fargelanda, Sweden, May 6, 1983.
(Phoenix's 1st choice, 11th overall, in 2001 Entry Draft).

			Regular Season					Playoffs				
Season	Club	League	GP	G	A	TP	PIM	GP	G	A	TP	PIM
99-2000	MoDo-18	Swede-Jr.	4	0	2	2	6					
	MoDo Jr.	Swede-Jr.	18	4	6	10	8					
2000-01	V. Frolunda Jr.	Swede-Jr.	11	3	7	10	12	4	1	2	3	6
	Vastra Frolunda	Sweden	31	3	2	5	6	5	0	0	0	2
2001-02	Calgary Hitmen	WHL	58	19	31	50	51	4	1	1	2	8
2002-03	Calgary Hitmen	WHL	63	34	43	77	95	5	1	3	4	4
	Springfield Falcons	AHL	2	1	0	1	0	6	2	0	2	12

SKINNER, Brett (SKIH-nuhr, BREHT) VAN.

Defense. Shoots left. 6'1", 170 lbs. Born, Brandon, Man., June 28, 1983.
(Vancouver's 3rd choice, 68th overall, in 2002 Entry Draft).

			Regular Season					Playoffs				
Season	Club	League	GP	G	A	TP	PIM	GP	G	A	TP	PIM
1998-99	Brandon Kings	MMBHL	29	3	18	21	20					
99-2000	Brandon Kings	MMHL	40	8	27	35	48					
2000-01	Trail Smoke Eaters	BCHL	59	11	24	35	43					
2001-02	Des Moines	USHL	44	9	38	47	25	3	0	1	1	0
2002-03	U. of Denver	WCHA	37	4	13	17	27					

MMBHL First All-Star Team (1999) • MMHL First All-Star Team (2000) • USHL First All-Star Team (2002) • USHL Defenseman of the Year (2002)

SKLADANY, Frantisek (sklah-DAH-nee, FRAN-tih-shehk) COL.

Left wing. Shoots left. 6', 185 lbs. Born, Martin, Czech., April 22, 1982.
(Colorado's 4th choice, 143rd overall, in 2001 Entry Draft).

			Regular Season					Playoffs				
Season	Club	League	GP	G	A	TP	PIM	GP	G	A	TP	PIM
1998-99	Martin	Slovakia	1	0	0	0	0					
99-2000	Martin Jr.	Slovak-Jr.	STATISTICS NOT AVAILABLE									
	Martin	Slovak-2	13	1	4	5	2					
2000-01	Boston University	H-East	35	4	5	9	4					
2001-02	Boston University	H-East	33	13	13	26	23					
2002-03	Boston University	H-East	41	14	21	35	34					

SKLENAR, Jaroslav (SKLEH-nahr, YAHR-oh-slav) TOR.

Right wing. Shoots right. 6', 167 lbs. Born, Ivancice, Czech., November 22, 1982.
(Toronto's 8th choice, 183rd overall, in 2001 Entry Draft).

			Regular Season					Playoffs				
Season	Club	League	GP	G	A	TP	PIM	GP	G	A	TP	PIM
99-2000	Trinec Jr.	Czech-Jr.	32	5	6	11	2					
2000-01	HC Ytong Brno Jr.	Czech-Jr.	26	10	11	21	22					
	HC Ytong Brno	Czech-3	21	4	4	8	6					
2001-02	Znojmo	Czech	4	0	0	0	2					
	HC Ytong Brno	Czech-2	5	0	0	0	4					
	Rosice	Czech-2	8	3	1	4	0					
2002-03	Znojmo	Czech	10	0	0	0	0					
	HK 36 Skalica	Slovakia	13	0	0	0	0					
	Trebic	Czech-2	8	0	1	1	2					
	HC Hvezda Brno	Czech-2	1	0	0	0	0					

SKOLNEY, Wade (SKOHL-nee, WAYD) **PHI.**

Defense. Shoots right. 6', 185 lbs. Born, Wynyard, Sask., June 24, 1981.

			Regular Season					Playoffs				
Season	Club	League	GP	G	A	TP	PIM	GP	G	A	TP	PIM
1997-98	Brandon	WHL	42	1	11	12	49	3	0	0	0	0
1998-99	Brandon	WHL	39	3	10	13	60	5	0	1	1	16
99-2000	Brandon	WHL	13	0	2	2	23	....	....	....	....	....
2000-01	Brandon	WHL	28	2	9	11	37	....	....	....	....	....
2001-02	Brandon	WHL	50	4	12	16	179	19	2	7	9	56
2002-03	Philadelphia	AHL	68	2	7	9	102	....	....	....	....	....

Signed as a free agent by **Philadelphia**, May 20, 2002.

SKOOG, Simon (SKOOG, SEE-muhn) **ST.L.**

Defense. Shoots left. 6'2", 218 lbs. Born, Solvesborg, Sweden, February 17, 1983.
(St. Louis' 8th choice, 283rd overall, in 2001 Entry Draft).

			Regular Season					Playoffs				
Season	Club	League	GP	G	A	TP	PIM	GP	G	A	TP	PIM
99-2000	Malmo IF Jr.	Swede-Jr.	4	0	0	0	0	....	....	....	....	....
2000-01	Morrums GoIS IK	Swede-2	27	0	1	1	12	....	....	....	....	....
2001-02	Morrums GoIS IK	Swede-2	53	3	8	11	46	....	....	....	....	....
2002-03	Morrums GoIS IK	Swede-2	39	2	4	6	38	2	0	1	1	4

SKRLAC, Rob (SKUHR-lak, RAWB)

Left wing. Shoots left. 6'5", 245 lbs. Born, Port McNeill, B.C., June 10, 1976.
(Buffalo's 11th choice, 224th overall, in 1995 Entry Draft).

			Regular Season					Playoffs				
Season	Club	League	GP	G	A	TP	PIM	GP	G	A	TP	PIM
1993-94	Richmond	BCAHA	49	44	55	99	56	....	....	....	....	....
1994-95	Kamloops Blazers	WHL	23	0	1	1	177	....	....	....	....	....
1995-96	Kamloops Blazers	WHL	63	1	4	5	216	13	0	0	0	52
1996-97	Kamloops Blazers	WHL	61	8	10	18	278	5	0	0	0	35
1997-98	Albany River Rats	AHL	53	0	2	2	256	....	....	....	....	....
1998-99	Albany River Rats	AHL	61	1	1	2	213	1	0	0	0	0
99-2000	Albany River Rats	AHL	37	0	0	0	115	....	....	....	....	....
2000-01	Albany River Rats	AHL	38	0	0	0	105	....	....	....	....	....
2001-02	Albany River Rats	AHL	2	0	0	0	22	....	....	....	....	....
	Mississippi	ECHL	29	1	3	4	161	....	....	....	....	....
	Portland Pirates	AHL	33	0	3	3	87	....	....	....	....	....
2002-03	Albany River Rats	AHL	42	2	3	5	165	....	....	....	....	....

Signed as a free agent by **New Jersey**, June 17, 1997.

SLATER, Jim (SLAY-tuhr, JIHM) **ATL.**

Center. Shoots left. 6', 182 lbs. Born, Petoskey, MI, December 9, 1982.
(Atlanta's 2nd choice, 30th overall, in 2002 Entry Draft).

			Regular Season					Playoffs				
Season	Club	League	GP	G	A	TP	PIM	GP	G	A	TP	PIM
1998-99	Cleveland Barons	NAJHL	50	13	20	33	58	2	0	0	0	2
99-2000	Cleveland Barons	NAJHL	56	35	50	85	129	3	1	3	4	4
2000-01	Cleveland Barons	NAJHL	48	27	37	64	122	6	6	6	12	6
2001-02	Michigan State	CCHA	37	11	21	32	50	....	....	....	....	....
2002-03	Michigan State	CCHA	37	18	26	44	26	....	....	....	....	....

NAJHL First All-Star Team (2000, 2001) • CCHA All-Rookie Team (2002) • CCHA First All-Star Team (2003)

SLOAN, Tyler (SLOHN, TIGH-luhr) **CBJ**

Defense. Shoots left. 6'4", 190 lbs. Born, Calgary, Alta., March 15, 1981.

			Regular Season					Playoffs				
Season	Club	League	GP	G	A	TP	PIM	GP	G	A	TP	PIM
1997-98	Calgary Buffaloes	AMHL	36	2	11	13	24	10	0	4	4	2
1998-99	Calgary Royals	AJHL	STATISTICS NOT AVAILABLE									
99-2000	Calgary Royals	AJHL	45	5	26	31	80	....	....	....	....	....
2000-01	Kamloops Blazers	WHL	70	5	28	33	146	4	0	0	0	4
2001-02	Kamloops Blazers	WHL	70	3	29	32	89	4	0	0	0	15
	Syracuse Crunch	AHL	2	0	0	0	5	....	....	....	....	....
2002-03	Syracuse Crunch	AHL	39	2	1	3	46	....	....	....	....	....
	Dayton Bombers	ECHL	14	1	2	3	22	....	....	....	....	....

AJHL First All-Star Team (1999)

Signed as a free agent by **Columbus**, September 24, 2000.

SLOVAK, Tomas (SLOHW-vahk, TAW-mawsh) **COL.**

Defense. Shoots right. 6'1", 203 lbs. Born, Kosice, Czech., April 5, 1983.
(Nashville's 3rd choice, 42nd overall, in 2001 Entry Draft).

			Regular Season					Playoffs				
Season	Club	League	GP	G	A	TP	PIM	GP	G	A	TP	PIM
99-2000	HC Kosice	Slovakia	2	0	0	0	0	....	....	....	....	....
2000-01	HC Kosice	Slovakia	43	5	5	10	28	3	1	0	1	2
2001-02	Kelowna Rockets	WHL	53	2	24	26	41	15	0	0	0	8
2002-03	Kelowna Rockets	WHL	65	18	53	71	86	19	2	*20	22	26

WHL West First All-Star Team (2003)

Traded to **Colorado** by **Nashville** for Sergei Soin, June 21, 2003.

SMABY, Matt (SMA-bee, MAT) **T.B.**

Defense. Shoots left. 6'5", 202 lbs. Born, Minneapolis, MN, October 14, 1984.
(Tampa Bay's 2nd choice, 41st overall, in 2003 Entry Draft).

			Regular Season					Playoffs				
Season	Club	League	GP	G	A	TP	PIM	GP	G	A	TP	PIM
2001-02	Shat.-St. Mary's	Hi-School	65	7	18	25	134	....	....	....	....	....
2002-03	Shat.-St. Mary's	Hi-School	57	3	20	23	114	....	....	....	....	....

• Signed Letter of Intent to attend **North Dakota** (WCHA), December 2, 2002.

SMITH, Jeff (SMIHTH, JEHF) **PHI.**

Left wing. Shoots left. 6'6", 212 lbs. Born, Regina, Sask., January 2, 1981.

			Regular Season					Playoffs				
Season	Club	League	GP	G	A	TP	PIM	GP	G	A	TP	PIM
1998-99	Red Deer Rebels	WHL	25	0	0	0	0	....	....	....	....	....
	Reg. Pat Cdns.	SMHL	35	28	19	47	71	....	....	....	....	....
99-2000	Red Deer Rebels	WHL	63	9	6	15	74	....	....	....	....	....
2000-01	Red Deer Rebels	WHL	72	22	11	33	187	....	....	....	....	....
2001-02	Red Deer Rebels	WHL	69	9	15	24	236	23	6	6	12	30
2002-03	Trenton Titans	ECHL	35	1	7	8	103	1	0	0	0	4
	Philadelphia	AHL	11	1	0	1	22	....	....	....	....	....

Signed as a free agent by **Philadelphia**, August 20, 2002.

SMITH, Kenny (SMIHTH, KEHN-nee) **EDM.**

Defense. Shoots right. 6'2", 209 lbs. Born, Stoneham, MA, December 31, 1981.
(Edmonton's 4th choice, 84th overall, in 2001 Entry Draft).

			Regular Season					Playoffs				
Season	Club	League	GP	G	A	TP	PIM	GP	G	A	TP	PIM
1998-99	U.S. National U-17	USDP	29	2	5	7	32	....	....	....	....	....
99-2000	U.S. National U-18	USDP	27	4	6	10	77	....	....	....	....	....
2000-01	Harvard Crimson	ECAC	21	0	2	2	37	....	....	....	....	....
2001-02	Harvard Crimson	ECAC	33	3	10	13	48	....	....	....	....	....
2002-03	Harvard Crimson	ECAC	33	4	11	15	52	....	....	....	....	....

SMITH, Marcus (SMIHTH, MAHR-kuhs) **PHX.**

Defense. Shoots right. 6', 192 lbs. Born, Denver, CO, January 14, 1983.
(Phoenix's 10th choice, 249th overall, in 2002 Entry Draft).

			Regular Season					Playoffs				
Season	Club	League	GP	G	A	TP	PIM	GP	G	A	TP	PIM
99-2000	Mississauga	OHL	15	1	2	3	0	....	....	....	....	....
2000-01	Kitchener Rangers	OHL	59	4	13	17	43	....	....	....	....	....
2001-02	Kitchener Rangers	OHL	65	6	25	31	63	4	1	0	1	8
2002-03	Kitchener Rangers	OHL	67	2	30	32	82	15	2	8	10	6

SMITH, Nathan (SMIHTH, NAY-thun) **VAN.**

Center. Shoots left. 6'2", 192 lbs. Born, Edmonton, Alta., February 9, 1982.
(Vancouver's 1st choice, 23rd overall, in 2000 Entry Draft).

			Regular Season					Playoffs				
Season	Club	League	GP	G	A	TP	PIM	GP	G	A	TP	PIM
1997-98	Sherwood Park	AMHL	35	15	13	28	24	....	....	....	....	....
1998-99	Swift Current	WHL	47	5	8	13	26	....	....	....	....	....
99-2000	Swift Current	WHL	70	21	28	49	72	12	1	6	7	4
2000-01	Swift Current	WHL	67	28	62	90	78	19	4	3	7	20
2001-02	Swift Current	WHL	47	22	38	60	52	12	3	6	9	18
2002-03	Manitoba Moose	AHL	53	9	8	17	30	14	1	3	4	25

SMITH, Tim (SMIHTH, TIHM) **VAN.**

Center. Shoots left. 5'9", 160 lbs. Born, Whitecourt, Alta., July 21, 1981.
(Vancouver's 7th choice, 272nd overall, in 2000 Entry Draft).

			Regular Season					Playoffs				
Season	Club	League	GP	G	A	TP	PIM	GP	G	A	TP	PIM
1997-98	Lebret Eagles	SJHL	36	6	7	13	12	....	....	....	....	....
1998-99	Spokane Chiefs	WHL	57	5	20	25	21	....	....	....	....	....
99-2000	Spokane Chiefs	WHL	71	26	70	96	65	15	7	7	14	32
2000-01	Spokane Chiefs	WHL	38	19	37	56	65	....	....	....	....	....
	Swift Current	WHL	30	12	22	34	38	19	10	14	24	38
2001-02	Swift Current	WHL	67	28	47	75	123	12	7	6	13	20
2002-03	Manitoba Moose	AHL	3	0	0	0	0	....	....	....	....	....
	Columbia Inferno	ECHL	68	22	37	59	44	17	5	11	16	16

SOCHOR, Jan (soh-KHAWR, YAN) **TOR.**

Left wing. Shoots right. 6', 198 lbs. Born, Usti nad Labem, Czech., January 17, 1980.
(Toronto's 6th choice, 161st overall, in 1999 Entry Draft).

			Regular Season					Playoffs				
Season	Club	League	GP	G	A	TP	PIM	GP	G	A	TP	PIM
1996-97	HC Slavia Praha Jr.	Czech-Jr.	26	11	12	23	....	....	....	....	....	....
1997-98	HC Slavia Praha Jr.	Czech-Jr.	33	26	12	38	....	....	....	....	....	....
	HC Slavia Praha	Czech	14	1	1	2	2	1	0	0	0	0
1998-99	HC Slavia Praha Jr.	Czech-Jr.	7	2	1	3	2	....	....	....	....	....
	HC Slavia Praha	Czech	47	10	10	20	14	....	....	....	....	....
99-2000	HC Slavia Praha Jr.	Czech-Jr.	12	5	5	10	6	....	....	....	....	....
	HC Slavia Praha	Czech	39	7	11	18	37	....	....	....	....	....
	Slovan Labem	Czech-2	6	2	3	5	8	....	....	....	....	....
2000-01	Vsetin Jr.	Czech-Jr.	8	5	3	8	0	....	....	....	....	....
	HC Slovnaft Vsetin	Czech	41	5	4	9	28	3	0	0	0	0
2001-02	Vsetin	Czech	27	4	0	4	8	....	....	....	....	....
2002-03	Vsetin	Czech	17	2	0	2	10	....	....	....	....	....
	SK Kaden	Czech-2	18	4	6	10	10	....	....	....	....	....

SODERBERG, Anders (SOH-dehr-buhrg, AN-duhrs) **BOS.**

Right wing. Shoots right. 5'6", 161 lbs. Born, Ornskoldsvik, Sweden, October 7, 1975.
(Boston's 10th choice, 234th overall, in 1996 Entry Draft).

			Regular Season					Playoffs				
Season	Club	League	GP	G	A	TP	PIM	GP	G	A	TP	PIM
1992-93	MoDo Jr.	Swede-Jr.	13	6	12	18	2	....	....	....	....	....
	MoDo	Sweden	1	0	0	0	0	....	....	....	....	....
1993-94	MoDo Jr.	Swede-Jr.	9	8	5	13	10	....	....	....	....	....
	MoDo	Sweden	19	0	0	0	2	9	0	0	0	0
1994-95	MoDo	Sweden	38	9	14	23	2	....	....	....	....	....
1995-96	MoDo	Sweden	40	10	18	28	10	8	3	3	6	0
1996-97	MoDo	Sweden	39	9	13	22	16	....	....	....	....	....
1997-98	MoDo	Sweden	44	15	10	25	4	9	5	1	6	2
1998-99	MoDo	Sweden	49	6	15	21	18	13	3	6	9	4
99-2000	MoDo	Sweden	43	15	10	25	18	9	1	2	3	0
2000-01	MoDo	Sweden	42	11	4	15	12	6	1	6	7	0
2001-02	MoDo	Sweden	30	6	9	15	6	11	0	0	0	0
2002-03	MoDo	Sweden	49	10	19	29	4	6	0	3	3	0

SODERSTROM, Christian (SAW-duhr-struhm, KRIHS-tyehn) **DET.**

Left wing. Shoots left. 6'1", 176 lbs. Born, Sundsvall, Sweden, October 13, 1980.
(Detroit's 9th choice, 262nd overall, in 2002 Entry Draft).

			Regular Season					Playoffs				
Season	Club	League	GP	G	A	TP	PIM	GP	G	A	TP	PIM
1997-98	Timra IK Jr.	Swede-Jr.	27	7	10	17	22	....	....	....	....	....
1998-99	Timra IK Jr.	Swede-Jr.	STATISTICS NOT AVAILABLE									
	Timra IK	Sweden-2	3	0	1	1	2	....	....	....	....	....
99-2000	Timra IK Jr.	Swede-Jr.	3	4	3	7	0	....	....	....	....	....
	Timra IK	Sweden-2	29	5	3	8	2	....	....	....	....	....
	Timra IK	Sweden-Q	14	3	3	6	2	10	1	0	1	2
2000-01	Timra IK	Sweden	46	6	6	12	16	....	....	....	....	....
2001-02	Timra IK	Sweden	48	8	8	16	16	....	....	....	....	....
	Timra IK	Sweden-Q	....	....	....	....	....	9	0	1	1	4
2002-03	Timra IK	Sweden	44	5	10	15	6	10	1	2	3	2

SOIN, Sergei (SOY-ihn, SAIR-gay) NSH.

Center/Left wing. Shoots left. 6', 175 lbs. Born, Moscow, USSR, March 31, 1982.
(Colorado's 3rd choice, 50th overall, in 2000 Entry Draft).

			Regular Season					Playoffs				
Season	Club	League	GP	G	A	TP	PIM	GP	G	A	TP	PIM
1997-98	Krylja Sovetov 2	Russia-3	2	0	0	0	0	....	....	....	....	....
1998-99	Krylja Sovetov	Russia	34	1	4	5	12	....	....	....	....	....
99-2000	Krylja Sovetov	Russia-2	33	8	7	5	24	....	....	....	....	....
2000-01	Krylja Sovetov 2	Russia-3	8	2	3	5	12	....	....	....	....	....
	Krylja Sovetov	Russia-2	30	8	5	13	10	....	....	....	....	....
2001-02	Krylja Sovetov 2	Russia-3	5	2	6	8	20	....	....	....	....	....
	Krylja Sovetov	Russia	41	5	7	12	8	....	....	....	....	....
2002-03	Krylja Sovetov	Russia	49	8	6	14	40	....	....	....	....	....

Traded to **Nashville** by **Colorado** for Tomas Slovak, June 21, 2003.

SOMERVUORI, Eero (soh-muhr-VOH-ree, AIR-oh) T.B.

Right wing. Shoots right. 5'10", 167 lbs. Born, Jarvenpaa, Finland, February 7, 1979.
(Tampa Bay's 9th choice, 170th overall, in 1997 Entry Draft).

			Regular Season					Playoffs				
Season	Club	League	GP	G	A	TP	PIM	GP	G	A	TP	PIM
1993-94	Jokerit Helsinki-C	Finn-Jr.	29	23	31	54	16	....	....	....	....	....
1994-95	Jokerit Helsinki-C	Finn-Jr.	17	23	16	39	8	6	7	3	10	2
	Jokerit Helsinki-B	Finn-Jr.	15	8	10	18	4	....	....	....	....	....
	Jokerit Helsinki Jr.	Finn-Jr.	10	1	1	2	2	1	0	1	1	0
1995-96	Jokerit Helsinki Jr.	Finn-Jr.	28	14	12	26	10	9	4	1	5	4
	Jokerit Helsinki-B	Finn-Jr.	13	10	13	23	6	....	....	....	....	....
	Haukat Jarvenpaa	Finland-2	1	0	0	0	0	....	....	....	....	....
	Jokerit Helsinki	Finland	6	1	2	3	0	....	....	....	....	....
1996-97	Jokerit Helsinki Jr.	Finn-Jr.	28	20	19	39	30	5	3	0	3	4
	Jokerit Helsinki	Finland	35	1	1	2	2	5	0	0	0	0
	Jokerit Helsinki	EuroHL	3	0	0	0	0	2	2	0	0	0
1997-98	Jokerit Helsinki	Finland	42	3	7	10	12	8	2	1	3	6
	Jokerit Helsinki	EuroHL	5	0	0	0	0	....	....	....	....	....
	Jokerit Helsinki Jr.	Finn-Jr.	14	4	8	12	2	....	....	....	....	....
1998-99	Jokerit Helsinki	Finland	50	7	8	15	24	3	1	0	1	6
	Jokerit Helsinki	EuroHL	6	0	0	0	0	1	0	0	0	0
	Jokerit Helsinki Jr.	Finn-Jr.	4	1	1	2	2	4	3	0	3	2
99-2000	Jokerit Helsinki	Finland	54	6	6	12	10	11	1	0	1	0
2000-01	HPK Hameenlinna	Finland	56	14	6	20	35	....	....	....	....	....
2001-02	HPK Hameenlinna	Finland	56	25	23	48	34	8	2	2	4	6
2002-03	HPK Hameenlinna	Finland	56	21	24	45	42	13	2	3	5	0

SOUCY, J.F. (SOO-cee, JAY-EHF) T.B.

Center. Shoots left. 6'3", 180 lbs. Born, Riviere Du Loup, Que., March 25, 1983.
(Tampa Bay's 10th choice, 252nd overall, in 2001 Entry Draft).

			Regular Season					Playoffs				
Season	Club	League	GP	G	A	TP	PIM	GP	G	A	TP	PIM
1998-99	Levis	QAAA	42	6	17	23	82	....	....	....	....	....
99-2000	Val-d'Or Foreurs	QMJHL	55	1	4	5	9	....	....	....	....	....
2000-01	Val-d'Or Foreurs	QMJHL	38	3	4	7	57	....	....	....	....	....
	Montreal Rocket	QMJHL	27	3	8	11	37	....	....	....	....	....
2001-02	Montreal Rocket	QMJHL	49	8	13	21	94	7	0	2	2	8
2002-03	Montreal Rocket	QMJHL	65	24	31	55	168	7	0	2	2	24

SOUZA, Mike (SOO-zah, MIGHK)

Left wing. Shoots left. 6'1", 210 lbs. Born, Melrose, MA, January 28, 1978.
(Chicago's 4th choice, 67th overall, in 1997 Entry Draft).

			Regular Season					Playoffs				
Season	Club	League	GP	G	A	TP	PIM	GP	G	A	TP	PIM
1992-93	Wakefield High	Hi-School	20	22	13	35	....	....	....	....	....	....
1993-94	Wakefield High	Hi-School	22	28	34	62	....	....	....	....	....	....
1994-95	Wakefield High	Hi-School	21	22	31	53	....	....	....	....	....	....
1995-96	Wakefield High	Hi-School	21	25	31	56	22	....	....	....	....	....
1996-97	New Hampshire	H-East	39	15	11	26	20	....	....	....	....	....
1997-98	New Hampshire	H-East	38	13	12	25	36	....	....	....	....	....
1998-99	New Hampshire	H-East	41	23	42	65	38	....	....	....	....	....
99-2000	New Hampshire	H-East	38	15	25	40	58	....	....	....	....	....
2000-01	Norfolk Admirals	AHL	75	14	17	31	44	3	0	0	0	2
2001-02	Norfolk Admirals	AHL	66	20	11	31	58	....	....	....	....	....
2002-03	Norfolk Admirals	AHL	5	2	2	4	7	....	....	....	....	....
	Bridgeport	AHL	59	7	15	22	89	9	0	1	1	12

NCAA Championship All-Tournament Team (1999) • Hockey East Second All-Star Team (2000)

SPANG, Dan (SPANG, DAN) S.J.

Defense. Shoots left. 6', 200 lbs. Born, Winchester, MA, August 18, 1983.
(San Jose's 2nd choice, 52nd overall, in 2002 Entry Draft).

			Regular Season					Playoffs				
Season	Club	League	GP	G	A	TP	PIM	GP	G	A	TP	PIM
2000-01	Winchester High	Hi-School	24	8	37	45	14	....	....	....	....	....
2001-02	Winchester High	Hi-School	6	9	8	17	14	....	....	....	....	....
2002-03	Boston University	H-East	27	3	6	9	14	....	....	....	....	....

• Missed majority of 2001-02 season recovering from head injuries suffered in automobile accident, October 2001.

SPENCE, Russell (SPEHNS, RUH-suhl) PHX.

Center. Shoots right. 6'3", 200 lbs. Born, Portage La Prairie, Man., January 1, 1982.
(Phoenix's 11th choice, 280th overall, in 2002 Entry Draft).

			Regular Season					Playoffs				
Season	Club	League	GP	G	A	TP	PIM	GP	G	A	TP	PIM
1998/00	Portage Terriers	MJHL	95	31	41	72	....	....	....	....	....	....
2000-01	Portage Terriers	MJHL	57	26	24	50	....	....	....	....	....	....
2001-02	OCN Blizzard	MJHL	55	29	51	80	37	15	7	7	14	6
2002-03	Alaska-Fairbanks	CCHA	23	2	9	11	8	....	....	....	....	....

MJHL First All-Star Team (2002)

SPENCER, Steve (SPEHN-suhr, STEEV) NSH.

Defense. Shoots left. 6'3", 220 lbs. Born, Regina, Sask., June 16, 1982.
(Nashville's 8th choice, 266th overall, in 2002 Entry Draft).

			Regular Season					Playoffs				
Season	Club	League	GP	G	A	TP	PIM	GP	G	A	TP	PIM
2000-01	La Ronge	SJHL	48	3	6	9	176	....	....	....	....	....
2001-02	Swift Current	WHL	65	1	4	5	226	11	0	0	0	36
2002-03	Swift Current	WHL	72	2	2	4	187	4	0	0	0	17

SPILLER, Matthew (SPIHL-uhr, MA-thew) PHX.

Defense. Shoots left. 6'5", 225 lbs. Born, Daysland, Alta., February 7, 1983.
(Phoenix's 2nd choice, 31st overall, in 2001 Entry Draft).

			Regular Season					Playoffs				
Season	Club	League	GP	G	A	TP	PIM	GP	G	A	TP	PIM
1998-99	East Central	AMHL	36	8	19	27	140	....	....	....	....	....
99-2000	Seattle	WHL	60	1	10	11	108	7	0	0	0	25
2000-01	Seattle	WHL	71	4	7	11	174	....	....	....	....	....
2001-02	Seattle	WHL	72	8	23	31	168	1	0	0	0	4
2002-03	Seattle	WHL	68	11	24	35	198	15	2	7	9	36

SPRUKTS, Janis (SPRUKTS, YAN-ish) FLA.

Center. Shoots left. 6'3", 224 lbs. Born, Riga, Latvia, January 31, 1982.
(Florida's 7th choice, 234th overall, in 2000 Entry Draft).

			Regular Season					Playoffs				
Season	Club	League	GP	G	A	TP	PIM	GP	G	A	TP	PIM
99-2000	Lukko Rauma Jr.	Finn-Jr.	26	2	5	7	6	3	0	0	0	0
	Essamika Jr.	EEHL-2	2	4	4	8	0	....	....	....	....	....
2000-01	Lukko Rauma Jr.	Finn-Jr.	36	15	22	37	24	3	0	0	0	0
	Lukko Rauma	Finland	9	0	0	0	2	....	....	....	....	....
2001-02	Acadie-Bathurst	QMJHL	63	35	44	79	46	16	14	8	22	12
	Sport Vassa	Finland-2	21	5	6	11	8	....	....	....	....	....
2002-03	Sport Vassa	Finland-2	21	5	6	11	8	....	....	....	....	....
	Acadie-Bathurst	QMJHL	30	9	29	38	12	11	3	5	8	0

• Released by **Sport Vassa** (Finland-2) and returned to **Acadie-Bathurst** (QMJHL), January 3, 2003.

SRDINKO, Jan (suhr-DIHN-koh, YAN) N.J.

Defense. Shoots left. 5'11", 195 lbs. Born, Vsetin, Czech., February 22, 1974.
(New Jersey's 8th choice, 241st overall, in 1997 Entry Draft).

			Regular Season					Playoffs				
Season	Club	League	GP	G	A	TP	PIM	GP	G	A	TP	PIM
1995-96	HC Petra Vsetin	Czech	31	0	3	3	....	9	0	0	0	....
1996-97	HC Petra Vsetin	Czech	49	2	8	10	71	10	0	3	3	29
1997-98	HC Petra Vsetin	Czech	47	1	4	5	95	10	0	3	3	4
	HC Petra Vsetin	EuroHL	9	0	1	1	4	....	....	....	....	....
1998-99	HC Slovnaft Vsetin	Czech	50	2	7	9	58	12	0	1	1	....
99-2000	HC Slovnaft Vsetin	Czech	48	3	10	13	50	9	2	0	2	29
2000-01	HC Slovnaft Vsetin	Czech	47	8	9	17	81	14	1	1	2	24
2001-02	HC Sparta Praha	Czech	50	6	5	11	100	2	0	0	0	0
2002-03	HC Sparta Praha	Czech	51	3	4	7	44	10	0	1	1	14

STAAL, Eric (STAHL, AIR-ihk) CAR.

Center. Shoots left. 6'3", 182 lbs. Born, Thunder Bay, Ont., October 29, 1984.
(Carolina's 1st choice, 2nd overall, in 2003 Entry Draft).

			Regular Season					Playoffs				
Season	Club	League	GP	G	A	TP	PIM	GP	G	A	TP	PIM
2000-01	Peterborough	OHL	63	19	30	49	23	7	2	5	7	4
2001-02	Peterborough	OHL	56	23	39	62	40	6	3	6	9	10
2002-03	Peterborough	OHL	66	39	59	98	36	7	9	5	14	6

OHL Second All-Star Team (2003) • Canadian Major Junior First All-Star Team (2003)

STAAL, Kim (STOHL, KIHM) MTL.

Center. Shoots right. 6', 185 lbs. Born, Herlev, Denmark, March 10, 1978.
(Montreal's 4th choice, 92nd overall, in 1996 Entry Draft).

			Regular Season					Playoffs				
Season	Club	League	GP	G	A	TP	PIM	GP	G	A	TP	PIM
1994-95	Malmo IF Jr.	Swede-Jr.	17	4	2	6	4	....	....	....	....	....
1995-96	Malmo IF Jr.	Swede-Jr.	30	24	20	44	14	....	....	....	....	....
1996-97	Malmo IF Jr.	Swede-Jr.	3	6	4	10	2	....	....	....	....	....
	Malmo IF	Sweden	4	0	1	1	2	....	....	....	....	....
1997-98	Malmo IF Jr.	Swede-Jr.	20	13	11	24	36	....	....	....	....	....
	Malmo IF	Sweden	13	0	1	1	1	....	....	....	....	....
1998-99	Malmo IF	Sweden	48	1	5	6	14	4	0	0	0	0
99-2000	Malmo IF	Sweden	50	14	10	24	24	6	1	1	2	4
2000-01	Malmo IF	Sweden	48	16	15	31	32	9	4	2	6	4
2001-02	MoDo	Sweden	49	14	23	37	16	12	3	7	10	2
2002-03	MoDo	Sweden	14	4	5	9	4	6	1	0	1	0
	Ornskoldviks SK	Swede-2	2	3	0	3	0	....	....	....	....	....

STALS, Juris (STAHLS, YOO-rihs) NYR

Left wing. Shoots left. 6'3", 187 lbs. Born, Riga, Latvia, August 4, 1982.
(NY Rangers' 11th choice, 269th overall, in 2001 Entry Draft).

			Regular Season					Playoffs				
Season	Club	League	GP	G	A	TP	PIM	GP	G	A	TP	PIM
99-2000	Lukko Rauma Jr.	Finn-Jr.	2	1	0	1	2	....	....	....	....	....
2000-01	Lukko Rauma Jr.	Finn-Jr.	45	23	22	45	26	3	1	0	1	0
2001-02	Sarnia Sting	OHL	60	23	22	45	12	5	0	1	1	2
2002-03	Sport Vassa	Finland-2	23	3	3	6	16	....	....	....	....	....
	Owen Sound	OHL	25	8	15	23	14	4	0	4	4	4
	Hartford Wolf Pack	AHL	2	0	1	1	0	....	....	....	....	....

STASTNY, Yan (STAS-nee, YAHN) BOS.

Center. Shoots left. 5'11", 175 lbs. Born, Quebec City, Que., September 30, 1982.
(Boston's 6th choice, 259th overall, in 2002 Entry Draft).

			Regular Season					Playoffs				
Season	Club	League	GP	G	A	TP	PIM	GP	G	A	TP	PIM
99-2000	St. Louis Sting	NAJHL	45	12	23	35	77	....	....	....	....	....
2000-01	St. Louis Sting	NAJHL	6	0	2	2	23	....	....	....	....	....
	Omaha Lancers	USHL	44	17	14	31	101	11	6	6	12	12
2001-02	Notre Dame	CCHA	33	6	11	17	38	....	....	....	....	....
2002-03	U. of Notre Dame	CCHA	39	14	9	23	44	....	....	....	....	....

STATE, Jeff (STAYT, JEHF) NYR

Defense. Shoots right. 6'6", 235 lbs. Born, Tonowanda, NY, September 17, 1979.

			Regular Season					Playoffs				
Season	Club	League	GP	G	A	TP	PIM	GP	G	A	TP	PIM
1997-98	Omaha Lancers	USHL	47	2	4	6	59	6	0	0	0	12
1998-99	Dubuque	USHL	54	2	4	6	113	2	0	0	0	2
99-2000	Burlington	OPJHL	44	12	18	30	50	....	....	....	....	....
2000-01	Merrimack College	H-East	35	1	2	3	58	....	....	....	....	....
2001-02	Merrimack College	H-East	35	0	9	9	84	....	....	....	....	....
2002-03	Hartford Wolf Pack	AHL	39	1	3	4	103	....	....	....	....	....
	Charlotte	ECHL	29	1	3	4	65	....	....	....	....	....

Signed as a free agent by **NY Rangers**, July 11, 2002.

STECKEL, Dave (STEH-kuhl, DAYV) L.A.

Center. Shoots left. 6'5", 200 lbs. Born, Westbend, WI, March 15, 1982.
(Los Angeles' 2nd choice, 30th overall, in 2001 Entry Draft).

			Regular Season					Playoffs				
Season	Club	League	GP	G	A	TP	PIM	GP	G	A	TP	PIM
1998-99	U.S. National U-17	USDP	51	3	14	17	18	....	....	....	....	....
	U.S. National U-18	USDP	2	0	0	0	2	....	....	....	....	....
99-2000	U.S. National U-18	USDP	52	13	13	26	94	....	....	....	....	....
2000-01	Ohio State	CCHA	33	17	18	35	80	....	....	....	....	....
2001-02	Ohio State	CCHA	36	6	16	22	75	....	....	....	....	....
2002-03	Ohio State	CCHA	36	10	8	18	50	....	....	....	....	....

CCHA All-Rookie Team (2001)

STEEN, Alexander (STEEN, al-ehx-AN-duhr) TOR.

Center. Shoots left. 5'11", 183 lbs. Born, Winnipeg, Man., March 1, 1984.
(Toronto's 1st choice, 24th overall, in 2002 Entry Draft).

			Regular Season					Playoffs				
Season	Club	League	GP	G	A	TP	PIM	GP	G	A	TP	PIM
99-2000	V. Frolunda Jr.	Swede-Jr.	14	3	5	8	16	....	....	....	....	....
	V. Frolunda-18	Swede-Jr.		STATISTICS NOT AVAILABLE								
2000-01	V. Frolunda Jr.	Swede-Jr.	23	11	12	23	15	3	1	0	1	2
	V. Frolunda-18	Swede-Jr.	6	3	3	6	9	....	....	....	....	....
2001-02	V. Frolunda Jr.	Swede-Jr.	23	21	17	38	47	2	1	1	2	2
	Vastra Frolunda	Sweden	26	0	3	3	14	10	1	2	3	0
2002-03	Vastra Frolunda	Sweden	45	5	10	15	18	16	2	3	5	4
	V. Frolunda Jr.	Swede-Jr.	2	0	2	2	0	....	....	....	....	....

STEEN, Calle (STEEN, CAL-lee) DET.

Right wing. Shoots left. 5'11", 198 lbs. Born, Stockholm, Sweden, May 16, 1980.
(Detroit's 6th choice, 142nd overall, in 1998 Entry Draft).

			Regular Season					Playoffs				
Season	Club	League	GP	G	A	TP	PIM	GP	G	A	TP	PIM
1995-96	Hammarby Jr.	Swede-Jr.	5	0	0	0	0	....	....	....	....	....
1996-97	Hammarby Jr.	Swede-Jr.	24	4	9	13	....	....	....	....	....	....
1997-98	Hammarby	Swede-2	21	1	3	4	22	....	....	....	....	....
1998-99	Hammarby	Swede-2	33	4	16	20	28	5	0	2	2	6
99-2000	Mora IK	Swede-2	32	4	4	8	48	9	0	2	2	10
2000-01	Bofors IK	Swede-2	31	4	7	11	69	....	....	....	....	....
	JYP Jyvaskyla	Finland	5	0	0	0	0	....	....	....	....	....
2001-02	Bofors IK	Swede-2	53	12	22	34	78	6	2	2	4	12
2002-03	Bofors IK	Swede-2	27	12	17	29	71	....	....	....	....	....
	Bofors IK	Swede-Q	6	2	3	5	41	....	....	....	....	....
	Farjestad	Sweden	11	0	2	2	2	12	1	5	6	12

STEEVES, Ryan (STEEVZ, RIGH-uhn) COL.

Center/Left wing. Shoots left. 6', 195 lbs. Born, Ottawa, Ont., December 31, 1982.
(Colorado's 8th choice, 227th overall, in 2002 Entry Draft).

			Regular Season					Playoffs				
Season	Club	League	GP	G	A	TP	PIM	GP	G	A	TP	PIM
1998-99	Ottawa Jr. Sens	OCJHL	51	17	12	29	45	....	....	....	....	....
99-2000	Ottawa Jr. Sens	OCJHL	55	36	39	75	87	....	....	....	....	....
2000-01	Yale University	ECAC	23	3	2	5	10	....	....	....	....	....
2001-02	Yale University	ECAC	31	9	13	22	20	....	....	....	....	....
2002-03	Yale University	ECAC	32	15	23	38	36	....	....	....	....	....

STEHLIK, Richard (SHTEH-lihk, RIH-chard) NSH.

Defense. Shoots left. 6'4", 245 lbs. Born, Skalica, Czech., June 22, 1984.
(Nashville's 5th choice, 76th overall, in 2003 Entry Draft).

			Regular Season					Playoffs				
Season	Club	League	GP	G	A	TP	PIM	GP	G	A	TP	PIM
99-2000	HK 36 Skalica Jr.	Slovak-Jr.	50	10	5	15	....	....	....	....	....	....
2000-01	HK 36 Skalica	Slovak	45	1	1	2	14	3	0	0	0	2
2001-02	HK 36 Skalica	Slovak	35	1	0	1	12	....	....	....	....	....
2002-03	Sherbrooke	QMJHL	43	8	16	24	105	12	1	5	6	20

STEMPNIAK, Lee (STEHMP-nee-ak, LEE) ST.L.

Right wing. Shoots right. 6', 190 lbs. Born, Buffalo, NY, February 4, 1983.
(St. Louis' 7th choice, 148th overall, in 2003 Entry Draft).

			Regular Season					Playoffs				
Season	Club	League	GP	G	A	TP	PIM	GP	G	A	TP	PIM
2000-01	Buffalo Lightning	OPJHL	48	34	51	86	36	....	....	....	....	....
2001-02	Dartmouth	ECAC	32	12	9	21	8	....	....	....	....	....
2002-03	Dartmouth	ECAC	34	21	28	49	32	....	....	....	....	....

STEPHENSON, Shay (STEE-vehn-suhn, SHAY) CAR.

Left wing. Shoots left. 6'4", 200 lbs. Born, Outlook, Sask., September 13, 1983.
(Carolina's 7th choice, 198th overall, in 2003 Entry Draft).

			Regular Season					Playoffs				
Season	Club	League	GP	G	A	TP	PIM	GP	G	A	TP	PIM
99-2000	Notre Dame	SMHL	42	23	7	30	46	....	....	....	....	....
2000-01	Red Deer Rebels	WHL	44	1	4	5	30	22	0	0	0	15
2001-02	Red Deer Rebels	WHL	59	9	10	19	55	23	0	3	3	14
2002-03	Red Deer Rebels	WHL	67	17	15	32	84	23	6	5	11	33

• Re-entered NHL Entry Draft. Originally Edmonton's 11th choice, 278th overall, in 2001 Entry Draft.

STEPP, Joel (STEHP, JOHL) ANA.

Center. Shoots left. 6', 185 lbs. Born, Estevan, Sask., February 11, 1983.
(Anaheim's 3rd choice, 69th overall, in 2001 Entry Draft).

			Regular Season					Playoffs				
Season	Club	League	GP	G	A	TP	PIM	GP	G	A	TP	PIM
1998-99	Estevan	SMBHL	60	65	70	135	120	....	....	....	....	....
	Red Deer Rebels	WHL	2	0	0	0	0	....	....	....	....	....
99-2000	Red Deer Rebels	WHL	65	11	13	24	59	4	1	0	1	8
2000-01	Red Deer Rebels	WHL	70	24	13	37	89	22	6	3	9	24
2001-02	Red Deer Rebels	WHL	70	27	26	53	59	23	11	11	22	24
2002-03	Red Deer Rebels	WHL	24	4	11	15	18	23	6	7	13	26

• Missed majority of 2002-03 season recovering from wrist surgery, September 12, 2002.

STERLING, Brett (STUHR-lihng, BRET) ATL.

Left wing. Shoots left. 5'7", 163 lbs. Born, Los Angeles, CA, April 24, 1984.
(Atlanta's 5th choice, 145th overall, in 2003 Entry Draft).

			Regular Season					Playoffs				
Season	Club	League	GP	G	A	TP	PIM	GP	G	A	TP	PIM
99-2000	L.A. Jr. Kings	SCAHA	35	45	25	70	....	....	....	....	....	....
2000-01	U.S. National U-17	USDP	60	26	36	62	66	....	....	....	....	....
2001-02	U.S. National U-18	USDP	50	29	19	48	36	....	....	....	....	....
2002-03	Colorado College	WCHA	36	27	11	38	30	....	....	....	....	....

WCHA All-Rookie Team (2003)

STEVENSON, Grant (STEE-vehn-suhn, GRANT) S.J.

Center. Shoots right. 5'11", 170 lbs. Born, Spruce Grove, Alta., October 15, 1981.

			Regular Season					Playoffs				
Season	Club	League	GP	G	A	TP	PIM	GP	G	A	TP	PIM
2000-01	Grand Prairie	AJHL	53	24	49	73	62	15	7	2	9	38
2001-02	Minnesota State	WCHA	38	8	8	16	36	....	....	....	....	....
2002-03	Minnesota State	WCHA	38	27	36	63	38	....	....	....	....	....

WCHA First All-Star Team (2003) • NCAA West Second All-American Team (2003)

Signed as a free agent by **San Jose**, April 18, 2003.

STEWART, Anthony (STEW-ahrt, AN-toh-nee) FLA.

Center. Shoots right. 6'1", 225 lbs. Born, Lasalle, Que., January 5, 1985.
(Florida's 2nd choice, 25th overall, in 2003 Entry Draft).

			Regular Season					Playoffs				
Season	Club	League	GP	G	A	TP	PIM	GP	G	A	TP	PIM
2000-01	North York	MTHL	34	30	70	100	....	....	....	....	....	....
2001-02	Kingston	OHL	65	19	24	43	12	1	0	0	0	0
2002-03	Kingston	OHL	68	32	38	70	47	....	....	....	....	....

STEWART, Danny (STEW-ahrt, DA-nee) MTL.

Left wing. Shoots left. 6', 173 lbs. Born, Charlottetown, PEI, April 23, 1985.
(Montreal's 6th choice, 123rd overall, in 2003 Entry Draft).

			Regular Season					Playoffs				
Season	Club	League	GP	G	A	TP	PIM	GP	G	A	TP	PIM
2001-02	Rimouski Oceanic	QMJHL	63	9	6	15	71	4	0	0	0	0
2002-03	Rimouski Oceanic	QMJHL	65	19	21	40	144	....	....	....	....	....

STEWART, Karl (STEW-ahrt, KARL) ATL.

Center. Shoots left. 5'10", 175 lbs. Born, Aurora, Ont., June 30, 1983.

			Regular Season					Playoffs				
Season	Club	League	GP	G	A	TP	PIM	GP	G	A	TP	PIM
2000-01	Plymouth Whalers	OHL	68	9	14	23	87	19	3	4	7	14
2001-02	Plymouth Whalers	OHL	65	20	23	43	104	6	0	2	2	21
2002-03	Plymouth Whalers	OHL	68	35	50	85	120	17	7	10	17	31

Signed as a free agent by **Atlanta**, September 28, 2001.

STONE, Ryan (STOHN, RIGH-uhn) PIT.

Center. Shoots left. 6'1", 199 lbs. Born, Calgary, Alta., March 20, 1985.
(Pittsburgh's 2nd choice, 32nd overall, in 2003 Entry Draft).

			Regular Season					Playoffs				
Season	Club	League	GP	G	A	TP	PIM	GP	G	A	TP	PIM
2000-01	Cgy. North Stars	AMHL	34	37	28	55	90	....	....	....	....	....
2001-02	Brandon	WHL	65	11	27	38	128	19	0	3	3	39
2002-03	Brandon	WHL	54	14	31	45	158	12	4	2	6	20

STONKUS, Alexei (STAWN-kuhs, al-EHX-ay) NYI

Defense. Shoots left. 5'11", 175 lbs. Born, Yaroslavl, USSR, May 6, 1984.
(NY Islanders' 4th choice, 189th overall, in 2002 Entry Draft).

			Regular Season					Playoffs				
Season	Club	League	GP	G	A	TP	PIM	GP	G	A	TP	PIM
2001-02	Yaroslavl 2	Russia-3	12	3	3	6	8	....	....	....	....	....
	Elektrostal 2	Russia-3	4	1	0	1	6	....	....	....	....	....
	Elektrostal	Russia-2	31	1	3	4	26	....	....	....	....	....
2002-03	Yaroslavl	Russia	11	0	0	0	2	....	....	....	....	....

STORTINI, Zachery (stohr-TEE-nee, ZA-kuh-ree) EDM.

Right wing. Shoots right. 6'3", 216 lbs. Born, Elliot Lake, Ont., September 11, 1985.
(Edmonton's 5th choice, 94th overall, in 2003 Entry Draft).

			Regular Season					Playoffs				
Season	Club	League	GP	G	A	TP	PIM	GP	G	A	TP	PIM
2000-01	Newmarket	OPJHL	34	3	10	13	68	....	....	....	....	....
2001-02	Sudbury Wolves	OHL	65	8	6	14	187	5	1	0	1	24
2002-03	Sudbury Wolves	OHL	62	13	16	29	222	....	....	....	....	....

STRACHAN, Tyson (STRAWN, TIGH-suhn) CAR.

Defense. Shoots right. 6'3", 205 lbs. Born, Melfort, Sask., October 30, 1984.
(Carolina's 6th choice, 137th overall, in 2003 Entry Draft).

			Regular Season					Playoffs				
Season	Club	League	GP	G	A	TP	PIM	GP	G	A	TP	PIM
2001-02	Tisdale	SMHL	42	5	18	23	70	....	....	....	....	....
2002-03	Vernon Vipers	BCHL	56	6	22	28	99	....	....	....	....	....

• Signed Letter of Intent to attend **Ohio State** (CCHA), February 22, 2003.

STRBAK, Martin (SHTUHR-bak, MAHR-tehn) L.A.

Defense. Shoots left. 6'2", 200 lbs. Born, Presov, Czech., January 15, 1975.
(Los Angeles' 10th choice, 224th overall, in 1993 Entry Draft).

			Regular Season					Playoffs				
Season	Club	League	GP	G	A	TP	PIM	GP	G	A	TP	PIM
2000-01	Vsetin	Czech	49	2	6	8	46	14	2	1	3	35
2001-02	Vsetin	Czech	33	8	9	17	46	....	....	....	....	....
2002-03	HPK Hameenlinna	Finland	20	4	9	13	68	13	2	3	5	8
	Yaroslavl	Russia	27	0	6	6	28	....	....	....	....	....

STREIT, Martin (STRIGHT, MAHR-tihn) CBJ

Right wing. Shoots right. 6'2", 202 lbs. Born, Vyskov, Czech., February 2, 1977.
(Philadelphia's 7th choice, 178th overall, in 1995 Entry Draft).

			Regular Season					Playoffs				
Season	Club	League	GP	G	A	TP	PIM	GP	G	A	TP	PIM
1995-96	HC Olomouc Jr.	Czech-Jr.	19	10	6	16	....	....	....	....	....	....
	HC Olomouc	Czech	10	0	0	0	....	....	....	....	....	....
1996-97	HC Olomouc	Czech	18	1	2	3	14	....	....	....	....	....
1997-98	HC Karlovy Vary	Czech	48	5	13	18	24	....	....	....	....	....
1998-99	HC Karlovy Vary	Czech	48	9	4	13	34	....	....	....	....	....
99-2000	HC Karlovy Vary	Czech	18	0	2	2	20	....	....	....	....	....
	HC Vitkovice	Czech	31	3	6	9	28	....	....	....	....	....
2000-01	HC Karlovy Vary	Czech	14	0	1	1	12	....	....	....	....	....
	HC Femax Havirov	Czech	11	0	0	0	6	....	....	....	....	....
2001-02	Vsetin	Czech	35	3	4	7	65	....	....	....	....	....
2002-03	Vsetin	Czech	47	8	5	13	48	4	0	0	0	2

Selected by **Columbus** from **Philadelphia** in Expansion Draft, June 23, 2000.

STROSHEIN, Garret (STROH-shighn, GAIR-reht) WSH.

Right wing. Shoots right. 6'7", 245 lbs. Born, Edmonton, Alta., April 4, 1980.

Season	Club	League	Regular Season GP	G	A	TP	PIM	Playoffs GP	G	A	TP	PIM
2000-01	San Diego Gulls	WCHL	3	0	0	0	5	....	....	....	....	....
2001-02	Mobile Mysticks	ECHL	3	0	0	0	13	....	....	....	....	....
	San Diego Gulls	WCHL	24	0	0	0	90	....	....	....	....	....
	Fresno Falcons	WCHL	20	1	0	1	67	....	....	....	....	....
	Bakersfield	WCHL	....	....	....	....	....	4	0	0	0	2
2002-03	Richmond	ECHL	2	0	0	0	7	....	....	....	....	....
	Portland Pirates	WHL	28	0	1	1	86	2	0	0	0	6

Signed as a free agent by **Washington**, July 14, 2003.

STUART, Colin (STEW-ahrt, CAW-lihn) ATL.

Center. Shoots left. 6'1", 195 lbs. Born, Rochester, MN, July 8, 1982.
(Atlanta's 5th choice, 135th overall, in 2001 Entry Draft).

Season	Club	League	Regular Season GP	G	A	TP	PIM	Playoffs GP	G	A	TP	PIM
1998-99	Lourdes High	Hi-School	23	22	32	54	....	....	....	....	....	....
99-2000	Lincoln Stars	USHL	53	18	19	37	38	9	1	3	4	2
2000-01	Colorado College	WCHA	41	2	7	9	26	....	....	....	....	....
2001-02	Colorado College	WCHA	43	13	9	22	34	....	....	....	....	....
2002-03	Colorado College	WCHA	42	13	11	24	56	....	....	....	....	....

STUART, Mark (STEW-ahrt, MAHRK) BOS.

Defense. Shoots left. 6'1", 209 lbs. Born, Rochester, MN, April 27, 1984.
(Boston's 1st choice, 21st overall, in 2003 Entry Draft).

Season	Club	League	Regular Season GP	G	A	TP	PIM	Playoffs GP	G	A	TP	PIM
99-2000	Lourdes High	Hi-School	28	19	22	41	....	....	....	....	....	....
2000-01	U.S. National U-17	USDP	64	3	16	19	120	....	....	....	....	....
2001-02	U.S. National U-18	USDP	61	9	11	20	25	....	....	....	....	....
	United States	Nt-Team	15	3	4	7	51	....	....	....	....	....
2002-03	Colorado College	WCHA	38	3	17	20	81	....	....	....	....	....

WCHA All-Rookie Team (2003)

STUSSI, Rene (SHTOO-see, REH-nay) ANA.

Center. Shoots right. 5'11", 183 lbs. Born, Muri, Switz., December 13, 1978.
(Anaheim's 7th choice, 209th overall, in 1997 Entry Draft).

Season	Club	League	Regular Season GP	G	A	TP	PIM	Playoffs GP	G	A	TP	PIM
1995-96	HC Thurgau	Swiss-2	34	2	4	6	10	7	3	0	3	2
1996-97	HC Thurgau	Swiss-2	42	20	31	51	24	8	5	4	9	4
1997-98	Kloten Flyers Jr.	Swiss-Jr.	1	5	0	5	0	....	....	....	....	....
	EHC Bulach	Swiss-2	4	3	5	8	20	....	....	....	....	....
	EHC Kloten	Swiss	38	9	8	17	10	7	1	0	1	4
1998-99	EHC Kloten	Swiss	36	5	5	10	14	....	....	....	....	....
	ZSC Lions Zurich	Swiss	7	1	1	2	6	7	1	1	2	4
99-2000	EV Zug	Swiss	45	7	5	12	13	9	0	1	1	0
2000-01	EHC Chur	Swiss	36	7	7	14	26	11	1	1	2	26
2001-02	EHC Chur	Swiss	21	3	2	5	2	....	....	....	....	....
	EHC Basel	Swiss-2	16	11	11	22	2	....	....	....	....	....
	HC Ajoie	Swiss-2	....	....	....	....	....	8	1	7	8	0
2002-03	EHC Basel	Swiss-2	38	22	26	48	8	15	6	12	18	8

STUTZEL, Mike (STUHT-zuhl, MIGHK) PHX.

Left wing. Shoots left. 6'2", 205 lbs. Born, Victoria, B.C., February 28, 1979.

Season	Club	League	Regular Season GP	G	A	TP	PIM	Playoffs GP	G	A	TP	PIM
1997-98	Powell River Kings	BCHL	24	7	5	12	38	....	....	....	....	....
	Prince George	BCHL	28	13	22	35	20	9	4	1	5	18
1998-99	Prince George	BCHL	STATISTICS NOT AVAILABLE									
99-2000	Northern Michigan	CCHA	29	3	6	9	44	....	....	....	....	....
2000-01	Northern Michigan	CCHA	16	3	5	8	6	....	....	....	....	....
2001-02	Northern Michigan	CCHA	40	16	17	33	20	....	....	....	....	....
2002-03	Northern Michigan	CCHA	41	27	15	42	50	....	....	....	....	....

Signed as a free agent by **Phoenix**, April 10, 2003.

SUBBOTIN, Dmitri (soo-BOH-tihn, dih-MEE-tree) CBJ

Left wing. Shoots left. 6'1", 183 lbs. Born, Tomsk, USSR, October 20, 1977.
(NY Rangers' 3rd choice, 76th overall, in 1996 Entry Draft).

Season	Club	League	Regular Season GP	G	A	TP	PIM	Playoffs GP	G	A	TP	PIM
1993-94	Yekaterinburg	CIS	12	0	3	3	4	....	....	....	....	....
1994-95	Yekaterinburg	CIS	52	9	6	15	75	2	0	0	0	2
1995-96	CSKA Moscow	CIS	41	6	5	11	62	3	0	0	0	0
1996-97	HC CSKA	Russia-2	8	1	0	1	8	....	....	....	....	....
	HC CSKA	Russia	17	5	3	8	22	2	0	0	0	2
1997-98	HC CSKA	Russia	16	1	1	2	47	....	....	....	....	....
1998-99	Dynamo Moscow	Russia	1	0	1	1	0	....	....	....	....	....
	Lada Togliatti	Russia	31	8	3	11	47	7	0	0	0	4
99-2000	Lada Togliatti	Russia	27	10	4	14	26	7	1	1	2	4
	Lada Togliatti 2	Russia-3	2	0	1	1	0	....	....	....	....	....
2000-01	Dynamo Moscow	Russia	39	11	15	26	48	....	....	....	....	....
2001-02	Magnitogorsk	Russia	38	8	3	11	18	9	0	2	2	10
2002-03	Cherepovets	Russia	10	0	1	1	31	....	....	....	....	....
	CSKA Moscow	Russia	20	3	9	12	6	....	....	....	....	....

Selected by **Columbus** from **NY Rangers** in Expansion Draft, June 23, 2000.

SUGLOBOV, Aleksander (suh-GLOH-bahf, al-ehx-AN-duhr) N.J.

Right wing. Shoots left. 6', 175 lbs. Born, Elektrostal, USSR, January 15, 1982.
(New Jersey's 3rd choice, 56th overall, in 2000 Entry Draft).

Season	Club	League	Regular Season GP	G	A	TP	PIM	Playoffs GP	G	A	TP	PIM
1998-99	Spartak Mos. 2	Russia-4	1	0	0	0	0	....	....	....	....	....
	Spartak Moscow	Russia	1	0	0	0	0	....	....	....	....	....
99-2000	Yaroslavl 2	Russia-3	38	23	10	33		....	....	....	....	....
2000-01	SKA St. Petersburg	Russia	8	1	0	1	6	....	....	....	....	....
	Ufa	Russia	6	0	0	0	4	....	....	....	....	....
	Yaroslavl	Russia	4	0	0	0	2	11	1	2	3	6
2001-02	Yaroslavl 2	Russia-3	6	5	2	7	20	....	....	....	....	....
	Yaroslavl	Russia	25	4	2	6	26	5	1	1	2	18
2002-03	Nizhnekamsk	Russia	6	0	0	0	4	....	....	....	....	....
	Yaroslavl	Russia	17	4	2	6	12	5	1	0	1	2

SULLIVAN, Brian (suh-LIH-vuhn, BRIGH-uhn) DAL.

Defense. Shoots left. 6'3", 185 lbs. Born, Marshfield, MA, June 27, 1980.
(Dallas' 9th choice, 243rd overall, in 1999 Entry Draft).

Season	Club	League	Regular Season GP	G	A	TP	PIM	Playoffs GP	G	A	TP	PIM
1997-98	Thayer Academy	Hi-School	26	0	5	5	17	....	....	....	....	....
1998-99	Thayer Academy	Hi-School	21	0	7	7	10	....	....	....	....	....
99-2000	Northeastern	H-East	23	0	1	1	8	....	....	....	....	....
2000-01	Northeastern	H-East	34	1	2	3	37	....	....	....	....	....
2001-02	Northeastern	H-East	6	0	0	0	2	....	....	....	....	....
2002-03	Northeastern	H-East	32	1	7	8	4	....	....	....	....	....

SULLIVAN, Jeff (SUHL-lih-vahn, JEHF)

Defense. Shoots left. 6'1", 185 lbs. Born, St. John's, Nfld., September 18, 1978.
(Ottawa's 5th choice, 146th overall, in 1997 Entry Draft).

Season	Club	League	Regular Season GP	G	A	TP	PIM	Playoffs GP	G	A	TP	PIM
1994-95	St. John's Capitals	NFAHA	40	10	15	25	120	....	....	....	....	....
1995-96	East Hants	MJrHL	52	15	20	35	270	....	....	....	....	....
1996-97	Granby Predateurs	QMJHL	25	4	8	12	47	....	....	....	....	....
	Halifax	QMJHL	45	4	23	27	200	18	0	5	5	96
1997-98	Halifax	QMJHL	69	9	27	36	377	5	0	1	1	21
1998-99	Halifax	QMJHL	69	7	30	37	320	5	1	1	2	14
99-2000	Saint John Flames	AHL	9	0	3	3	16	....	....	....	....	....
	Johnstown Chiefs	ECHL	58	2	8	10	181	7	0	2	2	32
2000-01	Johnstown Chiefs	ECHL	69	2	9	11	302	4	0	0	0	9
	Kentucky	AHL	1	0	0	0	4	....	....	....	....	....
	Saint John Flames	AHL	2	0	0	0	0	....	....	....	....	....
2001-02	Saint John Flames	AHL	41	1	1	2	96	....	....	....	....	....
	Johnstown Chiefs	ECHL	36	3	5	8	155	5	0	1	1	20
2002-03	Saint John Flames	AHL	6	0	0	0	8	....	....	....	....	....
	Johnstown Chiefs	ECHL	58	5	11	16	196	....	....	....	....	....

QMJHL All-Rookie Team (1997)

SULZER, Alexander (ZUHLT-suhr, ahl-ehx-AN-duhr) NSH.

Defense. Shoots left. 6'1", 204 lbs. Born, Kaufbeuren, West Germany, May 30, 1984.
(Nashville's 7th choice, 92nd overall, in 2003 Entry Draft).

Season	Club	League	Regular Season GP	G	A	TP	PIM	Playoffs GP	G	A	TP	PIM
2000-01	ESV Kaufbeuren	German-3	38	3	6	9	20	....	....	....	....	....
	Kaufbeuren Jr.	German-Jr.	1	0	2	2	2	....	....	....	....	....
2001-02	ESV Kaufbeuren	German-3	19	1	9	10	14	....	....	....	....	....
	Kaufbeuren Jr.	German-Jr.	1	0	0	0	4	....	....	....	....	....
2002-03	ESV Kaufbeuren	German-2	26	5	3	8	38	1	0	1	1	4
	Hamburg Freezers	Germany	18	0	1	1	18	5	0	0	0	12

SUTER, Ryan (SOO-tuhr, RIGH-uhn) NSH.

Defense. Shoots left. 6'1", 183 lbs. Born, Madison, WI, January 21, 1985.
(Nashville's 1st choice, 7th overall, in 2003 Entry Draft).

Season	Club	League	Regular Season GP	G	A	TP	PIM	Playoffs GP	G	A	TP	PIM
2000-01	Culver Academy	Hi-School	26	13	32	45	....	....	....	....	....	....
2001-02	U.S. National U-17	USDP	37	4	23	27		....	....	....	....	....
	U.S. National U-18	USDP	34	2	10	12	75	....	....	....	....	....
	U.S. National Team	Nt-Team	19	3	13	16	24	....	....	....	....	....
2002-03	U.S. National U-18	USDP	51	9	22	31	136	....	....	....	....	....

• Signed Letter of Intent to attend **University of Wisconsin** (WCHA), May 30, 2002.

SUTTER, Shaun (SUH-tuhr, SHAWN)

Right wing. Shoots right. 6'1", 185 lbs. Born, Red Deer, Alta., June 2, 1980.
(Calgary's 4th choice, 102nd overall, in 1998 Entry Draft).

Season	Club	League	Regular Season GP	G	A	TP	PIM	Playoffs GP	G	A	TP	PIM
1995-96	Red Deer	AMHL	23	4	6	10	62	....	....	....	....	....
1996-97	Red Deer	AMHL	33	15	24	39	143	....	....	....	....	....
	Lethbridge	WHL	1	0	0	0	0	....	....	....	....	....
1997-98	Lethbridge	WHL	69	11	9	20	146	4	0	0	0	4
1998-99	Lethbridge	WHL	35	8	4	12	43	....	....	....	....	....
	Medicine Hat	WHL	23	9	5	14	38	....	....	....	....	....
99-2000	Medicine Hat	WHL	29	1	7	8	43	....	....	....	....	....
	Calgary Hitmen	WHL	6	0	1	1	8	....	....	....	....	....
2000-01	Calgary Hitmen	WHL	63	29	35	64	102	12	1	2	3	12
	Saint John Flames	AHL	1	0	0	0	0	....	....	....	....	....
2001-02	Saint John Flames	AHL	11	0	2	2	10	....	....	....	....	....
	Johnstown Chiefs	ECHL	34	13	7	20	34	8	0	1	1	4
2002-03	Saint John Flames	AHL	25	7	4	11	14	....	....	....	....	....
	Johnstown Chiefs	ECHL	9	7	3	10	4	....	....	....	....	....

SVAGROVSKY, David (shva-GRAWF-skee, DAY-vihd) COL.

Right wing. Shoots right. 6'3", 205 lbs. Born, Prague, Czech., December 21, 1984.
(Colorado's 2nd choice, 131st overall, in 2003 Entry Draft).

Season	Club	League	Regular Season GP	G	A	TP	PIM	Playoffs GP	G	A	TP	PIM
99-2000	HC Slavia Praha Jr.	Czech-Jr.	31	1	3	4	12	....	....	....	....	....
2000-01	HC Slavia Praha Jr.	Czech-Jr.	48	20	29	49	82	7	5	1	6	10
2001-02	HC Slavia Praha Jr.	Czech-Jr.	44	7	6	13	38	....	....	....	....	....
2002-03	Seattle	WHL	68	17	25	42	47	15	4	6	10	12

SVATOS, Marek (SVA-tohsh, MAIR-ehk) COL.

Right wing. Shoots right. 5'9", 170 lbs. Born, Kosice, Czech., July 17, 1982.
(Colorado's 10th choice, 227th overall, in 2001 Entry Draft).

Season	Club	League	Regular Season GP	G	A	TP	PIM	Playoffs GP	G	A	TP	PIM
99-2000	HC Kosice Jr.	Slovak-Jr.	39	43	30	73	28	....	....	....	....	....
	HC Kosice	Slovakia	19	2	2	4	0	....	....	....	....	....
2000-01	Kootenay Ice	WHL	39	23	18	41	47	11	7	2	9	26
2001-02	Kootenay Ice	WHL	53	38	39	77	58	21	12	6	18	40
2002-03	Hershey Bears	AHL	30	9	4	13	10	....	....	....	....	....

WHL West Second All-Star Team (2002)

• Missed majority of 2002-03 season recovering from shoulder injury that required surgery, January 28, 2003.

SVENSK, Mikael (SVEHNSK, mih-KIGH-ehl) EDM.

Defense. Shoots right. 6'2", 191 lbs. Born, Gällstad, Sweden, February 28, 1983.
(Edmonton's 7th choice, 185th overall, in 2001 Entry Draft).

			Regular Season					Playoffs				
Season	Club	League	GP	G	A	TP	PIM	GP	G	A	TP	PIM
99-2000	V. Frolunda-18	Swede-Jr.	18	2	6	8	6	2	0	0	0	2
	V. Frolunda Jr.	Swede-Jr.	10	1	1	2	12	2	0	0	0	0
2000-01	V. Frolunda-18	Swede-Jr.	6	0	1	1	4	3	0	1	1	2
	V. Frolunda Jr.	Swede-Jr.	15	1	0	1	4	....	....	....	....	....
2001-02	V. Frolunda Jr.	Swede-Jr.	34	4	1	5	16	5	1	0	1	2
2002-03	Vastra Frolunda	Sweden	17	0	0	0	0	3	0	0	0	0
	V. Frolunda Jr.	Swede-Jr.	25	1	3	4	10	6	1	0	1	4

SVENSSON, Jimmie (SVEHN-sohn, JIH-mee) DET.

Center. Shoots left. 6'1", 183 lbs. Born, Vasteras, Sweden, February 25, 1982.
(Detroit's 9th choice, 228th overall, in 2000 Entry Draft).

			Regular Season					Playoffs				
Season	Club	League	GP	G	A	TP	PIM	GP	G	A	TP	PIM
99-2000	Vasteras IK-18	Swede-Jr.	5	1	3	4	20	....	....	....	....	....
	Vasteras IK Jr.	Swede-Jr.	29	10	2	12	121	....	....	....	....	....
2000-01	Malmo IF Jr.	Swede-Jr.	23	3	1	4	74	....	....	....	....	....
2001-02	Malmo IF Jr.	Swede-Jr.	38	18	10	28	105	5	0	1	1	10
2002-03	IF Troja/Ljungby	Swede-2	52	13	8	21	139	....	....	....	....	....

SWANSON, Jeremy (SWAWN-suhn, JAIR-eh-mee) FLA.

Defense. Shoots left. 6', 199 lbs. Born, Nipigon, Ont., June 21, 1984.
(Florida's choice, 169th overall, in 2002 Entry Draft).

			Regular Season					Playoffs				
Season	Club	League	GP	G	A	TP	PIM	GP	G	A	TP	PIM
99-2000	Thunder Bay Kings	TBMHL	48	8	16	24	19	....	....	....	....	....
2000-01	Sault Ste. Marie	OHL	54	1	6	7	60	....	....	....	....	....
2001-02	Barrie Colts	OHL	67	8	16	24	78	20	1	4	5	12
2002-03	Barrie Colts	OHL	68	7	34	41	129	....	....	....	....	....

TABACEK, Jan (tah-BA-chehk, YAN) ANA.

Defense. Shoots left. 5'11", 169 lbs. Born, Martin, Czech., April 7, 1980.
(Anaheim's 8th choice, 170th overall, in 2001 Entry Draft).

			Regular Season					Playoffs				
Season	Club	League	GP	G	A	TP	PIM	GP	G	A	TP	PIM
1997-98	MHC Martin Jr.	Slovak-Jr.	25	1	4	5	70	....	....	....	....	....
1998-99	MHC Martin	Slovakia	2	1	0	1	0	....	....	....	....	....
99-2000	MHC Martin	Slovak-2	35	1	7	8	22	....	....	....	....	....
2000-01	MHC Martin	Slovakia	44	8	5	13	62	3	1	2	3	0
2001-02	Slov. Bratislava	Slovakia	45	3	7	10	30	19	1	0	1	16
2002-03	Cincinnati	AHL	12	0	0	0	8	....	....	....	....	....
	Dayton Bombers	ECHL	2	0	1	1	16	....	....	....	....	....

TALBOT, Maxime (TAL-buht, MAX-eem) PIT.

Center. Shoots left. 5'11", 176 lbs. Born, Lemoyne, Que., February 11, 1984.
(Pittsburgh's 9th choice, 234th overall, in 2002 Entry Draft).

			Regular Season					Playoffs				
Season	Club	League	GP	G	A	TP	PIM	GP	G	A	TP	PIM
99-2000	Antoine-Girouard	QAAA	42	19	21	40	32	7	3	6	9	0
2000-01	Rouyn-Noranda	QMJHL	40	9	15	24	78	....	....	....	....	....
	Hull Olympiques	QMJHL	24	6	7	13	60	5	1	0	1	2
2001-02	Hull Olympiques	QMJHL	65	24	36	60	174	12	4	6	10	51
2002-03	Hull Olympiques	QMJHL	69	46	58	104	130	20	14	*30	*44	33

QMJHL Second All-Star Team (2003)

TALLACKSON, Barry (TAL-ak-suhn, BAIR-ee) N.J.

Right wing. Shoots right. 6'4", 196 lbs. Born, Grafton, ND, April 14, 1983.
(New Jersey's 2nd choice, 53rd overall, in 2002 Entry Draft).

			Regular Season					Playoffs				
Season	Club	League	GP	G	A	TP	PIM	GP	G	A	TP	PIM
99-2000	U.S. National U-17	USDP	53	14	6	20	90	....	....	....	....	....
2000-01	U.S. National U-18	USDP	63	23	24	47	77	....	....	....	....	....
2001-02	U. of Minnesota	WCHA	44	13	10	23	44	....	....	....	....	....
2002-03	U. of Minnesota	WCHA	32	9	14	23	18	....	....	....	....	....

TAMBELLINI, Jeff (tam-buh-LEE-nee, JEHF) L.A.

Left wing. Shoots left. 5'11", 186 lbs. Born, Calgary, Alta., April 13, 1984.
(Los Angeles' 3rd choice, 27th overall, in 2003 Entry Draft).

			Regular Season					Playoffs				
Season	Club	League	GP	G	A	TP	PIM	GP	G	A	TP	PIM
99-2000	Poco Buckeroos	PIJHL	41	30	34	64	....	....	....	....	....	....
2000-01	Chilliwack Chiefs	BCHL	54	21	30	51	13	....	....	....	....	....
2001-02	Chilliwack Chiefs	BCHL	34	46	71	117	23	29	27	27	54	....
2002-03	U. of Michigan	CCHA	43	26	19	45	24	....	....	....	....	....

PIJHL First All-Star Team (2000) • PIJHL Rookie of the Year (2000) • BCHL First All-Star Team (2002) • BCHL MVP (2002) • Canadian Junior "A" Player of the Year (2002) • CCHA All-Rookie Team (2003) • CCHA Second All-Star Team (2003) • CCHA Rookie of the Year (2003)

TARATUKHIN, Andrei (tahr-a-TOO-khin, AN-dray) CGY.

Center. Shoots left. 6', 198 lbs. Born, Omsk, USSR, February 22, 1983.
(Calgary's 2nd choice, 41st overall, in 2001 Entry Draft).

			Regular Season					Playoffs				
Season	Club	League	GP	G	A	TP	PIM	GP	G	A	TP	PIM
1998-99	Omsk 2	Russia-4	1	0	0	0	0	....	....	....	....	....
99-2000	Omsk 2	Russia-3	27	10	6	16	16	....	....	....	....	....
	Avangard Omsk	Russia	....	....	....	....	....	1	1	0	1	0
2000-01	Omsk 2	Russia-3	41	19	28	47	69	....	....	....	....	....
2001-02	Mostovik Kurgan	Russia-2	44	13	22	35	30	....	....	....	....	....
	Yaroslavl 2	Russia-3	5	5	2	7	12	....	....	....	....	....
2002-03	Avangard Omsk	Russia	21	0	1	1	4	7	1	0	1	18
	Omsk 2	Russia-3	15	4	13	17	20	....	....	....	....	....

TARDIF, Jamie (tahr-DIHF, JAY-mee) CGY.

Right wing. Shoots right. 6', 207 lbs. Born, Welland, Ont., January 23, 1985.
(Calgary's 4th choice, 112th overall, in 2003 Entry Draft).

			Regular Season					Playoffs				
Season	Club	League	GP	G	A	TP	PIM	GP	G	A	TP	PIM
2001-02	Peterborough	OHL	64	22	22	44	30	6	0	1	1	2
2002-03	Peterborough	OHL	68	31	29	60	32	7	3	4	7	0

TARKIR, Zach (TAHR-kihr, ZAK) N.J.

Defense. Shoots right. 6', 180 lbs. Born, Fresno, CA, June 28, 1984.
(New Jersey's 4th choice, 167th overall, in 2003 Entry Draft).

			Regular Season					Playoffs				
Season	Club	League	GP	G	A	TP	PIM	GP	G	A	TP	PIM
2000-01	Spokane Braves	KIJHL		STATISTICS NOT AVAILABLE								
2001-02	Great Falls	AWHL	24	3	5	8	....	8	0	3	3	....
2002-03	Chilliwack Chiefs	BCHL	53	5	28	33	86	....	....	....	....	....

• Signed Letter of Intent to attend **Northern Michigan** (CCHA), April 24, 2003.

TARVAINEN, Jussi (tahr-VIGH-nehn, YU-see) EDM.

Right wing. Shoots right. 6'3", 215 lbs. Born, Lahti, Finland, May 31, 1976.
(Edmonton's 7th choice, 95th overall, in 1994 Entry Draft).

			Regular Season					Playoffs				
Season	Club	League	GP	G	A	TP	PIM	GP	G	A	TP	PIM
1991-92	KalPa Kuopio-C	Finn-Jr.	3	0	3	3	4	....	....	....	....	....
1992-93	KalPa Kuopio-B	Finn-Jr.	18	13	9	22	38	....	....	....	....	....
	KalPa Kuopio Jr.	Finn-Jr.	17	3	6	9	35	....	....	....	....	....
1993-94	KalPa Kuopio Jr.	Finn-Jr.	16	9	14	23	12	....	....	....	....	....
	Junkkarit	Finland-2	1	0	0	0	0	....	....	....	....	....
	KalPa Kuopio	Finland	42	3	4	7	20	....	....	....	....	....
1994-95	KalPa Kuopio Jr.	Finn-Jr.	3	4	0	4	2	....	....	....	....	....
	KalPa Kuopio	Finland	45	10	7	17	34	3	0	0	0	2
1995-96	KalPa Kuopio Jr.	Finn-Jr.	3	2	3	5	10	7	3	4	7	12
	KalPa Kuopio	Finland	47	8	11	19	50	....	....	....	....	....
1996-97	KalPa Kuopio	Finland	49	14	26	40	62	....	....	....	....	....
	KalPa Kuopio Jr.	Finn-Jr.	....	....	....	....	....	1	0	0	0	2
	KalPa Kuopio	Finland-2	....	....	....	....	....	6	4	3	7	4
1997-98	JYP Jyvaskyla	Finland	43	12	26	38	59	....	....	....	....	....
1998-99	JYP Jyvaskyla	Finland	54	17	24	41	84	3	0	0	0	8
99-2000	Tappara Tampere	Finland	52	20	27	47	91	4	1	0	1	2
2000-01	Tappara Tampere	Finland	56	23	32	55	36	10	*8	2	10	2
2001-02	Tappara Tampere	Finland	56	24	26	50	42	10	4	3	7	0
2002-03	Tappara Tampere	Finland	56	14	21	35	24	15	*7	2	9	4

TATARINOV, Alexander (ta-TAHR-ee-nahf, al-ehx-AN-duhr) PHX.

Right wing. Shoots left. 5'11", 176 lbs. Born, Sverdlovsk, USSR, April 14, 1982.
(Phoenix's 2nd choice, 53rd overall, in 2000 Entry Draft).

			Regular Season					Playoffs				
Season	Club	League	GP	G	A	TP	PIM	GP	G	A	TP	PIM
1998-99	Yaroslavl 2	Russia-3	32	11	10	21	89	....	....	....	....	....
	Spartak Moscow	Russia	3	0	0	0	0	....	....	....	....	....
99-2000	Yaroslavl 2	Russia-3	35	12	12	24	36	....	....	....	....	....
2000-01	Kristall Saratov	Russia-2	24	3	3	6	8	....	....	....	....	....
	Yaroslavl	Russia	2	0	1	1	0	1	0	0	0	0
2001-02	Yaroslavl	Russia	21	4	3	7	8	....	....	....	....	....
	Amur Khabarovsk	Russia	11	0	0	0	0	....	....	....	....	....
	Yaroslavl 2	Russia-3	5	5	2	7	12	....	....	....	....	....
2002-03	Perm	Russia	31	6	5	11	16	....	....	....	....	....

TATICEK, Petr (TA-tih-chehk, PEE-tuhr) FLA.

Center. Shoots left. 6'3", 195 lbs. Born, Rakovnik, Czech., September 22, 1983.
(Florida's 2nd choice, 9th overall, in 2002 Entry Draft).

			Regular Season					Playoffs				
Season	Club	League	GP	G	A	TP	PIM	GP	G	A	TP	PIM
99-2000	Kladno Jr.	Czech-Jr.	48	11	16	27	26	....	....	....	....	....
	HC Velvana Kladno	Czech	4	0	0	0	4	....	....	....	....	....
2000-01	Kladno Jr.	Czech-Jr.	30	7	12	19	54	....	....	....	....	....
	Kladno	Czech	3	0	0	0	0	....	....	....	....	....
2001-02	Sault Ste. Marie	OHL	60	21	42	63	32	6	3	3	6	4
2002-03	Sault Ste. Marie	OHL	54	12	45	57	44	4	1	0	1	0

TAYLOR, Adam (TAY-lohr, A-duhm) CAR.

Center. Shoots right. 6', 190 lbs. Born, Courtenay, B.C., June 24, 1984.
(Carolina's 4th choice, 224th overall, in 2002 Entry Draft).

			Regular Season					Playoffs				
Season	Club	League	GP	G	A	TP	PIM	GP	G	A	TP	PIM
2000-01	Kootenay Ice	WHL	36	1	2	3	17	1	0	0	0	0
2001-02	Kootenay Ice	WHL	72	11	23	34	119	19	3	4	7	15
2002-03	Kootenay Ice	WHL	72	14	28	42	69	11	3	2	5	14

TAYLOR, Jake (TAY-lohr, JAIK) NYR

Defense. Shoots right. 6'4", 203 lbs. Born, Rochester, MN, August 1, 1983.
(NY Rangers' 5th choice, 177th overall, in 2002 Entry Draft).

			Regular Season					Playoffs				
Season	Club	League	GP	G	A	TP	PIM	GP	G	A	TP	PIM
2000-01	Rochester High	Hi-School	29	9	15	24	34	....	....	....	....	....
	Green Bay	USHL	5	0	0	0	8	....	....	....	....	....
2001-02	Green Bay	USHL	56	1	2	3	147	7	0	0	0	11
2002-03	Green Bay	USHL	60	8	8	16	160	....	....	....	....	....

• Signed Letter of Intent to attend **U. of Minnesota** (WCHA).

TERESCHENKO, Alexei (teh-REH-shehn-koh, al-EHX-ay) DAL.

Center. Shoots left. 5'11", 176 lbs. Born, Mozhaisk, USSR, December 16, 1980.
(Dallas' 4th choice, 91st overall, in 2000 Entry Draft).

			Regular Season					Playoffs				
Season	Club	League	GP	G	A	TP	PIM	GP	G	A	TP	PIM
1996-97	DynamoMoscow2	Russia-3	9	0	0	0	2	....	....	....	....	....
1997-98	Dynamo Moscow	Russia	26	6	7	13	30	....	....	....	....	....
1998-99	DynamoMoscow2	Russia-3	28	4	17	21	20	....	....	....	....	....
	THC Tver	Russia-2	12	3	4	7	4	....	....	....	....	....
	Dynamo Moscow	Russia	1	0	1	1	0	2	0	0	0	0
99-2000	Dynamo Moscow	Russia	27	1	1	2	10	17	1	1	2	8
2000-01	Dynamo Moscow	Russia	39	3	2	5	18	....	....	....	....	....
2001-02	Yaroslavl 2	Russia-3	1	0	0	0	0	....	....	....	....	....
	Dynamo Moscow	Russia	40	3	6	9	20	3	0	0	0	0
2002-03	Dynamo Moscow	Russia	40	7	9	16	14	5	1	0	1	2

TERNAVSKY, Artem (tuhr-NAV-skee, ahr-TEHM) WSH.

Defense. Shoots left. 6'3", 213 lbs. Born, Magnitogorsk, USSR, June 2, 1983.
(Washington's 4th choice, 160th overall, in 2001 Entry Draft).

			Regular Season					Playoffs				
Season	Club	League	GP	G	A	TP	PIM	GP	G	A	TP	PIM
99-2000	CSKA Moscow Jr.	Russia-Jr.	2	0	1	1	0	....	....	....	....	....
	HC CSKA 2	Russia-3	25	0	4	4	42	....	....	....	....	....
2000-01	Sherbrooke	QMJHL	65	3	15	18	143	....	....	....	....	....
2001-02	Mostovik Kurgan	Russia-2	25	0	0	0	46	....	....	....	....	....
2002-03	Sibir Novosibirsk	Russia	42	1	1	2	20	....	....	....	....	....

TESSIER, Michael (teh-SEE-ay, MIGH-kuhl) BUF.

Left wing. Shoots left. 6'2", 180 lbs. Born, Granby, Que., August 14, 1984.
(Buffalo's 3rd choice, 76th overall, in 2002 Entry Draft).

			Regular Season					Playoffs				
Season	Club	League	GP	G	A	TP	PIM	GP	G	A	TP	PIM
99-2000	Antoine-Girouard	QAAA	38	18	22	40	22	7	5	3	8	6
2000-01	Acadie-Bathurst	QMJHL	55	4	8	12	110	13	1	0	1	2
2001-02	Acadie-Bathurst	QMJHL	66	22	48	70	83	14	5	7	12	12
2002-03	Acadie-Bathurst	QMJHL	62	20	30	50	114	11	6	11	17	10

THINEL, Marc-Andre (tih-nehl, MAHRK-AWN-dray) MTL.

Right wing. Shoots left. 6', 178 lbs. Born, St-Jerome, Que., March 24, 1981.
(Montreal's 6th choice, 145th overall, in 1999 Entry Draft).

			Regular Season					Playoffs				
Season	Club	League	GP	G	A	TP	PIM	GP	G	A	TP	PIM
1996-97	Laval Laurentide	QAAA	40	12	10	22	....	13	0	5	5	....
1997-98	Victoriaville Tigres	QMJHL	58	7	10	17	20	6	0	3	3	4
1998-99	Victoriaville Tigres	QMJHL	66	45	58	103	16	6	5	3	8	4
99-2000	Victoriaville Tigres	QMJHL	71	59	73	132	55	6	5	6	11	18
2000-01	Victoriaville Tigres	QMJHL	70	62	88	150	101	13	12	13	25	18
2001-02	Quebec Citadelles	AHL	73	6	4	10	8	2	0	0	0	0
2002-03	Utah Grizzlies	AHL	44	5	15	20	10	2	0	0	0	0
	Lexington	ECHL	27	14	14	28	6	....	....	....	....	....

QMJHL First All-Star Team (2000) • QMJHL Second All-Star Team (2001)

THORBURN, Chris (THOHR-buhrn, KRIHS) BUF.

Center. Shoots right. 6'3", 207 lbs. Born, Sault Ste. Marie, Ont., June 3, 1983.
(Buffalo's 3rd choice, 50th overall, in 2001 Entry Draft).

			Regular Season					Playoffs				
Season	Club	League	GP	G	A	TP	PIM	GP	G	A	TP	PIM
1998-99	Elliot Lake Vikings	NOJHA	40	21	12	33	28	....	....	....	....	....
99-2000	North Bay	OHL	56	12	8	20	33	6	0	2	2	0
2000-01	North Bay	OHL	66	22	32	54	64	4	0	1	1	9
2001-02	North Bay	OHL	67	15	43	58	112	5	1	2	3	8
2002-03	Saginaw Spirit	OHL	37	19	19	38	68	....	....	....	....	....
	Plymouth Whalers	OHL	27	11	22	33	56	18	11	9	20	10

TIMONEN, Jussi (TEEM-oh-nehn, YU-see) PHI.

Defense. Shoots left. 6', 200 lbs. Born, Kuopio, Finland, June 29, 1983.
(Philadelphia's 3rd choice, 146th overall, in 2001 Entry Draft).

			Regular Season					Playoffs				
Season	Club	League	GP	G	A	TP	PIM	GP	G	A	TP	PIM
99-2000	KalPa Kuopio Jr.	Finn-Jr.	33	4	2	6	16	4	0	0	0	4
2000-01	Kalpa Kuopio-B	Finn-Jr.	38	6	7	13	22	....	....	....	....	....
	KalPa Kuopio Jr.	Finn-Jr.	1	0	1	1	0	....	....	....	....	....
2001-02	KalPa Kuopio Jr.	Finn-Jr.	10	1	1	2	10	....	....	....	....	....
	Kalpa Kuopio	Finland-2	41	3	8	11	10	8	0	2	2	0
2002-03	TPS Turku	Finland	39	1	0	1	10	7	0	2	2	4
	TuTu Turku	Finland-2	3	0	0	0	0	....	....	....	....	....

TJARNQVIST, Mathias (TUH-yahrn-kvihst, MAT-ee-uhs) DAL.

Right wing. Shoots left. 6'1", 183 lbs. Born, Umea, Sweden, April 15, 1979.
(Dallas' 3rd choice, 96th overall, in 1999 Entry Draft).

			Regular Season					Playoffs				
Season	Club	League	GP	G	A	TP	PIM	GP	G	A	TP	PIM
1995-96	Rogle Jr.	Swede-Jr.	4	2	0	2	0	....	....	....	....	....
1996-97	Rogle Jr.	Swede-Jr.	18	5	8	13	....	....	....	....	....	....
	Rogle	Swede-2	15	1	4	5	4	....	....	....	....	....
1997-98	Rogle	Swede-2	31	12	11	23	30	....	....	....	....	....
1998-99	Rogle	Swede-2	34	18	16	34	44	5	4	1	5	4
99-2000	Djurgarden	Sweden	50	12	12	24	20	13	3	2	5	16
2000-01	Djurgarden	Sweden	47	11	8	19	53	16	1	2	3	6
2001-02	Djurgarden	Sweden	6	0	1	1	4	2	0	0	0	2
2002-03	Djurgarden	Sweden	38	11	13	24	30	9	4	1	5	12

TJUTIN, Fedor (TYOO-tihn, feh-DUHR) NYR

Defense. Shoots left. 6'2", 196 lbs. Born, Izhevsk, USSR, July 19, 1983.
(NY Rangers' 2nd choice, 40th overall, in 2001 Entry Draft).

			Regular Season					Playoffs				
Season	Club	League	GP	G	A	TP	PIM	GP	G	A	TP	PIM
1998-99	Magnitogorsk 2	Russia-4	7	0	1	1	2	....	....	....	....	....
99-2000	Izhstal Izhevsk 2	Russia-3	38	11	8	19	68	....	....	....	....	....
	Izhstal Izhevsk	Russia-2	10	0	1	1	12	....	....	....	....	....
2000-01	SKA St. Petersburg	Russia	34	2	4	6	20	....	....	....	....	....
2001-02	Guelph Storm	OHL	53	19	40	59	54	9	2	8	10	8
2002-03	SKA St. Petersburg	Russia	10	1	1	2	16	....	....	....	....	....
	Ak Bars Kazan	Russia	10	0	0	0	8	5	0	0	0	4

TKACHENKO, Ivan (t'kuh-CHEHN-koh, ee-VAHN) CBJ

Left wing. Shoots left. 5'10", 183 lbs. Born, Yaroslavl, USSR, November 9, 1979.
(Columbus' 5th choice, 98th overall, in 2002 Entry Draft).

			Regular Season					Playoffs				
Season	Club	League	GP	G	A	TP	PIM	GP	G	A	TP	PIM
1997-98	Yaroslavl 2	Russia-2	STATISTICS NOT AVAILABLE									
	Torpedo Yaroslavl	Russia	....	....	....	....	....	1	0	0	0	0
1998-99	Yaroslavl 2	Russia-3	28	15	13	28	26	....	....	....	....	....
99-2000	Yaroslavl 2	Russia-3	1	1	0	1	0	....	....	....	....	....
	Motor Zavolzhje	Russia-2	43	15	14	29	22	....	....	....	....	....
	Nizhnekamsk 2	Russia-3	8	6	3	9	24	....	....	....	....	....
	Nizhnekamsk	Russia	5	1	0	1	0	4	0	1	1	0
2000-01	Nizhnekamsk	Russia	28	2	2	4	14	4	0	1	1	0
2001-02	Yaroslavl 2	Russia-3	1	0	1	1	2	....	....	....	....	....
	Yaroslavl	Russia	44	13	20	33	57	9	5	2	7	4
2002-03	Yaroslavl	Russia	44	11	6	17	57	10	2	3	5	6

TOFFEY, John (TAW-fee, JAWN) T.B.

Center. Shoots left. 6'3", 200 lbs. Born, Barnstable, MA, November 26, 1982.
(Tampa Bay's 13th choice, 287th overall, in 2002 Entry Draft).

			Regular Season					Playoffs				
Season	Club	League	GP	G	A	TP	PIM	GP	G	A	TP	PIM
2000-01	St. Sebastian's	Hi-School	22	22	24	46	....	....	....	....	....	....
2001-02	Ohio State	CCHA	24	2	3	5	4	....	....	....	....	....
2002-03	Walpole Stars	EJHL	19	7	8	15	10	....	....	....	....	....

• Compiled three-year totals of 65-29-27-56 for **St. Sebastian's** (Hi-School) between 1997-2000.

TOLKUNOV, Dmitri (tohl-ku-NAWF, di-MEE-tree) FLA.

Defense. Shoots right. 6'2", 200 lbs. Born, Kiev, USSR, May 5, 1979.

			Regular Season					Playoffs				
Season	Club	League	GP	G	A	TP	PIM	GP	G	A	TP	PIM
1996-97	Hull Olympiques	QMJHL	34	3	8	11	99	....	....	....	....	....
	Beauport Harfangs	QMJHL	27	3	7	10	18	4	0	1	1	4
1997-98	Quebec Remparts	QMJHL	66	10	25	35	81	14	3	9	12	22
1998-99	Quebec Rafales	QMJHL	69	11	57	68	110	13	2	7	9	22
99-2000	Cleveland	IHL	65	3	12	15	54	8	0	0	0	2
2000-01	Norfolk Admirals	AHL	78	5	18	23	93	9	0	1	1	4
2001-02	Norfolk Admirals	AHL	51	1	18	19	20	4	0	0	0	2
2002-03	Norfolk Admirals	AHL	47	1	17	18	39	....	....	....	....	....

QMJHL Second All-Star Team (1999)

Signed as a free agent by **Chicago**, October 8, 1998. Traded to **Florida** by **Chicago** for NY Islanders' 9th round choice (previously acquired by Florida – later traded to San Jose – San Jose selected Carter Lee) in 2003 Entry Draft, June 21, 2003,

TOLLEFSEN, Ole-Kristian (TOHL-uhf-suhn, OH-lay-KRIHS-tyahn) CBJ

Defense. Shoots left. 6'2", 200 lbs. Born, Oslo, Norway, March 29, 1984.
(Columbus' 3rd choice, 65th overall, in 2002 Entry Draft).

			Regular Season					Playoffs				
Season	Club	League	GP	G	A	TP	PIM	GP	G	A	TP	PIM
2000-01	Lillehammer IK	Norway	4	0	0	0	2	....	....	....	....	....
2001-02	Lillehammer IK	Norway	37	1	5	6	63	6	1	1	2	10
	Lillehammer IK	Norge-Jr.	....	....	....	....	....	1	0	2	2	4
2002-03	Brandon	WHL	43	6	14	20	73	17	0	2	2	38

TOLSA, Jari (TOHL-suh, YA-ree) DET.

Center. Shoots left. 6', 172 lbs. Born, Goteborg, Sweden, April 20, 1981.
(Detroit's 1st choice, 120th overall, in 1999 Entry Draft).

			Regular Season					Playoffs				
Season	Club	League	GP	G	A	TP	PIM	GP	G	A	TP	PIM
1997-98	V. Frolunda Jr.	Swede-Jr.	26	18	25	43	30	....	....	....	....	....
1998-99	V. Frolunda Jr.	Swede-Jr.	35	16	21	37	51	4	1	3	4	2
99-2000	V. Frolunda Jr.	Swede-Jr.	33	12	47	59	43	6	3	8	11	4
	Vastra Frolunda	Sweden	10	0	0	0	0	....	....	....	....	....
2000-01	V. Frolunda Jr.	Swede-Jr.	11	4	6	10	8	2	2	4	6	4
	Molndals HK	Swede-2	1	0	2	2	0	....	....	....	....	....
	Vastra Frolunda	Sweden	42	2	5	7	18	5	0	0	0	0
2001-02	Vastra Frolunda	Sweden	48	8	16	24	18	10	0	0	0	4
2002-03	Vastra Frolunda	Sweden	43	9	14	23	24	16	4	1	5	8

TOMICA, Marek (TAW-miht-suh, MAIR-ehk) DAL.

Left wing. Shoots left. 6', 178 lbs. Born, Prague, Czech., January 1, 1981.
(Dallas' 10th choice, 285th overall, in 2001 Entry Draft).

			Regular Season					Playoffs				
Season	Club	League	GP	G	A	TP	PIM	GP	G	A	TP	PIM
99-2000	HC Slavia Praha Jr.	Czech-Jr.	41	13	8	21	16	7	2	3	5	0
	HC Slavia Praha	Czech	13	0	0	0	2	....	....	....	....	....
2000-01	HC Slavia Praha Jr.	Czech-Jr.	5	2	2	4	4	....	....	....	....	....
	Beroun	Czech-2	8	0	2	2	2	....	....	....	....	....
	HC Mlada Boleslav	Czech-3	2	0	0	0	6	....	....	....	....	....
	HC Slavia Praha	Czech	37	3	9	12	8	11	0	0	0	0
2001-02	HC Slavia Praha	Czech	49	6	8	14	14	8	0	0	0	4
	HC Slavia Praha Jr.	Czech-Jr.	5	2	3	5	0	....	....	....	....	....
2002-03	HC Slavia Praha	Czech	32	1	3	4	14	13	0	1	1	10

TOOTOO, Jordin (TOO-TOO, JOHR-dihn) NSH.

Right wing. Shoots right. 5'9", 195 lbs. Born, Churchill, Man., February 2, 1983.
(Nashville's 6th choice, 98th overall, in 2001 Entry Draft).

			Regular Season					Playoffs				
Season	Club	League	GP	G	A	TP	PIM	GP	G	A	TP	PIM
1998-99	OCN Blizzard	MJHL	47	16	21	37	251	....	....	....	....	....
99-2000	Brandon	WHL	45	6	10	16	214	....	....	....	....	....
2000-01	Brandon	WHL	60	20	28	48	172	6	2	4	6	18
2001-02	Brandon	WHL	64	32	39	71	272	16	4	3	7	*58
2002-03	Brandon	WHL	51	35	39	74	216	17	6	3	9	49

WHL East First All-Star Team (2003)

TRAVIS, Dan (TRA-vihs, DAN) FLA.

Right wing. Shoots right. 6'3", 220 lbs. Born, Concord, NH, November 26, 1983.
(Florida's 7th choice, 141st overall, in 2003 Entry Draft).

			Regular Season					Playoffs				
Season	Club	League	GP	G	A	TP	PIM	GP	G	A	TP	PIM
2002-03	Deerfield Academy	Hi-School	STATISTICS NOT AVAILABLE									

• Signed Letter of Intent to attend **New Hampshire** (H-East), July 29, 2002.

TREILLE, Yorick (TRAYL, YOH-rihk) CHI.

Right wing. Shoots right. 6'3", 213 lbs. Born, Cannes, France, July 15, 1980.
(Chicago's 7th choice, 195th overall, in 1999 Entry Draft).

			Regular Season					Playoffs				
Season	Club	League	GP	G	A	TP	PIM	GP	G	A	TP	PIM
1997-98	Notre Dame	SJHL	54	18	28	46	42	....	....	....	....	....
1998-99	U. Mass-Lowell	H-East	30	6	5	11	24	....	....	....	....	....
99-2000	U. Mass-Lowell	H-East	33	10	12	22	34	....	....	....	....	....
2000-01	U. Mass-Lowell	H-East	31	10	14	24	35	....	....	....	....	....
2001-02	U. Mass-Lowell	H-East	30	10	16	26	24	....	....	....	....	....
2002-03	HIFK Helsinki	Finland	5	0	1	1	4	....	....	....	....	....
	Norfolk Admirals	AHL	27	3	2	5	25	....	....	....	....	....

TROJOVSKY, Matej (troh-YAWV-skee, MAH-tehzh) CAR.

Defense. Shoots left. 6'5", 220 lbs. Born, Plzen, Czech., October 12, 1984.
(Carolina's 5th choice, 130th overall, in 2003 Entry Draft).

			Regular Season					Playoffs				
Season	Club	League	GP	G	A	TP	PIM	GP	G	A	TP	PIM
99-2000	Plzen Jr.	Czech-Jr.	36	2	13	15	58	5	0	1	1	2
2000-01	Lincoln Stars	USHL	17	1	0	1	29	....	....	....	....	....
2001-02	Regina Pats	WHL	67	3	10	13	154	6	0	1	1	18
2002-03	Regina Pats	WHL	70	3	6	9	229	5	0	0	0	6

TROLIGA, Tomas (TROH-lih-guh, TAW-mash) ST.L.

Center. Shoots right. 6'4", 200 lbs. Born, Presov, Czech., April 24, 1984.
(St. Louis' 3rd choice, 89th overall, in 2002 Entry Draft).

			Regular Season					Playoffs				
Season	Club	League	GP	G	A	TP	PIM	GP	G	A	TP	PIM
99-2000	HK VTJ Presov Jr.	Slovak-Jr.	39	6	1	7	56	....	....	....	....	....
2000-01	HK VTJ Presov Jr.	Slovak-Jr.	30	14	16	30	108	....	....	....	....	....
	HK VTJ Presov	Slovak-2	7	1	0	1	8	....	....	....	....	....
2001-02	Nova Ves Jr.	Slovak-Jr.	STATISTICS NOT AVAILABLE									
	Spisska Nova Ves	Slovak-2	11	2	5	7	0	....	....	....	....	....
2002-03	HC Kosice	Slovakia	29	1	1	2	16	....	....	....	....	....
	MHC Martin	Slovakia	11	1	2	3	18	4	0	0	0	6

TROSCHINSKY, Andrei (troh-SCHIHN-skee, AN-dray) ST.L.

Center. Shoots left. 6'5", 227 lbs. Born, Ust-Kamenogorsk, USSR, February 14, 1978.
(St. Louis' 5th choice, 170th overall, in 1998 Entry Draft).

			Regular Season					Playoffs				
Season	Club	League	GP	G	A	TP	PIM	GP	G	A	TP	PIM
1996-97	Ust-Kamenogorsk	Russia-2	9	1	1	2	8	....	....	....	....	....
1997-98	Ust-Kamenogorsk	Russia-2	47	10	16	26	34	....	....	....	....	....
1998-99	Ust-Kamenog. 2	Russia-4	4	4	4	8	6	....	....	....	....	....
	Ust-Kamenog. 2	Russia-4	42	11	21	32	62	....	....	....	....	....
99-2000	Ust-Kamenog. 2	Russia-3	50	20	46	66	....	....	....	....	....	....
2000-01	Worcester IceCats	AHL	78	17	28	45	32	11	2	2	4	2
2001-02	Worcester IceCats	AHL	70	13	10	23	32	2	0	0	0	0
2002-03	Magnitogorsk	Russia	1	0	0	0	0	....	....	....	....	....

TRUBACHEV, Yuri (troo-bah-CHEHV, YOO-ree) CGY.

Center. Shoots left. 5'9", 187 lbs. Born, Cherepovets, USSR, March 9, 1983.
(Calgary's 7th choice, 164th overall, in 2001 Entry Draft).

			Regular Season					Playoffs				
Season	Club	League	GP	G	A	TP	PIM	GP	G	A	TP	PIM
1997-98	Cherepovets 2	Russia-3	1	0	0	0	0	....	....	....	....	....
1998-99	Cherepovets 3	Russia-4	9	5	1	6	0	....	....	....	....	....
	Cherepovets 2	Russia-3	2	0	0	0	0	....	....	....	....	....
99-2000	Cherepovets 2	Russia-3	42	13	19	32	76	....	....	....	....	....
2000-01	SKA St. Petersburg	Russia	34	6	5	11	24	....	....	....	....	....
2001-02	Cherepovets 2	Russia-3	5	3	3	6	2	....	....	....	....	....
	Cherepovets	Russia	32	2	1	3	6	4	0	2	2	0
2002-03	Cherepovets	Russia	48	5	7	12	26	12	1	2	3	6

TUKIO, Arto (TOO-kee-oh, AHR-toh) NYI

Defense. Shoots left. 5'10", 176 lbs. Born, Tampere, Finland, April 4, 1981.
(NY Islanders' 3rd choice, 101st overall, in 2000 Entry Draft).

			Regular Season					Playoffs				
Season	Club	League	GP	G	A	TP	PIM	GP	G	A	TP	PIM
1995-96	Ilves Tampere-C	Finn-Jr.	28	3	5	8	20	....	....	....	....	....
1996-97	Ilves Tampere-C	Finn-Jr.	6	1	3	4	4	....	....	....	....	....
	Ilves Tampere-B	Finn-Jr.	20	0	2	2	6	1	1	0	1	0
1997-98	Ilves Tampere-B	Finn-Jr.	39	7	7	14	64	....	....	....	....	....
	Ilves Tampere Jr.	Finn-Jr.	....	....	....	....	....	4	1	0	1	4
1998-99	Ilves Tampere-B	Finn-Jr.	10	1	5	6	18	....	....	....	....	....
	Ilves Tampere Jr.	Finn-Jr.	18	1	4	5	12	10	0	0	0	2
99-2000	Ilves Tampere Jr.	Finn-Jr.	11	2	1	3	24	....	....	....	....	....
	Hermes Kokkola	Finland-2	1	0	0	0	0	....	....	....	....	....
	Ilves Tampere	Finland	42	2	1	3	20	3	0	0	0	0
2000-01	Ilves Tampere Jr.	Finn-Jr.	3	1	1	2	0	....	....	....	....	....
	Ilves Tampere	Finland	43	5	10	15	26	7	2	1	3	4
2001-02	Ilves Tampere	Finland	47	8	9	17	28	3	0	1	1	0
2002-03	Jokerit Helsinki	Finland	49	6	10	16	26	9	0	1	1	4

TUMA, Martin (TOO-ma, MAHR-tehn) FLA.

Defense. Shoots left. 6'4", 209 lbs. Born, Most, Czech., September 14, 1985.
(Florida's 8th choice, 162nd overall, in 2003 Entry Draft).

			Regular Season					Playoffs				
Season	Club	League	GP	G	A	TP	PIM	GP	G	A	TP	PIM
2000-01	Litvinov Jr.	Czech-Jr.	45	4	12	16	62	6	0	3	3	8
2001-02	Litvinov Jr.	Czech-Jr.	39	2	1	3	104	2	0	0	0	0
	Litvinov	Czech	1	0	0	0	2	....	....	....	....	....
2002-03	Litvinov Jr.	Czech-Jr.	34	1	3	4	123	....	....	....	....	....

TUNIK, Yevgeny (TOO-nihk, yehv-GEH-nee) NYI

Center. Shoots left. 6'2", 198 lbs. Born, Kraskovo, USSR, November 17, 1984.
(NY Islanders' 3rd choice, 53rd overall, in 2003 Entry Draft).

			Regular Season					Playoffs				
Season	Club	League	GP	G	A	TP	PIM	GP	G	A	TP	PIM
99-2000	Elektrostal 2	Russia-3	3	0	0	0	4	....	....	....	....	....
2000-01	Elektrostal	Russia-2	8	2	0	2	2	....	....	....	....	....
2001-02	Elektrostal 2	Russia-3	14	13	6	19	18	....	....	....	....	....
	Elektrostal	Russia-2	22	5	0	5	8	....	....	....	....	....
2002-03	Elektrostal	Russia-2	42	14	10	24	24	....	....	....	....	....
	Elektrostal 2	Russia-3	1	0	0	0	0	....	....	....	....	....

TUOKKO, Marco (too-OH-koh, MAHR-koh) DAL.

Center. Shoots left. 6', 185 lbs. Born, Raisio, Finland, March 27, 1979.
(Dallas' 9th choice, 219th overall, in 2000 Entry Draft).

			Regular Season					Playoffs				
Season	Club	League	GP	G	A	TP	PIM	GP	G	A	TP	PIM
1995-96	TPS Turku-B	Finn-Jr.	31	9	13	22	49	3	1	0	1	0
	Kiekko-67 Turku	Finland-2	1	0	0	0	0	....	....	....	....	....
1996-97	TPS Turku-B	Finn-Jr.	5	1	3	4	0	6	1	6	7	4
	TPS Turku Jr.	Finn-Jr.	30	8	7	15	32	....	....	....	....	....
	Kiekko-67 Turku	Finland-2	6	3	1	4	31	....	....	....	....	....
1997-98	TPS Turku Jr.	Finn-Jr.	26	5	13	18	77	7	1	4	5	14
1998-99	TPS Turku Jr.	Finn-Jr.	1	0	0	0	0	....	....	....	....	....
	TPS Turku	Finland	48	5	4	9	24	10	0	1	1	10
99-2000	TPS Turku	Finland	54	10	10	20	73	11	2	2	4	6
2000-01	TPS Turku	Finland	53	5	11	16	54	10	2	2	4	16
2001-02	TPS Turku	Finland	42	2	9	11	69	8	1	1	2	4
2002-03	TPS Turku	Finland	41	5	4	9	42	7	1	1	2	2

TURON, David (TUHR-awn, DAY-vihd) TOR.

Defense. Shoots right. 6'3", 202 lbs. Born, Havirov, Czech., October 4, 1983.
(Toronto's 5th choice, 122nd overall, in 2002 Entry Draft).

			Regular Season					Playoffs				
Season	Club	League	GP	G	A	TP	PIM	GP	G	A	TP	PIM
99-2000	SK Karvina Jr.	Czech-Jr.	2	0	0	0	0	....	....	....	....	....
	Havirov Jr.	Czech-Jr.	41	14	11	25	54	....	....	....	....	....
2000-01	Havirov Jr.	Czech-Jr.	43	12	7	19	26	....	....	....	....	....
	HC Femax Havirov	Czech	4	0	0	0	4	....	....	....	....	....
2001-02	Havirov Jr.	Czech-Jr.	41	5	11	16	75	....	....	....	....	....
	HC Femax Havirov	Czech	14	0	1	1	10	....	....	....	....	....
2002-03	Portland	WHL	36	3	6	9	38	7	0	2	2	0

• Missed majority of 2002-03 season recovering from shoulder injury suffered in training camp, September 26, 2002.

TVRDON, Roman (t-vahr-DAWN, ROH-muhn) WSH.

Center. Shoots left. 6'1", 189 lbs. Born, Trencin, Czech., January 29, 1981.
(Washington's 6th choice, 132nd overall, in 1999 Entry Draft).

			Regular Season					Playoffs				
Season	Club	League	GP	G	A	TP	PIM	GP	G	A	TP	PIM
1997-98	Dukla Trencin Jr.	Slovak-Jr.	48	4	12	16	39	....	....	....	....	....
1998-99	Dukla Trencin Jr.	Slovak-Jr.	49	23	23	46	20	6	4	4	8	4
99-2000	Spokane Chiefs	WHL	69	26	44	70	40	15	4	7	11	16
2000-01	Spokane Chiefs	WHL	62	28	34	62	55	12	5	11	16	0
2001-02	Portland Pirates	AHL	49	5	9	14	22	....	....	....	....	....
2002-03	Portland Pirates	AHL	35	5	4	9	17	....	....	....	....	....

• Missed majority of 2002-03 season recovering from shoulder injury suffered in game vs. Saint John (AHL), December 28, 2002.

UCHEVATOV, Victor (oo-cheh-VA-tawf, VIHK-tohr) N.J.

Defense. Shoots left. 6'4", 225 lbs. Born, Angarsk, USSR, February 10, 1983.
(New Jersey's 4th choice, 60th overall, in 2001 Entry Draft).

			Regular Season					Playoffs				
Season	Club	League	GP	G	A	TP	PIM	GP	G	A	TP	PIM
2000-01	Yaroslavl 2	Russia-3	28	1	1	2	74	....	....	....	....	....
2001-02	Albany River Rats	AHL	64	0	2	2	50	....	....	....	....	....
2002-03	Albany River Rats	AHL	55	0	2	2	27	....	....	....	....	....

UJCIK, Viktor (OOY-chehk, VIHK-tohr) MTL.

Right wing. Shoots left. 5'11", 194 lbs. Born, Jihlava, Czech., May 24, 1972.
(Montreal's 8th choice, 266th overall, in 2001 Entry Draft).

			Regular Season					Playoffs				
Season	Club	League	GP	G	A	TP	PIM	GP	G	A	TP	PIM
1990-91	Dukla Jihlava	Czech	2	0	0	0	0	....	....	....	....	....
1991-92	Dukla Jihlava	Czech	35	10	9	19	32	8	3	4	7	0
1992-93	Dukla Jihlava	Czech	30	16	16	32	....	....	....	....	....	....
1993-94	HC Dukla Jihlava	Czech	44	17	30	47	....	4	3	3	6	....
1994-95	HC Dukla Jihlava	Czech	42	20	16	36	65	2	1	2	3	2
1995-96	HC Slavia Praha	Czech	39	*37	19	56	59	7	8	4	12	6
1996-97	HC Slavia Praha	Czech	40	26	21	47	41	3	1	1	2	2
1997-98	HC Slavia Praha	Czech	17	13	8	21	12	....	....	....	....	....
	HC Zele. Trinec	Czech	31	21	22	43	63	13	8	10	18	4
1998-99	HC Zele. Trinec	Czech	44	20	23	43	55	10	4	4	8	18
99-2000	HC Ocelari Trinec	Czech	42	14	20	34	32	4	1	0	1	28
2000-01	HC Ocelari Trinec	Czech	31	8	12	20	20	....	....	....	....	....
	HC Slavia Praha	Czech	19	9	9	18	8	11	8	8	16	10
2001-02	HC Slavia Praha	Czech	52	25	23	48	51	9	3	0	3	6
2002-03	HC Keramika Plzen	Czech	23	12	5	17	41	....	....	....	....	....
	HC Sparta Praha	Czech	26	11	6	17	14	10	3	5	8	6

ULMER, Layne (UHL-muhr, LAYN) NYR

Center. Shoots left. 6'1", 205 lbs. Born, North Battleford, Sask., September 14, 1980.
(Ottawa's 8th choice, 209th overall, in 1999 Entry Draft).

			Regular Season					Playoffs				
Season	Club	League	GP	G	A	TP	PIM	GP	G	A	TP	PIM
1996-97	Swift Current	SMHL	43	35	49	84	31	....	....	....	....	....
1997-98	Swift Current	WHL	50	8	9	17	23	12	3	1	4	0
1998-99	Swift Current	WHL	72	40	35	75	34	6	2	1	3	4
99-2000	Swift Current	WHL	71	50	54	104	66	12	12	6	18	16
2000-01	Swift Current	WHL	68	*63	56	119	75	19	7	3	10	20
2001-02	Hartford Wolf Pack	AHL	22	0	5	5	17	....	....	....	....	....
	Charlotte	ECHL	38	18	17	35	12	5	2	2	4	4
2002-03	Hartford Wolf Pack	AHL	68	12	20	32	16	2	0	0	0	0

WHL East First All-Star Team (2000, 2001)

Signed as a free agent by **NY Rangers**, June 13, 2001.

UMBERGER, R.J. (UHM-buhr-guhr, AHR-JAY) VAN.

Center. Shoots left. 6'2", 200 lbs. Born, Pittsburgh, PA, May 3, 1982.
(Vancouver's 1st choice, 16th overall, in 2001 Entry Draft).

			Regular Season					Playoffs				
Season	Club	League	GP	G	A	TP	PIM	GP	G	A	TP	PIM
1997-98	Plum Mustangs	Hi-School	26	*60	*56	*116	....	....	....	....	....	....
1998-99	U.S. National U-17	USDP	50	29	29	58	....	....	....	....	....	....
99-2000	U.S. National U-18	USDP	57	33	35	68	20	....	....	....	....	....
2000-01	Ohio State	CCHA	32	14	23	37	18	....	....	....	....	....
2001-02	Ohio State	CCHA	37	18	21	39	31	....	....	....	....	....
2002-03	Ohio State	CCHA	43	26	27	53	16	....	....	....	....	....

CCHA All-Rookie Team (2001) • CCHA Rookie of the Year (2001) • CCHA First All-Star Team (2003) • NCAA West Second All-American Team (2003)

UPPER, Dmitri (OO-puhr, dih-MEE-tree) NYI

Center. Shoots right. 6'1", 185 lbs. Born, Ust-Kamenogorsk, USSR, July 27, 1978.
(NY Islanders' 5th choice, 136th overall, in 2000 Entry Draft).

			Regular Season					Playoffs				
Season	Club	League	GP	G	A	TP	PIM	GP	G	A	TP	PIM
1997-98	Ust-Kamenogorsk	Russia-2	47	16	12	28	44	....	....	....	....	....
1998-99	Ust-Kamenog. 2	Russia-4	29	10	11	21	44	....	....	....	....	....
	Nizhny Novgorod	Russia-2	28	10	16	26	65	....	....	....	....	....
99-2000	Nizhny Novgorod	Russia	36	14	6	20	50	5	1	1	2	4
2000-01	Nizhny Novgorod	Russia	6	0	2	2	4	....	....	....	....	....
	Ak Bars Kazan	Russia	31	7	4	11	6	1	0	0	0	0
2001-02	Spartak Moscow	Russia	51	16	9	25	74	....	....	....	....	....
2002-03	Spartak Moscow	Russia	43	7	13	20	63	....	....	....	....	....

URQUHART, Cory (UHRK-hahrt, KOHR-ee) **MTL.**

Center. Shoots left. 6'2", 195 lbs. Born, Halifax, N.S., October 1, 1984.
(Montreal's 2nd choice, 40th overall, in 2003 Entry Draft).

			Regular Season					Playoffs				
Season	Club	League	GP	G	A	TP	PIM	GP	G	A	TP	PIM
99-2000	Dalhousie	NSMHL	21	15	14	29	12	....	....	....	....	....
2000-01	Quebec Remparts	QMJHL	60	25	24	49	32	2	0	0	0	2
2001-02	Quebec Remparts	QMJHL	36	8	10	18	4	....	....	....	....	....
	Montreal Rocket	QMJHL	34	9	9	18	6	7	3	2	5	0
2002-03	Montreal Rocket	QMJHL	71	35	43	78	28	7	9	6	15	6

USTRNUL, Libor (OOS-tuhr-nuhl, LEE-bohr) **ATL.**

Defense. Shoots left. 6'5", 230 lbs. Born, Steruberk, Czech., February 20, 1982.
(Atlanta's 3rd choice, 42nd overall, in 2000 Entry Draft).

			Regular Season					Playoffs				
Season	Club	League	GP	G	A	TP	PIM	GP	G	A	TP	PIM
1997-98	HC Olomouc Jr.	Czech-Jr.	45	2	11	13	54	....	....	....	....	....
1998-99	Thunder Bay Flyers	USHL	52	2	5	7	65	18	1	4	5	95
99-2000	Plymouth Whalers	OHL	68	0	15	15	208	23	0	3	3	29
2000-01	Plymouth Whalers	OHL	35	3	13	16	66	19	1	4	5	19
2001-02	Plymouth Whalers	OHL	43	1	8	9	84	2	0	0	0	6
	Chicago Wolves	AHL	1	0	0	0	0	1	0	0	0	5
2002-03	Chicago Wolves	AHL	40	1	1	2	94	6	0	0	0	0

UTKIN, Dmitri (OOT-kihn, dih-MEE-tree) **BOS.**

Left wing. Shoots left. 6', 169 lbs. Born, Yaroslavl, USSR, June 10, 1984.
(Boston's 5th choice, 228th overall, in 2002 Entry Draft).

			Regular Season					Playoffs				
Season	Club	League	GP	G	A	TP	PIM	GP	G	A	TP	PIM
2000-01	Yaroslavl 2	Russia-3	49	12	1	13	10	....	....	....	....	....
2001-02	Yaroslavl 2	Russia-3	32	15	7	22	33	....	....	....	....	....
2002-03	Yaroslavl	Russia	4	0	1	1	0	....	....	....	....	....

VAGNER, Martin (VAHG-nuhr, MAHR-tihn) **DAL.**

Defense. Shoots left. 6'1", 214 lbs. Born, Jaromer, Czech., March 16, 1984.
(Dallas' 1st choice, 26th overall, in 2002 Entry Draft).

			Regular Season					Playoffs				
Season	Club	League	GP	G	A	TP	PIM	GP	G	A	TP	PIM
99-2000	Sparta Praha Jr.	Czech-Jr.	46	2	8	10	34	....	....	....	....	....
2000-01	Pardubice Jr.	Czech-Jr.	53	2	12	14	46	....	....	....	....	....
2001-02	Hull Olympiques	QMJHL	64	6	28	34	81	8	0	1	1	10
2002-03	Hull Olympiques	QMJHL	53	1	12	13	98	20	1	4	5	38

QMJHL All-Rookie Team (2002)

VALCAK, Patrik (VAHL-chahk, PAT-rihk) **BOS.**

Center. Shoots left. 6'1", 185 lbs. Born, Ostrava, Czech., December 16, 1984.
(Boston's 6th choice, 129th overall, in 2003 Entry Draft).

			Regular Season					Playoffs				
Season	Club	League	GP	G	A	TP	PIM	GP	G	A	TP	PIM
2000-01	Sareza Ostrava Jr.	Czech-Jr.	44	13	16	29	34	....	....	....	....	....
2001-02	Sareza Ostrava Jr.	Czech-Jr.	45	9	16	25	44	....	....	....	....	....
2002-03	Sareza Ostrava Jr.	Czech-Jr.	38	14	18	32	131	....	....	....	....	....

VALDIX, Andreas (VAHL-dihx, an-DRAY-uhs) **WSH.**

Left wing. Shoots left. 5'11", 167 lbs. Born, Malmo, Sweden, December 6, 1984.
(Washington's 3rd choice, 109th overall, in 2003 Entry Draft).

			Regular Season					Playoffs				
Season	Club	League	GP	G	A	TP	PIM	GP	G	A	TP	PIM
99-2000	Malmo IF Jr.	Swede-Jr.	14	3	7	10	39	....	....	....	....	....
2000-01	Malmo IF Jr.	Swede-Jr.	28	7	7	14	24	....	....	....	....	....
2001-02	Malmo Jr.	Swede-Jr.	39	13	13	26	86	7	0	3	3	6
	Malmo IF	Sweden	1	0	0	0	0	....	....	....	....	....
2002-03	Malmo	Sweden	39	2	0	2	10	....	....	....	....	....
	Malmo Jr.	Swede-Jr.	11	10	12	22	16	6	2	5	7	8

VALEEV, Igor (val-AY-ehv, EE-gohr) **ST.L.**

Right wing. Shoots left. 5'11", 195 lbs. Born, Sneginsk, USSR, January 9, 1981.
(St. Louis' 3rd choice, 122nd overall, in 2001 Entry Draft).

			Regular Season					Playoffs				
Season	Club	League	GP	G	A	TP	PIM	GP	G	A	TP	PIM
1998-99	Lethbridge	WHL	8	2	3	5	13	....	....	....	....	....
	Saskatoon Blades	WHL	23	2	2	4	36	....	....	....	....	....
99-2000	Swift Current	WHL	36	7	5	12	78	4	0	1	1	22
2000-01	North Bay	OHL	62	17	61	78	175	4	0	1	1	22
	Muskegon Fury	UHL	....	....	....	....	....	3	0	1	1	2
2001-02	Worcester IceCats	AHL	29	3	6	9	72	....	....	....	....	....
2002-03	Worcester IceCats	AHL	72	6	12	18	153	3	0	0	0	2

• Missed majority of 2001-02 season recovering from head injury suffered in game vs. Springfield (AHL), December 14, 2001.

VALETTE, Craig (va-LEHT, KRAIG) **S.J.**

Center. Shoots left. 6', 200 lbs. Born, Shellbrook, Sask., October 7, 1982.

			Regular Season					Playoffs				
Season	Club	League	GP	G	A	TP	PIM	GP	G	A	TP	PIM
99-2000	Saskatoon Blades	WHL	47	2	1	3	25	3	0	0	0	0
2000-01	Saskatoon Blades	WHL	24	2	0	2	19	....	....	....	....	....
	Portland	WHL	39	8	6	14	39	16	0	2	2	27
2001-02	Portland	WHL	67	8	14	22	160	7	2	1	3	6
2002-03	Portland	WHL	71	30	26	56	192	7	5	4	9	18

Signed as a free agent by **San Jose**, April 4, 2003.

VALTONEN, Tomek (VAL-tuh-nehn, Toh-MEHK) **DET.**

Left wing. Shoots left. 6'1", 198 lbs. Born, Piotrkow Trybunalski, Poland, January 8, 1980.
(Detroit's 3rd choice, 56th overall, in 1998 Entry Draft).

			Regular Season					Playoffs				
Season	Club	League	GP	G	A	TP	PIM	GP	G	A	TP	PIM
1995-96	Ilves Tampere-C	Finn-Jr.	9	3	3	6	24	....	....	....	....	....
	Ilves Tampere-B	Finn-Jr.	11	7	7	14	28	....	....	....	....	....
	Ilves Tampere Jr.	Finn-Jr.	....	....	....	....	....	1	0	0	0	0
1996-97	Ilves Tampere-B	Finn-Jr.	26	10	9	19	82	3	0	1	1	6
	Ilves Tampere Jr.	Finn-Jr.	1	0	0	0	0	....	....	....	....	....
1997-98	JoKP Joensuu Jr.	Finn-Jr.	3	0	0	0	12	....	....	....	....	....
	JoKP Joensuu	Finland-2	6	1	2	3	39	....	....	....	....	....
	Ilves Tampere Jr.	Finn-Jr.	13	3	2	5	36	....	....	....	....	....
	Ilves Tampere	Finland	19	1	0	1	14	3	0	0	0	0
	Ilves Tampere-B	Finn-Jr.	....	....	....	....	....	7	0	2	2	16
1998-99	Plymouth Whalers	OHL	43	8	16	24	53	7	1	0	1	0
99-2000	Jokerit Helsinki	Finland	41	0	3	3	63	9	1	0	1	8
2000-01	Jokerit Helsinki	Finland	45	3	2	5	138	3	0	0	0	0
2001-02	Jokerit Helsinki	Finland	55	4	4	8	65	11	2	1	3	2
2002-03	Jokerit Helsinki	Finland	51	5	9	14	38	10	1	1	2	4

VAN DER GULIK, David (VAN-DUHR-GOO-lihk, DAY-vihd) **CGY.**

Right wing. Shoots left. 5'11", 175 lbs. Born, Abbotsford, B.C., April 20, 1983.
(Calgary's 10th choice, 206th overall, in 2002 Entry Draft).

			Regular Season					Playoffs				
Season	Club	League	GP	G	A	TP	PIM	GP	G	A	TP	PIM
99-2000	Chilliwack Chiefs	BCHL	41	35	46	81	....	....	....	....	....	....
2000-01	Chilliwack Chiefs	BCHL	60	42	38	80	....	....	....	....	....	....
2001-02	Chilliwack Chiefs	BCHL	56	38	62	100	90	13	8	11	19	....
2002-03	Boston University	H-East	40	10	10	20	56	....	....	....	....	....

Hockey East All-Rookie Team (2003)

VAN HOOF, Jeremy (van-HOOF, JAIR-reh-mee) **T.B.**

Defense. Shoots left. 6'2", 208 lbs. Born, Lindsay, Ont., August 12, 1981.
(Tampa Bay's 9th choice, 222nd overall, in 2001 Entry Draft).

			Regular Season					Playoffs				
Season	Club	League	GP	G	A	TP	PIM	GP	G	A	TP	PIM
1997-98	Lindsay Muskies	OPJHL	50	2	8	10	40	....	....	....	....	....
1998-99	Ottawa 67's	OHL	54	0	13	13	46	5	1	0	1	2
99-2000	Ottawa 67's	OHL	66	4	14	18	71	11	1	0	1	12
2000-01	Ottawa 67's	OHL	65	1	14	15	49	20	3	4	7	27
2001-02	Pensacola	ECHL	72	2	14	16	86	3	0	0	0	9
2002-03	Pensacola	ECHL	66	4	5	9	51	4	0	1	1	4
	Springfield Falcons	AHL	4	0	0	0	6	....	....	....	....	....

• Re-entered NHL Entry Draft. Originally Pittsburgh's 3rd choice, 57th overall, in 1999 Entry Draft.

VANDERMEER, Peter (VAN-duhr-meer, PEE-tuhr) **PHI.**

Left wing. Shoots left. 6', 205 lbs. Born, , Alta., October 14, 1975.

			Regular Season					Playoffs				
Season	Club	League	GP	G	A	TP	PIM	GP	G	A	TP	PIM
1992-93	Red Deer	AMHL	34	26	30	56	172	....	....	....	....	....
	Red Deer Rebels	WHL	2	0	0	0	2	....	....	....	....	....
1993-94	Red Deer Rebels	WHL	54	4	9	13	170	....	....	....	....	....
1994-95	Red Deer Rebels	WHL	61	16	16	32	218	....	....	....	....	....
1995-96	Red Deer Rebels	WHL	63	21	40	61	207	....	....	....	....	....
1996-97	Columbus Chill	ECHL	30	6	11	17	195	7	2	1	3	26
1997-98	Columbus Chill	ECHL	20	4	7	11	78	....	....	....	....	....
	Richmond	ECHL	18	2	5	7	165	....	....	....	....	....
	Rochester	AHL	30	4	2	6	140	4	1	0	1	13
1998-99	Binghamton	UHL	62	15	21	36	*390	5	2	2	4	0
	Rochester	AHL	2	1	0	1	16	16	1	0	1	38
99-2000	Richmond	ECHL	58	31	25	56	*457	3	0	1	1	20
	Wilkes-Barre	AHL	4	0	0	0	7	....	....	....	....	....
	Providence Bruins	AHL	....	....	....	....	....	9	0	3	3	2
2000-01	Providence Bruins	AHL	62	19	18	37	240	4	0	0	0	16
2001-02	Trenton Titans	ECHL	2	0	1	1	2	....	....	....	....	....
	Philadelphia	AHL	61	5	1	6	313	5	0	0	0	8
2002-03	Philadelphia	AHL	77	5	8	13	335	....	....	....	....	....

Signed as a free agent by **Philadelphia**, July 6, 2001.

VANEK, Thomas (VAH-nehk, TAW-muhs) **BUF.**

Left wing. Shoots right. 6'2", 208 lbs. Born, Vienna, Austria, January 19, 1984.
(Buffalo's 1st choice, 5th overall, in 2003 Entry Draft).

			Regular Season					Playoffs				
Season	Club	League	GP	G	A	TP	PIM	GP	G	A	TP	PIM
99-2000	Sioux Falls	USHL	35	15	18	33	12	3	0	1	1	0
2000-01	Sioux Falls	USHL	20	19	10	29	15	8	5	4	9	2
2001-02	Sioux Falls	USHL	53	46	45	91	54	3	0	0	0	9
2002-03	U. of Minnesota	WCHA	45	31	31	62	60	....	....	....	....	....

USHL First All-Star Team (2002) • USHL MVP (2002) • WCHA All-Rookie Team (2003) • WCHA Second All-Star Team (2003) • WCHA Rookie of the Year (2003) • NCAA Championship All-Tournament Team (2003) • NCAA Tournament MVP (2003)

VANNELLI, Michael (vuh-NEHL-ee, MIGH-kuhl) **ATL.**

Defense. Shoots right. 6'2", 190 lbs. Born, St. Paul, MN, October 2, 1983.
(Atlanta's 4th choice, 136th overall, in 2003 Entry Draft).

			Regular Season					Playoffs				
Season	Club	League	GP	G	A	TP	PIM	GP	G	A	TP	PIM
2001-02	Cretin-Durham	Hi-School	28	0	5	5	16	....	....	....	....	....
	Sioux Falls	USHL	37	0	5	5	24	....	....	....	....	....
2002-03	Sioux Falls	USHL	60	13	34	47	88	....	....	....	....	....

USHL First All-Star Team (2003)

• Signed Letter of Intent to attend **U. of Minnesota** (WCHA), November 2, 2002.

VAN OENE, Darren (van OH-uhn, DAIR-rehn) **BOS.**

Left wing. Shoots left. 6'4", 216 lbs. Born, Edmonton, Alta., January 18, 1978.
(Buffalo's 3rd choice, 33rd overall, in 1996 Entry Draft).

			Regular Season					Playoffs				
Season	Club	League	GP	G	A	TP	PIM	GP	G	A	TP	PIM
1993-94	Edmonton SSAC	AMHL	34	15	16	31	121	....	....	....	....	....
1994-95	Brandon	WHL	58	5	13	18	106	18	1	1	2	34
1995-96	Brandon	WHL	47	10	18	28	126	18	1	6	7	*78
1996-97	Brandon	WHL	56	21	27	48	139	6	2	3	5	19
1997-98	Brandon	WHL	51	23	24	47	161	18	6	8	14	51
1998-99	Rochester	AHL	73	11	20	31	143	12	2	4	6	8
99-2000	Rochester	AHL	80	20	18	38	153	21	1	3	4	24
2000-01	Rochester	AHL	64	10	12	22	147	4	1	0	1	4
2001-02	Rochester	AHL	52	8	6	14	73	2	0	0	0	4
2002-03	Providence Bruins	AHL	78	11	17	28	109	4	0	0	0	21

Signed as a free agent by **Boston**, July 29, 2002.

VAS, Janos (VAHSH, YAH-nohsh) DAL.

Left wing. Shoots left. 6'1", 183 lbs. Born, Dunaferr, Hungary, January 29, 1984.
(Dallas' 2nd choice, 32nd overall, in 2002 Entry Draft).

			Regular Season					Playoffs				
Season	Club	League	GP	G	A	TP	PIM	GP	G	A	TP	PIM
99-2000	Dunaferr SE	Hungary	2	2	0	0	0	....	....	....	....	....
2000-01	Malmo IF Jr.	Swede-Jr.	23	4	4	8	12	....	....	....	....	....
	Malmo IF 18	Swede-Jr.	3	2	0	2	4	....	....	....	....	....
2001-02	Malmo IF Jr.	Swede-Jr.	36	15	19	34	52	7	8	2	10	4
2002-03	Malmo IF Jr.	Swede-Jr.	17	5	12	17	14	....	....	....	....	....
	IK Pantern	Swede-2	STATISTICS NOT AVAILABLE									
	IF Troja/Ljunby	Swede-2	17	2	2	4	20	....	....	....	....	....
	Malmo	Sweden	14	1	0	1	2	....	....	....	....	....

VAUCLAIR, Julien (voh-KLAIR, JEW-lee-ehn) OTT.

Defense. Shoots left. 6', 205 lbs. Born, Delemont, Switz., October 2, 1979.
(Ottawa's 4th choice, 74th overall, in 1998 Entry Draft).

			Regular Season					Playoffs				
Season	Club	League	GP	G	A	TP	PIM	GP	G	A	TP	PIM
1995-96	HC Ajoie	Swiss-3	20	4	10	14	....	....	....	....	....	....
1996-97	HC Ajoie	Swiss-2	40	0	6	6	24	9	0	2	2	8
1997-98	HC Lugano	Swiss	36	1	2	3	12	7	0	0	0	25
1998-99	HC Lugano	Swiss	38	0	3	3	8	....	....	....	....	....
99-2000	HC Lugano	Swiss	45	3	3	6	16	14	0	0	0	0
2000-01	HC Lugano	Swiss	42	3	4	7	57	18	0	1	1	4
2001-02	Grand Rapids	AHL	71	5	14	19	18	4	0	1	1	4
	Switzerland	Olympics	4	1	0	1	2	....	....	....	....	....
2002-03	Binghamton	AHL	67	6	16	22	30	14	0	1	1	8

VAVRA, Josef (VAHV-rah, YOH-zuhf) OTT.

Left wing. Shoots left. 6', 199 lbs. Born, Valasske Mezirici, Czech., March 17, 1984.
(Ottawa's 7th choice, 246th overall, in 2002 Entry Draft).

			Regular Season					Playoffs				
Season	Club	League	GP	G	A	TP	PIM	GP	G	A	TP	PIM
99-2000	HC Vsetin-16	Czech-Jr.	50	25	21	46	90	....	....	....	....	....
2000-01	HC Vsetin-16	Czech-Jr.	32	22	33	55	99	....	....	....	....	....
	Vsetin Jr.	Czech-Jr.	11	0	2	2	2	....	....	....	....	....
2001-02	Vsetin Jr.	Czech-Jr.	35	3	12	15	39	....	....	....	....	....
2002-03	Tri-City Americans	WHL	37	2	5	7	26	....	....	....	....	....

• Missed majority of 2002-03 season recovering from knee injury suffered in game vs. Portland (WHL), November 6, 2002.

VENALAINEN, Sami (veh-na-LIGH-nehn, SA-mee) PHX.

Right wing. Shoots right. 5'11", 183 lbs. Born, Kangasala, Finland, October 14, 1981.
(Phoenix's 7th choice, 249th overall, in 2000 Entry Draft).

			Regular Season					Playoffs				
Season	Club	League	GP	G	A	TP	PIM	GP	G	A	TP	PIM
1996-97	Tappara-C	Finn-Jr.	32	21	17	38	31	4	2	1	3	0
1997-98	Tappara-C	Finn-Jr.	2	2	0	2	6	6	4	5	9	6
	Tappara-B	Finn-Jr.	33	18	7	25	12	....	....	....	....	....
1998-99	Tappara-B	Finn-Jr.	31	27	17	44	45	....	....	....	....	....
	Tappara Jr.	Finn-Jr.	10	3	2	5	29	....	....	....	....	....
99-2000	Tappara Jr.	Finn-Jr.	37	8	9	17	18	....	....	....	....	....
2000-01	Tappara Jr.	Finn-Jr.	21	6	13	19	12	9	3	1	4	0
	Tappara Tampere	Finland	36	0	1	1	2	1	0	0	0	0
2001-02	Tappara Tampere	Finland	56	5	8	13	24	10	0	1	1	8
2002-03	Tappara Tampere	Finland	55	5	9	14	48	13	0	0	0	10

VERENIKIN, Sergei (veh-rih-NEE-kihn, SAIR-gay) OTT.

Right wing. Shoots left. 5'11", 187 lbs. Born, Yaroslavl, USSR, September 8, 1979.
(Ottawa's 9th choice, 223rd overall, in 1998 Entry Draft).

			Regular Season					Playoffs				
Season	Club	League	GP	G	A	TP	PIM	GP	G	A	TP	PIM
1997-98	Yaroslavl 2	Russia-2	44	11	4	15	100	....	....	....	....	....
	Torpedo Yaroslavl	Russia	3	0	0	0	0	....	....	....	....	....
1998-99	Torpedo Yaroslavl	Russia	37	2	5	7	16	8	0	0	0	18
99-2000	Torpedo Yaroslavl	Russia	25	4	1	5	18	4	0	0	0	2
2000-01	Magnitogorsk	Russia	31	1	0	1	14	....	....	....	....	....
2001-02	Perm	Russia	47	6	4	10	26	....	....	....	....	....
2002-03	Khimik	Russia-2	7	0	2	2	6	....	....	....	....	....

VERMETTE, Antoine (vuhr-MEHT, AN-twuhn) OTT.

Center. Shoots left. 6'1", 184 lbs. Born, St-Agapit, Que., July 20, 1982.
(Ottawa's 3rd choice, 55th overall, in 2000 Entry Draft).

			Regular Season					Playoffs				
Season	Club	League	GP	G	A	TP	PIM	GP	G	A	TP	PIM
1997-98	Quebec Select	QAHA	19	11	20	31	36	....	....	....	....	....
	Levis-Lauzon	QAAA	8	1	1	2	4	1	0	0	0	0
1998-99	Quebec Remparts	QMJHL	57	9	17	26	32	13	0	0	0	2
99-2000	Victoriaville Tigres	QMJHL	71	30	41	71	87	6	0	1	1	6
2000-01	Victoriaville Tigres	QMJHL	71	57	62	119	102	9	4	6	10	14
2001-02	Victoriaville Tigres	QMJHL	4	0	2	2	6	22	10	16	26	10
2002-03	Binghamton	AHL	80	34	28	62	57	14	2	9	11	10

AHL All-Rookie Team (2003)

• Missed majority of 2001-02 season recovering from neck injury suffered at Team Canada Jr. Selection Camp, June 3, 2001.

VEROT, Darcy (vuhr-AWT, DAHR-see)

Left wing. Shoots left. 6', 202 lbs. Born, Radville, Sask., July 13, 1976.

			Regular Season					Playoffs				
Season	Club	League	GP	G	A	TP	PIM	GP	G	A	TP	PIM
1994-95	Weyburn	SJHL	57	8	18	26	240	16	5	2	7	50
1995-96	Weyburn	SJHL	64	15	30	45	191	3	1	0	1	20
1996-97	Weyburn	SJHL	61	26	51	77	218	13	3	8	11	24
1997-98	Lake Charles	WPHL	68	11	26	37	269	4	0	1	1	25
1998-99	Lake Charles	WPHL	68	17	23	40	236	9	2	4	6	53
99-2000	Wheeling Nailers	ECHL	44	7	12	19	240	....	....	....	....	....
	Wilkes-Barre	AHL	23	5	5	10	96	....	....	....	....	....
2000-01	Wilkes-Barre	AHL	78	10	15	25	347	21	2	3	5	40
2001-02	Wilkes-Barre	AHL	71	6	10	16	387	....	....	....	....	....
2002-03	Saint John Flames	AHL	73	5	11	16	299	....	....	....	....	....

Signed as a free agent by **Wilkes-Barre** (AHL), February 25, 2000. Signed as a free agent by **Pittsburgh**, July 28, 2000. Signed as a free agent by **Calgary**, July 9, 2002.

VIHKO, Joonas (VIH-koh, YOO-nuhs) ANA.

Center. Shoots right. 5'9", 176 lbs. Born, Helsinki, Finland, April 6, 1981.
(Anaheim's 4th choice, 103rd overall, in 2002 Entry Draft).

			Regular Season					Playoffs				
Season	Club	League	GP	G	A	TP	PIM	GP	G	A	TP	PIM
1998-99	HIFK Helsinki Jr.	Finn-Jr.	32	15	14	29	10	3	1	1	2	0
99-2000	HIFK Helsinki Jr.	Finn-Jr.	38	12	15	27	36	3	0	0	0	0
2000-01	HIFK Helsinki Jr.	Finn-Jr.	27	23	17	40	85	7	5	2	7	18
	HIFK Helsinki	Finland	3	0	0	0	2	....	....	....	....	....
2001-02	HIFK Helsinki	Finland	48	13	11	24	89	....	....	....	....	....
	HIFK Helsinki Jr.	Finn-Jr.	....	....	....	....	....	2	0	2	2	4
2002-03	HIFK Helsinki	Finland	50	14	11	25	20	1	0	0	0	2

VIITANEN, Mikko (vee-EE-tan-ehn, MEE-koh) COL.

Defense. Shoots left. 6'3", 220 lbs. Born, Rajamaki, Finland, February 18, 1982.
(Colorado's 6th choice, 149th overall, in 2001 Entry Draft).

			Regular Season					Playoffs				
Season	Club	League	GP	G	A	TP	PIM	GP	G	A	TP	PIM
1998-99	HPK-B	Finn-Jr.	36	3	6	9	40	....	....	....	....	....
	HPK Jr.	Finn-Jr.	1	0	0	0	0	....	....	....	....	....
99-2000	Chicago Freeze	NAJHL	53	4	6	10	126	....	....	....	....	....
2000-01	Ahmat Jr.	Finn-Jr.	9	3	4	7	41	....	....	....	....	....
	Ahmat Hyvinkaa	Finland-2	41	3	9	12	66	3	0	0	0	0
2001-02	Blues Espoo Jr.	Finn-Jr.	10	1	3	4	16	....	....	....	....	....
	Blues Espoo	Finland	3	0	0	0	6	....	....	....	....	....
	Jukurit Mikkeli	Finland-2	21	0	3	3	26	....	....	....	....	....
2002-03	KJT Jarvenpaa	Finland-2	9	0	1	1	56	....	....	....	....	....
	Blues Espoo	Finland	1	0	0	0	0	....	....	....	....	....

VIKINGSTAD, Tore (VIH-kihng-stahd, TOO-reh) ST.L.

Left wing. Shoots left. 6'4", 204 lbs. Born, Stavenger, Norway, October 8, 1975.
(St. Louis' 5th choice, 180th overall, in 1999 Entry Draft).

			Regular Season					Playoffs				
Season	Club	League	GP	G	A	TP	PIM	GP	G	A	TP	PIM
1994-95	Viking	Norway	28	5	3	8	8	....	....	....	....	....
1995-96	Viking	Norway	27	12	11	23	....	....	....	....	....	....
1996-97	Stjernen	Norway	42	23	35	58	20	....	....	....	....	....
1997-98	Stjernen	Norway	42	26	31	57	18	....	....	....	....	....
1998-99	Farjestad	Sweden	49	9	11	20	18	4	2	3	5	0
99-2000	Farjestad	Sweden	47	8	19	27	26	7	3	0	3	6
2000-01	Leksands IF	Sweden	41	10	15	25	24	....	....	....	....	....
2001-02	DEG Metro Stars	Germany	58	18	30	48	6	....	....	....	....	....
2002-03	DEG Metro Stars	Germany	45	13	18	31	40	5	1	0	1	0

VISHNYAKOV, Albert (vihsh-nyeh-KAWF, al-BAIRT) T.B.

Wing. Shoots right. 6', 185 lbs. Born, Almyetevsk, USSR, December 30, 1983.
(Tampa Bay's 9th choice, 273rd overall, in 2003 Entry Draft).

			Regular Season					Playoffs				
Season	Club	League	GP	G	A	TP	PIM	GP	G	A	TP	PIM
99-2000	Almetjevsk 2	Russia-3	41	11	5	16	68	....	....	....	....	....
2000-01	Almetjevsk	Russia-2	29	0	0	0	2	....	....	....	....	....
2001-02	Ak Bars Kazan	Russia	9	0	1	1	2	....	....	....	....	....
	Nizhny Novgorod	Russia	6	1	0	1	0	....	....	....	....	....
	Nizhny Novgorod 2	Russia-3	4	2	2	4	10	....	....	....	....	....
2002-03	Ak Bars Kazan	Russia	47	7	6	13	47	5	1	0	1	0

VLCEK, Ladislav (vuhl-CHEHK, LA-dih-dlav) DAL.

Right wing. Shoots left. 5'11", 184 lbs. Born, Kladno, Czech., September 26, 1981.
(Dallas' 8th choice, 192nd overall, in 2000 Entry Draft).

			Regular Season					Playoffs				
Season	Club	League	GP	G	A	TP	PIM	GP	G	A	TP	PIM
1998-99	Kladno Jr.	Czech-Jr.	46	13	27	40	....	....	....	....	....	....
	HC Velvana Kladno	Czech	4	0	1	1	0	....	....	....	....	....
99-2000	Kladno Jr.	Czech-Jr.	34	16	15	31	16	....	....	....	....	....
	HC CKD Slany	Czech-3	4	3	0	3	0	....	....	....	....	....
	Kralupy	Czech-3	1	0	1	1	0	5	2	2	4	4
	HC Velvana Kladno	Czech	21	3	2	5	4	....	....	....	....	....
2000-01	Kladno	Czech	45	6	10	16	22	....	....	....	....	....
2001-02	Kladno	Czech	20	3	1	4	14	....	....	....	....	....
	HC Ocelari Trinec	Czech	28	3	6	9	18	6	1	0	1	2
2002-03	HC Hame Zlin	Czech	13	2	1	3	0	....	....	....	....	....
	Karlovy Vary	Czech	12	1	0	1	2	....	....	....	....	....
	Beroun	Czech-2	12	3	3	6	12	....	....	....	....	....
	Beroun	Czech-Q	6	0	2	2	2	....	....	....	....	....

VODRAZKA, Jan (voh-DRAZ-kuh, YAHN)

Defense. Shoots left. 6'1", 200 lbs. Born, Plzen, Czech., November 10, 1976.

			Regular Season					Playoffs				
Season	Club	League	GP	G	A	TP	PIM	GP	G	A	TP	PIM
1994-95	HC Plzen Jr.	Czech-Jr.	STATISTICS NOT AVAILABLE									
1995-96	Detroit Whalers	OHL	47	5	11	16	117	17	2	3	5	29
1996-97	Detroit Whalers	OHL	61	7	21	28	238	5	0	1	1	17
	Richmond	ECHL	4	0	0	0	12	7	0	1	1	36
1997-98	Milwaukee	IHL	10	0	0	0	32	....	....	....	....	....
	Madison Monsters	UHL	55	3	15	18	224	6	1	1	2	36
1998-99	Pee Dee Pride	ECHL	64	8	12	20	262	13	0	0	0	56
99-2000	Kansas City Blades	IHL	66	2	8	10	280	....	....	....	....	....
2000-01	Kansas City Blades	IHL	65	3	11	14	227	....	....	....	....	....
	Kentucky	AHL	6	0	0	0	31	....	....	....	....	....
2001-02	Florida Everblades	ECHL	4	0	0	0	6	....	....	....	....	....
	Lowell	AHL	49	1	3	4	152	5	0	0	0	2
2002-03	Saint John Flames	AHL	80	1	4	5	169	....	....	....	....	....

Signed as a free agent by **Milwaukee** (IHL), October 5, 1997. Signed as a free agent by **Kansas City** (IHL), September 15, 1999. Signed as a free agent by **Lowell** (AHL), August 10, 2001. Signed as a free agent by **Calgary**, September 9, 2002.

VOLKOV, Konstantin (VOHL-kahv, kawn-stuhn-TIHN) TOR.

Right wing. Shoots left. 6', 174 lbs. Born, Kolpino, USSR, February 7, 1985.
(Toronto's 3rd choice, 125th overall, in 2003 Entry Draft).

			Regular Season					Playoffs				
Season	Club	League	GP	G	A	TP	PIM	GP	G	A	TP	PIM
2001-02	Dynamo Moscow 2	Russia-3	21	3	7	10	10	....	....	....	....	....
2002-03	Dynamo Moscow 2	Russia-3	29	13	17	30	2	....	....	....	....	....

VOLRAB, Daniel (VOHL-rab, DAN-yehl) DAL.

Center. Shoots left. 6', 182 lbs. Born, Decin, Czech., March 11, 1983.
(Dallas' 4th choice, 126th overall, in 2001 Entry Draft).

			Regular Season					Playoffs				
Season	Club	League	GP	G	A	TP	PIM	GP	G	A	TP	PIM
1994-95	HC Decin-14	Czech-Jr.	28	16	15	31	....	....	....	....	....	....
1995-96	HC Decin-14	Czech-Jr.	28	32	15	47	....	....	....	....	....	....
1996-97	Litvinov-14	Czech-Jr.	3	10	1	11	....	....	....	....	....	....
	Litvinov-18	Czech-Jr.	32	24	24	48	....	....	....	....	....	....
1997-98	Litvinov-18	Czech-Jr.	10	8	7	15	....	....	....	....	....	....
	Litvinov-Jr.	Czech-Jr.	35	4	3	7	....	....	....	....	....	....
1998-99	Litvinov Jr.	Czech-Jr.	7	1	1	2	....	....	....	....	....	....
	Sparta Praha Jr.	Czech-Jr.	37	23	20	43	....	....	....	....	....	....
99-2000	Sparta Praha Jr.	Czech-Jr.	39	33	25	58	18	7	4	6	10	2
2000-01	Sparta Praha Jr.	Czech-Jr.	27	9	10	19	30	2	1	0	1	0
	HC Sparta Praha	Czech	1	0	0	0	0	....	....	....	....	....
2001-02	Saskatoon Blades	WHL	72	13	28	41	61	7	1	1	2	6
2002-03	Saskatoon Blades	WHL	72	13	22	35	55	6	2	3	5	4

VONDRKA, Michal (VOHND-rah-ka, MEE-khahl) BUF.

Left wing. Shoots right. 6', 178 lbs. Born, Ceske Budejovice, Czech., May 17, 1983.
(Buffalo's 5th choice, 155th overall, in 2001 Entry Draft).

			Regular Season					Playoffs				
Season	Club	League	GP	G	A	TP	PIM	GP	G	A	TP	PIM
1998-99	C. Budejovice-18	Czech-Jr.	50	28	15	43	....	....	....	....	....	....
99-2000	C. Budejovice Jr.	Czech-Jr.	31	12	7	19	16	....	....	....	....	....
2000-01	C. Budejovice Jr.	Czech-Jr.	37	9	14	23	37	....	....	....	....	....
	Ceske Budejovice	Czech	8	1	0	1	2	....	....	....	....	....
	Hradec Kralove	Czech-2	1	0	1	1	2	....	....	....	....	....
2001-02	C. Budejovice Jr.	Czech-Jr.	14	3	9	12	8	....	....	....	....	....
	IHC Pisek	Czech-2	2	1	0	1	0	....	....	....	....	....
	Ceske Budejovice	Czech	33	1	1	2	2	....	....	....	....	....
2002-03	Ceske Budejovice	Czech	27	1	3	4	4	3	0	0	0	0
	C. Budejovice Jr.	Czech-Jr.	7	4	1	5	4	....	....	....	....	....
	IHC Pisek	Czech-2	20	4	2	6	39	3	1	0	1	0

VOROBIEV, Pavel (voh-roh-BEE-ehf, PAH-vehl) CHI.

Right wing. Shoots left. 6', 183 lbs. Born, Karaganda, USSR, May 5, 1982.
(Chicago's 2nd choice, 11th overall, in 2000 Entry Draft).

			Regular Season					Playoffs				
Season	Club	League	GP	G	A	TP	PIM	GP	G	A	TP	PIM
1996-97	Molot-Perm 2	Russia-3	2	0	0	0	0	....	....	....	....	....
1997-98	Yaroslavl 2	Russia-2	16	2	0	2	6	....	....	....	....	....
1998-99	Yaroslavl 2	Russia-3	17	0	1	1	0	....	....	....	....	....
99-2000	Yaroslavl 2	Russia-3	40	19	15	34	20	....	....	....	....	....
	Torpedo Yaroslavl	Russia	8	2	0	2	4	10	2	2	4	0
2000-01	Yaroslavl	Russia	36	8	8	16	28	10	4	1	5	8
2001-02	Yaroslavl	Russia	9	3	2	5	6	7	0	0	0	4
2002-03	Yaroslavl	Russia	44	10	18	28	10	7	0	1	1	2

VOROS, Aaron (VOH-ruhs, AIR-uhn) N.J.

Center. Shoots left. 6'3", 178 lbs. Born, Vancouver, B.C., July 2, 1981.
(New Jersey's 10th choice, 229th overall, in 2001 Entry Draft).

			Regular Season					Playoffs				
Season	Club	League	GP	G	A	TP	PIM	GP	G	A	TP	PIM
1998-99	Nor-West Caps	PIJHL	STATISTICS NOT AVAILABLE									
99-2000	Victoria Salsa	BCHL	58	14	21	35	285	....	....	....	....	....
2000-01	Victoria Salsa	BCHL	57	34	34	68	....	30	16	15	31	....
2001-02	Alaska-Fairbanks	CCHA	37	18	12	30	*101	....	....	....	....	....
2002-03	Alaska-Fairbanks	CCHA	16	2	5	7	42	....	....	....	....	....

BCHL Coastal Conference Second All-Star Team (2001) • CCHA All-Rookie Team (2002)
Missed majority of 2002-03 season recovering from leg surgery, January 30, 2003.

VOSTRIKOV, Artem (VAWS-trih-kawv, ahr-TEHM) CBJ

Center. Shoots left. 6'1", 175 lbs. Born, Togliatti, Russia, March 23, 1983.
(Columbus' 8th choice, 187th overall, in 2001 Entry Draft).

			Regular Season					Playoffs				
Season	Club	League	GP	G	A	TP	PIM	GP	G	A	TP	PIM
99-2000	Lada Togliatti 2	Russia-3	STATISTICS NOT AVAILABLE									
2000-01	Lada Togliatti 2	Russia-3	STATISTICS NOT AVAILABLE									
2001-02	Lada Togliatti	Russia	12	1	1	2	0	....	....	....	....	....
	CSK VVS Samara	Russia-2	23	1	4	5	40	....	....	....	....	....
2002-03	Spartak Moscow	Russia	20	2	3	5	0	....	....	....	....	....

VRANA, Petr (vuh-RA-nuh, PEE-tuhr) N.J.

Left wing. Shoots left. 5'10", 175 lbs. Born, Sternberk, Czech., March 29, 1985.
(New Jersey's 2nd choice, 42nd overall, in 2003 Entry Draft).

			Regular Season					Playoffs				
Season	Club	League	GP	G	A	TP	PIM	GP	G	A	TP	PIM
99-2000	HC Olomouc Jr.	Czech-Jr.	43	12	18	30	24	....	....	....	....	....
2000-01	HC Olomouc Jr.	Czech-Jr.	41	38	48	86	32	3	1	3	4	6
2001-02	Havirov-16	Czech-A	6	10	9	19	....	....	....	....	....	....
	Havirov-Jr.	Czech-Jr.	38	11	12	23	....	....	....	....	....	....
	HC Femax Havirov	Czech	6	0	0	0	4	....	....	....	....	....
2002-03	Halifax	QMJHL	72	37	46	83	32	24	5	15	20	12

QMJHL All-Rookie Team (2003) • QMJHL Rookie of the Year (2003)

VYDARENY, Rene (vih-DAH-reh-nay, REH-nay) VAN.

Defense. Shoots left. 6'1", 198 lbs. Born, Bratislava, Czech., May 6, 1981.
(Vancouver's 3rd choice, 69th overall, in 1999 Entry Draft).

			Regular Season					Playoffs				
Season	Club	League	GP	G	A	TP	PIM	GP	G	A	TP	PIM
1997-98	S. Bratislava Jr.	Slovak-Jr.	50	5	14	19	26	....	....	....	....	....
1998-99	S. Bratislava Jr.	Slovak-Jr.	42	4	7	11	65	2	0	0	0	2
	HK Kabat Trnava	Slovak-2	20	1	6	7	6	....	....	....	....	....
99-2000	Rimouski Oceanic	QMJHL	51	7	23	30	41	14	2	2	4	20
2000-01	Kansas City Blades	IHL	39	0	1	1	25	....	....	....	....	....
2001-02	Manitoba Moose	AHL	61	3	11	14	15	7	0	2	2	4
	Columbia Inferno	ECHL	10	2	1	3	9	....	....	....	....	....
2002-03	Manitoba Moose	AHL	71	2	8	10	46	14	0	2	2	16

• Missed majority of 2000-01 season due to dispute over ownership of playing rights between **Vancouver** and **HC Bratislava** (Slovakia), November 28, 2000.

WALLIN, Viktor (WAHL-in, VIHK-tohr) ANA.

Defense. Shoots left. 6'3", 200 lbs. Born, Jonkoping, Sweden, January 17, 1980.
(Anaheim's 3rd choice, 112th overall, in 1998 Entry Draft).

			Regular Season					Playoffs				
Season	Club	League	GP	G	A	TP	PIM	GP	G	A	TP	PIM
1996-97	HV 71 Jr.	Swede-Jr.	16	1	2	3	....	....	....	....	....	....
1997-98	HV 71 Jr.	Swede-Jr.	28	9	15	24	42	....	....	....	....	....
1998-99	HV 71 Jonkoping	Sweden	23	0	0	0	4	....	....	....	....	....
99-2000	HV 71 Jr.	Swede-Jr.	6	3	1	4	2	....	....	....	....	....
	HV 71 Jonkoping	Sweden	43	2	2	4	16	6	1	1	2	4
2000-01	HV 71 Jonkoping	Sweden	5	0	1	1	2	....	....	....	....	....
2001-02	Timra IK	Sweden	35	0	3	3	18	....	....	....	....	....
	Timra IK	Swede-Q	10	0	1	1	9	....	....	....	....	....
2002-03	AIK Solna	Swede-2	50	3	15	18	34	4	0	0	0	4

WALSH, Brendan (WAHLSH, BREHN-duhn)

Right wing. Shoots right. 5'9", 181 lbs. Born, Dorchester, MA, October 22, 1974.

			Regular Season					Playoffs				
Season	Club	League	GP	G	A	TP	PIM	GP	G	A	TP	PIM
1995-96	Boston University	H-East	38	8	16	24	90	....	....	....	....	....
1996-97	Boston University	H-East	27	5	8	13	83	....	....	....	....	....
1997-98	U. of Maine	H-East	DID NOT PLAY – TRANSFERRED COLLEGES									
1998-99	U. of Maine	H-East	30	7	13	20	58	....	....	....	....	....
99-2000	U. of Maine	H-East	39	9	21	30	*106	....	....	....	....	....
2000-01	Jackson Bandits	ECHL	25	3	6	9	179	....	....	....	....	....
	Cleveland	IHL	10	1	1	2	45	4	0	0	0	11
2001-02	Wheeling Nailers	ECHL	29	7	15	22	168	....	....	....	....	....
	Wilkes-Barre	AHL	29	2	2	4	184	....	....	....	....	....
2002-03	San Antonio	AHL	48	2	5	7	202	3	0	1	1	0
	Atlantic City	ECHL	6	0	2	2	40	....	....	....	....	....

Signed as a free agent by **Minnesota**, May 18, 2000.

WALSH, Mike (WAHLSH, MIGHK) NYR

Left wing. Shoots left. 6'2", 194 lbs. Born, Royal Oak, MI, March 4, 1983.
(NY Rangers' 4th choice, 143rd overall, in 2002 Entry Draft).

			Regular Season					Playoffs				
Season	Club	League	GP	G	A	TP	PIM	GP	G	A	TP	PIM
2000-01	Det. Compuware	NAJHL	50	10	12	22	59	3	1	0	1	4
2001-02	Det. Compuware	NAJHL	53	25	25	49	69	6	4	2	6	8
2002-03	U. of Notre Dame	CCHA	23	1	1	2	14	....	....	....	....	....

WALSH, Tom (WAHLSH, TAWM) S.J.

Defense. Shoots left. 6', 190 lbs. Born, Arlington, MA, April 22, 1983.
(San Jose's 5th choice, 163rd overall, in 2002 Entry Draft).

			Regular Season					Playoffs				
Season	Club	League	GP	G	A	TP	PIM	GP	G	A	TP	PIM
2001-02	Deerfield Academy	Hi-School	21	3	18	21	8	....	....	....	....	....
2002-03	Harvard Crimson	ECAC	32	1	6	7	30	....	....	....	....	....

WARREN, Morgan (WAWR-ihn, MOHR-gan)

Right wing. Shoots right. 6'2", 193 lbs. Born, Summerside, P.E.I., March 6, 1980.
(Toronto's 5th choice, 126th overall, in 1998 Entry Draft).

			Regular Season					Playoffs				
Season	Club	League	GP	G	A	TP	PIM	GP	G	A	TP	PIM
1996-97	Quinte Hawks	MTJHL	49	32	38	70	65	....	....	....	....	....
1997-98	Moncton Wildcats	QMJHL	58	11	10	21	80	10	2	2	4	2
1998-99	Moncton Wildcats	QMJHL	48	20	16	36	68	1	0	0	0	2
99-2000	Moncton Wildcats	QMJHL	65	29	36	65	53	16	7	5	12	4
2000-01	St. John's	AHL	57	2	10	12	16	4	0	0	0	0
2001-02	St. John's	AHL	80	11	14	25	46	11	0	0	0	8
2002-03	St. John's	AHL	58	8	8	16	16	....	....	....	....	....

WATSON, Dan (WAWT-suhn, DAN)

Defense. Shoots right. 6'2", 220 lbs. Born, Glencoe, Ont., October 5, 1979.

			Regular Season					Playoffs				
Season	Club	League	GP	G	A	TP	PIM	GP	G	A	TP	PIM
1995-96	Strathroy Rockets	OJHL-B	46	6	13	19	12	....	....	....	....	....
1996-97	Strathroy Rockets	OJHL-B	49	5	25	30	33	....	....	....	....	....
	Sarnia Sting	OHL	10	0	2	2	7	....	....	....	....	....
1997-98	Sarnia Sting	OHL	66	6	15	21	19	5	0	1	1	4
1998-99	Sarnia Sting	OHL	68	2	18	20	27	6	0	0	0	4
99-2000	Sarnia Sting	OHL	68	1	15	16	40	7	0	0	0	4
2000-01	Elmira Jackals	UHL	1	0	0	0	0	....	....	....	....	....
	Syracuse Crunch	AHL	59	3	4	7	12	4	0	0	0	6
2001-02	Dayton Bombers	ECHL	4	0	0	0	6	....	....	....	....	....
	Syracuse Crunch	AHL	53	1	3	4	25	....	....	....	....	....
2002-03	Syracuse Crunch	AHL	50	2	7	9	36	....	....	....	....	....
	Cleveland Barons	AHL	17	2	4	6	12	....	....	....	....	....

Signed as a free agent by **Columbus**, May 29, 2000.

WATSON, Greg (WAWT-suhn, GREHG) OTT.

Center. Shoots left. 6'2", 198 lbs. Born, Eastend, Sask., March 2, 1983.
(Florida's 3rd choice, 34th overall, in 2001 Entry Draft).

			Regular Season					Playoffs				
Season	Club	League	GP	G	A	TP	PIM	GP	G	A	TP	PIM
1998-99	Calgary Buffaloes	AMHL	71	23	23	46	120	....	....	....	....	....
	Prince Albert	WHL	2	0	0	0	5	....	....	....	....	....
99-2000	Prince Albert	WHL	67	10	5	15	63	6	0	2	2	2
2000-01	Prince Albert	WHL	71	22	28	50	72	....	....	....	....	....
2001-02	Prince Albert	WHL	51	22	30	52	88	....	....	....	....	....
2002-03	Prince Albert	WHL	39	11	15	26	58	....	....	....	....	....
	Brandon	WHL	30	6	14	20	37	17	3	8	11	12

Traded to **Ottawa** by **Florida** with Billy Thompson for Jani Hurme, October 1, 2002.

WAUGH, Geoff (WAW, JEHF) DAL.

Defense. Shoots right. 6'3", 210 lbs. Born, Winnipeg, Man., August 25, 1983.
(Dallas' 6th choice, 78th overall, in 2002 Entry Draft).

			Regular Season					Playoffs				
Season	Club	League	GP	G	A	TP	PIM	GP	G	A	TP	PIM
2000-01	Kindersley Klippers	SJHL	57	2	5	7	74	....	....	....	....	....
2001-02	Kindersley Klippers	SJHL	59	4	21	25	125	18	0	8	8	59
2002-03	Northern Michigan	CCHA	39	0	7	7	41	....	....	....	....	....

SJHL West First All-Star Team (2002)

WEBER, Shea (WEH-buhr, SHAY) NSH.

Defense. Shoots right. 6'3", 195 lbs. Born, Sicamous, B.C., August 14, 1985.
(Nashville's 4th choice, 49th overall, in 2003 Entry Draft).

			Regular Season					Playoffs				
Season	Club	League	GP	G	A	TP	PIM	GP	G	A	TP	PIM
2001-02	Sicamous Eagles	KIJHL	47	9	33	42	87	....	....	....	....	....
	Kelowna Rockets	WHL	5	0	0	0	0	....	....	....	....	....
2002-03	Kelowna Rockets	WHL	70	2	16	18	167	19	1	4	5	26

WELCH, Dan (WEHLCH, DAN) L.A.

Right wing. Shoots right. 5'10", 199 lbs. Born, Lansing, MI, February 23, 1981.
(Los Angeles' 9th choice, 245th overall, in 2000 Entry Draft).

			Regular Season					Playoffs				
Season	Club	League	GP	G	A	TP	PIM	GP	G	A	TP	PIM
1996/99	Hastings Huskies	Hi-School	90	76	123	199	....	....	....	....	....	....
99-2000	U. of Minnesota	WCHA	36	6	8	14	31	....	....	....	....	....
2000-01	Omaha Lancers	USHL	52	30	27	57	103	12	9	13	22	20
2001-02	U. of Minnesota	WCHA	19	4	7	11	12	....	....	....	....	....
	Omaha Lancers	USHL	7	4	2	6	8	....	....	....	....	....
2002-03	U. of Minnesota	WCHA	18	5	5	10	12	....	....	....	....	....
	Manchester	AHL	42	3	9	12	22	3	0	0	0	0

• Statistics for **Hastings** (Hi-School) are career totals for 1996-1999 seasons. • Ruled academically ineligible to play 2000-01 WCHA season by U. of Minnesota (WCHA). • Dismissed from U. of Minnesota (WCHA) hockey program for academic violations, January 3, 2003.

WELCH, Noah (WEHLCH, NOH-ah) PIT.

Defense. Shoots left. 6'4", 212 lbs. Born, Brighton, MA, August 26, 1982.
(Pittsburgh's 2nd choice, 54th overall, in 2001 Entry Draft).

			Regular Season					Playoffs				
Season	Club	League	GP	G	A	TP	PIM	GP	G	A	TP	PIM
99-2000	St. Sebastian's	Hi-School	26	4	11	15	35	....	....	....	....	....
	Eastern-Mass	MBAHL	4	0	3	3	6	....	....	....	....	....
2000-01	St. Sebastian's	Hi-School	30	11	20	31	37	....	....	....	....	....
2001-02	Harvard Crimson	ECAC	27	5	6	11	56	....	....	....	....	....
2002-03	Harvard Crimson	ECAC	34	6	22	28	70	....	....	....	....	....

ECAC All-Rookie Team (2002) • NCAA East Second All-American Team (2003)

WELLAR, Patrick (WEHL-uhr, PAT-rihk) WSH.

Defense. Shoots left. 6'3", 210 lbs. Born, Carrot River, Sask., April 12, 1983.
(Washington's 5th choice, 77th overall, in 2002 Entry Draft).

			Regular Season					Playoffs				
Season	Club	League	GP	G	A	TP	PIM	GP	G	A	TP	PIM
99-2000	Sask. Contacts	SMHL	44	5	15	20	120	....	....	....	....	....
	Portland	WHL	1	0	0	0	0	....	....	....	....	....
2000-01	Portland	WHL	57	2	7	9	65	10	0	1	1	13
2001-02	Portland	WHL	61	3	10	13	125	7	0	2	2	4
2002-03	Portland	WHL	11	1	4	5	31	....	....	....	....	....
	Calgary Hitmen	WHL	49	3	11	14	88	5	0	0	0	15

WELLER, Craig (WEH-luhr, KRAIG) NYR

Defense. Shoots right. 6'3", 195 lbs. Born, Calgary, Alta., January 17, 1981.
(St. Louis' 6th choice, 167th overall, in 2000 Entry Draft).

			Regular Season					Playoffs				
Season	Club	League	GP	G	A	TP	PIM	GP	G	A	TP	PIM
1997-98	Calgary Flames	AMHL	33	2	10	12	65	3	0	1	1	2
1998-99	Calgary Canucks	AJHL	49	4	14	18	80	13	0	1	1	10
99-2000	Calgary Canucks	AJHL	53	3	14	17	100	4	0	0	0	4
2000-01	U. Minn-Duluth	WCHA	6	0	1	1	0	....	....	....	....	....
	Kootenay Ice	WHL	30	1	5	6	40	11	0	2	2	26
2001-02	Kootenay Ice	WHL	69	5	13	18	127	22	3	7	10	27
2002-03	Hartford Wolf Pack	AHL	11	0	0	0	8	2	0	0	0	0
	Charlotte	ECHL	48	3	11	14	84	....	....	....	....	....

WHL West Second All-Star Team (2002)

• Left **Minnesota-Duluth** (WCHA) and signed as a free agent by **Kootenay** (WHL), January 7, 2001. Signed as a free agent by **NY Rangers**, July 11, 2002.

WELLWOOD, Kyle (WEHL-wud, KIGHL) TOR.

Center. Shoots right. 5'10", 190 lbs. Born, Windsor, Ont., May 16, 1983.
(Toronto's 6th choice, 134th overall, in 2001 Entry Draft).

			Regular Season					Playoffs				
Season	Club	League	GP	G	A	TP	PIM	GP	G	A	TP	PIM
1998-99	Tecumseh	OJHL-B	51	22	41	63	12	....	....	....	....	....
99-2000	Belleville Bulls	OHL	65	14	37	51	14	16	3	7	10	6
2000-01	Belleville Bulls	OHL	68	35	*83	*118	24	10	3	16	19	4
2001-02	Belleville Bulls	OHL	28	16	24	40	4	....	....	....	....	....
	Windsor Spitfires	OHL	26	14	21	35	0	16	12	12	24	0
2002-03	Windsor Spitfires	OHL	57	41	59	100	0	7	5	9	14	0

OHL First All-Star Team (2001)

WENNERBERG, Mattias (VEH-nuhr-buhrg, MA-tee-uhs) CHI.

Center. Shoots left. 5'11", 191 lbs. Born, Uma, Sweden, August 6, 1981.
(Chicago's 6th choice, 194th overall, in 1999 Entry Draft).

			Regular Season					Playoffs				
Season	Club	League	GP	G	A	TP	PIM	GP	G	A	TP	PIM
1996-97	Vilhelmina HC	Swede-4	20	7	12	19	14	....	....	....	....	....
1997-98	MoDo Jr.	Swede-Jr.	30	10	17	27	....	....	....	....	....	....
1998-99	MoDo Jr.	Swede-Jr.	43	13	12	25	....	....	....	....	....	....
99-2000	MoDo Jr.	Swede-Jr.	32	14	6	20	102	....	....	....	....	....
2000-01	Bodens IK	Swede-2	34	9	4	13	36	....	....	....	....	....
2001-02	IF Bjorkloven Umea	Swede-2	21	8	10	18	43	....	....	....	....	....
	MoDo	Sweden	24	2	2	4	16	13	4	4	8	*39
2002-03	MoDo	Sweden	50	17	8	25	30	6	0	0	0	2

WERNER, Steve (WUHR-nuhr, STEEV) WSH.

Right wing. Shoots right. 6', 197 lbs. Born, Washington, DC, August 8, 1984.
(Washington's 2nd choice, 83rd overall, in 2003 Entry Draft).

			Regular Season					Playoffs				
Season	Club	League	GP	G	A	TP	PIM	GP	G	A	TP	PIM
99-2000	Wsh. Jr. Capitals	MetroHL	42	32	45	77	....	....	....	....	....	....
2000-01	U.S. National U-17	USDP	69	12	23	35	26	....	....	....	....	....
2001-02	U.S. National U-18	USDP	54	16	20	36	42	....	....	....	....	....
2002-03	Massachusetts	H-East	37	16	22	38	4	....	....	....	....	....

WESTRUM, Erik (WEHST-ruhm, AIR-ihk) PHX.

Center. Shoots left. 6', 204 lbs. Born, Minneapolis, MN, July 26, 1979.
(Phoenix's 9th choice, 187th overall, in 1998 Entry Draft).

			Regular Season					Playoffs				
Season	Club	League	GP	G	A	TP	PIM	GP	G	A	TP	PIM
1995/97	Apple Valley	Hi-School	78	56	84	140	....	....	....	....	....	....
1997-98	U. of Minnesota	WCHA	39	6	12	18	43	....	....	....	....	....
1998-99	U. of Minnesota	WCHA	41	10	26	36	81	....	....	....	....	....
99-2000	U. of Minnesota	WCHA	39	27	26	53	99	....	....	....	....	....
2000-01	U. of Minnesota	WCHA	42	26	35	61	84	....	....	....	....	....
2001-02	Springfield Falcons	AHL	73	13	29	42	116	....	....	....	....	....
2002-03	Springfield Falcons	AHL	70	10	22	32	65	6	0	4	4	6

• Statistics for **Apple Valley** (Hi-School) are career totals for 1995-1997 seasons. • WCHA Second All-Star Team (2001)

WHITE, Ian (WIGHT, EE-uhn) TOR.

Defense. Shoots right. 5'10", 185 lbs. Born, Winnipeg, Man., June 4, 1984.
(Toronto's 6th choice, 191st overall, in 2002 Entry Draft).

			Regular Season					Playoffs				
Season	Club	League	GP	G	A	TP	PIM	GP	G	A	TP	PIM
2000-01	Swift Current	WHL	69	12	31	43	24	....	....	....	....	....
2001-02	Swift Current	WHL	70	32	47	79	40	12	4	5	9	12
2002-03	Swift Current	WHL	64	24	44	68	44	4	0	4	4	0

WHL East Second All-Star Team (2002) • WHL East First All-Star Team (2003)

WHITNEY, Ryan (WIHT-nee, RIGH-uhn) PIT.

Defense. Shoots left. 6'4", 202 lbs. Born, Boston, MA, February 19, 1983.
(Pittsburgh's 1st choice, 5th overall, in 2002 Entry Draft).

			Regular Season					Playoffs				
Season	Club	League	GP	G	A	TP	PIM	GP	G	A	TP	PIM
99-2000	Thayer Academy	Hi-School	22	5	33	38	....	....	....	....	....	....
2000-01	U.S. National U-17	USDP	60	9	31	40	86	....	....	....	....	....
2001-02	Boston University	H-East	35	4	17	21	46	....	....	....	....	....
2002-03	Boston University	H-East	34	3	10	13	48	....	....	....	....	....

Hockey East All-Rookie Team (2002)

WICHSER, Adrian (WIH-shuhr, A-dree-uhn) FLA.

Center. Shoots left. 6', 180 lbs. Born, Winterthur, Switz., March 18, 1980.
(Florida's 9th choice, 231st overall, in 1998 Entry Draft).

			Regular Season					Playoffs				
Season	Club	League	GP	G	A	TP	PIM	GP	G	A	TP	PIM
1997-98	EHC Kloten	Swiss	35	6	5	11	31	7	0	1	1	8
1998-99	EHC Kloten	Swiss	40	11	14	25	14	9	7	0	7	8
	Kloten Flyers Jr.	Swiss-Jr.	....	....	....	....	....	1	1	2	3	2
99-2000	EHC Kloten	Swiss	33	8	15	23	12	6	2	1	3	0
2000-01	EHC Kloten	Swiss	31	9	9	18	12	9	2	3	5	0
2001-02	Kloten Flyers	Swiss	41	18	27	45	16	11	4	4	8	2
2002-03	HC Lugano	Swiss	44	*26	17	43	4	15	2	2	4	2

WIDEMAN, Dennis (WIGHD-muhn, DEH-nihs) BUF.

Defense. Shoots right. 6', 200 lbs. Born, Kitchener, Ont., March 20, 1983.
(Buffalo's 9th choice, 241st overall, in 2002 Entry Draft).

			Regular Season					Playoffs				
Season	Club	League	GP	G	A	TP	PIM	GP	G	A	TP	PIM
1998-99	Elmira Sugar Kings	OJHL-B	47	18	30	48	142	....	....	....	....	....
99-2000	Sudbury Wolves	OHL	63	10	26	36	64	12	1	2	3	22
2000-01	Sudbury Wolves	OHL	25	7	11	18	37	....	....	....	....	....
	London Knights	OHL	24	8	8	16	38	5	0	4	4	6
2001-02	London Knights	OHL	65	27	42	69	141	12	4	9	13	26
2002-03	London Knights	OHL	55	20	27	47	83	14	6	6	12	10

WIDING, Daniel (VEE-dihng, DAN-yehl) NSH.

Right wing. Shoots right. 6'1", 197 lbs. Born, Gavle, Sweden, April 13, 1982.
(Nashville's 2nd choice, 36th overall, in 2000 Entry Draft).

			Regular Season					Playoffs				
Season	Club	League	GP	G	A	TP	PIM	GP	G	A	TP	PIM
99-2000	Leksands IF-18	Swede-Jr.	6	2	1	3	20	....	....	....	....	....
	Leksands IF Jr.	Swede-Jr.	34	15	12	27	65	2	1	0	1	4
	Leksands IF	Sweden	3	0	0	0	2	....	....	....	....	....
2000-01	Leksands IF Jr.	Swede-Jr.	6	2	3	5	31	....	....	....	....	....
	Leksands IF	Sweden	40	6	5	11	18	....	....	....	....	....
2001-02	Leksands IF Jr.	Swede-Jr.	3	2	6	8	2	....	....	....	....	....
	Leksands IF	Swede-2	55	12	12	24	92	....	....	....	....	....
2002-03	Leksands IF	Sweden	47	2	2	4	8	5	0	0	0	2
	Leksands IF Jr.	Swede-Jr.	2	0	1	1	4	....	....	....	....	....

WILFORD, Marty (WIHL-fohrd, MAHR-tee)

Defense. Shoots left. 6'1", 216 lbs. Born, Cobourg, Ont., April 17, 1977.
(Chicago's 7th choice, 149th overall, in 1995 Entry Draft).

			Regular Season					Playoffs				
Season	Club	League	GP	G	A	TP	PIM	GP	G	A	TP	PIM
1993-94	Peterborough	OPJHL	40	3	19	22	*107	....	....	....	....	....
1994-95	Oshawa Generals	OHL	63	1	6	7	95	7	1	1	2	4
1995-96	Oshawa Generals	OHL	65	3	24	27	107	5	0	1	1	4
1996-97	Oshawa Generals	OHL	62	19	43	62	126	16	2	18	20	28
1997-98	Columbus Chill	ECHL	46	8	27	35	123	....	....	....	....	....
	Indianapolis Ice	IHL	26	0	4	4	16	....	....	....	....	....
1998-99	Indianapolis Ice	IHL	80	3	13	16	116	7	0	1	1	16
99-2000	Cleveland	IHL	7	0	3	3	24	....	....	....	....	....
	Houston Aeros	IHL	45	0	9	9	30	11	2	2	4	18
2000-01	Norfolk Admirals	AHL	80	7	41	48	102	9	1	5	6	8
2001-02	Milwaukee	AHL	8	1	3	4	12	....	....	....	....	....
	St. John's	AHL	60	4	21	25	70	....	....	....	....	....
	Hartford Wolf Pack	AHL	9	0	2	2	2	10	3	3	6	4
2002-03	Norfolk Admirals	AHL	80	13	35	48	87	9	0	3	3	16

OHL Second All-Star Team (1997)

Traded to **Toronto** by **Chicago** for Shawn Thornton, September 30, 2001. Traded to **Nashville** by **Toronto** with D.J. Smith for Marc Moro, March 1, 2002.

WINCHESTER, Brad (WIHN-chehst-uhr, BRAD) EDM.

Left wing. Shoots left. 6'5", 215 lbs. Born, Madison, WI, March 1, 1981.
(Edmonton's 2nd choice, 35th overall, in 2000 Entry Draft).

			Regular Season					Playoffs				
Season	Club	League	GP	G	A	TP	PIM	GP	G	A	TP	PIM
1997-98	U.S. National U-18	USDP	74	22	23	45	162	....	....	....	....	....
1998-99	U.S. National U-18	USDP	65	21	23	44	103	....	....	....	....	....
99-2000	U. of Wisconsin	WCHA	33	9	9	18	48	....	....	....	....	....
2000-01	U. of Wisconsin	WCHA	41	7	9	16	71	....	....	....	....	....
2001-02	U. of Wisconsin	WCHA	38	14	20	34	38	....	....	....	....	....
2002-03	U. of Wisconsin	WCHA	38	10	6	16	58	....	....	....	....	....

WISNIEWSKI, James (wihs-NEHV-skee, JAYMS) **CHI.**

Defense. Shoots right. 5'11", 197 lbs. Born, Canton, MI, February 21, 1984.
(Chicago's 5th choice, 156th overall, in 2002 Entry Draft).

			Regular Season					Playoffs				
Season	Club	League	GP	G	A	TP	PIM	GP	G	A	TP	PIM
99-2000	Det. Compuware	NAJHL	50	5	11	16	67	5	0	3	3	4
2000-01	Plymouth Whalers	OHL	53	6	23	29	72	19	3	10	13	34
2001-02	Plymouth Whalers	OHL	62	11	25	36	100	6	1	2	3	6
2002-03	Plymouth Whalers	OHL	52	18	34	52	60	18	2	10	12	14

WOODFORD, Mike (WUD-fohrd, MIGHK) **FLA.**

Right wing. Shoots right. 5'11", 185 lbs. Born, Boston, MA, October 4, 1981.
(Florida's 6th choice, 117th overall, in 2001 Entry Draft).

			Regular Season					Playoffs				
Season	Club	League	GP	G	A	TP	PIM	GP	G	A	TP	PIM
99-2000	Cushing Academy	Hi-School	31	35	35	70	60	....	....	....	....	....
2000-01	Cushing Academy	Hi-School	36	34	39	73	68	....	....	....	....	....
2001-02	U. of Michigan	CCHA	43	8	11	19	46	....	....	....	....	....
2002-03	U. of Michigan	CCHA	37	5	12	17	73	....	....	....	....	....

WOYWITKA, Jeff (WOI-wiht-ka, JEHF) **PHI.**

Defense. Shoots left. 6'2", 209 lbs. Born, Vermilion, Alta., September 1, 1983.
(Philadelphia's 1st choice, 27th overall, in 2001 Entry Draft).

			Regular Season					Playoffs				
Season	Club	League	GP	G	A	TP	PIM	GP	G	A	TP	PIM
1998-99	Wainwright	AAHA	26	7	15	22	60	....	....	....	....	....
99-2000	Red Deer Rebels	WHL	67	4	12	16	40	4	0	3	3	2
2000-01	Red Deer Rebels	WHL	72	7	28	35	113	22	2	8	10	25
2001-02	Red Deer Rebels	WHL	72	14	23	37	109	23	2	10	12	22
2002-03	Red Deer Rebels	WHL	57	16	36	52	65	23	1	9	10	25

WHL East Second All-Star Team (2002) • WHL East First All-Star Team (2003)

YACHMENEV, Denis (YATCH-muh-nehv, DEH-nihs) **FLA.**

Left wing. Shoots left. 6'1", 185 lbs. Born, Chelyabinsk, USSR, June 4, 1984.
(Florida's 9th choice, 200th overall, in 2002 Entry Draft).

			Regular Season					Playoffs				
Season	Club	League	GP	G	A	TP	PIM	GP	G	A	TP	PIM
2000-01	Chelyabinsk 2	Russia-3	36	40	27	67	....	....	....	....	....	....
2001-02	North Bay	OHL	65	17	12	29	32	5	2	0	2	0
2002-03	Saginaw Spirit	OHL	68	17	28	45	69	....	....	....	....	....

YAKUBOV, Mikhail (yuh-KOO-bahf, mih-KIGH-eel) **CHI.**

Center. Shoots left. 6'3", 204 lbs. Born, Barnaul, USSR, February 16, 1982.
(Chicago's 1st choice, 10th overall, in 2000 Entry Draft).

			Regular Season					Playoffs				
Season	Club	League	GP	G	A	TP	PIM	GP	G	A	TP	PIM
1997-98	Lada Togliatti 2	Russia-3	7	0	0	0	0	....	....	....	....	....
1998-99	Lada Togliatti 2	Russia-4	38	11	4	15	32	....	....	....	....	....
99-2000	Lada Togliatti 2	Russia-3	26	12	19	31	14	....	....	....	....	....
2000-01	Lada Togliatti	Russia	25	0	0	0	4	4	0	0	0	0
2001-02	Red Deer Rebels	WHL	71	32	57	89	54	23	14	9	23	28
2002-03	Norfolk Admirals	AHL	62	6	5	11	36	9	0	0	0	8

WHL East Second All-Star Team (2002)

YERSHOV, Andrei (yuhr-SHAWF, AWN-dray) **CHI.**

Defense. Shoots left. 6', 216 lbs. Born, Voskresensk, USSR, August 22, 1976.
(Chicago's 9th choice, 240th overall, in 1998 Entry Draft).

			Regular Season					Playoffs				
Season	Club	League	GP	G	A	TP	PIM	GP	G	A	TP	PIM
1994-95	Voskresensk	CIS	16	0	0	0	6	....	....	....	....	....
1995-96	Voskresensk	CIS	18	1	0	1	28	....	....	....	....	....
1996-97	Voskresensk	Russia	23	3	1	4	32	2	0	0	0	2
1997-98	Voskresensk	Russia	45	5	8	13	60	....	....	....	....	....
1998-99	Voskresensk	Russia	33	6	6	12	88	....	....	....	....	....
99-2000	Lada Togliatti	Russia	10	0	1	1	12	4	0	0	0	6
2000-01	Vityaz Podolsk	Russia	30	1	5	6	32	....	....	....	....	....
2001-02	Voskresensk	Russia-2	62	18	15	33	101	....	....	....	....	....
	Voskresensk 2	Russia-3	1	0	1	1	4	....	....	....	....	....
2002-03	Voskresensk	Russia-2	46	3	8	11	36	....	....	....	....	....

YTFELDT, David (YOOT-fehld, DAY-vihd) **VAN.**

Defense. Shoots left. 6'1", 187 lbs. Born, Ornskoldsvik, Sweden, September 29, 1979.
(Vancouver's 6th choice, 136th overall, in 1998 Entry Draft).

			Regular Season					Playoffs				
Season	Club	League	GP	G	A	TP	PIM	GP	G	A	TP	PIM
1996-97	Leksands IF Jr.	Swede-Jr.	25	3	5	8	....	....	....	....	....	....
1997-98	Leksands IF Jr.	Swede-Jr.	23	13	10	23	101	....	....	....	....	....
	Leksands IF	Sweden	10	0	0	0	2	....	....	....	....	....
1998-99	Leksands IF	Sweden	39	0	4	4	65	4	0	1	1	4
99-2000	Leksands IF	Sweden	50	3	9	12	72	....	....	....	....	....
2000-01	V. Frolunda Jr.	Swede-Jr.	2	2	1	3	0	....	....	....	....	....
	JYP Jyvaskyla	Finland	11	0	4	4	26	....	....	....	....	....
	Vastra Frolunda	Sweden	9	0	1	1	8	5	0	1	1	4
2001-02	Linkopings HC	Sweden	8	0	0	0	4	....	....	....	....	....
2002-03	Nykoping	Swede-2	15	5	6	11	30	....	....	....	....	....

• Name when drafted was David Jonsson.

ZAINULLIN, Ruslan (zihj-NOO-luhn, roos-LAHN) **CGY.**

Right wing. Shoots left. 6'2", 202 lbs. Born, Kazan, USSR, February 14, 1982.
(Tampa Bay's 2nd choice, 34th overall, in 2000 Entry Draft).

			Regular Season					Playoffs				
Season	Club	League	GP	G	A	TP	PIM	GP	G	A	TP	PIM
1997-98	Ak Bars Kazan 2	Russia-3	27	0	1	1	2	....	....	....	....	....
1998-99	Ak Bars Kazan 2	Russia-4	36	13	8	21	22	....	....	....	....	....
99-2000	Ak Bars Kazan 2	Russia-3	12	13	6	19	....	....	....	....	....	....
	Ak Bars Kazan	Russia	14	1	1	2	4	....	....	....	....	....
2000-01	Ak Bars Kazan	Russia	29	1	3	4	14	1	0	0	0	0
2001-02	Ak Bars Kazan	Russia	21	0	2	2	8	3	0	0	0	2
2002-03	Ak Bars Kazan	Russia	4	0	1	1	2	....	....	....	....	....
	Nizhnekamsk	Russia	13	1	1	2	8	....	....	....	....	....

Traded to **Phoenix** by **Tampa Bay** with Mike Johnson, Paul Mara and NY Islanders' 2nd round choice (previously acquired, Phoenix selected Matthew Spiller) in 2001 Entry Draft for Nikolai Khabibulin and Stan Neckar, March 5, 2001. Rights traded to **Atlanta** by **Phoenix** with Kirill Safronov and Phoenix's 4th round choice (Patrick Dwyer) in 2002 Entry Draft for Darcy Hordichuk and Atlanta's 4th (Lance Monych) and 5th (John Zeiler) round choices in 2002 Entry Draft, March 19, 2002. Traded to **Calgary** by **Atlanta** for Marc Savard, November 15, 2002.

ZAKHAROV, Konstantin (za-KHAHR-awv, kawn-stuhn-TIHN) **ST.L.**

Left wing. Shoots right. 6'1", 185 lbs. Born, Minsk, USSR, May 2, 1985.
(St. Louis' 5th choice, 101st overall, in 2003 Entry Draft).

			Regular Season					Playoffs				
Season	Club	League	GP	G	A	TP	PIM	GP	G	A	TP	PIM
2000-01	Yunost Minsk	Belarus	19	11	7	18	40	....	....	....	....	....
2001-02	Yunost Minsk	Belarus	16	7	5	12	39	....	....	....	....	....
2002-03	HC Gomel	Belarus	19	8	19	27	18	....	....	....	....	....
	HC Gomel	EEHL	14	2	4	6	10	....	....	....	....	....
	Yunost Minsk	Belarus	17	18	19	37	34	....	....	....	....	....

ZANON, Greg (ZA-nuhn, GREHG) **OTT.**

Defense. Shoots left. 5'11", 200 lbs. Born, Burnaby, B.C., June 5, 1980.
(Ottawa's 6th choice, 156th overall, in 2000 Entry Draft).

			Regular Season					Playoffs				
Season	Club	League	GP	G	A	TP	PIM	GP	G	A	TP	PIM
1995-96	Burnaby Beavers	BCAHA	49	16	27	43	142	....	....	....	....	....
1996-97	Victoria Salsa	BCHL	53	4	13	17	124	....	....	....	....	....
1997-98	Victoria Salsa	BCHL	59	11	21	32	108	7	0	2	2	10
1998-99	South Surrey	BCHL	59	17	54	71	154	....	....	....	....	....
99-2000	Nebraska-Omaha	CCHA	42	3	26	29	56	....	....	....	....	....
2000-01	Nebraska-Omaha	CCHA	39	12	16	28	64	....	....	....	....	....
2001-02	Nebraska-Omaha	CCHA	41	9	16	25	54	....	....	....	....	....
2002-03	Nebraska-Omaha	CCHA	32	6	19	25	44	....	....	....	....	....

CCHA First All-Star Team (2001) • NCAA West Second All-American Team (2001, 2002) • CCHA Second All-Star Team (2002)

ZAVORAL, Vaclav (ZA-vohr-uhl, VATS-lahf) **TOR.**

Defense. Shoots left. 6'3", 213 lbs. Born, Teplice, Czech., May 22, 1981.
(Toronto's 5th choice, 151st overall, in 1999 Entry Draft).

			Regular Season					Playoffs				
Season	Club	League	GP	G	A	TP	PIM	GP	G	A	TP	PIM
1997-98	Litvinov Jr.	Czech-Jr.	46	0	5	5	....	....	....	....	....	....
1998-99	Litvinov Jr.	Czech-Jr.	43	2	10	12	....	....	....	....	....	....
	Litvinov	Czech	1	0	1	1	2	....	....	....	....	....
99-2000	Sault Ste. Marie	OHL	57	3	11	14	89	14	0	2	2	28
2000-01	Sault Ste. Marie	OHL	55	4	6	10	116	....	....	....	....	....
2001-02	Flint Generals	UHL	65	2	13	15	123	5	0	0	0	12
2002-03	Memphis	CHL	53	2	2	4	143	....	....	....	....	....

ZEILER, John (ZIGH-luhr, JAWN) **PHX.**

Right wing. Shoots right. 6', 193 lbs. Born, Pittsburgh, PA, November 21, 1982.
(Phoenix's 7th choice, 132nd overall, in 2002 Entry Draft).

			Regular Season					Playoffs				
Season	Club	League	GP	G	A	TP	PIM	GP	G	A	TP	PIM
99-2000	Pittsburgh Hornets	PAHA	27	17	15	32	94	....	....	....	....	....
2000-01	Sioux City	USHL	56	8	20	28	45	2	0	0	0	26
2001-02	Sioux City	USHL	60	23	27	50	116	12	2	3	5	25
2002-03	St. Lawrence	ECAC	37	10	17	27	28	....	....	....	....	....

ECAC All-Rookie Team (2003)

ZHERDEV, Nikolai (ZHAIR-dehv, nih-koh-LIGH) **CBJ**

Wing. Shoots right. 6', 176 lbs. Born, Kiev, USSR, November 5, 1984.
(Columbus' 1st choice, 4th overall, in 2003 Entry Draft).

			Regular Season					Playoffs				
Season	Club	League	GP	G	A	TP	PIM	GP	G	A	TP	PIM
99-2000	Elektrostal 2	Russia-3	21	10	7	17	26	....	....	....	....	....
2000-01	Elektrostal	Russia-2	18	5	8	13	12	....	....	....	....	....
2001-02	Elektrostal	Russia-2	53	13	15	28	62	....	....	....	....	....
	Elektrostal 2	Russia-3	1	1	0	1	4	....	....	....	....	....
2002-03	CSKA Moscow	Russia	44	12	12	24	34	....	....	....	....	....

ZHVACHKIN, Leonid (ZNVAHCH-kihn, lay-oh-NEED) **NYR**

Defense. Shoots left. 6'3", 189 lbs. Born, Tula, USSR, February 24, 1983.
(NY Rangers' 9th choice, 230th overall, in 2001 Entry Draft).

			Regular Season					Playoffs				
Season	Club	League	GP	G	A	TP	PIM	GP	G	A	TP	PIM
99-2000	HC CSKA 2	Russia-3	9	0	1	1	12	....	....	....	....	....
2000-01	Vityaz Podolsk 2	Russia-3	STATISTICS NOT AVAILABLE									
2001-02	Guelph Storm	OHL	62	2	2	4	58	9	0	0	0	5
2002-03	Guelph Storm	OHL	25	0	2	2	34	....	....	....	....	....
	Barrie Colts	OHL	31	0	1	1	35	6	0	0	0	6

ZIB, Lukas (ZIHB, LOO-kahsh) **EDM.**

Defense. Shoots left. 6'1", 200 lbs. Born, Ceske Budejovice, Czech., February 24, 1977.
(Edmonton's 3rd choice, 57th overall, in 1995 Entry Draft).

			Regular Season					Playoffs				
Season	Club	League	GP	G	A	TP	PIM	GP	G	A	TP	PIM
1994-95	Ceske Budejovice	Czech	13	2	0	2	16	9	1	0	1	6
1995-96	C. Budejovice Jr.	Czech-Jr.	11	5	1	6	....	....	....	....	....	....
	Ceske Budejovice	Czech	10	1	0	1	....	2	0	0	0	....
1996-97	Ceske Budejovice	Czech	13	0	0	0	4	2	0	0	0	0
1997-98	Ceske Budejovice	Czech	47	5	6	11	22	....	....	....	....	....
1998-99	Ceske Budejovice	Czech	24	1	4	5	18	....	....	....	....	....
99-2000	Ceske Budejovice	Czech	38	3	6	9	10	1	0	0	0	0
2000-01	Ceske Budejovice	Czech	22	2	3	5	16	....	....	....	....	....
	Zlin	Czech	19	4	3	7	8	....	....	....	....	....
2001-02	HC Karlovy Vary	Czech	36	4	10	14	20	....	....	....	....	....
	Blues Espoo	Finland	5	0	0	0	2	....	....	....	....	....
2002-03	Schwenningen	Germany	49	3	11	14	52	6	1	2	3	6
	Schwenningen	German-Q	6	1	2	3	6	....	....	....	....	....

ZIDLICKY, Marek (zhihd-LIHTS-kee, MAIR-ehk) **NSH.**

Defense. Shoots right. 5'11", 187 lbs. Born, Most, Czech., February 3, 1977.
(NY Rangers' 6th choice, 176th overall, in 2001 Entry Draft).

			Regular Season					Playoffs				
Season	Club	League	GP	G	A	TP	PIM	GP	G	A	TP	PIM
1994-95	HC Kladno	Czech	30	2	2	4	38	11	1	1	2	10
1995-96	HC Poldi Kladno	Czech	37	4	5	9	74	7	1	1	2	8
1996-97	HC Poldi Kladno	Czech	49	5	16	21	60	2	0	0	0	0
1997-98	HC Velvana Kladno	Czech	51	2	13	15	121	....	....	....	....	....
1998-99	HC Velvana Kladno	Czech	50	10	12	22	94	....	....	....	....	....
99-2000	HIFK Helsinki	EuroHL	4	2	2	4	10	1	0	0	0	0
	HIFK Helsinki	Finland	47	4	16	20	66	9	3	2	5	24
2000-01	HIFK Helsinki	Finland	51	12	25	37	146	5	0	1	1	6
2001-02	HIFK Helsinki	Finland	56	11	29	40	107	....	....	....	....	....
2002-03	HIFK Helsinki	Finland	54	10	37	47	79	4	0	0	0	4

Traded to **Nashville** by NY Rangers with Rem Murray and Tomas Kloucek for Mike Dunham, December 12, 2002.

ZIMAKOV, Sergei   (zih-MAH-kahv, SAIR-gay)   **WSH.**

Defense. Shoots left. 6'1", 194 lbs.   Born, Moscow, USSR, January 15, 1978.
(Washington's 4th choice, 58th overall, in 1996 Entry Draft).

				Regular Season						Playoffs			
Season	Club	League	GP	G	A	TP	PIM		GP	G	A	TP	PIM
1994-95	Omaha Lancers	USHL	48	14	46	60	22		....	....	....	....	....
1995-96	Krylja Sovetov	CIS	49	2	7	9	36		....	....	....	....	....
1996-97	Krylja Sovetov	Russia	39	4	3	7	57		2	0	0	0	0
1997-98	Krylja Sovetov	Russia	42	4	1	5	48		....	....	....	....	....
1998-99	Ak Bars Kazan	Russia	28	1	0	1	6		8	0	1	1	6
99-2000	Perm	Russia	31	1	2	3	34		3	0	1	1	0
2000-01	CSKA Moscow 2	Russia-3	3	2	2	4	2		....	....	....	....	....
	CSKA Moscow	Russia	26	1	5	6	28		....	....	....	....	....
2001-02	CSKA Moscow	Russia	42	3	10	13	74		....	....	....	....	....
2002-03	Ufa	Russia	11	0	0	0	8		....	....	....	....	....

ZINGER, Dwayne   (ZIHN-guhr, DWAYN)   **WSH.**

Defense. Shoots left. 6'4", 225 lbs.   Born, Coronation, Alta., July 5, 1976.

				Regular Season						Playoffs			
Season	Club	League	GP	G	A	TP	PIM		GP	G	A	TP	PIM
1995-96	Melville	SJHL	64	7	17	24	....		....	....	....	....	....
1996-97	Alaska-Fairbanks	CCHA	32	1	5	6	45		....	....	....	....	....
1997-98	Alaska-Fairbanks	CCHA	32	1	3	4	91		....	....	....	....	....
1998-99	Alaska-Fairbanks	CCHA	33	4	14	18	42		....	....	....	....	....
99-2000	Alaska-Fairbanks	CCHA	34	10	4	14	34		....	....	....	....	....
	Cincinnati	AHL	13	0	2	2	33		....	....	....	....	....
2000-01	Cincinnati	AHL	68	6	9	15	120		4	1	1	2	2
2001-02	Cincinnati	AHL	67	6	13	19	156		3	0	1	1	2
2002-03	Portland Pirates	AHL	65	1	7	8	67		3	0	0	0	2

SJHL First All-Star Team (1996)

Signed as a free agent by **Detroit**, March 13, 2000. Signed as a free agent by **Washington**, July 9, 2002.

ZINGONI, Peter   (zihn-GOH-nee, PEE-tuhr)   **CBJ**

Center. Shoots left. 6', 180 lbs.   Born, Bridgeport, CT, April 28, 1981.
(Columbus' 8th choice, 231st overall, in 2000 Entry Draft).

				Regular Season						Playoffs			
Season	Club	League	GP	G	A	TP	PIM		GP	G	A	TP	PIM
1998-99	New England	EJHL	40	26	22	48	....		....	....	....	....	....
99-2000	New England	EJHL	40	39	38	77	85		3	1	1	2	0
2000-01	Providence College	H-East	28	2	6	8	38		....	....	....	....	....
2001-02	Providence College	H-East	31	7	10	17	27		....	....	....	....	....
2002-03	Providence College	H-East	32	12	13	25	26		....	....	....	....	....

ZINOVJEV, Sergei   (zih-NOH-vee-ehv, SAIR-gay)   **BOS.**

Center/Left wing. Shoots left. 5'10", 178 lbs.   Born, Novokuznetsk, USSR, March 4, 1980.
(Boston's 6th choice, 73rd overall, in 2000 Entry Draft).

				Regular Season						Playoffs			
Season	Club	League	GP	G	A	TP	PIM		GP	G	A	TP	PIM
1997-98	Novokuznetsk 2	Russia-3	40	7	7	14	36		....	....	....	....	....
	Novokuznetsk	Russia-2	2	1	0	1	0		....	....	....	....	....
1998-99	Novokuznetsk 2	Russia-4	4	0	1	1	8		....	....	....	....	....
	Magnitogorsk	Russia	31	2	4	6	14		3	0	0	0	0
99-2000	Magnitogorsk	Russia	28	0	2	2	16		....	....	....	....	....
2000-01	Yaroslavl	Russia	27	2	10	12	36		....	....	....	....	....
	Ufa	Russia	8	4	5	9	6		....	....	....	....	....
2001-02	Spartak Moscow	Russia	51	12	18	30	43		5	1	1	2	6
2002-03	Ak Bars Kazan	Russia	47	14	17	31	50		....	....	....	....	....

ZOTKIN, Alexei   (ZOHT-kihn, al-EHX-ay)   **CHI.**

Left wing. Shoots left. 6', 200 lbs.   Born, Magnitogorsk, USSR, February 5, 1982.
(Chicago's 7th choice, 119th overall, in 2001 Entry Draft).

				Regular Season						Playoffs			
Season	Club	League	GP	G	A	TP	PIM		GP	G	A	TP	PIM
1997-98	Magnitogorsk 2	Russia-3	2	0	1	1	2		....	....	....	....	....
1998-99	Magnitogorsk 2	Russia-4	23	5	1	6	20		....	....	....	....	....
99-2000	Magnitogorsk 2	Russia-3	38	22	27	49	86		....	....	....	....	....
	Magnitogorsk	Russia	1	0	0	0	0		....	....	....	....	....
2000-01	Magnitogorsk 2	Russia-3	5	6	2	8	26		12	1	1	2	20
	Magnitogorsk	Russia	40	2	3	5	34		....	....	....	....	....
2001-02	Magnitogorsk	Russia	25	3	0	3	10		8	0	1	1	2
2002-03	Magnitogorsk	Russia	35	3	3	6	38		....	....	....	....	....

Late Additions to Player Register

TORONTO MAPLE LEAFS GENERAL MANAGER

FERGUSON, JOHN
General Manager, Toronto Maple Leafs.
Born in Winnipeg, Man., July 7, 1967.

The Toronto Maple Leafs announced John S. Ferguson as their general manager on August 29, 2003. Previously, he worked in the front office of the St. Louis Blues starting as the assistant general manager in 1997-98. He was promoted to vice president and director of hockey operations on February 26, 2001. Ferguson also held the title of president and general manger of the AHL's Worcester IceCats, the Blues' top minor league affiliate. He worked closely with general manager Larry Pleau in managing all facets of the Blues' hockey operations. Ferguson analyzed and negotiated player contracts, coordinated the Blues' pro scouting department and oversaw amateur scouting. Prior to joining the Blues he was a player agent where he was responsible for negotiating player contracts, product endorsements and player recruitment.

Ferguson spent two summers working at the National Hockey League's New York office in the hockey operations and legal departments where he gained valuable experience analyzing NHL standard player contracts, the salary arbitration process and the NHL Collective Bargaining Agreement. Ferguson was a member of the Ottawa Senators scouting staff from 1993 to 1996.

On the ice, Ferguson was co-captain of the hockey team at Providence College where he graduated with a degree in business administration in 1989. He played professionally for four seasons with the Montreal Canadiens and Ottawa Senators organizations. He was the assistant captain of the 1991-92 AHL regular-season champion Fredericton Canadiens, and won that team's "Unsung Hero" award two straight years.

Immediately following his pro hockey career, he enrolled at Suffolk University Law School and graduated three years later. He was admitted to the Massachusetts State Bar in 1996.

His father–also named John–was a member of five Stanley Cup championship teams with Montreal and later served as general manager of the New York Rangers and Winnipeg Jets and as director of player personnel for the Ottawa Senators.

FREE AGENT SIGNINGS

BOILEAU, Patrick – Signed as a free agent by Pittsburgh, August 28, 2003.
HLAVAC, Jan – Signed as a fgree agent by NY Rangers, August 28, 2003.
RUCINSKY, Martin – Signed as a fgree agent by NY Rangers, August 28, 2003.
VALICEVIC, Rob – Signed as a free agent by Anaheim, August 28, 2003.

League Abbreviations

AAHA	Alberta Amateur Hockey Association	Hi-School	High School (also H.S.)	OPJHL	Ontario Provincial Junior A Hockey League
AAHL	Alaska Amateur Hockey League	IEL	Internationale Eishockey Liga	OUAA	Ontario Universities Athletic Association
ACHL	Atlantic Coast Hockey League	IHL	International Hockey League	QAAA	Quebec Amateur Athletic Association
AFHL	American Frontier Hockey League	IJHL	Interstate Junior Hockey League	QAHA	Quebec Amateur Hockey Association
AHL	American Hockey League	KIDHL	Kootenay International Junior B Hockey League	QJHL	Quebec Junior Hockey League
AJHL	Alberta Junior Hockey Leagues	MAAC	Metro Atlantic Athletic Conference	QMJHL	Quebec Major Junior Hockey League
Alpenliga	Alpenliga (Austria, Italy, Slovenia 1994-1999)	MAHA	Manitoba Amateur Hockey Association	PCJHL	Pacific Coast Junior Hockey League
AMBHL	Alberta Major Bantam Hockey League	MBHL	Metropolitan Boston Hockey League	PIJHL	Pacific International Junior Hockey League
AMHL	Alberta Midget AAA Hockey League	MEHL	Midwest Elite Hockey League	RAMHL	Rural Alberta Midget Hockey League
AUAA	Atlantic University Athletic Association	MIAC	Minnesota Intercollegiate Athletic Conference	RMJHL	Rocky Mountain Junior Hockey League
AWHL	American West Hockey League	MJHL	Manitoba Junior Hockey League	SAHA	Saskatchewan Amateur Hockey Association
BCAHA	British Columbia Amateur Hockey Association	MJrHL	Maritime Junior Major Hockey League	SBHL	Saskatchewan Bantam Hockey League
BCHL	British Columbia (Junior) Hockey League (also BCJHL)	MMHL	Manitoba Midget AAA Hockey League	SJHL	Saskatchewan Junior Hockey League
CCHA	Central Collegiate Hockey Association	MNHL	Michigan National Hockey League	SMHL	Saskatchewan Midget AAA Hockey League
CEGEP	Quebec College Prep	MTJHL	Metropolitan Toronto Junior Hockey League	SSJHL	Southern Saskatchewan Junior B Hockey League
CHA	College Hockey America	MTHL	Metro Toronto Hockey League	SunHL	Sunshine Hockey League
CHL	Central Hockey League	NAJHL	North American Junior Hockey League	TBAHA	Thunder Bay Amateur Hockey Association
CIS	Commonwealth of Independent States	Nat-Team	National Team (also Nt.-Team)	TBJHL	Thunder Bay Junior Hockey League
ColHL	Colonial Hockey League	NBAHA	New Brunswick Amateur Hockey Association	TBMHL	Thunder Bay Midget Hockey League
CWUAA	Canadian Western University Athletic Association	NCAA	National Collegiate Athletic Association	UHL	United Hockey League
ECAC	Eastern College Athletic Conference	NEJHL	New England Junior Hockey League	USAHA	United States Amateur Hockey Association
ECHL	East Coast Hockey League	NFAHA	Newfoundland Amateur Hockey Association	USDP	United States National Development Program
EEHL	Eastern European Hockey League	NHL	National Hockey League	USHL	United States (Junior A) Hockey League
EJHL	Eastern Junior Hockey League	NOHA	Northern Ontario Hockey Association	VIJHL	Vancouver Island Junior Hockey League
EuroHL	European Hockey League	NOJHL	Northern Ontario Junior Hockey League	WCHA	Western Collegiate Hockey Association
Exhib.	Exhibition Games, Series or Season	NSMHL	Nova Scotia Midget AAA Hockey League	WCHL	West Coast Hockey League
G.N.	Great Northern	OCJHL	Ontario Central Junior A Hockey League	WHA	World Hockey Association
GPAC	Great Plains Athletic Conference	OHL	Ontario Hockey League	WHL	Western Hockey League
GTHL	Greater Toronto Hockey League	OJHL-B	Ontario Junior B Hockey Leagues	WNYHA	Western New York Hockey Association
H-East	Hockey East	OMHA	Ontario Minor Hockey Association	WPHL	Western Professional Hockey League
HJHL	Heritage Junior Hockey League	OMJHL	Ontario Major Junior Hockey League	WSJHL	Western States Junior Hockey League

2003-04 NHL Player Register

Note: The 2003-04 NHL Player Register lists forwards and defensemen only. Goaltenders are listed separately. The NHL Player Register lists every skater who played in the NHL in 2002-03 plus additional players with NHL experience. Trades and roster changes are current as of August 25, 2003.

Abbreviations: A – assists; **F%** – faceoff winning percentage; **G** – goals; **GP** – games played; **GT** – game-tying goals scored; **GW** – game-winning goals scored; **Min** – average time on ice; **PIM** – penalties in minutes; **+/–** – plus/minus rating; **PP** – powerplay goals scored; **Pts** – points; **S** – shots on goal; **S%** – shooting percentage; **SH** – shorthand goal scored; **TF** – Total faceoffs taken; ***** – league-leading total; **♦** – member of Stanley Cup-winning team.

Prospect Register begins on page 267.
Goaltender Register begins on page 574.
League abbreviations are listed on page 335.

ABID, Ramzi (a-BIHD, RAM-zee) PIT.

Left wing. Shoots left. 6'2", 210 lbs. Born, Montreal, Que., March 24, 1980. Phoenix's 3rd choice, 85th overall, in 2000 Entry Draft.

Season	Club	League	GP	G	A	Pts	PIM	PP	SH	GW	S	%	+/-	TF	F%	Min	GP	G	A	Pts	PIM	PP	SH	GW	Min
1995-96	Richelieu Riverains	QAAA	42	10	14	24	18	....	....	....	....	....	....	....	....	....	4	1	2	3	2	....	....	....	....
1996-97	Chicoutimi	QMJHL	65	13	24	37	141	....	....	....	....	....	....	....	....	....	21	2	12	14	28	....	....	....	....
1997-98	Chicoutimi	QMJHL	68	50	*85	*135	266	....	....	....	....	....	....	....	....	....	6	3	4	7	10	....	....	....	....
1998-99	Chicoutimi	QMJHL	21	11	15	26	97	....	....	....	....	....	....	....	....	....									
	Acadie-Bathurst	QMJHL	24	14	22	36	102	....	....	....	....	....	....	....	....	....	23	14	20	34	*84	....	....	....	....
99-2000	Acadie-Bathurst	QMJHL	13	10	11	21	61	....	....	....	....	....	....	....	....	....									
	Halifax	QMJHL	59	57	80	137	148	....	....	....	....	....	....	....	....	....	10	10	13	23	18	....	....	....	....
2000-01	Springfield	AHL	17	6	4	10	38	....	....	....	....	....	....	....	....	....									
2001-02	Springfield	AHL	66	18	25	43	214	....	....	....	....	....	....	....	....	....									
2002-03	**Phoenix**	**NHL**	30	10	8	18	30	4	0	3	52	19.2	1	1100.0		12:30									
	Springfield	AHL	27	15	10	25	50	....	....	....	....	....	....	....	....	....									
	Pittsburgh	**NHL**	3	0	0	0	2	0	0	0	7	0.0	-5	1	0.0	17:33									
	NHL Totals		33	10	8	18	32	4	0	3	59	16.9		2	50.0	12:58									

• Re-entered NHL Entry Draft. Originally Colorado's 5th choice, 28th overall, in 1998 Entry Draft.
Michel Briere Trophy (QMJHL MVP) (1998) • Jean Beliveau Trophy (QMJHL Leading Scorer) (1998) • QMJHL First All-Star Team (1998, 2000) • Canadian Major Junior First All-Star Team (2000) • Ed Chynoweth Trophy (Memorial Cup Leading Scorer) (2000)
• Missed majority of 2000-01 season recovering from wrist injury originally suffered in game vs. Louisville (AHL), October 27, 2000. Traded to **Pittsburgh** by **Phoenix** with Dan Focht and Guillaume Lefebvre for Jan Hrdina and Francois Leroux, March 11, 2003.

ADAMS, Bryan (A-duhms, BRIGH-uhn)

Center. Shoots left. 6', 185 lbs. Born, Fort St. James, B.C., March 20, 1977.

Season	Club	League	GP	G	A	Pts	PIM	PP	SH	GW	S	%	+/-	TF	F%	Min	GP	G	A	Pts	PIM	PP	SH	GW	Min
1994-95	Prince George	RMJHL	48	37	53	90	...	....	....	....	....	....	....	....	....	....									
1995-96	Michigan State	CCHA	42	3	8	11	12	....	....	....	....	....	....	....	....	....									
1996-97	Michigan State	CCHA	29	7	7	14	51	....	....	....	....	....	....	....	....	....									
1997-98	Michigan State	CCHA	31	9	21	30	39	....	....	....	....	....	....	....	....	....									
1998-99	Michigan State	CCHA	42	21	16	37	56	....	....	....	....	....	....	....	....	....									
99-2000	**Atlanta**	**NHL**	2	0	0	0	0	0	0	0	1	0.0	-1	0	0.0	10:57									
	Orlando	IHL	64	16	18	34	27	....	....	....	....	....	....	....	....	....	4	0	1	1	6	....	....	....	....
2000-01	**Atlanta**	**NHL**	9	0	1	1	2	0	0	0	3	0.0	-4	1	0.0	9:37									
	Orlando	IHL	61	18	28	46	43	....	....	....	....	....	....	....	....	....	16	3	4	7	20	....	....	....	....
2001-02	Chicago Wolves	AHL	64	10	17	27	25	....	....	....	....	....	....	....	....	....	5	0	0	0	2	....	....	....	....
2002-03	Grand Rapids	AHL	74	8	17	25	37	....	....	....	....	....	....	....	....	....	13	2	0	2	4	....	....	....	....
	NHL Totals		11	0	1	1	2	0	0	0	4	0.0		1	0.0	9:51									

Signed as a free agent by **Atlanta**, July 6, 1999. Signed as a free agent by **Detroit**, August 5, 2002.

ADAMS, Craig (A-duhms, KRAYG) CAR.

Right wing. Shoots right. 6', 200 lbs. Born, Seria, Brunei, April 26, 1977. Hartford's 9th choice, 223rd overall, in 1996 Entry Draft.

Season	Club	League	GP	G	A	Pts	PIM	PP	SH	GW	S	%	+/-	TF	F%	Min	GP	G	A	Pts	PIM	PP	SH	GW	Min
1994-95	Calgary Canucks	AJHL	STATISTICS NOT AVAILABLE																					
1995-96	Harvard Crimson	ECAC	34	8	9	17	56	....	....	....	....	....	....	....	....	....									
1996-97	Harvard Crimson	ECAC	32	6	4	10	36	....	....	....	....	....	....	....	....	....									
1997-98	Harvard Crimson	ECAC	12	6	6	12	12	....	....	....	....	....	....	....	....	....									
1998-99	Harvard Crimson	ECAC	31	9	14	23	53	....	....	....	....	....	....	....	....	....									
99-2000	Cincinnati	IHL	73	12	12	24	124	....	....	....	....	....	....	....	....	....	8	0	1	1	14	....	....	....	....
2000-01	**Carolina**	**NHL**	44	1	0	1	20	0	0	0	15	6.7	-7	4	25.0	4:30	3	0	0	0	0	0	0	0	3:45
	Cincinnati	IHL	4	0	1	1	9	....	....	....	....	....	....	....	....	....	1	0	0	0	2	....	....	....	....
2001-02	**Carolina**	**NHL**	33	0	1	1	38	0	0	0	17	0.0	2	9	33.3	5:54	1	0	0	0	0	0	0	0	7:41
	Lowell	AHL	22	5	4	9	51	....	....	....	....	....	....	....	....	....									
2002-03	**Carolina**	**NHL**	81	6	12	18	71	1	0	1	107	5.6	-11	20	35.0	12:12									
	NHL Totals		158	7	13	20	129	1	0	1	139	5.0		33	33.3	8:44	4	0	0	0	0	0	0	0	4:44

Rights transferred to **Carolina** after **Hartford** franchise relocated, June 25, 1997. • Missed majority of 1997-98 season recovering from shoulder injury suffered in game vs. University of Wisconsin (WCHA), December 27, 1997.

ADAMS, Kevyn (A-duhms, KEH-vihn) CAR.

Center. Shoots right. 6'1", 195 lbs. Born, Washington, DC, October 8, 1974. Boston's 1st choice, 25th overall, in 1993 Entry Draft.

Season	Club	League	GP	G	A	Pts	PIM	PP	SH	GW	S	%	+/-	TF	F%	Min	GP	G	A	Pts	PIM	PP	SH	GW	Min
1990-91	Niagara Scenics	NAJHL	55	17	20	37	24	....	....	....	....	....	....	....	....	....									
1991-92	Niagara Scenics	NAJHL	40	25	33	58	51	....	....	....	....	....	....	....	....	....									
1992-93	Miami-Ohio	CCHA	40	17	15	32	18	....	....	....	....	....	....	....	....	....									
1993-94	Miami-Ohio	CCHA	36	15	28	43	24	....	....	....	....	....	....	....	....	....									
1994-95	Miami-Ohio	CCHA	38	20	29	49	30	....	....	....	....	....	....	....	....	....									
1995-96	Miami-Ohio	CCHA	36	17	30	47	30	....	....	....	....	....	....	....	....	....									
1996-97	Grand Rapids	IHL	82	22	25	47	47	....	....	....	....	....	....	....	....	....	5	1	1	2	4	....	....	....	....

			Regular Season														Playoffs								
Season	Club	League	GP	G	A	Pts	PIM	PP	SH	GW	S	%	+/-	TF	F%	Min	GP	G	A	Pts	PIM	PP	SH	GW	Min
1997-98	Toronto	NHL	5	0	0	0	7	0	0	0	3	0.0	0												
	St. John's	AHL	59	17	20	37	99										4	0	0	0	4				
1998-99	Toronto	NHL	1	0	0	0	0	0	0	0	1	0.0	0	9	44.4	7:56	7	0	2	2	14	0	0	0	11:18
	St. John's	AHL	80	15	35	50	85										5	2	0	2	4				
99-2000	Toronto	NHL	52	5	8	13	39	0	0	0	70	7.1	-7	604	56.5	12:23	12	1	0	1	7	0	1	0	11:06
	St. John's	AHL	23	6	11	17	24																		
2000-01	Columbus	NHL	66	8	12	20	52	0	0	1	84	9.5	-4	1152	57.4	15:18									
	Florida	NHL	12	3	6	9	2	0	0	2	21	14.3	7	198	47.5	17:25									
2001-02	Florida	NHL	44	4	8	12	28	0	0	1	71	5.6	-3	572	57.9	13:21									
	Carolina	NHL	33	2	3	5	15	0	0	1	37	5.4	-2	187	58.8	9:05	23	1	0	1	4	0	0	0	7:29
2002-03	Carolina	NHL	77	9	9	18	57	0	0	0	169	5.3	-8	1018	53.1	14:39									
	NHL Totals		290	31	46	77	200	0	0	5	456	6.8		3740	55.6	13:38	42	2	2	4	25	0	1	0	9:09

CCHA Second All-Star Team (1995)

Signed as a free agent by **Toronto**, August 7, 1997. Selected by **Columbus** from **Toronto** in Expansion Draft, June 23, 2000. Traded to **Florida** by **Columbus** with Columbus's 4th round choice (Mike Woodford) in 2001 Entry Draft for Ray Whitney and future considerations, March 13, 2001. Traded to **Carolina** by **Florida** with Bret Hedican, Tomas Malec and future considerations for Sandis Ozolinsh and Byron Ritchie, January 16, 2002.

AFANASENKOV, Dmitry
(a-fahn-A-sehn-kahv, dih-MEE-tree) **T.B.**

Left wing. Shoots right. 6'2", 200 lbs. Born, Arkhangelsk, USSR, May 12, 1980. Tampa Bay's 3rd choice, 72nd overall, in 1998 Entry Draft.

Season	Club	League	GP	G	A	Pts	PIM	PP	SH	GW	S	%	+/-	TF	F%	Min	GP	G	A	Pts	PIM	PP	SH	GW	Min
1995-96	Yaroslavl Jr.	CIS-Jr.	35	28	16	44	8																		
	Yaroslavl	CIS	25	10	5	15	10																		
1996-97	Yaroslavl 2	Russia-3	45	20	15	35	14																		
1997-98	Yaroslavl	Russia	48	14	7	21	20																		
1998-99	Moncton Wildcats	QMJHL	15	5	5	10	12																		
	Sherbrooke	QMJHL	51	23	30	53	22										13	10	6	16	6				
99-2000	Sherbrooke	QMJHL	60	56	43	99	70										5	3	2	5	4				
2000-01	Tampa Bay	NHL	9	1	1	2	4	0	0	0	8	12.5	1	7	28.6	11:24									
	Detroit Vipers	IHL	65	15	22	37	26																		
2001-02	Tampa Bay	NHL	5	0	0	0	0	0	0	0	1	0.0	-1	0	0.0	4:54									
	Springfield	AHL	28	4	5	9	4																		
	Grand Rapids	AHL	18	1	2	3	2																		
2002-03	Springfield	AHL	41	4	9	13	25																		
	Kloten Flyers	Swiss															5	1	1	2	0				
	NHL Totals		14	1	1	2	4	0	0	0	9	11.1		7	28.6	9:05									

• Assigned to **Kloten** (Swiss) by **Tampa Bay**, February 19, 2003.

AFINOGENOV, Maxim
(ah-fihn-ah-GEHN-ahf, mahx-EEM) **BUF.**

Right wing. Shoots left. 6', 190 lbs. Born, Moscow, USSR, September 4, 1979. Buffalo's 3rd choice, 69th overall, in 1997 Entry Draft.

Season	Club	League	GP	G	A	Pts	PIM	PP	SH	GW	S	%	+/-	TF	F%	Min	GP	G	A	Pts	PIM	PP	SH	GW	Min
1996-97	Dynamo Moscow	Russia	29	6	5	11	10										4	0	2	2	0				
	Dynamo Moscow	EuroHL	3	0	0	0	0										3	1	0	1	4				
1997-98	Dynamo Moscow	Russia	35	10	5	15	53																		
	Dynamo Moscow	EuroHL	6	3	1	4	27																		
1998-99	Dynamo Moscow	Russia	38	8	13	21	24										16	*10	6	*16	14				
	Dynamo Moscow	EuroHL	5	3	5	8	29										4	2	1	3	27				
99-2000	Buffalo	NHL	65	16	18	34	41	2	0	2	128	12.5	-4	0	0.0	13:09	5	0	1	1	2	0	0	0	12:53
	Rochester	AHL	15	6	12	18	8										8	3	1	4	4				
2000-01	Buffalo	NHL	78	14	22	36	40	3	0	5	190	7.4	1	2	0.0	14:32	11	2	3	5	4	0	0	0	10:56
2001-02	Buffalo	NHL	81	21	19	40	69	3	1	0	234	9.0	-9	1	100.0	15:22									
	Russia	Olympics	6	2	2	4	4																		
2002-03	Buffalo	NHL	35	5	6	11	21	2	0	2	77	6.5	-12	4	50.0	13:24									
	NHL Totals		259	56	65	121	171	10	1	9	629	8.9		7	42.9	14:18	16	2	4	6	6	0	0	0	11:32

• Missed majority of 2002-03 season recovering from head injury suffered in training camp, October 8, 2002.

AITKEN, Johnathan
(ATE-kin, JAWN-uh-thuhn) **CHI.**

Defense. Shoots left. 6'4", 230 lbs. Born, Edmonton, Alta., May 24, 1978. Boston's 1st choice, 8th overall, in 1996 Entry Draft.

Season	Club	League	GP	G	A	Pts	PIM	PP	SH	GW	S	%	+/-	TF	F%	Min	GP	G	A	Pts	PIM	PP	SH	GW	Min
1993-94	Sherwood Park	AMHL	31	4	9	13	54																		
1994-95	Medicine Hat	WHL	53	0	5	5	71										5	0	0	0	0				
1995-96	Medicine Hat	WHL	71	6	14	20	131										5	1	0	1	6				
1996-97	Brandon	WHL	65	4	18	22	211										6	0	0	0	4				
1997-98	Brandon	WHL	69	9	25	34	183										18	0	8	8	67				
1998-99	Providence Bruins	AHL	65	2	9	11	92										13	0	0	0	17				
99-2000	Boston	NHL	3	0	0	0	0	0	0	0	2	0.0	-3	0	0.0	18:57									
	Providence Bruins	AHL	70	2	12	14	121										11	1	0	1	26				
2000-01	HC Sparta Praha	Czech	24	0	3	3	62																		
2001-02	Norfolk Admirals	AHL	28	0	1	1	43										4	0	0	0	2				
	Jackson Bandits	ECHL	43	1	9	10	141																		
2002-03	Norfolk Admirals	AHL	80	1	7	8	207										9	2	1	3	18				
	NHL Totals		3	0	0	0	0	0	0	0	2	0.0		0	0.0	18:57									

WHL East Second All-Star Team (1998)

Signed as a free agent by **Norfolk** (AHL), September 6, 2001. Signed as a free agent by **Chicago**, May 22, 2002.

ALATALO, Mika
(a-luh-TAH-loh, MEE-kuh)

Left wing. Shoots left. 6', 202 lbs. Born, Oulu, Finland, June 11, 1971. Winnipeg's 11th choice, 203rd overall, in 1990 Entry Draft.

Season	Club	League	GP	G	A	Pts	PIM	PP	SH	GW	S	%	+/-	TF	F%	Min	GP	G	A	Pts	PIM	PP	SH	GW	Min
1988-89	KooKoo Kouvola	Finland	34	8	6	14	10																		
1989-90	KooKoo Kouvola	Finland	41	3	5	8	22																		
1990-91	Lukko Rauma	Finland	39	10	1	11	10																		
1991-92	Lukko Rauma	Finland	43	20	17	37	32										2	0	0	0	0				
1992-93	Lukko Rauma	Finland	48	16	19	35	38										3	0	0	0	0				
1993-94	Lukko Rauma	Finland	45	19	15	34	77										9	2	2	4	4				
	Finland	Olympics	7	2	1	3	2																		
1994-95	TPS Turku	Finland	44	23	13	36	79										13	2	5	7	8				
1995-96	TPS Turku	Finland	49	19	18	37	44										11	3	4	7	8				
1996-97	Lulea HF	Sweden	50	19	18	37	54										10	2	3	5	22				
	Lulea HF	EuroHL	6	4	3	7	4																		
1997-98	Lulea HF	Sweden	45	14	10	24	22										2	0	0	0	0				
	Lulea HF	EuroHL	6	2	1	3	6																		
1998-99	TPS Turku	Finland	53	14	23	37	44										10	6	3	9	6				
99-2000	Phoenix	NHL	82	10	17	27	36	1	0	1	107	9.3	-3	3	0.0	12:37	5	0	0	0	2	0	0	0	8:23
2000-01	Phoenix	NHL	70	7	12	19	22	0	0	1	64	10.9	1	2	0.0	10:59									
2001-02	TPS Turku	Finland	56	20	22	42	95										8	1	1	2	12				
2002-03	TPS Turku	Finland	55	13	16	29	68										7	3	2	5	28				
	NHL Totals		152	17	29	46	58	1	0	2	171	9.9		5	0.0	11:52	5	0	0	0	2	0	0	0	8:23

Rights transferred to **Phoenix** after **Winnipeg** franchise relocated, July 1, 1996. Signed as a free agent by **TPS Turku** (Finland), May 25, 2001.

ALBELIN, Tommy
(AHL-buh-LEEN,TAW-mee) **N.J.**

Defense. Shoots left. 6'2", 195 lbs. Born, Stockholm, Sweden, May 21, 1964. Quebec's 7th choice, 158th overall, in 1983 Entry Draft.

Season	Club	League	GP	G	A	Pts	PIM	PP	SH	GW	S	%	+/-	TF	F%	Min	GP	G	A	Pts	PIM	PP	SH	GW	Min
1980-81	Stocksunds IF	Swede-3	18	6	1	7																			
1981-82	Stocksunds IF	Swede-3	22	6	2	8																			
1982-83	Djurgarden	Sweden	19	2	5	7	4										6	1	0	1	2				
1983-84	Djurgarden	Sweden	30	9	5	14	26										4	0	1	1	2				
1984-85	Djurgarden	Sweden	32	9	8	17	22										8	2	1	3	4				
1985-86	Djurgarden	Sweden	35	4	8	12	26																		
1986-87	Djurgarden	Sweden	33	7	5	12	49										2	0	0	0	0				
1987-88	Quebec	NHL	60	3	23	26	47	0	0	0	98	3.1	-7												

			Regular Season														Playoffs								
Season	Club	League	GP	G	A	Pts	PIM	PP	SH	GW	S	%	+/-	TF	F%	Min	GP	G	A	Pts	PIM	PP	SH	GW	Min
1988-89	**Quebec**	**NHL**	**14**	**2**	**4**	**6**	**27**	**1**	**0**	**1**	**16**	**12.5**	**–6**												
	Halifax Citadels	AHL	8	2	5	7	4																		
	New Jersey	**NHL**	**46**	**7**	**24**	**31**	**40**	**1**	**1**	**1**	**82**	**8.5**	**18**												
1989-90	**New Jersey**	**NHL**	**68**	**6**	**23**	**29**	**63**	**4**	**0**	**0**	**125**	**4.8**	**–1**												
1990-91	**New Jersey**	**NHL**	**47**	**2**	**12**	**14**	**44**	**1**	**0**	**0**	**66**	**3.0**	**1**				**3**	**0**	**1**	**1**	**2**	**0**	**0**	**0**	
	Utica Devils	AHL	14	4	2	6	10																		
1991-92	**New Jersey**	**NHL**	**19**	**0**	**4**	**4**	**4**	**0**	**0**	**0**	**18**	**0.0**	**7**				**1**	**1**	**1**	**2**	**0**	**0**	**0**	**0**	
	Utica Devils	AHL	11	4	6	10	4																		
1992-93	**New Jersey**	**NHL**	**36**	**1**	**5**	**6**	**14**	**1**	**0**	**1**	**33**	**3.0**	**0**				**5**	**2**	**0**	**2**	**0**	**1**	**0**	**1**	
1993-94	**New Jersey**	**NHL**	**62**	**2**	**17**	**19**	**36**	**1**	**0**	**1**	**62**	**3.2**	**20**				**20**	**2**	**5**	**7**	**14**	**1**	**0**	**1**	
	Albany River Rats	AHL	4	0	2	2	17																		
1994-95♦	**New Jersey**	**NHL**	**48**	**5**	**10**	**15**	**20**	**2**	**0**	**0**	**60**	**8.3**	**9**				**20**	**1**	**7**	**8**	**2**	**0**	**0**	**0**	
1995-96	**New Jersey**	**NHL**	**53**	**1**	**12**	**13**	**14**	**0**	**0**	**0**	**90**	**1.1**	**0**												
	Calgary	**NHL**	**20**	**0**	**1**	**1**	**4**	**0**	**0**	**0**	**31**	**0.0**	**1**				**4**	**0**	**0**	**0**	**0**	**0**	**0**	**0**	
1996-97	**Calgary**	**NHL**	**72**	**4**	**11**	**15**	**14**	**2**	**0**	**0**	**103**	**3.9**	**–8**												
1997-98	**Calgary**	**NHL**	**69**	**2**	**17**	**19**	**32**	**1**	**0**	**2**	**88**	**2.3**	**9**												
	Sweden	Olympics	3	0	0	0	4																		
1998-99	**Calgary**	**NHL**	**60**	**1**	**5**	**6**	**8**	**0**	**0**	**0**	**54**	**1.9**	**–11**	**1**	**0.0**	**19:08**									
99-2000	**Calgary**	**NHL**	**41**	**4**	**6**	**10**	**12**	**1**	**1**	**1**	**37**	**10.8**	**–3**	**0**	**0.0**	**21:35**									
2000-01	**Calgary**	**NHL**	**77**	**1**	**19**	**20**	**22**	**1**	**0**	**0**	**69**	**1.4**	**2**	**0**	**0.0**	**20:53**									
2001-02	**New Jersey**	**NHL**	**42**	**1**	**3**	**4**	**4**	**0**	**0**	**1**	**33**	**3.0**	**0**	**0**	**0.0**	**13:20**	**6**	**0**	**0**	**0**	**0**	**0**	**0**	**0**	**14:11**
2002-03♦	**New Jersey**	**NHL**	**37**	**1**	**6**	**7**	**6**	**0**	**1**	**0**	**30**	**3.3**	**10**	**0**	**0.0**	**15:13**	**16**	**1**	**0**	**1**	**2**	**0**	**0**	**0**	**14:18**
	Albany River Rats	AHL	5	0	2	2	2																		
	NHL Totals		**871**	**43**	**202**	**245**	**411**	**16**	**3**	**8**	**1095**	**3.9**		**1**	**0.0**	**18:32**	**75**	**7**	**14**	**21**	**20**	**2**	**0**	**2**	**14:16**

Traded to **New Jersey** by **Quebec** for New Jersey's 4th round choice (Niklas Andersson) in 1989 Entry Draft, December 12, 1988. Traded to **Calgary** by **New Jersey** with Cale Hulse and Jocelyn Lemieux for Phil Housley and Dan Keczmer, February 26, 1996. Signed as a free agent by **New Jersey**, July 9, 2001.

ALEXEEV, Nikita

(uh-LEHX-ee-ehv, nih-KEE-tuh) **T.B.**

Right wing. Shoots left. 6'5", 210 lbs. Born, Murmansk, USSR, December 27, 1981. Tampa Bay's 1st choice, 8th overall, in 2000 Entry Draft.

1996-97	Krylja Sovetov Jr.	Russia-Jr.	45	4	6	10	8																		
1997-98	Krylja Sovetov 2	Russia-3	61	11	4	15	36																		
1998-99	Erie Otters	OHL	61	17	18	35	14										5	1	1	2	4				
99-2000	Erie Otters	OHL	64	24	29	53	42										13	4	3	7	6				
2000-01	Erie Otters	OHL	64	31	41	72	45										12	7	7	14	12				
2001-02	**Tampa Bay**	**NHL**	**44**	**4**	**4**	**8**	**8**	**1**	**0**	**1**	**47**	**8.5**	**–9**	**0**	**0.0**	**11:26**									
	Springfield	AHL	35	5	9	14	16																		
2002-03	**Tampa Bay**	**NHL**	**37**	**4**	**2**	**6**	**8**	**1**	**0**	**1**	**52**	**7.7**	**–6**	**3**	**33.3**	**11:31**	**11**	**1**	**0**	**1**	**0**	**0**	**0**	**0**	**10:12**
	Springfield	AHL	36	7	5	12	8																		
	NHL Totals		**81**	**8**	**6**	**14**	**16**	**2**	**0**	**2**	**99**	**8.1**		**3**	**33.3**	**11:28**	**11**	**1**	**0**	**1**	**0**	**0**	**0**	**0**	**10:12**

ALFREDSSON, Daniel

(AHL-frehd-suhn, DAN-yehl) **OTT.**

Right wing. Shoots right. 5'11", 199 lbs. Born, Goteborg, Sweden, December 11, 1972. Ottawa's 5th choice, 133rd overall, in 1994 Entry Draft.

1990-91	IF Molndal	Swede-2	3	0	0	0	2										8	4	4	8	4				
1991-92	IF Molndal	Swede-2	32	12	8	20	43																		
1992-93	Vastra Frolunda	Sweden	20	1	5	6	8																		
1993-94	Vastra Frolunda	Sweden	39	20	10	30	18										4	1	1	2					
1994-95	Vastra Frolunda	Sweden	22	7	11	18	22																		
1995-96	**Ottawa**	**NHL**	**82**	**26**	**35**	**61**	**28**	**8**	**2**	**3**	**212**	**12.3**	**–18**												
1996-97	**Ottawa**	**NHL**	**76**	**24**	**47**	**71**	**30**	**11**	**1**	**1**	**247**	**9.7**	**5**				**7**	**5**	**2**	**7**	**6**	**3**	**0**	**2**	
1997-98	**Ottawa**	**NHL**	**55**	**17**	**28**	**45**	**18**	**7**	**0**	**7**	**149**	**11.4**	**7**				**11**	**7**	**2**	**9**	**20**	**2**	**1**	**1**	
	Sweden	Olympics	4	2	3	5	2																		
1998-99	**Ottawa**	**NHL**	**58**	**11**	**22**	**33**	**14**	**3**	**0**	**5**	**163**	**6.7**	**8**	**7**	**57.1**	**17:22**	**4**	**1**	**2**	**3**	**4**	**1**	**0**	**0**	**22:23**
99-2000	**Ottawa**	**NHL**	**57**	**21**	**38**	**59**	**28**	**4**	**2**	**0**	**164**	**12.8**	**11**	**3**	**66.7**	**18:45**	**6**	**1**	**3**	**4**	**2**	**1**	**0**	**0**	**20:22**
2000-01	**Ottawa**	**NHL**	**68**	**24**	**46**	**70**	**30**	**10**	**0**	**3**	**206**	**11.7**	**11**	**8**	**50.0**	**18:47**	**4**	**1**	**0**	**1**	**2**	**0**	**0**	**0**	**21:20**
2001-02	**Ottawa**	**NHL**	**78**	**37**	**34**	**71**	**45**	**9**	**1**	**4**	**243**	**15.2**	**3**	**30**	**30.0**	**20:19**	**12**	**7**	**6**	**13**	**4**	**3**	**0**	**3**	**21:43**
	Sweden	Olympics	4	1	4	5	2																		
2002-03	**Ottawa**	**NHL**	**78**	**27**	**51**	**78**	**42**	**9**	**0**	**6**	**240**	**11.3**	**15**	**40**	**40.0**	**19:32**	**18**	**4**	**4**	**8**	**12**	**4**	**0**	**1**	**17:60**
	NHL Totals		**552**	**187**	**301**	**488**	**235**	**61**	**6**	**29**	**1624**	**11.5**		**88**	**39.8**	**19:04**	**62**	**26**	**19**	**45**	**50**	**14**	**1**	**7**	**20:02**

NHL All-Rookie Team (1996) • Calder Memorial Trophy (1996)
Played in NHL All-Star Game (1996, 1997, 1998)

ALLEN, Bobby

(AHL-lehn, BAW-bee) **EDM.**

Defense. Shoots left. 6'1", 205 lbs. Born, Braintree, MA, November 14, 1978. Boston's 2nd choice, 52nd overall, in 1998 Entry Draft.

1996-97	Cushing Academy	Hi-School	36	11	33	44	28																		
1997-98	Boston College	H-East	40	7	21	28	49																		
1998-99	Boston College	H-East	43	9	23	32	34																		
99-2000	Boston College	H-East	42	4	23	27	40																		
2000-01	Boston College	H-East	42	5	18	23	28																		
2001-02	Providence Bruins	AHL	49	5	10	15	18																		
	Hamilton	AHL	10	1	6	7	0										14	0	3	3	6				
2002-03	**Edmonton**	**NHL**	**1**	**0**	**0**	**0**	**0**	**0**	**0**	**0**	**0**	**0.0**	**0**	**0**	**0.0**	**2:53**									
	Hamilton	AHL	56	1	12	13	24										23	0	5	5	10				
	NHL Totals		**1**	**0**	**0**	**0**	**0**	**0**	**0**	**0**	**0**	**0.0**		**0**	**0.0**	**2:53**									

Hockey East Second All-Star Team (2000) • Hockey East First All-Star Team (2001) • NCAA East First All-American Team (2001)
Traded to **Edmonton** by **Boston** for Sean Brown, March 19, 2002.

ALLEN, Bryan

(AHL-lehn, BRIGH-uhn) **VAN.**

Defense. Shoots left. 6'4", 215 lbs. Born, Kingston, Ont., August 21, 1980. Vancouver's 1st choice, 4th overall, in 1998 Entry Draft.

1995-96	Ernestown Jets	OJHL-C	36	1	16	17	71																		
1996-97	Oshawa Generals	OHL	60	2	4	6	76										18	1	3	4	26				
1997-98	Oshawa Generals	OHL	48	6	13	19	126										5	0	5	5	18				
1998-99	Oshawa Generals	OHL	37	7	15	22	77										15	0	3	3	26				
99-2000	Oshawa Generals	OHL	3	0	2	2	12										3	0	0	0	13				
	Syracuse Crunch	AHL	9	1	1	2	11										2	0	0	0	2				
2000-01	**Vancouver**	**NHL**	**6**	**0**	**0**	**0**	**0**	**0**	**0**	**0**	**2**	**0.0**	**0**	**0**	**0.0**	**9:20**	**2**	**0**	**0**	**0**	**2**	**0**	**0**	**0**	**13:47**
	Kansas City	IHL	75	5	20	25	99																		
2001-02	**Vancouver**	**NHL**	**11**	**0**	**0**	**0**	**6**	**0**	**0**	**0**	**4**	**0.0**	**1**	**0**	**0.0**	**10:47**									
	Manitoba Moose	AHL	68	7	18	25	121										5	0	1	1	8				
2002-03	Manitoba Moose	AHL	7	0	1	1	4																		
	Vancouver	**NHL**	**48**	**5**	**3**	**8**	**73**	**0**	**0**	**1**	**43**	**11.6**	**8**	**0**	**0.0**	**12:56**	**1**	**0**	**0**	**0**	**2**	**0**	**0**	**0**	**10:35**
	NHL Totals		**65**	**5**	**3**	**8**	**79**	**0**	**0**	**1**	**49**	**10.2**		**0**	**0.0**	**12:14**	**3**	**0**	**0**	**0**	**4**	**0**	**0**	**0**	**12:43**

OHL First All-Star Team (1999)
Missed majority of 1999-2000 season recovering from knee injury suffered in training camp, September 21, 1999.

ALLISON, Jamie

(AHL-lih-sohn, JAY-mee)

Defense. Shoots left. 6'1", 200 lbs. Born, Lindsay, Ont., May 13, 1975. Calgary's 2nd choice, 44th overall, in 1993 Entry Draft.

1990-91	Waterloo Siskins	OJHL-B	38	3	8	11	91																		
1991-92	Windsor Spitfires	OHL	59	4	8	12	70										4	1	1	2	2				
1992-93	Detroit	OHL	61	0	13	13	64										15	2	5	7	23				
1993-94	Detroit	OHL	40	2	22	24	69										17	2	9	11	35				
1994-95	Detroit	OHL	50	1	14	15	119										18	2	7	9	35				
	Calgary	**NHL**	**1**	**0**	**0**	**0**	**0**	**0**	**0**	**0**	**0**	**0.0**	**0**												
1995-96	Saint John Flames	AHL	71	3	16	19	223										14	0	2	2	16				

			Regular Season														Playoffs								
Season	Club	League	GP	G	A	Pts	PIM	PP	SH	GW	S	%	+/-	TF	F%	Min	GP	G	A	Pts	PIM	PP	SH	GW	Min
1996-97	**Calgary**	**NHL**	**20**	**0**	**0**	**0**	**35**	**0**	**0**	**0**	**8**	**0.0**	**–4**												
	Saint John Flames	AHL	46	3	6	9	139										5	0	1	1	4				
1997-98	**Calgary**	**NHL**	**43**	**3**	**8**	**11**	**104**	**0**	**0**	**1**	**27**	**11.1**	**3**												
	Saint John Flames	AHL	16	0	5	5	49																		
1998-99	Saint John Flames	AHL	5	0	0	0	23																		
	Chicago	**NHL**	**39**	**2**	**2**	**4**	**62**	**0**	**0**	**0**	**24**	**8.3**	**0**	**0**	**0.0**	**14:01**									
	Indianapolis Ice	IHL	3	1	0	1	10																		
99-2000	**Chicago**	**NHL**	**59**	**1**	**3**	**4**	**102**	**0**	**0**	**0**	**24**	**4.2**	**–5**	**0**	**0.0**	**14:14**									
2000-01	**Chicago**	**NHL**	**44**	**1**	**3**	**4**	**53**	**0**	**0**	**0**	**16**	**6.3**	**7**	**1**	**100.0**	**14:33**									
2001-02	**Calgary**	**NHL**	**37**	**0**	**2**	**2**	**24**	**0**	**0**	**0**	**14**	**0.0**	**–3**	**2**	**0.0**	**7:44**									
	Columbus	**NHL**	**7**	**0**	**0**	**0**	**28**	**0**	**0**	**0**	**2**	**0.0**	**–4**	**0**	**0.0**	**11:23**									
2002-03	**Columbus**	**NHL**	**48**	**0**	**1**	**1**	**99**	**0**	**0**	**0**	**23**	**0.0**	**–15**	**1**	**100.0**	**11:57**									
	NHL Totals		**298**	**7**	**19**	**26**	**507**	**0**	**0**	**1**	**138**	**5.1**		**4**	**50.0**	**12:41**									

Traded to **Chicago** by **Calgary** with Marty McInnis and Erik Andersson for Jeff Shantz and Steve Dubinsky, October 27, 1998. Claimed by **Calgary** from **Chicago** in Waiver Draft, September 28, 2001. Traded to **Columbus** by **Calgary** for Blake Sloan, March 19, 2002.

ALLISON, Jason

(AHL-lih-sohn, JAY-suhn) **L.A.**

Center. Shoots right. 6'3", 215 lbs. Born, North York, Ont., May 29, 1975. Washington's 2nd choice, 17th overall, in 1993 Entry Draft.

			Regular Season														Playoffs								
Season	Club	League	GP	G	A	Pts	PIM	PP	SH	GW	S	%	+/-	TF	F%	Min	GP	G	A	Pts	PIM	PP	SH	GW	Min
1990-91	North York	MTJHL	63	53	41	94																			
1991-92	London Knights	OHL	65	11	19	30	15										7	0	0	0	0				
1992-93	London Knights	OHL	66	42	76	118	50										12	7	13	20	8				
1993-94	London Knights	OHL	56	55	87	*142	68										5	2	13	15	13				
	Washington	**NHL**	**2**	**0**	**1**	**1**	**0**	**0**	**0**	**0**	**5**	**0.0**	**1**												
	Portland Pirates	AHL															6	2	1	3	0				
1994-95	London Knights	OHL	15	15	21	36	43																		
	Washington	**NHL**	**12**	**2**	**1**	**3**	**6**	**2**	**0**	**0**	**9**	**22.2**	**–3**												
	Portland Pirates	AHL	8	5	4	9	2										7	3	8	11	2				
1995-96	**Washington**	**NHL**	**19**	**0**	**3**	**3**	**2**	**0**	**0**	**0**	**18**	**0.0**	**–3**												
	Portland Pirates	AHL	57	28	41	69	42										6	1	6	7	9				
1996-97	**Washington**	**NHL**	**53**	**5**	**17**	**22**	**25**	**1**	**0**	**1**	**71**	**7.0**	**–3**												
	Boston	**NHL**	**19**	**3**	**9**	**12**	**9**	**1**	**0**	**0**	**28**	**10.7**	**–3**												
1997-98	**Boston**	**NHL**	**81**	**33**	**50**	**83**	**60**	**5**	**0**	**8**	**158**	**20.9**	**33**				**6**	**2**	**6**	**8**	**4**	**1**	**0**	**0**	
1998-99	**Boston**	**NHL**	**82**	**23**	**53**	**76**	**68**	**5**	**1**	**3**	**158**	**14.6**	**5**	**1760**	**52.2**	**22:23**	**12**	**2**	**9**	**11**	**6**	**1**	**0**	**0**	**25:36**
99-2000	**Boston**	**NHL**	**37**	**10**	**18**	**28**	**20**	**3**	**0**	**1**	**66**	**15.2**	**5**	**100**	**60.0**	**21:33**									
2000-01	**Boston**	**NHL**	**82**	**36**	**59**	**95**	**85**	**11**	**3**	**6**	**185**	**19.5**	**–8**	**1897**	**51.9**	**23:21**									
2001-02	**Los Angeles**	**NHL**	**73**	**19**	**55**	**74**	**68**	**5**	**0**	**2**	**139**	**13.7**	**2**	**1698**	**54.5**	**21:47**	**7**	**3**	**3**	**6**	**4**	**0**	**0**	**1**	**22:26**
2002-03	**Los Angeles**	**NHL**	**26**	**6**	**22**	**28**	**22**	**2**	**0**	**3**	**46**	**13.0**	**9**	**538**	**50.9**	**21:36**									
	NHL Totals		**486**	**137**	**288**	**425**	**365**	**35**	**4**	**24**	**883**	**15.5**		**5993**	**52.8**	**22:20**	**25**	**7**	**18**	**25**	**14**	**2**	**0**	**1**	**24:26**

OHL First All-Star Team (1994) • OHL MVP (1994) • Canadian Major Junior First All-Star Team (1994) • Canadian Major Junior Player of the Year (1994)

Played in NHL All-Star Game (2001)

Traded to **Boston** by **Washington** with Jim Carey, Anson Carter and Washington's 3rd round choice (Lee Goren) in 1997 Entry Draft for Bill Ranford, Adam Oates and Rick Tocchet, March 1, 1997. • Missed majority of 1999-2000 season recovering from thumb injury suffered in game vs. NY Islanders, January 8, 2000. Traded to **Los Angeles** by **Boston** with Mikko Eloranta for Jozef Stumpel and Glen Murray, October 24, 2001. • Missed majority of 2002-03 season recovering from knee (October 29, 2002 vs. Atlanta) and hip (January 25, 2003 vs. New Jersey) injuries.

AMONTE, Tony

(uh-MAHN-tee, TOH-nee) **PHI.**

Right wing. Shoots left. 6', 200 lbs. Born, Hingham, MA, August 2, 1970. NY Rangers' 3rd choice, 68th overall, in 1988 Entry Draft.

			Regular Season														Playoffs								
Season	Club	League	GP	G	A	Pts	PIM	PP	SH	GW	S	%	+/-	TF	F%	Min	GP	G	A	Pts	PIM	PP	SH	GW	Min
1985-86	Thayer Academy	Hi-School	2	0	0	0	0																		
1986-87	Thayer Academy	Hi-School	25	25	32	57																			
1987-88	Thayer Academy	Hi-School	28	30	38	68																			
1988-89	Thayer Academy	Hi-School	25	35	38	73																			
1989-90	Boston University	H-East	41	25	33	58	52																		
1990-91	Boston University	H-East	38	31	37	68	82																		
	NY Rangers	**NHL**															**2**	**0**	**2**	**2**	**2**	**0**	**0**	**0**	
1991-92	**NY Rangers**	**NHL**	**79**	**35**	**34**	**69**	**55**	**9**	**0**	**4**	**234**	**15.0**	**12**				**13**	**3**	**6**	**9**	**2**	**2**	**0**	**0**	
1992-93	**NY Rangers**	**NHL**	**83**	**33**	**43**	**76**	**49**	**13**	**0**	**4**	**270**	**12.2**	**0**												
1993-94	**NY Rangers**	**NHL**	**72**	**16**	**22**	**38**	**31**	**3**	**0**	**4**	**179**	**8.9**	**5**												
	Chicago	**NHL**	**7**	**1**	**3**	**4**	**6**	**1**	**0**	**0**	**16**	**6.3**	**–5**				**6**	**4**	**2**	**6**	**4**	**1**	**0**	**1**	
1994-95	HC Fassa	Euroliga	14	22	16	38	10																		
	HC Fassa	EuroHL	2	5	1	6	0																		
	Chicago	**NHL**	**48**	**15**	**20**	**35**	**41**	**6**	**1**	**3**	**105**	**14.3**	**7**				**16**	**3**	**3**	**6**	**10**	**0**	**0**	**0**	
1995-96	**Chicago**	**NHL**	**81**	**31**	**32**	**63**	**62**	**5**	**4**	**5**	**216**	**14.4**	**10**				**7**	**2**	**4**	**6**	**6**	**1**	**0**	**0**	
1996-97	**Chicago**	**NHL**	**81**	**41**	**36**	**77**	**64**	**9**	**2**	**4**	**266**	**15.4**	**35**				**6**	**4**	**2**	**6**	**8**	**0**	**0**	**0**	
1997-98	**Chicago**	**NHL**	**82**	**31**	**42**	**73**	**66**	**7**	**3**	**5**	**296**	**10.5**	**21**												
	United States	Olympics	4	0	1	1	4																		
1998-99	**Chicago**	**NHL**	**82**	**44**	**31**	**75**	**60**	**14**	**3**	**8**	**256**	**17.2**	**0**	**8**	**12.5**	**22:12**									
99-2000	**Chicago**	**NHL**	**82**	**43**	**41**	**84**	**48**	**11**	**5**	**2**	**260**	**16.5**	**10**	**22**	**22.7**	**21:54**									
2000-01	**Chicago**	**NHL**	**82**	**35**	**29**	**64**	**54**	**9**	**1**	**3**	**256**	**13.7**	**–22**	**27**	**40.7**	**22:09**									
2001-02	**Chicago**	**NHL**	**82**	**27**	**39**	**66**	**67**	**6**	**1**	**4**	**232**	**11.6**	**11**	**30**	**43.3**	**21:18**	**5**	**0**	**1**	**1**	**4**	**0**	**0**	**0**	**18:43**
	United States	Olympics	6	2	2	4	0																		
2002-03	**Phoenix**	**NHL**	**59**	**13**	**23**	**36**	**26**	**6**	**0**	**3**	**170**	**7.6**	**–12**	**53**	**35.9**	**19:27**									
	Philadelphia	**NHL**	**13**	**7**	**8**	**15**	**2**	**1**	**1**	**2**	**37**	**18.9**	**12**	**3**	**33.3**	**17:39**	**13**	**1**	**6**	**7**	**4**	**0**	**0**	**0**	**19:16**
	NHL Totals		**933**	**372**	**403**	**775**	**631**	**100**	**21**	**51**	**2793**	**13.3**		**143**	**35.0**	**21:23**	**68**	**17**	**26**	**43**	**40**	**4**	**0**	**1**	**19:07**

Hockey East Second All-Star Team (1991) • NCAA Championship All-Tournament Team (1991) • NHL All-Rookie Team (1992)

Played in NHL All-Star Game (1997, 1998, 1999, 2000, 2001)

• Missed majority of 1985-86 season recovering from knee injury, October, 1985. Traded to **Chicago** by **NY Rangers** with the rights to Matt Oates for Stephane Matteau and Brian Noonan, March 21, 1994. Signed as a free agent by **Phoenix**, July 12, 2002. Traded to **Philadelphia** by **Phoenix** for Guillaume Lefebvre, Atlanta's 3rd round choice (previously acquired, Phoenix selected Tyler Redenbach) in 2003 Entry Draft and Philadelphia's 2nd round choice in 2004 Entry Draft, March 10, 2003.

ANDERSSON, Jonas

(AN-duhr-suhn, JOH-nas) **NSH.**

Right wing. Shoots left. 6'3", 202 lbs. Born, Stockholm, Sweden, February 24, 1981. Nashville's 2nd choice, 33rd overall, in 1999 Entry Draft.

			Regular Season														Playoffs								
Season	Club	League	GP	G	A	Pts	PIM	PP	SH	GW	S	%	+/-	TF	F%	Min	GP	G	A	Pts	PIM	PP	SH	GW	Min
1997-98	AIK Solna Jr.	Swede-Jr.	33	14	16	30	32																		
1998-99	AIK Solna Jr.	Swede-Jr.	16	3	7	10	18																		
	London Knights	Britain	12	2	3	5	0																		
99-2000	North Bay	OHL	67	31	36	67	27										6	2	2	4	2				
	Milwaukee	IHL	2	1	0	1	0										2	0	0	0	2				
2000-01	Milwaukee	IHL	52	6	7	13	44										5	0	0	0	2				
2001-02	**Nashville**	**NHL**	**5**	**0**	**0**	**0**	**2**	**0**	**0**	**0**	**4**	**0.0**	**–2**	**0**	**0.0**	**9:06**									
	Milwaukee	AHL	71	13	17	30	19																		
2002-03	Milwaukee	AHL	49	7	4	11	12										5	0	1	1	4				
	NHL Totals		**5**	**0**	**0**	**0**	**2**	**0**	**0**	**0**	**4**	**0.0**		**0**	**0.0**	**9:06**									

ANDERSSON, Niklas

(AN-duhr-suhn, NIHK-las)

Left wing. Shoots left. 5'9", 180 lbs. Born, Kungalv, Sweden, May 20, 1971. Quebec's 5th choice, 68th overall, in 1989 Entry Draft.

			Regular Season														Playoffs								
Season	Club	League	GP	G	A	Pts	PIM	PP	SH	GW	S	%	+/-	TF	F%	Min	GP	G	A	Pts	PIM	PP	SH	GW	Min
1987-88	Vastra Frolunda	Swede-2	15	5	4	9	6										8	6	4	10	4				
1988-89	Vastra Frolunda	Swede-2	30	12	24	36	24										10	4	6	10	4				
1989-90	Vastra Frolunda	Sweden	38	10	21	31	14																		
1990-91	Vastra Frolunda	Sweden	39	14	25	39	38										10	6	3	9	24				
1991-92	Halifax Citadels	AHL	57	8	26	34	41																		
1992-93	**Quebec**	**NHL**	**3**	**0**	**1**	**1**	**2**	**0**	**0**	**0**	**4**	**0.0**	**0**												
	Halifax Citadels	AHL	76	32	50	82	42																		
1993-94	Cornwall Aces	AHL	42	18	34	52	8																		
1994-95	Denver Grizzlies	IHL	66	22	39	61	28										15	8	13	21	10				
1995-96	**NY Islanders**	**NHL**	**47**	**14**	**12**	**26**	**12**	**3**	**2**	**1**	**89**	**15.7**	**–3**												
	Utah Grizzlies	IHL	30	13	22	35	25																		
1996-97	**NY Islanders**	**NHL**	**74**	**12**	**31**	**43**	**57**	**1**	**1**	**1**	**122**	**9.8**	**4**												

			Regular Season														Playoffs								
Season	Club	League	GP	G	A	Pts	PIM	PP	SH	GW	S	%	+/-	TF	F%	Min	GP	G	A	Pts	PIM	PP	SH	GW	Min
1997-98	**San Jose**	**NHL**	**5**	**0**	**0**	**0**	**2**	**0**	**0**	**0**	**6**	**0.0**	**–1**	....	....	....	....	....	....	....	....	....	....	....	....
	Kentucky	AHL	37	10	28	38	54	....	....	....	....	....	....	....	....	....	....	....	....	....	....	....	....	....	....
	Utah Grizzlies	IHL	21	6	20	26	24	....	....	....	....	....	....	....	....	....	4	3	1	4	4	....	....	....	....
1998-99	Chicago Wolves	IHL	65	17	47	64	49	....	....	....	....	....	....	....	....	....	10	2	2	4	10	....	....	....	....
99-2000	**NY Islanders**	**NHL**	**17**	**3**	**7**	**10**	**8**	**1**	**0**	**0**	**24**	**12.5**	**–3**	**0**	**0.0**	**13:19**	....	....	....	....	....	....	....	....	....
	Chicago Wolves	IHL	52	20	21	41	59	....	....	....	....	....	....	....	....	....	9	6	1	7	4	....	....	....	....
	Nashville	**NHL**	**7**	**0**	**1**	**1**	**0**	**0**	**0**	**0**	**7**	**0.0**	**0**	**0**	**0.0**	**12:50**	....	....	....	....	....	....	....	....	....
2000-01	**Calgary**	**NHL**	**11**	**0**	**1**	**1**	**4**	**0**	**0**	**0**	**8**	**0.0**	**0**	**4**	**25.0**	**11:10**	....	....	....	....	....	....	....	....	....
	Chicago Wolves	IHL	66	33	39	72	81	....	....	....	....	....	....	....	....	....	16	1	*14	15	14	....	....	....	....
2001-02	Vastra Frolunda	Sweden	41	14	32	46	64	....	....	....	....	....	....	....	....	....	7	0	2	2	6	....	....	....	....
2002-03	Vastra Frolunda	Sweden	49	24	18	42	59	....	....	....	....	....	....	....	....	....	15	3	7	10	8	....	....	....	....
	NHL Totals		**164**	**29**	**53**	**82**	**85**	**5**	**3**	**2**	**260**	**11.2**		**4**	**25.0**	**12:33**	....	....	....	....	....	....	....	....	....

IHL Second All-Star Team (2000) • IHL First All-Star Team (2001)

Signed as a free agent by **NY Islanders**, July 15, 1994. Signed as a free agent by **San Jose**, September 17, 1997. Signed as a free agent by **Toronto**, September 4, 1998. Traded to **NY Islanders** by **Toronto** for Craig Charron, August 17, 1999. Claimed on waivers by **Nashville** from **NY Islanders**, January 20, 2000. Claimed on waivers by **NY Islanders** from **Nashville**, February 19, 2000. Signed as a free agent by **Calgary**, August 29, 2000. Signed as a free agent by **Vastra Frolunda** (Sweden), May 23, 2001.

ANDREYCHUK, Dave

(AN-druh-chuhk, DAYV) **T.B.**

Left wing. Shoots right. 6'4", 220 lbs. Born, Hamilton, Ont., September 29, 1963. Buffalo's 3rd choice, 16th overall, in 1982 Entry Draft.

1979-80	Hamilton Hawks	OMHA	21	25	24	49	....	....	....	....	....	....	....	....	....	....	....	....	....	....	....	....	....	....	....
1980-81	Oshawa Generals	OMJHL	67	22	22	44	80	....	....	....	....	....	....	....	....	....	10	3	2	5	20	....	....	....	....
1981-82	Oshawa Generals	OHL	67	57	43	100	71	....	....	....	....	....	....	....	....	....	3	1	4	5	16	....	....	....	....
1982-83	Oshawa Generals	OHL	14	8	24	32	6	....	....	....	....	....	....	....	....	....	....	....	....	....	....	....	....	....	....
	Buffalo	**NHL**	**43**	**14**	**23**	**37**	**16**	**3**	**0**	**1**	**66**	**21.2**	**6**	....	....	....	**4**	**1**	**0**	**1**	**4**	**0**	**0**	**0**	....
1983-84	**Buffalo**	**NHL**	**78**	**38**	**42**	**80**	**42**	**10**	**0**	**7**	**178**	**21.3**	**20**	....	....	....	**2**	**0**	**1**	**1**	**2**	**0**	**0**	**0**	....
1984-85	**Buffalo**	**NHL**	**64**	**31**	**30**	**61**	**54**	**14**	**0**	**2**	**153**	**20.3**	**–4**	....	....	....	**5**	**4**	**2**	**6**	**4**	**0**	**0**	**2**	....
1985-86	**Buffalo**	**NHL**	**80**	**36**	**51**	**87**	**61**	**12**	**0**	**3**	**225**	**16.0**	**3**	....	....	....	....	....	....	....	....	....	....	....	....
1986-87	**Buffalo**	**NHL**	**77**	**25**	**48**	**73**	**46**	**13**	**0**	**2**	**255**	**9.8**	**2**	....	....	....	....	....	....	....	....	....	....	....	....
1987-88	**Buffalo**	**NHL**	**80**	**30**	**48**	**78**	**112**	**15**	**0**	**5**	**253**	**11.9**	**1**	....	....	....	**6**	**2**	**4**	**6**	**0**	**1**	**0**	**0**	....
1988-89	**Buffalo**	**NHL**	**56**	**28**	**24**	**52**	**40**	**7**	**0**	**3**	**145**	**19.3**	**0**	....	....	....	**5**	**0**	**3**	**3**	**0**	**0**	**0**	**0**	....
1989-90	**Buffalo**	**NHL**	**73**	**40**	**42**	**82**	**42**	**18**	**0**	**3**	**206**	**19.4**	**6**	....	....	....	**6**	**2**	**5**	**7**	**2**	**1**	**0**	**0**	....
1990-91	**Buffalo**	**NHL**	**80**	**36**	**33**	**69**	**32**	**13**	**0**	**4**	**234**	**15.4**	**11**	....	....	....	**6**	**2**	**2**	**4**	**8**	**1**	**0**	**0**	....
1991-92	**Buffalo**	**NHL**	**80**	**41**	**50**	**91**	**71**	**28**	**0**	**2**	**337**	**12.2**	**–9**	....	....	....	**7**	**1**	**3**	**4**	**12**	**0**	**0**	**0**	....
1992-93	**Buffalo**	**NHL**	**52**	**29**	**32**	**61**	**48**	**20**	**0**	**2**	**171**	**17.0**	**–8**	....	....	....	....	....	....	....	....	....	....	....	....
	Toronto	**NHL**	**31**	**25**	**13**	**38**	**8**	**12**	**0**	**2**	**139**	**18.0**	**12**	....	....	....	**21**	**12**	**7**	**19**	**35**	**4**	**0**	**3**	....
1993-94	**Toronto**	**NHL**	**83**	**53**	**46**	**99**	**98**	**21**	**5**	**8**	**333**	**15.9**	**22**	....	....	....	**18**	**5**	**5**	**10**	**16**	**3**	**1**	**0**	....
1994-95	**Toronto**	**NHL**	**48**	**22**	**16**	**38**	**34**	**8**	**0**	**2**	**168**	**13.1**	**–7**	....	....	....	**7**	**3**	**2**	**5**	**25**	**2**	**0**	**0**	....
1995-96	**Toronto**	**NHL**	**61**	**20**	**24**	**44**	**54**	**12**	**2**	**3**	**200**	**10.0**	**–11**	....	....	....	....	....	....	....	....	....	....	....	....
	New Jersey	**NHL**	**15**	**8**	**5**	**13**	**10**	**2**	**0**	**0**	**41**	**19.5**	**2**	....	....	....	....	....	....	....	....	....	....	....	....
1996-97	**New Jersey**	**NHL**	**82**	**27**	**34**	**61**	**48**	**4**	**1**	**2**	**233**	**11.6**	**38**	....	....	....	**1**	**0**	**0**	**0**	**0**	**0**	**0**	**0**	....
1997-98	**New Jersey**	**NHL**	**75**	**14**	**34**	**48**	**26**	**4**	**0**	**2**	**180**	**7.8**	**19**	....	....	....	**6**	**1**	**0**	**1**	**4**	**1**	**0**	**0**	....
1998-99	**New Jersey**	**NHL**	**52**	**15**	**13**	**28**	**20**	**4**	**0**	**3**	**110**	**13.6**	**1**	**9**	**44.4**	**15:32**	**4**	**2**	**0**	**2**	**4**	**0**	**0**	**0**	**10:40**
99-2000	**Boston**	**NHL**	**63**	**19**	**14**	**33**	**28**	**7**	**0**	**2**	**192**	**9.9**	**–11**	**446**	**52.0**	**19:50**	....	....	....	....	....	....	....	....	....
	Colorado	**NHL**	**14**	**1**	**2**	**3**	**2**	**1**	**0**	**1**	**41**	**2.4**	**–9**	**15**	**60.0**	**17:16**	**17**	**3**	**2**	**5**	**18**	**2**	**0**	**0**	**16:22**
2000-01	**Buffalo**	**NHL**	**74**	**20**	**13**	**33**	**32**	**8**	**0**	**4**	**119**	**16.8**	**0**	**187**	**49.7**	**11:60**	**13**	**1**	**2**	**3**	**4**	**1**	**0**	**0**	**11:04**
2001-02	**Tampa Bay**	**NHL**	**82**	**21**	**17**	**38**	**109**	**9**	**1**	**5**	**161**	**13.0**	**–12**	**1393**	**53.0**	**16:26**	....	....	....	....	....	....	....	....	....
2002-03	**Tampa Bay**	**NHL**	**72**	**20**	**14**	**34**	**34**	**15**	**0**	**3**	**170**	**11.8**	**–12**	**1117**	**58.4**	**16:27**	**11**	**3**	**3**	**6**	**10**	**1**	**0**	**1**	**21:23**
	NHL Totals		**1515**	**613**	**668**	**1281**	**1067**	***260**	**9**	**71**	**4310**	**14.2**		**3167**	**54.6**	**16:01**	**139**	**42**	**41**	**83**	**148**	**17**	**1**	**6**	**15:33**

Played in NHL All-Star Game (1990, 1994)

Traded to **Toronto** by **Buffalo** with Daren Puppa and Buffalo's 1st round choice (Kenny Jonsson) in 1993 Entry Draft for Grant Fuhr and Toronto's 5th round choice (Kevin Popp) in 1995 Entry Draft, February 2, 1993. Traded to **New Jersey** by **Toronto** for New Jersey's 2nd round choice (Marek Posmyk) in 1996 Entry Draft and New Jersey's 3rd round choice (later traded back to New Jersey – New Jersey selected Andre Lakos) in 1999 Entry Draft, March 13, 1996. Signed as a free agent by Boston, July 29, 1999. Traded to **Colorado** by **Boston** with Raymond Bourque for Brian Rolston, Martin Grenier, Samuel Pahlsson and New Jersey's 1st round choice (previously acquired, Boston selected Martin Samuelsson) in 2000 Entry Draft, March 6, 2000. Signed as a free agent by **Buffalo**, July 13, 2000. Signed as a free agent by **Tampa Bay**, July 13, 2001.

ANTROPOV, Nik

(an-TROH-pahv, NIHK) **TOR.**

Center. Shoots left. 6'6", 220 lbs. Born, Vost, USSR, February 18, 1980. Toronto's 1st choice, 10th overall, in 1998 Entry Draft.

1995-96	Ust-Kamenog. Jr.	CIS-Jr.	20	18	20	38	30	....	....	....	....	....	....	....	....	....	....	....	....	....	....	....	....	....	....
1996-97	Ust-Kamenogorsk	Russia-2	8	2	1	3	6	....	....	....	....	....	....	....	....	....	....	....	....	....	....	....	....	....	....
1997-98	Ust-Kamenogorsk	Russia-2	42	15	24	39	62	....	....	....	....	....	....	....	....	....	....	....	....	....	....	....	....	....	....
1998-99	Dynamo Moscow	Russia	30	5	9	14	30	....	....	....	....	....	....	....	....	....	11	0	1	1	4	....	....	....	....
99-2000	**Toronto**	**NHL**	**66**	**12**	**18**	**30**	**41**	**0**	**0**	**2**	**89**	**13.5**	**14**	**501**	**46.3**	**12:48**	**3**	**0**	**0**	**0**	**4**	**0**	**0**	**0**	**10:14**
	St. John's	AHL	2	0	0	0	4	....	....	....	....	....	....	....	....	....	....	....	....	....	....	....	....	....	....
2000-01	**Toronto**	**NHL**	**52**	**6**	**11**	**17**	**30**	**0**	**0**	**1**	**71**	**8.5**	**5**	**431**	**44.3**	**10:02**	**9**	**2**	**1**	**3**	**12**	**1**	**0**	**1**	**11:04**
2001-02	**Toronto**	**NHL**	**11**	**1**	**1**	**2**	**4**	**0**	**0**	**0**	**12**	**8.3**	**–1**	**31**	**38.7**	**8:57**	....	....	....	....	....	....	....	....	....
	St. John's	AHL	34	11	24	35	47	....	....	....	....	....	....	....	....	....	....	....	....	....	....	....	....	....	....
2002-03	**Toronto**	**NHL**	**72**	**16**	**29**	**45**	**124**	**2**	**1**	**6**	**102**	**15.7**	**11**	**621**	**40.1**	**14:60**	**3**	**0**	**0**	**0**	**0**	**0**	**0**	**0**	**19:17**
	NHL Totals		**201**	**35**	**59**	**94**	**199**	**2**	**1**	**9**	**274**	**12.8**		**1584**	**43.2**	**12:40**	**15**	**2**	**1**	**3**	**16**	**1**	**0**	**1**	**12:32**

ARKHIPOV, Denis

(AHR-kih-pahv, DIHN-ihs) **NSH.**

Center. Shoots left. 6'3", 214 lbs. Born, Kazan, USSR, May 19, 1979. Nashville's 2nd choice, 60th overall, in 1998 Entry Draft.

1994-95	Ak Bars Kazan Jr.	CIS-Jr.	40	20	12	32	10	....	....	....	....	....	....	....	....	....	....	....	....	....	....	....	....	....	....
1995-96	Ak Bars Kazan Jr.	CIS-Jr.	40	15	8	23	30	....	....	....	....	....	....	....	....	....	....	....	....	....	....	....	....	....	....
	Ak Bars Kazan	CIS	15	10	8	18	10	....	....	....	....	....	....	....	....	....	....	....	....	....	....	....	....	....	....
1996-97	Ak Bars Kazan 2	Russia-3	50	17	23	40	20	....	....	....	....	....	....	....	....	....	....	....	....	....	....	....	....	....	....
	Ak Bars Kazan	Russia	1	1	0	1	0	....	....	....	....	....	....	....	....	....	....	....	....	....	....	....	....	....	....
1997-98	Ak Bars Kazan	Russia	29	2	2	4	2	....	....	....	....	....	....	....	....	....	....	....	....	....	....	....	....	....	....
1998-99	Ak Bars Kazan	Russia	34	12	1	13	22	....	....	....	....	....	....	....	....	....	9	2	3	5	6	....	....	....	....
	Ak Bars Kazan	EuroHL	4	0	0	0	0	....	....	....	....	....	....	....	....	....	1	0	0	0	0	....	....	....	....
99-2000	Ak Bars Kazan	Russia	32	7	9	16	14	....	....	....	....	....	....	....	....	....	18	5	5	10	6	....	....	....	....
2000-01	**Nashville**	**NHL**	**40**	**6**	**7**	**13**	**4**	**0**	**0**	**0**	**42**	**14.3**	**0**	**299**	**43.8**	**9:56**	....	....	....	....	....	....	....	....	....
	Milwaukee	IHL	40	9	8	17	11	....	....	....	....	....	....	....	....	....	....	....	....	....	....	....	....	....	....
2001-02	**Nashville**	**NHL**	**82**	**20**	**22**	**42**	**16**	**7**	**0**	**6**	**118**	**16.9**	**–18**	**1108**	**44.8**	**15:43**	....	....	....	....	....	....	....	....	....
2002-03	**Nashville**	**NHL**	**79**	**11**	**24**	**35**	**32**	**3**	**0**	**1**	**148**	**7.4**	**–18**	**1069**	**46.7**	**15:09**	....	....	....	....	....	....	....	....	....
	NHL Totals		**201**	**37**	**53**	**90**	**52**	**10**	**0**	**7**	**308**	**12.0**		**2476**	**45.5**	**14:20**	....	....	....	....	....	....	....	....	....

ARMSTRONG, Derek

(ahrm-STRAWNG, DEHR-ehk) **L.A.**

Center. Shoots right. 6', 195 lbs. Born, Ottawa, Ont., April 23, 1973. NY Islanders' 5th choice, 128th overall, in 1992 Entry Draft.

1989-90	Hawkesbury	OCJHL	48	8	10	18	30	....	....	....	....	....	....	....	....	....	....	....	....	....	....	....	....	....	....
1990-91	Hawkesbury	OCJHL	54	27	45	72	49	....	....	....	....	....	....	....	....	....	....	....	....	....	....	....	....	....	....
	Sudbury Wolves	OHL	2	0	2	2	0	....	....	....	....	....	....	....	....	....	....	....	....	....	....	....	....	....	....
1991-92	Sudbury Wolves	OHL	66	31	54	85	22	....	....	....	....	....	....	....	....	....	9	2	2	4	2	....	....	....	....
1992-93	Sudbury Wolves	OHL	66	44	62	106	56	....	....	....	....	....	....	....	....	....	14	9	10	19	26	....	....	....	....
1993-94	**NY Islanders**	**NHL**	**1**	**0**	**0**	**0**	**0**	**0**	**0**	**0**	**2**	**0.0**	**0**	....	....	....	....	....	....	....	....	....	....	....	....
	Salt Lake	IHL	76	23	35	58	61	....	....	....	....	....	....	....	....	....	....	....	....	....	....	....	....	....	....
1994-95	Denver Grizzlies	IHL	59	13	18	31	65	....	....	....	....	....	....	....	....	....	6	0	2	2	0	....	....	....	....
1995-96	**NY Islanders**	**NHL**	**19**	**1**	**3**	**4**	**14**	**0**	**0**	**0**	**23**	**4.3**	**–6**	....	....	....	....	....	....	....	....	....	....	....	....
	Worcester IceCats	AHL	51	11	15	26	33	....	....	....	....	....	....	....	....	....	4	2	1	3	0	....	....	....	....
1996-97	**NY Islanders**	**NHL**	**50**	**6**	**7**	**13**	**33**	**0**	**0**	**2**	**36**	**16.7**	**–8**	....	....	....	....	....	....	....	....	....	....	....	....
	Utah Grizzlies	IHL	17	4	8	12	10	....	....	....	....	....	....	....	....	....	6	0	4	4	4	....	....	....	....
1997-98	**Ottawa**	**NHL**	**9**	**2**	**0**	**2**	**9**	**0**	**0**	**1**	**8**	**25.0**	**1**	....	....	....	....	....	....	....	....	....	....	....	....
	Detroit Vipers	IHL	10	0	1	1	2	....	....	....	....	....	....	....	....	....	....	....	....	....	....	....	....	....	....
	Hartford	AHL	54	16	30	46	40	....	....	....	....	....	....	....	....	....	15	2	6	8	22	....	....	....	....
1998-99	**NY Rangers**	**NHL**	**3**	**0**	**0**	**0**	**0**	**0**	**0**	**0**	**1**	**0.0**	**0**	**0**	**0.0**	**2:50**	....	....	....	....	....	....	....	....	....
	Hartford	AHL	59	29	51	80	73	....	....	....	....	....	....	....	....	....	7	5	4	9	10	....	....	....	....
99-2000	**NY Rangers**	**NHL**	**1**	**0**	**0**	**0**	**0**	**0**	**0**	**0**	**1**	**0.0**	**0**	**3**	**33.3**	**3:10**	....	....	....	....	....	....	....	....	....
	Hartford	AHL	77	28	54	82	101	....	....	....	....	....	....	....	....	....	23	7	16	23	24	....	....	....	....

			Regular Season														Playoffs								
Season	Club	League	GP	G	A	Pts	PIM	PP	SH	GW	S	%	+/-	TF	F%	Min	GP	G	A	Pts	PIM	PP	SH	GW	Min
2000-01	NY Rangers	NHL	3	0	0	0	0	0	0	0	6	0.0	0	30	50.0	11:22	....	....	....	....	....	....	....	....	....
	Hartford	AHL	75	32	*69	*101	73	....	....	....	....	....	....	....	....	....	5	0	6	6	6	....	....	....	....
2001-02	SC Bern	Swiss	44	17	36	53	62	....	....	....	....	....	....	....	....	....	6	3	5	8	8	....	....	....	....
2002-03	Los Angeles	NHL	66	12	26	38	30	2	0	1	106	11.3	5	708	50.0	15:40	....	....	....	....	....	....	....	....	....
	Manchester	AHL	2	3	0	3	4	....	....	....	....	....	....	....	....	....	....	....	....	....	....	....	....	....	....
	NHL Totals		152	21	36	57	86	2	0	4	183	11.5		741	49.9	14:48	....	....	....	....	....	....	....	....	....

AHL Second All-Star Team (2000) • AHL First All-Star Team (2001) • John P. Sollenberger Trophy (Top Scorer – AHL) (2001) • Les Cunningham Award (MVP – AHL) (2001)

Signed as a free agent by **Ottawa**, July 28, 1997. Loaned to **Hartford** (AHL) by **Ottawa**, October 28, 1997. Signed as a free agent by **NY Rangers**, August 10, 1998. Signed as a free agent by **SC Bern** (Swiss) with NY Rangers retaining NHL rights, July 18, 2001. Traded to **Los Angeles** by **NY Rangers** for Los Angeles' 6th round choice (Chris Holt) in 2003 Entry Draft, July 16, 2002.

ARNASON, Tyler

(AHR-na-suhn, TIGH-luhr) **CHI.**

Center. Shoots left. 5'11", 198 lbs. Born, Oklahoma City, OK, March 16, 1979. Chicago's 6th choice, 183rd overall, in 1998 Entry Draft.

Season	Club	League	GP	G	A	Pts	PIM	PP	SH	GW	S	%	+/-	TF	F%	Min	GP	G	A	Pts	PIM	PP	SH	GW	Min
1996-97	Winnipeg South	MJHL	50	35	50	85	15	....	....	....	....	....	....	....	....	....	6	3	3	6	18	....	....	....	....
1997-98	Fargo-Moorhead	USHL	52	37	45	82	16	....	....	....	....	....	....	....	....	....	4	1	1	2	2	....	....	....	....
1998-99	St. Cloud State	WCHA	38	14	17	31	16	....	....	....	....	....	....	....	....	....	....	....	....	....	....	....	....	....	....
99-2000	St. Cloud State	WCHA	39	19	30	49	18	....	....	....	....	....	....	....	....	....	....	....	....	....	....	....	....	....	....
2000-01	St. Cloud State	WCHA	41	28	28	56	14	....	....	....	....	....	....	....	....	....	....	....	....	....	....	....	....	....	....
2001-02	Chicago	NHL	21	3	1	4	4	0	0	0	19	15.8	–3	112	41.1	9:28	3	0	0	0	0	0	0	0	7:43
	Norfolk Admirals	AHL	60	26	30	56	42	....	....	....	....	....	....	....	....	....	....	....	....	....	....	....	....	....	....
2002-03	Chicago	NHL	82	19	20	39	20	3	0	6	178	10.7	7	626	40.3	14:30	....	....	....	....	....	....	....	....	....
	NHL Totals		103	22	21	43	24	3	0	6	197	11.2		738	40.4	13:29	3	0	0	0	0	0	0	0	7:43

MJHL Rookie of the Year (1997) • USHL First All-Star Team (1998) • WCHA All-Rookie Team (1999) • WCHA Second All-Star Team (2000) • AHL All-Rookie Team (2002) • Dudley "Red" Garrett Memorial Trophy (Top Rookie – AHL) (2002) • NHL All-Rookie Team (2003)

ARNOTT, Jason

(AHR-niht, JAY-suhn) **DAL.**

Center. Shoots right. 6'4", 225 lbs. Born, Collingwood, Ont., October 11, 1974. Edmonton's 1st choice, 7th overall, in 1993 Entry Draft.

Season	Club	League	GP	G	A	Pts	PIM	PP	SH	GW	S	%	+/-	TF	F%	Min	GP	G	A	Pts	PIM	PP	SH	GW	Min
1989-90	Stayner Siskins	OJHL-C	34	21	31	52	12	....	....	....	....	....	....	....	....	....	....	....	....	....	....	....	....	....	....
1990-91	Lindsay Bears	OJHL-B	42	17	44	61	10	....	....	....	....	....	....	....	....	....	8	9	8	17	6	....	....	....	....
1991-92	Oshawa Generals	OHL	57	9	15	24	12	....	....	....	....	....	....	....	....	....	....	....	....	....	....	....	....	....	....
1992-93	Oshawa Generals	OHL	56	41	57	98	74	....	....	....	....	....	....	....	....	....	13	9	9	18	20	....	....	....	....
1993-94	Edmonton	NHL	78	33	35	68	104	10	0	4	194	17.0	1	....	....	....	....	....	....	....	....	....	....	....	....
1994-95	Edmonton	NHL	42	15	22	37	128	7	0	1	156	9.6	–14	....	....	....	....	....	....	....	....	....	....	....	....
1995-96	Edmonton	NHL	64	28	31	59	87	8	0	5	244	11.5	–6	....	....	....	....	....	....	....	....	....	....	....	....
1996-97	Edmonton	NHL	67	19	38	57	92	10	1	2	248	7.7	–21	....	....	....	12	3	6	9	18	1	0	0	....
1997-98	Edmonton	NHL	35	5	13	18	78	1	0	0	100	5.0	–16	....	....	....	....	....	....	....	....	....	....	....	....
	New Jersey	NHL	35	5	10	15	21	3	0	2	99	5.1	–8	....	....	....	5	0	2	2	0	0	0	0	....
1998-99	New Jersey	NHL	74	27	27	54	79	8	0	3	200	13.5	10	872	49.3	15:24	7	2	2	4	4	1	0	0	16:48
99-2000♦	New Jersey	NHL	76	22	34	56	51	7	0	4	244	9.0	22	1172	46.9	17:05	23	8	12	20	18	3	0	1	16:29
2000-01	New Jersey	NHL	54	21	34	55	75	8	0	3	138	15.2	23	760	49.6	16:12	23	8	7	15	16	5	0	0	15:49
2001-02	New Jersey	NHL	63	22	19	41	59	8	0	1	169	13.0	3	934	47.8	17:13	....	....	....	....	....	....	....	....	....
	Dallas	NHL	10	3	1	4	6	2	0	2	28	10.7	–1	77	52.0	18:13	....	....	....	....	....	....	....	....	....
2002-03	Dallas	NHL	72	23	24	47	51	7	0	6	169	13.6	9	1130	53.3	16:12	11	3	2	5	6	1	0	0	15:35
	NHL Totals		670	223	288	511	831	79	1	33	1989	11.2		4945	49.4	16:28	81	24	31	55	62	11	0	1	16:07

NHL All-Rookie Team (1994)

Played in NHL All-Star Game (1997)

Traded to **New Jersey** by **Edmonton** with Bryan Muir for Valeri Zelepukin and Bill Guerin, January 4, 1998. Traded to **Dallas** by **New Jersey** with Randy McKay and New Jersey's 1st round choice (later traded to Columbus – later traded to Buffalo – Buffalo selected Dan Paille) in 2002 Entry Draft for Joe Nieuwendyk and Jamie Langenbrunner, March 19, 2002.

ARVEDSON, Magnus

(AHR-vehd-suhn, MAGH-nuhs)

Left wing. Shoots left. 6'2", 198 lbs. Born, Karlstad, Sweden, November 25, 1971. Ottawa's 4th choice, 119th overall, in 1997 Entry Draft.

Season	Club	League	GP	G	A	Pts	PIM	PP	SH	GW	S	%	+/-	TF	F%	Min	GP	G	A	Pts	PIM	PP	SH	GW	Min
1990-91	Orebro IK	Swede-2	29	7	11	18	12	....	....	....	....	....	....	....	....	....	2	0	1	1	2	....	....	....	....
1991-92	Orebro IK	Swede-2	32	12	21	33	30	....	....	....	....	....	....	....	....	....	7	4	4	8	4	....	....	....	....
1992-93	Orebro IK	Swede-2	36	11	18	29	34	....	....	....	....	....	....	....	....	....	6	2	1	3	0	....	....	....	....
1993-94	Farjestad	Sweden	16	1	7	8	10	....	....	....	....	....	....	....	....	....	....	....	....	....	....	....	....	....	....
1994-95	Farjestad Jr.	Swede-Jr.	1	0	0	0	0	....	....	....	....	....	....	....	....	....	....	....	....	....	....	....	....	....	....
	Farjestad	Sweden	36	1	6	7	45	....	....	....	....	....	....	....	....	....	4	0	0	0	6	....	....	....	....
1995-96	Farjestad	Sweden	40	10	14	24	40	....	....	....	....	....	....	....	....	....	8	0	3	3	10	....	....	....	....
1996-97	Farjestad	Sweden	48	13	11	24	36	....	....	....	....	....	....	....	....	....	14	4	7	11	8	....	....	....	....
	Farjestad	EuroHL	5	1	0	1	2	....	....	....	....	....	....	....	....	....	2	0	1	1	2	....	....	....	....
1997-98	Ottawa	NHL	61	11	15	26	36	0	1	0	90	12.2	2	....	....	....	11	0	1	1	6	0	0	0	....
1998-99	Ottawa	NHL	80	21	26	47	50	0	4	6	136	15.4	33	25	20.0	17:08	3	0	1	1	2	0	0	0	21:32
99-2000	Ottawa	NHL	47	15	13	28	36	1	1	4	91	16.5	4	11	45.5	18:04	6	0	0	0	6	0	0	0	17:25
2000-01	Ottawa	NHL	51	17	16	33	24	1	2	4	79	21.5	23	7	28.6	16:01	2	0	0	0	0	0	0	0	16:20
2001-02	Ottawa	NHL	74	12	27	39	35	0	0	1	121	9.9	27	8	37.5	17:44	12	2	1	3	4	0	0	0	17:00
	Sweden	Olympics	4	0	0	0	0	....	....	....	....	....	....	....	....	....	....	....	....	....	....	....	....	....	....
2002-03	Ottawa	NHL	80	16	21	37	48	2	0	4	138	11.6	13	30	36.7	17:54	18	1	5	6	16	0	0	0	15:35
	NHL Totals		393	92	118	210	229	4	8	19	655	14.0		81	32.1	17:25	52	3	8	11	34	0	0	0	16:44

ASHAM, Arron

(ASH-uhm, AIR-ruhn) **NYI**

Right wing. Shoots right. 5'11", 209 lbs. Born, Portage La Prairie, Man., April 13, 1978. Montreal's 3rd choice, 71st overall, in 1996 Entry Draft.

Season	Club	League	GP	G	A	Pts	PIM	PP	SH	GW	S	%	+/-	TF	F%	Min	GP	G	A	Pts	PIM	PP	SH	GW	Min
1993-94	Portage	MAHA	21	18	19	37	82	....	....	....	....	....	....	....	....	....	....	....	....	....	....	....	....	....	....
1994-95	Red Deer Rebels	WHL	62	11	16	27	126	....	....	....	....	....	....	....	....	....	....	....	....	....	....	....	....	....	....
1995-96	Red Deer Rebels	WHL	70	32	45	77	174	....	....	....	....	....	....	....	....	....	10	6	3	9	20	....	....	....	....
1996-97	Red Deer Rebels	WHL	67	45	51	96	149	....	....	....	....	....	....	....	....	....	16	12	14	26	36	....	....	....	....
1997-98	Red Deer Rebels	WHL	67	43	49	92	153	....	....	....	....	....	....	....	....	....	5	0	2	2	8	....	....	....	....
	Fredericton	AHL	2	1	1	2	0	....	....	....	....	....	....	....	....	....	2	0	1	1	0	....	....	....	....
1998-99	Montreal	NHL	7	0	0	0	0	0	0	0	5	0.0	–4	0	0.0	7:27	....	....	....	....	....	....	....	....	....
	Fredericton	AHL	60	16	18	34	118	....	....	....	....	....	....	....	....	....	13	8	6	14	11	....	....	....	....
99-2000	Montreal	NHL	33	4	2	6	24	0	1	1	29	13.8	–7	1	0.0	10:14	....	....	....	....	....	....	....	....	....
	Quebec Citadelles	AHL	13	4	5	9	32	....	....	....	....	....	....	....	....	....	2	0	0	0	2	....	....	....	....
2000-01	Montreal	NHL	46	2	3	5	59	0	0	0	32	6.3	–9	3	100.0	8:28	....	....	....	....	....	....	....	....	....
	Quebec Citadelles	AHL	15	7	9	16	51	....	....	....	....	....	....	....	....	....	7	1	2	3	2	....	....	....	....
2001-02	Montreal	NHL	35	5	4	9	55	0	0	0	30	16.7	7	4	25.0	8:13	3	0	1	1	0	0	0	0	5:39
	Quebec Citadelles	AHL	24	9	14	23	35	....	....	....	....	....	....	....	....	....	....	....	....	....	....	....	....	....	....
2002-03	NY Islanders	NHL	78	15	19	34	57	4	0	1	114	13.2	1	17	41.2	12:13	5	0	0	0	16	0	0	0	15:09
	NHL Totals		199	26	28	54	195	4	1	2	210	12.4		25	44.0	10:09	8	0	1	1	16	0	0	0	11:35

Traded to **NY Islanders** by **Montreal** with Montreal's 5th round choice (Marcus Paulsson) in 2002 Entry Draft for Mariusz Czerkawski, June 22, 2002.

ASTASHENKO, Kaspars

(ahs-tuh-SHEHN-koh, KAHS-pars)

Defense/Wing. Shoots left. 6'2", 183 lbs. Born, Riga, Latvia, February 17, 1975. Tampa Bay's 5th choice, 127th overall, in 1999 Entry Draft.

Season	Club	League	GP	G	A	Pts	PIM	PP	SH	GW	S	%	+/-	TF	F%	Min	GP	G	A	Pts	PIM	PP	SH	GW	Min
1993-94	Pardaugava Riga	CIS	4	0	0	0	10	....	....	....	....	....	....	....	....	....	....	....	....	....	....	....	....	....	....
1994-95	Pardaugava Riga	CIS	25	0	0	0	24	....	....	....	....	....	....	....	....	....	....	....	....	....	....	....	....	....	....
1995-96	CSKA Moscow	CIS	26	0	1	1	10	....	....	....	....	....	....	....	....	....	....	....	....	....	....	....	....	....	....
1996-97	HC CSKA	Russia	41	0	0	0	48	....	....	....	....	....	....	....	....	....	2	0	1	1	4	....	....	....	....
1997-98	HC CSKA	Russia	25	1	3	4	6	....	....	....	....	....	....	....	....	....	....	....	....	....	....	....	....	....	....
1998-99	Cincinnati	IHL	74	3	11	14	166	....	....	....	....	....	....	....	....	....	3	0	2	2	6	....	....	....	....
	Dayton Bombers	ECHL	2	0	1	1	4	....	....	....	....	....	....	....	....	....	....	....	....	....	....	....	....	....	....
99-2000	Tampa Bay	NHL	8	0	1	1	4	0	0	0	3	0.0	–2	0	0.0	16:48	....	....	....	....	....	....	....	....	....
	Detroit Vipers	IHL	51	1	10	11	86	....	....	....	....	....	....	....	....	....	....	....	....	....	....	....	....	....	....
	Long Beach	IHL	14	0	3	3	10	....	....	....	....	....	....	....	....	....	....	....	....	....	....	....	....	....	....
2000-01	Tampa Bay	NHL	15	1	1	2	4	0	0	0	4	25.0	–4	0	0.0	6:50	....	....	....	....	....	....	....	....	....
	Detroit Vipers	IHL	51	6	10	16	58	....	....	....	....	....	....	....	....	....	....	....	....	....	....	....	....	....	....

			Regular Season														Playoffs								
Season	Club	League	GP	G	A	Pts	PIM	PP	SH	GW	S	%	+/-	TF	F%	Min	GP	G	A	Pts	PIM	PP	SH	GW	Min
2001-02	Springfield	AHL	11	0	2	2	15																		
	Lowell	AHL	37	2	8	10	39										5	1	1	2	2				
	Latvia	Olympics	1	0	0	0	0																		
2002-03	Lowell	AHL	47	6	11	17	60																		
	NHL Totals		**23**	**1**	**2**	**3**	**8**	**0**	**0**	**0**	**7**	**14.3**		**0**	**0.0**	**10:18**									

Traded to **Carolina** by **Tampa Bay** for Harlan Pratt, December 28, 2001.

AUBIN, Serge

(oh-BEHN, SAIRZH)

Left wing. Shoots left. 6'1", 194 lbs. Born, Val-d'Or, Que., February 15, 1975. Pittsburgh's 9th choice, 161st overall, in 1994 Entry Draft.

1990-91	Abitibi Forestiers	QAAA	27	2	4	6	10																		
1991-92	Abitibi Forestiers	QAAA	42	28	32	60	36										1	0	1	1	0				
1992-93	Drummondville	QMJHL	65	16	34	50	30										8	0	1	1	16				
1993-94	Granby Bisons	QMJHL	63	42	32	74	80										7	2	3	5	8				
1994-95	Granby Bisons	QMJHL	60	37	73	110	55										11	8	15	23	4				
1995-96	Hampton Roads	ECHL	62	24	62	86	74										3	1	4	5	10				
	Cleveland	IHL	2	0	0	0	0										2	0	0	0	0				
1996-97	Cleveland	IHL	57	9	16	25	38										2	0	0	0	0				
1997-98	Syracuse Crunch	AHL	55	6	14	20	57																		
	Hershey Bears	AHL	5	2	1	3	0										7	1	3	4	6				
1998-99	Hershey Bears	AHL	64	30	39	69	58										3	0	1	1	2				
	Colorado	**NHL**	**1**	**0**	**0**	**0**	**0**	**0**	**0**	**0**	**1**	**0.0**	**0**	**1**	**0.0**	**4:16**									
99-2000	**Colorado**	**NHL**	**15**	**2**	**1**	**3**	**6**	**0**	**0**	**1**	**14**	**14.3**	**1**	**79**	**50.6**	**6:37**	**17**	**0**	**1**	**1**	**6**	**0**	**0**	**0**	**5:06**
	Hershey Bears	AHL	58	42	38	80	56																		
2000-01	**Columbus**	**NHL**	**81**	**13**	**17**	**30**	**107**	**0**	**0**	**2**	**110**	**11.8**	**–20**	**1346**	**51.3**	**16:20**									
2001-02	**Columbus**	**NHL**	**71**	**8**	**8**	**16**	**32**	**1**	**0**	**1**	**86**	**9.3**	**–20**	**780**	**50.5**	**15:30**									
2002-03	**Colorado**	**NHL**	**66**	**4**	**6**	**10**	**64**	**0**	**0**	**1**	**62**	**6.5**	**–2**	**613**	**50.2**	**11:58**	**5**	**0**	**0**	**0**	**4**	**0**	**0**	**0**	**5:25**
	NHL Totals		**234**	**27**	**32**	**59**	**209**	**1**	**0**	**5**	**273**	**9.9**		**2819**	**50.8**	**14:10**	**22**	**0**	**1**	**1**	**10**	**0**	**0**	**0**	**5:10**

AHL First All-Star Team (2000)

Signed as a free agent by **Hershey** (AHL), July 24, 1998. Signed as a free agent by **Colorado**, December 22, 1998. Signed as a free agent by **Columbus**, July 11, 2000.

AUCOIN, Adrian

(oh-KOIN, AY-dree-an) **NYI**

Defense. Shoots right. 6'2", 214 lbs. Born, Ottawa, Ont., July 3, 1973. Vancouver's 7th choice, 117th overall, in 1992 Entry Draft.

1989-90	Nepean Raiders	OCJHL	54	2	14	16	95										4	0	1	1					
1990-91	Nepean Raiders	OCJHL	56	17	33	50	125																		
1991-92	Boston University	H-East	32	2	10	12	60																		
1992-93	Team Canada	Nat-Tm	42	8	10	18	71																		
1993-94	Team Canada	Nat-Tm	59	5	12	17	80																		
	Canada	Olympics	4	0	0	0	2																		
	Hamilton	AHL	13	1	2	3	19										4	0	2	2	6				
1994-95	Syracuse Crunch	AHL	71	13	18	31	52																		
	Vancouver	**NHL**	**1**	**1**	**0**	**1**	**0**	**0**	**0**	**0**	**2**	**50.0**	**1**				**4**	**1**	**0**	**1**	**0**	**1**	**0**	**0**	
1995-96	**Vancouver**	**NHL**	**49**	**4**	**14**	**18**	**34**	**2**	**0**	**0**	**85**	**4.7**	**8**				**6**	**0**	**0**	**0**	**2**	**0**	**0**	**0**	
	Syracuse Crunch	AHL	29	5	13	18	47																		
1996-97	**Vancouver**	**NHL**	**70**	**5**	**16**	**21**	**63**	**1**	**0**	**0**	**116**	**4.3**	**0**												
1997-98	**Vancouver**	**NHL**	**35**	**3**	**3**	**6**	**21**	**1**	**0**	**1**	**44**	**6.8**	**–4**												
1998-99	**Vancouver**	**NHL**	**82**	**23**	**11**	**34**	**77**	**18**	**2**	**3**	**174**	**13.2**	**–14**	**1**	**100.0**	**23:52**									
99-2000	**Vancouver**	**NHL**	**57**	**10**	**14**	**24**	**30**	**4**	**0**	**1**	**126**	**7.9**	**7**	**0**	**0.0**	**23:06**									
2000-01	**Vancouver**	**NHL**	**47**	**3**	**13**	**16**	**20**	**1**	**0**	**0**	**99**	**3.0**	**13**	**0**	**0.0**	**18:21**									
	Tampa Bay	**NHL**	**26**	**1**	**11**	**12**	**25**	**1**	**0**	**0**	**60**	**1.7**	**–8**	**0**	**0.0**	**23:34**									
2001-02	**NY Islanders**	**NHL**	**81**	**12**	**22**	**34**	**62**	**7**	**0**	**1**	**232**	**5.2**	**23**	**0**	**0.0**	**28:54**	**7**	**2**	**5**	**7**	**4**	**2**	**0**	**0**	**32:19**
2002-03	**NY Islanders**	**NHL**	**73**	**8**	**27**	**35**	**70**	**5**	**0**	**1**	**175**	**4.6**	**–5**	**0**	**0.0**	**29:01**	**5**	**1**	**2**	**3**	**4**	**0**	**0**	**0**	**31:43**
	NHL Totals		**521**	**70**	**131**	**201**	**402**	**40**	**2**	**7**	**1113**	**6.3**		**1**	**100.0**	**25:09**	**22**	**4**	**7**	**11**	**10**	**3**	**0**	**0**	**32:04**

• Missed majority of 1997-98 season recovering from ankle (October 4, 1997 vs. Anaheim) and groin (November 1, 1997 vs. Pittsburgh) injuries. Traded to **Tampa Bay** by **Vancouver** with Vancouver's 2nd round choice (Alexander Polushin) in 2001 Entry Draft for Dan Cloutier, February 7, 2001. Traded to **NY Islanders** by **Tampa Bay** with Alexander Kharitonov for Mathieu Biron and NY Islanders' 2nd round choice (later traded to Washington – later traded to Vancouver – Vancouver selected Denis Grot) in 2002 Entry Draft, June 22, 2001.

AUDETTE, Donald

(aw-DEHT, DAW-nohld) **MTL.**

Right wing. Shoots right. 5'8", 190 lbs. Born, Laval, Que., September 23, 1969. Buffalo's 8th choice, 183rd overall, in 1989 Entry Draft.

1985-86	Laval Laurentide	QAAA	41	32	38	70	51										8	5	9	14	10				
1986-87	Laval Titan	QMJHL	66	17	22	39	36										14	2	6	8	10				
1987-88	Laval Titan	QMJHL	63	48	61	109	56										14	7	12	19	20				
1988-89	Laval Titan	QMJHL	70	76	85	161	123										17	17	12	29	43				
1989-90	Rochester	AHL	70	42	46	88	78										15	9	8	17	29				
	Buffalo	**NHL**															**2**	**0**	**0**	**0**	**0**	**0**	**0**	**0**	
1990-91	**Buffalo**	**NHL**	**8**	**4**	**3**	**7**	**4**	**2**	**0**	**1**	**17**	**23.5**	**–1**												
	Rochester	AHL	5	4	0	4	2																		
1991-92	**Buffalo**	**NHL**	**63**	**31**	**17**	**48**	**75**	**5**	**0**	**6**	**153**	**20.3**	**–1**												
1992-93	**Buffalo**	**NHL**	**44**	**12**	**7**	**19**	**51**	**2**	**0**	**0**	**92**	**13.0**	**–8**				**8**	**2**	**2**	**4**	**6**	**0**	**0**	**0**	
	Rochester	AHL	6	8	4	12	10																		
1993-94	**Buffalo**	**NHL**	**77**	**29**	**30**	**59**	**41**	**16**	**1**	**4**	**207**	**14.0**	**2**				**7**	**0**	**1**	**1**	**6**	**0**	**0**	**0**	
1994-95	**Buffalo**	**NHL**	**46**	**24**	**13**	**37**	**27**	**13**	**0**	**7**	**124**	**19.4**	**–3**				**5**	**1**	**1**	**2**	**4**	**1**	**0**	**0**	
1995-96	**Buffalo**	**NHL**	**23**	**12**	**13**	**25**	**18**	**8**	**0**	**1**	**92**	**13.0**	**0**												
1996-97	**Buffalo**	**NHL**	**73**	**28**	**22**	**50**	**48**	**8**	**0**	**5**	**182**	**15.4**	**–6**				**11**	**4**	**5**	**9**	**6**	**3**	**0**	**0**	
1997-98	**Buffalo**	**NHL**	**75**	**24**	**20**	**44**	**59**	**10**	**0**	**5**	**198**	**12.1**	**10**				**15**	**5**	**8**	**13**	**10**	**3**	**0**	**2**	
1998-99	**Los Angeles**	**NHL**	**49**	**18**	**18**	**36**	**51**	**6**	**0**	**2**	**152**	**11.8**	**7**	**4**	**50.0**	**16:50**									
99-2000	**Los Angeles**	**NHL**	**49**	**12**	**20**	**32**	**45**	**1**	**0**	**3**	**112**	**10.7**	**6**	**4**	**50.0**	**14:56**									
	Atlanta	**NHL**	**14**	**7**	**4**	**11**	**12**	**0**	**1**	**1**	**50**	**14.0**	**–4**	**0**	**0.0**	**21:35**									
2000-01	**Atlanta**	**NHL**	**64**	**32**	**39**	**71**	**64**	**13**	**1**	**2**	**187**	**17.1**	**–3**	**7**	**57.1**	**20:18**									
	Buffalo	**NHL**	**12**	**2**	**6**	**8**	**12**	**1**	**0**	**1**	**38**	**5.3**	**1**	**1**	**0.0**	**17:25**	**13**	**3**	**6**	**9**	**4**	**0**	**0**	**0**	**17:06**
2001-02	**Dallas**	**NHL**	**20**	**4**	**8**	**12**	**12**	**3**	**0**	**2**	**49**	**8.2**	**2**	**2**	**50.0**	**12:26**									
	Montreal	**NHL**	**13**	**1**	**5**	**6**	**8**	**0**	**0**	**1**	**33**	**3.0**	**1**	**1**	**100.0**	**17:42**	**12**	**6**	**4**	**10**	**10**	**2**	**0**	**2**	**15:32**
2002-03	**Montreal**	**NHL**	**54**	**11**	**12**	**23**	**19**	**4**	**0**	**4**	**118**	**9.3**	**–7**	**6**	**33.3**	**15:30**									
	Hamilton	AHL	11	5	5	10	8																		
	NHL Totals		**684**	**251**	**237**	**488**	**546**	**92**	**3**	**45**	**1804**	**13.9**		**25**	**48.0**	**17:02**	**73**	**21**	**27**	**48**	**46**	**9**	**0**	**4**	**16:21**

QMJHL First All-Star Team (1989) • AHL First All-Star Team (1990) • Dudley "Red" Garret Memorial Trophy (Top Rookie – AHL) (1990)

Played in NHL ALL-Star Game (2001)

• Missed majority of 1990-91 season recovering from knee injury suffered in game vs. Edmonton, November 16, 1990. • Missed majority of 1995-96 season recovering from knee injury suffered in training camp, September 23, 1995. Traded to **Los Angeles** by **Buffalo** for Los Angeles' 2nd round choice (Milan Bartovic) in 1999 Entry Draft, December 18, 1998. Traded to **Atlanta** by **Los Angeles** with Frantisek Kaberle for Kelly Buchberger and Nelson Emerson, March 13, 2000. Traded to **Buffalo** by **Atlanta** for the rights to Kamil Piros and Buffalo's 4th round choice (later traded to St. Louis – St. Louis selected Igor Valeyev) in 2001 Entry Draft, March 13, 2001. Signed as a free agent by **Dallas**, July 2, 2001. Traded to **Montreal** by **Dallas** with Shaun Van Allen for Martin Rucinsky and Benoit Brunet, November 21, 2001. • Missed majority of 2001-02 season recovering from wrist injury suffered in game vs. NY Rangers, December 1, 2001.

AULIN, Jared

(AW-lihn, JAIR-ehd) **L.A.**

Center/Right wing. Shoots right. 6', 192 lbs. Born, Calgary, Alta., March 15, 1982. Colorado's 2nd choice, 47th overall, in 2000 Entry Draft.

1997-98	Airdrie Xtreme	AAHA	55	42	61	103	60																		
	Kamloops Blazers	WHL	2	0	0	0	0																		
1998-99	Kamloops Blazers	WHL	55	7	19	26	23										13	1	3	4	2				
99-2000	Kamloops Blazers	WHL	57	17	38	55	70										4	0	1	1	6				
2000-01	Kamloops Blazers	WHL	70	31	*77	108	62										4	0	2	2	0				
2001-02	Kamloops Blazers	WHL	46	33	34	67	80										4	1	2	3	2				
2002-03	**Los Angeles**	**NHL**	**17**	**2**	**2**	**4**	**0**	**1**	**0**	**0**	**21**	**9.5**	**–3**	**92**	**41.3**	**9:55**									
	Manchester	AHL	44	12	32	44	21										3	0	4	4	0				
	NHL Totals		**17**	**2**	**2**	**4**	**0**	**1**	**0**	**0**	**21**	**9.5**		**92**	**41.3**	**9:55**									

WHL West First All-Star Team (2001, 2002)

Traded to **Los Angeles** by **Colorado** to complete transaction that sent Rob Blake and Steve Reinprecht to Colorado (February 21, 2001), March 22, 2001.

AVERY, Sean

(AY-vuhr-ee, SHAWN) **L.A.**

Center. Shoots left. 5'10", 185 lbs. Born, Pickering, Ont., April 10, 1980.

Season	Club	League	Regular Season GP	G	A	Pts	PIM	PP	SH	GW	S	%	+/-	TF	F%	Min	Playoffs GP	G	A	Pts	PIM	PP	SH	GW	Min
1995-96	Markham	OMHA	70	34	81	115	180	....	....	....	....	....	....	....	....	....	....	....	....	....	....	....	....	....	....
	Markham Waxers	OJHL	1	0	0	0	4	....	....	....	....	....	....	....	....	....	....	....	....	....	....	....	....	....	....
1996-97	Owen Sound	OHL	58	10	21	31	86	....	....	....	....	....	....	....	....	....	4	1	0	1	4	....	....	....	....
1997-98	Owen Sound	OHL	47	13	41	54	105	....	....	....	....	....	....	....	....	....	....	....	....	....	....	....	....	....	....
1998-99	Owen Sound	OHL	28	22	23	45	70	....	....	....	....	....	....	....	....	....	....	....	....	....	....	....	....	....	....
	Kingston	OHL	33	14	25	39	88	....	....	....	....	....	....	....	....	....	5	1	3	4	13	....	....	....	....
99-2000	Kingston	OHL	55	28	56	84	215	....	....	....	....	....	....	....	....	....	5	2	2	4	26	....	....	....	....
2000-01	Cincinnati	AHL	58	8	15	23	304	....	....	....	....	....	....	....	....	....	4	1	0	1	19	....	....	....	....
2001-02	**Detroit**	**NHL**	**36**	**2**	**2**	**4**	**68**	**0**	**0**	**1**	**30**	**6.7**	**1**	**299**	**51.8**	**7:51**	....	....	....	....	....	....	....	....	....
	Cincinnati	AHL	36	14	7	21	106	....	....	....	....	....	....	....	....	....	....	....	....	....	....	....	....	....	....
2002-03	**Detroit**	**NHL**	**39**	**5**	**6**	**11**	**120**	**0**	**0**	**2**	**40**	**12.5**	**7**	**224**	**58.0**	**7:03**	....	....	....	....	....	....	....	....	....
	Grand Rapids	AHL	15	6	6	12	82	....	....	....	....	....	....	....	....	....	....	....	....	....	....	....	....	....	....
	Los Angeles	**NHL**	**12**	**1**	**3**	**4**	**33**	**0**	**0**	**0**	**19**	**5.3**	**0**	**49**	**46.9**	**13:50**	....	....	....	....	....	....	....	....	....
	Manchester	AHL	....	....	....	....	....	....	....	....	....	....	....	....	....	....	3	2	1	3	8	....	....	....	....
	NHL Totals		**87**	**8**	**11**	**19**	**221**	**0**	**0**	**3**	**89**	**9.0**		**572**	**53.8**	**8:19**	....	....	....	....	....	....	....	....	....

Signed as a free agent by **Detroit**, September 21, 1999. Traded to **Los Angeles** by **Detroit** with Maxim Kuznetsov, Detroit's 1st round choice (Jeff Tambellini) in 2003 Entry Draft and Detroit's 2nd round choice in 2004 Entry Draft for Mathieu Schneider, March 11, 2003.

AXELSSON, P.J.

(AHX-ehl-suhn, PEE-jay) **BOS.**

Left wing. Shoots left. 6'1", 184 lbs. Born, Kungalv, Sweden, February 26, 1975. Boston's 7th choice, 177th overall, in 1995 Entry Draft.

Season	Club	League	GP	G	A	Pts	PIM	PP	SH	GW	S	%	+/-	TF	F%	Min	GP	G	A	Pts	PIM	PP	SH	GW	Min
1992-93	V. Frolunda Jr.	Swede-Jr.	16	9	5	14	12	....	....	....	....	....	....	....	....	....	....	....	....	....	....	....	....	....	....
	Vastra Frolunda	Sweden	1	0	0	0	0	....	....	....	....	....	....	....	....	....	....	....	....	....	....	....	....	....	....
1993-94	Vastra Frolunda	Sweden	11	0	0	0	4	....	....	....	....	....	....	....	....	....	4	0	0	0	0	....	....	....	....
1994-95	V. Frolunda Jr.	Swede-Jr.	19	16	9	25	22	....	....	....	....	....	....	....	....	....	....	....	....	....	....	....	....	....	....
	Vastra Frolunda	Sweden	11	2	1	3	6	....	....	....	....	....	....	....	....	....	5	0	0	0	0	....	....	....	....
1995-96	Vastra Frolunda	Sweden	36	15	5	20	10	....	....	....	....	....	....	....	....	....	13	3	0	3	10	....	....	....	....
1996-97	Vastra Frolunda	Sweden	50	19	15	34	34	....	....	....	....	....	....	....	....	....	3	0	2	2	0	....	....	....	....
	Vastra Frolunda	EuroHL	3	1	1	2	0	....	....	....	....	....	....	....	....	....	3	0	0	0	2	....	....	....	....
1997-98	**Boston**	**NHL**	**82**	**8**	**19**	**27**	**38**	**2**	**0**	**1**	**144**	**5.6**	**−14**	....	....	....	**6**	**1**	**0**	**1**	**0**	**0**	**0**	**0**	....
1998-99	**Boston**	**NHL**	**77**	**7**	**10**	**17**	**18**	**0**	**0**	**2**	**146**	**4.8**	**−14**	**8**	**75.0**	**16:38**	**12**	**1**	**1**	**2**	**4**	**0**	**0**	**0**	**15:11**
99-2000	**Boston**	**NHL**	**81**	**10**	**16**	**26**	**24**	**0**	**0**	**4**	**186**	**5.4**	**1**	**22**	**27.3**	**16:43**	....	....	....	....	....	....	....	....	....
2000-01	**Boston**	**NHL**	**81**	**8**	**15**	**23**	**27**	**0**	**0**	**2**	**146**	**5.5**	**−12**	**41**	**36.6**	**12:30**	....	....	....	....	....	....	....	....	....
2001-02	**Boston**	**NHL**	**78**	**7**	**17**	**24**	**16**	**0**	**2**	**0**	**127**	**5.5**	**6**	**17**	**35.3**	**14:42**	**6**	**2**	**1**	**3**	**6**	**0**	**1**	**1**	**16:48**
	Sweden	Olympics	4	0	0	0	2	....	....	....	....	....	....	....	....	....	....	....	....	....	....	....	....	....	....
2002-03	**Boston**	**NHL**	**66**	**17**	**19**	**36**	**24**	**2**	**2**	**1**	**122**	**13.9**	**8**	**17**	**23.5**	**16:37**	**5**	**0**	**0**	**0**	**6**	**0**	**0**	**0**	**13:23**
	NHL Totals		**465**	**57**	**96**	**153**	**147**	**4**	**4**	**10**	**871**	**6.5**		**105**	**35.2**	**15:23**	**29**	**4**	**2**	**6**	**16**	**0**	**1**	**1**	**15:13**

BABENKO, Yuri

(bah-BEHN-koh, EW-ree)

Center. Shoots left. 6'1", 200 lbs. Born, Penza, USSR, January 2, 1978. Colorado's 2nd choice, 51st overall, in 1996 Entry Draft.

Season	Club	League	GP	G	A	Pts	PIM	PP	SH	GW	S	%	+/-	TF	F%	Min	GP	G	A	Pts	PIM	PP	SH	GW	Min
1995-96	Krylja Sovetov	CIS	21	0	0	0	16	....	....	....	....	....	....	....	....	....	....	....	....	....	....	....	....	....	....
1996-97	Krylja Sovetov 2	Russia-3	26	8	10	18	24	....	....	....	....	....	....	....	....	....	....	....	....	....	....	....	....	....	....
	HC CSKA	Russia-2	24	3	3	6	12	....	....	....	....	....	....	....	....	....	....	....	....	....	....	....	....	....	....
	Krylja Sovetov	Russia	4	1	0	1	4	....	....	....	....	....	....	....	....	....	....	....	....	....	....	....	....	....	....
1997-98	Plymouth Whalers	OHL	59	22	34	56	22	....	....	....	....	....	....	....	....	....	15	3	7	10	24	....	....	....	....
1998-99	Hershey Bears	AHL	74	11	15	26	47	....	....	....	....	....	....	....	....	....	2	0	1	1	0	....	....	....	....
99-2000	Hershey Bears	AHL	75	20	25	45	53	....	....	....	....	....	....	....	....	....	14	4	3	7	37	....	....	....	....
2000-01	**Colorado**	**NHL**	**3**	**0**	**0**	**0**	**0**	**0**	**0**	**0**	**2**	**0.0**	**0**	**26**	**23.1**	**10:34**	....	....	....	....	....	....	....	....	....
	Hershey Bears	AHL	71	17	18	35	80	....	....	....	....	....	....	....	....	....	12	2	1	3	6	....	....	....	....
2001-02	Hershey Bears	AHL	67	7	23	30	95	....	....	....	....	....	....	....	....	....	8	2	2	4	6	....	....	....	....
2002-03	Dynamo Moscow	Russia	35	3	8	11	52	....	....	....	....	....	....	....	....	....	2	0	0	0	2	....	....	....	....
	NHL Totals		**3**	**0**	**0**	**0**	**0**	**0**	**0**	**0**	**2**	**0.0**		**26**	**23.1**	**10:34**	....	....	....	....	....	....	....	....	....

Signed as a free agent by **Dynamo Moscow** (Russia), July 9, 2002.

BACKMAN, Christian

(BAK-man, KRIH-stan) **ST.L.**

Defense. Shoots left. 6'4", 198 lbs. Born, Alingsas, Sweden, April 28, 1980. St. Louis' 1st choice, 24th overall, in 1998 Entry Draft.

Season	Club	League	GP	G	A	Pts	PIM	PP	SH	GW	S	%	+/-	TF	F%	Min	GP	G	A	Pts	PIM	PP	SH	GW	Min
1996-97	V. Frolunda Jr.	Swede-Jr.	26	2	5	7	16	....	....	....	....	....	....	....	....	....	....	....	....	....	....	....	....	....	....
1997-98	V. Frolunda-18	Swede-Jr.	4	4	1	5	2	....	....	....	....	....	....	....	....	....	5	2	2	4	2	....	....	....	....
	V. Frolunda Jr.	Swede-Jr.	28	5	14	19	12	....	....	....	....	....	....	....	....	....	2	0	1	1	4	....	....	....	....
1998-99	V. Frolunda Jr.	Swede-Jr.	4	0	2	2	4	....	....	....	....	....	....	....	....	....	....	....	....	....	....	....	....	....	....
	Vastra Frolunda	Sweden	49	0	4	4	4	....	....	....	....	....	....	....	....	....	4	0	0	0	0	....	....	....	....
99-2000	V. Frolunda Jr.	Swede-Jr.	5	1	1	2	0	....	....	....	....	....	....	....	....	....	3	1	1	2	0	....	....	....	....
	Gislaveds IK	Swede-2	21	5	2	7	8	....	....	....	....	....	....	....	....	....	....	....	....	....	....	....	....	....	....
	Vastra Frolunda	Sweden	27	1	0	1	14	....	....	....	....	....	....	....	....	....	5	0	0	0	0	....	....	....	....
2000-01	Vastra Frolunda	Sweden	50	1	10	11	32	....	....	....	....	....	....	....	....	....	3	0	2	2	2	....	....	....	....
2001-02	Vastra Frolunda	Sweden	44	7	4	11	38	....	....	....	....	....	....	....	....	....	10	0	0	0	8	....	....	....	....
2002-03	**St. Louis**	**NHL**	**4**	**0**	**0**	**0**	**0**	**0**	**0**	**0**	**4**	**0.0**	**−3**	**0**	**0.0**	**12:22**	....	....	....	....	....	....	....	....	....
	Worcester IceCats	AHL	72	8	19	27	66	....	....	....	....	....	....	....	....	....	3	0	1	1	5	....	....	....	....
	NHL Totals		**4**	**0**	**0**	**0**	**0**	**0**	**0**	**0**	**4**	**0.0**		**0**	**0.0**	**12:22**	....	....	....	....	....	....	....	....	....

BALA, Chris

(BA-la, KRIHS) **MIN.**

Left wing. Shoots left. 6'1", 196 lbs. Born, Alexandria, VA, September 24, 1978. Ottawa's 3rd choice, 58th overall, in 1998 Entry Draft.

Season	Club	League	GP	G	A	Pts	PIM	PP	SH	GW	S	%	+/-	TF	F%	Min	GP	G	A	Pts	PIM	PP	SH	GW	Min
1996-97	Hill-Murray	Hi-School	23	28	33	61	36	....	....	....	....	....	....	....	....	....	....	....	....	....	....	....	....	....	....
1997-98	Harvard Crimson	ECAC	33	16	14	30	23	....	....	....	....	....	....	....	....	....	....	....	....	....	....	....	....	....	....
1998-99	Harvard Crimson	ECAC	28	5	10	15	16	....	....	....	....	....	....	....	....	....	....	....	....	....	....	....	....	....	....
99-2000	Harvard Crimson	ECAC	30	10	14	24	18	....	....	....	....	....	....	....	....	....	....	....	....	....	....	....	....	....	....
2000-01	Harvard Crimson	ECAC	32	14	16	30	24	....	....	....	....	....	....	....	....	....	....	....	....	....	....	....	....	....	....
2001-02	**Ottawa**	**NHL**	**6**	**0**	**1**	**1**	**0**	**0**	**0**	**0**	**2**	**0.0**	**1**	**0**	**0.0**	**5:43**	....	....	....	....	....	....	....	....	....
	Grand Rapids	AHL	70	21	16	37	9	....	....	....	....	....	....	....	....	....	4	0	1	1	0	....	....	....	....
2002-03	Binghamton	AHL	51	6	18	24	20	....	....	....	....	....	....	....	....	....	14	2	5	7	4	....	....	....	....
	NHL Totals		**6**	**0**	**1**	**1**	**0**	**0**	**0**	**0**	**2**	**0.0**		**0**	**0.0**	**5:43**	....	....	....	....	....	....	....	....	....

Traded to **Nashville** by **Ottawa** for Peter Smrek, June 26, 2003. Traded to **Minnesota** by **Nashville** for Curtis Murphy, June 26, 2003.

BALMOCHNYKH, Maxim

(bahl-MAWCH-nihky, mahx-EEM) **N.J.**

Left wing. Shoots left. 6'1", 210 lbs. Born, Lipetsk, USSR, March 7, 1979. Anaheim's 2nd choice, 45th overall, in 1997 Entry Draft.

Season	Club	League	GP	G	A	Pts	PIM	PP	SH	GW	S	%	+/-	TF	F%	Min	GP	G	A	Pts	PIM	PP	SH	GW	Min
1994-95	HC Lipetsk	CIS-2	3	0	1	1	4	....	....	....	....	....	....	....	....	....	....	....	....	....	....	....	....	....	....
1995-96	HC Lipetsk	CIS-2	40	15	5	20	60	....	....	....	....	....	....	....	....	....	....	....	....	....	....	....	....	....	....
1996-97	Lada Togliatti	Russia	18	6	1	7	22	....	....	....	....	....	....	....	....	....	....	....	....	....	....	....	....	....	....
1997-98	Lada Togliatti	Russia	37	10	4	14	46	....	....	....	....	....	....	....	....	....	....	....	....	....	....	....	....	....	....
	Chelyabinsk	Russia	2	0	0	0	2	....	....	....	....	....	....	....	....	....	....	....	....	....	....	....	....	....	....
1998-99	Lada Togliatti	Russia	15	2	1	3	10	....	....	....	....	....	....	....	....	....	4	0	1	1	8	....	....	....	....
	Quebec Remparts	QMJHL	21	9	22	31	38	....	....	....	....	....	....	....	....	....	....	....	....	....	....	....	....	....	....
99-2000	**Anaheim**	**NHL**	**6**	**0**	**1**	**1**	**2**	**0**	**0**	**0**	**6**	**0.0**	**2**	**0**	**0.0**	**6:44**	....	....	....	....	....	....	....	....	....
	Cincinnati	AHL	40	9	12	21	82	....	....	....	....	....	....	....	....	....	....	....	....	....	....	....	....	....	....
2000-01	Cincinnati	AHL	65	6	9	15	45	....	....	....	....	....	....	....	....	....	....	....	....	....	....	....	....	....	....
2001-02	Cincinnati	AHL	23	6	4	10	33	....	....	....	....	....	....	....	....	....	....	....	....	....	....	....	....	....	....
2002-03	Cherepovets	Russia	12	1	2	3	31	....	....	....	....	....	....	....	....	....	....	....	....	....	....	....	....	....	....
	NHL Totals		**6**	**0**	**1**	**1**	**2**	**0**	**0**	**0**	**6**	**0.0**		**0**	**0.0**	**6:44**	....	....	....	....	....	....	....	....	....

Traded to **New Jersey** by **Anaheim** with Jeff Friesen and Oleg Tverdovsky for Petr Sykora, Mike Commodore, Jean-Francois Damphousse and Igor Pohanka, July 6, 2002.

							Regular Season											Playoffs							
Season	Club	League	GP	G	A	Pts	PIM	PP	SH	GW	S	%	+/-	TF	F%	Min	GP	G	A	Pts	PIM	PP	SH	GW	Min

BANCROFT, Steve (BAN-crawft, STEEV)

Defense. Shoots left. 6'1", 214 lbs. Born, Toronto, Ont., October 6, 1970. Toronto's 3rd choice, 21st overall, in 1989 Entry Draft.

Season	Club	League	GP	G	A	Pts	PIM	PP	SH	GW	S	%	+/-	TF	F%	Min	GP	G	A	Pts	PIM	PP	SH	GW	Min
1985-86	Madoc	OJHL-C	7	1	0	1	21	....	....	....	....	....	....				....	....	....	....	....	....	....	....	....
	Trenton Bobcats	OJHL-B	16	1	5	6	16	....	....	....	....	....	....				....	....	....	....	....	....	....	....	....
1986-87	St. Catharines	OJHL-B	11	5	8	13	20	....	....	....	....	....	....				....	....	....	....	....	....	....	....	....
	Trenton Bobcats	OJHL-B	13	2	3	5	45	....	....	....	....	....	....				....	....	....	....	....	....	....	....	....
1987-88	Belleville Bulls	OHL	56	1	8	9	42	....	....	....	....	....	....				....	....	....	....	....	....	....	....	....
1988-89	Belleville Bulls	OHL	66	7	30	37	99	....	....	....	....	....	....				5	0	2	2	10				
1989-90	Belleville Bulls	OHL	53	10	33	43	135	....	....	....	....	....	....				11	3	9	12	38				
1990-91	Newmarket Saints	AHL	9	0	3	3	22	....	....	....	....	....	....				....	....	....	....	....				
	Maine Mariners	AHL	53	2	12	14	46	....	....	....	....	....	....				2	0	0	0	2				
1991-92	Maine Mariners	AHL	26	1	3	4	45	....	....	....	....	....	....				....	....	....	....	....				
	Indianapolis Ice	IHL	36	8	23	31	49	....	....	....	....	....	....				....	....	....	....	....				
1992-93	**Chicago**	**NHL**	1	0	0	0	0	0	0	0	0	0.0	0				....	....	....	....	....				
	Indianapolis Ice	IHL	53	10	35	45	138	....	....	....	....	....	....				5	0	0	0	16				
	Moncton Hawks	AHL	21	3	13	16	16	....	....	....	....	....	....				....	....	....	....	....				
1993-94	Cleveland	IHL	33	2	12	14	58	....	....	....	....	....	....				....	....	....	....	....				
1994-95	Detroit Vipers	IHL	6	1	3	4	0	....	....	....	....	....	....				....	....	....	....	....				
	Fort Wayne	IHL	50	7	17	24	100	....	....	....	....	....	....				5	0	3	3	8				
	St. John's	AHL	4	2	0	2	2	....	....	....	....	....	....				....	....	....	....	....				
1995-96	Los Angeles	IHL	15	3	10	13	22	....	....	....	....	....	....				....	....	....	....	....				
	Chicago Wolves	IHL	64	9	41	50	91	....	....	....	....	....	....				9	1	7	8	22				
1996-97	Chicago Wolves	IHL	39	6	10	16	66	....	....	....	....	....	....				....	....	....	....	....				
	Las Vegas	IHL	36	9	28	37	64	....	....	....	....	....	....				3	0	0	0	2				
1997-98	Las Vegas	IHL	70	15	44	59	148	....	....	....	....	....	....				19	2	11	13	30				
	Saint John Flames	AHL	9	0	4	4	12	....	....	....	....	....	....				....	....	....	....	....				
1998-99	Saint John Flames	AHL	8	1	4	5	22	....	....	....	....	....	....				15	0	6	6	28				
	Providence Bruins	AHL	62	7	34	41	78	....	....	....	....	....	....				....	....	....	....	....				
99-2000	Cincinnati	IHL	39	6	14	20	37	....	....	....	....	....	....				10	2	6	8	40				
	Houston Aeros	IHL	37	2	18	20	47	....	....	....	....	....	....				....	....	....	....	....				
2000-01	Kentucky	AHL	80	23	50	73	162	....	....	....	....	....	....				3	0	2	2	8				
2001-02	**San Jose**	**NHL**	5	0	1	1	2	0	0	0	5	0.0	-2	0	0.0	10:24	....	....	....	....	....				
	Cleveland Barons	AHL	72	6	38	44	226	....	....	....	....	....	....				....	....	....	....	....				
2002-03	Worcester IceCats	AHL	21	4	6	10	32	....	....	....	....	....	....				14	0	0	0	12				
	Binghamton	AHL	29	1	11	12	40	....	....	....	....	....	....				....	....	....	....	....				
	NHL Totals		6	0	1	1	2	0	0	0	5	0.0		0	0.0	10:24	....	....	....	....	....				

AHL First All-Star Team (2001)

Traded to **Boston** by **Toronto** for Rob Cimetta, November 9, 1990. Traded to **Chicago** by **Boston** with Boston's 11th round choice (later traded to Winnipeg – Winnipeg selected Russ Hewson) in 1993 Entry Draft for Chicago's 11th round choice (Evgeny Pavlov) in 1992 Entry Draft, January 8, 1992. Traded to **Winnipeg** by **Chicago** with future considerations for Troy Murray, February 11, 1993. Claimed by **Florida** from **Winnipeg** in Expansion Draft, June 24, 1993. Signed as a free agent by **Pittsburgh**, August 2, 1993. Signed as a free agent by **Los Angeles** (IHL), August 30, 1995. Signed as a free agent by **Carolina**, August 4, 1999. Traded to **Houston** (IHL) by **Cincinnati** (IHL) for Brian Felsner with Carolina retaining his NHL rights, January 19, 2000. Signed as a free agent by **San Jose**, August 10, 2000. Signed as a free agent by **St. Louis**, July 16, 2002.

BANHAM, Frank (BAN-ham, FRANK) **PHX.**

Right wing. Shoots right. 6', 190 lbs. Born, Calahoo, Alta., April 14, 1975. Washington's 4th choice, 147th overall, in 1993 Entry Draft.

Season	Club	League	GP	G	A	Pts	PIM	PP	SH	GW	S	%	+/-	TF	F%	Min	GP	G	A	Pts	PIM	PP	SH	GW	Min
1991-92	Fernie Ghostriders	RMJHL	47	45	45	90	120	....	....	....	....	....	....				9	2	7	9	8				
1992-93	Saskatoon Blades	WHL	71	29	33	62	55	....	....	....	....	....	....				16	8	11	19	36				
1993-94	Saskatoon Blades	WHL	65	28	39	67	99	....	....	....	....	....	....				8	2	6	8	12				
1994-95	Saskatoon Blades	WHL	70	50	39	89	63	....	....	....	....	....	....				4	6	0	6	2				
1995-96	Saskatoon Blades	WHL	72	*83	69	152	116	....	....	....	....	....	....				7	1	1	2	2				
	Baltimore Bandits	AHL	9	1	4	5	0	....	....	....	....	....	....				....	....	....	....	....				
1996-97	**Anaheim**	**NHL**	3	0	0	0	0	0	0	0	1	0.0	-2				....	....	....	....	....				
	Baltimore Bandits	AHL	21	11	13	24	4	....	....	....	....	....	....				....	....	....	....	....				
1997-98	**Anaheim**	**NHL**	21	9	2	11	12	1	0	0	43	20.9	-6				....	....	....	....	....				
	Cincinnati	AHL	35	7	8	15	39	....	....	....	....	....	....				3	0	1	1	0				
1998-99	Cincinnati	AHL	66	22	27	49	20	....	....	....	....	....	....				....	....	....	....	....				
99-2000	**Anaheim**	**NHL**	3	0	0	0	2	0	0	0	4	0.0	0	5	40.0	6:47	....	....	....	....	....				
	Cincinnati	AHL	72	19	22	41	58	....	....	....	....	....	....				....	....	....	....	....				
2000-01	Blues Espoo	Finland	56	24	27	51	70	....	....	....	....	....	....				12	*8	1	9	22				
2001-02	Jokerit Helsinki	Finland	52	22	16	38	38	....	....	....	....	....	....				....	....	....	....	....				
2002-03	Jokerit Helsinki	Finland	17	3	4	7	12	....	....	....	....	....	....				....	....	....	....	....				
	Phoenix	**NHL**	5	0	0	0	2	0	0	0	5	0.0	-1	1	0.0	7:52	....	....	....	....	....				
	Springfield	AHL	62	23	17	40	36	....	....	....	....	....	....				6	2	1	3	2				
	NHL Totals		32	9	2	11	16	1	0	0	53	17.0		6	33.3	7:27	....	....	....	....	....				

WHL East First All-Star Team (1996)

Signed as a free agent by **Anaheim**, January 27, 1996. Signed as a free agent by **Jokerit Helsinki** (Finland), April 24, 2001. Signed as a free agent by **Phoenix**, November 7, 2002.

BANNISTER, Drew (BAN-nihs-stuhr, DREW)

Defense. Shoots right. 6'2", 200 lbs. Born, Belleville, Ont., September 4, 1974. Tampa Bay's 2nd choice, 26th overall, in 1992 Entry Draft.

Season	Club	League	GP	G	A	Pts	PIM	PP	SH	GW	S	%	+/-	TF	F%	Min	GP	G	A	Pts	PIM	PP	SH	GW	Min
1989-90	Sudbury Legion	NOHA	26	13	14	27	98	....	....	....	....	....	....				....	....	....	....	....				
1990-91	Sault Ste. Marie	OHL	41	2	8	10	51	....	....	....	....	....	....				4	0	0	0	4				
1991-92	Sault Ste. Marie	OHL	64	4	21	25	122	....	....	....	....	....	....				16	3	10	13	36				
1992-93	Sault Ste. Marie	OHL	59	5	28	33	114	....	....	....	....	....	....				18	2	7	9	12				
1993-94	Sault Ste. Marie	OHL	58	7	43	50	108	....	....	....	....	....	....				14	6	9	15	20				
1994-95	Atlanta Knights	IHL	72	5	7	12	74	....	....	....	....	....	....				5	0	2	2	22				
1995-96	**Tampa Bay**	**NHL**	13	0	1	1	4	0	0	0	10	0.0	-1				....	....	....	....	....				
	Atlanta Knights	IHL	61	3	13	16	105	....	....	....	....	....	....				3	0	0	0	4				
1996-97	**Tampa Bay**	**NHL**	64	4	13	17	44	1	0	0	57	7.0	-21				....	....	....	....	....				
	Edmonton	**NHL**	1	0	1	1	0	0	0	0	2	0.0	-2				12	0	0	0	30	0	0	0	....
1997-98	**Edmonton**	**NHL**	34	0	2	2	42	0	0	0	27	0.0	-7				....	....	....	....	....				
	Anaheim	**NHL**	27	0	6	6	47	0	0	0	23	0.0	-2				....	....	....	....	....				
1998-99	Las Vegas	IHL	16	2	1	3	73	....	....	....	....	....	....				....	....	....	....	....				
	Tampa Bay	**NHL**	21	1	2	3	24	0	0	0	29	3.4	-4	0	0.0	15:49	....	....	....	....	....				
99-2000	Hartford	AHL	44	6	14	20	121	....	....	....	....	....	....				18	2	9	11	53				
2000-01	**NY Rangers**	**NHL**	3	0	0	0	0	0	0	0	3	0.0	-1	0	0.0	10:47	....	....	....	....	....				
	Hartford	AHL	73	9	30	39	143	....	....	....	....	....	....				5	0	2	2	6				
2001-02	**Anaheim**	**NHL**	1	0	0	0	0	0	0	0	1	0.0	0	0	0.0	13:19	....	....	....	....	....				
	Cincinnati	AHL	30	1	10	11	57	....	....	....	....	....	....				3	0	1	1	6				
2002-03	Karpat Oulu	Finland	41	2	12	14	81	....	....	....	....	....	....				14	2	0	2	*42				
	NHL Totals		164	5	25	30	161	1	0	0	152	3.3		0	0.0	15:07	12	0	0	0	30	0	0	0	....

Memorial Cup All-Star Team (1993) • OHL Second All-Star Team (1994)

Traded to **Edmonton** by **Tampa Bay** with Tampa Bay's 6th round choice (Peter Sarno) in 1997 Entry Draft for Jeff Norton, March 18, 1997. Traded to **Anaheim** by **Edmonton** for Bobby Dollas, January 9, 1998. Traded to **Tampa Bay** by **Anaheim** for Tampa Bay's 5th round choice (Peter Podhradsky) in 2000 Entry Draft, December 10, 1998. Signed as a free agent by **NY Rangers**, October 3, 1999. Signed as a free agent by **Anaheim**, July 27, 2001. • Missed majority of 2001-02 season recovering from shoulder injury suffered in game vs. Utah (AHL), November 30, 2001. Signed as a free agent by **Karpat Oulu** (Finland), October 20, 2002.

BARNABY, Matthew (BAHR-na-BEE, MA-thew) **NYR**

Right wing. Shoots left. 6', 189 lbs. Born, Ottawa, Ont., May 4, 1973. Buffalo's 5th choice, 83rd overall, in 1992 Entry Draft.

Season	Club	League	GP	G	A	Pts	PIM	PP	SH	GW	S	%	+/-	TF	F%	Min	GP	G	A	Pts	PIM	PP	SH	GW	Min
1989-90	Hull Frontaliers	QAHA	50	43	50	93	149	....	....	....	....	....	....				....	....	....	....	....				
	L'Outaouais	QAAA	2	0	0	0	0	....	....	....	....	....	....				....	....	....	....	....				
1990-91	Beauport	QMJHL	52	9	5	14	262	....	....	....	....	....	....				....	....	....	....	....				
1991-92	Beauport	QMJHL	63	29	37	66	*476	....	....	....	....	....	....				....	....	....	....	....				
1992-93	Victoriaville Tigres	QMJHL	65	44	67	111	*448	....	....	....	....	....	....				6	2	4	6	44				
	Buffalo	**NHL**	2	1	0	1	10	1	0	0	8	12.5	0				1	0	1	1	4	0	0	0	
1993-94	**Buffalo**	**NHL**	35	2	4	6	106	1	0	0	13	15.4	-7				3	0	0	0	17	0	0	0	
	Rochester	AHL	42	10	32	42	153	....	....	....	....	....	....				....	....	....	....	....				

Season	Club	League	GP	G	A	Pts	PIM	PP	SH	GW	S	%	+/-	TF	F%	Min	GP	G	A	Pts	PIM	PP	SH	GW	Min
			Regular Season														Playoffs								
1994-95	Rochester	AHL	56	21	29	50	274	....	....	....	....	....	....	....	....	....	....	....	....	....	....	....	....	....	....
	Buffalo	NHL	23	1	1	2	116	0	0	0	27	3.7	–2	....	....	....	....	....	....	....	....	....	....	....	....
1995-96	Buffalo	NHL	73	15	16	31	*335	0	0	0	131	11.5	–2	....	....	....	....	....	....	....	....	....	....	....	....
1996-97	Buffalo	NHL	68	19	24	43	249	2	0	1	121	15.7	16	....	....	....	8	0	4	4	36	0	0	0	....
1997-98	Buffalo	NHL	72	5	20	25	289	0	0	2	96	5.2	8	....	....	....	15	7	6	13	22	3	0	1	....
1998-99	Buffalo	NHL	44	4	14	18	143	0	0	3	52	7.7	–2	6	16.7	13:56	....	....	....	....	....	....	....	....	....
	Pittsburgh	NHL	18	2	2	4	34	1	0	0	27	7.4	–10	3	66.7	13:33	13	0	0	0	35	0	0	0	10:27
99-2000	Pittsburgh	NHL	64	12	12	24	197	0	0	3	80	15.0	3	75	44.0	12:38	11	0	2	2	29	0	0	0	13:41
2000-01	Pittsburgh	NHL	47	1	4	5	*168	0	0	0	38	2.6	–7	15	33.3	7:49	....	....	....	....	....	....	....	....	....
	Tampa Bay	NHL	29	4	4	8	*97	1	0	0	29	13.8	–3	1	100.0	12:34	....	....	....	....	....	....	....	....	....
2001-02	Tampa Bay	NHL	29	0	0	0	70	0	0	0	13	0.0	–7	1	0.0	7:54	....	....	....	....	....	....	....	....	....
	NY Rangers	NHL	48	8	13	21	144	0	0	1	56	14.3	–3	12	33.3	11:24	....	....	....	....	....	....	....	....	....
2002-03	NY Rangers	NHL	79	14	22	36	142	1	0	1	104	13.5	9	5	40.0	12:60	....	....	....	....	....	....	....	....	....
	NHL Totals		631	88	136	224	2100	7	0	11	795	11.1		118	40.7	11:44	51	7	13	20	143	3	0	1	11:56

Traded to **Pittsburgh** by **Buffalo** for Stu Barnes, March 11, 1999. Traded to **Tampa Bay** by **Pittsburgh** for Wayne Primeau, February 1, 2001. Traded to **NY Rangers** by **Tampa Bay** for Zdeno Ciger, December 12, 2001.

BARNES, Stu

(BAHRNZ, STEW) **DAL.**

Center. Shoots right. 5'11", 180 lbs. Born, Spruce Grove, Alta., December 25, 1970. Winnipeg's 1st choice, 4th overall, in 1989 Entry Draft.

1986-87	St. Albert Saints	AJHL	53	41	34	*75	103	....	....	....	....	....	....	....	....	....	19	7	15	22	....	....	....	....	....
1987-88	New Westminster	WHL	71	37	64	101	88	....	....	....	....	....	....	....	....	....	5	2	3	5	6	....	....	....	....
1988-89	Tri-City	WHL	70	59	82	141	117	....	....	....	....	....	....	....	....	....	7	6	5	11	10	....	....	....	....
1989-90	Tri-City	WHL	63	52	92	144	165	....	....	....	....	....	....	....	....	....	7	1	5	6	26	....	....	....	....
1990-91	Team Canada	Nat-Tm	53	22	27	49	68	....	....	....	....	....	....	....	....	....	....	....	....	....	....	....	....	....	....
1991-92	Winnipeg	NHL	46	8	9	17	26	4	0	0	75	10.7	–2	....	....	....	....	....	....	....	....	....	....	....	....
	Moncton Hawks	AHL	30	13	19	32	10	....	....	....	....	....	....	....	....	....	11	3	9	12	6	....	....	....	....
1992-93	Winnipeg	NHL	38	12	10	22	10	3	0	3	73	16.4	–3	....	....	....	6	1	3	4	2	0	0	0	....
	Moncton Hawks	AHL	42	23	31	54	58	....	....	....	....	....	....	....	....	....	....	....	....	....	....	....	....	....	....
1993-94	Winnipeg	NHL	18	5	4	9	8	2	0	0	24	20.8	–1	....	....	....	....	....	....	....	....	....	....	....	....
	Florida	NHL	59	18	20	38	30	6	1	3	148	12.2	5	....	....	....	....	....	....	....	....	....	....	....	....
1994-95	Florida	NHL	41	10	19	29	8	1	0	2	93	10.8	7	....	....	....	....	....	....	....	....	....	....	....	....
1995-96	Florida	NHL	72	19	25	44	46	8	0	5	158	12.0	–12	....	....	....	22	6	10	16	4	2	0	2	....
1996-97	Florida	NHL	19	2	8	10	10	1	0	0	44	4.5	–3	....	....	....	....	....	....	....	....	....	....	....	....
	Pittsburgh	NHL	62	17	22	39	16	4	0	3	132	12.9	–20	....	....	....	5	0	1	1	0	0	0	0	....
1997-98	Pittsburgh	NHL	78	30	35	65	30	15	1	5	196	15.3	15	....	....	....	6	3	3	6	2	0	0	1	....
1998-99	Pittsburgh	NHL	64	20	12	32	20	13	0	3	155	12.9	–12	720	51.9	17:52	....	....	....	....	....	....	....	....	....
	Buffalo	NHL	17	0	4	4	10	0	0	0	25	0.0	1	236	51.3	18:20	21	7	3	10	6	4	0	1	14:40
99-2000	Buffalo	NHL	82	20	25	45	16	8	2	2	137	14.6	–3	778	48.5	17:23	5	3	0	3	2	2	0	1	17:02
2000-01	Buffalo	NHL	75	19	24	43	26	3	2	5	160	11.9	–2	1470	48.3	19:06	13	4	4	8	2	2	0	2	18:30
2001-02	Buffalo	NHL	68	17	31	48	26	5	0	4	127	13.4	6	984	47.2	18:35	....	....	....	....	....	....	....	....	....
2002-03	Buffalo	NHL	68	11	21	32	20	2	1	2	124	8.9	–13	923	49.0	18:29	....	....	....	....	....	....	....	....	....
	Dallas	NHL	13	2	5	7	8	2	0	1	25	8.0	2	76	44.7	17:23	12	2	3	5	0	0	0	2	19:06
	NHL Totals		820	210	274	484	310	77	7	38	1696	12.4		5187	48.8	18:15	90	26	27	53	18	10	0	9	16:55

WHL West Second All-Star Team (1988, 1989) • WHL Rookie of the Year (1988) • WHL MVP (1989)

Traded to **Florida** by **Winnipeg** with St. Louis' 6th round choice (previously acquired, later traded to Edmonton – later traded back to Winnipeg – Winnipeg selected Chris Kibermanis) in 1994 Entry Draft for Randy Gilhen, November 25, 1993. Traded to **Pittsburgh** by **Florida** with Jason Woolley for Chris Wells, November 19, 1996. Traded to **Buffalo** by **Pittsburgh** for Matthew Barnaby, March 11, 1999. Traded to **Dallas** by **Buffalo** for Michael Ryan and Dallas's 2nd round choice (Branislav Fabry) in 2003 Entry Draft, March 10, 2003.

BARNEY, Scott

(BAHR-nee, SKAWT) **L.A.**

Center. Shoots right. 6'4", 208 lbs. Born, Oshawa, Ont., March 27, 1979. Los Angeles' 3rd choice, 29th overall, in 1997 Entry Draft.

1994-95	North York	MTJHL	41	16	19	35	88	....	....	....	....	....	....	....	....	....	....	....	....	....	....	....	....	....	....
1995-96	Peterborough	OHL	60	22	24	46	52	....	....	....	....	....	....	....	....	....	24	6	8	14	38	....	....	....	....
1996-97	Peterborough	OHL	64	21	33	54	110	....	....	....	....	....	....	....	....	....	9	0	3	3	16	....	....	....	....
1997-98	Peterborough	OHL	62	44	32	76	60	....	....	....	....	....	....	....	....	....	4	1	0	1	6	....	....	....	....
1998-99	Peterborough	OHL	44	41	26	67	80	....	....	....	....	....	....	....	....	....	5	4	1	5	4	....	....	....	....
	Springfield	AHL	5	0	0	0	2	....	....	....	....	....	....	....	....	....	1	0	0	0	2	....	....	....	....
99-2000			DID NOT PLAY – INJURED																						
2000-01			DID NOT PLAY – INJURED																						
2001-02			DID NOT PLAY – INJURED																						
2002-03	Los Angeles	NHL	5	0	0	0	0	0	0	0	5	0.0	–1	0	0.0	9:04	....	....	....	....	....	....	....	....	....
	Manchester	AHL	57	13	5	18	74	....	....	....	....	....	....	....	....	....	....	....	....	....	....	....	....	....	....
	NHL Totals		5	0	0	0	0	0	0	0	5	0.0		0	0.0	9:04	....	....	....	....	....	....	....	....	....

• Missed entire 1999-2000, 2000-01 and 2001-02 seasons recovering from back injury suffered in training camp, September 28, 1999.

BARON, Murray

(BAIR-uhn, MUHR-ray) **VAN.**

Defense. Shoots left. 6'3", 215 lbs. Born, Prince George, B.C., June 1, 1967. Philadelphia's 7th choice, 167th overall, in 1986 Entry Draft.

1984-85	Vernon Lakers	BCJHL	37	5	9	14	93	....	....	....	....	....	....	....	....	....	13	5	6	11	107	....	....	....	....
1985-86	Vernon Lakers	BCJHL	46	12	32	44	179	....	....	....	....	....	....	....	....	....	7	1	2	3	13	....	....	....	....
1986-87	North Dakota	WCHA	41	4	10	14	62	....	....	....	....	....	....	....	....	....	....	....	....	....	....	....	....	....	....
1987-88	North Dakota	WCHA	41	1	10	11	95	....	....	....	....	....	....	....	....	....	....	....	....	....	....	....	....	....	....
1988-89	North Dakota	WCHA	40	2	6	8	92	....	....	....	....	....	....	....	....	....	....	....	....	....	....	....	....	....	....
	Hershey Bears	AHL	9	0	3	3	8	....	....	....	....	....	....	....	....	....	....	....	....	....	....	....	....	....	....
1989-90	Philadelphia	NHL	16	2	2	4	12	0	0	0	18	11.1	–1	....	....	....	....	....	....	....	....	....	....	....	....
	Hershey Bears	AHL	50	0	10	10	101	....	....	....	....	....	....	....	....	....	....	....	....	....	....	....	....	....	....
1990-91	Philadelphia	NHL	67	8	8	16	74	3	0	1	86	9.3	–3	....	....	....	....	....	....	....	....	....	....	....	....
	Hershey Bears	AHL	6	2	3	5	0	....	....	....	....	....	....	....	....	....	....	....	....	....	....	....	....	....	....
1991-92	St. Louis	NHL	67	3	8	11	94	0	0	0	55	5.5	–3	....	....	....	2	0	0	0	2	0	0	0	....
1992-93	St. Louis	NHL	53	2	2	4	59	0	0	1	42	4.8	–5	....	....	....	11	0	0	0	12	0	0	0	....
1993-94	St. Louis	NHL	77	5	9	14	123	0	0	0	73	6.8	–14	....	....	....	4	0	0	0	10	0	0	0	....
1994-95	St. Louis	NHL	39	0	5	5	93	0	0	0	28	0.0	9	....	....	....	7	1	1	2	2	0	0	0	....
1995-96	St. Louis	NHL	82	2	9	11	190	0	0	0	86	2.3	3	....	....	....	13	1	0	1	20	0	1	0	....
1996-97	St. Louis	NHL	11	0	2	2	11	0	0	0	7	0.0	–4	....	....	....	....	....	....	....	....	....	....	....	....
	Montreal	NHL	60	1	5	6	107	0	0	0	52	1.9	–16	....	....	....	....	....	....	....	....	....	....	....	....
	Phoenix	NHL	8	0	0	0	4	0	0	0	5	0.0	0	....	....	....	1	0	0	0	0	0	0	0	....
1997-98	Phoenix	NHL	45	1	5	6	106	0	0	0	23	4.3	–10	....	....	....	6	0	2	2	6	0	0	0	....
1998-99	Vancouver	NHL	81	2	6	8	115	0	0	0	53	3.8	–23	0	0.0	18:14	....	....	....	....	....	....	....	....	....
99-2000	Vancouver	NHL	81	2	10	12	67	0	0	0	48	4.2	8	2	50.0	21:36	....	....	....	....	....	....	....	....	....
2000-01	Vancouver	NHL	82	3	8	11	63	0	0	1	56	5.4	–13	3	66.7	19:24	4	0	0	0	0	0	0	0	22:16
2001-02	Vancouver	NHL	61	1	6	7	68	0	0	0	38	2.6	8	2	50.0	16:57	6	0	1	1	10	0	0	0	12:30
2002-03	Vancouver	NHL	78	2	4	6	62	0	0	0	34	5.9	13	0	0.0	17:01	14	0	4	4	10	0	0	0	17:34
	NHL Totals		908	34	89	123	1248	3	0	3	704	4.8		7	57.1	18:45	68	2	8	10	72	0	1	0	17:05

Traded to **St. Louis** by **Philadelphia** with Ron Sutter for Dan Quinn and Rod Brind'Amour, September 22, 1991. Traded to **Montreal** by **St. Louis** with Shayne Corson and St. Louis' 5th round choice (Gennady Razin) in 1997 Entry Draft for Pierre Turgeon, Rory Fitzpatrick and Craig Conroy, October 29, 1996. Traded to **Phoenix** by **Montreal** with Chris Murray for Dave Manson, March 18, 1997. Signed as a free agent by **Vancouver**, July 14, 1998.

BARTECKO, Lubos

(bahr-TESHK-oh, LOO-bohsh)

Left wing. Shoots left. 5'11", 200 lbs. Born, Kezmarok, Czech., July 14, 1976.

1994-95	Poprad	Slovakia	3	1	0	1	0	....	....	....	....	....	....	....	....	....	....	....	....	....	....	....	....	....	....
1995-96	Chicoutimi	QMJHL	70	32	41	73	50	....	....	....	....	....	....	....	....	....	17	8	15	23	10	....	....	....	....
1996-97	Drummondville	QMJHL	58	40	51	91	49	....	....	....	....	....	....	....	....	....	8	1	8	9	4	....	....	....	....
1997-98	Worcester IceCats	AHL	34	10	12	22	24	....	....	....	....	....	....	....	....	....	10	4	2	6	2	....	....	....	....
1998-99	HC SKP Poprad	Slovakia	1	1	0	1	0	....	....	....	....	....	....	....	....	....	....	....	....	....	....	....	....	....	....
	St. Louis	NHL	32	5	11	16	6	0	0	1	37	13.5	4	0	0.0	13:13	5	0	0	0	2	0	0	0	13:29
	Worcester IceCats	AHL	49	14	24	38	22	....	....	....	....	....	....	....	....	....	....	....	....	....	....	....	....	....	....
99-2000	St. Louis	NHL	67	16	23	39	51	3	0	3	75	21.3	24	10	50.0	13:33	7	1	1	2	0	0	0	0	12:02
	Worcester IceCats	AHL	12	4	7	11	4	....	....	....	....	....	....	....	....	....	....	....	....	....	....	....	....	....	....

			Regular Season														Playoffs								
Season	Club	League	GP	G	A	Pts	PIM	PP	SH	GW	S	%	+/-	TF	F%	Min	GP	G	A	Pts	PIM	PP	SH	GW	Min
2000-01	**St. Louis**	**NHL**	**50**	**5**	**8**	**13**	**12**	**0**	**0**	**3**	**51**	**9.8**	**–1**	**2**	**50.0**	**10:25**	....	....	....	....	....	....	....	....	....
2001-02	**Atlanta**	**NHL**	**71**	**13**	**14**	**27**	**30**	**1**	**0**	**0**	**96**	**13.5**	**–15**	**4**	**25.0**	**14:28**	....	....	....	....	....	....	....	....	....
	Slovakia	Olympics	4	0	1	1	0	....	....	....	....	....	....	....	....	....	....	....	....	....	....	....	....	....	....
2002-03	**Atlanta**	**NHL**	**37**	**7**	**9**	**16**	**8**	**0**	**0**	**1**	**54**	**13.0**	**3**	**6**	**100.0**	**12:31**	....	....	....	....	....	....	....	....	....
	NHL Totals		**257**	**46**	**65**	**111**	**107**	**4**	**0**	**8**	**313**	**14.7**		**22**	**59.1**	**13:00**	**12**	**1**	**1**	**2**	**2**	**0**	**0**	**0**	**12:39**

Signed as a free agent by **St. Louis**, October 3, 1997. Traded to **Atlanta** by **St. Louis** for Buffalo's 4th round choice (previously acquired, St. Louis selected Igor Valeyev) in 2001 Entry Draft, June 23, 2001. • Missed majority of 2002-03 season recovering from wrist (November 2, 2002 vs. Florida) and groin (January 13, 2003 vs. Philadelphia) injuries.

BARTOVIC, Milan

(BAHR-tuh-vihch, MIH-lan) **BUF.**

Right wing. Shoots left. 5'11", 192 lbs. Born, Trencin, Czech., April 9, 1981. Buffalo's 2nd choice, 35th overall, in 1999 Entry Draft.

Season	Club	League	GP	G	A	Pts	PIM	PP	SH	GW	S	%	+/-	TF	F%	Min	GP	G	A	Pts	PIM	PP	SH	GW	Min
1997-98	Dukla Trencin Jr.	Slovak-Jr.	26	2	6	8	27	....	....	....	....	....	....	....	....	....	....	....	....	....	....	....	....	....	....
1998-99	Dukla Trencin Jr.	Slovak-Jr.	46	36	35	71	62	....	....	....	....	....	....	....	....	....	6	9	3	12	10	....	....	....	....
99-2000	Tri-City	WHL	18	8	9	17	12	....	....	....	....	....	....	....	....	....	....	....	....	....	....	....	....	....	....
	Brandon	WHL	38	18	22	40	28	....	....	....	....	....	....	....	....	....	....	....	....	....	....	....	....	....	....
2000-01	Brandon	WHL	34	15	25	40	40	....	....	....	....	....	....	....	....	....	6	1	2	3	8	....	....	....	....
	Rochester	AHL	2	1	1	2	0	....	....	....	....	....	....	....	....	....	4	0	1	1	2	....	....	....	....
2001-02	Rochester	AHL	73	15	11	26	56	....	....	....	....	....	....	....	....	....	2	0	0	0	0	....	....	....	....
2002-03	**Buffalo**	**NHL**	**3**	**1**	**0**	**1**	**0**	**0**	**0**	**0**	**5**	**20.0**	**0**	**1**	**100.0**	**9:52**	....	....	....	....	....	....	....	....	....
	Rochester	AHL	74	18	10	28	84	....	....	....	....	....	....	....	....	....	3	0	0	0	0	....	....	....	....
	NHL Totals		**3**	**1**	**0**	**1**	**0**	**0**	**0**	**0**	**5**	**20.0**		**1**	**100.0**	**9:52**	....	....	....	....	....	....	....	....	....

• Missed majority of 2000-01 season recovering from shoulder injury suffered in game vs. Red Deer (WHL), October 10, 2000.

BAST, Ryan

(BAST, RIGH-yuhn)

Defense. Shoots left. 6'2", 190 lbs. Born, Spruce Grove, Alta., August 27, 1975.

Season	Club	League	GP	G	A	Pts	PIM	PP	SH	GW	S	%	+/-	TF	F%	Min	GP	G	A	Pts	PIM	PP	SH	GW	Min
1992-93	St. Albert Raiders	AMHL	35	1	18	19	51	....	....	....	....	....	....	....	....	....	....	....	....	....	....	....	....	....	....
1993-94	Portland	WHL	6	0	0	0	4	....	....	....	....	....	....	....	....	....	....	....	....	....	....	....	....	....	....
	Prince Albert	WHL	47	2	8	10	139	....	....	....	....	....	....	....	....	....	....	....	....	....	....	....	....	....	....
1994-95	Prince Albert	WHL	42	1	10	11	149	....	....	....	....	....	....	....	....	....	14	0	3	3	13	....	....	....	....
1995-96	Prince Albert	WHL	44	7	15	22	129	....	....	....	....	....	....	....	....	....	....	....	....	....	....	....	....	....	....
	Calgary Hitmen	WHL	3	0	0	0	24	....	....	....	....	....	....	....	....	....	....	....	....	....	....	....	....	....	....
	Swift Current	WHL	25	2	3	5	50	....	....	....	....	....	....	....	....	....	6	1	0	1	21	....	....	....	....
1996-97	Las Vegas	IHL	49	2	3	5	266	....	....	....	....	....	....	....	....	....	....	....	....	....	....	....	....	....	....
	Toledo Storm	ECHL	12	2	2	4	75	....	....	....	....	....	....	....	....	....	....	....	....	....	....	....	....	....	....
	Saint John Flames	AHL	12	0	0	0	21	....	....	....	....	....	....	....	....	....	5	0	0	0	4	....	....	....	....
1997-98	Saint John Flames	AHL	77	3	8	11	187	....	....	....	....	....	....	....	....	....	21	0	1	1	55	....	....	....	....
1998-99	Saint John Flames	AHL	2	0	0	0	5	....	....	....	....	....	....	....	....	....	....	....	....	....	....	....	....	....	....
	Philadelphia	**NHL**	**2**	**0**	**1**	**1**	**0**	**0**	**0**	**0**	**1**	**0.0**	**0**	**0**	**0.0**	**13:24**	....	....	....	....	....	....	....	....	....
	Philadelphia	AHL	69	0	11	11	160	....	....	....	....	....	....	....	....	....	16	0	0	0	30	....	....	....	....
99-2000	Philadelphia	AHL	71	1	9	10	198	....	....	....	....	....	....	....	....	....	5	0	0	0	6	....	....	....	....
2000-01	Hartford	AHL	50	1	1	2	146	....	....	....	....	....	....	....	....	....	....	....	....	....	....	....	....	....	....
2001-02	Pee Dee Pride	ECHL	16	0	4	4	32	....	....	....	....	....	....	....	....	....	....	....	....	....	....	....	....	....	....
	Lowell	AHL	59	1	7	8	88	....	....	....	....	....	....	....	....	....	5	0	1	1	4	....	....	....	....
2002-03	Lowell	AHL	45	1	0	1	68	....	....	....	....	....	....	....	....	....	....	....	....	....	....	....	....	....	....
	Philadelphia	AHL	11	0	1	1	21	....	....	....	....	....	....	....	....	....	....	....	....	....	....	....	....	....	....
	Hartford	AHL	18	0	3	3	18	....	....	....	....	....	....	....	....	....	2	0	0	0	2	....	....	....	....
	NHL Totals		**2**	**0**	**1**	**1**	**0**	**0**	**0**	**0**	**1**	**0.0**		**0**	**0.0**	**13:24**	....	....	....	....	....	....	....	....	....

AHL Second All-Star Team (1998)

Signed as a free agent by **Las Vegas** (IHL), September 30, 1996. Traded to **Saint John** (AHL) by **Las Vegas** (IHL) for loan of Sasha Lakovic, March 20, 1997. Signed as a free agent by **Philadelphia**, May 18, 1998. • Calgary Flames filed official protest contesting Philadelphia's signing of Bast under the contention that he was property of AHL's Saint John Flames, May 20, 1998. • NHL ruled that Bast was not under contract to Calgary since he was never drafted and had no NHL clause in contract, May 22, 1998. NHL also ruled that Bast was not property of Philadelphia because Flyers' contract offer exceeded NHL rookie salary cap, May 22, 1998. A compromise was reached that traded Bast to **Philadelphia** by **Calgary** with Calgary's 8th round choice (David Nystrom) in 1999 Entry Draft for Philadelphia's 3rd round choice (later traded to NY Rangers – NY Rangers selected Patrick Aufiero) in 1999 Entry Draft, October 13, 1998. Signed as a free agent by **Hartford** (AHL), September 18, 2000. Signed as a free agent by **Lowell** (AHL), November 24, 2001. Signed as a free agent by **Carolina**, July 16, 2002. Traded to **Philadelphia** by **Carolina** with Sami Kapanen for Pavel Brendl and Bruno St. Jacques, February 7, 2003.

BATES, Shawn

(BAYTS, SHAWN) **NYI**

Center. Shoots right. 6', 205 lbs. Born, Melrose, MA, April 3, 1975. Boston's 4th choice, 103rd overall, in 1993 Entry Draft.

Season	Club	League	GP	G	A	Pts	PIM	PP	SH	GW	S	%	+/-	TF	F%	Min	GP	G	A	Pts	PIM	PP	SH	GW	Min
1990-91	Medford	Hi-School	22	18	43	61	6	....	....	....	....	....	....	....	....	....	....	....	....	....	....	....	....	....	....
1991-92	Medford	Hi-School	22	38	41	79	10	....	....	....	....	....	....	....	....	....	....	....	....	....	....	....	....	....	....
1992-93	Medford	Hi-School	25	49	46	95	20	....	....	....	....	....	....	....	....	....	....	....	....	....	....	....	....	....	....
1993-94	Boston University	H-East	41	10	19	29	24	....	....	....	....	....	....	....	....	....	....	....	....	....	....	....	....	....	....
1994-95	Boston University	H-East	38	18	12	30	48	....	....	....	....	....	....	....	....	....	....	....	....	....	....	....	....	....	....
1995-96	Boston University	H-East	40	28	22	50	54	....	....	....	....	....	....	....	....	....	....	....	....	....	....	....	....	....	....
1996-97	Boston University	H-East	41	17	18	35	64	....	....	....	....	....	....	....	....	....	....	....	....	....	....	....	....	....	....
1997-98	**Boston**	**NHL**	**13**	**2**	**0**	**2**	**2**	**0**	**0**	**0**	**12**	**16.7**	**–3**	....	....	....	....	....	....	....	....	....	....	....	....
	Providence Bruins	AHL	50	15	19	34	22	....	....	....	....	....	....	....	....	....	....	....	....	....	....	....	....	....	....
1998-99	**Boston**	**NHL**	**33**	**5**	**4**	**9**	**2**	**0**	**0**	**0**	**30**	**16.7**	**3**	**178**	**51.1**	**8:35**	**12**	**0**	**0**	**0**	**4**	**0**	**0**	**0**	**5:12**
	Providence Bruins	AHL	37	25	21	46	39	....	....	....	....	....	....	....	....	....	....	....	....	....	....	....	....	....	....
99-2000	**Boston**	**NHL**	**44**	**5**	**7**	**12**	**14**	**0**	**0**	**1**	**65**	**7.7**	**–17**	**460**	**47.0**	**10:52**	....	....	....	....	....	....	....	....	....
2000-01	**Boston**	**NHL**	**45**	**2**	**3**	**5**	**26**	**0**	**0**	**0**	**59**	**3.4**	**–12**	**413**	**50.6**	**9:19**	....	....	....	....	....	....	....	....	....
	Providence Bruins	AHL	11	5	8	13	12	....	....	....	....	....	....	....	....	....	8	2	6	8	8	....	....	....	....
2001-02	**NY Islanders**	**NHL**	**71**	**17**	**35**	**52**	**30**	**1**	**4**	**4**	**150**	**11.3**	**18**	**306**	**49.4**	**18:45**	**7**	**2**	**4**	**6**	**11**	**1**	**0**	**1**	**20:27**
2002-03	**NY Islanders**	**NHL**	**74**	**13**	**29**	**42**	**52**	**1**	**6**	**1**	**126**	**10.3**	**–9**	**398**	**57.0**	**18:26**	**5**	**1**	**0**	**1**	**0**	**1**	**0**	**0**	**18:36**
	NHL Totals		**280**	**44**	**78**	**122**	**126**	**2**	**10**	**6**	**442**	**10.0**		**1755**	**50.9**	**14:31**	**24**	**3**	**4**	**7**	**15**	**2**	**0**	**1**	**12:26**

NCAA Championship All-Tournament Team (1995)

Signed as a free agent by **NY Islanders**, July 8, 2001.

BATTAGLIA, Bates

(buh-TAG-lee-ah, BAYTS) **COL.**

Left wing. Shoots left. 6'2", 205 lbs. Born, Chicago, IL, December 13, 1975. Anaheim's 6th choice, 132nd overall, in 1994 Entry Draft.

Season	Club	League	GP	G	A	Pts	PIM	PP	SH	GW	S	%	+/-	TF	F%	Min	GP	G	A	Pts	PIM	PP	SH	GW	Min
1992-93	Team Illinois	MEHL	60	42	42	84	68	....	....	....	....	....	....	....	....	....	....	....	....	....	....	....	....	....	....
1993-94	Caledon	MTJHL	44	15	33	48	104	....	....	....	....	....	....	....	....	....	....	....	....	....	....	....	....	....	....
1994-95	Lake Superior	CCHA	38	6	14	20	34	....	....	....	....	....	....	....	....	....	....	....	....	....	....	....	....	....	....
1995-96	Lake Superior	CCHA	40	13	22	35	48	....	....	....	....	....	....	....	....	....	....	....	....	....	....	....	....	....	....
1996-97	Lake Superior	CCHA	38	12	27	39	80	....	....	....	....	....	....	....	....	....	....	....	....	....	....	....	....	....	....
1997-98	**Carolina**	**NHL**	**33**	**2**	**4**	**6**	**10**	**0**	**0**	**1**	**21**	**9.5**	**–1**	....	....	....	....	....	....	....	....	....	....	....	....
	New Haven	AHL	48	15	21	36	48	....	....	....	....	....	....	....	....	....	1	0	0	0	0	....	....	....	....
1998-99	**Carolina**	**NHL**	**60**	**7**	**11**	**18**	**97**	**0**	**0**	**0**	**52**	**13.5**	**7**	**144**	**39.6**	**9:53**	**6**	**0**	**3**	**3**	**8**	**0**	**0**	**0**	**15:21**
99-2000	**Carolina**	**NHL**	**77**	**16**	**18**	**34**	**39**	**3**	**0**	**3**	**86**	**18.6**	**20**	**23**	**26.1**	**15:12**	....	....	....	....	....	....	....	....	....
2000-01	**Carolina**	**NHL**	**80**	**12**	**15**	**27**	**76**	**2**	**0**	**3**	**133**	**9.0**	**–14**	**5**	**60.0**	**14:28**	**6**	**0**	**2**	**2**	**2**	**0**	**0**	**0**	**11:25**
2001-02	**Carolina**	**NHL**	**82**	**21**	**25**	**46**	**44**	**5**	**1**	**2**	**167**	**12.6**	**–6**	**12**	**33.3**	**19:05**	**23**	**5**	**9**	**14**	**14**	**1**	**0**	**1**	**20:42**
2002-03	**Carolina**	**NHL**	**70**	**5**	**14**	**19**	**90**	**0**	**1**	**1**	**96**	**5.2**	**–17**	**16**	**25.0**	**18:39**	....	....	....	....	....	....	....	....	....
	Colorado	**NHL**	**13**	**1**	**5**	**6**	**10**	**1**	**0**	**1**	**27**	**3.7**	**–2**	**3**	**0.0**	**15:19**	**7**	**0**	**2**	**2**	**4**	**0**	**0**	**0**	**14:39**
	NHL Totals		**415**	**64**	**92**	**156**	**366**	**11**	**2**	**11**	**582**	**11.0**		**203**	**36.5**	**15:41**	**42**	**5**	**16**	**21**	**28**	**1**	**0**	**1**	**17:36**

Traded to **Hartford** by **Anaheim** with Anaheim's 4th round choice (Josef Vasicek) in 1998 Entry Draft for Mark Janssens, March 18, 1997. Rights transferred to **Carolina** after **Hartford** franchise relocated, June 25, 1997. Traded to **Colorado** by **Carolina** for Radim Vrbata, March 11, 2003.

BAUMGARTNER, Nolan

(BAWM-gahrt-nuhr, NOH-lan) **VAN.**

Defense. Shoots right. 6'2", 205 lbs. Born, Calgary, Alta., March 23, 1976. Washington's 1st choice, 10th overall, in 1994 Entry Draft.

Season	Club	League	GP	G	A	Pts	PIM	PP	SH	GW	S	%	+/-	TF	F%	Min	GP	G	A	Pts	PIM	PP	SH	GW	Min
1991-92	Calgary Flames	AMHL	39	11	29	40	40	....	....	....	....	....	....	....	....	....	....	....	....	....	....	....	....	....	....
1992-93	Kamloops Blazers	WHL	43	0	5	5	30	....	....	....	....	....	....	....	....	....	11	1	1	2	0	....	....	....	....
1993-94	Kamloops Blazers	WHL	69	13	42	55	109	....	....	....	....	....	....	....	....	....	19	3	14	17	33	....	....	....	....
1994-95	Kamloops Blazers	WHL	62	8	36	44	71	....	....	....	....	....	....	....	....	....	21	4	13	17	16	....	....	....	....
1995-96	Kamloops Blazers	WHL	28	13	15	28	45	....	....	....	....	....	....	....	....	....	16	1	9	10	26	....	....	....	....
	Washington	**NHL**	**1**	**0**	**0**	**0**	**0**	**0**	**0**	**0**	**0**	**0.0**	**–1**	....	....	....	**1**	**0**	**0**	**0**	**10**	**0**	**0**	**0**	....

			Regular Season														Playoffs								
Season	Club	League	GP	G	A	Pts	PIM	PP	SH	GW	S	%	+/-	TF	F%	Min	GP	G	A	Pts	PIM	PP	SH	GW	Min
1996-97	Portland Pirates	AHL	8	2	2	4	4	....	....	....	....	....	....	....	....	....	....	....	....	....	....	....	....	....	....
1997-98	**Washington**	**NHL**	**4**	**0**	**1**	**1**	**0**	**0**	**0**	**0**	**4**	**0.0**	**0**	....	....	....	....	....	....	....	....	....	....	....	....
	Portland Pirates	AHL	70	2	24	26	70	....	....	....	....	....	....	....	....	....	10	1	4	5	10	....	....	....	....
1998-99	**Washington**	**NHL**	**5**	**0**	**0**	**0**	**0**	**0**	**0**	**0**	**1**	**0.0**	**–3**	**0**	**0.0**	**8:41**	....	....	....	....	....	....	....	....	....
	Portland Pirates	AHL	38	5	14	19	62	....	....	....	....	....	....	....	....	....	....	....	....	....	....	....	....	....	....
99-2000	**Washington**	**NHL**	**8**	**0**	**1**	**1**	**2**	**0**	**0**	**0**	**6**	**0.0**	**1**	**0**	**0.0**	**10:31**	....	....	....	....	....	....	....	....	....
	Portland Pirates	AHL	71	5	18	23	56	....	....	....	....	....	....	....	....	....	4	1	2	3	10	....	....	....	....
2000-01	**Chicago**	**NHL**	**8**	**0**	**0**	**0**	**6**	**0**	**0**	**0**	**7**	**0.0**	**–4**	**2**	**50.0**	**12:40**	....	....	....	....	....	....	....	....	....
	Norfolk Admirals	AHL	63	5	28	33	75	....	....	....	....	....	....	....	....	....	9	2	3	5	11	....	....	....	....
2001-02	Norfolk Admirals	AHL	76	10	24	34	72	....	....	....	....	....	....	....	....	....	4	0	1	1	2	....	....	....	....
2002-03	**Vancouver**	**NHL**	**8**	**1**	**2**	**3**	**4**	**1**	**0**	**0**	**7**	**14.3**	**4**	**0**	**0.0**	**11:36**	**2**	**0**	**0**	**0**	**0**	**0**	**0**	**0**	**11:06**
	Manitoba Moose	AHL	59	8	31	39	82	....	....	....	....	....	....	....	....	....	1	0	0	0	4	....	....	....	....
	NHL Totals		**34**	**1**	**4**	**5**	**12**	**1**	**0**	**0**	**25**	**4.0**		**2**	**50.0**	**11:05**	**3**	**0**	**0**	**0**	**10**	**0**	**0**	**0**	**11:06**

Memorial Cup All-Star Team (1994, 1995) • WHL West First All-Star Team (1995, 1996) • Canadian Major Junior First All-Star Team (1995) • Canadian Major Junior Defenseman of the Year (1995)
Traded to **Chicago** by **Washington** for Remi Royer, July 20, 2000. Signed as a free agent by **Vancouver**, July 11, 2002.

BAYDA, Ryan (BAY-duh, RIGH-uhn) CAR.

Left wing. Shoots left. 5'11", 185 lbs. Born, Saskatoon, Sask., December 9, 1980. Carolina's 2nd choice, 80th overall, in 2000 Entry Draft.

Season	Club	League	GP	G	A	Pts	PIM	PP	SH	GW	S	%	+/-	TF	F%	Min	GP	G	A	Pts	PIM	PP	SH	GW	Min
1995-96	Saskatoon Flyers	SMHL	60	85	74	159	85	....	....	....	....	....	....	....	....	....	....	....	....	....	....	....	....	....	....
1996-97	Sask. Contacts	SMHL	44	22	23	45	18	....	....	....	....	....	....	....	....	....	....	....	....	....	....	....	....	....	....
1997-98	Sask. Contacts	SMHL	41	29	49	78	103	....	....	....	....	....	....	....	....	....	....	....	....	....	....	....	....	....	....
1998-99	Vernon Vipers	BCHL	45	24	58	82	15	....	....	....	....	....	....	....	....	....	....	....	....	....	....	....	....	....	....
99-2000	North Dakota	WCHA	44	17	23	40	30	....	....	....	....	....	....	....	....	....	....	....	....	....	....	....	....	....	....
2000-01	North Dakota	WCHA	46	25	34	59	48	....	....	....	....	....	....	....	....	....	....	....	....	....	....	....	....	....	....
2001-02	North Dakota	WCHA	37	19	28	47	52	....	....	....	....	....	....	....	....	....	....	....	....	....	....	....	....	....	....
	Lowell	AHL	3	1	1	2	0	....	....	....	....	....	....	....	....	....	5	3	0	3	0	....	....	....	....
2002-03	**Carolina**	**NHL**	**25**	**4**	**10**	**14**	**16**	**0**	**0**	**1**	**49**	**8.2**	**–5**	**2**	**100.0**	**17:15**	....	....	....	....	....	....	....	....	....
	Lowell	AHL	53	11	32	43	32	....	....	....	....	....	....	....	....	....	....	....	....	....	....	....	....	....	....
	NHL Totals		**25**	**4**	**10**	**14**	**16**	**0**	**0**	**1**	**49**	**8.2**		**2**	**100.0**	**17:15**	....	....	....	....	....	....	....	....	....

BCHL Rookie of the Year (1999) • WCHA All-Rookie Team (2000) • WCHA Second All-Star Team (2001, 2002)

BEAUCHEMIN, Francois (boh-sheh-MEH, frahn-SWUH) MTL.

Defense. Shoots left. 6', 206 lbs. Born, Sorel, Que., June 4, 1980. Montreal's 3rd choice, 75th overall, in 1998 Entry Draft.

Season	Club	League	GP	G	A	Pts	PIM	PP	SH	GW	S	%	+/-	TF	F%	Min	GP	G	A	Pts	PIM	PP	SH	GW	Min
1995-96	Richelieu Riverains	QAAA	40	9	23	32	59	....	....	....	....	....	....	....	....	....	....	....	....	....	....	....	....	....	....
1996-97	Laval Titan	QMJHL	66	7	21	28	132	....	....	....	....	....	....	....	....	....	3	0	0	0	2	....	....	....	....
1997-98	Laval Titan	QMJHL	70	12	35	47	132	....	....	....	....	....	....	....	....	....	16	1	3	4	23	....	....	....	....
1998-99	Acadie-Bathurst	QMJHL	31	4	17	21	53	....	....	....	....	....	....	....	....	....	23	2	16	18	55	....	....	....	....
99-2000	Acadie-Bathurst	QMJHL	38	11	36	47	64	....	....	....	....	....	....	....	....	....	....	....	....	....	....	....	....	....	....
	Moncton Wildcats	QMJHL	33	8	31	39	35	....	....	....	....	....	....	....	....	....	16	2	11	13	14	....	....	....	....
2000-01	Quebec Citadelles	AHL	56	3	6	9	44	....	....	....	....	....	....	....	....	....	....	....	....	....	....	....	....	....	....
2001-02	Quebec Citadelles	AHL	56	8	11	19	88	....	....	....	....	....	....	....	....	....	3	0	1	1	0	....	....	....	....
	Mississippi	ECHL	7	1	3	4	2	....	....	....	....	....	....	....	....	....	....	....	....	....	....	....	....	....	....
2002-03	**Montreal**	**NHL**	**1**	**0**	**0**	**0**	**0**	**0**	**0**	**0**	**1**	**0.0**	**–1**	**0**	**0.0**	**17:11**	....	....	....	....	....	....	....	....	....
	Hamilton	AHL	75	7	21	28	92	....	....	....	....	....	....	....	....	....	23	1	9	10	16	....	....	....	....
	NHL Totals		**1**	**0**	**0**	**0**	**0**	**0**	**0**	**0**	**1**	**0.0**		**0**	**0.0**	**17:11**	....	....	....	....	....	....	....	....	....

QMJHL All-Rookie Team (1997) • QMJHL Second All-Star Team (2000)

BEAUDOIN, Eric (boh-DWEH, AIR-ihk) FLA.

Left wing. Shoots left. 6'5", 210 lbs. Born, Ottawa, Ont., May 3, 1980. Tampa Bay's 4th choice, 92nd overall, in 1998 Entry Draft.

Season	Club	League	GP	G	A	Pts	PIM	PP	SH	GW	S	%	+/-	TF	F%	Min	GP	G	A	Pts	PIM	PP	SH	GW	Min
1996-97	Ottawa Jr. Sens	OCJHL	54	12	19	31	55	....	....	....	....	....	....	....	....	....	....	....	....	....	....	....	....	....	....
1997-98	Guelph Storm	OHL	62	9	13	22	43	....	....	....	....	....	....	....	....	....	12	3	2	5	4	....	....	....	....
1998-99	Guelph Storm	OHL	66	28	43	71	79	....	....	....	....	....	....	....	....	....	11	5	3	8	12	....	....	....	....
99-2000	Guelph Storm	OHL	68	38	34	72	126	....	....	....	....	....	....	....	....	....	6	3	0	3	2	....	....	....	....
2000-01	Louisville Panthers	AHL	71	15	10	25	78	....	....	....	....	....	....	....	....	....	....	....	....	....	....	....	....	....	....
2001-02	**Florida**	**NHL**	**8**	**1**	**3**	**4**	**4**	**0**	**0**	**1**	**11**	**9.1**	**–2**	**1**	**0.0**	**17:27**	....	....	....	....	....	....	....	....	....
	Utah Grizzlies	AHL	44	5	16	21	83	....	....	....	....	....	....	....	....	....	....	....	....	....	....	....	....	....	....
2002-03	**Florida**	**NHL**	**15**	**0**	**1**	**1**	**25**	**0**	**0**	**0**	**11**	**0.0**	**–7**	**27**	**29.6**	**9:52**	....	....	....	....	....	....	....	....	....
	San Antonio	AHL	41	14	23	37	36	....	....	....	....	....	....	....	....	....	3	1	0	1	0	....	....	....	....
	NHL Totals		**23**	**1**	**4**	**5**	**29**	**0**	**0**	**1**	**22**	**4.5**		**28**	**28.6**	**12:30**	....	....	....	....	....	....	....	....	....

Traded to **Florida** by **Tampa Bay** for Florida's 7th round choice (Marek Priechodsky) in 2000 Entry Draft, June 1, 2000.

BEDNAR, Jaroslav (BEHD-nahr, YA-roh-slahv) FLA.

Right wing. Shoots right. 6', 198 lbs. Born, Prague, Czech., November 8, 1976. Los Angeles' 4th choice, 51st overall, in 2001 Entry Draft.

Season	Club	League	GP	G	A	Pts	PIM	PP	SH	GW	S	%	+/-	TF	F%	Min	GP	G	A	Pts	PIM	PP	SH	GW	Min
1994-95	HC Slavia Praha	Czech	20	6	7	13	4	....	....	....	....	....	....	....	....	....	3	0	0	0	0	....	....	....	....
1995-96	HC Slavia Praha	Czech	20	3	1	4	6	....	....	....	....	....	....	....	....	....	3	0	0	0	0	....	....	....	....
1996-97	HC Slavia Praha	Czech	45	18	12	30	18	....	....	....	....	....	....	....	....	....	....	....	....	....	....	....	....	....	....
1997-98	HC Slavia Praha	Czech	14	2	5	7	6	....	....	....	....	....	....	....	....	....	....	....	....	....	....	....	....	....	....
	Plzen	Czech	34	26	15	41	16	....	....	....	....	....	....	....	....	....	5	2	4	6	4	....	....	....	....
	Plzen	EuroHL	....	....	....	....	....	....	....	....	....	....	....	....	....	....	5	4	2	6	4	....	....	....	....
1998-99	HC Sparta Praha	Czech	52	23	14	37	30	....	....	....	....	....	....	....	....	....	8	5	2	7	0	....	....	....	....
99-2000	JYP Jyvaskyla	Finland	53	34	28	62	56	....	....	....	....	....	....	....	....	....	....	....	....	....	....	....	....	....	....
2000-01	HIFK Helsinki	Finland	56	*32	28	60	51	....	....	....	....	....	....	....	....	....	5	3	1	4	0	....	....	....	....
2001-02	**Los Angeles**	**NHL**	**22**	**4**	**2**	**6**	**8**	**1**	**0**	**2**	**20**	**20.0**	**–4**	**2**	**50.0**	**10:42**	**3**	**0**	**0**	**0**	**0**	**0**	**0**	**0**	**11:48**
	Manchester	AHL	48	16	21	37	16	....	....	....	....	....	....	....	....	....	....	....	....	....	....	....	....	....	....
2002-03	**Los Angeles**	**NHL**	**15**	**0**	**9**	**9**	**4**	**0**	**0**	**0**	**29**	**0.0**	**3**	**7**	**57.1**	**13:60**	....	....	....	....	....	....	....	....	....
	Florida	**NHL**	**52**	**5**	**13**	**18**	**14**	**2**	**0**	**1**	**66**	**7.6**	**–2**	**42**	**42.9**	**14:09**	....	....	....	....	....	....	....	....	....
	NHL Totals		**89**	**9**	**24**	**33**	**26**	**3**	**0**	**3**	**115**	**7.8**		**51**	**45.1**	**13:16**	**3**	**0**	**0**	**0**	**0**	**0**	**0**	**0**	**11:48**

Traded to **Florida** by **Los Angeles** with Andreas Lilja for Dmitry Yushkevich and NY Islanders' 5th round choice (previously acquired, Los Angeles selected Brady Murray) in 2003 Entry Draft, November 26, 2002.

BEECH, Kris (BEECH, KRIHS) PIT.

Center. Shoots left. 6'2", 209 lbs. Born, Salmon Arm, B.C., February 5, 1981. Washington's 1st choice, 7th overall, in 1999 Entry Draft.

Season	Club	League	GP	G	A	Pts	PIM	PP	SH	GW	S	%	+/-	TF	F%	Min	GP	G	A	Pts	PIM	PP	SH	GW	Min
1996-97	Sicamous Eagles	KIJHL	49	34	36	70	80	....	....	....	....	....	....	....	....	....	....	....	....	....	....	....	....	....	....
	Calgary Hitmen	WHL	8	1	1	2	0	....	....	....	....	....	....	....	....	....	....	....	....	....	....	....	....	....	....
1997-98	Calgary Hitmen	WHL	58	10	25	35	24	....	....	....	....	....	....	....	....	....	12	4	5	9	32	....	....	....	....
1998-99	Calgary Hitmen	WHL	68	26	41	67	103	....	....	....	....	....	....	....	....	....	6	1	4	5	8	....	....	....	....
99-2000	Calgary Hitmen	WHL	66	32	54	86	99	....	....	....	....	....	....	....	....	....	5	3	5	8	16	....	....	....	....
2000-01	**Washington**	**NHL**	**4**	**0**	**0**	**0**	**2**	**0**	**0**	**0**	**0**	**0.0**	**–2**	**25**	**36.0**	**7:29**	....	....	....	....	....	....	....	....	....
	Calgary Hitmen	WHL	40	22	44	66	103	....	....	....	....	....	....	....	....	....	10	2	8	10	26	....	....	....	....
2001-02	**Pittsburgh**	**NHL**	**79**	**10**	**15**	**25**	**45**	**2**	**0**	**0**	**126**	**7.9**	**–25**	**604**	**45.2**	**13:33**	....	....	....	....	....	....	....	....	....
2002-03	Wilkes-Barre	AHL	50	19	24	43	76	....	....	....	....	....	....	....	....	....	5	1	1	2	0	....	....	....	....
	Pittsburgh	**NHL**	**12**	**0**	**1**	**1**	**6**	**0**	**0**	**0**	**6**	**0.0**	**–3**	**96**	**42.7**	**10:34**	....	....	....	....	....	....	....	....	....
	NHL Totals		**95**	**10**	**16**	**26**	**53**	**2**	**0**	**0**	**132**	**7.6**		**725**	**44.6**	**12:56**	....	....	....	....	....	....	....	....	....

Returned to **Calgary** (WHL) by **Washington**, October 24, 2000. Traded to **Pittsburgh** by **Washington** with Michal Sivek, Ross Lupaschuk and future considerations for Jaromir Jagr and Frantisek Kucera, July 11, 2001.

BEGIN, Steve
(bay-ZHIN, STEEV) **BUF.**

Center. Shoots left. 5'11", 190 lbs. Born, Trois-Rivieres, Que., June 14, 1978. Calgary's 3rd choice, 40th overall, in 1996 Entry Draft.

			Regular Season														Playoffs								
Season	Club	League	GP	G	A	Pts	PIM	PP	SH	GW	S	%	+/-	TF	F%	Min	GP	G	A	Pts	PIM	PP	SH	GW	Min
1993-94	Cap-d-Madeleine	QAAA	8	0	1	1	6										2	0	0	0	0				
1994-95	Cap-d-Madeleine	QAAA	35	9	15	24	48										3	0	0	0	2				
1995-96	Val-d'Or Foreurs	QMJHL	64	13	23	36	218										13	1	3	4	33				
1996-97	Val-d'Or Foreurs	QMJHL	58	13	33	46	229										10	0	3	3	8				
	Saint John Flames	AHL															4	0	2	2	6				
1997-98	Val-d'Or Foreurs	QMJHL	35	18	17	35	73										15	2	12	14	34				
	Calgary	NHL	5	0	0	0	23	0	0	0	2	0.0	0												
1998-99	Saint John Flames	AHL	73	11	9	20	156										7	2	0	2	18				
99-2000	Calgary	NHL	13	1	1	2	18	0	0	0	3	33.3	–3	19	47.4	7:13									
	Saint John Flames	AHL	47	13	12	25	99																		
2000-01	Calgary	NHL	4	0	0	0	21	0	0	0	3	0.0	0	0	0.0	6:04									
	Saint John Flames	AHL	58	14	14	28	109										19	10	7	17	18				
2001-02	Calgary	NHL	51	7	5	12	79	1	0	0	65	10.8	–3	129	53.5	9:25									
2002-03	Calgary	NHL	50	3	1	4	51	0	0	1	59	5.1	–7	50	60.0	9:13									
	NHL Totals		123	11	7	18	192	1	0	1	132	8.3		198	54.5	8:59									

Jack A. Butterfield Trophy (Playoff MVP – AHL) (2001)

Traded to **Buffalo** by **Calgary** with Chris Drury for Steve Reinprecht and Rhett Warrener, July 3, 2003.

BEKAR, Derek
(BEH-kahr, DAIR-ehk) **NYI**

Left wing. Shoots left. 6'3", 197 lbs. Born, Burnaby, B.C., September 15, 1975. St. Louis' 7th choice, 205th overall, in 1995 Entry Draft.

Season	Club	League	GP	G	A	Pts	PIM	PP	SH	GW	S	%	+/-	TF	F%	Min	GP	G	A	Pts	PIM	PP	SH	GW	Min
1992-93	Notre Dame	SMHL	29	25	24	49	68																		
1993-94	Notre Dame	SJHL	62	20	31	51	77																		
1994-95	Powell River	BCJHL	46	33	29	62	35																		
1995-96	New Hampshire	H-East	34	15	18	33	4																		
1996-97	New Hampshire	H-East	39	18	21	39	34																		
1997-98	New Hampshire	H-East	35	32	28	60	46																		
1998-99	Worcester IceCats	AHL	51	16	20	36	6										4	0	0	0	0				
99-2000	St. Louis	NHL	1	0	0	0	0	0	0	0	0	0.0	0	0	0.0	5:14									
	Worcester IceCats	AHL	71	21	19	40	26										7	0	3	3	2				
2000-01	Worcester IceCats	AHL	18	5	2	7	10																		
	Portland Pirates	AHL	58	19	16	35	49										3	0	0	0	0				
2001-02	Manchester	AHL	74	27	20	47	42										5	1	4	5	2				
2002-03	Los Angeles	NHL	6	0	0	0	4	0	0	0	4	0.0	–1	1	0.0	7:29									
	Manchester	AHL	51	19	19	38	49										3	0	0	0	2				
	NHL Totals		7	0	0	0	4	0	0	0	4	0.0		1	0.0	7:10									

Hockey East Second All-Star Team (1998)

Traded to **Washington** by **St. Louis** for Mike Peluso, November 29, 2000. Signed as a free agent by **Los Angeles**, September 25, 2001. Signed as a free agent by **NY Islanders**, July, 2003.

BELAK, Wade
(BEE-lak, WAYD) **TOR.**

Defense/Right wing. Shoots right. 6'5", 221 lbs. Born, Saskatoon, Sask., July 3, 1976. Quebec's 1st choice, 12th overall, in 1994 Entry Draft.

Season	Club	League	GP	G	A	Pts	PIM	PP	SH	GW	S	%	+/-	TF	F%	Min	GP	G	A	Pts	PIM	PP	SH	GW	Min
1991-92	North Battleford	SMBHL	57	6	20	26	186																		
1992-93	North Battleford	SJHL	50	5	15	20	146																		
	Saskatoon Blades	WHL	7	0	0	0	23										7	0	0	0	0				
1993-94	Saskatoon Blades	WHL	69	4	13	17	226										16	2	2	4	43				
1994-95	Saskatoon Blades	WHL	72	4	14	18	290										9	0	0	0	36				
	Cornwall Aces	AHL															11	1	2	3	40				
1995-96	Saskatoon Blades	WHL	63	3	15	18	207										4	0	0	0	9				
	Cornwall Aces	AHL	5	0	0	0	18										2	0	0	0	2				
1996-97	Colorado	NHL	5	0	0	0	11	0	0	0	1	0.0	–1												
	Hershey Bears	AHL	65	1	7	8	320										16	0	1	1	61				
1997-98	Colorado	NHL	8	1	1	2	27	0	0	1	2	50.0	–3												
	Hershey Bears	AHL	11	0	0	0	30																		
1998-99	Colorado	NHL	22	0	0	0	71	0	0	0	5	0.0	–2	0	0.0	6:48									
	Hershey Bears	AHL	17	0	1	1	49																		
	Calgary	NHL	9	0	1	1	23	0	0	0	2	0.0	3	0	0.0	10:46									
	Saint John Flames	AHL	12	0	2	2	43										6	0	1	1	23				
99-2000	Calgary	NHL	40	0	2	2	122	0	0	0	11	0.0	–4	1	0.0	7:33									
2000-01	Calgary	NHL	23	0	0	0	79	0	0	0	8	0.0	–2	0	0.0	6:54									
	Toronto	NHL	16	1	1	2	31	0	0	0	8	12.5	–4	0	0.0	13:38									
2001-02	Toronto	NHL	63	1	3	4	142	0	0	0	47	2.1	2	0	0.0	9:14	16	1	0	1	18	0	0	0	7:28
2002-03	Toronto	NHL	55	3	6	9	196	0	0	0	33	9.1	–2	0	0.0	10:50	2	0	0	0	4	0	0	0	8:21
	NHL Totals		241	6	14	20	702	0	0	1	117	5.1		1	0.0	9:14	18	1	0	1	22	0	0	0	7:34

Rights transferred to **Colorado** after **Quebec** franchise relocated, June 21, 1995. Traded to **Calgary** by **Colorado** with Rene Corbet, Robyn Regehr and Colorado's 2nd round compensatory choice (Jarret Stoll) in 2000 Entry Draft for Theoren Fleury and Chris Dingman, February 28, 1999. • Missed majority of 1999-2000 and 2000-01 seasons recovering from shoulder injury suffered in game vs. Colorado, February 10, 2000. Claimed on waivers by **Toronto** from **Calgary**, February 16, 2001.

BELANGER, Eric
(buh-LAWN-zhay, AIR-ihk) **L.A.**

Center. Shoots left. 6', 185 lbs. Born, Sherbrooke, Que., December 16, 1977. Los Angeles' 5th choice, 96th overall, in 1996 Entry Draft.

Season	Club	League	GP	G	A	Pts	PIM	PP	SH	GW	S	%	+/-	TF	F%	Min	GP	G	A	Pts	PIM	PP	SH	GW	Min
1993-94	Magog	QAAA	32	19	24	43	24										13	5	6	11	36				
1994-95	Beauport	QMJHL	71	12	28	40	24										18	5	9	14	25				
1995-96	Beauport	QMJHL	59	35	48	83	18										20	13	14	27	6				
1996-97	Beauport	QMJHL	31	13	37	50	30																		
	Rimouski Oceanic	QMJHL	31	26	41	67	36										4	2	3	5	10				
1997-98	Fredericton	AHL	56	17	34	51	28										4	2	1	3	2				
1998-99	Springfield	AHL	33	8	18	26	10										3	0	1	1	2				
	Long Beach	IHL	1	0	0	0	0																		
99-2000	Lowell	AHL	65	15	25	40	20										7	3	3	6	2				
	Mohawk Valley	UHL	3	0	0	0	0																		
2000-01	Los Angeles	NHL	62	9	12	21	16	1	2	1	80	11.3	14	849	56.4	13:25	13	1	4	5	2	0	0	1	13:47
	Lowell	AHL	13	8	10	18	4																		
2001-02	Los Angeles	NHL	53	8	16	24	21	2	1	1	67	11.9	2	882	57.7	14:33	7	0	0	0	4	0	0	0	12:57
2002-03	Los Angeles	NHL	62	16	19	35	26	0	3	1	114	14.0	–5	1143	51.8	17:42									
	NHL Totals		177	33	47	80	63	3	6	3	261	12.6		2874	55.0	15:15	20	1	4	5	6	0	0	1	13:30

BELANGER, Francis
(buh-LAWN-zhay, FRAN-sihs)

Left wing. Shoots left. 6'3", 228 lbs. Born, Bellefeuille, Que., January 15, 1978. Philadelphia's 5th choice, 124th overall, in 1998 Entry Draft.

Season	Club	League	GP	G	A	Pts	PIM	PP	SH	GW	S	%	+/-	TF	F%	Min	GP	G	A	Pts	PIM	PP	SH	GW	Min
1994-95	Laval Laurentide	QAAA	25	11	8	19	78																		
1995-96	Hull Olympiques	QMJHL	1	0	0	0	0																		
1996-97	Hull Olympiques	QMJHL	53	13	13	26	134										8	2	2	4	57				
1997-98	Hull Olympiques	QMJHL	33	22	23	45	133																		
	Rimouski Oceanic	QMJHL	30	18	10	28	248										17	14	8	22	61				
1998-99	Philadelphia	AHL	58	13	13	26	242										16	4	3	7	16				
99-2000	Philadelphia	AHL	35	5	6	11	112																		
	Trenton Titans	ECHL	9	1	1	2	29																		
2000-01	Philadelphia	AHL	13	1	3	4	32																		
	Montreal	NHL	10	0	0	0	29	0	0	0	2	0.0	–3	0	0.0	4:30									
	Quebec Citadelles	AHL	22	15	4	19	101										9	2	5	7	20				
2001-02	Quebec Citadelles	AHL	69	15	26	41	165										3	1	1	2	0				
2002-03	Cincinnati	AHL	40	4	10	14	50																		
	NHL Totals		10	0	0	0	29	0	0	0	2	0.0		0	0.0	4:30									

Signed as a free agent by **Montreal**, February 15, 2001. Signed as a free agent by **Anaheim**, August 22, 2002. • Missed majority of 2002-03 season recovering from shoulder (January 11, 2003 vs. Rochester) and wrist (March 12, 2003 vs. Chicago) injuries.

BELANGER, Ken

(buh-LAWN-zhay, KEHN)

Left wing. Shoots left. 6'4", 225 lbs. Born, Sault Ste. Marie, Ont., May 14, 1974. Hartford's 7th choice, 153rd overall, in 1992 Entry Draft.

			Regular Season														Playoffs								
Season	Club	League	GP	G	A	Pts	PIM	PP	SH	GW	S	%	+/-	TF	F%	Min	GP	G	A	Pts	PIM	PP	SH	GW	Min
1990-91	Soo Legion	NOHA	43	24	29	53	169	....	....	....	....	....	....	....	....	....	....	....	....	....	....	....	....	....	....
1991-92	Ottawa 67's	OHL	51	4	4	8	174	....	....	....	....	....	....	....	....	....	11	0	0	0	24	....	....	....	....
1992-93	Ottawa 67's	OHL	34	6	12	18	139	....	....	....	....	....	....	....	....	....	....	....	....	....	....	....	....	....	....
	Guelph Storm	OHL	29	10	14	24	86	....	....	....	....	....	....	....	....	....	5	2	1	3	14	....	....	....	....
1993-94	Guelph Storm	OHL	55	11	22	33	185	....	....	....	....	....	....	....	....	....	9	2	3	5	30	....	....	....	....
1994-95	St. John's	AHL	47	5	5	10	246	....	....	....	....	....	....	....	....	....	4	0	0	0	30	....	....	....	....
	Toronto	**NHL**	**3**	**0**	**0**	**0**	**9**	**0**	**0**	**0**	**1**	**0.0**	**0**	....	....	....	....	....	....	....	....	....	....	....	....
1995-96	St. John's	AHL	40	16	14	30	222	....	....	....	....	....	....	....	....	....	....	....	....	....	....	....	....	....	....
	NY Islanders	**NHL**	**7**	**0**	**0**	**0**	**27**	**0**	**0**	**0**	**0**	**0.0**	**-2**	....	....	....	....	....	....	....	....	....	....	....	....
1996-97	**NY Islanders**	**NHL**	**18**	**0**	**2**	**2**	**102**	**0**	**0**	**0**	**5**	**0.0**	**-1**	....	....	....	....	....	....	....	....	....	....	....	....
	Kentucky	AHL	38	10	12	22	164	....	....	....	....	....	....	....	....	....	4	0	1	1	27	....	....	....	....
1997-98	**NY Islanders**	**NHL**	**37**	**3**	**1**	**4**	**101**	**0**	**0**	**1**	**10**	**30.0**	**1**	....	....	....	....	....	....	....	....	....	....	....	....
1998-99	**NY Islanders**	**NHL**	**9**	**1**	**1**	**2**	**30**	**0**	**0**	**0**	**3**	**33.3**	**1**	**0**	**0.0**	**5:05**	....	....	....	....	....	....	....	....	....
	Boston	**NHL**	**45**	**1**	**4**	**5**	**152**	**0**	**0**	**0**	**16**	**6.3**	**-2**	**1**	**0.0**	**4:38**	**12**	**1**	**0**	**1**	**16**	**0**	**0**	**0**	**5:11**
99-2000	**Boston**	**NHL**	**37**	**2**	**2**	**4**	**44**	**0**	**0**	**0**	**20**	**10.0**	**-4**	**1**	**0.0**	**5:17**	....	....	....	....	....	....	....	....	....
2000-01	**Boston**	**NHL**	**40**	**2**	**2**	**4**	**121**	**0**	**0**	**1**	**35**	**5.7**	**-6**	**1**	**100.0**	**7:06**	....	....	....	....	....	....	....	....	....
	Providence Bruins	AHL	10	1	4	5	47	....	....	....	....	....	....	....	....	....	2	0	0	0	4	....	....	....	....
2001-02	**Los Angeles**	**NHL**	**43**	**2**	**0**	**2**	**85**	**0**	**0**	**0**	**22**	**9.1**	**-5**	**0**	**0.0**	**4:22**	....	....	....	....	....	....	....	....	....
2002-03	**Los Angeles**	**NHL**	**4**	**0**	**0**	**0**	**17**	**0**	**0**	**0**	**0**	**0.0**	**0**	**0**	**0.0**	**4:03**	....	....	....	....	....	....	....	....	....
	NHL Totals		**243**	**11**	**12**	**23**	**688**	**0**	**0**	**2**	**112**	**9.8**		**3**	**33.3**	**5:16**	**12**	**1**	**0**	**1**	**16**	**0**	**0**	**0**	**5:11**

Traded to **Toronto** by **Hartford** for Toronto's 9th round choice (Matt Ball) in 1994 Entry Draft, March 18, 1994. Traded to **NY Islanders** by **Toronto** with Damian Rhodes for future considerations (Kirk Muller and Don Beaupre, January 23, 1996), January 23, 1996. Traded to **Boston** by **NY Islanders** for Ted Donato, November 7, 1998. • Missed majority of 1999-2000 season recovering from head injury suffered in game vs. Toronto, November 11, 1999. Signed as a free agent by **Los Angeles**, July 2, 2001. • Missed majority of 2002-03 season recovering from head injury suffered in game vs. San Jose, November 5, 2002.

BELL, Mark

(BEHL, MAWRK) **CHI.**

Center. Shoots left. 6'3", 205 lbs. Born, St. Paul's, Ont., August 5, 1980. Chicago's 1st choice, 8th overall, in 1998 Entry Draft.

			Regular Season														Playoffs								
Season	Club	League	GP	G	A	Pts	PIM	PP	SH	GW	S	%	+/-	TF	F%	Min	GP	G	A	Pts	PIM	PP	SH	GW	Min
1995-96	Stratford Cullitons	OJHL-B	47	8	15	23	32	....	....	....	....	....	....	....	....	....	....	....	....	....	....	....	....	....	....
1996-97	Ottawa 67's	OHL	65	8	12	20	40	....	....	....	....	....	....	....	....	....	24	4	7	11	13	....	....	....	....
1997-98	Ottawa 67's	OHL	55	34	26	60	87	....	....	....	....	....	....	....	....	....	13	6	5	11	14	....	....	....	....
1998-99	Ottawa 67's	OHL	44	29	26	55	69	....	....	....	....	....	....	....	....	....	9	6	5	11	8	....	....	....	....
99-2000	Ottawa 67's	OHL	48	34	38	72	95	....	....	....	....	....	....	....	....	....	2	0	1	1	0	....	....	....	....
2000-01	**Chicago**	**NHL**	**13**	**0**	**1**	**1**	**4**	**0**	**0**	**0**	**14**	**0.0**	**0**	**141**	**48.9**	**12:00**	....	....	....	....	....	....	....	....	....
	Norfolk Admirals	AHL	61	15	27	42	126	....	....	....	....	....	....	....	....	....	9	4	3	7	10	....	....	....	....
2001-02	**Chicago**	**NHL**	**80**	**12**	**16**	**28**	**124**	**1**	**0**	**1**	**120**	**10.0**	**-6**	**47**	**42.6**	**12:39**	**5**	**0**	**0**	**0**	**8**	**0**	**0**	**0**	**9:18**
2002-03	**Chicago**	**NHL**	**82**	**14**	**15**	**29**	**113**	**0**	**2**	**0**	**127**	**11.0**	**0**	**377**	**52.5**	**14:04**	....	....	....	....	....	....	....	....	....
	NHL Totals		**175**	**26**	**32**	**58**	**241**	**1**	**2**	**1**	**261**	**10.0**		**565**	**50.8**	**13:16**	**5**	**0**	**0**	**0**	**8**	**0**	**0**	**0**	**9:18**

BELLEFEUILLE, Blake

(BEHL-fay, BLAYK)

Center. Shoots right. 5'10", 208 lbs. Born, Framingham, MA, December 27, 1977.

			Regular Season														Playoffs								
Season	Club	League	GP	G	A	Pts	PIM	PP	SH	GW	S	%	+/-	TF	F%	Min	GP	G	A	Pts	PIM	PP	SH	GW	Min
1994-95	Framingham	Hi-School	30	42	50	92	....	....	....	....	....	....	....	....	....	....	....	....	....	....	....	....	....	....	....
1995-96	Framingham	Hi-School	30	31	60	91	....	....	....	....	....	....	....	....	....	....	....	....	....	....	....	....	....	....	....
1996-97	Boston College	H-East	34	16	19	35	20	....	....	....	....	....	....	....	....	....	....	....	....	....	....	....	....	....	....
1997-98	Boston College	H-East	41	19	20	39	35	....	....	....	....	....	....	....	....	....	....	....	....	....	....	....	....	....	....
1998-99	Boston College	H-East	43	24	25	49	80	....	....	....	....	....	....	....	....	....	....	....	....	....	....	....	....	....	....
99-2000	Boston College	H-East	39	18	31	49	28	....	....	....	....	....	....	....	....	....	....	....	....	....	....	....	....	....	....
2000-01	Syracuse Crunch	AHL	50	5	5	10	18	....	....	....	....	....	....	....	....	....	5	0	0	0	0	....	....	....	....
2001-02	**Columbus**	**NHL**	**2**	**0**	**1**	**1**	**0**	**0**	**0**	**0**	**2**	**0.0**	**1**	**15**	**60.0**	**8:21**	....	....	....	....	....	....	....	....	....
	Syracuse Crunch	AHL	75	11	19	30	33	....	....	....	....	....	....	....	....	....	4	2	0	2	0	....	....	....	....
2002-03	**Columbus**	**NHL**	**3**	**0**	**0**	**0**	**0**	**0**	**0**	**0**	**0**	**0.0**	**0**	**17**	**64.7**	**7:01**	....	....	....	....	....	....	....	....	....
	Syracuse Crunch	AHL	63	12	19	31	44	....	....	....	....	....	....	....	....	....	....	....	....	....	....	....	....	....	....
	NHL Totals		**5**	**0**	**1**	**1**	**0**	**0**	**0**	**0**	**2**	**0.0**		**32**	**62.5**	**7:33**	....	....	....	....	....	....	....	....	....

• All-time leading scorer in Massachusetts High School history with career totals of 120-182-302. • Hockey East Second All-Star Team (2000)

Signed as a free agent by **Columbus**, May 26, 2000.

BENYSEK, Ladislav

(BEHN-ih-sihk, LAD-ihs-SLAHV)

Defense. Shoots left. 6'2", 190 lbs. Born, Olomouc, Czech., March 24, 1975. Edmonton's 16th choice, 266th overall, in 1994 Entry Draft.

			Regular Season														Playoffs								
Season	Club	League	GP	G	A	Pts	PIM	PP	SH	GW	S	%	+/-	TF	F%	Min	GP	G	A	Pts	PIM	PP	SH	GW	Min
1992-93	HC Olomouc	Czech	3	0	0	0	0	....	....	....	....	....	....	....	....	....	....	....	....	....	....	....	....	....	....
1993-94	HC Olomouc Jr.	Czech-Jr.	STATISTICS NOT AVAILABLE																						
1994-95	Cape Breton	AHL	58	2	7	9	54	....	....	....	....	....	....	....	....	....	....	....	....	....	....	....	....	....	....
1995-96	HC Olomouc	Czech	33	1	4	5	....	....	....	....	....	....	....	....	....	....	4	0	0	0	....	....	....	....	....
1996-97	HC Olomouc	Czech	14	0	1	1	8	....	....	....	....	....	....	....	....	....	....	....	....	....	....	....	....	....	....
	HC Sparta Praha	Czech	36	5	5	10	28	....	....	....	....	....	....	....	....	....	5	0	1	1	2	....	....	....	....
	HC Sparta Praha	EuroHL	3	0	0	0	4	....	....	....	....	....	....	....	....	....	4	0	0	0	0	....	....	....	....
1997-98	HC Sparta Praha	Czech	1	0	0	0	0	....	....	....	....	....	....	....	....	....	....	....	....	....	....	....	....	....	....
	Edmonton	**NHL**	**2**	**0**	**0**	**0**	**0**	....	....	....	....	....	....	....	....	....	....	....	....	....	....	....	....	....	....
	Hamilton	AHL	53	2	14	16	29	....	....	....	....	....	....	....	....	....	9	1	1	2	2	....	....	....	....
1998-99	HC Sparta Praha	Czech	52	8	11	19	47	....	....	....	....	....	....	....	....	....	8	0	1	1	....	....	....	....	....
	HC Sparta Praha	EuroHL	7	0	0	0	2	....	....	....	....	....	....	....	....	....	2	0	0	0	0	....	....	....	....
99-2000	HC Sparta Praha	Czech	51	1	5	6	45	....	....	....	....	....	....	....	....	....	9	0	0	0	4	....	....	....	....
	HC Sparta Praha	EuroHL	5	1	1	2	6	....	....	....	....	....	....	....	....	....	4	0	0	0	4	....	....	....	....
2000-01	**Minnesota**	**NHL**	**71**	**2**	**5**	**7**	**38**	**1**	**0**	**0**	**48**	**4.2**	**-11**	**0**	**0.0**	**18:25**	....	....	....	....	....	....	....	....	....
2001-02	**Minnesota**	**NHL**	**74**	**1**	**7**	**8**	**28**	**0**	**0**	**0**	**44**	**2.3**	**-12**	**1**	**100.0**	**19:09**	....	....	....	....	....	....	....	....	....
2002-03	**Minnesota**	**NHL**	**14**	**0**	**0**	**0**	**8**	**0**	**0**	**0**	**7**	**0.0**	**-3**	**0**	**0.0**	**11:26**	....	....	....	....	....	....	....	....	....
	Houston Aeros	AHL	39	0	4	4	23	....	....	....	....	....	....	....	....	....	18	0	3	3	6	....	....	....	....
	NHL Totals		**161**	**3**	**12**	**15**	**74**	**1**	**0**	**0**	**99**	**3.0**		**1**	**100.0**	**18:09**	....	....	....	....	....	....	....	....	....

Claimed by **Anaheim** from **Edmonton** in Waiver Draft, September 27, 1999. Selected by **Minnesota** from **Anaheim** in Expansion Draft, June 23, 2000.

BERARD, Bryan

(buh-RAHRD, BRIGH-uhn)

Defense. Shoots left. 6'2", 219 lbs. Born, Woonsocket, RI, March 5, 1977. Ottawa's 1st choice, 1st overall, in 1995 Entry Draft.

			Regular Season														Playoffs								
Season	Club	League	GP	G	A	Pts	PIM	PP	SH	GW	S	%	+/-	TF	F%	Min	GP	G	A	Pts	PIM	PP	SH	GW	Min
1991-92	Mount St. Charles	Hi-School	15	3	15	18	4	....	....	....	....	....	....	....	....	....	....	....	....	....	....	....	....	....	....
1992-93	Mount St. Charles	Hi-School	15	8	12	20	18	....	....	....	....	....	....	....	....	....	....	....	....	....	....	....	....	....	....
1993-94	Mount St. Charles	Hi-School	15	11	26	37	4.5	....	....	....	....	....	....	....	....	....	4	3	3	6	6	....	....	....	....
1994-95	Detroit	OHL	58	20	55	75	97	....	....	....	....	....	....	....	....	....	21	4	20	24	38	....	....	....	....
1995-96	Detroit	OHL	56	31	58	89	116	....	....	....	....	....	....	....	....	....	17	7	18	25	41	....	....	....	....
1996-97	**NY Islanders**	**NHL**	**82**	**8**	**40**	**48**	**86**	**3**	**0**	**1**	**172**	**4.7**	**1**	....	....	....	....	....	....	....	....	....	....	....	....
1997-98	**NY Islanders**	**NHL**	**75**	**14**	**32**	**46**	**59**	**8**	**1**	**2**	**192**	**7.3**	**-32**	....	....	....	....	....	....	....	....	....	....	....	....
	United States	Olympics	2	0	0	0	0	....	....	....	....	....	....	....	....	....	....	....	....	....	....	....	....	....	....
1998-99	**NY Islanders**	**NHL**	**31**	**4**	**11**	**15**	**26**	**2**	**0**	**3**	**72**	**5.6**	**-6**	**0**	**0.0**	**24:45**	....	....	....	....	....	....	....	....	....
	Toronto	**NHL**	**38**	**5**	**14**	**19**	**22**	**2**	**0**	**2**	**63**	**7.9**	**7**	**0**	**0.0**	**22:38**	**17**	**1**	**8**	**9**	**8**	**1**	**0**	**0**	**21:11**
99-2000	**Toronto**	**NHL**	**64**	**3**	**27**	**30**	**42**	**1**	**0**	**0**	**98**	**3.1**	**11**	**0**	**0.0**	**19:34**	....	....	....	....	....	....	....	....	....
2000-01	**Toronto**	**NHL**	DID NOT PLAY – INJURED																						
2001-02	**NY Rangers**	**NHL**	**82**	**2**	**21**	**23**	**60**	**0**	**0**	**0**	**132**	**1.5**	**-1**	**0**	**0.0**	**19:38**	....	....	....	....	....	....	....	....	....
2002-03	**Boston**	**NHL**	**80**	**10**	**28**	**38**	**64**	**4**	**0**	**1**	**205**	**4.9**	**-4**	**0**	**0.0**	**21:21**	**3**	**1**	**0**	**1**	**2**	**0**	**0**	**0**	**21:50**
	NHL Totals		**452**	**46**	**173**	**219**	**359**	**20**	**1**	**9**	**934**	**4.9**		**0**	**0.0**	**21:01**	**20**	**2**	**8**	**10**	**10**	**1**	**0**	**0**	**21:17**

OHL All-Rookie Team (1995) • OHL First All-Star Team (1995, 1996) • OHL Rookie of the Year (1995) • Canadian Major Junior First All-Star Team (1995, 1996) • Canadian Major Junior Rookie of the Year (1995) • Canadian Major Junior Defenseman of the Year (1996) • NHL All-Rookie Team (1997) • Calder Memorial Trophy (1997)

Traded to **NY Islanders** by **Ottawa** with Don Beaupre and Martin Straka for Damian Rhodes and Wade Redden, January 23, 1996. Traded to **Toronto** by **NY Islanders** with NY Islanders' 6th round choice (Jan Sochor) in 1999 Entry Draft for Felix Potvin and Toronto's 6th round choice (later traded to Tampa Bay – Tampa Bay selected Fedor Fedorov) in 1999 Entry Draft, January 9, 1999. • Missed remainder of 1999-2000 season and entire 2000-01 season recovering from eye injury suffered in game vs. Ottawa, March 11, 2000. Signed as a free agent by **NY Rangers**, October 5, 2001. Signed as a free agent by **Boston**, August 13, 2002.

BEREHOWSKY, Drake
(beh-reh-HOW-skee, DRAYK)

Defense. Shoots right. 6'2", 225 lbs. Born, Toronto, Ont., January 3, 1972. Toronto's 1st choice, 10th overall, in 1990 Entry Draft.

			Regular Season														Playoffs								
Season	Club	League	GP	G	A	Pts	PIM	PP	SH	GW	S	%	+/-	TF	F%	Min	GP	G	A	Pts	PIM	PP	SH	GW	Min
1987-88	Barrie Colts	OJHL-B	40	10	36	46	81	....	....	....	....	....	....	....	....	....	....	....	....	....	....	....	....	....	....
1988-89	Kingston Raiders	OHL	63	7	39	46	85	....	....	....	....	....	....	....	....	....	....	....	....	....	....	....	....	....	....
1989-90	Kingston	OHL	9	3	11	14	28	....	....	....	....	....	....	....	....	....	....	....	....	....	....	....	....	....	....
1990-91	**Toronto**	**NHL**	**8**	**0**	**1**	**1**	**25**	**0**	**0**	**0**	**4**	**0.0**	**–6**	....	....	....	....	....	....	....	....	....	....	....	....
	Kingston	OHL	13	5	13	18	38	....	....	....	....	....	....	....	....	....	....	....	....	....	....	....	....	....	....
	North Bay	OHL	26	7	23	30	51	....	....	....	....	....	....	....	....	....	10	2	7	9	21	....	....	....	....
1991-92	North Bay	OHL	62	19	63	82	147	....	....	....	....	....	....	....	....	....	21	7	24	31	22	....	....	....	....
	Toronto	**NHL**	**1**	**0**	**0**	**0**	**0**	**0**	**0**	**0**	**0**	**0.0**	**0**	....	....	....	....	....	....	....	....	....	....	....	....
	St. John's	AHL	....	....	....	....	....	....	....	....	....	....	....	....	....	....	6	0	5	5	21	....	....	....	....
1992-93	**Toronto**	**NHL**	**41**	**4**	**15**	**19**	**61**	**1**	**0**	**1**	**41**	**9.8**	**1**	....	....	....	....	....	....	....	....	....	....	....	....
	St. John's	AHL	28	10	17	27	38	....	....	....	....	....	....	....	....	....	....	....	....	....	....	....	....	....	....
1993-94	**Toronto**	**NHL**	**49**	**2**	**8**	**10**	**63**	**2**	**0**	**2**	**29**	**6.9**	**–3**	....	....	....	....	....	....	....	....	....	....	....	....
	St. John's	AHL	18	3	12	15	40	....	....	....	....	....	....	....	....	....	....	....	....	....	....	....	....	....	....
1994-95	**Toronto**	**NHL**	**25**	**0**	**2**	**2**	**15**	**0**	**0**	**0**	**12**	**0.0**	**–10**	....	....	....	....	....	....	....	....	....	....	....	....
	Pittsburgh	**NHL**	**4**	**0**	**0**	**0**	**13**	**0**	**0**	**0**	**2**	**0.0**	**1**	....	....	....	**1**	**0**	**0**	**0**	**0**	**0**	**0**	**0**	....
1995-96	**Pittsburgh**	**NHL**	**1**	**0**	**0**	**0**	**0**	**0**	**0**	**0**	**0**	**0.0**	**1**	....	....	....	....	....	....	....	....	....	....	....	....
	Cleveland	IHL	74	6	28	34	141	....	....	....	....	....	....	....	....	....	3	0	3	3	6	....	....	....	....
1996-97	Carolina	AHL	49	2	15	17	55	....	....	....	....	....	....	....	....	....	....	....	....	....	....	....	....	....	....
	San Antonio	IHL	16	3	4	7	36	....	....	....	....	....	....	....	....	....	....	....	....	....	....	....	....	....	....
1997-98	**Edmonton**	**NHL**	**67**	**1**	**6**	**7**	**169**	**1**	**0**	**1**	**58**	**1.7**	**1**	....	....	....	**12**	**1**	**2**	**3**	**14**	**0**	**0**	**1**	....
	Hamilton	AHL	8	2	0	2	21	....	....	....	....	....	....	....	....	....	....	....	....	....	....	....	....	....	....
1998-99	**Nashville**	**NHL**	**74**	**2**	**15**	**17**	**140**	**0**	**0**	**0**	**79**	**2.5**	**–9**	**1**	**100.0**	**21:43**	....	....	....	....	....	....	....	....	....
99-2000	**Nashville**	**NHL**	**79**	**12**	**20**	**32**	**87**	**5**	**0**	**1**	**102**	**11.8**	**–4**	**0**	**0.0**	**22:39**	....	....	....	....	....	....	....	....	....
2000-01	**Nashville**	**NHL**	**66**	**6**	**18**	**24**	**100**	**3**	**0**	**1**	**94**	**6.4**	**–9**	**1**	**0.0**	**21:38**	....	....	....	....	....	....	....	....	....
	Vancouver	**NHL**	**14**	**1**	**1**	**2**	**21**	**1**	**0**	**0**	**13**	**7.7**	**0**	**0**	**0.0**	**17:10**	**4**	**0**	**0**	**0**	**12**	**0**	**0**	**0**	**14:20**
2001-02	**Vancouver**	**NHL**	**25**	**1**	**2**	**3**	**18**	**0**	**0**	**1**	**15**	**6.7**	**–5**	**1**	**0.0**	**13:28**	....	....	....	....	....	....	....	....	....
	Phoenix	**NHL**	**32**	**1**	**4**	**5**	**42**	**0**	**0**	**0**	**23**	**4.3**	**5**	**0**	**0.0**	**12:20**	**5**	**0**	**1**	**1**	**4**	**0**	**0**	**0**	**13:00**
2002-03	**Phoenix**	**NHL**	**7**	**1**	**2**	**3**	**27**	**0**	**0**	**0**	**8**	**12.5**	**0**	**0**	**0.0**	**10:52**	....	....	....	....	....	....	....	....	....
	Springfield	AHL	2	0	0	0	0	....	....	....	....	....	....	....	....	....	....	....	....	....	....	....	....	....	....
	NHL Totals		**493**	**31**	**94**	**125**	**781**	**13**	**0**	**7**	**480**	**6.5**		**3**	**33.3**	**19:46**	**22**	**1**	**3**	**4**	**30**	**0**	**0**	**1**	**13:36**

OHL First All-Star Team (1992) • Canadian Major Junior Defenseman of the Year (1992)

Traded to **Pittsburgh** by **Toronto** for Grant Jennings, April 7, 1995. Signed as a free agent by **Edmonton**, September 30, 1997. Traded to **Nashville** by **Edmonton** with Eric Fichaud and Greg de Vries for Mikhail Shtalenkov and Jim Dowd, October 1, 1998. Traded to **Vancouver** by **Nashville** for Atlanta's 2nd round choice (previously acquired, Nashville selected Timofei Shishkanov) in 2001 Entry Draft, March 9, 2001. Traded to **Phoenix** by **Vancouver** with Denis Pederson for Todd Warriner, Trevor Letowski, Tyler Bouck and Phoenix's 3rd round choice (later traded back to Phoenix – Phoenix selected Dimitri Pestunov) in 2003 Entry Draft, December 28, 2001. • Missed majority of 2002-03 season recovering from knee injury suffered in training camp, September 24, 2002.

BERENZWEIG, Bubba
(BAIR-ehn-zwighg, BUH-buh) **DAL.**

Defense. Shoots left. 6'1", 217 lbs. Born, Arlington Heights, IL, August 8, 1977. NY Islanders' 5th choice, 109th overall, in 1996 Entry Draft.

1992-93	Loomis-Chaffee	Hi-School	22	5	13	18	....	....	....	....	....	....	....	....	....	....	....	....	....	....	....	....	....	....	....
1993-94	Loomis-Chaffee	Hi-School	22	12	27	39	....	....	....	....	....	....	....	....	....	....	....	....	....	....	....	....	....	....	....
1994-95	Loomis-Chaffee	Hi-School	23	19	23	42	10	....	....	....	....	....	....	....	....	....	....	....	....	....	....	....	....	....	....
1995-96	U. of Michigan	CCHA	42	4	8	12	4	....	....	....	....	....	....	....	....	....	....	....	....	....	....	....	....	....	....
1996-97	U. of Michigan	CCHA	38	7	12	19	49	....	....	....	....	....	....	....	....	....	....	....	....	....	....	....	....	....	....
1997-98	U. of Michigan	CCHA	45	8	11	19	32	....	....	....	....	....	....	....	....	....	....	....	....	....	....	....	....	....	....
1998-99	U. of Michigan	CCHA	42	7	24	31	38	....	....	....	....	....	....	....	....	....	....	....	....	....	....	....	....	....	....
99-2000	**Nashville**	**NHL**	**2**	**0**	**0**	**0**	**0**	**0**	**0**	**0**	**3**	**0.0**	**–1**	**0**	**0.0**	**17:31**	....	....	....	....	....	....	....	....	....
	Milwaukee	IHL	79	4	23	27	48	....	....	....	....	....	....	....	....	....	3	1	2	3	0	....	....	....	....
2000-01	**Nashville**	**NHL**	**5**	**0**	**0**	**0**	**0**	**0**	**0**	**0**	**0**	**0.0**	**0**	**0**	**0.0**	**11:57**	....	....	....	....	....	....	....	....	....
	Milwaukee	IHL	72	10	26	36	38	....	....	....	....	....	....	....	....	....	5	0	4	4	4	....	....	....	....
2001-02	**Nashville**	**NHL**	**26**	**3**	**7**	**10**	**14**	**0**	**0**	**1**	**27**	**11.1**	**–3**	**1**	**0.0**	**13:45**	....	....	....	....	....	....	....	....	....
	Milwaukee	AHL	23	2	5	7	23	....	....	....	....	....	....	....	....	....	....	....	....	....	....	....	....	....	....
2002-03	**Nashville**	**NHL**	**4**	**0**	**0**	**0**	**0**	**0**	**0**	**0**	**5**	**0.0**	**0**	**0**	**0.0**	**17:47**	....	....	....	....	....	....	....	....	....
	Milwaukee	AHL	48	6	11	17	26	....	....	....	....	....	....	....	....	....	....	....	....	....	....	....	....	....	....
	Utah Grizzlies	AHL	26	6	11	17	4	....	....	....	....	....	....	....	....	....	....	....	....	....	....	....	....	....	....
	NHL Totals		**37**	**3**	**7**	**10**	**14**	**0**	**0**	**1**	**35**	**8.6**		**1**	**0.0**	**14:08**	....	....	....	....	....	....	....	....	....

CCHA Second All-Star Team (1998) • NCAA Championship All-Tournament Team (1998) • Ken McKenzie Trophy (Outstanding U.S.- Born Player – IHL) (2000) • IHL Second All-Star Team (2001)

Traded to **Nashville** by **NY Islanders** for Nashville's 4th round choice (Johan Halvardsson) in 1999 Entry Draft, April 14, 1999. Traded to **Dallas** by **Nashvlle** with future considerations for Jon Sim, February 17, 2003.

BEREZIN, Sergei
(BEH-reh-zihn, SAIR-gay)

Left wing. Shoots right. 5'10", 200 lbs. Born, Voskresensk, USSR, November 5, 1971. Toronto's 8th choice, 256th overall, in 1994 Entry Draft.

1990-91	Voskresensk	USSR	30	6	2	8	4	....	....	....	....	....	....	....	....	....	....	....	....	....	....	....	....	....	....
1991-92	Voskresensk	CIS	36	7	5	12	10	....	....	....	....	....	....	....	....	....	....	....	....	....	....	....	....	....	....
1992-93	Voskresensk	CIS	38	9	3	12	12	....	....	....	....	....	....	....	....	....	2	1	0	1	0	....	....	....	....
1993-94	Voskresensk	CIS	40	31	10	41	16	....	....	....	....	....	....	....	....	....	3	2	0	2	2	....	....	....	....
	Russia	Olympics	8	3	2	5	2	....	....	....	....	....	....	....	....	....	....	....	....	....	....	....	....	....	....
1994-95	Kolner Haie	Germany	43	*38	19	57	8	....	....	....	....	....	....	....	....	....	18	*17	8	25	14	....	....	....	....
1995-96	Kolner Haie	Germany	45	*49	31	80	8	....	....	....	....	....	....	....	....	....	14	*13	9	22	10	....	....	....	....
1996-97	**Toronto**	**NHL**	**73**	**25**	**16**	**41**	**2**	**7**	**0**	**2**	**177**	**14.1**	**–3**	....	....	....	....	....	....	....	....	....	....	....	....
1997-98	**Toronto**	**NHL**	**68**	**16**	**15**	**31**	**10**	**3**	**0**	**3**	**167**	**9.6**	**–3**	....	....	....	....	....	....	....	....	....	....	....	....
1998-99	**Toronto**	**NHL**	**76**	**37**	**22**	**59**	**12**	**9**	**1**	**4**	**263**	**14.1**	**16**	**26**	**57.7**	**15:32**	**17**	**6**	**6**	**12**	**4**	**2**	**0**	**2**	**17:09**
99-2000	**Toronto**	**NHL**	**61**	**26**	**13**	**39**	**2**	**5**	**0**	**4**	**241**	**10.8**	**8**	**11**	**45.5**	**16:52**	**12**	**4**	**4**	**8**	**0**	**0**	**0**	**1**	**17:31**
2000-01	**Toronto**	**NHL**	**79**	**22**	**28**	**50**	**8**	**10**	**0**	**3**	**256**	**8.6**	**2**	**4**	**75.0**	**15:41**	**11**	**2**	**5**	**7**	**2**	**0**	**0**	**2**	**14:46**
2001-02	**Phoenix**	**NHL**	**41**	**7**	**9**	**16**	**4**	**1**	**0**	**4**	**120**	**5.8**	**–1**	**2**	**50.0**	**15:33**	....	....	....	....	....	....	....	....	....
	Montreal	**NHL**	**29**	**4**	**6**	**10**	**4**	**3**	**0**	**1**	**80**	**5.0**	**3**	**2**	**0.0**	**14:01**	**6**	**1**	**1**	**2**	**0**	**1**	**0**	**0**	**14:02**
2002-03	**Chicago**	**NHL**	**66**	**18**	**13**	**31**	**8**	**5**	**0**	**0**	**171**	**10.5**	**–3**	**15**	**46.7**	**16:18**	....	....	....	....	....	....	....	....	....
	Washington	**NHL**	**9**	**5**	**4**	**9**	**4**	**0**	**0**	**2**	**28**	**17.9**	**10**	**1**	**0.0**	**15:41**	**6**	**0**	**1**	**1**	**0**	**0**	**0**	**0**	**11:52**
	NHL Totals		**502**	**160**	**126**	**286**	**54**	**43**	**1**	**23**	**1503**	**10.6**		**61**	**50.8**	**15:49**	**52**	**13**	**17**	**30**	**6**	**3**	**0**	**5**	**15:46**

NHL All-Rookie Team (1997)

Traded to **Phoenix** by **Toronto** for Mikael Renberg, June 23, 2001. Traded to **Montreal** by **Phoenix** for Brian Savage, Montreal's 3rd round choice (Matt Jones) in 2002 Entry Draft and future considerations, January 25, 2002. Traded to **Chicago** by **Montreal** for Chicago's 4th round choice in 2004 Entry Draft, June 30, 2002. Traded to **Washington** by **Chicago** for Washington's 4th round choice in 2004 Entry Draft, March 11, 2003.

BERG, Aki
(BUHRG, AH-kee) **TOR.**

Defense. Shoots left. 6'3", 213 lbs. Born, Turku, Finland, July 28, 1977. Los Angeles' 1st choice, 3rd overall, in 1995 Entry Draft.

1992-93	TPS Turku Jr.	Finn-Jr.	39	18	24	42	24	....	....	....	....	....	....	....	....	....	....	....	....	....	....	....	....	....	....
1993-94	TPS Turku Jr.	Finn-Jr.	21	3	11	14	24	....	....	....	....	....	....	....	....	....	7	0	0	0	10	....	....	....	....
	Kiekko-67 Turku	Finland-2	12	1	1	2	16	....	....	....	....	....	....	....	....	....	....	....	....	....	....	....	....	....	....
	TPS Turku	Finland	6	0	3	3	4	....	....	....	....	....	....	....	....	....	....	....	....	....	....	....	....	....	....
1994-95	TPS Turku Jr.	Finn-Jr.	8	1	0	1	30	....	....	....	....	....	....	....	....	....	....	....	....	....	....	....	....	....	....
	Kiekko-67 Turku	Finland-2	21	3	9	12	24	....	....	....	....	....	....	....	....	....	7	0	0	0	10	....	....	....	....
	TPS Turku	Finland	5	0	0	0	4	....	....	....	....	....	....	....	....	....	....	....	....	....	....	....	....	....	....
1995-96	**Los Angeles**	**NHL**	**51**	**0**	**7**	**7**	**29**	**0**	**0**	**0**	**56**	**0.0**	**–13**	....	....	....	....	....	....	....	....	....	....	....	....
	Phoenix	IHL	20	0	3	3	18	....	....	....	....	....	....	....	....	....	2	0	0	0	4	....	....	....	....
1996-97	**Los Angeles**	**NHL**	**41**	**2**	**6**	**8**	**24**	**2**	**0**	**0**	**65**	**3.1**	**–9**	....	....	....	....	....	....	....	....	....	....	....	....
	Phoenix	IHL	23	1	3	4	21	....	....	....	....	....	....	....	....	....	....	....	....	....	....	....	....	....	....
1997-98	**Los Angeles**	**NHL**	**72**	**0**	**8**	**8**	**61**	**0**	**0**	**0**	**58**	**0.0**	**3**	....	....	....	**4**	**0**	**3**	**3**	**0**	**0**	**0**	**0**	....
	Finland	Olympics	6	0	0	0	6	....	....	....	....	....	....	....	....	....	....	....	....	....	....	....	....	....	....
1998-99	TPS Turku	Finland	48	8	7	15	137	....	....	....	....	....	....	....	....	....	9	1	1	2	45	....	....	....	....
99-2000	**Los Angeles**	**NHL**	**70**	**3**	**13**	**16**	**45**	**0**	**0**	**0**	**70**	**4.3**	**–1**	**0**	**0.0**	**16:39**	**2**	**0**	**0**	**0**	**2**	**0**	**0**	**0**	**15:03**
2000-01	**Los Angeles**	**NHL**	**47**	**0**	**4**	**4**	**43**	**0**	**0**	**0**	**31**	**0.0**	**3**	**0**	**0.0**	**14:54**	....	....	....	....	....	....	....	....	....
	Toronto	**NHL**	**12**	**3**	**0**	**3**	**2**	**3**	**0**	**1**	**12**	**25.0**	**–6**	**0**	**0.0**	**18:13**	**11**	**0**	**2**	**2**	**4**	**0**	**0**	**0**	**16:31**

Season	Club	League	Regular Season GP	G	A	Pts	PIM	PP	SH	GW	S	%	+/-	TF	F%	Min	Playoffs GP	G	A	Pts	PIM	PP	SH	GW	Min
2001-02	**Toronto**	**NHL**	**81**	**1**	**10**	**11**	**46**	**0**	**0**	**0**	**66**	**1.5**	**14**	**1**	**100.0**	**18:43**	**20**	**0**	**1**	**1**	**37**	**0**	**0**	**0**	**18:25**
	Finland	Olympics	4	1	0	1	2																		
2002-03	**Toronto**	**NHL**	**78**	**4**	**7**	**11**	**28**	**0**	**0**	**2**	**49**	**8.2**	**3**	**0**	**0.0**	**15:02**	**7**	**1**	**1**	**2**	**2**	**0**	**0**	**0**	**19:45**
	NHL Totals		**452**	**13**	**55**	**68**	**278**	**5**	**0**	**3**	**407**	**3.2**		**1**	**100.0**	**16:34**	**44**	**1**	**7**	**8**	**45**	**0**	**0**	**0**	**17:57**

Traded to **Toronto** by **Los Angeles** for Adam Mair and Toronto's 2nd round choice (Mike Cammalleri) in 2001 Entry Draft, March 13, 2001.

BERGERON, Marc-Andre

(BAIR-zhur-uhn, MAHRK-AWN-dray) **EDM.**

Defense. Shoots left. 5'9", 190 lbs. Born, St-Louis-de-France, Que., October 13, 1980.

Season	Club	League	GP	G	A	Pts	PIM	PP	SH	GW	S	%	+/-	TF	F%	Min	GP	G	A	Pts	PIM	PP	SH	GW	Min
1996-97	Cap-de-Madelaine	QAAA	4	0	1	1	0										2	0	0	0	0				
1997-98	Baie-Comeau	QMJHL	40	6	14	20	48																		
1998-99	Baie-Comeau	QMJHL	46	8	14	22	57																		
	Shawinigan	QMJHL	24	6	7	13	66										5	2	2	4	24				
99-2000	Shawinigan	QMJHL	70	24	50	74	173										13	4	7	11	45				
2000-01	Shawinigan	QMJHL	69	42	59	101	185										10	4	11	15	24				
2001-02	Hamilton	AHL	50	2	13	15	61										9	1	4	5	8				
2002-03	**Edmonton**	**NHL**	**5**	**1**	**1**	**2**	**9**	**0**	**0**	**0**	**5**	**20.0**	**2**	**0**	**0.0**	**16:30**	**1**	**0**	**1**	**1**	**0**	**0**	**0**	**0**	**19:20**
	Hamilton	AHL	66	8	31	39	73										20	0	7	7	25				
	NHL Totals		**5**	**1**	**1**	**2**	**9**	**0**	**0**	**0**	**5**	**20.0**		**0**	**0.0**	**16:30**	**1**	**0**	**1**	**1**	**0**	**0**	**0**	**0**	**19:20**

QMJHL First All-Star Team (2001) • Canadian Major Junior First All-Star Team (2001) • Canadian Major Junior Defenseman of the Year (2001) • AHL Second All-Star Team (2003)

Signed as a free agent by **Edmonton**, July 20, 2001.

BERGEVIN, Marc

(BUHR-zheh-vihn, MAHRK) **PIT.**

Defense. Shoots left. 6'1", 209 lbs. Born, Montreal, Que., August 11, 1965. Chicago's 3rd choice, 60th overall, in 1983 Entry Draft.

Season	Club	League	GP	G	A	Pts	PIM	PP	SH	GW	S	%	+/-	TF	F%	Min	GP	G	A	Pts	PIM	PP	SH	GW	Min
1981-82	Mtl-Concordia	QAAA	44	10	20	30	54										5	0	2	2	4				
1982-83	Chicoutimi	QMJHL	64	3	27	30	113																		
1983-84	Chicoutimi	QMJHL	70	10	35	45	125																		
	Springfield	AHL	7	0	1	1	2																		
1984-85	**Chicago**	**NHL**	**60**	**0**	**6**	**6**	**54**	**0**	**0**	**0**	**41**	**0.0**	**–9**				**6**	**0**	**3**	**3**	**2**	**0**	**0**	**0**	
	Springfield	AHL															4	0	0	0	0				
1985-86	**Chicago**	**NHL**	**71**	**7**	**7**	**14**	**60**	**0**	**0**	**1**	**50**	**14.0**	**0**				**3**	**0**	**0**	**0**	**0**	**0**	**0**	**0**	
1986-87	**Chicago**	**NHL**	**66**	**4**	**10**	**14**	**66**	**0**	**0**	**0**	**56**	**7.1**	**4**				**3**	**1**	**0**	**1**	**2**	**0**	**0**	**0**	
1987-88	**Chicago**	**NHL**	**58**	**1**	**6**	**7**	**85**	**0**	**0**	**0**	**51**	**2.0**	**–19**												
	Saginaw Hawks	IHL	10	2	7	9	20																		
1988-89	**Chicago**	**NHL**	**11**	**0**	**0**	**0**	**18**	**0**	**0**	**0**	**9**	**0.0**	**–3**												
	NY Islanders	**NHL**	**58**	**2**	**13**	**15**	**62**	**1**	**0**	**0**	**56**	**3.6**	**2**												
1989-90	**NY Islanders**	**NHL**	**18**	**0**	**4**	**4**	**30**	**0**	**0**	**0**	**12**	**0.0**	**–8**												
	Springfield	AHL	47	7	16	23	66										17	2	11	13	16				
1990-91	Capital District	AHL	7	0	5	5	6																		
	Hartford	**NHL**	**4**	**0**	**0**	**0**	**4**	**0**	**0**	**0**	**2**	**0.0**	**–3**												
	Springfield	AHL	58	4	23	27	85										18	0	7	7	26				
1991-92	**Hartford**	**NHL**	**75**	**7**	**17**	**24**	**64**	**4**	**1**	**1**	**96**	**7.3**	**–13**				**5**	**0**	**0**	**0**	**2**	**0**	**0**	**0**	
1992-93	**Tampa Bay**	**NHL**	**78**	**2**	**12**	**14**	**66**	**0**	**0**	**0**	**69**	**2.9**	**–16**												
1993-94	**Tampa Bay**	**NHL**	**83**	**1**	**15**	**16**	**87**	**0**	**0**	**1**	**76**	**1.3**	**–5**												
1994-95	**Tampa Bay**	**NHL**	**44**	**2**	**4**	**6**	**51**	**0**	**1**	**0**	**32**	**6.3**	**–6**												
1995-96	**Detroit**	**NHL**	**70**	**1**	**9**	**10**	**33**	**0**	**0**	**0**	**26**	**3.8**	**7**				**17**	**1**	**0**	**1**	**14**	**1**	**0**	**0**	
1996-97	**St. Louis**	**NHL**	**82**	**0**	**4**	**4**	**53**	**0**	**0**	**0**	**30**	**0.0**	**–9**				**6**	**1**	**0**	**1**	**8**	**0**	**0**	**0**	
1997-98	**St. Louis**	**NHL**	**81**	**3**	**7**	**10**	**90**	**0**	**0**	**0**	**40**	**7.5**	**–2**				**10**	**0**	**1**	**1**	**8**	**0**	**0**	**0**	
1998-99	**St. Louis**	**NHL**	**52**	**1**	**1**	**2**	**99**	**0**	**0**	**0**	**40**	**2.5**	**–14**	**0**	**0.0**	**16:09**									
99-2000	**St. Louis**	**NHL**	**81**	**1**	**8**	**9**	**75**	**0**	**0**	**0**	**54**	**1.9**	**27**	**0**	**0.0**	**21:16**	**7**	**0**	**1**	**1**	**6**	**0**	**0**	**0**	**19:05**
2000-01	**St. Louis**	**NHL**	**2**	**0**	**0**	**0**	**0**	**0**	**0**	**0**	**1**	**0.0**	**1**	**0**	**0.0**	**14:51**									
	Pittsburgh	**NHL**	**36**	**1**	**4**	**5**	**26**	**0**	**0**	**0**	**11**	**9.1**	**5**	**0**	**0.0**	**16:57**	**12**	**0**	**1**	**1**	**2**	**0**	**0**	**0**	**18:22**
2001-02	**St. Louis**	**NHL**	**30**	**0**	**3**	**3**	**2**	**0**	**0**	**0**	**13**	**0.0**	**6**	**0**	**0.0**	**12:15**	**7**	**0**	**0**	**0**	**4**	**0**	**0**	**0**	**14:36**
	Worcester IceCats	AHL	2	0	0	0	0																		
2002-03	**Pittsburgh**	**NHL**	**69**	**2**	**5**	**7**	**36**	**0**	**0**	**0**	**27**	**7.4**	**–9**	**0**	**0.0**	**18:46**									
	Tampa Bay	**NHL**	**1**	**0**	**0**	**0**	**0**	**0**	**0**	**0**	**0**	**0.0**	**–2**	**0**	**0.0**	**18:26**									
	NHL Totals		**1130**	**35**	**135**	**170**	**1061**	**5**	**2**	**3**	**792**	**4.4**		**0**	**0.0**	**18:01**	**76**	**3**	**6**	**9**	**48**	**1**	**0**	**0**	**17:32**

Traded to **NY Islanders** by **Chicago** with Gary Nylund for Steve Konroyd and Bob Bassen, November 25, 1988. Traded to **Hartford** by **NY Islanders** for Hartford's 5th round choice (Ryan Duthie) in 1992 Entry Draft, October 30, 1990. Signed as a free agent by **Tampa Bay**, July 9, 1992. Traded to **Detroit** by **Tampa Bay** with Ben Hankinson for Shawn Burr and Detroit's 3rd round choice (later traded to Boston – Boston selected Jason Doyle) in 1996 Entry Draft, August 17, 1995. Signed as a free agent by **St. Louis**, July 31, 1996. Traded to **Pittsburgh** by **St. Louis** for Dan Trebil, December 28, 2000. • Missed majority of 2000-01 season recovering from thumb (October 5, 2000 vs. Phoenix) and knee (February 23, 2001 vs. Detroit) injuries. Signed as a free agent by **St. Louis**, November 6, 2001. Signed as a free agent by **Pittsburgh**, July 18, 2002. Traded to **Tampa Bay** by **Pittsburgh** for Brian Holzinger, March 11, 2003. Traded to **Pittsburgh** by **Tampa Bay** for NY Rangers' 9th round choice (previouslly acquired, Tampa Bay selected Albert Vishnyakov) in 2003 Entry Draft, May 12, 2003.

BERGLUND, Christian

(BUHRG-luhnd, KRIH-stan) **N.J.**

Left wing. Shoots left. 5'11", 190 lbs. Born, Orebro, Sweden, March 12, 1980. New Jersey's 3rd choice, 37th overall, in 1998 Entry Draft.

Season	Club	League	GP	G	A	Pts	PIM	PP	SH	GW	S	%	+/-	TF	F%	Min	GP	G	A	Pts	PIM	PP	SH	GW	Min
1994-95	Kariskoga IK	Swede-4	20	14	13	27																			
1995-96	Kristinehamn SK	Swede-3	23	8	8	16	12																		
1996-97	Farjestad Jr.	Swede-Jr.	21	2	3	5	24																		
1997-98	Farjestad Jr.	Swede-Jr.	29	23	19	42	88										2	0	0	0	0				
	Farjestad	Sweden	1	0	0	0	0																		
1998-99	Farjestad Jr.	Swede-Jr.	5	3	4	7	22																		
	Farjestad	Sweden	37	2	4	6	37										4	1	0	1	4				
99-2000	Farjestad Jr.	Swede-Jr.	5	3	5	8	8																		
	Bofors IK	Swede-2	6	2	0	2	12																		
	Farjestad	Sweden	43	8	6	14	44										7	2	1	3	10				
2000-01	Farjestad	Sweden	49	17	20	37	*142										16	7	7	14	22				
2001-02	**New Jersey**	**NHL**	**15**	**2**	**7**	**9**	**8**	**0**	**0**	**0**	**22**	**9.1**	**–3**	**2**	**50.0**	**12:26**	**3**	**0**	**0**	**0**	**2**	**0**	**0**	**0**	**11:31**
	Albany River Rats	AHL	60	21	26	47	69																		
2002-03	**New Jersey**	**NHL**	**38**	**4**	**5**	**9**	**20**	**0**	**0**	**0**	**50**	**8.0**	**3**	**11**	**9.1**	**10:11**									
	Albany River Rats	AHL	26	6	14	20	57																		
	NHL Totals		**53**	**6**	**12**	**18**	**28**	**0**	**0**	**0**	**72**	**8.3**		**13**	**15.4**	**10:49**	**3**	**0**	**0**	**0**	**2**	**0**	**0**	**0**	**11:31**

BERRY, Rick

(BAIR-ree, RIHK) **WSH.**

Defense. Shoots left. 6'2", 210 lbs. Born, Birtle, Man., November 4, 1978. Colorado's 3rd choice, 55th overall, in 1997 Entry Draft.

Season	Club	League	GP	G	A	Pts	PIM	PP	SH	GW	S	%	+/-	TF	F%	Min	GP	G	A	Pts	PIM	PP	SH	GW	Min
1994-95	Yellowhead Pass	MMHL	33	12	19	31	90																		
1995-96	Seattle	WHL	59	4	9	13	103										1	0	0	0	0				
1996-97	Seattle	WHL	72	12	21	33	125										15	3	7	10	23				
1997-98	Seattle	WHL	37	5	12	17	100																		
	Spokane Chiefs	WHL	22	4	9	13	31										17	1	4	5	26				
1998-99	Hershey Bears	AHL	62	2	6	8	153																		
99-2000	Hershey Bears	AHL	64	9	16	25	148										13	2	3	5	24				
2000-01	**Colorado**	**NHL**	**19**	**0**	**4**	**4**	**38**	**0**	**0**	**0**	**10**	**0.0**	**5**	**0**	**0.0**	**12:08**									
	Hershey Bears	AHL	48	6	17	23	87										12	2	2	4	18				
2001-02	**Colorado**	**NHL**	**57**	**0**	**0**	**0**	**60**	**0**	**0**	**0**	**29**	**0.0**	**1**	**0**	**0.0**	**9:29**									
	Pittsburgh	**NHL**	**13**	**0**	**2**	**2**	**21**	**0**	**0**	**0**	**20**	**0.0**	**–4**	**0**	**0.0**	**19:39**									
2002-03	**Washington**	**NHL**	**43**	**2**	**1**	**3**	**87**	**0**	**0**	**1**	**40**	**5.0**	**–3**	**0**	**0.0**	**12:58**									
	NHL Totals		**132**	**2**	**7**	**9**	**206**	**0**	**0**	**1**	**99**	**2.0**		**0**	**0.0**	**12:00**									

Traded to **Pittsburgh** by **Colorado** with Ville Nieminen for Darius Kasparaitis, March 19, 2002. Claimed by **Washington** from **Pittsburgh** in Waiver Draft, October 4, 2002.

BERTUZZI, Todd
(buhr-TOO-zee, TAWD) **VAN.**

Right wing. Shoots left. 6'3", 235 lbs. Born, Sudbury, Ont., February 2, 1975. NY Islanders' 1st choice, 23rd overall, in 1993 Entry Draft.

			Regular Season														Playoffs								
Season	Club	League	GP	G	A	Pts	PIM	PP	SH	GW	S	%	+/-	TF	F%	Min	GP	G	A	Pts	PIM	PP	SH	GW	Min
1990-91	Sudbury Legion	NOHA	48	25	46	71	247	....	....	....	....	....	....	....	....	....	....	....	....	....	....	....	....	....	....
	Sud. Cub Wolves	NOJHA	3	3	2	5	10	....	....	....	....	....	....	....	....	....	....	....	....	....	....	....	....	....	....
1991-92	Guelph Storm	OHL	47	7	14	21	145	....	....	....	....	....	....	....	....	....	....	....	....	....	....	....	....	....	....
1992-93	Guelph Storm	OHL	59	27	32	59	164	....	....	....	....	....	....	....	....	....	5	2	2	4	6	....	....	....	....
1993-94	Guelph Storm	OHL	61	28	54	82	165	....	....	....	....	....	....	....	....	....	9	2	6	8	30	....	....	....	....
1994-95	Guelph Storm	OHL	62	54	65	119	58	....	....	....	....	....	....	....	....	....	14	*15	18	33	41	....	....	....	....
1995-96	**NY Islanders**	**NHL**	**76**	**18**	**21**	**39**	**83**	**4**	**0**	**2**	**127**	**14.2**	**–14**	....	....	....	....	....	....	....	....	....	....	....	....
1996-97	**NY Islanders**	**NHL**	**64**	**10**	**13**	**23**	**68**	**3**	**0**	**1**	**79**	**12.7**	**–3**	....	....	....	....	....	....	....	....	....	....	....	....
	Utah Grizzlies	IHL	13	5	5	10	16	....	....	....	....	....	....	....	....	....	....	....	....	....	....	....	....	....	....
1997-98	**NY Islanders**	**NHL**	**52**	**7**	**11**	**18**	**58**	**1**	**0**	**1**	**63**	**11.1**	**–19**	....	....	....	....	....	....	....	....	....	....	....	....
	Vancouver	**NHL**	**22**	**6**	**9**	**15**	**63**	**1**	**1**	**1**	**39**	**15.4**	**2**	....	....	....	....	....	....	....	....	....	....	....	....
1998-99	**Vancouver**	**NHL**	**32**	**8**	**8**	**16**	**44**	**1**	**0**	**3**	**72**	**11.1**	**–6**	**191**	**43.5**	**18:28**	....	....	....	....	....	....	....	....	....
99-2000	**Vancouver**	**NHL**	**80**	**25**	**25**	**50**	**126**	**4**	**0**	**2**	**173**	**14.5**	**–2**	**476**	**46.6**	**15:24**	....	....	....	....	....	....	....	....	....
2000-01	**Vancouver**	**NHL**	**79**	**25**	**30**	**55**	**93**	**14**	**0**	**3**	**203**	**12.3**	**–18**	**84**	**45.2**	**17:13**	**4**	**2**	**2**	**4**	**8**	**0**	**0**	**0**	**19:01**
2001-02	**Vancouver**	**NHL**	**72**	**36**	**49**	**85**	**110**	**14**	**0**	**3**	**203**	**17.7**	**21**	**151**	**49.0**	**19:40**	**6**	**2**	**2**	**4**	**14**	**1**	**0**	**0**	**21:49**
2002-03	**Vancouver**	**NHL**	**82**	**46**	**51**	**97**	**144**	**25**	**0**	**7**	**243**	**18.9**	**2**	**208**	**47.1**	**20:34**	**14**	**2**	**4**	**6**	***60**	**0**	**0**	**0**	**21:05**
	NHL Totals		**559**	**181**	**217**	**398**	**789**	**67**	**1**	**23**	**1202**	**15.1**		**1110**	**46.4**	**18:13**	**24**	**6**	**8**	**14**	**82**	**1**	**0**	**0**	**20:55**

OHL Second All-Star team (1995) • NHL First All-Star Team (2003)

Played in NHL All-Star Game (2003)

Traded to **Vancouver** by **NY Islanders** with Bryan McCabe and NY Islanders' 3rd round choice (Jarkko Ruutu) in 1998 Entry Draft for Trevor Linden, February 6, 1998. • Missed majority of 1998-99 season recovering from leg injury suffered in game vs. Washington, November 1, 1998.

BERUBE, Craig
(buh-ROO-bee, KRAYG)

Left wing. Shoots left. 6'1", 210 lbs. Born, Calahoo, Alta., December 17, 1965.

			Regular Season														Playoffs								
Season	Club	League	GP	G	A	Pts	PIM	PP	SH	GW	S	%	+/-	TF	F%	Min	GP	G	A	Pts	PIM	PP	SH	GW	Min
1982-83	Williams Lake	PCJHL	33	9	24	33	99	....	....	....	....	....	....	....	....	....	....	....	....	....	....	....	....	....	....
	Kamloops	WHL	4	0	0	0	0	....	....	....	....	....	....	....	....	....	....	....	....	....	....	....	....	....	....
1983-84	New Westminster	WHL	70	11	20	31	104	....	....	....	....	....	....	....	....	....	8	1	2	3	5	....	....	....	....
1984-85	New Westminster	WHL	70	25	44	69	191	....	....	....	....	....	....	....	....	....	10	3	2	5	4	....	....	....	....
1985-86	Kamloops Blazers	WHL	32	17	14	31	119	....	....	....	....	....	....	....	....	....	....	....	....	....	....	....	....	....	....
	Medicine Hat	WHL	34	14	16	30	95	....	....	....	....	....	....	....	....	....	25	7	8	15	102	....	....	....	....
1986-87	**Philadelphia**	**NHL**	**7**	**0**	**0**	**0**	**57**	**0**	**0**	**0**	**4**	**0.0**	**2**	....	....	....	**5**	**0**	**0**	**0**	**17**	**0**	**0**	**0**	....
	Hershey Bears	AHL	63	7	17	24	325	....	....	....	....	....	....	....	....	....	....	....	....	....	....	....	....	....	....
1987-88	**Philadelphia**	**NHL**	**27**	**3**	**2**	**5**	**108**	**0**	**0**	**2**	**13**	**23.1**	**1**	....	....	....	....	....	....	....	....	....	....	....	....
	Hershey Bears	AHL	31	5	9	14	119	....	....	....	....	....	....	....	....	....	....	....	....	....	....	....	....	....	....
1988-89	**Philadelphia**	**NHL**	**53**	**1**	**1**	**2**	**199**	**0**	**0**	**0**	**31**	**3.2**	**–15**	....	....	....	**16**	**0**	**0**	**0**	**56**	**0**	**0**	**0**	....
	Hershey Bears	AHL	7	0	2	2	19	....	....	....	....	....	....	....	....	....	....	....	....	....	....	....	....	....	....
1989-90	**Philadelphia**	**NHL**	**74**	**4**	**14**	**18**	**291**	**0**	**0**	**0**	**52**	**7.7**	**–7**	....	....	....	....	....	....	....	....	....	....	....	....
1990-91	**Philadelphia**	**NHL**	**74**	**8**	**9**	**17**	**293**	**0**	**0**	**0**	**46**	**17.4**	**–6**	....	....	....	....	....	....	....	....	....	....	....	....
1991-92	**Toronto**	**NHL**	**40**	**5**	**7**	**12**	**109**	**1**	**0**	**1**	**42**	**11.9**	**–2**	....	....	....	....	....	....	....	....	....	....	....	....
	Calgary	**NHL**	**36**	**1**	**4**	**5**	**155**	**0**	**0**	**0**	**27**	**3.7**	**–3**	....	....	....	....	....	....	....	....	....	....	....	....
1992-93	**Calgary**	**NHL**	**77**	**4**	**8**	**12**	**209**	**0**	**0**	**2**	**58**	**6.9**	**–6**	....	....	....	**6**	**0**	**1**	**1**	**21**	**0**	**0**	**0**	....
1993-94	**Washington**	**NHL**	**84**	**7**	**7**	**14**	**305**	**0**	**0**	**0**	**48**	**14.6**	**–4**	....	....	....	**8**	**0**	**0**	**0**	**21**	**0**	**0**	**0**	....
1994-95	**Washington**	**NHL**	**43**	**2**	**4**	**6**	**173**	**0**	**0**	**0**	**22**	**9.1**	**–5**	....	....	....	**7**	**0**	**0**	**0**	**29**	**0**	**0**	**0**	....
1995-96	**Washington**	**NHL**	**50**	**2**	**10**	**12**	**151**	**1**	**0**	**1**	**28**	**7.1**	**1**	....	....	....	**2**	**0**	**0**	**0**	**19**	**0**	**0**	**0**	....
1996-97	**Washington**	**NHL**	**80**	**4**	**3**	**7**	**218**	**0**	**0**	**1**	**55**	**7.3**	**–11**	....	....	....	....	....	....	....	....	....	....	....	....
1997-98	**Washington**	**NHL**	**74**	**6**	**9**	**15**	**189**	**0**	**0**	**0**	**68**	**8.8**	**–3**	....	....	....	**21**	**1**	**0**	**1**	**21**	**0**	**0**	**1**	....
1998-99	**Washington**	**NHL**	**66**	**5**	**4**	**9**	**166**	**0**	**0**	**0**	**45**	**11.1**	**–7**	**14**	**42.9**	**6:47**	....	....	....	....	....	....	....	....	....
	Philadelphia	**NHL**	**11**	**0**	**0**	**0**	**28**	**0**	**0**	**0**	**7**	**0.0**	**–3**	**0**	**0.0**	**8:15**	**6**	**1**	**0**	**1**	**4**	**0**	**0**	**0**	**7:02**
99-2000	**Philadelphia**	**NHL**	**77**	**4**	**8**	**12**	**162**	**0**	**0**	**0**	**63**	**6.3**	**3**	**4**	**25.0**	**8:00**	**18**	**1**	**0**	**1**	**23**	**0**	**0**	**1**	**8:47**
2000-01	**Washington**	**NHL**	**22**	**0**	**1**	**1**	**18**	**0**	**0**	**0**	**8**	**0.0**	**–3**	**0**	**0.0**	**5:34**	....	....	....	....	....	....	....	....	....
	NY Islanders	**NHL**	**38**	**0**	**2**	**2**	**54**	**0**	**0**	**0**	**27**	**0.0**	**–5**	**11**	**45.5**	**6:02**	....	....	....	....	....	....	....	....	....
2001-02	**Calgary**	**NHL**	**66**	**3**	**1**	**4**	**164**	**1**	**0**	**0**	**34**	**8.8**	**–2**	**28**	**53.6**	**6:31**	....	....	....	....	....	....	....	....	....
2002-03	**Calgary**	**NHL**	**55**	**2**	**4**	**6**	**100**	**0**	**0**	**1**	**21**	**9.5**	**–6**	**27**	**29.6**	**5:16**	....	....	....	....	....	....	....	....	....
	NHL Totals		**1054**	**61**	**98**	**159**	**3149**	**3**	**0**	**8**	**699**	**8.7**		**84**	**41.7**	**6:39**	**89**	**3**	**1**	**4**	**211**	**0**	**0**	**2**	**8:21**

Signed as a free agent by **Philadelphia**, March 19, 1986. Traded to **Edmonton** by **Philadelphia** with Craig Fisher and Scott Mellanby for Dave Brown, Corey Foster and Jari Kurri, May 30, 1991. Traded to **Toronto** by **Edmonton** with Grant Fuhr and Glenn Anderson for Vincent Damphousse, Peter Ing, Scott Thornton and Luke Richardson, September 19, 1991. Traded to **Calgary** by **Toronto** with Alexander Godynyuk, Gary Leeman, Michel Petit and Jeff Reese for Doug Gilmour, Jamie Macoun, Ric Nattress, Rick Wamsley and Kent Manderville, January 2, 1992. Traded to **Washington** by **Calgary** for Washington's 5th round choice (Darryl Lafrance) in 1993 Entry Draft, June 26, 1993. Traded to **Philadelphia** by **Washington** for cash, March 23, 1999. Signed as a free agent by **Washington**, July 7, 2000. Traded to **NY Islanders** by **Washington** for Vancouver's 9th round choice (previously acquired, Washington selected Robert Muller) in 2001 Entry Draft, January 11, 2001. Signed as a free agent by **Calgary**, September 18, 2001.

BETTS, Blair
(BEHTS, BLAIR) **CGY.**

Center. Shoots left. 6'1", 200 lbs. Born, Edmonton, Alta., February 16, 1980. Calgary's 2nd choice, 33rd overall, in 1998 Entry Draft.

			Regular Season														Playoffs								
Season	Club	League	GP	G	A	Pts	PIM	PP	SH	GW	S	%	+/-	TF	F%	Min	GP	G	A	Pts	PIM	PP	SH	GW	Min
1995-96	Sherwood Park	AMHL	34	22	19	41	69	....	....	....	....	....	....	....	....	....	....	....	....	....	....	....	....	....	....
1996-97	Prince George	WHL	58	12	18	30	19	....	....	....	....	....	....	....	....	....	15	2	2	4	6	....	....	....	....
1997-98	Prince George	WHL	71	35	41	76	38	....	....	....	....	....	....	....	....	....	11	4	6	10	8	....	....	....	....
1998-99	Prince George	WHL	42	20	22	42	39	....	....	....	....	....	....	....	....	....	7	3	2	5	8	....	....	....	....
99-2000	Prince George	WHL	44	24	35	59	38	....	....	....	....	....	....	....	....	....	13	11	11	22	6	....	....	....	....
2000-01	Saint John Flames	AHL	75	13	15	28	28	....	....	....	....	....	....	....	....	....	19	2	3	5	4	....	....	....	....
2001-02	**Calgary**	**NHL**	**6**	**1**	**0**	**1**	**2**	**0**	**0**	**1**	**4**	**25.0**	**–1**	**39**	**48.7**	**7:05**	....	....	....	....	....	....	....	....	....
	Saint John Flames	AHL	67	20	29	49	10	....	....	....	....	....	....	....	....	....	....	....	....	....	....	....	....	....	....
2002-03	**Calgary**	**NHL**	**9**	**1**	**3**	**4**	**0**	**0**	**0**	**0**	**16**	**6.3**	**3**	**71**	**53.5**	**11:33**	....	....	....	....	....	....	....	....	....
	Saint John Flames	AHL	19	6	7	13	6	....	....	....	....	....	....	....	....	....	....	....	....	....	....	....	....	....	....
	NHL Totals		**15**	**2**	**3**	**5**	**2**	**0**	**0**	**1**	**20**	**10.0**		**110**	**51.8**	**9:46**	....	....	....	....	....	....	....	....	....

• Missed majority of 2002-03 season recovering from shoulder injury suffered in training camp, September 27, 2002.

BICANEK, Radim
(BEE-chah-nehk, RA-dihm)

Defense. Shoots left. 6'1", 209 lbs. Born, Uherske Hradiste, Czech., January 18, 1975. Ottawa's 2nd choice, 27th overall, in 1993 Entry Draft.

			Regular Season														Playoffs								
Season	Club	League	GP	G	A	Pts	PIM	PP	SH	GW	S	%	+/-	TF	F%	Min	GP	G	A	Pts	PIM	PP	SH	GW	Min
1992-93	Dukla Jihlava	Czech	43	2	3	5	....	....	....	....	....	....	....	....	....	....	....	....	....	....	....	....	....	....	....
1993-94	Belleville Bulls	OHL	63	16	27	43	49	....	....	....	....	....	....	....	....	....	12	2	8	10	21	....	....	....	....
1994-95	Belleville Bulls	OHL	49	13	26	39	61	....	....	....	....	....	....	....	....	....	16	6	5	11	30	....	....	....	....
	Ottawa	**NHL**	**6**	**0**	**0**	**0**	**0**	**0**	**0**	**0**	**6**	**0.0**	**3**	....	....	....	....	....	....	....	....	....	....	....	....
	P.E.I. Senators	AHL	....	....	....	....	....	....	....	....	....	....	....	....	....	....	3	0	1	1	0	....	....	....	....
1995-96	P.E.I. Senators	AHL	74	7	19	26	87	....	....	....	....	....	....	....	....	....	5	0	2	2	6	....	....	....	....
1996-97	**Ottawa**	**NHL**	**21**	**0**	**1**	**1**	**8**	**0**	**0**	**0**	**27**	**0.0**	**–4**	....	....	....	**7**	**0**	**0**	**0**	**8**	**0**	**0**	**0**	....
	Worcester IceCats	AHL	44	1	15	16	22	....	....	....	....	....	....	....	....	....	....	....	....	....	....	....	....	....	....
1997-98	**Ottawa**	**NHL**	**1**	**0**	**0**	**0**	**0**	**0**	**0**	**0**	**0**	**0.0**	**0**	....	....	....	....	....	....	....	....	....	....	....	....
	Detroit Vipers	IHL	9	1	3	4	16	....	....	....	....	....	....	....	....	....	....	....	....	....	....	....	....	....	....
	Manitoba Moose	IHL	42	1	7	8	52	....	....	....	....	....	....	....	....	....	....	....	....	....	....	....	....	....	....
1998-99	**Ottawa**	**NHL**	**7**	**0**	**0**	**0**	**4**	**0**	**0**	**0**	**6**	**0.0**	**–1**	**0**	**0.0**	**10:51**	....	....	....	....	....	....	....	....	....
	Grand Rapids	IHL	46	8	17	25	48	....	....	....	....	....	....	....	....	....	....	....	....	....	....	....	....	....	....
	Chicago	**NHL**	**7**	**0**	**0**	**0**	**6**	**0**	**0**	**0**	**7**	**0.0**	**–3**	**0**	**0.0**	**15:57**	....	....	....	....	....	....	....	....	....
99-2000	**Chicago**	**NHL**	**11**	**0**	**3**	**3**	**4**	**0**	**0**	**0**	**8**	**0.0**	**7**	**0**	**0.0**	**18:27**	....	....	....	....	....	....	....	....	....
	Cleveland	IHL	70	5	27	32	125	....	....	....	....	....	....	....	....	....	9	2	2	4	8	....	....	....	....
2000-01	**Columbus**	**NHL**	**9**	**0**	**2**	**2**	**6**	**0**	**0**	**0**	**11**	**0.0**	**1**	**1**	**100.0**	**17:08**	....	....	....	....	....	....	....	....	....
	Syracuse Crunch	AHL	68	22	43	65	124	....	....	....	....	....	....	....	....	....	5	4	2	6	2	....	....	....	....
2001-02	**Columbus**	**NHL**	**60**	**1**	**5**	**6**	**34**	**0**	**0**	**0**	**43**	**2.3**	**–15**	**0**	**0.0**	**13:32**	....	....	....	....	....	....	....	....	....
2002-03	Syracuse Crunch	AHL	56	6	17	23	111	....	....	....	....	....	....	....	....	....	....	....	....	....	....	....	....	....	....
	Binghamton	AHL	21	3	10	13	42	....	....	....	....	....	....	....	....	....	14	2	4	6	26	....	....	....	....
	NHL Totals		**122**	**1**	**11**	**12**	**62**	**0**	**0**	**0**	**108**	**0.9**		**1**	**100.0**	**14:26**	**7**	**0**	**0**	**0**	**8**	**0**	**0**	**0**	....

AHL Second All-Star Team (2001)

Traded to **Chicago** by **Ottawa** for Los Angeles' 6th round choice (previously acquired, Ottawa selected Martin Prusek) in 1999 Entry Draft, March 12, 1999. Selected by **Columbus** from **Chicago** in Expansion Draft, June 23, 2000.

BICEK, Jiri
(bee-SEHK, YEH-ree) **N.J.**

Right wing. Shoots left. 5'10", 195 lbs. Born, Kosice, Czech., December 3, 1978. New Jersey's 4th choice, 131st overall, in 1997 Entry Draft.

Season	Club	League	GP	G	A	Pts	PIM	PP	SH	GW	S	%	+/-	TF	F%	Min	Playoffs GP	G	A	Pts	PIM	PP	SH	GW	Min
1994-95	HC Kosice Jr.	Slovak-Jr.	42	38	36	74	18																		
1995-96	HC Kosice	Slovakia	30	10	15	25	16										9	2	4	6	0				
1996-97	HC Kosice	Slovakia	44	11	14	25	20										7	1	3	4					
1997-98	Albany River Rats	AHL	50	10	10	20	22										13	1	6	7	4				
1998-99	Albany River Rats	AHL	79	15	45	60	102										5	2	2	4	2				
99-2000	Albany River Rats	AHL	80	7	36	43	51										4	0	2	2	0				
2000-01	New Jersey	NHL	5	1	0	1	4	0	0	0	10	10.0	0	0	0.0	13:04									
	Albany River Rats	AHL	73	12	29	41	73																		
2001-02	New Jersey	NHL	1	0	0	0	0	0	0	0	2	0.0	–1	0	0.0	13:10									
	Albany River Rats	AHL	62	15	19	34	45																		
2002-03 ♦	New Jersey	NHL	44	5	6	11	25	1	0	1	63	7.9	7	3	0.0	11:48	5	0	0	0	0	0	0	0	8:10
	Albany River Rats	AHL	24	4	10	14	28																		
	NHL Totals		50	6	6	12	29	1	0	1	75	8.0		3	0.0	11:57	5	0	0	0	0	0	0	0	8:10

BIRON, Mathieu
(BEE-rawn, mat-yoo) **FLA.**

Defense. Shoots right. 6'6", 220 lbs. Born, Lac-St-Charles, Que., April 29, 1980. Los Angeles' 1st choice, 21st overall, in 1998 Entry Draft.

Season	Club	League	GP	G	A	Pts	PIM	PP	SH	GW	S	%	+/-	TF	F%	Min	Playoffs GP	G	A	Pts	PIM	PP	SH	GW	Min
1996-97	Ste-Foy	QAAA	40	4	22	26	49										10	3	4	7					
1997-98	Shawinigan	QMJHL	59	8	28	36	60										6	0	1	1	10				
1998-99	Shawinigan	QMJHL	69	13	32	45	116										6	0	2	2	6				
99-2000	NY Islanders	NHL	60	4	4	8	38	2	0	2	70	5.7	–13	2	0.0	15:02									
2000-01	NY Islanders	NHL	14	0	1	1	12	0	0	0	10	0.0	2	0	0.0	12:21									
	Lowell	AHL	22	1	3	4	17																		
	Springfield	AHL	34	0	6	6	18																		
2001-02	Tampa Bay	NHL	36	0	0	0	12	0	0	0	35	0.0	–16	0	0.0	14:47									
	Springfield	AHL	35	4	9	13	16																		
2002-03	San Antonio	AHL	43	3	8	11	58																		
	Florida	NHL	34	1	8	9	14	0	1	0	52	1.9	–18	0	0.0	21:08									
	NHL Totals		144	5	13	18	76	2	1	2	167	3.0		2	0.0	16:09									

Traded to **NY Islanders** by **Los Angeles** with Olli Jokinen, Josh Green and Los Angeles' 1st round choice (Taylor Pyatt) in 1999 Entry Draft for Ziggy Palffy, Brian Smolinski, Marcel Cousineau and New Jersey's 4th round choice (previously acquired, Los Angeles selected Daniel Johansson) in 1999 Entry Draft, June 20, 1999. Traded to **Tampa Bay** by **NY Islanders** with NY Islanders' 2nd round choice (later traded to Washington – later traded to Vancouver – Vancouver selected Denis Grot) in 2002 Entry Draft for Adrian Aucoin and Alexander Kharitonov, June 22, 2001. Claimed by **Columbus** from **Tampa Bay** in Waiver Draft, October 4, 2002. Traded to **Florida** by **Columbus** for Petr Tenkrat, October 4, 2002.

BLAKE, Jason
(BLAYK, JAY-suhn) **NYI**

Center. Shoots left. 5'10", 180 lbs. Born, Moorhead, MN, September 2, 1973.

Season	Club	League	GP	G	A	Pts	PIM	PP	SH	GW	S	%	+/-	TF	F%	Min	Playoffs GP	G	A	Pts	PIM	PP	SH	GW	Min
1991-92	Moorhead Spuds	Hi-School	25	30	30	60																			
1992-93	Waterloo	USHL	45	24	27	51	107																		
1993-94	Waterloo	USHL	47	50	50	100	76																		
1994-95	Ferris State	CCHA	36	16	16	32	46																		
1995-96	North Dakota	CCHA	DID NOT PLAY – TRANSFERRED COLLEGES																						
1996-97	North Dakota	WCHA	43	19	32	51	44																		
1997-98	North Dakota	WCHA	38	24	27	51	62																		
1998-99	North Dakota	WCHA	38	*28	*41	*69	49																		
	Los Angeles	NHL	1	1	0	1	0	0	0	0	5	20.0	1	14	35.7	17:13									
	Orlando	IHL	5	3	5	8	6										13	3	4	7	20				
99-2000	Los Angeles	NHL	64	5	18	23	26	0	0	1	131	3.8	4	269	43.9	11:17	3	0	0	0	0	0	0	0	9:35
	Long Beach	IHL	7	3	6	9	2																		
2000-01	Los Angeles	NHL	17	1	3	4	10	0	0	0	27	3.7	–8	13	61.5	10:03									
	Lowell	AHL	2	0	1	1	2																		
	NY Islanders	NHL	30	4	8	12	24	1	1	0	73	5.5	–12	118	44.1	15:43									
2001-02	NY Islanders	NHL	82	8	10	18	36	0	0	1	136	5.9	–11	23	43.5	12:54	7	0	1	1	13	0	0	0	12:13
2002-03	NY Islanders	NHL	81	25	30	55	58	3	1	4	253	9.9	16	22	18.2	17:38	5	0	1	1	2	0	0	0	19:39
	NHL Totals		275	44	69	113	154	4	2	6	625	7.0		459	42.9	14:04	15	0	2	2	15	0	0	0	14:10

WCHA First All-Star Team (1997, 1998, 1999) • NCAA West Second All-American Team (1998) • WCHA Player of the Year (1999) • NCAA West First All-American Team (1999)

Signed as a free agent by **Los Angeles**, April 20, 1999. Traded to **NY Islanders** by **Los Angeles** for NY Islanders' 5th round choice (Joel Andresen) in 2002 Entry Draft, January 3, 2001.

BLAKE, Rob
(BLAYK, RAWB) **COL.**

Defense. Shoots right. 6'4", 225 lbs. Born, Simcoe, Ont., December 10, 1969. Los Angeles' 4th choice, 70th overall, in 1988 Entry Draft.

Season	Club	League	GP	G	A	Pts	PIM	PP	SH	GW	S	%	+/-	TF	F%	Min	Playoffs GP	G	A	Pts	PIM	PP	SH	GW	Min
1985-86	Brantford Classics	OJHL-B	39	3	13	16	43																		
1986-87	Stratford Cullitons	OJHL-B	31	11	20	31	115																		
1987-88	Bowling Green	CCHA	43	5	8	13	88																		
1988-89	Bowling Green	CCHA	46	11	21	32	140																		
1989-90	Bowling Green	CCHA	42	23	36	59	140																		
	Los Angeles	NHL	4	0	0	0	4	0	0	0	3	0.0	0				8	1	3	4	4	1	0	0	
1990-91	Los Angeles	NHL	75	12	34	46	125	9	0	2	150	8.0	3				12	1	4	5	26	1	0	0	
1991-92	Los Angeles	NHL	57	7	13	20	102	5	0	0	131	5.3	–5				6	2	1	3	12	0	0	0	
1992-93	Los Angeles	NHL	76	16	43	59	152	10	0	4	243	6.6	18				23	4	6	10	46	1	1	0	
1993-94	Los Angeles	NHL	84	20	48	68	137	7	0	6	304	6.6	–7												
1994-95	Los Angeles	NHL	24	4	7	11	38	4	0	1	76	5.3	–16												
1995-96	Los Angeles	NHL	6	1	2	3	8	0	0	0	13	7.7	0												
1996-97	Los Angeles	NHL	62	8	23	31	82	4	0	1	169	4.7	–28												
1997-98	Los Angeles	NHL	81	23	27	50	94	11	0	4	261	8.8	–3				4	0	0	0	6	0	0	0	
	Canada	Olympics	6	1	1	2	2																		
1998-99	Los Angeles	NHL	62	12	23	35	128	5	1	2	216	5.6	–7	0	0.0	24:52									
99-2000	Los Angeles	NHL	77	18	39	57	112	12	0	5	327	5.5	10	0	0.0	28:30	4	0	2	2	4	0	0	0	30:10
2000-01	Los Angeles	NHL	54	17	32	49	69	9	0	1	223	7.6	–8	0	0.0	28:11									
	♦ Colorado	NHL	13	2	8	10	8	1	0	1	44	4.5	11	0	0.0	26:03	23	6	13	19	16	3	0	0	29:26
2001-02	Colorado	NHL	75	16	40	56	58	10	0	2	229	7.0	16	0	0.0	27:35	20	6	6	12	16	1	0	0	26:38
	Canada	Olympics	6	1	2	3	2																		
2002-03	Colorado	NHL	79	17	28	45	57	8	2	3	269	6.3	20	0	0.0	26:21	7	1	2	3	8	0	0	0	27:28
	NHL Totals		829	173	367	540	1174	95	3	32	2658	6.5		0	0.0	27:04	107	21	37	58	138	7	1	0	28:12

CCHA Second All-Star Team (1989) • CCHA First All-Star Team (1990) • NCAA West First All-American Team (1990) • NHL All-Rookie Team (1991) • NHL First All-Star Team (1998) • James Norris Memorial Trophy (1998) • NHL Second All-Star Team (2000, 2001, 2002)

Played in NHL All-Star Game (1994, 1999, 2000, 2001, 2002, 2003)

• Missed majority of 1995-96 season recovering from knee injury suffered in game vs. Washington, October 20, 1995. Traded to **Colorado** by **Los Angeles** with Steve Reinprecht for Adam Deadmarsh, Aaron Miller, a player to be named later (Jared Aulin, March 22, 2001), Colorado's 1st round choice (Dave Steckel) in 2001 Entry Draft and 1st round choice (Brian Boyle) in 2003 Entry Draft, February 21, 2001.

BLATNY, Zdenek
(BLAT-nee, z-DEHN-ehk) **ATL.**

Left wing. Shoots left. 6'1", 190 lbs. Born, Brno, Czech., January 14, 1981. Atlanta's 3rd choice, 68th overall, in 1999 Entry Draft.

Season	Club	League	GP	G	A	Pts	PIM	PP	SH	GW	S	%	+/-	TF	F%	Min	Playoffs GP	G	A	Pts	PIM	PP	SH	GW	Min
1997-98	Kometa Brno Jr.	Czech-Jr.	42	22	21	43	40																		
1998-99	Seattle	WHL	44	18	15	33	25										11	4	0	4	24				
99-2000	Seattle	WHL	7	4	5	9	12																		
	Kootenay Ice	WHL	61	43	39	82	119										21	10	*17	27	46				
2000-01	Kootenay Ice	WHL	58	37	48	85	120										11	8	10	18	24				
2001-02	Chicago Wolves	AHL	41	4	3	7	30										3	2	0	2	0				
	Greenville	ECHL	12	5	5	10	17										9	2	8	10	14				

			Regular Season														Playoffs								
Season	Club	League	GP	G	A	Pts	PIM	PP	SH	GW	S	%	+/-	TF	F%	Min	GP	G	A	Pts	PIM	PP	SH	GW	Min
2002-03	Atlanta	NHL	4	0	0	0	0	0	0	0	2	0.0	−1	0	0.0	10:31	....	....	....	....	....	....	....	....	....
	Chicago Wolves	AHL	72	12	9	21	62	....	....	....	....	....	....	....	....	....	9	0	2	2	20	....	....	....	....
	NHL Totals		4	0	0	0	0	0	0	0	2	0.0		0	0.0	10:31	....	....	....	....	....	....	....	....	....

WHL East Second All-Star Team (2000)

BLOUIN, Sylvain

(bluh-WHEN, SIHL-veh) **MTL.**

Left wing. Shoots left. 6'2", 215 lbs. Born, Montreal, Que., May 21, 1974. NY Rangers' 5th choice, 104th overall, in 1994 Entry Draft.

Season	Club	League	GP	G	A	Pts	PIM	PP	SH	GW	S	%	+/-	TF	F%	Min	GP	G	A	Pts	PIM	PP	SH	GW	Min
1991-92	Laval Titan	QMJHL	28	0	0	0	23	....	....	....	....	....	....	....	....	....	9	0	0	0	35	....	....	....	....
1992-93	Laval Titan	QMJHL	68	0	10	10	373	....	....	....	....	....	....	....	....	....	13	1	0	1	*66	....	....	....	....
1993-94	Laval Titan	QMJHL	62	18	22	40	*492	....	....	....	....	....	....	....	....	....	21	4	13	17	*177	....	....	....	....
1994-95	Chicago Wolves	IHL	1	0	0	0	2	....	....	....	....	....	....	....	....	....	....	....	....	....	....	....	....	....	....
	Charlotte	ECHL	50	5	7	12	280	....	....	....	....	....	....	....	....	....	3	0	0	0	6	....	....	....	....
	Binghamton	AHL	10	1	0	1	46	....	....	....	....	....	....	....	....	....	2	0	0	0	24	....	....	....	....
1995-96	Binghamton	AHL	71	5	8	13	*352	....	....	....	....	....	....	....	....	....	4	0	3	3	4	....	....	....	....
1996-97	NY Rangers	NHL	6	0	0	0	18	0	0	0	1	0.0	−1	....	....	....	....	....	....	....	....	....	....	....	....
	Binghamton	AHL	62	13	17	30	301	....	....	....	....	....	....	....	....	....	4	2	1	3	16	....	....	....	....
1997-98	NY Rangers	NHL	1	0	0	0	5	0	0	0	0	0.0	0	....	....	....	....	....	....	....	....	....	....	....	....
	Hartford	AHL	53	8	9	17	286	....	....	....	....	....	....	....	....	....	9	0	1	1	63	....	....	....	....
1998-99	Montreal	NHL	5	0	0	0	19	0	0	0	1	0.0	0	0	0.0	3:37	....	....	....	....	....	....	....	....	....
	Fredericton	AHL	67	6	10	16	333	....	....	....	....	....	....	....	....	....	15	2	0	2	*87	....	....	....	....
99-2000	Worcester IceCats	AHL	70	16	18	34	337	....	....	....	....	....	....	....	....	....	8	3	5	8	30	....	....	....	....
2000-01	Minnesota	NHL	41	3	2	5	117	0	0	0	37	8.1	−5	2	100.0	9:54	....	....	....	....	....	....	....	....	....
2001-02	Minnesota	NHL	43	0	2	2	130	0	0	0	28	0.0	−11	0	0.0	9:51	....	....	....	....	....	....	....	....	....
2002-03	Minnesota	NHL	2	0	0	0	4	0	0	0	1	0.0	0	1	0.0	7:38	....	....	....	....	....	....	....	....	....
	Montreal	NHL	17	0	0	0	43	0	0	0	3	0.0	−3	0	0.0	3:36	....	....	....	....	....	....	....	....	....
	Hamilton	AHL	19	2	4	6	39	....	....	....	....	....	....	....	....	....	11	1	1	2	28	....	....	....	....
	NHL Totals		115	3	4	7	336	0	0	0	71	4.2		3	66.7	8:34	....	....	....	....	....	....	....	....	....

Traded to **Montreal** by **NY Rangers** with NY Rangers' 6th round choice (later traded to Phoenix – Phoenix selected Erik Lewerstrom) in 1999 Entry Draft for Peter Popovic, June 30, 1998. Signed as a free agent by **St. Louis**, August 25, 1999. Signed as a free agent by **Montreal**, July 7, 2000. Claimed by **Minnesota** from **Montreal** in Waiver Draft, September 29, 2000. • Missed majority of 2000-01 season recovering from shoulder injury suffered in game vs. Chicago, December 7, 2000. Traded to **Montreal** by **Minnesota** for Montreal's 7th round choice (Grigory Misharin) in 2003 Entry Draft, October 31, 2002.

BOGUNIECKI, Eric

(BOH-guhn-ih-kee, AIR-ihk) **ST.L.**

Center. Shoots right. 5'8", 192 lbs. Born, New Haven, CT, May 6, 1975. St. Louis' 6th choice, 193rd overall, in 1993 Entry Draft.

Season	Club	League	GP	G	A	Pts	PIM	PP	SH	GW	S	%	+/-	TF	F%	Min	GP	G	A	Pts	PIM	PP	SH	GW	Min
1992-93	Westminster High	Hi-School	24	30	24	54	55	....	....	....	....	....	....	....	....	....	....	....	....	....	....	....	....	....	....
1993-94	New Hampshire	H-East	40	17	16	33	66	....	....	....	....	....	....	....	....	....	....	....	....	....	....	....	....	....	....
1994-95	New Hampshire	H-East	34	12	16	28	62	....	....	....	....	....	....	....	....	....	....	....	....	....	....	....	....	....	....
1995-96	New Hampshire	H-East	32	23	28	51	46	....	....	....	....	....	....	....	....	....	....	....	....	....	....	....	....	....	....
1996-97	New Hampshire	H-East	36	26	31	57	58	....	....	....	....	....	....	....	....	....	....	....	....	....	....	....	....	....	....
1997-98	Dayton Bombers	ECHL	26	19	18	37	36	....	....	....	....	....	....	....	....	....	....	....	....	....	....	....	....	....	....
	Fort Wayne	IHL	35	4	8	12	29	....	....	....	....	....	....	....	....	....	4	1	2	3	10	....	....	....	....
1998-99	Fort Wayne	IHL	72	32	34	66	100	....	....	....	....	....	....	....	....	....	2	0	1	1	2	....	....	....	....
99-2000	Florida	NHL	4	0	0	0	2	0	0	0	5	0.0	−1	25	36.0	8:35	....	....	....	....	....	....	....	....	....
	Louisville Panthers	AHL	57	33	42	75	148	....	....	....	....	....	....	....	....	....	4	3	2	5	20	....	....	....	....
2000-01	Louisville Panthers	AHL	28	13	12	25	56	....	....	....	....	....	....	....	....	....	....	....	....	....	....	....	....	....	....
	St. Louis	NHL	1	0	0	0	0	0	0	0	1	0.0	−1	0	0.0	13:44	....	....	....	....	....	....	....	....	....
	Worcester IceCats	AHL	45	17	28	45	100	....	....	....	....	....	....	....	....	....	9	3	2	5	10	....	....	....	....
2001-02	St. Louis	NHL	8	0	1	1	4	0	0	0	10	0.0	−2	21	38.1	11:42	1	0	1	1	0	0	0	0	8:01
	Worcester IceCats	AHL	63	*38	46	84	181	....	....	....	....	....	....	....	....	....	3	2	0	2	4	....	....	....	....
2002-03	St. Louis	NHL	80	22	27	49	38	3	1	5	117	18.8	22	5	40.0	14:00	7	1	2	3	2	1	0	0	13:09
	NHL Totals		93	22	28	50	44	3	1	5	133	16.5		51	37.3	13:34	8	1	3	4	2	1	0	0	12:30

Hockey East Second All-Star Team (1997) • AHL First All-Star Team (2002) • Les Cunningham Plaque (MVP – AHL) (2002)

Signed as a free agent by **Florida**, July 7, 1999. Traded to **St. Louis** by **Florida** for Andrei Podkonicky, December 17, 2000.

BOILEAU, Patrick

(BWOI-loh, PA-trihk)

Defense. Shoots right. 6', 202 lbs. Born, Montreal, Que., February 22, 1975. Washington's 3rd choice, 69th overall, in 1993 Entry Draft.

Season	Club	League	GP	G	A	Pts	PIM	PP	SH	GW	S	%	+/-	TF	F%	Min	GP	G	A	Pts	PIM	PP	SH	GW	Min
1990-91	Laval Laurentide	QAAA	3	0	1	1	0	....	....	....	....	....	....	....	....	....	....	....	....	....	....	....	....	....	....
1991-92	Laval Laurentide	QAAA	42	9	36	45	94	....	....	....	....	....	....	....	....	....	12	3	5	8	10	....	....	....	....
1992-93	Laval Titan	QMJHL	69	4	19	23	73	....	....	....	....	....	....	....	....	....	13	1	2	3	10	....	....	....	....
1993-94	Laval Titan	QMJHL	64	13	57	70	56	....	....	....	....	....	....	....	....	....	21	1	7	8	24	....	....	....	....
1994-95	Laval Titan	QMJHL	38	8	25	33	46	....	....	....	....	....	....	....	....	....	20	4	16	20	24	....	....	....	....
1995-96	Portland Pirates	AHL	78	10	28	38	41	....	....	....	....	....	....	....	....	....	19	1	3	4	12	....	....	....	....
1996-97	Washington	NHL	1	0	0	0	0	0	0	0	0	0.0	0	....	....	....	....	....	....	....	....	....	....	....	....
	Portland Pirates	AHL	67	16	28	44	63	....	....	....	....	....	....	....	....	....	5	1	1	2	4	....	....	....	....
1997-98	Portland Pirates	AHL	47	6	21	27	53	....	....	....	....	....	....	....	....	....	10	0	1	1	8	....	....	....	....
1998-99	Washington	NHL	4	0	1	1	2	0	0	0	7	0.0	−4	0	0.0	15:56	....	....	....	....	....	....	....	....	....
	Portland Pirates	AHL	52	6	18	24	52	....	....	....	....	....	....	....	....	....	....	....	....	....	....	....	....	....	....
	Indianapolis Ice	IHL	29	8	13	21	27	....	....	....	....	....	....	....	....	....	4	0	1	1	2	....	....	....	....
99-2000	Portland Pirates	AHL	63	2	15	17	61	....	....	....	....	....	....	....	....	....	4	0	0	0	4	....	....	....	....
2000-01	Portland Pirates	AHL	77	6	14	20	50	....	....	....	....	....	....	....	....	....	3	0	0	0	8	....	....	....	....
2001-02	Washington	NHL	2	0	0	0	2	0	0	0	0	0.0	−1	0	0.0	11:52	....	....	....	....	....	....	....	....	....
	Portland Pirates	AHL	75	17	19	36	43	....	....	....	....	....	....	....	....	....	....	....	....	....	....	....	....	....	....
2002-03	Grand Rapids	AHL	23	2	11	13	39	....	....	....	....	....	....	....	....	....	....	....	....	....	....	....	....	....	....
	Detroit	NHL	25	2	6	8	14	0	0	1	18	11.1	8	0	0.0	13:58	....	....	....	....	....	....	....	....	....
	NHL Totals		32	2	7	9	18	0	0	1	25	8.0		0	0.0	14:05	....	....	....	....	....	....	....	....	....

Canadian Major Junior Scholastic Player of the Year (1994)

Loaned to **Indianapolis** (IHL) by **Washington** (Portland-AHL), February 4, 1999. Signed as a free agent by **Detroit**, August 5, 2002.

BOMBARDIR, Brad

(bawm-bahr-DEER, BRAD) **MIN.**

Defense. Shoots left. 6'1", 205 lbs. Born, Powell River, B.C., May 5, 1972. New Jersey's 5th choice, 56th overall, in 1990 Entry Draft.

Season	Club	League	GP	G	A	Pts	PIM	PP	SH	GW	S	%	+/-	TF	F%	Min	GP	G	A	Pts	PIM	PP	SH	GW	Min
1988-89	Powell River	BCJHL	30	6	5	11	24	....	....	....	....	....	....	....	....	....	6	0	0	0	0	....	....	....	....
1989-90	Powell River	BCJHL	60	10	35	45	93	....	....	....	....	....	....	....	....	....	8	2	3	5	4	....	....	....	....
1990-91	North Dakota	WCHA	33	3	6	9	18	....	....	....	....	....	....	....	....	....	....	....	....	....	....	....	....	....	....
1991-92	North Dakota	WCHA	35	3	14	17	54	....	....	....	....	....	....	....	....	....	....	....	....	....	....	....	....	....	....
1992-93	North Dakota	WCHA	38	8	15	23	34	....	....	....	....	....	....	....	....	....	....	....	....	....	....	....	....	....	....
1993-94	North Dakota	WCHA	38	5	17	22	38	....	....	....	....	....	....	....	....	....	....	....	....	....	....	....	....	....	....
1994-95	Albany River Rats	AHL	77	5	22	27	22	....	....	....	....	....	....	....	....	....	14	0	3	3	6	....	....	....	....
1995-96	Albany River Rats	AHL	80	6	25	31	63	....	....	....	....	....	....	....	....	....	3	0	1	1	4	....	....	....	....
1996-97	Albany River Rats	AHL	32	0	8	8	6	....	....	....	....	....	....	....	....	....	16	1	3	4	8	....	....	....	....
1997-98	New Jersey	NHL	43	1	5	6	8	0	0	0	16	6.3	11	....	....	....	....	....	....	....	....	....	....	....	....
	Albany River Rats	AHL	5	0	0	0	0	....	....	....	....	....	....	....	....	....	....	....	....	....	....	....	....	....	....
1998-99	New Jersey	NHL	56	1	7	8	16	0	0	0	47	2.1	−4	1	0.0	15:03	5	0	0	0	0	0	0	0	16:03
99-2000◆	New Jersey	NHL	32	3	1	4	6	0	0	0	24	12.5	−6	0	0.0	15:54	1	0	0	0	0	0	0	0	18:55
2000-01	Minnesota	NHL	70	0	15	15	42	0	0	0	81	0.0	−6	1	0.0	20:50	....	....	....	....	....	....	....	....	....
2001-02	Minnesota	NHL	28	1	2	3	14	1	0	0	24	4.2	−6	0	0.0	20:33	....	....	....	....	....	....	....	....	....
2002-03	Minnesota	NHL	58	1	14	15	16	1	0	0	55	1.8	15	0	0.0	22:01	4	0	0	0	0	0	0	0	14:52
	NHL Totals		287	7	44	51	102	2	0	0	247	2.8		2	0.0	19:06	10	0	0	0	0	0	0	0	15:52

AHL Second All-Star Team (1996)

• Missed majority of 1999-2000 season recovering from esophagus injury suffered in game vs. Philadelphia, October 30, 1999. Traded to **Minnesota** by **New Jersey** for Chris Terreri and Minnesota's 9th round choice (later traded to Tampa Bay – Tampa Bay selected Thomas Ziegler) in 2000 Entry Draft, June 23, 2000. • Missed majority of 2001-02 season recovering from ankle injury suffered in game vs. San Jose, October 16, 2001.

BONDRA, Peter
(BAWN-druh, PEE-tuhr) **WSH.**

Right wing. Shoots left. 6', 200 lbs. Born, Luck, USSR, February 7, 1968. Washington's 9th choice, 156th overall, in 1990 Entry Draft.

Season	Club	League	GP	G	A	Pts	PIM	PP	SH	GW	S	%	+/-	TF	F%	Min	PO GP	PO G	PO A	PO Pts	PO PIM	PO PP	PO SH	PO GW	PO Min
1986-87	VSZ Kosice	Czech	32	4	5	9	24	....	....	....	....	....	....	....	....	....	....	....	....	....	....	....	....	....	....
1987-88	VSZ Kosice	Czech	45	27	11	38	20	....	....	....	....	....	....	....	....	....	....	....	....	....	....	....	....	....	....
1988-89	VSZ Kosice	Czech	40	30	10	40	20	....	....	....	....	....	....	....	....	....	....	....	....	....	....	....	....	....	....
1989-90	VSZ Kosice	Czech	44	29	17	46	....	....	....	....	....	....	....	....	....	....	5	7	2	9	....	....	....	....	....
1990-91	Washington	NHL	54	12	16	28	47	4	0	1	95	12.6	-10	....	....	....	4	0	1	1	2	0	0	0	....
1991-92	Washington	NHL	71	28	28	56	42	4	0	3	158	17.7	16	....	....	....	7	6	2	8	4	1	0	0	....
1992-93	Washington	NHL	83	37	48	85	70	10	0	7	239	15.5	8	....	....	....	6	0	6	6	0	0	0	0	....
1993-94	Washington	NHL	69	24	19	43	40	4	0	2	200	12.0	22	....	....	....	9	2	4	6	4	0	0	1	....
1994-95	HC Kosice	Slovakia	2	1	0	1	0	....	....	....	....	....	....	....	....	....	....	....	....	....	....	....	....	....	....
	Washington	NHL	47	*34	9	43	24	12	6	3	177	19.2	9	....	....	....	7	5	3	8	10	2	0	1	....
1995-96	Detroit Vipers	IHL	7	8	1	9	0	....	....	....	....	....	....	....	....	....	....	....	....	....	....	....	....	....	....
	Washington	NHL	67	52	28	80	40	11	4	7	322	16.1	18	....	....	....	6	3	2	5	8	2	0	1	....
1996-97	Washington	NHL	77	46	31	77	72	10	4	3	314	14.6	7	....	....	....	....	....	....	....	....	....	....	....	....
1997-98	Washington	NHL	76	*52	26	78	44	11	5	13	284	18.3	14	....	....	....	17	7	5	12	12	3	0	2	....
	Slovakia	Olympics	2	1	0	1	25	....	....	....	....	....	....	....	....	....	....	....	....	....	....	....	....	....	....
1998-99	Washington	NHL	66	31	24	55	56	6	3	5	284	10.9	-1	1	0.0	20:35	....	....	....	....	....	....	....	....	....
99-2000	Washington	NHL	62	21	17	38	30	5	3	5	187	11.2	5	2	50.0	18:48	5	1	1	2	4	1	0	0	17:30
2000-01	Washington	NHL	82	45	36	81	60	22	4	8	305	14.8	8	2	50.0	20:48	6	2	0	2	2	2	0	1	24:55
2001-02	Washington	NHL	77	39	31	70	80	17	1	8	333	11.7	-2	2	50.0	21:43	....	....	....	....	....	....	....	....	....
2002-03	Washington	NHL	76	30	26	56	52	9	2	4	256	11.7	-3	13	30.8	18:53	6	4	2	6	8	2	0	0	22:39
	NHL Totals		907	451	339	790	657	125	32	69	3154	14.3		20	35.0	20:13	73	30	26	56	54	13	0	6	21:56

Played in NHL All-Star Game (1993, 1996, 1997, 1998, 1999)

BONK, Radek
(BOHNK, RA-dehk) **OTT.**

Center. Shoots left. 6'3", 220 lbs. Born, Krnov, Czech., January 9, 1976. Ottawa's 1st choice, 3rd overall, in 1994 Entry Draft.

Season	Club	League	GP	G	A	Pts	PIM	PP	SH	GW	S	%	+/-	TF	F%	Min	PO GP	PO G	PO A	PO Pts	PO PIM	PO PP	PO SH	PO GW	PO Min
1990-91	Slezan Opava Jr.	Czech-Jr.	35	47	42	89	25	....	....	....	....	....	....	....	....	....	....	....	....	....	....	....	....	....	....
1991-92	AC ZPS Zlin Jr.	Czech-Jr.	45	47	36	83	30	....	....	....	....	....	....	....	....	....	....	....	....	....	....	....	....	....	....
1992-93	AC ZPS Zlin	Czech	30	5	5	10	10	....	....	....	....	....	....	....	....	....	....	....	....	....	....	....	....	....	....
1993-94	Las Vegas	IHL	76	42	45	87	208	....	....	....	....	....	....	....	....	....	5	1	2	3	10	....	....	....	....
1994-95	Las Vegas	IHL	33	7	13	20	62	....	....	....	....	....	....	....	....	....	....	....	....	....	....	....	....	....	....
	Ottawa	NHL	42	3	8	11	28	1	0	0	40	7.5	-5	....	....	....	....	....	....	....	....	....	....	....	....
	P.E.I. Senators	AHL	....	....	....	....	....	....	....	....	....	....	....	....	....	....	1	0	0	0	0	....	....	....	....
1995-96	Ottawa	NHL	76	16	19	35	36	5	0	1	161	9.9	-5	....	....	....	....	....	....	....	....	....	....	....	....
1996-97	Ottawa	NHL	53	5	13	18	14	0	1	0	82	6.1	-4	....	....	....	7	0	1	1	4	0	0	0	....
1997-98	Ottawa	NHL	65	7	9	16	16	1	0	0	93	7.5	-13	....	....	....	5	0	0	0	2	0	0	0	....
1998-99	Ottawa	NHL	81	16	16	32	48	0	1	6	110	14.5	15	1184	50.1	13:44	4	0	0	0	6	0	0	0	16:16
99-2000	Pardubice	Czech	3	1	0	1	4	....	....	....	....	....	....	....	....	....	....	....	....	....	....	....	....	....	....
	Ottawa	NHL	80	23	37	60	53	10	0	5	167	13.8	-2	1654	52.0	18:14	6	0	0	0	8	0	0	0	15:37
2000-01	Ottawa	NHL	74	23	36	59	52	5	2	3	139	16.5	27	1506	51.2	18:16	2	0	0	0	2	0	0	0	14:32
2001-02	Ottawa	NHL	82	25	45	70	52	6	2	5	170	14.7	3	1530	51.0	17:57	12	3	7	10	6	2	0	1	18:53
2002-03	Ottawa	NHL	70	22	32	54	36	11	0	4	146	15.1	6	1218	46.2	17:32	18	6	5	11	10	2	0	0	17:43
	NHL Totals		623	140	215	355	335	39	6	24	1108	12.6		7092	50.3	17:07	54	9	13	22	38	4	0	1	17:27

Garry F. Longman Memorial Trophy (Top Rookie – IHL) (1994)
Played in NHL All-Star Game (2000, 2001)

BONNI, Ryan
(baw-NEE, RIGH-uhn)

Defense. Shoots left. 6'4", 190 lbs. Born, Winnipeg, Man., February 18, 1979. Vancouver's 2nd choice, 34th overall, in 1997 Entry Draft.

Season	Club	League	GP	G	A	Pts	PIM	PP	SH	GW	S	%	+/-	TF	F%	Min	PO GP	PO G	PO A	PO Pts	PO PIM	PO PP	PO SH	PO GW	PO Min
1994-95	Winnipeg Sharks	MMHL	24	3	19	22	59	....	....	....	....	....	....	....	....	....	....	....	....	....	....	....	....	....	....
1995-96	Saskatoon Blades	WHL	63	1	7	8	78	....	....	....	....	....	....	....	....	....	3	0	0	0	0	....	....	....	....
1996-97	Saskatoon Blades	WHL	69	11	19	30	219	....	....	....	....	....	....	....	....	....	....	....	....	....	....	....	....	....	....
1997-98	Saskatoon Blades	WHL	42	5	14	19	100	....	....	....	....	....	....	....	....	....	....	....	....	....	....	....	....	....	....
1998-99	Saskatoon Blades	WHL	51	6	26	32	211	....	....	....	....	....	....	....	....	....	....	....	....	....	....	....	....	....	....
	Red Deer Rebels	WHL	20	3	10	13	41	....	....	....	....	....	....	....	....	....	9	0	4	4	25	....	....	....	....
99-2000	Vancouver	NHL	3	0	0	0	0	0	0	0	1	0.0	-1	0	0.0	9:37	....	....	....	....	....	....	....	....	....
	Syracuse Crunch	AHL	71	5	13	18	125	....	....	....	....	....	....	....	....	....	2	0	1	1	2	....	....	....	....
2000-01	Kansas City	IHL	80	2	9	11	127	....	....	....	....	....	....	....	....	....	....	....	....	....	....	....	....	....	....
2001-02	Manitoba Moose	AHL	11	0	1	1	33	....	....	....	....	....	....	....	....	....	2	0	0	0	2	....	....	....	....
	Columbia Inferno	ECHL	46	3	18	21	128	....	....	....	....	....	....	....	....	....	4	0	4	4	10	....	....	....	....
2002-03	St. John's	AHL	61	1	8	9	86	....	....	....	....	....	....	....	....	....	....	....	....	....	....	....	....	....	....
	NHL Totals		3	0	0	0	0	0	0	0	1	0.0		0	0.0	9:37	....	....	....	....	....	....	....	....	....

Traded to **Toronto** by **Vancouver** for Toronto's 8th round choice (Sergei Topol) in 2003 Entry Draft, June 25, 2002.

BONVIE, Dennis
(BOHN-vee, DEHN-his)

Right wing. Shoots right. 5'11", 205 lbs. Born, Antigonish, N.S., July 23, 1973.

Season	Club	League	GP	G	A	Pts	PIM	PP	SH	GW	S	%	+/-	TF	F%	Min	PO GP	PO G	PO A	PO Pts	PO PIM	PO PP	PO SH	PO GW	PO Min
1989-90	Antigonish	NSMHL	50	15	30	45	52	....	....	....	....	....	....	....	....	....	....	....	....	....	....	....	....	....	....
1990-91	Antigonish	MJrHL	40	1	8	9	347	....	....	....	....	....	....	....	....	....	....	....	....	....	....	....	....	....	....
1991-92	Kitchener Rangers	OHL	7	1	1	2	23	....	....	....	....	....	....	....	....	....	....	....	....	....	....	....	....	....	....
	North Bay	OHL	49	0	12	12	261	....	....	....	....	....	....	....	....	....	21	0	1	1	91	....	....	....	....
1992-93	North Bay	OHL	64	3	21	24	*316	....	....	....	....	....	....	....	....	....	5	0	0	0	34	....	....	....	....
1993-94	Cape Breton	AHL	63	1	10	11	278	....	....	....	....	....	....	....	....	....	4	0	0	0	11	....	....	....	....
1994-95	Cape Breton	AHL	74	5	15	20	422	....	....	....	....	....	....	....	....	....	....	....	....	....	....	....	....	....	....
	Edmonton	NHL	2	0	0	0	0	0	0	0	0	0.0	0	....	....	....	....	....	....	....	....	....	....	....	....
1995-96	Edmonton	NHL	8	0	0	0	47	0	0	0	0	0.0	-3	....	....	....	....	....	....	....	....	....	....	....	....
	Cape Breton	AHL	38	13	14	27	269	....	....	....	....	....	....	....	....	....	....	....	....	....	....	....	....	....	....
1996-97	Hamilton	AHL	73	9	20	29	*522	....	....	....	....	....	....	....	....	....	22	3	11	14	*91	....	....	....	....
1997-98	Edmonton	NHL	4	0	0	0	27	0	0	0	0	0.0	0	....	....	....	....	....	....	....	....	....	....	....	....
	Hamilton	AHL	57	11	19	30	295	....	....	....	....	....	....	....	....	....	9	0	5	5	18	....	....	....	....
1998-99	Chicago	NHL	11	0	0	0	44	0	0	0	1	0.0	-4	0	0.0	3:59	....	....	....	....	....	....	....	....	....
	Portland Pirates	AHL	3	1	0	1	16	....	....	....	....	....	....	....	....	....	....	....	....	....	....	....	....	....	....
	Philadelphia	AHL	37	4	10	14	158	....	....	....	....	....	....	....	....	....	14	3	3	6	26	....	....	....	....
99-2000	Pittsburgh	NHL	28	0	0	0	80	0	0	0	6	0.0	-2	0	0.0	3:14	....	....	....	....	....	....	....	....	....
	Wilkes-Barre	AHL	42	5	26	31	243	....	....	....	....	....	....	....	....	....	....	....	....	....	....	....	....	....	....
2000-01	Pittsburgh	NHL	3	0	0	0	0	0	0	0	1	0.0	-1	0	0.0	3:30	....	....	....	....	....	....	....	....	....
	Wilkes-Barre	AHL	65	5	18	23	221	....	....	....	....	....	....	....	....	....	21	0	4	4	35	....	....	....	....
2001-02	Boston	NHL	23	1	2	3	84	0	0	0	5	20.0	3	0	0.0	5:05	1	0	0	0	0	0	0	0	3:07
	Providence Bruins	AHL	55	8	8	16	290	....	....	....	....	....	....	....	....	....	....	....	....	....	....	....	....	....	....
2002-03	Ottawa	NHL	12	0	0	0	29	0	0	0	3	0.0	-1	0	0.0	3:05	....	....	....	....	....	....	....	....	....
	Binghamton	AHL	51	7	3	10	311	....	....	....	....	....	....	....	....	....	14	2	4	6	*85	....	....	....	....
	NHL Totals		91	1	2	3	311	0	0	0	16	6.3		0	0.0	3:53	1	0	0	0	0	0	0	0	3:07

Signed as a free agent by **Edmonton**, August 25, 1994. Claimed by **Chicago** from **Edmonton** in Waiver Draft, October 5, 1998. Traded to **Philadelphia** by **Chicago** for Frank Bialowas, January 8, 1999. Signed as a free agent by **Pittsburgh**, September 20, 1999. Signed as a free agent by **Boston**, October 5, 2001. Signed as a free agent by **Ottawa**, August 26, 2002.

BORDELEAU, Sebastien
(BOHR-duh-loh, SEH-bas-tyehn)

Center. Shoots right. 5'11", 185 lbs. Born, Vancouver, B.C., February 15, 1975. Montreal's 3rd choice, 73rd overall, in 1993 Entry Draft.

Season	Club	League	GP	G	A	Pts	PIM	PP	SH	GW	S	%	+/-	TF	F%	Min	PO GP	PO G	PO A	PO Pts	PO PIM	PO PP	PO SH	PO GW	PO Min
1990-91	Laval Laurentide	QAAA	39	27	36	63	....	....	....	....	....	....	....	....	....	....	....	....	....	....	....	....	....	....	....
1991-92	Hull Olympiques	QMJHL	62	26	32	58	91	....	....	....	....	....	....	....	....	....	5	0	3	3	23	....	....	....	....
1992-93	Hull Olympiques	QMJHL	60	18	39	57	95	....	....	....	....	....	....	....	....	....	10	3	8	11	20	....	....	....	....
1993-94	Hull Olympiques	QMJHL	60	26	57	83	147	....	....	....	....	....	....	....	....	....	17	6	14	20	26	....	....	....	....
1994-95	Hull Olympiques	QMJHL	68	52	76	128	142	....	....	....	....	....	....	....	....	....	18	*13	19	*32	25	....	....	....	....
	Fredericton	AHL	....	....	....	....	....	....	....	....	....	....	....	....	....	....	1	0	0	0	0	....	....	....	....
1995-96	Montreal	NHL	4	0	0	0	0	0	0	0	0	0.0	-1	....	....	....	....	....	....	....	....	....	....	....	....
	Fredericton	AHL	43	17	29	46	68	....	....	....	....	....	....	....	....	....	7	0	2	2	8	....	....	....	....

			Regular Season														Playoffs								
Season	Club	League	GP	G	A	Pts	PIM	PP	SH	GW	S	%	+/-	TF	F%	Min	GP	G	A	Pts	PIM	PP	SH	GW	Min
1996-97	Montreal	NHL	28	2	9	11	2	0	0	0	27	7.4	-3												
	Fredericton	AHL	34	18	22	40	50																		
1997-98	Montreal	NHL	53	6	8	14	36	2	1	0	55	10.9	5				5	0	0	0	2	0	0	0	
1998-99	Nashville	NHL	72	16	24	40	26	1	2	3	168	9.5	-14	1368	57.1	15:18									
99-2000	Nashville	NHL	60	10	13	23	30	0	2	1	127	7.9	-12	942	54.4	13:56									
2000-01	Nashville	NHL	14	2	3	5	14	0	0	0	20	10.0	-4	192	59.4	12:40									
	Worcester IceCats	AHL	2	0	2	2	9										11	1	7	8	23				
2001-02	Minnesota	NHL	14	1	4	5	8	0	0	0	25	4.0	-1	115	59.1	13:35									
	Houston Aeros	AHL	16	4	7	11	23																		
	Phoenix	NHL	6	0	0	0	2	0	0	0	3	0.0	-1	35	51.4	7:46									
	Springfield	AHL	34	9	10	19	54																		
2002-03	SC Bern	Swiss	41	21	27	48	158										13	4	5	9	10				
	NHL Totals		251	37	61	98	118	3	5	4	425	8.7		2652	56.3	14:10	5	0	0	0	2	0	0	0	

QMJHL All-Rookie Team (1992) • QMJHL First All-Star Team (1995)

Traded to **Nashville** by **Montreal** for future considerations, June 26, 1998. • Missed majority of 2000-01 season recovering from abdominal injury suffered in game vs. Detroit, November 18, 2000. Claimed on waivers by **St. Louis** from **Nashville**, March 13, 2001. Claimed by **Minnesota** from **St. Louis** in Waiver Draft, September 28, 2001. Traded to **Phoenix** by **Minnesota** for David Cullen, January 4, 2002.

BOTTERILL, Jason

(BOH-tuhr-ihl, JAY-suhn) **BUF.**

Left wing. Shoots left. 6'4", 220 lbs. Born, Edmonton, Alta., May 19, 1976. Dallas' 1st choice, 20th overall, in 1994 Entry Draft.

Season	Club	League	GP	G	A	Pts	PIM	PP	SH	GW	S	%	+/-	TF	F%	Min	GP	G	A	Pts	PIM	PP	SH	GW	Min
1992-93	St. Paul's Prep	Hi-School	22	22	26	48																			
1993-94	U. of Michigan	CCHA	36	20	19	39	94																		
1994-95	U. of Michigan	CCHA	34	14	14	28	117																		
1995-96	U. of Michigan	CCHA	37	*32	25	57	*143																		
1996-97	U. of Michigan	CCHA	42	*37	24	61	129																		
1997-98	Dallas	NHL	4	0	0	0	19	0	0	0	2	0.0	-1												
	Michigan	IHL	50	11	11	22	82										4	0	0	0	5				
1998-99	Dallas	NHL	17	0	0	0	23	0	0	0	8	0.0	-2	0	0.0	8:19									
	Michigan	IHL	56	13	25	38	106										5	2	1	3	4				
99-2000	Atlanta	NHL	25	1	4	5	17	0	0	1	17	5.9	-7	2	50.0	11:16									
	Orlando	IHL	17	7	8	15	27																		
	Calgary	NHL	2	0	0	0	0	0	0	0	2	0.0	-4	0	0.0	8:00									
	Saint John Flames	AHL	21	3	4	7	39										3	0	0	0	19				
2000-01	Saint John Flames	AHL	60	13	20	33	101										19	2	7	9	30				
2001-02	Calgary	NHL	4	1	0	1	2	1	0	1	4	25.0	-3	0	0.0	9:26									
	Saint John Flames	AHL	71	21	21	42	121																		
2002-03	Buffalo	NHL	17	1	4	5	14	1	0	0	20	5.0	1	5	40.0	10:48									
	Rochester	AHL	64	37	22	59	105										3	1	1	2	21				
	NHL Totals		69	3	8	11	75	2	0	2	53	5.7		7	42.9	10:10									

CCHA Second All-Star Team (1996) • NCAA West Second All-American Team (1997)

Traded to **Atlanta** by **Dallas** for Jamie Pushor, July 15, 1999. Traded to **Calgary** by **Atlanta** with Darryl Shannon for Hnat Domenichelli and Dmitri Vlasenkov, February 11, 2000. Signed as a free agent by **Buffalo**, August 12, 2002.

BOUCHARD, Joel

(BOO-shahrd, JOHL) **BUF.**

Defense. Shoots left. 6'1", 209 lbs. Born, Montreal, Que., January 23, 1974. Calgary's 7th choice, 129th overall, in 1992 Entry Draft.

Season	Club	League	GP	G	A	Pts	PIM	PP	SH	GW	S	%	+/-	TF	F%	Min	GP	G	A	Pts	PIM	PP	SH	GW	Min
1989-90	Mtl-Bourassa	QAAA	41	7	17	24	10										1	1	0	1	0				
1990-91	Longueuil	QMJHL	53	3	19	22	34										8	1	0	1	11				
1991-92	Verdun	QMJHL	70	9	20	29	55										19	1	7	8	20				
1992-93	Verdun	QMJHL	60	10	49	59	126										4	0	2	2	4				
1993-94	Verdun	QMJHL	60	15	55	70	62										4	1	0	1	6				
	Saint John Flames	AHL	1	0	0	0	0										2	0	0	0	0				
1994-95	Saint John Flames	AHL	77	6	25	31	63										5	1	0	1	4				
	Calgary	NHL	2	0	0	0	0	0	0	0	0	0.0	0												
1995-96	Calgary	NHL	4	0	0	0	4	0	0	0	0	0.0	0												
	Saint John Flames	AHL	74	8	25	33	104										16	1	4	5	10				
1996-97	Calgary	NHL	76	4	5	9	49	0	1	0	61	6.6	-23												
1997-98	Calgary	NHL	44	5	7	12	57	0	1	1	51	9.8	0												
	Saint John Flames	AHL	3	2	1	3	6																		
1998-99	Nashville	NHL	64	4	11	15	60	0	0	0	78	5.1	-10	0	0.0	22:34									
99-2000	Nashville	NHL	52	1	4	5	23	0	0	0	60	1.7	-11	0	0.0	18:41									
	Dallas	NHL	2	0	0	0	2	0	0	0	1	0.0	1	0	0.0	9:45									
2000-01	Grand Rapids	IHL	19	3	9	12	8																		
	Phoenix	NHL	32	1	2	3	22	0	0	0	26	3.8	-8	0	0.0	14:28									
2001-02	New Jersey	NHL	1	0	1	1	0	0	0	0	0	0.0	1	0	0.0	19:26									
	Albany River Rats	AHL	70	9	22	31	28																		
2002-03	NY Rangers	NHL	27	5	7	12	14	1	0	2	41	12.2	6	0	0.0	20:07									
	Hartford	AHL	22	6	14	20	22																		
	Pittsburgh	NHL	7	0	1	1	0	0	0	0	6	0.0	-6	0	0.0	21:49									
	NHL Totals		311	20	38	58	231	1	2	3	324	6.2		0	0.0	19:32									

QMJHL First All-Star Team (1994)

Claimed by **Nashville** from **Calgary** in Expansion Draft, June 26, 1998. Claimed on waivers by **Dallas** from **Nashville**, March 14, 2000. Signed as a free agent by **Phoenix**, August 31, 2000. Signed as a free agent by **New Jersey**, October 25, 2001. Signed as a free agent by **NY Rangers**, August 5, 2002. Traded to **Pittsburgh** by **NY Rangers** with Richard Lintner, Rico Fata , Mikael Samuelsson and future considerations for Mike Wilson, Alex Kovalev, Janne Laukkanen and Dan LaCouture, February 10, 2003. Signed as a free agent by **Buffalo**, July 12, 2003.

BOUCHARD, Pierre-Marc

(BOO-shahrd, PEE-air- MAHRK) **MIN.**

Center. Shoots left. 5'10", 165 lbs. Born, Sherbrooke, Que., April 27, 1984. Minnesota's 1st choice, 8th overall, in 2002 Entry Draft.

Season	Club	League	GP	G	A	Pts	PIM	PP	SH	GW	S	%	+/-	TF	F%	Min	GP	G	A	Pts	PIM	PP	SH	GW	Min
1998-99	Mtl.-Bourassa	QAHA	28	23	41	64																			
99-2000	Charles-Lemoyne	QAAA	42	28	*45	*74	20										9	4	8	12	6				
2000-01	Chicoutimi	QMJHL	67	38	57	95	20										6	5	8	13	0				
2001-02	Chicoutimi	QMJHL	69	46	*94	*140	54										4	2	3	5	4				
2002-03	Minnesota	NHL	50	7	13	20	18	5	0	1	53	13.2	1	474	40.7	13:16	5	0	1	1	2	0	0	0	13:15
	NHL Totals		50	7	13	20	18	5	0	1	53	13.2		474	40.7	13:16	5	0	1	1	2	0	0	0	13:15

QAAA First All-Star Team (2000) • QMJHL Rookie of the Year (2001) • QMJHL First All-Star Team (2002) • Canadian Major Junior First All-Star Team (2002) • Canadian Major Junior Player of the Year (2002)

BOUCHER, Philippe

(boo-SHAY, fihl-EEP) **DAL.**

Defense. Shoots right. 6'2", 221 lbs. Born, Ste-Apollinaire, Que., March 24, 1973. Buffalo's 1st choice, 13th overall, in 1991 Entry Draft.

Season	Club	League	GP	G	A	Pts	PIM	PP	SH	GW	S	%	+/-	TF	F%	Min	GP	G	A	Pts	PIM	PP	SH	GW	Min
1988-89	Ste-Foy	QAAA	5	0	0	0	2																		
1989-90	Ste-Foy	QAAA	42	26	60	86	76										12	6	*19	25	16				
1990-91	Granby Bisons	QMJHL	69	21	46	67	92																		
1991-92	Granby Bisons	QMJHL	49	22	37	59	47																		
	Laval Titan	QMJHL	16	7	11	18	36										10	5	6	11	8				
1992-93	Laval Titan	QMJHL	16	12	15	27	37										13	6	15	21	12				
	Buffalo	NHL	18	0	4	4	14	0	0	0	28	0.0	1												
	Rochester	AHL	5	4	3	7	8										3	0	1	1	2				
1993-94	Buffalo	NHL	38	6	8	14	29	4	0	1	67	9.0	-1				7	1	1	2	2	1	0	0	
	Rochester	AHL	31	10	22	32	51																		
1994-95	Rochester	AHL	43	14	27	41	26																		
	Buffalo	NHL	9	1	4	5	0	0	0	0	15	6.7	6												
	Los Angeles	NHL	6	1	0	1	4	0	0	0	15	6.7	-3												
1995-96	Los Angeles	NHL	53	7	16	23	31	5	0	1	145	4.8	-26												
	Phoenix	IHL	10	4	3	7	4																		
1996-97	Los Angeles	NHL	60	7	18	25	25	2	0	1	159	4.4	0												
1997-98	Los Angeles	NHL	45	6	10	16	49	1	0	0	80	7.5	6												
	Long Beach	IHL	2	0	1	1	4																		
1998-99	Los Angeles	NHL	45	2	6	8	32	1	0	0	87	2.3	-12	0	0.0	17:51									

Season	Club	League	GP	G	A	Pts	PIM	PP	SH	GW	S	%	+/-	TF	F%	Min	GP	G	A	Pts	PIM	PP	SH	GW	Min
			Regular Season														Playoffs								
99-2000	**Los Angeles**	**NHL**	**1**	**0**	**0**	**0**	**0**	**0**	**0**	**0**	**3**	**0.0**	**0**	**0**	**0.0**	**17:04**									
	Long Beach	IHL	14	4	11	15	8										6	0	9	9	8				
2000-01	**Los Angeles**	**NHL**	**22**	**2**	**4**	**6**	**20**	**2**	**0**	**0**	**40**	**5.0**	**4**	**0**	**0.0**	**18:25**	**13**	**0**	**1**	**1**	**2**	**0**	**0**	**0**	**15:48**
	Manitoba Moose	IHL	45	10	22	32	39																		
2001-02	**Los Angeles**	**NHL**	**80**	**7**	**23**	**30**	**94**	**4**	**0**	**2**	**198**	**3.5**	**0**	**0**	**0.0**	**21:36**	**5**	**0**	**1**	**1**	**2**	**0**	**0**	**0**	**19:31**
2002-03	**Dallas**	**NHL**	**80**	**7**	**20**	**27**	**94**	**1**	**1**	**3**	**137**	**5.1**	**28**	**1**	**0.0**	**20:29**	**11**	**1**	**2**	**3**	**11**	**0**	**0**	**0**	**21:28**
	NHL Totals		**457**	**46**	**113**	**159**	**392**	**20**	**1**	**8**	**974**	**4.7**		**1**	**0.0**	**20:08**	**36**	**2**	**5**	**7**	**17**	**1**	**0**	**0**	**18:36**

QMJHL Second All-Star Team (1991, 1992) • QMJHL Defensive Rookie of the Year (1991) • Canadian Major Junior Rookie of the Year (1991)

Traded to **Los Angeles** by **Buffalo** with Denis Tsygurov and Grant Fuhr for Alexei Zhitnik, Robb Stauber, Charlie Huddy and Los Angeles' 5th round choice (Marian Menhart) in 1995 Entry Draft, February 14, 1995. • Missed majority of 1999-2000 season recovering from foot injury suffered in training camp, September, 1999. Signed as a free agent by **Dallas**, July 2, 2002.

BOUCK, Tyler

(BOWK, TIGH-luhr) **VAN.**

Center. Shoots left. 6', 196 lbs. Born, Camrose, Alta., January 13, 1980. Dallas' 2nd choice, 57th overall, in 1998 Entry Draft.

Season	Club	League	GP	G	A	Pts	PIM	PP	SH	GW	S	%	+/-	TF	F%	Min	GP	G	A	Pts	PIM	PP	SH	GW	Min
1995-96	Sherwood Park	AMHL	22	10	21	31	58																		
1996-97	Prince George	WHL	12	0	2	2	11																		
1997-98	Prince George	WHL	65	11	26	37	90										11	1	0	1	21				
1998-99	Prince George	WHL	56	22	25	47	178										2	0	2	2	10				
99-2000	Prince George	WHL	57	30	33	63	183										13	6	13	19	36				
2000-01	**Dallas**	**NHL**	**48**	**2**	**5**	**7**	**29**	**0**	**0**	**1**	**41**	**4.9**	**−3**	**1**	**0.0**	**8:59**	**1**	**0**	**0**	**0**	**0**	**0**	**0**	**0**	**9:02**
	Utah Grizzlies	IHL	24	2	6	8	39																		
2001-02	**Phoenix**	**NHL**	**7**	**0**	**0**	**0**	**4**	**0**	**0**	**0**	**3**	**0.0**	**−1**	**0**	**0.0**	**6:54**									
	Springfield	AHL	21	1	2	3	33																		
	Manitoba Moose	AHL	20	4	4	8	25																		
2002-03	Manitoba Moose	AHL	76	10	28	38	103										14	2	2	4	10				
	NHL Totals		**55**	**2**	**5**	**7**	**33**	**0**	**0**	**1**	**44**	**4.5**		**1**	**0.0**	**8:43**	**1**	**0**	**0**	**0**	**0**	**0**	**0**	**0**	**9:02**

WHL West First All-Star Team (2000)

Traded to **Phoenix** by **Dallas** for Jyrki Lumme, June 23, 2001. Traded to **Vancouver** by **Phoenix** with Todd Warriner, Trevor Letowski and Phoenix's 3rd round choice (later traded back to Phoenix – Phoenix selected Dimitri Pestunov) in 2003 Entry Draft for Drake Berehowsky and Denis Pederson, December 28, 2001.

BOUGHNER, Bob

(BOOG-nuhr, BAWB) **CAR.**

Defense. Shoots right. 6', 203 lbs. Born, Windsor, Ont., March 8, 1971. Detroit's 2nd choice, 32nd overall, in 1989 Entry Draft.

Season	Club	League	GP	G	A	Pts	PIM	PP	SH	GW	S	%	+/-	TF	F%	Min	GP	G	A	Pts	PIM	PP	SH	GW	Min
1986-87	Belle River	OJHL-C	37	3	11	14	88																		
1987-88	St. Mary's Lincolns	OJHL-B	36	4	18	22	177																		
1988-89	Sault Ste. Marie	OHL	64	6	15	21	182																		
1989-90	Sault Ste. Marie	OHL	49	7	23	30	122																		
1990-91	Sault Ste. Marie	OHL	64	13	33	46	156										14	2	9	11	35				
1991-92	Toledo Storm	ECHL	28	3	10	13	79										5	2	0	2	15				
	Adirondack	AHL	1	0	0	0	7																		
1992-93	Adirondack	AHL	69	1	16	17	190																		
1993-94	Adirondack	AHL	72	8	14	22	292										10	1	1	2	18				
1994-95	Cincinnati	IHL	81	2	14	16	192										10	0	0	0	18				
1995-96	Carolina	AHL	46	2	15	17	127																		
	Buffalo	**NHL**	**31**	**0**	**1**	**1**	**104**	**0**	**0**	**0**	**14**	**0.0**	**3**												
1996-97	**Buffalo**	**NHL**	**77**	**1**	**7**	**8**	**225**	**0**	**0**	**0**	**34**	**2.9**	**12**				**11**	**0**	**1**	**1**	**9**	**0**	**0**	**0**	
1997-98	**Buffalo**	**NHL**	**69**	**1**	**3**	**4**	**165**	**0**	**0**	**0**	**26**	**3.8**	**5**				**14**	**0**	**4**	**4**	**15**	**0**	**0**	**0**	
1998-99	**Nashville**	**NHL**	**79**	**3**	**10**	**13**	**137**	**0**	**0**	**1**	**59**	**5.1**	**−6**	**0**	**0.0**	**18:31**									
99-2000	**Nashville**	**NHL**	**62**	**2**	**4**	**6**	**97**	**0**	**0**	**0**	**32**	**6.3**	**−13**	**0**	**0.0**	**17:20**									
	Pittsburgh	**NHL**	**11**	**1**	**0**	**1**	**69**	**1**	**0**	**1**	**8**	**12.5**	**2**	**0**	**0.0**	**17:05**	**11**	**0**	**2**	**2**	**15**	**0**	**0**	**0**	**18:40**
2000-01	**Pittsburgh**	**NHL**	**58**	**1**	**3**	**4**	**147**	**0**	**0**	**0**	**46**	**2.2**	**18**	**0**	**0.0**	**16:30**	**18**	**0**	**1**	**1**	**22**	**0**	**0**	**0**	**17:08**
2001-02	**Calgary**	**NHL**	**79**	**2**	**4**	**6**	**170**	**0**	**0**	**0**	**58**	**3.4**	**9**	**0**	**0.0**	**18:43**									
2002-03	**Calgary**	**NHL**	**69**	**3**	**14**	**17**	**126**	**0**	**0**	**1**	**62**	**4.8**	**5**	**0**	**0.0**	**19:51**									
	NHL Totals		**535**	**14**	**46**	**60**	**1240**	**1**	**0**	**3**	**339**	**4.1**		**0**	**0.0**	**18:14**	**54**	**0**	**8**	**8**	**61**	**0**	**0**	**0**	**17:43**

Signed as a free agent by **Florida**, July 25, 1994. Traded to **Buffalo** by **Florida** for Buffalo's 3rd round choice (Chris Allen) in 1996 Entry Draft, February 1, 1996. Claimed by **Nashville** from **Buffalo** in Expansion Draft, June 26, 1998. Traded to **Pittsburgh** by **Nashville** for Pavel Skrbek, March 13, 2000. Signed as a free agent by **Calgary**, July 2, 2001. Traded to **Carolina** by **Calgary** for Carolina's 4th round choice in 2004 Entry Draft and future considerations, July 16, 2003.

BOUILLON, Francis

(BOO-liawn, FRAN-sihs) **MTL.**

Defense. Shoots left. 5'8", 194 lbs. Born, New York, NY, October 17, 1975.

Season	Club	League	GP	G	A	Pts	PIM	PP	SH	GW	S	%	+/-	TF	F%	Min	GP	G	A	Pts	PIM	PP	SH	GW	Min
1991-92	Mtl-Bourassa	QAAA	42	2	5	7	28										9	1	0	1	6				
1992-93	Laval Titan	QMJHL	46	0	7	7	45																		
1993-94	Laval Titan	QMJHL	68	3	15	18	129										19	2	9	11	48				
1994-95	Laval Titan	QMJHL	72	8	25	33	115										20	3	11	14	21				
1995-96	Granby	QMJHL	68	11	35	46	156										21	2	12	14	30				
1996-97	Wheeling Nailers	ECHL	69	10	32	42	77										3	0	2	2	10				
1997-98	Quebec Rafales	IHL	71	8	27	35	76																		
1998-99	Fredericton	AHL	79	19	36	55	174										5	2	1	3	0				
99-2000	**Montreal**	**NHL**	**74**	**3**	**13**	**16**	**38**	**2**	**0**	**1**	**76**	**3.9**	**−7**	**1**	**0.0**	**15:52**									
2000-01	**Montreal**	**NHL**	**29**	**0**	**6**	**6**	**26**	**0**	**0**	**0**	**24**	**0.0**	**3**	**0**	**0.0**	**13:24**									
	Quebec Citadelles	AHL	4	0	0	0	0																		
2001-02	**Montreal**	**NHL**	**28**	**0**	**5**	**5**	**33**	**0**	**0**	**0**	**24**	**0.0**	**−5**	**0**	**0.0**	**18:47**									
	Quebec Citadelles	AHL	38	8	14	22	30																		
2002-03	**Nashville**	**NHL**	**4**	**0**	**0**	**0**	**2**	**0**	**0**	**0**	**0**	**0.0**	**−1**	**0**	**0.0**	**12:52**									
	Montreal	**NHL**	**20**	**3**	**1**	**4**	**2**	**0**	**1**	**0**	**30**	**10.0**	**−1**	**0**	**0.0**	**20:24**									
	Hamilton	AHL	29	1	12	13	31																		
	NHL Totals		**155**	**6**	**25**	**31**	**101**	**2**	**1**	**1**	**154**	**3.9**		**1**	**0.0**	**16:26**									

Signed as a free agent by **Montreal**, August 18, 1998. • Missed majority of 2000-01 season recovering from ankle injury suffered in game vs. Calgary, December 31, 2000. Claimed by **Nashville** from **Montreal** in Waiver Draft, October 4, 2002. Claimed on waivers by **Montreal** from **Nashville**, October 25, 2002.

BOULERICE, Jesse

(BOO-luhr-ighs, JEHS-see) **CAR.**

Right wing. Shoots right. 6'2", 203 lbs. Born, Plattsburgh, NY, August 10, 1978. Philadelphia's 4th choice, 133rd overall, in 1996 Entry Draft.

Season	Club	League	GP	G	A	Pts	PIM	PP	SH	GW	S	%	+/-	TF	F%	Min	GP	G	A	Pts	PIM	PP	SH	GW	Min
1994-95	Hawkesbury	OCJHL	46	1	8	9	160																		
1995-96	Detroit	OHL	64	2	5	7	150										16	0	0	0	12				
1996-97	Detroit	OHL	33	10	14	24	209																		
1997-98	Plymouth Whalers	OHL	53	20	23	43	170										13	2	4	6	35				
1998-99	Philadelphia	AHL	24	1	2	3	82																		
	New Orleans	ECHL	12	0	1	1	38																		
99-2000	Philadelphia	AHL	40	3	4	7	85										4	0	2	2	4				
	Trenton Titans	ECHL	25	8	8	16	90																		
2000-01	Philadelphia	AHL	60	3	4	7	256										10	1	1	2	28				
2001-02	**Philadelphia**	**NHL**	**3**	**0**	**0**	**0**	**5**	**0**	**0**	**0**	**1**	**0.0**	**−1**	**0**	**0.0**	**4:18**									
	Philadelphia	AHL	41	2	5	7	204																		
	Lowell	AHL	15	2	4	6	80										5	0	2	2	6				
2002-03	**Carolina**	**NHL**	**48**	**2**	**1**	**3**	**108**	**0**	**0**	**0**	**12**	**16.7**	**−2**	**0**	**0.0**	**3:54**									
	NHL Totals		**51**	**2**	**1**	**3**	**113**	**0**	**0**	**0**	**13**	**15.4**		**0**	**0.0**	**3:55**									

Traded to **Carolina** by **Philadelphia** for Greg Koehler, February 13, 2002.

BOULTON, Eric

(BOHL-tuhn, AIR-ihk) **BUF.**

Left wing. Shoots left. 6', 222 lbs. Born, Halifax, N.S., August 17, 1976. NY Rangers' 12th choice, 234th overall, in 1994 Entry Draft.

Season	Club	League	GP	G	A	Pts	PIM	PP	SH	GW	S	%	+/-	TF	F%	Min	GP	G	A	Pts	PIM	PP	SH	GW	Min
1992-93	Cole Harbour	MJrHL	44	12	15	27	212																		
1993-94	Oshawa Generals	OHL	45	4	3	7	149										5	0	0	0	16				
1994-95	Oshawa Generals	OHL	27	7	5	12	125																		
	Sarnia Sting	OHL	24	3	7	10	134										4	0	1	1	10				
1995-96	Sarnia Sting	OHL	66	14	29	43	243										9	0	3	3	29				

Season	Club	League	GP	G	A	Pts	PIM	PP	SH	GW	S	%	+/-	TF	F%	Min	Playoffs GP	G	A	Pts	PIM	PP	SH	GW	Min
1996-97	Binghamton	AHL	23	2	3	5	67										3	0	0	0	4				
	Charlotte	ECHL	44	14	11	25	325										3	0	1	1	6				
1997-98	Charlotte	ECHL	53	11	16	27	202										4	1	0	1	0				
	Fort Wayne	IHL	8	0	2	2	42																		
1998-99	Kentucky	AHL	34	3	3	6	154										10	0	1	1	36				
	Florida Everblades	ECHL	26	9	13	22	143																		
	Houston Aeros	IHL	7	1	0	1	41																		
99-2000	Rochester	AHL	76	2	2	4	276										18	2	1	3	53				
2000-01	**Buffalo**	**NHL**	**35**	**1**	**2**	**3**	**94**	**0**	**0**	**0**	**20**	**5.0**	**–1**	**2**	**0.0**	**5:42**									
2001-02	**Buffalo**	**NHL**	**35**	**2**	**3**	**5**	**129**	**0**	**0**	**1**	**21**	**9.5**	**–1**	**0**	**0.0**	**6:08**									
2002-03	**Buffalo**	**NHL**	**58**	**1**	**5**	**6**	**178**	**0**	**0**	**0**	**33**	**3.0**	**1**	**6**	**33.3**	**6:35**									
	NHL Totals		**128**	**4**	**10**	**14**	**401**	**0**	**0**	**1**	**74**	**5.4**		**8**	**25.0**	**6:13**									

Signed as a free agent by **Buffalo**, September 14, 1999.

BOUMEDIENNE, Josef

(BOO-mih-dyehn, JOH-sehf) **WSH.**

Defense. Shoots left. 6'1", 200 lbs. Born, Stockholm, Sweden, January 12, 1978. New Jersey's 7th choice, 91st overall, in 1996 Entry Draft.

Season	Club	League	GP	G	A	Pts	PIM	PP	SH	GW	S	%	+/-	TF	F%	Min	Playoffs GP	G	A	Pts	PIM	PP	SH	GW	Min
1994-95	Huddinge IK Jr.	Swede-Jr.	10	0	2	2	57																		
1995-96	Huddinge IK Jr.	Swede-Jr.	25	2	4	6	66																		
	Huddinge IK	Swede-2	7	0	0	0	14																		
1996-97	Sodertalje SK	Sweden	32	1	1	2	32																		
1997-98	Sodertalje SK	Sweden	26	3	3	6	28																		
1998-99	Tappara Tampere	Finland	51	6	8	14	119																		
99-2000	Tappara Tampere	Finland	50	8	24	32	160																		
2000-01	Albany River Rats	AHL	79	8	28	36	117										4	1	2	3	10				
2001-02	**New Jersey**	**NHL**	**1**	**1**	**0**	**1**	**2**	**0**	**0**	**0**	**1**	**100.0**	**–1**	**0**	**0.0**	**20:23**									
	Albany River Rats	AHL	9	0	3	3	10																		
	Tampa Bay	**NHL**	**3**	**0**	**0**	**0**	**4**	**0**	**0**	**0**	**0**	**0.0**	**–1**	**0**	**0.0**	**10:58**									
	Springfield	AHL	53	7	25	32	57																		
2002-03	Binghamton	AHL	26	2	15	17	62																		
	Washington	**NHL**	**6**	**1**	**0**	**1**	**0**	**0**	**0**	**1**	**7**	**14.3**	**–1**	**0**	**0.0**	**19:33**									
	Portland Pirates	AHL	44	8	22	30	77																		
	NHL Totals		**10**	**2**	**0**	**2**	**6**	**0**	**0**	**1**	**8**	**25.0**		**0**	**0.0**	**17:03**									

Traded to **Tampa Bay** by **New Jersey** with Sascha Goc and the rights to Anton But for Andrei Zyuzin, November 9, 2001. Traded to **Ottawa** by **Tampa Bay** for Ottawa's 7th round choice (Fredrik Norrena) in 2002 Entry Draft, June 23, 2002. Traded to **Washington** by **Ottawa** for Dean Melanson, December 16, 2002.

BOUWMEESTER, Jay

(BOW-mee-stuhr, JAY) **FLA.**

Defense. Shoots left. 6'4", 210 lbs. Born, Edmonton, Alta., September 27, 1983. Florida's 1st choice, 3rd overall, in 2002 Entry Draft.

Season	Club	League	GP	G	A	Pts	PIM	PP	SH	GW	S	%	+/-	TF	F%	Min	Playoffs GP	G	A	Pts	PIM	PP	SH	GW	Min
1998-99	Edmonton SSAC	AMHL	32	14	29	43	36																		
	Medicine Hat	WHL	8	2	1	3	2																		
99-2000	Medicine Hat	WHL	64	13	21	34	26																		
2000-01	Medicine Hat	WHL	61	14	39	53	44																		
2001-02	Medicine Hat	WHL	61	11	50	61	42																		
2002-03	**Florida**	**NHL**	**82**	**4**	**12**	**16**	**14**	**2**	**0**	**0**	**110**	**3.6**	**–29**	**0**	**0.0**	**20:09**									
	NHL Totals		**82**	**4**	**12**	**16**	**14**	**2**	**0**	**0**	**110**	**3.6**		**0**	**0.0**	**20:09**									

WHL East First All-Star Team (2002) • NHL All-Rookie Team (2003)

BOYLE, Dan

(BOIL, DAN) **T.B.**

Defense. Shoots right. 5'11", 190 lbs. Born, Ottawa, Ont., July 12, 1976.

Season	Club	League	GP	G	A	Pts	PIM	PP	SH	GW	S	%	+/-	TF	F%	Min	Playoffs GP	G	A	Pts	PIM	PP	SH	GW	Min
1992-93	Gloucester	OCJHL	55	22	51	73	60																		
1993-94	Gloucester	OCJHL	53	27	54	81	155																		
1994-95	Miami-Ohio	CCHA	35	8	18	26	24																		
1995-96	Miami-Ohio	CCHA	36	7	20	27	70																		
1996-97	Miami-Ohio	CCHA	40	11	43	54	52																		
1997-98	Miami-Ohio	CCHA	37	14	26	40	58																		
1998-99	**Florida**	**NHL**	**22**	**3**	**5**	**8**	**6**	**1**	**0**	**1**	**31**	**9.7**	**0**	**1**	**100.0**	**18:50**									
	Kentucky	AHL	53	8	34	42	87										12	3	5	8	16				
99-2000	**Florida**	**NHL**	**13**	**0**	**3**	**3**	**4**	**0**	**0**	**0**	**9**	**0.0**	**–2**	**0**	**0.0**	**16:57**									
	Louisville Panthers	AHL	58	14	38	52	75										4	0	2	2	8				
2000-01	**Florida**	**NHL**	**69**	**4**	**18**	**22**	**28**	**1**	**0**	**0**	**83**	**4.8**	**–14**	**0**	**0.0**	**16:56**									
	Louisville Panthers	AHL	6	0	5	5	12																		
2001-02	**Florida**	**NHL**	**25**	**3**	**3**	**6**	**12**	**1**	**0**	**0**	**31**	**9.7**	**–1**	**2**	**50.0**	**15:40**									
	Tampa Bay	**NHL**	**41**	**5**	**15**	**20**	**27**	**2**	**0**	**1**	**68**	**7.4**	**–15**	**0**	**0.0**	**22:28**									
2002-03	**Tampa Bay**	**NHL**	**77**	**13**	**40**	**53**	**44**	**8**	**0**	**1**	**136**	**9.6**	**9**	**2**	**0.0**	**24:31**	**11**	**0**	**7**	**7**	**6**	**0**	**0**	**0**	**27:45**
	NHL Totals		**247**	**28**	**84**	**112**	**121**	**13**	**0**	**3**	**358**	**7.8**		**5**	**40.0**	**20:15**	**11**	**0**	**7**	**7**	**6**	**0**	**0**	**0**	**27:45**

CCHA First All-Star Team (1997, 1998) • NCAA West First All-American Team (1997, 1998) • AHL Second All-Star Team (1999, 2000)

Signed as a free agent by **Florida**, March 30, 1998. Traded to **Tampa Bay** by **Florida** for Tampa Bay's 5th round choice (Martin Tuma) in 2003 Entry Draft, January 7, 2002.

BOYNTON, Nick

(BOIN-tuhn, NIHK) **BOS.**

Defense. Shoots right. 6'2", 210 lbs. Born, Nobleton, Ont., January 14, 1979. Boston's 1st choice, 21st overall, in 1999 Entry Draft.

Season	Club	League	GP	G	A	Pts	PIM	PP	SH	GW	S	%	+/-	TF	F%	Min	Playoffs GP	G	A	Pts	PIM	PP	SH	GW	Min
1993-94	Caledon	MTJHL	4	0	1	1	0																		
1994-95	Caledon	MTJHL	44	10	35	45	139																		
1995-96	Ottawa 67's	OHL	64	10	14	24	90										4	0	3	3	10				
1996-97	Ottawa 67's	OHL	63	13	51	64	143										24	4	*24	28	38				
1997-98	Ottawa 67's	OHL	40	7	31	38	94										13	0	4	4	24				
1998-99	Ottawa 67's	OHL	51	11	48	59	83										9	1	9	10	18				
99-2000	**Boston**	**NHL**	**5**	**0**	**0**	**0**	**0**	**0**	**0**	**0**	**6**	**0.0**	**–5**	**0**	**0.0**	**21:21**									
	Providence Bruins	AHL	53	5	14	19	66										12	1	0	1	6				
2000-01	**Boston**	**NHL**	**1**	**0**	**0**	**0**	**0**	**0**	**0**	**0**	**1**	**0.0**	**–1**	**0**	**0.0**	**14:27**									
	Providence Bruins	AHL	78	6	27	33	105										17	0	2	2	35				
2001-02	**Boston**	**NHL**	**80**	**4**	**14**	**18**	**107**	**0**	**0**	**1**	**136**	**2.9**	**18**	**0**	**0.0**	**18:30**	**6**	**1**	**2**	**3**	**8**	**0**	**0**	**0**	**21:30**
2002-03	**Boston**	**NHL**	**78**	**7**	**17**	**24**	**99**	**0**	**1**	**2**	**160**	**4.4**	**8**	**1**	**0.0**	**22:41**	**5**	**0**	**1**	**1**	**4**	**0**	**0**	**0**	**23:22**
	NHL Totals		**164**	**11**	**31**	**42**	**206**	**0**	**1**	**3**	**303**	**3.6**		**1**	**0.0**	**20:33**	**11**	**1**	**3**	**4**	**12**	**0**	**0**	**0**	**22:21**

• Re-entered NHL Entry Draft. Originally Washington's 1st choice, 9th overall, in 1997 Entry Draft.

OHL All-Rookie Team (1996) • Memorial Cup All-Star Team (1999) • Stafford Smythe Memorial Trophy (Memorial Cup MVP) (1999) • NHL All-Rookie Team (2002)

BRADLEY, Matt

(BRAD-lee, MAT) **PIT.**

Right wing. Shoots right. 6'2", 195 lbs. Born, Stittsville, Ont., June 13, 1978. San Jose's 4th choice, 102nd overall, in 1996 Entry Draft.

Season	Club	League	GP	G	A	Pts	PIM	PP	SH	GW	S	%	+/-	TF	F%	Min	Playoffs GP	G	A	Pts	PIM	PP	SH	GW	Min
1994-95	Cumberland	OCJHL	49	13	20	33	18																		
1995-96	Kingston	OHL	55	10	14	24	17										6	0	1	1	6				
1996-97	Kingston	OHL	65	24	24	48	41										5	0	4	4	2				
	Kentucky	AHL	1	0	1	1	0																		
1997-98	Kingston	OHL	55	33	50	83	24										8	3	4	7	7				
1998-99	Kentucky	AHL	79	23	20	43	57										10	1	4	5	4				
99-2000	Kentucky	AHL	80	22	19	41	81										9	6	3	9	9				
2000-01	**San Jose**	**NHL**	**21**	**1**	**1**	**2**	**19**	**0**	**0**	**0**	**16**	**6.3**	**0**	**0**	**0.0**	**6:58**									
	Kentucky	AHL	22	5	8	13	16										1	1	0	1	5				
2001-02	**San Jose**	**NHL**	**54**	**9**	**13**	**22**	**43**	**0**	**0**	**2**	**63**	**14.3**	**22**	**2**	**0.0**	**8:27**	**10**	**0**	**0**	**0**	**0**	**0**	**0**	**0**	**5:16**
2002-03	**San Jose**	**NHL**	**46**	**2**	**3**	**5**	**37**	**0**	**0**	**0**	**21**	**9.5**	**–1**	**1**	**0.0**	**7:54**									
	NHL Totals		**121**	**12**	**17**	**29**	**99**	**0**	**0**	**2**	**100**	**12.0**		**3**	**0.0**	**7:59**	**10**	**0**	**0**	**0**	**0**	**0**	**0**	**0**	**5:16**

William Hanley Award (Most Gentlemanly Player – OHL) (1998)

• Suffered season-ending wrist injury in game vs. Montreal, March 6, 2003. Traded to **Pittsburgh** by **San Jose** for Wayne Primeau, March 11, 2003.

BRASHEAR, Donald

(bra-SHEER, DAWN-ohld) **PHI.**

Left wing. Shoots left. 6'2", 235 lbs. Born, Bedford, IN, January 7, 1972.

			Regular Season														Playoffs								
Season	Club	League	GP	G	A	Pts	PIM	PP	SH	GW	S	%	+/-	TF	F%	Min	GP	G	A	Pts	PIM	PP	SH	GW	Min
1988-89	Ste-Foy	QAAA	10	1	2	3	10																		
1989-90	Longueuil	QMJHL	64	12	14	26	169										7	0	0	0	11				
1990-91	Longueuil	QMJHL	68	12	26	38	195										8	0	3	3	33				
1991-92	Verdun	QMJHL	65	18	24	42	283										18	4	2	6	98				
1992-93	Fredericton	AHL	76	11	3	14	261										5	0	0	0	8				
1993-94	**Montreal**	**NHL**	**14**	**2**	**2**	**4**	**34**	**0**	**0**	**0**	**15**	**13.3**	**0**				**2**	**0**	**0**	**0**	**0**	**0**	**0**	**0**	
	Fredericton	AHL	62	38	28	66	250																		
1994-95	Fredericton	AHL	29	10	9	19	182										17	7	5	12	77				
	Montreal	**NHL**	**20**	**1**	**1**	**2**	**63**	**0**	**0**	**1**	**10**	**10.0**	**–5**												
1995-96	**Montreal**	**NHL**	**67**	**0**	**4**	**4**	**223**	**0**	**0**	**0**	**25**	**0.0**	**–10**				**6**	**0**	**0**	**0**	**2**	**0**	**0**	**0**	
1996-97	**Montreal**	**NHL**	**10**	**0**	**0**	**0**	**38**	**0**	**0**	**0**	**6**	**0.0**	**–2**												
	Vancouver	**NHL**	**59**	**8**	**5**	**13**	**207**	**0**	**0**	**2**	**55**	**14.5**	**–6**												
1997-98	**Vancouver**	**NHL**	**77**	**9**	**9**	**18**	***372**	**0**	**0**	**1**	**64**	**14.1**	**–9**												
1998-99	**Vancouver**	**NHL**	**82**	**8**	**10**	**18**	**209**	**2**	**0**	**1**	**112**	**7.1**	**–25**	**6**	**16.7**	**13:25**									
99-2000	**Vancouver**	**NHL**	**60**	**11**	**2**	**13**	**136**	**1**	**0**	**3**	**83**	**13.3**	**–9**	**11**	**36.4**	**13:07**									
2000-01	**Vancouver**	**NHL**	**79**	**9**	**19**	**28**	**145**	**0**	**0**	**1**	**127**	**7.1**	**0**	**6**	**16.7**	**13:27**	**4**	**0**	**0**	**0**	**0**	**0**	**0**	**0**	**14:47**
2001-02	**Vancouver**	**NHL**	**31**	**5**	**8**	**13**	**90**	**1**	**0**	**0**	**45**	**11.1**	**–8**	**4**	**25.0**	**13:58**									
	Philadelphia	**NHL**	**50**	**4**	**15**	**19**	**109**	**0**	**0**	**2**	**62**	**6.5**	**0**	**1**	**0.0**	**12:60**	**5**	**0**	**0**	**0**	**19**	**0**	**0**	**0**	**9:55**
2002-03	**Philadelphia**	**NHL**	**80**	**8**	**17**	**25**	**161**	**0**	**0**	**1**	**99**	**8.1**	**5**	**27**	**33.3**	**13:23**	**13**	**1**	**2**	**3**	**21**	**0**	**0**	**0**	**11:09**
	NHL Totals		**629**	**65**	**92**	**157**	**1787**	**4**	**0**	**12**	**703**	**9.2**		**55**	**29.1**	**13:21**	**30**	**1**	**2**	**3**	**42**	**0**	**0**	**0**	**11:32**

Signed as a free agent by **Montreal**, July 28, 1992. Traded to **Vancouver** by **Montreal** for Jassen Cullimore, November 13, 1996. Traded to **Philadelphia** by **Vancouver** with Vancouver's 6th round choice (later traded to Columbus – Columbus selected Jaroslav Balastik) in 2002 Entry Draft for Jan Hlavac and Tampa Bay's 3rd round choice (previously acquired, Vancouver selected Brett Skinner) in 2002 Entry Draft, December 17, 2001.

BRENDL, Pavel

(BREHN-duhl, PAH-vehl) **CAR.**

Right wing. Shoots right. 6'1", 206 lbs. Born, Opocno, Czech., March 23, 1981. NY Rangers' 1st choice, 4th overall, in 1999 Entry Draft.

			Regular Season														Playoffs								
Season	Club	League	GP	G	A	Pts	PIM	PP	SH	GW	S	%	+/-	TF	F%	Min	GP	G	A	Pts	PIM	PP	SH	GW	Min
1996-97	HC Olomouc Jr.	Czech-Jr.	40	35	17	52																			
1997-98	HC Olomouc Jr.	Czech-Jr.	38	29	23	52																			
	HC Olomouc	Czech-2	12	1	1	2																			
1998-99	Calgary Hitmen	WHL	68	*73	61	*134	40										20	*21	*25	*46	18				
99-2000	Calgary Hitmen	WHL	61	*59	52	111	94										10	7	12	19	8				
	Hartford	AHL															2	0	0	0	0				
2000-01	Calgary Hitmen	WHL	49	40	35	75	66										10	7	6	13	6				
2001-02	Philadelphia	AHL	64	15	22	37	22										5	4	1	5	0				
	Philadelphia	**NHL**	**8**	**1**	**0**	**1**	**2**	**0**	**0**	**0**	**6**	**16.7**	**–1**	**21**	**19.1**	**8:59**	**2**	**0**	**0**	**0**	**0**	**0**	**0**	**0**	**11:28**
2002-03	**Philadelphia**	**NHL**	**42**	**5**	**7**	**12**	**4**	**1**	**0**	**1**	**80**	**6.3**	**8**	**9**	**22.2**	**10:19**									
	Carolina	**NHL**	**8**	**0**	**1**	**1**	**2**	**0**	**0**	**0**	**14**	**0.0**	**–3**	**2**	**50.0**	**15:05**									
	NHL Totals		**58**	**6**	**8**	**14**	**8**	**1**	**0**	**1**	**100**	**6.0**		**32**	**21.9**	**10:48**	**2**	**0**	**0**	**0**	**0**	**0**	**0**	**0**	**11:28**

WHL East First All-Star Team (1999) • Canadian Major Junior First All-Star Team (1999) • Canadian Major Junior Rookie of the Year (1999) • Memorial Cup All-Star Team (1999) • WHL East Second All-Star Team (2000)

Traded to **Philadelphia** by **NY Rangers** with Jan Hlavac, Kim Johnsson and NY Rangers' 3rd round choice (Stefan Ruzicka) in 2003 Entry Draft for Eric Lindros, August 20, 2001. Traded to **Carolina** by **Philadelphia** with Bruno St. Jacques for Sami Kapanen and Ryan Bast, February 7, 2003.

BRENNAN, Kip

(BREHN-nan, KIHP) **L.A.**

Left wing. Shoots left. 6'4", 228 lbs. Born, Kingston, Ont., August 27, 1980. Los Angeles' 4th choice, 103rd overall, in 1998 Entry Draft.

			Regular Season														Playoffs								
Season	Club	League	GP	G	A	Pts	PIM	PP	SH	GW	S	%	+/-	TF	F%	Min	GP	G	A	Pts	PIM	PP	SH	GW	Min
1995-96	St. Michael's B	MTJHL	40	0	11	11	155																		
1996-97	Windsor Spitfires	OHL	42	0	10	10	156										5	0	1	1	16				
1997-98	Windsor Spitfires	OHL	24	0	7	7	103																		
	Sudbury Wolves	OHL	24	0	3	3	85																		
1998-99	Sudbury Wolves	OHL	38	9	12	21	160																		
99-2000	Sudbury Wolves	OHL	55	16	16	32	228										12	3	3	6	67				
2000-01	Lowell	AHL	23	2	3	5	117																		
	Sudbury Wolves	OHL	27	7	14	21	94										12	5	6	11	*92				
2001-02	**Los Angeles**	**NHL**	**4**	**0**	**0**	**0**	**22**	**0**	**0**	**0**	**0**	**0.0**	**1**	**0**	**0.0**	**4:40**									
	Manchester	AHL	44	4	1	5	269										4	0	1	1	26				
2002-03	**Los Angeles**	**NHL**	**19**	**0**	**0**	**0**	**57**	**0**	**0**	**0**	**6**	**0.0**	**0**	**2**	**0.0**	**4:52**									
	Manchester	AHL	35	3	2	5	195										3	0	0	0	0				
	NHL Totals		**23**	**0**	**0**	**0**	**79**	**0**	**0**	**0**	**6**	**0.0**		**2**	**0.0**	**4:50**									

BRENNAN, Rich

(BREHN-nan, RIHCH) **BOS.**

Defense. Shoots right. 6'2", 200 lbs. Born, Schenectady, NY, November 26, 1972. Quebec's 3rd choice, 46th overall, in 1991 Entry Draft.

			Regular Season														Playoffs								
Season	Club	League	GP	G	A	Pts	PIM	PP	SH	GW	S	%	+/-	TF	F%	Min	GP	G	A	Pts	PIM	PP	SH	GW	Min
1988-89	Albany	Hi-School	25	17	30	47	57																		
1989-90	Tabor Academy	Hi-School	33	12	14	26	68																		
1990-91	Tabor Academy	Hi-School	34	13	37	50	91																		
1991-92	Boston University	H-East	30	4	13	17	50																		
1992-93	Boston University	H-East	40	9	11	20	68																		
1993-94	Boston University	H-East	41	8	27	35	82																		
1994-95	Boston University	H-East	31	5	22	27	56																		
1995-96	Brantford Smoke	ColHL	5	1	2	3	2																		
	Cornwall Aces	AHL	36	4	8	12	61										7	0	0	0	6				
1996-97	**Colorado**	**NHL**	**2**	**0**	**0**	**0**	**0**	**0**	**0**	**0**	**0**	**0.0**	**0**												
	Hershey Bears	AHL	74	11	45	56	88										23	2	*16	18	22				
1997-98	**San Jose**	**NHL**	**11**	**1**	**2**	**3**	**2**	**1**	**0**	**0**	**24**	**4.2**	**–4**												
	Kentucky	AHL	42	11	17	28	71																		
	Hartford	AHL	9	2	4	6	12										15	4	5	9	14				
1998-99	**NY Rangers**	**NHL**	**24**	**1**	**3**	**4**	**23**	**0**	**0**	**0**	**36**	**2.8**	**–4**	**0**	**0.0**	**13:02**									
	Hartford	AHL	47	4	24	28	42																		
99-2000	Lowell	AHL	67	15	30	45	110										7	1	5	6	0				
2000-01	**Los Angeles**	**NHL**	**2**	**0**	**0**	**0**	**0**	**0**	**0**	**0**	**1**	**0.0**	**–3**	**0**	**0.0**	**14:44**									
	Lowell	AHL	69	10	31	41	146																		
2001-02	**Nashville**	**NHL**	**4**	**0**	**0**	**0**	**2**	**0**	**0**	**0**	**0**	**0.0**	**0**	**0**	**0.0**	**14:31**									
	Milwaukee	AHL	23	4	8	12	27																		
	Manchester	AHL	16	2	5	7	6										5	1	1	2	16				
2002-03	**Boston**	**NHL**	**7**	**0**	**1**	**1**	**6**	**0**	**0**	**0**	**12**	**0.0**	**3**	**0**	**0.0**	**13:37**									
	Providence Bruins	AHL	41	3	29	32	51																		
	NHL Totals		**50**	**2**	**6**	**8**	**33**	**1**	**0**	**0**	**73**	**2.7**		**0**	**0.0**	**13:24**									

Hockey East First All-Star Team (1994) • NCAA East Second All-American Team (1994)

Rights transferred to **Colorado** after **Quebec** franchise relocated, June 21, 1995. Signed as a free agent by **San Jose**, July 9, 1997. Traded to **NY Rangers** by **San Jose** for Jason Muzzatti, March 24, 1998. Signed as a free agent by **Nashville**, September 23, 1999. Claimed by **Los Angeles** from **Nashville** in Waiver Draft, September 27, 1999. Signed as a free agent by **Nashville**, August 8, 2001. Traded to **Los Angeles** by **Nashville** for Brett Hauer, December 19, 2001. Signed as a free agent by **Boston**, July 18, 2002.

BREWER, Eric

(BREW-uhr, AIR-ihk) **EDM.**

Defense. Shoots left. 6'3", 220 lbs. Born, Vernon, B.C., April 17, 1979. NY Islanders' 2nd choice, 5th overall, in 1997 Entry Draft.

			Regular Season														Playoffs								
Season	Club	League	GP	G	A	Pts	PIM	PP	SH	GW	S	%	+/-	TF	F%	Min	GP	G	A	Pts	PIM	PP	SH	GW	Min
1994-95	Kamloops	BCAHA	40	19	19	38	62																		
1995-96	Prince George	WHL	63	4	10	14	25																		
1996-97	Prince George	WHL	71	5	24	29	81										15	2	4	6	16				
1997-98	Prince George	WHL	34	5	28	33	45										11	4	2	6	19				
1998-99	**NY Islanders**	**NHL**	**63**	**5**	**6**	**11**	**32**	**2**	**0**	**0**	**63**	**7.9**	**–14**	**0**	**0.0**	**15:28**									
99-2000	**NY Islanders**	**NHL**	**26**	**0**	**2**	**2**	**20**	**0**	**0**	**0**	**30**	**0.0**	**–11**	**0**	**0.0**	**18:33**									
	Lowell	AHL	25	2	2	4	26										7	0	0	0	0				
2000-01	**Edmonton**	**NHL**	**77**	**7**	**14**	**21**	**53**	**2**	**0**	**2**	**91**	**7.7**	**15**	**0**	**0.0**	**18:31**	**6**	**1**	**5**	**6**	**2**	**1**	**0**	**0**	**28:11**

			Regular Season														Playoffs								
Season	Club	League	GP	G	A	Pts	PIM	PP	SH	GW	S	%	+/-	TF	F%	Min	GP	G	A	Pts	PIM	PP	SH	GW	Min
2001-02	**Edmonton**	**NHL**	**81**	**7**	**18**	**25**	**45**	**6**	**0**	**2**	**165**	**4.2**	**-5**	**0**	**0.0**	**23:56**	....	....	....	....	....	....	....	....	....
	Canada	Olympics	6	2	0	2	0	....	....	....	....	....	....	....	....	....	....	....	....	....	....	....	....	....	....
2002-03	**Edmonton**	**NHL**	**80**	**8**	**21**	**29**	**45**	**1**	**0**	**1**	**147**	**5.4**	**-11**	**1**	**100.0**	**24:56**	**6**	**1**	**3**	**4**	**6**	**0**	**0**	**0**	**25:31**
	NHL Totals		**327**	**27**	**61**	**88**	**195**	**11**	**0**	**5**	**496**	**5.4**		**1**	**100.0**	**20:50**	**12**	**2**	**8**	**10**	**8**	**1**	**0**	**0**	**26:51**

WHL West Second All-Star Team (1998)
Played in NHL All-Star Game (2003)
Traded to **Edmonton** by **NY Islanders** with Josh Green and NY Islanders' 2nd round choice (Brad Winchester) in 2000 Entry Draft for Roman Hamrlik, June 24, 2000.

BRIERE, Daniel
(bree-AIR, DAN-yehl) **BUF.**

Center. Shoots right. 5'10", 178 lbs. Born, Gatineau, Que., October 6, 1977. Phoenix's 2nd choice, 24th overall, in 1996 Entry Draft.

Season	Club	League	GP	G	A	Pts	PIM	PP	SH	GW	S	%	+/-	TF	F%	Min	GP	G	A	Pts	PIM	PP	SH	GW	Min
1992-93	Abitibi Regents	QAAA	42	24	30	54	28	....	....	....	....	....	....	....	....	....	3	0	3	3	8	....	....	....	....
1993-94	Gatineau	QAAA	44	56	47	103	56	....	....	....	....	....	....	....	....	....	....	....	....	....	....	....	....	....	....
1994-95	Drummondville	QMJHL	72	51	72	123	54	....	....	....	....	....	....	....	....	....	4	2	3	5	2	....	....	....	....
1995-96	Drummondville	QMJHL	67	*67	*96	*163	84	....	....	....	....	....	....	....	....	....	6	6	12	18	8	....	....	....	....
1996-97	Drummondville	QMJHL	59	52	78	130	94	....	....	....	....	....	....	....	....	....	8	7	7	14	14	....	....	....	....
1997-98	**Phoenix**	**NHL**	**5**	**1**	**0**	**1**	**2**	**0**	**0**	**0**	**4**	**25.0**	**1**	....	....	....	....	....	....	....	....	....	....	....	....
	Springfield	AHL	68	36	56	92	42	....	....	....	....	....	....	....	....	....	4	1	2	3	4	....	....	....	....
1998-99	**Phoenix**	**NHL**	**64**	**8**	**14**	**22**	**30**	**2**	**0**	**2**	**90**	**8.9**	**-3**	**484**	**47.5**	**11:13**	....	....	....	....	....	....	....	....	....
	Las Vegas	IHL	1	1	1	2	0	....	....	....	....	....	....	....	....	....	....	....	....	....	....	....	....	....	....
	Springfield	AHL	13	2	6	8	20	....	....	....	....	....	....	....	....	....	3	0	1	1	2	....	....	....	....
99-2000	**Phoenix**	**NHL**	**13**	**1**	**1**	**2**	**0**	**0**	**0**	**0**	**9**	**11.1**	**0**	**65**	**49.2**	**7:41**	**1**	**0**	**0**	**0**	**0**	**0**	**0**	**0**	**6:16**
	Springfield	AHL	58	29	42	71	56	....	....	....	....	....	....	....	....	....	....	....	....	....	....	....	....	....	....
2000-01	**Phoenix**	**NHL**	**30**	**11**	**4**	**15**	**12**	**9**	**0**	**1**	**43**	**25.6**	**-2**	**210**	**50.0**	**10:50**	....	....	....	....	....	....	....	....	....
	Springfield	AHL	30	21	25	46	30	....	....	....	....	....	....	....	....	....	....	....	....	....	....	....	....	....	....
2001-02	**Phoenix**	**NHL**	**78**	**32**	**28**	**60**	**52**	**12**	**0**	**5**	**149**	**21.5**	**6**	**951**	**51.8**	**15:44**	**5**	**2**	**1**	**3**	**2**	**1**	**0**	**1**	**16:25**
2002-03	**Phoenix**	**NHL**	**68**	**17**	**29**	**46**	**50**	**4**	**0**	**3**	**142**	**12.0**	**-21**	**1108**	**52.5**	**17:02**	....	....	....	....	....	....	....	....	....
	Buffalo	**NHL**	**14**	**7**	**5**	**12**	**12**	**5**	**0**	**1**	**39**	**17.9**	**1**	**206**	**50.0**	**17:49**	....	....	....	....	....	....	....	....	....
	NHL Totals		**272**	**77**	**81**	**158**	**158**	**32**	**0**	**12**	**476**	**16.2**		**3024**	**51.1**	**14:09**	**6**	**2**	**1**	**3**	**2**	**1**	**0**	**1**	**14:43**

QMJHL All-Rookie Team (1995) • QMJHL Offensive Rookie of the Year (1995) • QMJHL Second All-Star Team (1996, 1997) • AHL First All-Star Team (1998) • Dudley "Red" Garrett Memorial Trophy (Top Rookie – AHL) (1998)
Traded to **Buffalo** by **Phoenix** with Phoenix's 3rd round choice in 2004 Entry Draft for Chris Gratton and Buffalo's 4th round choice in 2004 Entry Draft, March 10, 2003.

BRIGLEY, Travis
(BRIH-glee), TRA-vihs) **COL.**

Left wing. Shoots left. 6', 205 lbs. Born, Coronation, Alta., June 16, 1977. Calgary's 2nd choice, 39th overall, in 1996 Entry Draft.

Season	Club	League	GP	G	A	Pts	PIM	PP	SH	GW	S	%	+/-	TF	F%	Min	GP	G	A	Pts	PIM	PP	SH	GW	Min
1992-93	Leduc Oil Barons	AMHL	32	36	24	60	56	....	....	....	....	....	....	....	....	....	....	....	....	....	....	....	....	....	....
1993-94	Leduc Oil Barons	AMHL	34	29	44	73	141	....	....	....	....	....	....	....	....	....	....	....	....	....	....	....	....	....	....
	Lethbridge	WHL	1	0	0	0	0	....	....	....	....	....	....	....	....	....	....	....	....	....	....	....	....	....	....
1994-95	Lethbridge	WHL	64	14	18	32	14	....	....	....	....	....	....	....	....	....	....	....	....	....	....	....	....	....	....
1995-96	Lethbridge	WHL	69	34	43	77	94	....	....	....	....	....	....	....	....	....	4	2	3	5	8	....	....	....	....
1996-97	Lethbridge	WHL	71	43	47	90	56	....	....	....	....	....	....	....	....	....	19	9	9	18	31	....	....	....	....
1997-98	**Calgary**	**NHL**	**2**	**0**	**0**	**0**	**2**	**0**	**0**	**0**	**1**	**0.0**	**0**	....	....	....	....	....	....	....	....	....	....	....	....
	Saint John Flames	AHL	79	17	15	32	28	....	....	....	....	....	....	....	....	....	8	0	0	0	0	....	....	....	....
1998-99	Saint John Flames	AHL	74	15	35	50	48	....	....	....	....	....	....	....	....	....	7	3	1	4	2	....	....	....	....
99-2000	**Calgary**	**NHL**	**17**	**0**	**2**	**2**	**4**	**0**	**0**	**0**	**17**	**0.0**	**-6**	**2**	**0.0**	**14:14**	....	....	....	....	....	....	....	....	....
	Saint John Flames	AHL	9	3	1	4	4	....	....	....	....	....	....	....	....	....	....	....	....	....	....	....	....	....	....
	Detroit Vipers	IHL	29	6	10	16	24	....	....	....	....	....	....	....	....	....	....	....	....	....	....	....	....	....	....
	Philadelphia	AHL	15	2	2	4	15	....	....	....	....	....	....	....	....	....	5	1	0	1	4	....	....	....	....
2000-01	Knoxville Speed	UHL	4	2	4	6	4	....	....	....	....	....	....	....	....	....	....	....	....	....	....	....	....	....	....
	Cardiff Devils	Britain	12	5	9	14	6	....	....	....	....	....	....	....	....	....	....	....	....	....	....	....	....	....	....
	Louisville Panthers	AHL	49	14	21	35	34	....	....	....	....	....	....	....	....	....	....	....	....	....	....	....	....	....	....
2001-02	Macon Whoopee	ECHL	8	4	3	7	2	....	....	....	....	....	....	....	....	....	....	....	....	....	....	....	....	....	....
	Cincinnati	AHL	70	22	21	43	40	....	....	....	....	....	....	....	....	....	3	2	0	2	0	....	....	....	....
2002-03	Cincinnati	AHL	64	18	27	45	58	....	....	....	....	....	....	....	....	....	....	....	....	....	....	....	....	....	....
	Hershey Bears	AHL	13	3	5	8	4	....	....	....	....	....	....	....	....	....	5	1	2	3	2	....	....	....	....
	NHL Totals		**19**	**0**	**2**	**2**	**6**	**0**	**0**	**0**	**18**	**0.0**		**2**	**0.0**	**14:14**	....	....	....	....	....	....	....	....	....

Traded to **Philadelphia** by **Calgary** with Calgary's 6th round choice (Andrei Razin) in 2001 Entry Draft for Marc Bureau, March 6, 2000. Signed as a free agent by **Cardiff** (Britain), November 3, 2000. Signed as a free agent by **Florida**, December 16, 2000. Signed as a free agent by **Anaheim**, January 22, 2002. Traded to **Colorado** by **Anaheim** for future considerations, August 12, 2003.

BRIMANIS, Aris
(brih-MAN-ihs, AR-ihs) **ST.L.**

Defense. Shoots right. 6'3", 215 lbs. Born, Cleveland, OH, March 14, 1972. Philadelphia's 3rd choice, 86th overall, in 1991 Entry Draft.

Season	Club	League	GP	G	A	Pts	PIM	PP	SH	GW	S	%	+/-	TF	F%	Min	GP	G	A	Pts	PIM	PP	SH	GW	Min
1988-89	Culver Eagles	Hi-School	38	10	13	23	24	....	....	....	....	....	....	....	....	....	....	....	....	....	....	....	....	....	....
1989-90	Culver Eagles	Hi-School	37	15	10	25	52	....	....	....	....	....	....	....	....	....	....	....	....	....	....	....	....	....	....
1990-91	Bowling Green	CCHA	38	3	6	9	42	....	....	....	....	....	....	....	....	....	....	....	....	....	....	....	....	....	....
1991-92	Bowling Green	CCHA	32	2	9	11	38	....	....	....	....	....	....	....	....	....	....	....	....	....	....	....	....	....	....
1992-93	Brandon	WHL	71	8	50	58	110	....	....	....	....	....	....	....	....	....	4	2	1	3	7	....	....	....	....
1993-94	**Philadelphia**	**NHL**	**1**	**0**	**0**	**0**	**0**	**0**	**0**	**0**	**1**	**0.0**	**-1**	....	....	....	....	....	....	....	....	....	....	....	....
	Hershey Bears	AHL	75	8	15	23	65	....	....	....	....	....	....	....	....	....	11	2	3	5	12	....	....	....	....
1994-95	Hershey Bears	AHL	76	8	17	25	68	....	....	....	....	....	....	....	....	....	6	1	1	2	14	....	....	....	....
1995-96	**Philadelphia**	**NHL**	**17**	**0**	**2**	**2**	**12**	**0**	**0**	**0**	**11**	**0.0**	**-1**	....	....	....	....	....	....	....	....	....	....	....	....
	Hershey Bears	AHL	54	9	22	31	64	....	....	....	....	....	....	....	....	....	5	1	2	3	4	....	....	....	....
1996-97	**Philadelphia**	**NHL**	**3**	**0**	**1**	**1**	**0**	**0**	**0**	**0**	**1**	**0.0**	**0**	....	....	....	....	....	....	....	....	....	....	....	....
	Philadelphia	AHL	65	14	18	32	69	....	....	....	....	....	....	....	....	....	10	2	2	4	13	....	....	....	....
1997-98	Philadelphia	AHL	30	1	11	12	26	....	....	....	....	....	....	....	....	....	....	....	....	....	....	....	....	....	....
	Michigan	IHL	35	3	9	12	24	....	....	....	....	....	....	....	....	....	4	1	0	1	4	....	....	....	....
1998-99	Grand Rapids	IHL	66	16	21	37	70	....	....	....	....	....	....	....	....	....	....	....	....	....	....	....	....	....	....
	Fredericton	AHL	8	2	4	6	6	....	....	....	....	....	....	....	....	....	15	3	10	13	18	....	....	....	....
99-2000	**NY Islanders**	**NHL**	**18**	**2**	**1**	**3**	**6**	**2**	**0**	**0**	**16**	**12.5**	**-5**	**1**	**0.0**	**19:60**	....	....	....	....	....	....	....	....	....
	Kansas City	IHL	46	5	17	22	28	....	....	....	....	....	....	....	....	....	....	....	....	....	....	....	....	....	....
	Providence Bruins	AHL	7	0	2	2	2	....	....	....	....	....	....	....	....	....	14	3	4	7	10	....	....	....	....
2000-01	**NY Islanders**	**NHL**	**56**	**0**	**8**	**8**	**26**	**0**	**0**	**0**	**66**	**0.0**	**-12**	**0**	**0.0**	**15:36**	....	....	....	....	....	....	....	....	....
	Chicago Wolves	IHL	20	2	2	4	14	....	....	....	....	....	....	....	....	....	16	3	1	4	8	....	....	....	....
2001-02	**Anaheim**	**NHL**	**5**	**0**	**0**	**0**	**9**	**0**	**0**	**0**	**2**	**0.0**	**-1**	**0**	**0.0**	**9:31**	....	....	....	....	....	....	....	....	....
	Cincinnati	AHL	72	2	9	11	44	....	....	....	....	....	....	....	....	....	3	1	0	1	0	....	....	....	....
2002-03	Worcester IceCats	AHL	38	8	13	21	51	....	....	....	....	....	....	....	....	....	3	0	0	0	2	....	....	....	....
	NHL Totals		**100**	**2**	**12**	**14**	**53**	**2**	**0**	**0**	**97**	**2.1**		**1**	**0.0**	**16:13**	....	....	....	....	....	....	....	....	....

Signed as a free agent by **NY Islanders**, August 16, 1999. Loaned to **Providence** (AHL) by **NY Islanders**, March 14, 2000. Signed as a free agent by **Anaheim**, August 1, 2001. Signed as a free agent by **St. Louis**, August 15, 2002. • Missed majority of 2002-03 season recovering from leg injury suffered in game vs. Utah (AHL), December 20, 2002.

BRIND'AMOUR, Rod
(BRIHND-uh-MOHR, RAWD) **CAR.**

Center. Shoots left. 6'1", 200 lbs. Born, Ottawa, Ont., August 9, 1970. St. Louis' 1st choice, 9th overall, in 1988 Entry Draft.

Season	Club	League	GP	G	A	Pts	PIM	PP	SH	GW	S	%	+/-	TF	F%	Min	GP	G	A	Pts	PIM	PP	SH	GW	Min
1986-87	Notre Dame	SMHL	33	38	50	88	66	....	....	....	....	....	....	....	....	....	....	....	....	....	....	....	....	....	....
1987-88	Notre Dame	SJHL	56	46	61	107	136	....	....	....	....	....	....	....	....	....	....	....	....	....	....	....	....	....	....
1988-89	Michigan State	CCHA	42	27	32	59	63	....	....	....	....	....	....	....	....	....	....	....	....	....	....	....	....	....	....
	St. Louis	**NHL**	....	....	....	....	....	....	....	....	....	....	....	....	....	....	**5**	**2**	**0**	**2**	**4**	**0**	**0**	**0**	....
1989-90	**St. Louis**	**NHL**	**79**	**26**	**35**	**61**	**46**	**10**	**0**	**1**	**160**	**16.3**	**23**	....	....	....	**12**	**5**	**8**	**13**	**6**	**1**	**0**	**0**	....
1990-91	**St. Louis**	**NHL**	**78**	**17**	**32**	**49**	**93**	**4**	**0**	**3**	**169**	**10.1**	**2**	....	....	....	**13**	**2**	**5**	**7**	**10**	**1**	**0**	**0**	....
1991-92	**Philadelphia**	**NHL**	**80**	**33**	**44**	**77**	**100**	**8**	**4**	**5**	**202**	**16.3**	**-3**	....	....	....	....	....	....	....	....	....	....	....	....
1992-93	**Philadelphia**	**NHL**	**81**	**37**	**49**	**86**	**89**	**13**	**4**	**4**	**206**	**18.0**	**-8**	....	....	....	....	....	....	....	....	....	....	....	....
1993-94	**Philadelphia**	**NHL**	**84**	**35**	**62**	**97**	**85**	**14**	**1**	**4**	**230**	**15.2**	**-9**	....	....	....	....	....	....	....	....	....	....	....	....
1994-95	**Philadelphia**	**NHL**	**48**	**12**	**27**	**39**	**33**	**4**	**1**	**2**	**86**	**14.0**	**-4**	....	....	....	**15**	**6**	**9**	**15**	**8**	**2**	**1**	**1**	....
1995-96	**Philadelphia**	**NHL**	**82**	**26**	**61**	**87**	**110**	**4**	**4**	**5**	**213**	**12.2**	**20**	....	....	....	**12**	**2**	**5**	**7**	**6**	**1**	**0**	**0**	....
1996-97	**Philadelphia**	**NHL**	**82**	**27**	**32**	**59**	**41**	**8**	**2**	**3**	**205**	**13.2**	**2**	....	....	....	**19**	***13**	**8**	**21**	**10**	**4**	**2**	**1**	....
1997-98	**Philadelphia**	**NHL**	**82**	**36**	**38**	**74**	**54**	**10**	**2**	**8**	**205**	**17.6**	**-2**	....	....	....	**5**	**2**	**2**	**4**	**7**	**0**	**0**	**0**	....
	Canada	Olympics	6	1	2	3	0	....	....	....	....	....	....	....	....	....	....	....	....	....	....	....	....	....	....
1998-99	**Philadelphia**	**NHL**	**82**	**24**	**50**	**74**	**47**	**10**	**0**	**3**	**191**	**12.6**	**3**	**1773**	**56.5**	**21:29**	**6**	**1**	**3**	**4**	**0**	**0**	**0**	**0**	**25:08**

			Regular Season														Playoffs								
Season	Club	League	GP	G	A	Pts	PIM	PP	SH	GW	S	%	+/-	TF	F%	Min	GP	G	A	Pts	PIM	PP	SH	GW	Min
99-2000	**Philadelphia**	**NHL**	**12**	**5**	**3**	**8**	**4**	**4**	**0**	**0**	**26**	**19.2**	**−1**	**291**	**60.5**	**20:50**									
	Carolina	**NHL**	**33**	**4**	**10**	**14**	**22**	**0**	**1**	**1**	**61**	**6.6**	**−12**	**704**	**55.5**	**20:35**	....	....	....	....	....	....	....	....	....
2000-01	**Carolina**	**NHL**	**79**	**20**	**36**	**56**	**47**	**5**	**1**	**5**	**163**	**12.3**	**−7**	**1907**	**60.4**	**22:07**	**6**	**1**	**3**	**4**	**6**	**0**	**0**	**1**	**23:27**
2001-02	**Carolina**	**NHL**	**81**	**23**	**32**	**55**	**40**	**5**	**2**	**5**	**162**	**14.2**	**3**	**2058**	**59.2**	**22:07**	**23**	**4**	**8**	**12**	**16**	**2**	**1**	**1**	**24:52**
2002-03	**Carolina**	**NHL**	**48**	**14**	**23**	**37**	**37**	**7**	**1**	**0**	**110**	**12.7**	**−9**	**1242**	**56.5**	**23:46**	....	....	....	....	....	....	....	....	....
	NHL Totals		**1031**	**339**	**534**	**873**	**848**	**106**	**23**	**49**	**2389**	**14.2**		**7975**	**58.2**	**22:00**	**116**	**38**	**51**	**89**	**73**	**11**	**4**	**4**	**24:41**

CCHA Rookie of the Year (1989) • NHL All-Rookie Team (1990)

Played in NHL All-Star Game (1992)

Traded to **Philadelphia** by **St. Louis** with Dan Quinn for Ron Sutter and Murray Baron, September 22, 1991. Traded to **Carolina** by **Philadelphia** with Jean-Marc Pelletier and Philadelphia's 2nd round choice (later traded to Colorado – Colorado selected Agris Saviels) in 2000 Entry Draft for Keith Primeau and Carolina's 5th round choice (later traded to NY Islanders – NY Islanders selected Kristofer Ottosson) in 2000 Entry Draft, January 23, 2000.

BRISEBOIS, Patrice

(BREES-bwah, pa-TREEZ) **MTL.**

Defense. Shoots right. 6'2", 203 lbs. Born, Montreal, Que., January 27, 1971. Montreal's 2nd choice, 30th overall, in 1989 Entry Draft.

1986-87	Mtl-Bourassa	QAAA	39	15	19	34	66	....	....	....	....	....	....	....	....	....	....	....	....	....	....	....	....	....	....
1987-88	Laval Titan	QMJHL	48	10	34	44	95	....	....	....	....	....	....	....	....	....	6	0	2	2	2	....	....	....	....
1988-89	Laval Titan	QMJHL	50	20	45	65	95	....	....	....	....	....	....	....	....	....	17	8	14	22	45	....	....	....	....
1989-90	Laval Titan	QMJHL	56	18	70	88	108	....	....	....	....	....	....	....	....	....	13	7	9	16	26	....	....	....	....
1990-91	Drummondville	QMJHL	54	17	44	61	72	....	....	....	....	....	....	....	....	....	14	6	18	24	49	....	....	....	....
	Montreal	**NHL**	**10**	**0**	**2**	**2**	**4**	**0**	**0**	**0**	**11**	**0.0**	**1**	....	....	....	....	....	....	....	....	....	....	....	....
1991-92	**Montreal**	**NHL**	**26**	**2**	**8**	**10**	**20**	**0**	**0**	**1**	**37**	**5.4**	**9**	....	....	....	**11**	**2**	**4**	**6**	**6**	**1**	**0**	**1**	....
	Fredericton	AHL	53	12	27	39	51	....	....	....	....	....	....	....	....	....	....	....	....	....	....	....	....	....	....
1992-93♦	**Montreal**	**NHL**	**70**	**10**	**21**	**31**	**79**	**4**	**0**	**2**	**123**	**8.1**	**6**	....	....	....	**20**	**0**	**4**	**4**	**18**	**0**	**0**	**0**	....
1993-94	**Montreal**	**NHL**	**53**	**2**	**21**	**23**	**63**	**1**	**0**	**0**	**71**	**2.8**	**5**	....	....	....	**7**	**0**	**4**	**4**	**6**	**0**	**0**	**0**	....
1994-95	**Montreal**	**NHL**	**35**	**4**	**8**	**12**	**26**	**0**	**0**	**2**	**67**	**6.0**	**−2**	....	....	....	....	....	....	....	....	....	....	....	....
1995-96	**Montreal**	**NHL**	**69**	**9**	**27**	**36**	**65**	**3**	**0**	**1**	**127**	**7.1**	**10**	....	....	....	**6**	**1**	**2**	**3**	**6**	**0**	**0**	**0**	....
1996-97	**Montreal**	**NHL**	**49**	**2**	**13**	**15**	**24**	**0**	**0**	**1**	**72**	**2.8**	**−7**	....	....	....	**3**	**1**	**1**	**2**	**24**	**0**	**0**	**1**	....
1997-98	**Montreal**	**NHL**	**79**	**10**	**27**	**37**	**67**	**5**	**0**	**1**	**125**	**8.0**	**16**	....	....	....	**10**	**1**	**0**	**1**	**0**	**0**	**0**	**0**	....
1998-99	**Montreal**	**NHL**	**54**	**3**	**9**	**12**	**28**	**1**	**0**	**1**	**90**	**3.3**	**−8**	**0**	**0.0**	**22:26**	....	....	....	....	....	....	....	....	....
99-2000	**Montreal**	**NHL**	**54**	**10**	**25**	**35**	**18**	**5**	**0**	**2**	**88**	**11.4**	**−1**	**0**	**0.0**	**23:14**	....	....	....	....	....	....	....	....	....
2000-01	**Montreal**	**NHL**	**77**	**15**	**21**	**36**	**28**	**11**	**0**	**4**	**178**	**8.4**	**−31**	**1**	**100.0**	**24:43**	....	....	....	....	....	....	....	....	....
2001-02	**Montreal**	**NHL**	**71**	**4**	**29**	**33**	**25**	**2**	**1**	**1**	**95**	**4.2**	**9**	**0**	**0.0**	**23:53**	**10**	**1**	**1**	**2**	**2**	**0**	**0**	**0**	**22:05**
2002-03	**Montreal**	**NHL**	**73**	**4**	**25**	**29**	**32**	**1**	**0**	**1**	**105**	**3.8**	**−14**	**0**	**0.0**	**23:23**	....	....	....	....	....	....	....	....	....
	NHL Totals		**720**	**75**	**236**	**311**	**479**	**33**	**1**	**17**	**1189**	**6.3**		**1**	**100.0**	**23:37**	**67**	**6**	**16**	**22**	**62**	**1**	**0**	**2**	**22:05**

QMJHL Second All-Star Team (1990) • QMJHL First All-Star Team (1991) • Canadian Major Junior Defenseman of the Year (1991) • Memorial Cup All-Star Team (1991)

BROWN, Brad

(BROWN, BRAD) **MIN.**

Defense. Shoots right. 6'4", 220 lbs. Born, Baie Verte, Nfld., December 27, 1975. Montreal's 1st choice, 18th overall, in 1994 Entry Draft.

1990-91	Tor. Red Wings	MTHL	80	15	45	60	105	....	....	....	....	....	....	....	....	....	....	....	....	....	....	....	....	....	....
	St. Michael's B	OJHL-B	2	0	0	0	0	....	....	....	....	....	....	....	....	....	....	....	....	....	....	....	....	....	....
1991-92	North Bay	OHL	49	2	9	11	170	....	....	....	....	....	....	....	....	....	18	0	6	6	43	....	....	....	....
1992-93	North Bay	OHL	61	4	9	13	228	....	....	....	....	....	....	....	....	....	2	0	2	2	13	....	....	....	....
1993-94	North Bay	OHL	66	8	24	32	196	....	....	....	....	....	....	....	....	....	18	3	12	15	33	....	....	....	....
1994-95	North Bay	OHL	64	8	38	46	172	....	....	....	....	....	....	....	....	....	6	1	4	5	8	....	....	....	....
1995-96	Barrie Colts	OHL	27	3	13	16	82	....	....	....	....	....	....	....	....	....	....	....	....	....	....	....	....	....	....
	Fredericton	AHL	38	0	3	3	148	....	....	....	....	....	....	....	....	....	10	2	1	3	6	....	....	....	....
1996-97	**Montreal**	**NHL**	**8**	**0**	**0**	**0**	**22**	**0**	**0**	**0**	**0**	**0.0**	**−1**	....	....	....	....	....	....	....	....	....	....	....	....
	Fredericton	AHL	64	3	7	10	368	....	....	....	....	....	....	....	....	....	....	....	....	....	....	....	....	....	....
1997-98	Fredericton	AHL	64	1	8	9	297	....	....	....	....	....	....	....	....	....	4	0	0	0	29	....	....	....	....
1998-99	**Montreal**	**NHL**	**5**	**0**	**0**	**0**	**21**	**0**	**0**	**0**	**0**	**0.0**	**0**	**0**	**0.0**	**6:02**	....	....	....	....	....	....	....	....	....
	Chicago	**NHL**	**61**	**1**	**7**	**8**	**184**	**0**	**0**	**0**	**26**	**3.8**	**−4**	**0**	**0.0**	**15:08**	....	....	....	....	....	....	....	....	....
99-2000	**Chicago**	**NHL**	**57**	**0**	**9**	**9**	**134**	**0**	**0**	**0**	**15**	**0.0**	**−1**	**0**	**0.0**	**14:12**	....	....	....	....	....	....	....	....	....
2000-01	**NY Rangers**	**NHL**	**48**	**1**	**3**	**4**	**107**	**0**	**0**	**0**	**14**	**7.1**	**0**	**0**	**0.0**	**14:31**	....	....	....	....	....	....	....	....	....
2001-02	**Minnesota**	**NHL**	**51**	**0**	**4**	**4**	**123**	**0**	**0**	**0**	**23**	**0.0**	**−11**	**0**	**0.0**	**15:54**	....	....	....	....	....	....	....	....	....
2002-03	**Minnesota**	**NHL**	**57**	**0**	**1**	**1**	**90**	**0**	**0**	**0**	**10**	**0.0**	**−1**	**0**	**0.0**	**9:14**	**11**	**0**	**0**	**0**	**16**	**0**	**0**	**0**	**8:23**
	NHL Totals		**287**	**2**	**24**	**26**	**681**	**0**	**0**	**0**	**88**	**2.3**		**0**	**0.0**	**13:36**	**11**	**0**	**0**	**0**	**16**	**0**	**0**	**0**	**8:23**

OHL All-Rookie Team (1992)

Traded to **Chicago** by **Montreal** with Jocelyn Thibault and Dave Manson for Jeff Hackett, Eric Weinrich, Alain Nasreddine and Tampa Bay's 4th round choice (previously acquired, Montreal selected Chris Dyment) in 1999 Entry Draft, November 16, 1998. Traded to **NY Rangers** by **Chicago** with Michal Grosek for future considerations, October 5, 2000. Signed as a free agent by **Minnesota**, July 31, 2001.

BROWN, Curtis

(BROWN, KUHR-tihs) **BUF.**

Center/Left wing. Shoots left. 6', 197 lbs. Born, Unity, Sask., February 12, 1976. Buffalo's 2nd choice, 43rd overall, in 1994 Entry Draft.

1990-91	Unity Bantams	SMHL	60	93	104	197	55	....	....	....	....	....	....	....	....	....	....	....	....	....	....	....	....	....	....
1991-92	Moose Jaw	SMHL	36	35	30	65	44	....	....	....	....	....	....	....	....	....	....	....	....	....	....	....	....	....	....
1992-93	Moose Jaw	WHL	71	13	16	29	30	....	....	....	....	....	....	....	....	....	....	....	....	....	....	....	....	....	....
1993-94	Moose Jaw	WHL	72	27	38	65	82	....	....	....	....	....	....	....	....	....	....	....	....	....	....	....	....	....	....
1994-95	Moose Jaw	WHL	70	51	53	104	63	....	....	....	....	....	....	....	....	....	10	8	7	15	20	....	....	....	....
	Buffalo	**NHL**	**1**	**1**	**1**	**2**	**2**	**0**	**0**	**0**	**4**	**25.0**	**2**	....	....	....	....	....	....	....	....	....	....	....	....
1995-96	Moose Jaw	WHL	25	20	18	38	30	....	....	....	....	....	....	....	....	....	....	....	....	....	....	....	....	....	....
	Prince Albert	WHL	19	12	21	33	8	....	....	....	....	....	....	....	....	....	18	10	15	25	18	....	....	....	....
	Buffalo	**NHL**	**4**	**0**	**0**	**0**	**0**	**0**	**0**	**0**	**1**	**0.0**	**0**	....	....	....	....	....	....	....	....	....	....	....	....
	Rochester	AHL	....	....	....	....	....	....	....	....	....	....	....	....	....	....	12	0	1	1	2	....	....	....	....
1996-97	**Buffalo**	**NHL**	**28**	**4**	**3**	**7**	**18**	**0**	**0**	**1**	**31**	**12.9**	**4**	....	....	....	....	....	....	....	....	....	....	....	....
	Rochester	AHL	51	22	21	43	30	....	....	....	....	....	....	....	....	....	10	4	6	10	4	....	....	....	....
1997-98	**Buffalo**	**NHL**	**63**	**12**	**12**	**24**	**34**	**1**	**1**	**2**	**91**	**13.2**	**11**	....	....	....	**13**	**1**	**2**	**3**	**10**	**1**	**0**	**0**	....
1998-99	**Buffalo**	**NHL**	**78**	**16**	**31**	**47**	**56**	**5**	**1**	**3**	**128**	**12.5**	**23**	**1198**	**45.0**	**17:30**	**21**	**7**	**6**	**13**	**10**	**3**	**0**	**3**	**18:51**
99-2000	**Buffalo**	**NHL**	**74**	**22**	**29**	**51**	**42**	**5**	**0**	**4**	**149**	**14.8**	**19**	**1318**	**48.6**	**18:11**	**5**	**1**	**3**	**4**	**6**	**1**	**0**	**0**	**17:11**
2000-01	**Buffalo**	**NHL**	**70**	**10**	**22**	**32**	**34**	**2**	**1**	**0**	**105**	**9.5**	**15**	**1159**	**50.4**	**16:34**	**13**	**5**	**0**	**5**	**8**	**0**	**2**	**1**	**18:14**
2001-02	**Buffalo**	**NHL**	**82**	**20**	**17**	**37**	**32**	**4**	**1**	**5**	**171**	**11.7**	**−4**	**1608**	**49.0**	**17:48**	....	....	....	....	....	....	....	....	....
2002-03	**Buffalo**	**NHL**	**74**	**15**	**16**	**31**	**40**	**3**	**4**	**4**	**144**	**10.4**	**4**	**1387**	**49.5**	**16:53**	....	....	....	....	....	....	....	....	....
	NHL Totals		**474**	**100**	**131**	**231**	**258**	**20**	**8**	**19**	**824**	**12.1**		**6670**	**48.5**	**17:24**	**52**	**14**	**11**	**25**	**34**	**5**	**2**	**4**	**18:26**

WHL East First All-Star Team (1995) • WHL East Second All-Star Team (1996)

BROWN, Mike

(BROWN, MIGHK)

Left wing. Shoots left. 6'5", 185 lbs. Born, Surrey, B.C., April 27, 1979. Florida's 1st choice, 20th overall, in 1997 Entry Draft.

1993-94	Penticton	BCJHL	50	52	48	100	100	....	....	....	....	....	....	....	....	....	....	....	....	....	....	....	....	....	....
1994-95	Merritt	BCJHL	45	3	4	7	145	....	....	....	....	....	....	....	....	....	....	....	....	....	....	....	....	....	....
1995-96	Red Deer Rebels	WHL	62	4	5	9	125	....	....	....	....	....	....	....	....	....	10	0	0	0	18	....	....	....	....
1996-97	Red Deer Rebels	WHL	70	19	13	32	243	....	....	....	....	....	....	....	....	....	16	1	2	3	47	....	....	....	....
1997-98	Kamloops Blazers	WHL	72	23	33	56	305	....	....	....	....	....	....	....	....	....	7	2	1	3	22	....	....	....	....
1998-99	Kamloops Blazers	WHL	69	28	16	44	*285	....	....	....	....	....	....	....	....	....	15	3	7	10	*68	....	....	....	....
99-2000	Syracuse Crunch	AHL	71	13	18	31	284	....	....	....	....	....	....	....	....	....	4	0	0	0	0	....	....	....	....
2000-01	**Vancouver**	**NHL**	**1**	**0**	**0**	**0**	**5**	**0**	**0**	**0**	**1**	**0.0**	**0**	**0**	**0.0**	**4:48**	....	....	....	....	....	....	....	....	....
	Kansas City	IHL	78	14	13	27	214	....	....	....	....	....	....	....	....	....	....	....	....	....	....	....	....	....	....
2001-02	**Vancouver**	**NHL**	**15**	**0**	**0**	**0**	**72**	**0**	**0**	**0**	**2**	**0.0**	**1**	**0**	**0.0**	**3:29**	....	....	....	....	....	....	....	....	....
	Manitoba Moose	AHL	31	7	9	16	155	....	....	....	....	....	....	....	....	....	6	0	1	1	16	....	....	....	....
2002-03	**Anaheim**	**NHL**	**16**	**1**	**1**	**2**	**44**	**0**	**0**	**1**	**8**	**12.5**	**0**	**0**	**0.0**	**0:00**	....	....	....	....	....	....	....	....	**0:00**
	Cincinnati	AHL	27	3	3	6	85	....	....	....	....	....	....	....	....	....	....	....	....	....	....	....	....	....	....
	NHL Totals		**32**	**1**	**1**	**2**	**121**	**0**	**0**	**1**	**11**	**9.1**		**0**	**0.0**	**1:47**	....	....	....	....	....	....	....	....	....

Traded to **Vancouver** by **Florida** with Ed Jovanovski, Dave Gagner, Kevin Weekes and Florida's 1st round choice (Nathan Smith) in 2000 Entry Draft for Pavel Bure, Bret Hedican, Brad Ference and Vancouver's 3rd round choice (Robert Fried) in 2000 Entry Draft, January 17, 1999. Claimed on waivers by **Anaheim** from **Vancouver**, October 11, 2002.

BROWN, Sean

(BROWN, SHAWN) **N.J.**

Defense. Shoots left. 6'3", 210 lbs. Born, Oshawa, Ont., November 5, 1976. Boston's 2nd choice, 21st overall, in 1995 Entry Draft.

Season	Club	League	GP	G	A	Pts	PIM	PP	SH	GW	S	%	+/-	TF	F%	Min	GP	G	A	Pts	PIM	PP	SH	GW	Min
			Regular Season														Playoffs								
1992-93	Oshawa	OJHL-B	15	0	1	1	9	....	....	....	....	....	....	....	....	....	....	....	....	....	....	....	....	....	....
1993-94	Wellington Dukes	MTJHL	32	5	14	19	165	....	....	....	....	....	....	....	....	....	....	....	....	....	....	....	....	....	....
	Belleville Bulls	OHL	28	1	2	3	53	....	....	....	....	....	....	....	....	....	8	0	0	0	17	....	....	....	....
1994-95	Belleville Bulls	OHL	58	2	16	18	200	....	....	....	....	....	....	....	....	....	16	4	2	6	*67	....	....	....	....
1995-96	Belleville Bulls	OHL	37	10	23	33	150	....	....	....	....	....	....	....	....	....	....	....	....	....	....	....	....	....	....
	Sarnia Sting	OHL	26	8	17	25	112	....	....	....	....	....	....	....	....	....	10	1	0	1	38	....	....	....	....
1996-97	**Edmonton**	**NHL**	**5**	**0**	**0**	**0**	**4**	**0**	**0**	**0**	**2**	**0.0**	**–1**	....	....	....	....	....	....	....	....	....	....	....	....
	Hamilton	AHL	61	1	7	8	238	....	....	....	....	....	....	....	....	....	19	1	0	1	47	....	....	....	....
1997-98	**Edmonton**	**NHL**	**18**	**0**	**1**	**1**	**43**	**0**	**0**	**0**	**9**	**0.0**	**–1**	....	....	....	....	....	....	....	....	....	....	....	....
	Hamilton	AHL	43	4	6	10	166	....	....	....	....	....	....	....	....	....	6	0	2	2	38	....	....	....	....
1998-99	**Edmonton**	**NHL**	**51**	**0**	**7**	**7**	**188**	**0**	**0**	**0**	**27**	**0.0**	**1**	**0**	**0.0**	**12:14**	**1**	**0**	**0**	**0**	**10**	**0**	**0**	**0**	**7:33**
99-2000	**Edmonton**	**NHL**	**72**	**4**	**8**	**12**	**192**	**0**	**0**	**2**	**36**	**11.1**	**1**	**0**	**0.0**	**12:41**	**3**	**0**	**0**	**0**	**23**	**0**	**0**	**0**	**6:12**
2000-01	**Edmonton**	**NHL**	**62**	**2**	**3**	**5**	**110**	**0**	**0**	**0**	**30**	**6.7**	**2**	**0**	**0.0**	**11:07**	....	....	....	....	....	....	....	....	....
2001-02	**Edmonton**	**NHL**	**61**	**6**	**4**	**10**	**127**	**3**	**0**	**1**	**58**	**10.3**	**8**	**0**	**0.0**	**12:36**	....	....	....	....	....	....	....	....	....
	Boston	**NHL**	**12**	**0**	**1**	**1**	**47**	**0**	**0**	**0**	**6**	**0.0**	**–1**	**0**	**0.0**	**16:22**	**4**	**0**	**0**	**0**	**2**	**0**	**0**	**0**	**5:49**
2002-03	**Boston**	**NHL**	**69**	**1**	**5**	**6**	**117**	**0**	**0**	**0**	**39**	**2.6**	**–6**	**2**	**50.0**	**6:26**	....	....	....	....	....	....	....	....	....
	NHL Totals		**350**	**13**	**29**	**42**	**828**	**3**	**0**	**3**	**207**	**6.3**		**2**	**50.0**	**11:07**	**8**	**0**	**0**	**0**	**35**	**0**	**0**	**0**	**6:11**

OHL Second All-Star Team (1996)

Rights traded to **Edmonton** by **Boston** with Mariusz Czerkawski and Boston's 1st round choice (Matthieu Descoteaux) in 1996 Entry Draft for Bill Ranford, January 11, 1996. Traded to **Boston** by **Edmonton** for Bobby Allen, March 19, 2002. Signed as a free agent by **New Jersey**, July 24, 2003.

BRULE, Steve

(broo-LAY, STEEV)

Right wing. Shoots right. 6', 200 lbs. Born, Montreal, Que., January 15, 1975. New Jersey's 6th choice, 143rd overall, in 1993 Entry Draft.

Season	Club	League	GP	G	A	Pts	PIM	PP	SH	GW	S	%	+/-	TF	F%	Min	GP	G	A	Pts	PIM	PP	SH	GW	Min
1990-91	L'est Cantonniers	QAHA	32	25	30	55	20	....	....	....	....	....	....	....	....	....	....	....	....	....	....	....	....	....	....
1991-92	Mtl-Bourassa	QAAA	40	33	37	70	46	....	....	....	....	....	....	....	....	....	9	9	7	16	10	....	....	....	....
1992-93	St-Jean Lynx	QMJHL	70	33	47	80	46	....	....	....	....	....	....	....	....	....	4	0	0	0	9	....	....	....	....
1993-94	St-Jean Lynx	QMJHL	66	41	64	105	46	....	....	....	....	....	....	....	....	....	5	2	1	3	0	....	....	....	....
1994-95	St-Jean Lynx	QMJHL	69	44	64	108	42	....	....	....	....	....	....	....	....	....	7	3	4	7	8	....	....	....	....
	Albany River Rats	AHL	3	1	4	5	0	....	....	....	....	....	....	....	....	....	14	9	5	14	4	....	....	....	....
1995-96	Albany River Rats	AHL	80	30	21	51	37	....	....	....	....	....	....	....	....	....	4	0	0	0	17	....	....	....	....
1996-97	Albany River Rats	AHL	79	28	48	76	27	....	....	....	....	....	....	....	....	....	16	7	7	14	12	....	....	....	....
1997-98	Albany River Rats	AHL	80	34	43	77	34	....	....	....	....	....	....	....	....	....	13	8	3	11	4	....	....	....	....
1998-99	Albany River Rats	AHL	78	32	52	84	35	....	....	....	....	....	....	....	....	....	5	3	1	4	4	....	....	....	....
99-2000	Albany River Rats	AHL	75	30	46	76	18	....	....	....	....	....	....	....	....	....	5	1	2	3	0	....	....	....	....
	♦ New Jersey	**NHL**	....	....	....	....	....	....	....	....	....	....	....	....	....	....	**1**	**0**	**0**	**0**	**0**	**0**	**0**	**0**	**13:00**
2000-01	Manitoba Moose	IHL	78	21	48	69	22	....	....	....	....	....	....	....	....	....	13	3	10	13	12	....	....	....	....
2001-02	Cincinnati	AHL	77	21	42	63	50	....	....	....	....	....	....	....	....	....	3	0	1	1	0	....	....	....	....
2002-03	**Colorado**	**NHL**	**2**	**0**	**0**	**0**	**0**	**0**	**0**	**0**	**2**	**0.0**	**0**	**0**	**0.0**	**9:06**	....	....	....	....	....	....	....	....	....
	Hershey Bears	AHL	49	18	19	37	30	....	....	....	....	....	....	....	....	....	5	4	0	4	8	....	....	....	....
	NHL Totals		**2**	**0**	**0**	**0**	**0**	**0**	**0**	**0**	**2**	**0.0**		**0**	**0.0**	**9:06**	**1**	**0**	**0**	**0**	**0**	**0**	**0**	**0**	**13:00**

QMJHL All-Rookie Team (1993) • QMJHL Offensive Rookie of the Year (1993) • QMJHL Second All-Star Team (1995)

Signed as a free agent by **Detroit**, July 20, 2000. Signed as a free agent by **Colorado**, July 22, 2002.

BRUNETTE, Andrew

(broo-NEHT, AN-droo) **MIN.**

Left wing. Shoots left. 6'1", 210 lbs. Born, Sudbury, Ont., August 24, 1973. Washington's 6th choice, 174th overall, in 1993 Entry Draft.

Season	Club	League	GP	G	A	Pts	PIM	PP	SH	GW	S	%	+/-	TF	F%	Min	GP	G	A	Pts	PIM	PP	SH	GW	Min
1989-90	Rayside-Balfour	NOHA	32	38	*65	*103	....	....	....	....	....	....	....	....	....	....	....	....	....	....	....	....	....	....	....
	Rayside-Balfour	NOJHA	4	1	1	2	0	....	....	....	....	....	....	....	....	....	....	....	....	....	....	....	....	....	....
1990-91	Owen Sound	OHL	63	15	20	35	15	....	....	....	....	....	....	....	....	....	....	....	....	....	....	....	....	....	....
1991-92	Owen Sound	OHL	66	51	47	98	42	....	....	....	....	....	....	....	....	....	5	5	0	5	8	....	....	....	....
1992-93	Owen Sound	OHL	66	*62	*100	*162	91	....	....	....	....	....	....	....	....	....	8	8	6	14	16	....	....	....	....
1993-94	Portland Pirates	AHL	23	9	11	20	10	....	....	....	....	....	....	....	....	....	2	0	1	1	0	....	....	....	....
	Providence Bruins	AHL	3	0	0	0	0	....	....	....	....	....	....	....	....	....	....	....	....	....	....	....	....	....	....
	Hampton Roads	ECHL	20	12	18	30	32	....	....	....	....	....	....	....	....	....	7	7	6	13	18	....	....	....	....
1994-95	Portland Pirates	AHL	79	30	50	80	53	....	....	....	....	....	....	....	....	....	7	3	3	6	10	....	....	....	....
1995-96	**Washington**	**NHL**	**11**	**3**	**3**	**6**	**0**	**0**	**0**	**1**	**16**	**18.8**	**5**	....	....	....	**6**	**1**	**3**	**4**	**0**	**0**	**0**	**0**	....
	Portland Pirates	AHL	69	28	66	94	125	....	....	....	....	....	....	....	....	....	20	11	18	29	15	....	....	....	....
1996-97	**Washington**	**NHL**	**23**	**4**	**7**	**11**	**12**	**2**	**0**	**0**	**23**	**17.4**	**–3**	....	....	....	....	....	....	....	....	....	....	....	....
	Portland Pirates	AHL	50	22	51	73	48	....	....	....	....	....	....	....	....	....	5	1	2	3	0	....	....	....	....
1997-98	**Washington**	**NHL**	**28**	**11**	**12**	**23**	**12**	**4**	**0**	**2**	**42**	**26.2**	**2**	....	....	....	....	....	....	....	....	....	....	....	....
	Portland Pirates	AHL	43	21	46	67	64	....	....	....	....	....	....	....	....	....	10	1	11	12	12	....	....	....	....
1998-99	**Nashville**	**NHL**	**77**	**11**	**20**	**31**	**26**	**7**	**0**	**1**	**65**	**16.9**	**–10**	**8**	**50.0**	**13:13**	....	....	....	....	....	....	....	....	....
99-2000	**Atlanta**	**NHL**	**81**	**23**	**27**	**50**	**30**	**9**	**0**	**2**	**107**	**21.5**	**–32**	**8**	**25.0**	**15:42**	....	....	....	....	....	....	....	....	....
2000-01	**Atlanta**	**NHL**	**77**	**15**	**44**	**59**	**26**	**6**	**0**	**4**	**104**	**14.4**	**–5**	**11**	**54.6**	**16:58**	....	....	....	....	....	....	....	....	....
2001-02	**Minnesota**	**NHL**	**81**	**21**	**48**	**69**	**18**	**10**	**0**	**2**	**106**	**19.8**	**–4**	**111**	**58.6**	**16:02**	....	....	....	....	....	....	....	....	....
2002-03	**Minnesota**	**NHL**	**82**	**18**	**28**	**46**	**30**	**9**	**0**	**2**	**97**	**18.6**	**–10**	**59**	**44.1**	**14:29**	**18**	**7**	**6**	**13**	**4**	**4**	**0**	**1**	**14:60**
	NHL Totals		**460**	**106**	**189**	**295**	**154**	**47**	**0**	**14**	**560**	**18.9**		**197**	**52.3**	**15:17**	**24**	**8**	**9**	**17**	**4**	**4**	**0**	**1**	**14:60**

OHL First All-Star Team (1993) • Canadian Major Junior Second All-Star Team (1993) • AHL Second All-Star Team (1995)

Claimed by **Nashville** from **Washington** in Expansion Draft, June 26, 1998. Traded to **Atlanta** by **Nashville** for Atlanta's 5th round choice (Matt Hendricks) in 2000 Entry Draft, June 21, 1999. Signed as a free agent by **Minnesota**, July 17, 2001.

BRYLIN, Sergei

(BRIH-lin, SAIR-gay) **N.J.**

Center. Shoots left. 5'10", 190 lbs. Born, Moscow, USSR, January 13, 1974. New Jersey's 2nd choice, 42nd overall, in 1992 Entry Draft.

Season	Club	League	GP	G	A	Pts	PIM	PP	SH	GW	S	%	+/-	TF	F%	Min	GP	G	A	Pts	PIM	PP	SH	GW	Min
1991-92	CSKA Moscow	CIS	44	1	6	7	4	....	....	....	....	....	....	....	....	....	....	....	....	....	....	....	....	....	....
1992-93	CSKA Moscow	CIS	42	5	4	9	36	....	....	....	....	....	....	....	....	....	....	....	....	....	....	....	....	....	....
1993-94	CSKA Moscow	CIS	39	4	6	10	36	....	....	....	....	....	....	....	....	....	3	1	0	1	2	....	....	....	....
	Russian Penguins	IHL	13	4	5	9	18	....	....	....	....	....	....	....	....	....	....	....	....	....	....	....	....	....	....
1994-95	Albany River Rats	AHL	63	19	35	54	78	....	....	....	....	....	....	....	....	....	....	....	....	....	....	....	....	....	....
	♦ New Jersey	**NHL**	**26**	**6**	**8**	**14**	**8**	**0**	**0**	**0**	**41**	**14.6**	**12**	....	....	....	**12**	**1**	**2**	**3**	**4**	**0**	**0**	**0**	....
1995-96	**New Jersey**	**NHL**	**50**	**4**	**5**	**9**	**26**	**0**	**0**	**1**	**51**	**7.8**	**–2**	....	....	....	....	....	....	....	....	....	....	....	....
1996-97	**New Jersey**	**NHL**	**29**	**2**	**2**	**4**	**20**	**0**	**0**	**0**	**34**	**5.9**	**–13**	....	....	....	....	....	....	....	....	....	....	....	....
	Albany River Rats	AHL	43	17	24	41	38	....	....	....	....	....	....	....	....	....	16	4	8	12	12	....	....	....	....
1997-98	**New Jersey**	**NHL**	**18**	**2**	**3**	**5**	**0**	**0**	**0**	**0**	**20**	**10.0**	**4**	....	....	....	....	....	....	....	....	....	....	....	....
	Albany River Rats	AHL	44	21	22	43	60	....	....	....	....	....	....	....	....	....	....	....	....	....	....	....	....	....	....
1998-99	**New Jersey**	**NHL**	**47**	**5**	**10**	**15**	**28**	**3**	**0**	**1**	**51**	**9.8**	**8**	**184**	**50.5**	**12:55**	**5**	**3**	**1**	**4**	**4**	**1**	**0**	**1**	**18:21**
99-2000♦	**New Jersey**	**NHL**	**64**	**9**	**11**	**20**	**20**	**1**	**0**	**1**	**84**	**10.7**	**0**	**72**	**41.7**	**13:23**	**17**	**3**	**5**	**8**	**0**	**0**	**0**	**0**	**13:02**
2000-01	**New Jersey**	**NHL**	**75**	**23**	**29**	**52**	**24**	**3**	**1**	**0**	**130**	**17.7**	**25**	**43**	**44.2**	**15:31**	**20**	**3**	**4**	**7**	**6**	**1**	**0**	**1**	**13:07**
2001-02	**New Jersey**	**NHL**	**76**	**16**	**28**	**44**	**10**	**5**	**0**	**3**	**133**	**12.0**	**21**	**17**	**47.1**	**17:11**	**6**	**0**	**2**	**2**	**2**	**0**	**0**	**0**	**19:05**
2002-03♦	**New Jersey**	**NHL**	**52**	**11**	**8**	**19**	**16**	**3**	**1**	**1**	**86**	**12.8**	**–2**	**90**	**32.2**	**16:11**	**19**	**1**	**3**	**4**	**8**	**0**	**0**	**1**	**17:03**
	NHL Totals		**437**	**78**	**104**	**182**	**152**	**15**	**2**	**7**	**630**	**12.4**		**406**	**44.1**	**15:12**	**79**	**11**	**17**	**28**	**24**	**2**	**0**	**3**	**15:08**

BUCHBERGER, Kelly

(BUK-buhr-guhr, KEHL-lee) **PIT.**

Right wing. Shoots left. 6'2", 210 lbs. Born, Langenburg, Sask., December 2, 1966. Edmonton's 8th choice, 188th overall, in 1985 Entry Draft.

Season	Club	League	GP	G	A	Pts	PIM	PP	SH	GW	S	%	+/-	TF	F%	Min	GP	G	A	Pts	PIM	PP	SH	GW	Min
1983-84	Melville	SJHL	60	14	11	25	139	....	....	....	....	....	....	....	....	....	....	....	....	....	....	....	....	....	....
1984-85	Moose Jaw	WHL	51	12	17	29	114	....	....	....	....	....	....	....	....	....	....	....	....	....	....	....	....	....	....
1985-86	Moose Jaw	WHL	72	14	22	36	206	....	....	....	....	....	....	....	....	....	13	11	4	15	37	....	....	....	....
1986-87	Nova Scotia Oilers	AHL	70	12	20	32	257	....	....	....	....	....	....	....	....	....	5	0	1	1	23	....	....	....	....
	♦ Edmonton	**NHL**	....	....	....	....	....	....	....	....	....	....	....	....	....	....	**3**	**0**	**1**	**1**	**5**	**0**	**0**	**0**	....
1987-88	**Edmonton**	**NHL**	**19**	**1**	**0**	**1**	**81**	**0**	**0**	**0**	**10**	**10.0**	**–1**	....	....	....	....	....	....	....	....	....	....	....	....
	Nova Scotia Oilers	AHL	49	21	23	44	206	....	....	....	....	....	....	....	....	....	2	0	0	0	11	....	....	....	....
1988-89	**Edmonton**	**NHL**	**66**	**5**	**9**	**14**	**234**	**1**	**0**	**1**	**57**	**8.8**	**–14**	....	....	....	....	....	....	....	....	....	....	....	....
1989-90♦	**Edmonton**	**NHL**	**55**	**2**	**6**	**8**	**168**	**0**	**0**	**2**	**35**	**5.7**	**–8**	....	....	....	**19**	**0**	**5**	**5**	**13**	**0**	**0**	**0**	....
1990-91	**Edmonton**	**NHL**	**64**	**3**	**1**	**4**	**160**	**0**	**0**	**2**	**54**	**5.6**	**–6**	....	....	....	**12**	**2**	**1**	**3**	**25**	**0**	**0**	**0**	....

Season	Club	League	GP	G	A	Pts	PIM	PP	SH	GW	S	%	+/-	TF	F%	Min	GP	G	A	Pts	PIM	PP	SH	GW	Min
			Regular Season														Playoffs								
1991-92	Edmonton	NHL	79	20	24	44	157	0	4	3	90	22.2	9	....	....	....	16	1	4	5	32	0	0	0	....
1992-93	Edmonton	NHL	83	12	18	30	133	1	2	3	92	13.0	–27	....	....	....	....	....	....	....	....	....	....	....	....
1993-94	Edmonton	NHL	84	3	18	21	199	0	0	0	93	3.2	–20	....	....	....	....	....	....	....	....	....	....	....	....
1994-95	Edmonton	NHL	48	7	17	24	82	2	1	5	73	9.6	0	....	....	....	....	....	....	....	....	....	....	....	....
1995-96	Edmonton	NHL	82	11	14	25	184	0	2	3	119	9.2	–20	....	....	....	....	....	....	....	....	....	....	....	....
1996-97	Edmonton	NHL	81	8	30	38	159	0	0	3	78	10.3	4	....	....	....	12	5	2	7	16	0	0	1	....
1997-98	Edmonton	NHL	82	6	17	23	122	1	1	1	86	7.0	–10	....	....	....	12	1	2	3	25	0	0	0	....
1998-99	Edmonton	NHL	52	4	4	8	68	0	2	1	29	13.8	–6	23	26.1	11:49	4	0	0	0	0	0	0	0	10:06
99-2000	Atlanta	NHL	68	5	12	17	139	0	0	0	56	8.9	–34	577	45.6	16:21	....	....	....	....	....	....	....	....	....
	Los Angeles	NHL	13	2	1	3	13	0	0	0	20	10.0	–2	6	16.7	14:43	4	0	0	0	4	0	0	0	8:56
2000-01	Los Angeles	NHL	82	6	14	20	75	0	0	1	66	9.1	–10	155	40.7	14:26	8	1	0	1	2	0	0	0	9:58
2001-02	Los Angeles	NHL	74	6	7	13	105	0	0	1	39	15.4	–13	126	41.3	10:21	7	0	0	0	7	0	0	0	8:48
2002-03	Phoenix	NHL	79	3	9	12	109	0	1	0	32	9.4	0	784	43.1	9:59	....	....	....	....	....	....	....	....	....
	NHL Totals		**1111**	**104**	**201**	**305**	**2188**	**5**	**13**	**26**	**1029**	**10.1**		**1671**	**43.3**	**12:39**	**97**	**10**	**15**	**25**	**129**	**0**	**0**	**1**	**9:27**

Claimed by **Atlanta** from **Edmonton** in Expansion Draft, June 25, 1999. Traded to **Los Angeles** by **Atlanta** with Nelson Emerson for Donald Audette and Frantisek Kaberle, March 13, 2000. Signed as a free agent by **Phoenix**, July 7, 2002. Signed as a free agent by **Pittsburgh**, July 31, 2003.

BULIS, Jan

(BOO-lihs, YAHN) **MTL.**

Center. Shoots left. 6'2", 201 lbs. Born, Pardubice, Czech., March 18, 1978. Washington's 3rd choice, 43rd overall, in 1996 Entry Draft.

Season	Club	League	GP	G	A	Pts	PIM	PP	SH	GW	S	%	+/-	TF	F%	Min	GP	G	A	Pts	PIM	PP	SH	GW	Min
1993-94	HC Pardubice Jr.	Czech-Jr.	25	16	11	27	....	....	....	....	....	....	....	....	....	....	....	....	....	....	....	....	....	....	....
1994-95	Kelowna Spartans	BCJHL	51	23	25	48	36	....	....	....	....	....	....	....	....	....	17	7	9	16	0	....	....	....	....
1995-96	Barrie Colts	OHL	59	29	30	59	22	....	....	....	....	....	....	....	....	....	7	2	3	5	2	....	....	....	....
1996-97	Barrie Colts	OHL	64	42	61	103	42	....	....	....	....	....	....	....	....	....	9	3	7	10	10	....	....	....	....
1997-98	Kingston	OHL	2	0	1	1	0	....	....	....	....	....	....	....	....	....	12	8	10	18	12	....	....	....	....
	Washington	NHL	48	5	11	16	18	0	0	0	37	13.5	–5	....	....	....	....	....	....	....	....	....	....	....	....
	Portland Pirates	AHL	3	1	4	5	12	....	....	....	....	....	....	....	....	....	....	....	....	....	....	....	....	....	....
1998-99	Washington	NHL	38	7	16	23	6	3	0	3	57	12.3	3	599	48.9	14:27	....	....	....	....	....	....	....	....	....
	Cincinnati	IHL	10	2	2	4	14	....	....	....	....	....	....	....	....	....	....	....	....	....	....	....	....	....	....
99-2000	Washington	NHL	56	9	22	31	30	0	0	1	92	9.8	7	609	45.5	13:55	....	....	....	....	....	....	....	....	....
2000-01	Washington	NHL	39	5	13	18	26	1	0	0	41	12.2	0	224	46.9	11:53	....	....	....	....	....	....	....	....	....
	Portland Pirates	AHL	4	0	2	2	0	....	....	....	....	....	....	....	....	....	....	....	....	....	....	....	....	....	....
	Montreal	NHL	12	0	5	5	0	0	0	0	20	0.0	–1	230	48.3	18:25	....	....	....	....	....	....	....	....	....
2001-02	Montreal	NHL	53	9	10	19	8	1	0	3	87	10.3	–2	156	43.0	13:34	6	0	0	0	6	0	0	0	12:25
2002-03	Montreal	NHL	82	16	24	40	30	0	0	2	160	10.0	9	153	42.5	15:42	....	....	....	....	....	....	....	....	....
	NHL Totals		**328**	**51**	**101**	**152**	**118**	**5**	**0**	**9**	**494**	**10.3**		**1971**	**46.6**	**14:21**	**6**	**0**	**0**	**0**	**6**	**0**	**0**	**0**	**12:25**

Traded to **Montreal** by **Washington** with Richard Zednik and Washington's 1st round choice (Alexander Perezhogin) in 2001 Entry Draft for Trevor Linden, Dainius Zubrus and New Jersey's 2nd round choice (previously acquired, later traded to Tampa Bay – Tampa Bay selected Andreas Holmqvist) in 2001 Entry Draft, March 13, 2001.

BURE, Pavel

(boo-RAY, PAH-vehl) **NYR**

Right wing. Shoots left. 5'10", 189 lbs. Born, Moscow, USSR, March 31, 1971. Vancouver's 4th choice, 113th overall, in 1989 Entry Draft.

Season	Club	League	GP	G	A	Pts	PIM	PP	SH	GW	S	%	+/-	TF	F%	Min	GP	G	A	Pts	PIM	PP	SH	GW	Min
1987-88	CSKA Moscow	USSR	5	1	1	2	0	....	....	....	....	....	....	....	....	....	....	....	....	....	....	....	....	....	....
1988-89	CSKA Moscow	USSR	32	17	9	26	8	....	....	....	....	....	....	....	....	....	....	....	....	....	....	....	....	....	....
1989-90	CSKA Moscow	USSR	46	14	10	24	20	....	....	....	....	....	....	....	....	....	....	....	....	....	....	....	....	....	....
1990-91	CSKA Moscow	USSR	44	35	11	46	24	....	....	....	....	....	....	....	....	....	....	....	....	....	....	....	....	....	....
1991-92	Vancouver	NHL	65	34	26	60	30	7	3	6	268	12.7	0	....	....	....	13	6	4	10	14	0	0	0	....
1992-93	Vancouver	NHL	83	60	50	110	69	13	7	9	407	14.7	35	....	....	....	12	5	7	12	8	0	0	1	....
1993-94	Vancouver	NHL	76	*60	47	107	86	25	4	9	374	16.0	1	....	....	....	24	*16	15	31	40	3	0	2	....
1994-95	EV Landshut	Germany	1	3	0	3	2	....	....	....	....	....	....	....	....	....	....	....	....	....	....	....	....	....	....
	Spartak Moscow	CIS	1	2	0	2	2	....	....	....	....	....	....	....	....	....	....	....	....	....	....	....	....	....	....
	Vancouver	NHL	44	20	23	43	47	6	2	2	198	10.1	–8	....	....	....	11	7	6	13	10	2	2	0	....
1995-96	Vancouver	NHL	15	6	7	13	8	1	1	0	78	7.7	–2	....	....	....	....	....	....	....	....	....	....	....	....
1996-97	Vancouver	NHL	63	23	32	55	40	4	1	2	265	8.7	–14	....	....	....	....	....	....	....	....	....	....	....	....
1997-98	Vancouver	NHL	82	51	39	90	48	13	6	4	329	15.5	5	....	....	....	....	....	....	....	....	....	....	....	....
	Russia	Olympics	6	*9	0	9	2	....	....	....	....	....	....	....	....	....	....	....	....	....	....	....	....	....	....
1998-99	Florida	NHL	11	13	3	16	4	5	1	0	44	29.5	3	1	0.0	21:41	....	....	....	....	....	....	....	....	....
99-2000	Florida	NHL	74	*58	36	94	16	11	2	14	360	16.1	25	1	0.0	24:23	4	1	3	4	2	1	0	0	23:58
2000-01	Florida	NHL	82	*59	33	92	58	19	5	8	384	15.4	–2	5	20.0	26:52	....	....	....	....	....	....	....	....	....
2001-02	Florida	NHL	56	22	27	49	56	9	1	1	238	9.2	–14	7	28.6	25:18	....	....	....	....	....	....	....	....	....
	Russia	Olympics	6	2	1	3	8	....	....	....	....	....	....	....	....	....	....	....	....	....	....	....	....	....	....
	NY Rangers	NHL	12	12	8	20	6	3	0	1	49	24.5	9	1	0.0	23:43	....	....	....	....	....	....	....	....	....
2002-03	NY Rangers	NHL	39	19	11	30	16	5	1	3	136	14.0	4	3	0.0	18:56	....	....	....	....	....	....	....	....	....
	NHL Totals		**702**	**437**	**342**	**779**	**484**	**121**	**34**	**59**	**3130**	**14.0**		**18**	**16.7**	**24:24**	**64**	**35**	**35**	**70**	**74**	**6**	**2**	**3**	**23:58**

Calder Memorial Trophy (1992) • NHL First All-Star Team (1994) • Best Forward at Olympic Games (1998) • NHL Second All-Star Team (2000, 2001) • Maurice "Rocket" Richard Trophy (2000, 2001)

Played in NHL All-Star Game (1993, 1994, 1997, 1998, 2000, 2001)

Traded to **Florida** by **Vancouver** with Bret Hedican, Brad Ference and Vancouver's 3rd round choice (Robert Fried) in 2000 Entry Draft for Ed Jovanovski, Dave Gagner, Mike Brown, Kevin Weekes and Florida's 1st round choice (Nathan Smith) in 2000 Entry Draft, January 17, 1999. • Missed majority of 1998-99 season after demanding trade (August 10, 1998) and recovering from knee injury suffered in game vs. Pittsburgh, February 5, 1999. Traded to **NY Rangers** by **Florida** with Florida's 2nd round choice (Lee Falardeau) in 2002 Entry Draft for Igor Ulanov, Filip Novak, NY Rangers' 1st (later traded to Calgary – Calgary selected Eric Nystrom) and 2nd (Rob Globke) round choices in 2002 Entry Draft and NY Rangers' 4th round choice (later traded to Atlanta- Atlanta selected Guillaume Desbiens) in 2003 Entry Draft, March 18, 2002. • Missed majority of 2002-03 season recovering from knee injury originally suffered in game vs. Buffalo, December 6, 2002.

BURE, Valeri

(boo-RAY, VAL-uhr-ee) **FLA.**

Right wing. Shoots right. 5'10", 185 lbs. Born, Moscow, USSR, June 13, 1974. Montreal's 2nd choice, 33rd overall, in 1992 Entry Draft.

Season	Club	League	GP	G	A	Pts	PIM	PP	SH	GW	S	%	+/-	TF	F%	Min	GP	G	A	Pts	PIM	PP	SH	GW	Min
1990-91	CSKA Moscow	USSR	3	0	0	0	0	....	....	....	....	....	....	....	....	....	....	....	....	....	....	....	....	....	....
1991-92	Spokane Chiefs	WHL	53	27	22	49	78	....	....	....	....	....	....	....	....	....	10	11	6	17	10	....	....	....	....
1992-93	Spokane Chiefs	WHL	66	68	79	147	49	....	....	....	....	....	....	....	....	....	9	6	11	17	14	....	....	....	....
1993-94	Spokane Chiefs	WHL	59	40	62	102	48	....	....	....	....	....	....	....	....	....	3	5	3	8	2	....	....	....	....
1994-95	Fredericton	AHL	45	23	25	48	32	....	....	....	....	....	....	....	....	....	....	....	....	....	....	....	....	....	....
	Montreal	NHL	24	3	1	4	6	0	0	1	39	7.7	–1	....	....	....	....	....	....	....	....	....	....	....	....
1995-96	Montreal	NHL	77	22	20	42	28	5	0	1	143	15.4	10	....	....	....	6	0	1	1	6	0	0	0	....
1996-97	Montreal	NHL	64	14	21	35	6	4	0	2	131	10.7	4	....	....	....	5	0	1	1	2	0	0	0	....
1997-98	Montreal	NHL	50	7	22	29	33	2	0	1	134	5.2	–5	....	....	....	....	....	....	....	....	....	....	....	....
	Calgary	NHL	16	5	4	9	2	0	0	1	45	11.1	0	....	....	....	....	....	....	....	....	....	....	....	....
	Russia	Olympics	6	1	0	1	0	....	....	....	....	....	....	....	....	....	....	....	....	....	....	....	....	....	....
1998-99	Calgary	NHL	80	26	27	53	22	7	0	4	260	10.0	0	15	40.0	16:11	....	....	....	....	....	....	....	....	....
99-2000	Calgary	NHL	82	35	40	75	50	13	0	6	308	11.4	–7	8	25.0	20:58	....	....	....	....	....	....	....	....	....
2000-01	Calgary	NHL	78	27	28	55	26	16	0	2	276	9.8	–21	9	11.1	19:01	....	....	....	....	....	....	....	....	....
2001-02	Florida	NHL	31	8	10	18	12	2	0	1	100	8.0	–3	30	33.3	18:36	....	....	....	....	....	....	....	....	....
	Russia	Olympics	6	1	0	1	2	....	....	....	....	....	....	....	....	....	....	....	....	....	....	....	....	....	....
2002-03	Florida	NHL	46	5	21	26	10	3	0	2	150	3.3	–11	19	31.6	18:38	....	....	....	....	....	....	....	....	....
	St. Louis	NHL	5	0	2	2	0	0	0	0	11	0.0	–2	0	0.0	15:11	6	0	2	2	8	0	0	0	11:14
	NHL Totals		**553**	**152**	**196**	**348**	**195**	**52**	**0**	**21**	**1597**	**9.5**		**81**	**30.9**	**18:39**	**17**	**0**	**4**	**4**	**16**	**0**	**0**	**0**	**11:14**

WHL West First All-Star Team (1993) • WHL West Second All-Star Team (1994)

Played in NHL All-Star Game (2000)

Traded to **Calgary** by **Montreal** with Montreal's 4th round choice (Shaun Sutter) in 1998 Entry Draft for Jonas Hoglund and Zarley Zalapski, February 1, 1998. Traded to **Florida** by **Calgary** with Jason Wiemer for Rob Niedermayer and Philadelphia's 2nd round choice (previously acquired, Calgary selected Andrei Medvedev) in 2001 Entry Draft, June 24, 2001. • Missed majority of 2001-02 season recovering from knee injury suffered in game vs. Vancouver, October 16, 2001. Traded to **St. Louis** by **Florida** with future considerations for Mike Van Ryn, March 11, 2003. Claimed on waivers by **Florida**, June 26, 2003.

BUTENSCHON, Sven
(BUH-tehn-shohn, SVEHN) **NYI**

Defense. Shoots left. 6'4", 215 lbs. Born, Itzehoe, West Germany, March 22, 1976. Pittsburgh's 3rd choice, 57th overall, in 1994 Entry Draft.

Season	Club	League	Regular Season GP	G	A	Pts	PIM	PP	SH	GW	S	%	+/-	TF	F%	Min	Playoffs GP	G	A	Pts	PIM	PP	SH	GW	Min
1991-92	Eastman Selects	MMHL	36	2	10	12	110	....	....	....	....	....	....	....	....	....	....	....	....	....	....	....	....	....	....
1992-93	Eastman Selects	MMHL	35	14	22	36	101	....	....	....	....	....	....	....	....	....	....	....	....	....	....	....	....	....	....
1993-94	Brandon	WHL	70	3	19	22	51	....	....	....	....	....	....	....	....	....	4	0	0	0	6	....	....	....	....
1994-95	Brandon	WHL	21	1	5	6	44	....	....	....	....	....	....	....	....	....	18	1	2	3	11	....	....	....	....
1995-96	Brandon	WHL	70	4	37	41	99	....	....	....	....	....	....	....	....	....	19	1	12	13	18	....	....	....	....
1996-97	Cleveland	IHL	75	3	12	15	68	....	....	....	....	....	....	....	....	....	10	0	1	1	4	....	....	....	....
1997-98	**Pittsburgh**	**NHL**	**8**	**0**	**0**	**0**	**6**	**0**	**0**	**0**	**4**	**0.0**	**–1**	....	....	....	....	....	....	....	....	....	....	....	....
	Syracuse Crunch	AHL	65	14	23	37	66	....	....	....	....	....	....	....	....	....	5	1	2	3	0	....	....	....	....
1998-99	**Pittsburgh**	**NHL**	**17**	**0**	**0**	**0**	**6**	**0**	**0**	**0**	**8**	**0.0**	**–7**	**0**	**0.0**	**13:08**	....	....	....	....	....	....	....	....	....
	Houston Aeros	IHL	57	1	4	5	81	....	....	....	....	....	....	....	....	....	....	....	....	....	....	....	....	....	....
99-2000	**Pittsburgh**	**NHL**	**3**	**0**	**0**	**0**	**0**	**0**	**0**	**0**	**2**	**0.0**	**3**	**0**	**0.0**	**16:25**	....	....	....	....	....	....	....	....	....
	Wilkes-Barre	AHL	75	19	21	40	101	....	....	....	....	....	....	....	....	....	....	....	....	....	....	....	....	....	....
2000-01	**Pittsburgh**	**NHL**	**5**	**0**	**1**	**1**	**2**	**0**	**0**	**0**	**6**	**0.0**	**1**	**0**	**0.0**	**17:51**	....	....	....	....	....	....	....	....	....
	Wilkes-Barre	AHL	55	7	28	35	85	....	....	....	....	....	....	....	....	....	....	....	....	....	....	....	....	....	....
	Edmonton	**NHL**	**7**	**1**	**1**	**2**	**2**	**0**	**0**	**0**	**3**	**33.3**	**2**	**0**	**0.0**	**11:07**	....	....	....	....	....	....	....	....	....
2001-02	**Edmonton**	**NHL**	**14**	**0**	**0**	**0**	**4**	**0**	**0**	**0**	**8**	**0.0**	**0**	**0**	**0.0**	**9:39**	....	....	....	....	....	....	....	....	....
	Hamilton	AHL	61	9	35	44	88	....	....	....	....	....	....	....	....	....	....	....	....	....	....	....	....	....	....
2002-03	**NY Islanders**	**NHL**	**37**	**0**	**4**	**4**	**26**	**0**	**0**	**0**	**19**	**0.0**	**–6**	**0**	**0.0**	**12:26**	....	....	....	....	....	....	....	....	....
	Bridgeport	AHL	36	3	13	16	58	....	....	....	....	....	....	....	....	....	9	3	6	9	6	....	....	....	....
	NHL Totals		**91**	**1**	**6**	**7**	**46**	**0**	**0**	**0**	**50**	**2.0**		**0**	**0.0**	**12:28**	....	....	....	....	....	....	....	....	....

Traded to **Edmonton** by **Pittsburgh** for Dan LaCouture, March 13, 2001. Signed as a free agent by **Florida**, July 9, 2002. Traded to **NY Islanders** by **Florida** for Juraj Kolnik and NY Islanders' 9th round choice (later traded to San Jose – San Jose selected Carter Lee) in 2003 Entry Draft, October 11, 2003.

BUTSAYEV, Yuri
(buht-SIGH-ehv, YOO-ree) **ATL.**

Left wing. Shoots left. 6', 195 lbs. Born, Togliatti, USSR, October 11, 1978. Detroit's 1st choice, 49th overall, in 1997 Entry Draft.

Season	Club	League	Regular Season GP	G	A	Pts	PIM	PP	SH	GW	S	%	+/-	TF	F%	Min	Playoffs GP	G	A	Pts	PIM	PP	SH	GW	Min
1995-96	Lada Togliatti 2	CIS-2	35	19	7	26	....	....	....	....	....	....	....	....	....	....	....	....	....	....	....	....	....	....	....
	Lada Togliatti	CIS	1	0	0	0	0	....	....	....	....	....	....	....	....	....	....	....	....	....	....	....	....	....	....
1996-97	Lada Togliatti	Russia	42	13	11	24	38	....	....	....	....	....	....	....	....	....	11	2	2	4	8	....	....	....	....
1997-98	Lada Togliatti	Russia	44	8	9	17	63	....	....	....	....	....	....	....	....	....	....	....	....	....	....	....	....	....	....
	Lada Togliatti	EuroHL	6	2	0	2	8	....	....	....	....	....	....	....	....	....	....	....	....	....	....	....	....	....	....
1998-99	Dynamo Moscow	Russia	1	0	1	1	0	....	....	....	....	....	....	....	....	....	....	....	....	....	....	....	....	....	....
	Lada Togliatti	Russia	39	10	7	17	55	....	....	....	....	....	....	....	....	....	7	1	2	3	14	....	....	....	....
99-2000	**Detroit**	**NHL**	**57**	**5**	**3**	**8**	**12**	**0**	**0**	**0**	**46**	**10.9**	**–6**	**22**	**40.9**	**9:36**	....	....	....	....	....	....	....	....	....
	Cincinnati	AHL	9	0	1	1	0	....	....	....	....	....	....	....	....	....	....	....	....	....	....	....	....	....	....
2000-01	**Detroit**	**NHL**	**15**	**1**	**1**	**2**	**4**	**0**	**0**	**0**	**18**	**5.6**	**–2**	**6**	**33.3**	**9:09**	....	....	....	....	....	....	....	....	....
	Cincinnati	AHL	54	29	17	46	26	....	....	....	....	....	....	....	....	....	4	0	2	2	2	....	....	....	....
2001-02	**Detroit**	**NHL**	**3**	**0**	**0**	**0**	**0**	**0**	**0**	**0**	**4**	**0.0**	**–1**	**0**	**0.0**	**9:44**	....	....	....	....	....	....	....	....	....
	Cincinnati	AHL	61	21	23	44	44	....	....	....	....	....	....	....	....	....	....	....	....	....	....	....	....	....	....
	Atlanta	**NHL**	**8**	**2**	**0**	**2**	**4**	**0**	**0**	**0**	**6**	**33.3**	**1**	**1**	**100.0**	**13:28**	....	....	....	....	....	....	....	....	....
	Chicago Wolves	AHL	4	1	1	2	0	....	....	....	....	....	....	....	....	....	22	7	4	11	20	....	....	....	....
2002-03	**Atlanta**	**NHL**	**16**	**2**	**0**	**2**	**8**	**0**	**0**	**0**	**21**	**9.5**	**–5**	**26**	**30.8**	**12:05**	....	....	....	....	....	....	....	....	....
	Chicago Wolves	AHL	7	6	3	9	0	....	....	....	....	....	....	....	....	....	....	....	....	....	....	....	....	....	....
	Yaroslavl	Russia	19	2	5	7	37	....	....	....	....	....	....	....	....	....	10	2	3	5	4	....	....	....	....
	NHL Totals		**99**	**10**	**4**	**14**	**28**	**0**	**0**	**0**	**95**	**10.5**		**55**	**36.4**	**10:15**	....	....	....	....	....	....	....	....	....

Traded to **Atlanta** by **Detroit** with Detroit's 3rd round choice (later traded to Columbus – Columbus selected Jeff Genovy) in 2002 Entry Draft for Jiri Slegr, March 19, 2002. • Assigned to **Yaroslavl** (Russia) by **Atlanta**, November 22, 2002.

BUZEK, Petr
(BOO-zehk, PEE-tuhr) **CGY.**

Defense. Shoots left. 6'1", 220 lbs. Born, Jihlava, Czech., April 26, 1977. Dallas' 3rd choice, 63rd overall, in 1995 Entry Draft.

Season	Club	League	Regular Season GP	G	A	Pts	PIM	PP	SH	GW	S	%	+/-	TF	F%	Min	Playoffs GP	G	A	Pts	PIM	PP	SH	GW	Min
1993-94	Dukla Jihlava Jr.	Czech-Jr.	3	0	0	0	....	....	....	....	....	....	....	....	....	....	....	....	....	....	....	....	....	....	....
1994-95	HC Dukla Jihlava	Czech	43	2	5	7	47	....	....	....	....	....	....	....	....	....	2	0	0	0	2	....	....	....	....
1995-96	Michigan	IHL	DID NOT PLAY – INJURED																						
1996-97	Michigan	IHL	67	4	6	10	48	....	....	....	....	....	....	....	....	....	....	....	....	....	....	....	....	....	....
1997-98	**Dallas**	**NHL**	**2**	**0**	**0**	**0**	**2**	**0**	**0**	**0**	**0**	**0.0**	**1**	....	....	....	....	....	....	....	....	....	....	....	....
	Michigan	IHL	60	10	15	25	58	....	....	....	....	....	....	....	....	....	2	0	1	1	17	....	....	....	....
1998-99	**Dallas**	**NHL**	**2**	**0**	**0**	**0**	**2**	**0**	**0**	**0**	**0**	**0.0**	**0**	**0**	**0.0**	**13:50**	....	....	....	....	....	....	....	....	....
	Michigan	IHL	74	5	14	19	68	....	....	....	....	....	....	....	....	....	5	0	0	0	10	....	....	....	....
99-2000	**Atlanta**	**NHL**	**63**	**5**	**14**	**19**	**41**	**3**	**0**	**0**	**90**	**5.6**	**–22**	**0**	**0.0**	**18:24**	....	....	....	....	....	....	....	....	....
2000-01	**Atlanta**	**NHL**	**5**	**0**	**0**	**0**	**8**	**0**	**0**	**0**	**11**	**0.0**	**2**	**0**	**0.0**	**17:26**	....	....	....	....	....	....	....	....	....
2001-02	**Atlanta**	**NHL**	**9**	**0**	**0**	**0**	**13**	**0**	**0**	**0**	**2**	**0.0**	**–4**	**0**	**0.0**	**15:58**	....	....	....	....	....	....	....	....	....
	Chicago Wolves	AHL	4	0	1	1	2	....	....	....	....	....	....	....	....	....	....	....	....	....	....	....	....	....	....
	Calgary	**NHL**	**32**	**1**	**3**	**4**	**14**	**0**	**0**	**0**	**34**	**2.9**	**4**	**0**	**0.0**	**17:12**	....	....	....	....	....	....	....	....	....
2002-03	**Calgary**	**NHL**	**44**	**3**	**5**	**8**	**14**	**3**	**0**	**0**	**48**	**6.3**	**–6**	**0**	**0.0**	**14:22**	....	....	....	....	....	....	....	....	....
	NHL Totals		**157**	**9**	**22**	**31**	**94**	**6**	**0**	**0**	**185**	**4.9**		**0**	**0.0**	**16:47**	....	....	....	....	....	....	....	....	....

Played in NHL All-Star Game (2000)

• Missed entire 1995-96 season recovering from injuries suffered in automobile accident, July, 1995. Claimed by **Atlanta** from **Dallas** in Expansion Draft, June 25, 1999. • Missed majority of 2000-01 season recovering from neck injury suffered in game vs. Anaheim, October 17, 2000. Traded to **Calgary** by **Atlanta** for Jeff Cowan and the rights to Kurtis Foster, December 18, 2001.

BYKOV, Dmitri
(BEE-kawv, dih-MEE-tree)

Defense. Shoots left. 5'10", 169 lbs. Born, Izhevsk, USSR, May 5, 1977. Detroit's 6th choice, 258th overall, in 2001 Entry Draft.

Season	Club	League	Regular Season GP	G	A	Pts	PIM	PP	SH	GW	S	%	+/-	TF	F%	Min	Playoffs GP	G	A	Pts	PIM	PP	SH	GW	Min
1995-96	CSK VVS Samara	CIS	50	1	2	3	39	....	....	....	....	....	....	....	....	....	....	....	....	....	....	....	....	....	....
1996-97	CSK VVS Samara	Russia	44	1	6	7	20	....	....	....	....	....	....	....	....	....	2	0	0	0	2	....	....	....	....
1997-98	Lada Togliatti	Russia	9	0	1	1	4	....	....	....	....	....	....	....	....	....	....	....	....	....	....	....	....	....	....
	CSK VVS Samara	Russia	27	0	5	5	14	....	....	....	....	....	....	....	....	....	....	....	....	....	....	....	....	....	....
	Yaroslavl	Russia	10	1	2	3	6	....	....	....	....	....	....	....	....	....	7	0	1	1	10	....	....	....	....
1998-99	Lada Togliatti	Russia	39	0	6	6	24	....	....	....	....	....	....	....	....	....	7	1	0	1	8	....	....	....	....
	CSK VVS Samara	Russia	2	0	0	0	0	....	....	....	....	....	....	....	....	....	....	....	....	....	....	....	....	....	....
99-2000	Ak Bars Kazan	Russia	35	3	8	11	18	....	....	....	....	....	....	....	....	....	18	0	2	2	8	....	....	....	....
	Ak Bars Kazan 2	Russia-3	3	0	1	1	4	....	....	....	....	....	....	....	....	....	....	....	....	....	....	....	....	....	....
2000-01	Ak Bars Kazan	Russia	39	3	8	11	28	....	....	....	....	....	....	....	....	....	4	0	1	1	4	....	....	....	....
2001-02	Ak Bars Kazan	Russia	44	1	1	2	38	....	....	....	....	....	....	....	....	....	11	0	0	0	4	....	....	....	....
2002-03	**Detroit**	**NHL**	**71**	**2**	**10**	**12**	**43**	**1**	**0**	**0**	**58**	**3.4**	**1**	**2**	**100.0**	**18:22**	**4**	**0**	**0**	**0**	**0**	**0**	**0**	**0**	**11:14**
	NHL Totals		**71**	**2**	**10**	**12**	**43**	**1**	**0**	**0**	**58**	**3.4**		**2**	**100.0**	**18:22**	**4**	**0**	**0**	**0**	**0**	**0**	**0**	**0**	**11:14**

BYLSMA, Dan
(BIGHL-zmah, DAN) **ANA.**

Right wing. Shoots left. 6'2", 212 lbs. Born, Grand Haven, MI, September 19, 1970. Winnipeg's 7th choice, 109th overall, in 1989 Entry Draft.

Season	Club	League	Regular Season GP	G	A	Pts	PIM	PP	SH	GW	S	%	+/-	TF	F%	Min	Playoffs GP	G	A	Pts	PIM	PP	SH	GW	Min
1986-87	Oakville Blades	OJHL-B	10	4	9	13	21	....	....	....	....	....	....	....	....	....	....	....	....	....	....	....	....	....	....
	St. Mary's Lincolns	OJHL-B	27	14	28	42	21	....	....	....	....	....	....	....	....	....	....	....	....	....	....	....	....	....	....
1987-88	St. Mary's Lincolns	OJHL-B	40	30	39	69	33	....	....	....	....	....	....	....	....	....	8	8	18	26	....	....	....	....	....
1988-89	Bowling Green	CCHA	32	3	7	10	10	....	....	....	....	....	....	....	....	....	....	....	....	....	....	....	....	....	....
1989-90	Bowling Green	CCHA	44	13	17	30	30	....	....	....	....	....	....	....	....	....	....	....	....	....	....	....	....	....	....
1990-91	Bowling Green	CCHA	40	9	12	21	48	....	....	....	....	....	....	....	....	....	....	....	....	....	....	....	....	....	....
1991-92	Bowling Green	CCHA	34	11	14	25	24	....	....	....	....	....	....	....	....	....	....	....	....	....	....	....	....	....	....
1992-93	Greensboro	ECHL	60	25	35	60	66	....	....	....	....	....	....	....	....	....	1	0	1	1	10	....	....	....	....
	Rochester	AHL	2	0	1	1	0	....	....	....	....	....	....	....	....	....	....	....	....	....	....	....	....	....	....
1993-94	Greensboro	ECHL	25	14	16	30	52	....	....	....	....	....	....	....	....	....	....	....	....	....	....	....	....	....	....
	Albany River Rats	AHL	3	0	1	1	2	....	....	....	....	....	....	....	....	....	....	....	....	....	....	....	....	....	....
	Moncton Hawks	AHL	50	12	16	28	25	....	....	....	....	....	....	....	....	....	21	3	4	7	31	....	....	....	....
1994-95	Phoenix	IHL	81	19	23	42	41	....	....	....	....	....	....	....	....	....	9	4	4	8	4	....	....	....	....
1995-96	**Los Angeles**	**NHL**	**4**	**0**	**0**	**0**	**0**	**0**	**0**	**0**	**6**	**0.0**	**0**	....	....	....	....	....	....	....	....	....	....	....	....
	Phoenix	IHL	78	22	20	42	48	....	....	....	....	....	....	....	....	....	4	1	0	1	2	....	....	....	....
1996-97	**Los Angeles**	**NHL**	**79**	**3**	**6**	**9**	**32**	**0**	**0**	**0**	**86**	**3.5**	**–15**	....	....	....	....	....	....	....	....	....	....	....	....

Season	Club	League	GP	G	A	Pts	PIM	PP	SH	GW	S	%	+/-	TF	F%	Min	GP	G	A	Pts	PIM	PP	SH	GW	Min
			Regular Season														Playoffs								
1997-98	**Los Angeles**	**NHL**	**65**	**3**	**9**	**12**	**33**	**0**	**0**	**0**	**57**	**5.3**	**9**	....	....	....	**2**	**0**	**0**	**0**	**0**	**0**	**0**	**0**	....
	Long Beach	IHL	8	2	3	5	0	....	....	....	....	....	....	....	....	....	....	....	....	....	....	....	....	....	....
1998-99	**Los Angeles**	**NHL**	**8**	**0**	**0**	**0**	**2**	**0**	**0**	**0**	**3**	**0.0**	**–1**	**0**	**0.0**	**9:51**	....	....	....	....	....	....	....	....	....
	Springfield	AHL	2	0	2	2	2	....	....	....	....	....	....	....	....	....	....	....	....	....	....	....	....	....	....
	Long Beach	IHL	58	10	8	18	53	....	....	....	....	....	....	....	....	....	4	0	0	0	8	....	....	....	....
99-2000	**Los Angeles**	**NHL**	**64**	**3**	**6**	**9**	**55**	**0**	**1**	**0**	**43**	**7.0**	**–2**	**62**	**43.6**	**10:23**	**3**	**0**	**0**	**0**	**0**	**0**	**0**	**0**	**10:21**
	Long Beach	IHL	6	0	3	3	2	....	....	....	....	....	....	....	....	....	....	....	....	....	....	....	....	....	....
	Lowell	AHL	2	1	1	2	2	....	....	....	....	....	....	....	....	....	....	....	....	....	....	....	....	....	....
2000-01	**Anaheim**	**NHL**	**82**	**1**	**9**	**10**	**22**	**0**	**0**	**0**	**50**	**2.0**	**–12**	**10**	**50.0**	**11:45**	....	....	....	....	....	....	....	....	....
2001-02	**Anaheim**	**NHL**	**77**	**8**	**9**	**17**	**28**	**0**	**1**	**2**	**72**	**11.1**	**5**	**257**	**42.4**	**11:36**	....	....	....	....	....	....	....	....	....
2002-03	**Anaheim**	**NHL**	**39**	**1**	**4**	**5**	**12**	**0**	**0**	**0**	**23**	**4.3**	**–1**	**28**	**53.6**	**9:29**	**11**	**0**	**1**	**1**	**2**	**0**	**0**	**0**	**9:44**
	NHL Totals		**418**	**19**	**43**	**62**	**184**	**0**	**2**	**2**	**340**	**5.6**		**357**	**43.7**	**10:60**	**16**	**0**	**1**	**1**	**2**	**0**	**0**	**0**	**9:52**

Signed as a free agent by **Los Angeles**, July 7, 1994. Signed as a free agent by **Anaheim**, July 13, 2000. • Missed majority of 2002-03 season recovering from knee (January 28, 2003 vs. San Jose) and head (February 9, 2003 vs. Carolina) injuries.

CAIRNS, Eric

(KAIRNZ, AIR-ihk) **NYI**

Defense. Shoots left. 6'6", 230 lbs. Born, Oakville, Ont., June 27, 1974. NY Rangers' 3rd choice, 72nd overall, in 1992 Entry Draft.

1990-91	Burlington	OJHL-B	37	5	16	21	120	....	....	....	....	....	....	....	....	....	....	....	....	....	....	....	....	....	....
1991-92	Detroit	OHL	64	1	11	12	237	....	....	....	....	....	....	....	....	....	7	0	0	0	31	....	....	....	....
1992-93	Detroit	OHL	64	3	13	16	194	....	....	....	....	....	....	....	....	....	15	0	3	3	24	....	....	....	....
1993-94	Detroit	OHL	59	7	35	42	204	....	....	....	....	....	....	....	....	....	17	0	4	4	46	....	....	....	....
1994-95	Birmingham Bulls	ECHL	11	1	3	4	49	....	....	....	....	....	....	....	....	....	....	....	....	....	....	....	....	....	....
	Binghamton	AHL	27	0	3	3	134	....	....	....	....	....	....	....	....	....	9	1	1	2	28	....	....	....	....
1995-96	Binghamton	AHL	46	1	13	14	192	....	....	....	....	....	....	....	....	....	4	0	0	0	37	....	....	....	....
	Charlotte	ECHL	6	0	1	1	34	....	....	....	....	....	....	....	....	....	....	....	....	....	....	....	....	....	....
1996-97	**NY Rangers**	**NHL**	**40**	**0**	**1**	**1**	**147**	**0**	**0**	**0**	**17**	**0.0**	**–7**	....	....	....	**3**	**0**	**0**	**0**	**0**	**0**	**0**	**0**	....
	Binghamton	AHL	10	1	1	2	96	....	....	....	....	....	....	....	....	....	....	....	....	....	....	....	....	....	....
1997-98	**NY Rangers**	**NHL**	**39**	**0**	**3**	**3**	**92**	**0**	**0**	**0**	**17**	**0.0**	**–3**	....	....	....	....	....	....	....	....	....	....	....	....
	Hartford	AHL	7	1	2	3	43	....	....	....	....	....	....	....	....	....	....	....	....	....	....	....	....	....	....
1998-99	Hartford	AHL	11	0	2	2	49	....	....	....	....	....	....	....	....	....	....	....	....	....	....	....	....	....	....
	NY Islanders	**NHL**	**9**	**0**	**3**	**3**	**23**	**0**	**0**	**0**	**2**	**0.0**	**1**	**0**	**0.0**	**10:15**	....	....	....	....	....	....	....	....	....
	Lowell	AHL	24	0	0	0	91	....	....	....	....	....	....	....	....	....	3	1	0	1	32	....	....	....	....
99-2000	**NY Islanders**	**NHL**	**67**	**2**	**7**	**9**	**196**	**0**	**0**	**0**	**55**	**3.6**	**–5**	**0**	**0.0**	**17:43**	....	....	....	....	....	....	....	....	....
	Providence Bruins	AHL	4	1	1	2	14	....	....	....	....	....	....	....	....	....	....	....	....	....	....	....	....	....	....
2000-01	**NY Islanders**	**NHL**	**45**	**2**	**2**	**4**	**106**	**0**	**0**	**0**	**21**	**9.5**	**–18**	**1**	**0.0**	**16:24**	....	....	....	....	....	....	....	....	....
2001-02	**NY Islanders**	**NHL**	**74**	**2**	**5**	**7**	**176**	**0**	**0**	**1**	**34**	**5.9**	**–2**	**0**	**0.0**	**11:09**	**7**	**0**	**0**	**0**	**15**	**0**	**0**	**0**	**13:54**
2002-03	**NY Islanders**	**NHL**	**60**	**1**	**4**	**5**	**124**	**0**	**0**	**0**	**31**	**3.2**	**–7**	**0**	**0.0**	**11:50**	**5**	**0**	**0**	**0**	**13**	**0**	**0**	**0**	**6:02**
	NHL Totals		**334**	**7**	**25**	**32**	**864**	**0**	**0**	**1**	**177**	**4.0**		**1**	**0.0**	**13:56**	**15**	**0**	**0**	**0**	**28**	**0**	**0**	**0**	**10:38**

Claimed on waivers by **NY Islanders** from **NY Rangers**, December 22, 1998.

CAJANEK, Petr

(chuh-YA-nihk, PEE-tuhr) **ST.L.**

Right wing. Shoots left. 5'11", 176 lbs. Born, Gottwaldov, Czech., August 18, 1975. St. Louis' 6th choice, 253rd overall, in 2001 Entry Draft.

1993-94	AC ZPS Zlin	Czech	34	5	4	9	....	....	....	....	....	....	....	....	....	....	3	0	0	0	....	....	....	....	....
1994-95	AC ZPS Zlin	Czech	35	7	9	16	8	....	....	....	....	....	....	....	....	....	12	2	6	8	4	....	....	....	....
1995-96	AC ZPS Zlin	Czech	36	8	11	19	32	....	....	....	....	....	....	....	....	....	8	2	6	8	8	....	....	....	....
1996-97	AC ZPS Zlin	Czech	50	9	30	39	46	....	....	....	....	....	....	....	....	....	....	....	....	....	....	....	....	....	....
1997-98	Zlin	Czech	46	19	27	46	117	....	....	....	....	....	....	....	....	....	....	....	....	....	....	....	....	....	....
1998-99	Zlin	Czech	49	15	33	48	123	....	....	....	....	....	....	....	....	....	11	5	7	12	12	....	....	....	....
99-2000	Zlin	Czech	50	23	34	57	66	....	....	....	....	....	....	....	....	....	4	1	0	1	0	....	....	....	....
2000-01	Zlin	Czech	52	18	31	49	105	....	....	....	....	....	....	....	....	....	6	0	4	4	22	....	....	....	....
2001-02	Zlin	Czech	49	20	44	64	64	....	....	....	....	....	....	....	....	....	11	5	7	12	10	....	....	....	....
	Czech Republic	Olympics	4	0	0	0	0	....	....	....	....	....	....	....	....	....	....	....	....	....	....	....	....	....	....
2002-03	**St. Louis**	**NHL**	**51**	**9**	**29**	**38**	**20**	**2**	**2**	**1**	**90**	**10.0**	**16**	**793**	**48.4**	**15:56**	**2**	**0**	**0**	**0**	**2**	**0**	**0**	**0**	**11:07**
	NHL Totals		**51**	**9**	**29**	**38**	**20**	**2**	**2**	**1**	**90**	**10.0**		**793**	**48.4**	**15:56**	**2**	**0**	**0**	**0**	**2**	**0**	**0**	**0**	**11:07**

CALDER, Kyle

(KAWL-dehr, KIGHL) **CHI.**

Left wing. Shoots left. 5'11", 180 lbs. Born, Mannville, Alta., January 5, 1979. Chicago's 7th choice, 130th overall, in 1997 Entry Draft.

1994-95	Leduc Oil Barons	AMHL	27	25	32	57	22	....	....	....	....	....	....	....	....	....	....	....	....	....	....	....	....	....	....
1995-96	Regina Pats	WHL	27	1	7	8	10	....	....	....	....	....	....	....	....	....	11	0	0	0	0	....	....	....	....
1996-97	Regina Pats	WHL	62	25	34	59	17	....	....	....	....	....	....	....	....	....	5	3	0	3	6	....	....	....	....
1997-98	Regina Pats	WHL	62	27	50	77	58	....	....	....	....	....	....	....	....	....	2	0	1	1	0	....	....	....	....
1998-99	Regina Pats	WHL	34	23	28	51	29	....	....	....	....	....	....	....	....	....	....	....	....	....	....	....	....	....	....
	Kamloops Blazers	WHL	27	19	18	37	30	....	....	....	....	....	....	....	....	....	15	6	10	16	6	....	....	....	....
99-2000	**Chicago**	**NHL**	**8**	**1**	**1**	**2**	**2**	**0**	**0**	**0**	**5**	**20.0**	**–3**	**2**	**0.0**	**9:59**	....	....	....	....	....	....	....	....	....
	Cleveland	IHL	74	14	22	36	43	....	....	....	....	....	....	....	....	....	9	2	2	4	14	....	....	....	....
2000-01	**Chicago**	**NHL**	**43**	**5**	**10**	**15**	**14**	**0**	**0**	**1**	**63**	**7.9**	**–4**	**2**	**0.0**	**12:43**	....	....	....	....	....	....	....	....	....
	Norfolk Admirals	AHL	37	12	15	27	21	....	....	....	....	....	....	....	....	....	9	2	6	8	2	....	....	....	....
2001-02	**Chicago**	**NHL**	**81**	**17**	**36**	**53**	**47**	**6**	**0**	**3**	**133**	**12.8**	**8**	**0**	**0.0**	**16:33**	**5**	**2**	**0**	**2**	**2**	**1**	**0**	**0**	**16:45**
2002-03	**Chicago**	**NHL**	**82**	**15**	**27**	**42**	**40**	**7**	**0**	**2**	**164**	**9.1**	**–6**	**4**	**25.0**	**16:43**	....	....	....	....	....	....	....	....	....
	NHL Totals		**214**	**38**	**74**	**112**	**103**	**13**	**0**	**6**	**365**	**10.4**		**8**	**12.5**	**15:36**	**5**	**2**	**0**	**2**	**2**	**1**	**0**	**0**	**16:45**

CAMMALLERI, Michael

(kam-UH-LAIR-ee, MIGHK-uhl)) **L.A.**

Center. Shoots left. 5'9", 180 lbs. Born, Richmond Hill, Ont., June 8, 1982. Los Angeles' 3rd choice, 49th overall, in 2001 Entry Draft.

1997-98	Bramalea Blues	OPJHL	46	36	52	88	30	....	....	....	....	....	....	....	....	....	....	....	....	....	....	....	....	....	....
1998-99	Bramalea Blues	OPJHL	41	31	72	103	51	....	....	....	....	....	....	....	....	....	....	....	....	....	....	....	....	....	....
99-2000	U. of Michigan	CCHA	39	13	13	26	32	....	....	....	....	....	....	....	....	....	....	....	....	....	....	....	....	....	....
2000-01	U. of Michigan	CCHA	42	*29	32	61	24	....	....	....	....	....	....	....	....	....	....	....	....	....	....	....	....	....	....
2001-02	U. of Michigan	CCHA	29	23	21	44	28	....	....	....	....	....	....	....	....	....	....	....	....	....	....	....	....	....	....
2002-03	**Los Angeles**	**NHL**	**28**	**5**	**3**	**8**	**22**	**2**	**0**	**2**	**40**	**12.5**	**–4**	**253**	**51.4**	**14:05**	....	....	....	....	....	....	....	....	....
	Manchester	AHL	13	5	15	20	12	....	....	....	....	....	....	....	....	....	....	....	....	....	....	....	....	....	....
	NHL Totals		**28**	**5**	**3**	**8**	**22**	**2**	**0**	**2**	**40**	**12.5**		**253**	**51.4**	**14:05**	....	....	....	....	....	....	....	....	....

OPJHL Rookie of the Year (1998) • CCHA First All-Star Team (2001) • NCAA West Second All-American Team (2001) • CCHA Second All-Star Team (2002) • NCAA West First All-American Team (2002)
• Missed majority of 2002-03 season recovering from head injury suffered in game vs. San Jose, January 28, 2003.

CAMPBELL, Brian

(KAM-behl, BRIGH-uhn) **BUF.**

Defense. Shoots left. 6', 190 lbs. Born, Strathroy, Ont., May 23, 1979. Buffalo's 7th choice, 156th overall, in 1997 Entry Draft.

1994-95	Petrolia Oil Barons	OJHL-B	49	11	27	38	43	....	....	....	....	....	....	....	....	....	....	....	....	....	....	....	....	....	....
1995-96	Ottawa 67's	OHL	66	5	22	27	23	....	....	....	....	....	....	....	....	....	4	0	1	1	2	....	....	....	....
1996-97	Ottawa 67's	OHL	66	7	36	43	12	....	....	....	....	....	....	....	....	....	24	2	11	13	8	....	....	....	....
1997-98	Ottawa 67's	OHL	66	14	39	53	31	....	....	....	....	....	....	....	....	....	13	1	14	15	0	....	....	....	....
1998-99	Ottawa 67's	OHL	62	12	75	87	27	....	....	....	....	....	....	....	....	....	9	2	10	12	6	....	....	....	....
	Ottawa 67's	M-Cup	5	1	3	4	2	....	....	....	....	....	....	....	....	....	....	....	....	....	....	....	....	....	....
	Rochester	AHL	....	....	....	....	....	....	....	....	....	....	....	....	....	....	2	0	0	0	0	....	....	....	....
99-2000	**Buffalo**	**NHL**	**12**	**1**	**4**	**5**	**4**	**0**	**0**	**0**	**10**	**10.0**	**–2**	**0**	**0.0**	**15:48**	....	....	....	....	....	....	....	....	....
	Rochester	AHL	67	2	24	26	22	....	....	....	....	....	....	....	....	....	21	0	3	3	0	....	....	....	....
2000-01	**Buffalo**	**NHL**	**8**	**0**	**0**	**0**	**2**	**0**	**0**	**0**	**7**	**0.0**	**–2**	**0**	**0.0**	**15:40**	....	....	....	....	....	....	....	....	....
	Rochester	AHL	65	7	25	32	24	....	....	....	....	....	....	....	....	....	4	0	1	1	0	....	....	....	....
2001-02	**Buffalo**	**NHL**	**29**	**3**	**3**	**6**	**12**	**0**	**0**	**0**	**30**	**10.0**	**0**	**1**	**0.0**	**15:18**	....	....	....	....	....	....	....	....	....
	Rochester	AHL	45	2	35	37	13	....	....	....	....	....	....	....	....	....	....	....	....	....	....	....	....	....	....
2002-03	**Buffalo**	**NHL**	**65**	**2**	**17**	**19**	**20**	**0**	**0**	**1**	**90**	**2.2**	**–8**	**1**	**0.0**	**18:40**	....	....	....	....	....	....	....	....	....
	NHL Totals		**114**	**6**	**24**	**30**	**38**	**0**	**0**	**1**	**137**	**4.4**		**2**	**0.0**	**17:18**	....	....	....	....	....	....	....	....	....

OHL First All-Star Team (1999) • OHL MVP (1999) • Canadian Major Junior First All-Star Team (1999) • Canadian Major Junior Player of the Year (1999) • George Parsons Trophy (Memorial Cup Most Sportsmanlike Player) (1999)

CAMPBELL, Jim

(KAM-behl, JIHM)

Right wing. Shoots right. 6'2", 205 lbs. Born, Worcester, MA, April 3, 1973. Montreal's 2nd choice, 28th overall, in 1991 Entry Draft.

			Regular Season														Playoffs								
Season	Club	League	GP	G	A	Pts	PIM	PP	SH	GW	S	%	+/-	TF	F%	Min	GP	G	A	Pts	PIM	PP	SH	GW	Min
1988-89	Northfield Prep	Hi-School	12	12	8	20	6																		
1989-90	Northfield Prep	Hi-School	8	14	7	21	8																		
1990-91	Lawrence Prep	Hi-School	26	36	47	83	26																		
1991-92	Hull Olympiques	QMJHL	64	41	44	85	51										6	7	3	10	8				
1992-93	Hull Olympiques	QMJHL	50	42	29	71	66										8	11	4	15	43				
1993-94	Team USA	Nat-Tm	56	24	33	57	59																		
	United States	Olympics	8	0	0	0	6																		
	Fredericton	AHL	19	6	17	23	6																		
1994-95	Fredericton	AHL	77	27	24	51	103										12	0	7	7	8				
1995-96	Fredericton	AHL	44	28	23	51	24																		
	Anaheim	**NHL**	**16**	**2**	**3**	**5**	**36**	**1**	**0**	**0**	**25**	**8.0**	**0**												
	Baltimore Bandits	AHL	16	13	7	20	8										12	7	5	12	10				
1996-97	**St. Louis**	**NHL**	**68**	**23**	**20**	**43**	**68**	**5**	**0**	**6**	**169**	**13.6**	**3**				**4**	**1**	**0**	**1**	**6**	**1**	**0**	**0**	
1997-98	**St. Louis**	**NHL**	**76**	**22**	**19**	**41**	**55**	**7**	**0**	**6**	**147**	**15.0**	**0**				**10**	**7**	**3**	**10**	**12**	**4**	**0**	**2**	
1998-99	**St. Louis**	**NHL**	**55**	**4**	**21**	**25**	**41**	**1**	**0**	**0**	**99**	**4.0**	**-8**	**7**	**42.9**	**13:34**									
99-2000	Manitoba Moose	IHL	10	1	3	4	10																		
	St. Louis	**NHL**	**2**	**0**	**0**	**0**	**9**	**0**	**0**	**0**	**6**	**0.0**	**0**	**0**	**0.0**	**15:17**									
	Worcester IceCats	AHL	66	31	34	65	88										9	1	2	3	6				
2000-01	**Montreal**	**NHL**	**57**	**9**	**11**	**20**	**53**	**6**	**0**	**1**	**81**	**11.1**	**-3**	**14**	**42.9**	**10:19**									
	Quebec Citadelles	AHL	3	5	0	5	6																		
2001-02	**Chicago**	**NHL**	**9**	**1**	**1**	**2**	**4**	**0**	**0**	**0**	**12**	**8.3**	**-3**	**1**	**0.0**	**13:21**									
	Norfolk Admirals	AHL	44	11	14	25	26										4	3	1	4	2				
2002-03	**Florida**	**NHL**	**1**	**0**	**0**	**0**	**0**	**0**	**0**	**0**	**3**	**0.0**	**0**	**1**	**0.0**	**8:56**									
	San Antonio	AHL	64	16	37	53	55										1	0	0	0	0				
	NHL Totals		**284**	**61**	**75**	**136**	**266**	**20**	**0**	**13**	**542**	**11.3**		**23**	**39.1**	**12:03**	**14**	**8**	**3**	**11**	**18**	**5**	**0**	**2**	....

NHL All-Rookie Team (1997)

Traded to **Anaheim** by **Montreal** for Robert Dirk, January 21, 1996. Signed as a free agent by **St. Louis**, July 11, 1996. Loaned to **Manitoba** (IHL) by **St. Louis**, October 4, 1999 and recalled November 1, 1999. Signed as a free agent by **Montreal**, August 21, 2000. Signed as a free agent by **Chicago**, November 19, 2001. Signed as a free agent by **Florida**, July 19, 2002.

CARNEY, Keith

(KAHRN-nee, KEETH) **ANA.**

Defense. Shoots left. 6'2", 211 lbs. Born, Providence, RI, February 3, 1970. Buffalo's 3rd choice, 76th overall, in 1988 Entry Draft.

			Regular Season														Playoffs								
Season	Club	League	GP	G	A	Pts	PIM	PP	SH	GW	S	%	+/-	TF	F%	Min	GP	G	A	Pts	PIM	PP	SH	GW	Min
1987-88	Mount St. Charles	Hi-School	23	12	43	55	....																		
1988-89	U. of Maine	H-East	40	4	22	26	24																		
1989-90	U. of Maine	H-East	41	3	41	44	43																		
1990-91	U. of Maine	H-East	40	7	49	56	38																		
1991-92	Team USA	Nat-Tm	49	2	17	19	16																		
	Buffalo	**NHL**	**14**	**1**	**2**	**3**	**18**	**1**	**0**	**0**	**17**	**5.9**	**-3**				**7**	**0**	**3**	**3**	**0**	**0**	**0**	**0**	
	Rochester	AHL	24	1	10	11	2										2	0	2	2	0				
1992-93	**Buffalo**	**NHL**	**30**	**2**	**4**	**6**	**55**	**0**	**0**	**1**	**26**	**7.7**	**3**				**8**	**0**	**3**	**3**	**6**	**0**	**0**	**0**	
	Rochester	AHL	41	5	21	26	32																		
1993-94	**Buffalo**	**NHL**	**7**	**1**	**3**	**4**	**4**	**0**	**0**	**0**	**6**	**16.7**	**-1**												
	Chicago	**NHL**	**30**	**3**	**5**	**8**	**35**	**0**	**0**	**0**	**31**	**9.7**	**15**				**6**	**0**	**1**	**1**	**4**	**0**	**0**	**0**	
	Indianapolis Ice	IHL	28	0	14	14	20																		
1994-95	**Chicago**	**NHL**	**18**	**1**	**0**	**1**	**11**	**0**	**0**	**1**	**14**	**7.1**	**-1**				**4**	**0**	**1**	**1**	**0**	**0**	**0**	**0**	
1995-96	**Chicago**	**NHL**	**82**	**5**	**14**	**19**	**94**	**1**	**0**	**1**	**69**	**7.2**	**31**				**10**	**0**	**3**	**3**	**4**	**0**	**0**	**0**	
1996-97	**Chicago**	**NHL**	**81**	**3**	**15**	**18**	**62**	**0**	**0**	**1**	**77**	**3.9**	**26**				**6**	**1**	**1**	**2**	**2**	**0**	**0**	**0**	
1997-98	**Chicago**	**NHL**	**60**	**2**	**13**	**15**	**73**	**0**	**1**	**0**	**53**	**3.8**	**-7**												
	United States	Olympics	4	0	0	0	2																		
	Phoenix	**NHL**	**20**	**1**	**6**	**7**	**18**	**1**	**0**	**0**	**18**	**5.6**	**5**				**6**	**0**	**0**	**0**	**4**	**0**	**0**	**0**	
1998-99	**Phoenix**	**NHL**	**82**	**2**	**14**	**16**	**62**	**0**	**2**	**0**	**62**	**3.2**	**15**	**0**	**0.0**	**22:46**	**7**	**1**	**2**	**3**	**10**	**0**	**0**	**0**	**23:59**
99-2000	**Phoenix**	**NHL**	**82**	**4**	**20**	**24**	**87**	**0**	**0**	**1**	**73**	**5.5**	**11**	**0**	**0.0**	**21:12**	**5**	**0**	**0**	**0**	**17**	**0**	**0**	**0**	**22:38**
2000-01	**Phoenix**	**NHL**	**82**	**2**	**14**	**16**	**86**	**0**	**0**	**0**	**65**	**3.1**	**15**	**0**	**0.0**	**20:53**									
2001-02	**Anaheim**	**NHL**	**60**	**5**	**9**	**14**	**30**	**0**	**0**	**1**	**66**	**7.6**	**14**	**0**	**0.0**	**20:47**									
2002-03	**Anaheim**	**NHL**	**81**	**4**	**18**	**22**	**65**	**0**	**0**	**1**	**87**	**4.6**	**8**	**0**	**0.0**	**0:00**	**21**	**0**	**4**	**4**	**16**	**0**	**0**	**0**	
	NHL Totals		**729**	**36**	**137**	**173**	**700**	**3**	**3**	**7**	**664**	**5.4**		**0**	**0.0**	**16:58**	**80**	**2**	**18**	**20**	**63**	**0**	**0**	**0**	**23:25**

Hockey East Second All-Star Team (1990) • NCAA East Second All-American Team (1990) • Hockey East First All-Star Team (1991) • NCAA East First All-American Team (1991)

Traded to **Chicago** by **Buffalo** with Buffalo's 6th round choice (Marc Magliarditi) in 1995 Entry Draft for Craig Muni and Chicago's 5th round choice (Daniel Bienvenue) in 1995 Entry Draft, October 26, 1993. Traded to **Phoenix** by **Chicago** with Jim Cummins for Chad Kilger and Jayson More, March 4, 1998. Traded to **Anaheim** by **Phoenix** for Calgary's 2nd round choice (previously acquired, later traded back to Calgary – Calgary selected Andrei Taratukhin) in 2001 Entry Draft, June 19, 2001.

CARTER, Anson

(KAHR-tuhr, AN-sohn) **NYR**

Right wing. Shoots right. 6'1", 200 lbs. Born, Toronto, Ont., June 6, 1974. Quebec's 11th choice, 220th overall, in 1992 Entry Draft.

			Regular Season														Playoffs								
Season	Club	League	GP	G	A	Pts	PIM	PP	SH	GW	S	%	+/-	TF	F%	Min	GP	G	A	Pts	PIM	PP	SH	GW	Min
1989-90	Don Mills	MTHL	40	15	47	62	105																		
1990-91	Don Mills	MTHL	67	69	73	142	43																		
1991-92	Wexford Raiders	MTJHL	42	18	22	40	24																		
1992-93	Michigan State	CCHA	34	15	7	22	20																		
1993-94	Michigan State	CCHA	39	30	24	54	36																		
1994-95	Michigan State	CCHA	39	34	17	51	40																		
1995-96	Michigan State	CCHA	42	23	20	43	36																		
1996-97	**Washington**	**NHL**	**19**	**3**	**2**	**5**	**7**	**1**	**0**	**1**	**28**	**10.7**	**0**												
	Portland Pirates	AHL	27	19	19	38	11																		
	Boston	**NHL**	**19**	**8**	**5**	**13**	**2**	**1**	**1**	**1**	**51**	**15.7**	**-7**												
1997-98	**Boston**	**NHL**	**78**	**16**	**27**	**43**	**31**	**6**	**0**	**4**	**179**	**8.9**	**7**				**6**	**1**	**1**	**2**	**0**	**0**	**0**	**0**	
1998-99	Utah Grizzlies	IHL	6	1	1	2	0																		
	Boston	**NHL**	**55**	**24**	**16**	**40**	**22**	**6**	**0**	**6**	**123**	**19.5**	**7**	**172**	**43.0**	**18:44**	**12**	**4**	**3**	**7**	**0**	**1**	**0**	**1**	**21:31**
99-2000	**Boston**	**NHL**	**59**	**22**	**25**	**47**	**14**	**4**	**0**	**1**	**144**	**15.3**	**8**	**793**	**48.2**	**20:31**									
2000-01	**Edmonton**	**NHL**	**61**	**16**	**26**	**42**	**23**	**7**	**1**	**4**	**102**	**15.7**	**1**	**80**	**47.5**	**18:13**	**6**	**3**	**1**	**4**	**4**	**1**	**0**	**1**	**19:42**
2001-02	**Edmonton**	**NHL**	**82**	**28**	**32**	**60**	**25**	**12**	**0**	**6**	**181**	**15.5**	**3**	**316**	**46.5**	**19:18**									
2002-03	**Edmonton**	**NHL**	**68**	**25**	**30**	**55**	**20**	**10**	**0**	**1**	**176**	**14.2**	**-11**	**217**	**43.8**	**19:39**									
	NY Rangers	**NHL**	**11**	**1**	**4**	**5**	**6**	**0**	**0**	**0**	**17**	**5.9**	**0**	**5**	**20.0**	**17:49**									
	NHL Totals		**452**	**143**	**167**	**310**	**150**	**47**	**2**	**24**	**1001**	**14.3**		**1583**	**46.6**	**19:15**	**24**	**8**	**5**	**13**	**4**	**2**	**0**	**2**	**20:54**

CCHA First All-Star Team (1994, 1995) • NCAA West Second All-American Team (1995) • CCHA Second All-Star Team (1996)

Rights transferred to **Colorado** after **Quebec** franchise relocated, June 21, 1995. Traded to **Washington** by **Colorado** for Washington's 4th round choice (Ben Storey) in 1996 Entry Draft, April 3, 1996. Traded to **Boston** by **Washington** with Jim Carey, Jason Allison and Washington's 3rd round choice (Lee Goren) in 1997 Entry Draft for Bill Ranford, Adam Oates and Rick Tocchet, March 1, 1997. Signed as a free agent by **Utah** (IHL) with Boston retaining NHL rights, October 20, 1998. Traded to **Edmonton** by **Boston** with Boston's 1st (Ales Hemsky) and 2nd (Doug Lynch) round choices in 2001 Entry Draft for Bill Guerin and future considerations, November 15, 2000. Traded to **NY Rangers** by **Edmonton** with Ales Pisa for Radek Dvorak and Cory Cross, March 11, 2003.

CASSELS, Andrew

(KAS-uhls, AN-droo) **CBJ**

Center. Shoots left. 6'1", 185 lbs. Born, Bramalea, Ont., July 23, 1969. Montreal's 1st choice, 17th overall, in 1987 Entry Draft.

			Regular Season														Playoffs								
Season	Club	League	GP	G	A	Pts	PIM	PP	SH	GW	S	%	+/-	TF	F%	Min	GP	G	A	Pts	PIM	PP	SH	GW	Min
1985-86	Bramalea Blues	OPJHL	33	18	25	43	26																		
1986-87	Ottawa 67's	OHL	66	26	66	92	28										11	5	9	14	7				
1987-88	Ottawa 67's	OHL	61	48	*103	*151	39										16	8	*24	*32	13				
1988-89	Ottawa 67's	OHL	56	37	97	134	66										12	5	10	15	10				
1989-90	**Montreal**	**NHL**	**6**	**2**	**0**	**2**	**2**	**0**	**0**	**1**	**5**	**40.0**	**1**												
	Sherbrooke	AHL	55	22	45	67	25										12	2	11	13	6				
1990-91	**Montreal**	**NHL**	**54**	**6**	**19**	**25**	**20**	**1**	**0**	**3**	**55**	**10.9**	**2**				**8**	**0**	**2**	**2**	**2**	**0**	**0**	**0**	
1991-92	**Hartford**	**NHL**	**67**	**11**	**30**	**41**	**18**	**2**	**2**	**3**	**99**	**11.1**	**3**				**7**	**2**	**4**	**6**	**6**	**1**	**0**	**0**	
1992-93	**Hartford**	**NHL**	**84**	**21**	**64**	**85**	**62**	**8**	**3**	**1**	**134**	**15.7**	**-11**												
1993-94	**Hartford**	**NHL**	**79**	**16**	**42**	**58**	**37**	**8**	**1**	**3**	**126**	**12.7**	**-21**												
1994-95	**Hartford**	**NHL**	**46**	**7**	**30**	**37**	**18**	**1**	**0**	**1**	**74**	**9.5**	**-3**												
1995-96	**Hartford**	**NHL**	**81**	**20**	**43**	**63**	**39**	**6**	**0**	**1**	**135**	**14.8**	**8**												
1996-97	**Hartford**	**NHL**	**81**	**22**	**44**	**66**	**46**	**8**	**0**	**2**	**142**	**15.5**	**-16**												
1997-98	**Calgary**	**NHL**	**81**	**17**	**27**	**44**	**32**	**6**	**1**	**2**	**138**	**12.3**	**-7**												
1998-99	**Calgary**	**NHL**	**70**	**12**	**25**	**37**	**18**	**4**	**1**	**3**	**97**	**12.4**	**-12**	**1322**	**51.1**	**18:58**									
99-2000	**Vancouver**	**NHL**	**79**	**17**	**45**	**62**	**16**	**6**	**0**	**1**	**109**	**15.6**	**8**	**1127**	**48.3**	**19:19**									

			Regular Season														Playoffs								
Season	Club	League	GP	G	A	Pts	PIM	PP	SH	GW	S	%	+/-	TF	F%	Min	GP	G	A	Pts	PIM	PP	SH	GW	Min
2000-01	Vancouver	NHL	66	12	44	56	10	2	0	1	104	11.5	1	1164	49.9	19:22	....	....	....	....	....	....	....	....	....
2001-02	Vancouver	NHL	53	11	39	50	22	7	0	1	64	17.2	5	866	50.4	17:27	6	2	1	3	0	1	0	0	16:55
2002-03	Columbus	NHL	79	20	48	68	30	9	1	5	113	17.7	–4	1649	48.8	19:52	....	....	....	....	....	....	....	....	....
	NHL Totals		**926**	**194**	**500**	**694**	**370**	**68**	**9**	**28**	**1395**	**13.9**		**6128**	**49.6**	**19:06**	**21**	**4**	**7**	**11**	**8**	**2**	**0**	**0**	**16:55**

OHL Rookie of the Year (1987) • OHL First All-Star Team (1988,1989) • OHL MVP (1988)

Traded to **Hartford** by **Montreal** for Hartford's 2nd round choice (Valeri Bure) in 1992 Entry Draft, September 17, 1991. Transferred to **Carolina** after **Hartford** franchise relocated, June 25, 1997. Traded to **Calgary** by **Carolina** with Jean-Sebastien Giguere for Gary Roberts and Trevor Kidd, August 25, 1997. Signed as a free agent by **Vancouver**, August 19, 1999. Signed as a free agent by **Columbus**, August 15, 2002.

CHAPMAN, Brian

BUF.

Defense. Shoots left. 6'1", 195 lbs. Born, Brockville, Ont., February 10, 1968. Hartford's 3rd choice, 74th overall, in 1986 Entry Draft.

Season	Club	League	GP	G	A	Pts	PIM	PP	SH	GW	S	%	+/-	TF	F%	Min	GP	G	A	Pts	PIM	PP	SH	GW	Min
1984-85	Brockville Braves	OCJHL	50	11	32	43	145	....	....	....	....	....	....	....	....	....	....	....	....	....	....	....	....	....	....
1985-86	Belleville Bulls	OHL	66	6	31	37	168	....	....	....	....	....	....	....	....	....	24	2	6	8	54	....	....	....	....
1986-87	Belleville Bulls	OHL	54	4	32	36	142	....	....	....	....	....	....	....	....	....	6	1	1	2	10	....	....	....	....
	Binghamton	AHL	....	....	....	....	....	....	....	....	....	....	....	....	....	....	1	0	0	0	0	....	....	....	....
1987-88	Belleville Bulls	OHL	63	11	57	68	180	....	....	....	....	....	....	....	....	....	6	1	4	5	13	....	....	....	....
1988-89	Binghamton	AHL	71	5	25	30	216	....	....	....	....	....	....	....	....	....	....	....	....	....	....	....	....	....	....
1989-90	Binghamton	AHL	68	2	15	17	180	....	....	....	....	....	....	....	....	....	....	....	....	....	....	....	....	....	....
1990-91	**Hartford**	**NHL**	**3**	**0**	**0**	**0**	**29**	**0**	**0**	**0**	**0**	**0.0**	**0**	....	....	....	....	....	....	....	....	....	....	....	....
	Springfield	AHL	60	4	23	27	200	....	....	....	....	....	....	....	....	....	18	1	4	5	62	....	....	....	....
1991-92	Springfield	AHL	73	3	26	29	245	....	....	....	....	....	....	....	....	....	10	2	2	4	25	....	....	....	....
1992-93	Springfield	AHL	72	17	34	51	212	....	....	....	....	....	....	....	....	....	15	2	5	7	43	....	....	....	....
1993-94	Phoenix	IHL	78	6	35	41	280	....	....	....	....	....	....	....	....	....	....	....	....	....	....	....	....	....	....
1994-95	Phoenix	IHL	60	2	23	25	181	....	....	....	....	....	....	....	....	....	9	1	5	6	31	....	....	....	....
1995-96	Phoenix	IHL	66	8	11	19	187	....	....	....	....	....	....	....	....	....	4	0	1	1	14	....	....	....	....
1996-97	Phoenix	IHL	69	9	16	25	109	....	....	....	....	....	....	....	....	....	....	....	....	....	....	....	....	....	....
	Long Beach	IHL	14	1	7	8	67	....	....	....	....	....	....	....	....	....	17	0	3	3	38	....	....	....	....
1997-98	Long Beach	IHL	6	0	1	1	15	....	....	....	....	....	....	....	....	....	....	....	....	....	....	....	....	....	....
	Manitoba Moose	IHL	77	3	25	28	159	....	....	....	....	....	....	....	....	....	3	0	0	0	10	....	....	....	....
1998-99	Manitoba Moose	IHL	76	3	15	18	127	....	....	....	....	....	....	....	....	....	5	0	0	0	12	....	....	....	....
99-2000	Manitoba Moose	IHL	80	7	30	37	153	....	....	....	....	....	....	....	....	....	2	0	0	0	2	....	....	....	....
2000-01	Manitoba Moose	IHL	82	5	21	26	126	....	....	....	....	....	....	....	....	....	13	1	2	3	12	....	....	....	....
2001-02	Manitoba Moose	AHL	72	2	30	32	95	....	....	....	....	....	....	....	....	....	7	0	5	5	4	....	....	....	....
2002-03	Manitoba Moose	AHL	60	3	14	17	65	....	....	....	....	....	....	....	....	....	14	0	2	2	20	....	....	....	....
	NHL Totals		**3**	**0**	**0**	**0**	**29**	**0**	**0**	**0**	**0**	**0.0**		....	....	....	....	....	....	....	....	....	....	....	....

Signed as a free agent by **Los Angeles**, July 15, 1993. Traded to **Manitoba** (IHL) by **Long Beach** (IHL) for Russ Romaniuk, October 16, 1997. Signed as a free agent by **Buffalo**, August 21, 2003.

CHARA, Zdeno

(CHAH-rah, ZDEH-noh) **OTT.**

Defense. Shoots left. 6'9", 260 lbs. Born, Trencin, Czech., March 18, 1977. NY Islanders' 3rd choice, 56th overall, in 1996 Entry Draft.

Season	Club	League	GP	G	A	Pts	PIM	PP	SH	GW	S	%	+/-	TF	F%	Min	GP	G	A	Pts	PIM	PP	SH	GW	Min
1994-95	Dukla Trencin-B	Slovak-Jr.	30	22	22	44	113	....	....	....	....	....	....	....	....	....	....	....	....	....	....	....	....	....	....
	Dukla Trencin Jr.	Slovak-Jr.	2	0	0	0	0	....	....	....	....	....	....	....	....	....	....	....	....	....	....	....	....	....	....
1995-96	Dukla Trencin Jr.	Slovak-Jr.	22	1	13	14	80	....	....	....	....	....	....	....	....	....	....	....	....	....	....	....	....	....	....
	HK VTJ Piestany	Slovak-2	10	1	3	4	10	....	....	....	....	....	....	....	....	....	....	....	....	....	....	....	....	....	....
	Sparta Praha Jr.	Czech-Jr.	15	1	2	3	42	....	....	....	....	....	....	....	....	....	....	....	....	....	....	....	....	....	....
	HC Sparta Praha	Czech	1	0	0	0	0	....	....	....	....	....	....	....	....	....	....	....	....	....	....	....	....	....	....
1996-97	Prince George	WHL	49	3	19	22	120	....	....	....	....	....	....	....	....	....	15	1	7	8	45	....	....	....	....
1997-98	**NY Islanders**	**NHL**	**25**	**0**	**1**	**1**	**50**	**0**	**0**	**0**	**10**	**0.0**	**1**	....	....	....	....	....	....	....	....	....	....	....	....
	Kentucky	AHL	48	4	9	13	125	....	....	....	....	....	....	....	....	....	1	0	0	0	4	....	....	....	....
1998-99	**NY Islanders**	**NHL**	**59**	**2**	**6**	**8**	**83**	**0**	**1**	**0**	**56**	**3.6**	**–8**	**0**	**0.0**	**18:54**	....	....	....	....	....	....	....	....	....
	Lowell	AHL	23	2	2	4	47	....	....	....	....	....	....	....	....	....	....	....	....	....	....	....	....	....	....
99-2000	**NY Islanders**	**NHL**	**65**	**2**	**9**	**11**	**57**	**0**	**0**	**1**	**47**	**4.3**	**–27**	**0**	**0.0**	**22:52**	....	....	....	....	....	....	....	....	....
2000-01	**NY Islanders**	**NHL**	**82**	**2**	**7**	**9**	**157**	**0**	**1**	**0**	**83**	**2.4**	**–27**	**0**	**0.0**	**22:20**	....	....	....	....	....	....	....	....	....
2001-02	Dukla Trencin	Slovakia	8	2	2	4	32	....	....	....	....	....	....	....	....	....	....	....	....	....	....	....	....	....	....
	Ottawa	**NHL**	**75**	**10**	**13**	**23**	**156**	**4**	**1**	**2**	**105**	**9.5**	**30**	**0**	**0.0**	**22:16**	**10**	**0**	**1**	**1**	**12**	**0**	**0**	**0**	**26:07**
2002-03	**Ottawa**	**NHL**	**74**	**9**	**30**	**39**	**116**	**3**	**0**	**2**	**168**	**5.4**	**29**	**0**	**0.0**	**24:57**	**18**	**1**	**6**	**7**	**14**	**0**	**0**	**0**	**25:07**
	NHL Totals		**380**	**25**	**66**	**91**	**619**	**7**	**3**	**5**	**469**	**5.3**		**0**	**0.0**	**22:24**	**28**	**1**	**7**	**8**	**26**	**0**	**0**	**0**	**25:28**

Played in NHL All-Star Game (2003)

Traded to **Ottawa** by **NY Islanders** with Bill Muckalt and NY Islanders' 1st round choice (Jason Spezza) in 2001 Entry Draft for Alexei Yashin, June 23, 2001.

CHARTRAND, Brad

(SHAR-trand, BRAD) **L.A.**

Center. Shoots left. 5'11", 185 lbs. Born, Winnipeg, Man., December 14, 1974.

Season	Club	League	GP	G	A	Pts	PIM	PP	SH	GW	S	%	+/-	TF	F%	Min	GP	G	A	Pts	PIM	PP	SH	GW	Min
1988-89	Winnipeg Hawks	MMHL	24	30	50	80	40	....	....	....	....	....	....	....	....	....	....	....	....	....	....	....	....	....	....
1989-90	Winnipeg Hawks	MMHL	24	26	55	81	40	....	....	....	....	....	....	....	....	....	....	....	....	....	....	....	....	....	....
1990-91	Winnipeg Hawks	MMHL	34	26	45	71	40	....	....	....	....	....	....	....	....	....	....	....	....	....	....	....	....	....	....
1991-92	St. James	MJHL	45	24	25	49	32	....	....	....	....	....	....	....	....	....	....	....	....	....	....	....	....	....	....
1992-93	Cornell Big Red	ECAC	26	10	6	16	16	....	....	....	....	....	....	....	....	....	....	....	....	....	....	....	....	....	....
1993-94	Cornell Big Red	ECAC	30	4	14	18	48	....	....	....	....	....	....	....	....	....	....	....	....	....	....	....	....	....	....
1994-95	Cornell Big Red	ECAC	28	9	9	18	10	....	....	....	....	....	....	....	....	....	....	....	....	....	....	....	....	....	....
1995-96	Cornell Big Red	ECAC	34	24	19	43	16	....	....	....	....	....	....	....	....	....	....	....	....	....	....	....	....	....	....
1996-97	Team Canada	Nat-Tm	54	10	14	24	42	....	....	....	....	....	....	....	....	....	....	....	....	....	....	....	....	....	....
1997-98	Team Canada	Nat-Tm	60	24	30	54	47	....	....	....	....	....	....	....	....	....	....	....	....	....	....	....	....	....	....
	Rapperswil	Swiss	8	2	3	5	4	....	....	....	....	....	....	....	....	....	....	....	....	....	....	....	....	....	....
1998-99	St. John's	AHL	64	16	14	30	48	....	....	....	....	....	....	....	....	....	5	0	2	2	2	....	....	....	....
99-2000	**Los Angeles**	**NHL**	**50**	**6**	**6**	**12**	**17**	**0**	**1**	**3**	**51**	**11.8**	**4**	**62**	**53.2**	**11:03**	**4**	**0**	**0**	**0**	**6**	**0**	**0**	**0**	**8:09**
	Lowell	AHL	16	5	10	15	8	....	....	....	....	....	....	....	....	....	....	....	....	....	....	....	....	....	....
	Long Beach	IHL	1	0	0	0	0	....	....	....	....	....	....	....	....	....	3	0	0	0	0	....	....	....	....
2000-01	**Los Angeles**	**NHL**	**4**	**1**	**0**	**1**	**2**	**0**	**0**	**1**	**6**	**16.7**	**–2**	**0**	**0.0**	**11:37**	....	....	....	....	....	....	....	....	....
	Lowell	AHL	72	17	34	51	44	....	....	....	....	....	....	....	....	....	4	0	1	1	8	....	....	....	....
2001-02	**Los Angeles**	**NHL**	**46**	**7**	**9**	**16**	**40**	**0**	**0**	**1**	**49**	**14.3**	**5**	**481**	**53.2**	**12:05**	**7**	**1**	**1**	**2**	**2**	**0**	**0**	**1**	**11:07**
	Manchester	AHL	22	10	12	22	31	....	....	....	....	....	....	....	....	....	....	....	....	....	....	....	....	....	....
2002-03	**Los Angeles**	**NHL**	**62**	**8**	**6**	**14**	**33**	**0**	**1**	**2**	**64**	**12.5**	**–10**	**623**	**51.4**	**12:14**	....	....	....	....	....	....	....	....	....
	NHL Totals		**162**	**22**	**21**	**43**	**92**	**0**	**2**	**7**	**170**	**12.9**		**1166**	**52.2**	**11:49**	**11**	**1**	**1**	**2**	**8**	**0**	**0**	**1**	**10:03**

Signed as a free agent by **Los Angeles**, July 15, 1999. Loaned to **Lowell** (AHL) by **Los Angeles**, January 26, 2000.

CHEBATURKIN, Vladimir

(cheh-bah-TOOR-kihn)

Defense. Shoots left. 6'2", 226 lbs. Born, Tyumen, USSR, April 23, 1975. NY Islanders' 3rd choice, 66th overall, in 1993 Entry Draft.

Season	Club	League	GP	G	A	Pts	PIM	PP	SH	GW	S	%	+/-	TF	F%	Min	GP	G	A	Pts	PIM	PP	SH	GW	Min
1993-94	Kristall Elektrostal	CIS-2	42	4	4	8	38	....	....	....	....	....	....	....	....	....	....	....	....	....	....	....	....	....	....
1994-95	Kristall Elektrostal	CIS	52	2	6	8	90	....	....	....	....	....	....	....	....	....	....	....	....	....	....	....	....	....	....
1995-96	Kristall Elektrostal	CIS	44	1	6	7	30	....	....	....	....	....	....	....	....	....	....	....	....	....	....	....	....	....	....
1996-97	Utah Grizzlies	IHL	68	0	4	4	34	....	....	....	....	....	....	....	....	....	1	0	0	0	0	....	....	....	....
1997-98	**NY Islanders**	**NHL**	**2**	**0**	**2**	**2**	**0**	**0**	**0**	**0**	**0**	**0.0**	**–1**	....	....	....	....	....	....	....	....	....	....	....	....
	Kentucky	AHL	54	6	8	14	52	....	....	....	....	....	....	....	....	....	2	0	0	0	4	....	....	....	....
1998-99	**NY Islanders**	**NHL**	**8**	**0**	**0**	**0**	**12**	**0**	**0**	**0**	**4**	**0.0**	**6**	**0**	**0.0**	**17:12**	....	....	....	....	....	....	....	....	....
	Lowell	AHL	69	2	12	14	85	....	....	....	....	....	....	....	....	....	3	0	0	0	0	....	....	....	....
99-2000	**NY Islanders**	**NHL**	**17**	**1**	**1**	**2**	**8**	**0**	**0**	**0**	**9**	**11.1**	**–3**	**0**	**0.0**	**16:57**	....	....	....	....	....	....	....	....	....
	Lowell	AHL	63	1	8	9	118	....	....	....	....	....	....	....	....	....	7	0	4	4	11	....	....	....	....
2000-01	**St. Louis**	**NHL**	**22**	**1**	**2**	**3**	**26**	**0**	**0**	**0**	**5**	**20.0**	**5**	**0**	**0.0**	**13:09**	....	....	....	....	....	....	....	....	....
	Worcester IceCats	AHL	33	0	7	7	73	....	....	....	....	....	....	....	....	....	10	1	0	1	10	....	....	....	....
2001-02	**Chicago**	**NHL**	**13**	**0**	**2**	**2**	**6**	**0**	**0**	**0**	**8**	**0.0**	**0**	**0**	**0.0**	**12:42**	**3**	**0**	**0**	**0**	**2**	**0**	**0**	**0**	**11:39**
	Norfolk Admirals	AHL	57	2	8	10	78	....	....	....	....	....	....	....	....	....	....	....	....	....	....	....	....	....	....
2002-03	Hartford	AHL	53	4	3	7	88	....	....	....	....	....	....	....	....	....	....	....	....	....	....	....	....	....	....
	NHL Totals		**62**	**2**	**7**	**9**	**52**	**0**	**0**	**0**	**26**	**7.7**		**0**	**0.0**	**14:40**	**3**	**0**	**0**	**0**	**2**	**0**	**0**	**0**	**11:39**

Signed as a free agent by **St. Louis**, June 9, 2000. Signed as a free agent by **Chicago**, September 5, 2001. Signed as a free agent by **NY Rangers**, July 18, 2002.

CHEECHOO, Jonathan

(CHEE-choo, JAWN-ah-thuhn) **S.J.**

Right wing. Shoots right. 6', 205 lbs. Born, Moose Factory, Ont., July 15, 1980. San Jose's 2nd choice, 29th overall, in 1998 Entry Draft.

			Regular Season														Playoffs								
Season	Club	League	GP	G	A	Pts	PIM	PP	SH	GW	S	%	+/-	TF	F%	Min	GP	G	A	Pts	PIM	PP	SH	GW	Min
1996-97	Kitchener	OJHL-B	43	35	41	76	33																		
1997-98	Belleville Bulls	OHL	64	31	45	76	62										10	4	2	6	10				
1998-99	Belleville Bulls	OHL	63	35	47	82	74										21	15	15	30	27				
99-2000	Belleville Bulls	OHL	66	45	46	91	102										16	5	12	17	16				
2000-01	Kentucky	AHL	75	32	34	66	63										3	0	0	0	0				
2001-02	Cleveland Barons	AHL	53	21	25	46	54																		
2002-03	**San Jose**	**NHL**	**66**	**9**	**7**	**16**	**39**	**0**	**0**	**3**	**94**	**9.6**	**−5**	**8**	**37.5**	**10:43**									
	Cleveland Barons	AHL	9	3	4	7	16																		
	NHL Totals		**66**	**9**	**7**	**16**	**39**	**0**	**0**	**3**	**94**	**9.6**		**8**	**37.5**	**10:43**									

OHL All-Rookie Team (1998)

CHELIOS, Chris

(CHELL-EE-ohs, KRIHS) **DET.**

Defense. Shoots right. 6'1", 190 lbs. Born, Chicago, IL, January 25, 1962. Montreal's 5th choice, 40th overall, in 1981 Entry Draft.

Season	Club	League	GP	G	A	Pts	PIM	PP	SH	GW	S	%	+/-	TF	F%	Min	GP	G	A	Pts	PIM	PP	SH	GW	Min
1979-80	Moose Jaw	SJHL	53	12	31	43	118																		
1980-81	Moose Jaw	SJHL	54	23	64	87	175																		
1981-82	U. of Wisconsin	WCHA	43	6	43	49	50																		
1982-83	U. of Wisconsin	WCHA	26	9	17	26	50																		
1983-84	Team USA	Nat-Tm	60	14	35	49	58																		
	United States	Olympics	6	0	4	4	8																		
	Montreal	**NHL**	**12**	**0**	**2**	**2**	**12**	**0**	**0**	**0**	**23**	**0.0**	**−5**				**15**	**1**	**9**	**10**	**17**	**1**	**0**	**0**	
1984-85	**Montreal**	**NHL**	**74**	**9**	**55**	**64**	**87**	**2**	**1**	**0**	**199**	**4.5**	**11**				**9**	**2**	**8**	**10**	**17**	**2**	**0**	**0**	
1985-86♦	**Montreal**	**NHL**	**41**	**8**	**26**	**34**	**67**	**2**	**0**	**0**	**101**	**7.9**	**4**				**20**	**2**	**9**	**11**	**49**	**1**	**0**	**0**	
1986-87	**Montreal**	**NHL**	**71**	**11**	**33**	**44**	**124**	**6**	**0**	**2**	**141**	**7.8**	**−5**				**17**	**4**	**9**	**13**	**38**	**2**	**1**	**0**	
1987-88	**Montreal**	**NHL**	**71**	**20**	**41**	**61**	**172**	**10**	**1**	**5**	**199**	**10.1**	**14**				**11**	**3**	**1**	**4**	**29**	**1**	**0**	**0**	
1988-89	**Montreal**	**NHL**	**80**	**15**	**58**	**73**	**185**	**8**	**0**	**6**	**206**	**7.3**	**35**				**21**	**4**	**15**	**19**	**28**	**1**	**0**	**2**	
1989-90	**Montreal**	**NHL**	**53**	**9**	**22**	**31**	**136**	**1**	**2**	**1**	**123**	**7.3**	**20**				**5**	**0**	**1**	**1**	**8**	**0**	**0**	**0**	
1990-91	**Chicago**	**NHL**	**77**	**12**	**52**	**64**	**192**	**5**	**2**	**2**	**187**	**6.4**	**23**				**6**	**1**	**7**	**8**	**46**	**1**	**0**	**0**	
1991-92	**Chicago**	**NHL**	**80**	**9**	**47**	**56**	**245**	**2**	**2**	**2**	**239**	**3.8**	**24**				**18**	**6**	**15**	**21**	**37**	**3**	**0**	**1**	
1992-93	**Chicago**	**NHL**	**84**	**15**	**58**	**73**	**282**	**8**	**0**	**2**	**290**	**5.2**	**14**				**4**	**0**	**2**	**2**	**14**	**0**	**0**	**0**	
1993-94	**Chicago**	**NHL**	**76**	**16**	**44**	**60**	**212**	**7**	**1**	**2**	**219**	**7.3**	**12**				**6**	**1**	**1**	**2**	**8**	**1**	**0**	**0**	
1994-95	EHC Biel-Bienne	Swiss	3	0	3	3	4																		
	Chicago	**NHL**	**48**	**5**	**33**	**38**	**72**	**3**	**1**	**0**	**166**	**3.0**	**17**				**16**	**4**	**7**	**11**	**12**	**0**	**1**	**3**	
1995-96	**Chicago**	**NHL**	**81**	**14**	**58**	**72**	**140**	**7**	**0**	**3**	**219**	**6.4**	**25**				**9**	**0**	**3**	**3**	**8**	**0**	**0**	**0**	
1996-97	**Chicago**	**NHL**	**72**	**10**	**38**	**48**	**112**	**2**	**0**	**2**	**194**	**5.2**	**16**				**6**	**0**	**1**	**1**	**8**	**0**	**0**	**0**	
1997-98	**Chicago**	**NHL**	**81**	**3**	**39**	**42**	**151**	**1**	**0**	**0**	**205**	**1.5**	**−7**												
	United States	Olympics	4	2	0	2	2																		
1998-99	**Chicago**	**NHL**	**65**	**8**	**26**	**34**	**89**	**2**	**1**	**0**	**172**	**4.7**	**−4**	**4**	**25.0**	**27:19**									
	Detroit	**NHL**	**10**	**1**	**1**	**2**	**4**	**1**	**0**	**1**	**15**	**6.7**	**5**	**0**	**0.0**	**22:21**	**10**	**0**	**4**	**4**	**14**	**0**	**0**	**0**	**27:15**
99-2000	**Detroit**	**NHL**	**81**	**3**	**31**	**34**	**103**	**0**	**0**	**0**	**135**	**2.2**	**48**	**0**	**0.0**	**25:16**	**9**	**0**	**1**	**1**	**8**	**0**	**0**	**0**	**24:06**
2000-01	**Detroit**	**NHL**	**24**	**0**	**3**	**3**	**45**	**0**	**0**	**0**	**26**	**0.0**	**4**	**0**	**0.0**	**22:51**	**5**	**1**	**0**	**1**	**2**	**0**	**0**	**0**	**19:41**
2001-02♦	**Detroit**	**NHL**	**79**	**6**	**33**	**39**	**126**	**1**	**0**	**1**	**128**	**4.7**	**40**	**0**	**0.0**	**25:18**	**23**	**1**	**13**	**14**	**44**	**1**	**0**	**0**	**26:22**
	United States	Olympics	6	1	0	1	4																		
2002-03	**Detroit**	**NHL**	**66**	**2**	**17**	**19**	**78**	**0**	**1**	**1**	**92**	**2.2**	**4**	**0**	**0.0**	**24:15**	**4**	**0**	**0**	**0**	**2**	**0**	**0**	**0**	**25:43**
	NHL Totals		**1326**	**176**	**717**	**893**	**2634**	**68**	**12**	**30**	**3279**	**5.4**		**4**	**25.0**	**25:13**	**214**	**30**	**106**	**136**	**389**	**14**	**2**	**6**	**25:26**

WCHA Second All-Star Team (1983) • NCAA Championship All-Tournament Team (1983) • NHL All-Rookie Team (1985) • NHL First All-Star Team (1989, 1993, 1995, 1996, 2002) • James Norris Memorial Trophy (1989, 1993, 1996) • NHL Second All-Star Team (1991, 1997)

Played in NHL All-Star Game (1985, 1990, 1991, 1992, 1993, 1994, 1996, 1997, 1998, 2000, 2002)

Traded to **Chicago** by **Montreal** with Montreal's 2nd round choice (Michael Pomichter) in 1991 Entry Draft for Denis Savard, June 29, 1990. Traded to **Detroit** by **Chicago** for Anders Eriksson and Detroit's 1st round choices in 1999 (Steve McCarthy) and 2001 (Adam Munro) Entry Drafts, March 23, 1999. • Missed majority of 2000-01 season recovering from knee injury suffered in game vs. Dallas, November 17, 2000.

CHIMERA, Jason

(chihm-AIR-a, JAY-suhn) **EDM.**

Left wing. Shoots left. 6'2", 204 lbs. Born, Edmonton, Alta., May 2, 1979. Edmonton's 5th choice, 121st overall, in 1997 Entry Draft.

Season	Club	League	GP	G	A	Pts	PIM	PP	SH	GW	S	%	+/-	TF	F%	Min	GP	G	A	Pts	PIM	PP	SH	GW	Min
1994-95	Edmonton Pats	AMHL	33	27	31	58	42																		
1995-96	Edmonton Pats	AMHL	34	23	24	47	44																		
1996-97	Medicine Hat	WHL	71	16	23	39	64										4	0	1	1	4				
1997-98	Medicine Hat	WHL	72	34	32	66	93																		
	Hamilton	AHL	4	0	0	0	8																		
1998-99	Medicine Hat	WHL	37	18	22	40	84																		
	Brandon	WHL	21	14	12	26	32										5	4	1	5	8				
99-2000	Hamilton	AHL	78	15	13	28	77										10	0	2	2	12				
2000-01	**Edmonton**	**NHL**	**1**	**0**	**0**	**0**	**0**	**0**	**0**	**0**	**0**	**0.0**	**0**	**0**	**0.0**	**6:58**									
	Hamilton	AHL	78	29	25	54	93																		
2001-02	**Edmonton**	**NHL**	**3**	**1**	**0**	**1**	**0**	**0**	**0**	**0**	**3**	**33.3**	**−3**	**0**	**0.0**	**12:44**									
	Hamilton	AHL	77	26	51	77	158										15	4	6	10	10				
2002-03	**Edmonton**	**NHL**	**66**	**14**	**9**	**23**	**36**	**0**	**1**	**4**	**90**	**15.6**	**−2**	**11**	**54.6**	**10:46**	**2**	**0**	**2**	**2**	**0**	**0**	**0**	**0**	**10:54**
	NHL Totals		**70**	**15**	**9**	**24**	**36**	**0**	**1**	**4**	**93**	**16.1**		**11**	**54.5**	**10:47**	**2**	**0**	**2**	**2**	**0**	**0**	**0**	**0**	**10:54**

AHL First All-Star Team (2002)

CHISTOV, Stanislav

(chihs-TAHV, STAHN-his-LAHV) **ANA.**

Left wing. Shoots right. 5'10", 178 lbs. Born, Chelyabinsk, USSR, April 17, 1983. Anaheim's 1st choice, 5th overall, in 2001 Entry Draft.

Season	Club	League	GP	G	A	Pts	PIM	PP	SH	GW	S	%	+/-	TF	F%	Min	GP	G	A	Pts	PIM	PP	SH	GW	Min
1998-99	Chelyabinsk 2	Russia-4	1	0	0	0	0																		
	Georgetown	OPJHL	14	10	7	17	21																		
99-2000	Omsk Jr.	Russia-Jr.	5	4	3	7	8																		
	Omsk 2	Russia-3	18	12	4	16	24																		
	Novokuznetsk	Russia	9	7	4	11	18																		
	Avangard Omsk	Russia	3	1	0	1	2																		
2000-01	Omsk 2	Russia-3	8	5	4	9	2																		
	Avangard Omsk	Russia	24	4	8	12	12										5	0	0	0	2				
2001-02	Avangard Omsk	Russia	9	0	0	0	4																		
	CSKA Moscow 2	Russia-3	1	1	2	3	0																		
2002-03	**Anaheim**	**NHL**	**79**	**12**	**18**	**30**	**54**	**3**	**0**	**2**	**114**	**10.5**	**4**	**3**	**0.0**	**13:35**	**21**	**4**	**2**	**6**	**8**	**0**	**0**	**1**	**13:22**
	NHL Totals		**79**	**12**	**18**	**30**	**54**	**3**	**0**	**2**	**114**	**10.5**		**3**	**0.0**	**13:35**	**21**	**4**	**2**	**6**	**8**	**0**	**0**	**1**	**13:22**

CHOUINARD, Eric

(shwee-NAHR, AIR-ihk) **PHI.**

Left wing. Shoots left. 6'3", 215 lbs. Born, Atlanta, GA, July 8, 1980. Montreal's 1st choice, 16th overall, in 1998 Entry Draft.

Season	Club	League	GP	G	A	Pts	PIM	PP	SH	GW	S	%	+/-	TF	F%	Min	GP	G	A	Pts	PIM	PP	SH	GW	Min
1995-96	Magog	QAHA	22	12	14	26	12																		
	Ste-Foy	QAAA	17	2	5	7											15	7	12	19	12				
1996-97	Ste-Foy	QAAA	40	29	41	70	40										10	14	9	23					
1997-98	Quebec Remparts	QMJHL	68	41	42	83	18										14	7	10	17	6				
1998-99	Quebec Remparts	QMJHL	62	50	59	109	56										13	8	10	18	8				
	Fredericton	AHL															6	3	2	5	0				
99-2000	Quebec Remparts	QMJHL	50	57	47	104	105										11	14	4	18	8				
2000-01	**Montreal**	**NHL**	**13**	**1**	**3**	**4**	**0**	**1**	**0**	**0**	**11**	**9.1**	**0**	**31**	**54.8**	**10:59**									
	Quebec Citadelles	AHL	48	12	21	33	6										9	2	0	2	2				
2001-02	Quebec Citadelles	AHL	65	19	23	42	18										2	0	0	0	0				
2002-03	Utah Grizzlies	AHL	32	12	12	24	16																		
	Philadelphia	**NHL**	**28**	**4**	**4**	**8**	**8**	**1**	**0**	**0**	**45**	**8.9**	**2**	**12**	**33.3**	**9:38**									
	NHL Totals		**41**	**5**	**7**	**12**	**8**	**2**	**0**	**0**	**56**	**8.9**		**43**	**48.8**	**10:04**									

Traded to **Philadelphia** by **Montreal** for Philadelphia's 2nd round choice (Maxim Lapierre) in 2003 Entry Draft, January 29, 2003.

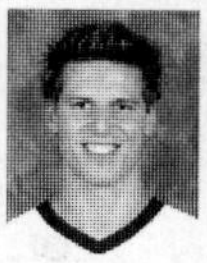

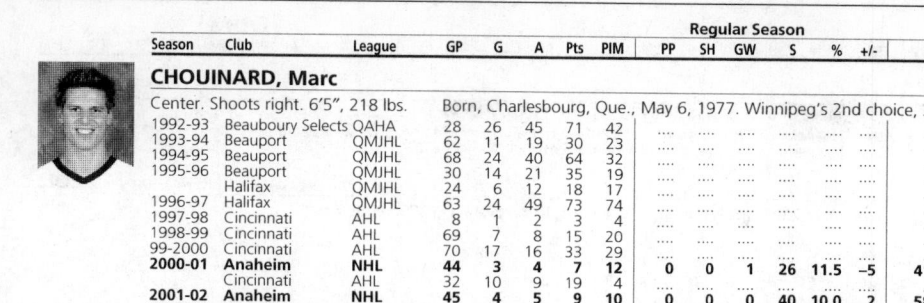

CHOUINARD, Marc

(shwee-NAHR, MAHRK) **MIN.**

Center. Shoots right. 6'5", 218 lbs. Born, Charlesbourg, Que., May 6, 1977. Winnipeg's 2nd choice, 32nd overall, in 1995 Entry Draft.

Season	Club	League	GP	G	A	Pts	PIM	PP	SH	GW	S	%	+/-	TF	F%	Min	Playoffs GP	G	A	Pts	PIM	PP	SH	GW	Min
1992-93	Beauboury Selects	QAHA	28	26	45	71	42	....	....	....	....	....	....	....	....	....	....	....	....	....	....	....	....	....	....
1993-94	Beauport	QMJHL	62	11	19	30	23	....	....	....	....	....	....	....	....	....	13	2	5	7	2	....	....	....	....
1994-95	Beauport	QMJHL	68	24	40	64	32	....	....	....	....	....	....	....	....	....	18	1	6	7	4	....	....	....	....
1995-96	Beauport	QMJHL	30	14	21	35	19	....	....	....	....	....	....	....	....	....	....	....	....	....	....	....	....	....	....
	Halifax	QMJHL	24	6	12	18	17	....	....	....	....	....	....	....	....	....	6	2	1	3	2	....	....	....	....
1996-97	Halifax	QMJHL	63	24	49	73	74	....	....	....	....	....	....	....	....	....	18	9	16	25	12	....	....	....	....
1997-98	Cincinnati	AHL	8	1	2	3	4	....	....	....	....	....	....	....	....	....	....	....	....	....	....	....	....	....	....
1998-99	Cincinnati	AHL	69	7	8	15	20	....	....	....	....	....	....	....	....	....	3	0	0	0	4	....	....	....	....
99-2000	Cincinnati	AHL	70	17	16	33	29	....	....	....	....	....	....	....	....	....	....	....	....	....	....	....	....	....	....
2000-01	**Anaheim**	**NHL**	**44**	**3**	**4**	**7**	**12**	**0**	**0**	**1**	**26**	**11.5**	**-5**	**414**	**60.9**	**7:50**	....	....	....	....	....	....	....	....	....
	Cincinnati	AHL	32	10	9	19	4	....	....	....	....	....	....	....	....	....	....	....	....	....	....	....	....	....	....
2001-02	**Anaheim**	**NHL**	**45**	**4**	**5**	**9**	**10**	**0**	**0**	**0**	**40**	**10.0**	**2**	**581**	**54.9**	**10:36**	....	....	....	....	....	....	....	....	....
2002-03	**Anaheim**	**NHL**	**70**	**3**	**4**	**7**	**40**	**0**	**1**	**0**	**52**	**5.8**	**-9**	**662**	**54.5**	**9:25**	**15**	**1**	**0**	**1**	**0**	**0**	**0**	**0**	**7:16**
	NHL Totals		**159**	**10**	**13**	**23**	**62**	**0**	**1**	**1**	**118**	**8.5**		**1657**	**56.2**	**9:19**	**15**	**1**	**0**	**1**	**0**	**0**	**0**	**0**	**7:16**

Traded to **Anaheim** by **Winnipeg** with Teemu Selanne and Winnipeg's 4th round choice (later traded to Toronto – later traded to Montreal – Montreal selected Kim Staal) in 1996 Entry Draft for Chad Kilger, Oleg Tverdovsky and Anaheim's 3rd round choice (Per-Anton Lundstrom) in 1996 Entry Draft, February 7, 1996. Signed as a free agent by **Minnesota**, July 28, 2003.

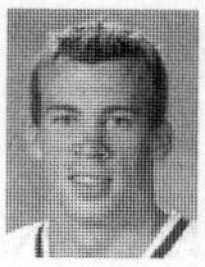

CHRISTIE, Ryan

(KRIHS-tee, RIGH-yuhn)

Left wing. Shoots left. 6'3", 200 lbs. Born, Beamsville, Ont., July 3, 1978. Dallas' 4th choice, 112th overall, in 1996 Entry Draft.

Season	Club	League	GP	G	A	Pts	PIM	PP	SH	GW	S	%	+/-	TF	F%	Min	Playoffs GP	G	A	Pts	PIM	PP	SH	GW	Min
1994-95	St. Catharines	OJHL-B	40	10	11	21	96	....	....	....	....	....	....	....	....	....	....	....	....	....	....	....	....	....	....
1995-96	Owen Sound	OHL	66	29	17	46	93	....	....	....	....	....	....	....	....	....	6	1	1	2	0	....	....	....	....
1996-97	Owen Sound	OHL	66	23	29	52	136	....	....	....	....	....	....	....	....	....	4	1	1	2	8	....	....	....	....
1997-98	Owen Sound	OHL	66	39	41	80	208	....	....	....	....	....	....	....	....	....	11	3	5	8	13	....	....	....	....
1998-99	Michigan	IHL	48	4	5	9	74	....	....	....	....	....	....	....	....	....	3	1	1	2	2	....	....	....	....
99-2000	**Dallas**	**NHL**	**5**	**0**	**0**	**0**	**0**	**0**	**0**	**0**	**1**	**0.0**	**-1**	**0**	**0.0**	**2:29**	....	....	....	....	....	....	....	....	....
	Michigan	IHL	76	24	25	49	140	....	....	....	....	....	....	....	....	....	....	....	....	....	....	....	....	....	....
2000-01	Utah Grizzlies	IHL	69	22	16	38	88	....	....	....	....	....	....	....	....	....	....	....	....	....	....	....	....	....	....
2001-02	**Calgary**	**NHL**	**2**	**0**	**0**	**0**	**0**	**0**	**0**	**0**	**0**	**0.0**	**-1**	**0**	**0.0**	**6:10**	....	....	....	....	....	....	....	....	....
	Saint John Flames	AHL	77	21	18	39	61	....	....	....	....	....	....	....	....	....	....	....	....	....	....	....	....	....	....
2002-03	Saint John Flames	AHL	67	10	14	24	84	....	....	....	....	....	....	....	....	....	....	....	....	....	....	....	....	....	....
	NHL Totals		**7**	**0**	**0**	**0**	**0**	**0**	**0**	**0**	**1**	**0.0**		**0**	**0.0**	**3:32**	....	....	....	....	....	....	....	....	....

Signed as a free agent by **Calgary**, July 1, 2001.

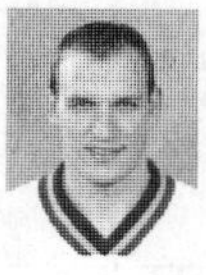

CHUBAROV, Artem

(choo-BAH-rahf, AHR-tehm) **VAN.**

Center. Shoots left. 6'1", 189 lbs. Born, Gorky, USSR, December 12, 1979. Vancouver's 2nd choice, 31st overall, in 1998 Entry Draft.

Season	Club	League	GP	G	A	Pts	PIM	PP	SH	GW	S	%	+/-	TF	F%	Min	Playoffs GP	G	A	Pts	PIM	PP	SH	GW	Min
1994-95	Niz. Novgorod Jr.	CIS-Jr.	60	20	30	50	20	....	....	....	....	....	....	....	....	....	....	....	....	....	....	....	....	....	....
1995-96	Niz. Novgorod Jr.	CIS-Jr.	60	22	25	47	20	....	....	....	....	....	....	....	....	....	....	....	....	....	....	....	....	....	....
1996-97	Niz. Novgorod 2	Russia-3	40	24	5	29	16	....	....	....	....	....	....	....	....	....	....	....	....	....	....	....	....	....	....
	Nizhny Novgorod	Russia	15	1	1	2	8	....	....	....	....	....	....	....	....	....	....	....	....	....	....	....	....	....	....
1997-98	Dynamo Moscow	Russia	30	1	4	5	4	....	....	....	....	....	....	....	....	....	....	....	....	....	....	....	....	....	....
1998-99	Dynamo Moscow	Russia	34	8	2	10	10	....	....	....	....	....	....	....	....	....	12	0	0	0	4	....	....	....	....
99-2000	**Vancouver**	**NHL**	**49**	**1**	**8**	**9**	**10**	**0**	**0**	**1**	**53**	**1.9**	**-4**	**488**	**48.0**	**11:43**	....	....	....	....	....	....	....	....	....
	Syracuse Crunch	AHL	14	7	6	13	4	....	....	....	....	....	....	....	....	....	1	0	0	0	0	....	....	....	....
2000-01	**Vancouver**	**NHL**	**1**	**0**	**0**	**0**	**0**	**0**	**0**	**0**	**0**	**0.0**	**-1**	**17**	**52.9**	**15:08**	....	....	....	....	....	....	....	....	....
	Kansas City	IHL	10	7	4	11	12	....	....	....	....	....	....	....	....	....	....	....	....	....	....	....	....	....	....
2001-02	**Vancouver**	**NHL**	**51**	**5**	**5**	**10**	**10**	**0**	**0**	**3**	**73**	**6.8**	**-3**	**517**	**53.6**	**12:37**	**6**	**0**	**1**	**1**	**0**	**0**	**0**	**0**	**14:44**
	Manitoba Moose	AHL	19	7	12	19	4	....	....	....	....	....	....	....	....	....	....	....	....	....	....	....	....	....	....
2002-03	**Vancouver**	**NHL**	**62**	**7**	**13**	**20**	**6**	**1**	**0**	**1**	**78**	**9.0**	**4**	**862**	**50.8**	**14:21**	**14**	**0**	**2**	**2**	**4**	**0**	**0**	**0**	**14:56**
	NHL Totals		**163**	**13**	**26**	**39**	**26**	**1**	**0**	**5**	**204**	**6.4**		**1884**	**50.8**	**13:01**	**20**	**0**	**3**	**3**	**4**	**0**	**0**	**0**	**14:52**

• Missed majority of 2000-01 season recovering from shoulder injury suffered in game vs. Manitoba (IHL), November 15, 2000.

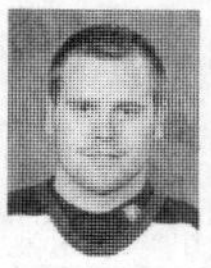

CIBAK, Martin

(TSEE-bak, MAHR-tihn) **T.B.**

Center. Shoots left. 6'1", 195 lbs. Born, Liptovsky Mikulas, Czech., May 17, 1980. Tampa Bay's 11th choice, 252nd overall, in 1998 Entry Draft.

Season	Club	League	GP	G	A	Pts	PIM	PP	SH	GW	S	%	+/-	TF	F%	Min	Playoffs GP	G	A	Pts	PIM	PP	SH	GW	Min
1995-96	L. Mikulas Jr.	Slovak-Jr.	48	38	35	73	....	....	....	....	....	....	....	....	....	....	....	....	....	....	....	....	....	....	....
1996-97	L. Mikulas Jr.	Slovak-Jr.	45	22	18	40	....	....	....	....	....	....	....	....	....	....	....	....	....	....	....	....	....	....	....
1997-98	L. Mikulas Jr.	Slovak-Jr.	42	31	21	52	....	....	....	....	....	....	....	....	....	....	....	....	....	....	....	....	....	....	....
	Liptov. Mikulas	Slovakia	28	1	3	4	10	....	....	....	....	....	....	....	....	....	....	....	....	....	....	....	....	....	....
1998-99	Medicine Hat	WHL	66	21	26	47	72	....	....	....	....	....	....	....	....	....	....	....	....	....	....	....	....	....	....
99-2000	Medicine Hat	WHL	58	16	29	45	77	....	....	....	....	....	....	....	....	....	....	....	....	....	....	....	....	....	....
2000-01	Detroit Vipers	IHL	79	10	28	38	88	....	....	....	....	....	....	....	....	....	....	....	....	....	....	....	....	....	....
2001-02	**Tampa Bay**	**NHL**	**26**	**1**	**5**	**6**	**8**	**0**	**0**	**0**	**22**	**4.5**	**-6**	**85**	**34.1**	**11:08**	....	....	....	....	....	....	....	....	....
	Springfield	AHL	52	5	9	14	44	....	....	....	....	....	....	....	....	....	....	....	....	....	....	....	....	....	....
2002-03	Springfield	AHL	62	5	15	20	78	....	....	....	....	....	....	....	....	....	6	1	2	3	4	....	....	....	....
	NHL Totals		**26**	**1**	**5**	**6**	**8**	**0**	**0**	**0**	**22**	**4.5**		**85**	**34.1**	**11:08**	....	....	....	....	....	....	....	....	....

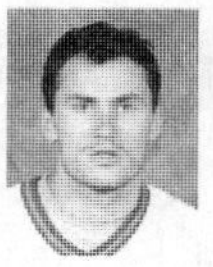

CIERNIK, Ivan

(CHAIR-nihk, ee-VAHN)

Right wing. Shoots left. 6'1", 234 lbs. Born, Levice, Czech., October 30, 1977. Ottawa's 6th choice, 216th overall, in 1996 Entry Draft.

Season	Club	League	GP	G	A	Pts	PIM	PP	SH	GW	S	%	+/-	TF	F%	Min	Playoffs GP	G	A	Pts	PIM	PP	SH	GW	Min
1994-95	HC Nitra Jr.	Slovak-Jr.	30	22	15	37	36	....	....	....	....	....	....	....	....	....	....	....	....	....	....	....	....	....	....
	HC Nitra	Slovakia	7	1	0	1	2	....	....	....	....	....	....	....	....	....	....	....	....	....	....	....	....	....	....
1995-96	HC Nitra	Slovakia	35	9	7	16	36	....	....	....	....	....	....	....	....	....	8	3	3	6	....	....	....	....	....
1996-97	Nitra	Slovakia	41	11	19	30	....	....	....	....	....	....	....	....	....	....	....	....	....	....	....	....	....	....	....
1997-98	**Ottawa**	**NHL**	**2**	**0**	**0**	**0**	**0**	**0**	**0**	**0**	**0**	**0.0**	**0**	....	....	....	....	....	....	....	....	....	....	....	....
	Worcester IceCats	AHL	53	9	12	21	38	....	....	....	....	....	....	....	....	....	1	0	0	0	2	....	....	....	....
1998-99	Adirondack	AHL	21	1	4	5	4	....	....	....	....	....	....	....	....	....	....	....	....	....	....	....	....	....	....
	Cincinnati	AHL	32	10	3	13	10	....	....	....	....	....	....	....	....	....	2	0	0	0	2	....	....	....	....
99-2000	Grand Rapids	IHL	66	13	12	25	64	....	....	....	....	....	....	....	....	....	6	0	6	6	2	....	....	....	....
2000-01	**Ottawa**	**NHL**	**4**	**2**	**0**	**2**	**2**	**0**	**0**	**0**	**7**	**28.6**	**2**	**0**	**0.0**	**7:41**	....	....	....	....	....	....	....	....	....
	Grand Rapids	IHL	66	27	38	65	53	....	....	....	....	....	....	....	....	....	10	5	6	11	26	....	....	....	....
2001-02	**Ottawa**	**NHL**	**23**	**1**	**2**	**3**	**4**	**0**	**0**	**0**	**18**	**5.6**	**0**	**7**	**71.4**	**7:51**	....	....	....	....	....	....	....	....	....
	Grand Rapids	AHL	2	2	1	3	0	....	....	....	....	....	....	....	....	....	....	....	....	....	....	....	....	....	....
	Washington	**NHL**	**6**	**0**	**1**	**1**	**2**	**0**	**0**	**0**	**5**	**0.0**	**0**	**0**	**0.0**	**9:15**	....	....	....	....	....	....	....	....	....
	Portland Pirates	AHL	26	10	5	15	28	....	....	....	....	....	....	....	....	....	....	....	....	....	....	....	....	....	....
2002-03	**Washington**	**NHL**	**47**	**8**	**10**	**18**	**24**	**0**	**0**	**2**	**61**	**13.1**	**6**	**9**	**33.3**	**11:48**	**2**	**0**	**1**	**1**	**6**	**0**	**0**	**0**	**9:09**
	Portland Pirates	AHL	13	4	6	10	6	....	....	....	....	....	....	....	....	....	....	....	....	....	....	....	....	....	....
	NHL Totals		**82**	**11**	**13**	**24**	**32**	**0**	**0**	**2**	**91**	**12.1**		**16**	**50.0**	**10:16**	**2**	**0**	**1**	**1**	**6**	**0**	**0**	**0**	**9:09**

Loaned to **Cincinnati** (AHL) by **Ottawa** with Ratislav Pavlikovsky and Erich Goldmann, January 12, 1999. Claimed on waivers by **Washington** from **Ottawa**, January 19, 2002.

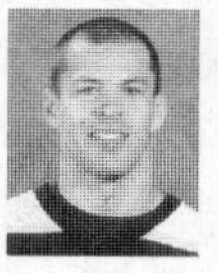

CISAR, Marian

(SIH-sahr, MAIR-eean) **NSH.**

Right wing. Shoots right. 6', 197 lbs. Born, Bratislava, Czech., February 25, 1978. Los Angeles' 2nd choice, 37th overall, in 1996 Entry Draft.

Season	Club	League	GP	G	A	Pts	PIM	PP	SH	GW	S	%	+/-	TF	F%	Min	Playoffs GP	G	A	Pts	PIM	PP	SH	GW	Min
1994-95	S. Bratislava Jr.	Slovak-Jr.	38	42	28	70	16	....	....	....	....	....	....	....	....	....	....	....	....	....	....	....	....	....	....
1995-96	S. Bratislava Jr.	Slovak-Jr.	16	26	17	43	2	....	....	....	....	....	....	....	....	....	....	....	....	....	....	....	....	....	....
	Slov. Bratislava	Slovakia	13	3	3	6	0	....	....	....	....	....	....	....	....	....	6	3	0	3	0	....	....	....	....
1996-97	Spokane Chiefs	WHL	70	31	35	66	52	....	....	....	....	....	....	....	....	....	9	6	2	8	4	....	....	....	....
1997-98	Spokane Chiefs	WHL	52	33	40	73	34	....	....	....	....	....	....	....	....	....	18	8	5	13	8	....	....	....	....
1998-99	Milwaukee	IHL	51	11	17	28	31	....	....	....	....	....	....	....	....	....	2	0	0	0	12	....	....	....	....
99-2000	**Nashville**	**NHL**	**3**	**0**	**0**	**0**	**4**	**0**	**0**	**0**	**2**	**0.0**	**-2**	**0**	**0.0**	**8:18**	....	....	....	....	....	....	....	....	....
	Milwaukee	IHL	78	20	32	52	82	....	....	....	....	....	....	....	....	....	1	0	0	0	0	....	....	....	....
2000-01	**Nashville**	**NHL**	**60**	**12**	**15**	**27**	**45**	**5**	**0**	**1**	**97**	**12.4**	**-7**	**0**	**0.0**	**13:10**	....	....	....	....	....	....	....	....	....
	Milwaukee	IHL	15	4	7	11	4	....	....	....	....	....	....	....	....	....	....	....	....	....	....	....	....	....	....
2001-02	**Nashville**	**NHL**	**10**	**1**	**2**	**3**	**8**	**1**	**0**	**0**	**16**	**6.3**	**-3**	**1**	**100.0**	**12:55**	....	....	....	....	....	....	....	....	....
	Milwaukee	AHL	2	1	0	1	2	....	....	....	....	....	....	....	....	....	....	....	....	....	....	....	....	....	....

			Regular Season														Playoffs								
Season	Club	League	GP	G	A	Pts	PIM	PP	SH	GW	S	%	+/-	TF	F%	Min	GP	G	A	Pts	PIM	PP	SH	GW	Min
2002-03	HC Znojemsti	Czech	9	2	0	2	4	....	....	....	....	....	....	....	....	....	....	....	....	....	....	....	....	....	....
	Lukko Rauma	Finland	26	6	8	14	6	....	....	....	....	....	....	....	....	....	....	....	....	....	....	....	....	....	....
	NHL Totals		**73**	**13**	**17**	**30**	**57**	**6**	**0**	**1**	**115**	**11.3**		**1**	**100.0**	**12:56**	....	....	....	....	....	....	....	....	....

Traded to **Nashville** by **Los Angeles** for future considerations, June 1, 1998. • Missed remainder of 2001-02 season after suffering head iinjury in game vs. Milwaukee (AHL), November 23, 2001.Signed as a free agent by **HC Znojemsti** (Czech) with Nashville retaining NHL rights, July 22, 2002. Signed as a free agent by **Nurnberg** (Germany), May 21, 2003.

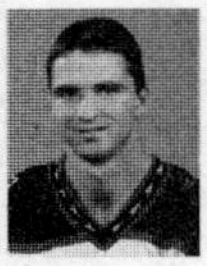

CLARK, Brett

(KLAHRK, BREHT) **COL.**

Defense. Shoots left. 6'1", 195 lbs. Born, Wapella, Sask., December 23, 1976. Montreal's 7th choice, 154th overall, in 1996 Entry Draft.

Season	Club	League	GP	G	A	Pts	PIM	PP	SH	GW	S	%	+/-	TF	F%	Min	GP	G	A	Pts	PIM	PP	SH	GW	Min
1994-95	Melville	SJHL	62	19	32	51	77	....	....	....	....	....	....	....	....	....	....	....	....	....	....	....	....	....	....
1995-96	U. of Maine	H-East	39	7	31	38	22	....	....	....	....	....	....	....	....	....	....	....	....	....	....	....	....	....	....
1996-97	Team Canada	Nat-Tm	57	6	21	27	52	....	....	....	....	....	....	....	....	....	....	....	....	....	....	....	....	....	....
1997-98	**Montreal**	**NHL**	**41**	**1**	**0**	**1**	**20**	**0**	**0**	**0**	**26**	**3.8**	**–3**	....	....	....	....	....	....	....	....	....	....	....	....
	Fredericton	AHL	20	0	6	6	6	....	....	....	....	....	....	....	....	....	4	0	1	1	17	....	....	....	....
1998-99	**Montreal**	**NHL**	**61**	**2**	**2**	**4**	**16**	**0**	**0**	**0**	**36**	**5.6**	**–3**	**0**	**0.0**	**13:11**	....	....	....	....	....	....	....	....	....
	Fredericton	AHL	3	1	0	1	0	....	....	....	....	....	....	....	....	....	....	....	....	....	....	....	....	....	....
99-2000	**Atlanta**	**NHL**	**14**	**0**	**1**	**1**	**4**	**0**	**0**	**0**	**13**	**0.0**	**–12**	**0**	**0.0**	**16:51**	....	....	....	....	....	....	....	....	....
	Orlando	IHL	63	9	17	26	31	....	....	....	....	....	....	....	....	....	6	0	1	1	0	....	....	....	....
2000-01	**Atlanta**	**NHL**	**28**	**1**	**2**	**3**	**14**	**0**	**0**	**0**	**35**	**2.9**	**–12**	**0**	**0.0**	**18:02**	....	....	....	....	....	....	....	....	....
	Orlando	IHL	43	2	9	11	32	....	....	....	....	....	....	....	....	....	15	1	6	7	2	....	....	....	....
2001-02	**Atlanta**	**NHL**	**2**	**0**	**0**	**0**	**0**	**0**	**0**	**0**	**0**	**0.0**	**–3**	**1**	**100.0**	**15:32**	....	....	....	....	....	....	....	....	....
	Chicago Wolves	AHL	42	3	17	20	18	....	....	....	....	....	....	....	....	....	....	....	....	....	....	....	....	....	....
	Hershey Bears	AHL	32	7	9	16	12	....	....	....	....	....	....	....	....	....	8	0	2	2	6	....	....	....	....
2002-03	Hershey Bears	AHL	80	8	27	35	26	....	....	....	....	....	....	....	....	....	5	0	4	4	4	....	....	....	....
	NHL Totals		**146**	**4**	**5**	**9**	**54**	**0**	**0**	**0**	**110**	**3.6**		**1**	**100.0**	**15:01**	....	....	....	....	....	....	....	....	....

Claimed by **Atlanta** from **Montreal** in Expansion Draft, June 25, 1999. Traded to **Colorado** by **Atlanta** for Frederic Cassivi, January 24, 2002.

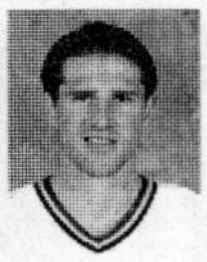

CLARK, Chris

(KLAHRK, KRIHS) **CGY.**

Right wing. Shoots right. 6', 200 lbs. Born, South Windsor, CT, March 8, 1976. Calgary's 3rd choice, 77th overall, in 1994 Entry Draft.

Season	Club	League	GP	G	A	Pts	PIM	PP	SH	GW	S	%	+/-	TF	F%	Min	GP	G	A	Pts	PIM	PP	SH	GW	Min
1990-91	South Windsor	Hi-School	23	16	15	31	24	....	....	....	....	....	....	....	....	....	....	....	....	....	....	....	....	....	....
1991-92	Springfield	NEJHL	49	21	29	50	56	....	....	....	....	....	....	....	....	....	....	....	....	....	....	....	....	....	....
1992-93	Springfield	NEJHL	43	17	60	77	120	....	....	....	....	....	....	....	....	....	....	....	....	....	....	....	....	....	....
1993-94	Springfield	NEJHL	35	31	26	57	185	....	....	....	....	....	....	....	....	....	....	....	....	....	....	....	....	....	....
1994-95	Clarkson Knights	ECAC	32	12	11	23	92	....	....	....	....	....	....	....	....	....	....	....	....	....	....	....	....	....	....
1995-96	Clarkson Knights	ECAC	38	10	8	18	108	....	....	....	....	....	....	....	....	....	....	....	....	....	....	....	....	....	....
1996-97	Clarkson Knights	ECAC	37	23	25	48	*86	....	....	....	....	....	....	....	....	....	....	....	....	....	....	....	....	....	....
1997-98	Clarkson Knights	ECAC	35	18	21	39	*106	....	....	....	....	....	....	....	....	....	....	....	....	....	....	....	....	....	....
1998-99	Saint John Flames	AHL	73	13	27	40	123	....	....	....	....	....	....	....	....	....	7	2	4	6	15	....	....	....	....
99-2000	**Calgary**	**NHL**	**22**	**0**	**1**	**1**	**14**	**0**	**0**	**0**	**17**	**0.0**	**–3**	**0**	**0.0**	**9:02**	....	....	....	....	....	....	....	....	....
	Saint John Flames	AHL	48	16	17	33	134	....	....	....	....	....	....	....	....	....	....	....	....	....	....	....	....	....	....
2000-01	**Calgary**	**NHL**	**29**	**5**	**1**	**6**	**38**	**1**	**0**	**0**	**43**	**11.6**	**0**	**3**	**33.3**	**11:56**	....	....	....	....	....	....	....	....	....
	Saint John Flames	AHL	48	18	17	35	131	....	....	....	....	....	....	....	....	....	18	4	10	14	49	....	....	....	....
2001-02	**Calgary**	**NHL**	**64**	**10**	**7**	**17**	**79**	**2**	**1**	**4**	**109**	**9.2**	**–12**	**21**	**33.3**	**13:57**	....	....	....	....	....	....	....	....	....
2002-03	**Calgary**	**NHL**	**81**	**10**	**12**	**22**	**126**	**2**	**0**	**2**	**156**	**6.4**	**–11**	**40**	**32.5**	**14:24**	....	....	....	....	....	....	....	....	....
	NHL Totals		**196**	**25**	**21**	**46**	**257**	**5**	**1**	**6**	**325**	**7.7**		**64**	**32.8**	**13:17**	....	....	....	....	....	....	....	....	....

ECAC Second All-Star Team (1998)

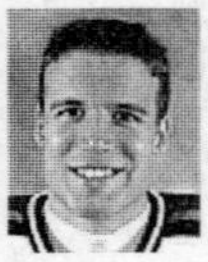

CLARKE, Dale

(KLAHRK, DAIL)

Defense. Shoots right. 6'2", 193 lbs. Born, Belleville, Ont., March 23, 1978.

Season	Club	League	GP	G	A	Pts	PIM	PP	SH	GW	S	%	+/-	TF	F%	Min	GP	G	A	Pts	PIM	PP	SH	GW	Min
1994-95	Wellington Dukes	MTJHL	48	2	13	15	18	....	....	....	....	....	....	....	....	....	....	....	....	....	....	....	....	....	....
1995-96	Wellington Dukes	MTJHL	51	6	24	30	78	....	....	....	....	....	....	....	....	....	....	....	....	....	....	....	....	....	....
1996-97	St. Lawrence	ECAC	34	1	6	7	20	....	....	....	....	....	....	....	....	....	....	....	....	....	....	....	....	....	....
1997-98	St. Lawrence	ECAC	33	1	6	7	66	....	....	....	....	....	....	....	....	....	....	....	....	....	....	....	....	....	....
1998-99	St. Lawrence	ECAC	39	3	13	16	44	....	....	....	....	....	....	....	....	....	....	....	....	....	....	....	....	....	....
99-2000	St. Lawrence	ECAC	36	6	17	23	24	....	....	....	....	....	....	....	....	....	....	....	....	....	....	....	....	....	....
	Worcester IceCats	AHL	....	....	....	....	....	....	....	....	....	....	....	....	....	....	2	0	0	0	0	....	....	....	....
2000-01	**St. Louis**	**NHL**	**3**	**0**	**0**	**0**	**0**	**0**	**0**	**0**	**5**	**0.0**	**1**	**0**	**0.0**	**13:38**	....	....	....	....	....	....	....	....	....
	Peoria Rivermen	ECHL	2	1	0	1	0	....	....	....	....	....	....	....	....	....	....	....	....	....	....	....	....	....	....
	Worcester IceCats	AHL	67	7	25	32	26	....	....	....	....	....	....	....	....	....	1	0	0	0	0	....	....	....	....
2001-02	Worcester IceCats	AHL	72	2	10	12	32	....	....	....	....	....	....	....	....	....	....	....	....	....	....	....	....	....	....
2002-03	Cincinnati	AHL	13	1	6	7	6	....	....	....	....	....	....	....	....	....	....	....	....	....	....	....	....	....	....
	Hershey Bears	AHL	33	1	5	6	12	....	....	....	....	....	....	....	....	....	....	....	....	....	....	....	....	....	....
	NHL Totals		**3**	**0**	**0**	**0**	**0**	**0**	**0**	**0**	**5**	**0.0**		**0**	**0.0**	**13:38**	....	....	....	....	....	....	....	....	....

Signed as a free agent by **St. Louis**, July 24, 1999. Traded to **Colorado** by **St. Louis** for future considerations, December 5, 2002.

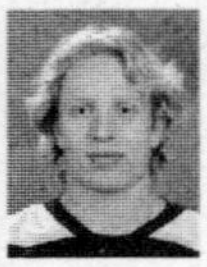

CLASSEN, Greg

(KLAW-sihn, GREHG) **NSH.**

Center. Shoots left. 6'1", 200 lbs. Born, Aylsham, Sask., August 24, 1977.

Season	Club	League	GP	G	A	Pts	PIM	PP	SH	GW	S	%	+/-	TF	F%	Min	GP	G	A	Pts	PIM	PP	SH	GW	Min
1997-98	Nipawin Hawks	SJHL	59	32	50	82	50	....	....	....	....	....	....	....	....	....	14	8	13	21	6	....	....	....	....
1998-99	Merrimack	H-East	36	14	11	25	28	....	....	....	....	....	....	....	....	....	....	....	....	....	....	....	....	....	....
99-2000	Merrimack	H-East	36	14	16	30	16	....	....	....	....	....	....	....	....	....	....	....	....	....	....	....	....	....	....
	Milwaukee	IHL	11	1	0	1	2	....	....	....	....	....	....	....	....	....	2	0	0	0	2	....	....	....	....
2000-01	**Nashville**	**NHL**	**27**	**2**	**4**	**6**	**14**	**1**	**0**	**0**	**18**	**11.1**	**–4**	**195**	**42.1**	**10:16**	....	....	....	....	....	....	....	....	....
	Milwaukee	IHL	23	5	10	15	31	....	....	....	....	....	....	....	....	....	5	0	0	0	0	....	....	....	....
2001-02	**Nashville**	**NHL**	**55**	**5**	**6**	**11**	**30**	**0**	**1**	**0**	**32**	**15.6**	**1**	**389**	**43.2**	**10:09**	....	....	....	....	....	....	....	....	....
	Milwaukee	AHL	8	2	4	6	12	....	....	....	....	....	....	....	....	....	....	....	....	....	....	....	....	....	....
2002-03	**Nashville**	**NHL**	**8**	**0**	**0**	**0**	**4**	**0**	**0**	**0**	**2**	**0.0**	**–3**	**65**	**52.3**	**10:02**	....	....	....	....	....	....	....	....	....
	Milwaukee	AHL	72	20	28	48	61	....	....	....	....	....	....	....	....	....	6	1	1	2	4	....	....	....	....
	NHL Totals		**90**	**7**	**10**	**17**	**48**	**1**	**1**	**0**	**52**	**13.5**		**649**	**43.8**	**10:10**	....	....	....	....	....	....	....	....	....

Hockey East All-Rookie Team (1999)

Signed as a free agent by **Nashville**, March 27, 2000.

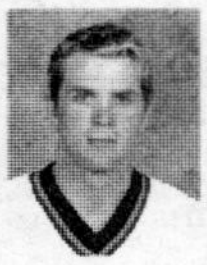

CLEARY, Daniel

(KLIH-ree, DAN-yehl) **PHX.**

Right wing. Shoots left. 6', 203 lbs. Born, Carbonear, Nfld., December 18, 1978. Chicago's 1st choice, 13th overall, in 1997 Entry Draft.

Season	Club	League	GP	G	A	Pts	PIM	PP	SH	GW	S	%	+/-	TF	F%	Min	GP	G	A	Pts	PIM	PP	SH	GW	Min
1993-94	Kingston	MTJHL	41	18	28	46	33	....	....	....	....	....	....	....	....	....	2	0	1	1	0	....	....	....	....
1994-95	Belleville Bulls	OHL	62	26	55	81	62	....	....	....	....	....	....	....	....	....	16	7	10	17	23	....	....	....	....
1995-96	Belleville Bulls	OHL	64	53	62	115	74	....	....	....	....	....	....	....	....	....	14	10	17	27	40	....	....	....	....
1996-97	Belleville Bulls	OHL	64	32	48	80	88	....	....	....	....	....	....	....	....	....	6	3	4	7	6	....	....	....	....
1997-98	Belleville Bulls	OHL	30	16	31	47	14	....	....	....	....	....	....	....	....	....	10	6	*17	*23	10	....	....	....	....
	Chicago	**NHL**	**6**	**0**	**0**	**0**	**0**	**0**	**0**	**0**	**4**	**0.0**	**–2**	....	....	....	....	....	....	....	....	....	....	....	....
	Indianapolis Ice	IHL	4	2	1	3	6	....	....	....	....	....	....	....	....	....	....	....	....	....	....	....	....	....	....
1998-99	**Chicago**	**NHL**	**35**	**4**	**5**	**9**	**24**	**0**	**0**	**0**	**49**	**8.2**	**–1**	**13**	**46.2**	**14:21**	....	....	....	....	....	....	....	....	....
	Portland Pirates	AHL	30	9	17	26	74	....	....	....	....	....	....	....	....	....	....	....	....	....	....	....	....	....	....
	Hamilton	AHL	9	0	1	1	7	....	....	....	....	....	....	....	....	....	3	0	0	0	0	....	....	....	....
99-2000	**Edmonton**	**NHL**	**17**	**3**	**2**	**5**	**8**	**0**	**0**	**1**	**18**	**16.7**	**–1**	**1**	**100.0**	**9:44**	**4**	**0**	**1**	**1**	**2**	**0**	**0**	**0**	**8:39**
	Hamilton	AHL	58	22	52	74	108	....	....	....	....	....	....	....	....	....	5	2	3	5	18	....	....	....	....
2000-01	**Edmonton**	**NHL**	**81**	**14**	**21**	**35**	**37**	**2**	**0**	**2**	**107**	**13.1**	**5**	**13**	**23.1**	**12:58**	**6**	**1**	**1**	**2**	**8**	**1**	**0**	**0**	**14:09**
2001-02	**Edmonton**	**NHL**	**65**	**10**	**19**	**29**	**51**	**2**	**1**	**1**	**75**	**13.3**	**–1**	**5**	**60.0**	**12:43**	....	....	....	....	....	....	....	....	....
2002-03	**Edmonton**	**NHL**	**57**	**4**	**13**	**17**	**31**	**0**	**0**	**1**	**89**	**4.5**	**5**	**5**	**40.0**	**11:58**	....	....	....	....	....	....	....	....	....
	NHL Totals		**261**	**35**	**60**	**95**	**151**	**4**	**1**	**5**	**342**	**10.2**		**37**	**40.5**	**12:39**	**10**	**1**	**2**	**3**	**10**	**1**	**0**	**0**	**11:57**

OHL All-Rookie Team (1995) • OHL First All-Star Team (1996, 1997) • AHL Second All-Star Team (2000)

Traded to **Edmonton** by **Chicago** with Chad Kilger, Ethan Moreau and Christian Laflamme for Boris Mironov, Dean McAmmond and Jonas Elofsson, March 20, 1999. Signed as a free agent by **Phoenix**, July 15, 2003.

			Regular Season														Playoffs								
Season	Club	League	GP	G	A	Pts	PIM	PP	SH	GW	S	%	+/-	TF	F%	Min	GP	G	A	Pts	PIM	PP	SH	GW	Min

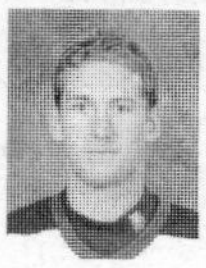

CLYMER, Ben

(KLIH-mehr, BEHN) **T.B.**

Left wing. Shoots right. 6'1", 199 lbs. Born, Bloomington, MN, April 11, 1978. Boston's 3rd choice, 27th overall, in 1997 Entry Draft.

Season	Club	League	GP	G	A	Pts	PIM	PP	SH	GW	S	%	+/-	TF	F%	Min	GP	G	A	Pts	PIM	PP	SH	GW	Min
1993-94	Jefferson Jaguars	Hi-School	23	3	7	10	20	....	....	....	....	....	....	....	....	....	....	....	....	....	....	....	....	....	....
1994-95	Jefferson Jaguars	Hi-School	28	11	22	33	36	....	....	....	....	....	....	....	....	....	....	....	....	....	....	....	....	....	....
1995-96	Jefferson Jaguars	Hi-School	18	12	34	46	34	....	....	....	....	....	....	....	....	....	5	0	6	6	6	....	....	....	....
1996-97	U. of Minnesota	WCHA	29	7	13	20	64	....	....	....	....	....	....	....	....	....	....	....	....	....	....	....	....	....	....
1997-98	U. of Minnesota	WCHA	1	0	0	0	2	....	....	....	....	....	....	....	....	....	....	....	....	....	....	....	....	....	....
1998-99	Seattle	WHL	70	12	44	56	93	....	....	....	....	....	....	....	....	....	11	1	5	6	12	....	....	....	....
99-2000	**Tampa Bay**	**NHL**	**60**	**2**	**6**	**8**	**87**	**2**	**0**	**0**	**98**	**2.0**	**–26**	**3**	**66.7**	**19:37**	....	....	....	....	....	....	....	....	....
	Detroit Vipers	IHL	19	1	9	10	30	....	....	....	....	....	....	....	....	....	....	....	....	....	....	....	....	....	....
2000-01	**Tampa Bay**	**NHL**	**23**	**5**	**1**	**6**	**21**	**3**	**0**	**0**	**25**	**20.0**	**–7**	**8**	**25.0**	**13:03**	....	....	....	....	....	....	....	....	....
	Detroit Vipers	IHL	53	5	8	13	88	....	....	....	....	....	....	....	....	....	....	....	....	....	....	....	....	....	....
2001-02	**Tampa Bay**	**NHL**	**81**	**14**	**20**	**34**	**36**	**4**	**0**	**2**	**151**	**9.3**	**–10**	**14**	**28.6**	**17:26**	....	....	....	....	....	....	....	....	....
2002-03	**Tampa Bay**	**NHL**	**65**	**6**	**12**	**18**	**57**	**1**	**0**	**1**	**103**	**5.8**	**–2**	**15**	**0.0**	**13:39**	**11**	**0**	**2**	**2**	**6**	**0**	**0**	**0**	**13:30**
	NHL Totals		**229**	**27**	**39**	**66**	**201**	**10**	**0**	**3**	**377**	**7.2**		**40**	**20.0**	**16:30**	**11**	**0**	**2**	**2**	**6**	**0**	**0**	**0**	**13:30**

• Missed majority of 1997-98 season recovering from shoulder injury suffered in game vs. U. of Michigan (CCHA), October 10, 1997. Signed as a free agent by **Tampa Bay**, October 2, 1999.

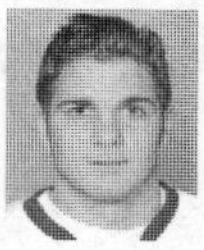

COLAIACOVO, Carlo

(koh-lee-A-KOH-voh, KAR-loh) **TOR.**

Defense. Shoots left. 6'1", 188 lbs. Born, Toronto, Ont., January 27, 1983. Toronto's 1st choice, 17th overall, in 2001 Entry Draft.

Season	Club	League	GP	G	A	Pts	PIM	PP	SH	GW	S	%	+/-	TF	F%	Min	GP	G	A	Pts	PIM	PP	SH	GW	Min
1998-99	Mississauga Reps	GTHL	44	10	12	23	28	....	....	....	....	....	....	....	....	....	....	....	....	....	....	....	....	....	....
99-2000	Erie Otters	OHL	52	4	18	22	12	....	....	....	....	....	....	....	....	....	13	2	4	6	9	....	....	....	....
2000-01	Erie Otters	OHL	62	12	27	39	59	....	....	....	....	....	....	....	....	....	14	4	7	11	16	....	....	....	....
2001-02	Erie Otters	OHL	60	13	27	40	49	....	....	....	....	....	....	....	....	....	21	7	10	17	20	....	....	....	....
2002-03	**Toronto**	**NHL**	**2**	**0**	**1**	**1**	**0**	**0**	**0**	**0**	**1**	**0.0**	**0**	**0**	**0.0**	**13:43**	....	....	....	....	....	....	....	....	....
	Erie Otters	OHL	35	14	21	35	12	....	....	....	....	....	....	....	....	....	....	....	....	....	....	....	....	....	....
	NHL Totals		**2**	**0**	**1**	**1**	**0**	**0**	**0**	**0**	**1**	**0.0**		**0**	**0.0**	**13:43**	....	....	....	....	....	....	....	....	....

OHL Second All-Star Team (2002, 2003)

• Returned to **Erie** (OHL) by **Toronto**, November 10, 2002.

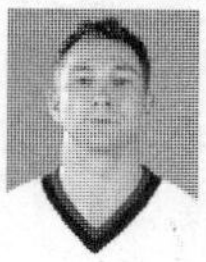

COLE, Erik

(KOHL, AIR-ihk) **CAR.**

Left wing. Shoots left. 6'2", 200 lbs. Born, Oswego, NY, November 6, 1978. Carolina's 3rd choice, 71st overall, in 1998 Entry Draft.

Season	Club	League	GP	G	A	Pts	PIM	PP	SH	GW	S	%	+/-	TF	F%	Min	GP	G	A	Pts	PIM	PP	SH	GW	Min
1995-96	Oswego	Hi-School	40	49	41	90	....	....	....	....	....	....	....	....	....	....	....	....	....	....	....	....	....	....	....
1996-97	Des Moines	USHL	48	30	34	64	140	....	....	....	....	....	....	....	....	....	5	2	0	2	6	....	....	....	....
1997-98	Clarkson Knights	ECAC	34	11	20	31	55	....	....	....	....	....	....	....	....	....	....	....	....	....	....	....	....	....	....
1998-99	Clarkson Knights	ECAC	36	*22	20	42	50	....	....	....	....	....	....	....	....	....	....	....	....	....	....	....	....	....	....
99-2000	Clarkson Knights	ECAC	33	19	11	30	46	....	....	....	....	....	....	....	....	....	....	....	....	....	....	....	....	....	....
	Cincinnati	IHL	9	4	3	7	2	....	....	....	....	....	....	....	....	....	7	1	1	2	2	....	....	....	....
2000-01	Cincinnati	IHL	69	23	20	43	28	....	....	....	....	....	....	....	....	....	5	1	0	1	2	....	....	....	....
2001-02	**Carolina**	**NHL**	**81**	**16**	**24**	**40**	**35**	**3**	**0**	**2**	**159**	**10.1**	**–10**	**17**	**47.1**	**16:04**	**23**	**6**	**3**	**9**	**30**	**1**	**0**	**1**	**18:27**
2002-03	**Carolina**	**NHL**	**53**	**14**	**13**	**27**	**72**	**6**	**2**	**3**	**125**	**11.2**	**1**	**56**	**39.3**	**17:08**	....	....	....	....	....	....	....	....	....
	NHL Totals		**134**	**30**	**37**	**67**	**107**	**9**	**2**	**5**	**284**	**10.6**		**73**	**41.1**	**16:29**	**23**	**6**	**3**	**9**	**30**	**1**	**0**	**1**	**18:27**

ECAC Rookie of the Year (1998) (co-winner - Willie Mitchell) • ECAC First All-Star Team (1999) • NCAA East Second All-American Team (1999) • ECAC Second All-Star Team (2000)

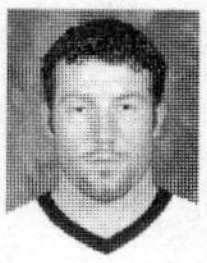

COMMODORE, Mike

(KAWM-uh-dohr, MIGHK) **CGY.**

Defense. Shoots right. 6'4", 230 lbs. Born, Fort Saskatchewan, Alta., November 7, 1979. New Jersey's 2nd choice, 42nd overall, in 1999 Entry Draft.

Season	Club	League	GP	G	A	Pts	PIM	PP	SH	GW	S	%	+/-	TF	F%	Min	GP	G	A	Pts	PIM	PP	SH	GW	Min
1996-97	Ft. Saskatchewan	AJHL	51	3	8	11	244	....	....	....	....	....	....	....	....	....	....	....	....	....	....	....	....	....	....
1997-98	North Dakota	WCHA	29	0	5	5	74	....	....	....	....	....	....	....	....	....	....	....	....	....	....	....	....	....	....
1998-99	North Dakota	WCHA	39	5	8	13	154	....	....	....	....	....	....	....	....	....	....	....	....	....	....	....	....	....	....
99-2000	North Dakota	WCHA	38	5	7	12	*154	....	....	....	....	....	....	....	....	....	....	....	....	....	....	....	....	....	....
2000-01	**New Jersey**	**NHL**	**20**	**1**	**4**	**5**	**14**	**0**	**0**	**0**	**11**	**9.1**	**5**	**0**	**0.0**	**12:46**	....	....	....	....	....	....	....	....	....
	Albany River Rats	AHL	41	2	5	7	59	....	....	....	....	....	....	....	....	....	....	....	....	....	....	....	....	....	....
2001-02	**New Jersey**	**NHL**	**37**	**0**	**1**	**1**	**30**	**0**	**0**	**0**	**22**	**0.0**	**–12**	**0**	**0.0**	**12:37**	....	....	....	....	....	....	....	....	....
	Albany River Rats	AHL	14	0	3	3	31	....	....	....	....	....	....	....	....	....	....	....	....	....	....	....	....	....	....
2002-03	Cincinnati	AHL	61	2	9	11	210	....	....	....	....	....	....	....	....	....	....	....	....	....	....	....	....	....	....
	Calgary	**NHL**	**6**	**0**	**1**	**1**	**19**	**0**	**0**	**0**	**5**	**0.0**	**2**	**0**	**0.0**	**11:35**	....	....	....	....	....	....	....	....	....
	Saint John Flames	AHL	7	0	3	3	18	....	....	....	....	....	....	....	....	....	....	....	....	....	....	....	....	....	....
	NHL Totals		**63**	**1**	**6**	**7**	**63**	**0**	**0**	**0**	**38**	**2.6**		**0**	**0.0**	**12:34**	....	....	....	....	....	....	....	....	....

NCAA Championship All-Tournament Team (2000)

Traded to **Anaheim** by **New Jersey** with Petr Sykora, Jean-Francois Damphousse and Igor Pohanka for Jeff Friesen, Oleg Tverdovsky and Maxim Balmochnykh, July 6, 2002. Traded to **Calgary** by **Anaheim** with Jean-Francois Damphousse for Rob Niedermayer, March 11, 2003.

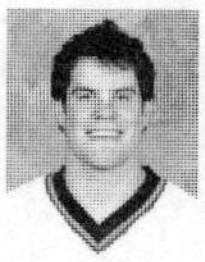

COMRIE, Mike

(KAWM-ree, MIGHK) **EDM.**

Center. Shoots left. 5'9", 178 lbs. Born, Edmonton, Alta., September 11, 1980. Edmonton's 5th choice, 91st overall, in 1999 Entry Draft.

Season	Club	League	GP	G	A	Pts	PIM	PP	SH	GW	S	%	+/-	TF	F%	Min	GP	G	A	Pts	PIM	PP	SH	GW	Min
1995-96	Edmonton SSAC	AMHL	33	51	52	103	....	....	....	....	....	....	....	....	....	....	....	....	....	....	....	....	....	....	....
1996-97	St. Albert Saints	AJHL	63	37	41	78	44	....	....	....	....	....	....	....	....	....	....	....	....	....	....	....	....	....	....
1997-98	St. Albert Saints	AJHL	58	*60	*78	*138	134	....	....	....	....	....	....	....	....	....	19	*24	*24	*48	51	....	....	....	....
1998-99	U. of Michigan	CCHA	42	19	25	44	38	....	....	....	....	....	....	....	....	....	....	....	....	....	....	....	....	....	....
99-2000	U. of Michigan	CCHA	40	24	35	59	95	....	....	....	....	....	....	....	....	....	....	....	....	....	....	....	....	....	....
2000-01	Kootenay Ice	WHL	37	39	40	79	79	....	....	....	....	....	....	....	....	....	....	....	....	....	....	....	....	....	....
	Edmonton	**NHL**	**41**	**8**	**14**	**22**	**14**	**3**	**0**	**1**	**62**	**12.9**	**6**	**372**	**43.3**	**11:23**	**6**	**1**	**2**	**3**	**0**	**1**	**0**	**1**	**14:60**
2001-02	**Edmonton**	**NHL**	**82**	**33**	**27**	**60**	**45**	**8**	**0**	**5**	**170**	**19.4**	**16**	**1198**	**47.3**	**17:32**	....	....	....	....	....	....	....	....	....
2002-03	**Edmonton**	**NHL**	**69**	**20**	**31**	**51**	**90**	**8**	**0**	**6**	**170**	**11.8**	**–18**	**1069**	**47.1**	**17:51**	**6**	**1**	**0**	**1**	**10**	**0**	**0**	**0**	**13:07**
	NHL Totals		**192**	**61**	**72**	**133**	**149**	**19**	**0**	**12**	**402**	**15.2**		**2639**	**46.6**	**16:20**	**12**	**2**	**2**	**4**	**10**	**1**	**0**	**1**	**14:03**

AJHL Rookie of the Year (1997) • AJHL MVP (1998) • Canadian Junior "A" Player of the Year (1998) • CCHA All-Rookie Team (1999) • CCHA First All-Star Team (1999) • CCHA Rookie of the Year (1999) • CCHA First All-Star Team (2000) • NCAA West Second All-American Team (2000)

• Left **University of Michigan** (CCHA) and signed as a free agent by **Kootenay** (WHL), August 23, 2000. • Left **Kootenay** (WHL) and signed with **Edmonton**, December 30, 2000.

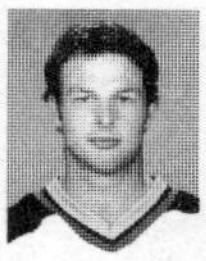

CONNOLLY, Tim

(KAHN-noh-lee, TIHM) **BUF.**

Center. Shoots right. 6'1", 182 lbs. Born, Syracuse, NY, May 7, 1981. NY Islanders' 1st choice, 5th overall, in 1999 Entry Draft.

Season	Club	League	GP	G	A	Pts	PIM	PP	SH	GW	S	%	+/-	TF	F%	Min	GP	G	A	Pts	PIM	PP	SH	GW	Min
1996-97	Syracuse	MTJHL	50	42	62	104	34	....	....	....	....	....	....	....	....	....	....	....	....	....	....	....	....	....	....
1997-98	Erie Otters	OHL	59	30	32	62	32	....	....	....	....	....	....	....	....	....	7	1	6	7	6	....	....	....	....
1998-99	Erie Otters	OHL	46	34	34	68	50	....	....	....	....	....	....	....	....	....	....	....	....	....	....	....	....	....	....
99-2000	**NY Islanders**	**NHL**	**81**	**14**	**20**	**34**	**44**	**2**	**1**	**1**	**114**	**12.3**	**–25**	**786**	**36.3**	**16:18**	....	....	....	....	....	....	....	....	....
2000-01	**NY Islanders**	**NHL**	**82**	**10**	**31**	**41**	**42**	**5**	**0**	**0**	**171**	**5.8**	**–14**	**989**	**41.7**	**20:02**	....	....	....	....	....	....	....	....	....
2001-02	**Buffalo**	**NHL**	**82**	**10**	**35**	**45**	**34**	**3**	**0**	**3**	**126**	**7.9**	**4**	**1074**	**39.6**	**16:58**	....	....	....	....	....	....	....	....	....
2002-03	**Buffalo**	**NHL**	**80**	**12**	**13**	**25**	**32**	**6**	**0**	**2**	**159**	**7.5**	**–28**	**845**	**42.8**	**15:60**	....	....	....	....	....	....	....	....	....
	NHL Totals		**325**	**46**	**99**	**145**	**152**	**16**	**1**	**6**	**570**	**8.1**		**3694**	**40.2**	**17:20**	....	....	....	....	....	....	....	....	....

Traded to **Buffalo** by **NY Islanders** with Taylor Pyatt for Michael Peca, June 24, 2001.

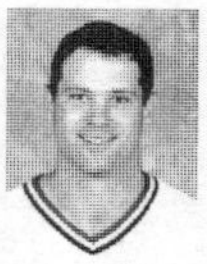

CONROY, Craig

(KAWN-roi, KRAYG) **CGY.**

Center. Shoots right. 6'2", 197 lbs. Born, Potsdam, NY, September 4, 1971. Montreal's 7th choice, 123rd overall, in 1990 Entry Draft.

Season	Club	League	GP	G	A	Pts	PIM	PP	SH	GW	S	%	+/-	TF	F%	Min	GP	G	A	Pts	PIM	PP	SH	GW	Min
1989-90	Northfield Prep	Hi-School	31	33	43	76	....	....	....	....	....	....	....	....	....	....	....	....	....	....	....	....	....	....	....
1990-91	Clarkson Knights	ECAC	40	8	21	29	24	....	....	....	....	....	....	....	....	....	....	....	....	....	....	....	....	....	....
1991-92	Clarkson Knights	ECAC	31	19	17	36	36	....	....	....	....	....	....	....	....	....	....	....	....	....	....	....	....	....	....
1992-93	Clarkson Knights	ECAC	35	10	23	33	26	....	....	....	....	....	....	....	....	....	....	....	....	....	....	....	....	....	....
1993-94	Clarkson Knights	ECAC	34	26	*40	*66	46	....	....	....	....	....	....	....	....	....	....	....	....	....	....	....	....	....	....
1994-95	Fredericton	AHL	55	26	18	44	29	....	....	....	....	....	....	....	....	....	11	7	3	10	6	....	....	....	....
	Montreal	**NHL**	**6**	**1**	**0**	**1**	**0**	**0**	**0**	**0**	**4**	**25.0**	**–1**	....	....	....	....	....	....	....	....	....	....	....	....
1995-96	**Montreal**	**NHL**	**7**	**0**	**0**	**0**	**2**	**0**	**0**	**0**	**1**	**0.0**	**–4**	....	....	....	....	....	....	....	....	....	....	....	....
	Fredericton	AHL	67	31	38	69	65	....	....	....	....	....	....	....	....	....	10	5	7	12	6	....	....	....	....

			Regular Season														Playoffs								
Season	**Club**	**League**	**GP**	**G**	**A**	**Pts**	**PIM**	**PP**	**SH**	**GW**	**S**	**%**	**+/-**	**TF**	**F%**	**Min**	**GP**	**G**	**A**	**Pts**	**PIM**	**PP**	**SH**	**GW**	**Min**
1996-97	Fredericton	AHL	9	10	6	16	10	....	....	....	....	....	....	....	....	....	....	....	....	....	....	....	....	....	....
	St. Louis	**NHL**	**61**	**6**	**11**	**17**	**43**	**0**	**0**	**1**	**74**	**8.1**	**0**	....	....	....	**6**	**0**	**0**	**0**	**8**	**0**	**0**	**0**	....
	Worcester IceCats	AHL	5	5	6	11	2	....	....	....	....	....	....	....	....	....	....	....	....	....	....	....	....	....	....
1997-98	**St. Louis**	**NHL**	**81**	**14**	**29**	**43**	**46**	**0**	**3**	**1**	**118**	**11.9**	**20**	....	....	....	**10**	**1**	**2**	**3**	**8**	**0**	**0**	**1**	....
1998-99	**St. Louis**	**NHL**	**69**	**14**	**25**	**39**	**38**	**0**	**1**	**1**	**134**	**10.4**	**14**	**1190**	**54.6**	**16:39**	**13**	**2**	**1**	**3**	**6**	**0**	**0**	**0**	**15:09**
99-2000	**St. Louis**	**NHL**	**79**	**12**	**15**	**27**	**36**	**1**	**2**	**3**	**98**	**12.2**	**5**	**1339**	**53.6**	**14:48**	**7**	**0**	**2**	**2**	**2**	**0**	**0**	**0**	**13:13**
2000-01	**St. Louis**	**NHL**	**69**	**11**	**14**	**25**	**46**	**0**	**3**	**2**	**101**	**10.9**	**2**	**729**	**55.1**	**14:01**	....	....	....	....	....	....	....	....	....
	Calgary	**NHL**	**14**	**3**	**4**	**7**	**14**	**0**	**1**	**0**	**32**	**9.4**	**0**	**264**	**52.7**	**18:08**	....	....	....	....	....	....	....	....	....
2001-02	**Calgary**	**NHL**	**81**	**27**	**48**	**75**	**32**	**7**	**2**	**4**	**146**	**18.5**	**24**	**1654**	**54.3**	**20:56**	....	....	....	....	....	....	....	....	....
2002-03	**Calgary**	**NHL**	**79**	**22**	**37**	**59**	**36**	**5**	**0**	**2**	**143**	**15.4**	**–4**	**1579**	**57.0**	**19:47**	....	....	....	....	....	....	....	....	....
	NHL Totals		**546**	**110**	**183**	**293**	**293**	**13**	**12**	**14**	**851**	**12.9**		**6755**	**54.9**	**17:23**	**36**	**3**	**5**	**8**	**24**	**0**	**0**	**1**	**14:28**

ECAC First All-Star Team (1994) • NCAA East First All-American Team (1994) • NCAA Final Four All-Tournament Team (1994)

Traded to **St. Louis** by **Montreal** with Pierre Turgeon and Rory Fitzpatrick for Murray Baron, Shayne Corson and St. Louis' 5th round choice (Gennady Razin) in 1997 Entry Draft, October 29, 1996. Traded to **Calgary** by **St. Louis** with St. Louis' 7th round choice (David Moss) in 2001 Entry Draft for Cory Stillman, March 13, 2001.

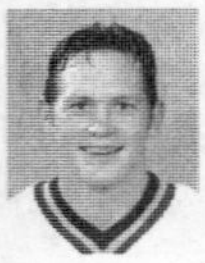

COOKE, Matt

(KUK, MAT) **VAN.**

Center. Shoots left. 5'11", 205 lbs. Born, Belleville, Ont., September 7, 1978. Vancouver's 8th choice, 144th overall, in 1997 Entry Draft.

Season	Club	League	GP	G	A	Pts	PIM	PP	SH	GW	S	%	+/-	TF	F%	Min	GP	G	A	Pts	PIM	PP	SH	GW	Min
1994-95	Wellington Dukes	MTJHL	46	9	23	32	62	....	....	....	....	....	....	....	....	....	....	....	....	....	....	....	....	....	....
1995-96	Windsor Spitfires	OHL	61	8	11	19	102	....	....	....	....	....	....	....	....	....	7	1	3	4	6	....	....	....	....
1996-97	Windsor Spitfires	OHL	65	45	50	95	146	....	....	....	....	....	....	....	....	....	5	5	5	10	10	....	....	....	....
1997-98	Windsor Spitfires	OHL	23	14	19	33	50	....	....	....	....	....	....	....	....	....	....	....	....	....	....	....	....	....	....
	Kingston	OHL	25	8	13	21	49	....	....	....	....	....	....	....	....	....	12	8	8	16	20	....	....	....	....
1998-99	**Vancouver**	**NHL**	**30**	**0**	**2**	**2**	**27**	**0**	**0**	**0**	**22**	**0.0**	**–12**	**189**	**40.2**	**8:07**	....	....	....	....	....	....	....	....	....
	Syracuse Crunch	AHL	37	15	18	33	119	....	....	....	....	....	....	....	....	....	....	....	....	....	....	....	....	....	....
99-2000	**Vancouver**	**NHL**	**51**	**5**	**7**	**12**	**39**	**0**	**1**	**1**	**58**	**8.6**	**3**	**71**	**39.4**	**11:48**	....	....	....	....	....	....	....	....	....
	Syracuse Crunch	AHL	18	5	8	13	27	....	....	....	....	....	....	....	....	....	....	....	....	....	....	....	....	....	....
2000-01	**Vancouver**	**NHL**	**81**	**14**	**13**	**27**	**94**	**0**	**2**	**0**	**121**	**11.6**	**5**	**321**	**43.0**	**14:35**	**4**	**0**	**0**	**0**	**4**	**0**	**0**	**0**	**12:04**
2001-02	**Vancouver**	**NHL**	**82**	**13**	**20**	**33**	**111**	**1**	**0**	**2**	**103**	**12.6**	**4**	**28**	**32.1**	**14:03**	**6**	**3**	**2**	**5**	**0**	**1**	**0**	**0**	**15:09**
2002-03	**Vancouver**	**NHL**	**82**	**15**	**27**	**42**	**82**	**1**	**4**	**0**	**118**	**12.7**	**21**	**31**	**35.5**	**13:24**	**14**	**2**	**1**	**3**	**12**	**0**	**0**	**0**	**14:06**
	NHL Totals		**326**	**47**	**69**	**116**	**353**	**2**	**7**	**3**	**422**	**11.1**		**640**	**40.9**	**13:07**	**24**	**5**	**3**	**8**	**16**	**1**	**0**	**0**	**14:02**

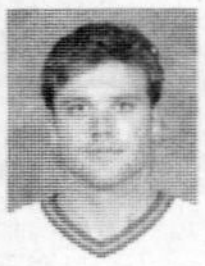

CORRINET, Chris

(KOHR-rih-neht, KRIHS)

Right wing. Shoots right. 6'3", 220 lbs. Born, Derby, CT, October 29, 1978. Washington's 4th choice, 107th overall, in 1998 Entry Draft.

Season	Club	League	GP	G	A	Pts	PIM	PP	SH	GW	S	%	+/-	TF	F%	Min	GP	G	A	Pts	PIM	PP	SH	GW	Min
1996-97	Deerfield	Hi-School	16	6	15	21	10	....	....	....	....	....	....	....	....	....	....	....	....	....	....	....	....	....	....
1997-98	Princeton	ECAC	31	3	6	9	22	....	....	....	....	....	....	....	....	....	....	....	....	....	....	....	....	....	....
1998-99	Princeton	ECAC	32	10	6	16	38	....	....	....	....	....	....	....	....	....	....	....	....	....	....	....	....	....	....
99-2000	Princeton	ECAC	30	10	14	24	41	....	....	....	....	....	....	....	....	....	....	....	....	....	....	....	....	....	....
2000-01	Princeton	ECAC	31	13	12	25	30	....	....	....	....	....	....	....	....	....	....	....	....	....	....	....	....	....	....
	Portland Pirates	AHL	6	0	1	1	4	....	....	....	....	....	....	....	....	....	2	1	0	1	0	....	....	....	....
2001-02	**Washington**	**NHL**	**8**	**0**	**1**	**1**	**6**	**0**	**0**	**0**	**8**	**0.0**	**–4**	**0**	**0.0**	**10:04**	....	....	....	....	....	....	....	....	....
	Portland Pirates	AHL	51	15	18	33	64	....	....	....	....	....	....	....	....	....	....	....	....	....	....	....	....	....	....
2002-03	Portland Pirates	AHL	33	0	3	3	23	....	....	....	....	....	....	....	....	....	....	....	....	....	....	....	....	....	....
	Philadelphia	AHL	1	0	0	0	0	....	....	....	....	....	....	....	....	....	....	....	....	....	....	....	....	....	....
	Worcester IceCats	AHL	28	6	12	18	27	....	....	....	....	....	....	....	....	....	3	0	2	2	2	....	....	....	....
	NHL Totals		**8**	**0**	**1**	**1**	**6**	**0**	**0**	**0**	**8**	**0.0**		**0**	**0.0**	**10:04**	....	....	....	....	....	....	....	....	....

Signed to a professional try-out contract by **Philadelphia** (AHL) following release by **Washington**, January 31, 2003. Signed to a professional try-out contract by **Worcester** (AHL) following release by **Philadelphia** (AHL), February 4, 2003.

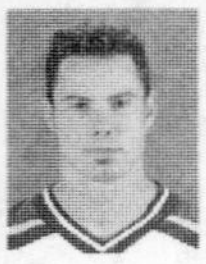

CORSO, Daniel

(KOHR-soh, DAN-yehl)

Center. Shoots left. 5'10", 187 lbs. Born, Montreal, Que., April 3, 1978. St. Louis' 6th choice, 169th overall, in 1996 Entry Draft.

Season	Club	League	GP	G	A	Pts	PIM	PP	SH	GW	S	%	+/-	TF	F%	Min	GP	G	A	Pts	PIM	PP	SH	GW	Min
1993-94	Magog	QAAA	36	17	22	39	....	....	....	....	....	....	....	....	....	....	12	10	12	22	....	....	....	....	....
1994-95	Victoriaville Tigres	QMJHL	65	27	26	53	6	....	....	....	....	....	....	....	....	....	4	2	5	7	2	....	....	....	....
1995-96	Victoriaville Tigres	QMJHL	65	49	65	114	77	....	....	....	....	....	....	....	....	....	12	6	7	13	4	....	....	....	....
1996-97	Victoriaville Tigres	QMJHL	54	51	68	119	50	....	....	....	....	....	....	....	....	....	....	....	....	....	....	....	....	....	....
1997-98	Victoriaville Tigres	QMJHL	35	24	51	75	20	....	....	....	....	....	....	....	....	....	3	1	1	2	2	....	....	....	....
1998-99	Worcester IceCats	AHL	63	14	14	28	26	....	....	....	....	....	....	....	....	....	....	....	....	....	....	....	....	....	....
99-2000	Worcester IceCats	AHL	71	21	34	55	19	....	....	....	....	....	....	....	....	....	9	2	3	5	10	....	....	....	....
2000-01	**St. Louis**	**NHL**	**28**	**10**	**3**	**13**	**14**	**5**	**0**	**4**	**42**	**23.8**	**0**	**296**	**56.1**	**13:56**	**12**	**0**	**1**	**1**	**0**	**0**	**0**	**0**	**8:52**
	Worcester IceCats	AHL	52	19	37	56	47	....	....	....	....	....	....	....	....	....	....	....	....	....	....	....	....	....	....
2001-02	**St. Louis**	**NHL**	**41**	**4**	**7**	**11**	**6**	**1**	**0**	**2**	**25**	**16.0**	**3**	**423**	**54.9**	**11:13**	**2**	**0**	**0**	**0**	**0**	**0**	**0**	**0**	**8:51**
2002-03	**St. Louis**	**NHL**	**1**	**0**	**0**	**0**	**0**	**0**	**0**	**0**	**0**	**0.0**	**–1**	**8**	**50.0**	**7:44**	....	....	....	....	....	....	....	....	....
	Worcester IceCats	AHL	1	0	0	0	0	....	....	....	....	....	....	....	....	....	....	....	....	....	....	....	....	....	....
	NHL Totals		**70**	**14**	**10**	**24**	**20**	**6**	**0**	**6**	**67**	**20.9**		**727**	**55.3**	**12:15**	**14**	**0**	**1**	**1**	**0**	**0**	**0**	**0**	**8:52**

QMJHL All-Rookie Team (1995) • QMJHL First All-Star Team (1997) • QMJHL MVP (1997)

• Spent majority of 2001-02 season on practice roster, October 22, 2001. • Missed majority of 2002-03 season recovering from shoulder injury.

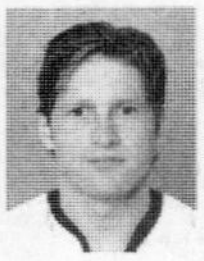

CORSON, Shayne

(KOHR-sohn, SHAYN)

Left wing. Shoots left. 6'1", 202 lbs. Born, Barrie, Ont., August 13, 1966. Montreal's 2nd choice, 8th overall, in 1984 Entry Draft.

Season	Club	League	GP	G	A	Pts	PIM	PP	SH	GW	S	%	+/-	TF	F%	Min	GP	G	A	Pts	PIM	PP	SH	GW	Min
1982-83	Barrie Colts	OJHL-B	23	13	29	42	87	....	....	....	....	....	....	....	....	....	....	....	....	....	....	....	....	....	....
1983-84	Brantford	OHL	66	25	46	71	165	....	....	....	....	....	....	....	....	....	6	4	1	5	26	....	....	....	....
1984-85	Hamilton	OHL	54	27	63	90	154	....	....	....	....	....	....	....	....	....	11	3	7	10	19	....	....	....	....
1985-86	Hamilton	OHL	47	41	57	98	153	....	....	....	....	....	....	....	....	....	....	....	....	....	....	....	....	....	....
	Montreal	**NHL**	**3**	**0**	**0**	**0**	**2**	**0**	**0**	**0**	**1**	**0.0**	**–3**	....	....	....	....	....	....	....	....	....	....	....	....
1986-87	**Montreal**	**NHL**	**55**	**12**	**11**	**23**	**144**	**0**	**1**	**3**	**69**	**17.4**	**10**	....	....	....	**17**	**6**	**5**	**11**	**30**	**1**	**1**	**1**	....
1987-88	**Montreal**	**NHL**	**71**	**12**	**27**	**39**	**152**	**2**	**0**	**2**	**90**	**13.3**	**22**	....	....	....	**3**	**1**	**0**	**1**	**12**	**0**	**0**	**0**	....
1988-89	**Montreal**	**NHL**	**80**	**26**	**24**	**50**	**193**	**10**	**0**	**3**	**133**	**19.5**	**–1**	....	....	....	**21**	**4**	**5**	**9**	**65**	**2**	**0**	**2**	....
1989-90	**Montreal**	**NHL**	**76**	**31**	**44**	**75**	**144**	**7**	**0**	**6**	**192**	**16.1**	**33**	....	....	....	**11**	**2**	**8**	**10**	**20**	**0**	**0**	**0**	....
1990-91	**Montreal**	**NHL**	**71**	**23**	**24**	**47**	**138**	**7**	**0**	**2**	**164**	**14.0**	**9**	....	....	....	**13**	**9**	**6**	**15**	**36**	**4**	**1**	**3**	....
1991-92	**Montreal**	**NHL**	**64**	**17**	**36**	**53**	**118**	**3**	**0**	**2**	**165**	**10.3**	**15**	....	....	....	**10**	**2**	**5**	**7**	**15**	**0**	**0**	**0**	....
1992-93	**Edmonton**	**NHL**	**80**	**16**	**31**	**47**	**209**	**9**	**2**	**1**	**164**	**9.8**	**–19**	....	....	....	....	....	....	....	....	....	....	....	....
1993-94	**Edmonton**	**NHL**	**64**	**25**	**29**	**54**	**118**	**11**	**0**	**3**	**171**	**14.6**	**–8**	....	....	....	....	....	....	....	....	....	....	....	....
1994-95	**Edmonton**	**NHL**	**48**	**12**	**24**	**36**	**86**	**2**	**0**	**1**	**131**	**9.2**	**–17**	....	....	....	....	....	....	....	....	....	....	....	....
1995-96	**St. Louis**	**NHL**	**77**	**18**	**28**	**46**	**192**	**13**	**0**	**0**	**150**	**12.0**	**3**	....	....	....	**13**	**8**	**6**	**14**	**22**	**6**	**1**	**1**	....
1996-97	**St. Louis**	**NHL**	**11**	**2**	**1**	**3**	**24**	**1**	**0**	**0**	**19**	**10.5**	**–4**	....	....	....	....	....	....	....	....	....	....	....	....
	Montreal	**NHL**	**47**	**6**	**15**	**21**	**80**	**2**	**0**	**2**	**96**	**6.3**	**–5**	....	....	....	**5**	**1**	**0**	**1**	**4**	**0**	**1**	**0**	....
1997-98	**Montreal**	**NHL**	**62**	**21**	**34**	**55**	**108**	**14**	**1**	**1**	**142**	**14.8**	**2**	....	....	....	**10**	**3**	**6**	**9**	**26**	**1**	**0**	**1**	....
	Canada	Olympics	6	1	1	2	2	....	....	....	....	....	....	....	....	....	....	....	....	....	....	....	....	....	....
1998-99	**Montreal**	**NHL**	**63**	**12**	**20**	**32**	**147**	**7**	**0**	**4**	**142**	**8.5**	**–10**	**184**	**45.1**	**20:42**	....	....	....	....	....	....	....	....	....
99-2000	**Montreal**	**NHL**	**70**	**8**	**20**	**28**	**115**	**2**	**0**	**1**	**121**	**6.6**	**–2**	**445**	**43.4**	**19:05**	....	....	....	....	....	....	....	....	....
2000-01	**Toronto**	**NHL**	**77**	**8**	**18**	**26**	**189**	**0**	**0**	**2**	**102**	**7.8**	**1**	**602**	**48.8**	**15:50**	**11**	**1**	**1**	**2**	**14**	**0**	**0**	**0**	**18:59**
2001-02	**Toronto**	**NHL**	**74**	**12**	**21**	**33**	**120**	**0**	**1**	**1**	**111**	**10.8**	**11**	**598**	**45.5**	**17:04**	**19**	**1**	**6**	**7**	**33**	**0**	**0**	**0**	**21:04**
2002-03	**Toronto**	**NHL**	**46**	**7**	**8**	**15**	**49**	**0**	**0**	**0**	**69**	**10.1**	**–5**	**202**	**44.6**	**15:02**	**2**	**0**	**0**	**0**	**2**	**0**	**0**	**0**	**9:42**
	NHL Totals		**1139**	**268**	**415**	**683**	**2328**	**90**	**5**	**34**	**2232**	**12.0**		**2031**	**45.9**	**17:37**	**135**	**38**	**48**	**86**	**279**	**14**	**4**	**8**	**19:38**

Played in NHL All-Star Game (1990, 1994, 1998)

Traded to **Edmonton** by **Montreal** with Brent Gilchrist and Vladimir Vujtek for Vincent Damphousse and Edmonton's 4th round choice (Adam Wiesel) in 1993 Entry Draft, August 27, 1992. Signed as a free agent by **St. Louis**, July 28, 1995. Traded to **Montreal** by **St. Louis** with Murray Baron and St. Louis' 5th round choice (Gennady Razin) in 1997 Entry Draft for Pierre Turgeon, Rory Fitzpatrick and Craig Conroy, October 29, 1996. Signed as a free agent by **Toronto**, July 4, 2000. • Officially announced retirement, April 15, 2003.

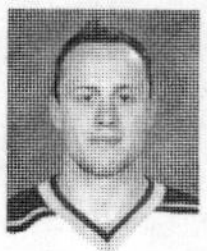

CORVO, Joe

(KOHR-voh, JOH-sehf) **L.A.**

Defense. Shoots right. 6'1", 205 lbs. Born, Oak Park, IL, June 20, 1977. Los Angeles' 4th choice, 83rd overall, in 1997 Entry Draft.

			Regular Season														Playoffs								
Season	Club	League	GP	G	A	Pts	PIM	PP	SH	GW	S	%	+/-	TF	F%	Min	GP	G	A	Pts	PIM	PP	SH	GW	Min
1995-96	West-Michigan	CCHA	41	5	25	30	38	....	....	....	....	....	....	....	....	....	....	....	....	....	....	....	....	....	....
1996-97	West-Michigan	CCHA	32	12	21	33	85	....	....	....	....	....	....	....	....	....	....	....	....	....	....	....	....	....	....
1997-98	West-Michigan	CCHA	32	5	12	17	93	....	....	....	....	....	....	....	....	....	....	....	....	....	....	....	....	....	....
1998-99	Springfield	AHL	50	5	15	20	32	....	....	....	....	....	....	....	....	....	....	....	....	....	....	....	....	....	....
	Hampton Roads	ECHL	5	0	0	0	15	....	....	....	....	....	....	....	....	....	4	0	1	1	0	....	....	....	....
99-2000			DID NOT PLAY																						
2000-01	Lowell	AHL	77	10	23	33	31	....	....	....	....	....	....	....	....	....	4	3	1	4	0	....	....	....	....
2001-02	Manchester	AHL	80	13	37	50	30	....	....	....	....	....	....	....	....	....	5	0	5	5	0	....	....	....	....
2002-03	Manchester	AHL	26	8	18	26	8	....	....	....	....	....	....	....	....	....	3	0	0	0	0	....	....	....	....
	Los Angeles	**NHL**	**50**	**5**	**7**	**12**	**14**	**2**	**0**	**0**	**84**	**6.0**	**2**	**0**	**0.0**	**18:37**	....	....	....	....	....	....	....	....	....
	NHL Totals		**50**	**5**	**7**	**12**	**14**	**2**	**0**	**0**	**84**	**6.0**		**0**	**0.0**	**18:37**	....	....	....	....	....	....	....	....	....

CCHA All-Rookie Team (1996) • CCHA Second All-Star Team (1997)

• Missed entire 1999-2000 season after failing to come to contract terms with **Los Angeles.**

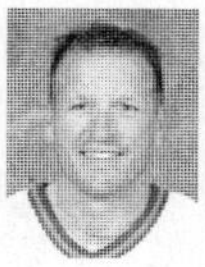

COTE, Sylvain

(KOH-tay, SIHL-vayn)

Defense. Shoots right. 5'11", 201 lbs. Born, Quebec City, Que., January 19, 1966. Hartford's 1st choice, 11th overall, in 1984 Entry Draft.

			Regular Season														Playoffs								
Season	Club	League	GP	G	A	Pts	PIM	PP	SH	GW	S	%	+/-	TF	F%	Min	GP	G	A	Pts	PIM	PP	SH	GW	Min
1981-82	Ste-Foy	QAAA	46	18	29	47	117	....	....	....	....	....	....	....	....	....	5	0	3	3	8	....	....	....	....
1982-83	Quebec Remparts	QMJHL	66	10	24	34	50	....	....	....	....	....	....	....	....	....	....	....	....	....	....	....	....	....	....
1983-84	Quebec Remparts	QMJHL	66	15	50	65	89	....	....	....	....	....	....	....	....	....	5	1	1	2	0	....	....	....	....
1984-85	**Hartford**	**NHL**	**67**	**3**	**9**	**12**	**17**	**1**	**0**	**1**	**90**	**3.3**	**-30**	....	....	....	....	....	....	....	....	....	....	....	....
1985-86	Hull Olympiques	QMJHL	26	10	33	43	14	....	....	....	....	....	....	....	....	....	13	6	*28	34	22	....	....	....	....
	Hartford	**NHL**	**2**	**0**	**0**	**0**	**0**	**0**	**0**	**0**	**0**	**0.0**	**1**	....	....	....	....	....	....	....	....	....	....	....	....
	Binghamton	AHL	12	2	4	6	0	....	....	....	....	....	....	....	....	....	....	....	....	....	....	....	....	....	....
1986-87	**Hartford**	**NHL**	**67**	**2**	**8**	**10**	**20**	**0**	**0**	**0**	**100**	**2.0**	**11**	....	....	....	**2**	**0**	**2**	**2**	**2**	**0**	**0**	**0**	....
1987-88	**Hartford**	**NHL**	**67**	**7**	**21**	**28**	**30**	**0**	**1**	**0**	**142**	**4.9**	**-8**	....	....	....	**6**	**1**	**1**	**2**	**4**	**1**	**0**	**0**	....
1988-89	**Hartford**	**NHL**	**78**	**8**	**9**	**17**	**49**	**1**	**0**	**0**	**130**	**6.2**	**-7**	....	....	....	**3**	**0**	**1**	**1**	**4**	**0**	**0**	**0**	....
1989-90	**Hartford**	**NHL**	**28**	**4**	**2**	**6**	**14**	**1**	**0**	**1**	**50**	**8.0**	**2**	....	....	....	**5**	**0**	**0**	**0**	**2**	**0**	**0**	**0**	....
1990-91	**Hartford**	**NHL**	**73**	**7**	**12**	**19**	**17**	**1**	**0**	**0**	**154**	**4.5**	**-17**	....	....	....	**6**	**0**	**2**	**2**	**2**	**0**	**0**	**0**	....
1991-92	**Washington**	**NHL**	**78**	**11**	**29**	**40**	**31**	**6**	**0**	**2**	**151**	**7.3**	**7**	....	....	....	**7**	**1**	**2**	**3**	**4**	**0**	**0**	**0**	....
1992-93	**Washington**	**NHL**	**77**	**21**	**29**	**50**	**34**	**8**	**2**	**3**	**206**	**10.2**	**28**	....	....	....	**6**	**1**	**1**	**2**	**4**	**0**	**0**	**0**	....
1993-94	**Washington**	**NHL**	**84**	**16**	**35**	**51**	**66**	**3**	**2**	**2**	**212**	**7.5**	**30**	....	....	....	**9**	**1**	**8**	**9**	**6**	**0**	**0**	**0**	....
1994-95	**Washington**	**NHL**	**47**	**5**	**14**	**19**	**53**	**1**	**0**	**2**	**124**	**4.0**	**2**	....	....	....	**7**	**1**	**3**	**4**	**2**	**0**	**0**	**0**	....
1995-96	**Washington**	**NHL**	**81**	**5**	**33**	**38**	**40**	**3**	**0**	**2**	**212**	**2.4**	**5**	....	....	....	**6**	**2**	**0**	**2**	**12**	**1**	**0**	**0**	....
1996-97	**Washington**	**NHL**	**57**	**6**	**18**	**24**	**28**	**2**	**0**	**0**	**131**	**4.6**	**11**	....	....	....	....	....	....	....	....	....	....	....	....
1997-98	**Washington**	**NHL**	**59**	**1**	**15**	**16**	**36**	**0**	**0**	**0**	**83**	**1.2**	**-5**	....	....	....	....	....	....	....	....	....	....	....	....
	Toronto	**NHL**	**12**	**3**	**6**	**9**	**6**	**1**	**0**	**1**	**20**	**15.0**	**2**	....	....	....	....	....	....	....	....	....	....	....	....
1998-99	**Toronto**	**NHL**	**79**	**5**	**24**	**29**	**28**	**0**	**0**	**1**	**119**	**4.2**	**22**	**1**	**0.0**	**21:04**	**17**	**2**	**1**	**3**	**10**	**0**	**0**	**0**	**19:49**
99-2000	**Toronto**	**NHL**	**3**	**0**	**1**	**1**	**0**	**0**	**0**	**0**	**3**	**0.0**	**1**	**0**	**0.0**	**21:40**	....	....	....	....	....	....	....	....	....
	Chicago	**NHL**	**45**	**6**	**18**	**24**	**14**	**5**	**0**	**2**	**78**	**7.7**	**-4**	**1**	**100.0**	**23:22**	....	....	....	....	....	....	....	....	....
	Dallas	**NHL**	**28**	**2**	**8**	**10**	**14**	**0**	**0**	**0**	**47**	**4.3**	**6**	**0**	**0.0**	**18:10**	**23**	**2**	**1**	**3**	**8**	**2**	**0**	**0**	**16:54**
2000-01	**Washington**	**NHL**	**68**	**7**	**11**	**18**	**18**	**1**	**1**	**1**	**86**	**8.1**	**-3**	**0**	**0.0**	**17:47**	**5**	**0**	**0**	**0**	**2**	**0**	**0**	**0**	**21:11**
2001-02	**Washington**	**NHL**	**70**	**3**	**11**	**14**	**26**	**1**	**0**	**2**	**101**	**3.0**	**-15**	**0**	**0.0**	**19:44**	....	....	....	....	....	....	....	....	....
2002-03	**Washington**	**NHL**	**1**	**0**	**0**	**0**	**4**	**0**	**0**	**0**	**0**	**0.0**	**0**	**0**	**0.0**	**4:12**	....	....	....	....	....	....	....	....	....
	NHL Totals		**1171**	**122**	**313**	**435**	**545**	**35**	**6**	**20**	**2239**	**5.4**		**2**	**50.0**	**20:01**	**102**	**11**	**22**	**33**	**62**	**4**	**0**	**0**	**18:28**

QMJHL Second All-Star Team (1984) • QMJHL First All-Star Team (1986)

Traded to **Washington** by **Hartford** for Washington's 2nd round choice (Andrei Nikolishin) in 1992 Entry Draft, September 8, 1991. Traded to **Toronto** by **Washington** for Jeff Brown, March 24, 1998. Traded to **Chicago** by **Toronto** for Chicago's 2nd round choice (Karel Pilar) in 2001 Entry Draft, October 8, 1999. Traded to **Dallas** by **Chicago** with Dave Manson for Kevin Dean, Derek Plante and Dallas' 2nd round choice (Matt Keith) in 2001 Entry Draft, February 8, 2000. Signed as a free agent by **Washington**, July 7, 2000. • Released by **Washington**, November 12, 2002.

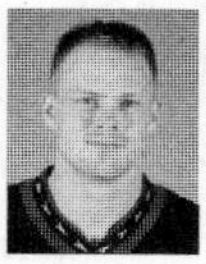

COWAN, Jeff

(KOW-an, JEHF) **ATL.**

Left wing. Shoots left. 6'2", 210 lbs. Born, Scarborough, Ont., September 27, 1976.

			Regular Season														Playoffs								
Season	Club	League	GP	G	A	Pts	PIM	PP	SH	GW	S	%	+/-	TF	F%	Min	GP	G	A	Pts	PIM	PP	SH	GW	Min
1992-93	Guelph Platers	OJHL-B	45	8	8	16	22	....	....	....	....	....	....	....	....	....	....	....	....	....	....	....	....	....	....
1993-94	Guelph Platers	OJHL-B	43	30	26	56	96	....	....	....	....	....	....	....	....	....	....	....	....	....	....	....	....	....	....
	Guelph Storm	OHL	17	1	0	1	5	....	....	....	....	....	....	....	....	....	....	....	....	....	....	....	....	....	....
1994-95	Guelph Storm	OHL	51	10	7	17	14	....	....	....	....	....	....	....	....	....	14	1	1	2	0	....	....	....	....
1995-96	Barrie Colts	OHL	66	38	14	52	29	....	....	....	....	....	....	....	....	....	5	1	2	3	6	....	....	....	....
1996-97	Saint John Flames	AHL	22	5	5	10	8	....	....	....	....	....	....	....	....	....	....	....	....	....	....	....	....	....	....
	Roanoke Express	ECHL	47	21	13	34	42	....	....	....	....	....	....	....	....	....	....	....	....	....	....	....	....	....	....
1997-98	Saint John Flames	AHL	69	15	13	28	23	....	....	....	....	....	....	....	....	....	13	4	1	5	14	....	....	....	....
1998-99	Saint John Flames	AHL	71	7	12	19	117	....	....	....	....	....	....	....	....	....	4	0	1	1	10	....	....	....	....
99-2000	**Calgary**	**NHL**	**13**	**4**	**1**	**5**	**16**	**0**	**0**	**0**	**26**	**15.4**	**2**	**0**	**0.0**	**10:22**	....	....	....	....	....	....	....	....	....
	Saint John Flames	AHL	47	15	10	25	77	....	....	....	....	....	....	....	....	....	....	....	....	....	....	....	....	....	....
2000-01	**Calgary**	**NHL**	**51**	**9**	**4**	**13**	**74**	**2**	**0**	**1**	**48**	**18.8**	**-8**	**5**	**20.0**	**9:06**	....	....	....	....	....	....	....	....	....
2001-02	**Calgary**	**NHL**	**19**	**1**	**0**	**1**	**40**	**0**	**0**	**1**	**13**	**7.7**	**-3**	**2**	**50.0**	**7:44**	....	....	....	....	....	....	....	....	....
	Atlanta	**NHL**	**38**	**4**	**1**	**5**	**50**	**0**	**0**	**1**	**51**	**7.8**	**-11**	**5**	**20.0**	**12:27**	....	....	....	....	....	....	....	....	....
2002-03	**Atlanta**	**NHL**	**66**	**3**	**5**	**8**	**115**	**0**	**0**	**0**	**52**	**5.8**	**-15**	**10**	**30.0**	**8:24**	....	....	....	....	....	....	....	....	....
	NHL Totals		**187**	**21**	**11**	**32**	**295**	**2**	**0**	**3**	**190**	**11.1**		**22**	**27.3**	**9:29**	....	....	....	....	....	....	....	....	....

Signed as a free agent by **Calgary**, October 2, 1995. Traded to **Atlanta** by **Calgary** with the rights to Kurtis Foster for Petr Buzek, December 18, 2001.

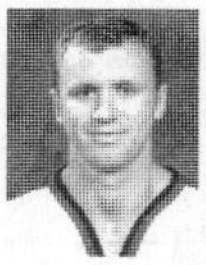

CRAIG, Mike

(KRAYG, MIGHK)

Right wing. Shoots right. 6'1", 185 lbs. Born, London, Ont., June 6, 1971. Minnesota's 2nd choice, 28th overall, in 1989 Entry Draft.

			Regular Season														Playoffs								
Season	Club	League	GP	G	A	Pts	PIM	PP	SH	GW	S	%	+/-	TF	F%	Min	GP	G	A	Pts	PIM	PP	SH	GW	Min
1986-87	Woodstock	OJHL-C	32	29	19	48	64	....	....	....	....	....	....	....	....	....	....	....	....	....	....	....	....	....	....
1987-88	Oshawa Generals	OHL	61	6	10	16	39	....	....	....	....	....	....	....	....	....	7	7	0	1	11	....	....	....	....
1988-89	Oshawa Generals	OHL	63	36	36	72	34	....	....	....	....	....	....	....	....	....	6	3	1	4	6	....	....	....	....
1989-90	Oshawa Generals	OHL	43	36	40	76	85	....	....	....	....	....	....	....	....	....	17	10	16	26	46	....	....	....	....
1990-91	**Minnesota**	**NHL**	**39**	**8**	**4**	**12**	**32**	**1**	**0**	**2**	**59**	**13.6**	**-11**	....	....	....	**10**	**1**	**1**	**2**	**20**	**1**	**0**	**1**	....
1991-92	**Minnesota**	**NHL**	**67**	**15**	**16**	**31**	**155**	**4**	**0**	**4**	**136**	**11.0**	**-12**	....	....	....	**4**	**1**	**0**	**1**	**7**	**0**	**0**	**0**	....
1992-93	**Minnesota**	**NHL**	**70**	**15**	**23**	**38**	**106**	**7**	**0**	**0**	**131**	**11.5**	**-11**	....	....	....	....	....	....	....	....	....	....	....	....
1993-94	**Dallas**	**NHL**	**72**	**13**	**24**	**37**	**139**	**3**	**0**	**2**	**150**	**8.7**	**-14**	....	....	....	**4**	**0**	**0**	**0**	**2**	**0**	**0**	**0**	....
1994-95	**Toronto**	**NHL**	**37**	**5**	**5**	**10**	**12**	**1**	**0**	**1**	**61**	**8.2**	**-21**	....	....	....	**2**	**0**	**1**	**1**	**2**	**0**	**0**	**0**	....
1995-96	**Toronto**	**NHL**	**70**	**8**	**12**	**20**	**42**	**1**	**0**	**1**	**108**	**7.4**	**-8**	....	....	....	**6**	**0**	**0**	**0**	**18**	**0**	**0**	**0**	....
1996-97	**Toronto**	**NHL**	**65**	**7**	**13**	**20**	**62**	**1**	**0**	**0**	**128**	**5.5**	**-20**	....	....	....	....	....	....	....	....	....	....	....	....
1997-98	San Antonio	IHL	12	4	1	5	18	....	....	....	....	....	....	....	....	....	....	....	....	....	....	....	....	....	....
	Kansas City	IHL	59	14	33	47	68	....	....	....	....	....	....	....	....	....	11	5	5	10	28	....	....	....	....
1998-99	**San Jose**	**NHL**	**1**	**0**	**0**	**0**	**0**	**0**	**0**	**0**	**1**	**0.0**	**-1**	**0**	**0.0**	**11:25**	....	....	....	....	....	....	....	....	....
	Kentucky	AHL	52	27	17	44	72	....	....	....	....	....	....	....	....	....	12	5	4	9	18	....	....	....	....
99-2000	Kentucky	AHL	76	39	39	78	116	....	....	....	....	....	....	....	....	....	9	5	5	10	14	....	....	....	....
2000-01	Hershey Bears	AHL	57	21	22	43	73	....	....	....	....	....	....	....	....	....	12	3	2	5	20	....	....	....	....
2001-02	**San Jose**	**NHL**	**2**	**0**	**0**	**0**	**2**	**0**	**0**	**0**	**2**	**0.0**	**0**	**0**	**0.0**	**7:57**	....	....	....	....	....	....	....	....	....
	Cleveland Barons	AHL	69	35	25	60	87	....	....	....	....	....	....	....	....	....	....	....	....	....	....	....	....	....	....
2002-03	SC Langnau	Swiss	44	17	17	34	97	....	....	....	....	....	....	....	....	....	....	....	....	....	....	....	....	....	....
	NHL Totals		**423**	**71**	**97**	**168**	**550**	**18**	**0**	**10**	**776**	**9.1**		**0**	**0.0**	**9:06**	**26**	**2**	**2**	**4**	**49**	**1**	**0**	**1**	....

Transferred to **Dallas** after **Minnesota** franchise relocated, June 9, 1993. Signed as a free agent by **Toronto**, July 29, 1994. Signed as a free agent by **San Jose**, July 13, 1998. Signed as a free agent by **Colorado**, August 2, 2000. Signed as a free agent by **San Jose**, September 6, 2001. Signed as a free agent by **SC Langnau** (Swiss), May 1, 2002.

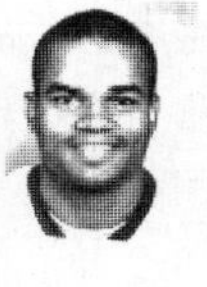

CRAIGHEAD, John

(KRAIG-hehd, JAWN)

Right wing. Shoots right. 6', 195 lbs. Born, Vancouver, B.C., November 23, 1971.

			Regular Season														Playoffs								
Season	Club	League	GP	G	A	Pts	PIM	PP	SH	GW	S	%	+/-	TF	F%	Min	GP	G	A	Pts	PIM	PP	SH	GW	Min
1990-91	Burnaby	PCJHL	22	10	32	42	259	....	....	....	....	....	....	....	....	....	....	....	....	....	....	....	....	....	....
	New Westminster	BCJHL	3	0	0	0	12	....	....	....	....	....	....	....	....	....	....	....	....	....	....	....	....	....	....
1991-92	West Palm Beach	SunHL	39	12	17	29	160	....	....	....	....	....	....	....	....	....	....	....	....	....	....	....	....	....	....
	South Surrey	BCJHL	13	7	6	13	38	....	....	....	....	....	....	....	....	....	....	....	....	....	....	....	....	....	....
	Chilliwack Chiefs	BCJHL	25	12	16	28	116	....	....	....	....	....	....	....	....	....	....	....	....	....	....	....	....	....	....

			Regular Season														Playoffs								
Season	Club	League	GP	G	A	Pts	PIM	PP	SH	GW	S	%	+/-	TF	F%	Min	GP	G	A	Pts	PIM	PP	SH	GW	Min
1992-93	West Palm Beach	SunHL	36	12	9	21	158	....	....	....	....	....	....	....	....	....	....	....	....	....	....	....	....	....	....
	Louisville	ECHL	5	1	0	1	33	....	....	....	....	....	....	....	....	....	....	....	....	....	....	....	....	....	....
1993-94	Huntington	ECHL	9	4	2	6	44	....	....	....	....	....	....	....	....	....	....	....	....	....	....	....	....	....	....
	Richmond	ECHL	28	18	12	30	89	....	....	....	....	....	....	....	....	....	....	....	....	....	....	....	....	....	....
1994-95	Detroit Vipers	IHL	44	5	7	12	285	....	....	....	....	....	....	....	....	....	3	0	1	1	4	....	....	....	....
1995-96	Detroit Vipers	IHL	63	7	9	16	368	....	....	....	....	....	....	....	....	....	10	2	3	5	28	....	....	....	....
1996-97	**Toronto**	**NHL**	**5**	**0**	**0**	**0**	**10**	**0**	**0**	**0**	**0**	**0.0**	**0**	....	....	....	....	....	....	....	....	....	....	....	....
	St. John's	AHL	53	9	10	19	318	....	....	....	....	....	....	....	....	....	7	1	1	2	22	....	....	....	....
1997-98	Cleveland	IHL	49	9	7	16	233	....	....	....	....	....	....	....	....	....	....	....	....	....	....	....	....	....	....
	Quebec Rafales	IHL	13	2	2	4	73	....	....	....	....	....	....	....	....	....	....	....	....	....	....	....	....	....	....
1998-99	Nurnberg	Germany	34	4	6	10	144	....	....	....	....	....	....	....	....	....	13	1	4	5	*60	....	....	....	....
99-2000	Nurnberg	Germany	59	20	18	38	208	....	....	....	....	....	....	....	....	....	....	....	....	....	....	....	....	....	....
2000-01	Nurnberg	Germany	49	7	11	18	152	....	....	....	....	....	....	....	....	....	4	0	0	0	12	....	....	....	....
2001-02	Oberhausen	Germany	49	10	12	22	226	....	....	....	....	....	....	....	....	....	....	....	....	....	....	....	....	....	....
2002-03	Manitoba Moose	AHL	47	5	10	15	109	....	....	....	....	....	....	....	....	....	14	0	2	2	32	....	....	....	....
	NHL Totals		**5**	**0**	**0**	**0**	**10**	**0**	**0**	**0**	**0**	**0.0**		....	....	....	....	....	....	....	....	....	....	....	....

Signed as a free agent by **Toronto**, July 22, 1996.

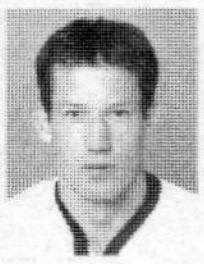

CROSS, Cory

(KRAWS, KOHR-ee) **EDM.**

Defense. Shoots left. 6'5", 220 lbs. Born, Lloydminster, Alta., January 3, 1971. Tampa Bay's 1st choice, 1st overall, in 1992 Supplemental Draft.

Season	Club	League	GP	G	A	Pts	PIM	PP	SH	GW	S	%	+/-	TF	F%	Min	GP	G	A	Pts	PIM	PP	SH	GW	Min
1990-91	U. of Alberta	CWUAA	20	2	5	7	16	....	....	....	....	....	....	....	....	....	....	....	....	....	....	....	....	....	....
1991-92	U. of Alberta	CWUAA	41	4	11	15	82	....	....	....	....	....	....	....	....	....	....	....	....	....	....	....	....	....	....
1992-93	U. of Alberta	CWUAA	43	11	28	39	107	....	....	....	....	....	....	....	....	....	....	....	....	....	....	....	....	....	....
	Atlanta Knights	IHL	7	0	1	1	2	....	....	....	....	....	....	....	....	....	4	0	0	0	6	....	....	....	....
1993-94	**Tampa Bay**	**NHL**	**5**	**0**	**0**	**0**	**6**	**0**	**0**	**0**	**5**	**0.0**	**–3**	....	....	....	....	....	....	....	....	....	....	....	....
	Atlanta Knights	IHL	70	4	14	18	72	....	....	....	....	....	....	....	....	....	9	1	2	3	14	....	....	....	....
1994-95	Atlanta Knights	IHL	41	5	10	15	67	....	....	....	....	....	....	....	....	....	....	....	....	....	....	....	....	....	....
	Tampa Bay	**NHL**	**43**	**1**	**5**	**6**	**41**	**0**	**0**	**1**	**35**	**2.9**	**–6**	....	....	....	....	....	....	....	....	....	....	....	....
1995-96	**Tampa Bay**	**NHL**	**75**	**2**	**14**	**16**	**66**	**0**	**0**	**0**	**57**	**3.5**	**4**	....	....	....	**6**	**0**	**0**	**0**	**22**	**0**	**0**	**0**	....
1996-97	**Tampa Bay**	**NHL**	**72**	**4**	**5**	**9**	**95**	**0**	**0**	**2**	**75**	**5.3**	**6**	....	....	....	....	....	....	....	....	....	....	....	....
1997-98	**Tampa Bay**	**NHL**	**74**	**3**	**6**	**9**	**77**	**0**	**1**	**0**	**72**	**4.2**	**–24**	....	....	....	....	....	....	....	....	....	....	....	....
1998-99	**Tampa Bay**	**NHL**	**67**	**2**	**16**	**18**	**92**	**0**	**0**	**0**	**96**	**2.1**	**–25**	**0**	**0.0**	**22:38**	....	....	....	....	....	....	....	....	....
99-2000	**Toronto**	**NHL**	**71**	**4**	**11**	**15**	**64**	**0**	**0**	**1**	**60**	**6.7**	**13**	**0**	**0.0**	**15:59**	**12**	**0**	**2**	**2**	**2**	**0**	**0**	**0**	**15:21**
2000-01	**Toronto**	**NHL**	**41**	**3**	**5**	**8**	**50**	**1**	**0**	**1**	**34**	**8.8**	**7**	**0**	**0.0**	**18:00**	**11**	**2**	**1**	**3**	**10**	**0**	**0**	**1**	**16:05**
2001-02	**Toronto**	**NHL**	**50**	**3**	**9**	**12**	**54**	**0**	**0**	**1**	**39**	**7.7**	**11**	**0**	**0.0**	**15:18**	**12**	**0**	**0**	**0**	**8**	**0**	**0**	**0**	**17:00**
2002-03	Hartford	AHL	2	0	0	0	2	....	....	....	....	....	....	....	....	....	....	....	....	....	....	....	....	....	....
	NY Rangers	**NHL**	**26**	**0**	**4**	**4**	**16**	**0**	**0**	**0**	**18**	**0.0**	**13**	**1**	**0.0**	**17:12**	....	....	....	....	....	....	....	....	....
	Edmonton	**NHL**	**11**	**2**	**3**	**5**	**8**	**1**	**0**	**1**	**11**	**18.2**	**3**	**0**	**0.0**	**17:51**	**6**	**0**	**1**	**1**	**20**	**0**	**0**	**0**	**20:37**
	NHL Totals		**535**	**24**	**78**	**102**	**569**	**2**	**1**	**7**	**502**	**4.8**		**1**	**0.0**	**18:02**	**47**	**2**	**4**	**6**	**62**	**0**	**0**	**1**	**16:48**

Traded to **Toronto** by **Tampa Bay** with Tampa Bay's 7th round choice (Ivan Kolozvary) in 2001 Entry Draft for Fredrik Modin, October 1, 1999. Signed as a free agent by **NY Rangers**, December 17, 2002. Traded to **Edmonton** by **NY Rangers** with Radek Dvorak for Anson Carter and Ales Pisa, March 11, 2003.

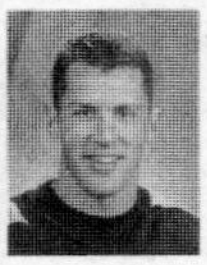

CROZIER, Greg

(KROH-zhuhr, GREHG) **N.J.**

Left wing. Shoots left. 6'3", 200 lbs. Born, Calgary, Alta., July 6, 1976. Pittsburgh's 4th choice, 73rd overall, in 1994 Entry Draft.

Season	Club	League	GP	G	A	Pts	PIM	PP	SH	GW	S	%	+/-	TF	F%	Min	GP	G	A	Pts	PIM	PP	SH	GW	Min
1991-92	Amherst Broncos	Hi-School	46	61	47	108	47	....	....	....	....	....	....	....	....	....	....	....	....	....	....	....	....	....	....
1992-93	Lawrence School	Hi-School	22	22	14	36	....	....	....	....	....	....	....	....	....	....	....	....	....	....	....	....	....	....	....
1993-94	Lawrence School	Hi-School	18	22	26	48	12	....	....	....	....	....	....	....	....	....	....	....	....	....	....	....	....	....	....
1994-95	Lawrence School	Hi-School	31	45	32	77	22	....	....	....	....	....	....	....	....	....	....	....	....	....	....	....	....	....	....
1995-96	U. of Michigan	CCHA	42	14	10	24	46	....	....	....	....	....	....	....	....	....	....	....	....	....	....	....	....	....	....
1996-97	U. of Michigan	CCHA	31	5	15	20	45	....	....	....	....	....	....	....	....	....	....	....	....	....	....	....	....	....	....
1997-98	U. of Michigan	CCHA	45	12	10	22	26	....	....	....	....	....	....	....	....	....	....	....	....	....	....	....	....	....	....
1998-99	U. of Michigan	CCHA	39	7	6	13	63	....	....	....	....	....	....	....	....	....	....	....	....	....	....	....	....	....	....
99-2000	Wilkes-Barre	AHL	71	22	22	44	33	....	....	....	....	....	....	....	....	....	....	....	....	....	....	....	....	....	....
2000-01	**Pittsburgh**	**NHL**	**1**	**0**	**0**	**0**	**0**	**0**	**0**	**0**	**0**	**0.0**	**0**	**0**	**0.0**	**4:10**	....	....	....	....	....	....	....	....	....
	Wilkes-Barre	AHL	77	24	36	60	81	....	....	....	....	....	....	....	....	....	21	6	5	11	16	....	....	....	....
2001-02	Providence Bruins	AHL	54	5	6	11	62	....	....	....	....	....	....	....	....	....	....	....	....	....	....	....	....	....	....
	Houston Aeros	AHL	10	1	5	6	10	....	....	....	....	....	....	....	....	....	14	2	1	3	26	....	....	....	....
2002-03	Houston Aeros	AHL	7	0	1	1	6	....	....	....	....	....	....	....	....	....	....	....	....	....	....	....	....	....	....
	Albany River Rats	AHL	56	19	19	38	46	....	....	....	....	....	....	....	....	....	....	....	....	....	....	....	....	....	....
	NHL Totals		**1**	**0**	**0**	**0**	**0**	**0**	**0**	**0**	**0**	**0.0**		**0**	**0.0**	**4:10**	....	....	....	....	....	....	....	....	....

Signed as a free agent by **Boston**, August 8, 2001. Traded to **Minnesota** by **Boston** for Darryl Laplante, March 19, 2002. Signed as a free agent by **New Jersey**, August, 2003.

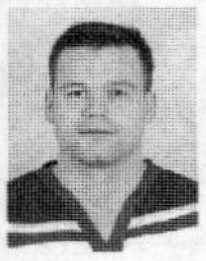

CULLEN, David

(KUH-lehn, DAY-vihd)

Defense. Shoots right. 6'2", 209 lbs. Born, St. Catharines, Ont., December 30, 1976.

Season	Club	League	GP	G	A	Pts	PIM	PP	SH	GW	S	%	+/-	TF	F%	Min	GP	G	A	Pts	PIM	PP	SH	GW	Min
1992-93	Thorold	OJHL-B	34	4	6	10	28	....	....	....	....	....	....	....	....	....	....	....	....	....	....	....	....	....	....
1993-94	Thorold	OJHL-B	40	10	35	45	26	....	....	....	....	....	....	....	....	....	....	....	....	....	....	....	....	....	....
1994-95	Thorold	OJHL-B	36	16	30	46	12	....	....	....	....	....	....	....	....	....	....	....	....	....	....	....	....	....	....
1995-96	U. of Maine	H-East	34	2	4	6	22	....	....	....	....	....	....	....	....	....	....	....	....	....	....	....	....	....	....
1996-97	U. of Maine	H-East	35	5	25	30	8	....	....	....	....	....	....	....	....	....	....	....	....	....	....	....	....	....	....
1997-98	U. of Maine	H-East	36	10	27	37	24	....	....	....	....	....	....	....	....	....	....	....	....	....	....	....	....	....	....
1998-99	U. of Maine	H-East	41	11	33	44	24	....	....	....	....	....	....	....	....	....	....	....	....	....	....	....	....	....	....
99-2000	Springfield	AHL	78	10	21	31	57	....	....	....	....	....	....	....	....	....	2	0	0	0	2	....	....	....	....
2000-01	Springfield	AHL	69	13	29	42	40	....	....	....	....	....	....	....	....	....	....	....	....	....	....	....	....	....	....
	Phoenix	**NHL**	**2**	**0**	**0**	**0**	**0**	**0**	**0**	**0**	**0**	**0.0**	**1**	**0**	**0.0**	**12:25**	....	....	....	....	....	....	....	....	....
2001-02	**Phoenix**	**NHL**	**14**	**0**	**0**	**0**	**6**	**0**	**0**	**0**	**3**	**0.0**	**–5**	**0**	**0.0**	**12:21**	....	....	....	....	....	....	....	....	....
	Springfield	AHL	15	1	4	5	4	....	....	....	....	....	....	....	....	....	....	....	....	....	....	....	....	....	....
	Minnesota	**NHL**	**3**	**0**	**0**	**0**	**0**	**0**	**0**	**0**	**0**	**0.0**	**–3**	**0**	**0.0**	**14:02**	....	....	....	....	....	....	....	....	....
	Houston Aeros	AHL	38	5	15	20	4	....	....	....	....	....	....	....	....	....	13	0	6	6	6	....	....	....	....
2002-03	Houston Aeros	AHL	72	2	27	29	42	....	....	....	....	....	....	....	....	....	23	3	4	7	14	....	....	....	....
	NHL Totals		**19**	**0**	**0**	**0**	**6**	**0**	**0**	**0**	**3**	**0.0**		**0**	**0.0**	**12:37**	....	....	....	....	....	....	....	....	....

Hockey East First All-Star Team (1999) • NCAA East First All-American Team (1999) • NCAA Championship All-Tournament Team (1999)

Signed as a free agent by **Phoenix**, April 16, 1999. Traded to **Minnesota** by **Phoenix** for Sebastien Bordeleau, January 4, 2002.

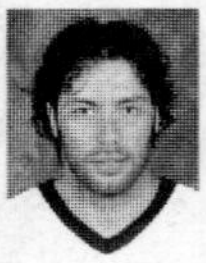

CULLEN, Matt

(KUH-lehn, MAT) **FLA.**

Center. Shoots left. 6'2", 199 lbs. Born, Virginia, MN, November 2, 1976. Anaheim's 2nd choice, 35th overall, in 1996 Entry Draft.

Season	Club	League	GP	G	A	Pts	PIM	PP	SH	GW	S	%	+/-	TF	F%	Min	GP	G	A	Pts	PIM	PP	SH	GW	Min
1994-95	Moorhead Spuds	Hi-School	28	47	42	89	78	....	....	....	....	....	....	....	....	....	....	....	....	....	....	....	....	....	....
1995-96	St. Cloud State	WCHA	39	12	29	41	28	....	....	....	....	....	....	....	....	....	....	....	....	....	....	....	....	....	....
1996-97	St. Cloud State	WCHA	36	15	30	45	70	....	....	....	....	....	....	....	....	....	....	....	....	....	....	....	....	....	....
	Baltimore Bandits	AHL	6	3	3	6	7	....	....	....	....	....	....	....	....	....	3	0	2	2	0	....	....	....	....
1997-98	**Anaheim**	**NHL**	**61**	**6**	**21**	**27**	**23**	**2**	**0**	**0**	**75**	**8.0**	**–4**	....	....	....	....	....	....	....	....	....	....	....	....
	Cincinnati	AHL	18	15	12	27	2	....	....	....	....	....	....	....	....	....	....	....	....	....	....	....	....	....	....
1998-99	**Anaheim**	**NHL**	**75**	**11**	**14**	**25**	**47**	**5**	**1**	**1**	**112**	**9.8**	**–12**	**1047**	**47.7**	**15:31**	**4**	**0**	**0**	**0**	**0**	**0**	**0**	**0**	**15:30**
	Cincinnati	AHL	3	1	2	3	8	....	....	....	....	....	....	....	....	....	....	....	....	....	....	....	....	....	....
99-2000	**Anaheim**	**NHL**	**80**	**13**	**26**	**39**	**24**	**1**	**0**	**1**	**137**	**9.5**	**5**	**1247**	**44.6**	**16:54**	....	....	....	....	....	....	....	....	....
2000-01	**Anaheim**	**NHL**	**82**	**10**	**30**	**40**	**38**	**4**	**0**	**1**	**159**	**6.3**	**–23**	**1478**	**48.0**	**18:15**	....	....	....	....	....	....	....	....	....
2001-02	**Anaheim**	**NHL**	**79**	**18**	**30**	**48**	**24**	**3**	**1**	**4**	**164**	**11.0**	**–1**	**1283**	**51.4**	**17:01**	....	....	....	....	....	....	....	....	....
2002-03	**Anaheim**	**NHL**	**50**	**7**	**14**	**21**	**12**	**1**	**0**	**1**	**77**	**9.1**	**–4**	**271**	**50.6**	**14:18**	....	....	....	....	....	....	....	....	....
	Florida	**NHL**	**30**	**6**	**6**	**12**	**22**	**2**	**1**	**1**	**54**	**11.1**	**–4**	**423**	**47.3**	**14:43**	....	....	....	....	....	....	....	....	....
	NHL Totals		**457**	**71**	**141**	**212**	**190**	**18**	**3**	**9**	**778**	**9.1**		**5749**	**48.0**	**16:27**	**4**	**0**	**0**	**0**	**0**	**0**	**0**	**0**	**15:30**

WCHA Second All-Star Team (1997)

Traded to **Florida** by **Anaheim** with Pavel Trnka and Anaheim's 4th round choice (James Pemberton) in 2003 Entry Draft for Sandis Ozolinsh and Lance Ward, January 30, 2003.

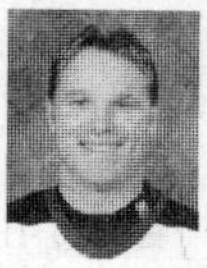

CULLIMORE, Jassen

(KUHL-ih-mohr, JAY-sehn) **T.B.**

Defense. Shoots left. 6'5", 244 lbs. Born, Simcoe, Ont., December 4, 1972. Vancouver's 2nd choice, 29th overall, in 1991 Entry Draft.

			Regular Season														Playoffs								
Season	Club	League	GP	G	A	Pts	PIM	PP	SH	GW	S	%	+/-	TF	F%	Min	GP	G	A	Pts	PIM	PP	SH	GW	Min
1986-87	Caledonia	OJHL-C	18	2	0	2	9																		
1987-88	Simcoe Rams	OJHL-C	35	11	14	25	92																		
1988-89	Peterboro B's	OJHL-B	29	11	17	28	88																		
	Peterborough	OHL	20	2	1	3	6																		
1989-90	Peterborough	OHL	59	2	6	8	61										11	0	2	2	8				
1990-91	Peterborough	OHL	62	8	16	24	74										4	1	0	1	7				
1991-92	Peterborough	OHL	54	9	37	46	65										10	3	6	9	8				
1992-93	Hamilton	AHL	56	5	7	12	60																		
1993-94	Hamilton	AHL	71	8	20	28	86										3	0	1	1	2				
1994-95	Syracuse Crunch	AHL	33	2	7	9	66																		
	Vancouver	NHL	34	1	2	3	39	0	0	0	30	3.3	−2				11	0	0	0	12	0	0	0	
1995-96	Vancouver	NHL	27	1	1	2	21	0	0	1	12	8.3	4												
1996-97	Vancouver	NHL	3	0	0	0	2	0	0	0	2	0.0	−2												
	Montreal	NHL	49	2	6	8	42	0	1	1	52	3.8	4				2	0	0	0	2	0	0	0	
1997-98	Montreal	NHL	3	0	0	0	4	0	0	0	1	0.0	0												
	Fredericton	AHL	5	1	0	1	8																		
	Tampa Bay	NHL	25	1	2	3	22	1	0	0	17	5.9	−4												
1998-99	Tampa Bay	NHL	78	5	12	17	81	1	1	1	73	6.8	−22	0	0.0	20:14									
99-2000	Providence Bruins	AHL	16	5	10	15	31																		
	Tampa Bay	NHL	46	1	1	2	66	0	0	0	23	4.3	−12	2	0.0	15:38									
2000-01	Tampa Bay	NHL	74	1	6	7	80	0	0	0	56	1.8	−6	0	0.0	19:43									
2001-02	Tampa Bay	NHL	78	4	9	13	58	0	0	1	84	4.8	−1	0	0.0	20:07									
2002-03	Tampa Bay	NHL	28	1	3	4	31	0	0	0	23	4.3	3	0	0.0	18:25	11	1	1	2	4	0	0	0	22:11
	NHL Totals		445	17	42	59	446	2	2	4	373	4.6		2	0.0	19:13	24	1	1	2	18	0	0	0	22:11

OHL Second All-Star Team (1992)

Traded to **Montreal** by **Vancouver** for Donald Brashear, November 13, 1996. Claimed on waivers by **Tampa Bay** from **Montreal**, January 22, 1998. Loaned to **Providence** (AHL) by **Tampa Bay**, October 1, 1999. • Missed majority of 2002-03 season recovering from elbow injury suffered in game vs. Vancouver, November 29, 2002.

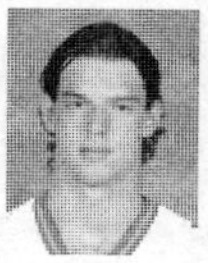

CUTTA, Jakub

(KOO-tuh, YA-kuhb) **WSH.**

Defense. Shoots left. 6'3", 217 lbs. Born, Jablonec nad Nisou, Czech., December 29, 1981. Washington's 3rd choice, 61st overall, in 2000 Entry Draft.

Season	Club	League	GP	G	A	Pts	PIM	PP	SH	GW	S	%	+/-	TF	F%	Min	GP	G	A	Pts	PIM	PP	SH	GW	Min
1997-98	HC Liberec Jr.	Czech-Jr.	29	3	13	16	70																		
1998-99	Swift Current	WHL	59	3	3	6	63																		
99-2000	Swift Current	WHL	71	2	12	14	114										12	0	2	2	24				
2000-01	Washington	NHL	3	0	0	0	0	0	0	0	1	0.0	−1	0	0.0	11:33									
	Swift Current	WHL	47	5	8	13	102										16	1	3	4	32				
2001-02	Washington	NHL	2	0	0	0	0	0	0	0	2	0.0	−3	0	0.0	16:02									
	Portland Pirates	AHL	56	1	3	4	69																		
2002-03	Portland Pirates	AHL	66	3	12	15	106										3	0	0	0	2				
	NHL Totals		5	0	0	0	0	0	0	0	3	0.0		0	0.0	13:20									

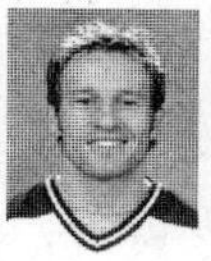

CZERKAWSKI, Mariusz

(chehr-KAWV-skee, MAIR-ee-UHZ) **NYI**

Right wing. Shoots left. 6', 200 lbs. Born, Radomsko, Poland, April 13, 1972. Boston's 5th choice, 106th overall, in 1991 Entry Draft.

Season	Club	League	GP	G	A	Pts	PIM	PP	SH	GW	S	%	+/-	TF	F%	Min	GP	G	A	Pts	PIM	PP	SH	GW	Min
1990-91	GKS Tychy	Poland	24	25	15	40																			
1991-92	Djurgarden	Sweden	39	8	5	13	4										3	0	0	0	2				
	Poland	Olympics	5	0	1	1	4																		
1992-93	Hammarby	Swede-2	32	*39	30	*69	74										13	*16	7	*23	34				
1993-94	Djurgarden	Sweden	39	13	21	34	20										6	3	1	4	2				
	Boston	NHL	4	2	1	3	0	1	0	0	11	18.2	−2				13	3	3	6	4	1	0	0	
1994-95	Kiekko Espoo	Finland	7	9	3	12	10																		
	Boston	NHL	47	12	14	26	31	1	0	2	126	9.5	4				5	1	0	1	0	0	0	0	
1995-96	Boston	NHL	33	5	6	11	10	1	0	0	63	7.9	−11												
	Edmonton	NHL	37	12	17	29	8	2	0	1	79	15.2	7												
1996-97	Edmonton	NHL	76	26	21	47	16	4	0	3	182	14.3	0				12	2	1	3	10	0	0	0	
1997-98	NY Islanders	NHL	68	12	13	25	23	2	0	1	136	8.8	11												
1998-99	NY Islanders	NHL	78	21	17	38	14	4	0	1	205	10.2	−10	2	0.0	14:18									
99-2000	NY Islanders	NHL	79	35	35	70	34	16	0	4	276	12.7	−16	4	25.0	17:45									
2000-01	NY Islanders	NHL	82	30	32	62	48	10	1	0	287	10.5	−24	8	50.0	18:44									
2001-02	NY Islanders	NHL	82	22	29	51	48	6	0	6	169	13.0	−8	10	10.0	15:58	7	2	2	4	4	1	0	0	12:58
2002-03	Montreal	NHL	43	5	9	14	16	1	0	0	77	6.5	−7	2	0.0	13:10									
	Hamilton	AHL	20	8	12	20	12										6	1	3	4	6				
	NHL Totals		629	182	194	376	248	48	1	18	1611	11.3		26	23.1	16:17	37	8	6	14	18	2	0	0	12:58

Played in NHL All-Star Game (2000)

Traded to **Edmonton** by **Boston** with Sean Brown and Boston's 1st round choice (Matthieu Descoteaux) in 1996 Entry Draft for Bill Ranford, January 11, 1996. Traded to **NY Islanders** by **Edmonton** for Dan LaCouture, August 25, 1997. Traded to **Montreal** by **NY Islanders** for Arron Asham and Montreal's 5th round choice (Marcus Paulsson) in 2002 Entry Draft, June 22, 2002. Signed as a free agent by **NY Islanders**, July 17, 2003.

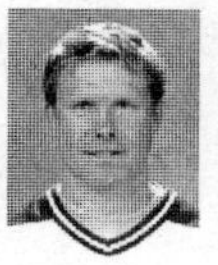

DACKELL, Andreas

(DA-kuhl, an-DRAY-uhs) **MTL.**

Right wing. Shoots right. 5'11", 194 lbs. Born, Gavle, Sweden, December 29, 1972. Ottawa's 3rd choice, 136th overall, in 1996 Entry Draft.

Season	Club	League	GP	G	A	Pts	PIM	PP	SH	GW	S	%	+/-	TF	F%	Min	GP	G	A	Pts	PIM	PP	SH	GW	Min
1990-91	Brynas IF Gavle	Sweden	3	0	1	1	2																		
1991-92	Brynas IF Gavle Jr.	Swede-Jr.	26	17	24	41	42										2	3	1	4	2				
	Brynas IF Gavle	Sweden	4	0	0	0	2										2	0	1	1	4				
1992-93	Brynas IF Gavle	Sweden	40	12	15	27	12										10	4	5	9	2				
1993-94	Brynas IF Gavle	Sweden	38	12	17	29	47										7	2	2	4	8				
	Sweden	Olympics	4	0	0	0	0																		
1994-95	Brynas IF Gavle	Sweden	39	17	16	33	34										14	3	3	6	14				
1995-96	Brynas IF Gavle	Sweden	40	25	22	47	79										10	9	6	15	12				
1996-97	Ottawa	NHL	79	12	19	31	8	2	0	3	79	15.2	−6				7	1	0	1	0	0	0	0	
1997-98	Ottawa	NHL	82	15	18	33	24	3	2	2	130	11.5	−11				11	1	1	2	2	1	0	0	
1998-99	Ottawa	NHL	77	15	35	50	30	6	0	3	107	14.0	9	5	40.0	17:18	4	0	1	1	0	0	0	0	18:49
99-2000	Ottawa	NHL	82	10	25	35	18	0	0	1	99	10.1	5	1	100.0	16:17	6	2	1	3	2	0	0	1	18:14
2000-01	Ottawa	NHL	81	13	18	31	24	1	0	3	72	18.1	7	13	15.4	14:02	4	0	0	0	0	0	0	0	12:19
2001-02	Montreal	NHL	79	15	18	33	24	2	3	2	83	18.1	−3	16	31.3	17:14	12	1	2	3	6	0	0	0	16:21
2002-03	Montreal	NHL	73	7	18	25	24	0	0	1	74	9.5	−5	18	27.8	14:53									
	NHL Totals		553	87	151	238	152	14	5	15	644	13.5		53	28.3	15:57	44	5	5	10	10	1	0	1	16:33

Traded to **Montreal** by **Ottawa** for Montreal's 8th round choice (Neil Petruic) in 2001 Entry Draft, June 24, 2001.

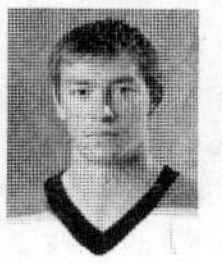

DAGENAIS, Pierre

(da-ZHUH-nay, PEE-air) **MTL.**

Right wing. Shoots left. 6'5", 215 lbs. Born, Blainville, Que., March 4, 1978. New Jersey's 6th choice, 105th overall, in 1998 Entry Draft.

Season	Club	League	GP	G	A	Pts	PIM	PP	SH	GW	S	%	+/-	TF	F%	Min	GP	G	A	Pts	PIM	PP	SH	GW	Min
1994-95	Laval Laurentide	QAAA	34	28	14	42	68										13	10	9	19	32				
1995-96	Moncton Alpines	QMJHL	67	43	25	68	59																		
1996-97	Moncton Wildcats	QMJHL	6	4	2	6	0																		
	Laval Titan	QMJHL	37	16	14	30	40																		
	Rouyn-Noranda	QMJHL	27	21	8	29	22																		
1997-98	Rouyn-Noranda	QMJHL	60	*66	67	133	50										6	6	2	8	2				
1998-99	Albany River Rats	AHL	69	17	13	30	37										4	0	0	0	0				
99-2000	Albany River Rats	AHL	80	35	30	65	47										5	1	0	1	14				
2000-01	New Jersey	NHL	9	3	2	5	6	1	0	1	20	15.0	1	8	37.5	12:22									
	Albany River Rats	AHL	69	34	28	62	52																		
2001-02	New Jersey	NHL	16	3	3	6	4	1	0	1	30	10.0	−5	5	40.0	10:54									
	Albany River Rats	AHL	6	0	2	2	2																		
	Florida	NHL	26	7	1	8	4	2	0	0	47	14.9	−5	4	75.0	11:04									
	Utah Grizzlies	AHL	4	1	1	2	2																		

			Regular Season														Playoffs								
Season	Club	League	GP	G	A	Pts	PIM	PP	SH	GW	S	%	+/-	TF	F%	Min	GP	G	A	Pts	PIM	PP	SH	GW	Min
2002-03	Florida	NHL	9	0	0	0	4	0	0	0	5	0.0	–1	0	0.0	6:01	....	....	....	....	....	....	....	....	....
	San Antonio	AHL	49	21	14	35	28	....	....	....	....	....	....	....	....	....	3	2	0	2	2	....	....	....	....
	NHL Totals		60	13	6	19	18	4	0	2	102	12.7		17	47.1	10:28	....	....	....	....	....	....	....	....	....

• Re-entered NHL Entry Draft. Originally New Jersey's 4th choice, 47th overall, in 1996 Entry Draft.

QMJHL All-Rookie Team (1996) • QMJHL Second All-Star Team (1998) • AHL Second All-Star Team (2001)

Claimed on waivers by **Florida** from **New Jersey**, January 12, 2002. Signed as a free agent by **Montreal**, July 4, 2003.

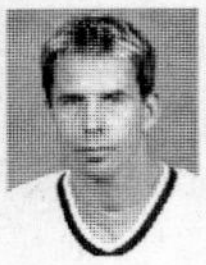

DAHLEN, Ulf

(DAH-lehn, UHLF)

Left wing. Shoots left. 6'2", 199 lbs. Born, Ostersund, Sweden, January 12, 1967. NY Rangers' 1st choice, 7th overall, in 1985 Entry Draft.

1983-84	Ostersund IK	Swede-2	36	15	11	26	10	....	....	....	....	....	....	....	....	....	....	....	....	....	....	....	....	....	....
1984-85	Ostersunds IK	Swede-2	31	27	*26	*53	20	....	....	....	....	....	....	....	....	....	5	6	0	6	4	....	....	....	....
1985-86	Bjorkloven	Sweden	22	4	3	7	8	....	....	....	....	....	....	....	....	....	....	....	....	....	....	....	....	....	....
1986-87	Bjorkloven	Sweden	31	9	12	21	20	....	....	....	....	....	....	....	....	....	6	6	2	8	4	....	....	....	....
1987-88	NY Rangers	NHL	70	29	23	52	26	11	0	4	159	18.2	5	....	....	....	....	....	....	....	....	....	....	....	....
	Colorado Rangers	IHL	2	2	2	4	0	....	....	....	....	....	....	....	....	....	....	....	....	....	....	....	....	....	....
1988-89	NY Rangers	NHL	56	24	19	43	50	8	0	1	147	16.3	–6	....	....	....	4	0	0	0	0	0	0	0	....
1989-90	NY Rangers	NHL	63	18	18	36	30	13	0	4	111	16.2	–4	....	....	....	....	....	....	....	....	....	....	....	....
	Minnesota	NHL	13	2	4	6	0	0	0	0	24	8.3	1	....	....	....	7	1	4	5	2	0	0	0	....
1990-91	Minnesota	NHL	66	21	18	39	6	4	0	3	133	15.8	7	....	....	....	15	2	6	8	4	0	0	0	....
1991-92	Minnesota	NHL	79	36	30	66	10	16	1	5	216	16.7	–5	....	....	....	7	0	3	3	2	0	0	0	....
1992-93	Minnesota	NHL	83	35	39	74	6	13	0	6	223	15.7	–20	....	....	....	....	....	....	....	....	....	....	....	....
1993-94	Dallas	NHL	65	19	38	57	10	12	0	3	147	12.9	–1	....	....	....	....	....	....	....	....	....	....	....	....
	San Jose	NHL	13	6	6	12	0	3	0	2	43	14.0	0	....	....	....	14	6	2	8	0	3	0	1	....
1994-95	San Jose	NHL	46	11	23	34	11	4	1	4	85	12.9	–2	....	....	....	11	5	4	9	0	3	0	1	....
1995-96	San Jose	NHL	59	16	12	28	27	5	0	2	103	15.5	–21	....	....	....	....	....	....	....	....	....	....	....	....
1996-97	San Jose	NHL	43	8	11	19	8	3	0	1	78	10.3	–11	....	....	....	....	....	....	....	....	....	....	....	....
	Chicago	NHL	30	6	8	14	10	1	0	3	53	11.3	9	....	....	....	5	0	1	1	0	0	0	0	....
1997-98	HV 71 Jonkoping	Sweden	29	9	22	31	16	....	....	....	....	....	....	....	....	....	5	1	3	4	12	....	....	....	....
	Sweden	Olympics	4	1	0	1	2	....	....	....	....	....	....	....	....	....	....	....	....	....	....	....	....	....	....
1998-99	HV 71 Jonkoping	Sweden	25	14	15	29	4	....	....	....	....	....	....	....	....	....	....	....	....	....	....	....	....	....	....
99-2000	Washington	NHL	75	15	23	38	8	5	0	4	106	14.2	11	115	48.7	12:40	5	0	1	1	2	0	0	0	12:28
2000-01	Washington	NHL	73	15	33	48	6	6	0	2	145	10.3	11	6	66.7	14:48	6	0	1	1	2	0	0	0	15:58
2001-02	Washington	NHL	69	23	29	52	8	7	0	4	141	16.3	–5	54	61.1	16:09	....	....	....	....	....	....	....	....	....
	Sweden	Olympics	4	1	2	3	0	....	....	....	....	....	....	....	....	....	....	....	....	....	....	....	....	....	....
2002-03	Dallas	NHL	63	17	20	37	14	9	0	1	100	17.0	11	18	50.0	13:49	11	1	3	4	0	1	0	0	12:54
	NHL Totals		966	301	354	655	230	120	2	49	2014	14.9		193	52.8	14:20	85	15	25	40	12	7	0	2	13:38

Traded to **Minnesota** by **NY Rangers** with Los Angeles' 4th round choice (previously acquired, Minnesota selected Cal McGowan) in 1990 Entry Draft for Mike Gartner, March 6, 1990. Transferred to **Dallas** after **Minnesota** franchise relocated, June 9, 1993. Traded to **San Jose** by **Dallas** with Dallas' 7th round choice (Brad Mehalko) in 1995 Entry Draft for Doug Zmolek and Mike Lalor, March 19, 1994. Traded to **Chicago** by **San Jose** with Chris Terreri and Michal Sykora for Ed Belfour, January 25, 1997. Signed as a free agent by **Washington**, August 16, 1999. Signed as a free agent by **Dallas**, August 13, 2002.

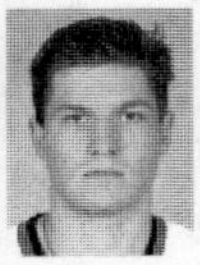

DAHLMAN, Toni

(DAHL-muhn, TOH-nee)

Right wing. Shoots right. 6', 193 lbs. Born, Helsinki, Finland, September 3, 1979. Ottawa's 12th choice, 286th overall, in 2001 Entry Draft.

1996-97	Karhu-Kissat Jr.	Finn-Jr.	24	22	18	30	6	....	....	....	....	....	....	....	....	....	....	....	....	....	....	....	....	....	....
1997-98	Jokerit Helsinki Jr.	Finn-Jr.	21	13	11	24	14	....	....	....	....	....	....	....	....	....	7	2	2	4	0	....	....	....	....
1998-99	Jokerit Helsinki Jr.	Finn-Jr.	33	10	22	32	6	....	....	....	....	....	....	....	....	....	9	4	3	7	2	....	....	....	....
	Jokerit Helsinki	Finland	5	0	0	0	0	....	....	....	....	....	....	....	....	....	3	0	1	1	0	....	....	....	....
99-2000	Jokerit Helsinki Jr.	Finn-Jr.	12	6	8	14	4	....	....	....	....	....	....	....	....	....	12	7	7	14	4	....	....	....	....
	Hermes Kokkola	Finland-2	23	6	3	9	4	....	....	....	....	....	....	....	....	....	....	....	....	....	....	....	....	....	....
	Jokerit Helsinki	Finland	1	0	0	0	0	....	....	....	....	....	....	....	....	....	....	....	....	....	....	....	....	....	....
2000-01	Ilves Tampere	Finland	56	10	18	28	16	....	....	....	....	....	....	....	....	....	9	3	2	5	2	....	....	....	....
2001-02	Ottawa	NHL	10	0	1	1	0	0	0	0	5	0.0	–1	0	0.0	7:04	....	....	....	....	....	....	....	....	....
	Grand Rapids	AHL	50	6	8	14	25	....	....	....	....	....	....	....	....	....	4	0	0	0	0	....	....	....	....
2002-03	Ottawa	NHL	12	1	0	1	0	0	0	1	5	20.0	–1	1	100.0	6:10	....	....	....	....	....	....	....	....	....
	Binghamton	AHL	59	6	18	24	14	....	....	....	....	....	....	....	....	....	5	0	0	0	14	....	....	....	....
	NHL Totals		22	1	1	2	0	0	0	1	10	10.0		1	100.0	6:34	....	....	....	....	....	....	....	....	....

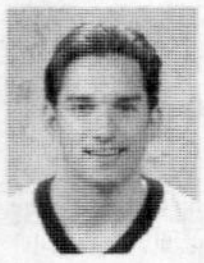

DAIGLE, Alexandre

(DAYG, al-EHX-an-dreh)

Center. Shoots left. 6', 195 lbs. Born, Montreal, Que., February 7, 1975. Ottawa's 1st choice, 1st overall, in 1993 Entry Draft.

1990-91	Laval Laurentide	QAAA	42	*50	*60	*110	98	....	....	....	....	....	....	....	....	....	13	5	9	14	23	....	....	....	....
1991-92	Victoriaville Tigres	QMJHL	66	35	75	110	63	....	....	....	....	....	....	....	....	....	....	....	....	....	....	....	....	....	....
1992-93	Victoriaville Tigres	QMJHL	53	45	92	137	85	....	....	....	....	....	....	....	....	....	6	5	6	11	4	....	....	....	....
1993-94	Ottawa	NHL	84	20	31	51	40	4	0	2	168	11.9	–45	....	....	....	....	....	....	....	....	....	....	....	....
1994-95	Victoriaville Tigres	QMJHL	18	14	20	34	16	....	....	....	....	....	....	....	....	....	....	....	....	....	....	....	....	....	....
	Ottawa	NHL	47	16	21	37	14	4	1	2	105	15.2	–22	....	....	....	....	....	....	....	....	....	....	....	....
1995-96	Ottawa	NHL	50	5	12	17	24	1	0	0	77	6.5	–30	....	....	....	....	....	....	....	....	....	....	....	....
1996-97	Ottawa	NHL	82	26	25	51	33	4	0	5	203	12.8	–33	....	....	....	7	0	0	0	2	0	0	0	....
1997-98	Ottawa	NHL	38	7	9	16	8	4	0	2	68	10.3	–7	....	....	....	....	....	....	....	....	....	....	....	....
	Philadelphia	NHL	37	9	17	26	6	4	0	3	78	11.5	–1	....	....	....	5	0	2	2	0	0	0	0	....
1998-99	Philadelphia	NHL	31	3	2	5	2	1	0	1	26	11.5	–1	53	39.6	7:59	....	....	....	....	....	....	....	....	....
	Tampa Bay	NHL	32	6	6	12	2	3	0	0	56	10.7	–12	4	50.0	13:59	....	....	....	....	....	....	....	....	....
99-2000	NY Rangers	NHL	58	8	18	26	23	1	0	1	52	15.4	–5	339	53.1	10:59	....	....	....	....	....	....	....	....	....
	Hartford	AHL	16	6	13	19	4	....	....	....	....	....	....	....	....	....	....	....	....	....	....	....	....	....	....
2000-01			OUT OF HOCKEY – RETIRED																						
2001-02			OUT OF HOCKEY – RETIRED																						
2002-03	Pittsburgh	NHL	33	4	3	7	8	1	0	0	48	8.3	–10	24	33.3	10:57	....	....	....	....	....	....	....	....	....
	Wilkes-Barre	AHL	40	9	29	38	18	....	....	....	....	....	....	....	....	....	4	0	1	1	0	....	....	....	....
	NHL Totals		492	104	144	248	160	27	1	16	881	11.8		420	50.2	10:60	12	0	2	2	2	0	0	0	....

QMJHL Second All-Star Team (1992) • QMJHL Offensive Rookie of the Year (1992) • Canadian Major Junior Rookie of the Year (1992) • QMJHL First All-Star Team (1993)

Traded to **Philadelphia** by **Ottawa** for Vaclav Prospal, Pat Falloon and Dallas' 2nd round choice (previously acquired, Ottawa selected Chris Bala) in 1998 Entry Draft, January 17, 1998. Traded to **Edmonton** by **Philadelphia** for Andrei Kovalenko, January 29, 1999. Traded to **Tampa Bay** by **Edmonton** for Alexander Selivanov, January 29, 1999. Traded to **NY Rangers** by **Tampa Bay** for cash, October 3, 1999. Signed to a free agent tryout contract by **Pittsburgh**, August 13, 2002.

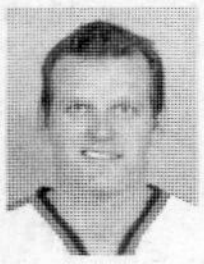

DAMPHOUSSE, Vincent

(DAHM-fooz, VIHN-seht) **S.J.**

Center. Shoots left. 6'1", 200 lbs. Born, Montreal, Que., December 17, 1967. Toronto's 1st choice, 6th overall, in 1986 Entry Draft.

1982-83	Mtl-Bourassa	QAAA	48	33	45	78	22	....	....	....	....	....	....	....	....	....	10	4	4	8	12	....	....	....	....
1983-84	Laval Voisins	QMJHL	66	29	36	65	25	....	....	....	....	....	....	....	....	....	....	....	....	....	....	....	....	....	....
1984-85	Laval Voisins	QMJHL	68	35	68	103	62	....	....	....	....	....	....	....	....	....	....	....	....	....	....	....	....	....	....
1985-86	Laval Titan	QMJHL	69	45	110	155	70	....	....	....	....	....	....	....	....	....	14	9	27	36	12	....	....	....	....
1986-87	Toronto	NHL	80	21	25	46	26	4	0	1	142	14.8	–6	....	....	....	12	1	5	6	8	1	0	0	....
1987-88	Toronto	NHL	75	12	36	48	40	1	0	2	111	10.8	2	....	....	....	6	0	1	1	10	0	0	0	....
1988-89	Toronto	NHL	80	26	42	68	75	6	0	4	190	13.7	–8	....	....	....	....	....	....	....	....	....	....	....	....
1989-90	Toronto	NHL	80	33	61	94	56	9	0	5	229	14.4	2	....	....	....	5	0	2	2	2	0	0	0	....
1990-91	Toronto	NHL	79	26	47	73	65	10	1	4	247	10.5	–31	....	....	....	....	....	....	....	....	....	....	....	....
1991-92	Edmonton	NHL	80	38	51	89	53	12	1	8	247	15.4	10	....	....	....	16	6	8	14	8	1	0	0	....
1992-93♦	Montreal	NHL	84	39	58	97	98	9	3	8	287	13.6	5	....	....	....	20	11	12	23	16	5	0	3	....
1993-94	Montreal	NHL	84	40	51	91	75	13	0	10	274	14.6	0	....	....	....	7	1	2	3	8	0	0	0	....
1994-95	Ratingen	Germany	11	5	7	12	24	....	....	....	....	....	....	....	....	....	....	....	....	....	....	....	....	....	....
	Montreal	NHL	48	10	30	40	42	4	0	4	123	8.1	15	....	....	....	....	....	....	....	....	....	....	....	....
1995-96	Montreal	NHL	80	38	56	94	158	11	4	3	254	15.0	5	....	....	....	6	4	4	8	0	0	1	2	....
1996-97	Montreal	NHL	82	27	54	81	82	7	2	3	244	11.1	–6	....	....	....	5	0	0	0	2	0	0	0	....
1997-98	Montreal	NHL	76	18	41	59	58	2	1	5	164	11.0	14	....	....	....	10	3	6	9	22	1	0	0	....
1998-99	Montreal	NHL	65	12	24	36	46	3	2	2	147	8.2	–7	1425	48.4	20:27	....	....	....	....	....	....	....	....	....
	San Jose	NHL	12	7	6	13	4	3	0	1	43	16.3	3	230	51.3	19:21	6	3	2	5	6	0	2	0	22:58
99-2000	San Jose	NHL	82	21	49	70	58	3	1	1	204	10.3	4	1642	49.0	20:26	12	1	7	8	16	1	0	0	22:14
2000-01	San Jose	NHL	45	9	37	46	62	4	0	3	101	8.9	17	1027	52.7	20:49	6	2	1	3	14	0	1	0	20:22

			Regular Season														Playoffs								
Season	Club	League	GP	G	A	Pts	PIM	PP	SH	GW	S	%	+/-	TF	F%	Min	GP	G	A	Pts	PIM	PP	SH	GW	Min
2001-02	San Jose	NHL	82	20	38	58	60	7	2	4	172	11.6	8	1690	49.9	19:38	12	2	6	8	12	1	0	0	19:14
2002-03	San Jose	NHL	82	23	38	61	66	15	0	6	176	13.1	−13	1301	51.7	19:09	....	....	....	....	....	....	....	....	....
	NHL Totals		1296	420	744	1164	1124	123	17	74	3355	12.5		7315	50.1	19:59	123	34	56	90	124	10	4	5	21:03

QMJHL Second All-Star Team (1986)

Played in NHL All-Star Game (1991, 1992, 2002)

Traded to **Edmonton** by **Toronto** with Peter Ing, Scott Thornton and Luke Richardson for Grant Fuhr, Glenn Anderson and Craig Berube, September 19, 1991. Traded to **Montreal** by **Edmonton** with Edmonton's 4th round choice (Adam Wiesel) in 1993 Entry Draft for Shayne Corson, Brent Gilchrist and Vladimir Vujtek, August 27, 1992. Traded to **San Jose** by **Montreal** for Phoenix's 5th round choice (previously acquired, Montreal selected Marc-Andre Thinel) in 1999 Entry Draft, San Jose's 1st round choice (Marcel Hossa) in 2000 Entry Draft and 2nd round choice (later traded to Columbus – Columbus selected Kiel McLeod) in 2001 Entry Draft, March 23, 1999.

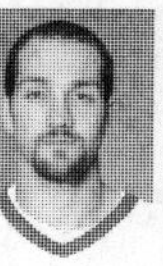

DANDENAULT, Mathieu

(DAHN-deh-noh, MAT-yoo) **DET.**

Right wing/Defense. Shoots right. 6', 200 lbs. Born, Sherbrooke, Que., February 3, 1976. Detroit's 2nd choice, 49th overall, in 1994 Entry Draft.

Season	Club	League	GP	G	A	Pts	PIM	PP	SH	GW	S	%	+/-	TF	F%	Min	GP	G	A	Pts	PIM	PP	SH	GW	Min
1990-91	Gloucester	OMHA	44	52	50	102	30	....	....	....	....	....	....	....	....	....	....	....	....	....	....	....	....	....	....
1991-92	Vanier Voyageurs	OCJHL	33	27	31	58	20	....	....	....	....	....	....	....	....	....	....	....	....	....	....	....	....	....	....
	Gloucester	OCJHL	6	3	4	7	0	....	....	....	....	....	....	....	....	....	....	....	....	....	....	....	....	....	....
1992-93	Gloucester	OCJHL	55	11	26	37	64	....	....	....	....	....	....	....	....	....	....	....	....	....	....	....	....	....	....
1993-94	Sherbrooke	QMJHL	67	17	36	53	67	....	....	....	....	....	....	....	....	....	12	4	10	14	12	....	....	....	....
1994-95	Sherbrooke	QMJHL	67	37	70	107	76	....	....	....	....	....	....	....	....	....	7	1	7	8	10	....	....	....	....
1995-96	**Detroit**	**NHL**	**34**	**5**	**7**	**12**	**6**	**1**	**0**	**0**	**32**	**15.6**	**6**	....	....	....	....	....	....	....	....	....	....	....	....
	Adirondack	AHL	4	0	0	0	0	....	....	....	....	....	....	....	....	....	....	....	....	....	....	....	....	....	....
1996-97♦	**Detroit**	**NHL**	**65**	**3**	**9**	**12**	**28**	**0**	**0**	**0**	**81**	**3.7**	**−10**	....	....	....	....	....	....	....	....	....	....	....	....
1997-98♦	**Detroit**	**NHL**	**68**	**5**	**12**	**17**	**43**	**0**	**0**	**0**	**75**	**6.7**	**5**	....	....	....	**3**	**1**	**0**	**1**	**0**	**1**	**0**	**0**	....
1998-99	**Detroit**	**NHL**	**75**	**4**	**10**	**14**	**59**	**0**	**0**	**0**	**94**	**4.3**	**17**	**3**	**0.0**	**15:10**	**10**	**0**	**1**	**1**	**0**	**0**	**0**	**0**	**11:51**
99-2000	**Detroit**	**NHL**	**81**	**6**	**12**	**18**	**20**	**0**	**0**	**0**	**98**	**6.1**	**−12**	**1**	**100.0**	**12:10**	**6**	**0**	**0**	**0**	**2**	**0**	**0**	**0**	**8:31**
2000-01	**Detroit**	**NHL**	**73**	**10**	**15**	**25**	**38**	**2**	**0**	**2**	**95**	**10.5**	**11**	**0**	**0.0**	**16:06**	**6**	**0**	**1**	**1**	**0**	**0**	**0**	**0**	**14:11**
2001-02♦	**Detroit**	**NHL**	**81**	**8**	**12**	**20**	**44**	**2**	**0**	**3**	**97**	**8.2**	**−5**	**1**	**0.0**	**16:43**	**23**	**1**	**2**	**3**	**8**	**0**	**1**	**0**	**13:29**
2002-03	**Detroit**	**NHL**	**74**	**4**	**15**	**19**	**64**	**1**	**0**	**0**	**74**	**5.4**	**25**	**0**	**0.0**	**19:08**	**4**	**0**	**0**	**0**	**2**	**0**	**0**	**0**	**25:51**
	NHL Totals		**551**	**45**	**92**	**137**	**302**	**6**	**0**	**5**	**646**	**7.0**		**5**	**20.0**	**15:48**	**52**	**2**	**4**	**6**	**12**	**1**	**1**	**0**	**13:38**

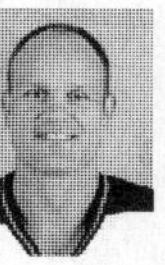

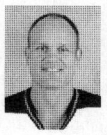

DANEYKO, Ken

(DAN-ee-KOH, KEHN)

Defense. Shoots left. 6'1", 215 lbs. Born, Windsor, Ont., April 17, 1964. New Jersey's 2nd choice, 18th overall, in 1982 Entry Draft.

Season	Club	League	GP	G	A	Pts	PIM	PP	SH	GW	S	%	+/-	TF	F%	Min	GP	G	A	Pts	PIM	PP	SH	GW	Min
1980-81	St. Albert Saints	AJHL	1	0	0	0	4	....	....	....	....	....	....	....	....	....	....	....	....	....	....	....	....	....	....
	Spokane Flyers	WHL	62	6	13	19	140	....	....	....	....	....	....	....	....	....	4	0	0	0	6	....	....	....	....
1981-82	Spokane Flyers	WHL	26	1	11	12	147	....	....	....	....	....	....	....	....	....	....	....	....	....	....	....	....	....	....
	Seattle Breakers	WHL	38	1	22	23	151	....	....	....	....	....	....	....	....	....	14	1	9	10	49	....	....	....	....
1982-83	Seattle Breakers	WHL	69	17	43	60	150	....	....	....	....	....	....	....	....	....	4	1	3	4	14	....	....	....	....
1983-84	Kamloops	WHL	19	6	28	34	52	....	....	....	....	....	....	....	....	....	17	4	9	13	28	....	....	....	....
	New Jersey	**NHL**	**11**	**1**	**4**	**5**	**17**	**0**	**0**	**0**	**17**	**5.9**	**−1**	....	....	....	....	....	....	....	....	....	....	....	....
1984-85	**New Jersey**	**NHL**	**1**	**0**	**0**	**0**	**10**	**0**	**0**	**0**	**1**	**0.0**	**−1**	....	....	....	....	....	....	....	....	....	....	....	....
	Maine Mariners	AHL	80	4	9	13	206	....	....	....	....	....	....	....	....	....	11	1	3	4	36	....	....	....	....
1985-86	**New Jersey**	**NHL**	**44**	**0**	**10**	**10**	**100**	**0**	**0**	**0**	**48**	**0.0**	**0**	....	....	....	....	....	....	....	....	....	....	....	....
	Maine Mariners	AHL	21	3	2	5	75	....	....	....	....	....	....	....	....	....	....	....	....	....	....	....	....	....	....
1986-87	**New Jersey**	**NHL**	**79**	**2**	**12**	**14**	**183**	**0**	**0**	**0**	**113**	**1.8**	**−13**	....	....	....	....	....	....	....	....	....	....	....	....
1987-88	**New Jersey**	**NHL**	**80**	**5**	**7**	**12**	**239**	**1**	**0**	**0**	**82**	**6.1**	**−3**	....	....	....	**20**	**1**	**6**	**7**	**83**	**0**	**0**	**1**	....
1988-89	**New Jersey**	**NHL**	**80**	**5**	**5**	**10**	**283**	**1**	**0**	**0**	**108**	**4.6**	**−22**	....	....	....	....	....	....	....	....	....	....	....	....
1989-90	**New Jersey**	**NHL**	**74**	**6**	**15**	**21**	**219**	**0**	**1**	**1**	**64**	**9.4**	**15**	....	....	....	**6**	**2**	**0**	**2**	**21**	**0**	**0**	**0**	....
1990-91	**New Jersey**	**NHL**	**80**	**4**	**16**	**20**	**249**	**1**	**2**	**1**	**106**	**3.8**	**−10**	....	....	....	**7**	**0**	**1**	**1**	**10**	**0**	**0**	**0**	....
1991-92	**New Jersey**	**NHL**	**80**	**1**	**7**	**8**	**170**	**0**	**0**	**0**	**57**	**1.8**	**7**	....	....	....	**7**	**0**	**3**	**3**	**16**	**0**	**0**	**0**	....
1992-93	**New Jersey**	**NHL**	**84**	**2**	**11**	**13**	**236**	**0**	**0**	**0**	**71**	**2.8**	**4**	....	....	....	**5**	**0**	**0**	**0**	**8**	**0**	**0**	**0**	....
1993-94	**New Jersey**	**NHL**	**78**	**1**	**9**	**10**	**176**	**0**	**0**	**1**	**60**	**1.7**	**27**	....	....	....	**20**	**0**	**1**	**1**	**45**	**0**	**0**	**0**	....
1994-95♦	**New Jersey**	**NHL**	**25**	**1**	**2**	**3**	**54**	**0**	**0**	**0**	**27**	**3.7**	**4**	....	....	....	**20**	**1**	**0**	**1**	**22**	**0**	**0**	**0**	....
1995-96	**New Jersey**	**NHL**	**80**	**2**	**4**	**6**	**115**	**0**	**0**	**0**	**67**	**3.0**	**−10**	....	....	....	....	....	....	....	....	....	....	....	....
1996-97	**New Jersey**	**NHL**	**77**	**2**	**7**	**9**	**70**	**0**	**0**	**0**	**63**	**3.2**	**24**	....	....	....	**10**	**0**	**0**	**0**	**28**	**0**	**0**	**0**	....
1997-98	**New Jersey**	**NHL**	**37**	**0**	**1**	**1**	**57**	**0**	**0**	**0**	**18**	**0.0**	**3**	....	....	....	**6**	**0**	**1**	**1**	**10**	**0**	**0**	**0**	....
1998-99	**New Jersey**	**NHL**	**82**	**2**	**9**	**11**	**63**	**0**	**0**	**0**	**63**	**3.2**	**27**	**1**	**0.0**	**20:03**	**7**	**0**	**0**	**0**	**8**	**0**	**0**	**0**	**18:01**
99-2000♦	**New Jersey**	**NHL**	**78**	**0**	**6**	**6**	**98**	**0**	**0**	**0**	**74**	**0.0**	**13**	**0**	**0.0**	**18:06**	**23**	**1**	**2**	**3**	**14**	**0**	**0**	**0**	**17:52**
2000-01	**New Jersey**	**NHL**	**77**	**0**	**4**	**4**	**87**	**0**	**0**	**0**	**50**	**0.0**	**8**	**0**	**0.0**	**17:17**	**25**	**0**	**3**	**3**	**21**	**0**	**0**	**0**	**16:41**
2001-02	**New Jersey**	**NHL**	**67**	**0**	**6**	**6**	**60**	**0**	**0**	**0**	**44**	**0.0**	**2**	**0**	**0.0**	**15:31**	**6**	**0**	**0**	**0**	**8**	**0**	**0**	**0**	**16:49**
2002-03♦	**New Jersey**	**NHL**	**69**	**2**	**7**	**9**	**33**	**0**	**0**	**0**	**38**	**5.3**	**6**	**1**	**100.0**	**15:37**	**13**	**0**	**0**	**0**	**2**	**0**	**0**	**0**	**13:44**
	NHL Totals		**1283**	**36**	**142**	**178**	**2519**	**3**	**3**	**3**	**1171**	**3.1**		**2**	**50.0**	**17:26**	**175**	**5**	**17**	**22**	**296**	**0**	**0**	**1**	**16:40**

Bill Masterton Memorial Trophy (2000)

• Missed majority of 1997-98 season after voluntarily entering NHL/NHLPA substance abuse program, November 6, 1997. • Officially announced retirement, July 11, 2003.

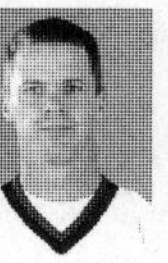

DANIELS, Jeff

(DAN-yehls, JEHF) **CAR.**

Left wing. Shoots left. 6'1", 200 lbs. Born, Oshawa, Ont., June 24, 1968. Pittsburgh's 6th choice, 109th overall, in 1986 Entry Draft.

Season	Club	League	GP	G	A	Pts	PIM	PP	SH	GW	S	%	+/-	TF	F%	Min	GP	G	A	Pts	PIM	PP	SH	GW	Min
1983-84	Oshawa	OJHL-B	57	59	72	131	22	....	....	....	....	....	....	....	....	....	....	....	....	....	....	....	....	....	....
1984-85	Oshawa	OJHL-B	7	7	2	9	11	....	....	....	....	....	....	....	....	....	....	....	....	....	....	....	....	....	....
	Oshawa Generals	OHL	59	7	11	18	16	....	....	....	....	....	....	....	....	....	....	....	....	....	....	....	....	....	....
1985-86	Oshawa Generals	OHL	62	13	19	32	23	....	....	....	....	....	....	....	....	....	6	0	1	1	0	....	....	....	....
1986-87	Oshawa Generals	OHL	54	14	9	23	22	....	....	....	....	....	....	....	....	....	15	3	2	5	5	....	....	....	....
1987-88	Oshawa Generals	OHL	64	29	39	68	59	....	....	....	....	....	....	....	....	....	4	2	3	5	0	....	....	....	....
1988-89	Muskegon	IHL	58	21	21	42	58	....	....	....	....	....	....	....	....	....	11	3	5	8	11	....	....	....	....
1989-90	Muskegon	IHL	80	30	47	77	39	....	....	....	....	....	....	....	....	....	6	1	1	2	7	....	....	....	....
1990-91	**Pittsburgh**	**NHL**	**11**	**0**	**2**	**2**	**2**	**0**	**0**	**0**	**6**	**0.0**	**0**	....	....	....	....	....	....	....	....	....	....	....	....
	Muskegon	IHL	62	23	29	52	18	....	....	....	....	....	....	....	....	....	5	1	3	4	2	....	....	....	....
1991-92♦	**Pittsburgh**	**NHL**	**2**	**0**	**0**	**0**	**0**	**0**	**0**	**0**	**0**	**0.0**	**0**	....	....	....	....	....	....	....	....	....	....	....	....
	Muskegon	IHL	44	19	16	35	38	....	....	....	....	....	....	....	....	....	10	5	4	9	9	....	....	....	....
1992-93	**Pittsburgh**	**NHL**	**58**	**5**	**4**	**9**	**14**	**0**	**0**	**1**	**30**	**16.7**	**−5**	....	....	....	**12**	**3**	**2**	**5**	**0**	**0**	**0**	**1**	....
	Cleveland	IHL	3	2	1	3	0	....	....	....	....	....	....	....	....	....	....	....	....	....	....	....	....	....	....
1993-94	**Pittsburgh**	**NHL**	**63**	**3**	**5**	**8**	**20**	**0**	**0**	**1**	**46**	**6.5**	**−1**	....	....	....	....	....	....	....	....	....	....	....	....
	Florida	**NHL**	**7**	**0**	**0**	**0**	**0**	**0**	**0**	**0**	**6**	**0.0**	**0**	....	....	....	....	....	....	....	....	....	....	....	....
1994-95	**Florida**	**NHL**	**3**	**0**	**0**	**0**	**0**	**0**	**0**	**0**	**0**	**0.0**	**0**	....	....	....	....	....	....	....	....	....	....	....	....
	Detroit Vipers	IHL	25	8	12	20	6	....	....	....	....	....	....	....	....	....	5	1	0	1	0	....	....	....	....
1995-96	Springfield	AHL	72	22	20	42	32	....	....	....	....	....	....	....	....	....	10	3	0	3	2	....	....	....	....
1996-97	**Hartford**	**NHL**	**10**	**0**	**2**	**2**	**0**	**0**	**0**	**0**	**6**	**0.0**	**2**	....	....	....	....	....	....	....	....	....	....	....	....
	Springfield	AHL	38	18	14	32	19	....	....	....	....	....	....	....	....	....	16	7	3	10	4	....	....	....	....
1997-98	**Carolina**	**NHL**	**2**	**0**	**0**	**0**	**0**	**0**	**0**	**0**	**1**	**0.0**	**0**	....	....	....	....	....	....	....	....	....	....	....	....
	New Haven	AHL	71	24	27	51	34	....	....	....	....	....	....	....	....	....	3	0	1	1	0	....	....	....	....
1998-99	**Nashville**	**NHL**	**9**	**1**	**3**	**4**	**2**	**0**	**0**	**0**	**8**	**12.5**	**−1**	**1**	**0.0**	**10:56**	....	....	....	....	....	....	....	....	....
	Milwaukee	IHL	62	12	31	43	19	....	....	....	....	....	....	....	....	....	2	1	1	2	0	....	....	....	....
99-2000	**Carolina**	**NHL**	**69**	**3**	**4**	**7**	**10**	**0**	**0**	**0**	**28**	**10.7**	**−8**	**47**	**46.8**	**7:42**	....	....	....	....	....	....	....	....	....
2000-01	**Carolina**	**NHL**	**67**	**1**	**1**	**2**	**15**	**0**	**0**	**0**	**42**	**2.4**	**−3**	**125**	**53.6**	**7:30**	**6**	**0**	**2**	**2**	**2**	**0**	**0**	**0**	**12:19**
2001-02	**Carolina**	**NHL**	**65**	**4**	**1**	**5**	**12**	**0**	**1**	**0**	**40**	**10.0**	**−6**	**178**	**46.6**	**8:07**	**23**	**0**	**1**	**1**	**0**	**0**	**0**	**0**	**7:16**
2002-03	**Carolina**	**NHL**	**59**	**0**	**4**	**4**	**8**	**0**	**0**	**0**	**41**	**0.0**	**−9**	**107**	**40.2**	**8:25**	....	....	....	....	....	....	....	....	....
	NHL Totals		**425**	**17**	**26**	**43**	**83**	**0**	**1**	**2**	**254**	**6.7**		**458**	**46.9**	**8:01**	**41**	**3**	**5**	**8**	**2**	**0**	**0**	**1**	**8:19**

Traded to **Florida** by **Pittsburgh** for Greg Hawgood, March 19, 1994. Signed as a free agent by **Hartford**, August 18, 1995. Transferred to **Carolina** after **Hartford** franchise relocated, June 25, 1997. Claimed by **Nashville** from **Carolina** in Expansion Draft, June 26, 1998. Signed as a free agent by **Carolina**, August 31, 1999.

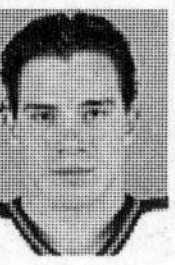

DANTON, Mike

(DAHN-tuhn, MIGHK) **ST.L.**

Center. Shoots right. 5'9", 190 lbs. Born, Brampton, Ont., October 21, 1980. New Jersey's 8th choice, 135th overall, in 2000 Entry Draft.

Season	Club	League	GP	G	A	Pts	PIM	PP	SH	GW	S	%	+/-	TF	F%	Min	GP	G	A	Pts	PIM	PP	SH	GW	Min
1996-97	Quinte Hawks	MTJHL	35	10	18	28	281	....	....	....	....	....	....	....	....	....	....	....	....	....	....	....	....	....	....
1997-98	Sarnia Sting	OHL	12	6	1	7	37	....	....	....	....	....	....	....	....	....	....	....	....	....	....	....	....	....	....
	St. Michael's	OHL	18	4	6	10	77	....	....	....	....	....	....	....	....	....	....	....	....	....	....	....	....	....	....
1998-99	St. Michael's	OHL	27	18	22	40	116	....	....	....	....	....	....	....	....	....	....	....	....	....	....	....	....	....	....
	Barrie Colts	OHL	26	15	20	35	62	....	....	....	....	....	....	....	....	....	9	6	5	11	38	....	....	....	....
99-2000	Barrie Colts	OHL	58	34	53	87	203	....	....	....	....	....	....	....	....	....	25	7	16	23	*107	....	....	....	....

			Regular Season														Playoffs								
Season	Club	League	GP	G	A	Pts	PIM	PP	SH	GW	S	%	+/-	TF	F%	Min	GP	G	A	Pts	PIM	PP	SH	GW	Min
2000-01	**New Jersey**	**NHL**	**2**	**0**	**0**	**0**	**6**	**0**	**0**	**0**	**3**	**0.0**	**0**	**6**	**50.0**	**7:52**	....	....	....	....	....	....	....	....	....
	Albany River Rats	AHL	69	19	15	34	195	....	....	....	....	....	....	....	....	....	....	....	....	....	....	....	....	....	....
2001-02	Albany River Rats	AHL	DID NOT PLAY – SUSPENDED																						
2002-03	**New Jersey**	**NHL**	**17**	**2**	**0**	**2**	**35**	**0**	**0**	**0**	**18**	**11.1**	**0**	**111**	**39.6**	**8:59**	....	....	....	....	....	....	....	....	....
	NHL Totals		**19**	**2**	**0**	**2**	**41**	**0**	**0**	**0**	**21**	**9.5**		**117**	**40.2**	**8:52**	....	....	....	....	....	....	....	....	....

• Legally changed last name from **Jefferson** to **Danton**, July 25, 2002.

• Suspended for 2001-02 season by New Jersey for refusing to report to Albany (AHL), October 2, 2001. • Missed majority of 2002-03 season after being suspended by New Jersey for refusing to report to Albany (AHL), December 3, 2002. Traded to **St. Louis** by **New Jersey** with New Jersey's 3rd round choice (Konstantin Zakharov) in 2003 Entry Draft for St. Louis's 3rd round choice (Ivan Khomutov) in 2003 Entry Draft, June 21, 2003.

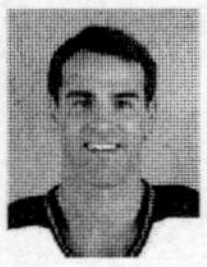

DARBY, Craig
(DAHR-bee, KRAYG) **N.J.**

Center. Shoots right. 6'4", 205 lbs. Born, Oneida, NY, September 26, 1972. Montreal's 3rd choice, 43rd overall, in 1991 Entry Draft.

1987-88	Albany	Hi-School	29	11	27	38	....	....	....	....	....	....	....	....	....	....	....	....	....	....	....	....	....	....	....
1988-89	Albany	Hi-School	29	36	40	*76	....	....	....	....	....	....	....	....	....	....	....	....	....	....	....	....	....	....	....
1989-90	Albany	Hi-School	29	32	53	85	....	....	....	....	....	....	....	....	....	....	....	....	....	....	....	....	....	....	....
1990-91	Albany	Hi-School	29	33	61	*94	....	....	....	....	....	....	....	....	....	....	4	8	1	9	....	....	....	....	....
1991-92	Providence	H-East	35	17	24	41	47	....	....	....	....	....	....	....	....	....	....	....	....	....	....	....	....	....	....
1992-93	Providence	H-East	35	11	21	32	62	....	....	....	....	....	....	....	....	....	....	....	....	....	....	....	....	....	....
1993-94	Fredericton	AHL	66	23	33	56	51	....	....	....	....	....	....	....	....	....	....	....	....	....	....	....	....	....	....
1994-95	Fredericton	AHL	64	21	47	68	82	....	....	....	....	....	....	....	....	....	....	....	....	....	....	....	....	....	....
	Montreal	**NHL**	**10**	**0**	**2**	**2**	**0**	**0**	**0**	**0**	**4**	**0.0**	**–5**	....	....	....	....	....	....	....	....	....	....	....	....
	NY Islanders	**NHL**	**3**	**0**	**0**	**0**	**0**	**0**	**0**	**0**	**1**	**0.0**	**–1**	....	....	....	....	....	....	....	....	....	....	....	....
1995-96	**NY Islanders**	**NHL**	**10**	**0**	**2**	**2**	**0**	**0**	**0**	**0**	**1**	**0.0**	**–1**	....	....	....	....	....	....	....	....	....	....	....	....
	Worcester IceCats	AHL	68	22	28	50	47	....	....	....	....	....	....	....	....	....	4	1	1	2	2	....	....	....	....
1996-97	**Philadelphia**	**NHL**	**9**	**1**	**4**	**5**	**2**	**0**	**1**	**0**	**13**	**7.7**	**2**	....	....	....	....	....	....	....	....	....	....	....	....
	Philadelphia	AHL	59	26	33	59	24	....	....	....	....	....	....	....	....	....	10	3	6	9	0	....	....	....	....
1997-98	**Philadelphia**	**NHL**	**3**	**1**	**0**	**1**	**0**	**0**	**0**	**0**	**3**	**33.3**	**0**	....	....	....	....	....	....	....	....	....	....	....	....
	Philadelphia	AHL	77	*42	45	87	34	....	....	....	....	....	....	....	....	....	20	5	9	14	4	....	....	....	....
1998-99	Milwaukee	IHL	81	32	22	54	33	....	....	....	....	....	....	....	....	....	2	3	0	3	0	....	....	....	....
99-2000	**Montreal**	**NHL**	**76**	**7**	**10**	**17**	**14**	**0**	**1**	**2**	**90**	**7.8**	**–14**	**1068**	**48.3**	**13:45**	....	....	....	....	....	....	....	....	....
2000-01	**Montreal**	**NHL**	**78**	**12**	**16**	**28**	**16**	**0**	**1**	**0**	**97**	**12.4**	**–17**	**1214**	**46.9**	**15:53**	....	....	....	....	....	....	....	....	....
2001-02	**Montreal**	**NHL**	**2**	**0**	**0**	**0**	**0**	**0**	**0**	**0**	**0**	**0.0**	**0**	**10**	**30.0**	**5:20**	....	....	....	....	....	....	....	....	....
	Quebec Citadelles	AHL	66	16	55	71	18	....	....	....	....	....	....	....	....	....	3	2	1	3	0	....	....	....	....
2002-03	**New Jersey**	**NHL**	**3**	**0**	**1**	**1**	**0**	**0**	**0**	**0**	**1**	**0.0**	**–1**	**21**	**47.6**	**10:36**	....	....	....	....	....	....	....	....	....
	Albany River Rats	AHL	76	23	51	74	42	....	....	....	....	....	....	....	....	....	....	....	....	....	....	....	....	....	....
	NHL Totals		**194**	**21**	**35**	**56**	**32**	**0**	**3**	**2**	**210**	**10.0**		**2313**	**47.5**	**14:38**	....	....	....	....	....	....	....	....	....

Hockey East Rookie of the Year (1992) (co-winner - Ian Moran) • AHL First All-Star Team (1998) • AHL Second All-Star Team (2003)

Traded to **NY Islanders** by **Montreal** with Kirk Muller and Mathieu Schneider for Pierre Turgeon and Vladimir Malakhov, April 5, 1995. Claimed on waivers by **Philadelphia** from **NY Islanders**, June 4, 1996. Claimed by **Nashville** from **Philadelphia** in Expansion Draft, June 26, 1998. Signed as a free agent by **Montreal**, August 4, 1999. Signed as a free agent by **New Jersey**, July 12, 2002.

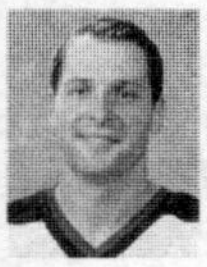

DARCHE, Mathieu
(DAHRSH, MATH-you)

Left wing. Shoots left. 6'1", 210 lbs. Born, St. Laurent, Que., November 26, 1976.

1995-96	Choate-Rosemary	Hi-School	STATISTICS NOT AVAILABLE																						
1996-97	McGill Redmen	OUAA	23	1	2	3	27	....	....	....	....	....	....	....	....	....	....	....	....	....	....	....	....	....	....
1997-98	McGill Redmen	OUAA	40	28	17	45	69	....	....	....	....	....	....	....	....	....	....	....	....	....	....	....	....	....	....
1998-99	McGill Redmen	OUAA	32	16	24	40	60	....	....	....	....	....	....	....	....	....	....	....	....	....	....	....	....	....	....
99-2000	McGill Redmen	OUAA	33	31	41	*72	38	....	....	....	....	....	....	....	....	....	5	2	8	10	16	....	....	....	....
2000-01	**Columbus**	**NHL**	**9**	**0**	**0**	**0**	**0**	**0**	**0**	**0**	**9**	**0.0**	**–4**	**1**	**0.0**	**10:07**	....	....	....	....	....	....	....	....	....
	Syracuse Crunch	AHL	66	16	24	40	21	....	....	....	....	....	....	....	....	....	5	0	1	1	4	....	....	....	....
2001-02	**Columbus**	**NHL**	**14**	**1**	**1**	**2**	**6**	**0**	**0**	**0**	**15**	**6.7**	**–5**	**3**	**33.3**	**9:49**	....	....	....	....	....	....	....	....	....
	Syracuse Crunch	AHL	63	22	23	45	26	....	....	....	....	....	....	....	....	....	10	2	5	7	2	....	....	....	....
2002-03	**Columbus**	**NHL**	**1**	**0**	**0**	**0**	**0**	**0**	**0**	**0**	**0**	**0.0**	**–1**	**0**	**0.0**	**6:57**	....	....	....	....	....	....	....	....	....
	Syracuse Crunch	AHL	76	32	32	64	38	....	....	....	....	....	....	....	....	....	....	....	....	....	....	....	....	....	....
	NHL Totals		**24**	**1**	**1**	**2**	**6**	**0**	**0**	**0**	**24**	**4.2**		**4**	**25.0**	**9:49**	....	....	....	....	....	....	....	....	....

• Played CIAU Football (1996-97) • OUAA East Second All-Star Team (1998) • OUAA East First All-Star Team (1999) • OUAA First All-Star Team (2000) • CIAU All-Canadian Team (2000) • Randy Gregg Trophy (Athletics and Academics) (2000)

Signed as a free agent by **Columbus**, May 16, 2000.

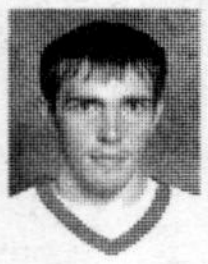

DATSYUK, Pavel
(daht-SOOK, PAH-vehl) **DET.**

Center. Shoots left. 5'11", 180 lbs. Born, Sverdlovsk, USSR, July 20, 1978. Detroit's 8th choice, 171st overall, in 1998 Entry Draft.

1996-97	Yekaterinburg	Russia-Q	18	2	2	4	4	....	....	....	....	....	....	....	....	....	....	....	....	....	....	....	....	....	....
	Yekaterinburg	Russia-Q	36	12	10	22	12	....	....	....	....	....	....	....	....	....	....	....	....	....	....	....	....	....	....
1997-98	Yekaterinburg	Russia	24	3	5	8	4	....	....	....	....	....	....	....	....	....	....	....	....	....	....	....	....	....	....
	Yekaterinburg	Russia	22	7	8	15	4	....	....	....	....	....	....	....	....	....	....	....	....	....	....	....	....	....	....
1998-99	Yekaterinburg 2	Russia-4	10	14	14	28	4	....	....	....	....	....	....	....	....	....	....	....	....	....	....	....	....	....	....
	Yekaterinburg	Russia-2	35	21	23	44	14	....	....	....	....	....	....	....	....	....	9	3	7	10	10	....	....	....	....
99-2000	Yekaterinburg	Russia	15	1	3	4	4	....	....	....	....	....	....	....	....	....	....	....	....	....	....	....	....	....	....
2000-01	Ak Bars Kazan	Russia	42	9	18	27	10	....	....	....	....	....	....	....	....	....	4	0	1	1	2	....	....	....	....
2001-02♦	**Detroit**	**NHL**	**70**	**11**	**24**	**35**	**4**	**2**	**0**	**1**	**79**	**13.9**	**4**	**794**	**47.7**	**13:39**	**21**	**3**	**3**	**6**	**2**	**1**	**0**	**1**	**10:40**
	Russia	Olympics	6	1	2	3	0	....	....	....	....	....	....	....	....	....	....	....	....	....	....	....	....	....	....
2002-03	**Detroit**	**NHL**	**64**	**12**	**39**	**51**	**16**	**1**	**0**	**1**	**82**	**14.6**	**20**	**778**	**48.2**	**15:28**	**4**	**0**	**0**	**0**	**0**	**0**	**0**	**0**	**18:48**
	NHL Totals		**134**	**23**	**63**	**86**	**20**	**3**	**0**	**2**	**161**	**14.3**		**1572**	**48.0**	**14:31**	**25**	**3**	**3**	**6**	**2**	**1**	**0**	**1**	**11:58**

• Spent majority of 1999-2000 season on **Ak Bars Kazan** (Russia) reserve squad.

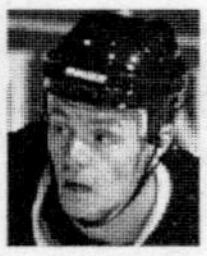

DAVIDSON, Matt
(DAY-vihd-SOHN, MAT) **CGY.**

Right wing. Shoots right. 6'3", 196 lbs. Born, Flin Flon, Man., August 9, 1977. Buffalo's 5th choice, 94th overall, in 1995 Entry Draft.

1992-93	Sask. Contacts	SMHL	36	14	18	32	36	....	....	....	....	....	....	....	....	....	....	....	....	....	....	....	....	....	....
1993-94	Portland	WHL	59	4	12	16	18	....	....	....	....	....	....	....	....	....	10	0	0	0	4	....	....	....	....
1994-95	Portland	WHL	72	17	20	37	51	....	....	....	....	....	....	....	....	....	9	1	3	4	0	....	....	....	....
1995-96	Portland	WHL	70	24	26	50	96	....	....	....	....	....	....	....	....	....	7	2	2	4	2	....	....	....	....
1996-97	Portland	WHL	72	44	27	71	47	....	....	....	....	....	....	....	....	....	6	0	1	1	2	....	....	....	....
1997-98	Rochester	AHL	72	15	12	27	12	....	....	....	....	....	....	....	....	....	3	1	0	1	2	....	....	....	....
1998-99	Rochester	AHL	80	26	15	41	44	....	....	....	....	....	....	....	....	....	18	2	1	3	6	....	....	....	....
99-2000	Rochester	AHL	80	12	20	32	30	....	....	....	....	....	....	....	....	....	19	4	2	6	8	....	....	....	....
2000-01	**Columbus**	**NHL**	**5**	**0**	**0**	**0**	**0**	**0**	**0**	**0**	**2**	**0.0**	**2**	**0**	**0.0**	**7:14**	....	....	....	....	....	....	....	....	....
	Syracuse Crunch	AHL	72	14	11	25	24	....	....	....	....	....	....	....	....	....	5	1	2	3	2	....	....	....	....
2001-02	**Columbus**	**NHL**	**17**	**1**	**2**	**3**	**10**	**0**	**0**	**0**	**18**	**5.6**	**–11**	**7**	**0.0**	**14:34**	....	....	....	....	....	....	....	....	....
	Syracuse Crunch	AHL	47	9	11	20	64	....	....	....	....	....	....	....	....	....	8	1	3	4	4	....	....	....	....
2002-03	**Columbus**	**NHL**	**34**	**4**	**5**	**9**	**18**	**0**	**0**	**0**	**28**	**14.3**	**–12**	**7**	**28.6**	**11:49**	....	....	....	....	....	....	....	....	....
	Syracuse Crunch	AHL	48	18	16	34	26	....	....	....	....	....	....	....	....	....	....	....	....	....	....	....	....	....	....
	NHL Totals		**56**	**5**	**7**	**12**	**28**	**0**	**0**	**0**	**48**	**10.4**		**14**	**14.3**	**12:14**	....	....	....	....	....	....	....	....	....

Traded to **Columbus** by **Buffalo** with Jean-Luc Grand-Pierre, San Jose's 5th round choice (previously acquired, Columbus selected Tyler Kolarik) in 2000 Entry Draft and Buffalo's 5th round choice (later traded to Calgary – later traded to Detroit – Detroit selected Andreas Jamtin) in 2001 Entry Draft to complete Expansion Draft agreement which had Columbus select Geoff Sanderson and Dwayne Roloson from Buffalo, June 23, 2000. Signed as a free agent by **Calgary**, July 15, 2003.

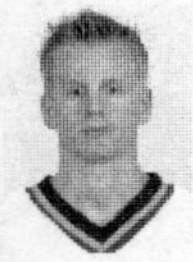

DAVIDSSON, Johan
(DAH-vihd-suhn, YOH-hahn) **VAN.**

Center. Shoots right. 6'1", 190 lbs. Born, Jonkoping, Sweden, January 6, 1976. Anaheim's 2nd choice, 28th overall, in 1994 Entry Draft.

1992-93	HV 71 Jonkoping	Sweden	8	1	0	1	0	....	....	....	....	....	....	....	....	....	....	....	....	....	....	....	....	....	....
1993-94	HV 71 Jr.	Swede-Jr.	5	2	3	5	0	....	....	....	....	....	....	....	....	....	....	....	....	....	....	....	....	....	....
	HV 71 Jonkoping	Sweden	38	2	5	7	4	....	....	....	....	....	....	....	....	....	....	....	....	....	....	....	....	....	....
1994-95	HV 71 Jr.	Swede-Jr.	3	4	1	5	0	....	....	....	....	....	....	....	....	....	....	....	....	....	....	....	....	....	....
	HV 71 Jonkoping	Sweden	37	4	7	11	20	....	....	....	....	....	....	....	....	....	13	3	2	5	0	....	....	....	....
1995-96	HV 71 Jonkoping	Sweden	39	7	11	18	20	....	....	....	....	....	....	....	....	....	4	0	2	2	0	....	....	....	....
1996-97	HV 71 Jonkoping	Sweden	50	18	21	39	18	....	....	....	....	....	....	....	....	....	5	0	3	3	2	....	....	....	....

Season	Club	League	Regular Season GP	G	A	Pts	PIM	PP	SH	GW	S	%	+/-	TF	F%	Min	Playoffs GP	G	A	Pts	PIM	PP	SH	GW	Min
1997-98	HIFK Helsinki	Finland	43	10	30	40	8										9	3	10	13	0				
1998-99	**Anaheim**	**NHL**	**64**	**3**	**5**	**8**	**14**	**1**	**0**	**1**	**48**	**6.3**	**–9**	**516**	**37.0**	**10:37**	**1**	**0**	**0**	**0**	**0**	**0**	**0**	**0**	**7:20**
	Cincinnati	AHL	9	1	6	7	2																		
99-2000	**Anaheim**	**NHL**	**5**	**1**	**0**	**1**	**2**	**0**	**0**	**1**	**8**	**12.5**	**0**	**38**	**42.1**	**10:42**									
	Cincinnati	AHL	56	9	31	40	24																		
	NY Islanders	**NHL**	**14**	**2**	**4**	**6**	**0**	**0**	**0**	**0**	**21**	**9.5**	**0**	**130**	**40.0**	**11:32**									
2000-01	Blues Espoo	Finland	35	12	17	29	34																		
2001-02	HV 71 Jonkoping	Sweden	50	13	27	40	24										8	2	3	5	2				
2002-03	HV 71 Jonkoping	Sweden	50	16	26	42	4										7	0	3	3	2				
	NHL Totals		**83**	**6**	**9**	**15**	**16**	**1**	**0**	**2**	**77**	**7.8**		**684**	**37.9**	**10:47**	**1**	**0**	**0**	**0**	**0**	**0**	**0**	**0**	**7:20**

Traded to **NY Islanders** by **Anaheim** with future considerations for Jorgen Jonsson, March 11, 2000. Signed as a free agent by **Vancouver**, September 6, 2000.

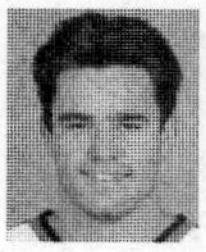

DAVISON, Rob

(DAY-vihs-ohn, RAWB) **S.J.**

Defense. Shoots left. 6'2", 225 lbs. Born, St. Catharines, Ont., May 1, 1980. San Jose's 4th choice, 98th overall, in 1998 Entry Draft.

Season	Club	League	GP	G	A	Pts	PIM	PP	SH	GW	S	%	+/-	TF	F%	Min	GP	G	A	Pts	PIM	PP	SH	GW	Min
1995-96	St. Michael's B	OJHL-B	21	0	0	0	21																		
1996-97	St. Michael's B	OJHL-B	45	2	6	8	93																		
1997-98	North Bay	OHL	59	0	11	11	200																		
1998-99	North Bay	OHL	59	2	17	19	150										4	0	1	1	12				
99-2000	North Bay	OHL	67	4	6	10	194										6	0	1	1	8				
2000-01	Kentucky	AHL	72	0	4	4	230										3	0	0	0	0				
2001-02	Cleveland Barons	AHL	70	1	3	4	206																		
2002-03	**San Jose**	**NHL**	**15**	**1**	**2**	**3**	**22**	**0**	**0**	**0**	**15**	**6.7**	**4**	**0**	**0.0**	**17:53**									
	Cleveland Barons	AHL	42	1	3	4	82																		
	NHL Totals		**15**	**1**	**2**	**3**	**22**	**0**	**0**	**0**	**15**	**6.7**		**0**	**0.0**	**17:53**									

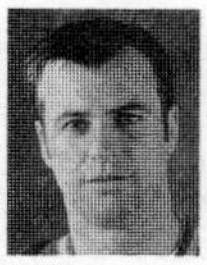

DAW, Jeff

(DAW, JEHF)

Center. Shoots right. 6'3", 190 lbs. Born, Carlisle, Ont., February 28, 1972.

Season	Club	League	GP	G	A	Pts	PIM	PP	SH	GW	S	%	+/-	TF	F%	Min	GP	G	A	Pts	PIM	PP	SH	GW	Min
1989-90	Milton Merchants	OPJHL	42	19	29	48	2																		
1990-91	Milton Merchants	OPJHL	34	21	41	62	22																		
1991-92	Milton Merchants	OPJHL	41	33	33	66	20																		
1992-93	U. Mass-Lowell	H-East	37	12	18	30	14																		
1993-94	U. Mass-Lowell	H-East	40	6	12	18	12																		
1994-95	U. Mass-Lowell	H-East	40	27	15	42	24																		
1995-96	U. Mass-Lowell	H-East	40	23	28	51	10																		
1996-97	Wheeling Nailers	ECHL	13	3	8	11	26																		
	Hamilton	AHL	56	11	8	19	39										19	4	5	9	0				
1997-98	Hamilton	AHL	79	28	35	63	20										9	6	3	9	0				
1998-99	Hamilton	AHL	66	18	29	47	10										11	0	3	3	4				
99-2000	Cleveland	IHL	9	4	1	5	2																		
	Houston Aeros	IHL	44	9	8	17	12																		
	Lowell	AHL	10	0	5	5	4										7	1	2	3	6				
2000-01	Lowell	AHL	65	28	28	56	33										3	0	1	1	2				
	Cleveland	IHL	8	2	3	5	2																		
2001-02	**Colorado**	**NHL**	**1**	**0**	**1**	**1**	**0**	**0**	**0**	**0**	**2**	**0.0**	**0**	**0**	**0.0**	**12:34**									
	Hershey Bears	AHL	79	26	25	51	22										8	1	1	2	4				
2002-03	Lowell	AHL	51	14	16	30	18																		
	Springfield	AHL	12	2	4	6	2										6	0	2	2	2				
	NHL Totals		**1**	**0**	**1**	**1**	**0**	**0**	**0**	**0**	**2**	**0.0**		**0**	**0.0**	**12:34**									

Signed as a free agent by **Edmonton**, August 1, 1996. Signed as a free agent by **Chicago**, July 22, 1999. Traded to **Lowell** (AHL) by **Houston** (IHL) with Chicago retaining NHL rights for Dave Hymovitz, March 17, 2000. Selected by **Minnesota** from **Chicago** in Expansion Draft, June 23, 2000. Signed as a free agent by **Colorado**, July 23, 2001. Signed as a free agent by **Carolina**, August 27, 2002. Traded to **Toronto** by **Carolina** for future considerations, May 29, 2003.

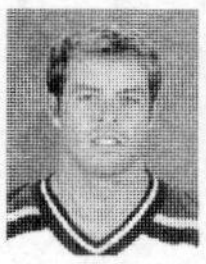

DAWE, Jason

(DAW, JAY-suhn)

Right wing. Shoots left. 5'10", 189 lbs. Born, North York, Ont., May 29, 1973. Buffalo's 2nd choice, 35th overall, in 1991 Entry Draft.

Season	Club	League	GP	G	A	Pts	PIM	PP	SH	GW	S	%	+/-	TF	F%	Min	GP	G	A	Pts	PIM	PP	SH	GW	Min
1988-89	Don Mills	MTHL	44	35	28	63	103																		
1989-90	Peterborough	OHL	50	15	18	33	19										12	4	7	11	4				
1990-91	Peterborough	OHL	66	43	27	70	43										4	3	1	4	0				
1991-92	Peterborough	OHL	66	53	55	108	55										4	5	0	5	0				
1992-93	Peterborough	OHL	59	58	68	126	80										21	18	33	51	18				
	Rochester	AHL															3	1	0	1	0				
1993-94	**Buffalo**	**NHL**	**32**	**6**	**7**	**13**	**12**	**3**	**0**	**1**	**35**	**17.1**	**1**				**6**	**0**	**1**	**1**	**6**	**0**	**0**	**0**	
	Rochester	AHL	48	22	14	36	44																		
1994-95	Rochester	AHL	44	27	19	46	24																		
	Buffalo	**NHL**	**42**	**7**	**4**	**11**	**19**	**0**	**1**	**2**	**51**	**13.7**	**–6**				**5**	**2**	**1**	**3**	**6**	**0**	**0**	**0**	
1995-96	**Buffalo**	**NHL**	**67**	**25**	**25**	**50**	**33**	**8**	**1**	**0**	**130**	**19.2**	**–8**												
	Rochester	AHL	7	5	4	9	2																		
1996-97	**Buffalo**	**NHL**	**81**	**22**	**26**	**48**	**32**	**4**	**1**	**3**	**136**	**16.2**	**14**				**11**	**2**	**1**	**3**	**6**	**0**	**0**	**0**	
1997-98	**Buffalo**	**NHL**	**68**	**19**	**17**	**36**	**36**	**4**	**1**	**3**	**115**	**16.5**	**10**												
	NY Islanders	**NHL**	**13**	**1**	**2**	**3**	**6**	**0**	**0**	**0**	**19**	**5.3**	**–2**												
1998-99	**NY Islanders**	**NHL**	**22**	**2**	**3**	**5**	**8**	**0**	**0**	**0**	**29**	**6.9**	**0**	**4**	**25.0**	**11:55**									
	Montreal	**NHL**	**37**	**4**	**5**	**9**	**14**	**1**	**0**	**1**	**52**	**7.7**	**0**	**4**	**0.0**	**11:00**									
99-2000	Milwaukee	IHL	41	11	13	24	24																		
	NY Rangers	**NHL**	**3**	**0**	**1**	**1**	**2**	**0**	**0**	**0**	**8**	**0.0**	**0**	**1**	**100.0**	**13:35**									
	Hartford	AHL	27	9	9	18	24										21	10	7	17	37				
2000-01	Hartford	AHL	4	2	0	2	2																		
2001-02	**NY Rangers**	**NHL**	**1**	**0**	**0**	**0**	**0**	**0**	**0**	**0**	**1**	**0.0**	**–1**	**0**	**0.0**	**9:21**									
	Hartford	AHL	79	28	37	65	46										9	4	0	4	15				
2002-03	Worcester IceCats	AHL	71	17	28	45	47										3	0	0	0	5				
	NHL Totals		**366**	**86**	**90**	**176**	**162**	**20**	**4**	**10**	**576**	**14.9**		**9**	**22.2**	**11:25**	**22**	**4**	**3**	**7**	**18**	**0**	**0**	**0**	

OHL First All-Star Team (1993) • Canadian Major Junior Second All-Star Team (1993) • George Parsons Trophy (Memorial Cup Most Sportsmanlike Player) (1993)

Traded to **NY Islanders** by **Buffalo** for Jason Holland and Paul Kruse, March 24, 1998. Claimed on waivers by **Montreal** from **NY Islanders**, December 15, 1998. Signed as a free agent by **Nashville**, October 2, 1999. Traded to **NY Rangers** by **Nashville** for John Namestnikov, February 3, 2000. • Missed majority of 2000-01 season recovering from ankle injury suffered in game vs. Springfield (AHL), October 6, 2000. Signed as a free agent by **St. Louis**, July 23, 2002.

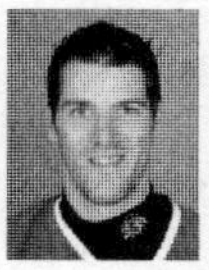

DAZE, Eric

(dah-ZAY, AIR-ihk) **CHI.**

Right wing. Shoots left. 6'6", 234 lbs. Born, Montreal, Que., July 2, 1975. Chicago's 5th choice, 90th overall, in 1993 Entry Draft.

Season	Club	League	GP	G	A	Pts	PIM	PP	SH	GW	S	%	+/-	TF	F%	Min	GP	G	A	Pts	PIM	PP	SH	GW	Min
1990-91	Laval Laurentide	QAHA	30	25	20	45	30																		
1991-92	Laval Laurentide	QAAA	35	30	29	59	40										12	8	10	18	8				
1992-93	Beauport	QMJHL	68	19	36	55	24																		
1993-94	Beauport	QMJHL	66	59	48	107	31										15	16	8	24	2				
1994-95	Beauport	QMJHL	57	54	45	99	20										16	9	12	21	23				
	Chicago	**NHL**	**4**	**1**	**1**	**2**	**2**	**0**	**0**	**0**	**1**	**100.0**	**2**				**16**	**0**	**1**	**1**	**4**	**0**	**0**	**0**	
1995-96	**Chicago**	**NHL**	**80**	**30**	**23**	**53**	**18**	**2**	**0**	**2**	**167**	**18.0**	**16**				**10**	**3**	**5**	**8**	**0**	**0**	**0**	**1**	
1996-97	**Chicago**	**NHL**	**71**	**22**	**19**	**41**	**16**	**11**	**0**	**4**	**176**	**12.5**	**–4**				**6**	**2**	**1**	**3**	**2**	**0**	**0**	**0**	
1997-98	**Chicago**	**NHL**	**80**	**31**	**11**	**42**	**22**	**10**	**0**	**7**	**216**	**14.4**	**4**												
1998-99	**Chicago**	**NHL**	**72**	**22**	**20**	**42**	**22**	**8**	**0**	**2**	**189**	**11.6**	**–13**	**4**	**0.0**	**16:16**									
99-2000	**Chicago**	**NHL**	**59**	**23**	**13**	**36**	**28**	**6**	**0**	**1**	**143**	**16.1**	**–16**	**9**	**22.2**	**16:15**									
2000-01	**Chicago**	**NHL**	**79**	**33**	**24**	**57**	**16**	**9**	**1**	**8**	**205**	**16.1**	**1**	**3**	**33.3**	**17:45**									
2001-02	**Chicago**	**NHL**	**82**	**38**	**32**	**70**	**36**	**12**	**0**	**5**	**264**	**14.4**	**17**	**5**	**0.0**	**17:07**	**5**	**0**	**0**	**0**	**2**	**0**	**0**	**0**	**17:12**
2002-03	**Chicago**	**NHL**	**54**	**22**	**22**	**44**	**14**	**3**	**0**	**5**	**170**	**12.9**	**10**	**4**	**25.0**	**16:17**									
	NHL Totals		**581**	**222**	**165**	**387**	**174**	**61**	**1**	**34**	**1531**	**14.5**		**25**	**16.0**	**16:48**	**37**	**5**	**7**	**12**	**8**	**0**	**0**	**1**	**17:12**

QMJHL First All-Star Team (1994, 1995) • Canadian Major Junior Most Sportsmanlike Player of the Year (1995) • NHL All-Rookie Team (1996)

Played in NHL All-Star Game (2002)

						Regular Season												Playoffs							
Season	Club	League	GP	G	A	Pts	PIM	PP	SH	GW	S	%	+/-	TF	F%	Min	GP	G	A	Pts	PIM	PP	SH	GW	Min

DEADMARSH, Adam (DEHD-mahrsh, A-duhm) L.A.

Right wing. Shoots right. 6', 205 lbs.   Born, Trail, B.C., May 10, 1975. Quebec's 2nd choice, 14th overall, in 1993 Entry Draft.

Season	Club	League	GP	G	A	Pts	PIM	PP	SH	GW	S	%	+/-	TF	F%	Min	GP	G	A	Pts	PIM	PP	SH	GW	Min
1990-91	Beaver Valley	KIJHL	35	28	44	72	95	....	....	....	....	....	....	....	....	....	....	....	....	....	....	....	....	....	....
1991-92	Portland	WHL	68	30	30	60	81	....	....	....	....	....	....	....	....	....	6	3	3	6	13	....	....	....	....
1992-93	Portland	WHL	58	33	36	69	126	....	....	....	....	....	....	....	....	....	16	7	8	15	29	....	....	....	....
1993-94	Portland	WHL	65	43	56	99	212	....	....	....	....	....	....	....	....	....	10	9	8	17	33	....	....	....	....
1994-95	Portland	WHL	29	28	20	48	129	....	....	....	....	....	....	....	....	....	....	....	....	....	....	....	....	....	....
	Quebec	**NHL**	48	9	8	17	56	0	0	0	48	18.8	16				6	0	1	1	0	0	0	0	
1995-96♦	Colorado	NHL	78	21	27	48	142	3	0	2	151	13.9	20				22	5	12	17	25	1	0	0	
1996-97	Colorado	NHL	78	33	27	60	136	10	3	4	198	16.7	8				17	3	6	9	24	1	0	1	
1997-98	Colorado	NHL	73	22	21	43	125	10	0	6	187	11.8	0				7	2	0	2	4	1	0	0	
	United States	Olympic	4	0	1	0	1	....	....	....	....	....	....				....	....	....	....	....	....	....	....	
1998-99	Colorado	NHL	66	22	27	49	99	10	0	3	152	14.5	−2	621	45.9	20:46	19	8	4	12	20	3	0	0	18:51
99-2000	Colorado	NHL	71	18	27	45	106	5	0	4	153	11.8	−10	430	46.5	20:27	17	4	11	15	21	1	0	1	18:47
2000-01	Colorado	NHL	39	13	13	26	59	7	0	2	86	15.1	−2	56	55.4	17:38	....	....	....	....	....	....	....	....	
	Los Angeles	**NHL**	18	4	2	6	4	0	0	0	40	10.0	3	21	57.1	18:47	13	3	3	6	4	0	0	2	20:09
2001-02	Los Angeles	NHL	76	29	33	62	71	12	0	5	139	20.9	8	60	38.3	19:17	4	1	3	4	2	0	0	0	18:51
	United States	Olympic	6	1	1	2	2	....	....	....	....	....	....				....	....	....	....	....	....	....	....	
2002-03	Los Angeles	NHL	20	13	4	17	21	4	0	1	55	23.6	2	26	46.2	19:18	....	....	....	....	....	....	....	....	
	NHL Totals		567	184	189	373	819	61	3	27	1209	15.2		1214	46.4	19:39	105	26	40	66	100	7	0	4	19:09

Transferred to **Colorado** after **Quebec** franchise relocated, June 21, 1995. Traded to **Los Angeles** by **Colorado** with Aaron Miller, a player to be named later (Jared Aulin, March 22, 2001), Colorado's 1st round choice (Dave Steckel) in 2001 Entry Draft and Colorado's 1st round choice (Brian Boyle) in 2003 Entry Draft for Rob Blake and Steve Reinprecht, February 21, 2001. • Missed majority of 2002-03 season recovering from head injury suffered in game vs. Phoenix, December 15, 2002.

DeBRUSK, Louie (duh-BRUHSK, LEW-ee)

Left wing. Shoots left. 6'2", 238 lbs.   Born, Cambridge, Ont., March 19, 1971. NY Rangers' 4th choice, 49th overall, in 1989 Entry Draft.

Season	Club	League	GP	G	A	Pts	PIM	PP	SH	GW	S	%	+/-	TF	F%	Min	GP	G	A	Pts	PIM	PP	SH	GW	Min
1986-87	Port Elgin Huskies	OJHL-C	10	2	1	3	4	....	....	....	....	....	....				....	....	....	....	....	....	....	....	
1987-88	Stratford Cullitons	OJHL-B	45	13	14	27	205	....	....	....	....	....	....				....	....	....	....	....	....	....	....	
1988-89	London Knights	OHL	59	11	11	22	149	....	....	....	....	....	....				19	1	1	2	43	....	....	....	
1989-90	London Knights	OHL	61	21	19	40	198	....	....	....	....	....	....				6	2	2	4	24	....	....	....	
1990-91	London Knights	OHL	61	31	33	64	*223	....	....	....	....	....	....				7	2	2	4	14	....	....	....	
	Binghamton	AHL	2	0	0	0	7	....	....	....	....	....	....				2	0	0	0	9	....	....	....	
1991-92	**Edmonton**	**NHL**	25	2	1	3	124	0	0	1	7	28.6	4				....	....	....	....	....	....	....	....	
	Cape Breton	AHL	28	2	2	4	73	....	....	....	....	....	....				....	....	....	....	....	....	....	....	
1992-93	Edmonton	NHL	51	8	2	10	205	0	0	1	33	24.2	−16				....	....	....	....	....	....	....	....	
1993-94	Edmonton	NHL	48	4	6	10	185	0	0	0	27	14.8	−9				....	....	....	....	....	....	....	....	
	Cape Breton	AHL	5	3	1	4	58	....	....	....	....	....	....				....	....	....	....	....	....	....	....	
1994-95	Edmonton	NHL	34	2	0	2	93	0	0	0	14	14.3	−4				....	....	....	....	....	....	....	....	
1995-96	Edmonton	NHL	38	1	3	4	96	0	0	0	17	5.9	−7				....	....	....	....	....	....	....	....	
1996-97	Edmonton	NHL	32	2	0	2	94	0	0	0	10	20.0	−6				6	0	0	0	4	0	0	0	
1997-98	**Tampa Bay**	**NHL**	54	1	2	3	166	0	0	0	14	7.1	−2				....	....	....	....	....	....	....	....	
	San Antonio	IHL	17	7	4	11	130	....	....	....	....	....	....				....	....	....	....	....	....	....	....	
1998-99	**Phoenix**	**NHL**	15	0	0	0	34	0	0	0	6	0.0	−2	0	0.0	5:57	6	2	0	2	6	0	0	0	8:06
	Las Vegas	IHL	26	3	6	9	160	....	....	....	....	....	....				....	....	....	....	....	....	....	....	
	Springfield	AHL	3	1	0	1	0	....	....	....	....	....	....				....	....	....	....	....	....	....	....	
	Long Beach	IHL	24	5	5	10	134	....	....	....	....	....	....				....	....	....	....	....	....	....	....	
99-2000	Phoenix	NHL	61	4	3	7	78	0	0	0	24	16.7	1	0	0.0	5:21	3	0	0	0	0	0	0	0	2:27
2000-01	Phoenix	NHL	39	0	0	0	79	0	0	0	12	0.0	−5	0	0.0	4:49	....	....	....	....	....	....	....	....	
2001-02	Quebec Citadelles	AHL	9	0	0	0	44	....	....	....	....	....	....				....	....	....	....	....	....	....	....	
	Hamilton	AHL	20	3	5	8	42	....	....	....	....	....	....				13	1	0	1	30	....	....	....	
2002-03	**Chicago**	**NHL**	4	0	0	0	7	0	0	0	0	0.0	0	0	0.0	6:09	....	....	....	....	....	....	....	....	
	Norfolk Admirals	AHL	20	1	0	1	10	....	....	....	....	....	....				....	....	....	....	....	....	....	....	
	NHL Totals		401	24	17	41	1161	0	0	2	164	14.6		0	0.0	5:17	15	2	0	2	10	0	0	0	6:13

Traded to **Edmonton** by **NY Rangers** with Bernie Nicholls and Steven Rice for Mark Messier and future considerations (Jeff Beukeboom for David Shaw, November 12, 1991), October 4, 1991. Signed as a free agent by **Tampa Bay**, September 23, 1997. Traded to **Phoenix** by **Tampa Bay** with Tampa Bay's 5th round choice (Jay Leach) in 1998 Entry Draft for Craig Janney, June 11, 1998. Signed to 25-game tryout contract by **Quebec** (AHL), November 25, 2001. Released by **Quebec** (AHL) and signed as a free agent by **Hamilton** (AHL), December 21, 2001. Signed as a free agent by **Chicago**, August 30, 2002. • Spent majority of 2002-03 season with **Norfolk** (AHL) as a healthy reserve. • Officially announced retirement, April 27, 2003.

DEFAUW, Brad (duh-FOU, BRAD) CAR.

Left wing. Shoots left. 6'2", 220 lbs.   Born, Edina, MN, November 10, 1977. Carolina's 2nd choice, 28th overall, in 1997 Entry Draft.

Season	Club	League	GP	G	A	Pts	PIM	PP	SH	GW	S	%	+/-	TF	F%	Min	GP	G	A	Pts	PIM	PP	SH	GW	Min
1995-96	Apple Valley	Hi-School	28	21	34	55	14	....	....	....	....	....	....				....	....	....	....	....	....	....	....	
1996-97	North Dakota	WCHA	37	7	6	13	39	....	....	....	....	....	....				....	....	....	....	....	....	....	....	
1997-98	North Dakota	WCHA	36	9	11	20	34	....	....	....	....	....	....				....	....	....	....	....	....	....	....	
1998-99	North Dakota	WCHA	34	11	12	23	64	....	....	....	....	....	....				....	....	....	....	....	....	....	....	
99-2000	North Dakota	WCHA	43	13	9	22	52	....	....	....	....	....	....				....	....	....	....	....	....	....	....	
2000-01	Cincinnati	IHL	82	20	31	51	39	....	....	....	....	....	....				4	2	0	2	8	....	....	....	
2001-02	Lowell	AHL	63	17	21	38	29	....	....	....	....	....	....				5	2	1	3	6	....	....	....	
2002-03	**Carolina**	**NHL**	9	3	0	3	2	1	0	1	19	15.8	−2	0	0.0	13:45	....	....	....	....	....	....	....	....	
	Lowell	AHL	61	11	12	23	48	....	....	....	....	....	....				....	....	....	....	....	....	....	....	
	NHL Totals		9	3	0	3	2	1	0	1	19	15.8		0	0.0	13:45									

DELMORE, Andy (DEHL-mohr, AN-dee) BUF.

Defense. Shoots right. 6'1", 200 lbs.   Born, LaSalle, Ont., December 26, 1976.

Season	Club	League	GP	G	A	Pts	PIM	PP	SH	GW	S	%	+/-	TF	F%	Min	GP	G	A	Pts	PIM	PP	SH	GW	Min
1992-93	Chatham	OJHL-B	47	4	21	25	38	....	....	....	....	....	....				....	....	....	....	....	....	....	....	
1993-94	North Bay	OHL	45	2	7	9	33	....	....	....	....	....	....				17	0	0	0	2	....	....	....	
1994-95	North Bay	OHL	40	2	14	16	21	....	....	....	....	....	....				3	0	0	0	4	....	....	....	
	Sarnia Sting	OHL	27	5	13	18	27	....	....	....	....	....	....				10	3	7	10	2	....	....	....	
1995-96	Sarnia Sting	OHL	64	21	38	59	45	....	....	....	....	....	....				12	2	10	12	10	....	....	....	
1996-97	Sarnia Sting	OHL	64	18	60	78	39	....	....	....	....	....	....				....	....	....	....	....	....	....	....	
	Fredericton	AHL	4	0	1	1	0	....	....	....	....	....	....				18	4	4	8	21	....	....	....	
1997-98	Philadelphia	AHL	73	9	30	39	46	....	....	....	....	....	....				15	1	4	5	6	....	....	....	
1998-99	**Philadelphia**	**NHL**	2	0	1	1	0	0	0	0	2	0.0	−1	0	0.0	20:42	....	....	....	....	....	....	....	....	
	Philadelphia	AHL	70	5	18	23	51	....	....	....	....	....	....				18	5	2	7	14	1	0	1	17:33
99-2000	Philadelphia	NHL	27	2	5	7	8	0	0	1	55	3.6	−1	0	0.0	17:17									
	Philadelphia	AHL	39	12	14	26	31	....	....	....	....	....	....				2	1	0	1	2	0	0	1	15:19
2000-01	Philadelphia	NHL	66	5	9	14	16	2	0	0	119	4.2	2	0	0.0	17:39	....	....	....	....	....	....	....	....	
2001-02	Nashville	NHL	73	16	22	38	22	11	0	3	175	9.1	−13	0	0.0	19:40	....	....	....	....	....	....	....	....	
2002-03	Nashville	NHL	71	18	16	34	28	14	0	6	149	12.1	−17	0	0.0	17:05	....	....	....	....	....	....	....	....	
	NHL Totals		239	41	53	94	74	27	0	10	500	8.2		0	0.0	18:05	20	6	2	8	16	1	0	2	17:19

OHL First All-Star Team (1997)

Signed as a free agent by **Philadelphia**, June 9, 1997. Traded to **Nashville** by **Philadelphia** for Nashville's 3rd round choice (later traded to Phoenix – Phoenix selected Joe Callahan) in 2002 Entry Draft, July 31, 2001. Traded to **Buffalo** by **Nashville** for Buffalo's 3rd round choice in 2004 Entry Draft, June 27, 2003.

DEMITRA, Pavol (deh-MEET-rah, PAH-vohl) ST.L.

Left wing. Shoots left. 6', 206 lbs.   Born, Dubnica, Czech., November 29, 1974. Ottawa's 9th choice, 227th overall, in 1993 Entry Draft.

Season	Club	League	GP	G	A	Pts	PIM	PP	SH	GW	S	%	+/-	TF	F%	Min	GP	G	A	Pts	PIM	PP	SH	GW	Min
1991-92	Dubnica	Czech-2	28	13	10	23	12	....	....	....	....	....	....				....	....	....	....	....	....	....	....	
1992-93	CAPEH Dubnica	Czech-2	4	3	0	3	....	....	....	....	....	....	....				....	....	....	....	....	....	....	....	
	Dukla Trencin	Czech	46	11	17	28	0	....	....	....	....	....	....				....	....	....	....	....	....	....	....	
1993-94	**Ottawa**	**NHL**	12	1	1	2	4	1	0	0	10	10.0	−7				....	....	....	....	....	....	....	....	
	P.E.I. Senators	AHL	41	18	23	41	8	....	....	....	....	....	....				....	....	....	....	....	....	....	....	
1994-95	P.E.I. Senators	AHL	61	26	48	74	23	....	....	....	....	....	....				5	0	7	7	0	....	....	....	
	Ottawa	**NHL**	16	4	3	7	0	1	0	0	21	19.0	−4				....	....	....	....	....	....	....	....	
1995-96	Ottawa	NHL	31	7	10	17	6	2	0	1	66	10.6	−3				....	....	....	....	....	....	....	....	
	P.E.I. Senators	AHL	48	28	53	81	44	....	....	....	....	....	....				....	....	....	....	....	....	....	....	

			Regular Season														Playoffs								
Season	Club	League	GP	G	A	Pts	PIM	PP	SH	GW	S	%	+/-	TF	F%	Min	GP	G	A	Pts	PIM	PP	SH	GW	Min
1996-97	Dukla Trencin	Slovakia	1	1	1	2	....	....	....	....	....	....	....	....	....	....	....	....	....	....	....	....	....	....	....
	Las Vegas	IHL	22	8	13	21	10	....	....	....	....	....	....	....	....	....	....	....	....	....	....	....	....	....	....
	St. Louis	NHL	8	3	0	3	2	2	0	1	15	20.0	0	....	....	....	6	1	3	4	6	0	0	0	....
	Grand Rapids	IHL	42	20	30	50	24	....	....	....	....	....	....	....	....	....	....	....	....	....	....	....	....	....	....
1997-98	St. Louis	NHL	61	22	30	52	22	4	4	6	147	15.0	11	....	....	....	10	3	3	6	2	0	0	0	....
1998-99	St. Louis	NHL	82	37	52	89	16	14	0	10	259	14.3	13	250	44.0	20:10	13	5	4	9	4	3	0	1	19:10
99-2000	St. Louis	NHL	71	28	47	75	8	8	0	4	241	11.6	34	41	39.0	19:13	....	....	....	....	....	....	....	....	....
2000-01	St. Louis	NHL	44	20	25	45	16	5	0	5	124	16.1	27	8	37.5	18:03	15	2	4	6	2	0	0	1	18:13
2001-02	St. Louis	NHL	82	35	43	78	46	11	0	10	212	16.5	13	1224	48.1	19:11	10	4	7	11	6	2	1	1	19:45
	Slovakia	Olympics	2	1	2	3	2	....	....	....	....	....	....	....	....	....	....	....	....	....	....	....	....	....	....
2002-03	St. Louis	NHL	78	36	57	93	32	11	0	4	205	17.6	0	1253	46.1	19:47	7	2	4	6	2	1	0	0	18:20
	NHL Totals		485	193	268	461	152	59	4	41	1300	14.8		2776	46.7	19:25	61	17	25	42	22	6	1	3	18:51

Lady Byng Trophy (2000)
Played in NHL All-Star Game (1999, 2000, 2002)
Traded to **St. Louis** by **Ottawa** for Christer Olsson, November 27, 1996.

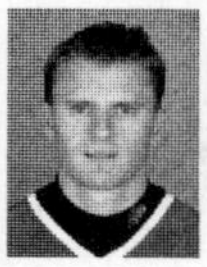

DEMPSEY, Nathan (DEHMP-see, NAY-thun) CHI.

Defense. Shoots right. 6', 190 lbs. Born, Spruce Grove, Alta., July 14, 1974. Toronto's 12th choice, 245th overall, in 1992 Entry Draft.

1990-91	St. Albert Saints	AMHL	34	11	20	31	73	....	....	....	....	....	....	....	....	....	....	....	....	....	....	....	....	....	....
1991-92	Regina Pats	WHL	70	4	22	26	72	....	....	....	....	....	....	....	....	....	....	....	....	....	....	....	....	....	....
1992-93	Regina Pats	WHL	72	12	29	41	95	....	....	....	....	....	....	....	....	....	13	3	8	11	14	....	....	....	....
	St. John's	AHL	....	....	....	....	....	....	....	....	....	....	....	....	....	....	2	0	0	0	0	....	....	....	....
1993-94	Regina Pats	WHL	56	14	36	50	100	....	....	....	....	....	....	....	....	....	4	0	0	0	4	....	....	....	....
1994-95	St. John's	AHL	74	7	30	37	91	....	....	....	....	....	....	....	....	....	5	1	0	1	11	....	....	....	....
1995-96	St. John's	AHL	73	5	15	20	103	....	....	....	....	....	....	....	....	....	4	1	0	1	9	....	....	....	....
1996-97	Toronto	NHL	14	1	1	2	2	0	0	0	11	9.1	–2	....	....	....	....	....	....	....	....	....	....	....	....
	St. John's	AHL	52	8	18	26	108	....	....	....	....	....	....	....	....	....	6	1	0	1	4	....	....	....	....
1997-98	St. John's	AHL	68	12	16	28	85	....	....	....	....	....	....	....	....	....	4	0	0	0	0	....	....	....	....
1998-99	St. John's	AHL	67	2	29	31	70	....	....	....	....	....	....	....	....	....	5	0	1	1	2	....	....	....	....
99-2000	Toronto	NHL	6	0	2	2	2	0	0	0	3	0.0	2	1	0.0	13:40	....	....	....	....	....	....	....	....	....
	St. John's	AHL	44	15	12	27	40	....	....	....	....	....	....	....	....	....	....	....	....	....	....	....	....	....	....
2000-01	Toronto	NHL	25	1	9	10	4	1	0	0	31	3.2	13	0	0.0	15:53	....	....	....	....	....	....	....	....	....
	St. John's	AHL	55	11	28	39	60	....	....	....	....	....	....	....	....	....	4	0	4	4	8	....	....	....	....
2001-02	Toronto	NHL	3	0	0	0	0	0	0	0	3	0.0	1	0	0.0	13:60	6	0	2	2	0	0	0	0	14:30
	St. John's	AHL	75	13	48	61	66	....	....	....	....	....	....	....	....	....	11	1	5	6	8	....	....	....	....
2002-03	Chicago	NHL	67	5	23	28	26	1	0	2	124	4.0	–7	0	0.0	20:55	....	....	....	....	....	....	....	....	....
	NHL Totals		115	7	35	42	34	2	0	2	172	4.1		1	0.0	19:02	6	0	2	2	0	0	0	0	14:30

WHL East Second All-Star Team (1994) • AHL Second All-Star Team (2002) • Fred Hunt Memorial Trophy (Sportsmanship – AHL) (2002)
Signed as a free agent by **Chicago**, July 12, 2002.

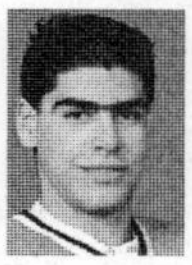

DESCOTEAUX, Matthieu (DAY-koh-toh, MAT-yoo)

Defense. Shoots left. 6'3", 216 lbs. Born, Pierreville, Que., September 23, 1977. Edmonton's 2nd choice, 19th overall, in 1996 Entry Draft.

1993-94	Cap-d-Madeleine	QAAA	43	2	5	7	26	....	....	....	....	....	....	....	....	....	....	....	....	....	....	....	....	....	....
1994-95	Shawinigan	QMJHL	50	3	2	5	28	....	....	....	....	....	....	....	....	....	15	1	1	2	19	....	....	....	....
1995-96	Shawinigan	QMJHL	69	2	13	15	129	....	....	....	....	....	....	....	....	....	6	0	0	0	6	....	....	....	....
1996-97	Shawinigan	QMJHL	38	6	18	24	121	....	....	....	....	....	....	....	....	....	....	....	....	....	....	....	....	....	....
	Hull Olympiques	QMJHL	32	6	19	25	34	....	....	....	....	....	....	....	....	....	14	1	8	9	29	....	....	....	....
1997-98	Hamilton	AHL	67	2	8	10	70	....	....	....	....	....	....	....	....	....	2	0	0	0	0	....	....	....	....
1998-99	Hamilton	AHL	74	6	12	18	49	....	....	....	....	....	....	....	....	....	4	0	0	0	0	....	....	....	....
99-2000	Hamilton	AHL	49	5	7	12	29	....	....	....	....	....	....	....	....	....	....	....	....	....	....	....	....	....	....
	Quebec Citadelles	AHL	12	0	6	6	6	....	....	....	....	....	....	....	....	....	2	0	1	1	0	....	....	....	....
2000-01	Montreal	NHL	5	1	1	2	4	1	0	0	6	16.7	–2	0	0.0	15:10	....	....	....	....	....	....	....	....	....
	Quebec Citadelles	AHL	73	16	27	43	38	....	....	....	....	....	....	....	....	....	7	0	3	3	4	....	....	....	....
2001-02	Quebec Citadelles	AHL	65	6	14	20	34	....	....	....	....	....	....	....	....	....	3	1	2	3	0	....	....	....	....
2002-03	Utah Grizzlies	AHL	48	3	3	6	47	....	....	....	....	....	....	....	....	....	....	....	....	....	....	....	....	....	....
	NHL Totals		5	1	1	2	4	1	0	0	6	16.7		0	0.0	15:10	....	....	....	....	....	....	....	....	....

Traded to **Montreal** by **Edmonton** with Christian Laflamme for Igor Ulanov and Alain Nasreddine, March 9, 2000.

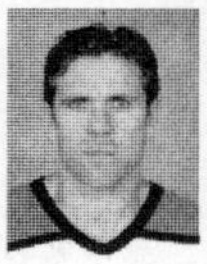

DESJARDINS, Eric (deh-ZHAHR-dai, AIR-ihk) PHI.

Defense. Shoots right. 6'1", 205 lbs. Born, Rouyn, Que., June 14, 1969. Montreal's 3rd choice, 38th overall, in 1987 Entry Draft.

1985-86	Laval Laurentide	QAAA	42	6	30	36	54	....	....	....	....	....	....	....	....	....	8	2	10	12	14	....	....	....	....
1986-87	Granby Bisons	QMJHL	66	14	24	38	178	....	....	....	....	....	....	....	....	....	8	3	2	5	10	....	....	....	....
1987-88	Granby Bisons	QMJHL	62	18	49	67	138	....	....	....	....	....	....	....	....	....	5	0	3	3	10	....	....	....	....
	Sherbrooke	AHL	3	0	0	0	6	....	....	....	....	....	....	....	....	....	4	0	2	2	2	....	....	....	....
1988-89	Montreal	NHL	36	2	12	14	26	1	0	0	39	5.1	9	....	....	....	14	1	1	2	6	1	0	0	....
1989-90	Montreal	NHL	55	3	13	16	51	1	0	0	48	6.3	1	....	....	....	6	0	0	0	10	0	0	0	....
1990-91	Montreal	NHL	62	7	18	25	27	0	0	1	114	6.1	7	....	....	....	13	1	4	5	8	1	0	0	....
1991-92	Montreal	NHL	77	6	32	38	50	4	0	2	141	4.3	17	....	....	....	11	3	3	6	4	1	0	0	....
1992-93♦	Montreal	NHL	82	13	32	45	98	7	0	1	163	8.0	20	....	....	....	20	4	10	14	23	1	0	1	....
1993-94	Montreal	NHL	84	12	23	35	97	6	1	3	193	6.2	–1	....	....	....	7	0	2	2	4	0	0	0	....
1994-95	Montreal	NHL	9	0	6	6	2	0	0	0	14	0.0	2	....	....	....	....	....	....	....	....	....	....	....	....
	Philadelphia	NHL	34	5	18	23	12	1	0	1	79	6.3	10	....	....	....	15	4	4	8	10	1	0	2	....
1995-96	Philadelphia	NHL	80	7	40	47	45	5	0	2	184	3.8	19	....	....	....	12	0	6	6	2	0	0	0	....
1996-97	Philadelphia	NHL	82	12	34	46	50	5	1	1	183	6.6	25	....	....	....	19	2	8	10	12	0	0	0	....
1997-98	Philadelphia	NHL	77	6	27	33	36	2	1	0	150	4.0	11	....	....	....	5	0	1	1	0	0	0	0	....
	Canada	Olympics	6	0	0	0	2	....	....	....	....	....	....	....	....	....	....	....	....	....	....	....	....	....	....
1998-99	Philadelphia	NHL	68	15	36	51	38	6	0	2	190	7.9	18	0	0.0	25:48	6	2	2	4	4	1	0	1	26:40
99-2000	Philadelphia	NHL	81	14	41	55	32	8	0	4	207	6.8	20	1	0.0	27:01	18	2	10	12	2	1	0	1	28:00
2000-01	Philadelphia	NHL	79	15	33	48	50	6	1	4	187	8.0	–3	3	100.0	26:27	6	1	1	2	0	0	0	0	27:49
2001-02	Philadelphia	NHL	65	6	19	25	24	2	1	0	117	5.1	–1	2	0.0	22:12	5	0	1	1	2	0	0	0	22:30
2002-03	Philadelphia	NHL	79	8	24	32	35	1	0	2	197	4.1	30	0	0.0	22:55	5	2	1	3	0	0	0	0	27:38
	NHL Totals		1050	131	408	539	673	55	5	23	2206	5.9		6	50.0	24:58	162	22	54	76	87	7	0	5	27:02

QMJHL Second All-Star Team (1987) • QMJHL First All-Star Team (1988) • NHL Second All-Star Team (1999, 2000)
Played in NHL All-Star Game (1992, 1996, 2000)
Traded to **Philadelphia** by **Montreal** with Gilbert Dionne and John LeClair for Mark Recchi and Philadelphia's 3rd round choice (Martin Hohenberger) in 1995 Entry Draft, February 9, 1995.

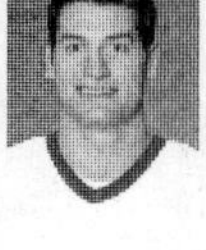

DEVEREAUX, Boyd (DEH-vuhr-oh, BOID) DET.

Center. Shoots left. 6'2", 195 lbs. Born, Seaforth, Ont., April 16, 1978. Edmonton's 1st choice, 6th overall, in 1996 Entry Draft.

1992-93	Seaforth Sailors	OJHL-D	34	7	20	27	13	....	....	....	....	....	....	....	....	....	....	....	....	....	....	....	....	....	....
1993-94	Stratford Cullitons	OJHL-B	46	12	27	39	8	....	....	....	....	....	....	....	....	....	....	....	....	....	....	....	....	....	....
1994-95	Stratford Cullitons	OJHL-B	45	31	74	105	21	....	....	....	....	....	....	....	....	....	....	....	....	....	....	....	....	....	....
1995-96	Kitchener Rangers	OHL	66	20	38	58	35	....	....	....	....	....	....	....	....	....	12	3	7	10	4	....	....	....	....
1996-97	Kitchener Rangers	OHL	54	28	41	69	37	....	....	....	....	....	....	....	....	....	13	4	11	15	8	....	....	....	....
	Hamilton	AHL	....	....	....	....	....	....	....	....	....	....	....	....	....	....	1	0	1	1	0	....	....	....	....
1997-98	Edmonton	NHL	38	1	4	5	6	0	0	0	27	3.7	–5	....	....	....	....	....	....	....	....	....	....	....	....
	Hamilton	AHL	14	5	6	11	6	....	....	....	....	....	....	....	....	....	9	1	1	2	8	....	....	....	....
1998-99	Edmonton	NHL	61	6	8	14	23	0	1	4	39	15.4	2	409	42.8	10:09	1	0	0	0	0	0	0	0	32:46
	Hamilton	AHL	7	4	6	10	2	....	....	....	....	....	....	....	....	....	8	0	3	3	4	....	....	....	....
99-2000	Edmonton	NHL	76	8	19	27	20	0	1	2	108	7.4	7	241	34.9	12:36	....	....	....	....	....	....	....	....	....
2000-01	Detroit	NHL	55	5	6	11	14	0	0	0	66	7.6	1	124	37.1	10:08	2	0	0	0	0	0	0	0	10:39

			Regular Season														Playoffs								
Season	Club	League	GP	G	A	Pts	PIM	PP	SH	GW	S	%	+/-	TF	F%	Min	GP	G	A	Pts	PIM	PP	SH	GW	Min
2001-02 ♦	Detroit	NHL	79	9	16	25	24	0	0	2	116	7.8	9	12	33.3	11:30	21	2	4	6	4	0	0	0	10:58
2002-03	Detroit	NHL	61	3	9	12	16	0	0	1	72	4.2	4	7	42.9	9:26									
	NHL Totals		370	32	62	94	103	0	2	9	428	7.5		793	39.3	10:54	24	2	4	6	4	0	0	0	11:51

Canadian Major Junior Scholastic Player of the Year (1996)

Signed as a free agent by **Detroit**, August 23, 2000.

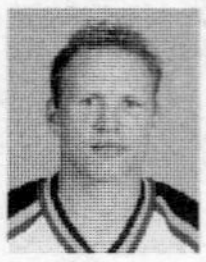

de VRIES, Greg

(deh-VREES, GREHG) **NYR**

Defense. Shoots left. 6'3", 215 lbs. Born, Sundridge, Ont., January 4, 1973.

			Regular Season														Playoffs								
Season	Club	League	GP	G	A	Pts	PIM	PP	SH	GW	S	%	+/-	TF	F%	Min	GP	G	A	Pts	PIM	PP	SH	GW	Min
1988-89	Cortina Astros	OMHA	35	28	40	68																			
1989-90	Aurora Eagles	OJHL	42	1	16	17	32																		
1990-91	Stratford Cullitons	OJHL-B	40	8	32	40	120										3	2	1	3	20				
1991-92	Thorold Eagles	OJHL-B	3	0	0	0	0																		
	Bowling Green	CCHA	24	0	3	3	20																		
1992-93	Niagara Falls	OHL	62	3	23	26	86										4	0	1	1	6				
1993-94	Niagara Falls	OHL	64	5	40	45	135																		
	Cape Breton	AHL	9	0	0	0	11										1	0	0	0	0				
1994-95	Cape Breton	AHL	77	5	19	24	68																		
1995-96	**Edmonton**	**NHL**	**13**	**1**	**1**	**2**	**12**	**0**	**0**	**0**	**8**	**12.5**	**–2**												
	Cape Breton	AHL	58	9	30	39	174																		
1996-97	**Edmonton**	**NHL**	**37**	**0**	**4**	**4**	**52**	**0**	**0**	**0**	**31**	**0.0**	**–2**				**12**	**0**	**1**	**1**	**8**	**0**	**0**	**0**	
	Hamilton	AHL	34	4	14	18	26																		
1997-98	**Edmonton**	**NHL**	**65**	**7**	**4**	**11**	**80**	**1**	**0**	**0**	**53**	**13.2**	**–17**				**7**	**0**	**0**	**0**	**21**	**0**	**0**	**0**	
1998-99	**Nashville**	**NHL**	**6**	**0**	**0**	**0**	**4**	**0**	**0**	**0**	**1**	**1.0**	**–4**	**0**	**0.0**	**18:11**									
	Colorado	**NHL**	**67**	**1**	**3**	**4**	**60**	**0**	**0**	**0**	**56**	**56.0**	**–3**	**1**	**100.0**	**16:23**	**19**	**0**	**2**	**2**	**22**	**0**	**0**	**0**	**12:09**
99-2000	**Colorado**	**NHL**	**69**	**2**	**7**	**9**	**73**	**0**	**0**	**0**	**40**	**5.0**	**–7**	**0**	**0.0**	**14:59**	**5**	**0**	**0**	**0**	**4**	**0**	**0**	**0**	**8:09**
2000-01 ♦	**Colorado**	**NHL**	**79**	**5**	**12**	**17**	**51**	**0**	**0**	**0**	**76**	**6.6**	**23**	**0**	**0.0**	**17:06**	**23**	**0**	**1**	**1**	**20**	**0**	**0**	**0**	**14:17**
2001-02	**Colorado**	**NHL**	**82**	**8**	**12**	**20**	**57**	**1**	**1**	**3**	**148**	**5.4**	**18**	**1**	**0.0**	**23:03**	**21**	**4**	**9**	**13**	**2**	**0**	**0**	**1**	**24:12**
2002-03	**Colorado**	**NHL**	**82**	**6**	**26**	**32**	**70**	**0**	**0**	**2**	**112**	**5.4**	**15**	**1**	**100.0**	**22:15**	**7**	**2**	**0**	**2**	**0**	**0**	**0**	**0**	**22:11**
	NHL Totals		**500**	**30**	**69**	**99**	**459**	**2**	**1**	**5**	**525**	**5.7**		**3**	**66.7**	**18:59**	**94**	**6**	**13**	**19**	**77**	**0**	**0**	**1**	**16:51**

Signed as a free agent by **Edmonton**, March 20, 1994. Traded to **Nashville** by **Edmonton** with Eric Fichaud and Drake Berehowsky for Mikhail Shtalenkov and Jim Dowd, October 1, 1998. Traded to **Colorado** by **Nashville** for Colorado's 2nd round choice (Ed Hill) in 1999 Entry Draft, October 24, 1998. Signed as a free agent by **NY Rangers**, July 14, 2003.

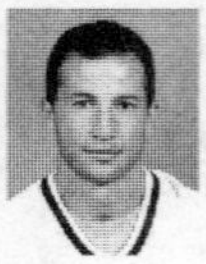

DiMAIO, Rob

(duh-MIGH-oh, RAWB) **DAL.**

Right wing. Shoots right. 5'10", 190 lbs. Born, Calgary, Alta., February 19, 1968. NY Islanders' 6th choice, 118th overall, in 1987 Entry Draft.

			Regular Season														Playoffs								
Season	Club	League	GP	G	A	Pts	PIM	PP	SH	GW	S	%	+/-	TF	F%	Min	GP	G	A	Pts	PIM	PP	SH	GW	Min
1984-85	Kamloops Blazers	WHL	55	9	18	27	29										7	1	3	4	2				
1985-86	Kamloops Blazers	WHL	6	1	0	1	0																		
	Medicine Hat	WHL	55	20	30	50	82										22	6	6	12	39				
1986-87	Medicine Hat	WHL	70	27	43	70	130										20	7	11	18	46				
1987-88	Medicine Hat	WHL	54	47	43	90	120										14	12	19	*31	59				
1988-89	**NY Islanders**	**NHL**	**16**	**1**	**0**	**1**	**30**	**0**	**0**	**1**	**16**	**6.3**	**–6**												
	Springfield	AHL	40	13	18	31	67																		
1989-90	**NY Islanders**	**NHL**	**7**	**0**	**0**	**0**	**2**	**0**	**0**	**0**	**2**	**0.0**	**0**				**1**	**1**	**0**	**1**	**4**	**0**	**0**	**0**	
	Springfield	AHL	54	25	27	52	69										16	4	7	11	45				
1990-91	**NY Islanders**	**NHL**	**1**	**0**	**0**	**0**	**0**	**0**	**0**	**0**	**0**	**0.0**	**0**												
	Capital District	AHL	12	3	4	7	22																		
1991-92	**NY Islanders**	**NHL**	**50**	**5**	**2**	**7**	**43**	**0**	**2**	**0**	**43**	**11.6**	**–23**												
1992-93	**Tampa Bay**	**NHL**	**54**	**9**	**15**	**24**	**62**	**2**	**0**	**0**	**75**	**12.0**	**0**												
1993-94	**Tampa Bay**	**NHL**	**39**	**8**	**7**	**15**	**40**	**2**	**0**	**1**	**51**	**15.7**	**–5**												
	Philadelphia	**NHL**	**14**	**3**	**5**	**8**	**6**	**0**	**0**	**1**	**30**	**10.0**	**1**												
1994-95	**Philadelphia**	**NHL**	**36**	**3**	**1**	**4**	**53**	**0**	**0**	**0**	**34**	**8.8**	**8**				**15**	**2**	**4**	**6**	**4**	**0**	**1**	**1**	
1995-96	**Philadelphia**	**NHL**	**59**	**6**	**15**	**21**	**58**	**1**	**1**	**0**	**49**	**12.2**	**0**				**3**	**0**	**0**	**0**	**0**	**0**	**0**	**0**	
1996-97	**Boston**	**NHL**	**72**	**13**	**15**	**28**	**82**	**0**	**3**	**2**	**152**	**8.6**	**–21**												
1997-98	**Boston**	**NHL**	**79**	**10**	**17**	**27**	**82**	**0**	**0**	**4**	**112**	**8.9**	**–13**				**6**	**1**	**0**	**1**	**8**	**0**	**0**	**0**	
1998-99	**Boston**	**NHL**	**71**	**7**	**14**	**21**	**95**	**1**	**0**	**0**	**121**	**5.8**	**–14**	**83**	**45.8**	**16:41**	**12**	**2**	**0**	**2**	**8**	**0**	**0**	**1**	**16:50**
99-2000	**Boston**	**NHL**	**50**	**5**	**16**	**21**	**42**	**0**	**0**	**0**	**93**	**5.4**	**–1**	**278**	**44.2**	**16:47**									
	NY Rangers	**NHL**	**12**	**1**	**3**	**4**	**8**	**0**	**0**	**0**	**18**	**5.6**	**–8**	**1**	**0.0**	**15:30**									
2000-01	**Carolina**	**NHL**	**74**	**6**	**18**	**24**	**54**	**0**	**2**	**1**	**99**	**6.1**	**–14**	**46**	**43.5**	**14:58**	**6**	**0**	**0**	**0**	**4**	**0**	**0**	**0**	**14:30**
2001-02	**Dallas**	**NHL**	**61**	**6**	**6**	**12**	**25**	**0**	**2**	**2**	**63**	**9.5**	**–2**	**76**	**44.7**	**10:52**									
	Utah Grizzlies	AHL	3	1	1	2	0																		
2002-03	**Dallas**	**NHL**	**69**	**10**	**9**	**19**	**76**	**0**	**0**	**2**	**81**	**12.3**	**18**	**49**	**44.9**	**12:58**	**12**	**1**	**4**	**5**	**10**	**0**	**0**	**0**	**15:50**
	NHL Totals		**764**	**93**	**143**	**236**	**758**	**6**	**10**	**14**	**1039**	**9.0**		**533**	**44.5**	**14:28**	**55**	**7**	**8**	**15**	**38**	**0**	**1**	**2**	**15:58**

Stafford Smythe Memorial Trophy (Memorial Cup MVP) (1988)

Claimed by **Tampa Bay** from **NY Islanders** in Expansion Draft, June 18, 1992. Traded to **Philadelphia** by **Tampa Bay** for Jim Cummins and Philadelphia's 4th round choice (later traded back to Philadelphia – Philadelphia selected Radovan Somik) in 1995 Entry Draft, March 18, 1994. Claimed by **San Jose** from **Philadelphia** in Waiver Draft, September 30, 1996. Traded to **Boston** by **San Jose** for Boston's 5th round choice (Adam Nittel) in 1997 Entry Draft, September 30, 1996. Traded to **NY Rangers** by **Boston** for Mike Knuble, March 10, 2000. Traded to **Carolina** by **NY Rangers** with Darren Langdon for Sandy McCarthy and Carolina's 4th round choice (Bryce Lampman) in 2001 Entry Draft, August 4, 2000. Signed as a free agent by **Dallas**, July 1, 2001.

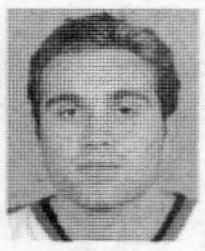

DIMITRAKOS, Niko

(DIH-mih-tra-kohs, NIK-oh) **S.J.**

Right wing. Shoots right. 5'11", 190 lbs. Born, Boston, MA, May 21, 1979. San Jose's 4th choice, 155th overall, in 1999 Entry Draft.

			Regular Season														Playoffs								
Season	Club	League	GP	G	A	Pts	PIM	PP	SH	GW	S	%	+/-	TF	F%	Min	GP	G	A	Pts	PIM	PP	SH	GW	Min
1994-95	Matignon	Hi-School	23	10	12	22																			
1995-96	Matignon	Hi-School	25	12	28	40																			
1996-97	Matignon	Hi-School	25	23	32	55																			
1997-98	Avon Old Farms	Hi-School	26	27	28	55																			
1998-99	U. of Maine	H-East	35	8	19	27	33																		
99-2000	U. of Maine	H-East	32	11	16	27	16																		
2000-01	U. of Maine	H-East	29	11	14	25	43																		
2001-02	U. of Maine	H-East	43	20	31	51	44																		
2002-03	**San Jose**	**NHL**	**21**	**6**	**7**	**13**	**8**	**3**	**0**	**0**	**34**	**17.6**	**–7**	**2**	**50.0**	**14:15**									
	Cleveland Barons	AHL	55	15	29	44	30																		
	NHL Totals		**21**	**6**	**7**	**13**	**8**	**3**	**0**	**0**	**34**	**17.6**		**2**	**50.0**	**14:15**									

NCAA Championship All-Tournament Team (1999) • Hockey East Second All-Star Team (2002)

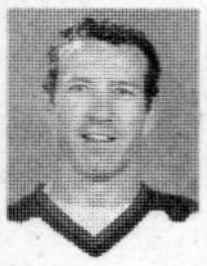

DINEEN, Kevin

(DIH-neen, KEH-vihn)

Right wing. Shoots right. 5'11", 198 lbs. Born, Quebec City, Que., October 28, 1963. Hartford's 3rd choice, 56th overall, in 1982 Entry Draft.

			Regular Season														Playoffs								
Season	Club	League	GP	G	A	Pts	PIM	PP	SH	GW	S	%	+/-	TF	F%	Min	GP	G	A	Pts	PIM	PP	SH	GW	Min
1980-81	St. Michael's B	OJHL-B	40	15	28	43	167																		
1981-82	U. of Denver	WCHA	26	10	10	20	70																		
1982-83	U. of Denver	WCHA	36	16	13	29	108																		
1983-84	Team Canada	Nat-Tm	52	5	11	16	2																		
	Canada	Olympics	7	0	0	0	8																		
1984-85	**Hartford**	**NHL**	**57**	**25**	**16**	**41**	**120**	**8**	**4**	**2**	**141**	**17.7**	**–6**												
	Binghamton	AHL	25	15	8	23	41																		
1985-86	**Hartford**	**NHL**	**57**	**33**	**35**	**68**	**124**	**6**	**0**	**8**	**167**	**19.8**	**16**				**10**	**6**	**7**	**13**	**18**	**1**	**0**	**2**	
1986-87	**Hartford**	**NHL**	**78**	**40**	**39**	**79**	**110**	**11**	**0**	**7**	**234**	**17.1**	**7**				**6**	**2**	**1**	**3**	**31**	**1**	**0**	**0**	
1987-88	**Hartford**	**NHL**	**74**	**25**	**25**	**50**	**217**	**5**	**0**	**4**	**223**	**11.2**	**–14**				**6**	**4**	**4**	**8**	**8**	**1**	**0**	**1**	
1988-89	**Hartford**	**NHL**	**79**	**45**	**44**	**89**	**167**	**20**	**1**	**4**	**294**	**15.3**	**–6**				**4**	**1**	**0**	**1**	**10**	**0**	**0**	**0**	
1989-90	**Hartford**	**NHL**	**67**	**25**	**41**	**66**	**164**	**8**	**2**	**2**	**214**	**11.7**	**7**				**6**	**3**	**2**	**5**	**18**	**0**	**0**	**1**	
1990-91	**Hartford**	**NHL**	**61**	**17**	**30**	**47**	**104**	**4**	**0**	**2**	**161**	**10.6**	**–15**				**6**	**1**	**0**	**1**	**16**	**0**	**0**	**0**	
1991-92	**Hartford**	**NHL**	**16**	**4**	**2**	**6**	**23**	**1**	**0**	**1**	**28**	**14.3**	**–6**												
	Philadelphia	**NHL**	**64**	**26**	**30**	**56**	**130**	**5**	**3**	**4**	**197**	**13.2**	**1**												
1992-93	**Philadelphia**	**NHL**	**83**	**35**	**28**	**63**	**201**	**6**	**3**	**7**	**241**	**14.5**	**14**												
1993-94	**Philadelphia**	**NHL**	**71**	**19**	**23**	**42**	**113**	**5**	**1**	**2**	**156**	**12.2**	**–9**												
1994-95	Houston Aeros	IHL	17	6	4	10	42																		
	Philadelphia	**NHL**	**40**	**8**	**5**	**13**	**39**	**4**	**0**	**2**	**55**	**14.5**	**–1**				**15**	**6**	**4**	**10**	**18**	**1**	**0**	**1**	
1995-96	**Philadelphia**	**NHL**	**26**	**0**	**2**	**2**	**50**	**0**	**0**	**0**	**31**	**0.0**	**–8**												
	Hartford	**NHL**	**20**	**2**	**7**	**9**	**67**	**0**	**0**	**0**	**35**	**5.7**	**7**												
1996-97	**Hartford**	**NHL**	**78**	**19**	**29**	**48**	**141**	**8**	**0**	**5**	**185**	**10.3**	**–6**												

							Regular Season										Playoffs								
Season	Club	League	GP	G	A	Pts	PIM	PP	SH	GW	S	%	+/-	TF	F%	Min	GP	G	A	Pts	PIM	PP	SH	GW	Min
1997-98	**Carolina**	**NHL**	**54**	**7**	**16**	**23**	**105**	**0**	**0**	**1**	**96**	**7.3**	**-7**	....	....	....	....	....	....	....	....	....	....	....	....
1998-99	**Carolina**	**NHL**	**67**	**8**	**10**	**18**	**97**	**0**	**0**	**1**	**86**	**9.3**	**5**	**6**	**16.7**	**9:58**	**6**	**0**	**0**	**0**	**8**	**0**	**0**	**0**	**8:01**
99-2000	**Ottawa**	**NHL**	**67**	**4**	**8**	**12**	**57**	**0**	**0**	**1**	**71**	**5.6**	**2**	**10**	**50.0**	**9:31**	....	....	....	....	....	....	....	....	....
2000-01	**Columbus**	**NHL**	**66**	**8**	**7**	**15**	**126**	**0**	**0**	**3**	**74**	**10.8**	**2**	**13**	**30.8**	**10:37**	....	....	....	....	....	....	....	....	....
2001-02	**Columbus**	**NHL**	**59**	**5**	**8**	**13**	**62**	**0**	**0**	**0**	**73**	**6.8**	**-6**	**9**	**11.1**	**10:07**	....	....	....	....	....	....	....	....	....
2002-03	**Columbus**	**NHL**	**4**	**0**	**0**	**0**	**12**	**0**	**0**	**0**	**7**	**0.0**	**0**	**4**	**50.0**	**10:40**	....	....	....	....	....	....	....	....	....
	NHL Totals		**1188**	**355**	**405**	**760**	**2229**	**91**	**14**	**56**	**2769**	**12.8**		**42**	**31.0**	**10:04**	**59**	**23**	**18**	**41**	**127**	**4**	**0**	**5**	**8:01**

Bud Light/NHL Man of the Year Award (1991)

Played in NHL All-Star Game (1988, 1989)

Traded to **Philadelphia** by **Hartford** for Murray Craven and Philadelphia's 4th round choice (Kevin Smyth) in 1992 Entry Draft, November 13, 1991. Traded to **Hartford** by **Philadelphia** for Hartford/Carolina's 3rd (Kris Mallette) and 7th (later traded back to Hartford/Carolina – Carolina selected Andrew Merrick) round choices in 1997 Entry Draft, December 28, 1995. Transferred to **Carolina** after **Hartford** franchise relocated, June 25, 1997. Signed as a free agent by **Ottawa**, September 1, 1999. Selected by **Columbus** from **Ottawa** in Expansion Draft, June 23, 2000. • Officially announced retirement, November 5, 2002.

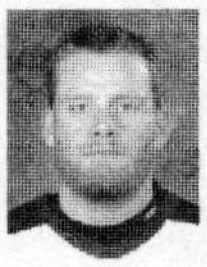

DINGMAN, Chris
(DIHNG-man, KRIHS) **T.B.**

Left wing. Shoots left. 6'4", 225 lbs. Born, Edmonton, Alta., July 6, 1976. Calgary's 1st choice, 19th overall, in 1994 Entry Draft.

Season	Club	League	GP	G	A	Pts	PIM	PP	SH	GW	S	%	+/-	TF	F%	Min	GP	G	A	Pts	PIM	PP	SH	GW	Min
1991-92	Edm. Mercurys	AMHL	36	23	18	41	72	....	....	....	....	....	....	....	....	....	....	....	....	....	....	....	....	....	....
1992-93	Brandon	WHL	50	10	17	27	64	....	....	....	....	....	....	....	....	....	4	0	0	0	0	....	....	....	....
1993-94	Brandon	WHL	45	21	20	41	77	....	....	....	....	....	....	....	....	....	13	1	7	8	39	....	....	....	....
1994-95	Brandon	WHL	66	40	43	83	201	....	....	....	....	....	....	....	....	....	3	1	0	1	9	....	....	....	....
1995-96	Brandon	WHL	40	16	29	45	109	....	....	....	....	....	....	....	....	....	19	12	11	23	60	....	....	....	....
	Saint John Flames	AHL	....	....	....	....	....	....	....	....	....	....	....	....	....	....	1	0	0	0	0	....	....	....	....
1996-97	Saint John Flames	AHL	71	5	6	11	195	....	....	....	....	....	....	....	....	....	....	....	....	....	....	....	....	....	....
1997-98	**Calgary**	**NHL**	**70**	**3**	**3**	**6**	**149**	**1**	**0**	**0**	**47**	**6.4**	**-11**	....	....	....	....	....	....	....	....	....	....	....	....
1998-99	**Calgary**	**NHL**	**2**	**0**	**0**	**0**	**17**	**0**	**0**	**0**	**1**	**0.0**	**-2**	**0**	**0.0**	**8:11**	....	....	....	....	....	....	....	....	....
	Saint John Flames	AHL	50	5	7	12	140	....	....	....	....	....	....	....	....	....	....	....	....	....	....	....	....	....	....
	Colorado	**NHL**	**1**	**0**	**0**	**0**	**7**	**0**	**0**	**0**	**0**	**0.0**	**0**	**0**	**0.0**	**0:30**	....	....	....	....	....	....	....	....	....
	Hershey Bears	AHL	17	1	3	4	102	....	....	....	....	....	....	....	....	....	5	0	2	2	6	....	....	....	....
99-2000	**Colorado**	**NHL**	**68**	**8**	**3**	**11**	**132**	**2**	**0**	**1**	**54**	**14.8**	**-2**	**2**	**0.0**	**6:29**	....	....	....	....	....	....	....	....	....
2000-01♦	**Colorado**	**NHL**	**41**	**1**	**1**	**2**	**108**	**0**	**0**	**0**	**33**	**3.0**	**-3**	**0**	**0.0**	**6:26**	**16**	**0**	**4**	**4**	**14**	**0**	**0**	**0**	**6:18**
2001-02	**Carolina**	**NHL**	**30**	**0**	**1**	**1**	**77**	**0**	**0**	**0**	**17**	**0.0**	**-2**	**2**	**100.0**	**6:54**	....	....	....	....	....	....	....	....	....
	Tampa Bay	**NHL**	**14**	**0**	**4**	**4**	**26**	**0**	**0**	**0**	**24**	**0.0**	**-8**	**0**	**0.0**	**10:43**	....	....	....	....	....	....	....	....	....
2002-03	**Tampa Bay**	**NHL**	**51**	**2**	**1**	**3**	**91**	**0**	**0**	**0**	**41**	**4.9**	**-11**	**3**	**33.3**	**9:34**	**10**	**1**	**0**	**1**	**4**	**0**	**0**	**0**	**12:45**
	NHL Totals		**277**	**14**	**13**	**27**	**607**	**3**	**0**	**1**	**217**	**6.5**		**7**	**42.9**	**7:34**	**26**	**1**	**4**	**5**	**18**	**0**	**0**	**0**	**8:47**

Traded to **Colorado** by **Calgary** with Theoren Fleury for Rene Corbet, Wade Belak, Robyn Regehr and Colorado's 2nd round compensatory choice (Jarret Stoll) in 2000 Entry Draft, February 28, 1999. • Missed majority of 2000-01 season recovering from knee injury suffered in game vs. Ottawa, November 15, 2000. Traded to **Carolina** by **Colorado** for Carolina's 5th round choice (Mikko Viitanen) in 2001 Entry Draft, June 24, 2001. Traded to **Tampa Bay** by **Carolina** with Shane Willis for Kevin Weekes, March 5, 2002.

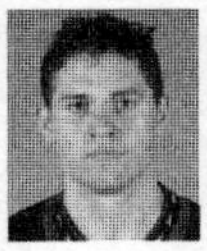

DiPENTA, Joe
(DIH-pehn-tah, JOH) **ATL.**

Defense. Shoots left. 6'2", 235 lbs. Born, Barrie, Ont., February 25, 1979. Florida's 2nd choice, 61st overall, in 1998 Entry Draft.

Season	Club	League	GP	G	A	Pts	PIM	PP	SH	GW	S	%	+/-	TF	F%	Min	GP	G	A	Pts	PIM	PP	SH	GW	Min
1996-97	Smiths Falls Bears	OCJHL	54	13	22	35	92	....	....	....	....	....	....	....	....	....	....	....	....	....	....	....	....	....	....
1997-98	Boston University	H-East	38	2	16	18	50	....	....	....	....	....	....	....	....	....	....	....	....	....	....	....	....	....	....
1998-99	Boston University	H-East	36	2	15	17	72	....	....	....	....	....	....	....	....	....	....	....	....	....	....	....	....	....	....
99-2000	Halifax	QMJHL	63	13	43	56	83	....	....	....	....	....	....	....	....	....	10	3	4	7	26	....	....	....	....
2000-01	Philadelphia	AHL	71	3	5	8	65	....	....	....	....	....	....	....	....	....	10	1	2	3	15	....	....	....	....
2001-02	Philadelphia	AHL	61	2	4	6	71	....	....	....	....	....	....	....	....	....	....	....	....	....	....	....	....	....	....
	Chicago Wolves	AHL	15	0	2	2	15	....	....	....	....	....	....	....	....	....	25	1	3	4	22	....	....	....	....
2002-03	**Atlanta**	**NHL**	**3**	**1**	**1**	**2**	**0**	**0**	**0**	**0**	**2**	**50.0**	**3**	**0**	**0.0**	**15:47**	....	....	....	....	....	....	....	....	....
	Chicago Wolves	AHL	76	2	17	19	107	....	....	....	....	....	....	....	....	....	9	0	1	1	7	....	....	....	....
	NHL Totals		**3**	**1**	**1**	**2**	**0**	**0**	**0**	**0**	**2**	**50.0**		**0**	**0.0**	**15:47**	....	....	....	....	....	....	....	....	....

• Left **Boston U.** (H-East) and signed with **Halifax** (QMJHL), May 2, 1999. Signed as a free agent by **Philadelphia**, July 12, 2000. Traded to **Atlanta** by **Philadelphia** for Jarrod Skalde, March 5, 2002.

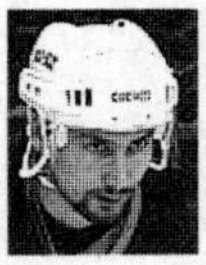

DIVISEK, Tomas
(DIH-vih-sehk, TOH-mahs) **PHI.**

Center. Shoots left. 6'2", 204 lbs. Born, Most, Czech., July 19, 1979. Philadelphia's 9th choice, 195th overall, in 1998 Entry Draft.

Season	Club	League	GP	G	A	Pts	PIM	PP	SH	GW	S	%	+/-	TF	F%	Min	GP	G	A	Pts	PIM	PP	SH	GW	Min
1995-96	Slavia Praha Jr.	Czech-Jr.	36	20	27	47	12	....	....	....	....	....	....	....	....	....	....	....	....	....	....	....	....	....	....
1996-97	Slavia Praha Jr.	Czech-Jr.	41	17	25	42	18	....	....	....	....	....	....	....	....	....	....	....	....	....	....	....	....	....	....
	HC Slavia Praha	Czech	1	0	0	0	0	....	....	....	....	....	....	....	....	....	....	....	....	....	....	....	....	....	....
1997-98	Slavia Praha Jr.	Czech-Jr.	27	20	16	36	12	....	....	....	....	....	....	....	....	....	....	....	....	....	....	....	....	....	....
	HC Slavia Praha	Czech	22	2	0	2	8	....	....	....	....	....	....	....	....	....	....	....	....	....	....	....	....	....	....
1998-99	HC Slavia Praha	Czech	45	8	4	12	26	....	....	....	....	....	....	....	....	....	....	....	....	....	....	....	....	....	....
99-2000	Philadelphia	AHL	59	18	31	49	30	....	....	....	....	....	....	....	....	....	5	0	3	3	2	....	....	....	....
2000-01	**Philadelphia**	**NHL**	**2**	**0**	**0**	**0**	**0**	**0**	**0**	**0**	**2**	**0.0**	**-1**	**0**	**0.0**	**11:30**	....	....	....	....	....	....	....	....	....
	Philadelphia	AHL	45	10	22	32	33	....	....	....	....	....	....	....	....	....	10	4	9	13	4	....	....	....	....
2001-02	**Philadelphia**	**NHL**	**3**	**1**	**0**	**1**	**0**	**0**	**0**	**1**	**3**	**33.3**	**1**	**28**	**50.0**	**8:12**	....	....	....	....	....	....	....	....	....
	Philadelphia	AHL	65	13	18	31	54	....	....	....	....	....	....	....	....	....	....	....	....	....	....	....	....	....	....
	Springfield	AHL	9	2	1	3	8	....	....	....	....	....	....	....	....	....	....	....	....	....	....	....	....	....	....
2002-03	HC Pardubice	Czech	34	16	14	30	22	....	....	....	....	....	....	....	....	....	15	2	4	6	12	....	....	....	....
	Hradec Kralove	Czech-2	1	2	0	2	10	....	....	....	....	....	....	....	....	....	....	....	....	....	....	....	....	....	....
	NHL Totals		**5**	**1**	**0**	**1**	**0**	**0**	**0**	**1**	**5**	**20.0**		**28**	**50.0**	**9:31**	....	....	....	....	....	....	....	....	....

Signed as a free agent by **HC Pardubice** (Czech) with Philadelphia retaining NHL rights, July 23, 2002.

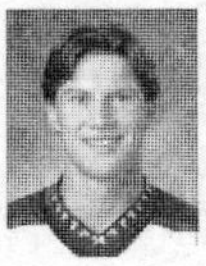

DOAN, Shane
(DOHN, SHAYN) **PHX.**

Right wing. Shoots right. 6'2", 216 lbs. Born, Halkirk, Alta., October 10, 1976. Winnipeg's 1st choice, 7th overall, in 1995 Entry Draft.

Season	Club	League	GP	G	A	Pts	PIM	PP	SH	GW	S	%	+/-	TF	F%	Min	GP	G	A	Pts	PIM	PP	SH	GW	Min
1991-92	Killam Selects	AAHA	56	80	84	164	74	....	....	....	....	....	....	....	....	....	....	....	....	....	....	....	....	....	....
1992-93	Kamloops Blazers	WHL	51	7	12	19	65	....	....	....	....	....	....	....	....	....	13	0	1	1	8	....	....	....	....
1993-94	Kamloops Blazers	WHL	52	24	24	48	88	....	....	....	....	....	....	....	....	....	....	....	....	....	....	....	....	....	....
1994-95	Kamloops Blazers	WHL	71	37	57	94	106	....	....	....	....	....	....	....	....	....	21	6	10	16	16	....	....	....	....
1995-96	**Winnipeg**	**NHL**	**74**	**7**	**10**	**17**	**101**	**1**	**0**	**3**	**106**	**6.6**	**-9**	....	....	....	**6**	**0**	**0**	**0**	**6**	**0**	**0**	**0**	....
1996-97	**Phoenix**	**NHL**	**63**	**4**	**8**	**12**	**49**	**0**	**0**	**0**	**100**	**4.0**	**-3**	....	....	....	**4**	**0**	**0**	**0**	**2**	**0**	**0**	**0**	....
1997-98	**Phoenix**	**NHL**	**33**	**5**	**6**	**11**	**35**	**0**	**0**	**3**	**42**	**11.9**	**-3**	....	....	....	**6**	**1**	**0**	**1**	**6**	**0**	**0**	**0**	....
	Springfield	AHL	39	21	21	42	64	....	....	....	....	....	....	....	....	....	....	....	....	....	....	....	....	....	....
1998-99	**Phoenix**	**NHL**	**79**	**6**	**16**	**22**	**54**	**0**	**0**	**0**	**156**	**3.8**	**-5**	**6**	**16.7**	**12:42**	**7**	**2**	**2**	**4**	**6**	**0**	**0**	**2**	**17:58**
99-2000	**Phoenix**	**NHL**	**81**	**26**	**25**	**51**	**66**	**1**	**1**	**4**	**221**	**11.8**	**6**	**25**	**36.0**	**16:51**	**4**	**1**	**2**	**3**	**8**	**1**	**0**	**0**	**18:11**
2000-01	**Phoenix**	**NHL**	**76**	**26**	**37**	**63**	**89**	**6**	**1**	**6**	**220**	**11.8**	**0**	**15**	**40.0**	**19:32**	....	....	....	....	....	....	....	....	....
2001-02	**Phoenix**	**NHL**	**81**	**20**	**29**	**49**	**61**	**6**	**0**	**2**	**205**	**9.8**	**11**	**52**	**44.2**	**18:10**	**5**	**2**	**2**	**4**	**6**	**0**	**0**	**0**	**17:21**
2002-03	**Phoenix**	**NHL**	**82**	**21**	**37**	**58**	**86**	**7**	**0**	**2**	**225**	**9.3**	**3**	**623**	**39.8**	**18:47**	....	....	....	....	....	....	....	....	....
	NHL Totals		**569**	**115**	**168**	**283**	**541**	**21**	**2**	**20**	**1275**	**9.0**		**721**	**39.8**	**17:12**	**32**	**6**	**6**	**12**	**34**	**1**	**0**	**2**	**17:49**

Memorial Cup All-Star Team (1995) • Stafford Smythe Memorial Trophy (Memorial Cup MVP) (1995)

Transferred to **Phoenix** after **Winnipeg** franchise relocated, July 1, 1996.

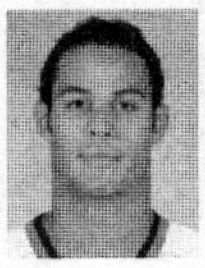

DOIG, Jason
(DOIG, JAY-suhn) **WSH.**

Defense. Shoots right. 6'3", 228 lbs. Born, Montreal, Que., January 29, 1977. Winnipeg's 3rd choice, 34th overall, in 1995 Entry Draft.

Season	Club	League	GP	G	A	Pts	PIM	PP	SH	GW	S	%	+/-	TF	F%	Min	GP	G	A	Pts	PIM	PP	SH	GW	Min
1990-91	North Shore	QAHA	31	30	33	63	53	....	....	....	....	....	....	....	....	....	....	....	....	....	....	....	....	....	....
1991-92	North Shore	QAHA	29	11	11	22	20	....	....	....	....	....	....	....	....	....	....	....	....	....	....	....	....	....	....
1992-93	Lac St-Louis Lions	QAAA	35	11	16	27	40	....	....	....	....	....	....	....	....	....	7	5	5	10	16	....	....	....	....
1993-94	St-Jean Lynx	QMJHL	63	8	17	25	65	....	....	....	....	....	....	....	....	....	5	0	2	2	2	....	....	....	....
1994-95	Laval Titan	QMJHL	55	13	42	55	259	....	....	....	....	....	....	....	....	....	20	4	13	17	39	....	....	....	....
1995-96	Laval Titan	QMJHL	5	3	6	9	20	....	....	....	....	....	....	....	....	....	....	....	....	....	....	....	....	....	....
	Granby	QMJHL	24	4	30	34	91	....	....	....	....	....	....	....	....	....	20	10	22	32	*110	....	....	....	....
	Winnipeg	**NHL**	**15**	**1**	**1**	**2**	**28**	**0**	**0**	**0**	**7**	**14.3**	**-2**	....	....	....	....	....	....	....	....	....	....	....	....
	Springfield	AHL	5	0	0	0	28	....	....	....	....	....	....	....	....	....	....	....	....	....	....	....	....	....	....
1996-97	Granby	QMJHL	39	14	33	47	211	....	....	....	....	....	....	....	....	....	5	0	4	4	27	....	....	....	....
	Las Vegas	IHL	6	0	1	1	19	....	....	....	....	....	....	....	....	....	....	....	....	....	....	....	....	....	....
	Springfield	AHL	5	0	3	3	2	....	....	....	....	....	....	....	....	....	17	1	4	5	37	....	....	....	....

			Regular Season														Playoffs								
Season	Club	League	GP	G	A	Pts	PIM	PP	SH	GW	S	%	+/-	TF	F%	Min	GP	G	A	Pts	PIM	PP	SH	GW	Min
1997-98	**Phoenix**	**NHL**	**4**	**0**	**1**	**1**	**12**	**0**	**0**	**0**	**1**	**0.0**	**–4**												
	Springfield	AHL	46	2	25	27	153										3	0	0	0	2				
1998-99	**Phoenix**	**NHL**	**9**	**0**	**1**	**1**	**10**	**0**	**0**	**0**	**0**	**0.0**	**2**	**0**	**0.0**	**5:08**									
	Springfield	AHL	32	3	5	8	67																		
	Hartford	AHL	8	1	4	5	40										7	1	1	2	39				
99-2000	**NY Rangers**	**NHL**	**7**	**0**	**1**	**1**	**22**	**0**	**0**	**0**	**3**	**0.0**	**–2**	**0**	**0.0**	**8:50**									
	Hartford	AHL	27	3	11	14	70										21	1	5	6	20				
2000-01	**NY Rangers**	**NHL**	**3**	**0**	**0**	**0**	**0**	**0**	**0**	**0**	**1**	**0.0**	**0**	**0**	**0.0**	**6:35**									
	Hartford	AHL	52	4	20	24	178										5	0	1	1	4				
2001-02	Grand Rapids	AHL	57	1	17	18	103										5	0	0	0	18				
2002-03	**Washington**	**NHL**	**55**	**3**	**5**	**8**	**108**	**0**	**0**	**1**	**41**	**7.3**	**–3**	**1**	**0.0**	**14:11**	**6**	**0**	**1**	**1**	**6**	**0**	**0**	**0**	**16:52**
	Portland Pirates	AHL	21	1	4	5	66																		
	NHL Totals		**93**	**4**	**9**	**13**	**180**	**0**	**0**	**1**	**53**	**7.5**		**1**	**0.0**	**12:16**	**6**	**0**	**1**	**1**	**6**	**0**	**0**	**0**	**16:52**

QMJHL All-Rookie Team (1994) • Memorial Cup All-Star Team (1996)

Transferred to **Phoenix** after **Winnipeg** franchise relocated, July 1, 1996. Traded to **NY Rangers** by **Phoenix** with Phoenix's 6th round choice (Jay Dardis) in 1999 Entry Draft for Stan Neckar, March 23, 1999. Traded to **Ottawa** by **NY Rangers** with Jeff Ulmer for Sean Gagnon, June 29, 2001. Signed as free agent by **Washington**, September 12, 2002.

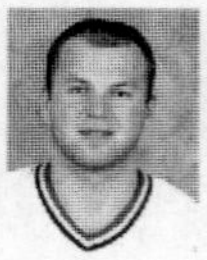

DOME, Robert

(doh-MAY, RAW-buhrt) **CGY.**

Right wing. Shoots left. 6', 210 lbs. Born, Skalica, Czech., January 29, 1979. Pittsburgh's 1st choice, 17th overall, in 1997 Entry Draft.

Season	Club	League	GP	G	A	Pts	PIM	PP	SH	GW	S	%	+/-	TF	F%	Min	GP	G	A	Pts	PIM	PP	SH	GW	Min
1994-95	Dukla Trencin Jr.	Slovak-Jr.	36	36	43	79	39																		
1995-96	Utah Grizzlies	IHL	56	10	9	19	28																		
1996-97	Long Beach	IHL	13	4	6	10	14																		
	Las Vegas	IHL	43	10	7	17	22																		
1997-98	**Pittsburgh**	**NHL**	**30**	**5**	**2**	**7**	**12**	**1**	**0**	**0**	**29**	**17.2**	**–1**												
	Syracuse Crunch	AHL	36	21	25	46	77																		
1998-99	Syracuse Crunch	AHL	48	18	17	35	70																		
	Houston Aeros	IHL	20	2	4	6	24																		
99-2000	**Pittsburgh**	**NHL**	**22**	**2**	**5**	**7**	**0**	**0**	**0**	**0**	**27**	**7.4**	**1**	**5**	**40.0**	**9:51**									
	Wilkes-Barre	AHL	51	12	26	38	83																		
2000-01	Kladno	Czech	29	9	12	21	57																		
	HC Ocelari Trinec	Czech	5	0	3	3	4																		
2001-02	Wilkes-Barre	AHL	39	9	8	17	53																		
2002-03	**Calgary**	**NHL**	**1**	**0**	**0**	**0**	**0**	**0**	**0**	**0**	**1**	**0.0**	**0**	**0**	**0.0**	**8:16**									
	Saint John Flames	AHL	56	27	29	56	41																		
	NHL Totals		**53**	**7**	**7**	**14**	**12**	**1**	**0**	**0**	**57**	**12.3**		**5**	**40.0**	**9:47**									

• Missed majority of 2001-02 season recovering from heel injury suffered during off-season training, July 10, 2001. Signed as a free agent by **Calgary**, July 17, 2002.

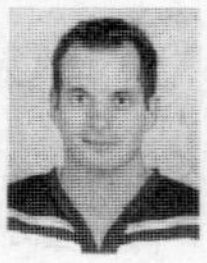

DOMENICHELLI, Hnat

(daw-meh-CHEHL-ee, NAT)

Left wing. Shoots left. 6', 195 lbs. Born, Edmonton, Alta., February 17, 1976. Hartford's 2nd choice, 83rd overall, in 1994 Entry Draft.

Season	Club	League	GP	G	A	Pts	PIM	PP	SH	GW	S	%	+/-	TF	F%	Min	GP	G	A	Pts	PIM	PP	SH	GW	Min
1991-92	Edmonton Freeze	AMHL	34	34	49	83	101																		
1992-93	Kamloops Blazers	WHL	45	12	8	20	15										11	1	1	2	2				
1993-94	Kamloops Blazers	WHL	69	27	40	67	31										19	10	12	22	0				
1994-95	Kamloops Blazers	WHL	72	52	62	114	34										19	9	9	18	9				
1995-96	Kamloops Blazers	WHL	62	59	89	148	37										16	7	9	16	29				
1996-97	**Hartford**	**NHL**	**13**	**2**	**1**	**3**	**7**	**1**	**0**	**0**	**14**	**14.3**	**–4**												
	Springfield	AHL	39	24	24	48	12																		
	Calgary	**NHL**	**10**	**1**	**2**	**3**	**2**	**1**	**0**	**0**	**16**	**6.3**	**1**												
	Saint John Flames	AHL	1	1	1	2	0										5	5	0	5	2				
1997-98	**Calgary**	**NHL**	**31**	**9**	**7**	**16**	**6**	**1**	**0**	**1**	**70**	**12.9**	**4**												
	Saint John Flames	AHL	48	33	13	46	24										19	7	8	15	14				
1998-99	**Calgary**	**NHL**	**23**	**5**	**5**	**10**	**11**	**3**	**0**	**0**	**45**	**11.1**	**–4**	**3**	**0.0**	**12:59**									
	Saint John Flames	AHL	51	25	21	46	26										7	4	4	8	2				
99-2000	**Calgary**	**NHL**	**32**	**5**	**9**	**14**	**12**	**1**	**0**	**1**	**57**	**8.8**	**0**	**78**	**46.2**	**12:39**									
	Saint John Flames	AHL	12	6	7	13	8																		
	Atlanta	**NHL**	**27**	**6**	**9**	**15**	**4**	**0**	**0**	**0**	**68**	**8.8**	**–21**	**9**	**55.6**	**16:55**									
2000-01	**Atlanta**	**NHL**	**63**	**15**	**12**	**27**	**18**	**4**	**0**	**1**	**150**	**10.0**	**–9**	**24**	**37.5**	**14:21**									
2001-02	**Atlanta**	**NHL**	**40**	**8**	**11**	**19**	**34**	**1**	**0**	**1**	**87**	**9.2**	**–18**	**9**	**33.3**	**14:51**									
	Minnesota	**NHL**	**27**	**1**	**5**	**6**	**10**	**0**	**0**	**0**	**57**	**1.8**	**–5**	**10**	**30.0**	**12:40**									
2002-03	**Minnesota**	**NHL**	**1**	**0**	**0**	**0**	**0**	**0**	**0**	**0**	**1**	**0.0**	**0**	**0**	**0.0**	**11:11**									
	Houston Aeros	AHL	62	29	34	63	58										23	6	8	14	8				
	NHL Totals		**267**	**52**	**61**	**113**	**104**	**12**	**0**	**4**	**565**	**9.2**		**133**	**42.1**	**14:08**									

WHL West Second All-Star Team (1995) • WHL West First All-Star Team (1996) • Canadian Major Junior First All-Star Team (1996) • Canadian Major Junior Most Sportsmanlike Player of the Year (1996)

Traded to **Calgary** by **Hartford** with Glen Featherstone, New Jersey's 2nd round choice (previously acquired, Calgary selected Dimitri Kokorev) in 1997 Entry Draft and Vancouver's 3rd round choice (previously acquired, Calgary selected Paul Manning) in 1998 Entry Draft for Steve Chiasson and Colorado's 3rd round choice (previously acquired, Carolina selected Francis Lessard) in 1997 Entry Draft, March 5, 1997. Traded to **Atlanta** by **Calgary** with Dmitri Vlasenkov for Darryl Shannon and Jason Botterill, February 11, 2000. Traded to **Minnesota** by **Atlanta** for Andy Sutton, January 22, 2002.

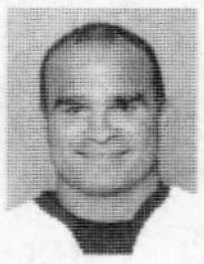

DOMI, Tie

(DOH-mee, TIGH) **TOR.**

Right wing. Shoots right. 5'10", 213 lbs. Born, Windsor, Ont., November 1, 1969. Toronto's 2nd choice, 27th overall, in 1988 Entry Draft.

Season	Club	League	GP	G	A	Pts	PIM	PP	SH	GW	S	%	+/-	TF	F%	Min	GP	G	A	Pts	PIM	PP	SH	GW	Min
1984-85	Belle River	OJHL-C	28	7	5	12	98																		
1985-86	Windsor Bulldogs	OJHL-B	42	8	17	25	*346																		
1986-87	Peterboro B's	OJHL-B	2	0	0	0	10																		
	Peterborough	OHL	18	1	1	2	79																		
1987-88	Peterborough	OHL	60	22	21	43	*292										12	3	9	12	24				
1988-89	Peterborough	OHL	43	14	16	30	175										17	10	9	19	*70				
1989-90	**Toronto**	**NHL**	**2**	**0**	**0**	**0**	**42**	**0**	**0**	**0**	**0**	**0.0**	**0**												
	Newmarket Saints	AHL	57	14	11	25	285																		
1990-91	**NY Rangers**	**NHL**	**28**	**1**	**0**	**1**	**185**	**0**	**0**	**0**	**5**	**20.0**	**–5**												
	Binghamton	AHL	25	11	6	17	219										7	3	2	5	16				
1991-92	**NY Rangers**	**NHL**	**42**	**2**	**4**	**6**	**246**	**0**	**0**	**1**	**20**	**10.0**	**–4**				**6**	**1**	**1**	**2**	**32**	**0**	**0**	**0**	
1992-93	**NY Rangers**	**NHL**	**12**	**2**	**0**	**2**	**95**	**0**	**0**	**0**	**11**	**18.2**	**–1**												
	Winnipeg	**NHL**	**49**	**3**	**10**	**13**	**249**	**0**	**0**	**0**	**29**	**10.3**	**2**				**6**	**1**	**0**	**1**	**23**	**0**	**0**	**0**	
1993-94	**Winnipeg**	**NHL**	**81**	**8**	**11**	**19**	***347**	**0**	**0**	**1**	**98**	**8.2**	**–8**												
1994-95	**Winnipeg**	**NHL**	**31**	**4**	**4**	**8**	**128**	**0**	**0**	**0**	**34**	**11.8**	**–6**												
	Toronto	**NHL**	**9**	**0**	**1**	**1**	**31**	**0**	**0**	**0**	**12**	**0.0**	**1**				**7**	**1**	**0**	**1**	**0**	**0**	**0**	**0**	
1995-96	**Toronto**	**NHL**	**72**	**7**	**6**	**13**	**297**	**0**	**0**	**1**	**61**	**11.5**	**–3**				**6**	**0**	**2**	**2**	**4**	**0**	**0**	**0**	
1996-97	**Toronto**	**NHL**	**80**	**11**	**17**	**28**	**275**	**2**	**0**	**1**	**98**	**11.2**	**–17**												
1997-98	**Toronto**	**NHL**	**80**	**4**	**10**	**14**	**365**	**0**	**0**	**0**	**72**	**5.6**	**–5**												
1998-99	**Toronto**	**NHL**	**72**	**8**	**14**	**22**	**198**	**0**	**0**	**1**	**65**	**12.3**	**5**	**9**	**44.4**	**9:42**	**14**	**0**	**2**	**2**	**24**	**0**	**0**	**0**	**6:58**
99-2000	**Toronto**	**NHL**	**70**	**5**	**9**	**14**	**198**	**0**	**0**	**2**	**64**	**7.8**	**–5**	**4**	**25.0**	**9:58**	**12**	**0**	**1**	**1**	**20**	**0**	**0**	**0**	**6:40**
2000-01	**Toronto**	**NHL**	**82**	**13**	**7**	**20**	**214**	**1**	**0**	**1**	**60**	**21.7**	**2**	**5**	**80.0**	**8:23**	**8**	**0**	**1**	**1**	**20**	**0**	**0**	**0**	**8:27**
2001-02	**Toronto**	**NHL**	**74**	**9**	**10**	**19**	**157**	**0**	**0**	**2**	**93**	**9.7**	**3**	**22**	**45.5**	**10:20**	**19**	**1**	**3**	**4**	***61**	**0**	**0**	**1**	**11:15**
2002-03	**Toronto**	**NHL**	**79**	**15**	**14**	**29**	**171**	**4**	**0**	**0**	**91**	**16.5**	**–1**	**21**	**19.1**	**10:56**	**7**	**1**	**0**	**1**	**13**	**0**	**0**	**1**	**14:47**
	NHL Totals		**863**	**92**	**117**	**209**	**3198**	**7**	**0**	**10**	**813**	**11.3**		**61**	**37.7**	**9:51**	**85**	**5**	**10**	**15**	**197**	**0**	**0**	**1**	**9:23**

Traded to **NY Rangers** by **Toronto** with Mark LaForest for Greg Johnston, June 28, 1990. Traded to **Winnipeg** by **NY Rangers** with Kris King for Ed Olczyk, December 28, 1992. Traded to **Toronto** by **Winnipeg** for Mike Eastwood and Toronto's 3rd round choice (Brad Isbister) in 1995 Entry Draft, April 7, 1995. Traded to **Nashville** by **Toronto** for Nashville's 8th round choice (Shaun Landolt) in 2003 Entry Draft, June 30, 2002. Signed as a free agent by **Toronto**, July 14, 2002.

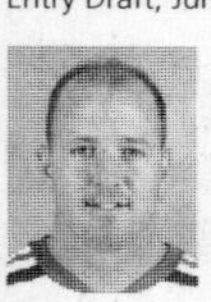

DONATO, Ted

(duh-NAH-toh, TEHD) **BOS.**

Left wing. Shoots left. 5'10", 180 lbs. Born, Boston, MA, April 28, 1969. Boston's 6th choice, 98th overall, in 1987 Entry Draft.

Season	Club	League	GP	G	A	Pts	PIM	PP	SH	GW	S	%	+/-	TF	F%	Min	GP	G	A	Pts	PIM	PP	SH	GW	Min
1986-87	Catholic Memorial	Hi-School	22	29	34	63	30																		
1987-88	Harvard Crimson	ECAC	28	12	14	26	24																		
1988-89	Harvard Crimson	ECAC	34	14	37	51	30																		
1989-90	Harvard Crimson	ECAC	16	5	6	11	34																		
1990-91	Harvard Crimson	ECAC	27	19	*37	56	26																		

			Regular Season														Playoffs								
Season	Club	League	GP	G	A	Pts	PIM	PP	SH	GW	S	%	+/-	TF	F%	Min	GP	G	A	Pts	PIM	PP	SH	GW	Min
1991-92	Team USA	Nat-Tm	52	11	22	33	24	....	....	....	....	....	....	....	....	....	....	....	....	....	....	....	....	....	....
	United States	Olympics	8	4	3	7	8	....	....	....	....	....	....	....	....	....	....	....	....	....	....	....	....	....	....
	Boston	**NHL**	**10**	**1**	**2**	**3**	**8**	**0**	**0**	**0**	**13**	**7.7**	**–1**	....	....	....	**15**	**3**	**4**	**7**	**4**	**0**	**0**	**1**	....
1992-93	**Boston**	**NHL**	**82**	**15**	**20**	**35**	**61**	**3**	**2**	**5**	**118**	**12.7**	**2**	....	....	....	**4**	**0**	**1**	**1**	**0**	**0**	**0**	**0**	....
1993-94	**Boston**	**NHL**	**84**	**22**	**32**	**54**	**59**	**9**	**2**	**1**	**158**	**13.9**	**0**	....	....	....	**13**	**4**	**2**	**6**	**10**	**2**	**0**	**1**	....
1994-95	TuTo Turku	Finland	14	5	5	10	47	....	....	....	....	....	....	....	....	....	....	....	....	....	....	....	....	....	....
	Boston	**NHL**	**47**	**10**	**10**	**20**	**10**	**1**	**0**	**1**	**71**	**14.1**	**3**	....	....	....	**5**	**0**	**0**	**0**	**4**	**0**	**0**	**0**	....
1995-96	**Boston**	**NHL**	**82**	**23**	**26**	**49**	**46**	**7**	**0**	**1**	**152**	**15.1**	**6**	....	....	....	**5**	**1**	**2**	**3**	**2**	**1**	**0**	**0**	....
1996-97	**Boston**	**NHL**	**67**	**25**	**26**	**51**	**37**	**6**	**2**	**2**	**172**	**14.5**	**–9**	....	....	....	....	....	....	....	....	....	....	....	....
1997-98	**Boston**	**NHL**	**79**	**16**	**23**	**39**	**54**	**3**	**0**	**5**	**129**	**12.4**	**6**	....	....	....	**5**	**0**	**0**	**0**	**2**	**0**	**0**	**0**	....
1998-99	**Boston**	**NHL**	**14**	**1**	**3**	**4**	**4**	**0**	**0**	**0**	**22**	**4.5**	**0**	**18**	**44.4**	**15:21**	....	....	....	....	....	....	....	....	....
	NY Islanders	**NHL**	**55**	**7**	**11**	**18**	**27**	**2**	**0**	**0**	**68**	**10.3**	**–10**	**142**	**45.8**	**12:09**	....	....	....	....	....	....	....	....	....
	Ottawa	**NHL**	**13**	**3**	**2**	**5**	**10**	**1**	**0**	**0**	**16**	**18.8**	**2**	**4**	**25.0**	**11:10**	**1**	**0**	**0**	**0**	**0**	**0**	**0**	**0**	**5:38**
99-2000	**Anaheim**	**NHL**	**81**	**11**	**19**	**30**	**26**	**2**	**0**	**3**	**138**	**8.0**	**–3**	**212**	**41.5**	**14:35**	....	....	....	....	....	....	....	....	....
2000-01	**Dallas**	**NHL**	**65**	**8**	**17**	**25**	**26**	**1**	**0**	**3**	**71**	**11.3**	**6**	**16**	**37.5**	**10:13**	**8**	**0**	**1**	**1**	**0**	**0**	**0**	**0**	**10:24**
2001-02	**NY Islanders**	**NHL**	**1**	**0**	**0**	**0**	**0**	**0**	**0**	**0**	**1**	**0.0**	**–1**	**0**	**0.0**	**7:55**	....	....	....	....	....	....	....	....	....
	Bridgeport	AHL	1	0	0	0	0	....	....	....	....	....	....	....	....	....	....	....	....	....	....	....	....	....	....
	St. Louis	**NHL**	**2**	**0**	**0**	**0**	**2**	**0**	**0**	**0**	**0**	**0.0**	**–2**	**15**	**53.3**	**9:17**	....	....	....	....	....	....	....	....	....
	Los Angeles	**NHL**	**2**	**0**	**0**	**0**	**2**	**0**	**0**	**0**	**1**	**0.0**	**–2**	**10**	**20.0**	**7:20**	....	....	....	....	....	....	....	....	....
	Manchester	AHL	36	18	25	43	19	....	....	....	....	....	....	....	....	....	5	1	3	4	0	....	....	....	....
2002-03	**NY Rangers**	**NHL**	**49**	**2**	**1**	**3**	**6**	**0**	**0**	**0**	**30**	**6.7**	**–1**	**290**	**47.9**	**8:33**	....	....	....	....	....	....	....	....	....
	Hartford	AHL	18	8	12	20	14	....	....	....	....	....	....	....	....	....	....	....	....	....	....	....	....	....	....
	NHL Totals		**733**	**144**	**192**	**336**	**378**	**35**	**6**	**21**	**1160**	**12.4**		**707**	**44.8**	**11:49**	**56**	**8**	**10**	**18**	**22**	**3**	**0**	**2**	**9:53**

NCAA Championship All-Tournament Team (1989) • NCAA Championship Tournament MVP (1989) • ECAC First All-Star Team (1991)

Traded to **NY Islanders** by **Boston** for Ken Belanger, November 7, 1998. Traded to **Ottawa** by **NY Islanders** for Ottawa's 4th round choice (later traded to Phoenix – Phoenix selected Preston Mizzi) in 1999 Entry Draft, March 20, 1999. Traded to **Anaheim** by **Ottawa** with the rights to Antti-Jussi Niemi for Patrick Lalime, June 18, 1999. Signed as a free agent agent by **Dallas**, August 17, 2000. Signed as a free agent by **NY Islanders**, January 16, 2002. Claimed on waivers by **Los Angeles** from **NY Islanders**, January 28, 2002. Claimed on waivers by **St. Louis** from **Los Angeles**, March 6, 2002. Claimed on waivers by **Los Angeles** from **St. Louis**, March 19, 2002. • Missed majority of 2001-02 season recovering from shoulder injury suffered in game vs. St. John's (AHL), January 9, 2002. Signed as a free agent by **NY Rangers**, July 8, 2002. Signed as a free agent by **Boston**, July 22, 2003.

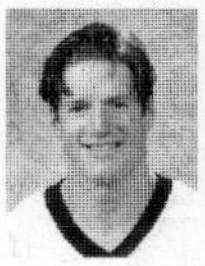

DONOVAN, Shean

(DAW-nuh-vuhn, SHAWN) **CGY.**

Right wing. Shoots right. 6'2", 200 lbs. Born, Timmins, Ont., January 22, 1975. San Jose's 2nd choice, 28th overall, in 1993 Entry Draft.

Season	Club	League	GP	G	A	Pts	PIM	PP	SH	GW	S	%	+/-	TF	F%	Min	GP	G	A	Pts	PIM	PP	SH	GW	Min
1990-91	Kanata Valley	OCJHL	44	8	5	13	8	....	....	....	....	....	....	....	....	....	....	....	....	....	....	....	....	....	....
1991-92	Ottawa 67's	OHL	58	11	8	19	14	....	....	....	....	....	....	....	....	....	11	1	0	1	5	....	....	....	....
1992-93	Ottawa 67's	OHL	66	29	23	52	33	....	....	....	....	....	....	....	....	....	....	....	....	....	....	....	....	....	....
1993-94	Ottawa 67's	OHL	62	35	49	84	63	....	....	....	....	....	....	....	....	....	17	10	11	21	14	....	....	....	....
1994-95	Ottawa 67's	OHL	29	22	19	41	41	....	....	....	....	....	....	....	....	....	....	....	....	....	....	....	....	....	....
	San Jose	**NHL**	**14**	**0**	**0**	**0**	**6**	**0**	**0**	**0**	**13**	**0.0**	**–6**	....	....	....	**7**	**0**	**1**	**1**	**6**	**0**	**0**	**0**	....
	Kansas City	IHL	5	0	2	2	7	....	....	....	....	....	....	....	....	....	14	5	3	8	23	....	....	....	....
1995-96	**San Jose**	**NHL**	**74**	**13**	**8**	**21**	**39**	**0**	**1**	**2**	**73**	**17.8**	**–17**	....	....	....	....	....	....	....	....	....	....	....	....
	Kansas City	IHL	4	0	0	0	8	....	....	....	....	....	....	....	....	....	5	0	0	0	8	....	....	....	....
1996-97	**San Jose**	**NHL**	**73**	**9**	**6**	**15**	**42**	**0**	**1**	**0**	**115**	**7.8**	**–18**	....	....	....	....	....	....	....	....	....	....	....	....
	Kentucky	AHL	3	1	3	4	18	....	....	....	....	....	....	....	....	....	....	....	....	....	....	....	....	....	....
1997-98	**San Jose**	**NHL**	**20**	**3**	**3**	**6**	**22**	**0**	**0**	**0**	**24**	**12.5**	**3**	....	....	....	....	....	....	....	....	....	....	....	....
	Colorado	**NHL**	**47**	**5**	**7**	**12**	**48**	**0**	**0**	**0**	**57**	**8.8**	**3**	....	....	....	....	....	....	....	....	....	....	....	....
1998-99	**Colorado**	**NHL**	**68**	**7**	**12**	**19**	**37**	**1**	**0**	**1**	**81**	**8.6**	**4**	**9**	**22.2**	**8:46**	**5**	**0**	**0**	**0**	**2**	**0**	**0**	**0**	**4:55**
99-2000	**Colorado**	**NHL**	**18**	**1**	**0**	**1**	**8**	**0**	**0**	**0**	**13**	**7.7**	**–4**	**1**	**0.0**	**5:20**	....	....	....	....	....	....	....	....	....
	Atlanta	**NHL**	**33**	**4**	**7**	**11**	**18**	**1**	**0**	**1**	**53**	**7.5**	**–13**	**22**	**31.8**	**14:19**	....	....	....	....	....	....	....	....	....
2000-01	**Atlanta**	**NHL**	**63**	**12**	**11**	**23**	**47**	**1**	**3**	**1**	**93**	**12.9**	**–14**	**218**	**45.9**	**14:03**	....	....	....	....	....	....	....	....	....
2001-02	**Atlanta**	**NHL**	**48**	**6**	**6**	**12**	**40**	**1**	**0**	**2**	**64**	**9.4**	**–16**	**12**	**50.0**	**13:30**	....	....	....	....	....	....	....	....	....
	Pittsburgh	**NHL**	**13**	**2**	**1**	**3**	**4**	**0**	**0**	**0**	**18**	**11.1**	**–5**	**4**	**0.0**	**14:34**	....	....	....	....	....	....	....	....	....
2002-03	**Pittsburgh**	**NHL**	**52**	**4**	**5**	**9**	**30**	**0**	**1**	**0**	**66**	**6.1**	**–6**	**37**	**24.3**	**13:01**	....	....	....	....	....	....	....	....	....
	Calgary	**NHL**	**13**	**1**	**2**	**3**	**7**	**0**	**0**	**1**	**22**	**4.5**	**–2**	**3**	**66.7**	**15:39**	....	....	....	....	....	....	....	....	....
	NHL Totals		**536**	**67**	**68**	**135**	**348**	**4**	**6**	**8**	**692**	**9.7**		**306**	**41.2**	**12:14**	**12**	**0**	**1**	**1**	**8**	**0**	**0**	**0**	**4:55**

Traded to **Colorado** by **San Jose** with San Jose's 1st round choice (Alex Tanguay) in 1998 Entry Draft for Mike Ricci and Colorado's 2nd round choice (later traded to Buffalo – Buffalo selected Jaroslav Kristek), in 1998 Entry Draft, November 21, 1997. Traded to **Atlanta** by **Colorado** for Rick Tabaracci, December 8, 1999. Claimed on waivers by **Pittsburgh** from **Atlanta**, March 15, 2002. Traded to **Calgary** by **Pittsburgh** for Micki Dupont and Mathias Johansson, March 11, 2003.

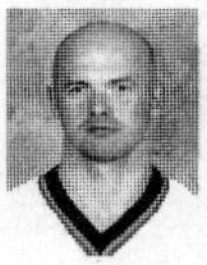

DOPITA, Jiri

(doh-PEE-tuh, YIH-ree)

Center. Shoots left. 6'4", 210 lbs. Born, Sumperk, Czech., December 2, 1968. NY Islanders' 4th choice, 123rd overall, in 1998 Entry Draft.

Season	Club	League	GP	G	A	Pts	PIM	PP	SH	GW	S	%	+/-	TF	F%	Min	GP	G	A	Pts	PIM	PP	SH	GW	Min
1989-90	Dukla Jihlava	Czech	5	1	2	3	0	....	....	....	....	....	....	....	....	....	....	....	....	....	....	....	....	....	....
1990-91	TJ DS Olomouc	Czech	42	11	13	24	26	....	....	....	....	....	....	....	....	....	....	....	....	....	....	....	....	....	....
1991-92	TJ DS Olomouc	Czech	38	24	20	44	28	....	....	....	....	....	....	....	....	....	3	1	4	5	0	....	....	....	....
1992-93	HC Olomouc	Czech	28	12	17	29	16	....	....	....	....	....	....	....	....	....	....	....	....	....	....	....	....	....	....
	Eisbaren Berlin	Germany	11	7	8	15	49	....	....	....	....	....	....	....	....	....	4	3	5	8	5	....	....	....	....
1993-94	Eisbaren Berlin	Germany	42	23	21	44	52	....	....	....	....	....	....	....	....	....	....	....	....	....	....	....	....	....	....
	HC Olomouc	Czech	....	....	....	....	....	....	....	....	....	....	....	....	....	....	12	4	7	11	....	....	....	....	....
1994-95	Eisbaren Berlin	Germany	42	28	40	68	55	....	....	....	....	....	....	....	....	....	....	....	....	....	....	....	....	....	....
1995-96	HC Petra Vsetin	Czech	38	19	20	39	20	....	....	....	....	....	....	....	....	....	13	9	11	20	10	....	....	....	....
1996-97	HC Petra Vsetin	Czech	52	*30	31	61	55	....	....	....	....	....	....	....	....	....	10	7	4	11	22	....	....	....	....
1997-98	HC Petra Vsetin	Czech	52	21	34	55	64	....	....	....	....	....	....	....	....	....	10	*12	6	18	4	....	....	....	....
	HC Petra Vsetin	EuroHL	6	2	4	6	4	....	....	....	....	....	....	....	....	....	....	....	....	....	....	....	....	....	....
1998-99	HC Slovnaft Vsetin	Czech	50	19	32	51	43	....	....	....	....	....	....	....	....	....	12	1	6	7	....	....	....	....	....
99-2000	HC Slovnaft Vsetin	Czech	49	*30	29	59	83	....	....	....	....	....	....	....	....	....	9	0	4	4	6	....	....	....	....
	HC Slovnaft Vsetin	EuroHL	3	0	2	2	2	....	....	....	....	....	....	....	....	....	....	....	....	....	....	....	....	....	....
2000-01	HC Slovnaft Vsetin	Czech	46	19	31	50	53	....	....	....	....	....	....	....	....	....	14	8	*13	*21	18	....	....	....	....
2001-02	**Philadelphia**	**NHL**	**52**	**11**	**16**	**27**	**8**	**3**	**0**	**2**	**79**	**13.9**	**9**	**705**	**48.7**	**15:14**	....	....	....	....	....	....	....	....	....
	Czech Republic	Olympics	4	2	2	4	2	....	....	....	....	....	....	....	....	....	....	....	....	....	....	....	....	....	....
2002-03	**Edmonton**	**NHL**	**21**	**1**	**5**	**6**	**11**	**0**	**0**	**1**	**23**	**4.3**	**–4**	**316**	**52.9**	**13:49**	....	....	....	....	....	....	....	....	....
	NHL Totals		**73**	**12**	**21**	**33**	**19**	**3**	**0**	**3**	**102**	**11.8**		**1021**	**50.0**	**14:50**	....	....	....	....	....	....	....	....	....

• Re-entered NHL Entry Draft. Originally Boston's 4th choice, 133rd overall, in 1992 Entry Draft.

Rights traded to **Florida** by **NY Islanders** for San Jose's 5th round choice (previously acquired, NY Islanders selected Adam Johnson) in 1999 Entry Draft, June 26, 1999. Rights traded to **Philadelphia** by **Florida** for Philadelphia's 2nd round choice (later traded to Calgary – Calgary selected Andrei Medvedev) in 2001 Entry Draft, June 23, 2001. Traded to **Edmonton** by **Philadelphia** for Edmonton's 3rd round choice (Ryan Potulny) in 2003 Entry Draft and future considerations, June 19, 2002. Signed as a free agent by **HC Olomouc** (Czech) after securing release from **Edmonton**, February 3, 2003.

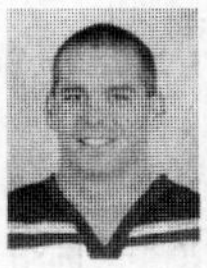

DOWD, Jim

(DOWD, JIHM) **MIN.**

Center. Shoots right. 6'1", 190 lbs. Born, Brick, NJ, December 25, 1968. New Jersey's 7th choice, 149th overall, in 1987 Entry Draft.

Season	Club	League	GP	G	A	Pts	PIM	PP	SH	GW	S	%	+/-	TF	F%	Min	GP	G	A	Pts	PIM	PP	SH	GW	Min
1983-84	Brick High	Hi-School	20	19	30	49	....	....	....	....	....	....	....	....	....	....	....	....	....	....	....	....	....	....	....
1984-85	Brick High	Hi-School	24	58	55	113	....	....	....	....	....	....	....	....	....	....	....	....	....	....	....	....	....	....	....
1985-86	Brick High	Hi-School	24	47	51	98	....	....	....	....	....	....	....	....	....	....	....	....	....	....	....	....	....	....	....
1986-87	Brick High	Hi-School	24	22	33	55	....	....	....	....	....	....	....	....	....	....	....	....	....	....	....	....	....	....	....
1987-88	Lake Superior	CCHA	45	18	27	45	16	....	....	....	....	....	....	....	....	....	....	....	....	....	....	....	....	....	....
1988-89	Lake Superior	CCHA	46	24	35	59	40	....	....	....	....	....	....	....	....	....	....	....	....	....	....	....	....	....	....
1989-90	Lake Superior	CCHA	46	25	*67	92	30	....	....	....	....	....	....	....	....	....	....	....	....	....	....	....	....	....	....
1990-91	Lake Superior	CCHA	44	24	*54	*78	53	....	....	....	....	....	....	....	....	....	....	....	....	....	....	....	....	....	....
1991-92	**New Jersey**	**NHL**	**1**	**0**	**0**	**0**	**0**	**0**	**0**	**0**	**0**	**0.0**	**0**	....	....	....	....	....	....	....	....	....	....	....	....
	Utica Devils	AHL	78	17	42	59	47	....	....	....	....	....	....	....	....	....	4	2	2	4	4	....	....	....	....
1992-93	**New Jersey**	**NHL**	**1**	**0**	**0**	**0**	**0**	**0**	**0**	**0**	**1**	**0.0**	**–1**	....	....	....	....	....	....	....	....	....	....	....	....
	Utica Devils	AHL	78	27	45	72	62	....	....	....	....	....	....	....	....	....	5	1	7	8	10	....	....	....	....
1993-94	**New Jersey**	**NHL**	**15**	**5**	**10**	**15**	**0**	**2**	**0**	**0**	**26**	**19.2**	**8**	....	....	....	**19**	**2**	**6**	**8**	**8**	**0**	**0**	**0**	....
	Albany River Rats	AHL	58	26	37	63	76	....	....	....	....	....	....	....	....	....	....	....	....	....	....	....	....	....	....
1994-95♦	**New Jersey**	**NHL**	**10**	**1**	**4**	**5**	**0**	**1**	**0**	**0**	**14**	**7.1**	**–5**	....	....	....	**11**	**2**	**1**	**3**	**8**	**0**	**0**	**1**	....
1995-96	**New Jersey**	**NHL**	**28**	**4**	**9**	**13**	**17**	**0**	**0**	**0**	**41**	**9.8**	**–1**	....	....	....	....	....	....	....	....	....	....	....	....
	Vancouver	**NHL**	**38**	**1**	**6**	**7**	**6**	**0**	**0**	**0**	**35**	**2.9**	**–8**	....	....	....	**1**	**0**	**0**	**0**	**0**	**0**	**0**	**0**	....
1996-97	**NY Islanders**	**NHL**	**3**	**0**	**0**	**0**	**0**	**0**	**0**	**0**	**0**	**0.0**	**–1**	....	....	....	....	....	....	....	....	....	....	....	....
	Utah Grizzlies	IHL	48	10	21	31	27	....	....	....	....	....	....	....	....	....	....	....	....	....	....	....	....	....	....
	Saint John Flames	AHL	24	5	11	16	18	....	....	....	....	....	....	....	....	....	5	1	2	3	0	....	....	....	....

Season	Club	League	GP	G	A	Pts	PIM	PP	SH	GW	S	%	+/-	TF	F%	Min	GP	G	A	Pts	PIM	PP	SH	GW	Min
			Regular Season														Playoffs								
1997-98	**Calgary**	**NHL**	**48**	**6**	**8**	**14**	**12**	**0**	**1**	**0**	**58**	**10.3**	**10**												
	Saint John Flames	AHL	35	8	30	38	20										19	3	13	16	10				
1998-99	**Edmonton**	**NHL**	**1**	**0**	**0**	**0**	**0**	**0**	**0**	**0**	**1**	**0.0**	**0**	**7**	**14.3**	**9:47**									
	Hamilton	AHL	51	15	29	44	82										11	3	6	9	8				
99-2000	**Edmonton**	**NHL**	**69**	**5**	**18**	**23**	**45**	**2**	**0**	**1**	**103**	**4.9**	**10**	**720**	**54.0**	**13:08**	**5**	**2**	**1**	**3**	**4**	**0**	**0**	**0**	**15:22**
2000-01	**Minnesota**	**NHL**	**68**	**7**	**22**	**29**	**80**	**0**	**0**	**0**	**92**	**7.6**	**–6**	**1154**	**50.7**	**17:50**									
2001-02	**Minnesota**	**NHL**	**82**	**13**	**30**	**43**	**54**	**5**	**0**	**1**	**111**	**11.7**	**–14**	**1243**	**52.9**	**15:34**									
2002-03	**Minnesota**	**NHL**	**78**	**8**	**17**	**25**	**31**	**3**	**1**	**2**	**78**	**10.3**	**–1**	**930**	**47.9**	**13:03**	**15**	**0**	**2**	**2**	**0**	**0**	**0**	**0**	**12:58**
	NHL Totals		**442**	**50**	**124**	**174**	**245**	**13**	**2**	**4**	**560**	**8.9**		**4054**	**51.3**	**14:51**	**51**	**6**	**10**	**16**	**20**	**0**	**0**	**1**	**13:34**

CCHA Second All-Star Team (1990) • NCAA West Second All-American Team (1990) • CCHA First All-Star Team (1991) • CCHA Player of the Year (1991) • NCAA West First All-American Team (1991)

• Missed majority of 1994-95 season recovering from shoulder injury suffered in game vs. Quebec, February 2, 1995. Traded to **Hartford** by **New Jersey** with New Jersey's 2nd round choice (later traded to Calgary – Calgary selected Dmitri Kokorev) in 1997 Entry Draft for Jocelyn Lemieux and Hartford's 2nd round choice (later traded to Dallas – Dallas selected John Erskine) in 1998 Entry Draft, December 19, 1995. Traded to **Vancouver** by **Hartford** with Frantisek Kucera and Hartford's 2nd round choice (Ryan Bonni) in 1997 Entry Draft for Jeff Brown and Vancouver's 3rd round choice (later traded to Calgary – Calgary selected Paul Manning) in 1998 Entry Draft, December 19, 1995. Claimed by **NY Islanders** from **Vancouver** in Waiver Draft, September 30, 1996. Signed as a free agent by **Calgary**, August, 1997. Traded to **Nashville** by **Calgary** for future considerations, June 26, 1998. Traded to **Edmonton** by **Nashville** with Mikhail Shtalenkov for Eric Fichaud, Drake Berehowsky and Greg de Vries, October 1, 1998. Selected by **Minnesota** from **Edmonton** in Expansion Draft, June 23, 2000.

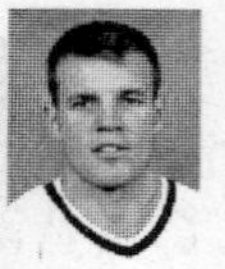

DOWNEY, Aaron

(DOW-nee, AIR-ruhn) **DAL.**

Right wing. Shoots right. 6'1", 216 lbs. Born, Shelburne, Ont., August 27, 1974.

Season	Club	League	GP	G	A	Pts	PIM	PP	SH	GW	S	%	+/-	TF	F%	Min	GP	G	A	Pts	PIM	PP	SH	GW	Min
1990-91	Grand Valley	OJHL-C	27	6	8	14	57																		
1991-92	Collingwood	OJHL-B	40	9	8	17	111																		
1992-93	Guelph Storm	OHL	53	3	3	6	88										5	1	0	1	0				
1993-94	Cole Harbour	NSMHL	35	8	20	28	210																		
1994-95	Cole Harbour	NSMHL	40	10	31	41	320																		
1995-96	Hampton Roads	ECHL	65	12	11	23	354																		
1996-97	Manitoba Moose	IHL	2	0	0	0	17																		
	Portland Pirates	AHL	3	0	0	0	19																		
	Hampton Roads	ECHL	64	8	8	16	338										9	0	3	3	26				
1997-98	Providence Bruins	AHL	78	5	10	15	*407																		
1998-99	Providence Bruins	AHL	75	10	12	22	*401										19	1	1	2	46				
99-2000	**Boston**	**NHL**	**1**	**0**	**0**	**0**	**0**	**0**	**0**	**0**	**0**	**0.0**	**0**	**0**	**0.0**	**8:31**									
	Providence Bruins	AHL	47	6	4	10	221										14	1	0	1	24				
2000-01	**Chicago**	**NHL**	**3**	**0**	**0**	**0**	**6**	**0**	**0**	**0**	**2**	**0.0**	**–1**	**0**	**0.0**	**5:30**									
	Norfolk Admirals	AHL	67	6	15	21	234										9	0	0	0	4				
2001-02	**Chicago**	**NHL**	**36**	**1**	**0**	**1**	**76**	**0**	**0**	**1**	**10**	**10.0**	**–2**	**0**	**0.0**	**5:06**	**4**	**0**	**0**	**0**	**8**	**0**	**0**	**0**	**6:29**
	Norfolk Admirals	AHL	12	0	2	2	21																		
2002-03	**Dallas**	**NHL**	**43**	**1**	**1**	**2**	**69**	**0**	**0**	**0**	**14**	**7.1**	**1**	**0**	**0.0**	**4:47**									
	NHL Totals		**83**	**2**	**1**	**3**	**151**	**0**	**0**	**1**	**26**	**7.7**		**0**	**0.0**	**4:59**	**4**	**0**	**0**	**0**	**8**	**0**	**0**	**0**	**6:29**

Signed as a free agent by **Boston**, January 20, 1998. Signed as a free agent by **Chicago**, August 13, 2000. Signed as a free agent by **Dallas**, July 3, 2002.

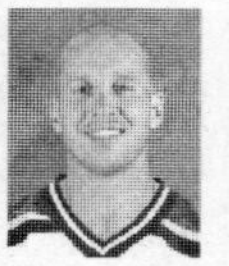

DRAKE, Dallas

(DRAYK, DAL-uhs) **ST.L.**

Right wing. Shoots left. 6'1", 190 lbs. Born, Trail, B.C., February 4, 1969. Detroit's 6th choice, 116th overall, in 1989 Entry Draft.

Season	Club	League	GP	G	A	Pts	PIM	PP	SH	GW	S	%	+/-	TF	F%	Min	GP	G	A	Pts	PIM	PP	SH	GW	Min
1984-85	Rossland	KIJHL	30	13	37	50																			
1985-86	Rossland	KIJHL	41	53	73	126																			
1986-87	Rossland	KIJHL	40	55	80	135																			
1987-88	Vernon Lakers	BCJHL	47	39	85	124	50										11	9	17	26	30				
1988-89	North-Michigan	WCHA	38	17	22	39	22										7	1	2	3	4				
1989-90	North-Michigan	WCHA	36	13	24	37	42																		
1990-91	North-Michigan	WCHA	44	22	36	58	89																		
1991-92	North-Michigan	WCHA	38	*39	41	*80	46																		
1992-93	**Detroit**	**NHL**	**72**	**18**	**26**	**44**	**93**	**3**	**2**	**5**	**89**	**20.2**	**15**				**7**	**3**	**3**	**6**	**6**	**1**	**0**	**0**	
1993-94	**Detroit**	**NHL**	**47**	**10**	**22**	**32**	**37**	**0**	**1**	**2**	**78**	**12.8**	**5**												
	Adirondack	AHL	1	2	0	2	0																		
	Winnipeg	**NHL**	**15**	**3**	**5**	**8**	**12**	**1**	**1**	**1**	**34**	**8.8**	**–6**												
1994-95	**Winnipeg**	**NHL**	**43**	**8**	**18**	**26**	**30**	**0**	**0**	**1**	**66**	**12.1**	**–6**												
1995-96	**Winnipeg**	**NHL**	**69**	**19**	**20**	**39**	**36**	**4**	**4**	**2**	**121**	**15.7**	**–7**				**3**	**0**	**0**	**0**	**0**	**0**	**0**	**0**	
1996-97	**Phoenix**	**NHL**	**63**	**17**	**19**	**36**	**52**	**5**	**1**	**1**	**113**	**15.0**	**–11**				**7**	**0**	**1**	**1**	**2**	**0**	**0**	**0**	
1997-98	**Phoenix**	**NHL**	**60**	**11**	**29**	**40**	**71**	**3**	**0**	**2**	**112**	**9.8**	**17**				**4**	**0**	**1**	**1**	**2**	**0**	**0**	**0**	
1998-99	**Phoenix**	**NHL**	**53**	**9**	**22**	**31**	**65**	**0**	**0**	**3**	**105**	**8.6**	**17**	**5**	**60.0**	**15:38**	**7**	**4**	**3**	**7**	**4**	**2**	**0**	**1**	**19:51**
99-2000	**Phoenix**	**NHL**	**79**	**15**	**30**	**45**	**62**	**0**	**2**	**5**	**127**	**11.8**	**11**	**4**	**25.0**	**15:48**	**5**	**0**	**1**	**1**	**4**	**0**	**0**	**0**	**15:30**
2000-01	**St. Louis**	**NHL**	**82**	**12**	**29**	**41**	**71**	**2**	**0**	**3**	**142**	**8.5**	**18**	**11**	**45.5**	**14:44**	**15**	**4**	**2**	**6**	**16**	**0**	**1**	**1**	**14:08**
2001-02	**St. Louis**	**NHL**	**80**	**11**	**15**	**26**	**87**	**1**	**3**	**2**	**116**	**9.5**	**8**	**92**	**32.6**	**13:26**	**8**	**0**	**0**	**0**	**8**	**0**	**0**	**0**	**11:59**
2002-03	**St. Louis**	**NHL**	**80**	**20**	**10**	**30**	**66**	**4**	**1**	**2**	**113**	**17.7**	**–7**	**56**	**39.3**	**14:48**	**7**	**1**	**4**	**5**	**23**	**0**	**0**	**1**	**13:04**
	NHL Totals		**743**	**153**	**245**	**398**	**682**	**23**	**15**	**29**	**1216**	**12.6**		**168**	**36.3**	**14:49**	**63**	**12**	**15**	**27**	**65**	**3**	**1**	**3**	**14:40**

WCHA First All-Star Team (1992) • NCAA West First All-American Team (1992)

Traded to **Winnipeg** by **Detroit** with Tim Cheveldae for Bob Essensa and Sergei Bautin, March 8, 1994. Transferred to **Phoenix** after **Winnipeg** franchise relocated, July 1, 1996. Selected by **Minnesota** from **Phoenix** in Expansion Draft, June 23, 2000. Signed as a free agent by **St. Louis**, July 1, 2000.

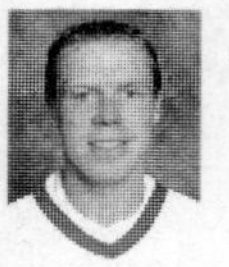

DRAPER, Kris

(DRAY-puhr, KRIHS) **DET.**

Center. Shoots left. 5'11", 190 lbs. Born, Toronto, Ont., May 24, 1971. Winnipeg's 4th choice, 62nd overall, in 1989 Entry Draft.

Season	Club	League	GP	G	A	Pts	PIM	PP	SH	GW	S	%	+/-	TF	F%	Min	GP	G	A	Pts	PIM	PP	SH	GW	Min
1987-88	Don Mills	MTHL	40	35	32	67	46																		
1988-89	Team Canada	Nat-Tm	60	11	15	26	16																		
1989-90	Team Canada	Nat-Tm	61	12	22	34	44																		
1990-91	Ottawa 67's	OHL	39	19	42	61	35										17	8	11	19	20				
	Winnipeg	**NHL**	**3**	**1**	**0**	**1**	**5**	**0**	**0**	**0**	**1**	**100.0**	**0**												
	Moncton Hawks	AHL	7	2	1	3	2																		
1991-92	**Winnipeg**	**NHL**	**10**	**2**	**0**	**2**	**2**	**0**	**0**	**0**	**19**	**10.5**	**0**				**2**	**0**	**0**	**0**	**0**	**0**	**0**	**0**	
	Moncton Hawks	AHL	61	11	18	29	113										4	0	1	1	6				
1992-93	**Winnipeg**	**NHL**	**7**	**0**	**0**	**0**	**2**	**0**	**0**	**0**	**5**	**0.0**	**–6**												
	Moncton Hawks	AHL	67	12	23	35	40										5	2	2	4	18				
1993-94	**Detroit**	**NHL**	**39**	**5**	**8**	**13**	**31**	**0**	**1**	**0**	**55**	**9.1**	**11**				**7**	**2**	**2**	**4**	**4**	**0**	**1**	**0**	
	Adirondack	AHL	46	20	23	43	49																		
1994-95	**Detroit**	**NHL**	**36**	**2**	**6**	**8**	**22**	**0**	**0**	**0**	**44**	**4.5**	**1**				**18**	**4**	**1**	**5**	**12**	**0**	**1**	**1**	
1995-96	**Detroit**	**NHL**	**52**	**7**	**9**	**16**	**32**	**0**	**1**	**0**	**51**	**13.7**	**2**				**18**	**4**	**2**	**6**	**18**	**0**	**1**	**0**	
1996-97♦	**Detroit**	**NHL**	**76**	**8**	**5**	**13**	**73**	**1**	**0**	**1**	**85**	**9.4**	**–11**				**20**	**2**	**4**	**6**	**12**	**0**	**1**	**0**	
1997-98♦	**Detroit**	**NHL**	**64**	**13**	**10**	**23**	**45**	**1**	**0**	**4**	**96**	**13.5**	**5**				**19**	**1**	**3**	**4**	**12**	**0**	**0**	**1**	
1998-99	**Detroit**	**NHL**	**80**	**4**	**14**	**18**	**79**	**0**	**1**	**1**	**78**	**5.1**	**2**	**887**	**54.6**	**12:43**	**10**	**0**	**1**	**1**	**6**	**0**	**0**	**0**	**11:35**
99-2000	**Detroit**	**NHL**	**51**	**5**	**7**	**12**	**28**	**0**	**0**	**3**	**76**	**6.6**	**3**	**380**	**57.6**	**13:33**	**9**	**2**	**0**	**2**	**6**	**0**	**0**	**0**	**12:26**
2000-01	**Detroit**	**NHL**	**75**	**8**	**17**	**25**	**38**	**0**	**1**	**1**	**123**	**6.5**	**17**	**997**	**56.5**	**13:26**	**6**	**0**	**1**	**1**	**2**	**0**	**0**	**0**	**16:08**
2001-02♦	**Detroit**	**NHL**	**82**	**15**	**15**	**30**	**56**	**0**	**2**	**3**	**137**	**10.9**	**26**	**756**	**53.2**	**15:35**	**23**	**2**	**3**	**5**	**20**	**0**	**0**	**0**	**17:00**
2002-03	**Detroit**	**NHL**	**82**	**14**	**21**	**35**	**82**	**0**	**1**	**2**	**142**	**9.9**	**6**	**1059**	**56.9**	**16:12**	**4**	**0**	**0**	**0**	**4**	**0**	**0**	**0**	**17:29**
	NHL Totals		**657**	**84**	**112**	**196**	**495**	**2**	**7**	**15**	**912**	**9.2**		**4079**	**55.7**	**14:23**	**136**	**17**	**17**	**34**	**96**	**0**	**4**	**2**	**15:06**

Traded to **Detroit** by **Winnipeg** for future considerations, June 30, 1993.

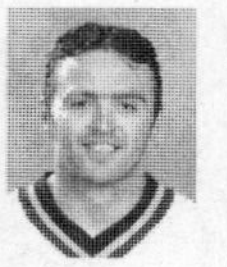

DRUKEN, Harold

(DROO-kehn, HAIR-ohld) **TOR.**

Center. Shoots left. 6', 200 lbs. Born, St. John's, Nfld., January 26, 1979. Vancouver's 3rd choice, 36th overall, in 1997 Entry Draft.

Season	Club	League	GP	G	A	Pts	PIM	PP	SH	GW	S	%	+/-	TF	F%	Min	GP	G	A	Pts	PIM	PP	SH	GW	Min
1995-96	Noble-Greenough	Hi-School	30	37	28	65	28																		
1996-97	Detroit	OHL	63	27	31	58	14										5	3	2	5	0				
1997-98	Plymouth Whalers	OHL	64	38	44	82	12										15	9	11	20	4				
1998-99	Plymouth Whalers	OHL	60	*58	45	103	34										11	9	12	21	14				
99-2000	**Vancouver**	**NHL**	**33**	**7**	**9**	**16**	**10**	**2**	**0**	**0**	**69**	**10.1**	**14**	**307**	**47.9**	**13:01**									
	Syracuse Crunch	AHL	47	20	25	45	32										4	1	2	3	6				
2000-01	**Vancouver**	**NHL**	**55**	**15**	**15**	**30**	**14**	**6**	**0**	**3**	**82**	**18.3**	**2**	**598**	**43.8**	**11:59**	**4**	**0**	**1**	**1**	**0**	**0**	**0**	**0**	**13:43**
	Kansas City	IHL	15	5	9	14	20																		
2001-02	**Vancouver**	**NHL**	**27**	**4**	**4**	**8**	**6**	**1**	**0**	**2**	**33**	**12.1**	**–1**	**269**	**54.7**	**11:09**									
	Manitoba Moose	AHL	11	2	9	11	4																		

			Regular Season														Playoffs								
Season	Club	League	GP	G	A	Pts	PIM	PP	SH	GW	S	%	+/-	TF	F%	Min	GP	G	A	Pts	PIM	PP	SH	GW	Min
2002-03	**Vancouver**	**NHL**	**3**	**1**	**1**	**2**	**0**	**0**	**0**	**0**	**3**	**33.3**	**−1**	**21**	**47.6**	**8:48**	....	....	....	....	....	....	....	....	....
	Carolina	**NHL**	**10**	**0**	**1**	**1**	**2**	**0**	**0**	**0**	**3**	**0.0**	**−1**	**31**	**41.9**	**4:03**	....	....	....	....	....	....	....	....	....
	Toronto	**NHL**	**5**	**0**	**2**	**2**	**2**	**0**	**0**	**0**	**8**	**0.0**	**1**	**25**	**44.0**	**12:50**	....	....	....	....	....	....	....	....	....
	St. John's	AHL	6	0	3	3	2	....	....	....	....	....	....	....	....	....	....	....	....	....	....	....	....	....	....
	Carolina	**NHL**	**4**	**0**	**0**	**0**	**0**	**0**	**0**	**0**	**2**	**0.0**	**0**	**8**	**75.0**	**3:52**	....	....	....	....	....	....	....	....	....
	Lowell	AHL	24	8	10	18	8	....	....	....	....	....	....	....	....	....	....	....	....	....	....	....	....	....	....
	NHL Totals		**137**	**27**	**32**	**59**	**34**	**9**	**0**	**5**	**200**	**13.5**		**1259**	**47.3**	**11:13**	**4**	**0**	**1**	**1**	**0**	**0**	**0**	**0**	**13:43**

OHL All-Rookie Team (1997) • OHL Second All-Star Team (1999)

Missed majority of 2001-02 season recovering from ankle injury suffered in game vs. Dallas, December 2, 2001. Traded to **Carolina** by **Vancouver** with Jan Hlavac for Darren Langdon and Marek Malik, November 1, 2002. Claimed on waivers by **Toronto** from **Carolina**, December 11, 2002. Claimed on waivers by **Carolina** from **Toronto**, January 17, 2003. Traded to **Toronto** by **Carolina** for Allan Rourke, May 29, 2003.

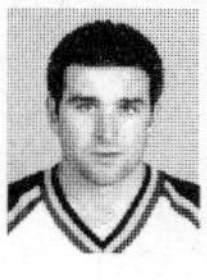

DRURY, Chris

(DROO-ree, KRIHS) **BUF.**

Center. Shoots right. 5'10", 180 lbs. Born, Trumbull, CT, August 20, 1976. Quebec's 5th choice, 72nd overall, in 1994 Entry Draft.

Season	Club	League	GP	G	A	Pts	PIM	PP	SH	GW	S	%	+/-	TF	F%	Min	GP	G	A	Pts	PIM	PP	SH	GW	Min
1991-92	Fairfield Prep	Hi-School	25	22	27	49	....	....	....	....	....	....	....	....	....	....	....	....	....	....	....	....	....	....	....
1992-93	Fairfield Prep	Hi-School	24	25	32	57	15	....	....	....	....	....	....	....	....	....	....	....	....	....	....	....	....	....	....
1993-94	Fairfield Prep	Hi-School	24	37	18	55	....	....	....	....	....	....	....	....	....	....	....	....	....	....	....	....	....	....	....
1994-95	Boston University	H-East	39	12	15	27	38	....	....	....	....	....	....	....	....	....	....	....	....	....	....	....	....	....	....
1995-96	Boston University	H-East	37	35	33	*68	46	....	....	....	....	....	....	....	....	....	....	....	....	....	....	....	....	....	....
1996-97	Boston University	H-East	41	*38	24	62	64	....	....	....	....	....	....	....	....	....	....	....	....	....	....	....	....	....	....
1997-98	Boston University	H-East	38	28	29	57	88	....	....	....	....	....	....	....	....	....	....	....	....	....	....	....	....	....	....
1998-99	**Colorado**	**NHL**	**79**	**20**	**24**	**44**	**62**	**6**	**0**	**3**	**138**	**14.5**	**9**	**418**	**46.9**	**13:15**	**19**	**6**	**2**	**8**	**4**	**0**	**0**	**4**	**11:28**
99-2000	**Colorado**	**NHL**	**82**	**20**	**47**	**67**	**42**	**7**	**0**	**2**	**213**	**9.4**	**8**	**1321**	**53.1**	**18:33**	**17**	**4**	**10**	**14**	**4**	**1**	**0**	**2**	**18:30**
2000-01♦	**Colorado**	**NHL**	**71**	**24**	**41**	**65**	**47**	**11**	**0**	**5**	**204**	**11.8**	**6**	**552**	**55.1**	**18:03**	**23**	**11**	**5**	**16**	**4**	**2**	**0**	**2**	**19:06**
2001-02	**Colorado**	**NHL**	**82**	**21**	**25**	**46**	**38**	**5**	**0**	**6**	**236**	**8.9**	**1**	**1139**	**53.2**	**17:57**	**21**	**5**	**7**	**12**	**10**	**1**	**0**	**3**	**17:01**
	United States	Olympics	6	0	0	0	0	....	....	....	....	....	....	....	....	....	....	....	....	....	....	....	....	....	....
2002-03	**Calgary**	**NHL**	**80**	**23**	**30**	**53**	**33**	**5**	**1**	**5**	**224**	**10.3**	**−9**	**942**	**53.8**	**18:33**	....	....	....	....	....	....	....	....	....
	NHL Totals		**394**	**108**	**167**	**275**	**222**	**34**	**1**	**21**	**1015**	**10.6**		**4372**	**52.9**	**17:16**	**80**	**26**	**24**	**50**	**22**	**4**	**0**	**11**	**16:37**

Hockey East Second All-Star Team (1996, 1997) • NCAA East Second All-American Team (1996) • Hockey East Player of the Year (1997, 1998) • NCAA East First All-American Team (1997, 1998) • NCAA Championship All-Tournament Team (1997) • Hockey East First All-Star Team (1998) • Hobey Baker Memorial Award (Top U.S. Collegiate Player) (1998) • NHL All-Rookie Team (1999) • Calder Memorial Trophy (1999)

Rights transferred to **Colorado** after **Quebec** franchise relocated, June 21, 1995. Traded to **Calgary** by **Colorado** with Stephane Yelle for Derek Morris, Jeff Shantz and Dean McAmmond, October 1, 2002. Traded to **Buffalo** by **Calgary** with Steve Begin for Steve Reinprecht and Rhett Warrener, July 3, 2003.

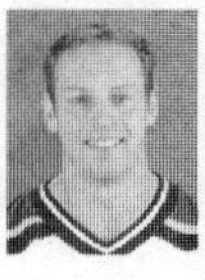

DUBINSKY, Steve

(doo-BIHN-skee, STEEV)

Center. Shoots left. 6', 190 lbs. Born, Montreal, Que., July 9, 1970. Chicago's 9th choice, 226th overall, in 1990 Entry Draft.

Season	Club	League	GP	G	A	Pts	PIM	PP	SH	GW	S	%	+/-	TF	F%	Min	GP	G	A	Pts	PIM	PP	SH	GW	Min
1989-90	Clarkson Knights	ECAC	35	7	10	17	24	....	....	....	....	....	....	....	....	....	....	....	....	....	....	....	....	....	....
1990-91	Clarkson Knights	ECAC	39	13	23	36	26	....	....	....	....	....	....	....	....	....	....	....	....	....	....	....	....	....	....
1991-92	Clarkson Knights	ECAC	32	20	31	51	40	....	....	....	....	....	....	....	....	....	....	....	....	....	....	....	....	....	....
1992-93	Clarkson Knights	ECAC	35	18	26	44	58	....	....	....	....	....	....	....	....	....	....	....	....	....	....	....	....	....	....
1993-94	**Chicago**	**NHL**	**27**	**2**	**6**	**8**	**16**	**0**	**0**	**0**	**20**	**10.0**	**1**	....	....	....	**6**	**0**	**0**	**0**	**10**	**0**	**0**	**0**	....
	Indianapolis Ice	IHL	54	15	25	40	63	....	....	....	....	....	....	....	....	....	....	....	....	....	....	....	....	....	....
1994-95	**Chicago**	**NHL**	**16**	**0**	**0**	**0**	**8**	**0**	**0**	**0**	**16**	**0.0**	**−5**	....	....	....	....	....	....	....	....	....	....	....	....
	Indianapolis Ice	IHL	62	16	11	27	29	....	....	....	....	....	....	....	....	....	....	....	....	....	....	....	....	....	....
1995-96	**Chicago**	**NHL**	**43**	**2**	**3**	**5**	**14**	**0**	**0**	**0**	**33**	**6.1**	**3**	....	....	....	....	....	....	....	....	....	....	....	....
	Indianapolis Ice	IHL	16	8	8	16	10	....	....	....	....	....	....	....	....	....	....	....	....	....	....	....	....	....	....
1996-97	**Chicago**	**NHL**	**5**	**0**	**0**	**0**	**0**	**0**	**0**	**0**	**4**	**0.0**	**2**	....	....	....	**4**	**1**	**0**	**1**	**4**	**0**	**0**	**0**	....
	Indianapolis Ice	IHL	77	32	40	72	53	....	....	....	....	....	....	....	....	....	1	3	1	4	0	....	....	....	....
1997-98	**Chicago**	**NHL**	**82**	**5**	**13**	**18**	**57**	**0**	**1**	**0**	**112**	**4.5**	**−6**	....	....	....	....	....	....	....	....	....	....	....	....
1998-99	**Chicago**	**NHL**	**1**	**0**	**0**	**0**	**0**	**0**	**0**	**0**	**1**	**0.0**	**0**	**5**	**60.0**	**5:11**	....	....	....	....	....	....	....	....	....
	Calgary	**NHL**	**61**	**4**	**10**	**14**	**14**	**0**	**2**	**0**	**69**	**5.8**	**−7**	**223**	**46.6**	**14:38**	....	....	....	....	....	....	....	....	....
99-2000	**Calgary**	**NHL**	**23**	**0**	**1**	**1**	**4**	**0**	**0**	**0**	**29**	**0.0**	**−12**	**207**	**49.3**	**12:05**	....	....	....	....	....	....	....	....	....
2000-01	**Chicago**	**NHL**	**60**	**6**	**4**	**10**	**33**	**0**	**1**	**0**	**70**	**8.6**	**−4**	**714**	**56.7**	**10:60**	....	....	....	....	....	....	....	....	....
	Norfolk Admirals	AHL	14	6	5	11	4	....	....	....	....	....	....	....	....	....	....	....	....	....	....	....	....	....	....
2001-02	**Chicago**	**NHL**	**3**	**1**	**0**	**1**	**4**	**0**	**0**	**1**	**6**	**16.7**	**1**	**1**	**100.0**	**11:50**	....	....	....	....	....	....	....	....	....
	Norfolk Admirals	AHL	16	7	3	10	6	....	....	....	....	....	....	....	....	....	....	....	....	....	....	....	....	....	....
	Nashville	**NHL**	**26**	**5**	**2**	**7**	**10**	**0**	**0**	**0**	**42**	**11.9**	**−2**	**270**	**56.3**	**15:54**	....	....	....	....	....	....	....	....	....
	Milwaukee	AHL	36	13	13	26	16	....	....	....	....	....	....	....	....	....	....	....	....	....	....	....	....	....	....
2002-03	**St. Louis**	**NHL**	**28**	**0**	**6**	**6**	**4**	**0**	**0**	**0**	**23**	**0.0**	**3**	**268**	**56.7**	**10:45**	....	....	....	....	....	....	....	....	....
	Worcester IceCats	AHL	6	1	5	6	4	....	....	....	....	....	....	....	....	....	....	....	....	....	....	....	....	....	....
	NHL Totals		**375**	**25**	**45**	**70**	**164**	**0**	**4**	**1**	**425**	**5.9**		**1688**	**54.4**	**12:48**	**10**	**1**	**0**	**1**	**14**	**0**	**0**	**0**	....

Traded to **Calgary** by **Chicago** with Jeff Shantz for Marty McInnis, Jamie Allison and Eric Andersson, October 27, 1998. • Missed remainder of 1999-2000 season recovering from knee injury suffered in game vs. Chicago, December 12, 1999. Signed as a free agent by **Chicago**, August 25, 2000. Traded to **Nashville** by **Chicago** for future considerations, February 6, 2002. Signed as a free agent by **St. Louis**, July 16, 2002. • Missed majority of 2002-03 season recovering from illness and head injury suffered in game vs. Pittsburgh, February 22, 2003.

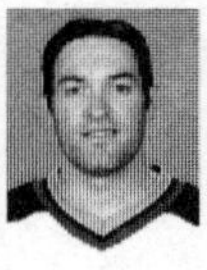

DUMONT, J.P.

(DOO-mawnt, JAY-pee) **BUF.**

Right wing. Shoots left. 6'1", 205 lbs. Born, Montreal, Que., April 1, 1978. NY Islanders' 1st choice, 3rd overall, in 1996 Entry Draft.

Season	Club	League	GP	G	A	Pts	PIM	PP	SH	GW	S	%	+/-	TF	F%	Min	GP	G	A	Pts	PIM	PP	SH	GW	Min
1993-94	Mtl-Bourassa	QAAA	44	27	20	47	44	....	....	....	....	....	....	....	....	....	4	2	3	5	4	....	....	....	....
1994-95	Val-d'Or Foreurs	QMJHL	48	5	14	19	24	....	....	....	....	....	....	....	....	....	....	....	....	....	....	....	....	....	....
1995-96	Val-d'Or Foreurs	QMJHL	66	48	57	105	109	....	....	....	....	....	....	....	....	....	13	12	8	20	22	....	....	....	....
1996-97	Val-d'Or Foreurs	QMJHL	62	44	64	108	86	....	....	....	....	....	....	....	....	....	13	9	7	16	12	....	....	....	....
1997-98	Val-d'Or Foreurs	QMJHL	55	57	42	99	63	....	....	....	....	....	....	....	....	....	19	31	15	46	18	....	....	....	....
1998-99	**Chicago**	**NHL**	**25**	**9**	**6**	**15**	**10**	**0**	**0**	**2**	**42**	**21.4**	**7**	**10**	**50.0**	**14:14**	....	....	....	....	....	....	....	....	....
	Portland Pirates	AHL	50	32	14	46	39	....	....	....	....	....	....	....	....	....	....	....	....	....	....	....	....	....	....
	Chicago Wolves	IHL	....	....	....	....	....	....	....	....	....	....	....	....	....	....	10	4	1	5	6	....	....	....	....
99-2000	**Chicago**	**NHL**	**47**	**10**	**8**	**18**	**18**	**0**	**0**	**1**	**86**	**11.6**	**−6**	**12**	**33.3**	**12:54**	....	....	....	....	....	....	....	....	....
	Cleveland	IHL	7	5	2	7	8	....	....	....	....	....	....	....	....	....	....	....	....	....	....	....	....	....	....
	Rochester	AHL	13	7	10	17	18	....	....	....	....	....	....	....	....	....	21	14	7	21	32	....	....	....	....
2000-01	**Buffalo**	**NHL**	**79**	**23**	**28**	**51**	**54**	**9**	**0**	**5**	**156**	**14.7**	**1**	**3**	**33.3**	**15:01**	**13**	**4**	**3**	**7**	**8**	**0**	**0**	**0**	**14:32**
2001-02	**Buffalo**	**NHL**	**76**	**23**	**21**	**44**	**42**	**7**	**0**	**3**	**154**	**14.9**	**−10**	**4**	**50.0**	**15:14**	....	....	....	....	....	....	....	....	....
2002-03	**Buffalo**	**NHL**	**76**	**14**	**21**	**35**	**44**	**2**	**0**	**2**	**135**	**10.4**	**−14**	**15**	**20.0**	**15:04**	....	....	....	....	....	....	....	....	....
	NHL Totals		**303**	**79**	**84**	**163**	**168**	**18**	**0**	**13**	**573**	**13.8**		**44**	**34.1**	**14:41**	**13**	**4**	**3**	**7**	**8**	**0**	**0**	**0**	**14:32**

QMJHL Second All-Star Team (1997)

Rights traded to **Chicago** by **NY Islanders** with Chicago's 5th round choice (later traded to Philadelphia – Philadelphia selected Francis Belanger) in 1998 Entry Draft for Dmitri Nabokov, May 30, 1998. Traded to **Buffalo** by **Chicago** with Doug Gilmour for Michal Grosek, March 10, 2000.

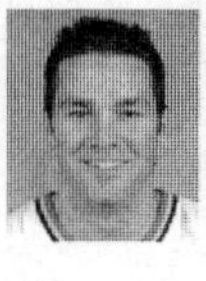

DuPONT, Micki

(DOO-pawnt, MIH-kee)

Defense. Shoots right. 5'9", 186 lbs. Born, Calgary, Alta., April 15, 1980. Calgary's 9th choice, 270th overall, in 2000 Entry Draft.

Season	Club	League	GP	G	A	Pts	PIM	PP	SH	GW	S	%	+/-	TF	F%	Min	GP	G	A	Pts	PIM	PP	SH	GW	Min
1995-96	Calgary Blazers	AMHL	35	10	35	45	68	....	....	....	....	....	....	....	....	....	....	....	....	....	....	....	....	....	....
1996-97	Kamloops Blazers	WHL	59	8	27	35	39	....	....	....	....	....	....	....	....	....	5	0	4	4	8	....	....	....	....
1997-98	Kamloops Blazers	WHL	71	13	41	54	91	....	....	....	....	....	....	....	....	....	7	0	1	1	10	....	....	....	....
1998-99	Kamloops Blazers	WHL	59	8	27	35	110	....	....	....	....	....	....	....	....	....	15	2	8	10	22	....	....	....	....
99-2000	Kamloops Blazers	WHL	70	26	62	88	156	....	....	....	....	....	....	....	....	....	4	0	2	2	17	....	....	....	....
	Long Beach	IHL	1	0	0	0	0	....	....	....	....	....	....	....	....	....	....	....	....	....	....	....	....	....	....
	San Diego Gulls	WCHL	....	....	....	....	....	....	....	....	....	....	....	....	....	....	7	2	2	4	0	....	....	....	....
2000-01	Saint John Flames	AHL	67	8	21	29	28	....	....	....	....	....	....	....	....	....	19	1	9	10	14	....	....	....	....
2001-02	**Calgary**	**NHL**	**2**	**0**	**0**	**0**	**2**	**0**	**0**	**0**	**2**	**0.0**	**0**	**0**	**0.0**	**14:44**	....	....	....	....	....	....	....	....	....
	Saint John Flames	AHL	77	7	33	40	77	....	....	....	....	....	....	....	....	....	....	....	....	....	....	....	....	....	....
2002-03	**Calgary**	**NHL**	**16**	**1**	**2**	**3**	**4**	**0**	**0**	**0**	**27**	**3.7**	**−5**	**0**	**0.0**	**16:45**	....	....	....	....	....	....	....	....	....
	Saint John Flames	AHL	44	12	21	33	73	....	....	....	....	....	....	....	....	....	....	....	....	....	....	....	....	....	....
	Wilkes-Barre	AHL	14	1	4	5	16	....	....	....	....	....	....	....	....	....	6	3	0	3	21	....	....	....	....
	NHL Totals		**18**	**1**	**2**	**3**	**6**	**0**	**0**	**0**	**29**	**3.4**		**0**	**0.0**	**16:31**	....	....	....	....	....	....	....	....	....

Traded to **Pittsburgh** by **Calgary** with Mathias Johansson for Shean Donovan, March 11, 2003.

			Regular Season														Playoffs							
Season	Club	League	GP	G	A	Pts	PIM	PP	SH	GW	S	%	+/-	TF	F%	Min	GP	G	A	Pts	PIM	PP	SH	GW	Min

DUPUIS, Pascal
(doo-PWEE, pas-KAL)   **MIN.**

Left wing. Shoots left. 6', 196 lbs.   Born, Laval, Que., April 7, 1979.

Season	Club	League	GP	G	A	Pts	PIM	PP	SH	GW	S	%	+/-	TF	F%	Min	GP	G	A	Pts	PIM	PP	SH	GW	Min
1995-96	Laval Laurentide	QAAA	41	10	15	25	....	....	....	....	....	....	....	....	....	....	14	11	11	22	....				
1996-97	Rouyn-Noranda	QMJHL	44	9	15	24	20	....	....	....	....	....	....	....	....	....	....								
1997-98	Rouyn-Noranda	QMJHL	39	9	17	26	36	....	....	....	....	....	....	....	....	....	....								
	Shawinigan	QMJHL	28	7	13	20	10	....	....	....	....	....	....	....	....	....	6	2	0	2	4				
1998-99	Shawinigan	QMJHL	57	30	42	72	118	....	....	....	....	....	....	....	....	....	6	1	8	9	18				
99-2000	Shawinigan	QMJHL	61	50	55	105	99	....	....	....	....	....	....	....	....	....	13	*15	7	22	4				
2000-01	**Minnesota**	**NHL**	4	1	0	1	4	1	0	0	8	12.5	0	0	0.0	15:36	....							
	Cleveland	IHL	70	19	24	43	37	....	....	....	....	....	....	....	....	....	4	0	0	0	0				
2001-02	**Minnesota**	**NHL**	76	15	12	27	16	3	2	0	154	9.7	–10	40	32.5	15:08	....							
2002-03	**Minnesota**	**NHL**	80	20	28	48	44	6	0	4	183	10.9	17	186	40.9	17:30	16	4	4	8	8	2	0	1	16:58
	NHL Totals		160	36	40	76	64	10	2	4	345	10.4		226	39.4	16:20	16	4	4	8	8	2	0	1	16:58

Signed as a free agent by **Minnesota**, August 18, 2000.

DVORAK, Radek
(duh-VOHR-ak, RA-dehk)   **EDM.**

Right wing. Shoots right. 6'2", 200 lbs.   Born, Tabor, Czech., March 9, 1977. Florida's 1st choice, 10th overall, in 1995 Entry Draft.

Season	Club	League	GP	G	A	Pts	PIM	PP	SH	GW	S	%	+/-	TF	F%	Min	GP	G	A	Pts	PIM	PP	SH	GW	Min
1992-93	C. Budejovice Jr.	Czech-Jr.	35	44	46	90	....	....	....	....	....	....	....	....	....	....	....								
1993-94	C. Budejovice Jr.	Czech-Jr.	20	17	18	35	....	....	....	....	....	....	....	....	....	....	....								
	Ceske Budejovice	Czech	8	0	0	0	0	....	....	....	....	....	....	....	....	....	9	5	1	6	....				
1994-95	Ceske Budejovice	Czech	10	3	5	8	2	....	....	....	....	....	....	....	....	....	....								
1995-96	**Florida**	**NHL**	77	13	14	27	20	0	0	4	126	10.3	5	....	....	....	16	1	3	4	0	0	0	0	
1996-97	**Florida**	**NHL**	78	18	21	39	30	2	0	1	139	12.9	–2	....	....	....	3	0	0	0	0	0	0	0	
1997-98	**Florida**	**NHL**	64	12	24	36	33	2	3	0	112	10.7	–1	....	....	....	....								
1998-99	**Florida**	**NHL**	82	19	24	43	29	0	4	0	182	10.4	7	98	46.9	16:13	....								
99-2000	**Florida**	**NHL**	35	7	10	17	6	0	0	1	67	10.4	5	16	37.5	15:25	....								
	NY Rangers	**NHL**	46	11	22	33	10	2	1	0	90	12.2	0	34	35.3	18:24	....								
2000-01	**NY Rangers**	**NHL**	82	31	36	67	20	5	2	3	230	13.5	9	20	30.0	19:04	....								
2001-02	**NY Rangers**	**NHL**	65	17	20	37	14	3	3	1	210	8.1	–20	5	0.0	19:44	....								
	Czech Republic	Olympics	4	0	0	0	0	....	....	....	....	....	....	....	....	....	....								
2002-03	**NY Rangers**	**NHL**	63	6	21	27	16	2	0	0	134	4.5	–3	9	44.4	15:42	....								
	Edmonton	**NHL**	12	4	4	8	14	1	0	0	32	12.5	–3	1	0.0	16:07	4	1	0	1	0	0	0	1	15:05
	NHL Totals		604	138	196	334	192	17	13	10	1322	10.4		183	40.4	17:31	23	2	3	5	0	0	0	1	15:05

Traded to **San Jose** by **Florida** for Mike Vernon and San Jose's 3rd round choice (Sean O'Connor) in 2000 Entry Draft, December 30, 1999. Traded to **NY Rangers** by **San Jose** for Todd Harvey and NY Rangers' 4th round choice (Dimitri Patzold) in 2001 Entry Draft, December 30, 1999. Traded to **Edmonton** by **NY Rangers** with Cory Cross for Anson Carter and Ales Pisa, March 11, 2003.

DWYER, Gordie
(DWIGH-uhr, GOHR-dee)   **MTL.**

Left wing. Shoots left. 6'3", 215 lbs.   Born, Dalhousie, N.B., January 25, 1978. Montreal's 5th choice, 152nd overall, in 1998 Entry Draft.

Season	Club	League	GP	G	A	Pts	PIM	PP	SH	GW	S	%	+/-	TF	F%	Min	GP	G	A	Pts	PIM	PP	SH	GW	Min
1993-94	Magog	QAAA	42	7	15	22	62	....	....	....	....	....	....	....	....	....	4	2	1	3	0				
1994-95	Hull Olympiques	QMJHL	57	3	7	10	204	....	....	....	....	....	....	....	....	....	17	1	3	4	54				
1995-96	Hull Olympiques	QMJHL	25	5	9	14	199	....	....	....	....	....	....	....	....	....	....								
	Laval Titan	QMJHL	22	5	17	22	72	....	....	....	....	....	....	....	....	....	....								
	Beauport	QMJHL	22	4	9	13	87	....	....	....	....	....	....	....	....	....	20	3	5	8	104				
1996-97	Drummondville	QMJHL	66	21	48	69	393	....	....	....	....	....	....	....	....	....	8	6	1	7	39				
1997-98	Quebec Remparts	QMJHL	59	18	27	45	365	....	....	....	....	....	....	....	....	....	14	4	9	13	67				
1998-99	Fredericton	AHL	14	0	0	0	46	....	....	....	....	....	....	....	....	....	....								
	New Orleans	ECHL	36	1	3	4	163	....	....	....	....	....	....	....	....	....	11	0	0	0	27				
99-2000	Quebec Citadelles	AHL	7	0	0	0	37	....	....	....	....	....	....	....	....	....	....								
	Tampa Bay	**NHL**	24	0	1	1	135	0	0	0	7	0.0	–6	0	0.0	4:57	....								
	Detroit Vipers	IHL	27	0	2	2	147	....	....	....	....	....	....	....	....	....	....								
2000-01	**Tampa Bay**	**NHL**	28	0	1	1	96	0	0	0	12	0.0	–7	2	50.0	5:47	....								
	Detroit Vipers	IHL	24	2	3	5	169	....	....	....	....	....	....	....	....	....	....								
2001-02	**Tampa Bay**	**NHL**	26	0	2	2	60	0	0	0	6	0.0	–4	0	0.0	5:05	....								
	Springfield	AHL	17	1	3	4	80	....	....	....	....	....	....	....	....	....	....								
2002-03	**NY Rangers**	**NHL**	17	0	1	1	50	0	0	0	8	0.0	–1	1	0.0	6:28	....								
	Hartford	AHL	15	3	2	5	117	....	....	....	....	....	....	....	....	....	....								
	Montreal	**NHL**	11	0	0	0	46	0	0	0	2	0.0	–2	2	50.0	7:33	....								
	NHL Totals		106	0	5	5	387	0	0	0	35	0.0		5	40.0	5:43	....								

• Re-entered NHL Entry Draft. Originally St. Louis' 2nd choice, 67th overall, in 1996 Entry Draft.

Traded to **Tampa Bay** by **Montreal** for Mike McBain, November 26, 1999. Traded to **NY Rangers** by **Tampa Bay** for Boyd Kane, October 10, 2002. Claimed on waivers by **Montreal** from **NY Rangers**, February 21, 2003.

DYKHUIS, Karl
(DIGH-kowz, KAHRL)   **MTL.**

Defense. Shoots left. 6'3", 214 lbs.   Born, Sept-Iles, Que., July 8, 1972. Chicago's 1st choice, 16th overall, in 1990 Entry Draft.

Season	Club	League	GP	G	A	Pts	PIM	PP	SH	GW	S	%	+/-	TF	F%	Min	GP	G	A	Pts	PIM	PP	SH	GW	Min
1987-88	Lac St-Jean	QAAA	37	2	12	14	....	....	....	....	....	....	....	....	....	....	2	0	1	1	2				
1988-89	Hull Olympiques	QMJHL	63	2	29	31	59	....	....	....	....	....	....	....	....	....	9	1	9	10	6				
1989-90	Hull Olympiques	QMJHL	69	10	46	56	119	....	....	....	....	....	....	....	....	....	11	2	5	7	2				
1990-91	Team Canada	Nat-Tm	37	2	9	11	16	....	....	....	....	....	....	....	....	....	....								
	Longueuil	QMJHL	3	1	4	5	6	....	....	....	....	....	....	....	....	....	8	2	5	7	6				
1991-92	Team Canada	Nat-Tm	29	1	2	3	16	....	....	....	....	....	....	....	....	....	....								
	Verdun	QMJHL	29	5	19	24	55	....	....	....	....	....	....	....	....	....	17	0	12	12	14				
	Chicago	**NHL**	6	1	3	4	4	1	0	0	12	8.3	–1	....	....	....	....								
1992-93	**Chicago**	**NHL**	12	0	5	5	0	0	0	0	10	0.0	2	....	....	....	....								
	Indianapolis Ice	IHL	59	5	18	23	76	....	....	....	....	....	....	....	....	....	5	1	1	2	8				
1993-94	Indianapolis Ice	IHL	73	7	25	32	132	....	....	....	....	....	....	....	....	....	....								
1994-95	Indianapolis Ice	IHL	52	2	21	23	63	....	....	....	....	....	....	....	....	....	....								
	Philadelphia	**NHL**	33	2	6	8	37	1	0	1	46	4.3	7	....	....	....	15	4	4	8	14	2	0	2	
	Hershey Bears	AHL	1	0	0	0	0	....	....	....	....	....	....	....	....	....	....								
1995-96	**Philadelphia**	**NHL**	82	5	15	20	101	1	0	0	104	4.8	12	....	....	....	12	2	2	4	22	1	0	0	
1996-97	**Philadelphia**	**NHL**	62	4	15	19	35	2	0	1	101	4.0	6	....	....	....	18	0	3	3	2	0	0	0	
1997-98	**Tampa Bay**	**NHL**	78	5	9	14	110	0	1	0	91	5.5	–8	....	....	....	....								
1998-99	**Tampa Bay**	**NHL**	33	2	1	3	18	0	0	0	27	7.4	–21	0	0.0	20:14	....								
	Philadelphia	**NHL**	45	2	4	6	32	0	0	0	61	3.3	–2	0	0.0	18:15	5	1	0	1	0	0	0	0	18:05
99-2000	**Philadelphia**	**NHL**	5	0	1	1	6	0	0	0	5	0.0	–2	0	0.0	14:54	....								
	Montreal	**NHL**	67	7	12	19	40	3	1	0	64	10.9	–3	0	0.0	19:53	....								
2000-01	**Montreal**	**NHL**	67	8	9	17	44	2	0	1	66	12.1	9	4	100.0	15:40	....								
2001-02	**Montreal**	**NHL**	80	5	7	12	32	0	0	1	85	5.9	16	0	0.0	19:54	12	1	1	2	8	0	0	0	18:39
2002-03	**Montreal**	**NHL**	65	1	4	5	34	0	0	0	24	4.2	–5	1	0.0	14:60	....								
	NHL Totals		635	42	91	133	493	11	2	4	696	6.0		5	80.0	17:59	62	8	10	18	50	3	0	2	18:29

QMJHL All-Rookie Team (1989) • QMJHL Defensive Rookie of the Year (1989) • QMJHL First All-Star Team (1990)

Traded to **Philadelphia** by **Chicago** for Bob Wilkie and Philadelphia's 5th round choice (Kyle Calder) in 1997 Entry Draft, February 16, 1995. Traded to **Tampa Bay** by **Philadelphia** with Mikael Renberg for Philadelphia's 1st round choices (previously acquired) in 1998 (Simon Gagne), 1999 (Maxime Ouellet), 2000 (Justin Williams) and 2001 (later traded to Ottawa – Ottawa selected Tim Gleason) Entry Drafts, August 20, 1997. Traded to **Philadelphia** by **Tampa Bay** for Petr Svoboda, December 28, 1998. Traded to **Montreal** by **Philadelphia** for cash, October 20, 1999.

EAKINS, Dallas
(EE-kins, DAL-las)   **VAN.**

Defense. Shoots left. 6'2", 195 lbs.   Born, Dade City, FL, February 27, 1967. Washington's 11th choice, 208th overall, in 1985 Entry Draft.

Season	Club	League	GP	G	A	Pts	PIM	PP	SH	GW	S	%	+/-	TF	F%	Min	GP	G	A	Pts	PIM	PP	SH	GW	Min
1983-84	Peterboro AA	OMHA	29	7	20	27	67	....	....	....	....	....	....	....	....	....	....								
	Peterborough	OJHL-B	5	0	3	3	4	....	....	....	....	....	....	....	....	....	....								
1984-85	Peterborough	OHL	48	0	8	8	96	....	....	....	....	....	....	....	....	....	7	0	0	0	18				
1985-86	Peterborough	OHL	60	6	16	22	134	....	....	....	....	....	....	....	....	....	16	0	1	1	30				
1986-87	Peterborough	OHL	54	3	11	14	145	....	....	....	....	....	....	....	....	....	12	1	4	5	37				
1987-88	Peterborough	OHL	64	11	27	38	129	....	....	....	....	....	....	....	....	....	12	3	12	15	16				
1988-89	Baltimore	AHL	62	0	10	10	139	....	....	....	....	....	....	....	....	....	....								
1989-90	Moncton Hawks	AHL	75	2	11	13	189	....	....	....	....	....	....	....	....	....	....								
1990-91	Moncton Hawks	AHL	75	1	13	13	132	....	....	....	....	....	....	....	....	....	9	0	1	1	44				

			Regular Season														Playoffs								
Season	Club	League	GP	G	A	Pts	PIM	PP	SH	GW	S	%	+/-	TF	F%	Min	GP	G	A	Pts	PIM	PP	SH	GW	Min
1991-92	Moncton Hawks	AHL	67	3	13	16	136	....	....	....	....	....	....	....	....	....	11	2	1	3	16	....	....	....	....
1992-93	**Winnipeg**	**NHL**	14	0	2	2	38	0	0	0	9	0.0	2	....	....	....	....	....	....	....	....	....	....	....	....
	Moncton Hawks	AHL	55	4	6	10	132	....	....	....	....	....	....	....	....	....	....	....	....	....	....	....	....	....	....
1993-94	**Florida**	**NHL**	1	0	0	0	0	0	0	0	2	0.0	0	....	....	....	....	....	....	....	....	....	....	....	....
	Cincinnati	IHL	80	1	18	19	143	....	....	....	....	....	....	....	....	....	8	0	1	1	41	....	....	....	....
1994-95	Cincinnati	IHL	59	6	12	18	69	....	....	....	....	....	....	....	....	....	....	....	....	....	....	....	....	....	....
	Florida	**NHL**	17	0	1	1	35	0	0	0	3	0.0	2	....	....	....	....	....	....	....	....	....	....	....	....
1995-96	**St. Louis**	**NHL**	16	0	1	1	34	0	0	0	6	0.0	–2	....	....	....	....	....	....	....	....	....	....	....	....
	Worcester IceCats	AHL	4	0	0	0	12	....	....	....	....	....	....	....	....	....	....	....	....	....	....	....	....	....	....
	Winnipeg	**NHL**	2	0	0	0	0	0	0	0	0	0.0	1	....	....	....	....	....	....	....	....	....	....	....	....
1996-97	**Phoenix**	**NHL**	4	0	0	0	10	0	0	0	2	0.0	–3	....	....	....	....	....	....	....	....	....	....	....	....
	Springfield	AHL	38	6	7	13	63	....	....	....	....	....	....	....	....	....	....	....	....	....	....	....	....	....	....
	NY Rangers	**NHL**	3	0	0	0	6	0	0	0	2	0.0	–1	....	....	....	4	0	0	0	4	0	0	0	....
	Binghamton	AHL	19	1	7	8	15	....	....	....	....	....	....	....	....	....	....	....	....	....	....	....	....	....	....
1997-98	**Florida**	**NHL**	23	0	1	1	44	0	0	0	16	0.0	1	....	....	....	....	....	....	....	....	....	....	....	....
	New Haven	AHL	4	0	1	1	7	....	....	....	....	....	....	....	....	....	....	....	....	....	....	....	....	....	....
1998-99	**Toronto**	**NHL**	18	0	2	2	24	0	0	0	11	0.0	3	0	0.0	16:28	1	0	0	0	0	0	0	0	2:28
	Chicago Wolves	IHL	2	0	0	0	0	....	....	....	....	....	....	....	....	....	....	....	....	....	....	....	....	....	....
	St. John's	AHL	20	3	7	10	16	....	....	....	....	....	....	....	....	....	5	0	1	1	6	....	....	....	....
99-2000	**NY Islanders**	**NHL**	2	0	1	1	2	0	0	0	4	0.0	3	0	0.0	21:28	....	....	....	....	....	....	....	....	....
	Chicago Wolves	IHL	68	5	26	31	99	....	....	....	....	....	....	....	....	....	16	1	4	5	16	....	....	....	....
2000-01	**Calgary**	**NHL**	17	0	1	1	11	0	0	0	4	0.0	–1	0	0.0	12:18	....	....	....	....	....	....	....	....	....
	Chicago Wolves	IHL	64	3	16	19	49	....	....	....	....	....	....	....	....	....	14	0	0	0	24	....	....	....	....
2001-02	**Calgary**	**NHL**	3	0	0	0	4	0	0	0	0	0.0	1	0	0.0	14:21	....	....	....	....	....	....	....	....	....
	Chicago Wolves	AHL	54	2	15	17	58	....	....	....	....	....	....	....	....	....	25	0	6	6	53	....	....	....	....
2002-03	Chicago Wolves	AHL	72	4	11	15	84	....	....	....	....	....	....	....	....	....	9	1	0	1	31	....	....	....	....
	NHL Totals		**120**	**0**	**9**	**9**	**208**	**0**	**0**	**0**	**59**	**0.0**		**0**	**0.0**	**14:47**	**5**	**0**	**0**	**0**	**4**	**0**	**0**	**0**	**2:28**

IHL Second All-Star Team (2000)

Signed as a free agent by **Winnipeg**, October 17, 1989. Signed as a free agent by **Florida**, July 8, 1993. Traded to **St. Louis** by **Florida** for St. Louis' 4th round choice (Ivan Novoseltsev) in 1997 Entry Draft, September 28, 1995. Claimed on waivers by **Winnipeg** from **St. Louis**, March 20, 1996. Transferred to **Phoenix** after **Winnipeg** franchise relocated, July 1, 1996. Traded to **NY Rangers** by **Phoenix** with Mike Eastwood for Jayson More, February 6, 1997. Signed as a free agent by **Florida**, July 30, 1997. Signed as a free agent by **Toronto**, July 28, 1998. Signed as a free agent by **NY Islanders**, August 12, 1999. Traded to **Chicago** by **NY Islanders** for future considerations, March 3, 2000. Signed as a free agent by **Calgary**, July 27, 2000. Signed as a free agent by **Atlanta**, July 23, 2002. Signed as a free agent by **Vancouver**, August 6, 2003.

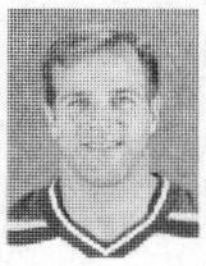

EASTWOOD, Mike

(EEST-wuhd, MIGHK) **PIT.**

Center. Shoots right. 6'3", 216 lbs. Born, Ottawa, Ont., July 1, 1967. Toronto's 5th choice, 91st overall, in 1987 Entry Draft.

Season	Club	League	GP	G	A	Pts	PIM	PP	SH	GW	S	%	+/-	TF	F%	Min	GP	G	A	Pts	PIM	PP	SH	GW	Min
1984-85	Nepean Raiders	OCJHL	46	10	13	23	18	....	....	....	....	....	....	....	....	....	....	....	....	....	....	....	....	....	....
1985-86	Nepean Raiders	OCJHL	7	4	2	6	6	....	....	....	....	....	....	....	....	....	....	....	....	....	....	....	....	....	....
1986-87	Pembroke	OCJHL	54	58	45	103	62	....	....	....	....	....	....	....	....	....	23	36	11	47	32	....	....	....	....
1987-88	West-Michigan	CCHA	42	5	8	13	14	....	....	....	....	....	....	....	....	....	....	....	....	....	....	....	....	....	....
1988-89	West-Michigan	CCHA	40	10	13	23	87	....	....	....	....	....	....	....	....	....	....	....	....	....	....	....	....	....	....
1989-90	West-Michigan	CCHA	40	25	27	52	36	....	....	....	....	....	....	....	....	....	....	....	....	....	....	....	....	....	....
1990-91	West-Michigan	CCHA	42	29	32	61	84	....	....	....	....	....	....	....	....	....	....	....	....	....	....	....	....	....	....
1991-92	**Toronto**	**NHL**	9	0	2	2	4	0	0	0	6	0.0	–4	....	....	....	....	....	....	....	....	....	....	....	....
	St. John's	AHL	61	18	25	43	28	....	....	....	....	....	....	....	....	....	16	9	10	19	16	....	....	....	....
1992-93	**Toronto**	**NHL**	12	1	6	7	21	0	0	0	11	9.1	–2	....	....	....	10	1	2	3	8	0	0	0	....
	St. John's	AHL	60	24	35	59	32	....	....	....	....	....	....	....	....	....	....	....	....	....	....	....	....	....	....
1993-94	**Toronto**	**NHL**	54	8	10	18	28	1	0	2	41	19.5	2	....	....	....	18	3	2	5	12	1	0	1	....
1994-95	**Toronto**	**NHL**	36	5	5	10	32	0	0	0	38	13.2	–12	....	....	....	....	....	....	....	....	....	....	....	....
	Winnipeg	**NHL**	13	3	6	9	4	0	0	0	17	17.6	3	....	....	....	....	....	....	....	....	....	....	....	....
1995-96	**Winnipeg**	**NHL**	80	14	14	28	20	2	0	3	94	14.9	–14	....	....	....	6	0	1	1	2	0	0	0	....
1996-97	**Phoenix**	**NHL**	33	1	3	4	4	0	0	0	22	4.5	–3	....	....	....	....	....	....	....	....	....	....	....	....
	NY Rangers	**NHL**	27	1	7	8	10	0	0	0	22	4.5	2	....	....	....	15	1	2	3	22	0	0	0	....
1997-98	**NY Rangers**	**NHL**	48	5	5	10	16	0	0	0	34	14.7	–2	....	....	....	....	....	....	....	....	....	....	....	....
	St. Louis	**NHL**	10	1	0	1	6	0	0	1	4	25.0	0	....	....	....	3	1	0	1	0	0	0	1	....
1998-99	**St. Louis**	**NHL**	82	9	21	30	36	0	0	0	76	11.8	6	1235	56.6	14:59	13	1	1	2	6	0	0	0	16:02
99-2000	**St. Louis**	**NHL**	79	19	15	34	32	1	3	3	83	22.9	5	872	52.2	15:08	7	1	1	2	6	0	0	0	13:28
2000-01	**St. Louis**	**NHL**	77	6	17	23	28	0	2	1	51	11.8	4	1230	53.4	14:08	15	0	2	2	2	0	0	0	15:13
2001-02	**St. Louis**	**NHL**	71	7	10	17	41	0	0	2	60	11.7	–2	1110	53.8	12:55	10	0	0	0	6	0	0	0	15:32
2002-03	**St. Louis**	**NHL**	17	1	3	4	8	1	0	0	7	14.3	1	203	42.9	10:44	....	....	....	....	....	....	....	....	....
	Chicago	**NHL**	53	2	10	12	24	0	0	0	32	6.3	–6	713	53.3	12:54	....	....	....	....	....	....	....	....	....
	NHL Totals		**701**	**83**	**134**	**217**	**314**	**5**	**5**	**12**	**598**	**13.9**		**5363**	**53.6**	**13:59**	**97**	**8**	**11**	**19**	**64**	**1**	**0**	**2**	**15:15**

CCHA Second All-Star Team (1991)

Traded to **Winnipeg** by **Toronto** with Toronto's 3rd round choice (Brad Isbister) in 1995 Entry Draft for Tie Domi, April 7, 1995. Transferred to **Phoenix** after **Winnipeg** franchise relocated, July 1, 1996. Traded to **NY Rangers** by **Phoenix** with Dallas Eakins for Jayson More, February 6, 1997. Traded to **St. Louis** by **NY Rangers** for Harry York, March 24, 1998. Claimed on waivers by **Chicago** from **St. Louis**, December 11, 2002. Signed as a free agent by **Pittsburgh**, July 31, 2003.

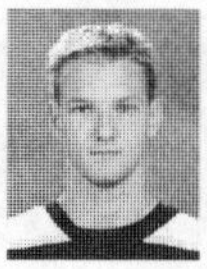

EATON, Mark

(EE-tohn, MAHRK) **NSH.**

Defense. Shoots left. 6'2", 208 lbs. Born, Wilmington, DE, May 6, 1977.

Season	Club	League	GP	G	A	Pts	PIM	PP	SH	GW	S	%	+/-	TF	F%	Min	GP	G	A	Pts	PIM	PP	SH	GW	Min
1995-96	Waterloo	USHL	50	4	21	25	....	....	....	....	....	....	....	....	....	....	....	....	....	....	....	....	....	....	....
1996-97	Waterloo	USHL	50	6	32	38	62	....	....	....	....	....	....	....	....	....	....	....	....	....	....	....	....	....	....
1997-98	U. of Notre Dame	CCHA	41	12	17	29	32	....	....	....	....	....	....	....	....	....	....	....	....	....	....	....	....	....	....
1998-99	Philadelphia	AHL	74	9	27	36	38	....	....	....	....	....	....	....	....	....	16	4	8	12	0	....	....	....	....
99-2000	**Philadelphia**	**NHL**	27	1	1	2	8	0	0	1	25	4.0	1	0	0.0	18:17	7	0	0	0	0	0	0	0	13:36
	Philadelphia	AHL	47	9	17	26	6	....	....	....	....	....	....	....	....	....	....	....	....	....	....	....	....	....	....
2000-01	**Nashville**	**NHL**	34	3	8	11	14	1	0	1	32	9.4	7	0	0.0	17:13	....	....	....	....	....	....	....	....	....
	Milwaukee	IHL	34	3	12	15	27	....	....	....	....	....	....	....	....	....	....	....	....	....	....	....	....	....	....
2001-02	**Nashville**	**NHL**	58	3	5	8	24	0	0	0	52	5.8	–12	0	0.0	17:12	....	....	....	....	....	....	....	....	....
2002-03	**Nashville**	**NHL**	50	2	7	9	22	0	0	0	52	3.8	1	0	0.0	15:45	....	....	....	....	....	....	....	....	....
	Milwaukee	AHL	3	1	0	1	2	....	....	....	....	....	....	....	....	....	....	....	....	....	....	....	....	....	....
	NHL Totals		**169**	**9**	**21**	**30**	**68**	**1**	**0**	**2**	**161**	**5.6**		**0**	**0.0**	**16:57**	**7**	**0**	**0**	**0**	**0**	**0**	**0**	**0**	**13:36**

USHL Second All-Star Team (1997) • Curt Hammer Award (Most Gentlemanly Player – USHL) (1997) • CCHA Rookie of the Year (1998)

Signed as a free agent by **Philadelphia**, August 4, 1998. Traded to **Nashville** by **Philadelphia** for Detroit's 3rd round choice (previously acquired, Philadelphia selected Patrick Sharp) in 2001 Entry Draft, September 29, 2000.

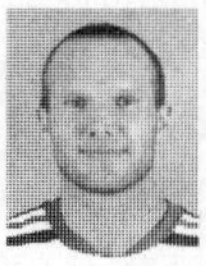

EKMAN, Nils

(EHK-mahn, NIHLS) **S.J.**

Left wing. Shoots left. 5'11", 185 lbs. Born, Stockholm, Sweden, March 11, 1976. Calgary's 6th choice, 107th overall, in 1994 Entry Draft.

Season	Club	League	GP	G	A	Pts	PIM	PP	SH	GW	S	%	+/-	TF	F%	Min	GP	G	A	Pts	PIM	PP	SH	GW	Min
1993-94	Hammarby Jr.	Swede-Jr.	11	4	5	9	14	....	....	....	....	....	....	....	....	....	....	....	....	....	....	....	....	....	....
	Hammarby	Swede-2	18	7	2	9	4	....	....	....	....	....	....	....	....	....	....	....	....	....	....	....	....	....	....
1994-95	Hammarby Jr.	Swede-Jr.	2	2	1	3	0	....	....	....	....	....	....	....	....	....	....	....	....	....	....	....	....	....	....
	Hammarby	Swede-2	32	10	8	18	18	....	....	....	....	....	....	....	....	....	....	....	....	....	....	....	....	....	....
1995-96	Hammarby	Swede-2	26	9	7	16	53	....	....	....	....	....	....	....	....	....	1	0	0	0	0	....	....	....	....
1996-97	Kiekko Espoo	Finland	50	24	19	43	60	....	....	....	....	....	....	....	....	....	4	2	0	2	4	....	....	....	....
1997-98	Kiekko Espoo	Finland	43	14	14	28	86	....	....	....	....	....	....	....	....	....	7	2	2	4	27	....	....	....	....
	Saint John Flames	AHL	....	....	....	....	....	....	....	....	....	....	....	....	....	....	1	0	0	0	2	....	....	....	....
1998-99	Blues Espoo	Finland	52	20	14	34	96	....	....	....	....	....	....	....	....	....	3	1	1	2	6	....	....	....	....
99-2000	Detroit Vipers	IHL	10	7	2	9	8	....	....	....	....	....	....	....	....	....	....	....	....	....	....	....	....	....	....
	Tampa Bay	**NHL**	28	2	2	4	36	1	0	0	42	4.8	–8	3	0.0	11:12	....	....	....	....	....	....	....	....	....
	Long Beach	IHL	27	11	12	23	26	....	....	....	....	....	....	....	....	....	5	3	3	6	4	....	....	....	....
2000-01	**Tampa Bay**	**NHL**	43	9	11	20	40	2	1	1	72	12.5	–15	16	37.5	15:45	....	....	....	....	....	....	....	....	....
	Detroit Vipers	IHL	33	22	14	36	63	....	....	....	....	....	....	....	....	....	....	....	....	....	....	....	....	....	....
2001-02	Djurgarden	Sweden	38	16	15	31	57	....	....	....	....	....	....	....	....	....	4	1	0	1	32	....	....	....	....
2002-03	Hartford	AHL	57	30	36	66	73	....	....	....	....	....	....	....	....	....	2	0	2	2	4	....	....	....	....
	NHL Totals		**71**	**11**	**13**	**24**	**76**	**3**	**1**	**1**	**114**	**9.6**		**19**	**31.6**	**13:57**	....	....	....	....	....	....	....	....	....

Garry F. Longman Memorial Trophy (Top Rookie – IHL) (2000)

Traded to **Tampa Bay** by **Calgary** with Calgary's 4th round choice (later traded to NY Islanders – NY Islanders selected Vladimir Gorbunov) in 2000 Entry Draft for Andreas Johansson, November 20, 1999. Traded to **NY Rangers** by **Tampa Bay** with Kyle Freadrich for Tim Taylor, June 30, 2001. Traded to **San Jose** by **NY Rangers** for Chad Wiseman, August 12, 2003.

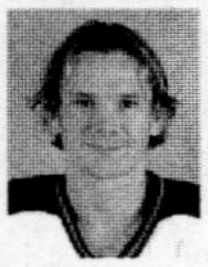

ELIAS, Patrik
(ehl-EE-ahsh, PA-trihk) **N.J.**

Center. Shoots left. 6'1", 195 lbs. Born, Trebic, Czech., April 13, 1976. New Jersey's 2nd choice, 51st overall, in 1994 Entry Draft.

			Regular Season														Playoffs								
Season	Club	League	GP	G	A	Pts	PIM	PP	SH	GW	S	%	+/-	TF	F%	Min	GP	G	A	Pts	PIM	PP	SH	GW	Min
1992-93	Poldi Kladno	Czech	2	0	0	0	....	....	....	....	....	....	....	....	....	....	....	....	....	....	....	....	....	....	....
1993-94	HC Kladno	Czech	15	1	2	3	....	....	....	....	....	....	....	....	....	....	11	2	2	4	....	....	....	....	....
1994-95	HC Kladno	Czech	28	4	3	7	37	....	....	....	....	....	....	....	....	....	7	1	2	3	12	....	....	....	....
1995-96	**New Jersey**	**NHL**	**1**	**0**	**0**	**0**	**0**	**0**	**0**	**0**	**2**	**0.0**	**–1**	....	....	....	....	....	....	....	....	....	....	....	....
	Albany River Rats	AHL	74	27	36	63	83	....	....	....	....	....	....	....	....	....	4	1	1	2	2	....	....	....	....
1996-97	**New Jersey**	**NHL**	**17**	**2**	**3**	**5**	**2**	**0**	**0**	**0**	**23**	**8.7**	**–4**	....	....	....	**8**	**2**	**3**	**5**	**4**	**1**	**0**	**0**	....
	Albany River Rats	AHL	57	24	43	67	76	....	....	....	....	....	....	....	....	....	6	1	2	3	8	....	....	....	....
1997-98	**New Jersey**	**NHL**	**74**	**18**	**19**	**37**	**28**	**5**	**0**	**6**	**147**	**12.2**	**18**	....	....	....	**4**	**0**	**1**	**1**	**0**	**0**	**0**	**0**	....
	Albany River Rats	AHL	3	3	0	3	2	....	....	....	....	....	....	....	....	....	....	....	....	....	....	....	....	....	....
1998-99	**New Jersey**	**NHL**	**74**	**17**	**33**	**50**	**34**	**3**	**0**	**2**	**157**	**10.8**	**19**	**99**	**38.4**	**15:50**	**7**	**0**	**5**	**5**	**6**	**0**	**0**	**0**	**18:07**
99-2000	Trebic	Czech-2	2	2	1	3	2	....	....	....	....	....	....	....	....	....	....	....	....	....	....	....	....	....	....
	Pardubice	Czech	5	1	4	5	31	....	....	....	....	....	....	....	....	....	....	....	....	....	....	....	....	....	....
	♦ New Jersey	**NHL**	**72**	**35**	**37**	**72**	**58**	**9**	**0**	**9**	**183**	**19.1**	**16**	**134**	**45.5**	**17:28**	**23**	**7**	***13**	**20**	**9**	**2**	**1**	**1**	**17:44**
2000-01	**New Jersey**	**NHL**	**82**	**40**	**56**	**96**	**51**	**8**	**3**	**6**	**220**	**18.2**	**45**	**155**	**41.3**	**18:44**	**25**	**9**	**14**	**23**	**10**	**3**	**1**	**2**	**18:14**
2001-02	**New Jersey**	**NHL**	**75**	**29**	**32**	**61**	**36**	**8**	**1**	**8**	**199**	**14.6**	**4**	**128**	**45.3**	**18:57**	**6**	**2**	**4**	**6**	**6**	**2**	**0**	**0**	**20:33**
	Czech Republic	Olympics	4	1	1	2	0	....	....	....	....	....	....	....	....	....	....	....	....	....	....	....	....	....	....
2002-03	**♦ New Jersey**	**NHL**	**81**	**28**	**29**	**57**	**22**	**6**	**0**	**4**	**255**	**11.0**	**17**	**427**	**43.8**	**18:05**	**24**	**5**	**8**	**13**	**26**	**2**	**0**	**2**	**17:14**
	NHL Totals		**476**	**169**	**209**	**378**	**231**	**39**	**4**	**35**	**1186**	**14.2**		**943**	**43.3**	**17:50**	**97**	**25**	**48**	**73**	**61**	**10**	**2**	**5**	**17:58**

NHL All-Rookie Team (1998) • NHL First All-Star Team (2001)
Played in NHL All-Star Game (2000, 2002)

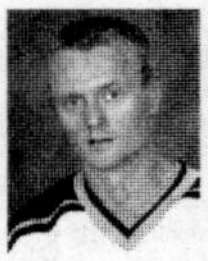

ELORANTA, Mikko
(ehl-oh-RAN-tuh, MEE-koh)

Left wing. Shoots left. 6', 190 lbs. Born, Turku, Finland, August 24, 1972. Boston's 9th choice, 247th overall, in 1999 Entry Draft.

Season	Club	League	GP	G	A	Pts	PIM	PP	SH	GW	S	%	+/-	TF	F%	Min	GP	G	A	Pts	PIM	PP	SH	GW	Min
1989-90	TPS Turku Jr.	Finn-Jr.	2	0	0	0	0	....	....	....	....	....	....	....	....	....	....	....	....	....	....	....	....	....	....
1990-91	TPS Turku Jr.	Finn-Jr.	35	8	8	16	18	....	....	....	....	....	....	....	....	....	....	....	....	....	....	....	....	....	....
1991-92	TPS Turku Jr.	Finn-Jr.	19	3	1	4	8	....	....	....	....	....	....	....	....	....	8	0	0	0	0	....	....	....	....
1992-93	TPS Turku Jr.	Finn-Jr.	31	11	6	17	20	....	....	....	....	....	....	....	....	....	6	0	4	4	6	....	....	....	....
1993-94	Kiekko-67 Turku	Finland-2	45	3	4	7	24	....	....	....	....	....	....	....	....	....	....	....	....	....	....	....	....	....	....
1994-95	Kiekko-67 Turku	Finland-2	47	18	14	32	52	....	....	....	....	....	....	....	....	....	3	3	0	3	4	....	....	....	....
1995-96	Kiekko-67 Turku	Finland-2	8	6	7	13	2	....	....	....	....	....	....	....	....	....	....	....	....	....	....	....	....	....	....
	Ilves Tampere	Finland	43	18	15	33	86	....	....	....	....	....	....	....	....	....	3	0	2	2	2	....	....	....	....
1996-97	TPS Turku	EuroHL	6	3	1	4	6	....	....	....	....	....	....	....	....	....	1	0	0	0	0	....	....	....	....
	TPS Turku	Finland	31	6	15	21	52	....	....	....	....	....	....	....	....	....	10	5	2	7	6	....	....	....	....
1997-98	TPS Turku	EuroHL	3	1	0	1	12	....	....	....	....	....	....	....	....	....	....	....	....	....	....	....	....	....	....
	TPS Turku	Finland	46	23	14	37	82	....	....	....	....	....	....	....	....	....	2	0	0	0	8	....	....	....	....
1998-99	TPS Turku	Finland	52	19	21	40	103	....	....	....	....	....	....	....	....	....	10	1	6	7	26	....	....	....	....
99-2000	**Boston**	**NHL**	**50**	**6**	**12**	**18**	**36**	**1**	**0**	**0**	**59**	**10.2**	**–10**	**77**	**35.1**	**12:18**	....	....	....	....	....	....	....	....	....
2000-01	**Boston**	**NHL**	**62**	**12**	**11**	**23**	**38**	**1**	**1**	**2**	**89**	**13.5**	**2**	**82**	**23.2**	**10:26**	....	....	....	....	....	....	....	....	....
2001-02	**Boston**	**NHL**	**6**	**0**	**0**	**0**	**2**	**0**	**0**	**0**	**15**	**0.0**	**–1**	**8**	**25.0**	**16:12**	....	....	....	....	....	....	....	....	....
	Los Angeles	**NHL**	**71**	**9**	**9**	**18**	**54**	**1**	**0**	**2**	**121**	**7.4**	**0**	**1**	**100.0**	**11:27**	**7**	**1**	**1**	**2**	**2**	**0**	**0**	**0**	**12:02**
	Finland	Olympics	4	2	0	2	2	....	....	....	....	....	....	....	....	....	....	....	....	....	....	....	....	....	....
2002-03	**Los Angeles**	**NHL**	**75**	**5**	**12**	**17**	**56**	**1**	**0**	**1**	**96**	**5.2**	**–15**	**14**	**42.9**	**12:50**	....	....	....	....	....	....	....	....	....
	NHL Totals		**264**	**32**	**44**	**76**	**186**	**4**	**1**	**5**	**380**	**8.4**		**182**	**30.2**	**11:52**	**7**	**1**	**1**	**2**	**2**	**0**	**0**	**0**	**12:02**

Traded to **Los Angeles** by **Boston** with Jason Allison for Jozef Stumpel and Glen Murray, October 24, 2001.

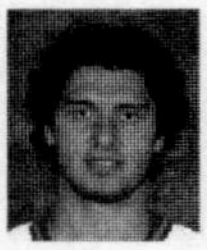

EMINGER, Steve
(EH-mihn-juhr, STEEV) **WSH.**

Defense. Shoots right. 6'1", 196 lbs. Born, Woodbridge, Ont., October 31, 1983. Washington's 1st choice, 12th overall, in 2002 Entry Draft.

Season	Club	League	GP	G	A	Pts	PIM	PP	SH	GW	S	%	+/-	TF	F%	Min	GP	G	A	Pts	PIM	PP	SH	GW	Min
1997-98	Vaughan Rangers	OMHA	STATISTICS NOT AVAILABLE																						
1998-99	Bramalea Blues	OPJHL	47	6	9	15	81	....	....	....	....	....	....	....	....	....	....	....	....	....	....	....	....	....	....
99-2000	Kitchener Rangers	OHL	50	2	14	16	74	....	....	....	....	....	....	....	....	....	5	0	0	0	0	....	....	....	....
2000-01	Kitchener Rangers	OHL	54	6	26	32	66	....	....	....	....	....	....	....	....	....	....	....	....	....	....	....	....	....	....
2001-02	Kitchener Rangers	OHL	64	19	39	58	93	....	....	....	....	....	....	....	....	....	4	0	2	2	10	....	....	....	....
2002-03	**Washington**	**NHL**	**17**	**0**	**2**	**2**	**24**	**0**	**0**	**0**	**6**	**0.0**	**–3**	**0**	**0.0**	**10:08**	....	....	....	....	....	....	....	....	....
	Kitchener Rangers	OHL	23	2	27	29	40	....	....	....	....	....	....	....	....	....	21	3	8	11	44	....	....	....	....
	NHL Totals		**17**	**0**	**2**	**2**	**24**	**0**	**0**	**0**	**6**	**0.0**		**0**	**0.0**	**10:08**	....	....	....	....	....	....	....	....	....

OHL Second All-Star Team (2002, 2003) • Memorial Cup All-Star Team (2003)

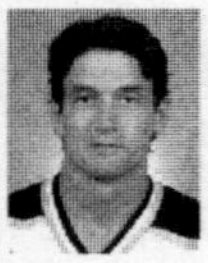

EMMONS, John
(eh-mohns, JAWN)

Center. Shoots left. 6'1", 203 lbs. Born, San Jose, CA, August 17, 1974. Calgary's 7th choice, 122nd overall, in 1993 Entry Draft.

Season	Club	League	GP	G	A	Pts	PIM	PP	SH	GW	S	%	+/-	TF	F%	Min	GP	G	A	Pts	PIM	PP	SH	GW	Min
1990-91	New Canaan	Hi-School	20	19	37	56	20	....	....	....	....	....	....	....	....	....	....	....	....	....	....	....	....	....	....
1991-92	New Canaan	Hi-School	22	24	49	73	24	....	....	....	....	....	....	....	....	....	....	....	....	....	....	....	....	....	....
1992-93	Yale University	ECAC	28	3	5	8	66	....	....	....	....	....	....	....	....	....	....	....	....	....	....	....	....	....	....
1993-94	Yale University	ECAC	25	5	12	17	66	....	....	....	....	....	....	....	....	....	....	....	....	....	....	....	....	....	....
1994-95	Yale University	ECAC	28	4	16	20	57	....	....	....	....	....	....	....	....	....	....	....	....	....	....	....	....	....	....
1995-96	Yale University	ECAC	31	8	20	28	124	....	....	....	....	....	....	....	....	....	....	....	....	....	....	....	....	....	....
1996-97	Dayton Bombers	ECHL	69	20	37	57	62	....	....	....	....	....	....	....	....	....	4	0	1	1	2	....	....	....	....
	Fort Wayne	IHL	1	0	0	0	0	....	....	....	....	....	....	....	....	....	....	....	....	....	....	....	....	....	....
1997-98	Michigan	IHL	81	9	25	34	85	....	....	....	....	....	....	....	....	....	4	1	1	2	10	....	....	....	....
1998-99	Detroit Vipers	IHL	75	13	22	35	172	....	....	....	....	....	....	....	....	....	11	4	5	9	22	....	....	....	....
99-2000	**Ottawa**	**NHL**	**10**	**0**	**0**	**0**	**6**	**0**	**0**	**0**	**3**	**0.0**	**–2**	**62**	**58.1**	**7:27**	....	....	....	....	....	....	....	....	....
	Grand Rapids	IHL	64	10	16	26	78	....	....	....	....	....	....	....	....	....	16	1	4	5	28	....	....	....	....
200u-01	**Ottawa**	**NHL**	**41**	**1**	**1**	**2**	**20**	**0**	**0**	**0**	**28**	**3.6**	**–5**	**315**	**51.4**	**7:46**	....	....	....	....	....	....	....	....	....
	Grand Rapids	IHL	9	1	0	1	4	....	....	....	....	....	....	....	....	....	....	....	....	....	....	....	....	....	....
	Tampa Bay	**NHL**	**12**	**1**	**1**	**2**	**22**	**0**	**0**	**0**	**9**	**11.1**	**0**	**160**	**52.5**	**13:07**	....	....	....	....	....	....	....	....	....
2001-02	**Boston**	**NHL**	**22**	**0**	**2**	**2**	**16**	**0**	**0**	**0**	**20**	**0.0**	**–4**	**153**	**56.9**	**8:04**	....	....	....	....	....	....	....	....	....
	Providence Bruins	AHL	46	4	8	12	32	....	....	....	....	....	....	....	....	....	2	1	1	2	0	....	....	....	....
2002-03	Eisbaren Berlin	Germany	29	2	7	9	49	....	....	....	....	....	....	....	....	....	9	3	2	5	4	....	....	....	....
	NHL Totals		**85**	**2**	**4**	**6**	**64**	**0**	**0**	**0**	**60**	**3.3**		**690**	**53.5**	**8:34**	....	....	....	....	....	....	....	....	....

Signed as a free agent by **Ottawa**, August 7, 1998. Traded to **Tampa Bay** by **Ottawa** for Craig Millar, March 13, 2001. Signed as a free agent by **Boston**, August 8, 2001. Signed as a free agent by **Eisbaren Berlin** (Germany), November 25, 2002.

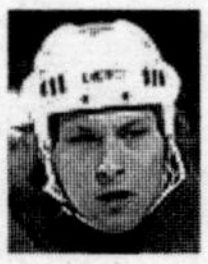

ENDICOTT, Shane
(ehn-DIH-kawt, SHAYN) **PIT.**

Center. Shoots left. 6'4", 214 lbs. Born, Saskatoon, Sask., December 21, 1981. Pittsburgh's 2nd choice, 52nd overall, in 2000 Entry Draft.

Season	Club	League	GP	G	A	Pts	PIM	PP	SH	GW	S	%	+/-	TF	F%	Min	GP	G	A	Pts	PIM	PP	SH	GW	Min
1997-98	Sask. Contacts	SMHL	43	31	32	63	42	....	....	....	....	....	....	....	....	....	....	....	....	....	....	....	....	....	....
	Seattle	WHL	....	....	....	....	....	....	....	....	....	....	....	....	....	....	5	0	0	0	0	....	....	....	....
1998-99	Seattle	WHL	72	13	26	39	27	....	....	....	....	....	....	....	....	....	11	0	1	1	0	....	....	....	....
99-2000	Seattle	WHL	70	23	32	55	62	....	....	....	....	....	....	....	....	....	7	1	6	7	6	....	....	....	....
2000-01	Seattle	WHL	72	36	43	79	86	....	....	....	....	....	....	....	....	....	9	4	5	9	12	....	....	....	....
2001-02	**Pittsburgh**	**NHL**	**4**	**0**	**1**	**1**	**4**	**0**	**0**	**0**	**2**	**0.0**	**–1**	**18**	**33.3**	**8:28**	....	....	....	....	....	....	....	....	....
	Wilkes-Barre	AHL	63	19	20	39	46	....	....	....	....	....	....	....	....	....	....	....	....	....	....	....	....	....	....
2002-03	Wilkes-Barre	AHL	74	13	26	39	68	....	....	....	....	....	....	....	....	....	6	0	2	2	4	....	....	....	....
	NHL Totals		**4**	**0**	**1**	**1**	**4**	**0**	**0**	**0**	**2**	**0.0**		**18**	**33.3**	**8:28**	....	....	....	....	....	....	....	....	....

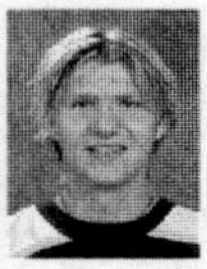

ERAT, Martin
(EE-rat, mahr-TIHN) **NSH.**

Left wing. Shoots left. 6', 195 lbs. Born, Trebic, Czech., August 28, 1981. Nashville's 12th choice, 191st overall, in 1999 Entry Draft.

Season	Club	League	GP	G	A	Pts	PIM	PP	SH	GW	S	%	+/-	TF	F%	Min	GP	G	A	Pts	PIM	PP	SH	GW	Min
1997-98	Zlin Jr.	Czech-Jr.	46	35	30	65	....	....	....	....	....	....	....	....	....	....	....	....	....	....	....	....	....	....	....
1998-99	Zlin Jr.	Czech-Jr.	35	21	23	44	....	....	....	....	....	....	....	....	....	....	....	....	....	....	....	....	....	....	....
	Zlin	Czech	5	0	0	0	2	....	....	....	....	....	....	....	....	....	....	....	....	....	....	....	....	....	....
99-2000	Saskatoon Blades	WHL	66	27	26	53	82	....	....	....	....	....	....	....	....	....	11	4	8	12	16	....	....	....	....
2000-01	Saskatoon Blades	WHL	31	19	35	54	48	....	....	....	....	....	....	....	....	....	....	....	....	....	....	....	....	....	....
	Red Deer Rebels	WHL	17	4	24	28	24	....	....	....	....	....	....	....	....	....	22	*15	*21	*36	32	....	....	....	....

			Regular Season														Playoffs								
Season	Club	League	GP	G	A	Pts	PIM	PP	SH	GW	S	%	+/-	TF	F%	Min	GP	G	A	Pts	PIM	PP	SH	GW	Min
2001-02	Nashville	NHL	80	9	24	33	32	2	0	2	84	10.7	–11	3	66.7	13:10									
2002-03	Nashville	NHL	27	1	7	8	14	1	0	0	39	2.6	–9	1	0.0	12:47									
	Milwaukee	AHL	45	10	22	32	41										6	5	4	9	4				
	NHL Totals		107	10	31	41	46	3	0	2	123	8.1		4	50.0	13:04									

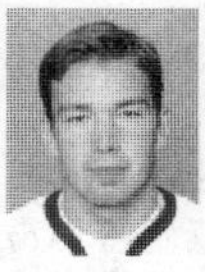

ERIKSSON, Anders

(AIR-ihk-suhn, AND-uhrs)

Defense. Shoots left. 6’2”, 220 lbs. Born, Bollnas, Sweden, January 9, 1975. Detroit’s 1st choice, 22nd overall, in 1993 Entry Draft.

			Regular Season														Playoffs								
Season	Club	League	GP	G	A	Pts	PIM	PP	SH	GW	S	%	+/-	TF	F%	Min	GP	G	A	Pts	PIM	PP	SH	GW	Min
1992-93	MoDo Jr.	Swede-Jr.	10	5	3	8	14																		
	MoDo	Sweden	20	0	2	2	2										1	0	0	0	0				
1993-94	MoDo Jr.	Swede-Jr.	3	1	2	3	34																		
	MoDo	Sweden	38	2	8	10	42										11	0	0	0	8				
1994-95	MoDo	Sweden	39	3	6	9	54																		
1995-96	Detroit	NHL	1	0	0	0	2	0	0	0	0	0.0	1				3	0	0	0	0	0	0	0	
	Adirondack	AHL	75	6	36	42	64										3	0	0	0	0				
1996-97	Detroit	NHL	23	0	6	6	10	0	0	0	27	0.0	5												
	Adirondack	AHL	44	3	25	28	36										4	0	1	1	4				
1997-98♦	Detroit	NHL	66	7	14	21	32	1	0	2	91	7.7	21				18	0	5	5	16	0	0	0	
1998-99	Detroit	NHL	61	2	10	12	34	0	0	1	67	3.0	5	0	0.0	15:54									
	Chicago	NHL	11	0	8	8	0	0	0	0	12	0.0	6	0	0.0	22:51									
99-2000	Chicago	NHL	73	3	25	28	20	0	0	1	86	3.5	4	1	100.0	21:03									
2000-01	Chicago	NHL	13	2	3	5	2	1	0	0	19	10.5	–4	0	0.0	21:20									
	Florida	NHL	60	0	21	21	28	0	0	0	80	0.0	2	1	0.0	21:02									
2001-02	Toronto	NHL	34	0	2	2	12	0	0	0	31	0.0	–1	0	0.0	15:55	10	0	0	0	0	0	0	0	17:24
	St. John’s	AHL	25	4	6	10	14										11	0	5	5	6				
2002-03	Toronto	NHL	4	0	0	0	0	0	0	0	7	0.0	1	0	0.0	19:02									
	St. John’s	AHL	72	5	34	39	133																		
	NHL Totals		346	14	89	103	140	2	0	4	420	3.3		2	50.0	19:12	31	0	5	5	16	0	0	0	17:24

Traded to **Chicago** by **Detroit** with Detroit’s 1st round choices in 1999 (Steve McCarthy) and 2001 (Adam Munro) Entry Drafts for Chris Chelios, March 23, 1999. Traded to **Florida** by **Chicago** for Jaroslav Spacek, November 6, 2000. Signed as a free agent by **Toronto**, July 9, 2001.

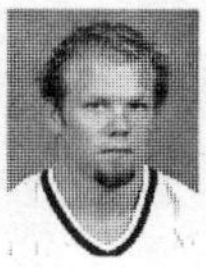

ERSKINE, John

(AIR-skign, JAWN) **DAL.**

Defense. Shoots left. 6’4”, 215 lbs. Born, Kingston, Ont., June 26, 1980. Dallas’ 1st choice, 39th overall, in 1998 Entry Draft.

			Regular Season														Playoffs								
Season	Club	League	GP	G	A	Pts	PIM	PP	SH	GW	S	%	+/-	TF	F%	Min	GP	G	A	Pts	PIM	PP	SH	GW	Min
1996-97	Quinte Hawks	MTJHL	48	4	16	20	241																		
1997-98	London Knights	OHL	55	0	9	9	205										16	0	5	5	25				
1998-99	London Knights	OHL	57	8	12	20	208										25	5	10	15	38				
99-2000	London Knights	OHL	58	12	31	43	177																		
2000-01	Utah Grizzlies	IHL	77	1	8	9	284																		
2001-02	Dallas	NHL	33	0	1	1	62	0	0	0	16	0.0	–8	0	0.0	10:44									
	Utah Grizzlies	AHL	39	2	6	8	118										3	0	0	0	10				
2002-03	Dallas	NHL	16	2	0	2	29	0	0	0	12	16.7	1	0	0.0	10:45									
	Utah Grizzlies	AHL	52	2	8	10	274										1	0	1	1	15				
	NHL Totals		49	2	1	3	91	0	0	0	28	7.1		0	0.0	10:45									

OHL First All-Star Team (2000)

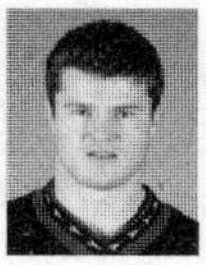

EXELBY, Garnet

(EHX-uhl-bee, GAHR-neht) **ATL.**

Defense. Shoots left. 6’1”, 210 lbs. Born, Craik, Sask., August 16, 1981. Atlanta’s 9th choice, 217th overall, in 1999 Entry Draft.

			Regular Season														Playoffs								
Season	Club	League	GP	G	A	Pts	PIM	PP	SH	GW	S	%	+/-	TF	F%	Min	GP	G	A	Pts	PIM	PP	SH	GW	Min
1997-98	Winnipeg South	MJHL	46	5	11	16	110																		
1998-99	Saskatoon Blades	WHL	61	5	3	8	91																		
99-2000	Saskatoon Blades	WHL	63	1	8	9	79										11	0	2	2	21				
2000-01	Saskatoon Blades	WHL	43	5	10	15	110																		
	Regina Pats	WHL	22	2	8	10	51										6	0	2	2	2				
2001-02	Chicago Wolves	AHL	75	3	4	7	257										25	0	4	4	49				
2002-03	Chicago Wolves	AHL	53	3	6	9	140										9	0	1	1	27				
	Atlanta	NHL	15	0	2	2	41	0	0	0	9	0.0	0	0	0.0	18:04									
	NHL Totals		15	0	2	2	41	0	0	0	9	0.0		0	0.0	18:04									

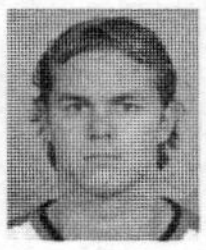

FAHEY, Jim

(FA-hee, JIHM) **S.J.**

Defense. Shoots right. 6’, 215 lbs. Born, Boston, MA, May 11, 1979. San Jose’s 9th choice, 212th overall, in 1998 Entry Draft.

			Regular Season														Playoffs								
Season	Club	League	GP	G	A	Pts	PIM	PP	SH	GW	S	%	+/-	TF	F%	Min	GP	G	A	Pts	PIM	PP	SH	GW	Min
1997-98	Catholic Memorial	Hi-School	24	12	32	44	28																		
1998-99	Northeastern	H-East	32	5	13	18	34																		
99-2000	Northeastern	H-East	36	3	17	20	62																		
2000-01	Northeastern	H-East	36	4	23	27	48																		
2001-02	Northeastern	H-East	39	14	32	46	50																		
2002-03	San Jose	NHL	43	1	19	20	33	0	0	0	66	1.5	–3	1	100.0	18:20									
	Cleveland Barons	AHL	25	3	14	17	42																		
	NHL Totals		43	1	19	20	33	0	0	0	66	1.5		1	100.0	18:20									

Hockey East Second All-Star Team (2001) • Hockey East First All-Star Team (2002)

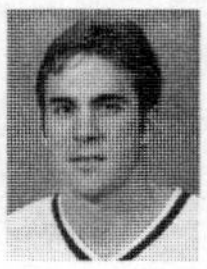

FAIRCHILD, Kelly

(FAIR-chighld, KEHL-lee)

Center. Shoots left. 5’11”, 180 lbs. Born, Hibbing, MN, April 9, 1973. Los Angeles’ 6th choice, 152nd overall, in 1991 Entry Draft.

			Regular Season														Playoffs								
Season	Club	League	GP	G	A	Pts	PIM	PP	SH	GW	S	%	+/-	TF	F%	Min	GP	G	A	Pts	PIM	PP	SH	GW	Min
1988-89	Hibbing High	Hi-School	22	9	8	17	24																		
1989-90	Grand Rapids	Hi-School	28	12	17	29	73																		
1990-91	Grand Rapids	Hi-School	28	28	45	73	25																		
1991-92	U. of Wisconsin	WCHA	37	11	10	21	45																		
1992-93	U. of Wisconsin	WCHA	42	25	29	54	54																		
1993-94	U. of Wisconsin	WCHA	42	20	44	*64	81																		
1994-95	St. John’s	AHL	53	27	23	50	51										4	0	2	2	4				
1995-96	Toronto	NHL	1	0	1	1	2	0	0	0	1	0.0	1												
	St. John’s	AHL	78	29	49	78	85										2	0	1	1	4				
1996-97	Toronto	NHL	22	0	2	2	2	0	0	0	14	0.0	–5												
	St. John’s	AHL	29	9	22	31	36																		
	Orlando	IHL	25	9	6	15	20										9	6	5	11	16				
1997-98	St. John’s	AHL	17	5	2	7	24																		
	Orlando	IHL	22	2	6	8	20																		
	Milwaukee	IHL	40	20	24	44	32										10	5	2	7	4				
1998-99	Dallas	NHL	1	0	0	0	0	0	0	0	4	0.0	0	12	25.0	12:37									
	Michigan	IHL	74	17	33	50	88										5	2	2	4	16				
99-2000	Michigan	IHL	78	21	41	62	89																		
2000-01	Hershey Bears	AHL	70	23	40	63	68										12	2	9	11	10				
2001-02	Colorado	NHL	10	2	0	2	2	0	0	0	6	33.3	1	32	43.8	6:35									
	Hershey Bears	AHL	63	22	25	47	92										8	2	1	3	6				
2002-03	Eisbaren Berlin	Germany	51	20	32	52	74										9	3	3	6	20				
	NHL Totals		34	2	3	5	6	0	0	0	25	8.0		44	38.6	7:08									

WCHA First All-Star Team (1994)

Traded to **Toronto** by **Los Angeles** with Dixon Ward, Guy Leveque and Shayne Toporowski for Eric Lacroix, Chris Snell and Toronto’s 4th round choice (Eric Belanger) in 1996 Entry Draft, October 3, 1994. Traded to **Milwaukee** (IHL) by **Orlando** (IHL) with Dave McIntyre for Sean McCann and Dave Mackey, January 11, 1998. Signed as a free agent by **Dallas**, July 2, 1998. Signed as a free agent by **Colorado**, August 29, 2000. Signed as a free agent by **Eisbaren Berlin** (Germany) with **Colorado** retaining NHL rights, July 28, 2002.

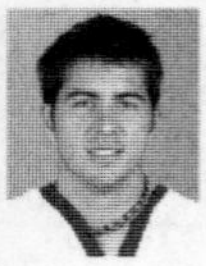

FARKAS, Jeff

(FAHR-kuhs, JEHF)

Right wing. Shoots left. 6', 185 lbs. Born, Amherst, NY, January 24, 1978. Toronto's 1st choice, 57th overall, in 1997 Entry Draft.

			Regular Season														Playoffs								
Season	Club	League	GP	G	A	Pts	PIM	PP	SH	GW	S	%	+/-	TF	F%	Min	GP	G	A	Pts	PIM	PP	SH	GW	Min
1993-94	Nichols High	Hi-School	28	27	57	84	25	....	....	....	....	....	....	....	....	....	....	....	....	....	....	....	....	....	....
1994-95	Niagara Scenics	EJHL	47	54	55	99	70	....	....	....	....	....	....	....	....	....	....	....	....	....	....	....	....	....	....
1995-96	Niagara Scenics	MTJHL	47	42	70	112	75	....	....	....	....	....	....	....	....	....	....	....	....	....	....	....	....	....	....
1996-97	Boston College	H-East	35	13	23	36	34	....	....	....	....	....	....	....	....	....	....	....	....	....	....	....	....	....	....
1997-98	Boston College	H-East	40	11	28	39	42	....	....	....	....	....	....	....	....	....	....	....	....	....	....	....	....	....	....
1998-99	Boston College	H-East	43	32	25	57	56	....	....	....	....	....	....	....	....	....	....	....	....	....	....	....	....	....	....
99-2000	Boston College	H-East	41	32	26	*58	61	....	....	....	....	....	....	....	....	....	....	....	....	....	....	....	....	....	....
	Toronto	**NHL**	....	....	....	....	....	....	....	....	....	....	....	....	....	....	**3**	**1**	**0**	**1**	**0**	**0**	**0**	**0**	**12:49**
2000-01	**Toronto**	**NHL**	**2**	**0**	**0**	**0**	**2**	**0**	**0**	**0**	**1**	**0.0**	**–1**	**0**	**0.0**	**14:09**	....	....	....	....	....	....	....	....	....
	St. John's	AHL	77	28	40	68	62	....	....	....	....	....	....	....	....	....	4	1	2	3	4	....	....	....	....
2001-02	**Toronto**	**NHL**	**6**	**0**	**2**	**2**	**4**	**0**	**0**	**0**	**3**	**0.0**	**1**	**1**	**0.0**	**9:37**	**2**	**0**	**0**	**0**	**0**	**0**	**0**	**0**	**1:34**
	St. John's	AHL	71	16	34	50	49	....	....	....	....	....	....	....	....	....	4	0	0	0	0	....	....	....	....
2002-03	Manitoba Moose	AHL	39	11	14	25	28	....	....	....	....	....	....	....	....	....	....	....	....	....	....	....	....	....	....
	Atlanta	**NHL**	**3**	**0**	**0**	**0**	**0**	**0**	**0**	**0**	**5**	**0.0**	**–1**	**2**	**50.0**	**13:32**	....	....	....	....	....	....	....	....	....
	Chicago Wolves	AHL	24	5	12	17	14	....	....	....	....	....	....	....	....	....	....	....	....	....	....	....	....	....	....
	NHL Totals		**11**	**0**	**2**	**2**	**6**	**0**	**0**	**0**	**9**	**0.0**		**3**	**33.3**	**11:30**	**5**	**1**	**0**	**1**	**0**	**0**	**0**	**0**	**8:19**

Hockey East First All-Star Team (2000) • NCAA East First All-American Team (2000) • NCAA Championship All-Tournament Team (2000)

Traded to **Vancouver** by **Toronto** for Josh Holden, June 23, 2002. Traded to **Atlanta** by **Vancouver** for Chris Herperger and Chris Nielsen, January 20, 2003.

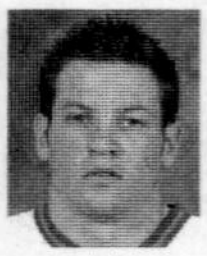

FARRELL, Mike

(FAIR-uhl, MIGHK) **NSH.**

Right wing. Shoots right. 6', 222 lbs. Born, Edina, MN, October 20, 1978. Washington's 9th choice, 220th overall, in 1998 Entry Draft.

			Regular Season														Playoffs								
Season	Club	League	GP	G	A	Pts	PIM	PP	SH	GW	S	%	+/-	TF	F%	Min	GP	G	A	Pts	PIM	PP	SH	GW	Min
1996-97	Culver Eagles	Hi-School	STATISTICS NOT AVAILABLE																						
1997-98	Providence	H-East	33	5	8	13	32	....	....	....	....	....	....	....	....	....	....	....	....	....	....	....	....	....	....
1998-99	Providence	H-East	29	3	12	15	51	....	....	....	....	....	....	....	....	....	....	....	....	....	....	....	....	....	....
99-2000	Providence	H-East	36	3	6	9	71	....	....	....	....	....	....	....	....	....	....	....	....	....	....	....	....	....	....
	Portland Pirates	AHL	7	2	0	2	0	....	....	....	....	....	....	....	....	....	4	0	1	1	0	....	....	....	....
2000-01	Portland Pirates	AHL	79	6	18	24	61	....	....	....	....	....	....	....	....	....	3	0	2	2	2	....	....	....	....
2001-02	**Washington**	**NHL**	**8**	**0**	**0**	**0**	**0**	**0**	**0**	**0**	**1**	**0.0**	**–1**	**0**	**0.0**	**5:35**	....	....	....	....	....	....	....	....	....
	Portland Pirates	AHL	61	12	15	27	62	....	....	....	....	....	....	....	....	....	....	....	....	....	....	....	....	....	....
2002-03	**Washington**	**NHL**	**4**	**0**	**0**	**0**	**2**	**0**	**0**	**0**	**2**	**0.0**	**1**	**0**	**0.0**	**2:48**	....	....	....	....	....	....	....	....	....
	Portland Pirates	AHL	68	12	12	24	107	....	....	....	....	....	....	....	....	....	3	0	1	1	0	....	....	....	....
	NHL Totals		**12**	**0**	**0**	**0**	**2**	**0**	**0**	**0**	**3**	**0.0**		**0**	**0.0**	**4:40**	....	....	....	....	....	....	....	....	....

Traded to **Nashville** by **Washington** for Alexander Riazantsev, July 14, 2003.

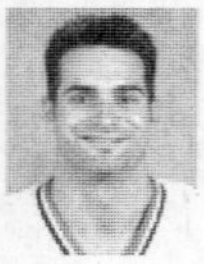

FATA, Rico

(FA-tuh, REE-koh) **PIT.**

Right wing. Shoots left. 6', 200 lbs. Born, Sault Ste. Marie, Ont., February 12, 1980. Calgary's 1st choice, 6th overall, in 1998 Entry Draft.

			Regular Season														Playoffs								
Season	Club	League	GP	G	A	Pts	PIM	PP	SH	GW	S	%	+/-	TF	F%	Min	GP	G	A	Pts	PIM	PP	SH	GW	Min
1994-95	Soo Legion	NOHA	51	52	51	103	....	....	....	....	....	....	....	....	....	....	....	....	....	....	....	....	....	....	....
1995-96	Sault Ste. Marie	OHL	62	11	15	26	52	....	....	....	....	....	....	....	....	....	4	0	0	0	0	....	....	....	....
1996-97	London Knights	OHL	59	19	34	53	76	....	....	....	....	....	....	....	....	....	....	....	....	....	....	....	....	....	....
1997-98	London Knights	OHL	64	43	33	76	110	....	....	....	....	....	....	....	....	....	16	9	5	14	*49	....	....	....	....
1998-99	**Calgary**	**NHL**	**20**	**0**	**1**	**1**	**4**	**0**	**0**	**0**	**13**	**0.0**	**0**	**2**	**50.0**	**7:36**	....	....	....	....	....	....	....	....	....
	London Knights	OHL	23	15	18	33	41	....	....	....	....	....	....	....	....	....	25	10	12	22	42	....	....	....	....
99-2000	**Calgary**	**NHL**	**2**	**0**	**0**	**0**	**0**	**0**	**0**	**0**	**0**	**0.0**	**–1**	**0**	**0.0**	**10:06**	....	....	....	....	....	....	....	....	....
	Saint John Flames	AHL	76	29	29	58	65	....	....	....	....	....	....	....	....	....	3	0	0	0	4	....	....	....	....
2000-01	**Calgary**	**NHL**	**5**	**0**	**0**	**0**	**6**	**0**	**0**	**0**	**6**	**0.0**	**–3**	**0**	**0.0**	**9:25**	....	....	....	....	....	....	....	....	....
	Saint John Flames	AHL	70	23	29	52	129	....	....	....	....	....	....	....	....	....	19	2	3	5	22	....	....	....	....
2001-02	**NY Rangers**	**NHL**	**10**	**0**	**0**	**0**	**0**	**0**	**0**	**0**	**8**	**0.0**	**–2**	**55**	**47.3**	**8:31**	....	....	....	....	....	....	....	....	....
	Hartford	AHL	61	35	36	71	36	....	....	....	....	....	....	....	....	....	10	2	5	7	4	....	....	....	....
2002-03	**NY Rangers**	**NHL**	**36**	**2**	**4**	**6**	**6**	**0**	**0**	**0**	**30**	**6.7**	**–1**	**30**	**50.0**	**7:16**	....	....	....	....	....	....	....	....	....
	Hartford	AHL	9	8	6	14	6	....	....	....	....	....	....	....	....	....	....	....	....	....	....	....	....	....	....
	Pittsburgh	**NHL**	**27**	**5**	**8**	**13**	**10**	**0**	**0**	**0**	**49**	**10.2**	**–6**	**87**	**49.4**	**17:46**	....	....	....	....	....	....	....	....	....
	NHL Totals		**100**	**7**	**13**	**20**	**26**	**0**	**0**	**0**	**106**	**6.6**		**174**	**48.9**	**10:28**	....	....	....	....	....	....	....	....	....

AHL Second All-Star Team (2002)

• Returned to **London** (OHL) by **Calgary** following WJC-A tournament, January 10, 1999. Claimed on waivers by **NY Rangers** from **Calgary**, October 3, 2001. Traded to **Pittsburgh** by **NY Rangers** with Joel Bouchard, Richard Lintner, Mikael Samuelsson and future considerations for Mike Wilson, Alex Kovalev, Janne Laukkanen and Dan LaCouture, February 10, 2003.

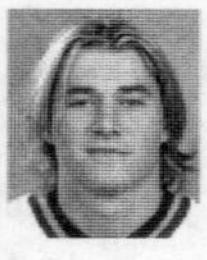

FEDOROV, Fedor

(FEH-duh-rahf, feh-DUHR) **VAN.**

Center. Shoots left. 6'3", 202 lbs. Born, Appatity, USSR, June 11, 1981. Vancouver's 2nd choice, 66th overall, in 2001 Entry Draft.

			Regular Season														Playoffs								
Season	Club	League	GP	G	A	Pts	PIM	PP	SH	GW	S	%	+/-	TF	F%	Min	GP	G	A	Pts	PIM	PP	SH	GW	Min
1997-98	Det. Caesars	MNHL	13	3	7	10	18	....	....	....	....	....	....	....	....	....	....	....	....	....	....	....	....	....	....
1998-99	Port Huron	UHL	42	2	5	7	20	....	....	....	....	....	....	....	....	....	....	....	....	....	....	....	....	....	....
99-2000	Windsor Spitfires	OHL	60	7	10	17	115	....	....	....	....	....	....	....	....	....	12	1	0	1	4	....	....	....	....
2000-01	Sudbury Wolves	OHL	67	33	45	78	88	....	....	....	....	....	....	....	....	....	12	4	6	10	36	....	....	....	....
2001-02	Manitoba Moose	AHL	8	2	1	3	6	....	....	....	....	....	....	....	....	....	....	....	....	....	....	....	....	....	....
	Columbia Inferno	ECHL	2	0	2	2	0	....	....	....	....	....	....	....	....	....	....	....	....	....	....	....	....	....	....
2002-03	**Vancouver**	**NHL**	**7**	**0**	**1**	**1**	**4**	**0**	**0**	**0**	**2**	**0.0**	**0**	**26**	**46.2**	**9:10**	....	....	....	....	....	....	....	....	....
	Manitoba Moose	AHL	50	10	13	23	61	....	....	....	....	....	....	....	....	....	3	1	2	3	0	....	....	....	....
	NHL Totals		**7**	**0**	**1**	**1**	**4**	**0**	**0**	**0**	**2**	**0.0**		**26**	**46.2**	**9:10**	....	....	....	....	....	....	....	....	....

• Re-entered NHL Entry Draft. Originally Tampa Bay's 7th choice, 182nd overall, in 1999 Entry Draft.

Signed as an underage free agent by **Detroit** (IHL), August 5, 1998. Released by **Detroit** (IHL), September 30, 1998. Signed as an underage free agent by **Port Huron** (UHL), October 1, 1998. • Missed majority of 2001-02 season recovering from eye injury suffered in game vs. Macon (ECHL), November 17, 2001.

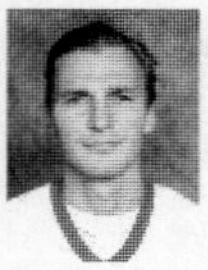

FEDOROV, Sergei

(FEH-duh-rahf, SAIR-gay) **ANA.**

Center. Shoots left. 6'1", 200 lbs. Born, Pskov, USSR, December 13, 1969. Detroit's 4th choice, 74th overall, in 1989 Entry Draft.

			Regular Season														Playoffs								
Season	Club	League	GP	G	A	Pts	PIM	PP	SH	GW	S	%	+/-	TF	F%	Min	GP	G	A	Pts	PIM	PP	SH	GW	Min
1985-86	Dynamo Minsk	USSR-2	15	6	1	7	10	....	....	....	....	....	....	....	....	....	....	....	....	....	....	....	....	....	....
1986-87	CSKA Moscow	USSR	29	6	6	12	12	....	....	....	....	....	....	....	....	....	....	....	....	....	....	....	....	....	....
1987-88	CSKA Moscow	USSR	48	7	9	16	20	....	....	....	....	....	....	....	....	....	....	....	....	....	....	....	....	....	....
1988-89	CSKA Moscow	USSR	44	9	8	17	35	....	....	....	....	....	....	....	....	....	....	....	....	....	....	....	....	....	....
1989-90	CSKA Moscow	USSR	48	19	10	29	22	....	....	....	....	....	....	....	....	....	....	....	....	....	....	....	....	....	....
1990-91	**Detroit**	**NHL**	**77**	**31**	**48**	**79**	**66**	**11**	**3**	**5**	**259**	**12.0**	**11**	....	....	....	**7**	**1**	**5**	**6**	**4**	**0**	**0**	**1**	....
1991-92	**Detroit**	**NHL**	**80**	**32**	**54**	**86**	**72**	**7**	**2**	**5**	**249**	**12.9**	**26**	....	....	....	**11**	**5**	**5**	**10**	**8**	**1**	**2**	**1**	....
1992-93	**Detroit**	**NHL**	**73**	**34**	**53**	**87**	**72**	**13**	**4**	**3**	**217**	**15.7**	**33**	....	....	....	**7**	**3**	**6**	**9**	**23**	**1**	**1**	**0**	....
1993-94	**Detroit**	**NHL**	**82**	**56**	**64**	**120**	**34**	**13**	**4**	**10**	**337**	**16.6**	**48**	....	....	....	**7**	**1**	**7**	**8**	**6**	**0**	**0**	**0**	....
1994-95	**Detroit**	**NHL**	**42**	**20**	**30**	**50**	**24**	**7**	**3**	**5**	**147**	**13.6**	**6**	....	....	....	**17**	**7**	***17**	***24**	**6**	**3**	**0**	**0**	....
1995-96	**Detroit**	**NHL**	**78**	**39**	**68**	**107**	**48**	**11**	**3**	**11**	**306**	**12.7**	**49**	....	....	....	**19**	**2**	***18**	**20**	**10**	**0**	**0**	**2**	....
1996-97♦	**Detroit**	**NHL**	**74**	**30**	**33**	**63**	**30**	**9**	**2**	**4**	**273**	**11.0**	**29**	....	....	....	**20**	**8**	**12**	**20**	**12**	**3**	**0**	**4**	....
1997-98	Russia	Olympics	6	1	5	6	8	....	....	....	....	....	....	....	....	....	....	....	....	....	....	....	....	....	....
	♦ Detroit	**NHL**	**21**	**6**	**11**	**17**	**25**	**2**	**0**	**2**	**68**	**8.8**	**10**	....	....	....	**22**	***10**	**10**	**20**	**12**	**2**	**1**	**1**	....
1998-99	**Detroit**	**NHL**	**77**	**26**	**37**	**63**	**66**	**6**	**2**	**3**	**224**	**11.6**	**9**	**1414**	**51.7**	**19:21**	**10**	**1**	**8**	**9**	**8**	**0**	**0**	**0**	**19:54**
99-2000	**Detroit**	**NHL**	**68**	**27**	**35**	**62**	**22**	**4**	**4**	**7**	**263**	**10.3**	**8**	**1274**	**53.8**	**20:05**	**9**	**4**	**4**	**8**	**4**	**2**	**0**	**1**	**20:48**
2000-01	**Detroit**	**NHL**	**75**	**32**	**37**	**69**	**40**	**14**	**2**	**7**	**268**	**11.9**	**12**	**1601**	**55.8**	**21:05**	**6**	**2**	**5**	**7**	**0**	**1**	**0**	**1**	**22:19**
2001-02♦	**Detroit**	**NHL**	**81**	**31**	**37**	**68**	**36**	**10**	**0**	**6**	**256**	**12.1**	**20**	**1160**	**51.7**	**19:33**	**23**	**5**	**14**	**19**	**20**	**2**	**1**	**0**	**22:20**
	Russia	Olympics	6	2	2	4	4	....	....	....	....	....	....	....	....	....	....	....	....	....	....	....	....	....	....
2002-03	**Detroit**	**NHL**	**80**	**36**	**47**	**83**	**52**	**10**	**2**	**11**	**281**	**12.8**	**15**	**1580**	**53.4**	**21:11**	**4**	**1**	**2**	**3**	**0**	**0**	**0**	**0**	**22:07**
	NHL Totals		**908**	**400**	**554**	**954**	**587**	**117**	**31**	**79**	**3148**	**12.7**		**7029**	**53.4**	**20:15**	**162**	**50**	**113**	**163**	**113**	**15**	**5**	**11**	**21:35**

NHL All-Rookie Team (1991) • NHL First All-Star Team (1994) • Frank J. Selke Trophy (1994, 1996) • Lester B. Pearson Award (1994) • Hart Trophy (1994)

Played in NHL All-Star Game (1992, 1994, 1996, 2001, 2002, 2003)

• Missed majority of 1997-98 season after failing to come to contract terms with **Detroit**. Signed as a free agent by **Anaheim**, July 19, 2003.

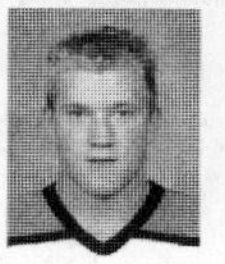

FEDORUK, Todd

(FEH-duh-ruhk, TAWD) **PHI.**

Left wing. Shoots left. 6'2", 235 lbs. Born, Redwater, Alta., February 13, 1979. Philadelphia's 6th choice, 164th overall, in 1997 Entry Draft.

			Regular Season														Playoffs								
Season	Club	League	GP	G	A	Pts	PIM	PP	SH	GW	S	%	+/-	TF	F%	Min	GP	G	A	Pts	PIM	PP	SH	GW	Min
1994-95	Ft. Saskatchewan	AMHL	STATISTICS NOT AVAILABLE																						
1995-96	Kelowna Rockets	WHL	44	1	1	2	83	....	....	....	....	....	....	....	....	....	4	0	0	0	6	....	....	....	....
1996-97	Kelowna Rockets	WHL	31	1	5	6	87	....	....	....	....	....	....	....	....	....	6	0	0	0	13	....	....	....	....
1997-98	Kelowna Rockets	WHL	31	3	5	8	120	....	....	....	....	....	....	....	....	....	....	....	....	....	....	....	....	....	....
	Regina Pats	WHL	21	4	3	7	80	....	....	....	....	....	....	....	....	....	9	1	2	3	23	....	....	....	....
1998-99	Regina Pats	WHL	39	12	12	24	107	....	....	....	....	....	....	....	....	....	....	....	....	....	....	....	....	....	....
	Prince Albert	WHL	28	6	4	10	75	....	....	....	....	....	....	....	....	....	13	1	6	7	49	....	....	....	....
99-2000	Trenton Titans	ECHL	18	2	5	7	118	....	....	....	....	....	....	....	....	....	....	....	....	....	....	....	....	....	....
	Philadelphia	AHL	19	1	2	3	40	....	....	....	....	....	....	....	....	....	5	0	1	1	2	....	....	....	....
2000-01	**Philadelphia**	**NHL**	**53**	**5**	**5**	**10**	**109**	**0**	**0**	**0**	**28**	**17.9**	**0**	**0**	**0.0**	**7:02**	**2**	**0**	**0**	**0**	**20**	**0**	**0**	**0**	**5:57**
	Philadelphia	AHL	14	0	1	1	49	....	....	....	....	....	....	....	....	....	....	....	....	....	....	....	....	....	....
2001-02	**Philadelphia**	**NHL**	**55**	**3**	**4**	**7**	**141**	**0**	**0**	**0**	**21**	**14.3**	**–2**	**5**	**0.0**	**6:21**	**3**	**0**	**0**	**0**	**0**	**0**	**0**	**0**	**2:46**
	Philadelphia	AHL	7	0	1	1	54	....	....	....	....	....	....	....	....	....	....	....	....	....	....	....	....	....	....
2002-03	**Philadelphia**	**NHL**	**63**	**1**	**5**	**6**	**105**	**0**	**0**	**0**	**33**	**3.0**	**1**	**1**	**0.0**	**6:30**	**1**	**0**	**0**	**0**	**0**	**0**	**0**	**0**	**4:52**
	NHL Totals		**171**	**9**	**14**	**23**	**355**	**0**	**0**	**0**	**82**	**11.0**		**6**	**0.0**	**6:37**	**6**	**0**	**0**	**0**	**20**	**0**	**0**	**0**	**4:10**

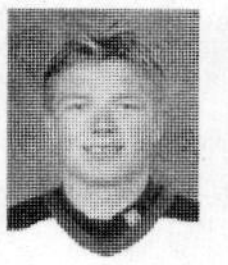

FEDOTENKO, Ruslan

(feh-doh-TEHN-koh, roos-LAHN) **T.B.**

Left wing. Shoots left. 6'2", 195 lbs. Born, Kiev, Ukraine, January 18, 1979.

			Regular Season														Playoffs								
Season	Club	League	GP	G	A	Pts	PIM	PP	SH	GW	S	%	+/-	TF	F%	Min	GP	G	A	Pts	PIM	PP	SH	GW	Min
1997-98	Melfort Mustangs	SJHL	68	35	31	66	55	....	....	....	....	....	....	....	....	....	....	....	....	....	....	....	....	....	....
1998-99	Sioux City	USHL	55	43	34	77	139	....	....	....	....	....	....	....	....	....	5	5	1	6	9	....	....	....	....
99-2000	Trenton Titans	ECHL	8	5	3	8	9	....	....	....	....	....	....	....	....	....	....	....	....	....	....	....	....	....	....
	Philadelphia	AHL	67	16	34	50	42	....	....	....	....	....	....	....	....	....	2	0	0	0	0	....	....	....	....
2000-01	**Philadelphia**	**NHL**	**74**	**16**	**20**	**36**	**72**	**3**	**0**	**4**	**119**	**13.4**	**8**	**7**	**71.4**	**14:38**	**6**	**0**	**1**	**1**	**4**	**0**	**0**	**0**	**11:18**
	Philadelphia	AHL	8	1	0	1	8	....	....	....	....	....	....	....	....	....	....	....	....	....	....	....	....	....	....
2001-02	**Philadelphia**	**NHL**	**78**	**17**	**9**	**26**	**43**	**0**	**1**	**3**	**121**	**14.0**	**15**	**41**	**43.9**	**13:56**	**5**	**1**	**0**	**1**	**2**	**0**	**0**	**1**	**14:11**
	Ukraine	Olympics	1	1	0	1	4	....	....	....	....	....	....	....	....	....	....	....	....	....	....	....	....	....	....
2002-03	**Tampa Bay**	**NHL**	**76**	**19**	**13**	**32**	**44**	**6**	**0**	**6**	**114**	**16.7**	**–7**	**90**	**48.9**	**16:01**	**11**	**0**	**1**	**1**	**2**	**0**	**0**	**1**	**13:58**
	NHL Totals		**228**	**52**	**42**	**94**	**159**	**9**	**1**	**13**	**354**	**14.7**		**138**	**48.6**	**14:51**	**22**	**1**	**2**	**3**	**8**	**0**	**0**	**1**	**13:17**

Signed as a free agent by **Philadelphia**, August 3, 1999. Traded to **Tampa Bay** by **Philadelphia** with Tampa Bay's 2nd round choice (previously acquired, later traded to Dallas – Dallas selected Tobias Stephan) in 2002 Entry Draft and Phoenix's 2nd round choice (previously acquired, later traded to San Jose – San Jose selected Dan Spang) in 2002 Entry Draft for Tampa Bay's 1st round choice (Joni Pitkanen) in 2002 Entry Draft, June 21, 2002.

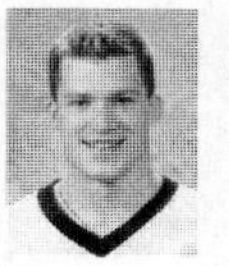

FERENCE, Andrew

(fuhr-EHNS, AN-droo) **CGY.**

Defense. Shoots left. 5'10", 196 lbs. Born, Edmonton, Alta., March 17, 1979. Pittsburgh's 8th choice, 208th overall, in 1997 Entry Draft.

			Regular Season														Playoffs								
Season	Club	League	GP	G	A	Pts	PIM	PP	SH	GW	S	%	+/-	TF	F%	Min	GP	G	A	Pts	PIM	PP	SH	GW	Min
1994-95	Sherwood Park	AMHL	31	4	14	18	74	....	....	....	....	....	....	....	....	....	....	....	....	....	....	....	....	....	....
	Portland	WHL	2	0	0	0	4	....	....	....	....	....	....	....	....	....	....	....	....	....	....	....	....	....	....
1995-96	Portland	WHL	72	9	31	40	159	....	....	....	....	....	....	....	....	....	7	1	3	4	12	....	....	....	....
1996-97	Portland	WHL	72	12	32	44	163	....	....	....	....	....	....	....	....	....	6	1	2	3	12	....	....	....	....
1997-98	Portland	WHL	72	11	57	68	142	....	....	....	....	....	....	....	....	....	16	2	18	20	28	....	....	....	....
1998-99	Portland	WHL	40	11	21	32	104	....	....	....	....	....	....	....	....	....	4	1	4	5	10	....	....	....	....
	Kansas City	IHL	5	1	2	3	4	....	....	....	....	....	....	....	....	....	3	0	0	0	9	....	....	....	....
99-2000	**Pittsburgh**	**NHL**	**30**	**2**	**4**	**6**	**20**	**0**	**0**	**1**	**26**	**7.7**	**3**	**0**	**0.0**	**16:19**	....	....	....	....	....	....	....	....	....
	Wilkes-Barre	AHL	44	8	20	28	58	....	....	....	....	....	....	....	....	....	....	....	....	....	....	....	....	....	....
2000-01	**Pittsburgh**	**NHL**	**36**	**4**	**11**	**15**	**28**	**1**	**0**	**1**	**47**	**8.5**	**6**	**0**	**0.0**	**18:51**	**18**	**3**	**7**	**10**	**16**	**1**	**0**	**1**	**22:02**
	Wilkes-Barre	AHL	43	6	18	24	95	....	....	....	....	....	....	....	....	....	3	1	0	1	12	....	....	....	....
2001-02	**Pittsburgh**	**NHL**	**75**	**4**	**7**	**11**	**73**	**1**	**0**	**0**	**82**	**4.9**	**–12**	**2**	**0.0**	**18:34**	....	....	....	....	....	....	....	....	....
2002-03	**Pittsburgh**	**NHL**	**22**	**1**	**3**	**4**	**36**	**1**	**0**	**0**	**22**	**4.5**	**–16**	**1**	**100.0**	**19:33**	....	....	....	....	....	....	....	....	....
	Wilkes-Barre	AHL	1	0	0	0	2	....	....	....	....	....	....	....	....	....	....	....	....	....	....	....	....	....	....
	Calgary	**NHL**	**16**	**0**	**4**	**4**	**6**	**0**	**0**	**0**	**17**	**0.0**	**1**	**0**	**0.0**	**17:38**	....	....	....	....	....	....	....	....	....
	NHL Totals		**179**	**11**	**29**	**40**	**163**	**3**	**0**	**2**	**194**	**5.7**		**3**	**33.3**	**18:17**	**18**	**3**	**7**	**10**	**16**	**1**	**0**	**1**	**22:02**

WHL West First All-Star Team (1998) • WHL West Second All-Star Team (1999)

• Missed majority of 2002-03 season recovering from groin (November 18, 2002 vs. Montreal) and ankle (March 20, 2003 vs. Los Angeles) injuries. Traded to **Calgary** by **Pittsburgh** for future considerations, February 10, 2003.

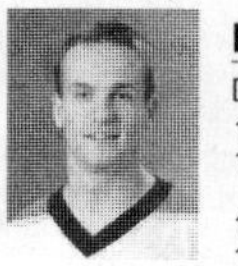

FERENCE, Brad

(FAIR-ehns, BRAD) **PHX.**

Defense. Shoots right. 6'3", 210 lbs. Born, Calgary, Alta., April 2, 1979. Vancouver's 1st choice, 10th overall, in 1997 Entry Draft.

			Regular Season														Playoffs								
Season	Club	League	GP	G	A	Pts	PIM	PP	SH	GW	S	%	+/-	TF	F%	Min	GP	G	A	Pts	PIM	PP	SH	GW	Min
1994-95	Calgary Royals	ABHL	60	19	47	66	220	....	....	....	....	....	....	....	....	....	....	....	....	....	....	....	....	....	....
1995-96	Calgary Royals	ABHL	22	7	21	28	140	....	....	....	....	....	....	....	....	....	....	....	....	....	....	....	....	....	....
	Spokane Chiefs	WHL	5	0	2	2	18	....	....	....	....	....	....	....	....	....	....	....	....	....	....	....	....	....	....
1996-97	Spokane Chiefs	WHL	67	6	20	26	324	....	....	....	....	....	....	....	....	....	9	0	4	4	21	....	....	....	....
1997-98	Spokane Chiefs	WHL	54	9	30	39	213	....	....	....	....	....	....	....	....	....	18	0	7	7	59	....	....	....	....
1998-99	Spokane Chiefs	WHL	31	3	22	25	125	....	....	....	....	....	....	....	....	....	....	....	....	....	....	....	....	....	....
	Tri-City	WHL	20	6	15	21	116	....	....	....	....	....	....	....	....	....	12	1	9	10	63	....	....	....	....
99-2000	**Florida**	**NHL**	**13**	**0**	**2**	**2**	**46**	**0**	**0**	**0**	**10**	**0.0**	**2**	**0**	**0.0**	**13:40**	....	....	....	....	....	....	....	....	....
	Louisville Panthers	AHL	58	2	7	9	231	....	....	....	....	....	....	....	....	....	2	0	0	0	2	....	....	....	....
2000-01	**Florida**	**NHL**	**14**	**0**	**1**	**1**	**14**	**0**	**0**	**0**	**5**	**0.0**	**–10**	**0**	**0.0**	**13:03**	....	....	....	....	....	....	....	....	....
	Louisville Panthers	AHL	52	3	21	24	200	....	....	....	....	....	....	....	....	....	....	....	....	....	....	....	....	....	....
2001-02	**Florida**	**NHL**	**80**	**2**	**15**	**17**	**254**	**0**	**0**	**0**	**65**	**3.1**	**–13**	**1**	**0.0**	**19:44**	....	....	....	....	....	....	....	....	....
2002-03	**Florida**	**NHL**	**60**	**2**	**6**	**8**	**118**	**0**	**0**	**0**	**41**	**4.9**	**2**	**0**	**0.0**	**15:58**	....	....	....	....	....	....	....	....	....
	Phoenix	**NHL**	**15**	**0**	**1**	**1**	**28**	**0**	**0**	**0**	**8**	**0.0**	**–5**	**0**	**0.0**	**16:33**	....	....	....	....	....	....	....	....	....
	NHL Totals		**182**	**4**	**25**	**29**	**460**	**0**	**0**	**0**	**129**	**3.1**		**1**	**0.0**	**17:17**	....	....	....	....	....	....	....	....	....

Memorial Cup All-Star Team (1998)

Traded to **Florida** by **Vancouver** with Pavel Bure, Bret Hedican and Vancouver's 3rd round choice (Robert Fried) in 2000 Entry Draft for Ed Jovanovski, Dave Gagner, Mike Brown, Kevin Weekes and Florida's 1st round choice (Nathan Smith) in 2000 Entry Draft, January 17, 1999. Traded to **Phoenix** by **Florida** for Darcy Hordichuk and Phoenix's 2nd round choice (later traded to Tampa Bay – Tampa Bay selected Matt Smaby) in 2003 Entry Draft, March 8, 2003.

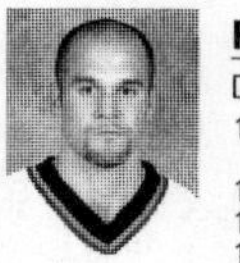

FERGUSON, Scott

(fuhr-GUH-sohn, SKAWT) **EDM.**

Defense. Shoots left. 6'1", 195 lbs. Born, Camrose, Alta., January 6, 1973.

			Regular Season														Playoffs								
Season	Club	League	GP	G	A	Pts	PIM	PP	SH	GW	S	%	+/-	TF	F%	Min	GP	G	A	Pts	PIM	PP	SH	GW	Min
1990-91	Sherwood Park	AJHL	32	2	9	11	91	....	....	....	....	....	....	....	....	....	....	....	....	....	....	....	....	....	....
	Kamloops Blazers	WHL	4	0	0	0	0	....	....	....	....	....	....	....	....	....	....	....	....	....	....	....	....	....	....
1991-92	Kamloops Blazers	WHL	62	4	10	14	138	....	....	....	....	....	....	....	....	....	12	0	2	2	21	....	....	....	....
1992-93	Kamloops Blazers	WHL	71	4	19	23	206	....	....	....	....	....	....	....	....	....	13	0	2	2	24	....	....	....	....
1993-94	Kamloops Blazers	WHL	68	5	49	54	180	....	....	....	....	....	....	....	....	....	19	5	11	16	48	....	....	....	....
1994-95	Cape Breton	AHL	58	4	6	10	103	....	....	....	....	....	....	....	....	....	....	....	....	....	....	....	....	....	....
	Wheeling	ECHL	5	1	5	6	16	....	....	....	....	....	....	....	....	....	....	....	....	....	....	....	....	....	....
1995-96	Cape Breton	AHL	80	5	16	21	196	....	....	....	....	....	....	....	....	....	....	....	....	....	....	....	....	....	....
1996-97	Hamilton	AHL	74	6	14	20	115	....	....	....	....	....	....	....	....	....	21	5	7	12	59	....	....	....	....
1997-98	**Edmonton**	**NHL**	**1**	**0**	**0**	**0**	**0**	**0**	**0**	**0**	**0**	**0.0**	**1**	....	....	....	....	....	....	....	....	....	....	....	....
	Hamilton	AHL	77	7	17	24	150	....	....	....	....	....	....	....	....	....	9	0	3	3	16	....	....	....	....
1998-99	**Anaheim**	**NHL**	**2**	**0**	**1**	**1**	**0**	**0**	**0**	**0**	**1**	**0.0**	**0**	**0**	**0.0**	**15:09**	....	....	....	....	....	....	....	....	....
	Cincinnati	AHL	78	4	31	35	59	....	....	....	....	....	....	....	....	....	3	0	0	0	4	....	....	....	....
99-2000	Cincinnati	AHL	77	7	25	32	166	....	....	....	....	....	....	....	....	....	....	....	....	....	....	....	....	....	....
2000-01	**Edmonton**	**NHL**	**20**	**0**	**1**	**1**	**13**	**0**	**0**	**0**	**8**	**0.0**	**2**	**0**	**0.0**	**10:55**	**6**	**0**	**0**	**0**	**0**	**0**	**0**	**0**	**8:21**
	Hamilton	AHL	42	3	18	21	79	....	....	....	....	....	....	....	....	....	....	....	....	....	....	....	....	....	....
2001-02	**Edmonton**	**NHL**	**50**	**3**	**2**	**5**	**75**	**0**	**0**	**0**	**27**	**11.1**	**11**	**0**	**0.0**	**13:40**	....	....	....	....	....	....	....	....	....
2002-03	**Edmonton**	**NHL**	**78**	**3**	**5**	**8**	**120**	**0**	**0**	**0**	**45**	**6.7**	**11**	**1**	**100.0**	**0:00**	**5**	**0**	**0**	**0**	**8**	**0**	**0**	**0**	....
	NHL Totals		**151**	**6**	**9**	**15**	**208**	**0**	**0**	**0**	**81**	**7.4**		**1**	**0.0**	**6:13**	**11**	**0**	**0**	**0**	**8**	**0**	**0**	**0**	**8:21**

WHL West Second All-Star Team (1994)

Signed as a free agent by **Edmonton**, June 2, 1994. Traded to **Ottawa** by **Edmonton** for Frantisek Musil, March 9, 1998. Signed as a free agent by **Anaheim**, July 27, 1998. Signed as a free agent by **Edmonton**, July 5, 2000.

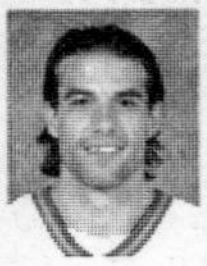

FERRARO, Chris

(fuh-RAHR-oh, KRIHS) **PHX.**

Center. Shoots right. 5'9", 175 lbs. Born, Port Jefferson, NY, January 24, 1973. NY Rangers' 4th choice, 85th overall, in 1992 Entry Draft.

			Regular Season														Playoffs								
Season	Club	League	GP	G	A	Pts	PIM	PP	SH	GW	S	%	+/-	TF	F%	Min	GP	G	A	Pts	PIM	PP	SH	GW	Min
1990-91	Dubuque	USHL	45	53	44	97	84										8	3	9	12	12				
1991-92	Dubuque	USHL	20	30	19	49	52																		
	Waterloo	USHL	18	19	31	50	54										4	5	6	11	14				
1992-93	U. of Maine	H-East	39	25	26	51	46																		
1993-94	U. of Maine	H-East	4	0	1	1	8																		
	Team USA	Nat-Tm	48	8	34	42	58																		
1994-95	Atlanta Knights	IHL	54	13	14	27	72																		
	Binghamton	AHL	13	6	4	10	38										10	2	3	5	16				
1995-96	**NY Rangers**	**NHL**	**2**	**1**	**0**	**1**	**0**	**1**	**0**	**0**	**4**	**25.0**	**-3**												
	Binghamton	AHL	77	32	67	99	208										4	4	2	6	13				
1996-97	**NY Rangers**	**NHL**	**12**	**1**	**1**	**2**	**6**	**0**	**0**	**0**	**23**	**4.3**	**1**												
	Binghamton	AHL	53	29	34	63	94																		
1997-98	**Pittsburgh**	**NHL**	**46**	**3**	**4**	**7**	**43**	**0**	**0**	**0**	**42**	**7.1**	**-2**												
1998-99	**Edmonton**	**NHL**	**2**	**1**	**0**	**1**	**0**	**0**	**0**	**0**	**1**	**100.0**	**1**	**19**	**52.6**	**8:33**									
	Hamilton	AHL	72	35	41	76	104										11	8	5	13	20				
99-2000	**NY Islanders**	**NHL**	**11**	**1**	**3**	**4**	**8**	**0**	**0**	**0**	**15**	**6.7**	**1**	**92**	**50.0**	**9:30**									
	Providence Bruins	AHL	21	9	9	18	32																		
	Chicago Wolves	IHL	25	7	18	25	40										16	5	8	13	14				
2000-01	Albany River Rats	AHL	74	24	42	66	111																		
2001-02	**Washington**	**NHL**	**1**	**0**	**1**	**1**	**0**	**0**	**0**	**0**	**4**	**0.0**	**0**	**2**	**0.0**	**15:17**									
	Portland Pirates	AHL	2	1	1	2	6																		
2002-03	Portland Pirates	AHL	57	19	32	51	121										3	0	1	1	6				
	NHL Totals		**74**	**7**	**9**	**16**	**57**	**1**	**0**	**0**	**89**	**7.9**		**113**	**49.6**	**9:47**									

Fred Hunt Memorial Trophy (Sportsmanship – AHL) (2003) (co-winner - Eric Healey)

Claimed on waivers by **Pittsburgh** from **NY Rangers**, October 1, 1997. Signed as a free agent by **Edmonton**, August 13, 1998. Signed as a free agent by **NY Islanders**, July 22, 1999. Signed as a free agent by **New Jersey**, July 20, 2000. Traded to **Washington** by **New Jersey** for future considerations, August 22, 2001. • Missed majority of 2001-02 season after being granted personal leave of absence by Washington, October 15, 2001. Signed as a free agent by **Phoenix**, July 17, 2003.

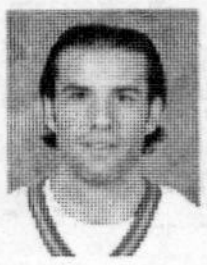

FERRARO, Peter

(fuh-RAHR-oh, PEE-tuhr) **PHX.**

Left wing. Shoots right. 5'10", 180 lbs. Born, Port Jefferson, NY, January 24, 1973. NY Rangers' 1st choice, 24th overall, in 1992 Entry Draft.

Season	Club	League	GP	G	A	Pts	PIM	PP	SH	GW	S	%	+/-	TF	F%	Min	GP	G	A	Pts	PIM	PP	SH	GW	Min
1990-91	Dubuque	USHL	29	21	31	52	83										8	7	5	12	10				
1991-92	Dubuque	USHL	21	25	25	50	92																		
	Waterloo	USHL	21	23	28	51	76										4	8	5	13	16				
1992-93	U. of Maine	H-East	36	18	32	50	106																		
1993-94	U. of Maine	H-East	4	3	6	9	16																		
	Team USA	Nat-Tm	60	30	34	64	87																		
	United States	Olympics	8	6	0	6	6																		
1994-95	Atlanta Knights	IHL	61	15	24	39	118																		
	Binghamton	AHL	12	2	6	8	67										11	4	3	7	51				
1995-96	**NY Rangers**	**NHL**	**5**	**0**	**1**	**1**	**0**	**0**	**0**	**0**	**6**	**0.0**	**-5**												
	Binghamton	AHL	68	48	53	101	157										4	1	6	7	22				
1996-97	**NY Rangers**	**NHL**	**2**	**0**	**0**	**0**	**0**	**0**	**0**	**0**	**3**	**0.0**	**0**				**2**	**0**	**0**	**0**	**0**	**0**	**0**	**0**	
	Binghamton	AHL	75	38	39	77	171										4	3	1	4	18				
1997-98	**Pittsburgh**	**NHL**	**29**	**3**	**4**	**7**	**12**	**0**	**0**	**0**	**34**	**8.8**	**-2**												
	NY Rangers	**NHL**	**1**	**0**	**0**	**0**	**2**	**0**	**0**	**0**	**3**	**0.0**	**-2**												
	Hartford	AHL	36	17	23	40	54										15	8	6	14	59				
1998-99	**Boston**	**NHL**	**46**	**6**	**8**	**14**	**44**	**1**	**0**	**1**	**61**	**9.8**	**10**	**70**	**37.1**	**10:12**									
	Providence Bruins	AHL	16	15	10	25	14										19	9	12	21	38				
99-2000	**Boston**	**NHL**	**5**	**0**	**1**	**1**	**0**	**0**	**0**	**0**	**3**	**0.0**	**-1**	**19**	**47.4**	**8:11**									
	Providence Bruins	AHL	48	21	25	46	98										13	5	7	12	14				
2000-01	Providence Bruins	AHL	78	26	45	71	109										17	4	5	9	34				
2001-02	**Washington**	**NHL**	**4**	**0**	**1**	**1**	**0**	**0**	**0**	**0**	**3**	**0.0**	**-1**	**0**	**0.0**	**12:54**									
	Portland Pirates	AHL	67	21	37	58	119																		
2002-03	Portland Pirates	AHL	59	22	41	63	123										3	0	2	2	16				
	NHL Totals		**92**	**9**	**15**	**24**	**58**	**1**	**0**	**1**	**113**	**8.0**		**89**	**39.3**	**10:13**	**2**	**0**	**0**	**0**	**0**	**0**	**0**	**0**	

AHL First All-Star Team (1996) • Jack A. Butterfield Trophy (Playoff MVP – AHL) (1999)

Claimed on waivers by **Pittsburgh** from **NY Rangers**, October 1, 1997. Claimed on waivers by **NY Rangers** from **Pittsburgh**, January 9, 1998. Signed as a free agent by **Boston**, August 5, 1998. Claimed by **Atlanta** from **Boston** in Expansion Draft, June 25, 1999. Traded to **Boston** by **Atlanta** for Randy Robitaille, June 25, 1999. Signed as a free agent by **Washington**, August 1, 2001. Signed as a free agent by **Phoenix**, July 17, 2003.

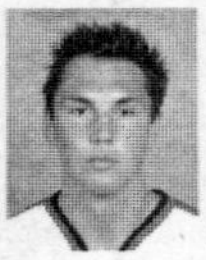

FIBIGER, Jesse

(feh-BEH-gehr, JEH-see) **S.J.**

Defense. Shoots left. 6'3", 210 lbs. Born, Victoria, B.C., April 4, 1978. Anaheim's 5th choice, 178th overall, in 1998 Entry Draft.

Season	Club	League	GP	G	A	Pts	PIM	PP	SH	GW	S	%	+/-	TF	F%	Min	GP	G	A	Pts	PIM	PP	SH	GW	Min
1996-97	Victoria Salsa	BCHL	53	6	18	24	88																		
1997-98	U. Minn-Duluth	WCHA	40	3	6	9	82																		
1998-99	U. Minn-Duluth	WCHA	36	4	16	20	61																		
99-2000	U. Minn-Duluth	WCHA	37	4	6	10	83																		
2000-01	U. Minn-Duluth	WCHA	37	0	8	8	56																		
2001-02	Cleveland Barons	AHL	79	6	12	18	94																		
2002-03	**San Jose**	**NHL**	**16**	**0**	**0**	**0**	**2**	**0**	**0**	**0**	**2**	**0.0**	**-5**	**0**	**0.0**	**6:05**									
	Cleveland Barons	AHL	59	3	11	14	63																		
	NHL Totals		**16**	**0**	**0**	**0**	**2**	**0**	**0**	**0**	**2**	**0.0**		**0**	**0.0**	**6:05**									

Signed as a free agent by **San Jose**, August 15, 2001.

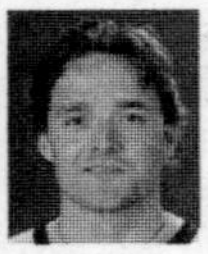

FIDDLER, Vernon

(FIHD-luhr, VUHR-nuhn) **NSH.**

Center. Shoots left. 5'11", 197 lbs. Born, Edmonton, Alta., May 9, 1980.

Season	Club	League	GP	G	A	Pts	PIM	PP	SH	GW	S	%	+/-	TF	F%	Min	GP	G	A	Pts	PIM	PP	SH	GW	Min
1997-98	Kelowna Rockets	WHL	65	10	11	21	31										7	0	1	1	4				
1998-99	Kelowna Rockets	WHL	68	22	21	43	82										6	2	0	2	8				
99-2000	Kelowna Rockets	WHL	64	20	28	48	60										5	1	3	4	4				
2000-01	Kelowna Rockets	WHL	3	0	2	2	0																		
	Medicine Hat	WHL	67	33	38	71	100																		
	Arkansas	ECHL	3	0	1	1	2										5	3	0	3	5				
2001-02	Roanoke Express	ECHL	44	27	28	55	71																		
	Norfolk Admirals	AHL	38	8	5	13	28										4	1	3	4	2				
2002-03	**Nashville**	**NHL**	**19**	**4**	**2**	**6**	**14**	**0**	**0**	**1**	**20**	**20.0**	**2**	**171**	**53.8**	**9:40**									
	Milwaukee	AHL	54	8	16	24	70										6	1	2	3	14				
	NHL Totals		**19**	**4**	**2**	**6**	**14**	**0**	**0**	**1**	**20**	**20.0**		**171**	**53.8**	**9:40**									

ECHL All-Rookie Team (2002)

Signed as a free agent by **Arkansas** (ECHL), March 31, 2001. Traded to **Roanoke** (ECHL) by **Arkansas** (ECHL) for Calvin Elfring, August 11, 2001. Signed as a free agent by **Nashville**, May 6, 2002.

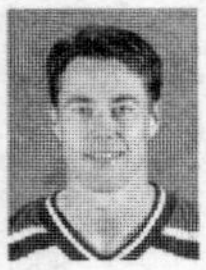

FINLEY, Jeff

(FIHN-lee, JEHF) **ST.L.**

Defense. Shoots left. 6'2", 205 lbs. Born, Edmonton, Alta., April 14, 1967. NY Islanders' 4th choice, 55th overall, in 1985 Entry Draft.

Season	Club	League	GP	G	A	Pts	PIM	PP	SH	GW	S	%	+/-	TF	F%	Min	GP	G	A	Pts	PIM	PP	SH	GW	Min
1983-84	Summerland	BCJHL	49	0	21	21	14																		
	Portland	WHL	5	0	0	0	5										5	0	1	1	4				
1984-85	Portland	WHL	69	6	44	50	57										6	1	2	3	2				
1985-86	Portland	WHL	70	11	59	70	83										15	1	7	8	16				
1986-87	Portland	WHL	72	13	53	66	113										20	1	*21	22	27				
1987-88	**NY Islanders**	**NHL**	**10**	**0**	**5**	**5**	**15**	**0**	**0**	**0**	**9**	**0.0**	**5**				**1**	**0**	**0**	**0**	**2**	**0**	**0**	**0**	
	Springfield	AHL	52	5	18	23	50																		
1988-89	**NY Islanders**	**NHL**	**4**	**0**	**0**	**0**	**6**	**0**	**0**	**0**	**1**	**0.0**	**1**												
	Springfield	AHL	65	3	16	19	55																		
1989-90	**NY Islanders**	**NHL**	**11**	**0**	**1**	**1**	**0**	**0**	**0**	**0**	**7**	**0.0**	**0**				**5**	**0**	**2**	**2**	**2**	**0**	**0**	**0**	
	Springfield	AHL	57	1	15	16	41										13	1	4	5	23				

Season	Club	League	Regular Season														Playoffs								
			GP	G	A	Pts	PIM	PP	SH	GW	S	%	+/-	TF	F%	Min	GP	G	A	Pts	PIM	PP	SH	GW	Min
1990-91	**NY Islanders**	**NHL**	**11**	**0**	**0**	**0**	**4**	**0**	**0**	**0**	**0**	**0.0**	**–1**	....	....	....	....	....	....	....	....	....	....	....	....
	Capital District	AHL	67	10	34	44	34	....	....	....	....	....	....	....	....	....	....	....	....	....	....	....	....	....	....
1991-92	**NY Islanders**	**NHL**	**51**	**1**	**10**	**11**	**26**	**0**	**0**	**0**	**25**	**4.0**	**–6**	....	....	....	....	....	....	....	....	....	....	....	....
	Capital District	AHL	20	1	9	10	6	....	....	....	....	....	....	....	....	....	....	....	....	....	....	....	....	....	....
1992-93	Capital District	AHL	61	6	29	35	34	....	....	....	....	....	....	....	....	....	4	0	1	1	0	....	....	....	....
1993-94	**Philadelphia**	**NHL**	**55**	**1**	**8**	**9**	**24**	**0**	**0**	**0**	**43**	**2.3**	**16**	....	....	....	....	....	....	....	....	....	....	....	....
1994-95	Hershey Bears	AHL	36	2	9	11	33	....	....	....	....	....	....	....	....	....	6	0	1	1	8	....	....	....	....
1995-96	**Winnipeg**	**NHL**	**65**	**1**	**5**	**6**	**81**	**0**	**0**	**0**	**27**	**3.7**	**–2**	....	....	....	**6**	**0**	**0**	**0**	**4**	**0**	**0**	**0**	....
	Springfield	AHL	14	3	12	15	22	....	....	....	....	....	....	....	....	....	....	....	....	....	....	....	....	....	....
1996-97	**Phoenix**	**NHL**	**65**	**3**	**7**	**10**	**40**	**1**	**0**	**1**	**38**	**7.9**	**–8**	....	....	....	**1**	**0**	**0**	**0**	**2**	**0**	**0**	**0**	....
1997-98	**NY Rangers**	**NHL**	**63**	**1**	**6**	**7**	**55**	**0**	**0**	**0**	**32**	**3.1**	**–3**	....	....	....	....	....	....	....	....	....	....	....	....
1998-99	**NY Rangers**	**NHL**	**2**	**0**	**0**	**0**	**0**	**0**	**0**	**0**	**0**	**0.0**	**–1**	**0**	**0.0**	**11:40**	....	....	....	....	....	....	....	....	....
	Hartford	AHL	42	2	10	12	28	....	....	....	....	....	....	....	....	....	....	....	....	....	....	....	....	....	....
	St. Louis	**NHL**	**30**	**1**	**2**	**3**	**20**	**0**	**0**	**0**	**16**	**6.3**	**12**	**0**	**0.0**	**17:36**	**13**	**1**	**2**	**3**	**8**	**0**	**0**	**1**	**20:10**
99-2000	**St. Louis**	**NHL**	**74**	**2**	**8**	**10**	**38**	**0**	**0**	**2**	**31**	**6.5**	**26**	**1**	**100.0**	**17:49**	**7**	**0**	**2**	**2**	**4**	**0**	**0**	**0**	**17:21**
2000-01	**St. Louis**	**NHL**	**72**	**2**	**8**	**10**	**38**	**0**	**0**	**0**	**35**	**5.7**	**7**	**1**	**0.0**	**18:53**	**2**	**0**	**0**	**0**	**0**	**0**	**0**	**0**	**3:24**
2001-02	**St. Louis**	**NHL**	**78**	**0**	**6**	**6**	**30**	**0**	**0**	**0**	**39**	**0.0**	**12**	**0**	**0.0**	**18:31**	**10**	**0**	**0**	**0**	**8**	**0**	**0**	**0**	**18:02**
2002-03	**St. Louis**	**NHL**	**64**	**1**	**3**	**4**	**46**	**0**	**0**	**1**	**30**	**3.3**	**–2**	**0**	**0.0**	**15:37**	**6**	**0**	**0**	**0**	**6**	**0**	**0**	**0**	**15:11**
	NHL Totals		**655**	**13**	**69**	**82**	**423**	**1**	**0**	**4**	**333**	**3.9**		**2**	**50.0**	**17:44**	**51**	**1**	**6**	**7**	**36**	**0**	**0**	**1**	**17:25**

Rights traded to **Ottawa** by **NY Islanders** for Chris Luongo, June 30, 1993. Signed as a free agent by **Philadelphia**, July 30, 1993. Traded to **Winnipeg** by **Philadelphia** for Russ Romaniuk, June 27, 1995. Transferred to **Phoenix** after **Winnipeg** franchise relocated, July 1, 1996. Signed as a free agent by **NY Rangers**, August 18, 1997. Traded to **St. Louis** by **NY Rangers** with Geoff Smith for future considerations (Chris Kenady, February 22, 1999), February 13, 1999.

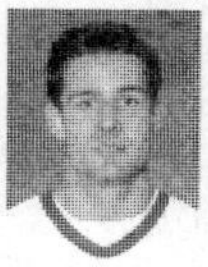

FISCHER, Jiri

(FIH-shuhr, YIH-ree) **DET.**

Defense. Shoots left. 6'5", 225 lbs. Born, Horovice, Czech., July 31, 1980. Detroit's 1st choice, 25th overall, in 1998 Entry Draft.

1995-96	Kladno Jr.	Czech-Jr.	39	6	10	16	....	....	....	....	....	....	....	....	....	....	....	....	....	....	....	....	....	....	....
1996-97	Kladno Jr.	Czech-Jr.	38	7	21	28	....	....	....	....	....	....	....	....	....	....	....	....	....	....	....	....	....	....	....
1997-98	Hull Olympiques	QMJHL	70	3	19	22	112	....	....	....	....	....	....	....	....	....	11	1	4	5	16	....	....	....	....
1998-99	Hull Olympiques	QMJHL	65	22	56	78	141	....	....	....	....	....	....	....	....	....	23	6	17	23	44	....	....	....	....
99-2000	**Detroit**	**NHL**	**52**	**0**	**8**	**8**	**45**	**0**	**0**	**0**	**41**	**0.0**	**1**	**0**	**0.0**	**10:51**	....	....	....	....	....	....	....	....	....
	Cincinnati	AHL	7	0	2	2	10	....	....	....	....	....	....	....	....	....	....	....	....	....	....	....	....	....	....
2000-01	**Detroit**	**NHL**	**55**	**1**	**8**	**9**	**59**	**0**	**0**	**0**	**64**	**1.6**	**3**	**0**	**0.0**	**16:46**	**5**	**0**	**0**	**0**	**9**	**0**	**0**	**0**	**16:25**
	Cincinnati	AHL	18	2	6	8	22	....	....	....	....	....	....	....	....	....	....	....	....	....	....	....	....	....	....
2001-02♦	**Detroit**	**NHL**	**80**	**2**	**8**	**10**	**67**	**0**	**0**	**1**	**103**	**1.9**	**17**	**0**	**0.0**	**17:10**	**22**	**3**	**3**	**6**	**30**	**0**	**0**	**1**	**19:41**
2002-03	**Detroit**	**NHL**	**15**	**1**	**5**	**6**	**16**	**0**	**0**	**0**	**19**	**5.3**	**0**	**0**	**0.0**	**21:24**	....	....	....	....	....	....	....	....	....
	NHL Totals		**202**	**4**	**29**	**33**	**187**	**0**	**0**	**1**	**227**	**1.8**		**0**	**0.0**	**15:45**	**27**	**3**	**3**	**6**	**39**	**0**	**0**	**1**	**19:05**

QMJHL First All-Star Team (1999)

• Missed majority of 2002-03 season recovering from knee injury suffered in game vs. Nashville, November 12, 2002.

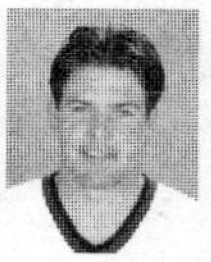

FISHER, Mike

(FIH-shuhr, MIGHK) **OTT.**

Center. Shoots right. 6'1", 200 lbs. Born, Peterborough, Ont., June 5, 1980. Ottawa's 2nd choice, 44th overall, in 1998 Entry Draft.

1996-97	Peterborough	OPJHL	51	26	30	56	35	....	....	....	....	....	....	....	....	....	....	....	....	....	....	....	....	....	....
1997-98	Sudbury Wolves	OHL	66	24	25	49	65	....	....	....	....	....	....	....	....	....	9	2	2	4	13	....	....	....	....
1998-99	Sudbury Wolves	OHL	68	41	65	106	55	....	....	....	....	....	....	....	....	....	4	2	1	3	4	....	....	....	....
99-2000	**Ottawa**	**NHL**	**32**	**4**	**5**	**9**	**15**	**0**	**0**	**1**	**49**	**8.2**	**–6**	**356**	**47.8**	**12:57**	....	....	....	....	....	....	....	....	....
2000-01	**Ottawa**	**NHL**	**60**	**7**	**12**	**19**	**46**	**0**	**0**	**3**	**83**	**8.4**	**–1**	**709**	**50.2**	**11:38**	**4**	**0**	**1**	**1**	**4**	**0**	**0**	**0**	**13:41**
2001-02	**Ottawa**	**NHL**	**58**	**15**	**9**	**24**	**55**	**0**	**3**	**4**	**123**	**12.2**	**8**	**848**	**48.7**	**14:05**	**10**	**2**	**1**	**3**	**0**	**0**	**0**	**0**	**16:17**
2002-03	**Ottawa**	**NHL**	**74**	**18**	**20**	**38**	**54**	**5**	**1**	**3**	**142**	**12.7**	**13**	**1077**	**48.1**	**15:59**	**18**	**2**	**2**	**4**	**16**	**0**	**1**	**1**	**16:58**
	NHL Totals		**224**	**44**	**46**	**90**	**170**	**5**	**4**	**11**	**397**	**11.1**		**2990**	**48.7**	**13:54**	**32**	**4**	**4**	**8**	**20**	**0**	**1**	**1**	**16:20**

• Missed majority of 1999-2000 season recovering from knee injury suffered in game vs. Boston, December 30, 1999.

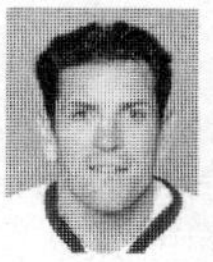

FITZGERALD, Tom

(FIHTZ-jair-uhld, TAWM) **TOR.**

Right wing. Shoots right. 6', 190 lbs. Born, Billerica, MA, August 28, 1968. NY Islanders' 1st choice, 17th overall, in 1986 Entry Draft.

1984-85	Austin Mustangs	Hi-School	18	20	21	41	....	....	....	....	....	....	....	....	....	....	....	....	....	....	....	....	....	....	....
1985-86	Austin Mustangs	Hi-School	24	35	38	73	....	....	....	....	....	....	....	....	....	....	....	....	....	....	....	....	....	....	....
1986-87	Providence	H-East	27	8	14	22	22	....	....	....	....	....	....	....	....	....	....	....	....	....	....	....	....	....	....
1987-88	Providence	H-East	36	19	15	34	50	....	....	....	....	....	....	....	....	....	....	....	....	....	....	....	....	....	....
1988-89	**NY Islanders**	**NHL**	**23**	**3**	**5**	**8**	**10**	**0**	**0**	**1**	**24**	**12.5**	**1**	....	....	....	....	....	....	....	....	....	....	....	....
	Springfield	AHL	61	24	18	42	43	....	....	....	....	....	....	....	....	....	....	....	....	....	....	....	....	....	....
1989-90	**NY Islanders**	**NHL**	**19**	**2**	**5**	**7**	**4**	**0**	**0**	**1**	**24**	**8.3**	**–3**	....	....	....	**4**	**1**	**0**	**1**	**4**	**0**	**0**	**0**	....
	Springfield	AHL	53	30	23	53	32	....	....	....	....	....	....	....	....	....	14	2	9	11	13	....	....	....	....
1990-91	**NY Islanders**	**NHL**	**41**	**5**	**5**	**10**	**24**	**0**	**0**	**2**	**60**	**8.3**	**–9**	....	....	....	....	....	....	....	....	....	....	....	....
	Capital District	AHL	27	7	7	14	50	....	....	....	....	....	....	....	....	....	....	....	....	....	....	....	....	....	....
1991-92	**NY Islanders**	**NHL**	**45**	**6**	**11**	**17**	**28**	**0**	**2**	**2**	**71**	**8.5**	**–3**	....	....	....	....	....	....	....	....	....	....	....	....
	Capital District	AHL	4	1	1	2	4	....	....	....	....	....	....	....	....	....	....	....	....	....	....	....	....	....	....
1992-93	**NY Islanders**	**NHL**	**77**	**9**	**18**	**27**	**34**	**0**	**3**	**1**	**83**	**10.8**	**–2**	....	....	....	**18**	**2**	**5**	**7**	**18**	**0**	**0**	**0**	....
1993-94	**Florida**	**NHL**	**83**	**18**	**14**	**32**	**54**	**0**	**3**	**1**	**144**	**12.5**	**–3**	....	....	....	....	....	....	....	....	....	....	....	....
1994-95	**Florida**	**NHL**	**48**	**3**	**13**	**16**	**31**	**0**	**0**	**0**	**78**	**3.8**	**–3**	....	....	....	....	....	....	....	....	....	....	....	....
1995-96	**Florida**	**NHL**	**82**	**13**	**21**	**34**	**75**	**1**	**6**	**2**	**141**	**9.2**	**–3**	....	....	....	**22**	**4**	**4**	**8**	**34**	**0**	**0**	**2**	....
1996-97	**Florida**	**NHL**	**71**	**10**	**14**	**24**	**64**	**0**	**2**	**1**	**135**	**7.4**	**7**	....	....	....	**5**	**0**	**1**	**1**	**0**	**0**	**0**	**0**	....
1997-98	**Florida**	**NHL**	**69**	**10**	**5**	**15**	**57**	**0**	**1**	**1**	**105**	**9.5**	**–4**	....	....	....	....	....	....	....	....	....	....	....	....
	Colorado	**NHL**	**11**	**2**	**1**	**3**	**22**	**0**	**1**	**0**	**14**	**14.3**	**0**	....	....	....	**7**	**0**	**1**	**1**	**20**	**0**	**0**	**0**	....
1998-99	**Nashville**	**NHL**	**80**	**13**	**19**	**32**	**48**	**0**	**0**	**1**	**180**	**7.2**	**–18**	**155**	**52.3**	**17:17**	....	....	....	....	....	....	....	....	....
99-2000	**Nashville**	**NHL**	**82**	**13**	**9**	**22**	**66**	**0**	**3**	**1**	**119**	**10.9**	**–18**	**264**	**51.9**	**13:57**	....	....	....	....	....	....	....	....	....
2000-01	**Nashville**	**NHL**	**82**	**9**	**9**	**18**	**71**	**0**	**2**	**2**	**135**	**6.7**	**–5**	**458**	**54.6**	**14:58**	....	....	....	....	....	....	....	....	....
2001-02	**Nashville**	**NHL**	**63**	**7**	**9**	**16**	**33**	**0**	**1**	**0**	**101**	**6.9**	**–4**	**525**	**48.4**	**14:15**	....	....	....	....	....	....	....	....	....
	Chicago	**NHL**	**15**	**1**	**3**	**4**	**6**	**0**	**1**	**0**	**24**	**4.2**	**–3**	**110**	**50.0**	**16:16**	**5**	**0**	**0**	**0**	**4**	**0**	**0**	**0**	**15:15**
2002-03	**Toronto**	**NHL**	**66**	**4**	**13**	**17**	**57**	**0**	**0**	**0**	**89**	**4.5**	**10**	**90**	**50.0**	**12:07**	**7**	**0**	**1**	**1**	**4**	**0**	**0**	**0**	**18:11**
	NHL Totals		**957**	**128**	**174**	**302**	**684**	**1**	**25**	**16**	**1527**	**8.4**		**1602**	**51.3**	**14:41**	**68**	**7**	**12**	**19**	**84**	**0**	**0**	**2**	**16:58**

Claimed by **Florida** from **NY Islanders** in Expansion Draft, June 24, 1993. Traded to **Colorado** by **Florida** for the rights to Mark Parrish and Anaheim's 3rd round choice (previously acquired, Florida selected Lance Ward) in 1998 Entry Draft, March 24, 1998. Signed as a free agent by **Nashville**, July 6, 1998. Traded to **Chicago** by **Nashville** for Chicago's 4th round choice (later traded to Anaheim – Anaheim selected Nathan Saunders) in 2003 Entry Draft and future considerations, March 13, 2002. Signed as a free agent by **Toronto**, July 17, 2002.

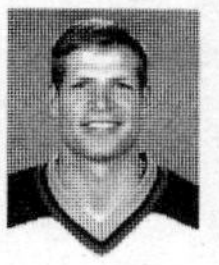

FITZPATRICK, Rory

(fitz-PA-trihk, ROHR-ee) **BUF.**

Defense. Shoots right. 6'2", 215 lbs. Born, Rochester, NY, January 11, 1975. Montreal's 2nd choice, 47th overall, in 1993 Entry Draft.

1990-91	Rochester	NAJHL	40	0	5	5	....	....	....	....	....	....	....	....	....	....	....	....	....	....	....	....	....	....	....
1991-92	Rochester	NAJHL	28	8	28	36	141	....	....	....	....	....	....	....	....	....	....	....	....	....	....	....	....	....	....
1992-93	Sudbury Wolves	OHL	58	4	20	24	68	....	....	....	....	....	....	....	....	....	14	0	0	0	17	....	....	....	....
1993-94	Sudbury Wolves	OHL	65	12	34	46	112	....	....	....	....	....	....	....	....	....	10	2	5	7	10	....	....	....	....
1994-95	Sudbury Wolves	OHL	56	12	36	48	72	....	....	....	....	....	....	....	....	....	18	3	15	18	21	....	....	....	....
	Fredericton	AHL	....	....	....	....	....	....	....	....	....	....	....	....	....	....	10	1	2	3	5	....	....	....	....
1995-96	**Montreal**	**NHL**	**42**	**0**	**2**	**2**	**18**	**0**	**0**	**0**	**31**	**0.0**	**–7**	....	....	....	**6**	**1**	**1**	**2**	**0**	**0**	**0**	**0**	....
	Fredericton	AHL	18	4	6	10	36	....	....	....	....	....	....	....	....	....	....	....	....	....	....	....	....	....	....
1996-97	**Montreal**	**NHL**	**6**	**0**	**1**	**1**	**6**	**0**	**0**	**0**	**5**	**0.0**	**–2**	....	....	....	....	....	....	....	....	....	....	....	....
	St. Louis	**NHL**	**2**	**0**	**0**	**0**	**2**	**0**	**0**	**0**	**1**	**0.0**	**–2**	....	....	....	....	....	....	....	....	....	....	....	....
	Worcester IceCats	AHL	49	4	13	17	78	....	....	....	....	....	....	....	....	....	5	1	2	3	0	....	....	....	....
1997-98	Worcester IceCats	AHL	62	8	22	30	111	....	....	....	....	....	....	....	....	....	11	0	3	3	26	....	....	....	....
1998-99	**St. Louis**	**NHL**	**1**	**0**	**0**	**0**	**2**	**0**	**0**	**0**	**0**	**0.0**	**–3**	**0**	**0.0**	**4:49**	....	....	....	....	....	....	....	....	....
	Worcester IceCats	AHL	53	5	16	21	82	....	....	....	....	....	....	....	....	....	4	0	1	1	17	....	....	....	....
99-2000	Worcester IceCats	AHL	28	0	5	5	48	....	....	....	....	....	....	....	....	....	....	....	....	....	....	....	....	....	....
	Milwaukee	IHL	27	2	1	3	27	....	....	....	....	....	....	....	....	....	3	0	2	2	2	....	....	....	....
2000-01	**Nashville**	**NHL**	**2**	**0**	**0**	**0**	**2**	**0**	**0**	**0**	**0**	**0.0**	**–2**	**0**	**0.0**	**9:47**	....	....	....	....	....	....	....	....	....
	Milwaukee	IHL	22	0	2	2	32	....	....	....	....	....	....	....	....	....	....	....	....	....	....	....	....	....	....
	Hamilton	AHL	34	3	17	20	29	....	....	....	....	....	....	....	....	....	....	....	....	....	....	....	....	....	....
2001-02	**Buffalo**	**NHL**	**5**	**0**	**0**	**0**	**4**	**0**	**0**	**0**	**2**	**0.0**	**–2**	**0**	**0.0**	**11:54**	....	....	....	....	....	....	....	....	....
	Rochester	AHL	60	4	8	12	83	....	....	....	....	....	....	....	....	....	2	0	1	1	0	....	....	....	....

			Regular Season														Playoffs								
Season	Club	League	GP	G	A	Pts	PIM	PP	SH	GW	S	%	+/-	TF	F%	Min	GP	G	A	Pts	PIM	PP	SH	GW	Min
2002-03	**Buffalo**	**NHL**	**36**	**1**	**3**	**4**	**16**	**0**	**0**	**0**	**29**	**3.4**	**–7**	**0**	**0.0**	**17:02**	....	....	....	....	....	....	....	....	....
	Rochester	AHL	41	5	11	16	65	....	....	....	....	....	....	....	....	....	....	....	....	....	....	....	....	....	....
	NHL Totals		**94**	**1**	**6**	**7**	**50**	**0**	**0**	**0**	**68**	**1.5**		**0**	**0.0**	**15:50**	**6**	**1**	**1**	**2**	**0**	**0**	**0**	**0**	....

OHL All-Rookie Team (1993)

Traded to **St. Louis** by **Montreal** with Pierre Turgeon and Craig Conroy for Murray Baron, Shayne Corson and St. Louis' 5th round choice (Gennady Razin) in 1997 Entry Draft, October 29, 1996. Claimed by **Boston** from **St. Louis** in Waiver Draft, October 5, 1998. Claimed on waivers by **St. Louis** from **Boston**, October 7, 1998. Traded to **Nashville** by **St. Louis** for Dan Keczmer, February 9, 2000. Traded to **Edmonton** by **Nashville** for future considerations, January 12, 2001. Signed as a free agent by **Buffalo**, August 14, 2001.

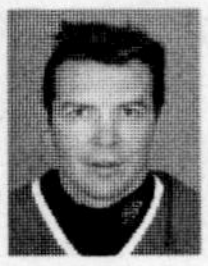

FLEURY, Theoren

(FLUH-ree, THAIR-ihn) **CHI.**

Right wing. Shoots right. 5'6", 182 lbs. Born, Oxbow, Sask., June 29, 1968. Calgary's 9th choice, 166th overall, in 1987 Entry Draft.

Season	Club	League	GP	G	A	Pts	PIM	PP	SH	GW	S	%	+/-	TF	F%	Min	GP	G	A	Pts	PIM	PP	SH	GW	Min
1983-84	St. James	MJHL	22	33	31	64	88	....	....	....	....	....	....	....	....	....	....	....	....	....	....	....	....	....	....
1984-85	Moose Jaw	WHL	71	29	46	75	82	....	....	....	....	....	....	....	....	....	....	....	....	....	....	....	....	....	....
1985-86	Moose Jaw	WHL	72	43	65	108	124	....	....	....	....	....	....	....	....	....	13	7	13	20	16	....	....	....	....
1986-87	Moose Jaw	WHL	66	61	68	129	110	....	....	....	....	....	....	....	....	....	9	7	9	16	34	....	....	....	....
1987-88	Moose Jaw	WHL	65	68	92	*160	235	....	....	....	....	....	....	....	....	....	....	....	....	....	....	....	....	....	....
	Salt Lake	IHL	2	3	4	7	7	....	....	....	....	....	....	....	....	....	8	11	5	16	16	....	....	....	....
1988-89♦	**Calgary**	**NHL**	**36**	**14**	**20**	**34**	**46**	**5**	**0**	**3**	**89**	**15.7**	**5**	....	....	....	**22**	**5**	**6**	**11**	**24**	**3**	**0**	**3**	....
	Salt Lake	IHL	40	37	37	74	81	....	....	....	....	....	....	....	....	....	....	....	....	....	....	....	....	....	....
1989-90	**Calgary**	**NHL**	**80**	**31**	**35**	**66**	**157**	**9**	**3**	**6**	**200**	**15.5**	**22**	....	....	....	**6**	**2**	**3**	**5**	**10**	**0**	**0**	**0**	....
1990-91	**Calgary**	**NHL**	**79**	**51**	**53**	**104**	**136**	**9**	**7**	**9**	**249**	**20.5**	**48**	....	....	....	**7**	**2**	**5**	**7**	**14**	**0**	**0**	**1**	....
1991-92	**Calgary**	**NHL**	**80**	**33**	**40**	**73**	**133**	**11**	**1**	**6**	**225**	**14.7**	**0**	....	....	....	....	....	....	....	....	....	....	....	....
1992-93	**Calgary**	**NHL**	**83**	**34**	**66**	**100**	**88**	**12**	**2**	**4**	**250**	**13.6**	**14**	....	....	....	**6**	**5**	**7**	**12**	**27**	**3**	**1**	**0**	....
1993-94	**Calgary**	**NHL**	**83**	**40**	**45**	**85**	**186**	**16**	**1**	**6**	**278**	**14.4**	**30**	....	....	....	**7**	**6**	**4**	**10**	**5**	**1**	**0**	**2**	....
1994-95	Tappara Tampere	Finland	10	8	9	17	22	....	....	....	....	....	....	....	....	....	....	....	....	....	....	....	....	....	....
	Calgary	**NHL**	**47**	**29**	**29**	**58**	**112**	**9**	**2**	**5**	**173**	**16.8**	**6**	....	....	....	**7**	**7**	**7**	**14**	**2**	**2**	**1**	**0**	....
1995-96	**Calgary**	**NHL**	**80**	**46**	**50**	**96**	**112**	**17**	**5**	**4**	**353**	**13.0**	**17**	....	....	....	**4**	**2**	**1**	**3**	**14**	**0**	**0**	**0**	....
1996-97	**Calgary**	**NHL**	**81**	**29**	**38**	**67**	**104**	**9**	**2**	**3**	**336**	**8.6**	**–12**	....	....	....	....	....	....	....	....	....	....	....	....
1997-98	**Calgary**	**NHL**	**82**	**27**	**51**	**78**	**197**	**3**	**2**	**4**	**282**	**9.6**	**0**	....	....	....	....	....	....	....	....	....	....	....	....
	Canada	Olympics	6	1	3	4	2	....	....	....	....	....	....	....	....	....	....	....	....	....	....	....	....	....	....
1998-99	**Calgary**	**NHL**	**60**	**30**	**39**	**69**	**68**	**7**	**3**	**3**	**250**	**12.0**	**18**	**517**	**59.2**	**23:33**	....	....	....	....	....	....	....	....	....
	Colorado	**NHL**	**15**	**10**	**14**	**24**	**18**	**1**	**0**	**2**	**51**	**19.6**	**8**	**150**	**58.7**	**22:33**	**18**	**5**	**12**	**17**	**20**	**2**	**0**	**0**	**22:17**
99-2000	**NY Rangers**	**NHL**	**80**	**15**	**49**	**64**	**68**	**1**	**0**	**1**	**246**	**6.1**	**–4**	**490**	**56.5**	**19:41**	....	....	....	....	....	....	....	....	....
2000-01	**NY Rangers**	**NHL**	**62**	**30**	**44**	**74**	**122**	**8**	**7**	**3**	**238**	**12.6**	**0**	**139**	**47.5**	**21:47**	....	....	....	....	....	....	....	....	....
2001-02	**NY Rangers**	**NHL**	**82**	**24**	**39**	**63**	**216**	**7**	**0**	**5**	**267**	**9.0**	**0**	**170**	**47.7**	**20:48**	....	....	....	....	....	....	....	....	....
	Canada	Olympics	6	0	2	2	6	....	....	....	....	....	....	....	....	....	....	....	....	....	....	....	....	....	....
2002-03	**Chicago**	**NHL**	**54**	**12**	**21**	**33**	**77**	**1**	**0**	**3**	**124**	**9.7**	**–7**	**346**	**53.8**	**16:45**	....	....	....	....	....	....	....	....	....
	NHL Totals		**1084**	**455**	**633**	**1088**	**1840**	**125**	**35**	**67**	**3611**	**12.6**		**1812**	**55.4**	**20:39**	**77**	**34**	**45**	**79**	**116**	**11**	**2**	**6**	**22:17**

WHL East First All-Star Team (1987) • WHL East Second All-Star Team (1988) • Shared Alka-Seltzer Plus Award with Marty McSorley (1991) • NHL Second All-Star Team (1995)

Played in NHL All-Star Game (1991, 1992, 1996, 1997, 1998, 1999, 2001)

Traded to **Colorado** by **Calgary** with Chris Dingman for Rene Corbet, Wade Belak, Robyn Regehr and Colorado's 2nd round compensatory choice (Jarret Stoll) in 2000 Entry Draft, February 28, 1999. Signed as a free agent by **NY Rangers**, July 8, 1999. Traded to **San Jose** by **NY Rangers** to complete transaction that sent San Jose's 6th round choice (Kim Hirschovits) in 2002 Entry Draft for NY Rangers' 6th round choice in 2003 Entry Draft (June 23, 2002), June 26, 2002. Signed as a free agent by **Chicago**, August 15, 2002. • Suspended indefinitely by NHL for violating terms of his substance abuse aftercare program, October 8, 2002. • Reinstated by NHL and cleared to return to active duty, December 5, 2002. • Suspended indefinitely by NHL for violating terms of his substance abuse aftercare program, April 11, 2003.

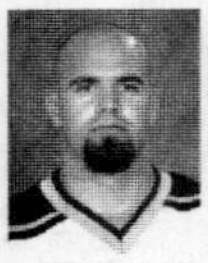

FLINN, Ryan

(FLIHN, RIGH-yan) **L.A.**

Left wing. Shoots left. 6'5", 248 lbs. Born, Halifax, N.S., April 20, 1980. New Jersey's 8th choice, 143rd overall, in 1998 Entry Draft.

Season	Club	League	GP	G	A	Pts	PIM	PP	SH	GW	S	%	+/-	TF	F%	Min	GP	G	A	Pts	PIM	PP	SH	GW	Min
1996-97	Laval Titan	QMJHL	23	3	2	5	56	....	....	....	....	....	....	....	....	....	2	0	0	0	0	....	....	....	....
1997-98	Laval Titan	QMJHL	59	4	12	16	217	....	....	....	....	....	....	....	....	....	15	1	0	1	63	....	....	....	....
1998-99	Acadie-Bathurst	QMJHL	44	3	4	7	195	....	....	....	....	....	....	....	....	....	23	2	0	2	37	....	....	....	....
99-2000	Halifax	QMJHL	67	14	19	33	365	....	....	....	....	....	....	....	....	....	....	....	....	....	....	....	....	....	....
2000-01	Cape Breton	QMJHL	57	16	17	33	280	....	....	....	....	....	....	....	....	....	9	1	1	2	43	....	....	....	....
2001-02	Reading Royals	ECHL	20	1	3	4	130	....	....	....	....	....	....	....	....	....	....	....	....	....	....	....	....	....	....
	Los Angeles	**NHL**	**10**	**0**	**0**	**0**	**51**	**0**	**0**	**0**	**2**	**0.0**	**0**	**0**	**0.0**	**3:29**	....	....	....	....	....	....	....	....	....
	Manchester	AHL	37	0	1	1	113	....	....	....	....	....	....	....	....	....	1	0	0	0	0	....	....	....	....
2002-03	**Los Angeles**	**NHL**	**19**	**1**	**0**	**1**	**28**	**0**	**0**	**0**	**13**	**7.7**	**0**	**0**	**0.0**	**5:28**	....	....	....	....	....	....	....	....	....
	Manchester	AHL	27	2	2	4	95	....	....	....	....	....	....	....	....	....	....	....	....	....	....	....	....	....	....
	NHL Totals		**29**	**1**	**0**	**1**	**79**	**0**	**0**	**0**	**15**	**6.7**		**0**	**0.0**	**4:47**	....	....	....	....	....	....	....	....	....

Signed as a free agent by **Los Angeles**, January 8, 2002.

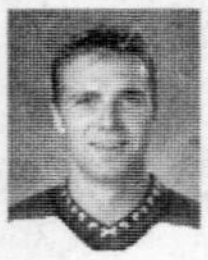

FOCHT, Dan

(FOHKT, DAN) **PIT.**

Defense. Shoots left. 6'6", 234 lbs. Born, Regina, Sask., December 31, 1977. Phoenix's 1st choice, 11th overall, in 1996 Entry Draft.

Season	Club	League	GP	G	A	Pts	PIM	PP	SH	GW	S	%	+/-	TF	F%	Min	GP	G	A	Pts	PIM	PP	SH	GW	Min
1994-95	Saskatoon Blazers	SMHL	33	6	12	18	98	....	....	....	....	....	....	....	....	....	....	....	....	....	....	....	....	....	....
1995-96	Tri-City	WHL	63	6	12	18	161	....	....	....	....	....	....	....	....	....	11	1	1	2	23	....	....	....	....
1996-97	Tri-City	WHL	28	0	5	5	92	....	....	....	....	....	....	....	....	....	....	....	....	....	....	....	....	....	....
	Regina Pats	WHL	22	2	2	4	59	....	....	....	....	....	....	....	....	....	5	0	2	2	8	....	....	....	....
	Springfield	AHL	1	0	0	0	2	....	....	....	....	....	....	....	....	....	....	....	....	....	....	....	....	....	....
1997-98	Springfield	AHL	61	2	5	7	125	....	....	....	....	....	....	....	....	....	3	0	0	0	4	....	....	....	....
1998-99	Mississippi	ECHL	2	0	0	0	6	....	....	....	....	....	....	....	....	....	....	....	....	....	....	....	....	....	....
	Springfield	AHL	30	0	2	2	58	....	....	....	....	....	....	....	....	....	3	1	0	1	10	....	....	....	....
99-2000	Jokerit Helsinki	Finland	2	0	0	0	0	....	....	....	....	....	....	....	....	....	....	....	....	....	....	....	....	....	....
	Mississippi	ECHL	4	0	1	1	0	....	....	....	....	....	....	....	....	....	....	....	....	....	....	....	....	....	....
	Springfield	AHL	44	2	9	11	86	....	....	....	....	....	....	....	....	....	5	0	1	1	2	....	....	....	....
2000-01	Springfield	AHL	69	0	6	6	156	....	....	....	....	....	....	....	....	....	....	....	....	....	....	....	....	....	....
2001-02	**Phoenix**	**NHL**	**8**	**0**	**0**	**0**	**11**	**0**	**0**	**0**	**5**	**0.0**	**0**	**0**	**0.0**	**12:25**	**1**	**0**	**1**	**1**	**0**	**0**	**0**	**0**	**8:20**
	Springfield	AHL	56	2	8	10	134	....	....	....	....	....	....	....	....	....	....	....	....	....	....	....	....	....	....
2002-03	**Phoenix**	**NHL**	**10**	**0**	**0**	**0**	**10**	**0**	**0**	**0**	**1**	**0.0**	**–2**	**0**	**0.0**	**8:40**	....	....	....	....	....	....	....	....	....
	Springfield	AHL	37	2	7	9	80	....	....	....	....	....	....	....	....	....	....	....	....	....	....	....	....	....	....
	Pittsburgh	**NHL**	**12**	**0**	**3**	**3**	**19**	**0**	**0**	**0**	**11**	**0.0**	**–7**	**1**	**0.0**	**18:14**	....	....	....	....	....	....	....	....	....
	NHL Totals		**30**	**0**	**3**	**3**	**40**	**0**	**0**	**0**	**17**	**0.0**		**1**	**0.0**	**13:29**	**1**	**0**	**1**	**1**	**0**	**0**	**0**	**0**	**8:20**

Traded to **Pittsburgh** by **Phoenix** with Ramzi Abid and Guillaume Lefebvre for Jan Hrdina and Francois Leroux, March 11, 2003.

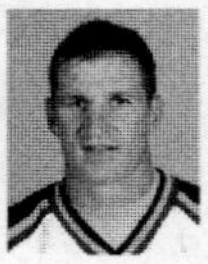

FOOTE, Adam

(FUT, A-duhm) **COL.**

Defense. Shoots right. 6'2", 215 lbs. Born, Toronto, Ont., July 10, 1971. Quebec's 2nd choice, 22nd overall, in 1989 Entry Draft.

Season	Club	League	GP	G	A	Pts	PIM	PP	SH	GW	S	%	+/-	TF	F%	Min	GP	G	A	Pts	PIM	PP	SH	GW	Min
1987-88	Whitby Midgets	OMHA	65	25	43	68	108	....	....	....	....	....	....	....	....	....	....	....	....	....	....	....	....	....	....
1988-89	Sault Ste. Marie	OHL	66	7	32	39	120	....	....	....	....	....	....	....	....	....	....	....	....	....	....	....	....	....	....
1989-90	Sault Ste. Marie	OHL	61	12	43	55	199	....	....	....	....	....	....	....	....	....	....	....	....	....	....	....	....	....	....
1990-91	Sault Ste. Marie	OHL	59	18	51	69	93	....	....	....	....	....	....	....	....	....	14	5	12	17	28	....	....	....	....
1991-92	**Quebec**	**NHL**	**46**	**2**	**5**	**7**	**44**	**0**	**0**	**0**	**55**	**3.6**	**–4**	....	....	....	....	....	....	....	....	....	....	....	....
	Halifax Citadels	AHL	6	0	1	1	2	....	....	....	....	....	....	....	....	....	....	....	....	....	....	....	....	....	....
1992-93	**Quebec**	**NHL**	**81**	**4**	**12**	**16**	**168**	**0**	**1**	**0**	**54**	**7.4**	**6**	....	....	....	**6**	**0**	**1**	**1**	**2**	**0**	**0**	**0**	....
1993-94	**Quebec**	**NHL**	**45**	**2**	**6**	**8**	**67**	**0**	**0**	**0**	**42**	**4.8**	**3**	....	....	....	....	....	....	....	....	....	....	....	....
1994-95	**Quebec**	**NHL**	**35**	**0**	**7**	**7**	**52**	**0**	**0**	**0**	**24**	**0.0**	**17**	....	....	....	**6**	**0**	**1**	**1**	**14**	**0**	**0**	**0**	....
1995-96♦	**Colorado**	**NHL**	**73**	**5**	**11**	**16**	**88**	**1**	**0**	**1**	**49**	**10.2**	**27**	....	....	....	**22**	**1**	**3**	**4**	**36**	**0**	**0**	**0**	....
1996-97	**Colorado**	**NHL**	**78**	**2**	**19**	**21**	**135**	**0**	**0**	**0**	**60**	**3.3**	**16**	....	....	....	**17**	**0**	**4**	**4**	**62**	**0**	**0**	**0**	....
1997-98	**Colorado**	**NHL**	**77**	**3**	**14**	**17**	**124**	**0**	**0**	**1**	**64**	**4.7**	**–3**	....	....	....	**7**	**0**	**0**	**0**	**23**	**0**	**0**	**0**	....
	Canada	Olympics	6	0	1	1	4	....	....	....	....	....	....	....	....	....	....	....	....	....	....	....	....	....	....
1998-99	**Colorado**	**NHL**	**64**	**5**	**16**	**21**	**92**	**3**	**0**	**0**	**83**	**6.0**	**20**	**0**	**0.0**	**24:50**	**19**	**2**	**3**	**5**	**24**	**1**	**0**	**0**	**28:34**
99-2000	**Colorado**	**NHL**	**59**	**5**	**13**	**18**	**98**	**1**	**0**	**2**	**63**	**7.9**	**5**	**0**	**0.0**	**25:51**	**16**	**0**	**7**	**7**	**28**	**0**	**0**	**0**	**26:05**
2000-01♦	**Colorado**	**NHL**	**35**	**3**	**12**	**15**	**42**	**1**	**1**	**1**	**59**	**5.1**	**6**	**0**	**0.0**	**25:22**	**23**	**3**	**4**	**7**	***47**	**1**	**0**	**1**	**28:22**

Season	Club	League	Regular Season GP	G	A	Pts	PIM	PP	SH	GW	S	%	+/-	TF	F%	Min	Playoffs GP	G	A	Pts	PIM	PP	SH	GW	Min
2001-02	Colorado	NHL	55	5	22	27	55	1	1	0	85	5.9	7	0	0.0	25:59	21	1	6	7	28	0	0	0	27:46
	Canada	Olympics	6	1	0	1	2	....	....	....	....	....	....	....	....	....	....	....	....	....	....	....	....	....	....
2002-03	Colorado	NHL	78	11	20	31	88	3	0	2	106	10.4	30	0	0.0	25:43	6	0	1	1	8	0	0	0	24:12
	NHL Totals		726	47	157	204	1053	10	3	7	744	6.3		0	0.0	25:33	143	7	30	37	272	2	0	1	27:32

OHL First All-Star Team (1991)

Transferred to **Colorado** after **Quebec** franchise relocated, June 21, 1995. • Missed majority of 2000-01 season recovering from shoulder injury suffered in game vs. Carolina, January 6, 2001.

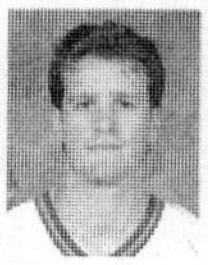

FORBES, Colin
(FOHRBS, COHL-ihn)

Center. Shoots left. 6'3", 205 lbs. Born, New Westminster, B.C., February 16, 1976. Philadelphia's 5th choice, 166th overall, in 1994 Entry Draft.

Season	Club	League	GP	G	A	Pts	PIM	PP	SH	GW	S	%	+/-	TF	F%	Min	GP	G	A	Pts	PIM	PP	SH	GW	Min
1993-94	Sherwood Park	AJHL	47	18	22	40	76	....	....	....	....	....	....	....	....	....	....	....	....	....	....	....	....	....	....
1994-95	Portland	WHL	72	24	31	55	108	....	....	....	....	....	....	....	....	....	9	1	3	4	10	....	....	....	....
1995-96	Portland	WHL	72	33	44	77	137	....	....	....	....	....	....	....	....	....	7	2	5	7	14	....	....	....	....
	Hershey Bears	AHL	2	1	0	1	2	....	....	....	....	....	....	....	....	....	4	0	2	2	2	....	....	....	....
1996-97	Philadelphia	NHL	3	1	0	1	0	0	0	0	3	33.3	0	....	....	....	3	0	0	0	0	0	0	0	....
	Philadelphia	AHL	74	21	28	49	108	....	....	....	....	....	....	....	....	....	10	5	5	10	33	....	....	....	....
1997-98	Philadelphia	NHL	63	12	7	19	59	2	0	2	93	12.9	2	....	....	....	5	0	0	0	2	0	0	0	....
	Philadelphia	AHL	13	7	4	11	22	....	....	....	....	....	....	....	....	....	....	....	....	....	....	....	....	....	....
1998-99	Philadelphia	NHL	66	9	7	16	51	0	0	4	92	9.8	0	2	50.0	12:35	....	....	....	....	....	....	....	....	....
	Tampa Bay	NHL	14	3	1	4	10	0	1	0	25	12.0	–5	0	0.0	17:30	....	....	....	....	....	....	....	....	....
99-2000	Tampa Bay	NHL	8	0	0	0	18	0	0	0	3	0.0	–4	1	0.0	8:53	....	....	....	....	....	....	....	....	....
	Ottawa	NHL	45	2	5	7	12	0	0	0	54	3.7	–1	82	47.6	8:34	5	1	0	1	14	0	0	0	6:48
2000-01	Ottawa	NHL	39	0	1	1	31	0	0	0	26	0.0	–3	10	40.0	6:10	....	....	....	....	....	....	....	....	....
	NY Rangers	NHL	19	1	4	5	15	0	0	0	20	5.0	–3	1	0.0	7:52	....	....	....	....	....	....	....	....	....
2001-02	Utah Grizzlies	AHL	4	0	0	0	21	....	....	....	....	....	....	....	....	....	....	....	....	....	....	....	....	....	....
	Washington	NHL	38	5	3	8	15	0	1	1	49	10.2	–2	253	44.7	11:01	....	....	....	....	....	....	....	....	....
	Portland Pirates	AHL	14	4	5	9	18	....	....	....	....	....	....	....	....	....	....	....	....	....	....	....	....	....	....
2002-03	Washington	NHL	5	0	0	0	0	0	0	0	3	0.0	–2	12	50.0	9:38	....	....	....	....	....	....	....	....	....
	Portland Pirates	AHL	69	22	38	60	73	....	....	....	....	....	....	....	....	....	3	2	2	4	4	....	....	....	....
	NHL Totals		300	33	28	61	211	2	2	7	368	9.0		361	45.2	10:13	13	1	0	1	16	0	0	0	6:48

Traded to **Tampa Bay** by **Philadelphia** with Philadelphia's 4th round choice (Michal Lanicek) in 1999 Entry Draft for Mikael Andersson and Sandy McCarthy, March 20, 1999. Traded to **Ottawa** by **Tampa Bay** for Bruce Gardiner, November 11, 1999. Traded to **NY Rangers** by **Ottawa** for Eric Lacroix, March 1, 2001. Signed as a free agent by **Washington**, January 8, 2002.

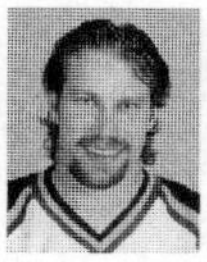

FORSBERG, Peter
(FOHRS-buhrg, PEE-tuhr) **COL.**

Center. Shoots left. 6', 205 lbs. Born, Ornskoldsvik, Sweden, July 20, 1973. Philadelphia's 1st choice, 6th overall, in 1991 Entry Draft.

Season	Club	League	GP	G	A	Pts	PIM	PP	SH	GW	S	%	+/-	TF	F%	Min	GP	G	A	Pts	PIM	PP	SH	GW	Min
1989-90	MoDo Jr.	Swede-Jr.	30	15	12	27	42	....	....	....	....	....	....	....	....	....	....	....	....	....	....	....	....	....	....
	MoDo	Sweden	1	0	1	1	4	....	....	....	....	....	....	....	....	....	....	....	....	....	....	....	....	....	....
1990-91	MoDo Jr.	Swede-Jr.	39	38	64	102	56	....	....	....	....	....	....	....	....	....	....	....	....	....	....	....	....	....	....
	MoDo	Sweden	23	7	10	17	22	....	....	....	....	....	....	....	....	....	....	....	....	....	....	....	....	....	....
1991-92	MoDo	Sweden	39	9	18	27	78	....	....	....	....	....	....	....	....	....	....	....	....	....	....	....	....	....	....
1992-93	MoDo Jr.	Swede-Jr.	2	0	3	3	4	....	....	....	....	....	....	....	....	....	....	....	....	....	....	....	....	....	....
	MoDo	Sweden	39	23	24	47	92	....	....	....	....	....	....	....	....	....	3	4	1	5	0	....	....	....	....
1993-94	MoDo	Sweden	39	18	26	44	82	....	....	....	....	....	....	....	....	....	11	9	7	16	14	....	....	....	....
	Sweden	Olympics	8	2	6	8	6	....	....	....	....	....	....	....	....	....	....	....	....	....	....	....	....	....	....
1994-95	MoDo	Sweden	11	5	9	14	20	....	....	....	....	....	....	....	....	....	....	....	....	....	....	....	....	....	....
	Quebec	NHL	47	15	35	50	16	3	0	3	86	17.4	17	....	....	....	6	2	4	6	4	1	0	0	....
1995-96♦	Colorado	NHL	82	30	86	116	47	7	3	3	217	13.8	26	....	....	....	22	10	11	21	18	3	0	1	....
1996-97	Colorado	NHL	65	28	58	86	73	5	4	4	188	14.9	31	....	....	....	14	5	12	17	10	3	0	0	....
1997-98	Colorado	NHL	72	25	66	91	94	7	3	7	202	12.4	6	....	....	....	7	6	5	11	12	2	0	0	....
	Sweden	Olympics	4	1	4	5	6	....	....	....	....	....	....	....	....	....	....	....	....	....	....	....	....	....	....
1998-99	Colorado	NHL	78	30	67	97	108	9	2	7	217	13.8	27	895	54.4	23:29	19	8	16	*24	31	1	1	0	21:39
99-2000	Colorado	NHL	49	14	37	51	52	3	0	2	105	13.3	9	519	46.6	20:55	16	7	8	15	12	2	1	4	20:59
2000-01♦	Colorado	NHL	73	27	62	89	54	12	2	5	178	15.2	23	755	46.6	20:48	11	4	10	14	6	1	0	2	21:55
2001-02	Colorado	NHL	....	....	....	....	....	....	....	....	....	....	....	....	....	....	20	9	*18	*27	20	0	0	4	18:10
2002-03	Colorado	NHL	75	29	*77	*106	70	8	0	2	166	17.5	52	709	47.0	19:20	7	2	6	8	6	1	0	0	20:01
	NHL Totals		541	198	488	686	514	54	14	33	1359	14.6		2878	49.1	21:11	122	53	90	143	119	14	2	11	20:26

NHL All-Rookie Team (1995) • Calder Memorial Trophy (1995) • NHL First All-Star Team (1998, 1999, 2003) • Art Ross Trophy (2003) • Hart Trophy (2003)

Played in NHL All-Star Game (1996, 1998, 1999, 2001, 2003)

Traded to **Quebec** by **Philadelphia** with Steve Duchesne, Kerry Huffman, Mike Ricci, Ron Hextall, Philadelphia's 1st round choice (Jocelyn Thibault) in 1993 Entry Draft, $15,000,000 and future considerations (Chris Simon and Philadelphia's 1st round choice (later traded to Toronto – later traded to Washington – Washington selected Nolan Baumgartner) in 1994 Entry Draft, July 21, 1992) for Eric Lindros, June 30, 1992. Transferred to **Colorado** after **Quebec** franchise relocated, June 21, 1995. • Missed entire 2001-02 regular season recovering from spleen injury suffered in game vs. Los Angeles, May 9, 2001 and ankle injury suffered in practice, January 10, 2002.

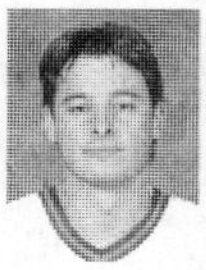

FORTIN, Jean-Francois
(fohr-TEHN, ZHAWN-fran-SWUH) **WSH.**

Defense. Shoots right. 6'2", 205 lbs. Born, Laval, Que., March 15, 1979. Washington's 2nd choice, 35th overall, in 1997 Entry Draft.

Season	Club	League	GP	G	A	Pts	PIM	PP	SH	GW	S	%	+/-	TF	F%	Min	GP	G	A	Pts	PIM	PP	SH	GW	Min
1993-94	Laval Laurentide	QAHA	31	8	20	28	32	....	....	....	....	....	....	....	....	....	....	....	....	....	....	....	....	....	....
1994-95	Abitibi Forestiers	QAAA	44	2	14	16	34	....	....	....	....	....	....	....	....	....	10	2	2	4	....	....	....	....	....
1995-96	Sherbrooke	QMJHL	69	7	15	22	40	....	....	....	....	....	....	....	....	....	7	2	6	8	2	....	....	....	....
1996-97	Sherbrooke	QMJHL	59	7	30	37	89	....	....	....	....	....	....	....	....	....	2	0	1	1	14	....	....	....	....
1997-98	Sherbrooke	QMJHL	55	12	25	37	37	....	....	....	....	....	....	....	....	....	....	....	....	....	....	....	....	....	....
1998-99	Sherbrooke	QMJHL	64	17	33	50	78	....	....	....	....	....	....	....	....	....	12	5	13	18	20	....	....	....	....
99-2000	Portland Pirates	AHL	43	3	5	8	44	....	....	....	....	....	....	....	....	....	2	0	0	0	0	....	....	....	....
	Hampton Roads	ECHL	7	0	2	2	0	....	....	....	....	....	....	....	....	....	....	....	....	....	....	....	....	....	....
2000-01	Portland Pirates	AHL	32	1	7	8	22	....	....	....	....	....	....	....	....	....	1	0	0	0	0	....	....	....	....
	Richmond	ECHL	15	0	4	4	2	....	....	....	....	....	....	....	....	....	....	....	....	....	....	....	....	....	....
2001-02	Washington	NHL	36	1	3	4	20	0	0	0	24	4.2	–1	1	100.0	19:25	....	....	....	....	....	....	....	....	....
	Portland Pirates	AHL	44	4	9	13	20	....	....	....	....	....	....	....	....	....	....	....	....	....	....	....	....	....	....
2002-03	Washington	NHL	33	0	1	1	22	0	0	0	20	0.0	–3	0	0.0	15:14	....	....	....	....	....	....	....	....	....
	Portland Pirates	AHL	10	2	1	3	17	....	....	....	....	....	....	....	....	....	....	....	....	....	....	....	....	....	....
	NHL Totals		69	1	4	5	42	0	0	0	44	2.3		1	100.0	17:25	....	....	....	....	....	....	....	....	....

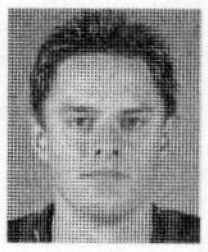

FOSTER, Kurtis
(FAW-stuhr, KUHR-this) **ATL.**

Defense. Shoots right. 6'5", 230 lbs. Born, Carp, Ont., November 24, 1981. Calgary's 2nd choice, 40th overall, in 2000 Entry Draft.

Season	Club	League	GP	G	A	Pts	PIM	PP	SH	GW	S	%	+/-	TF	F%	Min	GP	G	A	Pts	PIM	PP	SH	GW	Min
1997-98	Ottawa Valley	ODMHA	36	7	18	25	88	....	....	....	....	....	....	....	....	....	....	....	....	....	....	....	....	....	....
	Peterborough	OHL	39	1	1	2	45	....	....	....	....	....	....	....	....	....	4	0	0	0	2	....	....	....	....
1998-99	Peterborough	OHL	54	2	13	15	59	....	....	....	....	....	....	....	....	....	5	0	0	0	6	....	....	....	....
99-2000	Peterborough	OHL	68	6	18	24	116	....	....	....	....	....	....	....	....	....	5	1	2	3	4	....	....	....	....
2000-01	Peterborough	OHL	62	17	24	41	78	....	....	....	....	....	....	....	....	....	7	1	1	2	10	....	....	....	....
2001-02	Peterborough	OHL	33	10	4	14	58	....	....	....	....	....	....	....	....	....	....	....	....	....	....	....	....	....	....
	Chicago Wolves	AHL	39	6	9	15	59	....	....	....	....	....	....	....	....	....	14	1	1	2	21	....	....	....	....
2002-03	Atlanta	NHL	2	0	0	0	0	0	0	0	1	0.0	–2	0	0.0	11:06	....	....	....	....	....	....	....	....	....
	Chicago Wolves	AHL	75	15	27	42	159	....	....	....	....	....	....	....	....	....	9	1	3	4	14	....	....	....	....
	NHL Totals		2	0	0	0	0	0	0	0	1	0.0		0	0.0	11:06	....	....	....	....	....	....	....	....	....

Rights traded to **Atlanta** by **Calgary** with Jeff Cowan for Petr Buzek, December 18, 2001.

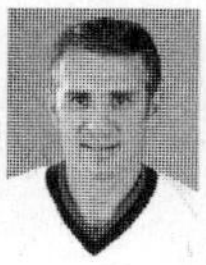

FRANCIS, Ron
(FRAN-sihs, RAWN) **CAR.**

Center. Shoots left. 6'3", 200 lbs. Born, Sault Ste. Marie, Ont., March 1, 1963. Hartford's 1st choice, 4th overall, in 1981 Entry Draft.

Season	Club	League	GP	G	A	Pts	PIM	PP	SH	GW	S	%	+/-	TF	F%	Min	GP	G	A	Pts	PIM	PP	SH	GW	Min
1979-80	Soo Legion	NOHA	45	57	92	149	....	....	....	....	....	....	....	....	....	....	....	....	....	....	....	....	....	....	....
1980-81	Sault Ste. Marie	OMJHL	64	26	43	69	33	....	....	....	....	....	....	....	....	....	19	7	8	15	34	....	....	....	....
1981-82	Sault Ste. Marie	OHL	25	18	30	48	46	....	....	....	....	....	....	....	....	....	....	....	....	....	....	....	....	....	....
	Hartford	NHL	59	25	43	68	51	12	0	1	163	15.3	–13	....	....	....	....	....	....	....	....	....	....	....	....
1982-83	Hartford	NHL	79	31	59	90	60	4	2	4	212	14.6	–25	....	....	....	....	....	....	....	....	....	....	....	....
1983-84	Hartford	NHL	72	23	60	83	45	5	0	5	202	11.4	–10	....	....	....	....	....	....	....	....	....	....	....	....
1984-85	Hartford	NHL	80	24	57	81	66	4	0	1	195	12.3	–23	....	....	....	....	....	....	....	....	....	....	....	....
1985-86	Hartford	NHL	53	24	53	77	24	7	1	4	120	20.0	8	....	....	....	10	1	2	3	4	0	0	0	....

			Regular Season														Playoffs								
Season	Club	League	GP	G	A	Pts	PIM	PP	SH	GW	S	%	+/-	TF	F%	Min	GP	G	A	Pts	PIM	PP	SH	GW	Min
1986-87	Hartford	NHL	75	30	63	93	45	7	0	7	189	15.9	10	....	....	....	6	2	2	4	6	1	0	0	....
1987-88	Hartford	NHL	80	25	50	75	87	11	1	3	172	14.5	–8	....	....	....	6	2	5	7	2	1	0	0	....
1988-89	Hartford	NHL	69	29	48	77	36	8	0	4	156	18.6	4	....	....	....	4	0	2	2	0	0	0	0	....
1989-90	Hartford	NHL	80	32	69	101	73	15	1	5	170	18.8	13	....	....	....	7	3	3	6	8	1	0	0	....
1990-91	Hartford	NHL	67	21	55	76	51	10	1	6	149	14.1	–2	....	....	....	....	....	....	....	....	....	....	....	....
	♦ Pittsburgh	NHL	14	2	9	11	21	0	0	1	25	8.0	0	....	....	....	24	7	10	17	24	0	0	4	....
1991-92 ♦	Pittsburgh	NHL	70	21	33	54	30	5	1	2	121	17.4	–7	....	....	....	21	8	*19	27	6	2	0	2	....
1992-93	Pittsburgh	NHL	84	24	76	100	68	9	2	4	215	11.2	6	....	....	....	12	6	11	17	19	1	0	1	....
1993-94	Pittsburgh	NHL	82	27	66	93	62	8	0	2	216	12.5	–3	....	....	....	6	0	2	2	6	0	0	0	....
1994-95	Pittsburgh	NHL	44	11	*48	59	18	3	0	1	94	11.7	30	....	....	....	12	6	13	19	4	2	0	0	....
1995-96	Pittsburgh	NHL	77	27	*92	119	56	12	1	4	158	17.1	25	....	....	....	11	3	6	9	4	2	0	1	....
1996-97	Pittsburgh	NHL	81	27	63	90	20	10	1	2	183	14.8	7	....	....	....	5	1	2	3	2	1	0	0	....
1997-98	Pittsburgh	NHL	81	25	62	87	20	7	0	5	189	13.2	12	....	....	....	6	1	5	6	2	0	0	0	....
1998-99	Carolina	NHL	82	21	31	52	34	8	0	2	133	15.8	–2	1589	51.5	21:55	3	0	1	1	0	0	0	0	16:27
99-2000	Carolina	NHL	78	23	50	73	18	7	0	4	150	15.3	10	1566	53.3	21:58	....	....	....	....	....	....	....	....	....
2000-01	Carolina	NHL	82	15	50	65	32	7	0	4	130	11.5	–15	1271	57.5	20:15	3	0	0	0	0	0	0	0	13:21
2001-02	Carolina	NHL	80	27	50	77	18	14	0	5	165	16.4	4	1136	58.9	20:41	23	6	10	16	6	4	0	3	21:03
2002-03	Carolina	NHL	82	22	35	57	30	8	1	1	156	14.1	–22	880	52.5	19:56	....	....	....	....	....	....	....	....	....
	NHL Totals		1651	536	1222	1758	965	181	12	77	3663	14.6		6442	54.6	20:57	159	46	93	139	93	15	0	11	19:47

Alka-Seltzer Plus Award (1995) • Frank J. Selke Trophy (1995) • Lady Byng Trophy (1995, 1998, 2002) • King Clancy Memorial Trophy (2002)
Played in NHL All-Star Game (1983, 1985, 1990, 1996)
Traded to **Pittsburgh** by **Hartford** with Grant Jennings and Ulf Samuelsson for John Cullen, Jeff Parker and Zarley Zalapski, March 4, 1991. Signed as a free agent by **Carolina**, July 13, 1998.

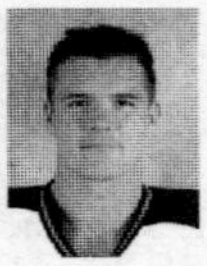

FRIESEN, Jeff (FREE-zuhn, JEHF) N.J.

Left wing. Shoots left. 6', 215 lbs. Born, Meadow Lake, Sask., August 5, 1976. San Jose's 1st choice, 11th overall, in 1994 Entry Draft.

1991-92	Sask. Contacts	SMHL	35	37	51	88	75	....	....	....	....	....	....	....	....	....	....	....	....	....	....	....	....	....	....
	Regina Pats	WHL	4	3	1	4	2	....	....	....	....	....	....	....	....	....	....	....	....	....	....	....	....	....	....
1992-93	Regina Pats	WHL	70	45	38	83	23	....	....	....	....	....	....	....	....	....	13	7	10	17	8	....	....	....	....
1993-94	Regina Pats	WHL	66	51	67	118	48	....	....	....	....	....	....	....	....	....	4	3	2	5	2	....	....	....	....
1994-95	Regina Pats	WHL	25	21	23	44	22	....	....	....	....	....	....	....	....	....	....	....	....	....	....	....	....	....	....
	San Jose	NHL	48	15	10	25	14	5	1	2	86	17.4	–8	....	....	....	11	1	5	6	4	0	0	0	....
1995-96	San Jose	NHL	79	15	31	46	42	2	0	0	123	12.2	–19	....	....	....	....	....	....	....	....	....	....	....	....
1996-97	San Jose	NHL	82	28	34	62	75	6	2	5	200	14.0	–8	....	....	....	....	....	....	....	....	....	....	....	....
1997-98	San Jose	NHL	79	31	32	63	40	7	6	7	186	16.7	8	....	....	....	6	0	1	1	2	0	0	0	....
1998-99	San Jose	NHL	78	22	35	57	42	10	1	3	215	10.2	3	24	33.3	19:25	6	2	2	4	14	1	0	0	22:22
99-2000	San Jose	NHL	82	26	35	61	47	11	3	7	191	13.6	–2	3	66.7	19:48	11	2	2	4	10	0	0	0	17:21
2000-01	San Jose	NHL	64	12	24	36	56	2	0	1	120	10.0	7	7	28.6	18:51	....	....	....	....	....	....	....	....	....
	Anaheim	NHL	15	2	10	12	10	2	0	0	29	6.9	–2	43	55.8	21:28	....	....	....	....	....	....	....	....	....
2001-02	Anaheim	NHL	81	17	26	43	44	1	1	0	161	10.6	–1	45	48.9	17:59	....	....	....	....	....	....	....	....	....
2002-03 ♦	New Jersey	NHL	81	23	28	51	26	3	0	4	179	12.8	23	11	45.5	15:33	24	10	4	14	6	1	0	4	16:02
	NHL Totals		689	191	265	456	396	49	14	29	1490	12.8		133	47.4	18:25	58	15	14	29	36	2	0	4	17:19

WHL Rookie of the Year (1993) • Canadian Major Junior Rookie of the Year (1993) • NHL All-Rookie Team (1995)
Traded to **Anaheim** by **San Jose** with Steve Shields and San Jose's 2nd round choice (later traded to Dallas – Dallas selected Vojtech Polak) in 2003 Entry Draft for Teemu Selanne, March 5, 2001. Traded to **New Jersey** by **Anaheim** with Oleg Tverdovsky and Maxim Balmochnykh for Petr Sykora, Mike Commodore, Jean-Francois Damphousse and Igor Pohanka, July 6, 2002.

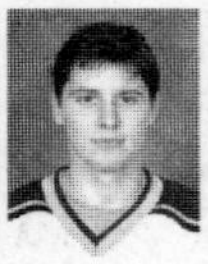

FROLOV, Alexander (froh-LAHF, al-ehx-AN-duhr) L.A.

Left wing. Shoots right. 6'4", 195 lbs. Born, Moscow, USSR, June 19, 1982. Los Angeles' 1st choice, 20th overall, in 2000 Entry Draft.

1998-99	Spartak Moscow	Russia	1	0	0	0	0	....	....	....	....	....	....	....	....	....	....	....	....	....	....	....	....	....	....
99-2000	Yaroslavl 2	Russia-3	36	27	13	40	30	....	....	....	....	....	....	....	....	....	....	....	....	....	....	....	....	....	....
2000-01	Spartak Moscow	Russia-2	44	20	19	39	8	....	....	....	....	....	....	....	....	....	....	....	....	....	....	....	....	....	....
2001-02	Krylja Sovetov 2	Russia-3	2	0	0	0	4	....	....	....	....	....	....	....	....	....	....	....	....	....	....	....	....	....	....
	Krylja Sovetov	Russia	43	18	12	30	16	....	....	....	....	....	....	....	....	....	3	1	0	1	0	....	....	....	....
2002-03	Los Angeles	NHL	79	14	17	31	34	1	0	3	141	9.9	12	9	22.2	14:23	....	....	....	....	....	....	....	....	....
	NHL Totals		79	14	17	31	34	1	0	3	141	9.9		9	22.2	14:23	....	....	....	....	....	....	....	....	....

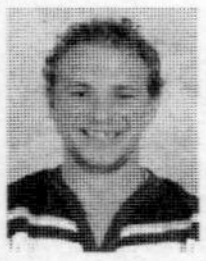

GABORIK, Marian (GA-bohr-ihk, MAIR-ee-uhn) MIN.

Right wing. Shoots left. 6'1", 190 lbs. Born, Trencin, Czech., February 14, 1982. Minnesota's 1st choice, 3rd overall, in 2000 Entry Draft.

1997-98	Dukla Trencin Jr.	Slovak-Jr.	36	37	22	59	28	....	....	....	....	....	....	....	....	....	....	....	....	....	....	....	....	....	....
	Dukla Trencin	Slovakia	1	1	0	1	0	....	....	....	....	....	....	....	....	....	....	....	....	....	....	....	....	....	....
1998-99	Dukla Trencin	Slovakia	33	11	9	20	6	....	....	....	....	....	....	....	....	....	3	1	0	1	2	....	....	....	....
99-2000	Dukla Trencin	Slovakia	50	25	21	46	34	....	....	....	....	....	....	....	....	....	5	1	2	3	2	....	....	....	....
2000-01	Minnesota	NHL	71	18	18	36	32	6	0	3	179	10.1	–6	3	33.3	15:26	....	....	....	....	....	....	....	....	....
2001-02	Minnesota	NHL	78	30	37	67	34	10	0	4	221	13.6	0	4	25.0	16:47	....	....	....	....	....	....	....	....	....
2002-03	Minnesota	NHL	81	30	35	65	46	5	1	8	280	10.7	12	16	25.0	17:24	18	9	8	17	6	4	0	0	18:12
	NHL Totals		230	78	90	168	112	21	1	15	680	11.5		23	26.1	16:35	18	9	8	17	6	4	0	0	18:12

Played in NHL All-Star Game (2003)

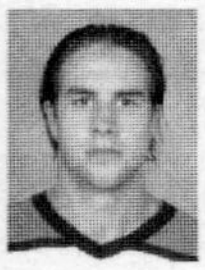

GAGNE, Simon (GAH-nyay, see-MOHN) PHI.

Left wing. Shoots left. 6', 190 lbs. Born, Ste-Foy, Que., February 29, 1980. Philadelphia's 1st choice, 22nd overall, in 1998 Entry Draft.

1995-96	Ste-Foy	QAAA	27	13	9	22	18	....	....	....	....	....	....	....	....	....	15	7	8	15	8	....	....	....	....
1996-97	Beauport	QMJHL	51	9	22	31	49	....	....	....	....	....	....	....	....	....	....	....	....	....	....	....	....	....	....
1997-98	Quebec Remparts	QMJHL	53	30	39	69	26	....	....	....	....	....	....	....	....	....	12	11	5	16	23	....	....	....	....
1998-99	Quebec Remparts	QMJHL	61	50	70	120	42	....	....	....	....	....	....	....	....	....	13	9	8	17	4	....	....	....	....
99-2000	Philadelphia	NHL	80	20	28	48	22	8	1	4	159	12.6	11	443	42.2	14:59	17	5	5	10	2	2	0	1	16:46
2000-01	Philadelphia	NHL	69	27	32	59	18	6	0	7	191	14.1	24	21	28.6	18:05	6	3	0	3	0	2	0	0	19:09
2001-02	Philadelphia	NHL	79	33	33	66	32	4	1	7	199	16.6	31	6	83.3	18:09	5	0	0	0	2	0	0	0	19:16
	Canada	Olympics	6	1	3	4	0	....	....	....	....	....	....	....	....	....	....	....	....	....	....	....	....	....	....
2002-03	Philadelphia	NHL	46	9	18	27	16	1	1	3	115	7.8	20	70	42.9	17:24	13	4	1	5	6	0	1	1	18:13
	NHL Totals		274	89	111	200	88	19	3	21	664	13.4		540	42.2	17:05	41	12	6	18	10	4	1	2	17:53

QMJHL Second All-Star Team (1999) • NHL All-Rookie Team (2000)
Played in NHL ALL-Star Game (2001)

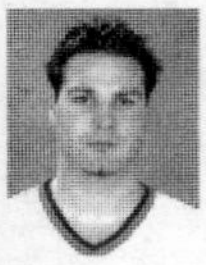

GAGNON, Sean (gah-NYAWN, SHAWN)

Defense. Shoots left. 6'2", 219 lbs. Born, Sault Ste. Marie, Ont., September 11, 1973.

1990-91	Soo Elks	NOHA	46	21	26	47	218	....	....	....	....	....	....	....	....	....	....	....	....	....	....	....	....	....	....
1991-92	Sud. N. Wolves	NOJHA	13	10	13	23	34	....	....	....	....	....	....	....	....	....	....	....	....	....	....	....	....	....	....
	Sudbury Wolves	OHL	44	3	4	7	60	....	....	....	....	....	....	....	....	....	5	0	1	1	0	....	....	....	....
1992-93	Sudbury Wolves	OHL	6	1	1	2	16	....	....	....	....	....	....	....	....	....	....	....	....	....	....	....	....	....	....
	Ottawa 67's	OHL	33	2	10	12	68	....	....	....	....	....	....	....	....	....	....	....	....	....	....	....	....	....	....
	Sault Ste. Marie	OHL	24	1	5	6	65	....	....	....	....	....	....	....	....	....	15	2	2	4	25	....	....	....	....
1993-94	Sault Ste. Marie	OHL	42	4	12	16	147	....	....	....	....	....	....	....	....	....	14	1	1	2	52	....	....	....	....
1994-95	Dayton Bombers	ECHL	68	9	23	32	339	....	....	....	....	....	....	....	....	....	8	0	3	3	69	....	....	....	....
1995-96	Dayton Bombers	ECHL	68	7	22	29	326	....	....	....	....	....	....	....	....	....	3	0	1	1	33	....	....	....	....
1996-97	Fort Wayne	IHL	72	7	7	14	*457	....	....	....	....	....	....	....	....	....	....	....	....	....	....	....	....	....	....
1997-98	Phoenix	NHL	5	0	1	1	14	0	0	0	3	0.0	1	....	....	....	....	....	....	....	....	....	....	....	....
	Springfield	AHL	54	4	13	17	330	....	....	....	....	....	....	....	....	....	2	0	1	1	17	....	....	....	....
1998-99	Phoenix	NHL	2	0	0	0	7	0	0	0	1	0.0	–2	0	0.0	7:56	....	....	....	....	....	....	....	....	....
	Springfield	AHL	68	8	14	22	331	....	....	....	....	....	....	....	....	....	3	0	0	0	14	....	....	....	....
99-2000	Jokerit Helsinki	Finland	42	3	5	8	183	....	....	....	....	....	....	....	....	....	11	4	1	5	22	....	....	....	....
2000-01	Ottawa	NHL	5	0	0	0	13	0	0	0	0	0.0	0	0	0.0	10:45	....	....	....	....	....	....	....	....	....
	Grand Rapids	IHL	70	4	16	20	226	....	....	....	....	....	....	....	....	....	10	2	3	5	30	....	....	....	....

Season	Club	League	GP	G	A	Pts	PIM	PP	SH	GW	S	%	+/-	TF	F%	Min	GP	G	A	Pts	PIM	PP	SH	GW	Min
			Regular Season														Playoffs								
2001-02	Hartford	AHL	42	3	5	8	200	....	....	....	....	....	....	....	....	....	....	....	....	....	....	....	....	....	....
2002-03	San Antonio	AHL	42	3	6	9	157	....	....	....	....	....	....	....	....	....	3	0	0	0	4	....	....	....	....
	NHL Totals		**12**	**0**	**1**	**1**	**34**	**0**	**0**	**0**	**4**	**0.0**		**0**	**0.0**	**9:57**	....	....	....	....	....	....	....	....	....

Signed as a free agent by **Phoenix**, May 14, 1997. Signed as a free agent by **Ottawa**, July 7, 2000. Traded to **NY Rangers** by **Ottawa** for Jason Doig and Jeff Ulmer, June 29, 2001. Signed as a free agent by **San Antonio** (AHL), December 18, 2002.

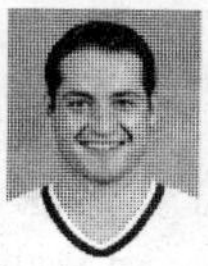

GAINEY, Steve

(GAY-nee, STEEV) **DAL.**

Left wing. Shoots left. 6'1", 192 lbs. Born, Montreal, Que., January 26, 1979. Dallas' 3rd choice, 77th overall, in 1997 Entry Draft.

Season	Club	League	GP	G	A	Pts	PIM	PP	SH	GW	S	%	+/-	TF	F%	Min	GP	G	A	Pts	PIM	PP	SH	GW	Min
1995-96	Kamloops Blazers	WHL	49	1	4	5	40	....	....	....	....	....	....	....	....	....	3	0	0	0	0	....	....	....	....
1996-97	Kamloops Blazers	WHL	60	9	18	27	60	....	....	....	....	....	....	....	....	....	2	0	0	0	9	....	....	....	....
1997-98	Kamloops Blazers	WHL	68	21	34	55	93	....	....	....	....	....	....	....	....	....	7	1	7	8	15	....	....	....	....
1998-99	Kamloops Blazers	WHL	68	30	34	64	155	....	....	....	....	....	....	....	....	....	15	5	4	9	38	....	....	....	....
99-2000	Fort Wayne	UHL	1	0	0	0	0	....	....	....	....	....	....	....	....	....	....	....	....	....	....	....	....	....	....
	Michigan	IHL	58	8	10	18	41	....	....	....	....	....	....	....	....	....	....	....	....	....	....	....	....	....	....
2000-01	**Dallas**	**NHL**	**1**	**0**	**0**	**0**	**0**	**0**	**0**	**0**	**0**	**0.0**	**0**	**0**	**0.0**	**2:21**	....	....	....	....	....	....	....	....	....
	Utah Grizzlies	IHL	61	7	7	14	167	....	....	....	....	....	....	....	....	....	....	....	....	....	....	....	....	....	....
2001-02	**Dallas**	**NHL**	**5**	**0**	**1**	**1**	**7**	**0**	**0**	**0**	**1**	**0.0**	**–1**	**0**	**0.0**	**7:24**	....	....	....	....	....	....	....	....	....
	Utah Grizzlies	AHL	58	16	18	34	87	....	....	....	....	....	....	....	....	....	....	....	....	....	....	....	....	....	....
2002-03	Utah Grizzlies	AHL	68	9	17	26	106	....	....	....	....	....	....	....	....	....	2	0	0	0	11	....	....	....	....
	NHL Totals		**6**	**0**	**1**	**1**	**7**	**0**	**0**	**0**	**1**	**0.0**		**0**	**0.0**	**6:34**	....	....	....	....	....	....	....	....	....

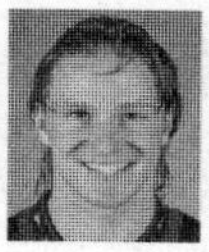

GAMACHE, Simon

(ga-MOHSH, see-MOHN) **ATL.**

Center. Shoots left. 5'9", 185 lbs. Born, Thetford Mines, Que., January 3, 1981. Atlanta's 14th choice, 290th overall, in 2000 Entry Draft.

Season	Club	League	GP	G	A	Pts	PIM	PP	SH	GW	S	%	+/-	TF	F%	Min	GP	G	A	Pts	PIM	PP	SH	GW	Min
1997-98	Levis-Lauzon	QAAA	42	28	26	54	....	....	....	....	....	....	....	....	....	....	4	1	1	2	....	....	....	....	....
1998-99	Val-d'Or Foreurs	QMJHL	70	19	43	62	54	....	....	....	....	....	....	....	....	....	6	1	2	3	4	....	....	....	....
99-2000	Val-d'Or Foreurs	QMJHL	72	64	79	143	74	....	....	....	....	....	....	....	....	....	....	....	....	....	....	....	....	....	....
2000-01	Val-d'Or Foreurs	QMJHL	72	*74	*110	*184	70	....	....	....	....	....	....	....	....	....	21	*22	*35	*57	18	....	....	....	....
2001-02	Chicago Wolves	AHL	26	2	4	6	11	....	....	....	....	....	....	....	....	....	....	....	....	....	....	....	....	....	....
	Greenville	ECHL	31	19	19	38	35	....	....	....	....	....	....	....	....	....	17	*15	9	*24	22	....	....	....	....
2002-03	**Atlanta**	**NHL**	**2**	**0**	**0**	**0**	**2**	**0**	**0**	**0**	**3**	**0.0**	**–1**	**0**	**0.0**	**12:37**	....	....	....	....	....	....	....	....	....
	Chicago Wolves	AHL	76	35	42	77	37	....	....	....	....	....	....	....	....	....	9	7	2	9	4	....	....	....	....
	NHL Totals		**2**	**0**	**0**	**0**	**2**	**0**	**0**	**0**	**3**	**0.0**		**0**	**0.0**	**12:37**	....	....	....	....	....	....	....	....	....

Canadian Major Junior Second All-Star Team (2000) • QMJHL First All-Star Team (2001) • Michel Briere Trophy (MVP – QMJHL) (2001) • Canadian Major Junior First All-Star Team (2001) • Canadian Major Junior Player of the Year (2001) • Sheetrock CHL Top Scorer Award (2001) • Memorial Cup All-Star Team (2001) • Ed Chynoweth Trophy (Memorial Cup Leading Scorer) (2001) • ECHL All-Rookie Team (2002) • ECHL Playoff MVP (2002) (co-winner - Tyrone Garner)

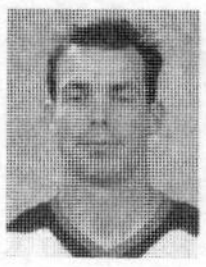

GARDINER, Bruce

(gahr-DIHN-uhr, BREWS)

Right wing. Shoots right. 6'1", 193 lbs. Born, Barrie, Ont., February 11, 1972. St. Louis' 6th choice, 131st overall, in 1991 Entry Draft.

Season	Club	League	GP	G	A	Pts	PIM	PP	SH	GW	S	%	+/-	TF	F%	Min	GP	G	A	Pts	PIM	PP	SH	GW	Min
1988-89	Barrie Colts	OJHL-B	41	17	28	45	29	....	....	....	....	....	....	....	....	....	....	....	....	....	....	....	....	....	....
1989-90	Barrie Colts	OJHL-B	40	19	26	45	89	....	....	....	....	....	....	....	....	....	13	10	11	21	32	....	....	....	....
1990-91	Colgate	ECAC	27	4	9	13	72	....	....	....	....	....	....	....	....	....	....	....	....	....	....	....	....	....	....
1991-92	Colgate	ECAC	23	7	8	15	77	....	....	....	....	....	....	....	....	....	....	....	....	....	....	....	....	....	....
1992-93	Colgate	ECAC	33	17	12	29	64	....	....	....	....	....	....	....	....	....	....	....	....	....	....	....	....	....	....
1993-94	Colgate	ECAC	33	23	23	46	68	....	....	....	....	....	....	....	....	....	....	....	....	....	....	....	....	....	....
	Peoria Rivermen	IHL	3	0	0	0	0	....	....	....	....	....	....	....	....	....	....	....	....	....	....	....	....	....	....
1994-95	P.E.I. Senators	AHL	72	17	20	37	132	....	....	....	....	....	....	....	....	....	7	4	1	5	4	....	....	....	....
1995-96	P.E.I. Senators	AHL	38	11	13	24	87	....	....	....	....	....	....	....	....	....	5	2	4	6	4	....	....	....	....
1996-97	**Ottawa**	**NHL**	**67**	**11**	**10**	**21**	**49**	**0**	**1**	**2**	**94**	**11.7**	**4**	....	....	....	**7**	**0**	**1**	**1**	**2**	**0**	**0**	**0**	....
1997-98	**Ottawa**	**NHL**	**55**	**7**	**11**	**18**	**50**	**0**	**0**	**0**	**64**	**10.9**	**2**	....	....	....	**11**	**1**	**3**	**4**	**2**	**0**	**0**	**1**	....
1998-99	**Ottawa**	**NHL**	**59**	**4**	**8**	**12**	**43**	**0**	**0**	**1**	**70**	**5.7**	**6**	**278**	**45.7**	**12:52**	**3**	**0**	**0**	**0**	**4**	**0**	**0**	**0**	**11:21**
99-2000	**Ottawa**	**NHL**	**10**	**0**	**3**	**3**	**4**	**0**	**0**	**0**	**18**	**0.0**	**1**	**62**	**59.7**	**13:24**	....	....	....	....	....	....	....	....	....
	Tampa Bay	**NHL**	**41**	**3**	**6**	**9**	**37**	**0**	**0**	**0**	**30**	**10.0**	**–21**	**330**	**56.4**	**13:36**	....	....	....	....	....	....	....	....	....
2000-01	**Columbus**	**NHL**	**73**	**7**	**15**	**22**	**78**	**0**	**0**	**1**	**60**	**11.7**	**–1**	**505**	**51.5**	**14:36**	....	....	....	....	....	....	....	....	....
2001-02	**New Jersey**	**NHL**	**7**	**2**	**1**	**3**	**2**	**1**	**0**	**0**	**10**	**20.0**	**–1**	**9**	**44.4**	**13:16**	....	....	....	....	....	....	....	....	....
	Albany River Rats	AHL	45	5	18	23	71	....	....	....	....	....	....	....	....	....	....	....	....	....	....	....	....	....	....
2002-03	Lada Togliatti	Russia	30	4	8	12	106	....	....	....	....	....	....	....	....	....	10	1	0	1	20	....	....	....	....
	NHL Totals		**312**	**34**	**54**	**88**	**263**	**1**	**1**	**4**	**346**	**9.8**		**1184**	**51.9**	**13:44**	**21**	**1**	**4**	**5**	**8**	**0**	**0**	**1**	**11:21**

ECAC Second All-Star Team (1994)

Signed as a free agent by **Ottawa**, June 14, 1994. Traded to **Tampa Bay** by **Ottawa** for Colin Forbes, November 11, 1999. Selected by **Columbus** from **Tampa Bay** in Expansion Draft, June 23, 2000. Signed as a free agent by **New Jersey**, October 21, 2001.

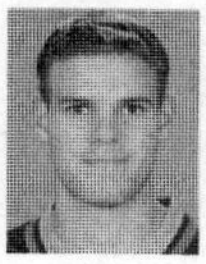

GAUSTAD, Paul

(GAW-stad, PAWL) **BUF.**

Center. Shoots left. 6'4", 217 lbs. Born, Fargo, ND, February 3, 1982. Buffalo's 6th choice, 220th overall, in 2000 Entry Draft.

Season	Club	League	GP	G	A	Pts	PIM	PP	SH	GW	S	%	+/-	TF	F%	Min	GP	G	A	Pts	PIM	PP	SH	GW	Min
1998-99	Portland Hawks	USAHA	45	47	53	100	81	....	....	....	....	....	....	....	....	....	....	....	....	....	....	....	....	....	....
99-2000	Portland	WHL	56	6	8	14	110	....	....	....	....	....	....	....	....	....	....	....	....	....	....	....	....	....	....
2000-01	Portland	WHL	70	11	30	41	168	....	....	....	....	....	....	....	....	....	16	10	6	16	59	....	....	....	....
2001-02	Portland	WHL	72	36	44	80	202	....	....	....	....	....	....	....	....	....	6	3	1	4	16	....	....	....	....
2002-03	**Buffalo**	**NHL**	**1**	**0**	**0**	**0**	**0**	**0**	**0**	**0**	**0**	**0.0**	**0**	**7**	**42.9**	**5:48**	....	....	....	....	....	....	....	....	....
	Rochester	AHL	80	14	39	53	137	....	....	....	....	....	....	....	....	....	3	0	0	0	4	....	....	....	....
	NHL Totals		**1**	**0**	**0**	**0**	**0**	**0**	**0**	**0**	**0**	**0.0**		**7**	**42.9**	**5:48**	....	....	....	....	....	....	....	....	....

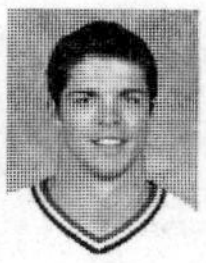

GAUTHIER, Denis

(GOH-tyay, DEH-nihs) **CGY.**

Defense. Shoots left. 6'2", 224 lbs. Born, Montreal, Que., October 1, 1976. Calgary's 1st choice, 20th overall, in 1995 Entry Draft.

Season	Club	League	GP	G	A	Pts	PIM	PP	SH	GW	S	%	+/-	TF	F%	Min	GP	G	A	Pts	PIM	PP	SH	GW	Min
1991-92	St-Jean-de-Rich.	QAHA	STATISTICS NOT AVAILABLE																						
1992-93	Drummondville	QMJHL	61	1	7	8	136	....	....	....	....	....	....	....	....	....	10	0	5	5	40	....	....	....	....
1993-94	Drummondville	QMJHL	60	0	7	7	176	....	....	....	....	....	....	....	....	....	9	2	0	2	41	....	....	....	....
1994-95	Drummondville	QMJHL	64	9	31	40	190	....	....	....	....	....	....	....	....	....	4	0	5	5	12	....	....	....	....
1995-96	Drummondville	QMJHL	53	25	49	74	140	....	....	....	....	....	....	....	....	....	6	4	4	8	32	....	....	....	....
	Saint John Flames	AHL	5	2	0	2	8	....	....	....	....	....	....	....	....	....	16	1	6	7	20	....	....	....	....
1996-97	Saint John Flames	AHL	73	3	28	31	74	....	....	....	....	....	....	....	....	....	5	0	0	0	6	....	....	....	....
1997-98	**Calgary**	**NHL**	**10**	**0**	**0**	**0**	**16**	**0**	**0**	**0**	**3**	**0.0**	**–5**	....	....	....	....	....	....	....	....	....	....	....	....
	Saint John Flames	AHL	68	4	20	24	154	....	....	....	....	....	....	....	....	....	21	0	4	4	83	....	....	....	....
1998-99	**Calgary**	**NHL**	**55**	**3**	**4**	**7**	**68**	**0**	**0**	**0**	**40**	**7.5**	**3**	**0**	**0.0**	**12:41**	....	....	....	....	....	....	....	....	....
	Saint John Flames	AHL	16	0	3	3	31	....	....	....	....	....	....	....	....	....	....	....	....	....	....	....	....	....	....
99-2000	**Calgary**	**NHL**	**39**	**1**	**1**	**2**	**50**	**0**	**0**	**0**	**29**	**3.4**	**–4**	**0**	**0.0**	**19:21**	....	....	....	....	....	....	....	....	....
2000-01	**Calgary**	**NHL**	**62**	**2**	**6**	**8**	**78**	**0**	**0**	**0**	**33**	**6.1**	**3**	**0**	**0.0**	**16:37**	....	....	....	....	....	....	....	....	....
2001-02	**Calgary**	**NHL**	**66**	**5**	**8**	**13**	**91**	**0**	**1**	**2**	**76**	**6.6**	**9**	**0**	**0.0**	**19:19**	....	....	....	....	....	....	....	....	....
2002-03	**Calgary**	**NHL**	**72**	**1**	**11**	**12**	**99**	**0**	**0**	**1**	**50**	**2.0**	**5**	**0**	**0.0**	**19:52**	....	....	....	....	....	....	....	....	....
	NHL Totals		**304**	**12**	**30**	**42**	**402**	**0**	**1**	**3**	**231**	**5.2**		**0**	**0.0**	**17:39**	....	....	....	....	....	....	....	....	....

QMJHL First All-Star Team (1996) • Canadian Major Junior First All-Star Team (1996)

• Missed majority of 1999-2000 season recovering from hip injury suffered in game vs. St. Louis, February 1, 2000.

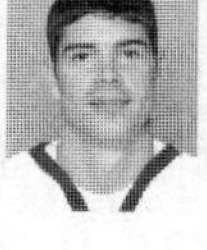

GAVEY, Aaron

(GAY-vee, AIR-ruhn) **TOR.**

Center. Shoots left. 6'2", 189 lbs. Born, Sudbury, Ont., February 22, 1974. Tampa Bay's 4th choice, 74th overall, in 1992 Entry Draft.

Season	Club	League	GP	G	A	Pts	PIM	PP	SH	GW	S	%	+/-	TF	F%	Min	GP	G	A	Pts	PIM	PP	SH	GW	Min
1990-91	Peterborough	OPJHL	42	26	30	56	68	....	....	....	....	....	....	....	....	....	....	....	....	....	....	....	....	....	....
1991-92	Sault Ste. Marie	OHL	48	7	11	18	27	....	....	....	....	....	....	....	....	....	19	5	1	6	10	....	....	....	....
1992-93	Sault Ste. Marie	OHL	62	45	39	84	116	....	....	....	....	....	....	....	....	....	18	5	9	14	36	....	....	....	....
1993-94	Sault Ste. Marie	OHL	60	42	60	102	116	....	....	....	....	....	....	....	....	....	14	11	10	21	22	....	....	....	....
1994-95	Atlanta Knights	IHL	66	18	17	35	85	....	....	....	....	....	....	....	....	....	5	0	1	1	9	....	....	....	....
1995-96	**Tampa Bay**	**NHL**	**73**	**8**	**4**	**12**	**56**	**1**	**1**	**2**	**65**	**12.3**	**–6**	....	....	....	**6**	**0**	**0**	**0**	**4**	**0**	**0**	**0**	....
1996-97	**Tampa Bay**	**NHL**	**16**	**1**	**2**	**3**	**12**	**0**	**0**	**0**	**8**	**12.5**	**–1**	....	....	....	....	....	....	....	....	....	....	....	....
	Calgary	**NHL**	**41**	**7**	**9**	**16**	**34**	**3**	**0**	**1**	**54**	**13.0**	**–11**	....	....	....	....	....	....	....	....	....	....	....	....

			Regular Season														Playoffs								
Season	Club	League	GP	G	A	Pts	PIM	PP	SH	GW	S	%	+/-	TF	F%	Min	GP	G	A	Pts	PIM	PP	SH	GW	Min
1997-98	**Calgary**	**NHL**	26	2	3	5	24	0	0	1	27	7.4	–5	....	....	....	....	....	....	....	....	....	....	....	....
	Saint John Flames	AHL	8	4	3	7	28	....	....	....	....	....	....	....	....	....	....	....	....	....	....	....	....	....	....
1998-99	**Dallas**	**NHL**	7	0	0	0	10	0	0	0	4	0.0	–1	43	48.8	8:09	....	....	....	....	....	....	....	....	....
	Michigan	IHL	67	24	33	57	128	....	....	....	....	....	....	....	....	....	5	2	3	5	4	....	....	....	....
99-2000	**Dallas**	**NHL**	41	7	6	13	44	1	0	2	39	17.9	0	263	51.7	9:55	13	1	2	3	10	0	0	1	6:09
	Michigan	IHL	28	14	15	29	73	....	....	....	....	....	....	....	....	....	....	....	....	....	....	....	....	....	....
2000-01	**Minnesota**	**NHL**	75	10	14	24	52	1	0	2	100	10.0	–8	584	43.5	14:00	....	....	....	....	....	....	....	....	....
2001-02	**Minnesota**	**NHL**	71	6	11	17	38	1	0	0	75	8.0	–21	254	42.5	11:55	....	....	....	....	....	....	....	....	....
2002-03	**Toronto**	**NHL**	5	0	1	1	0	0	0	0	8	0.0	1	31	48.4	11:19	....	....	....	....	....	....	....	....	....
	St. John's	AHL	70	14	29	43	83	....	....	....	....	....	....	....	....	....	....	....	....	....	....	....	....	....	....
	NHL Totals		355	41	50	91	270	7	1	8	380	10.8		1175	45.4	12:08	19	1	2	3	14	0	0	1	6:09

Traded to **Calgary** by **Tampa Bay** for Rick Tabaracci, November 19, 1996. Traded to **Dallas** by **Calgary** for Bob Bassen, July 14, 1998. Traded to **Minnesota** by **Dallas** with Pavel Patera, Dallas' 8th round choice (Eric Johansson) in 2000 Entry Draft and Minnesota's 4th round choice (previously acquired, later traded to Los Angeles – Los Angeles selected Aaron Rome) in 2002 Entry Draft for Brad Lukowich and Minnesota's 3rd (Yared Hagos) and 9th (Dale Sullivan) round choices in 2001 Entry Draft, June 25, 2000. Signed as a free agent by **Toronto**, July 24, 2002.

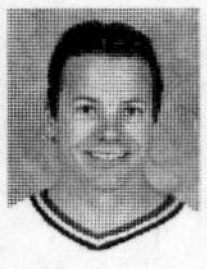

GELINAS, Martin

(ZHEHL-in-nuh, MAHR-tihn) **CGY.**

Left wing. Shoots left. 5'11", 195 lbs. Born, Shawinigan, Que., June 5, 1970. Los Angeles' 1st choice, 7th overall, in 1988 Entry Draft.

Season	Club	League	GP	G	A	Pts	PIM	PP	SH	GW	S	%	+/-	TF	F%	Min	GP	G	A	Pts	PIM	PP	SH	GW	Min
1985-86	Noranda Aces	NOHA	5	1	1	2	0	....	....	....	....	....	....	....	....	....	....	....	....	....	....	....	....	....	....
1986-87	L'est Cantonniers	QAAA	41	36	42	78	36	....	....	....	....	....	....	....	....	....	7	7	5	12	2	....	....	....	....
1987-88	Hull Olympiques	QMJHL	65	63	68	131	74	....	....	....	....	....	....	....	....	....	17	15	18	33	32	....	....	....	....
1988-89	Hull Olympiques	QMJHL	41	38	39	77	31	....	....	....	....	....	....	....	....	....	9	5	4	9	14	....	....	....	....
	Edmonton	**NHL**	6	1	2	3	0	0	0	0	14	7.1	–1	....	....	....	....	....	....	....	....	....	....	....	....
1989-90♦	**Edmonton**	**NHL**	46	17	8	25	30	5	0	2	71	23.9	0	....	....	....	20	2	3	5	6	0	0	0	....
1990-91	**Edmonton**	**NHL**	73	20	20	40	34	4	0	2	124	16.1	–7	....	....	....	18	3	6	9	25	0	0	1	....
1991-92	**Edmonton**	**NHL**	68	11	18	29	62	1	0	0	94	11.7	14	....	....	....	15	1	3	4	10	0	0	0	....
1992-93	**Edmonton**	**NHL**	65	11	12	23	30	0	0	1	93	11.8	3	....	....	....	....	....	....	....	....	....	....	....	....
1993-94	**Quebec**	**NHL**	31	6	6	12	8	0	0	0	53	11.3	–2	....	....	....	....	....	....	....	....	....	....	....	....
	Vancouver	**NHL**	33	8	8	16	26	3	0	1	54	14.8	–6	....	....	....	24	5	4	9	14	2	0	1	....
1994-95	**Vancouver**	**NHL**	46	13	10	23	36	1	0	4	75	17.3	8	....	....	....	3	0	1	1	0	0	0	0	....
1995-96	**Vancouver**	**NHL**	81	30	26	56	59	3	4	5	181	16.6	8	....	....	....	6	1	1	2	12	1	0	0	....
1996-97	**Vancouver**	**NHL**	74	35	33	68	42	6	1	3	177	19.8	6	....	....	....	....	....	....	....	....	....	....	....	....
1997-98	**Vancouver**	**NHL**	24	4	4	8	10	1	1	1	49	8.2	–6	....	....	....	....	....	....	....	....	....	....	....	....
	Carolina	**NHL**	40	12	14	26	30	2	1	4	98	12.2	1	....	....	....	....	....	....	....	....	....	....	....	....
1998-99	**Carolina**	**NHL**	76	13	15	28	67	0	0	2	111	11.7	3	6	50.0	13:13	6	0	3	3	2	0	0	0	19:33
99-2000	**Carolina**	**NHL**	81	14	16	30	40	3	0	0	139	10.1	–10	5	40.0	13:39	....	....	....	....	....	....	....	....	....
2000-01	**Carolina**	**NHL**	79	23	29	52	59	6	1	4	170	13.5	–4	6	0.0	17:54	6	0	1	1	6	0	0	0	17:51
2001-02	**Carolina**	**NHL**	72	13	16	29	30	3	0	1	121	10.7	–1	13	23.1	16:05	23	3	4	7	10	0	0	1	14:16
2002-03	**Calgary**	**NHL**	81	21	31	52	51	6	0	3	152	13.8	–3	96	51.0	16:33	....	....	....	....	....	....	....	....	....
	NHL Totals		976	252	268	520	614	44	8	33	1776	14.2		126	45.2	15:29	121	15	26	41	85	3	0	3	15:47

QMJHL First All-Star Team (1988) • QMJHL Offensive Rookie of the Year (1988) • Canadian Major Junior Rookie of the Year (1988) • George Parsons Trophy (Memorial Cup Most Sportsmanlike Player) (1988)

Traded to **Edmonton** by **Los Angeles** with Jimmy Carson and Los Angeles' 1st round choices in 1989 (later traded to New Jersey – New Jersey selected Jason Miller), 1991 (Martin Rucinsky) and 1993 (Nick Stajduhar) Entry Drafts and cash for Wayne Gretzky, Mike Krushelnyski and Marty McSorley, August 9, 1988. Traded to **Quebec** by **Edmonton** with Edmonton's 6th round choice (Nicholas Checco) in 1993 Entry Draft for Scott Pearson, June 20, 1993. Claimed on waivers by **Vancouver** from **Quebec**, January 15, 1994. Traded to **Carolina** by **Vancouver** with Kirk McLean for Sean Burke, Geoff Sanderson and Enrico Ciccone, January 3, 1998. Signed as a free agent by **Calgary**, July 2, 2002.

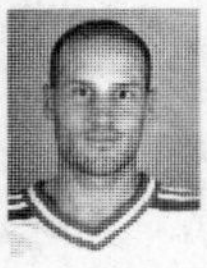

GERNANDER, Ken

(guhr-NAN-duhr, KEHN) **NYR**

Right wing. Shoots left. 5'10", 175 lbs. Born, Coleraine, MN, June 30, 1969. Winnipeg's 4th choice, 96th overall, in 1987 Entry Draft.

Season	Club	League	GP	G	A	Pts	PIM	PP	SH	GW	S	%	+/-	TF	F%	Min	GP	G	A	Pts	PIM	PP	SH	GW	Min
1985-86	Greenway Raiders	Hi-School	23	14	23	37	....	....	....	....	....	....	....	....	....	....	....	....	....	....	....	....	....	....	....
1986-87	Greenway Raiders	Hi-School	26	35	34	69	....	....	....	....	....	....	....	....	....	....	....	....	....	....	....	....	....	....	....
1987-88	U. of Minnesota	WCHA	44	14	14	28	14	....	....	....	....	....	....	....	....	....	....	....	....	....	....	....	....	....	....
1988-89	U. of Minnesota	WCHA	44	9	11	20	2	....	....	....	....	....	....	....	....	....	....	....	....	....	....	....	....	....	....
1989-90	U. of Minnesota	WCHA	44	32	17	49	24	....	....	....	....	....	....	....	....	....	....	....	....	....	....	....	....	....	....
1990-91	U. of Minnesota	WCHA	44	23	20	43	24	....	....	....	....	....	....	....	....	....	....	....	....	....	....	....	....	....	....
1991-92	Fort Wayne	IHL	13	7	6	13	2	....	....	....	....	....	....	....	....	....	....	....	....	....	....	....	....	....	....
	Moncton Hawks	AHL	43	8	18	26	9	....	....	....	....	....	....	....	....	....	8	1	1	2	2	....	....	....	....
1992-93	Moncton Hawks	AHL	71	18	29	47	20	....	....	....	....	....	....	....	....	....	5	1	4	5	0	....	....	....	....
1993-94	Moncton Hawks	AHL	71	22	25	47	12	....	....	....	....	....	....	....	....	....	19	6	1	7	0	....	....	....	....
1994-95	Binghamton	AHL	80	28	25	53	24	....	....	....	....	....	....	....	....	....	11	2	2	4	6	....	....	....	....
1995-96	**NY Rangers**	**NHL**	10	2	3	5	4	2	0	0	10	20.0	–3	....	....	....	6	0	0	0	0	0	0	0	....
	Binghamton	AHL	63	44	29	73	38	....	....	....	....	....	....	....	....	....	....	....	....	....	....	....	....	....	....
1996-97	Binghamton	AHL	46	13	18	31	30	....	....	....	....	....	....	....	....	....	2	0	1	1	0	....	....	....	....
	NY Rangers	**NHL**	....	....	....	....	....	....	....	....	....	....	....	....	....	....	9	0	0	0	0	0	0	0	....
1997-98	Hartford	AHL	80	35	28	63	26	....	....	....	....	....	....	....	....	....	12	5	6	11	4	....	....	....	....
1998-99	Hartford	AHL	70	23	26	49	32	....	....	....	....	....	....	....	....	....	7	1	2	3	2	....	....	....	....
99-2000	Hartford	AHL	79	28	29	57	24	....	....	....	....	....	....	....	....	....	23	5	5	10	0	....	....	....	....
2000-01	Hartford	AHL	80	22	27	49	39	....	....	....	....	....	....	....	....	....	2	0	0	0	0	....	....	....	....
2001-02	Hartford	AHL	75	18	31	49	19	....	....	....	....	....	....	....	....	....	10	1	3	4	4	....	....	....	....
2002-03	Hartford	AHL	72	17	19	36	22	....	....	....	....	....	....	....	....	....	2	0	0	0	0	....	....	....	....
	NHL Totals		10	2	3	5	4	2	0	0	10	20.0		....	....	....	15	0	0	0	0	0	0	0	....

Fred Hunt Memorial Trophy (Sportsmanship – AHL) (1996)

Signed as a free agent by **NY Rangers**, July 4, 1994.

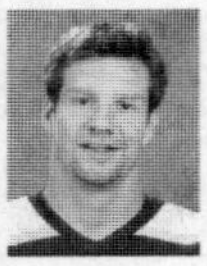

GILCHRIST, Brent

(GIHL-chrihst, BREHNT)

Left wing. Shoots left. 5'11", 180 lbs. Born, Moose Jaw, Sask., April 3, 1967. Montreal's 6th choice, 79th overall, in 1985 Entry Draft.

Season	Club	League	GP	G	A	Pts	PIM	PP	SH	GW	S	%	+/-	TF	F%	Min	GP	G	A	Pts	PIM	PP	SH	GW	Min
1983-84	Kelowna Wings	WHL	69	16	11	27	16	....	....	....	....	....	....	....	....	....	....	....	....	....	....	....	....	....	....
1984-85	Kelowna Wings	WHL	51	35	38	73	58	....	....	....	....	....	....	....	....	....	6	5	2	7	8	....	....	....	....
1985-86	Spokane Chiefs	WHL	52	45	45	90	57	....	....	....	....	....	....	....	....	....	9	6	7	13	19	....	....	....	....
1986-87	Spokane Chiefs	WHL	46	45	55	100	71	....	....	....	....	....	....	....	....	....	5	2	7	9	6	....	....	....	....
	Sherbrooke	AHL	....	....	....	....	....	....	....	....	....	....	....	....	....	....	10	2	7	9	2	....	....	....	....
1987-88	Sherbrooke	AHL	77	26	48	74	83	....	....	....	....	....	....	....	....	....	6	1	3	4	6	....	....	....	....
1988-89	**Montreal**	**NHL**	49	8	16	24	16	0	0	2	68	11.8	9	....	....	....	9	1	1	2	10	0	0	0	....
	Sherbrooke	AHL	7	6	5	11	7	....	....	....	....	....	....	....	....	....	....	....	....	....	....	....	....	....	....
1989-90	**Montreal**	**NHL**	57	9	15	24	28	1	0	0	80	11.3	3	....	....	....	8	2	0	2	2	0	0	0	....
1990-91	**Montreal**	**NHL**	51	6	9	15	10	1	0	1	81	7.4	–3	....	....	....	13	5	3	8	6	0	0	1	....
1991-92	**Montreal**	**NHL**	79	23	27	50	57	2	0	3	146	15.8	29	....	....	....	11	2	4	6	6	1	0	0	....
1992-93	**Edmonton**	**NHL**	60	10	10	20	47	2	0	0	94	10.6	–10	....	....	....	....	....	....	....	....	....	....	....	....
	Minnesota	**NHL**	8	0	1	1	2	0	0	0	12	0.0	–2	....	....	....	....	....	....	....	....	....	....	....	....
1993-94	**Dallas**	**NHL**	76	17	14	31	31	3	1	5	103	16.5	0	....	....	....	9	3	1	4	2	1	0	0	....
1994-95	**Dallas**	**NHL**	32	9	4	13	16	1	3	1	70	12.9	–3	....	....	....	5	0	1	1	2	0	0	0	....
1995-96	**Dallas**	**NHL**	77	20	22	42	36	6	1	2	164	12.2	–11	....	....	....	....	....	....	....	....	....	....	....	....
1996-97	**Dallas**	**NHL**	67	10	20	30	24	2	0	2	116	8.6	6	....	....	....	6	2	2	4	2	0	0	0	....
1997-98♦	**Detroit**	**NHL**	61	13	14	27	40	5	0	3	124	10.5	4	....	....	....	15	2	1	3	12	0	0	0	....
1998-99	**Detroit**	**NHL**	5	1	0	1	0	0	0	1	4	25.0	–1	28	42.9	11:58	3	0	0	0	0	0	0	0	7:53
99-2000	**Detroit**	**NHL**	24	4	2	6	24	0	0	0	33	12.1	1	180	50.0	11:19	6	0	0	0	6	0	0	0	8:54
2000-01	**Detroit**	**NHL**	60	1	8	9	41	0	0	0	75	1.3	–8	401	50.9	11:41	5	0	1	1	0	0	0	0	10:24
2001-02	**Detroit**	**NHL**	19	1	1	2	8	0	0	1	24	4.2	–3	118	53.4	9:22	....	....	....	....	....	....	....	....	....
	Dallas	**NHL**	26	2	5	7	6	0	0	0	29	6.9	–6	141	48.9	12:35	....	....	....	....	....	....	....	....	....
2002-03	**Nashville**	**NHL**	41	1	2	3	14	0	0	0	41	2.4	–11	25	32.0	10:46	....	....	....	....	....	....	....	....	....
	NHL Totals		792	135	170	305	400	23	5	21	1264	10.7		893	49.9	11:19	90	17	14	31	48	2	0	1	9:13

Traded to **Edmonton** by **Montreal** with Shayne Corson and Vladimir Vujtek for Vincent Damphousse and Edmonton's 4th round choice (Adam Wiesel) in 1993 Entry Draft, August 27, 1992. Traded to **Minnesota** by **Edmonton** for Todd Elik, March 5, 1993. Transferred to **Dallas** after **Minnesota** franchise relocated, June 9, 1993. Signed as a free agent by **Detroit**, August 1, 1997. Claimed by **Tampa Bay** from **Detroit** in Waiver Draft, October 5, 1998. Traded to **Detroit** by **Tampa Bay** for future considerations, October 5, 1998. • Missed majority of 1998-99 and 1999-2000 seasons recovering from hernia surgery, September 22, 1998. Claimed on waivers by **Dallas** from **Detroit**, February 13, 2002. Signed as a free agent by **Nashville**, July 11, 2002. • Missed majority of 2002-03 season recovering from back injury suffered in game vs. Edmonton, January 18, 2003.

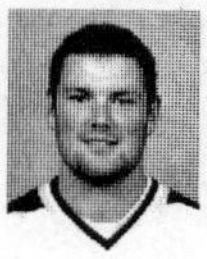

GILL, Hal

(GIHL, HAL) **BOS.**

Defense. Shoots left. 6'7", 250 lbs. Born, Concord, MA, April 6, 1975. Boston's 8th choice, 207th overall, in 1993 Entry Draft.

			Regular Season														Playoffs								
Season	Club	League	GP	G	A	Pts	PIM	PP	SH	GW	S	%	+/-	TF	F%	Min	GP	G	A	Pts	PIM	PP	SH	GW	Min
1992-93	Nashoba High	Hi-School	20	25	25	50	....	....	....	....	....	....	....	....	....	....	....	....	....	....	....	....	....	....	....
1993-94	Providence	H-East	31	1	2	3	26	....	....	....	....	....	....	....	....	....	....	....	....	....	....	....	....	....	....
1994-95	Providence	H-East	26	1	3	4	22	....	....	....	....	....	....	....	....	....	....	....	....	....	....	....	....	....	....
1995-96	Providence	H-East	39	5	12	17	54	....	....	....	....	....	....	....	....	....	....	....	....	....	....	....	....	....	....
1996-97	Providence	H-East	35	5	16	21	52	....	....	....	....	....	....	....	....	....	....	....	....	....	....	....	....	....	....
1997-98	Boston	NHL	68	2	4	6	47	0	0	0	56	3.6	4	....	....	....	6	0	0	0	4	0	0	0	....
	Providence Bruins	AHL	4	1	0	1	23	....	....	....	....	....	....	....	....	....	....	....	....	....	....	....	....	....	....
1998-99	Boston	NHL	80	3	7	10	63	0	0	2	102	2.9	–10	1	100.0	20:54	12	0	0	0	14	0	0	0	20:41
99-2000	Boston	NHL	81	3	9	12	51	0	0	0	120	2.5	0	0	0.0	17:15	....	....	....	....	....	....	....	....	....
2000-01	Boston	NHL	80	1	10	11	71	0	0	0	79	1.3	–2	0	0.0	18:21	....	....	....	....	....	....	....	....	....
2001-02	Boston	NHL	79	4	18	22	77	0	0	0	137	2.9	16	0	0.0	24:13	6	0	1	1	2	0	0	0	23:04
2002-03	Boston	NHL	76	4	13	17	56	0	0	0	114	3.5	21	0	0.0	20:42	5	0	0	0	4	0	0	0	20:19
	NHL Totals		464	17	61	78	365	0	0	2	608	2.8		1	100.0	20:16	29	0	1	1	24	0	0	0	21:14

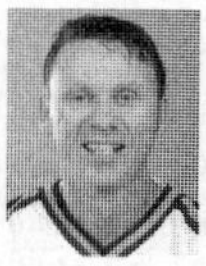

GILL, Todd

(GIHL, TAWD) **FLA.**

Defense. Shoots left. 6', 180 lbs. Born, Cardinal, Ont., November 9, 1965. Toronto's 2nd choice, 25th overall, in 1984 Entry Draft.

			Regular Season														Playoffs								
Season	Club	League	GP	G	A	Pts	PIM	PP	SH	GW	S	%	+/-	TF	F%	Min	GP	G	A	Pts	PIM	PP	SH	GW	Min
1980-81	Cardinal Broncos	OHA-B	35	10	14	24	65	....	....	....	....	....	....	....	....	....	....	....	....	....	....	....	....	....	....
1981-82	Brockville Braves	OCJHL	48	5	16	21	169	....	....	....	....	....	....	....	....	....	....	....	....	....	....	....	....	....	....
1982-83	Windsor Spitfires	OHL	70	12	24	36	108	....	....	....	....	....	....	....	....	....	3	0	0	0	11	....	....	....	....
1983-84	Windsor Spitfires	OHL	68	9	48	57	184	....	....	....	....	....	....	....	....	....	3	1	1	2	10	....	....	....	....
1984-85	Windsor Spitfires	OHL	53	17	40	57	148	....	....	....	....	....	....	....	....	....	4	0	1	1	14	....	....	....	....
	Toronto	NHL	10	1	0	1	13	0	0	0	9	11.1	–1	....	....	....	....	....	....	....	....	....	....	....	....
1985-86	Toronto	NHL	15	1	2	3	28	0	0	0	9	11.1	0	....	....	....	1	0	0	0	0	0	0	0	....
	St. Catharines	AHL	58	8	25	33	90	....	....	....	....	....	....	....	....	....	10	1	6	7	17	....	....	....	....
1986-87	Toronto	NHL	61	4	27	31	92	1	0	0	51	7.8	–3	....	....	....	13	2	2	4	42	0	0	0	....
	Newmarket Saints	AHL	11	1	8	9	33	....	....	....	....	....	....	....	....	....	....	....	....	....	....	....	....	....	....
1987-88	Toronto	NHL	65	8	17	25	131	1	0	3	109	7.3	–20	....	....	....	6	1	3	4	20	1	0	0	....
	Newmarket Saints	AHL	2	0	1	1	2	....	....	....	....	....	....	....	....	....	....	....	....	....	....	....	....	....	....
1988-89	Toronto	NHL	59	11	14	25	72	0	0	1	92	12.0	–3	....	....	....	....	....	....	....	....	....	....	....	....
1989-90	Toronto	NHL	48	1	14	15	92	0	0	0	44	2.3	–8	....	....	....	5	0	3	3	16	0	0	0	....
1990-91	Toronto	NHL	72	2	22	24	113	0	0	0	90	2.2	–4	....	....	....	....	....	....	....	....	....	....	....	....
1991-92	Toronto	NHL	74	2	15	17	91	1	0	0	82	2.4	–22	....	....	....	....	....	....	....	....	....	....	....	....
1992-93	Toronto	NHL	69	11	32	43	66	5	0	2	113	9.7	4	....	....	....	21	1	10	11	26	0	0	0	....
1993-94	Toronto	NHL	45	4	24	28	44	2	0	1	74	5.4	8	....	....	....	18	1	5	6	37	0	0	1	....
1994-95	Toronto	NHL	47	7	25	32	64	3	1	2	82	8.5	–8	....	....	....	7	0	3	3	6	0	0	0	....
1995-96	Toronto	NHL	74	7	18	25	116	1	0	2	109	6.4	–15	....	....	....	6	0	0	0	24	0	0	0	....
1996-97	San Jose	NHL	79	0	21	21	101	0	0	0	101	0.0	–20	....	....	....	....	....	....	....	....	....	....	....	....
1997-98	San Jose	NHL	64	8	13	21	31	4	0	1	100	8.0	–13	....	....	....	....	....	....	....	....	....	....	....	....
	St. Louis	NHL	11	5	4	9	10	3	0	1	22	22.7	2	....	....	....	10	2	2	4	10	1	1	0	....
1998-99	St. Louis	NHL	28	2	3	5	16	1	0	0	36	5.6	–6	0	0.0	17:36	....	....	....	....	....	....	....	....	....
	Detroit	NHL	23	2	2	4	11	0	0	1	25	8.0	–4	0	0.0	18:45	2	0	1	1	0	0	0	0	21:19
99-2000	Phoenix	NHL	41	1	6	7	30	0	0	1	41	2.4	–10	0	0.0	16:07	....	....	....	....	....	....	....	....	....
	Detroit	NHL	13	2	0	2	15	0	0	1	20	10.0	2	1	100.0	15:31	9	0	1	1	4	0	0	0	10:02
2000-01	Detroit	NHL	68	3	8	11	53	0	1	0	66	4.5	17	2	0.0	18:36	5	0	0	0	8	0	0	0	17:03
	Cincinnati	AHL	2	0	1	1	2	....	....	....	....	....	....	....	....	....	....	....	....	....	....	....	....	....	....
2001-02	Colorado	NHL	36	0	4	4	25	0	0	0	26	0.0	3	0	0.0	12:44	....	....	....	....	....	....	....	....	....
2002-03	Springfield	AHL	15	1	5	6	20	....	....	....	....	....	....	....	....	....	....	....	....	....	....	....	....	....	....
	Chicago	NHL	5	0	1	1	0	0	0	0	9	0.0	3	0	0.0	19:31	....	....	....	....	....	....	....	....	....
	Norfolk Admirals	AHL	9	0	3	3	10	....	....	....	....	....	....	....	....	....	9	2	5	7	10	....	....	....	....
	NHL Totals		1007	82	272	354	1214	22	2	16	1310	6.3		3	33.3	16:51	103	7	30	37	193	2	1	1	13:38

Traded to **San Jose** by **Toronto** for Jamie Baker and San Jose's 5th round choice (Peter Cava) in 1996 Entry Draft, June 14, 1996. Traded to **St. Louis** by **San Jose** for Joe Murphy, March 24, 1998. Claimed on waivers by **Detroit** from **St. Louis**, December 30, 1998. Signed as a free agent by **Phoenix**, July 21, 1999. Traded to **Detroit** by **Phoenix** for Philippe Audet, March 13, 2000. Signed as a free agent by **Colorado**, July 24, 2001. • Released by **Colorado**, February 12, 2002. Signed as a free agent by **Chicago**, March 5, 2003. Signed as a free agent by **Florida**, August 20, 2003.

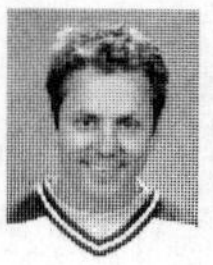

GILMOUR, Doug

(GIHL-mohr, DUHG)

Center. Shoots left. 5'11", 177 lbs. Born, Kingston, Ont., June 25, 1963. St. Louis' 4th choice, 134th overall, in 1982 Entry Draft.

			Regular Season														Playoffs								
Season	Club	League	GP	G	A	Pts	PIM	PP	SH	GW	S	%	+/-	TF	F%	Min	GP	G	A	Pts	PIM	PP	SH	GW	Min
1979-80	Kingston	OHA-B	15	2	5	7	26	....	....	....	....	....	....	....	....	....	....	....	....	....	....	....	....	....	....
	Belleville Bobcats	OHA-B	25	9	14	23	18	....	....	....	....	....	....	....	....	....	....	....	....	....	....	....	....	....	....
1980-81	Cornwall Royals	QMJHL	51	12	23	35	35	....	....	....	....	....	....	....	....	....	19	8	13	21	6	....	....	....	....
1981-82	Cornwall Royals	OHL	67	46	73	119	42	....	....	....	....	....	....	....	....	....	5	6	9	15	2	....	....	....	....
1982-83	Cornwall Royals	OHL	68	70	*107	*177	62	....	....	....	....	....	....	....	....	....	8	8	10	18	16	....	....	....	....
1983-84	St. Louis	NHL	80	25	28	53	57	3	1	1	157	15.9	6	....	....	....	11	2	9	11	10	1	0	1	....
1984-85	St. Louis	NHL	78	21	36	57	49	3	1	3	162	13.0	3	....	....	....	3	1	1	2	2	0	0	0	....
1985-86	St. Louis	NHL	74	25	28	53	41	2	1	5	183	13.7	–3	....	....	....	19	9	12	*21	25	1	2	2	....
1986-87	St. Louis	NHL	80	42	63	105	58	17	1	2	207	20.3	–2	....	....	....	6	2	2	4	16	1	0	1	....
1987-88	St. Louis	NHL	72	36	50	86	59	19	2	4	163	22.1	–13	....	....	....	10	3	14	17	18	1	0	0	....
1988-89 ♦	Calgary	NHL	72	26	59	85	44	11	0	5	161	16.1	45	....	....	....	22	11	11	22	20	3	0	3	....
1989-90	Calgary	NHL	78	24	67	91	54	12	1	3	152	15.8	20	....	....	....	6	3	1	4	8	0	0	1	....
1990-91	Calgary	NHL	78	20	61	81	144	2	2	5	135	14.8	27	....	....	....	7	1	1	2	0	0	0	1	....
1991-92	Calgary	NHL	38	11	27	38	46	4	1	1	64	17.2	12	....	....	....	....	....	....	....	....	....	....	....	....
	Toronto	NHL	40	15	34	49	32	6	0	3	104	14.4	13	....	....	....	....	....	....	....	....	....	....	....	....
1992-93	Toronto	NHL	83	32	95	127	100	15	3	2	211	15.2	32	....	....	....	21	10	*25	35	30	4	0	1	....
1993-94	Toronto	NHL	83	27	84	111	105	10	1	3	167	16.2	25	....	....	....	18	6	22	28	42	5	0	1	....
1994-95	Rapperswil	Swiss	9	2	13	15	16	....	....	....	....	....	....	....	....	....	....	....	....	....	....	....	....	....	....
	Toronto	NHL	44	10	23	33	26	3	0	1	73	13.7	–5	....	....	....	7	0	6	6	6	0	0	0	....
1995-96	Toronto	NHL	81	32	40	72	77	10	2	3	180	17.8	–5	....	....	....	6	1	7	8	12	1	0	0	....
1996-97	Toronto	NHL	61	15	45	60	46	2	1	1	103	14.6	–5	....	....	....	....	....	....	....	....	....	....	....	....
	New Jersey	NHL	20	7	15	22	22	2	0	0	40	17.5	7	....	....	....	10	0	4	4	14	0	0	0	....
1997-98	New Jersey	NHL	63	13	40	53	68	3	0	5	94	13.8	10	....	....	....	6	5	2	7	4	1	0	1	....
1998-99	Chicago	NHL	72	16	40	56	56	7	1	4	110	14.5	–16	1619	53.6	22:29	....	....	....	....	....	....	....	....	....
99-2000	Chicago	NHL	63	22	34	56	51	8	0	3	100	22.0	–12	941	53.7	19:59	....	....	....	....	....	....	....	....	....
	Buffalo	NHL	11	3	14	17	12	2	0	0	13	23.1	3	35	51.4	18:58	5	0	1	1	0	0	0	0	13:38
2000-01	Buffalo	NHL	71	7	31	38	70	4	0	0	91	7.7	3	429	51.1	18:02	13	2	4	6	12	1	0	1	17:47
2001-02	Montreal	NHL	70	10	31	41	48	5	0	2	78	12.8	–7	1241	51.1	18:39	12	4	6	10	16	1	0	0	20:01
2002-03	Montreal	NHL	61	11	19	30	36	3	0	0	85	12.9	–6	361	49.9	16:45	....	....	....	....	....	....	....	....	....
	Toronto	NHL	1	0	0	0	0	0	0	0	0	0.0	0	1	0.0	4:51	....	....	....	....	....	....	....	....	....
	NHL Totals		1474	450	964	1414	1301	153	18	56	2833	15.9		4627	52.4	19:12	182	60	128	188	235	20	2	13	17:59

OHL First All-Star Team (1983) • OHL MVP (1983) • Frank J. Selke Trophy (1993)

Played in NHL All-Star Game (1993, 1994)

Traded to **Calgary** by **St. Louis** with Mark Hunter, Steve Bozek and Michael Dark for Mike Bullard, Craig Coxe and Tim Corkery, September 6, 1988. Traded to **Toronto** by **Calgary** with Jamie Macoun, Ric Nattress, Kent Manderville and Rick Wamsley for Gary Leeman, Alexander Godynyuk, Jeff Reese, Michel Petit and Craig Berube, January 2, 1992. Traded to **New Jersey** by **Toronto** with Dave Ellett and New Jersey's 3rd round choice (previously acquired, New Jersey selected Andre Lakos) in 1999 Entry Draft for Jason Smith, Steve Sullivan and the rights to Alyn McCauley, February 25, 1997. Signed as a free agent by **Chicago**, July 28, 1998. Traded to **Buffalo** by **Chicago** with J.P. Dumont for Michal Grosek, March 10, 2000. Signed as a free agent by **Montreal**, October 5, 2001. Traded to **Toronto** by **Montreal** for Toronto's 6th round choice (Mark Flood) in 2003 Entry Draft, March 11, 2003.

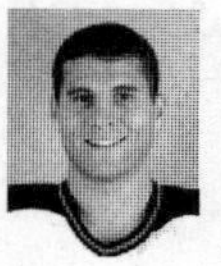

GIONTA, Brian

(jee-OHN-tuh, BRIGH-uhn) **N.J.**

Right wing. Shoots right. 5'7", 175 lbs. Born, Rochester, NY, January 18, 1979. New Jersey's 4th choice, 82nd overall, in 1998 Entry Draft.

			Regular Season														Playoffs								
Season	Club	League	GP	G	A	Pts	PIM	PP	SH	GW	S	%	+/-	TF	F%	Min	GP	G	A	Pts	PIM	PP	SH	GW	Min
1994-95	Rochester	NEJHL	28	*52	37	*89	....	....	....	....	....	....	....	....	....	....	....	....	....	....	....	....	....	....	....
1995-96	Niagara Scenics	MTJHL	51	47	44	91	59	....	....	....	....	....	....	....	....	....	....	....	....	....	....	....	....	....	....
1996-97	Niagara Scenics	MTJHL	50	57	70	127	101	....	....	....	....	....	....	....	....	....	6	6	11	17	21	....	....	....	....
1997-98	Boston College	H-East	40	30	32	62	44	....	....	....	....	....	....	....	....	....	....	....	....	....	....	....	....	....	....
1998-99	Boston College	H-East	39	27	33	60	46	....	....	....	....	....	....	....	....	....	....	....	....	....	....	....	....	....	....
99-2000	Boston College	H-East	42	*33	23	56	66	....	....	....	....	....	....	....	....	....	....	....	....	....	....	....	....	....	....
2000-01	Boston College	H-East	43	*33	21	*54	47	....	....	....	....	....	....	....	....	....	....	....	....	....	....	....	....	....	....

			Regular Season														Playoffs								
Season	Club	League	GP	G	A	Pts	PIM	PP	SH	GW	S	%	+/-	TF	F%	Min	GP	G	A	Pts	PIM	PP	SH	GW	Min
2001-02	**New Jersey**	**NHL**	**33**	**4**	**7**	**11**	**8**	**0**	**0**	**0**	**58**	**6.9**	**10**	**36**	**44.4**	**13:25**	**6**	**2**	**2**	**4**	**0**	**0**	**1**	**2**	**17:08**
	Albany River Rats	AHL	37	9	16	25	18	....	....	....	....	....	....	....	....	....	....	....	....	....	....	....	....	....	....
2002-03♦	**New Jersey**	**NHL**	**58**	**12**	**13**	**25**	**23**	**2**	**0**	**3**	**129**	**9.3**	**5**	**14**	**57.1**	**14:48**	**24**	**1**	**8**	**9**	**6**	**0**	**0**	**0**	**14:31**
	NHL Totals		**91**	**16**	**20**	**36**	**31**	**2**	**0**	**3**	**187**	**8.6**		**50**	**48.0**	**14:18**	**30**	**3**	**10**	**13**	**6**	**0**	**1**	**2**	**15:03**

MTJHL Player of the Year (1997) • Hockey East Rookie of the Year (1998) • Hockey East Second All-Star Team (1998) • NCAA East Second All-American Team (1998) • • Hockey East First All-Star Team (1999, 2000, 2001) • NCAA East First All-American Team (1999, 2000, 2001) • Hockey East Player of the Year (2001) • Walter Brown Award (New England's Outstanding American-born College player) (2001) (co-winner - Ty Conklin)

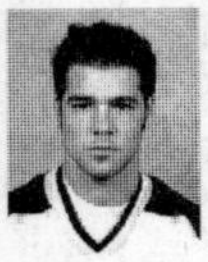

GIRARD, Jonathan

(zhih-RAHR, JAWN-ah-thuhn) **BOS.**

Defense. Shoots right. 5'11", 201 lbs. Born, Joliette, Que., May 27, 1980. Boston's 1st choice, 48th overall, in 1998 Entry Draft.

Season	Club	League	GP	G	A	Pts	PIM	PP	SH	GW	S	%	+/-	TF	F%	Min	GP	G	A	Pts	PIM	PP	SH	GW	Min
1995-96	Laval Laurentide	QAAA	39	11	22	33	44	....	....	....	....	....	....	....	....	....	16	4	11	15	16	....	....	....	....
1996-97	Laval Titan	QMJHL	39	11	23	34	13	....	....	....	....	....	....	....	....	....	3	0	3	3	0	....	....	....	....
1997-98	Laval Titan	QMJHL	64	20	47	67	44	....	....	....	....	....	....	....	....	....	16	2	16	18	13	....	....	....	....
1998-99	Acadie-Bathurst	QMJHL	50	9	58	67	60	....	....	....	....	....	....	....	....	....	23	13	18	31	22	....	....	....	....
	Boston	**NHL**	**3**	**0**	**0**	**0**	**0**	**0**	**0**	**0**	**3**	**0.0**	**1**	**0**	**0.0**	**9:28**	....	....	....	....	....	....	....	....	....
99-2000	**Boston**	**NHL**	**23**	**1**	**2**	**3**	**2**	**0**	**0**	**0**	**17**	**5.9**	**–1**	**0**	**0.0**	**9:32**	....	....	....	....	....	....	....	....	....
	Moncton Wildcats	QMJHL	26	10	25	35	36	....	....	....	....	....	....	....	....	....	16	3	15	18	36	....	....	....	....
	Providence Bruins	AHL	5	0	1	1	0	....	....	....	....	....	....	....	....	....	....	....	....	....	....	....	....	....	....
2000-01	**Boston**	**NHL**	**31**	**3**	**13**	**16**	**14**	**2**	**0**	**1**	**42**	**7.1**	**2**	**0**	**0.0**	**16:32**	....	....	....	....	....	....	....	....	....
	Providence Bruins	AHL	39	3	21	24	6	....	....	....	....	....	....	....	....	....	17	0	5	5	4	....	....	....	....
2001-02	**Boston**	**NHL**	**20**	**0**	**3**	**3**	**9**	**0**	**0**	**0**	**28**	**0.0**	**0**	**0**	**0.0**	**14:43**	**1**	**0**	**0**	**0**	**2**	**0**	**0**	**0**	**10:06**
	Providence Bruins	AHL	59	6	31	37	36	....	....	....	....	....	....	....	....	....	2	0	0	0	2	....	....	....	....
2002-03	**Boston**	**NHL**	**73**	**6**	**16**	**22**	**21**	**2**	**0**	**2**	**123**	**4.9**	**4**	**0**	**0.0**	**20:50**	**2**	**0**	**1**	**1**	**0**	**0**	**0**	**0**	**16:40**
	NHL Totals		**150**	**10**	**34**	**44**	**46**	**4**	**0**	**3**	**213**	**4.7**		**0**	**0.0**	**17:10**	**3**	**0**	**1**	**1**	**2**	**0**	**0**	**0**	**14:28**

QMJHL All-Rookie Team (1997) • QMJHL Second All-Star Team (1998) • QMJHL First All-Star Team (1999, 2000)

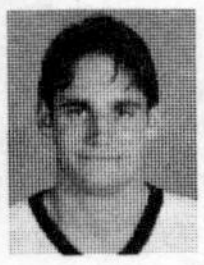

GIROUX, Raymond

(zhih-ROO, ray-MAWN) **N.J.**

Defense. Shoots left. 6'1", 190 lbs. Born, North Bay, Ont., July 20, 1976. Philadelphia's 7th choice, 202nd overall, in 1994 Entry Draft.

Season	Club	League	GP	G	A	Pts	PIM	PP	SH	GW	S	%	+/-	TF	F%	Min	GP	G	A	Pts	PIM	PP	SH	GW	Min
1992-93	Powassan Hawks	NOJHA	45	8	18	26	117	....	....	....	....	....	....	....	....	....	....	....	....	....	....	....	....	....	....
1993-94	Powassan Hawks	NOJHA	36	10	40	50	42	....	....	....	....	....	....	....	....	....	....	....	....	....	....	....	....	....	....
1994-95	Yale Bulldogs	ECAC	27	1	3	4	8	....	....	....	....	....	....	....	....	....	....	....	....	....	....	....	....	....	....
1995-96	Yale Bulldogs	ECAC	30	3	16	19	36	....	....	....	....	....	....	....	....	....	....	....	....	....	....	....	....	....	....
1996-97	Yale Bulldogs	ECAC	32	9	12	21	38	....	....	....	....	....	....	....	....	....	....	....	....	....	....	....	....	....	....
1997-98	Yale Bulldogs	ECAC	35	9	*30	39	62	....	....	....	....	....	....	....	....	....	....	....	....	....	....	....	....	....	....
1998-99	Lowell	AHL	59	13	19	32	92	....	....	....	....	....	....	....	....	....	3	1	1	2	0	....	....	....	....
99-2000	**NY Islanders**	**NHL**	**14**	**0**	**9**	**9**	**10**	**0**	**0**	**0**	**24**	**0.0**	**0**	**9**	**22.2**	**14:40**	....	....	....	....	....	....	....	....	....
	Lowell	AHL	49	12	21	33	34	....	....	....	....	....	....	....	....	....	7	0	0	0	2	....	....	....	....
2000-01	HIFK Helsinki	Finland	22	3	9	12	34	....	....	....	....	....	....	....	....	....	....	....	....	....	....	....	....	....	....
	AIK Solna	Sweden	9	0	1	1	16	....	....	....	....	....	....	....	....	....	....	....	....	....	....	....	....	....	....
	Jokerit Helsinki	Finland	24	4	9	13	16	....	....	....	....	....	....	....	....	....	5	0	0	0	0	....	....	....	....
2001-02	**NY Islanders**	**NHL**	**2**	**0**	**0**	**0**	**2**	**0**	**0**	**0**	**2**	**0.0**	**–1**	**0**	**0.0**	**12:18**	....	....	....	....	....	....	....	....	....
	Bridgeport	AHL	79	13	40	53	73	....	....	....	....	....	....	....	....	....	19	1	7	8	20	....	....	....	....
2002-03	**New Jersey**	**NHL**	**11**	**0**	**1**	**1**	**6**	**0**	**0**	**0**	**20**	**0.0**	**–2**	**0**	**0.0**	**18:18**	....	....	....	....	....	....	....	....	....
	Albany River Rats	AHL	67	11	38	49	49	....	....	....	....	....	....	....	....	....	....	....	....	....	....	....	....	....	....
	NHL Totals		**27**	**0**	**10**	**10**	**18**	**0**	**0**	**0**	**46**	**0.0**		**9**	**22.2**	**15:58**	....	....	....	....	....	....	....	....	....

ECAC First All-Star Team (1998) • NCAA East First All-American Team (1998) • AHL First All-Star Team (2003)

Rights traded to **NY Islanders** by **Philadelphia** for NY Islanders' 6th round choice (later traded to Montreal – Montreal selected Scott Selig) in 2000 Entry Draft, August 25, 1998. Signed as a free agent by **New Jersey**, July 12, 2002.

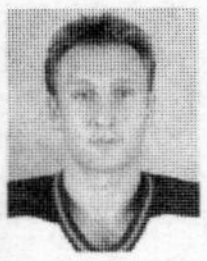

GOC, Sascha

(GAWCH, SA-shah) **T.B.**

Defense. Shoots right. 6'2", 225 lbs. Born, Calw, West Germany, April 17, 1979. New Jersey's 5th choice, 159th overall, in 1997 Entry Draft.

Season	Club	League	GP	G	A	Pts	PIM	PP	SH	GW	S	%	+/-	TF	F%	Min	GP	G	A	Pts	PIM	PP	SH	GW	Min
1995-96	Schwenningen Jr.	Ger.-Jr.	11	3	6	9	77	....	....	....	....	....	....	....	....	....	....	....	....	....	....	....	....	....	....
	Schwenningen	Germany	1	0	0	0	0	....	....	....	....	....	....	....	....	....	....	....	....	....	....	....	....	....	....
1996-97	Schwenningen	Germany	41	3	1	4	28	....	....	....	....	....	....	....	....	....	5	0	0	0	0	....	....	....	....
1997-98	Schwenningen	Germany	49	5	5	10	45	....	....	....	....	....	....	....	....	....	....	....	....	....	....	....	....	....	....
1998-99	Albany River Rats	AHL	55	1	12	13	24	....	....	....	....	....	....	....	....	....	2	0	0	0	0	....	....	....	....
99-2000	Albany River Rats	AHL	64	9	22	31	35	....	....	....	....	....	....	....	....	....	5	2	0	2	6	....	....	....	....
2000-01	**New Jersey**	**NHL**	**11**	**0**	**0**	**0**	**4**	**0**	**0**	**0**	**7**	**0.0**	**7**	**0**	**0.0**	**13:37**	....	....	....	....	....	....	....	....	....
	Albany River Rats	AHL	55	10	29	39	49	....	....	....	....	....	....	....	....	....	....	....	....	....	....	....	....	....	....
2001-02	**New Jersey**	**NHL**	**2**	**0**	**0**	**0**	**0**	**0**	**0**	**0**	**2**	**0.0**	**–2**	**0**	**0.0**	**19:21**	....	....	....	....	....	....	....	....	....
	Albany River Rats	AHL	10	0	5	5	12	....	....	....	....	....	....	....	....	....	....	....	....	....	....	....	....	....	....
	Tampa Bay	**NHL**	**9**	**0**	**0**	**0**	**0**	**0**	**0**	**0**	**2**	**0.0**	**0**	**0**	**0.0**	**5:32**	....	....	....	....	....	....	....	....	....
	Springfield	AHL	36	3	9	12	30	....	....	....	....	....	....	....	....	....	....	....	....	....	....	....	....	....	....
2002-03	Adler Mannheim	Germany	49	1	3	4	87	....	....	....	....	....	....	....	....	....	7	1	0	1	*41	....	....	....	....
	NHL Totals		**22**	**0**	**0**	**0**	**4**	**0**	**0**	**0**	**11**	**0.0**		**0**	**0.0**	**10:50**	....	....	....	....	....	....	....	....	....

Traded to **Tampa Bay** by **New Jersey** with Josef Boumedienne and the rights to Anton But for Andrei Zyuzin, November 9, 2001. Signed as a free agent by **Adler Mannheim** (Germany), April 23, 2002.

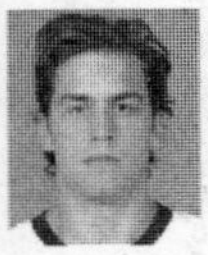

GODARD, Eric

(GAW-duhrd, AIR-ihk) **NYI**

Right wing. Shoots right. 6'4", 227 lbs. Born, Vernon, B.C., March 7, 1980.

Season	Club	League	GP	G	A	Pts	PIM	PP	SH	GW	S	%	+/-	TF	F%	Min	GP	G	A	Pts	PIM	PP	SH	GW	Min
1997-98	Lethbridge	WHL	7	0	0	0	26	....	....	....	....	....	....	....	....	....	2	0	0	0	0	....	....	....	....
1998-99	Lethbridge	WHL	66	2	5	7	213	....	....	....	....	....	....	....	....	....	4	0	0	0	14	....	....	....	....
99-2000	Lethbridge	WHL	60	3	5	8	*310	....	....	....	....	....	....	....	....	....	....	....	....	....	....	....	....	....	....
	Louisville Panthers	AHL	4	0	1	1	16	....	....	....	....	....	....	....	....	....	....	....	....	....	....	....	....	....	....
2000-01	Louisville Panthers	AHL	45	0	0	0	132	....	....	....	....	....	....	....	....	....	....	....	....	....	....	....	....	....	....
2001-02	Bridgeport	AHL	67	1	4	5	198	....	....	....	....	....	....	....	....	....	20	0	4	4	30	....	....	....	....
2002-03	**NY Islanders**	**NHL**	**19**	**0**	**0**	**0**	**48**	**0**	**0**	**0**	**6**	**0.0**	**–3**	**0**	**0.0**	**4:32**	**2**	**0**	**1**	**1**	**4**	**0**	**0**	**0**	**1:09**
	Bridgeport	AHL	46	2	2	4	199	....	....	....	....	....	....	....	....	....	6	0	0	0	16	....	....	....	....
	NHL Totals		**19**	**0**	**0**	**0**	**48**	**0**	**0**	**0**	**6**	**0.0**		**0**	**0.0**	**4:32**	**2**	**0**	**1**	**1**	**4**	**0**	**0**	**0**	**1:09**

Signed as a free agent by **Florida**, September 24, 1999. Traded to **NY Islanders** by **Florida** for Florida's 3rd round choice (previously acquired, Florida selected Gregory Campbell) in 2002 Entry Draft, June 22, 2002.

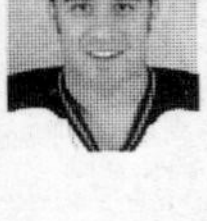

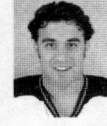

GOMEZ, Scott

(GOH-mehz, SKAWT) **N.J.**

Center. Shoots left. 5'11", 200 lbs. Born, Anchorage, AK, December 23, 1979. New Jersey's 2nd choice, 27th overall, in 1998 Entry Draft.

Season	Club	League	GP	G	A	Pts	PIM	PP	SH	GW	S	%	+/-	TF	F%	Min	GP	G	A	Pts	PIM	PP	SH	GW	Min
1994-95	East High	Hi-School	28	30	48	78	....	....	....	....	....	....	....	....	....	....	....	....	....	....	....	....	....	....	....
1995-96	East High	Hi-School	27	*56	49	*101	....	....	....	....	....	....	....	....	....	....	....	....	....	....	....	....	....	....	....
	Anchorage	AAHL	40	*70	*67	*137	44	....	....	....	....	....	....	....	....	....	....	....	....	....	....	....	....	....	....
1996-97	South Surrey	BCHL	56	48	76	124	94	....	....	....	....	....	....	....	....	....	21	18	23	41	57	....	....	....	....
1997-98	Tri-City	WHL	45	12	37	49	57	....	....	....	....	....	....	....	....	....	....	....	....	....	....	....	....	....	....
1998-99	Tri-City	WHL	58	30	*78	108	55	....	....	....	....	....	....	....	....	....	10	6	13	19	31	....	....	....	....
99-2000♦	**New Jersey**	**NHL**	**82**	**19**	**51**	**70**	**78**	**7**	**0**	**1**	**204**	**9.3**	**14**	**341**	**44.6**	**16:21**	**23**	**4**	**6**	**10**	**4**	**1**	**0**	**2**	**14:08**
2000-01	**New Jersey**	**NHL**	**76**	**14**	**49**	**63**	**46**	**2**	**0**	**4**	**155**	**9.0**	**–1**	**1010**	**44.6**	**15:46**	**25**	**5**	**9**	**14**	**24**	**0**	**0**	**0**	**16:06**
2001-02	**New Jersey**	**NHL**	**76**	**10**	**38**	**48**	**36**	**1**	**0**	**1**	**156**	**6.4**	**–4**	**628**	**48.7**	**16:46**	....	....	....	....	....	....	....	....	....
2002-03♦	**New Jersey**	**NHL**	**80**	**13**	**42**	**55**	**48**	**2**	**0**	**4**	**205**	**6.3**	**17**	**864**	**47.5**	**16:01**	**24**	**3**	**9**	**12**	**2**	**0**	**0**	**0**	**13:45**
	NHL Totals		**314**	**56**	**180**	**236**	**208**	**12**	**0**	**10**	**720**	**7.8**		**2843**	**46.4**	**16:13**	**72**	**12**	**24**	**36**	**30**	**1**	**0**	**2**	**14:41**

BCHL All-Rookie Team (1997) • WHL West First All-Star Team (1999) • NHL All-Rookie Team (2000) • Calder Memorial Trophy (2000)

Played in NHL All-Star Game (2000)

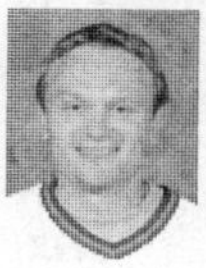

GONCHAR, Sergei

(gohn-CHAR, SAIR-gay) **WSH.**

Defense. Shoots left. 6'2", 208 lbs. Born, Chelyabinsk, USSR, April 13, 1974. Washington's 1st choice, 14th overall, in 1992 Entry Draft.

			Regular Season														Playoffs								
Season	Club	League	GP	G	A	Pts	PIM	PP	SH	GW	S	%	+/-	TF	F%	Min	GP	G	A	Pts	PIM	PP	SH	GW	Min
1991-92	Chelyabinsk	CIS	31	1	0	1	6	....	....	....	....	....	....	....	....	....	....	....	....	....	....	....	....	....	....
1992-93	Dynamo Moscow	CIS	31	1	3	4	70	....	....	....	....	....	....	....	....	....	10	0	0	0	12	....	....	....	....
1993-94	Dynamo Moscow	CIS	44	4	5	9	36	....	....	....	....	....	....	....	....	....	10	0	3	3	14	....	....	....	....
	Portland Pirates	AHL	....	....	....	....	....	....	....	....	....	....	....	....	....	....	2	0	0	0	0	....	....	....	....
1994-95	Portland Pirates	AHL	61	10	32	42	67	....	....	....	....	....	....	....	....	....	....	....	....	....	....	....	....	....	....
	Washington	**NHL**	31	2	5	7	22	0	0	0	38	5.3	4	....	....	....	7	2	2	4	2	0	0	1	....
1995-96	**Washington**	**NHL**	78	15	26	41	60	4	0	4	139	10.8	25	....	....	....	6	2	4	6	4	1	0	0	....
1996-97	**Washington**	**NHL**	57	13	17	30	36	3	0	3	129	10.1	−11	....	....	....	....	....	....	....	....	....	....	....	....
1997-98	Lada Togliatti	Russia	7	3	2	5	4	....	....	....	....	....	....	....	....	....	....	....	....	....	....	....	....	....	....
	Lada Togliatti	EuroHL	1	1	0	1	2	....	....	....	....	....	....	....	....	....	....	....	....	....	....	....	....	....	....
	Washington	**NHL**	72	5	16	21	66	2	0	0	134	3.7	2	....	....	....	21	7	4	11	30	3	1	2	....
	Russia	Olympics	6	0	2	2	0	....	....	....	....	....	....	....	....	....	....	....	....	....	....	....	....	....	....
1998-99	**Washington**	**NHL**	53	21	10	31	57	13	1	3	180	11.7	1	0	0.0	23:55	....	....	....	....	....	....	....	....	....
99-2000	**Washington**	**NHL**	73	18	36	54	52	5	0	3	181	9.9	26	0	0.0	21:46	5	1	0	1	6	0	0	0	19:58
2000-01	**Washington**	**NHL**	76	19	38	57	70	8	0	2	241	7.9	12	1	100.0	22:26	6	1	3	4	2	1	0	0	19:45
2001-02	**Washington**	**NHL**	76	26	33	59	58	7	0	2	216	12.0	−1	1	100.0	23:51	....	....	....	....	....	....	....	....	....
	Russia	Olympics	6	0	0	0	2	....	....	....	....	....	....	....	....	....	....	....	....	....	....	....	....	....	....
2002-03	**Washington**	**NHL**	82	18	49	67	52	7	0	2	224	8.0	13	0	0.0	26:35	6	0	5	5	4	0	0	0	29:00
	NHL Totals		598	137	230	367	473	49	1	19	1482	9.2		2	100.0	23:46	51	13	18	31	48	5	1	3	23:05

NHL Second All-Star Team (2002, 2003)

Played in NHL All-Star Game (2001, 2002, 2003)

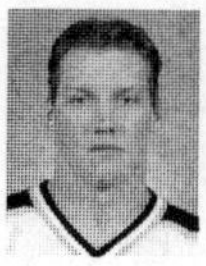

GOREN, Lee

(GOH-rehn, LEE) **FLA.**

Right wing. Shoots right. 6'3", 207 lbs. Born, Winnipeg, Man., December 26, 1977. Boston's 5th choice, 63rd overall, in 1997 Entry Draft.

			Regular Season														Playoffs								
Season	Club	League	GP	G	A	Pts	PIM	PP	SH	GW	S	%	+/-	TF	F%	Min	GP	G	A	Pts	PIM	PP	SH	GW	Min
1994-95	Wpg. Warriors	MMHL	31	19	31	50	50	....	....	....	....	....	....	....	....	....	....	....	....	....	....	....	....	....	....
1995-96	Minot Top Guns	SJHL	56	25	35	61	....	....	....	....	....	....	....	....	....	....	12	5	20	25	....	....	....	....	....
	Saskatoon Blades	WHL	2	0	0	0	2	....	....	....	....	....	....	....	....	....	....	....	....	....	....	....	....	....	....
1996-97	North Dakota	WCHA		DID NOT PLAY – FRESHMAN																					
1997-98	North Dakota	WCHA	29	3	13	16	26	....	....	....	....	....	....	....	....	....	....	....	....	....	....	....	....	....	....
1998-99	North Dakota	WCHA	38	26	19	45	20	....	....	....	....	....	....	....	....	....	....	....	....	....	....	....	....	....	....
99-2000	North Dakota	WCHA	44	*34	29	63	42	....	....	....	....	....	....	....	....	....	....	....	....	....	....	....	....	....	....
2000-01	**Boston**	**NHL**	21	2	0	2	7	1	0	0	9	22.2	−3	21	38.1	4:24	....	....	....	....	....	....	....	....	....
	Providence Bruins	AHL	54	15	18	33	72	....	....	....	....	....	....	....	....	....	17	5	2	7	11	....	....	....	....
2001-02	Providence Bruins	AHL	71	11	26	37	121	....	....	....	....	....	....	....	....	....	2	0	0	0	0	....	....	....	....
2002-03	**Boston**	**NHL**	14	2	1	3	7	2	0	0	15	13.3	−2	0	0.0	8:15	5	0	0	0	5	0	0	0	6:29
	Providence Bruins	AHL	65	32	37	69	106	....	....	....	....	....	....	....	....	....	3	0	1	1	0	....	....	....	....
	NHL Totals		35	4	1	5	14	3	0	0	24	16.7		21	38.1	5:56	5	0	0	0	5	0	0	0	6:29

WCHA Second All-Star Team (2000) • NCAA West Second All-American Team (2000) • NCAA Championship All-Tournament Team (2000) • NCAA Championship Tournament MVP (2000)

• Ruled ineligible to play during 1996-97 season by NCAA due to appearance with **Saskatoon** (WHL) in 1995-96 season.Signed as a free agent by **Florida**, July 24, 2003.

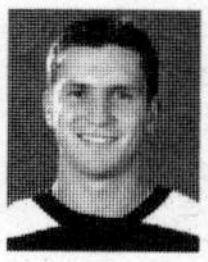

GOSSELIN, David

(GAH-sih-lihn, DAY-vihd) **DAL.**

Right wing. Shoots right. 6'1", 205 lbs. Born, Levis, Que., June 22, 1977. New Jersey's 4th choice, 78th overall, in 1995 Entry Draft.

			Regular Season														Playoffs								
Season	Club	League	GP	G	A	Pts	PIM	PP	SH	GW	S	%	+/-	TF	F%	Min	GP	G	A	Pts	PIM	PP	SH	GW	Min
1992-93	Richelieu Riverains	QAAA	40	5	12	17	24	....	....	....	....	....	....	....	....	....	4	0	0	0	2	....	....	....	....
1993-94	Richelieu Riverains	QAAA	44	26	19	45	62	....	....	....	....	....	....	....	....	....	4	2	1	3	0	....	....	....	....
1994-95	Sherbrooke	QMJHL	58	8	8	16	36	....	....	....	....	....	....	....	....	....	7	0	0	0	2	....	....	....	....
1995-96	Sherbrooke	QMJHL	55	24	24	48	147	....	....	....	....	....	....	....	....	....	7	2	2	4	4	....	....	....	....
1996-97	Sherbrooke	QMJHL	23	11	15	26	52	....	....	....	....	....	....	....	....	....	....	....	....	....	....	....	....	....	....
	Chicoutimi	QMJHL	28	16	33	49	65	....	....	....	....	....	....	....	....	....	12	9	7	16	16	....	....	....	....
1997-98	Chicoutimi	QMJHL	69	46	64	110	139	....	....	....	....	....	....	....	....	....	6	1	4	5	8	....	....	....	....
1998-99	Milwaukee	IHL	74	17	11	28	78	....	....	....	....	....	....	....	....	....	2	0	2	2	2	....	....	....	....
99-2000	**Nashville**	**NHL**	10	2	1	3	6	0	0	0	14	14.3	−4	0	0.0	9:16	....	....	....	....	....	....	....	....	....
	Milwaukee	IHL	70	21	20	41	118	....	....	....	....	....	....	....	....	....	3	0	0	0	10	....	....	....	....
2000-01	Milwaukee	IHL	32	5	9	14	56	....	....	....	....	....	....	....	....	....	....	....	....	....	....	....	....	....	....
2001-02	**Nashville**	**NHL**	3	0	0	0	5	0	0	0	0	0.0	−1	0	0.0	7:05	....	....	....	....	....	....	....	....	....
	Milwaukee	AHL	66	11	21	32	112	....	....	....	....	....	....	....	....	....	....	....	....	....	....	....	....	....	....
2002-03	Utah Grizzlies	AHL	80	12	22	34	141	....	....	....	....	....	....	....	....	....	2	0	1	1	6	....	....	....	....
	NHL Totals		13	2	1	3	11	0	0	0	14	14.3		0	0.0	8:46	....	....	....	....	....	....	....	....	....

Signed as a free agent by **Nashville**, July 1, 1998. • Missed majority of 2000-01 season recovering from knee injury suffered in game vs. Grand Rapids (IHL), December 28, 2000. Traded to **Dallas** by **Nashville** with Nashville's 5th round choice (Eero Kilpelainen) in 2003 Entry Draft for Ed Belfour and Cameron Mann, June 29, 2002.

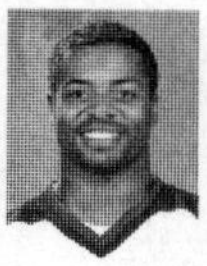

GRAND-PIERRE, Jean-Luc

(GRAHN pee-AIR, ZHAHN-LOOK) **CBJ**

Defense. Shoots right. 6'3", 223 lbs. Born, Montreal, Que., February 2, 1977. St. Louis' 6th choice, 179th overall, in 1995 Entry Draft.

			Regular Season														Playoffs								
Season	Club	League	GP	G	A	Pts	PIM	PP	SH	GW	S	%	+/-	TF	F%	Min	GP	G	A	Pts	PIM	PP	SH	GW	Min
1992-93	Lac St-Louis Lions	QAAA	1	0	0	0	2	....	....	....	....	....	....	....	....	....	....	....	....	....	....	....	....	....	....
1993-94	Beauport	QMJHL	46	1	4	5	27	....	....	....	....	....	....	....	....	....	1	0	0	0	0	....	....	....	....
1994-95	Val-d'Or Foreurs	QMJHL	59	10	13	23	126	....	....	....	....	....	....	....	....	....	....	....	....	....	....	....	....	....	....
1995-96	Val-d'Or Foreurs	QMJHL	67	13	21	34	209	....	....	....	....	....	....	....	....	....	13	1	4	5	47	....	....	....	....
1996-97	Val-d'Or Foreurs	QMJHL	58	9	24	33	186	....	....	....	....	....	....	....	....	....	13	5	8	13	46	....	....	....	....
1997-98	Rochester	AHL	75	4	6	10	211	....	....	....	....	....	....	....	....	....	4	0	0	0	2	....	....	....	....
1998-99	**Buffalo**	**NHL**	16	0	1	1	17	0	0	0	11	0.0	0	0	0.0	13:36	....	....	....	....	....	....	....	....	....
	Rochester	AHL	55	5	4	9	90	....	....	....	....	....	....	....	....	....	....	....	....	....	....	....	....	....	....
99-2000	**Buffalo**	**NHL**	11	0	0	0	15	0	0	0	11	0.0	−1	0	0.0	15:11	4	0	0	0	4	0	0	0	17:34
	Rochester	AHL	62	5	8	13	124	....	....	....	....	....	....	....	....	....	17	0	1	1	40	....	....	....	....
2000-01	**Columbus**	**NHL**	64	1	4	5	73	0	0	0	33	3.0	−6	0	0.0	12:51	....	....	....	....	....	....	....	....	....
2001-02	**Columbus**	**NHL**	81	2	6	8	90	0	0	0	62	3.2	−28	3	0.0	15:20	....	....	....	....	....	....	....	....	....
2002-03	**Columbus**	**NHL**	41	1	0	1	64	0	0	0	32	3.1	−6	0	0.0	13:38	....	....	....	....	....	....	....	....	....
	Syracuse Crunch	AHL	2	1	0	1	6	....	....	....	....	....	....	....	....	....	....	....	....	....	....	....	....	....	....
	NHL Totals		213	4	11	15	259	0	0	0	149	2.7		3	0.0	14:08	4	0	0	0	4	0	0	0	17:34

Traded to **Buffalo** by **St. Louis** with Ottawa's 2nd round choice (previously acquired, Buffalo selected Cory Sarich) in 1996 Entry Draft and St. Louis' 3rd round choice (Maxim Afinogenov) in 1997 Entry Draft for Yuri Khmylev and Buffalo's 8th round choice (Andrei Podkonicky) in 1996 Entry Draft, March 20, 1996. Traded to **Columbus** by **Buffalo** with Matt Davidson, San Jose's 5th round choice (previously acquired, Columbus selected Tyler Kolarik) in 2000 Entry Draft and Buffalo's 5th round choice (later traded to Calgary – later traded to Detroit – Detroit selected Andreas Jamtin) in 2001 Entry Draft to complete Expansion Draft agreement which had Columbus select Geoff Sanderson and Dwayne Roloson from Buffalo, June 23, 2000.

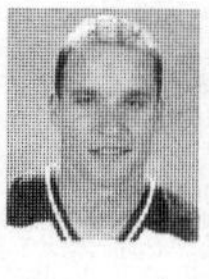

GRATTON, Benoit

(grah-TOHN, BEHN-wah) **MTL.**

Center. Shoots left. 5'11", 194 lbs. Born, Montreal, Que., December 28, 1976. Washington's 6th choice, 105th overall, in 1995 Entry Draft.

			Regular Season														Playoffs								
Season	Club	League	GP	G	A	Pts	PIM	PP	SH	GW	S	%	+/-	TF	F%	Min	GP	G	A	Pts	PIM	PP	SH	GW	Min
1992-93	Laval Laurentide	QAAA	40	19	38	57	74	....	....	....	....	....	....	....	....	....	13	1	9	10	27	....	....	....	....
1993-94	Laval Titan	QMJHL	51	9	14	23	70	....	....	....	....	....	....	....	....	....	20	2	1	3	19	....	....	....	....
1994-95	Laval Titan	QMJHL	71	30	58	88	199	....	....	....	....	....	....	....	....	....	20	8	*21	29	42	....	....	....	....
1995-96	Laval Titan	QMJHL	38	21	39	60	130	....	....	....	....	....	....	....	....	....	....	....	....	....	....	....	....	....	....
	Granby	QMJHL	27	12	46	58	97	....	....	....	....	....	....	....	....	....	21	13	26	39	68	....	....	....	....
1996-97	Portland Pirates	AHL	76	6	40	46	140	....	....	....	....	....	....	....	....	....	5	2	1	3	14	....	....	....	....
1997-98	**Washington**	**NHL**	6	0	1	1	6	0	0	0	5	0.0	1	....	....	....	....	....	....	....	....	....	....	....	....
	Portland Pirates	AHL	58	19	31	50	137	....	....	....	....	....	....	....	....	....	8	4	2	6	24	....	....	....	....
1998-99	**Washington**	**NHL**	16	4	3	7	16	0	0	0	24	16.7	−1	136	54.4	13:28	....	....	....	....	....	....	....	....	....
	Portland Pirates	AHL	64	18	42	60	135	....	....	....	....	....	....	....	....	....	....	....	....	....	....	....	....	....	....
99-2000	**Calgary**	**NHL**	10	0	2	2	10	0	0	0	4	0.0	1	68	63.2	8:15	....	....	....	....	....	....	....	....	....
	Saint John Flames	AHL	65	17	49	66	137	....	....	....	....	....	....	....	....	....	3	0	1	1	4	....	....	....	....
2000-01	**Calgary**	**NHL**	14	1	3	4	14	0	0	0	13	7.7	0	105	63.8	9:11	....	....	....	....	....	....	....	....	....
	Saint John Flames	AHL	53	10	36	46	153	....	....	....	....	....	....	....	....	....	....	....	....	....	....	....	....	....	....

			Regular Season														Playoffs								
Season	Club	League	GP	G	A	Pts	PIM	PP	SH	GW	S	%	+/-	TF	F%	Min	GP	G	A	Pts	PIM	PP	SH	GW	Min
2001-02	Montreal	NHL	8	1	0	1	8	0	0	0	8	12.5	–1	98	63.3	9:51	....	....	....	....	....	....	....	....	....
	Quebec Citadelles	AHL	35	10	19	29	70	....	....	....	....	....	....	....	....	....	3	2	3	5	10	....	....	....	....
2002-03	Hamilton	AHL	43	21	39	60	78	....	....	....	....	....	....	....	....	....	22	2	*15	17	73	....	....	....	....
	NHL Totals		54	6	9	15	54	0	0	0	54	11.1		407	60.4	10:32	....	....	....	....	....	....	....	....	....

Traded to **Calgary** by **Washington** for Steve Shirreffs, August 18, 1999. Claimed on waivers by **Montreal** from **Calgary**, April 11, 2001.

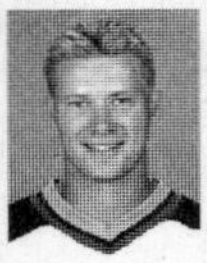

GRATTON, Chris

(GRA-tuhn, KRIHS) **PHX.**

Center. Shoots left. 6'4", 225 lbs. Born, Brantford, Ont., July 5, 1975. Tampa Bay's 1st choice, 3rd overall, in 1993 Entry Draft.

Season	Club	League	GP	G	A	Pts	PIM	PP	SH	GW	S	%	+/-	TF	F%	Min	GP	G	A	Pts	PIM	PP	SH	GW	Min
1989-90	Brantford Classics	OJHL-B	1	0	2	2	2	....	....	....	....	....	....	....	....	....	....	....	....	....	....	....	....	....	....
1990-91	Brantford Classics	OJHL-B	31	30	30	60	28	....	....	....	....	....	....	....	....	....	....	....	....	....	....	....	....	....	....
1991-92	Kingston	OHL	62	27	39	66	37	....	....	....	....	....	....	....	....	....	....	....	....	....	....	....	....	....	....
1992-93	Kingston	OHL	58	55	54	109	125	....	....	....	....	....	....	....	....	....	16	11	18	29	42	....	....	....	....
1993-94	Tampa Bay	NHL	84	13	29	42	123	5	1	2	161	8.1	–25	....	....	....	....	....	....	....	....	....	....	....	....
1994-95	Tampa Bay	NHL	46	7	20	27	89	2	0	0	91	7.7	–2	....	....	....	....	....	....	....	....	....	....	....	....
1995-96	Tampa Bay	NHL	82	17	21	38	105	7	0	3	183	9.3	–13	....	....	....	6	0	2	2	27	0	0	0	....
1996-97	Tampa Bay	NHL	82	30	32	62	201	9	0	4	230	13.0	–28	....	....	....	....	....	....	....	....	....	....	....	....
1997-98	Philadelphia	NHL	82	22	40	62	159	5	0	2	182	12.1	11	....	....	....	5	2	0	2	10	0	0	0	....
1998-99	Philadelphia	NHL	26	1	7	8	41	0	0	0	54	1.9	–8	38	42.1	14:25	....	....	....	....	....	....	....	....	....
	Tampa Bay	NHL	52	7	19	26	102	1	0	1	127	5.5	–20	1032	53.9	18:20	....	....	....	....	....	....	....	....	....
99-2000	Tampa Bay	NHL	58	14	27	41	121	4	0	1	168	8.3	–24	1341	55.9	20:03	....	....	....	....	....	....	....	....	....
	Buffalo	NHL	14	1	7	8	15	0	0	0	34	2.9	1	256	54.3	16:40	5	0	1	1	4	0	0	0	14:56
2000-01	Buffalo	NHL	82	19	21	40	102	5	0	5	156	12.2	0	1161	57.3	14:37	13	6	4	10	14	2	0	1	12:33
2001-02	Buffalo	NHL	82	15	24	39	75	1	0	5	139	10.8	0	1297	53.8	14:57	....	....	....	....	....	....	....	....	....
2002-03	Buffalo	NHL	66	15	29	44	86	4	0	2	187	8.0	–5	1099	58.9	16:26	....	....	....	....	....	....	....	....	....
	Phoenix	NHL	14	0	1	1	21	0	0	0	28	0.0	–11	231	57.1	17:12	....	....	....	....	....	....	....	....	....
	NHL Totals		770	161	277	438	1240	43	1	25	1740	9.3		6455	55.8	16:26	29	8	7	15	55	2	0	1	13:13

OHL All-Rookie Team (1992) • OHL Rookie of the Year (1992)

Signed as a free agent by **Philadelphia**, August 14, 1997. Traded to **Tampa Bay** by **Philadelphia** with Mike Sillinger for Mikael Renberg and Daymond Langkow, December 12, 1998. Traded to **Buffalo** by **Tampa Bay** with Tampa Bay's 2nd round choice (Derek Roy) in 2001 Entry Draft for Cory Sarich, Wayne Primeau, Brian Holzinger and Buffalo's 3rd round choice (Alexander Kharitonov) in 2000 Entry Draft, March 9, 2000. Traded to **Phoenix** by **Buffalo** with Buffalo's 4th round choice in 2004 Entry Draft for Daniel Briere and Phoenix's 3rd round choice in 2004 Entry Draft, March 10, 2003.

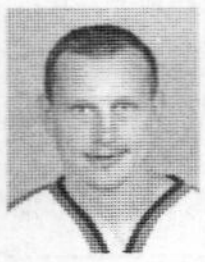

GRAVES, Adam

(GRAYVS, A-duhm) **S.J.**

Left wing. Shoots left. 6', 205 lbs. Born, Toronto, Ont., April 12, 1968. Detroit's 2nd choice, 22nd overall, in 1986 Entry Draft.

Season	Club	League	GP	G	A	Pts	PIM	PP	SH	GW	S	%	+/-	TF	F%	Min	GP	G	A	Pts	PIM	PP	SH	GW	Min
1984-85	King City Dukes	OJHL-B	25	23	33	56	29	....	....	....	....	....	....	....	....	....	....	....	....	....	....	....	....	....	....
1985-86	Windsor Spitfires	OHL	62	27	37	64	35	....	....	....	....	....	....	....	....	....	16	5	11	16	10	....	....	....	....
1986-87	Windsor Spitfires	OHL	66	45	55	100	70	....	....	....	....	....	....	....	....	....	14	9	8	17	32	....	....	....	....
	Adirondack	AHL	....	....	....	....	....	....	....	....	....	....	....	....	....	....	5	0	1	1	0	....	....	....	....
1987-88	Windsor Spitfires	OHL	37	28	32	60	107	....	....	....	....	....	....	....	....	....	12	14	18	*32	16	....	....	....	....
	Detroit	NHL	9	0	1	1	8	0	0	0	9	0.0	–2	....	....	....	....	....	....	....	....	....	....	....	....
1988-89	Detroit	NHL	56	7	5	12	60	0	0	1	60	11.7	–5	....	....	....	5	0	0	0	4	0	0	0	....
	Adirondack	AHL	14	10	11	21	28	....	....	....	....	....	....	....	....	....	14	11	7	18	17	....	....	....	....
1989-90	Detroit	NHL	13	0	1	1	13	0	0	0	10	0.0	–5	....	....	....	....	....	....	....	....	....	....	....	....
	♦ Edmonton	NHL	63	9	12	21	123	1	0	1	84	10.7	5	....	....	....	22	5	6	11	17	0	0	1	....
1990-91	Edmonton	NHL	76	7	18	25	127	2	0	1	126	5.6	–21	....	....	....	18	2	4	6	22	0	0	0	....
1991-92	NY Rangers	NHL	80	26	33	59	139	4	4	4	228	11.4	19	....	....	....	10	5	3	8	22	1	0	1	....
1992-93	NY Rangers	NHL	84	36	29	65	148	12	1	6	275	13.1	–4	....	....	....	....	....	....	....	....	....	....	....	....
1993-94♦	NY Rangers	NHL	84	52	27	79	127	20	4	4	291	17.9	27	....	....	....	23	10	7	17	24	3	0	0	....
1994-95	NY Rangers	NHL	47	17	14	31	51	9	0	3	185	9.2	9	....	....	....	10	4	4	8	8	2	0	0	....
1995-96	NY Rangers	NHL	82	22	36	58	100	9	1	2	266	8.3	18	....	....	....	10	7	1	8	4	6	0	2	....
1996-97	NY Rangers	NHL	82	33	28	61	66	10	4	3	269	12.3	10	....	....	....	15	2	1	3	12	1	0	2	....
1997-98	NY Rangers	NHL	72	23	12	35	41	10	0	2	226	10.2	–30	....	....	....	....	....	....	....	....	....	....	....	....
1998-99	NY Rangers	NHL	82	38	15	53	47	14	2	7	239	15.9	–12	347	51.3	20:33	....	....	....	....	....	....	....	....	....
99-2000	NY Rangers	NHL	77	23	17	40	14	11	0	4	194	11.9	–15	51	49.0	18:46	....	....	....	....	....	....	....	....	....
2000-01	NY Rangers	NHL	82	10	16	26	77	1	0	1	136	7.4	–16	98	55.1	15:44	....	....	....	....	....	....	....	....	....
2001-02	San Jose	NHL	81	17	14	31	51	1	3	1	139	12.2	11	24	41.7	15:47	12	3	1	4	6	0	0	2	14:16
2002-03	San Jose	NHL	82	9	9	18	32	1	0	0	118	7.6	–14	30	46.7	13:03	....	....	....	....	....	....	....	....	....
	NHL Totals		1152	329	287	616	1224	105	19	40	2855	11.5		550	51.1	16:45	125	38	27	65	119	13	0	8	14:16

NHL Second All-Star Team (1994) • King Clancy Memorial Trophy (1994) • Bill Masterton Memorial Trophy (2001)

Played in NHL All-Star Game (1994)

Traded to **Edmonton** by **Detroit** with Petr Klima, Joe Murphy and Jeff Sharples for Jimmy Carson, Kevin McClelland and Edmonton's 5th round choice (later traded to Montreal – Montreal selected Brad Layzell) in 1991 Entry Draft, November 2, 1989. Signed as a free agent by **NY Rangers**, September 3, 1991. Traded to **San Jose** by **NY Rangers** with future considerations for Mikael Samuelsson and Christian Gosselin, June 24, 2001.

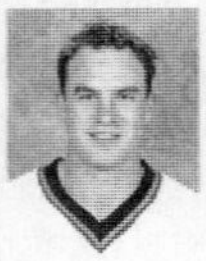

GREEN, Josh

(GREEN, JAWSH) **CGY.**

Left wing. Shoots left. 6'4", 212 lbs. Born, Camrose, Alta., November 16, 1977. Los Angeles' 1st choice, 30th overall, in 1996 Entry Draft.

Season	Club	League	GP	G	A	Pts	PIM	PP	SH	GW	S	%	+/-	TF	F%	Min	GP	G	A	Pts	PIM	PP	SH	GW	Min
1992-93	Camrose Kodiacs	ABHL	60	55	45	100	80	....	....	....	....	....	....	....	....	....	....	....	....	....	....	....	....	....	....
1993-94	Medicine Hat	WHL	63	22	22	44	43	....	....	....	....	....	....	....	....	....	3	0	0	0	4	....	....	....	....
1994-95	Medicine Hat	WHL	68	32	23	55	64	....	....	....	....	....	....	....	....	....	5	5	1	6	2	....	....	....	....
1995-96	Medicine Hat	WHL	46	18	25	43	55	....	....	....	....	....	....	....	....	....	5	2	2	4	4	....	....	....	....
1996-97	Medicine Hat	WHL	51	25	32	57	61	....	....	....	....	....	....	....	....	....	....	....	....	....	....	....	....	....	....
	Swift Current	WHL	23	10	15	25	33	....	....	....	....	....	....	....	....	....	10	9	7	16	19	....	....	....	....
1997-98	Swift Current	WHL	5	9	1	10	9	....	....	....	....	....	....	....	....	....	....	....	....	....	....	....	....	....	....
	Portland	WHL	26	26	18	44	27	....	....	....	....	....	....	....	....	....	....	....	....	....	....	....	....	....	....
	Fredericton	AHL	43	16	15	31	14	....	....	....	....	....	....	....	....	....	4	1	3	4	6	....	....	....	....
1998-99	Los Angeles	NHL	27	1	3	4	8	1	0	0	35	2.9	–5	2	50.0	11:44	....	....	....	....	....	....	....	....	....
	Springfield	AHL	41	15	15	30	29	....	....	....	....	....	....	....	....	....	....	....	....	....	....	....	....	....	....
99-2000	NY Islanders	NHL	49	12	14	26	41	2	0	3	109	11.0	–7	12	50.0	13:36	....	....	....	....	....	....	....	....	....
	Lowell	AHL	17	6	2	8	19	....	....	....	....	....	....	....	....	....	....	....	....	....	....	....	....	....	....
2000-01	Hamilton	AHL	2	2	0	2	2	....	....	....	....	....	....	....	....	....	....	....	....	....	....	....	....	....	....
	Edmonton	NHL	....	....	....	....	....	....	....	....	....	....	....	....	....	....	3	0	0	0	0	0	0	0	7:55
2001-02	Edmonton	NHL	61	10	5	15	52	1	0	1	78	12.8	9	18	38.9	10:05	....	....	....	....	....	....	....	....	....
2002-03	Edmonton	NHL	20	0	2	2	12	0	0	0	20	0.0	–3	5	0.0	10:22	....	....	....	....	....	....	....	....	....
	NY Rangers	NHL	4	0	0	0	2	0	0	0	3	0.0	–1	0	0.0	9:06	....	....	....	....	....	....	....	....	....
	Washington	NHL	21	1	2	3	7	0	0	0	20	5.0	1	3	0.0	8:07	....	....	....	....	....	....	....	....	....
	NHL Totals		182	24	26	50	122	4	0	4	265	9.1		40	35.0	11:03	3	0	0	0	0	0	0	0	7:55

Traded to **NY Islanders** by **Los Angeles** with Olli Jokinen, Mathieu Biron and Los Angeles' 1st round choice (Taylor Pyatt) in 1999 Entry Draft for Ziggy Palffy, Brian Smolinski, Marcel Cousineau and New Jersey's 4th round choice (previously acquired, Los Angeles selected Daniel Johansson) in 1999 Entry Draft, June 20, 1999. Traded to **Edmonton** by **NY Islanders** with Eric Brewer and NY Islanders' 2nd round choice (Brad Winchester) in 2000 Entry Draft for Roman Hamrlik, June 24, 2000. • Missed majority of 2000-01 season recovering from shoulder injury suffered in game vs. Detroit, October 10, 2000. Traded to **NY Rangers** by **Edmonton** for future considerations, December 12, 2002. Claimed on waivers by **Washington** from **NY Rangers**, January 15, 2003. Signed as a free agent by **Calgary**, July 17, 2003.

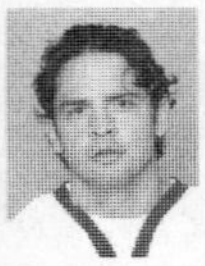

GREEN, Travis

(GREEN, TRA-vihs) **TOR.**

Center. Shoots right. 6'2", 200 lbs. Born, Castlegar, B.C., December 20, 1970. NY Islanders' 2nd choice, 23rd overall, in 1989 Entry Draft.

Season	Club	League	GP	G	A	Pts	PIM	PP	SH	GW	S	%	+/-	TF	F%	Min	GP	G	A	Pts	PIM	PP	SH	GW	Min
1985-86	Castlegar Rebels	KIJHL	35	30	40	70	41	....	....	....	....	....	....	....	....	....	....	....	....	....	....	....	....	....	....
1986-87	Spokane Chiefs	WHL	64	8	17	25	27	....	....	....	....	....	....	....	....	....	3	0	0	0	0	....	....	....	....
1987-88	Spokane Chiefs	WHL	72	33	54	87	42	....	....	....	....	....	....	....	....	....	15	10	10	20	13	....	....	....	....
1988-89	Spokane Chiefs	WHL	75	51	51	102	79	....	....	....	....	....	....	....	....	....	....	....	....	....	....	....	....	....	....
1989-90	Spokane Chiefs	WHL	50	45	44	89	80	....	....	....	....	....	....	....	....	....	....	....	....	....	....	....	....	....	....
	Medicine Hat	WHL	25	15	24	39	19	....	....	....	....	....	....	....	....	....	3	0	0	0	2	....	....	....	....
1990-91	Capital District	AHL	73	21	34	55	26	....	....	....	....	....	....	....	....	....	....	....	....	....	....	....	....	....	....
1991-92	Capital District	AHL	71	23	27	50	10	....	....	....	....	....	....	....	....	....	7	0	4	4	21	....	....	....	....
1992-93	NY Islanders	NHL	61	7	18	25	43	1	0	0	115	6.1	4	....	....	....	12	3	1	4	6	0	0	0	....
	Capital District	AHL	20	12	11	23	39	....	....	....	....	....	....	....	....	....	....	....	....	....	....	....	....	....	....
1993-94	NY Islanders	NHL	83	18	22	40	44	1	0	2	164	11.0	16	....	....	....	4	0	0	0	2	0	0	0	....
1994-95	NY Islanders	NHL	42	5	7	12	25	0	0	0	59	8.5	–10	....	....	....	....	....	....	....	....	....	....	....	....
1995-96	NY Islanders	NHL	69	25	45	70	42	14	1	2	186	13.4	–20	....	....	....	....	....	....	....	....	....	....	....	....

Season	Club	League	Regular Season														Playoffs								
			GP	G	A	Pts	PIM	PP	SH	GW	S	%	+/-	TF	F%	Min	GP	G	A	Pts	PIM	PP	SH	GW	Min
1996-97	NY Islanders	NHL	79	23	41	64	38	10	0	3	177	13.0	–5												
1997-98	NY Islanders	NHL	54	14	12	26	66	8	0	2	99	14.1	–19												
	Anaheim	NHL	22	5	11	16	16	1	0	0	42	11.9	–10												
1998-99	Anaheim	NHL	79	13	17	30	81	3	1	2	165	7.9	–7	1325	52.8	17:17	4	0	1	1	4	0	0	0	15:02
99-2000	Phoenix	NHL	78	25	21	46	45	6	0	2	157	15.9	–4	1322	55.6	16:36	5	2	1	3	2	0	0	0	17:23
2000-01	Phoenix	NHL	69	13	15	28	63	3	0	0	113	11.5	–11	1135	54.9	16:05									
2001-02	Toronto	NHL	82	11	23	34	61	3	0	2	119	9.2	13	647	54.1	14:32	20	3	6	9	34	0	0	1	20:34
2002-03	Toronto	NHL	75	12	12	24	67	2	1	3	86	14.0	2	802	53.5	12:57	4	2	1	3	4	0	1	1	18:08
	NHL Totals		**793**	**171**	**244**	**415**	**591**	**52**	**3**	**18**	**1482**	**11.5**		**5231**	**54.2**	**15:29**	**49**	**10**	**10**	**20**	**52**	**0**	**1**	**2**	**19:07**

Traded to **Anaheim** by **NY Islanders** with Doug Houda and Tony Tuzzolino for Joe Sacco, J.J. Daigneault and Mark Janssens, February 6, 1998. Traded to **Phoenix** by **Anaheim** with Anaheim's 1st round choice (Scott Kelman) in 1999 Entry Draft for Oleg Tverdovsky, June 26, 1999. Traded to **Toronto** by **Phoenix** with Robert Reichel and Craig Mills for Danny Markov, June 12, 2001.

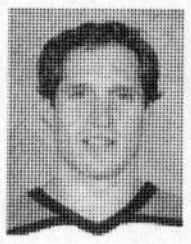

GREIG, Mark

(GREG, MAHRK)

Right wing. Shoots right. 5'11", 190 lbs. Born, High River, Alta., January 25, 1970. Hartford's 1st choice, 15th overall, in 1990 Entry Draft.

1985-86	Blackie Bisons	AAHA	31	12	43	55	44																		
1986-87	Cgy. North Stars	AMHL	18	9	28	37	30																		
	Calgary Wranglers	WHL	5	0	0	0	0																		
1987-88	Lethbridge	WHL	65	9	18	27	38																		
1988-89	Lethbridge	WHL	71	36	72	108	113										8	5	5	10	16				
1989-90	Lethbridge	WHL	65	55	80	135	149										18	11	21	32	35				
1990-91	Hartford	NHL	4	0	0	0	0	0	0	0	1	0.0	–1												
	Springfield	AHL	73	32	55	87	73										17	2	6	8	22				
1991-92	Hartford	NHL	17	0	5	5	6	0	0	0	18	0.0	7												
	Springfield	AHL	50	20	27	47	38										9	1	1	2	20				
1992-93	Hartford	NHL	22	1	7	8	27	0	0	0	16	6.3	–11												
	Springfield	AHL	55	20	38	58	86																		
1993-94	Hartford	NHL	31	4	5	9	31	0	0	0	41	9.8	–6												
	Springfield	AHL	4	0	4	4	21																		
	Toronto	NHL	13	2	2	4	10	0	0	0	14	14.3	1												
	St. John's	AHL	9	4	6	10	0										11	4	2	6	26				
1994-95	Saint John Flames	AHL	67	31	50	81	82										2	0	1	1	0				
	Calgary	NHL	8	1	1	2	2	0	0	0	5	20.0	1												
1995-96	Atlanta Knights	IHL	71	25	48	73	104										3	2	1	3	4				
1996-97	Quebec Rafales	IHL	5	1	2	3	0																		
	Houston Aeros	IHL	59	12	30	42	59										13	5	8	13	2				
1997-98	Grand Rapids	IHL	69	26	36	62	103										3	0	4	4	4				
1998-99	Philadelphia	NHL	7	1	3	4	2	0	0	0	9	11.1	1	0	0.0	9:55	2	0	1	1	0	0	0	0	10:28
	Philadelphia	AHL	67	23	46	69	102										7	1	5	6	14				
99-2000	Philadelphia	NHL	11	3	2	5	6	0	0	1	14	21.4	0	1	0.0	11:19	3	0	0	0	0	0	0	0	9:28
	Philadelphia	AHL	68	34	48	82	116										5	3	2	5	6				
2000-01	Philadelphia	NHL	7	1	1	2	4	0	0	0	7	14.3	–2	0	0.0	14:23									
	Philadelphia	AHL	74	31	57	88	98										10	6	5	11	4				
2001-02	Philadelphia	AHL	66	22	37	59	105										5	0	4	4	6				
2002-03	Philadelphia	NHL	5	0	1	1	2	0	0	0	2	0.0	1	0	0.0	5:02									
	Philadelphia	AHL	73	30	44	74	127																		
	NHL Totals		**125**	**13**	**27**	**40**	**90**	**0**	**0**	**1**	**127**	**10.2**		**1**	**0.0**	**10:40**	**5**	**0**	**1**	**1**	**0**	**0**	**0**	**0**	**9:52**

WHL East First All-Star Team (1990) • AHL First All-Star Team (2001)

Traded to **Toronto** by **Hartford** with Hartford's 6th round choice (Doug Bonner) in 1995 Entry Draft for Ted Crowley, January 25, 1994. Signed as a free agent by **Calgary**, August 9, 1994. Signed as a free agent by **Philadelphia**, July 28, 1998.

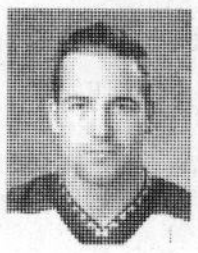

GRENIER, Martin

(GREH-nyay, MAHR-tihn) **VAN.**

Defense. Shoots left. 6'5", 245 lbs. Born, Laval, Que., November 2, 1980. Colorado's 2nd choice, 45th overall, in 1999 Entry Draft.

1996-97	Laval Laurentide	QAAA	34	3	16	19	117										13	0	4	4					
1997-98	Quebec Remparts	QMJHL	61	4	11	15	202										14	0	2	2	36				
1998-99	Quebec Remparts	QMJHL	60	7	18	25	*479										13	0	4	4	29				
99-2000	Quebec Remparts	QMJHL	67	11	35	46	302										7	1	4	5	27				
2000-01	Quebec Remparts	QMJHL	26	5	16	21	82																		
	Victoriaville Tigres	QMJHL	28	9	19	28	108										13	2	8	10	51				
2001-02	Phoenix	NHL	5	0	0	0	5	0	0	0	1	0.0	0	1	100.0	5:56									
	Springfield	AHL	69	2	6	8	241																		
2002-03	Phoenix	NHL	3	0	0	0	0	0	0	0	0	0.0	–1	0	0.0	6:11									
	Springfield	AHL	73	2	10	12	232										6	0	1	1	12				
	NHL Totals		**8**	**0**	**0**	**0**	**5**	**0**	**0**	**0**	**1**	**0.0**		**1**	**100.0**	**6:02**									

Traded to **Boston** by **Colorado** with Brian Rolston, Samuel Pahlsson and New Jersey's 1st round choice (previously acquired, Boston selected Martin Samuelsson) in 2000 Entry Draft for Raymond Bourque and Dave Andreychuk, March 6, 2000. Signed as a free agent by **Phoenix**, June 27, 2001. Traded to **Vancouver** by **Phoenix** for Bryan Helmer, July 25, 2003.

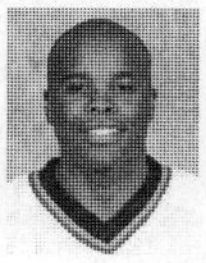

GRIER, Mike

(GREER, MIGHK) **WSH.**

Right wing. Shoots right. 6'1", 227 lbs. Born, Detroit, MI, January 5, 1975. St. Louis' 7th choice, 219th overall, in 1993 Entry Draft.

1992-93	St. Sebastian's	Hi-School	22	16	27	43	32																		
1993-94	Boston University	H-East	39	9	9	18	56																		
1994-95	Boston University	H-East	37	*29	26	55	85																		
1995-96	Boston University	H-East	38	21	25	46	82																		
1996-97	Edmonton	NHL	79	15	17	32	45	4	0	2	89	16.9	7				12	3	1	4	4	1	0	1	
1997-98	Edmonton	NHL	66	9	6	15	73	1	0	1	90	10.0	–3				12	2	2	4	13	0	0	1	
1998-99	Edmonton	NHL	82	20	24	44	54	3	2	1	143	14.0	5	34	20.6	15:57	4	1	1	2	6	0	0	0	23:26
99-2000	Edmonton	NHL	65	9	22	31	68	0	3	2	115	7.8	9	32	46.8	15:45									
2000-01	Edmonton	NHL	74	20	16	36	20	2	3	2	124	16.1	11	36	38.9	16:44	6	0	0	0	8	0	0	0	21:23
2001-02	Edmonton	NHL	82	8	17	25	32	0	2	3	112	7.1	1	38	47.4	15:01									
2002-03	Washington	NHL	82	15	17	32	36	2	2	2	133	11.3	–14	98	43.9	17:48	6	1	1	2	2	0	0	0	17:59
	NHL Totals		**530**	**96**	**119**	**215**	**328**	**12**	**12**	**13**	**806**	**11.9**		**238**	**40.8**	**16:16**	**40**	**7**	**5**	**12**	**33**	**1**	**0**	**2**	**20:37**

Hockey East First All-Star Team (1995) • NCAA East First All-American Team (1995)

Rights traded to **Edmonton** by **St. Louis** with Curtis Joseph for St. Louis' 1st round choices in 1996 (previously acquired, St. Louis selected Marty Reasoner) and 1997 (previously acquired, later traded to Los Angeles – Los Angeles selected Matt Zultek) Entry Drafts, August 4, 1995. Traded to **Washington** by **Edmonton** for Washington's 2nd round choice (later traded to NY Islanders – NY Islanders selected Evgeni Tunik) in 2003 Entry Draft and Vancouver's 3rd round choice (previously acquired, Edmonton selected Zachery Stortini) in 2003 Entry Draft, October 7, 2002.

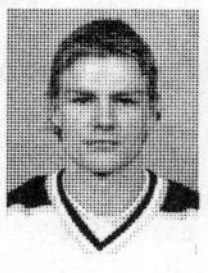

GROSEK, Michal

(GROH-shehk, MIHK-al) **BOS.**

Left wing. Shoots right. 6'2", 207 lbs. Born, Vyskov, Czech., June 1, 1975. Winnipeg's 7th choice, 145th overall, in 1993 Entry Draft.

1992-93	AC ZPS Zlin	Czech	17	1	3	4																			
1993-94	Tacoma Rockets	WHL	30	25	20	45	106										7	2	2	4	30				
	Winnipeg	NHL	3	1	0	1	0	0	0	0	4	25.0	–1												
	Moncton Hawks	AHL	20	1	2	3	47										2	0	0	0	0				
1994-95	Springfield	AHL	45	10	22	32	98																		
	Winnipeg	NHL	24	2	2	4	21	0	0	1	27	7.4	–3												
1995-96	Winnipeg	NHL	1	0	0	0	0	0	0	0	1	0.0	–1												
	Springfield	AHL	39	16	19	35	68																		
	Buffalo	NHL	22	6	4	10	31	2	0	1	33	18.2	0												
1996-97	Buffalo	NHL	82	15	21	36	71	1	0	2	117	12.8	25				12	3	3	6	8	0	0	0	
1997-98	Buffalo	NHL	67	10	20	30	60	2	0	1	114	8.8	9				15	6	4	10	28	2	0	3	
1998-99	Buffalo	NHL	76	20	30	50	102	4	0	3	140	14.3	21	5	60.0	17:14	13	0	4	4	28	0	0	0	11:51
99-2000	Buffalo	NHL	61	11	23	34	35	2	0	2	96	11.5	12	8	25.0	16:17									
	Chicago	NHL	14	2	4	6	12	1	0	0	18	11.1	–1	1	0.0	13:06									
2000-01	NY Rangers	NHL	65	9	11	20	61	2	0	0	84	10.7	–10	14	28.6	11:05									
	Hartford	AHL	12	8	7	15	12																		

			Regular Season														Playoffs								
Season	Club	League	GP	G	A	Pts	PIM	PP	SH	GW	S	%	+/-	TF	F%	Min	GP	G	A	Pts	PIM	PP	SH	GW	Min
2001-02	NY Rangers	NHL	15	3	2	5	12	0	0	0	23	13.0	–3	2	0.0	12:24	....	....	....	....	....	....	....	....	....
	Hartford	AHL	48	14	30	44	167	....	....	....	....	....	....	....	....	....	....	....	....	....	....	....	....	....	....
2002-03	Boston	NHL	63	2	18	20	71	0	0	1	74	2.7	2	95	43.2	10:43	5	0	0	0	13	0	0	0	6:12
	NHL Totals		493	81	135	216	476	14	0	11	731	11.1		125	40.0	13:50	45	9	11	20	77	2	0	3	10:17

Traded to **Buffalo** by **Winnipeg** with Darryl Shannon for Craig Muni, February 15, 1996. Traded to **Chicago** by **Buffalo** for Doug Gilmour, J.P. Dumont and future considerations, March 10, 2000. Traded to **NY Rangers** by **Chicago** with Brad Brown for future considerations, October 5, 2000. Signed as a free agent by **Boston**, July 16, 2002.

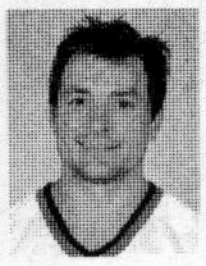

GRUDEN, John

(GROO-duhn, JAWN) **WSH.**

Defense. Shoots left. 6', 203 lbs. Born, Virginia, MN, June 4, 1970. Boston's 7th choice, 168th overall, in 1990 Entry Draft.

Season	Club	League	GP	G	A	Pts	PIM	PP	SH	GW	S	%	+/-	TF	F%	Min	GP	G	A	Pts	PIM	PP	SH	GW	Min
1989-90	Waterloo	USHL	47	7	39	46	35	....	....	....	....	....	....	....	....	....	....	....	....	....	....	....	....	....	....
1990-91	Ferris State	CCHA	37	4	11	15	27	....	....	....	....	....	....	....	....	....	....	....	....	....	....	....	....	....	....
1991-92	Ferris State	CCHA	37	9	14	23	24	....	....	....	....	....	....	....	....	....	....	....	....	....	....	....	....	....	....
1992-93	Ferris State	CCHA	41	16	14	30	58	....	....	....	....	....	....	....	....	....	....	....	....	....	....	....	....	....	....
1993-94	Ferris State	CCHA	38	11	25	36	52	....	....	....	....	....	....	....	....	....	....	....	....	....	....	....	....	....	....
	Boston	NHL	7	0	1	1	2	0	0	0	8	0.0	–3	....	....	....	....	....	....	....	....	....	....	....	....
1994-95	Boston	NHL	38	0	6	6	22	0	0	0	30	0.0	3	....	....	....	....	....	....	....	....	....	....	....	....
	Providence Bruins	AHL	1	0	1	1	0	....	....	....	....	....	....	....	....	....	....	....	....	....	....	....	....	....	....
1995-96	Boston	NHL	14	0	0	0	4	0	0	0	12	0.0	–3	....	....	....	3	0	1	1	0	0	0	0	....
	Providence Bruins	AHL	39	5	19	24	29	....	....	....	....	....	....	....	....	....	....	....	....	....	....	....	....	....	....
1996-97	Providence Bruins	AHL	78	18	27	45	52	....	....	....	....	....	....	....	....	....	10	3	6	9	4	....	....	....	....
1997-98	Detroit Vipers	IHL	76	13	42	55	74	....	....	....	....	....	....	....	....	....	21	1	8	9	14	....	....	....	....
1998-99	Ottawa	NHL	13	0	1	1	8	0	0	0	10	0.0	0	0	0.0	13:07	....	....	....	....	....	....	....	....	....
	Detroit Vipers	IHL	59	10	28	38	52	....	....	....	....	....	....	....	....	....	10	0	1	1	6	....	....	....	....
99-2000	Ottawa	NHL	9	0	0	0	4	0	0	0	3	0.0	0	0	0.0	16:29	....	....	....	....	....	....	....	....	....
	Grand Rapids	IHL	50	5	17	22	24	....	....	....	....	....	....	....	....	....	12	1	4	5	8	....	....	....	....
2000-01	Grand Rapids	IHL	34	2	6	8	18	....	....	....	....	....	....	....	....	....	10	1	4	5	8	....	....	....	....
2001-02	Grand Rapids	AHL	57	3	14	17	48	....	....	....	....	....	....	....	....	....	5	1	0	1	2	....	....	....	....
2002-03	Eisbaren Berlin	Germany	38	6	25	31	34	....	....	....	....	....	....	....	....	....	9	2	6	8	4	....	....	....	....
	NHL Totals		81	0	8	8	40	0	0	0	63	0.0		0	0.0	14:30	3	0	1	1	0	0	0	0	....

CCHA First All-Star Team (1994) • NCAA West First All-American Team (1994) • IHL Second All-Star Team (1998) • AHL First All-Star Team (2002)

Signed as a free agent by **Ottawa**, August 7, 1998. • Missed majority of 2000-01 season recovering from shoulder injury suffered in training camp, October 1, 2000. Signed as a free agent by **Eisbaren Berlin** (Germany), May 3, 2002. Signed as a free agent by **Washington**, August, 2003.

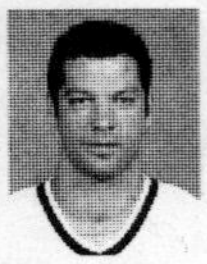

GUERIN, Bill

(GAIR-ihn, BIHL) **DAL.**

Right wing. Shoots right. 6'2", 210 lbs. Born, Worcester, MA, November 9, 1970. New Jersey's 1st choice, 5th overall, in 1989 Entry Draft.

Season	Club	League	GP	G	A	Pts	PIM	PP	SH	GW	S	%	+/-	TF	F%	Min	GP	G	A	Pts	PIM	PP	SH	GW	Min
1985-86	Springfield	NEJHL	48	26	19	45	71	....	....	....	....	....	....	....	....	....	....	....	....	....	....	....	....	....	....
1986-87	Springfield	NEJHL	32	34	20	54	40	....	....	....	....	....	....	....	....	....	....	....	....	....	....	....	....	....	....
1987-88	Springfield	NEJHL	38	31	44	75	146	....	....	....	....	....	....	....	....	....	....	....	....	....	....	....	....	....	....
1988-89	Springfield	NEJHL	31	32	35	67	90	....	....	....	....	....	....	....	....	....	....	....	....	....	....	....	....	....	....
1989-90	Boston College	H-East	39	14	11	25	54	....	....	....	....	....	....	....	....	....	....	....	....	....	....	....	....	....	....
1990-91	Boston College	H-East	38	26	19	45	102	....	....	....	....	....	....	....	....	....	....	....	....	....	....	....	....	....	....
1991-92	Team USA	Nat-Tm	46	12	15	27	67	....	....	....	....	....	....	....	....	....	....	....	....	....	....	....	....	....	....
	New Jersey	NHL	5	0	1	1	9	0	0	0	8	0.0	1	....	....	....	6	3	0	3	4	0	0	0	....
	Utica Devils	AHL	22	13	10	23	6	....	....	....	....	....	....	....	....	....	4	1	3	4	14	....	....	....	....
1992-93	New Jersey	NHL	65	14	20	34	63	0	0	2	123	11.4	14	....	....	....	5	1	1	2	4	0	0	0	....
	Utica Devils	AHL	18	10	7	17	47	....	....	....	....	....	....	....	....	....	....	....	....	....	....	....	....	....	....
1993-94	New Jersey	NHL	81	25	19	44	101	2	0	3	195	12.8	14	....	....	....	17	2	1	3	35	0	0	1	....
1994-95 ♦	New Jersey	NHL	48	12	13	25	72	4	0	3	96	12.5	6	....	....	....	20	3	8	11	30	1	0	0	....
1995-96	New Jersey	NHL	80	23	30	53	116	8	0	6	216	10.6	7	....	....	....	....	....	....	....	....	....	....	....	....
1996-97	New Jersey	NHL	82	29	18	47	95	7	0	9	177	16.4	–2	....	....	....	8	2	1	3	18	1	0	1	....
1997-98	New Jersey	NHL	19	5	5	10	13	1	0	2	48	10.4	0	....	....	....	....	....	....	....	....	....	....	....	....
	Edmonton	NHL	40	13	16	29	80	8	0	2	130	10.0	1	....	....	....	12	7	1	8	17	4	0	0	....
	United States	Olympics	4	0	3	3	2	....	....	....	....	....	....	....	....	....	....	....	....	....	....	....	....	....	....
1998-99	Edmonton	NHL	80	30	34	64	133	13	0	2	261	11.5	7	74	40.5	19:42	3	0	2	2	2	0	0	0	26:14
99-2000	Edmonton	NHL	70	24	22	46	123	11	0	2	188	12.8	4	13	46.2	18:01	5	3	2	5	9	1	0	0	17:55
2000-01	Edmonton	NHL	21	12	10	22	18	4	0	1	64	18.8	11	0	0.0	19:49	....	....	....	....	....	....	....	....	....
	Boston	NHL	64	28	35	63	122	7	1	4	225	12.4	–4	36	41.7	22:43	....	....	....	....	....	....	....	....	....
2001-02	Boston	NHL	78	41	25	66	91	10	1	7	355	11.5	–1	17	52.9	20:45	6	4	2	6	6	3	0	0	21:17
	United States	Olympics	6	4	0	4	4	....	....	....	....	....	....	....	....	....	....	....	....	....	....	....	....	....	....
2002-03	Dallas	NHL	64	25	25	50	113	11	0	2	229	10.9	5	20	25.0	18:33	4	0	0	0	4	0	0	0	8:34
	NHL Totals		797	281	273	554	1149	86	2	45	2315	12.1		160	40.6	19:56	86	25	18	43	129	10	0	2	18:21

NHL Second All-Star Team (2002)

Played in NHL All-Star Game (2001, 2003)

Traded to **Edmonton** by **New Jersey** with Valeri Zelepukin for Jason Arnott and Bryan Muir, January 4, 1998. Traded to **Boston** by **Edmonton** for Anson Carter, Boston's 1st (Ales Hemsky) and 2nd (Doug Lynch) round choices in 2001 Entry Draft and future considerations, November 15, 2000. Signed as a free agent by **Dallas**, July 3, 2002.

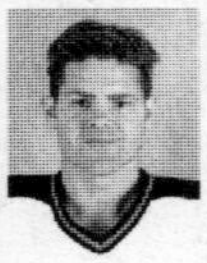

GUOLLA, Steve

(GUH-wah-lah, STEEV) **N.J.**

Center. Shoots left. 6', 190 lbs. Born, Scarborough, Ont., March 15, 1973. Ottawa's 1st choice, 3rd overall, in 1994 Supplemental Draft.

Season	Club	League	GP	G	A	Pts	PIM	PP	SH	GW	S	%	+/-	TF	F%	Min	GP	G	A	Pts	PIM	PP	SH	GW	Min
1988-89	Tor. Red Wings	MTHL	25	14	20	34	....	....	....	....	....	....	....	....	....	....	....	....	....	....	....	....	....	....	....
1989-90	Tor. Red Wings	MTHL	40	42	47	89	....	....	....	....	....	....	....	....	....	....	....	....	....	....	....	....	....	....	....
1990-91	Wexford Raiders	MTJHL	44	34	44	78	34	....	....	....	....	....	....	....	....	....	12	12	16	28	....	....	....	....	....
1991-92	Michigan State	CCHA	33	4	9	13	8	....	....	....	....	....	....	....	....	....	....	....	....	....	....	....	....	....	....
1992-93	Michigan State	CCHA	39	19	35	54	6	....	....	....	....	....	....	....	....	....	....	....	....	....	....	....	....	....	....
1993-94	Michigan State	CCHA	41	23	46	69	16	....	....	....	....	....	....	....	....	....	....	....	....	....	....	....	....	....	....
1994-95	Michigan State	CCHA	40	16	35	51	16	....	....	....	....	....	....	....	....	....	....	....	....	....	....	....	....	....	....
1995-96	P.E.I. Senators	AHL	72	32	48	80	28	....	....	....	....	....	....	....	....	....	3	0	0	0	0	....	....	....	....
1996-97	San Jose	NHL	43	13	8	21	14	2	0	1	81	16.0	–10	....	....	....	....	....	....	....	....	....	....	....	....
	Kentucky	AHL	34	22	22	44	10	....	....	....	....	....	....	....	....	....	4	2	1	3	0	....	....	....	....
1997-98	San Jose	NHL	7	1	1	2	0	0	0	0	9	11.1	–2	....	....	....	....	....	....	....	....	....	....	....	....
	Kentucky	AHL	69	37	63	100	45	....	....	....	....	....	....	....	....	....	3	0	0	0	0	....	....	....	....
1998-99	San Jose	NHL	14	2	2	4	6	0	0	1	22	9.1	3	172	36.6	13:54	....	....	....	....	....	....	....	....	....
	Kentucky	AHL	53	29	47	76	33	....	....	....	....	....	....	....	....	....	....	....	....	....	....	....	....	....	....
99-2000	Tampa Bay	NHL	46	6	10	16	11	2	0	0	52	11.5	2	155	45.8	11:26	....	....	....	....	....	....	....	....	....
	Atlanta	NHL	20	4	9	13	4	2	0	0	34	11.8	–13	345	42.6	17:47	....	....	....	....	....	....	....	....	....
2000-01	Atlanta	NHL	63	12	16	28	23	2	0	3	96	12.5	–6	859	47.7	14:41	....	....	....	....	....	....	....	....	....
2001-02	Albany River Rats	AHL	68	25	35	60	27	....	....	....	....	....	....	....	....	....	....	....	....	....	....	....	....	....	....
2002-03	New Jersey	NHL	12	2	0	2	2	0	0	0	6	33.3	1	61	41.0	7:60	....	....	....	....	....	....	....	....	....
	Albany River Rats	AHL	22	11	17	28	4	....	....	....	....	....	....	....	....	....	....	....	....	....	....	....	....	....	....
	NHL Totals		205	40	46	86	60	8	0	5	300	13.3		1592	45.0	13:32	....	....	....	....	....	....	....	....	....

CCHA Second All-Star Team (1994) • NCAA West Second All-American Team (1994) • AHL Second All-Star Team (1998, 1999) • Les Cunningham Award (MVP – AHL) (1998)

Signed as a free agent by **San Jose**, August 22, 1996. Traded to **Tampa Bay** by **San Jose** with Bill Houlder, Shawn Burr and Andrei Zyuzin for Niklas Sundstrom and NY Rangers' 3rd round choice (previously acquired, later traded to Chicago – Chicago selected Igor Radulov) in 2000 Entry Draft, August 4, 1999. Claimed on waivers by **Atlanta** from **Tampa Bay**, March 1, 2000. Signed as a free agent by **New Jersey**, October 21, 2001. • Missed majority of 2002-03 season recovering from back injury suffered in game vs. NY Islanders, November 27, 2002.

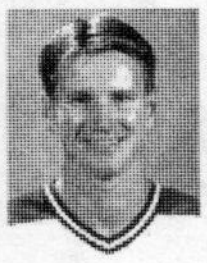

GUREN, Miloslav

(GOO-rihn, MEER-oh-slahf) **MTL.**

Defense. Shoots left. 6'2", 215 lbs. Born, Uherske Hradiste, Czech., September 24, 1976. Montreal's 2nd choice, 60th overall, in 1995 Entry Draft.

Season	Club	League	GP	G	A	Pts	PIM	PP	SH	GW	S	%	+/-	TF	F%	Min	GP	G	A	Pts	PIM	PP	SH	GW	Min
1993-94	AC ZPS Zlin	Czech	22	1	5	6	....	....	....	....	....	....	....	....	....	....	3	0	0	0	....	....	....	....	....
1994-95	AC ZPS Zlin	Czech	32	3	7	10	10	....	....	....	....	....	....	....	....	....	12	1	0	1	6	....	....	....	....
1995-96	AC ZPS Zlin	Czech	28	1	2	3	....	....	....	....	....	....	....	....	....	....	7	1	0	1	....	....	....	....	....
1996-97	Fredericton	AHL	79	6	26	32	26	....	....	....	....	....	....	....	....	....	....	....	....	....	....	....	....	....	....
1997-98	Fredericton	AHL	78	15	36	51	36	....	....	....	....	....	....	....	....	....	4	1	2	3	0	....	....	....	....
1998-99	Montreal	NHL	12	0	1	1	4	0	0	0	11	0.0	–1	0	0.0	12:02	....	....	....	....	....	....	....	....	....
	Fredericton	AHL	63	5	16	21	24	....	....	....	....	....	....	....	....	....	15	4	7	11	10	....	....	....	....
99-2000	Montreal	NHL	24	1	2	3	12	1	0	0	20	5.0	–5	0	0.0	15:14	....	....	....	....	....	....	....	....	....
	Quebec Citadelles	AHL	29	5	12	17	16	....	....	....	....	....	....	....	....	....	3	0	0	0	2	....	....	....	....

			Regular Season														Playoffs								
Season	**Club**	**League**	**GP**	**G**	**A**	**Pts**	**PIM**	**PP**	**SH**	**GW**	**S**	**%**	**+/-**	**TF**	**F%**	**Min**	**GP**	**G**	**A**	**Pts**	**PIM**	**PP**	**SH**	**GW**	**Min**
2000-01	Quebec Citadelles	AHL	75	11	40	51	24	....	....	....	....	....	....	....	....	....	8	4	2	6	6	....	....	....	....
2001-02	HC Ocelari Trinec	Czech	52	2	9	11	44	....	....	....	....	....	....	....	....	....	6	1	2	3	9	....	....	....	....
2002-03	CSKA Moscow	Russia	39	2	7	9	14	....	....	....	....	....	....	....	....	....	....	....	....	....	....	....	....	....	....
	NHL Totals		**36**	**1**	**3**	**4**	**16**	**1**	**0**	**0**	**31**	**3.2**		**0**	**0.0**	**14:10**	....	....	....	....	....	....	....	....	....

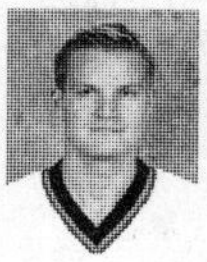

HAAKANA, Kari

(HA-kuh-nuh, KAH-ree) **EDM.**

Defense. Shoots left. 6'1", 222 lbs. Born, Outokumpu, Finland, November 8, 1973. Edmonton's 9th choice, 248th overall, in 2001 Entry Draft.

Season	Club	League	GP	G	A	Pts	PIM	PP	SH	GW	S	%	+/-	TF	F%	Min	GP	G	A	Pts	PIM	PP	SH	GW	Min
1990-91	Kiekko Espoo Jr.	Finn-Jr.	36	3	3	6	34	....	....	....	....	....	....	....	....	....	....	....	....	....	....	....	....	....	....
	Kiekko Espoo	Finland-2	4	0	1	1	0	....	....	....	....	....	....	....	....	....	....	....	....	....	....	....	....	....	....
1991-92	Kiekko Espoo Jr.	Finn-Jr.	26	0	4	4	34	....	....	....	....	....	....	....	....	....	....	....	....	....	....	....	....	....	....
1992-93	Lukko Rauma Jr.	Finn-Jr.	36	4	16	20	60	....	....	....	....	....	....	....	....	....	....	....	....	....	....	....	....	....	....
	Lukko Rauma	Finland	4	0	0	0	0	....	....	....	....	....	....	....	....	....	....	....	....	....	....	....	....	....	....
1993-94	Kiekko Espoo Jr.	Finn-Jr.	5	0	2	2	2	....	....	....	....	....	....	....	....	....	....	....	....	....	....	....	....	....	....
	Kiekko Espoo	Finland	47	3	2	5	40	....	....	....	....	....	....	....	....	....	....	....	....	....	....	....	....	....	....
1994-95	Kiekko Espoo	Finland	48	4	3	7	54	....	....	....	....	....	....	....	....	....	4	0	0	0	0	....	....	....	....
1995-96	Kiekko Espoo	Finland	45	1	7	8	48	....	....	....	....	....	....	....	....	....	....	....	....	....	....	....	....	....	....
1996-97	Kiekko Espoo	Finland	48	0	12	12	69	....	....	....	....	....	....	....	....	....	....	....	....	....	....	....	....	....	....
1997-98	Kiekko Espoo	Finland	47	4	1	5	59	....	....	....	....	....	....	....	....	....	8	0	1	1	6	....	....	....	....
1998-99	Rosenheim	Germany	51	1	9	10	58	....	....	....	....	....	....	....	....	....	....	....	....	....	....	....	....	....	....
99-2000	Rosenheim	Germany	51	3	5	8	46	....	....	....	....	....	....	....	....	....	10	1	4	5	28	....	....	....	....
2000-01	Jokerit Helsinki	Finland	52	2	8	10	98	....	....	....	....	....	....	....	....	....	5	0	0	0	2	....	....	....	....
2001-02	Hamilton	AHL	6	0	2	2	25	....	....	....	....	....	....	....	....	....	....	....	....	....	....	....	....	....	....
	Jokerit Helsinki	Finland	36	0	3	3	40	....	....	....	....	....	....	....	....	....	12	2	2	4	2	....	....	....	....
2002-03	**Edmonton**	**NHL**	**13**	**0**	**0**	**0**	**4**	**0**	**0**	**0**	**2**	**0.0**	**–2**	**0**	**0.0**	**7:55**	....	....	....	....	....	....	....	....	....
	Hamilton	AHL	12	0	4	4	12	....	....	....	....	....	....	....	....	....	14	1	2	3	6	....	....	....	....
	NHL Totals		**13**	**0**	**0**	**0**	**4**	**0**	**0**	**0**	**2**	**0.0**		**0**	**0.0**	**7:55**	....	....	....	....	....	....	....	....	....

Missed majority of 2002-03 season recovering from rib injury suffered in game vs. Vancouver, December 26, 2002.

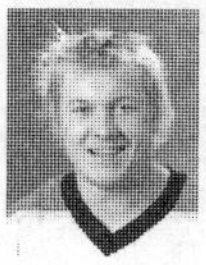

HAGMAN, Niklas

(HAG-muhn, NIHK-las) **FLA.**

Left wing. Shoots left. 6', 200 lbs. Born, Espoo, Finland, December 5, 1979. Florida's 3rd choice, 70th overall, in 1999 Entry Draft.

Season	Club	League	GP	G	A	Pts	PIM	PP	SH	GW	S	%	+/-	TF	F%	Min	GP	G	A	Pts	PIM	PP	SH	GW	Min
1994-95	HIFK Helsinki-C	Finn-Jr.	28	30	15	45	40	....	....	....	....	....	....	....	....	....	4	2	0	2	6	....	....	....	....
1995-96	HIFK Helsinki-B	Finn-Jr.	26	12	21	33	32	....	....	....	....	....	....	....	....	....	4	3	0	3	2	....	....	....	....
	HIFK Helsinki Jr.	Finn-Jr.	12	3	1	4	0	....	....	....	....	....	....	....	....	....	....	....	....	....	....	....	....	....	....
1996-97	HIFK Helsinki Jr.	Finn-Jr.	30	13	12	25	30	....	....	....	....	....	....	....	....	....	4	1	1	2	0	....	....	....	....
1997-98	HIFK Helsinki Jr.	Finn-Jr.	26	9	5	14	16	....	....	....	....	....	....	....	....	....	....	....	....	....	....	....	....	....	....
	HIFK Helsinki	Finland	8	1	0	1	0	....	....	....	....	....	....	....	....	....	....	....	....	....	....	....	....	....	....
	HIFK Helsinki-B	Finn-Jr.	1	0	1	1	0	....	....	....	....	....	....	....	....	....	....	....	....	....	....	....	....	....	....
1998-99	HIFK Helsinki Jr.	Finn-Jr.	14	4	9	13	43	....	....	....	....	....	....	....	....	....	....	....	....	....	....	....	....	....	....
	HIFK Helsinki	Finland	17	1	1	2	14	....	....	....	....	....	....	....	....	....	....	....	....	....	....	....	....	....	....
	HIFK Helsinki	EuroHL	1	0	1	1	0	....	....	....	....	....	....	....	....	....	....	....	....	....	....	....	....	....	....
	Blues Espoo	Finland	14	1	1	2	2	....	....	....	....	....	....	....	....	....	4	1	0	1	0	....	....	....	....
99-2000	Karpat Oulu	Finland-2	41	17	18	35	12	....	....	....	....	....	....	....	....	....	7	4	2	6	....	....	....	....	....
2000-01	Karpat Oulu	Finland	56	28	18	46	32	....	....	....	....	....	....	....	....	....	8	3	1	4	0	....	....	....	....
2001-02	**Florida**	**NHL**	**78**	**10**	**18**	**28**	**8**	**0**	**1**	**2**	**134**	**7.5**	**–6**	**32**	**28.1**	**13:50**	....	....	....	....	....	....	....	....	....
	Finland	Olympics	4	1	2	3	0	....	....	....	....	....	....	....	....	....	....	....	....	....	....	....	....	....	....
2002-03	**Florida**	**NHL**	**80**	**8**	**15**	**23**	**20**	**2**	**0**	**0**	**132**	**6.1**	**–8**	**17**	**11.8**	**13:31**	....	....	....	....	....	....	....	....	....
	NHL Totals		**158**	**18**	**33**	**51**	**28**	**2**	**1**	**2**	**266**	**6.8**		**49**	**22.4**	**13:40**	....	....	....	....	....	....	....	....	....

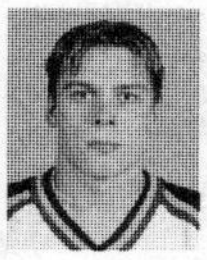

HAHL, Riku

(HAHL, REE-koo) **COL.**

Center. Shoots left. 6', 190 lbs. Born, Hameenlinna, Finland, November 1, 1980. Colorado's 9th choice, 183rd overall, in 1999 Entry Draft.

Season	Club	League	GP	G	A	Pts	PIM	PP	SH	GW	S	%	+/-	TF	F%	Min	GP	G	A	Pts	PIM	PP	SH	GW	Min
1995-96	HPK-C	Finn-Jr.	32	18	30	48	28	....	....	....	....	....	....	....	....	....	....	....	....	....	....	....	....	....	....
1996-97	HPK-B	Finn-Jr.	32	19	24	43	22	....	....	....	....	....	....	....	....	....	....	....	....	....	....	....	....	....	....
	HPK Jr.	Finn-Jr.	2	0	1	1	2	....	....	....	....	....	....	....	....	....	6	2	0	2	2	....	....	....	....
1997-98	HPK-B	Finn-Jr.	10	5	14	19	6	....	....	....	....	....	....	....	....	....	....	....	....	....	....	....	....	....	....
	HPK Jr.	Finn-Jr.	35	13	6	19	12	....	....	....	....	....	....	....	....	....	....	....	....	....	....	....	....	....	....
1998-99	HPK Jr.	Finn-Jr.	6	0	2	2	6	....	....	....	....	....	....	....	....	....	....	....	....	....	....	....	....	....	....
	HPK Hameenlinna	Finland	28	0	1	1	0	....	....	....	....	....	....	....	....	....	8	0	0	0	2	....	....	....	....
99-2000	HPK Jr.	Finn-Jr.	12	1	6	7	8	....	....	....	....	....	....	....	....	....	9	5	4	9	16	....	....	....	....
	HPK Hameenlinna	Finland	50	4	3	7	18	....	....	....	....	....	....	....	....	....	8	0	0	0	2	....	....	....	....
2000-01	HPK Jr.	Finn-Jr.	2	1	3	4	0	....	....	....	....	....	....	....	....	....	....	....	....	....	....	....	....	....	....
	HPK Hameenlinna	Finland	55	3	9	12	32	....	....	....	....	....	....	....	....	....	....	....	....	....	....	....	....	....	....
2001-02	**Colorado**	**NHL**	**22**	**2**	**3**	**5**	**14**	**0**	**0**	**1**	**17**	**11.8**	**1**	**94**	**35.1**	**9:26**	**21**	**1**	**2**	**3**	**0**	**0**	**0**	**0**	**7:31**
	Hershey Bears	AHL	52	6	17	23	16	....	....	....	....	....	....	....	....	....	....	....	....	....	....	....	....	....	....
2002-03	**Colorado**	**NHL**	**42**	**3**	**4**	**7**	**12**	**0**	**0**	**0**	**61**	**4.9**	**3**	**69**	**37.7**	**11:03**	**6**	**0**	**2**	**2**	**2**	**0**	**0**	**0**	**13:49**
	Hershey Bears	AHL	28	7	7	14	17	....	....	....	....	....	....	....	....	....	....	....	....	....	....	....	....	....	....
	NHL Totals		**64**	**5**	**7**	**12**	**26**	**0**	**0**	**1**	**78**	**6.4**		**163**	**36.2**	**10:30**	**27**	**1**	**4**	**5**	**2**	**0**	**0**	**0**	**8:55**

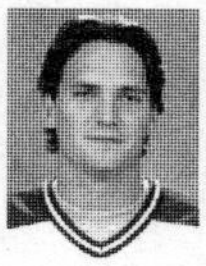

HAINSEY, Ron

(HAYN-zee, RAWN) **MTL.**

Defense. Shoots left. 6'3", 200 lbs. Born, Bolton, CT, March 24, 1981. Montreal's 1st choice, 13th overall, in 2000 Entry Draft.

Season	Club	League	GP	G	A	Pts	PIM	PP	SH	GW	S	%	+/-	TF	F%	Min	GP	G	A	Pts	PIM	PP	SH	GW	Min
1997-98	U.S. National U-18	USDP	66	6	15	21	44	....	....	....	....	....	....	....	....	....	....	....	....	....	....	....	....	....	....
1998-99	U.S. National U-18	USDP	48	5	12	17	45	....	....	....	....	....	....	....	....	....	....	....	....	....	....	....	....	....	....
99-2000	U. Mass-Lowell	H-East	30	3	8	11	20	....	....	....	....	....	....	....	....	....	....	....	....	....	....	....	....	....	....
2000-01	U. Mass-Lowell	H-East	33	10	26	36	51	....	....	....	....	....	....	....	....	....	....	....	....	....	....	....	....	....	....
	Quebec Citadelles	AHL	4	1	0	1	0	....	....	....	....	....	....	....	....	....	1	0	0	0	0	....	....	....	....
2001-02	Quebec Citadelles	AHL	63	7	24	31	26	....	....	....	....	....	....	....	....	....	3	0	0	0	0	....	....	....	....
2002-03	**Montreal**	**NHL**	**21**	**0**	**0**	**0**	**2**	**0**	**0**	**0**	**12**	**0.0**	**–1**	**0**	**0.0**	**12:25**	....	....	....	....	....	....	....	....	....
	Hamilton	AHL	33	2	11	13	26	....	....	....	....	....	....	....	....	....	23	1	10	11	20	....	....	....	....
	NHL Totals		**21**	**0**	**0**	**0**	**2**	**0**	**0**	**0**	**12**	**0.0**		**0**	**0.0**	**12:25**	....	....	....	....	....	....	....	....	....

Hockey East First All-Star Team (2001) • NCAA East Second All-American Team (2001) • AHL All-Rookie Team (2002)

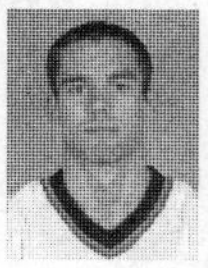

HAJT, Chris

(HIGHT, KRIHS) **WSH.**

Defense. Shoots left. 6'3", 206 lbs. Born, Saskatoon, Sask., July 5, 1978. Edmonton's 3rd choice, 32nd overall, in 1996 Entry Draft.

Season	Club	League	GP	G	A	Pts	PIM	PP	SH	GW	S	%	+/-	TF	F%	Min	GP	G	A	Pts	PIM	PP	SH	GW	Min
1993-94	Amherst Knights	WNYHA	38	8	20	28	16	....	....	....	....	....	....	....	....	....	....	....	....	....	....	....	....	....	....
1994-95	Guelph Storm	OHL	57	1	7	8	35	....	....	....	....	....	....	....	....	....	14	0	2	2	9	....	....	....	....
1995-96	Guelph Storm	OHL	63	8	27	35	69	....	....	....	....	....	....	....	....	....	16	0	6	6	13	....	....	....	....
1996-97	Guelph Storm	OHL	58	11	15	26	62	....	....	....	....	....	....	....	....	....	18	0	8	8	25	....	....	....	....
1997-98	Guelph Storm	OHL	44	2	21	23	46	....	....	....	....	....	....	....	....	....	12	1	5	6	11	....	....	....	....
1998-99	Hamilton	AHL	64	0	4	4	36	....	....	....	....	....	....	....	....	....	....	....	....	....	....	....	....	....	....
99-2000	Hamilton	AHL	54	0	8	8	30	....	....	....	....	....	....	....	....	....	10	0	2	2	0	....	....	....	....
2000-01	**Edmonton**	**NHL**	**1**	**0**	**0**	**0**	**0**	**0**	**0**	**0**	**0**	**0.0**	**–1**	**0**	**0.0**	**7:38**	....	....	....	....	....	....	....	....	....
	Hamilton	AHL	70	0	10	10	48	....	....	....	....	....	....	....	....	....	....	....	....	....	....	....	....	....	....
2001-02	Hamilton	AHL	39	2	3	5	34	....	....	....	....	....	....	....	....	....	15	1	2	3	8	....	....	....	....
2002-03	Portland Pirates	AHL	71	11	15	26	61	....	....	....	....	....	....	....	....	....	1	0	0	0	2	....	....	....	....
	NHL Totals		**1**	**0**	**0**	**0**	**0**	**0**	**0**	**0**	**0**	**0.0**		**0**	**0.0**	**7:38**	....	....	....	....	....	....	....	....	....

OHL Second All-Star Team (1998)

Signed as a free agent by **Washington**, July 23, 2002.

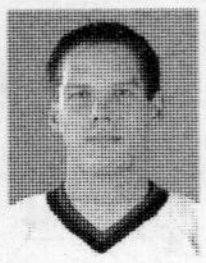

HALKO, Steven
(HAL-koh, STEE-vehn)

Defense. Shoots right. 6'1", 200 lbs. Born, Etobicoke, Ont., March 8, 1974. Hartford's 10th choice, 225th overall, in 1992 Entry Draft.

			Regular Season														Playoffs								
Season	Club	League	GP	G	A	Pts	PIM	PP	SH	GW	S	%	+/-	TF	F%	Min	GP	G	A	Pts	PIM	PP	SH	GW	Min
1989-90	Newmarket	OJHL-B	30	3	5	8	16	....	....	....	....	....	....	....	....	....	....	....	....	....	....	....	....	....	....
1990-91	Newmarket	OJHL-B	35	2	13	15	37	....	....	....	....	....	....	....	....	....	....	....	....	....	....	....	....	....	....
	Markham	OJHL-B	8	4	3	7	2	....	....	....	....	....	....	....	....	....	....	....	....	....	....	....	....	....	....
1991-92	Thornhill Islanders	MTJHL	44	15	46	61	43	....	....	....	....	....	....	....	....	....	....	....	....	....	....	....	....	....	....
1992-93	U. of Michigan	CCHA	39	1	12	13	12	....	....	....	....	....	....	....	....	....	....	....	....	....	....	....	....	....	....
1993-94	U. of Michigan	CCHA	41	2	13	15	32	....	....	....	....	....	....	....	....	....	....	....	....	....	....	....	....	....	....
1994-95	U. of Michigan	CCHA	39	2	14	16	20	....	....	....	....	....	....	....	....	....	....	....	....	....	....	....	....	....	....
1995-96	U. of Michigan	CCHA	43	4	16	20	32	....	....	....	....	....	....	....	....	....	....	....	....	....	....	....	....	....	....
1996-97	Springfield	AHL	70	1	5	6	37	....	....	....	....	....	....	....	....	....	11	0	2	2	8	....	....	....	....
1997-98	**Carolina**	**NHL**	**18**	**0**	**2**	**2**	**10**	**0**	**0**	**0**	**7**	**0.0**	**–1**	....	....	....	....	....	....	....	....	....	....	....	....
	New Haven	AHL	65	1	19	20	44	....	....	....	....	....	....	....	....	....	1	0	0	0	0	....	....	....	....
1998-99	**Carolina**	**NHL**	**20**	**0**	**3**	**3**	**24**	**0**	**0**	**0**	**6**	**0.0**	**5**	**0**	**0.0**	**15:57**	**4**	**0**	**0**	**0**	**2**	**0**	**0**	**0**	**18:57**
	New Haven	AHL	42	2	7	9	58	....	....	....	....	....	....	....	....	....	....	....	....	....	....	....	....	....	....
99-2000	**Carolina**	**NHL**	**58**	**0**	**8**	**8**	**25**	**0**	**0**	**0**	**54**	**0.0**	**0**	**1**	**100.0**	**16:43**	....	....	....	....	....	....	....	....	....
2000-01	**Carolina**	**NHL**	**48**	**0**	**1**	**1**	**6**	**0**	**0**	**0**	**24**	**0.0**	**–10**	**0**	**0.0**	**13:27**	....	....	....	....	....	....	....	....	....
2001-02	**Carolina**	**NHL**	**5**	**0**	**1**	**1**	**6**	**0**	**0**	**0**	**0**	**0.0**	**3**	**0**	**0.0**	**9:43**	....	....	....	....	....	....	....	....	....
	Worcester IceCats	AHL	43	3	5	8	15	....	....	....	....	....	....	....	....	....	3	0	1	1	0	....	....	....	....
2002-03	**Carolina**	**NHL**	**6**	**0**	**0**	**0**	**0**	**0**	**0**	**0**	**5**	**0.0**	**1**	**0**	**0.0**	**10:14**	....	....	....	....	....	....	....	....	....
	Lowell	AHL	71	4	22	26	34	....	....	....	....	....	....	....	....	....	....	....	....	....	....	....	....	....	....
	NHL Totals		**155**	**0**	**15**	**15**	**71**	**0**	**0**	**0**	**96**	**0.0**		**1**	**100.0**	**14:55**	**4**	**0**	**0**	**0**	**2**	**0**	**0**	**0**	**18:57**

CCHA Second All-Star Team (1995, 1996) • NCAA Championship All-Tournament Team (1996)

Transferred to **Carolina** after **Hartford** franchise relocated, June 25, 1997. Traded to **St. Louis** by **Carolina** with Carolina's 4th round choice (later traded to Atlanta – Atlanta selected Lane Manson) in 2002 Entry Draft for Sean Hill, December 5, 2001. Signed as a free agent by **Carolina**, August 5, 2002.

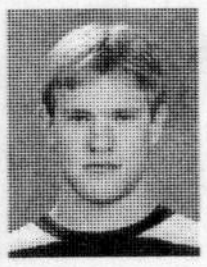

HALL, Adam
(HAWL, A-dam) **NSH.**

Right wing. Shoots right. 6'3", 205 lbs. Born, Kalamazoo, MI, August 14, 1980. Nashville's 3rd choice, 52nd overall, in 1999 Entry Draft.

			Regular Season														Playoffs								
Season	Club	League	GP	G	A	Pts	PIM	PP	SH	GW	S	%	+/-	TF	F%	Min	GP	G	A	Pts	PIM	PP	SH	GW	Min
1996-97	Bramalea Blues	OPJHL	43	9	14	23	92	....	....	....	....	....	....	....	....	....	....	....	....	....	....	....	....	....	....
1997-98	U.S. National U-18	USDP	71	42	23	65	63	....	....	....	....	....	....	....	....	....	....	....	....	....	....	....	....	....	....
1998-99	Michigan State	CCHA	36	16	7	23	74	....	....	....	....	....	....	....	....	....	....	....	....	....	....	....	....	....	....
99-2000	Michigan State	CCHA	40	*26	13	39	38	....	....	....	....	....	....	....	....	....	....	....	....	....	....	....	....	....	....
2000-01	Michigan State	CCHA	42	18	12	30	42	....	....	....	....	....	....	....	....	....	....	....	....	....	....	....	....	....	....
2001-02	Michigan State	CCHA	41	19	15	34	36	....	....	....	....	....	....	....	....	....	....	....	....	....	....	....	....	....	....
	Nashville	**NHL**	**1**	**0**	**1**	**1**	**0**	**0**	**0**	**0**	**2**	**0.0**	**0**	**0**	**0.0**	**14:04**	....	....	....	....	....	....	....	....	....
	Milwaukee	AHL	6	2	2	4	4	....	....	....	....	....	....	....	....	....	....	....	....	....	....	....	....	....	....
2002-03	**Nashville**	**NHL**	**79**	**16**	**12**	**28**	**31**	**8**	**0**	**2**	**146**	**11.0**	**–8**	**17**	**52.9**	**14:09**	....	....	....	....	....	....	....	....	....
	Milwaukee	AHL	1	0	0	0	2	....	....	....	....	....	....	....	....	....	....	....	....	....	....	....	....	....	....
	NHL Totals		**80**	**16**	**13**	**29**	**31**	**8**	**0**	**2**	**148**	**10.8**		**17**	**52.9**	**14:09**	....	....	....	....	....	....	....	....	....

CCHA Second All-Star Team (2000)

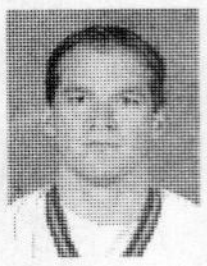

HALPERN, Jeff
(HAL-pehrn, JEHF) **WSH.**

Center. Shoots right. 6', 201 lbs. Born, Potomac, MD, May 3, 1976.

			Regular Season														Playoffs								
Season	Club	League	GP	G	A	Pts	PIM	PP	SH	GW	S	%	+/-	TF	F%	Min	GP	G	A	Pts	PIM	PP	SH	GW	Min
1994-95	Stratford Cullitons	OJHL-B	44	29	54	83	43	....	....	....	....	....	....	....	....	....	....	....	....	....	....	....	....	....	....
1995-96	Princeton	ECAC	29	3	11	14	30	....	....	....	....	....	....	....	....	....	....	....	....	....	....	....	....	....	....
1996-97	Princeton	ECAC	33	7	24	31	35	....	....	....	....	....	....	....	....	....	....	....	....	....	....	....	....	....	....
1997-98	Princeton	ECAC	36	*28	25	*53	46	....	....	....	....	....	....	....	....	....	....	....	....	....	....	....	....	....	....
1998-99	Princeton	ECAC	33	*22	22	44	32	....	....	....	....	....	....	....	....	....	....	....	....	....	....	....	....	....	....
	Portland Pirates	AHL	6	2	1	3	4	....	....	....	....	....	....	....	....	....	....	....	....	....	....	....	....	....	....
99-2000	**Washington**	**NHL**	**79**	**18**	**11**	**29**	**39**	**4**	**4**	**1**	**108**	**16.7**	**21**	**812**	**51.1**	**13:14**	**5**	**2**	**1**	**3**	**0**	**1**	**0**	**1**	**15:16**
2000-01	**Washington**	**NHL**	**80**	**21**	**21**	**42**	**60**	**2**	**1**	**5**	**110**	**19.1**	**13**	**1293**	**52.4**	**16:08**	**6**	**2**	**3**	**5**	**17**	**1**	**0**	**1**	**20:01**
2001-02	**Washington**	**NHL**	**48**	**5**	**14**	**19**	**29**	**0**	**0**	**4**	**74**	**6.8**	**–9**	**661**	**56.0**	**15:19**	....	....	....	....	....	....	....	....	....
2002-03	**Washington**	**NHL**	**82**	**13**	**21**	**34**	**88**	**1**	**2**	**2**	**126**	**10.3**	**6**	**1492**	**54.1**	**17:25**	**6**	**0**	**1**	**1**	**2**	**0**	**0**	**0**	**19:59**
	NHL Totals		**289**	**57**	**67**	**124**	**216**	**7**	**7**	**12**	**418**	**13.6**		**4258**	**53.3**	**15:34**	**17**	**4**	**5**	**9**	**19**	**2**	**0**	**2**	**18:37**

ECAC Second All-Star Team (1998, 1999)

Signed as a free agent by **Washington**, March 29, 1999.

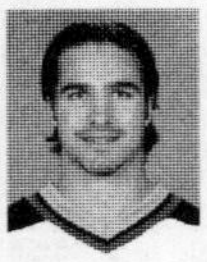

HAMEL, Denis
(ha-MEHL, deh-NEE) **OTT.**

Left wing. Shoots left. 6'1", 201 lbs. Born, Lachute, Que., May 10, 1977. St. Louis' 5th choice, 153rd overall, in 1995 Entry Draft.

			Regular Season														Playoffs								
Season	Club	League	GP	G	A	Pts	PIM	PP	SH	GW	S	%	+/-	TF	F%	Min	GP	G	A	Pts	PIM	PP	SH	GW	Min
1992-93	Lachute Regents	QAAA	32	18	24	42		....	....	....	....	....	....	....	....	....	....	....	....	....	....	....	....	....	....
1993-94	Lac St-Louis Lions	QAAA	28	10	11	21	50	....	....	....	....	....	....	....	....	....	....	....	....	....	....	....	....	....	....
	Abitibi Foresters	QAAA	15	5	7	12	29	....	....	....	....	....	....	....	....	....	5	0	3	3	16	....	....	....	....
1994-95	Chicoutimi	QMJHL	66	15	12	27	155	....	....	....	....	....	....	....	....	....	12	2	0	2	27	....	....	....	....
1995-96	Chicoutimi	QMJHL	65	40	49	89	199	....	....	....	....	....	....	....	....	....	17	10	14	24	64	....	....	....	....
1996-97	Chicoutimi	QMJHL	70	50	50	100	357	....	....	....	....	....	....	....	....	....	20	15	10	25	58	....	....	....	....
1997-98	Rochester	AHL	74	10	15	25	98	....	....	....	....	....	....	....	....	....	4	1	2	3	0	....	....	....	....
1998-99	Rochester	AHL	74	16	17	33	121	....	....	....	....	....	....	....	....	....	20	3	4	7	10	....	....	....	....
99-2000	**Buffalo**	**NHL**	**3**	**1**	**0**	**1**	**0**	**0**	**0**	**0**	**3**	**33.3**	**–1**	**0**	**0.0**	**9:45**	....	....	....	....	....	....	....	....	....
	Rochester	AHL	76	34	24	58	122	....	....	....	....	....	....	....	....	....	21	6	7	13	49	....	....	....	....
2000-01	**Buffalo**	**NHL**	**41**	**8**	**3**	**11**	**22**	**1**	**1**	**3**	**55**	**14.5**	**–2**	**171**	**33.9**	**10:58**	....	....	....	....	....	....	....	....	....
2001-02	**Buffalo**	**NHL**	**61**	**2**	**6**	**8**	**28**	**0**	**0**	**0**	**80**	**2.5**	**–1**	**94**	**39.4**	**10:60**	....	....	....	....	....	....	....	....	....
2002-03	**Buffalo**	**NHL**	**25**	**2**	**0**	**2**	**17**	**0**	**0**	**1**	**41**	**4.9**	**–4**	**4**	**25.0**	**12:40**	....	....	....	....	....	....	....	....	....
	Rochester	AHL	48	27	20	47	64	....	....	....	....	....	....	....	....	....	3	3	2	5	4	....	....	....	....
	NHL Totals		**130**	**13**	**9**	**22**	**67**	**1**	**1**	**4**	**179**	**7.3**		**269**	**35.7**	**11:17**	....	....	....	....	....	....	....	....	....

QMJHL All-Rookie Team (1995)

Traded to **Buffalo** by **St. Louis** for Charlie Huddy and Buffalo's 7th round choice (Daniel Corso) in 1996 Entry Draft, March 19, 1996. • Missed majority of 2000-01 season recovering from knee injury suffered in game vs. NY Islanders, January 27, 2001. Signed as a free agent by **Ottawa**, July 5, 2003.

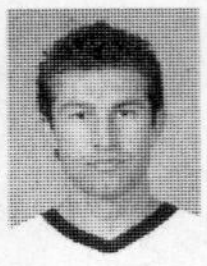

HAMRLIK, Roman
(HAHM-reh-lik, ROH-muhn) **NYI**

Defense. Shoots left. 6'2", 200 lbs. Born, Zlin, Czech., April 12, 1974. Tampa Bay's 1st choice, 1st overall, in 1992 Entry Draft.

			Regular Season														Playoffs								
Season	Club	League	GP	G	A	Pts	PIM	PP	SH	GW	S	%	+/-	TF	F%	Min	GP	G	A	Pts	PIM	PP	SH	GW	Min
1990-91	AC ZPS Zlin	Czech	14	2	2	4	18	....	....	....	....	....	....	....	....	....	....	....	....	....	....	....	....	....	....
1991-92	AC ZPS Zlin	Czech	34	5	5	10	50	....	....	....	....	....	....	....	....	....	....	....	....	....	....	....	....	....	....
1992-93	**Tampa Bay**	**NHL**	**67**	**6**	**15**	**21**	**71**	**1**	**0**	**1**	**113**	**5.3**	**–21**	....	....	....	....	....	....	....	....	....	....	....	....
	Atlanta Knights	IHL	2	1	1	2	2	....	....	....	....	....	....	....	....	....	....	....	....	....	....	....	....	....	....
1993-94	**Tampa Bay**	**NHL**	**64**	**3**	**18**	**21**	**135**	**0**	**0**	**0**	**158**	**1.9**	**–14**	....	....	....	....	....	....	....	....	....	....	....	....
1994-95	AC ZPS Zlin	Czech	2	1	0	1	10	....	....	....	....	....	....	....	....	....	....	....	....	....	....	....	....	....	....
	Tampa Bay	**NHL**	**48**	**12**	**11**	**23**	**86**	**7**	**1**	**2**	**134**	**9.0**	**–18**	....	....	....	....	....	....	....	....	....	....	....	....
1995-96	**Tampa Bay**	**NHL**	**82**	**16**	**49**	**65**	**103**	**12**	**0**	**2**	**281**	**5.7**	**–24**	....	....	....	**5**	**0**	**1**	**1**	**4**	**0**	**0**	**0**	
1996-97	**Tampa Bay**	**NHL**	**79**	**12**	**28**	**40**	**57**	**6**	**0**	**0**	**238**	**5.0**	**–29**	....	....	....	....	....	....	....	....	....	....	....	....
1997-98	**Tampa Bay**	**NHL**	**37**	**3**	**12**	**15**	**22**	**1**	**0**	**0**	**86**	**3.5**	**–18**	....	....	....	....	....	....	....	....	....	....	....	....
	Edmonton	**NHL**	**41**	**6**	**20**	**26**	**48**	**4**	**1**	**3**	**112**	**5.4**	**3**	....	....	....	**12**	**0**	**6**	**6**	**12**	**0**	**0**	**0**	
	Czech Republic	Olympics	6	1	0	1	2	....	....	....	....	....	....	....	....	....	....	....	....	....	....	....	....	....	....
1998-99	**Edmonton**	**NHL**	**75**	**8**	**24**	**32**	**70**	**3**	**0**	**0**	**172**	**4.7**	**9**	**0**	**0.0**	**23:49**	**3**	**0**	**0**	**0**	**2**	**0**	**0**	**0**	**16:23**
99-2000	Zlin	Czech	6	0	3	3	4	....	....	....	....	....	....	....	....	....	....	....	....	....	....	....	....	....	....
	Edmonton	**NHL**	**80**	**8**	**37**	**45**	**68**	**5**	**0**	**0**	**180**	**4.4**	**1**	**0**	**0.0**	**25:18**	**5**	**0**	**1**	**1**	**4**	**0**	**0**	**0**	**24:44**
2000-01	**NY Islanders**	**NHL**	**76**	**16**	**30**	**46**	**92**	**5**	**1**	**4**	**232**	**6.9**	**–20**	**1**	**100.0**	**25:12**	....	....	....	....	....	....	....	....	....
2001-02	**NY Islanders**	**NHL**	**70**	**11**	**26**	**37**	**78**	**4**	**1**	**1**	**169**	**6.5**	**7**	**1**	**0.0**	**25:32**	**7**	**1**	**6**	**7**	**6**	**0**	**0**	**0**	**29:09**
	Czech Republic	Olympics	4	0	1	1	2	....	....	....	....	....	....	....	....	....	....	....	....	....	....	....	....	....	....
2002-03	**NY Islanders**	**NHL**	**73**	**9**	**32**	**41**	**87**	**3**	**0**	**2**	**151**	**6.0**	**21**	**0**	**0.0**	**26:34**	**5**	**0**	**2**	**2**	**2**	**0**	**0**	**0**	**29:24**
	NHL Totals		**792**	**110**	**302**	**412**	**917**	**51**	**4**	**15**	**2026**	**5.4**		**2**	**50.0**	**25:16**	**37**	**1**	**16**	**17**	**30**	**0**	**0**	**0**	**26:12**

Played in NHL All-Star Game (1996, 1999, 2003)

Traded to **Edmonton** by **Tampa Bay** with Paul Comrie for Bryan Marchment, Steve Kelly and Jason Bonsignore, December 30, 1997. Traded to **NY Islanders** by **Edmonton** for Eric Brewer, Josh Green and NY Islanders' 2nd round choice (Brad Winchester) in 2000 Entry Draft, June 24, 2000.

Regular Season / Playoffs

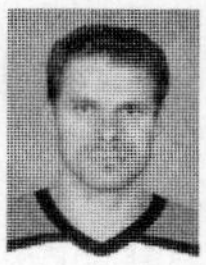

HANDZUS, Michal

(HAHND-zuhs, MEE-chal) **PHI.**

Center. Shoots left. 6'5", 217 lbs. Born, Banska Bystrica, Czech., March 11, 1977. St. Louis' 3rd choice, 101st overall, in 1995 Entry Draft.

Season	Club	League	GP	G	A	Pts	PIM	PP	SH	GW	S	%	+/-	TF	F%	Min	GP	G	A	Pts	PIM	PP	SH	GW	Min
1993-94	B. Bystrica Jr.	Slovak-Jr.	40	23	36	59																			
1994-95	Banska Bystrica	Slovak-2	22	15	14	29	10																		
1995-96	Banska Bystrica	Slovakia	19	3	1	4	8																		
1996-97	HC SKP PS Poprad	Slovakia	44	15	18	33																			
1997-98	Worcester IceCats	AHL	69	27	36	63	54										11	2	6	8	10				
1998-99	**St. Louis**	**NHL**	**66**	**4**	**12**	**16**	**30**	**0**	**0**	**0**	**78**	**5.1**	**–9**	**794**	**49.9**	**14:48**	**11**	**0**	**2**	**2**	**8**	**0**	**0**	**0**	**16:52**
99-2000	**St. Louis**	**NHL**	**81**	**25**	**28**	**53**	**44**	**3**	**4**	**5**	**166**	**15.1**	**19**	**1243**	**51.5**	**17:43**	**7**	**0**	**3**	**3**	**6**	**0**	**0**	**0**	**16:35**
2000-01	**St. Louis**	**NHL**	**36**	**10**	**14**	**24**	**12**	**3**	**2**	**2**	**58**	**17.2**	**11**	**581**	**50.6**	**17:60**									
	Phoenix	**NHL**	**10**	**4**	**4**	**8**	**21**	**0**	**1**	**0**	**14**	**28.6**	**5**	**111**	**60.4**	**15:26**									
2001-02	**Phoenix**	**NHL**	**79**	**15**	**30**	**45**	**34**	**3**	**1**	**1**	**94**	**16.0**	**–8**	**1227**	**48.7**	**16:09**	**5**	**0**	**0**	**0**	**2**	**0**	**0**	**0**	**15:01**
	Slovakia	Olympics	2	1	0	1	6																		
2002-03	**Philadelphia**	**NHL**	**82**	**23**	**21**	**44**	**46**	**1**	**1**	**9**	**133**	**17.3**	**13**	**1350**	**52.3**	**17:33**	**13**	**2**	**6**	**8**	**6**	**0**	**0**	**1**	**18:23**
	NHL Totals		**354**	**81**	**109**	**190**	**187**	**10**	**9**	**17**	**543**	**14.9**		**5306**	**50.9**	**16:45**	**36**	**2**	**11**	**13**	**22**	**0**	**0**	**1**	**17:06**

Traded to **Phoenix** by **St. Louis** with Ladislav Nagy, the rights to Jeff Taffe and St. Louis' 1st round choice (Ben Eager) in 2002 Entry Draft for Keith Tkachuk, March 13, 2001. Traded to **Philadelphia** by **Phoenix** with Robert Esche for Brian Boucher and Nashville's 3rd round choice (previously acquired, Phoenix selected Joe Callahan) in 2002 Entry Draft, June 12, 2002.

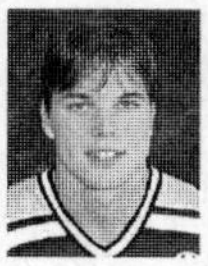

HANKINSON, Casey

(HAN-kihn-suhn, KAY-see) **ANA.**

Left wing. Shoots left. 6'1", 187 lbs. Born, Edina, MN, May 8, 1976. Chicago's 9th choice, 201st overall, in 1995 Entry Draft.

Season	Club	League	GP	G	A	Pts	PIM	PP	SH	GW	S	%	+/-	TF	F%	Min	GP	G	A	Pts	PIM	PP	SH	GW	Min
1992-93	Edina Hornets	Hi-School	25	20	26	46																			
1993-94	Edina Hornets	Hi-School	24	21	20	41	50																		
1994-95	U. of Minnesota	WCHA	33	7	1	8	86																		
1995-96	U. of Minnesota	WCHA	39	16	19	35	101																		
1996-97	U. of Minnesota	WCHA	42	17	24	41	79																		
1997-98	U. of Minnesota	WCHA	35	10	12	22	81																		
1998-99	Portland Pirates	AHL	72	10	13	23	106																		
99-2000	Cleveland	IHL	82	7	22	29	140										2	0	0	0	2				
2000-01	**Chicago**	**NHL**	**11**	**0**	**1**	**1**	**9**	**0**	**0**	**0**	**15**	**0.0**	**–3**	**0**	**0.0**	**9:46**									
	Norfolk Admirals	AHL	69	30	21	51	74										9	5	4	9	2				
2001-02	**Chicago**	**NHL**	**3**	**0**	**0**	**0**	**0**	**0**	**0**	**0**	**1**	**0.0**	**–2**	**6**	**33.3**	**8:38**									
	Norfolk Admirals	AHL	72	19	30	49	85										4	1	2	3	0				
2002-03	Norfolk Admirals	AHL	78	27	28	55	59										9	4	3	7	10				
	NHL Totals		**14**	**0**	**1**	**1**	**9**	**0**	**0**	**0**	**16**	**0.0**		**6**	**33.3**	**9:31**									

Signed as a free agent by **Anaheim**, July 25, 2003.

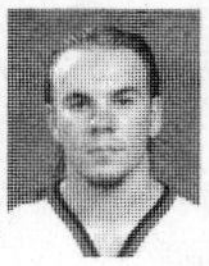

HANNAN, Scott

(HAN-nan, SKAWT) **S.J.**

Defense. Shoots left. 6'2", 220 lbs. Born, Richmond, B.C., January 23, 1979. San Jose's 2nd choice, 23rd overall, in 1997 Entry Draft.

Season	Club	League	GP	G	A	Pts	PIM	PP	SH	GW	S	%	+/-	TF	F%	Min	GP	G	A	Pts	PIM	PP	SH	GW	Min
1994-95	Surrey Wolves	BCAHA	70	54	54	108	200																		
	Tacoma Rockets	WHL	2	0	0	0	0																		
1995-96	Kelowna Rockets	WHL	69	4	5	9	76										6	0	1	1	4				
1996-97	Kelowna Rockets	WHL	70	17	26	43	101										6	0	0	0	8				
1997-98	Kelowna Rockets	WHL	47	10	30	40	70										7	2	7	9	14				
1998-99	**San Jose**	**NHL**	**5**	**0**	**2**	**2**	**6**	**0**	**0**	**0**	**4**	**0.0**	**0**	**0**	**0.0**	**7:15**									
	Kelowna Rockets	WHL	47	15	30	45	92										6	1	2	3	14				
	Kentucky	AHL	2	0	0	0	2										12	0	2	2	10				
99-2000	**San Jose**	**NHL**	**30**	**1**	**2**	**3**	**10**	**0**	**0**	**0**	**28**	**3.6**	**7**	**1**	**0.0**	**17:09**	**1**	**0**	**1**	**1**	**0**	**0**	**0**	**0**	**18:14**
	Kentucky	AHL	41	5	12	17	40																		
2000-01	**San Jose**	**NHL**	**75**	**3**	**14**	**17**	**51**	**0**	**0**	**1**	**96**	**3.1**	**10**	**0**	**0.0**	**19:02**	**6**	**0**	**1**	**1**	**6**	**0**	**0**	**0**	**25:10**
2001-02	**San Jose**	**NHL**	**75**	**2**	**12**	**14**	**57**	**0**	**0**	**1**	**68**	**2.9**	**10**	**1**	**100.0**	**20:19**	**12**	**0**	**2**	**2**	**12**	**0**	**0**	**0**	**20:46**
2002-03	**San Jose**	**NHL**	**81**	**3**	**19**	**22**	**61**	**1**	**0**	**0**	**103**	**2.9**	**0**	**3**	**33.3**	**24:16**									
	NHL Totals		**266**	**9**	**49**	**58**	**185**	**1**	**0**	**2**	**299**	**3.0**		**5**	**40.0**	**20:33**	**19**	**0**	**4**	**4**	**18**	**0**	**0**	**0**	**22:01**

WHL West First All-Star Team (1999)

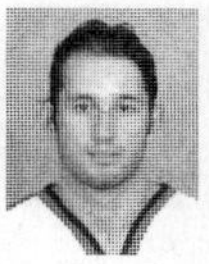

HANSEN, Tavis

(HAN-sehn, TA-vihs) **S.J.**

Right wing. Shoots right. 6'1", 205 lbs. Born, Prince Albert, Sask., June 17, 1975. Winnipeg's 3rd choice, 58th overall, in 1994 Entry Draft.

Season	Club	League	GP	G	A	Pts	PIM	PP	SH	GW	S	%	+/-	TF	F%	Min	GP	G	A	Pts	PIM	PP	SH	GW	Min
1992-93	Shellbrook	SMHL	42	42	63	105	107																		
1993-94	Tacoma Rockets	WHL	71	23	31	54	122										8	1	3	4	17				
1994-95	Tacoma Rockets	WHL	71	32	41	73	142										4	1	1	2	8				
	Winnipeg	**NHL**	**1**	**0**	**0**	**0**	**0**	**0**	**0**	**0**	**0**	**0.0**	**0**												
1995-96	Springfield	AHL	67	6	16	22	85										5	1	2	3	2				
1996-97	**Phoenix**	**NHL**	**1**	**0**	**0**	**0**	**0**	**0**	**0**	**0**	**0**	**0.0**	**0**												
	Springfield	AHL	12	3	1	4	23																		
1997-98	Springfield	AHL	73	20	14	34	70										4	1	2	3	18				
1998-99	**Phoenix**	**NHL**	**20**	**2**	**1**	**3**	**12**	**0**	**0**	**0**	**14**	**14.3**	**–4**	**5**	**80.0**	**8:07**	**2**	**0**	**0**	**0**	**0**	**0**	**0**	**0**	**3:45**
	Springfield	AHL	63	23	11	34	85										3	0	1	1	5				
99-2000	**Phoenix**	**NHL**	**5**	**0**	**0**	**0**	**0**	**0**	**0**	**0**	**2**	**0.0**	**0**	**0**	**0.0**	**4:17**									
	Springfield	AHL	59	21	27	48	164										5	2	1	3	4				
2000-01	**Phoenix**	**NHL**	**7**	**0**	**0**	**0**	**4**	**0**	**0**	**0**	**2**	**0.0**	**–1**	**1**	**100.0**	**5:05**									
	Springfield	AHL	24	6	10	16	81																		
2001-02	Hershey Bears	AHL	35	9	6	15	50										8	0	3	3	8				
2002-03	Cleveland Barons	AHL	80	23	21	44	81																		
	NHL Totals		**34**	**2**	**1**	**3**	**16**	**0**	**0**	**0**	**18**	**11.1**		**6**	**83.3**	**6:51**	**2**	**0**	**0**	**0**	**0**	**0**	**0**	**0**	**3:45**

Transferred to **Phoenix** after **Winnipeg** franchise relocated, July 1, 1996. • Missed majority of 2000-01 and 2001-02 seasons recovering from arm injury suffered in game vs. Hershey (AHL), February 3, 2001. Signed as a free agent by **Hershey** (AHL), January 16, 2002. Signed as a free agent by **San Jose**, September 5, 2002.

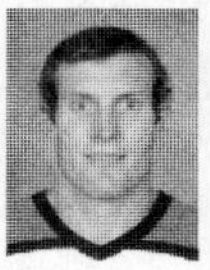

HARLOCK, David

(HAHR-lahk, DAY-vihd)

Defense. Shoots left. 6'2", 215 lbs. Born, Toronto, Ont., March 16, 1971. New Jersey's 2nd choice, 24th overall, in 1990 Entry Draft.

Season	Club	League	GP	G	A	Pts	PIM	PP	SH	GW	S	%	+/-	TF	F%	Min	GP	G	A	Pts	PIM	PP	SH	GW	Min
1986-87	Tor. Red Wings	MTHL	86	17	55	72	60																		
1987-88	Tor. Red Wings	MTHL	70	16	56	72	100																		
	Henry Carr	MTJHL	3	0	0	0	4																		
1988-89	St. Michael's B	OJHL-B	25	4	16	20	34										27	3	12	15	14				
1989-90	U. of Michigan	CCHA	42	2	13	15	44																		
1990-91	U. of Michigan	CCHA	39	2	8	10	70																		
1991-92	U. of Michigan	CCHA	44	1	6	7	80																		
1992-93	U. of Michigan	CCHA	38	3	9	12	58																		
1993-94	Team Canada	Nat-Tm	41	0	3	3	28																		
	Canada	Olympics	8	0	0	0	8																		
	Toronto	**NHL**	**6**	**0**	**0**	**0**	**0**	**0**	**0**	**0**	**2**	**0.0**	**–2**												
	St. John's	AHL	10	0	3	3	2										9	0	0	0	6				
1994-95	St. John's	AHL	58	0	6	6	44										5	0	0	0	0				
	Toronto	**NHL**	**1**	**0**	**0**	**0**	**0**	**0**	**0**	**0**	**0**	**0.0**	**–1**												
1995-96	**Toronto**	**NHL**	**1**	**0**	**0**	**0**	**0**	**0**	**0**	**0**	**0**	**0.0**	**0**												
	St. John's	AHL	77	0	12	12	92										4	0	1	1	2				
1996-97	San Antonio	IHL	69	3	10	13	82										9	0	0	0	10				
1997-98	**Washington**	**NHL**	**6**	**0**	**0**	**0**	**4**	**0**	**0**	**0**	**2**	**0.0**	**2**												
	Portland Pirates	AHL	71	3	15	18	66										10	2	2	4	6				
1998-99	**NY Islanders**	**NHL**	**70**	**2**	**6**	**8**	**68**	**0**	**0**	**0**	**35**	**5.7**	**–16**	**0**	**0.0**	**18:15**									
99-2000	**Atlanta**	**NHL**	**44**	**0**	**6**	**6**	**36**	**0**	**0**	**0**	**29**	**0.0**	**–8**	**0**	**0.0**	**19:41**									
2000-01	**Atlanta**	**NHL**	**65**	**0**	**1**	**1**	**62**	**0**	**0**	**0**	**26**	**0.0**	**–28**	**0**	**0.0**	**17:04**									

			Regular Season														Playoffs								
Season	Club	League	GP	G	A	Pts	PIM	PP	SH	GW	S	%	+/-	TF	F%	Min	GP	G	A	Pts	PIM	PP	SH	GW	Min
2001-02	Atlanta	NHL	19	0	1	1	18	0	0	0	12	0.0	–2	0	0.0	14:55	....	....	....	....	....	....	....	....	....
	Chicago Wolves	AHL	24	2	9	11	28	....	....	....	....	....	....	....	....	....	....	....	....	....	....	....	....	....	....
	Philadelphia	AHL	11	0	4	4	14	....	....	....	....	....	....	....	....	....	5	0	1	1	4	....	....	....	....
2002-03	Philadelphia	AHL	59	2	18	20	83	....	....	....	....	....	....	....	....	....	....	....	....	....	....	....	....	....	....
	NHL Totals		212	2	14	16	188	0	0	0	106	1.9		0	0.0	17:52	....	....	....	....	....	....	....	....	....

Signed as a free agent by **Toronto**, August 20, 1993. Signed as a free agent by **Washington**, August 20, 1997. Signed as a free agent by **NY Islanders**, August 24, 1998. Claimed by **Atlanta** from **NY Islanders** in Expansion Draft, June 25, 1999. Traded to **Philadelphia** by **Atlanta** with Atlanta's 3rd (later traded to Phoenix – Phoenix selected Tyler Redenbach) and 7th (later traded to San Jose – San Jose selected Joe Pavelski) round choices in 2003 Entry Draft for Francis Lessard, March 15, 2002.

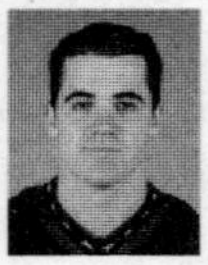

HARTIGAN, Mark
(HAHR-tih-guhn, MAHRK) **CBJ**

Center. Shoots left. 6', 200 lbs. Born, Fort St. John, B.C., October 15, 1977.

1996-97	Weyburn	SJHL	52	44	32	76	....	....	....	....	....	....	....	....	....	....	....	....	....	....	....	....	....	....	....
1997-98	Weyburn	SJHL	62	*59	46	*105	81	....	....	....	....	....	....	....	....	....	23	17	21	38	10	....	....	....	....
1998-99	St. Cloud State	WCHA	DID NOT PLAY – FRESHMAN																						
99-2000	St. Cloud State	WCHA	37	22	20	42	24	....	....	....	....	....	....	....	....	....	....	....	....	....	....	....	....	....	....
2000-01	St. Cloud State	WCHA	40	27	21	48	20	....	....	....	....	....	....	....	....	....	....	....	....	....	....	....	....	....	....
2001-02	St. Cloud State	WCHA	42	*37	38	75	42	....	....	....	....	....	....	....	....	....	....	....	....	....	....	....	....	....	....
	Atlanta	NHL	2	0	0	0	2	0	0	0	3	0.0	–2	18	38.9	13:16	....	....	....	....	....	....	....	....	....
2002-03	Atlanta	NHL	23	5	2	7	6	1	0	0	25	20.0	–8	220	47.3	10:52	....	....	....	....	....	....	....	....	....
	Chicago Wolves	AHL	55	15	31	46	43	....	....	....	....	....	....	....	....	....	9	1	2	3	10	....	....	....	....
	NHL Totals		25	5	2	7	8	1	0	0	28	17.9		238	46.6	11:03	....	....	....	....	....	....	....	....	....

SJHL First All-Star Team (1998) • SJHL Player of the Year (1998) • Royal Bank Cup MVP (1998) • WCHA First All-Star Team (2002) • WCHA Player of the Year (2002)

Signed as a free agent by **Atlanta**, March 27, 2002. Signed as a free agent by **Columbus**, July 15, 2003.

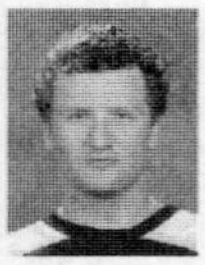

HARTNELL, Scott
(HAHRT-nuhl, SKAWT) **NSH.**

Left wing. Shoots left. 6'2", 205 lbs. Born, Regina, Sask., April 18, 1982. Nashville's 1st choice, 6th overall, in 2000 Entry Draft.

1997-98	Lloydminster	AJHL	56	9	25	34	82	....	....	....	....	....	....	....	....	....	4	2	1	3	8	....	....	....	....
	Prince Albert	WHL	1	0	1	1	2	....	....	....	....	....	....	....	....	....	....	....	....	....	....	....	....	....	....
1998-99	Prince Albert	WHL	65	10	34	44	104	....	....	....	....	....	....	....	....	....	14	0	5	5	22	....	....	....	....
99-2000	Prince Albert	WHL	62	27	55	82	124	....	....	....	....	....	....	....	....	....	6	3	2	5	6	....	....	....	....
2000-01	Nashville	NHL	75	2	14	16	48	0	0	0	92	2.2	–8	3	33.3	10:54	....	....	....	....	....	....	....	....	....
2001-02	Nashville	NHL	75	14	27	41	111	3	0	4	162	8.6	5	12	25.0	16:58	....	....	....	....	....	....	....	....	....
2002-03	Nashville	NHL	82	12	22	34	101	2	0	2	221	5.4	–3	23	30.4	15:17	....	....	....	....	....	....	....	....	....
	NHL Totals		232	28	63	91	260	5	0	6	475	5.9		38	28.9	14:25	....	....	....	....	....	....	....	....	....

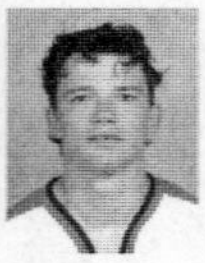

HARVEY, Todd
(HAHR-vee, TAWD) **S.J.**

Right wing/Center. Shoots right. 6', 200 lbs. Born, Hamilton, Ont., February 17, 1975. Dallas' 1st choice, 9th overall, in 1993 Entry Draft.

1989-90	Cambridge	OJHL-B	41	35	27	62	213	....	....	....	....	....	....	....	....	....	....	....	....	....	....	....	....	....	....
1990-91	Cambridge	OJHL-B	35	32	39	71	174	....	....	....	....	....	....	....	....	....	....	....	....	....	....	....	....	....	....
1991-92	Detroit	OHL	58	21	43	64	141	....	....	....	....	....	....	....	....	....	7	3	5	8	30	....	....	....	....
1992-93	Detroit	OHL	55	50	50	100	83	....	....	....	....	....	....	....	....	....	15	9	12	21	39	....	....	....	....
1993-94	Detroit	OHL	49	34	51	85	75	....	....	....	....	....	....	....	....	....	17	10	12	22	26	....	....	....	....
1994-95	Detroit	OHL	11	8	14	22	12	....	....	....	....	....	....	....	....	....	....	....	....	....	....	....	....	....	....
	Dallas	NHL	40	11	9	20	67	2	0	1	64	17.2	–3	....	....	....	5	0	0	0	8	0	0	0	....
1995-96	Dallas	NHL	69	9	20	29	136	3	0	1	101	8.9	–13	....	....	....	....	....	....	....	....	....	....	....	....
	Michigan	IHL	5	1	3	4	8	....	....	....	....	....	....	....	....	....	....	....	....	....	....	....	....	....	....
1996-97	Dallas	NHL	71	9	22	31	142	1	0	2	99	9.1	19	....	....	....	7	0	1	1	10	0	0	0	....
1997-98	Dallas	NHL	59	9	10	19	104	0	0	1	88	10.2	5	....	....	....	....	....	....	....	....	....	....	....	....
1998-99	NY Rangers	NHL	37	11	17	28	72	6	0	2	58	19.0	–1	175	50.3	17:19	....	....	....	....	....	....	....	....	....
99-2000	NY Rangers	NHL	31	3	3	6	62	0	0	0	31	9.7	–9	173	49.1	12:21	....	....	....	....	....	....	....	....	....
	San Jose	NHL	40	8	4	12	78	2	0	0	59	13.6	–2	44	43.2	12:55	12	1	0	1	8	1	0	0	10:47
2000-01	San Jose	NHL	69	10	11	21	72	1	0	2	66	15.2	6	98	40.8	11:05	6	0	0	0	8	0	0	0	6:59
2001-02	San Jose	NHL	69	9	13	22	73	0	0	1	66	13.6	16	223	48.4	9:47	12	0	2	2	12	0	0	0	7:32
2002-03	San Jose	NHL	76	3	16	19	74	0	0	0	64	4.7	5	119	44.5	9:57	....	....	....	....	....	....	....	....	....
	NHL Totals		561	82	125	207	880	15	0	10	696	11.8		832	47.2	11:36	42	1	3	4	46	1	0	0	8:43

OHL All-Rookie Team (1992)

Traded to **NY Rangers** by **Dallas** with Bob Errey and Dallas' 4th round choice (Boyd Kane) in 1998 Entry Draft for Brian Skrudland, Mike Keane and NY Rangers' 6th round choice (Pavel Patera) in 1998 Entry Draft, March 24, 1998. Traded to **San Jose** by **NY Rangers** with NY Rangers' 4th round choice (Dimitri Patzold) in 2001 Entry Draft for Radek Dvorak, December 30, 1999.

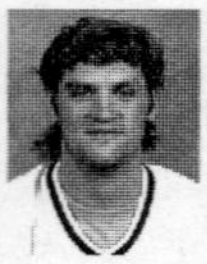

HATCHER, Derian
(HAT-chuhr, DAIR-ee-an) **DET.**

Defense. Shoots left. 6'5", 235 lbs. Born, Sterling Hts., MI, June 4, 1972. Minnesota's 1st choice, 8th overall, in 1990 Entry Draft.

1987-88	Detroit GPD	MNHL	25	5	13	18	52	....	....	....	....	....	....	....	....	....	....	....	....	....	....	....	....	....	....
1988-89	Detroit GPD	MNHL	51	19	35	54	100	....	....	....	....	....	....	....	....	....	....	....	....	....	....	....	....	....	....
1989-90	North Bay	OHL	64	14	38	52	81	....	....	....	....	....	....	....	....	....	5	2	3	5	8	....	....	....	....
1990-91	North Bay	OHL	64	13	49	62	163	....	....	....	....	....	....	....	....	....	10	2	10	12	28	....	....	....	....
1991-92	Minnesota	NHL	43	8	4	12	88	0	0	2	51	15.7	7	....	....	....	5	0	2	2	8	0	0	0	....
1992-93	Minnesota	NHL	67	4	15	19	178	0	0	1	73	5.5	–27	....	....	....	....	....	....	....	....	....	....	....	....
	Kalamazoo Wings	IHL	2	1	2	3	21	....	....	....	....	....	....	....	....	....	....	....	....	....	....	....	....	....	....
1993-94	Dallas	NHL	83	12	19	31	211	2	1	2	132	9.1	19	....	....	....	9	0	2	2	14	0	0	0	....
1994-95	Dallas	NHL	43	5	11	16	105	2	0	2	74	6.8	3	....	....	....	....	....	....	....	....	....	....	....	....
1995-96	Dallas	NHL	79	8	23	31	129	2	0	1	125	6.4	–12	....	....	....	....	....	....	....	....	....	....	....	....
1996-97	Dallas	NHL	63	3	19	22	97	0	0	0	96	3.1	8	....	....	....	7	0	2	2	20	0	0	0	....
1997-98	Dallas	NHL	70	6	25	31	132	3	0	2	74	8.1	9	....	....	....	17	3	3	6	39	2	0	0	....
	United States	Olympics	4	0	0	0	0	....	....	....	....	....	....	....	....	....	....	....	....	....	....	....	....	....	....
1998-99♦	Dallas	NHL	80	9	21	30	102	3	0	2	125	7.2	21	0	0.0	24:44	18	1	6	7	24	0	0	0	29:06
99-2000	Dallas	NHL	57	2	22	24	68	0	0	0	90	2.2	6	0	0.0	27:33	23	1	3	4	29	0	0	0	27:40
2000-01	Dallas	NHL	80	2	21	23	77	1	0	2	97	2.1	5	0	0.0	25:53	10	0	1	1	16	0	0	0	28:53
2001-02	Dallas	NHL	80	4	21	25	87	1	0	0	111	3.6	12	0	0.0	26:40	....	....	....	....	....	....	....	....	....
2002-03	Dallas	NHL	82	8	22	30	106	1	1	2	159	5.0	37	0	0.0	25:51	11	1	2	3	33	0	0	0	30:02
	NHL Totals		827	71	223	294	1380	15	2	16	1207	5.9		0	0.0	26:03	100	6	21	27	183	2	0	0	28:42

NHL Second All-Star Team (2003)

Played in NHL All-Star Game (1997)

Transferred to **Dallas** after **Minnesota** franchise relocated, June 9, 1993. Signed as a free agent by **Detroit**, July 3, 2003.

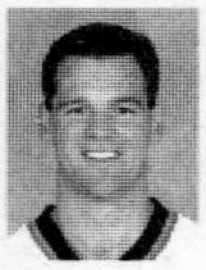

HAUER, Brett
(HOW-uhr, BREHT)

Defense. Shoots right. 6'2", 210 lbs. Born, Richfield, MN, July 11, 1971. Vancouver's 3rd choice, 71st overall, in 1989 Entry Draft.

1987-88	Richfield Spartans	Hi-School	24	3	3	6	....	....	....	....	....	....	....	....	....	....	....	....	....	....	....	....	....	....	....
1988-89	Richfield Spartans	Hi-School	24	8	15	23	70	....	....	....	....	....	....	....	....	....	....	....	....	....	....	....	....	....	....
1989-90	U. Minn-Duluth	WCHA	37	2	6	8	44	....	....	....	....	....	....	....	....	....	....	....	....	....	....	....	....	....	....
1990-91	U. Minn-Duluth	WCHA	30	1	7	8	54	....	....	....	....	....	....	....	....	....	....	....	....	....	....	....	....	....	....
1991-92	U. Minn-Duluth	WCHA	33	8	14	22	40	....	....	....	....	....	....	....	....	....	....	....	....	....	....	....	....	....	....
1992-93	U. Minn-Duluth	WCHA	40	10	46	56	52	....	....	....	....	....	....	....	....	....	....	....	....	....	....	....	....	....	....
1993-94	Team USA	Nat-Tm	57	6	14	20	88	....	....	....	....	....	....	....	....	....	....	....	....	....	....	....	....	....	....
	United States	Olympics	8	0	0	0	10	....	....	....	....	....	....	....	....	....	....	....	....	....	....	....	....	....	....
	Las Vegas	IHL	21	0	7	7	8	....	....	....	....	....	....	....	....	....	1	0	0	0	0	....	....	....	....
1994-95	AIK Solna	Swede-2	37	1	3	4	38	....	....	....	....	....	....	....	....	....	....	....	....	....	....	....	....	....	....
1995-96	Edmonton	NHL	29	4	2	6	30	2	0	1	53	7.5	–11	....	....	....	....	....	....	....	....	....	....	....	....
	Cape Breton	AHL	17	3	5	8	29	....	....	....	....	....	....	....	....	....	....	....	....	....	....	....	....	....	....
1996-97	Chicago Wolves	IHL	81	10	30	40	50	....	....	....	....	....	....	....	....	....	4	2	0	2	4	....	....	....	....
1997-98	Manitoba Moose	IHL	82	13	48	61	58	....	....	....	....	....	....	....	....	....	3	0	0	0	2	....	....	....	....
1998-99	Manitoba Moose	IHL	81	15	56	71	66	....	....	....	....	....	....	....	....	....	5	0	5	5	4	....	....	....	....
99-2000	Edmonton	NHL	5	0	2	2	2	0	0	0	8	0.0	–2	0	0.0	14:48	....	....	....	....	....	....	....	....	....
	Manitoba Moose	IHL	77	13	47	60	92	....	....	....	....	....	....	....	....	....	2	0	1	1	2	....	....	....	....
2000-01	Manitoba Moose	IHL	82	17	42	59	52	....	....	....	....	....	....	....	....	....	13	1	9	10	12	....	....	....	....

Season	Club	League	GP	G	A	Pts	PIM	PP	SH	GW	S	%	+/-	TF	F%	Min	Playoffs GP	G	A	Pts	PIM	PP	SH	GW	Min
2001-02	Manchester	AHL	29	2	11	13	38	....	....	....	....	....	....	....	....	....	....	....	....	....	....	....	....	....	....
	Nashville	**NHL**	**3**	**0**	**0**	**0**	**6**	**0**	**0**	**0**	**2**	**0.0**	**–3**	**0**	**0.0**	**10:29**	....	....	....	....	....	....	....	....	....
	Milwaukee	AHL	48	6	21	27	14	....	....	....	....	....	....	....	....	....	....	....	....	....	....	....	....	....	....
2002-03	Geneve-Servette	Swiss	44	10	16	26	24	....	....	....	....	....	....	....	....	....	6	0	1	1	8	....	....	....	....
	NHL Totals		**37**	**4**	**4**	**8**	**38**	**2**	**0**	**1**	**63**	**6.3**		**0**	**0.0**	**13:11**	....	....	....	....	....	....	....	....	....

WCHA First All-Star Team (1993) • NCAA West First All-American Team (1993) • IHL First All-Star Team (1999, 2000, 2001) • Govenors' Trophy (Top Defenseman – IHL) (2000, 2001)

Signed as a free agent by **Las Vegas** (IHL), February 15, 1994. Traded to **Edmonton** by **Vancouver** for Edmonton's 7th round choice (Larry Shapley) in 1997 Entry Draft, August 24, 1995. Signed as a free agent by **Manitoba** (IHL), September 15, 1997. Signed as a free agent by **Los Angeles**, July 8, 2001. Traded to **Nashville** by **Los Angeles** for Rich Brennan, December 19, 2001. Signed as a free agent by **Geneve-Servette** (Swiss), July 11, 2002.

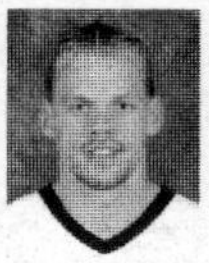

HAVELID, Niclas

(HAHV-lihd, NIHK-lahs) **ANA.**

Defense. Shoots left. 5'11", 196 lbs. Born, Stockholm, Sweden, April 12, 1973. Anaheim's 2nd choice, 83rd overall, in 1999 Entry Draft.

Season	Club	League	GP	G	A	Pts	PIM	PP	SH	GW	S	%	+/-	TF	F%	Min	Playoffs GP	G	A	Pts	PIM	PP	SH	GW	Min
1988-89	Enkopings SK	Swede-3	7	0	1	1	0	....	....	....	....	....	....	....	....	....	....	....	....	....	....	....	....	....	....
1989-90	Enkopings SK	Swede-3	24	1	2	3	28	....	....	....	....	....	....	....	....	....	....	....	....	....	....	....	....	....	....
1990-91	RA-73	Swede-2	30	2	3	5	22	....	....	....	....	....	....	....	....	....	....	....	....	....	....	....	....	....	....
1991-92	AIK Solna	Sweden	10	0	0	0	2	....	....	....	....	....	....	....	....	....	....	....	....	....	....	....	....	....	....
1992-93	AIK Solna	Sweden	30	1	2	3	22	....	....	....	....	....	....	....	....	....	3	0	0	0	2	....	....	....	....
1993-94	AIK Solna	Swede-2	22	3	9	12	14	....	....	....	....	....	....	....	....	....	....	....	....	....	....	....	....	....	....
1994-95	AIK Solna	Swede-2	40	3	7	10	38	....	....	....	....	....	....	....	....	....	....	....	....	....	....	....	....	....	....
1995-96	AIK Solna	Sweden	40	5	6	11	30	....	....	....	....	....	....	....	....	....	....	....	....	....	....	....	....	....	....
1996-97	AIK Solna	Sweden	49	3	6	9	42	....	....	....	....	....	....	....	....	....	7	1	2	3	8	....	....	....	....
1997-98	AIK Solna	Sweden	43	8	4	12	42	....	....	....	....	....	....	....	....	....	10	1	3	4	39	....	....	....	....
1998-99	Malmo IF	Sweden	50	10	12	22	42	....	....	....	....	....	....	....	....	....	8	0	4	4	10	....	....	....	....
99-2000	**Anaheim**	**NHL**	**50**	**2**	**7**	**9**	**20**	**0**	**0**	**2**	**70**	**2.9**	**0**	**1**	**0.0**	**19:10**	....	....	....	....	....	....	....	....	....
	Cincinnati	AHL	2	0	0	0	0	....	....	....	....	....	....	....	....	....	....	....	....	....	....	....	....	....	....
2000-01	**Anaheim**	**NHL**	**47**	**4**	**10**	**14**	**34**	**2**	**0**	**1**	**69**	**5.8**	**–6**	**4**	**0.0**	**21:51**	....	....	....	....	....	....	....	....	....
2001-02	**Anaheim**	**NHL**	**52**	**1**	**2**	**3**	**40**	**0**	**0**	**0**	**45**	**2.2**	**–13**	**1**	**0.0**	**17:01**	....	....	....	....	....	....	....	....	....
2002-03	**Anaheim**	**NHL**	**82**	**11**	**22**	**33**	**30**	**4**	**0**	**5**	**169**	**6.5**	**5**	**3**	**0.0**	**22:30**	**21**	**0**	**4**	**4**	**2**	**0**	**0**	**0**	**25:41**
	NHL Totals		**231**	**18**	**41**	**59**	**124**	**6**	**0**	**8**	**353**	**5.1**		**9**	**0.0**	**20:25**	**21**	**0**	**4**	**4**	**2**	**0**	**0**	**0**	**25:41**

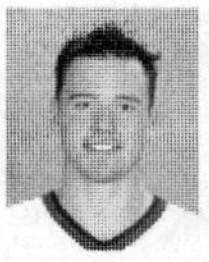

HAVLAT, Martin

(HAHV-lat, MAHR-tihn) **OTT.**

Left wing. Shoots left. 6'1", 190 lbs. Born, Mlada Boleslav, Czech., April 19, 1981. Ottawa's 1st choice, 26th overall, in 1999 Entry Draft.

Season	Club	League	GP	G	A	Pts	PIM	PP	SH	GW	S	%	+/-	TF	F%	Min	Playoffs GP	G	A	Pts	PIM	PP	SH	GW	Min
1997-98	Ytong Brno Jr.	Czech-Jr.	32	38	29	67	....	....	....	....	....	....	....	....	....	....	....	....	....	....	....	....	....	....	....
1998-99	Trinec Jr.	Czech-Jr.	31	28	23	51	....	....	....	....	....	....	....	....	....	....	....	....	....	....	....	....	....	....	....
	Trinec	Czech	24	2	3	5	4	....	....	....	....	....	....	....	....	....	8	0	0	0	....	....	....	....	....
99-2000	HC Ocelari Trinec	Czech	46	13	29	42	42	....	....	....	....	....	....	....	....	....	4	0	2	2	8	....	....	....	....
2000-01	**Ottawa**	**NHL**	**73**	**19**	**23**	**42**	**20**	**7**	**0**	**5**	**133**	**14.3**	**8**	**40**	**30.0**	**13:47**	**4**	**0**	**0**	**0**	**2**	**0**	**0**	**0**	**14:04**
2001-02	**Ottawa**	**NHL**	**72**	**22**	**28**	**50**	**66**	**9**	**0**	**6**	**145**	**15.2**	**–7**	**15**	**40.0**	**14:46**	**12**	**2**	**5**	**7**	**14**	**2**	**0**	**2**	**16:19**
	Czech Republic	Olympics	4	3	1	4	27	....	....	....	....	....	....	....	....	....	....	....	....	....	....	....	....	....	....
2002-03	**Ottawa**	**NHL**	**67**	**24**	**35**	**59**	**30**	**9**	**0**	**4**	**179**	**13.4**	**20**	**7**	**14.3**	**16:27**	**18**	**5**	**6**	**11**	**14**	**1**	**0**	**2**	**16:27**
	NHL Totals		**212**	**65**	**86**	**151**	**116**	**25**	**0**	**15**	**457**	**14.2**		**62**	**30.6**	**14:57**	**34**	**7**	**11**	**18**	**30**	**3**	**0**	**4**	**16:07**

NHL All-Rookie Team (2001)

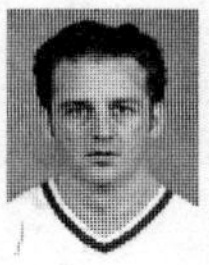

HAWGOOD, Greg

(HAW-guhd, GREHG)

Defense. Shoots left. 5'10", 190 lbs. Born, Edmonton, Alta., August 10, 1968. Boston's 9th choice, 202nd overall, in 1986 Entry Draft.

Season	Club	League	GP	G	A	Pts	PIM	PP	SH	GW	S	%	+/-	TF	F%	Min	Playoffs GP	G	A	Pts	PIM	PP	SH	GW	Min
1983-84	Kamloops	WHL	49	10	23	33	39	....	....	....	....	....	....	....	....	....	6	0	2	2	2	....	....	....	....
1984-85	Kamloops Blazers	WHL	66	25	40	65	72	....	....	....	....	....	....	....	....	....	15	3	15	18	15	....	....	....	....
1985-86	Kamloops Blazers	WHL	71	34	85	119	86	....	....	....	....	....	....	....	....	....	16	9	22	31	16	....	....	....	....
1986-87	Kamloops Blazers	WHL	61	30	93	123	139	....	....	....	....	....	....	....	....	....	13	7	16	23	18	....	....	....	....
1987-88	Kamloops Blazers	WHL	63	48	85	133	142	....	....	....	....	....	....	....	....	....	16	10	16	26	33	....	....	....	....
	Boston	**NHL**	**1**	**0**	**0**	**0**	**0**	**0**	**0**	**0**	**1**	**0.0**	**–1**	....	....	....	**3**	**1**	**0**	**1**	**0**	**0**	**0**	**0**	....
1988-89	**Boston**	**NHL**	**56**	**16**	**24**	**40**	**84**	**5**	**0**	**0**	**132**	**12.1**	**4**	....	....	....	**10**	**0**	**2**	**2**	**2**	**0**	**0**	**0**	....
	Maine Mariners	AHL	21	2	9	11	41	....	....	....	....	....	....	....	....	....	....	....	....	....	....	....	....	....	....
1989-90	**Boston**	**NHL**	**77**	**11**	**27**	**38**	**76**	**2**	**0**	**1**	**127**	**8.7**	**12**	....	....	....	**15**	**1**	**3**	**4**	**12**	**1**	**0**	**0**	....
1990-91	HC Asiago	Italy	2	3	0	3	9	....	....	....	....	....	....	....	....	....	....	....	....	....	....	....	....	....	....
	Maine Mariners	AHL	5	0	1	1	13	....	....	....	....	....	....	....	....	....	....	....	....	....	....	....	....	....	....
	Edmonton	**NHL**	**6**	**0**	**1**	**1**	**6**	**0**	**0**	**0**	**9**	**0.0**	**–2**	....	....	....	....	....	....	....	....	....	....	....	....
	Cape Breton	AHL	55	10	32	42	73	....	....	....	....	....	....	....	....	....	4	0	3	3	23	....	....	....	....
1991-92	**Edmonton**	**NHL**	**20**	**2**	**11**	**13**	**22**	**0**	**0**	**0**	**24**	**8.3**	**19**	....	....	....	**13**	**0**	**3**	**3**	**23**	**0**	**0**	**0**	....
	Cape Breton	AHL	56	20	55	75	26	....	....	....	....	....	....	....	....	....	3	2	2	4	0	....	....	....	....
1992-93	**Edmonton**	**NHL**	**29**	**5**	**13**	**18**	**35**	**2**	**0**	**0**	**47**	**10.6**	**–1**	....	....	....	....	....	....	....	....	....	....	....	....
	Philadelphia	**NHL**	**40**	**6**	**22**	**28**	**39**	**5**	**0**	**1**	**91**	**6.6**	**–7**	....	....	....	....	....	....	....	....	....	....	....	....
1993-94	**Philadelphia**	**NHL**	**19**	**3**	**12**	**15**	**19**	**3**	**0**	**0**	**37**	**8.1**	**2**	....	....	....	....	....	....	....	....	....	....	....	....
	Florida	**NHL**	**33**	**2**	**14**	**16**	**9**	**0**	**0**	**1**	**55**	**3.6**	**8**	....	....	....	....	....	....	....	....	....	....	....	....
	Pittsburgh	**NHL**	**12**	**1**	**2**	**3**	**8**	**1**	**0**	**1**	**20**	**5.0**	**–1**	....	....	....	**1**	**0**	**0**	**0**	**0**	**0**	**0**	**0**	....
1994-95	**Pittsburgh**	**NHL**	**21**	**1**	**4**	**5**	**25**	**1**	**0**	**0**	**17**	**5.9**	**2**	....	....	....	....	....	....	....	....	....	....	....	....
	Cleveland	IHL	....	....	....	....	....	....	....	....	....	....	....	....	....	....	3	1	0	1	4	....	....	....	....
1995-96	Las Vegas	IHL	78	20	65	85	101	....	....	....	....	....	....	....	....	....	15	5	11	16	24	....	....	....	....
1996-97	**San Jose**	**NHL**	**63**	**6**	**12**	**18**	**69**	**3**	**0**	**0**	**83**	**7.2**	**–22**	....	....	....	....	....	....	....	....	....	....	....	....
1997-98	Kolner Haie	Germany	4	0	1	1	16	....	....	....	....	....	....	....	....	....	....	....	....	....	....	....	....	....	....
	Kolner Haie	EuroHL	1	0	0	0	2	....	....	....	....	....	....	....	....	....	....	....	....	....	....	....	....	....	....
	Houston Aeros	IHL	81	19	52	71	75	....	....	....	....	....	....	....	....	....	4	0	4	4	0	....	....	....	....
1998-99	Houston Aeros	IHL	76	17	57	74	90	....	....	....	....	....	....	....	....	....	19	4	8	12	24	....	....	....	....
99-2000	**Vancouver**	**NHL**	**79**	**5**	**17**	**22**	**26**	**2**	**0**	**0**	**70**	**7.1**	**5**	**2**	**50.0**	**17:11**	....	....	....	....	....	....	....	....	....
2000-01	**Vancouver**	**NHL**	**16**	**2**	**5**	**7**	**6**	**1**	**0**	**1**	**16**	**12.5**	**8**	**1**	**0.0**	**14:55**	....	....	....	....	....	....	....	....	....
	Kansas City	IHL	46	6	16	22	21	....	....	....	....	....	....	....	....	....	....	....	....	....	....	....	....	....	....
2001-02	**Dallas**	**NHL**	**2**	**0**	**0**	**0**	**2**	**0**	**0**	**0**	**1**	**0.0**	**0**	**0**	**0.0**	**6:21**	....	....	....	....	....	....	....	....	....
	Utah Grizzlies	AHL	67	18	43	61	83	....	....	....	....	....	....	....	....	....	5	0	2	2	2	....	....	....	....
2002-03	Utah Grizzlies	AHL	70	15	42	57	76	....	....	....	....	....	....	....	....	....	2	1	0	1	14	....	....	....	....
	NHL Totals		**474**	**60**	**164**	**224**	**426**	**25**	**0**	**5**	**730**	**8.2**		**3**	**33.3**	**16:35**	**42**	**2**	**8**	**10**	**37**	**1**	**0**	**0**	....

WHL West First All-Star Team (1986, 1987, 1988) • Canadian Major Junior Defenseman of the Year (1988) • AHL First All-Star Team (1992) • Eddie Shore Award (Top Defenseman – AHL) (1992) • IHL First All-Star Team (1996, 1998, 1999) • Governors' Trophy (Top Defenseman – IHL) (1996, 1999) • AHL Second All-Star Team (2002)

Traded to **Edmonton** by **Boston** for Vladimir Ruzicka, October 22, 1990. Traded to **Philadelphia** by **Edmonton** with Josef Beranek for Brian Benning, January 16, 1993. Traded to **Florida** by **Philadelphia** for cash, November 30, 1993. Traded to **Pittsburgh** by **Florida** for Jeff Daniels, March 19, 1994. Signed as a free agent by **San Jose**, September 25, 1996. Signed as a free agent by **Vancouver**, September 30, 1999. Signed as a free agent by **Dallas**, July 17, 2001.

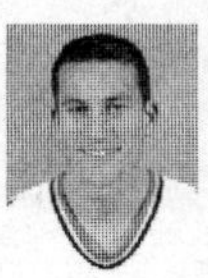

HAY, Dwayne

(HAY, DWAYN)

Left wing. Shoots left. 6'1", 203 lbs. Born, London, Ont., February 11, 1977. Washington's 3rd choice, 43rd overall, in 1995 Entry Draft.

Season	Club	League	GP	G	A	Pts	PIM	PP	SH	GW	S	%	+/-	TF	F%	Min	Playoffs GP	G	A	Pts	PIM	PP	SH	GW	Min
1991-92	London Travellers	OMHA	86	70	56	126	104	....	....	....	....	....	....	....	....	....	....	....	....	....	....	....	....	....	....
1992-93	Listowel Cyclones	OJHL-B	50	19	33	52	40	....	....	....	....	....	....	....	....	....	....	....	....	....	....	....	....	....	....
1993-94	Listowel Cyclones	OJHL-B	48	10	24	34	56	....	....	....	....	....	....	....	....	....	....	....	....	....	....	....	....	....	....
1994-95	Guelph Storm	OHL	65	26	28	54	37	....	....	....	....	....	....	....	....	....	14	5	7	12	6	....	....	....	....
1995-96	Guelph Storm	OHL	60	28	30	58	49	....	....	....	....	....	....	....	....	....	16	4	9	13	18	....	....	....	....
1996-97	Guelph Storm	OHL	32	17	17	34	21	....	....	....	....	....	....	....	....	....	11	4	6	10	0	....	....	....	....
1997-98	**Washington**	**NHL**	**2**	**0**	**0**	**0**	**2**	**0**	**0**	**0**	**1**	**0.0**	**0**	....	....	....	....	....	....	....	....	....	....	....	....
	Portland Pirates	AHL	58	6	7	13	35	....	....	....	....	....	....	....	....	....	....	....	....	....	....	....	....	....	....
	New Haven	AHL	10	3	2	5	4	....	....	....	....	....	....	....	....	....	2	0	0	0	0	....	....	....	....
1998-99	**Florida**	**NHL**	**9**	**0**	**0**	**0**	**0**	**0**	**0**	**0**	**3**	**0.0**	**–1**	**1**	**0.0**	**6:35**	....	....	....	....	....	....	....	....	....
	New Haven	AHL	46	18	17	35	22	....	....	....	....	....	....	....	....	....	....	....	....	....	....	....	....	....	....
99-2000	**Florida**	**NHL**	**6**	**0**	**0**	**0**	**2**	**0**	**0**	**0**	**3**	**0.0**	**–2**	**0**	**0.0**	**6:36**	....	....	....	....	....	....	....	....	....
	Louisville Panthers	AHL	41	11	20	31	18	....	....	....	....	....	....	....	....	....	....	....	....	....	....	....	....	....	....
	Tampa Bay	**NHL**	**13**	**1**	**1**	**2**	**2**	**0**	**0**	**0**	**11**	**9.1**	**0**	**1**	**0.0**	**6:04**	....	....	....	....	....	....	....	....	....
2000-01	**Calgary**	**NHL**	**49**	**1**	**3**	**4**	**16**	**0**	**0**	**0**	**39**	**2.6**	**–4**	**6**	**16.7**	**8:24**	....	....	....	....	....	....	....	....	....

			Regular Season														Playoffs								
Season	Club	League	GP	G	A	Pts	PIM	PP	SH	GW	S	%	+/-	TF	F%	Min	GP	G	A	Pts	PIM	PP	SH	GW	Min
2001-02	Saint John Flames	AHL	70	5	12	17	39	....	....	....	....	....	....	....	....	....	....	....	....	....	....	....	....	....	....
2002-03	St. John's	AHL	51	10	19	29	31	....	....	....	....	....	....	....	....	....	....	....	....	....	....	....	....	....	....
	NHL Totals		**79**	**2**	**4**	**6**	**22**	**0**	**0**	**0**	**57**	**3.5**		**8**	**12.5**	**7:39**	....	....	....	....	....	....	....	....	....

Traded to **Florida** by **Washington** with future considerations for Esa Tikkanen, March 9, 1998. Traded to **Tampa Bay** by **Florida** with Ryan Johnson for Mike Sillinger, March 14, 2000. Claimed on waivers by **Calgary** from **Tampa Bay**, October 3, 2000. Signed as a free agent by **Toronto**, November 30, 2002.

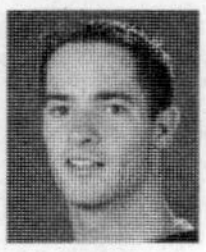

HAYDAR, Darren (HAY-duhr, DAIR-ehn) NSH.

Right wing. Shoots left. 5'9", 170 lbs. Born, Toronto, Ont., October 22, 1979. Nashville's 14th choice, 248th overall, in 1999 Entry Draft.

Season	Club	League	GP	G	A	Pts	PIM	PP	SH	GW	S	%	+/-	TF	F%	Min	GP	G	A	Pts	PIM	PP	SH	GW	Min
1995-96	Milton Merchants	OPJHL	6	1	2	3	4	....	....	....	....	....	....	....	....	....	....	....	....	....	....	....	....	....	....
1996-97	Milton Merchants	OPJHL	51	32	68	100	68	....	....	....	....	....	....	....	....	....	....	....	....	....	....	....	....	....	....
1997-98	Milton Merchants	OPJHL	51	*71	*69	*140	65	....	....	....	....	....	....	....	....	....	....	....	....	....	....	....	....	....	....
1998-99	New Hampshire	H-East	41	31	30	61	34	....	....	....	....	....	....	....	....	....	....	....	....	....	....	....	....	....	....
99-2000	New Hampshire	H-East	38	22	19	41	42	....	....	....	....	....	....	....	....	....	....	....	....	....	....	....	....	....	....
2000-01	New Hampshire	H-East	39	18	23	41	38	....	....	....	....	....	....	....	....	....	....	....	....	....	....	....	....	....	....
2001-02	New Hampshire	H-East	40	31	*45	*76	28	....	....	....	....	....	....	....	....	....	....	....	....	....	....	....	....	....	....
2002-03	**Nashville**	**NHL**	**2**	**0**	**0**	**0**	**0**	**0**	**0**	**0**	**1**	**0.0**	**–1**	**0**	**0.0**	**8:54**	....	....	....	....	....	....	....	....	....
	Milwaukee	AHL	75	29	46	75	36	....	....	....	....	....	....	....	....	....	6	1	4	5	2	....	....	....	....
	NHL Totals		**2**	**0**	**0**	**0**	**0**	**0**	**0**	**0**	**1**	**0.0**		**0**	**0.0**	**8:54**	....	....	....	....	....	....	....	....	....

OPJHL First All-Star Team (1998) • OPJHL Player of the Year (1998) • Hockey East Second All-Star Team (1999, 2000) • Hockey East Rookie of the Year (1999) • Hockey East First All-Star Team (2002) • AHL All-Rookie Team (2003) • Dudley "Red" Garrett Memorial Trophy (Top Rookie – AHL) (2003)

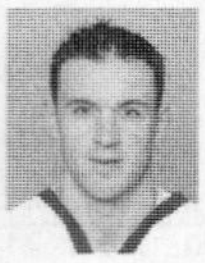

HEALEY, Paul (HEE-lee, PAWL) NYR

Left wing. Shoots right. 6'2", 198 lbs. Born, Edmonton, Alta., March 20, 1975. Philadelphia's 7th choice, 192nd overall, in 1993 Entry Draft.

Season	Club	League	GP	G	A	Pts	PIM	PP	SH	GW	S	%	+/-	TF	F%	Min	GP	G	A	Pts	PIM	PP	SH	GW	Min
1991-92	Ft. Saskatchewan	AJHL	52	11	19	30	40	....	....	....	....	....	....	....	....	....	....	....	....	....	....	....	....	....	....
1992-93	Prince Albert	WHL	72	12	20	32	66	....	....	....	....	....	....	....	....	....	....	....	....	....	....	....	....	....	....
1993-94	Prince Albert	WHL	63	23	26	49	70	....	....	....	....	....	....	....	....	....	....	....	....	....	....	....	....	....	....
1994-95	Prince Albert	WHL	71	43	50	93	67	....	....	....	....	....	....	....	....	....	12	3	4	7	2	....	....	....	....
1995-96	Hershey Bears	AHL	60	7	15	22	35	....	....	....	....	....	....	....	....	....	....	....	....	....	....	....	....	....	....
1996-97	**Philadelphia**	**NHL**	**2**	**0**	**0**	**0**	**0**	**0**	**0**	**0**	**0**	**0.0**	**0**	....	....	....	....	....	....	....	....	....	....	....	....
	Philadelphia	AHL	64	21	19	40	56	....	....	....	....	....	....	....	....	....	10	4	1	5	10	....	....	....	....
1997-98	**Philadelphia**	**NHL**	**4**	**0**	**0**	**0**	**12**	**0**	**0**	**0**	**0**	**0.0**	**0**	....	....	....	....	....	....	....	....	....	....	....	....
	Philadelphia	AHL	71	34	18	52	48	....	....	....	....	....	....	....	....	....	20	6	2	8	4	....	....	....	....
1998-99	Philadelphia	AHL	72	26	20	46	39	....	....	....	....	....	....	....	....	....	15	4	6	10	11	....	....	....	....
99-2000	Milwaukee	IHL	76	21	18	39	28	....	....	....	....	....	....	....	....	....	3	1	2	3	0	....	....	....	....
2000-01	Hamilton	AHL	79	39	32	71	34	....	....	....	....	....	....	....	....	....	....	....	....	....	....	....	....	....	....
2001-02	**Toronto**	**NHL**	**21**	**3**	**7**	**10**	**2**	**0**	**0**	**0**	**29**	**10.3**	**7**	**5**	**60.0**	**11:03**	**18**	**0**	**1**	**1**	**2**	**0**	**0**	**0**	**9:01**
	St. John's	AHL	58	27	29	56	30	....	....	....	....	....	....	....	....	....	2	1	1	2	8	....	....	....	....
2002-03	**Toronto**	**NHL**	**44**	**3**	**7**	**10**	**16**	**1**	**0**	**0**	**43**	**7.0**	**8**	**13**	**38.5**	**12:00**	**4**	**0**	**1**	**1**	**2**	**0**	**0**	**0**	**9:14**
	St. John's	AHL	17	6	10	16	12	....	....	....	....	....	....	....	....	....	....	....	....	....	....	....	....	....	....
	NHL Totals		**71**	**6**	**14**	**20**	**30**	**1**	**0**	**0**	**72**	**8.3**		**18**	**44.4**	**11:42**	**22**	**0**	**2**	**2**	**4**	**0**	**0**	**0**	**9:03**

WHL East Second All-Star Team (1995)

Traded to **Nashville** by **Philadelphia** for Matt Henderson, September 27, 1999. Signed as a free agent by **Edmonton**, August 31, 2000. Signed as a free agent by **Toronto**, July 24, 2001. Signed as a free agent by **NY Rangers**, July 28, 2003.

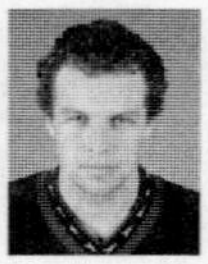

HEATLEY, Dany (HEET-lee, DA-nee) ATL.

Right wing. Shoots left. 6'3", 215 lbs. Born, Freiburg, West Germany, January 21, 1981. Atlanta's 1st choice, 2nd overall, in 2000 Entry Draft.

Season	Club	League	GP	G	A	Pts	PIM	PP	SH	GW	S	%	+/-	TF	F%	Min	GP	G	A	Pts	PIM	PP	SH	GW	Min
1996-97	Calgary Blazers	AMHL	25	30	42	72	26	....	....	....	....	....	....	....	....	....	....	....	....	....	....	....	....	....	....
1997-98	Calgary Buffaloes	AMHL	36	39	42	*91	34	....	....	....	....	....	....	....	....	....	10	10	12	*22	30	....	....	....	....
1998-99	Calgary Canucks	AJHL	60	*70	56	*126	91	....	....	....	....	....	....	....	....	....	13	*22	13	*35	6	....	....	....	....
99-2000	U. of Wisconsin	WCHA	38	28	28	56	32	....	....	....	....	....	....	....	....	....	....	....	....	....	....	....	....	....	....
2000-01	U. of Wisconsin	WCHA	39	24	33	57	74	....	....	....	....	....	....	....	....	....	....	....	....	....	....	....	....	....	....
2001-02	**Atlanta**	**NHL**	**82**	**26**	**41**	**67**	**56**	**7**	**0**	**4**	**202**	**12.9**	**–19**	**116**	**32.8**	**19:53**	....	....	....	....	....	....	....	....	....
2002-03	**Atlanta**	**NHL**	**77**	**41**	**48**	**89**	**58**	**19**	**1**	**6**	**252**	**16.3**	**–8**	**49**	**36.7**	**21:57**	....	....	....	....	....	....	....	....	....
	NHL Totals		**159**	**67**	**89**	**156**	**114**	**26**	**1**	**10**	**454**	**14.8**		**165**	**33.9**	**20:53**	....	....	....	....	....	....	....	....	....

Air Canada Cup MVP (1997) • AJHL Player of the Year (1999) • Canadian Junior "A" Player of the Year (1999) • WCHA First All-Star Team (2000) • WCHA Rookie of the Year (2000) • NCAA West Second All-American Team (2000) • WCHA Second All-Star Team (2001) • NCAA West First All-American Team (2001) • NHL All-Rookie Team (2002) • Calder Memorial Trophy (2002)

Played in NHL All-Star Game (2003)

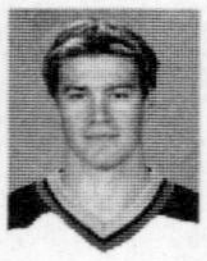

HECHT, Jochen (HEHKHT, YOH-khehn) BUF.

Left wing. Shoots left. 6'1", 200 lbs. Born, Mannheim, West Germany, June 21, 1977. St. Louis' 1st choice, 49th overall, in 1995 Entry Draft.

Season	Club	League	GP	G	A	Pts	PIM	PP	SH	GW	S	%	+/-	TF	F%	Min	GP	G	A	Pts	PIM	PP	SH	GW	Min
1993-94	Mannheim Jr.	Ger.-Jr.	28	27	13	40	103	....	....	....	....	....	....	....	....	....	....	....	....	....	....	....	....	....	....
1994-95	Adler Mannheim	Germany	43	11	12	23	68	....	....	....	....	....	....	....	....	....	10	5	4	9	12	....	....	....	....
1995-96	Adler Mannheim	Germany	44	12	16	28	68	....	....	....	....	....	....	....	....	....	8	3	2	5	6	....	....	....	....
1996-97	Adler Mannheim	Germany	46	21	21	42	36	....	....	....	....	....	....	....	....	....	9	3	3	6	4	....	....	....	....
1997-98	Adler Mannheim	Germany	44	7	19	26	42	....	....	....	....	....	....	....	....	....	10	1	1	2	14	....	....	....	....
	Adler Mannheim	EuroHL	5	0	4	4	8	....	....	....	....	....	....	....	....	....	....	....	....	....	....	....	....	....	....
	Germany	Olympics	4	1	0	1	6	....	....	....	....	....	....	....	....	....	....	....	....	....	....	....	....	....	....
1998-99	**St. Louis**	**NHL**	**3**	**0**	**0**	**0**	**0**	**0**	**0**	**0**	**4**	**0.0**	**–2**	**19**	**21.1**	**13:16**	**5**	**2**	**0**	**2**	**0**	**0**	**0**	**0**	**16:40**
	Worcester IceCats	AHL	74	21	35	56	48	....	....	....	....	....	....	....	....	....	4	1	1	2	2	....	....	....	....
99-2000	**St. Louis**	**NHL**	**63**	**13**	**21**	**34**	**28**	**5**	**0**	**1**	**140**	**9.3**	**20**	**75**	**49.3**	**15:25**	**7**	**4**	**6**	**10**	**2**	**1**	**0**	**1**	**17:02**
2000-01	**St. Louis**	**NHL**	**72**	**19**	**25**	**44**	**48**	**8**	**3**	**1**	**208**	**9.1**	**11**	**160**	**43.8**	**17:56**	**15**	**2**	**4**	**6**	**4**	**0**	**0**	**0**	**17:19**
2001-02	**Edmonton**	**NHL**	**82**	**16**	**24**	**40**	**60**	**5**	**0**	**3**	**211**	**7.6**	**4**	**26**	**53.9**	**14:60**	....	....	....	....	....	....	....	....	....
	Germany	Olympics	4	1	1	2	2	....	....	....	....	....	....	....	....	....	....	....	....	....	....	....	....	....	....
2002-03	**Buffalo**	**NHL**	**49**	**10**	**16**	**26**	**30**	**2**	**0**	**2**	**145**	**6.9**	**4**	**33**	**30.3**	**17:55**	....	....	....	....	....	....	....	....	....
	NHL Totals		**269**	**58**	**86**	**144**	**166**	**20**	**3**	**7**	**708**	**8.2**		**313**	**43.1**	**16:24**	**27**	**8**	**10**	**18**	**6**	**1**	**0**	**1**	**17:07**

Traded to **Edmonton** by **St. Louis** with Marty Reasoner and Jan Horacek for Doug Weight and Michel Riesen, July 1, 2001. Traded to **Buffalo** by **Edmonton** for Atlanta's 2nd round choice (previously acquired, Edmonton selected Jeff Deslauriers) in 2002 Entry Draft and Nashville's 2nd round choice (previously acquired, Edmonton selected Jarret Stoll) in 2002 Entry Draft, June 22, 2002.

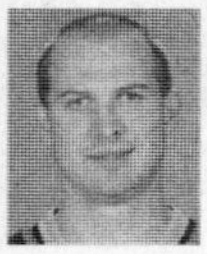

HECL, Radoslav (HEHT-suhl, RA-doh-slahf)

Defense. Shoots left. 6'1", 196 lbs. Born, Partizanske, Czech., October 11, 1974. Buffalo's 8th choice, 208th overall, in 2002 Entry Draft.

Season	Club	League	GP	G	A	Pts	PIM	PP	SH	GW	S	%	+/-	TF	F%	Min	GP	G	A	Pts	PIM	PP	SH	GW	Min
1995-96	HC Nitra	Cze-Rep	39	6	5	11	....	....	....	....	....	....	....	....	....	....	....	....	....	....	....	....	....	....	....
1996-97	Slovan Bratislava	EuroHL	4	0	0	0	0	....	....	....	....	....	....	....	....	....	2	0	0	0	0	....	....	....	....
	Slovan Bratislava	Slovakia	34	1	5	6	41	....	....	....	....	....	....	....	....	....	2	0	0	0	0	....	....	....	....
1997-98	Slovan Bratislava	EuroHL	6	2	1	3	6	....	....	....	....	....	....	....	....	....	2	0	0	0	0	....	....	....	....
	Slovan Bratislava	Slovakia	35	8	7	15	41	....	....	....	....	....	....	....	....	....	10	0	4	4	6	....	....	....	....
	Banska Bystrica	Slovak-2	5	1	0	1	16	....	....	....	....	....	....	....	....	....	....	....	....	....	....	....	....	....	....
1998-99	Slovan Bratislava	EuroHL	6	0	0	0	14	....	....	....	....	....	....	....	....	....	....	....	....	....	....	....	....	....	....
	Slovan Bratislava	Slovakia	40	5	10	15	61	....	....	....	....	....	....	....	....	....	10	2	4	6	31	....	....	....	....
99-2000	Slovan Bratislava	Slovakia	41	2	7	9	61	....	....	....	....	....	....	....	....	....	8	2	1	3	2	....	....	....	....
2000-01	Slovan Bratislava	Slovakia	25	2	5	7	6	....	....	....	....	....	....	....	....	....	6	1	1	2	18	....	....	....	....
2001-02	Slovan Bratislava	Slovakia	50	7	13	20	22	....	....	....	....	....	....	....	....	....	19	3	5	8	10	....	....	....	....
2002-03	**Buffalo**	**NHL**	**14**	**0**	**0**	**0**	**2**	**0**	**0**	**0**	**3**	**0.0**	**0**	**0**	**0.0**	**10:01**	....	....	....	....	....	....	....	....	....
	Rochester	AHL	58	6	14	20	41	....	....	....	....	....	....	....	....	....	3	0	0	0	2	....	....	....	....
	NHL Totals		**14**	**0**	**0**	**0**	**2**	**0**	**0**	**0**	**3**	**0.0**		**0**	**0.0**	**10:01**	....	....	....	....	....	....	....	....	....

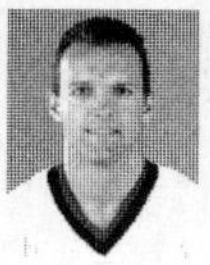

HEDICAN, Bret

(HEH-dih-kan, BREHT) **CAR.**

Defense. Shoots left. 6'2", 205 lbs. Born, St. Paul, MN, August 10, 1970. St. Louis' 10th choice, 198th overall, in 1988 Entry Draft.

			Regular Season															Playoffs								
Season	Club	League	GP	G	A	Pts	PIM	PP	SH	GW	S	%	+/-	TF	F%	Min	GP	G	A	Pts	PIM	PP	SH	GW	Min
1987-88	North St. Paul	Hi-School	23	15	19	34	16																		
1988-89	St. Cloud State	NCAA-3	28	5	3	8	28																		
1989-90	St. Cloud State	NCAA-3	36	4	17	21	37																		
1990-91	St. Cloud State	WCHA	41	21	26	47	26																		
1991-92	Team USA	Nat-Tm	54	1	8	9	59																		
	United States	Olympics	8	0	0	0	4																		
	St. Louis	**NHL**	**4**	**1**	**0**	**1**	**0**	**0**	**0**	**0**	**1**	**100.0**	**1**				**5**	**0**	**0**	**0**	**0**	**0**	**0**	**0**	
1992-93	**St. Louis**	**NHL**	**42**	**0**	**8**	**8**	**30**	**0**	**0**	**0**	**40**	**0.0**	**–2**				**10**	**0**	**0**	**0**	**14**	**0**	**0**	**0**	
	Peoria Rivermen	IHL	19	0	8	8	10																		
1993-94	**St. Louis**	**NHL**	**61**	**0**	**11**	**11**	**64**	**0**	**0**	**0**	**78**	**0.0**	**–8**												
	Vancouver	**NHL**	**8**	**0**	**1**	**1**	**0**	**0**	**0**	**0**	**10**	**0.0**	**1**				**24**	**1**	**6**	**7**	**16**	**0**	**0**	**0**	
1994-95	**Vancouver**	**NHL**	**45**	**2**	**11**	**13**	**34**	**0**	**0**	**0**	**56**	**3.6**	**–3**				**11**	**0**	**2**	**2**	**6**	**0**	**0**	**0**	
1995-96	**Vancouver**	**NHL**	**77**	**6**	**23**	**29**	**83**	**1**	**0**	**0**	**113**	**5.3**	**8**				**6**	**0**	**1**	**1**	**10**	**0**	**0**	**0**	
1996-97	**Vancouver**	**NHL**	**67**	**4**	**15**	**19**	**51**	**2**	**0**	**1**	**93**	**4.3**	**–3**												
1997-98	**Vancouver**	**NHL**	**71**	**3**	**24**	**27**	**79**	**1**	**0**	**0**	**84**	**3.6**	**3**												
1998-99	**Vancouver**	**NHL**	**42**	**2**	**11**	**13**	**34**	**0**	**2**	**0**	**52**	**3.8**	**7**	**0**	**0.0**	**18:40**									
	Florida	**NHL**	**25**	**3**	**7**	**10**	**17**	**0**	**0**	**1**	**38**	**7.9**	**–2**	**0**	**0.0**	**22:24**									
99-2000	**Florida**	**NHL**	**76**	**6**	**19**	**25**	**68**	**2**	**0**	**1**	**58**	**10.3**	**4**	**0**	**0.0**	**19:36**	**4**	**0**	**0**	**0**	**0**	**0**	**0**	**0**	**20:42**
2000-01	**Florida**	**NHL**	**70**	**5**	**15**	**20**	**72**	**4**	**0**	**1**	**104**	**4.8**	**–7**	**0**	**0.0**	**21:49**									
2001-02	**Florida**	**NHL**	**31**	**3**	**7**	**10**	**12**	**0**	**0**	**0**	**46**	**6.5**	**–4**	**0**	**0.0**	**24:27**									
	Carolina	**NHL**	**26**	**2**	**4**	**6**	**10**	**0**	**0**	**1**	**39**	**5.1**	**3**	**0**	**0.0**	**22:56**	**23**	**1**	**4**	**5**	**20**	**0**	**0**	**0**	**23:52**
2002-03	**Carolina**	**NHL**	**72**	**3**	**14**	**17**	**75**	**1**	**0**	**1**	**113**	**2.7**	**–24**	**0**	**0.0**	**23:02**									
	NHL Totals		**717**	**40**	**170**	**210**	**629**	**11**	**2**	**6**	**925**	**4.3**		**0**	**0.0**	**21:33**	**83**	**2**	**13**	**15**	**66**	**0**	**0**	**0**	**23:24**

WCHA First All-Star Team (1991)

Traded to **Vancouver** by **St. Louis** with Jeff Brown and Nathan LaFayette for Craig Janney, March 21, 1994. Traded to **Florida** by **Vancouver** with Pavel Bure, Brad Ference and Vancouver's 3rd round choice (Robert Fried) in 2000 Entry Draft for Ed Jovanovski, Dave Gagner, Mike Brown, Kevin Weekes and Florida's 1st round choice (Nathan Smith) in 2000 Entry Draft, January 17, 1999. Traded to **Carolina** by **Florida** with Kevyn Adams, Tomas Malec and a conditional 2nd round choice in 2003 Entry Draft for Sandis Ozolinsh and Byron Ritchie, January 16, 2002.

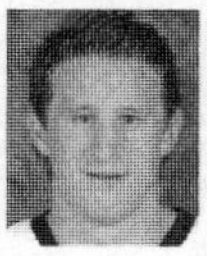

HEDSTROM, Jonathan

(HEHD-struhm, JAWN-ah-thuhn) **ANA.**

Right wing. Shoots left. 6', 200 lbs. Born, Skelleftea, Sweden, December 27, 1977. Toronto's 8th choice, 221st overall, in 1997 Entry Draft.

Season	Club	League	GP	G	A	Pts	PIM	PP	SH	GW	S	%	+/-	TF	F%	Min	GP	G	A	Pts	PIM	PP	SH	GW	Min
1995-96	Skelleftea AIK	Swede-2	7	0	0	0	0																		
1996-97	Skelleftea AIK Jr.	Swede-Jr.	9	4	4	8																			
	Skelleftea AIK	Swede-2	12	1	1	2	10										6	0	0	0	2				
1997-98	Skelleftea AIK Jr.	Swede-Jr.	1	0	0	0	2																		
	Skelleftea AIK	Swede-2	16	2	3	5																			
1998-99	Skelleftea AIK	Swede-2	36	15	28	43	74																		
99-2000	Lulea HF	Sweden	48	9	17	26	46										9	2	1	3	12				
2000-01	Lulea HF	Sweden	46	9	19	28	68										12	1	6	7	16				
2001-02	Lulea HF	Sweden	47	11	7	18	38										4	2	1	3	6				
2002-03	**Anaheim**	**NHL**	**4**	**0**	**0**	**0**	**0**	**0**	**0**	**0**	**3**	**0.0**	**–1**	**1**	**0.0**	**7:51**									
	Cincinnati	AHL	50	14	21	35	62																		
	NHL Totals		**4**	**0**	**0**	**0**	**0**	**0**	**0**	**0**	**3**	**0.0**		**1**	**0.0**	**7:51**									

Rights traded to **Anaheim** by **Toronto** for Anaheim's 6th (Vadim Sozinov) and 7th (Markus Seikola) round choices in 2000 Entry Draft, June 25, 2000.

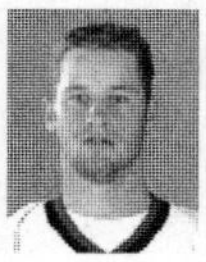

HEEREMA, Jeff

(HEER-eh-muh, JEHF) **CAR.**

Right wing. Shoots right. 6'1", 190 lbs. Born, Thunder Bay, Ont., January 17, 1980. Carolina's 1st choice, 11th overall, in 1998 Entry Draft.

Season	Club	League	GP	G	A	Pts	PIM	PP	SH	GW	S	%	+/-	TF	F%	Min	GP	G	A	Pts	PIM	PP	SH	GW	Min
1996-97	T. Bay Kings	TBMHL	54	42	29	71	112																		
1997-98	Sarnia Sting	OHL	63	32	40	72	88										5	4	1	5	10				
1998-99	Sarnia Sting	OHL	62	31	39	70	113										6	5	1	6	0				
99-2000	Sarnia Sting	OHL	67	36	41	77	62										7	4	2	6	10				
2000-01	Cincinnati	IHL	73	17	16	33	42										4	0	0	0	0				
2001-02	Lowell	AHL	76	33	37	70	90										5	2	3	5	2				
2002-03	**Carolina**	**NHL**	**10**	**3**	**0**	**3**	**2**	**1**	**0**	**0**	**16**	**18.8**	**–2**	**0**	**0.0**	**9:37**									
	Lowell	AHL	36	15	17	32	25																		
	NHL Totals		**10**	**3**	**0**	**3**	**2**	**1**	**0**	**0**	**16**	**18.8**		**0**	**0.0**	**9:37**									

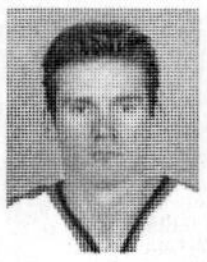

HEINS, Shawn

(HIGHNS, SHAWN)

Defense. Shoots left. 6'4", 210 lbs. Born, Eganville, Ont., December 24, 1973.

Season	Club	League	GP	G	A	Pts	PIM	PP	SH	GW	S	%	+/-	TF	F%	Min	GP	G	A	Pts	PIM	PP	SH	GW	Min
1991-92	Peterborough	OHL	49	1	1	2	73										7	0	0	0	5				
1992-93	Peterborough	OHL	5	0	0	0	10																		
	Windsor Spitfires	OHL	53	7	10	17	107																		
1993-94	Renfrew	NOJHA	32	16	34	50	250																		
1994-95	Renfrew	NOJHA	35	30	49	79	188																		
1995-96	Mobile Mysticks	ECHL	62	7	20	27	152																		
	Cape Breton	AHL	1	0	0	0	0																		
1996-97	Mobile Mysticks	ECHL	56	6	17	23	253										3	0	2	2	2				
	Kansas City	IHL	6	0	0	0	9																		
1997-98	Kansas City	IHL	82	22	28	50	303										11	1	0	1	49				
1998-99	Team Canada	Nat-Tm	36	5	16	21	66																		
	San Jose	**NHL**	**5**	**0**	**0**	**0**	**13**	**0**	**0**	**0**	**4**	**0.0**	**0**	**0**	**0.0**	**13:38**									
	Kentucky	AHL	18	2	2	4	108										12	2	7	9	10				
99-2000	**San Jose**	**NHL**	**1**	**0**	**0**	**0**	**2**	**0**	**0**	**0**	**1**	**0.0**	**–1**	**0**	**0.0**	**10:57**									
	Kentucky	AHL	69	11	52	63	238										9	3	3	6	44				
2000-01	**San Jose**	**NHL**	**38**	**3**	**4**	**7**	**57**	**2**	**0**	**0**	**45**	**6.7**	**2**	**0**	**0.0**	**10:15**	**2**	**0**	**0**	**0**	**0**	**0**	**0**	**0**	**7:31**
2001-02	**San Jose**	**NHL**	**17**	**0**	**2**	**2**	**24**	**0**	**0**	**0**	**20**	**0.0**	**1**	**0**	**0.0**	**9:46**									
2002-03	**San Jose**	**NHL**	**20**	**0**	**1**	**1**	**9**	**0**	**0**	**0**	**10**	**0.0**	**–2**	**0**	**0.0**	**8:32**									
	Pittsburgh	**NHL**	**27**	**1**	**1**	**2**	**33**	**0**	**0**	**1**	**28**	**3.6**	**–2**	**0**	**0.0**	**19:11**									
	NHL Totals		**108**	**4**	**8**	**12**	**138**	**2**	**0**	**1**	**108**	**3.7**		**0**	**0.0**	**12:15**	**2**	**0**	**0**	**0**	**0**	**0**	**0**	**0**	**7:31**

AHL First All-Star Team (2000)

Signed as a free agent by **San Jose**, January 5, 1997. • Missed majority of 2000-01 season recovering from head injury suffered in game vs. Chicago, February 14, 2001. • Missed majority of 2001-02 season recovering from knee (December 4, 2001 vs. Calgary) and jaw (January 19, 2002 vs. Colorado) injuries. Traded to **Pittsburgh** by **San Jose** for Pittsburgh's 5th round choice (Patrick Ehelechner) in 2003 Entry Draft, February 9, 2003.

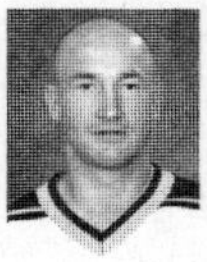

HEINZE, Steve

(HIGHNS, STEEV)

Right wing. Shoots right. 5'11", 202 lbs. Born, Lawrence, MA, January 30, 1970. Boston's 2nd choice, 60th overall, in 1988 Entry Draft.

Season	Club	League	GP	G	A	Pts	PIM	PP	SH	GW	S	%	+/-	TF	F%	Min	GP	G	A	Pts	PIM	PP	SH	GW	Min
1986-87	Lawrence School	Hi-School	23	26	24	50																			
1987-88	Lawrence School	Hi-School	23	30	25	55																			
1988-89	Boston College	H-East	36	26	23	49	26																		
1989-90	Boston College	H-East	40	27	36	63	41																		
1990-91	Boston College	H-East	35	21	26	47	35																		
1991-92	Team USA	Nat-Tm	49	18	15	33	38																		
	United States	Olympics	8	1	3	4	8																		
	Boston	**NHL**	**14**	**3**	**4**	**7**	**6**	**0**	**0**	**2**	**29**	**10.3**	**–1**				**7**	**0**	**3**	**3**	**17**	**0**	**0**	**0**	
1992-93	**Boston**	**NHL**	**73**	**18**	**13**	**31**	**24**	**0**	**2**	**4**	**146**	**12.3**	**20**				**4**	**1**	**1**	**2**	**2**	**0**	**0**	**0**	
1993-94	**Boston**	**NHL**	**77**	**10**	**11**	**21**	**32**	**0**	**2**	**1**	**183**	**5.5**	**–2**				**13**	**2**	**3**	**5**	**7**	**0**	**0**	**0**	
1994-95	**Boston**	**NHL**	**36**	**7**	**9**	**16**	**23**	**0**	**1**	**0**	**70**	**10.0**	**0**				**5**	**0**	**0**	**0**	**0**	**0**	**0**	**0**	
1995-96	**Boston**	**NHL**	**76**	**16**	**12**	**28**	**43**	**0**	**1**	**3**	**129**	**12.4**	**–3**				**5**	**1**	**1**	**2**	**4**	**0**	**1**	**0**	
1996-97	**Boston**	**NHL**	**30**	**17**	**8**	**25**	**27**	**4**	**2**	**2**	**96**	**17.7**	**–8**												
1997-98	**Boston**	**NHL**	**61**	**26**	**20**	**46**	**54**	**9**	**0**	**6**	**160**	**16.3**	**8**				**6**	**0**	**0**	**0**	**6**	**0**	**0**	**0**	
1998-99	**Boston**	**NHL**	**73**	**22**	**18**	**40**	**30**	**9**	**0**	**3**	**146**	**15.1**	**7**	**2**	**0.0**	**15:48**	**12**	**4**	**3**	**7**	**0**	**2**	**0**	**0**	**15:35**
99-2000	**Boston**	**NHL**	**75**	**12**	**13**	**25**	**36**	**2**	**0**	**2**	**145**	**8.3**	**–8**	**8**	**12.5**	**14:57**									
2000-01	**Columbus**	**NHL**	**65**	**22**	**20**	**42**	**38**	**14**	**0**	**3**	**125**	**17.6**	**–19**	**38**	**29.0**	**18:49**									
	Buffalo	**NHL**	**14**	**5**	**7**	**12**	**8**	**1**	**0**	**1**	**19**	**26.3**	**6**	**0**	**0.0**	**15:24**	**13**	**3**	**4**	**7**	**10**	**3**	**0**	**0**	**13:34**

Season	Club	League	GP	G	A	Pts	PIM	PP	SH	GW	S	%	+/-	TF	F%	Min	GP	G	A	Pts	PIM	PP	SH	GW	Min
			Regular Season														Playoffs								
2001-02	**Los Angeles**	**NHL**	**73**	**15**	**16**	**31**	**46**	**8**	**0**	**4**	**123**	**12.2**	**–15**	**4**	**50.0**	**15:47**	**4**	**0**	**0**	**0**	**2**	**0**	**0**	**0**	**10:22**
2002-03	**Los Angeles**	**NHL**	**27**	**5**	**7**	**12**	**12**	**1**	**0**	**0**	**44**	**11.4**	**–5**	**14**	**21.4**	**15:17**									
	Manchester	AHL	18	8	9	17	12																		
	NHL Totals		**694**	**178**	**158**	**336**	**379**	**48**	**8**	**31**	**1415**	**12.6**		**66**	**25.8**	**16:08**	**69**	**11**	**15**	**26**	**48**	**5**	**1**	**0**	**13:58**

Hockey East First All-Star Team (1990) • NCAA East First All-American Team (1990)

Selected by **Columbus** from **Boston** in Expansion Draft, June 23, 2000. Traded to **Buffalo** by **Columbus** for Buffalo's 3rd round choice (Per Mars) in 2001 Entry Draft, March 13, 2001. Signed as a free agent by **Los Angeles**, July 4, 2001.

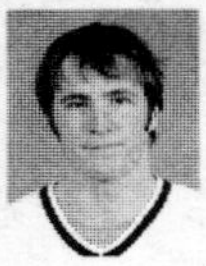

HEISTEN, Barrett (HIGH-stehn, BAIR-reht) DAL.

Left wing. Shoots left. 6'1", 200 lbs. Born, Anchorage, AK, March 19, 1980. Buffalo's 1st choice, 20th overall, in 1999 Entry Draft.

Season	Club	League	GP	G	A	Pts	PIM	PP	SH	GW	S	%	+/-	TF	F%	Min	GP	G	A	Pts	PIM	PP	SH	GW	Min
1996-97	Anchorage	AAHL	39	35	29	64																			
1997-98	U.S. National U-18	USDP	50	11	26	37	245																		
1998-99	U. of Maine	H-East	34	12	16	28	72																		
99-2000	U. of Maine	H-East	37	13	24	37	86																		
2000-01	Seattle	WHL	58	20	57	77	61										9	2	6	8	20				
2001-02	**NY Rangers**	**NHL**	**10**	**0**	**0**	**0**	**2**	**0**	**0**	**0**	**7**	**0.0**	**–4**	**7**	**28.6**	**7:36**									
	Hartford	AHL	49	9	9	18	60																		
	Utah Grizzlies	AHL	12	5	1	6	14										5	1	0	1	4				
2002-03	Utah Grizzlies	AHL	58	10	10	20	47										2	0	0	0	4				
	NHL Totals		**10**	**0**	**0**	**0**	**2**	**0**	**0**	**0**	**7**	**0.0**		**7**	**28.6**	**7:36**									

• Left **University of Maine** (H-East) and signed with **Seattle** (WHL) who had selected him 80th overall in 1998 WHL Bantam Draft, August 7, 2000. Signed as a free agent by **NY Rangers**, June 16, 2001. Traded to **Dallas** by **NY Rangers** with Manny Malhotra for Martin Rucinsky and Roman Lyashenko, March 12, 2002.

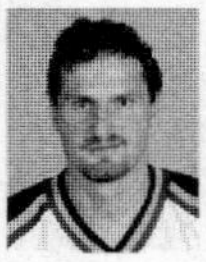

HEJDUK, Milan (HAY-dook, MEE-lan) COL.

Right wing. Shoots right. 5'11", 185 lbs. Born, Usti-nad-Labem, Czech., February 14, 1976. Quebec's 6th choice, 87th overall, in 1994 Entry Draft.

Season	Club	League	GP	G	A	Pts	PIM	PP	SH	GW	S	%	+/-	TF	F%	Min	GP	G	A	Pts	PIM	PP	SH	GW	Min
1993-94	HC Pardubice	Czech	22	6	3	9											10	5	1	6					
1994-95	HC Pardubice	Czech	43	11	13	24	6										6	3	1	4	0				
1995-96	Pardubice	Czech	37	13	7	20																			
1996-97	Pardubice	Czech	51	27	11	38	10										10	6	0	6	27				
1997-98	Pardubice	Czech	48	26	19	45	20										3	0	0	0	2				
	Czech Republic	Olympics	4	0	0	0	2																		
1998-99	**Colorado**	**NHL**	**82**	**14**	**34**	**48**	**26**	**4**	**0**	**5**	**178**	**7.9**	**8**	**2**	**50.0**	**15:45**	**16**	**6**	**6**	**12**	**4**	**1**	**0**	**3**	**15:53**
99-2000	**Colorado**	**NHL**	**82**	**36**	**36**	**72**	**16**	**13**	**0**	**9**	**228**	**15.8**	**14**	**3**	**100.0**	**19:58**	**17**	**5**	**4**	**9**	**6**	**3**	**0**	**1**	**19:56**
2000-01♦	**Colorado**	**NHL**	**80**	**41**	**38**	**79**	**36**	**12**	**1**	**9**	**213**	**19.2**	**32**	**3**	**33.3**	**19:52**	**23**	**7**	***16**	**23**	**6**	**4**	**0**	**1**	**21:33**
2001-02	**Colorado**	**NHL**	**62**	**21**	**23**	**44**	**24**	**7**	**1**	**5**	**139**	**15.1**	**0**	**5**	**40.0**	**20:11**	**16**	**3**	**3**	**6**	**4**	**1**	**0**	**0**	**18:24**
	Czech Republic	Olympics	4	1	0	1	0																		
2002-03	**Colorado**	**NHL**	**82**	***50**	**48**	**98**	**32**	**18**	**0**	**4**	**244**	**20.5**	**52**	**43**	**44.2**	**19:50**	**7**	**2**	**2**	**4**	**2**	**1**	**0**	**0**	**20:42**
	NHL Totals		**388**	**162**	**179**	**341**	**134**	**54**	**2**	**32**	**1002**	**16.2**		**56**	**46.4**	**19:04**	**79**	**23**	**31**	**54**	**22**	**10**	**0**	**5**	**19:21**

NHL All-Rookie Team (1999) • NHL Second All-Star Team (2003) • Maurice "Rocket" Richard Trophy (2003)

Played in NHL All-Star Game (2000, 2001)

Rights transferred to **Colorado** after **Quebec** franchise relocated, June 21, 1995.

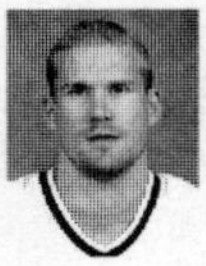

HELENIUS, Sami (huh-LEHN-ee-uhs, SA-mee)

Defense. Shoots left. 6'6", 230 lbs. Born, Helsinki, Finland, January 22, 1974. Calgary's 5th choice, 102nd overall, in 1992 Entry Draft.

Season	Club	League	GP	G	A	Pts	PIM	PP	SH	GW	S	%	+/-	TF	F%	Min	GP	G	A	Pts	PIM	PP	SH	GW	Min
1990-91	Jokerit Helsinki Jr.	Finn-Jr.	2	0	0	0	6																		
1991-92	Jokerit Helsinki Jr.	Finn-Jr.	14	3	3	6	24																		
	Jokerit Helsinki	Finland-2	13	4	4	8	24																		
1992-93	Jokerit Helsinki Jr.	Finn-Jr.	13	2	3	5	18																		
	Vantaa HT	Finland-2	21	3	2	5	50																		
	Jokerit Helsinki	Finland	1	0	0	0	0																		
1993-94	Reipas Lahti Jr.	Finn-Jr.	11	3	4	7	48																		
	Reipas Lahti	Finland	37	2	3	5	46																		
1994-95	Saint John Flames	AHL	69	2	5	7	217																		
1995-96	Saint John Flames	AHL	68	0	3	3	231										10	0	0	0	9				
1996-97	**Calgary**	**NHL**	**3**	**0**	**1**	**1**	**0**	**0**	**0**	**0**	**1**	**0.0**	**1**												
	Saint John Flames	AHL	72	5	10	15	218										2	0	0	0	0				
1997-98	Saint John Flames	AHL	63	1	2	3	185																		
	Las Vegas	IHL	10	0	1	1	19										4	0	0	0	25				
1998-99	**Calgary**	**NHL**	**4**	**0**	**0**	**0**	**8**	**0**	**0**	**0**	**1**	**0.0**	**–2**	**0**	**0.0**	**10:16**									
	Las Vegas	IHL	42	2	3	5	193																		
	Tampa Bay	**NHL**	**4**	**1**	**0**	**1**	**15**	**0**	**1**	**0**	**3**	**33.3**	**–3**	**0**	**0.0**	**16:53**									
	Chicago Wolves	IHL	4	0	0	0	11																		
	Hershey Bears	AHL	8	0	0	0	29										5	0	0	0	16				
99-2000	**Colorado**	**NHL**	**33**	**0**	**0**	**0**	**46**	**0**	**0**	**0**	**6**	**0.0**	**–5**	**0**	**0.0**	**7:04**									
	Hershey Bears	AHL	12	0	1	1	31										9	0	0	0	40				
2000-01	**Dallas**	**NHL**	**57**	**1**	**2**	**3**	**99**	**0**	**0**	**0**	**18**	**5.6**	**1**	**0**	**0.0**	**10:39**	**1**	**0**	**0**	**0**	**0**	**0**	**0**	**0**	**5:53**
2001-02	**Dallas**	**NHL**	**39**	**0**	**0**	**0**	**58**	**0**	**0**	**0**	**18**	**0.0**	**–4**	**0**	**0.0**	**9:41**									
2002-03	**Dallas**	**NHL**	**5**	**0**	**0**	**0**	**6**	**0**	**0**	**0**	**2**	**0.0**	**1**	**0**	**0.0**	**9:49**									
	Utah Grizzlies	AHL	4	0	0	0	14																		
	Chicago	**NHL**	**10**	**0**	**1**	**1**	**28**	**0**	**0**	**0**	**5**	**0.0**	**3**	**0**	**0.0**	**11:16**									
	NHL Totals		**155**	**2**	**4**	**6**	**260**	**0**	**1**	**0**	**54**	**3.7**		**0**	**0.0**	**9:47**	**1**	**0**	**0**	**0**	**0**	**0**	**0**	**0**	**5:53**

Traded to **Tampa Bay** by **Calgary** for future considerations, January 29, 1999. Traded to **Colorado** by **Tampa Bay** for future considerations, March 23, 1999. Signed as a free agent by **Dallas**, July 12, 2000. Signed as a free agent by **Jokerit Helsinki** (Finland) with Dallas retaining NHL rights, May 15, 2002. Traded to **Chicago** by **Dallas** with Dallas's 7th round choice in 2004 Entry Draft for Lyle Odelein, March 10, 2003. • Missed majority of 2002-03 season recovering from knee injury suffered in game vs. Chicago (AHL), January 11, 2003.

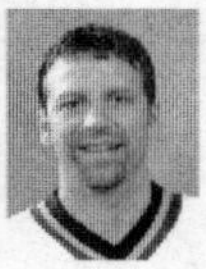

HELMER, Bryan (HEHL-muhr, BRIGH-uhn) PHX.

Defense. Shoots right. 6'1", 200 lbs. Born, Sault Ste. Marie, Ont., July 15, 1972.

Season	Club	League	GP	G	A	Pts	PIM	PP	SH	GW	S	%	+/-	TF	F%	Min	GP	G	A	Pts	PIM	PP	SH	GW	Min
1989-90	Wellington Dukes	MTJHL	44	4	20	24	204																		
	Belleville Bulls	OHL	6	0	1	1	0																		
1990-91	Wellington Dukes	MTJHL	50	11	14	25	109																		
1991-92	Wellington Dukes	MTJHL	42	17	31	48	66										3	2	1	3	0				
1992-93	Wellington Dukes	MTJHL	48	21	54	75	84										9	4	8	12	22				
1993-94	Albany River Rats	AHL	65	4	19	23	79										5	0	0	0	9				
1994-95	Albany River Rats	AHL	77	7	36	43	101										7	1	0	1	0				
1995-96	Albany River Rats	AHL	80	14	30	44	107										4	2	0	2	6				
1996-97	Albany River Rats	AHL	77	12	27	39	113										16	1	7	8	10				
1997-98	Albany River Rats	AHL	80	14	49	63	101										13	4	9	13	18				
1998-99	**Phoenix**	**NHL**	**11**	**0**	**0**	**0**	**23**	**0**	**0**	**0**	**11**	**0.0**	**2**	**0**	**0.0**	**7:43**									
	Las Vegas	IHL	8	1	3	4	28																		
	St. Louis	**NHL**	**29**	**0**	**4**	**4**	**19**	**0**	**0**	**0**	**38**	**0.0**	**3**	**1**	**100.0**	**19:08**									
	Worcester IceCats	AHL	16	7	8	15	18										4	0	0	0	12				
99-2000	**St. Louis**	**NHL**	**15**	**1**	**1**	**2**	**10**	**1**	**0**	**1**	**19**	**5.3**	**–3**	**0**	**0.0**	**16:15**									
	Worcester IceCats	AHL	54	10	25	35	124										9	1	4	5	10				
2000-01	Kansas City	IHL	42	4	15	19	76																		
	Vancouver	**NHL**	**20**	**2**	**4**	**6**	**18**	**0**	**0**	**0**	**28**	**7.1**	**0**	**0**	**0.0**	**16:51**									
2001-02	**Vancouver**	**NHL**	**40**	**5**	**5**	**10**	**53**	**2**	**0**	**1**	**43**	**11.6**	**10**	**0**	**0.0**	**12:04**	**6**	**0**	**0**	**0**	**0**	**0**	**0**	**0**	**9:09**
	Manitoba Moose	AHL	34	6	18	24	69																		
2002-03	**Vancouver**	**NHL**	**2**	**0**	**0**	**0**	**0**	**0**	**0**	**0**	**2**	**0.0**	**1**	**0**	**0.0**	**13:24**									
	Manitoba Moose	AHL	60	7	24	31	82										14	0	4	4	20				
	NHL Totals		**117**	**8**	**14**	**22**	**123**	**3**	**0**	**2**	**141**	**5.7**		**1**	**100.0**	**14:47**	**6**	**0**	**0**	**0**	**0**	**0**	**0**	**0**	**9:09**

AHL First All-Star Team (1998)

Signed as a free agent by **New Jersey**, July 10, 1994. Signed as a free agent by **Phoenix**, July 17, 1998. Claimed on waivers by **St. Louis** from **Phoenix**, December 19, 1998. Signed as a free agent by **Vancouver**, August 21, 2000. Traded to **Phoenix** by **Vancouver** for Martin Grenier, July 25, 2003.

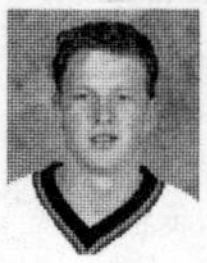

HEMSKY, Ales

(HEHM-skee, ahl-EHSH) **EDM.**

Right wing. Shoots right. 6', 192 lbs. Born, Pardubice, Czech., August 13, 1983. Edmonton's 1st choice, 13th overall, in 2001 Entry Draft.

			Regular Season														Playoffs								
Season	Club	League	GP	G	A	Pts	PIM	PP	SH	GW	S	%	+/-	TF	F%	Min	GP	G	A	Pts	PIM	PP	SH	GW	Min
99-2000	Pardubice Jr.	Czech-Jr.	45	20	36	56	54	....	....	....	....	....	....	....	....	....	7	4	14	18	36	....	....	....	....
	Pardubice	Czech	4	0	1	1	0	....	....	....	....	....	....	....	....	....	....	....	....	....	....	....	....	....	....
2000-01	Hull Olympiques	QMJHL	68	36	64	100	67	....	....	....	....	....	....	....	....	....	5	2	3	5	2	....	....	....	....
2001-02	Hull Olympiques	QMJHL	53	27	70	97	86	....	....	....	....	....	....	....	....	....	10	6	10	16	6	....	....	....	....
2002-03	**Edmonton**	**NHL**	**59**	**6**	**24**	**30**	**14**	**0**	**0**	**1**	**50**	**12.0**	**5**	**3**	**33.3**	**12:04**	**6**	**0**	**0**	**0**	**0**	**0**	**0**	**0**	**12:46**
	NHL Totals		**59**	**6**	**24**	**30**	**14**	**0**	**0**	**1**	**50**	**12.0**		**3**	**33.3**	**12:04**	**6**	**0**	**0**	**0**	**0**	**0**	**0**	**0**	**12:46**

QMJHL Second All-Star Team (2002)

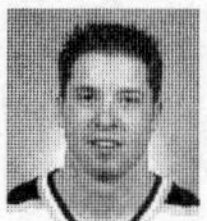

HENDERSON, Jay

(HEHN-duhr-SOHN, JAY)

Left wing. Shoots left. 5'11", 190 lbs. Born, Edmonton, Alta., September 17, 1978. Boston's 12th choice, 246th overall, in 1997 Entry Draft.

			Regular Season														Playoffs								
Season	Club	League	GP	G	A	Pts	PIM	PP	SH	GW	S	%	+/-	TF	F%	Min	GP	G	A	Pts	PIM	PP	SH	GW	Min
1993-94	Sherwood Park	AMBHL	31	12	21	33	36	....	....	....	....	....	....	....	....	....	....	....	....	....	....	....	....	....	....
1994-95	Red Deer Rebels	WHL	54	3	9	12	80	....	....	....	....	....	....	....	....	....	....	....	....	....	....	....	....	....	....
1995-96	Red Deer Rebels	WHL	71	15	13	28	139	....	....	....	....	....	....	....	....	....	10	1	1	2	11	....	....	....	....
1996-97	Edmonton Ice	WHL	66	28	32	60	127	....	....	....	....	....	....	....	....	....	....	....	....	....	....	....	....	....	....
1997-98	Edmonton Ice	WHL	72	49	45	94	130	....	....	....	....	....	....	....	....	....	....	....	....	....	....	....	....	....	....
	Providence Bruins	AHL	11	3	1	4	11	....	....	....	....	....	....	....	....	....	....	....	....	....	....	....	....	....	....
1998-99	**Boston**	**NHL**	**4**	**0**	**0**	**0**	**2**	**0**	**0**	**0**	**4**	**0.0**	**–1**	**0**	**0.0**	**5:39**	....	....	....	....	....	....	....	....	....
	Providence Bruins	AHL	55	7	9	16	172	....	....	....	....	....	....	....	....	....	2	0	0	0	2	....	....	....	....
99-2000	**Boston**	**NHL**	**16**	**1**	**3**	**4**	**9**	**0**	**0**	**0**	**18**	**5.6**	**1**	**2**	**0.0**	**5:22**	....	....	....	....	....	....	....	....	....
	Providence Bruins	AHL	60	18	27	45	200	....	....	....	....	....	....	....	....	....	14	1	2	3	16	....	....	....	....
2000-01	**Boston**	**NHL**	**13**	**0**	**0**	**0**	**26**	**0**	**0**	**0**	**12**	**0.0**	**–1**	**3**	**100.0**	**6:58**	....	....	....	....	....	....	....	....	....
	Providence Bruins	AHL	41	9	7	16	121	....	....	....	....	....	....	....	....	....	1	0	0	0	2	....	....	....	....
2002-03	Providence Bruins	AHL	39	7	13	20	152	....	....	....	....	....	....	....	....	....	....	....	....	....	....	....	....	....	....
	Hartford	AHL	14	3	4	7	27	....	....	....	....	....	....	....	....	....	....	....	....	....	....	....	....	....	....
	Houston Aeros	AHL	22	7	4	11	65	....	....	....	....	....	....	....	....	....	23	2	2	4	25	....	....	....	....
	NHL Totals		**33**	**1**	**3**	**4**	**37**	**0**	**0**	**0**	**34**	**2.9**		**5**	**60.0**	**6:02**	....	....	....	....	....	....	....	....	....

• Missed entire 2001-02 season recovering from knee injury suffered in pre-season game vs. Detroit, September 21, 2001. Traded to **NY Rangers** by **Boston** for Boston's 9th round choice in 2004 Entry Draft, January 17, 2003. Traded to **Minnesota** by **NY Rangers** for Cory Larose, February 20, 2003.

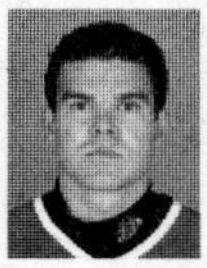

HENDERSON, Matt

(HEHN-duhr-SOHN, MAT)

Right wing. Shoots left. 6'1", 200 lbs. Born, White Bear Lake, MN, June 22, 1974.

			Regular Season														Playoffs								
Season	Club	League	GP	G	A	Pts	PIM	PP	SH	GW	S	%	+/-	TF	F%	Min	GP	G	A	Pts	PIM	PP	SH	GW	Min
1993-94	St. Paul Vulcans	USHL	48	27	24	51	....	....	....	....	....	....	....	....	....	....	....	....	....	....	....	....	....	....	....
1994-95	North Dakota	WCHA	19	1	3	4	16	....	....	....	....	....	....	....	....	....	....	....	....	....	....	....	....	....	....
1995-96	North Dakota	WCHA	36	9	10	19	34	....	....	....	....	....	....	....	....	....	2	0	1	1	0	....	....	....	....
1996-97	North Dakota	WCHA	42	14	17	31	71	....	....	....	....	....	....	....	....	....	7	5	4	9	10	....	....	....	....
1997-98	North Dakota	WCHA	38	24	14	38	74	....	....	....	....	....	....	....	....	....	5	2	2	4	4	....	....	....	....
1998-99	**Nashville**	**NHL**	**2**	**0**	**0**	**0**	**2**	**0**	**0**	**0**	**0**	**0.0**	**–1**	**0**	**0.0**	**6:23**	....	....	....	....	....	....	....	....	....
	Milwaukee	IHL	77	19	19	38	117	....	....	....	....	....	....	....	....	....	2	0	0	0	0	....	....	....	....
99-2000	Trenton Titans	ECHL	16	2	4	6	47	....	....	....	....	....	....	....	....	....	....	....	....	....	....	....	....	....	....
	Philadelphia	AHL	51	4	8	12	37	....	....	....	....	....	....	....	....	....	5	0	0	0	4	....	....	....	....
2000-01	Norfolk Admirals	AHL	78	14	24	38	80	....	....	....	....	....	....	....	....	....	9	1	1	2	16	....	....	....	....
2001-02	**Chicago**	**NHL**	**4**	**0**	**1**	**1**	**0**	**0**	**0**	**0**	**3**	**0.0**	**–1**	**0**	**0.0**	**7:08**	....	....	....	....	....	....	....	....	....
	Norfolk Admirals	AHL	74	21	28	49	90	....	....	....	....	....	....	....	....	....	4	0	0	0	6	....	....	....	....
2002-03	Norfolk Admirals	AHL	77	18	29	47	95	....	....	....	....	....	....	....	....	....	1	0	0	0	0	....	....	....	....
	NHL Totals		**6**	**0**	**1**	**1**	**2**	**0**	**0**	**0**	**3**	**0.0**		**0**	**0.0**	**6:53**	....	....	....	....	....	....	....	....	....

NCAA Championship All-Tournament Team (1997) • NCAA Championship Tournament MVP (1997)

Signed as a free agent by **Nashville**, July 14, 1998. Traded to **Philadelphia** by **Nashville** for Paul Healey, September 27, 1999. Signed as a free agent by **Chicago**, September 5, 2001.

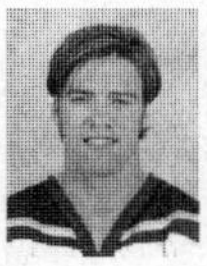

HENDRICKSON, Darby

(HEHN-drihk-SOHN, DAHR-bee) **MIN.**

Center. Shoots left. 6'1", 195 lbs. Born, Richfield, MN, August 28, 1972. Toronto's 3rd choice, 73rd overall, in 1990 Entry Draft.

			Regular Season														Playoffs								
Season	Club	League	GP	G	A	Pts	PIM	PP	SH	GW	S	%	+/-	TF	F%	Min	GP	G	A	Pts	PIM	PP	SH	GW	Min
1987-88	Richfield Spartans	Hi-School	22	12	9	21	10	....	....	....	....	....	....	....	....	....	....	....	....	....	....	....	....	....	....
1988-89	Richfield Spartans	Hi-School	22	22	20	42	12	....	....	....	....	....	....	....	....	....	....	....	....	....	....	....	....	....	....
1989-90	Richfield Spartans	Hi-School	24	23	27	50	49	....	....	....	....	....	....	....	....	....	....	....	....	....	....	....	....	....	....
1990-91	Richfield Spartans	Hi-School	27	32	29	61	....	....	....	....	....	....	....	....	....	....	....	....	....	....	....	....	....	....	....
1991-92	U. of Minnesota	WCHA	41	25	28	53	61	....	....	....	....	....	....	....	....	....	....	....	....	....	....	....	....	....	....
1992-93	U. of Minnesota	WCHA	31	12	15	27	35	....	....	....	....	....	....	....	....	....	....	....	....	....	....	....	....	....	....
1993-94	Team USA	Nat-Tm	59	12	16	28	30	....	....	....	....	....	....	....	....	....	....	....	....	....	....	....	....	....	....
	United States	Olympics	8	0	0	0	6	....	....	....	....	....	....	....	....	....	....	....	....	....	....	....	....	....	....
	Toronto	**NHL**	....	....	....	....	....	....	....	....	....	....	....	....	....	....	**2**	**0**	**0**	**0**	**0**	**0**	**0**	**0**	....
	St. John's	AHL	6	4	1	5	4	....	....	....	....	....	....	....	....	....	3	1	1	2	0	....	....	....	....
1994-95	St. John's	AHL	59	16	20	36	48	....	....	....	....	....	....	....	....	....	....	....	....	....	....	....	....	....	....
	Toronto	**NHL**	**8**	**0**	**1**	**1**	**4**	**0**	**0**	**0**	**4**	**0.0**	**0**	....	....	....	....	....	....	....	....	....	....	....	....
1995-96	**Toronto**	**NHL**	**46**	**6**	**6**	**12**	**47**	**0**	**0**	**0**	**43**	**14.0**	**–2**	....	....	....	....	....	....	....	....	....	....	....	....
	NY Islanders	**NHL**	**16**	**1**	**4**	**5**	**33**	**0**	**0**	**1**	**30**	**3.3**	**–6**	....	....	....	....	....	....	....	....	....	....	....	....
1996-97	**Toronto**	**NHL**	**64**	**11**	**6**	**17**	**47**	**0**	**1**	**0**	**105**	**10.5**	**–20**	....	....	....	....	....	....	....	....	....	....	....	....
	St. John's	AHL	12	5	4	9	21	....	....	....	....	....	....	....	....	....	....	....	....	....	....	....	....	....	....
1997-98	**Toronto**	**NHL**	**80**	**8**	**4**	**12**	**67**	**0**	**0**	**0**	**115**	**7.0**	**–20**	....	....	....	....	....	....	....	....	....	....	....	....
1998-99	**Toronto**	**NHL**	**35**	**2**	**3**	**5**	**30**	**0**	**0**	**0**	**34**	**5.9**	**–4**	**278**	**46.0**	**10:16**	....	....	....	....	....	....	....	....	....
	Vancouver	**NHL**	**27**	**2**	**2**	**4**	**22**	**1**	**0**	**0**	**36**	**5.6**	**–15**	**427**	**46.8**	**17:15**	....	....	....	....	....	....	....	....	....
99-2000	**Vancouver**	**NHL**	**40**	**5**	**4**	**9**	**14**	**0**	**1**	**1**	**39**	**12.8**	**–3**	**407**	**46.2**	**11:32**	....	....	....	....	....	....	....	....	....
	Syracuse Crunch	AHL	20	5	8	13	16	....	....	....	....	....	....	....	....	....	....	....	....	....	....	....	....	....	....
2000-01	**Minnesota**	**NHL**	**72**	**18**	**11**	**29**	**36**	**3**	**1**	**1**	**114**	**15.8**	**1**	**1119**	**45.2**	**15:50**	....	....	....	....	....	....	....	....	....
2001-02	**Minnesota**	**NHL**	**68**	**9**	**15**	**24**	**50**	**2**	**2**	**1**	**79**	**11.4**	**–22**	**1206**	**47.7**	**16:43**	....	....	....	....	....	....	....	....	....
2002-03	**Minnesota**	**NHL**	**28**	**1**	**5**	**6**	**8**	**0**	**0**	**0**	**34**	**2.9**	**–3**	**413**	**48.4**	**15:16**	**17**	**2**	**3**	**5**	**4**	**0**	**0**	**1**	**16:58**
	NHL Totals		**484**	**63**	**61**	**124**	**358**	**6**	**5**	**4**	**633**	**10.0**		**3850**	**46.7**	**14:47**	**19**	**2**	**3**	**5**	**4**	**0**	**0**	**1**	**16:58**

Minnesota High School Player of the Year (1991) • WCHA Rookie of the Year (1992)

Traded to **NY Islanders** by **Toronto** with Sean Haggerty, Kenny Jonsson and Toronto's 1st round choice (Roberto Luongo) in 1997 Entry Draft for Wendel Clark, Mathieu Schneider and D.J. Smith, March 13, 1996. Traded to **Toronto** by **NY Islanders** for Toronto's 5th round choice (Jiri Dopita) in 1998 Entry Draft, October 11, 1996. Traded to **Vancouver** by **Toronto** for Chris McAllister, February 16, 1999. Selected by **Minnesota** from **Vancouver** in Expansion Draft, June 23, 2000. • Missed majority of 2002-03 season recovering from arm injury suffered in training camp, September 24, 2002.

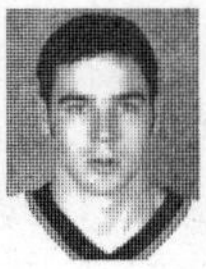

HENRY, Alex

(HEHN-ree, AL-ehx) **WSH.**

Left wing. Shoots left. 6'5", 220 lbs. Born, Elliot Lake, Ont., October 18, 1979. Edmonton's 2nd choice, 67th overall, in 1998 Entry Draft.

			Regular Season														Playoffs								
Season	Club	League	GP	G	A	Pts	PIM	PP	SH	GW	S	%	+/-	TF	F%	Min	GP	G	A	Pts	PIM	PP	SH	GW	Min
1995-96	Timmins Titans	NOHA	30	2	4	11	15	....	....	....	....	....	....	....	....	....	....	....	....	....	....	....	....	....	....
	Timmins	NOJHA	2	0	0	0	0	....	....	....	....	....	....	....	....	....	....	....	....	....	....	....	....	....	....
1996-97	London Knights	OHL	61	1	10	11	65	....	....	....	....	....	....	....	....	....	....	....	....	....	....	....	....	....	....
1997-98	London Knights	OHL	62	5	9	14	97	....	....	....	....	....	....	....	....	....	16	0	3	3	14	....	....	....	....
1998-99	London Knights	OHL	68	5	23	28	105	....	....	....	....	....	....	....	....	....	25	3	10	13	22	....	....	....	....
99-2000	Hamilton	AHL	60	1	0	1	69	....	....	....	....	....	....	....	....	....	....	....	....	....	....	....	....	....	....
2000-01	Hamilton	AHL	56	2	3	5	87	....	....	....	....	....	....	....	....	....	....	....	....	....	....	....	....	....	....
2001-02	Hamilton	AHL	69	4	8	12	143	....	....	....	....	....	....	....	....	....	15	1	2	3	16	....	....	....	....
2002-03	**Edmonton**	**NHL**	**3**	**0**	**0**	**0**	**0**	**0**	**0**	**0**	**0**	**0.0**	**–1**	**0**	**0.0**	**7:02**	....	....	....	....	....	....	....	....	....
	Washington	**NHL**	**38**	**0**	**0**	**0**	**80**	**0**	**0**	**0**	**8**	**0.0**	**–4**	**1**	**0.0**	**3:39**	....	....	....	....	....	....	....	....	....
	Portland Pirates	AHL	3	0	1	1	0	....	....	....	....	....	....	....	....	....	....	....	....	....	....	....	....	....	....
	NHL Totals		**41**	**0**	**0**	**0**	**80**	**0**	**0**	**0**	**8**	**0.0**		**1**	**0.0**	**3:54**	....	....	....	....	....	....	....	....	....

Claimed on waivers by **Washington** from **Edmonton**, October 24, 2002.

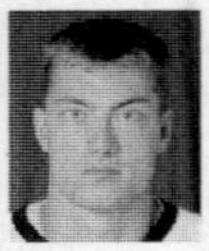

HENRY, Burke

(HEHN-ree, BUHRK) **CHI.**

Defense. Shoots left. 6'3", 206 lbs. Born, Ste. Rose, Man., January 21, 1979. NY Rangers' 3rd choice, 73rd overall, in 1997 Entry Draft.

			Regular Season														Playoffs								
Season	Club	League	GP	G	A	Pts	PIM	PP	SH	GW	S	%	+/-	TF	F%	Min	GP	G	A	Pts	PIM	PP	SH	GW	Min
1995-96	Brandon	WHL	50	6	11	17	58	....	....	....	....	....	....	....	....	....	19	0	4	4	19	....	....	....	....
1996-97	Brandon	WHL	55	6	25	31	81	....	....	....	....	....	....	....	....	....	6	1	3	4	4	....	....	....	....
1997-98	Brandon	WHL	72	18	65	83	153	....	....	....	....	....	....	....	....	....	18	3	16	19	37	....	....	....	....
1998-99	Brandon	WHL	68	18	58	76	151	....	....	....	....	....	....	....	....	....	5	1	6	7	9	....	....	....	....
99-2000	Hartford	AHL	64	3	12	15	47	....	....	....	....	....	....	....	....	....	5	0	0	0	2	....	....	....	....
2000-01	Hartford	AHL	80	8	30	38	133	....	....	....	....	....	....	....	....	....	5	0	0	0	2	....	....	....	....
2001-02	Saint John Flames	AHL	58	0	17	17	92	....	....	....	....	....	....	....	....	....	....	....	....	....	....	....	....	....	....
2002-03	Norfolk Admirals	AHL	60	6	22	28	121	....	....	....	....	....	....	....	....	....	9	1	2	3	9	....	....	....	....
	Chicago	**NHL**	**16**	**0**	**2**	**2**	**9**	**0**	**0**	**0**	**25**	**0.0**	**–13**	**0**	**0.0**	**18:32**	....	....	....	....	....	....	....	....	....
	NHL Totals		**16**	**0**	**2**	**2**	**9**	**0**	**0**	**0**	**25**	**0.0**		**0**	**0.0**	**18:32**	....	....	....	....	....	....	....	....	....

WHL East First All-Star Team (1998) • WHL East Second All-Star Team (1999)

Traded to **Calgary** by **NY Rangers** for Chris St. Croix, June 23, 2001. Signed as a free agent by **Norfolk** (AHL), October 9, 2002. Signed as a free agent by **Chicago**, December 11, 2002.

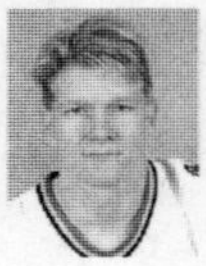

HENTUNEN, Jukka

(HEHN-too-nehn, YOO-kuh) **NSH.**

Right wing. Shoots right. 5'10", 194 lbs. Born, Joroinen, Finland, May 3, 1974. Calgary's 7th choice, 176th overall, in 2000 Entry Draft.

			Regular Season														Playoffs								
Season	Club	League	GP	G	A	Pts	PIM	PP	SH	GW	S	%	+/-	TF	F%	Min	GP	G	A	Pts	PIM	PP	SH	GW	Min
1993-94	Kiekko Warkaus	Finland-3	16	7	6	13	10	....	....	....	....	....	....	....	....	....	8	4	1	5	2	....	....	....	....
1994-95	Kiekko Warkaus	Finland-3	29	23	23	46	28	....	....	....	....	....	....	....	....	....	....	....	....	....	....	....	....	....	....
1995-96	Diskos Jyvaskyla	Finland-2	43	23	18	41	14	....	....	....	....	....	....	....	....	....	10	5	6	11	4	....	....	....	....
1996-97	Hermes Kokkola	Finland-2	35	10	13	23	43	....	....	....	....	....	....	....	....	....	3	1	0	1	0	....	....	....	....
1997-98	Hermes Kokkola	Finland-2	49	19	16	35	36	....	....	....	....	....	....	....	....	....	3	3	3	6	0	....	....	....	....
1998-99	Hermes Kokkola	Finland-2	1	0	0	0	0	....	....	....	....	....	....	....	....	....	....	....	....	....	....	....	....	....	....
	HPK Hameenlinna	Finland	41	13	21	34	32	....	....	....	....	....	....	....	....	....	8	1	4	5	12	....	....	....	....
99-2000	HPK Hameenlinna	Finland	53	17	28	45	76	....	....	....	....	....	....	....	....	....	8	4	2	6	12	....	....	....	....
2000-01	Jokerit Helsinki	Finland	56	27	28	55	24	....	....	....	....	....	....	....	....	....	5	1	0	1	4	....	....	....	....
2001-02	**Calgary**	**NHL**	**28**	**2**	**3**	**5**	**4**	**1**	**0**	**0**	**38**	**5.3**	**–9**	**0**	**0.0**	**11:09**	....	....	....	....	....	....	....	....	....
	Saint John Flames	AHL	9	3	3	6	0	....	....	....	....	....	....	....	....	....	....	....	....	....	....	....	....	....	....
	Nashville	**NHL**	**10**	**2**	**2**	**4**	**0**	**0**	**0**	**1**	**12**	**16.7**	**0**	**0**	**0.0**	**12:46**	....	....	....	....	....	....	....	....	....
2002-03	Jokerit Helsinki	Finland	48	11	11	22	28	....	....	....	....	....	....	....	....	....	10	4	2	6	0	....	....	....	....
	NHL Totals		**38**	**4**	**5**	**9**	**4**	**1**	**0**	**1**	**50**	**8.0**		**0**	**0.0**	**11:35**	....	....	....	....	....	....	....	....	....

Traded to **Nashville** by **Calgary** for a conditional choice in 2003 Entry Draft, March 17, 2002.

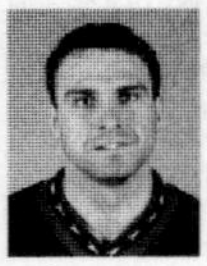

HERPERGER, Chris

(HUHR-puhr-GEHR, KRIHS) **VAN.**

Center. Shoots left. 6', 190 lbs. Born, Esterhazy, Sask., February 24, 1974. Philadelphia's 9th choice, 223rd overall, in 1992 Entry Draft.

			Regular Season														Playoffs								
Season	Club	League	GP	G	A	Pts	PIM	PP	SH	GW	S	%	+/-	TF	F%	Min	GP	G	A	Pts	PIM	PP	SH	GW	Min
1990-91	Swift Current	SMHL	STATISTICS NOT AVAILABLE																						
	Swift Current	WHL	10	0	1	1	5	....	....	....	....	....	....	....	....	....	....	....	....	....	....	....	....	....	....
1991-92	Swift Current	WHL	72	14	19	33	44	....	....	....	....	....	....	....	....	....	8	0	1	1	9	....	....	....	....
1992-93	Swift Current	WHL	20	9	7	16	31	....	....	....	....	....	....	....	....	....	....	....	....	....	....	....	....	....	....
	Seattle	WHL	46	20	11	31	30	....	....	....	....	....	....	....	....	....	5	1	1	2	6	....	....	....	....
1993-94	Seattle	WHL	71	44	51	95	110	....	....	....	....	....	....	....	....	....	9	12	10	22	12	....	....	....	....
1994-95	Seattle	WHL	59	49	52	101	106	....	....	....	....	....	....	....	....	....	4	4	0	4	6	....	....	....	....
	Hershey Bears	AHL	4	0	0	0	0	....	....	....	....	....	....	....	....	....	....	....	....	....	....	....	....	....	....
1995-96	Hershey Bears	AHL	46	8	12	20	36	....	....	....	....	....	....	....	....	....	....	....	....	....	....	....	....	....	....
	Baltimore Bandits	AHL	21	2	3	5	17	....	....	....	....	....	....	....	....	....	9	2	3	5	6	....	....	....	....
1996-97	Baltimore Bandits	AHL	67	19	22	41	88	....	....	....	....	....	....	....	....	....	3	0	0	0	0	....	....	....	....
1997-98	Team Canada	Nat-Tm	63	20	30	50	102	....	....	....	....	....	....	....	....	....	....	....	....	....	....	....	....	....	....
1998-99	Indianapolis Ice	IHL	79	19	29	48	81	....	....	....	....	....	....	....	....	....	7	0	4	4	4	....	....	....	....
99-2000	**Chicago**	**NHL**	**9**	**0**	**0**	**0**	**5**	**0**	**0**	**0**	**2**	**0.0**	**–2**	**52**	**55.8**	**7:39**	....	....	....	....	....	....	....	....	....
	Cleveland	IHL	73	22	26	48	122	....	....	....	....	....	....	....	....	....	9	3	3	6	8	....	....	....	....
2000-01	**Chicago**	**NHL**	**61**	**10**	**15**	**25**	**20**	**0**	**1**	**3**	**76**	**13.2**	**0**	**678**	**56.2**	**13:07**	....	....	....	....	....	....	....	....	....
	Norfolk Admirals	AHL	9	1	4	5	9	....	....	....	....	....	....	....	....	....	....	....	....	....	....	....	....	....	....
2001-02	**Ottawa**	**NHL**	**72**	**4**	**9**	**13**	**43**	**0**	**0**	**0**	**81**	**4.9**	**4**	**769**	**49.3**	**11:19**	....	....	....	....	....	....	....	....	....
2002-03	**Atlanta**	**NHL**	**27**	**4**	**1**	**5**	**7**	**0**	**0**	**0**	**26**	**15.4**	**–11**	**187**	**44.4**	**12:30**	....	....	....	....	....	....	....	....	....
	Chicago Wolves	AHL	7	1	1	2	14	....	....	....	....	....	....	....	....	....	....	....	....	....	....	....	....	....	....
	Manitoba Moose	AHL	15	6	6	12	12	....	....	....	....	....	....	....	....	....	....	....	....	....	....	....	....	....	....
	NHL Totals		**169**	**18**	**25**	**43**	**75**	**0**	**1**	**3**	**185**	**9.7**		**1686**	**51.7**	**11:58**	....	....	....	....	....	....	....	....	....

WHL West Second All-Star Team (1995)

Traded to **Anaheim** by **Philadelphia** with Winnipeg/Phoenix's 7th round choice (previously acquired, Anaheim selected Tony Mohagen) in 1997 Entry Draft for Bob Corkum, February 6, 1996. Signed as a free agent by **Chicago**, September 2, 1998. Signed as a free agent by **Ottawa**, July 13, 2001. Signed as a free agent by **Atlanta**, August 1, 2002. Traded to **Vancouver** by **Atlanta** with Chris Nielsen for Jeff Farkas, January 20, 2003.

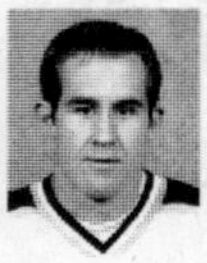

HERR, Matt

(HUHR, MAT) **BOS.**

Center. Shoots left. 6'2", 204 lbs. Born, Hackensack, NJ, May 26, 1976. Washington's 4th choice, 93rd overall, in 1994 Entry Draft.

			Regular Season														Playoffs								
Season	Club	League	GP	G	A	Pts	PIM	PP	SH	GW	S	%	+/-	TF	F%	Min	GP	G	A	Pts	PIM	PP	SH	GW	Min
1990-91	Hotchkiss High	Hi-School	26	9	5	14	....	....	....	....	....	....	....	....	....	....	....	....	....	....	....	....	....	....	....
1991-92	Hotchkiss High	Hi-School	25	17	16	33		....	....	....	....	....	....	....	....	....	....	....	....	....	....	....	....	....	....
1992-93	Hotchkiss High	Hi-School	24	48	30	78		....	....	....	....	....	....	....	....	....	....	....	....	....	....	....	....	....	....
1993-94	Hotchkiss High	Hi-School	24	28	19	47		....	....	....	....	....	....	....	....	....	....	....	....	....	....	....	....	....	....
1994-95	U. of Michigan	CCHA	37	11	8	19	51	....	....	....	....	....	....	....	....	....	3	1	0	1	4	....	....	....	....
1995-96	U. of Michigan	CCHA	40	18	13	31	55	....	....	....	....	....	....	....	....	....	7	0	4	4	0	....	....	....	....
1996-97	U. of Michigan	CCHA	43	29	23	52	67	....	....	....	....	....	....	....	....	....	6	2	2	4	8	....	....	....	....
1997-98	U. of Michigan	CCHA	31	14	17	31	62	....	....	....	....	....	....	....	....	....	....	....	....	....	....	....	....	....	....
1998-99	**Washington**	**NHL**	**30**	**2**	**2**	**4**	**8**	**1**	**0**	**0**	**40**	**5.0**	**–7**	**176**	**52.8**	**11:05**	....	....	....	....	....	....	....	....	....
	Portland Pirates	AHL	46	15	14	29	29	....	....	....	....	....	....	....	....	....	....	....	....	....	....	....	....	....	....
99-2000	Portland Pirates	AHL	77	22	21	43	51	....	....	....	....	....	....	....	....	....	4	1	1	2	4	....	....	....	....
2000-01	**Washington**	**NHL**	**22**	**2**	**3**	**5**	**17**	**0**	**0**	**1**	**20**	**10.0**	**3**	**2**	**100.0**	**8:09**	....	....	....	....	....	....	....	....	....
	Portland Pirates	AHL	40	21	13	34	58	....	....	....	....	....	....	....	....	....	....	....	....	....	....	....	....	....	....
	Philadelphia	AHL	11	2	4	6	18	....	....	....	....	....	....	....	....	....	9	2	1	3	8	....	....	....	....
2001-02	**Florida**	**NHL**	**3**	**0**	**0**	**0**	**0**	**0**	**0**	**0**	**1**	**0.0**	**–2**	**15**	**53.3**	**6:27**	....	....	....	....	....	....	....	....	....
	Hershey Bears	AHL	61	18	16	34	68	....	....	....	....	....	....	....	....	....	7	1	2	3	15	....	....	....	....
2002-03	**Boston**	**NHL**	**3**	**0**	**0**	**0**	**0**	**0**	**0**	**0**	**1**	**0.0**	**0**	**8**	**50.0**	**8:17**	....	....	....	....	....	....	....	....	....
	Providence Bruins	AHL	77	34	38	72	146	....	....	....	....	....	....	....	....	....	4	0	1	1	12	....	....	....	....
	NHL Totals		**58**	**4**	**5**	**9**	**25**	**1**	**0**	**1**	**62**	**6.5**		**201**	**53.2**	**9:35**	....	....	....	....	....	....	....	....	....

AHL First All-Star Team (2003)

Traded to **Philadelphia** by **Washington** for Dean Melanson, March 13, 2001. Signed as a free agent by **Florida**, August 21, 2001. Signed as a free agent by **Boston**, July 18, 2002.

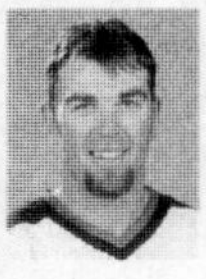

HEWARD, Jamie

(HEW-uhrd, JAY-mee)

Defense. Shoots right. 6'2", 207 lbs. Born, Regina, Sask., March 30, 1971. Pittsburgh's 1st choice, 16th overall, in 1989 Entry Draft.

			Regular Season														Playoffs								
Season	Club	League	GP	G	A	Pts	PIM	PP	SH	GW	S	%	+/-	TF	F%	Min	GP	G	A	Pts	PIM	PP	SH	GW	Min
1987-88	Regina Pats	WHL	68	10	17	27	17	....	....	....	....	....	....	....	....	....	4	1	1	2	2	....	....	....	....
1988-89	Regina Pats	WHL	52	31	28	59	29	....	....	....	....	....	....	....	....	....	....	....	....	....	....	....	....	....	....
1989-90	Regina Pats	WHL	72	14	44	58	42	....	....	....	....	....	....	....	....	....	11	2	2	4	10	....	....	....	....
1990-91	Regina Pats	WHL	71	23	61	84	41	....	....	....	....	....	....	....	....	....	8	2	9	11	6	....	....	....	....
1991-92	Muskegon	IHL	54	6	21	27	37	....	....	....	....	....	....	....	....	....	14	1	4	5	4	....	....	....	....
1992-93	Cleveland	IHL	58	9	18	27	64	....	....	....	....	....	....	....	....	....	....	....	....	....	....	....	....	....	....
1993-94	Cleveland	IHL	73	8	16	24	72	....	....	....	....	....	....	....	....	....	....	....	....	....	....	....	....	....	....
1994-95	Team Canada	Nat-Tm	51	11	35	46	32	....	....	....	....	....	....	....	....	....	....	....	....	....	....	....	....	....	....
1995-96	**Toronto**	**NHL**	**5**	**0**	**0**	**0**	**0**	**0**	**0**	**0**	**8**	**0.0**	**–1**	....	....	....	....	....	....	....	....	....	....	....	....
	St. John's	AHL	73	22	34	56	33	....	....	....	....	....	....	....	....	....	3	1	1	2	6	....	....	....	....
1996-97	**Toronto**	**NHL**	**20**	**1**	**4**	**5**	**6**	**0**	**0**	**0**	**23**	**4.3**	**–6**	....	....	....	....	....	....	....	....	....	....	....	....
	St. John's	AHL	27	8	19	27	26	....	....	....	....	....	....	....	....	....	9	1	3	4	6	....	....	....	....
1997-98	Philadelphia	AHL	72	17	48	65	54	....	....	....	....	....	....	....	....	....	20	3	16	19	10	....	....	....	....
1998-99	**Nashville**	**NHL**	**63**	**6**	**12**	**18**	**44**	**4**	**0**	**1**	**124**	**4.8**	**–24**	**0**	**0.0**	**16:12**	....	....	....	....	....	....	....	....	....
99-2000	**NY Islanders**	**NHL**	**54**	**6**	**11**	**17**	**26**	**2**	**0**	**1**	**92**	**6.5**	**–9**	**0**	**0.0**	**19:58**	....	....	....	....	....	....	....	....	....
2000-01	**Columbus**	**NHL**	**69**	**11**	**16**	**27**	**33**	**9**	**0**	**1**	**108**	**10.2**	**3**	**0**	**0.0**	**14:21**	....	....	....	....	....	....	....	....	....

			Regular Season														Playoffs								
Season	Club	League	GP	G	A	Pts	PIM	PP	SH	GW	S	%	+/-	TF	F%	Min	GP	G	A	Pts	PIM	PP	SH	GW	Min
2001-02	**Columbus**	**NHL**	**28**	**1**	**2**	**3**	**7**	**0**	**0**	**0**	**38**	**2.6**	**–9**	**1**	**100.0**	**14:04**	....	....	....	....	....	....	....	....	....
	Syracuse Crunch	AHL	14	3	10	13	6	....	....	....	....	....	....	....	....	....	10	0	4	4	6	....	....	....	....
2002-03	Geneve-Servette	Swiss	40	8	23	31	60	....	....	....	....	....	....	....	....	....	6	1	1	2	22	....	....	....	....
	NHL Totals		**239**	**25**	**45**	**70**	**116**	**15**	**0**	**3**	**393**	**6.4**		**1**	**100.0**	**16:17**	....	....	....	....	....	....	....	....	....

WHL East First All-Star Team (1991) • AHL First All-Star Team (1996, 1998) • Eddie Shore Award (Top Defenseman – AHL) (1998)

Signed as a free agent by **Toronto**, May 4, 1995. Signed as a free agent by **Philadelphia**, July 31, 1997. Signed as a free agent by **Nashville**, August 10, 1998. Signed as a free agent by **NY Islanders**, July 27, 1999. Claimed on waivers by **Columbus** from **NY Islanders**, May 26, 2000. Signed as a free agent by **Geneve-Servette** (Swiss), April 17, 2002.

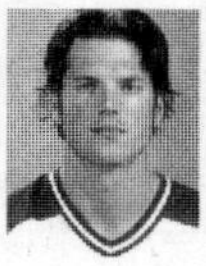

HIGGINS, Matt

(HIH-gihns, MAT)

Center. Shoots left. 6′2″, 190 lbs. Born, Calgary, Alta., October 29, 1977. Montreal's 1st choice, 18th overall, in 1996 Entry Draft.

Season	Club	League	GP	G	A	Pts	PIM	PP	SH	GW	S	%	+/-	TF	F%	Min	GP	G	A	Pts	PIM	PP	SH	GW	Min
1992-93	Vernon	BCAHA	70	53	76	129	54	....	....	....	....	....	....	....	....	....	....	....	....	....	....	....	....	....	....
1993-94	Moose Jaw	WHL	64	6	10	16	10	....	....	....	....	....	....	....	....	....	....	....	....	....	....	....	....	....	....
1994-95	Moose Jaw	WHL	72	36	34	70	26	....	....	....	....	....	....	....	....	....	10	1	2	3	2	....	....	....	....
1995-96	Moose Jaw	WHL	67	30	33	63	43	....	....	....	....	....	....	....	....	....	....	....	....	....	....	....	....	....	....
1996-97	Moose Jaw	WHL	71	33	57	90	51	....	....	....	....	....	....	....	....	....	12	3	5	8	2	....	....	....	....
1997-98	**Montreal**	**NHL**	**1**	**0**	**0**	**0**	**0**	**0**	**0**	**0**	**1**	**0.0**	**–1**	....	....	....	....	....	....	....	....	....	....	....	....
	Fredericton	AHL	50	5	22	27	12	....	....	....	....	....	....	....	....	....	4	1	2	3	2	....	....	....	....
1998-99	**Montreal**	**NHL**	**25**	**1**	**0**	**1**	**0**	**0**	**0**	**0**	**12**	**8.3**	**–2**	**108**	**45.4**	**5:41**	....	....	....	....	....	....	....	....	....
	Fredericton	AHL	11	3	4	7	6	....	....	....	....	....	....	....	....	....	5	0	2	2	0	....	....	....	....
99-2000	**Montreal**	**NHL**	**25**	**0**	**2**	**2**	**4**	**0**	**0**	**0**	**9**	**0.0**	**–6**	**145**	**48.3**	**7:57**	....	....	....	....	....	....	....	....	....
	Quebec Citadelles	AHL	29	1	15	16	21	....	....	....	....	....	....	....	....	....	....	....	....	....	....	....	....	....	....
2000-01	**Montreal**	**NHL**	**6**	**0**	**0**	**0**	**2**	**0**	**0**	**0**	**3**	**0.0**	**–2**	**40**	**47.5**	**9:27**	....	....	....	....	....	....	....	....	....
	Quebec Citadelles	AHL	66	10	18	28	18	....	....	....	....	....	....	....	....	....	8	0	1	1	4	....	....	....	....
2001-02	Bridgeport	AHL	43	13	19	32	24	....	....	....	....	....	....	....	....	....	15	1	0	1	6	....	....	....	....
2002-03	Bridgeport	AHL	45	11	12	23	30	....	....	....	....	....	....	....	....	....	2	0	0	0	2	....	....	....	....
	NHL Totals		**57**	**1**	**2**	**3**	**6**	**0**	**0**	**0**	**25**	**4.0**		**293**	**47.1**	**7:06**	....	....	....	....	....	....	....	....	....

Signed as a free agent by **Bridgeport** (AHL), December 26, 2001.

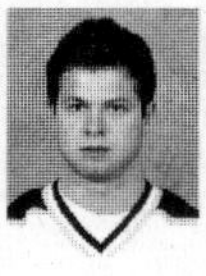

HILBERT, Andy

(HIHL-buhrt, AN-dee) **BOS.**

Center/Left wing. Shoots left. 5′11″, 190 lbs. Born, Lansing, MI, February 6, 1981. Boston's 3rd choice, 37th overall, in 2000 Entry Draft.

Season	Club	League	GP	G	A	Pts	PIM	PP	SH	GW	S	%	+/-	TF	F%	Min	GP	G	A	Pts	PIM	PP	SH	GW	Min
1997-98	U.S. National U-18	USDP	75	34	30	64	148	....	....	....	....	....	....	....	....	....	....	....	....	....	....	....	....	....	....
1998-99	U.S. National U-18	USDP	46	23	35	58	140	....	....	....	....	....	....	....	....	....	....	....	....	....	....	....	....	....	....
99-2000	U. of Michigan	CCHA	35	17	15	32	39	....	....	....	....	....	....	....	....	....	....	....	....	....	....	....	....	....	....
2000-01	U. of Michigan	CCHA	42	26	38	64	72	....	....	....	....	....	....	....	....	....	....	....	....	....	....	....	....	....	....
2001-02	**Boston**	**NHL**	**6**	**1**	**0**	**1**	**2**	**0**	**0**	**0**	**11**	**9.1**	**–2**	**4**	**50.0**	**11:34**	....	....	....	....	....	....	....	....	....
	Providence Bruins	AHL	72	26	27	53	74	....	....	....	....	....	....	....	....	....	2	0	0	0	2	....	....	....	....
2002-03	**Boston**	**NHL**	**14**	**0**	**3**	**3**	**7**	**0**	**0**	**0**	**22**	**0.0**	**–1**	**34**	**44.1**	**11:30**	....	....	....	....	....	....	....	....	....
	Providence Bruins	AHL	64	35	35	70	119	....	....	....	....	....	....	....	....	....	4	0	1	1	4	....	....	....	....
	NHL Totals		**20**	**1**	**3**	**4**	**9**	**0**	**0**	**0**	**33**	**3.0**		**38**	**44.7**	**11:31**	....	....	....	....	....	....	....	....	....

CCHA First All-Star Team (2001) • NCAA West First All-American Team (2001) • AHL All-Rookie Team (2002)

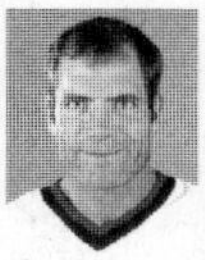

HILL, Sean

(HIHL, SHAWN) **CAR.**

Defense. Shoots right. 6′, 205 lbs. Born, Duluth, MN, February 14, 1970. Montreal's 9th choice, 167th overall, in 1988 Entry Draft.

Season	Club	League	GP	G	A	Pts	PIM	PP	SH	GW	S	%	+/-	TF	F%	Min	GP	G	A	Pts	PIM	PP	SH	GW	Min
1986-87	Lakefield Chiefs	OJHL-C	3	1	1	2	14	....	....	....	....	....	....	....	....	....	....	....	....	....	....	....	....	....	....
1987-88	East Duluth	Hi-School	24	10	17	27	....	....	....	....	....	....	....	....	....	....	....	....	....	....	....	....	....	....	....
1988-89	U. of Wisconsin	WCHA	45	2	23	25	69	....	....	....	....	....	....	....	....	....	....	....	....	....	....	....	....	....	....
1989-90	U. of Wisconsin	WCHA	42	14	39	53	78	....	....	....	....	....	....	....	....	....	....	....	....	....	....	....	....	....	....
1990-91	U. of Wisconsin	WCHA	37	19	32	51	122	....	....	....	....	....	....	....	....	....	....	....	....	....	....	....	....	....	....
	Montreal	**NHL**	....	....	....	....	....	....	....	....	....	....	....	....	....	....	**1**	**0**	**0**	**0**	**0**	**0**	**0**	**0**	....
	Fredericton	AHL	....	....	....	....	....	....	....	....	....	....	....	....	....	....	3	0	2	2	2	....	....	....	....
1991-92	Fredericton	AHL	42	7	20	27	65	....	....	....	....	....	....	....	....	....	7	1	3	4	6	....	....	....	....
	Team USA	Nat-Tm	12	4	3	7	16	....	....	....	....	....	....	....	....	....	....	....	....	....	....	....	....	....	....
	United States	Olympics	8	2	0	2	6	....	....	....	....	....	....	....	....	....	....	....	....	....	....	....	....	....	....
	Montreal	**NHL**	....	....	....	....	....	....	....	....	....	....	....	....	....	....	**4**	**1**	**0**	**1**	**2**	**0**	**0**	**0**	....
1992-93♦	**Montreal**	**NHL**	**31**	**2**	**6**	**8**	**54**	**1**	**0**	**1**	**37**	**5.4**	**–5**	....	....	....	**3**	**0**	**0**	**0**	**4**	**0**	**0**	**0**	....
	Fredericton	AHL	6	1	3	4	10	....	....	....	....	....	....	....	....	....	....	....	....	....	....	....	....	....	....
1993-94	**Anaheim**	**NHL**	**68**	**7**	**20**	**27**	**78**	**2**	**1**	**1**	**165**	**4.2**	**–12**	....	....	....	....	....	....	....	....	....	....	....	....
1994-95	**Ottawa**	**NHL**	**45**	**1**	**14**	**15**	**30**	**0**	**0**	**0**	**107**	**0.9**	**–11**	....	....	....	....	....	....	....	....	....	....	....	....
1995-96	**Ottawa**	**NHL**	**80**	**7**	**14**	**21**	**94**	**2**	**0**	**2**	**157**	**4.5**	**–26**	....	....	....	....	....	....	....	....	....	....	....	....
1996-97	**Ottawa**	**NHL**	**5**	**0**	**0**	**0**	**4**	**0**	**0**	**0**	**9**	**0.0**	**1**	....	....	....	....	....	....	....	....	....	....	....	....
1997-98	**Ottawa**	**NHL**	**13**	**1**	**1**	**2**	**6**	**0**	**0**	**0**	**16**	**6.3**	**–3**	....	....	....	....	....	....	....	....	....	....	....	....
	Carolina	**NHL**	**42**	**0**	**5**	**5**	**48**	**0**	**0**	**0**	**37**	**0.0**	**–2**	....	....	....	....	....	....	....	....	....	....	....	....
1998-99	**Carolina**	**NHL**	**54**	**0**	**10**	**10**	**48**	**0**	**0**	**0**	**44**	**0.0**	**9**	**0**	**0.0**	**19:02**	....	....	....	....	....	....	....	....	....
99-2000	**Carolina**	**NHL**	**62**	**13**	**31**	**44**	**59**	**8**	**0**	**2**	**150**	**8.7**	**3**	**1**	**0.0**	**24:31**	....	....	....	....	....	....	....	....	....
2000-01	**St. Louis**	**NHL**	**48**	**1**	**10**	**11**	**51**	**0**	**0**	**0**	**47**	**2.1**	**5**	**1**	**0.0**	**17:23**	**15**	**0**	**1**	**1**	**12**	**0**	**0**	**0**	**13:46**
2001-02	**St. Louis**	**NHL**	**23**	**0**	**3**	**3**	**28**	**0**	**0**	**0**	**29**	**0.0**	**1**	**0**	**0.0**	**15:56**	....	....	....	....	....	....	....	....	....
	Carolina	**NHL**	**49**	**7**	**23**	**30**	**61**	**4**	**0**	**2**	**116**	**6.0**	**–1**	**1**	**0.0**	**23:58**	**23**	**4**	**4**	**8**	**20**	**4**	**0**	**1**	**25:55**
2002-03	**Carolina**	**NHL**	**82**	**5**	**24**	**29**	**141**	**1**	**0**	**0**	**188**	**2.7**	**4**	**1**	**0.0**	**24:21**	....	....	....	....	....	....	....	....	....
	NHL Totals		**602**	**44**	**161**	**205**	**702**	**18**	**1**	**8**	**1102**	**4.0**		**4**	**0.0**	**21:46**	**46**	**5**	**5**	**10**	**38**	**4**	**0**	**1**	**21:07**

WCHA Second All-Star Team (1990, 1991) • NCAA West Second All-American Team (1991)

Claimed by **Anaheim** from **Montreal** in Expansion Draft, June 24, 1993. Traded to **Ottawa** by **Anaheim** with Anaheim's 9th round choice (Frederic Cassivi) in 1994 Entry Draft for Ottawa's 3rd round choice (later traded to Tampa Bay – Tampa Bay selected Vadim Epanchintsev) in 1994 Entry Draft, June 29, 1994. • Missed remainder of 1996-97 season recovering from knee injury suffered in game vs. New Jersey, October 18, 1996. Traded to **Carolina** by **Ottawa** for Chris Murray, November 18, 1997. Signed as a free agent by **St. Louis**, July 1, 2000. Traded to **Carolina** by **St. Louis** for Steve Halko and Carolina's 4th round choice (later traded to Atlanta – Atlanta selected Lane Manson) in 2002 Entry Draft, December 5, 2001.

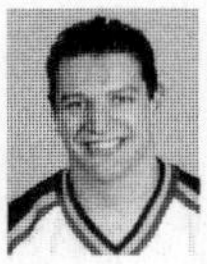

HINOTE, Dan

(HIGH-noht, DAN) **COL.**

Right wing. Shoots right. 6′, 190 lbs. Born, Leesburg, FL, January 30, 1977. Colorado's 9th choice, 167th overall, in 1996 Entry Draft.

Season	Club	League	GP	G	A	Pts	PIM	PP	SH	GW	S	%	+/-	TF	F%	Min	GP	G	A	Pts	PIM	PP	SH	GW	Min
1993-94	Elk River Elks	Hi-School	STATISTICS NOT AVAILABLE																						
1994-95	Army	NCAA	33	20	24	44	20	....	....	....	....	....	....	....	....	....	....	....	....	....	....	....	....	....	....
1995-96	Army	NCAA	34	21	24	45	22	....	....	....	....	....	....	....	....	....	....	....	....	....	....	....	....	....	....
1996-97	Oshawa Generals	OHL	60	15	13	28	58	....	....	....	....	....	....	....	....	....	18	4	5	9	8	....	....	....	....
1997-98	Oshawa Generals	OHL	35	12	15	27	39	....	....	....	....	....	....	....	....	....	5	2	2	4	7	....	....	....	....
	Hershey Bears	AHL	24	1	4	5	25	....	....	....	....	....	....	....	....	....	....	....	....	....	....	....	....	....	....
1998-99	Hershey Bears	AHL	65	4	16	20	95	....	....	....	....	....	....	....	....	....	5	3	1	4	6	....	....	....	....
99-2000	**Colorado**	**NHL**	**27**	**1**	**3**	**4**	**10**	**0**	**0**	**0**	**14**	**7.1**	**0**	**132**	**51.5**	**7:51**	....	....	....	....	....	....	....	....	....
	Hershey Bears	AHL	55	28	31	59	96	....	....	....	....	....	....	....	....	....	14	4	5	9	19	....	....	....	....
2000-01♦	**Colorado**	**NHL**	**76**	**5**	**10**	**15**	**51**	**1**	**0**	**1**	**69**	**7.2**	**1**	**506**	**49.8**	**10:21**	**23**	**2**	**4**	**6**	**21**	**0**	**0**	**0**	**8:22**
2001-02	**Colorado**	**NHL**	**58**	**6**	**6**	**12**	**39**	**0**	**1**	**3**	**75**	**8.0**	**8**	**267**	**51.3**	**12:27**	**19**	**1**	**2**	**3**	**9**	**0**	**0**	**0**	**10:46**
2002-03	**Colorado**	**NHL**	**60**	**6**	**4**	**10**	**49**	**0**	**0**	**3**	**65**	**9.2**	**4**	**218**	**46.8**	**10:36**	**7**	**1**	**2**	**3**	**2**	**0**	**0**	**0**	**14:19**
	NHL Totals		**221**	**18**	**23**	**41**	**149**	**1**	**1**	**7**	**223**	**8.1**		**1123**	**49.8**	**10:40**	**49**	**4**	**8**	**12**	**32**	**0**	**0**	**0**	**10:08**

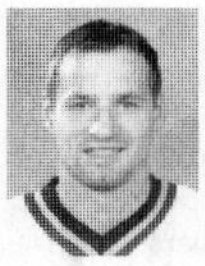

HLAVAC, Jan

(huh-LAH-vahch, YAHN)

Left wing. Shoots left. 6′, 185 lbs. Born, Prague, Czech., September 20, 1976. NY Islanders' 2nd choice, 28th overall, in 1995 Entry Draft.

Season	Club	League	GP	G	A	Pts	PIM	PP	SH	GW	S	%	+/-	TF	F%	Min	GP	G	A	Pts	PIM	PP	SH	GW	Min
1993-94	Sparta Praha Jr.	Czech-Jr.	27	12	15	27	....	....	....	....	....	....	....	....	....	....	....	....	....	....	....	....	....	....	....
	HC Sparta Praha	Czech	9	1	1	2	....	....	....	....	....	....	....	....	....	....	....	....	....	....	....	....	....	....	....
1994-95	HC Sparta Praha	Czech	38	7	6	13	18	....	....	....	....	....	....	....	....	....	5	0	2	2	0	....	....	....	....
1995-96	HC Sparta Praha	Czech	34	8	5	13	....	....	....	....	....	....	....	....	....	....	12	1	2	3	....	....	....	....	....
1996-97	HC Sparta Praha	Czech	38	8	13	21	24	....	....	....	....	....	....	....	....	....	10	5	2	7	2	....	....	....	....
	HC Sparta Praha	EuroHL	3	4	0	4	6	....	....	....	....	....	....	....	....	....	....	....	....	....	....	....	....	....	....
1997-98	HC Sparta Praha	Czech	48	17	30	47	40	....	....	....	....	....	....	....	....	....	5	1	0	1	2	....	....	....	....
	HC Sparta Praha	EuroHL	5	0	3	3	4	....	....	....	....	....	....	....	....	....	....	....	....	....	....	....	....	....	....
1998-99	HC Sparta Praha	Czech	49	*33	20	53	52	....	....	....	....	....	....	....	....	....	6	1	3	4	....	....	....	....	....
	HC Sparta Praha	EuroHL	5	4	2	6	0	....	....	....	....	....	....	....	....	....	1	1	1	2	0	....	....	....	....

Season	Club	League	GP	G	A	Pts	PIM	PP	SH	GW	S	%	+/-	TF	F%	Min	GP	G	A	Pts	PIM	PP	SH	GW	Min
								Regular Season									Playoffs								
99-2000	**NY Rangers**	**NHL**	**67**	**19**	**23**	**42**	**16**	**6**	**0**	**2**	**134**	**14.2**	**3**	**6**	**33.3**	**15:09**	....	....	....	....	....	....	....	....	....
	Hartford	AHL	3	1	0	1	0	....	....	....	....	....	....	....	....	....	....	....	....	....	....	....	....	....	....
2000-01	**NY Rangers**	**NHL**	**79**	**28**	**36**	**64**	**20**	**5**	**0**	**6**	**195**	**14.4**	**3**	**0**	**0.0**	**16:38**	....	....	....	....	....	....	....	....	....
2001-02	**Philadelphia**	**NHL**	**31**	**7**	**3**	**10**	**8**	**0**	**0**	**1**	**62**	**11.3**	**5**	**0**	**0.0**	**12:36**	....	....	....	....	....	....	....	....	....
	Vancouver	**NHL**	**46**	**9**	**12**	**21**	**10**	**1**	**0**	**2**	**70**	**12.9**	**4**	**2**	**100.0**	**14:46**	**5**	**0**	**1**	**1**	**0**	**0**	**0**	**0**	**9:38**
2002-03	**Vancouver**	**NHL**	**9**	**1**	**1**	**2**	**6**	**0**	**0**	**0**	**7**	**14.3**	**–1**	**0**	**0.0**	**10:51**	....	....	....	....	....	....	....	....	....
	Carolina	**NHL**	**52**	**9**	**15**	**24**	**22**	**6**	**0**	**1**	**116**	**7.8**	**–9**	**21**	**38.1**	**17:10**	....	....	....	....	....	....	....	....	....
	NHL Totals		**284**	**73**	**90**	**163**	**82**	**18**	**0**	**12**	**584**	**12.5**		**29**	**41.4**	**15:28**	**5**	**0**	**1**	**1**	**0**	**0**	**0**	**0**	**9:38**

Traded to **Calgary** by **NY Islanders** for Jorgen Jonsson, July 14, 1998. Rights traded to **NY Rangers** by **Calgary** with Calgary's 1st (Jamie Lundmark) and 3rd (later traded back to Calgary – Calgary selected Craig Andersson) round choices in 1999 Entry Draft for Marc Savard and NY Rangers' 1st round choice (Oleg Saprykin) in 1999 Entry Draft, June 26, 1999. Traded to **Philadelphia** by **NY Rangers** with Kim Johnsson, Pavel Brendl and NY Rangers' 3rd round choice (Stefan Ruzicka) in 2003 Entry Draft for Eric Lindros, August 20, 2001. Traded to **Vancouver** by **Philadelphia** with Tampa Bay's 3rd round choice (previously acquired, Vancouver selected Brett Skinner) in 2002 Entry Draft for Donald Brashear and Vancouver's 6th round choice (later traded to Columbus – Columbus selected Jaroslav Balastik) in 2002 Entry Draft, December 17, 2001. Traded to **Carolina** by **Vancouver** with Harold Druken for Darren Langdon and Marek Malik, November 1, 2002.

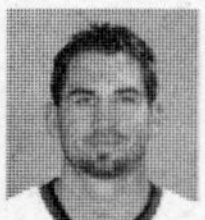

HNIDY, Shane (NIGH-dee, SHAYN) OTT.

Defense. Shoots right. 6'2", 204 lbs. Born, Neepawa, Man., November 8, 1975. Buffalo's 7th choice, 173rd overall, in 1994 Entry Draft.

Season	Club	League	GP	G	A	Pts	PIM	PP	SH	GW	S	%	+/-	TF	F%	Min	GP	G	A	Pts	PIM	PP	SH	GW	Min
1990-91	Yellowhead Pass	MMHL	36	9	11	20	92	....	....	....	....	....	....	....	....	....	....	....	....	....	....	....	....	....	....
1991-92	Swift Current	WHL	56	1	3	4	11	....	....	....	....	....	....	....	....	....	....	....	....	....	....	....	....	....	....
1992-93	Swift Current	WHL	45	5	12	17	62	....	....	....	....	....	....	....	....	....	4	0	0	0	0	....	....	....	....
	Prince Albert	WHL	27	2	10	12	43	....	....	....	....	....	....	....	....	....	....	....	....	....	....	....	....	....	....
1993-94	Prince Albert	WHL	69	7	26	33	113	....	....	....	....	....	....	....	....	....	....	....	....	....	....	....	....	....	....
1994-95	Prince Albert	WHL	72	5	29	34	169	....	....	....	....	....	....	....	....	....	15	4	7	11	29	....	....	....	....
1995-96	Prince Albert	WHL	58	11	42	53	100	....	....	....	....	....	....	....	....	....	18	4	11	15	34	....	....	....	....
1996-97	Baton Rouge	ECHL	21	3	10	13	50	....	....	....	....	....	....	....	....	....	....	....	....	....	....	....	....	....	....
	Saint John Flames	AHL	44	2	12	14	112	....	....	....	....	....	....	....	....	....	....	....	....	....	....	....	....	....	....
1997-98	Grand Rapids	IHL	77	6	12	18	210	....	....	....	....	....	....	....	....	....	3	0	2	2	23	....	....	....	....
1998-99	Adirondack	AHL	68	9	20	29	121	....	....	....	....	....	....	....	....	....	3	0	1	1	0	....	....	....	....
99-2000	Cincinnati	AHL	68	9	19	28	153	....	....	....	....	....	....	....	....	....	....	....	....	....	....	....	....	....	....
2000-01	**Ottawa**	**NHL**	**52**	**3**	**2**	**5**	**84**	**0**	**0**	**1**	**47**	**6.4**	**8**	**0**	**0.0**	**13:05**	**1**	**0**	**0**	**0**	**0**	**0**	**0**	**0**	**13:23**
	Grand Rapids	IHL	2	0	0	0	2	....	....	....	....	....	....	....	....	....	....	....	....	....	....	....	....	....	....
2001-02	**Ottawa**	**NHL**	**33**	**1**	**1**	**2**	**57**	**0**	**0**	**0**	**34**	**2.9**	**–10**	**0**	**0.0**	**16:56**	**12**	**1**	**1**	**2**	**12**	**0**	**0**	**0**	**16:00**
2002-03	**Ottawa**	**NHL**	**67**	**0**	**8**	**8**	**130**	**0**	**0**	**0**	**58**	**0.0**	**–1**	**1**	**0.0**	**13:55**	**1**	**0**	**0**	**0**	**0**	**0**	**0**	**0**	**9:38**
	NHL Totals		**152**	**4**	**11**	**15**	**271**	**0**	**0**	**1**	**139**	**2.9**		**1**	**0.0**	**14:17**	**14**	**1**	**1**	**2**	**12**	**0**	**0**	**0**	**15:22**

Signed as a free agent by **Detroit**, August 6, 1998. Traded to **Ottawa** by **Detroit** for Ottawa's 8th round choice (Todd Jackson) in 2000 Entry Draft, June 25, 2000. • Missed majority of 2001-02 season recovering from ankle injury suffered in game vs. Boston, December 26, 2001.

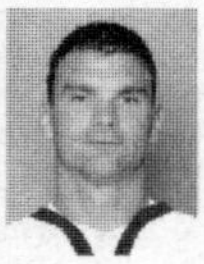

HOGLUND, Jonas (HOHG-lund, YOH-nuhs)

Left wing. Shoots right. 6'3", 215 lbs. Born, Hammaro, Sweden, August 29, 1972. Calgary's 11th choice, 222nd overall, in 1992 Entry Draft.

Season	Club	League	GP	G	A	Pts	PIM	PP	SH	GW	S	%	+/-	TF	F%	Min	GP	G	A	Pts	PIM	PP	SH	GW	Min
1990-91	Farjestad	Sweden	40	5	5	10	4	....	....	....	....	....	....	....	....	....	8	1	0	1	0	....	....	....	....
1991-92	Farjestad	Sweden	40	14	11	25	6	....	....	....	....	....	....	....	....	....	6	2	4	6	2	....	....	....	....
1992-93	Farjestad	Sweden	40	13	13	26	14	....	....	....	....	....	....	....	....	....	3	1	0	1	0	....	....	....	....
1993-94	Farjestad	Sweden	22	7	2	9	10	....	....	....	....	....	....	....	....	....	....	....	....	....	....	....	....	....	....
1994-95	Farjestad	Sweden	40	14	12	26	16	....	....	....	....	....	....	....	....	....	4	3	2	5	0	....	....	....	....
1995-96	Farjestad	Sweden	40	*32	11	43	18	....	....	....	....	....	....	....	....	....	8	2	1	3	6	....	....	....	....
1996-97	**Calgary**	**NHL**	**68**	**19**	**16**	**35**	**12**	**3**	**0**	**6**	**189**	**10.1**	**–4**	....	....	....	....	....	....	....	....	....	....	....	....
1997-98	**Calgary**	**NHL**	**50**	**6**	**8**	**14**	**16**	**0**	**0**	**0**	**124**	**4.8**	**–9**	....	....	....	....	....	....	....	....	....	....	....	....
	Montreal	**NHL**	**28**	**6**	**5**	**11**	**6**	**4**	**0**	**0**	**62**	**9.7**	**2**	....	....	....	**10**	**2**	**0**	**2**	**0**	**0**	**0**	**0**	....
1998-99	**Montreal**	**NHL**	**74**	**8**	**10**	**18**	**16**	**1**	**0**	**0**	**122**	**6.6**	**–5**	**17**	**29.4**	**11:50**	....	....	....	....	....	....	....	....	....
99-2000	**Toronto**	**NHL**	**82**	**29**	**27**	**56**	**10**	**9**	**1**	**3**	**215**	**13.5**	**–2**	**4**	**50.0**	**17:10**	**12**	**2**	**4**	**6**	**2**	**0**	**0**	**0**	**17:33**
2000-01	**Toronto**	**NHL**	**82**	**23**	**26**	**49**	**14**	**5**	**0**	**5**	**196**	**11.7**	**1**	**4**	**50.0**	**15:08**	**10**	**0**	**0**	**0**	**4**	**0**	**0**	**0**	**12:22**
2001-02	**Toronto**	**NHL**	**82**	**13**	**34**	**47**	**26**	**1**	**1**	**4**	**199**	**6.5**	**11**	**1**	**0.0**	**15:34**	**20**	**4**	**6**	**10**	**2**	**3**	**0**	**1**	**15:08**
2002-03	**Toronto**	**NHL**	**79**	**13**	**19**	**32**	**12**	**2**	**0**	**3**	**157**	**8.3**	**2**	**3**	**33.3**	**12:47**	**7**	**0**	**1**	**1**	**0**	**0**	**0**	**0**	**14:15**
	NHL Totals		**545**	**117**	**145**	**262**	**112**	**25**	**2**	**21**	**1264**	**9.3**		**29**	**34.5**	**14:34**	**59**	**8**	**11**	**19**	**8**	**3**	**0**	**1**	**15:02**

Traded to **Montreal** by **Calgary** with Zarley Zalapski for Valeri Bure and Montreal's 4th round choice (Shaun Sutter) in 1998 Entry Draft, February 1, 1998. Signed as a free agent by **Toronto**, July 13, 1999.

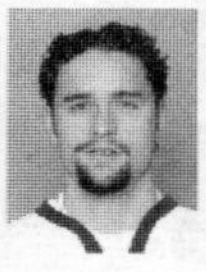

HOLDEN, Josh (HOHL-dehn, JAWSH) TOR.

Center. Shoots left. 6', 190 lbs. Born, Calgary, Alta., January 18, 1978. Vancouver's 1st choice, 12th overall, in 1996 Entry Draft.

Season	Club	League	GP	G	A	Pts	PIM	PP	SH	GW	S	%	+/-	TF	F%	Min	GP	G	A	Pts	PIM	PP	SH	GW	Min
1993-94	Calgary Buffaloes	AMHL	34	14	15	29	82	....	....	....	....	....	....	....	....	....	....	....	....	....	....	....	....	....	....
1994-95	Regina Pats	WHL	62	20	23	43	45	....	....	....	....	....	....	....	....	....	4	3	1	4	0	....	....	....	....
1995-96	Regina Pats	WHL	70	57	55	112	105	....	....	....	....	....	....	....	....	....	11	4	5	9	23	....	....	....	....
1996-97	Regina Pats	WHL	58	49	49	98	148	....	....	....	....	....	....	....	....	....	5	3	2	5	10	....	....	....	....
1997-98	Regina Pats	WHL	56	41	58	99	134	....	....	....	....	....	....	....	....	....	2	2	2	4	10	....	....	....	....
1998-99	**Vancouver**	**NHL**	**30**	**2**	**4**	**6**	**10**	**1**	**0**	**0**	**44**	**4.5**	**–10**	**269**	**39.0**	**12:44**	....	....	....	....	....	....	....	....	....
	Syracuse Crunch	AHL	38	14	15	29	48	....	....	....	....	....	....	....	....	....	....	....	....	....	....	....	....	....	....
99-2000	**Vancouver**	**NHL**	**6**	**1**	**5**	**6**	**2**	**0**	**0**	**0**	**5**	**20.0**	**2**	**42**	**42.9**	**10:25**	....	....	....	....	....	....	....	....	....
	Syracuse Crunch	AHL	45	19	32	51	113	....	....	....	....	....	....	....	....	....	4	1	0	1	10	....	....	....	....
2000-01	**Vancouver**	**NHL**	**10**	**1**	**0**	**1**	**0**	**0**	**0**	**0**	**12**	**8.3**	**0**	**85**	**35.3**	**9:27**	....	....	....	....	....	....	....	....	....
	Kansas City	IHL	60	27	26	53	136	....	....	....	....	....	....	....	....	....	....	....	....	....	....	....	....	....	....
2001-02	**Carolina**	**NHL**	**8**	**0**	**0**	**0**	**2**	**0**	**0**	**0**	**3**	**0.0**	**0**	**41**	**41.5**	**5:17**	....	....	....	....	....	....	....	....	....
	Manitoba Moose	AHL	68	16	17	33	187	....	....	....	....	....	....	....	....	....	7	1	1	2	4	....	....	....	....
2002-03	**Toronto**	**NHL**	**5**	**1**	**0**	**1**	**2**	**0**	**0**	**0**	**6**	**16.7**	**–2**	**0**	**0.0**	**8:06**	....	....	....	....	....	....	....	....	....
	St. John's	AHL	65	24	29	53	123	....	....	....	....	....	....	....	....	....	....	....	....	....	....	....	....	....	....
	NHL Totals		**59**	**5**	**9**	**14**	**16**	**1**	**0**	**0**	**70**	**7.1**		**437**	**38.9**	**10:32**	....	....	....	....	....	....	....	....	....

WHL East Second All-Star Team (1998)

Claimed by **Carolina** from **Vancouver** in Waiver Draft, September 28, 2001. Claimed on waivers by **Vancouver** from **Carolina**, October 25, 2001. Traded to **Toronto** by **Vancouver** for Jeff Farkas, June 23, 2002.

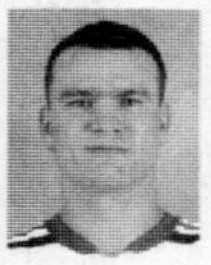

HOLIK, Bobby (HOH-leek, BAWB-ee) NYR

Center. Shoots right. 6'4", 230 lbs. Born, Jihlava, Czech., January 1, 1971. Hartford's 1st choice, 10th overall, in 1989 Entry Draft.

Season	Club	League	GP	G	A	Pts	PIM	PP	SH	GW	S	%	+/-	TF	F%	Min	GP	G	A	Pts	PIM	PP	SH	GW	Min
1987-88	Dukla Jihlava	Czech	31	5	9	14	16	....	....	....	....	....	....	....	....	....	....	....	....	....	....	....	....	....	....
1988-89	Dukla Jihlava	Czech	24	7	10	17	32	....	....	....	....	....	....	....	....	....	....	....	....	....	....	....	....	....	....
1989-90	Dukla Jihlava	Czech	42	15	26	41	....	....	....	....	....	....	....	....	....	....	....	....	....	....	....	....	....	....	....
1990-91	**Hartford**	**NHL**	**78**	**21**	**22**	**43**	**113**	**8**	**0**	**3**	**173**	**12.1**	**–3**	....	....	....	**6**	**0**	**0**	**0**	**7**	**0**	**0**	**0**	....
1991-92	**Hartford**	**NHL**	**76**	**21**	**24**	**45**	**44**	**1**	**0**	**2**	**207**	**10.1**	**4**	....	....	....	**7**	**0**	**1**	**1**	**6**	**0**	**0**	**0**	....
1992-93	**New Jersey**	**NHL**	**61**	**20**	**19**	**39**	**76**	**7**	**0**	**4**	**180**	**11.1**	**–6**	....	....	....	**5**	**1**	**1**	**2**	**6**	**0**	**0**	**0**	....
	Utica Devils	AHL	1	0	0	0	2	....	....	....	....	....	....	....	....	....	....	....	....	....	....	....	....	....	....
1993-94	**New Jersey**	**NHL**	**70**	**13**	**20**	**33**	**72**	**2**	**0**	**3**	**130**	**10.0**	**28**	....	....	....	**20**	**0**	**3**	**3**	**6**	**0**	**0**	**0**	....
1994-95♦	**New Jersey**	**NHL**	**48**	**10**	**10**	**20**	**18**	**0**	**0**	**2**	**84**	**11.9**	**9**	....	....	....	**20**	**4**	**4**	**8**	**22**	**2**	**0**	**1**	....
1995-96	**New Jersey**	**NHL**	**63**	**13**	**17**	**30**	**58**	**1**	**0**	**1**	**157**	**8.3**	**9**	....	....	....	....	....	....	....	....	....	....	....	....
1996-97	**New Jersey**	**NHL**	**82**	**23**	**39**	**62**	**54**	**5**	**0**	**6**	**192**	**12.0**	**24**	....	....	....	**10**	**2**	**3**	**5**	**4**	**1**	**0**	**0**	....
1997-98	**New Jersey**	**NHL**	**82**	**29**	**36**	**65**	**100**	**8**	**0**	**8**	**238**	**12.2**	**23**	....	....	....	**5**	**0**	**0**	**0**	**8**	**0**	**0**	**0**	....
1998-99	**New Jersey**	**NHL**	**78**	**27**	**37**	**64**	**119**	**5**	**0**	**8**	**253**	**10.7**	**16**	**1350**	**53.6**	**17:34**	**7**	**0**	**7**	**7**	**6**	**0**	**0**	**0**	**18:14**
99-2000♦	**New Jersey**	**NHL**	**79**	**23**	**23**	**46**	**106**	**7**	**0**	**4**	**257**	**8.9**	**7**	**1390**	**55.6**	**16:53**	**23**	**3**	**7**	**10**	**14**	**0**	**0**	**1**	**17:29**
2000-01	**New Jersey**	**NHL**	**80**	**15**	**35**	**50**	**97**	**3**	**0**	**3**	**206**	**7.3**	**19**	**1365**	**56.0**	**15:49**	**25**	**6**	**10**	**16**	**37**	**1**	**0**	**3**	**16:05**
2001-02	**New Jersey**	**NHL**	**81**	**25**	**29**	**54**	**97**	**6**	**0**	**3**	**270**	**9.3**	**7**	**1594**	**54.5**	**17:42**	**6**	**4**	**1**	**5**	**2**	**1**	**0**	**0**	**17:53**
2002-03	**NY Rangers**	**NHL**	**64**	**16**	**19**	**35**	**52**	**3**	**0**	**2**	**213**	**7.5**	**–1**	**1390**	**58.2**	**18:07**	....	....	....	....	....	....	....	....	....
	NHL Totals		**942**	**256**	**330**	**586**	**1006**	**56**	**0**	**49**	**2560**	**10.0**		**7089**	**55.6**	**17:11**	**134**	**20**	**37**	**57**	**118**	**5**	**0**	**5**	**17:02**

Played in NHL All-Star Game (1998, 1999)

Traded to **New Jersey** by **Hartford** with Hartford's 2nd round choice (Jay Pandolfo) in 1993 Entry Draft for Sean Burke and Eric Weinrich, August 28, 1992. Signed as a free agent by **NY Rangers**, July 1, 2002.

			Regular Season														Playoffs								
Season	Club	League	GP	G	A	Pts	PIM	PP	SH	GW	S	%	+/-	TF	F%	Min	GP	G	A	Pts	PIM	PP	SH	GW	Min

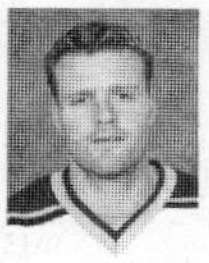

HOLLAND, Jason

(HAWL-land, JAY-suhn) **L.A.**

Defense. Shoots right. 6'3", 219 lbs. Born, Morinville, Alta., April 30, 1976. NY Islanders' 2nd choice, 38th overall, in 1994 Entry Draft.

Season	Club	League	GP	G	A	Pts	PIM	PP	SH	GW	S	%	+/-	TF	F%	Min	GP	G	A	Pts	PIM	PP	SH	GW	Min
1991-92	St. Albert Raiders	AMHL	38	9	29	38	94																		
1992-93	St. Albert Raiders	AMHL	31	11	25	36	36																		
	Kamloops Blazers	WHL	4	0	0	0	2																		
1993-94	Kamloops Blazers	WHL	59	14	15	29	80										18	2	3	5	4				
1994-95	Kamloops Blazers	WHL	71	9	32	41	65										21	2	7	9	9				
1995-96	Kamloops Blazers	WHL	63	24	33	57	98										16	4	9	13	22				
1996-97	**NY Islanders**	**NHL**	**4**	**1**	**0**	**1**	**0**	**0**	**0**	**0**	**3**	**33.3**	**1**												
	Kentucky	AHL	72	14	25	39	46										4	0	2	2	0				
1997-98	**NY Islanders**	**NHL**	**8**	**0**	**0**	**0**	**4**	**0**	**0**	**0**	**6**	**0.0**	**–4**												
	Kentucky	AHL	50	10	16	26	29																		
	Rochester	AHL	9	0	4	4	10										4	0	3	3	4				
1998-99	**Buffalo**	**NHL**	**3**	**0**	**0**	**0**	**8**	**0**	**0**	**0**	**2**	**0.0**	**–1**	**0**	**0.0**	**10:58**									
	Rochester	AHL	74	4	25	29	36										20	2	5	7	8				
99-2000	**Buffalo**	**NHL**	**9**	**0**	**1**	**1**	**0**	**0**	**0**	**0**	**8**	**0.0**	**0**	**0**	**0.0**	**15:31**	**1**	**0**	**0**	**0**	**0**	**0**	**0**	**0**	**15:41**
	Rochester	AHL	54	3	15	18	24										12	1	0	1	2				
2000-01	Rochester	AHL	63	4	19	23	45										4	1	0	1	0				
2001-02	**Los Angeles**	**NHL**	**3**	**0**	**0**	**0**	**0**	**0**	**0**	**0**	**1**	**0.0**	**–1**	**0**	**0.0**	**15:50**									
	Manchester	AHL	65	9	18	27	39										5	1	0	1	5				
2002-03	**Los Angeles**	**NHL**	**2**	**0**	**1**	**1**	**0**	**0**	**0**	**0**	**0**	**0.0**	**1**	**0**	**0.0**	**13:31**									
	Manchester	AHL	67	4	27	31	53										3	0	0	0	0				
	NHL Totals		**29**	**1**	**2**	**3**	**12**	**0**	**0**	**0**	**20**	**5.0**		**0**	**0.0**	**14:32**	**1**	**0**	**0**	**0**	**0**	**0**	**0**	**0**	**15:41**

Warwick Trophy (MVP – AMHL) (1993) • WHL West First All-Star Team (1996)

Traded to **Buffalo** by **NY Islanders** with Paul Kruse for Jason Dawe, March 24, 1998. Signed as a free agent by **Los Angeles**, August 23, 2001.

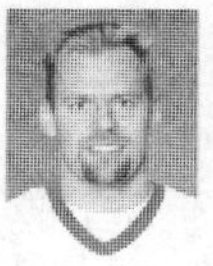

HOLMSTROM, Tomas

(HOHLM-struhm, TAW-mas) **DET.**

Left wing. Shoots left. 6', 200 lbs. Born, Pitea, Sweden, January 23, 1973. Detroit's 9th choice, 257th overall, in 1994 Entry Draft.

Season	Club	League	GP	G	A	Pts	PIM	PP	SH	GW	S	%	+/-	TF	F%	Min	GP	G	A	Pts	PIM	PP	SH	GW	Min
1989-90	Pitea HC	Swede-2	9	1	0	1	4																		
1990-91	Pitea HC	Swede-2	26	5	4	9	16																		
1991-92	Pitea HC	Swede-2	31	15	12	27	44																		
1992-93	Pitea HC	Swede-2	32	17	15	32	30																		
1993-94	Bodens IK	Swede-2	34	23	16	39	86										9	3	3	6	24				
1994-95	Lulea HF	Sweden	40	14	14	28	56										8	1	2	3	20				
1995-96	Lulea HF	Sweden	34	12	11	23	78										11	6	2	8	22				
1996-97♦	**Detroit**	**NHL**	**47**	**6**	**3**	**9**	**33**	**3**	**0**	**0**	**53**	**11.3**	**–10**				**1**	**0**	**0**	**0**	**0**	**0**	**0**	**0**	
	Adirondack	AHL	6	3	1	4	7																		
1997-98♦	**Detroit**	**NHL**	**57**	**5**	**17**	**22**	**44**	**1**	**0**	**1**	**48**	**10.4**	**6**				**22**	**7**	**12**	**19**	**16**	**2**	**0**	**0**	
1998-99	**Detroit**	**NHL**	**82**	**13**	**21**	**34**	**69**	**5**	**0**	**4**	**100**	**13.0**	**–11**	**0**	**0.0**	**12:22**	**10**	**4**	**3**	**7**	**4**	**2**	**0**	**1**	**12:32**
99-2000	**Detroit**	**NHL**	**72**	**13**	**22**	**35**	**43**	**4**	**0**	**1**	**71**	**18.3**	**4**	**0**	**0.0**	**12:06**	**9**	**3**	**1**	**4**	**16**	**1**	**0**	**1**	**11:42**
2000-01	**Detroit**	**NHL**	**73**	**16**	**24**	**40**	**40**	**9**	**0**	**2**	**74**	**21.6**	**–12**	**2**	**50.0**	**11:41**	**6**	**1**	**3**	**4**	**8**	**1**	**0**	**0**	**14:23**
2001-02♦	**Detroit**	**NHL**	**69**	**8**	**18**	**26**	**58**	**6**	**0**	**1**	**79**	**10.1**	**–12**	**2**	**0.0**	**12:23**	**23**	**8**	**3**	**11**	**8**	**3**	**0**	**2**	**11:31**
	Sweden	Olympics	4	1	0	1	0																		
2002-03	**Detroit**	**NHL**	**74**	**20**	**20**	**40**	**62**	**12**	**0**	**2**	**109**	**18.3**	**11**	**2**	**0.0**	**12:28**	**4**	**1**	**1**	**2**	**4**	**1**	**0**	**0**	**14:37**
	NHL Totals		**474**	**81**	**125**	**206**	**349**	**40**	**0**	**11**	**534**	**15.2**		**6**	**16.7**	**12:12**	**75**	**24**	**23**	**47**	**56**	**10**	**0**	**4**	**12:19**

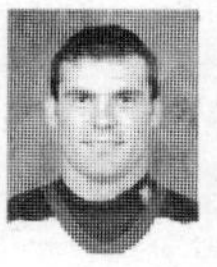

HOLZINGER, Brian

(HOHL-zihn-guhr, BRIGH-uhn) **PIT.**

Center. Shoots right. 5'11", 186 lbs. Born, Parma, OH, October 10, 1972. Buffalo's 7th choice, 124th overall, in 1991 Entry Draft.

Season	Club	League	GP	G	A	Pts	PIM	PP	SH	GW	S	%	+/-	TF	F%	Min	GP	G	A	Pts	PIM	PP	SH	GW	Min
1988-89	Padua High	Hi-School	35	73	65	138																			
1989-90	Det. Compuware	NAJHL	44	36	37	73																			
1990-91	Det. Compuware	NAJHL	37	45	41	86	16																		
1991-92	Bowling Green	CCHA	30	14	8	22	36																		
1992-93	Bowling Green	CCHA	41	31	26	57	44																		
1993-94	Bowling Green	CCHA	38	22	15	37	24																		
1994-95	Bowling Green	CCHA	38	35	33	68	42																		
	Buffalo	**NHL**	**4**	**0**	**3**	**3**	**0**	**0**	**0**	**0**	**3**	**0.0**	**2**				**4**	**2**	**1**	**3**	**2**	**1**	**0**	**0**	
1995-96	**Buffalo**	**NHL**	**58**	**10**	**10**	**20**	**37**	**5**	**0**	**1**	**71**	**14.1**	**–21**												
	Rochester	AHL	17	10	11	21	14										19	10	14	24	10				
1996-97	**Buffalo**	**NHL**	**81**	**22**	**29**	**51**	**54**	**2**	**2**	**6**	**142**	**15.5**	**9**				**12**	**2**	**5**	**7**	**8**	**0**	**1**	**0**	
1997-98	**Buffalo**	**NHL**	**69**	**14**	**21**	**35**	**36**	**4**	**2**	**1**	**116**	**12.1**	**–2**				**15**	**4**	**7**	**11**	**18**	**1**	**1**	**0**	
1998-99	**Buffalo**	**NHL**	**81**	**17**	**17**	**34**	**45**	**5**	**0**	**2**	**143**	**11.9**	**2**	**852**	**50.4**	**16:31**	**21**	**3**	**5**	**8**	**33**	**1**	**0**	**0**	**15:50**
99-2000	**Buffalo**	**NHL**	**59**	**7**	**17**	**24**	**30**	**0**	**1**	**2**	**81**	**8.6**	**4**	**839**	**45.7**	**14:38**									
	Tampa Bay	**NHL**	**14**	**3**	**3**	**6**	**21**	**1**	**1**	**0**	**23**	**13.0**	**–7**	**119**	**46.2**	**16:10**									
2000-01	**Tampa Bay**	**NHL**	**70**	**11**	**25**	**36**	**64**	**3**	**0**	**2**	**87**	**12.6**	**–9**	**775**	**47.4**	**16:03**									
2001-02	**Tampa Bay**	**NHL**	**23**	**1**	**2**	**3**	**4**	**0**	**0**	**0**	**20**	**5.0**	**–4**	**54**	**55.6**	**9:19**									
2002-03	**Tampa Bay**	**NHL**	**5**	**0**	**1**	**1**	**2**	**0**	**0**	**0**	**3**	**0.0**	**1**	**26**	**34.6**	**9:08**									
	Springfield	AHL	28	6	20	26	16																		
	Pittsburgh	**NHL**	**9**	**1**	**2**	**3**	**6**	**0**	**0**	**0**	**20**	**5.0**	**–6**	**161**	**47.8**	**16:24**									
	NHL Totals		**473**	**86**	**130**	**216**	**299**	**20**	**6**	**14**	**709**	**12.1**		**2826**	**47.8**	**15:10**	**52**	**11**	**18**	**29**	**61**	**3**	**2**	**0**	**15:50**

CCHA Second All-Star Team (1993) • CCHA First All-Star Team (1995) • CCHA Player of the Year (1995) • NCAA West First All-American Team (1995) • Hobey Baker Memorial Award (Top U.S. Collegiate Player) (1995)

Traded to **Tampa Bay** by **Buffalo** with Cory Sarich, Wayne Primeau and Buffalo's 3rd round choice (Alexander Kharitonov) in 2000 Entry Draft for Chris Gratton and Tampa Bay's 2nd round choice (Derek Roy) in 2001 Entry Draft, March 9, 2000. • Missed majority of 2001-02 season recovering from shoulder injury suffered in game vs. Florida, October 7, 2001. Traded to **Pittsburgh** by **Tampa Bay** for Marc Bergevin, March 11, 2003.

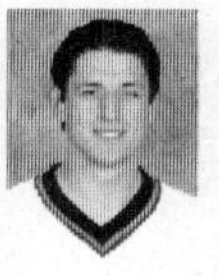

HORCOFF, Shawn

(HOHR-cuhf, SHAWN) **EDM.**

Center. Shoots left. 6'1", 204 lbs. Born, Trail, B.C., September 17, 1978. Edmonton's 3rd choice, 99th overall, in 1998 Entry Draft.

Season	Club	League	GP	G	A	Pts	PIM	PP	SH	GW	S	%	+/-	TF	F%	Min	GP	G	A	Pts	PIM	PP	SH	GW	Min
1994-95	Trail Smokies	RMJHL	47	50	46	96	26																		
1995-96	Chilliwack Chiefs	BCHL	58	49	96	*146	44																		
1996-97	Michigan State	CCHA	40	10	13	23	20																		
1997-98	Michigan State	CCHA	34	14	13	27	50																		
1998-99	Michigan State	CCHA	39	12	25	37	70																		
99-2000	Michigan State	CCHA	42	14	*51	*65	50																		
2000-01	**Edmonton**	**NHL**	**49**	**9**	**7**	**16**	**10**	**0**	**0**	**2**	**42**	**21.4**	**8**	**122**	**41.8**	**9:14**	**5**	**0**	**0**	**0**	**0**	**0**	**0**	**0**	**6:31**
	Hamilton	AHL	24	10	18	28	19																		
2001-02	**Edmonton**	**NHL**	**61**	**8**	**14**	**22**	**18**	**0**	**0**	**0**	**57**	**14.0**	**3**	**454**	**46.3**	**11:20**									
	Hamilton	AHL	2	1	2	3	6																		
2002-03	**Edmonton**	**NHL**	**78**	**12**	**21**	**33**	**55**	**2**	**0**	**3**	**98**	**12.2**	**10**	**301**	**42.9**	**13:30**	**6**	**3**	**1**	**4**	**6**	**0**	**0**	**1**	**15:27**
	NHL Totals		**188**	**29**	**42**	**71**	**83**	**2**	**0**	**5**	**197**	**14.7**		**877**	**44.5**	**11:41**	**11**	**3**	**1**	**4**	**6**	**0**	**0**	**1**	**11:23**

BCHL Player of the Year (1996) • Brett Hull Trophy (Top Scorer – BCHL) (1996) • BCHL First All-Star Team (1996) • CCHA First All-Star Team (2000) • CCHA Player of the Year (2000) • NCAA West First All-American Team (2000)

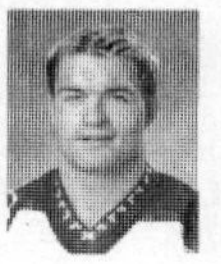

HORDICHUK, Darcy

(HOHR-dih-chuhk, DAHR-see) **FLA.**

Left wing. Shoots left. 6'1", 215 lbs. Born, Kamsack, Sask., August 10, 1980. Atlanta's 9th choice, 180th overall, in 2000 Entry Draft.

Season	Club	League	GP	G	A	Pts	PIM	PP	SH	GW	S	%	+/-	TF	F%	Min	GP	G	A	Pts	PIM	PP	SH	GW	Min
1996-97	Yorkton Mallers	SMHL	57	6	15	21	230																		
	Calgary Hitmen	WHL	3	0	0	0	2																		
1997-98	Dauphin Kings	MJHL	58	12	21	33	279																		
1998-99	Saskatoon Blades	WHL	66	3	2	5	246																		
99-2000	Saskatoon Blades	WHL	63	6	8	14	269										11	4	2	6	43				
2000-01	**Atlanta**	**NHL**	**11**	**0**	**0**	**0**	**38**	**0**	**0**	**0**	**6**	**0.0**	**–3**	**0**	**0.0**	**7:18**									
	Orlando	IHL	69	7	3	10	*369										16	3	3	6	*41				
2001-02	**Atlanta**	**NHL**	**33**	**1**	**1**	**2**	**127**	**0**	**0**	**0**	**8**	**12.5**	**–5**	**4**	**25.0**	**6:03**									
	Chicago Wolves	AHL	34	5	4	9	127																		
	Phoenix	**NHL**	**1**	**0**	**0**	**0**	**14**	**0**	**0**	**0**	**0**	**0.0**	**0**	**0**	**0.0**	**7:18**									

			Regular Season														Playoffs								
Season	Club	League	GP	G	A	Pts	PIM	PP	SH	GW	S	%	+/-	TF	F%	Min	GP	G	A	Pts	PIM	PP	SH	GW	Min
2002-03	**Phoenix**	**NHL**	25	0	0	0	82	0	0	0	5	0.0	–1	0	0.0	4:47	....	....	....	....	....	....	....	....	....
	Springfield	AHL	22	1	3	4	38	....	....	....	....	....	....	....	....	....	....	....	....	....	....	....	....	....	....
	Florida	**NHL**	3	0	0	0	15	0	0	0	2	0.0	–1	0	0.0	9:45	....	....	....	....	....	....	....	....	....
	NHL Totals		73	1	1	2	276	0	0	0	21	4.8		4	25.0	5:58	....	....	....	....	....	....	....	....	....

Traded to **Phoenix** by **Atlanta** with Atlanta's 4th (Lance Monych) and 5th (John Zeiler) round choices in 2002 Entry Draft for Kiril Safronov, the rights to Ruslan Zainullin and Phoenix's 4th round choice (Patrick Dwyer) in 2002 Entry Draft, March 19, 2002. Traded to **Florida** by **Phoenix** with Phoenix's 2nd round choice (later traded to Tampa Bay – Tampa Bay selected Matt Smaby) in 2003 Entry Draft for Brad Ference, March 8, 2003.

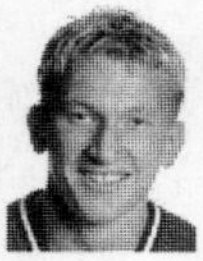

HOSSA, Marcel

(HOH-sah, MAHR-sehl) **MTL.**

Left wing. Shoots left. 6'2", 211 lbs. Born, Ilava, Czech., October 12, 1981. Montreal's 2nd choice, 16th overall, in 2000 Entry Draft.

Season	Club	League	GP	G	A	Pts	PIM	PP	SH	GW	S	%	+/-	TF	F%	Min	GP	G	A	Pts	PIM	PP	SH	GW	Min
1996-97	Dukla Trencin Jr.	Slovak-Jr.	45	30	21	51	30	....	....	....	....	....	....	....	....	....	....	....	....	....	....	....	....	....	....
1997-98	Dukla Trencin Jr.	Slovak-Jr.	39	11	38	49	44	....	....	....	....	....	....	....	....	....	....	....	....	....	....	....	....	....	....
1998-99	Portland	WHL	70	7	14	21	66	....	....	....	....	....	....	....	....	....	2	0	0	0	2	....	....	....	....
99-2000	Portland	WHL	60	24	29	53	58	....	....	....	....	....	....	....	....	....	....	....	....	....	....	....	....	....	....
2000-01	Portland	WHL	58	34	56	90	58	....	....	....	....	....	....	....	....	....	16	5	7	12	14	....	....	....	....
2001-02	**Montreal**	**NHL**	10	3	1	4	2	0	0	0	20	15.0	2	0	0.0	11:09	....	....	....	....	....	....	....	....	....
	Quebec Citadelles	AHL	50	17	15	32	24	....	....	....	....	....	....	....	....	....	3	0	0	0	4	....	....	....	....
2002-03	**Montreal**	**NHL**	34	6	7	13	14	2	0	1	51	11.8	3	4	50.0	13:58	....	....	....	....	....	....	....	....	....
	Hamilton	AHL	37	19	13	32	18	....	....	....	....	....	....	....	....	....	21	4	7	11	12	....	....	....	....
	NHL Totals		44	9	8	17	16	2	0	1	71	12.7		4	50.0	13:20	....	....	....	....	....	....	....	....	....

WHL West Second All-Star Team (2001)

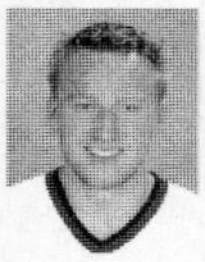

HOSSA, Marian

(HOH-sah, MAIR-ee-an) **OTT.**

Right wing. Shoots left. 6'1", 208 lbs. Born, Stara Lubovna, Czech., January 12, 1979. Ottawa's 1st choice, 12th overall, in 1997 Entry Draft.

Season	Club	League	GP	G	A	Pts	PIM	PP	SH	GW	S	%	+/-	TF	F%	Min	GP	G	A	Pts	PIM	PP	SH	GW	Min
1995-96	Dukla Trencin Jr.	Slovak-Jr.	53	42	49	91	26	....	....	....	....	....	....	....	....	....	....	....	....	....	....	....	....	....	....
1996-97	Dukla Trencin	Slovakia	46	25	19	44	33	....	....	....	....	....	....	....	....	....	7	5	5	10	....	....	....	....	....
1997-98	Portland	WHL	53	45	40	85	50	....	....	....	....	....	....	....	....	....	16	13	6	19	6	....	....	....	....
	Ottawa	**NHL**	7	0	1	1	0	0	0	0	10	0.0	–1	....	....	....	....	....	....	....	....	....	....	....	....
1998-99	**Ottawa**	**NHL**	60	15	15	30	37	1	0	2	124	12.1	18	4	25.0	13:59	4	0	2	2	4	0	0	0	16:45
99-2000	**Ottawa**	**NHL**	78	29	27	56	32	5	0	4	240	12.1	5	7	57.1	17:12	6	0	0	0	2	0	0	0	15:22
2000-01	**Ottawa**	**NHL**	81	32	43	75	44	11	2	7	249	12.9	19	14	42.9	18:01	4	1	1	2	4	0	0	0	19:01
2001-02	Dukla Trencin	Slovakia	8	3	4	7	16	....	....	....	....	....	....	....	....	....	....	....	....	....	....	....	....	....	....
	Ottawa	**NHL**	80	31	35	66	50	9	1	4	278	11.2	11	12	33.3	18:29	12	4	6	10	2	1	0	0	19:04
	Slovakia	Olympics	2	4	2	6	0	....	....	....	....	....	....	....	....	....	....	....	....	....	....	....	....	....	....
2002-03	**Ottawa**	**NHL**	80	45	35	80	34	14	0	10	229	19.7	8	19	36.8	18:31	18	5	11	16	6	3	0	1	18:41
	NHL Totals		386	152	156	308	197	40	3	27	1130	13.5		56	39.3	17:25	44	10	20	30	18	4	0	1	18:12

WHL West First All-Star Team (1998) • Canadian Major Junior First All-Star Team (1998) • Memorial Cup All-Star Team (1998) • NHL All-Rookie Team (1999)
Played in NHL All-Star Game (2001, 2003)

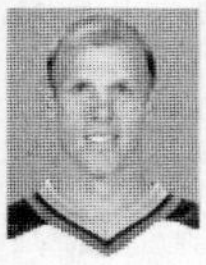

HOUDA, Doug

(HOO-duh, DUHG)

Defense. Shoots right. 6'2", 208 lbs. Born, Blairmore, Alta., June 3, 1966. Detroit's 2nd choice, 28th overall, in 1984 Entry Draft.

Season	Club	League	GP	G	A	Pts	PIM	PP	SH	GW	S	%	+/-	TF	F%	Min	GP	G	A	Pts	PIM	PP	SH	GW	Min
1982-83	Calgary Wranglers	WHL	71	5	23	28	99	....	....	....	....	....	....	....	....	....	16	1	3	4	44	....	....	....	....
1983-84	Calgary Wranglers	WHL	69	6	30	36	195	....	....	....	....	....	....	....	....	....	4	0	0	0	7	....	....	....	....
1984-85	Calgary Wranglers	WHL	65	20	54	74	182	....	....	....	....	....	....	....	....	....	8	3	4	7	29	....	....	....	....
	Kalamazoo Wings	IHL	....	....	....	....	....	....	....	....	....	....	....	....	....	....	7	0	2	2	10	....	....	....	....
1985-86	Calgary Wranglers	WHL	16	4	10	14	60	....	....	....	....	....	....	....	....	....	....	....	....	....	....	....	....	....	....
	Medicine Hat	WHL	35	9	23	32	80	....	....	....	....	....	....	....	....	....	25	4	19	23	64	....	....	....	....
	Detroit	**NHL**	6	0	0	0	4	0	0	0	5	0.0	–7	....	....	....	....	....	....	....	....	....	....	....	....
1986-87	Adirondack	AHL	77	6	23	29	142	....	....	....	....	....	....	....	....	....	11	1	8	9	50	....	....	....	....
1987-88	**Detroit**	**NHL**	11	1	1	2	10	0	0	0	10	10.0	0	....	....	....	....	....	....	....	....	....	....	....	....
	Adirondack	AHL	71	10	32	42	169	....	....	....	....	....	....	....	....	....	11	0	3	3	44	....	....	....	....
1988-89	**Detroit**	**NHL**	57	2	11	13	67	0	0	0	38	5.3	17	....	....	....	6	0	1	1	0	0	0	0	....
	Adirondack	AHL	7	0	3	3	8	....	....	....	....	....	....	....	....	....	....	....	....	....	....	....	....	....	....
1989-90	**Detroit**	**NHL**	73	2	9	11	127	0	0	0	59	3.4	–5	....	....	....	....	....	....	....	....	....	....	....	....
1990-91	**Detroit**	**NHL**	22	0	4	4	43	0	0	0	21	0.0	–2	....	....	....	....	....	....	....	....	....	....	....	....
	Adirondack	AHL	38	9	17	26	67	....	....	....	....	....	....	....	....	....	....	....	....	....	....	....	....	....	....
	Hartford	**NHL**	19	1	2	3	41	0	0	0	21	4.8	–3	....	....	....	6	0	0	0	8	0	0	0	....
1991-92	**Hartford**	**NHL**	56	3	6	9	125	1	0	1	40	7.5	–2	....	....	....	6	0	2	2	13	0	0	0	....
1992-93	**Hartford**	**NHL**	60	2	6	8	167	0	0	0	43	4.7	–19	....	....	....	....	....	....	....	....	....	....	....	....
1993-94	**Hartford**	**NHL**	7	0	0	0	23	0	0	0	1	0.0	–4	....	....	....	....	....	....	....	....	....	....	....	....
	Los Angeles	**NHL**	54	2	6	8	165	0	0	0	31	6.5	–15	....	....	....	....	....	....	....	....	....	....	....	....
1994-95	**Buffalo**	**NHL**	28	1	2	3	68	0	0	0	21	4.8	1	....	....	....	....	....	....	....	....	....	....	....	....
1995-96	**Buffalo**	**NHL**	38	1	3	4	52	0	0	0	21	4.8	3	....	....	....	....	....	....	....	....	....	....	....	....
	Rochester	AHL	21	1	6	7	41	....	....	....	....	....	....	....	....	....	19	3	5	8	30	....	....	....	....
1996-97	**NY Islanders**	**NHL**	70	2	8	10	99	0	0	0	29	6.9	1	....	....	....	....	....	....	....	....	....	....	....	....
	Utah Grizzlies	IHL	3	0	0	0	7	....	....	....	....	....	....	....	....	....	....	....	....	....	....	....	....	....	....
1997-98	**NY Islanders**	**NHL**	31	1	2	3	47	0	0	0	15	6.7	–6	....	....	....	....	....	....	....	....	....	....	....	....
	Anaheim	**NHL**	24	1	2	3	52	0	1	0	9	11.1	–5	....	....	....	....	....	....	....	....	....	....	....	....
1998-99	**Detroit**	**NHL**	3	0	1	1	0	0	0	0	1	0.0	–2	0	0.0	6:51	....	....	....	....	....	....	....	....	....
	Adirondack	AHL	73	7	21	28	122	....	....	....	....	....	....	....	....	....	3	0	1	1	4	....	....	....	....
99-2000	**Buffalo**	**NHL**	1	0	0	0	12	0	0	0	0	0.0	0	0	0.0	9:10	....	....	....	....	....	....	....	....	....
	Rochester	AHL	79	7	17	24	175	....	....	....	....	....	....	....	....	....	21	1	8	9	39	....	....	....	....
2000-01	Rochester	AHL	43	6	20	26	106	....	....	....	....	....	....	....	....	....	4	0	0	0	4	....	....	....	....
2001-02	Rochester	AHL	64	6	22	28	170	....	....	....	....	....	....	....	....	....	2	0	0	0	4	....	....	....	....
2002-03	**Buffalo**	**NHL**	1	0	0	0	2	0	0	0	1	0.0	–2	0	0.0	12:39	....	....	....	....	....	....	....	....	....
	Rochester	AHL	77	3	22	25	191	....	....	....	....	....	....	....	....	....	3	0	2	2	22	....	....	....	....
	NHL Totals		561	19	63	82	1104	1	1	1	366	5.2		0	0.0	8:28	18	0	3	3	21	0	0	0	....

WHL East Second All-Star Team (1985) • AHL First All-Star Team (1988)

Traded to **Hartford** by **Detroit** for Doug Crossman, February 20, 1991. Traded to **Los Angeles** by **Hartford** for Marc Potvin, November 3, 1993. Traded to **Buffalo** by **Los Angeles** for Sean O'Donnell, July 26, 1994. Signed as a free agent by **NY Islanders**, October 26, 1996. Traded to **Anaheim** by **NY Islanders** with Travis Green and Tony Tuzzolino for Joe Sacco, J.J. Daigneault and Mark Janssens, February 6, 1998. Traded to **Detroit** by **Anaheim** for future considerations, October 9, 1998. Signed as a free agent by **Buffalo**, July 13, 1999.

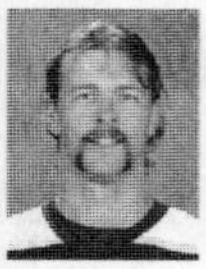

HOULDER, Bill

(HOHL-duhr, BIHL)

Defense. Shoots left. 6'2", 217 lbs. Born, Thunder Bay, Ont., March 11, 1967. Washington's 4th choice, 82nd overall, in 1985 Entry Draft.

Season	Club	League	GP	G	A	Pts	PIM	PP	SH	GW	S	%	+/-	TF	F%	Min	GP	G	A	Pts	PIM	PP	SH	GW	Min
1983-84	T. Bay Beavers	TBJHL	23	4	18	22	37	....	....	....	....	....	....	....	....	....	....	....	....	....	....	....	....	....	....
1984-85	North Bay	OHL	66	4	20	24	37	....	....	....	....	....	....	....	....	....	8	0	0	0	2	....	....	....	....
1985-86	North Bay	OHL	59	5	30	35	97	....	....	....	....	....	....	....	....	....	10	1	6	7	12	....	....	....	....
1986-87	North Bay	OHL	62	17	51	68	68	....	....	....	....	....	....	....	....	....	22	4	19	23	20	....	....	....	....
1987-88	**Washington**	**NHL**	30	1	2	3	10	0	0	0	20	5.0	–2	....	....	....	....	....	....	....	....	....	....	....	....
	Fort Wayne	IHL	43	10	14	24	32	....	....	....	....	....	....	....	....	....	....	....	....	....	....	....	....	....	....
1988-89	**Washington**	**NHL**	8	0	3	3	4	0	0	0	5	0.0	7	....	....	....	....	....	....	....	....	....	....	....	....
	Baltimore	AHL	65	10	36	46	50	....	....	....	....	....	....	....	....	....	....	....	....	....	....	....	....	....	....
1989-90	**Washington**	**NHL**	41	1	11	12	28	0	0	0	49	2.0	8	....	....	....	....	....	....	....	....	....	....	....	....
	Baltimore	AHL	26	3	7	10	12	....	....	....	....	....	....	....	....	....	7	0	2	2	2	....	....	....	....
1990-91	**Buffalo**	**NHL**	7	0	2	2	4	0	0	0	7	0.0	–2	....	....	....	....	....	....	....	....	....	....	....	....
	Rochester	AHL	69	13	53	66	28	....	....	....	....	....	....	....	....	....	15	5	13	18	4	....	....	....	....
1991-92	**Buffalo**	**NHL**	10	1	0	1	8	0	0	0	18	5.6	–2	....	....	....	....	....	....	....	....	....	....	....	....
	Rochester	AHL	42	8	26	34	16	....	....	....	....	....	....	....	....	....	16	5	6	11	4	....	....	....	....
1992-93	**Buffalo**	**NHL**	15	3	5	8	6	0	0	0	29	10.3	5	....	....	....	8	0	2	2	4	0	0	0	....
	San Diego Gulls	IHL	64	24	48	72	39	....	....	....	....	....	....	....	....	....	....	....	....	....	....	....	....	....	....
1993-94	**Anaheim**	**NHL**	80	14	25	39	40	3	0	3	187	7.5	–18	....	....	....	....	....	....	....	....	....	....	....	....
1994-95	**St. Louis**	**NHL**	41	5	13	18	20	1	0	0	59	8.5	16	....	....	....	4	1	1	2	0	0	0	0	....
1995-96	**Tampa Bay**	**NHL**	61	5	23	28	22	3	0	0	90	5.6	1	....	....	....	6	0	1	1	4	0	0	0	....
1996-97	**Tampa Bay**	**NHL**	79	4	21	25	30	0	0	2	116	3.4	16	....	....	....	....	....	....	....	....	....	....	....	....
1997-98	**San Jose**	**NHL**	82	7	25	32	48	4	0	2	102	6.9	13	....	....	....	6	1	2	3	2	0	0	0	....
1998-99	**San Jose**	**NHL**	76	9	23	32	40	7	0	5	115	7.8	8	0	0.0	22:08	6	3	0	3	4	3	0	0	24:59

Season	Club	League	GP	G	A	Pts	PIM	PP	SH	GW	S	%	+/-	TF	F%	Min	GP	G	A	Pts	PIM	PP	SH	GW	Min
			Regular Season														Playoffs								
99-2000	Tampa Bay	NHL	14	1	2	3	2	1	0	0	21	4.8	-3	1	100.0	21:29	....	....	....	....	....	....	....	....	....
	Nashville	NHL	57	2	12	14	24	1	0	1	68	2.9	-6	1	100.0	22:36	....	....	....	....	....	....	....	....	....
2000-01	Nashville	NHL	81	4	12	16	40	0	1	1	78	5.1	-7	2	0.0	21:12	....	....	....	....	....	....	....	....	....
2001-02	Nashville	NHL	82	0	8	8	40	0	0	0	44	0.0	-1	3	0.0	21:33	....	....	....	....	....	....	....	....	....
2002-03	Nashville	NHL	82	2	4	6	46	0	0	1	51	3.9	-2	2	0.0	19:07	....	....	....	....	....	....	....	....	....
	NHL Totals		846	59	191	250	412	20	1	15	1059	5.6		9	22.2	21:14	30	5	6	11	14	3	0	0	24:59

AHL First All-Star Team (1991) • Governor's Trophy (Top Defenseman – IHL) (1993) • IHL First All-Star Team (1993)

Traded to **Buffalo** by **Washington** for Shawn Anderson, September 30, 1990. Claimed by **Anaheim** from **Buffalo** in Expansion Draft, June 24, 1993. Traded to **St. Louis** by **Anaheim** for Jason Marshall, August 29, 1994. Signed as a free agent by **Tampa Bay**, July 26, 1995. Signed as a free agent by **San Jose**, July 16, 1997. Traded to **Tampa Bay** by **San Jose** with Andrei Zyuzin, Shawn Burr and Steve Guolla for Niklas Sundstrom and NY Rangers' 3rd round choice (previously acquired, later traded to Chicago – Chicago selected Igor Radulov) in 2000 Entry Draft, August 4, 1999. Claimed on waivers by **Nashville** from **Tampa Bay**, November 10, 1999.

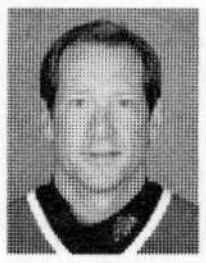

HOUSLEY, Phil

(HOWZ-lee, FIHL)

Defense. Shoots left. 5'10", 185 lbs. Born, St. Paul, MN, March 9, 1964. Buffalo's 1st choice, 6th overall, in 1982 Entry Draft.

Season	Club	League	GP	G	A	Pts	PIM	PP	SH	GW	S	%	+/-	TF	F%	Min	GP	G	A	Pts	PIM	PP	SH	GW	Min
1980-81	St. Paul Vulcans	USHL	6	7	7	14	6	....	....	....	....	....	....	....	....	....	10	5	5	10	0	....	....	....	....
1981-82	South St. Paul	Hi-School	22	31	34	65	18	....	....	....	....	....	....	....	....	....	....	....	....	....	....	....	....	....	....
1982-83	Buffalo	NHL	77	19	47	66	39	11	0	2	183	10.4	-4	....	....	....	10	3	4	7	2	1	0	0	....
1983-84	Buffalo	NHL	75	31	46	77	33	13	2	6	234	13.2	3	....	....	....	3	0	0	0	6	0	0	0	....
1984-85	Buffalo	NHL	73	16	53	69	28	3	0	4	188	8.5	15	....	....	....	5	3	2	5	2	0	0	0	....
1985-86	Buffalo	NHL	79	15	47	62	54	7	0	2	180	8.3	-9	....	....	....	....	....	....	....	....	....	....	....	....
1986-87	Buffalo	NHL	78	21	46	67	57	8	1	2	202	10.4	-2	....	....	....	....	....	....	....	....	....	....	....	....
1987-88	Buffalo	NHL	74	29	37	66	96	6	0	1	231	12.6	-17	....	....	....	6	2	4	6	6	1	0	0	....
1988-89	Buffalo	NHL	72	26	44	70	47	5	0	3	178	14.6	6	....	....	....	5	1	3	4	2	0	0	0	....
1989-90	Buffalo	NHL	80	21	60	81	32	8	1	4	201	10.4	11	....	....	....	6	1	4	5	4	1	0	0	....
1990-91	Winnipeg	NHL	78	23	53	76	24	12	1	3	206	11.2	-13	....	....	....	....	....	....	....	....	....	....	....	....
1991-92	Winnipeg	NHL	74	23	63	86	92	11	0	4	234	9.8	-5	....	....	....	7	1	4	5	0	1	0	1	....
1992-93	Winnipeg	NHL	80	18	79	97	52	6	0	2	249	7.2	-14	....	....	....	6	0	7	7	2	0	0	0	....
1993-94	St. Louis	NHL	26	7	15	22	12	4	0	1	60	11.7	-5	....	....	....	4	2	1	3	4	2	0	0	....
1994-95	Zurcher SC	Swiss	10	6	8	14	34	....	....	....	....	....	....	....	....	....	....	....	....	....	....	....	....	....	....
	Calgary	NHL	43	8	35	43	18	3	0	0	135	5.9	17	....	....	....	7	0	9	9	0	0	0	0	....
1995-96	Calgary	NHL	59	16	36	52	22	6	0	1	155	10.3	-2	....	....	....	....	....	....	....	....	....	....	....	....
	New Jersey	NHL	22	1	15	16	8	0	0	0	50	2.0	-4	....	....	....	....	....	....	....	....	....	....	....	....
1996-97	Washington	NHL	77	11	29	40	24	3	1	2	167	6.6	-10	....	....	....	....	....	....	....	....	....	....	....	....
1997-98	Washington	NHL	64	6	25	31	24	4	1	0	116	5.2	-10	....	....	....	18	0	4	4	4	0	0	0	....
1998-99	Calgary	NHL	79	11	43	54	52	4	0	1	193	5.7	14	0	0.0	20:52	....	....	....	....	....	....	....	....	....
99-2000	Calgary	NHL	78	11	44	55	24	5	0	2	176	6.3	-12	1	0.0	23:29	....	....	....	....	....	....	....	....	....
2000-01	Calgary	NHL	69	4	30	34	24	0	0	0	115	3.5	-15	0	0.0	18:10	....	....	....	....	....	....	....	....	....
2001-02	Chicago	NHL	80	15	24	39	34	8	0	6	218	6.9	-3	0	0.0	21:46	5	0	1	1	4	0	0	0	17:53
	United States	Olympics	6	1	4	5	0	....	....	....	....	....	....	....	....	....	....	....	....	....	....	....	....	....	....
2002-03	Chicago	NHL	57	6	23	29	24	2	0	2	134	4.5	7	1	100.0	19:23	....	....	....	....	....	....	....	....	....
	Toronto	NHL	1	0	0	0	2	0	0	0	3	0.0	-1	0	0.0	16:04	3	0	0	0	0	0	0	0	13:36
	NHL Totals		1495	338	894	1232	822	129	7	48	3808	8.9		2	50.0	20:52	85	13	43	56	36	6	0	1	16:17

NHL All-Rookie Team (1983) • NHL Second All-Star Team (1992)

Played in NHL All-Star Game (1984, 1989, 1990, 1991, 1992, 1993, 2000)

Traded to **Winnipeg** by **Buffalo** with Scott Arniel, Jeff Parker and Buffalo's 1st round choice (Keith Tkachuk) in 1990 Entry Draft for Dale Hawerchuk and Winnipeg's 1st round choice (Brad May) in 1990 Entry Draft, June 16, 1990. Traded to **St. Louis** by **Winnipeg** for Nelson Emerson and Stephane Quintal, September 24, 1993. Traded to **Calgary** by **St. Louis** with St. Louis' 2nd round choices in 1996 (Steve Begin) and 1997 (John Tripp) Entry Drafts for Al MacInnis and Calgary's 4th round choice (Didier Tremblay) in 1997 Entry Draft, July 4, 1994. Traded to **New Jersey** by **Calgary** with Dan Keczmer for Tommy Albelin, Cale Hulse and Jocelyn Lemieux, February 26, 1996. Signed as a free agent by **Washington**, July 22, 1996. Claimed on waivers by **Calgary** from **Washington**, July 21, 1998. Claimed by **Chicago** from **Calgary** in Waiver Draft, September 28, 2001. Traded to **Toronto** by **Chicago** for Toronto's 9th round choice (Chris Porter) in 2003 Entry Draft and Toronto's 4th round choice in 2004 Entry Draft, March 11, 2003.

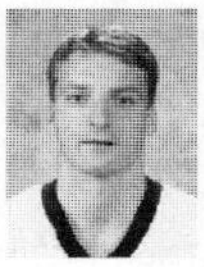

HRDINA, Jan

(huhr-DEE-nah, YAN) **PHX.**

Center. Shoots right. 6', 206 lbs. Born, Hradec Kralove, Czech., February 5, 1976. Pittsburgh's 4th choice, 128th overall, in 1995 Entry Draft.

Season	Club	League	GP	G	A	Pts	PIM	PP	SH	GW	S	%	+/-	TF	F%	Min	GP	G	A	Pts	PIM	PP	SH	GW	Min
1993-94	H. Kralove Jr.	Czech-Jr.	10	1	6	7	0	....	....	....	....	....	....	....	....	....	....	....	....	....	....	....	....	....	....
	Hradec Kralove	Czech	23	1	5	6	....	....	....	....	....	....	....	....	....	....	4	0	1	1	....	....	....	....	....
1994-95	Seattle	WHL	69	41	59	100	79	....	....	....	....	....	....	....	....	....	4	0	1	1	8	....	....	....	....
1995-96	Seattle	WHL	30	19	28	47	37	....	....	....	....	....	....	....	....	....	....	....	....	....	....	....	....	....	....
	Spokane Chiefs	WHL	18	10	16	26	25	....	....	....	....	....	....	....	....	....	18	5	14	19	49	....	....	....	....
1996-97	Cleveland	IHL	68	23	31	54	82	....	....	....	....	....	....	....	....	....	13	1	2	3	8	....	....	....	....
1997-98	Syracuse Crunch	AHL	72	20	24	44	82	....	....	....	....	....	....	....	....	....	5	1	3	4	10	....	....	....	....
1998-99	Pittsburgh	NHL	82	13	29	42	40	3	0	2	94	13.8	-2	1461	56.7	16:26	13	4	1	5	12	1	0	1	21:03
99-2000	Pittsburgh	NHL	70	13	33	46	43	3	0	1	84	15.5	13	1392	53.7	18:47	9	4	8	12	2	1	0	0	22:04
2000-01	Pittsburgh	NHL	78	15	28	43	48	3	0	1	89	16.9	19	1067	53.8	15:56	18	2	5	7	8	0	0	0	15:04
2001-02	Pittsburgh	NHL	79	24	33	57	50	6	0	6	115	20.9	-7	667	50.4	19:51	....	....	....	....	....	....	....	....	....
	Czech Republic	Olympics	4	0	0	0	0	....	....	....	....	....	....	....	....	....	....	....	....	....	....	....	....	....	....
2002-03	Pittsburgh	NHL	57	14	25	39	34	11	0	4	84	16.7	1	984	56.0	19:45	....	....	....	....	....	....	....	....	....
	Phoenix	NHL	4	0	4	4	8	0	0	0	2	0.0	3	70	60.0	18:12	....	....	....	....	....	....	....	....	....
	NHL Totals		370	79	152	231	223	26	0	14	468	16.9		5641	54.6	18:02	40	10	14	24	22	2	0	1	18:35

Traded to **Phoenix** by **Pittsburgh** with Francois Leroux for Ramzi Abid, Dan Focht and Guillaume Lefebvre, March 11, 2003.

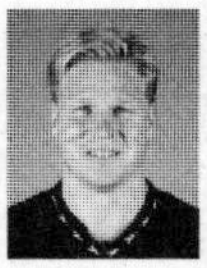

HRKAC, Tony

(HUHR-kuhz, TOH-nee)

Center. Shoots left. 5'10", 190 lbs. Born, Thunder Bay, Ont., July 7, 1966. St. Louis' 2nd choice, 32nd overall, in 1984 Entry Draft.

Season	Club	League	GP	G	A	Pts	PIM	PP	SH	GW	S	%	+/-	TF	F%	Min	GP	G	A	Pts	PIM	PP	SH	GW	Min
1983-84	Orillia Travelways	OPJHL	42	*52	54	*106	20	....	....	....	....	....	....	....	....	....	....	....	....	....	....	....	....	....	....
1984-85	North Dakota	WCHA	36	18	36	54	16	....	....	....	....	....	....	....	....	....	....	....	....	....	....	....	....	....	....
1985-86	Team Canada	Nat-Tm	62	19	30	49	36	....	....	....	....	....	....	....	....	....	....	....	....	....	....	....	....	....	....
1986-87	North Dakota	WCHA	48	46	70	116	48	....	....	....	....	....	....	....	....	....	....	....	....	....	....	....	....	....	....
	St. Louis	NHL	....	....	....	....	....	....	....	....	....	....	....	....	....	....	3	0	0	0	0	0	0	0	....
1987-88	St. Louis	NHL	67	11	37	48	22	2	1	3	86	12.8	5	....	....	....	10	6	1	7	4	3	1	1	....
1988-89	St. Louis	NHL	70	17	28	45	8	5	0	1	133	12.8	-10	....	....	....	4	1	1	2	0	0	0	1	....
1989-90	St. Louis	NHL	28	5	12	17	8	1	0	0	41	12.2	1	....	....	....	....	....	....	....	....	....	....	....	....
	Quebec	NHL	22	4	8	12	2	2	0	0	29	13.8	-5	....	....	....	....	....	....	....	....	....	....	....	....
	Halifax Citadels	AHL	20	12	21	33	4	....	....	....	....	....	....	....	....	....	6	5	9	14	4	....	....	....	....
1990-91	Quebec	NHL	70	16	32	48	16	6	0	0	122	13.1	-22	....	....	....	....	....	....	....	....	....	....	....	....
	Halifax Citadels	AHL	3	4	1	5	2	....	....	....	....	....	....	....	....	....	....	....	....	....	....	....	....	....	....
1991-92	San Jose	NHL	22	2	10	12	4	0	0	0	31	6.5	-2	....	....	....	....	....	....	....	....	....	....	....	....
	Chicago	NHL	18	1	2	3	6	0	0	0	22	4.5	4	....	....	....	3	0	0	0	2	0	0	0	....
1992-93	Indianapolis Ice	IHL	80	45	*87	*132	70	....	....	....	....	....	....	....	....	....	5	0	2	2	2	....	....	....	....
1993-94	St. Louis	NHL	36	6	5	11	8	1	1	1	43	14.0	-11	....	....	....	4	0	0	0	0	0	0	0	....
	Peoria Rivermen	IHL	45	30	51	81	25	....	....	....	....	....	....	....	....	....	1	1	2	3	0	....	....	....	....
1994-95	Milwaukee	IHL	71	24	67	91	26	....	....	....	....	....	....	....	....	....	15	4	9	13	16	....	....	....	....
1995-96	Milwaukee	IHL	43	14	28	42	18	....	....	....	....	....	....	....	....	....	5	1	3	4	4	....	....	....	....
1996-97	Milwaukee	IHL	81	27	61	88	20	....	....	....	....	....	....	....	....	....	3	1	1	2	2	....	....	....	....
1997-98	Dallas	NHL	13	5	3	8	0	3	0	0	14	35.7	0	....	....	....	....	....	....	....	....	....	....	....	....
	Michigan	IHL	20	7	15	22	6	....	....	....	....	....	....	....	....	....	....	....	....	....	....	....	....	....	....
	Edmonton	NHL	36	8	11	19	10	4	0	1	43	18.6	3	....	....	....	12	0	3	3	2	0	0	0	....
1998-99♦	Dallas	NHL	69	13	14	27	26	2	0	2	67	19.4	2	666	48.0	12:02	5	0	2	2	4	0	0	0	9:15
99-2000	NY Islanders	NHL	7	0	2	2	0	0	0	0	2	0.0	-1	34	35.3	11:22	....	....	....	....	....	....	....	....	....
	Anaheim	NHL	60	4	7	11	8	1	0	0	37	10.8	-2	536	50.8	9:04	....	....	....	....	....	....	....	....	....
2000-01	Anaheim	NHL	80	13	25	38	29	0	0	1	88	14.8	0	1072	50.7	13:46	....	....	....	....	....	....	....	....	....

			Regular Season														Playoffs								
Season	Club	League	GP	G	A	Pts	PIM	PP	SH	GW	S	%	+/-	TF	F%	Min	GP	G	A	Pts	PIM	PP	SH	GW	Min
2001-02	Atlanta	NHL	80	18	26	44	12	5	1	2	101	17.8	–12	935	47.5	17:29	....	....	....	....	....	....	....	....	....
2002-03	Atlanta	NHL	80	9	17	26	14	2	0	2	86	10.5	–16	1125	44.6	16:06	....	....	....	....	....	....	....	....	....
	NHL Totals		758	132	239	371	173	34	3	13	945	14.0		4368	47.9	13:56	41	7	7	14	12	3	1	2	9:15

WCHA First All-Star Team (1987) • WCHA Player of the Year (1987) • NCAA West First All-American Team (1987) • NCAA Championship All-Tournament Team (1987) • NCAA Championship Tournament MVP (1987) • Hobey Baker Memorial Award (Top U.S. Collegiate Player) (1987) • James Gatschene Memorial Trophy (MVP – IHL) (1993) • Leo P. Lamoureux Memorial Trophy (Top Scorer – IHL) (1993) • IHL First All-Star Team (1993)

Traded to **Quebec** by **St. Louis** with Greg Millen for Jeff Brown, December 13, 1989. Traded to **San Jose** by **Quebec** for Greg Paslawski, May 31, 1991. Traded to **Chicago** by **San Jose** for Chicago's 6th round choice (Fredrik Oduya) in 1993 Entry Draft, February 7, 1992. Signed as a free agent by **St. Louis**, July 30, 1993. Signed as a free agent by **Dallas**, August 12, 1997. Claimed on waivers by **Edmonton** from **Dallas**, January 6, 1998. Traded to **Pittsburgh** by **Edmonton** with Bobby Dollas for Josef Beranek, June 16, 1998. Claimed by **Nashville** from **Pittsburgh** in Expansion Draft, June 26, 1998. Traded to **Dallas** by **Nashville** for future considerations, July 9, 1998. Signed as a free agent by **NY Islanders**, July 29, 1999. Traded to **Anaheim** by **NY Islanders** with Dean Malkoc for Ted Drury, October 29, 1999. Signed as a free agent by **Atlanta**, July 25, 2001.

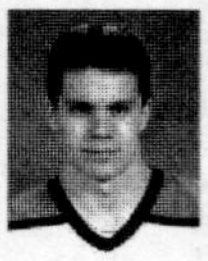

HUBACEK, Petr

(HOO-buh-chehk, PEE-tuhr) **NSH.**

Center. Shoots right. 6'2", 183 lbs. Born, Brno, Czech., September 2, 1979. Philadelphia's 11th choice, 243rd overall, in 1998 Entry Draft.

Season	Club	League	GP	G	A	Pts	PIM	PP	SH	GW	S	%	+/-	TF	F%	Min	GP	G	A	Pts	PIM	PP	SH	GW	Min
1997-98	Kometa Brno Jr.	Czech-Jr.	17	9	5	14	....	....	....	....	....	....	....	....	....	....	....	....	....	....	....	....	....	....	....
	HC Kometa Brno	Czech-2	48	6	10	16	....	....	....	....	....	....	....	....	....	....	....	....	....	....	....	....	....	....	....
1998-99	HC Vitkovice	Czech	25	0	4	4	2	....	....	....	....	....	....	....	....	....	4	0	0	0	....	....	....	....	....
99-2000	HC Vitkovice	Czech	48	11	12	23	81	....	....	....	....	....	....	....	....	....	....	....	....	....	....	....	....	....	....
2000-01	**Philadelphia**	**NHL**	**6**	**1**	**0**	**1**	**2**	**0**	**0**	**0**	**5**	**20.0**	**–1**	**39**	**25.6**	**11:20**	....	....	....	....	....	....	....	....	....
	Philadelphia	AHL	62	3	9	12	29	....	....	....	....	....	....	....	....	....	9	0	1	1	6	....	....	....	....
2001-02	Philadelphia	AHL	22	1	6	7	8	....	....	....	....	....	....	....	....	....	....	....	....	....	....	....	....	....	....
	Milwaukee	AHL	14	2	0	2	0	....	....	....	....	....	....	....	....	....	....	....	....	....	....	....	....	....	....
2002-03	HC Hame Zlin	Czech	44	4	15	19	14	....	....	....	....	....	....	....	....	....	....	....	....	....	....	....	....	....	....
	HC Vitkovice	Czech	7	1	4	5	10	....	....	....	....	....	....	....	....	....	6	1	0	1	16	....	....	....	....
	NHL Totals		**6**	**1**	**0**	**1**	**2**	**0**	**0**	**0**	**5**	**20.0**		**39**	**25.6**	**11:20**	....	....	....	....	....	....	....	....	....

Traded to **Nashville** by **Philadelphia** with Jason Beckett for Yves Sarault, January 11, 2002. Signed as a free agent by **HC Hame Zlin** (Czech) with Nashville retaining NHL rights, August 4, 2002.

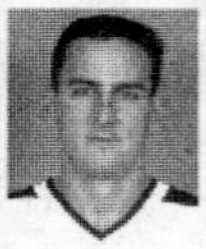

HULBIG, Joe

(HUHL-bihg, JOH) **N.J.**

Left wing. Shoots left. 6'3", 215 lbs. Born, Norwood, MA, September 29, 1973. Edmonton's 1st choice, 13th overall, in 1992 Entry Draft.

Season	Club	League	GP	G	A	Pts	PIM	PP	SH	GW	S	%	+/-	TF	F%	Min	GP	G	A	Pts	PIM	PP	SH	GW	Min
1989-90	St. Sebastian's	Hi-School	30	13	12	25	....	....	....	....	....	....	....	....	....	....	....	....	....	....	....	....	....	....	....
1990-91	St. Sebastian's	Hi-School	30	23	19	42	....	....	....	....	....	....	....	....	....	....	....	....	....	....	....	....	....	....	....
1991-92	St. Sebastian's	Hi-School	17	19	24	43	30	....	....	....	....	....	....	....	....	....	....	....	....	....	....	....	....	....	....
1992-93	Providence	H-East	26	3	13	16	22	....	....	....	....	....	....	....	....	....	....	....	....	....	....	....	....	....	....
1993-94	Providence	H-East	28	6	4	10	36	....	....	....	....	....	....	....	....	....	....	....	....	....	....	....	....	....	....
1994-95	Providence	H-East	37	14	21	35	36	....	....	....	....	....	....	....	....	....	....	....	....	....	....	....	....	....	....
1995-96	Providence	H-East	31	14	22	36	56	....	....	....	....	....	....	....	....	....	....	....	....	....	....	....	....	....	....
1996-97	**Edmonton**	**NHL**	**6**	**0**	**0**	**0**	**0**	**0**	**0**	**0**	**4**	**0.0**	**–1**	....	....	....	**6**	**0**	**1**	**1**	**2**	**0**	**0**	**0**	....
	Hamilton	AHL	73	18	28	46	59	....	....	....	....	....	....	....	....	....	16	6	10	16	6	....	....	....	....
1997-98	**Edmonton**	**NHL**	**17**	**2**	**2**	**4**	**2**	**0**	**0**	**1**	**8**	**25.0**	**–1**	....	....	....	....	....	....	....	....	....	....	....	....
	Hamilton	AHL	46	15	16	31	52	....	....	....	....	....	....	....	....	....	3	0	1	1	2	....	....	....	....
1998-99	**Edmonton**	**NHL**	**1**	**0**	**0**	**0**	**2**	**0**	**0**	**0**	**2**	**0.0**	**1**	**0**	**0.0**	**8:20**	....	....	....	....	....	....	....	....	....
	Hamilton	AHL	76	22	24	46	68	....	....	....	....	....	....	....	....	....	11	4	2	6	18	....	....	....	....
99-2000	**Boston**	**NHL**	**24**	**2**	**2**	**4**	**8**	**0**	**0**	**0**	**15**	**13.3**	**–8**	**2**	**0.0**	**8:18**	....	....	....	....	....	....	....	....	....
	Providence Bruins	AHL	15	4	5	9	17	....	....	....	....	....	....	....	....	....	....	....	....	....	....	....	....	....	....
2000-01	**Boston**	**NHL**	**7**	**0**	**0**	**0**	**4**	**0**	**0**	**0**	**0**	**0.0**	**–3**	**0**	**0.0**	**5:28**	....	....	....	....	....	....	....	....	....
	Providence Bruins	AHL	36	4	11	15	19	....	....	....	....	....	....	....	....	....	15	2	2	4	20	....	....	....	....
2001-02	Providence Bruins	AHL	54	8	10	18	41	....	....	....	....	....	....	....	....	....	....	....	....	....	....	....	....	....	....
	Worcester IceCats	AHL	7	0	3	3	2	....	....	....	....	....	....	....	....	....	3	1	0	1	7	....	....	....	....
2002-03	Albany River Rats	AHL	35	11	9	20	20	....	....	....	....	....	....	....	....	....	....	....	....	....	....	....	....	....	....
	NHL Totals		**55**	**4**	**4**	**8**	**16**	**0**	**0**	**1**	**29**	**13.8**		**2**	**0.0**	**7:41**	**6**	**0**	**1**	**1**	**2**	**0**	**0**	**0**	....

Signed as a free agent by **Boston**, July 23, 1999. • Missed majority of 2000-01 season recovering from head injury suffered in game vs. Ottawa, November 9, 2000. Signed as a free agent by **New Jersey**, October 1, 2002.

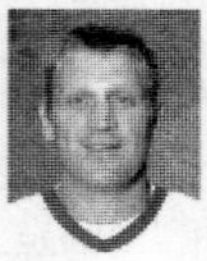

HULL, Brett

(HUHL, BREHT) **DET.**

Right wing. Shoots right. 5'11", 203 lbs. Born, Belleville, Ont., August 9, 1964. Calgary's 6th choice, 117th overall, in 1984 Entry Draft.

Season	Club	League	GP	G	A	Pts	PIM	PP	SH	GW	S	%	+/-	TF	F%	Min	GP	G	A	Pts	PIM	PP	SH	GW	Min
1982-83	Penticton Knights	BCJHL	50	48	56	104	27	....	....	....	....	....	....	....	....	....	....	....	....	....	....	....	....	....	....
1983-84	Penticton Knights	BCJHL	56	*105	83	*188	20	....	....	....	....	....	....	....	....	....	....	....	....	....	....	....	....	....	....
1984-85	U. Minn-Duluth	WCHA	48	32	28	60	24	....	....	....	....	....	....	....	....	....	....	....	....	....	....	....	....	....	....
1985-86	U. Minn-Duluth	WCHA	42	52	32	84	46	....	....	....	....	....	....	....	....	....	....	....	....	....	....	....	....	....	....
	Calgary	**NHL**	....	....	....	....	....	....	....	....	....	....	....	....	....	....	**2**	**0**	**0**	**0**	**0**	**0**	**0**	**0**	....
1986-87	**Calgary**	**NHL**	**5**	**1**	**0**	**1**	**0**	**0**	**0**	**1**	**5**	**20.0**	**–1**	....	....	....	**4**	**2**	**1**	**3**	**0**	**0**	**0**	**0**	....
	Moncton	AHL	67	50	42	92	16	....	....	....	....	....	....	....	....	....	3	2	2	4	2	....	....	....	....
1987-88	**Calgary**	**NHL**	**52**	**26**	**24**	**50**	**12**	**4**	**0**	**3**	**153**	**17.0**	**10**	....	....	....	....	....	....	....	....	....	....	....	....
	St. Louis	**NHL**	**13**	**6**	**8**	**14**	**4**	**2**	**0**	**0**	**58**	**10.3**	**4**	....	....	....	**10**	**7**	**2**	**9**	**4**	**4**	**0**	**3**	....
1988-89	**St. Louis**	**NHL**	**78**	**41**	**43**	**84**	**33**	**16**	**0**	**6**	**305**	**13.4**	**–17**	....	....	....	**10**	**5**	**5**	**10**	**6**	**1**	**0**	**2**	....
1989-90	**St. Louis**	**NHL**	**80**	***72**	**41**	**113**	**24**	**27**	**0**	**12**	**385**	**18.7**	**–1**	....	....	....	**12**	**13**	**8**	**21**	**17**	**7**	**0**	**3**	....
1990-91	**St. Louis**	**NHL**	**78**	***86**	**45**	**131**	**22**	**29**	**0**	**11**	**389**	**22.1**	**23**	....	....	....	**13**	**11**	**8**	**19**	**4**	**3**	**0**	**2**	....
1991-92	**St. Louis**	**NHL**	**73**	***70**	**39**	**109**	**48**	**20**	**5**	**9**	**408**	**17.2**	**–2**	....	....	....	**6**	**4**	**4**	**8**	**4**	**1**	**1**	**1**	....
1992-93	**St. Louis**	**NHL**	**80**	**54**	**47**	**101**	**41**	**29**	**0**	**2**	**390**	**13.8**	**–27**	....	....	....	**11**	**8**	**5**	**13**	**2**	**5**	**0**	**2**	....
1993-94	**St. Louis**	**NHL**	**81**	**57**	**40**	**97**	**38**	**25**	**3**	**6**	**392**	**14.5**	**–3**	....	....	....	**4**	**2**	**1**	**3**	**0**	**1**	**0**	**0**	....
1994-95	**St. Louis**	**NHL**	**48**	**29**	**21**	**50**	**10**	**9**	**3**	**6**	**200**	**14.5**	**13**	....	....	....	**7**	**6**	**2**	**8**	**0**	**2**	**0**	**0**	....
1995-96	**St. Louis**	**NHL**	**70**	**43**	**40**	**83**	**30**	**16**	**5**	**6**	**327**	**13.1**	**4**	....	....	....	**13**	**6**	**5**	**11**	**10**	**2**	**1**	**1**	....
1996-97	**St. Louis**	**NHL**	**77**	**42**	**40**	**82**	**10**	**12**	**2**	**6**	**302**	**13.9**	**–9**	....	....	....	**6**	**2**	**7**	**9**	**2**	**0**	**0**	**0**	....
1997-98	**St. Louis**	**NHL**	**66**	**27**	**45**	**72**	**26**	**10**	**0**	**6**	**211**	**12.8**	**–1**	....	....	....	**10**	**3**	**3**	**6**	**2**	**1**	**0**	**1**	....
	United States	Olympics	4	2	1	3	0	....	....	....	....	....	....	....	....	....	....	....	....	....	....	....	....	....	....
1998-99♦	**Dallas**	**NHL**	**60**	**32**	**26**	**58**	**30**	**15**	**0**	**11**	**192**	**16.7**	**19**	**12**	**50.0**	**17:24**	**22**	**8**	**7**	**15**	**4**	**3**	**0**	**2**	**18:29**
99-2000	**Dallas**	**NHL**	**79**	**24**	**35**	**59**	**43**	**11**	**0**	**3**	**223**	**10.8**	**–21**	**10**	**40.0**	**18:37**	**23**	***11**	***13**	***24**	**4**	**3**	**0**	**4**	**19:59**
2000-01	**Dallas**	**NHL**	**79**	**39**	**40**	**79**	**18**	**11**	**0**	**8**	**219**	**17.8**	**10**	**10**	**30.0**	**17:53**	**10**	**2**	**5**	**7**	**6**	**1**	**0**	**0**	**20:10**
2001-02♦	**Detroit**	**NHL**	**82**	**30**	**33**	**63**	**35**	**7**	**1**	**4**	**247**	**12.1**	**18**	**5**	**20.0**	**18:49**	**23**	***10**	**8**	**18**	**4**	**3**	**2**	**2**	**17:54**
	United States	Olympics	6	3	5	8	6	....	....	....	....	....	....	....	....	....	....	....	....	....	....	....	....	....	....
2002-03	**Detroit**	**NHL**	**82**	**37**	**39**	**76**	**22**	**12**	**1**	**4**	**262**	**14.1**	**11**	**18**	**38.9**	**18:07**	**4**	**0**	**1**	**1**	**0**	**0**	**0**	**0**	**20:17**
	NHL Totals		**1183**	**716**	**606**	**1322**	**446**	**255**	**20**	**104**	**4668**	**15.3**		**55**	**38.2**	**18:13**	**190**	**100**	**85**	**185**	**69**	**37**	**4**	**23**	**19:02**

BCJHL Interior Division First All-Star Team (1983, 1984) • WCHA Freshman of the Year (1985) • WCHA First All-Star Team (1986) • AHL First All-Star Team (1987) • Dudley "Red" Garrett Memorial Trophy (Top Rookie – AHL) (1987) • NHL First All-Star Team (1990, 1991, 1992) • Dodge Ram Tough Award (1990, 1991) • Lady Byng Trophy (1990) • ProSet/NHL Player of the Year Award (1991) • Lester B. Pearson Award (1991) • Hart Memorial Trophy (1991)

Played in NHL All-Star Game (1989, 1990, 1992, 1993, 1994, 1996, 1997, 2001)

Traded to **St. Louis** by **Calgary** with Steve Bozek for Rob Ramage and Rick Wamsley, March 7, 1988. Signed as a free agent by **Dallas**, July 3, 1998. Signed as a free agent by **Detroit**, August 22, 2001.

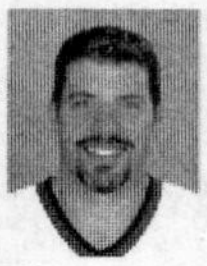

HULL, Jody

(HUHL, JOH-dee) **OTT.**

Right wing. Shoots right. 6'2", 195 lbs. Born, Petrolia, Ont., February 2, 1969. Hartford's 1st choice, 18th overall, in 1987 Entry Draft.

Season	Club	League	GP	G	A	Pts	PIM	PP	SH	GW	S	%	+/-	TF	F%	Min	GP	G	A	Pts	PIM	PP	SH	GW	Min
1984-85	Cambridge	OJHL-B	38	13	17	30	39	....	....	....	....	....	....	....	....	....	....	....	....	....	....	....	....	....	....
1985-86	Peterborough	OHL	61	20	22	42	29	....	....	....	....	....	....	....	....	....	16	1	5	6	4	....	....	....	....
1986-87	Peterborough	OHL	49	18	34	52	22	....	....	....	....	....	....	....	....	....	12	4	9	13	14	....	....	....	....
1987-88	Peterborough	OHL	60	50	44	94	33	....	....	....	....	....	....	....	....	....	12	10	8	18	8	....	....	....	....
1988-89	**Hartford**	**NHL**	**60**	**16**	**18**	**34**	**10**	**6**	**0**	**2**	**82**	**19.5**	**6**	....	....	....	**1**	**0**	**0**	**0**	**2**	**0**	**0**	**0**	....
1989-90	**Hartford**	**NHL**	**38**	**7**	**10**	**17**	**21**	**2**	**0**	**0**	**46**	**15.2**	**–6**	....	....	....	**5**	**0**	**1**	**1**	**2**	**0**	**0**	**0**	....
	Binghamton	AHL	21	7	10	17	6	....	....	....	....	....	....	....	....	....	....	....	....	....	....	....	....	....	....
1990-91	**NY Rangers**	**NHL**	**47**	**5**	**8**	**13**	**10**	**0**	**0**	**0**	**57**	**8.8**	**2**	....	....	....	....	....	....	....	....	....	....	....	....
1991-92	**NY Rangers**	**NHL**	**3**	**0**	**0**	**0**	**2**	**0**	**0**	**0**	**4**	**0.0**	**–4**	....	....	....	....	....	....	....	....	....	....	....	....
	Binghamton	AHL	69	34	31	65	28	....	....	....	....	....	....	....	....	....	11	5	2	7	4	....	....	....	....
1992-93	**Ottawa**	**NHL**	**69**	**13**	**21**	**34**	**14**	**5**	**1**	**0**	**134**	**9.7**	**–24**	....	....	....	....	....	....	....	....	....	....	....	....
1993-94	**Florida**	**NHL**	**69**	**13**	**13**	**26**	**8**	**0**	**1**	**5**	**100**	**13.0**	**6**	....	....	....	....	....	....	....	....	....	....	....	....
1994-95	**Florida**	**NHL**	**46**	**11**	**8**	**19**	**8**	**0**	**0**	**4**	**63**	**17.5**	**–1**	....	....	....	....	....	....	....	....	....	....	....	....
1995-96	**Florida**	**NHL**	**78**	**20**	**17**	**37**	**25**	**2**	**0**	**3**	**120**	**16.7**	**5**	....	....	....	**14**	**3**	**2**	**5**	**0**	**0**	**0**	**0**	....
1996-97	**Florida**	**NHL**	**67**	**10**	**6**	**16**	**4**	**0**	**1**	**2**	**92**	**10.9**	**1**	....	....	....	**5**	**0**	**0**	**0**	**0**	**0**	**0**	**0**	....

			Regular Season															Playoffs								
Season	Club	League	GP	G	A	Pts	PIM	PP	SH	GW	S	%	+/-	TF	F%	Min	GP	G	A	Pts	PIM	PP	SH	GW	Min
1997-98	**Florida**	**NHL**	**21**	**2**	**0**	**2**	**4**	**0**	**1**	**0**	**23**	**8.7**	**1**	....	....	....	....	....	....	....	....	....	....	....	....
	Tampa Bay	**NHL**	**28**	**2**	**4**	**6**	**4**	**0**	**0**	**2**	**28**	**7.1**	**2**	....	....	....	....	....	....	....	....	....	....	....	....
1998-99	**Philadelphia**	**NHL**	**72**	**3**	**11**	**14**	**12**	**0**	**0**	**1**	**73**	**4.1**	**−2**	**15**	**53.3**	**12:59**	**6**	**0**	**0**	**0**	**4**	**0**	**0**	**0**	**15:38**
99-2000	Orlando	IHL	1	0	0	0	0	....	....	....	....	....	....	....	....	....	....	....	....	....	....	....	....	....	....
	Philadelphia	**NHL**	**67**	**10**	**3**	**13**	**4**	**0**	**2**	**2**	**63**	**15.9**	**8**	**36**	**41.7**	**11:58**	**18**	**0**	**1**	**1**	**0**	**0**	**0**	**0**	**14:20**
2000-01	**Philadelphia**	**NHL**	**71**	**7**	**8**	**15**	**10**	**0**	**2**	**2**	**78**	**9.0**	**−1**	**83**	**36.1**	**13:13**	**6**	**0**	**0**	**0**	**4**	**0**	**0**	**0**	**13:04**
2001-02	**Ottawa**	**NHL**	**24**	**2**	**2**	**4**	**6**	**0**	**0**	**1**	**12**	**16.7**	**0**	**10**	**30.0**	**10:10**	**12**	**1**	**1**	**2**	**2**	**0**	**0**	**0**	**11:06**
	Grand Rapids	AHL	3	2	1	3	2	....	....	....	....	....	....	....	....	....	....	....	....	....	....	....	....	....	....
2002-03	**Ottawa**	**NHL**	**70**	**3**	**8**	**11**	**14**	**0**	**0**	**1**	**42**	**7.1**	**−3**	**38**	**26.3**	**10:32**	**2**	**0**	**0**	**0**	**0**	**0**	**0**	**0**	**8:17**
	NHL Totals		**830**	**124**	**137**	**261**	**156**	**15**	**8**	**25**	**1017**	**12.2**		**182**	**36.3**	**12:02**	**69**	**4**	**5**	**9**	**14**	**0**	**0**	**0**	**13:11**

OHL Second All-Star Team (1988)

Traded to **NY Rangers** by **Hartford** for Carey Wilson and NY Rangers' 3rd round choice (Michael Nylander) in the 1991 Entry Draft, July 9, 1990. Traded to **Ottawa** by **NY Rangers** for future considerations, July 28, 1992. Signed as a free agent by **Florida**, August 10, 1993. Traded to **Tampa Bay** by **Florida** with Mark Fitzpatrick for Dino Ciccarelli and Jeff Norton, January 15, 1998. Signed as a free agent by **Philadelphia**, October 7, 1998. Claimed by **Atlanta** from **Philadelphia** in Expansion Draft, June 25, 1999. Traded to **Philadelphia** by **Atlanta** for cash, October 15, 1999. Signed as a free agent by **Ottawa**, January 24, 2002.

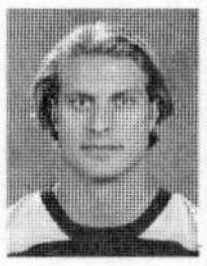

HULSE, Cale

(HUHLS, KAYL) **PHX.**

Defense. Shoots right. 6'3", 220 lbs. Born, Edmonton, Alta., November 10, 1973. New Jersey's 3rd choice, 66th overall, in 1992 Entry Draft.

1990-91	Calgary Royals	AJHL	49	3	23	26	220	....	....	....	....	....	....	....	....	....	....	....	....	....	....	....	....	....	....
1991-92	Portland	WHL	70	4	18	22	230	....	....	....	....	....	....	....	....	....	6	0	2	2	27	....	....	....	....
1992-93	Portland	WHL	72	10	26	36	284	....	....	....	....	....	....	....	....	....	16	4	4	8	65	....	....	....	....
1993-94	Albany River Rats	AHL	79	7	14	21	186	....	....	....	....	....	....	....	....	....	5	0	3	3	11	....	....	....	....
1994-95	Albany River Rats	AHL	77	5	13	18	215	....	....	....	....	....	....	....	....	....	12	1	1	2	17	....	....	....	....
1995-96	**New Jersey**	**NHL**	**8**	**0**	**0**	**0**	**15**	**0**	**0**	**0**	**5**	**0.0**	**−2**	....	....	....	....	....	....	....	....	....	....	....	....
	Albany River Rats	AHL	42	4	23	27	107	....	....	....	....	....	....	....	....	....	....	....	....	....	....	....	....	....	....
	Calgary	**NHL**	**3**	**0**	**0**	**0**	**5**	**0**	**0**	**0**	**4**	**0.0**	**3**	....	....	....	**1**	**0**	**0**	**0**	**0**	**0**	**0**	**0**	....
	Saint John Flames	AHL	13	2	7	9	39	....	....	....	....	....	....	....	....	....	....	....	....	....	....	....	....	....	....
1996-97	**Calgary**	**NHL**	**63**	**1**	**6**	**7**	**91**	**0**	**1**	**0**	**58**	**1.7**	**−2**	....	....	....	....	....	....	....	....	....	....	....	....
1997-98	**Calgary**	**NHL**	**79**	**5**	**22**	**27**	**169**	**1**	**1**	**0**	**117**	**4.3**	**1**	....	....	....	....	....	....	....	....	....	....	....	....
1998-99	**Calgary**	**NHL**	**73**	**3**	**9**	**12**	**117**	**0**	**0**	**0**	**83**	**3.6**	**−8**	**1**	**0.0**	**16:38**	....	....	....	....	....	....	....	....	....
99-2000	**Calgary**	**NHL**	**47**	**1**	**6**	**7**	**47**	**0**	**0**	**0**	**41**	**2.4**	**−11**	**1**	**100.0**	**12:38**	....	....	....	....	....	....	....	....	....
2000-01	**Nashville**	**NHL**	**82**	**1**	**7**	**8**	**128**	**0**	**0**	**1**	**93**	**1.1**	**−5**	**0**	**0.0**	**20:05**	....	....	....	....	....	....	....	....	....
2001-02	**Nashville**	**NHL**	**63**	**0**	**2**	**2**	**121**	**0**	**0**	**0**	**70**	**0.0**	**−18**	**0**	**0.0**	**18:51**	....	....	....	....	....	....	....	....	....
2002-03	**Nashville**	**NHL**	**80**	**2**	**6**	**8**	**121**	**0**	**0**	**1**	**82**	**2.4**	**−11**	**0**	**0.0**	**19:05**	....	....	....	....	....	....	....	....	....
	NHL Totals		**498**	**13**	**58**	**71**	**814**	**1**	**2**	**2**	**553**	**2.4**		**2**	**50.0**	**17:53**	**1**	**0**	**0**	**0**	**0**	**0**	**0**	**0**	....

Traded to **Calgary** by **New Jersey** with Tommy Albelin and Jocelyn Lemieux for Phil Housley and Dan Keczmer, February 26, 1996. Traded to **Nashville** by **Calgary** with Calgary's 3rd round choice (Denis Platonov) in 2001 Entry Draft for Sergei Krivokrasov, March 14, 2000. Signed as a free agent by **Phoenix**, July 10, 2003.

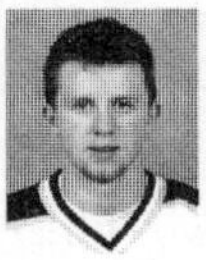

HUML, Ivan

(HUH-muhl, ee-VAHN) **BOS.**

Left wing. Shoots left. 6'2", 195 lbs. Born, Kladno, Czech., September 6, 1981. Boston's 4th choice, 59th overall, in 2000 Entry Draft.

1996-97	Kladno Jr.	Czech-Jr.	37	16	3	19	....	....	....	....	....	....	....	....	....	....	....	....	....	....	....	....	....	....	....
1997-98	Kladno Jr.	Czech-Jr.	46	37	24	61	....	....	....	....	....	....	....	....	....	....	....	....	....	....	....	....	....	....	....
	Kladno	Czech	1	0	0	0	0	....	....	....	....	....	....	....	....	....	....	....	....	....	....	....	....	....	....
1998-99	Kladno Jr.	Czech-Jr.	18	6	6	12	....	....	....	....	....	....	....	....	....	....	....	....	....	....	....	....	....	....	....
	Langley Hornets	BCHL	33	23	17	40	41	....	....	....	....	....	....	....	....	....	....	....	....	....	....	....	....	....	....
99-2000	Langley Hornets	BCHL	49	53	51	104	72	....	....	....	....	....	....	....	....	....	....	....	....	....	....	....	....	....	....
2000-01	Providence Bruins	AHL	79	13	6	19	28	....	....	....	....	....	....	....	....	....	17	0	0	0	2	....	....	....	....
2001-02	**Boston**	**NHL**	**1**	**0**	**1**	**1**	**0**	**0**	**0**	**0**	**2**	**0.0**	**2**	**0**	**0.0**	**15:43**	....	....	....	....	....	....	....	....	....
	Providence Bruins	AHL	76	28	19	47	75	....	....	....	....	....	....	....	....	....	2	0	0	0	0	....	....	....	....
2002-03	**Boston**	**NHL**	**41**	**6**	**11**	**17**	**30**	**0**	**0**	**2**	**75**	**8.0**	**3**	**22**	**45.5**	**12:46**	....	....	....	....	....	....	....	....	....
	Providence Bruins	AHL	30	10	16	26	42	....	....	....	....	....	....	....	....	....	4	2	0	2	0	....	....	....	....
	NHL Totals		**42**	**6**	**12**	**18**	**30**	**0**	**0**	**2**	**77**	**7.8**		**22**	**45.5**	**12:50**	....	....	....	....	....	....	....	....	....

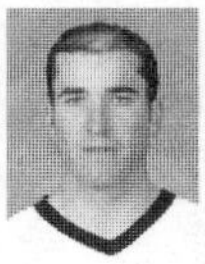

HUNTER, Trent

(HUHN-tuhr, TREHNT) **NYI**

Right wing. Shoots right. 6'3", 191 lbs. Born, Red Deer, Alta., July 5, 1980. Anaheim's 4th choice, 150th overall, in 1998 Entry Draft.

1996-97	Red Deer	AMHL	42	30	25	55	50	....	....	....	....	....	....	....	....	....	....	....	....	....	....	....	....	....	....
1997-98	Prince George	WHL	60	13	14	27	34	....	....	....	....	....	....	....	....	....	8	1	0	1	4	....	....	....	....
1998-99	Prince George	WHL	50	18	20	38	34	....	....	....	....	....	....	....	....	....	7	2	5	7	2	....	....	....	....
99-2000	Prince George	WHL	67	46	49	95	47	....	....	....	....	....	....	....	....	....	13	7	15	22	6	....	....	....	....
2000-01	Springfield	AHL	57	18	17	35	14	....	....	....	....	....	....	....	....	....	....	....	....	....	....	....	....	....	....
2001-02	Bridgeport	AHL	80	30	35	65	30	....	....	....	....	....	....	....	....	....	17	8	11	19	6	....	....	....	....
	NY Islanders	**NHL**	....	....	....	....	....	....	....	....	....	....	....	....	....	....	**4**	**1**	**1**	**2**	**2**	**0**	**0**	**0**	**11:13**
2002-03	**NY Islanders**	**NHL**	**8**	**0**	**4**	**4**	**4**	**0**	**0**	**0**	**19**	**0.0**	**5**	**1**	**0.0**	**12:13**	....	....	....	....	....	....	....	....	....
	Bridgeport	AHL	70	30	41	71	39	....	....	....	....	....	....	....	....	....	9	7	4	11	10	....	....	....	....
	NHL Totals		**8**	**0**	**4**	**4**	**4**	**0**	**0**	**0**	**19**	**0.0**		**1**	**0.0**	**12:13**	**4**	**1**	**1**	**2**	**2**	**0**	**0**	**0**	**11:13**

WHL West First All-Star Team (2000)

Traded to **NY Islanders** by **Anaheim** for Columbus' 4th round choice (previously acquired, Anaheim selected Jonas Ronnqvist) in 2000 Entry Draft, May 23, 2000.

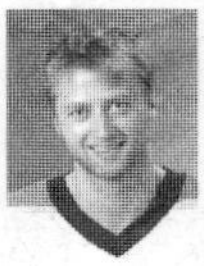

HUSELIUS, Kristian

(hoo-SAY-lee-oos, KRIHST-yan) **FLA.**

Left wing. Shoots left. 6'1", 190 lbs. Born, Osterhaninge, Sweden, November 10, 1978. Florida's 2nd choice, 47th overall, in 1997 Entry Draft.

1994-95	Hammarby Jr.	Swede-Jr.	17	6	2	8	2	....	....	....	....	....	....	....	....	....	....	....	....	....	....	....	....	....	....
1995-96	Hammarby Jr.	Swede-Jr.	25	13	8	21	14	....	....	....	....	....	....	....	....	....	....	....	....	....	....	....	....	....	....
	Hammarby	Swede-2	6	1	0	1	0	....	....	....	....	....	....	....	....	....	....	....	....	....	....	....	....	....	....
1996-97	Farjestad	Sweden	13	2	0	2	4	....	....	....	....	....	....	....	....	....	5	1	0	1	0	....	....	....	....
1997-98	Farjestad	Sweden	34	2	1	3	2	....	....	....	....	....	....	....	....	....	11	0	0	0	0	....	....	....	....
	Farjestad	EuroHL	5	2	3	5	0	....	....	....	....	....	....	....	....	....	....	....	....	....	....	....	....	....	....
1998-99	Farjestad	Sweden	28	4	4	8	4	....	....	....	....	....	....	....	....	....	....	....	....	....	....	....	....	....	....
	Farjestad	EuroHL	6	2	2	4	8	....	....	....	....	....	....	....	....	....	1	0	0	0	0	....	....	....	....
	Vastra Frolunda	Sweden	20	2	2	4	2	....	....	....	....	....	....	....	....	....	4	1	0	1	0	....	....	....	....
99-2000	Vastra Frolunda	Sweden	50	21	23	44	20	....	....	....	....	....	....	....	....	....	5	2	2	4	8	....	....	....	....
2000-01	Vastra Frolunda	Sweden	49	*32	*35	*67	26	....	....	....	....	....	....	....	....	....	5	4	5	9	14	....	....	....	....
2001-02	**Florida**	**NHL**	**79**	**23**	**22**	**45**	**14**	**6**	**1**	**3**	**169**	**13.6**	**−4**	**14**	**21.4**	**16:55**	....	....	....	....	....	....	....	....	....
2002-03	**Florida**	**NHL**	**78**	**20**	**23**	**43**	**20**	**3**	**0**	**3**	**187**	**10.7**	**−6**	**6**	**33.3**	**17:20**	....	....	....	....	....	....	....	....	....
	NHL Totals		**157**	**43**	**45**	**88**	**34**	**9**	**1**	**6**	**356**	**12.1**		**20**	**25.0**	**17:07**	....	....	....	....	....	....	....	....	....

NHL All-Rookie Team (2002)

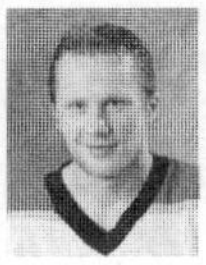

HYVONEN, Hannes

(HOO-voh-nuhn, HAH-nuhs) **CBJ**

Right wing. Shoots right. 6'2", 200 lbs. Born, Oulu, Finland, August 29, 1975. San Jose's 7th choice, 257th overall, in 1999 Entry Draft.

1993-94	Karpat Oulu Jr.	Finn-Jr.	35	15	13	28	26	....	....	....	....	....	....	....	....	....	3	0	0	0	0	....	....	....	....
	Karpat Oulu	Finland-2	3	3	1	4	2	....	....	....	....	....	....	....	....	....	....	....	....	....	....	....	....	....	....
1994-95	TPS Turku Jr.	Finn-Jr.	10	8	2	10	64	....	....	....	....	....	....	....	....	....	....	....	....	....	....	....	....	....	....
	Kiekko-67 Jr.	Finn-Jr.	1	1	0	1	0	....	....	....	....	....	....	....	....	....	....	....	....	....	....	....	....	....	....
	Kiekko-67 Turku	Finland-2	16	4	2	6	10	....	....	....	....	....	....	....	....	....	....	....	....	....	....	....	....	....	....
	TPS Turku	Finland	9	4	3	7	16	....	....	....	....	....	....	....	....	....	5	0	0	0	7	....	....	....	....
1995-96	Kiekko-67 Turku	Finland-2	2	1	0	1	8	....	....	....	....	....	....	....	....	....	....	....	....	....	....	....	....	....	....
	TPS Turku	Finland	30	11	5	16	49	....	....	....	....	....	....	....	....	....	7	0	1	1	28	....	....	....	....
1996-97	TPS Turku	Finland	41	10	5	15	48	....	....	....	....	....	....	....	....	....	10	4	2	6	14	....	....	....	....
1997-98	TPS Turku	Finland	29	2	6	8	71	....	....	....	....	....	....	....	....	....	2	0	0	0	0	....	....	....	....
1998-99	Blues Espoo	Finland	52	23	18	41	74	....	....	....	....	....	....	....	....	....	4	2	1	3	2	....	....	....	....
99-2000	Blues Espoo	Finland	18	5	2	7	*89	....	....	....	....	....	....	....	....	....	....	....	....	....	....	....	....	....	....
	HIFK Helsinki	Finland	22	2	2	4	*100	....	....	....	....	....	....	....	....	....	9	4	0	4	8	....	....	....	....
2000-01	HIFK Helsinki	Finland	56	14	12	26	34	....	....	....	....	....	....	....	....	....	5	0	0	0	8	....	....	....	....
2001-02	**San Jose**	**NHL**	**6**	**0**	**0**	**0**	**0**	**0**	**0**	**0**	**4**	**0.0**	**−2**	**0**	**0.0**	**5:40**	....	....	....	....	....	....	....	....	....
	Cleveland Barons	AHL	67	24	18	42	136	....	....	....	....	....	....	....	....	....	....	....	....	....	....	....	....	....	....

			Regular Season														Playoffs								
Season	Club	League	GP	G	A	Pts	PIM	PP	SH	GW	S	%	+/-	TF	F%	Min	GP	G	A	Pts	PIM	PP	SH	GW	Min
2002-03	Columbus	NHL	36	4	5	9	22	0	0	0	48	8.3	–11	8	25.0	10:02									
	Farjestad	Sweden	10	11	0	11	12										14	5	0	5	41				
	NHL Totals		42	4	5	9	22	0	0	0	52	7.7		8	25.0	9:25									

Traded to **Florida** by **San Jose** for Florida's 7th round choice (Jonathon Tremblay) in 2003 Entry Draft, July 16, 2002. Claimed on waivers by **Columbus** from **Florida**, October 5, 2002. • Loaned to **Farjestad** (Sweden) by **Columbus**, January 25, 2003.

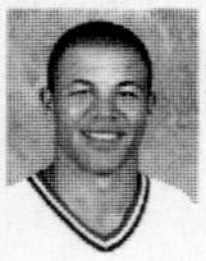

IGINLA, Jarome

(ih-GIHN-lah, jah-ROHM) **CGY.**

Right wing. Shoots right. 6'1", 208 lbs. Born, Edmonton, Alta., July 1, 1977. Dallas' 1st choice, 11th overall, in 1995 Entry Draft.

1991-92	St. Albert Raiders	AMHL	36	26	30	56	22																		
1992-93	St. Albert Raiders	AMHL	36	34	53	87	20																		
1993-94	Kamloops Blazers	WHL	48	6	23	29	33										19	3	6	9	10				
1994-95	Kamloops Blazers	WHL	72	33	38	71	111										21	7	11	18	34				
1995-96	Kamloops Blazers	WHL	63	63	73	136	120										16	16	13	29	44				
	Calgary	NHL															2	1	1	2	0	0	0	0	
1996-97	Calgary	NHL	82	21	29	50	37	8	1	3	169	12.4	–4												
1997-98	Calgary	NHL	70	13	19	32	29	0	2	1	154	8.4	–10												
1998-99	Calgary	NHL	82	28	23	51	58	7	0	4	211	13.3	1	111	51.4	16:30									
99-2000	Calgary	NHL	77	29	34	63	26	12	0	4	256	11.3	0	278	52.9	18:24									
2000-01	Calgary	NHL	77	31	40	71	62	10	0	4	229	13.5	–2	638	51.7	19:58									
2001-02	Calgary	NHL	82	*52	44	*96	77	16	1	7	311	16.7	27	308	55.2	22:22									
	Canada	Olympics	6	3	1	4	0																		
2002-03	Calgary	NHL	75	35	32	67	49	11	3	6	316	11.1	–10	90	43.3	21:26									
	NHL Totals		545	209	221	430	338	64	7	29	1646	12.7		1425	52.1	19:43	2	1	1	2	0	0	0	0	

George Parsons Trophy (Memorial Cup Most Sportsmanlike Player) (1995) • WHL West First All-Star Team (1996) • Canadian Major Junior First All-Star Team (1996) • NHL All-Rookie Team (1997) • NHL First All-Star Team (2002) • Maurice "Rocket" Richard Trophy (2002) • Art Ross Trophy (2002) • Lester B. Pearson Award (2002)

Played in NHL All-Star Game (2002, 2003)

Traded to **Calgary** by **Dallas** with Corey Millen for Joe Nieuwendyk, December 19, 1995.

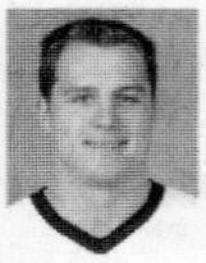

ISBISTER, Brad

(IHZ-bihs-tuhr, BRAD) **EDM.**

Left wing. Shoots right. 6'4", 220 lbs. Born, Edmonton, Alta., May 7, 1977. Winnipeg's 4th choice, 67th overall, in 1995 Entry Draft.

1992-93	Calgary Canucks	ABHL	35	24	25	49	74																		
1993-94	Portland	WHL	64	7	10	17	45										10	0	2	2	0				
1994-95	Portland	WHL	67	16	20	36	123																		
1995-96	Portland	WHL	71	45	44	89	184										7	2	4	6	20				
1996-97	Portland	WHL	24	15	18	33	45										6	2	1	3	16				
	Springfield	AHL	7	3	1	4	14										9	1	2	3	10				
1997-98	Phoenix	NHL	66	9	8	17	102	1	0	1	115	7.8	4				5	0	0	0	2	0	0	0	
	Springfield	AHL	9	8	2	10	36																		
1998-99	Phoenix	NHL	32	4	4	8	46	0	0	2	48	8.3	1	3	0.0	11:33									
	Springfield	AHL	4	1	1	2	12																		
	Las Vegas	IHL	2	0	0	0	9																		
99-2000	NY Islanders	NHL	64	22	20	42	100	9	0	1	135	16.3	–18	55	54.6	16:58									
2000-01	NY Islanders	NHL	51	18	14	32	59	7	1	4	129	14.0	–19	255	45.9	19:26									
2001-02	NY Islanders	NHL	79	17	21	38	113	4	0	2	142	12.0	1	71	45.1	15:18	3	1	1	2	17	1	0	1	12:33
2002-03	NY Islanders	NHL	53	10	13	23	34	2	0	2	90	11.1	–9	13	46.2	13:54									
	Edmonton	NHL	13	3	2	5	9	0	0	1	29	10.3	0	10	50.0	13:14	6	0	1	1	12	0	0	0	10:04
	NHL Totals		358	83	82	165	463	23	1	13	688	12.1		407	46.7	15:38	14	1	2	3	31	1	0	1	10:54

WHL West Second All-Star Team (1997)

Rights transferred to **Phoenix** after **Winnipeg** franchise relocated, July 1, 1996. Traded to **NY Islanders** by **Phoenix** with Phoenix's 3rd round choice (Brian Collins) in 1999 Entry Draft for Robert Reichel, NY Islanders' 3rd round choice (Jason Jaspers) in 1999 Entry Draft and Ottawa's 4th round choice (previously acquired, Phoenix selected Preston Mizzi) in 1999 Entry Draft, March 20, 1999. Traded to **Edmonton** by **NY Islanders** with Raffi Torres for Janne Niinimaa and Washington's 2nd round choice (previously acquired, NY Islanders selected Evgeni Tunik) in 2003 Entry Draft , March 11, 2003.

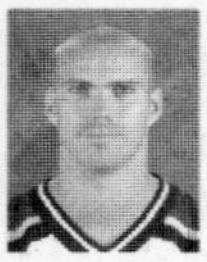

JACKMAN, Barret

(JAK-man, BAIR-reht) **ST.L.**

Defense. Shoots left. 6'1", 197 lbs. Born, Trail, B.C., March 5, 1981. St. Louis' 1st choice, 17th overall, in 1999 Entry Draft.

1996-97	Beaver Valley	VIJHL	32	22	25	47	180																		
1997-98	Regina Pats	WHL	68	2	11	13	224										9	0	3	3	32				
1998-99	Regina Pats	WHL	70	8	36	44	259																		
99-2000	Regina Pats	WHL	53	9	37	46	175										6	1	1	2	19				
	Worcester IceCats	AHL															2	0	0	0	13				
2000-01	Regina Pats	WHL	43	9	27	36	138										6	0	3	3	8				
2001-02	St. Louis	NHL	1	0	0	0	0	0	0	0	1	0.0	0	0	0.0	18:56	1	0	0	0	2	0	0	0	18:24
	Worcester IceCats	AHL	75	2	12	14	266										3	0	1	1	4				
2002-03	St. Louis	NHL	82	3	16	19	190	0	0	0	66	4.5	23	0	0.0	20:03	7	0	0	0	14	0	0	0	21:59
	NHL Totals		83	3	16	19	190	0	0	0	67	4.5		0	0.0	20:02	8	0	0	0	16	0	0	0	21:32

WHL East Second All-Star Team (2000) • AHL All-Rookie Team (2002) • NHL All-Rookie Team (2003) • Calder Memorial Trophy (2003)

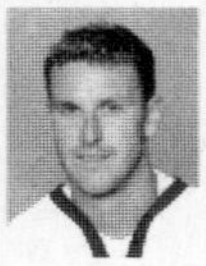

JACKMAN, Ric

(JAK-man, RIHK) **TOR.**

Defense. Shoots right. 6'2", 197 lbs. Born, Toronto, Ont., June 28, 1978. Dallas' 1st choice, 5th overall, in 1996 Entry Draft.

1993-94	Mississauga Sens	MTHL	81	35	53	88	156																		
1994-95	Mississauga Sens	MTHL	53	20	37	57	120																		
	Richmond Hill	OJHL	10	2	9	11	16																		
1995-96	Sault Ste. Marie	OHL	66	13	29	42	97										4	1	0	1	15				
1996-97	Sault Ste. Marie	OHL	53	13	34	47	116										10	2	6	8	24				
1997-98	Sault Ste. Marie	OHL	60	33	40	73	111																		
	Michigan	IHL	14	1	5	6	10										4	0	0	0	10				
1998-99	Michigan	IHL	71	13	17	30	106										5	0	4	4	6				
99-2000	Dallas	NHL	22	1	2	3	6	1	0	0	16	6.3	–1	0	0.0	8:06									
	Michigan	IHL	50	3	16	19	51																		
2000-01	Dallas	NHL	16	0	0	0	18	0	0	0	10	0.0	–6	0	0.0	8:51									
	Utah Grizzlies	IHL	57	9	19	28	24																		
2001-02	Boston	NHL	2	0	0	0	2	0	0	0	4	0.0	–1	0	0.0	13:26									
	Providence Bruins	AHL	9	0	1	1	8										2	0	0	0	2				
2002-03	Toronto	NHL	42	0	2	2	41	0	0	0	35	0.0	–10	0	0.0	13:59									
	St. John's	AHL	8	2	6	8	24																		
	NHL Totals		82	1	4	5	67	1	0	0	65	1.5		0	0.0	11:23									

OHL All-Rookie Team (1996) • OHL Second All-Star Team (1998)

Traded to **Boston** by **Dallas** for Cameron Mann, June 23, 2001. • Missed majority of 2001-02 season recovering from shoulder injury suffered in game vs. St. Louis, October 21, 2001. Traded to **Toronto** by **Boston** for the rights to Kris Vernarsky, May 13, 2002.

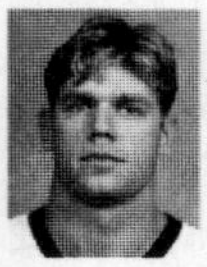

JACKSON, Dane

(JAK-sohn, DAYN)

Right wing. Shoots right. 6'1", 200 lbs. Born, Castlegar, B.C., May 17, 1970. Vancouver's 3rd choice, 44th overall, in 1988 Entry Draft.

1987-88	Vernon Lakers	BCJHL	49	24	30	54	95										13	7	10	17	49				
1988-89	North Dakota	WCHA	30	4	5	9	33																		
1989-90	North Dakota	WCHA	44	15	11	26	56																		
1990-91	North Dakota	WCHA	37	17	9	26	79																		
1991-92	North Dakota	WCHA	39	23	19	42	81																		
1992-93	Hamilton	AHL	68	23	20	43	59																		
1993-94	Vancouver	NHL	12	5	1	6	9	0	0	0	18	27.8	3												
	Hamilton	AHL	60	25	35	60	75										4	2	2	4	16				
1994-95	Syracuse Crunch	AHL	78	30	28	58	162																		
	Vancouver	NHL	3	1	0	1	4	0	0	0	6	16.7	0				6	0	0	0	10	0	0	0	
1995-96	Buffalo	NHL	22	5	4	9	41	0	0	1	20	25.0	3												
	Rochester	AHL	50	27	19	46	132										19	4	6	10	53				

			Regular Season														Playoffs								
Season	Club	League	GP	G	A	Pts	PIM	PP	SH	GW	S	%	+/-	TF	F%	Min	GP	G	A	Pts	PIM	PP	SH	GW	Min
1996-97	Rochester	AHL	78	24	34	58	111	....	....	....	....	....	....	....	....	....	10	7	4	11	14	....	....	....	....
1997-98	**NY Islanders**	**NHL**	**8**	**1**	**1**	**2**	**4**	**0**	**0**	**1**	**5**	**20.0**	**1**	....	....	....	....	....	....	....	....	....	....	....	....
	Rochester	AHL	28	10	13	23	55	....	....	....	....	....	....	....	....	....	3	2	2	4	4	....	....	....	....
1998-99	Lowell	AHL	80	16	27	43	103	....	....	....	....	....	....	....	....	....	3	0	1	1	16	....	....	....	....
99-2000	Rochester	AHL	21	6	9	15	8	....	....	....	....	....	....	....	....	....	....	....	....	....	....	....	....	....	....
2000-01	Rochester	AHL	69	16	12	28	104	....	....	....	....	....	....	....	....	....	4	1	1	2	4	....	....	....	....
2001-02	Manchester	AHL	76	16	21	37	93	....	....	....	....	....	....	....	....	....	5	1	0	1	9	....	....	....	....
2002-03	Manchester	AHL	63	6	14	20	80	....	....	....	....	....	....	....	....	....	3	0	1	1	0	....	....	....	....
	NHL Totals		**45**	**12**	**6**	**18**	**58**	**0**	**0**	**2**	**49**	**24.5**		....	....	....	**6**	**0**	**0**	**0**	**10**	**0**	**0**	**0**	....

Signed as a free agent by **Buffalo**, September 20, 1995. Signed as a free agent by **NY Islanders**, July 21, 1997. Signed as a free agent by **Rochester** (AHL), August 29, 1999. • Missed majority of 1999-2000 season recovering from knee injury suffered in game vs. Springfield (AHL), January 21, 2000. Signed as a free agent by **Manchester** (AHL), September 7, 2001.

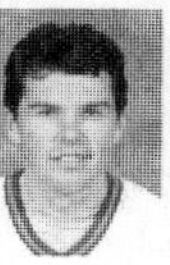

JAGR, Jaromir

(YAH-guhr, YAIR-oh-MEER) **WSH.**

Right wing. Shoots left. 6'2", 234 lbs. Born, Kladno, Czech., February 15, 1972. Pittsburgh's 1st choice, 5th overall, in 1990 Entry Draft.

1984-85	Kladno Jr.	Czech-Jr.	34	24	17	41	....	....	....	....	....	....	....	....	....	....	....	....	....	....	....	....	....	....	....
1985-86	Kladno Jr.	Czech-Jr.	36	41	29	70	....	....	....	....	....	....	....	....	....	....	....	....	....	....	....	....	....	....	....
1986-87	Kladno Jr.	Czech-Jr.	30	35	35	70	....	....	....	....	....	....	....	....	....	....	....	....	....	....	....	....	....	....	....
1987-88	Kladno Jr.	Czech-Jr.	35	57	27	84	....	....	....	....	....	....	....	....	....	....	....	....	....	....	....	....	....	....	....
1988-89	Kladno	Czech	29	3	3	6	4	....	....	....	....	....	....	....	....	....	10	5	7	12	0	....	....	....	....
1989-90	Poldi Kladno	Czech	42	22	28	50	....	....	....	....	....	....	....	....	....	....	9	*8	2	10	....	....	....	....	....
1990-91♦	**Pittsburgh**	**NHL**	**80**	**27**	**30**	**57**	**42**	**7**	**0**	**4**	**136**	**19.9**	**–4**	....	....	....	**24**	**3**	**10**	**13**	**6**	**1**	**0**	**1**	....
1991-92♦	**Pittsburgh**	**NHL**	**70**	**32**	**37**	**69**	**34**	**4**	**0**	**4**	**194**	**16.5**	**12**	....	....	....	**21**	**11**	**13**	**24**	**6**	**2**	**0**	**4**	....
1992-93	**Pittsburgh**	**NHL**	**81**	**34**	**60**	**94**	**61**	**10**	**1**	**9**	**242**	**14.0**	**30**	....	....	....	**12**	**5**	**4**	**9**	**23**	**1**	**0**	**1**	....
1993-94	**Pittsburgh**	**NHL**	**80**	**32**	**67**	**99**	**61**	**9**	**0**	**6**	**298**	**10.7**	**15**	....	....	....	**6**	**2**	**4**	**6**	**16**	**0**	**0**	**1**	....
1994-95	HC Kladno	Czech	11	8	14	22	10	....	....	....	....	....	....	....	....	....	....	....	....	....	....	....	....	....	....
	HC Bolzano	Euroliga	5	8	8	16	4	....	....	....	....	....	....	....	....	....	....	....	....	....	....	....	....	....	....
	HC Bolzano	Italy	1	0	0	0	0	....	....	....	....	....	....	....	....	....	....	....	....	....	....	....	....	....	....
	EHC Schalke	German-3	1	1	10	11	0	....	....	....	....	....	....	....	....	....	....	....	....	....	....	....	....	....	....
	Pittsburgh	**NHL**	**48**	**32**	**38**	***70**	**37**	**8**	**3**	**7**	**192**	**16.7**	**23**	....	....	....	**12**	**10**	**5**	**15**	**6**	**2**	**1**	**1**	....
1995-96	**Pittsburgh**	**NHL**	**82**	**62**	**87**	**149**	**96**	**20**	**1**	**12**	**403**	**15.4**	**31**	....	....	....	**18**	**11**	**12**	**23**	**18**	**5**	**1**	**1**	....
1996-97	**Pittsburgh**	**NHL**	**63**	**47**	**48**	**95**	**40**	**11**	**2**	**6**	**234**	**20.1**	**22**	....	....	....	**5**	**4**	**4**	**8**	**4**	**2**	**0**	**0**	....
1997-98	**Pittsburgh**	**NHL**	**77**	**35**	***67**	***102**	**64**	**7**	**0**	**8**	**262**	**13.4**	**17**	....	....	....	**6**	**4**	**5**	**9**	**2**	**1**	**0**	**0**	....
	Czech Republic	Olympics	6	1	4	5	2	....	....	....	....	....	....	....	....	....	....	....	....	....	....	....	....	....	....
1998-99	**Pittsburgh**	**NHL**	**81**	**44**	***83**	***127**	**66**	**10**	**1**	**7**	**343**	**12.8**	**17**	**4**	**50.0**	**25:51**	**9**	**5**	**7**	**12**	**16**	**1**	**0**	**1**	**25:32**
99-2000	**Pittsburgh**	**NHL**	**63**	**42**	**54**	***96**	**50**	**10**	**0**	**5**	**290**	**14.5**	**25**	**9**	**22.2**	**23:12**	**11**	**8**	**8**	**16**	**6**	**2**	**0**	**4**	**24:32**
2000-01	**Pittsburgh**	**NHL**	**81**	**52**	***69**	***121**	**42**	**14**	**1**	**10**	**317**	**16.4**	**19**	**2**	**0.0**	**23:19**	**16**	**2**	**10**	**12**	**18**	**2**	**0**	**0**	**22:15**
2001-02	**Washington**	**NHL**	**69**	**31**	**48**	**79**	**30**	**10**	**0**	**3**	**197**	**15.7**	**0**	**2**	**50.0**	**21:43**	....	....	....	....	....	....	....	....	....
	Czech Republic	Olympics	4	2	3	5	4	....	....	....	....	....	....	....	....	....	....	....	....	....	....	....	....	....	....
2002-03	**Washington**	**NHL**	**75**	**36**	**41**	**77**	**38**	**13**	**2**	**9**	**290**	**12.4**	**5**	**5**	**20.0**	**21:18**	**6**	**2**	**5**	**7**	**2**	**1**	**0**	**0**	**25:13**
	NHL Totals		**950**	**506**	**729**	**1235**	**661**	**133**	**11**	**90**	**3398**	**14.9**		**22**	**27.3**	**23:09**	**146**	**67**	**87**	**154**	**123**	**20**	**2**	**14**	**23:59**

NHL All-Rookie Team (1991) • NHL First All-Star Team (1995, 1996, 1998, 1999, 2000, 2001) • Art Ross Trophy (1995, 1998, 1999, 2000, 2001) • NHL Second All-Star Team (1997) • Lester B. Pearson Award (1999, 2000) • Hart Trophy (1999)

Played in NHL All-Star Game (1992, 1993, 1996, 1998, 1999, 2000, 2002, 2003)

Traded to **Washington** by **Pittsburgh** with Frantisek Kucera for Kris Beech, Michal Sivek, Ross Lupaschuk and future considerations, July 11, 2001.

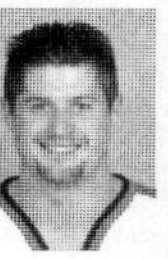

JAKOPIN, John

(JA-koh-pihn, JAWN) **NYR**

Defense. Shoots right. 6'5", 239 lbs. Born, Toronto, Ont., May 16, 1975. Detroit's 4th choice, 97th overall, in 1993 Entry Draft.

1992-93	St. Michael's B	MTJHL	45	9	21	30	42	....	....	....	....	....	....	....	....	....	13	3	2	5	4	....	....	....	....
1993-94	Merrimack	H-East	36	2	8	10	64	....	....	....	....	....	....	....	....	....	....	....	....	....	....	....	....	....	....
1994-95	Merrimack	H-East	37	4	10	14	42	....	....	....	....	....	....	....	....	....	....	....	....	....	....	....	....	....	....
1995-96	Merrimack	H-East	32	10	15	25	68	....	....	....	....	....	....	....	....	....	....	....	....	....	....	....	....	....	....
1996-97	Merrimack	H-East	31	4	12	16	68	....	....	....	....	....	....	....	....	....	....	....	....	....	....	....	....	....	....
	Adirondack	AHL	3	0	0	0	9	....	....	....	....	....	....	....	....	....	....	....	....	....	....	....	....	....	....
1997-98	**Florida**	**NHL**	**2**	**0**	**0**	**0**	**4**	**0**	**0**	**0**	**1**	**0.0**	**–3**	....	....	....	....	....	....	....	....	....	....	....	....
	New Haven	AHL	60	2	18	20	151	....	....	....	....	....	....	....	....	....	3	0	0	0	0	....	....	....	....
1998-99	**Florida**	**NHL**	**3**	**0**	**0**	**0**	**0**	**0**	**0**	**0**	**0**	**0.0**	**–1**	**0**	**0.0**	**13:32**	....	....	....	....	....	....	....	....	....
	New Haven	AHL	60	2	7	9	154	....	....	....	....	....	....	....	....	....	....	....	....	....	....	....	....	....	....
99-2000	**Florida**	**NHL**	**17**	**0**	**0**	**0**	**26**	**0**	**0**	**0**	**1**	**0.0**	**–2**	**0**	**0.0**	**11:58**	....	....	....	....	....	....	....	....	....
	Louisville Panthers	AHL	23	4	6	10	47	....	....	....	....	....	....	....	....	....	....	....	....	....	....	....	....	....	....
2000-01	**Florida**	**NHL**	**60**	**1**	**2**	**3**	**62**	**0**	**0**	**0**	**23**	**4.3**	**–4**	**2**	**50.0**	**12:54**	....	....	....	....	....	....	....	....	....
	Louisville Panthers	AHL	8	0	1	1	21	....	....	....	....	....	....	....	....	....	....	....	....	....	....	....	....	....	....
2001-02	**Pittsburgh**	**NHL**	**19**	**0**	**4**	**4**	**42**	**0**	**0**	**0**	**3**	**0.0**	**2**	**0**	**0.0**	**8:16**	....	....	....	....	....	....	....	....	....
	Wilkes-Barre	AHL	30	3	5	8	90	....	....	....	....	....	....	....	....	....	....	....	....	....	....	....	....	....	....
2002-03	**San Jose**	**NHL**	**12**	**0**	**0**	**0**	**11**	**0**	**0**	**0**	**3**	**0.0**	**0**	**0**	**0.0**	**8:11**	....	....	....	....	....	....	....	....	....
	Cleveland Barons	AHL	18	0	4	4	27	....	....	....	....	....	....	....	....	....	....	....	....	....	....	....	....	....	....
	NHL Totals		**113**	**1**	**6**	**7**	**145**	**0**	**0**	**0**	**31**	**3.2**		**2**	**50.0**	**11:28**	....	....	....	....	....	....	....	....	....

Signed as a free agent by **Florida**, May 14, 1997. • Missed majority of 1999-2000 season recovering from groin injury suffered in game vs. Carolina, February 1, 2000. Claimed on waivers by **Pittsburgh** from **Florida**, October 3, 2001. Signed as a free agent by **San Jose**, September 5, 2002. • Missed majority of 2002-03 season recovering from head injury suffered in game vs. Milwaukee (AHL), November 30, 2002. Signed as a free agent by **NY Rangers**, August 21, 2003.

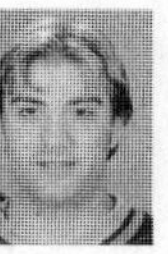

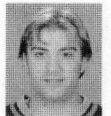

JANIK, Doug

(JAN-nihk, DUHG) **BUF.**

Defense. Shoots left. 6'2", 209 lbs. Born, Agawam, MA, March 26, 1980. Buffalo's 3rd choice, 55th overall, in 1999 Entry Draft.

1995-96	Springfield	NEJHL	48	16	38	54	....	....	....	....	....	....	....	....	....	....	....	....	....	....	....	....	....	....	....
1996-97	Springfield	NEJHL	39	12	24	36	22	....	....	....	....	....	....	....	....	....	11	5	9	14	10	....	....	....	....
1997-98	U.S. National U-18	USDP	65	8	26	34	105	....	....	....	....	....	....	....	....	....	....	....	....	....	....	....	....	....	....
1998-99	U. of Maine	H-East	35	3	13	16	44	....	....	....	....	....	....	....	....	....	....	....	....	....	....	....	....	....	....
99-2000	U. of Maine	H-East	36	6	14	20	54	....	....	....	....	....	....	....	....	....	....	....	....	....	....	....	....	....	....
2000-01	U. of Maine	H-East	39	3	15	18	52	....	....	....	....	....	....	....	....	....	....	....	....	....	....	....	....	....	....
2001-02	Rochester	AHL	80	6	17	23	100	....	....	....	....	....	....	....	....	....	2	0	0	0	0	....	....	....	....
2002-03	**Buffalo**	**NHL**	**6**	**0**	**0**	**0**	**2**	**0**	**0**	**0**	**1**	**0.0**	**1**	**0**	**0.0**	**7:42**	....	....	....	....	....	....	....	....	....
	Rochester	AHL	75	3	13	16	120	....	....	....	....	....	....	....	....	....	3	0	0	0	6	....	....	....	....
	NHL Totals		**6**	**0**	**0**	**0**	**2**	**0**	**0**	**0**	**1**	**0.0**		**0**	**0.0**	**7:42**	....	....	....	....	....	....	....	....	....

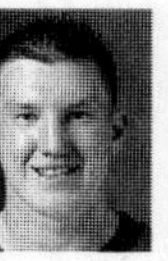

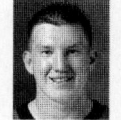

JARDINE, Ryan

(JAHR-dighn, RIGH-yan) **FLA.**

Left wing. Shoots left. 6', 210 lbs. Born, Ottawa, Ont., March 15, 1980. Florida's 4th choice, 89th overall, in 1998 Entry Draft.

1996-97	Kanata Valley	OCJHL	52	30	27	57	76	....	....	....	....	....	....	....	....	....	....	....	....	....	....	....	....	....	....
1997-98	Sault Ste. Marie	OHL	65	28	32	60	16	....	....	....	....	....	....	....	....	....	....	....	....	....	....	....	....	....	....
1998-99	Sault Ste. Marie	OHL	68	27	34	61	56	....	....	....	....	....	....	....	....	....	5	0	1	1	6	....	....	....	....
99-2000	Sault Ste. Marie	OHL	65	43	34	77	58	....	....	....	....	....	....	....	....	....	17	11	8	19	16	....	....	....	....
2000-01	Louisville Panthers	AHL	77	12	14	26	38	....	....	....	....	....	....	....	....	....	....	....	....	....	....	....	....	....	....
2001-02	**Florida**	**NHL**	**8**	**0**	**2**	**2**	**2**	**0**	**0**	**0**	**6**	**0.0**	**0**	**2**	**100.0**	**8:55**	....	....	....	....	....	....	....	....	....
	Utah Grizzlies	AHL	64	16	16	32	56	....	....	....	....	....	....	....	....	....	4	1	1	2	0	....	....	....	....
2002-03	San Antonio	AHL	64	14	17	31	37	....	....	....	....	....	....	....	....	....	3	1	0	1	0	....	....	....	....
	NHL Totals		**8**	**0**	**2**	**2**	**2**	**0**	**0**	**0**	**6**	**0.0**		**2**	**100.0**	**8:55**	....	....	....	....	....	....	....	....	....

OHL All-Rookie Team (1998)

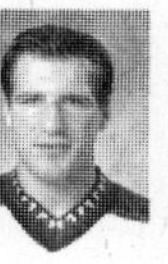

JASPERS, Jason

(JAS-puhrs, JAY-suhn) **PHX.**

Center. Shoots left. 5'11", 197 lbs. Born, Thunder Bay, Ont., April 8, 1981. Phoenix's 4th choice, 71st overall, in 1999 Entry Draft.

1996-97	Thunder Bay	TBAHA	70	51	69	120	67	....	....	....	....	....	....	....	....	....	....	....	....	....	....	....	....	....	....
1997-98	Thunder Bay	TBAHA	72	45	75	120	90	....	....	....	....	....	....	....	....	....	....	....	....	....	....	....	....	....	....
1998-99	Sudbury Wolves	OHL	68	28	33	61	81	....	....	....	....	....	....	....	....	....	4	2	1	3	13	....	....	....	....
99-2000	Sudbury Wolves	OHL	68	46	61	107	107	....	....	....	....	....	....	....	....	....	12	4	6	10	27	....	....	....	....
2000-01	Sudbury Wolves	OHL	63	42	42	84	77	....	....	....	....	....	....	....	....	....	12	3	16	19	18	....	....	....	....

Season	Club	League	GP	G	A	Pts	PIM	PP	SH	GW	S	%	+/-	TF	F%	Min	GP	G	A	Pts	PIM	PP	SH	GW	Min
			Regular Season														Playoffs								
2001-02	Phoenix	NHL	4	0	1	1	4	0	0	0	1	0.0	–1	14	35.7	8:07									
	Springfield	AHL	71	25	23	48	55																		
2002-03	Phoenix	NHL	2	0	0	0	0	0	0	0	0	0.0	–1	14	57.1	7:17									
	Springfield	AHL	63	4	15	19	57										6	0	0	0	4				
	NHL Totals		6	0	1	1	4	0	0	0	1	0.0		28	46.4	7:50									

OHL Second All-Star Team (2000)

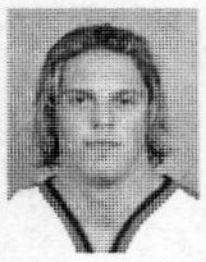

JILLSON, Jeff

(JIHL-sohn, JEHF) **BOS.**

Defense. Shoots right. 6'3", 220 lbs. Born, North Smithfield, RI, July 24, 1980. San Jose's 1st choice, 14th overall, in 1999 Entry Draft.

Season	Club	League	GP	G	A	Pts	PIM	PP	SH	GW	S	%	+/-	TF	F%	Min	GP	G	A	Pts	PIM	PP	SH	GW	Min
1995-96	Mount St. Charles	Hi-School	15	8	7	15	15										5	1	1	2	4				
1996-97	Mount St. Charles	Hi-School	15	16	14	30	20										4	0	4	4	6				
1997-98	Mount St. Charles	Hi-School	15	10	13	23	32										5	4	5	9	6				
1998-99	U. of Michigan	CCHA	38	5	19	24	71																		
99-2000	U. of Michigan	CCHA	38	8	26	34	115																		
2000-01	U. of Michigan	CCHA	43	10	20	30	74																		
2001-02	San Jose	NHL	48	5	13	18	29	3	0	2	47	10.6	2	0	0.0	14:36	4	0	0	0	0	0	0	0	5:45
	Cleveland Barons	AHL	27	2	13	15	45																		
2002-03	San Jose	NHL	26	0	6	6	9	0	0	0	22	0.0	–7	0	0.0	13:45									
	Cleveland Barons	AHL	19	3	5	8	12																		
	Providence Bruins	AHL	30	4	11	15	26										4	0	2	2	8				
	NHL Totals		74	5	19	24	38	3	0	2	69	7.2		0	0.0	14:18	4	0	0	0	0	0	0	0	5:45

Rhode Island All-State First All-Star Team (1996, 1997, 1998) • CCHA All-Rookie Team (1999) • CCHA First All-Star Team (2000, 2001) • NCAA West First All-American Team (2000) • NCAA West Second All-American Team (2001)

Traded to **Boston** by **San Jose** with Jeff Hackett for Kyle McLaren and Boston's 4th round choice in 2004 Entry Draft, January 23, 2003.

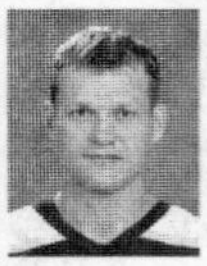

JOHANSSON, Andreas

(yoh-HAHN-suhn, ahn-DRAY-uhs) **NSH.**

Center. Shoots left. 6', 202 lbs. Born, Hofors, Sweden, May 19, 1973. NY Islanders' 7th choice, 136th overall, in 1991 Entry Draft.

Season	Club	League	GP	G	A	Pts	PIM	PP	SH	GW	S	%	+/-	TF	F%	Min	GP	G	A	Pts	PIM	PP	SH	GW	Min
1987-88	Bofors IK	Swede-3	1	0	0	0	0																		
1988-89	Bofors IK	Swede-3	28	19	11	30																			
1989-90	Falu IF	Swede-2	21	3	1	4	14																		
1990-91	Falu IF	Swede-2	31	12	10	22	38																		
1991-92	Farjestad	Sweden	30	3	1	4	10										6	0	0	0	4				
1992-93	Farjestad	Sweden	38	4	7	11	38										2	0	0	0	0				
1993-94	Farjestad	Sweden	37	11	16	27	24										3	1	4	5	2				
1994-95	Farjestad	Sweden	36	9	10	19	42										4	0	0	0	10				
1995-96	NY Islanders	NHL	3	0	1	1	0	0	0	0	6	0.0	1												
	Worcester IceCats	AHL	29	5	5	10	32																		
	Utah Grizzlies	IHL	22	4	13	17	28										12	0	5	5	6				
1996-97	NY Islanders	NHL	15	2	2	4	0	1	0	0	21	9.5	–6												
	Pittsburgh	NHL	27	2	7	9	20	0	0	0	38	5.3	–6												
	Cleveland	IHL	10	2	4	6	42										11	1	5	6	8				
1997-98	Pittsburgh	NHL	50	5	10	15	20	0	1	0	49	10.2	4				1	0	0	0	0	0	0	0	
	Sweden	Olympics	3	0	0	0	2																		
1998-99	Ottawa	NHL	69	21	16	37	34	7	0	6	144	14.6	1	9	22.2	14:39	2	0	0	0	0	0	0	0	14:13
99-2000	Tampa Bay	NHL	12	2	3	5	8	0	0	0	11	18.2	1	0	0.0	10:50									
	Calgary	NHL	28	3	7	10	14	1	0	0	47	6.4	–3	5	20.0	13:33									
2000-01	SC Bern	Swiss	40	15	29	44	94										7	5	4	9	0				
2001-02	NY Rangers	NHL	70	14	10	24	46	3	0	1	108	13.0	6	299	43.1	16:19									
2002-03	Nashville	NHL	56	20	17	37	22	10	0	0	124	16.1	–4	14	50.0	16:46									
	NHL Totals		330	69	73	142	164	22	1	7	548	12.6		327	42.5	15:19	3	0	0	0	0	0	0	0	14:13

Traded to **Pittsburgh** by **NY Islanders** with Darius Kasparaitis for Bryan Smolinski, November 17, 1996. Signed as a free agent by **Ottawa**, September 29, 1998. Traded to **Tampa Bay** by **Ottawa** for Rob Zamuner and Tampa Bay's 2nd round choice (later traded to Philadelphia – later traded back to Tampa Bay – later traded to Dallas – Dallas selected Tobias Stephan) in 2002 Entry Draft, June 29, 1999. Traded to **Calgary** by **Tampa Bay** for Nils Ekman and Calgary's 4th round choice (later traded to NY Islanders – NY Islanders selected Vladimir Gorbunov) in 2000 Entry Draft, November 13, 1999. • Missed majority of 1999-2000 season recovering from back injury suffered in game vs. Vancouver, January 2, 2000. Claimed by **NY Rangers** from **Calgary** in Waiver Draft, September 29, 2000. Signed as a free agent by **Nashville**, September 6, 2002.

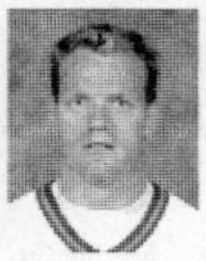

JOHANSSON, Calle

(yoh-HAHN-suhn, KAL-ee)

Defense. Shoots left. 5'11", 203 lbs. Born, Goteborg, Sweden, February 14, 1967. Buffalo's 1st choice, 14th overall, in 1985 Entry Draft.

Season	Club	League	GP	G	A	Pts	PIM	PP	SH	GW	S	%	+/-	TF	F%	Min	GP	G	A	Pts	PIM	PP	SH	GW	Min
1981-82	KBA-67	Swede-3	27	3	3	6																			
1982-83	KBA-67	Swede-3	29	12	11	23																			
1983-84	Vastra Frolunda	Sweden	28	4	4	8	10																		
1984-85	Vastra Frolunda	Swede-2	30	8	13	21	16																		
1985-86	Bjorkloven	Sweden	17	1	2	3	4																		
1986-87	Bjorkloven	Sweden	30	2	13	15	20										6	1	3	4	6				
1987-88	Buffalo	NHL	71	4	38	42	37	2	0	0	93	4.3	12				6	0	1	1	0	0	0	0	
1988-89	Buffalo	NHL	47	2	11	13	33	0	0	1	53	3.8	–7												
	Washington	NHL	12	1	7	8	4	1	0	0	22	4.5	1				6	1	2	3	0	1	0	0	
1989-90	Washington	NHL	70	8	31	39	25	4	0	2	103	7.8	7				15	1	6	7	4	0	0	0	
1990-91	Washington	NHL	80	11	41	52	23	2	1	2	128	8.6	–2				10	2	7	9	8	1	0	0	
1991-92	Washington	NHL	80	14	42	56	49	5	2	2	119	11.8	2				7	0	5	5	4	0	0	0	
1992-93	Washington	NHL	77	7	38	45	56	6	0	0	133	5.3	3				6	0	5	5	4	0	0	0	
1993-94	Washington	NHL	84	9	33	42	59	4	0	1	141	6.4	3				6	1	3	4	4	0	0	1	
1994-95	EHC Kloten	Swiss	5	1	2	3	8																		
	Washington	NHL	46	5	26	31	35	4	0	2	112	4.5	–6				7	3	1	4	0	1	0	0	
1995-96	Washington	NHL	78	10	25	35	50	4	0	0	182	5.5	13												
1996-97	Washington	NHL	65	6	11	17	16	2	0	0	133	4.5	–2												
1997-98	Washington	NHL	73	15	20	35	30	10	1	1	163	9.2	–11				21	2	8	10	16	0	0	0	
	Sweden	Olympics	4	0	0	0	2																		
1998-99	Washington	NHL	67	8	21	29	22	2	0	2	145	5.5	10	0	0.0	23:58									
99-2000	Washington	NHL	82	7	25	32	24	1	0	3	138	5.1	13	0	0.0	23:55	5	1	2	3	0	1	0	0	25:42
2000-01	Washington	NHL	76	7	29	36	26	5	0	0	154	4.5	11	0	0.0	23:44	6	1	2	3	2	0	0	0	23:41
2001-02	Washington	NHL	11	2	0	2	8	0	0	1	18	11.1	–4	0	0.0	21:14									
2002-03	Washington	NHL	82	3	12	15	22	1	0	0	77	3.9	9	1	0.0	21:45	6	0	1	1	0	0	0	0	19:15
	NHL Totals		1101	119	410	529	519	53	4	17	1914	6.2		1	0.0	23:14	101	12	43	55	42	4	0	1	22:42

NHL All-Rookie Team (1988)

Traded to **Washington** by **Buffalo** with Buffalo's 2nd round choice (Byron Dafoe) in 1989 Entry Draft for Clint Malarchuk, Grant Ledyard and Washington's 6th round choice (Brian Holzinger) in 1991 Entry Draft, March 7, 1989. • Missed majority of 2001-02 season recovering from rotator cuff injury suffered in game vs. Atlanta, November 10, 2001.

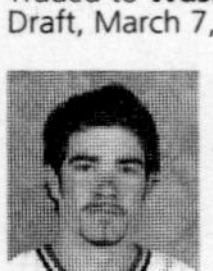

JOHANSSON, Mathias

(yoh-HAHN-suhn)

Center. Shoots left. 6'2", 185 lbs. Born, Oskarshamn, Sweden, February 22, 1974. Calgary's 3rd choice, 54th overall, in 1992 Entry Draft.

Season	Club	League	GP	G	A	Pts	PIM	PP	SH	GW	S	%	+/-	TF	F%	Min	GP	G	A	Pts	PIM	PP	SH	GW	Min
1990-91	Farjestad	Sweden	3	0	0	0	0																		
1991-92	Farjestad	Sweden	16	0	0	0	2										1	0	0	0	0				
1992-93	Grums IK	Swede-2	25	8	6	14	12																		
	Farjestad	Sweden	12	2	3	5	4										3	0	0	0	0				
1993-94	Farjestad	Sweden	16	2	1	3	4																		
1994-95	Farjestad	Sweden	40	7	8	15	30										4	4	3	7	2				
1995-96	Farjestad	Sweden	40	8	21	29	10										8	2	1	3	4				
1996-97	Farjestad	Sweden	48	12	15	27	14										14	4	4	8	12				
	Farjestad	EuroHL	5	0	1	1	0																		
1997-98	Farjestad	Sweden	46	8	21	29	36										12	2	1	3	10				
	Farjestad	EuroHL	8	3	4	7	2																		
1998-99	Farjestad	Sweden	50	9	15	24	14										3	0	1	1	4				
	Farjestad	EuroHL	5	1	3	4	6										2	0	0	0	4				
99-2000	Farjestad	Sweden	49	20	19	39	40										7	2	1	3	4				
2000-01	Farjestad	Sweden	49	15	20	35	42										16	4	9	13	18				

Season	Club	League	Regular Season														Playoffs								
			GP	G	A	Pts	PIM	PP	SH	GW	S	%	+/-	TF	F%	Min	GP	G	A	Pts	PIM	PP	SH	GW	Min
2001-02	Farjestad	Sweden	50	4	11	15	22	....	....	....	....	....	....	....	....	....	10	6	1	7	8	....	....	....	....
	Sweden	Olympics	4	1	0	1	0	....	....	....	....	....	....	....	....	....	....	....	....	....	....	....	....	....	....
2002-03	**Calgary**	**NHL**	**46**	**4**	**5**	**9**	**12**	**1**	**0**	**0**	**54**	**7.4**	**–15**	**376**	**53.7**	**12:39**	....	....	....	....	....	....	....	....	....
	Pittsburgh	**NHL**	**12**	**1**	**5**	**6**	**4**	**1**	**0**	**0**	**16**	**6.3**	**1**	**174**	**42.0**	**17:04**	....	....	....	....	....	....	....	....	....
	NHL Totals		**58**	**5**	**10**	**15**	**16**	**2**	**0**	**0**	**70**	**7.1**		**550**	**50.0**	**13:34**	....	....	....	....	....	....	....	....	....

Traded to **Pittsburgh** by **Calgary** with Micki DuPont for Shean Donovan, March 11, 2003.

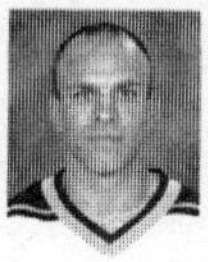

JOHNSON, Craig

(JAWN-suhn, KRAYG)

Left wing. Shoots left. 6'2", 200 lbs. Born, St. Paul, MN, March 18, 1972. St. Louis' 1st choice, 33rd overall, in 1990 Entry Draft.

1987-88	Hill-Murray	Hi-School	28	14	20	34	4	....	....	....	....	....	....	....	....	....	....	....	....	....	....	....	....	....	....
1988-89	Hill-Murray	Hi-School	24	22	30	52	10	....	....	....	....	....	....	....	....	....	....	....	....	....	....	....	....	....	....
1989-90	Hill-Murray	Hi-School	23	15	36	51	0	....	....	....	....	....	....	....	....	....	....	....	....	....	....	....	....	....	....
1990-91	U. of Minnesota	WCHA	33	13	18	31	34	....	....	....	....	....	....	....	....	....	....	....	....	....	....	....	....	....	....
1991-92	U. of Minnesota	WCHA	41	17	38	55	66	....	....	....	....	....	....	....	....	....	....	....	....	....	....	....	....	....	....
1992-93	U. of Minnesota	WCHA	42	22	24	46	70	....	....	....	....	....	....	....	....	....	....	....	....	....	....	....	....	....	....
	Jacksonville	SunHL	23	2	9	11	38	....	....	....	....	....	....	....	....	....	....	....	....	....	....	....	....	....	....
1993-94	Team USA	Nat-Tm	54	25	26	51	64	....	....	....	....	....	....	....	....	....	....	....	....	....	....	....	....	....	....
	United States	Olympics	8	0	4	4	4	....	....	....	....	....	....	....	....	....	....	....	....	....	....	....	....	....	....
1994-95	**St. Louis**	**NHL**	**15**	**3**	**3**	**6**	**6**	**0**	**0**	**0**	**19**	**15.8**	**4**	....	....	....	**1**	**0**	**0**	**0**	**2**	**0**	**0**	**0**	....
	Peoria Rivermen	IHL	16	2	6	8	25	....	....	....	....	....	....	....	....	....	9	0	4	4	10	....	....	....	....
1995-96	**St. Louis**	**NHL**	**49**	**8**	**7**	**15**	**30**	**1**	**0**	**0**	**69**	**11.6**	**–4**	....	....	....	....	....	....	....	....	....	....	....	....
	Worcester IceCats	AHL	5	3	0	3	2	....	....	....	....	....	....	....	....	....	....	....	....	....	....	....	....	....	....
	Los Angeles	**NHL**	**11**	**5**	**4**	**9**	**6**	**3**	**0**	**0**	**28**	**17.9**	**–4**	....	....	....	....	....	....	....	....	....	....	....	....
1996-97	**Los Angeles**	**NHL**	**31**	**4**	**3**	**7**	**26**	**1**	**0**	**0**	**30**	**13.3**	**–7**	....	....	....	....	....	....	....	....	....	....	....	....
1997-98	**Los Angeles**	**NHL**	**74**	**17**	**21**	**38**	**42**	**6**	**0**	**2**	**125**	**13.6**	**9**	....	....	....	**4**	**1**	**0**	**1**	**4**	**0**	**0**	**0**	....
1998-99	**Los Angeles**	**NHL**	**69**	**7**	**12**	**19**	**32**	**2**	**0**	**2**	**94**	**7.4**	**–12**	**2**	**50.0**	**12:02**	....	....	....	....	....	....	....	....	....
99-2000	**Los Angeles**	**NHL**	**76**	**9**	**14**	**23**	**28**	**1**	**0**	**1**	**106**	**8.5**	**–10**	**9**	**55.6**	**13:56**	**4**	**1**	**0**	**1**	**2**	**0**	**0**	**0**	**11:28**
2000-01	**Los Angeles**	**NHL**	**26**	**4**	**5**	**9**	**16**	**0**	**0**	**0**	**36**	**11.1**	**0**	**2**	**100.0**	**10:40**	....	....	....	....	....	....	....	....	....
2001-02	**Los Angeles**	**NHL**	**72**	**13**	**14**	**27**	**24**	**4**	**1**	**3**	**102**	**12.7**	**14**	**11**	**36.4**	**14:15**	**7**	**1**	**2**	**3**	**2**	**0**	**0**	**1**	**14:00**
2002-03	**Los Angeles**	**NHL**	**70**	**3**	**6**	**9**	**22**	**0**	**0**	**0**	**87**	**3.4**	**–13**	**28**	**32.1**	**14:05**	....	....	....	....	....	....	....	....	....
	NHL Totals		**493**	**73**	**89**	**162**	**232**	**18**	**1**	**8**	**696**	**10.5**		**52**	**40.4**	**13:21**	**16**	**3**	**2**	**5**	**10**	**0**	**0**	**1**	**13:05**

Traded to **Los Angeles** by **St. Louis** with Patrice Tardif, Roman Vopat, St. Louis' 5th round choice (Peter Hogan) in 1996 Entry Draft and St. Louis' 1st round choice (Matt Zultek) in 1997 Entry Draft for Wayne Gretzky, February 27, 1996. • Missed majority of 2000-01 season recovering from ankle injury suffered in game vs. San Jose, December 26, 2000.

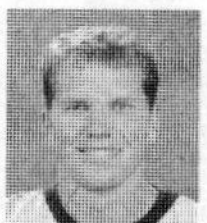

JOHNSON, Greg

(JAWN-suhn, GREHG) **NSH.**

Center. Shoots left. 5'11", 200 lbs. Born, Thunder Bay, Ont., March 16, 1971. Philadelphia's 1st choice, 33rd overall, in 1989 Entry Draft.

1988-89	Thunder Bay	USHL	47	32	64	96	4	....	....	....	....	....	....	....	....	....	12	5	13	18	0	....	....	....	....
1989-90	North Dakota	WCHA	44	17	38	55	11	....	....	....	....	....	....	....	....	....	....	....	....	....	....	....	....	....	....
1990-91	North Dakota	WCHA	38	18	*61	79	6	....	....	....	....	....	....	....	....	....	....	....	....	....	....	....	....	....	....
1991-92	North Dakota	WCHA	39	20	*54	74	8	....	....	....	....	....	....	....	....	....	....	....	....	....	....	....	....	....	....
1992-93	North Dakota	WCHA	34	19	45	64	18	....	....	....	....	....	....	....	....	....	....	....	....	....	....	....	....	....	....
	Team Canada	Nat-Tm	23	6	14	20	2	....	....	....	....	....	....	....	....	....	....	....	....	....	....	....	....	....	....
1993-94	**Detroit**	**NHL**	**52**	**6**	**11**	**17**	**22**	**1**	**1**	**0**	**48**	**12.5**	**–7**	....	....	....	**7**	**2**	**2**	**4**	**2**	**1**	**0**	**0**	....
	Adirondack	AHL	3	2	4	6	0	....	....	....	....	....	....	....	....	....	4	0	4	4	2	....	....	....	....
	Canada	Olympics	8	0	3	3	0	....	....	....	....	....	....	....	....	....	....	....	....	....	....	....	....	....	....
1994-95	**Detroit**	**NHL**	**22**	**3**	**5**	**8**	**14**	**2**	**0**	**0**	**32**	**9.4**	**1**	....	....	....	**1**	**0**	**0**	**0**	**0**	**0**	**0**	**0**	....
1995-96	**Detroit**	**NHL**	**60**	**18**	**22**	**40**	**30**	**5**	**0**	**2**	**87**	**20.7**	**6**	....	....	....	**13**	**3**	**1**	**4**	**8**	**0**	**0**	**0**	....
1996-97	**Detroit**	**NHL**	**43**	**6**	**10**	**16**	**12**	**0**	**0**	**0**	**56**	**10.7**	**–5**	....	....	....	....	....	....	....	....	....	....	....	....
	Pittsburgh	**NHL**	**32**	**7**	**9**	**16**	**14**	**1**	**0**	**0**	**52**	**13.5**	**–13**	....	....	....	**5**	**1**	**0**	**1**	**2**	**0**	**0**	**0**	....
1997-98	**Pittsburgh**	**NHL**	**5**	**1**	**0**	**1**	**2**	**0**	**0**	**0**	**4**	**25.0**	**0**	....	....	....	....	....	....	....	....	....	....	....	....
	Chicago	**NHL**	**69**	**11**	**22**	**33**	**38**	**4**	**0**	**3**	**85**	**12.9**	**–2**	....	....	....	....	....	....	....	....	....	....	....	....
1998-99	**Nashville**	**NHL**	**68**	**16**	**34**	**50**	**24**	**2**	**3**	**0**	**120**	**13.3**	**–8**	**1441**	**53.6**	**19:26**	....	....	....	....	....	....	....	....	....
99-2000	**Nashville**	**NHL**	**82**	**11**	**33**	**44**	**40**	**2**	**0**	**1**	**133**	**8.3**	**–15**	**1684**	**50.8**	**19:13**	....	....	....	....	....	....	....	....	....
2000-01	**Nashville**	**NHL**	**82**	**15**	**17**	**32**	**46**	**1**	**0**	**4**	**97**	**15.5**	**–6**	**1583**	**51.8**	**17:49**	....	....	....	....	....	....	....	....	....
2001-02	**Nashville**	**NHL**	**82**	**18**	**26**	**44**	**38**	**3**	**0**	**2**	**145**	**12.4**	**–14**	**1764**	**51.8**	**19:34**	....	....	....	....	....	....	....	....	....
2002-03	**Nashville**	**NHL**	**38**	**8**	**9**	**17**	**22**	**0**	**0**	**0**	**55**	**14.5**	**7**	**753**	**52.1**	**17:11**	....	....	....	....	....	....	....	....	....
	NHL Totals		**635**	**120**	**198**	**318**	**302**	**21**	**4**	**12**	**914**	**13.1**		**7225**	**51.9**	**18:48**	**26**	**6**	**3**	**9**	**12**	**1**	**0**	**0**	....

Centennial Cup All-Star Team (1989) • WCHA First All-Star Team (1991, 1992, 1993) • NCAA West First All-American Team (1991, 1993) • NCAA West Second All-American Team (1992)

Traded to **Detroit** by **Philadelphia** with Philadelphia's 5th round choice (Frederic Deschenes) in 1994 Entry Draft for Jim Cummins and Philadelphia's 4th round choice (previously acquired, later traded to Boston – Boston selected Charles Paquette) in 1993 Entry Draft, June 20, 1993. Traded to **Pittsburgh** by **Detroit** for Tomas Sandstrom, January 27, 1997. Traded to **Chicago** by **Pittsburgh** for Tuomas Gronman, October 27, 1997. Claimed by **Nashville** from **Chicago** in Expansion Draft, June 26, 1998. Missed majority of 2002-03 season recovering from head injury suffered in game vs. Vancouver, October 21, 2002.

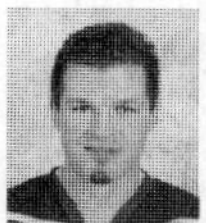

JOHNSON, Matt

(JAWN-suhn, MAT) **MIN.**

Left wing. Shoots left. 6'5", 235 lbs. Born, Welland, Ont., November 23, 1975. Los Angeles' 2nd choice, 33rd overall, in 1994 Entry Draft.

1991-92	Welland Aerostars	OJHL-B	38	6	19	25	214	....	....	....	....	....	....	....	....	....	....	....	....	....	....	....	....	....	....
	Ajax Axemen	MTJHL	1	0	0	0	0	....	....	....	....	....	....	....	....	....	....	....	....	....	....	....	....	....	....
1992-93	Peterborough	OHL	66	8	17	25	211	....	....	....	....	....	....	....	....	....	16	1	1	2	56	....	....	....	....
1993-94	Peterborough	OHL	50	13	24	37	233	....	....	....	....	....	....	....	....	....	....	....	....	....	....	....	....	....	....
1994-95	Peterborough	OHL	14	1	2	3	43	....	....	....	....	....	....	....	....	....	....	....	....	....	....	....	....	....	....
	Los Angeles	**NHL**	**14**	**1**	**0**	**1**	**102**	**0**	**0**	**0**	**4**	**25.0**	**0**	....	....	....	....	....	....	....	....	....	....	....	....
1995-96	**Los Angeles**	**NHL**	**1**	**0**	**0**	**0**	**5**	**0**	**0**	**0**	**1**	**0.0**	**0**	....	....	....	....	....	....	....	....	....	....	....	....
	Phoenix	IHL	29	4	4	8	87	....	....	....	....	....	....	....	....	....	....	....	....	....	....	....	....	....	....
1996-97	**Los Angeles**	**NHL**	**52**	**1**	**3**	**4**	**194**	**0**	**0**	**0**	**20**	**5.0**	**–4**	....	....	....	....	....	....	....	....	....	....	....	....
1997-98	**Los Angeles**	**NHL**	**66**	**2**	**4**	**6**	**249**	**0**	**0**	**0**	**18**	**11.1**	**–8**	....	....	....	**4**	**0**	**0**	**0**	**6**	**0**	**0**	**0**	....
1998-99	**Los Angeles**	**NHL**	**49**	**2**	**1**	**3**	**131**	**0**	**0**	**0**	**14**	**14.3**	**–5**	**1**	**0.0**	**5:55**	....	....	....	....	....	....	....	....	....
99-2000	**Atlanta**	**NHL**	**64**	**2**	**5**	**7**	**144**	**0**	**0**	**0**	**54**	**3.7**	**–11**	**1**	**100.0**	**8:25**	....	....	....	....	....	....	....	....	....
2000-01	**Minnesota**	**NHL**	**50**	**1**	**1**	**2**	**137**	**0**	**0**	**0**	**21**	**4.8**	**–6**	**1**	**100.0**	**7:43**	....	....	....	....	....	....	....	....	....
2001-02	**Minnesota**	**NHL**	**60**	**4**	**0**	**4**	**183**	**0**	**0**	**1**	**23**	**17.4**	**–13**	**1**	**100.0**	**7:23**	....	....	....	....	....	....	....	....	....
2002-03	**Minnesota**	**NHL**	**60**	**3**	**5**	**8**	**201**	**0**	**0**	**1**	**24**	**12.5**	**–8**	**5**	**40.0**	**7:24**	**12**	**0**	**0**	**0**	**25**	**0**	**0**	**0**	**6:39**
	NHL Totals		**416**	**16**	**19**	**35**	**1346**	**0**	**0**	**2**	**179**	**8.9**		**9**	**55.6**	**7:25**	**16**	**0**	**0**	**0**	**31**	**0**	**0**	**0**	**6:39**

OHL All-Rookie Team (1993)

Claimed by **Atlanta** from **Los Angeles** in Expansion Draft, June 25, 1999. Traded to **Minnesota** by **Atlanta** for San Jose's 3rd round choice (previously acquired, later traded to Pittsburgh, later traded to Columbus – Columbus selected Aaron Johnson) in 2001 Entry Draft, September 29, 2000.

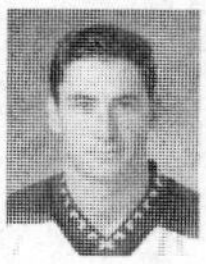

JOHNSON, Mike

(JAWN-suhn, MIGHK) **PHX.**

Right wing. Shoots right. 6'2", 201 lbs. Born, Scarborough, Ont., October 3, 1974.

1991-92	Hillcrest Summits	MTHL	45	43	66	109	....	....	....	....	....	....	....	....	....	....	20	10	19	29	....	....	....	....	....
1992-93	Aurora Eagles	MTJHL	48	25	40	65	18	....	....	....	....	....	....	....	....	....	7	7	15	22	....	....	....	....	....
1993-94	Bowling Green	CCHA	38	6	14	20	18	....	....	....	....	....	....	....	....	....	....	....	....	....	....	....	....	....	....
1994-95	Bowling Green	CCHA	37	16	33	49	35	....	....	....	....	....	....	....	....	....	....	....	....	....	....	....	....	....	....
1995-96	Bowling Green	CCHA	30	12	19	31	22	....	....	....	....	....	....	....	....	....	....	....	....	....	....	....	....	....	....
1996-97	Bowling Green	CCHA	38	30	32	62	46	....	....	....	....	....	....	....	....	....	....	....	....	....	....	....	....	....	....
	Toronto	**NHL**	**13**	**2**	**2**	**4**	**4**	**0**	**1**	**1**	**27**	**7.4**	**–2**	....	....	....	....	....	....	....	....	....	....	....	....
1997-98	**Toronto**	**NHL**	**82**	**15**	**32**	**47**	**24**	**5**	**0**	**0**	**143**	**10.5**	**–4**	....	....	....	....	....	....	....	....	....	....	....	....
1998-99	**Toronto**	**NHL**	**79**	**20**	**24**	**44**	**35**	**5**	**3**	**2**	**149**	**13.4**	**13**	**15**	**53.3**	**16:16**	**17**	**3**	**2**	**5**	**4**	**0**	**0**	**1**	**16:28**
99-2000	**Toronto**	**NHL**	**52**	**11**	**14**	**25**	**23**	**2**	**1**	**3**	**89**	**12.4**	**8**	**2**	**50.0**	**15:22**	....	....	....	....	....	....	....	....	....
	Tampa Bay	**NHL**	**28**	**10**	**12**	**22**	**4**	**4**	**0**	**0**	**43**	**23.3**	**–2**	**5**	**60.0**	**20:33**	....	....	....	....	....	....	....	....	....
2000-01	**Tampa Bay**	**NHL**	**64**	**11**	**27**	**38**	**38**	**3**	**1**	**0**	**107**	**10.3**	**–10**	**2**	**0.0**	**18:13**	....	....	....	....	....	....	....	....	....
	Phoenix	**NHL**	**12**	**2**	**3**	**5**	**4**	**1**	**0**	**0**	**17**	**11.8**	**0**	**0**	**0.0**	**12:12**	....	....	....	....	....	....	....	....	....

Season	Club	League	Regular Season GP	G	A	Pts	PIM	PP	SH	GW	S	%	+/-	TF	F%	Min	Playoffs GP	G	A	Pts	PIM	PP	SH	GW	Min
2001-02	Phoenix	NHL	57	5	22	27	28	1	2	0	73	6.8	14	13	30.8	15:49	5	1	1	2	6	0	0	0	14:45
2002-03	Phoenix	NHL	82	23	40	63	47	8	0	3	178	12.9	9	34	50.0	19:39	....	....	....	....	....	....	....	....	....
	NHL Totals		469	99	176	275	207	29	8	9	826	12.0		71	46.5	17:20	22	4	3	7	10	0	0	1	16:05

NHL All-Rookie Team (1998)

Signed as a free agent by **Toronto**, March 16, 1997. Traded to **Tampa Bay** by **Toronto** with Marek Posmyk, Toronto's 5th (Pavel Sedov) and 6th (Aaron Gionet) round choices in 2000 Entry Draft and future considerations for Darcy Tucker, Tampa Bay's 4th round choice (Miguel Delisle) in 2000 Entry Draft and future considerations, February 9, 2000. Traded to **Phoenix** by **Tampa Bay** with Paul Mara, Ruslan Zainullin and NY Islanders' 2nd round choice (previously acquired, Phoenix selected Matthew Spiller) in 2001 Entry Draft for Nikolai Khabibulin and Stan Neckar, March 5, 2001.

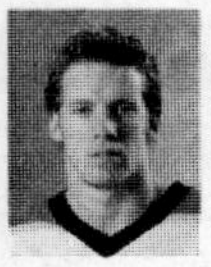

JOHNSON, Ryan

(JAWN-suhn, RIGH-yuhn) **ST.L.**

Center. Shoots left. 6'1", 200 lbs. Born, Thunder Bay, Ont., June 14, 1976. Florida's 4th choice, 36th overall, in 1994 Entry Draft.

Season	Club	League	GP	G	A	Pts	PIM	PP	SH	GW	S	%	+/-	TF	F%	Min	GP	G	A	Pts	PIM	PP	SH	GW	Min
1992-93	Thunder Bay	TBAHA	60	25	33	58	....	....	....	....	....	....	....	....	....	....	....	....	....	....	....	....	....	....	....
1993-94	Thunder Bay	USHL	48	14	36	50	28	....	....	....	....	....	....	....	....	....	....	....	....	....	....	....	....	....	....
1994-95	North Dakota	WCHA	38	6	22	28	39	....	....	....	....	....	....	....	....	....	....	....	....	....	....	....	....	....	....
1995-96	North Dakota	WCHA	21	2	17	19	14	....	....	....	....	....	....	....	....	....	....	....	....	....	....	....	....	....	....
	Team Canada	Nat-Tm	28	5	12	17	14	....	....	....	....	....	....	....	....	....	....	....	....	....	....	....	....	....	....
1996-97	Carolina	AHL	79	18	24	42	28	....	....	....	....	....	....	....	....	....	....	....	....	....	....	....	....	....	....
1997-98	Florida	NHL	10	0	2	2	0	0	0	0	6	0.0	–4	....	....	....	....	....	....	....	....	....	....	....	....
	New Haven	AHL	64	19	48	67	12	....	....	....	....	....	....	....	....	....	3	0	1	1	0	....	....	....	....
1998-99	Florida	NHL	1	1	0	1	0	0	0	0	1	100.0	0	16	37.5	15:26	....	....	....	....	....	....	....	....	....
	New Haven	AHL	37	8	19	27	18	....	....	....	....	....	....	....	....	....	....	....	....	....	....	....	....	....	....
99-2000	Florida	NHL	66	4	12	16	14	0	0	0	44	9.1	1	684	51.8	11:47	....	....	....	....	....	....	....	....	....
	Tampa Bay	NHL	14	0	2	2	2	0	0	0	5	0.0	–9	117	53.0	11:02	....	....	....	....	....	....	....	....	....
2000-01	Tampa Bay	NHL	80	7	14	21	44	1	0	0	71	9.9	–20	951	48.9	15:47	....	....	....	....	....	....	....	....	....
2001-02	Florida	NHL	29	1	3	4	10	0	0	0	24	4.2	–5	336	47.9	13:00	....	....	....	....	....	....	....	....	....
2002-03	Florida	NHL	58	2	5	7	26	0	0	0	54	3.7	–13	689	48.0	10:40	....	....	....	....	....	....	....	....	....
	St. Louis	NHL	17	0	0	0	12	0	0	0	13	0.0	0	180	51.7	10:34	6	0	2	2	6	0	0	0	8:14
	NHL Totals		275	15	38	53	108	1	0	0	218	6.9		2973	49.5	12:46	6	0	2	2	6	0	0	0	8:14

Traded to **Tampa Bay** by **Florida** with Dwayne Hay for Mike Sillinger, March 14, 2000. Traded to **Florida** by **Tampa Bay** with Tampa Bay's 6th round choice (later traded back to Tampa Bay – Tampa Bay selected Doug O'Brien) in 2003 Entry Draft for Vaclav Prospal, July 10, 2001. • Missed majority of 2001-02 season recovering from head injury suffered in game vs. St. Louis, December 22, 2001. Claimed on waivers by **St. Louis** from **Florida**, February 19, 2003.

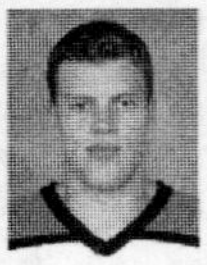

JOHNSSON, Kim

(YAWN-suhn, KIHM) **PHI.**

Defense. Shoots left. 6'1", 205 lbs. Born, Malmo, Sweden, March 16, 1976. NY Rangers' 15th choice, 286th overall, in 1994 Entry Draft.

Season	Club	League	GP	G	A	Pts	PIM	PP	SH	GW	S	%	+/-	TF	F%	Min	GP	G	A	Pts	PIM	PP	SH	GW	Min
1993-94	Malmo IF Jr.	Swede-Jr.	14	5	3	8	14	....	....	....	....	....	....	....	....	....	....	....	....	....	....	....	....	....	....
	Malmo IF	Sweden	2	0	0	0	0	....	....	....	....	....	....	....	....	....	....	....	....	....	....	....	....	....	....
1994-95	Malmo IF Jr.	Swede-Jr.	29	6	15	21	40	....	....	....	....	....	....	....	....	....	....	....	....	....	....	....	....	....	....
	Malmo IF	Sweden	13	0	0	0	4	....	....	....	....	....	....	....	....	....	1	0	0	0	0	....	....	....	....
1995-96	Malmo IF	Sweden	38	2	0	2	30	....	....	....	....	....	....	....	....	....	4	0	1	1	8	....	....	....	....
1996-97	Malmo IF	Sweden	49	4	9	13	42	....	....	....	....	....	....	....	....	....	4	0	0	0	2	....	....	....	....
1997-98	Malmo IF	Sweden	45	5	9	14	29	....	....	....	....	....	....	....	....	....	....	....	....	....	....	....	....	....	....
1998-99	Malmo IF	Sweden	49	9	8	17	76	....	....	....	....	....	....	....	....	....	8	2	3	5	12	....	....	....	....
99-2000	NY Rangers	NHL	76	6	15	21	46	1	0	1	101	5.9	–13	0	0.0	18:06	....	....	....	....	....	....	....	....	....
2000-01	NY Rangers	NHL	75	5	21	26	40	4	0	0	104	4.8	–3	0	0.0	21:16	....	....	....	....	....	....	....	....	....
2001-02	Philadelphia	NHL	82	11	30	41	42	5	0	1	150	7.3	12	0	0.0	23:02	5	0	0	0	2	0	0	0	22:48
	Sweden	Olympics	4	1	1	2	0	....	....	....	....	....	....	....	....	....	....	....	....	....	....	....	....	....	....
2002-03	Philadelphia	NHL	82	10	29	39	38	5	0	2	159	6.3	11	0	0.0	24:05	13	0	3	3	8	0	0	0	26:07
	NHL Totals		315	32	95	127	166	15	0	4	514	6.2		0	0.0	21:42	18	0	3	3	10	0	0	0	25:12

Traded to **Philadelphia** by **NY Rangers** with Jan Hlavac, Pavel Brendl and NY Rangers' 3rd round choice (Stefan Ruzicka) in 2003 Entry Draft for Eric Lindros, August 20, 2001.

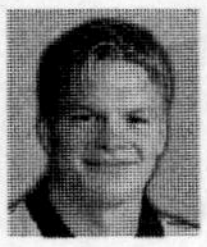

JOKELA, Mikko

(YOH-kih-lah, MIH-koh) **VAN.**

Defense. Shoots right. 6'1", 210 lbs. Born, Lappeenranta, Finland, March 4, 1980. New Jersey's 5th choice, 96th overall, in 1998 Entry Draft.

Season	Club	League	GP	G	A	Pts	PIM	PP	SH	GW	S	%	+/-	TF	F%	Min	GP	G	A	Pts	PIM	PP	SH	GW	Min
1994-95	KalPa Kuopio-C	Finn-Jr.	29	7	12	19	36	....	....	....	....	....	....	....	....	....	....	....	....	....	....	....	....	....	....
1995-96	KalPa Kuopio-C	Finn-Jr.	23	10	19	29	103	....	....	....	....	....	....	....	....	....	6	3	5	8	4	....	....	....	....
	KalPa Kuopio-B	Finn-Jr.	9	2	1	3	20	....	....	....	....	....	....	....	....	....	....	....	....	....	....	....	....	....	....
	KalPa Kuopio Jr.	Finn-Jr.	11	2	1	3	20	....	....	....	....	....	....	....	....	....	....	....	....	....	....	....	....	....	....
1996-97	KalPa Kuopio-B	Finn-Jr.	11	3	2	5	8	....	....	....	....	....	....	....	....	....	5	1	1	2	4	....	....	....	....
	KalPa Kuopio Jr.	Finn-Jr.	22	2	4	6	4	....	....	....	....	....	....	....	....	....	....	....	....	....	....	....	....	....	....
	KalPa Kuopio-B	Finn-Jr.	....	....	....	....	....	....	....	....	....	....	....	....	....	....	12	0	1	1	14	....	....	....	....
1997-98	HIFK Helsinki Jr.	Finn-Jr.	22	2	5	7	14	....	....	....	....	....	....	....	....	....	....	....	....	....	....	....	....	....	....
	Hermes Kokkola	Finland-2	6	0	1	1	2	....	....	....	....	....	....	....	....	....	....	....	....	....	....	....	....	....	....
	HIFK Helsinki	Finland	16	0	0	0	0	....	....	....	....	....	....	....	....	....	....	....	....	....	....	....	....	....	....
1998-99	KalPa Kuopio Jr.	Finn-Jr.	1	0	1	1	2	....	....	....	....	....	....	....	....	....	....	....	....	....	....	....	....	....	....
	KalPa Kuopio	Finland	42	1	2	3	18	....	....	....	....	....	....	....	....	....	....	....	....	....	....	....	....	....	....
	HIFK Helsinki	Finland	3	0	0	0	2	....	....	....	....	....	....	....	....	....	....	....	....	....	....	....	....	....	....
	KalPa Kuopio	Finland-2	....	....	....	....	....	....	....	....	....	....	....	....	....	....	6	0	0	0	2	....	....	....	....
99-2000	SaiPa	Finland	48	0	5	5	50	....	....	....	....	....	....	....	....	....	....	....	....	....	....	....	....	....	....
	SaiPa Jr.	Finn-Jr.	....	....	....	....	....	....	....	....	....	....	....	....	....	....	1	0	0	0	0	....	....	....	....
2000-01	SaiPa Jr.	Finn-Jr.	4	2	2	4	2	....	....	....	....	....	....	....	....	....	3	0	0	0	2	....	....	....	....
	KooKoo Kouvola	Finland-2	5	3	0	3	0	....	....	....	....	....	....	....	....	....	....	....	....	....	....	....	....	....	....
	SaiPa	Finland	50	1	0	1	24	....	....	....	....	....	....	....	....	....	....	....	....	....	....	....	....	....	....
2001-02	Albany River Rats	AHL	56	5	13	18	28	....	....	....	....	....	....	....	....	....	....	....	....	....	....	....	....	....	....
2002-03	Albany River Rats	AHL	44	8	11	19	35	....	....	....	....	....	....	....	....	....	....	....	....	....	....	....	....	....	....
	Vancouver	NHL	1	0	0	0	0	0	0	0	3	0.0	0	0	0.0	5:09	....	....	....	....	....	....	....	....	....
	Manitoba Moose	AHL	32	3	7	10	17	....	....	....	....	....	....	....	....	....	14	1	4	5	2	....	....	....	....
	NHL Totals		1	0	0	0	0	0	0	0	3	0.0		0	0.0	5:09	....	....	....	....	....	....	....	....	....

Traded to **Vancouver** by **New Jersey** for Steve Kariya, January 24, 2003.

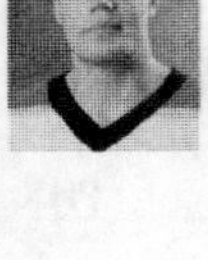

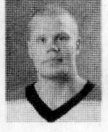

JOKINEN, Olli

(YOH-kih-nihn, OH-lee) **FLA.**

Center. Shoots left. 6'3", 205 lbs. Born, Kuopio, Finland, December 5, 1978. Los Angeles' 1st choice, 3rd overall, in 1997 Entry Draft.

Season	Club	League	GP	G	A	Pts	PIM	PP	SH	GW	S	%	+/-	TF	F%	Min	GP	G	A	Pts	PIM	PP	SH	GW	Min
1992-93	KalPa Kuopio-C	Finn-Jr.	14	8	3	11	12	....	....	....	....	....	....	....	....	....	....	....	....	....	....	....	....	....	....
1993-94	KalPa Kuopio-C	Finn-Jr.	31	27	25	52	62	....	....	....	....	....	....	....	....	....	....	....	....	....	....	....	....	....	....
1994-95	KalPa Kuopio-B	Finn-Jr.	12	9	14	23	46	....	....	....	....	....	....	....	....	....	....	....	....	....	....	....	....	....	....
	KalPa Kuopio Jr.	Finn-Jr.	6	0	1	1	6	....	....	....	....	....	....	....	....	....	....	....	....	....	....	....	....	....	....
1995-96	KalPa Kuopio Jr.	Finn-Jr.	25	20	14	34	47	....	....	....	....	....	....	....	....	....	7	4	4	8	20	....	....	....	....
	KalPa Kuopio	Finland	15	1	1	2	2	....	....	....	....	....	....	....	....	....	....	....	....	....	....	....	....	....	....
1996-97	HIFK Helsinki Jr.	Finn-Jr.	2	1	0	1	6	....	....	....	....	....	....	....	....	....	....	....	....	....	....	....	....	....	....
	HIFK Helsinki	Finland	50	14	27	41	88	....	....	....	....	....	....	....	....	....	....	....	....	....	....	....	....	....	....
1997-98	Los Angeles	NHL	8	0	0	0	6	0	0	0	12	0.0	–5	....	....	....	....	....	....	....	....	....	....	....	....
	HIFK Helsinki	Finland	30	11	28	39	8	....	....	....	....	....	....	....	....	....	9	*7	2	9	2	....	....	....	....
1998-99	Los Angeles	NHL	66	9	12	21	44	3	1	1	87	10.3	–10	779	43.9	14:42	....	....	....	....	....	....	....	....	....
	Springfield	AHL	9	3	6	9	6	....	....	....	....	....	....	....	....	....	....	....	....	....	....	....	....	....	....
99-2000	NY Islanders	NHL	82	11	10	21	80	1	2	3	138	8.0	0	841	46.1	16:15	....	....	....	....	....	....	....	....	....
2000-01	Florida	NHL	78	6	10	16	106	0	0	0	121	5.0	–22	638	42.3	13:23	....	....	....	....	....	....	....	....	....
2001-02	Florida	NHL	80	9	20	29	98	3	1	0	153	5.9	–16	1222	45.2	18:05	....	....	....	....	....	....	....	....	....
	Finland	Olympics	4	2	1	3	0	....	....	....	....	....	....	....	....	....	....	....	....	....	....	....	....	....	....
2002-03	Florida	NHL	81	36	29	65	79	13	3	6	240	15.0	–17	1925	46.7	22:02	....	....	....	....	....	....	....	....	....
	NHL Totals		395	71	81	152	413	20	7	10	751	9.5		5405	45.3	16:60	....	....	....	....	....	....	....	....	....

Played in NHL All-Star Game (2003)

Traded to **NY Islanders** by **Los Angeles** with Josh Green, Mathieu Biron and Los Angeles' 1st round choice (Taylor Pyatt) in 1999 Entry Draft for Ziggy Palffy, Brian Smolinski, Marcel Cousineau and New Jersey's 4th round choice (previously acquired, Los Angeles selected Daniel Johansson) in 1999 Entry Draft, June 20, 1999. Traded to **Florida** by **NY Islanders** with Roberto Luongo for Mark Parrish and Oleg Kvasha, June 24, 2000.

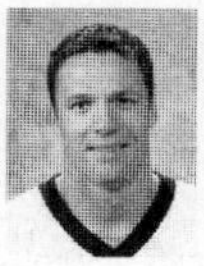

JONSSON, Hans

(YAWN-suhn, HANS)

Defense. Shoots left. 6'1", 205 lbs. Born, Jarved, Sweden, August 2, 1973. Pittsburgh's 11th choice, 286th overall, in 1993 Entry Draft.

Season	Club	League	GP	G	A	Pts	PIM	PP	SH	GW	S	%	+/-	TF	F%	Min	Playoffs GP	G	A	Pts	PIM	PP	SH	GW	Min
1991-92	Hasums IF	Swede-2	13	4	6	10	10	....	....	....	....	....	....	....	....	....	....	....	....	....	....	....	....	....	....
	MoDo	Sweden	6	0	1	1	4	....	....	....	....	....	....	....	....	....	....	....	....	....	....	....	....	....	....
1992-93	MoDo	Sweden	40	2	2	4	24	....	....	....	....	....	....	....	....	....	3	0	1	1	2	....	....	....	....
1993-94	MoDo	Sweden	23	4	1	5	18	....	....	....	....	....	....	....	....	....	10	0	1	1	12	....	....	....	....
1994-95	MoDo	Sweden	39	4	6	10	30	....	....	....	....	....	....	....	....	....	....	....	....	....	....	....	....	....	....
1995-96	MoDo	Sweden	36	10	6	16	30	....	....	....	....	....	....	....	....	....	8	2	1	3	24	....	....	....	....
1996-97	MoDo	Sweden	27	7	5	12	18	....	....	....	....	....	....	....	....	....	....	....	....	....	....	....	....	....	....
1997-98	MoDo	Sweden	40	8	6	14	40	....	....	....	....	....	....	....	....	....	8	1	1	2	12	....	....	....	....
1998-99	MoDo	Sweden	41	3	4	7	40	....	....	....	....	....	....	....	....	....	13	2	4	6	22	....	....	....	....
99-2000	**Pittsburgh**	**NHL**	**68**	**3**	**11**	**14**	**12**	**0**	**1**	**1**	**49**	**6.1**	**–5**	**0**	**0.0**	**18:34**	**11**	**0**	**1**	**1**	**6**	**0**	**0**	**0**	**23:16**
2000-01	**Pittsburgh**	**NHL**	**58**	**4**	**18**	**22**	**22**	**2**	**0**	**0**	**44**	**9.1**	**11**	**0**	**0.0**	**18:27**	**16**	**0**	**0**	**0**	**8**	**0**	**0**	**0**	**17:11**
2001-02	**Pittsburgh**	**NHL**	**53**	**2**	**5**	**7**	**22**	**2**	**0**	**0**	**37**	**5.4**	**–12**	**0**	**0.0**	**18:12**	....	....	....	....	....	....	....	....	....
2002-03	**Pittsburgh**	**NHL**	**63**	**1**	**4**	**5**	**36**	**0**	**0**	**0**	**40**	**2.5**	**–23**	**2**	**0.0**	**17:04**	....	....	....	....	....	....	....	....	....
	NHL Totals		**242**	**10**	**38**	**48**	**92**	**4**	**1**	**1**	**170**	**5.9**		**2**	**0.0**	**18:04**	**27**	**0**	**1**	**1**	**14**	**0**	**0**	**0**	**19:39**

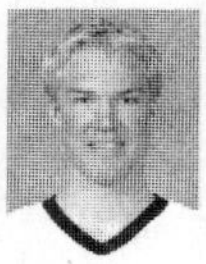

JONSSON, Kenny

(YAWN-suhn, KEHN-nee) **NYI**

Defense. Shoots left. 6'3", 217 lbs. Born, Angelholm, Sweden, October 6, 1974. Toronto's 1st choice, 12th overall, in 1993 Entry Draft.

Season	Club	League	GP	G	A	Pts	PIM	PP	SH	GW	S	%	+/-	TF	F%	Min	Playoffs GP	G	A	Pts	PIM	PP	SH	GW	Min
1991-92	Rogle	Swede-2	30	4	11	15	24	....	....	....	....	....	....	....	....	....	5	0	0	0	0	....	....	....	....
1992-93	Rogle Jr.	Swede-Jr.	2	1	2	3	25	....	....	....	....	....	....	....	....	....	....	....	....	....	....	....	....	....	....
	Rogle	Sweden	39	3	10	13	42	....	....	....	....	....	....	....	....	....	....	....	....	....	....	....	....	....	....
1993-94	Rogle	Sweden	36	4	13	17	40	....	....	....	....	....	....	....	....	....	3	1	1	2	2	....	....	....	....
	Sweden	Olympics	3	1	0	1	0	....	....	....	....	....	....	....	....	....	....	....	....	....	....	....	....	....	....
1994-95	Rogle	Sweden	8	3	1	4	20	....	....	....	....	....	....	....	....	....	....	....	....	....	....	....	....	....	....
	St. John's	AHL	10	2	5	7	2	....	....	....	....	....	....	....	....	....	....	....	....	....	....	....	....	....	....
	Toronto	**NHL**	**39**	**2**	**7**	**9**	**16**	**0**	**0**	**1**	**50**	**4.0**	**–8**	....	....	....	**4**	**0**	**0**	**0**	**0**	**0**	**0**	**0**	....
1995-96	**Toronto**	**NHL**	**50**	**4**	**22**	**26**	**22**	**3**	**0**	**1**	**90**	**4.4**	**12**	....	....	....	....	....	....	....	....	....	....	....	....
	NY Islanders	**NHL**	**16**	**0**	**4**	**4**	**10**	**0**	**0**	**0**	**40**	**0.0**	**–5**	....	....	....	....	....	....	....	....	....	....	....	....
1996-97	**NY Islanders**	**NHL**	**81**	**3**	**18**	**21**	**24**	**1**	**0**	**0**	**92**	**3.3**	**10**	....	....	....	....	....	....	....	....	....	....	....	....
1997-98	**NY Islanders**	**NHL**	**81**	**14**	**26**	**40**	**58**	**6**	**0**	**2**	**108**	**13.0**	**–2**	....	....	....	....	....	....	....	....	....	....	....	....
1998-99	**NY Islanders**	**NHL**	**63**	**8**	**18**	**26**	**34**	**6**	**0**	**0**	**91**	**8.8**	**–18**	**0**	**0.0**	**24:59**	....	....	....	....	....	....	....	....	....
99-2000	**NY Islanders**	**NHL**	**65**	**1**	**24**	**25**	**32**	**1**	**0**	**0**	**84**	**1.2**	**–15**	**0**	**0.0**	**24:29**	....	....	....	....	....	....	....	....	....
2000-01	**NY Islanders**	**NHL**	**65**	**8**	**21**	**29**	**30**	**5**	**0**	**0**	**91**	**8.8**	**–22**	**0**	**0.0**	**24:04**	....	....	....	....	....	....	....	....	....
2001-02	**NY Islanders**	**NHL**	**76**	**10**	**22**	**32**	**26**	**2**	**1**	**0**	**107**	**9.3**	**15**	**2**	**0.0**	**25:34**	**5**	**1**	**2**	**3**	**4**	**1**	**0**	**0**	**23:48**
	Sweden	Olympics	3	1	0	1	2	....	....	....	....	....	....	....	....	....	....	....	....	....	....	....	....	....	....
2002-03	**NY Islanders**	**NHL**	**71**	**8**	**18**	**26**	**24**	**3**	**1**	**0**	**108**	**7.4**	**–8**	**6**	**50.0**	**23:12**	**5**	**0**	**1**	**1**	**0**	**0**	**0**	**0**	**28:46**
	NHL Totals		**607**	**58**	**180**	**238**	**276**	**27**	**2**	**4**	**861**	**6.7**		**8**	**37.5**	**24:28**	**14**	**1**	**3**	**4**	**4**	**1**	**0**	**0**	**26:17**

NHL All-Rookie Team (1995)

Traded to **NY Islanders** by **Toronto** with Sean Haggerty, Darby Hendrickson and Toronto's 1st round choice (Roberto Luongo) in 1997 Entry Draft for Wendel Clark, Mathieu Schneider and D.J. Smith, March 13, 1996.

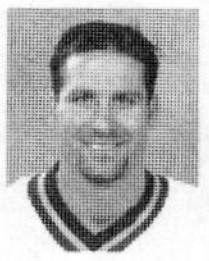

JOVANOVSKI, Ed

(joh-van-OHV-skee, EHD) **VAN.**

Defense. Shoots left. 6'2", 210 lbs. Born, Windsor, Ont., June 26, 1976. Florida's 1st choice, 1st overall, in 1994 Entry Draft.

Season	Club	League	GP	G	A	Pts	PIM	PP	SH	GW	S	%	+/-	TF	F%	Min	Playoffs GP	G	A	Pts	PIM	PP	SH	GW	Min
1991-92	Windsor	OMHA	50	25	40	65	88	....	....	....	....	....	....	....	....	....	....	....	....	....	....	....	....	....	....
1992-93	Windsor Bulldogs	OJHL-B	48	7	46	53	88	....	....	....	....	....	....	....	....	....	....	....	....	....	....	....	....	....	....
1993-94	Windsor Spitfires	OHL	62	15	36	51	221	....	....	....	....	....	....	....	....	....	4	0	0	0	15	....	....	....	....
1994-95	Windsor Spitfires	OHL	50	23	42	65	198	....	....	....	....	....	....	....	....	....	9	2	7	9	39	....	....	....	....
1995-96	**Florida**	**NHL**	**70**	**10**	**11**	**21**	**137**	**2**	**0**	**2**	**116**	**8.6**	**–3**	....	....	....	**22**	**1**	**8**	**9**	**52**	**0**	**0**	**0**	....
1996-97	**Florida**	**NHL**	**61**	**7**	**16**	**23**	**172**	**3**	**0**	**1**	**80**	**8.8**	**–1**	....	....	....	**5**	**0**	**0**	**0**	**4**	**0**	**0**	**0**	....
1997-98	**Florida**	**NHL**	**81**	**9**	**14**	**23**	**158**	**2**	**1**	**3**	**142**	**6.3**	**–12**	....	....	....	....	....	....	....	....	....	....	....	....
1998-99	**Florida**	**NHL**	**41**	**3**	**13**	**16**	**82**	**1**	**0**	**1**	**68**	**4.4**	**–4**	**0**	**0.0**	**22:35**	....	....	....	....	....	....	....	....	....
	Vancouver	**NHL**	**31**	**2**	**9**	**11**	**44**	**0**	**0**	**0**	**41**	**4.9**	**–5**	**0**	**0.0**	**21:16**	....	....	....	....	....	....	....	....	....
99-2000	**Vancouver**	**NHL**	**75**	**5**	**21**	**26**	**54**	**1**	**0**	**1**	**109**	**4.6**	**–3**	**0**	**0.0**	**24:03**	....	....	....	....	....	....	....	....	....
2000-01	**Vancouver**	**NHL**	**79**	**12**	**35**	**47**	**102**	**4**	**0**	**2**	**193**	**6.2**	**–1**	**0**	**0.0**	**24:57**	**4**	**1**	**1**	**2**	**0**	**0**	**0**	**0**	**25:54**
2001-02	**Vancouver**	**NHL**	**82**	**17**	**31**	**48**	**101**	**7**	**1**	**3**	**202**	**8.4**	**–7**	**0**	**0.0**	**25:11**	**6**	**1**	**4**	**5**	**8**	**1**	**0**	**0**	**25:48**
	Canada	Olympics	6	0	3	3	4	....	....	....	....	....	....	....	....	....	....	....	....	....	....	....	....	....	....
2002-03	**Vancouver**	**NHL**	**67**	**6**	**40**	**46**	**113**	**2**	**0**	**1**	**145**	**4.1**	**19**	**0**	**0.0**	**24:15**	**14**	**7**	**1**	**8**	**22**	**4**	**1**	**2**	**23:40**
	NHL Totals		**587**	**71**	**190**	**261**	**963**	**22**	**2**	**14**	**1096**	**6.5**		**0**	**0.0**	**24:08**	**51**	**10**	**14**	**24**	**86**	**5**	**1**	**2**	**24:34**

OHL All-Rookie Team (1994) • OHL Second All-Star Team (1994) • OHL First All-Star Team (1995) • NHL All-Rookie Team (1996)

Played in NHL All-Star Game (2001, 2002, 2003)

Traded to **Vancouver** by **Florida** with Dave Gagner, Mike Brown, Kevin Weekes and Florida's 1st round choice (Nathan Smith) in 2000 Entry Draft for Pavel Bure, Bret Hedican, Brad Ference and Vancouver's 3rd round choice (Robert Fried) in 2000 Entry Draft, January 17, 1999.

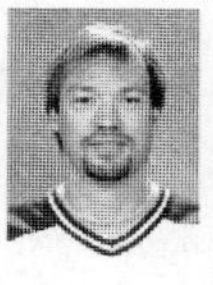

JUNEAU, Joe

(ZHOO-noh, JOH) **MTL.**

Center. Shoots left. 6', 195 lbs. Born, Pont-Rouge, Que., January 5, 1968. Boston's 3rd choice, 81st overall, in 1988 Entry Draft.

Season	Club	League	GP	G	A	Pts	PIM	PP	SH	GW	S	%	+/-	TF	F%	Min	Playoffs GP	G	A	Pts	PIM	PP	SH	GW	Min
1983-84	Ste-Foy	QAAA	30	3	7	10	24	....	....	....	....	....	....	....	....	....	12	3	11	14	4	....	....	....	....
1984-85	Ste-Foy	QAAA	41	25	46	71	60	....	....	....	....	....	....	....	....	....	13	9	15	24	20	....	....	....	....
1985-86	Levis-Lauzon	CEGEP	STATISTICS NOT AVAILABLE																						
1986-87	Levis-Lauzon	CEGEP	38	27	57	84	....	....	....	....	....	....	....	....	....	....	....	....	....	....	....	....	....	....	....
1987-88	RPI Engineers	ECAC	31	16	29	45	18	....	....	....	....	....	....	....	....	....	....	....	....	....	....	....	....	....	....
1988-89	RPI Engineers	ECAC	30	12	23	35	40	....	....	....	....	....	....	....	....	....	....	....	....	....	....	....	....	....	....
1989-90	RPI Engineers	ECAC	34	18	*52	*70	31	....	....	....	....	....	....	....	....	....	....	....	....	....	....	....	....	....	....
1990-91	RPI Engineers	ECAC	29	23	40	63	68	....	....	....	....	....	....	....	....	....	....	....	....	....	....	....	....	....	....
1991-92	Team Canada	Nat-Tm	60	20	49	69	35	....	....	....	....	....	....	....	....	....	....	....	....	....	....	....	....	....	....
	Canada	Olympics	8	6	*9	*15	4	....	....	....	....	....	....	....	....	....	....	....	....	....	....	....	....	....	....
	Boston	**NHL**	**14**	**5**	**14**	**19**	**4**	**2**	**0**	**0**	**38**	**13.2**	**6**	....	....	....	**15**	**4**	**8**	**12**	**21**	**2**	**0**	**0**	....
1992-93	**Boston**	**NHL**	**84**	**32**	**70**	**102**	**33**	**9**	**0**	**3**	**229**	**14.0**	**23**	....	....	....	**4**	**2**	**4**	**6**	**6**	**2**	**0**	**0**	....
1993-94	**Boston**	**NHL**	**63**	**14**	**58**	**72**	**35**	**4**	**0**	**2**	**142**	**9.9**	**11**	....	....	....	....	....	....	....	....	....	....	....	....
	Washington	**NHL**	**11**	**5**	**8**	**13**	**6**	**2**	**0**	**0**	**22**	**22.7**	**0**	....	....	....	**11**	**4**	**5**	**9**	**6**	**2**	**0**	**1**	....
1994-95	**Washington**	**NHL**	**44**	**5**	**38**	**43**	**8**	**3**	**0**	**0**	**70**	**7.1**	**–1**	....	....	....	**7**	**2**	**6**	**8**	**2**	**0**	**0**	**0**	....
1995-96	**Washington**	**NHL**	**80**	**14**	**50**	**64**	**30**	**7**	**2**	**2**	**176**	**8.0**	**–3**	....	....	....	**5**	**0**	**7**	**7**	**6**	**0**	**0**	**0**	....
1996-97	**Washington**	**NHL**	**58**	**15**	**27**	**42**	**8**	**9**	**1**	**3**	**124**	**12.1**	**–11**	....	....	....	....	....	....	....	....	....	....	....	....
1997-98	**Washington**	**NHL**	**56**	**9**	**22**	**31**	**26**	**4**	**1**	**1**	**87**	**10.3**	**–8**	....	....	....	**21**	**7**	**10**	**17**	**8**	**1**	**1**	**4**	....
1998-99	**Washington**	**NHL**	**63**	**14**	**27**	**41**	**20**	**2**	**1**	**3**	**142**	**9.9**	**–3**	**437**	**48.1**	**19:28**	....	....	....	....	....	....	....	....	....
	Buffalo	**NHL**	**9**	**1**	**1**	**2**	**2**	**0**	**0**	**0**	**8**	**12.5**	**–1**	**8**	**12.5**	**17:11**	**20**	**3**	**8**	**11**	**10**	**0**	**1**	**0**	**16:51**
99-2000	**Ottawa**	**NHL**	**65**	**13**	**24**	**37**	**22**	**2**	**0**	**2**	**126**	**10.3**	**3**	**830**	**51.6**	**18:28**	**6**	**2**	**1**	**3**	**0**	**0**	**0**	**0**	**18:21**
2000-01	**Phoenix**	**NHL**	**69**	**10**	**23**	**33**	**28**	**5**	**0**	**3**	**100**	**10.0**	**–2**	**210**	**50.5**	**17:25**	....	....	....	....	....	....	....	....	....
2001-02	**Montreal**	**NHL**	**70**	**8**	**28**	**36**	**10**	**1**	**0**	**1**	**96**	**8.3**	**–3**	**1337**	**48.6**	**18:37**	**12**	**1**	**4**	**5**	**6**	**0**	**0**	**0**	**19:15**
2002-03	**Montreal**	**NHL**	**72**	**6**	**16**	**22**	**20**	**0**	**0**	**2**	**88**	**6.8**	**–10**	**1235**	**52.4**	**16:46**	....	....	....	....	....	....	....	....	....
	NHL Totals		**758**	**151**	**406**	**557**	**252**	**50**	**5**	**22**	**1448**	**10.4**		**4057**	**50.3**	**18:05**	**101**	**25**	**53**	**78**	**65**	**7**	**2**	**5**	**17:50**

NCAA East First All-American Team (1990) • ECAC Second All-Star Team (1991) • NCAA East Second All-American Team (1991) • NHL All-Rookie Team (1993)

Traded to **Washington** by **Boston** for Al Iafrate, March 21, 1994. Traded to **Buffalo** by **Washington** with Washington's 3rd round choice (Tim Preston) in 1999 Entry Draft for Alexei Tezikov and Buffalo's 4th round compensatory choice (later traded to Calgary – Calgary selected Levente Szuper) in 2000 Entry Draft, March 22, 1999. Signed as a free agent by **Ottawa**, October 25, 1999. Selected by **Minnesota** from **Ottawa** in Expansion Draft, June 23, 2000. Traded to **Phoenix** by **Minnesota** for the rights to Rickard Wallin, June 23, 2000. Traded to **Montreal** by **Phoenix** for future considerations, June 15, 2001.

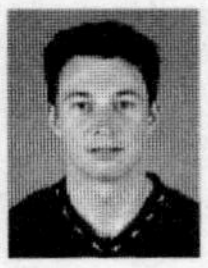

KABERLE, Frantisek
(KA-buhr-lay, FRAN-tih-sehk) **ATL.**

Defense. Shoots left. 6'1", 190 lbs. Born, Kladno, Czech., November 8, 1973. Los Angeles' 3rd choice, 76th overall, in 1999 Entry Draft.

			Regular Season														Playoffs								
Season	Club	League	GP	G	A	Pts	PIM	PP	SH	GW	S	%	+/-	TF	F%	Min	GP	G	A	Pts	PIM	PP	SH	GW	Min
1991-92	Poldi Kladno	Czech	37	1	4	5	8	....	....	....	....	....	....	....	....	....	8	0	1	1	0	....	....	....	....
1992-93	Poldi Kladno	Czech	40	4	5	9	....	....	....	....	....	....	....	....	....	....	9	2	4	6	....	....	....	....	....
1993-94	HC Kladno	Czech	41	4	16	20	....	....	....	....	....	....	....	....	....	....	11	1	1	2	....	....	....	....	....
1994-95	HC Kladno	Czech	40	7	17	24	20	....	....	....	....	....	....	....	....	....	8	0	3	3	12	....	....	....	....
1995-96	MoDo	Sweden	40	5	7	12	34	....	....	....	....	....	....	....	....	....	8	0	1	1	0	....	....	....	....
1996-97	MoDo	Sweden	50	3	11	14	28	....	....	....	....	....	....	....	....	....	....	....	....	....	....	....	....	....	....
1997-98	MoDo	Sweden	46	5	4	9	22	....	....	....	....	....	....	....	....	....	9	1	1	2	4	....	....	....	....
1998-99	MoDo	Sweden	45	15	18	33	4	....	....	....	....	....	....	....	....	....	13	2	5	7	8	....	....	....	....
99-2000	**Los Angeles**	**NHL**	**37**	**0**	**9**	**9**	**4**	**0**	**0**	**0**	**41**	**0.0**	**3**	**0**	**0.0**	**17:04**	....	....	....	....	....	....	....	....	....
	Long Beach	IHL	18	2	8	10	8	....	....	....	....	....	....	....	....	....	....	....	....	....	....	....	....	....	....
	Atlanta	**NHL**	**14**	**1**	**6**	**7**	**6**	**0**	**1**	**0**	**35**	**2.9**	**–13**	**0**	**0.0**	**24:39**	....	....	....	....	....	....	....	....	....
	Lowell	AHL	4	0	2	2	0	....	....	....	....	....	....	....	....	....	....	....	....	....	....	....	....	....	....
2000-01	**Atlanta**	**NHL**	**51**	**4**	**11**	**15**	**18**	**1**	**0**	**1**	**99**	**4.0**	**11**	**1**	**0.0**	**22:17**	....	....	....	....	....	....	....	....	....
2001-02	**Atlanta**	**NHL**	**61**	**5**	**20**	**25**	**24**	**1**	**0**	**0**	**82**	**6.1**	**–11**	**0**	**0.0**	**21:35**	....	....	....	....	....	....	....	....	....
2002-03	**Atlanta**	**NHL**	**79**	**7**	**19**	**26**	**32**	**3**	**1**	**2**	**105**	**6.7**	**–19**	**0**	**0.0**	**21:57**	....	....	....	....	....	....	....	....	....
	NHL Totals		**242**	**17**	**65**	**82**	**84**	**5**	**2**	**3**	**362**	**4.7**		**1**	**0.0**	**21:20**	....	....	....	....	....	....	....	....	....

Traded to **Atlanta** by **Los Angeles** with Donald Audette for Kelly Buchberger and Nelson Emerson, March 13, 2000.

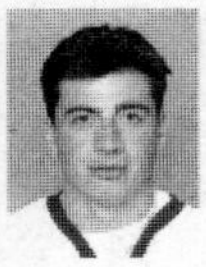

KABERLE, Tomas
(KA-buhr-lay, TAW-mas) **TOR.**

Defense. Shoots left. 6'1", 198 lbs. Born, Rakovnik, Czech., March 2, 1978. Toronto's 13th choice, 204th overall, in 1996 Entry Draft.

			Regular Season														Playoffs								
Season	Club	League	GP	G	A	Pts	PIM	PP	SH	GW	S	%	+/-	TF	F%	Min	GP	G	A	Pts	PIM	PP	SH	GW	Min
1994-95	HC Kladno Jr.	Czech-Jr.	37	7	10	17	....	....	....	....	....	....	....	....	....	....	....	....	....	....	....	....	....	....	....
	HC Kladno	Czech	4	0	1	1	0	....	....	....	....	....	....	....	....	....	....	....	....	....	....	....	....	....	....
1995-96	Kladno Jr.	Czech-Jr.	23	6	13	19	....	....	....	....	....	....	....	....	....	....	....	....	....	....	....	....	....	....	....
	HC Poldi Kladno	Czech	23	0	1	1	2	....	....	....	....	....	....	....	....	....	2	0	0	0	0	....	....	....	....
1996-97	HC Poldi Kladno	Czech	49	0	5	5	26	....	....	....	....	....	....	....	....	....	3	0	0	0	0	....	....	....	....
1997-98	Kladno	Czech	47	4	19	23	12	....	....	....	....	....	....	....	....	....	....	....	....	....	....	....	....	....	....
	St. John's	AHL	2	0	0	0	0	....	....	....	....	....	....	....	....	....	....	....	....	....	....	....	....	....	....
1998-99	**Toronto**	**NHL**	**57**	**4**	**18**	**22**	**12**	**0**	**0**	**2**	**71**	**5.6**	**3**	**0**	**0.0**	**18:42**	**14**	**0**	**3**	**3**	**2**	**0**	**0**	**0**	**17:10**
99-2000	**Toronto**	**NHL**	**82**	**7**	**33**	**40**	**24**	**2**	**0**	**0**	**82**	**8.5**	**3**	**0**	**0.0**	**22:55**	**12**	**1**	**4**	**5**	**0**	**0**	**0**	**1**	**23:01**
2000-01	**Toronto**	**NHL**	**82**	**6**	**39**	**45**	**24**	**0**	**0**	**1**	**96**	**6.3**	**10**	**2**	**0.0**	**22:41**	**11**	**1**	**3**	**4**	**0**	**0**	**0**	**1**	**21:33**
2001-02	Kladno	Czech	9	1	7	8	4	....	....	....	....	....	....	....	....	....	....	....	....	....	....	....	....	....	....
	Toronto	**NHL**	**69**	**10**	**29**	**39**	**2**	**5**	**0**	**3**	**85**	**11.8**	**5**	**2**	**100.0**	**25:00**	**20**	**2**	**8**	**10**	**16**	**0**	**0**	**0**	**28:40**
	Czech Republic	Olympics	4	0	1	1	2	....	....	....	....	....	....	....	....	....	....	....	....	....	....	....	....	....	....
2002-03	**Toronto**	**NHL**	**82**	**11**	**36**	**47**	**30**	**4**	**1**	**2**	**119**	**9.2**	**20**	**3**	**66.7**	**24:50**	**7**	**2**	**1**	**3**	**0**	**1**	**0**	**1**	**30:04**
	NHL Totals		**372**	**38**	**155**	**193**	**92**	**11**	**1**	**8**	**453**	**8.4**		**7**	**57.1**	**23:02**	**64**	**6**	**19**	**25**	**18**	**1**	**0**	**3**	**24:01**

Played in NHL All-Star Game (2002)

Signed as a restricted free agent by **Kladno** (Czech) with **Toronto** retaining NHL rights, September 29, 2001. • Re-signed by **Toronto**, October 30, 2001.

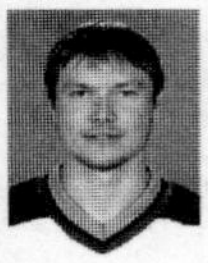

KALININ, Dmitri
(kah-LIHN-ihn, DIH-mih-TREE) **BUF.**

Defense. Shoots left. 6'3", 215 lbs. Born, Chelyabinsk, USSR, July 22, 1980. Buffalo's 1st choice, 18th overall, in 1998 Entry Draft.

			Regular Season														Playoffs								
Season	Club	League	GP	G	A	Pts	PIM	PP	SH	GW	S	%	+/-	TF	F%	Min	GP	G	A	Pts	PIM	PP	SH	GW	Min
1995-96	Chelyabinsk Jr.	CIS-Jr.	30	10	10	20	60	....	....	....	....	....	....	....	....	....	....	....	....	....	....	....	....	....	....
	Chelyabinsk	CIS	20	0	3	3	10	....	....	....	....	....	....	....	....	....	....	....	....	....	....	....	....	....	....
1996-97	Chelyabinsk 2	Russia-3	20	0	0	0	10	....	....	....	....	....	....	....	....	....	....	....	....	....	....	....	....	....	....
	Chelyabinsk	Russia	2	0	0	0	0	....	....	....	....	....	....	....	....	....	2	0	0	0	0	....	....	....	....
1997-98	Chelyabinsk	Russia	26	0	2	2	24	....	....	....	....	....	....	....	....	....	....	....	....	....	....	....	....	....	....
1998-99	Moncton Wildcats	QMJHL	39	7	18	25	44	....	....	....	....	....	....	....	....	....	4	1	1	2	0	....	....	....	....
	Rochester	AHL	3	0	1	1	14	....	....	....	....	....	....	....	....	....	7	0	0	0	6	....	....	....	....
99-2000	**Buffalo**	**NHL**	**4**	**0**	**0**	**0**	**4**	**0**	**0**	**0**	**3**	**0.0**	**0**	**0**	**0.0**	**16:53**	....	....	....	....	....	....	....	....	....
	Rochester	AHL	75	2	19	21	52	....	....	....	....	....	....	....	....	....	21	2	9	11	8	....	....	....	....
2000-01	**Buffalo**	**NHL**	**79**	**4**	**18**	**22**	**38**	**2**	**0**	**0**	**88**	**4.5**	**–2**	**1**	**100.0**	**19:50**	**13**	**0**	**2**	**2**	**4**	**0**	**0**	**0**	**20:05**
2001-02	**Buffalo**	**NHL**	**58**	**2**	**11**	**13**	**26**	**0**	**0**	**0**	**67**	**3.0**	**–6**	**0**	**0.0**	**18:03**	....	....	....	....	....	....	....	....	....
2002-03	**Buffalo**	**NHL**	**65**	**8**	**13**	**21**	**57**	**3**	**1**	**0**	**83**	**9.6**	**–7**	**0**	**0.0**	**21:41**	....	....	....	....	....	....	....	....	....
	Rochester	AHL	1	0	0	0	0	....	....	....	....	....	....	....	....	....	....	....	....	....	....	....	....	....	....
	NHL Totals		**206**	**14**	**42**	**56**	**125**	**5**	**1**	**0**	**241**	**5.8**		**1**	**100.0**	**19:51**	**13**	**0**	**2**	**2**	**4**	**0**	**0**	**0**	**20:05**

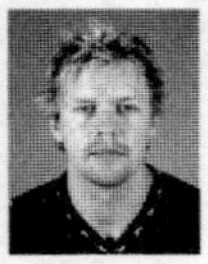

KALLIO, Tomi
(KAL-ee-oh, TAW-mee)

Right wing. Shoots left. 6', 190 lbs. Born, Turku, Finland, January 27, 1977. Colorado's 4th choice, 81st overall, in 1995 Entry Draft.

			Regular Season														Playoffs								
Season	Club	League	GP	G	A	Pts	PIM	PP	SH	GW	S	%	+/-	TF	F%	Min	GP	G	A	Pts	PIM	PP	SH	GW	Min
1992-93	TPS Turku-C	Finn-Jr.	39	39	34	73	18	....	....	....	....	....	....	....	....	....	....	....	....	....	....	....	....	....	....
1993-94	TPS Turku-B	Finn-Jr.	10	5	6	11	14	....	....	....	....	....	....	....	....	....	1	0	1	1	0	....	....	....	....
	TPS Turku Jr.	Finn-Jr.	33	9	7	16	16	....	....	....	....	....	....	....	....	....	6	0	1	1	2	....	....	....	....
1994-95	TPS Turku-B	Finn-Jr.	1	2	0	2	0	....	....	....	....	....	....	....	....	....	....	....	....	....	....	....	....	....	....
	TPS Turku Jr.	Finn-Jr.	14	5	12	17	24	....	....	....	....	....	....	....	....	....	....	....	....	....	....	....	....	....	....
	Kiekko-67 Turku	Finland-2	25	8	5	13	16	....	....	....	....	....	....	....	....	....	7	3	1	4	6	....	....	....	....
1995-96	TPS Turku Jr.	Finn-Jr.	8	8	3	11	14	....	....	....	....	....	....	....	....	....	....	....	....	....	....	....	....	....	....
	Kiekko-67 Turku	Finland-2	29	10	11	21	28	....	....	....	....	....	....	....	....	....	....	....	....	....	....	....	....	....	....
	TPS Turku	Finland	8	2	3	5	10	....	....	....	....	....	....	....	....	....	4	0	0	0	2	....	....	....	....
1996-97	TPS Turku	Finland	47	9	10	19	18	....	....	....	....	....	....	....	....	....	8	2	0	2	2	....	....	....	....
	TPS Turku	EuroHL	6	2	0	2	25	....	....	....	....	....	....	....	....	....	4	0	0	0	0	....	....	....	....
1997-98	TPS Turku	Finland	47	10	10	20	8	....	....	....	....	....	....	....	....	....	4	0	2	2	0	....	....	....	....
	TPS Turku	EuroHL	6	0	1	1	2	....	....	....	....	....	....	....	....	....	....	....	....	....	....	....	....	....	....
1998-99	TPS Turku	Finland	54	15	21	36	20	....	....	....	....	....	....	....	....	....	10	3	4	7	6	....	....	....	....
99-2000	TPS Turku	Finland	50	26	27	53	40	....	....	....	....	....	....	....	....	....	11	4	*9	13	4	....	....	....	....
	TPS Turku	EuroHL	5	2	1	3	0	....	....	....	....	....	....	....	....	....	5	5	3	8	2	....	....	....	....
2000-01	**Atlanta**	**NHL**	**56**	**14**	**13**	**27**	**22**	**2**	**0**	**2**	**115**	**12.2**	**–3**	**8**	**12.5**	**16:17**	....	....	....	....	....	....	....	....	....
2001-02	**Atlanta**	**NHL**	**60**	**8**	**14**	**22**	**12**	**1**	**0**	**0**	**102**	**7.8**	**–8**	**3**	**33.3**	**14:45**	....	....	....	....	....	....	....	....	....
	Finland	Olympics	4	1	2	3	2	....	....	....	....	....	....	....	....	....	....	....	....	....	....	....	....	....	....
2002-03	**Atlanta**	**NHL**	**5**	**0**	**2**	**2**	**4**	**0**	**0**	**0**	**3**	**0.0**	**–2**	**0**	**0.0**	**12:47**	....	....	....	....	....	....	....	....	....
	Columbus	**NHL**	**12**	**1**	**2**	**3**	**8**	**0**	**0**	**0**	**20**	**5.0**	**–7**	**2**	**50.0**	**14:52**	....	....	....	....	....	....	....	....	....
	Philadelphia	**NHL**	**7**	**1**	**0**	**1**	**2**	**0**	**0**	**0**	**5**	**20.0**	**–1**	**0**	**0.0**	**9:29**	....	....	....	....	....	....	....	....	....
	Vastra Frolunda	Sweden	10	6	8	14	10	....	....	....	....	....	....	....	....	....	16	*8	*8	*16	14	....	....	....	....
	NHL Totals		**140**	**24**	**31**	**55**	**48**	**3**	**0**	**2**	**245**	**9.8**		**13**	**23.1**	**15:02**	....	....	....	....	....	....	....	....	....

Claimed by **Atlanta** from **Colorado** in Expansion Draft, June 25, 1999. Traded to **Columbus** by **Atlanta** with Pauli Levokari for Chris Nielsen and Petteri Nummelin, December 2, 2002. Claimed on waivers by **Philadelphia** from **Columbus**, January 1, 2003. Signed as a free agent by **Vastra Frolunda** (Sweden) following release by **Philadelphia**, January 24, 2003.

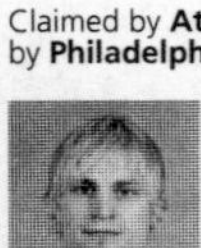

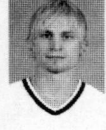

KAPANEN, Niko
(KA-pah-nehn, NEE-KOH) **DAL.**

Center. Shoots left. 5'9", 180 lbs. Born, Hattula, Finland, April 29, 1978. Dallas' 5th choice, 173rd overall, in 1998 Entry Draft.

			Regular Season														Playoffs								
Season	Club	League	GP	G	A	Pts	PIM	PP	SH	GW	S	%	+/-	TF	F%	Min	GP	G	A	Pts	PIM	PP	SH	GW	Min
1992-93	HPK-C	Finn-Jr.	14	14	6	20	2	....	....	....	....	....	....	....	....	....	....	....	....	....	....	....	....	....	....
1993-94	HPK-C	Finn-Jr.	2	0	1	1	0	....	....	....	....	....	....	....	....	....	....	....	....	....	....	....	....	....	....
	HPK Jr.	Finn-Jr.	31	17	33	50	34	....	....	....	....	....	....	....	....	....	....	....	....	....	....	....	....	....	....
1994-95	HPK-B	Finn-Jr.	37	19	44	63	40	....	....	....	....	....	....	....	....	....	....	....	....	....	....	....	....	....	....
1995-96	HPK-B	Finn-Jr.	10	6	6	12	8	....	....	....	....	....	....	....	....	....	....	....	....	....	....	....	....	....	....
	HPK Jr.	Finn-Jr.	26	15	22	37	34	....	....	....	....	....	....	....	....	....	....	....	....	....	....	....	....	....	....
	HPK Hameenlinna	Finland	7	1	0	1	0	....	....	....	....	....	....	....	....	....	....	....	....	....	....	....	....	....	....
1996-97	HPK Jr.	Finn-Jr.	5	1	7	8	2	....	....	....	....	....	....	....	....	....	2	0	1	1	2	....	....	....	....
	HPK Hameenlinna	Finland	41	6	9	15	12	....	....	....	....	....	....	....	....	....	10	4	5	9	2	....	....	....	....
	HPK Hameenlinna	EuroHL	6	3	0	3	4	....	....	....	....	....	....	....	....	....	1	0	0	0	0	....	....	....	....
1997-98	HPK Jr.	Finn-Jr.	2	1	1	2	0	....	....	....	....	....	....	....	....	....	....	....	....	....	....	....	....	....	....
	HPK Hameenlinna	Finland	48	8	18	26	44	....	....	....	....	....	....	....	....	....	....	....	....	....	....	....	....	....	....
1998-99	HPK Hameenlinna	Finland	53	14	29	43	49	....	....	....	....	....	....	....	....	....	8	3	4	7	4	....	....	....	....
99-2000	HPK Hameenlinna	Finland	53	20	28	48	40	....	....	....	....	....	....	....	....	....	8	1	9	10	4	....	....	....	....
2000-01	TPS Turku	Finland	56	11	21	32	20	....	....	....	....	....	....	....	....	....	10	2	1	3	4	....	....	....	....

Season	Club	League	GP	G	A	Pts	PIM	PP	SH	GW	S	%	+/-	TF	F%	Min	GP	G	A	Pts	PIM	PP	SH	GW	Min
			Regular Season														Playoffs								
2001-02	**Dallas**	**NHL**	**9**	**0**	**1**	**1**	**2**	**0**	**0**	**0**	**3**	**0.0**	**–1**	**59**	**40.7**	**9:44**	....	....	....	....	....	....	....	....	....
	Utah Grizzlies	AHL	59	13	28	41	40	....	....	....	....	....	....	....	....	....	5	2	1	3	0	....	....	....	....
2002-03	**Dallas**	**NHL**	**82**	**5**	**29**	**34**	**44**	**0**	**1**	**1**	**80**	**6.3**	**25**	**1111**	**47.5**	**14:39**	**12**	**4**	**3**	**7**	**12**	**0**	**1**	**0**	**16:03**
	NHL Totals		**91**	**5**	**30**	**35**	**46**	**0**	**1**	**1**	**83**	**6.0**		**1170**	**47.2**	**14:10**	**12**	**4**	**3**	**7**	**12**	**0**	**1**	**0**	**16:03**

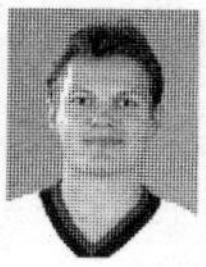

KAPANEN, Sami

(KA-pah-nehn, SA-mee) **PHI.**

Right wing. Shoots left. 5'10", 185 lbs. Born, Vantaa, Finland, June 14, 1973. Hartford's 4th choice, 87th overall, in 1995 Entry Draft.

1989-90	KalPa Kuopio Jr.	Finn-Jr.	30	14	13	27	4	....	....	....	....	....	....	....	....	....	....	....	....	....	....	....	....	....	....
1990-91	KalPa Kuopio Jr.	Finn-Jr.	31	9	27	36	10	....	....	....	....	....	....	....	....	....	....	....	....	....	....	....	....	....	....
	KalPa Kuopio	Finland	14	1	2	3	2	....	....	....	....	....	....	....	....	....	8	2	1	3	2	....	....	....	....
1991-92	KalPa Kuopio Jr.	Finn-Jr.	8	1	3	4	12	....	....	....	....	....	....	....	....	....	....	....	....	....	....	....	....	....	....
	KalPa Kuopio	Finland	42	15	10	25	8	....	....	....	....	....	....	....	....	....	....	....	....	....	....	....	....	....	....
1992-93	KalPa Kuopio Jr.	Finn-Jr.	7	11	14	25	2	....	....	....	....	....	....	....	....	....	....	....	....	....	....	....	....	....	....
	KalPa Kuopio	Finland	37	4	17	21	12	....	....	....	....	....	....	....	....	....	....	....	....	....	....	....	....	....	....
1993-94	KalPa Kuopio	Finland	48	23	32	55	16	....	....	....	....	....	....	....	....	....	....	....	....	....	....	....	....	....	....
	Finland	Olympics	8	1	0	1	2	....	....	....	....	....	....	....	....	....	....	....	....	....	....	....	....	....	....
1994-95	HIFK Helsinki	Finland	49	14	28	42	42	....	....	....	....	....	....	....	....	....	3	0	0	0	0	....	....	....	....
1995-96	**Hartford**	**NHL**	**35**	**5**	**4**	**9**	**6**	**0**	**0**	**0**	**46**	**10.9**	**0**	....	....	....	....	....	....	....	....	....	....	....	....
	Springfield	AHL	28	14	17	31	4	....	....	....	....	....	....	....	....	....	3	1	2	3	0	....	....	....	....
1996-97	**Hartford**	**NHL**	**45**	**13**	**12**	**25**	**2**	**3**	**0**	**2**	**82**	**15.9**	**6**	....	....	....	....	....	....	....	....	....	....	....	....
1997-98	**Carolina**	**NHL**	**81**	**26**	**37**	**63**	**16**	**4**	**0**	**5**	**190**	**13.7**	**9**	....	....	....	....	....	....	....	....	....	....	....	....
	Finland	Olympics	6	0	1	1	0	....	....	....	....	....	....	....	....	....	....	....	....	....	....	....	....	....	....
1998-99	**Carolina**	**NHL**	**81**	**24**	**35**	**59**	**10**	**5**	**0**	**7**	**254**	**9.4**	**–1**	**10**	**50.0**	**19:25**	**5**	**1**	**1**	**2**	**0**	**0**	**0**	**0**	**19:09**
99-2000	**Carolina**	**NHL**	**76**	**24**	**24**	**48**	**12**	**7**	**0**	**5**	**229**	**10.5**	**10**	**2**	**50.0**	**19:53**	....	....	....	....	....	....	....	....	....
2000-01	**Carolina**	**NHL**	**82**	**20**	**37**	**57**	**24**	**7**	**0**	**4**	**223**	**9.0**	**–12**	**6**	**16.7**	**18:56**	**6**	**2**	**3**	**5**	**0**	**1**	**0**	**0**	**20:13**
2001-02	**Carolina**	**NHL**	**77**	**27**	**42**	**69**	**23**	**11**	**0**	**4**	**248**	**10.9**	**9**	**7**	**14.3**	**20:38**	**23**	**1**	**8**	**9**	**6**	**0**	**0**	**0**	**20:03**
	Finland	Olympics	4	1	2	3	4	....	....	....	....	....	....	....	....	....	....	....	....	....	....	....	....	....	....
2002-03	**Carolina**	**NHL**	**43**	**6**	**12**	**18**	**12**	**3**	**0**	**1**	**108**	**5.6**	**–17**	**16**	**31.3**	**18:37**	....	....	....	....	....	....	....	....	....
	Philadelphia	**NHL**	**28**	**4**	**9**	**13**	**6**	**2**	**0**	**1**	**81**	**4.9**	**–1**	**5**	**40.0**	**19:21**	**13**	**4**	**3**	**7**	**6**	**2**	**0**	**0**	**20:12**
	NHL Totals		**548**	**149**	**212**	**361**	**111**	**42**	**0**	**29**	**1461**	**10.2**		**46**	**32.6**	**19:33**	**47**	**8**	**15**	**23**	**12**	**3**	**0**	**0**	**20:01**

Played in NHL All-Star Game (2000, 2002)

Transferred to **Carolina** after **Hartford** franchise relocated, June 25, 1997. Traded to **Philadelphia** by **Carolina** with Ryan Bast for Pavel Brendl and Bruno St. Jacques, February 7, 2003.

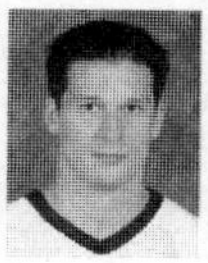

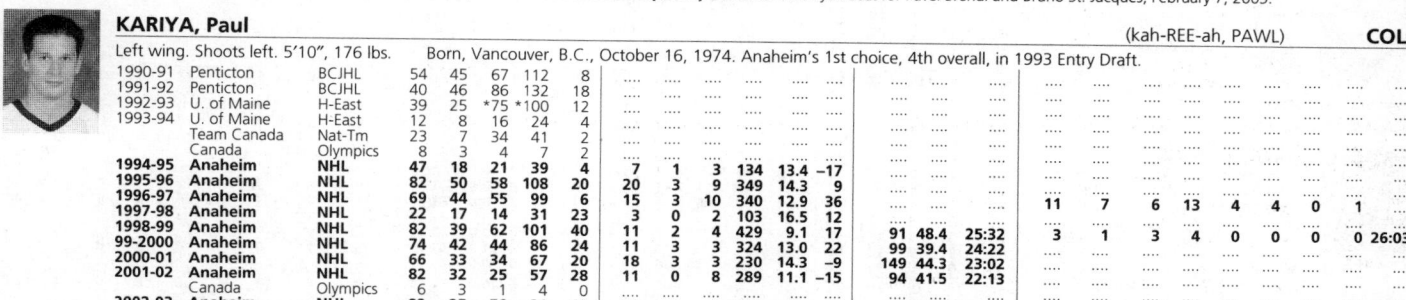

KARIYA, Paul

(kah-REE-ah, PAWL) **COL.**

Left wing. Shoots left. 5'10", 176 lbs. Born, Vancouver, B.C., October 16, 1974. Anaheim's 1st choice, 4th overall, in 1993 Entry Draft.

1990-91	Penticton	BCJHL	54	45	67	112	8	....	....	....	....	....	....	....	....	....	....	....	....	....	....	....	....	....	....
1991-92	Penticton	BCJHL	40	46	86	132	18	....	....	....	....	....	....	....	....	....	....	....	....	....	....	....	....	....	....
1992-93	U. of Maine	H-East	39	25	*75	*100	12	....	....	....	....	....	....	....	....	....	....	....	....	....	....	....	....	....	....
1993-94	U. of Maine	H-East	12	8	16	24	4	....	....	....	....	....	....	....	....	....	....	....	....	....	....	....	....	....	....
	Team Canada	Nat-Tm	23	7	34	41	2	....	....	....	....	....	....	....	....	....	....	....	....	....	....	....	....	....	....
	Canada	Olympics	8	3	4	7	2	....	....	....	....	....	....	....	....	....	....	....	....	....	....	....	....	....	....
1994-95	**Anaheim**	**NHL**	**47**	**18**	**21**	**39**	**4**	**7**	**1**	**3**	**134**	**13.4**	**–17**	....	....	....	....	....	....	....	....	....	....	....	....
1995-96	**Anaheim**	**NHL**	**82**	**50**	**58**	**108**	**20**	**20**	**3**	**9**	**349**	**14.3**	**9**	....	....	....	....	....	....	....	....	....	....	....	....
1996-97	**Anaheim**	**NHL**	**69**	**44**	**55**	**99**	**6**	**15**	**3**	**10**	**340**	**12.9**	**36**	....	....	....	**11**	**7**	**6**	**13**	**4**	**4**	**0**	**1**	
1997-98	**Anaheim**	**NHL**	**22**	**17**	**14**	**31**	**23**	**3**	**0**	**2**	**103**	**16.5**	**12**	....	....	....	....	....	....	....	....	....	....	....	....
1998-99	**Anaheim**	**NHL**	**82**	**39**	**62**	**101**	**40**	**11**	**2**	**4**	**429**	**9.1**	**17**	**91**	**48.4**	**25:32**	**3**	**1**	**3**	**4**	**0**	**0**	**0**	**0**	**26:03**
99-2000	**Anaheim**	**NHL**	**74**	**42**	**44**	**86**	**24**	**11**	**3**	**3**	**324**	**13.0**	**22**	**99**	**39.4**	**24:22**	....	....	....	....	....	....	....	....	....
2000-01	**Anaheim**	**NHL**	**66**	**33**	**34**	**67**	**20**	**18**	**3**	**3**	**230**	**14.3**	**–9**	**149**	**44.3**	**23:02**	....	....	....	....	....	....	....	....	....
2001-02	**Anaheim**	**NHL**	**82**	**32**	**25**	**57**	**28**	**11**	**0**	**8**	**289**	**11.1**	**–15**	**94**	**41.5**	**22:13**	....	....	....	....	....	....	....	....	....
	Canada	Olympics	6	3	1	4	0	....	....	....	....	....	....	....	....	....	....	....	....	....	....	....	....	....	....
2002-03	**Anaheim**	**NHL**	**82**	**25**	**56**	**81**	**48**	**11**	**1**	**2**	**257**	**9.7**	**–3**	**39**	**30.8**	**20:17**	**21**	**6**	**6**	**12**	**6**	**0**	**0**	**1**	**21:15**
	NHL Totals		**606**	**300**	**369**	**669**	**213**	**107**	**16**	**44**	**2455**	**12.2**		**472**	**42.4**	**23:04**	**35**	**14**	**15**	**29**	**10**	**4**	**0**	**2**	**21:51**

Hockey East First All-Star Team (1993) • Hockey East Rookie of the Year (1993) • Hockey East Player of the Year (1993) • NCAA East First All-American Team (1993) • NCAA Championship All-Tournament Team (1993) • Hobey Baker Memorial Award (Top U.S. Collegiate Player) (1993) • NHL All-Rookie Team (1995) • Lady Byng Trophy (1996, 1997) • NHL First All-Star Team (1996, 1997, 1999) • NHL Second All-Star Team (2000, 2003)

Played in NHL All-Star Game (1996, 1997, 1999, 2000, 2001, 2002, 2003)

• Missed majority of 1997-98 season after failing to come to contract terms with **Anaheim** and recovering from head injury suffered in game vs. San Jose, February 1, 1998. Signed as a free agent by **Colorado**, July 3, 2003.

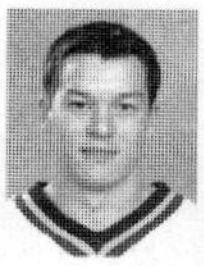

KARIYA, Steve

(kah-REE-ah, STEEV) **N.J.**

Left wing. Shoots right. 5'8", 170 lbs. Born, North Vancouver, B.C., December 22, 1977.

1994-95	Nanaimo Clippers	BCJHL	60	36	60	96	4	....	....	....	....	....	....	....	....	....	....	....	....	....	....	....	....	....	....
1995-96	U. of Maine	H-East	39	7	16	23	8	....	....	....	....	....	....	....	....	....	....	....	....	....	....	....	....	....	....
1996-97	U. of Maine	H-East	35	19	31	50	10	....	....	....	....	....	....	....	....	....	....	....	....	....	....	....	....	....	....
1997-98	U. of Maine	H-East	35	25	25	50	22	....	....	....	....	....	....	....	....	....	....	....	....	....	....	....	....	....	....
1998-99	U. of Maine	H-East	41	27	38	65	24	....	....	....	....	....	....	....	....	....	....	....	....	....	....	....	....	....	....
99-2000	**Vancouver**	**NHL**	**45**	**8**	**11**	**19**	**22**	**0**	**0**	**0**	**41**	**19.5**	**9**	**4**	**50.0**	**12:38**	....	....	....	....	....	....	....	....	....
	Syracuse Crunch	AHL	29	18	23	41	22	....	....	....	....	....	....	....	....	....	4	2	1	3	0	....	....	....	....
2000-01	**Vancouver**	**NHL**	**17**	**1**	**6**	**7**	**8**	**1**	**0**	**0**	**22**	**4.5**	**–1**	**0**	**0.0**	**11:42**	....	....	....	....	....	....	....	....	....
	Kansas City	IHL	43	15	29	44	51	....	....	....	....	....	....	....	....	....	....	....	....	....	....	....	....	....	....
2001-02	**Vancouver**	**NHL**	**3**	**0**	**1**	**1**	**2**	**0**	**0**	**0**	**0**	**0.0**	**–2**	**0**	**0.0**	**12:17**	....	....	....	....	....	....	....	....	....
	Manitoba Moose	AHL	67	25	37	62	48	....	....	....	....	....	....	....	....	....	7	1	2	3	2	....	....	....	....
2002-03	Manitoba Moose	AHL	38	14	14	28	18	....	....	....	....	....	....	....	....	....	....	....	....	....	....	....	....	....	....
	Albany River Rats	AHL	31	12	19	31	20	....	....	....	....	....	....	....	....	....	....	....	....	....	....	....	....	....	....
	NHL Totals		**65**	**9**	**18**	**27**	**32**	**1**	**0**	**0**	**63**	**14.3**		**4**	**50.0**	**12:23**	....	....	....	....	....	....	....	....	....

BCJHL First Team All-Star (1995) • BCJHL Most Sportsmanlike Player (1995) • Hockey East First All-Star Team (1999) • NCAA East First All-American Team (1999)

Signed as a free agent by **Vancouver**, April 21, 1999. Traded to **New Jersey** by **Vancouver** for Mikko Jokela, January 24, 2003.

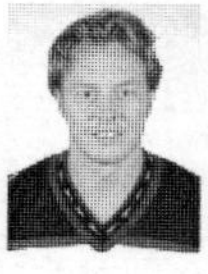

KARLSSON, Andreas

(KARLS-uhn, AN-dray-uhs)

Center. Shoots left. 6'4", 205 lbs. Born, Ludvika, Sweden, August 19, 1975. Calgary's 8th choice, 148th overall, in 1993 Entry Draft.

1992-93	Leksands IF	Sweden	13	0	0	0	6	....	....	....	....	....	....	....	....	....	....	....	....	....	....	....	....	....	....
1993-94	Leksands IF	Sweden	21	0	0	0	10	....	....	....	....	....	....	....	....	....	3	0	0	0	0	....	....	....	....
1994-95	Leksands IF Jr.	Swede-Jr.	3	3	3	6	0	....	....	....	....	....	....	....	....	....	....	....	....	....	....	....	....	....	....
	Leksands IF	Sweden	24	7	8	15	0	....	....	....	....	....	....	....	....	....	4	0	1	1	0	....	....	....	....
1995-96	Leksands IF Jr.	Swede-Jr.	2	4	1	5	6	....	....	....	....	....	....	....	....	....	....	....	....	....	....	....	....	....	....
	Leksands IF	Sweden	40	10	13	23	10	....	....	....	....	....	....	....	....	....	....	....	....	....	....	....	....	....	....
1996-97	Leksands IF	Sweden	49	13	11	24	39	....	....	....	....	....	....	....	....	....	9	2	0	2	2	....	....	....	....
1997-98	Leksands IF	Sweden	33	9	14	23	20	....	....	....	....	....	....	....	....	....	4	1	0	1	0	....	....	....	....
	Leksands IF	EuroHL	6	2	3	5	2	....	....	....	....	....	....	....	....	....	....	....	....	....	....	....	....	....	....
1998-99	Leksands IF	Sweden	49	18	15	33	18	....	....	....	....	....	....	....	....	....	4	1	0	1	6	....	....	....	....
	Leksands IF	EuroHL	6	1	3	4	2	....	....	....	....	....	....	....	....	....	2	1	1	2	2	....	....	....	....
99-2000	**Atlanta**	**NHL**	**51**	**5**	**9**	**14**	**14**	**1**	**0**	**0**	**74**	**6.8**	**–17**	**552**	**46.7**	**12:60**	....	....	....	....	....	....	....	....	....
	Orlando	IHL	18	5	5	10	6	....	....	....	....	....	....	....	....	....	....	....	....	....	....	....	....	....	....
2000-01	**Atlanta**	**NHL**	**60**	**5**	**11**	**16**	**16**	**0**	**1**	**0**	**83**	**6.0**	**–2**	**743**	**48.6**	**12:54**	....	....	....	....	....	....	....	....	....
2001-02	**Atlanta**	**NHL**	**42**	**1**	**7**	**8**	**20**	**0**	**0**	**0**	**41**	**2.4**	**–8**	**386**	**45.1**	**12:30**	....	....	....	....	....	....	....	....	....
	Chicago Wolves	AHL	16	6	14	20	11	....	....	....	....	....	....	....	....	....	23	7	14	21	6	....	....	....	....
2002-03	Chicago Wolves	AHL	41	12	20	32	16	....	....	....	....	....	....	....	....	....	9	1	3	4	4	....	....	....	....
	NHL Totals		**153**	**11**	**27**	**38**	**50**	**1**	**1**	**0**	**198**	**5.6**		**1681**	**47.2**	**12:49**	....	....	....	....	....	....	....	....	....

Traded to **Atlanta** by **Calgary** for future considerations, June 25, 1999.

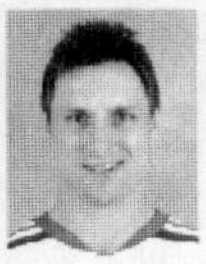

KARPA, Dave

(KAHR-puh, DAYV)

Defense. Shoots right. 6'1", 210 lbs. Born, Regina, Sask., May 7, 1971. Quebec's 4th choice, 68th overall, in 1991 Entry Draft.

			Regular Season														Playoffs								
Season	Club	League	GP	G	A	Pts	PIM	PP	SH	GW	S	%	+/-	TF	F%	Min	GP	G	A	Pts	PIM	PP	SH	GW	Min
1988-89	Notre Dame	SJHL	41	16	37	53	....	....	....	....	....	....	....	....	....	....	....	....	....	....	....	....	....	....	....
1989-90	Notre Dame	SJHL	43	9	19	28	271	....	....	....	....	....	....	....	....	....	....	....	....	....	....	....	....	....	....
1990-91	Ferris State	CCHA	41	6	19	25	109	....	....	....	....	....	....	....	....	....	....	....	....	....	....	....	....	....	....
1991-92	Ferris State	CCHA	34	7	12	19	124	....	....	....	....	....	....	....	....	....	....	....	....	....	....	....	....	....	....
	Quebec	NHL	4	0	0	0	14	0	0	0	2	0.0	2	....	....	....	....	....	....	....	....	....	....	....	....
	Halifax Citadels	AHL	2	0	0	0	4	....	....	....	....	....	....	....	....	....	....	....	....	....	....	....	....	....	....
1992-93	Quebec	NHL	12	0	1	1	13	0	0	0	2	0.0	-6	....	....	....	3	0	0	0	0	0	0	0	....
	Halifax Citadels	AHL	71	4	27	31	167	....	....	....	....	....	....	....	....	....	....	....	....	....	....	....	....	....	....
1993-94	Quebec	NHL	60	5	12	17	148	2	0	0	48	10.4	0	....	....	....	....	....	....	....	....	....	....	....	....
	Cornwall Aces	AHL	1	0	0	0	0	....	....	....	....	....	....	....	....	....	12	2	2	4	27	....	....	....	....
1994-95	Cornwall Aces	AHL	6	0	2	2	19	....	....	....	....	....	....	....	....	....	....	....	....	....	....	....	....	....	....
	Quebec	NHL	2	0	0	0	0	0	0	0	1	0.0	-1	....	....	....	....	....	....	....	....	....	....	....	....
	Anaheim	NHL	26	1	5	6	91	0	0	0	32	3.1	0	....	....	....	....	....	....	....	....	....	....	....	....
1995-96	Anaheim	NHL	72	3	16	19	270	0	1	1	62	4.8	-3	....	....	....	....	....	....	....	....	....	....	....	....
1996-97	Anaheim	NHL	69	2	11	13	210	0	0	1	90	2.2	11	....	....	....	8	1	1	2	20	0	0	1	....
1997-98	Anaheim	NHL	78	1	11	12	217	0	0	0	64	1.6	-3	....	....	....	....	....	....	....	....	....	....	....	....
1998-99	Carolina	NHL	33	0	2	2	55	0	0	0	21	0.0	1	0	0.0	16:55	2	0	0	0	2	0	0	0	12:06
99-2000	Carolina	NHL	27	1	4	5	52	0	0	0	24	4.2	9	0	0.0	17:21	....	....	....	....	....	....	....	....	....
	Cincinnati	IHL	39	1	8	9	147	....	....	....	....	....	....	....	....	....	....	....	....	....	....	....	....	....	....
2000-01	Carolina	NHL	80	4	6	10	159	2	0	0	69	5.8	-19	0	0.0	20:01	6	0	0	0	17	0	0	0	18:13
2001-02	NY Rangers	NHL	75	1	10	11	131	0	0	1	53	1.9	-9	0	0.0	16:54	....	....	....	....	....	....	....	....	....
2002-03	NY Rangers	NHL	19	0	2	2	14	0	0	0	13	0.0	-1	1	0.0	14:35	....	....	....	....	....	....	....	....	....
	Hartford	AHL	34	0	7	7	70	....	....	....	....	....	....	....	....	....	2	0	0	0	0	....	....	....	....
	NHL Totals		557	18	80	98	1374	4	1	3	481	3.7		1	0.0	17:50	19	1	1	2	39	0	0	1	16:41

Traded to **Anaheim** by **Quebec** for Anaheim's 4th round choice (later traded to St. Louis – St. Louis selected Jan Horacek) in 1997 Entry Draft, March 9, 1995. Traded to **Carolina** by **Anaheim** with Anaheim's 4th round choice (later traded to Atlanta – Atlanta selected Blake Robson) in 2000 Entry Draft for Stu Grimson and Kevin Haller, August 11, 1998. Signed as a free agent by **NY Rangers**, July 1, 2001.

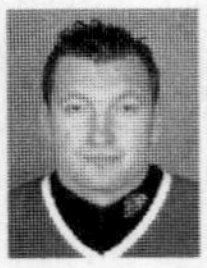

KARPOVTSEV, Alexander

(kar-POHV-tzehv, al-ehx-AN-duhr) **CHI.**

Defense. Shoots right. 6'3", 221 lbs. Born, Moscow, USSR, April 7, 1970. Quebec's 7th choice, 158th overall, in 1990 Entry Draft.

			Regular Season														Playoffs								
Season	Club	League	GP	G	A	Pts	PIM	PP	SH	GW	S	%	+/-	TF	F%	Min	GP	G	A	Pts	PIM	PP	SH	GW	Min
1989-90	Dynamo Moscow	USSR	35	1	1	2	27	....	....	....	....	....	....	....	....	....	....	....	....	....	....	....	....	....	....
1990-91	Dynamo Moscow	USSR	40	0	5	5	15	....	....	....	....	....	....	....	....	....	....	....	....	....	....	....	....	....	....
1991-92	Dynamo Moscow	CIS	35	4	2	6	26	....	....	....	....	....	....	....	....	....	....	....	....	....	....	....	....	....	....
1992-93	Dynamo Moscow	CIS	36	3	11	14	100	....	....	....	....	....	....	....	....	....	7	2	1	3	0	....	....	....	....
1993-94♦	NY Rangers	NHL	67	3	15	18	58	1	0	1	78	3.8	12	....	....	....	17	0	4	4	12	0	0	0	....
1994-95	Dynamo Moscow	CIS	13	0	2	2	10	....	....	....	....	....	....	....	....	....	....	....	....	....	....	....	....	....	....
	NY Rangers	NHL	47	4	8	12	30	1	0	1	82	4.9	-4	....	....	....	8	1	0	1	0	0	0	0	....
1995-96	NY Rangers	NHL	40	2	16	18	26	1	0	1	71	2.8	12	....	....	....	6	0	1	1	4	0	0	0	....
1996-97	NY Rangers	NHL	77	9	29	38	59	6	1	0	84	10.7	1	....	....	....	13	1	3	4	20	1	0	0	....
1997-98	NY Rangers	NHL	47	3	7	10	38	1	0	1	46	6.5	-1	....	....	....	....	....	....	....	....	....	....	....	....
1998-99	NY Rangers	NHL	2	1	0	1	0	0	0	0	4	25.0	1	0	0.0	22:38	....	....	....	....	....	....	....	....	....
	Toronto	NHL	56	2	25	27	52	1	0	1	61	3.3	38	0	0.0	20:58	14	1	3	4	12	1	0	0	19:44
99-2000	Toronto	NHL	69	3	14	17	54	3	0	0	51	5.9	9	2	0.0	20:14	11	0	3	3	4	0	0	0	21:04
2000-01	Dynamo Moscow	Russia	5	0	1	1	0	....	....	....	....	....	....	....	....	....	....	....	....	....	....	....	....	....	....
	Chicago	NHL	53	2	13	15	39	1	0	0	52	3.8	-4	0	0.0	20:28	....	....	....	....	....	....	....	....	....
2001-02	Chicago	NHL	65	1	9	10	40	0	1	0	40	2.5	10	3	33.3	20:40	5	1	0	1	0	0	0	1	20:53
2002-03	Chicago	NHL	40	4	10	14	12	3	0	1	36	11.1	-8	0	0.0	21:40	....	....	....	....	....	....	....	....	....
	NHL Totals		563	34	146	180	408	18	2	6	605	5.6		5	20.0	20:44	74	4	14	18	52	2	0	1	20:25

Traded to **NY Rangers** by **Quebec** for Mike Hurlbut, September 7, 1993. Traded to **Toronto** by **NY Rangers** with NY Rangers' 4th round choice (Mirko Murovic) in 1999 Entry Draft for Mathieu Schneider, October 14, 1998. Traded to **Chicago** by **Toronto** with Toronto's 4th round choice (Vladimir Gusev) in 2001 Entry Draft for Bryan McCabe, October 2, 2000. • Missed majority of 2002-03 season recovering from ankle (November 5, 2002 vs. Detroit) and cheekbone (February 20, 2003 vs. Phoenix) injuries.

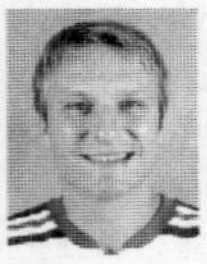

KASPARAITIS, Darius

(KAZ-puhr-IGH-tihz, DAIR-ee-uhs) **NYR**

Defense. Shoots left. 5'11", 212 lbs. Born, Elektrenai, USSR, October 16, 1972. NY Islanders' 1st choice, 5th overall, in 1992 Entry Draft.

			Regular Season														Playoffs								
Season	Club	League	GP	G	A	Pts	PIM	PP	SH	GW	S	%	+/-	TF	F%	Min	GP	G	A	Pts	PIM	PP	SH	GW	Min
1988-89	Dynamo Moscow	USSR	3	0	0	0	0	....	....	....	....	....	....	....	....	....	....	....	....	....	....	....	....	....	....
1989-90	Dynamo Moscow	USSR	1	0	0	0	0	....	....	....	....	....	....	....	....	....	....	....	....	....	....	....	....	....	....
1990-91	Dynamo Moscow	USSR	17	0	1	1	10	....	....	....	....	....	....	....	....	....	....	....	....	....	....	....	....	....	....
1991-92	Dynamo Moscow	CIS	31	2	10	12	14	....	....	....	....	....	....	....	....	....	....	....	....	....	....	....	....	....	....
1992-93	Dynamo Moscow	CIS	7	1	3	4	8	....	....	....	....	....	....	....	....	....	....	....	....	....	....	....	....	....	....
	NY Islanders	NHL	79	4	17	21	166	0	0	0	92	4.3	15	....	....	....	18	0	5	5	31	0	0	0	....
1993-94	NY Islanders	NHL	76	1	10	11	142	0	0	0	81	1.2	-6	....	....	....	4	0	0	0	8	0	0	0	....
1994-95	NY Islanders	NHL	13	0	1	1	22	0	0	0	8	0.0	-11	....	....	....	....	....	....	....	....	....	....	....	....
1995-96	NY Islanders	NHL	46	1	7	8	93	0	0	0	34	2.9	-12	....	....	....	....	....	....	....	....	....	....	....	....
1996-97	NY Islanders	NHL	18	0	5	5	16	0	0	0	12	0.0	-7	....	....	....	....	....	....	....	....	....	....	....	....
	Pittsburgh	NHL	57	2	16	18	84	0	0	0	46	4.3	24	....	....	....	5	0	0	0	6	0	0	0	....
1997-98	Pittsburgh	NHL	81	4	8	12	127	0	2	0	71	5.6	3	....	....	....	5	0	0	0	8	0	0	0	....
	Russia	Olympics	6	0	2	2	6	....	....	....	....	....	....	....	....	....	....	....	....	....	....	....	....	....	....
1998-99	Pittsburgh	NHL	48	1	4	5	70	0	0	0	32	3.1	12	0	0.0	16:01	....	....	....	....	....	....	....	....	....
99-2000	Pittsburgh	NHL	73	3	12	15	146	1	0	1	76	3.9	-12	0	0.0	18:07	11	1	1	2	10	0	0	0	21:39
2000-01	Pittsburgh	NHL	77	3	16	19	111	1	0	0	81	3.7	11	0	0.0	19:14	17	1	1	2	26	0	0	1	19:52
2001-02	Pittsburgh	NHL	69	2	12	14	123	0	0	0	75	2.7	-1	1	0.0	20:32	....	....	....	....	....	....	....	....	....
	Russia	Olympics	6	1	0	1	4	....	....	....	....	....	....	....	....	....	....	....	....	....	....	....	....	....	....
	Colorado	NHL	11	0	0	0	19	0	0	0	6	0.0	1	0	0.0	19:44	21	0	3	3	18	0	0	0	20:46
2002-03	NY Rangers	NHL	80	3	11	14	85	0	0	1	84	3.6	5	0	0.0	18:54	....	....	....	....	....	....	....	....	....
	NHL Totals		728	24	119	143	1204	2	2	2	698	3.4		1	0.0	18:46	81	2	10	12	107	0	0	1	20:39

Traded to **Pittsburgh** by **NY Islanders** with Andreas Johansson for Bryan Smolinski, November 17, 1996. Traded to **Colorado** by **Pittsburgh** for Ville Niemenen and Rick Berry, March 19, 2002. Signed as a free agent by **NY Rangers**, July 2, 2002.

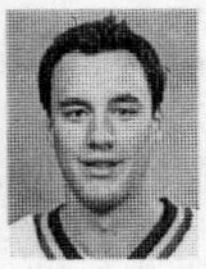

KAVANAGH, Pat

(KA-vuh-naw, PAT) **VAN.**

Right wing. Shoots right. 6'3", 192 lbs. Born, Ottawa, Ont., March 14, 1979. Philadelphia's 2nd choice, 50th overall, in 1997 Entry Draft.

			Regular Season														Playoffs								
Season	Club	League	GP	G	A	Pts	PIM	PP	SH	GW	S	%	+/-	TF	F%	Min	GP	G	A	Pts	PIM	PP	SH	GW	Min
1995-96	Kanata Valley	OCJHL	54	19	16	35	99	....	....	....	....	....	....	....	....	....	....	....	....	....	....	....	....	....	....
1996-97	Peterborough	OHL	43	6	8	14	53	....	....	....	....	....	....	....	....	....	11	1	1	2	12	....	....	....	....
1997-98	Peterborough	OHL	66	10	16	26	85	....	....	....	....	....	....	....	....	....	4	1	0	1	6	....	....	....	....
1998-99	Peterborough	OHL	68	26	43	69	118	....	....	....	....	....	....	....	....	....	5	0	5	5	10	....	....	....	....
99-2000	Syracuse Crunch	AHL	68	12	8	20	56	....	....	....	....	....	....	....	....	....	4	0	0	0	0	....	....	....	....
2000-01	Kansas City	IHL	78	26	15	41	86	....	....	....	....	....	....	....	....	....	....	....	....	....	....	....	....	....	....
	Vancouver	NHL	....	....	....	....	....	....	....	....	....	....	....	....	....	....	3	0	0	0	2	0	0	0	8:27
2001-02	Manitoba Moose	AHL	70	13	19	32	100	....	....	....	....	....	....	....	....	....	7	1	0	1	6	....	....	....	....
2002-03	Vancouver	NHL	3	1	0	1	2	0	0	1	4	25.0	2	27	37.0	10:23	....	....	....	....	....	....	....	....	....
	Manitoba Moose	AHL	63	15	15	30	96	....	....	....	....	....	....	....	....	....	14	7	4	11	20	....	....	....	....
	NHL Totals		3	1	0	1	2	0	0	1	4	25.0		27	37.0	10:23	3	0	0	0	2	0	0	0	8:27

Traded to **Vancouver** by **Philadelphia** for Vancouver's 6th round choice (Konstantin Rudenko) in 1999 Entry Draft, June 1, 1999.

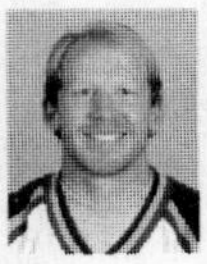

KEANE, Mike

(KEEN, MIGHK)

Right wing. Shoots right. 5'10", 185 lbs. Born, Winnipeg, Man., May 29, 1967.

			Regular Season														Playoffs								
Season	Club	League	GP	G	A	Pts	PIM	PP	SH	GW	S	%	+/-	TF	F%	Min	GP	G	A	Pts	PIM	PP	SH	GW	Min
1983-84	Wpg. Monarchs	MMHL	21	17	19	36	59	....	....	....	....	....	....	....	....	....	....	....	....	....	....	....	....	....	....
	Winnipeg	WHL	1	0	0	0	0	....	....	....	....	....	....	....	....	....	....	....	....	....	....	....	....	....	....
1984-85	Moose Jaw	WHL	65	17	26	43	141	....	....	....	....	....	....	....	....	....	....	....	....	....	....	....	....	....	....
1985-86	Moose Jaw	WHL	67	34	49	83	162	....	....	....	....	....	....	....	....	....	13	6	8	14	9	....	....	....	....
1986-87	Moose Jaw	WHL	53	25	45	70	107	....	....	....	....	....	....	....	....	....	9	3	9	12	11	....	....	....	....
	Sherbrooke	AHL	....	....	....	....	....	....	....	....	....	....	....	....	....	....	9	2	2	4	16	....	....	....	....
1987-88	Sherbrooke	AHL	78	25	43	68	70	....	....	....	....	....	....	....	....	....	6	1	1	2	18	....	....	....	....
1988-89	Montreal	NHL	69	16	19	35	69	5	0	1	90	17.8	9	....	....	....	21	4	3	7	17	2	0	0	....

			Regular Season														Playoffs								
Season	Club	League	GP	G	A	Pts	PIM	PP	SH	GW	S	%	+/-	TF	F%	Min	GP	G	A	Pts	PIM	PP	SH	GW	Min
1989-90	**Montreal**	**NHL**	**74**	**9**	**15**	**24**	**78**	**1**	**0**	**1**	**92**	**9.8**	**0**	....	....	....	**11**	**0**	**1**	**1**	**8**	**0**	**0**	**0**	....
1990-91	**Montreal**	**NHL**	**73**	**13**	**23**	**36**	**50**	**2**	**1**	**2**	**109**	**11.9**	**6**	....	....	....	**12**	**3**	**2**	**5**	**6**	**0**	**0**	**0**	....
1991-92	**Montreal**	**NHL**	**67**	**11**	**30**	**41**	**64**	**2**	**0**	**2**	**116**	**9.5**	**16**	....	....	....	**8**	**1**	**1**	**2**	**16**	**0**	**0**	**0**	....
1992-93 ♦	**Montreal**	**NHL**	**77**	**15**	**45**	**60**	**95**	**0**	**0**	**1**	**120**	**12.5**	**29**	....	....	....	**19**	**2**	**13**	**15**	**6**	**0**	**0**	**0**	....
1993-94	**Montreal**	**NHL**	**80**	**16**	**30**	**46**	**119**	**6**	**2**	**2**	**129**	**12.4**	**6**	....	....	....	**6**	**3**	**1**	**4**	**4**	**0**	**0**	**0**	....
1994-95	**Montreal**	**NHL**	**48**	**10**	**10**	**20**	**15**	**1**	**0**	**0**	**75**	**13.3**	**5**	....	....	....	....	....	....	....	....	....	....	....	....
1995-96	**Montreal**	**NHL**	**18**	**0**	**7**	**7**	**6**	**0**	**0**	**0**	**17**	**0.0**	**–6**	....	....	....	....	....	....	....	....	....	....	....	....
	♦ Colorado	**NHL**	**55**	**10**	**10**	**20**	**40**	**0**	**2**	**2**	**67**	**14.9**	**1**	....	....	....	**22**	**3**	**2**	**5**	**16**	**0**	**0**	**1**	....
1996-97	**Colorado**	**NHL**	**81**	**10**	**17**	**27**	**63**	**0**	**1**	**1**	**91**	**11.0**	**2**	....	....	....	**17**	**3**	**1**	**4**	**24**	**0**	**0**	**1**	....
1997-98	**NY Rangers**	**NHL**	**70**	**8**	**10**	**18**	**47**	**2**	**0**	**0**	**113**	**7.1**	**–12**	....	....	....	....	....	....	....	....	....	....	....	....
	Dallas	**NHL**	**13**	**2**	**3**	**5**	**5**	**0**	**0**	**1**	**15**	**13.3**	**0**	....	....	....	**17**	**4**	**4**	**8**	**0**	**0**	**1**	**1**	....
1998-99 ♦	**Dallas**	**NHL**	**81**	**6**	**23**	**29**	**62**	**1**	**1**	**1**	**106**	**5.7**	**–2**	**11**	**27.3**	**13:57**	**23**	**5**	**2**	**7**	**6**	**0**	**1**	**1**	**18:02**
99-2000	**Dallas**	**NHL**	**81**	**13**	**21**	**34**	**41**	**0**	**4**	**3**	**85**	**15.3**	**9**	**10**	**50.0**	**16:10**	**23**	**2**	**4**	**6**	**14**	**0**	**0**	**0**	**16:20**
2000-01	**Dallas**	**NHL**	**67**	**10**	**14**	**24**	**35**	**1**	**0**	**1**	**64**	**15.6**	**4**	**25**	**60.0**	**15:28**	**10**	**3**	**2**	**5**	**4**	**0**	**0**	**0**	**16:08**
2001-02	**St. Louis**	**NHL**	**56**	**4**	**6**	**10**	**22**	**1**	**0**	**0**	**47**	**8.5**	**–2**	**49**	**30.6**	**14:19**	....	....	....	....	....	....	....	....	....
	Colorado	**NHL**	**22**	**2**	**5**	**7**	**16**	**0**	**0**	**0**	**26**	**7.7**	**–2**	**42**	**31.0**	**16:55**	**18**	**1**	**4**	**5**	**8**	**0**	**0**	**0**	**16:18**
2002-03	**Colorado**	**NHL**	**65**	**5**	**5**	**10**	**34**	**0**	**1**	**1**	**35**	**14.3**	**0**	**102**	**19.6**	**12:15**	**6**	**0**	**0**	**0**	**2**	**0**	**0**	**0**	**7:57**
	NHL Totals		**1097**	**160**	**293**	**453**	**861**	**22**	**12**	**19**	**1397**	**11.5**		**239**	**29.7**	**14:38**	**213**	**34**	**40**	**74**	**131**	**2**	**2**	**4**	**16:10**

Signed as a free agent by **Montreal**, September 25, 1985. Traded to **Colorado** by **Montreal** with Patrick Roy for Andrei Kovalenko, Martin Rucinsky and Jocelyn Thibault, December 6, 1995. Signed as a free agent by **NY Rangers**, July 30, 1997. Traded to **Dallas** by **NY Rangers** with Brian Skrudland and NY Rangers' 6th round choice (Pavel Patera) in 1998 Entry Draft for Todd Harvey, Bob Errey and Dallas' 4th round choice (Boyd Kane) in 1998 Entry Draft, March 24, 1998. Signed as a free agent by **St. Louis**, July 10, 2001. Traded to **Colorado** by **St. Louis** for Shjon Podein, February 11, 2002.

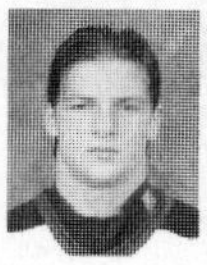

KEEFE, Sheldon

(KEEF, SHEHL-duhn) **T.B.**

Right wing. Shoots right. 5'11", 185 lbs. Born, Brampton, Ont., September 17, 1980. Tampa Bay's 1st choice, 47th overall, in 1999 Entry Draft.

1995-96	Tor. Young Nats	MTHL	45	66	71	137	....	....	....	....	....	....	....	....	....	....	....	....	....	....	....	....	....	....	....
1996-97	Quinte Hawks	MTJHL	44	21	23	44	41	....	....	....	....	....	....	....	....	....	....	....	....	....	....	....	....	....	....
	Bramalea Blues	OPJHL	8	0	3	3	4	....	....	....	....	....	....	....	....	....	....	....	....	....	....	....	....	....	....
1997-98	Caledon	MTJHL	43	41	40	81	117	....	....	....	....	....	....	....	....	....	13	15	8	23	....	....	....	....	....
1998-99	St. Michael's	OHL	38	37	37	74	80	....	....	....	....	....	....	....	....	....	....	....	....	....	....	....	....	....	....
	Barrie Colts	OHL	28	14	28	42	60	....	....	....	....	....	....	....	....	....	10	5	5	10	31	....	....	....	....
99-2000	Barrie Colts	OHL	66	48	*73	*121	95	....	....	....	....	....	....	....	....	....	25	10	13	23	41	....	....	....	....
2000-01	**Tampa Bay**	**NHL**	**49**	**4**	**0**	**4**	**38**	**0**	**0**	**0**	**32**	**12.5**	**–13**	**1**	**0.0**	**8:00**	....	....	....	....	....	....	....	....	....
	Detroit Vipers	IHL	13	7	5	12	23	....	....	....	....	....	....	....	....	....	....	....	....	....	....	....	....	....	....
2001-02	**Tampa Bay**	**NHL**	**39**	**6**	**7**	**13**	**16**	**0**	**0**	**1**	**52**	**11.5**	**–11**	**70**	**45.7**	**13:00**	....	....	....	....	....	....	....	....	....
	Springfield	AHL	24	9	9	18	26	....	....	....	....	....	....	....	....	....	....	....	....	....	....	....	....	....	....
2002-03	**Tampa Bay**	**NHL**	**37**	**2**	**5**	**7**	**24**	**0**	**0**	**0**	**51**	**3.9**	**–1**	**32**	**43.8**	**10:15**	....	....	....	....	....	....	....	....	....
	Springfield	AHL	33	16	15	31	28	....	....	....	....	....	....	....	....	....	6	0	0	0	4	....	....	....	....
	NHL Totals		**125**	**12**	**12**	**24**	**78**	**0**	**0**	**1**	**135**	**8.9**		**103**	**44.7**	**10:14**	....	....	....	....	....	....	....	....	....

OHL All-Rookie Team (1999) • OHL Rookie of the Year (1999) • OHL Second All-Star Team (2000) • Eddie Powers Memorial Trophy (Top Scorer – OHL) (2000) • Canadian Major Junior First All-Star Team (2000) • Memorial Cup All-Star Team (2000)

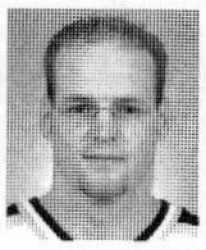

KELLEHER, Chris

(KEH-leh-huhr, KRIHS)

Defense. Shoots left. 6'1", 210 lbs. Born, Cambridge, MA, March 23, 1975. Pittsburgh's 5th choice, 130th overall, in 1993 Entry Draft.

1990-91	Belmont Hill	Hi-School	20	4	23	27	14	....	....	....	....	....	....	....	....	....	....	....	....	....	....	....	....	....	....
1991-92	St. Sebastian's	Hi-School	28	7	27	34	12	....	....	....	....	....	....	....	....	....	....	....	....	....	....	....	....	....	....
1992-93	St. Sebastian's	Hi-School	25	8	30	38	16	....	....	....	....	....	....	....	....	....	....	....	....	....	....	....	....	....	....
1993-94	St. Sebastian's	Hi-School	24	10	21	31	....	....	....	....	....	....	....	....	....	....	....	....	....	....	....	....	....	....	....
1994-95	Boston University	H-East	35	3	17	20	62	....	....	....	....	....	....	....	....	....	....	....	....	....	....	....	....	....	....
1995-96	Boston University	H-East	37	7	18	25	43	....	....	....	....	....	....	....	....	....	....	....	....	....	....	....	....	....	....
1996-97	Boston University	H-East	39	10	24	34	54	....	....	....	....	....	....	....	....	....	....	....	....	....	....	....	....	....	....
1997-98	Boston University	H-East	37	4	26	30	40	....	....	....	....	....	....	....	....	....	....	....	....	....	....	....	....	....	....
1998-99	Syracuse Crunch	AHL	45	1	4	5	43	....	....	....	....	....	....	....	....	....	....	....	....	....	....	....	....	....	....
99-2000	Wilkes-Barre	AHL	67	0	12	12	40	....	....	....	....	....	....	....	....	....	....	....	....	....	....	....	....	....	....
2000-01	Wilkes-Barre	AHL	66	6	13	19	37	....	....	....	....	....	....	....	....	....	21	7	18	*25	4	....	....	....	....
2001-02	**Boston**	**NHL**	**1**	**0**	**0**	**0**	**0**	**0**	**0**	**0**	**0**	**0.0**	**0**	**0**	**0.0**	**6:07**	....	....	....	....	....	....	....	....	....
	Providence Bruins	AHL	31	6	13	19	14	....	....	....	....	....	....	....	....	....	2	0	1	1	0	....	....	....	....
2002-03	Providence Bruins	AHL	72	8	27	35	50	....	....	....	....	....	....	....	....	....	4	0	1	1	0	....	....	....	....
	NHL Totals		**1**	**0**	**0**	**0**	**0**	**0**	**0**	**0**	**0**	**0.0**		**0**	**0.0**	**6:07**	....	....	....	....	....	....	....	....	....

NCAA East Second All-American Team (1997, 1998) • Hockey East Second All-Star Team (1998)

Signed as a free agent by **Boston**, July 24, 2001.

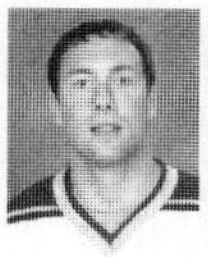

KELLY, Steve

(KEHL-lee, STEEV) **L.A.**

Center. Shoots left. 6'2", 205 lbs. Born, Vancouver, B.C., October 26, 1976. Edmonton's 1st choice, 6th overall, in 1995 Entry Draft.

1991-92	Westbank	BCAHA	30	25	60	85	75	....	....	....	....	....	....	....	....	....	....	....	....	....	....	....	....	....	....
1992-93	Prince Albert	WHL	65	11	9	20	75	....	....	....	....	....	....	....	....	....	....	....	....	....	....	....	....	....	....
1993-94	Prince Albert	WHL	65	19	42	61	106	....	....	....	....	....	....	....	....	....	....	....	....	....	....	....	....	....	....
1994-95	Prince Albert	WHL	68	31	41	72	153	....	....	....	....	....	....	....	....	....	15	7	9	16	35	....	....	....	....
1995-96	Prince Albert	WHL	70	27	74	101	203	....	....	....	....	....	....	....	....	....	18	13	18	31	47	....	....	....	....
1996-97	**Edmonton**	**NHL**	**8**	**1**	**0**	**1**	**6**	**0**	**0**	**1**	**6**	**16.7**	**–1**	....	....	....	**6**	**0**	**0**	**0**	**2**	**0**	**0**	**0**	....
	Hamilton	AHL	48	9	29	38	111	....	....	....	....	....	....	....	....	....	11	3	3	6	24	....	....	....	....
1997-98	**Edmonton**	**NHL**	**19**	**0**	**2**	**2**	**8**	**0**	**0**	**0**	**5**	**0.0**	**–4**	....	....	....	....	....	....	....	....	....	....	....	....
	Hamilton	AHL	11	2	8	10	18	....	....	....	....	....	....	....	....	....	....	....	....	....	....	....	....	....	....
	Tampa Bay	**NHL**	**24**	**2**	**1**	**3**	**15**	**1**	**0**	**0**	**17**	**11.8**	**–9**	....	....	....	....	....	....	....	....	....	....	....	....
	Milwaukee	IHL	5	0	1	1	19	....	....	....	....	....	....	....	....	....	....	....	....	....	....	....	....	....	....
	Cleveland	IHL	5	1	1	2	29	....	....	....	....	....	....	....	....	....	1	0	1	1	0	....	....	....	....
1998-99	**Tampa Bay**	**NHL**	**34**	**1**	**3**	**4**	**27**	**0**	**0**	**1**	**15**	**6.7**	**–15**	**11**	**54.5**	**10:51**	....	....	....	....	....	....	....	....	....
	Cleveland	IHL	18	6	7	13	36	....	....	....	....	....	....	....	....	....	....	....	....	....	....	....	....	....	....
99-2000	Detroit Vipers	IHL	1	0	0	0	4	....	....	....	....	....	....	....	....	....	....	....	....	....	....	....	....	....	....
	♦ New Jersey	**NHL**	**1**	**0**	**0**	**0**	**0**	**0**	**0**	**0**	**0**	**0.0**	**0**	**0**	**0.0**	**4:28**	**10**	**0**	**0**	**0**	**4**	**0**	**0**	**0**	**11:32**
	Albany River Rats	AHL	76	21	36	57	131	....	....	....	....	....	....	....	....	....	3	1	1	2	2	....	....	....	....
2000-01	**New Jersey**	**NHL**	**24**	**2**	**2**	**4**	**21**	**0**	**0**	**0**	**18**	**11.1**	**0**	**87**	**48.3**	**9:58**	....	....	....	....	....	....	....	....	....
	Los Angeles	**NHL**	**11**	**1**	**0**	**1**	**4**	**0**	**0**	**0**	**4**	**25.0**	**0**	**51**	**39.2**	**6:44**	**8**	**0**	**0**	**0**	**2**	**0**	**0**	**0**	**5:23**
2001-02	**Los Angeles**	**NHL**	**8**	**0**	**1**	**1**	**2**	**0**	**0**	**0**	**0**	**0.0**	**–1**	**44**	**36.4**	**6:52**	**1**	**0**	**0**	**0**	**0**	**0**	**0**	**0**	**5:54**
	Manchester	AHL	49	10	21	31	88	....	....	....	....	....	....	....	....	....	5	1	8	9	4	....	....	....	....
2002-03	**Los Angeles**	**NHL**	**15**	**2**	**3**	**5**	**0**	**0**	**0**	**1**	**14**	**14.3**	**–6**	**133**	**42.9**	**12:29**	....	....	....	....	....	....	....	....	....
	Manchester	AHL	54	19	44	63	144	....	....	....	....	....	....	....	....	....	3	0	1	1	0	....	....	....	....
	NHL Totals		**144**	**9**	**12**	**21**	**83**	**1**	**0**	**3**	**79**	**11.4**		**326**	**43.3**	**9:59**	**25**	**0**	**0**	**0**	**8**	**0**	**0**	**0**	**8:39**

Traded to **Tampa Bay** by **Edmonton** with Bryan Marchment and Jason Bonsignore for Roman Hamrlik and Paul Comrie, December 30, 1997. Traded to **New Jersey** by **Tampa Bay** for New Jersey's 7th round choice (Brian Eklund) in 2000 Entry Draft, October 7, 1999. Traded to **Los Angeles** by **New Jersey** to complete transaction that sent Bob Corkum to New Jersey (February 23, 2001), February 27, 2001. • Spent majority of 2000-01 season with New Jersey and Los Angeles as a healthy scratch.

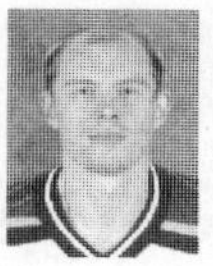

KHAVANOV, Alexander

(khuh-VAN-ahf, al-ehx-AN-duhr) **ST.L.**

Defense. Shoots left. 6'2", 205 lbs. Born, Moscow, USSR, January 30, 1972. St. Louis' 8th choice, 232nd overall, in 1999 Entry Draft.

1992-93	Birmingham Bulls	ECHL	19	0	3	3	14	....	....	....	....	....	....	....	....	....	....	....	....	....	....	....	....	....	....
	Raleigh Icecaps	ECHL	17	0	6	6	8	....	....	....	....	....	....	....	....	....	....	....	....	....	....	....	....	....	....
1993-94	St. Petersburg	CIS	41	1	2	3	24	....	....	....	....	....	....	....	....	....	....	....	....	....	....	....	....	....	....
1994-95	St. Petersburg	CIS	49	7	0	7	32	....	....	....	....	....	....	....	....	....	3	0	0	0	0	....	....	....	....
1995-96	St. Petersburg	CIS	32	1	5	6	41	....	....	....	....	....	....	....	....	....	....	....	....	....	....	....	....	....	....
	HPK Hameenlinna	Finland	16	0	2	2	4	....	....	....	....	....	....	....	....	....	9	0	0	0	0	....	....	....	....
1996-97	Cherepovets	Russia	39	3	8	11	56	....	....	....	....	....	....	....	....	....	3	1	0	1	4	....	....	....	....
1997-98	Cherepovets	Russia	44	3	5	8	46	....	....	....	....	....	....	....	....	....	....	....	....	....	....	....	....	....	....
1998-99	Dynamo Moscow	Russia	40	2	7	9	14	....	....	....	....	....	....	....	....	....	16	1	5	6	35	....	....	....	....
	Dynamo Moscow	EuroHL	5	0	1	1	2	....	....	....	....	....	....	....	....	....	6	0	0	0	4	....	....	....	....
99-2000	Dynamo Moscow	Russia	38	5	12	17	49	....	....	....	....	....	....	....	....	....	17	0	3	3	4	....	....	....	....
	Dynamo Moscow	EuroHL	6	2	0	2	0	....	....	....	....	....	....	....	....	....	....	....	....	....	....	....	....	....	....
2000-01	**St. Louis**	**NHL**	**74**	**7**	**16**	**23**	**52**	**2**	**0**	**0**	**92**	**7.6**	**16**	**0**	**0.0**	**20:54**	**15**	**3**	**2**	**5**	**14**	**1**	**0**	**0**	**21:16**

Season	Club	League	Regular Season GP	G	A	Pts	PIM	PP	SH	GW	S	%	+/-	TF	F%	Min	Playoffs GP	G	A	Pts	PIM	PP	SH	GW	Min
2001-02	**St. Louis**	**NHL**	**81**	**3**	**21**	**24**	**55**	**0**	**0**	**0**	**87**	**3.4**	**9**	**0**	**0.0**	**17:13**	**4**	**0**	**0**	**0**	**2**	**0**	**0**	**0**	**15:08**
2002-03	**St. Louis**	**NHL**	**81**	**8**	**25**	**33**	**48**	**2**	**1**	**2**	**90**	**8.9**	**–1**	**2**	**50.0**	**21:57**	**7**	**2**	**3**	**5**	**2**	**1**	**0**	**0**	**19:05**
	NHL Totals		**236**	**18**	**62**	**80**	**155**	**4**	**1**	**2**	**269**	**6.7**		**2**	**50.0**	**19:60**	**26**	**5**	**5**	**10**	**18**	**2**	**0**	**0**	**19:44**

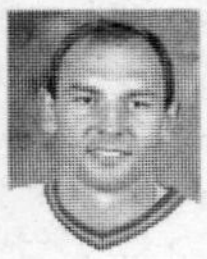

KHRISTICH, Dmitri

(KRIH-stihch, dih-MEE-tree)

Left wing/Center. Shoots right. 6'2", 195 lbs. Born, Kiev, USSR, July 23, 1969. Washington's 6th choice, 120th overall, in 1988 Entry Draft.

Season	Club	League	GP	G	A	Pts	PIM	PP	SH	GW	S	%	+/-	TF	F%	Min	GP	G	A	Pts	PIM	PP	SH	GW	Min
1985-86	Sokol Kiev	USSR	4	0	0	0	0	....	....	....	....	....	....	....	....	....	....	....	....	....	....	....	....	....	....
1986-87	Sokol Kiev	USSR	20	3	0	3	4	....	....	....	....	....	....	....	....	....	....	....	....	....	....	....	....	....	....
1987-88	Sokol Kiev	USSR	37	9	1	10	18	....	....	....	....	....	....	....	....	....	....	....	....	....	....	....	....	....	....
1988-89	Sokol Kiev	USSR	42	17	10	27	15	....	....	....	....	....	....	....	....	....	....	....	....	....	....	....	....	....	....
1989-90	Sokol Kiev	USSR	47	14	22	36	32	....	....	....	....	....	....	....	....	....	....	....	....	....	....	....	....	....	....
1990-91	Sokol Kiev	USSR	28	10	12	22	20	....	....	....	....	....	....	....	....	....	....	....	....	....	....	....	....	....	....
	Washington	**NHL**	**40**	**13**	**14**	**27**	**21**	**1**	**0**	**0**	**77**	**16.9**	**–1**	....	....	....	**11**	**1**	**3**	**4**	**6**	**0**	**0**	**0**	....
	Baltimore	AHL	3	0	0	0	0	....	....	....	....	....	....	....	....	....	....	....	....	....	....	....	....	....	....
1991-92	**Washington**	**NHL**	**80**	**36**	**37**	**73**	**35**	**14**	**1**	**7**	**188**	**19.1**	**24**	....	....	....	**7**	**3**	**2**	**5**	**15**	**3**	**0**	**1**	....
1992-93	**Washington**	**NHL**	**64**	**31**	**35**	**66**	**28**	**9**	**1**	**1**	**127**	**24.4**	**29**	....	....	....	**6**	**2**	**5**	**7**	**2**	**1**	**0**	**0**	....
1993-94	**Washington**	**NHL**	**83**	**29**	**29**	**58**	**73**	**10**	**0**	**4**	**195**	**14.9**	**–2**	....	....	....	**11**	**2**	**3**	**5**	**10**	**0**	**0**	**0**	....
1994-95	**Washington**	**NHL**	**48**	**12**	**14**	**26**	**41**	**8**	**0**	**2**	**92**	**13.0**	**0**	....	....	....	**7**	**1**	**4**	**5**	**0**	**0**	**0**	**0**	....
1995-96	**Los Angeles**	**NHL**	**76**	**27**	**37**	**64**	**44**	**12**	**0**	**3**	**204**	**13.2**	**0**	....	....	....	....	....	....	....	....	....	....	....	....
1996-97	**Los Angeles**	**NHL**	**75**	**19**	**37**	**56**	**38**	**3**	**0**	**2**	**135**	**14.1**	**8**	....	....	....	....	....	....	....	....	....	....	....	....
1997-98	**Boston**	**NHL**	**82**	**29**	**37**	**66**	**42**	**13**	**2**	**1**	**144**	**20.1**	**25**	....	....	....	**6**	**2**	**2**	**4**	**2**	**2**	**0**	**0**	....
1998-99	**Boston**	**NHL**	**79**	**29**	**42**	**71**	**48**	**13**	**1**	**6**	**144**	**20.1**	**11**	**76**	**44.7**	**19:46**	**12**	**3**	**4**	**7**	**6**	**0**	**0**	**1**	**19:55**
99-2000	**Toronto**	**NHL**	**53**	**12**	**18**	**30**	**24**	**3**	**0**	**0**	**79**	**15.2**	**8**	**84**	**45.2**	**16:10**	**12**	**1**	**2**	**3**	**0**	**1**	**0**	**0**	**16:06**
2000-01	**Toronto**	**NHL**	**27**	**3**	**6**	**9**	**8**	**2**	**0**	**0**	**23**	**13.0**	**8**	**129**	**41.9**	**15:01**	....	....	....	....	....	....	....	....	....
	Washington	**NHL**	**43**	**10**	**19**	**29**	**8**	**4**	**0**	**4**	**54**	**18.5**	**–8**	**3**	**33.3**	**14:53**	**3**	**0**	**0**	**0**	**0**	**0**	**0**	**0**	**6:50**
2001-02	**Washington**	**NHL**	**61**	**9**	**12**	**21**	**12**	**3**	**0**	**2**	**54**	**16.7**	**2**	**621**	**46.4**	**13:60**	....	....	....	....	....	....	....	....	....
	Ukraine	Olympics	2	2	0	2	0	....	....	....	....	....	....	....	....	....	....	....	....	....	....	....	....	....	....
2002-03	Magnitogorsk	Russia	31	9	12	21	20	....	....	....	....	....	....	....	....	....	3	0	0	0	4	....	....	....	....
	NHL Totals		**811**	**259**	**337**	**596**	**422**	**95**	**5**	**32**	**1516**	**17.1**		**913**	**45.5**	**16:25**	**75**	**15**	**25**	**40**	**41**	**7**	**0**	**2**	**16:46**

Played in NHL All-Star Game (1997, 1999)

Traded to **Los Angeles** by **Washington** with Byron Dafoe for Los Angeles' 1st round choice (Alexandre Volchkov) and Dallas' 4th round choice (previously acquired, Washington selected Justin Davis) in 1996 Entry Draft, July 8, 1995. Traded to **Boston** by **Los Angeles** with Byron Dafoe for Jozef Stumpel, Sandy Moger and Boston's 4th round choice (later traded to New Jersey – New Jersey selected Pierre Dagenais) in 1998 Entry Draft, August 29, 1997. Traded to **Toronto** by **Boston** for Toronto's 2nd round choice (Ivan Huml) in 2000 Entry Draft, October 20, 1999. Traded to **Washington** by **Toronto** for Tampa Bay's 3rd round choice (previously acquired, Toronto selected Brendan Bell) in 2001 Entry Draft, December 11, 2000.

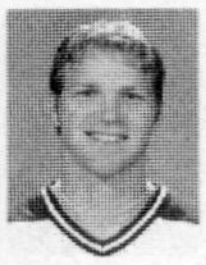

KILGER, Chad

(KIHL-guhr, CHAD) **MTL.**

Left wing. Shoots left. 6'4", 224 lbs. Born, Cornwall, Ont., November 27, 1976. Anaheim's 1st choice, 4th overall, in 1995 Entry Draft.

Season	Club	League	GP	G	A	Pts	PIM	PP	SH	GW	S	%	+/-	TF	F%	Min	GP	G	A	Pts	PIM	PP	SH	GW	Min
1992-93	Cornwall Colts	OCJHL	55	30	36	66	26	....	....	....	....	....	....	....	....	....	6	0	0	0	0	....	....	....	....
1993-94	Kingston	OHL	66	17	35	52	23	....	....	....	....	....	....	....	....	....	6	7	2	9	8	....	....	....	....
1994-95	Kingston	OHL	65	42	53	95	95	....	....	....	....	....	....	....	....	....	6	5	2	7	10	....	....	....	....
1995-96	**Anaheim**	**NHL**	**45**	**5**	**7**	**12**	**22**	**0**	**0**	**1**	**38**	**13.2**	**–2**	....	....	....	....	....	....	....	....	....	....	....	....
	Winnipeg	**NHL**	**29**	**2**	**3**	**5**	**12**	**0**	**0**	**0**	**19**	**10.5**	**–2**	....	....	....	**4**	**1**	**0**	**1**	**0**	**0**	**0**	**1**	....
1996-97	**Phoenix**	**NHL**	**24**	**4**	**3**	**7**	**13**	**1**	**0**	**0**	**30**	**13.3**	**–5**	....	....	....	....	....	....	....	....	....	....	....	....
	Springfield	AHL	52	17	28	45	36	....	....	....	....	....	....	....	....	....	16	5	7	12	56	....	....	....	....
1997-98	**Phoenix**	**NHL**	**10**	**0**	**1**	**1**	**4**	**0**	**0**	**0**	**9**	**0.0**	**–2**	....	....	....	....	....	....	....	....	....	....	....	....
	Springfield	AHL	35	14	14	28	33	....	....	....	....	....	....	....	....	....	....	....	....	....	....	....	....	....	....
	Chicago	**NHL**	**22**	**3**	**8**	**11**	**6**	**2**	**0**	**1**	**23**	**13.0**	**2**	....	....	....	....	....	....	....	....	....	....	....	....
1998-99	**Chicago**	**NHL**	**64**	**14**	**11**	**25**	**30**	**2**	**1**	**1**	**68**	**20.6**	**–1**	**488**	**56.6**	**14:03**	....	....	....	....	....	....	....	....	....
	Edmonton	**NHL**	**13**	**1**	**1**	**2**	**4**	**0**	**0**	**0**	**13**	**7.7**	**–3**	**82**	**53.7**	**11:22**	**4**	**0**	**0**	**0**	**4**	**0**	**0**	**0**	**12:59**
99-2000	**Edmonton**	**NHL**	**40**	**3**	**2**	**5**	**18**	**0**	**0**	**0**	**32**	**9.4**	**–6**	**269**	**48.0**	**8:33**	**3**	**0**	**0**	**0**	**0**	**0**	**0**	**0**	**8:01**
	Hamilton	AHL	7	4	2	6	4	....	....	....	....	....	....	....	....	....	....	....	....	....	....	....	....	....	....
2000-01	**Edmonton**	**NHL**	**34**	**5**	**2**	**7**	**17**	**1**	**0**	**0**	**28**	**17.9**	**–7**	**391**	**53.5**	**8:18**	....	....	....	....	....	....	....	....	....
	Montreal	**NHL**	**43**	**9**	**16**	**25**	**34**	**1**	**1**	**1**	**75**	**12.0**	**–1**	**319**	**52.4**	**17:57**	....	....	....	....	....	....	....	....	....
2001-02	**Montreal**	**NHL**	**75**	**8**	**15**	**23**	**27**	**0**	**1**	**2**	**87**	**9.2**	**–7**	**357**	**53.8**	**13:14**	**12**	**0**	**1**	**1**	**9**	**0**	**0**	**0**	**13:60**
2002-03	**Montreal**	**NHL**	**60**	**9**	**7**	**16**	**21**	**0**	**0**	**1**	**60**	**15.0**	**–4**	**208**	**46.6**	**10:42**	....	....	....	....	....	....	....	....	....
	NHL Totals		**459**	**63**	**76**	**139**	**208**	**7**	**3**	**7**	**482**	**13.1**		**2114**	**52.7**	**12:24**	**23**	**1**	**1**	**2**	**13**	**0**	**0**	**1**	**12:50**

Traded to **Winnipeg** by **Anaheim** with Oleg Tverdovsky and Anaheim's 3rd round choice (Per-Anton Lundstrom) in 1996 Entry Draft for Teemu Selanne, Marc Chouinard and Winnipeg's 4th round choice (later traded to Toronto – later traded to Montreal – Montreal selected Kim Staal) in 1996 Entry Draft, February 7, 1996. Transferred to **Phoenix** after **Winnipeg** franchise relocated, July 1, 1996. Traded to **Chicago** by **Phoenix** with Jayson More for Keith Carney and Jim Cummins, March 4, 1998. Traded to **Edmonton** by **Chicago** with Daniel Cleary, Ethan Moreau and Christian Laflamme for Boris Mironov, Dean McAmmond and Jonas Elofsson, March 20, 1999. Traded to **Montreal** by **Edmonton** for Sergei Zholtok, December 18, 2000.

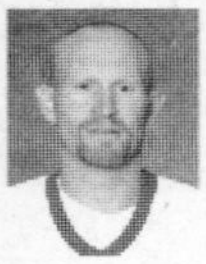

KING, Derek

(KIHNG, DAIR-ehk) **DET.**

Left wing. Shoots left. 6'1", 203 lbs. Born, Hamilton, Ont., February 11, 1967. NY Islanders' 2nd choice, 13th overall, in 1985 Entry Draft.

Season	Club	League	GP	G	A	Pts	PIM	PP	SH	GW	S	%	+/-	TF	F%	Min	GP	G	A	Pts	PIM	PP	SH	GW	Min
1982-83	Ham. Mtn. A's	OPJHL	8	1	2	3	0	....	....	....	....	....	....	....	....	....	....	....	....	....	....	....	....	....	....
1983-84	Ham. Mtn. A's	OPJHL	37	10	14	24	142	....	....	....	....	....	....	....	....	....	....	....	....	....	....	....	....	....	....
1984-85	Sault Ste. Marie	OHL	63	35	38	73	106	....	....	....	....	....	....	....	....	....	16	3	13	16	11	....	....	....	....
1985-86	Sault Ste. Marie	OHL	25	12	17	29	33	....	....	....	....	....	....	....	....	....	....	....	....	....	....	....	....	....	....
	Oshawa Generals	OHL	19	8	13	21	15	....	....	....	....	....	....	....	....	....	6	3	2	5	13	....	....	....	....
1986-87	Oshawa Generals	OHL	57	53	53	106	74	....	....	....	....	....	....	....	....	....	17	14	10	24	40	....	....	....	....
	NY Islanders	**NHL**	**2**	**0**	**0**	**0**	**0**	**0**	**0**	**0**	**5**	**0.0**	**0**	....	....	....	....	....	....	....	....	....	....	....	....
1987-88	**NY Islanders**	**NHL**	**55**	**12**	**24**	**36**	**30**	**1**	**0**	**4**	**94**	**12.8**	**7**	....	....	....	**5**	**0**	**2**	**2**	**2**	**0**	**0**	**0**	....
	Springfield	AHL	10	7	6	13	6	....	....	....	....	....	....	....	....	....	....	....	....	....	....	....	....	....	....
1988-89	**NY Islanders**	**NHL**	**60**	**14**	**29**	**43**	**14**	**4**	**0**	**0**	**103**	**13.6**	**10**	....	....	....	....	....	....	....	....	....	....	....	....
	Springfield	AHL	4	4	0	4	0	....	....	....	....	....	....	....	....	....	....	....	....	....	....	....	....	....	....
1989-90	**NY Islanders**	**NHL**	**46**	**13**	**27**	**40**	**20**	**5**	**0**	**1**	**91**	**14.3**	**2**	....	....	....	**4**	**0**	**0**	**0**	**4**	**0**	**0**	**0**	....
	Springfield	AHL	21	11	12	23	33	....	....	....	....	....	....	....	....	....	....	....	....	....	....	....	....	....	....
1990-91	**NY Islanders**	**NHL**	**66**	**19**	**26**	**45**	**44**	**2**	**0**	**2**	**130**	**14.6**	**1**	....	....	....	....	....	....	....	....	....	....	....	....
1991-92	**NY Islanders**	**NHL**	**80**	**40**	**38**	**78**	**46**	**21**	**0**	**6**	**189**	**21.2**	**–10**	....	....	....	....	....	....	....	....	....	....	....	....
1992-93	**NY Islanders**	**NHL**	**77**	**38**	**38**	**76**	**47**	**21**	**0**	**7**	**201**	**18.9**	**–4**	....	....	....	**18**	**3**	**11**	**14**	**14**	**0**	**0**	**0**	....
1993-94	**NY Islanders**	**NHL**	**78**	**30**	**40**	**70**	**59**	**10**	**0**	**7**	**171**	**17.5**	**18**	....	....	....	**4**	**0**	**1**	**1**	**0**	**0**	**0**	**0**	....
1994-95	**NY Islanders**	**NHL**	**43**	**10**	**16**	**26**	**41**	**7**	**0**	**0**	**118**	**8.5**	**–5**	....	....	....	....	....	....	....	....	....	....	....	....
1995-96	**NY Islanders**	**NHL**	**61**	**12**	**20**	**32**	**23**	**5**	**1**	**0**	**154**	**7.8**	**–10**	....	....	....	....	....	....	....	....	....	....	....	....
1996-97	**NY Islanders**	**NHL**	**70**	**23**	**30**	**53**	**20**	**5**	**0**	**3**	**153**	**15.0**	**–6**	....	....	....	....	....	....	....	....	....	....	....	....
	Hartford	**NHL**	**12**	**3**	**3**	**6**	**2**	**1**	**0**	**0**	**28**	**10.7**	**0**	....	....	....	....	....	....	....	....	....	....	....	....
1997-98	**Toronto**	**NHL**	**77**	**21**	**25**	**46**	**43**	**4**	**0**	**3**	**166**	**12.7**	**–7**	....	....	....	....	....	....	....	....	....	....	....	....
1998-99	**Toronto**	**NHL**	**81**	**24**	**28**	**52**	**20**	**8**	**0**	**4**	**150**	**16.0**	**15**	**1**	**0.0**	**14:02**	**16**	**1**	**3**	**4**	**4**	**0**	**0**	**0**	**15:05**
99-2000	**Toronto**	**NHL**	**3**	**0**	**0**	**0**	**2**	**0**	**0**	**0**	**4**	**0.0**	**–2**	**0**	**0.0**	**11:29**	....	....	....	....	....	....	....	....	....
	St. Louis	**NHL**	**19**	**2**	**7**	**9**	**6**	**1**	**0**	**0**	**29**	**6.9**	**0**	**0**	**0.0**	**12:44**	....	....	....	....	....	....	....	....	....
	Grand Rapids	IHL	52	19	30	49	25	....	....	....	....	....	....	....	....	....	17	7	8	15	8	....	....	....	....
2000-01	Grand Rapids	IHL	76	32	51	*83	19	....	....	....	....	....	....	....	....	....	10	5	5	10	4	....	....	....	....
2001-02	Munchen Barons	Germany	60	19	26	45	22	....	....	....	....	....	....	....	....	....	9	2	4	6	4	....	....	....	....
2002-03	Grand Rapids	AHL	59	13	28	41	20	....	....	....	....	....	....	....	....	....	15	4	10	14	6	....	....	....	....
	NHL Totals		**830**	**261**	**351**	**612**	**417**	**95**	**1**	**37**	**1786**	**14.6**		**1**	**0.0**	**13:43**	**47**	**4**	**17**	**21**	**24**	**0**	**0**	**0**	**15:05**

OHL Rookie of the Year (1985) • OHL First All-Star Team (1987) • IHL Second All-Star Team (2001) • Leo P. Lamoureux Memorial Trophy (Top Scorer – IHL) (2001) (tied with Steve Larouche)

Traded to **Hartford** by **NY Islanders** for Hartford's 5th round choice (Adam Edinger) in 1997 Entry Draft, March 18, 1997. Signed as a free agent by **Toronto**, July 4, 1997. Traded to **St. Louis** by **Toronto** for Tyler Harlton and future considerations, October 20, 1999. Signed as a free agent by **Ottawa**, August 10, 2000. Signed as a free agent with **Munchen** (Germany), July 13, 2001. Signed as a free agent by **Detroit**, July 24, 2002.

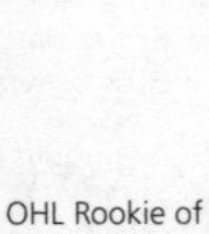

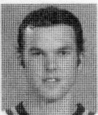

KING, Jason

(KIHNG, JAY-suhn) **VAN.**

Center. Shoots left. 6'1", 195 lbs. Born, Corner Brook, Nfld., September 14, 1981. Vancouver's 5th choice, 212th overall, in 2001 Entry Draft.

Season	Club	League	GP	G	A	Pts	PIM	PP	SH	GW	S	%	+/-	TF	F%	Min	GP	G	A	Pts	PIM	PP	SH	GW	Min
99-2000	Halifax	QMJHL	53	3	7	10	8	....	....	....	....	....	....	....	....	....	10	0	0	0	2	....	....	....	....
2000-01	Halifax	QMJHL	72	48	41	89	78	....	....	....	....	....	....	....	....	....	6	3	2	5	16	....	....	....	....
2001-02	Halifax	QMJHL	61	*63	36	99	39	....	....	....	....	....	....	....	....	....	13	9	8	17	13	....	....	....	....

			Regular Season														Playoffs								
Season	Club	League	GP	G	A	Pts	PIM	PP	SH	GW	S	%	+/-	TF	F%	Min	GP	G	A	Pts	PIM	PP	SH	GW	Min
2002-03	**Vancouver**	**NHL**	**8**	**0**	**2**	**2**	**0**	**0**	**0**	**0**	**12**	**0.0**	**0**	**0**	**0.0**	**11:17**									
	Manitoba Moose	AHL	67	20	20	40	15										14	4	3	7	14				
	NHL Totals		**8**	**0**	**2**	**2**	**0**	**0**	**0**	**0**	**12**	**0.0**		**0**	**0.0**	**11:17**									

QMJHL Second All-Star Team (2001)

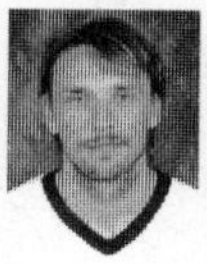

KJELLBERG, Patric

(SHEHL-buhrg, PA-trihk)

Right wing. Shoots left. 6'2", 210 lbs. Born, Trelleborg, Sweden, June 17, 1969. Montreal's 4th choice, 83rd overall, in 1988 Entry Draft.

Season	Club	League	GP	G	A	Pts	PIM	PP	SH	GW	S	%	+/-	TF	F%	Min	GP	G	A	Pts	PIM	PP	SH	GW	Min
1985-86	Falu IF	Swede-2	5	0	2	2	0																		
1986-87	Falu IF	Swede-2	32	11	13	24	16																		
1987-88	Falu IF	Swede-2	29	15	10	25	6																		
1988-89	AIK Solna	Sweden	25	7	9	16	8																		
1989-90	AIK Solna	Sweden	33	8	16	24	6										3	1	0	1	0				
1990-91	AIK Solna	Sweden	38	4	11	15	18																		
1991-92	AIK Solna	Sweden	40	20	13	33	14										3	1	0	1	2				
	Sweden	Olympics	8	1	3	4	0																		
1992-93	**Montreal**	**NHL**	**7**	**0**	**0**	**0**	**2**	**0**	**0**	**0**	**7**	**0.0**	**–3**												
	Fredericton	AHL	41	10	27	37	14										5	2	2	4	0				
1993-94	HV 71 Jonkoping	Sweden	40	11	17	28	18																		
	Sweden	Olympics	8	0	1	1	2																		
1994-95	HV 71 Jonkoping	Sweden	29	5	15	20	12																		
1995-96	Djurgarden	Sweden	40	9	7	16	10										4	0	2	2	2				
1996-97	Djurgarden	Sweden	49	29	11	40	18										4	2	3	5	4				
1997-98	Djurgarden	Sweden	46	*30	18	48	16										15	7	3	10	12				
1998-99	**Nashville**	**NHL**	**71**	**11**	**20**	**31**	**24**	**2**	**0**	**2**	**103**	**10.7**	**–13**	**83**	**37.3**	**17:41**									
99-2000	**Nashville**	**NHL**	**82**	**23**	**23**	**46**	**14**	**9**	**0**	**3**	**129**	**17.8**	**–11**	**22**	**31.8**	**18:12**									
2000-01	**Nashville**	**NHL**	**81**	**14**	**31**	**45**	**12**	**5**	**0**	**2**	**139**	**10.1**	**–2**	**9**	**33.3**	**17:39**									
2001-02	**Nashville**	**NHL**	**12**	**1**	**3**	**4**	**6**	**0**	**0**	**0**	**19**	**5.3**	**–3**	**1**	**0.0**	**16:50**									
	Anaheim	**NHL**	**65**	**7**	**8**	**15**	**10**	**4**	**0**	**0**	**69**	**10.1**	**–9**	**24**	**37.5**	**17:07**									
2002-03	**Anaheim**	**NHL**	**76**	**8**	**11**	**19**	**16**	**2**	**1**	**2**	**95**	**8.4**	**–9**	**14**	**57.1**	**15:38**	**10**	**0**	**0**	**0**	**0**	**0**	**0**	**0**	**10:30**
	NHL Totals		**394**	**64**	**96**	**160**	**84**	**22**	**1**	**9**	**561**	**11.4**		**153**	**37.9**	**17:16**	**10**	**0**	**0**	**0**	**0**	**0**	**0**	**0**	**10:30**

Signed as a free agent by **Nashville**, June 27, 1998. Traded to **Anaheim** by **Nashville** for Petr Tenkrat, November 1, 2001. • Officially announced retirement, June 6, 2003.

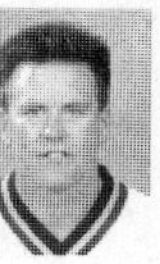

KLATT, Trent

(KLAT, TREHNT) **L.A.**

Right wing. Shoots right. 6'1", 210 lbs. Born, Robbinsdale, MN, January 30, 1971. Washington's 5th choice, 82nd overall, in 1989 Entry Draft.

Season	Club	League	GP	G	A	Pts	PIM	PP	SH	GW	S	%	+/-	TF	F%	Min	GP	G	A	Pts	PIM	PP	SH	GW	Min
1986-87	Osseo Orioles	Hi-School	22	9	27	36																			
1987-88	Osseo Orioles	Hi-School	22	19	17	36																			
1988-89	Osseo Orioles	Hi-School	22	24	39	63																			
1989-90	U. of Minnesota	WCHA	38	22	14	36	16																		
1990-91	U. of Minnesota	WCHA	39	16	28	44	58																		
1991-92	U. of Minnesota	WCHA	41	27	36	63	76																		
	Minnesota	**NHL**	**1**	**0**	**0**	**0**	**0**	**0**	**0**	**0**	**1**	**0.0**	**0**				**6**	**0**	**0**	**0**	**2**	**0**	**0**	**0**	
1992-93	**Minnesota**	**NHL**	**47**	**4**	**19**	**23**	**38**	**1**	**0**	**0**	**69**	**5.8**	**2**												
	Kalamazoo Wings	IHL	31	8	11	19	18																		
1993-94	**Dallas**	**NHL**	**61**	**14**	**24**	**38**	**30**	**3**	**0**	**2**	**86**	**16.3**	**13**				**9**	**2**	**1**	**3**	**4**	**1**	**0**	**0**	
	Kalamazoo Wings	IHL	6	3	2	5	4																		
1994-95	**Dallas**	**NHL**	**47**	**12**	**10**	**22**	**26**	**5**	**0**	**3**	**91**	**13.2**	**–2**				**5**	**1**	**0**	**1**	**0**	**1**	**0**	**0**	
1995-96	**Dallas**	**NHL**	**22**	**4**	**4**	**8**	**23**	**0**	**0**	**1**	**37**	**10.8**	**0**												
	Michigan	IHL	2	1	2	3	5																		
	Philadelphia	**NHL**	**49**	**3**	**8**	**11**	**21**	**0**	**0**	**1**	**64**	**4.7**	**2**				**12**	**4**	**1**	**5**	**0**	**0**	**0**	**0**	
1996-97	**Philadelphia**	**NHL**	**76**	**24**	**21**	**45**	**20**	**5**	**5**	**5**	**131**	**18.3**	**9**				**19**	**4**	**3**	**7**	**12**	**0**	**0**	**2**	
1997-98	**Philadelphia**	**NHL**	**82**	**14**	**28**	**42**	**16**	**5**	**0**	**3**	**143**	**9.8**	**2**				**5**	**0**	**0**	**0**	**0**	**0**	**0**	**0**	
1998-99	**Philadelphia**	**NHL**	**2**	**0**	**0**	**0**	**0**	**0**	**0**	**0**	**2**	**0.0**	**0**	**0**	**0.0**	**11:11**									
	Vancouver	**NHL**	**73**	**4**	**10**	**14**	**12**	**0**	**0**	**0**	**58**	**6.9**	**–3**	**37**	**32.4**	**11:21**									
99-2000	**Vancouver**	**NHL**	**47**	**10**	**10**	**20**	**26**	**8**	**0**	**0**	**100**	**10.0**	**–8**	**19**	**63.2**	**16:04**									
	Syracuse Crunch	AHL	24	13	10	23	6																		
2000-01	**Vancouver**	**NHL**	**77**	**13**	**20**	**33**	**31**	**3**	**0**	**1**	**140**	**9.3**	**8**	**75**	**50.7**	**13:33**	**4**	**3**	**0**	**3**	**0**	**2**	**0**	**0**	**15:54**
2001-02	**Vancouver**	**NHL**	**34**	**8**	**7**	**15**	**10**	**2**	**1**	**3**	**67**	**11.9**	**9**	**101**	**54.5**	**15:27**									
2002-03	**Vancouver**	**NHL**	**82**	**16**	**13**	**29**	**8**	**3**	**0**	**2**	**127**	**12.6**	**10**	**47**	**40.4**	**12:25**	**14**	**2**	**4**	**6**	**2**	**2**	**0**	**1**	**12:42**
	NHL Totals		**700**	**126**	**174**	**300**	**261**	**35**	**6**	**21**	**1116**	**11.3**		**279**	**48.7**	**13:19**	**74**	**16**	**9**	**25**	**20**	**6**	**0**	**3**	**13:25**

Minnesota High School Player of the Year (1989)

Traded to **Minnesota** by **Washington** with Steve Maltais for Shawn Chambers, June 21, 1991. Transferred to **Dallas** after **Minnesota** franchise relocated, June 9, 1993. Traded to **Philadelphia** by **Dallas** for Brent Fedyk, December 13, 1995. Traded to **Vancouver** by **Philadelphia** for Vancouver's 6th round choice (later traded to Atlanta – Atlanta selected Jeff Dwyer) in 2000 Entry Draft, October 19, 1998. • Missed majority of 2001-02 season recovering from abdominal injury suffered in game vs. Ottawa, November 20, 2001. Signed as a free agent by **Los Angeles**, July 7, 2003.

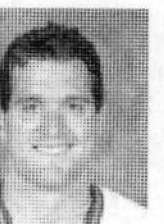

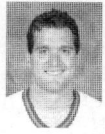

KLEE, Ken

(KLEE, KEHN)

Defense. Shoots right. 6', 210 lbs. Born, Indianapolis, IN, April 24, 1971. Washington's 11th choice, 177th overall, in 1990 Entry Draft.

Season	Club	League	GP	G	A	Pts	PIM	PP	SH	GW	S	%	+/-	TF	F%	Min	GP	G	A	Pts	PIM	PP	SH	GW	Min
1988-89	St. Michael's B	OJHL-B	40	9	23	32	64										27	5	12	17	54				
1989-90	Bowling Green	CCHA	39	0	5	5	52																		
1990-91	Bowling Green	CCHA	37	7	28	35	50																		
1991-92	Bowling Green	CCHA	10	0	1	1	14																		
1992-93	Baltimore	AHL	77	4	14	18	93										7	0	1	1	15				
1993-94	Portland Pirates	AHL	65	2	9	11	87										17	1	2	3	14				
1994-95	Portland Pirates	AHL	49	5	7	12	89																		
	Washington	**NHL**	**23**	**3**	**1**	**4**	**41**	**0**	**0**	**0**	**18**	**16.7**	**2**				**7**	**0**	**0**	**0**	**4**	**0**	**0**	**0**	
1995-96	**Washington**	**NHL**	**66**	**8**	**3**	**11**	**60**	**0**	**1**	**2**	**76**	**10.5**	**–1**				**1**	**0**	**0**	**0**	**0**	**0**	**0**	**0**	
1996-97	**Washington**	**NHL**	**80**	**3**	**8**	**11**	**115**	**0**	**0**	**2**	**108**	**2.8**	**–5**												
1997-98	**Washington**	**NHL**	**51**	**4**	**2**	**6**	**46**	**0**	**0**	**1**	**44**	**9.1**	**–3**				**9**	**1**	**0**	**1**	**10**	**0**	**0**	**0**	
1998-99	**Washington**	**NHL**	**78**	**7**	**13**	**20**	**80**	**0**	**0**	**1**	**132**	**5.3**	**–9**	**0**	**0.0**	**19:07**									
99-2000	**Washington**	**NHL**	**80**	**7**	**13**	**20**	**79**	**0**	**0**	**2**	**113**	**6.2**	**8**	**0**	**0.0**	**20:29**	**5**	**0**	**1**	**1**	**10**	**0**	**0**	**0**	**21:38**
2000-01	**Washington**	**NHL**	**54**	**2**	**4**	**6**	**60**	**0**	**0**	**0**	**58**	**3.4**	**–5**	**0**	**0.0**	**17:15**	**6**	**0**	**1**	**1**	**8**	**0**	**0**	**0**	**13:47**
2001-02	**Washington**	**NHL**	**68**	**8**	**8**	**16**	**38**	**2**	**0**	**3**	**85**	**9.4**	**4**	**2**	**0.0**	**19:24**									
2002-03	**Washington**	**NHL**	**70**	**1**	**16**	**17**	**89**	**0**	**0**	**0**	**67**	**1.5**	**22**	**0**	**0.0**	**21:49**	**6**	**0**	**0**	**0**	**6**	**0**	**0**	**0**	**23:11**
	NHL Totals		**570**	**43**	**68**	**111**	**608**	**2**	**1**	**11**	**701**	**6.1**		**2**	**0.0**	**19:44**	**34**	**1**	**2**	**3**	**38**	**0**	**0**	**0**	**19:25**

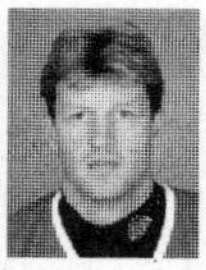

KLEMM, Jon

(KLEHM, JAWN) **CHI.**

Defense. Shoots right. 6'2", 200 lbs. Born, Cranbrook, B.C., January 8, 1970.

Season	Club	League	GP	G	A	Pts	PIM	PP	SH	GW	S	%	+/-	TF	F%	Min	GP	G	A	Pts	PIM	PP	SH	GW	Min
1986-87	Cranbrook Colts	KIJHL	59	20	51	71	54																		
1987-88	Seattle	WHL	68	6	7	13	24																		
1988-89	Seattle	WHL	2	1	1	2	0																		
	Spokane Chiefs	WHL	66	6	34	40	42																		
1989-90	Spokane Chiefs	WHL	66	3	28	31	100										6	1	1	2	5				
1990-91	Spokane Chiefs	WHL	72	7	58	65	65										15	3	6	9	8				
1991-92	**Quebec**	**NHL**	**4**	**0**	**1**	**1**	**0**	**0**	**0**	**0**	**2**	**0.0**	**2**												
	Halifax Citadels	AHL	70	6	13	19	40																		
1992-93	Halifax Citadels	AHL	80	3	20	23	32																		
1993-94	**Quebec**	**NHL**	**7**	**0**	**0**	**0**	**4**	**0**	**0**	**0**	**11**	**0.0**	**–1**												
	Cornwall Aces	AHL	66	4	26	30	78										13	1	2	3	6				
1994-95	Cornwall Aces	AHL	65	6	13	19	84																		
	Quebec	**NHL**	**4**	**1**	**0**	**1**	**2**	**0**	**0**	**0**	**5**	**20.0**	**3**												
1995-96♦	**Colorado**	**NHL**	**56**	**3**	**12**	**15**	**20**	**0**	**1**	**1**	**61**	**4.9**	**12**				**15**	**2**	**1**	**3**	**0**	**1**	**0**	**0**	
1996-97	**Colorado**	**NHL**	**80**	**9**	**15**	**24**	**37**	**1**	**2**	**1**	**103**	**8.7**	**12**				**17**	**1**	**1**	**2**	**6**	**0**	**0**	**0**	
1997-98	**Colorado**	**NHL**	**67**	**6**	**8**	**14**	**30**	**0**	**0**	**0**	**60**	**10.0**	**–3**				**4**	**0**	**0**	**0**	**0**	**0**	**0**	**0**	
1998-99	**Colorado**	**NHL**	**39**	**1**	**2**	**3**	**31**	**0**	**0**	**0**	**28**	**3.6**	**4**	**14**	**35.7**	**13:43**	**19**	**0**	**1**	**1**	**10**	**0**	**0**	**0**	**8:32**
99-2000	**Colorado**	**NHL**	**73**	**5**	**7**	**12**	**34**	**0**	**0**	**0**	**64**	**7.8**	**26**	**17**	**47.1**	**17:22**	**17**	**2**	**1**	**3**	**9**	**0**	**0**	**0**	**14:25**
2000-01♦	**Colorado**	**NHL**	**78**	**4**	**11**	**15**	**54**	**2**	**0**	**2**	**97**	**4.1**	**22**	**1**	**100.0**	**19:56**	**22**	**1**	**2**	**3**	**16**	**0**	**0**	**1**	**16:15**

			Regular Season														Playoffs								
Season	Club	League	GP	G	A	Pts	PIM	PP	SH	GW	S	%	+/-	TF	F%	Min	GP	G	A	Pts	PIM	PP	SH	GW	Min
2001-02	**Chicago**	**NHL**	82	4	16	20	42	2	0	1	111	3.6	−3	1	0.0	23:50	5	0	1	1	4	0	0	0	21:58
2002-03	**Chicago**	**NHL**	70	2	14	16	44	1	0	1	74	2.7	−9	2	0.0	21:57	....	....	....	....	....	....	....	....	....
	NHL Totals		560	35	86	121	298	6	3	6	616	5.7		35	40.0	20:01	99	6	7	13	45	1	0	1	13:53

WHL West Second All-Star Team (1991)

Signed as a free agent by **Quebec**, May 14, 1991. Transferred to **Colorado** after **Quebec** franchise relocated, June 21, 1995. • Missed majority of 1998-99 season recovering from knee injury suffered in game vs. Phoenix, November 10, 1998. Signed as a free agent by **Chicago**, July 1, 2001.

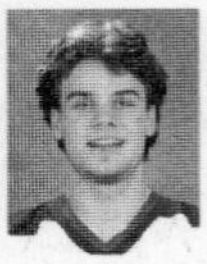

KLESLA, Rostislav
(KLEHS-luh, RAHS-tih-slav) **CBJ**

Defense. Shoots left. 6'3", 206 lbs. Born, Novy Jicin, Czech., March 21, 1982. Columbus' 1st choice, 4th overall, in 2000 Entry Draft.

Season	Club	League	GP	G	A	Pts	PIM	PP	SH	GW	S	%	+/-	TF	F%	Min	GP	G	A	Pts	PIM	PP	SH	GW	Min
1997-98	HC Opava Jr.	Czech-Jr.	38	11	18	29	87	....	....	....	....	....	....	....	....	....	8	2	2	4	0	....	....	....	....
1998-99	Sioux City	USHL	54	4	12	16	100	....	....	....	....	....	....	....	....	....	5	2	0	2	2	....	....	....	....
99-2000	Brampton	OHL	67	16	29	45	174	....	....	....	....	....	....	....	....	....	6	1	1	2	21	....	....	....	....
2000-01	**Columbus**	**NHL**	8	2	0	2	6	0	0	0	10	20.0	−1	0	0.0	18:25	....	....	....	....	....	....	....	....	....
	Brampton	OHL	45	18	36	54	59	....	....	....	....	....	....	....	....	....	9	2	9	11	26	....	....	....	....
2001-02	**Columbus**	**NHL**	75	8	8	16	74	1	0	0	102	7.8	−6	0	0.0	18:52	....	....	....	....	....	....	....	....	....
2002-03	**Columbus**	**NHL**	72	2	14	16	71	0	0	0	89	2.2	−22	0	0.0	18:45	....	....	....	....	....	....	....	....	....
	NHL Totals		155	12	22	34	151	1	0	0	201	6.0		0	0.0	18:47	....	....	....	....	....	....	....	....	....

OHL All-Rookie Team (2000) • Canadian Major Junior All-Rookie Team (2000) • OHL First All-Star Team (2001) • NHL All-Rookie Team (2002)

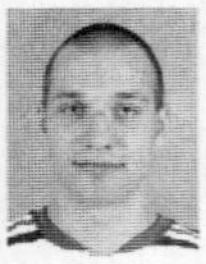

KLOUCEK, Tomas
(KLOH-chehk, TAW-mahsh) **NSH.**

Defense. Shoots left. 6'3", 225 lbs. Born, Prague, Czech., March 7, 1980. NY Rangers' 6th choice, 131st overall, in 1998 Entry Draft.

Season	Club	League	GP	G	A	Pts	PIM	PP	SH	GW	S	%	+/-	TF	F%	Min	GP	G	A	Pts	PIM	PP	SH	GW	Min
1995-96	Slavia Praha Jr.	Czech-Jr.	40	2	8	10	....	....	....	....	....	....	....	....	....	....	....	....	....	....	....	....	....	....	....
1996-97	Slavia Praha Jr.	Czech-Jr.	43	4	14	18	44	....	....	....	....	....	....	....	....	....	....	....	....	....	....	....	....	....	....
1997-98	Slavia Praha Jr.	Czech-Jr.	43	1	9	10	....	....	....	....	....	....	....	....	....	....	....	....	....	....	....	....	....	....	....
1998-99	Cape Breton	QMJHL	59	4	17	21	162	....	....	....	....	....	....	....	....	....	2	0	0	0	4	....	....	....	....
99-2000	Hartford	AHL	73	2	8	10	113	....	....	....	....	....	....	....	....	....	23	0	4	4	18	....	....	....	....
2000-01	**NY Rangers**	**NHL**	43	1	4	5	74	0	0	0	22	4.5	−3	0	0.0	16:43	....	....	....	....	....	....	....	....	....
	Hartford	AHL	21	0	2	2	44	....	....	....	....	....	....	....	....	....	....	....	....	....	....	....	....	....	....
2001-02	**NY Rangers**	**NHL**	52	1	3	4	137	0	0	0	21	4.8	−2	1	0.0	11:58	....	....	....	....	....	....	....	....	....
	Hartford	AHL	9	0	2	2	27	....	....	....	....	....	....	....	....	....	10	1	1	2	8	....	....	....	....
2002-03	Hartford	AHL	20	3	4	7	102	....	....	....	....	....	....	....	....	....	....	....	....	....	....	....	....	....	....
	Nashville	**NHL**	3	0	0	0	2	0	0	0	1	0.0	1	0	0.0	9:45	....	....	....	....	....	....	....	....	....
	Milwaukee	AHL	34	0	6	6	80	....	....	....	....	....	....	....	....	....	....	....	....	....	....	....	....	....	....
	NHL Totals		98	2	7	9	213	0	0	0	44	4.5		1	0.0	13:59	....	....	....	....	....	....	....	....	....

Traded to **Nashville** by **NY Rangers** with Rem Murray and Marek Zidlicky for Mike Dunham, December 12, 2002.

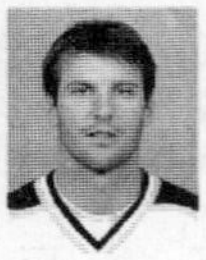

KNUBLE, Mike
(kuh-NOO-buhl, MIGHK) **BOS.**

Right wing. Shoots right. 6'3", 228 lbs. Born, Toronto, Ont., July 4, 1972. Detroit's 4th choice, 76th overall, in 1991 Entry Draft.

Season	Club	League	GP	G	A	Pts	PIM	PP	SH	GW	S	%	+/-	TF	F%	Min	GP	G	A	Pts	PIM	PP	SH	GW	Min
1988-89	East Kentwood	Hi-School	28	52	37	89	60	....	....	....	....	....	....	....	....	....	....	....	....	....	....	....	....	....	....
1989-90	East Kentwood	Hi-School	29	63	40	103	40	....	....	....	....	....	....	....	....	....	....	....	....	....	....	....	....	....	....
1990-91	Kalamazoo	NAJHL	36	18	24	42	30	....	....	....	....	....	....	....	....	....	....	....	....	....	....	....	....	....	....
1991-92	U. of Michigan	CCHA	43	7	8	15	48	....	....	....	....	....	....	....	....	....	....	....	....	....	....	....	....	....	....
1992-93	U. of Michigan	CCHA	39	26	16	42	57	....	....	....	....	....	....	....	....	....	....	....	....	....	....	....	....	....	....
1993-94	U. of Michigan	CCHA	41	32	26	58	71	....	....	....	....	....	....	....	....	....	....	....	....	....	....	....	....	....	....
1994-95	U. of Michigan	CCHA	34	*38	22	60	62	....	....	....	....	....	....	....	....	....	....	....	....	....	....	....	....	....	....
	Adirondack	AHL	....	....	....	....	....	....	....	....	....	....	....	....	....	....	3	0	0	0	0	....	....	....	....
1995-96	Adirondack	AHL	80	22	23	45	59	....	....	....	....	....	....	....	....	....	3	1	0	1	0	....	....	....	....
1996-97	**Detroit**	**NHL**	9	1	0	1	0	0	0	0	10	10.0	−1	....	....	....	....	....	....	....	....	....	....	....	....
	Adirondack	AHL	68	28	35	63	54	....	....	....	....	....	....	....	....	....	....	....	....	....	....	....	....	....	....
1997-98♦	**Detroit**	**NHL**	53	7	6	13	16	0	0	0	54	13.0	2	....	....	....	3	0	1	1	0	0	0	0	....
1998-99	**NY Rangers**	**NHL**	82	15	20	35	26	3	0	1	113	13.3	−7	1	100.0	14:52	....	....	....	....	....	....	....	....	....
99-2000	**NY Rangers**	**NHL**	59	9	5	14	18	1	0	1	50	18.0	−5	9	55.6	10:39	....	....	....	....	....	....	....	....	....
	Boston	**NHL**	14	3	3	6	8	1	0	1	28	10.7	−2	3	0.0	19:29	....	....	....	....	....	....	....	....	....
2000-01	**Boston**	**NHL**	82	7	13	20	37	0	1	1	92	7.6	0	115	31.3	10:34	....	....	....	....	....	....	....	....	....
2001-02	**Boston**	**NHL**	54	8	6	14	42	0	0	2	77	10.4	9	27	44.4	9:45	2	0	0	0	0	0	0	0	3:30
2002-03	**Boston**	**NHL**	75	30	29	59	45	9	0	4	185	16.2	18	34	44.1	17:24	5	0	2	2	2	0	0	0	17:35
	NHL Totals		428	80	82	162	192	14	1	10	609	13.1		189	36.5	13:10	10	0	3	3	2	0	0	0	13:33

CCHA Second All-Star Team (1994, 1995) • NCAA West Second All-American Team (1995)

Traded to **NY Rangers** by **Detroit** for NY Rangers' 2nd round choice (Tomas Kopecky) in 2000 Entry Draft, October 1, 1998. Traded to **Boston** by **NY Rangers** for Rob DiMaio, March 10, 2000.

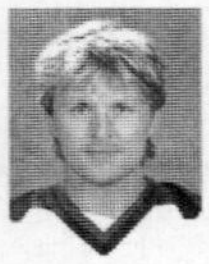

KNUTSEN, Espen
(kuh-NOOT-suhn, EHS-pehn) **CBJ**

Center. Shoots left. 5'11", 188 lbs. Born, Oslo, Norway, January 12, 1972. Hartford's 9th choice, 204th overall, in 1990 Entry Draft.

Season	Club	League	GP	G	A	Pts	PIM	PP	SH	GW	S	%	+/-	TF	F%	Min	GP	G	A	Pts	PIM	PP	SH	GW	Min
1988-89	Valerengen Jr.	Nor-Jr.	36	14	7	21	18	....	....	....	....	....	....	....	....	....	....	....	....	....	....	....	....	....	....
1989-90	Valerengen IF Oslo	Norway	40	25	28	53	44	....	....	....	....	....	....	....	....	....	....	....	....	....	....	....	....	....	....
1990-91	Valerengen IF Oslo	Norway	31	30	24	54	42	....	....	....	....	....	....	....	....	....	5	3	4	7	....	....	....	....	....
1991-92	Valerengen IF Oslo	Norway	30	28	26	54	37	....	....	....	....	....	....	....	....	....	8	7	8	15	....	....	....	....	....
1992-93	Valerengen IF Oslo	Norway	13	11	13	24	4	....	....	....	....	....	....	....	....	....	....	....	....	....	....	....	....	....	....
1993-94	Valerengen IF Oslo	Norway	38	32	26	58	20	....	....	....	....	....	....	....	....	....	....	....	....	....	....	....	....	....	....
	Norway	Olympics	7	1	3	4	2	....	....	....	....	....	....	....	....	....	....	....	....	....	....	....	....	....	....
1994-95	Djurgarden	Sweden	30	6	14	20	18	....	....	....	....	....	....	....	....	....	3	0	1	1	0	....	....	....	....
1995-96	Djurgarden	Sweden	32	10	23	33	50	....	....	....	....	....	....	....	....	....	4	1	0	1	2	....	....	....	....
1996-97	Djurgarden	Sweden	39	16	33	49	20	....	....	....	....	....	....	....	....	....	4	2	4	6	6	....	....	....	....
1997-98	**Anaheim**	**NHL**	19	3	0	3	6	1	0	0	21	14.3	−10	....	....	....	....	....	....	....	....	....	....	....	....
	Cincinnati	AHL	41	4	13	17	18	....	....	....	....	....	....	....	....	....	....	....	....	....	....	....	....	....	....
1998-99	Djurgarden	Sweden	39	18	24	42	32	....	....	....	....	....	....	....	....	....	4	0	1	1	2	....	....	....	....
	Djurgarden	EuroHL	4	2	2	4	2	....	....	....	....	....	....	....	....	....	....	....	....	....	....	....	....	....	....
99-2000	Djurgarden	Sweden	48	18	35	53	65	....	....	....	....	....	....	....	....	....	13	5	*16	*21	2	....	....	....	....
2000-01	**Columbus**	**NHL**	66	11	42	53	30	2	0	0	62	17.7	−3	125	52.8	15:59	....	....	....	....	....	....	....	....	....
2001-02	**Columbus**	**NHL**	77	11	31	42	47	5	2	1	102	10.8	−28	500	46.4	20:15	....	....	....	....	....	....	....	....	....
2002-03	**Columbus**	**NHL**	31	5	4	9	20	3	0	1	28	17.9	−15	325	39.4	16:44	....	....	....	....	....	....	....	....	....
	NHL Totals		193	30	77	107	103	11	2	2	213	14.1		950	44.8	18:00	....	....	....	....	....	....	....	....	....

Played in NHL All-Star Game (2002)

Rights traded to **Anaheim** by **Hartford** for Kevin Brown, October 1, 1996. Traded to **Columbus** by **Anaheim** for Columbus' 4th round choice (Vladmir Korsunov) in 2001 Entry Draft, May 25, 2000. • Missed majority of 2002-03 season recovering from groin (November 5, 2002 vs. Washington) and wrist (March 13, 2003 vs. Colorado) injuries.

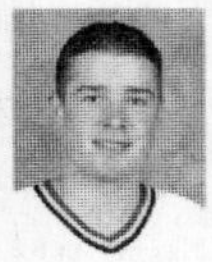

KOBASEW, Chuck
(KOH-buh-soo, CHUK) **CGY.**

Center. Shoots left. 5'11", 195 lbs. Born, Osoyoos, B.C., April 17, 1982. Calgary's 1st choice, 14th overall, in 2001 Entry Draft.

Season	Club	League	GP	G	A	Pts	PIM	PP	SH	GW	S	%	+/-	TF	F%	Min	GP	G	A	Pts	PIM	PP	SH	GW	Min
1997-98	Osoyoos Heat	KIJHL	6	2	2	4	2	....	....	....	....	....	....	....	....	....	....	....	....	....	....	....	....	....	....
1998-99	Osoyoos Heat	KIJHL	23	25	24	49	....	....	....	....	....	....	....	....	....	....	....	....	....	....	....	....	....	....	....
	Penticton	BCHL	30	11	17	28	18	....	....	....	....	....	....	....	....	....	....	....	....	....	....	....	....	....	....
99-2000	Penticton	BCHL	58	*54	52	106	83	....	....	....	....	....	....	....	....	....	....	....	....	....	....	....	....	....	....
2000-01	Boston College	H-East	43	27	22	49	38	....	....	....	....	....	....	....	....	....	....	....	....	....	....	....	....	....	....
2001-02	Kelowna Rockets	WHL	55	41	21	62	114	....	....	....	....	....	....	....	....	....	15	10	5	15	22	....	....	....	....
2002-03	**Calgary**	**NHL**	23	4	2	6	8	1	0	1	29	13.8	−3	5	0.0	11:48	....	....	....	....	....	....	....	....	....
	Saint John Flames	AHL	48	21	12	33	61	....	....	....	....	....	....	....	....	....	....	....	....	....	....	....	....	....	....
	NHL Totals		23	4	2	6	8	1	0	1	29	13.8		5	0.0	11:48	....	....	....	....	....	....	....	....	....

BCHL First All-Star Team (2000) • BCHL Interior Division MVP (2000) • Hockey East Second All-Star Team (2001) • Hockey East Rookie of the Year (2001) • NCAA Championship All-Tournament Team (2001) • NCAA Championship Tournament MVP (2001)

• Left **Boston College** (H-East) and signed with **Kelowna** (WHL), August 13, 2001.

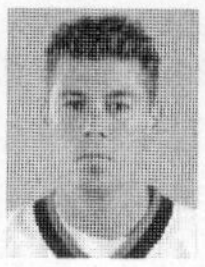

KOEHLER, Greg

(KEE-luhr, GREHG)

Center. Shoots left. 6'2", 195 lbs. Born, Scarborough, Ont., February 27, 1975.

			Regular Season														Playoffs								
Season	Club	League	GP	G	A	Pts	PIM	PP	SH	GW	S	%	+/-	TF	F%	Min	GP	G	A	Pts	PIM	PP	SH	GW	Min
1992-93	Niagara Falls	OJHL-B	40	24	19	43	125	....	....	....	....	....	....	....	....	....	....	....	....	....	....	....	....	....	....
1993-94	North York	MTJHL	49	27	47	74	179	....	....	....	....	....	....	....	....	....	....	....	....	....	....	....	....	....	....
1994-95	North York	MTJHL	47	28	43	71	126	....	....	....	....	....	....	....	....	....	....	....	....	....	....	....	....	....	....
1995-96	Brampton	MTJHL	49	33	64	97	87	....	....	....	....	....	....	....	....	....	....	....	....	....	....	....	....	....	....
1996-97	U. Mass-Lowell	H-East	37	16	20	36	49	....	....	....	....	....	....	....	....	....	....	....	....	....	....	....	....	....	....
1997-98	U. Mass-Lowell	H-East	33	20	17	37	62	....	....	....	....	....	....	....	....	....	....	....	....	....	....	....	....	....	....
	New Haven	AHL	3	0	0	0	2	....	....	....	....	....	....	....	....	....	....	....	....	....	....	....	....	....	....
1998-99	New Haven	AHL	26	4	0	4	29	....	....	....	....	....	....	....	....	....	....	....	....	....	....	....	....	....	....
	Florida Everblades	ECHL	29	13	14	27	62	....	....	....	....	....	....	....	....	....	6	2	3	5	12	....	....	....	....
99-2000	Cincinnati	IHL	74	12	13	25	157	....	....	....	....	....	....	....	....	....	8	0	3	3	14	....	....	....	....
2000-01	**Carolina**	**NHL**	**1**	**0**	**0**	**0**	**0**	**0**	**0**	**0**	**0**	**0.0**	**0**	**0**	**0.0**	**0:46**	....	....	....	....	....	....	....	....	....
	Cincinnati	IHL	80	35	36	71	122	....	....	....	....	....	....	....	....	....	5	2	2	4	6	....	....	....	....
2001-02	Lowell	AHL	56	18	18	36	58	....	....	....	....	....	....	....	....	....	....	....	....	....	....	....	....	....	....
	Philadelphia	AHL	22	8	4	12	34	....	....	....	....	....	....	....	....	....	5	1	2	3	6	....	....	....	....
2002-03	Milwaukee	AHL	43	16	10	26	51	....	....	....	....	....	....	....	....	....	....	....	....	....	....	....	....	....	....
	Manchester	AHL	13	1	13	14	26	....	....	....	....	....	....	....	....	....	....	....	....	....	....	....	....	....	....
	NHL Totals		**1**	**0**	**0**	**0**	**0**	**0**	**0**	**0**	**0**	**0.0**		**0**	**0.0**	**0:46**	....	....	....	....	....	....	....	....	....

Hockey East All-Rookie Team (1997) • Hockey East Rookie of the Year (1997) • IHL Second All-Star Team (2001)

Signed as a free agent by **Carolina**, March 31, 1998. Traded to **Philadelphia** by **Carolina** for Jesse Boulerice, February 13, 2002. Signed as a free agent by **Nashville**, July 15, 2002. Traded to **Los Angeles** by **Nashville** for future considerations, February 4, 2003.

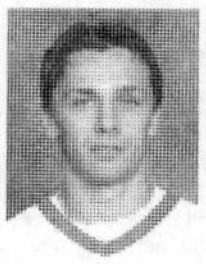

KOHN, Ladislav

(KOHN, LA-dih-slahf)

Right wing. Shoots left. 5'11", 194 lbs. Born, Uherske Hradiste, Czech., March 4, 1975. Calgary's 9th choice, 175th overall, in 1994 Entry Draft.

			Regular Season														Playoffs								
Season	Club	League	GP	G	A	Pts	PIM	PP	SH	GW	S	%	+/-	TF	F%	Min	GP	G	A	Pts	PIM	PP	SH	GW	Min
1993-94	Brandon	WHL	2	0	0	0	0	....	....	....	....	....	....	....	....	....	....	....	....	....	....	....	....	....	....
	Swift Current	WHL	69	33	35	68	68	....	....	....	....	....	....	....	....	....	7	5	4	9	8	....	....	....	....
1994-95	Swift Current	WHL	65	32	60	92	122	....	....	....	....	....	....	....	....	....	6	2	6	8	14	....	....	....	....
	Saint John Flames	AHL	1	0	0	0	0	....	....	....	....	....	....	....	....	....	....	....	....	....	....	....	....	....	....
1995-96	**Calgary**	**NHL**	**5**	**1**	**0**	**1**	**2**	**0**	**0**	**0**	**8**	**12.5**	**–1**	....	....	....	....	....	....	....	....	....	....	....	....
	Saint John Flames	AHL	73	28	45	73	97	....	....	....	....	....	....	....	....	....	16	6	5	11	12	....	....	....	....
1996-97	Saint John Flames	AHL	76	28	29	57	81	....	....	....	....	....	....	....	....	....	5	0	0	0	0	....	....	....	....
1997-98	**Calgary**	**NHL**	**4**	**0**	**1**	**1**	**0**	**0**	**0**	**0**	**2**	**0.0**	**2**	....	....	....	....	....	....	....	....	....	....	....	....
	Saint John Flames	AHL	65	25	31	56	90	....	....	....	....	....	....	....	....	....	21	14	6	20	20	....	....	....	....
1998-99	**Toronto**	**NHL**	**16**	**1**	**3**	**4**	**4**	**0**	**0**	**0**	**23**	**4.3**	**1**	**16**	**18.8**	**12:34**	**2**	**0**	**0**	**0**	**5**	**0**	**0**	**0**	**4:25**
	St. John's	AHL	61	27	42	69	90	....	....	....	....	....	....	....	....	....	....	....	....	....	....	....	....	....	....
99-2000	**Anaheim**	**NHL**	**77**	**5**	**16**	**21**	**27**	**1**	**0**	**1**	**123**	**4.1**	**–17**	**15**	**33.3**	**12:06**	....	....	....	....	....	....	....	....	....
2000-01	**Anaheim**	**NHL**	**51**	**4**	**3**	**7**	**42**	**0**	**1**	**0**	**86**	**4.7**	**–15**	**45**	**26.7**	**10:59**	....	....	....	....	....	....	....	....	....
	Atlanta	**NHL**	**26**	**3**	**4**	**7**	**44**	**0**	**1**	**0**	**43**	**7.0**	**–12**	**16**	**37.5**	**13:38**	....	....	....	....	....	....	....	....	....
2001-02	Cincinnati	AHL	4	0	0	0	9	....	....	....	....	....	....	....	....	....	....	....	....	....	....	....	....	....	....
	Detroit	**NHL**	**4**	**0**	**0**	**0**	**4**	**0**	**0**	**0**	**2**	**0.0**	**0**	**0**	**0.0**	**5:13**	....	....	....	....	....	....	....	....	....
	Blues Espoo	Finland	40	22	13	35	103	....	....	....	....	....	....	....	....	....	3	0	0	0	14	....	....	....	....
2002-03	**Calgary**	**NHL**	**3**	**0**	**1**	**1**	**2**	**0**	**0**	**0**	**3**	**0.0**	**1**	**2**	**50.0**	**8:53**	....	....	....	....	....	....	....	....	....
	Saint John Flames	AHL	35	8	19	27	30	....	....	....	....	....	....	....	....	....	....	....	....	....	....	....	....	....	....
	Philadelphia	AHL	15	4	7	11	2	....	....	....	....	....	....	....	....	....	....	....	....	....	....	....	....	....	....
	NHL Totals		**186**	**14**	**28**	**42**	**125**	**1**	**2**	**1**	**290**	**4.8**		**94**	**28.7**	**11:50**	**2**	**0**	**0**	**0**	**5**	**0**	**0**	**0**	**4:25**

Traded to **Toronto** by **Calgary** for David Cooper, July 2, 1998. Claimed by **Atlanta** from **Toronto** in Waiver Draft, September 27, 1999. Traded to **Anaheim** by **Atlanta** for Anaheim's 8th round choice (Evan Nielsen) in 2000 Entry Draft, September 27, 1999. Traded to **Atlanta** by **Anaheim** for Sergei Vyshedkevich and Scott Langkow, February 9, 2001. Signed as a free agent by **Detroit** with player option to return to Finland, October 22, 2001. Traded to **Calgary** by **Detroit** for future considerations, September 10, 2002.

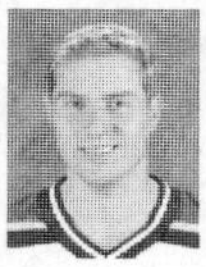

KOIVISTO, Tom

(KOI-vihs-toh, TAWM) **ST.L.**

Defense. Shoots right. 5'10", 194 lbs. Born, Turku, Finland, June 4, 1974. St. Louis' 8th choice, 253rd overall, in 2002 Entry Draft.

			Regular Season														Playoffs								
Season	Club	League	GP	G	A	Pts	PIM	PP	SH	GW	S	%	+/-	TF	F%	Min	GP	G	A	Pts	PIM	PP	SH	GW	Min
1991-92	TPS Turku Jr.	Finn-Jr.	36	4	9	13	40	....	....	....	....	....	....	....	....	....	8	1	3	4	12	....	....	....	....
1992-93	TPS Turku Jr.	Finn-Jr.	21	10	8	18	30	....	....	....	....	....	....	....	....	....	5	1	1	2	6	....	....	....	....
	Kiekoo-67 Turku	Finland-2	16	0	4	4	4	....	....	....	....	....	....	....	....	....	....	....	....	....	....	....	....	....	....
	TPS Turku	Fiinland	1	0	0	0	0	....	....	....	....	....	....	....	....	....	1	0	0	0	0	....	....	....	....
1993-94	TPS Turku Jr.	Finn-Jr.	10	4	5	9	16	....	....	....	....	....	....	....	....	....	7	0	5	5	8	....	....	....	....
	Kiekko-67 Turku	Finland-2	16	4	12	16	2	....	....	....	....	....	....	....	....	....	....	....	....	....	....	....	....	....	....
	TPS Turku	Finland	18	2	5	7	4	....	....	....	....	....	....	....	....	....	1	0	1	1	2	....	....	....	....
1994-95	TPS Turku Jr.	Finn-Jr.	5	0	2	2	8	....	....	....	....	....	....	....	....	....	....	....	....	....	....	....	....	....	....
	Kiekko-67 Turku	Finland-2	14	7	3	10	6	....	....	....	....	....	....	....	....	....	....	....	....	....	....	....	....	....	....
	TPS Turku	Finland	4	0	0	0	4	....	....	....	....	....	....	....	....	....	....	....	....	....	....	....	....	....	....
	HPK Hameenlina	Finland	25	3	3	6	16	....	....	....	....	....	....	....	....	....	....	....	....	....	....	....	....	....	....
1995-96	HPK Hameenlina	Finland	50	8	11	19	52	....	....	....	....	....	....	....	....	....	9	1	2	3	6	....	....	....	....
1996-97	HPK Hameenlina	Finland	46	18	17	35	50	....	....	....	....	....	....	....	....	....	10	4	2	6	6	....	....	....	....
1997-98	HPK Hameenlina	EuroHL	3	1	0	1	0	....	....	....	....	....	....	....	....	....	....	....	....	....	....	....	....	....	....
	HPK Hameenlina	Finland	23	6	6	12	28	....	....	....	....	....	....	....	....	....	....	....	....	....	....	....	....	....	....
1998-99	HPK Hameenlina	Finland	52	13	26	39	91	....	....	....	....	....	....	....	....	....	8	5	1	6	14	....	....	....	....
99-2000	Jokerit Helsinki	Finland	43	8	20	28	58	....	....	....	....	....	....	....	....	....	11	2	1	3	2	....	....	....	....
2000-01	Jokerit Helsinki	Finland	47	8	15	23	36	....	....	....	....	....	....	....	....	....	5	0	0	0	2	....	....	....	....
2001-02	Jokerit Helsinki	Finland	43	8	14	22	30	....	....	....	....	....	....	....	....	....	12	3	8	11	2	....	....	....	....
2002-03	**St. Louis**	**NHL**	**22**	**2**	**4**	**6**	**10**	**0**	**0**	**1**	**26**	**7.7**	**1**	**0**	**0.0**	**16:44**	....	....	....	....	....	....	....	....	....
	Worcester IceCats	AHL	47	4	13	17	32	....	....	....	....	....	....	....	....	....	3	0	0	0	0	....	....	....	....
	NHL Totals		**22**	**2**	**4**	**6**	**10**	**0**	**0**	**1**	**26**	**7.7**		**0**	**0.0**	**16:44**	....	....	....	....	....	....	....	....	....

Finnish Elite League All-Star Team (2002) • Finnish Elite League Best Defenseman (2002)

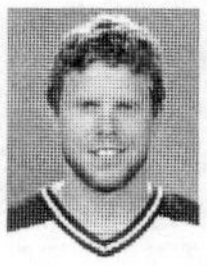

KOIVU, Saku

(KOI-voo, SA-koo) **MTL.**

Center. Shoots left. 5'10", 181 lbs. Born, Turku, Finland, November 23, 1974. Montreal's 1st choice, 21st overall, in 1993 Entry Draft.

			Regular Season														Playoffs								
Season	Club	League	GP	G	A	Pts	PIM	PP	SH	GW	S	%	+/-	TF	F%	Min	GP	G	A	Pts	PIM	PP	SH	GW	Min
1990-91	TPS Turku-B	Finn-Jr.	24	20	28	48	26	....	....	....	....	....	....	....	....	....	....	....	....	....	....	....	....	....	....
1991-92	TPS Turku-B	Finn-Jr.	12	3	7	10	6	....	....	....	....	....	....	....	....	....	....	....	....	....	....	....	....	....	....
	TPS Turku Jr.	Finn-Jr.	34	25	28	53	57	....	....	....	....	....	....	....	....	....	8	5	*9	*14	6	....	....	....	....
1992-93	TPS Turku	Finland	46	3	7	10	28	....	....	....	....	....	....	....	....	....	11	3	2	5	2	....	....	....	....
1993-94	TPS Turku	Finland	47	23	30	53	42	....	....	....	....	....	....	....	....	....	11	4	8	12	16	....	....	....	....
	Finland	Olympics	8	4	3	7	12	....	....	....	....	....	....	....	....	....	....	....	....	....	....	....	....	....	....
1994-95	TPS Turku	Finland	45	27	*47	*74	73	....	....	....	....	....	....	....	....	....	13	*7	10	17	16	....	....	....	....
1995-96	**Montreal**	**NHL**	**82**	**20**	**25**	**45**	**40**	**8**	**3**	**2**	**136**	**14.7**	**–7**	....	....	....	**6**	**3**	**1**	**4**	**8**	**0**	**0**	**0**	....
1996-97	**Montreal**	**NHL**	**50**	**17**	**39**	**56**	**38**	**5**	**0**	**3**	**135**	**12.6**	**7**	....	....	....	**5**	**1**	**3**	**4**	**10**	**0**	**0**	**0**	....
1997-98	**Montreal**	**NHL**	**69**	**14**	**43**	**57**	**48**	**2**	**2**	**3**	**145**	**9.7**	**8**	....	....	....	**6**	**2**	**3**	**5**	**2**	**1**	**0**	**0**	....
	Finland	Olympics	6	2	*8	*10	4	....	....	....	....	....	....	....	....	....	....	....	....	....	....	....	....	....	....
1998-99	**Montreal**	**NHL**	**65**	**14**	**30**	**44**	**38**	**4**	**2**	**0**	**145**	**9.7**	**–7**	**1427**	**52.6**	**20:02**	....	....	....	....	....	....	....	....	....
99-2000	**Montreal**	**NHL**	**24**	**3**	**18**	**21**	**14**	**1**	**0**	**0**	**53**	**5.7**	**7**	**495**	**52.9**	**19:13**	....	....	....	....	....	....	....	....	....
2000-01	**Montreal**	**NHL**	**54**	**17**	**30**	**47**	**40**	**7**	**0**	**3**	**113**	**15.0**	**2**	**1092**	**47.6**	**21:23**	....	....	....	....	....	....	....	....	....
2001-02	**Montreal**	**NHL**	**3**	**0**	**2**	**2**	**0**	**0**	**0**	**0**	**2**	**0.0**	**0**	**13**	**61.5**	**13:57**	**12**	**4**	**6**	**10**	**4**	**1**	**0**	**1**	**15:54**
2002-03	**Montreal**	**NHL**	**82**	**21**	**50**	**71**	**72**	**5**	**1**	**5**	**147**	**14.3**	**5**	**1566**	**49.6**	**19:14**	....	....	....	....	....	....	....	....	....
	NHL Totals		**429**	**106**	**237**	**343**	**290**	**32**	**8**	**16**	**876**	**12.1**		**4593**	**50.5**	**19:54**	**29**	**10**	**13**	**23**	**24**	**2**	**0**	**1**	**15:54**

Bill Masterton Memorial Trophy (2002)

Played in NHL All-Star Game (1998)

Missed majority of 1999-2000 season recovering from shoulder injury suffered in game vs. NY Rangers, October 30, 1999. • Missed majority of 2001-02 season recovering from non-Hodgkins lymphoma, September 6, 2001.

			Regular Season														Playoffs								
Season	Club	League	GP	G	A	Pts	PIM	PP	SH	GW	S	%	+/-	TF	F%	Min	GP	G	A	Pts	PIM	PP	SH	GW	Min

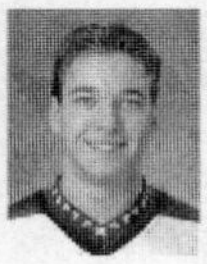

KOLANOS, Krystofer
(koh-LA-nohs, KRIHS) **PHX.**

Center. Shoots right. 6'3", 201 lbs. Born, Calgary, Alta., July 27, 1981. Phoenix's 1st choice, 19th overall, in 2000 Entry Draft.

Season	Club	League	GP	G	A	Pts	PIM	PP	SH	GW	S	%	+/-	TF	F%	Min	GP	G	A	Pts	PIM	PP	SH	GW	Min
1996-97	Calgary Flames	AAHA	24	24	35	59	....	....	....	....	....	....	....	....	....	....	....	....	....	....	....	....	....	....	....
1997-98	Calgary Buffaloes	AMHL	34	34	43	77	29	....	....	....	....	....	....	....	....	....	....	....	....	....	....	....	....	....	....
1998-99	Calgary Royals	AJHL	58	43	67	110	98	....	....	....	....	....	....	....	....	....	....	....	....	....	....	....	....	....	....
99-2000	Boston College	H-East	42	16	16	32	48	....	....	....	....	....	....	....	....	....	....	....	....	....	....	....	....	....	....
2000-01	Boston College	H-East	41	25	25	50	54	....	....	....	....	....	....	....	....	....	....	....	....	....	....	....	....	....	....
2001-02	**Phoenix**	**NHL**	**57**	**11**	**11**	**22**	**48**	**0**	**0**	**5**	**81**	**13.6**	**6**	**703**	**46.4**	**13:05**	**2**	**0**	**0**	**0**	**6**	**0**	**0**	**0**	**11:12**
2002-03	**Phoenix**	**NHL**	**2**	**0**	**0**	**0**	**0**	**0**	**0**	**0**	**8**	**0.0**	**0**	**16**	**31.3**	**14:06**	....	....	....	....	....	....	....	....	....
	NHL Totals		**59**	**11**	**11**	**22**	**48**	**0**	**0**	**5**	**89**	**12.4**		**719**	**46.0**	**13:07**	**2**	**0**	**0**	**0**	**6**	**0**	**0**	**0**	**11:12**

AJHL First All-Star Team (1999) • AJHL Rookie of the Year (1999) • Hockey East All-Rookie Team (2000) • Hockey East Second All-Star Team (2001) • NCAA East Second All-American Team (2001) • NCAA Championship All-Tournament Team (2001)

Missed majority of 2002-03 season recovering from head injury originally suffered in game vs. **Pittsburgh**, March 20, 2002.

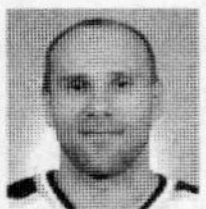

KOLARIK, Pavel
(koh-LAHR-ihk, PAH-vehl)

Defense. Shoots left. 6'1", 207 lbs. Born, Vyskov, Czech., October 24, 1972. Boston's 11th choice, 268th overall, in 2000 Entry Draft.

Season	Club	League	GP	G	A	Pts	PIM	PP	SH	GW	S	%	+/-	TF	F%	Min	GP	G	A	Pts	PIM	PP	SH	GW	Min
1994-95	H+S Beroun	Czech-2	STATISTICS NOT AVAILABLE																						
	HC Kladno	Czech	....	....	....	....	....	....	....	....	....	....	....	....	....	....	1	0	0	0	0	....	....	....	....
1995-96	H+S Beroun	Czech-2	STATISTICS NOT AVAILABLE																						
1996-97	HC Slavia Praha	Czech	27	1	2	3	10	....	....	....	....	....	....	....	....	....	3	0	0	0	2	....	....	....	....
1997-98	HC Slavia Praha	Czech	51	0	4	4	24	....	....	....	....	....	....	....	....	....	5	0	0	0	2	....	....	....	....
1998-99	HC Slavia Praha	Czech	51	1	8	9	44	....	....	....	....	....	....	....	....	....	....	....	....	....	....	....	....	....	....
99-2000	HC Slavia Praha	Czech	52	5	3	8	38	....	....	....	....	....	....	....	....	....	....	....	....	....	....	....	....	....	....
2000-01	**Boston**	**NHL**	**10**	**0**	**0**	**0**	**4**	**0**	**0**	**0**	**1**	**0.0**	**–2**	**0**	**0.0**	**8:49**	....	....	....	....	....	....	....	....	....
	Providence Bruins	AHL	51	5	6	11	14	....	....	....	....	....	....	....	....	....	17	0	4	4	4	....	....	....	....
2001-02	**Boston**	**NHL**	**13**	**0**	**0**	**0**	**6**	**0**	**0**	**0**	**6**	**0.0**	**0**	**0**	**0.0**	**6:45**	....	....	....	....	....	....	....	....	....
	Providence Bruins	AHL	47	3	4	7	10	....	....	....	....	....	....	....	....	....	2	0	0	0	2	....	....	....	....
2002-03	HC Slavia Praha	Czech	52	7	4	11	22	....	....	....	....	....	....	....	....	....	17	2	1	3	10	....	....	....	....
	NHL Totals		**23**	**0**	**0**	**0**	**10**	**0**	**0**	**0**	**7**	**0.0**		**0**	**0.0**	**7:39**	....	....	....	....	....	....	....	....	....

Signed as a free agent by **HC Slavia Praha** (Czech), August 23, 2002.

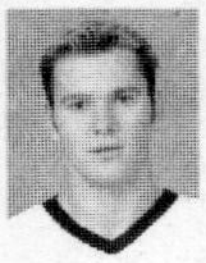

KOLNIK, Juraj
(KOHL-nihk, YEW-igh) **FLA.**

Right wing. Shoots right. 5'10", 190 lbs. Born, Nitra, Czech., November 13, 1980. NY Islanders' 7th choice, 101st overall, in 1999 Entry Draft.

Season	Club	League	GP	G	A	Pts	PIM	PP	SH	GW	S	%	+/-	TF	F%	Min	GP	G	A	Pts	PIM	PP	SH	GW	Min
1997-98	Nitra Jr.	Slovak-Jr.	26	28	16	44	50	....	....	....	....	....	....	....	....	....	....	....	....	....	....	....	....	....	....
	Nitra	Slovakia	28	1	3	4	6	....	....	....	....	....	....	....	....	....	....	....	....	....	....	....	....	....	....
1998-99	Quebec Remparts	QMJHL	12	6	5	11	6	....	....	....	....	....	....	....	....	....	....	....	....	....	....	....	....	....	....
	Rimouski Oceanic	QMJHL	50	36	37	73	34	....	....	....	....	....	....	....	....	....	11	9	6	15	6	....	....	....	....
99-2000	Rimouski Oceanic	QMJHL	47	53	53	106	53	....	....	....	....	....	....	....	....	....	14	10	17	27	16	....	....	....	....
2000-01	**NY Islanders**	**NHL**	**29**	**4**	**3**	**7**	**12**	**0**	**0**	**0**	**38**	**10.5**	**–8**	**1**	**100.0**	**10:28**	....	....	....	....	....	....	....	....	....
	Lowell	AHL	25	2	6	8	18	....	....	....	....	....	....	....	....	....	....	....	....	....	....	....	....	....	....
	Springfield	AHL	29	15	20	35	20	....	....	....	....	....	....	....	....	....	....	....	....	....	....	....	....	....	....
2001-02	**NY Islanders**	**NHL**	**7**	**2**	**0**	**2**	**0**	**1**	**0**	**0**	**10**	**20.0**	**–2**	**1**	**0.0**	**7:57**	....	....	....	....	....	....	....	....	....
	Bridgeport	AHL	67	18	30	48	40	....	....	....	....	....	....	....	....	....	20	7	14	21	17	....	....	....	....
2002-03	**Florida**	**NHL**	**10**	**0**	**1**	**1**	**0**	**0**	**0**	**0**	**14**	**0.0**	**1**	**1**	**0.0**	**10:33**	....	....	....	....	....	....	....	....	....
	San Antonio	AHL	65	25	15	40	36	....	....	....	....	....	....	....	....	....	3	0	1	1	4	....	....	....	....
	NHL Totals		**46**	**6**	**4**	**10**	**12**	**1**	**0**	**0**	**62**	**9.7**		**3**	**33.3**	**10:06**	....	....	....	....	....	....	....	....	....

Memorial Cup All-Star Team (2000)

Traded to **Florida** by **NY Islanders** with NY Islanders' 9th round choice (later traded to San Jose – San Jose selected Carter Lee) in 2003 Entry Draft for Sven Butenschon, October 11, 2002.

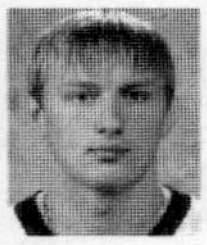

KOLTSOV, Konstantin
(kohlt-SAHV, kawn-stuhn-TEEN) **PIT.**

Right wing. Shoots left. 6', 201 lbs. Born, Minsk, USSR, April 17, 1981. Pittsburgh's 1st choice, 18th overall, in 1999 Entry Draft.

Season	Club	League	GP	G	A	Pts	PIM	PP	SH	GW	S	%	+/-	TF	F%	Min	GP	G	A	Pts	PIM	PP	SH	GW	Min
1997-98	Cherepovets 2	Russia-3	44	11	12	23	16	....	....	....	....	....	....	....	....	....	....	....	....	....	....	....	....	....	....
	Cherepovets	Russia	2	0	0	0	2	....	....	....	....	....	....	....	....	....	....	....	....	....	....	....	....	....	....
1998-99	Cherepovets 3	Russia-4	2	0	1	1	2	....	....	....	....	....	....	....	....	....	....	....	....	....	....	....	....	....	....
	Cherepovets 2	Russia-3	11	1	4	5	18	....	....	....	....	....	....	....	....	....	....	....	....	....	....	....	....	....	....
	Cherepovets	Russia	33	3	0	3	8	....	....	....	....	....	....	....	....	....	1	0	0	0	2	....	....	....	....
99-2000	Magnitogorsk	Russia	30	3	4	7	12	....	....	....	....	....	....	....	....	....	11	1	1	2	6	....	....	....	....
2000-01	Ak Bars Kazan	Russia	24	7	8	15	10	....	....	....	....	....	....	....	....	....	2	0	0	0	4	....	....	....	....
2001-02	Ak Bars Kazan	Russia	10	1	2	3	2	....	....	....	....	....	....	....	....	....	....	....	....	....	....	....	....	....	....
	Spartak Mos. 2	Russia-3	2	0	1	1	0	....	....	....	....	....	....	....	....	....	....	....	....	....	....	....	....	....	....
	Spartak Moscow	Russia	23	1	0	1	12	....	....	....	....	....	....	....	....	....	....	....	....	....	....	....	....	....	....
2002-03	**Pittsburgh**	**NHL**	**2**	**0**	**0**	**0**	**0**	**0**	**0**	**0**	**4**	**0.0**	**–2**	**0**	**0.0**	**13:06**	....	....	....	....	....	....	....	....	....
	Wilkes-Barre	AHL	65	9	21	30	41	....	....	....	....	....	....	....	....	....	6	2	4	6	4	....	....	....	....
	NHL Totals		**2**	**0**	**0**	**0**	**0**	**0**	**0**	**0**	**4**	**0.0**		**0**	**0.0**	**13:06**	....	....	....	....	....	....	....	....	....

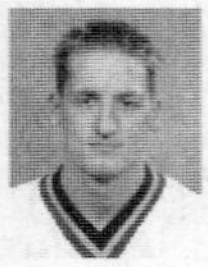

KOMARNISKI, Zenith
(KOH-mahr-NIHS-kee, ZEE-nihth) **VAN.**

Left wing. Shoots left. 6', 200 lbs. Born, Edmonton, Alta., August 13, 1978. Vancouver's 2nd choice, 75th overall, in 1996 Entry Draft.

Season	Club	League	GP	G	A	Pts	PIM	PP	SH	GW	S	%	+/-	TF	F%	Min	GP	G	A	Pts	PIM	PP	SH	GW	Min
1993-94	Ft. Saskatchewan	AMHL	32	14	32	46	42	....	....	....	....	....	....	....	....	....	....	....	....	....	....	....	....	....	....
1994-95	Tri-City	WHL	66	5	19	24	110	....	....	....	....	....	....	....	....	....	17	1	2	3	47	....	....	....	....
1995-96	Tri-City	WHL	42	5	21	26	85	....	....	....	....	....	....	....	....	....	....	....	....	....	....	....	....	....	....
1996-97	Tri-City	WHL	58	12	44	56	112	....	....	....	....	....	....	....	....	....	....	....	....	....	....	....	....	....	....
1997-98	Tri-City	WHL	3	0	4	4	18	....	....	....	....	....	....	....	....	....	....	....	....	....	....	....	....	....	....
	Spokane Chiefs	WHL	43	7	20	27	90	....	....	....	....	....	....	....	....	....	18	4	6	10	49	....	....	....	....
1998-99	Syracuse Crunch	AHL	58	9	19	28	89	....	....	....	....	....	....	....	....	....	....	....	....	....	....	....	....	....	....
99-2000	**Vancouver**	**NHL**	**18**	**1**	**1**	**2**	**8**	**0**	**0**	**0**	**21**	**4.8**	**–1**	**0**	**0.0**	**16:11**	....	....	....	....	....	....	....	....	....
	Syracuse Crunch	AHL	42	4	12	16	130	....	....	....	....	....	....	....	....	....	4	2	0	2	6	....	....	....	....
2000-01	Kansas City	IHL	70	7	22	29	191	....	....	....	....	....	....	....	....	....	....	....	....	....	....	....	....	....	....
2001-02	Manitoba Moose	AHL	77	5	20	25	153	....	....	....	....	....	....	....	....	....	7	0	2	2	13	....	....	....	....
2002-03	**Vancouver**	**NHL**	**1**	**0**	**0**	**0**	**2**	**0**	**0**	**0**	**0**	**0.0**	**0**	**0**	**0.0**	**6:25**	....	....	....	....	....	....	....	....	....
	Manitoba Moose	AHL	53	15	8	23	94	....	....	....	....	....	....	....	....	....	13	2	2	4	30	....	....	....	....
	NHL Totals		**19**	**1**	**1**	**2**	**10**	**0**	**0**	**0**	**21**	**4.8**		**0**	**0.0**	**15:40**	....	....	....	....	....	....	....	....	....

WHL West First All-Star Team (1997)

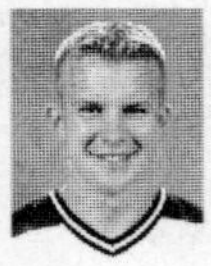

KOMISAREK, Mike
(koh-mih-SAIR-ehk, MIGHK) **MTL.**

Defense. Shoots right. 6'4", 240 lbs. Born, Islip Terrace, NY, January 19, 1982. Montreal's 1st choice, 7th overall, in 2001 Entry Draft.

Season	Club	League	GP	G	A	Pts	PIM	PP	SH	GW	S	%	+/-	TF	F%	Min	GP	G	A	Pts	PIM	PP	SH	GW	Min
1998-99	New England	EJHL	53	17	24	51	....	....	....	....	....	....	....	....	....	....	....	....	....	....	....	....	....	....	....
99-2000	U.S. National U-18	USDP	51	5	8	13	124	....	....	....	....	....	....	....	....	....	....	....	....	....	....	....	....	....	....
2000-01	U. of Michigan	CCHA	41	4	12	16	77	....	....	....	....	....	....	....	....	....	....	....	....	....	....	....	....	....	....
2001-02	U. of Michigan	CCHA	40	11	19	30	70	....	....	....	....	....	....	....	....	....	....	....	....	....	....	....	....	....	....
2002-03	**Montreal**	**NHL**	**21**	**0**	**1**	**1**	**28**	**0**	**0**	**0**	**26**	**0.0**	**–6**	**0**	**0.0**	**16:42**	....	....	....	....	....	....	....	....	....
	Hamilton	AHL	56	5	25	30	79	....	....	....	....	....	....	....	....	....	23	1	5	6	60	....	....	....	....
	NHL Totals		**21**	**0**	**1**	**1**	**28**	**0**	**0**	**0**	**26**	**0.0**		**0**	**0.0**	**16:42**	....	....	....	....	....	....	....	....	....

CCHA First All-Star Team (2002) • NCAA West First All-American Team (2002) • AHL All-Rookie Team (2003)

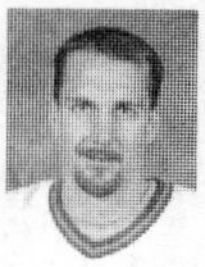

KONOWALCHUK, Steve

(kahn-uh-WAHL-chuhk, STEEV) **WSH.**

Left wing. Shoots left. 6'2", 207 lbs. Born, Salt Lake City, UT, November 11, 1972. Washington's 5th choice, 58th overall, in 1991 Entry Draft.

			Regular Season														Playoffs								
Season	Club	League	GP	G	A	Pts	PIM	PP	SH	GW	S	%	+/-	TF	F%	Min	GP	G	A	Pts	PIM	PP	SH	GW	Min
1989-90	Prince Albert	SMHL	36	30	28	58	22	....	....	....	....	....	....	....	....	....	....	....	....	....	....	....	....	....	....
1990-91	Portland	WHL	72	43	49	92	78	....	....	....	....	....	....	....	....	....	....	....	....	....	....	....	....	....	....
1991-92	Portland	WHL	64	51	53	104	95	....	....	....	....	....	....	....	....	....	6	3	6	9	12	....	....	....	....
	Washington	**NHL**	**1**	**0**	**0**	**0**	**0**	**0**	**0**	**0**	**1**	**0.0**	**0**	....	....	....	....	....	....	....	....	....	....	....	....
	Baltimore	AHL	3	1	1	2	0	....	....	....	....	....	....	....	....	....	....	....	....	....	....	....	....	....	....
1992-93	**Washington**	**NHL**	**36**	**4**	**7**	**11**	**16**	**1**	**0**	**1**	**34**	**11.8**	**4**	....	....	....	**2**	**0**	**1**	**1**	**0**	**0**	**0**	**0**	....
	Baltimore	AHL	37	18	28	46	74	....	....	....	....	....	....	....	....	....	....	....	....	....	....	....	....	....	....
1993-94	**Washington**	**NHL**	**62**	**12**	**14**	**26**	**33**	**0**	**0**	**0**	**63**	**19.0**	**9**	....	....	....	**11**	**0**	**1**	**1**	**10**	**0**	**0**	**0**	....
	Portland Pirates	AHL	8	11	4	15	4	....	....	....	....	....	....	....	....	....	....	....	....	....	....	....	....	....	....
1994-95	**Washington**	**NHL**	**46**	**11**	**14**	**25**	**44**	**3**	**3**	**3**	**88**	**12.5**	**7**	....	....	....	**7**	**2**	**5**	**7**	**12**	**0**	**1**	**0**	....
1995-96	**Washington**	**NHL**	**70**	**23**	**22**	**45**	**92**	**7**	**1**	**3**	**197**	**11.7**	**13**	....	....	....	**2**	**0**	**2**	**2**	**0**	**0**	**0**	**0**	....
1996-97	**Washington**	**NHL**	**78**	**17**	**25**	**42**	**67**	**2**	**1**	**3**	**155**	**11.0**	**–3**	....	....	....	....	....	....	....	....	....	....	....	....
1997-98	**Washington**	**NHL**	**80**	**10**	**24**	**34**	**80**	**2**	**0**	**2**	**131**	**7.6**	**9**	....	....	....	....	....	....	....	....	....	....	....	....
1998-99	**Washington**	**NHL**	**45**	**12**	**12**	**24**	**26**	**4**	**1**	**2**	**98**	**12.2**	**0**	**124**	**51.6**	**17:50**	....	....	....	....	....	....	....	....	....
99-2000	**Washington**	**NHL**	**82**	**16**	**27**	**43**	**80**	**3**	**0**	**1**	**146**	**11.0**	**19**	**147**	**49.7**	**17:36**	**5**	**1**	**0**	**1**	**2**	**0**	**1**	**0**	**17:25**
2000-01	**Washington**	**NHL**	**82**	**24**	**23**	**47**	**87**	**6**	**0**	**5**	**163**	**14.7**	**8**	**91**	**55.0**	**17:04**	**6**	**2**	**3**	**5**	**14**	**2**	**0**	**0**	**19:39**
2001-02	**Washington**	**NHL**	**28**	**2**	**12**	**14**	**23**	**0**	**0**	**0**	**36**	**5.6**	**–2**	**64**	**56.3**	**16:29**	....	....	....	....	....	....	....	....	....
2002-03	**Washington**	**NHL**	**77**	**15**	**15**	**30**	**71**	**2**	**0**	**3**	**119**	**12.6**	**3**	**92**	**44.6**	**16:42**	**6**	**0**	**0**	**0**	**6**	**0**	**0**	**0**	**16:07**
	NHL Totals		**687**	**146**	**195**	**341**	**619**	**30**	**6**	**23**	**1231**	**11.9**		**518**	**51.0**	**17:11**	**39**	**5**	**12**	**17**	**44**	**2**	**2**	**0**	**17:45**

WHL West First All-Star Team (1992) • WHL MVP (1992)

• Missed majority of 2001-02 season recovering from shoulder injury suffered in game vs. Los Angeles, October 16, 2001.

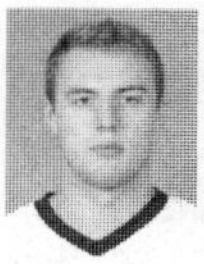

KOROLEV, Evgeny

(KOH-roh-lehv, ehv-GEHN-ee) **NYI**

Defense. Shoots left. 6'1", 214 lbs. Born, Moscow, USSR, July 24, 1978. NY Islanders' 6th choice, 182nd overall, in 1998 Entry Draft.

Season	Club	League	GP	G	A	Pts	PIM	PP	SH	GW	S	%	+/-	TF	F%	Min	GP	G	A	Pts	PIM	PP	SH	GW	Min
1995-96	Peterborough	OHL	60	2	12	14	60	....	....	....	....	....	....	....	....	....	6	0	0	0	2	....	....	....	....
1996-97	Peterborough	OHL	64	5	17	22	60	....	....	....	....	....	....	....	....	....	11	1	1	2	8	....	....	....	....
1997-98	Peterborough	OHL	37	5	21	26	39	....	....	....	....	....	....	....	....	....	....	....	....	....	....	....	....	....	....
	London Knights	OHL	27	4	10	14	36	....	....	....	....	....	....	....	....	....	15	2	7	9	29	....	....	....	....
1998-99	Roanoke Express	ECHL	2	0	1	1	0	....	....	....	....	....	....	....	....	....	....	....	....	....	....	....	....	....	....
	Lowell	AHL	54	2	6	8	48	....	....	....	....	....	....	....	....	....	2	0	1	1	0	....	....	....	....
99-2000	**NY Islanders**	**NHL**	**17**	**1**	**2**	**3**	**8**	**0**	**0**	**0**	**7**	**14.3**	**–10**	**0**	**0.0**	**16:12**	....	....	....	....	....	....	....	....	....
	Lowell	AHL	57	1	10	11	61	....	....	....	....	....	....	....	....	....	6	0	0	0	4	....	....	....	....
2000-01	**NY Islanders**	**NHL**	**8**	**0**	**0**	**0**	**6**	**0**	**0**	**0**	**11**	**0.0**	**0**	**0**	**0.0**	**16:40**	....	....	....	....	....	....	....	....	....
	Chicago Wolves	IHL	4	0	1	1	0	....	....	....	....	....	....	....	....	....	....	....	....	....	....	....	....	....	....
	Louisville Panthers	AHL	36	2	14	16	68	....	....	....	....	....	....	....	....	....	....	....	....	....	....	....	....	....	....
2001-02	**NY Islanders**	**NHL**	**17**	**0**	**2**	**2**	**6**	**0**	**0**	**0**	**9**	**0.0**	**0**	**0**	**0.0**	**10:22**	**2**	**0**	**0**	**0**	**0**	**0**	**0**	**0**	**5:35**
	Bridgeport	AHL	53	5	8	13	30	....	....	....	....	....	....	....	....	....	....	....	....	....	....	....	....	....	....
2002-03	Yaroslavl	Russia	16	1	2	3	22	....	....	....	....	....	....	....	....	....	8	0	0	0	6	....	....	....	....
	NHL Totals		**42**	**1**	**4**	**5**	**20**	**0**	**0**	**0**	**27**	**3.7**		**0**	**0.0**	**13:56**	**2**	**0**	**0**	**0**	**0**	**0**	**0**	**0**	**5:35**

• Re-entered NHL Entry Draft. Originally NY Islanders' 9th choice, 192nd overall, in 1996 Entry Draft.
Signed as a free agent by **Yaroslavl** (Russia), October 14, 2002.

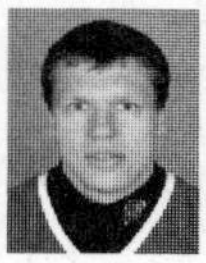

KOROLEV, Igor

(KOH-roh-lehv, EE-gohr) **CHI.**

Center. Shoots left. 6'1", 190 lbs. Born, Moscow, USSR, September 6, 1970. St. Louis' 1st choice, 38th overall, in 1992 Entry Draft.

Season	Club	League	GP	G	A	Pts	PIM	PP	SH	GW	S	%	+/-	TF	F%	Min	GP	G	A	Pts	PIM	PP	SH	GW	Min
1988-89	Dynamo Moscow	USSR	1	0	0	0	2	....	....	....	....	....	....	....	....	....	....	....	....	....	....	....	....	....	....
1989-90	Dynamo Moscow	USSR	17	3	2	5	2	....	....	....	....	....	....	....	....	....	....	....	....	....	....	....	....	....	....
1990-91	Dynamo Moscow	USSR	38	12	4	16	12	....	....	....	....	....	....	....	....	....	....	....	....	....	....	....	....	....	....
1991-92	Dynamo Moscow	CIS	39	15	12	27	16	....	....	....	....	....	....	....	....	....	....	....	....	....	....	....	....	....	....
1992-93	Dynamo Moscow	CIS	5	1	2	3	4	....	....	....	....	....	....	....	....	....	....	....	....	....	....	....	....	....	....
	St. Louis	**NHL**	**74**	**4**	**23**	**27**	**20**	**2**	**0**	**0**	**76**	**5.3**	**–1**	....	....	....	**3**	**0**	**0**	**0**	**0**	**0**	**0**	**0**	....
1993-94	**St. Louis**	**NHL**	**73**	**6**	**10**	**16**	**40**	**0**	**0**	**1**	**93**	**6.5**	**–12**	....	....	....	**2**	**0**	**0**	**0**	**0**	**0**	**0**	**0**	....
1994-95	Dynamo Moscow	CIS	13	4	6	10	18	....	....	....	....	....	....	....	....	....	....	....	....	....	....	....	....	....	....
	Winnipeg	**NHL**	**45**	**8**	**22**	**30**	**10**	**1**	**0**	**1**	**85**	**9.4**	**1**	....	....	....	....	....	....	....	....	....	....	....	....
1995-96	**Winnipeg**	**NHL**	**73**	**22**	**29**	**51**	**42**	**8**	**0**	**5**	**165**	**13.3**	**1**	....	....	....	**6**	**0**	**3**	**3**	**0**	**0**	**0**	**0**	....
1996-97	**Phoenix**	**NHL**	**41**	**3**	**7**	**10**	**28**	**2**	**0**	**0**	**41**	**7.3**	**–5**	....	....	....	**1**	**0**	**0**	**0**	**0**	**0**	**0**	**0**	....
	Michigan	IHL	4	2	2	4	0	....	....	....	....	....	....	....	....	....	....	....	....	....	....	....	....	....	....
	Phoenix	IHL	4	2	6	8	4	....	....	....	....	....	....	....	....	....	....	....	....	....	....	....	....	....	....
1997-98	**Toronto**	**NHL**	**78**	**17**	**22**	**39**	**22**	**6**	**3**	**5**	**97**	**17.5**	**–18**	....	....	....	....	....	....	....	....	....	....	....	....
1998-99	**Toronto**	**NHL**	**66**	**13**	**34**	**47**	**46**	**1**	**0**	**2**	**99**	**13.1**	**11**	**973**	**42.0**	**18:06**	**1**	**0**	**0**	**0**	**0**	**0**	**0**	**0**	**7:42**
99-2000	**Toronto**	**NHL**	**80**	**20**	**26**	**46**	**22**	**5**	**3**	**4**	**101**	**19.8**	**12**	**964**	**41.3**	**17:56**	**12**	**0**	**4**	**4**	**6**	**0**	**0**	**0**	**18:56**
2000-01	**Toronto**	**NHL**	**73**	**10**	**19**	**29**	**28**	**2**	**0**	**0**	**78**	**12.8**	**3**	**569**	**42.5**	**15:41**	**11**	**0**	**0**	**0**	**0**	**0**	**0**	**0**	**17:43**
2001-02	**Chicago**	**NHL**	**82**	**9**	**20**	**29**	**20**	**0**	**1**	**1**	**78**	**11.5**	**–5**	**1166**	**41.1**	**16:49**	**5**	**0**	**1**	**1**	**0**	**0**	**0**	**0**	**15:50**
2002-03	**Chicago**	**NHL**	**48**	**4**	**5**	**9**	**30**	**1**	**0**	**1**	**32**	**12.5**	**–1**	**375**	**42.4**	**13:39**	....	....	....	....	....	....	....	....	....
	Norfolk Admirals	AHL	14	4	3	7	0	....	....	....	....	....	....	....	....	....	9	2	4	6	4	....	....	....	....
	NHL Totals		**733**	**116**	**217**	**333**	**308**	**28**	**7**	**20**	**945**	**12.3**		**4047**	**41.7**	**16:39**	**41**	**0**	**8**	**8**	**6**	**0**	**0**	**0**	**17:33**

Claimed by **Winnipeg** from **St. Louis** in NHL Waiver Draft, January 18, 1995. Transferred to **Phoenix** after **Winnipeg** franchise relocated, July 1, 1996. Signed as a free agent by **Toronto**, September 29, 1997. Traded to **Chicago** by **Toronto** for Philadelphia's 3rd round choice (previously acquired, Toronto selected Nicolas Corbeil) in 2001 Entry Draft, June 23, 2001.

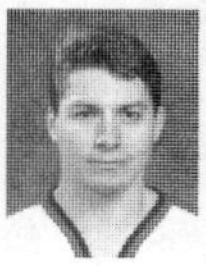

KOROLYUK, Alexander

(koh-roh-LYUHK, al-ehx-AN-duhr) **S.J.**

Left wing. Shoots left. 5'9", 195 lbs. Born, Moscow, USSR, January 15, 1976. San Jose's 6th choice, 141st overall, in 1994 Entry Draft.

Season	Club	League	GP	G	A	Pts	PIM	PP	SH	GW	S	%	+/-	TF	F%	Min	GP	G	A	Pts	PIM	PP	SH	GW	Min
1993-94	Krylja Sovetov	CIS	22	4	4	8	20	....	....	....	....	....	....	....	....	....	3	1	0	1	4	....	....	....	....
1994-95	Krylja Sovetov	CIS	52	16	13	29	62	....	....	....	....	....	....	....	....	....	4	1	2	3	4	....	....	....	....
1995-96	Krylja Sovetov	CIS	50	30	19	49	77	....	....	....	....	....	....	....	....	....	....	....	....	....	....	....	....	....	....
1996-97	Krylja Sovetov	Russia	17	8	5	13	46	....	....	....	....	....	....	....	....	....	....	....	....	....	....	....	....	....	....
	Manitoba Moose	IHL	42	20	16	36	71	....	....	....	....	....	....	....	....	....	....	....	....	....	....	....	....	....	....
1997-98	**San Jose**	**NHL**	**19**	**2**	**3**	**5**	**6**	**1**	**0**	**0**	**23**	**8.7**	**–5**	....	....	....	....	....	....	....	....	....	....	....	....
	Kentucky	AHL	44	16	23	39	96	....	....	....	....	....	....	....	....	....	3	0	0	0	0	....	....	....	....
1998-99	**San Jose**	**NHL**	**55**	**12**	**18**	**30**	**26**	**2**	**0**	**0**	**96**	**12.5**	**3**	**4**	**50.0**	**13:53**	**6**	**1**	**3**	**4**	**2**	**0**	**0**	**1**	**11:01**
	Kentucky	AHL	23	9	13	22	16	....	....	....	....	....	....	....	....	....	....	....	....	....	....	....	....	....	....
99-2000	**San Jose**	**NHL**	**57**	**14**	**21**	**35**	**35**	**3**	**0**	**1**	**124**	**11.3**	**4**	**1**	**100.0**	**13:36**	**9**	**0**	**3**	**3**	**6**	**0**	**0**	**0**	**11:37**
2000-01	Ak Bars Kazan	Russia	6	0	5	5	4	....	....	....	....	....	....	....	....	....	....	....	....	....	....	....	....	....	....
	San Jose	**NHL**	**70**	**12**	**13**	**25**	**41**	**3**	**0**	**1**	**140**	**8.6**	**2**	**30**	**33.3**	**11:56**	**2**	**0**	**0**	**0**	**0**	**0**	**0**	**0**	**8:11**
2001-02	**San Jose**	**NHL**	**32**	**3**	**7**	**10**	**14**	**0**	**0**	**1**	**49**	**6.1**	**2**	**10**	**30.0**	**12:16**	....	....	....	....	....	....	....	....	....
2002-03	Ak Bars Kazan	Russia	45	14	17	31	46	....	....	....	....	....	....	....	....	....	4	0	0	0	0	....	....	....	....
	NHL Totals		**233**	**43**	**62**	**105**	**122**	**9**	**0**	**3**	**432**	**10.0**		**45**	**35.6**	**12:56**	**17**	**1**	**6**	**7**	**8**	**0**	**0**	**1**	**10:60**

• Spent majority of 2001-02 season on practice roster. Signed as a free agent by **Ak Bars Kazan** (Russia) with San Jose retaining NHL rights, July 9, 2002.

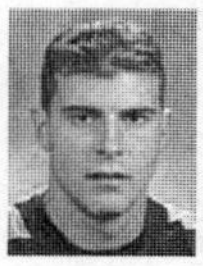

KOSTOPOULOS, Tom

(kaw-STAWP-oh-lihs, TAWM) **PIT.**

Right wing. Shoots right. 6', 200 lbs. Born, Mississauga, Ont., January 24, 1979. Pittsburgh's 9th choice, 204th overall, in 1999 Entry Draft.

Season	Club	League	GP	G	A	Pts	PIM	PP	SH	GW	S	%	+/-	TF	F%	Min	GP	G	A	Pts	PIM	PP	SH	GW	Min
1995-96	Brampton	OPJHL	24	9	9	18	28	....	....	....	....	....	....	....	....	....	....	....	....	....	....	....	....	....	....
1996-97	London Knights	OHL	64	13	12	25	67	....	....	....	....	....	....	....	....	....	....	....	....	....	....	....	....	....	....
1997-98	London Knights	OHL	66	24	26	50	108	....	....	....	....	....	....	....	....	....	16	6	4	10	26	....	....	....	....
1998-99	London Knights	OHL	66	27	60	87	114	....	....	....	....	....	....	....	....	....	25	19	16	35	32	....	....	....	....
99-2000	Wilkes-Barre	AHL	76	26	32	58	121	....	....	....	....	....	....	....	....	....	....	....	....	....	....	....	....	....	....
2000-01	Wilkes-Barre	AHL	80	16	36	52	120	....	....	....	....	....	....	....	....	....	21	3	9	12	6	....	....	....	....
2001-02	**Pittsburgh**	**NHL**	**11**	**1**	**2**	**3**	**9**	**0**	**0**	**0**	**8**	**12.5**	**–1**	**0**	**0.0**	**12:03**	....	....	....	....	....	....	....	....	....
	Wilkes-Barre	AHL	70	27	26	53	112	....	....	....	....	....	....	....	....	....	....	....	....	....	....	....	....	....	....
2002-03	**Pittsburgh**	**NHL**	**8**	**0**	**1**	**1**	**0**	**0**	**0**	**0**	**6**	**0.0**	**–4**	**2**	**0.0**	**4:33**	....	....	....	....	....	....	....	....	....
	Wilkes-Barre	AHL	71	21	42	63	131	....	....	....	....	....	....	....	....	....	6	1	2	3	7	....	....	....	....
	NHL Totals		**19**	**1**	**3**	**4**	**9**	**0**	**0**	**0**	**14**	**7.1**		**2**	**0.0**	**8:53**	....	....	....	....	....	....	....	....	....

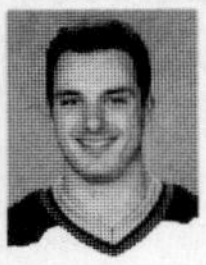

KOTALIK, Ales
(KOH-tahl-eek, ALehsh) **BUF.**

Right wing. Shoots right. 6'1", 217 lbs. Born, Jindrichuv Hradec, Czech., December 23, 1978. Buffalo's 7th choice, 164th overall, in 1998 Entry Draft.

			Regular Season														Playoffs								
Season	Club	League	GP	G	A	Pts	PIM	PP	SH	GW	S	%	+/-	TF	F%	Min	GP	G	A	Pts	PIM	PP	SH	GW	Min
1993-94	C. Budejovice Jr.	Czech-Jr.	28	12	12	24																			
1994-95	C. Budejovice Jr.	Czech-Jr.	36	26	17	43																			
1995-96	C. Budejovice Jr.	Czech-Jr.	28	6	7	13																			
1996-97	C. Budejovice Jr.	Czech-Jr.	36	15	16	31	24																		
1997-98	Ceske Budejovice	Czech	47	9	7	16	14																		
1998-99	Ceske Budejovice	Czech	41	8	13	21	16										3	0	0	0					
99-2000	Ceske Budejovice	Czech	43	7	12	19	34										3	0	1	1	6				
2000-01	Ceske Budejovice	Czech	52	19	29	48	54																		
2001-02	Rochester	AHL	68	18	25	43	55										1	0	0	0	0				
	Buffalo	**NHL**	**13**	**1**	**3**	**4**	**2**	**0**	**0**	**0**	**21**	**4.8**	**–1**	**11**	**27.3**	**12:35**									
2002-03	**Buffalo**	**NHL**	**68**	**21**	**14**	**35**	**30**	**4**	**0**	**2**	**138**	**15.2**	**–2**	**37**	**51.4**	**15:15**									
	Rochester	AHL	8	0	2	2	4																		
	NHL Totals		**81**	**22**	**17**	**39**	**32**	**4**	**0**	**2**	**159**	**13.8**		**48**	**45.8**	**14:49**									

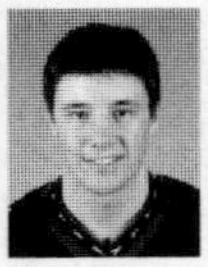

KOVALCHUK, Ilya
(koh-vuhl-CHOOK, IHL-yah) **ATL.**

Left wing. Shoots right. 6'2", 235 lbs. Born, Tver, USSR, April 15, 1983. Atlanta's 1st choice, 1st overall, in 2001 Entry Draft.

99-2000	Spartak Moscow	Russia-2	49	12	5	17	75																		
	Spartak Mos. 2	Russia-3	2	2	1	3	14																		
2000-01	Spartak Moscow	Russia-2	51	42	22	64	112																		
2001-02	**Atlanta**	**NHL**	**65**	**29**	**22**	**51**	**28**	**7**	**0**	**4**	**184**	**15.8**	**–19**	**6**	**16.7**	**18:32**									
	Russia	Olympics	6	1	2	3	14																		
2002-03	**Atlanta**	**NHL**	**81**	**38**	**29**	**67**	**57**	**9**	**0**	**3**	**257**	**14.8**	**–24**	**15**	**40.0**	**19:27**									
	NHL Totals		**146**	**67**	**51**	**118**	**85**	**16**	**0**	**7**	**441**	**15.2**		**21**	**33.3**	**19:02**									

NHL All-Rookie Team (2002)

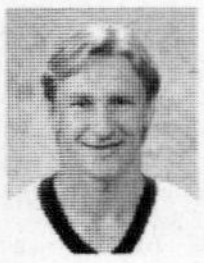

KOVALEV, Alex
(koh-VAH-lehv, al-EHX) **NYR**

Right wing. Shoots left. 6'1", 220 lbs. Born, Togliatti, USSR, February 24, 1973. NY Rangers' 1st choice, 15th overall, in 1991 Entry Draft.

1989-90	Dynamo Moscow	USSR	1	0	0	0	0																		
1990-91	Dynamo Moscow	USSR	18	1	2	3	4																		
1991-92	Dynamo Moscow	CIS	33	16	9	25	20																		
	Russia	Olympics	8	1	2	3	14																		
1992-93	**NY Rangers**	**NHL**	**65**	**20**	**18**	**38**	**79**	**3**	**0**	**3**	**134**	**14.9**	**–10**												
	Binghamton	AHL	13	13	11	24	35										9	3	5	8	14				
1993-94♦	**NY Rangers**	**NHL**	**76**	**23**	**33**	**56**	**154**	**7**	**0**	**3**	**184**	**12.5**	**18**				**23**	**9**	**12**	**21**	**18**	**5**	**0**	**2**	
1994-95	Lada Togliatti	CIS	12	8	8	16	49																		
	NY Rangers	**NHL**	**48**	**13**	**15**	**28**	**30**	**1**	**1**	**1**	**103**	**12.6**	**–6**				**10**	**4**	**7**	**11**	**10**	**0**	**0**	**0**	
1995-96	**NY Rangers**	**NHL**	**81**	**24**	**34**	**58**	**98**	**8**	**1**	**7**	**206**	**11.7**	**5**				**11**	**3**	**4**	**7**	**14**	**0**	**0**	**1**	
1996-97	**NY Rangers**	**NHL**	**45**	**13**	**22**	**35**	**42**	**1**	**0**	**0**	**110**	**11.8**	**11**												
1997-98	**NY Rangers**	**NHL**	**73**	**23**	**30**	**53**	**44**	**8**	**0**	**3**	**173**	**13.3**	**–22**												
1998-99	**NY Rangers**	**NHL**	**14**	**3**	**4**	**7**	**12**	**1**	**0**	**1**	**35**	**8.6**	**–6**	**18**	**44.4**	**19:53**									
	Pittsburgh	**NHL**	**63**	**20**	**26**	**46**	**37**	**5**	**1**	**4**	**156**	**12.8**	**8**	**226**	**43.4**	**20:30**	**10**	**5**	**7**	**12**	**14**	**0**	**0**	**1**	**20:24**
99-2000	**Pittsburgh**	**NHL**	**82**	**26**	**40**	**66**	**94**	**9**	**2**	**4**	**254**	**10.2**	**–3**	**306**	**47.4**	**22:53**	**11**	**1**	**5**	**6**	**10**	**0**	**0**	**0**	**26:35**
2000-01	**Pittsburgh**	**NHL**	**79**	**44**	**51**	**95**	**96**	**12**	**2**	**9**	**307**	**14.3**	**12**	**255**	**40.0**	**23:35**	**18**	**5**	**5**	**10**	**16**	**1**	**0**	**0**	**20:57**
2001-02	**Pittsburgh**	**NHL**	**67**	**32**	**44**	**76**	**80**	**8**	**1**	**3**	**266**	**12.0**	**2**	**179**	**45.3**	**24:03**									
	Russia	Olympics	6	3	1	4	4																		
2002-03	**Pittsburgh**	**NHL**	**54**	**27**	**37**	**64**	**50**	**8**	**0**	**1**	**212**	**12.7**	**–11**	**19**	**31.6**	**24:03**									
	NY Rangers	**NHL**	**24**	**10**	**3**	**13**	**20**	**3**	**0**	**2**	**59**	**16.9**	**2**	**19**	**42.1**	**20:09**									
	NHL Totals		**771**	**278**	**357**	**635**	**836**	**74**	**8**	**41**	**2199**	**12.6**		**1022**	**43.8**	**22:43**	**83**	**27**	**40**	**67**	**82**	**6**	**0**	**4**	**22:24**

Played in NHL All-Star Game (2001, 2003)

Traded to **Pittsburgh** by **NY Rangers** with Harry York for Petr Nedved, Chris Tamer and Sean Pronger, November 25, 1998. Traded to **NY Rangers** by **Pittsburgh** with Mike Wilson, Janne Laukkanen and Dan LaCouture for Joel Bouchard, Richard Lintner, Rico Fata, Mikael Samuelsson and future considerations, February 10, 2003.

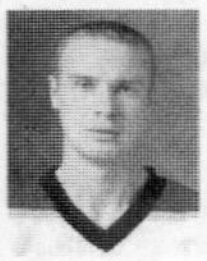

KOZLOV, Viktor
(KAHS-lahf, VIHK-tohr) **FLA.**

Center. Shoots right. 6'5", 225 lbs. Born, Togliatti, USSR, February 14, 1975. San Jose's 1st choice, 6th overall, in 1993 Entry Draft.

1990-91	Lada Togliatti	USSR-2	2	2	0	2	0																		
1991-92	Lada Togliatti	CIS	3	0	0	0	0																		
1992-93	Dynamo Moscow	CIS	30	6	5	11	4										10	3	0	3	0				
1993-94	Dynamo Moscow	CIS	42	16	9	25	14										7	3	2	5	0				
1994-95	Dynamo Moscow	CIS	3	1	1	2	2																		
	San Jose	**NHL**	**16**	**2**	**0**	**2**	**2**	**0**	**0**	**0**	**23**	**8.7**	**–5**												
	Kansas City	IHL	4	1	1	2	0										13	4	5	9	12				
1995-96	**San Jose**	**NHL**	**62**	**6**	**13**	**19**	**6**	**1**	**0**	**0**	**107**	**5.6**	**–15**												
	Kansas City	IHL	15	4	7	11	12																		
1996-97	**San Jose**	**NHL**	**78**	**16**	**25**	**41**	**40**	**4**	**0**	**4**	**184**	**8.7**	**–16**												
1997-98	**San Jose**	**NHL**	**18**	**5**	**2**	**7**	**2**	**2**	**0**	**0**	**51**	**9.8**	**–2**												
	Florida	**NHL**	**46**	**12**	**11**	**23**	**14**	**3**	**2**	**0**	**114**	**10.5**	**–1**												
1998-99	**Florida**	**NHL**	**65**	**16**	**35**	**51**	**24**	**5**	**1**	**1**	**209**	**7.7**	**13**	**985**	**41.2**	**19:03**									
99-2000	**Florida**	**NHL**	**80**	**17**	**53**	**70**	**16**	**6**	**0**	**2**	**223**	**7.6**	**24**	**1616**	**42.9**	**19:27**	**4**	**0**	**1**	**1**	**0**	**0**	**0**	**0**	**16:05**
2000-01	**Florida**	**NHL**	**51**	**14**	**23**	**37**	**10**	**6**	**0**	**2**	**139**	**10.1**	**–4**	**817**	**41.6**	**18:23**									
2001-02	**Florida**	**NHL**	**50**	**9**	**18**	**27**	**20**	**6**	**0**	**1**	**143**	**6.3**	**–16**	**840**	**43.1**	**19:54**									
2002-03	**Florida**	**NHL**	**74**	**22**	**34**	**56**	**18**	**7**	**1**	**1**	**232**	**9.5**	**–8**	**404**	**42.8**	**22:35**									
	NHL Totals		**540**	**119**	**214**	**333**	**152**	**40**	**4**	**11**	**1425**	**8.4**		**4662**	**42.3**	**19:60**	**4**	**0**	**1**	**1**	**0**	**0**	**0**	**0**	**16:05**

Played in NHL All-Star Game (2000)

Traded to **Florida** by **San Jose** with Florida's 5th round choice (previously acquired, Florida selected Jaroslav Spacek) in 1998 Entry Draft for Dave Lowry and Florida's 1st round choice (later traded to Tampa Bay – Tampa Bay selected Vincent Lecavalier) in 1998 Entry Draft, November 13, 1997.

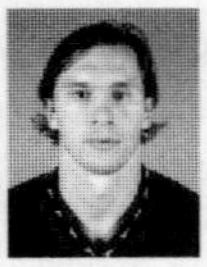

KOZLOV, Vyacheslav
(KAHS-lahf, VYACH-ih-slav) **ATL.**

Right wing. Shoots left. 5'10", 185 lbs. Born, Voskresensk, USSR, May 3, 1972. Detroit's 2nd choice, 45th overall, in 1990 Entry Draft.

1987-88	Voskresensk	USSR	2	0	0	0	0																		
1988-89	Voskresensk	USSR	14	0	1	1	2																		
1989-90	Voskresensk	USSR	45	14	12	26	38																		
1990-91	Voskresensk	USSR	45	11	13	24	46																		
1991-92	CSKA Moscow	CIS	11	6	5	11	12																		
	Detroit	**NHL**	**7**	**0**	**2**	**2**	**2**	**0**	**0**	**0**	**9**	**0.0**	**–2**												
1992-93	**Detroit**	**NHL**	**17**	**4**	**1**	**5**	**14**	**0**	**0**	**0**	**26**	**15.4**	**–1**				**4**	**0**	**2**	**2**	**2**	**0**	**0**	**0**	
	Adirondack	AHL	45	23	36	59	54										4	1	1	2	4				
1993-94	**Detroit**	**NHL**	**77**	**34**	**39**	**73**	**50**	**8**	**2**	**6**	**202**	**16.8**	**27**				**7**	**2**	**5**	**7**	**12**	**0**	**0**	**0**	
	Adirondack	AHL	3	0	1	1	15																		
1994-95	CSKA Moscow	CIS	10	3	4	7	14																		
	Detroit	**NHL**	**46**	**13**	**20**	**33**	**45**	**5**	**0**	**3**	**97**	**13.4**	**12**				**18**	**9**	**7**	**16**	**10**	**1**	**0**	**4**	
1995-96	**Detroit**	**NHL**	**82**	**36**	**37**	**73**	**70**	**9**	**0**	**7**	**237**	**15.2**	**33**				**19**	**5**	**7**	**12**	**10**	**2**	**0**	**1**	
1996-97♦	**Detroit**	**NHL**	**75**	**23**	**22**	**45**	**46**	**3**	**0**	**6**	**211**	**10.9**	**21**				**20**	**8**	**5**	**13**	**14**	**4**	**0**	**2**	
1997-98♦	**Detroit**	**NHL**	**80**	**25**	**27**	**52**	**46**	**6**	**0**	**1**	**221**	**11.3**	**14**				**22**	**6**	**8**	**14**	**10**	**1**	**0**	**4**	
1998-99	**Detroit**	**NHL**	**79**	**29**	**29**	**58**	**45**	**6**	**1**	**4**	**209**	**13.9**	**10**	**38**	**36.8**	**16:02**	**10**	**6**	**1**	**7**	**4**	**3**	**0**	**0**	**14:44**
99-2000	**Detroit**	**NHL**	**72**	**18**	**18**	**36**	**28**	**4**	**0**	**3**	**165**	**10.9**	**11**	**28**	**35.7**	**15:30**	**8**	**2**	**1**	**3**	**12**	**1**	**0**	**1**	**12:20**
2000-01	**Detroit**	**NHL**	**72**	**20**	**18**	**38**	**30**	**4**	**0**	**5**	**187**	**10.7**	**9**	**51**	**47.1**	**14:43**	**6**	**4**	**1**	**5**	**2**	**2**	**0**	**0**	**16:27**

			Regular Season														Playoffs								
Season	Club	League	GP	G	A	Pts	PIM	PP	SH	GW	S	%	+/-	TF	F%	Min	GP	G	A	Pts	PIM	PP	SH	GW	Min
2001-02	Buffalo	NHL	38	9	13	22	16	3	0	1	68	13.2	0	24	41.7	16:31									
2002-03	Atlanta	NHL	79	21	49	70	66	9	1	2	185	11.4	-10	67	34.3	20:01									
	NHL Totals		**724**	**232**	**275**	**507**	**458**	**57**	**4**	**38**	**1817**	**12.8**		**208**	**38.9**	**16:37**	**114**	**42**	**37**	**79**	**76**	**14**	**0**	**12**	**14:22**

Traded to **Buffalo** by **Detroit** with Detroit's 1st round choice (later traded to Columbus – later traded to Atlanta – Atlanta selected Jim Slater) in 2002 Entry Draft and future considerations for Dominik Hasek, July 1, 2001. • Missed majority of 2001-02 season recovering from Achilles tendon injury suffered in game vs. Columbus, December 31, 2001. Traded to **Atlanta** by **Buffalo** with Buffalo's 2nd round choice (later traded to Nashville – Nashville selected Konstantin Glazachev) in 2003 Entry Draft for Atlanta's 2nd (later traded to Florida – Florida selected Kamil Kreps) and 3rd (later traded to Phoenix – Phoenix selected Tyler Redenbach) round choices in 2003 Entry Draft, June 22, 2002.

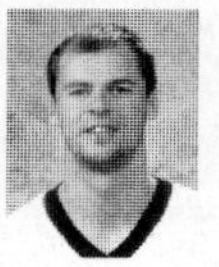

KRAFT, Milan
(KRAFT, MIH-lan) **PIT.**

Center. Shoots right. 6'3", 214 lbs. Born, Plzen, Czech., January 17, 1980. Pittsburgh's 1st choice, 23rd overall, in 1998 Entry Draft.

Season	Club	League	GP	G	A	Pts	PIM	PP	SH	GW	S	%	+/-	TF	F%	Min	GP	G	A	Pts	PIM	PP	SH	GW	Min
1995-96	HC ZKZ Plzen Jr.	Czech-Jr.	49	54	41	95																			
1996-97	HC ZKZ Plzen Jr.	Czech-Jr.	29	24	12	36																			
	HC ZKZ Plzen	Czech	9	0	1	1	2																		
1997-98	Plzen Jr.	Czech-Jr.	24	22	21	43	12																		
	Plzen	Czech	16	0	5	5	0										1	0	0	0	0				
1998-99	Prince Albert	WHL	68	40	46	86	32										14	7	13	20	6				
99-2000	Prince Albert	WHL	56	34	35	69	42										6	4	1	5	4				
2000-01	**Pittsburgh**	**NHL**	**42**	**7**	**7**	**14**	**8**	**1**	**1**	**1**	**63**	**11.1**	**-6**	**427**	**37.9**	**11:41**	**8**	**0**	**0**	**0**	**2**	**0**	**0**	**0**	**12:13**
	Wilkes-Barre	AHL	40	21	23	44	27										14	12	7	19	6				
2001-02	**Pittsburgh**	**NHL**	**68**	**8**	**8**	**16**	**16**	**1**	**0**	**2**	**103**	**7.8**	**-9**	**766**	**44.7**	**12:29**									
	Wilkes-Barre	AHL	8	4	4	8	10																		
2002-03	**Pittsburgh**	**NHL**	**31**	**7**	**5**	**12**	**10**	**0**	**0**	**1**	**50**	**14.0**	**-8**	**392**	**43.1**	**13:56**									
	Wilkes-Barre	AHL	40	13	24	37	28										6	2	4	6	4				
	NHL Totals		**141**	**22**	**20**	**42**	**34**	**2**	**1**	**4**	**216**	**10.2**		**1585**	**42.5**	**12:34**	**8**	**0**	**0**	**0**	**2**	**0**	**0**	**0**	**12:13**

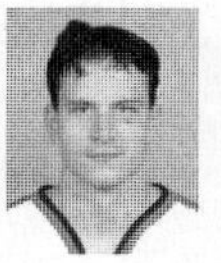

KRAFT, Ryan
(KRAFT, RIGH-uhn) **NYI**

Center. Shoots left. 5'9", 181 lbs. Born, Bottineau, ND, November 7, 1975. San Jose's 11th choice, 194th overall, in 1995 Entry Draft.

Season	Club	League	GP	G	A	Pts	PIM	PP	SH	GW	S	%	+/-	TF	F%	Min	GP	G	A	Pts	PIM	PP	SH	GW	Min
1993-94	Moorhead Spuds	Hi-School	25	40	45	85																			
1994-95	U. of Minnesota	WCHA	44	13	33	46	44																		
1995-96	U. of Minnesota	WCHA	41	13	24	37	24																		
1996-97	U. of Minnesota	WCHA	42	25	21	46	37																		
1997-98	U. of Minnesota	WCHA	32	11	26	37	16																		
1998-99	Richmond	ECHL	63	28	36	64	35										18	10	10	20	4				
99-2000	Richmond	ECHL	44	32	35	67	32																		
	Cleveland	IHL	1	0	1	1	0																		
	Kentucky	AHL	15	7	6	13	2										5	3	1	4	0				
2000-01	Kentucky	AHL	77	38	50	88	36										3	2	0	2	0				
2001-02	Cleveland Barons	AHL	63	19	41	60	42																		
2002-03	**San Jose**	**NHL**	**7**	**0**	**1**	**1**	**0**	**0**	**0**	**0**	**1**	**0.0**	**2**	**41**	**34.2**	**8:33**									
	Cleveland Barons	AHL	53	14	27	41	12																		
	NHL Totals		**7**	**0**	**1**	**1**	**0**	**0**	**0**	**0**	**1**	**0.0**		**41**	**34.1**	**8:33**									

WCHA All-Rookie Team (1995) • WCHA All-Academic Team (1996) • AHL Second All-Star Team (2001) • Dudley "Red" Garrett Memorial Trophy (Top Rookie – AHL) (2001)

Signed as a free agent by **NY Islanders**, July 8, 2003.

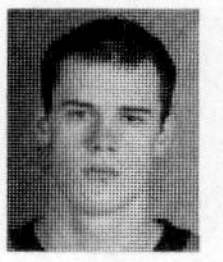

KRAJICEK, Lukas
(KRIGH-ee-chehk, LOO-kahsh) **FLA.**

Defense. Shoots left. 6'2", 185 lbs. Born, Prostejov, Czech., March 11, 1983. Florida's 2nd choice, 24th overall, in 2001 Entry Draft.

Season	Club	League	GP	G	A	Pts	PIM	PP	SH	GW	S	%	+/-	TF	F%	Min	GP	G	A	Pts	PIM	PP	SH	GW	Min
1998-99	Zlin Jr.	Czech-Jr.	48	8	18	26	40																		
99-2000	Det. Compuware	NAJHL	53	5	22	27	61										5	0	1	1	18				
2000-01	Peterborough	OHL	61	8	27	35	53										7	0	5	5	0				
2001-02	**Florida**	**NHL**	**5**	**0**	**0**	**0**	**0**	**0**	**0**	**0**	**3**	**0.0**	**0**	**0**	**0.0**	**13:23**									
	Peterborough	OHL	55	10	32	42	56										6	0	5	5	6				
2002-03	Peterborough	OHL	52	11	42	53	42										7	0	3	3	0				
	San Antonio	AHL	3	0	1	1	0										3	0	0	0	0				
	NHL Totals		**5**	**0**	**0**	**0**	**0**	**0**	**0**	**0**	**3**	**0.0**		**0**	**0.0**	**13:23**									

OHL All-Rookie Team (2001) • OHL First All-Star Team (2003)

• Returned to **Peterborough** (OHL) by **Florida**, October 28, 2001.

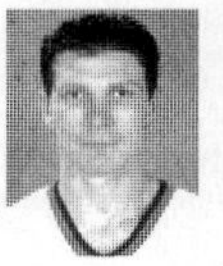

KRAVCHUK, Igor
(krahv-CHOOK, EE-gohr)

Defense. Shoots left. 6'1", 218 lbs. Born, Ufa, USSR, September 13, 1966. Chicago's 5th choice, 71st overall, in 1991 Entry Draft.

Season	Club	League	GP	G	A	Pts	PIM	PP	SH	GW	S	%	+/-	TF	F%	Min	GP	G	A	Pts	PIM	PP	SH	GW	Min
1984-85	Ufa	USSR-2	50	3	2	5	22																		
1985-86	Ufa	USSR	21	2	2	4	6																		
1986-87	Ufa	USSR	22	0	1	1	8																		
1987-88	CSKA Moscow	USSR	48	1	8	9	12																		
	Soviet Union	Olympics	6	1	0	1	0																		
1988-89	CSKA Moscow	USSR	22	3	3	6	2																		
1989-90	CSKA Moscow	USSR	48	1	3	4	16																		
1990-91	CSKA Moscow	USSR	41	6	5	11	16																		
1991-92	CSKA Moscow	CIS	30	3	8	11	6																		
	Russia	Olympics	8	3	2	5	6																		
	Chicago	**NHL**	**18**	**1**	**8**	**9**	**4**	**0**	**0**	**1**	**40**	**2.5**	**-3**				**18**	**2**	**6**	**8**	**8**	**1**	**0**	**0**	
1992-93	**Chicago**	**NHL**	**38**	**6**	**9**	**15**	**30**	**3**	**0**	**0**	**101**	**5.9**	**11**												
	Edmonton	**NHL**	**17**	**4**	**8**	**12**	**2**	**1**	**0**	**0**	**42**	**9.5**	**-8**												
1993-94	**Edmonton**	**NHL**	**81**	**12**	**38**	**50**	**16**	**5**	**0**	**2**	**197**	**6.1**	**-12**												
1994-95	**Edmonton**	**NHL**	**36**	**7**	**11**	**18**	**29**	**3**	**1**	**0**	**93**	**7.5**	**-15**												
1995-96	**Edmonton**	**NHL**	**26**	**4**	**4**	**8**	**10**	**3**	**0**	**0**	**59**	**6.8**	**-13**												
	St. Louis	**NHL**	**40**	**3**	**12**	**15**	**24**	**0**	**0**	**1**	**114**	**2.6**	**-6**				**10**	**1**	**5**	**6**	**4**	**0**	**0**	**1**	
1996-97	**St. Louis**	**NHL**	**82**	**4**	**24**	**28**	**35**	**1**	**0**	**0**	**142**	**2.8**	**7**				**2**	**0**	**0**	**0**	**2**	**0**	**0**	**0**	
1997-98	**Ottawa**	**NHL**	**81**	**8**	**27**	**35**	**8**	**3**	**1**	**1**	**191**	**4.2**	**-19**				**11**	**2**	**3**	**5**	**4**	**0**	**0**	**0**	
	Russia	Olympics	6	0	2	2	2																		
1998-99	**Ottawa**	**NHL**	**79**	**4**	**21**	**25**	**32**	**3**	**0**	**0**	**171**	**2.3**	**14**	**0**	**0.0**	**23:51**	**4**	**0**	**0**	**0**	**0**	**0**	**0**	**0**	**23:07**
99-2000	**Ottawa**	**NHL**	**64**	**6**	**12**	**18**	**20**	**5**	**0**	**1**	**126**	**4.8**	**-5**	**0**	**0.0**	**20:41**	**6**	**1**	**1**	**2**	**0**	**0**	**0**	**0**	**25:49**
2000-01	**Ottawa**	**NHL**	**15**	**1**	**5**	**6**	**14**	**0**	**0**	**1**	**13**	**7.7**	**4**	**0**	**0.0**	**20:41**									
	Calgary	**NHL**	**37**	**0**	**8**	**8**	**4**	**0**	**0**	**0**	**54**	**0.0**	**-12**	**0**	**0.0**	**23:43**									
2001-02	**Calgary**	**NHL**	**78**	**4**	**22**	**26**	**19**	**1**	**0**	**1**	**135**	**3.0**	**3**	**0**	**0.0**	**18:32**									
	Russia	Olympics	6	0	2	2	0																		
2002-03	**Florida**	**NHL**	**7**	**0**	**1**	**1**	**4**	**0**	**0**	**0**	**8**	**0.0**	**-3**	**0**	**0.0**	**18:46**									
	NHL Totals		**699**	**64**	**210**	**274**	**251**	**28**	**2**	**8**	**1486**	**4.3**		**0**	**0.0**	**21:20**	**51**	**6**	**15**	**21**	**18**	**1**	**0**	**1**	**24:44**

Played in NHL All-Star Game (1999)

Traded to **Edmonton** by **Chicago** with Dean McAmmond for Joe Murphy, February 24, 1993. Traded to **St. Louis** by **Edmonton** with Ken Sutton for Jeff Norton and Donald Dufresne, January 4, 1996. Traded to **Ottawa** by **St. Louis** for Steve Duchesne, August 25, 1997. Claimed on waivers by **Calgary** from **Ottawa**, November 10, 2000. Signed as a free agent by **Florida**, March 11, 2003.

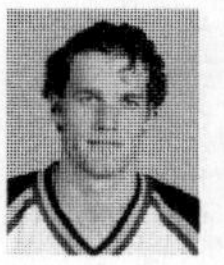

KRESTANOVICH, Jordan
(KREH-sta-noh-vihtch, JOHR-dan) **COL.**

Left wing. Shoots left. 6'1", 170 lbs. Born, Langley, B.C., June 14, 1981. Colorado's 7th choice, 152nd overall, in 1999 Entry Draft.

Season	Club	League	GP	G	A	Pts	PIM	PP	SH	GW	S	%	+/-	TF	F%	Min	GP	G	A	Pts	PIM	PP	SH	GW	Min
1996-97	Surrey Chiefs	BCAHA	55	79	81	160																			
1997-98	Calgary Hitmen	WHL	22	1	0	1	0										13	0	0	0	0				
1998-99	Calgary Hitmen	WHL	62	6	13	19	10										20	3	8	11	4				
99-2000	Calgary Hitmen	WHL	72	19	24	43	22										13	7	7	14	4				
	Hershey Bears	AHL															1	0	0	0	0				
2000-01	Calgary Hitmen	WHL	70	40	60	100	32										12	8	4	12	8				
	Hershey Bears	AHL															2	0	0	0	0				
2001-02	**Colorado**	**NHL**	**8**	**0**	**2**	**2**	**0**	**0**	**0**	**0**	**6**	**0.0**	**1**	**0**	**0.0**	**8:34**									
	Hershey Bears	AHL	68	12	22	34	18										8	1	0	1	0				
2002-03	Hershey Bears	AHL	70	13	21	34	24										4	0	1	1	2				
	NHL Totals		**8**	**0**	**2**	**2**	**0**	**0**	**0**	**0**	**6**	**0.0**		**0**	**0.0**	**8:34**									

			Regular Season														Playoffs								
Season	Club	League	GP	G	A	Pts	PIM	PP	SH	GW	S	%	+/-	TF	F%	Min	GP	G	A	Pts	PIM	PP	SH	GW	Min

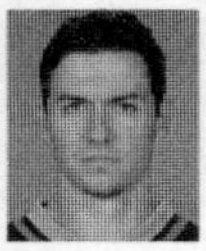

KRISTEK, Jaroslav

(KRIHSH-tehk, YAH-roh-slahv) **BUF.**

Right wing. Shoots left. 6'1", 188 lbs. Born, Zlin, Czech., March 16, 1980. Buffalo's 4th choice, 50th overall, in 1998 Entry Draft.

1995-96	AC ZPS Zlin Jr.	Czech-Jr.	34	33	20	53	....	....	....	....	....	....	....	....	....	....	....	....	....	....	....	....	....	....	....
1996-97	AC ZPS Zlin Jr.	Czech-Jr.	44	28	27	55	....	....	....	....	....	....	....	....	....	....	....	....	....	....	....	....	....	....	....
1997-98	Zlin Jr.	Czech-Jr.	7	8	5	13	....	....	....	....	....	....	....	....	....	....	....	....	....	....	....	....	....	....	....
	HC Prostejov	Czech-2	4	0	0	0	....	....	....	....	....	....	....	....	....	....	....	....	....	....	....	....	....	....	....
	Zlin	Czech	37	2	8	10	20	....	....	....	....	....	....	....	....	....	....	....	....	....	....	....	....	....	....
1998-99	Tri-City	WHL	70	38	48	86	55	....	....	....	....	....	....	....	....	....	12	4	3	7	2	....	....	....	....
99-2000	Tri-City	WHL	45	26	25	51	16	....	....	....	....	....	....	....	....	....	2	0	0	0	0	....	....	....	....
2000-01	Rochester	AHL	35	5	3	8	20	....	....	....	....	....	....	....	....	....	....	....	....	....	....	....	....	....	....
2001-02	Rochester	AHL	43	3	6	9	20	....	....	....	....	....	....	....	....	....	1	0	0	0	0	....	....	....	....
2002-03	**Buffalo**	**NHL**	**6**	**0**	**0**	**0**	**4**	**0**	**0**	**0**	**4**	**0.0**	**–2**	**0**	**0.0**	**11:37**	....	....	....	....	....	....	....	....	....
	Rochester	AHL	47	15	17	32	24	....	....	....	....	....	....	....	....	....	....	....	....	....	....	....	....	....	....
	NHL Totals		**6**	**0**	**0**	**0**	**4**	**0**	**0**	**0**	**4**	**0.0**		**0**	**0.0**	**11:37**	....	....	....	....	....	....	....	....	....

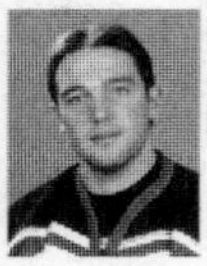

KRIVOKRASOV, Sergei

(krih-vuh-KRA-sahf, SAIR-gay)

Right wing. Shoots left. 5'11", 185 lbs. Born, Angarsk, USSR, April 15, 1974. Chicago's 1st choice, 12th overall, in 1992 Entry Draft.

1990-91	CSKA Moscow	USSR	41	4	0	4	8	....	....	....	....	....	....	....	....	....	....	....	....	....	....	....	....	....	....
1991-92	CSKA Moscow	CIS	42	10	8	18	35	....	....	....	....	....	....	....	....	....	....	....	....	....	....	....	....	....	....
1992-93	**Chicago**	**NHL**	**4**	**0**	**0**	**0**	**2**	**0**	**0**	**0**	**0**	**0.0**	**–2**	....	....	....	....	....	....	....	....	....	....	....	....
	Indianapolis Ice	IHL	78	36	33	69	157	....	....	....	....	....	....	....	....	....	5	3	1	4	2	....	....	....	....
1993-94	**Chicago**	**NHL**	**9**	**1**	**0**	**1**	**4**	**0**	**0**	**0**	**7**	**14.3**	**–2**	....	....	....	....	....	....	....	....	....	....	....	....
	Indianapolis Ice	IHL	53	19	26	45	145	....	....	....	....	....	....	....	....	....	....	....	....	....	....	....	....	....	....
1994-95	Indianapolis Ice	IHL	29	12	15	27	41	....	....	....	....	....	....	....	....	....	....	....	....	....	....	....	....	....	....
	Chicago	**NHL**	**41**	**12**	**7**	**19**	**33**	**6**	**0**	**2**	**72**	**16.7**	**9**	....	....	....	**10**	**0**	**0**	**0**	**8**	**0**	**0**	**0**	....
1995-96	**Chicago**	**NHL**	**46**	**6**	**10**	**16**	**32**	**0**	**0**	**1**	**52**	**11.5**	**10**	....	....	....	**5**	**1**	**0**	**1**	**2**	**0**	**0**	**1**	....
	Indianapolis Ice	IHL	9	4	5	9	28	....	....	....	....	....	....	....	....	....	....	....	....	....	....	....	....	....	....
1996-97	**Chicago**	**NHL**	**67**	**13**	**11**	**24**	**42**	**2**	**0**	**3**	**104**	**12.5**	**–1**	....	....	....	**6**	**1**	**0**	**1**	**4**	**0**	**0**	**0**	....
1997-98	**Chicago**	**NHL**	**58**	**10**	**13**	**23**	**33**	**1**	**0**	**2**	**127**	**7.9**	**–1**	....	....	....	....	....	....	....	....	....	....	....	....
	Russia	Olympics	6	0	0	0	4	....	....	....	....	....	....	....	....	....	....	....	....	....	....	....	....	....	....
1998-99	**Nashville**	**NHL**	**70**	**25**	**23**	**48**	**42**	**10**	**0**	**6**	**208**	**12.0**	**–5**	**0**	**0.0**	**16:08**	....	....	....	....	....	....	....	....	....
99-2000	**Nashville**	**NHL**	**63**	**9**	**17**	**26**	**40**	**3**	**0**	**2**	**132**	**6.8**	**–7**	**1**	**0.0**	**13:08**	....	....	....	....	....	....	....	....	....
	Calgary	**NHL**	**12**	**1**	**10**	**11**	**4**	**0**	**0**	**0**	**27**	**3.7**	**2**	**0**	**0.0**	**13:22**	....	....	....	....	....	....	....	....	....
2000-01	**Minnesota**	**NHL**	**54**	**7**	**15**	**22**	**20**	**2**	**0**	**1**	**107**	**6.5**	**–1**	**3**	**0.0**	**13:05**	....	....	....	....	....	....	....	....	....
2001-02	**Minnesota**	**NHL**	**9**	**1**	**1**	**2**	**17**	**0**	**0**	**1**	**13**	**7.7**	**–1**	**0**	**0.0**	**12:13**	....	....	....	....	....	....	....	....	....
	Anaheim	**NHL**	**17**	**1**	**2**	**3**	**19**	**0**	**0**	**0**	**38**	**2.6**	**–1**	**5**	**60.0**	**12:05**	....	....	....	....	....	....	....	....	....
	Cincinnati	AHL	15	3	5	8	27	....	....	....	....	....	....	....	....	....	1	0	0	0	2	....	....	....	....
2002-03	Amur Khabarovsk	Russia	51	16	18	34	87	....	....	....	....	....	....	....	....	....	....	....	....	....	....	....	....	....	....
	NHL Totals		**450**	**86**	**109**	**195**	**288**	**24**	**0**	**18**	**887**	**9.7**		**9**	**33.3**	**13:57**	**21**	**2**	**0**	**2**	**14**	**0**	**0**	**1**	....

Played in NHL All-Star Game (1999)

Traded to **Nashville** by **Chicago** for future considerations, June 26, 1998. Traded to **Calgary** by **Nashville** for Cale Hulse and Calgary's 3rd round choice (Denis Platonov) in 2001 Entry Draft, March 14, 2000. Selected by **Minnesota** from **Calgary** in Expansion Draft, June 23, 2000. Traded to **Anaheim** by **Minnesota** for Anaheim's 7th round choice (Niklas Eckerblom) in 2002 Entry Draft and a conditional choice in 2003 Entry Draft, November 1, 2001. Signed as a free agent by **Amur Khabarovsk** (Russia), July 14, 2002.

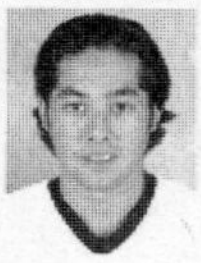

KROG, Jason

(KROHG, JAY-suhn) **ANA.**

Center. Shoots right. 5'11", 191 lbs. Born, Fernie, B.C., October 9, 1975.

1992-93	Chilliwack Chiefs	BCJHL	52	30	27	57	52	....	....	....	....	....	....	....	....	....	....	....	....	....	....	....	....	....	....
1993-94	Chilliwack Chiefs	BCJHL	42	19	36	55	20	....	....	....	....	....	....	....	....	....	....	....	....	....	....	....	....	....	....
1994-95	Chilliwack Chiefs	BCJHL	60	47	81	128	36	....	....	....	....	....	....	....	....	....	....	....	....	....	....	....	....	....	....
1995-96	New Hampshire	H-East	34	4	16	20	20	....	....	....	....	....	....	....	....	....	....	....	....	....	....	....	....	....	....
1996-97	New Hampshire	H-East	39	23	*44	*67	28	....	....	....	....	....	....	....	....	....	....	....	....	....	....	....	....	....	....
1997-98	New Hampshire	H-East	38	*33	33	66	44	....	....	....	....	....	....	....	....	....	....	....	....	....	....	....	....	....	....
1998-99	New Hampshire	H-East	41	*34	*51	*85	38	....	....	....	....	....	....	....	....	....	....	....	....	....	....	....	....	....	....
99-2000	**NY Islanders**	**NHL**	**17**	**2**	**4**	**6**	**6**	**1**	**0**	**0**	**22**	**9.1**	**–1**	**81**	**53.1**	**10:03**	....	....	....	....	....	....	....	....	....
	Lowell	AHL	45	6	21	27	22	....	....	....	....	....	....	....	....	....	....	....	....	....	....	....	....	....	....
	Providence Bruins	AHL	11	9	8	17	4	....	....	....	....	....	....	....	....	....	6	2	2	4	0	....	....	....	....
2000-01	**NY Islanders**	**NHL**	**9**	**0**	**3**	**3**	**0**	**0**	**0**	**0**	**7**	**0.0**	**4**	**60**	**48.3**	**10:32**	....	....	....	....	....	....	....	....	....
	Lowell	AHL	26	11	16	27	6	....	....	....	....	....	....	....	....	....	....	....	....	....	....	....	....	....	....
	Springfield	AHL	24	7	23	30	4	....	....	....	....	....	....	....	....	....	....	....	....	....	....	....	....	....	....
2001-02	**NY Islanders**	**NHL**	**2**	**0**	**0**	**0**	**0**	**0**	**0**	**0**	**0**	**0.0**	**0**	**13**	**46.2**	**6:40**	....	....	....	....	....	....	....	....	....
	Bridgeport	AHL	64	26	36	62	13	....	....	....	....	....	....	....	....	....	20	10	13	23	8	....	....	....	....
2002-03	**Anaheim**	**NHL**	**67**	**10**	**15**	**25**	**12**	**0**	**1**	**1**	**92**	**10.9**	**1**	**634**	**60.4**	**13:47**	**21**	**3**	**1**	**4**	**4**	**0**	**0**	**0**	**12:10**
	Cincinnati	AHL	9	3	4	7	6	....	....	....	....	....	....	....	....	....	....	....	....	....	....	....	....	....	....
	NHL Totals		**95**	**12**	**22**	**34**	**18**	**1**	**1**	**1**	**121**	**9.9**		**788**	**58.5**	**12:40**	**21**	**3**	**1**	**4**	**4**	**0**	**0**	**0**	**12:10**

Hockey East All-Star Team (1997) • NCAA East Second All-American Team (1997) • Hockey East First All-Star Team (1998, 1999) • Hockey East Player of the Year (1999) • NCAA East First All-American Team (1999) • NCAA Championship All-Tournament Team (1999) • Hobey Baker Memorial Award (Top U.S. Collegiate Player) (1999)

Signed as a free agent by **NY Islanders**, May 14, 1999. Loaned to **Providence** (AHL) by **NY Islanders**, March 1, 2000. Signed as a free agent by **Anaheim**, July 17, 2002.

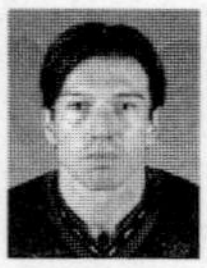

KRUPP, Uwe

(KROOP, OO-VAY)

Defense. Shoots right. 6'6", 235 lbs. Born, Cologne, West Germany, June 24, 1965. Buffalo's 13th choice, 223rd overall, in 1983 Entry Draft.

1982-83	Kolner EC	Germany	11	0	0	0	0	....	....	....	....	....	....	....	....	....	....	....	....	....	....	....	....	....	....
1983-84	Kolner EC	Germany	26	0	4	4	22	....	....	....	....	....	....	....	....	....	....	....	....	....	....	....	....	....	....
1984-85	Kolner EC	Germany	31	7	7	14	....	....	....	....	....	....	....	....	....	....	9	4	1	5	....	....	....	....	....
1985-86	Kolner EC	Germany	35	6	18	24	83	....	....	....	....	....	....	....	....	....	10	4	3	7	....	....	....	....	....
1986-87	**Buffalo**	**NHL**	**26**	**1**	**4**	**5**	**23**	**0**	**0**	**0**	**34**	**2.9**	**–9**	....	....	....	....	....	....	....	....	....	....	....	....
	Rochester	AHL	42	3	19	22	50	....	....	....	....	....	....	....	....	....	17	1	11	12	16	....	....	....	....
1987-88	**Buffalo**	**NHL**	**75**	**2**	**9**	**11**	**151**	**0**	**0**	**0**	**84**	**2.4**	**–1**	....	....	....	**6**	**0**	**0**	**0**	**15**	**0**	**0**	**0**	....
1988-89	**Buffalo**	**NHL**	**70**	**5**	**13**	**18**	**55**	**0**	**1**	**0**	**51**	**9.8**	**0**	....	....	....	**5**	**0**	**1**	**1**	**4**	**0**	**0**	**0**	....
1989-90	**Buffalo**	**NHL**	**74**	**3**	**20**	**23**	**85**	**0**	**1**	**1**	**69**	**4.3**	**15**	....	....	....	**6**	**0**	**0**	**0**	**4**	**0**	**0**	**0**	....
1990-91	**Buffalo**	**NHL**	**74**	**12**	**32**	**44**	**66**	**6**	**0**	**0**	**138**	**8.7**	**14**	....	....	....	**6**	**1**	**1**	**2**	**6**	**1**	**0**	**0**	....
1991-92	**Buffalo**	**NHL**	**8**	**2**	**0**	**2**	**6**	**0**	**0**	**0**	**13**	**15.4**	**0**	....	....	....	....	....	....	....	....	....	....	....	....
	NY Islanders	**NHL**	**59**	**6**	**29**	**35**	**43**	**2**	**0**	**0**	**115**	**5.2**	**13**	....	....	....	....	....	....	....	....	....	....	....	....
1992-93	**NY Islanders**	**NHL**	**80**	**9**	**29**	**38**	**67**	**2**	**0**	**2**	**116**	**7.8**	**6**	....	....	....	**18**	**1**	**5**	**6**	**12**	**0**	**0**	**0**	....
1993-94	**NY Islanders**	**NHL**	**41**	**7**	**14**	**21**	**30**	**3**	**0**	**0**	**82**	**8.5**	**11**	....	....	....	**4**	**0**	**1**	**1**	**4**	**0**	**0**	**0**	....
1994-95	EV Landshut	Germany	5	1	2	3	6	....	....	....	....	....	....	....	....	....	....	....	....	....	....	....	....	....	....
	Quebec	**NHL**	**44**	**6**	**17**	**23**	**20**	**3**	**0**	**1**	**102**	**5.9**	**14**	....	....	....	**5**	**0**	**2**	**2**	**2**	**0**	**0**	**0**	....
1995-96♦	**Colorado**	**NHL**	**6**	**0**	**3**	**3**	**4**	**0**	**0**	**0**	**9**	**0.0**	**4**	....	....	....	**22**	**4**	**12**	**16**	**33**	**1**	**0**	**2**	....
1996-97	**Colorado**	**NHL**	**60**	**4**	**17**	**21**	**48**	**2**	**0**	**1**	**107**	**3.7**	**12**	....	....	....	....	....	....	....	....	....	....	....	....
1997-98	**Colorado**	**NHL**	**78**	**9**	**22**	**31**	**38**	**5**	**0**	**2**	**149**	**6.0**	**21**	....	....	....	**7**	**0**	**1**	**1**	**4**	**0**	**0**	**0**	....
	Germany	Olympics	2	0	2	2	4	....	....	....	....	....	....	....	....	....	....	....	....	....	....	....	....	....	....
1998-99	**Detroit**	**NHL**	**22**	**3**	**2**	**5**	**6**	**0**	**0**	**0**	**32**	**9.4**	**0**	**0**	**0.0**	**21:23**	....	....	....	....	....	....	....	....	....
99-2000	**Detroit**	**NHL**	DID NOT PLAY – INJURED																						
2000-01	**Detroit**	**NHL**	DID NOT PLAY – INJURED																						
2001-02	**Detroit**	**NHL**	**8**	**0**	**1**	**1**	**8**	**0**	**0**	**0**	**9**	**0.0**	**–1**	**0**	**0.0**	**17:03**	**2**	**0**	**0**	**0**	**2**	**0**	**0**	**0**	**20:00**
2002-03	**Atlanta**	**NHL**	**4**	**0**	**0**	**0**	**10**	**0**	**0**	**0**	**1**	**0.0**	**–2**	**0**	**0.0**	**15:19**	....	....	....	....	....	....	....	....	....
	NHL Totals		**729**	**69**	**212**	**281**	**660**	**23**	**2**	**7**	**1111**	**6.2**		**0**	**0.0**	**19:39**	**81**	**6**	**23**	**29**	**86**	**2**	**0**	**2**	**20:00**

Played in NHL All-Star Game (1991)

Traded to **NY Islanders** by **Buffalo** with Pierre Turgeon, Benoit Hogue and Dave McLlwain for Pat LaFontaine, Randy Hillier, Randy Wood and NY Islanders' 4th round choice (Dean Melanson) in 1992 Entry Draft, October 25, 1991. Traded to **Quebec** by **NY Islanders** with NY Islanders' 1st round choice (Wade Belak) in 1994 Entry Draft for Ron Sutter and Quebec's 1st round choice (Brett Lindros) in 1994 Entry Draft, June 28, 1994. Transferred to **Colorado** after **Quebec** franchise relocated, June 21, 1995. Claimed by **Nashville** from **Colorado** in Expansion Draft, June 26, 1998. Signed as a free agent by **Detroit**, July 7, 1998. • Missed remainder of 1998-99 season and entire 1999-2000 and 2000-01 seasons recovering from back injury suffered prior to game vs. Phoenix, December 19, 1998. Signed as a free agent by **Atlanta**, July 19, 2002. • Missed majority of 2002-03 season recovering from back surgery, November 6, 2002. • Officially announced retirement, April 27, 2003.

Season	Club	League	Regular Season														Playoffs								
Season	Club	League	GP	G	A	Pts	PIM	PP	SH	GW	S	%	+/-	TF	F%	Min	GP	G	A	Pts	PIM	PP	SH	GW	Min

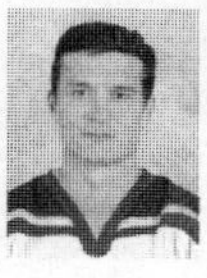

KUBA, Filip

(KOO-bah, FIHL-ihp) **MIN.**

Defense. Shoots left. 6'3", 205 lbs. Born, Ostrava, Czech., December 29, 1976. Florida's 8th choice, 192nd overall, in 1995 Entry Draft.

1994-95	HC Vitkovice Jr.	Czech-Jr.	35	10	15	25	....	....	....	....	....	....	....	....	....	....	....	....	....	....	....	....	....	....	....
	HC Vitkovice	Czech	....	....	....	....	....	....	....	....	....	....	....	....	....	....	4	0	0	0	2	....	....	....	....
1995-96	HC Vitkovice	Czech	19	0	1	1	....	....	....	....	....	....	....	....	....	....	....	....	....	....	....	....	....	....	....
1996-97	Carolina	AHL	51	0	12	12	38	....	....	....	....	....	....	....	....	....	....	....	....	....	....	....	....	....	....
1997-98	New Haven	AHL	77	4	13	17	58	....	....	....	....	....	....	....	....	....	3	1	1	2	0	....	....	....	....
1998-99	**Florida**	**NHL**	**5**	**0**	**1**	**1**	**0**	**0**	**0**	**0**	**5**	**0.0**	**2**	**0**	**0.0**	**22:29**	....	....	....	....	....	....	....	....	....
	Kentucky	AHL	45	2	8	10	33	....	....	....	....	....	....	....	....	....	10	0	1	1	4	....	....	....	....
99-2000	**Florida**	**NHL**	**13**	**1**	**5**	**6**	**2**	**1**	**0**	**1**	**16**	**6.3**	**–3**	**0**	**0.0**	**13:52**	....	....	....	....	....	....	....	....	....
	Houston Aeros	IHL	27	3	6	9	13	....	....	....	....	....	....	....	....	....	11	1	2	3	4	....	....	....	....
2000-01	**Minnesota**	**NHL**	**75**	**9**	**21**	**30**	**28**	**4**	**0**	**4**	**141**	**6.4**	**–6**	**1**	**0.0**	**24:16**	....	....	....	....	....	....	....	....	....
2001-02	**Minnesota**	**NHL**	**62**	**5**	**19**	**24**	**32**	**3**	**0**	**1**	**101**	**5.0**	**–6**	**0**	**0.0**	**25:30**	....	....	....	....	....	....	....	....	....
2002-03	**Minnesota**	**NHL**	**78**	**8**	**21**	**29**	**29**	**4**	**2**	**1**	**129**	**6.2**	**0**	**1**	**0.0**	**23:56**	**18**	**3**	**5**	**8**	**24**	**3**	**0**	**0**	**26:46**
	NHL Totals		**233**	**23**	**67**	**90**	**91**	**12**	**2**	**7**	**392**	**5.9**		**2**	**0.0**	**23:52**	**18**	**3**	**5**	**8**	**24**	**3**	**0**	**0**	**26:46**

Traded to **Calgary** by **Florida** for Rocky Thompson, March 16, 2000. Selected by **Minnesota** from **Calgary** in Expansion Draft, June 23, 2000.

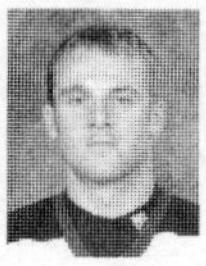

KUBINA, Pavel

(koo-BEE-nuh, PAH-vehl) **T.B.**

Defense. Shoots right. 6'4", 230 lbs. Born, Celadna, Czech., April 15, 1977. Tampa Bay's 6th choice, 179th overall, in 1996 Entry Draft.

1993-94	HC Vitkovice Jr.	Czech-Jr.	35	4	3	7	....	....	....	....	....	....	....	....	....	....	....	....	....	....	....	....	....	....	....
	HC Vitkovice	Czech	1	0	0	0	....	....	....	....	....	....	....	....	....	....	....	....	....	....	....	....	....	....	....
1994-95	HC Vitkovice Jr.	Czech-Jr.	20	6	10	16	....	....	....	....	....	....	....	....	....	....	....	....	....	....	....	....	....	....	....
	HC Vitkovice	Czech	8	2	0	2	10	....	....	....	....	....	....	....	....	....	4	0	0	0	0	....	....	....	....
1995-96	HC Vitkovice Jr.	Czech-Jr.	16	5	10	15	....	....	....	....	....	....	....	....	....	....	....	....	....	....	....	....	....	....	....
	HC Vitkovice	Czech	33	3	4	7	32	....	....	....	....	....	....	....	....	....	4	0	0	0	0	....	....	....	....
1996-97	HC Vitkovice	Czech	1	0	0	0	0	....	....	....	....	....	....	....	....	....	....	....	....	....	....	....	....	....	....
	Moose Jaw	WHL	61	12	32	44	116	....	....	....	....	....	....	....	....	....	11	2	5	7	27	....	....	....	....
1997-98	**Tampa Bay**	**NHL**	**10**	**1**	**2**	**3**	**22**	**0**	**0**	**0**	**8**	**12.5**	**–1**	....	....	....	....	....	....	....	....	....	....	....	....
	Adirondack	AHL	55	4	8	12	86	....	....	....	....	....	....	....	....	....	1	1	0	1	14	....	....	....	....
1998-99	**Tampa Bay**	**NHL**	**68**	**9**	**12**	**21**	**80**	**3**	**1**	**1**	**119**	**7.6**	**–33**	**2**	**0.0**	**22:47**	....	....	....	....	....	....	....	....	....
	Cleveland	IHL	6	2	2	4	16	....	....	....	....	....	....	....	....	....	....	....	....	....	....	....	....	....	....
99-2000	**Tampa Bay**	**NHL**	**69**	**8**	**18**	**26**	**93**	**6**	**0**	**3**	**128**	**6.3**	**–19**	**0**	**0.0**	**22:32**	....	....	....	....	....	....	....	....	....
2000-01	**Tampa Bay**	**NHL**	**70**	**11**	**19**	**30**	**103**	**6**	**1**	**1**	**128**	**8.6**	**–14**	**2**	**0.0**	**24:06**	....	....	....	....	....	....	....	....	....
2001-02	**Tampa Bay**	**NHL**	**82**	**11**	**23**	**34**	**106**	**5**	**2**	**3**	**189**	**5.8**	**–22**	**1**	**100.0**	**23:39**	....	....	....	....	....	....	....	....	....
	Czech Republic	Olympics	4	0	1	1	0	....	....	....	....	....	....	....	....	....	....	....	....	....	....	....	....	....	....
2002-03	**Tampa Bay**	**NHL**	**75**	**3**	**19**	**22**	**78**	**0**	**0**	**0**	**139**	**2.2**	**–7**	**1**	**0.0**	**21:24**	**11**	**0**	**0**	**0**	**12**	**0**	**0**	**0**	**24:52**
	NHL Totals		**374**	**43**	**93**	**136**	**482**	**20**	**4**	**8**	**711**	**6.0**		**6**	**16.7**	**22:54**	**11**	**0**	**0**	**0**	**12**	**0**	**0**	**0**	**24:52**

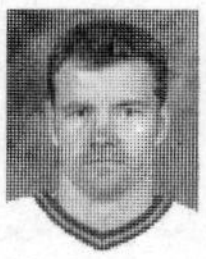

KUCERA, Frantisek

(koo-CHAIR-uh, FRAN-tih-sehk)

Defense. Shoots right. 6'2", 205 lbs. Born, Prague, Czech., February 3, 1968. Chicago's 3rd choice, 77th overall, in 1986 Entry Draft.

1985-86	Sparta CKD Praha	Czech	15	0	0	0	....	....	....	....	....	....	....	....	....	....	....	....	....	....	....	....	....	....	....
1986-87	Sparta CKD Praha	Czech	40	5	2	7	14	....	....	....	....	....	....	....	....	....	....	....	....	....	....	....	....	....	....
1987-88	Sparta CKD Praha	Czech	46	7	2	9	30	....	....	....	....	....	....	....	....	....	....	....	....	....	....	....	....	....	....
1988-89	Dukla Jihlava	Czech	45	10	9	19	28	....	....	....	....	....	....	....	....	....	....	....	....	....	....	....	....	....	....
1989-90	Dukla Jihlava	Czech	42	8	10	18	....	....	....	....	....	....	....	....	....	....	1	1	0	1	....	....	....	....	....
1990-91	**Chicago**	**NHL**	**40**	**2**	**12**	**14**	**32**	**1**	**0**	**0**	**65**	**3.1**	**3**	....	....	....	....	....	....	....	....	....	....	....	....
	Indianapolis Ice	IHL	35	8	19	27	23	....	....	....	....	....	....	....	....	....	7	0	1	1	15	....	....	....	....
1991-92	**Chicago**	**NHL**	**61**	**3**	**10**	**13**	**36**	**1**	**0**	**1**	**82**	**3.7**	**3**	....	....	....	**6**	**0**	**0**	**0**	**0**	**0**	**0**	**0**	....
	Indianapolis Ice	IHL	7	1	2	3	4	....	....	....	....	....	....	....	....	....	....	....	....	....	....	....	....	....	....
1992-93	**Chicago**	**NHL**	**71**	**5**	**14**	**19**	**59**	**1**	**0**	**1**	**117**	**4.3**	**7**	....	....	....	....	....	....	....	....	....	....	....	....
1993-94	**Chicago**	**NHL**	**60**	**4**	**13**	**17**	**34**	**2**	**0**	**0**	**90**	**4.4**	**9**	....	....	....	....	....	....	....	....	....	....	....	....
	Hartford	**NHL**	**16**	**1**	**3**	**4**	**14**	**1**	**0**	**0**	**32**	**3.1**	**–12**	....	....	....	....	....	....	....	....	....	....	....	....
1994-95	HC Sparta Praha	Czech	16	1	2	3	14	....	....	....	....	....	....	....	....	....	....	....	....	....	....	....	....	....	....
	Hartford	**NHL**	**48**	**3**	**17**	**20**	**30**	**0**	**0**	**1**	**73**	**4.1**	**3**	....	....	....	....	....	....	....	....	....	....	....	....
1995-96	**Hartford**	**NHL**	**30**	**2**	**6**	**8**	**10**	**0**	**0**	**1**	**43**	**4.7**	**–3**	....	....	....	....	....	....	....	....	....	....	....	....
	Vancouver	**NHL**	**24**	**1**	**0**	**1**	**10**	**0**	**0**	**0**	**34**	**2.9**	**5**	....	....	....	**6**	**0**	**1**	**1**	**0**	**0**	**0**	**0**	....
1996-97	**Vancouver**	**NHL**	**2**	**0**	**0**	**0**	**0**	**0**	**0**	**0**	**3**	**0.0**	**0**	....	....	....	....	....	....	....	....	....	....	....	....
	Syracuse Crunch	AHL	42	6	29	35	36	....	....	....	....	....	....	....	....	....	....	....	....	....	....	....	....	....	....
	Houston Aeros	IHL	12	0	3	3	20	....	....	....	....	....	....	....	....	....	....	....	....	....	....	....	....	....	....
	Philadelphia	**NHL**	**2**	**0**	**0**	**0**	**2**	**0**	**0**	**0**	**2**	**0.0**	**–2**	....	....	....	....	....	....	....	....	....	....	....	....
	Philadelphia	AHL	9	1	5	6	2	....	....	....	....	....	....	....	....	....	10	1	6	7	20	....	....	....	....
1997-98	HC Sparta Praha	Czech	43	8	12	20	49	....	....	....	....	....	....	....	....	....	9	3	1	4	*53	....	....	....	....
	HC Sparta Praha	EuroHL	4	0	1	1	2	....	....	....	....	....	....	....	....	....	....	....	....	....	....	....	....	....	....
	Czech Republic	Olympics	6	0	0	0	0	....	....	....	....	....	....	....	....	....	....	....	....	....	....	....	....	....	....
1998-99	HC Sparta Praha	Czech	42	3	12	15	92	....	....	....	....	....	....	....	....	....	8	0	2	2	....	....	....	....	....
	HC Sparta Praha	EuroHL	6	0	2	2	10	....	....	....	....	....	....	....	....	....	2	0	0	0	2	....	....	....	....
99-2000	HC Sparta Praha	Czech	51	7	26	33	40	....	....	....	....	....	....	....	....	....	9	1	9	10	4	....	....	....	....
	HC Sparta Praha	EuroHL	6	0	2	2	4	....	....	....	....	....	....	....	....	....	4	0	1	1	2	....	....	....	....
2000-01	**Columbus**	**NHL**	**48**	**2**	**5**	**7**	**12**	**0**	**0**	**0**	**51**	**3.9**	**–5**	**0**	**0.0**	**17:42**	....	....	....	....	....	....	....	....	....
	Pittsburgh	**NHL**	**7**	**0**	**2**	**2**	**0**	**0**	**0**	**0**	**9**	**0.0**	**–2**	**0**	**0.0**	**16:28**	....	....	....	....	....	....	....	....	....
2001-02	HC Sparta Praha	Czech	10	2	2	4	2	....	....	....	....	....	....	....	....	....	....	....	....	....	....	....	....	....	....
	Washington	**NHL**	**56**	**1**	**13**	**14**	**12**	**0**	**0**	**0**	**67**	**1.5**	**7**	**0**	**0.0**	**20:39**	....	....	....	....	....	....	....	....	....
2002-03	HC Slavia Praha	Czech	44	4	15	19	26	....	....	....	....	....	....	....	....	....	6	0	1	1	0	....	....	....	....
	NHL Totals		**465**	**24**	**95**	**119**	**251**	**6**	**0**	**4**	**668**	**3.6**		**0**	**0.0**	**19:07**	**12**	**0**	**1**	**1**	**0**	**0**	**0**	**0**	....

Traded to **Hartford** by **Chicago** with Jocelyn Lemieux for Gary Suter, Randy Cunneyworth and Hartford's 3rd round choice (later traded to Vancouver – Vancouver selected Larry Courville) in 1995 Entry Draft, March 11, 1994. Traded to **Vancouver** by **Hartford** with Jim Dowd and Hartford's 2nd round choice (Ryan Bonni) in 1997 Entry Draft for Jeff Brown and Vancouver's 3rd round choice (later traded to Calgary – Calgary selected Paul Manning) in 1998 Entry Draft, December 19, 1995. Traded to **Philadelphia** by **Vancouver** for future considerations, March 18, 1997. Signed as a free agent by **Columbus**, July 7, 2000. Traded to **Pittsburgh** by **Columbus** for Pittsburgh's 6th round choice (Scott Horvath) in 2001 Entry Draft, March 13, 2001. Traded to **Washington** by **Pittsburgh** with Jaromir Jagr for Kris Beech, Michal Sivek, Ross Lupaschuk and future considerations, July 11, 2001. Signed as a free agent by **HC Slavia Praha** (Czech), June 11, 2002.

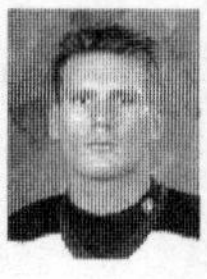

KUDROC, Kristian

(KOO-drawch, KRIHS-tan) **FLA.**

Defense. Shoots right. 6'7", 255 lbs. Born, Michalovce, Czech., May 21, 1981. NY Islanders' 4th choice, 28th overall, in 1999 Entry Draft.

1997-98	Michalovce Jr.	Slovak-Jr.	47	7	4	11	66	....	....	....	....	....	....	....	....	....	....	....	....	....	....	....	....	....	....
	Michalovce	Slovak-2	4	0	0	0	0	....	....	....	....	....	....	....	....	....	....	....	....	....	....	....	....	....	....
1998-99	Michalovce	Slovak-2	17	0	3	3	12	....	....	....	....	....	....	....	....	....	....	....	....	....	....	....	....	....	....
99-2000	Quebec Remparts	QMJHL	57	9	22	31	172	....	....	....	....	....	....	....	....	....	11	2	5	7	29	....	....	....	....
2000-01	**Tampa Bay**	**NHL**	**22**	**2**	**2**	**4**	**36**	**0**	**0**	**1**	**12**	**16.7**	**0**	**0**	**0.0**	**9:09**	....	....	....	....	....	....	....	....	....
	Detroit Vipers	IHL	44	4	3	7	80	....	....	....	....	....	....	....	....	....	....	....	....	....	....	....	....	....	....
2001-02	**Tampa Bay**	**NHL**	**2**	**0**	**0**	**0**	**0**	**0**	**0**	**0**	**0**	**0.0**	**0**	**0**	**0.0**	**7:49**	....	....	....	....	....	....	....	....	....
	Springfield	AHL	55	0	8	8	126	....	....	....	....	....	....	....	....	....	....	....	....	....	....	....	....	....	....
	Philadelphia	AHL	10	0	3	3	14	....	....	....	....	....	....	....	....	....	5	1	1	2	21	....	....	....	....
2002-03	Springfield	AHL	35	0	4	4	58	....	....	....	....	....	....	....	....	....	....	....	....	....	....	....	....	....	....
	NHL Totals		**24**	**2**	**2**	**4**	**36**	**0**	**0**	**1**	**12**	**16.7**		**0**	**0.0**	**9:02**									

Traded to **Tampa Bay** by **NY Islanders** with Kevin Weekes and NY Islanders' 2nd round choice (later traded to Phoenix – Phoenix selected Matthew Spiller) in 2001 Entry Draft for Tampa Bay's 1st round choice (Raffi Torres) in 2000 Entry Draft, Calgary's 4th round choice (previously acquired, NY Islanders selected Vladimir Gorbunov) in 2000 Entry Draft and NY Islanders' 7th round choice (previously acquired, NY Islanders selected Ryan Caldwell) in 2000 Entry Draft, June 24, 2000. • Missed majority of 2002-03 season recovering from head injury suffered in game vs. Providence (AHL), October 2, 2002. Signed as a free agent by **Florida**, July 3, 2003.

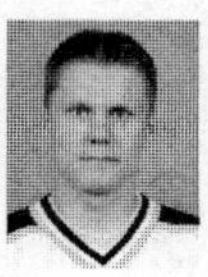

KULTANEN, Jarno

(kuhl-TAH-nuhn, YAR-noh) **BOS.**

Defense. Shoots left. 6'2", 198 lbs. Born, Luumaki, Finland, January 8, 1973. Boston's 8th choice, 174th overall, in 2000 Entry Draft.

1991-92	KooKoo Jr.	Finn-Jr.	22	7	17	24	28	....	....	....	....	....	....	....	....	....	....	....	....	....	....	....	....	....	....
	KooKoo Kouvola	Finland-2	1	0	0	0	0	....	....	....	....	....	....	....	....	....	....	....	....	....	....	....	....	....	....
1992-93	KooKoo Jr.	Finn-Jr.	11	6	5	11	8	....	....	....	....	....	....	....	....	....	....	....	....	....	....	....	....	....	....
	KooKoo Kouvola	Finland-2	27	1	1	2	33	....	....	....	....	....	....	....	....	....	....	....	....	....	....	....	....	....	....
	Centers	Finland-2	1	1	0	1	0	....	....	....	....	....	....	....	....	....	....	....	....	....	....	....	....	....	....

			Regular Season														Playoffs								
Season	Club	League	GP	G	A	Pts	PIM	PP	SH	GW	S	%	+/-	TF	F%	Min	GP	G	A	Pts	PIM	PP	SH	GW	Min
1993-94	KooKoo Jr.	Finn-Jr.	3	1	0	1	2	....	....	....	....	....	....	....	....	....	....	....	....	....	....	....	....	....	....
	KooKoo Kouvola	Finland-2	45	7	10	17	42	....	....	....	....	....	....	....	....	....	....	....	....	....	....	....	....	....	....
1994-95	KalPa Kuopio	Finland	47	5	12	17	26	....	....	....	....	....	....	....	....	....	3	0	0	0	8	....	....	....	....
1995-96	KalPa Kuopio	Finland	49	4	10	14	42	....	....	....	....	....	....	....	....	....	....	....	....	....	....	....	....	....	....
1996-97	HIFK Helsinki	Finland	24	1	3	4	6	....	....	....	....	....	....	....	....	....	....	....	....	....	....	....	....	....	....
1997-98	HIFK Helsinki	Finland	25	0	1	1	20	....	....	....	....	....	....	....	....	....	8	0	1	1	2	....	....	....	....
1998-99	HIFK Helsinki	Finland	51	6	6	12	53	....	....	....	....	....	....	....	....	....	10	1	0	1	27	....	....	....	....
	HIFK Helsinki	EuroHL	5	1	0	1	4	....	....	....	....	....	....	....	....	....	4	0	1	1	2	....	....	....	....
99-2000	HIFK Helsinki	Finland	46	6	8	14	51	....	....	....	....	....	....	....	....	....	9	0	0	0	6	....	....	....	....
	HIFK Helsinki	EuroHL	5	2	2	4	31	....	....	....	....	....	....	....	....	....	2	0	0	0	2	....	....	....	....
2000-01	**Boston**	**NHL**	**62**	**2**	**8**	**10**	**26**	**0**	**0**	**1**	**76**	**2.6**	**–3**	**0**	**0.0**	**19:29**	....	....	....	....	....	....	....	....	....
2001-02	**Boston**	**NHL**	**38**	**0**	**3**	**3**	**33**	**0**	**0**	**0**	**31**	**0.0**	**–1**	**0**	**0.0**	**12:58**	....	....	....	....	....	....	....	....	....
2002-03	**Boston**	**NHL**	**2**	**0**	**0**	**0**	**0**	**0**	**0**	**0**	**3**	**0.0**	**1**	**0**	**0.0**	**10:16**	....	....	....	....	....	....	....	....	....
	Providence Bruins	AHL	59	9	25	34	35	....	....	....	....	....	....	....	....	....	4	0	0	0	6	....	....	....	....
	NHL Totals		**102**	**2**	**11**	**13**	**59**	**0**	**0**	**1**	**110**	**1.8**		**0**	**0.0**	**16:52**	....	....	....	....	....	....	....	....	....

• Missed majority of 2001-02 season recovering from knee injury suffered in game vs. Minnesota, October 8, 2001.

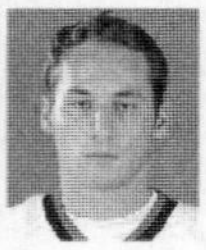

KURKA, Tomas (KUHR-kuh, TAW-mahsh) CAR.

Left wing. Shoots left. 5'11", 190 lbs. Born, Most, Czech., December 14, 1981. Carolina's 1st choice, 32nd overall, in 2000 Entry Draft.

Season	Club	League	GP	G	A	Pts	PIM	PP	SH	GW	S	%	+/-	TF	F%	Min	GP	G	A	Pts	PIM	PP	SH	GW	Min
1996-97	Litvinov Jr.	Czech-Jr.	38	25	20	45	20	....	....	....	....	....	....	....	....	....	....	....	....	....	....	....	....	....	....
1997-98	Litvinov Jr.	Czech-Jr.	44	38	23	61	90	....	....	....	....	....	....	....	....	....	....	....	....	....	....	....	....	....	....
1998-99	Litvinov Jr.	Czech-Jr.	42	23	16	39	47	....	....	....	....	....	....	....	....	....	....	....	....	....	....	....	....	....	....
	Litvinov	Czech	6	0	0	0	0	....	....	....	....	....	....	....	....	....	....	....	....	....	....	....	....	....	....
99-2000	Plymouth Whalers	OHL	64	36	28	64	37	....	....	....	....	....	....	....	....	....	17	7	6	13	6	....	....	....	....
2000-01	Plymouth Whalers	OHL	47	15	29	44	20	....	....	....	....	....	....	....	....	....	16	8	13	21	13	....	....	....	....
2001-02	Lowell	AHL	71	13	15	28	24	....	....	....	....	....	....	....	....	....	5	1	1	2	2	....	....	....	....
2002-03	**Carolina**	**NHL**	**14**	**3**	**2**	**5**	**2**	**0**	**0**	**0**	**22**	**13.6**	**1**	**4**	**50.0**	**14:59**	....	....	....	....	....	....	....	....	....
	Lowell	AHL	61	17	12	29	10	....	....	....	....	....	....	....	....	....	....	....	....	....	....	....	....	....	....
	NHL Totals		**14**	**3**	**2**	**5**	**2**	**0**	**0**	**0**	**22**	**13.6**		**4**	**50.0**	**14:59**	....	....	....	....	....	....	....	....	....

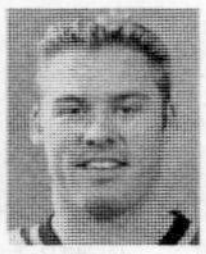

KURTZ, Justin (KUHRTZ, JUHS-tihn)

Defense. Shoots left. 6', 188 lbs. Born, Winnipeg, Man., January 14, 1977. Winnipeg's 5th choice, 84th overall, in 1995 Entry Draft.

Season	Club	League	GP	G	A	Pts	PIM	PP	SH	GW	S	%	+/-	TF	F%	Min	GP	G	A	Pts	PIM	PP	SH	GW	Min
1993-94	Brandon	WHL	63	3	13	16	37	....	....	....	....	....	....	....	....	....	14	1	3	4	24	....	....	....	....
1994-95	Brandon	WHL	65	8	34	42	75	....	....	....	....	....	....	....	....	....	18	2	2	4	26	....	....	....	....
1995-96	Brandon	WHL	53	19	55	74	107	....	....	....	....	....	....	....	....	....	18	4	6	10	37	....	....	....	....
1996-97	Brandon	WHL	59	24	44	68	85	....	....	....	....	....	....	....	....	....	6	3	2	5	4	....	....	....	....
1997-98	Las Vegas	IHL	63	11	11	22	62	....	....	....	....	....	....	....	....	....	....	....	....	....	....	....	....	....	....
	Saint John Flames	AHL	4	0	0	0	6	....	....	....	....	....	....	....	....	....	6	0	0	0	0	....	....	....	....
1998-99	Louisiana	ECHL	6	1	4	5	6	....	....	....	....	....	....	....	....	....	....	....	....	....	....	....	....	....	....
	Manitoba Moose	IHL	38	4	6	10	40	....	....	....	....	....	....	....	....	....	5	0	0	0	4	....	....	....	....
99-2000	Manitoba Moose	IHL	66	3	15	18	94	....	....	....	....	....	....	....	....	....	2	0	0	0	0	....	....	....	....
2000-01	Manitoba Moose	IHL	69	8	22	30	62	....	....	....	....	....	....	....	....	....	13	2	3	5	12	....	....	....	....
2001-02	**Vancouver**	**NHL**	**27**	**3**	**5**	**8**	**14**	**2**	**0**	**0**	**30**	**10.0**	**–4**	**0**	**0.0**	**15:58**	....	....	....	....	....	....	....	....	....
	Manitoba Moose	AHL	52	10	29	39	64	....	....	....	....	....	....	....	....	....	7	0	4	4	4	....	....	....	....
2002-03	Manitoba Moose	AHL	71	11	29	40	65	....	....	....	....	....	....	....	....	....	14	3	4	7	17	....	....	....	....
	NHL Totals		**27**	**3**	**5**	**8**	**14**	**2**	**0**	**0**	**30**	**10.0**		**0**	**0.0**	**15:58**	....	....	....	....	....	....	....	....	....

WHL East Second All-Star Team (1996)

Signed as a free agent by **Vancouver**, October 15, 2001.

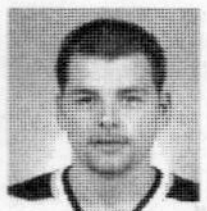

KUTLAK, Zdenek (KUHT-lak, zuh-DEHN-ehk) BOS.

Defense. Shoots left. 6'3", 221 lbs. Born, Budejovice, Czech., February 13, 1980. Boston's 10th choice, 237th overall, in 2000 Entry Draft.

Season	Club	League	GP	G	A	Pts	PIM	PP	SH	GW	S	%	+/-	TF	F%	Min	GP	G	A	Pts	PIM	PP	SH	GW	Min
1996-97	C. Budejovice Jr.	Czech-Jr.	45	8	11	19	20	....	....	....	....	....	....	....	....	....	....	....	....	....	....	....	....	....	....
1997-98	C. Budejovice Jr.	Czech-Jr.	43	1	6	7	30	....	....	....	....	....	....	....	....	....	....	....	....	....	....	....	....	....	....
1998-99	C. Budejovice Jr.	Czech-Jr.	31	6	14	20	20	....	....	....	....	....	....	....	....	....	....	....	....	....	....	....	....	....	....
	Ceske Budejovice	Czech	22	1	3	4	4	....	....	....	....	....	....	....	....	....	3	0	0	0	0	....	....	....	....
99-2000	C. Budejovice Jr.	Czech-Jr.	8	4	2	6	26	....	....	....	....	....	....	....	....	....	....	....	....	....	....	....	....	....	....
	JindrichuvHradec	Czech-3	4	1	1	2	0	....	....	....	....	....	....	....	....	....	....	....	....	....	....	....	....	....	....
	IHC Pisek	Czech-2	3	1	0	1	0	....	....	....	....	....	....	....	....	....	2	0	0	0	2	....	....	....	....
	Ceske Budejovice	Czech	28	1	0	1	2	....	....	....	....	....	....	....	....	....	1	0	0	0	0	....	....	....	....
2000-01	**Boston**	**NHL**	**10**	**0**	**2**	**2**	**4**	**0**	**0**	**0**	**7**	**0.0**	**–3**	**0**	**0.0**	**16:05**	....	....	....	....	....	....	....	....	....
	Providence Bruins	AHL	62	4	5	9	16	....	....	....	....	....	....	....	....	....	....	....	....	....	....	....	....	....	....
2001-02	Providence Bruins	AHL	80	5	15	20	73	....	....	....	....	....	....	....	....	....	2	0	0	0	0	....	....	....	....
2002-03	**Boston**	**NHL**	**4**	**1**	**0**	**1**	**0**	**0**	**0**	**0**	**1**	**100.0**	**0**	**0**	**0.0**	**5:16**	....	....	....	....	....	....	....	....	....
	Providence Bruins	AHL	68	4	12	16	52	....	....	....	....	....	....	....	....	....	4	1	0	1	2	....	....	....	....
	NHL Totals		**14**	**1**	**2**	**3**	**4**	**0**	**0**	**0**	**8**	**12.5**		**0**	**0.0**	**12:60**	....	....	....	....	....	....	....	....	....

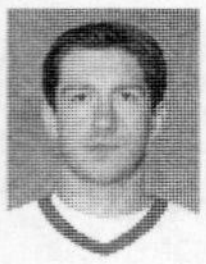

KUZNETSOV, Maxim (kooz-NEHT-zahv, MAX-ihm) L.A.

Defense. Shoots left. 6'5", 230 lbs. Born, Pavlodar, USSR, March 24, 1977. Detroit's 1st choice, 26th overall, in 1995 Entry Draft.

Season	Club	League	GP	G	A	Pts	PIM	PP	SH	GW	S	%	+/-	TF	F%	Min	GP	G	A	Pts	PIM	PP	SH	GW	Min
1994-95	Dynamo Moscow	CIS	11	0	0	0	8	....	....	....	....	....	....	....	....	....	....	....	....	....	....	....	....	....	....
1995-96	Dynamo Moscow	CIS	9	1	1	2	22	....	....	....	....	....	....	....	....	....	4	0	0	0	0	....	....	....	....
1996-97	Dynamo Moscow	Russia	23	0	2	2	16	....	....	....	....	....	....	....	....	....	....	....	....	....	....	....	....	....	....
	Adirondack	AHL	2	0	1	1	6	....	....	....	....	....	....	....	....	....	2	0	0	0	0	....	....	....	....
1997-98	Adirondack	AHL	51	5	5	10	43	....	....	....	....	....	....	....	....	....	3	0	1	1	4	....	....	....	....
1998-99	Adirondack	AHL	60	0	4	4	30	....	....	....	....	....	....	....	....	....	3	0	0	0	0	....	....	....	....
99-2000	Cincinnati	AHL	47	2	9	11	36	....	....	....	....	....	....	....	....	....	....	....	....	....	....	....	....	....	....
2000-01	**Detroit**	**NHL**	**25**	**1**	**2**	**3**	**23**	**0**	**0**	**0**	**17**	**5.9**	**–1**	**1**	**0.0**	**9:28**	....	....	....	....	....	....	....	....	....
2001-02	**Detroit**	**NHL**	**39**	**1**	**2**	**3**	**40**	**0**	**0**	**0**	**27**	**3.7**	**0**	**0**	**0.0**	**11:51**	....	....	....	....	....	....	....	....	....
	Cincinnati	AHL	7	1	0	1	4	....	....	....	....	....	....	....	....	....	....	....	....	....	....	....	....	....	....
2002-03	**Detroit**	**NHL**	**53**	**0**	**3**	**3**	**54**	**0**	**0**	**0**	**32**	**0.0**	**0**	**1**	**100.0**	**13:10**	....	....	....	....	....	....	....	....	....
	Los Angeles	**NHL**	**3**	**0**	**0**	**0**	**0**	**0**	**0**	**0**	**1**	**0.0**	**1**	**0**	**0.0**	**16:37**	....	....	....	....	....	....	....	....	....
	NHL Totals		**120**	**2**	**7**	**9**	**117**	**0**	**0**	**0**	**77**	**2.6**		**2**	**50.0**	**12:03**	....	....	....	....	....	....	....	....	....

• Missed majority of 2000-01 season recovering from knee injury suffered in game vs. Vancouver, November 24, 2000. Traded to **Los Angeles** by **Detroit** with Sean Avery, Detroit's 1st round choice (Jeff Tambellini) in 2003 Entry Draft and Detroit's 2nd round choice in 2004 Entry Draft for Mathieu Schneider, March 11, 2003.

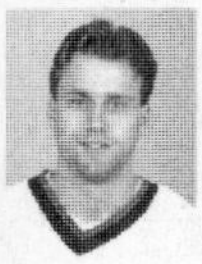

KUZNIK, Greg (kooz-NIHK, GREHG)

Defense. Shoots left. 6', 185 lbs. Born, Prince George, B.C., June 12, 1978. Hartford's 7th choice, 171st overall, in 1996 Entry Draft.

Season	Club	League	GP	G	A	Pts	PIM	PP	SH	GW	S	%	+/-	TF	F%	Min	GP	G	A	Pts	PIM	PP	SH	GW	Min
1994-95	Royal City	BCJHL	45	2	13	15	83	....	....	....	....	....	....	....	....	....	....	....	....	....	....	....	....	....	....
1995-96	Seattle	WHL	70	2	13	15	149	....	....	....	....	....	....	....	....	....	5	0	0	0	6	....	....	....	....
1996-97	Seattle	WHL	70	4	9	13	161	....	....	....	....	....	....	....	....	....	14	0	2	2	26	....	....	....	....
1997-98	Seattle	WHL	72	5	12	17	197	....	....	....	....	....	....	....	....	....	5	0	0	0	4	....	....	....	....
1998-99	New Haven	AHL	27	1	0	1	33	....	....	....	....	....	....	....	....	....	....	....	....	....	....	....	....	....	....
	Florida Everblades	ECHL	50	6	8	14	110	....	....	....	....	....	....	....	....	....	5	1	0	1	0	....	....	....	....
99-2000	Cincinnati	IHL	46	0	3	3	53	....	....	....	....	....	....	....	....	....	4	0	0	0	4	....	....	....	....
	Dayton Bombers	ECHL	7	1	0	1	16	....	....	....	....	....	....	....	....	....	....	....	....	....	....	....	....	....	....
	Florida Everblades	ECHL	9	1	4	5	6	....	....	....	....	....	....	....	....	....	3	0	0	0	2	....	....	....	....
2000-01	**Carolina**	**NHL**	**1**	**0**	**0**	**0**	**0**	**0**	**0**	**0**	**0**	**0.0**	**0**	**0**	**0.0**	**7:32**	....	....	....	....	....	....	....	....	....
	Cincinnati	IHL	73	0	7	7	72	....	....	....	....	....	....	....	....	....	5	0	1	1	4	....	....	....	....
2001-02	Lowell	AHL	58	3	8	11	40	....	....	....	....	....	....	....	....	....	5	0	0	0	8	....	....	....	....
2002-03	Lowell	AHL	61	2	3	5	74	....	....	....	....	....	....	....	....	....	....	....	....	....	....	....	....	....	....
	NHL Totals		**1**	**0**	**0**	**0**	**0**	**0**	**0**	**0**	**0**	**0.0**		**0**	**0.0**	**7:32**	....	....	....	....	....	....	....	....	....

Transferred to **Carolina** after **Hartford** franchise relocated, June 25, 1997.

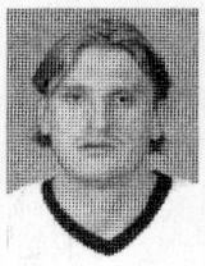

KVASHA, Oleg

(kuh-VAH-shah, OH-lehg) **NYI**

Left wing/Center. Shoots right. 6'5", 230 lbs. Born, Moscow, USSR, July 26, 1978. Florida's 3rd choice, 65th overall, in 1996 Entry Draft.

			Regular Season														Playoffs								
Season	Club	League	GP	G	A	Pts	PIM	PP	SH	GW	S	%	+/-	TF	F%	Min	GP	G	A	Pts	PIM	PP	SH	GW	Min
1995-96	CSKA Moscow	CIS	38	2	3	5	14	....	....	....	....	....	....	....	....	....	2	0	0	0	0	....	....	....	....
1996-97	HC CSKA	Russia	44	20	22	42	115	....	....	....	....	....	....	....	....	....	....	....	....	....	....	....	....	....	....
1997-98	New Haven	AHL	57	13	16	29	46	....	....	....	....	....	....	....	....	....	3	2	1	3	0	....	....	....	....
1998-99	**Florida**	**NHL**	**68**	**12**	**13**	**25**	**45**	**4**	**0**	**2**	**138**	**8.7**	**5**	**373**	**28.4**	**12:48**	....	....	....	....	....	....	....	....	....
99-2000	**Florida**	**NHL**	**78**	**5**	**20**	**25**	**34**	**2**	**0**	**0**	**110**	**4.5**	**3**	**553**	**34.9**	**11:24**	**4**	**0**	**0**	**0**	**0**	**0**	**0**	**0**	**10:17**
2000-01	**NY Islanders**	**NHL**	**62**	**11**	**9**	**20**	**46**	**0**	**0**	**0**	**118**	**9.3**	**–15**	**627**	**43.7**	**14:56**	....	....	....	....	....	....	....	....	....
2001-02	**NY Islanders**	**NHL**	**71**	**13**	**25**	**38**	**80**	**2**	**0**	**3**	**119**	**10.9**	**–4**	**456**	**47.4**	**14:12**	**7**	**0**	**1**	**1**	**6**	**0**	**0**	**0**	**15:17**
	Russia	Olympics	5	0	0	0	0	....	....	....	....	....	....	....	....	....	....	....	....	....	....	....	....	....	....
2002-03	**NY Islanders**	**NHL**	**69**	**12**	**14**	**26**	**44**	**0**	**1**	**2**	**121**	**9.9**	**4**	**256**	**43.0**	**13:03**	**5**	**0**	**1**	**1**	**2**	**0**	**0**	**0**	**16:26**
	NHL Totals		**348**	**53**	**81**	**134**	**249**	**8**	**1**	**7**	**606**	**8.7**		**2265**	**39.7**	**13:12**	**16**	**0**	**2**	**2**	**8**	**0**	**0**	**0**	**14:24**

Traded to **NY Islanders** by **Florida** with Mark Parrish for Roberto Luongo and Olli Jokinen, June 24, 2000.

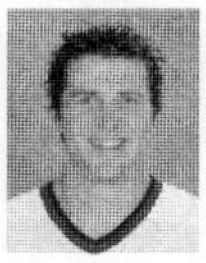

KWIATKOWSKI, Joel

(KWEE-at-KOW-skee, JOHL)

Defense. Shoots left. 6'2", 210 lbs. Born, Kindersley, Sask., March 22, 1977. Dallas' 7th choice, 194th overall, in 1996 Entry Draft.

Season	Club	League	GP	G	A	Pts	PIM	PP	SH	GW	S	%	+/-	TF	F%	Min	GP	G	A	Pts	PIM	PP	SH	GW	Min
1994-95	Tacoma Rockets	WHL	70	4	13	17	66	....	....	....	....	....	....	....	....	....	4	0	0	0	2	....	....	....	....
	North Battleford	SJHL	51	3	14	17	89	....	....	....	....	....	....	....	....	....	....	....	....	....	....	....	....	....	....
1995-96	Kelowna Rockets	WHL	40	6	17	23	85	....	....	....	....	....	....	....	....	....	....	....	....	....	....	....	....	....	....
	Prince George	WHL	32	6	11	17	48	....	....	....	....	....	....	....	....	....	....	....	....	....	....	....	....	....	....
1996-97	Prince George	WHL	72	15	37	52	94	....	....	....	....	....	....	....	....	....	15	4	2	6	24	....	....	....	....
1997-98	Prince George	WHL	62	21	43	64	65	....	....	....	....	....	....	....	....	....	11	3	6	9	6	....	....	....	....
1998-99	Cincinnati	AHL	80	12	21	33	48	....	....	....	....	....	....	....	....	....	3	2	0	2	0	....	....	....	....
99-2000	Cincinnati	AHL	70	4	22	26	28	....	....	....	....	....	....	....	....	....	....	....	....	....	....	....	....	....	....
2000-01	Grand Rapids	IHL	77	4	17	21	58	....	....	....	....	....	....	....	....	....	10	1	0	1	4	....	....	....	....
	Ottawa	**NHL**	**4**	**1**	**0**	**1**	**0**	**0**	**0**	**0**	**2**	**50.0**	**1**	**0**	**0.0**	**12:04**	....	....	....	....	....	....	....	....	....
2001-02	**Ottawa**	**NHL**	**11**	**0**	**0**	**0**	**12**	**0**	**0**	**0**	**9**	**0.0**	**5**	**0**	**0.0**	**13:41**	....	....	....	....	....	....	....	....	....
	Grand Rapids	AHL	65	8	21	29	94	....	....	....	....	....	....	....	....	....	5	1	2	3	12	....	....	....	....
2002-03	**Ottawa**	**NHL**	**20**	**0**	**2**	**2**	**6**	**0**	**0**	**0**	**28**	**0.0**	**2**	**2**	**0.0**	**12:13**	....	....	....	....	....	....	....	....	....
	Binghamton	AHL	1	0	0	0	2	....	....	....	....	....	....	....	....	....	....	....	....	....	....	....	....	....	....
	Washington	**NHL**	**34**	**0**	**3**	**3**	**12**	**0**	**0**	**0**	**28**	**0.0**	**1**	**2**	**0.0**	**15:32**	**6**	**0**	**0**	**0**	**2**	**0**	**0**	**0**	**17:48**
	NHL Totals		**69**	**1**	**5**	**6**	**30**	**0**	**0**	**0**	**67**	**1.5**		**4**	**0.0**	**14:05**	**6**	**0**	**0**	**0**	**2**	**0**	**0**	**0**	**17:48**

WHL West Second All-Star Team (1997) • WHL West First All-Star Team (1998)

Signed as a free agent by **Anaheim**, June 18, 1998. Traded to **Ottawa** by **Anaheim** for Patrick Traverse, June 12, 2000. Traded to **Washington** by **Ottawa** for Washington's 9th round choice (later traded back to Washington – Washington selected Mark Olafson) in 2003 Entry Draft, January 15, 2003.

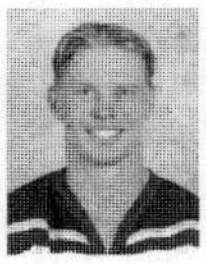

LAAKSONEN, Antti

(lah-AHK-soh-nehn, AHN-tee) **MIN.**

Left wing. Shoots left. 6', 180 lbs. Born, Tammela, Finland, October 3, 1973. Boston's 10th choice, 191st overall, in 1997 Entry Draft.

Season	Club	League	GP	G	A	Pts	PIM	PP	SH	GW	S	%	+/-	TF	F%	Min	GP	G	A	Pts	PIM	PP	SH	GW	Min
1991-92	FoPS Forssa Jr.	Finn-Jr.	24	19	23	42	22	....	....	....	....	....	....	....	....	....	....	....	....	....	....	....	....	....	....
	FoPS Forssa	Finland-2	41	16	15	31	8	....	....	....	....	....	....	....	....	....	....	....	....	....	....	....	....	....	....
1992-93	FoPS Forssa Jr.	Finn-Jr.	9	5	3	8	10	....	....	....	....	....	....	....	....	....	....	....	....	....	....	....	....	....	....
	FoPS Forssa	Finland-2	34	11	19	30	36	....	....	....	....	....	....	....	....	....	....	....	....	....	....	....	....	....	....
	HPK Jr.	Finn-Jr.	1	1	1	2	0	....	....	....	....	....	....	....	....	....	....	....	....	....	....	....	....	....	....
	HPK Hameenlinna	Finland	2	0	0	0	0	....	....	....	....	....	....	....	....	....	....	....	....	....	....	....	....	....	....
1993-94	U. of Denver	WCHA	36	12	9	21	38	....	....	....	....	....	....	....	....	....	....	....	....	....	....	....	....	....	....
1994-95	U. of Denver	WCHA	40	17	18	35	42	....	....	....	....	....	....	....	....	....	....	....	....	....	....	....	....	....	....
1995-96	U. of Denver	WCHA	39	25	28	53	71	....	....	....	....	....	....	....	....	....	....	....	....	....	....	....	....	....	....
1996-97	U. of Denver	WCHA	39	21	17	38	63	....	....	....	....	....	....	....	....	....	....	....	....	....	....	....	....	....	....
1997-98	Providence Bruins	AHL	38	3	2	5	14	....	....	....	....	....	....	....	....	....	....	....	....	....	....	....	....	....	....
	Charlotte	ECHL	15	4	3	7	12	....	....	....	....	....	....	....	....	....	6	0	3	3	0	....	....	....	....
1998-99	**Boston**	**NHL**	**11**	**1**	**2**	**3**	**2**	**0**	**0**	**0**	**8**	**12.5**	**–1**	**0**	**0.0**	**9:20**	....	....	....	....	....	....	....	....	....
	Providence Bruins	AHL	66	25	33	58	52	....	....	....	....	....	....	....	....	....	19	7	2	9	28	....	....	....	....
99-2000	**Boston**	**NHL**	**27**	**6**	**3**	**9**	**2**	**0**	**0**	**1**	**23**	**26.1**	**3**	**3**	**66.7**	**7:50**	....	....	....	....	....	....	....	....	....
	Providence Bruins	AHL	40	10	12	22	57	....	....	....	....	....	....	....	....	....	14	5	4	9	4	....	....	....	....
2000-01	**Minnesota**	**NHL**	**82**	**12**	**16**	**28**	**24**	**0**	**2**	**1**	**129**	**9.3**	**–7**	**15**	**26.7**	**16:27**	....	....	....	....	....	....	....	....	....
2001-02	**Minnesota**	**NHL**	**82**	**16**	**17**	**33**	**22**	**0**	**0**	**1**	**104**	**15.4**	**–5**	**19**	**42.1**	**16:20**	....	....	....	....	....	....	....	....	....
2002-03	**Minnesota**	**NHL**	**82**	**15**	**16**	**31**	**26**	**1**	**2**	**4**	**106**	**14.2**	**4**	**51**	**29.4**	**15:55**	**16**	**1**	**3**	**4**	**4**	**0**	**0**	**0**	**16:34**
	NHL Totals		**284**	**50**	**54**	**104**	**76**	**1**	**4**	**7**	**370**	**13.5**		**88**	**33.0**	**15:10**	**16**	**1**	**3**	**4**	**4**	**0**	**0**	**0**	**16:34**

WCHA Second All-Star Team (1996)

Signed as a free agent by **Minnesota**, July 14, 2000.

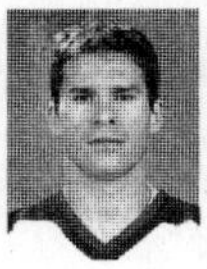

LACHANCE, Scott

(lah-CHANTS, SKAWT) **CBJ**

Defense. Shoots left. 6'1", 215 lbs. Born, Charlottesville, VA, October 22, 1972. NY Islanders' 1st choice, 4th overall, in 1991 Entry Draft.

Season	Club	League	GP	G	A	Pts	PIM	PP	SH	GW	S	%	+/-	TF	F%	Min	GP	G	A	Pts	PIM	PP	SH	GW	Min
1988-89	Springfield	NEJHL	36	8	28	36	20	....	....	....	....	....	....	....	....	....	....	....	....	....	....	....	....	....	....
1989-90	Springfield	NEJHL	34	25	41	66	62	....	....	....	....	....	....	....	....	....	....	....	....	....	....	....	....	....	....
1990-91	Boston University	H-East	31	5	19	24	48	....	....	....	....	....	....	....	....	....	....	....	....	....	....	....	....	....	....
1991-92	Team USA	Nat-Tm	36	1	10	11	34	....	....	....	....	....	....	....	....	....	....	....	....	....	....	....	....	....	....
	United States	Olympics	8	0	1	1	6	....	....	....	....	....	....	....	....	....	....	....	....	....	....	....	....	....	....
	NY Islanders	**NHL**	**17**	**1**	**4**	**5**	**9**	**0**	**0**	**0**	**20**	**5.0**	**13**	....	....	....	....	....	....	....	....	....	....	....	....
1992-93	**NY Islanders**	**NHL**	**75**	**7**	**17**	**24**	**67**	**0**	**1**	**2**	**62**	**11.3**	**–1**	....	....	....	....	....	....	....	....	....	....	....	....
1993-94	**NY Islanders**	**NHL**	**74**	**3**	**11**	**14**	**70**	**0**	**0**	**1**	**59**	**5.1**	**–5**	....	....	....	**3**	**0**	**0**	**0**	**0**	**0**	**0**	**0**	....
1994-95	**NY Islanders**	**NHL**	**26**	**6**	**7**	**13**	**26**	**3**	**0**	**0**	**56**	**10.7**	**2**	....	....	....	....	....	....	....	....	....	....	....	....
1995-96	**NY Islanders**	**NHL**	**55**	**3**	**10**	**13**	**54**	**1**	**0**	**0**	**81**	**3.7**	**–19**	....	....	....	....	....	....	....	....	....	....	....	....
1996-97	**NY Islanders**	**NHL**	**81**	**3**	**11**	**14**	**47**	**1**	**0**	**0**	**97**	**3.1**	**–7**	....	....	....	....	....	....	....	....	....	....	....	....
1997-98	**NY Islanders**	**NHL**	**63**	**2**	**11**	**13**	**45**	**1**	**0**	**0**	**62**	**3.2**	**–11**	....	....	....	....	....	....	....	....	....	....	....	....
1998-99	**NY Islanders**	**NHL**	**59**	**1**	**8**	**9**	**30**	**1**	**0**	**0**	**37**	**2.7**	**–19**	**0**	**0.0**	**21:34**	....	....	....	....	....	....	....	....	....
	Montreal	**NHL**	**17**	**1**	**1**	**2**	**11**	**0**	**0**	**0**	**22**	**4.5**	**–2**	**0**	**0.0**	**22:29**	....	....	....	....	....	....	....	....	....
99-2000	**Montreal**	**NHL**	**57**	**0**	**6**	**6**	**22**	**0**	**0**	**0**	**41**	**0.0**	**–4**	**0**	**0.0**	**17:47**	....	....	....	....	....	....	....	....	....
2000-01	**Vancouver**	**NHL**	**76**	**3**	**11**	**14**	**46**	**0**	**0**	**0**	**55**	**5.5**	**5**	**0**	**0.0**	**19:26**	**2**	**0**	**1**	**1**	**2**	**0**	**0**	**0**	**13:09**
2001-02	**Vancouver**	**NHL**	**81**	**1**	**10**	**11**	**50**	**0**	**0**	**0**	**48**	**2.1**	**15**	**2**	**100.0**	**20:02**	**6**	**1**	**1**	**2**	**4**	**0**	**0**	**1**	**20:33**
2002-03	**Columbus**	**NHL**	**61**	**0**	**1**	**1**	**46**	**0**	**0**	**0**	**35**	**0.0**	**–20**	**0**	**0.0**	**20:01**	....	....	....	....	....	....	....	....	....
	NHL Totals		**742**	**31**	**108**	**139**	**523**	**7**	**1**	**3**	**675**	**4.6**		**2**	**100.0**	**19:55**	**11**	**1**	**2**	**3**	**6**	**0**	**0**	**1**	**18:41**

Played in NHL All-Star Game (1997)

Traded to **Montreal** by **NY Islanders** for Montreal's 3rd round choice (Mattias Weinhandl) in 1999 Entry Draft, March 9, 1999. Signed as a free agent by **Vancouver**, August 13, 2000. Signed as a free agent by **Columbus**, July 4, 2002.

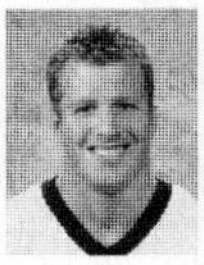

LaCOUTURE, Dan

(LA-koo-TUHR, DAN) **NYR**

Left wing. Shoots left. 6'2", 208 lbs. Born, Hyannis, MA, April 18, 1977. NY Islanders' 2nd choice, 29th overall, in 1996 Entry Draft.

Season	Club	League	GP	G	A	Pts	PIM	PP	SH	GW	S	%	+/-	TF	F%	Min	GP	G	A	Pts	PIM	PP	SH	GW	Min
1992-93	Natick Redmen	Hi-School	20	38	34	72	46	....	....	....	....	....	....	....	....	....	....	....	....	....	....	....	....	....	....
1993-94	Natick Redmen	Hi-School	21	52	49	101	58	....	....	....	....	....	....	....	....	....	....	....	....	....	....	....	....	....	....
1994-95	Springfield Jr. Pics	NEJHL	52	44	56	100	98	....	....	....	....	....	....	....	....	....	....	....	....	....	....	....	....	....	....
1995-96	Springfield Jr. Pics	NAJHL	41	36	41	77	87	....	....	....	....	....	....	....	....	....	13	12	13	25	23	....	....	....	....
1996-97	Boston University	H-East	31	13	12	25	18	....	....	....	....	....	....	....	....	....	....	....	....	....	....	....	....	....	....
1997-98	Hamilton	AHL	77	15	10	25	31	....	....	....	....	....	....	....	....	....	5	1	0	1	0	....	....	....	....
1998-99	**Edmonton**	**NHL**	**3**	**0**	**0**	**0**	**0**	**0**	**0**	**0**	**0**	**0.0**	**1**	**0**	**0.0**	**6:30**	....	....	....	....	....	....	....	....	....
	Hamilton	AHL	72	17	14	31	73	....	....	....	....	....	....	....	....	....	9	2	1	3	2	....	....	....	....
99-2000	**Edmonton**	**NHL**	**5**	**0**	**0**	**0**	**10**	**0**	**0**	**0**	**2**	**0.0**	**0**	**0**	**0.0**	**7:02**	**1**	**0**	**0**	**0**	**0**	**0**	**0**	**0**	**2:05**
	Hamilton	AHL	70	23	17	40	85	....	....	....	....	....	....	....	....	....	6	2	1	3	0	....	....	....	....
2000-01	**Edmonton**	**NHL**	**37**	**2**	**4**	**6**	**29**	**0**	**0**	**1**	**22**	**9.1**	**–2**	**5**	**20.0**	**7:06**	....	....	....	....	....	....	....	....	....
	Pittsburgh	**NHL**	**11**	**0**	**0**	**0**	**14**	**0**	**0**	**0**	**1**	**0.0**	**0**	**1**	**100.0**	**5:57**	**5**	**0**	**0**	**0**	**2**	**0**	**0**	**0**	**5:46**
2001-02	**Pittsburgh**	**NHL**	**82**	**6**	**11**	**17**	**71**	**0**	**1**	**0**	**77**	**7.8**	**–19**	**21**	**38.1**	**13:16**	....	....	....	....	....	....	....	....	....

			Regular Season														Playoffs								
Season	Club	League	GP	G	A	Pts	PIM	PP	SH	GW	S	%	+/-	TF	F%	Min	GP	G	A	Pts	PIM	PP	SH	GW	Min
2002-03	Pittsburgh	NHL	44	2	2	4	72	0	0	0	30	6.7	–8	5	80.0	9:13	....	....	....	....	....	....	....	....	....
	NY Rangers	NHL	24	1	4	5	0	0	0	0	17	5.9	4	1	0.0	10:18	....	....	....	....	....	....	....	....	....
	NHL Totals		206	11	21	32	196	0	1	1	149	7.4		33	42.4	10:19	6	0	0	0	2	0	0	0	5:09

Traded to **Edmonton** by **NY Islanders** for Mariusz Czerkawski, August 25, 1997. Traded to **Pittsburgh** by **Edmonton** for Sven Butenschon, March 13, 2001. Traded to **NY Rangers** by **Pittsburgh** with Mike Wilson, Alex Kovalev and Janne Laukkanen for Joel Bouchard, Richard Lintner, Rico Fata, Mikael Samuelsson and future considerations, February 10, 2003.

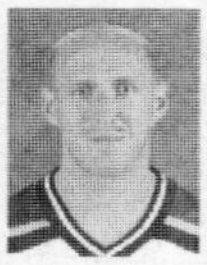

LAFLAMME, Christian

(lah-FLAM, KRIHS-tan) **ST.L.**

Defense. Shoots right. 6'1", 206 lbs. Born, St-Charles, Que., November 24, 1976. Chicago's 2nd choice, 45th overall, in 1995 Entry Draft.

Season	Club	League	GP	G	A	Pts	PIM	PP	SH	GW	S	%	+/-	TF	F%	Min	GP	G	A	Pts	PIM	PP	SH	GW	Min
1991-92	Ste-Foy	QAAA	42	5	27	32	100	....	....	....	....	....	....	....	....	....	8	1	2	3	14	....	....	....	....
1992-93	Verdun	QMJHL	69	2	17	19	85	....	....	....	....	....	....	....	....	....	3	0	2	2	6	....	....	....	....
1993-94	Verdun	QMJHL	72	4	34	38	85	....	....	....	....	....	....	....	....	....	4	0	3	3	4	....	....	....	....
1994-95	Beauport	QMJHL	67	6	41	47	82	....	....	....	....	....	....	....	....	....	8	1	4	5	6	....	....	....	....
1995-96	Beauport	QMJHL	41	13	23	36	63	....	....	....	....	....	....	....	....	....	20	7	17	24	32	....	....	....	....
1996-97	Chicago	NHL	4	0	1	1	2	0	0	0	3	0.0	3	....	....	....	....	....	....	....	....	....	....	....	....
	Indianapolis Ice	IHL	62	5	15	20	60	....	....	....	....	....	....	....	....	....	4	1	1	2	16	....	....	....	....
1997-98	Chicago	NHL	72	0	11	11	59	0	0	0	75	0.0	14	....	....	....	....	....	....	....	....	....	....	....	....
1998-99	Chicago	NHL	62	2	11	13	70	0	0	0	53	3.8	0	0	0.0	18:51	....	....	....	....	....	....	....	....	....
	Portland Pirates	AHL	2	0	1	1	2	....	....	....	....	....	....	....	....	....	....	....	....	....	....	....	....	....	....
	Edmonton	NHL	11	0	1	1	0	0	0	0	15	0.0	–3	0	0.0	16:33	4	0	1	1	2	0	0	0	21:51
99-2000	Edmonton	NHL	50	0	5	5	32	0	0	0	18	0.0	–4	5	40.0	13:40	....	....	....	....	....	....	....	....	....
	Montreal	NHL	15	0	2	2	8	0	0	0	6	0.0	–5	0	0.0	14:32	....	....	....	....	....	....	....	....	....
2000-01	Montreal	NHL	39	0	3	3	42	0	0	0	16	0.0	–11	1	0.0	12:04	....	....	....	....	....	....	....	....	....
2001-02	St. Louis	NHL	8	0	1	1	4	0	0	0	6	0.0	3	0	0.0	13:54	....	....	....	....	....	....	....	....	....
	Worcester IceCats	AHL	62	2	17	19	52	....	....	....	....	....	....	....	....	....	....	....	....	....	....	....	....	....	....
2002-03	St. Louis	NHL	47	0	9	9	45	0	0	0	44	0.0	1	0	0.0	15:10	5	0	0	0	4	0	0	0	12:28
	Worcester IceCats	AHL	8	0	4	4	6	....	....	....	....	....	....	....	....	....	....	....	....	....	....	....	....	....	....
	NHL Totals		308	2	44	46	262	0	0	0	236	0.8		6	33.3	15:17	9	0	1	1	6	0	0	0	16:38

QMJHL All-Rookie Team (1993) • QMJHL Second All-Star Team (1995)

Traded to **Edmonton** by **Chicago** with Daniel Cleary, Ethan Moreau and Chad Kilger for Boris Mironov, Dean McAmmond and Jonas Elofsson, March 20, 1999. Traded to **Montreal** by **Edmonton** with Matthieu Descoteaux for Igor Ulanov and Alain Nasreddine, March 9, 2000. • Missed majority of 2000-01 season recovering from groin injury suffered in game vs. Calgary, December 13, 2000. Signed as a free agent by **St. Louis**, August 21, 2001.

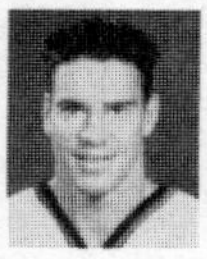

LANDRY, Eric

(LAN-dree, AIR-ihk)

Center. Shoots left. 5'10", 184 lbs. Born, Gatineau, Que., January 20, 1975.

Season	Club	League	GP	G	A	Pts	PIM	PP	SH	GW	S	%	+/-	TF	F%	Min	GP	G	A	Pts	PIM	PP	SH	GW	Min
1992-93	Abitibi Forestiers	QAAA	40	15	11	26	98	....	....	....	....	....	....	....	....	....	1	0	0	0	19	....	....	....	....
1993-94	St-Hyacinthe	QMJHL	69	42	34	76	128	....	....	....	....	....	....	....	....	....	7	4	2	6	13	....	....	....	....
1994-95	St-Hyacinthe	QMJHL	68	38	36	74	249	....	....	....	....	....	....	....	....	....	5	2	1	3	10	....	....	....	....
1995-96	Cape Breton	AHL	74	19	33	52	187	....	....	....	....	....	....	....	....	....	....	....	....	....	....	....	....	....	....
1996-97	Hamilton	AHL	74	15	17	32	139	....	....	....	....	....	....	....	....	....	22	6	7	13	43	....	....	....	....
1997-98	Calgary	NHL	12	1	0	1	4	0	0	0	7	14.3	–2	....	....	....	....	....	....	....	....	....	....	....	....
	Saint John Flames	AHL	61	17	21	38	194	....	....	....	....	....	....	....	....	....	20	4	6	10	58	....	....	....	....
1998-99	Calgary	NHL	3	0	1	1	0	0	0	0	1	0.0	1	15	46.7	9:54	....	....	....	....	....	....	....	....	....
	Saint John Flames	AHL	56	19	22	41	158	....	....	....	....	....	....	....	....	....	7	2	5	7	12	....	....	....	....
99-2000	Kentucky	AHL	79	35	31	66	170	....	....	....	....	....	....	....	....	....	9	3	6	9	2	....	....	....	....
2000-01	Montreal	NHL	51	4	7	11	43	2	0	0	54	7.4	–9	510	52.8	9:19	....	....	....	....	....	....	....	....	....
	Quebec Citadelles	AHL	27	14	18	32	90	....	....	....	....	....	....	....	....	....	9	4	4	8	35	....	....	....	....
2001-02	Montreal	NHL	2	0	1	1	0	0	0	0	0	0.0	2	1	0.0	7:34	....	....	....	....	....	....	....	....	....
	Quebec Citadelles	AHL	63	32	43	75	125	....	....	....	....	....	....	....	....	....	3	1	1	2	16	....	....	....	....
2002-03	Utah Grizzlies	AHL	73	26	36	62	119	....	....	....	....	....	....	....	....	....	2	0	1	1	2	....	....	....	....
	NHL Totals		68	5	9	14	47	2	0	0	62	8.1		526	52.5	9:17	....	....	....	....	....	....	....	....	....

QMJHL All-Rookie Team (1994)

Signed as a free agent by **Calgary**, August 20, 1997. Traded to **San Jose** by **Calgary** for Fredrik Oduya, July 12, 1999. Signed as a free agent by **Montreal**, July 7, 2000. Signed as a free agent by **HC Lausanne** (Swiss), April 9, 2003.

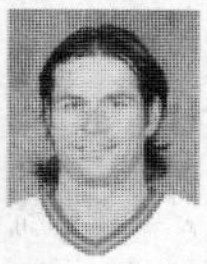

LANG, Robert

(LANG, RAW-buhrt) **WSH.**

Center. Shoots right. 6'2", 216 lbs. Born, Teplice, Czech., December 19, 1970. Los Angeles' 6th choice, 133rd overall, in 1990 Entry Draft.

Season	Club	League	GP	G	A	Pts	PIM	PP	SH	GW	S	%	+/-	TF	F%	Min	GP	G	A	Pts	PIM	PP	SH	GW	Min
1988-89	CHZ Litvinov	Czech	7	3	2	5	0	....	....	....	....	....	....	....	....	....	....	....	....	....	....	....	....	....	....
1989-90	CHZ Litvinov	Czech	32	8	7	15	....	....	....	....	....	....	....	....	....	....	8	3	3	6	....	....	....	....	....
1990-91	CHZ Litvinov	Czech	56	26	26	52	38	....	....	....	....	....	....	....	....	....	....	....	....	....	....	....	....	....	....
1991-92	CHZ Litvinov	Czech	43	12	31	43	34	....	....	....	....	....	....	....	....	....	....	....	....	....	....	....	....	....	....
	Czechoslovakia	Olympics	8	5	8	13	8	....	....	....	....	....	....	....	....	....	....	....	....	....	....	....	....	....	....
1992-93	Los Angeles	NHL	11	0	5	5	2	0	0	0	3	0.0	–3	....	....	....	....	....	....	....	....	....	....	....	....
	Phoenix	IHL	38	9	21	30	20	....	....	....	....	....	....	....	....	....	....	....	....	....	....	....	....	....	....
1993-94	Los Angeles	NHL	32	9	10	19	10	0	0	0	41	22.0	7	....	....	....	....	....	....	....	....	....	....	....	....
	Phoenix	IHL	44	11	24	35	34	....	....	....	....	....	....	....	....	....	....	....	....	....	....	....	....	....	....
1994-95	Litvinov	Czech	16	4	19	23	28	....	....	....	....	....	....	....	....	....	....	....	....	....	....	....	....	....	....
	Los Angeles	NHL	36	4	8	12	4	0	0	0	38	10.5	–7	....	....	....	....	....	....	....	....	....	....	....	....
1995-96	Los Angeles	NHL	68	6	16	22	10	0	2	0	71	8.5	–15	....	....	....	....	....	....	....	....	....	....	....	....
1996-97	HC Sparta Praha	Czech	38	14	27	41	30	....	....	....	....	....	....	....	....	....	5	1	2	3	4	....	....	....	....
	HC Sparta Praha	EuroHL	4	2	2	4	0	....	....	....	....	....	....	....	....	....	4	2	1	3	2	....	....	....	....
1997-98	Boston	NHL	3	0	0	0	2	0	0	0	2	0.0	1	....	....	....	....	....	....	....	....	....	....	....	....
	Pittsburgh	NHL	51	9	13	22	14	1	1	2	64	14.1	6	....	....	....	6	0	3	3	2	0	0	0	....
	Czech Republic	Olympics	6	0	3	3	0	....	....	....	....	....	....	....	....	....	....	....	....	....	....	....	....	....	....
	Houston Aeros	IHL	9	1	7	8	4	....	....	....	....	....	....	....	....	....	....	....	....	....	....	....	....	....	....
1998-99	Pittsburgh	NHL	72	21	23	44	24	7	0	3	137	15.3	–10	964	44.8	16:24	12	0	2	2	0	0	0	0	13:58
99-2000	Pittsburgh	NHL	78	23	42	65	14	13	0	5	142	16.2	–9	1433	50.7	19:22	11	3	3	6	0	2	0	0	21:42
2000-01	Pittsburgh	NHL	82	32	48	80	28	10	0	2	177	18.1	20	1348	43.9	20:24	16	4	4	8	4	0	0	0	19:21
2001-02	Pittsburgh	NHL	62	18	32	50	16	5	1	3	175	10.3	9	1172	46.3	22:56	....	....	....	....	....	....	....	....	....
	Czech Republic	Olympics	4	1	2	3	2	....	....	....	....	....	....	....	....	....	....	....	....	....	....	....	....	....	....
2002-03	Washington	NHL	82	22	47	69	22	10	0	2	146	15.1	12	1069	45.9	18:47	6	2	1	3	2	0	0	1	21:55
	NHL Totals		577	144	244	388	146	46	4	17	996	14.5		5986	46.5	19:29	51	9	13	22	8	2	0	1	18:50

Signed as a free agent by **Pittsburgh**, September 2, 1997. Claimed by **Boston** from **Pittsburgh** in Waiver Draft, September 28, 1997. Claimed on waivers by **Pittsburgh** from **Boston**, October 25, 1997. Signed as a free agent by **Washington**, July 1, 2002.

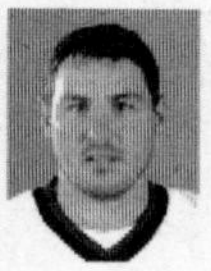

LANGDON, Darren

(LAING-duhn, DAIR-uhn) **VAN.**

Left wing. Shoots left. 6'1", 205 lbs. Born, Deer Lake, Nfld., January 8, 1971.

Season	Club	League	GP	G	A	Pts	PIM	PP	SH	GW	S	%	+/-	TF	F%	Min	GP	G	A	Pts	PIM	PP	SH	GW	Min
1991-92	Summerside	MJrHL	44	34	49	83	441	....	....	....	....	....	....	....	....	....	....	....	....	....	....	....	....	....	....
1992-93	Binghamton	AHL	18	3	4	7	115	....	....	....	....	....	....	....	....	....	8	0	1	1	14	....	....	....	....
	Dayton Bombers	ECHL	54	23	22	45	429	....	....	....	....	....	....	....	....	....	3	0	1	1	40	....	....	....	....
1993-94	Binghamton	AHL	54	2	7	9	327	....	....	....	....	....	....	....	....	....	....	....	....	....	....	....	....	....	....
1994-95	Binghamton	AHL	55	6	14	20	296	....	....	....	....	....	....	....	....	....	11	1	3	4	*84	....	....	....	....
	NY Rangers	NHL	18	1	1	2	62	0	0	0	6	16.7	0	....	....	....	....	....	....	....	....	....	....	....	....
1995-96	NY Rangers	NHL	64	7	4	11	175	0	0	1	29	24.1	2	....	....	....	2	0	0	0	0	0	0	0	....
	Binghamton	AHL	1	0	0	0	12	....	....	....	....	....	....	....	....	....	....	....	....	....	....	....	....	....	....
1996-97	NY Rangers	NHL	60	3	6	9	195	0	0	1	24	12.5	–1	....	....	....	10	0	0	0	2	0	0	0	....
1997-98	NY Rangers	NHL	70	3	3	6	197	0	0	0	15	20.0	0	....	....	....	....	....	....	....	....	....	....	....	....
1998-99	NY Rangers	NHL	44	0	0	0	80	0	0	0	8	0.0	–3	0	0.0	3:33	....	....	....	....	....	....	....	....	....
99-2000	NY Rangers	NHL	21	0	1	1	26	0	0	0	13	0.0	–2	0	0.0	5:36	....	....	....	....	....	....	....	....	....
2000-01	Carolina	NHL	54	0	2	2	94	0	0	0	6	0.0	–4	2	100.0	3:21	4	0	0	0	12	0	0	0	3:31
2001-02	Carolina	NHL	58	2	1	3	106	0	0	1	12	16.7	2	1	100.0	4:11	....	....	....	....	....	....	....	....	....

			Regular Season														Playoffs								
Season	**Club**	**League**	**GP**	**G**	**A**	**Pts**	**PIM**	**PP**	**SH**	**GW**	**S**	**%**	**+/-**	**TF**	**F%**	**Min**	**GP**	**G**	**A**	**Pts**	**PIM**	**PP**	**SH**	**GW**	**Min**
2002-03	**Carolina**	**NHL**	**9**	**0**	**0**	**0**	**16**	**0**	**0**	**0**	**4**	**0.0**	**0**	**0**	**0.0**	**2:45**	....	....	....	....	....	....	....	....	....
	Vancouver	**NHL**	**45**	**0**	**1**	**1**	**143**	**0**	**0**	**0**	**15**	**0.0**	**–2**	**1**	**0.0**	**5:26**	....	....	....	....	....	....	....	....	....
	NHL Totals		**443**	**16**	**19**	**35**	**1094**	**0**	**0**	**3**	**132**	**12.1**		**4**	**75.0**	**4:11**	**16**	**0**	**0**	**0**	**14**	**0**	**0**	**0**	**3:31**

Signed as a free agent by **NY Rangers**, August 16, 1993. • Missed majority of 1999-2000 season recovering from hernia injury suffered in game vs. New Jersey, December 1, 1999. Traded to **Carolina** by **NY Rangers** with Rob DiMaio for Sandy McCarthy and Carolina's 4th round choice (Bryce Lampman) in 2001 Entry Draft, August 4, 2000. Traded to **Vancouver** by **Carolina** with Marek Malik for Jan Hlavac and Harold Druken, November 1, 2002.

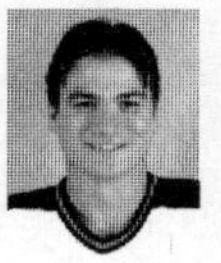

LANGENBRUNNER, Jamie

(lan-gehn-BRUH-nuhr, JAY-mee) **N.J.**

Right wing. Shoots right. 6'1", 200 lbs. Born, Duluth, MN, July 24, 1975. Dallas' 2nd choice, 35th overall, in 1993 Entry Draft.

Season	Club	League	GP	G	A	Pts	PIM	PP	SH	GW	S	%	+/-	TF	F%	Min	GP	G	A	Pts	PIM	PP	SH	GW	Min
1990-91	Cloquet High	Hi-School	20	6	16	22	8	....	....	....	....	....	....	....	....	....	....	....	....	....	....	....	....	....	....
1991-92	Cloquet High	Hi-School	23	16	23	39	24	....	....	....	....	....	....	....	....	....	....	....	....	....	....	....	....	....	....
1992-93	Cloquet High	Hi-School	27	27	62	89	18	....	....	....	....	....	....	....	....	....	....	....	....	....	....	....	....	....	....
1993-94	Peterborough	OHL	62	33	58	91	53	....	....	....	....	....	....	....	....	....	7	4	6	10	2	....	....	....	....
1994-95	Peterborough	OHL	62	42	57	99	84	....	....	....	....	....	....	....	....	....	11	8	14	22	12	....	....	....	....
	Dallas	**NHL**	**2**	**0**	**0**	**0**	**2**	**0**	**0**	**0**	**1**	**0.0**	**0**	....	....	....	....	....	....	....	....	....	....	....	....
	Kalamazoo Wings	IHL	....	....	....	....	....	....	....	....	....	....	....	....	....	....	11	1	3	4	2	....	....	....	....
1995-96	**Dallas**	**NHL**	**12**	**2**	**2**	**4**	**6**	**1**	**0**	**0**	**15**	**13.3**	**–2**	....	....	....	....	....	....	....	....	....	....	....	....
	Michigan	IHL	59	25	40	65	129	....	....	....	....	....	....	....	....	....	10	3	10	13	8	....	....	....	....
1996-97	**Dallas**	**NHL**	**76**	**13**	**26**	**39**	**51**	**3**	**0**	**3**	**112**	**11.6**	**–2**	....	....	....	**5**	**1**	**1**	**2**	**14**	**0**	**0**	**1**	....
1997-98	**Dallas**	**NHL**	**81**	**23**	**29**	**52**	**61**	**8**	**0**	**6**	**159**	**14.5**	**9**	....	....	....	**16**	**1**	**4**	**5**	**14**	**0**	**0**	**1**	....
	United States	Olympics	3	0	0	0	4	....	....	....	....	....	....	....	....	....	....	....	....	....	....	....	....	....	....
1998-99♦	**Dallas**	**NHL**	**75**	**12**	**33**	**45**	**62**	**4**	**0**	**1**	**145**	**8.3**	**10**	**217**	**46.1**	**15:51**	**23**	**10**	**7**	**17**	**16**	**4**	**0**	**3**	**17:43**
99-2000	**Dallas**	**NHL**	**65**	**18**	**21**	**39**	**68**	**4**	**2**	**6**	**153**	**11.8**	**16**	**40**	**50.0**	**17:33**	**15**	**1**	**7**	**8**	**18**	**1**	**0**	**0**	**15:28**
2000-01	**Dallas**	**NHL**	**53**	**12**	**18**	**30**	**57**	**3**	**2**	**4**	**104**	**11.5**	**4**	**316**	**45.3**	**16:30**	**10**	**2**	**2**	**4**	**6**	**0**	**0**	**1**	**19:26**
2001-02	**Dallas**	**NHL**	**68**	**10**	**16**	**26**	**54**	**0**	**1**	**2**	**132**	**7.6**	**–11**	**120**	**45.0**	**15:45**	....	....	....	....	....	....	....	....	....
	New Jersey	**NHL**	**14**	**3**	**3**	**6**	**23**	**0**	**0**	**2**	**31**	**9.7**	**2**	**2**	**50.0**	**15:27**	**5**	**0**	**1**	**1**	**8**	**0**	**0**	**0**	**14:57**
2002-03♦	**New Jersey**	**NHL**	**78**	**22**	**33**	**55**	**65**	**5**	**1**	**5**	**197**	**11.2**	**17**	**72**	**47.2**	**17:48**	**24**	***11**	**7**	***18**	**16**	**1**	**0**	**4**	**17:34**
	NHL Totals		**524**	**115**	**181**	**296**	**449**	**28**	**6**	**29**	**1049**	**11.0**		**767**	**45.9**	**16:39**	**98**	**26**	**29**	**55**	**92**	**6**	**0**	**10**	**17:16**

Traded to **New Jersey** by **Dallas** with Joe Nieuwendyk for Jason Arnott, Randy McKay and New Jersey's 1st round choice (later traded to Columbus – later traded to Buffalo – Buffalo selected Dan Paille) in 2002 Entry Draft, March 19, 2002.

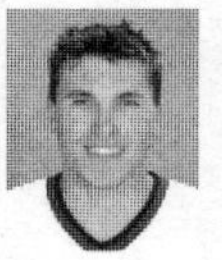

LANGFELD, Josh

(LANG-fehld, JAWSH) **OTT.**

Right wing. Shoots right. 6'3", 216 lbs. Born, Fridley, MN, July 17, 1977. Ottawa's 3rd choice, 66th overall, in 1997 Entry Draft.

Season	Club	League	GP	G	A	Pts	PIM	PP	SH	GW	S	%	+/-	TF	F%	Min	GP	G	A	Pts	PIM	PP	SH	GW	Min
1995-96	Great Falls	AFJHL	45	45	40	85	105	....	....	....	....	....	....	....	....	....	....	....	....	....	....	....	....	....	....
1996-97	Lincoln Stars	USHL	38	35	23	58	100	....	....	....	....	....	....	....	....	....	14	8	*13	*21	42	....	....	....	....
1997-98	U. of Michigan	CCHA	46	19	17	36	66	....	....	....	....	....	....	....	....	....	....	....	....	....	....	....	....	....	....
1998-99	U. of Michigan	CCHA	41	21	14	35	84	....	....	....	....	....	....	....	....	....	....	....	....	....	....	....	....	....	....
99-2000	U. of Michigan	CCHA	39	9	21	30	56	....	....	....	....	....	....	....	....	....	....	....	....	....	....	....	....	....	....
2000-01	U. of Michigan	CCHA	42	16	12	28	44	....	....	....	....	....	....	....	....	....	....	....	....	....	....	....	....	....	....
2001-02	**Ottawa**	**NHL**	**1**	**0**	**0**	**0**	**2**	**0**	**0**	**0**	**5**	**0.0**	**0**	**0**	**0.0**	**8:15**	....	....	....	....	....	....	....	....	....
	Grand Rapids	AHL	68	21	16	37	29	....	....	....	....	....	....	....	....	....	5	2	0	2	0	....	....	....	....
2002-03	**Ottawa**	**NHL**	**12**	**0**	**1**	**1**	**4**	**0**	**0**	**0**	**16**	**0.0**	**2**	**0**	**0.0**	**11:11**	....	....	....	....	....	....	....	....	....
	Binghamton	AHL	59	14	21	35	38	....	....	....	....	....	....	....	....	....	13	5	3	8	8	....	....	....	....
	NHL Totals		**13**	**0**	**1**	**1**	**6**	**0**	**0**	**0**	**21**	**0.0**		**0**	**0.0**	**10:57**	....	....	....	....	....	....	....	....	....

NCAA Championship All-Tournament Team (1998)

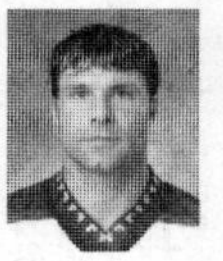

LANGKOW, Daymond

(LAING-kow, DAY-muhn) **PHX.**

Center. Shoots left. 5'11", 192 lbs. Born, Edmonton, Alta., September 27, 1976. Tampa Bay's 1st choice, 5th overall, in 1995 Entry Draft.

Season	Club	League	GP	G	A	Pts	PIM	PP	SH	GW	S	%	+/-	TF	F%	Min	GP	G	A	Pts	PIM	PP	SH	GW	Min
1991-92	Edmonton Pats	AMHL	35	36	45	81	100	....	....	....	....	....	....	....	....	....	....	....	....	....	....	....	....	....	....
	Tri-City	WHL	1	0	0	0	0	....	....	....	....	....	....	....	....	....	....	....	....	....	....	....	....	....	....
1992-93	Tri-City	WHL	64	22	42	64	100	....	....	....	....	....	....	....	....	....	4	1	0	1	4	....	....	....	....
1993-94	Tri-City	WHL	61	40	43	83	174	....	....	....	....	....	....	....	....	....	4	2	2	4	15	....	....	....	....
1994-95	Tri-City	WHL	72	*67	73	*140	142	....	....	....	....	....	....	....	....	....	17	12	15	27	52	....	....	....	....
1995-96	Tri-City	WHL	48	30	61	91	103	....	....	....	....	....	....	....	....	....	11	14	13	27	20	....	....	....	....
	Tampa Bay	**NHL**	**4**	**0**	**1**	**1**	**0**	**0**	**0**	**0**	**4**	**0.0**	**–1**	....	....	....	....	....	....	....	....	....	....	....	....
1996-97	**Tampa Bay**	**NHL**	**79**	**15**	**13**	**28**	**35**	**3**	**1**	**1**	**170**	**8.8**	**1**	....	....	....	....	....	....	....	....	....	....	....	....
	Adirondack	AHL	2	1	1	2	0	....	....	....	....	....	....	....	....	....	....	....	....	....	....	....	....	....	....
1997-98	**Tampa Bay**	**NHL**	**68**	**8**	**14**	**22**	**62**	**2**	**0**	**1**	**156**	**5.1**	**–9**	....	....	....	....	....	....	....	....	....	....	....	....
1998-99	**Tampa Bay**	**NHL**	**22**	**4**	**6**	**10**	**15**	**1**	**0**	**1**	**40**	**10.0**	**0**	**399**	**48.4**	**17:10**	....	....	....	....	....	....	....	....	....
	Cleveland	IHL	4	1	1	2	18	....	....	....	....	....	....	....	....	....	....	....	....	....	....	....	....	....	....
	Philadelphia	**NHL**	**56**	**10**	**13**	**23**	**24**	**3**	**1**	**1**	**109**	**9.2**	**–8**	**738**	**48.0**	**15:12**	**6**	**0**	**2**	**2**	**2**	**0**	**0**	**0**	**16:50**
99-2000	**Philadelphia**	**NHL**	**82**	**18**	**32**	**50**	**56**	**5**	**0**	**7**	**222**	**8.1**	**1**	**1263**	**45.1**	**16:57**	**16**	**5**	**5**	**10**	**23**	**1**	**1**	**2**	**20:03**
2000-01	**Philadelphia**	**NHL**	**71**	**13**	**41**	**54**	**50**	**3**	**0**	**2**	**190**	**6.8**	**12**	**1181**	**47.2**	**18:38**	**6**	**2**	**4**	**6**	**2**	**1**	**0**	**0**	**20:17**
2001-02	**Phoenix**	**NHL**	**80**	**27**	**35**	**62**	**36**	**6**	**3**	**2**	**171**	**15.8**	**18**	**1379**	**46.2**	**19:11**	**5**	**1**	**0**	**1**	**0**	**0**	**0**	**0**	**21:06**
2002-03	**Phoenix**	**NHL**	**82**	**20**	**32**	**52**	**56**	**4**	**2**	**2**	**196**	**10.2**	**20**	**1972**	**46.5**	**20:60**	....	....	....	....	....	....	....	....	....
	NHL Totals		**544**	**115**	**187**	**302**	**334**	**27**	**7**	**17**	**1258**	**9.1**		**6932**	**46.6**	**18:19**	**33**	**8**	**11**	**19**	**27**	**2**	**1**	**2**	**19:40**

WHL West First All-Star Team (1995) • Canadian Major Junior First All-Star Team (1995) • WHL West Second All-Star Team (1996)

Traded to **Philadelphia** by **Tampa Bay** with Mikael Renberg for Chris Gratton and Mike Sillinger, December 12, 1998. Traded to **Phoenix** by **Philadelphia** for Phoenix's 2nd round choice (later traded to Tampa Bay – later traded to San Jose – San Jose selected Dan Spang) in 2002 Entry Draft and Phoenix's 1st round choice (Jeff Carter) in 2003 Entry Draft, July 2, 2001.

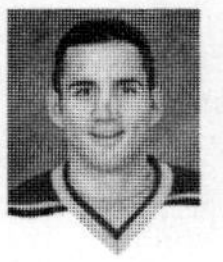

LAPERRIERE, Ian

(luh-PAIR-ee-YAIR, EE-ihn) **L.A.**

Right wing. Shoots right. 6'1", 201 lbs. Born, Montreal, Que., January 19, 1974. St. Louis' 6th choice, 158th overall, in 1992 Entry Draft.

Season	Club	League	GP	G	A	Pts	PIM	PP	SH	GW	S	%	+/-	TF	F%	Min	GP	G	A	Pts	PIM	PP	SH	GW	Min
1989-90	Mtl-Bourassa	QAAA	22	4	10	14	10	....	....	....	....	....	....	....	....	....	3	0	1	1	6	....	....	....	....
1990-91	Drummondville	QMJHL	65	19	29	48	117	....	....	....	....	....	....	....	....	....	14	2	9	11	48	....	....	....	....
1991-92	Drummondville	QMJHL	70	28	49	77	160	....	....	....	....	....	....	....	....	....	4	2	2	4	9	....	....	....	....
1992-93	Drummondville	QMJHL	60	44	*96	140	188	....	....	....	....	....	....	....	....	....	10	6	13	19	20	....	....	....	....
1993-94	Drummondville	QMJHL	62	41	72	113	150	....	....	....	....	....	....	....	....	....	9	4	6	10	35	....	....	....	....
	St. Louis	**NHL**	**1**	**0**	**0**	**0**	**0**	**0**	**0**	**0**	**1**	**0.0**	**0**	....	....	....	....	....	....	....	....	....	....	....	....
	Peoria Rivermen	IHL	....	....	....	....	....	....	....	....	....	....	....	....	....	....	5	1	3	4	2	....	....	....	....
1994-95	Peoria Rivermen	IHL	51	16	32	48	111	....	....	....	....	....	....	....	....	....	....	....	....	....	....	....	....	....	....
	St. Louis	**NHL**	**37**	**13**	**14**	**27**	**85**	**1**	**0**	**1**	**53**	**24.5**	**12**	....	....	....	**7**	**0**	**4**	**4**	**21**	**0**	**0**	**0**	....
1995-96	**St. Louis**	**NHL**	**33**	**3**	**6**	**9**	**87**	**1**	**0**	**1**	**31**	**9.7**	**–4**	....	....	....	....	....	....	....	....	....	....	....	....
	Worcester IceCats	AHL	3	2	1	3	22	....	....	....	....	....	....	....	....	....	....	....	....	....	....	....	....	....	....
	NY Rangers	**NHL**	**28**	**1**	**2**	**3**	**53**	**0**	**0**	**0**	**21**	**4.8**	**–5**	....	....	....	....	....	....	....	....	....	....	....	....
	Los Angeles	**NHL**	**10**	**2**	**3**	**5**	**15**	**0**	**0**	**0**	**18**	**11.1**	**–2**	....	....	....	....	....	....	....	....	....	....	....	....
1996-97	**Los Angeles**	**NHL**	**62**	**8**	**15**	**23**	**102**	**0**	**1**	**2**	**84**	**9.5**	**–25**	....	....	....	....	....	....	....	....	....	....	....	....
1997-98	**Los Angeles**	**NHL**	**77**	**6**	**15**	**21**	**131**	**0**	**1**	**1**	**74**	**8.1**	**0**	....	....	....	**4**	**1**	**0**	**1**	**6**	**0**	**0**	**0**	....
1998-99	**Los Angeles**	**NHL**	**72**	**3**	**10**	**13**	**138**	**0**	**0**	**1**	**62**	**4.8**	**–5**	**643**	**47.3**	**11:47**	....	....	....	....	....	....	....	....	....
99-2000	**Los Angeles**	**NHL**	**79**	**9**	**13**	**22**	**185**	**0**	**0**	**1**	**87**	**10.3**	**–14**	**1111**	**53.7**	**13:15**	**4**	**0**	**0**	**0**	**2**	**0**	**0**	**0**	**10:21**
2000-01	**Los Angeles**	**NHL**	**79**	**8**	**10**	**18**	**141**	**0**	**0**	**0**	**60**	**13.3**	**5**	**297**	**51.9**	**12:02**	**13**	**1**	**2**	**3**	**12**	**0**	**0**	**0**	**14:01**
2001-02	**Los Angeles**	**NHL**	**81**	**8**	**14**	**22**	**125**	**0**	**0**	**3**	**89**	**9.0**	**5**	**134**	**49.3**	**13:45**	**7**	**0**	**1**	**1**	**9**	**0**	**0**	**0**	**14:18**
2002-03	**Los Angeles**	**NHL**	**73**	**7**	**12**	**19**	**122**	**1**	**1**	**1**	**85**	**8.2**	**–9**	**317**	**49.2**	**15:46**	....	....	....	....	....	....	....	....	....
	NHL Totals		**632**	**68**	**114**	**182**	**1184**	**3**	**3**	**11**	**665**	**10.2**		**2502**	**51.0**	**13:19**	**35**	**2**	**7**	**9**	**50**	**0**	**0**	**0**	**13:29**

QMJHL Second All-Star Team (1993)

Traded to **NY Rangers** by **St. Louis** for Stephane Matteau, December 28, 1995. Traded to **Los Angeles** by **NY Rangers** with Ray Ferraro, Mattias Norstrom, Nathan LaFayette and NY Rangers' 4th round choice (Sean Blanchard) in 1997 Entry Draft for Marty McSorley, Jari Kurri and Shane Churla, March 14, 1996.

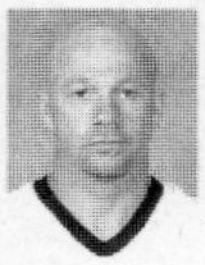

LAPOINTE, Claude

(luh-POYNT, KLOHD) **PHI.**

Left wing/Center. Shoots left. 5'9", 188 lbs. Born, Lachine, Que., October 11, 1968. Quebec's 12th choice, 234th overall, in 1988 Entry Draft.

			Regular Season														Playoffs								
Season	Club	League	GP	G	A	Pts	PIM	PP	SH	GW	S	%	+/-	TF	F%	Min	GP	G	A	Pts	PIM	PP	SH	GW	Min
1983-84	Lac St-Louis Lions	QAAA	42	28	29	57	42										8	3	7	10	8				
1984-85	Lac St-Louis Lions	QAAA	42	20	32	52	66										11	4	8	12	16				
1985-86	Trois-Rivieres	QMJHL	63	14	32	46	70										9	5	6	11	4				
1986-87	Trois-Rivieres	QMJHL	70	47	57	104	123																		
1987-88	Laval Titan	QMJHL	69	37	83	120	143										13	2	17	19	53				
1988-89	Laval Titan	QMJHL	63	32	72	104	158										17	5	14	19	66				
1989-90	Halifax Citadels	AHL	63	18	19	37	51										6	1	1	2	34				
1990-91	Quebec	NHL	13	2	2	4	4	0	0	0	7	28.6	3												
	Halifax Citadels	AHL	43	17	17	34	46																		
1991-92	Quebec	NHL	78	13	20	33	86	0	2	2	95	13.7	–8												
1992-93	Quebec	NHL	74	10	26	36	98	0	0	1	91	11.0	5				6	2	4	6	8	0	0	0	
1993-94	Quebec	NHL	59	11	17	28	70	1	1	1	73	15.1	2												
1994-95	Quebec	NHL	29	4	8	12	41	0	0	0	40	10.0	5				5	0	0	0	8	0	0	0	
1995-96	Colorado	NHL	3	0	0	0	0	0	0	0	0	0.0	–1												
	Calgary	NHL	32	4	5	9	20	0	2	1	44	9.1	2				2	0	0	0	0	0	0	0	
	Saint John Flames	AHL	12	5	3	8	10																		
1996-97	NY Islanders	NHL	73	13	5	18	49	0	3	3	80	16.3	–12												
	Utah Grizzlies	IHL	9	7	6	13	14																		
1997-98	NY Islanders	NHL	78	10	10	20	47	0	1	3	82	12.2	–9												
1998-99	NY Islanders	NHL	82	14	23	37	62	2	2	1	134	10.4	–19	1218	56.6	19:21									
99-2000	NY Islanders	NHL	76	15	16	31	60	2	1	3	129	11.6	–22	1284	54.0	19:39									
2000-01	NY Islanders	NHL	80	9	23	32	56	1	1	1	94	9.6	–2	1074	50.4	18:40									
2001-02	NY Islanders	NHL	80	9	12	21	60	0	3	0	74	12.2	–9	907	54.6	13:05	7	0	0	0	14	0	0	0	13:20
2002-03	NY Islanders	NHL	66	6	6	12	20	0	0	1	67	9.0	–3	686	55.0	12:16									
	Philadelphia	NHL	14	2	2	4	16	0	0	0	20	10.0	5	107	63.6	11:05	13	2	3	5	14	0	0	0	13:15
	NHL Totals		837	122	175	297	689	6	16	17	1030	11.8		5276	54.3	16:33	33	4	7	11	44	0	0	0	13:17

Transferred to **Colorado** after **Quebec** franchise relocated, June 21, 1995. Traded to **Calgary** by **Colorado** for Calgary's 7th round choice (Sami Pahlsson) in 1996 Entry Draft, November 1, 1995. Signed as a free agent by **NY Islanders**, August 14, 1996. Traded to **Philadelphia** by **NY Islanders** for Philadelphia's 5th round choice (later traded to Pittsburgh – Pittsburgh selected Evgeni Isakov) in 2003 Entry Draft, March 9, 2003.

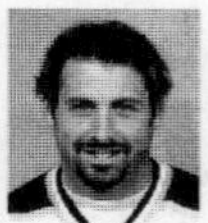

LAPOINTE, Martin

(luh-POYNT, MAHR-tihn) **BOS.**

Right wing. Shoots right. 5'11", 215 lbs. Born, Ville St-Pierre, Que., September 12, 1973. Detroit's 1st choice, 10th overall, in 1991 Entry Draft.

			Regular Season														Playoffs								
Season	Club	League	GP	G	A	Pts	PIM	PP	SH	GW	S	%	+/-	TF	F%	Min	GP	G	A	Pts	PIM	PP	SH	GW	Min
1988-89	Lac St-Louis Lions	QAAA	42	39	45	84	46										3	6	2	8	4				
1989-90	Laval Titan	QMJHL	65	42	54	96	77										14	8	17	25	54				
1990-91	Laval Titan	QMJHL	64	44	54	98	66										13	7	14	21	26				
1991-92	Laval Titan	QMJHL	31	25	30	55	84										10	4	10	14	32				
	Detroit	NHL	4	0	1	1	5	0	0	0	2	0.0	2				3	0	1	1	4	0	0	0	
	Adirondack	AHL															8	2	2	4	4				
1992-93	Laval Titan	QMJHL	35	38	51	89	41										13	*13	*17	*30	22				
	Detroit	NHL	3	0	0	0	0	0	0	0	2	0.0	–2												
	Adirondack	AHL	8	1	2	3	9																		
1993-94	Detroit	NHL	50	8	8	16	55	2	0	0	45	17.8	7				4	0	0	0	6	0	0	0	
	Adirondack	AHL	28	25	21	46	47										4	1	1	2	8				
1994-95	Adirondack	AHL	39	29	16	45	80																		
	Detroit	NHL	39	4	6	10	73	0	0	1	46	8.7	1				2	0	1	1	8	0	0	0	
1995-96	Detroit	NHL	58	6	3	9	93	1	0	0	76	7.9	0				11	1	2	3	12	0	0	0	
1996-97♦	Detroit	NHL	78	16	17	33	167	5	1	1	149	10.7	–14				20	4	8	12	60	1	0	1	
1997-98♦	Detroit	NHL	79	15	19	34	106	4	0	3	154	9.7	0				21	9	6	15	20	2	1	1	
1998-99	Detroit	NHL	77	16	13	29	141	7	1	4	153	10.5	7	217	47.9	15:06	10	0	2	2	20	0	0	0	11:43
99-2000	Detroit	NHL	82	16	25	41	121	1	1	2	127	12.6	17	287	54.4	14:43	9	3	1	4	20	2	0	1	14:28
2000-01	Detroit	NHL	82	27	30	57	127	13	0	8	181	14.9	3	461	53.2	16:06	6	0	1	1	8	0	0	0	16:53
2001-02	Boston	NHL	68	17	23	40	101	4	0	2	141	12.1	12	222	53.6	17:22	6	1	2	3	12	1	0	1	16:58
2002-03	Boston	NHL	59	8	10	18	87	1	0	1	110	7.3	–19	52	48.1	15:22	5	1	0	1	14	0	0	0	14:39
	NHL Totals		679	133	155	288	1076	38	3	22	1186	11.2		1239	52.4	15:42	97	19	24	43	184	6	1	4	14:33

QMJHL First All-Star Team (1990, 1993) • QMJHL Offensive Rookie of the Year) (1990) • QMJHL Second All-Star Team (1991) • Memorial Cup All-Star Team (1993)

Signed as a free agent by **Boston**, July 2, 2001.

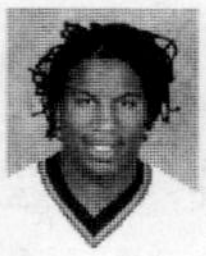

LARAQUE, Georges

(luh-RAK, zhawrzh) **EDM.**

Right wing. Shoots right. 6'3", 245 lbs. Born, Montreal, Que., December 7, 1976. Edmonton's 2nd choice, 31st overall, in 1995 Entry Draft.

			Regular Season														Playoffs								
Season	Club	League	GP	G	A	Pts	PIM	PP	SH	GW	S	%	+/-	TF	F%	Min	GP	G	A	Pts	PIM	PP	SH	GW	Min
1991-92	Mtl-Bourassa	QAHA	28	20	20	40	30																		
1992-93	Mtl-Bourassa	QAAA	37	8	20	28	50										3	1	2	3	2				
1993-94	St-Jean Lynx	QMJHL	70	11	11	22	142										4	0	0	0	7				
1994-95	St-Jean Lynx	QMJHL	62	19	22	41	259										7	1	1	2	42				
1995-96	Laval Titan	QMJHL	11	8	13	21	76																		
	St-Hyacinthe	QMJHL	8	3	4	7	59																		
	Granby	QMJHL	22	9	7	16	125										18	7	6	13	104				
1996-97	Hamilton	AHL	73	14	20	34	179										15	1	3	4	12				
1997-98	Edmonton	NHL	11	0	0	0	59	0	0	0	4	0.0	–4												
	Hamilton	AHL	46	10	20	30	154										3	0	0	0	11				
1998-99	Edmonton	NHL	39	3	2	5	57	0	0	0	17	17.6	–1	0	0.0	5:31	4	0	0	0	2	0	0	0	7:35
	Hamilton	AHL	25	6	8	14	93																		
99-2000	Edmonton	NHL	76	8	8	16	123	0	0	0	56	14.3	5	0	0.0	8:28	5	0	1	1	6	0	0	0	9:14
2000-01	Edmonton	NHL	82	13	16	29	148	1	0	1	73	17.8	5	0	0.0	9:03	6	1	1	2	8	0	0	0	9:54
2001-02	Edmonton	NHL	80	5	14	19	157	1	0	1	95	5.3	6	0	0.0	9:48									
2002-03	Edmonton	NHL	64	6	7	13	110	0	0	2	46	13.0	–4	0	0.0	9:15	6	1	3	4	4	0	0	0	12:11
	NHL Totals		352	35	47	82	654	2	0	4	291	12.0		0	0.0	8:44	21	2	5	7	20	0	0	0	9:57

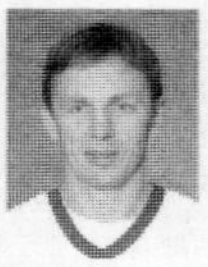

LARIONOV, Igor

(LAIR-ee-AH-nohv, EE-gohr) **DET.**

Center. Shoots left. 5'9", 170 lbs. Born, Voskresensk, USSR, December 3, 1960. Vancouver's 11th choice, 214th overall, in 1985 Entry Draft.

			Regular Season														Playoffs								
Season	Club	League	GP	G	A	Pts	PIM	PP	SH	GW	S	%	+/-	TF	F%	Min	GP	G	A	Pts	PIM	PP	SH	GW	Min
1977-78	Voskresensk	USSR	6	3	0	3	4																		
1978-79	Voskresensk	USSR	32	3	4	7	12																		
1979-80	Voskresensk	USSR	42	11	7	18	24																		
1980-81	Voskresensk	USSR	43	22	23	45	36																		
1981-82	CSKA Moscow	USSR	46	31	22	53	6																		
1982-83	CSKA Moscow	USSR	44	20	19	39	20																		
1983-84	CSKA Moscow	USSR	43	15	26	41	30																		
	Soviet Union	Olympics	6	1	4	5	6																		
1984-85	CSKA Moscow	USSR	40	18	28	46	20																		
1985-86	CSKA Moscow	USSR	40	21	31	52	33																		
1986-87	CSKA Moscow	USSR	39	20	26	46	34																		
1987-88	CSKA Moscow	USSR	51	25	32	57	54																		
	Soviet Union	Olympics	8	4	*9	13	4																		
1988-89	CSKA Moscow	USSR	31	15	12	27	22																		
1989-90	Vancouver	NHL	74	17	27	44	20	8	0	2	118	14.4	–5												
1990-91	Vancouver	NHL	64	13	21	34	14	1	1	0	66	19.7	–3				6	1	0	1	6	0	0	0	
1991-92	Vancouver	NHL	72	21	44	65	54	10	3	4	97	21.6	7				13	3	7	10	4	1	0	0	
1992-93	HC Lugano	Swiss	24	10	19	29	44										8	3	15	18	0				
1993-94	San Jose	NHL	60	18	38	56	40	3	2	2	72	25.0	20				14	5	13	18	10	0	0	0	
1994-95	San Jose	NHL	33	4	20	24	14	0	0	1	69	5.8	–3				11	1	8	9	2	0	0	0	
1995-96	San Jose	NHL	4	1	1	2	0	1	0	0	5	20.0	–6												
	Detroit	NHL	69	21	50	71	34	9	1	5	108	19.4	37				19	6	7	13	6	3	0	2	
1996-97♦	Detroit	NHL	64	12	42	54	26	2	1	4	95	12.6	31				20	4	8	12	8	3	0	1	
1997-98♦	Detroit	NHL	69	8	39	47	40	3	0	2	93	8.6	14				22	3	10	13	12	0	0	0	
1998-99	Detroit	NHL	75	14	49	63	48	4	2	2	83	16.9	13	867	49.8	17:20	7	0	2	2	0	0	0	0	13:51
99-2000	Detroit	NHL	79	9	38	47	28	3	0	4	69	13.0	13	729	43.6	16:05	9	1	2	3	6	1	0	0	14:10

			Regular Season														Playoffs								
Season	Club	League	GP	G	A	Pts	PIM	PP	SH	GW	S	%	+/-	TF	F%	Min	GP	G	A	Pts	PIM	PP	SH	GW	Min
2000-01	Florida	NHL	26	5	6	11	10	2	0	0	15	33.3	-11	299	48.8	16:33	....	....	....	....	....	....	....	....	....
	Detroit	NHL	39	4	25	29	28	2	0	1	31	12.9	6	311	44.4	16:36	6	1	3	4	2	1	0	0	17:06
2001-02♦	Detroit	NHL	70	11	32	43	50	4	0	1	50	22.0	-5	653	43.3	14:28	18	5	6	11	4	0	0	1	13:58
	Russia	Olympics	6	0	3	3	4	....	....	....	....	....	....	....	....	....	....	....	....	....	....	....	....	....	....
2002-03	Detroit	NHL	74	10	33	43	48	5	0	3	50	20.0	-7	454	43.0	13:55	4	0	1	1	0	0	0	0	15:11
	NHL Totals		872	168	465	633	454	57	10	31	1021	16.5		3313	45.6	15:40	149	30	67	97	60	9	0	4	14:31

USSR First All-Star Team (1983, 1986, 1987, 1988) • USSR Player of the Year (1988)

Played in NHL All-Star Game (1998)

Claimed by **San Jose** from **Vancouver** in Waiver Draft, October 4, 1992. Traded to **Detroit** by **San Jose** for Ray Sheppard, October 24, 1995. Signed as a free agent by **Florida**, July 1, 2000. Traded to **Detroit** by **Florida** for Yan Golubovsky, December 28, 2000.

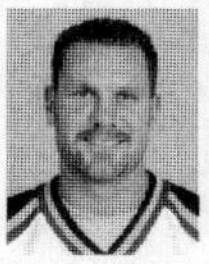

LARSEN, Brad (LARH-sehn, BRAD) COL.

Left wing. Shoots left. 6', 200 lbs. Born, Nakusp, B.C., June 28, 1977. Colorado's 5th choice, 87th overall, in 1997 Entry Draft.

1992-93	Nelson	RMJHL	42	31	37	68	164	....	....	....	....	....	....	....	....	....	....	....	....	....	....	....	....	....	....
1993-94	Swift Current	WHL	64	15	18	33	32	....	....	....	....	....	....	....	....	....	7	1	2	3	4	....	....	....	....
1994-95	Swift Current	WHL	62	24	33	57	73	....	....	....	....	....	....	....	....	....	6	0	1	1	2	....	....	....	....
1995-96	Swift Current	WHL	51	30	47	77	67	....	....	....	....	....	....	....	....	....	6	3	2	5	13	....	....	....	....
1996-97	Swift Current	WHL	61	36	46	82	61	....	....	....	....	....	....	....	....	....	....	....	....	....	....	....	....	....	....
1997-98	Colorado	NHL	1	0	0	0	0	0	0	0	0	0.0	0	....	....	....	....	....	....	....	....	....	....	....	....
	Hershey Bears	AHL	65	12	10	22	80	....	....	....	....	....	....	....	....	....	7	3	2	5	2	....	....	....	....
1998-99	Hershey Bears	AHL	18	3	4	7	11	....	....	....	....	....	....	....	....	....	5	0	1	1	6	....	....	....	....
99-2000	Hershey Bears	AHL	52	13	26	39	66	....	....	....	....	....	....	....	....	....	14	5	2	7	29	....	....	....	....
2000-01	Colorado	NHL	9	0	0	0	0	0	0	0	3	0.0	1	14	57.1	9:17	....	....	....	....	....	....	....	....	....
	Hershey Bears	AHL	67	21	25	46	93	....	....	....	....	....	....	....	....	....	10	1	3	4	6	....	....	....	....
2001-02	Colorado	NHL	50	2	7	9	47	1	0	0	38	5.3	4	71	54.9	8:07	21	1	1	2	13	0	0	0	7:07
2002-03	Colorado	NHL	6	0	3	3	2	0	0	0	6	0.0	3	31	41.9	8:17	....	....	....	....	....	....	....	....	....
	Hershey Bears	AHL	25	3	6	9	25	....	....	....	....	....	....	....	....	....	4	1	1	2	8	....	....	....	....
	NHL Totals		66	2	10	12	49	1	0	0	47	4.3		116	51.7	8:18	21	1	1	2	13	0	0	0	7:07

• Re-entered NHL Entry Draft. Originally Ottawa's 3rd choice, 53rd overall, in 1995 Entry Draft.

WHL East Second All-Star Team (1997)

Rights traded to **Colorado** by **Ottawa** for Janne Laukkanen, January 26, 1996. • Missed majority of 1998-99 season recovering from abdominal injury suffered in game vs. Albany (AHL), November 20, 1998. Missed majority of 2002-03 season recovering from groin (October 27, 2002 vs. Minnesota) and back (December 11, 2002) injuries.

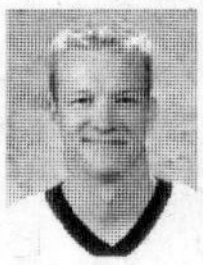

LAUKKANEN, Janne (LOW-kah-nehn, YAN-nee) T.B.

Defense. Shoots left. 6'1", 196 lbs. Born, Lahti, Finland, March 19, 1970. Quebec's 8th choice, 156th overall, in 1991 Entry Draft.

1986-87	K. Reipas Jr.	Finn-Jr.	1	0	0	0	0	....	....	....	....	....	....	....	....	....	....	....	....	....	....	....	....	....	....
1987-88	K. Reipas-B	Finn-Jr.	20	5	5	10	48	....	....	....	....	....	....	....	....	....	....	....	....	....	....	....	....	....	....
1988-89	Army Jr.	Finn-Jr.	6	0	1	1	6	....	....	....	....	....	....	....	....	....	....	....	....	....	....	....	....	....	....
	Hockey-Reipas	Finland-2	33	1	7	8	24	....	....	....	....	....	....	....	....	....	....	....	....	....	....	....	....	....	....
1989-90	H. Reipas Jr.	Finn-Jr.	2	2	2	4	2	....	....	....	....	....	....	....	....	....	....	....	....	....	....	....	....	....	....
	Hockey-Reipas	Finland-2	44	8	22	30	60	....	....	....	....	....	....	....	....	....	....	....	....	....	....	....	....	....	....
1990-91	Reipas Lahti	Finland	44	8	14	22	56	....	....	....	....	....	....	....	....	....	....	....	....	....	....	....	....	....	....
1991-92	HPK Hameenlinna	Finland	43	5	14	19	62	....	....	....	....	....	....	....	....	....	....	....	....	....	....	....	....	....	....
	Finland	Olympics	8	0	1	1	6	....	....	....	....	....	....	....	....	....	....	....	....	....	....	....	....	....	....
1992-93	HPK Hameenlinna	Finland	47	8	21	29	76	....	....	....	....	....	....	....	....	....	12	1	4	5	10	....	....	....	....
1993-94	HPK Hameenlinna	Finland	48	5	24	29	46	....	....	....	....	....	....	....	....	....	....	....	....	....	....	....	....	....	....
	Finland	Olympics	8	0	2	2	12	....	....	....	....	....	....	....	....	....	....	....	....	....	....	....	....	....	....
	Ceske Budejovice	Czech	....	....	....	....	....	....	....	....	....	....	....	....	....	....	3	0	1	1	0	....	....	....	....
1994-95	Cornwall Aces	AHL	55	8	26	34	41	....	....	....	....	....	....	....	....	....	....	....	....	....	....	....	....	....	....
	Quebec	NHL	11	0	3	3	4	0	0	0	12	0.0	3	....	....	....	6	1	0	1	2	0	0	0	
1995-96	Colorado	NHL	3	1	0	1	0	1	0	0	4	25.0	-1	....	....	....	....	....	....	....	....	....	....	....	....
	Cornwall Aces	AHL	35	7	20	27	60	....	....	....	....	....	....	....	....	....	....	....	....	....	....	....	....	....	....
	Ottawa	NHL	20	0	2	2	14	0	0	0	31	0.0	0	....	....	....	....	....	....	....	....	....	....	....	....
1996-97	Ottawa	NHL	76	3	18	21	76	2	0	0	109	2.8	-14	....	....	....	7	0	1	1	6	0	0	0	
1997-98	Ottawa	NHL	60	4	17	21	64	2	0	2	69	5.8	-15	....	....	....	11	2	2	4	8	1	0	1	
	Finland	Olympics	6	0	0	0	4	....	....	....	....	....	....	....	....	....	....	....	....	....	....	....	....	....	....
1998-99	Ottawa	NHL	50	1	11	12	40	0	0	0	46	2.2	18	0	0.0	18:37	4	0	0	0	4	0	0	0	17:28
99-2000	Ottawa	NHL	60	1	11	12	55	0	0	0	62	1.6	14	0	0.0	19:47	....	....	....	....	....	....	....	....	....
	Pittsburgh	NHL	11	1	7	8	12	1	0	0	19	5.3	3	0	0.0	16:55	11	2	4	6	10	1	0	1	23:52
2000-01	Pittsburgh	NHL	50	3	17	20	34	0	0	0	58	5.2	9	0	0.0	18:28	18	2	2	4	14	1	0	0	19:18
2001-02	Pittsburgh	NHL	47	6	7	13	28	3	0	1	66	9.1	-18	0	0.0	17:51	....	....	....	....	....	....	....	....	....
2002-03	Pittsburgh	NHL	17	1	6	7	8	0	0	0	10	10.0	-3	0	0.0	16:51	....	....	....	....	....	....	....	....	....
	Hartford	AHL	5	0	3	3	2	....	....	....	....	....	....	....	....	....	....	....	....	....	....	....	....	....	....
	Tampa Bay	NHL	2	1	0	1	0	0	0	0	2	50.0	1	0	0.0	18:15	2	0	0	0	2	0	0	0	22:27
	NHL Totals		407	22	99	121	335	9	0	3	488	4.5		0	0.0	18:31	59	7	9	16	46	3	0	2	20:42

Transferred to **Colorado** after **Quebec** franchise relocated, June 21, 1995. Traded to **Ottawa** by **Colorado** for the rights to Brad Larsen, January 26, 1996. Traded to **Pittsburgh** by **Ottawa** with Ron Tugnutt for Tom Barrasso, March 14, 2000. • Missed majority of 2002-03 season recovering from hip injury suffered in game vs. San Jose, December 12, 2002. Traded to **NY Rangers** by **Pittsburgh** with Mike Wilson, Alex Kovalev and Dan LaCouture for Joel Bouchard, Richard Lintner, Rico Fata, Mikael Samuelsson and future considerations, February 10, 2003. Claimed on waivers by **Tampa Bay** from **NY Rangers**, March 11, 2003.

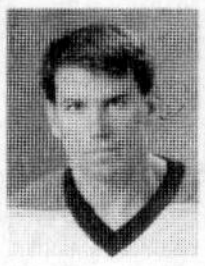

LAUS, Paul (LOWZ, PAWL) FLA.

Defense. Shoots right. 6'1", 215 lbs. Born, Beamsville, Ont., September 26, 1970. Pittsburgh's 2nd choice, 37th overall, in 1989 Entry Draft.

1986-87	St. Catharines	OJHL-B	40	1	8	9	56	....	....	....	....	....	....	....	....	....	....	....	....	....	....	....	....	....	....
1987-88	Hamilton	OHL	56	1	9	10	171	....	....	....	....	....	....	....	....	....	14	0	0	0	28	....	....	....	....
1988-89	Niagara Falls	OHL	49	1	10	11	225	....	....	....	....	....	....	....	....	....	15	0	5	5	56	....	....	....	....
1989-90	Niagara Falls	OHL	60	13	35	48	231	....	....	....	....	....	....	....	....	....	16	6	16	22	71	....	....	....	....
1990-91	Albany Choppers	IHL	7	0	0	0	7	....	....	....	....	....	....	....	....	....	....	....	....	....	....	....	....	....	....
	Knoxville	ECHL	20	6	12	18	83	....	....	....	....	....	....	....	....	....	....	....	....	....	....	....	....	....	....
	Muskegon	IHL	35	3	4	7	103	....	....	....	....	....	....	....	....	....	4	0	0	0	13	....	....	....	....
1991-92	Muskegon	IHL	75	0	21	21	248	....	....	....	....	....	....	....	....	....	14	2	5	7	70	....	....	....	....
1992-93	Cleveland	IHL	76	8	18	26	427	....	....	....	....	....	....	....	....	....	4	1	0	1	27	....	....	....	....
1993-94	Florida	NHL	39	2	0	2	109	0	0	1	15	13.3	9	....	....	....	....	....	....	....	....	....	....	....	....
1994-95	Florida	NHL	37	0	7	7	138	0	0	0	18	0.0	12	....	....	....	....	....	....	....	....	....	....	....	....
1995-96	Florida	NHL	78	3	6	9	236	0	0	0	45	6.7	-2	....	....	....	21	2	6	8	*62	0	0	0	
1996-97	Florida	NHL	77	0	12	12	313	0	0	0	63	0.0	13	....	....	....	5	0	1	1	4	0	0	0	
1997-98	Florida	NHL	77	0	11	11	293	0	0	0	64	0.0	-5	....	....	....	....	....	....	....	....	....	....	....	....
1998-99	Florida	NHL	75	1	9	10	218	0	0	0	54	1.9	-1	0	0.0	11:09	....	....	....	....	....	....	....	....	....
99-2000	Florida	NHL	77	3	8	11	172	0	0	0	44	6.8	-1	1	0.0	7:37	4	0	0	0	8	0	0	0	10:22
2000-01	Florida	NHL	25	1	2	3	66	0	0	0	18	5.6	5	0	0.0	14:22	....	....	....	....	....	....	....	....	....
2001-02	Florida	NHL	45	4	3	7	157	0	1	0	39	10.3	1	0	0.0	14:10	....	....	....	....	....	....	....	....	....
2002-03		DID NOT PLAY – INJURED																							
	NHL Totals		530	14	58	72	1702	0	1	1	360	3.9		1	0.0	10:54	30	2	7	9	74	0	0	0	10:22

Claimed by **Florida** from **Pittsburgh** in Expansion Draft, June 24, 1993. • Missed majority of 2000-01 season recovering from hernia injury suffered in game vs. Carolina, November 15, 2000. • Missed entire 2002-03 season recovering from wrist injury suffered in game vs. Montreal, January 20, 2002.

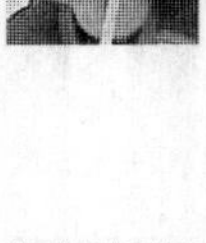

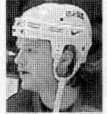

LAW, Kirby (LAW, KUHR-bee) PHI.

Right wing. Shoots right. 6'1", 185 lbs. Born, McCreary, Man., March 11, 1977.

1991-92	McCreary	MAHA	60	89	103	192	60	....	....	....	....	....	....	....	....	....	....	....	....	....	....	....	....	....	....
1992-93	Dauphin Kings	MJHL	48	20	15	35	8	....	....	....	....	....	....	....	....	....	....	....	....	....	....	....	....	....	....
1993-94	Saskatoon Blades	WHL	66	9	11	20	39	....	....	....	....	....	....	....	....	....	16	0	0	0	6	....	....	....	....
1994-95	Saskatoon Blades	WHL	46	10	15	25	44	....	....	....	....	....	....	....	....	....	....	....	....	....	....	....	....	....	....
	Lethbridge	WHL	24	4	10	14	38	....	....	....	....	....	....	....	....	....	....	....	....	....	....	....	....	....	....
1995-96	Lethbridge	WHL	71	17	45	62	133	....	....	....	....	....	....	....	....	....	4	0	0	0	12	....	....	....	....
1996-97	Lethbridge	WHL	72	39	52	91	200	....	....	....	....	....	....	....	....	....	19	4	14	18	60	....	....	....	....
1997-98	Brandon	WHL	49	34	44	78	153	....	....	....	....	....	....	....	....	....	9	3	3	6	41	....	....	....	....

			Regular Season														Playoffs								
Season	Club	League	GP	G	A	Pts	PIM	PP	SH	GW	S	%	+/-	TF	F%	Min	GP	G	A	Pts	PIM	PP	SH	GW	Min
1998-99	Orlando	IHL	67	18	13	31	136																		
	Adirondack	AHL	11	2	3	5	40										3	1	0	1	2				
99-2000	Louisville Panthers	AHL	66	31	21	52	173																		
	Orlando	IHL	1	1	0	1	0																		
	Philadelphia	AHL	12	1	4	5	6										5	2	0	2	2				
2000-01	**Philadelphia**	**NHL**	**1**	**0**	**0**	**0**	**0**	**0**	**0**	**0**	**0**	**0.0**	**–1**	**0**	**0.0**	**3:23**									
	Philadelphia	AHL	78	27	34	61	150										10	1	6	7	16				
2001-02	Philadelphia	AHL	71	18	24	42	102										5	0	0	0	0				
2002-03	Philadelphia	AHL	74	22	19	41	166																		
	Philadelphia	**NHL**	**2**	**0**	**0**	**0**	**2**	**0**	**0**	**0**	**0**	**0.0**	**0**	**0**	**0.0**	**1:41**									
	NHL Totals		**3**	**0**	**0**	**0**	**2**	**0**	**0**	**0**	**0**	**0.0**		**0**	**0.0**	**2:15**									

Signed as a free agent by **Atlanta**, July 27, 1999. Traded to **Philadelphia** by **Atlanta** for Vancouver's 6th round choice (previously acquired, Atlanta selected Jeff Dwyer) in 2000 Entry Draft and Philadelphia's 6th round choice (Pasi Nurminen) in 2001 Entry Draft, March 14, 2000.

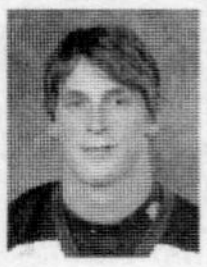

LECAVALIER, Vincent

(luh-KAV-uhl-YAY, VIHN-sihnt) **T.B.**

Center. Shoots left. 6'4", 205 lbs. Born, Ile Bizard, Que., April 21, 1980. Tampa Bay's 1st choice, 1st overall, in 1998 Entry Draft.

Season	Club	League	GP	G	A	Pts	PIM	PP	SH	GW	S	%	+/-	TF	F%	Min	GP	G	A	Pts	PIM	PP	SH	GW	Min
1995-96	Notre Dame	SMHL	22	52	52	104																			
1996-97	Rimouski Oceanic	QMJHL	64	42	61	103	38										4	4	3	7	2				
1997-98	Rimouski Oceanic	QMJHL	58	44	71	115	117										18	*15	*26	*41	46				
1998-99	**Tampa Bay**	**NHL**	**82**	**13**	**15**	**28**	**23**	**2**	**0**	**2**	**125**	**10.4**	**–19**	**953**	**40.3**	**13:40**									
99-2000	**Tampa Bay**	**NHL**	**80**	**25**	**42**	**67**	**43**	**6**	**0**	**3**	**166**	**15.1**	**–25**	**1288**	**44.4**	**19:18**									
2000-01	**Tampa Bay**	**NHL**	**68**	**23**	**28**	**51**	**66**	**7**	**0**	**3**	**165**	**13.9**	**–26**	**1278**	**44.9**	**19:57**									
2001-02	**Tampa Bay**	**NHL**	**76**	**20**	**17**	**37**	**61**	**5**	**0**	**3**	**164**	**12.2**	**–18**	**931**	**41.5**	**17:09**									
2002-03	**Tampa Bay**	**NHL**	**80**	**33**	**45**	**78**	**39**	**11**	**2**	**3**	**274**	**12.0**	**0**	**1200**	**43.9**	**19:33**	**11**	**3**	**3**	**6**	**22**	**1**	**0**	**1**	**22:36**
	NHL Totals		**386**	**114**	**147**	**261**	**232**	**31**	**2**	**14**	**894**	**12.8**		**5650**	**43.2**	**17:51**	**11**	**3**	**3**	**6**	**22**	**1**	**0**	**1**	**22:36**

QMJHL All-Rookie Team (1997) • QMJHL Offensive Rookie of the Year (1997) • Canadian Major Junior Rookie of the Year (1997) • QMJHL First All-Star Team (1998) • Canadian Major Junior First All-Star Team (1998)

Played in NHL All-Star Game (2003)

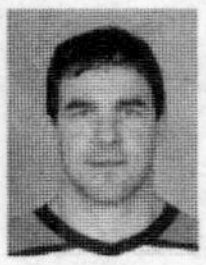

LeCLAIR, John

(luh-KLAIR, JAWN) **PHI.**

Left wing. Shoots left. 6'3", 226 lbs. Born, St. Albans, VT, July 5, 1969. Montreal's 2nd choice, 33rd overall, in 1987 Entry Draft.

Season	Club	League	GP	G	A	Pts	PIM	PP	SH	GW	S	%	+/-	TF	F%	Min	GP	G	A	Pts	PIM	PP	SH	GW	Min
1985-86	Bellows	Hi-School	22	41	28	69	14																		
1986-87	Bellows	Hi-School	23	44	40	84	14																		
1987-88	U. of Vermont	ECAC	31	12	22	34	62																		
1988-89	U. of Vermont	ECAC	18	9	12	21	40																		
1989-90	U. of Vermont	ECAC	10	10	6	16	38																		
1990-91	U. of Vermont	ECAC	33	25	20	45	58																		
	Montreal	**NHL**	**10**	**2**	**5**	**7**	**2**	**0**	**0**	**1**	**12**	**16.7**	**1**				**3**	**0**	**0**	**0**	**0**	**0**	**0**	**0**	
1991-92	**Montreal**	**NHL**	**59**	**8**	**11**	**19**	**14**	**3**	**0**	**0**	**73**	**11.0**	**5**				**8**	**1**	**1**	**2**	**4**	**0**	**0**	**0**	
	Fredericton	AHL	8	7	7	14	10										2	0	0	0	4				
1992-93♦	**Montreal**	**NHL**	**72**	**19**	**25**	**44**	**33**	**2**	**0**	**2**	**139**	**13.7**	**11**				**20**	**4**	**6**	**10**	**14**	**0**	**0**	**3**	
1993-94	**Montreal**	**NHL**	**74**	**19**	**24**	**43**	**32**	**1**	**0**	**1**	**153**	**12.4**	**17**				**7**	**2**	**1**	**3**	**8**	**1**	**0**	**0**	
1994-95	**Montreal**	**NHL**	**9**	**1**	**4**	**5**	**10**	**1**	**0**	**0**	**18**	**5.6**	**–1**												
	Philadelphia	**NHL**	**37**	**25**	**24**	**49**	**20**	**5**	**0**	**7**	**113**	**22.1**	**21**				**15**	**5**	**7**	**12**	**4**	**1**	**0**	**1**	
1995-96	**Philadelphia**	**NHL**	**82**	**51**	**46**	**97**	**64**	**19**	**0**	**10**	**270**	**18.9**	**21**				**11**	**6**	**5**	**11**	**6**	**4**	**0**	**1**	
1996-97	**Philadelphia**	**NHL**	**82**	**50**	**47**	**97**	**58**	**10**	**0**	**5**	**324**	**15.4**	**44**				**19**	**9**	**12**	**21**	**10**	**4**	**0**	**3**	
1997-98	**Philadelphia**	**NHL**	**82**	**51**	**36**	**87**	**32**	**16**	**0**	**9**	**303**	**16.8**	**30**				**5**	**1**	**1**	**2**	**8**	**1**	**0**	**1**	
	United States	Olympics	4	0	1	1	0																		
1998-99	**Philadelphia**	**NHL**	**76**	**43**	**47**	**90**	**30**	**16**	**0**	**7**	**246**	**17.5**	**36**	**7**	**14.3**	**21:03**	**6**	**3**	**0**	**3**	**12**	**2**	**0**	**0**	**20:14**
99-2000	**Philadelphia**	**NHL**	**82**	**40**	**37**	**77**	**36**	**13**	**0**	**7**	**249**	**16.1**	**8**	**7**	**28.6**	**20:18**	**18**	**6**	**7**	**13**	**6**	**4**	**0**	**2**	**21:16**
2000-01	**Philadelphia**	**NHL**	**16**	**7**	**5**	**12**	**0**	**3**	**0**	**2**	**48**	**14.6**	**2**	**0**	**0.0**	**19:06**	**6**	**1**	**2**	**3**	**2**	**0**	**0**	**0**	**19:34**
2001-02	**Philadelphia**	**NHL**	**82**	**25**	**26**	**51**	**30**	**4**	**0**	**6**	**220**	**11.4**	**5**	**4**	**75.0**	**17:30**	**5**	**0**	**0**	**0**	**2**	**0**	**0**	**0**	**17:18**
	United States	Olympics	6	*6	1	7	2																		
2002-03	**Philadelphia**	**NHL**	**35**	**18**	**10**	**28**	**16**	**8**	**0**	**4**	**99**	**18.2**	**10**	**3**	**66.7**	**16:09**	**13**	**2**	**3**	**5**	**10**	**1**	**0**	**0**	**17:09**
	NHL Totals		**798**	**359**	**347**	**706**	**377**	**101**	**0**	**61**	**2267**	**15.8**		**21**	**38.1**	**19:08**	**136**	**40**	**45**	**85**	**86**	**18**	**0**	**11**	**19:24**

ECAC Second All-Star Team (1991) • NHL First All-Star Team (1995, 1998) • NHL Second All-Star Team (1996, 1997, 1999) • Bud Light Plus/Minus Award (1997) • Bud Ice Plus/Minus Award (1999)

Played in NHL All-Star Game (1996, 1997, 1998, 1999, 2000)

• Missed majority of 1989-90 season recovering from knee surgery, January 20, 1990. Traded to **Philadelphia** by **Montreal** with Eric Desjardins and Gilbert Dionne for Mark Recchi and Philadelphia's 3rd round choice (Martin Hohenberger) in 1995 Entry Draft, February 9, 1995. • Missed majority of 2000-01 season recovering from back injury suffered in game vs. Boston, October 7, 2000. • Missed majority of 2002-03 season recovering from shoulder injury suffered in game vs. St. Louis, November 27, 2002.

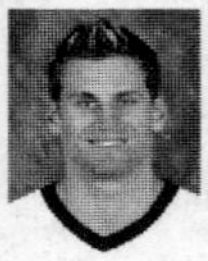

LECLERC, Mike

(luh-KLUHRK, MIGHK) **ANA.**

Left wing. Shoots left. 6'2", 208 lbs. Born, Winnipeg, Man., November 10, 1976. Anaheim's 3rd choice, 55th overall, in 1995 Entry Draft.

Season	Club	League	GP	G	A	Pts	PIM	PP	SH	GW	S	%	+/-	TF	F%	Min	GP	G	A	Pts	PIM	PP	SH	GW	Min
1991-92	St. Boniface	MJHL	43	16	12	28	25																		
	Victoria Cougars	WHL	2	0	0	0	0																		
1992-93	Victoria Cougars	WHL	70	4	11	15	118																		
1993-94	Victoria Cougars	WHL	68	29	11	40	112																		
1994-95	Prince George	WHL	43	20	36	56	78																		
	Brandon	WHL	23	5	8	13	50										18	10	6	16	33				
1995-96	Brandon	WHL	71	58	53	111	161										19	6	19	25	25				
1996-97	**Anaheim**	**NHL**	**5**	**1**	**1**	**2**	**0**	**0**	**0**	**1**	**3**	**33.3**	**2**				**1**	**0**	**0**	**0**	**0**	**0**	**0**	**0**	
	Baltimore Bandits	AHL	71	29	27	56	134																		
1997-98	**Anaheim**	**NHL**	**7**	**0**	**0**	**0**	**6**	**0**	**0**	**0**	**11**	**0.0**	**–6**												
	Cincinnati	AHL	48	18	22	40	83																		
1998-99	**Anaheim**	**NHL**	**7**	**0**	**0**	**0**	**4**	**0**	**0**	**0**	**1**	**0.0**	**–2**	**0**	**0.0**	**5:52**	**1**	**0**	**0**	**0**	**0**	**0**	**0**	**0**	**15:02**
	Cincinnati	AHL	65	25	28	53	153										3	0	1	1	19				
99-2000	**Anaheim**	**NHL**	**69**	**8**	**11**	**19**	**70**	**0**	**0**	**2**	**105**	**7.6**	**–15**	**1**	**0.0**	**12:08**									
2000-01	**Anaheim**	**NHL**	**54**	**15**	**20**	**35**	**26**	**3**	**0**	**3**	**130**	**11.5**	**–1**	**5**	**20.0**	**17:35**									
2001-02	**Anaheim**	**NHL**	**82**	**20**	**24**	**44**	**107**	**8**	**0**	**4**	**178**	**11.2**	**–12**	**10**	**50.0**	**17:23**									
2002-03	**Anaheim**	**NHL**	**57**	**9**	**19**	**28**	**34**	**1**	**0**	**4**	**122**	**7.4**	**–8**	**17**	**29.4**	**16:56**	**21**	**2**	**9**	**11**	**12**	**1**	**0**	**2**	**19:02**
	NHL Totals		**281**	**53**	**75**	**128**	**247**	**12**	**0**	**14**	**550**	**9.6**		**33**	**33.3**	**15:41**	**23**	**2**	**9**	**11**	**12**	**1**	**0**	**2**	**18:51**

WHL East Second All-Star Team (1996)

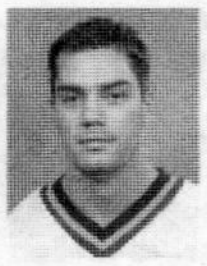

LEEB, Brad

(LEEB, BRAD) **TOR.**

Right wing. Shoots right. 5'11", 187 lbs. Born, Red Deer, Alta., August 27, 1979.

Season	Club	League	GP	G	A	Pts	PIM	PP	SH	GW	S	%	+/-	TF	F%	Min	GP	G	A	Pts	PIM	PP	SH	GW	Min
1994-95	Red Deer	AMHL	36	31	14	45	93																		
	Red Deer Rebels	WHL	3	0	0	0	4																		
1995-96	Red Deer Rebels	WHL	38	3	6	9	30										10	2	0	2	11				
1996-97	Red Deer Rebels	WHL	70	15	20	35	76										16	3	3	6	6				
1997-98	Red Deer Rebels	WHL	63	23	23	46	88										3	2	0	2	2				
1998-99	Red Deer Rebels	WHL	64	32	47	79	84										9	5	9	14	10				
99-2000	**Vancouver**	**NHL**	**2**	**0**	**0**	**0**	**2**	**0**	**0**	**0**	**3**	**0.0**	**–2**	**0**	**0.0**	**12:07**									
	Syracuse Crunch	AHL	61	19	18	37	50										4	0	0	0	6				
2000-01	Kansas City	IHL	53	18	16	34	53																		
2001-02	**Vancouver**	**NHL**	**2**	**0**	**0**	**0**	**0**	**0**	**0**	**0**	**1**	**0.0**	**1**	**0**	**0.0**	**9:35**									
	Manitoba Moose	AHL	60	17	15	32	45																		
2002-03	St. John's	AHL	79	35	26	61	78																		
	NHL Totals		**4**	**0**	**0**	**0**	**2**	**0**	**0**	**0**	**4**	**0.0**		**0**	**0.0**	**10:51**									

WHL East Second All-Star Team (1999)

Signed as a free agent by **Vancouver**, October 8, 1999. Traded to **Toronto** by **Vancouver** for Tomas Mojzis, September 4, 2002.

LEETCH, Brian
(LEECH, BRIGH-uhn) **NYR**

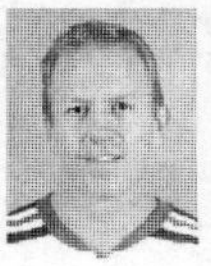

Defense. Shoots left. 6'1", 190 lbs. Born, Corpus Christi, TX, March 3, 1968. NY Rangers' 1st choice, 9th overall, in 1986 Entry Draft.

			Regular Season														Playoffs								
Season	Club	League	GP	G	A	Pts	PIM	PP	SH	GW	S	%	+/-	TF	F%	Min	GP	G	A	Pts	PIM	PP	SH	GW	Min
1983-84	Avon Old Farms	Hi-School	28	52	49	101	24	....	....	....	....	....	....	....	....	....	....	....	....	....	....	....	....	....	....
1984-85	Avon Old Farms	Hi-School	26	30	46	76	15	....	....	....	....	....	....	....	....	....	....	....	....	....	....	....	....	....	....
1985-86	Avon Old Farms	Hi-School	28	40	44	84	18	....	....	....	....	....	....	....	....	....	....	....	....	....	....	....	....	....	....
1986-87	Boston College	H-East	37	9	38	47	10	....	....	....	....	....	....	....	....	....	....	....	....	....	....	....	....	....	....
1987-88	Team USA	Nat-Tm	50	13	61	74	38	....	....	....	....	....	....	....	....	....	....	....	....	....	....	....	....	....	....
	United States	Olympics	6	1	5	6	4	....	....	....	....	....	....	....	....	....	....	....	....	....	....	....	....	....	....
	NY Rangers	**NHL**	**17**	**2**	**12**	**14**	**0**	**1**	**0**	**1**	**40**	**5.0**	**5**	....	....	....	....	....	....	....	....	....	....	....	....
1988-89	**NY Rangers**	**NHL**	**68**	**23**	**48**	**71**	**50**	**8**	**3**	**1**	**268**	**8.6**	**8**	....	....	....	**4**	**3**	**2**	**5**	**2**	**2**	**0**	**0**	....
1989-90	**NY Rangers**	**NHL**	**72**	**11**	**45**	**56**	**26**	**5**	**0**	**2**	**222**	**5.0**	**–18**	....	....	....	....	....	....	....	....	....	....	....	....
1990-91	**NY Rangers**	**NHL**	**80**	**16**	**72**	**88**	**42**	**6**	**0**	**4**	**206**	**7.8**	**2**	....	....	....	**6**	**1**	**3**	**4**	**0**	**0**	**0**	**0**	....
1991-92	**NY Rangers**	**NHL**	**80**	**22**	**80**	**102**	**26**	**10**	**1**	**3**	**245**	**9.0**	**25**	....	....	....	**13**	**4**	**11**	**15**	**4**	**1**	**1**	**0**	....
1992-93	**NY Rangers**	**NHL**	**36**	**6**	**30**	**36**	**26**	**2**	**1**	**1**	**150**	**4.0**	**2**	....	....	....	....	....	....	....	....	....	....	....	....
1993-94♦	**NY Rangers**	**NHL**	**84**	**23**	**56**	**79**	**67**	**17**	**1**	**4**	**328**	**7.0**	**28**	....	....	....	**23**	**11**	***23**	***34**	**6**	**4**	**0**	**4**	....
1994-95	**NY Rangers**	**NHL**	**48**	**9**	**32**	**41**	**18**	**3**	**0**	**2**	**182**	**4.9**	**0**	....	....	....	**10**	**6**	**8**	**14**	**8**	**3**	**0**	**1**	....
1995-96	**NY Rangers**	**NHL**	**82**	**15**	**70**	**85**	**30**	**7**	**0**	**3**	**276**	**5.4**	**12**	....	....	....	**11**	**1**	**6**	**7**	**4**	**1**	**0**	**0**	....
1996-97	**NY Rangers**	**NHL**	**82**	**20**	**58**	**78**	**40**	**9**	**0**	**2**	**256**	**7.8**	**31**	....	....	....	**15**	**2**	**8**	**10**	**6**	**1**	**0**	**1**	....
1997-98	**NY Rangers**	**NHL**	**76**	**17**	**33**	**50**	**32**	**11**	**0**	**2**	**230**	**7.4**	**–36**	....	....	....	....	....	....	....	....	....	....	....	....
	United States	Olympics	4	1	1	2	0	....	....	....	....	....	....	....	....	....	....	....	....	....	....	....	....	....	....
1998-99	**NY Rangers**	**NHL**	**82**	**13**	**42**	**55**	**42**	**4**	**0**	**1**	**184**	**7.1**	**–7**	**0**	**0.0**	**29:52**	....	....	....	....	....	....	....	....	....
99-2000	**NY Rangers**	**NHL**	**50**	**7**	**19**	**26**	**20**	**3**	**0**	**2**	**124**	**5.6**	**–16**	**0**	**0.0**	**26:57**	....	....	....	....	....	....	....	....	....
2000-01	**NY Rangers**	**NHL**	**82**	**21**	**58**	**79**	**34**	**10**	**1**	**3**	**241**	**8.7**	**–18**	**0**	**0.0**	**29:21**	....	....	....	....	....	....	....	....	....
2001-02	**NY Rangers**	**NHL**	**82**	**10**	**45**	**55**	**28**	**1**	**0**	**3**	**202**	**5.0**	**14**	**0**	**0.0**	**25:52**	....	....	....	....	....	....	....	....	....
	United States	Olympics	6	0	5	5	0	....	....	....	....	....	....	....	....	....	....	....	....	....	....	....	....	....	....
2002-03	**NY Rangers**	**NHL**	**51**	**12**	**18**	**30**	**20**	**5**	**0**	**2**	**150**	**8.0**	**–3**	**0**	**0.0**	**26:06**	....	....	....	....	....	....	....	....	....
	NHL Totals		**1072**	**227**	**718**	**945**	**501**	**102**	**7**	**36**	**3304**	**6.9**		**0**	**0.0**	**27:49**	**82**	**28**	**61**	**89**	**30**	**12**	**1**	**6**	....

Hockey East First All-Star Team (1987) • Hockey East Rookie of the Year (1987) • Hockey East Player of the Year (1987) • NCAA East First All-American Team (1987) • NHL All-Rookie Team (1989) • Calder Memorial Trophy (1989) • NHL Second All-Star Team (1991, 1994, 1996) • James Norris Memorial Trophy (1992, 1997) • NHL First All-Star Team (1992, 1997) • Conn Smythe Trophy (1994)

Played in NHL All-Star Game (1990, 1991, 1992, 1994, 1996, 1997, 1998, 2001, 2002)

Rights traded to **Edmonton** by **NY Rangers** for Jussi Markkanen and future considerations, June 30, 2003. Signed as a free agent by **NY Rangers**, July 30, 2003.

LEFEBVRE, Guillaume
(luh-FAYV, GEE-ohm) **PIT.**

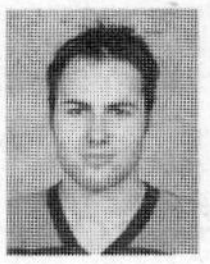

Left wing. Shoots left. 6'1", 200 lbs. Born, Amos, Que., May 7, 1981. Philadelphia's 6th choice, 227th overall, in 2000 Entry Draft.

Season	Club	League	GP	G	A	Pts	PIM	PP	SH	GW	S	%	+/-	TF	F%	Min	GP	G	A	Pts	PIM	PP	SH	GW	Min
1996-97	Amos Forestiers	QAAA	40	7	12	19	14	....	....	....	....	....	....	....	....	....	....	....	....	....	....	....	....	....	....
1997-98	Amos Forestiers	QAAA	42	12	16	28	100	....	....	....	....	....	....	....	....	....	6	4	5	9	....	....	....	....	....
1998-99	Shawinigan	QMJHL	40	3	1	4	49	....	....	....	....	....	....	....	....	....	....	....	....	....	....	....	....	....	....
	Cape Breton	QMJHL	24	2	7	9	13	....	....	....	....	....	....	....	....	....	5	0	1	1	0	....	....	....	....
99-2000	Cape Breton	QMJHL	44	26	28	54	82	....	....	....	....	....	....	....	....	....	....	....	....	....	....	....	....	....	....
	Quebec Remparts	QMJHL	2	3	1	4	0	....	....	....	....	....	....	....	....	....	....	....	....	....	....	....	....	....	....
	Rouyn-Noranda	QMJHL	25	4	11	15	39	....	....	....	....	....	....	....	....	....	11	4	0	4	25	....	....	....	....
2000-01	Rouyn-Noranda	QMJHL	61	24	43	67	160	....	....	....	....	....	....	....	....	....	9	3	1	4	22	....	....	....	....
	Philadelphia	AHL	....	....	....	....	....	....	....	....	....	....	....	....	....	....	9	0	1	1	2	....	....	....	....
2001-02	**Philadelphia**	**NHL**	**3**	**0**	**0**	**0**	**0**	**0**	**0**	**0**	**3**	**0.0**	**–1**	**0**	**0.0**	**5:55**	....	....	....	....	....	....	....	....	....
	Philadelphia	AHL	78	19	15	34	111	....	....	....	....	....	....	....	....	....	5	0	0	0	4	....	....	....	....
2002-03	**Philadelphia**	**NHL**	**14**	**0**	**0**	**0**	**4**	**0**	**0**	**0**	**5**	**0.0**	**1**	**0**	**0.0**	**7:27**	....	....	....	....	....	....	....	....	....
	Philadelphia	AHL	47	7	6	13	113	....	....	....	....	....	....	....	....	....	....	....	....	....	....	....	....	....	....
	Pittsburgh	**NHL**	**12**	**2**	**4**	**6**	**0**	**0**	**0**	**0**	**14**	**14.3**	**1**	**1**	**100.0**	**17:30**	....	....	....	....	....	....	....	....	....
	Wilkes-Barre	AHL	1	1	0	1	0	....	....	....	....	....	....	....	....	....	5	0	0	0	6	....	....	....	....
	NHL Totals		**29**	**2**	**4**	**6**	**4**	**0**	**0**	**0**	**22**	**9.1**		**1**	**100.0**	**11:27**	....	....	....	....	....	....	....	....	....

Traded to **Phoenix** by **Philadelphia** with Atlanta's 3rd round choice (previously acquired, Phoenix selected Tyler Redenbach) in 2003 Entry Draft and Philadelphia's 2nd round choice in 2004 Entry Draft for Tony Amonte, March 10, 2003. Traded to **Pittsburgh** by **Phoenix** with Ramzi Abid and Dan Focht for Jan Hrdina and Francois Leroux, March 11, 2003.

LEFEBVRE, Sylvain
(luh-FAYV, SIHL-veh)

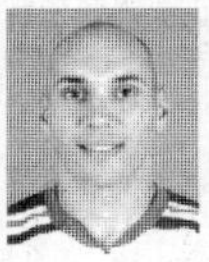

Defense. Shoots left. 6'2", 205 lbs. Born, Richmond, Que., October 14, 1967.

Season	Club	League	GP	G	A	Pts	PIM	PP	SH	GW	S	%	+/-	TF	F%	Min	GP	G	A	Pts	PIM	PP	SH	GW	Min
1983-84	Cantons	QAAA	1	0	0	0	0	....	....	....	....	....	....	....	....	....	2	1	0	1	2	....	....	....	....
1984-85	Laval Voisins	QMJHL	66	7	5	12	31	....	....	....	....	....	....	....	....	....	....	....	....	....	....	....	....	....	....
1985-86	Laval Titan	QMJHL	71	8	17	25	48	....	....	....	....	....	....	....	....	....	14	1	0	1	25	....	....	....	....
1986-87	Laval Titan	QMJHL	70	10	36	46	44	....	....	....	....	....	....	....	....	....	15	1	6	7	12	....	....	....	....
1987-88	Sherbrooke	AHL	79	3	24	27	73	....	....	....	....	....	....	....	....	....	6	2	3	5	4	....	....	....	....
1988-89	Sherbrooke	AHL	77	15	32	47	119	....	....	....	....	....	....	....	....	....	6	1	3	4	4	....	....	....	....
1989-90	**Montreal**	**NHL**	**68**	**3**	**10**	**13**	**61**	**0**	**0**	**0**	**89**	**3.4**	**18**	....	....	....	**6**	**0**	**0**	**0**	**2**	**0**	**0**	**0**	....
1990-91	**Montreal**	**NHL**	**63**	**5**	**18**	**23**	**30**	**1**	**0**	**1**	**76**	**6.6**	**–11**	....	....	....	**11**	**1**	**0**	**1**	**6**	**0**	**0**	**0**	....
1991-92	**Montreal**	**NHL**	**69**	**3**	**14**	**17**	**91**	**0**	**0**	**0**	**85**	**3.5**	**9**	....	....	....	**2**	**0**	**0**	**0**	**2**	**0**	**0**	**0**	....
1992-93	**Toronto**	**NHL**	**81**	**2**	**12**	**14**	**90**	**0**	**0**	**0**	**81**	**2.5**	**8**	....	....	....	**21**	**3**	**3**	**6**	**20**	**0**	**0**	**0**	....
1993-94	**Toronto**	**NHL**	**84**	**2**	**9**	**11**	**79**	**0**	**0**	**0**	**96**	**2.1**	**33**	....	....	....	**18**	**0**	**3**	**3**	**16**	**0**	**0**	**0**	....
1994-95	**Quebec**	**NHL**	**48**	**2**	**11**	**13**	**17**	**0**	**0**	**0**	**81**	**2.5**	**13**	....	....	....	**6**	**0**	**2**	**2**	**2**	**0**	**0**	**0**	....
1995-96♦	**Colorado**	**NHL**	**75**	**5**	**11**	**16**	**49**	**2**	**0**	**0**	**115**	**4.3**	**26**	....	....	....	**22**	**0**	**5**	**5**	**12**	**0**	**0**	**0**	....
1996-97	**Colorado**	**NHL**	**71**	**2**	**11**	**13**	**30**	**1**	**0**	**0**	**77**	**2.6**	**12**	....	....	....	**17**	**0**	**0**	**0**	**25**	**0**	**0**	**0**	....
1997-98	**Colorado**	**NHL**	**81**	**0**	**10**	**10**	**48**	**0**	**0**	**0**	**66**	**0.0**	**2**	....	....	....	**7**	**0**	**0**	**0**	**4**	**0**	**0**	**0**	....
1998-99	**Colorado**	**NHL**	**76**	**2**	**18**	**20**	**48**	**0**	**0**	**0**	**64**	**3.1**	**18**	**0**	**0.0**	**20:56**	**19**	**0**	**1**	**1**	**12**	**0**	**0**	**0**	**22:45**
99-2000	**NY Rangers**	**NHL**	**82**	**2**	**10**	**12**	**43**	**0**	**0**	**0**	**67**	**3.0**	**–13**	**0**	**0.0**	**18:36**	....	....	....	....	....	....	....	....	....
2000-01	**NY Rangers**	**NHL**	**71**	**2**	**13**	**15**	**55**	**0**	**0**	**0**	**39**	**5.1**	**3**	**0**	**0.0**	**18:10**	....	....	....	....	....	....	....	....	....
2001-02	**NY Rangers**	**NHL**	**41**	**0**	**5**	**5**	**23**	**0**	**0**	**0**	**20**	**0.0**	**–3**	**0**	**0.0**	**16:38**	....	....	....	....	....	....	....	....	....
	Hartford	AHL	15	0	5	5	11	....	....	....	....	....	....	....	....	....	....	....	....	....	....	....	....	....	....
2002-03	**NY Rangers**	**NHL**	**35**	**0**	**2**	**2**	**10**	**0**	**0**	**0**	**14**	**0.0**	**–7**	**3**	**33.3**	**15:17**	....	....	....	....	....	....	....	....	....
	NHL Totals		**945**	**30**	**154**	**184**	**674**	**4**	**0**	**1**	**970**	**3.1**		**3**	**33.3**	**18:26**	**129**	**4**	**14**	**18**	**101**	**0**	**0**	**0**	**22:45**

AHL Second All-Star Team (1989)

Signed as a free agent by **Montreal**, September 24, 1986. Traded to **Toronto** by **Montreal** for Toronto's 3rd round choice (Martin Belanger) in 1994 Entry Draft, August 20, 1992. Traded to **Quebec** by **Toronto** with Wendel Clark, Landon Wilson and Toronto's 1st round choice (Jeffrey Kealty) in 1994 Entry Draft for Mats Sundin, Garth Butcher, Todd Warriner and Philadelphia's 1st round choice (previously acquired, later traded to Washington – Washington selected Nolan Baumgartner) in 1994 Entry Draft, June 28, 1994. Transferred to **Colorado** after **Quebec** franchise relocated, June 21, 1995. Signed as a free agent by **NY Rangers**, July 22, 1999. • Missed majority of 2002-03 season recovering from finger injury suffered in game vs. Chicago, December 11, 2002.

LEGWAND, David
(LEHG-wuhnd, DAY-vihd) **NSH.**

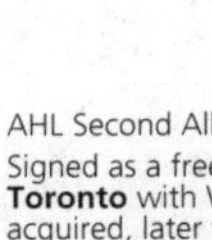

Center. Shoots left. 6'2", 190 lbs. Born, Detroit, MI, August 17, 1980. Nashville's 1st choice, 2nd overall, in 1998 Entry Draft.

Season	Club	League	GP	G	A	Pts	PIM	PP	SH	GW	S	%	+/-	TF	F%	Min	GP	G	A	Pts	PIM	PP	SH	GW	Min
1996-97	Det. Compuware	MNHL	44	21	41	62	58	....	....	....	....	....	....	....	....	....	....	....	....	....	....	....	....	....	....
1997-98	Plymouth Whalers	OHL	59	54	51	105	56	....	....	....	....	....	....	....	....	....	15	8	12	20	24	....	....	....	....
1998-99	Plymouth Whalers	OHL	55	31	49	80	65	....	....	....	....	....	....	....	....	....	11	3	8	11	8	....	....	....	....
	Nashville	**NHL**	**1**	**0**	**0**	**0**	**0**	**0**	**0**	**0**	**2**	**0.0**	**0**	**9**	**55.6**	**12:50**	....	....	....	....	....	....	....	....	....
99-2000	**Nashville**	**NHL**	**71**	**13**	**15**	**28**	**30**	**4**	**0**	**2**	**111**	**11.7**	**–6**	**637**	**41.6**	**14:43**	....	....	....	....	....	....	....	....	....
2000-01	**Nashville**	**NHL**	**81**	**13**	**28**	**41**	**38**	**3**	**0**	**3**	**172**	**7.6**	**1**	**888**	**40.3**	**15:14**	....	....	....	....	....	....	....	....	....
2001-02	**Nashville**	**NHL**	**63**	**11**	**19**	**30**	**54**	**1**	**1**	**1**	**121**	**9.1**	**1**	**843**	**40.5**	**16:25**	....	....	....	....	....	....	....	....	....
2002-03	**Nashville**	**NHL**	**64**	**17**	**31**	**48**	**34**	**3**	**1**	**4**	**167**	**10.2**	**–2**	**1095**	**46.6**	**19:14**	....	....	....	....	....	....	....	....	....
	NHL Totals		**280**	**54**	**93**	**147**	**156**	**11**	**2**	**10**	**573**	**9.4**		**3472**	**42.6**	**16:17**	....	....	....	....	....	....	....	....	....

OHL All-Rookie Team (1998) • OHL First All-Star Team (1998) • OHL Rookie of the Year (1998) • OHL MVP (1998) • Canadian Major Junior Rookie of the Year (1998)

LEHTINEN, Jere
(LEH-tih-nehn, YUH-ree) **DAL.**

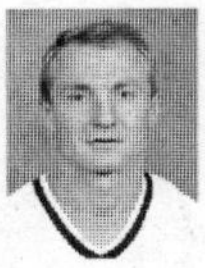

Right wing. Shoots right. 6', 200 lbs. Born, Espoo, Finland, June 24, 1973. Minnesota's 3rd choice, 88th overall, in 1992 Entry Draft.

Season	Club	League	GP	G	A	Pts	PIM	PP	SH	GW	S	%	+/-	TF	F%	Min	GP	G	A	Pts	PIM	PP	SH	GW	Min
1989-90	Kiekko-67 Jr.	Finn-Jr.	32	23	23	46	6	....	....	....	....	....	....	....	....	....	5	0	3	3	0	....	....	....	....
1990-91	Kiekko Espoo Jr.	Finn-Jr.	3	3	1	4	0	....	....	....	....	....	....	....	....	....	....	....	....	....	....	....	....	....	....
	Kiekko Espoo	Finland-2	32	15	9	24	12	....	....	....	....	....	....	....	....	....	....	....	....	....	....	....	....	....	....
1991-92	Kiekko-67 Jr.	Finn-Jr.	8	5	4	9	2	....	....	....	....	....	....	....	....	....	....	....	....	....	....	....	....	....	....
	Kiekko Espoo	Finland-2	43	32	17	49	6	....	....	....	....	....	....	....	....	....	....	....	....	....	....	....	....	....	....

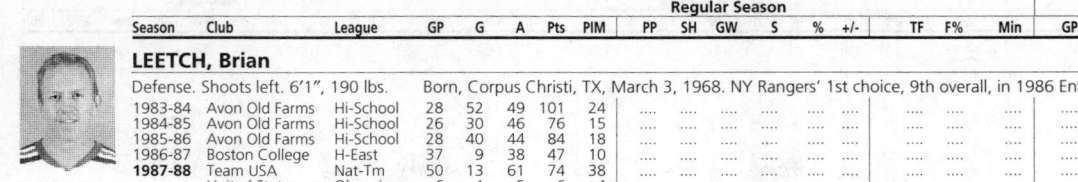

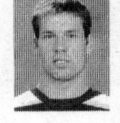

			Regular Season														Playoffs								
Season	Club	League	GP	G	A	Pts	PIM	PP	SH	GW	S	%	+/-	TF	F%	Min	GP	G	A	Pts	PIM	PP	SH	GW	Min
1992-93	Kiekko-67 Jr.	Finn-Jr.	4	5	3	8	8	....	....	....	....	....	....	....	....	....	....	....	....	....	....	....	....	....	....
	Kiekko Espoo	Finland	45	13	14	27	6	....	....	....	....	....	....	....	....	....	....	....	....	....	....	....	....	....	....
1993-94	TPS Turku	Finland	42	19	20	39	6	....	....	....	....	....	....	....	....	....	11	*11	2	13	*2	....	....	....	....
	Finland	Olympics	8	3	0	3	0	....	....	....	....	....	....	....	....	....	....	....	....	....	....	....	....	....	....
1994-95	TPS Turku	Finland	39	19	23	42	33	....	....	....	....	....	....	....	....	....	13	*8	6	14	4	....	....	....	....
1995-96	**Dallas**	**NHL**	**57**	**6**	**22**	**28**	**16**	**0**	**0**	**1**	**109**	**5.5**	**5**	....	....	....	....	....	....	....	....	....	....	....	....
	Michigan	IHL	1	1	0	1	0	....	....	....	....	....	....	....	....	....	....	....	....	....	....	....	....	....	....
1996-97	**Dallas**	**NHL**	**63**	**16**	**27**	**43**	**2**	**3**	**1**	**2**	**134**	**11.9**	**26**	....	....	....	**7**	**2**	**2**	**4**	**0**	**0**	**0**	**0**	....
1997-98	**Dallas**	**NHL**	**72**	**23**	**19**	**42**	**20**	**7**	**2**	**6**	**201**	**11.4**	**19**	....	....	....	**12**	**3**	**5**	**8**	**2**	**1**	**0**	**0**	....
	Finland	Olympics	6	4	2	6	2	....	....	....	....	....	....	....	....	....	....	....	....	....	....	....	....	....	....
1998-99 ♦	**Dallas**	**NHL**	**74**	**20**	**32**	**52**	**18**	**7**	**1**	**2**	**173**	**11.6**	**29**	**9**	**33.3**	**19:36**	**23**	**10**	**3**	**13**	**2**	**1**	**1**	**0**	**21:09**
99-2000	**Dallas**	**NHL**	**17**	**3**	**5**	**8**	**0**	**0**	**0**	**1**	**29**	**10.3**	**1**	**0**	**0.0**	**17:31**	**13**	**1**	**5**	**6**	**2**	**0**	**0**	**0**	**21:15**
2000-01	**Dallas**	**NHL**	**74**	**20**	**25**	**45**	**24**	**7**	**0**	**1**	**148**	**13.5**	**14**	**7**	**28.6**	**19:17**	**10**	**1**	**0**	**1**	**2**	**0**	**0**	**0**	**20:13**
2001-02	**Dallas**	**NHL**	**73**	**25**	**24**	**49**	**14**	**7**	**1**	**4**	**198**	**12.6**	**27**	**18**	**22.2**	**19:50**	....	....	....	....	....	....	....	....	....
	Finland	Olympics	4	1	2	3	2	....	....	....	....	....	....	....	....	....	....	....	....	....	....	....	....	....	....
2002-03	**Dallas**	**NHL**	**80**	**31**	**17**	**48**	**20**	**5**	**0**	**3**	**238**	**13.0**	**39**	**36**	**22.2**	**18:47**	**12**	**3**	**2**	**5**	**0**	**1**	**0**	**1**	**21:12**
	NHL Totals		**510**	**144**	**171**	**315**	**114**	**36**	**5**	**20**	**1230**	**11.7**		**70**	**24.3**	**19:16**	**77**	**20**	**17**	**37**	**8**	**3**	**1**	**1**	**21:01**

Frank J. Selke Trophy (1998, 1999, 2003)

Played in NHL All-Star Game (1998)

Rights transferred to **Dallas** after **Minnesota** franchise relocated, June 9, 1993. • Missed majority of 1999-2000 season recovering from leg injury suffered in game vs. Nashville, October 16, 1999.

LEMIEUX, Claude

(lehm-YOO, KLOHD) **DAL.**

Right wing. Shoots right. 6'1", 227 lbs. Born, Buckingham, Que., July 16, 1965. Montreal's 2nd choice, 26th overall, in 1983 Entry Draft.

Season	Club	League	GP	G	A	Pts	PIM	PP	SH	GW	S	%	+/-	TF	F%	Min	GP	G	A	Pts	PIM	PP	SH	GW	Min
1981-82	Richelieu Riverains	QAAA	48	24	48	72	96	....	....	....	....	....	....	....	....	....	8	10	13	23	14	....	....	....	....
1982-83	Trois-Rivieres	QMJHL	62	28	38	66	187	....	....	....	....	....	....	....	....	....	4	1	0	1	30	....	....	....	....
1983-84	Verdun Juniors	QMJHL	51	41	45	86	225	....	....	....	....	....	....	....	....	....	9	8	12	20	63	....	....	....	....
	Montreal	**NHL**	**8**	**1**	**1**	**2**	**12**	**0**	**0**	**0**	**7**	**14.3**	**–2**	....	....	....	....	....	....	....	....	....	....	....	....
	Nova Scotia	AHL	....	....	....	....	....	....	....	....	....	....	....	....	....	....	2	1	0	1	0	....	....	....	....
1984-85	Verdun	QMJHL	52	58	66	124	152	....	....	....	....	....	....	....	....	....	14	23	17	40	38	....	....	....	....
	Montreal	**NHL**	**1**	**0**	**1**	**1**	**7**	**0**	**0**	**0**	**0**	**0.0**	**1**	....	....	....	....	....	....	....	....	....	....	....	....
1985-86 ♦	**Montreal**	**NHL**	**10**	**1**	**2**	**3**	**22**	**1**	**0**	**0**	**16**	**6.3**	**–6**	....	....	....	**20**	**10**	**6**	**16**	**68**	**4**	**0**	**4**	....
	Sherbrooke	AHL	58	21	32	53	145	....	....	....	....	....	....	....	....	....	....	....	....	....	....	....	....	....	....
1986-87	**Montreal**	**NHL**	**76**	**27**	**26**	**53**	**156**	**5**	**0**	**1**	**184**	**14.7**	**0**	....	....	....	**17**	**4**	**9**	**13**	**41**	**2**	**0**	**0**	....
1987-88	**Montreal**	**NHL**	**78**	**31**	**30**	**61**	**137**	**6**	**0**	**3**	**241**	**12.9**	**16**	....	....	....	**11**	**3**	**2**	**5**	**20**	**0**	**0**	**2**	....
1988-89	**Montreal**	**NHL**	**69**	**29**	**22**	**51**	**136**	**7**	**0**	**3**	**220**	**13.2**	**14**	....	....	....	**18**	**4**	**3**	**7**	**58**	**0**	**0**	**1**	....
1989-90	**Montreal**	**NHL**	**39**	**8**	**10**	**18**	**106**	**3**	**0**	**1**	**104**	**7.7**	**–8**	....	....	....	**11**	**1**	**3**	**4**	**38**	**0**	**0**	**1**	....
1990-91	**New Jersey**	**NHL**	**78**	**30**	**17**	**47**	**105**	**10**	**0**	**2**	**271**	**11.1**	**–8**	....	....	....	**7**	**4**	**0**	**4**	**34**	**2**	**0**	**1**	....
1991-92	**New Jersey**	**NHL**	**74**	**41**	**27**	**68**	**109**	**13**	**1**	**8**	**296**	**13.9**	**9**	....	....	....	**7**	**4**	**3**	**7**	**26**	**1**	**0**	**0**	....
1992-93	**New Jersey**	**NHL**	**77**	**30**	**51**	**81**	**155**	**13**	**0**	**3**	**311**	**9.6**	**3**	....	....	....	**5**	**2**	**0**	**2**	**19**	**1**	**0**	**0**	....
1993-94	**New Jersey**	**NHL**	**79**	**18**	**26**	**44**	**86**	**5**	**0**	**5**	**181**	**9.9**	**13**	....	....	....	**20**	**7**	**11**	**18**	**44**	**0**	**0**	**2**	....
1994-95 ♦	**New Jersey**	**NHL**	**45**	**6**	**13**	**19**	**86**	**1**	**0**	**1**	**117**	**5.1**	**2**	....	....	....	**20**	***13**	**3**	**16**	**20**	**0**	**0**	**3**	....
1995-96 ♦	**Colorado**	**NHL**	**79**	**39**	**32**	**71**	**117**	**9**	**2**	**10**	**315**	**12.4**	**14**	....	....	....	**19**	**5**	**7**	**12**	**55**	**3**	**0**	**0**	....
1996-97	**Colorado**	**NHL**	**45**	**11**	**17**	**28**	**43**	**5**	**0**	**4**	**168**	**6.5**	**–4**	....	....	....	**17**	***13**	**10**	**23**	**32**	**4**	**0**	**4**	....
1997-98	**Colorado**	**NHL**	**78**	**26**	**27**	**53**	**115**	**11**	**1**	**1**	**261**	**10.0**	**–7**	....	....	....	**7**	**3**	**3**	**6**	**8**	**1**	**0**	**1**	....
1998-99	**Colorado**	**NHL**	**82**	**27**	**24**	**51**	**102**	**11**	**0**	**8**	**292**	**9.2**	**0**	**43**	**41.9**	**21:14**	**19**	**3**	**11**	**14**	**26**	**1**	**0**	**0**	**19:28**
99-2000	**Colorado**	**NHL**	**13**	**3**	**6**	**9**	**4**	**0**	**0**	**0**	**36**	**8.3**	**0**	**2**	**50.0**	**18:40**	....	....	....	....	....	....	....	....	....
	♦ New Jersey	**NHL**	**70**	**17**	**21**	**38**	**86**	**7**	**0**	**3**	**221**	**7.7**	**–3**	**49**	**28.6**	**17:55**	**23**	**4**	**6**	**10**	**28**	**1**	**0**	**0**	**18:59**
2000-01	**Phoenix**	**NHL**	**46**	**10**	**16**	**26**	**58**	**2**	**0**	**1**	**99**	**10.1**	**1**	**28**	**21.4**	**17:12**	....	....	....	....	....	....	....	....	....
2001-02	**Phoenix**	**NHL**	**82**	**16**	**25**	**41**	**70**	**4**	**1**	**3**	**174**	**9.2**	**–5**	**49**	**28.6**	**17:12**	**5**	**0**	**0**	**0**	**2**	**0**	**0**	**0**	**16:58**
2002-03	**Phoenix**	**NHL**	**36**	**6**	**8**	**14**	**30**	**1**	**1**	**0**	**74**	**8.1**	**–3**	**295**	**46.8**	**14:02**	....	....	....	....	....	....	....	....	....
	Dallas	**NHL**	**32**	**2**	**4**	**6**	**14**	**0**	**0**	**0**	**45**	**4.4**	**–9**	**35**	**48.6**	**13:14**	**7**	**0**	**1**	**1**	**10**	**0**	**0**	**0**	**11:24**
	NHL Totals		**1197**	**379**	**406**	**785**	**1756**	**114**	**6**	**57**	**3633**	**10.4**		**501**	**41.5**	**17:38**	**233**	**80**	**78**	**158**	**529**	**20**	**0**	**19**	**17:59**

QMJHL Second All-Star Team (1984) • QMJHL First All-Star Team (1985) • Conn Smythe Trophy (1995)

• Missed majority of 1989-90 season recovering from abdominal injury suffered in game vs. Boston, October 9, 1989. Traded to **New Jersey** by **Montreal** for Sylvain Turgeon, September 4, 1990. Traded to **NY Islanders** by **New Jersey** for Steve Thomas, October 3, 1995. Traded to **Colorado** by **NY Islanders** for Wendel Clark, October 3, 1995. Traded to **New Jersey** by **Colorado** with Colorado's 1st (David Hale) and 2nd (Matt DeMarchi) round choices in 2000 Entry Draft for Brian Rolston and New Jersey's 1st round choice (later traded to Boston – Boston selected Martin Samuelsson) in 2000 Entry Draft, November 3, 1999. Signed as a free agent by **Phoenix**, December 5, 2000. Traded to **Dallas** by **Phoenix** for Scott Pellerin and future considerations, January 16, 2003.

LEMIEUX, Mario

(lehm-YOO, MAHR-ee-oh) **PIT.**

Center. Shoots right. 6'4", 230 lbs. Born, Montreal, Que., October 5, 1965. Pittsburgh's 1st choice, 1st overall, in 1984 Entry Draft.

Season	Club	League	GP	G	A	Pts	PIM	PP	SH	GW	S	%	+/-	TF	F%	Min	GP	G	A	Pts	PIM	PP	SH	GW	Min
1980-81	Mtl-Concordia	QAAA	47	62	62	124	127	....	....	....	....	....	....	....	....	....	3	2	5	7	8	....	....	....	....
1981-82	Laval Voisins	QMJHL	64	30	66	96	22	....	....	....	....	....	....	....	....	....	18	5	9	14	31	....	....	....	....
1982-83	Laval Voisins	QMJHL	66	84	100	184	76	....	....	....	....	....	....	....	....	....	12	14	18	32	18	....	....	....	....
1983-84	Laval Voisins	QMJHL	70	*133	*149	*282	92	....	....	....	....	....	....	....	....	....	14	*29	*23	*52	29	....	....	....	....
1984-85	**Pittsburgh**	**NHL**	**73**	**43**	**57**	**100**	**54**	**11**	**0**	**2**	**209**	**20.6**	**–35**	....	....	....	....	....	....	....	....	....	....	....	....
1985-86	**Pittsburgh**	**NHL**	**79**	**48**	**93**	**141**	**43**	**17**	**0**	**4**	**276**	**17.4**	**–6**	....	....	....	....	....	....	....	....	....	....	....	....
1986-87	**Pittsburgh**	**NHL**	**63**	**54**	**53**	**107**	**57**	**19**	**0**	**4**	**267**	**20.2**	**13**	....	....	....	....	....	....	....	....	....	....	....	....
1987-88	**Pittsburgh**	**NHL**	**77**	***70**	**98**	***168**	**92**	**22**	**10**	**7**	**382**	**18.3**	**23**	....	....	....	....	....	....	....	....	....	....	....	....
1988-89	**Pittsburgh**	**NHL**	**76**	***85**	***114**	***199**	**100**	**31**	**13**	**8**	**313**	**27.2**	**41**	....	....	....	**11**	**12**	**7**	**19**	**16**	**7**	**1**	**0**	....
1989-90	**Pittsburgh**	**NHL**	**59**	**45**	**78**	**123**	**78**	**14**	**3**	**4**	**226**	**19.9**	**–18**	....	....	....	....	....	....	....	....	....	....	....	....
1990-91 ♦	**Pittsburgh**	**NHL**	**26**	**19**	**26**	**45**	**30**	**6**	**1**	**2**	**89**	**21.3**	**8**	....	....	....	**23**	**16**	***28**	***44**	**16**	**6**	**2**	**0**	....
1991-92 ♦	**Pittsburgh**	**NHL**	**64**	**44**	**87**	***131**	**94**	**12**	**4**	**5**	**249**	**17.7**	**27**	....	....	....	**15**	***16**	**18**	***34**	**2**	**8**	**2**	**5**	....
1992-93	**Pittsburgh**	**NHL**	**60**	**69**	**91**	***160**	**38**	**16**	**6**	**10**	**286**	**24.1**	**55**	....	....	....	**11**	**8**	**10**	**18**	**10**	**3**	**1**	**1**	....
1993-94	**Pittsburgh**	**NHL**	**22**	**17**	**20**	**37**	**32**	**7**	**0**	**4**	**92**	**18.5**	**–2**	....	....	....	**6**	**4**	**3**	**7**	**2**	**1**	**0**	**0**	....
1994-95	**Pittsburgh**	**NHL**	DID NOT PLAY																						
1995-96	**Pittsburgh**	**NHL**	**70**	***69**	***92**	***161**	**54**	**31**	**8**	**8**	**338**	**20.4**	**10**	....	....	....	**18**	**11**	**16**	**27**	**33**	**3**	**1**	**2**	....
1996-97	**Pittsburgh**	**NHL**	**76**	**50**	***72**	***122**	**65**	**15**	**3**	**7**	**327**	**15.3**	**27**	....	....	....	**5**	**3**	**3**	**6**	**4**	**0**	**0**	**0**	....
1997-98			OUT OF HOCKEY – RETIRED																						
1998-99			OUT OF HOCKEY – RETIRED																						
99-2000			OUT OF HOCKEY – RETIRED																						
2000-01	**Pittsburgh**	**NHL**	**43**	**35**	**41**	**76**	**18**	**16**	**1**	**5**	**171**	**20.5**	**15**	**852**	**52.1**	**24:20**	**18**	**6**	**11**	**17**	**4**	**1**	**0**	**3**	**24:35**
2001-02	**Pittsburgh**	**NHL**	**24**	**6**	**25**	**31**	**14**	**2**	**0**	**0**	**75**	**8.0**	**0**	**354**	**44.6**	**22:16**	....	....	....	....	....	....	....	....	....
	Canada	Olympics	5	2	4	6	0	....	....	....	....	....	....	....	....	....	....	....	....	....	....	....	....	....	....
2002-03	**Pittsburgh**	**NHL**	**67**	**28**	**63**	**91**	**43**	**14**	**0**	**4**	**235**	**11.9**	**–25**	**1029**	**46.1**	**23:05**	....	....	....	....	....	....	....	....	....
	NHL Totals		**879**	**682**	**1010**	**1692**	**812**	**233**	**49**	**74**	**3535**	**19.3**		**2235**	**48.1**	**23:20**	**107**	**76**	**96**	**172**	**87**	**29**	**7**	**11**	**24:35**

QMJHL Second All-Star Team (1983) • QMJHL First All-Star Team (1984) • QMJHL MVP (1984) • Canadian Major Junior Player of the Year (1984) • NHL All-Rookie Team (1985) • Calder Memorial Trophy (1985) • NHL Second All-Star Team (1986, 1987, 1992, 2001) • Lester B. Pearson Award (1986, 1988, 1993, 1996) • Canada Cup All-Star Team (1987) • NHL First All-Star Team (1988, 1989, 1993, 1996, 1997) • Dodge Performance of the Year Award (1988) • Dodge Performer of the Year Award (1988, 1989) • Art Ross Trophy (1988, 1989, 1992, 1993, 1996, 1997) • Hart Trophy (1988, 1993, 1996) • Dodge Ram Tough Award (1989) • Conn Smythe Trophy (1991, 1992) • ProSet/NHL Player of the Year Award (1992) • Alka-Seltzer Plus Award (1993) • Bill Masterton Memorial Trophy (1993) • Lester Patrick Trophy (2000)

Played in NHL All-Star Game (1985, 1986, 1988, 1989, 1990, 1992, 1996, 1997, 2001, 2002)

• Missed remainder of 1989-90 and majority of 1990-91 seasons recovering from back injury suffered in game vs. NY Rangers, February 14, 1989. • Missed remainder of 1992-93 season after being diagnosed with Hodgkin's Disease, January 12, 1993. • Missed majority of 1993-94 season recovering from back injury suffered in game vs. Chicago, November 11, 1993. • Missed entire 1994-95 season recovering from effects of treatment for Hodgkin's Disease and back injury suffered in game vs. NY Rangers, March 12, 1994. • Became third player (Gordie Howe, Guy Lafleur) to appear in NHL game after being inducted into Hockey Hall of Fame, December 27, 2000. • Missed majority of 2001-02 season recovering from hip injury suffered in game vs. Anaheim, October 6, 2001.

LEOPOLD, Jordan

(LEE-oh-pohld, JOHR-dan) **CGY.**

Defense. Shoots left. 6', 193 lbs. Born, Golden Valley, MN, August 3, 1980. Anaheim's 1st choice, 44th overall, in 1999 Entry Draft.

Season	Club	League	GP	G	A	Pts	PIM	PP	SH	GW	S	%	+/-	TF	F%	Min	GP	G	A	Pts	PIM	PP	SH	GW	Min
1995-96	Armstrong	Hi-School	19	11	14	25	30	....	....	....	....	....	....	....	....	....	....	....	....	....	....	....	....	....	....
1996-97	Armstrong	Hi-School	30	24	36	60	....	....	....	....	....	....	....	....	....	....	....	....	....	....	....	....	....	....	....
1997-98	U.S. National U-18	USDP	60	11	12	23	16	....	....	....	....	....	....	....	....	....	....	....	....	....	....	....	....	....	....
1998-99	U. of Minnesota	WCHA	39	7	16	23	20	....	....	....	....	....	....	....	....	....	....	....	....	....	....	....	....	....	....
99-2000	U. of Minnesota	WCHA	39	6	18	24	20	....	....	....	....	....	....	....	....	....	....	....	....	....	....	....	....	....	....
2000-01	U. of Minnesota	WCHA	42	12	37	49	38	....	....	....	....	....	....	....	....	....	....	....	....	....	....	....	....	....	....
2001-02	U. of Minnesota	WCHA	44	20	28	48	28	....	....	....	....	....	....	....	....	....	....	....	....	....	....	....	....	....	....

			Regular Season														Playoffs								
Season	Club	League	GP	G	A	Pts	PIM	PP	SH	GW	S	%	+/-	TF	F%	Min	GP	G	A	Pts	PIM	PP	SH	GW	Min
2002-03	**Calgary**	**NHL**	**58**	**4**	**10**	**14**	**12**	**3**	**0**	**0**	**78**	**5.1**	**–15**	**0**	**0.0**	**20:36**									
	Saint John Flames	AHL	3	1	2	3	0																		
	NHL Totals		**58**	**4**	**10**	**14**	**12**	**3**	**0**	**0**	**78**	**5.1**		**0**	**0.0**	**20:36**									

WCHA All-Rookie Team (1999) • WCHA Second All-Star Team (2000) • WCHA First All-Star Team (2001, 2002) • NCAA West First All-American Team (2001) • Hobey Baker Memorial Award (Top U.S. Collegiate Player) (2002)

Traded to **Calgary** by **Anaheim** for Andrei Nazarov and Calgary's 2nd round choice (later traded to Phoenix – later traded back to Calgary – Calgary selected Andrei Taratukhin) in 2001 Entry Draft, September 26, 2000.

LEROUX, Francois

(leh-ROO, FRAN-swuh) **PHX.**

Defense. Shoots left. 6'6", 247 lbs. Born, Ste-Adele, Que., April 18, 1970. Edmonton's 1st choice, 19th overall, in 1988 Entry Draft.

Season	Club	League	GP	G	A	Pts	PIM	PP	SH	GW	S	%	+/-	TF	F%	Min	GP	G	A	Pts	PIM	PP	SH	GW	Min
1986-87	Laval Laurentide	QAAA	42	5	11	16	76										8	0	1	1	12				
1987-88	St-Jean Castors	QMJHL	58	3	8	11	143										7	2	0	2	21				
1988-89	St-Jean Castors	QMJHL	57	8	34	42	185																		
	Edmonton	**NHL**	**2**	**0**	**0**	**0**	**0**	**0**	**0**	**0**	**0**	**0.0**	**1**												
1989-90	Victoriaville Tigres	QMJHL	54	4	33	37	169																		
	Edmonton	**NHL**	**3**	**0**	**1**	**1**	**0**	**0**	**0**	**0**	**0**	**0.0**	**–2**												
1990-91	**Edmonton**	**NHL**	**1**	**0**	**2**	**2**	**0**	**0**	**0**	**0**	**1**	**0.0**	**1**												
	Cape Breton	AHL	71	2	7	9	124										4	0	1	1	19				
1991-92	**Edmonton**	**NHL**	**4**	**0**	**0**	**0**	**7**	**0**	**0**	**0**	**0**	**0.0**	**–1**												
	Cape Breton	AHL	61	7	22	29	114										5	0	0	0	8				
1992-93	**Edmonton**	**NHL**	**1**	**0**	**0**	**0**	**4**	**0**	**0**	**0**	**0**	**0.0**	**0**												
	Cape Breton	AHL	55	10	24	34	139										16	0	5	5	29				
1993-94	**Ottawa**	**NHL**	**23**	**0**	**1**	**1**	**70**	**0**	**0**	**0**	**8**	**0.0**	**–4**												
	P.E.I. Senators	AHL	25	4	6	10	52																		
1994-95	P.E.I. Senators	AHL	45	4	14	18	137																		
	Pittsburgh	**NHL**	**40**	**0**	**2**	**2**	**114**	**0**	**0**	**0**	**19**	**0.0**	**7**				**12**	**0**	**2**	**2**	**14**	**0**	**0**	**0**	
1995-96	**Pittsburgh**	**NHL**	**66**	**2**	**9**	**11**	**161**	**0**	**0**	**0**	**43**	**4.7**	**2**				**18**	**1**	**1**	**2**	**20**	**0**	**0**	**1**	
1996-97	**Pittsburgh**	**NHL**	**59**	**0**	**3**	**3**	**81**	**0**	**0**	**0**	**5**	**0.0**	**–3**				**3**	**0**	**0**	**0**	**0**	**0**	**0**	**0**	
1997-98	**Colorado**	**NHL**	**50**	**1**	**2**	**3**	**140**	**0**	**0**	**0**	**14**	**7.1**	**–3**												
1998-99	Grand Rapids	IHL	13	1	1	2	22																		
99-2000	Springfield	AHL	64	3	6	9	162										5	0	0	0	2				
2000-01	Springfield	AHL	65	4	6	10	180																		
2001-02	Berlin Capitals	Germany	56	1	10	11	110																		
2002-03	Wilkes-Barre	AHL	57	1	3	4	124																		
	Springfield	AHL	6	0	0	0	0										6	0	1	1	2				
	NHL Totals		**249**	**3**	**20**	**23**	**577**	**0**	**0**	**0**	**90**	**3.3**					**33**	**1**	**3**	**4**	**34**	**0**	**0**	**1**	

Claimed on waivers by **Ottawa** from **Edmonton**, October 6, 1993. Claimed by **Pittsburgh** from **Ottawa** in Waiver Draft, January 18, 1995. Traded to **Colorado** by **Pittsburgh** for Colorado's 3rd round choice (David Cameron) in 1998 Entry Draft, September 28, 1997. Signed as a free agent by **Grand Rapids** (IHL), February 18, 1999. Signed as a free agent by **Phoenix**, July 20, 1999.Signed as a free agent by **Berlin Capitals** (Germany), July 17, 2001. Signed as a free agent by **Pittsburgh**, July 16, 2002. Traded to **Phoenix** by **Pittsburgh** with Jan Hrdina for Ramzi Abid, Dan Focht and Guillaume Lefebvre, March 11, 2003.

LESCHYSHYN, Curtis

(luh-SIH-shuhn, KUHR-tihs) **OTT.**

Defense. Shoots left. 6'1", 207 lbs. Born, Thompson, Man., September 21, 1969. Quebec's 1st choice, 3rd overall, in 1988 Entry Draft.

Season	Club	League	GP	G	A	Pts	PIM	PP	SH	GW	S	%	+/-	TF	F%	Min	GP	G	A	Pts	PIM	PP	SH	GW	Min
1985-86	Saskatoon Blazers	SMHL	34	9	34	43	52																		
	Saskatoon Blades	WHL	1	0	0	0	0																		
1986-87	Saskatoon Blades	WHL	70	14	26	40	107										11	1	5	6	14				
1987-88	Saskatoon Blades	WHL	56	14	41	55	86										10	2	5	7	16				
1988-89	**Quebec**	**NHL**	**71**	**4**	**9**	**13**	**71**	**1**	**1**	**0**	**58**	**6.9**	**–32**												
1989-90	**Quebec**	**NHL**	**68**	**2**	**6**	**8**	**44**	**1**	**0**	**0**	**42**	**4.8**	**–41**												
1990-91	**Quebec**	**NHL**	**55**	**3**	**7**	**10**	**49**	**2**	**0**	**1**	**57**	**5.3**	**–19**												
1991-92	**Quebec**	**NHL**	**42**	**5**	**12**	**17**	**42**	**3**	**0**	**1**	**61**	**8.2**	**–28**												
	Halifax Citadels	AHL	6	0	2	2	4																		
1992-93	**Quebec**	**NHL**	**82**	**9**	**23**	**32**	**61**	**4**	**0**	**2**	**73**	**12.3**	**25**				**6**	**1**	**1**	**2**	**6**	**1**	**0**	**0**	
1993-94	**Quebec**	**NHL**	**72**	**5**	**17**	**22**	**65**	**3**	**0**	**2**	**97**	**5.2**	**–2**												
1994-95	**Quebec**	**NHL**	**44**	**2**	**13**	**15**	**20**	**0**	**0**	**0**	**43**	**4.7**	**29**				**3**	**0**	**1**	**1**	**4**	**0**	**0**	**0**	
1995-96♦	**Colorado**	**NHL**	**77**	**4**	**15**	**19**	**73**	**0**	**0**	**1**	**76**	**5.3**	**32**				**17**	**1**	**2**	**3**	**8**	**0**	**0**	**0**	
1996-97	**Colorado**	**NHL**	**11**	**0**	**5**	**5**	**6**	**0**	**0**	**0**	**8**	**0.0**	**1**												
	Washington	**NHL**	**2**	**0**	**0**	**0**	**2**	**0**	**0**	**0**	**0**	**0.0**	**0**												
	Hartford	**NHL**	**64**	**4**	**13**	**17**	**30**	**1**	**1**	**1**	**94**	**4.3**	**–19**												
1997-98	**Carolina**	**NHL**	**73**	**2**	**10**	**12**	**45**	**1**	**0**	**1**	**53**	**3.8**	**–2**												
1998-99	**Carolina**	**NHL**	**65**	**2**	**7**	**9**	**50**	**0**	**0**	**0**	**35**	**5.7**	**–1**	**0**	**0.0**	**19:18**	**6**	**0**	**0**	**0**	**6**	**0**	**0**	**0**	**24:07**
99-2000	**Carolina**	**NHL**	**53**	**0**	**2**	**2**	**14**	**0**	**0**	**0**	**31**	**0.0**	**–19**	**0**	**0.0**	**17:47**									
2000-01	**Minnesota**	**NHL**	**54**	**2**	**3**	**5**	**19**	**1**	**0**	**1**	**43**	**4.7**	**–2**	**0**	**0.0**	**19:31**									
	Ottawa	**NHL**	**11**	**0**	**4**	**4**	**0**	**0**	**0**	**0**	**8**	**0.0**	**7**	**0**	**0.0**	**19:04**	**4**	**0**	**0**	**0**	**0**	**0**	**0**	**0**	**21:05**
2001-02	**Ottawa**	**NHL**	**79**	**1**	**9**	**10**	**44**	**0**	**0**	**0**	**59**	**1.7**	**–5**	**0**	**0.0**	**18:28**	**12**	**0**	**1**	**1**	**0**	**0**	**0**	**0**	**16:49**
2002-03	**Ottawa**	**NHL**	**54**	**1**	**6**	**7**	**18**	**0**	**0**	**0**	**30**	**3.3**	**11**	**0**	**0.0**	**15:13**	**18**	**0**	**1**	**1**	**10**	**0**	**0**	**0**	**14:11**
	NHL Totals		**977**	**46**	**161**	**207**	**653**	**17**	**2**	**10**	**868**	**5.3**		**0**	**0.0**	**18:10**	**66**	**2**	**6**	**8**	**34**	**1**	**0**	**0**	**17:09**

WHL East First All-Star Team (1988)

Transferred to **Colorado** after **Quebec** franchise relcoated, June 21, 1995. Traded to **Washington** by **Colorado** with Chris Simon for Keith Jones, Washington's 1st (Scott Parker) and 4th (later traded back to Washington – Washington selected Krys Barch) round choices in 1998 Entry Draft, November 2, 1996. Traded to **Hartford** by **Washington** for Andrei Nikolishin, November 9, 1996. Transferred to **Carolina** after **Hartford** franchise relocated, June 25, 1997. Selected by **Minnesota** from **Carolina** in Expansion Draft, June 23, 2000. Traded to **Ottawa** by **Minnesota** for Ottawa's 3rd round choice (Stephane Veilleux) in 2001 Entry Draft and future considerations, March 13, 2001.

LESSARD, Francis

(leh-SAHR, FRAN-sihs) **ATL.**

Right wing. Shoots right. 6'2", 220 lbs. Born, Montreal, Que., May 30, 1979. Carolina's 3rd choice, 80th overall, in 1997 Entry Draft.

Season	Club	League	GP	G	A	Pts	PIM	PP	SH	GW	S	%	+/-	TF	F%	Min	GP	G	A	Pts	PIM	PP	SH	GW	Min
1995-96	Laval Laurentide	QAAA	41	5	7	12	73																		
1996-97	Val-d'Or Foreurs	QMJHL	66	1	9	10	287																		
1997-98	Val-d'Or Foreurs	QMJHL	63	3	20	23	338										19	1	6	7	*101				
1998-99	Drummondville	QMJHL	53	12	36	48	295																		
99-2000	Philadelphia	AHL	78	4	8	12	416										5	0	1	1	7				
2000-01	Philadelphia	AHL	64	3	7	10	330										10	0	0	0	33				
2001-02	Philadelphia	AHL	60	0	6	6	251																		
	Atlanta	**NHL**	**5**	**0**	**0**	**0**	**26**	**0**	**0**	**0**	**2**	**0.0**	**0**	**0**	**0.0**	**12:45**									
	Chicago Wolves	AHL	7	2	1	3	34										15	0	1	1	40				
2002-03	**Atlanta**	**NHL**	**18**	**0**	**2**	**2**	**61**	**0**	**0**	**0**	**7**	**0.0**	**1**	**0**	**0.0**	**5:40**									
	Chicago Wolves	AHL	50	2	5	7	194										1	0	0	0	0				
	NHL Totals		**23**	**0**	**2**	**2**	**87**	**0**	**0**	**0**	**9**	**0.0**		**0**	**0.0**	**7:12**									

Memorial Cup All-Star Team (1998)

Traded to **Philadelphia** by **Carolina** for Philadelphia's 8th round choice (Antti Jokella) in 1999 Entry Draft, May 25, 1999. Traded to **Atlanta** by **Philadelphia** for David Harlock and Atlanta's 3rd (later traded to Phoenix – Phoenix selected Tyler Redenbach) and 7th (later traded to San Jose – San Jose selected Joe Pavelski) round choices in 2003 Entry Draft, March 15, 2002.

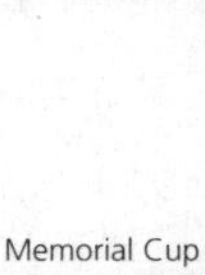

LETANG, Alan

(leh-TANG, A-luhn) **NYI**

Defense. Shoots left. 6'1", 201 lbs. Born, Renfrew, Ont., September 4, 1975. Montreal's 10th choice, 203rd overall, in 1993 Entry Draft.

Season	Club	League	GP	G	A	Pts	PIM	PP	SH	GW	S	%	+/-	TF	F%	Min	GP	G	A	Pts	PIM	PP	SH	GW	Min
1990-91	Ottawa Valley	ODMHA	32	3	26	29	16																		
1991-92	Cornwall Royals	OHL	47	1	4	5	16										6	0	0	0	2				
1992-93	Newmarket	OHL	66	1	25	26	14										6	0	3	3	2				
1993-94	Newmarket	OHL	58	3	21	24	30																		
1994-95	Sarnia Sting	OHL	62	5	36	41	35										4	2	2	4	6				
1995-96	Fredericton	AHL	71	0	26	26	40										10	0	3	3	4				
1996-97	Fredericton	AHL	60	2	9	11	8																		
1997-98	Kaufbeurer Adler	Germany	15	1	5	6	8																		
	SC Langnau	Swiss-2	11	4	3	7	6																		
	Augsburg	Germany	17	0	1	1	4																		
1998-99	Team Canada	Nat-Tm	41	3	9	12	20																		
	EV Zug	Swiss	....	....	....	....	....										9	0	4	4	4				
	Michigan	IHL	12	3	3	6	0										5	0	2	2	0				

			Regular Season														Playoffs								
Season	Club	League	GP	G	A	Pts	PIM	PP	SH	GW	S	%	+/-	TF	F%	Min	GP	G	A	Pts	PIM	PP	SH	GW	Min
99-2000	Dallas	NHL	8	0	0	0	2	0	0	0	1	0.0	–5	0	0.0	9:57	....	....	....	....	....	....	....	....	....
	Michigan	IHL	51	1	12	13	30	....	....	....	....	....	....	....	....	....	....	....	....	....	....	....	....	....	....
2000-01	Utah Grizzlies	IHL	79	6	24	30	26	....	....	....	....	....	....	....	....	....	....	....	....	....	....	....	....	....	....
2001-02	Calgary	NHL	2	0	0	0	0	0	0	0	0	0.0	–2	0	0.0	11:06	....	....	....	....	....	....	....	....	....
	Saint John Flames	AHL	61	4	24	28	33	....	....	....	....	....	....	....	....	....	....	....	....	....	....	....	....	....	....
2002-03	NY Islanders	NHL	4	0	0	0	0	0	0	0	2	0.0	–1	0	0.0	13:28	....	....	....	....	....	....	....	....	....
	Bridgeport	AHL	70	3	21	24	21	....	....	....	....	....	....	....	....	....	8	1	0	1	0	....	....	....	....
	NHL Totals		14	0	0	0	2	0	0	0	3	0.0		0	0.0	11:07	....	....	....	....	....	....	....	....	....

Signed as a free agent by **Dallas**, March 22, 1999. Signed as a free agent by **Calgary**, August 22, 2001. Signed as a free agent by **NY Islanders**, July 18, 2002.

LETOWSKI, Trevor

(leh-TOW-skee, TREH-vuhr) **CBJ**

Right wing. Shoots right. 5'10", 176 lbs. Born, Thunder Bay, Ont., April 5, 1977. Phoenix's 6th choice, 174th overall, in 1996 Entry Draft.

Season	Club	League	GP	G	A	Pts	PIM	PP	SH	GW	S	%	+/-	TF	F%	Min	GP	G	A	Pts	PIM	PP	SH	GW	Min
1993-94	T. Bay Kings	TBMHL	64	41	60	101	48	....	....	....	....	....	....	....	....	....	....	....	....	....	....	....	....	....	....
1994-95	Sarnia Sting	OHL	66	22	19	41	33	....	....	....	....	....	....	....	....	....	4	0	1	1	9	....	....	....	....
1995-96	Sarnia Sting	OHL	66	36	63	99	66	....	....	....	....	....	....	....	....	....	10	9	5	14	10	....	....	....	....
1996-97	Sarnia Sting	OHL	55	35	73	108	51	....	....	....	....	....	....	....	....	....	12	9	12	21	20	....	....	....	....
1997-98	Springfield	AHL	75	11	20	31	26	....	....	....	....	....	....	....	....	....	4	1	0	1	2	....	....	....	....
1998-99	Phoenix	NHL	14	2	2	4	2	0	0	0	8	25.0	1	49	55.1	6:01	....	....	....	....	....	....	....	....	....
	Springfield	AHL	67	32	35	67	46	....	....	....	....	....	....	....	....	....	3	1	0	1	2	....	....	....	....
99-2000	Phoenix	NHL	82	19	20	39	20	3	4	3	125	15.2	2	692	47.7	16:03	5	1	1	2	4	0	0	0	15:52
2000-01	Phoenix	NHL	77	7	15	22	32	0	1	3	110	6.4	–2	726	46.1	16:20	....	....	....	....	....	....	....	....	....
2001-02	Phoenix	NHL	33	2	6	8	4	0	0	0	43	4.7	2	250	52.4	14:27	....	....	....	....	....	....	....	....	....
	Vancouver	NHL	42	7	10	17	15	1	0	0	65	10.8	2	111	44.1	12:47	6	0	1	1	8	0	0	0	11:49
2002-03	Vancouver	NHL	78	11	14	25	36	1	1	2	136	8.1	8	70	41.4	12:26	6	0	1	1	0	0	0	0	9:39
	NHL Totals		326	48	67	115	109	5	6	8	487	9.9		1898	47.5	14:14	17	1	3	4	12	0	0	0	12:15

Traded to **Vancouver** by **Phoenix** with Todd Warriner, Tyler Bouck and Phoenix's 3rd round choice (later traded back to Phoenix – Phoenix selected Dimitri Pestunov) in 2003 Entry Draft for Drake Berehowsky and Denis Pederson, December 28, 2001. Signed as a free agent by **Columbus**, July 3, 2003.

LIDSTROM, Nicklas

(LID-struhm, NIHK-las) **DET.**

Defense. Shoots left. 6'2", 185 lbs. Born, Vasteras, Sweden, April 28, 1970. Detroit's 3rd choice, 53rd overall, in 1989 Entry Draft.

Season	Club	League	GP	G	A	Pts	PIM	PP	SH	GW	S	%	+/-	TF	F%	Min	GP	G	A	Pts	PIM	PP	SH	GW	Min
1987-88	Vasteras IK	Swede-2	3	0	0	0	0	....	....	....	....	....	....	....	....	....	5	0	0	0	6	....	....	....	....
1988-89	Vasteras IK	Sweden	34	1	6	7	4	....	....	....	....	....	....	....	....	....	5	0	2	2	0	....	....	....	....
1989-90	Vasteras IK	Sweden	39	8	8	16	14	....	....	....	....	....	....	....	....	....	2	0	1	1	2	....	....	....	....
1990-91	Vasteras IK	Sweden	38	4	19	23	2	....	....	....	....	....	....	....	....	....	4	0	0	0	4	....	....	....	....
1991-92	Detroit	NHL	80	11	49	60	22	5	0	1	168	6.5	36	....	....	....	11	1	2	3	0	1	0	0	....
1992-93	Detroit	NHL	84	7	34	41	28	3	0	2	156	4.5	7	....	....	....	7	1	0	1	0	1	0	0	....
1993-94	Detroit	NHL	84	10	46	56	26	4	0	3	200	5.0	43	....	....	....	7	3	2	5	0	1	1	0	....
1994-95	Vasteras IK	Sweden	13	2	10	12	4	....	....	....	....	....	....	....	....	....	....	....	....	....	....	....	....	....	....
	Detroit	NHL	43	10	16	26	6	7	0	0	90	11.1	15	....	....	....	18	4	12	16	8	3	0	2	....
1995-96	Detroit	NHL	81	17	50	67	20	8	1	1	211	8.1	29	....	....	....	19	5	9	14	10	1	0	0	....
1996-97♦	Detroit	NHL	79	15	42	57	30	8	0	1	214	7.0	11	....	....	....	20	2	6	8	2	0	0	0	....
1997-98♦	Detroit	NHL	80	17	42	59	18	7	1	1	205	8.3	22	....	....	....	22	6	13	19	8	2	0	2	....
	Sweden	Olympics	4	1	1	2	2	....	....	....	....	....	....	....	....	....	....	....	....	....	....	....	....	....	....
1998-99	Detroit	NHL	81	14	43	57	14	6	2	3	205	6.8	14	0	0.0	26:31	10	2	9	11	4	2	0	0	30:21
99-2000	Detroit	NHL	81	20	53	73	18	9	4	3	218	9.2	19	0	0.0	28:45	9	2	4	6	4	1	0	0	30:28
2000-01	Detroit	NHL	82	15	56	71	18	8	0	0	272	5.5	9	0	0.0	28:27	6	1	7	8	0	0	0	0	29:17
2001-02♦	Detroit	NHL	78	9	50	59	20	6	0	0	215	4.2	13	0	0.0	28:49	23	5	11	16	2	2	1	2	31:10
	Sweden	Olympics	4	1	5	6	0	....	....	....	....	....	....	....	....	....	....	....	....	....	....	....	....	....	....
2002-03	Detroit	NHL	82	18	44	62	38	8	1	4	175	10.3	40	0	0.0	29:20	4	0	2	2	0	0	0	0	33:35
	NHL Totals		935	163	525	688	258	79	9	19	2329	7.0		0	0.0	28:22	156	32	77	109	38	14	2	6	30:52

NHL All-Rookie Team (1992) • NHL First All-Star Team (1998, 1999, 2000, 2001, 2002, 2003) • James Norris Memorial Trophy (2001, 2002, 2003) • Conn Smythe Trophy (2002)
Played in NHL All-Star Game (1996, 1998, 1999, 2000, 2001, 2002, 2003)

LILJA, Andreas

(LIHL-yuh, an-DRAY-uhs) **FLA.**

Defense. Shoots left. 6'3", 228 lbs. Born, Landskrona, Sweden, July 13, 1975. Los Angeles' 2nd choice, 54th overall, in 2000 Entry Draft.

Season	Club	League	GP	G	A	Pts	PIM	PP	SH	GW	S	%	+/-	TF	F%	Min	GP	G	A	Pts	PIM	PP	SH	GW	Min
1993-94	Malmo IF Jr.	Swede-Jr.	14	3	7	10	38	....	....	....	....	....	....	....	....	....	....	....	....	....	....	....	....	....	....
1994-95	Malmo IF Jr.	Swede-Jr.	30	7	13	20	82	....	....	....	....	....	....	....	....	....	....	....	....	....	....	....	....	....	....
	Malmo IF	Sweden	3	0	0	0	2	....	....	....	....	....	....	....	....	....	....	....	....	....	....	....	....	....	....
1995-96	Malmo IF Jr.	Swede-Jr.	3	0	1	1	6	....	....	....	....	....	....	....	....	....	....	....	....	....	....	....	....	....	....
	Malmo IF	Sweden	40	1	5	6	63	....	....	....	....	....	....	....	....	....	5	0	1	1	2	....	....	....	....
1996-97	Malmo IF	Sweden	47	1	0	1	22	....	....	....	....	....	....	....	....	....	4	0	0	0	10	....	....	....	....
1997-98	Malmo IF	Swede-2	11	6	5	11	24	....	....	....	....	....	....	....	....	....	....	....	....	....	....	....	....	....	....
	Malmo IF	Sweden	10	0	0	0	0	....	....	....	....	....	....	....	....	....	....	....	....	....	....	....	....	....	....
	Mora IK	Swede-2	13	1	4	5	30	....	....	....	....	....	....	....	....	....	4	1	0	1	14	....	....	....	....
1998-99	Malmo IF	Sweden	41	0	3	3	44	....	....	....	....	....	....	....	....	....	1	0	0	0	4	....	....	....	....
99-2000	Malmo IF	Sweden	49	8	11	19	88	....	....	....	....	....	....	....	....	....	6	0	0	0	8	....	....	....	....
2000-01	Los Angeles	NHL	2	0	0	0	4	0	0	0	1	0.0	–2	0	0.0	12:22	1	0	0	0	0	0	0	0	6:56
	Lowell	AHL	61	7	29	36	149	....	....	....	....	....	....	....	....	....	4	0	6	6	6	....	....	....	....
2001-02	Los Angeles	NHL	26	1	4	5	22	1	0	0	12	8.3	3	0	0.0	11:27	5	0	0	0	6	0	0	0	10:26
	Manchester	AHL	4	0	1	1	4	....	....	....	....	....	....	....	....	....	....	....	....	....	....	....	....	....	....
2002-03	Los Angeles	NHL	17	0	3	3	14	0	0	0	13	0.0	5	0	0.0	20:04	....	....	....	....	....	....	....	....	....
	Florida	NHL	56	4	8	12	56	0	0	0	59	6.8	8	0	0.0	19:11	....	....	....	....	....	....	....	....	....
	NHL Totals		101	5	15	20	96	1	0	0	85	5.9		0	0.0	17:12	6	0	0	0	6	0	0	0	9:51

• Spent majority of 2001-02 season on practice roster. Traded to **Florida** by **Los Angeles** with Jaroslav Bednar for Dmitry Yushkevich and Florida's 5th round choice (previously acquired, Los Angeles selected Brady Murray) in 2003 Entry Draft, Novermber 26, 2002.

LINDEN, Trevor

(LIHND-dehn, TREH-vohr) **VAN.**

Right wing. Shoots right. 6'4", 215 lbs. Born, Medicine Hat, Alta., April 11, 1970. Vancouver's 1st choice, 2nd overall, in 1988 Entry Draft.

Season	Club	League	GP	G	A	Pts	PIM	PP	SH	GW	S	%	+/-	TF	F%	Min	GP	G	A	Pts	PIM	PP	SH	GW	Min
1985-86	Medicine Hat	AMHL	40	14	22	36	14	....	....	....	....	....	....	....	....	....	....	....	....	....	....	....	....	....	....
	Medicine Hat	WHL	5	2	0	2	0	....	....	....	....	....	....	....	....	....	....	....	....	....	....	....	....	....	....
1986-87	Medicine Hat	WHL	72	14	22	36	59	....	....	....	....	....	....	....	....	....	20	5	4	9	17	....	....	....	....
1987-88	Medicine Hat	WHL	67	46	64	110	76	....	....	....	....	....	....	....	....	....	16	*13	12	25	19	....	....	....	....
1988-89	Vancouver	NHL	80	30	29	59	41	10	1	2	186	16.1	–10	....	....	....	7	3	4	7	8	2	1	0	....
1989-90	Vancouver	NHL	73	21	30	51	43	6	2	3	171	12.3	–17	....	....	....	....	....	....	....	....	....	....	....	....
1990-91	Vancouver	NHL	80	33	37	70	65	16	2	4	229	14.4	–25	....	....	....	6	0	7	7	2	0	0	0	....
1991-92	Vancouver	NHL	80	31	44	75	101	6	1	6	201	15.4	3	....	....	....	13	4	8	12	6	2	0	1	....
1992-93	Vancouver	NHL	84	33	39	72	64	8	0	3	209	15.8	19	....	....	....	12	5	8	13	16	2	0	1	....
1993-94	Vancouver	NHL	84	32	29	61	73	10	2	3	234	13.7	6	....	....	....	24	12	13	25	18	5	1	1	....
1994-95	Vancouver	NHL	48	18	22	40	40	9	0	1	129	14.0	–5	....	....	....	11	2	6	8	12	1	0	0	....
1995-96	Vancouver	NHL	82	33	47	80	42	12	1	2	202	16.3	6	....	....	....	6	4	4	8	6	2	0	0	....
1996-97	Vancouver	NHL	49	9	31	40	27	2	2	2	84	10.7	5	....	....	....	....	....	....	....	....	....	....	....	....
1997-98	Vancouver	NHL	42	7	14	21	49	2	0	1	74	9.5	–13	....	....	....	....	....	....	....	....	....	....	....	....
	NY Islanders	NHL	25	10	7	17	33	3	2	1	59	16.9	–1	....	....	....	....	....	....	....	....	....	....	....	....
	Canada	Olympics	6	1	0	1	10	....	....	....	....	....	....	....	....	....	....	....	....	....	....	....	....	....	....
1998-99	NY Islanders	NHL	82	18	29	47	32	8	1	1	167	10.8	–14	261	50.2	21:29	....	....	....	....	....	....	....	....	....
99-2000	Montreal	NHL	50	13	17	30	34	4	0	3	87	14.9	–3	860	56.3	17:51	....	....	....	....	....	....	....	....	....
2000-01	Montreal	NHL	57	12	21	33	52	6	0	3	96	12.5	–2	1142	52.7	20:47	....	....	....	....	....	....	....	....	....
	Washington	NHL	12	3	1	4	8	0	0	0	30	10.0	2	75	60.0	18:03	6	0	4	4	14	0	0	0	22:41

			Regular Season														Playoffs								
Season	Club	League	GP	G	A	Pts	PIM	PP	SH	GW	S	%	+/-	TF	F%	Min	GP	G	A	Pts	PIM	PP	SH	GW	Min
2001-02	Washington	NHL	16	1	2	3	6	1	0	0	19	5.3	−2	71	49.3	16:06	....	....	....	....	....	....	....	....	....
	Vancouver	NHL	64	12	22	34	65	2	0	2	122	9.8	−3	1190	53.4	19:23	6	1	4	5	0	0	0	0	19:36
2002-03	Vancouver	NHL	71	19	22	41	30	4	1	1	116	16.4	−1	568	54.4	15:52	14	1	2	3	10	0	1	0	17:38
	NHL Totals		1079	335	443	778	805	109	15	38	2415	13.9		4167	53.8	18:59	105	32	60	92	92	14	3	3	19:15

• Family name was originally Van der Linden • WHL East Second All-Star Team (1988) • NHL All-Rookie Team (1989) • King Clancy Memorial Trophy (1997)

Played in NHL All-Star Game (1991, 1992)

Traded to **NY Islanders** by **Vancouver** for Todd Bertuzzi, Bryan McCabe and NY Islanders' 3rd round choice (Jarkko Ruutu) in 1998 Entry Draft, February 6, 1998. Traded to **Montreal** by **NY Islanders** for Montreal's 1st round choice (Branislav Mezei) in 1999 Entry Draft, May 29, 1999. Traded to **Washington** by **Montreal** with Dainius Zubrus and New Jersey's 2nd round choice (previously acquired, later traded to Tampa Bay – Tampa Bay selected Andreas Holmqvist) in 2001 Entry Draft for Richard Zednik, Jan Bulis and Washington's 1st round choice (Alexander Perezhogin) in 2001 Entry Draft, March 13, 2001. Traded to **Vancouver** by **Washington** with NY Islanders' 2nd round choice (previously acquired, Vancouver selected Denis Grot) in 2002 Entry Draft for Vancouver's 1st round choice (Boyd Gordon) in 2002 Entry Draft and Vancouver's 3rd round choice (later traded to Edmonton – Edmonton selected Zachery Stortini) in 2003 Entry Draft, November 10, 2001.

LINDGREN, Mats

(LIHND-gruhn, MAHTS) **VAN.**

Center/Left wing. Shoots left. 6'2", 202 lbs. Born, Skelleftea, Sweden, October 1, 1974. Winnipeg's 1st choice, 15th overall, in 1993 Entry Draft.

1990-91	Skelleftea AIK	Swede-2	10	0	1	1	0	....	....	....	....	....	....	....	....	....	....	....	....	....	....	....	....	....	....
1991-92	Skelleftea AIK	Swede-2	29	14	18	32	12	....	....	....	....	....	....	....	....	....	3	3	2	5	2	....	....	....	....
1992-93	Skelleftea AIK	Swede-2	32	20	18	38	18	....	....	....	....	....	....	....	....	....	3	0	0	0	2	....	....	....	....
1993-94	Farjestad	Sweden	22	11	6	17	26	....	....	....	....	....	....	....	....	....	....	....	....	....	....	....	....	....	....
1994-95	Farjestad	Sweden	37	17	15	32	20	....	....	....	....	....	....	....	....	....	3	0	0	0	4	....	....	....	....
1995-96	Cape Breton	AHL	13	7	5	12	6	....	....	....	....	....	....	....	....	....	....	....	....	....	....	....	....	....	....
1996-97	Edmonton	NHL	69	11	14	25	12	2	3	1	71	15.5	−7	....	....	....	12	0	4	4	0	0	0	0	....
	Hamilton	AHL	9	6	7	13	6	....	....	....	....	....	....	....	....	....	....	....	....	....	....	....	....	....	....
1997-98	Edmonton	NHL	82	13	13	26	42	1	3	3	131	9.9	0	....	....	....	12	1	1	2	10	0	0	0	....
	Sweden	Olympics	4	0	0	0	2	....	....	....	....	....	....	....	....	....	....	....	....	....	....	....	....	....	....
1998-99	Edmonton	NHL	48	5	12	17	22	0	1	0	53	9.4	4	363	47.9	11:31	....	....	....	....	....	....	....	....	....
	NY Islanders	NHL	12	5	3	8	2	3	0	1	30	16.7	2	180	48.9	20:08	....	....	....	....	....	....	....	....	....
99-2000	NY Islanders	NHL	43	9	7	16	24	1	0	1	68	13.2	0	551	49.2	19:17	....	....	....	....	....	....	....	....	....
2000-01	NY Islanders	NHL	20	3	4	7	10	0	2	0	34	8.8	4	176	48.3	15:14	....	....	....	....	....	....	....	....	....
2001-02	NY Islanders	NHL	59	3	12	15	16	0	0	1	35	8.6	0	237	59.1	8:21	....	....	....	....	....	....	....	....	....
2002-03	Vancouver	NHL	54	5	9	14	18	0	2	1	51	9.8	−2	763	54.5	13:54	....	....	....	....	....	....	....	....	....
	Manitoba Moose	AHL	4	0	1	1	6	....	....	....	....	....	....	....	....	....	....	....	....	....	....	....	....	....	....
	NHL Totals		387	54	74	128	146	7	11	8	473	11.4		2270	51.7	13:26	24	1	5	6	10	0	0	0	....

Traded to **Edmonton** by **Winnipeg** with Boris Mironov, Winnipeg's 1st round choice (Jason Bonsignore) in 1994 Entry Draft and Florida's 4th round choice (previously acquired, Edmonton selected Adam Copeland) in 1994 Entry Draft for Dave Manson and St. Louis' 6th round choice (previously acquired, Winnipeg selected Chris Kibermanis) in 1994 Entry Draft, March 15, 1994. Traded to **NY Islanders** by **Edmonton** with Edmonton's 8th round choice (Radek Martinek) in 1999 Entry Draft for Tommy Salo, March 20, 1999. • Missed majority of 2000-01 season recovering from shoulder injury suffered in game vs. Anaheim, November 25, 2000. Signed as a free agent by **Vancouver**, November 3, 2002.

LINDROS, Eric

(LIHND-rahz, AIR-ihk) **NYR**

Center. Shoots right. 6'4", 240 lbs. Born, London, Ont., February 28, 1973. Quebec's 1st choice, 1st overall, in 1991 Entry Draft.

1988-89	St. Michael's B	OJHL-B	37	24	43	67	193	....	....	....	....	....	....	....	....	....	27	23	25	48	155	....	....	....	....
1989-90	Det. Compuware	NAJHL	14	23	29	52	123	....	....	....	....	....	....	....	....	....	....	....	....	....	....	....	....	....	....
	Oshawa Generals	OHL	25	17	19	36	61	....	....	....	....	....	....	....	....	....	17	18	18	36	76	....	....	....	....
1990-91	Oshawa Generals	OHL	57	*71	78	*149	189	....	....	....	....	....	....	....	....	....	16	*18	20	*38	*93	....	....	....	....
1991-92	Oshawa Generals	OHL	13	9	22	31	54	....	....	....	....	....	....	....	....	....	....	....	....	....	....	....	....	....	....
	Team Canada	Nat-Tm	24	19	16	35	34	....	....	....	....	....	....	....	....	....	....	....	....	....	....	....	....	....	....
	Canada	Olympics	8	5	6	11	5	....	....	....	....	....	....	....	....	....	....	....	....	....	....	....	....	....	....
1992-93	Philadelphia	NHL	61	41	34	75	147	8	1	5	180	22.8	28	....	....	....	....	....	....	....	....	....	....	....	....
1993-94	Philadelphia	NHL	65	44	53	97	103	13	2	9	197	22.3	16	....	....	....	....	....	....	....	....	....	....	....	....
1994-95	Philadelphia	NHL	46	29	41	*70	60	7	0	4	144	20.1	27	....	....	....	12	4	11	15	18	0	0	1	....
1995-96	Philadelphia	NHL	73	47	68	115	163	15	0	4	294	16.0	26	....	....	....	12	6	6	12	43	3	0	2	....
1996-97	Philadelphia	NHL	52	32	47	79	136	9	0	7	198	16.2	31	....	....	....	19	12	14	*26	40	4	0	1	....
1997-98	Philadelphia	NHL	63	30	41	71	134	10	1	4	202	14.9	14	....	....	....	5	1	2	3	17	0	0	0	....
	Canada	Olympics	6	2	3	5	2	....	....	....	....	....	....	....	....	....	....	....	....	....	....	....	....	....	....
1998-99	Philadelphia	NHL	71	40	53	93	120	10	1	2	242	16.5	35	1529	60.0	22:56	....	....	....	....	....	....	....	....	....
99-2000	Philadelphia	NHL	55	27	32	59	83	10	1	2	187	14.4	11	1318	57.8	22:02	2	1	0	1	0	0	0	0	8:26
2000-01	Philadelphia	NHL	DID NOT PLAY																						
2001-02	NY Rangers	NHL	72	37	36	73	138	12	1	4	196	18.9	19	1707	54.4	21:03	....	....	....	....	....	....	....	....	....
	Canada	Olympics	6	1	0	1	8	....	....	....	....	....	....	....	....	....	....	....	....	....	....	....	....	....	....
2002-03	NY Rangers	NHL	81	19	34	53	141	9	0	3	235	8.1	5	778	53.0	20:15	....	....	....	....	....	....	....	....	....
	NHL Totals		639	346	439	785	1225	103	7	44	2075	16.7		5332	56.6	21:29	50	24	33	57	118	7	0	4	8:26

Memorial Cup All-Star Team (1990) • OHL First All-Star Team (1991) • OHL MVP (1991) • Canadian Major Junior Player of the Year (1991) • NHL All-Rookie Team (1993) • NHL First All-Star Team (1995) • Lester B. Pearson Award (1995) • Hart Trophy (1995) • NHL Second All-Star Team (1996)

Played in NHL All-Star Game (1994, 1996, 1997, 1998, 1999, 2000)

Traded to **Philadelphia** by **Quebec** for Peter Forsberg, Steve Duchesne, Kerry Huffman, Mike Ricci, Ron Hextall, Philadelphia's 1st round choice (Jocelyn Thibault) in 1993 Entry Draft, $15,000,000 and future considerations (Chris Simon and Philadelphia's 1st round choice (later traded to Toronto – later traded to Washington – Washington selected Nolan Baumgartner) in 1994 Entry Draft, July 21, 1992), June 30, 1992. • Missed entire 2000-01 season recovering from head injury suffered in game vs. New Jersey, May 26, 2000 and contract dispute with Philadelphia Flyers management. Traded to **NY Rangers** by **Philadelphia** for Kim Johnsson, Jan Havac, Pavel Brendl and NY Rangers' 3rd round choice (Stefan Ruzicka) in 2003 Entry Draft, August 20, 2001.

LINDSAY, Bill

(LIHND-see, BIHL) **ATL.**

Right wing. Shoots left. 6', 195 lbs. Born, Fernie, B.C., May 17, 1971. Quebec's 6th choice, 103rd overall, in 1991 Entry Draft.

1988-89	Vernon Lakers	BCJHL	56	24	29	53	166	....	....	....	....	....	....	....	....	....	....	....	....	....	....	....	....	....	....
1989-90	Tri-City	WHL	72	40	45	85	84	....	....	....	....	....	....	....	....	....	7	3	0	3	17	....	....	....	....
1990-91	Tri-City	WHL	63	46	47	93	151	....	....	....	....	....	....	....	....	....	5	3	6	9	10	....	....	....	....
1991-92	Tri-City	WHL	42	34	59	93	81	....	....	....	....	....	....	....	....	....	3	2	3	5	16	....	....	....	....
	Quebec	NHL	23	2	4	6	14	0	0	1	35	5.7	−6	....	....	....	....	....	....	....	....	....	....	....	....
1992-93	Quebec	NHL	44	4	9	13	16	0	0	0	58	6.9	0	....	....	....	....	....	....	....	....	....	....	....	....
	Halifax Citadels	AHL	20	11	13	24	18	....	....	....	....	....	....	....	....	....	....	....	....	....	....	....	....	....	....
1993-94	Florida	NHL	84	6	6	12	97	0	0	0	90	6.7	−2	....	....	....	....	....	....	....	....	....	....	....	....
1994-95	Florida	NHL	48	10	9	19	46	0	1	0	63	15.9	1	....	....	....	....	....	....	....	....	....	....	....	....
1995-96	Florida	NHL	73	12	22	34	57	0	3	2	118	10.2	13	....	....	....	22	5	5	10	18	0	1	1	....
1996-97	Florida	NHL	81	11	23	34	120	0	1	3	168	6.5	1	....	....	....	3	0	1	1	8	0	0	0	....
1997-98	Florida	NHL	82	12	16	28	80	0	2	5	150	8.0	−2	....	....	....	....	....	....	....	....	....	....	....	....
1998-99	Florida	NHL	75	12	15	27	92	0	1	2	135	8.9	−1	57	40.4	13:37	....	....	....	....	....	....	....	....	....
99-2000	Calgary	NHL	80	8	12	20	86	0	0	2	147	5.4	−7	28	39.3	12:55	....	....	....	....	....	....	....	....	....
2000-01	Calgary	NHL	52	1	9	10	97	0	0	0	57	1.8	−8	9	55.6	10:32	....	....	....	....	....	....	....	....	....
	San Jose	NHL	16	0	4	4	29	0	0	0	14	0.0	2	2	0.0	9:16	6	0	0	0	16	0	0	0	6:40
2001-02	Florida	NHL	63	4	7	11	117	0	0	1	63	6.3	−11	124	44.4	9:40	....	....	....	....	....	....	....	....	....
	Montreal	NHL	13	1	3	4	23	0	0	0	14	7.1	0	26	53.9	10:10	11	2	2	4	2	0	0	0	6:58
2002-03	Montreal	NHL	19	0	2	2	23	0	0	0	7	0.0	−1	21	42.9	5:20	....	....	....	....	....	....	....	....	....
	Hamilton	AHL	28	6	12	18	89	....	....	....	....	....	....	....	....	....	23	10	3	13	31	....	....	....	....
	NHL Totals		753	83	141	224	897	0	8	16	1119	7.4		267	43.8	11:18	42	7	8	15	44	0	1	1	6:52

WHL West Second All-Star Team (1992)

Claimed by **Florida** from **Quebec** in Expansion Draft, June 24, 1993. Traded to **Calgary** by **Florida** for Todd Simpson, September 30, 1999. Traded to **San Jose** by **Calgary** for Minnesota's 8th round choice (previously acquired, Calgary selected Joe Campbell) in 2001 Entry Draft, March 6, 2001. Signed as a free agent by **Florida**, August 23, 2001. Claimed on waivers by **Montreal** from **Florida**, March 19, 2002. Signed as a free agent by **Atlanta**, August 25, 2003.

LING, David

(LIHNG, DAY-vihd) **CBJ**

Right wing. Shoots right. 5'10", 204 lbs. Born, Halifax, N.S., January 9, 1975. Quebec's 9th choice, 179th overall, in 1993 Entry Draft.

1991-92	Charlottetown	MJrHL	30	33	42	75	270	....	....	....	....	....	....	....	....	....	....	....	....	....	....	....	....	....	....
	St. Michael's B	OJHL-B	8	5	14	19	25	....	....	....	....	....	....	....	....	....	....	....	....	....	....	....	....	....	....
1992-93	Kingston	OHL	64	17	46	63	275	....	....	....	....	....	....	....	....	....	16	3	12	15	*72	....	....	....	....
1993-94	Kingston	OHL	61	37	40	77	*254	....	....	....	....	....	....	....	....	....	6	4	2	6	16	....	....	....	....
1994-95	Kingston	OHL	62	*61	74	135	136	....	....	....	....	....	....	....	....	....	6	7	8	15	12	....	....	....	....
1995-96	Saint John Flames	AHL	75	24	32	56	179	....	....	....	....	....	....	....	....	....	9	0	5	5	12	....	....	....	....

			Regular Season														Playoffs								
Season	Club	League	GP	G	A	Pts	PIM	PP	SH	GW	S	%	+/-	TF	F%	Min	GP	G	A	Pts	PIM	PP	SH	GW	Min
1996-97	Saint John Flames	AHL	5	0	2	2	19	....	....	....	....	....	....	....	....	....	....	....	....	....	....	....	....	....	....
	Montreal	NHL	2	0	0	0	0	0	0	0	0	0.0	0	....	....	....	....	....	....	....	....	....	....	....	....
	Fredericton	AHL	48	22	36	58	229	....	....	....	....	....	....	....	....	....	....	....	....	....	....	....	....	....	....
1997-98	Montreal	NHL	1	0	0	0	0	0	0	0	1	0.0	–1	....	....	....	....	....	....	....	....	....	....	....	....
	Fredericton	AHL	67	25	41	66	148	....	....	....	....	....	....	....	....	....	....	....	....	....	....	....	....	....	....
	Indianapolis Ice	IHL	12	8	6	14	30	....	....	....	....	....	....	....	....	....	5	4	1	5	31	....	....	....	....
1998-99	Kansas City	IHL	82	30	42	72	112	....	....	....	....	....	....	....	....	....	3	1	0	1	20	....	....	....	....
99-2000	Kansas City	IHL	82	35	48	83	210	....	....	....	....	....	....	....	....	....	....	....	....	....	....	....	....	....	....
2000-01	Utah Grizzlies	IHL	79	15	28	43	202	....	....	....	....	....	....	....	....	....	....	....	....	....	....	....	....	....	....
2001-02	Syracuse Crunch	AHL	71	19	41	60	240	....	....	....	....	....	....	....	....	....	10	5	5	10	16	....	....	....	....
	Columbus	NHL	5	0	0	0	7	0	0	0	5	0.0	–1	1	0.0	9:47	....	....	....	....	....	....	....	....	....
2002-03	Columbus	NHL	35	3	2	5	86	0	0	0	37	8.1	–6	15	40.0	7:56	....	....	....	....	....	....	....	....	....
	Syracuse Crunch	AHL	46	7	34	41	129	....	....	....	....	....	....	....	....	....	....	....	....	....	....	....	....	....	....
	NHL Totals		43	3	2	5	93	0	0	0	43	7.0		16	37.5	8:10	....	....	....	....	....	....	....	....	....

OHL First All-Star Team (1995) • OHL MVP (1995) • Canadian Major Junior First All-Star Team (1995) • Canadian Major Junior Player of the Year (1995) • IHL First All-Star Team (2000)

Rights transferred to **Colorado** after **Quebec** franchise relocated, June 21, 1995. Traded to **Calgary** by **Colorado** with Colorado's 9th round choice (Steve Shirreffs) in 1995 Entry Draft for Calgary's 9th round choice (Chris George) in 1995 Entry Draft, July 7, 1995. Traded to **Montreal** by **Calgary** with Calgary's 6th round choice (Gordie Dwyer) in 1998 Entry Draft for Scott Fraser, October 24, 1996. Traded to **Chicago** by **Montreal** for Martin Gendron, March 14, 1998. Signed as a free agent by **Kansas City** (IHL) with Chicago retaining NHL rights, September 3, 1998. Traded to **Dallas** by **Chicago** for future considerations, August 11, 2000. Signed as a free agent by **Columbus**, July 7, 2001.

LINTNER, Richard

(LIHNT-nuhr, RIH-chahrd)

Defense. Shoots right. 6'3", 212 lbs. Born, Trencin, Czech., November 15, 1977. Phoenix's 4th choice, 119th overall, in 1996 Entry Draft.

			Regular Season														Playoffs								
Season	Club	League	GP	G	A	Pts	PIM	PP	SH	GW	S	%	+/-	TF	F%	Min	GP	G	A	Pts	PIM	PP	SH	GW	Min
1994-95	Dukla Trencin Jr.	Slovak-Jr.	42	12	13	25	20	....	....	....	....	....	....	....	....	....	....	....	....	....	....	....	....	....	....
1995-96	Dukla Trencin Jr.	Slovak-Jr.	30	15	17	32	210	....	....	....	....	....	....	....	....	....	....	....	....	....	....	....	....	....	....
	Dukla Trencin	Slovakia	2	0	0	0	0	....	....	....	....	....	....	....	....	....	....	....	....	....	....	....	....	....	....
1996-97	Nova Ves	Slovakia	35	2	1	3	....	....	....	....	....	....	....	....	....	....	....	....	....	....	....	....	....	....	....
	MoDo Jr.	Swede-Jr.	20	6	11	17	....	....	....	....	....	....	....	....	....	....	....	....	....	....	....	....	....	....	....
1997-98	Springfield	AHL	71	6	9	15	61	....	....	....	....	....	....	....	....	....	3	1	1	2	4	....	....	....	....
1998-99	MoDo Jr.	Swede-Jr.	2	1	0	1	0	....	....	....	....	....	....	....	....	....	....	....	....	....	....	....	....	....	....
	Springfield	AHL	8	0	1	1	16	....	....	....	....	....	....	....	....	....	....	....	....	....	....	....	....	....	....
	Milwaukee	IHL	66	9	16	25	75	....	....	....	....	....	....	....	....	....	....	....	....	....	....	....	....	....	....
99-2000	Nashville	NHL	33	1	5	6	22	0	0	0	58	1.7	–6	0	0.0	14:51	....	....	....	....	....	....	....	....	....
	Milwaukee	IHL	31	13	8	21	37	....	....	....	....	....	....	....	....	....	....	....	....	....	....	....	....	....	....
2000-01	Nashville	NHL	50	3	5	8	22	1	0	0	81	3.7	2	0	0.0	13:05	....	....	....	....	....	....	....	....	....
2001-02	MoDo	Sweden	28	12	9	21	85	....	....	....	....	....	....	....	....	....	14	3	0	3	8	....	....	....	....
	Dukla Trencin	Slovakia	6	2	0	2	0	....	....	....	....	....	....	....	....	....	....	....	....	....	....	....	....	....	....
	Slovakia	Olympics	4	1	1	2	0	....	....	....	....	....	....	....	....	....	....	....	....	....	....	....	....	....	....
2002-03	NY Rangers	NHL	10	1	0	1	0	1	0	0	9	11.1	–5	0	0.0	14:20	....	....	....	....	....	....	....	....	....
	Hartford	AHL	26	6	15	21	30	....	....	....	....	....	....	....	....	....	....	....	....	....	....	....	....	....	....
	Pittsburgh	NHL	19	3	2	5	10	1	0	0	36	8.3	–9	0	0.0	18:59	....	....	....	....	....	....	....	....	....
	Wilkes-Barre	AHL	6	1	4	5	2	....	....	....	....	....	....	....	....	....	....	....	....	....	....	....	....	....	....
	NHL Totals		112	8	12	20	54	3	0	0	184	4.3		0	0.0	14:43	....	....	....	....	....	....	....	....	....

Traded to **Nashville** by **Phoenix** with Cliff Ronning for future considerations, October 31, 1998. Signed as a free agent by **Dukla Trencin** (Slovakia) with Nashville retaining NHL rights, October 17, 2001. Traded to **NY Rangers** by **Nashville** for Peter Smrek, March 19, 2002. Traded to **Pittsburgh** by **NY Rangers** with Joel Bouchard, Rico Fata, Mikael Samuelsson and future considerations for Mike Wilson, Alex Kovalev, Janne Laukkanen and Dan LaCouture, February 10, 2003.

LOW, Reed

(LOH, REED) **ST.L.**

Right wing. Shoots right. 6'3", 222 lbs. Born, Moose Jaw, Sask., June 21, 1976. St. Louis' 7th choice, 177th overall, in 1996 Entry Draft.

			Regular Season														Playoffs								
Season	Club	League	GP	G	A	Pts	PIM	PP	SH	GW	S	%	+/-	TF	F%	Min	GP	G	A	Pts	PIM	PP	SH	GW	Min
1994-95	Minot Top Guns	SJHL	STATISTICS NOT AVAILABLE																						
	Regina Pats	WHL	2	0	0	0	5	....	....	....	....	....	....	....	....	....	....	....	....	....	....	....	....	....	....
1995-96	Moose Jaw	WHL	61	12	7	19	221	....	....	....	....	....	....	....	....	....	....	....	....	....	....	....	....	....	....
1996-97	Moose Jaw	WHL	62	16	11	27	228	....	....	....	....	....	....	....	....	....	12	2	1	3	50	....	....	....	....
1997-98	Worcester IceCats	AHL	17	1	1	2	75	....	....	....	....	....	....	....	....	....	3	0	0	0	0	....	....	....	....
	Baton Rouge	ECHL	39	4	2	6	145	....	....	....	....	....	....	....	....	....	....	....	....	....	....	....	....	....	....
1998-99	Worcester IceCats	AHL	77	5	6	11	239	....	....	....	....	....	....	....	....	....	4	0	0	0	2	....	....	....	....
99-2000	Worcester IceCats	AHL	80	12	16	28	203	....	....	....	....	....	....	....	....	....	9	1	3	4	16	....	....	....	....
2000-01	St. Louis	NHL	56	1	5	6	159	0	0	0	31	3.2	4	2	50.0	6:17	....	....	....	....	....	....	....	....	....
2001-02	St. Louis	NHL	58	0	5	5	160	0	0	0	25	0.0	–3	0	0.0	5:22	....	....	....	....	....	....	....	....	....
2002-03	St. Louis	NHL	79	2	4	6	234	0	0	1	48	4.2	3	14	71.4	6:19	....	....	....	....	....	....	....	....	....
	NHL Totals		193	3	14	17	553	0	0	1	104	2.9		16	68.8	6:01	....	....	....	....	....	....	....	....	....

LOWRY, Dave

(LOW-ree, DAYV)

Left wing. Shoots left. 6'1", 195 lbs. Born, Sudbury, Ont., February 14, 1965. Vancouver's 6th choice, 114th overall, in 1983 Entry Draft.

			Regular Season														Playoffs								
Season	Club	League	GP	G	A	Pts	PIM	PP	SH	GW	S	%	+/-	TF	F%	Min	GP	G	A	Pts	PIM	PP	SH	GW	Min
1981-82	Nepean	ODMHA	60	50	64	114	46	....	....	....	....	....	....	....	....	....	....	....	....	....	....	....	....	....	....
1982-83	London Knights	OHL	42	11	16	27	48	....	....	....	....	....	....	....	....	....	3	0	0	0	14	....	....	....	....
1983-84	London Knights	OHL	66	29	47	76	125	....	....	....	....	....	....	....	....	....	8	6	6	12	41	....	....	....	....
1984-85	London Knights	OHL	61	60	60	120	94	....	....	....	....	....	....	....	....	....	8	6	5	11	10	....	....	....	....
1985-86	Vancouver	NHL	73	10	8	18	143	1	0	1	66	15.2	–21	....	....	....	3	0	0	0	0	0	0	0	....
1986-87	Vancouver	NHL	70	8	10	18	176	0	0	1	74	10.8	–23	....	....	....	....	....	....	....	....	....	....	....	....
1987-88	Vancouver	NHL	22	1	3	4	38	0	0	0	14	7.1	–2	....	....	....	....	....	....	....	....	....	....	....	....
	Fredericton	AHL	46	18	27	45	59	....	....	....	....	....	....	....	....	....	14	7	3	10	72	....	....	....	....
1988-89	St. Louis	NHL	21	3	3	6	11	0	1	0	22	13.6	1	....	....	....	10	0	5	5	4	0	0	0	....
	Peoria Rivermen	IHL	58	31	35	66	45	....	....	....	....	....	....	....	....	....	....	....	....	....	....	....	....	....	....
1989-90	St. Louis	NHL	78	19	6	25	75	0	2	1	98	19.4	1	....	....	....	12	2	1	3	39	0	0	0	....
1990-91	St. Louis	NHL	79	19	21	40	168	0	2	5	123	15.4	19	....	....	....	13	1	4	5	35	0	0	0	....
1991-92	St. Louis	NHL	75	7	13	20	77	0	0	1	85	8.2	–11	....	....	....	6	0	1	1	20	0	0	0	....
1992-93	St. Louis	NHL	58	5	8	13	101	0	0	0	59	8.5	–18	....	....	....	11	2	0	2	14	0	1	0	....
1993-94	Florida	NHL	80	15	22	37	64	3	0	3	122	12.3	–4	....	....	....	....	....	....	....	....	....	....	....	....
1994-95	Florida	NHL	45	10	10	20	25	2	0	3	70	14.3	–3	....	....	....	....	....	....	....	....	....	....	....	....
1995-96	Florida	NHL	63	10	14	24	36	0	0	1	83	12.0	–2	....	....	....	22	10	7	17	39	4	0	2	....
1996-97	Florida	NHL	77	15	14	29	51	2	0	2	96	15.6	2	....	....	....	5	0	0	0	0	0	0	0	....
1997-98	Florida	NHL	7	0	0	0	2	0	0	0	4	0.0	–1	....	....	....	....	....	....	....	....	....	....	....	....
	San Jose	NHL	50	4	4	8	51	0	0	1	47	8.5	0	....	....	....	6	0	0	0	18	0	0	0	....
1998-99	San Jose	NHL	61	6	9	15	24	2	0	0	58	10.3	–5	6	50.0	9:14	1	0	0	0	0	0	0	0	8:37
99-2000	San Jose	NHL	32	1	4	5	18	0	0	0	25	4.0	1	1	100.0	9:11	12	1	2	3	6	0	0	0	12:13
2000-01	Calgary	NHL	79	18	17	35	47	5	0	5	108	16.7	–2	20	20.0	15:57	....	....	....	....	....	....	....	....	....
2001-02	Calgary	NHL	62	7	6	13	51	2	1	1	74	9.5	–20	15	26.7	14:58	....	....	....	....	....	....	....	....	....
2002-03	Calgary	NHL	34	5	14	19	22	1	0	0	40	12.5	4	13	15.4	14:18	....	....	....	....	....	....	....	....	....
	Saint John Flames	AHL	22	3	6	9	16	....	....	....	....	....	....	....	....	....	....	....	....	....	....	....	....	....	....
	NHL Totals		1066	163	186	349	1180	18	6	25	1268	12.9		55	25.5	13:10	101	16	20	36	175	4	1	2	11:56

OHL First All-Star Team (1985)

Traded to **St. Louis** by **Vancouver** for Ernie Vargas, September 29, 1988. Claimed by **Florida** from **St. Louis** in Expansion Draft, June 24, 1993. Traded to **San Jose** by **Florida** with Florida's 1st round choice (later traded to Tampa Bay – Tampa Bay selected Vincent Lecavalier) in 1998 Entry Draft for Viktor Kozlov and Florida's 5th round choice (previously acquired, Florida selected Jaroslav Spacek) in 1998 Entry Draft, November 13, 1997. • Missed majority of 1999-2000 season recovering from shoulder injury suffered in game vs. Montreal, November 23, 1999. Signed as a free agent by **Calgary**, July 24, 2000.

LOYNS, Lynn

(LOINZ, LIHN) **S.J.**

Left wing. Shoots left. 5'11", 200 lbs. Born, Naicam, Sask., February 21, 1981.

			Regular Season														Playoffs								
Season	Club	League	GP	G	A	Pts	PIM	PP	SH	GW	S	%	+/-	TF	F%	Min	GP	G	A	Pts	PIM	PP	SH	GW	Min
1997-98	Spokane Chiefs	WHL	49	1	12	13	8	....	....	....	....	....	....	....	....	....	13	1	4	5	2	....	....	....	....
1998-99	Spokane Chiefs	WHL	72	20	30	50	43	....	....	....	....	....	....	....	....	....	....	....	....	....	....	....	....	....	....
99-2000	Spokane Chiefs	WHL	71	20	29	49	47	....	....	....	....	....	....	....	....	....	14	3	2	5	12	....	....	....	....
2000-01	Spokane Chiefs	WHL	66	31	42	73	81	....	....	....	....	....	....	....	....	....	....	....	....	....	....	....	....	....	....
2001-02	Cleveland Barons	AHL	76	9	9	18	81	....	....	....	....	....	....	....	....	....	....	....	....	....	....	....	....	....	....

			Regular Season														Playoffs								
Season	Club	League	GP	G	A	Pts	PIM	PP	SH	GW	S	%	+/-	TF	F%	Min	GP	G	A	Pts	PIM	PP	SH	GW	Min
2002-03	San Jose	NHL	19	3	0	3	19	0	0	0	12	25.0	–4	1	0.0	7:50	....	....	....	....	....	....	....	....	....
	Cleveland Barons	AHL	36	7	8	15	39	....	....	....	....	....	....	....	....	....	....	....	....	....	....	....	....	....	....
	NHL Totals		19	3	0	3	19	0	0	0	12	25.0		1	0.0	7:50	....	....	....	....	....	....	....	....	....

Signed as a free agent by **San Jose**, October 3, 2001.

LUKOWICH, Brad

(loo-KUH-which, BRAD) **T.B.**

Defense. Shoots left. 6'1", 200 lbs. Born, Cranbrook, B.C., August 12, 1976. NY Islanders' 4th choice, 90th overall, in 1994 Entry Draft.

Season	Club	League	GP	G	A	Pts	PIM	PP	SH	GW	S	%	+/-	TF	F%	Min	GP	G	A	Pts	PIM	PP	SH	GW	Min
1992-93	Cranbrook Colts	RMJHL	54	21	41	62	162	....	....	....	....	....	....	....	....	....	....	....	....	....	....	....	....	....	....
	Kamloops Blazers	WHL	1	0	0	0	0	....	....	....	....	....	....	....	....	....	....	....	....	....	....	....	....	....	....
1993-94	Kamloops Blazers	WHL	42	5	11	16	166	....	....	....	....	....	....	....	....	....	16	0	1	1	35	....	....	....	....
1994-95	Kamloops Blazers	WHL	63	10	35	45	125	....	....	....	....	....	....	....	....	....	18	0	7	7	21	....	....	....	....
1995-96	Kamloops Blazers	WHL	65	14	55	69	114	....	....	....	....	....	....	....	....	....	13	2	10	12	29	....	....	....	....
1996-97	Michigan	IHL	69	2	6	8	77	....	....	....	....	....	....	....	....	....	4	0	1	1	2	....	....	....	....
1997-98	Dallas	NHL	4	0	1	1	2	0	0	0	2	0.0	–2	....	....	....	....	....	....	....	....	....	....	....	....
	Michigan	IHL	60	6	27	33	104	....	....	....	....	....	....	....	....	....	4	0	4	4	14	....	....	....	....
1998-99	Dallas	NHL	14	1	2	3	19	0	0	0	8	12.5	3	0	0.0	16:18	8	0	1	1	4	0	0	0	9:60
	Michigan	IHL	67	8	21	29	95	....	....	....	....	....	....	....	....	....	....	....	....	....	....	....	....	....	....
99-2000	Dallas	NHL	60	3	1	4	50	0	0	1	33	9.1	–14	1	0.0	11:44	....	....	....	....	....	....	....	....	....
2000-01	Dallas	NHL	80	4	10	14	76	0	0	2	43	9.3	28	1	100.0	14:48	10	1	0	1	4	0	0	0	17:28
2001-02	Dallas	NHL	66	1	6	7	40	0	0	0	56	1.8	–1	0	0.0	13:14	....	....	....	....	....	....	....	....	....
2002-03	Tampa Bay	NHL	70	1	14	15	46	0	0	0	52	1.9	4	1	0.0	17:34	9	0	1	1	2	0	0	0	17:48
	NHL Totals		294	10	34	44	233	0	0	3	194	5.2		3	33.3	14:33	27	1	2	3	10	0	0	0	15:22

Traded to **Dallas** by **NY Islanders** for Dallas' 3rd round choice (Robert Schnabel) in 1997 Entry Draft, June 1, 1996. Traded to **Minnesota** by **Dallas** with Manny Fernandez for Minnesota's 3rd round choice (Joel Lundqvist) in 2000 Entry Draft and 4th round choice (later traded back to Minnesota – later traded to Los Angeles – Los Angeles selected Aaron Rome) in 2002 Entry Draft, June 12, 2000. Traded to **Dallas** by **Minnesota** with Minnesota's 3rd (Yared Hagos) and 9th (Dale Sullivan) round choices in 2001 Entry Draft for Aaron Gavey, Pavel Patera, Dallas' 8th round choice (Eric Johansson) in 2000 Entry Draft and Minnesota's 4th round choice (previously acquired, later traded to Los Angeles – Los Angeles selected Aaron Rome) in 2002 Entry Draft, June 25, 2000. Traded to **Tampa Bay** by **Dallas** with Dallas' 7th round choice (Jay Rosehill) in 2003 Entry Draft for Tampa Bay's 2nd round choice (previously acquired, later traded back to Tampa Bay – later traded to Dallas – Dallas selected Tobias Stephan) in 2002 Entry Draft, June 22, 2002.

LUMME, Jyrki

(LOO-may, YUHR-kee)

Defense. Shoots left. 6'1", 209 lbs. Born, Tampere, Finland, July 16, 1966. Montreal's 3rd choice, 57th overall, in 1986 Entry Draft.

Season	Club	League	GP	G	A	Pts	PIM	PP	SH	GW	S	%	+/-	TF	F%	Min	GP	G	A	Pts	PIM	PP	SH	GW	Min
1983-84	KooVee Jr.	Finn-Jr.	28	5	4	9	61	....	....	....	....	....	....	....	....	....	....	....	....	....	....	....	....	....	....
1984-85	KooVee Tampere	Finland-3	30	6	4	10	44	....	....	....	....	....	....	....	....	....	....	....	....	....	....	....	....	....	....
1985-86	Ilves Tampere Jr.	Finn-Jr.	6	3	3	6	6	....	....	....	....	....	....	....	....	....	4	0	0	0	8	....	....	....	....
	Ilves Tampere	Finland	31	1	4	5	4	....	....	....	....	....	....	....	....	....	....	....	....	....	....	....	....	....	....
1986-87	Ilves Tampere Jr.	Finn-Jr.	1	0	1	1	6	....	....	....	....	....	....	....	....	....	1	1	0	1	6	....	....	....	....
	Ilves Tampere	Finland	43	12	12	24	52	....	....	....	....	....	....	....	....	....	4	0	1	1	2	....	....	....	....
1987-88	Ilves Tampere	Finland	43	8	22	30	75	....	....	....	....	....	....	....	....	....	....	....	....	....	....	....	....	....	....
	Finland	Olympics	6	0	1	1	2	....	....	....	....	....	....	....	....	....	....	....	....	....	....	....	....	....	....
1988-89	Montreal	NHL	21	1	3	4	10	1	0	0	18	5.6	3	....	....	....	....	....	....	....	....	....	....	....	....
	Sherbrooke	AHL	26	4	11	15	10	....	....	....	....	....	....	....	....	....	6	1	3	4	4	....	....	....	....
1989-90	Montreal	NHL	54	1	19	20	41	0	0	0	79	1.3	17	....	....	....	....	....	....	....	....	....	....	....	....
	Vancouver	NHL	11	3	7	10	8	0	0	1	30	10.0	0	....	....	....	....	....	....	....	....	....	....	....	....
1990-91	Vancouver	NHL	80	5	27	32	59	1	0	0	157	3.2	–15	....	....	....	6	2	3	5	0	1	1	0	....
1991-92	Vancouver	NHL	75	12	32	44	65	3	1	1	106	11.3	25	....	....	....	13	2	3	5	4	1	0	1	....
1992-93	Vancouver	NHL	74	8	36	44	55	3	2	1	123	6.5	30	....	....	....	12	0	5	5	6	0	0	0	....
1993-94	Vancouver	NHL	83	13	42	55	50	1	3	3	161	8.1	3	....	....	....	24	2	11	13	16	2	0	1	....
1994-95	Ilves Tampere	Finland	12	4	4	8	24	....	....	....	....	....	....	....	....	....	....	....	....	....	....	....	....	....	....
	Vancouver	NHL	36	5	12	17	26	3	0	1	78	6.4	4	....	....	....	11	2	6	8	8	1	0	0	....
1995-96	Vancouver	NHL	80	17	37	54	50	8	0	2	192	8.9	–9	....	....	....	6	1	3	4	2	1	0	0	....
1996-97	Vancouver	NHL	66	11	24	35	32	5	0	2	107	10.3	8	....	....	....	....	....	....	....	....	....	....	....	....
1997-98	Vancouver	NHL	74	9	21	30	34	4	0	1	117	7.7	–25	....	....	....	....	....	....	....	....	....	....	....	....
	Finland	Olympics	6	1	0	1	16	....	....	....	....	....	....	....	....	....	....	....	....	....	....	....	....	....	....
1998-99	Phoenix	NHL	60	7	21	28	34	1	0	4	121	5.8	5	0	0.0	23:20	7	0	1	1	6	0	0	0	26:57
99-2000	Phoenix	NHL	74	8	32	40	44	4	0	3	142	5.6	9	0	0.0	23:36	5	0	1	1	2	0	0	0	28:13
2000-01	Phoenix	NHL	58	4	21	25	44	0	0	0	77	5.2	3	0	0.0	21:44	....	....	....	....	....	....	....	....	....
2001-02	Dallas	NHL	15	0	1	1	4	0	0	0	12	0.0	–5	0	0.0	13:40	....	....	....	....	....	....	....	....	....
	Toronto	NHL	51	4	8	12	18	1	2	1	61	6.6	13	0	0.0	19:57	14	0	0	0	4	0	0	0	20:09
	Finland	Olympics	4	0	1	1	0	....	....	....	....	....	....	....	....	....	....	....	....	....	....	....	....	....	....
2002-03	Toronto	NHL	73	6	11	17	46	1	0	3	72	8.3	10	0	0.0	20:37	7	0	2	2	4	0	0	0	20:17
	NHL Totals		985	114	354	468	620	36	8	23	1653	6.9		0	0.0	21:33	105	9	35	44	52	6	1	2	22:51

Traded to **Vancouver** by **Montreal** for St. Louis' 2nd round choice (previously acquired, Montreal selected Craig Darby) in 1991 Entry Draft, March 6, 1990. Signed as a free agent by **Phoenix**, July 3, 1998. Traded to **Dallas** by **Phoenix** for Tyler Bouck, June 23, 2001. Traded to **Toronto** by **Dallas** for Dave Manson, November 21, 2001.

LUNDMARK, Jamie

(LUHND-mahrk, JAY-mee) **NYR**

Center. Shoots right. 6', 174 lbs. Born, Edmonton, Alta., January 16, 1981. NY Rangers' 2nd choice, 9th overall, in 1999 Entry Draft.

Season	Club	League	GP	G	A	Pts	PIM	PP	SH	GW	S	%	+/-	TF	F%	Min	GP	G	A	Pts	PIM	PP	SH	GW	Min
1996-97	St. Albert Saints	AJHL	35	10	9	19	8	....	....	....	....	....	....	....	....	....	....	....	....	....	....	....	....	....	....
1997-98	St. Albert Saints	AJHL	57	33	58	91	171	....	....	....	....	....	....	....	....	....	19	13	18	31	5	....	....	....	....
1998-99	Moose Jaw	WHL	70	40	51	91	121	....	....	....	....	....	....	....	....	....	11	5	4	9	24	....	....	....	....
99-2000	Moose Jaw	WHL	37	21	27	48	33	....	....	....	....	....	....	....	....	....	....	....	....	....	....	....	....	....	....
2000-01	Seattle	WHL	52	35	42	77	49	....	....	....	....	....	....	....	....	....	9	4	4	8	16	....	....	....	....
2001-02	Hartford	AHL	79	27	32	59	56	....	....	....	....	....	....	....	....	....	10	3	4	7	16	....	....	....	....
2002-03	NY Rangers	NHL	55	8	11	19	16	0	0	0	78	10.3	–3	62	43.6	12:04	....	....	....	....	....	....	....	....	....
	Hartford	AHL	22	9	9	18	18	....	....	....	....	....	....	....	....	....	2	0	0	0	0	....	....	....	....
	NHL Totals		55	8	11	19	16	0	0	0	78	10.3		62	43.5	12:04	....	....	....	....	....	....	....	....	....

WHL All-Rookie Team (1999) • WHL East Second All-Star Team (1999) • WHL West First All-Star Team (2001)

LUPASCHUK, Ross

(LOO-puhs-chuhk, RAWS) **PIT.**

Defense. Shoots right. 6'1", 218 lbs. Born, Edmonton, Alta., January 19, 1981. Washington's 4th choice, 34th overall, in 1999 Entry Draft.

Season	Club	League	GP	G	A	Pts	PIM	PP	SH	GW	S	%	+/-	TF	F%	Min	GP	G	A	Pts	PIM	PP	SH	GW	Min
1996-97	Edmonton Mets	AJHL	65	5	22	27	87	....	....	....	....	....	....	....	....	....	....	....	....	....	....	....	....	....	....
1997-98	Prince Albert	WHL	67	6	12	18	170	....	....	....	....	....	....	....	....	....	....	....	....	....	....	....	....	....	....
1998-99	Prince Albert	WHL	67	8	20	28	127	....	....	....	....	....	....	....	....	....	14	4	9	13	16	....	....	....	....
99-2000	Prince Albert	WHL	22	8	8	16	42	....	....	....	....	....	....	....	....	....	....	....	....	....	....	....	....	....	....
	Red Deer Rebels	WHL	46	13	27	40	116	....	....	....	....	....	....	....	....	....	4	0	1	1	10	....	....	....	....
2000-01	Red Deer Rebels	WHL	65	28	37	65	135	....	....	....	....	....	....	....	....	....	22	5	10	15	54	....	....	....	....
2001-02	Wilkes-Barre	AHL	72	9	20	29	91	....	....	....	....	....	....	....	....	....	....	....	....	....	....	....	....	....	....
2002-03	Pittsburgh	NHL	3	0	0	0	4	0	0	0	3	0.0	–3	0	0.0	16:20	....	....	....	....	....	....	....	....	....
	Wilkes-Barre	AHL	74	18	18	36	101	....	....	....	....	....	....	....	....	....	4	0	2	2	20	....	....	....	....
	NHL Totals		3	0	0	0	4	0	0	0	3	0.0		0	0.0	16:20	....	....	....	....	....	....	....	....	....

WHL East Second All-Star Team (2001) • Memorial Cup All-Star Team (2001)

Traded to **Pittsburgh** by **Washington** with Kris Beech, Michal Sivek and future considerations for Jaromir Jagr and Frantisek Kucera, July 11, 2001.

LYASHENKO, Roman

(LIGH-a-SHEHN-koh, ROH-muhn)

Center. Shoots right. 6', 189 lbs. Born, Murmansk, Russia, May 2, 1979. Dallas' 2nd choice, 52nd overall, in 1997 Entry Draft.

Season	Club	League	GP	G	A	Pts	PIM	PP	SH	GW	S	%	+/-	TF	F%	Min	GP	G	A	Pts	PIM	PP	SH	GW	Min
1995-96	Yaroslavl	CIS	60	7	10	17	12	....	....	....	....	....	....	....	....	....	....	....	....	....	....	....	....	....	....
1996-97	Yaroslavl 2	Russia-3	2	1	1	2	8	....	....	....	....	....	....	....	....	....	....	....	....	....	....	....	....	....	....
	Yaroslavl	Russia	42	5	7	12	16	....	....	....	....	....	....	....	....	....	9	3	0	3	6	....	....	....	....
1997-98	Yaroslavl	Russia	46	7	6	13	28	....	....	....	....	....	....	....	....	....	....	....	....	....	....	....	....	....	....
	Yaroslavl	EuroHL	10	1	1	2	2	....	....	....	....	....	....	....	....	....	....	....	....	....	....	....	....	....	....
1998-99	Yaroslavl	Russia	42	10	9	19	51	....	....	....	....	....	....	....	....	....	9	0	4	4	8	....	....	....	....
99-2000	Dallas	NHL	58	6	6	12	10	0	0	1	51	11.8	–2	339	45.7	10:56	16	2	1	3	0	0	0	2	8:25
	Michigan	IHL	9	3	2	5	8	....	....	....	....	....	....	....	....	....	....	....	....	....	....	....	....	....	....
2000-01	Dallas	NHL	60	6	3	9	45	0	0	1	48	12.5	–1	418	43.3	9:35	1	0	0	0	0	0	0	0	4:00
	Utah Grizzlies	IHL	6	0	1	1	2	....	....	....	....	....	....	....	....	....	....	....	....	....	....	....	....	....	....

			Regular Season														Playoffs								
Season	Club	League	GP	G	A	Pts	PIM	PP	SH	GW	S	%	+/-	TF	F%	Min	GP	G	A	Pts	PIM	PP	SH	GW	Min
2001-02	Dallas	NHL	4	0	0	0	0	0	0	0	3	0.0	–2	25	44.0	7:42									
	Utah Grizzlies	AHL	58	11	25	36	37																		
	NY Rangers	NHL	15	2	0	2	0	0	0	0	13	15.4	0	99	41.4	7:50									
	Hartford	AHL															4	1	1	2	2				
2002-03	NY Rangers	NHL	2	0	0	0	0	0	0	0	4	0.0	–2	11	54.6	11:47									
	Hartford	AHL	71	23	35	58	44										2	1	1	2	0				
	NHL Totals		139	14	9	23	55	0	0	2	119	11.8		892	44.2	9:56	17	2	1	3	0	0	0	2	8:10

Traded to **NY Rangers** by **Dallas** with Martin Rucinsky for Manny Malhotra and Barrett Heisten, March 12, 2002. • Died July 6, 2003.

LYDMAN, Toni
(LEED-man, TOH-nee) **CGY.**

Defense. Shoots left. 6'1", 202 lbs. Born, Lahti, Finland, September 25, 1977. Calgary's 5th choice, 89th overall, in 1996 Entry Draft.

1992-93	Reipas Lahti-C	Finn-Jr.	36	10	9	19	22																		
1993-94	Reipas Lahti-B	Finn-Jr.	9	3	1	4	4																		
	Reipas Lahti Jr.	Finn-Jr.	1	0	0	0	0																		
1994-95	Reipas Lahti-B	Finn-Jr.	9	7	4	11	12																		
	Reipas Lahti-B	Finn-Jr.	26	6	4	10	10																		
1995-96	Reipas Lahti Jr.	Finn-Jr.	9	2	2	4	6																		
	Reipas Lahti	Finland	39	5	2	7	30										3	0	1	1	0				
1996-97	Tappara Tampere	Finland	49	1	2	3	65										3	0	0	0	6				
1997-98	Tappara Tampere	Finland	48	4	10	14	48										4	0	2	2	0				
1998-99	HIFK Helsinki	Finland	42	4	7	11	36										11	0	3	3	2				
	HIFK Helsinki	EuroHL	6	0	2	2	29										4	1							
99-2000	HIFK Helsinki	Finland	46	4	18	22	36										9	0	4	4	6				
2000-01	Calgary	NHL	62	3	16	19	30	1	0	0	80	3.8	–7	0	0.0	20:36									
2001-02	Calgary	NHL	79	6	22	28	52	1	0	0	126	4.8	–8	0	0.0	21:10									
2002-03	Calgary	NHL	81	6	20	26	28	3	0	0	143	4.2	–7	0	0.0	25:47									
	NHL Totals		222	15	58	73	110	5	0	0	349	4.3		0	0.0	22:41									

MacDONALD, Craig
(MAK-DAWN-uhld, KRAYG) **FLA.**

Left wing. Shoots left. 6'1", 195 lbs. Born, Antigonish, N.S., April 7, 1977. Hartford's 3rd choice, 88th overall, in 1996 Entry Draft.

1994-95	Lawrence School	Hi-School	30	25	52	77	10																		
1995-96	Harvard Crimson	ECAC	34	7	10	17	10																		
1996-97	Harvard Crimson	ECAC	32	6	10	16	20																		
1997-98	Team Canada	Nat-Tm	58	18	29	47	38																		
1998-99	Carolina	NHL	11	0	0	0	0	0	0	0	5	0.0	0	2	100.0	2:29	1	0	0	0	0	0	0	0	2:46
	New Haven	AHL	62	17	31	48	77																		
99-2000	Cincinnati	IHL	78	12	24	36	76										11	4	1	5	8				
2000-01	Cincinnati	IHL	82	20	28	48	104										5	0	1	1	6				
2001-02	Carolina	NHL	12	1	1	2	0	0	0	0	15	6.7	–1	19	47.4	10:11	4	0	0	0	2	0	0	0	4:42
	Lowell	AHL	64	19	22	41	61																		
2002-03	Carolina	NHL	35	1	3	4	20	0	0	0	43	2.3	–3	72	55.6	9:21									
	Lowell	AHL	27	7	20	27	38																		
	NHL Totals		58	2	4	6	20	0	0	0	63	3.2		93	54.8	8:13	5	0	0	0	2	0	0	0	4:19

Rights transferred to **Carolina** after **Hartford** franchise relocated, June 25, 1997. Signed as a free agent by **Florida**, August 14, 2003.

MacINNIS, Al
(MAK-IHN-his, AL) **ST.L.**

Defense. Shoots right. 6'2", 204 lbs. Born, Inverness, N.S., July 11, 1963. Calgary's 1st choice, 15th overall, in 1981 Entry Draft.

1979-80	Regina Blues	SJHL	59	20	28	48	110																		
1980-81	Kitchener Rangers	OMJHL	47	11	28	39	59										18	4	12	16	20				
1981-82	Kitchener Rangers	OHL	59	25	50	75	145										15	5	10	15	44				
	Calgary	NHL	2	0	0	0	0	0	0	0	2	0.0	0												
1982-83	Kitchener Rangers	OHL	51	38	46	84	67										8	3	8	11	9				
	Calgary	NHL	14	1	3	4	9	0	0	0	7	14.3	0												
1983-84	Calgary	NHL	51	11	34	45	42	7	0	2	160	6.9	0				11	2	12	14	13	2	0	1	
	Colorado Flames	CHL	19	5	14	19	22																		
1984-85	Calgary	NHL	67	14	52	66	75	8	0	0	259	5.4	7				4	1	2	3	8	1	0	0	
1985-86	Calgary	NHL	77	11	57	68	76	4	0	0	241	4.6	38				21	4	*15	19	30	2	0	0	
1986-87	Calgary	NHL	79	20	56	76	97	7	0	2	262	7.6	20				4	1	0	1	0	1	0	0	
1987-88	Calgary	NHL	80	25	58	83	114	7	2	2	245	10.2	13				7	3	6	9	18	2	0	0	
1988-89 ♦	Calgary	NHL	79	16	58	74	136	8	0	3	277	5.8	38				22	7	*24	*31	46	5	0	4	
1989-90	Calgary	NHL	79	28	62	90	82	14	1	3	304	9.2	20				6	2	3	5	8	1	0	0	
1990-91	Calgary	NHL	78	28	75	103	90	17	0	1	305	9.2	42				7	2	3	5	8	2	0	0	
1991-92	Calgary	NHL	72	20	57	77	83	11	0	0	304	6.6	13												
1992-93	Calgary	NHL	50	11	43	54	61	7	0	4	201	5.5	15				6	1	6	7	10	1	0	0	
1993-94	Calgary	NHL	75	28	54	82	95	12	1	5	324	8.6	35				7	2	6	8	12	1	0	0	
1994-95	St. Louis	NHL	32	8	20	28	43	2	0	0	110	7.3	19				7	1	5	6	10	0	0	0	
1995-96	St. Louis	NHL	82	17	44	61	88	9	1	1	317	5.4	5				13	3	4	7	20	1	0	0	
1996-97	St. Louis	NHL	72	13	30	43	65	6	1	1	296	4.4	2				6	1	2	3	4	1	0	0	
1997-98	St. Louis	NHL	71	19	30	49	80	9	1	2	227	8.4	6				8	2	6	8	12	1	0	0	
	Canada	Olympics	6	2	0	2	2																		
1998-99	St. Louis	NHL	82	20	42	62	70	11	1	2	314	6.4	33	0	0.0	29:07	13	4	8	12	20	2	0	0	35:14
99-2000	St. Louis	NHL	61	11	28	39	34	6	0	7	245	4.5	20	0	0.0	26:07	7	1	3	4	14	1	0	0	28:52
2000-01	St. Louis	NHL	59	12	42	54	52	6	1	3	218	5.5	23	0	0.0	26:32	15	2	8	10	18	2	0	0	30:46
2001-02	St. Louis	NHL	71	11	35	46	52	6	0	4	231	4.8	3	0	0.0	26:56	10	0	7	7	4	0	0	0	29:03
	Canada	Olympics	6	0	0	0	8																		
2002-03	St. Louis	NHL	80	16	52	68	61	9	1	2	299	5.4	22	2	100.0	26:55	3	0	1	1	0	0	0	0	12:41
	NHL Totals		1413	340	932	1272	1505	166	10	44	5148	6.6		2	100.0	27:14	177	39	121	160	255	26	0	5	30:13

OHL First All-Star Team (1982, 1983) • NHL Second All-Star Team (1987, 1989, 1994) • Conn Smythe Trophy (1989) • NHL First All-Star Team (1990, 1991, 1999, 2003) • James Norris Memorial Trophy (1999)

Played in NHL All-Star Game (1985, 1988, 1990, 1991, 1992, 1994, 1996, 1997, 1998, 1999, 2000, 2003)

Traded to **St. Louis** by **Calgary** with Calgary's 4th round choice (Didier Tremblay) in 1997 Entry Draft for Phil Housley and St. Louis' 2nd round choices in 1996 (Steve Begin) and 1997 (John Tripp) Entry Drafts, July 4, 1994.

MacKENZIE, Derek
(muh-KEHN-zee, DAIR-ehk) **ATL.**

Center. Shoots left. 5'11", 175 lbs. Born, Sudbury, Ont., June 11, 1981. Atlanta's 6th choice, 128th overall, in 1999 Entry Draft.

1996-97	Rayside-Balfour	NOJHA	40	23	32	55	40																		
1997-98	Sudbury Wolves	OHL	59	9	11	20	26																		
1998-99	Sudbury Wolves	OHL	68	22	65	87	74										4	2	4	6	2				
99-2000	Sudbury Wolves	OHL	68	24	33	57	110										12	5	9	14	16				
2000-01	Sudbury Wolves	OHL	62	40	49	89	89										12	6	8	14	16				
2001-02	Atlanta	NHL	1	0	0	0	2	0	0	0	1	0.0	–1	16	56.3	13:51									
	Chicago Wolves	AHL	68	13	12	25	80										25	4	2	6	20				
2002-03	Chicago Wolves	AHL	80	14	18	32	97										9	0	0	0	4				
	NHL Totals		1	0	0	0	2	0	0	0	1	0.0		16	56.3	13:51									

MacLEAN, Don
(mihk-LAYN, DAWN) **CBJ**

Center. Shoots left. 6'2", 199 lbs. Born, Sydney, N.S., January 14, 1977. Los Angeles' 2nd choice, 33rd overall, in 1995 Entry Draft.

1992-93	Halifax Hawks	NSMHL	27	15	25	40	34																		
1993-94	Halifax Hawks	NSMHL	25	35	35	70	151																		
1994-95	Beauport	QMJHL	64	15	27	42	37										17	4	4	8	6				
1995-96	Beauport	QMJHL	1	0	1	1	0																		
	Laval Titan	QMJHL	21	17	11	28	29																		
	Hull Olympiques	QMJHL	39	26	34	60	44										17	6	7	13	14				
1996-97	Hull Olympiques	QMJHL	69	34	47	81	67										14	11	10	21	39				

			Regular Season														Playoffs								
Season	Club	League	GP	G	A	Pts	PIM	PP	SH	GW	S	%	+/-	TF	F%	Min	GP	G	A	Pts	PIM	PP	SH	GW	Min
1997-98	**Los Angeles**	**NHL**	**22**	**5**	**2**	**7**	**4**	**2**	**0**	**0**	**25**	**20.0**	**−1**												
	Fredericton	AHL	39	9	5	14	32										4	1	3	4	2				
1998-99	Springfield	AHL	41	5	14	19	31																		
	Grand Rapids	IHL	28	6	13	19	8																		
99-2000	Lowell	AHL	40	11	17	28	18																		
	St. John's	AHL	21	14	12	26	8																		
2000-01	**Toronto**	**NHL**	**3**	**0**	**1**	**1**	**2**	**0**	**0**	**0**	**2**	**0.0**	**−2**	**33**	**54.6**	**9:48**									
	St. John's	AHL	61	26	34	60	48										4	2	1	3	2				
2001-02	St. John's	AHL	75	33	*54	*87	49										9	5	5	10	6				
	Toronto	**NHL**															**3**	**0**	**0**	**0**	**0**	**0**	**0**	**0**	**1:39**
2002-03	Syracuse Crunch	AHL	17	9	9	18	6																		
	NHL Totals		**25**	**5**	**3**	**8**	**6**	**2**	**0**	**0**	**27**	**18.5**		**33**	**54.5**	**9:48**	**3**	**0**	**0**	**0**	**0**	**0**	**0**	**0**	**1:39**

John P. Sollenberger Trophy (Top Scorer – AHL) (2002)

Traded to **Toronto** by **Los Angeles** for Craig Charron, February 23, 2000. Signed as a free agent by **Columbus**, July 17, 2002. • Missed majority of 2002-03 season recovering from neck surgery, September 16, 2002.

MacNEIL, Ian

(muhk-NEEL, EE-an) **PHI.**

Center. Shoots left. 6'2", 190 lbs. Born, Halifax, N.S., April 27, 1977. Hartford's 3rd choice, 85th overall, in 1995 Entry Draft.

Season	Club	League	GP	G	A	Pts	PIM	PP	SH	GW	S	%	+/-	TF	F%	Min	GP	G	A	Pts	PIM	PP	SH	GW	Min
1993-94	Whitby Lions	OMHA	50	30	22	52	102																		
1994-95	Oshawa Generals	OHL	60	7	21	28	62										7	0	2	2	0				
1995-96	Oshawa Generals	OHL	49	15	17	32	54										5	1	2	3	8				
1996-97	Oshawa Generals	OHL	64	23	20	43	96										18	2	3	5	37				
1997-98	New Haven	AHL	68	12	21	33	67										3	1	0	1	10				
1998-99	New Haven	AHL	47	6	4	10	62																		
99-2000	Cincinnati	IHL	81	19	18	37	100										11	3	2	5	25				
2000-01	Cincinnati	IHL	82	17	22	39	139										5	0	1	1	4				
2001-02	Lowell	AHL	79	14	20	34	128										2	0	1	1	4				
2002-03	**Philadelphia**	**NHL**	**2**	**0**	**0**	**0**	**0**	**0**	**0**	**0**	**2**	**0.0**	**1**	**0**	**0.0**	**10:08**									
	Philadelphia	AHL	71	10	13	23	132																		
	NHL Totals		**2**	**0**	**0**	**0**	**0**	**0**	**0**	**0**	**2**	**0.0**		**0**	**0.0**	**10:08**									

Rights transferred to **Carolina** after **Hartford** franchise relocated, June 25, 1997. Signed as a free agent by **Philadelphia**, July 2, 2002.

MADDEN, John

(MA-dehn, JAWN) **N.J.**

Center. Shoots left. 5'11", 190 lbs. Born, Barrie, Ont., May 4, 1973.

Season	Club	League	GP	G	A	Pts	PIM	PP	SH	GW	S	%	+/-	TF	F%	Min	GP	G	A	Pts	PIM	PP	SH	GW	Min
1989-90	Alliston Hornets	OJHL-C	31	24	25	49	26																		
1990-91	Alliston Hornets	OJHL-C	14	15	21	36	10																		
	Barrie Colts	OJHL-B	1	0	0	0	0																		
1991-92	Barrie Colts	OJHL-B	42	50	54	104	46										13	10	9	19	14				
1992-93	Barrie Colts	OJHL-B	43	49	75	124	62																		
1993-94	U. of Michigan	CCHA	36	6	11	17	14																		
1994-95	U. of Michigan	CCHA	39	21	22	43	8																		
1995-96	U. of Michigan	CCHA	43	27	30	57	45																		
1996-97	U. of Michigan	CCHA	42	26	37	63	56																		
1997-98	Albany River Rats	AHL	74	20	36	56	40										13	3	13	16	14				
1998-99	**New Jersey**	**NHL**	**4**	**0**	**1**	**1**	**0**	**0**	**0**	**0**	**4**	**0.0**	**−2**	**0**	**0.0**	**9:13**									
	Albany River Rats	AHL	75	38	60	98	44										5	2	2	4	6				
99-2000♦	**New Jersey**	**NHL**	**74**	**16**	**9**	**25**	**6**	**0**	**6**	**3**	**115**	**13.9**	**7**	**770**	**47.5**	**11:40**	**20**	**3**	**4**	**7**	**0**	**0**	**1**	**2**	**15:30**
2000-01	**New Jersey**	**NHL**	**80**	**23**	**15**	**38**	**12**	**0**	**3**	**4**	**163**	**14.1**	**24**	**974**	**46.6**	**15:35**	**25**	**4**	**3**	**7**	**6**	**0**	**0**	**0**	**15:15**
2001-02	**New Jersey**	**NHL**	**82**	**15**	**8**	**23**	**25**	**0**	**0**	**2**	**170**	**8.8**	**6**	**1001**	**47.0**	**15:36**	**6**	**0**	**0**	**0**	**0**	**0**	**0**	**0**	**17:25**
2002-03♦	**New Jersey**	**NHL**	**80**	**19**	**22**	**41**	**26**	**2**	**2**	**3**	**207**	**9.2**	**13**	**1502**	**50.9**	**18:18**	**24**	**6**	**10**	**16**	**2**	**2**	**1**	**1**	**19:38**
	NHL Totals		**320**	**73**	**55**	**128**	**69**	**2**	**11**	**12**	**659**	**11.1**		**4247**	**48.4**	**15:17**	**75**	**13**	**17**	**30**	**8**	**2**	**2**	**3**	**16:54**

CCHA First All-Star Team (1997) • NCAA West First All-American Team (1997) • Frank J. Selke Trophy (2001)

Signed as a free agent by **New Jersey**, June 26, 1997.

MAIR, Adam

(MAIR, A-duhm) **BUF.**

Center. Shoots right. 6'2", 215 lbs. Born, Hamilton, Ont., February 15, 1979. Toronto's 2nd choice, 84th overall, in 1997 Entry Draft.

Season	Club	League	GP	G	A	Pts	PIM	PP	SH	GW	S	%	+/-	TF	F%	Min	GP	G	A	Pts	PIM	PP	SH	GW	Min
1994-95	Ohsweken	OJHL-B	39	21	23	44	91																		
1995-96	Owen Sound	OHL	62	12	15	27	63										6	0	0	0	2				
1996-97	Owen Sound	OHL	65	16	35	51	113										4	1	0	1	2				
1997-98	Owen Sound	OHL	56	25	27	52	179										11	6	3	9	31				
1998-99	Owen Sound	OHL	43	23	41	64	109										16	10	10	20	*47				
	St. John's	AHL															3	1	0	1	6				
	Toronto	**NHL**															**5**	**1**	**0**	**1**	**14**	**0**	**0**	**0**	**5:37**
99-2000	**Toronto**	**NHL**	**8**	**1**	**0**	**1**	**6**	**0**	**0**	**0**	**7**	**14.3**	**−1**	**9**	**33.3**	**11:33**	**5**	**0**	**0**	**0**	**8**	**0**	**0**	**0**	**10:15**
	St. John's	AHL	66	22	27	49	124																		
2000-01	**Toronto**	**NHL**	**16**	**0**	**2**	**2**	**14**	**0**	**0**	**0**	**17**	**0.0**	**3**	**56**	**51.8**	**9:00**									
	St. John's	AHL	47	18	27	45	69																		
	Los Angeles	**NHL**	**10**	**0**	**0**	**0**	**6**	**0**	**0**	**0**	**5**	**0.0**	**−3**	**21**	**61.9**	**6:14**									
2001-02	**Los Angeles**	**NHL**	**18**	**1**	**1**	**2**	**57**	**0**	**0**	**0**	**10**	**10.0**	**1**	**31**	**58.1**	**7:11**									
	Manchester	AHL	27	10	9	19	48										5	5	1	6	10				
2002-03	**Buffalo**	**NHL**	**79**	**6**	**11**	**17**	**146**	**0**	**1**	**1**	**83**	**7.2**	**−4**	**572**	**51.2**	**10:37**									
	NHL Totals		**131**	**8**	**14**	**22**	**229**	**0**	**1**	**1**	**122**	**6.6**		**689**	**51.7**	**9:40**	**10**	**1**	**0**	**1**	**22**	**0**	**0**	**0**	**7:56**

Traded to **Los Angeles** by **Toronto** with Toronto's 2nd round choice (Mike Cammalleri) in 2001 Entry Draft for Aki Berg, March 13, 2001. Traded to **Buffalo** by **Los Angeles** with Los Angeles' 5th round choice (Thomas Morrow) in 2003 Entry Draft for Erik Rasmussen, July 24, 2002.

MAJESKY, Ivan

(migh-EHV-skee, EE-vahn) **ATL.**

Defense. Shoots right. 6'5", 225 lbs. Born, Banska Bystrica, Czech., September 2, 1976. Florida's 12th choice, 267th overall, in 2001 Entry Draft.

Season	Club	League	GP	G	A	Pts	PIM	PP	SH	GW	S	%	+/-	TF	F%	Min	GP	G	A	Pts	PIM	PP	SH	GW	Min
1995-96	Banska Bystrica	Slovakia	17	0	0	0	18																		
1996-97	Banska Bystrica	Slovakia	49	2	4	6																			
1997-98	Banska Bystrica	Slovak-2	43	6	7	13	50																		
1998-99	Banska Bystrica	Slovak-2	48	7	7	14	68																		
	HKm Zvolen	Slovakia															6	0	2	2	2				
99-2000	HKm Zvolen	Slovakia	51	7	9	16	68										10	0	4	4	2				
2000-01	Ilves Tampere	Finland	54	2	14	16	99										9	0	1	1	6				
2001-02	Ilves Tampere	Finland	44	6	6	12	84																		
	Slovakia	Olympics	4	0	1	1	4																		
2002-03	**Florida**	**NHL**	**82**	**4**	**8**	**12**	**92**	**0**	**0**	**2**	**52**	**7.7**	**−18**	**0**	**0.0**	**20:53**									
	NHL Totals		**82**	**4**	**8**	**12**	**92**	**0**	**0**	**2**	**52**	**7.7**		**0**	**0.0**	**20:53**									

Traded to **Atlanta** by **Florida** for Atlanta's 2nd round choice (Kamil Kreps) in 2003 Entry Draft, June 21, 2003.

MALAKHOV, Vladimir

(mah-LAH-kahf, vla-DIH-meer) **NYR**

Defense. Shoots left. 6'4", 230 lbs. Born, Sverdlovsk, USSR, August 30, 1968. NY Islanders' 12th choice, 191st overall, in 1989 Entry Draft.

Season	Club	League	GP	G	A	Pts	PIM	PP	SH	GW	S	%	+/-	TF	F%	Min	GP	G	A	Pts	PIM	PP	SH	GW	Min
1986-87	Spartak Moscow	USSR	22	0	1	1	12																		
1987-88	Spartak Moscow	USSR	28	2	2	4	26																		
1988-89	CSKA Moscow	USSR	34	6	2	8	16																		
1989-90	CSKA Moscow	USSR	48	2	10	12	34																		
1990-91	CSKA Moscow	USSR	46	5	13	18	22																		
1991-92	CSKA Moscow	CIS	40	1	9	10	12																		
	Russia	Olympics	8	3	0	3	4																		
1992-93	**NY Islanders**	**NHL**	**64**	**14**	**38**	**52**	**59**	**7**	**0**	**0**	**178**	**7.9**	**14**				**17**	**3**	**6**	**9**	**12**	**0**	**0**	**0**	
	Capital District	AHL	3	2	1	3	11																		
1993-94	**NY Islanders**	**NHL**	**76**	**10**	**47**	**57**	**80**	**4**	**0**	**2**	**235**	**4.3**	**29**				**4**	**0**	**0**	**0**	**6**	**0**	**0**	**0**	
1994-95	**NY Islanders**	**NHL**	**26**	**3**	**13**	**16**	**32**	**1**	**0**	**0**	**61**	**4.9**	**−1**												
	Montreal	**NHL**	**14**	**1**	**4**	**5**	**14**	**0**	**0**	**0**	**30**	**3.3**	**−2**												

			Regular Season														Playoffs								
Season	Club	League	GP	G	A	Pts	PIM	PP	SH	GW	S	%	+/-	TF	F%	Min	GP	G	A	Pts	PIM	PP	SH	GW	Min
1995-96	Montreal	NHL	61	5	23	28	79	2	0	0	122	4.1	7	....	....	....	....	....	....	....	....	....	....	....	....
1996-97	Montreal	NHL	65	10	20	30	43	5	0	1	177	5.6	3	....	....	....	5	0	0	0	6	0	0	0	....
1997-98	Montreal	NHL	74	13	31	44	70	8	0	2	166	7.8	16	....	....	....	9	3	4	7	10	2	0	0	....
1998-99	Montreal	NHL	62	13	21	34	77	8	0	3	143	9.1	–7	0	0.0	23:29	....	....	....	....	....	....	....	....	....
99-2000	Montreal	NHL	7	0	0	0	4	0	0	0	7	0.0	0	0	0.0	21:20	....	....	....	....	....	....	....	....	....
	♦ New Jersey	NHL	17	1	4	5	19	1	0	1	11	9.1	1	0	0.0	20:18	23	1	4	5	18	1	0	0	19:31
2000-01	NY Rangers	NHL	3	0	2	2	4	0	0	0	6	0.0	0	0	0.0	19:07	....	....	....	....	....	....	....	....	....
2001-02	NY Rangers	NHL	81	6	22	28	83	1	0	0	145	4.1	10	1	100.0	22:48	....	....	....	....	....	....	....	....	....
	Russia	Olympics	6	1	3	4	4	....	....	....	....	....	....	....	....	....	....	....	....	....	....	....	....	....	....
2002-03	NY Rangers	NHL	71	3	14	17	52	1	0	0	131	2.3	–7	0	0.0	21:24	....	....	....	....	....	....	....	....	....
	NHL Totals		621	79	239	318	616	38	0	9	1412	5.6		1	100.0	22:18	58	7	14	21	52	3	0	0	19:31

NHL All-Rookie Team (1993)

Traded to **Montreal** by **NY Islanders** with Pierre Turgeon for Kirk Muller, Mathieu Schneider and Craig Darby, April 5, 1995. • Missed majority of 1999-2000 season recovering from knee injury suffered in exhibition game vs. Boston, September 27, 1999. Traded to **New Jersey** by **Montreal** for Sheldon Souray, Josh DeWolf and New Jersey's 2nd round choice (later traded to Washington – later traded to Tampa Bay – Tampa Bay selected Andreas Holmqvist) in 2001 Entry Draft, March 1, 2000. Signed as a free agent by **NY Rangers**, July 10, 2000. • Missed majority of 2000-01 season recovering from knee injury suffered in game vs. Montreal, November 11, 2000.

MALEC, Tomas
(MA-lehts, TAW-mahsh) **CAR.**

Defense. Shoots left. 6'2", 195 lbs. Born, Skalica, Czech., May 13, 1982. Florida's 4th choice, 64th overall, in 2001 Entry Draft.

Season	Club	League	GP	G	A	Pts	PIM	PP	SH	GW	S	%	+/-	TF	F%	Min	GP	G	A	Pts	PIM	PP	SH	GW	Min
99-2000	HK 36 Skalica Jr.	Slovak-Jr.	46	6	5	11	150	....	....	....	....	....	....	....	....	....	....	....	....	....	....	....	....	....	....
2000-01	Rimouski Oceanic	QMJHL	64	13	50	63	198	....	....	....	....	....	....	....	....	....	11	0	11	11	26	....	....	....	....
2001-02	Rimouski Oceanic	QMJHL	51	14	32	46	164	....	....	....	....	....	....	....	....	....	7	3	1	4	10	....	....	....	....
	Lowell	AHL	....	....	....	....	....	....	....	....	....	....	....	....	....	....	4	0	0	0	4	....	....	....	....
2002-03	Carolina	NHL	41	0	2	2	43	0	0	0	30	0.0	–5	1	100.0	11:13	....	....	....	....	....	....	....	....	....
	Lowell	AHL	30	0	4	4	50	....	....	....	....	....	....	....	....	....	....	....	....	....	....	....	....	....	....
	NHL Totals		41	0	2	2	43	0	0	0	30	0.0		1	100.0	11:13	....	....	....	....	....	....	....	....	....

Traded to **Carolina** by **Florida** with Bret Hedican, Kevyn Adams and a conditional 2nd round choice in 2003 Entry Draft for Sandis Ozolinsh and Byron Ritchie, January 16, 2002.

MALHOTRA, Manny
(mal-HOH-truh, MAHN-ee) **DAL.**

Center. Shoots left. 6'2", 215 lbs. Born, Mississauga, Ont., May 18, 1980. NY Rangers' 1st choice, 7th overall, in 1998 Entry Draft.

Season	Club	League	GP	G	A	Pts	PIM	PP	SH	GW	S	%	+/-	TF	F%	Min	GP	G	A	Pts	PIM	PP	SH	GW	Min
1995-96	Mississauga Reps	MTHL	54	27	44	71	62	....	....	....	....	....	....	....	....	....	....	....	....	....	....	....	....	....	....
1996-97	Guelph Storm	OHL	61	16	28	44	26	....	....	....	....	....	....	....	....	....	18	7	7	14	11	....	....	....	....
1997-98	Guelph Storm	OHL	57	16	35	51	29	....	....	....	....	....	....	....	....	....	12	7	6	13	8	....	....	....	....
1998-99	NY Rangers	NHL	73	8	8	16	13	1	0	2	61	13.1	–2	588	43.9	8:36	....	....	....	....	....	....	....	....	....
99-2000	NY Rangers	NHL	27	0	0	0	4	0	0	0	18	0.0	–6	132	44.7	6:42	....	....	....	....	....	....	....	....	....
	Guelph Storm	OHL	5	2	2	4	4	....	....	....	....	....	....	....	....	....	6	0	2	2	4	....	....	....	....
	Hartford	AHL	12	1	5	6	2	....	....	....	....	....	....	....	....	....	23	1	2	3	10	....	....	....	....
2000-01	NY Rangers	NHL	50	4	8	12	31	0	0	2	46	8.7	–10	248	44.4	9:03	....	....	....	....	....	....	....	....	....
	Hartford	AHL	28	5	6	11	69	....	....	....	....	....	....	....	....	....	5	0	0	0	0	....	....	....	....
2001-02	NY Rangers	NHL	56	7	6	13	42	0	1	1	41	17.1	–1	310	42.9	10:14	....	....	....	....	....	....	....	....	....
	Dallas	NHL	16	1	0	1	5	0	0	0	19	5.3	–3	121	48.8	10:37	....	....	....	....	....	....	....	....	....
2002-03	Dallas	NHL	59	3	7	10	42	0	0	1	62	4.8	–2	447	47.0	9:22	5	1	0	1	0	0	0	0	8:13
	NHL Totals		281	23	29	52	137	1	1	6	247	9.3		1846	44.9	9:06	5	1	0	1	0	0	0	0	8:13

Memorial Cup All-Star Team (1998) • George Parsons Trophy (Memorial Cup Most Sportsmanlike Player) (1998)

Traded to **Dallas** by **NY Rangers** with Barrett Heisten for Martin Rucinsky and Roman Lyashenko, March 12, 2002.

MALIK, Marek
(MAW-leck, MAIR-ehk) **VAN.**

Defense. Shoots left. 6'5", 215 lbs. Born, Ostrava, Czech., June 24, 1975. Hartford's 2nd choice, 72nd overall, in 1993 Entry Draft.

Season	Club	League	GP	G	A	Pts	PIM	PP	SH	GW	S	%	+/-	TF	F%	Min	GP	G	A	Pts	PIM	PP	SH	GW	Min
1992-93	TJ Vitkovice Jr.	Czech-Jr.	20	5	10	15	16	....	....	....	....	....	....	....	....	....	....	....	....	....	....	....	....	....	....
1993-94	HC Vitkovice	Czech	38	3	3	6	0	....	....	....	....	....	....	....	....	....	3	0	1	1	0	....	....	....	....
1994-95	Springfield	AHL	58	11	30	41	91	....	....	....	....	....	....	....	....	....	....	....	....	....	....	....	....	....	....
	Hartford	NHL	1	0	1	1	0	0	0	0	0	0.0	1	....	....	....	....	....	....	....	....	....	....	....	....
1995-96	Hartford	NHL	7	0	0	0	4	0	0	0	2	0.0	–3	....	....	....	....	....	....	....	....	....	....	....	....
	Springfield	AHL	68	8	14	22	135	....	....	....	....	....	....	....	....	....	8	1	3	4	20	....	....	....	....
1996-97	Hartford	NHL	47	1	5	6	50	0	0	1	33	3.0	5	....	....	....	....	....	....	....	....	....	....	....	....
	Springfield	AHL	3	0	3	3	4	....	....	....	....	....	....	....	....	....	....	....	....	....	....	....	....	....	....
1997-98	Malmo IF	Sweden	37	1	5	6	21	....	....	....	....	....	....	....	....	....	....	....	....	....	....	....	....	....	....
1998-99	HC Vitkovice	Czech	1	1	0	1	6	....	....	....	....	....	....	....	....	....	....	....	....	....	....	....	....	....	....
	Carolina	NHL	52	2	9	11	36	1	0	0	36	5.6	–6	0	0.0	21:14	4	0	0	0	4	0	0	0	11:26
	New Haven	AHL	21	2	8	10	28	....	....	....	....	....	....	....	....	....	....	....	....	....	....	....	....	....	....
99-2000	Carolina	NHL	57	4	10	14	63	0	0	1	57	7.0	13	0	0.0	18:00	....	....	....	....	....	....	....	....	....
2000-01	Carolina	NHL	61	6	14	20	34	1	0	1	72	8.3	–4	0	0.0	19:36	3	0	0	0	6	0	0	0	19:37
2001-02	Carolina	NHL	82	4	19	23	88	0	0	0	91	4.4	8	0	0.0	20:29	23	0	3	3	18	0	0	0	18:09
2002-03	Carolina	NHL	10	0	2	2	16	0	0	0	9	0.0	–3	0	0.0	17:02	....	....	....	....	....	....	....	....	....
	Vancouver	NHL	69	7	11	18	52	1	1	2	68	10.3	23	1	0.0	18:06	14	1	1	2	10	1	0	0	16:06
	NHL Totals		386	24	71	95	343	3	1	5	368	6.5		1	0.0	19:24	44	1	4	5	38	1	0	0	16:59

Transferred to **Carolina** after **Hartford** franchise relocated, June 25, 1997. Traded to **Vancouver** by **Carolina** with Darren Langdon for Jan Hlavac and Harold Druken, November 1, 2002.

MALTAIS, Steve
(MAHL-tay, STEEV)

Left wing. Shoots left. 6'2", 205 lbs. Born, Arvida, Que., January 25, 1969. Washington's 2nd choice, 57th overall, in 1987 Entry Draft.

Season	Club	League	GP	G	A	Pts	PIM	PP	SH	GW	S	%	+/-	TF	F%	Min	GP	G	A	Pts	PIM	PP	SH	GW	Min
1985-86	Wexford Raiders	MTHL	33	35	19	54	38	....	....	....	....	....	....	....	....	....	....	....	....	....	....	....	....	....	....
	Wexford Raiders	MTJHL	1	1	0	1	0	....	....	....	....	....	....	....	....	....	....	....	....	....	....	....	....	....	....
1986-87	Cornwall Royals	OHL	65	32	12	44	29	....	....	....	....	....	....	....	....	....	5	0	0	0	2	....	....	....	....
1987-88	Cornwall Royals	OHL	59	39	46	85	30	....	....	....	....	....	....	....	....	....	11	9	6	15	33	....	....	....	....
1988-89	Cornwall Royals	OHL	58	53	70	123	67	....	....	....	....	....	....	....	....	....	18	14	16	30	16	....	....	....	....
	Fort Wayne	IHL	....	....	....	....	....	....	....	....	....	....	....	....	....	....	4	2	1	3	0	....	....	....	....
1989-90	Washington	NHL	8	0	0	0	2	0	0	0	11	0.0	–2	....	....	....	1	0	0	0	0	0	0	0	....
	Baltimore	AHL	67	29	37	66	54	....	....	....	....	....	....	....	....	....	12	6	10	16	6	....	....	....	....
1990-91	Washington	NHL	7	0	0	0	2	0	0	0	3	0.0	–1	....	....	....	....	....	....	....	....	....	....	....	....
	Baltimore	AHL	73	36	43	79	97	....	....	....	....	....	....	....	....	....	6	1	4	5	10	....	....	....	....
1991-92	Minnesota	NHL	12	2	1	3	2	0	0	0	6	33.3	–1	....	....	....	....	....	....	....	....	....	....	....	....
	Kalamazoo Wings	IHL	48	25	31	56	51	....	....	....	....	....	....	....	....	....	....	....	....	....	....	....	....	....	....
	Halifax Citadels	AHL	10	3	3	6	0	....	....	....	....	....	....	....	....	....	....	....	....	....	....	....	....	....	....
1992-93	Tampa Bay	NHL	63	7	13	20	35	4	0	1	96	7.3	–20	....	....	....	....	....	....	....	....	....	....	....	....
	Atlanta Knights	IHL	16	14	10	24	22	....	....	....	....	....	....	....	....	....	....	....	....	....	....	....	....	....	....
1993-94	Detroit	NHL	4	0	1	1	0	0	0	0	2	0.0	–1	....	....	....	....	....	....	....	....	....	....	....	....
	Adirondack	AHL	73	35	49	84	79	....	....	....	....	....	....	....	....	....	12	5	11	16	14	....	....	....	....
1994-95	Chicago Wolves	IHL	79	*57	40	97	145	....	....	....	....	....	....	....	....	....	3	1	1	2	0	....	....	....	....
1995-96	Chicago Wolves	IHL	81	56	66	122	161	....	....	....	....	....	....	....	....	....	9	7	7	14	20	....	....	....	....
1996-97	Chicago Wolves	IHL	81	*60	54	114	62	....	....	....	....	....	....	....	....	....	4	2	0	2	4	....	....	....	....
1997-98	Chicago Wolves	IHL	82	*46	57	103	120	....	....	....	....	....	....	....	....	....	22	8	11	19	28	....	....	....	....
1998-99	Chicago Wolves	IHL	82	*56	44	100	164	....	....	....	....	....	....	....	....	....	10	4	6	10	2	....	....	....	....
99-2000	Chicago Wolves	IHL	82	*44	46	*90	78	....	....	....	....	....	....	....	....	....	16	9	4	13	14	....	....	....	....
2000-01	Columbus	NHL	26	0	3	3	12	0	0	0	30	0.0	–9	2	0.0	11:57	....	....	....	....	....	....	....	....	....
	Chicago Wolves	IHL	50	25	26	51	57	....	....	....	....	....	....	....	....	....	16	7	10	17	2	....	....	....	....
2001-02	Chicago Wolves	AHL	67	31	32	63	62	....	....	....	....	....	....	....	....	....	25	*12	10	22	22	....	....	....	....
2002-03	Chicago Wolves	AHL	79	30	*56	*86	86	....	....	....	....	....	....	....	....	....	9	3	5	8	12	....	....	....	....
	NHL Totals		120	9	18	27	53	4	0	1	148	6.1		2	0.0	11:57	1	0	0	0	0	0	0	0	....

OHL Second All-Star Team (1989) • IHL First All-Star Team (1995, 1999, 2000) • IHL Second All-Star Team (1996, 1997) • Leo P. Lamoureux Memorial Trophy (Top Scorer – IHL) (2000) • John P. Sollenberger Trophy (Top Scorer – AHL) (2003)

Traded to **Minnesota** by **Washington** with Trent Klatt for Shawn Chambers, June 21, 1991. Traded to **Quebec** by **Minnesota** for Kip Miller, March 8, 1992. Claimed by **Tampa Bay** from **Quebec** in Expansion Draft, June 18, 1992. Traded to **Detroit** by **Tampa Bay** for Dennis Vial, June 8, 1993. Signed as a free agent by **Chicago** (IHL), September 8, 1994. Signed as a free agent by **Columbus**, October 6, 2000.

MALTBY, Kirk

(MAHLT-bee, KUHRK) **DET.**

Right wing. Shoots right. 6', 180 lbs. Born, Guelph, Ont., December 22, 1972. Edmonton's 4th choice, 65th overall, in 1992 Entry Draft.

			Regular Season														Playoffs								
Season	Club	League	GP	G	A	Pts	PIM	PP	SH	GW	S	%	+/-	TF	F%	Min	GP	G	A	Pts	PIM	PP	SH	GW	Min
1988-89	Cambridge	OJHL-B	48	28	18	46	138	....	....	....	....	....	....	....	....	....	....	....	....	....	....	....	....	....	....
1989-90	Owen Sound	OHL	61	12	15	27	90	....	....	....	....	....	....	....	....	....	12	1	6	7	15	....	....	....	....
1990-91	Owen Sound	OHL	66	34	32	66	100	....	....	....	....	....	....	....	....	....	....	....	....	....	....	....	....	....	....
1991-92	Owen Sound	OHL	66	50	41	91	99	....	....	....	....	....	....	....	....	....	5	3	3	6	18	....	....	....	....
1992-93	Cape Breton	AHL	73	22	23	45	130	....	....	....	....	....	....	....	....	....	16	3	3	6	45	....	....	....	....
1993-94	**Edmonton**	**NHL**	**68**	**11**	**8**	**19**	**74**	**0**	**1**	**1**	**89**	**12.4**	**–2**	....	....	....	....	....	....	....	....	....	....	....	....
1994-95	**Edmonton**	**NHL**	**47**	**8**	**3**	**11**	**49**	**0**	**2**	**1**	**73**	**11.0**	**–11**	....	....	....	....	....	....	....	....	....	....	....	....
1995-96	**Edmonton**	**NHL**	**49**	**2**	**6**	**8**	**61**	**0**	**0**	**1**	**51**	**3.9**	**–16**	....	....	....	....	....	....	....	....	....	....	....	....
	Cape Breton	AHL	4	1	2	3	6	....	....	....	....	....	....	....	....	....	....	....	....	....	....	....	....	....	....
	Detroit	**NHL**	**6**	**1**	**0**	**1**	**6**	**0**	**0**	**0**	**4**	**25.0**	**0**	....	....	....	**8**	**0**	**1**	**1**	**4**	**0**	**0**	**0**	....
1996-97♦	**Detroit**	**NHL**	**66**	**3**	**5**	**8**	**75**	**0**	**0**	**0**	**62**	**4.8**	**3**	....	....	....	**20**	**5**	**2**	**7**	**24**	**0**	**1**	**1**	....
1997-98♦	**Detroit**	**NHL**	**65**	**14**	**9**	**23**	**89**	**2**	**1**	**3**	**106**	**13.2**	**11**	....	....	....	**22**	**3**	**1**	**4**	**30**	**0**	**1**	**0**	....
1998-99	**Detroit**	**NHL**	**53**	**8**	**6**	**14**	**34**	**0**	**1**	**2**	**76**	**10.5**	**–6**	**10**	**40.0**	**13:13**	**10**	**1**	**0**	**1**	**8**	**0**	**0**	**1**	**11:32**
99-2000	**Detroit**	**NHL**	**41**	**6**	**8**	**14**	**24**	**0**	**2**	**1**	**71**	**8.5**	**1**	**2**	**50.0**	**13:30**	**8**	**0**	**1**	**1**	**4**	**0**	**0**	**0**	**13:45**
2000-01	**Detroit**	**NHL**	**79**	**12**	**7**	**19**	**22**	**1**	**3**	**3**	**119**	**10.1**	**16**	**14**	**35.7**	**14:17**	**6**	**0**	**0**	**0**	**6**	**0**	**0**	**0**	**15:23**
2001-02♦	**Detroit**	**NHL**	**82**	**9**	**15**	**24**	**40**	**0**	**1**	**5**	**108**	**8.3**	**15**	**38**	**47.4**	**13:23**	**23**	**3**	**3**	**6**	**32**	**0**	**2**	**0**	**16:34**
2002-03	**Detroit**	**NHL**	**82**	**14**	**23**	**37**	**91**	**0**	**4**	**1**	**116**	**12.1**	**17**	**43**	**37.2**	**16:10**	**4**	**0**	**0**	**0**	**4**	**0**	**0**	**0**	**17:18**
	NHL Totals		**638**	**88**	**90**	**178**	**565**	**3**	**15**	**18**	**875**	**10.1**		**107**	**41.1**	**14:16**	**101**	**12**	**8**	**20**	**112**	**0**	**4**	**2**	**15:03**

Traded to **Detroit** by **Edmonton** for Dan McGillis, March 20, 1996. • Missed majority of 1999-2000 season recovering from hernia injury suffered in game vs. Dallas, October 5, 1999.

MANDERVILLE, Kent

(MAN-duhr-VIHL, KEHNT)

Center. Shoots left. 6'3", 200 lbs. Born, Edmonton, Alta., April 12, 1971. Calgary's 1st choice, 24th overall, in 1989 Entry Draft.

			Regular Season														Playoffs								
Season	Club	League	GP	G	A	Pts	PIM	PP	SH	GW	S	%	+/-	TF	F%	Min	GP	G	A	Pts	PIM	PP	SH	GW	Min
1987-88	Notre Dame	SMHL	32	22	18	40	42	....	....	....	....	....	....	....	....	....	....	....	....	....	....	....	....	....	....
1988-89	Notre Dame	SJHL	58	39	36	75	165	....	....	....	....	....	....	....	....	....	....	....	....	....	....	....	....	....	....
1989-90	Cornell Big Red	ECAC	26	11	15	26	28	....	....	....	....	....	....	....	....	....	....	....	....	....	....	....	....	....	....
1990-91	Cornell Big Red	ECAC	28	17	14	31	60	....	....	....	....	....	....	....	....	....	....	....	....	....	....	....	....	....	....
1991-92	Team Canada	Nat-Tm	63	16	24	40	78	....	....	....	....	....	....	....	....	....	....	....	....	....	....	....	....	....	....
	Canada	Olympics	8	1	2	3	0	....	....	....	....	....	....	....	....	....	....	....	....	....	....	....	....	....	....
	Toronto	**NHL**	**15**	**0**	**4**	**4**	**0**	**0**	**0**	**0**	**14**	**0.0**	**1**	....	....	....	....	....	....	....	....	....	....	....	....
	St. John's	AHL	....	....	....	....	....	....	....	....	....	....	....	....	....	....	12	5	9	14	14	....	....	....	....
1992-93	**Toronto**	**NHL**	**18**	**1**	**1**	**2**	**17**	**0**	**0**	**1**	**15**	**6.7**	**–9**	....	....	....	**18**	**1**	**0**	**1**	**8**	**0**	**0**	**0**	....
	St. John's	AHL	56	19	28	47	86	....	....	....	....	....	....	....	....	....	2	0	2	2	0	....	....	....	....
1993-94	**Toronto**	**NHL**	**67**	**7**	**9**	**16**	**63**	**0**	**0**	**1**	**81**	**8.6**	**5**	....	....	....	**12**	**1**	**0**	**1**	**4**	**0**	**1**	**0**	....
1994-95	**Toronto**	**NHL**	**36**	**0**	**1**	**1**	**22**	**0**	**0**	**0**	**43**	**0.0**	**–2**	....	....	....	**7**	**0**	**0**	**0**	**6**	**0**	**0**	**0**	....
1995-96	**Edmonton**	**NHL**	**37**	**3**	**5**	**8**	**38**	**0**	**2**	**0**	**63**	**4.8**	**–5**	....	....	....	....	....	....	....	....	....	....	....	....
	St. John's	AHL	27	16	12	28	26	....	....	....	....	....	....	....	....	....	....	....	....	....	....	....	....	....	....
1996-97	**Hartford**	**NHL**	**44**	**6**	**5**	**11**	**18**	**0**	**0**	**1**	**51**	**11.8**	**3**	....	....	....	....	....	....	....	....	....	....	....	....
	Springfield	AHL	23	5	20	25	18	....	....	....	....	....	....	....	....	....	....	....	....	....	....	....	....	....	....
1997-98	**Carolina**	**NHL**	**77**	**4**	**4**	**8**	**31**	**0**	**0**	**0**	**80**	**5.0**	**–6**	....	....	....	....	....	....	....	....	....	....	....	....
1998-99	**Carolina**	**NHL**	**81**	**5**	**11**	**16**	**38**	**0**	**0**	**0**	**71**	**7.0**	**9**	**609**	**46.3**	**8:07**	**6**	**0**	**0**	**0**	**2**	**0**	**0**	**0**	**9:58**
99-2000	**Carolina**	**NHL**	**56**	**1**	**4**	**5**	**12**	**0**	**0**	**1**	**45**	**2.2**	**–8**	**399**	**47.1**	**8:15**	....	....	....	....	....	....	....	....	....
	Philadelphia	**NHL**	**13**	**0**	**3**	**3**	**4**	**0**	**0**	**0**	**17**	**0.0**	**2**	**148**	**54.1**	**11:56**	**18**	**0**	**1**	**1**	**22**	**0**	**0**	**0**	**13:47**
2000-01	**Philadelphia**	**NHL**	**82**	**5**	**10**	**15**	**47**	**0**	**3**	**2**	**136**	**3.7**	**–2**	**813**	**47.9**	**12:38**	**6**	**1**	**2**	**3**	**2**	**0**	**0**	**0**	**12:44**
2001-02	**Philadelphia**	**NHL**	**34**	**2**	**5**	**7**	**8**	**0**	**0**	**0**	**39**	**5.1**	**2**	**178**	**43.8**	**8:51**	....	....	....	....	....	....	....	....	....
	Pittsburgh	**NHL**	**4**	**1**	**0**	**1**	**4**	**0**	**0**	**0**	**4**	**25.0**	**1**	**57**	**45.6**	**12:43**	....	....	....	....	....	....	....	....	....
2002-03	**Pittsburgh**	**NHL**	**82**	**2**	**5**	**7**	**46**	**0**	**0**	**1**	**72**	**2.8**	**–22**	**550**	**48.9**	**11:05**	....	....	....	....	....	....	....	....	....
	NHL Totals		**646**	**37**	**67**	**104**	**348**	**0**	**5**	**7**	**731**	**5.1**		**2754**	**47.6**	**10:09**	**67**	**3**	**3**	**6**	**44**	**0**	**1**	**0**	**12:49**

ECAC Rookie of the Year (1990)

Traded to **Toronto** by **Calgary** with Doug Gilmour, Jamie Macoun, Rick Wamsley and Ric Nattress for Gary Leeman, Alexander Godynyuk, Jeff Reese, Michel Petit and Craig Berube, January 2, 1992. Traded to **Edmonton** by **Toronto** for Peter White and Edmonton's 4th round choice (Jason Sessa) in 1996 Entry Draft, December 4, 1995. Signed as a free agent by **Hartford**, October 2, 1996. Transferred to **Carolina** after **Hartford** franchise relocated, June 25, 1997. Traded to **Philadelphia** by **Carolina** for Sandy McCarthy, March 14, 2000. • Missed majority of 2001-02 season recovering from ankle injury suffered in game vs. Montreal, October 27, 2001. Traded to **Pittsburgh** by **Philadelphia** for Billy Tibbetts, March 17, 2002.

MANLOW, Eric

(MAN-low, AIR-ihk) **NYI**

Center. Shoots left. 6', 180 lbs. Born, Belleville, Ont., April 7, 1975. Chicago's 2nd choice, 50th overall, in 1993 Entry Draft.

			Regular Season														Playoffs								
Season	Club	League	GP	G	A	Pts	PIM	PP	SH	GW	S	%	+/-	TF	F%	Min	GP	G	A	Pts	PIM	PP	SH	GW	Min
1990-91	Peterborough	OMHA	59	67	51	118	90	....	....	....	....	....	....	....	....	....	....	....	....	....	....	....	....	....	....
	Peterborough	OJHL-B	1	0	0	0	0	....	....	....	....	....	....	....	....	....	....	....	....	....	....	....	....	....	....
1991-92	Kitchener Rangers	OHL	59	12	20	32	17	....	....	....	....	....	....	....	....	....	14	2	5	7	10	....	....	....	....
1992-93	Kitchener Rangers	OHL	53	26	21	47	31	....	....	....	....	....	....	....	....	....	4	0	1	1	2	....	....	....	....
1993-94	Kitchener Rangers	OHL	49	28	32	60	25	....	....	....	....	....	....	....	....	....	3	0	1	1	4	....	....	....	....
1994-95	Kitchener Rangers	OHL	44	25	29	54	26	....	....	....	....	....	....	....	....	....	....	....	....	....	....	....	....	....	....
	Detroit	OHL	16	4	16	20	11	....	....	....	....	....	....	....	....	....	21	11	10	21	18	....	....	....	....
1995-96	Indianapolis Ice	IHL	75	6	11	17	32	....	....	....	....	....	....	....	....	....	4	0	1	1	4	....	....	....	....
1996-97	Baltimore Bandits	AHL	36	6	6	12	13	....	....	....	....	....	....	....	....	....	3	0	0	0	0	....	....	....	....
	Columbus Chill	ECHL	32	18	18	36	20	....	....	....	....	....	....	....	....	....	....	....	....	....	....	....	....	....	....
1997-98	Indianapolis Ice	IHL	60	8	11	19	25	....	....	....	....	....	....	....	....	....	3	1	0	1	0	....	....	....	....
1998-99	Long Beach	IHL	51	9	19	28	30	....	....	....	....	....	....	....	....	....	8	0	0	0	8	....	....	....	....
	Florida Everblades	ECHL	18	8	15	23	11	....	....	....	....	....	....	....	....	....	....	....	....	....	....	....	....	....	....
99-2000	Florida Everblades	ECHL	26	14	24	38	24	....	....	....	....	....	....	....	....	....	....	....	....	....	....	....	....	....	....
	Providence Bruins	AHL	46	17	16	33	14	....	....	....	....	....	....	....	....	....	14	6	8	14	8	....	....	....	....
2000-01	**Boston**	**NHL**	**8**	**0**	**1**	**1**	**2**	**0**	**0**	**0**	**3**	**0.0**	**0**	**61**	**50.8**	**7:26**	....	....	....	....	....	....	....	....	....
	Providence Bruins	AHL	60	16	51	67	18	....	....	....	....	....	....	....	....	....	17	6	7	13	6	....	....	....	....
2001-02	**Boston**	**NHL**	**3**	**0**	**0**	**0**	**0**	**0**	**0**	**0**	**2**	**0.0**	**0**	**16**	**31.3**	**6:05**	....	....	....	....	....	....	....	....	....
	Providence Bruins	AHL	70	13	35	48	30	....	....	....	....	....	....	....	....	....	2	0	0	0	2	....	....	....	....
2002-03	**NY Islanders**	**NHL**	**8**	**2**	**1**	**3**	**4**	**1**	**0**	**0**	**7**	**28.6**	**2**	**84**	**54.8**	**12:27**	....	....	....	....	....	....	....	....	....
	Bridgeport	AHL	62	19	40	59	58	....	....	....	....	....	....	....	....	....	9	0	6	6	2	....	....	....	....
	NHL Totals		**19**	**2**	**2**	**4**	**6**	**1**	**0**	**0**	**12**	**16.7**		**161**	**50.9**	**9:20**	....	....	....	....	....	....	....	....	....

Signed as a free agent by **Providence** (AHL), January 24, 2000. Signed as a free agent by **Boston**, July 11, 2000. Signed as a free agent by **NY Islanders**, July 21, 2002.

MANN, Cameron

(MAN, CAM-uhr-ROHN)

Right wing. Shoots right. 6', 195 lbs. Born, Thompson, Man., April 20, 1977. Boston's 5th choice, 99th overall, in 1995 Entry Draft.

			Regular Season														Playoffs								
Season	Club	League	GP	G	A	Pts	PIM	PP	SH	GW	S	%	+/-	TF	F%	Min	GP	G	A	Pts	PIM	PP	SH	GW	Min
1992-93	Kenora Thistles	NOJHA	35	23	24	47	49	....	....	....	....	....	....	....	....	....	....	....	....	....	....	....	....	....	....
1993-94	Peterborough	OPJHL	16	3	14	17	23	....	....	....	....	....	....	....	....	....	....	....	....	....	....	....	....	....	....
	Peterborough	OHL	49	8	17	25	18	....	....	....	....	....	....	....	....	....	7	1	1	2	2	....	....	....	....
1994-95	Peterborough	OHL	64	19	24	43	40	....	....	....	....	....	....	....	....	....	11	3	8	11	4	....	....	....	....
1995-96	Peterborough	OHL	66	42	60	102	108	....	....	....	....	....	....	....	....	....	24	*27	16	*43	33	....	....	....	....
1996-97	Peterborough	OHL	51	33	50	83	91	....	....	....	....	....	....	....	....	....	11	10	18	28	16	....	....	....	....
1997-98	**Boston**	**NHL**	**9**	**0**	**1**	**1**	**4**	**0**	**0**	**0**	**6**	**0.0**	**1**	....	....	....	....	....	....	....	....	....	....	....	....
	Providence Bruins	AHL	71	21	26	47	99	....	....	....	....	....	....	....	....	....	....	....	....	....	....	....	....	....	....
1998-99	**Boston**	**NHL**	**33**	**5**	**2**	**7**	**17**	**1**	**0**	**1**	**42**	**11.9**	**0**	**22**	**36.4**	**10:40**	**1**	**0**	**0**	**0**	**0**	**0**	**0**	**0**	**1:48**
	Providence Bruins	AHL	43	21	25	46	65	....	....	....	....	....	....	....	....	....	11	7	7	14	4	....	....	....	....
99-2000	**Boston**	**NHL**	**32**	**8**	**4**	**12**	**13**	**1**	**0**	**0**	**48**	**16.7**	**–6**	**16**	**25.0**	**12:50**	....	....	....	....	....	....	....	....	....
	Providence Bruins	AHL	29	7	12	19	45	....	....	....	....	....	....	....	....	....	11	6	7	13	0	....	....	....	....
2000-01	**Boston**	**NHL**	**15**	**1**	**3**	**4**	**6**	**0**	**0**	**0**	**17**	**5.9**	**0**	**1**	**0.0**	**8:29**	....	....	....	....	....	....	....	....	....
	Providence Bruins	AHL	39	24	23	47	59	....	....	....	....	....	....	....	....	....	....	....	....	....	....	....	....	....	....
2001-02	Utah Grizzlies	AHL	61	19	32	51	83	....	....	....	....	....	....	....	....	....	5	0	0	0	6	....	....	....	....
2002-03	**Nashville**	**NHL**	**4**	**0**	**0**	**0**	**0**	**0**	**0**	**0**	**5**	**0.0**	**–2**	**0**	**0.0**	**5:53**	....	....	....	....	....	....	....	....	....
	Milwaukee	AHL	59	26	31	57	75	....	....	....	....	....	....	....	....	....	6	3	3	6	0	....	....	....	....
	NHL Totals		**93**	**14**	**10**	**24**	**40**	**2**	**0**	**1**	**118**	**11.9**		**39**	**30.8**	**10:53**	**1**	**0**	**0**	**0**	**0**	**0**	**0**	**0**	**1:48**

OHL First All-Star Team (1996, 1997) • Memorial Cup All-Star Team (1996) • Stafford Smythe Memorial Trophy (Memorial Cup MVP) (1996)

Traded to **Dallas** by **Boston** for Richard Jackman, June 23, 2001. Traded to **Nashville** by **Dallas** with Ed Belfour for David Gosselin and Nashville's 5th round choice (Eero Kilpelainen) in 2003 Entry Draft, June 29, 2002.

MANNING, Paul

(MAN-nihng, PAWL) **CBJ**

Defense. Shoots left. 6'4", 205 lbs. Born, Red Deer, Alta., April 15, 1979. Calgary's 3rd choice, 62nd overall, in 1998 Entry Draft.

Season	Club	League	GP	G	A	Pts	PIM	PP	SH	GW	S	%	+/-	TF	F%	Min	Playoffs GP	G	A	Pts	PIM	PP	SH	GW	Min
1995-96	Red Deer	AMHL	32	8	32	40																			
1996-97	Red Deer Vipers	HJHL	36	9	33	42																			
1997-98	Colorado College	WCHA	30	1	5	6	16																		
1998-99	Colorado College	WCHA	41	3	10	13	75																		
99-2000	Colorado College	WCHA	39	6	17	23	26																		
2000-01	Colorado College	WCHA	34	2	28	30	48																		
2001-02	Syracuse Crunch	AHL	35	1	4	5	16																		
	Elmira Jackals	UHL	1	1	0	1	0																		
2002-03	**Columbus**	**NHL**	**8**	**0**	**0**	**0**	**2**	**0**	**0**	**0**	**4**	**0.0**	**0**	**0**	**0.0**	**13:02**									
	Syracuse Crunch	AHL	52	2	5	7	37																		
	NHL Totals		**8**	**0**	**0**	**0**	**2**	**0**	**0**	**0**	**4**	**0.0**		**0**	**0.0**	**13:02**									

WCHA Second All-Star Team (2001)

Rights traded to **Columbus** by **Calgary** for Buffalo's 5th round choice (previously acquired, later traded to Detroit – Detroit selected Andreas Jamtin) in 2001 Entry Draft, June 24, 2001.

MAPLETOFT, Justin

(MAPLE-tawft, JUH-stihn) **NYI**

Center. Shoots left. 6'1", 180 lbs. Born, Lloydminster, Sask., January 11, 1981. NY Islanders' 9th choice, 130th overall, in 1999 Entry Draft.

Season	Club	League	GP	G	A	Pts	PIM	PP	SH	GW	S	%	+/-	TF	F%	Min	Playoffs GP	G	A	Pts	PIM	PP	SH	GW	Min
1996-97	Calgary Royals	AMHL	36	25	36	51																			
	Red Deer Rebels	WHL	2	0	0	0	0																		
1997-98	Red Deer Rebels	WHL	65	9	4	13	41																		
1998-99	Red Deer Rebels	WHL	72	24	22	46	81																		
99-2000	Red Deer Rebels	WHL	72	39	57	96	135											4	2	1	3	28				
2000-01	Red Deer Rebels	WHL	70	43	*77	*120	111											22	13	*21	34	59				
2001-02	Bridgeport	AHL	80	13	20	33	60											20	7	10	17	23				
2002-03	**NY Islanders**	**NHL**	**11**	**2**	**2**	**4**	**2**	**1**	**0**	**0**	**12**	**16.7**	**−1**	**138**	**41.3**	**12:17**	**2**	**0**	**0**	**0**	**0**	**0**	**0**	**0**	**7:23**
	Bridgeport	AHL	63	13	26	39	47											7	1	2	3	6				
	NHL Totals		**11**	**2**	**2**	**4**	**2**	**1**	**0**	**0**	**12**	**16.7**		**138**	**41.3**	**12:17**	**2**	**0**	**0**	**0**	**0**	**0**	**0**	**0**	**7:23**

WHL East First All-Star Team (2000, 2001) • Canadian Major Junior First All-Star Team (2001)

MARA, Paul

(MAIR-uh, PAWL) **PHX.**

Defense. Shoots left. 6'4", 217 lbs. Born, Ridgewood, NJ, September 7, 1979. Tampa Bay's 1st choice, 7th overall, in 1997 Entry Draft.

Season	Club	League	GP	G	A	Pts	PIM	PP	SH	GW	S	%	+/-	TF	F%	Min	Playoffs GP	G	A	Pts	PIM	PP	SH	GW	Min
1994-95	Belmont Hill	Hi-School	28	5	17	22	28																		
1995-96	Belmont Hill	Hi-School	28	18	20	38	40																		
1996-97	Sudbury Wolves	OHL	44	9	34	43	61																		
1997-98	Sudbury Wolves	OHL	25	8	18	26	79																		
	Plymouth Whalers	OHL	25	8	15	23	30											15	3	14	17	30				
1998-99	Plymouth Whalers	OHL	52	13	41	54	95											11	5	7	12	28				
	Tampa Bay	**NHL**	**1**	**1**	**1**	**2**	**0**	**1**	**0**	**0**	**1**	**100.0**	**−3**	**0**	**0.0**	**19:34**									
99-2000	**Tampa Bay**	**NHL**	**54**	**7**	**11**	**18**	**73**	**4**	**0**	**1**	**78**	**9.0**	**−27**	**0**	**0.0**	**22:13**									
	Detroit Vipers	IHL	15	3	5	8	22																		
2000-01	**Tampa Bay**	**NHL**	**46**	**6**	**10**	**16**	**40**	**2**	**0**	**1**	**58**	**10.3**	**−17**	**0**	**0.0**	**23:06**									
	Detroit Vipers	IHL	10	3	3	6	22																		
	Phoenix	**NHL**	**16**	**0**	**4**	**4**	**14**	**0**	**0**	**0**	**20**	**0.0**	**1**	**0**	**0.0**	**19:22**									
2001-02	**Phoenix**	**NHL**	**75**	**7**	**17**	**24**	**58**	**2**	**0**	**0**	**112**	**6.3**	**−6**	**2**	**100.0**	**21:34**	**5**	**0**	**0**	**0**	**4**	**0**	**0**	**0**	**22:57**
2002-03	**Phoenix**	**NHL**	**73**	**10**	**15**	**25**	**78**	**1**	**0**	**0**	**95**	**10.5**	**−7**	**1**	**0.0**	**21:06**									
	NHL Totals		**265**	**31**	**58**	**89**	**263**	**10**	**0**	**2**	**364**	**8.5**		**3**	**66.7**	**21:42**	**5**	**0**	**0**	**0**	**4**	**0**	**0**	**0**	**22:57**

Traded to **Phoenix** by **Tampa Bay** with Mike Johnson, Ruslan Zainullin and NY Islanders' 2nd round choice (previously acquired, Phoenix selected Matthew Spiller) in 2001 Entry Draft for Nikolai Khabibulin and Stan Neckar, March 5, 2001.

MARCHANT, Todd

(mahr-SHAHNT, TAWD) **CBJ**

Center. Shoots left. 5'10", 178 lbs. Born, Buffalo, NY, August 12, 1973. NY Rangers' 8th choice, 164th overall, in 1993 Entry Draft.

Season	Club	League	GP	G	A	Pts	PIM	PP	SH	GW	S	%	+/-	TF	F%	Min	Playoffs GP	G	A	Pts	PIM	PP	SH	GW	Min
1990-91	Niagara Scenics	NAJHL	37	31	47	78																			
1991-92	Clarkson Knights	ECAC	32	20	12	32	32																		
1992-93	Clarkson Knights	ECAC	33	18	28	46	38																		
1993-94	Team USA	Nat-Tm	59	28	39	67	48																		
	United States	Olympics	8	1	1	2	6																		
	NY Rangers	**NHL**	**1**	**0**	**0**	**0**	**0**	**0**	**0**	**0**	**1**	**0.0**	**−1**												
	Binghamton	AHL	8	2	7	9	6																		
	Edmonton	**NHL**	**3**	**0**	**1**	**1**	**2**	**0**	**0**	**0**	**5**	**0.0**	**−1**												
	Cape Breton	AHL	3	1	4	5	2											5	1	1	2	0				
1994-95	Cape Breton	AHL	38	22	25	47	25																		
	Edmonton	**NHL**	**45**	**13**	**14**	**27**	**32**	**3**	**2**	**2**	**95**	**13.7**	**−3**												
1995-96	**Edmonton**	**NHL**	**81**	**19**	**19**	**38**	**66**	**2**	**3**	**2**	**221**	**8.6**	**−19**												
1996-97	**Edmonton**	**NHL**	**79**	**14**	**19**	**33**	**44**	**0**	**4**	**3**	**202**	**6.9**	**11**				**12**	**4**	**2**	**6**	**12**	**0**	**3**	**1**	
1997-98	**Edmonton**	**NHL**	**76**	**14**	**21**	**35**	**71**	**2**	**1**	**3**	**194**	**7.2**	**9**				**12**	**1**	**1**	**2**	**10**	**0**	**0**	**0**	
1998-99	**Edmonton**	**NHL**	**82**	**14**	**22**	**36**	**65**	**3**	**1**	**2**	**183**	**7.7**	**3**	**1449**	**50.0**	**16:47**	**4**	**1**	**1**	**2**	**12**	**0**	**0**	**0**	**24:21**
99-2000	**Edmonton**	**NHL**	**82**	**17**	**23**	**40**	**70**	**0**	**1**	**0**	**170**	**10.0**	**7**	**1593**	**52.9**	**17:08**	**3**	**1**	**0**	**1**	**2**	**0**	**0**	**0**	**18:07**
2000-01	**Edmonton**	**NHL**	**71**	**13**	**26**	**39**	**51**	**0**	**4**	**2**	**113**	**11.5**	**1**	**1549**	**53.8**	**17:54**	**6**	**0**	**0**	**0**	**4**	**0**	**0**	**0**	**22:57**
2001-02	**Edmonton**	**NHL**	**82**	**12**	**22**	**34**	**41**	**0**	**3**	**1**	**124**	**9.7**	**7**	**1523**	**52.4**	**16:58**									
2002-03	**Edmonton**	**NHL**	**77**	**20**	**40**	**60**	**48**	**7**	**1**	**3**	**146**	**13.7**	**13**	**1336**	**58.0**	**19:54**	**6**	**0**	**2**	**2**	**2**	**0**	**0**	**0**	**20:03**
	NHL Totals		**679**	**136**	**207**	**343**	**490**	**17**	**20**	**18**	**1454**	**9.4**		**7450**	**53.4**	**17:42**	**43**	**7**	**6**	**13**	**42**	**0**	**3**	**1**	**21:34**

ECAC Second All-Star Team (1993)

Traded to **Edmonton** by **NY Rangers** for Craig MacTavish, March 21, 1994. Signed as a free agent by **Columbus**, July 3, 2003.

MARCHMENT, Bryan

(MAHRCH-mehnt, BRIGH-uhn) **TOR.**

Defense. Shoots left. 6'1", 200 lbs. Born, Scarborough, Ont., May 1, 1969. Winnipeg's 1st choice, 16th overall, in 1987 Entry Draft.

Season	Club	League	GP	G	A	Pts	PIM	PP	SH	GW	S	%	+/-	TF	F%	Min	Playoffs GP	G	A	Pts	PIM	PP	SH	GW	Min
1984-85	Tor. Young Nats	MTHL	69	14	35	49	229																		
1985-86	Belleville Bulls	OHL	57	5	15	20	225										21	0	7	7	83				
1986-87	Belleville Bulls	OHL	52	6	38	44	238										6	0	4	4	17				
1987-88	Belleville Bulls	OHL	56	7	51	58	200										6	1	3	4	19				
1988-89	Belleville Bulls	OHL	43	14	36	50	118										5	0	1	1	12				
	Winnipeg	**NHL**	**2**	**0**	**0**	**0**	**2**	**0**	**0**	**0**	**1**	**0.0**	**0**												
1989-90	**Winnipeg**	**NHL**	**7**	**0**	**2**	**2**	**28**	**0**	**0**	**0**	**5**	**0.0**	**0**												
	Moncton Hawks	AHL	56	4	19	23	217																		
1990-91	**Winnipeg**	**NHL**	**28**	**2**	**2**	**4**	**91**	**0**	**0**	**0**	**24**	**8.3**	**−5**												
	Moncton Hawks	AHL	33	2	11	13	101																		
1991-92	**Chicago**	**NHL**	**58**	**5**	**10**	**15**	**168**	**2**	**0**	**0**	**55**	**9.1**	**−4**				**16**	**1**	**0**	**1**	**36**	**0**	**0**	**0**	
1992-93	**Chicago**	**NHL**	**78**	**5**	**15**	**20**	**313**	**1**	**0**	**1**	**75**	**6.7**	**15**				**4**	**0**	**0**	**0**	**12**	**0**	**0**	**0**	
1993-94	**Chicago**	**NHL**	**13**	**1**	**4**	**5**	**42**	**0**	**0**	**0**	**18**	**5.6**	**−2**												
	Hartford	**NHL**	**42**	**3**	**7**	**10**	**124**	**0**	**1**	**1**	**74**	**4.1**	**−12**												
1994-95	**Edmonton**	**NHL**	**40**	**1**	**5**	**6**	**184**	**0**	**0**	**0**	**57**	**1.8**	**−11**												
1995-96	**Edmonton**	**NHL**	**78**	**3**	**15**	**18**	**202**	**0**	**0**	**0**	**96**	**3.1**	**−7**												
1996-97	**Edmonton**	**NHL**	**71**	**3**	**13**	**16**	**132**	**1**	**0**	**0**	**89**	**3.4**	**13**				**3**	**0**	**0**	**0**	**4**	**0**	**0**	**0**	
1997-98	**Edmonton**	**NHL**	**27**	**0**	**4**	**4**	**58**	**0**	**0**	**0**	**23**	**0.0**	**−2**												
	Tampa Bay	**NHL**	**22**	**2**	**4**	**6**	**43**	**0**	**0**	**0**	**20**	**10.0**	**−3**												
	San Jose	**NHL**	**12**	**0**	**3**	**3**	**43**	**0**	**0**	**0**	**13**	**0.0**	**2**				**6**	**0**	**0**	**0**	**10**	**0**	**0**	**0**	
1998-99	**San Jose**	**NHL**	**59**	**2**	**6**	**8**	**101**	**0**	**0**	**0**	**49**	**4.1**	**−7**	**0**	**0.0**	**17:43**	**6**	**0**	**0**	**0**	**4**	**0**	**0**	**0**	**16:41**
99-2000	**San Jose**	**NHL**	**49**	**0**	**4**	**4**	**72**	**0**	**0**	**0**	**51**	**0.0**	**5**	**0**	**0.0**	**18:55**	**11**	**2**	**1**	**3**	**12**	**0**	**0**	**0**	**18:40**
2000-01	**San Jose**	**NHL**	**75**	**7**	**11**	**18**	**204**	**0**	**1**	**3**	**73**	**9.6**	**15**	**1**	**100.0**	**18:12**	**5**	**0**	**1**	**1**	**2**	**0**	**0**	**0**	**17:00**
2001-02	**San Jose**	**NHL**	**72**	**2**	**20**	**22**	**178**	**0**	**0**	**0**	**68**	**2.9**	**22**	**0**	**0.0**	**18:47**	**12**	**1**	**1**	**2**	**10**	**0**	**0**	**0**	**15:29**

Season	Club	League	GP	G	A	Pts	PIM	PP	SH	GW	S	%	+/-	TF	F%	Min	GP	G	A	Pts	PIM	PP	SH	GW	Min
			Regular Season														**Playoffs**								
2002-03	San Jose	NHL	67	2	9	11	108	0	0	0	66	3.0	-2	0	0.0	19:19									
	Colorado	NHL	14	0	3	3	33	0	0	0	18	0.0	4	0	0.0	16:42	7	0	0	0	4	0	0	0	16:02
	NHL Totals		814	38	137	175	2126	4	2	5	875	4.3		1	100.0	18:30	70	4	3	7	94	0	0	0	16:48

OHL Second All-Star Team (1989)

Traded to **Chicago** by **Winnipeg** with Chris Norton for Troy Murray and Warren Rychel, July 22, 1991. Traded to **Hartford** by **Chicago** with Steve Larmer for Eric Weinrich and Patrick Poulin, November 2, 1993. Transferred to **Edmonton** from **Hartford** as compensation for Hartford's signing of free agent Steven Rice, August 30, 1994. Traded to **Tampa Bay** by **Edmonton** with Steve Kelly and Jason Bonsignore for Roman Hamrlik and Paul Comrie, December 30, 1997. Traded to **San Jose** by **Tampa Bay** with David Shaw and Tampa Bay's 1st round choice (later traded to Nashville – Nashville selected David Legwand) in 1998 Entry Draft for Andrei Nazarov and Florida's 1st round choice (previously acquired, Tampa Bay selected Vincent Lecavallier) in 1998 Entry Draft, March 24, 1998. Traded to **Colorado** by **San Jose** for Colorado's 3rd (later traded to Calgary – Calgary selected Ryan Donally) and 5th (later traded back to Colorado – Colorado selected Brad Richardson) round choices in 2003 Entry Draft, March 8, 2003. Signed as a free agent by **Toronto**, July 11, 2003.

MARHA, Josef

(MAHR-hah, JOH-sehf)

Center. Shoots left. 6', 176 lbs. Born, Havlickuv Brod, Czech., June 2, 1976. Quebec's 3rd choice, 35th overall, in 1994 Entry Draft.

Season	Club	League	GP	G	A	Pts	PIM	PP	SH	GW	S	%	+/-	TF	F%	Min	GP	G	A	Pts	PIM	PP	SH	GW	Min
1991-92	Dukla Jihlava Jr.	Czech-Jr.	25	12	13	25	0																		
1992-93	Dukla Jihlava	Czech	7	2	2	4																			
1993-94	HC Dukla Jihlava	Czech	41	7	2	9											3	0	1	1					
1994-95	HC Dukla Jihlava	Czech	35	3	7	10	6																		
1995-96	Colorado	NHL	2	0	1	1	0	0	0	0	2	0.0	1												
	Cornwall Aces	AHL	74	18	30	48	30										8	1	2	3	10				
1996-97	Colorado	NHL	6	0	1	1	0	0	0	0	6	0.0	0												
	Hershey Bears	AHL	67	23	49	72	44										19	6	*16	*22	10				
1997-98	Colorado	NHL	11	2	5	7	4	0	0	0	10	20.0	0												
	Hershey Bears	AHL	55	6	46	52	30																		
	Anaheim	NHL	12	7	4	11	0	3	0	0	21	33.3	4												
1998-99	Anaheim	NHL	10	0	1	1	0	0	0	0	13	0.0	-4	107	40.2	12:02									
	Cincinnati	AHL	3	1	0	1	4																		
	Chicago	NHL	22	2	5	7	4	1	0	1	32	6.3	5	275	50.9	14:37									
	Portland Pirates	AHL	8	0	8	8	2																		
99-2000	Chicago	NHL	81	10	12	22	18	2	1	3	91	11.0	-10	1110	46.3	13:20									
2000-01	Chicago	NHL	15	0	3	3	6	0	0	0	17	0.0	-4	196	50.0	12:46									
	Norfolk Admirals	AHL	60	18	28	46	44										9	1	8	9	6				
2001-02	HC Davos	Swiss	44	19	15	34	38										16	6	9	15	8				
2002-03	HC Davos	Swiss	43	14	18	32	51										17	4	6	10	6				
	NHL Totals		159	21	32	53	32	6	1	4	192	10.9		1688	47.1	13:23									

Rights transferred to **Colorado** after **Quebec** franchise relocated, June 21, 1995. Traded to **Anaheim** by **Colorado** for Warren Rychel and Anaheim's 4th round choice (Sanny Lindstrom) in 1999 Entry Draft, March 24, 1998. Traded to **Chicago** by **Anaheim** for Chicago's 4th round choice (Alexandr Chagodayev) in 1999 Entry Draft, January 28, 1999. Signed as a free agent by **HC Davos** (Swiss), June 13, 2001.

MARKOV, Andrei

(MAHR-kahf, AHN-dray) **MTL.**

Defense. Shoots left. 6', 208 lbs. Born, Voskresensk, USSR, December 20, 1978. Montreal's 6th choice, 162nd overall, in 1998 Entry Draft.

Season	Club	League	GP	G	A	Pts	PIM	PP	SH	GW	S	%	+/-	TF	F%	Min	GP	G	A	Pts	PIM	PP	SH	GW	Min
1995-96	Voskresensk	CIS	38	0	0	0	14																		
1996-97	Voskresensk	Russia	43	8	4	12	32										2	1	1	2	0				
1997-98	Voskresensk	Russia	43	10	5	15	83																		
1998-99	Dynamo Moscow	Russia	38	10	11	21	32										16	3	6	9	6				
	Dynamo Moscow	EuroHL	12	7	5	12	12										6	2	2	4	4				
99-2000	Dynamo Moscow	Russia	29	11	12	23	28										17	4	3	7	8				
2000-01	Montreal	NHL	63	6	17	23	18	2	0	0	82	7.3	-6	2	50.0	16:53									
	Quebec Citadelles	AHL	14	0	5	5	4										7	1	1	2	2				
2001-02	Montreal	NHL	56	5	19	24	24	2	0	1	73	6.8	-1	0	0.0	17:15	12	1	3	4	8	0	0	1	15:53
	Quebec Citadelles	AHL	12	4	6	10	7																		
2002-03	Montreal	NHL	79	13	24	37	34	3	0	2	159	8.2	13	1	0.0	23:17									
	NHL Totals		198	24	60	84	76	7	0	3	314	7.6		3	33.3	19:33	12	1	3	4	8	0	0	1	15:53

MARKOV, Danny

(MAHR-kahf, DA-nee) **CAR.**

Defense. Shoots left. 6'1", 190 lbs. Born, Moscow, USSR, July 30, 1976. Toronto's 7th choice, 223rd overall, in 1995 Entry Draft.

Season	Club	League	GP	G	A	Pts	PIM	PP	SH	GW	S	%	+/-	TF	F%	Min	GP	G	A	Pts	PIM	PP	SH	GW	Min
1993-94	Spartak Moscow	CIS	13	1	0	1	6										1	0	0	0	0				
1994-95	Spartak Moscow	CIS	39	0	1	1	36																		
1995-96	Spartak Moscow	CIS	38	2	0	2	12										2	0	0	0	2				
1996-97	Spartak Moscow	Russia	39	3	6	9	41																		
	St. John's	AHL	10	2	4	6	18										11	2	6	8	14				
1997-98	Toronto	NHL	25	2	5	7	28	1	0	0	15	13.3	0												
	St. John's	AHL	52	3	23	26	124										2	0	1	1	0				
1998-99	Toronto	NHL	57	4	8	12	47	0	0	0	34	11.8	5	0	0.0	18:41	17	0	6	6	18	0	0	0	22:24
99-2000	Toronto	NHL	59	0	10	10	28	0	0	0	38	0.0	13	1	0.0	20:08	12	0	3	3	10	0	0	0	21:05
2000-01	Toronto	NHL	59	3	13	16	34	1	0	2	49	6.1	6	0	0.0	19:02	11	1	1	2	12	0	0	0	21:30
2001-02	Phoenix	NHL	72	6	30	36	67	4	0	1	103	5.8	-7	0	0.0	22:55									
	Russia	Olympics	5	0	1	1	0																		
2002-03	Phoenix	NHL	64	4	16	20	36	2	0	0	105	3.8	2	0	0.0	23:16									
	NHL Totals		336	19	82	101	240	8	0	3	344	5.5		1	0.0	20:57	40	1	10	11	40	0	0	0	21:45

Traded to **Phoenix** by **Toronto** for Robert Reichel, Travis Green and Craig Mills, June 12, 2001. Traded to **Carolina** by **Phoenix** for David Tanabe and Igor Knyazev, June 21, 2003.

MARLEAU, Patrick

(mahr-LOH, PAT-rihk) **S.J.**

Center. Shoots left. 6'2", 210 lbs. Born, Aneroid, Sask., September 15, 1979. San Jose's 1st choice, 2nd overall, in 1997 Entry Draft.

Season	Club	League	GP	G	A	Pts	PIM	PP	SH	GW	S	%	+/-	TF	F%	Min	GP	G	A	Pts	PIM	PP	SH	GW	Min
1993-94	Swift Current	SMHL	53	72	95	167																			
1994-95	Swift Current	SMHL	31	30	22	52	18																		
1995-96	Seattle	WHL	72	32	42	74	22										5	3	4	7	4				
1996-97	Seattle	WHL	71	51	74	125	37										15	7	16	23	12				
1997-98	San Jose	NHL	74	13	19	32	14	1	0	2	90	14.4	5				5	0	1	1	0	0	0	0	
1998-99	San Jose	NHL	81	21	24	45	24	4	0	4	134	15.7	10	1121	43.4	15:11	6	2	1	3	4	2	0	0	11:08
99-2000	San Jose	NHL	81	17	23	40	36	3	0	3	161	10.6	-9	851	42.0	14:11	5	1	1	2	2	1	0	0	11:51
2000-01	San Jose	NHL	81	25	27	52	22	5	0	6	146	17.1	7	1088	44.8	16:17	6	2	0	2	4	0	0	0	14:50
2001-02	San Jose	NHL	79	21	23	44	40	3	0	5	121	17.4	9	897	47.3	14:04	12	6	5	11	6	1	0	3	15:50
2002-03	San Jose	NHL	82	28	29	57	33	8	1	3	172	16.3	-10	1403	47.3	18:31									
	NHL Totals		478	125	145	270	169	24	1	23	824	15.2		5360	45.1	15:40	34	11	8	19	16	4	0	3	13:58

WHL West First All-Star Team (1997)

MARSHALL, Grant

(MAHR-shahl, GRANT) **N.J.**

Right wing. Shoots right. 6'1", 195 lbs. Born, Mississauga, Ont., June 9, 1973. Toronto's 2nd choice, 23rd overall, in 1992 Entry Draft.

Season	Club	League	GP	G	A	Pts	PIM	PP	SH	GW	S	%	+/-	TF	F%	Min	GP	G	A	Pts	PIM	PP	SH	GW	Min
1989-90	Tor. Young Nats	MTHL	39	15	28	43	56																		
1990-91	Ottawa 67's	OHL	26	6	11	17	25										1	0	0	0	0				
1991-92	Ottawa 67's	OHL	61	32	51	83	132										11	6	11	17	11				
1992-93	Ottawa 67's	OHL	30	14	29	43	83																		
	Newmarket	OHL	31	11	25	36	89										7	4	7	11	20				
	St. John's	AHL	2	0	0	0	0										2	0	0	0	2				
1993-94	St. John's	AHL	67	11	29	40	155										11	1	5	6	17				
1994-95	Kalamazoo Wings	IHL	61	17	29	46	96										16	9	3	12	27				
	Dallas	NHL	2	0	1	1	0	0	0	0	0	0.0	1												
1995-96	Dallas	NHL	70	9	19	28	111	0	0	0	62	14.5	0												
1996-97	Dallas	NHL	56	6	4	10	98	0	0	0	0	0.0	5				5	0	2	2	8	0	0	0	
1997-98	Dallas	NHL	72	9	10	19	96	3	0	1	91	9.9	-2				17	0	2	2	*47	0	0	0	
1998-99♦	Dallas	NHL	82	13	18	31	85	2	0	4	112	11.6	1	2	50.0	12:39	14	0	3	3	20	0	0	0	11:42
99-2000	Dallas	NHL	45	2	6	8	38	1	0	0	43	4.7	-5	3	0.0	11:19	14	0	1	1	4	0	0	0	10:08
2000-01	Dallas	NHL	75	13	24	37	64	4	0	1	93	14.0	1	16	56.3	11:05	9	0	0	0	0	0	0	0	11:15
2001-02	Columbus	NHL	81	15	18	33	86	6	0	4	152	9.9	-20	28	39.3	15:27									

			Regular Season														Playoffs								
Season	Club	League	GP	G	A	Pts	PIM	PP	SH	GW	S	%	+/-	TF	F%	Min	GP	G	A	Pts	PIM	PP	SH	GW	Min
2002-03	Columbus	NHL	66	8	20	28	71	3	0	2	96	8.3	–8	26	46.2	13:56	....	....	....	....	....	....	....	....	....
	♦ New Jersey	NHL	10	1	3	4	7	0	0	0	17	5.9	–3	1	100.0	11:38	24	6	2	8	8	2	0	1	14:30
	NHL Totals		559	76	123	199	656	19	0	12	666	11.4		76	44.7	12:60	83	6	10	16	87	2	0	1	12:23

• Missed majority of 1990-91 season recovering from neck injury suffered in game vs. Sudbury (OHL), December 4, 1990. Transferred to **Dallas** from **Toronto** with Peter Zezel as compensation for Toronto's signing of free agent Mike Craig, August 10, 1994. Traded to **Columbus** by **Dallas** for Columbus' 2nd round choice (Loui Eriksson) in 2003 Entry Draft, August 29, 2001. Traded to **New Jersey** by **Columbus** for future considerations, March 10, 2003.

MARSHALL, Jason

(MAHR-shahl, JAY-suhn) **MIN.**

Defense. Shoots right. 6'2", 200 lbs. Born, Cranbrook, B.C., February 22, 1971. St. Louis' 1st choice, 9th overall, in 1989 Entry Draft.

1987-88	Columbia Valley	RMJHL	40	4	28	32	150	....	....	....	....	....	....	....	....	....	....	....	....	....	....	....	....	....	....
1988-89	Vernon Lakers	BCJHL	48	10	30	40	197	....	....	....	....	....	....	....	....	....	31	6	6	12	14	....	....	....	....
1989-90	Team Canada	Nat-Tm	73	1	11	12	57	....	....	....	....	....	....	....	....	....	....	....	....	....	....	....	....	....	....
1990-91	Tri-City	WHL	59	10	34	44	236	....	....	....	....	....	....	....	....	....	7	1	2	3	20	....	....	....	....
	Peoria Rivermen	IHL	....	....	....	....	....	....	....	....	....	....	....	....	....	....	18	0	1	1	48	....	....	....	....
1991-92	St. Louis	NHL	2	1	0	1	4	0	0	0	2	50.0	0	....	....	....	....	....	....	....	....	....	....	....	....
	Peoria Rivermen	IHL	78	4	18	22	178	....	....	....	....	....	....	....	....	....	10	0	1	1	16	....	....	....	....
1992-93	Peoria Rivermen	IHL	77	4	16	20	229	....	....	....	....	....	....	....	....	....	4	0	0	0	20	....	....	....	....
1993-94	Team Canada	Nat-Tm	41	3	10	13	60	....	....	....	....	....	....	....	....	....	....	....	....	....	....	....	....	....	....
	Peoria Rivermen	IHL	20	1	1	2	72	....	....	....	....	....	....	....	....	....	3	2	0	2	2	....	....	....	....
1994-95	San Diego Gulls	IHL	80	7	18	25	218	....	....	....	....	....	....	....	....	....	5	0	1	1	8	....	....	....	....
	Anaheim	NHL	1	0	0	0	0	0	0	0	1	0.0	–2	....	....	....	....	....	....	....	....	....	....	....	....
1995-96	Anaheim	NHL	24	0	1	1	42	0	0	0	9	0.0	3	....	....	....	....	....	....	....	....	....	....	....	....
	Baltimore Bandits	AHL	57	1	13	14	150	....	....	....	....	....	....	....	....	....	....	....	....	....	....	....	....	....	....
1996-97	Anaheim	NHL	73	1	9	10	140	0	0	0	34	2.9	6	....	....	....	7	0	1	1	4	0	0	0	....
1997-98	Anaheim	NHL	72	3	6	9	189	1	0	0	68	4.4	–8	....	....	....	....	....	....	....	....	....	....	....	....
1998-99	Anaheim	NHL	72	1	7	8	142	0	0	0	63	1.6	–5	0	0.0	19:06	4	1	0	1	10	1	0	0	21:29
99-2000	Anaheim	NHL	55	0	3	3	88	0	0	0	41	0.0	–10	2	50.0	16:33	....	....	....	....	....	....	....	....	....
2000-01	Anaheim	NHL	50	3	4	7	105	2	1	1	38	7.9	–12	1	0.0	14:36	....	....	....	....	....	....	....	....	....
	Washington	NHL	5	0	0	0	17	0	0	0	5	0.0	–1	0	0.0	11:48	....	....	....	....	....	....	....	....	....
2001-02	Minnesota	NHL	80	5	6	11	148	1	0	0	73	6.8	–8	0	0.0	16:18	....	....	....	....	....	....	....	....	....
2002-03	Minnesota	NHL	45	1	5	6	69	0	0	0	40	2.5	4	7	28.6	11:24	15	1	1	2	16	0	0	1	10:50
	NHL Totals		479	15	41	56	944	4	1	1	374	4.0		10	30.0	15:56	26	2	2	4	30	1	0	1	13:05

Traded to **Anaheim** by **St. Louis** for Bill Houlder, August 29, 1994. Traded to **Washington** by **Anaheim** for Alexei Tezikov and Edmonton's 4th round choice (previously acquired, Anaheim selected Brandon Rogers) in 2001 Entry Draft, March 13, 2001. Signed as a free agent by **Minnesota**, July 2, 2001.

MARTINEK, Radek

(MAHR-tih-nehk, RA-dehk) **NYI**

Defense. Shoots right. 6'1", 200 lbs. Born, Havlickuv Brod, Czech., August 31, 1976. NY Islanders' 12th choice, 228th overall, in 1999 Entry Draft.

1996-97	Ceske Budejovice	Czech	52	3	5	8	40	....	....	....	....	....	....	....	....	....	5	0	1	1	2	....	....	....	....
1997-98	Ceske Budejovice	Czech	42	2	7	9	36	....	....	....	....	....	....	....	....	....	....	....	....	....	....	....	....	....	....
1998-99	Ceske Budejovice	Czech	52	12	13	25	50	....	....	....	....	....	....	....	....	....	3	0	2	2	....	....	....	....	....
99-2000	Ceske Budejovice	Czech	45	5	18	23	24	....	....	....	....	....	....	....	....	....	3	0	0	0	6	....	....	....	....
2000-01	Ceske Budejovice	Czech	44	8	10	18	45	....	....	....	....	....	....	....	....	....	....	....	....	....	....	....	....	....	....
2001-02	NY Islanders	NHL	23	1	4	5	16	0	0	1	25	4.0	5	0	0.0	21:07	....	....	....	....	....	....	....	....	....
2002-03	NY Islanders	NHL	66	2	11	13	26	0	0	1	67	3.0	15	0	0.0	17:15	4	0	0	0	4	0	0	0	10:16
	Bridgeport	AHL	3	0	3	3	2	....	....	....	....	....	....	....	....	....	....	....	....	....	....	....	....	....	....
	NHL Totals		89	3	15	18	42	0	0	2	92	3.3		0	0.0	18:15	4	0	0	0	4	0	0	0	10:16

• Missed majority of 2001-02 season recovering from knee injury suffered in game vs. NY Rangers, November 11, 2001.

MARTINS, Steve

(MAHR-tihns, STEEV) **ST.L.**

Center. Shoots left. 5'9", 185 lbs. Born, Gatineau, Que., April 13, 1972. Hartford's 1st choice, 5th overall, in 1994 Supplemental Draft.

1988-89	L'Outaouais	QAAA	38	18	33	51	70	....	....	....	....	....	....	....	....	....	....	....	....	....	....	....	....	....	....
1989-90	Choate-Rosemary	Hi-School	STATISTICS NOT AVAILABLE																						
1990-91	Choate-Rosemary	Hi-School	STATISTICS NOT AVAILABLE																						
1991-92	Harvard Crimson	ECAC	20	13	14	27	26	....	....	....	....	....	....	....	....	....	....	....	....	....	....	....	....	....	....
1992-93	Harvard Crimson	ECAC	18	6	8	14	40	....	....	....	....	....	....	....	....	....	....	....	....	....	....	....	....	....	....
1993-94	Harvard Crimson	ECAC	32	25	35	60	*93	....	....	....	....	....	....	....	....	....	....	....	....	....	....	....	....	....	....
1994-95	Harvard Crimson	ECAC	28	15	23	38	93	....	....	....	....	....	....	....	....	....	....	....	....	....	....	....	....	....	....
1995-96	Hartford	NHL	23	1	3	4	8	0	0	0	27	3.7	–3	....	....	....	....	....	....	....	....	....	....	....	....
	Springfield	AHL	30	9	20	29	10	....	....	....	....	....	....	....	....	....	....	....	....	....	....	....	....	....	....
1996-97	Hartford	NHL	2	0	1	1	0	0	0	0	2	0.0	0	....	....	....	....	....	....	....	....	....	....	....	....
	Springfield	AHL	63	12	31	43	78	....	....	....	....	....	....	....	....	....	17	1	3	4	26	....	....	....	....
1997-98	Carolina	NHL	3	0	0	0	0	0	0	0	0	0.0	0	....	....	....	....	....	....	....	....	....	....	....	....
	Chicago Wolves	IHL	78	20	41	61	122	....	....	....	....	....	....	....	....	....	21	6	14	20	28	....	....	....	....
1998-99	Ottawa	NHL	36	4	3	7	10	1	0	1	27	14.8	4	191	56.0	8:28	....	....	....	....	....	....	....	....	....
	Detroit Vipers	IHL	4	1	6	7	16	....	....	....	....	....	....	....	....	....	....	....	....	....	....	....	....	....	....
99-2000	Ottawa	NHL	2	1	0	1	0	0	0	0	3	33.3	–1	3	0.0	11:10	....	....	....	....	....	....	....	....	....
	Tampa Bay	NHL	57	5	7	12	37	0	1	1	62	8.1	–11	806	50.9	13:27	....	....	....	....	....	....	....	....	....
2000-01	Tampa Bay	NHL	20	1	1	2	13	0	0	0	18	5.6	–9	184	52.2	9:35	....	....	....	....	....	....	....	....	....
	Detroit Vipers	IHL	8	5	4	9	4	....	....	....	....	....	....	....	....	....	....	....	....	....	....	....	....	....	....
	NY Islanders	NHL	39	1	3	4	20	0	1	0	28	3.6	–7	302	58.0	9:41	....	....	....	....	....	....	....	....	....
	Chicago Wolves	IHL	5	1	2	3	0	....	....	....	....	....	....	....	....	....	16	1	6	7	22	....	....	....	....
2001-02	Ottawa	NHL	14	1	0	1	4	0	0	0	11	9.1	1	121	55.4	9:33	2	0	0	0	0	0	0	0	7:12
	Grand Rapids	AHL	51	10	21	31	66	....	....	....	....	....	....	....	....	....	3	0	0	0	0	....	....	....	....
2002-03	Ottawa	NHL	14	2	3	5	10	0	0	0	13	15.4	3	111	55.9	9:45	....	....	....	....	....	....	....	....	....
	Binghamton	AHL	26	5	11	16	31	....	....	....	....	....	....	....	....	....	....	....	....	....	....	....	....	....	....
	St. Louis	NHL	28	3	3	6	18	0	1	0	25	12.0	–8	369	54.7	13:38	2	0	1	1	0	0	0	0	9:23
	NHL Totals		238	19	24	43	120	1	3	2	216	8.8		2087	53.6	11:01	4	0	1	1	0	0	0	0	8:18

ECAC First All-Star Team (1994) • ECAC Player of the Year (1994) • NCAA East First All-American Team (1994) • NCAA Final Four All-Tournament Team (1994)

Transferred to **Carolina** after **Hartford** franchise relocated, June 25, 1997. Signed as a free agent by **Ottawa**, July 20, 1998. Claimed on waivers by **Tampa Bay** from **Ottawa**, October 29, 1999. Traded to **NY Islanders** by **Tampa Bay** for future considerations, January 3, 2001. Signed as a free agent by **Ottawa**, August 30, 2001. Claimed on waivers by **St. Louis** from **Ottawa**, January 15, 2003.

MATTE, Christian

(MA-tay, KRIH-stan)

Right wing. Shoots right. 6', 190 lbs. Born, Hull, Que., January 20, 1975. Quebec's 8th choice, 153rd overall, in 1993 Entry Draft.

1991-92	Abitibi Foresters	QAAA	42	18	27	45	30	....	....	....	....	....	....	....	....	....	4	1	0	1	0	....	....	....	....
1992-93	Granby Bisons	QMJHL	68	17	36	53	59	....	....	....	....	....	....	....	....	....	....	....	....	....	....	....	....	....	....
1993-94	Granby Bisons	QMJHL	59	50	47	97	103	....	....	....	....	....	....	....	....	....	7	5	5	10	12	....	....	....	....
	Cornwall Aces	AHL	1	0	0	0	0	....	....	....	....	....	....	....	....	....	....	....	....	....	....	....	....	....	....
1994-95	Granby Bisons	QMJHL	66	50	66	116	86	....	....	....	....	....	....	....	....	....	13	11	7	18	12	....	....	....	....
	Cornwall Aces	AHL	....	....	....	....	....	....	....	....	....	....	....	....	....	....	3	0	1	1	2	....	....	....	....
1995-96	Cornwall Aces	AHL	64	20	32	52	51	....	....	....	....	....	....	....	....	....	7	1	1	2	6	....	....	....	....
1996-97	Colorado	NHL	5	1	1	2	0	0	0	0	6	16.7	1	....	....	....	....	....	....	....	....	....	....	....	....
	Hershey Bears	AHL	49	18	18	36	78	....	....	....	....	....	....	....	....	....	22	8	3	11	25	....	....	....	....
1997-98	Colorado	NHL	5	0	0	0	6	0	0	0	5	0.0	0	....	....	....	....	....	....	....	....	....	....	....	....
	Hershey Bears	AHL	71	33	40	73	109	....	....	....	....	....	....	....	....	....	7	3	2	5	4	....	....	....	....
1998-99	Colorado	NHL	7	1	1	2	0	0	0	0	9	11.1	–2	13	30.8	7:45	....	....	....	....	....	....	....	....	....
	Hershey Bears	AHL	60	31	47	78	48	....	....	....	....	....	....	....	....	....	5	2	1	3	8	....	....	....	....
99-2000	Colorado	NHL	5	0	1	1	4	0	0	0	1	0.0	–2	2	0.0	8:37	....	....	....	....	....	....	....	....	....
	Hershey Bears	AHL	73	43	*61	*104	85	....	....	....	....	....	....	....	....	....	14	8	6	14	10	....	....	....	....
2000-01	Minnesota	NHL	3	0	0	0	2	0	0	0	8	0.0	0	0	0.0	13:21	....	....	....	....	....	....	....	....	....
	Cleveland	IHL	58	*38	29	67	59	....	....	....	....	....	....	....	....	....	4	1	1	2	0	....	....	....	....

Season	Club	League	Regular Season GP	G	A	Pts	PIM	PP	SH	GW	S	%	+/-	TF	F%	Min	Playoffs GP	G	A	Pts	PIM	PP	SH	GW	Min
2001-02	Rochester	AHL	72	22	29	51	48	....	....	....	....	....	....	....	....	....	2	0	0	0	0	....	....	....	....
2002-03	ZSC Lions Zurich	Swiss	44	22	25	47	49	....	....	....	....	....	....	....	....	....	12	5	3	8	14	....	....	....	....
	NHL Totals		**25**	**2**	**3**	**5**	**12**	**0**	**0**	**0**	**29**	**6.9**		**15**	**26.7**	**9:09**	....	....	....	....	....	....	....	....	....

QMJHL All-Rookie Team (1993) • QMJHL Second All-Star Team (1994) • AHL First All-Star Team (2000) • John P. Sollenberger Trophy (Top Scorer – AHL) (2000)

Rights transferred to **Colorado** after **Quebec** franchise relocated, June 21, 1995. Signed as a free agent by **Minnesota**, July 11, 2000. Signed as a free agent by **Buffalo**, August 2, 2001. Signed as a free agent by **ZSC Lions Zurich** (Swiss), June 14, 2002.

MATTEAU, Stephane

(mah-TOH, STEH-fan)

Left wing. Shoots left. 6'4", 215 lbs. Born, Rouyn-Noranda, Que., September 2, 1969. Calgary's 2nd choice, 25th overall, in 1987 Entry Draft.

Season	Club	League	GP	G	A	Pts	PIM	PP	SH	GW	S	%	+/-	TF	F%	Min	GP	G	A	Pts	PIM	PP	SH	GW	Min
1985-86	Hull Olympiques	QMJHL	60	6	8	14	19	....	....	....	....	....	....	....	....	....	4	0	0	0	0	....	....	....	....
1986-87	Hull Olympiques	QMJHL	69	27	48	75	113	....	....	....	....	....	....	....	....	....	8	3	7	10	8	....	....	....	....
1987-88	Hull Olympiques	QMJHL	57	17	40	57	179	....	....	....	....	....	....	....	....	....	18	5	14	19	94	....	....	....	....
1988-89	Hull Olympiques	QMJHL	59	44	45	89	202	....	....	....	....	....	....	....	....	....	9	8	6	14	30	....	....	....	....
	Salt Lake	IHL	....	....	....	....	....	....	....	....	....	....	....	....	....	....	9	0	4	4	13	....	....	....	....
1989-90	Salt Lake	IHL	81	23	35	58	130	....	....	....	....	....	....	....	....	....	10	6	3	9	38	....	....	....	....
1990-91	**Calgary**	**NHL**	**78**	**15**	**19**	**34**	**93**	**0**	**1**	**1**	**114**	**13.2**	**17**	....	....	....	**5**	**0**	**1**	**1**	**0**	**0**	**0**	**0**	....
1991-92	**Calgary**	**NHL**	**4**	**1**	**0**	**1**	**19**	**0**	**0**	**0**	**7**	**14.3**	**2**	....	....	....	....	....	....	....	....	....	....	....	....
	Chicago	**NHL**	**20**	**5**	**8**	**13**	**45**	**1**	**0**	**0**	**31**	**16.1**	**3**	....	....	....	**18**	**4**	**6**	**10**	**24**	**1**	**1**	**0**	....
1992-93	**Chicago**	**NHL**	**79**	**15**	**18**	**33**	**98**	**2**	**0**	**4**	**95**	**15.8**	**6**	....	....	....	**3**	**0**	**1**	**1**	**2**	**0**	**0**	**0**	....
1993-94	**Chicago**	**NHL**	**65**	**15**	**16**	**31**	**55**	**2**	**0**	**2**	**113**	**13.3**	**10**	....	....	....	....	....	....	....	....	....	....	....	....
	• **NY Rangers**	**NHL**	**12**	**4**	**3**	**7**	**2**	**1**	**0**	**0**	**22**	**18.2**	**5**	....	....	....	**23**	**6**	**3**	**9**	**20**	**1**	**0**	**2**	....
1994-95	**NY Rangers**	**NHL**	**41**	**3**	**5**	**8**	**25**	**0**	**0**	**0**	**37**	**8.1**	**–8**	....	....	....	**9**	**0**	**1**	**1**	**10**	**0**	**0**	**0**	....
1995-96	**NY Rangers**	**NHL**	**32**	**4**	**2**	**6**	**22**	**1**	**0**	**0**	**39**	**10.3**	**–4**	....	....	....	....	....	....	....	....	....	....	....	....
	St. Louis	**NHL**	**46**	**7**	**13**	**20**	**65**	**3**	**0**	**2**	**70**	**10.0**	**–4**	....	....	....	**11**	**0**	**2**	**2**	**8**	**0**	**0**	**0**	....
1996-97	**St. Louis**	**NHL**	**74**	**16**	**20**	**36**	**50**	**1**	**2**	**2**	**98**	**16.3**	**11**	....	....	....	**5**	**0**	**0**	**0**	**0**	**0**	**0**	**0**	....
1997-98	**San Jose**	**NHL**	**73**	**15**	**14**	**29**	**60**	**1**	**0**	**2**	**79**	**19.0**	**4**	....	....	....	**4**	**0**	**1**	**1**	**0**	**0**	**0**	**0**	....
1998-99	**San Jose**	**NHL**	**68**	**8**	**15**	**23**	**73**	**0**	**0**	**0**	**72**	**11.1**	**2**	**13**	**38.5**	**13:34**	**5**	**0**	**0**	**0**	**6**	**0**	**0**	**0**	**13:58**
99-2000	**San Jose**	**NHL**	**69**	**12**	**12**	**24**	**61**	**0**	**0**	**3**	**73**	**16.4**	**–3**	**8**	**50.0**	**11:52**	**10**	**0**	**2**	**2**	**8**	**0**	**0**	**0**	**13:16**
2000-01	**San Jose**	**NHL**	**80**	**13**	**19**	**32**	**32**	**1**	**0**	**3**	**81**	**16.0**	**5**	**61**	**37.7**	**10:55**	**6**	**1**	**3**	**4**	**0**	**0**	**0**	**0**	**13:10**
2001-02	**San Jose**	**NHL**	**55**	**7**	**4**	**11**	**15**	**1**	**1**	**0**	**43**	**16.3**	**4**	**12**	**50.0**	**9:09**	**10**	**1**	**2**	**3**	**2**	**0**	**0**	**0**	**7:23**
2002-03	**Florida**	**NHL**	**52**	**4**	**4**	**8**	**27**	**0**	**0**	**0**	**47**	**8.5**	**–9**	**19**	**36.8**	**10:46**	....	....	....	....	....	....	....	....	....
	San Antonio	AHL	3	0	0	0	4	....	....	....	....	....	....	....	....	....	....	....	....	....	....	....	....	....	....
	NHL Totals		**848**	**144**	**172**	**316**	**742**	**14**	**4**	**19**	**1021**	**14.1**		**113**	**39.8**	**11:21**	**109**	**12**	**22**	**34**	**80**	**2**	**1**	**2**	**11:28**

• Missed majority of 1991-92 season recovering from thigh injury suffered in game vs. Los Angeles, October 10, 1991. Traded to **Chicago** by **Calgary** for Trent Yawney, December 16, 1991. Traded to **NY Rangers** by **Chicago** with Brian Noonan for Tony Amonte and the rights to Matt Oates, March 21, 1994. Traded to **St. Louis** by **NY Rangers** for Ian Laperriere, December 28, 1995. Traded to **San Jose** by **St. Louis** for Darren Turcotte, July 24, 1997. Signed as a free agent by **Florida**, August 2, 2002.

MATTEUCCI, Mike

(ma-TEW-chee, MIGHK) **N.J.**

Defense. Shoots left. 6'3", 210 lbs. Born, Trail, B.C., December 27, 1971.

Season	Club	League	GP	G	A	Pts	PIM	PP	SH	GW	S	%	+/-	TF	F%	Min	GP	G	A	Pts	PIM	PP	SH	GW	Min
1991-92	Estevan Bruins	SJHL	STATISTICS NOT AVAILABLE																						
1992-93	Lake Superior	CCHA	19	1	3	4	16	....	....	....	....	....	....	....	....	....	....	....	....	....	....	....	....	....	....
1993-94	Lake Superior	CCHA	45	6	11	17	64	....	....	....	....	....	....	....	....	....	....	....	....	....	....	....	....	....	....
1994-95	Lake Superior	CCHA	38	3	11	14	52	....	....	....	....	....	....	....	....	....	....	....	....	....	....	....	....	....	....
1995-96	Lake Superior	CCHA	40	3	13	16	82	....	....	....	....	....	....	....	....	....	....	....	....	....	....	....	....	....	....
	Los Angeles	IHL	4	0	0	0	7	....	....	....	....	....	....	....	....	....	....	....	....	....	....	....	....	....	....
1996-97	Long Beach	IHL	81	4	4	8	254	....	....	....	....	....	....	....	....	....	18	0	1	1	42	....	....	....	....
1997-98	Long Beach	IHL	79	1	7	8	258	....	....	....	....	....	....	....	....	....	17	0	2	2	57	....	....	....	....
1998-99	Long Beach	IHL	79	3	9	12	253	....	....	....	....	....	....	....	....	....	8	0	1	1	12	....	....	....	....
99-2000	Long Beach	IHL	64	0	4	4	170	....	....	....	....	....	....	....	....	....	6	0	0	0	16	....	....	....	....
2000-01	**Minnesota**	**NHL**	**3**	**0**	**0**	**0**	**2**	**0**	**0**	**0**	**3**	**0.0**	**–2**	**1**	**100.0**	**11:29**	....	....	....	....	....	....	....	....	....
	Cleveland	IHL	69	0	7	7	189	....	....	....	....	....	....	....	....	....	4	0	0	0	15	....	....	....	....
2001-02	**Minnesota**	**NHL**	**3**	**0**	**0**	**0**	**2**	**0**	**0**	**0**	**0**	**0.0**	**1**	**0**	**0.0**	**10:06**	....	....	....	....	....	....	....	....	....
	Houston Aeros	AHL	69	3	10	13	128	....	....	....	....	....	....	....	....	....	14	1	1	2	33	....	....	....	....
2002-03	Albany River Rats	AHL	68	1	3	4	133	....	....	....	....	....	....	....	....	....	....	....	....	....	....	....	....	....	....
	NHL Totals		**6**	**0**	**0**	**0**	**4**	**0**	**0**	**0**	**3**	**0.0**		**1**	**100.0**	**10:48**	....	....	....	....	....	....	....	....	....

Signed as a free agent by **Edmonton**, September 10, 1998. Traded to **Boston** by **Edmonton** for Kay Whitmore, December 29, 1999. Signed as a free agent by **Minnesota**, July 20, 2000. Signed as a free agent by **New Jersey**, July 12, 2002.

MATVICHUK, Richard

(MAT-vih-chuhk, RIH-chahrd) **DAL.**

Defense. Shoots left. 6'2", 215 lbs. Born, Edmonton, Alta., February 5, 1973. Minnesota's 1st choice, 8th overall, in 1991 Entry Draft.

Season	Club	League	GP	G	A	Pts	PIM	PP	SH	GW	S	%	+/-	TF	F%	Min	GP	G	A	Pts	PIM	PP	SH	GW	Min
1988-89	Ft. Saskatchewan	AJHL	58	7	36	43	147	....	....	....	....	....	....	....	....	....	....	....	....	....	....	....	....	....	....
1989-90	Saskatoon Blades	WHL	56	8	24	32	126	....	....	....	....	....	....	....	....	....	10	2	8	10	16	....	....	....	....
1990-91	Saskatoon Blades	WHL	68	13	36	49	117	....	....	....	....	....	....	....	....	....	....	....	....	....	....	....	....	....	....
1991-92	Saskatoon Blades	WHL	58	14	40	54	126	....	....	....	....	....	....	....	....	....	22	1	9	10	61	....	....	....	....
1992-93	**Minnesota**	**NHL**	**53**	**2**	**3**	**5**	**26**	**1**	**0**	**0**	**51**	**3.9**	**–8**	....	....	....	....	....	....	....	....	....	....	....	....
	Kalamazoo Wings	IHL	3	0	1	1	6	....	....	....	....	....	....	....	....	....	....	....	....	....	....	....	....	....	....
1993-94	**Dallas**	**NHL**	**25**	**0**	**3**	**3**	**22**	**0**	**0**	**0**	**18**	**0.0**	**1**	....	....	....	**7**	**1**	**1**	**2**	**12**	**1**	**0**	**0**	....
	Kalamazoo Wings	IHL	43	8	17	25	84	....	....	....	....	....	....	....	....	....	....	....	....	....	....	....	....	....	....
1994-95	**Dallas**	**NHL**	**14**	**0**	**2**	**2**	**14**	**0**	**0**	**0**	**21**	**0.0**	**–7**	....	....	....	**5**	**0**	**2**	**2**	**4**	**0**	**0**	**0**	....
	Kalamazoo Wings	IHL	17	0	6	6	16	....	....	....	....	....	....	....	....	....	....	....	....	....	....	....	....	....	....
1995-96	**Dallas**	**NHL**	**73**	**6**	**16**	**22**	**71**	**0**	**0**	**1**	**81**	**7.4**	**4**	....	....	....	....	....	....	....	....	....	....	....	....
1996-97	**Dallas**	**NHL**	**57**	**5**	**7**	**12**	**87**	**0**	**2**	**0**	**83**	**6.0**	**1**	....	....	....	**7**	**0**	**1**	**1**	**20**	**0**	**0**	**0**	....
1997-98	**Dallas**	**NHL**	**74**	**3**	**15**	**18**	**63**	**0**	**0**	**0**	**71**	**4.2**	**7**	....	....	....	**16**	**1**	**1**	**2**	**14**	**0**	**0**	**0**	....
1998-99 •	**Dallas**	**NHL**	**64**	**3**	**9**	**12**	**51**	**1**	**0**	**0**	**54**	**5.6**	**23**	**0**	**0.0**	**21:19**	**22**	**1**	**5**	**6**	**20**	**0**	**0**	**0**	**22:40**
99-2000	**Dallas**	**NHL**	**70**	**4**	**21**	**25**	**42**	**0**	**0**	**1**	**73**	**5.5**	**7**	**0**	**0.0**	**24:27**	**23**	**2**	**5**	**7**	**14**	**0**	**0**	**0**	**25:51**
2000-01	**Dallas**	**NHL**	**78**	**4**	**16**	**20**	**62**	**2**	**0**	**1**	**85**	**4.7**	**5**	**1**	**100.0**	**22:53**	**10**	**0**	**0**	**0**	**14**	**0**	**0**	**0**	**22:43**
2001-02	**Dallas**	**NHL**	**82**	**9**	**12**	**21**	**52**	**4**	**0**	**2**	**109**	**8.3**	**11**	**1**	**0.0**	**23:47**	....	....	....	....	....	....	....	....	....
2002-03	**Dallas**	**NHL**	**68**	**1**	**5**	**6**	**58**	**0**	**0**	**1**	**59**	**1.7**	**1**	**3**	**0.0**	**19:23**	**12**	**0**	**3**	**3**	**8**	**0**	**0**	**0**	**19:55**
	NHL Totals		**658**	**37**	**109**	**146**	**548**	**8**	**2**	**6**	**705**	**5.2**		**5**	**20.0**	**22:28**	**102**	**5**	**18**	**23**	**106**	**1**	**0**	**0**	**23:17**

WHL East First All-Star Team (1992)

Transferred to **Dallas** after **Minnesota** franchise relocated, June 9, 1993.

MAY, Brad

(MAY, BRAD) **VAN.**

Left wing. Shoots left. 6'1", 217 lbs. Born, Toronto, Ont., November 29, 1971. Buffalo's 1st choice, 14th overall, in 1990 Entry Draft.

Season	Club	League	GP	G	A	Pts	PIM	PP	SH	GW	S	%	+/-	TF	F%	Min	GP	G	A	Pts	PIM	PP	SH	GW	Min
1987-88	Markham	OMHA	31	22	37	59	58	....	....	....	....	....	....	....	....	....	....	....	....	....	....	....	....	....	....
	Markham	MTJHL	6	1	1	2	21	....	....	....	....	....	....	....	....	....	....	....	....	....	....	....	....	....	....
1988-89	Niagara Falls	OHL	65	8	14	22	304	....	....	....	....	....	....	....	....	....	17	0	1	1	55	....	....	....	....
1989-90	Niagara Falls	OHL	61	32	58	90	223	....	....	....	....	....	....	....	....	....	16	9	13	22	64	....	....	....	....
1990-91	Niagara Falls	OHL	34	37	32	69	93	....	....	....	....	....	....	....	....	....	14	11	14	25	53	....	....	....	....
1991-92	**Buffalo**	**NHL**	**69**	**11**	**6**	**17**	**309**	**1**	**0**	**3**	**82**	**13.4**	**–12**	....	....	....	**7**	**1**	**4**	**5**	**2**	**0**	**0**	**1**	....
1992-93	**Buffalo**	**NHL**	**82**	**13**	**13**	**26**	**242**	**0**	**0**	**1**	**114**	**11.4**	**3**	....	....	....	**8**	**1**	**1**	**2**	**14**	**0**	**0**	**1**	....
1993-94	**Buffalo**	**NHL**	**84**	**18**	**27**	**45**	**171**	**3**	**0**	**3**	**166**	**10.8**	**–6**	....	....	....	**7**	**0**	**2**	**2**	**9**	**0**	**0**	**0**	....
1994-95	**Buffalo**	**NHL**	**33**	**3**	**3**	**6**	**87**	**1**	**0**	**0**	**42**	**7.1**	**5**	....	....	....	**4**	**0**	**0**	**0**	**2**	**0**	**0**	**0**	....
1995-96	**Buffalo**	**NHL**	**79**	**15**	**29**	**44**	**295**	**3**	**0**	**4**	**168**	**8.9**	**6**	....	....	....	....	....	....	....	....	....	....	....	....
1996-97	**Buffalo**	**NHL**	**42**	**3**	**4**	**7**	**106**	**1**	**0**	**1**	**75**	**4.0**	**–8**	....	....	....	**10**	**1**	**1**	**2**	**32**	**0**	**0**	**0**	....
1997-98	**Buffalo**	**NHL**	**36**	**4**	**7**	**11**	**113**	**0**	**0**	**0**	**41**	**9.8**	**2**	....	....	....	....	....	....	....	....	....	....	....	....
	Vancouver	**NHL**	**27**	**9**	**3**	**12**	**41**	**4**	**0**	**2**	**56**	**16.1**	**0**	....	....	....	....	....	....	....	....	....	....	....	....
1998-99	**Vancouver**	**NHL**	**66**	**6**	**11**	**17**	**102**	**1**	**0**	**1**	**91**	**6.6**	**–14**	**8**	**12.5**	**13:04**	....	....	....	....	....	....	....	....	....
99-2000	**Vancouver**	**NHL**	**59**	**9**	**7**	**16**	**90**	**0**	**0**	**3**	**66**	**13.6**	**–2**	**3**	**0.0**	**10:24**	....	....	....	....	....	....	....	....	....
2000-01	**Phoenix**	**NHL**	**62**	**11**	**14**	**25**	**107**	**0**	**0**	**0**	**83**	**13.3**	**10**	**3**	**33.3**	**11:11**	....	....	....	....	....	....	....	....	....
2001-02	**Phoenix**	**NHL**	**72**	**10**	**12**	**22**	**95**	**1**	**0**	**3**	**105**	**9.5**	**11**	**3**	**0.0**	**12:04**	**5**	**0**	**0**	**0**	**0**	**0**	**0**	**0**	**10:19**

			Regular Season														Playoffs								
Season	Club	League	GP	G	A	Pts	PIM	PP	SH	GW	S	%	+/-	TF	F%	Min	GP	G	A	Pts	PIM	PP	SH	GW	Min
2002-03	Phoenix	NHL	20	3	4	7	32	0	0	0	24	12.5	3	0	0.0	9:56	....	....	....	....	....	....	....	....	....
	Vancouver	NHL	3	0	0	0	10	0	0	0	1	0.0	1	0	0.0	7:48	14	0	0	0	15	0	0	0	7:24
	NHL Totals		734	115	140	255	1800	15	0	21	1114	10.3		17	11.8	11:34	55	3	8	11	74	0	0	2	8:11

OHL Second All-Star Team (1990, 1991)

• Missed majority of 1990-91 season recovering from knee injury suffered at Team Canada Juniors evaluation camp, August 21, 1990. Traded to **Vancouver** by **Buffalo** with Buffalo's 3rd round choice (later traded to Tampa Bay – Tampa Bay selected Jimmie Olvestad) in 1999 Entry Draft for Geoff Sanderson, February 4, 1998. Traded to **Phoenix** by **Vancouver** for future considerations, June 24, 2000. • Missed majority of 2002-03 season recovering from shoulder injury suffered in pre-season game vs. Vancouver, October 6, 2002. Traded to **Vancouver** by **Phoenix** for Phoenix's 3rd round choice (previously acquired, Phoenix selected Dimitri Pestunov) in 2003 Entry Draft, March 11, 2003.

MAYERS, Jamal
(MAI-uhrz, JUH-MAHL) **ST.L.**

Right wing. Shoots right. 6'1", 217 lbs. Born, Toronto, Ont., October 24, 1974. St. Louis' 3rd choice, 89th overall, in 1993 Entry Draft.

Season	Club	League	GP	G	A	Pts	PIM	PP	SH	GW	S	%	+/-	TF	F%	Min	GP	G	A	Pts	PIM	PP	SH	GW	Min
1990-91	Thornhill Rattlers	MTJHL	44	12	24	36	78	....	....	....	....	....	....	....	....	....	....	....	....	....	....	....	....	....	....
1991-92	Thornhill Rattlers	MTJHL	56	38	69	107	36	....	....	....	....	....	....	....	....	....	....	....	....	....	....	....	....	....	....
1992-93	West-Michigan	CCHA	38	8	17	25	26	....	....	....	....	....	....	....	....	....	....	....	....	....	....	....	....	....	....
1993-94	West-Michigan	CCHA	40	17	32	49	40	....	....	....	....	....	....	....	....	....	....	....	....	....	....	....	....	....	....
1994-95	West-Michigan	CCHA	39	13	32	45	40	....	....	....	....	....	....	....	....	....	....	....	....	....	....	....	....	....	....
1995-96	West-Michigan	CCHA	38	17	22	39	75	....	....	....	....	....	....	....	....	....	....	....	....	....	....	....	....	....	....
1996-97	St. Louis	NHL	6	0	1	1	2	0	0	0	7	0.0	–3	....	....	....	....	....	....	....	....	....	....	....	....
	Worcester IceCats	AHL	62	12	14	26	104	....	....	....	....	....	....	....	....	....	5	4	5	9	4	....	....	....	....
1997-98	Worcester IceCats	AHL	61	19	24	43	117	....	....	....	....	....	....	....	....	....	11	3	4	7	10	....	....	....	....
1998-99	St. Louis	NHL	34	4	5	9	40	0	0	0	48	8.3	–3	2	50.0	8:08	11	0	1	1	8	0	0	0	8:34
	Worcester IceCats	AHL	20	9	7	16	34	....	....	....	....	....	....	....	....	....	....	....	....	....	....	....	....	....	....
99-2000	St. Louis	NHL	79	7	10	17	90	0	0	0	99	7.1	0	77	52.0	9:46	7	0	4	4	2	0	0	0	10:42
2000-01	St. Louis	NHL	77	8	13	21	117	0	0	0	132	6.1	–3	273	51.3	11:04	15	2	3	5	8	0	0	0	11:28
2001-02	St. Louis	NHL	77	9	8	17	99	0	1	0	105	8.6	9	761	52.6	11:36	10	3	0	3	2	0	0	2	11:14
2002-03	St. Louis	NHL	15	2	5	7	8	0	0	0	26	7.7	1	111	51.4	14:21	....	....	....	....	....	....	....	....	....
	NHL Totals		288	30	42	72	356	0	1	0	417	7.2		1224	52.1	10:40	43	5	8	13	20	0	0	2	10:33

• Missed majority of 2002-03 season recovering from knee injury suffered in game vs. Calgary, November 16, 2002.

McALLISTER, Chris
(mih-KAL-ihs-tuhr, KRIHS) **COL.**

Defense. Shoots left. 6'8", 240 lbs. Born, Saskatoon, Sask., June 16, 1975. Vancouver's 1st choice, 40th overall, in 1995 Entry Draft.

Season	Club	League	GP	G	A	Pts	PIM	PP	SH	GW	S	%	+/-	TF	F%	Min	GP	G	A	Pts	PIM	PP	SH	GW	Min
1992-93	Saskatoon Royals	NSJHL	40	14	14	28	224	....	....	....	....	....	....	....	....	....	....	....	....	....	....	....	....	....	....
	Saskatoon Blades	WHL	4	0	0	0	2	....	....	....	....	....	....	....	....	....	....	....	....	....	....	....	....	....	....
1993-94	Humboldt	SJHL	50	3	5	8	150	....	....	....	....	....	....	....	....	....	....	....	....	....	....	....	....	....	....
	Saskatoon Blades	WHL	2	0	0	0	5	....	....	....	....	....	....	....	....	....	....	....	....	....	....	....	....	....	....
1994-95	Saskatoon Blades	WHL	65	2	8	10	134	....	....	....	....	....	....	....	....	....	10	0	0	0	28	....	....	....	....
1995-96	Syracuse Crunch	AHL	68	0	2	2	142	....	....	....	....	....	....	....	....	....	16	0	0	0	34	....	....	....	....
1996-97	Syracuse Crunch	AHL	43	3	1	4	108	....	....	....	....	....	....	....	....	....	3	0	0	0	6	....	....	....	....
1997-98	Vancouver	NHL	36	1	2	3	106	0	0	0	15	6.7	–12	....	....	....	....	....	....	....	....	....	....	....	....
	Syracuse Crunch	AHL	23	0	1	1	71	....	....	....	....	....	....	....	....	....	5	0	0	0	21	....	....	....	....
1998-99	Vancouver	NHL	28	1	1	2	63	0	0	0	6	16.7	–7	0	0.0	5:53	....	....	....	....	....	....	....	....	....
	Syracuse Crunch	AHL	5	0	0	0	24	....	....	....	....	....	....	....	....	....	....	....	....	....	....	....	....	....	....
	Toronto	NHL	20	0	2	2	39	0	0	0	12	0.0	4	0	0.0	13:59	6	0	1	1	4	0	0	0	12:60
99-2000	Toronto	NHL	36	0	3	3	68	0	0	0	12	0.0	–4	0	0.0	12:02	....	....	....	....	....	....	....	....	....
2000-01	Philadelphia	NHL	60	2	2	4	124	0	0	0	33	6.1	1	0	0.0	11:36	2	0	0	0	0	0	0	0	7:59
2001-02	Philadelphia	NHL	42	0	5	5	113	0	0	0	26	0.0	–7	0	0.0	9:12	....	....	....	....	....	....	....	....	....
2002-03	Philadelphia	NHL	19	0	0	0	21	0	0	0	9	0.0	–2	0	0.0	9:32	....	....	....	....	....	....	....	....	....
	Philadelphia	AHL	4	0	0	0	12	....	....	....	....	....	....	....	....	....	....	....	....	....	....	....	....	....	....
	Colorado	NHL	14	0	1	1	26	0	0	0	4	0.0	6	0	0.0	8:02	1	0	0	0	0	0	0	0	2:34
	NHL Totals		255	4	16	20	560	0	0	0	117	3.4		0	0.0	10:17	9	0	1	1	4	0	0	0	10:43

Traded to **Toronto** by **Vancouver** for Darby Hendrickson, February 16, 1999. Traded to **Philadelphia** by **Toronto** for the rights to Regan Kelly, September 26, 2000. Traded to **Colorado** by **Philadelphia** for Colorado's 6th round choice (Ville Hostikka) in 2003 Entry Draft, February 5, 2003.

McALPINE, Chris
(mih-KAL-pighn, KRIHS)

Defense. Shoots right. 6', 210 lbs. Born, Roseville, MN, December 1, 1971. New Jersey's 10th choice, 137th overall, in 1990 Entry Draft.

Season	Club	League	GP	G	A	Pts	PIM	PP	SH	GW	S	%	+/-	TF	F%	Min	GP	G	A	Pts	PIM	PP	SH	GW	Min
1989-90	Roseville High	Hi-School	25	15	13	28	....	....	....	....	....	....	....	....	....	....	....	....	....	....	....	....	....	....	....
1990-91	U. of Minnesota	WCHA	38	7	9	16	112	....	....	....	....	....	....	....	....	....	....	....	....	....	....	....	....	....	....
1991-92	U. of Minnesota	WCHA	39	3	9	12	126	....	....	....	....	....	....	....	....	....	....	....	....	....	....	....	....	....	....
1992-93	U. of Minnesota	WCHA	41	14	9	23	82	....	....	....	....	....	....	....	....	....	....	....	....	....	....	....	....	....	....
1993-94	U. of Minnesota	WCHA	36	12	18	30	121	....	....	....	....	....	....	....	....	....	....	....	....	....	....	....	....	....	....
1994-95	Albany River Rats	AHL	48	4	18	22	49	....	....	....	....	....	....	....	....	....	....	....	....	....	....	....	....	....	....
	♦ New Jersey	NHL	24	0	3	3	17	0	0	0	19	0.0	4	....	....	....	....	....	....	....	....	....	....	....	....
1995-96	Albany River Rats	AHL	57	5	14	19	72	....	....	....	....	....	....	....	....	....	4	0	0	0	13	....	....	....	....
1996-97	Albany River Rats	AHL	44	1	9	10	48	....	....	....	....	....	....	....	....	....	....	....	....	....	....	....	....	....	....
	St. Louis	NHL	15	0	0	0	24	0	0	0	3	0.0	–2	....	....	....	4	0	1	1	0	0	0	0	....
1997-98	St. Louis	NHL	54	3	7	10	36	0	0	0	35	8.6	14	....	....	....	10	0	0	0	16	0	0	0	....
1998-99	St. Louis	NHL	51	1	1	2	50	0	0	0	56	1.8	–10	0	0.0	12:51	13	0	0	0	2	0	0	0	6:34
99-2000	St. Louis	NHL	21	1	1	2	14	0	0	0	25	4.0	1	0	0.0	11:41	....	....	....	....	....	....	....	....	....
	Worcester IceCats	AHL	10	1	4	5	4	....	....	....	....	....	....	....	....	....	....	....	....	....	....	....	....	....	....
	Tampa Bay	NHL	10	1	1	2	10	0	0	0	5	20.0	–5	0	0.0	18:23	....	....	....	....	....	....	....	....	....
	Detroit Vipers	IHL	8	0	0	0	6	....	....	....	....	....	....	....	....	....	....	....	....	....	....	....	....	....	....
	Atlanta	NHL	3	0	0	0	2	0	0	0	4	0.0	–4	0	0.0	19:40	....	....	....	....	....	....	....	....	....
2000-01	Chicago	NHL	50	0	6	6	32	0	0	0	61	0.0	5	2	50.0	17:41	....	....	....	....	....	....	....	....	....
	Norfolk Admirals	AHL	13	4	7	11	6	....	....	....	....	....	....	....	....	....	....	....	....	....	....	....	....	....	....
2001-02	Chicago	NHL	40	0	3	3	36	0	0	0	40	0.0	8	0	0.0	15:22	1	0	0	0	0	0	0	0	8:38
	Norfolk Admirals	AHL	8	0	4	4	4	....	....	....	....	....	....	....	....	....	....	....	....	....	....	....	....	....	....
2002-03	Los Angeles	NHL	21	0	2	2	24	0	0	0	15	0.0	–4	0	0.0	12:42	....	....	....	....	....	....	....	....	....
	Manchester	AHL	3	0	0	0	0	....	....	....	....	....	....	....	....	....	....	....	....	....	....	....	....	....	....
	NHL Totals		289	6	24	30	245	0	0	0	263	2.3		2	50.0	14:50	28	0	1	1	18	0	0	0	6:43

WCHA First All-Star Team (1994) • NCAA West Second All-American Team (1994)

Traded to **St. Louis** by **New Jersey** with New Jersey's 9th round choice (James Desmarais) in 1999 Entry Draft for Peter Zezel, February 11, 1997. Traded to **Tampa Bay** by **St. Louis** with Rich Parent for Stephane Richer, January 13, 2000. Traded to **Atlanta** by **Tampa Bay** for Mikko Kuparinen, March 11, 2000. Signed as a free agent by **Chicago**, July 27, 2000. Signed as a free agent by **Los Angeles**, August 27, 2002. • Missed majority of 2002-03 season recovering from hernia injury suffered in game vs. San Jose, January 28, 2003.

McAMMOND, Dean
(MIHK-AM-uhnd, DEEN) **CGY.**

Left wing. Shoots left. 5'11", 193 lbs. Born, Grand Cache, Alta., June 15, 1973. Chicago's 1st choice, 22nd overall, in 1991 Entry Draft.

Season	Club	League	GP	G	A	Pts	PIM	PP	SH	GW	S	%	+/-	TF	F%	Min	GP	G	A	Pts	PIM	PP	SH	GW	Min
1988-89	St. Albert Raiders	AMHL	36	33	44	77	132	....	....	....	....	....	....	....	....	....	....	....	....	....	....	....	....	....	....
1989-90	Prince Albert	WHL	53	11	11	22	49	....	....	....	....	....	....	....	....	....	14	2	3	5	18	....	....	....	....
1990-91	Prince Albert	WHL	71	33	35	68	108	....	....	....	....	....	....	....	....	....	2	0	1	1	6	....	....	....	....
1991-92	Prince Albert	WHL	63	37	54	91	189	....	....	....	....	....	....	....	....	....	10	12	11	23	26	....	....	....	....
	Chicago	NHL	5	0	2	2	0	0	0	0	4	0.0	–2	....	....	....	3	0	0	0	2	0	0	0	....
1992-93	Prince Albert	WHL	30	19	29	48	44	....	....	....	....	....	....	....	....	....	....	....	....	....	....	....	....	....	....
	Swift Current	WHL	18	10	13	23	24	....	....	....	....	....	....	....	....	....	17	*16	19	35	20	....	....	....	....
1993-94	Edmonton	NHL	45	6	21	27	16	2	0	0	52	11.5	12	....	....	....	....	....	....	....	....	....	....	....	....
	Cape Breton	AHL	28	9	12	21	38	....	....	....	....	....	....	....	....	....	....	....	....	....	....	....	....	....	....
1994-95	Edmonton	NHL	6	0	0	0	0	0	0	0	3	0.0	–1	....	....	....	....	....	....	....	....	....	....	....	....
1995-96	Edmonton	NHL	53	15	15	30	23	4	0	0	79	19.0	6	....	....	....	....	....	....	....	....	....	....	....	....
	Cape Breton	AHL	22	9	15	24	55	....	....	....	....	....	....	....	....	....	....	....	....	....	....	....	....	....	....
1996-97	Edmonton	NHL	57	12	17	29	28	4	0	6	106	11.3	–15	....	....	....	....	....	....	....	....	....	....	....	....
1997-98	Edmonton	NHL	77	19	31	50	46	8	0	3	128	14.8	9	....	....	....	12	1	4	5	12	0	0	0	....
1998-99	Edmonton	NHL	65	9	16	25	36	1	0	0	122	7.4	5	26	38.5	14:15	....	....	....	....	....	....	....	....	....
	Chicago	NHL	12	1	4	5	2	0	0	1	16	6.3	3	37	48.6	15:43	....	....	....	....	....	....	....	....	....
99-2000	Chicago	NHL	76	14	18	32	72	1	0	1	118	11.9	11	257	39.7	16:25	....	....	....	....	....	....	....	....	....
2000-01	Chicago	NHL	61	10	16	26	43	1	0	1	95	10.5	4	23	43.5	15:30	....	....	....	....	....	....	....	....	....
	Philadelphia	NHL	10	1	1	2	0	1	0	0	17	5.9	–1	65	46.2	11:60	4	0	0	0	2	0	0	0	9:25

			Regular Season														Playoffs								
Season	Club	League	GP	G	A	Pts	PIM	PP	SH	GW	S	%	+/-	TF	F%	Min	GP	G	A	Pts	PIM	PP	SH	GW	Min
2001-02	**Calgary**	**NHL**	**73**	**21**	**30**	**51**	**60**	**7**	**0**	**4**	**152**	**13.8**	**2**	**143**	**55.2**	**18:56**	....	....	....	....	....	....	....	....	....
2002-03	**Colorado**	**NHL**	**41**	**10**	**8**	**18**	**10**	**2**	**0**	**2**	**72**	**13.9**	**1**	**9**	**55.6**	**14:24**	....	....	....	....	....	....	....	....	....
	NHL Totals		**581**	**118**	**179**	**297**	**336**	**31**	**0**	**18**	**964**	**12.2**		**560**	**45.4**	**15:59**	**19**	**1**	**4**	**5**	**16**	**0**	**0**	**0**	**9:25**

Traded to **Edmonton** by **Chicago** with Igor Kravchuk for Joe Murphy, February 24, 1993. Traded to **Chicago** by **Edmonton** with Boris Mironov and Jonas Elofsson for Chad Kilger, Daniel Cleary, Ethan Moreau and Christian Laflamme, March 20, 1999. Traded to **Philadelphia** by **Chicago** for Philadelphia's 3rd round choice (later traded to Toronto – Toronto selected Nicolas Corbeil) in 2001 Entry Draft, March 13, 2001. Traded to **Calgary** by **Philadelphia** for Calgary's 4th round choice (Rosario Ruggeri) in 2002 Entry Draft, June 24, 2001. Traded to **Colorado** by **Calgary** with Derek Morris and Jeff Shantz for Chris Drury and Stephane Yelle, October 1, 2002. Traded to **Calgary** by **Colorado** for Calgary's 5th round choice (Mark McCutcheon) in 2003 Entry Draft, March 11, 2003. • Ruled ineligible to play remainder of 2002-03 season by NHL due to transaction violation by Calgary, March 15, 2003.

McCABE, Bryan
(mih-KAYB, BRIGH-uhn) **TOR.**

Defense. Shoots left. 6'2", 220 lbs. Born, St. Catharines, Ont., June 8, 1975. NY Islanders' 2nd choice, 40th overall, in 1993 Entry Draft.

Season	Club	League	GP	G	A	Pts	PIM	PP	SH	GW	S	%	+/-	TF	F%	Min	GP	G	A	Pts	PIM	PP	SH	GW	Min
1990-91	Calgary Canucks	AMHL	33	14	34	48	55	....	....	....	....	....	....	....	....	....	....	....	....	....	....	....	....	....	....
1991-92	Medicine Hat	WHL	68	6	24	30	157	....	....	....	....	....	....	....	....	....	4	0	0	0	6	....	....	....	....
1992-93	Medicine Hat	WHL	14	0	13	13	83	....	....	....	....	....	....	....	....	....	....	....	....	....	....	....	....	....	....
	Spokane Chiefs	WHL	46	3	44	47	134	....	....	....	....	....	....	....	....	....	6	1	5	6	28	....	....	....	....
1993-94	Spokane Chiefs	WHL	64	22	62	84	218	....	....	....	....	....	....	....	....	....	3	0	4	4	4	....	....	....	....
1994-95	Spokane Chiefs	WHL	42	14	39	53	115	....	....	....	....	....	....	....	....	....	....	....	....	....	....	....	....	....	....
	Brandon	WHL	20	6	10	16	38	....	....	....	....	....	....	....	....	....	18	4	13	17	59	....	....	....	....
1995-96	**NY Islanders**	**NHL**	**82**	**7**	**16**	**23**	**156**	**3**	**0**	**1**	**130**	**5.4**	**–24**	....	....	....	....	....	....	....	....	....	....	....	....
1996-97	**NY Islanders**	**NHL**	**82**	**8**	**20**	**28**	**165**	**2**	**1**	**2**	**117**	**6.8**	**–2**	....	....	....	....	....	....	....	....	....	....	....	....
1997-98	**NY Islanders**	**NHL**	**56**	**3**	**9**	**12**	**145**	**1**	**0**	**0**	**81**	**3.7**	**9**	....	....	....	....	....	....	....	....	....	....	....	....
	Vancouver	**NHL**	**26**	**1**	**11**	**12**	**64**	**0**	**1**	**0**	**42**	**2.4**	**10**	....	....	....	....	....	....	....	....	....	....	....	....
1998-99	**Vancouver**	**NHL**	**69**	**7**	**14**	**21**	**120**	**1**	**2**	**0**	**98**	**7.1**	**–11**	**1**	**0.0**	**24:13**	....	....	....	....	....	....	....	....	....
99-2000	**Chicago**	**NHL**	**79**	**6**	**19**	**25**	**139**	**2**	**0**	**2**	**119**	**5.0**	**–8**	**1**	**0.0**	**23:23**	....	....	....	....	....	....	....	....	....
2000-01	**Toronto**	**NHL**	**82**	**5**	**24**	**29**	**123**	**3**	**0**	**2**	**159**	**3.1**	**16**	**0**	**0.0**	**23:49**	**11**	**2**	**3**	**5**	**16**	**1**	**0**	**0**	**23:56**
2001-02	**Toronto**	**NHL**	**82**	**17**	**26**	**43**	**129**	**8**	**0**	**1**	**157**	**10.8**	**16**	**1**	**0.0**	**24:34**	**20**	**5**	**5**	**10**	**30**	**3**	**0**	**1**	**29:33**
2002-03	**Toronto**	**NHL**	**75**	**6**	**18**	**24**	**135**	**3**	**0**	**1**	**149**	**4.0**	**9**	**1**	**0.0**	**23:39**	**7**	**0**	**3**	**3**	**10**	**0**	**0**	**0**	**27:28**
	NHL Totals		**633**	**60**	**157**	**217**	**1176**	**23**	**4**	**9**	**1052**	**5.7**		**4**	**0.0**	**23:56**	**38**	**7**	**11**	**18**	**56**	**4**	**0**	**1**	**27:32**

WHL West Second All-Star Team (1993) • WHL West First All-Star Team (1994) • WHL East First All-Star Team (1995) • Memorial Cup All-Star Team (1995)

Traded to **Vancouver** by **NY Islanders** with Todd Bertuzzi and NY Islanders' 3rd round choice (Jarkko Ruutu) in 1998 Entry Draft for Trevor Linden, February 6, 1998. Traded to **Chicago** by **Vancouver** with Vancouver's 1st round choice (Pavel Vorobiev) in 2000 Entry Draft for Chicago's 1st round choice (later traded to Tampa Bay – later traded to NY Rangers – NY Rangers selected Pavel Brendl) in 1999 Entry Draft, June 25, 1999. Traded to **Toronto** by **Chicago** for Alexander Karpovtsev and Toronto's 4th round choice (Vladimir Gusev) in 2001 Entry Draft, October 2, 2000.

McCARTHY, Sandy
(mih-KAHR-thee, SAN-dee) **BOS.**

Right wing. Shoots right. 6'3", 222 lbs. Born, Toronto, Ont., June 15, 1972. Calgary's 3rd choice, 52nd overall, in 1991 Entry Draft.

Season	Club	League	GP	G	A	Pts	PIM	PP	SH	GW	S	%	+/-	TF	F%	Min	GP	G	A	Pts	PIM	PP	SH	GW	Min
1987-88	Midland	OJHL-C	18	2	1	3	70	....	....	....	....	....	....	....	....	....	....	....	....	....	....	....	....	....	....
1988-89	Hawkesbury	OCJHL	42	4	11	15	139	....	....	....	....	....	....	....	....	....	....	....	....	....	....	....	....	....	....
1989-90	Laval Titan	QMJHL	65	10	11	21	269	....	....	....	....	....	....	....	....	....	14	3	3	6	60	....	....	....	....
1990-91	Laval Titan	QMJHL	68	21	19	40	297	....	....	....	....	....	....	....	....	....	13	6	5	11	67	....	....	....	....
1991-92	Laval Titan	QMJHL	62	39	51	90	326	....	....	....	....	....	....	....	....	....	8	4	5	9	81	....	....	....	....
1992-93	Salt Lake	IHL	77	18	20	38	220	....	....	....	....	....	....	....	....	....	....	....	....	....	....	....	....	....	....
1993-94	**Calgary**	**NHL**	**79**	**5**	**5**	**10**	**173**	**0**	**0**	**0**	**39**	**12.8**	**–3**	....	....	....	**7**	**0**	**0**	**0**	**34**	**0**	**0**	**0**	....
1994-95	**Calgary**	**NHL**	**37**	**5**	**3**	**8**	**101**	**0**	**0**	**2**	**29**	**17.2**	**1**	....	....	....	**6**	**0**	**1**	**1**	**17**	**0**	**0**	**0**	....
1995-96	**Calgary**	**NHL**	**75**	**9**	**7**	**16**	**173**	**3**	**0**	**1**	**98**	**9.2**	**–8**	....	....	....	**4**	**0**	**0**	**0**	**10**	**0**	**0**	**0**	....
1996-97	**Calgary**	**NHL**	**33**	**3**	**5**	**8**	**113**	**1**	**0**	**1**	**38**	**7.9**	**–8**	....	....	....	....	....	....	....	....	....	....	....	....
1997-98	**Calgary**	**NHL**	**52**	**8**	**5**	**13**	**170**	**1**	**0**	**1**	**68**	**11.8**	**–18**	....	....	....	....	....	....	....	....	....	....	....	....
	Tampa Bay	**NHL**	**14**	**0**	**5**	**5**	**71**	**0**	**0**	**0**	**26**	**0.0**	**–1**	....	....	....	....	....	....	....	....	....	....	....	....
1998-99	**Tampa Bay**	**NHL**	**67**	**5**	**7**	**12**	**135**	**1**	**0**	**0**	**89**	**5.6**	**–22**	**0**	**0.0**	**11:02**	....	....	....	....	....	....	....	....	....
	Philadelphia	**NHL**	**13**	**0**	**1**	**1**	**25**	**0**	**0**	**0**	**18**	**0.0**	**–2**	**2**	**50.0**	**11:09**	**6**	**0**	**1**	**1**	**0**	**0**	**0**	**0**	**6:33**
99-2000	**Philadelphia**	**NHL**	**58**	**6**	**5**	**11**	**111**	**1**	**0**	**0**	**68**	**8.8**	**–5**	**4**	**0.0**	**10:27**	....	....	....	....	....	....	....	....	....
	Carolina	**NHL**	**13**	**0**	**0**	**0**	**9**	**1**	**0**	**0**	**12**	**0.0**	**2**	**0**	**0.0**	**7:24**	....	....	....	....	....	....	....	....	....
2000-01	**NY Rangers**	**NHL**	**81**	**11**	**10**	**21**	**171**	**0**	**0**	**2**	**95**	**11.6**	**3**	**4**	**0.0**	**10:25**	....	....	....	....	....	....	....	....	....
2001-02	**NY Rangers**	**NHL**	**82**	**10**	**13**	**23**	**171**	**1**	**0**	**3**	**90**	**11.1**	**–8**	**6**	**50.0**	**8:29**	....	....	....	....	....	....	....	....	....
2002-03	**NY Rangers**	**NHL**	**82**	**6**	**9**	**15**	**81**	**0**	**0**	**1**	**81**	**7.4**	**–4**	**11**	**9.1**	**7:26**	....	....	....	....	....	....	....	....	....
	NHL Totals		**686**	**68**	**75**	**143**	**1504**	**8**	**0**	**11**	**751**	**9.1**		**27**	**18.5**	**9:26**	**23**	**0**	**2**	**2**	**61**	**0**	**0**	**0**	**6:33**

Traded to **Tampa Bay** by **Calgary** with Calgary's 3rd (Brad Richards) and 5th (Curtis Rich) round choices in 1998 Entry Draft for Jason Wiemer, March 24, 1998. Traded to **Philadelphia** by **Tampa Bay** with Mikael Andersson for Colin Forbes and Philadelphia's 4th round choice (Michal Lanicek) in 1999 Entry Draft, March 20, 1999. Traded to **Carolina** by **Philadelphia** for Kent Manderville, March 14, 2000. Traded to **NY Rangers** by **Carolina** with Carolina's' 4th round choice (Bryce Lampman) in 2001 Entry Draft for Darren Langdon and Rob DiMaio, August 4, 2000. Signed as a free agent by **Boston**, August 12, 2003.

McCARTHY, Steve
(mih-KAHR-thee, STEEV) **CHI.**

Defense. Shoots left. 6'1", 197 lbs. Born, Trail, B.C., February 3, 1981. Chicago's 1st choice, 23rd overall, in 1999 Entry Draft.

Season	Club	League	GP	G	A	Pts	PIM	PP	SH	GW	S	%	+/-	TF	F%	Min	GP	G	A	Pts	PIM	PP	SH	GW	Min
1996-97	Trail Smokies	BCHL	57	25	52	77	81	....	....	....	....	....	....	....	....	....	....	....	....	....	....	....	....	....	....
	Edmonton Ice	WHL	2	0	0	0	0	....	....	....	....	....	....	....	....	....	....	....	....	....	....	....	....	....	....
1997-98	Edmonton Ice	WHL	58	11	29	40	59	....	....	....	....	....	....	....	....	....	....	....	....	....	....	....	....	....	....
1998-99	Kootenay Ice	WHL	57	19	33	52	79	....	....	....	....	....	....	....	....	....	6	0	5	5	8	....	....	....	....
99-2000	**Chicago**	**NHL**	**5**	**1**	**1**	**2**	**4**	**1**	**0**	**0**	**4**	**25.0**	**0**	**0**	**0.0**	**15:09**	....	....	....	....	....	....	....	....	....
	Kootenay Ice	WHL	37	13	23	36	36	....	....	....	....	....	....	....	....	....	....	....	....	....	....	....	....	....	....
2000-01	**Chicago**	**NHL**	**44**	**0**	**5**	**5**	**8**	**0**	**0**	**0**	**32**	**0.0**	**–7**	**0**	**0.0**	**14:47**	....	....	....	....	....	....	....	....	....
	Norfolk Admirals	AHL	7	0	4	4	2	....	....	....	....	....	....	....	....	....	....	....	....	....	....	....	....	....	....
2001-02	**Chicago**	**NHL**	**3**	**0**	**0**	**0**	**2**	**0**	**0**	**0**	**2**	**0.0**	**–1**	**0**	**0.0**	**11:48**	....	....	....	....	....	....	....	....	....
	Norfolk Admirals	AHL	77	7	21	28	37	....	....	....	....	....	....	....	....	....	2	0	3	3	2	....	....	....	....
2002-03	**Chicago**	**NHL**	**57**	**1**	**4**	**5**	**23**	**0**	**0**	**0**	**55**	**1.8**	**–1**	**0**	**0.0**	**16:25**	....	....	....	....	....	....	....	....	....
	Norfolk Admirals	AHL	19	1	6	7	14	....	....	....	....	....	....	....	....	....	9	0	4	4	0	....	....	....	....
	NHL Totals		**109**	**2**	**10**	**12**	**37**	**1**	**0**	**0**	**93**	**2.2**		**0**	**0.0**	**15:34**	....	....	....	....	....	....	....	....	....

McCARTY, Darren
(mih-KAHR-tee, DAIR-ehn) **DET.**

Right wing. Shoots right. 6'1", 210 lbs. Born, Burnaby, B.C., April 1, 1972. Detroit's 2nd choice, 46th overall, in 1992 Entry Draft.

Season	Club	League	GP	G	A	Pts	PIM	PP	SH	GW	S	%	+/-	TF	F%	Min	GP	G	A	Pts	PIM	PP	SH	GW	Min
1988-89	Peterboro B's	OJHL-B	34	18	17	35	135	....	....	....	....	....	....	....	....	....	....	....	....	....	....	....	....	....	....
1989-90	Belleville Bulls	OHL	63	12	15	27	142	....	....	....	....	....	....	....	....	....	11	1	1	2	21	....	....	....	....
1990-91	Belleville Bulls	OHL	60	30	37	67	151	....	....	....	....	....	....	....	....	....	6	2	2	4	13	....	....	....	....
1991-92	Belleville Bulls	OHL	65	*55	72	127	177	....	....	....	....	....	....	....	....	....	5	1	4	5	13	....	....	....	....
1992-93	Adirondack	AHL	73	17	19	36	278	....	....	....	....	....	....	....	....	....	11	0	1	1	33	....	....	....	....
1993-94	**Detroit**	**NHL**	**67**	**9**	**17**	**26**	**181**	**0**	**0**	**2**	**81**	**11.1**	**12**	....	....	....	**7**	**2**	**2**	**4**	**8**	**0**	**0**	**0**	....
1994-95	**Detroit**	**NHL**	**31**	**5**	**8**	**13**	**88**	**1**	**0**	**2**	**27**	**18.5**	**5**	....	....	....	**18**	**3**	**2**	**5**	**14**	**0**	**0**	**0**	....
1995-96	**Detroit**	**NHL**	**63**	**15**	**14**	**29**	**158**	**8**	**0**	**1**	**102**	**14.7**	**14**	....	....	....	**19**	**3**	**2**	**5**	**20**	**0**	**0**	**1**	....
1996-97♦	**Detroit**	**NHL**	**68**	**19**	**30**	**49**	**126**	**5**	**0**	**6**	**171**	**11.1**	**14**	....	....	....	**20**	**3**	**4**	**7**	**34**	**0**	**0**	**2**	....
1997-98♦	**Detroit**	**NHL**	**71**	**15**	**22**	**37**	**157**	**5**	**1**	**2**	**166**	**9.0**	**0**	....	....	....	**22**	**3**	**8**	**11**	**34**	**0**	**0**	**1**	....
1998-99	**Detroit**	**NHL**	**69**	**14**	**26**	**40**	**108**	**6**	**0**	**1**	**140**	**10.0**	**10**	**15**	**33.3**	**17:04**	**10**	**1**	**1**	**2**	**23**	**0**	**0**	**0**	**13:04**
99-2000	**Detroit**	**NHL**	**24**	**6**	**6**	**12**	**48**	**0**	**0**	**1**	**40**	**15.0**	**1**	**1**	**0.0**	**13:40**	**9**	**0**	**1**	**1**	**12**	**0**	**0**	**0**	**14:09**
2000-01	**Detroit**	**NHL**	**72**	**12**	**10**	**22**	**123**	**1**	**1**	**3**	**118**	**10.2**	**–5**	**26**	**53.9**	**13:26**	**6**	**1**	**0**	**1**	**2**	**0**	**0**	**0**	**13:11**
2001-02♦	**Detroit**	**NHL**	**62**	**5**	**7**	**12**	**98**	**0**	**0**	**1**	**74**	**6.8**	**2**	**26**	**38.5**	**11:47**	**23**	**4**	**4**	**8**	**34**	**0**	**0**	**1**	**13:33**
2002-03	**Detroit**	**NHL**	**73**	**13**	**9**	**22**	**138**	**1**	**0**	**2**	**129**	**10.1**	**10**	**320**	**57.8**	**13:18**	**4**	**0**	**0**	**0**	**6**	**0**	**0**	**0**	**15:45**
	NHL Totals		**600**	**113**	**149**	**262**	**1225**	**27**	**2**	**21**	**1048**	**10.8**		**388**	**55.2**	**13:55**	**138**	**20**	**24**	**44**	**187**	**0**	**0**	**5**	**13:41**

OHL First All-Star Team (1992)

• Missed majority of 1999-2000 season recovering from hernia injury suffered in game vs. Dallas, November 10, 1999.

			Regular Season														Playoffs								
Season	Club	League	GP	G	A	Pts	PIM	PP	SH	GW	S	%	+/-	TF	F%	Min	GP	G	A	Pts	PIM	PP	SH	GW	Min

McCAULEY, Alyn

(mih-KAW-lee, AL-ihn) **S.J.**

Center. Shoots left. 5'11", 190 lbs. Born, Brockville, Ont., May 29, 1977. New Jersey's 5th choice, 79th overall, in 1995 Entry Draft.

Season	Club	League	GP	G	A	Pts	PIM	PP	SH	GW	S	%	+/-	TF	F%	Min	GP	G	A	Pts	PIM	PP	SH	GW	Min
1991-92	Kingston	OCJHL	37	5	17	22	6	....	....	....	....	....	....	....	....	....	....	....	....	....	....	....	....	....	....
1992-93	Kingston	OCJHL	38	31	29	60	18	....	....	....	....	....	....	....	....	....	....	....	....	....	....	....	....	....	....
1993-94	Ottawa 67's	OHL	38	13	23	36	10	....	....	....	....	....	....	....	....	....	13	5	14	19	4	....	....	....	....
1994-95	Ottawa 67's	OHL	65	16	38	54	20	....	....	....	....	....	....	....	....	....	....	....	....	....	....	....	....	....	....
1995-96	Ottawa 67's	OHL	55	34	48	82	24	....	....	....	....	....	....	....	....	....	2	0	0	0	0	....	....	....	....
1996-97	Ottawa 67's	OHL	50	*56	56	112	16	....	....	....	....	....	....	....	....	....	22	14	22	36	14	....	....	....	....
	St. John's	AHL	....	....	....	....	....	....	....	....	....	....	....	....	....	....	3	0	1	1	0	....	....	....	....
1997-98	**Toronto**	**NHL**	**60**	**6**	**10**	**16**	**6**	**0**	**0**	**1**	**77**	**7.8**	**–7**	....	....	....	....	....	....	....	....	....	....	....	....
1998-99	**Toronto**	**NHL**	**39**	**9**	**15**	**24**	**2**	**1**	**0**	**1**	**76**	**11.8**	**7**	**591**	**46.4**	**15:10**	....	....	....	....	....	....	....	....	....
99-2000	**Toronto**	**NHL**	**45**	**5**	**5**	**10**	**10**	**1**	**0**	**0**	**41**	**12.2**	**–6**	**450**	**47.8**	**10:46**	**5**	**0**	**0**	**0**	**6**	**0**	**0**	**0**	**7:51**
	St. John's	AHL	5	1	1	2	0	....	....	....	....	....	....	....	....	....	....	....	....	....	....	....	....	....	....
2000-01	**Toronto**	**NHL**	**14**	**1**	**0**	**1**	**0**	**0**	**0**	**0**	**13**	**7.7**	**0**	**139**	**46.8**	**10:28**	**10**	**0**	**0**	**0**	**2**	**0**	**0**	**0**	**9:34**
	St. John's	AHL	47	16	28	44	12	....	....	....	....	....	....	....	....	....	....	....	....	....	....	....	....	....	....
2001-02	**Toronto**	**NHL**	**82**	**6**	**10**	**16**	**18**	**0**	**1**	**1**	**95**	**6.3**	**10**	**951**	**48.1**	**11:24**	**20**	**5**	**10**	**15**	**4**	**1**	**0**	**2**	**19:12**
2002-03	**Toronto**	**NHL**	**64**	**6**	**9**	**15**	**16**	**0**	**0**	**0**	**79**	**7.6**	**3**	**515**	**44.5**	**12:54**	....	....	....	....	....	....	....	....	....
	San Jose	**NHL**	**16**	**3**	**7**	**10**	**4**	**3**	**0**	**0**	**29**	**10.3**	**–2**	**81**	**50.6**	**17:29**	....	....	....	....	....	....	....	....	....
	NHL Totals		**320**	**36**	**56**	**92**	**56**	**5**	**1**	**3**	**410**	**8.8**		**2727**	**47.0**	**12:33**	**35**	**5**	**10**	**15**	**12**	**1**	**0**	**2**	**14:49**

OHL First All-Star Team (1996, 1997) • OHL MVP (1996, 1997) • Canadian Major Junior First All-Star Team (1997) • Canadian Major Junior Player of the Year (1997)

Rights traded to **Toronto** by **New Jersey** with Jason Smith and Steve Sullivan for Doug Gilmour, Dave Ellett and New Jersey's 3rd round choice (previously acquired, New Jersey selected Andre Lakos) in 1999 Entry Draft, February 25, 1997. Traded to **San Jose** by **Toronto** with Brad Boyes and Toronto's 1st round choice (later traded to Boston – Boston selected Mark Stuart) in 2003 Entry Draft for Owen Nolan, March 5, 2003.

McDONALD, Andy

(mihk-DAW-nuhld, AN-dee) **ANA.**

Center. Shoots left. 5'10", 186 lbs. Born, Strathroy, Ont., August 25, 1977.

Season	Club	League	GP	G	A	Pts	PIM	PP	SH	GW	S	%	+/-	TF	F%	Min	GP	G	A	Pts	PIM	PP	SH	GW	Min
1993-94	Strathroy Rockets	OJHL-B	7	2	2	4	0	....	....	....	....	....	....	....	....	....	....	....	....	....	....	....	....	....	....
1994-95	Strathroy Rockets	OJHL-B	50	32	41	73	24	....	....	....	....	....	....	....	....	....	....	....	....	....	....	....	....	....	....
1995-96	Strathroy Rockets	OJHL-B	52	31	56	87	103	....	....	....	....	....	....	....	....	....	....	....	....	....	....	....	....	....	....
1996-97	Colgate	ECAC	33	9	10	19	16	....	....	....	....	....	....	....	....	....	....	....	....	....	....	....	....	....	....
1997-98	Colgate	ECAC	35	13	19	32	26	....	....	....	....	....	....	....	....	....	....	....	....	....	....	....	....	....	....
1998-99	Colgate	ECAC	35	20	26	46	42	....	....	....	....	....	....	....	....	....	....	....	....	....	....	....	....	....	....
99-2000	Colgate	ECAC	34	25	*33	*58	49	....	....	....	....	....	....	....	....	....	....	....	....	....	....	....	....	....	....
2000-01	**Anaheim**	**NHL**	**16**	**1**	**0**	**1**	**6**	**0**	**0**	**0**	**21**	**4.8**	**0**	**139**	**48.9**	**11:11**	....	....	....	....	....	....	....	....	....
	Cincinnati	AHL	46	15	25	40	21	....	....	....	....	....	....	....	....	....	3	0	1	1	2	....	....	....	....
2001-02	**Anaheim**	**NHL**	**53**	**7**	**21**	**28**	**10**	**2**	**0**	**3**	**79**	**8.9**	**2**	**818**	**53.7**	**15:59**	....	....	....	....	....	....	....	....	....
	Cincinnati	AHL	21	7	25	32	6	....	....	....	....	....	....	....	....	....	....	....	....	....	....	....	....	....	....
2002-03	**Anaheim**	**NHL**	**46**	**10**	**11**	**21**	**14**	**3**	**0**	**1**	**92**	**10.9**	**–1**	**604**	**56.0**	**18:31**	....	....	....	....	....	....	....	....	....
	NHL Totals		**115**	**18**	**32**	**50**	**30**	**5**	**0**	**4**	**192**	**9.4**		**1561**	**54.1**	**16:20**	....	....	....	....	....	....	....	....	....

OJHL-B Player of the Year (1996) • ECAC Second All-Star Team (1999) • ECAC First All-Star Team (2000) • NCAA East First All-American Team (2000)

Signed as a free agent by **Anaheim**, April 3, 2000.

McDONELL, Kent

(MAHK-dah-NEHL, KEHNT) **CBJ**

Right wing. Shoots right. 6'2", 205 lbs. Born, Williamstown, Ont., March 1, 1979. Detroit's 3rd choice, 181st overall, in 1999 Entry Draft.

Season	Club	League	GP	G	A	Pts	PIM	PP	SH	GW	S	%	+/-	TF	F%	Min	GP	G	A	Pts	PIM	PP	SH	GW	Min
1995-96	Cornwall Colts	OCJHL	33	21	14	35	64	....	....	....	....	....	....	....	....	....	....	....	....	....	....	....	....	....	....
1996-97	Guelph Storm	OHL	56	7	5	12	57	....	....	....	....	....	....	....	....	....	16	0	2	2	4	....	....	....	....
1997-98	Guelph Storm	OHL	64	28	23	51	76	....	....	....	....	....	....	....	....	....	12	7	4	11	18	....	....	....	....
1998-99	Guelph Storm	OHL	60	31	38	69	110	....	....	....	....	....	....	....	....	....	11	4	3	7	36	....	....	....	....
99-2000	Guelph Storm	OHL	56	35	35	70	100	....	....	....	....	....	....	....	....	....	6	1	4	5	6	....	....	....	....
2000-01	Dayton Bombers	ECHL	28	16	9	25	94	....	....	....	....	....	....	....	....	....	3	0	0	0	4	....	....	....	....
	Syracuse Crunch	AHL	32	3	3	6	36	....	....	....	....	....	....	....	....	....	3	1	0	1	0	....	....	....	....
2001-02	Syracuse Crunch	AHL	72	18	13	31	122	....	....	....	....	....	....	....	....	....	3	0	2	2	0	....	....	....	....
2002-03	**Columbus**	**NHL**	**3**	**0**	**0**	**0**	**0**	**0**	**0**	**0**	**4**	**0.0**	**–1**	**0**	**0.0**	**8:40**	....	....	....	....	....	....	....	....	....
	Syracuse Crunch	AHL	72	14	24	38	93	....	....	....	....	....	....	....	....	....	....	....	....	....	....	....	....	....	....
	NHL Totals		**3**	**0**	**0**	**0**	**0**	**0**	**0**	**0**	**4**	**0.0**		**0**	**0.0**	**8:40**	....	....	....	....	....	....	....	....	....

• Re-entered NHL Entry Draft. Originally Carolina's 9th choice, 225th overall, in 1997 Entry Draft.

Traded to **Columbus** by **Detroit** for Columbus's 6th round choice (Andreas Sundin) in 2003 Entry Draft, August 14, 2000.

McEACHERN, Shawn

(muh-GEH-kruhn, SHAWN) **ATL.**

Right wing. Shoots left. 5'11", 200 lbs. Born, Waltham, MA, February 28, 1969. Pittsburgh's 6th choice, 110th overall, in 1987 Entry Draft.

Season	Club	League	GP	G	A	Pts	PIM	PP	SH	GW	S	%	+/-	TF	F%	Min	GP	G	A	Pts	PIM	PP	SH	GW	Min
1985-86	Matignon	Hi-School	20	32	20	52	....	....	....	....	....	....	....	....	....	....	....	....	....	....	....	....	....	....	....
1986-87	Matignon	Hi-School	16	29	28	57	....	....	....	....	....	....	....	....	....	....	....	....	....	....	....	....	....	....	....
1987-88	Matignon	Hi-School	22	52	40	92	....	....	....	....	....	....	....	....	....	....	....	....	....	....	....	....	....	....	....
1988-89	Boston University	H-East	36	20	28	48	32	....	....	....	....	....	....	....	....	....	....	....	....	....	....	....	....	....	....
1989-90	Boston University	H-East	43	25	31	56	78	....	....	....	....	....	....	....	....	....	....	....	....	....	....	....	....	....	....
1990-91	Boston University	H-East	41	34	48	82	43	....	....	....	....	....	....	....	....	....	....	....	....	....	....	....	....	....	....
1991-92	Team USA	Nat-Tm	57	26	23	49	38	....	....	....	....	....	....	....	....	....	....	....	....	....	....	....	....	....	....
	United States	Olympics	8	1	0	1	10	....	....	....	....	....	....	....	....	....	....	....	....	....	....	....	....	....	....
	◆ **Pittsburgh**	**NHL**	**15**	**0**	**4**	**4**	**0**	**0**	**0**	**0**	**14**	**0.0**	**1**	....	....	....	**19**	**2**	**7**	**9**	**4**	**0**	**0**	**0**	....
1992-93	**Pittsburgh**	**NHL**	**84**	**28**	**33**	**61**	**46**	**7**	**0**	**6**	**196**	**14.3**	**21**	....	....	....	**12**	**3**	**2**	**5**	**10**	**0**	**0**	**1**	....
1993-94	**Los Angeles**	**NHL**	**49**	**8**	**13**	**21**	**24**	**0**	**3**	**0**	**81**	**9.9**	**1**	....	....	....	....	....	....	....	....	....	....	....	....
	Pittsburgh	**NHL**	**27**	**12**	**9**	**21**	**10**	**0**	**2**	**1**	**78**	**15.4**	**13**	....	....	....	**6**	**1**	**0**	**1**	**2**	**0**	**0**	**0**	....
1994-95	Kiekko Espoo	Finland	8	1	3	4	6	....	....	....	....	....	....	....	....	....	....	....	....	....	....	....	....	....	....
	Pittsburgh	**NHL**	**44**	**13**	**13**	**26**	**22**	**1**	**2**	**1**	**97**	**13.4**	**4**	....	....	....	**11**	**0**	**2**	**2**	**8**	**0**	**0**	**0**	....
1995-96	**Boston**	**NHL**	**82**	**24**	**29**	**53**	**34**	**3**	**2**	**3**	**238**	**10.1**	**–5**	....	....	....	**5**	**2**	**1**	**3**	**8**	**0**	**0**	**0**	....
1996-97	**Ottawa**	**NHL**	**65**	**11**	**20**	**31**	**18**	**0**	**1**	**2**	**150**	**7.3**	**–5**	....	....	....	**7**	**2**	**0**	**2**	**8**	**1**	**0**	**0**	....
1997-98	**Ottawa**	**NHL**	**81**	**24**	**24**	**48**	**42**	**8**	**2**	**4**	**229**	**10.5**	**1**	....	....	....	**11**	**0**	**4**	**4**	**8**	**0**	**0**	**0**	....
1998-99	**Ottawa**	**NHL**	**77**	**31**	**25**	**56**	**46**	**7**	**0**	**4**	**223**	**13.9**	**8**	**441**	**48.5**	**18:45**	**4**	**2**	**0**	**2**	**6**	**1**	**0**	**0**	**21:51**
99-2000	**Ottawa**	**NHL**	**69**	**29**	**22**	**51**	**24**	**10**	**0**	**4**	**219**	**13.2**	**2**	**54**	**50.0**	**17:50**	**6**	**0**	**3**	**3**	**4**	**0**	**0**	**0**	**18:08**
2000-01	**Ottawa**	**NHL**	**82**	**32**	**40**	**72**	**62**	**9**	**0**	**1**	**231**	**13.9**	**10**	**420**	**48.8**	**18:25**	**4**	**0**	**2**	**2**	**2**	**0**	**0**	**0**	**20:49**
2001-02	**Ottawa**	**NHL**	**80**	**15**	**31**	**46**	**52**	**5**	**0**	**3**	**196**	**7.7**	**9**	**210**	**52.4**	**17:40**	**12**	**0**	**4**	**4**	**2**	**0**	**0**	**0**	**16:59**
2002-03	**Atlanta**	**NHL**	**46**	**10**	**16**	**26**	**28**	**4**	**1**	**1**	**120**	**8.3**	**–27**	**154**	**43.5**	**19:18**	....	....	....	....	....	....	....	....	....
	NHL Totals		**801**	**237**	**279**	**516**	**408**	**54**	**13**	**30**	**2072**	**11.4**		**1279**	**48.7**	**18:19**	**97**	**12**	**25**	**37**	**62**	**2**	**0**	**1**	**18:35**

Hockey East Second All-Star Team (1990) • Hockey East First All-Star Team (1991) • NCAA East First All-American Team (1991)

Traded to **Los Angeles** by **Pittsburgh** for Marty McSorley, August 27, 1993. Traded to **Pittsburgh** by **Los Angeles** with Tomas Sandstrom for Marty McSorley and Jim Paek, February 16, 1994. Traded to **Boston** by **Pittsburgh** with Kevin Stevens for Glen Murray, Bryan Smolinski and Boston's 3rd round choice (Boyd Kane) in 1996 Entry Draft, August 2, 1995. Traded to **Ottawa** by **Boston** for Trent McCleary and Ottawa's 3rd round choice (Eric Naud) in 1996 Entry Draft, June 22, 1996. Traded to **Atlanta** by **Ottawa** with Ottawa's 6th round choice in 2004 Entry Draft for Brian Pothier, June 29, 2002.

McGILLIS, Dan

(MIHK-gihl-his, DAN) **BOS.**

Defense. Shoots left. 6'2", 230 lbs. Born, Hawkesbury, Ont., July 1, 1972. Detroit's 10th choice, 238th overall, in 1992 Entry Draft.

Season	Club	League	GP	G	A	Pts	PIM	PP	SH	GW	S	%	+/-	TF	F%	Min	GP	G	A	Pts	PIM	PP	SH	GW	Min
1989-90	Hawkesbury	OCJHL	55	2	1	3	52	....	....	....	....	....	....	....	....	....	....	....	....	....	....	....	....	....	....
1990-91	Hawkesbury	OCJHL	56	8	22	30	92	....	....	....	....	....	....	....	....	....	....	....	....	....	....	....	....	....	....
1991-92	Hawkesbury	OCJHL	36	5	19	24	106	....	....	....	....	....	....	....	....	....	....	....	....	....	....	....	....	....	....
1992-93	Northeastern	H-East	35	5	12	17	42	....	....	....	....	....	....	....	....	....	....	....	....	....	....	....	....	....	....
1993-94	Northeastern	H-East	38	4	25	29	82	....	....	....	....	....	....	....	....	....	....	....	....	....	....	....	....	....	....
1994-95	Northeastern	H-East	34	9	22	31	70	....	....	....	....	....	....	....	....	....	....	....	....	....	....	....	....	....	....
1995-96	Northeastern	H-East	34	12	24	36	50	....	....	....	....	....	....	....	....	....	....	....	....	....	....	....	....	....	....
1996-97	**Edmonton**	**NHL**	**73**	**6**	**16**	**22**	**52**	**2**	**1**	**2**	**139**	**4.3**	**2**	....	....	....	**12**	**0**	**5**	**5**	**24**	**0**	**0**	**0**	....
1997-98	**Edmonton**	**NHL**	**67**	**10**	**15**	**25**	**74**	**5**	**0**	**3**	**119**	**8.4**	**–17**	....	....	....	....	....	....	....	....	....	....	....	....
	Philadelphia	**NHL**	**13**	**1**	**5**	**6**	**35**	**1**	**0**	**0**	**18**	**5.6**	**–4**	....	....	....	**5**	**1**	**2**	**3**	**10**	**1**	**0**	**0**	....
1998-99	**Philadelphia**	**NHL**	**78**	**8**	**37**	**45**	**61**	**6**	**0**	**4**	**164**	**4.9**	**16**	**0**	**0.0**	**21:41**	**6**	**0**	**1**	**1**	**12**	**0**	**0**	**0**	**19:36**
99-2000	**Philadelphia**	**NHL**	**68**	**4**	**14**	**18**	**55**	**3**	**0**	**1**	**128**	**3.1**	**16**	**0**	**0.0**	**20:04**	**18**	**2**	**6**	**8**	**12**	**0**	**0**	**0**	**24:42**
2000-01	**Philadelphia**	**NHL**	**82**	**14**	**35**	**49**	**86**	**4**	**0**	**4**	**207**	**6.8**	**13**	**1**	**0.0**	**23:23**	**6**	**1**	**0**	**1**	**6**	**0**	**1**	**0**	**24:12**
2001-02	**Philadelphia**	**NHL**	**75**	**5**	**14**	**19**	**46**	**2**	**0**	**1**	**147**	**3.4**	**17**	**0**	**0.0**	**21:04**	**5**	**1**	**0**	**1**	**8**	**1**	**0**	**0**	**20:27**

			Regular Season														Playoffs								
Season	Club	League	GP	G	A	Pts	PIM	PP	SH	GW	S	%	+/-	TF	F%	Min	GP	G	A	Pts	PIM	PP	SH	GW	Min
2002-03	Philadelphia	NHL	24	0	3	3	20	0	0	0	41	0.0	7	0	0.0	18:13	....	....	....	....	....	....	....	....	....
	San Jose	NHL	37	3	13	16	30	2	0	0	71	4.2	–6	0	0.0	21:54	....	....	....	....	....	....	....	....	....
	Boston	NHL	10	0	1	1	10	0	0	0	18	0.0	2	0	0.0	21:15	5	3	0	3	2	2	0	1	18:54
	NHL Totals		527	51	153	204	469	25	1	15	1052	4.8		1	0.0	21:26	57	8	14	22	74	4	1	1	22:36

Hockey East First All-Star Team (1995, 1996) • NCAA East First All-American Team (1996)

Traded to **Edmonton** by **Detroit** for Kirk Maltby, March 20, 1996. Traded to **Philadelphia** by **Edmonton** with Edmonton's 2nd round choice (Jason Beckett) in 1998 Entry Draft for Janne Niinimaa, March 24, 1998. Traded to **San Jose** by **Philadelphia** for Marcus Ragnarsson, December 6, 2002. Traded to **Boston** by **San Jose** for Boston's 2nd round choice (later traded to NY Rangers – NY Rangers selected Ivan Baranka) in 2003 Entry Draft, March 11, 2003.

McINNIS, Marty

(MAK-ih-nihs, MAHR-tee)

Right wing. Shoots right. 5'11", 187 lbs. Born, Hingham, MA, June 2, 1970. NY Islanders' 10th choice, 163rd overall, in 1988 Entry Draft.

Season	Club	League	GP	G	A	Pts	PIM	PP	SH	GW	S	%	+/-	TF	F%	Min	GP	G	A	Pts	PIM	PP	SH	GW	Min
1986-87	Milton Academy	Hi-School	25	21	19	40	....	....	....	....	....	....	....	....	....	....	....	....	....	....	....	....	....	....	....
1987-88	Milton Academy	Hi-School	25	26	25	51	....	....	....	....	....	....	....	....	....	....	....	....	....	....	....	....	....	....	....
1988-89	Boston College	H-East	39	13	19	32	8	....	....	....	....	....	....	....	....	....	....	....	....	....	....	....	....	....	....
1989-90	Boston College	H-East	41	24	29	53	43	....	....	....	....	....	....	....	....	....	....	....	....	....	....	....	....	....	....
1990-91	Boston College	H-East	38	21	36	57	40	....	....	....	....	....	....	....	....	....	....	....	....	....	....	....	....	....	....
1991-92	Team USA	Nat-Tm	54	15	19	34	20	....	....	....	....	....	....	....	....	....	....	....	....	....	....	....	....	....	....
	United States	Olympics	8	5	2	7	4	....	....	....	....	....	....	....	....	....	....	....	....	....	....	....	....	....	....
	NY Islanders	**NHL**	**15**	**3**	**5**	**8**	**0**	**0**	**0**	**0**	**24**	**12.5**	**6**	....	....	....	....	....	....	....	....	....	....	....	....
1992-93	**NY Islanders**	**NHL**	**56**	**10**	**20**	**30**	**24**	**0**	**1**	**0**	**60**	**16.7**	**7**	....	....	....	**3**	**0**	**1**	**1**	**0**	**0**	**0**	**0**	....
	Capital District	AHL	10	4	12	16	2	....	....	....	....	....	....	....	....	....	....	....	....	....	....	....	....	....	....
1993-94	**NY Islanders**	**NHL**	**81**	**25**	**31**	**56**	**24**	**3**	**5**	**3**	**136**	**18.4**	**31**	....	....	....	**4**	**0**	**0**	**0**	**0**	**0**	**0**	**0**	....
1994-95	**NY Islanders**	**NHL**	**41**	**9**	**7**	**16**	**8**	**0**	**0**	**1**	**68**	**13.2**	**–1**	....	....	....	....	....	....	....	....	....	....	....	....
1995-96	**NY Islanders**	**NHL**	**74**	**12**	**34**	**46**	**39**	**2**	**0**	**1**	**167**	**7.2**	**–11**	....	....	....	....	....	....	....	....	....	....	....	....
1996-97	**NY Islanders**	**NHL**	**70**	**20**	**22**	**42**	**20**	**4**	**1**	**4**	**163**	**12.3**	**–7**	....	....	....	....	....	....	....	....	....	....	....	....
	Calgary	**NHL**	**10**	**3**	**4**	**7**	**2**	**1**	**0**	**0**	**19**	**15.8**	**–1**	....	....	....	....	....	....	....	....	....	....	....	....
1997-98	**Calgary**	**NHL**	**75**	**19**	**25**	**44**	**34**	**5**	**4**	**0**	**128**	**14.8**	**1**	....	....	....	....	....	....	....	....	....	....	....	....
1998-99	**Calgary**	**NHL**	**6**	**1**	**1**	**2**	**6**	**0**	**0**	**0**	**7**	**14.3**	**–1**	**28**	**32.1**	**13:51**	....	....	....	....	....	....	....	....	....
	Anaheim	**NHL**	**75**	**18**	**34**	**52**	**36**	**11**	**1**	**5**	**139**	**12.9**	**–14**	**390**	**46.9**	**18:59**	**4**	**2**	**0**	**2**	**2**	**2**	**0**	**0**	**21:07**
99-2000	**Anaheim**	**NHL**	**62**	**10**	**18**	**28**	**26**	**2**	**1**	**2**	**129**	**7.8**	**–4**	**355**	**50.1**	**19:04**	....	....	....	....	....	....	....	....	....
2000-01	**Anaheim**	**NHL**	**75**	**20**	**22**	**42**	**40**	**10**	**0**	**1**	**136**	**14.7**	**–21**	**605**	**47.1**	**18:30**	....	....	....	....	....	....	....	....	....
2001-02	**Anaheim**	**NHL**	**60**	**9**	**14**	**23**	**25**	**2**	**0**	**0**	**131**	**6.9**	**–14**	**150**	**48.7**	**15:18**	....	....	....	....	....	....	....	....	....
	Boston	**NHL**	**19**	**2**	**3**	**5**	**8**	**0**	**0**	**1**	**26**	**7.7**	**–1**	**204**	**41.2**	**17:42**	**6**	**0**	**1**	**1**	**0**	**0**	**0**	**0**	**7:21**
2002-03	**Boston**	**NHL**	**77**	**9**	**10**	**19**	**38**	**0**	**0**	**1**	**121**	**7.4**	**–11**	**345**	**42.6**	**14:14**	**5**	**1**	**0**	**1**	**2**	**0**	**0**	**0**	**14:29**
	NHL Totals		**796**	**170**	**250**	**420**	**330**	**40**	**13**	**19**	**1454**	**11.7**		**2077**	**46.2**	**17:11**	**22**	**3**	**2**	**5**	**4**	**2**	**0**	**0**	**13:24**

Traded to **Calgary** by **NY Islanders** with Tyrone Garner and Calgary's 6th round choice (previously acquired, Calgary selected Ilja Demidov) in 1997 Entry Draft for Robert Reichel, March 18, 1997. Traded to **Chicago** by **Calgary** with Eric Andersson and Jamie Allison for Jeff Shantz and Steve Dubinsky, October 27, 1998. Traded to **Anaheim** by **Chicago** for Toronto's 4th round choice (previously acquired, later traded to Washington – Washington selected Ryan Vanbuskirk) in 2000 Entry Draft, October 27, 1998. Traded to **Boston by Anaheim** for Boston's 3rd round choice (later traded to Nashville – later traded to Detroit – Detroit selected Valtteri Filppula) in 2002 Entry Draft, March 6, 2002.

McKAY, Randy

(mih-KAY, RAN-dee)

Right wing. Shoots right. 6'2", 210 lbs. Born, Montreal, Que., January 25, 1967. Detroit's 6th choice, 113th overall, in 1985 Entry Draft.

Season	Club	League	GP	G	A	Pts	PIM	PP	SH	GW	S	%	+/-	TF	F%	Min	GP	G	A	Pts	PIM	PP	SH	GW	Min
1983-84	Lac St-Louis Lions	QAAA	38	18	28	46	62	....	....	....	....	....	....	....	....	....	11	6	10	16	8	....	....	....	....
1984-85	Michigan Tech	WCHA	25	4	5	9	32	....	....	....	....	....	....	....	....	....	....	....	....	....	....	....	....	....	....
1985-86	Michigan Tech	WCHA	40	12	22	34	46	....	....	....	....	....	....	....	....	....	....	....	....	....	....	....	....	....	....
1986-87	Michigan Tech	WCHA	39	5	11	16	46	....	....	....	....	....	....	....	....	....	....	....	....	....	....	....	....	....	....
1987-88	Michigan Tech	WCHA	41	17	24	41	70	....	....	....	....	....	....	....	....	....	....	....	....	....	....	....	....	....	....
	Adirondack	AHL	10	0	3	3	12	....	....	....	....	....	....	....	....	....	6	0	4	4	0	....	....	....	....
1988-89	**Detroit**	**NHL**	**3**	**0**	**0**	**0**	**0**	**0**	**0**	**0**	**2**	**0.0**	**–1**	....	....	....	**2**	**0**	**0**	**0**	**2**	**0**	**0**	**0**	....
	Adirondack	AHL	58	29	34	63	170	....	....	....	....	....	....	....	....	....	14	4	7	11	60	....	....	....	....
1989-90	**Detroit**	**NHL**	**33**	**3**	**6**	**9**	**51**	**0**	**0**	**0**	**33**	**9.1**	**1**	....	....	....	....	....	....	....	....	....	....	....	....
	Adirondack	AHL	36	16	23	39	99	....	....	....	....	....	....	....	....	....	6	3	0	3	35	....	....	....	....
1990-91	**Detroit**	**NHL**	**47**	**1**	**7**	**8**	**183**	**0**	**0**	**0**	**22**	**4.5**	**–15**	....	....	....	**5**	**0**	**1**	**1**	**41**	**0**	**0**	**0**	....
1991-92	**New Jersey**	**NHL**	**80**	**17**	**16**	**33**	**246**	**2**	**0**	**1**	**111**	**15.3**	**6**	....	....	....	**7**	**1**	**3**	**4**	**10**	**1**	**0**	**0**	....
1992-93	**New Jersey**	**NHL**	**73**	**11**	**11**	**22**	**206**	**1**	**0**	**2**	**94**	**11.7**	**0**	....	....	....	**5**	**0**	**0**	**0**	**16**	**0**	**0**	**0**	....
1993-94	**New Jersey**	**NHL**	**78**	**12**	**15**	**27**	**244**	**0**	**0**	**1**	**77**	**15.6**	**24**	....	....	....	**20**	**1**	**2**	**3**	**24**	**0**	**0**	**0**	....
1994-95♦	**New Jersey**	**NHL**	**33**	**5**	**7**	**12**	**44**	**0**	**0**	**0**	**44**	**11.4**	**10**	....	....	....	**19**	**8**	**4**	**12**	**11**	**2**	**0**	**2**	....
1995-96	**New Jersey**	**NHL**	**76**	**11**	**10**	**21**	**145**	**3**	**0**	**3**	**97**	**11.3**	**7**	....	....	....	....	....	....	....	....	....	....	....	....
1996-97	**New Jersey**	**NHL**	**77**	**9**	**18**	**27**	**109**	**0**	**0**	**2**	**92**	**9.8**	**15**	....	....	....	**10**	**1**	**1**	**2**	**0**	**0**	**0**	**0**	....
1997-98	**New Jersey**	**NHL**	**74**	**24**	**24**	**48**	**86**	**8**	**0**	**5**	**141**	**17.0**	**30**	....	....	....	**6**	**0**	**1**	**1**	**0**	**0**	**0**	**0**	....
1998-99	**New Jersey**	**NHL**	**70**	**17**	**20**	**37**	**143**	**3**	**0**	**5**	**136**	**12.5**	**10**	**1**	**0.0**	**16:06**	**7**	**3**	**2**	**5**	**2**	**0**	**0**	**1**	**17:06**
99-2000♦	**New Jersey**	**NHL**	**67**	**16**	**23**	**39**	**80**	**3**	**0**	**4**	**116**	**13.8**	**8**	**2**	**0.0**	**15:39**	**23**	**0**	**6**	**6**	**9**	**0**	**0**	**0**	**11:39**
2000-01	**New Jersey**	**NHL**	**77**	**23**	**20**	**43**	**50**	**12**	**0**	**5**	**120**	**19.2**	**3**	**2**	**50.0**	**13:58**	**19**	**6**	**3**	**9**	**8**	**2**	**0**	**1**	**14:27**
2001-02	**New Jersey**	**NHL**	**55**	**6**	**7**	**13**	**65**	**3**	**0**	**1**	**63**	**9.5**	**2**	**2**	**0.0**	**13:15**	....	....	....	....	....	....	....	....	....
	Dallas	**NHL**	**14**	**1**	**4**	**5**	**7**	**0**	**0**	**0**	**10**	**10.0**	**2**	**1**	**0.0**	**12:02**	....	....	....	....	....	....	....	....	....
2002-03	**Montreal**	**NHL**	**75**	**6**	**13**	**19**	**72**	**2**	**0**	**0**	**52**	**11.5**	**–14**	**17**	**23.5**	**11:03**	....	....	....	....	....	....	....	....	....
	NHL Totals		**932**	**162**	**201**	**363**	**1731**	**37**	**0**	**29**	**1210**	**13.4**		**25**	**20.0**	**13:54**	**123**	**20**	**23**	**43**	**123**	**5**	**0**	**4**	**13:31**

Transferred to **New Jersey** by **Detroit** with Dave Barr as compensation for Detroit's signing of free agent Troy Crowder, September 9, 1991. Traded to **Dallas** by **New Jersey** with Jason Arnott and New Jersey's 1st round choice (later traded to Columbus – later traded to Buffalo – Buffalo selected Dan Paille) in 2002 Entry Draft for Joe Nieuwendyk and Jamie Langenbrunner, March 19, 2002. Signed as a free agent by **Montreal**, July 4, 2002.

McKEE, Jay

(mih-KEE, JAY) **BUF.**

Defense. Shoots left. 6'4", 212 lbs. Born, Kingston, Ont., September 8, 1977. Buffalo's 1st choice, 14th overall, in 1995 Entry Draft.

Season	Club	League	GP	G	A	Pts	PIM	PP	SH	GW	S	%	+/-	TF	F%	Min	GP	G	A	Pts	PIM	PP	SH	GW	Min
1992-93	Ernestown Jets	OJHL-C	36	0	17	17	37	....	....	....	....	....	....	....	....	....	....	....	....	....	....	....	....	....	....
	Kingston	MTJHL	2	0	0	0	0	....	....	....	....	....	....	....	....	....	....	....	....	....	....	....	....	....	....
1993-94	Sudbury Wolves	OHL	51	0	1	1	51	....	....	....	....	....	....	....	....	....	3	0	0	0	0	....	....	....	....
1994-95	Sudbury Wolves	OHL	39	6	6	12	91	....	....	....	....	....	....	....	....	....	....	....	....	....	....	....	....	....	....
	Niagara Falls	OHL	26	3	13	16	60	....	....	....	....	....	....	....	....	....	6	2	3	5	10	....	....	....	....
1995-96	Niagara Falls	OHL	64	5	41	46	129	....	....	....	....	....	....	....	....	....	10	1	5	6	16	....	....	....	....
	Buffalo	**NHL**	**1**	**0**	**1**	**1**	**2**	**0**	**0**	**0**	**2**	**0.0**	**1**	....	....	....	....	....	....	....	....	....	....	....	....
	Rochester	AHL	4	0	1	1	15	....	....	....	....	....	....	....	....	....	....	....	....	....	....	....	....	....	....
1996-97	**Buffalo**	**NHL**	**43**	**1**	**9**	**10**	**35**	**0**	**0**	**0**	**29**	**3.4**	**3**	....	....	....	**3**	**0**	**0**	**0**	**0**	**0**	**0**	**0**	....
	Rochester	AHL	7	2	5	7	4	....	....	....	....	....	....	....	....	....	....	....	....	....	....	....	....	....	....
1997-98	**Buffalo**	**NHL**	**56**	**1**	**13**	**14**	**42**	**0**	**0**	**0**	**55**	**1.8**	**–1**	....	....	....	**1**	**0**	**0**	**0**	**0**	**0**	**0**	**0**	....
	Rochester	AHL	13	1	7	8	11	....	....	....	....	....	....	....	....	....	....	....	....	....	....	....	....	....	....
1998-99	**Buffalo**	**NHL**	**72**	**0**	**6**	**6**	**75**	**0**	**0**	**0**	**57**	**0.0**	**20**	**0**	**0.0**	**20:28**	**21**	**0**	**3**	**3**	**24**	**0**	**0**	**0**	**22:31**
99-2000	**Buffalo**	**NHL**	**78**	**5**	**12**	**17**	**50**	**1**	**0**	**1**	**84**	**6.0**	**5**	**0**	**0.0**	**20:58**	**1**	**0**	**0**	**0**	**0**	**0**	**0**	**0**	**17:57**
2000-01	**Buffalo**	**NHL**	**74**	**1**	**10**	**11**	**76**	**0**	**0**	**0**	**62**	**1.6**	**9**	**2**	**0.0**	**19:24**	**8**	**1**	**0**	**1**	**6**	**0**	**0**	**1**	**19:23**
2001-02	**Buffalo**	**NHL**	**81**	**2**	**11**	**13**	**43**	**0**	**0**	**1**	**50**	**4.0**	**18**	**0**	**0.0**	**19:26**	....	....	....	....	....	....	....	....	....
2002-03	**Buffalo**	**NHL**	**59**	**0**	**5**	**5**	**49**	**0**	**0**	**0**	**44**	**0.0**	**–16**	**0**	**0.0**	**18:45**	....	....	....	....	....	....	....	....	....
	NHL Totals		**464**	**10**	**67**	**77**	**372**	**1**	**0**	**2**	**383**	**2.6**		**2**	**0.0**	**19:51**	**34**	**1**	**3**	**4**	**30**	**0**	**0**	**1**	**21:32**

OHL Second All-Star Team (1996)

McKENNA, Steve

(mih-KEHN-ah, STEEV) **PIT.**

Left wing. Shoots left. 6'8", 252 lbs. Born, Toronto, Ont., August 21, 1973.

Season	Club	League	GP	G	A	Pts	PIM	PP	SH	GW	S	%	+/-	TF	F%	Min	GP	G	A	Pts	PIM	PP	SH	GW	Min
1991-92	Cambridge	OJHL-B	48	21	23	44	173	....	....	....	....	....	....	....	....	....	....	....	....	....	....	....	....	....	....
1992-93	Notre Dame	SJHL	STATISTICS NOT AVAILABLE																						
1993-94	Merrimack	H-East	37	1	2	3	74	....	....	....	....	....	....	....	....	....	....	....	....	....	....	....	....	....	....
1994-95	Merrimack	H-East	37	1	9	10	74	....	....	....	....	....	....	....	....	....	....	....	....	....	....	....	....	....	....
1995-96	Merrimack	H-East	33	3	11	14	67	....	....	....	....	....	....	....	....	....	....	....	....	....	....	....	....	....	....
1996-97	**Los Angeles**	**NHL**	**9**	**0**	**0**	**0**	**37**	**0**	**0**	**0**	**6**	**0.0**	**1**	....	....	....	....	....	....	....	....	....	....	....	....
	Phoenix	IHL	66	6	5	11	187	....	....	....	....	....	....	....	....	....	....	....	....	....	....	....	....	....	....
1997-98	**Los Angeles**	**NHL**	**62**	**4**	**4**	**8**	**150**	**1**	**0**	**0**	**42**	**9.5**	**–9**	....	....	....	**3**	**0**	**1**	**1**	**8**	**0**	**0**	**0**	....
	Fredericton	AHL	6	2	1	3	48	....	....	....	....	....	....	....	....	....	....	....	....	....	....	....	....	....	....
1998-99	**Los Angeles**	**NHL**	**20**	**1**	**0**	**1**	**36**	**0**	**0**	**0**	**12**	**8.3**	**–3**	**0**	**0.0**	**8:24**	....	....	....	....	....	....	....	....	....
99-2000	**Los Angeles**	**NHL**	**46**	**0**	**5**	**5**	**125**	**0**	**0**	**0**	**14**	**0.0**	**3**	**1**	**0.0**	**4:53**	....	....	....	....	....	....	....	....	....

			Regular Season														Playoffs								
Season	Club	League	GP	G	A	Pts	PIM	PP	SH	GW	S	%	+/-	TF	F%	Min	GP	G	A	Pts	PIM	PP	SH	GW	Min
2000-01	Minnesota	NHL	20	1	1	2	19	0	0	0	12	8.3	0	0	0.0	7:59	....	....	....	....	....	....	....	....	....
	Pittsburgh	NHL	34	0	0	0	100	0	0	0	7	0.0	–4	0	0.0	3:16	....	....	....	....	....	....	....	....	....
2001-02	NY Rangers	NHL	54	2	1	3	144	1	0	1	17	11.8	0	2	0.0	3:59	....	....	....	....	....	....	....	....	....
	Hartford	AHL	3	0	0	0	11	....	....	....	....	....	....	....	....	....	....	....	....	....	....	....	....	....	....
2002-03	Pittsburgh	NHL	79	9	1	10	128	5	0	3	59	15.3	–18	1	0.0	7:45	....	....	....	....	....	....	....	....	....
	NHL Totals		324	17	12	29	739	7	0	4	169	10.1		4	0.0	5:54	3	0	1	1	8	0	0	0	....

Signed as a free agent by **Los Angeles**, May 23, 1996. Selected by **Minnesota** from **Los Angeles** in Expansion Draft, June 23, 2000. Traded to **Pittsburgh** by **Minnesota** for Roman Simicek, January 13, 2001. Signed as a free agent by **NY Rangers**, August 28, 2001. Signed as a free agent by **Pittsburgh**, July 12, 2002.

McKENZIE, Jim

(MIHK-ehn-zee, JIHM) **NSH.**

Left wing. Shoots left. 6'4", 230 lbs. Born, Gull Lake, Sask., November 3, 1969. Hartford's 3rd choice, 73rd overall, in 1989 Entry Draft.

Season	Club	League	GP	G	A	Pts	PIM	PP	SH	GW	S	%	+/-	TF	F%	Min	GP	G	A	Pts	PIM	PP	SH	GW	Min
1985-86	Moose Jaw	SMHL	36	18	26	44	89	....	....	....	....	....	....	....	....	....	....	....	....	....	....	....	....	....	....
	Moose Jaw	WHL	3	0	2	2	0	....	....	....	....	....	....	....	....	....	....	....	....	....	....	....	....	....	....
1986-87	Moose Jaw	WHL	65	5	3	8	125	....	....	....	....	....	....	....	....	....	9	0	0	0	7	....	....	....	....
1987-88	Moose Jaw	WHL	62	1	17	18	134	....	....	....	....	....	....	....	....	....	....	....	....	....	....	....	....	....	....
1988-89	Victoria Cougars	WHL	67	15	27	42	176	....	....	....	....	....	....	....	....	....	8	1	4	5	30	....	....	....	....
1989-90	Hartford	NHL	5	0	0	0	4	0	0	0	0	0.0	0	....	....	....	....	....	....	....	....	....	....	....	....
	Binghamton	AHL	56	4	12	16	149	....	....	....	....	....	....	....	....	....	....	....	....	....	....	....	....	....	....
1990-91	Hartford	NHL	41	4	3	7	108	0	0	0	16	25.0	–7	....	....	....	6	0	0	0	8	0	0	0	....
	Springfield	AHL	24	3	4	7	102	....	....	....	....	....	....	....	....	....	....	....	....	....	....	....	....	....	....
1991-92	Hartford	NHL	67	5	1	6	87	0	0	0	34	14.7	–6	....	....	....	....	....	....	....	....	....	....	....	....
1992-93	Hartford	NHL	64	3	6	9	202	0	0	0	36	8.3	–10	....	....	....	....	....	....	....	....	....	....	....	....
1993-94	Hartford	NHL	26	1	2	3	67	0	0	0	9	11.1	–6	....	....	....	....	....	....	....	....	....	....	....	....
	Dallas	NHL	34	2	3	5	63	0	0	1	18	11.1	4	....	....	....	....	....	....	....	....	....	....	....	....
	Pittsburgh	NHL	11	0	0	0	16	0	0	0	6	0.0	–5	....	....	....	3	0	0	0	0	0	0	0	....
1994-95	Pittsburgh	NHL	39	2	1	3	63	0	0	1	16	12.5	–7	....	....	....	5	0	0	0	4	0	0	0	....
1995-96	Winnipeg	NHL	73	4	2	6	202	0	0	0	28	14.3	–4	....	....	....	1	0	0	0	2	0	0	0	....
1996-97	Phoenix	NHL	65	5	3	8	200	0	0	1	38	13.2	–5	....	....	....	7	0	0	0	2	0	0	0	....
1997-98	Phoenix	NHL	64	3	4	7	146	0	0	0	35	8.6	–7	....	....	....	1	0	0	0	0	0	0	0	....
1998-99	Anaheim	NHL	73	5	4	9	99	1	0	1	59	8.5	–18	8	50.0	10:22	4	0	0	0	4	0	0	0	6:58
99-2000	Anaheim	NHL	31	3	3	6	48	0	0	0	22	13.6	–5	2	0.0	10:26	....	....	....	....	....	....	....	....	....
	Washington	NHL	30	1	2	3	16	0	0	0	10	10.0	0	0	0.0	6:22	1	0	0	0	0	0	0	0	0:17
2000-01	New Jersey	NHL	53	2	2	4	119	0	0	0	32	6.3	0	0	0.0	7:56	3	0	0	0	2	0	0	0	5:42
2001-02	New Jersey	NHL	67	3	5	8	123	1	0	0	33	9.1	0	3	0.0	7:19	6	0	0	0	2	0	0	0	9:47
2002-03♦	New Jersey	NHL	76	4	8	12	88	0	0	2	42	9.5	3	5	60.0	7:42	13	0	0	0	14	0	0	0	7:60
	NHL Totals		819	47	49	96	1651	2	0	6	434	10.8		18	38.9	8:23	50	0	0	0	38	0	0	0	7:42

Traded to **Florida** by **Hartford** for Alexander Godynyuk, December 16, 1993. Traded to **Dallas** by **Florida** for Dallas' 4th round choice (later traded to Ottawa – Ottawa selected Kevin Bolibruck) in 1995 Entry Draft, December 16, 1993. Traded to **Pittsburgh** by **Dallas** for Mike Needham, March 21, 1994. Signed as a free agent by **NY Islanders**, August 2, 1995. Claimed by **Winnipeg** from **NY Islanders** in Waiver Draft, October 2, 1995. Transferred to **Phoenix** after **Winnipeg** franchise relocated, July 1, 1996. Traded to **Anaheim** by **Phoenix** for Jean-Francois Jomphe, June 18, 1998. Claimed on waivers by **Washington** from **Anaheim**, January 20, 2000. Signed as a free agent by **New Jersey**, July 3, 2000. Signed as a free agent by **Nashville**, July 22, 2003.

McLAREN, Kyle

(mih-KLAIR-uhn, KIGHL) **S.J.**

Defense. Shoots left. 6'4", 230 lbs. Born, Humboldt, Sask., June 18, 1977. Boston's 1st choice, 9th overall, in 1995 Entry Draft.

Season	Club	League	GP	G	A	Pts	PIM	PP	SH	GW	S	%	+/-	TF	F%	Min	GP	G	A	Pts	PIM	PP	SH	GW	Min
1992-93	Lethbridge	AMHL	60	28	28	56	84	....	....	....	....	....	....	....	....	....	....	....	....	....	....	....	....	....	....
1993-94	Tacoma Rockets	WHL	62	1	9	10	53	....	....	....	....	....	....	....	....	....	6	1	4	5	6	....	....	....	....
1994-95	Tacoma Rockets	WHL	47	13	19	32	68	....	....	....	....	....	....	....	....	....	4	1	1	2	4	....	....	....	....
1995-96	Boston	NHL	74	5	12	17	73	0	0	0	74	6.8	16	....	....	....	5	0	0	0	14	0	0	0	....
1996-97	Boston	NHL	58	5	9	14	54	0	0	1	68	7.4	–9	....	....	....	....	....	....	....	....	....	....	....	....
1997-98	Boston	NHL	66	5	20	25	56	2	0	0	101	5.0	13	....	....	....	6	1	0	1	4	1	0	0	....
1998-99	Boston	NHL	52	6	18	24	48	3	0	0	97	6.2	1	0	0.0	23:25	12	0	3	3	10	0	0	0	26:45
99-2000	Boston	NHL	71	8	11	19	67	2	0	3	142	5.6	–4	5	40.0	23:18	....	....	....	....	....	....	....	....	....
2000-01	Boston	NHL	58	5	12	17	53	2	0	0	91	5.5	–5	4	50.0	24:14	....	....	....	....	....	....	....	....	....
2001-02	Boston	NHL	38	0	8	8	19	0	0	0	57	0.0	–4	1	0.0	19:21	4	0	0	0	20	0	0	0	18:37
2002-03	San Jose	NHL	33	0	8	8	30	0	0	0	43	0.0	–10	0	0.0	22:40	....	....	....	....	....	....	....	....	....
	NHL Totals		450	34	98	132	400	9	0	4	673	5.1		10	40.0	22:51	27	1	3	4	48	1	0	0	24:43

NHL All-Rookie Team (1996)

• Missed majority of 2001-02 season recovering from chest (October 10, 2001 vs. Minnesota) and wrist (December 26, 2001 vs. Ottawa) injuries. •Missed majority of 2002-03 season in contract dispute with Boston. Traded to **San Jose** by **Boston** with Boston's 4th round choice in 2004 Entry Draft for Jeff Hackett and Jeff Jillson, January 23, 2003.

McLEAN, Brett

(mihk-LAYN, BREHT) **CHI.**

Center. Shoots left. 5'11", 194 lbs. Born, Comox, B.C., August 14, 1978. Dallas' 9th choice, 242nd overall, in 1997 Entry Draft.

Season	Club	League	GP	G	A	Pts	PIM	PP	SH	GW	S	%	+/-	TF	F%	Min	GP	G	A	Pts	PIM	PP	SH	GW	Min
1993-94	Notre Dame	SMBHL	71	109	124	233	70	....	....	....	....	....	....	....	....	....	....	....	....	....	....	....	....	....	....
1994-95	Tacoma Rockets	WHL	67	11	23	34	33	....	....	....	....	....	....	....	....	....	4	0	1	1	0	....	....	....	....
1995-96	Kelowna Rockets	WHL	71	37	42	79	60	....	....	....	....	....	....	....	....	....	6	2	2	4	6	....	....	....	....
1996-97	Kelowna Rockets	WHL	72	44	60	104	98	....	....	....	....	....	....	....	....	....	6	4	2	6	12	....	....	....	....
1997-98	Kelowna Rockets	WHL	54	42	45	87	91	....	....	....	....	....	....	....	....	....	7	4	5	9	17	....	....	....	....
1998-99	Kelowna Rockets	WHL	44	32	38	70	46	....	....	....	....	....	....	....	....	....	....	....	....	....	....	....	....	....	....
	Brandon	WHL	21	15	16	31	20	....	....	....	....	....	....	....	....	....	5	1	6	7	8	....	....	....	....
	Cincinnati	AHL	7	0	3	3	6	....	....	....	....	....	....	....	....	....	....	....	....	....	....	....	....	....	....
99-2000	Johnstown Chiefs	ECHL	8	4	7	11	6	....	....	....	....	....	....	....	....	....	....	....	....	....	....	....	....	....	....
	Saint John Flames	AHL	72	15	23	38	115	....	....	....	....	....	....	....	....	....	3	0	1	1	2	....	....	....	....
2000-01	Cleveland	IHL	74	20	24	44	54	....	....	....	....	....	....	....	....	....	4	0	0	0	18	....	....	....	....
2001-02	Houston Aeros	AHL	78	24	21	45	71	....	....	....	....	....	....	....	....	....	14	1	6	7	12	....	....	....	....
2002-03	Chicago	NHL	2	0	0	0	0	0	0	0	1	0.0	–1	19	26.3	10:47	....	....	....	....	....	....	....	....	....
	Norfolk Admirals	AHL	77	23	38	61	60	....	....	....	....	....	....	....	....	....	9	2	6	8	9	....	....	....	....
	NHL Totals		2	0	0	0	0	0	0	0	1	0.0		19	26.3	10:47	....	....	....	....	....	....	....	....	....

WHL West Second All-Star Team (1998)

Signed as a free agent by **Calgary**, September, 1999. Signed as a free agent by **Minnesota**, July 13, 2000. Signed as a free agent by **Chicago**, July 23, 2002.

McMORROW, Sean

(muhk-MOHR-roh, SHAWN) **BUF.**

Left wing. Shoots right. 6'4", 214 lbs. Born, Vancouver, B.C., January 19, 1982. Buffalo's 7th choice, 258th overall, in 2000 Entry Draft.

Season	Club	League	GP	G	A	Pts	PIM	PP	SH	GW	S	%	+/-	TF	F%	Min	GP	G	A	Pts	PIM	PP	SH	GW	Min
1998-99	Pickering Panthers	OPJHL	35	2	10	12	175	....	....	....	....	....	....	....	....	....	....	....	....	....	....	....	....	....	....
99-2000	Sarnia Sting	OHL	31	0	1	1	75	....	....	....	....	....	....	....	....	....	....	....	....	....	....	....	....	....	....
	Kitchener Rangers	OHL	31	0	1	1	67	....	....	....	....	....	....	....	....	....	4	0	0	0	12	....	....	....	....
2000-01	Mississauga	OHL	13	0	0	0	34	....	....	....	....	....	....	....	....	....	....	....	....	....	....	....	....	....	....
	Kingston	OHL	7	0	1	1	22	....	....	....	....	....	....	....	....	....	....	....	....	....	....	....	....	....	....
	London Knights	OHL	29	0	3	3	75	....	....	....	....	....	....	....	....	....	5	0	0	0	0	....	....	....	....
2001-02	London Knights	OHL	38	0	1	1	107	....	....	....	....	....	....	....	....	....	....	....	....	....	....	....	....	....	....
	Oshawa Generals	OHL	27	6	1	7	63	....	....	....	....	....	....	....	....	....	5	1	0	1	12	....	....	....	....
2002-03	Buffalo	NHL	1	0	0	0	0	0	0	0	0	0.0	0	0	0.0	1:27	....	....	....	....	....	....	....	....	....
	Rochester	AHL	64	0	1	1	315	....	....	....	....	....	....	....	....	....	3	0	0	0	17	....	....	....	....
	NHL Totals		1	0	0	0	0	0	0	0	0	0.0		0	0.0	1:27	....	....	....	....	....	....	....	....	....

MELANSON, Dean

(meh-LAHN-suhn, DEEN)

Defense. Shoots right. 5'11", 190 lbs. Born, Antigonish, N.S., November 19, 1973. Buffalo's 4th choice, 80th overall, in 1992 Entry Draft.

Season	Club	League	GP	G	A	Pts	PIM	PP	SH	GW	S	%	+/-	TF	F%	Min	GP	G	A	Pts	PIM	PP	SH	GW	Min
1989-90	Antigonish	MJrHL	STATISTICS NOT AVAILABLE																						
1990-91	St-Hyacinthe	QMJHL	69	10	17	27	110	....	....	....	....	....	....	....	....	....	4	0	1	1	2	....	....	....	....
1991-92	St-Hyacinthe	QMJHL	42	8	19	27	158	....	....	....	....	....	....	....	....	....	6	1	2	3	25	....	....	....	....
1992-93	St-Hyacinthe	QMJHL	57	13	29	42	253	....	....	....	....	....	....	....	....	....	....	....	....	....	....	....	....	....	....
	Rochester	AHL	8	0	1	1	6	....	....	....	....	....	....	....	....	....	14	1	6	7	18	....	....	....	....
1993-94	Rochester	AHL	80	1	21	22	138	....	....	....	....	....	....	....	....	....	4	0	1	1	2	....	....	....	....
1994-95	Rochester	AHL	43	4	7	11	84	....	....	....	....	....	....	....	....	....	....	....	....	....	....	....	....	....	....
	Buffalo	NHL	5	0	0	0	4	0	0	0	1	0.0	–1	....	....	....	....	....	....	....	....	....	....	....	....
1995-96	Rochester	AHL	70	3	13	16	204	....	....	....	....	....	....	....	....	....	14	3	3	6	22	....	....	....	....

			Regular Season														Playoffs								
Season	Club	League	GP	G	A	Pts	PIM	PP	SH	GW	S	%	+/-	TF	F%	Min	GP	G	A	Pts	PIM	PP	SH	GW	Min
1996-97	Quebec Rafales	IHL	72	3	21	24	95	....	....	....	....	....	....	....	....	....	7	0	2	2	12	....	....	....	....
1997-98	Rochester	AHL	73	7	9	16	228	....	....	....	....	....	....	....	....	....	4	0	2	2	0	....	....	....	....
1998-99	Rochester	AHL	79	7	27	34	192	....	....	....	....	....	....	....	....	....	17	3	2	5	32	....	....	....	....
99-2000	Philadelphia	AHL	58	11	25	36	178	....	....	....	....	....	....	....	....	....	4	2	3	5	10	....	....	....	....
2000-01	Philadelphia	AHL	15	1	4	5	48	....	....	....	....	....	....	....	....	....	....	....	....	....	....	....	....	....	....
	Chicago Wolves	IHL	42	1	7	8	80	....	....	....	....	....	....	....	....	....	....	....	....	....	....	....	....	....	....
	Portland Pirates	AHL	13	1	4	5	14	....	....	....	....	....	....	....	....	....	2	0	0	0	10	....	....	....	....
2001-02	**Washington**	**NHL**	**4**	**0**	**0**	**0**	**4**	**0**	**0**	**0**	**6**	**0.0**	**1**	**0**	**0.0**	**12:36**	....	....	....	....	....	....	....	....	....
	Portland Pirates	AHL	70	2	14	16	140	....	....	....	....	....	....	....	....	....	....	....	....	....	....	....	....	....	....
2002-03	Portland Pirates	AHL	23	1	4	5	40	....	....	....	....	....	....	....	....	....	....	....	....	....	....	....	....	....	....
	Binghamton	AHL	35	4	3	7	93	....	....	....	....	....	....	....	....	....	13	0	1	1	48	....	....	....	....
	NHL Totals		**9**	**0**	**0**	**0**	**8**	**0**	**0**	**0**	**7**	**0.0**		**0**	**0.0**	**12:36**	....	....	....	....	....	....	....	....	....

QMJHL All-Rookie Team (1991)

Signed as a free agent by **Philadelphia**, July 22, 1999. Traded to **Washington** by **Philadelphia** for Matt Herr, March 13, 2001. Traded to **Ottawa** by **Washington** for Josef Boumedienne, December 16, 2002.

MELICHAR, Josef

(mehl-ee-KHAHR, YOH-sehf) **PIT.**

Defense. Shoots left. 6'2", 221 lbs. Born, Ceske Budejovice, Czech., January 20, 1979. Pittsburgh's 3rd choice, 71st overall, in 1997 Entry Draft.

Season	Club	League	GP	G	A	Pts	PIM	PP	SH	GW	S	%	+/-	TF	F%	Min	GP	G	A	Pts	PIM	PP	SH	GW	Min
1995-96	C. Budejovice Jr.	Czech-Jr.	38	3	4	7	....	....	....	....	....	....	....	....	....	....	....	....	....	....	....	....	....	....	....
1996-97	C. Budejovice Jr.	Czech-Jr.	41	2	3	5	10	....	....	....	....	....	....	....	....	....	....	....	....	....	....	....	....	....	....
1997-98	Tri-City	WHL	67	9	24	33	154	....	....	....	....	....	....	....	....	....	....	....	....	....	....	....	....	....	....
1998-99	Tri-City	WHL	65	8	28	36	125	....	....	....	....	....	....	....	....	....	11	1	0	1	15	....	....	....	....
99-2000	Wilkes-Barre	AHL	80	3	9	12	126	....	....	....	....	....	....	....	....	....	....	....	....	....	....	....	....	....	....
2000-01	**Pittsburgh**	**NHL**	**18**	**0**	**2**	**2**	**21**	**0**	**0**	**0**	**9**	**0.0**	**–5**	**0**	**0.0**	**14:54**	....	....	....	....	....	....	....	....	....
	Wilkes-Barre	AHL	46	2	5	7	69	....	....	....	....	....	....	....	....	....	21	0	5	5	6	....	....	....	....
2001-02	**Pittsburgh**	**NHL**	**60**	**0**	**3**	**3**	**68**	**0**	**0**	**0**	**46**	**0.0**	**–1**	**0**	**0.0**	**16:46**	....	....	....	....	....	....	....	....	....
2002-03	**Pittsburgh**	**NHL**	**8**	**0**	**0**	**0**	**2**	**0**	**0**	**0**	**6**	**0.0**	**–2**	**0**	**0.0**	**15:19**	....	....	....	....	....	....	....	....	....
	NHL Totals		**86**	**0**	**5**	**5**	**91**	**0**	**0**	**0**	**61**	**0.0**		**0**	**0.0**	**16:15**	....	....	....	....	....	....	....	....	....

Missed majority of 2002-03 season recovering from shoulder injury suffered in game vs. Boston, October 13, 2002.

MELLANBY, Scott

(MEH-lihn-bee, SKAWT) **ST.L.**

Right wing. Shoots right. 6'1", 205 lbs. Born, Montreal, Que., June 11, 1966. Philadelphia's 2nd choice, 27th overall, in 1984 Entry Draft.

Season	Club	League	GP	G	A	Pts	PIM	PP	SH	GW	S	%	+/-	TF	F%	Min	GP	G	A	Pts	PIM	PP	SH	GW	Min
1982-83	Don Mills	MTHL	72	66	52	118	38	....	....	....	....	....	....	....	....	....	....	....	....	....	....	....	....	....	....
1983-84	Henry Carr	MTJHL	39	37	37	74	97	....	....	....	....	....	....	....	....	....	....	....	....	....	....	....	....	....	....
1984-85	U. of Wisconsin	WCHA	40	14	24	38	60	....	....	....	....	....	....	....	....	....	....	....	....	....	....	....	....	....	....
1985-86	U. of Wisconsin	WCHA	32	21	23	44	89	....	....	....	....	....	....	....	....	....	....	....	....	....	....	....	....	....	....
	Philadelphia	**NHL**	**2**	**0**	**0**	**0**	**0**	**0**	**0**	**0**	**0**	**0.0**	**–1**	....	....	....	....	....	....	....	....	....	....	....	....
1986-87	**Philadelphia**	**NHL**	**71**	**11**	**21**	**32**	**94**	**1**	**0**	**0**	**118**	**9.3**	**8**	....	....	....	**24**	**5**	**5**	**10**	**46**	**0**	**0**	**1**	....
1987-88	**Philadelphia**	**NHL**	**75**	**25**	**26**	**51**	**185**	**7**	**0**	**2**	**190**	**13.2**	**–7**	....	....	....	**7**	**0**	**1**	**1**	**16**	**0**	**0**	**0**	....
1988-89	**Philadelphia**	**NHL**	**76**	**21**	**29**	**50**	**183**	**11**	**0**	**3**	**202**	**10.4**	**–13**	....	....	....	**19**	**4**	**5**	**9**	**28**	**0**	**0**	**0**	....
1989-90	**Philadelphia**	**NHL**	**57**	**6**	**17**	**23**	**77**	**0**	**0**	**1**	**104**	**5.8**	**–4**	....	....	....	....	....	....	....	....	....	....	....	....
1990-91	**Philadelphia**	**NHL**	**74**	**20**	**21**	**41**	**155**	**5**	**0**	**6**	**165**	**12.1**	**8**	....	....	....	....	....	....	....	....	....	....	....	....
1991-92	**Edmonton**	**NHL**	**80**	**23**	**27**	**50**	**197**	**7**	**0**	**5**	**159**	**14.5**	**5**	....	....	....	**16**	**2**	**1**	**3**	**29**	**1**	**0**	**1**	....
1992-93	**Edmonton**	**NHL**	**69**	**15**	**17**	**32**	**147**	**6**	**0**	**3**	**114**	**13.2**	**–4**	....	....	....	....	....	....	....	....	....	....	....	....
1993-94	**Florida**	**NHL**	**80**	**30**	**30**	**60**	**149**	**17**	**0**	**4**	**204**	**14.7**	**0**	....	....	....	....	....	....	....	....	....	....	....	....
1994-95	**Florida**	**NHL**	**48**	**13**	**12**	**25**	**90**	**4**	**0**	**5**	**130**	**10.0**	**–16**	....	....	....	....	....	....	....	....	....	....	....	....
1995-96	**Florida**	**NHL**	**79**	**32**	**38**	**70**	**160**	**19**	**0**	**3**	**225**	**14.2**	**4**	....	....	....	**22**	**3**	**6**	**9**	**44**	**2**	**0**	**0**	....
1996-97	**Florida**	**NHL**	**82**	**27**	**29**	**56**	**170**	**9**	**1**	**4**	**221**	**12.2**	**7**	....	....	....	**5**	**0**	**2**	**2**	**4**	**0**	**0**	**0**	....
1997-98	**Florida**	**NHL**	**79**	**15**	**24**	**39**	**127**	**6**	**0**	**1**	**188**	**8.0**	**–14**	....	....	....	....	....	....	....	....	....	....	....	....
1998-99	**Florida**	**NHL**	**67**	**18**	**27**	**45**	**85**	**4**	**0**	**3**	**136**	**13.2**	**5**	**11**	**27.3**	**16:14**	....	....	....	....	....	....	....	....	....
99-2000	**Florida**	**NHL**	**77**	**18**	**28**	**46**	**126**	**6**	**0**	**2**	**134**	**13.4**	**14**	**20**	**60.0**	**14:51**	**4**	**0**	**1**	**1**	**2**	**0**	**0**	**0**	**13:09**
2000-01	**Florida**	**NHL**	**40**	**4**	**9**	**13**	**46**	**1**	**0**	**0**	**58**	**6.9**	**–13**	**4**	**50.0**	**14:59**	....	....	....	....	....	....	....	....	....
	St. Louis	**NHL**	**23**	**7**	**1**	**8**	**25**	**2**	**0**	**0**	**37**	**18.9**	**0**	**1**	**0.0**	**15:00**	**15**	**3**	**3**	**6**	**17**	**2**	**0**	**0**	**14:43**
2001-02	**St. Louis**	**NHL**	**64**	**15**	**26**	**41**	**93**	**8**	**0**	**2**	**137**	**10.9**	**–5**	**3**	**0.0**	**15:40**	**10**	**7**	**3**	**10**	**18**	**4**	**0**	**1**	**17:54**
2002-03	**St. Louis**	**NHL**	**80**	**26**	**31**	**57**	**176**	**13**	**0**	**4**	**132**	**19.7**	**1**	**11**	**45.5**	**16:39**	**6**	**0**	**1**	**1**	**10**	**0**	**0**	**0**	**16:18**
	NHL Totals		**1223**	**326**	**413**	**739**	**2285**	**126**	**1**	**48**	**2654**	**12.3**		**50**	**44.0**	**15:42**	**128**	**24**	**28**	**52**	**214**	**9**	**0**	**3**	**15:43**

Played in NHL All-Star Game (1996)

Traded to **Edmonton** by **Philadelphia** with Craig Fisher and Craig Berube for Dave Brown, Corey Foster and Jari Kurri, May 30, 1991. Claimed by **Florida** from **Edmonton** in Expansion Draft, June 24, 1993. Traded to **St. Louis** by **Florida** for rights to Dave Morisset and St. Louis' 5th round choice (Vince Bellissimo) in 2002 Entry Draft, February 9, 2001.

MELOCHE, Eric

(muh-LAWSH, AIR-ihk) **PIT.**

Right wing. Shoots right. 5'10", 197 lbs. Born, Montreal, Que., May 1, 1976. Pittsburgh's 7th choice, 186th overall, in 1996 Entry Draft.

Season	Club	League	GP	G	A	Pts	PIM	PP	SH	GW	S	%	+/-	TF	F%	Min	GP	G	A	Pts	PIM	PP	SH	GW	Min
1994-95	Cornwall Colts	OCJHL	40	7	15	22	51	....	....	....	....	....	....	....	....	....	....	....	....	....	....	....	....	....	....
1995-96	Cornwall Colts	OCJHL	64	68	53	121	162	....	....	....	....	....	....	....	....	....	....	....	....	....	....	....	....	....	....
1996-97	Ohio State	CCHA	39	12	11	23	78	....	....	....	....	....	....	....	....	....	....	....	....	....	....	....	....	....	....
1997-98	Ohio State	CCHA	42	26	22	48	86	....	....	....	....	....	....	....	....	....	....	....	....	....	....	....	....	....	....
1998-99	Ohio State	CCHA	35	11	16	27	87	....	....	....	....	....	....	....	....	....	....	....	....	....	....	....	....	....	....
99-2000	Ohio State	CCHA	36	20	11	31	*138	....	....	....	....	....	....	....	....	....	....	....	....	....	....	....	....	....	....
2000-01	Wilkes-Barre	AHL	79	20	20	40	72	....	....	....	....	....	....	....	....	....	21	6	10	16	17	....	....	....	....
2001-02	**Pittsburgh**	**NHL**	**23**	**0**	**1**	**1**	**8**	**0**	**0**	**0**	**29**	**0.0**	**–7**	**4**	**0.0**	**10:10**	....	....	....	....	....	....	....	....	....
	Wilkes-Barre	AHL	55	13	14	27	91	....	....	....	....	....	....	....	....	....	....	....	....	....	....	....	....	....	....
2002-03	**Pittsburgh**	**NHL**	**13**	**5**	**1**	**6**	**4**	**2**	**0**	**1**	**34**	**14.7**	**–2**	**27**	**55.6**	**0:00**	....	....	....	....	....	....	....	....	....
	Wilkes-Barre	AHL	59	12	17	29	95	....	....	....	....	....	....	....	....	....	6	1	0	1	20	....	....	....	....
	NHL Totals		**36**	**5**	**2**	**7**	**12**	**2**	**0**	**1**	**63**	**7.9**		**31**	**0.0**	**6:30**	....	....	....	....	....	....	....	....	....

MESSIER, Eric

(MEHS-see-ay, AIR-ihk) **FLA.**

Left wing. Shoots left. 6'2", 195 lbs. Born, Drummondville, Que., October 29, 1973.

Season	Club	League	GP	G	A	Pts	PIM	PP	SH	GW	S	%	+/-	TF	F%	Min	GP	G	A	Pts	PIM	PP	SH	GW	Min
1990-91	Swift Textile	QAHA	STATISTICS NOT AVAILABLE																						
	Mtl-Bourassa	QAAA	3	0	1	1	0	....	....	....	....	....	....	....	....	....	2	0	0	0	0	....	....	....	....
1991-92	Trois-Rivieres	QMJHL	58	2	10	12	28	....	....	....	....	....	....	....	....	....	15	2	2	4	13	....	....	....	....
1992-93	Sherbrooke	QMJHL	51	4	17	21	82	....	....	....	....	....	....	....	....	....	15	0	4	4	18	....	....	....	....
1993-94	Sherbrooke	QMJHL	67	4	24	28	69	....	....	....	....	....	....	....	....	....	12	1	7	8	14	....	....	....	....
1994-95	U. Quebec T-R	OUAA	13	8	5	13	20	....	....	....	....	....	....	....	....	....	4	0	3	3	8	....	....	....	....
1995-96	Cornwall Aces	AHL	72	5	9	14	111	....	....	....	....	....	....	....	....	....	8	1	1	2	20	....	....	....	....
1996-97	**Colorado**	**NHL**	**21**	**0**	**0**	**0**	**4**	**0**	**0**	**0**	**11**	**0.0**	**7**	....	....	....	**6**	**0**	**0**	**0**	**4**	**0**	**0**	**0**	....
	Hershey Bears	AHL	55	16	26	42	69	....	....	....	....	....	....	....	....	....	9	3	8	11	14	....	....	....	....
1997-98	**Colorado**	**NHL**	**62**	**4**	**12**	**16**	**20**	**0**	**0**	**0**	**66**	**6.1**	**4**	....	....	....	....	....	....	....	....	....	....	....	....
1998-99	**Colorado**	**NHL**	**31**	**4**	**2**	**6**	**14**	**1**	**0**	**1**	**30**	**13.3**	**0**	**0**	**0.0**	**13:43**	**3**	**0**	**0**	**0**	**0**	**0**	**0**	**0**	**4:40**
	Hershey Bears	AHL	6	1	3	4	4	....	....	....	....	....	....	....	....	....	....	....	....	....	....	....	....	....	....
99-2000	**Colorado**	**NHL**	**61**	**3**	**6**	**9**	**24**	**1**	**0**	**0**	**28**	**10.7**	**0**	**4**	**25.0**	**10:27**	**14**	**0**	**1**	**1**	**4**	**0**	**0**	**0**	**4:55**
2000-01 ♦	**Colorado**	**NHL**	**64**	**5**	**7**	**12**	**26**	**0**	**0**	**1**	**60**	**8.3**	**–3**	**9**	**44.4**	**12:16**	**23**	**2**	**2**	**4**	**14**	**0**	**0**	**0**	**16:16**
2001-02	**Colorado**	**NHL**	**74**	**5**	**10**	**15**	**26**	**0**	**0**	**3**	**84**	**6.0**	**–5**	**8**	**25.0**	**15:15**	**21**	**1**	**2**	**3**	**0**	**0**	**0**	**0**	**16:34**
2002-03	**Colorado**	**NHL**	**72**	**4**	**10**	**14**	**16**	**0**	**1**	**1**	**52**	**7.7**	**–2**	**17**	**17.7**	**12:20**	**5**	**0**	**0**	**0**	**0**	**0**	**0**	**0**	**6:57**
	NHL Totals		**385**	**25**	**47**	**72**	**130**	**2**	**1**	**6**	**331**	**7.6**		**38**	**26.3**	**12:48**	**72**	**3**	**5**	**8**	**22**	**0**	**0**	**0**	**12:43**

QMJHL Second All-Star Team (1994)

Signed as a free agent by **Colorado**, June 14, 1995. • Missed majority of 1998-99 season recovering from elbow injury suffered in game vs. Ottawa, October 10, 1998. Traded to **Florida** by **Colorado** with Vaclav Nedorost for Peter Worrell and Florida's 2nd round choice in 2004 Entry Draft, July 19, 2003.

MESSIER, Mark
(MEHS-see-ay, MAHRK)

Center. Shoots left. 6'1", 210 lbs. Born, Edmonton, Alta., January 18, 1961. Edmonton's 2nd choice, 48th overall, in 1979 Entry Draft.

			Regular Season														Playoffs								
Season	Club	League	GP	G	A	Pts	PIM	PP	SH	GW	S	%	+/-	TF	F%	Min	GP	G	A	Pts	PIM	PP	SH	GW	Min
1976-77	Spruce Grove	AJHL	57	27	39	66	91																		
1977-78	St. Albert Saints	AJHL	54	25	49	74	194																		
	Portland	WHL															7	4	1	5	2				
1978-79	St. Albert Saints	AJHL	17	15	18	33	64																		
	Indianapolis	WHA	5	0	0	0	0																		
	Cincinnati	WHA	47	1	10	11	58																		
1979-80	**Edmonton**	**NHL**	**75**	**12**	**21**	**33**	**120**	**1**	**1**	**1**	**113**	**10.6**	**–10**				**3**	**1**	**2**	**3**	**2**	**0**	**1**	**0**	
	Houston Apollos	CHL	4	0	3	3	4																		
1980-81	**Edmonton**	**NHL**	**72**	**23**	**40**	**63**	**102**	**4**	**0**	**1**	**179**	**12.8**	**–12**				**9**	**2**	**5**	**7**	**13**	**0**	**0**	**0**	
1981-82	**Edmonton**	**NHL**	**78**	**50**	**38**	**88**	**119**	**10**	**0**	**3**	**235**	**21.3**	**21**				**5**	**1**	**2**	**3**	**8**	**0**	**0**	**0**	
1982-83	**Edmonton**	**NHL**	**77**	**48**	**58**	**106**	**72**	**12**	**1**	**2**	**237**	**20.3**	**19**				**15**	**15**	**6**	**21**	**14**	**4**	**2**	**0**	
1983-84♦	**Edmonton**	**NHL**	**73**	**37**	**64**	**101**	**165**	**7**	**4**	**7**	**219**	**16.9**	**40**				**19**	**8**	**18**	**26**	**19**	**1**	**1**	**2**	
1984-85♦	**Edmonton**	**NHL**	**55**	**23**	**31**	**54**	**57**	**4**	**5**	**1**	**136**	**16.9**	**8**				**18**	**12**	**13**	**25**	**12**	**1**	**1**	**1**	
1985-86	**Edmonton**	**NHL**	**63**	**35**	**49**	**84**	**68**	**10**	**5**	**7**	**201**	**17.4**	**36**				**10**	**4**	**6**	**10**	**18**	**0**	**2**	**0**	
1986-87♦	**Edmonton**	**NHL**	**77**	**37**	**70**	**107**	**73**	**7**	**4**	**5**	**208**	**17.8**	**21**				**21**	**12**	**16**	**28**	**16**	**1**	**2**	**1**	
1987-88♦	**Edmonton**	**NHL**	**77**	**37**	**74**	**111**	**103**	**12**	**3**	**7**	**182**	**20.3**	**21**				**19**	**11**	**23**	**34**	**29**	**7**	**1**	**0**	
1988-89	**Edmonton**	**NHL**	**72**	**33**	**61**	**94**	**130**	**6**	**6**	**4**	**164**	**20.1**	**–5**				**7**	**1**	**11**	**12**	**8**	**0**	**0**	**0**	
1989-90♦	**Edmonton**	**NHL**	**79**	**45**	**84**	**129**	**79**	**13**	**6**	**3**	**211**	**21.3**	**19**				**22**	**9**	***22**	***31**	**20**	**1**	**1**	**1**	
1990-91	**Edmonton**	**NHL**	**53**	**12**	**52**	**64**	**34**	**3**	**1**	**2**	**109**	**11.0**	**15**				**18**	**4**	**11**	**15**	**16**	**1**	**0**	**0**	
1991-92	**NY Rangers**	**NHL**	**79**	**35**	**72**	**107**	**76**	**12**	**4**	**6**	**212**	**16.5**	**31**				**11**	**7**	**7**	**14**	**6**	**2**	**2**	**0**	
1992-93	**NY Rangers**	**NHL**	**75**	**25**	**66**	**91**	**72**	**7**	**2**	**2**	**215**	**11.6**	**–6**												
1993-94♦	**NY Rangers**	**NHL**	**76**	**26**	**58**	**84**	**76**	**6**	**2**	**5**	**216**	**12.0**	**25**				**23**	**12**	**18**	**30**	**33**	**2**	**1**	**4**	
1994-95	**NY Rangers**	**NHL**	**46**	**14**	**39**	**53**	**40**	**3**	**3**	**2**	**126**	**11.1**	**8**				**10**	**3**	**10**	**13**	**8**	**2**	**0**	**1**	
1995-96	**NY Rangers**	**NHL**	**74**	**47**	**52**	**99**	**122**	**14**	**1**	**5**	**241**	**19.5**	**29**				**11**	**4**	**7**	**11**	**16**	**2**	**0**	**1**	
1996-97	**NY Rangers**	**NHL**	**71**	**36**	**48**	**84**	**88**	**7**	**5**	**9**	**227**	**15.9**	**12**				**15**	**3**	**9**	**12**	**6**	**0**	**0**	**1**	
1997-98	**Vancouver**	**NHL**	**82**	**22**	**38**	**60**	**58**	**8**	**2**	**2**	**139**	**15.8**	**–10**												
1998-99	**Vancouver**	**NHL**	**59**	**13**	**35**	**48**	**33**	**4**	**2**	**2**	**97**	**13.4**	**–12**	**1536**	**53.9**	**22:36**									
99-2000	**Vancouver**	**NHL**	**66**	**17**	**37**	**54**	**30**	**6**	**0**	**4**	**131**	**13.0**	**–15**	**1684**	**56.8**	**21:12**									
2000-01	**NY Rangers**	**NHL**	**82**	**24**	**43**	**67**	**89**	**12**	**3**	**2**	**131**	**18.3**	**–25**	**1879**	**55.5**	**19:14**									
2001-02	**NY Rangers**	**NHL**	**41**	**7**	**16**	**23**	**32**	**2**	**0**	**2**	**69**	**10.1**	**–1**	**787**	**53.6**	**18:31**									
2002-03	**NY Rangers**	**NHL**	**78**	**18**	**22**	**40**	**30**	**8**	**1**	**5**	**117**	**15.4**	**–2**	**1280**	**52.9**	**18:38**									
	NHL Totals		**1680**	**676**	**1168**	**1844**	**1868**	**178**	**61**	**89**	**4115**	**16.4**		**7166**	**54.8**	**20:00**	**236**	**109**	**186**	**295**	**244**	**24**	**14**	**12**	

NHL First All-Star Team (1982, 1983, 1990, 1992) • NHL Second All-Star Team (1984) • Conn Smythe Trophy (1984) • Lester B. Pearson Award (1990, 1992) • Hart Trophy (1990, 1992)

Played in NHL All-Star Game (1982, 1983, 1984, 1986, 1988, 1989, 1990, 1991, 1992, 1994, 1996, 1997, 1998, 2000)

Signed as an underage free agent by **Indianapolis** (WHA) to a 10-game tryout contract, November 5, 1978. Signed as a free agent by **Cincinnati** (WHA) after **Indianapolis** (WHA) franchise folded, December, 1978. Traded to **NY Rangers** by **Edmonton** with future considerations (Jeff Beukeboom for David Shaw, November 12, 1991) for Bernie Nicholls, Steven Rice and Louie DeBrusk, October 4, 1991. Signed as a free agent by **Vancouver**, July 30, 1997. Signed as a free agent by **NY Rangers**, July 13, 2000. • Missed majority of 2001-02 season recovering from back injury suffered in game vs. Toronto, December 8, 2001. Rights traded to **San Jose** by **NY Rangers** for future considerations, June 30, 2003.

METROPOLIT, Glen
(MEH-troh-poh-LIHT, GLEHN)

Center. Shoots right. 5'10", 200 lbs. Born, Toronto, Ont., June 25, 1974.

1992-93	Richmond Hill	MTJHL	43	27	36	63	36																		
1993-94	Richmond Hill	MTJHL	49	38	62	100	83																		
1994-95	Vernon Vipers	BCJHL	60	43	74	117	92																		
1995-96	Nashville Knights	ECHL	58	30	31	61	62										5	3	8	11	2				
	Atlanta Knights	IHL	1	0	0	0	0																		
1996-97	Pensacola	ECHL	54	35	47	82	45										12	9	16	25	28				
	Quebec Rafales	IHL	22	5	4	9	14										5	0	0	0	2				
1997-98	Grand Rapids	IHL	79	20	35	55	90										3	1	1	2	0				
1998-99	Grand Rapids	IHL	77	28	53	81	92																		
99-2000	**Washington**	**NHL**	**30**	**6**	**13**	**19**	**4**	**1**	**0**	**1**	**57**	**10.5**	**5**	**37**	**46.0**	**13:17**	**2**	**0**	**0**	**0**	**2**	**0**	**0**	**0**	**7:07**
	Portland Pirates	AHL	48	18	42	60	73										1	1	0	1	0				
2000-01	**Washington**	**NHL**	**15**	**1**	**5**	**6**	**10**	**0**	**0**	**0**	**20**	**5.0**	**–2**	**3**	**33.3**	**11:50**	**1**	**0**	**0**	**0**	**0**	**0**	**0**	**0**	**7:03**
	Portland Pirates	AHL	51	25	42	67	59																		
2001-02	**Tampa Bay**	**NHL**	**2**	**0**	**0**	**0**	**0**	**0**	**0**	**0**	**1**	**0.0**	**–2**	**2**	**50.0**	**10:26**									
	Washington	**NHL**	**33**	**1**	**16**	**17**	**6**	**0**	**0**	**0**	**51**	**2.0**	**3**	**145**	**49.7**	**14:24**									
	Portland Pirates	AHL	32	17	22	39	20																		
2002-03	**Washington**	**NHL**	**23**	**2**	**3**	**5**	**6**	**0**	**0**	**1**	**22**	**9.1**	**4**	**99**	**49.5**	**10:07**									
	Portland Pirates	AHL	33	7	23	30	23										3	1	1	2	0				
	NHL Totals		**103**	**10**	**37**	**47**	**26**	**1**	**0**	**2**	**151**	**6.6**		**286**	**49.0**	**12:40**	**3**	**0**	**0**	**0**	**2**	**0**	**0**	**0**	**7:05**

Signed as a free agent by **Washington**, July 19, 1999. Claimed by **Tampa Bay** from **Washington** in Waiver Draft, September 28, 2001. Claimed on waivers by **Washington** from **Tampa Bay**, October 20, 2001. Signed as a free agent by **Jokerit Helsinki** (Finland), April 22, 2003.

MEZEI, Branislav
(MEH-tzay, BRAN-ih-slav) **FLA.**

Defense. Shoots left. 6'5", 236 lbs. Born, Nitra, Czech., October 8, 1980. NY Islanders' 3rd choice, 10th overall, in 1999 Entry Draft.

1996-97	HC Nitra Jr.	Slovak-Jr.	40	8	17	25	42																		
1997-98	Belleville Bulls	OHL	53	3	5	8	58										8	0	2	2	8				
1998-99	Belleville Bulls	OHL	60	5	18	23	90										18	0	4	4	29				
99-2000	Belleville Bulls	OHL	58	7	21	28	99										6	0	3	3	10				
2000-01	**NY Islanders**	**NHL**	**42**	**1**	**4**	**5**	**53**	**0**	**0**	**0**	**29**	**3.4**	**–5**	**0**	**0.0**	**14:48**									
	Lowell	AHL	20	0	3	3	28																		
2001-02	**NY Islanders**	**NHL**	**24**	**0**	**2**	**2**	**12**	**0**	**0**	**0**	**4**	**0.0**	**2**	**0**	**0.0**	**8:28**									
	Bridgeport	AHL	59	1	9	10	137										20	0	1	1	48				
2002-03	**Florida**	**NHL**	**11**	**2**	**0**	**2**	**10**	**0**	**0**	**1**	**10**	**20.0**	**–2**	**0**	**0.0**	**18:22**									
	San Antonio	AHL	1	0	0	0	0										3	0	0	0	0				
	NHL Totals		**77**	**3**	**6**	**9**	**75**	**0**	**0**	**1**	**43**	**7.0**		**0**	**0.0**	**13:20**									

OHL First All-Star Team (2000)

Traded to **Florida** by **NY Islanders** for Jason Wiemer, July 3, 2002. • Missed majority of 2002-03 season recovering from ankle (October 12, 2002 vs. Atlanta) and foot (January 1, 2003 vs. New Jersey) injuries.

MILLER, Aaron
(MIHL-luhr, AIR-ruhn) **L.A.**

Defense. Shoots right. 6'4", 200 lbs. Born, Buffalo, NY, August 11, 1971. NY Rangers' 6th choice, 88th overall, in 1989 Entry Draft.

1987-88	Niagara Scenics	NAJHL	30	4	9	13	2																		
1988-89	Niagara Scenics	NAJHL	59	24	38	62	60																		
1989-90	U. of Vermont	ECAC	31	1	15	16	24																		
1990-91	U. of Vermont	ECAC	30	3	7	10	22																		
1991-92	U. of Vermont	ECAC	31	3	16	19	28																		
1992-93	U. of Vermont	ECAC	30	4	13	17	16																		
1993-94	**Quebec**	**NHL**	**1**	**0**	**0**	**0**	**0**	**0**	**0**	**0**	**0**	**0.0**	**–1**												
	Cornwall Aces	AHL	64	4	10	14	49										13	0	2	2	10				
1994-95	Cornwall Aces	AHL	76	4	18	22	69																		
	Quebec	**NHL**	**9**	**0**	**3**	**3**	**6**	**0**	**0**	**0**	**12**	**0.0**	**2**												
1995-96	**Colorado**	**NHL**	**5**	**0**	**0**	**0**	**0**	**0**	**0**	**0**	**2**	**0.0**	**0**												
	Cornwall Aces	AHL	62	4	23	27	77										8	0	1	1	6				
1996-97	**Colorado**	**NHL**	**56**	**5**	**12**	**17**	**15**	**0**	**0**	**3**	**47**	**10.6**	**15**				**17**	**1**	**2**	**3**	**10**	**0**	**0**	**0**	
1997-98	**Colorado**	**NHL**	**55**	**2**	**2**	**4**	**51**	**0**	**0**	**0**	**29**	**6.9**	**0**				**7**	**0**	**0**	**0**	**8**	**0**	**0**	**0**	
1998-99	**Colorado**	**NHL**	**76**	**5**	**13**	**18**	**42**	**1**	**0**	**2**	**87**	**5.7**	**3**	**0**	**0.0**	**21:49**	**19**	**1**	**5**	**6**	**10**	**0**	**0**	**0**	**21:13**
99-2000	**Colorado**	**NHL**	**53**	**1**	**7**	**8**	**36**	**0**	**0**	**0**	**44**	**2.3**	**3**	**0**	**0.0**	**19:05**	**17**	**1**	**1**	**2**	**6**	**0**	**0**	**0**	**19:12**
2000-01	**Colorado**	**NHL**	**56**	**4**	**9**	**13**	**29**	**0**	**0**	**0**	**49**	**8.2**	**19**	**0**	**0.0**	**18:25**									
	Los Angeles	**NHL**	**13**	**0**	**5**	**5**	**14**	**0**	**0**	**0**	**10**	**0.0**	**3**	**1**	**0.0**	**22:44**	**13**	**0**	**1**	**1**	**6**	**0**	**0**	**0**	**22:02**

			Regular Season														Playoffs								
Season	Club	League	GP	G	A	Pts	PIM	PP	SH	GW	S	%	+/-	TF	F%	Min	GP	G	A	Pts	PIM	PP	SH	GW	Min
2001-02	Los Angeles	NHL	74	5	12	17	54	0	1	3	75	6.7	14	0	0.0	22:21	7	0	0	0	0	0	0	0	26:28
	United States	Olympics	6	0	0	0	4																		
2002-03	Los Angeles	NHL	49	1	5	6	24	0	0	0	34	2.9	−7	1	100.0	21:30									
	NHL Totals		447	23	68	91	271	1	1	8	389	5.9		2	50.0	20:53	80	3	9	12	40	0	0	0	21:27

ECAC First All-Star Team (1993) • NCAA East Second All-American Team (1993)

Traded to **Quebec** by **NY Rangers** with NY Rangers' 5th round choice (Bill Lindsay) in 1991 Entry Draft for Joe Cirella, January 17, 1991. Transferred to **Colorado** after **Quebec** franchise relocated, June 21, 1995. Traded to **Los Angeles** by **Colorado** with Adam Deadmarsh, a player to be named later (Jared Aulin, March 22, 2001), Colorado's 1st round choice (Dave Steckel) in 2001 Entry Draft and Colorado's 1st round choice (Brian Boyle) in 2003 Entry Draft for Rob Blake and Steve Reinprecht, February 21, 2001.

MILLER, Kevin

(MIHL-luhr, KEH-vihn) **DET.**

Center. Shoots right. 5'11", 190 lbs. Born, Lansing, MI, September 2, 1965. NY Rangers' 10th choice, 202nd overall, in 1984 Entry Draft.

Season	Club	League	GP	G	A	Pts	PIM	PP	SH	GW	S	%	+/-	TF	F%	Min	GP	G	A	Pts	PIM	PP	SH	GW	Min
1983-84	Redford Royals	GLJHL	44	28	57	85																			
1984-85	Michigan State	CCHA	44	11	29	40	84																		
1985-86	Michigan State	CCHA	45	19	52	71	112																		
1986-87	Michigan State	CCHA	42	25	56	81	63																		
1987-88	Michigan State	CCHA	9	6	3	9	18																		
	Team USA	Nat-Tm	48	31	32	63	33																		
	United States	Olympics	5	1	3	4	4																		
1988-89	NY Rangers	NHL	24	3	5	8	2	0	0	1	40	7.5	−1												
	Denver Rangers	IHL	55	29	47	76	19										4	2	1	3	2				
1989-90	NY Rangers	NHL	16	0	5	5	2	0	0	0	9	0.0	−1				1	0	0	0	0	0	0	0	
	Flint Spirits	IHL	48	19	23	42	41																		
1990-91	NY Rangers	NHL	63	17	27	44	63	1	2	3	113	15.0	1												
	Detroit	NHL	11	5	2	7	4	0	1	0	23	21.7	−4				7	3	2	5	20	0	1	0	
1991-92	Detroit	NHL	80	20	26	46	53	3	1	4	130	15.4	6				9	0	2	2	4	0	0	0	
1992-93	Washington	NHL	10	0	3	3	35	0	0	0	10	0.0	−4												
	St. Louis	NHL	72	24	22	46	65	8	3	4	153	15.7	6				10	0	3	3	11	0	0	0	
1993-94	St. Louis	NHL	75	23	25	48	83	6	3	5	154	14.9	6				3	1	0	1	4	0	1	0	
1994-95	St. Louis	NHL	15	2	5	7	0	0	0	0	19	10.5	4												
	San Jose	NHL	21	6	7	13	13	1	1	2	41	14.6	0				6	0	0	0	2	0	0	0	
1995-96	San Jose	NHL	68	22	20	42	41	2	2	2	146	15.1	−8												
	Pittsburgh	NHL	13	6	5	11	4	1	0	0	33	18.2	4				18	3	2	5	8	0	0	0	
1996-97	Chicago	NHL	69	14	17	31	41	5	1	2	139	10.1	−10				6	0	1	1	0	0	0	0	
1997-98	Chicago	NHL	37	4	7	11	8	0	0	1	37	10.8	−4												
	Indianapolis Ice	IHL	26	11	11	22	41										2	1	1	2	0				
1998-99	NY Islanders	NHL	33	1	5	6	13	0	0	0	37	2.7	−5	114	49.1	10:19									
	Chicago Wolves	IHL	30	11	20	31	8										10	2	7	9	22				
99-2000	Ottawa	NHL	9	3	2	5	2	1	0	2	11	27.3	1	34	41.2	8:10	1	0	0	0	0	0	0	0	4:33
	Grand Rapids	IHL	63	20	34	54	51										17	*11	7	*18	30				
2000-01	HC Davos	Swiss	36	*29	27	56	61										4	3	0	3	2				
2001-02	HC Davos	Swiss	43	23	18	41	78										16	4	10	14	12				
2002-03	HC Davos	Swiss	44	14	24	38	40										17	8	3	11	4				
	NHL Totals		616	150	183	333	429	28	14	26	1095	13.7		148	47.3	9:51	61	7	10	17	49	0	2	0	4:33

Traded to **Detroit** by **NY Rangers** with Jim Cummins and Dennis Vial for Joe Kocur and Per Djoos, March 5, 1991. Traded to **Washington** by **Detroit** for Dino Ciccarelli, June 20, 1992. Traded to **St. Louis** by **Washington** for Paul Cavallini, November 2, 1992. Traded to **San Jose** by **St. Louis** for Todd Elik, March 23, 1995. Traded to **Pittsburgh** by **San Jose** for Pittsburgh's 5th round choice (later traded to Boston – Boston selected Elias Abrahamsson) in 1996 Entry Draft , March 20, 1996. Signed as a free agent by **Chicago**, July 18, 1996. Signed as a free agent by **NY Islanders**, October 9, 1998. Signed as a free agent by **Ottawa**, August 24, 1999. Signed as a free agent by **HC Davos** (Swiss), July 26, 2000. Signed as a free agent by **Detroit**, July, 2003.

MILLER, Kip

(MIHL-luhr, KIHP) **WSH.**

Center. Shoots left. 5'10", 190 lbs. Born, Lansing, MI, June 11, 1969. Quebec's 4th choice, 72nd overall, in 1987 Entry Draft.

Season	Club	League	GP	G	A	Pts	PIM	PP	SH	GW	S	%	+/-	TF	F%	Min	GP	G	A	Pts	PIM	PP	SH	GW	Min
1984-85	Det. Compuware	MNHL	65	69	63	132																			
1985-86	Det. Compuware	GLJHL	30	25	28	53																			
1986-87	Michigan State	CCHA	41	20	19	39	92																		
1987-88	Michigan State	CCHA	39	16	25	41	51																		
1988-89	Michigan State	CCHA	47	32	45	77	94																		
1989-90	Michigan State	CCHA	45	*48	53	*101	60																		
1990-91	Quebec	NHL	13	4	3	7	7	0	0	0	16	25.0	−1												
	Halifax Citadels	AHL	66	36	33	69	40																		
1991-92	Quebec	NHL	36	5	10	15	12	1	0	2	46	10.9	−21												
	Halifax Citadels	AHL	24	9	17	26	8																		
	Minnesota	NHL	3	1	2	3	2	1	0	0	3	33.3	−1												
	Kalamazoo Wings	IHL	6	1	8	9	4										12	3	9	12	12				
1992-93	Kalamazoo Wings	IHL	61	17	39	56	59																		
1993-94	San Jose	NHL	11	2	2	4	6	0	0	0	21	9.5	−1												
	Kansas City	IHL	71	38	54	92	51																		
1994-95	Denver Grizzlies	IHL	71	46	60	106	54										17	*15	14	29	8				
	NY Islanders	NHL	8	0	1	1	0	0	0	0	11	0.0	1												
1995-96	Chicago	NHL	10	1	4	5	2	0	0	0	12	8.3	1												
	Indianapolis Ice	IHL	73	32	59	91	46										5	2	6	8	2				
1996-97	Chicago Wolves	IHL	43	11	41	52	32																		
	Indianapolis Ice	IHL	37	17	24	41	18										4	2	2	4	2				
1997-98	Utah Grizzlies	IHL	72	38	59	97	30										4	3	2	5	10				
	NY Islanders	NHL	9	1	3	4	2	0	0	0	11	9.1	−2												
1998-99	Pittsburgh	NHL	77	19	23	42	22	1	0	4	125	15.2	1	150	44.7	16:55	13	2	7	9	19	1	0	0	18:56
99-2000	Pittsburgh	NHL	44	4	15	19	10	0	0	1	50	8.0	−1	132	40.2	14:18									
	Anaheim	NHL	30	6	17	23	4	2	0	1	32	18.8	1	7	42.9	13:44									
2000-01	Pittsburgh	NHL	33	3	8	11	6	1	0	0	38	7.9	0	61	50.8	9:46									
	Grand Rapids	IHL	34	16	19	35	12										10	5	8	13	2				
2001-02	Grand Rapids	AHL	41	21	35	56	27																		
	NY Islanders	NHL	37	7	17	24	6	2	0	1	52	13.5	2	119	58.8	14:07	7	4	2	6	2	2	0	1	11:14
2002-03	Washington	NHL	72	12	38	50	18	3	0	4	89	13.5	−1	171	49.7	14:58	5	0	2	2	2	0	0	0	10:36
	NHL Totals		383	65	143	208	97	11	0	13	506	12.8		640	48.3	14:34	25	6	11	17	23	3	0	1	15:07

CCHA First All-Star Team (1989, 1990) • CCHA Player of the Year (1990) • NCAA West First All-American Team (1989, 1990) • Hobey Baker Memorial Award (Top U.S. Collegiate Player) (1990)

Traded to **Minnesota** by **Quebec** for Steve Maltais, March 8, 1992. Signed as a free agent by **San Jose**, August 10, 1993. Signed as a free agent by **NY Islanders**, July 7, 1994. Signed as a free agent by **Chicago**, July 21, 1995. Signed as a free agent by **NY Islanders**, November 26, 1997. Claimed by **Pittsburgh** from **NY Islanders** in Waiver Draft, October 5, 1998. Traded to **Anaheim** by **Pittsburgh** for Anaheim's 9th round choice (Roman Simicek) in 2000 Entry Draft, January 29, 2000. Signed as a free agent by **Pittsburgh**, September 24, 2000. Signed as a free agent by **Grand Rapids** (AHL), May 31, 2001. Signed as a free agent by **NY Islanders**, January 16, 2002. Signed as a free agent by **Washington**, July 9, 2002.

MILLEY, Norm

(MIHL-lee, NOHR-man) **BUF.**

Right wing. Shoots right. 6', 200 lbs. Born, Toronto, Ont., February 14, 1980. Buffalo's 3rd choice, 47th overall, in 1998 Entry Draft.

Season	Club	League	GP	G	A	Pts	PIM	PP	SH	GW	S	%	+/-	TF	F%	Min	GP	G	A	Pts	PIM	PP	SH	GW	Min
1995-96	Tor. Red Wings	MTHL	42	42	36	78																			
	St. Michael's B	OJHL-B	5	2	1	3	0																		
1996-97	Sudbury Wolves	OHL	61	30	32	62	15																		
1997-98	Sudbury Wolves	OHL	62	33	41	74	48										10	0	1	1	4				
1998-99	Sudbury Wolves	OHL	68	52	68	120	47										4	2	3	5	4				
99-2000	Sudbury Wolves	OHL	68	*52	60	112	47										12	8	11	19	6				
2000-01	Rochester	AHL	77	20	27	47	56										4	0	0	0	2				
2001-02	Buffalo	NHL	5	0	1	1	0	0	0	0	10	0.0	0	1	0.0	13:12									
	Rochester	AHL	74	20	18	38	20										2	0	3	3	6				
2002-03	Buffalo	NHL	8	0	2	2	6	0	0	0	8	0.0	−2	2	50.0	10:41									
	Rochester	AHL	67	16	32	48	39										3	2	0	2	2				
	NHL Totals		13	0	3	3	6	0	0	0	18	0.0		3	33.3	11:39									

OHL All-Rookie Team (1997) • OHL Second All-Star Team (1999) • OHL First All-Star Team (2000) • Canadian Major Junior First All-Star Team (2000)

MILLS, Craig

(MIHLS, KRAYG)

Right wing. Shoots right. 6', 190 lbs. Born, Toronto, Ont., August 27, 1976. Winnipeg's 5th choice, 108th overall, in 1994 Entry Draft.

			Regular Season														Playoffs								
Season	Club	League	GP	G	A	Pts	PIM	PP	SH	GW	S	%	+/-	TF	F%	Min	GP	G	A	Pts	PIM	PP	SH	GW	Min
1992-93	St. Michael's B	MTJHL	44	9	21	30	42	....	....	....	....	....	....	....	....	....	15	1	6	7	8	....	....	....	....
1993-94	Belleville Bulls	OHL	63	15	18	33	88	....	....	....	....	....	....	....	....	....	12	2	1	3	11	....	....	....	....
1994-95	Belleville Bulls	OHL	62	39	41	80	104	....	....	....	....	....	....	....	....	....	13	7	9	16	8	....	....	....	....
1995-96	Belleville Bulls	OHL	48	10	19	29	113	....	....	....	....	....	....	....	....	....	14	4	5	9	32	....	....	....	....
	Winnipeg	**NHL**	**4**	**0**	**2**	**2**	**0**	**0**	**0**	**0**	**0**	**0.0**	**0**	....	....	....	**1**	**0**	**0**	**0**	**0**	**0**	**0**	**0**	....
	Springfield	AHL	....	....	....	....	....	....	....	....	....	....	....	....	....	....	2	0	0	0	0	....	....	....	....
1996-97	Indianapolis Ice	IHL	80	12	7	19	199	....	....	....	....	....	....	....	....	....	4	0	0	0	4	....	....	....	....
1997-98	**Chicago**	**NHL**	**20**	**0**	**3**	**3**	**34**	**0**	**0**	**0**	**5**	**0.0**	**1**	....	....	....	....	....	....	....	....	....	....	....	....
	Indianapolis Ice	IHL	42	8	11	19	119	....	....	....	....	....	....	....	....	....	5	0	0	0	27	....	....	....	....
1998-99	**Chicago**	**NHL**	**7**	**0**	**0**	**0**	**2**	**0**	**0**	**0**	**1**	**0.0**	**−2**	**0**	**0.0**	**5:48**	....	....	....	....	....	....	....	....	....
	Chicago Wolves	IHL	5	0	0	0	14	....	....	....	....	....	....	....	....	....	....	....	....	....	....	....	....	....	....
	Portland Pirates	AHL	48	7	11	18	59	....	....	....	....	....	....	....	....	....	....	....	....	....	....	....	....	....	....
	Indianapolis Ice	IHL	12	2	3	5	14	....	....	....	....	....	....	....	....	....	6	1	0	1	5	....	....	....	....
99-2000	Springfield	AHL	78	10	13	23	151	....	....	....	....	....	....	....	....	....	5	2	1	3	6	....	....	....	....
2000-01	Springfield	AHL	64	8	5	13	131	....	....	....	....	....	....	....	....	....	....	....	....	....	....	....	....	....	....
2001-02	St. John's	AHL	74	10	21	31	137	....	....	....	....	....	....	....	....	....	11	3	3	6	22	....	....	....	....
2002-03	St. John's	AHL	65	10	16	26	121	....	....	....	....	....	....	....	....	....	....	....	....	....	....	....	....	....	....
	NHL Totals		**31**	**0**	**5**	**5**	**36**	**0**	**0**	**0**	**6**	**0.0**		**0**	**0.0**	**5:48**	**1**	**0**	**0**	**0**	**0**	**0**	**0**	**0**	....

Canadian Major Junior Humanitarian Player of the Year (1996)

Rights transferred to **Phoenix** after **Winnipeg** franchise relocated, July 1, 1996. Traded to **Chicago** by **Phoenix** with Alexei Zhamnov and Phoenix's 1st round choice (Ty Jones) in 1997 Entry Draft for Jeremy Roenick, August 16, 1996. Traded to **Phoenix** by **Chicago** for cash, September 11, 1999. Traded to **Toronto** by **Phoenix** with Robert Reichel and Travis Green for Danny Markov, June 12, 2001.

MIRONOV, Boris

(mih-RAWN-ohv, BOHR-ihs) **NYR**

Defense. Shoots right. 6'3", 223 lbs. Born, Moscow, USSR, March 21, 1972. Winnipeg's 2nd choice, 27th overall, in 1992 Entry Draft.

			Regular Season														Playoffs								
Season	Club	League	GP	G	A	Pts	PIM	PP	SH	GW	S	%	+/-	TF	F%	Min	GP	G	A	Pts	PIM	PP	SH	GW	Min
1988-89	CSKA Moscow	USSR	1	0	0	0	0	....	....	....	....	....	....	....	....	....	....	....	....	....	....	....	....	....	....
1989-90	CSKA Moscow	USSR	7	0	0	0	0	....	....	....	....	....	....	....	....	....	....	....	....	....	....	....	....	....	....
1990-91	CSKA Moscow	USSR	36	1	5	6	16	....	....	....	....	....	....	....	....	....	....	....	....	....	....	....	....	....	....
1991-92	CSKA Moscow	CIS	36	2	1	3	22	....	....	....	....	....	....	....	....	....	....	....	....	....	....	....	....	....	....
1992-93	CSKA Moscow	CIS	19	0	5	5	20	....	....	....	....	....	....	....	....	....	....	....	....	....	....	....	....	....	....
1993-94	**Winnipeg**	**NHL**	**65**	**7**	**22**	**29**	**96**	**5**	**0**	**0**	**122**	**5.7**	**−29**	....	....	....	....	....	....	....	....	....	....	....	....
	Edmonton	**NHL**	**14**	**0**	**2**	**2**	**14**	**0**	**0**	**0**	**23**	**0.0**	**−4**	....	....	....	....	....	....	....	....	....	....	....	....
1994-95	**Edmonton**	**NHL**	**29**	**1**	**7**	**8**	**40**	**0**	**0**	**0**	**48**	**2.1**	**−9**	....	....	....	....	....	....	....	....	....	....	....	....
	Cape Breton	AHL	4	2	5	7	23	....	....	....	....	....	....	....	....	....	....	....	....	....	....	....	....	....	....
1995-96	**Edmonton**	**NHL**	**78**	**8**	**24**	**32**	**101**	**7**	**0**	**1**	**158**	**5.1**	**−23**	....	....	....	....	....	....	....	....	....	....	....	....
1996-97	**Edmonton**	**NHL**	**55**	**6**	**26**	**32**	**85**	**2**	**0**	**1**	**147**	**4.1**	**2**	....	....	....	**12**	**2**	**8**	**10**	**16**	**2**	**0**	**0**	....
1997-98	**Edmonton**	**NHL**	**81**	**16**	**30**	**46**	**100**	**10**	**1**	**1**	**203**	**7.9**	**−8**	....	....	....	**12**	**3**	**3**	**6**	**27**	**1**	**0**	**1**	....
	Russia	Olympics	6	0	2	2	2	....	....	....	....	....	....	....	....	....	....	....	....	....	....	....	....	....	....
1998-99	**Edmonton**	**NHL**	**63**	**11**	**29**	**40**	**104**	**5**	**0**	**4**	**138**	**8.0**	**6**	**0**	**0.0**	**25:55**	....	....	....	....	....	....	....	....	....
	Chicago	**NHL**	**12**	**0**	**9**	**9**	**27**	**0**	**0**	**0**	**35**	**0.0**	**7**	**0**	**0.0**	**24:17**	....	....	....	....	....	....	....	....	....
99-2000	**Chicago**	**NHL**	**58**	**9**	**28**	**37**	**72**	**4**	**2**	**1**	**144**	**6.3**	**−3**	**1**	**100.0**	**24:53**	....	....	....	....	....	....	....	....	....
2000-01	**Chicago**	**NHL**	**66**	**5**	**17**	**22**	**42**	**3**	**0**	**0**	**143**	**3.5**	**−14**	**0**	**0.0**	**22:05**	....	....	....	....	....	....	....	....	....
2001-02	**Chicago**	**NHL**	**64**	**4**	**14**	**18**	**68**	**0**	**0**	**1**	**129**	**3.1**	**15**	**0**	**0.0**	**22:43**	**1**	**0**	**0**	**0**	**2**	**0**	**0**	**0**	**5:41**
	Russia	Olympics	6	1	0	1	2	....	....	....	....	....	....	....	....	....	....	....	....	....	....	....	....	....	....
2002-03	**Chicago**	**NHL**	**20**	**3**	**1**	**4**	**22**	**1**	**0**	**0**	**14**	**21.4**	**−1**	**0**	**0.0**	**19:12**	....	....	....	....	....	....	....	....	....
	NY Rangers	**NHL**	**36**	**3**	**9**	**12**	**34**	**1**	**0**	**0**	**56**	**5.4**	**3**	**0**	**0.0**	**20:35**	....	....	....	....	....	....	....	....	....
	NHL Totals		**641**	**73**	**218**	**291**	**805**	**38**	**3**	**9**	**1360**	**5.4**		**1**	**100.0**	**23:13**	**25**	**5**	**11**	**16**	**45**	**3**	**0**	**1**	**5:41**

NHL All-Rookie Team (1994)

Traded to **Edmonton** by **Winnipeg** with Mats Lindgren, Winnipeg's 1st round choice (Jason Bonsignore) in 1994 Entry Draft and Florida's 4th round choice (previously acquired, Edmonton selected Adam Copeland) in 1994 Entry Draft for Dave Manson and St. Louis' 6th round choice (previously acquired, Winnipeg selected Chris Kibermanis) in 1994 Entry Draft, March 15, 1994. Traded to **Chicago** by **Edmonton** with Dean McAmmond and Jonas Elofsson for Chad Kilger, Daniel Cleary, Ethan Moreau and Christian Laflamme, March 20, 1999. Traded to **NY Rangers** by **Chicago** for future considerations, January 8, 2003.

MITCHELL, Willie

(MIHT-chehl, WIHL-lee) **MIN.**

Defense. Shoots left. 6'3", 205 lbs. Born, Port McNeill, B.C., April 23, 1977. New Jersey's 12th choice, 199th overall, in 1996 Entry Draft.

			Regular Season														Playoffs								
Season	Club	League	GP	G	A	Pts	PIM	PP	SH	GW	S	%	+/-	TF	F%	Min	GP	G	A	Pts	PIM	PP	SH	GW	Min
1993-94	Notre Dame	SMHL	31	4	11	15	81	....	....	....	....	....	....	....	....	....	....	....	....	....	....	....	....	....	....
1994-95	Kelowna Spartans	BCHL	42	3	8	11	71	....	....	....	....	....	....	....	....	....	....	....	....	....	....	....	....	....	....
1995-96	Melfort Mustangs	SJHL	19	2	6	8	....	....	....	....	....	....	....	....	....	....	14	0	2	2	12	....	....	....	....
1996-97	Melfort Mustangs	SJHL	64	14	42	56	227	....	....	....	....	....	....	....	....	....	4	0	1	1	23	....	....	....	....
1997-98	Clarkson Knights	ECAC	34	9	17	26	105	....	....	....	....	....	....	....	....	....	....	....	....	....	....	....	....	....	....
1998-99	Clarkson Knights	ECAC	34	10	19	29	40	....	....	....	....	....	....	....	....	....	....	....	....	....	....	....	....	....	....
	Albany River Rats	AHL	6	1	3	4	29	....	....	....	....	....	....	....	....	....	....	....	....	....	....	....	....	....	....
99-2000	**New Jersey**	**NHL**	**2**	**0**	**0**	**0**	**0**	**0**	**0**	**0**	**2**	**0.0**	**1**	**0**	**0.0**	**16:04**	....	....	....	....	....	....	....	....	....
	Albany River Rats	AHL	63	5	14	19	71	....	....	....	....	....	....	....	....	....	5	1	2	3	4	....	....	....	....
2000-01	**New Jersey**	**NHL**	**16**	**0**	**2**	**2**	**29**	**0**	**0**	**0**	**14**	**0.0**	**0**	**0**	**0.0**	**14:52**	....	....	....	....	....	....	....	....	....
	Albany River Rats	AHL	41	3	13	16	94	....	....	....	....	....	....	....	....	....	....	....	....	....	....	....	....	....	....
	Minnesota	**NHL**	**17**	**1**	**7**	**8**	**11**	**0**	**0**	**0**	**16**	**6.3**	**4**	**0**	**0.0**	**20:49**	....	....	....	....	....	....	....	....	....
2001-02	**Minnesota**	**NHL**	**68**	**3**	**10**	**13**	**68**	**0**	**0**	**1**	**67**	**4.5**	**−16**	**0**	**0.0**	**21:25**	....	....	....	....	....	....	....	....	....
2002-03	**Minnesota**	**NHL**	**69**	**2**	**12**	**14**	**84**	**0**	**1**	**1**	**67**	**3.0**	**13**	**0**	**0.0**	**21:28**	**18**	**1**	**3**	**4**	**14**	**0**	**0**	**0**	**24:48**
	NHL Totals		**172**	**6**	**31**	**37**	**192**	**0**	**1**	**2**	**166**	**3.6**		**0**	**0.0**	**20:43**	**18**	**1**	**3**	**4**	**14**	**0**	**0**	**0**	**24:48**

SJHL First All-Star Team (1997) • SJHL Top Defenseman Award (1997) • ECAC Second All-Star Team (1998) • ECAC Rookie of the Year (1998) (co-winner - Erik Cole) • ECAC First All-Star Team (1999) • NCAA East Second All-American Team (1999)

Traded to **Minnesota** by **New Jersey** for Sean O'Donnell, March 4, 2001.

MODANO, Mike

(moh-DA-noh, MIGHK) **DAL.**

Center. Shoots left. 6'3", 205 lbs. Born, Livonia, MI, June 7, 1970. Minnesota's 1st choice, 1st overall, in 1988 Entry Draft.

			Regular Season														Playoffs								
Season	Club	League	GP	G	A	Pts	PIM	PP	SH	GW	S	%	+/-	TF	F%	Min	GP	G	A	Pts	PIM	PP	SH	GW	Min
1985-86	Det. Compuware	MNHL	69	66	65	131	32	....	....	....	....	....	....	....	....	....	....	....	....	....	....	....	....	....	....
1986-87	Prince Albert	WHL	70	32	30	62	96	....	....	....	....	....	....	....	....	....	8	1	4	5	4	....	....	....	....
1987-88	Prince Albert	WHL	65	47	80	127	80	....	....	....	....	....	....	....	....	....	9	7	11	18	18	....	....	....	....
1988-89	Prince Albert	WHL	41	39	66	105	74	....	....	....	....	....	....	....	....	....	....	....	....	....	....	....	....	....	....
	Minnesota	**NHL**	....	....	....	....	....	....	....	....	....	....	....	....	....	....	**2**	**0**	**0**	**0**	**0**	**0**	**0**	**0**	....
1989-90	**Minnesota**	**NHL**	**80**	**29**	**46**	**75**	**63**	**12**	**0**	**2**	**172**	**16.9**	**−7**	....	....	....	**7**	**1**	**1**	**2**	**12**	**0**	**0**	**0**	....
1990-91	**Minnesota**	**NHL**	**79**	**28**	**36**	**64**	**65**	**9**	**0**	**2**	**232**	**12.1**	**2**	....	....	....	**23**	**8**	**12**	**20**	**16**	**3**	**0**	**1**	....
1991-92	**Minnesota**	**NHL**	**76**	**33**	**44**	**77**	**46**	**5**	**0**	**8**	**256**	**12.9**	**−9**	....	....	....	**7**	**3**	**2**	**5**	**4**	**1**	**0**	**0**	....
1992-93	**Minnesota**	**NHL**	**82**	**33**	**60**	**93**	**83**	**9**	**0**	**7**	**307**	**10.7**	**−7**	....	....	....	....	....	....	....	....	....	....	....	....
1993-94	**Dallas**	**NHL**	**76**	**50**	**43**	**93**	**54**	**18**	**0**	**4**	**281**	**17.8**	**−8**	....	....	....	**9**	**7**	**3**	**10**	**16**	**2**	**0**	**2**	....
1994-95	**Dallas**	**NHL**	**30**	**12**	**17**	**29**	**8**	**4**	**1**	**0**	**100**	**12.0**	**7**	....	....	....	....	....	....	....	....	....	....	....	....
1995-96	**Dallas**	**NHL**	**78**	**36**	**45**	**81**	**63**	**8**	**4**	**4**	**320**	**11.3**	**−12**	....	....	....	....	....	....	....	....	....	....	....	....
1996-97	**Dallas**	**NHL**	**80**	**35**	**48**	**83**	**42**	**9**	**5**	**9**	**291**	**12.0**	**43**	....	....	....	**7**	**4**	**1**	**5**	**0**	**1**	**1**	**2**	....
1997-98	**Dallas**	**NHL**	**52**	**21**	**38**	**59**	**32**	**7**	**5**	**2**	**191**	**11.0**	**25**	....	....	....	**17**	**4**	**10**	**14**	**12**	**1**	**0**	**1**	....
	United States	Olympics	4	2	0	2	0	....	....	....	....	....	....	....	....	....	....	....	....	....	....	....	....	....	....
1998-99♦	**Dallas**	**NHL**	**77**	**34**	**47**	**81**	**44**	**6**	**4**	**7**	**224**	**15.2**	**29**	**1572**	**51.1**	**20:50**	**23**	**5**	***18**	**23**	**16**	**1**	**1**	**1**	**24:40**
99-2000	**Dallas**	**NHL**	**77**	**38**	**43**	**81**	**48**	**11**	**1**	**8**	**188**	**20.2**	**0**	**1763**	**51.4**	**22:55**	**23**	**10**	***13**	**23**	**10**	**4**	**0**	**2**	**25:26**
2000-01	**Dallas**	**NHL**	**81**	**33**	**51**	**84**	**52**	**8**	**3**	**7**	**208**	**15.9**	**26**	**1791**	**52.0**	**22:24**	**9**	**3**	**4**	**7**	**0**	**2**	**0**	**0**	**25:43**
2001-02	**Dallas**	**NHL**	**78**	**34**	**43**	**77**	**38**	**6**	**2**	**5**	**219**	**15.5**	**14**	**1710**	**53.7**	**22:27**	....	....	....	....	....	....	....	....	....
	United States	Olympics	6	0	*6	6	4	....	....	....	....	....	....	....	....	....	....	....	....	....	....	....	....	....	....
2002-03	**Dallas**	**NHL**	**79**	**28**	**57**	**85**	**30**	**5**	**2**	**6**	**193**	**14.5**	**34**	**1808**	**51.4**	**20:53**	**12**	**5**	**10**	**15**	**4**	**1**	**0**	**2**	**23:53**
	NHL Totals		**1025**	**444**	**618**	**1062**	**668**	**117**	**27**	**71**	**3182**	**14.0**		**8644**	**51.9**	**21:54**	**139**	**50**	**74**	**124**	**90**	**16**	**2**	**11**	**24:56**

WHL East First All-Star Team (1989) • NHL All-Rookie Team (1990) • NHL Second All-Star Team (2000)

Played in NHL All-Star Game (1993, 1998, 1999, 2000, 2003)

Transferred to **Dallas** after **Minnesota** franchise relocated, June 9, 1993.

MODIN, Fredrik

(moh-DEEN, FREHD-rihk) **T.B.**

Left wing. Shoots left. 6'4", 225 lbs. Born, Sundsvall, Sweden, October 8, 1974. Toronto's 3rd choice, 64th overall, in 1994 Entry Draft.

Season	Club	League	GP	G	A	Pts	PIM	PP	SH	GW	S	%	+/-	TF	F%	Min	Playoffs GP	G	A	Pts	PIM	PP	SH	GW	Min
1991-92	Timra IK	Swede-2	11	1	0	1	0																		
1992-93	Timra IK	Swede-2	30	5	7	12	12										5	1	0	1	0				
1993-94	Timra IK	Swede-2	30	16	15	31	36										2	0	1	1	6				
1994-95	Brynas IF Gavle	Sweden	38	9	10	19	33										14	4	4	8	6				
1995-96	Brynas IF Gavle	Sweden	22	4	8	12	22																		
1996-97	Toronto	NHL	76	6	7	13	24	0	0	0	85	7.1	–14												
1997-98	Toronto	NHL	74	16	16	32	32	1	0	4	137	11.7	–5												
1998-99	Toronto	NHL	67	16	15	31	35	1	0	3	108	14.8	14	2	50.0	13:34	8	0	0	0	6	0	0	0	9:50
99-2000	Tampa Bay	NHL	80	22	26	48	18	3	0	5	167	13.2	–26	6	50.0	15:32									
2000-01	Tampa Bay	NHL	76	32	24	56	48	8	0	4	217	14.7	–1	21	42.9	17:15									
2001-02	Tampa Bay	NHL	54	14	17	31	27	2	0	4	141	9.9	0	25	40.0	19:05									
2002-03	Tampa Bay	NHL	76	17	23	40	43	2	1	4	179	9.5	7	35	28.6	17:35	11	2	0	2	18	0	0	0	19:18
	NHL Totals		503	123	128	251	227	17	1	24	1034	11.9		89	37.1	16:31	19	2	0	2	24	0	0	0	15:19

Played in NHL All-Star Game (2001)

Traded to **Tampa Bay** by **Toronto** for Cory Cross and Tampa Bay's 7th round choice (Ivan Kolozvary) in 2001 Entry Draft, October 1, 1999.

MODRY, Jaroslav

(MOH-dree, YAHRO-slahv) **L.A.**

Defense. Shoots left. 6'2", 220 lbs. Born, Ceske Budejovice, Czech., February 27, 1971. New Jersey's 11th choice, 179th overall, in 1990 Entry Draft.

Season	Club	League	GP	G	A	Pts	PIM	PP	SH	GW	S	%	+/-	TF	F%	Min	Playoffs GP	G	A	Pts	PIM	PP	SH	GW	Min
1987-88	Ceske Budejovice	Czech	3	0	0	0	0																		
1988-89	Ceske Budejovice	Czech	28	0	1	1	8																		
1989-90	Ceske Budejovice	Czech	41	2	2	4																			
1990-91	Dukla Trencin	Czech	33	1	9	10	6																		
1991-92	Ceske Budejovice	Czech-2	14	4	10	14																			
	Dukla Trencin	Czech	18	0	4	4	6																		
1992-93	Utica Devils	AHL	80	7	35	42	62										5	0	2	2	2				
1993-94	New Jersey	NHL	41	2	15	17	18	2	0	0	35	5.7	10												
	Albany River Rats	AHL	19	1	5	6	25																		
1994-95	Ceske Budejovice	Czech	19	1	3	4	30																		
	New Jersey	NHL	11	0	0	0	0	0	0	0	10	0.0	–1												
	Albany River Rats	AHL	18	5	6	11	14										14	3	3	6	4				
1995-96	Ottawa	NHL	64	4	14	18	38	1	0	1	89	4.5	–17												
	Los Angeles	NHL	9	0	3	3	6	0	0	0	17	0.0	–4												
1996-97	Los Angeles	NHL	30	3	3	6	25	1	1	0	32	9.4	–13												
	Phoenix	IHL	23	3	12	15	17																		
	Utah Grizzlies	IHL	11	1	4	5	20										7	0	1	1	6				
1997-98	Utah Grizzlies	IHL	74	12	21	33	72										4	0	2	2	6				
1998-99	Los Angeles	NHL	5	0	1	1	0	0	0	0	11	0.0	1	0	0.0	26:00									
	Long Beach	IHL	64	6	29	35	44										8	4	2	6	4				
99-2000	Los Angeles	NHL	26	5	4	9	18	5	0	1	32	15.6	–2	0	0.0	19:13	2	0	0	0	2	0	0	0	16:48
	Long Beach	IHL	11	2	4	6	8																		
2000-01	Los Angeles	NHL	63	4	15	19	48	0	0	0	72	5.6	16	0	0.0	18:22	10	1	0	1	4	1	0	1	16:08
2001-02	Los Angeles	NHL	80	4	38	42	65	4	0	0	119	3.4	–4	0	0.0	19:31	7	0	2	2	0	0	0	0	21:26
2002-03	Los Angeles	NHL	82	13	25	38	68	8	0	1	205	6.3	–13	1	0.0	22:39									
	NHL Totals		411	35	118	153	286	21	1	3	622	5.6		1	0.0	20:20	19	1	2	3	6	1	0	1	18:09

Played in NHL All-Star Game (2002)

Traded to **Ottawa** by **New Jersey** for Ottawa's 4th round choice (Alyn McCauley) in 1995 Entry Draft, July 8, 1995. Traded to **Los Angeles** by **Ottawa** with Ottawa's 8th round choice (Stephen Valiquette) in 1996 Entry Draft for Kevin Brown, March 20, 1996.

MOGILNY, Alexander

(moh-GIHL-nee, al-ehx-AN-duhr) **TOR.**

Right wing. Shoots left. 6', 209 lbs. Born, Khabarovsk, USSR, February 18, 1969. Buffalo's 4th choice, 89th overall, in 1988 Entry Draft.

Season	Club	League	GP	G	A	Pts	PIM	PP	SH	GW	S	%	+/-	TF	F%	Min	Playoffs GP	G	A	Pts	PIM	PP	SH	GW	Min
1986-87	CSKA Moscow	USSR	28	15	1	16	4																		
1987-88	CSKA Moscow	USSR	39	12	8	20	14																		
	Soviet Union	Olympics	6	3	2	5	2																		
1988-89	CSKA Moscow	USSR	31	11	11	22	24																		
1989-90	Buffalo	NHL	65	15	28	43	16	4	0	2	130	11.5	8				4	0	1	1	2	0	0	0	
1990-91	Buffalo	NHL	62	30	34	64	16	3	3	5	201	14.9	14				6	0	6	6	2	0	0	0	
1991-92	Buffalo	NHL	67	39	45	84	73	15	0	2	236	16.5	7				2	0	2	2	0	0	0	0	
1992-93	Buffalo	NHL	77	*76	51	127	40	27	0	11	360	21.1	7				7	7	3	10	6	2	0	0	
1993-94	Buffalo	NHL	66	32	47	79	22	17	0	7	258	12.4	8				7	4	2	6	6	1	0	0	
1994-95	Spartak Moscow	CIS	1	0	1	1	0																		
	Buffalo	NHL	44	19	28	47	36	12	0	2	148	12.8	0				5	3	2	5	2	0	0	0	
1995-96	Vancouver	NHL	79	55	52	107	16	10	5	6	292	18.8	14				6	1	8	9	8	0	0	0	
1996-97	Vancouver	NHL	76	31	42	73	18	7	1	4	174	17.8	9												
1997-98	Vancouver	NHL	51	18	27	45	36	5	4	1	118	15.3	–6												
1998-99	Vancouver	NHL	59	14	31	45	58	3	2	1	110	12.7	0	47	23.4	20:35									
99-2000	Vancouver	NHL	47	21	17	38	16	3	1	1	126	16.7	7	9	11.1	19:34									
	♦ New Jersey	NHL	12	3	3	6	4	2	0	0	35	8.6	–4	0	0.0	17:04	23	4	3	7	4	2	0	1	16:06
2000-01	New Jersey	NHL	75	43	40	83	43	12	0	7	240	17.9	10	11	36.4	16:53	25	5	11	16	8	1	0	2	16:42
2001-02	Toronto	NHL	66	24	33	57	8	5	0	4	188	12.8	1	5	40.0	17:38	20	8	3	11	8	2	0	2	19:23
2002-03	Toronto	NHL	73	33	46	79	12	5	3	9	165	20.0	4	18	33.3	20:03	6	5	2	7	4	0	1	0	21:43
	NHL Totals		919	453	524	977	414	130	19	62	2781	16.3		90	26.7	18:46	111	37	43	80	50	8	1	5	17:39

NHL Second All-Star Team (1993, 1996) • Lady Byng Trophy (2003)

Played in NHL All-Star Game (1992, 1993, 1994, 1996)

Traded to **Vancouver** by **Buffalo** with Buffalo's 5th round choice (Todd Norman) in 1995 Entry Draft for Michael Peca, Mike Wilson and Vancouver's 1st round choice (Jay McKee) in 1995 Entry Draft, July 8, 1995. Traded to **New Jersey** by **Vancouver** for Brendan Morrison and Denis Pederson, March 14, 2000. Signed as a free agent by **Toronto**, July 3, 2001.

MONTADOR, Steve

(MAWN-tuh-dohr, STEEV) **CGY.**

Defense. Shoots right. 6', 210 lbs. Born, Vancouver, B.C., December 21, 1979.

Season	Club	League	GP	G	A	Pts	PIM	PP	SH	GW	S	%	+/-	TF	F%	Min	Playoffs GP	G	A	Pts	PIM	PP	SH	GW	Min
1995-96	St. Michael's B	OPJHL	46	3	16	19	145																		
1996-97	North Bay	OHL	63	7	28	35	129																		
1997-98	North Bay	OHL	37	5	16	21	54																		
	Erie Otters	OHL	26	3	17	20	35										7	1	1	2	9				
1998-99	Erie Otters	OHL	61	9	33	42	114										5	0	2	2	4				
99-2000	Peterborough	OHL	64	14	42	56	97										5	0	2	2	4				
	Saint John Flames	AHL															2	0	0	0	0				
2000-01	Saint John Flames	AHL	58	1	6	7	95										19	0	8	8	13				
2001-02	Calgary	NHL	11	1	2	3	26	0	0	0	10	10.0	–2	0	0.0	12:12									
	Saint John Flames	AHL	67	9	16	25	107																		
2002-03	Calgary	NHL	50	1	1	2	114	0	0	0	64	1.6	–9	0	0.0	15:11									
	Saint John Flames	AHL	11	1	7	8	20																		
	NHL Totals		61	2	3	5	140	0	0	0	74	2.7		0	0.0	14:39									

Signed as a free agent by **Calgary**, April 10, 2000.

MONTGOMERY, Jim

(mawnt-GUHM-uhr-ee, JIHM)

Center. Shoots right. 5'10", 180 lbs. Born, Montreal, Que., June 30, 1969.

Season	Club	League	GP	G	A	Pts	PIM	PP	SH	GW	S	%	+/-	TF	F%	Min	Playoffs GP	G	A	Pts	PIM	PP	SH	GW	Min
1988-89	Pembroke	OCJHL	50	53	*101	154	112																		
1989-90	U. of Maine	H-East	45	26	34	60	35																		
1990-91	U. of Maine	H-East	43	24	*57	81	44																		
1991-92	U. of Maine	H-East	37	21	44	65	46																		
1992-93	U. of Maine	H-East	45	32	63	95	40																		
1993-94	St. Louis	NHL	67	6	14	20	44	0	0	1	67	9.0	–1												
	Peoria Rivermen	IHL	12	7	8	15	10																		

Season	Club	League	GP	G	A	Pts	PIM	PP	SH	GW	S	%	+/-	TF	F%	Min	GP	G	A	Pts	PIM	PP	SH	GW	Min
			Regular Season														Playoffs								
1994-95	**Montreal**	**NHL**	**5**	**0**	**0**	**0**	**2**	**0**	**0**	**0**	**3**	**0.0**	**–2**	....	....	....	....	....	....	....	....	....	....	....	....
	Philadelphia	**NHL**	**8**	**1**	**1**	**2**	**6**	**0**	**0**	**0**	**10**	**10.0**	**–2**	....	....	....	**7**	**1**	**0**	**1**	**2**	**0**	**0**	**0**	....
	Hershey Bears	AHL	16	8	6	14	14	....	....	....	....	....	....	....	....	....	6	3	2	5	25	....	....	....	....
1995-96	**Philadelphia**	**NHL**	**5**	**1**	**2**	**3**	**9**	**0**	**0**	**0**	**4**	**25.0**	**1**	....	....	....	**1**	**0**	**0**	**0**	**0**	**0**	**0**	**0**	....
	Hershey Bears	AHL	78	34	*71	105	95	....	....	....	....	....	....	....	....	....	4	3	2	5	6	....	....	....	....
1996-97	Kolner Haie	Germany	50	12	35	47	111	....	....	....	....	....	....	....	....	....	4	0	1	1	6	....	....	....	....
	Kolner Haie	EuroHL	6	0	1	1	16	....	....	....	....	....	....	....	....	....	....	....	....	....	....	....	....	....	....
1997-98	Philadelphia	AHL	68	19	43	62	75	....	....	....	....	....	....	....	....	....	20	*13	16	29	55	....	....	....	....
1998-99	Philadelphia	AHL	78	29	58	87	89	....	....	....	....	....	....	....	....	....	16	4	11	15	20	....	....	....	....
99-2000	Philadelphia	AHL	13	3	9	12	22	....	....	....	....	....	....	....	....	....	....	....	....	....	....	....	....	....	....
	Manitoba Moose	IHL	67	18	28	46	111	....	....	....	....	....	....	....	....	....	....	....	....	....	....	....	....	....	....
2000-01	**San Jose**	**NHL**	**28**	**1**	**6**	**7**	**19**	**1**	**0**	**0**	**17**	**5.9**	....	**0**	**0.0**	**0:00**	....	....	....	....	....	....	....	....	....
	Kentucky	AHL	55	22	52	74	44	....	....	....	....	....	....	....	....	....	3	1	2	3	5	....	....	....	....
2001-02	**Dallas**	**NHL**	**8**	**0**	**2**	**2**	**0**	**0**	**0**	**0**	**8**	**0.0**	**–1**	**38**	**63.2**	**8:35**	....	....	....	....	....	....	....	....	....
	Utah Grizzlies	AHL	71	28	43	71	90	....	....	....	....	....	....	....	....	....	5	0	1	1	23	....	....	....	....
2002-03	Utah Grizzlies	AHL	72	22	46	68	109	....	....	....	....	....	....	....	....	....	2	0	0	0	2	....	....	....	....
	NHL Totals		**121**	**9**	**25**	**34**	**80**	**1**	**0**	**1**	**109**	**8.3**		**38**	**63.2**	**1:54**	**8**	**1**	**0**	**1**	**2**	**0**	**0**	**0**	....

Hockey East Second All-Star Team (1991, 1992) • Hockey East First All-Star Team (1993) • NCAA East Second All-American Team (1993) • NCAA Championship All-Tournament Team (1993) • NCAA Championship Tournament MVP (1993) • AHL Second All-Star Team (1996)

Signed as a free agent by **St. Louis**, June 2, 1993. Traded to **Montreal** by **St. Louis** for Guy Carbonneau, August 19, 1994. Claimed on waivers by **Philadelphia** from **Montreal**, February 10, 1995. Signed as a free agent by **San Jose**, August 15, 2000. Signed as a free agent by **Dallas**, July 10, 2001.

MOORE, Steve

(MOOR, STEEV) **COL.**

Center. Shoots right. 6'2", 205 lbs. Born, Windsor, Ont., September 22, 1978. Colorado's 7th choice, 53rd overall, in 1998 Entry Draft.

Season	Club	League	GP	G	A	Pts	PIM	PP	SH	GW	S	%	+/-	TF	F%	Min	GP	G	A	Pts	PIM	PP	SH	GW	Min
1995-96	Thornhill Islanders	MTJHL	50	25	27	52	57	....	....	....	....	....	....	....	....	....	18	4	5	9	....	....	....	....	....
1996-97	Thornhill Islanders	MTJHL	50	34	52	86	52	....	....	....	....	....	....	....	....	....	13	10	11	21	2	....	....	....	....
1997-98	Harvard Crimson	ECAC	33	10	23	33	46	....	....	....	....	....	....	....	....	....	....	....	....	....	....	....	....	....	....
1998-99	Harvard Crimson	ECAC	30	18	13	31	34	....	....	....	....	....	....	....	....	....	....	....	....	....	....	....	....	....	....
99-2000	Harvard Crimson	ECAC	27	10	16	26	53	....	....	....	....	....	....	....	....	....	....	....	....	....	....	....	....	....	....
2000-01	Harvard Crimson	ECAC	32	7	26	33	43	....	....	....	....	....	....	....	....	....	....	....	....	....	....	....	....	....	....
2001-02	**Colorado**	**NHL**	**8**	**0**	**0**	**0**	**4**	**0**	**0**	**0**	**5**	**0.0**	**–4**	**33**	**51.5**	**7:05**	....	....	....	....	....	....	....	....	....
	Hershey Bears	AHL	68	10	17	27	31	....	....	....	....	....	....	....	....	....	8	0	1	1	6	....	....	....	....
2002-03	**Colorado**	**NHL**	**4**	**0**	**0**	**0**	**0**	**0**	**0**	**0**	**0**	**0.0**	**0**	**23**	**30.4**	**8:56**	....	....	....	....	....	....	....	....	....
	Hershey Bears	AHL	58	10	13	23	41	....	....	....	....	....	....	....	....	....	5	0	1	1	4	....	....	....	....
	NHL Totals		**12**	**0**	**0**	**0**	**4**	**0**	**0**	**0**	**5**	**0.0**		**56**	**42.9**	**7:42**	....	....	....	....	....	....	....	....	....

MORAN, Brad

(moh-RAN, BRAD) **CBJ**

Center. Shoots left. 5'11", 187 lbs. Born, Abbotsford, B.C., March 20, 1979. Buffalo's 8th choice, 191st overall, in 1998 Entry Draft.

Season	Club	League	GP	G	A	Pts	PIM	PP	SH	GW	S	%	+/-	TF	F%	Min	GP	G	A	Pts	PIM	PP	SH	GW	Min
1994-95	Abbotsford	BCAHA	56	66	93	159	40	....	....	....	....	....	....	....	....	....	....	....	....	....	....	....	....	....	....
1995-96	Calgary Hitmen	WHL	70	13	31	44	28	....	....	....	....	....	....	....	....	....	....	....	....	....	....	....	....	....	....
1996-97	Calgary Hitmen	WHL	72	30	36	66	61	....	....	....	....	....	....	....	....	....	....	....	....	....	....	....	....	....	....
1997-98	Calgary Hitmen	WHL	72	53	49	102	64	....	....	....	....	....	....	....	....	....	18	10	8	18	20	....	....	....	....
1998-99	Calgary Hitmen	WHL	71	60	58	118	96	....	....	....	....	....	....	....	....	....	21	17	*25	42	26	....	....	....	....
99-2000	Calgary Hitmen	WHL	72	48	*72	*120	84	....	....	....	....	....	....	....	....	....	13	7	15	22	18	....	....	....	....
2000-01	Syracuse Crunch	AHL	71	11	19	30	30	....	....	....	....	....	....	....	....	....	5	3	4	7	2	....	....	....	....
2001-02	**Columbus**	**NHL**	**3**	**0**	**0**	**0**	**0**	**0**	**0**	**0**	**2**	**0.0**	**0**	**22**	**40.9**	**7:39**	....	....	....	....	....	....	....	....	....
	Syracuse Crunch	AHL	64	25	24	49	51	....	....	....	....	....	....	....	....	....	10	5	8	13	2	....	....	....	....
2002-03	Syracuse Crunch	AHL	47	12	19	31	22	....	....	....	....	....	....	....	....	....	....	....	....	....	....	....	....	....	....
	NHL Totals		**3**	**0**	**0**	**0**	**0**	**0**	**0**	**0**	**2**	**0.0**		**22**	**40.9**	**7:39**	....	....	....	....	....	....	....	....	....

WHL East First All-Star Team (1999, 2000)

Signed as a free agent by **Columbus**, June 5, 2000.

MORAN, Ian

(moh-RAN, EE-an) **BOS.**

Defense. Shoots right. 6', 200 lbs. Born, Cleveland, OH, August 24, 1972. Pittsburgh's 5th choice, 107th overall, in 1990 Entry Draft.

Season	Club	League	GP	G	A	Pts	PIM	PP	SH	GW	S	%	+/-	TF	F%	Min	GP	G	A	Pts	PIM	PP	SH	GW	Min
1987-88	Belmont Hill	Hi-School	25	3	13	16	15	....	....	....	....	....	....	....	....	....	....	....	....	....	....	....	....	....	....
1988-89	Belmont Hill	Hi-School	23	7	25	32	8	....	....	....	....	....	....	....	....	....	....	....	....	....	....	....	....	....	....
1989-90	Belmont Hill	Hi-School	23	10	36	46	....	....	....	....	....	....	....	....	....	....	....	....	....	....	....	....	....	....	....
1990-91	Belmont Hill	Hi-School	23	7	44	51	12	....	....	....	....	....	....	....	....	....	....	....	....	....	....	....	....	....	....
1991-92	Boston College	H-East	30	2	16	18	44	....	....	....	....	....	....	....	....	....	....	....	....	....	....	....	....	....	....
1992-93	Boston College	H-East	31	8	12	20	32	....	....	....	....	....	....	....	....	....	....	....	....	....	....	....	....	....	....
1993-94	Team USA	Nat-Tm	50	8	15	23	69	....	....	....	....	....	....	....	....	....	....	....	....	....	....	....	....	....	....
	Cleveland	IHL	33	5	13	18	39	....	....	....	....	....	....	....	....	....	....	....	....	....	....	....	....	....	....
1994-95	Cleveland	IHL	64	7	31	38	94	....	....	....	....	....	....	....	....	....	4	0	1	1	2	....	....	....	....
	Pittsburgh	**NHL**	....	....	....	....	....	....	....	....	....	....	....	....	....	....	**8**	**0**	**0**	**0**	**0**	**0**	**0**	**0**	....
1995-96	**Pittsburgh**	**NHL**	**51**	**1**	**1**	**2**	**47**	**0**	**0**	**0**	**44**	**2.3**	**–1**	....	....	....	....	....	....	....	....	....	....	....	....
1996-97	**Pittsburgh**	**NHL**	**36**	**4**	**5**	**9**	**22**	**0**	**0**	**0**	**50**	**8.0**	**–11**	....	....	....	**5**	**1**	**2**	**3**	**4**	**0**	**0**	**0**	....
	Cleveland	IHL	36	6	23	29	26	....	....	....	....	....	....	....	....	....	....	....	....	....	....	....	....	....	....
1997-98	**Pittsburgh**	**NHL**	**37**	**1**	**6**	**7**	**19**	**0**	**0**	**1**	**33**	**3.0**	**0**	....	....	....	**6**	**0**	**0**	**0**	**2**	**0**	**0**	**0**	....
1998-99	**Pittsburgh**	**NHL**	**62**	**4**	**5**	**9**	**37**	**0**	**1**	**0**	**65**	**6.2**	**1**	**32**	**34.4**	**16:34**	**13**	**0**	**2**	**2**	**8**	**0**	**0**	**0**	**21:10**
99-2000	**Pittsburgh**	**NHL**	**73**	**4**	**8**	**12**	**28**	**0**	**0**	**0**	**58**	**6.9**	**–10**	**210**	**33.8**	**11:21**	**11**	**0**	**1**	**1**	**2**	**0**	**0**	**0**	**8:52**
2000-01	**Pittsburgh**	**NHL**	**40**	**3**	**4**	**7**	**28**	**0**	**0**	**1**	**73**	**4.1**	**5**	**4**	**25.0**	**17:42**	**18**	**0**	**1**	**1**	**4**	**0**	**0**	**0**	**15:54**
2001-02	**Pittsburgh**	**NHL**	**64**	**2**	**8**	**10**	**54**	**0**	**0**	**1**	**94**	**2.1**	**–11**	**2**	**100.0**	**19:60**	....	....	....	....	....	....	....	....	....
2002-03	**Pittsburgh**	**NHL**	**70**	**0**	**7**	**7**	**46**	**0**	**0**	**0**	**85**	**0.0**	**–17**	**4**	**75.0**	**18:37**	....	....	....	....	....	....	....	....	....
	Boston	**NHL**	**8**	**0**	**1**	**1**	**2**	**0**	**0**	**0**	**11**	**0.0**	**–1**	**1**	**100.0**	**16:22**	**5**	**0**	**1**	**1**	**4**	**0**	**0**	**0**	**18:24**
	NHL Totals		**441**	**19**	**45**	**64**	**283**	**0**	**1**	**3**	**513**	**3.7**		**253**	**35.2**	**16:39**	**66**	**1**	**7**	**8**	**24**	**0**	**0**	**0**	**15:59**

Hockey East All-Rookie Team (1992) • Hockey East Rookie of the Year (1992) (co-winner - Craig Darby)

• Missed majority of 1997-98 season recovering from knee injury suffered in training camp, September 30, 1997. • Missed majority of 2000-01 season recovering from hand injury originally suffered in game vs. Edmonton, November 11, 2000. Traded to **Boston** by **Pittsburgh** for Boston's 4th round choice (Paul Bissonnette) in 2003 Entry Draft, March 11, 2003.

MORAVEC, David

(muh-RAHV-ehts, DAY-vihd) **BUF.**

Right wing. Shoots left. 6', 180 lbs. Born, Vitkovice, Czech., March 24, 1973. Buffalo's 9th choice, 218th overall, in 1998 Entry Draft.

Season	Club	League	GP	G	A	Pts	PIM	PP	SH	GW	S	%	+/-	TF	F%	Min	GP	G	A	Pts	PIM	PP	SH	GW	Min
1994-95	HC Vitkovice	Czech	38	4	13	17	12	....	....	....	....	....	....	....	....	....	6	1	7	8	0	....	....	....	....
1995-96	HC Vitkovice	Czech	37	6	5	11	14	....	....	....	....	....	....	....	....	....	4	0	0	0	4	....	....	....	....
1996-97	HC Vitkovice	Czech	52	18	22	40	30	....	....	....	....	....	....	....	....	....	9	6	3	9	0	....	....	....	....
1997-98	HC Vitkovice	Czech	51	*38	26	64	28	....	....	....	....	....	....	....	....	....	11	6	9	15	8	....	....	....	....
1998-99	HC Vitkovice	Czech	50	21	22	43	44	....	....	....	....	....	....	....	....	....	4	1	1	2	....	....	....	....	....
99-2000	**Buffalo**	**NHL**	**1**	**0**	**0**	**0**	**0**	**0**	**0**	**0**	**2**	**0.0**	**–1**	**2**	**50.0**	**15:15**	....	....	....	....	....	....	....	....	....
	HC Vitkovice	Czech	38	11	18	29	34	....	....	....	....	....	....	....	....	....	....	....	....	....	....	....	....	....	....
2000-01	HC Vitkovice	Czech	51	15	20	35	34	....	....	....	....	....	....	....	....	....	10	4	6	10	4	....	....	....	....
2001-02	HC Vitkovice	Czech	46	18	26	44	32	....	....	....	....	....	....	....	....	....	14	7	7	14	2	....	....	....	....
2002-03	HC Vitkovice	Czech	52	18	35	53	50	....	....	....	....	....	....	....	....	....	6	2	1	3	4	....	....	....	....
	NHL Totals		**1**	**0**	**0**	**0**	**0**	**0**	**0**	**0**	**2**	**0.0**		**2**	**50.0**	**15:15**	....	....	....	....	....	....	....	....	....

MOREAU, Ethan

(moh-ROH, EE-than) **EDM.**

Left wing. Shoots left. 6'2", 209 lbs. Born, Huntsville, Ont., September 22, 1975. Chicago's 1st choice, 14th overall, in 1994 Entry Draft.

Season	Club	League	GP	G	A	Pts	PIM	PP	SH	GW	S	%	+/-	TF	F%	Min	GP	G	A	Pts	PIM	PP	SH	GW	Min
1990-91	Orillia Terriers	OPJHL	42	17	22	39	26	....	....	....	....	....	....	....	....	....	12	6	6	12	18	....	....	....	....
1991-92	Niagara Falls	OHL	62	20	35	55	39	....	....	....	....	....	....	....	....	....	17	4	6	10	4	....	....	....	....
1992-93	Niagara Falls	OHL	65	32	41	73	69	....	....	....	....	....	....	....	....	....	4	0	3	3	4	....	....	....	....
1993-94	Niagara Falls	OHL	59	44	54	98	100	....	....	....	....	....	....	....	....	....	....	....	....	....	....	....	....	....	....
1994-95	Niagara Falls	OHL	39	25	41	66	69	....	....	....	....	....	....	....	....	....	....	....	....	....	....	....	....	....	....
	Sudbury Wolves	OHL	23	13	17	30	22	....	....	....	....	....	....	....	....	....	18	6	12	18	26	....	....	....	....
1995-96	**Chicago**	**NHL**	**8**	**0**	**1**	**1**	**4**	**0**	**0**	**0**	**1**	**0.0**	**1**	....	....	....	....	....	....	....	....	....	....	....	....
	Indianapolis Ice	IHL	71	21	20	41	126	....	....	....	....	....	....	....	....	....	5	4	0	4	8	....	....	....	....
1996-97	**Chicago**	**NHL**	**82**	**15**	**16**	**31**	**123**	**0**	**0**	**1**	**114**	**13.2**	**13**	....	....	....	**6**	**1**	**0**	**1**	**9**	**0**	**0**	**0**	....

Season	Club	League	GP	G	A	Pts	PIM	PP	SH	GW	S	%	+/-	TF	F%	Min	GP	G	A	Pts	PIM	PP	SH	GW	Min
			Regular Season														Playoffs								
1997-98	**Chicago**	**NHL**	**54**	**9**	**9**	**18**	**73**	**2**	**0**	**0**	**87**	**10.3**	**0**	....	....	....	....	....	....	....	....	....	....	....	....
1998-99	**Chicago**	**NHL**	**66**	**9**	**6**	**15**	**84**	**0**	**0**	**1**	**80**	**11.3**	**-5**	**3**	**33.3**	**12:30**	....	....	....	....	....	....	....	....	....
	Edmonton	**NHL**	**14**	**1**	**5**	**6**	**8**	**0**	**0**	**1**	**16**	**6.3**	**2**	**1**	**0.0**	**11:47**	**4**	**0**	**3**	**3**	**6**	**0**	**0**	**0**	**17:26**
99-2000	**Edmonton**	**NHL**	**73**	**17**	**10**	**27**	**62**	**1**	**0**	**3**	**106**	**16.0**	**8**	**8**	**62.5**	**15:07**	**5**	**0**	**1**	**1**	**0**	**0**	**0**	**0**	**15:46**
2000-01	**Edmonton**	**NHL**	**68**	**9**	**10**	**19**	**90**	**0**	**1**	**3**	**97**	**9.3**	**-6**	**2**	**0.0**	**14:11**	**4**	**0**	**0**	**0**	**2**	**0**	**0**	**0**	**10:35**
2001-02	**Edmonton**	**NHL**	**80**	**11**	**5**	**16**	**81**	**0**	**2**	**1**	**129**	**8.5**	**4**	**11**	**54.6**	**12:43**	....	....	....	....	....	....	....	....	....
2002-03	**Edmonton**	**NHL**	**78**	**14**	**17**	**31**	**112**	**2**	**3**	**2**	**137**	**10.2**	**-7**	**25**	**12.0**	**13:30**	**6**	**0**	**1**	**1**	**16**	**0**	**0**	**0**	**12:23**
	NHL Totals		**523**	**85**	**79**	**164**	**637**	**5**	**6**	**12**	**767**	**11.1**		**50**	**30.0**	**13:32**	**25**	**1**	**5**	**6**	**33**	**0**	**0**	**0**	**13:57**

OHL All-Rookie Team (1992)

Traded to **Edmonton** by **Chicago** with Daniel Cleary, Chad Kilger and Christian Laflamme for Boris Mironov, Dean McAmmond and Jonas Elofsson, March 20, 1999.

MORGAN, Jason

(MOHR-gan, JAY-son) **CGY.**

Center. Shoots left. 6'1", 200 lbs. Born, St. John's, Nfld., October 9, 1976. Los Angeles' 5th choice, 118th overall, in 1995 Entry Draft.

Season	Club	League	GP	G	A	Pts	PIM	PP	SH	GW	S	%	+/-	TF	F%	Min	GP	G	A	Pts	PIM	PP	SH	GW	Min
1992-93	Kit. Rangers	OMHA	69	44	40	84	85	....	....	....	....	....	....	....	....	....	....	....	....	....	....	....	....	....	....
1993-94	Kitchener Rangers	OHL	65	6	15	21	16	....	....	....	....	....	....	....	....	....	5	1	0	1	0	....	....	....	....
1994-95	Kitchener Rangers	OHL	35	3	15	18	25	....	....	....	....	....	....	....	....	....	....	....	....	....	....	....	....	....	....
	Kingston	OHL	20	0	3	3	14	....	....	....	....	....	....	....	....	....	6	0	2	2	0	....	....	....	....
1995-96	Kingston	OHL	66	16	38	54	50	....	....	....	....	....	....	....	....	....	6	1	2	3	0	....	....	....	....
1996-97	**Los Angeles**	**NHL**	**3**	**0**	**0**	**0**	**0**	**0**	**0**	**0**	**4**	**0.0**	**-3**	....	....	....	....	....	....	....	....	....	....	....	....
	Phoenix	IHL	57	3	6	9	29	....	....	....	....	....	....	....	....	....	....	....	....	....	....	....	....	....	....
	Mississippi	ECHL	6	3	0	3	0	....	....	....	....	....	....	....	....	....	3	1	1	2	6	....	....	....	....
1997-98	**Los Angeles**	**NHL**	**11**	**1**	**0**	**1**	**4**	**0**	**0**	**0**	**5**	**20.0**	**-7**	....	....	....	....	....	....	....	....	....	....	....	....
	Springfield	AHL	58	13	22	35	66	....	....	....	....	....	....	....	....	....	3	1	0	1	18	....	....	....	....
1998-99	Long Beach	IHL	13	4	6	10	18	....	....	....	....	....	....	....	....	....	....	....	....	....	....	....	....	....	....
	Springfield	AHL	46	6	16	22	51	....	....	....	....	....	....	....	....	....	3	0	0	0	6	....	....	....	....
99-2000	Cincinnati	IHL	15	1	3	4	14	....	....	....	....	....	....	....	....	....	....	....	....	....	....	....	....	....	....
	Florida Everblades	ECHL	48	14	25	39	79	....	....	....	....	....	....	....	....	....	5	2	2	4	16	....	....	....	....
2000-01	Florida Everblades	ECHL	37	15	22	37	41	....	....	....	....	....	....	....	....	....	5	2	3	5	17	....	....	....	....
	Hamilton	AHL	11	2	0	2	10	....	....	....	....	....	....	....	....	....	....	....	....	....	....	....	....	....	....
	Springfield	AHL	16	1	4	5	19	....	....	....	....	....	....	....	....	....	....	....	....	....	....	....	....	....	....
	Saint John Flames	AHL	....	....	....	....	....	....	....	....	....	....	....	....	....	....	6	0	1	1	2	....	....	....	....
2001-02	Saint John Flames	AHL	76	17	20	37	69	....	....	....	....	....	....	....	....	....	....	....	....	....	....	....	....	....	....
2002-03	Saint John Flames	AHL	80	13	40	53	63	....	....	....	....	....	....	....	....	....	....	....	....	....	....	....	....	....	....
	NHL Totals		**14**	**1**	**0**	**1**	**4**	**0**	**0**	**0**	**9**	**11.1**		....	....	....	....	....	....	....	....	....	....	....	....

Signed to tryout contract by **Saint John** (AHL), April 22, 2001. Signed as a free agent by **Saint John** (AHL), August 28, 2001. Signed as a free agent by **Calgary**, July 11, 2002.

MORISSET, Dave

(moh-rih-SEHT, DAYV) **FLA.**

Right wing. Shoots right. 6'2", 195 lbs. Born, Langley, B.C., April 6, 1981. St. Louis' 2nd choice, 65th overall, in 2000 Entry Draft.

Season	Club	League	GP	G	A	Pts	PIM	PP	SH	GW	S	%	+/-	TF	F%	Min	GP	G	A	Pts	PIM	PP	SH	GW	Min
1997-98	Seattle	WHL	58	6	2	8	104	....	....	....	....	....	....	....	....	....	5	1	0	1	6	....	....	....	....
1998-99	Seattle	WHL	17	4	0	4	31	....	....	....	....	....	....	....	....	....	11	1	1	2	22	....	....	....	....
99-2000	Seattle	WHL	60	23	34	57	69	....	....	....	....	....	....	....	....	....	7	3	4	7	12	....	....	....	....
2000-01	Seattle	WHL	61	32	36	68	95	....	....	....	....	....	....	....	....	....	9	4	2	6	12	....	....	....	....
2001-02	**Florida**	**NHL**	**4**	**0**	**0**	**0**	**5**	**0**	**0**	**0**	**2**	**0.0**	**-7**	**1**	**0.0**	**11:21**	....	....	....	....	....	....	....	....	....
	Bridgeport	AHL	62	9	10	19	46	....	....	....	....	....	....	....	....	....	19	0	1	1	13	....	....	....	....
2002-03	San Antonio	AHL	30	3	3	6	13	....	....	....	....	....	....	....	....	....	....	....	....	....	....	....	....	....	....
	NHL Totals		**4**	**0**	**0**	**0**	**5**	**0**	**0**	**0**	**2**	**0.0**		**1**	**0.0**	**11:21**	....	....	....	....	....	....	....	....	....

• Missed majority of 1998-99 season recovering from shoulder injury suffered in practice, November, 1998. Rights traded to **Florida** by **St. Louis** with St. Louis' 5th round choice (Vince Bellissimo) in 2002 Entry Draft for Scott Mellanby, February 9, 2001.

MORO, Marc

(MOH-roh, MAHRK) **TOR.**

Defense. Shoots left. 6'1", 218 lbs. Born, Toronto, Ont., July 17, 1977. Ottawa's 2nd choice, 27th overall, in 1995 Entry Draft.

Season	Club	League	GP	G	A	Pts	PIM	PP	SH	GW	S	%	+/-	TF	F%	Min	GP	G	A	Pts	PIM	PP	SH	GW	Min
1992-93	Mississauga Sens	MTHL	42	9	18	27	56	....	....	....	....	....	....	....	....	....	....	....	....	....	....	....	....	....	....
	Mississauga Sens	MTJHL	2	0	0	0	0	....	....	....	....	....	....	....	....	....	....	....	....	....	....	....	....	....	....
1993-94	Kingston	MTJHL	12	0	2	2	10	....	....	....	....	....	....	....	....	....	....	....	....	....	....	....	....	....	....
	Kingston	OHL	43	0	3	3	81	....	....	....	....	....	....	....	....	....	....	....	....	....	....	....	....	....	....
1994-95	Kingston	OHL	64	4	12	16	255	....	....	....	....	....	....	....	....	....	6	0	0	0	23	....	....	....	....
1995-96	Kingston	OHL	66	4	17	21	261	....	....	....	....	....	....	....	....	....	6	0	0	0	12	....	....	....	....
	P.E.I. Senators	AHL	2	0	0	0	7	....	....	....	....	....	....	....	....	....	2	0	0	0	4	....	....	....	....
1996-97	Kingston	OHL	37	4	8	12	97	....	....	....	....	....	....	....	....	....	....	....	....	....	....	....	....	....	....
	Sault Ste. Marie	OHL	26	0	5	5	74	....	....	....	....	....	....	....	....	....	11	1	6	7	38	....	....	....	....
1997-98	**Anaheim**	**NHL**	**1**	**0**	**0**	**0**	**0**	**0**	**0**	**0**	**0**	**0.0**	**0**	....	....	....	....	....	....	....	....	....	....	....	....
	Cincinnati	AHL	74	1	6	7	181	....	....	....	....	....	....	....	....	....	....	....	....	....	....	....	....	....	....
1998-99	Milwaukee	IHL	80	0	5	5	264	....	....	....	....	....	....	....	....	....	2	0	0	0	4	....	....	....	....
99-2000	**Nashville**	**NHL**	**8**	**0**	**0**	**0**	**40**	**0**	**0**	**0**	**3**	**0.0**	**-3**	**0**	**0.0**	**10:55**	....	....	....	....	....	....	....	....	....
	Milwaukee	IHL	64	5	5	10	203	....	....	....	....	....	....	....	....	....	....	....	....	....	....	....	....	....	....
2000-01	**Nashville**	**NHL**	**6**	**0**	**0**	**0**	**12**	**0**	**0**	**0**	**1**	**0.0**	**1**	**0**	**0.0**	**3:34**	....	....	....	....	....	....	....	....	....
	Milwaukee	IHL	68	2	9	11	190	....	....	....	....	....	....	....	....	....	5	1	0	1	10	....	....	....	....
2001-02	**Nashville**	**NHL**	**13**	**0**	**0**	**0**	**23**	**0**	**0**	**0**	**7**	**0.0**	**-3**	**0**	**0.0**	**12:02**	....	....	....	....	....	....	....	....	....
	Milwaukee	AHL	41	1	8	9	81	....	....	....	....	....	....	....	....	....	....	....	....	....	....	....	....	....	....
	Toronto	**NHL**	**2**	**0**	**0**	**0**	**2**	**0**	**0**	**0**	**0**	**0.0**	**0**	**0**	**0.0**	**11:23**	....	....	....	....	....	....	....	....	....
	St. John's	AHL	7	1	0	1	21	....	....	....	....	....	....	....	....	....	....	....	....	....	....	....	....	....	....
2002-03	St. John's	AHL	68	3	8	11	128	....	....	....	....	....	....	....	....	....	....	....	....	....	....	....	....	....	....
	NHL Totals		**30**	**0**	**0**	**0**	**77**	**0**	**0**	**0**	**11**	**0.0**		**0**	**0.0**	**9:56**	....	....	....	....	....	....	....	....	....

Rights traded to **Anaheim** by **Ottawa** with Ted Drury for Jason York and Shaun Van Allen, October 1, 1996. Traded to **Nashville** by **Anaheim** with Chris Mason for Dominic Roussel, October 5, 1998. Traded to **Toronto** by **Nashville** for D.J. Smith and Marty Wilford, March 1, 2002.

MOROZOV, Aleksey

(moh-ROH-zohv, ah-LEHK-see) **PIT.**

Right wing. Shoots left. 6'1", 204 lbs. Born, Moscow, USSR, February 16, 1977. Pittsburgh's 1st choice, 24th overall, in 1995 Entry Draft.

Season	Club	League	GP	G	A	Pts	PIM	PP	SH	GW	S	%	+/-	TF	F%	Min	GP	G	A	Pts	PIM	PP	SH	GW	Min
1993-94	Krylja Sovetov	CIS	7	0	0	0	0	....	....	....	....	....	....	....	....	....	3	0	0	0	2	....	....	....	....
1994-95	Krylja Sovetov	CIS	48	15	12	27	53	....	....	....	....	....	....	....	....	....	4	0	3	3	0	....	....	....	....
1995-96	Krylja Sovetov	CIS	47	13	9	22	26	....	....	....	....	....	....	....	....	....	....	....	....	....	....	....	....	....	....
1996-97	Krylja Sovetov	Russia	44	21	11	32	32	....	....	....	....	....	....	....	....	....	2	0	1	1	2	....	....	....	....
1997-98	Krylja Sovetov	Russia	6	2	1	3	4	....	....	....	....	....	....	....	....	....	....	....	....	....	....	....	....	....	....
	Pittsburgh	**NHL**	**76**	**13**	**13**	**26**	**8**	**2**	**0**	**3**	**80**	**16.3**	**-4**	....	....	....	**6**	**0**	**1**	**1**	**2**	**0**	**0**	**0**	....
	Russia	Olympics	6	2	2	4	0	....	....	....	....	....	....	....	....	....	....	....	....	....	....	....	....	....	....
1998-99	**Pittsburgh**	**NHL**	**67**	**9**	**10**	**19**	**14**	**0**	**0**	**0**	**75**	**12.0**	**5**	**7**	**42.9**	**11:50**	**10**	**1**	**1**	**2**	**0**	**0**	**0**	**0**	**12:01**
99-2000	**Pittsburgh**	**NHL**	**68**	**12**	**19**	**31**	**14**	**0**	**1**	**0**	**101**	**11.9**	**12**	**27**	**33.3**	**13:51**	**5**	**0**	**0**	**0**	**0**	**0**	**0**	**0**	**11:48**
2000-01	**Pittsburgh**	**NHL**	**66**	**5**	**14**	**19**	**6**	**0**	**0**	**1**	**72**	**6.9**	**-8**	**19**	**42.1**	**10:41**	**18**	**3**	**3**	**6**	**6**	**0**	**1**	**0**	**14:59**
2001-02	**Pittsburgh**	**NHL**	**72**	**20**	**29**	**49**	**16**	**7**	**0**	**3**	**162**	**12.3**	**-7**	**1**	**100.0**	**16:42**	....	....	....	....	....	....	....	....	....
2002-03	**Pittsburgh**	**NHL**	**27**	**9**	**16**	**25**	**16**	**6**	**0**	**2**	**46**	**19.6**	**-3**	**0**	**0.0**	**18:42**	....	....	....	....	....	....	....	....	....
	NHL Totals		**376**	**68**	**101**	**169**	**74**	**15**	**1**	**9**	**536**	**12.7**		**54**	**38.9**	**13:50**	**39**	**4**	**5**	**9**	**8**	**0**	**1**	**0**	**13:36**

• Missed majority of 2002-03 season recovering from wrist injury suffered in game vs. Toronto, December 10, 2002.

MORRIS, Derek

(MOH-rihs, DAIR-ihk) **COL.**

Defense. Shoots right. 5'11", 210 lbs. Born, Edmonton, Alta., August 24, 1978. Calgary's 1st choice, 13th overall, in 1996 Entry Draft.

Season	Club	League	GP	G	A	Pts	PIM	PP	SH	GW	S	%	+/-	TF	F%	Min	GP	G	A	Pts	PIM	PP	SH	GW	Min
1994-95	Red Deer	AMHL	31	6	35	41	74	....	....	....	....	....	....	....	....	....	....	....	....	....	....	....	....	....	....
1995-96	Regina Pats	WHL	67	8	44	52	70	....	....	....	....	....	....	....	....	....	11	1	7	8	26	....	....	....	....
1996-97	Regina Pats	WHL	67	18	57	75	180	....	....	....	....	....	....	....	....	....	5	0	3	3	9	....	....	....	....
	Saint John Flames	AHL	7	0	3	3	7	....	....	....	....	....	....	....	....	....	5	0	3	3	7	....	....	....	....
1997-98	**Calgary**	**NHL**	**82**	**9**	**20**	**29**	**88**	**5**	**1**	**1**	**120**	**7.5**	**1**	....	....	....	....	....	....	....	....	....	....	....	....
1998-99	**Calgary**	**NHL**	**71**	**7**	**27**	**34**	**73**	**3**	**0**	**2**	**150**	**4.7**	**4**	**0**	**0.0**	**20:44**	....	....	....	....	....	....	....	....	....
99-2000	**Calgary**	**NHL**	**78**	**9**	**29**	**38**	**80**	**3**	**0**	**2**	**193**	**4.7**	**2**	**0**	**0.0**	**24:51**	....	....	....	....	....	....	....	....	....
2000-01	**Calgary**	**NHL**	**51**	**5**	**23**	**28**	**56**	**3**	**1**	**4**	**142**	**3.5**	**-15**	**0**	**0.0**	**25:51**	....	....	....	....	....	....	....	....	....
	Saint John Flames	AHL	3	1	2	3	2	....	....	....	....	....	....	....	....	....	....	....	....	....	....	....	....	....	....

						Regular Season											Playoffs								
Season	Club	League	GP	G	A	Pts	PIM	PP	SH	GW	S	%	+/-	TF	F%	Min	GP	G	A	Pts	PIM	PP	SH	GW	Min
2001-02	Calgary	NHL	61	4	30	34	88	2	0	1	166	2.4	–4	1	100.0	24:40	....	....	....	....	....	....	....	....	....
2002-03	Colorado	NHL	75	11	37	48	68	9	0	7	191	5.8	16	0	0.0	23:49	7	0	3	3	6	0	0	0	22:44
	NHL Totals		418	45	166	211	453	25	2	17	962	4.7		1	100.0	23:52	7	0	3	3	6	0	0	0	22:44

WHL East First All-Star Team (1997) • NHL All-Rookie Team (1998)

Traded to **Colorado** by **Calgary** with Jeff Shantz and Dean McAmmond for Chris Drury and Stephane Yelle, October 1, 2002.

MORRISON, Brendan (MOHR-ih-suhn, BREHN-duhn) VAN.

Center. Shoots left. 5'11", 190 lbs. Born, Pitt Meadows, B.C., August 15, 1975. New Jersey's 3rd choice, 39th overall, in 1993 Entry Draft.

1990-91	Ridge Meadows	BCAHA	77	126	127	253	88	....	....	....	....	....	....	....	....	....	....	....	....	....	....	....	....	....	....
1991-92	Ridge Meadows	BCAHA	55	56	111	167	56	....	....	....	....	....	....	....	....	....	....	....	....	....	....	....	....	....	....
1992-93	Penticton	BCJHL	56	35	59	94	45	....	....	....	....	....	....	....	....	....	....	....	....	....	....	....	....	....	....
1993-94	U. of Michigan	CCHA	38	20	28	48	24	....	....	....	....	....	....	....	....	....	5	2	7	9	2	....	....	....	....
1994-95	U. of Michigan	CCHA	39	23	*53	*76	42	....	....	....	....	....	....	....	....	....	5	1	11	12	6	....	....	....	....
1995-96	U. of Michigan	CCHA	35	28	44	*72	41	....	....	....	....	....	....	....	....	....	7	6	9	15	4	....	....	....	....
1996-97	U. of Michigan	CCHA	43	31	*57	*88	52	....	....	....	....	....	....	....	....	....	6	6	8	14	8	....	....	....	....
1997-98	New Jersey	NHL	11	5	4	9	0	0	0	1	19	26.3	3	....	....	....	3	0	1	1	0	0	0	0	....
	Albany River Rats	AHL	72	35	49	84	44	....	....	....	....	....	....	....	....	....	8	3	4	7	19	....	....	....	....
1998-99	New Jersey	NHL	76	13	33	46	18	5	0	2	111	11.7	–4	920	51.1	13:55	7	0	2	2	0	0	0	0	13:04
99-2000	Trebic	Czech-2	2	0	0	0	0	....	....	....	....	....	....	....	....	....	....	....	....	....	....	....	....	....	....
	Pardubice	Czech	6	5	2	7	2	....	....	....	....	....	....	....	....	....	....	....	....	....	....	....	....	....	....
	New Jersey	NHL	44	5	21	26	8	2	0	1	79	6.3	8	572	51.1	16:09	....	....	....	....	....	....	....	....	....
	Vancouver	NHL	12	2	7	9	10	0	0	0	17	11.8	4	48	54.2	14:41	....	....	....	....	....	....	....	....	....
2000-01	Vancouver	NHL	82	16	38	54	42	3	2	3	179	8.9	2	1685	50.1	18:22	4	1	2	3	0	1	0	0	20:49
2001-02	Vancouver	NHL	82	23	44	67	26	6	0	4	183	12.6	18	1307	49.9	19:21	6	0	2	2	6	0	0	0	19:44
2002-03	Vancouver	NHL	82	25	46	71	36	6	2	8	167	15.0	18	1585	48.3	21:13	14	4	7	11	18	1	0	1	20:18
	NHL Totals		389	89	193	282	140	22	4	19	755	11.8		6117	49.8	17:56	34	5	14	19	24	2	0	1	18:37

CCHA Rookie of the Year (1994) • CCHA First All-Star Team (1995, 1996, 1997) • NCAA West First All-American Team (1995, 1996, 1997) • CCHA Player of the Year (1996, 1997) • NCAA Championship All-Tournament Team (1996) • NCAA Championship Tournament MVP (1996) • Hobey Baker Memorial Award (Top U.S. Collegiate Player) (1997)

Traded to **Vancouver** by **New Jersey** with Denis Pederson for Alexander Mogilny, March 14, 2000.

MORRISONN, Shaone (MOHR-rih-sohn, SHAWN) BOS.

Defense. Shoots left. 6'3", 205 lbs. Born, Vancouver, B.C., December 23, 1982. Boston's 1st choice, 19th overall, in 2001 Entry Draft.

1997-98	Vancouver T-Birds	BCAHA	45	16	44	60	75	....	....	....	....	....	....	....	....	....	....	....	....	....	....	....	....	....	....
1998-99	South Surrey	BCHL	19	0	2	2	13	....	....	....	....	....	....	....	....	....	....	....	....	....	....	....	....	....	....
99-2000	Kamloops Blazers	WHL	57	1	6	7	80	....	....	....	....	....	....	....	....	....	4	0	0	0	6	....	....	....	....
2000-01	Kamloops Blazers	WHL	61	13	25	38	132	....	....	....	....	....	....	....	....	....	4	0	0	0	6	....	....	....	....
2001-02	Kamloops Blazers	WHL	61	11	26	37	106	....	....	....	....	....	....	....	....	....	4	0	2	2	2	....	....	....	....
2002-03	Boston	NHL	11	0	0	0	8	0	0	0	4	0.0	0	0	0.0	8:57	....	....	....	....	....	....	....	....	....
	Providence Bruins	AHL	60	5	16	21	103	....	....	....	....	....	....	....	....	....	4	0	0	0	6	....	....	....	....
	NHL Totals		11	0	0	0	8	0	0	0	4	0.0		0	0.0	8:57	....	....	....	....	....	....	....	....	....

MORROW, Brenden (MOHR-roh, BREHN-duhn) DAL.

Left wing. Shoots left. 5'11", 200 lbs. Born, Carlyle, Sask., January 16, 1979. Dallas' 1st choice, 25th overall, in 1997 Entry Draft.

1994-95	Estevan	SMBHL	60	117	72	189	45	....	....	....	....	....	....	....	....	....	....	....	....	....	....	....	....	....	....
1995-96	Portland	WHL	65	13	12	25	61	....	....	....	....	....	....	....	....	....	7	0	0	0	8	....	....	....	....
1996-97	Portland	WHL	71	39	49	88	178	....	....	....	....	....	....	....	....	....	6	2	1	3	4	....	....	....	....
1997-98	Portland	WHL	68	34	52	86	184	....	....	....	....	....	....	....	....	....	16	10	8	18	65	....	....	....	....
1998-99	Portland	WHL	61	41	44	85	248	....	....	....	....	....	....	....	....	....	4	0	4	4	18	....	....	....	....
99-2000	Dallas	NHL	64	14	19	33	81	3	0	3	113	12.4	8	25	48.0	15:51	21	2	4	6	22	1	0	0	15:04
	Michigan	IHL	9	2	0	2	18	....	....	....	....	....	....	....	....	....	....	....	....	....	....	....	....	....	....
2000-01	Dallas	NHL	82	20	24	44	128	7	0	6	121	16.5	18	22	45.5	15:29	10	0	3	3	12	0	0	0	16:60
2001-02	Dallas	NHL	72	17	18	35	109	4	0	3	102	16.7	12	39	41.0	16:52	....	....	....	....	....	....	....	....	....
2002-03	Dallas	NHL	71	21	22	43	134	2	3	4	105	20.0	20	29	27.6	15:43	12	3	5	8	16	2	0	0	21:03
	NHL Totals		289	72	83	155	452	16	3	16	441	16.3		115	40.0	15:58	43	5	12	17	50	3	0	0	17:11

WHL West First All-Star Team (1999)

MOTTAU, Mike (MAW-tuh, MIGHK) ANA.

Defense. Shoots left. 6', 192 lbs. Born, Quincy, MA, March 19, 1978. NY Rangers' 10th choice, 182nd overall, in 1997 Entry Draft.

1994-95	Thayer Academy	Hi-School	29	7	19	26	....	....	....	....	....	....	....	....	....	....	....	....	....	....	....	....	....	....	....
1995-96	Thayer Academy	Hi-School	31	6	20	26	14	....	....	....	....	....	....	....	....	....	....	....	....	....	....	....	....	....	....
1996-97	Boston College	H-East	38	5	18	23	77	....	....	....	....	....	....	....	....	....	....	....	....	....	....	....	....	....	....
1997-98	Boston College	H-East	40	13	36	49	50	....	....	....	....	....	....	....	....	....	....	....	....	....	....	....	....	....	....
1998-99	Boston College	H-East	43	3	39	42	44	....	....	....	....	....	....	....	....	....	....	....	....	....	....	....	....	....	....
	United States	WC-A	3	2	1	3	0	....	....	....	....	....	....	....	....	....	....	....	....	....	....	....	....	....	....
99-2000	Boston College	H-East	42	6	37	43	61	....	....	....	....	....	....	....	....	....	....	....	....	....	....	....	....	....	....
2000-01	NY Rangers	NHL	18	0	3	3	13	0	0	0	17	0.0	–6	0	0.0	15:18	....	....	....	....	....	....	....	....	....
	Hartford	AHL	61	10	33	43	45	....	....	....	....	....	....	....	....	....	5	0	1	1	19	....	....	....	....
2001-02	NY Rangers	NHL	1	0	0	0	0	0	0	0	0	0.0	0	0	0.0	6:20	....	....	....	....	....	....	....	....	....
	Hartford	AHL	80	9	42	51	56	....	....	....	....	....	....	....	....	....	10	0	5	5	4	....	....	....	....
2002-03	Hartford	AHL	29	1	18	19	24	....	....	....	....	....	....	....	....	....	....	....	....	....	....	....	....	....	....
	Calgary	NHL	4	0	0	0	0	0	0	0	0	0.0	–1	0	0.0	9:50	....	....	....	....	....	....	....	....	....
	Saint John Flames	AHL	32	5	12	17	14	....	....	....	....	....	....	....	....	....	....	....	....	....	....	....	....	....	....
	NHL Totals		23	0	3	3	13	0	0	0	17	0.0		0	0.0	13:57	....	....	....	....	....	....	....	....	....

Hockey East First All-Star Team (1998, 2000) • NCAA East Second All-American Team (1998) • NCAA Championship All-Tournament Team (1998, 2000) • Hockey East Second All-Star Team (1999) • NCAA East First All-American Team (1999, 2000) • Hockey East Player of the Year (2000) (co-winner - Ty Conklin) • Hobey Baker Memorial Award (Top U.S. Collegiate Player) (2000)

Traded to **Calgary** by **NY Rangers** for Calgary's 6th round choice (Ivan Dornic) in 2003 Entry Draft and future considerations, January 22, 2003. Signed as a free agent by **Anaheim**, July 25, 2003.

MOWERS, Mark (MAHW-uhrs, MAHRK) DET.

Center. Shoots right. 5'11", 187 lbs. Born, Whitesboro, NY, February 16, 1974.

1992-93	Saginaw Gears	NAJHL	39	31	39	70	....	....	....	....	....	....	....	....	....	....	....	....	....	....	....	....	....	....	....
1993-94	Dubuque	USHL	47	51	31	82	80	....	....	....	....	....	....	....	....	....	....	....	....	....	....	....	....	....	....
1994-95	New Hampshire	H-East	36	13	23	36	16	....	....	....	....	....	....	....	....	....	....	....	....	....	....	....	....	....	....
1995-96	New Hampshire	H-East	34	21	26	47	18	....	....	....	....	....	....	....	....	....	....	....	....	....	....	....	....	....	....
1996-97	New Hampshire	H-East	39	26	32	58	52	....	....	....	....	....	....	....	....	....	....	....	....	....	....	....	....	....	....
1997-98	New Hampshire	H-East	35	25	31	56	32	....	....	....	....	....	....	....	....	....	....	....	....	....	....	....	....	....	....
1998-99	Nashville	NHL	30	0	6	6	4	0	0	0	24	0.0	–4	241	49.0	9:22	....	....	....	....	....	....	....	....	....
	Milwaukee	IHL	51	14	22	36	24	....	....	....	....	....	....	....	....	....	1	0	0	0	0	....	....	....	....
99-2000	Nashville	NHL	41	4	5	9	10	0	0	0	50	8.0	0	312	45.2	10:58	....	....	....	....	....	....	....	....	....
	Milwaukee	IHL	23	11	15	26	34	....	....	....	....	....	....	....	....	....	....	....	....	....	....	....	....	....	....
2000-01	Milwaukee	IHL	63	25	25	50	54	....	....	....	....	....	....	....	....	....	5	1	2	3	2	....	....	....	....
2001-02	Nashville	NHL	14	1	2	3	2	0	0	0	5	20.0	–2	24	33.3	8:31	....	....	....	....	....	....	....	....	....
	Milwaukee	AHL	45	19	20	39	34	....	....	....	....	....	....	....	....	....	....	....	....	....	....	....	....	....	....
2002-03	Grand Rapids	AHL	78	34	47	81	47	....	....	....	....	....	....	....	....	....	15	3	4	7	4	....	....	....	....
	NHL Totals		85	5	13	18	16	0	0	0	79	6.3		577	46.3	9:60	....	....	....	....	....	....	....	....	....

Hockey East Rookie of the Year (1995) • Hockey East Second All-Star Team (1998) • NCAA East First All-American Team (1998) • Ken McKenzie Trophy (U.S. Born Rookie of the Year – IHL) (1999) • AHL Second All-Star Team (2003)

Signed as a free agent by **Nashville**, June 11, 1998. Signed as a free agent by **Detroit**, August 5, 2002.

MROZIK, Rick
(muh-ROH-zihk, RIHK) **BUF.**

Center. Shoots left. 6'2", 185 lbs. Born, Duluth, MN, January 2, 1975. Dallas' 4th choice, 136th overall, in 1993 Entry Draft.

			Regular Season														Playoffs								
Season	Club	League	GP	G	A	Pts	PIM	PP	SH	GW	S	%	+/-	TF	F%	Min	GP	G	A	Pts	PIM	PP	SH	GW	Min
1992-93	Cloquet High	Hi-School	28	9	38	47	12																		
1993-94	U. Minn-Duluth	WCHA	38	2	9	11	38																		
1994-95	U. Minn-Duluth	WCHA	3	0	0	0	2																		
1995-96	U. Minn-Duluth	WCHA	35	3	19	22	63																		
1996-97	U. Minn-Duluth	WCHA	38	11	23	34	56																		
1997-98	Portland Pirates	AHL	75	2	15	17	52										10	1	3	4	2				
1998-99	Portland Pirates	AHL	70	4	8	12	63																		
99-2000	Worcester IceCats	AHL	3	0	0	0	0																		
	Pee Dee Pride	ECHL	60	9	19	28	44										5	2	0	2	6				
	Syracuse Crunch	AHL	1	0	0	0	0																		
2000-01	Saint John Flames	AHL	76	5	11	16	26										19	1	1	2	6				
2001-02	Saint John Flames	AHL	55	2	5	7	27																		
2002-03	**Calgary**	**NHL**	**2**	**0**	**0**	**0**	**0**	**0**	**0**	**0**	**2**	**0.0**	**0**	**0**	**0.0**	**10:02**									
	Saint John Flames	AHL	68	2	10	12	46																		
	NHL Totals		**2**	**0**	**0**	**0**	**0**	**0**	**0**	**0**	**2**	**0.0**		**0**	**0.0**	**10:02**									

WCHA Second All-Star Team (1997)

Traded to **Washington** by **Dallas** with Mark Tinordi for Kevin Hatcher, January 18, 1995. Signed as a free agent by **Calgary**, August 6, 2001. Signed as a free agent by **Buffalo**, August 21, 2003.

MUCKALT, Bill
(MUH-kawlt, BIHL) **MIN.**

Right wing. Shoots right. 6'1", 200 lbs. Born, Surrey, B.C., July 15, 1974. Vancouver's 9th choice, 221st overall, in 1994 Entry Draft.

Season	Club	League	GP	G	A	Pts	PIM	PP	SH	GW	S	%	+/-	TF	F%	Min	GP	G	A	Pts	PIM	PP	SH	GW	Min
1991-92	Merritt	BCJHL	55	14	11	25	75																		
1992-93	Merritt	BCJHL	59	31	43	74	80																		
1993-94	Merritt	BCJHL	43	58	51	109	99																		
	Kelowna Spartans	BCJHL	15	12	10	22	20																		
1994-95	U. of Michigan	CCHA	39	19	18	37	42										5	1	1	2	6				
1995-96	U. of Michigan	CCHA	41	28	30	58	34										7	5	6	11	6				
1996-97	U. of Michigan	CCHA	36	26	38	64	69										6	5	9	14	2				
1997-98	U. of Michigan	CCHA	46	32	*35	*67	94																		
1998-99	**Vancouver**	**NHL**	**73**	**16**	**20**	**36**	**98**	**4**	**2**	**1**	**119**	**13.4**	**–9**	**68**	**55.9**	**15:24**									
99-2000	**Vancouver**	**NHL**	**33**	**4**	**8**	**12**	**17**	**1**	**0**	**1**	**53**	**7.5**	**6**	**6**	**50.0**	**14:34**									
	NY Islanders	**NHL**	**12**	**4**	**3**	**7**	**4**	**0**	**0**	**0**	**26**	**15.4**	**5**	**8**	**50.0**	**12:23**									
2000-01	**NY Islanders**	**NHL**	**60**	**11**	**15**	**26**	**33**	**1**	**0**	**2**	**90**	**12.2**	**–4**	**7**	**14.3**	**13:43**									
2001-02	**Ottawa**	**NHL**	**70**	**0**	**8**	**8**	**46**	**0**	**0**	**0**	**73**	**0.0**	**–3**	**13**	**69.2**	**9:46**									
2002-03	**Minnesota**	**NHL**	**8**	**5**	**3**	**8**	**6**	**0**	**0**	**0**	**13**	**38.5**	**5**	**6**	**50.0**	**13:00**	**5**	**0**	**0**	**0**	**0**	**0**	**0**	**0**	**11:15**
	NHL Totals		**256**	**40**	**57**	**97**	**204**	**6**	**2**	**4**	**374**	**10.7**		**108**	**53.7**	**13:08**	**5**	**0**	**0**	**0**	**0**	**0**	**0**	**0**	**11:15**

CCHA First All-Star Team (1998) • NCAA West First All-American Team (1998)

Traded to **NY Islanders** by **Vancouver** with Kevin Weekes and Dave Scatchard for Felix Potvin, NY Islanders' compensatory 2nd round choice (later traded to New Jersey – New Jersey selected Teemu Laine) in 2000 Entry Draft and NY Islanders' 3rd round choice (Thatcher Bell) in 2000 Entry Draft, December 19, 1999. • Missed majority of 1999-2000 season recovering from shoulder injury suffered in game vs. Tampa Bay, January 13, 2000. Traded to **Ottawa** by **NY Islanders** with Zdeno Chara and NY Islanders' 1st round choice (Jason Spezza) in 2001 Entry Draft for Alexei Yashin, June 23, 2001. Signed as a free agent by **Minnesota**, July 3, 2002. • Missed majority of 2002-03 season recovering from shoulder injury suffered in game vs. Calgary, October 22, 2002.

MUIR, Bryan
(MEWR, BRIGH-uhn) **L.A.**

Defense. Shoots left. 6'4", 220 lbs. Born, Winnipeg, Man., June 8, 1973.

Season	Club	League	GP	G	A	Pts	PIM	PP	SH	GW	S	%	+/-	TF	F%	Min	GP	G	A	Pts	PIM	PP	SH	GW	Min
1991-92	Wexford Raiders	MTJHL	44	3	19	22	35																		
1992-93	New Hampshire	H-East	26	1	2	3	24																		
1993-94	New Hampshire	H-East	40	0	4	4	48																		
1994-95	New Hampshire	H-East	28	9	9	18	46																		
1995-96	Team Canada	Nat-Tm	42	6	12	18	38																		
	Edmonton	**NHL**	**5**	**0**	**0**	**0**	**6**	**0**	**0**	**0**	**4**	**0.0**	**–4**												
1996-97	Hamilton	AHL	75	8	16	24	80										14	0	5	5	12				
	Edmonton	**NHL**															**5**	**0**	**0**	**0**	**4**	**0**	**0**	**0**	
1997-98	**Edmonton**	**NHL**	**7**	**0**	**0**	**0**	**17**	**0**	**0**	**0**	**6**	**0.0**	**0**												
	Hamilton	AHL	28	3	10	13	62																		
	Albany River Rats	AHL	41	3	10	13	67										13	3	0	3	12				
1998-99	**New Jersey**	**NHL**	**1**	**0**	**0**	**0**	**0**	**0**	**0**	**0**	**4**	**0.0**	**0**	**0**	**0.0**	**9:54**									
	Albany River Rats	AHL	10	0	0	0	29																		
	Chicago	**NHL**	**53**	**1**	**4**	**5**	**50**	**0**	**0**	**0**	**78**	**1.3**	**1**	**0**	**0.0**	**18:49**									
	Portland Pirates	AHL	2	1	1	2	2																		
99-2000	**Chicago**	**NHL**	**11**	**2**	**3**	**5**	**13**	**0**	**1**	**0**	**19**	**10.5**	**–1**	**0**	**0.0**	**17:54**									
	Tampa Bay	**NHL**	**30**	**1**	**1**	**2**	**32**	**0**	**0**	**0**	**32**	**3.1**	**–8**	**1**	**100.0**	**19:29**									
2000-01	**Tampa Bay**	**NHL**	**10**	**0**	**3**	**3**	**15**	**0**	**0**	**0**	**14**	**0.0**	**–7**	**1**	**0.0**	**18:34**									
	Detroit Vipers	IHL	21	5	7	12	36																		
	Colorado	**NHL**	**8**	**0**	**0**	**0**	**4**	**0**	**0**	**0**	**3**	**0.0**	**0**	**0**	**0.0**	**8:14**	**3**	**0**	**0**	**0**	**0**	**0**	**0**	**0**	**3:15**
	Hershey Bears	AHL	26	5	8	13	50																		
2001-02	**Colorado**	**NHL**	**22**	**1**	**1**	**2**	**9**	**0**	**0**	**0**	**26**	**3.8**	**1**	**0**	**0.0**	**10:20**	**21**	**0**	**0**	**0**	**2**	**0**	**0**	**0**	**5:39**
	Hershey Bears	AHL	59	10	16	26	133																		
2002-03	**Colorado**	**NHL**	**32**	**0**	**2**	**2**	**19**	**0**	**0**	**0**	**9**	**0.0**	**3**	**0**	**0.0**	**6:33**									
	Hershey Bears	AHL	36	9	12	21	75										5	2	6	8	6				
	NHL Totals		**179**	**5**	**14**	**19**	**165**	**0**	**1**	**0**	**195**	**2.6**		**2**	**50.0**	**14:50**	**29**	**0**	**0**	**0**	**6**	**0**	**0**	**0**	**5:21**

Signed to five-game amateur tryout contract by **Edmonton**, February 29, 1996. Signed as a free agent by **Edmonton**, April 30, 1996. Traded to **New Jersey** by **Edmonton** with Jason Arnott for Valeri Zelepukin and Bill Guerin, January 4, 1998. Traded to **Chicago** by **New Jersey** for Chicago's 3rd round choice (Michael Rupp) in 2000 Entry Draft. November 13, 1998. Traded to **Tampa Bay** by **Chicago** with Reid Simpson for Michael Nylander, November 12, 1999. • Missed majority of 1999-2000 season recovering from leg injury suffered in game vs. Atlanta, November 17, 1999. Traded to **Colorado** by **Tampa Bay** for Colorado's 8th round choice (Dmitri Bezrukov) in 2001 Entry Draft, January 23, 2001. Signed as a free agent by **Los Angeles**, July 31, 2003.

MULLER, Kirk
(MUHL-luhr, KUHRK)

Left wing. Shoots left. 6', 205 lbs. Born, Kingston, Ont., February 8, 1966. New Jersey's 1st choice, 2nd overall, in 1984 Entry Draft.

Season	Club	League	GP	G	A	Pts	PIM	PP	SH	GW	S	%	+/-	TF	F%	Min	GP	G	A	Pts	PIM	PP	SH	GW	Min
1980-81	Kingston	OHA-B	42	17	37	54	5																		
	Kingston	OMJHL	2	0	0	0	0																		
1981-82	Kingston	OHL	67	12	39	51	27										4	5	1	6	4				
1982-83	Guelph Platers	OHL	66	52	60	112	41																		
1983-84	Guelph Platers	OHL	49	31	63	94	27																		
	Canada	Olympics	6	2	1	3	0																		
1984-85	**New Jersey**	**NHL**	**80**	**17**	**37**	**54**	**69**	**9**	**1**	**0**	**157**	**10.8**	**–31**												
1985-86	**New Jersey**	**NHL**	**77**	**25**	**41**	**66**	**45**	**5**	**1**	**1**	**168**	**14.9**	**–20**												
1986-87	**New Jersey**	**NHL**	**79**	**26**	**50**	**76**	**75**	**10**	**1**	**4**	**193**	**13.5**	**–7**												
1987-88	**New Jersey**	**NHL**	**80**	**37**	**57**	**94**	**114**	**17**	**2**	**1**	**215**	**17.2**	**19**				**20**	**4**	**8**	**12**	**37**	**0**	**0**	**0**	
1988-89	**New Jersey**	**NHL**	**80**	**31**	**43**	**74**	**119**	**12**	**1**	**4**	**182**	**17.0**	**–23**												
1989-90	**New Jersey**	**NHL**	**80**	**30**	**56**	**86**	**74**	**9**	**0**	**6**	**200**	**15.0**	**–1**				**6**	**1**	**3**	**4**	**11**	**0**	**0**	**0**	
1990-91	**New Jersey**	**NHL**	**80**	**19**	**51**	**70**	**76**	**7**	**0**	**3**	**221**	**8.6**	**1**				**7**	**0**	**2**	**2**	**10**	**0**	**0**	**0**	
1991-92	**Montreal**	**NHL**	**78**	**36**	**41**	**77**	**86**	**15**	**1**	**7**	**191**	**18.8**	**15**				**11**	**4**	**3**	**7**	**31**	**2**	**1**	**1**	
1992-93♦	**Montreal**	**NHL**	**80**	**37**	**57**	**94**	**77**	**12**	**0**	**4**	**231**	**16.0**	**8**				**20**	**10**	**7**	**17**	**18**	**3**	**0**	**3**	
1993-94	**Montreal**	**NHL**	**76**	**23**	**34**	**57**	**96**	**9**	**2**	**3**	**168**	**13.7**	**–1**				**7**	**6**	**2**	**8**	**4**	**3**	**0**	**2**	
1994-95	**Montreal**	**NHL**	**33**	**8**	**11**	**19**	**33**	**3**	**0**	**1**	**81**	**9.9**	**–21**												
	NY Islanders	**NHL**	**12**	**3**	**5**	**8**	**14**	**1**	**1**	**1**	**16**	**18.8**	**3**												
1995-96	**NY Islanders**	**NHL**	**15**	**4**	**3**	**7**	**15**	**0**	**0**	**0**	**23**	**17.4**	**–10**												
	Toronto	**NHL**	**36**	**9**	**16**	**25**	**42**	**7**	**0**	**1**	**79**	**11.4**	**–3**				**6**	**3**	**2**	**5**	**0**	**2**	**0**	**0**	
1996-97	**Toronto**	**NHL**	**66**	**20**	**17**	**37**	**85**	**9**	**1**	**3**	**153**	**13.1**	**–23**												
	Florida	**NHL**	**10**	**1**	**2**	**3**	**4**	**1**	**0**	**1**	**21**	**4.8**	**–2**				**5**	**1**	**2**	**3**	**4**	**1**	**0**	**0**	
1997-98	**Florida**	**NHL**	**70**	**8**	**21**	**29**	**54**	**1**	**0**	**3**	**115**	**7.0**	**–14**												
1998-99	**Florida**	**NHL**	**82**	**4**	**11**	**15**	**49**	**0**	**0**	**1**	**107**	**3.7**	**–11**	**1157**	**49.1**	**14:28**									
99-2000	**Dallas**	**NHL**	**47**	**7**	**15**	**22**	**24**	**3**	**0**	**2**	**57**	**12.3**	**–3**	**443**	**48.5**	**16:24**	**23**	**2**	**3**	**5**	**18**	**0**	**0**	**1**	**11:56**
2000-01	**Dallas**	**NHL**	**55**	**1**	**9**	**10**	**26**	**0**	**0**	**0**	**54**	**1.9**	**–4**	**539**	**50.8**	**12:22**	**10**	**1**	**3**	**4**	**12**	**0**	**0**	**1**	**14:36**

			Regular Season														Playoffs								
Season	Club	League	GP	G	A	Pts	PIM	PP	SH	GW	S	%	+/-	TF	F%	Min	GP	G	A	Pts	PIM	PP	SH	GW	Min
2001-02	**Dallas**	**NHL**	**78**	**10**	**20**	**30**	**28**	**4**	**0**	**1**	**111**	**9.0**	**–12**	**511**	**49.7**	**13:48**	....	....	....	....	....	....	....	....	....
2002-03	**Dallas**	**NHL**	**55**	**1**	**5**	**6**	**18**	**0**	**0**	**0**	**48**	**2.1**	**–6**	**201**	**56.2**	**9:28**	**12**	**1**	**1**	**2**	**8**	**0**	**0**	**0**	**10:45**
	NHL Totals		**1349**	**357**	**602**	**959**	**1223**	**134**	**11**	**47**	**2791**	**12.8**		**2851**	**49.9**	**13:21**	**127**	**33**	**36**	**69**	**153**	**11**	**1**	**8**	**12:13**

Played in NHL All-Star Game (1985, 1986, 1988, 1990, 1992, 1993)

Traded to **Montreal** by **New Jersey** with Roland Melanson for Stephane Richer and Tom Chorske, September 20, 1991. Traded to **NY Islanders** by **Montreal** with Mathieu Schneider and Craig Darby for Pierre Turgeon and Vladimir Malakhov, April 5, 1995. Traded to **Toronto** by **NY Islanders** with Don Beaupre to complete transaction that sent Damian Rhodes and Ken Belanger to NY Islanders (January 23, 1996), January 23, 1996. Traded to **Florida** by **Toronto** for Jason Podollan, March 18, 1997. Signed as a free agent by **Dallas**, December 15, 1999. Claimed by **Columbus** from **Dallas** in Waiver Draft, September 28, 2001. Traded to **Dallas** by **Columbus** for the rights to Evgeny Petrochinin, September 28, 2001.

MURPHY, Curtis

(MUHR-fee, KUHR-this) **NSH.**

Defense. Shoots right. 5'8", 185 lbs. Born, Kerrobert, Sask., December 3, 1975.

Season	Club	League	GP	G	A	Pts	PIM	PP	SH	GW	S	%	+/-	TF	F%	Min	GP	G	A	Pts	PIM	PP	SH	GW	Min
1993-94	Nipawin Hawks	SJHL	60	21	33	54	....	....	....	....	....	....	....	....	....	....	....	....	....	....	....	....	....	....	....
1994-95	North Dakota	WCHA	33	6	10	16	28	....	....	....	....	....	....	....	....	....	....	....	....	....	....	....	....	....	....
1995-96	North Dakota	WCHA	38	6	12	18	58	....	....	....	....	....	....	....	....	....	....	....	....	....	....	....	....	....	....
1996-97	North Dakota	WCHA	43	12	30	42	36	....	....	....	....	....	....	....	....	....	....	....	....	....	....	....	....	....	....
1997-98	North Dakota	WCHA	39	8	34	42	78	....	....	....	....	....	....	....	....	....	....	....	....	....	....	....	....	....	....
1998-99	Orlando	IHL	80	22	35	57	60	....	....	....	....	....	....	....	....	....	17	4	5	9	16	....	....	....	....
99-2000	Orlando	IHL	81	8	43	51	59	....	....	....	....	....	....	....	....	....	6	0	2	2	6	....	....	....	....
2000-01	Orlando	IHL	51	19	30	49	55	....	....	....	....	....	....	....	....	....	10	2	9	11	12	....	....	....	....
2001-02	Houston Aeros	AHL	80	12	35	47	75	....	....	....	....	....	....	....	....	....	14	2	4	6	10	....	....	....	....
2002-03	**Minnesota**	**NHL**	**1**	**0**	**0**	**0**	**0**	**0**	**0**	**0**	**0**	**0.0**	**0**	**0**	**0.0**	**8:56**	....	....	....	....	....	....	....	....	....
	Houston Aeros	AHL	80	23	31	54	63	....	....	....	....	....	....	....	....	....	23	2	7	9	22	....	....	....	....
	NHL Totals		**1**	**0**	**0**	**0**	**0**	**0**	**0**	**0**	**0**	**0.0**		**0**	**0.0**	**8:56**	....	....	....	....	....	....	....	....	....

WCHA First All-Star Team (1997, 1998) • NCAA West Second All-American Team (1997) • WCHA Player of the Year (1998) • WCHA All-Tournament Team (1998) • NCAA West First All-American Team (1998) • IHL First All-Star Team (2001) • AHL First All-Star Team (2003) • Eddie Shore Award (Outstanding Defenseman – AHL) (2003)

Signed as a free agent by **Minnesota**, June 18, 2001. Traded to **Nashville** by **Minnesota** for Chris Bala, June 26, 2003.

MURRAY, Glen

(MUHR-ree, GLEHN) **BOS.**

Right wing. Shoots right. 6'3", 225 lbs. Born, Halifax, N.S., November 1, 1972. Boston's 1st choice, 18th overall, in 1991 Entry Draft.

Season	Club	League	GP	G	A	Pts	PIM	PP	SH	GW	S	%	+/-	TF	F%	Min	GP	G	A	Pts	PIM	PP	SH	GW	Min
1988-89	Bridgewater	NSMHL	45	50	56	106	62	....	....	....	....	....	....	....	....	....	....	....	....	....	....	....	....	....	....
1989-90	Sudbury Wolves	OHL	62	8	28	36	17	....	....	....	....	....	....	....	....	....	7	0	0	0	4	....	....	....	....
1990-91	Sudbury Wolves	OHL	66	27	38	65	82	....	....	....	....	....	....	....	....	....	5	8	4	12	10	....	....	....	....
1991-92	Sudbury Wolves	OHL	54	37	47	84	93	....	....	....	....	....	....	....	....	....	11	7	4	11	18	....	....	....	....
	Boston	**NHL**	**5**	**3**	**1**	**4**	**0**	**1**	**0**	**0**	**20**	**15.0**	**2**	....	....	....	**15**	**4**	**2**	**6**	**10**	**1**	**0**	**0**	....
1992-93	**Boston**	**NHL**	**27**	**3**	**4**	**7**	**8**	**2**	**0**	**1**	**28**	**10.7**	**–6**	....	....	....	....	....	....	....	....	....	....	....	....
	Providence Bruins	AHL	48	30	26	56	42	....	....	....	....	....	....	....	....	....	6	1	4	5	4	....	....	....	....
1993-94	**Boston**	**NHL**	**81**	**18**	**13**	**31**	**48**	**0**	**0**	**4**	**114**	**15.8**	**–1**	....	....	....	**13**	**4**	**5**	**9**	**14**	**0**	**0**	**0**	....
1994-95	**Boston**	**NHL**	**35**	**5**	**2**	**7**	**46**	**0**	**0**	**2**	**64**	**7.8**	**–11**	....	....	....	**2**	**0**	**0**	**0**	**2**	**0**	**0**	**0**	....
1995-96	**Pittsburgh**	**NHL**	**69**	**14**	**15**	**29**	**57**	**0**	**0**	**2**	**100**	**14.0**	**4**	....	....	....	**18**	**2**	**6**	**8**	**10**	**0**	**0**	**1**	....
1996-97	**Pittsburgh**	**NHL**	**66**	**11**	**11**	**22**	**24**	**3**	**0**	**1**	**127**	**8.7**	**–19**	....	....	....	....	....	....	....	....	....	....	....	....
	Los Angeles	**NHL**	**11**	**5**	**3**	**8**	**8**	**0**	**0**	**0**	**26**	**19.2**	**–2**	....	....	....	....	....	....	....	....	....	....	....	....
1997-98	**Los Angeles**	**NHL**	**81**	**29**	**31**	**60**	**54**	**7**	**3**	**7**	**193**	**15.0**	**6**	....	....	....	**4**	**2**	**0**	**2**	**6**	**0**	**0**	**0**	....
1998-99	**Los Angeles**	**NHL**	**61**	**16**	**15**	**31**	**36**	**3**	**3**	**3**	**173**	**9.2**	**–14**	**12**	**25.0**	**20:33**	....	....	....	....	....	....	....	....	....
99-2000	**Los Angeles**	**NHL**	**78**	**29**	**33**	**62**	**60**	**10**	**1**	**2**	**202**	**14.4**	**13**	**15**	**80.0**	**18:30**	**4**	**0**	**0**	**0**	**2**	**0**	**0**	**0**	**19:04**
2000-01	**Los Angeles**	**NHL**	**64**	**18**	**21**	**39**	**32**	**3**	**1**	**1**	**138**	**13.0**	**9**	**7**	**42.9**	**18:12**	**13**	**4**	**3**	**7**	**4**	**1**	**0**	**1**	**19:51**
2001-02	**Los Angeles**	**NHL**	**9**	**6**	**5**	**11**	**0**	**4**	**0**	**2**	**34**	**17.6**	**5**	**1**	**100.0**	**19:08**	....	....	....	....	....	....	....	....	....
	Boston	**NHL**	**73**	**35**	**25**	**60**	**40**	**5**	**0**	**7**	**212**	**16.5**	**26**	**39**	**23.1**	**19:50**	**6**	**1**	**4**	**5**	**4**	**0**	**0**	**0**	**18:02**
2002-03	**Boston**	**NHL**	**82**	**44**	**48**	**92**	**64**	**12**	**0**	**5**	**331**	**13.3**	**9**	**32**	**37.5**	**22:36**	**5**	**1**	**1**	**2**	**4**	**0**	**0**	**0**	**19:36**
	NHL Totals		**742**	**236**	**227**	**463**	**477**	**50**	**8**	**37**	**1762**	**13.4**		**106**	**37.7**	**19:59**	**80**	**18**	**21**	**39**	**56**	**2**	**0**	**2**	**19:18**

Played in NHL All-Star Game (2003)

Traded to **Pittsburgh** by **Boston** with Bryan Smolinski and Boston's 3rd round choice (Boyd Kane) in 1996 Entry Draft for Kevin Stevens and Shawn McEachern, August 2, 1995. Traded to **Los Angeles** by **Pittsburgh** for Ed Olczyk, March 18, 1997. Traded to **Boston** by **Los Angeles** with Jozef Stumpel for Jason Allison and Mikko Eloranta, October 24, 2001.

MURRAY, Marty

(MUHR-ree, MAHR-tee) **CAR.**

Center. Shoots left. 5'9", 180 lbs. Born, Lylton, Man., February 16, 1975. Calgary's 5th choice, 96th overall, in 1993 Entry Draft.

Season	Club	League	GP	G	A	Pts	PIM	PP	SH	GW	S	%	+/-	TF	F%	Min	GP	G	A	Pts	PIM	PP	SH	GW	Min
1990-91	S-W Cougars	MMHL	36	46	47	93	50	....	....	....	....	....	....	....	....	....	....	....	....	....	....	....	....	....	....
1991-92	Brandon	WHL	68	20	36	56	22	....	....	....	....	....	....	....	....	....	....	....	....	....	....	....	....	....	....
1992-93	Brandon	WHL	67	29	65	94	50	....	....	....	....	....	....	....	....	....	4	1	3	4	0	....	....	....	....
1993-94	Brandon	WHL	64	43	71	114	33	....	....	....	....	....	....	....	....	....	14	6	14	20	14	....	....	....	....
1994-95	Brandon	WHL	65	40	*88	128	53	....	....	....	....	....	....	....	....	....	18	9	*20	29	16	....	....	....	....
1995-96	**Calgary**	**NHL**	**15**	**3**	**3**	**6**	**0**	**2**	**0**	**0**	**22**	**13.6**	**–4**	....	....	....	....	....	....	....	....	....	....	....	....
	Saint John Flames	AHL	58	25	31	56	20	....	....	....	....	....	....	....	....	....	14	2	4	6	4	....	....	....	....
1996-97	**Calgary**	**NHL**	**2**	**0**	**0**	**0**	**4**	**0**	**0**	**0**	**2**	**0.0**	**0**	....	....	....	....	....	....	....	....	....	....	....	....
	Saint John Flames	AHL	67	19	39	58	40	....	....	....	....	....	....	....	....	....	5	2	3	5	4	....	....	....	....
1997-98	**Calgary**	**NHL**	**2**	**0**	**0**	**0**	**2**	**0**	**0**	**0**	**2**	**0.0**	**1**	....	....	....	....	....	....	....	....	....	....	....	....
	Saint John Flames	AHL	41	10	30	40	16	....	....	....	....	....	....	....	....	....	21	10	10	20	12	....	....	....	....
1998-99	EC Villacher SV	Alpenliga	33	26	41	67	12	....	....	....	....	....	....	....	....	....	....	....	....	....	....	....	....	....	....
	EC Villacher SV	Austria	17	13	17	30	6	....	....	....	....	....	....	....	....	....	6	1	4	5	0	....	....	....	....
99-2000	Kolner Haie	Germany	56	12	47	59	28	....	....	....	....	....	....	....	....	....	10	4	3	7	2	....	....	....	....
2000-01	**Calgary**	**NHL**	**7**	**0**	**0**	**0**	**0**	**0**	**0**	**0**	**6**	**0.0**	**–2**	**88**	**55.7**	**14:28**	....	....	....	....	....	....	....	....	....
	Saint John Flames	AHL	56	24	52	76	36	....	....	....	....	....	....	....	....	....	19	4	16	20	18	....	....	....	....
2001-02	**Philadelphia**	**NHL**	**74**	**12**	**15**	**27**	**10**	**1**	**1**	**2**	**109**	**11.0**	**10**	**913**	**50.7**	**13:56**	**5**	**0**	**1**	**1**	**0**	**0**	**0**	**0**	**13:14**
	Philadelphia	AHL	3	0	3	3	2	....	....	....	....	....	....	....	....	....	....	....	....	....	....	....	....	....	....
2002-03	**Philadelphia**	**NHL**	**76**	**11**	**15**	**26**	**13**	**1**	**1**	**0**	**105**	**10.5**	**–1**	**472**	**55.1**	**12:22**	**4**	**0**	**0**	**0**	**4**	**0**	**0**	**0**	**11:00**
	NHL Totals		**176**	**26**	**33**	**59**	**29**	**4**	**2**	**2**	**246**	**10.6**		**1473**	**52.4**	**13:12**	**9**	**0**	**1**	**1**	**4**	**0**	**0**	**0**	**12:15**

WHL East First All-Star Team (1994, 1995) • Canadian Major Junior Second All-Star Team (1994) • WHL MVP (1995)

Signed as a free agent by **Philadelphia**, July 9, 2001. Traded to **Carolina** by **Philadelphia** for Carolina's 6th round choice in 2004 Entry Draft, June 22, 2003.

MURRAY, Rem

(MUHR-ree, REHM) **NSH.**

Center/left wing. Shoots left. 6'2", 200 lbs. Born, Stratford, Ont., October 9, 1972. Los Angeles' 5th choice, 135th overall, in 1992 Entry Draft.

Season	Club	League	GP	G	A	Pts	PIM	PP	SH	GW	S	%	+/-	TF	F%	Min	GP	G	A	Pts	PIM	PP	SH	GW	Min
1989-90	Stratford Cullitons	OJHL-B	46	19	32	51	48	....	....	....	....	....	....	....	....	....	....	....	....	....	....	....	....	....	....
1990-91	Stratford Cullitons	OJHL-B	48	39	59	98	39	....	....	....	....	....	....	....	....	....	....	....	....	....	....	....	....	....	....
1991-92	Michigan State	CCHA	41	12	36	48	16	....	....	....	....	....	....	....	....	....	....	....	....	....	....	....	....	....	....
1992-93	Michigan State	CCHA	40	22	35	57	24	....	....	....	....	....	....	....	....	....	....	....	....	....	....	....	....	....	....
1993-94	Michigan State	CCHA	41	16	38	54	18	....	....	....	....	....	....	....	....	....	....	....	....	....	....	....	....	....	....
1994-95	Michigan State	CCHA	40	20	36	56	21	....	....	....	....	....	....	....	....	....	....	....	....	....	....	....	....	....	....
1995-96	Cape Breton	AHL	79	31	59	90	40	....	....	....	....	....	....	....	....	....	....	....	....	....	....	....	....	....	....
1996-97	**Edmonton**	**NHL**	**82**	**11**	**20**	**31**	**16**	**1**	**0**	**2**	**85**	**12.9**	**9**	....	....	....	**12**	**1**	**2**	**3**	**4**	**0**	**0**	**0**	....
1997-98	**Edmonton**	**NHL**	**61**	**9**	**9**	**18**	**39**	**2**	**2**	**0**	**59**	**15.3**	**–9**	....	....	....	**11**	**1**	**4**	**5**	**2**	**0**	**0**	**0**	....
1998-99	**Edmonton**	**NHL**	**78**	**21**	**18**	**39**	**20**	**4**	**1**	**4**	**116**	**18.1**	**4**	**1013**	**48.1**	**15:50**	**4**	**1**	**1**	**2**	**2**	**0**	**0**	**0**	**22:40**
99-2000	**Edmonton**	**NHL**	**44**	**9**	**5**	**14**	**8**	**2**	**0**	**3**	**65**	**13.8**	**–2**	**303**	**50.5**	**14:16**	**5**	**0**	**1**	**1**	**2**	**0**	**0**	**0**	**15:19**
2000-01	**Edmonton**	**NHL**	**82**	**15**	**21**	**36**	**24**	**1**	**3**	**3**	**122**	**12.3**	**5**	**694**	**49.3**	**15:21**	**6**	**2**	**0**	**2**	**6**	**1**	**0**	**0**	**18:10**
2001-02	**Edmonton**	**NHL**	**69**	**7**	**17**	**24**	**14**	**0**	**2**	**1**	**84**	**8.3**	**5**	**825**	**50.9**	**14:27**	....	....	....	....	....	....	....	....	....
	NY Rangers	**NHL**	**11**	**1**	**2**	**3**	**4**	**0**	**0**	**0**	**14**	**7.1**	**–9**	**151**	**51.7**	**15:51**	....	....	....	....	....	....	....	....	....
2002-03	**NY Rangers**	**NHL**	**32**	**6**	**6**	**12**	**4**	**1**	**1**	**1**	**62**	**9.7**	**–3**	**118**	**53.4**	**15:39**	....	....	....	....	....	....	....	....	....
	Nashville	**NHL**	**53**	**6**	**13**	**19**	**18**	**1**	**0**	**0**	**81**	**7.4**	**1**	**720**	**49.2**	**17:16**	....	....	....	....	....	....	....	....	....
	NHL Totals		**512**	**85**	**111**	**196**	**147**	**12**	**9**	**14**	**688**	**12.4**		**3824**	**49.6**	**15:28**	**38**	**5**	**8**	**13**	**16**	**1**	**0**	**0**	**18:25**

CCHA Second All-Star Team (1995)

Signed as a free agent by **Edmonton**, September 19, 1995. Traded to **NY Rangers** by **Edmonton** with Tom Poti for Mike York and NY Rangers' 4th round choice (Ivan Koltsov) in 2002 Entry Draft, March 19, 2002. Traded to **Nashville** by **NY Rangers** with Tomas Kloucek and Marek Zidlicky for Mike Dunham, December 12, 2002.

NAGY, Ladislav
(NA-gee, LA-dih-slahv) **PHX.**

Left wing. Shoots left. 5'11", 186 lbs. Born, Saca, Czech., June 1, 1979. St. Louis' 6th choice, 177th overall, in 1997 Entry Draft.

Season	Club	League	Regular Season														Playoffs								
			GP	G	A	Pts	PIM	PP	SH	GW	S	%	+/-	TF	F%	Min	GP	G	A	Pts	PIM	PP	SH	GW	Min
1996-97	HC Kosice Jr.	Slovak-Jr.	45	29	30	59	105																		
	HK Dragon Presov	Slovak-2	11	6	5	11																			
1997-98	HC Kosice	Slovakia	29	19	15	34	41										11	2	4	6	6				
1998-99	Halifax	QMJHL	63	71	55	126	148										5	3	3	6	18				
	Worcester IceCats	AHL															3	2	2	4	0				
99-2000	**St. Louis**	**NHL**	**11**	**2**	**4**	**6**	**2**	**1**	**0**	**0**	**15**	**13.3**	**2**	**6**	**33.3**	**12:19**	**6**	**1**	**1**	**2**	**0**	**0**	**0**	**0**	**13:28**
	Worcester IceCats	AHL	69	23	28	51	67										2	1	0	1	0				
2000-01	**St. Louis**	**NHL**	**40**	**8**	**8**	**16**	**20**	**2**	**0**	**2**	**59**	**13.6**	**-2**	**28**	**50.0**	**13:03**									
	Worcester IceCats	AHL	20	6	14	20	36																		
	Phoenix	**NHL**	**6**	**0**	**1**	**1**	**2**	**0**	**0**	**0**	**5**	**0.0**	**0**	**0**	**0.0**	**12:38**									
2001-02	**Phoenix**	**NHL**	**74**	**23**	**19**	**42**	**50**	**5**	**0**	**5**	**187**	**12.3**	**6**	**17**	**47.1**	**15:04**	**5**	**0**	**0**	**0**	**21**	**0**	**0**	**0**	**15:45**
2002-03	HC Kosice	Slovakia	1	2	1	3	0																		
	Phoenix	**NHL**	**80**	**22**	**35**	**57**	**92**	**8**	**0**	**6**	**209**	**10.5**	**17**	**41**	**34.2**	**17:28**									
	NHL Totals		**211**	**55**	**67**	**122**	**166**	**16**	**0**	**13**	**475**	**11.6**		**92**	**41.3**	**15:23**	**11**	**1**	**1**	**2**	**21**	**0**	**0**	**0**	**14:30**

Traded to **Phoenix** by **St. Louis** with Michal Handzus, the rights to Jeff Taffe and St. Louis' 1st round choice (Ben Eager) in 2002 Entry Draft for Keith Tkachuk, March 13, 2001.

NASH, Rick
(NASH, RIHK) **CBJ**

Left wing. Shoots left. 6'3", 188 lbs. Born, Brampton, Ont., June 16, 1984. Columbus' 1st choice, 1st overall, in 2002 Entry Draft.

Season	Club	League	Regular Season														Playoffs								
			GP	G	A	Pts	PIM	PP	SH	GW	S	%	+/-	TF	F%	Min	GP	G	A	Pts	PIM	PP	SH	GW	Min
99-2000	Tor. Marlboros	GTHL	34	61	54	115	34																		
2000-01	London Knights	OHL	58	31	35	66	56										4	3	3	6	8				
2001-02	London Knights	OHL	54	32	40	72	88										12	10	9	19	21				
2002-03	**Columbus**	**NHL**	**74**	**17**	**22**	**39**	**78**	**6**	**0**	**2**	**154**	**11.0**	**-27**	**14**	**35.7**	**13:57**									
	NHL Totals		**74**	**17**	**22**	**39**	**78**	**6**	**0**	**2**	**154**	**11.0**		**14**	**35.7**	**13:57**									

OHL All-Rookie Team (2001) • OHL Rookie of the Year (2001) • CHL All-Rookie Team (2001) • NHL All-Rookie Team (2003)

NASH, Tyson
(NASH, TIGH-sohn) **PHX.**

Left wing. Shoots left. 5'11", 194 lbs. Born, Edmonton, Alta., March 11, 1975. Vancouver's 10th choice, 247th overall, in 1994 Entry Draft.

Season	Club	League	Regular Season														Playoffs								
			GP	G	A	Pts	PIM	PP	SH	GW	S	%	+/-	TF	F%	Min	GP	G	A	Pts	PIM	PP	SH	GW	Min
1990-91	Sherwood Park	AMHL	40	17	28	43	63																		
1991-92	Kamloops Blazers	WHL	33	1	6	7	62										4	0	0	0	0				
1992-93	Kamloops Blazers	WHL	61	10	16	26	78										13	3	2	5	32				
1993-94	Kamloops Blazers	WHL	65	20	36	56	135										16	3	4	7	12				
1994-95	Kamloops Blazers	WHL	63	34	41	75	70										21	10	7	17	30				
1995-96	Syracuse Crunch	AHL	50	4	7	11	58										4	0	0	0	11				
	Raleigh IceCaps	ECHL	6	1	1	2	8																		
1996-97	Syracuse Crunch	AHL	77	17	17	34	105										3	0	2	2	0				
1997-98	Syracuse Crunch	AHL	74	20	20	40	184										5	0	2	2	28				
1998-99	**St. Louis**	**NHL**	**2**	**0**	**0**	**0**	**5**	**0**	**0**	**0**	**1**	**0.0**	**-1**	**0**	**0.0**	**7:44**	**1**	**0**	**0**	**0**	**2**	**0**	**0**	**0**	**6:25**
	Worcester IceCats	AHL	55	14	22	36	143										4	4	1	5	27				
99-2000	**St. Louis**	**NHL**	**66**	**4**	**9**	**13**	**150**	**0**	**1**	**1**	**68**	**5.9**	**6**	**0**	**0.0**	**8:35**	**6**	**1**	**0**	**1**	**24**	**0**	**0**	**0**	**8:36**
2000-01	**St. Louis**	**NHL**	**57**	**8**	**7**	**15**	**110**	**0**	**1**	**0**	**113**	**7.1**	**8**	**2**	**50.0**	**12:29**									
2001-02	**St. Louis**	**NHL**	**64**	**6**	**7**	**13**	**100**	**0**	**0**	**1**	**66**	**9.1**	**2**	**14**	**35.7**	**10:02**	**9**	**0**	**1**	**1**	**20**	**0**	**0**	**0**	**8:03**
2002-03	**St. Louis**	**NHL**	**66**	**6**	**3**	**9**	**114**	**1**	**0**	**2**	**77**	**7.8**	**0**	**9**	**11.1**	**9:53**	**7**	**2**	**1**	**3**	**6**	**0**	**0**	**0**	**9:05**
	NHL Totals		**255**	**24**	**26**	**50**	**479**	**1**	**2**	**4**	**325**	**7.4**		**25**	**28.0**	**10:09**	**23**	**3**	**2**	**5**	**52**	**0**	**0**	**0**	**8:26**

Signed as a free agent by **St. Louis**, July 14, 1998. Traded to **Phoenix** by **St. Louis** for Phoenix's 5th round choice (Lee Stempniak) in 2003 Enrey Draft, June 21, 2003.

NASLUND, Markus
(NAZ-luhnd, MAHR-kuhs) **VAN.**

Left wing. Shoots left. 5'11", 195 lbs. Born, Ornskoldsvik, Sweden, July 30, 1973. Pittsburgh's 1st choice, 16th overall, in 1991 Entry Draft.

Season	Club	League	Regular Season														Playoffs								
			GP	G	A	Pts	PIM	PP	SH	GW	S	%	+/-	TF	F%	Min	GP	G	A	Pts	PIM	PP	SH	GW	Min
1988-89	Ornskoldsviks IF	Swede-3	14	7	6	13																			
1989-90	MoDo Jr.	Swede-Jr.	33	43	35	78	20																		
1990-91	MoDo	Sweden	32	10	9	19	14																		
1991-92	MoDo	Sweden	39	22	18	40	54																		
1992-93	MoDo Jr.	Swede-Jr.	2	4	1	5	2																		
	MoDo	Sweden	39	22	17	39	67										3	3	2	5	0				
1993-94	**Pittsburgh**	**NHL**	**71**	**4**	**7**	**11**	**27**	**1**	**0**	**0**	**80**	**5.0**	**-3**												
	Cleveland	IHL	5	1	6	7	4																		
1994-95	**Pittsburgh**	**NHL**	**14**	**2**	**2**	**4**	**2**	**0**	**0**	**0**	**13**	**15.4**	**0**												
	Cleveland	IHL	7	3	4	7	6										4	1	3	4	8				
1995-96	**Pittsburgh**	**NHL**	**66**	**19**	**33**	**52**	**36**	**3**	**0**	**4**	**125**	**15.2**	**17**												
	Vancouver	**NHL**	**10**	**3**	**0**	**3**	**6**	**1**	**0**	**1**	**19**	**15.8**	**3**				**6**	**1**	**2**	**3**	**8**	**1**	**0**	**0**	
1996-97	**Vancouver**	**NHL**	**78**	**21**	**20**	**41**	**30**	**4**	**0**	**4**	**120**	**17.5**	**-15**												
1997-98	**Vancouver**	**NHL**	**76**	**14**	**20**	**34**	**56**	**2**	**1**	**0**	**106**	**13.2**	**5**												
1998-99	**Vancouver**	**NHL**	**80**	**36**	**30**	**66**	**74**	**15**	**2**	**3**	**205**	**17.6**	**-13**	**14**	**57.1**	**19:57**									
99-2000	**Vancouver**	**NHL**	**82**	**27**	**38**	**65**	**64**	**6**	**2**	**3**	**271**	**10.0**	**-5**	**13**	**46.2**	**20:13**									
2000-01	**Vancouver**	**NHL**	**72**	**41**	**34**	**75**	**58**	**18**	**1**	**5**	**277**	**14.8**	**-2**	**6**	**50.0**	**19:03**									
2001-02	**Vancouver**	**NHL**	**81**	**40**	**50**	**90**	**50**	**8**	**0**	**6**	**302**	**13.2**	**22**	**5**	**20.0**	**19:31**	**6**	**1**	**1**	**2**	**2**	**0**	**0**	**0**	**18:54**
	Sweden	Olympics	4	2	1	3	0																		
2002-03	**Vancouver**	**NHL**	**82**	**48**	**56**	**104**	**52**	**24**	**0**	**12**	**294**	**16.3**	**6**	**6**	**33.3**	**19:54**	**14**	**5**	**9**	**14**	**18**	**2**	**0**	**1**	**18:14**
	NHL Totals		**712**	**255**	**290**	**545**	**455**	**82**	**6**	**38**	**1812**	**14.1**		**44**	**45.5**	**19:44**	**26**	**7**	**12**	**19**	**28**	**3**	**0**	**1**	**18:26**

NHL First All-Star Team (2002, 2003) • Lester B. Pearson Award (2003)

Played in NHL All-Star Game (1999, 2001, 2002, 2003)

Traded to **Vancouver** by **Pittsburgh** for Alek Stojanov, March 20, 1996.

NASREDDINE, Alain
(NAS-ruh-deen, AL-eh) **NYI**

Defense. Shoots left. 6'1", 201 lbs. Born, Montreal, Que., July 10, 1975. Florida's 8th choice, 135th overall, in 1993 Entry Draft.

Season	Club	League	Regular Season														Playoffs								
			GP	G	A	Pts	PIM	PP	SH	GW	S	%	+/-	TF	F%	Min	GP	G	A	Pts	PIM	PP	SH	GW	Min
1990-91	Mtl-Bourassa	QAAA	35	10	25	35	50																		
1991-92	Drummondville	QMJHL	61	1	9	10	78										4	0	0	0	17				
1992-93	Drummondville	QMJHL	64	0	14	14	137										10	0	1	1	36				
1993-94	Chicoutimi	QMJHL	60	3	24	27	218										26	2	10	12	118				
1994-95	Chicoutimi	QMJHL	67	8	31	39	342										13	3	5	8	40				
1995-96	Carolina	AHL	63	0	5	5	245																		
1996-97	Carolina	AHL	26	0	4	4	109																		
	Indianapolis Ice	IHL	49	0	2	2	248										4	1	1	2	27				
1997-98	Indianapolis Ice	IHL	75	1	12	13	258										5	0	2	2	12				
1998-99	**Chicago**	**NHL**	**7**	**0**	**0**	**0**	**19**	**0**	**0**	**0**	**2**	**0.0**	**-2**	**0**	**0.0**	**12:11**									
	Portland Pirates	AHL	7	0	1	1	36																		
	Montreal	**NHL**	**8**	**0**	**0**	**0**	**33**	**0**	**0**	**0**	**1**	**0.0**	**1**	**0**	**0.0**	**8:12**									
	Fredericton	AHL	38	0	10	10	108										15	0	3	3	39				
99-2000	Quebec Citadelles	AHL	59	1	6	7	178																		
	Hamilton	AHL	11	0	0	0	12										10	1	1	2	14				
2000-01	Hamilton	AHL	74	4	14	18	164																		
2001-02	Hamilton	AHL	79	7	10	17	154										12	1	3	4	22				
2002-03	**NY Islanders**	**NHL**	**3**	**0**	**0**	**0**	**2**	**0**	**0**	**0**	**0**	**0.0**	**0**	**0**	**0.0**	**12:11**									
	Bridgeport	AHL	67	3	9	12	114										9	0	0	0	27				
	NHL Totals		**18**	**0**	**0**	**0**	**54**	**0**	**0**	**0**	**3**	**0.0**		**0**	**0.0**	**10:25**									

QMJHL Second All-Star Team (1995)

Traded to **Chicago** by **Florida** for Ivan Droppa, December 18, 1996. Traded to **Montreal** by **Chicago** with Jeff Hackett, Eric Weinrich and Tampa Bay's 4th round choice (previously acquired, Montreal selected Chris Dyment) in 1999 Entry Draft for Jocelyn Thibault, Dave Manson and Brad Brown, November 16, 1998. Traded to **Edmonton** by **Montreal** with Igor Ulanov for Christian Laflamme and Matthieu Descoteaux, March 9, 2000. Signed as a free agent by **NY Islanders**, September 6, 2002.

NAZAROV, Andrei

(nah-ZAH-rohv, AWN-dray) **PHX.**

Left wing. Shoots right. 6'5", 241 lbs. Born, Chelyabinsk, USSR, May 22, 1974. San Jose's 2nd choice, 10th overall, in 1992 Entry Draft.

			Regular Season														Playoffs								
Season	Club	League	GP	G	A	Pts	PIM	PP	SH	GW	S	%	+/-	TF	F%	Min	GP	G	A	Pts	PIM	PP	SH	GW	Min
1991-92	Dynamo Moscow	CIS	2	1	0	1	2	....	....	....	....	....	....	....	....	....	....	....	....	....	....	....	....	....	....
1992-93	Dynamo Moscow	CIS	42	8	2	10	79	....	....	....	....	....	....	....	....	....	10	1	1	2	8	....	....	....	....
1993-94	Dynamo Moscow	CIS	6	2	2	4	0	....	....	....	....	....	....	....	....	....	....	....	....	....	....	....	....	....	....
	San Jose	**NHL**	**1**	**0**	**0**	**0**	**0**	**0**	**0**	**0**	**0**	**0.0**	**0**	....	....	....	....	....	....	....	....	....	....	....	....
	Kansas City	IHL	71	15	18	33	64	....	....	....	....	....	....	....	....	....	....	....	....	....	....	....	....	....	....
1994-95	Kansas City	IHL	43	15	10	25	55	....	....	....	....	....	....	....	....	....	....	....	....	....	....	....	....	....	....
	San Jose	**NHL**	**26**	**3**	**5**	**8**	**94**	**0**	**0**	**0**	**19**	**15.8**	**–1**	....	....	....	**6**	**0**	**0**	**0**	**9**	**0**	**0**	**0**	....
1995-96	**San Jose**	**NHL**	**42**	**7**	**7**	**14**	**62**	**2**	**0**	**1**	**55**	**12.7**	**–15**	....	....	....	....	....	....	....	....	....	....	....	....
	Kansas City	IHL	27	4	6	10	118	....	....	....	....	....	....	....	....	....	2	0	0	0	2	....	....	....	....
1996-97	**San Jose**	**NHL**	**60**	**12**	**15**	**27**	**222**	**1**	**0**	**1**	**116**	**10.3**	**–4**	....	....	....	....	....	....	....	....	....	....	....	....
	Kentucky	AHL	3	1	2	3	4	....	....	....	....	....	....	....	....	....	....	....	....	....	....	....	....	....	....
1997-98	**San Jose**	**NHL**	**40**	**1**	**1**	**2**	**112**	**0**	**0**	**0**	**31**	**3.2**	**–4**	....	....	....	....	....	....	....	....	....	....	....	....
	Tampa Bay	**NHL**	**14**	**1**	**1**	**2**	**58**	**0**	**0**	**0**	**19**	**5.3**	**–9**	....	....	....	....	....	....	....	....	....	....	....	....
1998-99	**Tampa Bay**	**NHL**	**26**	**2**	**0**	**2**	**43**	**0**	**0**	**0**	**18**	**11.1**	**–5**	**4**	**50.0**	**8:13**	....	....	....	....	....	....	....	....	....
	Calgary	**NHL**	**36**	**5**	**9**	**14**	**30**	**0**	**0**	**2**	**53**	**9.4**	**1**	**0**	**0.0**	**14:31**	....	....	....	....	....	....	....	....	....
99-2000	**Calgary**	**NHL**	**76**	**10**	**22**	**32**	**78**	**1**	**0**	**1**	**110**	**9.1**	**3**	**2**	**100.0**	**11:44**	....	....	....	....	....	....	....	....	....
2000-01	**Anaheim**	**NHL**	**16**	**1**	**0**	**1**	**29**	**0**	**0**	**0**	**13**	**7.7**	**–9**	**2**	**50.0**	**8:42**	....	....	....	....	....	....	....	....	....
	Boston	**NHL**	**63**	**1**	**4**	**5**	**200**	**0**	**0**	**0**	**50**	**2.0**	**–14**	**14**	**21.4**	**8:12**	....	....	....	....	....	....	....	....	....
2001-02	**Boston**	**NHL**	**47**	**0**	**2**	**2**	**164**	**0**	**0**	**0**	**18**	**0.0**	**–2**	**1**	**100.0**	**3:10**	....	....	....	....	....	....	....	....	....
	Phoenix	**NHL**	**30**	**6**	**3**	**9**	**51**	**0**	**0**	**0**	**38**	**15.8**	**7**	**1**	**100.0**	**7:35**	**3**	**0**	**0**	**0**	**2**	**0**	**0**	**0**	**9:34**
2002-03	**Phoenix**	**NHL**	**59**	**3**	**0**	**3**	**135**	**2**	**0**	**0**	**35**	**8.6**	**–9**	**6**	**33.3**	**6:34**	....	....	....	....	....	....	....	....	....
	NHL Totals		**536**	**52**	**69**	**121**	**1278**	**6**	**0**	**5**	**575**	**9.0**		**30**	**40.0**	**8:38**	**9**	**0**	**0**	**0**	**11**	**0**	**0**	**0**	**9:34**

Traded to **Tampa Bay** by **San Jose** with Florida's 1st round choice (previously acquired, Tampa Bay selected Vincent Lecavalier) in 1998 Entry Draft for Bryan Marchment, David Shaw and Tampa Bay's 1st round choice (later traded to Nashville – Nashville selected David Legwand) in 1998 Entry Draft, March 24, 1998. Traded to **Calgary** by **Tampa Bay** for Michael Nylander, January 19, 1999. Traded to **Anaheim** by **Calgary** with Calgary's 2nd round choice (later traded to Phoenix – later traded back to Calgary – Calgary selected Andrei Taratukhin) in 2001 Entry Draft for Jordan Leopold, September 26, 2000. Traded to **Boston** by **Anaheim** with Patrick Traverse for Samuel Pahlsson, November 18, 2000. Traded to **Phoenix** by **Boston** for Phoenix's 5th round choice (Peter Hamerlik) in 2002 Entry Draft, January 25, 2002.

NECKAR, Stan

(NEHTS-kahzh, STAN)

Defense. Shoots left. 6'1", 214 lbs. Born, Ceske Budejovice, Czech., December 22, 1975. Ottawa's 2nd choice, 29th overall, in 1994 Entry Draft.

Season	Club	League	GP	G	A	Pts	PIM	PP	SH	GW	S	%	+/-	TF	F%	Min	GP	G	A	Pts	PIM	PP	SH	GW	Min
1991-92	C. Budejovice Jr.	Czech-Jr.	18	1	3	4	....	....	....	....	....	....	....	....	....	....	....	....	....	....	....	....	....	....	....
1992-93	Ceske Budejovice	Czech	42	2	9	11	12	....	....	....	....	....	....	....	....	....	....	....	....	....	....	....	....	....	....
1993-94	Ceske Budejovice	Czech	12	3	2	5	2	....	....	....	....	....	....	....	....	....	3	0	0	0	....	....	....	....	....
1994-95	Detroit Vipers	IHL	15	2	2	4	15	....	....	....	....	....	....	....	....	....	....	....	....	....	....	....	....	....	....
	Ottawa	**NHL**	**48**	**1**	**3**	**4**	**37**	**0**	**0**	**0**	**34**	**2.9**	**–20**	....	....	....	....	....	....	....	....	....	....	....	....
1995-96	**Ottawa**	**NHL**	**82**	**3**	**9**	**12**	**54**	**1**	**0**	**0**	**57**	**5.3**	**–16**	....	....	....	....	....	....	....	....	....	....	....	....
1996-97	**Ottawa**	**NHL**	**5**	**0**	**0**	**0**	**2**	**0**	**0**	**0**	**3**	**0.0**	**2**	....	....	....	....	....	....	....	....	....	....	....	....
1997-98	**Ottawa**	**NHL**	**60**	**2**	**2**	**4**	**31**	**0**	**0**	**0**	**43**	**4.7**	**–14**	....	....	....	**9**	**0**	**0**	**0**	**2**	**0**	**0**	**0**	....
1998-99	**Ottawa**	**NHL**	**3**	**0**	**2**	**2**	**0**	**0**	**0**	**0**	**2**	**0.0**	**–1**	**0**	**0.0**	**15:53**	....	....	....	....	....	....	....	....	....
	NY Rangers	**NHL**	**18**	**0**	**0**	**0**	**8**	**0**	**0**	**0**	**8**	**0.0**	**–1**	**0**	**0.0**	**13:46**	....	....	....	....	....	....	....	....	....
	Phoenix	**NHL**	**11**	**0**	**1**	**1**	**10**	**0**	**0**	**0**	**6**	**0.0**	**3**	**0**	**0.0**	**15:08**	**6**	**0**	**1**	**1**	**4**	**0**	**0**	**0**	**10:20**
99-2000	**Phoenix**	**NHL**	**66**	**2**	**8**	**10**	**36**	**0**	**0**	**0**	**34**	**5.9**	**1**	**0**	**0.0**	**14:27**	**5**	**0**	**0**	**0**	**0**	**0**	**0**	**0**	**11:28**
2000-01	**Phoenix**	**NHL**	**53**	**2**	**2**	**4**	**63**	**0**	**0**	**1**	**16**	**12.5**	**–2**	**0**	**0.0**	**15:26**	....	....	....	....	....	....	....	....	....
	Tampa Bay	**NHL**	**16**	**0**	**2**	**2**	**8**	**0**	**0**	**0**	**10**	**0.0**	**–1**	**0**	**0.0**	**18:33**	....	....	....	....	....	....	....	....	....
2001-02	**Tampa Bay**	**NHL**	**77**	**1**	**7**	**8**	**24**	**0**	**1**	**0**	**38**	**2.6**	**–18**	**0**	**0.0**	**20:31**	....	....	....	....	....	....	....	....	....
2002-03	**Tampa Bay**	**NHL**	**70**	**1**	**4**	**5**	**43**	**0**	**0**	**1**	**38**	**2.6**	**–6**	**0**	**0.0**	**18:42**	**7**	**0**	**2**	**2**	**2**	**0**	**0**	**0**	**18:35**
	NHL Totals		**509**	**12**	**40**	**52**	**316**	**1**	**1**	**2**	**289**	**4.2**		**0**	**0.0**	**17:16**	**27**	**0**	**3**	**3**	**8**	**0**	**0**	**0**	**13:51**

Traded to **NY Rangers** by **Ottawa** for Bill Berg and NY Rangers' 2nd round choice (later traded to Anaheim – Anaheim selected Jordan Leopold) in 1999 Entry Draft, November 27, 1998. Traded to **Phoenix** by **NY Rangers** for Jason Doig and Phoenix's 6th round choice (Jay Dardis) in 1999 Entry Draft, March 23, 1999. Traded to **Tampa Bay** by **Phoenix** with Nikolai Khabibulin for Mike Johnson, Paul Mara, Ruslan Zainullin and NY Islanders' 2nd round choice (previously acquired, Phoenix selected Matthew Spiller) in 2001 Entry Draft, March 5, 2001.

NEDOROST, Andrej

(NEHD-ohr-ohst, awn-DRAY) **CBJ**

Left wing. Shoots left. 6', 192 lbs. Born, Trencin, Czech., April 30, 1980. Columbus' 10th choice, 286th overall, in 2000 Entry Draft.

Season	Club	League	GP	G	A	Pts	PIM	PP	SH	GW	S	%	+/-	TF	F%	Min	GP	G	A	Pts	PIM	PP	SH	GW	Min
1996-96	Dukla Trencin Jr.	Slovak-Jr.	40	50	35	85	....	....	....	....	....	....	....	....	....	....	....	....	....	....	....	....	....	....	....
1996-97	Dukla Trencin Jr.	Slovak-Jr.	45	15	16	31	....	....	....	....	....	....	....	....	....	....	....	....	....	....	....	....	....	....	....
1997-98	Dukla Trencin Jr.	Slovak-Jr.	45	27	22	49	61	....	....	....	....	....	....	....	....	....	....	....	....	....	....	....	....	....	....
	Dukla Trencin	Slovakia	1	0	0	0	0	....	....	....	....	....	....	....	....	....	....	....	....	....	....	....	....	....	....
1998-99	Essen Jr.	Ger.-Jr.	17	37	18	55	43	....	....	....	....	....	....	....	....	....	....	....	....	....	....	....	....	....	....
	Essen	German-2	30	3	5	8	22	....	....	....	....	....	....	....	....	....	....	....	....	....	....	....	....	....	....
99-2000	Essen	Germany	66	7	5	12	44	....	....	....	....	....	....	....	....	....	....	....	....	....	....	....	....	....	....
2000-01	Plzen	Czech	33	10	8	18	22	....	....	....	....	....	....	....	....	....	....	....	....	....	....	....	....	....	....
2001-02	**Columbus**	**NHL**	**7**	**0**	**2**	**2**	**2**	**0**	**0**	**0**	**12**	**0.0**	**–3**	**1**	**100.0**	**12:56**	....	....	....	....	....	....	....	....	....
	Syracuse Crunch	AHL	37	5	13	18	28	....	....	....	....	....	....	....	....	....	10	1	3	4	4	....	....	....	....
2002-03	**Columbus**	**NHL**	**12**	**0**	**1**	**1**	**4**	**0**	**0**	**0**	**10**	**0.0**	**–6**	**30**	**36.7**	**9:15**	....	....	....	....	....	....	....	....	....
	Syracuse Crunch	AHL	63	14	19	33	85	....	....	....	....	....	....	....	....	....	....	....	....	....	....	....	....	....	....
	NHL Totals		**19**	**0**	**3**	**3**	**6**	**0**	**0**	**0**	**22**	**0.0**		**31**	**38.7**	**10:36**	....	....	....	....	....	....	....	....	....

NEDOROST, Vaclav

(neh-DOHR-uhst, VA-tslav) **FLA.**

Center. Shoots left. 6'1", 190 lbs. Born, Budejovice, Czech., March 16, 1982. Colorado's 1st choice, 14th overall, in 2000 Entry Draft.

Season	Club	League	GP	G	A	Pts	PIM	PP	SH	GW	S	%	+/-	TF	F%	Min	GP	G	A	Pts	PIM	PP	SH	GW	Min
1997-98	C. Budejovice Jr.	Czech-Jr.	43	30	23	53	20	....	....	....	....	....	....	....	....	....	....	....	....	....	....	....	....	....	....
1998-99	C. Budejovice Jr.	Czech-Jr.	39	6	15	21	20	....	....	....	....	....	....	....	....	....	....	....	....	....	....	....	....	....	....
	Ceske Budejovice	Czech	7	0	2	2	0	....	....	....	....	....	....	....	....	....	....	....	....	....	....	....	....	....	....
99-2000	C. Budejovice Jr.	Czech-Jr.	14	4	7	11	4	....	....	....	....	....	....	....	....	....	....	....	....	....	....	....	....	....	....
	Ceske Budejovice	Czech	38	8	6	14	6	....	....	....	....	....	....	....	....	....	....	....	....	....	....	....	....	....	....
2000-01	Ceske Budejovice	Czech	36	3	12	15	14	....	....	....	....	....	....	....	....	....	3	0	0	0	0	....	....	....	....
2001-02	**Colorado**	**NHL**	**25**	**2**	**2**	**4**	**2**	**1**	**0**	**0**	**22**	**9.1**	**–4**	**62**	**45.2**	**10:15**	....	....	....	....	....	....	....	....	....
	Hershey Bears	AHL	49	12	22	34	16	....	....	....	....	....	....	....	....	....	7	2	3	5	2	....	....	....	....
2002-03	**Colorado**	**NHL**	**42**	**4**	**5**	**9**	**20**	**1**	**0**	**0**	**35**	**11.4**	**8**	**151**	**44.4**	**10:29**	....	....	....	....	....	....	....	....	....
	Hershey Bears	AHL	5	3	2	5	0	....	....	....	....	....	....	....	....	....	5	2	2	4	0	....	....	....	....
	NHL Totals		**67**	**6**	**7**	**13**	**22**	**2**	**0**	**0**	**57**	**10.5**		**213**	**44.6**	**10:24**	....	....	....	....	....	....	....	....	....

Traded to **Florida** by **Colorado** with Eric Messier for Peter Worrell and Florida's 2nd round choice in 2004 Entry Draft, July 19, 2003.

NEDVED, Petr

(NEHD-VEHD, PEE-tuhr) **NYR**

Center. Shoots left. 6'3", 195 lbs. Born, Liberec, Czech., December 9, 1971. Vancouver's 1st choice, 2nd overall, in 1990 Entry Draft.

Season	Club	League	GP	G	A	Pts	PIM	PP	SH	GW	S	%	+/-	TF	F%	Min	GP	G	A	Pts	PIM	PP	SH	GW	Min
1988-89	CHZ Litvinov Jr.	Czech-Jr.	20	32	19	51	12	....	....	....	....	....	....	....	....	....	....	....	....	....	....	....	....	....	....
1989-90	Seattle	WHL	71	65	80	145	80	....	....	....	....	....	....	....	....	....	11	4	9	13	2	....	....	....	....
1990-91	**Vancouver**	**NHL**	**61**	**10**	**6**	**16**	**20**	**1**	**0**	**0**	**97**	**10.3**	**–21**	....	....	....	**6**	**0**	**1**	**1**	**0**	**0**	**0**	**0**	....
1991-92	**Vancouver**	**NHL**	**77**	**15**	**22**	**37**	**36**	**5**	**0**	**1**	**99**	**15.2**	**–3**	....	....	....	**10**	**1**	**4**	**5**	**16**	**0**	**0**	**0**	....
1992-93	**Vancouver**	**NHL**	**84**	**38**	**33**	**71**	**96**	**2**	**1**	**3**	**149**	**25.5**	**20**	....	....	....	**12**	**2**	**3**	**5**	**2**	**0**	**0**	**0**	....
1993-94	Team Canada	Nat-Tm	17	19	12	31	16	....	....	....	....	....	....	....	....	....	....	....	....	....	....	....	....	....	....
	Canada	Olympics	8	5	1	6	6	....	....	....	....	....	....	....	....	....	....	....	....	....	....	....	....	....	....
	St. Louis	**NHL**	**19**	**6**	**14**	**20**	**8**	**2**	**0**	**0**	**63**	**9.5**	**2**	....	....	....	**4**	**0**	**1**	**1**	**4**	**0**	**0**	**0**	....
1994-95	**NY Rangers**	**NHL**	**46**	**11**	**12**	**23**	**26**	**1**	**0**	**3**	**123**	**8.9**	**–1**	....	....	....	**10**	**3**	**2**	**5**	**6**	**2**	**0**	**0**	....
1995-96	**Pittsburgh**	**NHL**	**80**	**45**	**54**	**99**	**68**	**8**	**1**	**5**	**204**	**22.1**	**37**	....	....	....	**18**	**10**	**10**	**20**	**16**	**4**	**0**	**2**	....
1996-97	**Pittsburgh**	**NHL**	**74**	**33**	**38**	**71**	**66**	**12**	**3**	**4**	**189**	**17.5**	**–2**	....	....	....	**5**	**1**	**2**	**3**	**12**	**0**	**1**	**0**	....
1997-98	Stadion Liberec	Czech-2	2	0	3	3	....	....	....	....	....	....	....	....	....	....	....	....	....	....	....	....	....	....	....
	TJ Novy Jicin	Czech-3	7	9	16	25	....	....	....	....	....	....	....	....	....	....	....	....	....	....	....	....	....	....	....
	HC Sparta Praha	Czech	5	2	3	5	8	....	....	....	....	....	....	....	....	....	6	0	2	2	52	....	....	....	....
	Las Vegas	IHL	3	3	3	6	4	....	....	....	....	....	....	....	....	....	....	....	....	....	....	....	....	....	....
1998-99	Las Vegas	IHL	13	8	10	18	32	....	....	....	....	....	....	....	....	....	....	....	....	....	....	....	....	....	....
	NY Rangers	**NHL**	**56**	**20**	**27**	**47**	**50**	**9**	**1**	**3**	**153**	**13.1**	**–6**	**1069**	**52.5**	**20:31**	....	....	....	....	....	....	....	....	....
99-2000	**NY Rangers**	**NHL**	**76**	**24**	**44**	**68**	**40**	**6**	**2**	**4**	**201**	**11.9**	**2**	**1354**	**54.0**	**19:54**	....	....	....	....	....	....	....	....	....
2000-01	**NY Rangers**	**NHL**	**79**	**32**	**46**	**78**	**54**	**9**	**1**	**5**	**230**	**13.9**	**10**	**1349**	**49.7**	**20:16**	....	....	....	....	....	....	....	....	....

			Regular Season														Playoffs								
Season	Club	League	GP	G	A	Pts	PIM	PP	SH	GW	S	%	+/-	TF	F%	Min	GP	G	A	Pts	PIM	PP	SH	GW	Min
2001-02	Liberec	Czech-2	1	3	0	3	2																		
	NY Rangers	**NHL**	**78**	**21**	**25**	**46**	**36**	**6**	**1**	**3**	**175**	**12.0**	**–8**	**1402**	**52.1**	**19:22**									
2002-03	**NY Rangers**	**NHL**	**78**	**27**	**31**	**58**	**64**	**8**	**3**	**4**	**205**	**13.2**	**–4**	**1142**	**53.0**	**20:21**									
	NHL Totals		**808**	**282**	**352**	**634**	**564**	**69**	**13**	**35**	**1888**	**14.9**		**6316**	**52.2**	**20:03**	**65**	**17**	**23**	**40**	**56**	**6**	**1**	**2**	....

WHL Rookie of the Year (1990) • Canadian Major Junior Rookie of the Year (1990)

Signed as a free agent by **St. Louis**, March 5, 1994. Traded to **NY Rangers** by **St. Louis** for Esa Tikkanen and Doug Lidster, July 24, 1994. Traded to **Pittsburgh** by **NY Rangers** with Sergei Zubov for Luc Robitaille and Ulf Samuelsson, August 31, 1995. Traded to **NY Rangers** by **Pittsburgh** with Chris Tamer and Sean Pronger for Alex Kovalev and Harry York, November 25, 1998.

NEIL, Chris

(NEEL, KRIHS) **OTT.**

Right wing. Shoots right. 6', 213 lbs. Born, Markdale, Ont., June 18, 1979. Ottawa's 7th choice, 161st overall, in 1998 Entry Draft.

Season	Club	League	GP	G	A	Pts	PIM	PP	SH	GW	S	%	+/-	TF	F%	Min	GP	G	A	Pts	PIM	PP	SH	GW	Min
1995-96	Orangeville	OJHL-B	43	15	15	30	50																		
1996-97	North Bay	OHL	65	13	16	29	150																		
1997-98	North Bay	OHL	59	26	29	55	231																		
1998-99	North Bay	OHL	66	26	46	72	215										4	1	0	1	15				
99-2000	Mobile Mysticks	ECHL	4	0	2	2	39																		
	Grand Rapids	IHL	51	9	10	19	301										8	0	2	2	24				
2000-01	Grand Rapids	IHL	78	15	21	36	354										10	2	2	4	22				
2001-02	**Ottawa**	**NHL**	**72**	**10**	**7**	**17**	**231**	**1**	**0**	**0**	**56**	**17.9**	**5**	**0**	**0.0**	**8:22**	**12**	**0**	**0**	**0**	**12**	**0**	**0**	**0**	**7:12**
2002-03	**Ottawa**	**NHL**	**68**	**6**	**4**	**10**	**147**	**0**	**0**	**0**	**62**	**9.7**	**8**	**5**	**60.0**	**7:40**	**15**	**1**	**0**	**1**	**24**	**0**	**0**	**0**	**7:57**
	NHL Totals		**140**	**16**	**11**	**27**	**378**	**1**	**0**	**0**	**118**	**13.6**		**5**	**60.0**	**8:01**	**27**	**1**	**0**	**1**	**36**	**0**	**0**	**0**	**7:37**

NELSON, Jeff

(NEHL-sohn, JEHF)

Center. Shoots left. 5'11", 190 lbs. Born, Prince Albert, Sask., December 18, 1972. Washington's 4th choice, 36th overall, in 1991 Entry Draft.

Season	Club	League	GP	G	A	Pts	PIM	PP	SH	GW	S	%	+/-	TF	F%	Min	GP	G	A	Pts	PIM	PP	SH	GW	Min
1987-88	Prince Albert	SMHL	31	24	32	56	32																		
1988-89	Prince Albert	WHL	71	30	57	87	74										4	0	3	3	4				
1989-90	Prince Albert	WHL	72	28	69	97	79										14	2	11	13	10				
1990-91	Prince Albert	WHL	72	46	74	120	58										3	1	1	2	4				
1991-92	Prince Albert	WHL	64	48	65	113	84										9	7	14	21	18				
1992-93	Baltimore	AHL	72	14	38	52	12										7	1	3	4	2				
1993-94	Portland Pirates	AHL	80	34	73	107	92										17	10	5	15	20				
1994-95	Portland Pirates	AHL	64	33	50	83	57										7	1	4	5	8				
	Washington	**NHL**	**10**	**1**	**0**	**1**	**2**	**0**	**0**	**0**	**4**	**25.0**	**–2**												
1995-96	**Washington**	**NHL**	**33**	**0**	**7**	**7**	**16**	**0**	**0**	**0**	**21**	**0.0**	**3**				**3**	**0**	**0**	**0**	**4**	**0**	**0**	**0**	
	Portland Pirates	AHL	39	15	32	47	62																		
1996-97	Grand Rapids	IHL	82	34	55	89	85										5	0	4	4	4				
1997-98	Milwaukee	IHL	52	20	34	54	30										10	2	7	9	15				
1998-99	**Nashville**	**NHL**	**9**	**2**	**1**	**3**	**2**	**0**	**0**	**0**	**8**	**25.0**	**–1**	**138**	**55.1**	**16:09**									
	Milwaukee	IHL	70	20	31	51	66										2	0	0	0	0				
99-2000	Portland Pirates	AHL	73	24	30	54	38										1	0	0	0	0				
2000-01	Portland Pirates	AHL	80	18	37	55	63										3	0	2	2	6				
2001-02	Schwenningen	Germany	60	13	14	27	60																		
2002-03	Cleveland Barons	AHL	80	12	48	60	26																		
	NHL Totals		**52**	**3**	**8**	**11**	**20**	**0**	**0**	**0**	**33**	**9.1**		**138**	**55.1**	**16:09**	**3**	**0**	**0**	**0**	**4**	**0**	**0**	**0**	....

Canadian Major Junior Scholastic Player of the Year (1989, 1990) • WHL East Second All-Star Team (1991, 1992)

Signed as a free agent by **Grand Rapids** (IHL), September 9, 1996. Signed as a free agent by **Nashville**, August 19, 1998. Traded to **Washington** by **Nashville** for cash, June 21, 1999. Signed as a free agent by **Schwenningen** (Germany), July 17, 2001. Signed as a free agent by **San Jose**, September 5, 2002.

NEMCHINOV, Sergei

(nehm-CHEE-nahf, SAIR-gay)

Left wing. Shoots left. 6'1", 205 lbs. Born, Moscow, USSR, January 14, 1964. NY Rangers' 14th choice, 244th overall, in 1990 Entry Draft.

Season	Club	League	GP	G	A	Pts	PIM	PP	SH	GW	S	%	+/-	TF	F%	Min	GP	G	A	Pts	PIM	PP	SH	GW	Min
1981-82	Krylja Sovetov	USSR	15	1	0	1	0																		
1982-83	CSKA Moscow	USSR	11	0	0	0	2																		
1983-84	CSKA Moscow	USSR	20	6	5	11	4																		
1984-85	CSKA Moscow	USSR	31	2	4	6	4																		
1985-86	Krylja Sovetov	USSR	39	7	12	19	28																		
1986-87	Krylja Sovetov	USSR	40	13	9	22	24																		
1987-88	Krylja Sovetov	USSR	48	17	11	28	26																		
1988-89	Krylja Sovetov	USSR	43	15	14	29	28																		
1989-90	Krylja Sovetov	USSR	48	17	16	33	34																		
1990-91	Krylja Sovetov	USSR	46	21	24	45	30																		
1991-92	**NY Rangers**	**NHL**	**73**	**30**	**28**	**58**	**15**	**2**	**0**	**5**	**124**	**24.2**	**19**				**13**	**1**	**4**	**5**	**8**	**0**	**0**	**0**	
1992-93	**NY Rangers**	**NHL**	**81**	**23**	**31**	**54**	**34**	**0**	**1**	**3**	**144**	**16.0**	**15**												
1993-94♦	**NY Rangers**	**NHL**	**76**	**22**	**27**	**49**	**36**	**4**	**0**	**6**	**144**	**15.3**	**13**				**23**	**2**	**5**	**7**	**6**	**0**	**0**	**0**	
1994-95	**NY Rangers**	**NHL**	**47**	**7**	**6**	**13**	**16**	**0**	**0**	**3**	**67**	**10.4**	**–6**				**10**	**4**	**5**	**9**	**2**	**0**	**0**	**1**	
1995-96	**NY Rangers**	**NHL**	**78**	**17**	**15**	**32**	**38**	**0**	**0**	**2**	**118**	**14.4**	**9**				**6**	**0**	**1**	**1**	**2**	**0**	**0**	**0**	
1996-97	**NY Rangers**	**NHL**	**63**	**6**	**13**	**19**	**12**	**1**	**0**	**1**	**90**	**6.7**	**5**												
	Vancouver	**NHL**	**6**	**2**	**3**	**5**	**4**	**0**	**0**	**1**	**7**	**28.6**	**4**												
1997-98	**NY Islanders**	**NHL**	**74**	**10**	**19**	**29**	**24**	**2**	**1**	**1**	**94**	**10.6**	**3**												
	Russia	Olympics	6	1	0	1	0																		
1998-99	**NY Islanders**	**NHL**	**67**	**8**	**8**	**16**	**22**	**1**	**0**	**0**	**61**	**13.1**	**–17**	**606**	**42.4**	**14:21**									
	New Jersey	**NHL**	**10**	**4**	**0**	**4**	**6**	**1**	**0**	**1**	**13**	**30.8**	**4**	**38**	**52.6**	**15:36**	**4**	**0**	**0**	**0**	**0**	**0**	**0**	**0**	**10:38**
99-2000♦	**New Jersey**	**NHL**	**53**	**10**	**16**	**26**	**18**	**0**	**1**	**1**	**55**	**18.2**	**1**	**453**	**45.7**	**13:42**	**21**	**3**	**2**	**5**	**2**	**1**	**0**	**0**	**14:30**
2000-01	**New Jersey**	**NHL**	**65**	**8**	**22**	**30**	**16**	**1**	**0**	**2**	**70**	**11.4**	**11**	**649**	**48.1**	**13:13**	**25**	**1**	**3**	**4**	**4**	**0**	**0**	**0**	**11:42**
2001-02	**New Jersey**	**NHL**	**68**	**5**	**5**	**10**	**10**	**0**	**0**	**1**	**49**	**10.2**	**–9**	**497**	**42.7**	**11:09**	**3**	**0**	**0**	**0**	**0**	**0**	**0**	**0**	**8:20**
2002-03	Yaroslavl	Russia	27	5	6	11	26										10	0	5	5	10				
	NHL Totals		**761**	**152**	**193**	**345**	**251**	**12**	**3**	**27**	**1036**	**14.7**		**2243**	**44.9**	**13:10**	**105**	**11**	**20**	**31**	**24**	**1**	**0**	**1**	**12:32**

Traded to **Vancouver** by **NY Rangers** with Brian Noonan for Esa Tikkanen and Russ Courtnall, March 8, 1997. Signed as a free agent by **NY Islanders**, July 10, 1997. Traded to **New Jersey** by **NY Islanders** for New Jersey's 4th round choice (later traded to Los Angeles – Los Angeles selected Daniel Johansson) in 1999 Entry Draft, March 22, 1999.

NEMECEK, Jan

(NEHM-eh-chehk, YAHN) **L.A.**

Defense. Shoots Left. 6'1", 220 lbs. Born, Pisek, Czech., February 14, 1976. Los Angeles' 7th choice, 215th overall, in 1994 Entry Draft.

Season	Club	League	GP	G	A	Pts	PIM	PP	SH	GW	S	%	+/-	TF	F%	Min	GP	G	A	Pts	PIM	PP	SH	GW	Min
1992-93	Ceske Budejovice	Czech	15	0	0	0	....																		
1993-94	Ceske Budejovice	Czech	16	0	1	1	16																		
1994-95	Hull Olympiques	QMJHL	49	10	16	26	48										21	5	9	14	10				
1995-96	Hull Olympiques	QMJHL	57	17	49	66	58										17	2	13	15	10				
1996-97	Mississippi	ECHL	20	3	9	12	16										3	0	0	0	4				
	Phoenix	IHL	24	1	1	2	2																		
1997-98	Fredericton	AHL	65	7	24	31	43										2	0	0	0	0				
1998-99	**Los Angeles**	**NHL**	**6**	**1**	**0**	**1**	**4**	**0**	**0**	**1**	**8**	**12.5**	**–1**	**0**	**0.0**	**16:42**									
	Long Beach	IHL	66	5	16	21	42																		
99-2000	**Los Angeles**	**NHL**	**1**	**0**	**0**	**0**	**0**	**0**	**0**	**0**	**0**	**0.0**	**0**	**0**	**0.0**	**9:36**									
	Long Beach	IHL	71	9	15	24	22										6	1	0	1	4				
2000-01	Nurnberg	Germany	60	5	16	21	18										4	1	0	1	0				
2001-02	Nurnberg	Germany	60	6	18	24	18										4	0	3	3	2				
2002-03	Karlovy Vary	Czech	30	1	9	10	16																		
	KLH Chumotov	Czech-2	2	0	0	0	0																		
	NHL Totals		**7**	**1**	**0**	**1**	**4**	**0**	**0**	**1**	**8**	**12.5**		**0**	**0.0**	**15:41**	....	....	....	....	....	....	....	....	....

QMJHL Second All-Star Team (1996)

NICHOL, Scott
(NIH-KOHL, SKAWT) **CHI.**

Center. Shoots right. 5'8", 173 lbs. Born, Edmonton, Alta., December 31, 1974. Buffalo's 9th choice, 272nd overall, in 1993 Entry Draft.

			Regular Season														Playoffs								
Season	Club	League	GP	G	A	Pts	PIM	PP	SH	GW	S	%	+/-	TF	F%	Min	GP	G	A	Pts	PIM	PP	SH	GW	Min
1991-92	Calgary Flames	AMHL	23	26	16	42	132	....	....	....	....	....	....	....	....	....	....	....	....	....	....	....	....	....	....
1992-93	Portland	WHL	67	31	33	64	146	....	....	....	....	....	....	....	....	....	16	8	8	16	41	....	....	....	....
1993-94	Portland	WHL	65	40	53	93	144	....	....	....	....	....	....	....	....	....	10	3	8	11	16	....	....	....	....
1994-95	Rochester	AHL	71	11	16	27	136	....	....	....	....	....	....	....	....	....	5	0	3	3	14	....	....	....	....
1995-96	**Buffalo**	**NHL**	**2**	**0**	**0**	**0**	**10**	**0**	**0**	**0**	**4**	**0.0**	**0**	....	....	....	....	....	....	....	....	....	....	....	....
	Rochester	AHL	62	14	18	32	170	....	....	....	....	....	....	....	....	....	19	7	6	13	36	....	....	....	....
1996-97	Rochester	AHL	68	22	21	43	133	....	....	....	....	....	....	....	....	....	10	2	1	3	26	....	....	....	....
1997-98	**Buffalo**	**NHL**	**3**	**0**	**0**	**0**	**4**	**0**	**0**	**0**	**5**	**0.0**	**0**	....	....	....	....	....	....	....	....	....	....	....	....
	Rochester	AHL	35	13	7	20	113	....	....	....	....	....	....	....	....	....	....	....	....	....	....	....	....	....	....
1998-99	Rochester	AHL	52	13	20	33	120	....	....	....	....	....	....	....	....	....	....	....	....	....	....	....	....	....	....
99-2000	Rochester	AHL	37	7	11	18	141	....	....	....	....	....	....	....	....	....	....	....	....	....	....	....	....	....	....
2000-01	Detroit Vipers	IHL	67	7	24	31	198	....	....	....	....	....	....	....	....	....	....	....	....	....	....	....	....	....	....
2001-02	**Calgary**	**NHL**	**60**	**8**	**9**	**17**	**107**	**2**	**1**	**0**	**49**	**16.3**	**−9**	**458**	**53.1**	**12:41**	....	....	....	....	....	....	....	....	....
2002-03	**Calgary**	**NHL**	**68**	**5**	**5**	**10**	**149**	**0**	**1**	**0**	**66**	**7.6**	**−7**	**357**	**58.3**	**10:47**	....	....	....	....	....	....	....	....	....
	NHL Totals		**133**	**13**	**14**	**27**	**270**	**2**	**2**	**0**	**124**	**10.5**		**815**	**55.3**	**11:40**	....	....	....	....	....	....	....	....	....

• Missed majority of 1999-2000 season recovering from knee injury suffered in game vs. Saint John (AHL), February 16, 2000. Signed as a free agent by **Calgary**, July 1, 2001. Signed as a free agent by **Chicago**, July 1, 2003.

NICKULAS, Eric
(NICK-luhs, AIR-ihk)

Right wing. Shoots right. 5'11", 200 lbs. Born, Hyannis, MA, March 25, 1975. Boston's 3rd choice, 99th overall, in 1994 Entry Draft.

			Regular Season														Playoffs								
Season	Club	League	GP	G	A	Pts	PIM	PP	SH	GW	S	%	+/-	TF	F%	Min	GP	G	A	Pts	PIM	PP	SH	GW	Min
1991-92	Barnstable	Hi-School	24	30	25	55	....	....	....	....	....	....	....	....	....	....	....	....	....	....	....	....	....	....	....
1992-93	Tabor Academy	Hi-School	28	25	25	50	....	....	....	....	....	....	....	....	....	....	....	....	....	....	....	....	....	....	....
1993-94	Cushing Academy	Hi-School	25	46	36	82	....	....	....	....	....	....	....	....	....	....	....	....	....	....	....	....	....	....	....
1994-95	New Hampshire	H-East	33	15	9	24	32	....	....	....	....	....	....	....	....	....	....	....	....	....	....	....	....	....	....
1995-96	New Hampshire	H-East	34	26	12	38	66	....	....	....	....	....	....	....	....	....	....	....	....	....	....	....	....	....	....
1996-97	New Hampshire	H-East	39	29	22	51	80	....	....	....	....	....	....	....	....	....	....	....	....	....	....	....	....	....	....
1997-98	Orlando	IHL	76	22	9	31	77	....	....	....	....	....	....	....	....	....	6	0	0	0	10	....	....	....	....
1998-99	**Boston**	**NHL**	**2**	**0**	**0**	**0**	**0**	**0**	**0**	**0**	**0**	**0.0**	**0**	**0**	**0.0**	**3:27**	**1**	**0**	**0**	**0**	**2**	**0**	**0**	**0**	**4:35**
	Providence Bruins	AHL	75	31	27	58	83	....	....	....	....	....	....	....	....	....	18	8	12	20	33	....	....	....	....
99-2000	**Boston**	**NHL**	**20**	**5**	**6**	**11**	**12**	**1**	**0**	**0**	**28**	**17.9**	**−1**	**4**	**50.0**	**11:13**	....	....	....	....	....	....	....	....	....
	Providence Bruins	AHL	40	6	6	12	37	....	....	....	....	....	....	....	....	....	12	2	3	5	20	....	....	....	....
2000-01	**Boston**	**NHL**	**7**	**0**	**0**	**0**	**4**	**0**	**0**	**0**	**6**	**0.0**	**−2**	**1**	**100.0**	**7:07**	....	....	....	....	....	....	....	....	....
	Providence Bruins	AHL	62	20	23	43	100	....	....	....	....	....	....	....	....	....	12	4	4	8	24	....	....	....	....
2001-02	Worcester IceCats	AHL	54	11	25	36	48	....	....	....	....	....	....	....	....	....	3	0	1	1	2	....	....	....	....
2002-03	**St. Louis**	**NHL**	**8**	**0**	**1**	**1**	**6**	**0**	**0**	**0**	**3**	**0.0**	**−2**	**0**	**0.0**	**9:31**	....	....	....	....	....	....	....	....	....
	Worcester IceCats	AHL	39	17	16	33	40	....	....	....	....	....	....	....	....	....	3	0	0	0	2	....	....	....	....
	NHL Totals		**37**	**5**	**7**	**12**	**22**	**1**	**0**	**0**	**37**	**13.5**		**5**	**60.0**	**9:39**	**1**	**0**	**0**	**0**	**2**	**0**	**0**	**0**	**4:35**

Ken McKenzie Trophy (U.S. Born Rookie of the Year – IHL) (1998)

Signed as a free agent by **Worcester** (AHL), November 10, 2001. Signed as a free agent by **St. Louis**, July 16, 2002.

NIEDERMAYER, Rob
(NEE-duhr-MIGH-uhr, RAWB) **ANA.**

Center. Shoots left. 6'2", 204 lbs. Born, Cassiar, B.C., December 28, 1974. Florida's 1st choice, 5th overall, in 1993 Entry Draft.

			Regular Season														Playoffs								
Season	Club	League	GP	G	A	Pts	PIM	PP	SH	GW	S	%	+/-	TF	F%	Min	GP	G	A	Pts	PIM	PP	SH	GW	Min
1989-90	Cranbrook	BCAHA	35	42	40	82	30	....	....	....	....	....	....	....	....	....	....	....	....	....	....	....	....	....	....
1990-91	Medicine Hat	WHL	71	24	26	50	8	....	....	....	....	....	....	....	....	....	12	3	7	10	2	....	....	....	....
1991-92	Medicine Hat	WHL	71	32	46	78	77	....	....	....	....	....	....	....	....	....	4	2	3	5	2	....	....	....	....
1992-93	Medicine Hat	WHL	52	43	34	77	67	....	....	....	....	....	....	....	....	....	....	....	....	....	....	....	....	....	....
1993-94	**Florida**	**NHL**	**65**	**9**	**17**	**26**	**51**	**3**	**0**	**2**	**67**	**13.4**	**−11**	....	....	....	....	....	....	....	....	....	....	....	....
1994-95	Medicine Hat	WHL	13	9	15	24	14	....	....	....	....	....	....	....	....	....	....	....	....	....	....	....	....	....	....
	Florida	**NHL**	**48**	**4**	**6**	**10**	**36**	**1**	**0**	**0**	**58**	**6.9**	**−13**	....	....	....	....	....	....	....	....	....	....	....	....
1995-96	**Florida**	**NHL**	**82**	**26**	**35**	**61**	**107**	**11**	**0**	**6**	**155**	**16.8**	**1**	....	....	....	**22**	**5**	**3**	**8**	**12**	**2**	**0**	**2**	....
1996-97	**Florida**	**NHL**	**60**	**14**	**24**	**38**	**54**	**3**	**0**	**2**	**136**	**10.3**	**4**	....	....	....	**5**	**2**	**1**	**3**	**6**	**1**	**0**	**0**	....
1997-98	**Florida**	**NHL**	**33**	**8**	**7**	**15**	**41**	**5**	**0**	**2**	**64**	**12.5**	**−9**	....	....	....	....	....	....	....	....	....	....	....	....
1998-99	**Florida**	**NHL**	**82**	**18**	**33**	**51**	**50**	**6**	**1**	**3**	**142**	**12.7**	**−13**	**1895**	**47.1**	**21:17**	....	....	....	....	....	....	....	....	....
99-2000	**Florida**	**NHL**	**81**	**10**	**23**	**33**	**46**	**1**	**0**	**4**	**135**	**7.4**	**−5**	**1632**	**47.9**	**19:04**	**4**	**1**	**0**	**1**	**6**	**0**	**0**	**0**	**15:55**
2000-01	**Florida**	**NHL**	**67**	**12**	**20**	**32**	**50**	**3**	**1**	**0**	**115**	**10.4**	**−12**	**997**	**45.0**	**20:30**	....	....	....	....	....	....	....	....	....
2001-02	**Calgary**	**NHL**	**57**	**6**	**14**	**20**	**49**	**1**	**2**	**1**	**87**	**6.9**	**−15**	**777**	**48.4**	**18:01**	....	....	....	....	....	....	....	....	....
2002-03	**Calgary**	**NHL**	**54**	**8**	**10**	**18**	**42**	**2**	**0**	**1**	**104**	**7.7**	**−13**	**139**	**48.9**	**17:29**	....	....	....	....	....	....	....	....	....
	Anaheim	**NHL**	**12**	**2**	**2**	**4**	**15**	**1**	**0**	**0**	**21**	**9.5**	**3**	**14**	**42.9**	**15:21**	**21**	**3**	**7**	**10**	**18**	**0**	**2**	**0**	**23:35**
	NHL Totals		**641**	**117**	**191**	**308**	**541**	**37**	**4**	**21**	**1084**	**10.8**		**5454**	**47.2**	**19:19**	**52**	**11**	**11**	**22**	**42**	**3**	**2**	**2**	**22:21**

WHL East First All-Star Team (1993)

• Missed majority of 1997-98 season recovering from thumb (November 26, 1997 vs. Boston) and head (March 19, 1998 vs. Buffalo) injuries. Traded to **Calgary** by **Florida** with Philadelphia's 2nd round choice (previously acquired, Calgary selected Andrei Medvedev) in 2001 Entry Draft for Valeri Bure and Jason Wiemer, June 23, 2001. Traded to **Anaheim** by **Calgary** for Mike Commodore and Jean-Francois Damphousse, March 11, 2003.

NIEDERMAYER, Scott
(NEE-duhr-MIGH-uhr, SKAWT) **N.J.**

Defense. Shoots left. 6'1", 200 lbs. Born, Edmonton, Alta., August 31, 1973. New Jersey's 1st choice, 3rd overall, in 1991 Entry Draft.

			Regular Season														Playoffs								
Season	Club	League	GP	G	A	Pts	PIM	PP	SH	GW	S	%	+/-	TF	F%	Min	GP	G	A	Pts	PIM	PP	SH	GW	Min
1988-89	Cranbrook Blazers	BCAHA	62	55	37	92	100	....	....	....	....	....	....	....	....	....	....	....	....	....	....	....	....	....	....
1989-90	Kamloops Blazers	WHL	64	14	55	69	64	....	....	....	....	....	....	....	....	....	17	2	14	16	35	....	....	....	....
1990-91	Kamloops Blazers	WHL	57	26	56	82	52	....	....	....	....	....	....	....	....	....	....	....	....	....	....	....	....	....	....
1991-92	Kamloops Blazers	WHL	35	7	32	39	61	....	....	....	....	....	....	....	....	....	17	9	14	23	28	....	....	....	....
	New Jersey	**NHL**	**4**	**0**	**1**	**1**	**2**	**0**	**0**	**0**	**4**	**0.0**	**1**	....	....	....	....	....	....	....	....	....	....	....	....
1992-93	**New Jersey**	**NHL**	**80**	**11**	**29**	**40**	**47**	**5**	**0**	**0**	**131**	**8.4**	**8**	....	....	....	**5**	**0**	**3**	**3**	**2**	**0**	**0**	**0**	....
1993-94	**New Jersey**	**NHL**	**81**	**10**	**36**	**46**	**42**	**5**	**0**	**2**	**135**	**7.4**	**34**	....	....	....	**20**	**2**	**2**	**4**	**8**	**1**	**0**	**0**	....
1994-95◆	**New Jersey**	**NHL**	**48**	**4**	**15**	**19**	**18**	**4**	**0**	**0**	**52**	**7.7**	**19**	....	....	....	**20**	**4**	**7**	**11**	**10**	**2**	**0**	**1**	....
1995-96	**New Jersey**	**NHL**	**79**	**8**	**25**	**33**	**46**	**6**	**0**	**0**	**179**	**4.5**	**5**	....	....	....	....	....	....	....	....	....	....	....	....
1996-97	**New Jersey**	**NHL**	**81**	**5**	**30**	**35**	**64**	**3**	**0**	**3**	**159**	**3.1**	**−4**	....	....	....	**10**	**2**	**4**	**6**	**6**	**2**	**0**	**1**	....
1997-98	**New Jersey**	**NHL**	**81**	**14**	**43**	**57**	**27**	**11**	**0**	**1**	**175**	**8.0**	**5**	....	....	....	**6**	**0**	**2**	**2**	**4**	**0**	**0**	**0**	....
1998-99	Utah Grizzlies	IHL	5	0	2	2	0	....	....	....	....	....	....	....	....	....	....	....	....	....	....	....	....	....	....
	New Jersey	**NHL**	**72**	**11**	**35**	**46**	**26**	**1**	**1**	**3**	**161**	**6.8**	**16**	**13**	**15.4**	**24:40**	**7**	**1**	**3**	**4**	**18**	**1**	**0**	**0**	**25:30**
99-2000◆	**New Jersey**	**NHL**	**71**	**7**	**31**	**38**	**48**	**1**	**0**	**0**	**109**	**6.4**	**19**	**8**	**37.5**	**24:21**	**22**	**5**	**2**	**7**	**10**	**0**	**2**	**1**	**25:28**
2000-01	**New Jersey**	**NHL**	**57**	**6**	**29**	**35**	**22**	**1**	**0**	**5**	**87**	**6.9**	**14**	**5**	**0.0**	**23:19**	**21**	**0**	**6**	**6**	**14**	**0**	**0**	**0**	**23:53**
2001-02	**New Jersey**	**NHL**	**76**	**11**	**22**	**33**	**30**	**2**	**0**	**6**	**129**	**8.5**	**12**	**1**	**100.0**	**24:17**	**6**	**0**	**2**	**2**	**6**	**0**	**0**	**0**	**26:37**
	Canada	Olympics	6	1	1	2	4	....	....	....	....	....	....	....	....	....	....	....	....	....	....	....	....	....	....
2002-03◆	**New Jersey**	**NHL**	**81**	**11**	**28**	**39**	**62**	**3**	**0**	**3**	**164**	**6.7**	**23**	**1**	**0.0**	**24:30**	**24**	**2**	***16**	***18**	**16**	**1**	**0**	**0**	**26:07**
	NHL Totals		**811**	**98**	**324**	**422**	**434**	**42**	**1**	**23**	**1485**	**6.6**		**28**	**21.4**	**24:16**	**141**	**16**	**47**	**63**	**94**	**7**	**2**	**3**	**25:20**

WHL West First All-Star Team (1991, 1992) • Canadian Major Junior Scholastic Player of the Year (1991) • Memorial Cup All-Star Team (1992) • Stafford Smythe Memorial Trophy (Memorial Cup MVP) (1992) • NHL All-Rookie Team (1993) • NHL Second All-Star Team (1998)

Played in NHL All-Star Game (1998, 2001)

Signed to 25-game tryout contract by **Utah** (IHL) with **New Jersey** retaining NHL rights, October 19, 1998.

NIELSEN, Chris
(NEEL-sehn, KRIHS) **VAN.**

Right wing. Shoots right. 6'2", 204 lbs. Born, Moshi, Tanzania, February 16, 1980. NY Islanders' 2nd choice, 36th overall, in 1998 Entry Draft.

			Regular Season														Playoffs								
Season	Club	League	GP	G	A	Pts	PIM	PP	SH	GW	S	%	+/-	TF	F%	Min	GP	G	A	Pts	PIM	PP	SH	GW	Min
1995-96	S-W Cougars	MMHL	39	37	35	72	59	....	....	....	....	....	....	....	....	....	....	....	....	....	....	....	....	....	....
	Calgary Hitmen	WHL	6	0	0	0	0	....	....	....	....	....	....	....	....	....	....	....	....	....	....	....	....	....	....
1996-97	Calgary Hitmen	WHL	62	11	19	30	39	....	....	....	....	....	....	....	....	....	....	....	....	....	....	....	....	....	....
1997-98	Calgary Hitmen	WHL	68	22	29	51	31	....	....	....	....	....	....	....	....	....	18	2	4	6	10	....	....	....	....
1998-99	Calgary Hitmen	WHL	70	22	24	46	45	....	....	....	....	....	....	....	....	....	21	11	5	16	28	....	....	....	....
99-2000	Calgary Hitmen	WHL	62	38	31	69	86	....	....	....	....	....	....	....	....	....	13	14	9	23	20	....	....	....	....
2000-01	**Columbus**	**NHL**	**29**	**4**	**5**	**9**	**4**	**0**	**0**	**1**	**36**	**11.1**	**4**	**18**	**55.6**	**10:30**	....	....	....	....	....	....	....	....	....
	Syracuse Crunch	AHL	47	10	11	21	24	....	....	....	....	....	....	....	....	....	5	2	2	4	4	....	....	....	....
2001-02	**Columbus**	**NHL**	**23**	**2**	**3**	**5**	**4**	**0**	**0**	**1**	**28**	**7.1**	**−3**	**6**	**33.3**	**10:47**	....	....	....	....	....	....	....	....	....
	Syracuse Crunch	AHL	47	12	12	24	18	....	....	....	....	....	....	....	....	....	10	2	2	4	2	....	....	....	....

			Regular Season														Playoffs								
Season	Club	League	GP	G	A	Pts	PIM	PP	SH	GW	S	%	+/-	TF	F%	Min	GP	G	A	Pts	PIM	PP	SH	GW	Min
2002-03	Syracuse Crunch	AHL	19	1	3	4	8																		
	Chicago Wolves	AHL	18	3	4	7	4																		
	Manitoba Moose	AHL	33	3	10	13	13										14	1	2	3	16				
	NHL Totals		**52**	**6**	**8**	**14**	**8**	**0**	**0**	**2**	**64**	**9.4**		**24**	**50.0**	**10:38**									

Traded to **Columbus** by **NY Islanders** for Columbus' 4th (later traded to Anaheim – Anaheim selected Jonas Ronnqvist) and 9th (Dmitri Altarev) round choices in 2000 Entry Draft, May 11, 2000. Traded to **Atlanta** by **Columbus** with Petteri Nummelin for Tomi Kallio and Pauli Levokari, December 2, 2002. Traded to **Vancouver** by **Atlanta** with Chris Herperger for Jeff Farkas, January 20, 2003.

NIEMI, Antti-Jussi

(nee-mee, AN-tee-YOO-see)

Defense. Shoots left. 6'1", 195 lbs. Born, Vantaa, Finland, September 22, 1977. Ottawa's 2nd choice, 81st overall, in 1996 Entry Draft.

Season	Club	League	GP	G	A	Pts	PIM	PP	SH	GW	S	%	+/-	TF	F%	Min	GP	G	A	Pts	PIM	PP	SH	GW	Min
1992-93	Jokerit Helsinki-C	Finn-Jr.	38	9	23	32	54																		
	Jokerit Helsinki-B	Finn-Jr.	2	0	0	0	2																		
1993-94	Jokerit Helsinki-B	Finn-Jr.	13	1	1	2	8																		
	Jokerit Helsinki Jr.	Finn-Jr.	33	0	3	3	26																		
1994-95	Jokerit Helsinki-B	Finn-Jr.	10	3	5	8	42																		
	Jokerit Helsinki Jr.	Finn-Jr.	24	4	8	12	74																		
1995-96	Jokerit Helsinki Jr.	Finn-Jr.	34	11	18	29	56										8	0	4	4	39				
	Haukat Jarvenpaa	Finland-2	4	0	2	2	8																		
	Jokerit Helsinki	Finland	6	0	2	2	6										1	0	0	0	0				
1996-97	Jokerit Helsinki	Finland	44	2	9	11	38										9	0	2	2	2				
1997-98	Jokerit Helsinki	Finland	46	2	6	8	24										8	0	1	1	0				
	Jokerit Helsinki	EuroHL	6	0	1	1	6																		
1998-99	Jokerit Helsinki	Finland	53	3	7	10	107										3	0	0	0	2				
	Jokerit Helsinki	EuroHL	6	2	2	4	4										2	0	1	1	0				
99-2000	Jokerit Helsinki	Finland	53	8	8	16	79										11	0	3	3	6				
2000-01	**Anaheim**	**NHL**	**28**	**1**	**1**	**2**	**22**	**0**	**0**	**0**	**18**	**5.6**	**–6**	**0**	**0.0**	**15:56**									
	Cincinnati	AHL	36	3	8	11	26																		
2001-02	**Anaheim**	**NHL**	**1**	**0**	**0**	**0**	**0**	**0**	**0**	**0**	**0**	**0.0**	**–1**	**0**	**0.0**	**9:53**									
	Cincinnati	AHL	39	10	9	19	25										3	1	1	2	2				
2002-03	Jokerit Helsinki	Finland	48	6	11	17	42										1	0	0	0	0				
	NHL Totals		**29**	**1**	**1**	**2**	**22**	**0**	**0**	**0**	**18**	**5.6**		**0**	**0.0**	**15:44**									

Rights traded to **Anaheim** by **Ottawa** with Ted Donato for Patrick Lalime, June 18, 1999. Signed as a free agent by **Jokerit Helsinki** (Finland), August 13, 2002.

NIEMINEN, Ville

(nee-EHM-ih-nehn, VIHL-ee) **CHI.**

Left wing. Shoots left. 6', 200 lbs. Born, Tampere, Finland, April 6, 1977. Colorado's 4th choice, 78th overall, in 1997 Entry Draft.

Season	Club	League	GP	G	A	Pts	PIM	PP	SH	GW	S	%	+/-	TF	F%	Min	GP	G	A	Pts	PIM	PP	SH	GW	Min
1994-95	Tappara Jr.	Finn-Jr.	16	11	21	32	47																		
	Tappara Tampere	Finland	16	0	0	0	0																		
1995-96	Tappara Jr.	Finn-Jr.	20	20	23	43	63																		
	KooKoo Kouvola	Finland-2	7	2	1	3	4																		
	Tappara Tampere	Finland	4	0	1	1	8																		
1996-97	Tappara Tampere	Finland	49	10	13	23	120										3	1	0	1	8				
1997-98	Hershey Bears	AHL	74	14	22	36	85																		
1998-99	Hershey Bears	AHL	67	24	19	43	127										3	0	1	1	0				
99-2000	**Colorado**	**NHL**	**1**	**0**	**0**	**0**	**0**	**0**	**0**	**0**	**2**	**0.0**	**0**	**0**	**0.0**	**10:12**									
	Hershey Bears	AHL	74	21	30	51	54										9	2	4	6	6				
2000-01♦	**Colorado**	**NHL**	**50**	**14**	**8**	**22**	**38**	**2**	**0**	**3**	**68**	**20.6**	**8**	**3**	**33.3**	**12:26**	**23**	**4**	**6**	**10**	**20**	**3**	**0**	**1**	**14:10**
	Hershey Bears	AHL	28	10	11	21	48																		
2001-02	**Colorado**	**NHL**	**53**	**10**	**14**	**24**	**30**	**1**	**0**	**5**	**72**	**13.9**	**1**	**8**	**62.5**	**12:41**									
	Finland	Olympics	4	0	1	1	2																		
	Pittsburgh	**NHL**	**13**	**1**	**2**	**3**	**8**	**0**	**0**	**0**	**11**	**9.1**	**–2**	**0**	**0.0**	**16:10**									
2002-03	**Pittsburgh**	**NHL**	**75**	**9**	**12**	**21**	**93**	**0**	**2**	**1**	**86**	**10.5**	**–25**	**46**	**52.2**	**14:08**									
	NHL Totals		**192**	**34**	**36**	**70**	**169**	**3**	**2**	**9**	**239**	**14.2**		**57**	**52.6**	**13:25**	**23**	**4**	**6**	**10**	**20**	**3**	**0**	**1**	**14:10**

Traded to **Pittsburgh** by **Colorado** with Rick Berry for Darius Kasparaitis, March 19, 2002. Signed as a free agent by **Chicago**, July 29, 2003.

NIEUWENDYK, Joe

(NOO-ihn-DIGHK, JOH)

Center. Shoots left. 6'2", 205 lbs. Born, Oshawa, Ont., September 10, 1966. Calgary's 2nd choice, 27th overall, in 1985 Entry Draft.

Season	Club	League	GP	G	A	Pts	PIM	PP	SH	GW	S	%	+/-	TF	F%	Min	GP	G	A	Pts	PIM	PP	SH	GW	Min
1983-84	Pickering Panthers	MTJHL	38	30	28	58	35																		
1984-85	Cornell Big Red	ECAC	29	21	24	45	30																		
1985-86	Cornell Big Red	ECAC	29	26	28	54	67																		
1986-87	Cornell Big Red	ECAC	23	26	26	52	26																		
	Calgary	**NHL**	**9**	**5**	**1**	**6**	**0**	**2**	**0**	**1**	**16**	**31.3**	**0**				**6**	**2**	**2**	**4**	**0**	**0**	**0**	**0**	
1987-88	**Calgary**	**NHL**	**75**	**51**	**41**	**92**	**23**	**31**	**3**	**8**	**212**	**24.1**	**20**				**8**	**3**	**4**	**7**	**2**	**1**	**0**	**0**	
1988-89♦	**Calgary**	**NHL**	**77**	**51**	**31**	**82**	**40**	**19**	**3**	**11**	**215**	**23.7**	**26**				**22**	**10**	**4**	**14**	**10**	**6**	**0**	**1**	
1989-90	**Calgary**	**NHL**	**79**	**45**	**50**	**95**	**40**	**18**	**0**	**3**	**226**	**19.9**	**32**				**6**	**4**	**6**	**10**	**4**	**1**	**0**	**0**	
1990-91	**Calgary**	**NHL**	**79**	**45**	**40**	**85**	**36**	**22**	**4**	**1**	**222**	**20.3**	**19**				**7**	**4**	**1**	**5**	**10**	**2**	**0**	**0**	
1991-92	**Calgary**	**NHL**	**69**	**22**	**34**	**56**	**55**	**7**	**0**	**2**	**137**	**16.1**	**–1**												
1992-93	**Calgary**	**NHL**	**79**	**38**	**37**	**75**	**52**	**14**	**0**	**6**	**208**	**18.3**	**9**				**6**	**3**	**6**	**9**	**10**	**1**	**0**	**0**	
1993-94	**Calgary**	**NHL**	**64**	**36**	**39**	**75**	**51**	**14**	**1**	**7**	**191**	**18.8**	**19**				**6**	**2**	**2**	**4**	**0**	**1**	**0**	**0**	
1994-95	**Calgary**	**NHL**	**46**	**21**	**29**	**50**	**33**	**3**	**0**	**4**	**122**	**17.2**	**11**				**5**	**4**	**3**	**7**	**0**	**2**	**0**	**1**	
1995-96	**Dallas**	**NHL**	**52**	**14**	**18**	**32**	**41**	**8**	**0**	**3**	**138**	**10.1**	**–17**												
1996-97	**Dallas**	**NHL**	**66**	**30**	**21**	**51**	**32**	**8**	**0**	**2**	**173**	**17.3**	**–5**				**7**	**2**	**2**	**4**	**6**	**0**	**0**	**0**	
1997-98	**Dallas**	**NHL**	**73**	**39**	**30**	**69**	**30**	**14**	**0**	**11**	**203**	**19.2**	**16**				**1**	**1**	**0**	**1**	**0**	**0**	**0**	**0**	
	Canada	Olympics	6	2	3	5	2																		
1998-99♦	**Dallas**	**NHL**	**67**	**28**	**27**	**55**	**34**	**8**	**0**	**8**	**157**	**17.8**	**11**	**1170**	**63.2**	**15:33**	**23**	***11**	**10**	**21**	**19**	**3**	**0**	**6**	**18:27**
99-2000	**Dallas**	**NHL**	**48**	**15**	**19**	**34**	**26**	**7**	**0**	**2**	**110**	**13.6**	**–1**	**924**	**59.1**	**16:15**	**23**	**7**	**3**	**10**	**18**	**3**	**0**	**2**	**16:41**
2000-01	**Dallas**	**NHL**	**69**	**29**	**23**	**52**	**30**	**12**	**0**	**4**	**166**	**17.5**	**5**	**1262**	**57.2**	**16:11**	**7**	**4**	**0**	**4**	**4**	**1**	**0**	**1**	**15:50**
2001-02	**Dallas**	**NHL**	**67**	**23**	**24**	**47**	**18**	**6**	**0**	**5**	**157**	**14.6**	**–2**	**1345**	**59.6**	**16:59**									
	Canada	Olympics	6	1	1	2	0																		
	New Jersey	**NHL**	**14**	**2**	**9**	**11**	**4**	**0**	**0**	**1**	**32**	**6.3**	**2**	**275**	**55.3**	**16:22**	**5**	**0**	**1**	**1**	**0**	**0**	**0**	**0**	**19:22**
2002-03♦	**New Jersey**	**NHL**	**80**	**17**	**28**	**45**	**56**	**3**	**0**	**4**	**201**	**8.5**	**10**	**1383**	**58.5**	**16:45**	**17**	**3**	**6**	**9**	**4**	**1**	**0**	**0**	**15:03**
	NHL Totals		**1113**	**511**	**501**	**1012**	**601**	**196**	**11**	**83**	**2886**	**17.7**		**6359**	**59.3**	**16:22**	**149**	**60**	**50**	**110**	**87**	**22**	**0**	**11**	**16:57**

ECAC Rookie of the Year (1985) • ECAC First All-Star Team (1986, 1987) • NCAA East First All-American Team (1986, 1987) • ECAC Player of the Year (1987) • Calder Memorial Trophy (1988) • NHL All-Rookie Team (1988) • Dodge Ram Tough Award (1988) • King Clancy Memorial Trophy (1995) • Conn Smythe Trophy (1999)

Played in NHL All-Star Game (1988, 1989, 1990, 1994)

Traded to **Dallas** by **Calgary** for Corey Millen and Jarome Iginla, December 19, 1995. Traded to **New Jersey** by **Dallas** with Jamie Langenbrunner for Jason Arnott, Randy McKay and New Jersey's 1st round choice (later traded to Columbus – later traded to Buffalo – Buffalo selected Dan Paille) in 2002 Entry Draft, March 19, 2002.

NIINIMAA, Janne

(nihn-EE-mah, YAH-nee) **NYI**

Defense. Shoots left. 6'1", 220 lbs. Born, Raahe, Finland, May 22, 1975. Philadelphia's 1st choice, 36th overall, in 1993 Entry Draft.

Season	Club	League	GP	G	A	Pts	PIM	PP	SH	GW	S	%	+/-	TF	F%	Min	GP	G	A	Pts	PIM	PP	SH	GW	Min
1990-91	Karpat Oulu Jr.	Finn-Jr.	3	1	0	1	2																		
1991-92	Karpat Oulu Jr.	Finn-Jr.	3	0	0	0	4																		
	Karpat Oulu	Finland-2	41	2	11	13	49																		
1992-93	Karpat Oulu Jr.	Finn-Jr.	10	3	9	12	16																		
	KKP Kiimimki	Finland-3	1	0	2	2	4																		
	Karpat Oulu	Finland-2	29	2	3	5	14																		
1993-94	Jokerit Helsinki Jr.	Finn-Jr.	10	2	6	8	41																		
	Jokerit Helsinki	Finland	45	3	8	11	24										12	1	1	2	4				
1994-95	Jokerit Helsinki Jr.	Finn-Jr.	3	1	2	3	4																		
	Jokerit Helsinki	Finland	42	7	10	17	36										10	1	4	5	35				
1995-96	Jokerit Helsinki	Finland	49	5	15	20	79										11	0	2	2	12				
	Jokerit Helsinki Jr.	Finn-Jr.															2	3	4	7	6				
1996-97	**Philadelphia**	**NHL**	**77**	**4**	**40**	**44**	**58**	**1**	**0**	**2**	**141**	**2.8**	**12**				**19**	**1**	**12**	**13**	**16**	**1**	**0**	**1**	
1997-98	**Philadelphia**	**NHL**	**66**	**3**	**31**	**34**	**56**	**2**	**0**	**1**	**115**	**2.6**	**6**												
	Finland	Olympics	6	0	3	3	8																		
	Edmonton	**NHL**	**11**	**1**	**8**	**9**	**6**	**1**	**0**	**0**	**19**	**5.3**	**7**				**11**	**1**	**1**	**2**	**12**	**0**	**0**	**1**	
1998-99	**Edmonton**	**NHL**	**81**	**4**	**24**	**28**	**88**	**2**	**0**	**1**	**142**	**2.8**	**7**	**1**	**0.0**	**23:54**	**4**	**0**	**0**	**0**	**2**	**0**	**0**	**0**	**28:16**
99-2000	**Edmonton**	**NHL**	**81**	**8**	**25**	**33**	**89**	**2**	**2**	**0**	**133**	**6.0**	**14**	**0**	**0.0**	**24:28**	**5**	**0**	**2**	**2**	**2**	**0**	**0**	**0**	**21:39**

Season	Club	League	GP	G	A	Pts	PIM	PP	SH	GW	S	%	+/-	TF	F%	Min	GP	G	A	Pts	PIM	PP	SH	GW	Min
								Regular Season									Playoffs								
2000-01	Edmonton	NHL	82	12	34	46	90	8	0	1	122	9.8	6	0	0.0	25:20	6	0	2	2	6	0	0	0	28:33
2001-02	Edmonton	NHL	81	5	39	44	80	1	0	2	119	4.2	13	0	0.0	26:02	....	....	....	....	....	....	....	....	....
	Finland	Olympics	4	0	3	3	2	....	....	....	....	....	....	....	....	....	....	....	....	....	....	....	....	....	....
2002-03	Edmonton	NHL	63	4	24	28	66	2	0	0	90	4.4	–7	1	0.0	26:48	....	....	....	....	....	....	....	....	....
	NY Islanders	NHL	13	1	5	6	14	1	0	0	11	9.1	–2	0	0.0	23:02	5	0	1	1	12	0	0	0	23:32
	NHL Totals		555	42	230	272	547	20	2	7	892	4.7		2	0.0	25:10	50	2	18	20	50	1	0	2	25:31

NHL All-Rookie Team (1997)

Played in NHL All-Star Game (2001)

Traded to **Edmonton** by **Philadelphia** for Dan McGillis and Edmonton's 2nd round choice (Jason Beckett) in 1998 Entry Draft, March 24, 1998. Traded to **NY Islanders** by **Edmonton** with Washington's 2nd round choice (previously acquired, NY Islanders selected Evgeni Tunik) in 2003 Entry Draft for Brad Isbister and Raffi Torres, March 11, 2003.

NIKOLISHIN, Andrei

(nee-koh-LEE-shin, AWN-dray) **COL.**

Center. Shoots left. 6', 213 lbs. Born, Vorkuta, USSR, March 25, 1973. Hartford's 2nd choice, 47th overall, in 1992 Entry Draft.

Season	Club	League	GP	G	A	Pts	PIM	PP	SH	GW	S	%	+/-	TF	F%	Min	GP	G	A	Pts	PIM	PP	SH	GW	Min
1990-91	Dynamo Moscow	USSR	2	0	0	0	0	....	....	....	....	....	....	....	....	....	....	....	....	....	....	....	....	....	....
1991-92	Dynamo Moscow	CIS	18	1	0	1	4	....	....	....	....	....	....	....	....	....	....	....	....	....	....	....	....	....	....
1992-93	Dynamo Moscow	CIS	42	5	7	12	30	....	....	....	....	....	....	....	....	....	10	2	1	3	8	....	....	....	....
1993-94	Dynamo Moscow	CIS	41	8	12	20	30	....	....	....	....	....	....	....	....	....	9	1	3	4	4	....	....	....	....
	Russia	Olympics	8	2	5	7	6	....	....	....	....	....	....	....	....	....	....	....	....	....	....	....	....	....	....
1994-95	Dynamo Moscow	CIS	12	7	2	9	6	....	....	....	....	....	....	....	....	....	....	....	....	....	....	....	....	....	....
	Hartford	NHL	39	8	10	18	10	1	1	0	57	14.0	7	....	....	....	....	....	....	....	....	....	....	....	....
1995-96	Hartford	NHL	61	14	37	51	34	4	1	3	83	16.9	–2	....	....	....	....	....	....	....	....	....	....	....	....
1996-97	Hartford	NHL	12	2	5	7	2	0	0	0	25	8.0	–2	....	....	....	....	....	....	....	....	....	....	....	....
	Washington	NHL	59	7	14	21	30	1	0	0	73	9.6	5	....	....	....	....	....	....	....	....	....	....	....	....
1997-98	Washington	NHL	38	6	10	16	14	1	0	1	40	15.0	1	....	....	....	21	1	13	14	12	1	0	0	....
	Portland Pirates	AHL	2	0	0	0	2	....	....	....	....	....	....	....	....	....	....	....	....	....	....	....	....	....	....
1998-99	Dynamo Moscow	Russia	4	0	0	0	0	....	....	....	....	....	....	....	....	....	....	....	....	....	....	....	....	....	....
	Washington	NHL	73	8	27	35	28	0	1	1	121	6.6	0	1354	52.5	17:34	....	....	....	....	....	....	....	....	....
99-2000	Washington	NHL	76	11	14	25	28	0	2	2	98	11.2	6	1190	54.7	15:44	5	0	2	2	4	0	0	0	17:27
2000-01	Washington	NHL	81	13	25	38	34	4	0	2	145	9.0	9	1214	55.4	15:32	6	0	0	0	2	0	0	0	16:50
2001-02	Washington	NHL	80	13	23	36	40	1	0	0	143	9.1	–1	1445	55.7	17:23	....	....	....	....	....	....	....	....	....
	Russia	Olympics	6	0	1	1	6	....	....	....	....	....	....	....	....	....	....	....	....	....	....	....	....	....	....
2002-03	Chicago	NHL	60	6	15	21	26	0	1	0	73	8.2	–3	947	56.6	17:01	....	....	....	....	....	....	....	....	....
	NHL Totals		579	88	180	268	246	12	6	9	858	10.3		6150	54.9	16:37	32	1	15	16	18	1	0	0	17:06

Traded to **Washington** by **Hartford** for Curtis Leschyshyn, November 9, 1996. Traded to **Chicago** by **Washington** with Chris Simon for Michael Nylander, Chicago's 3rd round choice (Stephen Werner) in 2003 Entry Draft and future considerations, November 1, 2002. Traded to **Colorado** by **Chicago** for future considerations, June 21, 2003.

NILSON, Marcus

(NIHL-suhn, MAHR-kuhs) **FLA.**

Left wing. Shoots right. 6'2", 195 lbs. Born, Balsta, Sweden, March 1, 1978. Florida's 1st choice, 20th overall, in 1996 Entry Draft.

Season	Club	League	GP	G	A	Pts	PIM	PP	SH	GW	S	%	+/-	TF	F%	Min	GP	G	A	Pts	PIM	PP	SH	GW	Min
1994-95	Djurgarden Jr.	Swede-Jr.	24	7	8	15	22	....	....	....	....	....	....	....	....	....	....	....	....	....	....	....	....	....	....
1995-96	Djurgarden Jr.	Swede-Jr.	25	19	17	36	46	....	....	....	....	....	....	....	....	....	2	1	1	2	12	....	....	....	....
	Djurgarden	Sweden	12	0	0	0	0	....	....	....	....	....	....	....	....	....	1	0	0	0	0	....	....	....	....
1996-97	Djurgarden	Sweden	37	0	3	3	33	....	....	....	....	....	....	....	....	....	4	0	0	0	0	....	....	....	....
1997-98	Djurgarden	Sweden	41	4	7	11	18	....	....	....	....	....	....	....	....	....	15	2	1	3	16	....	....	....	....
1998-99	Florida	NHL	8	1	1	2	5	0	0	1	7	14.3	2	6	50.0	12:24	....	....	....	....	....	....	....	....	....
	New Haven	AHL	69	8	25	33	10	....	....	....	....	....	....	....	....	....	....	....	....	....	....	....	....	....	....
99-2000	Florida	NHL	9	0	2	2	2	0	0	0	6	0.0	2	14	64.3	7:56	....	....	....	....	....	....	....	....	....
	Louisville Panthers	AHL	64	9	23	32	52	....	....	....	....	....	....	....	....	....	4	0	0	0	2	....	....	....	....
2000-01	Florida	NHL	78	12	24	36	74	0	0	2	141	8.5	–3	169	40.8	15:46	....	....	....	....	....	....	....	....	....
2001-02	Florida	NHL	81	14	19	33	55	6	1	2	147	9.5	–14	539	43.8	16:31	....	....	....	....	....	....	....	....	....
2002-03	Florida	NHL	82	15	19	34	31	7	1	0	187	8.0	2	469	46.7	15:31	....	....	....	....	....	....	....	....	....
	NHL Totals		258	42	65	107	167	13	2	5	488	8.6		1197	44.8	15:33	....	....	....	....	....	....	....	....	....

NOLAN, Owen

(NOH-lan, OH-wehn) **TOR.**

Right wing. Shoots right. 6'1", 215 lbs. Born, Belfast, Ireland, February 12, 1972. Quebec's 1st choice, 1st overall, in 1990 Entry Draft.

Season	Club	League	GP	G	A	Pts	PIM	PP	SH	GW	S	%	+/-	TF	F%	Min	GP	G	A	Pts	PIM	PP	SH	GW	Min
1987-88	Thorold	OMHA	28	53	32	85	24	....	....	....	....	....	....	....	....	....	....	....	....	....	....	....	....	....	....
	Thorold	OJHL-B	3	1	0	1	2	....	....	....	....	....	....	....	....	....	....	....	....	....	....	....	....	....	....
1988-89	Cornwall Royals	OHL	62	34	25	59	213	....	....	....	....	....	....	....	....	....	18	5	11	16	41	....	....	....	....
1989-90	Cornwall Royals	OHL	58	51	59	110	240	....	....	....	....	....	....	....	....	....	6	7	5	12	26	....	....	....	....
1990-91	Quebec	NHL	59	3	10	13	109	0	0	0	54	5.6	–19	....	....	....	....	....	....	....	....	....	....	....	....
	Halifax Citadels	AHL	6	4	4	8	11	....	....	....	....	....	....	....	....	....	....	....	....	....	....	....	....	....	....
1991-92	Quebec	NHL	75	42	31	73	183	17	0	0	190	22.1	–9	....	....	....	....	....	....	....	....	....	....	....	....
1992-93	Quebec	NHL	73	36	41	77	185	15	0	4	241	14.9	–1	....	....	....	5	1	0	1	2	0	0	0	....
1993-94	Quebec	NHL	6	2	2	4	8	0	0	0	15	13.3	2	....	....	....	....	....	....	....	....	....	....	....	....
1994-95	Quebec	NHL	46	30	19	49	46	13	2	8	137	21.9	21	....	....	....	6	2	3	5	6	0	0	0	....
1995-96	Colorado	NHL	9	4	4	8	9	4	0	0	23	17.4	–3	....	....	....	....	....	....	....	....	....	....	....	....
	San Jose	NHL	72	29	32	61	137	12	1	2	184	15.8	–30	....	....	....	....	....	....	....	....	....	....	....	....
1996-97	San Jose	NHL	72	31	32	63	155	10	0	3	225	13.8	–19	....	....	....	....	....	....	....	....	....	....	....	....
1997-98	San Jose	NHL	75	14	27	41	144	3	1	1	192	7.3	–2	....	....	....	6	2	2	4	26	2	0	1	....
1998-99	San Jose	NHL	78	19	26	45	129	6	2	3	207	9.2	16	657	49.3	19:09	6	1	1	2	6	0	0	0	20:15
99-2000	San Jose	NHL	78	44	40	84	110	18	4	6	261	16.9	–1	357	50.7	21:07	10	8	2	10	6	2	2	3	22:14
2000-01	San Jose	NHL	57	24	25	49	75	10	1	4	191	12.6	0	407	46.9	21:49	6	1	1	2	8	0	0	1	22:45
2001-02	San Jose	NHL	75	23	43	66	93	8	2	2	217	10.6	7	545	47.0	19:23	12	3	6	9	8	0	0	0	19:46
	Canada	Olympics	6	0	3	3	2	....	....	....	....	....	....	....	....	....	....	....	....	....	....	....	....	....	....
2002-03	San Jose	NHL	61	22	20	42	91	8	3	4	192	11.5	–5	226	50.4	18:08	....	....	....	....	....	....	....	....	....
	Toronto	NHL	14	7	5	12	16	5	0	1	29	24.1	2	56	48.2	16:60	7	0	2	2	2	0	0	0	23:19
	NHL Totals		850	330	357	687	1490	129	16	38	2358	14.0		2248	48.6	19:47	58	18	17	35	64	4	2	5	21:29

OHL Rookie of the Year (1989) • OHL First All-Star Team (1990)

Played in NHL All-Star Game (1992, 1996, 1997, 2000, 2002)

• Missed majority of 1993-94 season recovering from shoulder injury suffered in game vs. Tampa Bay, November 13, 1993. Transferred to **Colorado** after **Quebec** franchise relocated, June 21, 1995. Traded to **San Jose** by **Colorado** for Sandis Ozolinsh, October 26, 1995. Traded to **Toronto** by **San Jose** for Alyn McCauley, Brad Boyes and Toronto's 1st round choice (later traded to Boston – Boston selected Mark Stuart) in 2003 Entry Draft, March 5, 2003.

NORDSTROM, Peter

(NOHRD-struhm, PEE-tuhr) **BOS.**

Center. Shoots left. 6'1", 200 lbs. Born, Munkfors, Sweden, July 26, 1974. Boston's 3rd choice, 78th overall, in 1998 Entry Draft.

Season	Club	League	GP	G	A	Pts	PIM	PP	SH	GW	S	%	+/-	TF	F%	Min	GP	G	A	Pts	PIM	PP	SH	GW	Min
1989-90	IFK Munkfors	Swede-3	21	2	1	3	8	....	....	....	....	....	....	....	....	....	....	....	....	....	....	....	....	....	....
1990-91	IFK Munkfors	Swede-3	32	10	18	28	20	....	....	....	....	....	....	....	....	....	....	....	....	....	....	....	....	....	....
1991-92	IFK Munkfors	Swede-3	31	12	20	32	42	....	....	....	....	....	....	....	....	....	....	....	....	....	....	....	....	....	....
1992-93	IFK Munkfors	Swede-3	35	19	11	30	44	....	....	....	....	....	....	....	....	....	....	....	....	....	....	....	....	....	....
1993-94	IFK Munkfors	Swede-3	31	17	26	43	87	....	....	....	....	....	....	....	....	....	....	....	....	....	....	....	....	....	....
1994-95	IFK Munkfors	Swede-2	21	8	17	25	30	....	....	....	....	....	....	....	....	....	....	....	....	....	....	....	....	....	....
	Leksands IF	Sweden	13	1	0	1	0	....	....	....	....	....	....	....	....	....	....	....	....	....	....	....	....	....	....
1995-96	Farjestad	Sweden	40	6	5	11	36	....	....	....	....	....	....	....	....	....	8	0	3	3	12	....	....	....	....
1996-97	Farjestad	Sweden	44	9	5	14	32	....	....	....	....	....	....	....	....	....	14	1	2	3	6	....	....	....	....
1997-98	Farjestad	Sweden	45	6	19	25	46	....	....	....	....	....	....	....	....	....	12	5	7	*12	8	....	....	....	....
1998-99	Farjestad	Sweden	21	4	4	8	14	....	....	....	....	....	....	....	....	....	4	1	1	2	2	....	....	....	....
	Farjestad	EuroHL	2	1	0	1	2	....	....	....	....	....	....	....	....	....	....	....	....	....	....	....	....	....	....
	Boston	NHL	2	0	0	0	0	0	0	0	0	0.0	–1	0	0.0	8:04	....	....	....	....	....	....	....	....	....
	Providence Bruins	AHL	13	2	1	3	2	....	....	....	....	....	....	....	....	....	....	....	....	....	....	....	....	....	....
99-2000	Farjestad	Sweden	45	8	14	22	48	....	....	....	....	....	....	....	....	....	7	0	3	3	2	....	....	....	....
2000-01	Farjestad	Sweden	49	7	15	22	59	....	....	....	....	....	....	....	....	....	16	2	6	8	30	....	....	....	....
2001-02	Farjestad	Sweden	45	5	18	23	56	....	....	....	....	....	....	....	....	....	9	3	3	6	4	....	....	....	....
2002-03	Farjestad	Sweden	44	13	17	30	59	....	....	....	....	....	....	....	....	....	14	5	5	10	10	....	....	....	....
	NHL Totals		2	0	0	0	0	0	0	0	0	0.0		0	0.0	8:04	....	....	....	....	....	....	....	....	....

NORSTROM, Mattias
(NOHR-struhm, MAT-tee-ahs) **L.A.**

Defense. Shoots left. 6'2", 201 lbs. Born, Stockholm, Sweden, January 2, 1972. NY Rangers' 2nd choice, 48th overall, in 1992 Entry Draft.

Season	Club	League	GP	G	A	Pts	PIM	PP	SH	GW	S	%	+/-	TF	F%	Min	Playoffs GP	G	A	Pts	PIM	PP	SH	GW	Min
1990-91	Mora IK	Swede-2	9	1	1	2	6										1	0	0	0	2				
1991-92	AIK Solna	Sweden	39	4	3	7	28										3	0	2	2	2				
1992-93	AIK Solna	Sweden	22	0	1	1	16																		
1993-94	**NY Rangers**	**NHL**	**9**	**0**	**2**	**2**	**6**	**0**	**0**	**0**	**3**	**0.0**	**0**												
	Binghamton	AHL	55	1	9	10	70																		
1994-95	Binghamton	AHL	63	9	10	19	91																		
	NY Rangers	**NHL**	**9**	**0**	**3**	**3**	**2**	**0**	**0**	**0**	**4**	**0.0**	**2**				**3**	**0**	**0**	**0**	**0**	**0**	**0**	**0**	
1995-96	**NY Rangers**	**NHL**	**25**	**2**	**1**	**3**	**22**	**0**	**0**	**0**	**17**	**11.8**	**5**												
	Los Angeles	**NHL**	**11**	**0**	**1**	**1**	**18**	**0**	**0**	**0**	**17**	**0.0**	**-8**												
1996-97	**Los Angeles**	**NHL**	**80**	**1**	**21**	**22**	**84**	**0**	**0**	**0**	**106**	**0.9**	**-4**												
1997-98	**Los Angeles**	**NHL**	**73**	**1**	**12**	**13**	**90**	**0**	**0**	**0**	**61**	**1.6**	**14**				**4**	**0**	**0**	**0**	**2**	**0**	**0**	**0**	
	Sweden	Olympics	4	0	1	1	2																		
1998-99	**Los Angeles**	**NHL**	**78**	**2**	**5**	**7**	**36**	**0**	**1**	**0**	**61**	**3.3**	**-10**	**1**	**0.0**	**20:20**									
99-2000	**Los Angeles**	**NHL**	**82**	**1**	**13**	**14**	**66**	**0**	**0**	**0**	**62**	**1.6**	**22**	**0**	**0.0**	**21:49**	**4**	**0**	**0**	**0**	**6**	**0**	**0**	**0**	**21:35**
2000-01	**Los Angeles**	**NHL**	**82**	**0**	**18**	**18**	**60**	**0**	**0**	**0**	**59**	**0.0**	**10**	**2**	**0.0**	**21:50**	**13**	**0**	**2**	**2**	**18**	**0**	**0**	**0**	**23:16**
2001-02	**Los Angeles**	**NHL**	**79**	**2**	**9**	**11**	**38**	**0**	**0**	**0**	**42**	**4.8**	**-2**	**0**	**0.0**	**23:01**	**7**	**0**	**0**	**0**	**4**	**0**	**0**	**0**	**23:24**
	Sweden	Olympics	4	0	0	0	0																		
2002-03	**Los Angeles**	**NHL**	**82**	**0**	**6**	**6**	**49**	**0**	**0**	**0**	**63**	**0.0**	**0**	**1**	**100.0**	**21:30**									
	NHL Totals		**610**	**9**	**91**	**100**	**471**	**0**	**1**	**0**	**495**	**1.8**		**4**	**25.0**	**21:42**	**31**	**0**	**2**	**2**	**30**	**0**	**0**	**0**	**23:02**

Played in NHL All-Star Game (1999)

Traded to **Los Angeles** by **NY Rangers** with Ray Ferraro, Ian Laperriere, Nathan Lafayette and NY Rangers' 4th round choice (Sean Blanchard) in 1997 Entry Draft for Marty McSorley, Jari Kurri and Shane Churla, March 14, 1996.

NORTON, Brad
(NOHR-tohn, BRAD) **L.A.**

Defense. Shoots left. 6'4", 235 lbs. Born, Cambridge, MA, February 13, 1975. Edmonton's 9th choice, 215th overall, in 1993 Entry Draft.

Season	Club	League	GP	G	A	Pts	PIM	PP	SH	GW	S	%	+/-	TF	F%	Min	Playoffs GP	G	A	Pts	PIM	PP	SH	GW	Min
1992-93	Cushing Academy	Hi-School	31	10	26	36																			
1993-94	Cushing Academy	Hi-School	STATISTICS NOT AVAILABLE																						
1994-95	U. Mass-Amherst	H-East	30	0	6	6	89																		
1995-96	U. Mass-Amherst	H-East	34	4	12	16	99																		
1996-97	U. Mass-Amherst	H-East	35	2	16	18	88																		
1997-98	U. Mass-Amherst	H-East	20	2	13	15	28																		
	Detroit Vipers	IHL	33	1	4	5	56										22	0	2	2	87				
1998-99	Hamilton	AHL	58	1	8	9	134										11	0	1	1	6				
99-2000	Hamilton	AHL	40	5	12	17	104										10	1	4	5	26				
2000-01	Hamilton	AHL	46	3	15	18	114																		
2001-02	**Florida**	**NHL**	**22**	**0**	**2**	**2**	**45**	**0**	**0**	**0**	**6**	**0.0**	**-2**	**1**	**0.0**	**9:15**									
	Hershey Bears	AHL	40	0	10	10	62										2	0	0	0	6				
2002-03	**Los Angeles**	**NHL**	**53**	**3**	**3**	**6**	**97**	**0**	**0**	**0**	**19**	**15.8**	**1**	**2**	**0.0**	**6:04**									
	NHL Totals		**75**	**3**	**5**	**8**	**142**	**0**	**0**	**0**	**25**	**12.0**		**3**	**0.0**	**7:00**									

Signed as a free agent by **Florida**, July 27, 2001. Signed as a free agent by **Los Angeles**, October, 8, 2002.

NOVOSELTSEV, Ivan
(noh-voh-SEHLT-sehv, ee-VAHN) **FLA.**

Right wing. Shoots left. 6'1", 210 lbs. Born, Golitsino, USSR, January 23, 1979. Florida's 5th choice, 95th overall, in 1997 Entry Draft.

Season	Club	League	GP	G	A	Pts	PIM	PP	SH	GW	S	%	+/-	TF	F%	Min	Playoffs GP	G	A	Pts	PIM	PP	SH	GW	Min
1995-96	Krylja Sovetov	CIS	1	0	0	0	2																		
1996-97	Krylja Sovetov 2	Russia-3	19	5	3	8	39																		
	Krylja Sovetov	Russia	30	0	3	3	18										2	0	0	0	4				
1997-98	Sarnia Sting	OHL	53	26	22	48	41										5	1	1	2	8				
1998-99	Sarnia Sting	OHL	68	57	39	96	45										5	2	4	6	6				
99-2000	**Florida**	**NHL**	**14**	**2**	**1**	**3**	**8**	**2**	**0**	**0**	**8**	**25.0**	**-3**	**1**	**100.0**	**10:29**									
	Louisville Panthers	AHL	47	14	21	35	22										4	1	0	1	6				
2000-01	**Florida**	**NHL**	**38**	**3**	**6**	**9**	**16**	**0**	**0**	**0**	**34**	**8.8**	**-5**	**1**	**0.0**	**10:44**									
	Louisville Panthers	AHL	34	2	10	12	8																		
2001-02	**Florida**	**NHL**	**70**	**13**	**16**	**29**	**44**	**1**	**1**	**5**	**109**	**11.9**	**-10**	**27**	**44.4**	**14:53**									
2002-03	**Florida**	**NHL**	**78**	**10**	**17**	**27**	**30**	**1**	**0**	**0**	**115**	**8.7**	**-16**	**39**	**30.8**	**15:02**									
	NHL Totals		**200**	**28**	**40**	**68**	**98**	**4**	**1**	**5**	**266**	**10.5**		**68**	**36.8**	**13:51**									

OHL First All-Star Team (1999)

NUMMELIN, Petteri
(NOO-muh-lihn, PEH-tuh-ree) **ATL.**

Defense. Shoots left. 5'10", 196 lbs. Born, Turku, Finland, November 25, 1972. Columbus' 3rd choice, 133rd overall, in 2000 Entry Draft.

Season	Club	League	GP	G	A	Pts	PIM	PP	SH	GW	S	%	+/-	TF	F%	Min	Playoffs GP	G	A	Pts	PIM	PP	SH	GW	Min
1988-89	TPS Turku Jr.	Finn-Jr.	11	2	3	5	2																		
1989-90	TPS Turku Jr.	Finn-Jr.	33	6	14	20	45																		
1990-91	TPS Turku Jr.	Finn-Jr.	35	20	16	36	28																		
	Kiekko-67 Turku	Finland-2	2	0	2	2	4																		
1991-92	Kiekko-67 Jr.	Finn-Jr.	13	16	15	31	28																		
	Kiekko-67 Turku	Finland-2	41	12	24	36	36																		
1992-93	TPS Turku Jr.	Finn-Jr.	1	1	0	1	0																		
	TPS Turku	Finland	3	0	0	0	8																		
	Reipas Lahti	Finland	20	5	8	13	20																		
	Kiekko-67 Turku	Finland-2	28	14	15	29	18																		
1993-94	TPS Turku	Finland	44	14	24	38	20										11	0	3	3	4				
1994-95	TPS Turku	Finland	48	10	17	27	32										11	4	3	7	0				
1995-96	Vastra Frolunda	Sweden	32	7	11	18	26										12	2	7	9	4				
1996-97	Vastra Frolunda	Sweden	44	20	14	34	39										2	0	1	1	0				
1997-98	HC Davos	Swiss	33	13	17	30	24										17	8	14	22	2				
1998-99	HC Davos	Swiss	44	11	42	53	22										4	0	2	2	2				
99-2000	HC Davos	Swiss	40	15	23	38	20										5	0	3	3	0				
2000-01	**Columbus**	**NHL**	**61**	**4**	**12**	**16**	**10**	**2**	**0**	**0**	**99**	**4.0**	**-11**	**1**	**0.0**	**17:14**									
2001-02	HC Lugano	Swiss	35	4	18	22	6										13	6	9	15	2				
2002-03	HC Lugano	Swiss	43	18	*39	*57	12										8	3	6	9	2				
	NHL Totals		**61**	**4**	**12**	**16**	**10**	**2**	**0**	**0**	**99**	**4.0**		**1**	**0.0**	**17:14**									

Traded to **Atlanta** by **Columbus** with Chris Nielsen for Tomi Kallio and Pauli Levokari, December 2, 2002.

NUMMINEN, Teppo
(NOO-mih-nehn, TEH-poh) **DAL.**

Defense. Shoots right. 6'2", 197 lbs. Born, Tampere, Finland, July 3, 1968. Winnipeg's 2nd choice, 29th overall, in 1986 Entry Draft.

Season	Club	League	GP	G	A	Pts	PIM	PP	SH	GW	S	%	+/-	TF	F%	Min	Playoffs GP	G	A	Pts	PIM	PP	SH	GW	Min
1984-85	Tappara Jr.	Finn-Jr.	30	14	17	31	10																		
	Whitby Lawmen	OPJHL	16	3	9	12	0																		
1985-86	Tappara Jr.	Finn-Jr.	2	0	0	0	0										3	0	1	1	2				
	Tappara Tampere	Finland	31	2	4	6	6										8	0	0	0	0				
1986-87	Tappara Tampere	Finland	44	9	9	18	16										9	4	1	5	4				
1987-88	Tappara Tampere	Finland	40	10	10	20	29										10	6	6	12	6				
	Finland	Olympics	6	1	4	5	0																		
1988-89	**Winnipeg**	**NHL**	**69**	**1**	**14**	**15**	**36**	**0**	**1**	**0**	**85**	**1.2**	**-11**												
1989-90	**Winnipeg**	**NHL**	**79**	**11**	**32**	**43**	**20**	**1**	**0**	**1**	**105**	**10.5**	**-4**				**7**	**1**	**2**	**3**	**10**	**0**	**0**	**0**	
1990-91	**Winnipeg**	**NHL**	**80**	**8**	**25**	**33**	**28**	**3**	**0**	**0**	**151**	**5.3**	**-15**												
1991-92	**Winnipeg**	**NHL**	**80**	**5**	**34**	**39**	**32**	**4**	**0**	**1**	**143**	**3.5**	**15**				**7**	**0**	**0**	**0**	**0**	**0**	**0**	**0**	
1992-93	**Winnipeg**	**NHL**	**66**	**7**	**30**	**37**	**33**	**3**	**1**	**0**	**103**	**6.8**	**4**				**6**	**1**	**1**	**2**	**2**	**1**	**0**	**0**	
1993-94	**Winnipeg**	**NHL**	**57**	**5**	**18**	**23**	**28**	**4**	**0**	**1**	**89**	**5.6**	**-23**												
1994-95	TuTo Turku	Finland	12	3	8	11	4																		
	Winnipeg	**NHL**	**42**	**5**	**16**	**21**	**16**	**2**	**0**	**0**	**86**	**5.8**	**12**												
1995-96	**Winnipeg**	**NHL**	**74**	**11**	**43**	**54**	**22**	**6**	**0**	**3**	**165**	**6.7**	**-4**				**6**	**0**	**0**	**0**	**2**	**0**	**0**	**0**	
1996-97	**Phoenix**	**NHL**	**82**	**2**	**25**	**27**	**28**	**0**	**0**	**0**	**135**	**1.5**	**-3**				**7**	**3**	**3**	**6**	**0**	**1**	**0**	**1**	
1997-98	**Phoenix**	**NHL**	**82**	**11**	**40**	**51**	**30**	**6**	**0**	**2**	**126**	**8.7**	**25**				**1**	**0**	**0**	**0**	**0**	**0**	**0**	**0**	
	Finland	Olympics	6	1	1	2	2																		

								Regular Season									Playoffs								
Season	Club	League	GP	G	A	Pts	PIM	PP	SH	GW	S	%	+/-	TF	F%	Min	GP	G	A	Pts	PIM	PP	SH	GW	Min
1998-99	**Phoenix**	**NHL**	**82**	**10**	**30**	**40**	**30**	**1**	**0**	**0**	**156**	**6.4**	**3**	**2**	**0.0**	**24:26**	**7**	**2**	**1**	**3**	**4**	**2**	**0**	**0**	**26:09**
99-2000	**Phoenix**	**NHL**	**79**	**8**	**34**	**42**	**16**	**2**	**0**	**2**	**126**	**6.3**	**21**	**1**	**0.0**	**23:37**	**5**	**1**	**1**	**2**	**0**	**0**	**0**	**0**	**23:11**
2000-01	**Phoenix**	**NHL**	**72**	**5**	**26**	**31**	**36**	**1**	**0**	**2**	**109**	**4.6**	**9**	**0**	**0.0**	**24:28**									
2001-02	**Phoenix**	**NHL**	**76**	**13**	**35**	**48**	**20**	**4**	**0**	**6**	**117**	**11.1**	**13**	**0**	**0.0**	**23:51**	**4**	**0**	**0**	**0**	**2**	**0**	**0**	**0**	**25:33**
	Finland	Olympics	4	0	1	1	0																		
2002-03	**Phoenix**	**NHL**	**78**	**6**	**24**	**30**	**30**	**2**	**0**	**1**	**108**	**5.6**	**0**	**0**	**0.0**	**23:51**									
	NHL Totals		**1098**	**108**	**426**	**534**	**405**	**39**	**2**	**19**	**1804**	**6.0**		**3**	**0.0**	**24:03**	**50**	**8**	**8**	**16**	**20**	**4**	**0**	**1**	**25:04**

Played in NHL All-Star Game (1999, 2000, 2001)

Transferred to **Phoenix** after **Winnipeg** franchise relocated, July 1, 1996. Traded to **Dallas** by **Phoenix** for Mike Sillinger, July 22, 2003.

NYLANDER, Michael (NEE-lan-duhr, MIGH-kuhl) WSH.

Center. Shoots left. 6'1", 195 lbs. Born, Stockholm, Sweden, October 3, 1972. Hartford's 4th choice, 59th overall, in 1991 Entry Draft.

								Regular Season									Playoffs								
Season	Club	League	GP	G	A	Pts	PIM	PP	SH	GW	S	%	+/-	TF	F%	Min	GP	G	A	Pts	PIM	PP	SH	GW	Min
1989-90	Huddinge IK	Swede-2	31	7	15	22	4										5	3	0	3	0				
1990-91	Huddinge IK	Swede-2	33	14	20	34	10										2	0	0	0	0				
1991-92	AIK Solna	Sweden	40	11	17	28	30										3	1	4	5	4				
1992-93	**Hartford**	**NHL**	**59**	**11**	**22**	**33**	**36**	**3**	**0**	**1**	**85**	**12.9**	**–7**												
	Springfield	AHL															3	3	3	6	2				
1993-94	**Hartford**	**NHL**	**58**	**11**	**33**	**44**	**24**	**4**	**0**	**1**	**74**	**14.9**	**–2**												
	Springfield	AHL	4	0	9	9	0																		
	Calgary	**NHL**	**15**	**2**	**9**	**11**	**6**	**0**	**0**	**0**	**21**	**9.5**	**10**				**3**	**0**	**0**	**0**	**0**	**0**	**0**	**0**	
1994-95	JyP HT Jyvaskyla	Finland	16	11	19	30	63																		
	Calgary	**NHL**	**6**	**0**	**1**	**1**	**2**	**0**	**0**	**0**	**2**	**0.0**	**1**				**6**	**0**	**6**	**6**	**2**	**0**	**0**	**0**	
1995-96	**Calgary**	**NHL**	**73**	**17**	**38**	**55**	**20**	**4**	**0**	**6**	**163**	**10.4**	**0**				**4**	**0**	**0**	**0**	**0**	**0**	**0**	**0**	
1996-97	HC Lugano	Swiss	36	12	43	55	28										8	3	8	11	8				
1997-98	**Calgary**	**NHL**	**65**	**13**	**23**	**36**	**24**	**0**	**0**	**2**	**117**	**11.1**	**10**												
	Sweden	Olympics	4	0	0	0	6																		
1998-99	**Calgary**	**NHL**	**9**	**2**	**3**	**5**	**2**	**1**	**0**	**0**	**7**	**28.6**	**1**	**25**	**60.0**	**11:10**									
	Tampa Bay	**NHL**	**24**	**2**	**7**	**9**	**6**	**0**	**0**	**0**	**26**	**7.7**	**–10**	**75**	**44.0**	**13:29**									
99-2000	**Tampa Bay**	**NHL**	**11**	**1**	**2**	**3**	**4**	**1**	**0**	**0**	**10**	**10.0**	**–3**	**35**	**57.1**	**10:32**									
	Chicago	**NHL**	**66**	**23**	**28**	**51**	**26**	**4**	**0**	**2**	**112**	**20.5**	**9**	**561**	**46.9**	**16:39**									
2000-01	**Chicago**	**NHL**	**82**	**25**	**39**	**64**	**32**	**4**	**0**	**5**	**176**	**14.2**	**7**	**1036**	**48.3**	**18:52**									
2001-02	**Chicago**	**NHL**	**82**	**15**	**46**	**61**	**50**	**6**	**0**	**2**	**158**	**9.5**	**28**	**974**	**50.2**	**15:33**	**5**	**0**	**3**	**3**	**2**	**0**	**0**	**0**	**15:20**
	Sweden	Olympics	4	1	2	3	0																		
2002-03	**Chicago**	**NHL**	**9**	**0**	**4**	**4**	**4**	**0**	**0**	**0**	**20**	**0.0**	**0**	**86**	**48.8**	**15:19**									
	Washington	**NHL**	**71**	**17**	**39**	**56**	**36**	**7**	**0**	**2**	**141**	**12.1**	**3**	**1005**	**47.4**	**18:41**	**6**	**3**	**2**	**5**	**8**	**1**	**0**	**1**	**16:45**
	NHL Totals		**630**	**139**	**294**	**433**	**272**	**34**	**0**	**21**	**1112**	**12.5**		**3797**	**48.4**	**16:44**	**24**	**3**	**11**	**14**	**12**	**1**	**0**	**1**	**16:06**

Traded to **Calgary** by **Hartford** with James Patrick and Zarley Zalapski for Gary Suter, Paul Ranheim and Ted Drury, March 10, 1994. • Missed majority of 1994-95 season recovering from wrist injury suffered in game vs. St. Louis, January 24, 1995. Traded to **Tampa Bay** by **Calgary** for Andrei Nazarov, January 19, 1999. Traded to **Chicago** by **Tampa Bay** for Bryan Muir and Reid Simpson, November 12, 1999. Traded to **Washington** by **Chicago** with Chicago's 3rd round choice (Stephen Werner) in 2003 Entry Draft and future considerations for Chris Simon and Andrei Nikolishin, November 1, 2002.

OATES, Adam (OHTS, A-duhm)

Center. Shoots right. 5'11", 190 lbs. Born, Weston, Ont., August 27, 1962.

								Regular Season									Playoffs								
Season	Club	League	GP	G	A	Pts	PIM	PP	SH	GW	S	%	+/-	TF	F%	Min	GP	G	A	Pts	PIM	PP	SH	GW	Min
1979-80	Port Credit Titans	OHA-B	34	30	36	66	41																		
	Markham Waxers	OHA-A	9	1	6	7	2																		
1980-81	Markham Waxers	OHA-A	43	36	53	89	89																		
1981-82	Markham Waxers	OJHL-A	40	59	110	169	....																		
1982-83	RPI Engineers	ECAC	22	9	33	42	8																		
1983-84	RPI Engineers	ECAC	38	26	57	83	15																		
1984-85	RPI Engineers	ECAC	38	31	60	91	29																		
1985-86	**Detroit**	**NHL**	**38**	**9**	**11**	**20**	**10**	**1**	**0**	**1**	**49**	**18.4**	**–24**												
	Adirondack	AHL	34	18	28	46	4										17	7	14	21	4				
1986-87	**Detroit**	**NHL**	**76**	**15**	**32**	**47**	**21**	**4**	**0**	**1**	**138**	**10.9**	**0**				**16**	**4**	**7**	**11**	**6**	**0**	**0**	**1**	
1987-88	**Detroit**	**NHL**	**63**	**14**	**40**	**54**	**20**	**3**	**0**	**3**	**111**	**12.6**	**16**				**16**	**8**	**12**	**20**	**6**	**4**	**0**	**1**	
1988-89	**Detroit**	**NHL**	**69**	**16**	**62**	**78**	**14**	**2**	**0**	**1**	**127**	**12.6**	**–1**				**6**	**0**	**8**	**8**	**2**	**0**	**0**	**0**	
1989-90	**St. Louis**	**NHL**	**80**	**23**	**79**	**102**	**30**	**6**	**2**	**3**	**168**	**13.7**	**9**				**12**	**2**	**12**	**14**	**4**	**1**	**0**	**0**	
1990-91	**St. Louis**	**NHL**	**61**	**25**	**90**	**115**	**29**	**3**	**1**	**3**	**139**	**18.0**	**15**				**13**	**7**	**13**	**20**	**10**	**2**	**0**	**1**	
1991-92	**St. Louis**	**NHL**	**54**	**10**	**59**	**69**	**12**	**3**	**0**	**3**	**118**	**8.5**	**–4**												
	Boston	**NHL**	**26**	**10**	**20**	**30**	**10**	**3**	**0**	**1**	**73**	**13.7**	**–5**				**15**	**5**	**14**	**19**	**4**	**3**	**0**	**2**	
1992-93	**Boston**	**NHL**	**84**	**45**	***97**	**142**	**32**	**24**	**1**	**11**	**254**	**17.7**	**15**				**4**	**0**	**9**	**9**	**4**	**0**	**0**	**0**	
1993-94	**Boston**	**NHL**	**77**	**32**	**80**	**112**	**45**	**16**	**2**	**3**	**197**	**16.2**	**10**				**13**	**3**	**9**	**12**	**8**	**2**	**0**	**0**	
1994-95	**Boston**	**NHL**	**48**	**12**	**41**	**53**	**8**	**4**	**1**	**2**	**109**	**11.0**	**–11**				**5**	**1**	**0**	**1**	**2**	**1**	**0**	**0**	
1995-96	**Boston**	**NHL**	**70**	**25**	**67**	**92**	**18**	**7**	**1**	**2**	**183**	**13.7**	**16**				**5**	**2**	**5**	**7**	**2**	**0**	**1**	**0**	
1996-97	**Boston**	**NHL**	**63**	**18**	**52**	**70**	**10**	**2**	**2**	**4**	**138**	**13.0**	**–3**												
	Washington	**NHL**	**17**	**4**	**8**	**12**	**4**	**1**	**0**	**1**	**22**	**18.2**	**–2**												
1997-98	**Washington**	**NHL**	**82**	**18**	**58**	**76**	**36**	**3**	**2**	**3**	**121**	**14.9**	**6**				**21**	**6**	**11**	**17**	**8**	**1**	**1**	**1**	
1998-99	**Washington**	**NHL**	**59**	**12**	**42**	**54**	**22**	**3**	**0**	**0**	**79**	**15.2**	**–1**	**1330**	**59.2**	**20:34**									
99-2000	**Washington**	**NHL**	**82**	**15**	**56**	**71**	**14**	**5**	**0**	**6**	**93**	**16.1**	**13**	**2176**	**56.8**	**22:20**	**5**	**0**	**3**	**3**	**4**	**0**	**0**	**0**	**25:06**
2000-01	**Washington**	**NHL**	**81**	**13**	***69**	**82**	**28**	**5**	**0**	**4**	**72**	**18.1**	**–9**	**1836**	**58.9**	**20:60**	**6**	**0**	**0**	**0**	**0**	**0**	**0**	**0**	**16:21**
2001-02	**Washington**	**NHL**	**66**	**11**	***57**	**68**	**22**	**3**	**0**	**1**	**85**	**12.9**	**–2**	**1642**	**56.5**	**22:06**									
	Philadelphia	**NHL**	**14**	**3**	***7**	**10**	**6**	**0**	**0**	**0**	**17**	**17.6**	**–2**	**323**	**55.7**	**20:51**	**5**	**0**	**2**	**2**	**0**	**0**	**0**	**0**	**21:53**
2002-03	**Anaheim**	**NHL**	**67**	**9**	**36**	**45**	**16**	**4**	**0**	**2**	**67**	**13.4**	**–1**	**1064**	**57.8**	**18:38**	**21**	**4**	**9**	**13**	**6**	**3**	**0**	**1**	**19:15**
	NHL Totals		**1277**	**339**	**1063**	**1402**	**407**	**102**	**12**	**55**	**2360**	**14.4**		**8371**	**57.7**	**20:59**	**163**	**42**	**114**	**156**	**66**	**17**	**2**	**7**	**19:56**

ECAC Second All-Star Team (1984) • NCAA East First All-American Team (1984, 1985) • ECAC First All-Star Team (1985) • NCAA Championship All-Tournament Team (1985) • NHL Second All-Star Team (1991)

Played in NHL All-Star Game (1991, 1992, 1993, 1994, 1997)

Signed as a free agent by **Detroit,** June 28, 1985. Traded to **St. Louis** by **Detroit** with Paul MacLean for Bernie Federko and Tony McKegney, June 15, 1989. Traded to **Boston** by **St. Louis** for Craig Janney and Stephane Quintal, February 7, 1992. Traded to **Washington** by **Boston** with Bill Ranford and Rick Tocchet for Jim Carey, Anson Carter, Jason Allison and Washington's 3rd round choice (Lee Goren) in 1997 Entry Draft, March 1, 1997. Traded to **Philadelphia** by **Washington** for Maxime Ouellet and Philadelphia's 1st (later traded to Dallas – Dallas selected Martin Vagner), 2nd (Maxime Daigneault) and 3rd (Derek Krestanovich) round choices in 2002 Entry Draft, March 19, 2002. Signed as a free agent by **Anaheim**, July 1, 2002.

OBSUT, Jaroslav (OHB-suht, YAHR-oh-slahv) VAN.

Defense. Shoots left. 6'1", 200 lbs. Born, Presov, Czech., September 3, 1976. Winnipeg's 9th choice, 188th overall, in 1995 Entry Draft.

								Regular Season									Playoffs								
Season	Club	League	GP	G	A	Pts	PIM	PP	SH	GW	S	%	+/-	TF	F%	Min	GP	G	A	Pts	PIM	PP	SH	GW	Min
1994-95	North Battleford	SJHL	55	21	30	51	126																		
1995-96	Swift Current	WHL	72	10	11	21	57										6	0	0	0	2				
1996-97	Edmonton Ice	WHL	13	2	9	11	4																		
	Medicine Hat	WHL	50	8	26	34	42										4	0	2	2	2				
	Toledo Storm	ECHL	3	1	0	1	0										5	0	1	1	6				
1997-98	Raleigh Icecaps	ECHL	60	6	26	32	46																		
	Syracuse Crunch	AHL	4	0	1	1	4																		
1998-99	Augusta Lynx	ECHL	41	11	25	36	42																		
	Manitoba Moose	IHL	2	0	0	0	0																		
	Worcester IceCats	AHL	31	2	8	10	14										4	0	1	1	2				
99-2000	Worcester IceCats	AHL	7	0	2	2	4																		
2000-01	**St. Louis**	**NHL**	**4**	**0**	**0**	**0**	**2**	**0**	**0**	**0**	**3**	**0.0**	**1**	**0**	**0.0**	**18:31**									
	Peoria Rivermen	ECHL	3	0	4	4	2																		
	Worcester IceCats	AHL	47	9	12	21	20										7	0	1	1	4				
2001-02	**Colorado**	**NHL**	**3**	**0**	**0**	**0**	**0**	**0**	**0**	**0**	**3**	**0.0**	**0**	**0**	**0.0**	**9:47**									
	Hershey Bears	AHL	58	3	22	25	48										8	0	2	2	2				
	Slovakia	Olympics	4	0	0	0	2																		
2002-03	Manitoba Moose	AHL	60	6	13	19	59										14	0	4	4	8				
	NHL Totals		**7**	**0**	**0**	**0**	**2**	**0**	**0**	**0**	**6**	**0.0**		**0**	**0.0**	**14:46**									

Signed as a free agent by **St. Louis**, April 26, 1999. • Missed majority of 1999-2000 season recovering from knee injury suffered in practice, October, 1999. Signed as a free agent by **Colorado**, August 11, 2001. Signed as a free agent by **Vancouver**, July 10, 2002.

ODELEIN, Lyle

(OH-duh-LIGHN, LIGHL)

Defense. Shoots right. 6', 210 lbs. Born, Quill Lake, Sask., July 21, 1968. Montreal's 8th choice, 141st overall, in 1986 Entry Draft.

			Regular Season														Playoffs								
Season	Club	League	GP	G	A	Pts	PIM	PP	SH	GW	S	%	+/-	TF	F%	Min	GP	G	A	Pts	PIM	PP	SH	GW	Min
1984-85	Regina Pat Cdns.	SMHL	26	12	13	25	30	....	....	....	....	....	....	....	....	....	....	....	....	....	....	....	....	....	....
1985-86	Moose Jaw	WHL	67	9	37	46	117	....	....	....	....	....	....	....	....	....	13	1	6	7	34	....	....	....	....
1986-87	Moose Jaw	WHL	59	9	50	59	70	....	....	....	....	....	....	....	....	....	9	2	5	7	26	....	....	....	....
1987-88	Moose Jaw	WHL	63	15	43	58	166	....	....	....	....	....	....	....	....	....	....	....	....	....	....	....	....	....	....
1988-89	Sherbrooke	AHL	33	3	4	7	120	....	....	....	....	....	....	....	....	....	3	0	2	2	5	....	....	....	....
	Peoria Rivermen	IHL	36	2	8	10	116	....	....	....	....	....	....	....	....	....	....	....	....	....	....	....	....	....	....
1989-90	**Montreal**	**NHL**	**8**	**0**	**2**	**2**	**33**	**0**	**0**	**0**	**1**	**0.0**	**–1**	....	....	....	....	....	....	....	....	....	....	....	....
	Sherbrooke	AHL	68	7	24	31	265	....	....	....	....	....	....	....	....	....	12	6	5	11	79	....	....	....	....
1990-91	**Montreal**	**NHL**	**52**	**0**	**2**	**2**	**259**	**0**	**0**	**0**	**25**	**0.0**	**7**	....	....	....	**12**	**0**	**0**	**0**	**54**	**0**	**0**	**0**	....
1991-92	**Montreal**	**NHL**	**71**	**1**	**7**	**8**	**212**	**0**	**0**	**0**	**43**	**2.3**	**15**	....	....	....	**7**	**0**	**0**	**0**	**11**	**0**	**0**	**0**	....
1992-93♦	**Montreal**	**NHL**	**83**	**2**	**14**	**16**	**205**	**0**	**0**	**0**	**79**	**2.5**	**35**	....	....	....	**20**	**1**	**5**	**6**	**30**	**0**	**0**	**0**	....
1993-94	**Montreal**	**NHL**	**79**	**11**	**29**	**40**	**276**	**6**	**0**	**2**	**116**	**9.5**	**8**	....	....	....	**7**	**0**	**0**	**0**	**17**	**0**	**0**	**0**	....
1994-95	**Montreal**	**NHL**	**48**	**3**	**7**	**10**	**152**	**0**	**0**	**0**	**74**	**4.1**	**–13**	....	....	....	....	....	....	....	....	....	....	....	....
1995-96	**Montreal**	**NHL**	**79**	**3**	**14**	**17**	**230**	**0**	**1**	**0**	**74**	**4.1**	**8**	....	....	....	**6**	**1**	**1**	**2**	**6**	**0**	**1**	**0**	....
1996-97	**New Jersey**	**NHL**	**79**	**3**	**13**	**16**	**110**	**1**	**0**	**2**	**93**	**3.2**	**16**	....	....	....	**10**	**2**	**2**	**4**	**19**	**1**	**0**	**0**	....
1997-98	**New Jersey**	**NHL**	**79**	**4**	**19**	**23**	**171**	**1**	**0**	**0**	**76**	**5.3**	**11**	....	....	....	**6**	**1**	**1**	**2**	**21**	**1**	**0**	**1**	....
1998-99	**New Jersey**	**NHL**	**70**	**5**	**26**	**31**	**114**	**1**	**0**	**0**	**101**	**5.0**	**6**	**0**	**0.0**	**19:53**	**7**	**0**	**3**	**3**	**10**	**0**	**0**	**0**	**18:28**
99-2000	**New Jersey**	**NHL**	**57**	**1**	**15**	**16**	**104**	**0**	**0**	**1**	**59**	**1.7**	**–10**	**0**	**0.0**	**16:42**	....	....	....	....	....	....	....	....	....
	Phoenix	**NHL**	**16**	**1**	**7**	**8**	**19**	**1**	**0**	**0**	**30**	**3.3**	**1**	**0**	**0.0**	**21:45**	**5**	**0**	**0**	**0**	**16**	**0**	**0**	**0**	**16:38**
2000-01	**Columbus**	**NHL**	**81**	**3**	**14**	**17**	**118**	**1**	**0**	**0**	**104**	**2.9**	**–16**	**0**	**0.0**	**21:31**	....	....	....	....	....	....	....	....	....
2001-02	**Columbus**	**NHL**	**65**	**2**	**14**	**16**	**89**	**0**	**0**	**0**	**76**	**2.6**	**–28**	**0**	**0.0**	**22:12**	....	....	....	....	....	....	....	....	....
	Chicago	**NHL**	**12**	**0**	**2**	**2**	**4**	**0**	**0**	**0**	**10**	**0.0**	**0**	**0**	**0.0**	**24:23**	**4**	**0**	**1**	**1**	**25**	**0**	**0**	**0**	**24:08**
2002-03	**Chicago**	**NHL**	**65**	**7**	**4**	**11**	**76**	**0**	**0**	**0**	**77**	**9.1**	**7**	**1**	**100.0**	**19:05**	....	....	....	....	....	....	....	....	....
	Dallas	**NHL**	**3**	**0**	**0**	**0**	**6**	**0**	**0**	**0**	**1**	**0.0**	**0**	**0**	**0.0**	**17:49**	**2**	**0**	**0**	**0**	**0**	**0**	**0**	**0**	**12:52**
	NHL Totals		**947**	**46**	**189**	**235**	**2178**	**11**	**1**	**5**	**1039**	**4.4**		**1**	**100.0**	**20:14**	**86**	**5**	**13**	**18**	**209**	**2**	**1**	**1**	**18:36**

Traded to **New Jersey** by **Montreal** for Stephane Richer, August 22, 1996. Traded to **Phoenix** by **New Jersey** for Deron Quint and Phoenix's 3rd round choice (later traded back to Phoenix – Phoenix selected Beat Forster) in 2001 Entry Draft, March 7, 2000. Selected by **Columbus** from **Phoenix** in Expansion Draft, June 23, 2000. Traded to **Chicago** by **Columbus** for Jaroslav Spacek and Chicago's 2nd round choice (Dan Fritsche) in 2003 Entry Draft, March 19, 2002. Traded to **Dallas** by **Chicago** for Sami Helenius and Dallas's 7th round choice in 2004 Entry Draft, March 10, 2003.

ODGERS, Jeff

(AWD-juhrs, JEHF)

Right wing. Shoots right. 5'11", 200 lbs. Born, Spy Hill, Sask., May 31, 1969.

			Regular Season														Playoffs								
Season	Club	League	GP	G	A	Pts	PIM	PP	SH	GW	S	%	+/-	TF	F%	Min	GP	G	A	Pts	PIM	PP	SH	GW	Min
1985-86	Saskatoon Blazers	SMHL	36	27	29	56	74	....	....	....	....	....	....	....	....	....	....	....	....	....	....	....	....	....	....
1986-87	Brandon	WHL	70	7	14	21	150	....	....	....	....	....	....	....	....	....	....	....	....	....	....	....	....	....	....
1987-88	Brandon	WHL	70	17	18	35	202	....	....	....	....	....	....	....	....	....	4	1	1	2	14	....	....	....	....
1988-89	Brandon	WHL	71	31	29	60	277	....	....	....	....	....	....	....	....	....	....	....	....	....	....	....	....	....	....
1989-90	Brandon	WHL	64	37	28	65	209	....	....	....	....	....	....	....	....	....	....	....	....	....	....	....	....	....	....
1990-91	Kansas City	IHL	77	12	19	31	318	....	....	....	....	....	....	....	....	....	....	....	....	....	....	....	....	....	....
1991-92	**San Jose**	**NHL**	**61**	**7**	**4**	**11**	**217**	**0**	**0**	**0**	**64**	**10.9**	**–21**	....	....	....	....	....	....	....	....	....	....	....	....
	Kansas City	IHL	12	2	2	4	56	....	....	....	....	....	....	....	....	....	4	2	1	3	0	....	....	....	....
1992-93	**San Jose**	**NHL**	**66**	**12**	**15**	**27**	**253**	**6**	**0**	**0**	**100**	**12.0**	**–26**	....	....	....	....	....	....	....	....	....	....	....	....
1993-94	**San Jose**	**NHL**	**81**	**13**	**8**	**21**	**222**	**7**	**0**	**0**	**73**	**17.8**	**–13**	....	....	....	**11**	**0**	**0**	**0**	**11**	**0**	**0**	**0**	....
1994-95	**San Jose**	**NHL**	**48**	**4**	**3**	**7**	**117**	**0**	**0**	**1**	**47**	**8.5**	**–8**	....	....	....	**11**	**1**	**1**	**2**	**23**	**0**	**0**	**0**	....
1995-96	**San Jose**	**NHL**	**78**	**12**	**4**	**16**	**192**	**0**	**0**	**1**	**84**	**14.3**	**–4**	....	....	....	....	....	....	....	....	....	....	....	....
1996-97	**Boston**	**NHL**	**80**	**7**	**8**	**15**	**197**	**1**	**0**	**1**	**84**	**8.3**	**–15**	....	....	....	....	....	....	....	....	....	....	....	....
1997-98	Providence Bruins	AHL	4	0	0	0	31	....	....	....	....	....	....	....	....	....	....	....	....	....	....	....	....	....	....
	Colorado	**NHL**	**68**	**5**	**8**	**13**	**213**	**0**	**0**	**0**	**47**	**10.6**	**5**	....	....	....	**6**	**0**	**0**	**0**	**25**	**0**	**0**	**0**	....
1998-99	**Colorado**	**NHL**	**75**	**2**	**3**	**5**	**259**	**1**	**0**	**0**	**39**	**5.1**	**–3**	**8**	**37.5**	**5:07**	**15**	**1**	**0**	**1**	**14**	**0**	**0**	**1**	**4:20**
99-2000	**Colorado**	**NHL**	**62**	**1**	**2**	**3**	**162**	**0**	**0**	**1**	**29**	**3.4**	**–7**	**2**	**50.0**	**5:23**	**4**	**0**	**0**	**0**	**0**	**0**	**0**	**0**	**2:38**
2000-01	**Atlanta**	**NHL**	**82**	**6**	**7**	**13**	**226**	**0**	**0**	**1**	**67**	**9.0**	**–8**	**2**	**50.0**	**8:39**	....	....	....	....	....	....	....	....	....
2001-02	**Atlanta**	**NHL**	**46**	**4**	**4**	**8**	**135**	**0**	**0**	**1**	**34**	**11.8**	**–3**	**5**	**20.0**	**8:37**	....	....	....	....	....	....	....	....	....
2002-03	**Atlanta**	**NHL**	**74**	**2**	**4**	**6**	**171**	**0**	**0**	**1**	**48**	**4.2**	**–13**	**4**	**25.0**	**7:48**	....	....	....	....	....	....	....	....	....
	NHL Totals		**821**	**75**	**70**	**145**	**2364**	**15**	**0**	**7**	**716**	**10.5**		**21**	**33.3**	**7:05**	**47**	**2**	**1**	**3**	**73**	**0**	**0**	**1**	**3:59**

Signed as a free agent by **San Jose**, September 3, 1991. Traded to **Boston** by **San Jose** with Pittsburgh's 5th round choice (previously acquired, Boston selected Elias Abrahamsson) in 1996 Entry Draft for Al Iafrate, June 21, 1996. Signed as a free agent by **Colorado**, October 24, 1997. Selected by **Minnesota** from **Colorado** in Expansion Draft, June 23, 2000. Claimed by **Atlanta** from **Minnesota** in Waiver Draft, September 29, 2000.

O'DONNELL, Sean

(oh-DOHN-ehl, SHAWN) **BOS.**

Defense. Shoots left. 6'3", 230 lbs. Born, Ottawa, Ont., October 13, 1971. Buffalo's 6th choice, 123rd overall, in 1991 Entry Draft.

			Regular Season														Playoffs								
Season	Club	League	GP	G	A	Pts	PIM	PP	SH	GW	S	%	+/-	TF	F%	Min	GP	G	A	Pts	PIM	PP	SH	GW	Min
1987-88	Kanata Valley	OCJHL	54	4	25	29	96	....	....	....	....	....	....	....	....	....	....	....	....	....	....	....	....	....	....
1988-89	Sudbury Wolves	OHL	56	1	9	10	49	....	....	....	....	....	....	....	....	....	....	....	....	....	....	....	....	....	....
1989-90	Sudbury Wolves	OHL	64	7	19	26	84	....	....	....	....	....	....	....	....	....	7	1	2	3	8	....	....	....	....
1990-91	Sudbury Wolves	OHL	66	8	23	31	114	....	....	....	....	....	....	....	....	....	5	1	4	5	10	....	....	....	....
1991-92	Rochester	AHL	73	4	9	13	193	....	....	....	....	....	....	....	....	....	16	1	2	3	21	....	....	....	....
1992-93	Rochester	AHL	74	3	18	21	203	....	....	....	....	....	....	....	....	....	17	1	6	7	38	....	....	....	....
1993-94	Rochester	AHL	64	2	10	12	242	....	....	....	....	....	....	....	....	....	4	0	1	1	21	....	....	....	....
1994-95	Phoenix	IHL	61	2	18	20	132	....	....	....	....	....	....	....	....	....	9	0	1	1	21	....	....	....	....
	Los Angeles	**NHL**	**15**	**0**	**2**	**2**	**49**	**0**	**0**	**0**	**12**	**0.0**	**–2**	....	....	....	....	....	....	....	....	....	....	....	....
1995-96	**Los Angeles**	**NHL**	**71**	**2**	**5**	**7**	**127**	**0**	**0**	**0**	**65**	**3.1**	**3**	....	....	....	....	....	....	....	....	....	....	....	....
1996-97	**Los Angeles**	**NHL**	**55**	**5**	**12**	**17**	**144**	**2**	**0**	**0**	**68**	**7.4**	**–13**	....	....	....	....	....	....	....	....	....	....	....	....
1997-98	**Los Angeles**	**NHL**	**80**	**2**	**15**	**17**	**179**	**0**	**0**	**1**	**71**	**2.8**	**7**	....	....	....	**4**	**1**	**0**	**1**	**36**	**0**	**0**	**0**	....
1998-99	**Los Angeles**	**NHL**	**80**	**1**	**13**	**14**	**186**	**0**	**0**	**0**	**64**	**1.6**	**1**	**0**	**0.0**	**19:10**	....	....	....	....	....	....	....	....	....
99-2000	**Los Angeles**	**NHL**	**80**	**2**	**12**	**14**	**114**	**0**	**0**	**1**	**51**	**3.9**	**4**	**0**	**0.0**	**17:41**	**4**	**1**	**0**	**1**	**4**	**0**	**0**	**0**	**16:26**
2000-01	**Minnesota**	**NHL**	**63**	**4**	**12**	**16**	**128**	**1**	**0**	**2**	**58**	**6.9**	**–2**	**12**	**50.0**	**23:00**	....	....	....	....	....	....	....	....	....
	New Jersey	**NHL**	**17**	**0**	**1**	**1**	**33**	**0**	**0**	**0**	**9**	**0.0**	**2**	**0**	**0.0**	**16:27**	**23**	**1**	**2**	**3**	**41**	**0**	**0**	**0**	**16:21**
2001-02	**Boston**	**NHL**	**80**	**3**	**22**	**25**	**89**	**1**	**0**	**2**	**112**	**2.7**	**27**	**0**	**0.0**	**24:50**	**6**	**0**	**2**	**2**	**4**	**0**	**0**	**0**	**24:57**
2002-03	**Boston**	**NHL**	**70**	**1**	**15**	**16**	**76**	**0**	**0**	**1**	**61**	**1.6**	**8**	**1**	**0.0**	**22:05**	....	....	....	....	....	....	....	....	....
	NHL Totals		**611**	**20**	**109**	**129**	**1125**	**4**	**0**	**7**	**571**	**3.5**		**13**	**46.2**	**21:03**	**37**	**3**	**4**	**7**	**85**	**0**	**0**	**0**	**17:55**

Traded to **Los Angeles** by **Buffalo** for Doug Houda, July 26, 1994. Selected by **Minnesota** from **Los Angeles** in Expansion Draft, June 23, 2000. Traded to **New Jersey** by **Minnesota** for Willie Mitchell, March 4, 2001. Signed as a free agent by **Boston**, July 2, 2001.

OHLUND, Mattias

(OH-luhnd, MAT-tee-ahs) **VAN.**

Defense. Shoots left. 6'2", 220 lbs. Born, Pitea, Sweden, September 9, 1976. Vancouver's 1st choice, 13th overall, in 1994 Entry Draft.

			Regular Season														Playoffs								
Season	Club	League	GP	G	A	Pts	PIM	PP	SH	GW	S	%	+/-	TF	F%	Min	GP	G	A	Pts	PIM	PP	SH	GW	Min
1992-93	Pitea HC	Swede-2	22	0	6	6	16	....	....	....	....	....	....	....	....	....	....	....	....	....	....	....	....	....	....
1993-94	Pitea HC	Swede-2	28	7	10	17	62	....	....	....	....	....	....	....	....	....	....	....	....	....	....	....	....	....	....
1994-95	Lulea HF	Sweden	34	6	10	16	34	....	....	....	....	....	....	....	....	....	9	4	0	4	16	....	....	....	....
1995-96	Lulea HF	Sweden	38	4	10	14	26	....	....	....	....	....	....	....	....	....	13	1	0	1	47	....	....	....	....
1996-97	Lulea HF	Sweden	47	7	9	16	38	....	....	....	....	....	....	....	....	....	10	1	2	3	8	....	....	....	....
	Lulea HF	EuroHL	6	0	3	3	0	....	....	....	....	....	....	....	....	....	....	....	....	....	....	....	....	....	....
1997-98	**Vancouver**	**NHL**	**77**	**7**	**23**	**30**	**76**	**1**	**0**	**0**	**172**	**4.1**	**3**	....	....	....	....	....	....	....	....	....	....	....	....
	Sweden	Olympics	4	0	1	1	4	....	....	....	....	....	....	....	....	....	....	....	....	....	....	....	....	....	....
1998-99	**Vancouver**	**NHL**	**74**	**9**	**26**	**35**	**83**	**2**	**1**	**1**	**129**	**7.0**	**–19**	**0**	**0.0**	**26:04**	....	....	....	....	....	....	....	....	....
99-2000	**Vancouver**	**NHL**	**42**	**4**	**16**	**20**	**24**	**2**	**1**	**1**	**63**	**6.3**	**6**	**0**	**0.0**	**27:41**	....	....	....	....	....	....	....	....	....
2000-01	**Vancouver**	**NHL**	**65**	**8**	**20**	**28**	**46**	**1**	**1**	**4**	**136**	**5.9**	**–16**	**0**	**0.0**	**25:00**	**4**	**1**	**3**	**4**	**6**	**1**	**0**	**0**	**26:32**
2001-02	**Vancouver**	**NHL**	**81**	**10**	**26**	**36**	**56**	**4**	**1**	**3**	**193**	**5.2**	**16**	**0**	**0.0**	**25:17**	**6**	**1**	**1**	**2**	**6**	**0**	**0**	**0**	**28:48**
	Sweden	Olympics	4	0	2	2	2	....	....	....	....	....	....	....	....	....	....	....	....	....	....	....	....	....	....
2002-03	**Vancouver**	**NHL**	**59**	**2**	**27**	**29**	**42**	**0**	**0**	**0**	**100**	**2.0**	**1**	**0**	**0.0**	**25:23**	**13**	**3**	**4**	**7**	**12**	**0**	**0**	**0**	**24:01**
	NHL Totals		**398**	**40**	**138**	**178**	**327**	**10**	**4**	**9**	**793**	**5.0**		**0**	**0.0**	**25:44**	**23**	**5**	**8**	**13**	**24**	**1**	**0**	**0**	**25:42**

NHL All-Rookie Team (1998)
Played in NHL All-Star Game (1999)

OLAUSSON, Fredrik

(OHL-ah-suhn, FREHD-rihk)

Defense. Shoots right. 6'2", 198 lbs. Born, Dadesjo, Sweden, October 5, 1966. Winnipeg's 4th choice, 81st overall, in 1985 Entry Draft.

			Regular Season														Playoffs								
Season	Club	League	GP	G	A	Pts	PIM	PP	SH	GW	S	%	+/-	TF	F%	Min	GP	G	A	Pts	PIM	PP	SH	GW	Min
1982-83	Nybro SK	Swede-2	31	4	4	8	12																		
1983-84	Nybro SK	Swede-2	28	8	14	22	32																		
1984-85	Farjestad	Sweden	29	5	12	17	22										3	1	0	1	0				
1985-86	Farjestad	Sweden	33	4	12	16	22										8	3	2	5	6				
1986-87	Winnipeg	NHL	72	7	29	36	24	1	0	2	119	5.9	–3				10	2	3	5	4	1	0	0	
1987-88	Winnipeg	NHL	38	5	10	15	18	2	0	2	65	7.7	3				5	1	1	2	0	0	0	0	
1988-89	Winnipeg	NHL	75	15	47	62	32	4	0	1	178	8.4	6												
1989-90	Winnipeg	NHL	77	9	46	55	32	3	0	0	147	6.1	–1				7	0	2	2	2	0	0	0	
1990-91	Winnipeg	NHL	71	12	29	41	24	5	0	0	168	7.1	–22												
1991-92	Winnipeg	NHL	77	20	42	62	34	13	1	2	227	8.8	–31				7	1	5	6	4	1	0	0	
1992-93	Winnipeg	NHL	68	16	41	57	22	11	0	3	165	9.7	–4				6	0	2	2	2	0	0	0	
1993-94	Winnipeg	NHL	18	2	5	7	10	1	0	0	41	4.9	–3												
	Edmonton	NHL	55	9	19	28	20	6	0	1	85	10.6	–4												
1994-95	EC Ehrwald	Austria	10	4	3	7	8																		
	Edmonton	NHL	33	0	10	10	20	0	0	0	52	0.0	–4												
1995-96	Edmonton	NHL	20	0	6	6	14	0	0	0	20	0.0	–14												
	Anaheim	NHL	36	2	16	18	24	1	0	0	63	3.2	7												
1996-97	Anaheim	NHL	20	2	9	11	8	1	0	0	35	5.7	–5												
	Pittsburgh	NHL	51	7	20	27	24	2	0	3	75	9.3	21				4	0	1	1	0	0	0	0	
1997-98	Pittsburgh	NHL	76	6	27	33	42	2	0	1	89	6.7	13				6	0	3	3	2	0	0	0	
1998-99	Anaheim	NHL	74	16	40	56	30	10	0	2	121	13.2	17	0	0.0	19:47	4	0	2	2	4	0	0	0	21:33
99-2000	Anaheim	NHL	70	15	19	34	28	8	0	1	120	12.5	–13	0	0.0	20:01									
2000-01	SC Bern	Swiss	43	12	15	27	28										4	1	4	5	0				
2001-02 ♦	Detroit	NHL	47	2	13	15	22	0	1	1	61	3.3	9	0	0.0	16:37	21	2	4	6	10	1	0	1	19:58
	Sweden	Olympics	4	0	0	0	2																		
2002-03	Anaheim	NHL	44	2	6	8	22	2	0	1	38	5.3	0	0	0.0	14:26	1	0	0	0	0	0	0	0	3:19
	NHL Totals		**1022**	**147**	**434**	**581**	**450**	**72**	**2**	**20**	**1869**	**7.9**		**0**	**0.0**	**18:13**	**71**	**6**	**23**	**29**	**28**	**3**	**0**	**1**	**19:34**

Traded to **Edmonton** by **Winnipeg** with Winnipeg's 7th round choice (Curtis Sheptak) in 1994 Entry Draft for Edmonton's 3rd round choice (Tavis Hansen) in 1994 Entry Draft, December 6, 1993. Claimed on waivers by **Anaheim** from **Edmonton**, January 16, 1996. Traded to **Pittsburgh** by **Anaheim** with Alex Hicks for Shawn Antoski and Dmitri Mironov, November 19, 1996. Signed as a free agent by **Anaheim**, August 28, 1998. Signed as a free agent by **Detroit**, May 24, 2001. Signed as a free agent by **Anaheim**, July 12, 2002.

OLIVER, David

(AWL-ih-vuhr, DAY-vihd) **DAL.**

Right wing. Shoots right. 6', 190 lbs. Born, Sechelt, B.C., April 17, 1971. Edmonton's 7th choice, 144th overall, in 1991 Entry Draft.

			Regular Season														Playoffs								
Season	Club	League	GP	G	A	Pts	PIM	PP	SH	GW	S	%	+/-	TF	F%	Min	GP	G	A	Pts	PIM	PP	SH	GW	Min
1988-89	Vernon Lakers	BCJHL	58	41	38	79	38																		
1989-90	Vernon Lakers	BCJHL	58	51	48	99	22																		
1990-91	U. of Michigan	CCHA	27	13	11	24	34																		
1991-92	U. of Michigan	CCHA	44	31	27	58	32																		
1992-93	U. of Michigan	CCHA	40	35	20	55	18																		
1993-94	U. of Michigan	CCHA	41	28	40	68	16																		
1994-95	Cape Breton	AHL	32	11	18	29	8																		
	Edmonton	NHL	44	16	14	30	20	10	0	0	79	20.3	–11												
1995-96	Edmonton	NHL	80	20	19	39	34	14	0	0	131	15.3	–22												
1996-97	Edmonton	NHL	17	1	2	3	4	0	0	0	22	4.5	–8												
	NY Rangers	NHL	14	2	1	3	4	0	0	0	13	15.4	3				3	0	0	0	0	0	0	0	
1997-98	Houston Aeros	IHL	78	38	27	65	60										4	3	0	3	4				
1998-99	Ottawa	NHL	17	2	5	7	4	0	0	0	18	11.1	1	3	33.3	10:34									
	Houston Aeros	IHL	37	18	17	35	30										19	10	6	16	22				
99-2000	Phoenix	NHL	9	1	0	1	2	1	0	0	6	16.7	0	0	0.0	7:38									
	Houston Aeros	IHL	45	16	11	27	40										11	3	4	7	8				
2000-01	Ottawa	NHL	7	0	0	0	2	0	0	0	2	0.0	0	0	0.0	5:37									
	Grand Rapids	IHL	51	14	17	31	35										10	6	2	8	8				
2001-02	Munchen Barons	Germany	59	20	14	34	30										9	2	2	4	6				
2002-03	Dallas	NHL	6	0	3	3	2	0	0	0	5	0.0	1	0	0.0	9:13	6	0	0	0	2	0	0	0	6:33
	Utah Grizzlies	AHL	37	11	14	25	14																		
	NHL Totals		**194**	**42**	**44**	**86**	**72**	**25**	**0**	**0**	**276**	**15.2**		**3**	**33.3**	**8:48**	**9**	**0**	**0**	**0**	**2**	**0**	**0**	**0**	**6:33**

CCHA Second All-Star Team (1993) • CCHA First All-Star Team (1994) • CCHA Player of the Year (1994) • NCAA West First All-American Team (1994)

Claimed on waivers by **NY Rangers** from **Edmonton**, February 21, 1997. Signed as a free agent by **Ottawa**, July 2, 1998. Signed as a free agent by **Phoenix**, July 20, 1999. Signed as a free agent by **Ottawa**, August 2, 2000. Signed as a free agent by **Dallas**, July 30, 2002.

OLIWA, Krzysztof

(oh-LEE-vuh, KHRIH-stahf) **CGY.**

Left wing. Shoots left. 6'5", 245 lbs. Born, Tychy, Poland, April 12, 1973. New Jersey's 4th choice, 65th overall, in 1993 Entry Draft.

			Regular Season														Playoffs								
Season	Club	League	GP	G	A	Pts	PIM	PP	SH	GW	S	%	+/-	TF	F%	Min	GP	G	A	Pts	PIM	PP	SH	GW	Min
1990-91	GKS Katowski Jr.	Pol.-Jr.	5	4	4	8	10																		
1991-92	GKS Tychy	Poland	10	3	7	10	6																		
1992-93	Welland Cougars	OJHL-B	30	13	21	34	127																		
1993-94	Albany River Rats	AHL	33	2	4	6	151																		
	Raleigh IceCaps	ECHL	15	0	2	2	65										9	0	0	0	35				
1994-95	Albany River Rats	AHL	20	1	1	2	77																		
	Saint John Flames	AHL	14	1	4	5	79																		
	Raleigh IceCaps	ECHL	5	0	2	2	32																		
	Detroit Vipers	IHL	4	0	1	1	24																		
1995-96	Albany River Rats	AHL	51	5	11	16	217																		
	Raleigh IceCaps	ECHL	9	1	0	1	53																		
1996-97	New Jersey	NHL	1	0	0	0	5	0	0	0	0	0.0	–1												
	Albany River Rats	AHL	60	13	14	27	322										15	7	1	8	49				
1997-98	New Jersey	NHL	73	2	3	5	295	0	0	2	53	3.8	3				6	0	0	0	23	0	0	0	
1998-99	New Jersey	NHL	64	5	7	12	240	0	0	1	59	8.5	4	1	0.0	7:02	1	0	0	0	2	0	0	0	2:35
99-2000 ♦	New Jersey	NHL	69	6	10	16	184	1	0	2	61	9.8	–2	3	66.7	6:45									
2000-01	Columbus	NHL	10	0	2	2	34	0	0	0	5	0.0	1	0	0.0	5:17									
	Pittsburgh	NHL	26	1	2	3	131	0	0	0	17	5.9	–4	1	100.0	4:58	5	0	0	0	16	0	0	0	2:14
2001-02	Pittsburgh	NHL	57	0	2	2	150	0	0	0	31	0.0	–5	0	0.0	5:35									
2002-03	NY Rangers	NHL	9	0	0	0	51	0	0	0	3	0.0	1	1	0.0	3:45									
	Hartford	AHL	15	0	1	1	30																		
	Boston	NHL	33	0	0	0	110	0	0	0	11	0.0	–4	1	0.0	3:58									
	NHL Totals		**342**	**14**	**26**	**40**	**1200**	**1**	**0**	**5**	**240**	**5.8**		**7**	**42.9**	**5:54**	**12**	**0**	**0**	**0**	**41**	**0**	**0**	**0**	**2:18**

• Born Krzystof Graboski

Traded to **Columbus** by **New Jersey** with future considerations (Deron Quint, June 23, 2000) for Columbus' 3rd round choice (Brandon Nolan) in 2001 Entry Draft and future considerations (Turner Stevenson, June 23, 2000), June 12, 2000. • Missed majority of 2000-2001 season recovering from arm injury suffered in game vs. Detroit, October 28, 2000. Traded to **Pittsburgh** by **Columbus** for San Jose's 3rd round choice (previously acquired, Columbus selected Aaron Johnson) in 2001 Entry Draft, January 14, 2001. Traded to **NY Rangers** by **Pittsburgh** for NY Rangers' 9th round choice (later traded to Tampa Bay – Tampa Bay selected Albert Vishnyakov) in 2003 Entry Draft, June 23, 2002. Traded to **Boston** by **NY Rangers** for Boston's 9th round choice in 2004 Entry Draft, January 6, 2003. Signed as a free agent by **Calgary**, July 30, 2003.

OLVESTAD, Jimmie

(OHL-vuh-stahd, JIHM-mee) **T.B.**

Left wing. Shoots left. 6'1", 189 lbs. Born, Stockholm, Sweden, February 16, 1980. Tampa Bay's 4th choice, 88th overall, in 1999 Entry Draft.

			Regular Season														Playoffs								
Season	Club	League	GP	G	A	Pts	PIM	PP	SH	GW	S	%	+/-	TF	F%	Min	GP	G	A	Pts	PIM	PP	SH	GW	Min
1996-97	Huddinge IK Jr.	Swede-Jr.	40	15	16	31																			
1997-98	Djurgarden Jr.	Swede-Jr.	10	3	3	6	10																		
	Huddinge IK	Swede-2	11	0	0	0	6																		
1998-99	Djurgarden	Sweden	44	2	4	6	18										4	0	0	0	8				
99-2000	Djurgarden	Sweden	50	6	3	9	34										13	1	2	3	12				
2000-01	Djurgarden	Sweden	50	7	8	15	79										16	7	2	9	14				
2001-02	Tampa Bay	NHL	74	3	11	14	24	0	0	0	99	3.0	3	14	28.6	13:60									
2002-03	Tampa Bay	NHL	37	0	3	3	16	0	0	0	30	0.0	–2	12	33.3	10:28									
	Springfield	AHL	6	0	1	1	13																		
	NHL Totals		**111**	**3**	**14**	**17**	**40**	**0**	**0**	**0**	**129**	**2.3**		**26**	**30.8**	**12:49**									

O'NEILL, Jeff

(OH-NEEL, JEHF) **CAR.**

Right wing. Shoots right. 6'1", 195 lbs. Born, Richmond Hill, Ont., February 23, 1976. Hartford's 1st choice, 5th overall, in 1994 Entry Draft.

			Regular Season														Playoffs								
Season	Club	League	GP	G	A	Pts	PIM	PP	SH	GW	S	%	+/-	TF	F%	Min	GP	G	A	Pts	PIM	PP	SH	GW	Min
1990-91	Richmond Hill	OMHA	78	56	134	190	....	....	....	....	....	....	....	....	....	....	....	....	....	....	....	....	....	....	....
1991-92	Thornhill	MTJHL	43	27	*53	80	48	....	....	....	....	....	....	....	....	....	....	....	....	....	....	....	....	....	....
1992-93	Guelph Storm	OHL	65	32	47	79	88	....	....	....	....	....	....	....	....	....	5	2	2	4	6	....	....	....	....
1993-94	Guelph Storm	OHL	66	45	81	126	95	....	....	....	....	....	....	....	....	....	9	2	11	13	31	....	....	....	....
1994-95	Guelph Storm	OHL	57	43	81	124	56	....	....	....	....	....	....	....	....	....	14	8	18	26	34	....	....	....	....
1995-96	**Hartford**	**NHL**	**65**	**8**	**19**	**27**	**40**	**1**	**0**	**1**	**65**	**12.3**	**–3**	....	....	....	....	....	....	....	....	....	....	....	....
1996-97	**Hartford**	**NHL**	**72**	**14**	**16**	**30**	**40**	**2**	**1**	**2**	**101**	**13.9**	**–24**	....	....	....	....	....	....	....	....	....	....	....	....
	Springfield	AHL	1	0	0	0	0	....	....	....	....	....	....	....	....	....	....	....	....	....	....	....	....	....	....
1997-98	**Carolina**	**NHL**	**74**	**19**	**20**	**39**	**67**	**7**	**1**	**4**	**114**	**16.7**	**–8**	....	....	....	....	....	....	....	....	....	....	....	....
1998-99	**Carolina**	**NHL**	**75**	**16**	**15**	**31**	**66**	**4**	**0**	**2**	**121**	**13.2**	**3**	**941**	**45.6**	**16:44**	**6**	**0**	**1**	**1**	**0**	**0**	**0**	**0**	**19:25**
99-2000	**Carolina**	**NHL**	**80**	**25**	**38**	**63**	**72**	**4**	**0**	**7**	**189**	**13.2**	**–9**	**1337**	**49.5**	**19:20**	....	....	....	....	....	....	....	....	....
2000-01	**Carolina**	**NHL**	**82**	**41**	**26**	**67**	**106**	**17**	**0**	**5**	**242**	**16.9**	**–18**	**726**	**50.0**	**18:20**	**6**	**1**	**2**	**3**	**10**	**0**	**0**	**1**	**17:33**
2001-02	**Carolina**	**NHL**	**76**	**31**	**33**	**64**	**63**	**11**	**0**	**6**	**272**	**11.4**	**–5**	**831**	**56.7**	**19:44**	**22**	**8**	**5**	**13**	**27**	**3**	**0**	**1**	**18:60**
2002-03	**Carolina**	**NHL**	**82**	**30**	**31**	**61**	**38**	**11**	**0**	**7**	**316**	**9.5**	**–21**	**986**	**54.1**	**19:09**	....	....	....	....	....	....	....	....	....
	NHL Totals		**606**	**184**	**198**	**382**	**492**	**57**	**2**	**34**	**1420**	**13.0**		**4821**	**51.0**	**18:40**	**34**	**9**	**8**	**17**	**37**	**3**	**0**	**2**	**18:49**

OHL All-Rookie Team (1993) • OHL Rookie of the Year (1993) • OHL First All-Star Team (1995)
Played in NHL All-Star Game (2003)
Transferred to **Carolina** after **Hartford** franchise relocated, June 25, 1997.

ORPIK, Brooks

(OHR-pihk, BRUKS) **PIT.**

Defense. Shoots left. 6'2", 224 lbs. Born, San Francisco, CA, September 26, 1980. Pittsburgh's 1st choice, 18th overall, in 2000 Entry Draft.

Season	Club	League	GP	G	A	Pts	PIM	PP	SH	GW	S	%	+/-	TF	F%	Min	GP	G	A	Pts	PIM	PP	SH	GW	Min
1996-97	Thayer Academy	Hi-School	20	4	1	5	....	....	....	....	....	....	....	....	....	....	....	....	....	....	....	....	....	....	....
1997-98	Thayer Academy	Hi-School	22	0	7	7	....	....	....	....	....	....	....	....	....	....	....	....	....	....	....	....	....	....	....
1998-99	Boston College	H-East	41	1	10	11	*96	....	....	....	....	....	....	....	....	....	....	....	....	....	....	....	....	....	....
99-2000	Boston College	H-East	38	1	9	10	102	....	....	....	....	....	....	....	....	....	....	....	....	....	....	....	....	....	....
2000-01	Boston College	H-East	40	0	20	20	*124	....	....	....	....	....	....	....	....	....	....	....	....	....	....	....	....	....	....
2001-02	Wilkes-Barre	AHL	78	2	18	20	99	....	....	....	....	....	....	....	....	....	....	....	....	....	....	....	....	....	....
2002-03	**Pittsburgh**	**NHL**	**6**	**0**	**0**	**0**	**2**	**0**	**0**	**0**	**2**	**0.0**	**–5**	**0**	**0.0**	**18:19**	....	....	....	....	....	....	....	....	....
	Wilkes-Barre	AHL	71	4	14	18	105	....	....	....	....	....	....	....	....	....	6	0	0	0	14	....	....	....	....
	NHL Totals		**6**	**0**	**0**	**0**	**2**	**0**	**0**	**0**	**2**	**0.0**		**0**	**0.0**	**18:19**	....	....	....	....	....	....	....	....	....

ORSZAGH, Vladimir

(OHR-sahg, VLAD-ih-meer) **NSH.**

Right wing. Shoots left. 5'11", 195 lbs. Born, Banska Bystrica, Czech., May 24, 1977. NY Islanders' 4th choice, 106th overall, in 1995 Entry Draft.

Season	Club	League	GP	G	A	Pts	PIM	PP	SH	GW	S	%	+/-	TF	F%	Min	GP	G	A	Pts	PIM	PP	SH	GW	Min
1993-94	B. Bystrica Jr.	Slovak-Jr.	38	38	27	65	....	....	....	....	....	....	....	....	....	....	....	....	....	....	....	....	....	....	....
1994-95	Banska Bystrica	Slovak-2	38	18	12	30	....	....	....	....	....	....	....	....	....	....	....	....	....	....	....	....	....	....	....
1995-96	Banska Bystrica	Slovakia	31	9	5	14	22	....	....	....	....	....	....	....	....	....	....	....	....	....	....	....	....	....	....
1996-97	Utah Grizzlies	IHL	68	12	15	27	30	....	....	....	....	....	....	....	....	....	3	0	1	1	4	....	....	....	....
1997-98	**NY Islanders**	**NHL**	**11**	**0**	**1**	**1**	**2**	**0**	**0**	**0**	**9**	**0.0**	**–3**	....	....	....	....	....	....	....	....	....	....	....	....
	Utah Grizzlies	IHL	62	13	10	23	60	....	....	....	....	....	....	....	....	....	4	2	0	2	0	....	....	....	....
1998-99	**NY Islanders**	**NHL**	**12**	**1**	**0**	**1**	**6**	**0**	**0**	**0**	**4**	**20.0**	**2**	**0**	**0.0**	**6:36**	....	....	....	....	....	....	....	....	....
	Lowell	AHL	68	18	23	41	57	....	....	....	....	....	....	....	....	....	3	2	2	4	2	....	....	....	....
99-2000	**NY Islanders**	**NHL**	**11**	**2**	**1**	**3**	**4**	**0**	**0**	**0**	**16**	**12.5**	**1**	**0**	**0.0**	**11:55**	....	....	....	....	....	....	....	....	....
	Lowell	AHL	55	8	12	20	22	....	....	....	....	....	....	....	....	....	7	3	3	6	2	....	....	....	....
2000-01	Djurgarden	Sweden	50	23	13	36	62	....	....	....	....	....	....	....	....	....	16	*7	3	10	20	....	....	....	....
2001-02	**Nashville**	**NHL**	**79**	**15**	**21**	**36**	**56**	**5**	**0**	**3**	**113**	**13.3**	**–15**	**10**	**20.0**	**16:04**	....	....	....	....	....	....	....	....	....
2002-03	**Nashville**	**NHL**	**78**	**16**	**16**	**32**	**38**	**3**	**0**	**3**	**152**	**10.5**	**–1**	**17**	**29.4**	**17:34**	....	....	....	....	....	....	....	....	....
	NHL Totals		**191**	**34**	**39**	**73**	**106**	**8**	**0**	**6**	**294**	**11.6**		**27**	**25.9**	**15:50**	....	....	....	....	....	....	....	....	....

Signed as a free agent by **Nashville**, May 30, 2001.

O'SULLIVAN, Chris

(oh-SUHL-lih-van, KRIHS)

Defense. Shoots left. 6'2", 205 lbs. Born, Dorchester, MA, May 15, 1974. Calgary's 2nd choice, 30th overall, in 1992 Entry Draft.

Season	Club	League	GP	G	A	Pts	PIM	PP	SH	GW	S	%	+/-	TF	F%	Min	GP	G	A	Pts	PIM	PP	SH	GW	Min
1991-92	Catholic Memorial	Hi-School	26	26	23	49	65	....	....	....	....	....	....	....	....	....	....	....	....	....	....	....	....	....	....
1992-93	Boston University	H-East	5	0	2	2	4	....	....	....	....	....	....	....	....	....	....	....	....	....	....	....	....	....	....
1993-94	Boston University	H-East	32	5	18	23	25	....	....	....	....	....	....	....	....	....	....	....	....	....	....	....	....	....	....
1994-95	Boston University	H-East	40	23	33	56	48	....	....	....	....	....	....	....	....	....	....	....	....	....	....	....	....	....	....
1995-96	Boston University	H-East	37	12	35	47	50	....	....	....	....	....	....	....	....	....	....	....	....	....	....	....	....	....	....
1996-97	**Calgary**	**NHL**	**27**	**2**	**8**	**10**	**2**	**1**	**0**	**1**	**41**	**4.9**	**0**	....	....	....	....	....	....	....	....	....	....	....	....
	Saint John Flames	AHL	29	3	8	11	17	....	....	....	....	....	....	....	....	....	5	0	4	4	0	....	....	....	....
1997-98	**Calgary**	**NHL**	**12**	**0**	**2**	**2**	**10**	**0**	**0**	**0**	**12**	**0.0**	**4**	....	....	....	....	....	....	....	....	....	....	....	....
	Saint John Flames	AHL	32	4	10	14	2	....	....	....	....	....	....	....	....	....	21	2	17	19	18	....	....	....	....
1998-99	**Calgary**	**NHL**	**10**	**0**	**1**	**1**	**2**	**0**	**0**	**0**	**10**	**0.0**	**–1**	**1**	**0.0**	**9:07**	....	....	....	....	....	....	....	....	....
	Saint John Flames	AHL	41	7	29	36	24	....	....	....	....	....	....	....	....	....	....	....	....	....	....	....	....	....	....
	Hartford	AHL	10	1	4	5	0	....	....	....	....	....	....	....	....	....	7	1	3	4	11	....	....	....	....
99-2000	**Vancouver**	**NHL**	**11**	**0**	**5**	**5**	**2**	**0**	**0**	**0**	**16**	**0.0**	**2**	**0**	**0.0**	**17:47**	....	....	....	....	....	....	....	....	....
	Syracuse Crunch	AHL	59	18	47	65	24	....	....	....	....	....	....	....	....	....	4	0	1	1	0	....	....	....	....
2000-01	Cincinnati	AHL	60	9	40	49	31	....	....	....	....	....	....	....	....	....	4	0	3	3	0	....	....	....	....
2001-02	Kloten Flyers	Swiss	39	7	16	23	34	....	....	....	....	....	....	....	....	....	6	1	2	3	12	....	....	....	....
2002-03	**Anaheim**	**NHL**	**2**	**0**	**1**	**1**	**0**	**0**	**0**	**0**	**3**	**0.0**	**0**	**0**	**0.0**	**12:46**	....	....	....	....	....	....	....	....	....
	Cincinnati	AHL	27	2	13	15	8	....	....	....	....	....	....	....	....	....	....	....	....	....	....	....	....	....	....
	NHL Totals		**62**	**2**	**17**	**19**	**16**	**1**	**0**	**1**	**82**	**2.4**		**1**	**0.0**	**13:35**	....	....	....	....	....	....	....	....	....

Hockey East First All-Star Team (1995) • NCAA East Second All-American Team (1995) • NCAA Championship All-Tournament Team (1995) • NCAA Championship Tournament MVP (1995)

• Missed majority of 1992-93 season recovering from neck injury suffered in game vs. Boston College (H-East), November 11, 1992. Traded to **NY Rangers** by **Calgary** for Lee Sorochan, March 23, 1999. Signed as a free agent by **Vancouver**, August 20, 1999. Signed as a free agent by **Anaheim**, July 20, 2000. Signed as a free agent by **Kloten** (Swiss), June 22, 2001. Signed as a free agent by **Anaheim**, July 22, 2002. • Missed majority of 2002-03 season recovering from neck injury suffered in game vs. Saint John (AHL), December 21, 2002.

OTT, Steve

(AWT, STEEV) **DAL.**

Center. Shoots left. 6', 160 lbs. Born, Summerside, P.E.I., August 19, 1982. Dallas' 1st choice, 25th overall, in 2000 Entry Draft.

Season	Club	League	GP	G	A	Pts	PIM	PP	SH	GW	S	%	+/-	TF	F%	Min	GP	G	A	Pts	PIM	PP	SH	GW	Min
1998-99	Leamington Flyers	OJHL-B	48	14	30	44	110	....	....	....	....	....	....	....	....	....	....	....	....	....	....	....	....	....	....
99-2000	Windsor Spitfires	OHL	66	23	39	62	131	....	....	....	....	....	....	....	....	....	12	3	5	8	21	....	....	....	....
2000-01	Windsor Spitfires	OHL	55	50	37	87	164	....	....	....	....	....	....	....	....	....	9	3	8	11	27	....	....	....	....
2001-02	Windsor Spitfires	OHL	53	43	45	88	178	....	....	....	....	....	....	....	....	....	14	6	10	16	49	....	....	....	....
2002-03	**Dallas**	**NHL**	**26**	**3**	**4**	**7**	**31**	**0**	**0**	**0**	**25**	**12.0**	**6**	**4**	**50.0**	**8:46**	**1**	**0**	**0**	**0**	**0**	**0**	**0**	**0**	**6:57**
	Utah Grizzlies	AHL	40	9	11	20	98	....	....	....	....	....	....	....	....	....	....	....	....	....	....	....	....	....	....
	NHL Totals		**26**	**3**	**4**	**7**	**31**	**0**	**0**	**0**	**25**	**12.0**		**4**	**50.0**	**8:46**	**1**	**0**	**0**	**0**	**0**	**0**	**0**	**0**	**6:57**

OHL Second All-Star Team (2002)

OZOLINSH, Sandis

(OH-zoh-LIHNCH, SAN-dihz) **ANA.**

Defense. Shoots left. 6'3", 215 lbs. Born, Riga, Latvia, August 3, 1972. San Jose's 3rd choice, 30th overall, in 1991 Entry Draft.

Season	Club	League	GP	G	A	Pts	PIM	PP	SH	GW	S	%	+/-	TF	F%	Min	GP	G	A	Pts	PIM	PP	SH	GW	Min
1990-91	Dynamo Riga	USSR	44	0	3	3	51	....	....	....	....	....	....	....	....	....	....	....	....	....	....	....	....	....	....
1991-92	Riga Stars	CIS	30	6	0	6	42	....	....	....	....	....	....	....	....	....	....	....	....	....	....	....	....	....	....
	Kansas City	IHL	34	6	9	15	20	....	....	....	....	....	....	....	....	....	15	2	5	7	22	....	....	....	....
1992-93	**San Jose**	**NHL**	**37**	**7**	**16**	**23**	**40**	**2**	**0**	**0**	**83**	**8.4**	**–9**	....	....	....	....	....	....	....	....	....	....	....	....
1993-94	**San Jose**	**NHL**	**81**	**26**	**38**	**64**	**24**	**4**	**0**	**3**	**157**	**16.6**	**16**	....	....	....	**14**	**0**	**10**	**10**	**8**	**0**	**0**	**0**	....
1994-95	**San Jose**	**NHL**	**48**	**9**	**16**	**25**	**30**	**3**	**1**	**2**	**83**	**10.8**	**–6**	....	....	....	**11**	**3**	**2**	**5**	**6**	**1**	**0**	**0**	....
1995-96	San Francisco	IHL	2	1	0	1	0	....	....	....	....	....	....	....	....	....	....	....	....	....	....	....	....	....	....
	San Jose	**NHL**	**7**	**1**	**3**	**4**	**4**	**1**	**0**	**0**	**21**	**4.8**	**2**	....	....	....	....	....	....	....	....	....	....	....	....
	◆ Colorado	**NHL**	**66**	**13**	**37**	**50**	**50**	**7**	**1**	**1**	**145**	**9.0**	**0**	....	....	....	**22**	**5**	**14**	**19**	**16**	**2**	**0**	**1**	....
1996-97	**Colorado**	**NHL**	**80**	**23**	**45**	**68**	**88**	**13**	**0**	**4**	**232**	**9.9**	**4**	....	....	....	**17**	**4**	**13**	**17**	**24**	**2**	**0**	**1**	....
1997-98	**Colorado**	**NHL**	**66**	**13**	**38**	**51**	**65**	**9**	**0**	**2**	**135**	**9.6**	**–12**	....	....	....	**7**	**0**	**7**	**7**	**14**	**0**	**0**	**0**	....
1998-99	**Colorado**	**NHL**	**39**	**7**	**25**	**32**	**22**	**4**	**0**	**3**	**81**	**8.6**	**10**	**0**	**0.0**	**22:06**	**19**	**4**	**8**	**12**	**22**	**3**	**0**	**1**	**22:24**

			Regular Season														Playoffs								
Season	Club	League	GP	G	A	Pts	PIM	PP	SH	GW	S	%	+/-	TF	F%	Min	GP	G	A	Pts	PIM	PP	SH	GW	Min
99-2000	**Colorado**	**NHL**	**82**	**16**	**36**	**52**	**46**	**6**	**0**	**1**	**210**	**7.6**	**17**	**0**	**0.0**	**22:41**	**17**	**5**	**5**	**10**	**20**	**3**	**0**	**1**	**18:35**
2000-01	**Carolina**	**NHL**	**72**	**12**	**32**	**44**	**71**	**4**	**2**	**2**	**145**	**8.3**	**–25**	**0**	**0.0**	**22:12**	**6**	**0**	**2**	**2**	**5**	**0**	**0**	**0**	**19:04**
2001-02	**Carolina**	**NHL**	**46**	**4**	**19**	**23**	**34**	**1**	**0**	**0**	**71**	**5.6**	**–4**	**0**	**0.0**	**19:30**	....	....	....	....	....	....	....	....	....
	Florida	**NHL**	**37**	**10**	**19**	**29**	**24**	**2**	**0**	**1**	**101**	**9.9**	**–3**	**0**	**0.0**	**30:30**	....	....	....	....	....	....	....	....	....
	Latvia	Olympics	1	0	4	4	0	....	....	....	....	....	....	....	....	....	....	....	....	....	....	....	....	....	....
2002-03	**Florida**	**NHL**	**51**	**7**	**19**	**26**	**40**	**5**	**0**	**2**	**83**	**8.4**	**–16**	**0**	**0.0**	**28:23**	....	....	....	....	....	....	....	....	....
	Anaheim	**NHL**	**31**	**5**	**13**	**18**	**16**	**1**	**0**	**1**	**54**	**9.3**	**10**	**0**	**0.0**	**22:08**	**21**	**2**	**6**	**8**	**10**	**0**	**0**	**1**	**23:37**
	NHL Totals		**743**	**153**	**356**	**509**	**554**	**62**	**4**	**22**	**1601**	**9.6**		**0**	**0.0**	**23:41**	**134**	**23**	**67**	**90**	**125**	**11**	**0**	**5**	**21:28**

NHL First All-Star Team (1997)

Played in NHL All-Star Game (1994, 1997, 1998, 2000, 2001, 2002, 2003)

• Missed majority of 1992-93 season recovering from knee injury suffered in game vs. Philadelphia, December 30, 1992. Traded to **Colorado** by **San Jose** for Owen Nolan, October 26, 1995. Traded to **Carolina** by **Colorado** with Columbus' 2nd round choice (previously acquired, Carolina selected Tomas Kurka) in 2000 Entry Draft for Nolan Pratt, Carolina's 1st (Vaclav Nedorost) and 2nd (Jared Aulin) round choices in 2000 Entry Draft and Philadelphia's 2nd round choice (previously acquired, Colorado selected Agris Saviels) in 2000 Entry Draft, June 24, 2000. Traded to **Florida** by **Carolina** with Byron Ritchie for Bret Hedican, Kevyn Adams, Tomas Malec and a conditional 2nd round choice in 2003 Entry Draft, January 16, 2002. Traded to **Anaheim** by **Florida** with Lance Ward for Pavel Trnka, Matt Cullen and Anaheim's 4th round choice (James Pemberton) in 2003 Entry Draft, January 30, 2003.

PAHLSSON, Samuel

(PAWL-suhn, SAM-ew-l) **ANA.**

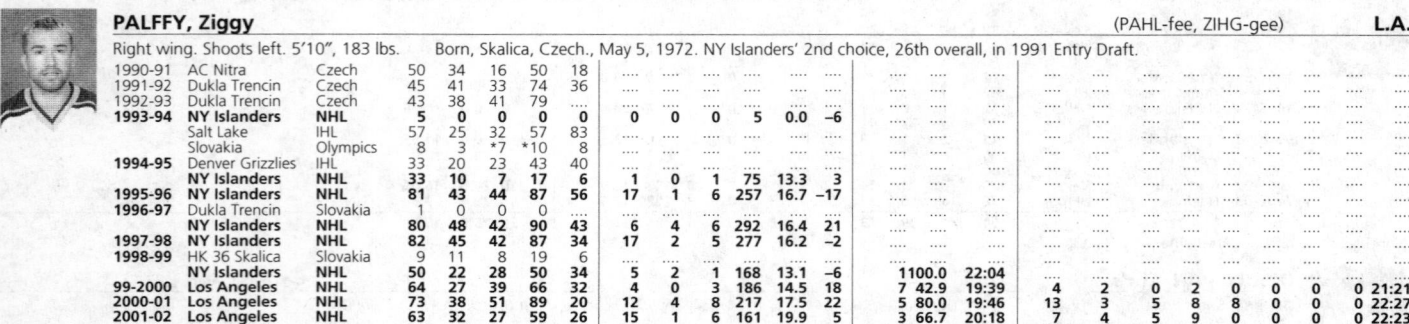

Center. Shoots left. 5'11", 212 lbs. Born, Ornskoldsvik, Sweden, December 17, 1977. Colorado's 10th choice, 176th overall, in 1996 Entry Draft.

Season	Club	League	GP	G	A	Pts	PIM	PP	SH	GW	S	%	+/-	TF	F%	Min	GP	G	A	Pts	PIM	PP	SH	GW	Min
1992-93	Ange IK	Swede-4	9	0	0	0	0	....	....	....	....	....	....	....	....	....	....	....	....	....	....	....	....	....	....
1993-94	Ange IK	Swede-4	STATISTICS NOT AVAILABLE																						
1994-95	MoDo Jr.	Swede-Jr.	30	10	11	21	26	....	....	....	....	....	....	....	....	....	....	....	....	....	....	....	....	....	....
	MoDo	Sweden	1	0	0	0	0	....	....	....	....	....	....	....	....	....	....	....	....	....	....	....	....	....	....
1995-96	MoDo Jr.	Swede-Jr.	5	2	6	8	2	....	....	....	....	....	....	....	....	....	....	....	....	....	....	....	....	....	....
	MoDo	Sweden	36	1	3	4	8	....	....	....	....	....	....	....	....	....	4	0	0	0	0	....	....	....	....
1996-97	MoDo	Sweden	49	8	9	17	83	....	....	....	....	....	....	....	....	....	....	....	....	....	....	....	....	....	....
1997-98	MoDo	Sweden	23	6	11	17	24	....	....	....	....	....	....	....	....	....	9	3	0	3	6	....	....	....	....
1998-99	MoDo	Sweden	50	17	17	34	44	....	....	....	....	....	....	....	....	....	13	3	3	6	10	....	....	....	....
99-2000	MoDo	Sweden	47	16	11	27	67	....	....	....	....	....	....	....	....	....	13	3	3	6	8	....	....	....	....
	MoDo	EuroHL	4	1	0	1	0	....	....	....	....	....	....	....	....	....	3	1	1	2	2	....	....	....	....
2000-01	**Boston**	**NHL**	**17**	**1**	**1**	**2**	**6**	**0**	**0**	**0**	**13**	**7.7**	**–5**	**239**	**40.2**	**14:19**	....	....	....	....	....	....	....	....	....
	Anaheim	**NHL**	**59**	**3**	**4**	**7**	**14**	**1**	**1**	**1**	**46**	**6.5**	**–9**	**867**	**45.1**	**14:14**	....	....	....	....	....	....	....	....	....
2001-02	**Anaheim**	**NHL**	**80**	**6**	**14**	**20**	**26**	**1**	**1**	**0**	**99**	**6.1**	**–16**	**1201**	**49.8**	**16:24**	....	....	....	....	....	....	....	....	....
2002-03	**Anaheim**	**NHL**	**34**	**4**	**11**	**15**	**18**	**0**	**1**	**2**	**28**	**14.3**	**10**	**118**	**52.5**	**13:20**	**21**	**2**	**4**	**6**	**12**	**0**	**0**	**0**	**16:41**
	Cincinnati	AHL	13	1	7	8	24	....	....	....	....	....	....	....	....	....	....	....	....	....	....	....	....	....	....
	NHL Totals		**190**	**14**	**30**	**44**	**64**	**2**	**3**	**3**	**186**	**7.5**		**2425**	**47.3**	**14:59**	**21**	**2**	**4**	**6**	**12**	**0**	**0**	**0**	**16:41**

Traded to **Boston** by **Colorado** with Brian Rolston, Martin Grenier and New Jersey's 1st round choice (previously acquired, Boston selected Martin Samuelsson) in 2000 Entry Draft for Raymond Bourque and Dave Andreychuk, March 6, 2000. Traded to **Anaheim** by **Boston** for Patrick Traverse and Andrei Nazarov, November 18, 2000.

PALFFY, Ziggy

(PAHL-fee, ZIHG-gee) **L.A.**

Right wing. Shoots left. 5'10", 183 lbs. Born, Skalica, Czech., May 5, 1972. NY Islanders' 2nd choice, 26th overall, in 1991 Entry Draft.

Season	Club	League	GP	G	A	Pts	PIM	PP	SH	GW	S	%	+/-	TF	F%	Min	GP	G	A	Pts	PIM	PP	SH	GW	Min
1990-91	AC Nitra	Czech	50	34	16	50	18	....	....	....	....	....	....	....	....	....	....	....	....	....	....	....	....	....	....
1991-92	Dukla Trencin	Czech	45	41	33	74	36	....	....	....	....	....	....	....	....	....	....	....	....	....	....	....	....	....	....
1992-93	Dukla Trencin	Czech	43	38	41	79	....	....	....	....	....	....	....	....	....	....	....	....	....	....	....	....	....	....	....
1993-94	**NY Islanders**	**NHL**	**5**	**0**	**0**	**0**	**0**	**0**	**0**	**0**	**5**	**0.0**	**–6**	....	....	....	....	....	....	....	....	....	....	....	....
	Salt Lake	IHL	57	25	32	57	83	....	....	....	....	....	....	....	....	....	....	....	....	....	....	....	....	....	....
	Slovakia	Olympics	8	3	*7	*10	8	....	....	....	....	....	....	....	....	....	....	....	....	....	....	....	....	....	....
1994-95	Denver Grizzlies	IHL	33	20	23	43	40	....	....	....	....	....	....	....	....	....	....	....	....	....	....	....	....	....	....
	NY Islanders	**NHL**	**33**	**10**	**7**	**17**	**6**	**1**	**0**	**1**	**75**	**13.3**	**3**	....	....	....	....	....	....	....	....	....	....	....	....
1995-96	**NY Islanders**	**NHL**	**81**	**43**	**44**	**87**	**56**	**17**	**1**	**6**	**257**	**16.7**	**–17**	....	....	....	....	....	....	....	....	....	....	....	....
1996-97	Dukla Trencin	Slovakia	1	0	0	0	....	....	....	....	....	....	....	....	....	....	....	....	....	....	....	....	....	....	....
	NY Islanders	**NHL**	**80**	**48**	**42**	**90**	**43**	**6**	**4**	**6**	**292**	**16.4**	**21**	....	....	....	....	....	....	....	....	....	....	....	....
1997-98	**NY Islanders**	**NHL**	**82**	**45**	**42**	**87**	**34**	**17**	**2**	**5**	**277**	**16.2**	**–2**	....	....	....	....	....	....	....	....	....	....	....	....
1998-99	HK 36 Skalica	Slovakia	9	11	8	19	6	....	....	....	....	....	....	....	....	....	....	....	....	....	....	....	....	....	....
	NY Islanders	**NHL**	**50**	**22**	**28**	**50**	**34**	**5**	**2**	**1**	**168**	**13.1**	**–6**	**1**	**100.0**	**22:04**	....	....	....	....	....	....	....	....	....
99-2000	**Los Angeles**	**NHL**	**64**	**27**	**39**	**66**	**32**	**4**	**0**	**3**	**186**	**14.5**	**18**	**7**	**42.9**	**19:39**	**4**	**2**	**0**	**2**	**0**	**0**	**0**	**0**	**21:21**
2000-01	**Los Angeles**	**NHL**	**73**	**38**	**51**	**89**	**20**	**12**	**4**	**8**	**217**	**17.5**	**22**	**5**	**80.0**	**19:46**	**13**	**3**	**5**	**8**	**8**	**0**	**0**	**0**	**22:27**
2001-02	**Los Angeles**	**NHL**	**63**	**32**	**27**	**59**	**26**	**15**	**1**	**6**	**161**	**19.9**	**5**	**3**	**66.7**	**20:18**	**7**	**4**	**5**	**9**	**0**	**0**	**0**	**0**	**22:23**
	Slovakia	Olympics	1	0	0	0	0	....	....	....	....	....	....	....	....	....	....	....	....	....	....	....	....	....	....
2002-03	**Los Angeles**	**NHL**	**76**	**37**	**48**	**85**	**47**	**10**	**2**	**5**	**277**	**13.4**	**22**	**10**	**30.0**	**22:27**	....	....	....	....	....	....	....	....	....
	NHL Totals		**607**	**302**	**328**	**630**	**298**	**87**	**16**	**41**	**1915**	**15.8**		**26**	**50.0**	**20:49**	**24**	**9**	**10**	**19**	**8**	**0**	**0**	**0**	**22:15**

Played in NHL All-Star Game (1998, 2001, 2002)

Traded to **Los Angeles** by **NY Islanders** with Brian Smolinski, Marcel Cousineau and New Jersey's 4th round choice (previously acquired, Los Angeles selected Daniel Johansson) in 1999 Entry Draft for Olli Jokinen, Josh Green, Mathieu Biron and Los Angeles' 1st round choice (Taylor Pyatt) in 1999 Entry Draft, June 20, 1999.

PANDOLFO, Jay

(pan-DAHL-foh, JAY) **N.J.**

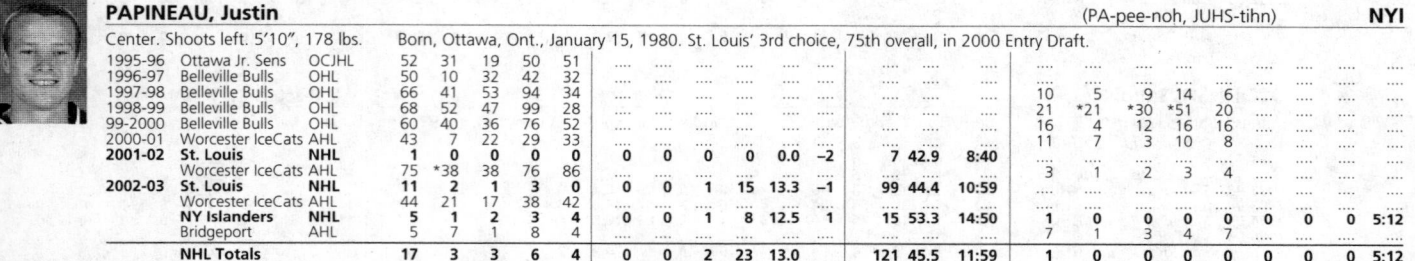

Left wing. Shoots left. 6'1", 190 lbs. Born, Winchester, MA, December 27, 1974. New Jersey's 2nd choice, 32nd overall, in 1993 Entry Draft.

Season	Club	League	GP	G	A	Pts	PIM	PP	SH	GW	S	%	+/-	TF	F%	Min	GP	G	A	Pts	PIM	PP	SH	GW	Min
1989-90	Burlington Prep	Hi-School	23	33	30	63	18	....	....	....	....	....	....	....	....	....	....	....	....	....	....	....	....	....	....
1990-91	Burlington Prep	Hi-School	20	19	27	46	10	....	....	....	....	....	....	....	....	....	....	....	....	....	....	....	....	....	....
1991-92	Burlington Prep	Hi-School	20	35	34	69	14	....	....	....	....	....	....	....	....	....	....	....	....	....	....	....	....	....	....
1992-93	Boston University	H-East	37	16	22	38	16	....	....	....	....	....	....	....	....	....	....	....	....	....	....	....	....	....	....
1993-94	Boston University	H-East	37	17	25	42	27	....	....	....	....	....	....	....	....	....	....	....	....	....	....	....	....	....	....
1994-95	Boston University	H-East	20	7	13	20	6	....	....	....	....	....	....	....	....	....	....	....	....	....	....	....	....	....	....
1995-96	Boston University	H-East	39	*38	29	67	6	....	....	....	....	....	....	....	....	....	....	....	....	....	....	....	....	....	....
	Albany River Rats	AHL	5	3	1	4	0	....	....	....	....	....	....	....	....	....	3	0	0	0	0	....	....	....	....
1996-97	**New Jersey**	**NHL**	**46**	**6**	**8**	**14**	**6**	**0**	**0**	**1**	**61**	**9.8**	**–1**	....	....	....	**6**	**0**	**1**	**1**	**0**	**0**	**0**	**0**	....
	Albany River Rats	AHL	12	3	9	12	0	....	....	....	....	....	....	....	....	....	....	....	....	....	....	....	....	....	....
1997-98	**New Jersey**	**NHL**	**23**	**1**	**3**	**4**	**4**	**0**	**0**	**0**	**23**	**4.3**	**–4**	....	....	....	**3**	**0**	**2**	**2**	**0**	**0**	**0**	**0**	....
	Albany River Rats	AHL	51	18	19	37	24	....	....	....	....	....	....	....	....	....	....	....	....	....	....	....	....	....	....
1998-99	**New Jersey**	**NHL**	**70**	**14**	**13**	**27**	**10**	**1**	**1**	**4**	**100**	**14.0**	**3**	**10**	**40.0**	**15:13**	**7**	**1**	**0**	**1**	**0**	**0**	**0**	**0**	**13:19**
99-2000♦	**New Jersey**	**NHL**	**71**	**7**	**8**	**15**	**4**	**0**	**0**	**0**	**86**	**8.1**	**0**	**19**	**47.4**	**13:25**	**23**	**0**	**5**	**5**	**0**	**0**	**0**	**0**	**15:35**
2000-01	**New Jersey**	**NHL**	**63**	**4**	**12**	**16**	**16**	**0**	**0**	**0**	**57**	**7.0**	**3**	**15**	**53.3**	**14:05**	**25**	**1**	**4**	**5**	**4**	**0**	**0**	**0**	**12:38**
2001-02	**New Jersey**	**NHL**	**65**	**4**	**10**	**14**	**15**	**0**	**1**	**0**	**72**	**5.6**	**12**	**12**	**41.7**	**13:59**	**6**	**0**	**0**	**0**	**0**	**0**	**0**	**0**	**16:11**
2002-03♦	**New Jersey**	**NHL**	**68**	**6**	**11**	**17**	**23**	**0**	**1**	**4**	**92**	**6.5**	**12**	**13**	**23.1**	**16:08**	**24**	**6**	**6**	**12**	**2**	**0**	**0**	**1**	**16:34**
	NHL Totals		**406**	**42**	**65**	**107**	**78**	**1**	**3**	**9**	**491**	**8.6**		**69**	**42.0**	**14:34**	**94**	**8**	**18**	**26**	**6**	**0**	**0**	**1**	**14:51**

Hockey East First All-Star Team (1996) • Hockey East Player of the Year (1996) • NCAA East First All-American Team (1996)

PAPINEAU, Justin

(PA-pee-noh, JUHS-tihn) **NYI**

Center. Shoots left. 5'10", 178 lbs. Born, Ottawa, Ont., January 15, 1980. St. Louis' 3rd choice, 75th overall, in 2000 Entry Draft.

Season	Club	League	GP	G	A	Pts	PIM	PP	SH	GW	S	%	+/-	TF	F%	Min	GP	G	A	Pts	PIM	PP	SH	GW	Min
1995-96	Ottawa Jr. Sens	OCJHL	52	31	19	50	51																		
1996-97	Belleville Bulls	OHL	50	10	32	42	32	....	....	....	....	....	....	....	....	....	....	....	....	....	....	....	....	....	....
1997-98	Belleville Bulls	OHL	66	41	53	94	34	....	....	....	....	....	....	....	....	....	10	5	9	14	6	....	....	....	....
1998-99	Belleville Bulls	OHL	68	52	47	99	28	....	....	....	....	....	....	....	....	....	21	*21	*30	*51	20	....	....	....	....
99-2000	Belleville Bulls	OHL	60	40	36	76	52	....	....	....	....	....	....	....	....	....	16	4	12	16	16	....	....	....	....
2000-01	Worcester IceCats	AHL	43	7	22	29	33	....	....	....	....	....	....	....	....	....	11	7	3	10	8	....	....	....	....
2001-02	**St. Louis**	**NHL**	**1**	**0**	**0**	**0**	**0**	**0**	**0**	**0**	**0**	**0.0**	**–2**	**7**	**42.9**	**8:40**	....	....	....	....	....	....	....	....	....
	Worcester IceCats	AHL	75	*38	38	76	86	....	....	....	....	....	....	....	....	....	3	1	2	3	4	....	....	....	....
2002-03	**St. Louis**	**NHL**	**11**	**2**	**1**	**3**	**0**	**0**	**0**	**1**	**15**	**13.3**	**–1**	**99**	**44.4**	**10:59**	....	....	....	....	....	....	....	....	....
	Worcester IceCats	AHL	44	21	17	38	42	....	....	....	....	....	....	....	....	....	....	....	....	....	....	....	....	....	....
	NY Islanders	**NHL**	**5**	**1**	**2**	**3**	**4**	**0**	**0**	**1**	**8**	**12.5**	**1**	**15**	**53.3**	**14:50**	**1**	**0**	**0**	**0**	**0**	**0**	**0**	**0**	**5:12**
	Bridgeport	AHL	5	7	1	8	4	....	....	....	....	....	....	....	....	....	7	1	3	4	7	....	....	....	....
	NHL Totals		**17**	**3**	**3**	**6**	**4**	**0**	**0**	**2**	**23**	**13.0**		**121**	**45.5**	**11:59**	**1**	**0**	**0**	**0**	**0**	**0**	**0**	**0**	**5:12**

• Re-entered NHL Entry Draft. Originally Los Angeles' 2nd choice, 46th overall, in 1998 Entry Draft.

Traded to **NY Islanders** by **St. Louis** with St. Louis' 2nd round choice (Jeremy Colliton) in 2003 Entry Draft for Chris Osgood and NY Islanders' 3rd round choice (Konstantin Barulin) in 2003 Entry Draft, March 11, 2003.

Season	Club	League	Regular Season GP	G	A	Pts	PIM	PP	SH	GW	S	%	+/-	TF	F%	Min	Playoffs GP	G	A	Pts	PIM	PP	SH	GW	Min

PARK, Richard

(PAHRK, RIH-chahrd) **MIN.**

Right wing. Shoots right. 5'11", 190 lbs. Born, Seoul, South Korea, May 27, 1976. Pittsburgh's 2nd choice, 50th overall, in 1994 Entry Draft.

Season	Club	League	GP	G	A	Pts	PIM	PP	SH	GW	S	%	+/-	TF	F%	Min	GP	G	A	Pts	PIM	PP	SH	GW	Min
1991-92	Tor. Young Nats	MTHL	76	49	58	107	91																		
1992-93	Belleville Bulls	OHL	66	23	38	61	38										5	0	0	0	14				
1993-94	Belleville Bulls	OHL	59	27	49	76	70										12	3	5	8	18				
1994-95	Belleville Bulls	OHL	45	28	51	79	35										16	9	18	27	12				
	Pittsburgh	**NHL**	**1**	**0**	**1**	**1**	**2**	**0**	**0**	**0**	**4**	**0.0**	**1**				**3**	**0**	**0**	**0**	**2**	**0**	**0**	**0**	
1995-96	Belleville Bulls	OHL	6	7	6	13	2										14	18	12	30	10				
	Pittsburgh	**NHL**	**56**	**4**	**6**	**10**	**36**	**0**	**1**	**1**	**62**	**6.5**	**3**				**1**	**0**	**0**	**0**	**0**	**0**	**0**	**0**	
1996-97	**Pittsburgh**	**NHL**	**1**	**0**	**0**	**0**	**0**	**0**	**0**	**0**	**1**	**0.0**	**–1**												
	Cleveland	IHL	50	12	15	27	30																		
	Anaheim	**NHL**	**11**	**1**	**1**	**2**	**10**	**0**	**0**	**0**	**9**	**11.1**	**0**				**11**	**0**	**1**	**1**	**2**	**0**	**0**	**0**	
1997-98	**Anaheim**	**NHL**	**15**	**0**	**2**	**2**	**8**	**0**	**0**	**0**	**14**	**0.0**	**–3**												
	Cincinnati	AHL	56	17	26	43	36																		
1998-99	**Philadelphia**	**NHL**	**7**	**0**	**0**	**0**	**0**	**0**	**0**	**0**	**5**	**0.0**	**–1**	**15**	**53.3**	**9:21**									
	Philadelphia	AHL	75	41	42	83	33										16	9	6	15	4				
99-2000	Utah Grizzlies	IHL	82	28	32	60	36										5	1	0	1	0				
2000-01	Cleveland	IHL	75	27	21	48	29										4	0	2	2	4				
2001-02	**Minnesota**	**NHL**	**63**	**10**	**15**	**25**	**10**	**2**	**1**	**2**	**115**	**8.7**	**–1**	**79**	**41.8**	**16:28**									
	Houston Aeros	AHL	13	4	10	14	6																		
2002-03	**Minnesota**	**NHL**	**81**	**14**	**10**	**24**	**16**	**2**	**2**	**3**	**149**	**9.4**	**–3**	**178**	**48.9**	**16:36**	**18**	**3**	**3**	**6**	**4**	**0**	**0**	**1**	**17:03**
	NHL Totals		**235**	**29**	**35**	**64**	**82**	**4**	**4**	**6**	**359**	**8.1**		**272**	**47.1**	**16:13**	**33**	**3**	**4**	**7**	**8**	**0**	**0**	**1**	**17:03**

OHL All-Rookie Team (1993) • AHL Second All-Star Team (1999)

Traded to **Anaheim** by **Pittsburgh** for Roman Oksiuta, March 18, 1997. Signed as a free agent by **Philadelphia**, August 24, 1998. Signed as a free agent by **Utah** (IHL), September 22, 1999. Signed as a free agent by **Minnesota**, June 6, 2000.

PARKER, Scott

(PAR-kuhr, SKAWT) **S.J.**

Right wing. Shoots right. 6'5", 230 lbs. Born, Hanford, CA, January 29, 1978. Colorado's 4th choice, 20th overall, in 1998 Entry Draft.

Season	Club	League	GP	G	A	Pts	PIM	PP	SH	GW	S	%	+/-	TF	F%	Min	GP	G	A	Pts	PIM	PP	SH	GW	Min
1993-94	Alaska Arctic Ice	AAHL	34	8	12	20	86																		
1994-95	Spokane Braves	KIJHL	43	7	21	28	128																		
1995-96	Kelowna Rockets	WHL	64	3	4	7	159										6	0	0	0	12				
1996-97	Kelowna Rockets	WHL	68	18	8	26	*330										6	0	2	2	4				
1997-98	Kelowna Rockets	WHL	71	30	22	52	243										7	6	0	6	23				
1998-99	**Colorado**	**NHL**	**27**	**0**	**0**	**0**	**71**	**0**	**0**	**0**	**3**	**0.0**	**–3**	**1**	**0.0**	**1:37**									
	Hershey Bears	AHL	32	4	3	7	143										4	0	0	0	6				
99-2000	Hershey Bears	AHL	68	12	7	19	206										11	1	1	2	56				
2000-01♦	**Colorado**	**NHL**	**69**	**2**	**3**	**5**	**155**	**0**	**0**	**1**	**35**	**5.7**	**–2**	**2**	**0.0**	**5:42**	**4**	**0**	**0**	**0**	**2**	**0**	**0**	**0**	**2:12**
2001-02	**Colorado**	**NHL**	**63**	**1**	**4**	**5**	**154**	**0**	**0**	**0**	**32**	**3.1**	**0**	**0**	**0.0**	**5:50**									
2002-03	**Colorado**	**NHL**	**43**	**1**	**3**	**4**	**82**	**0**	**0**	**0**	**20**	**5.0**	**6**	**0**	**0.0**	**6:15**	**1**	**0**	**0**	**0**	**2**	**0**	**0**	**0**	**1:44**
	NHL Totals		**202**	**4**	**10**	**14**	**462**	**0**	**0**	**1**	**90**	**4.4**		**3**	**0.0**	**5:19**	**5**	**0**	**0**	**0**	**4**	**0**	**0**	**0**	**2:06**

• Re-entered NHL Entry Draft. Originally New Jersey's 6th choice, 63rd overall, in 1996 Entry Draft.

Traded to **San Jose** by **Colorado** for Colorado's 5th round choice (previously acquired, Colorado selected Brad Richardson) in 2003 Entry Draft, June 21, 2003.

PARRISH, Mark

(PAIR-ihsh, MAHRK) **NYI**

Right wing. Shoots right. 5'11", 200 lbs. Born, Edina, MN, February 2, 1977. Colorado's 3rd choice, 79th overall, in 1996 Entry Draft.

Season	Club	League	GP	G	A	Pts	PIM	PP	SH	GW	S	%	+/-	TF	F%	Min	GP	G	A	Pts	PIM	PP	SH	GW	Min
1994-95	Jefferson Jaguars	Hi-School	27	40	20	60	42																		
1995-96	St. Cloud State	WCHA	39	15	13	28	30																		
1996-97	St. Cloud State	WCHA	35	*27	15	42	60																		
1997-98	Seattle	WHL	54	54	38	92	29										5	2	3	5	2				
	New Haven	AHL	1	1	0	1	2																		
1998-99	**Florida**	**NHL**	**73**	**24**	**13**	**37**	**25**	**5**	**0**	**5**	**129**	**18.6**	**–6**	**1**	**0.0**	**13:59**									
	New Haven	AHL	2	1	0	1	0																		
99-2000	**Florida**	**NHL**	**81**	**26**	**18**	**44**	**39**	**6**	**0**	**3**	**152**	**17.1**	**1**	**8**	**75.0**	**14:04**	**4**	**0**	**1**	**1**	**0**	**0**	**0**	**0**	**12:36**
2000-01	**NY Islanders**	**NHL**	**70**	**17**	**13**	**30**	**28**	**6**	**0**	**3**	**123**	**13.8**	**–27**	**3**	**33.3**	**15:27**									
2001-02	**NY Islanders**	**NHL**	**78**	**30**	**30**	**60**	**32**	**9**	**1**	**6**	**162**	**18.5**	**10**	**10**	**40.0**	**16:48**	**7**	**2**	**1**	**3**	**6**	**2**	**0**	**0**	**17:27**
2002-03	**NY Islanders**	**NHL**	**81**	**23**	**25**	**48**	**28**	**9**	**0**	**5**	**147**	**15.6**	**–11**	**9**	**44.4**	**16:12**	**5**	**1**	**0**	**1**	**4**	**1**	**0**	**0**	**16:02**
	NHL Totals		**383**	**120**	**99**	**219**	**152**	**35**	**1**	**22**	**713**	**16.8**		**31**	**48.4**	**15:19**	**16**	**3**	**2**	**5**	**10**	**3**	**0**	**0**	**15:48**

NCAA West Second All-American Team (1997) • WHL West First All-Star Team (1998)

Played in NHL All-Star Game (2002)

Rights traded to **Florida** by **Colorado** with Anaheim's 3rd round choice (previously acquired, Florida selected Lance Ward) in 1998 Entry Draft for Tom Fitzgerald, March 24, 1998. Traded to **NY Islanders** by **Florida** with Oleg Kvasha for Roberto Luongo and Olli Jokinen, June 24, 2000.

PARSSINEN, Timo

(pahr-SIH-nehn, TEE-moh)

Left wing. Shoots left. 5'10", 176 lbs. Born, Lohjan mlk., Finland, January 19, 1977. Anaheim's 4th choice, 102nd overall, in 2001 Entry Draft.

Season	Club	League	GP	G	A	Pts	PIM	PP	SH	GW	S	%	+/-	TF	F%	Min	GP	G	A	Pts	PIM	PP	SH	GW	Min
1994-95	TuTo Turku Jr.	Finn-Jr.	14	9	6	15	33																		
	TuTo Turku	Finland	1	1	0	1	0																		
1995-96	TuTo Turku Jr.	Finn-Jr.	14	18	15	33	12										11	12	6	18	36				
	TuTo Turku	Finland	7	0	0	0	4																		
1996-97	TuTo Turku	Finland-2	39	21	29	50	30																		
	TuTo Turku Jr.	Finn-Jr.															9	2	14	16	36				
1997-98	Hermes Kokkola	Finland-2	46	29	39	68	66										3	1	0	1	4				
1998-99	HPK Hameenlinna	Finland	46	15	24	39	46										8	2	3	5	8				
99-2000	HPK Hameenlinna	Finland	53	25	27	52	60										8	5	5	10	8				
2000-01	HPK Hameenlinna	Finland	54	18	31	49	48																		
2001-02	**Anaheim**	**NHL**	**17**	**0**	**3**	**3**	**2**	**0**	**0**	**0**	**16**	**0.0**	**0**	**1**	**100.0**	**11:44**									
	Cincinnati	AHL	49	14	24	38	22										3	0	2	2	0				
2002-03	HIFK Helsinki	Finland	55	16	31	47	41										4	2	0	2	0				
	NHL Totals		**17**	**0**	**3**	**3**	**2**	**0**	**0**	**0**	**16**	**0.0**		**1**	**100.0**	**11:44**									

PATRICK, James

(PAT-rihk, JAYMS) **BUF.**

Defense. Shoots right. 6'2", 202 lbs. Born, Winnipeg, Man., June 14, 1963. NY Rangers' 1st choice, 9th overall, in 1981 Entry Draft.

Season	Club	League	GP	G	A	Pts	PIM	PP	SH	GW	S	%	+/-	TF	F%	Min	GP	G	A	Pts	PIM	PP	SH	GW	Min
1980-81	Prince Albert	SJHL	59	21	61	82	162																		
1981-82	North Dakota	WCHA	42	5	24	29	26																		
1982-83	North Dakota	WCHA	36	12	36	48	29																		
1983-84	Team Canada	Nat-Tm	63	7	24	31	52																		
	Canada	Olympics	7	0	3	3	4																		
	NY Rangers	**NHL**	**12**	**1**	**7**	**8**	**2**	**0**	**0**	**0**	**15**	**6.7**	**6**				**5**	**0**	**3**	**3**	**2**	**0**	**0**	**0**	
1984-85	**NY Rangers**	**NHL**	**75**	**8**	**28**	**36**	**71**	**4**	**1**	**1**	**101**	**7.9**	**–17**				**3**	**0**	**0**	**0**	**4**	**0**	**0**	**0**	
1985-86	**NY Rangers**	**NHL**	**75**	**14**	**29**	**43**	**88**	**2**	**1**	**1**	**131**	**10.7**	**14**				**16**	**1**	**5**	**6**	**34**	**0**	**0**	**0**	
1986-87	**NY Rangers**	**NHL**	**78**	**10**	**45**	**55**	**62**	**5**	**0**	**0**	**143**	**7.0**	**13**				**6**	**1**	**2**	**3**	**2**	**1**	**0**	**1**	
1987-88	**NY Rangers**	**NHL**	**70**	**17**	**45**	**62**	**52**	**9**	**0**	**1**	**187**	**9.1**	**16**												
1988-89	**NY Rangers**	**NHL**	**68**	**11**	**36**	**47**	**41**	**6**	**0**	**2**	**147**	**7.5**	**3**				**4**	**0**	**1**	**1**	**2**	**0**	**0**	**0**	
1989-90	**NY Rangers**	**NHL**	**73**	**14**	**43**	**57**	**50**	**9**	**0**	**0**	**136**	**10.3**	**4**				**10**	**3**	**8**	**11**	**0**	**2**	**0**	**1**	
1990-91	**NY Rangers**	**NHL**	**74**	**10**	**49**	**59**	**58**	**6**	**0**	**2**	**138**	**7.2**	**–5**				**6**	**0**	**0**	**0**	**6**	**0**	**0**	**0**	
1991-92	**NY Rangers**	**NHL**	**80**	**14**	**57**	**71**	**54**	**6**	**0**	**1**	**148**	**9.5**	**34**				**13**	**0**	**7**	**7**	**12**	**0**	**0**	**0**	
1992-93	**NY Rangers**	**NHL**	**60**	**5**	**21**	**26**	**61**	**3**	**0**	**0**	**99**	**5.1**	**1**												
1993-94	**NY Rangers**	**NHL**	**6**	**0**	**3**	**3**	**2**	**0**	**0**	**0**	**6**	**0.0**	**1**												
	Hartford	**NHL**	**47**	**8**	**20**	**28**	**32**	**4**	**1**	**2**	**65**	**12.3**	**–12**												
	Calgary	**NHL**	**15**	**2**	**2**	**4**	**6**	**1**	**0**	**0**	**20**	**10.0**	**6**				**7**	**0**	**1**	**1**	**6**	**0**	**0**	**0**	
1994-95	**Calgary**	**NHL**	**43**	**0**	**10**	**10**	**14**	**0**	**0**	**0**	**43**	**0.0**	**–3**				**5**	**0**	**1**	**1**	**0**	**0**	**0**	**0**	
1995-96	**Calgary**	**NHL**	**80**	**3**	**32**	**35**	**30**	**1**	**0**	**0**	**116**	**2.6**	**3**				**4**	**0**	**0**	**0**	**2**	**0**	**0**	**0**	
1996-97	**Calgary**	**NHL**	**19**	**3**	**1**	**4**	**6**	**1**	**0**	**0**	**22**	**13.6**	**2**												
1997-98	**Calgary**	**NHL**	**60**	**6**	**11**	**17**	**26**	**1**	**0**	**1**	**57**	**10.5**	**–2**												
1998-99	**Buffalo**	**NHL**	**45**	**1**	**7**	**8**	**16**	**0**	**0**	**0**	**31**	**3.2**	**12**	**0**	**0.0**	**14:45**	**20**	**0**	**1**	**1**	**12**	**0**	**0**	**0**	**13:57**

			Regular Season														Playoffs								
Season	Club	League	GP	G	A	Pts	PIM	PP	SH	GW	S	%	+/-	TF	F%	Min	GP	G	A	Pts	PIM	PP	SH	GW	Min
99-2000	**Buffalo**	**NHL**	**66**	**5**	**8**	**13**	**22**	**0**	**0**	**3**	**40**	**12.5**	**8**	**0**	**0.0**	**15:59**	**5**	**0**	**1**	**1**	**2**	**0**	**0**	**0**	**15:23**
2000-01	**Buffalo**	**NHL**	**54**	**4**	**9**	**13**	**12**	**1**	**0**	**0**	**48**	**8.3**	**9**	**0**	**0.0**	**17:16**	**13**	**1**	**2**	**3**	**2**	**0**	**0**	**0**	**20:10**
2001-02	**Buffalo**	**NHL**	**56**	**5**	**8**	**13**	**16**	**1**	**0**	**0**	**45**	**11.1**	**3**	**0**	**0.0**	**16:27**									
2002-03	**Buffalo**	**NHL**	**69**	**4**	**12**	**16**	**26**	**2**	**0**	**1**	**63**	**6.3**	**–3**	**2**	**100.0**	**18:55**									
	NHL Totals		**1225**	**145**	**483**	**628**	**747**	**62**	**3**	**15**	**1801**	**8.1**		**2**	**100.0**	**16:49**	**117**	**6**	**32**	**38**	**86**	**3**	**0**	**2**	**16:16**

WCHA Second All-Star Team (1982) • WCHA Freshman of the Year (1982) • NCAA Chamionship All-Tournament Team (1982) • WCHA First All-Star Team (1983) • NCAA West All American Team (1983)

Traded to **Hartford** by **NY Rangers** with Darren Turcotte for Steve Larmer, Nick Kypreos, Barry Richter and Hartford's 6th round choice (Yuri Litvinov) in 1994 Entry Draft, November 2, 1993. Traded to **Calgary** by **Hartford** with Zarley Zalapski and Michael Nylander for Gary Suter, Paul Ranheim and Ted Drury, March 10, 1994. • Missed majority of 1996-97 season recovering from knee injury originally suffered in game vs. Pittsburgh, October 24, 1996. Signed as a free agent by **Buffalo**, October 7, 1998.

PAUL, Jeff

(PAWL, JEHF) **FLA.**

Defense. Shoots right. 6'3", 200 lbs. Born, London, Ont., March 1, 1978. Chicago's 2nd choice, 42nd overall, in 1996 Entry Draft.

1993-94	Woodstock Vets	OJHL-C	36	1	6	7	73																		
1994-95	Niagara Falls	OHL	57	3	10	13	64										6	0	2	2	0				
1995-96	Niagara Falls	OHL	48	1	7	8	81										10	0	4	4	37				
1996-97	Erie Otters	OHL	60	4	23	27	152										5	2	0	2	12				
1997-98	Erie Otters	OHL	48	3	17	20	108										7	0	2	2	13				
1998-99	Portland Pirates	AHL	6	0	0	0	4																		
	Indianapolis Ice	IHL	55	0	7	7	120										7	0	2	2	12				
99-2000	Cleveland	IHL	69	6	6	12	210										9	1	0	1	12				
2000-01	Norfolk Admirals	AHL	59	5	6	11	171										9	0	2	2	12				
2001-02	Hershey Bears	AHL	58	1	13	14	201										7	0	1	1	6				
2002-03	**Colorado**	**NHL**	**2**	**0**	**0**	**0**	**7**	**0**	**0**	**0**	**0**	**0.0**	**0**	**0**	**0.0**	**3:32**									
	Hershey Bears	AHL	50	2	3	5	123																		
	NHL Totals		**2**	**0**	**0**	**0**	**7**	**0**	**0**	**0**	**0**	**0.0**		**0**	**0.0**	**3:32**									

Signed as a free agent by **Colorado**, August 8, 2001. Signed as a free agent by **Florida**, August 19, 2003.

PAYER, Serge

(pie-YAY, SAIRZH) **FLA.**

Center. Shoots left. 6', 192 lbs. Born, Rockland, Ont., May 7, 1979.

1994-95	Cumberland Colts	ODMHA	42	37	46	83	55																		
1995-96	Kitchener Rangers	OHL	66	8	16	24	18										12	0	2	2	2				
1996-97	Kitchener Rangers	OHL	63	7	16	23	27										13	1	3	4	2				
1997-98	Kitchener Rangers	OHL	44	20	21	41	51										6	3	0	3	7				
1998-99	Kitchener Rangers	OHL	40	18	19	37	22																		
99-2000	Kitchener Rangers	OHL	44	10	26	36	53										5	0	3	3	6				
2000-01	**Florida**	**NHL**	**43**	**5**	**1**	**6**	**21**	**0**	**1**	**0**	**34**	**14.7**	**0**	**97**	**42.3**	**7:27**									
	Louisville Panthers	AHL	32	6	6	12	15																		
2001-02	Utah Grizzlies	AHL	20	6	2	8	9																		
2002-03	San Antonio	AHL	78	10	31	41	30										1	0	0	0	2				
	NHL Totals		**43**	**5**	**1**	**6**	**21**	**0**	**1**	**0**	**34**	**14.7**		**97**	**42.3**	**7:27**									

• Missed remainder of 1998-99 and majority of 1999-2000 seasons recovering from Guillian-Barre Syndrome, January 25, 1999. Signed as a free agent by **Florida**, September 30, 1997. • Missed majority of 2001-02 season recovering from back injury suffered in training camp, September, 2001.

PEAT, Stephen

(PEET, STEEV-vuhn) **WSH.**

Right wing. Shoots right. 6'3", 210 lbs. Born, Princeton, B.C., March 10, 1980. Anaheim's 2nd choice, 32nd overall, in 1998 Entry Draft.

1995-96	Langley Thunder	BCJHL	59	5	15	20	112																		
	Red Deer Rebels	WHL	1	0	0	0	0																		
1996-97	Red Deer Rebels	WHL	68	3	14	17	161										16	0	2	2	22				
1997-98	Red Deer Rebels	WHL	63	6	12	18	189										5	0	0	0	8				
1998-99	Red Deer Rebels	WHL	31	2	6	8	98																		
	Tri-City	WHL	5	0	0	0	19																		
99-2000	Tri-City	WHL	12	0	2	2	48																		
	Calgary Hitmen	WHL	23	0	8	8	100										13	0	1	1	33				
2000-01	Portland Pirates	AHL	6	0	0	0	16																		
2001-02	**Washington**	**NHL**	**38**	**2**	**2**	**4**	**85**	**0**	**0**	**0**	**11**	**18.2**	**–1**	**0**	**0.0**	**5:04**									
	Portland Pirates	AHL	17	2	2	4	57																		
2002-03	**Washington**	**NHL**	**27**	**1**	**0**	**1**	**57**	**0**	**0**	**0**	**7**	**14.3**	**–3**	**0**	**0.0**	**4:09**									
	Portland Pirates	AHL	18	0	0	0	52																		
	NHL Totals		**65**	**3**	**2**	**5**	**142**	**0**	**0**	**0**	**18**	**16.7**		**0**	**0.0**	**4:41**									

• Missed majority of 1999-2000 season recovering from injuries sustained off-ice, February 8, 2000. Rights traded to **Washington** by **Anaheim** for Washington's 4th round choice (later traded to Montreal – later traded to Pittsburgh – Pittsburgh selected Michel Ouellet) in 2000 Entry Draft, June 1, 2000. • Missed majority of 2000-01 recovering from groin injury suffered in training camp, September 29, 2000.

PECA, Michael

(PEH-kuh, MIGHK-uhl) **NYI**

Center. Shoots right. 5'11", 190 lbs. Born, Toronto, Ont., March 26, 1974. Vancouver's 2nd choice, 40th overall, in 1992 Entry Draft.

1989-90	Tor. Red Wings	MTHL	39	42	53	95	40																		
1990-91	Sudbury Wolves	OHL	62	14	27	41	24										5	1	0	1	7				
1991-92	Sudbury Wolves	OHL	39	16	34	50	61																		
	Ottawa 67's	OHL	27	8	17	25	32										11	6	10	16	6				
1992-93	Ottawa 67's	OHL	55	38	64	102	80																		
	Hamilton	AHL	9	6	3	9	11																		
1993-94	Ottawa 67's	OHL	55	50	63	113	101										17	7	22	29	30				
	Vancouver	**NHL**	**4**	**0**	**0**	**0**	**2**	**0**	**0**	**0**	**5**	**0.0**	**–1**												
1994-95	Syracuse Crunch	AHL	35	10	24	34	75																		
	Vancouver	**NHL**	**33**	**6**	**6**	**12**	**30**	**2**	**0**	**1**	**46**	**13.0**	**–6**				**5**	**0**	**1**	**1**	**8**	**0**	**0**	**0**	
1995-96	**Buffalo**	**NHL**	**68**	**11**	**20**	**31**	**67**	**4**	**3**	**1**	**109**	**10.1**	**–1**												
1996-97	**Buffalo**	**NHL**	**79**	**20**	**29**	**49**	**80**	**5**	**6**	**4**	**137**	**14.6**	**26**				**10**	**0**	**2**	**2**	**8**	**0**	**0**	**0**	
1997-98	**Buffalo**	**NHL**	**61**	**18**	**22**	**40**	**57**	**6**	**5**	**1**	**132**	**13.6**	**12**				**13**	**3**	**2**	**5**	**8**	**0**	**0**	**1**	
1998-99	**Buffalo**	**NHL**	**82**	**27**	**29**	**56**	**81**	**10**	**0**	**8**	**199**	**13.6**	**7**	**1855**	**49.4**	**20:44**	**21**	**5**	**8**	**13**	**18**	**2**	**1**	**0**	**22:28**
99-2000	**Buffalo**	**NHL**	**73**	**20**	**21**	**41**	**67**	**2**	**0**	**3**	**144**	**13.9**	**6**	**1604**	**48.6**	**19:57**	**5**	**0**	**1**	**1**	**4**	**0**	**0**	**0**	**18:42**
2000-01	**Buffalo**	**NHL**	DID NOT PLAY																						
2001-02	**NY Islanders**	**NHL**	**80**	**25**	**35**	**60**	**62**	**3**	**6**	**5**	**168**	**14.9**	**19**	**1804**	**52.4**	**20:14**	**5**	**1**	**0**	**1**	**2**	**0**	**0**	**0**	**16:15**
	Canada	Olympics	6	0	2	2	2																		
2002-03	**NY Islanders**	**NHL**	**66**	**13**	**29**	**42**	**43**	**4**	**2**	**2**	**117**	**11.1**	**–4**	**1315**	**53.0**	**18:57**	**5**	**0**	**0**	**0**	**4**	**0**	**0**	**0**	**20:10**
	NHL Totals		**546**	**140**	**191**	**331**	**489**	**36**	**22**	**25**	**1057**	**13.2**		**6578**	**50.7**	**20:01**	**64**	**9**	**14**	**23**	**52**	**2**	**1**	**1**	**20:45**

Frank J. Selke Trophy (1997, 2002)

Traded to **Buffalo** by **Vancouver** with Mike Wilson and Vancouver's 1st round choice (Jay McKee) in 1995 Entry Draft for Alexander Mogilny and Buffalo's 5th round choice (Todd Norman) in 1995 Entry Draft, July 8, 1995. • Missed entire 2000-01 season after failing to come to contract terms with **Buffalo**. Rights traded to **NY Islanders** by **Buffalo** for Tim Connolly and Taylor Pyatt, June 24, 2001.

PEDERSON, Denis

(PEE-duhr-suhn, DEH-nihs)

Center/Right wing. Shoots right. 6'2", 205 lbs. Born, Prince Albert, Sask., September 10, 1975. New Jersey's 1st choice, 13th overall, in 1993 Entry Draft.

1990-91	Prince Albert	SMHL	30	25	17	42	84																		
1991-92	Prince Albert	SMHL	21	33	25	58	40																		
	Prince Albert	WHL	10	0	0	0	6										7	0	1	1	13				
1992-93	Prince Albert	WHL	72	33	40	73	134																		
1993-94	Prince Albert	WHL	71	53	45	98	157																		
1994-95	Prince Albert	WHL	63	30	38	68	122										15	11	14	25	14				
	Albany River Rats	AHL															3	0	0	0	2				
1995-96	**New Jersey**	**NHL**	**10**	**3**	**1**	**4**	**0**	**1**	**0**	**2**	**6**	**50.0**	**–1**												
	Albany River Rats	AHL	68	28	43	71	104										4	1	2	3	0				
1996-97	**New Jersey**	**NHL**	**70**	**12**	**20**	**32**	**62**	**3**	**0**	**3**	**106**	**11.3**	**7**				**9**	**0**	**0**	**0**	**2**	**0**	**0**	**0**	
	Albany River Rats	AHL	3	1	3	4	7																		
1997-98	**New Jersey**	**NHL**	**80**	**15**	**13**	**28**	**97**	**7**	**0**	**1**	**135**	**11.1**	**–6**				**6**	**1**	**1**	**2**	**2**	**0**	**1**	**0**	
1998-99	**New Jersey**	**NHL**	**76**	**11**	**12**	**23**	**66**	**3**	**0**	**1**	**145**	**7.6**	**–10**	**540**	**42.8**	**15:19**	**3**	**0**	**1**	**1**	**0**	**0**	**0**	**0**	**9:36**

			Regular Season														Playoffs								
Season	Club	League	GP	G	A	Pts	PIM	PP	SH	GW	S	%	+/-	TF	F%	Min	GP	G	A	Pts	PIM	PP	SH	GW	Min
99-2000	**New Jersey**	**NHL**	**35**	**3**	**3**	**6**	**16**	**0**	**0**	**0**	**41**	**7.3**	**-7**	**125**	**48.8**	**10:42**									
	Vancouver	**NHL**	**12**	**3**	**2**	**5**	**2**	**0**	**0**	**1**	**15**	**20.0**	**1**	**70**	**45.7**	**12:41**									
2000-01	**Vancouver**	**NHL**	**61**	**4**	**8**	**12**	**65**	**0**	**1**	**3**	**70**	**5.7**	**0**	**351**	**42.7**	**11:42**	**4**	**0**	**1**	**1**	**4**	**0**	**0**	**0**	**15:53**
2001-02	**Vancouver**	**NHL**	**29**	**1**	**5**	**6**	**31**	**0**	**0**	**0**	**24**	**4.2**	**-2**	**142**	**47.2**	**8:18**									
	Phoenix	**NHL**	**19**	**1**	**1**	**2**	**20**	**0**	**0**	**0**	**18**	**5.6**	**-2**	**202**	**49.0**	**10:32**	**5**	**0**	**2**	**2**	**0**	**0**	**0**	**0**	**10:36**
2002-03	**Nashville**	**NHL**	**43**	**4**	**6**	**10**	**39**	**0**	**0**	**0**	**64**	**6.3**	**2**	**440**	**50.2**	**12:48**									
	NHL Totals		**435**	**57**	**71**	**128**	**398**	**14**	**1**	**11**	**624**	**9.1**		**1870**	**46.0**	**12:21**	**27**	**1**	**5**	**6**	**8**	**0**	**1**	**0**	**12:07**

WHL East Second All-Star Team (1994)

Traded to **Vancouver** by **New Jersey** with Brendan Morrison for Alexander Mogilny, March 14, 2000. Traded to **Phoenix** by **Vancouver** with Drake Berehowsky for Todd Warriner, Trevor Letowski, Tyler Bouck and Phoenix's 3rd round choice (later traded back to Phoenix – Phoenix selected Dimitri Pestunov) in 2003 Entry Draft, December 28, 2001. Signed as a free agent by **Nashville**, July 24, 2002.

PELLERIN, Scott

(PEHL-ih-rihn, SKAWT)

Left wing. Shoots left. 5'11", 190 lbs. Born, Shediac, N.B., January 9, 1970. New Jersey's 4th choice, 47th overall, in 1989 Entry Draft.

1985-86	Moncton Flyers	NBAHA	45	65	34	99	34																		
1986-87	Notre Dame	SMHL	72	62	68	130	98																		
1987-88	Notre Dame	SJHL	57	37	49	86	139																		
1988-89	U. of Maine	H-East	45	29	33	62	92																		
1989-90	U. of Maine	H-East	42	22	34	56	68																		
1990-91	U. of Maine	H-East	43	23	25	48	60																		
1991-92	U. of Maine	H-East	37	*32	25	57	54																		
	Utica Devils	AHL															3	1	0	1	0				
1992-93	**New Jersey**	**NHL**	**45**	**10**	**11**	**21**	**41**	**1**	**2**	**0**	**60**	**16.7**	**-1**												
	Utica Devils	AHL	27	15	18	33	33										2	0	1	1	0				
1993-94	**New Jersey**	**NHL**	**1**	**0**	**0**	**0**	**2**	**0**	**0**	**0**	**0**	**0.0**	**0**												
	Albany River Rats	AHL	73	28	46	74	84										5	2	1	3	11				
1994-95	Albany River Rats	AHL	74	23	33	56	95										14	6	4	10	8				
1995-96	**New Jersey**	**NHL**	**6**	**2**	**1**	**3**	**0**	**0**	**0**	**0**	**9**	**22.2**	**1**												
	Albany River Rats	AHL	75	35	47	82	142										4	0	3	3	10				
1996-97	**St. Louis**	**NHL**	**54**	**8**	**10**	**18**	**35**	**0**	**2**	**2**	**76**	**10.5**	**12**				**6**	**0**	**0**	**0**	**6**	**0**	**0**	**0**	
	Worcester IceCats	AHL	24	10	16	26	37																		
1997-98	**St. Louis**	**NHL**	**80**	**8**	**21**	**29**	**62**	**1**	**1**	**0**	**96**	**8.3**	**14**				**10**	**0**	**2**	**2**	**10**	**0**	**0**	**0**	
1998-99	**St. Louis**	**NHL**	**80**	**20**	**21**	**41**	**42**	**0**	**5**	**4**	**138**	**14.5**	**1**	**6**	**66.7**	**17:18**	**8**	**1**	**0**	**1**	**4**	**0**	**0**	**0**	**13:50**
99-2000	**St. Louis**	**NHL**	**80**	**8**	**15**	**23**	**48**	**0**	**2**	**2**	**120**	**6.7**	**9**	**6**	**16.7**	**14:47**	**7**	**0**	**0**	**0**	**2**	**0**	**0**	**0**	**14:55**
2000-01	**Minnesota**	**NHL**	**58**	**11**	**28**	**39**	**45**	**2**	**2**	**2**	**117**	**9.4**	**6**	**47**	**31.9**	**18:40**									
	Carolina	**NHL**	**19**	**0**	**5**	**5**	**6**	**0**	**0**	**0**	**21**	**0.0**	**-4**	**52**	**44.2**	**14:14**	**6**	**0**	**0**	**0**	**4**	**0**	**0**	**0**	**11:10**
2001-02	**Boston**	**NHL**	**35**	**1**	**5**	**6**	**6**	**0**	**0**	**0**	**41**	**2.4**	**-6**	**24**	**37.5**	**11:38**									
	Dallas	**NHL**	**33**	**3**	**5**	**8**	**15**	**0**	**0**	**0**	**22**	**13.6**	**-5**	**8**	**25.0**	**9:13**									
2002-03	**Dallas**	**NHL**	**20**	**1**	**3**	**4**	**8**	**1**	**0**	**0**	**20**	**5.0**	**-3**	**5**	**20.0**	**10:43**									
	Phoenix	**NHL**	**23**	**0**	**1**	**1**	**8**	**0**	**0**	**0**	**17**	**0.0**	**-5**	**12**	**58.3**	**9:32**									
	NHL Totals		**534**	**72**	**126**	**198**	**318**	**5**	**14**	**10**	**737**	**9.8**		**160**	**38.8**	**14:33**	**37**	**1**	**2**	**3**	**26**	**0**	**0**	**0**	**13:26**

Hockey East Rookie of the Year (co-winner - Rob Gaudreau (1989) • Hockey East First All-Star Team (1992) • Hockey East Player of the Year (1992) • NCAA East First All-American Team (1992) • Hobey Baker Memorial Award (Top U.S. Collegiate Player) (1992)

Signed as a free agent by **St. Louis**, July 10, 1996. Selected by **Minnesota** from **St. Louis** in Expansion Draft, June 23, 2000. Traded to **Carolina** by **Minnesota** for Askhat Rakhmatullin, Carolina's 3rd round choice (later traded to NY Rangers – NY Rangers selected Garth Murray) in 2001 Entry Draft and Carolina's compensatory 5th round choice (Armands Berzins) in 2002 Entry Draft, March 1, 2001. Signed as a free agent by **Boston**, July 26, 2001. Claimed on waivers by **Dallas** from **Boston**, January 12, 2002. Traded to **Phoenix** by **Dallas** with future considerations for Claude Lemieux, January 16, 2003.

PELTONEN, Ville

(PEHL-TOH-nen, VIHL-ee)

Left wing. Shoots left. 5'11", 188 lbs. Born, Vantaa, Finland, May 24, 1973. San Jose's 4th choice, 58th overall, in 1993 Entry Draft.

1990-91	HIFK Helsinki Jr.	Finn-Jr.	36	21	16	37	16										7	2	3	5	10				
1991-92	HIFK Helsinki Jr.	Finn-Jr.	37	28	23	51	28										4	0	2	2	0				
	HIFK Helsinki	Finland	6	0	0	0	0																		
1992-93	HIFK Helsinki Jr.	Finn-Jr.	2	4	2	6	4																		
	HIFK Helsinki	Finland	46	13	24	37	16										4	0	2	2	2				
1993-94	HIFK Helsinki	Finland	43	16	22	38	14										3	0	0	0	2				
	Finland	Olympics	8	4	3	7	0																		
1994-95	HIFK Helsinki	Finland	45	20	16	36	16										3	0	0	0	0				
1995-96	**San Jose**	**NHL**	**31**	**2**	**11**	**13**	**14**	**0**	**0**	**0**	**58**	**3.4**	**-7**												
	Kansas City	IHL	29	5	13	18	8																		
1996-97	**San Jose**	**NHL**	**28**	**2**	**3**	**5**	**0**	**1**	**0**	**0**	**35**	**5.7**	**-8**												
	Kentucky	AHL	40	22	30	52	21																		
1997-98	Vastra Frolunda	Sweden	45	22	29	*51	44										7	4	2	6	0				
	Finland	Olympics	6	2	1	3	6																		
1998-99	**Nashville**	**NHL**	**14**	**5**	**5**	**10**	**2**	**1**	**0**	**0**	**31**	**16.1**	**1**	**0**	**0.0**	**15:54**									
99-2000	**Nashville**	**NHL**	**79**	**6**	**22**	**28**	**22**	**2**	**0**	**2**	**125**	**4.8**	**-1**	**1**	**100.0**	**14:41**									
2000-01	**Nashville**	**NHL**	**23**	**3**	**1**	**4**	**2**	**0**	**0**	**0**	**38**	**7.9**	**-7**	**2**	**0.0**	**11:40**									
	Milwaukee	IHL	53	27	33	60	26										5	2	1	3	6				
2001-02	Jokerit Helsinki	Finland	30	11	18	29	8																		
2002-03	Jokerit Helsinki	Finland	49	23	19	42	14										10	4	6	10	0				
	NHL Totals		**175**	**18**	**42**	**60**	**40**	**4**	**0**	**2**	**287**	**6.3**		**3**	**33.3**	**14:14**									

IHL Second All-Star Team (2001)

Traded to **Nashville** by **San Jose** for Nashville's 5th round choice (later traded to Phoenix – Phoenix selected Josh Blackburn) in 1998 Entry Draft, June 26, 1998. • Missed majority of 1998-99 season recovering from shoulder surgery, December 10, 1998. Signed as a free agent by **Jokerit Helsinki** (Finland), April 26, 2001.

PELUSO, Mike

(puh-LOO-soh, MIGHK) **PHI.**

Right wing. Shoots right. 6'1", 208 lbs. Born, Bismarck, ND, September 2, 1974. Calgary's 12th choice, 253rd overall, in 1994 Entry Draft.

1993-94	Omaha Lancers	USHL	48	36	29	65	77																		
1994-95	U. Minn-Duluth	WCHA	38	11	23	34	38																		
1995-96	U. Minn-Duluth	WCHA	38	25	19	44	64																		
1996-97	U. Minn-Duluth	WCHA	37	20	20	40	53																		
1997-98	U. Minn-Duluth	WCHA	40	24	21	45	100																		
1998-99	Portland Pirates	AHL	26	7	6	13	6																		
99-2000	Portland Pirates	AHL	71	25	29	54	86										4	2	0	2	0				
2000-01	Portland Pirates	AHL	19	12	10	22	17																		
	Worcester IceCats	AHL	44	17	23	40	22										11	3	3	6	4				
2001-02	**Chicago**	**NHL**	**37**	**4**	**2**	**6**	**19**	**0**	**0**	**1**	**45**	**8.9**	**-3**	**1**	**0.0**	**9:17**									
	Norfolk Admirals	AHL	29	18	9	27	4										4	1	0	1	0				
2002-03	Norfolk Admirals	AHL	74	24	31	55	35										9	1	2	3	4				
	NHL Totals		**37**	**4**	**2**	**6**	**19**	**0**	**0**	**1**	**45**	**8.9**		**1**	**0.0**	**9:17**									

WCHA Second All-Star Team (1997)

Signed as a free agent by **Washington**, October 9, 1998. Traded to **St. Louis** by **Washington** for Derek Bekar, November 29, 2000. Signed as a free agent by **Chicago**, August 1, 2001. Signed as a free agent by **Philadelphia**, July 24, 2003.

PERREAULT, Yanic

(puh-ROH, YAH-nihk) **MTL.**

Center. Shoots left. 5'11", 185 lbs. Born, Sherbrooke, Que., April 4, 1971. Toronto's 1st choice, 47th overall, in 1991 Entry Draft.

1987-88	L'est Cantonniers	QAAA	42	*70	57	*127	14										8	12	10	22	6				
1988-89	Trois-Rivieres	QMJHL	70	53	55	108	48																		
1989-90	Trois-Rivieres	QMJHL	63	51	63	114	75										7	6	5	11	19				
1990-91	Trois-Rivieres	QMJHL	67	*87	98	*185	103										6	4	7	11	6				
1991-92	St. John's	AHL	62	38	38	76	19										16	7	8	15	4				
1992-93	St. John's	AHL	79	49	46	95	56										9	4	5	9	2				
1993-94	**Toronto**	**NHL**	**13**	**3**	**3**	**6**	**0**	**2**	**0**	**0**	**24**	**12.5**	**1**												
	St. John's	AHL	62	45	60	105	38										11	*12	6	18	14				
1994-95	Phoenix	IHL	68	51	48	99	52																		
	Los Angeles	**NHL**	**26**	**2**	**5**	**7**	**20**	**0**	**0**	**1**	**43**	**4.7**	**3**												

			Regular Season														Playoffs								
Season	Club	League	GP	G	A	Pts	PIM	PP	SH	GW	S	%	+/-	TF	F%	Min	GP	G	A	Pts	PIM	PP	SH	GW	Min
1995-96	**Los Angeles**	**NHL**	**78**	**25**	**24**	**49**	**16**	**8**	**3**	**7**	**175**	**14.3**	**–11**	....	....	....	....	....	....	....	....	....	....	....	....
1996-97	**Los Angeles**	**NHL**	**41**	**11**	**14**	**25**	**20**	**1**	**1**	**0**	**98**	**11.2**	**0**	....	....	....	....	....	....	....	....	....	....	....	....
1997-98	**Los Angeles**	**NHL**	**79**	**28**	**20**	**48**	**32**	**3**	**2**	**3**	**206**	**13.6**	**6**	....	....	....	**4**	**1**	**2**	**3**	**6**	**1**	**0**	**0**	....
1998-99	**Los Angeles**	**NHL**	**64**	**10**	**17**	**27**	**30**	**2**	**2**	**1**	**113**	**8.8**	**–3**	**1024**	**56.5**	**15:24**	....	....	....	....	....	....	....	....	....
	Toronto	**NHL**	**12**	**7**	**8**	**15**	**12**	**2**	**1**	**2**	**28**	**25.0**	**10**	**164**	**62.8**	**13:20**	**17**	**3**	**6**	**9**	**6**	**0**	**0**	**2**	**15:55**
99-2000	**Toronto**	**NHL**	**58**	**18**	**27**	**45**	**22**	**5**	**0**	**4**	**114**	**15.8**	**3**	**987**	**61.8**	**15:18**	**1**	**0**	**1**	**1**	**0**	**0**	**0**	**0**	**12:56**
2000-01	**Toronto**	**NHL**	**76**	**24**	**28**	**52**	**52**	**5**	**0**	**2**	**134**	**17.9**	**0**	**1055**	**62.7**	**14:01**	**11**	**2**	**3**	**5**	**4**	**1**	**0**	**1**	**12:20**
2001-02	**Montreal**	**NHL**	**82**	**27**	**29**	**56**	**40**	**6**	**0**	**7**	**156**	**17.3**	**–3**	**1485**	**61.3**	**16:47**	**11**	**3**	**5**	**8**	**0**	**2**	**0**	**1**	**13:05**
2002-03	**Montreal**	**NHL**	**73**	**24**	**22**	**46**	**30**	**7**	**0**	**4**	**145**	**16.6**	**–11**	**1156**	**62.9**	**16:05**	....	....	....	....	....	....	....	....	....
	NHL Totals		**602**	**179**	**197**	**376**	**274**	**41**	**9**	**31**	**1236**	**14.5**		**5871**	**61.1**	**15:29**	**44**	**9**	**17**	**26**	**16**	**4**	**0**	**4**	**14:05**

QMJHL All-Rookie Team (1989) • QMJHL Offensive Rookie of the Year (1989) • Canadian Major Junior Rookie of the Year (1989) • QMJHL First All-Star Team (1991) • QMJHL MVP (1991)

Traded to **Los Angeles** by **Toronto** for Los Angeles' 4th round choice (later traded to Philadelphia – later traded to Los Angeles – Los Angeles selected Mikael Simons) in 1996 Entry Draft, July 11, 1994. Traded to **Toronto** by **Los Angeles** for Jason Podollan and Toronto's 3rd round choice (Cory Campbell) in 1999 Entry Draft, March 23, 1999. Signed as a free agent by **Montreal**, July 4, 2001.

PERROTT, Nathan

(PEHR-roht, NAY-than) **TOR.**

Right wing. Shoots right. 6', 225 lbs. Born, Owen Sound, Ont., December 8, 1976. New Jersey's 2nd choice, 44th overall, in 1995 Entry Draft.

Season	Club	League	GP	G	A	Pts	PIM	PP	SH	GW	S	%	+/-	TF	F%	Min	GP	G	A	Pts	PIM	PP	SH	GW	Min
1992-93	Walkerton	OJHL-C	25	6	13	19	45	....	....	....	....	....	....	....	....	....	....	....	....	....	....	....	....	....	....
1993-94	St. Mary's Lincolns	OJHL-B	41	11	26	37	249	....	....	....	....	....	....	....	....	....	....	....	....	....	....	....	....	....	....
1994-95	Oshawa Generals	OHL	63	18	28	46	233	....	....	....	....	....	....	....	....	....	2	1	1	2	9	....	....	....	....
1995-96	Oshawa Generals	OHL	59	30	32	62	158	....	....	....	....	....	....	....	....	....	5	2	3	5	8	....	....	....	....
	Albany River Rats	AHL	4	0	0	0	12	....	....	....	....	....	....	....	....	....	....	....	....	....	....	....	....	....	....
1996-97	Oshawa Generals	OHL	5	1	0	1	17	....	....	....	....	....	....	....	....	....	....	....	....	....	....	....	....	....	....
	Sault Ste. Marie	OHL	37	18	23	41	120	....	....	....	....	....	....	....	....	....	11	5	5	10	60	....	....	....	....
1997-98	Indianapolis Ice	IHL	31	4	3	7	76	....	....	....	....	....	....	....	....	....	....	....	....	....	....	....	....	....	....
	Jacksonville	ECHL	30	6	8	14	135	....	....	....	....	....	....	....	....	....	....	....	....	....	....	....	....	....	....
1998-99	Indianapolis Ice	IHL	72	14	11	25	307	....	....	....	....	....	....	....	....	....	7	3	1	4	45	....	....	....	....
99-2000	Cleveland	IHL	65	12	9	21	248	....	....	....	....	....	....	....	....	....	9	2	1	3	19	....	....	....	....
2000-01	Norfolk Admirals	AHL	73	11	17	28	268	....	....	....	....	....	....	....	....	....	9	2	0	2	18	....	....	....	....
2001-02	Norfolk Admirals	AHL	2	0	0	0	5	....	....	....	....	....	....	....	....	....	....	....	....	....	....	....	....	....	....
	Nashville	**NHL**	**22**	**1**	**2**	**3**	**74**	**0**	**0**	**1**	**7**	**14.3**	**–1**	**1**	**0.0**	**4:55**	....	....	....	....	....	....	....	....	....
	Milwaukee	AHL	56	6	10	16	190	....	....	....	....	....	....	....	....	....	....	....	....	....	....	....	....	....	....
2002-03	**Nashville**	**NHL**	**1**	**0**	**0**	**0**	**5**	**0**	**0**	**0**	**0**	**0.0**	**0**	**0**	**0.0**	**4:13**	....	....	....	....	....	....	....	....	....
	Milwaukee	AHL	27	1	2	3	106	....	....	....	....	....	....	....	....	....	....	....	....	....	....	....	....	....	....
	St. John's	AHL	36	7	8	15	97	....	....	....	....	....	....	....	....	....	....	....	....	....	....	....	....	....	....
	NHL Totals		**23**	**1**	**2**	**3**	**79**	**0**	**0**	**1**	**7**	**14.3**		**1**	**0.0**	**4:53**	....	....	....	....	....	....	....	....	....

Signed as a free agent by **Chicago**, August 27, 1997. Traded to **Nashville** by **Chicago** for future considerations, October 9, 2001. Traded to **Toronto** by **Nashville** for Bob Wren, Decleber 31, 2002.

PERSSON, Ricard

(PAIR-suhn, RIH-kahrd)

Defense. Shoots left. 6'1", 201 lbs. Born, Ostersund, Sweden, August 24, 1969. New Jersey's 2nd choice, 23rd overall, in 1987 Entry Draft.

Season	Club	League	GP	G	A	Pts	PIM	PP	SH	GW	S	%	+/-	TF	F%	Min	GP	G	A	Pts	PIM	PP	SH	GW	Min
1984-85	Ostersunds IK	Swede-2	13	0	3	3	6	....	....	....	....	....	....	....	....	....	....	....	....	....	....	....	....	....	....
1985-86	Ostersunds IK	Swede-2	24	2	2	4	16	....	....	....	....	....	....	....	....	....	....	....	....	....	....	....	....	....	....
1986-87	Ostersunds IK	Swede-2	31	10	11	21	28	....	....	....	....	....	....	....	....	....	....	....	....	....	....	....	....	....	....
1987-88	Leksands IF	Sweden	31	2	0	2	8	....	....	....	....	....	....	....	....	....	2	0	1	1	2	....	....	....	....
1988-89	Leksands IF	Sweden	33	2	4	6	28	....	....	....	....	....	....	....	....	....	9	0	1	1	6	....	....	....	....
1989-90	Leksands IF	Sweden	43	9	10	19	62	....	....	....	....	....	....	....	....	....	3	0	0	0	6	....	....	....	....
1990-91	Leksands IF	Sweden	37	6	9	15	42	....	....	....	....	....	....	....	....	....	....	....	....	....	....	....	....	....	....
1991-92	Leksands IF	Sweden	21	0	7	7	28	....	....	....	....	....	....	....	....	....	....	....	....	....	....	....	....	....	....
1992-93	Leksands IF	Sweden	36	7	15	22	63	....	....	....	....	....	....	....	....	....	2	0	2	2	0	....	....	....	....
1993-94	Malmo IF	Sweden	40	11	9	20	38	....	....	....	....	....	....	....	....	....	11	2	0	2	12	....	....	....	....
1994-95	Malmo IF	Sweden	31	3	13	16	38	....	....	....	....	....	....	....	....	....	9	0	2	2	8	....	....	....	....
	Albany River Rats	AHL	3	0	0	0	0	....	....	....	....	....	....	....	....	....	9	3	5	8	7	....	....	....	....
1995-96	**New Jersey**	**NHL**	**12**	**2**	**1**	**3**	**8**	**1**	**0**	**0**	**41**	**4.9**	**5**	....	....	....	....	....	....	....	....	....	....	....	....
	Albany River Rats	AHL	67	15	31	46	59	....	....	....	....	....	....	....	....	....	4	0	0	0	7	....	....	....	....
1996-97	**New Jersey**	**NHL**	**1**	**0**	**0**	**0**	**0**	**0**	**0**	**0**	**2**	**0.0**	**0**	....	....	....	....	....	....	....	....	....	....	....	....
	Albany River Rats	AHL	13	1	4	5	8	....	....	....	....	....	....	....	....	....	....	....	....	....	....	....	....	....	....
	St. Louis	**NHL**	**53**	**4**	**8**	**12**	**45**	**1**	**0**	**0**	**68**	**5.9**	**–2**	....	....	....	**6**	**0**	**0**	**0**	**27**	**0**	**0**	**0**	....
1997-98	**St. Louis**	**NHL**	**1**	**0**	**0**	**0**	**0**	**0**	**0**	**0**	**0**	**0.0**	**0**	....	....	....	....	....	....	....	....	....	....	....	....
	Worcester IceCats	AHL	32	2	16	18	58	....	....	....	....	....	....	....	....	....	10	3	7	10	24	....	....	....	....
1998-99	**St. Louis**	**NHL**	**54**	**1**	**12**	**13**	**94**	**0**	**0**	**0**	**52**	**1.9**	**4**	**1**	**100.0**	**19:58**	**13**	**0**	**3**	**3**	**17**	**0**	**0**	**0**	**22:13**
	Worcester IceCats	AHL	19	6	4	10	42	....	....	....	....	....	....	....	....	....	....	....	....	....	....	....	....	....	....
99-2000	**St. Louis**	**NHL**	**41**	**0**	**8**	**8**	**38**	**0**	**0**	**0**	**30**	**0.0**	**–2**	**0**	**0.0**	**12:24**	**3**	**1**	**0**	**1**	**0**	**0**	**0**	**0**	**11:17**
	Worcester IceCats	AHL	2	0	1	1	0	....	....	....	....	....	....	....	....	....	....	....	....	....	....	....	....	....	....
2000-01	**Ottawa**	**NHL**	**33**	**1**	**8**	**9**	**35**	**0**	**0**	**1**	**43**	**2.3**	**8**	**0**	**0.0**	**17:06**	**2**	**0**	**0**	**0**	**0**	**0**	**0**	**0**	**11:37**
2001-02	**Ottawa**	**NHL**	**34**	**2**	**7**	**9**	**42**	**0**	**0**	**0**	**35**	**5.7**	**3**	**0**	**0.0**	**14:34**	**2**	**0**	**0**	**0**	**15**	**0**	**0**	**0**	**6:59**
2002-03	Eisbaren Berlin	Germany	42	11	24	35	80	....	....	....	....	....	....	....	....	....	9	1	5	6	2	....	....	....	....
	NHL Totals		**229**	**10**	**44**	**54**	**262**	**2**	**0**	**1**	**271**	**3.7**		**1**	**100.0**	**16:20**	**26**	**1**	**3**	**4**	**59**	**0**	**0**	**0**	**17:59**

Traded to **St. Louis** by **New Jersey** with Mike Peluso for Ken Sutton and St. Louis' 2nd round choice (Brett Clouthier) in 1999 Entry Draft, November 26, 1996. Signed as a free agent by **Ottawa**, July 12, 2000. • Missed majority of 2000-01 season recovering from ankle injury suffered in game vs. Pittsburgh, October 25, 2001. • Spent majority of 2001-02 season on **Ottawa** practice roster. Signed as a free agent by **Eisbaren Berlin** (Germany), August 8, 2002.

PETERSEN, Toby

(PEE-tuhr-sohn, TOH-bee) **PIT.**

Center. Shoots left. 5'9", 197 lbs. Born, Minneapolis, MN, October 27, 1978. Pittsburgh's 9th choice, 244th overall, in 1998 Entry Draft.

Season	Club	League	GP	G	A	Pts	PIM	PP	SH	GW	S	%	+/-	TF	F%	Min	GP	G	A	Pts	PIM	PP	SH	GW	Min
1995-96	Jefferson Jaguars	Hi-School	25	29	30	59	....	....	....	....	....	....	....	....	....	....	....	....	....	....	....	....	....	....	....
1996-97	Colorado College	WCHA	40	17	21	38	18	....	....	....	....	....	....	....	....	....	....	....	....	....	....	....	....	....	....
1997-98	Colorado College	WCHA	40	16	17	33	34	....	....	....	....	....	....	....	....	....	....	....	....	....	....	....	....	....	....
1998-99	Colorado College	WCHA	21	12	12	24	2	....	....	....	....	....	....	....	....	....	....	....	....	....	....	....	....	....	....
99-2000	Colorado College	WCHA	37	14	19	33	8	....	....	....	....	....	....	....	....	....	....	....	....	....	....	....	....	....	....
2000-01	**Pittsburgh**	**NHL**	**12**	**2**	**6**	**8**	**4**	**0**	**0**	**1**	**25**	**8.0**	**3**	**39**	**35.9**	**13:22**	....	....	....	....	....	....	....	....	....
	Wilkes-Barre	AHL	73	26	41	67	22	....	....	....	....	....	....	....	....	....	21	7	6	13	4	....	....	....	....
2001-02	**Pittsburgh**	**NHL**	**79**	**8**	**10**	**18**	**4**	**1**	**1**	**0**	**116**	**6.9**	**–15**	**338**	**45.6**	**12:16**	....	....	....	....	....	....	....	....	....
2002-03	Wilkes-Barre	AHL	80	31	35	66	24	....	....	....	....	....	....	....	....	....	6	1	3	4	4	....	....	....	....
	NHL Totals		**91**	**10**	**16**	**26**	**8**	**1**	**1**	**1**	**141**	**7.1**		**377**	**44.6**	**12:25**	....	....	....	....	....	....	....	....	....

Minnesota High School All-State, All-Metro and All-Conference Player of the Year (1996) • WCHA All-Rookie Team (1997)

PETROV, Oleg

(PEH-trahf, OH-lehg)

Right wing. Shoots left. 5'9", 172 lbs. Born, Moscow, USSR, April 18, 1971. Montreal's 9th choice, 127th overall, in 1991 Entry Draft.

Season	Club	League	GP	G	A	Pts	PIM	PP	SH	GW	S	%	+/-	TF	F%	Min	GP	G	A	Pts	PIM	PP	SH	GW	Min
1989-90	CSKA Moscow	USSR	30	4	7	11	4	....	....	....	....	....	....	....	....	....	....	....	....	....	....	....	....	....	....
1990-91	CSKA Moscow	USSR	43	7	4	11	8	....	....	....	....	....	....	....	....	....	....	....	....	....	....	....	....	....	....
1991-92	CSKA Moscow	CIS	42	10	16	26	8	....	....	....	....	....	....	....	....	....	....	....	....	....	....	....	....	....	....
1992-93	**Montreal**	**NHL**	**9**	**2**	**1**	**3**	**10**	**0**	**0**	**1**	**20**	**10.0**	**2**	....	....	....	**1**	**0**	**0**	**0**	**0**	**0**	**0**	**0**	....
	Fredericton	AHL	55	26	29	55	36	....	....	....	....	....	....	....	....	....	5	4	1	5	0	....	....	....	....
1993-94	**Montreal**	**NHL**	**55**	**12**	**15**	**27**	**2**	**1**	**0**	**1**	**107**	**11.2**	**7**	....	....	....	**2**	**0**	**0**	**0**	**0**	**0**	**0**	**0**	....
	Fredericton	AHL	23	8	20	28	18	....	....	....	....	....	....	....	....	....	....	....	....	....	....	....	....	....	....
1994-95	**Montreal**	**NHL**	**12**	**2**	**3**	**5**	**4**	**0**	**0**	**0**	**26**	**7.7**	**–7**	....	....	....	....	....	....	....	....	....	....	....	....
	Fredericton	AHL	17	7	11	18	12	....	....	....	....	....	....	....	....	....	17	5	6	11	10	....	....	....	....
1995-96	**Montreal**	**NHL**	**36**	**4**	**7**	**11**	**23**	**0**	**0**	**2**	**44**	**9.1**	**–9**	....	....	....	**5**	**0**	**1**	**1**	**0**	**0**	**0**	**0**	....
	Fredericton	AHL	22	12	18	30	71	....	....	....	....	....	....	....	....	....	6	2	6	8	0	....	....	....	....
1996-97	HC Ambri-Piotta	Swiss	45	24	28	52	44	....	....	....	....	....	....	....	....	....	....	....	....	....	....	....	....	....	....
	HC Merano	Italy	12	5	12	17	4	....	....	....	....	....	....	....	....	....	....	....	....	....	....	....	....	....	....
1997-98	HC Ambri-Piotta	Swiss	40	30	*63	*93	60	....	....	....	....	....	....	....	....	....	14	11	11	22	40	....	....	....	....
1998-99	HC Ambri-Piotta	Swiss	45	35	*52	*87	52	....	....	....	....	....	....	....	....	....	15	9	11	*20	32	....	....	....	....
99-2000	**Montreal**	**NHL**	**44**	**2**	**24**	**26**	**8**	**1**	**0**	**0**	**96**	**2.1**	**10**	**9**	**33.3**	**15:51**	....	....	....	....	....	....	....	....	....
	Quebec Citadelles	AHL	16	7	7	14	4	....	....	....	....	....	....	....	....	....	....	....	....	....	....	....	....	....	....
2000-01	**Montreal**	**NHL**	**81**	**17**	**30**	**47**	**24**	**4**	**2**	**1**	**158**	**10.8**	**–11**	**8**	**25.0**	**18:33**	....	....	....	....	....	....	....	....	....
2001-02	**Montreal**	**NHL**	**75**	**24**	**17**	**41**	**12**	**3**	**1**	**6**	**152**	**15.8**	**–4**	**4**	**25.0**	**18:56**	**12**	**1**	**5**	**6**	**2**	**0**	**0**	**1**	**19:55**

			Regular Season														Playoffs								
Season	Club	League	GP	G	A	Pts	PIM	PP	SH	GW	S	%	+/-	TF	F%	Min	GP	G	A	Pts	PIM	PP	SH	GW	Min
2002-03	**Montreal**	**NHL**	**53**	**7**	**16**	**23**	**16**	**2**	**0**	**2**	**87**	**8.0**	**–2**	**6**	**33.3**	**13:44**									
	Nashville	**NHL**	**17**	**2**	**2**	**4**	**2**	**0**	**0**	**0**	**37**	**5.4**	**–4**	**1**	**100.0**	**16:20**									
	NHL Totals		**382**	**72**	**115**	**187**	**101**	**11**	**3**	**13**	**727**	**9.9**		**28**	**32.1**	**17:08**	**20**	**1**	**6**	**7**	**2**	**0**	**0**	**1**	**19:55**

NHL All-Rookie Team (1994)

Signed as a free agent by **Montreal**, July 15, 1999. Traded to **Nashville** by **Montreal** for Nashville's 4th round choice (later traded to Washington – Washington selected Andreas Valdix) in 2003 Entry Draft, March 3, 2003.

PETROVICKY, Ronald

(PEHT-roh-vih-kee, RAW-nohld) **NYR**

Right wing. Shoots right. 5'11", 190 lbs. Born, Zilina, Czech., February 15, 1977. Calgary's 9th choice, 228th overall, in 1996 Entry Draft.

Season	Club	League	GP	G	A	Pts	PIM	PP	SH	GW	S	%	+/-	TF	F%	Min	GP	G	A	Pts	PIM	PP	SH	GW	Min
1993-94	Dukla Trencin Jr.	Slovak-Jr.	36	28	27	55	42																		
	Dukla Trencin	Slovakia	1	0	0	0	0																		
1994-95	Tri-City	WHL	39	4	11	15	86																		
	Prince George	WHL	21	4	6	10	37																		
1995-96	Prince George	WHL	39	19	21	40	61																		
1996-97	Prince George	WHL	72	32	37	69	119										15	4	9	13	31				
1997-98	Regina Pats	WHL	71	64	49	113	168										9	2	4	6	11				
1998-99	Saint John Flames	AHL	78	12	21	33	114										7	1	2	3	19				
99-2000	Saint John Flames	AHL	67	23	33	56	131										3	1	1	2	6				
2000-01	**Calgary**	**NHL**	**30**	**4**	**5**	**9**	**54**	**1**	**0**	**1**	**30**	**13.3**	**0**	**7**	**42.9**	**11:33**									
2001-02	**Calgary**	**NHL**	**77**	**5**	**7**	**12**	**85**	**1**	**0**	**1**	**78**	**6.4**	**0**	**28**	**46.4**	**11:42**									
2002-03	**NY Rangers**	**NHL**	**66**	**5**	**9**	**14**	**77**	**2**	**1**	**1**	**65**	**7.7**	**–12**	**52**	**42.3**	**12:25**									
	NHL Totals		**173**	**14**	**21**	**35**	**216**	**4**	**1**	**3**	**173**	**8.1**		**87**	**43.7**	**11:57**									

WHL East Second All-Star Team (1998)

• Missed majority of 2000-01 season recovering from wrist injury suffered in game vs. Detroit, October 5, 2000. Claimed by **NY Rangers** from **Calgary** in Waiver Draft, October 4, 2002.

PETTINEN, Tomi

(peh-TIHN-ehn, TAW-mee) **NYI**

Defense. Shoots left. 6'3", 220 lbs. Born, Ylojarvi, Finland, June 17, 1977. NY Islanders' 9th choice, 267th overall, in 2000 Entry Draft.

Season	Club	League	GP	G	A	Pts	PIM	PP	SH	GW	S	%	+/-	TF	F%	Min	GP	G	A	Pts	PIM	PP	SH	GW	Min
1993-94	Ilves Tampere-C	Finn-Jr.	31	2	2	4	4																		
1994-95	Ilves Tampere-B	Finn-Jr.	31	1	6	7	46										4	0	0	0	2				
	Ilves Tampere Jr.	Finn-Jr.	1	0	0	0	0																		
1995-96	KooVee Jr.	Finn-Jr.	21	0	0	0	64																		
	Ilves Tampere Jr.	Finn-Jr.	12	1	1	2	18																		
1996-97	Ilves Tampere Jr.	Finn-Jr.	26	3	8	11	44																		
	Ilves Tampere	Finland	16	1	0	1	12																		
1997-98	Ilves Tampere Jr.	Finn-Jr.	14	1	4	5	24																		
	Ilves Tampere	Finland	3	0	0	0	0																		
	Lukko Rauma Jr.	Finn-Jr.	11	2	6	8	14																		
	Lukko Rauma	Finland-2	4	0	0	0	2																		
	Lukko Rauma	Finland	27	0	2	2	16																		
1998-99	Hermes Kokkola	Finland-2	42	8	6	14	76										3	0	0	0	6				
	HIFK Helsinki	Finland	4	0	0	0	2																		
99-2000	Ilves Tampere	Finland	51	1	6	7	78										3	1	2	3	2				
2000-01	Ilves Tampere	Finland	56	2	2	4	86										9	0	0	0	4				
2001-02	Ilves Tampere	Finland	48	5	4	9	51										3	0	0	0	4				
	Bridgeport	AHL															9	0	1	1	0				
2002-03	**NY Islanders**	**NHL**	**2**	**0**	**0**	**0**	**0**	**0**	**0**	**0**	**0**	**0.0**	**1**	**0**	**0.0**	**11:34**									
	Bridgeport	AHL	75	1	8	9	56										9	0	0	0	17				
	NHL Totals		**2**	**0**	**0**	**0**	**0**	**0**	**0**	**0**	**0**	**0.0**		**0**	**0.0**	**11:34**									

PETTINGER, Matt

(PEH-tihn-juhr, MAT) **WSH.**

Left wing. Shoots left. 6'1", 205 lbs. Born, Edmonton, Alta., October 22, 1980. Washington's 2nd choice, 43rd overall, in 2000 Entry Draft.

Season	Club	League	GP	G	A	Pts	PIM	PP	SH	GW	S	%	+/-	TF	F%	Min	GP	G	A	Pts	PIM	PP	SH	GW	Min
1994-95	Victoria Racquet	BCAHA	55	52	48	100	41																		
1995-96	Victoria Racquet	BCAHA	60	80	65	145	45																		
1996-97	Victoria Salsa	BCHL	49	22	14	36	31																		
1997-98	Victoria Salsa	BCHL	55	22	20	42	56										7	5	1	6	8				
1998-99	U. of Denver	WCHA	33	6	14	20	44																		
99-2000	U. of Denver	WCHA	19	2	6	8	49																		
	Calgary Hitmen	WHL	27	14	6	20	41										11	2	6	8	30				
2000-01	**Washington**	**NHL**	**10**	**0**	**0**	**0**	**2**	**0**	**0**	**0**	**6**	**0.0**	**–1**	**2**	**50.0**	**7:47**									
	Portland Pirates	AHL	64	19	17	36	92										2	0	0	0	4				
2001-02	**Washington**	**NHL**	**61**	**7**	**3**	**10**	**44**	**1**	**0**	**1**	**73**	**9.6**	**–8**	**5**	**20.0**	**9:39**									
	Portland Pirates	AHL	9	3	3	6	24																		
2002-03	**Washington**	**NHL**	**1**	**0**	**0**	**0**	**0**	**0**	**0**	**0**	**0**	**0.0**	**0**	**1**	**0.0**	**3:30**									
	Portland Pirates	AHL	69	14	13	27	72										3	0	2	2	2				
	NHL Totals		**72**	**7**	**3**	**10**	**46**	**1**	**0**	**1**	**79**	**8.9**		**8**	**25.0**	**9:18**									

Left **U. of Denver** (WCHA) and signed as a free agent with **Calgary** (WHL), January 10, 2000.

PHILLIPS, Chris

(FIHL-ihps, KRIHS) **OTT.**

Defense. Shoots left. 6'3", 215 lbs. Born, Calgary, Alta., March 9, 1978. Ottawa's 1st choice, 1st overall, in 1996 Entry Draft.

Season	Club	League	GP	G	A	Pts	PIM	PP	SH	GW	S	%	+/-	TF	F%	Min	GP	G	A	Pts	PIM	PP	SH	GW	Min
1993-94	Fort McMurray	AJHL	56	6	16	22	72										10	0	3	3	16				
1994-95	Fort McMurray	AJHL	48	16	32	48	127										11	4	2	6	10				
1995-96	Prince Albert	WHL	61	10	30	40	97										18	2	12	14	30				
1996-97	Prince Albert	WHL	32	3	23	26	58																		
	Lethbridge	WHL	26	4	18	22	28										19	4	*21	25	20				
1997-98	**Ottawa**	**NHL**	**72**	**5**	**11**	**16**	**38**	**2**	**0**	**2**	**107**	**4.7**	**2**				**11**	**0**	**2**	**2**	**2**	**0**	**0**	**0**	
1998-99	**Ottawa**	**NHL**	**34**	**3**	**3**	**6**	**32**	**2**	**0**	**0**	**51**	**5.9**	**–5**	**0**	**0.0**	**18:06**	**3**	**0**	**0**	**0**	**0**	**0**	**0**	**0**	**13:50**
99-2000	**Ottawa**	**NHL**	**65**	**5**	**14**	**19**	**39**	**0**	**0**	**1**	**96**	**5.2**	**12**	**0**	**0.0**	**16:50**	**6**	**0**	**1**	**1**	**4**	**0**	**0**	**0**	**18:17**
2000-01	**Ottawa**	**NHL**	**73**	**2**	**12**	**14**	**31**	**2**	**0**	**0**	**77**	**2.6**	**8**	**1**	**0.0**	**21:28**	**1**	**1**	**0**	**1**	**0**	**0**	**0**	**0**	**20:52**
2001-02	**Ottawa**	**NHL**	**63**	**6**	**16**	**22**	**29**	**1**	**0**	**1**	**103**	**5.8**	**5**	**0**	**0.0**	**19:31**	**12**	**0**	**0**	**0**	**12**	**0**	**0**	**0**	**21:44**
2002-03	**Ottawa**	**NHL**	**78**	**3**	**16**	**19**	**71**	**2**	**0**	**1**	**97**	**3.1**	**7**	**0**	**0.0**	**20:13**	**18**	**2**	**4**	**6**	**12**	**0**	**0**	**1**	**21:36**
	NHL Totals		**385**	**24**	**72**	**96**	**240**	**9**	**0**	**5**	**531**	**4.5**		**1**	**0.0**	**19:26**	**51**	**3**	**7**	**10**	**30**	**0**	**0**	**1**	**20:33**

WHL East First All-Star Team (1997) • Canadian Major Junior First All-Star Team (1997)

• Missed majority of 1998-99 season recovering from ankle injury suffered in game vs. Buffalo, December 30, 1998.

PICARD, Michel

(PEE-cahr, mih-SHEHL) **DET.**

Left wing. Shoots left. 5'11", 190 lbs. Born, Beauport, Que., November 7, 1969. Hartford's 8th choice, 178th overall, in 1989 Entry Draft.

Season	Club	League	GP	G	A	Pts	PIM	PP	SH	GW	S	%	+/-	TF	F%	Min	GP	G	A	Pts	PIM	PP	SH	GW	Min
1985-86	Ste-Foy	QAAA	42	53	34	87																			
1986-87	Trois-Rivieres	QMJHL	66	33	35	68	53																		
1987-88	Trois-Rivieres	QMJHL	69	40	55	95	71																		
1988-89	Trois-Rivieres	QMJHL	66	59	81	140	170										4	1	3	4	2				
1989-90	Binghamton	AHL	67	16	24	40	98																		
1990-91	**Hartford**	**NHL**	**5**	**1**	**0**	**1**	**2**	**0**	**0**	**0**	**7**	**14.3**	**–2**												
	Springfield	AHL	77	*56	40	96	61										18	8	13	21	18				
1991-92	**Hartford**	**NHL**	**25**	**3**	**5**	**8**	**6**	**1**	**0**	**0**	**41**	**7.3**	**–2**												
	Springfield	AHL	40	21	17	38	44										11	2	0	2	34				
1992-93	**San Jose**	**NHL**	**25**	**4**	**0**	**4**	**24**	**2**	**0**	**0**	**32**	**12.5**	**–17**												
	Kansas City	IHL	33	7	10	17	51										12	3	2	5	20				
1993-94	Portland Pirates	AHL	61	41	44	85	99										17	11	10	21	22				
1994-95	P.E.I. Senators	AHL	57	32	57	89	58										8	4	4	8	6				
	Ottawa	**NHL**	**24**	**5**	**8**	**13**	**14**	**1**	**0**	**0**	**33**	**15.2**	**–1**												
1995-96	**Ottawa**	**NHL**	**17**	**2**	**6**	**8**	**10**	**0**	**0**	**1**	**21**	**9.5**	**–1**												
	P.E.I. Senators	AHL	55	37	45	82	79										5	5	1	6	2				
1996-97	Vastra Frolunda	Sweden	3	0	1	1	0																		
	Grand Rapids	IHL	82	46	55	101	58										5	2	0	2	10				

			Regular Season														Playoffs								
Season	Club	League	GP	G	A	Pts	PIM	PP	SH	GW	S	%	+/-	TF	F%	Min	GP	G	A	Pts	PIM	PP	SH	GW	Min
1997-98	Grand Rapids	IHL	58	28	41	69	42	....	....	....	....	....	....	....	....	....	....	....	....	....	....	....	....	....	....
	St. Louis	**NHL**	**16**	**1**	**8**	**9**	**29**	**0**	**0**	**0**	**19**	**5.3**	**3**	....	....	....	....	....	....	....	....	....	....	....	....
1998-99	**St. Louis**	**NHL**	**45**	**11**	**11**	**22**	**16**	**0**	**0**	**2**	**69**	**15.9**	**5**	**1**	**100.0**	**14:20**	**5**	**0**	**0**	**0**	**2**	**0**	**0**	**0**	**13:54**
	Grand Rapids	IHL	6	2	2	4	2	....	....	....	....	....	....	....	....	....	....	....	....	....	....	....	....	....	....
99-2000	Grand Rapids	IHL	65	33	35	68	50	....	....	....	....	....	....	....	....	....	17	8	10	*18	4	....	....	....	....
	Edmonton	**NHL**	**2**	**0**	**0**	**0**	**2**	**0**	**0**	**0**	**2**	**0.0**	**0**	**0**	**0.0**	**9:56**	....	....	....	....	....	....	....	....	....
2000-01	**Philadelphia**	**NHL**	**7**	**1**	**4**	**5**	**0**	**1**	**0**	**0**	**12**	**8.3**	**6**	**0**	**0.0**	**14:14**	....	....	....	....	....	....	....	....	....
	Philadelphia	AHL	72	31	39	70	22	....	....	....	....	....	....	....	....	....	10	4	5	9	4	....	....	....	....
2001-02	Adler Mannheim	Germany	60	24	28	52	30	....	....	....	....	....	....	....	....	....	12	*7	6	13	4	....	....	....	....
2002-03	Grand Rapids	AHL	78	32	52	84	34	....	....	....	....	....	....	....	....	....	15	3	1	4	8	....	....	....	....
	NHL Totals		**166**	**28**	**42**	**70**	**103**	**5**	**0**	**3**	**236**	**11.9**		**1**	**100.0**	**14:09**	**5**	**0**	**0**	**0**	**2**	**0**	**0**	**0**	**13:54**

QMJHL Second All-Star Team (1989) • AHL First All-Star Team (1991, 1995) • AHL Second All-Star Team (1994, 2003) • IHL First All-Star Team (1997)

Traded to **San Jose** by **Hartford** for future considerations (Yvon Corriveau, January 21, 1993), October 9, 1992. Signed as a free agent by **Portland** (AHL), September, 1993. Signed as a free agent by **Ottawa**, June 16, 1994. Traded to **Washington** by **Ottawa** for cash, May 21, 1996. Signed as a free agent by **St. Louis**, January 5, 1998. Signed as a free agent by **Edmonton**, December 2, 1999. Signed as a free agent by **Philadelphia**, August 14, 2000. Signed as a free agent by **Detroit**, July 15, 2002.

PILAR, Karel

(PEE-lahr, KAH-rehl) **TOR.**

Defense. Shoots right. 6'3", 207 lbs. Born, Prague, Czech., December 23, 1977. Toronto's 2nd choice, 39th overall, in 2001 Entry Draft.

99-2000	Litvinov	Czech	49	2	12	14	61	....	....	....	....	....	....	....	....	....	7	0	0	0	4	....	....	....	....
2000-01	Litvinov	Czech	52	12	26	38	52	....	....	....	....	....	....	....	....	....	4	1	1	2	25	....	....	....	....
2001-02	**Toronto**	**NHL**	**23**	**1**	**3**	**4**	**8**	**0**	**0**	**0**	**32**	**3.1**	**3**	**0**	**0.0**	**16:03**	**11**	**0**	**4**	**4**	**12**	**0**	**0**	**0**	**17:47**
	St. John's	AHL	52	10	14	24	26	....	....	....	....	....	....	....	....	....	....	....	....	....	....	....	....	....	....
2002-03	**Toronto**	**NHL**	**17**	**3**	**4**	**7**	**12**	**1**	**0**	**1**	**22**	**13.6**	**–7**	**0**	**0.0**	**18:29**	....	....	....	....	....	....	....	....	....
	St. John's	AHL	7	2	5	7	28	....	....	....	....	....	....	....	....	....	....	....	....	....	....	....	....	....	....
	NHL Totals		**40**	**4**	**7**	**11**	**20**	**1**	**0**	**1**	**54**	**7.4**		**0**	**0.0**	**17:05**	**11**	**0**	**4**	**4**	**12**	**0**	**0**	**0**	**17:47**

• Spent majority of 2002-03 season with Toronto as a healthy reserve.

PIRJETA, Lasse

(PEER-yeh-tuh, LAH-see) **CBJ**

Left wing. Shoots left. 6'3", 222 lbs. Born, Oulu, Finland, April 4, 1974. Columbus' 7th choice, 133rd overall, in 2002 Entry Draft.

1991-92	Tacoma Rockets	WHL	16	5	2	7	4	....	....	....	....	....	....	....	....	....	....	....	....	....	....	....	....	....	....
	Karpat Oulu Jr.	Finn-Jr.	7	1	4	5	8	....	....	....	....	....	....	....	....	....	....	....	....	....	....	....	....	....	....
	Karpat Oulu	Finland-2	2	0	0	0	0	....	....	....	....	....	....	....	....	....	....	....	....	....	....	....	....	....	....
1992-93	Karpat Oulu Jr.	Finn-Jr.	24	13	19	32	34	....	....	....	....	....	....	....	....	....	....	....	....	....	....	....	....	....	....
	Karpat Oulu	Finland-2	20	4	3	7	6	....	....	....	....	....	....	....	....	....	....	....	....	....	....	....	....	....	....
1993-94	TPS Turku Jr.	Finn-Jr.	6	2	2	4	2	....	....	....	....	....	....	....	....	....	4	6	2	8	2	....	....	....	....
	Kiekko-67 Turku	Finland-2	2	2	1	3	0	....	....	....	....	....	....	....	....	....	....	....	....	....	....	....	....	....	....
	TPS Turku	Finland	43	9	9	18	14	....	....	....	....	....	....	....	....	....	11	4	0	4	2	....	....	....	....
1994-95	TPS Turku Jr.	Finn-Jr.	1	0	0	0	0	....	....	....	....	....	....	....	....	....	....	....	....	....	....	....	....	....	....
	TPS Turku	Finland	49	7	13	20	64	....	....	....	....	....	....	....	....	....	8	0	1	1	29	....	....	....	....
1995-96	TPS Turku	Finland	45	13	14	27	34	....	....	....	....	....	....	....	....	....	11	6	3	9	4	....	....	....	....
1996-97	Vastra Frolunda	Sweden	50	14	8	22	36	....	....	....	....	....	....	....	....	....	3	0	1	1	4	....	....	....	....
	Vastra Frolunda	EuroHL	5	2	6	8	4	....	....	....	....	....	....	....	....	....	....	....	....	....	....	....	....	....	....
1997-98	Tappara Tampere	Finland	48	24	22	46	20	....	....	....	....	....	....	....	....	....	4	1	1	2	2	....	....	....	....
1998-99	Tappara Tampere	Finland	54	22	19	41	32	....	....	....	....	....	....	....	....	....	....	....	....	....	....	....	....	....	....
99-2000	HIFK Helsinki	Finland	54	18	25	43	24	....	....	....	....	....	....	....	....	....	9	2	3	5	10	....	....	....	....
	HIFK Helsinki	EuroHL	6	1	3	4	6	....	....	....	....	....	....	....	....	....	2	1	1	2	0	....	....	....	....
2000-01	HIFK Helsinki	Finland	55	15	18	33	24	....	....	....	....	....	....	....	....	....	....	....	....	....	....	....	....	....	....
2001-02	Karpat Oulu	Finland	55	15	26	41	24	....	....	....	....	....	....	....	....	....	4	2	2	4	2	....	....	....	....
2002-03	**Columbus**	**NHL**	**51**	**11**	**10**	**21**	**12**	**2**	**0**	**2**	**80**	**13.8**	**–4**	**327**	**43.1**	**11:28**	....	....	....	....	....	....	....	....	....
	NHL Totals		**51**	**11**	**10**	**21**	**12**	**2**	**0**	**2**	**80**	**13.8**		**327**	**43.1**	**11:28**	....	....	....	....	....	....	....	....	....

PIROS, Kamil

(PIH-ruhsh, KA-mihl) **ATL.**

Center. Shoots left. 6', 200 lbs. Born, Most, Czech., November 20, 1978. Buffalo's 9th choice, 212th overall, in 1997 Entry Draft.

1993-94	HC Banik Most Jr.	Czech-Jr.	16	12	10	22	....	....	....	....	....	....	....	....	....	....	....	....	....	....	....	....	....	....	....
	Litvinov Jr.	Czech-Jr.	22	6	13	19	....	....	....	....	....	....	....	....	....	....	....	....	....	....	....	....	....	....	....
1994-95	Litvinov Jr.	Czech-Jr.	40	27	16	43	....	....	....	....	....	....	....	....	....	....	....	....	....	....	....	....	....	....	....
1995-96	Litvinov Jr.	Czech-Jr.	42	16	13	29	....	....	....	....	....	....	....	....	....	....	....	....	....	....	....	....	....	....	....
1996-97	Litvinov Jr.	Czech-Jr.	3	2	1	3	....	....	....	....	....	....	....	....	....	....	....	....	....	....	....	....	....	....	....
	Litvinov	Czech	38	4	9	13	10	....	....	....	....	....	....	....	....	....	....	....	....	....	....	....	....	....	....
1997-98	Litvinov	Czech	14	0	1	1	2	....	....	....	....	....	....	....	....	....	....	....	....	....	....	....	....	....	....
	HC Vitkovice	Czech	26	2	9	11	14	....	....	....	....	....	....	....	....	....	....	....	....	....	....	....	....	....	....
1998-99	Litvinov	Czech	41	7	9	16	10	....	....	....	....	....	....	....	....	....	....	....	....	....	....	....	....	....	....
99-2000	Litvinov	Czech	40	8	8	16	18	....	....	....	....	....	....	....	....	....	7	0	3	3	2	....	....	....	....
2000-01	Litvinov	Czech	48	11	13	24	28	....	....	....	....	....	....	....	....	....	6	1	1	2	2	....	....	....	....
2001-02	**Atlanta**	**NHL**	**8**	**0**	**1**	**1**	**4**	**0**	**0**	**0**	**4**	**0.0**	**–2**	**81**	**32.1**	**12:12**	....	....	....	....	....	....	....	....	....
	Chicago Wolves	AHL	64	19	30	49	16	....	....	....	....	....	....	....	....	....	25	6	11	17	6	....	....	....	....
2002-03	**Atlanta**	**NHL**	**3**	**3**	**2**	**5**	**2**	**0**	**0**	**1**	**8**	**37.5**	**4**	**47**	**40.4**	**17:05**	....	....	....	....	....	....	....	....	....
	Chicago Wolves	AHL	51	10	9	19	16	....	....	....	....	....	....	....	....	....	9	1	0	1	4	....	....	....	....
	NHL Totals		**11**	**3**	**3**	**6**	**6**	**0**	**0**	**1**	**12**	**25.0**		**128**	**35.2**	**13:32**	....	....	....	....	....	....	....	....	....

Rights traded to **Atlanta** by **Buffalo** with Buffalo's 4th round choice (later traded to St. Louis – St. Louis selected Igor Valeyev) in 2001 Entry Draft for Donald Audette, March 13, 2001.

PISA, Ales

(PEE-sha, al-EHSH) **NYR**

Defense. Shoots left. 6', 195 lbs. Born, Pardibuce, Czech., January 2, 1977. Edmonton's 10th choice, 272nd overall, in 2001 Entry Draft.

1993-94	HC Pardubice	Czech	2	0	0	0	0	....	....	....	....	....	....	....	....	....	....	....	....	....	....	....	....	....	....
1994-95	HC Pardubice	Czech	22	0	0	0	18	....	....	....	....	....	....	....	....	....	2	0	0	0	0	....	....	....	....
1995-96	Pardubice	Czech	33	0	4	4	82	....	....	....	....	....	....	....	....	....	....	....	....	....	....	....	....	....	....
1996-97	Pardubice	Czech	41	4	2	6	70	....	....	....	....	....	....	....	....	....	6	0	2	2	6	....	....	....	....
1997-98	Pardubice	Czech	50	4	9	13	107	....	....	....	....	....	....	....	....	....	3	0	0	0	4	....	....	....	....
1998-99	Pardubice	Czech	48	7	12	19	74	....	....	....	....	....	....	....	....	....	3	0	1	1	....	....	....	....	....
99-2000	Pardubice	Czech	51	5	11	16	58	....	....	....	....	....	....	....	....	....	1	0	0	0	4	....	....	....	....
2000-01	Pardubice	Czech	47	10	13	23	75	....	....	....	....	....	....	....	....	....	7	2	2	4	4	....	....	....	....
2001-02	**Edmonton**	**NHL**	**2**	**0**	**0**	**0**	**2**	**0**	**0**	**0**	**3**	**0.0**	**0**	**0**	**0.0**	**15:02**	....	....	....	....	....	....	....	....	....
	Hamilton	AHL	52	6	12	18	62	....	....	....	....	....	....	....	....	....	14	1	4	5	8	....	....	....	....
2002-03	**Edmonton**	**NHL**	**48**	**1**	**3**	**4**	**24**	**1**	**0**	**0**	**34**	**2.9**	**11**	**0**	**0.0**	**12:56**	....	....	....	....	....	....	....	....	....
	Hamilton	AHL	7	0	1	1	14	....	....	....	....	....	....	....	....	....	....	....	....	....	....	....	....	....	....
	NY Rangers	**NHL**	**3**	**0**	**0**	**0**	**0**	**0**	**0**	**0**	**3**	**0.0**	**1**	**0**	**0.0**	**13:55**	....	....	....	....	....	....	....	....	....
	NHL Totals		**53**	**1**	**3**	**4**	**26**	**1**	**0**	**0**	**40**	**2.5**		**0**	**0.0**	**13:04**	....	....	....	....	....	....	....	....	....

Traded to **NY Rangers** by **Edmonton** with Anson Carter for Radek Dvorak and Cory Cross, March 11, 2003.

PISANI, Fernando

(pih-ZAN-ee, FUHR-nan-DOH) **EDM.**

Right wing. Shoots left. 6'1", 203 lbs. Born, Edmonton, Alta., December 27, 1976. Edmonton's 9th choice, 195th overall, in 1996 Entry Draft.

1993-94	St. Albert Saints	AJHL	50	6	21	27	24	....	....	....	....	....	....	....	....	....	....	....	....	....	....	....	....	....	....
1994-95	Bonnyville	AJHL	16	4	34	37	97	....	....	....	....	....	....	....	....	....	....	....	....	....	....	....	....	....	....
	St. Albert Saints	AJHL	40	26	21	47	16	....	....	....	....	....	....	....	....	....	....	....	....	....	....	....	....	....	....
1995-96	St. Albert Saints	AJHL	58	40	63	103	134	....	....	....	....	....	....	....	....	....	18	7	22	29	28	....	....	....	....
1996-97	Providence	H-East	35	12	18	30	36	....	....	....	....	....	....	....	....	....	....	....	....	....	....	....	....	....	....
1997-98	Providence	H-East	36	16	18	34	20	....	....	....	....	....	....	....	....	....	....	....	....	....	....	....	....	....	....
1998-99	Providence	H-East	38	14	37	51	42	....	....	....	....	....	....	....	....	....	....	....	....	....	....	....	....	....	....
99-2000	Providence	H-East	38	14	24	38	56	....	....	....	....	....	....	....	....	....	....	....	....	....	....	....	....	....	....
2000-01	Hamilton	AHL	52	12	13	25	28	....	....	....	....	....	....	....	....	....	....	....	....	....	....	....	....	....	....
2001-02	Hamilton	AHL	79	26	34	60	60	....	....	....	....	....	....	....	....	....	15	4	6	10	4	....	....	....	....
2002-03	**Edmonton**	**NHL**	**35**	**8**	**5**	**13**	**10**	**0**	**1**	**0**	**32**	**25.0**	**9**	**1**	**100.0**	**10:43**	**6**	**1**	**0**	**1**	**2**	**0**	**0**	**0**	**13:48**
	Hamilton	AHL	41	17	15	32	24	....	....	....	....	....	....	....	....	....	....	....	....	....	....	....	....	....	....
	NHL Totals		**35**	**8**	**5**	**13**	**10**	**0**	**1**	**0**	**32**	**25.0**		**1**	**100.0**	**10:43**	**6**	**1**	**0**	**1**	**2**	**0**	**0**	**0**	**13:48**

PITTIS, Domenic

(PIH-THIS, DOHM-ihn-ihk)

Center. Shoots left. 5'11", 190 lbs. Born, Calgary, Alta., October 1, 1974. Pittsburgh's 2nd choice, 52nd overall, in 1993 Entry Draft.

			Regular Season														Playoffs								
Season	Club	League	GP	G	A	Pts	PIM	PP	SH	GW	S	%	+/-	TF	F%	Min	GP	G	A	Pts	PIM	PP	SH	GW	Min
1990-91	Calgary Flames	AMHL	35	23	54	77	43																		
1991-92	Lethbridge	WHL	65	6	17	23	18										5	0	2	2	4				
1992-93	Lethbridge	WHL	66	46	73	119	69										4	3	3	6	8				
1993-94	Lethbridge	WHL	72	58	69	127	93										8	4	11	15	16				
1994-95	Cleveland	IHL	62	18	32	50	66										3	0	2	2	2				
1995-96	Cleveland	IHL	74	10	28	38	100										3	0	0	0	2				
1996-97	**Pittsburgh**	**NHL**	**1**	**0**	**0**	**0**	**0**	**0**	**0**	**0**	**0**	**0.0**	**–1**												
	Long Beach	IHL	65	23	43	66	91										18	5	9	14	26				
1997-98	Syracuse Crunch	AHL	75	23	41	64	90										5	1	3	4	4				
1998-99	**Buffalo**	**NHL**	**3**	**0**	**0**	**0**	**2**	**0**	**0**	**0**	**1**	**0.0**	**0**	**19**	**42.1**	**8:35**									
	Rochester	AHL	76	38	66	*104	108										20	7	*14	*21	40				
99-2000	**Buffalo**	**NHL**	**7**	**1**	**0**	**1**	**6**	**0**	**0**	**0**	**6**	**16.7**	**1**	**65**	**44.6**	**11:27**									
	Rochester	AHL	53	17	48	65	85										21	4	*26	*30	28				
2000-01	**Edmonton**	**NHL**	**47**	**4**	**5**	**9**	**49**	**0**	**0**	**2**	**42**	**9.5**	**–5**	**367**	**54.8**	**10:46**	**3**	**0**	**0**	**0**	**2**	**0**	**0**	**0**	**8:00**
2001-02	**Edmonton**	**NHL**	**22**	**0**	**6**	**6**	**8**	**0**	**0**	**0**	**18**	**0.0**	**–2**	**52**	**55.8**	**11:23**									
2002-03	**Nashville**	**NHL**	**2**	**0**	**0**	**0**	**2**	**0**	**0**	**0**	**1**	**0.0**	**0**	**6**	**16.7**	**4:60**									
	Milwaukee	AHL	30	11	21	32	65										6	2	4	6	8				
	NHL Totals		**82**	**5**	**11**	**16**	**67**	**0**	**0**	**2**	**68**	**7.4**		**509**	**52.7**	**10:46**	**3**	**0**	**0**	**0**	**2**	**0**	**0**	**0**	**8:00**

WHL East Second All-Star Team (1994) • John P. Sollenberger Trophy (Top Scorer – AHL) (1999)

Signed as a free agent by **Buffalo**, August 10, 1998. Signed as a free agent by **Edmonton**, July 25, 2000. • Missed majority of 2001-02 season recovering from head injury suffered in game vs. Nashvile, February 28, 2002. Signed as a free agent by **Nashville**, July 24, 2002. • Missed majority of 2002-03 season recovering from head injury suffered in game vs. San Jose, November 7, 2002.

PLETKA, Vaclav

(PLEHT-kuh, VA-tslav) **PHI.**

Right wing. Shoots left. 5'11", 182 lbs. Born, Mlada Boleslav, Czech., June 8, 1979. Philadelphia's 5th choice, 208th overall, in 1999 Entry Draft.

Season	Club	League	GP	G	A	Pts	PIM	PP	SH	GW	S	%	+/-	TF	F%	Min	GP	G	A	Pts	PIM	PP	SH	GW	Min
1995-96	Mlada Boleslav Jr.	Czech-Jr.	35	22	17	39																			
1996-97	Mlada Boleslav Jr.	Czech-Jr.	37	28	13	41																			
1997-98	Mlada Boleslav Jr.	Czech-Jr.	36	23	25	48																			
1998-99	Trinec Jr.	Czech-Jr.	20	11	5	16																			
	Trinec	Czech	50	15	11	26	20										10	2	1	3					
99-2000	HC Ocelari Trinec	Czech	51	28	21	49	62										4	2	2	4	2				
2000-01	Philadelphia	AHL	71	20	21	41	51										10	1	3	4	4				
2001-02	**Philadelphia**	**NHL**	**1**	**0**	**0**	**0**	**0**	**0**	**0**	**0**	**2**	**0.0**	**0**	**0**	**0.0**	**11:34**									
	Philadelphia	AHL	61	20	19	39	43																		
2002-03	HC Ocelari Trinec	Czech	47	20	24	44	58										12	3	2	5	18				
	NHL Totals		**1**	**0**	**0**	**0**	**0**	**0**	**0**	**0**	**2**	**0.0**		**0**	**0.0**	**11:34**									

Signed as a free agent by **HC Ocelari Trinec** (Czech), July 27, 2002.

POAPST, Steve

(POHPST, STEEV) **CHI.**

Defense. Shoots left. 6', 200 lbs. Born, Cornwall, Ont., January 3, 1969.

Season	Club	League	GP	G	A	Pts	PIM	PP	SH	GW	S	%	+/-	TF	F%	Min	GP	G	A	Pts	PIM	PP	SH	GW	Min
1986-87	Smiths Falls Bears	OCJHL	54	10	27	37	94																		
1987-88	Colgate	ECAC	32	3	13	16	22																		
1988-89	Colgate	ECAC	30	0	5	5	38																		
1989-90	Colgate	ECAC	38	4	15	19	54																		
1990-91	Colgate	ECAC	32	6	15	21	43																		
1991-92	Hampton Roads	ECHL	55	8	20	28	29										14	1	4	5	12				
1992-93	Hampton Roads	ECHL	63	10	35	45	57										4	0	1	1	4				
	Baltimore	AHL	7	0	1	1	4										7	0	3	3	6				
1993-94	Portland Pirates	AHL	78	14	21	35	47										12	0	3	3	8				
1994-95	Portland Pirates	AHL	71	8	22	30	60										7	0	1	1	16				
1995-96	**Washington**	**NHL**	**3**	**1**	**0**	**1**	**0**	**0**	**0**	**1**	**2**	**50.0**	**–1**				**6**	**0**	**0**	**0**	**0**	**0**	**0**	**0**	
	Portland Pirates	AHL	70	10	24	34	79										20	2	6	8	16				
1996-97	Portland Pirates	AHL	47	1	20	21	34										5	0	1	1	6				
1997-98	Portland Pirates	AHL	76	8	29	37	46										10	2	3	5	8				
1998-99	**Washington**	**NHL**	**22**	**0**	**0**	**0**	**8**	**0**	**0**	**0**	**11**	**0.0**	**–8**	**0**	**0.0**	**12:26**									
	Portland Pirates	AHL	54	3	21	24	36																		
99-2000	Portland Pirates	AHL	58	0	14	14	20										3	1	0	1	2				
2000-01	**Chicago**	**NHL**	**36**	**2**	**3**	**5**	**12**	**0**	**0**	**0**	**27**	**7.4**	**3**	**0**	**0.0**	**17:03**									
	Norfolk Admirals	AHL	37	1	8	9	14																		
2001-02	**Chicago**	**NHL**	**56**	**1**	**7**	**8**	**30**	**0**	**0**	**0**	**48**	**2.1**	**6**	**0**	**0.0**	**14:52**	**5**	**0**	**0**	**0**	**0**	**0**	**0**	**0**	**23:14**
2002-03	**Chicago**	**NHL**	**75**	**2**	**11**	**13**	**50**	**0**	**0**	**0**	**49**	**4.1**	**14**	**0**	**0.0**	**22:51**									
	NHL Totals		**192**	**6**	**21**	**27**	**100**	**0**	**0**	**1**	**137**	**4.4**		**0**	**0.0**	**18:10**	**11**	**0**	**0**	**0**	**0**	**0**	**0**	**0**	**23:14**

ECHL First All-Star Team (1993)

Signed as a free agent by **Washington**, February 4, 1995. Signed as a free agent by **Chicago**, July 27, 2000.

PODEIN, Shjon

(poh-DEEN, SHAWN)

Left wing. Shoots left. 6'2", 200 lbs. Born, Rochester, MN, March 5, 1968. Edmonton's 9th choice, 166th overall, in 1988 Entry Draft.

Season	Club	League	GP	G	A	Pts	PIM	PP	SH	GW	S	%	+/-	TF	F%	Min	GP	G	A	Pts	PIM	PP	SH	GW	Min
1985-86	John Marshall	Hi-School	25	34	30	64																			
1986-87	American Int'l.	NCAA-2	6	0	1	1	0																		
1987-88	U. Minn-Duluth	WCHA	30	4	4	8	48																		
1988-89	U. Minn-Duluth	WCHA	36	7	5	12	46																		
1989-90	U. Minn-Duluth	WCHA	35	21	18	39	36																		
1990-91	Cape Breton	AHL	63	14	15	29	65										4	0	0	0	5				
1991-92	Cape Breton	AHL	80	30	24	54	46										5	3	1	4	2				
1992-93	**Edmonton**	**NHL**	**40**	**13**	**6**	**19**	**25**	**2**	**1**	**1**	**64**	**20.3**	**–2**												
	Cape Breton	AHL	38	18	21	39	32										9	2	2	4	29				
1993-94	**Edmonton**	**NHL**	**28**	**3**	**5**	**8**	**8**	**0**	**0**	**0**	**26**	**11.5**	**3**												
	Cape Breton	AHL	5	4	4	8	4																		
1994-95	**Philadelphia**	**NHL**	**44**	**3**	**7**	**10**	**33**	**0**	**0**	**1**	**48**	**6.3**	**–2**				**15**	**1**	**3**	**4**	**10**	**0**	**0**	**0**	
1995-96	**Philadelphia**	**NHL**	**79**	**15**	**10**	**25**	**89**	**0**	**4**	**4**	**115**	**13.0**	**25**				**12**	**1**	**2**	**3**	**50**	**0**	**0**	**1**	
1996-97	**Philadelphia**	**NHL**	**82**	**14**	**18**	**32**	**41**	**0**	**0**	**4**	**153**	**9.2**	**7**				**19**	**4**	**3**	**7**	**16**	**0**	**0**	**1**	
1997-98	**Philadelphia**	**NHL**	**82**	**11**	**13**	**24**	**53**	**1**	**1**	**2**	**126**	**8.7**	**8**				**5**	**0**	**0**	**0**	**10**	**0**	**0**	**0**	
1998-99	**Philadelphia**	**NHL**	**14**	**1**	**0**	**1**	**0**	**0**	**0**	**0**	**26**	**3.8**	**–2**	**2**	**50.0**	**11:52**									
	Colorado	**NHL**	**41**	**2**	**6**	**8**	**24**	**0**	**0**	**0**	**49**	**4.1**	**–3**	**21**	**42.9**	**11:49**	**19**	**1**	**1**	**2**	**12**	**0**	**0**	**0**	**14:54**
99-2000	**Colorado**	**NHL**	**75**	**11**	**8**	**19**	**29**	**0**	**1**	**3**	**104**	**10.6**	**12**	**17**	**64.7**	**13:31**	**17**	**5**	**0**	**5**	**8**	**0**	**0**	**1**	**10:50**
2000-01 ♦	**Colorado**	**NHL**	**82**	**15**	**17**	**32**	**68**	**0**	**0**	**3**	**137**	**10.9**	**7**	**69**	**44.9**	**14:23**	**23**	**2**	**3**	**5**	**14**	**0**	**0**	**1**	**14:59**
2001-02	**Colorado**	**NHL**	**41**	**6**	**6**	**12**	**39**	**0**	**1**	**2**	**43**	**14.0**	**0**	**15**	**13.3**	**12:60**									
	St. Louis	**NHL**	**23**	**2**	**4**	**6**	**2**	**0**	**0**	**0**	**24**	**8.3**	**2**	**14**	**21.4**	**15:09**	**10**	**0**	**0**	**0**	**6**	**0**	**0**	**0**	**13:46**
2002-03	**St. Louis**	**NHL**	**68**	**4**	**6**	**10**	**28**	**1**	**0**	**0**	**52**	**7.7**	**7**	**190**	**46.3**	**10:54**	**7**	**0**	**1**	**1**	**6**	**0**	**0**	**0**	**10:30**
	NHL Totals		**699**	**100**	**106**	**206**	**439**	**4**	**8**	**20**	**967**	**10.3**		**328**	**44.2**	**12:59**	**127**	**14**	**13**	**27**	**132**	**0**	**0**	**4**	**13:28**

King Clancy Memorial Trophy (2001)

Signed as a free agent by **Philadelphia**, July 27, 1994. Traded to **Colorado** by **Philadelphia** for Keith Jones, November 12, 1998. Traded to **St. Louis** by **Colorado** for Mike Keane, February 11, 2002.

PODKONICKY, Andrej

(pohd-koh-NIHTZ-kee, AWN-dray) **WSH.**

Center. Shoots left. 6'2", 202 lbs. Born, Zvolen, Czech., May 9, 1978. St. Louis' 8th choice, 196th overall, in 1996 Entry Draft.

Season	Club	League	GP	G	A	Pts	PIM	PP	SH	GW	S	%	+/-	TF	F%	Min	GP	G	A	Pts	PIM	PP	SH	GW	Min
1994-95	HKm Zvolen	Slovak-2	17	0	4	4	6																		
1995-96	HKm Zvolen	Slovak-2	38	18	12	30	18																		
1996-97	Portland	WHL	71	25	46	71	127										6	1	1	2	8				
1997-98	Portland	WHL	64	30	44	74	81										16	4	12	16	20				
1998-99	Worcester IceCats	AHL	61	19	24	43	52										4	0	0	0	4				
99-2000	Worcester IceCats	AHL	77	16	25	41	68										9	2	5	7	6				

Season	Club	League	GP	G	A	Pts	PIM	PP	SH	GW	S	%	+/-	TF	F%	Min	GP	G	A	Pts	PIM	PP	SH	GW	Min
			Regular Season														Playoffs								
2000-01	Worcester IceCats	AHL	16	2	3	5	15	....	....	....	....	....	....	....	....	....	....	....	....	....	....	....	....	....	....
	Florida	**NHL**	**6**	**1**	**0**	**1**	**2**	**0**	**0**	**0**	**5**	**20.0**	**0**	**34**	**55.9**	**6:04**	....	....	....	....	....	....	....	....	....
	Louisville Panthers	AHL	41	6	10	16	31	....	....	....	....	....	....	....	....	....	....	....	....	....	....	....	....	....	....
2001-02	HIFK Helsinki	Finland	23	3	6	9	41	....	....	....	....	....	....	....	....	....	....	....	....	....	....	....	....	....	....
	Slov. Bratislava	Slovakia	16	11	2	13	2	....	....	....	....	....	....	....	....	....	19	4	7	11	49	....	....	....	....
2002-03	Iserlohn Roosters	Germany	52	18	15	33	54	....	....	....	....	....	....	....	....	....	....	....	....	....	....	....	....	....	....
	NHL Totals		**6**	**1**	**0**	**1**	**2**	**0**	**0**	**0**	**5**	**20.0**		**34**	**55.9**	**6:04**	....	....	....	....	....	....	....	....	....

Memorial Cup All-Star Team (1998) • Ed Chynoweth Award (Memorial Cup Top Scorer) (1998)

Traded to **Florida** by **St. Louis** for Eric Boguniecki, December 17, 2000. Signed as a free agent by **HIFK Helsinki** (Finland), August 14, 2001. Signed as a free agent by **Iserlohn** (Germany), August 3, 2002. Signed as a free agent by **Washington**, July 14, 2003.

PODOLLAN, Jason
(poh-DOH-luhn, JAY-suhn)

Right wing. Shoots right. 6'1", 198 lbs. Born, Vernon, B.C., February 18, 1976. Florida's 3rd choice, 31st overall, in 1994 Entry Draft.

Season	Club	League	GP	G	A	Pts	PIM	PP	SH	GW	S	%	+/-	TF	F%	Min	GP	G	A	Pts	PIM	PP	SH	GW	Min
1990-91	Sherwood Park	AMHL	61	105	111	216	133	....	....	....	....	....	....	....	....	....	....	....	....	....	....	....	....	....	....
1991-92	Penticton	BCJHL	59	20	26	46	66	....	....	....	....	....	....	....	....	....	....	....	....	....	....	....	....	....	....
	Spokane Chiefs	WHL	2	0	0	0	2	....	....	....	....	....	....	....	....	....	10	3	1	4	16	....	....	....	....
1992-93	Spokane Chiefs	WHL	72	36	33	69	108	....	....	....	....	....	....	....	....	....	10	4	4	8	14	....	....	....	....
1993-94	Spokane Chiefs	WHL	69	29	37	66	108	....	....	....	....	....	....	....	....	....	3	3	0	3	2	....	....	....	....
1994-95	Spokane Chiefs	WHL	72	43	41	84	102	....	....	....	....	....	....	....	....	....	11	5	7	12	18	....	....	....	....
	Cincinnati	IHL	....	....	....	....	....	....	....	....	....	....	....	....	....	....	3	0	0	0	2	....	....	....	....
1995-96	Spokane Chiefs	WHL	56	37	25	62	103	....	....	....	....	....	....	....	....	....	18	*21	12	33	28	....	....	....	....
1996-97	**Florida**	**NHL**	**19**	**1**	**1**	**2**	**4**	**1**	**0**	**0**	**20**	**5.0**	**–3**	....	....	....	....	....	....	....	....	....	....	....	....
	Carolina	AHL	39	21	25	46	36	....	....	....	....	....	....	....	....	....	....	....	....	....	....	....	....	....	....
	Toronto	**NHL**	**10**	**0**	**3**	**3**	**6**	**0**	**0**	**0**	**10**	**0.0**	**–2**	....	....	....	....	....	....	....	....	....	....	....	....
	St. John's	AHL	....	....	....	....	....	....	....	....	....	....	....	....	....	....	11	2	3	5	6	....	....	....	....
1997-98	St. John's	AHL	70	30	31	61	116	....	....	....	....	....	....	....	....	....	4	1	0	1	10	....	....	....	....
1998-99	**Toronto**	**NHL**	**4**	**0**	**0**	**0**	**0**	**0**	**0**	**0**	**2**	**0.0**	**0**	**0**	**0.0**	**6:29**	....	....	....	....	....	....	....	....	....
	St. John's	AHL	68	42	26	68	65	....	....	....	....	....	....	....	....	....	....	....	....	....	....	....	....	....	....
	Los Angeles	**NHL**	**6**	**0**	**0**	**0**	**5**	**0**	**0**	**0**	**7**	**0.0**	**–3**	**0**	**0.0**	**10:15**	....	....	....	....	....	....	....	....	....
	Long Beach	IHL	8	5	3	8	2	....	....	....	....	....	....	....	....	....	6	1	2	3	4	....	....	....	....
99-2000	**Los Angeles**	**NHL**	**1**	**0**	**1**	**1**	**2**	**0**	**0**	**0**	**2**	**0.0**	**0**	**0**	**0.0**	**16:13**	....	....	....	....	....	....	....	....	....
	Lowell	AHL	71	29	26	55	91	....	....	....	....	....	....	....	....	....	4	0	0	0	4	....	....	....	....
2000-01	Detroit Vipers	IHL	63	15	16	31	98	....	....	....	....	....	....	....	....	....	....	....	....	....	....	....	....	....	....
	Manitoba Moose	IHL	16	5	2	7	10	....	....	....	....	....	....	....	....	....	4	0	0	0	2	....	....	....	....
2001-02	**NY Islanders**	**NHL**	**1**	**0**	**0**	**0**	**2**	**0**	**0**	**0**	**1**	**0.0**	**0**	**0**	**0.0**	**4:10**	....	....	....	....	....	....	....	....	....
	Bridgeport	AHL	65	21	24	45	63	....	....	....	....	....	....	....	....	....	20	5	4	9	32	....	....	....	....
2002-03	Adler Mannheim	Germany	31	16	4	20	68	....	....	....	....	....	....	....	....	....	....	....	....	....	....	....	....	....	....
	NHL Totals		**41**	**1**	**5**	**6**	**19**	**1**	**0**	**0**	**42**	**2.4**		**0**	**0.0**	**8:59**	....	....	....	....	....	....	....	....	....

WHL West Second All-Star Team (1996)

Traded to **Toronto** by **Florida** for Kirk Muller, March 18, 1997. Traded to **Los Angeles** by **Toronto** with Toronto's 3rd round choice (Cory Campbell) in 1999 Entry Draft for Yanic Perreault, March 23, 1999. Claimed by **Tampa Bay** from **Los Angeles** in Waiver Draft, September 29, 2000. Signed as a free agent by **NY Islanders**, August 24, 2001. Signed as a free agent by **Adler Mannheim** (Germany), July 29, 2002.

PONIKAROVSKY, Alexei
(poh-NIH-kahr-ohv-skee, al-EHX-ay) **TOR.**

Left wing. Shoots left. 6'4", 220 lbs. Born, Kiev, USSR, April 9, 1980. Toronto's 4th choice, 87th overall, in 1998 Entry Draft.

Season	Club	League	GP	G	A	Pts	PIM	PP	SH	GW	S	%	+/-	TF	F%	Min	GP	G	A	Pts	PIM	PP	SH	GW	Min
1995-96	Dyno. Moscow Jr.	CIS-Jr.	70	14	10	24	20	....	....	....	....	....	....	....	....	....	....	....	....	....	....	....	....	....	....
1996-97	Dyno. Moscow Jr.	Russia-Jr.	60	12	15	27	30	....	....	....	....	....	....	....	....	....	....	....	....	....	....	....	....	....	....
	DynamoMoscow2	Russia-3	2	0	0	0	2	....	....	....	....	....	....	....	....	....	....	....	....	....	....	....	....	....	....
1997-98	Dynamo Moscow	Russia	24	1	2	3	30	....	....	....	....	....	....	....	....	....	....	....	....	....	....	....	....	....	....
1998-99	Krylja Sovetov	Russia	13	2	1	3	2	....	....	....	....	....	....	....	....	....	....	....	....	....	....	....	....	....	....
	Dynamo Moscow	Russia	....	....	....	....	....	....	....	....	....	....	....	....	....	....	3	0	0	0	2	....	....	....	....
99-2000	THC Tver	Russia-2	29	8	14	22	26	....	....	....	....	....	....	....	....	....	....	....	....	....	....	....	....	....	....
	Dynamo Moscow	Russia	19	1	0	1	8	....	....	....	....	....	....	....	....	....	1	0	0	0	0	....	....	....	....
	Dynamo Moscow	EuroHL	2	0	2	2	0	....	....	....	....	....	....	....	....	....	....	....	....	....	....	....	....	....	....
2000-01	**Toronto**	**NHL**	**22**	**1**	**3**	**4**	**14**	**0**	**0**	**0**	**21**	**4.8**	**–1**	**7**	**28.6**	**8:32**	....	....	....	....	....	....	....	....	....
	St. John's	AHL	49	12	24	36	44	....	....	....	....	....	....	....	....	....	4	0	0	0	4	....	....	....	....
2001-02	**Toronto**	**NHL**	**8**	**2**	**0**	**2**	**0**	**0**	**0**	**1**	**8**	**25.0**	**2**	**2**	**50.0**	**8:03**	**10**	**0**	**0**	**0**	**4**	**0**	**0**	**0**	**8:15**
	St. John's	AHL	72	21	27	48	74	....	....	....	....	....	....	....	....	....	5	2	1	3	8	....	....	....	....
	Ukraine	Olympics	4	1	1	2	6	....	....	....	....	....	....	....	....	....	....	....	....	....	....	....	....	....	....
2002-03	**Toronto**	**NHL**	**13**	**0**	**3**	**3**	**11**	**0**	**0**	**0**	**13**	**0.0**	**4**	**4**	**25.0**	**10:43**	....	....	....	....	....	....	....	....	....
	St. John's	AHL	63	24	22	46	68	....	....	....	....	....	....	....	....	....	....	....	....	....	....	....	....	....	....
	NHL Totals		**43**	**3**	**6**	**9**	**25**	**0**	**0**	**1**	**42**	**7.1**		**13**	**30.8**	**9:06**	**10**	**0**	**0**	**0**	**4**	**0**	**0**	**0**	**8:15**

POSMYK, Marek
(PAWZ-mihk, MAHR-ehk) **T.B.**

Defense. Shoots right. 6'5", 228 lbs. Born, Jihlava, Czech., September 15, 1978. Toronto's 1st choice, 36th overall, in 1996 Entry Draft.

Season	Club	League	GP	G	A	Pts	PIM	PP	SH	GW	S	%	+/-	TF	F%	Min	GP	G	A	Pts	PIM	PP	SH	GW	Min
1994-95	Dukla Jihlava Jr.	Czech-Jr.	16	1	3	4	....	....	....	....	....	....	....	....	....	....	....	....	....	....	....	....	....	....	....
1995-96	Dukla Jihlava Jr.	Czech-Jr.	16	6	5	11	....	....	....	....	....	....	....	....	....	....	....	....	....	....	....	....	....	....	....
	HC Dukla Jihlava	Czech	18	1	2	3	....	....	....	....	....	....	....	....	....	....	1	0	0	0	....	....	....	....	....
1996-97	HC Dukla Jihlava	Czech	24	1	7	8	44	....	....	....	....	....	....	....	....	....	....	....	....	....	....	....	....	....	....
	St. John's	AHL	2	0	0	0	2	....	....	....	....	....	....	....	....	....	....	....	....	....	....	....	....	....	....
1997-98	Sarnia Sting	OHL	48	8	16	24	94	....	....	....	....	....	....	....	....	....	5	0	2	2	6	....	....	....	....
	St. John's	AHL	3	0	0	0	4	....	....	....	....	....	....	....	....	....	....	....	....	....	....	....	....	....	....
1998-99	St. John's	AHL	41	1	0	1	36	....	....	....	....	....	....	....	....	....	....	....	....	....	....	....	....	....	....
99-2000	St. John's	AHL	38	1	6	7	57	....	....	....	....	....	....	....	....	....	....	....	....	....	....	....	....	....	....
	Tampa Bay	**NHL**	**18**	**1**	**2**	**3**	**20**	**0**	**0**	**0**	**22**	**4.5**	**1**	**1**	**100.0**	**13:12**	....	....	....	....	....	....	....	....	....
	Detroit Vipers	IHL	1	0	1	1	0	....	....	....	....	....	....	....	....	....	....	....	....	....	....	....	....	....	....
2000-01	**Tampa Bay**	**NHL**	**1**	**0**	**0**	**0**	**0**	**0**	**0**	**0**	**0**	**0.0**	**–1**	**0**	**0.0**	**13:27**	....	....	....	....	....	....	....	....	....
	Detroit Vipers	IHL	49	7	14	21	58	....	....	....	....	....	....	....	....	....	....	....	....	....	....	....	....	....	....
2001-02	Zlin	Czech	45	8	6	14	147	....	....	....	....	....	....	....	....	....	6	0	0	0	10	....	....	....	....
2002-03	HC Slavia Praha	Czech	41	0	4	4	20	....	....	....	....	....	....	....	....	....	17	4	3	7	34	....	....	....	....
	NHL Totals		**19**	**1**	**2**	**3**	**20**	**0**	**0**	**0**	**22**	**4.5**		**1**	**100.0**	**13:12**	....	....	....	....	....	....	....	....	....

Traded to **Tampa Bay** by **Toronto** with Mike Johnson, Toronto's 5th (Pavel Sedov) and 6th (Aaron Gionet) round choices in 2000 Entry Draft and future considerations for Darcy Tucker, Tampa Bay's 4th round choice (Miguel Delisle) in 2000 Entry Draft and future considerations, February 9, 2000. Signed as a free agent by **Zlin** (Czech) with Tampa Bay retaining NHL rights, August 12, 2001.

POTHIER, Brian
(POH-thee-uhr, BRIGH-uhn) **OTT.**

Defense. Shoots right. 6', 195 lbs. Born, New Bedford, MA, April 15, 1977.

Season	Club	League	GP	G	A	Pts	PIM	PP	SH	GW	S	%	+/-	TF	F%	Min	GP	G	A	Pts	PIM	PP	SH	GW	Min
1995-96	Northfield High	Hi-School	27	11	22	33	36	....	....	....	....	....	....	....	....	....	....	....	....	....	....	....	....	....	....
1996-97	RPI Engineers	ECAC	34	1	11	12	42	....	....	....	....	....	....	....	....	....	....	....	....	....	....	....	....	....	....
1997-98	RPI Engineers	ECAC	35	2	9	11	28	....	....	....	....	....	....	....	....	....	....	....	....	....	....	....	....	....	....
1998-99	RPI Engineers	ECAC	37	5	13	18	36	....	....	....	....	....	....	....	....	....	....	....	....	....	....	....	....	....	....
99-2000	RPI Engineers	ECAC	36	9	24	33	44	....	....	....	....	....	....	....	....	....	....	....	....	....	....	....	....	....	....
2000-01	**Atlanta**	**NHL**	**3**	**0**	**0**	**0**	**2**	**0**	**0**	**0**	**0**	**0.0**	**4**	**0**	**0.0**	**20:38**	....	....	....	....	....	....	....	....	....
	Orlando	IHL	76	12	29	41	69	....	....	....	....	....	....	....	....	....	16	3	5	8	11	....	....	....	....
2001-02	**Atlanta**	**NHL**	**33**	**3**	**6**	**9**	**22**	**1**	**0**	**1**	**65**	**4.6**	**–19**	**0**	**0.0**	**21:41**	....	....	....	....	....	....	....	....	....
	Chicago Wolves	AHL	39	6	13	19	30	....	....	....	....	....	....	....	....	....	....	....	....	....	....	....	....	....	....
2002-03	**Ottawa**	**NHL**	**14**	**2**	**4**	**6**	**6**	**0**	**0**	**1**	**23**	**8.7**	**11**	**0**	**0.0**	**15:23**	**1**	**0**	**0**	**0**	**2**	**0**	**0**	**0**	**13:11**
	Binghamton	AHL	68	7	40	47	58	....	....	....	....	....	....	....	....	....	8	2	8	10	4	....	....	....	....
	NHL Totals		**50**	**5**	**10**	**15**	**30**	**1**	**0**	**2**	**88**	**5.7**		**0**	**0.0**	**19:51**	**1**	**0**	**0**	**0**	**2**	**0**	**0**	**0**	**13:11**

ECAC Second All-Star Team (2000) • ECAC All-Tournament Team (2000) • NCAA East Second All-American Team (2000) • Garry F. Longman Memorial Trophy (Top Rookie – IHL) (2001) • AHL Second All-Star Team (2003)

Signed as a free agent by **Atlanta**, March 27, 2000. Traded to **Ottawa** by **Atlanta** for Shawn McEachern and Ottawa's 6th round choice in 2004 Entry Draft, June 29, 2002.

POTI, Tom

(POH-tee, TAWM) **NYR**

Defense. Shoots left. 6'3", 215 lbs. Born, Worcester, MA, March 22, 1977. Edmonton's 4th choice, 59th overall, in 1996 Entry Draft.

			Regular Season															Playoffs								
Season	Club	League	GP	G	A	Pts	PIM	PP	SH	GW	S	%	+/-	TF	F%	Min	GP	G	A	Pts	PIM	PP	SH	GW	Min
1992-93	St. Peter's High	Hi-School	55	25	46	71	....	....	....	....	....	....	....	....	....	....	....	....	....	....	....	....	....	....	....
1993-94	Cushing Academy	Hi-School	30	10	35	45	....	....	....	....	....	....	....	....	....	....	....	....	....	....	....	....	....	....	....
1994-95	Cushing Academy	Hi-School	36	17	54	71	35	....	....	....	....	....	....	....	....	....	....	....	....	....	....	....	....	....	....
	Central-Mass	MBAHL	8	8	10	18	....	....	....	....	....	....	....	....	....	....	....	....	....	....	....	....	....	....	....
1995-96	Cushing Academy	Hi-School	29	14	59	73	18	....	....	....	....	....	....	....	....	....	....	....	....	....	....	....	....	....	....
1996-97	Boston University	H-East	38	4	17	21	54	....	....	....	....	....	....	....	....	....	....	....	....	....	....	....	....	....	....
1997-98	Boston University	H-East	38	13	29	42	60	....	....	....	....	....	....	....	....	....	....	....	....	....	....	....	....	....	....
1998-99	**Edmonton**	**NHL**	**73**	**5**	**16**	**21**	**42**	**2**	**0**	**3**	**94**	**5.3**	**10**	**0**	**0.0**	**19:33**	**4**	**0**	**1**	**1**	**2**	**0**	**0**	**0**	**28:02**
99-2000	**Edmonton**	**NHL**	**76**	**9**	**26**	**35**	**65**	**2**	**1**	**1**	**125**	**7.2**	**8**	**0**	**0.0**	**24:10**	**5**	**0**	**1**	**1**	**0**	**0**	**0**	**0**	**23:53**
2000-01	**Edmonton**	**NHL**	**81**	**12**	**20**	**32**	**60**	**6**	**0**	**3**	**161**	**7.5**	**–4**	**0**	**0.0**	**22:44**	**6**	**0**	**2**	**2**	**2**	**0**	**0**	**0**	**20:25**
2001-02	**Edmonton**	**NHL**	**55**	**1**	**16**	**17**	**42**	**1**	**0**	**0**	**100**	**1.0**	**–6**	**0**	**0.0**	**24:32**	....	....	....	....	....	....	....	....	....
	United States	Olympics	6	0	1	1	4	....	....	....	....	....	....	....	....	....	....	....	....	....	....	....	....	....	....
	NY Rangers	**NHL**	**11**	**1**	**7**	**8**	**2**	**1**	**0**	**1**	**9**	**11.1**	**–4**	**0**	**0.0**	**21:45**	....	....	....	....	....	....	....	....	....
2002-03	**NY Rangers**	**NHL**	**80**	**11**	**37**	**48**	**58**	**3**	**0**	**2**	**148**	**7.4**	**–6**	**0**	**0.0**	**24:43**	....	....	....	....	....	....	....	....	....
	NHL Totals		**376**	**39**	**122**	**161**	**269**	**15**	**1**	**10**	**637**	**6.1**		**0**	**0.0**	**23:04**	**15**	**0**	**4**	**4**	**4**	**0**	**0**	**0**	**23:36**

NCAA Championship All-Tournament Team (1997) • Hockey East First All-Star Team (1998) • NCAA East First All-American Team (1998) • NHL All-Rookie Team (1999)

Played in NHL All-Star Game (2003)

Traded to **NY Rangers** by **Edmonton** with Rem Murray for Mike York and NY Rangers' 4th round choice (Ivan Koltsov) in 2002 Entry Draft, March 19, 2002.

PRATT, Nolan

(PRAT, NOH-lan) **T.B.**

Defense. Shoots left. 6'3", 200 lbs. Born, Fort McMurray, Alta., August 14, 1975. Hartford's 4th choice, 115th overall, in 1993 Entry Draft.

Season	Club	League	GP	G	A	Pts	PIM	PP	SH	GW	S	%	+/-	TF	F%	Min	GP	G	A	Pts	PIM	PP	SH	GW	Min
1991-92	Bonnyville	AJHL	33	3	7	10	57	....	....	....	....	....	....	....	....	....	....	....	....	....	....	....	....	....	....
	Portland	WHL	22	2	9	11	13	....	....	....	....	....	....	....	....	....	6	1	3	4	12	....	....	....	....
1992-93	Portland	WHL	70	4	19	23	97	....	....	....	....	....	....	....	....	....	16	2	7	9	31	....	....	....	....
1993-94	Portland	WHL	72	4	32	36	105	....	....	....	....	....	....	....	....	....	10	1	2	3	14	....	....	....	....
1994-95	Portland	WHL	72	6	37	43	196	....	....	....	....	....	....	....	....	....	9	1	6	7	10	....	....	....	....
1995-96	Springfield	AHL	62	2	6	8	72	....	....	....	....	....	....	....	....	....	2	0	0	0	0	....	....	....	....
	Richmond	ECHL	4	1	0	1	2	....	....	....	....	....	....	....	....	....	....	....	....	....	....	....	....	....	....
1996-97	**Hartford**	**NHL**	**9**	**0**	**2**	**2**	**6**	**0**	**0**	**0**	**4**	**0.0**	**0**	....	....	....	....	....	....	....	....	....	....	....	....
	Springfield	AHL	66	1	18	19	127	....	....	....	....	....	....	....	....	....	17	0	3	3	18	....	....	....	....
1997-98	**Carolina**	**NHL**	**23**	**0**	**2**	**2**	**44**	**0**	**0**	**0**	**11**	**0.0**	**–2**	....	....	....	....	....	....	....	....	....	....	....	....
	New Haven	AHL	54	3	15	18	135	....	....	....	....	....	....	....	....	....	....	....	....	....	....	....	....	....	....
1998-99	**Carolina**	**NHL**	**61**	**1**	**14**	**15**	**95**	**0**	**0**	**1**	**46**	**2.2**	**15**	**0**	**0.0**	**16:45**	**3**	**0**	**0**	**0**	**2**	**0**	**0**	**0**	**19:58**
99-2000	**Carolina**	**NHL**	**64**	**3**	**1**	**4**	**90**	**0**	**0**	**1**	**47**	**6.4**	**–22**	**0**	**0.0**	**19:10**	....	....	....	....	....	....	....	....	....
2000-01	**Colorado**	**NHL**	**46**	**1**	**2**	**3**	**40**	**0**	**0**	**1**	**26**	**3.8**	**2**	**1**	**0.0**	**9:50**	....	....	....	....	....	....	....	....	....
2001-02	**Tampa Bay**	**NHL**	**46**	**0**	**3**	**3**	**51**	**0**	**0**	**0**	**38**	**0.0**	**–4**	**1**	**0.0**	**18:25**	....	....	....	....	....	....	....	....	....
2002-03	**Tampa Bay**	**NHL**	**67**	**1**	**7**	**8**	**35**	**0**	**0**	**0**	**38**	**2.6**	**–6**	**0**	**0.0**	**17:34**	**4**	**0**	**1**	**1**	**0**	**0**	**0**	**0**	**21:01**
	NHL Totals		**316**	**6**	**31**	**37**	**361**	**0**	**0**	**3**	**210**	**2.9**		**2**	**0.0**	**16:38**	**7**	**0**	**1**	**1**	**2**	**0**	**0**	**0**	**20:34**

Transferred to **Carolina** after **Hartford** franchise relocated, June 25, 1997. Traded to **Colorado** by **Carolina** with Carolina's 1st (Vaclav Nedorost) and 2nd (Jared Aulin) round choices in 2000 Entry Draft and Philadelphia's 2nd round choice (previously acquired, Colorado selected Agris Saviels) in 2000 Entry Draft for Sandis Ozolinsh and Columbus' 2nd round choice (previously acquired, Carolina selected Tomas Kurka) in 2000 Entry Draft, June 24, 2000. Traded to **Tampa Bay** by **Colorado** for Los Angeles' 6th round choice (previously acquired, Colorado selected Scott Horvath) in 2001 Entry Draft, June 24, 2001.

PRIMEAU, Keith

(PREE-moh, KEETH) **PHI.**

Center. Shoots left. 6'5", 220 lbs. Born, Toronto, Ont., November 24, 1971. Detroit's 1st choice, 3rd overall, in 1990 Entry Draft.

Season	Club	League	GP	G	A	Pts	PIM	PP	SH	GW	S	%	+/-	TF	F%	Min	GP	G	A	Pts	PIM	PP	SH	GW	Min
1986-87	Whitby Flyers	OMHA	65	69	80	149	116	....	....	....	....	....	....	....	....	....	....	....	....	....	....	....	....	....	....
1987-88	Hamilton Kilty B's	OJHL-B	19	19	17	36	16	....	....	....	....	....	....	....	....	....	....	....	....	....	....	....	....	....	....
	Hamilton	OHL	47	6	6	12	69	....	....	....	....	....	....	....	....	....	11	0	2	2	2	....	....	....	....
1988-89	Niagara Falls	OHL	48	20	35	55	56	....	....	....	....	....	....	....	....	....	17	9	16	25	12	....	....	....	....
1989-90	Niagara Falls	OHL	65	*57	70	*127	97	....	....	....	....	....	....	....	....	....	16	*16	17	*33	49	....	....	....	....
1990-91	**Detroit**	**NHL**	**58**	**3**	**12**	**15**	**106**	**0**	**0**	**1**	**33**	**9.1**	**–12**	....	....	....	**5**	**1**	**1**	**2**	**25**	**0**	**0**	**0**	....
	Adirondack	AHL	6	3	5	8	8	....	....	....	....	....	....	....	....	....	....	....	....	....	....	....	....	....	....
1991-92	**Detroit**	**NHL**	**35**	**6**	**10**	**16**	**83**	**0**	**0**	**0**	**27**	**22.2**	**9**	....	....	....	**11**	**0**	**0**	**0**	**14**	**0**	**0**	**0**	....
	Adirondack	AHL	42	21	24	45	89	....	....	....	....	....	....	....	....	....	9	1	7	8	27	....	....	....	....
1992-93	**Detroit**	**NHL**	**73**	**15**	**17**	**32**	**152**	**4**	**1**	**2**	**75**	**20.0**	**–6**	....	....	....	**7**	**0**	**2**	**2**	**26**	**0**	**0**	**0**	....
1993-94	**Detroit**	**NHL**	**78**	**31**	**42**	**73**	**173**	**7**	**3**	**4**	**155**	**20.0**	**34**	....	....	....	**7**	**0**	**2**	**2**	**6**	**0**	**0**	**0**	....
1994-95	**Detroit**	**NHL**	**45**	**15**	**27**	**42**	**99**	**1**	**0**	**3**	**96**	**15.6**	**17**	....	....	....	**17**	**4**	**5**	**9**	**45**	**2**	**0**	**0**	....
1995-96	**Detroit**	**NHL**	**74**	**27**	**25**	**52**	**168**	**6**	**2**	**7**	**150**	**18.0**	**19**	....	....	....	**17**	**1**	**4**	**5**	**28**	**0**	**0**	**0**	....
1996-97	**Hartford**	**NHL**	**75**	**26**	**25**	**51**	**161**	**6**	**3**	**2**	**169**	**15.4**	**–3**	....	....	....	....	....	....	....	....	....	....	....	....
1997-98	**Carolina**	**NHL**	**81**	**26**	**37**	**63**	**110**	**7**	**3**	**2**	**180**	**14.4**	**19**	....	....	....	....	....	....	....	....	....	....	....	....
	Canada	Olympics	6	2	1	3	4	....	....	....	....	....	....	....	....	....	....	....	....	....	....	....	....	....	....
1998-99	**Carolina**	**NHL**	**78**	**30**	**32**	**62**	**75**	**9**	**1**	**5**	**178**	**16.9**	**8**	**1823**	**53.5**	**21:21**	**6**	**0**	**3**	**3**	**6**	**0**	**0**	**0**	**24:35**
99-2000	**Philadelphia**	**NHL**	**23**	**7**	**10**	**17**	**31**	**1**	**0**	**1**	**51**	**13.7**	**10**	**478**	**54.2**	**17:38**	**18**	**2**	**11**	**13**	**13**	**0**	**0**	**1**	**20:25**
2000-01	**Philadelphia**	**NHL**	**71**	**34**	**39**	**73**	**76**	**11**	**0**	**4**	**165**	**20.6**	**17**	**1811**	**53.5**	**19:58**	**4**	**0**	**3**	**3**	**8**	**0**	**0**	**0**	**19:44**
2001-02	**Philadelphia**	**NHL**	**75**	**19**	**29**	**48**	**128**	**5**	**0**	**3**	**151**	**12.6**	**–3**	**1595**	**51.3**	**17:60**	**5**	**0**	**0**	**0**	**6**	**0**	**0**	**0**	**17:20**
2002-03	**Philadelphia**	**NHL**	**80**	**19**	**27**	**46**	**93**	**6**	**0**	**4**	**171**	**11.1**	**4**	**1613**	**51.4**	**19:16**	**13**	**1**	**1**	**2**	**14**	**0**	**0**	**0**	**20:21**
	NHL Totals		**846**	**258**	**332**	**590**	**1455**	**63**	**13**	**38**	**1601**	**16.1**		**7320**	**52.6**	**19:31**	**110**	**9**	**32**	**41**	**191**	**2**	**0**	**1**	**20:33**

OHL Second All-Star Team (1990)

Played in NHL All-Star Game (1999)

Traded to **Hartford** by **Detroit** with Paul Coffey and Detroit's 1st round choice (Nikos Tselios) in 1997 Entry Draft for Brendan Shanahan and Brian Glynn, October 9, 1996. Transferred to **Carolina** after **Hartford** franchise relocated, June 25, 1997. • Missed majority of 1999-2000 season after failing to come to contract terms with **Carolina**. Traded to **Philadelphia** by **Carolina** with Carolina's 5th round choice (later traded to NY Islanders – NY Islanders selected Kristofer Ottosson) in 2000 Entry Draft for Rod Brind'Amour, Jean-Marc Pelletier and Philadelphia's 2nd round choice (later traded to Colorado – Colorado selected Agris Saviels) in 2000 Entry Draft, January 23, 2000.

PRIMEAU, Wayne

(PREE-moh, WAYN) **S.J.**

Center. Shoots left. 6'3", 220 lbs. Born, Scarborough, Ont., June 4, 1976. Buffalo's 1st choice, 17th overall, in 1994 Entry Draft.

Season	Club	League	GP	G	A	Pts	PIM	PP	SH	GW	S	%	+/-	TF	F%	Min	GP	G	A	Pts	PIM	PP	SH	GW	Min
1991-92	Whitby Flyers	OMHA	63	36	50	86	96	....	....	....	....	....	....	....	....	....	....	....	....	....	....	....	....	....	....
1992-93	Owen Sound	OHL	66	10	27	37	108	....	....	....	....	....	....	....	....	....	8	1	4	5	0	....	....	....	....
1993-94	Owen Sound	OHL	65	25	50	75	75	....	....	....	....	....	....	....	....	....	9	1	6	7	8	....	....	....	....
1994-95	Owen Sound	OHL	66	34	62	96	84	....	....	....	....	....	....	....	....	....	10	4	9	13	15	....	....	....	....
	Buffalo	**NHL**	**1**	**1**	**0**	**1**	**0**	**0**	**0**	**1**	**2**	**50.0**	**–2**	....	....	....	....	....	....	....	....	....	....	....	....
1995-96	Owen Sound	OHL	28	15	29	44	52	....	....	....	....	....	....	....	....	....	....	....	....	....	....	....	....	....	....
	Oshawa Generals	OHL	24	12	13	25	33	....	....	....	....	....	....	....	....	....	3	2	3	5	2	....	....	....	....
	Buffalo	**NHL**	**2**	**0**	**0**	**0**	**0**	**0**	**0**	**0**	**0**	**0.0**	**0**	....	....	....	....	....	....	....	....	....	....	....	....
	Rochester	AHL	8	2	3	5	6	....	....	....	....	....	....	....	....	....	17	3	1	4	11	....	....	....	....
1996-97	**Buffalo**	**NHL**	**45**	**2**	**4**	**6**	**64**	**1**	**0**	**0**	**25**	**8.0**	**–2**	....	....	....	**9**	**0**	**0**	**0**	**6**	**0**	**0**	**0**	....
	Rochester	AHL	24	9	5	14	27	....	....	....	....	....	....	....	....	....	1	0	0	0	0	....	....	....	....
1997-98	**Buffalo**	**NHL**	**69**	**6**	**6**	**12**	**87**	**2**	**0**	**1**	**51**	**11.8**	**9**	....	....	....	**14**	**1**	**3**	**4**	**6**	**0**	**0**	**0**	....
1998-99	**Buffalo**	**NHL**	**67**	**5**	**8**	**13**	**38**	**0**	**0**	**0**	**55**	**9.1**	**–6**	**529**	**48.6**	**10:19**	**19**	**3**	**4**	**7**	**6**	**1**	**0**	**0**	**13:29**
99-2000	**Buffalo**	**NHL**	**41**	**5**	**7**	**12**	**38**	**2**	**0**	**1**	**40**	**12.5**	**–8**	**430**	**45.6**	**11:03**	....	....	....	....	....	....	....	....	....
	Tampa Bay	**NHL**	**17**	**2**	**3**	**5**	**25**	**0**	**0**	**0**	**35**	**5.7**	**–4**	**290**	**45.5**	**14:21**	....	....	....	....	....	....	....	....	....
2000-01	**Tampa Bay**	**NHL**	**47**	**2**	**13**	**15**	**77**	**0**	**0**	**0**	**47**	**4.3**	**–17**	**630**	**52.2**	**14:11**	....	....	....	....	....	....	....	....	....
	Pittsburgh	**NHL**	**28**	**1**	**6**	**7**	**54**	**0**	**0**	**0**	**30**	**3.3**	**0**	**318**	**51.3**	**12:45**	**18**	**1**	**3**	**4**	**2**	**0**	**0**	**0**	**15:06**
2001-02	**Pittsburgh**	**NHL**	**33**	**3**	**7**	**10**	**18**	**0**	**1**	**0**	**28**	**10.7**	**–1**	**519**	**53.2**	**12:38**	....	....	....	....	....	....	....	....	....
2002-03	**Pittsburgh**	**NHL**	**70**	**5**	**11**	**16**	**55**	**1**	**0**	**0**	**101**	**5.0**	**–30**	**1240**	**50.4**	**16:17**	....	....	....	....	....	....	....	....	....
	San Jose	**NHL**	**7**	**1**	**1**	**2**	**0**	**0**	**0**	**0**	**13**	**7.7**	**2**	**98**	**45.9**	**15:59**	....	....	....	....	....	....	....	....	....
	NHL Totals		**427**	**33**	**66**	**99**	**456**	**6**	**1**	**3**	**427**	**7.7**		**4054**	**49.9**	**13:10**	**60**	**5**	**10**	**15**	**20**	**1**	**0**	**0**	**14:16**

Traded to **Tampa Bay** by **Buffalo** with Cory Sarich, Brian Holzinger and Buffalo's 3rd round choice (Alexander Kharitonov) in 2000 Entry Draft for Chris Gratton and Tampa Bay's 2nd round choice (Derek Roy) in 2001 Entry Draft, March 9, 2000. Traded to **Pittsburgh** by **Tampa Bay** for Matthew Barnaby, February 1, 2001. • Missed majority of 2001-02 season recovering from knee injury suffered in game vs. Buffalo, January 8, 2002. Traded to **San Jose** by **Pittsburgh** for Matt Bradley, March 11, 2003.

PRONGER, Chris (PRAHN-guhr, KRIHS) ST.L.

Defense. Shoots left. 6'6", 220 lbs. Born, Dryden, Ont., October 10, 1974. Hartford's 1st choice, 2nd overall, in 1993 Entry Draft.

			Regular Season														Playoffs								
Season	Club	League	GP	G	A	Pts	PIM	PP	SH	GW	S	%	+/-	TF	F%	Min	GP	G	A	Pts	PIM	PP	SH	GW	Min
1990-91	Stratford Cullitons	OJHL-B	48	15	37	52	132	....	....	....	....	....	....	....	....	....	....	....	....	....	....	....	....	....	....
1991-92	Peterborough	OHL	63	17	45	62	90	....	....	....	....	....	....	....	....	....	10	1	8	9	28	....	....	....	....
1992-93	Peterborough	OHL	61	15	62	77	108	....	....	....	....	....	....	....	....	....	21	15	25	40	51	....	....	....	....
1993-94	**Hartford**	**NHL**	**81**	**5**	**25**	**30**	**113**	**2**	**0**	**0**	**174**	**2.9**	**–3**	....	....	....	....	....	....	....	....	....	....	....	....
1994-95	**Hartford**	**NHL**	**43**	**5**	**9**	**14**	**54**	**3**	**0**	**1**	**94**	**5.3**	**–12**	....	....	....	....	....	....	....	....	....	....	....	....
1995-96	**St. Louis**	**NHL**	**78**	**7**	**18**	**25**	**110**	**3**	**1**	**1**	**138**	**5.1**	**–18**	....	....	....	**13**	**1**	**5**	**6**	**16**	**0**	**0**	**0**	....
1996-97	**St. Louis**	**NHL**	**79**	**11**	**24**	**35**	**143**	**4**	**0**	**0**	**147**	**7.5**	**15**	....	....	....	**6**	**1**	**1**	**2**	**22**	**0**	**0**	**0**	....
1997-98	**St. Louis**	**NHL**	**81**	**9**	**27**	**36**	**180**	**1**	**0**	**2**	**145**	**6.2**	**47**	....	....	....	**10**	**1**	**9**	**10**	**26**	**0**	**0**	**0**	....
	Canada	Olympics	6	0	0	0	4	....	....	....	....	....	....	....	....	....	....	....	....	....	....	....	....	....	....
1998-99	**St. Louis**	**NHL**	**67**	**13**	**33**	**46**	**113**	**8**	**0**	**0**	**172**	**7.6**	**3**	**0**	**0.0**	**30:36**	**13**	**1**	**4**	**5**	**28**	**1**	**0**	**0**	**35:53**
99-2000	**St. Louis**	**NHL**	**79**	**14**	**48**	**62**	**92**	**8**	**0**	**3**	**192**	**7.3**	**52**	**1**	**0.0**	**30:14**	**7**	**3**	**4**	**7**	**32**	**2**	**0**	**2**	**30:14**
2000-01	**St. Louis**	**NHL**	**51**	**8**	**39**	**47**	**75**	**4**	**0**	**0**	**121**	**6.6**	**21**	**0**	**0.0**	**27:45**	**15**	**1**	**7**	**8**	**32**	**0**	**0**	**0**	**33:50**
2001-02	**St. Louis**	**NHL**	**78**	**7**	**40**	**47**	**120**	**4**	**1**	**3**	**204**	**3.4**	**23**	**0**	**0.0**	**29:28**	**9**	**1**	**7**	**8**	**24**	**0**	**0**	**0**	**27:51**
	Canada	Olympics	6	0	1	1	2	....	....	....	....	....	....	....	....	....	....	....	....	....	....	....	....	....	....
2002-03	**St. Louis**	**NHL**	**5**	**1**	**3**	**4**	**10**	**0**	**0**	**0**	**11**	**9.1**	**–2**	**1**	**0.0**	**21:39**	**7**	**1**	**3**	**4**	**14**	**0**	**0**	**0**	**24:36**
	NHL Totals		**642**	**80**	**266**	**346**	**1010**	**37**	**2**	**10**	**1398**	**5.7**		**2**	**0.0**	**29:30**	**80**	**10**	**40**	**50**	**194**	**3**	**0**	**2**	**31:32**

OHL All-Rookie Team (1992) • OHL First All-Star Team (1993) • Canadian Major Junior First All-Star Team (1993) • Canadian Major Junior Defenseman of the Year (1993) • NHL All-Rookie Team (1994) • NHL Second All-Star Team (1998) • Bud Ice Plus/Minus Award (1998) • NHL First All-Star Team (2000) • Bud Light Plus/Minus Award (2000) • James Norris Memorial Trophy (2000) • Hart Trophy (2000)

Played in NHL All-Star Game (1999, 2000, 2002)

Traded to **St. Louis** by **Hartford** for Brendan Shanahan, July 27, 1995. • Missed majority of 2002-03 season recovering from wrist and knee surgery, September 10, 2002.

PRONGER, Sean (PRAHN-guhr, SHAWN) CBJ

Center. Shoots left. 6'3", 209 lbs. Born, Thunder Bay, Ont., November 30, 1972. Vancouver's 3rd choice, 51st overall, in 1991 Entry Draft.

			Regular Season														Playoffs								
Season	Club	League	GP	G	A	Pts	PIM	PP	SH	GW	S	%	+/-	TF	F%	Min	GP	G	A	Pts	PIM	PP	SH	GW	Min
1988-89	Kenora Boise	NOJHA	33	38	30	68	....	....	....	....	....	....	....	....	....	....	....	....	....	....	....	....	....	....	....
1989-90	Thunder Bay	USHL	48	18	34	52	61	....	....	....	....	....	....	....	....	....	....	....	....	....	....	....	....	....	....
1990-91	Bowling Green	CCHA	40	3	7	10	30	....	....	....	....	....	....	....	....	....	....	....	....	....	....	....	....	....	....
1991-92	Bowling Green	CCHA	34	9	7	16	28	....	....	....	....	....	....	....	....	....	....	....	....	....	....	....	....	....	....
1992-93	Bowling Green	CCHA	39	23	23	46	35	....	....	....	....	....	....	....	....	....	....	....	....	....	....	....	....	....	....
1993-94	Bowling Green	CCHA	38	17	17	34	38	....	....	....	....	....	....	....	....	....	....	....	....	....	....	....	....	....	....
1994-95	Knoxville	ECHL	34	18	23	41	55	....	....	....	....	....	....	....	....	....	....	....	....	....	....	....	....	....	....
	Greensboro	ECHL	2	0	2	2	0	....	....	....	....	....	....	....	....	....	....	....	....	....	....	....	....	....	....
	San Diego Gulls	IHL	8	0	0	0	2	....	....	....	....	....	....	....	....	....	....	....	....	....	....	....	....	....	....
1995-96	**Anaheim**	**NHL**	**7**	**0**	**1**	**1**	**6**	**0**	**0**	**0**	**3**	**0.0**	**0**	....	....	....	....	....	....	....	....	....	....	....	....
	Baltimore Bandits	AHL	72	16	17	33	61	....	....	....	....	....	....	....	....	....	12	3	7	10	16	....	....	....	....
1996-97	**Anaheim**	**NHL**	**39**	**7**	**7**	**14**	**20**	**1**	**0**	**1**	**43**	**16.3**	**6**	....	....	....	**9**	**0**	**2**	**2**	**4**	**0**	**0**	**0**	....
	Baltimore Bandits	AHL	41	26	17	43	17	....	....	....	....	....	....	....	....	....	....	....	....	....	....	....	....	....	....
1997-98	**Anaheim**	**NHL**	**62**	**5**	**15**	**20**	**30**	**1**	**0**	**2**	**68**	**7.4**	**–9**	....	....	....	....	....	....	....	....	....	....	....	....
	Pittsburgh	**NHL**	**5**	**1**	**0**	**1**	**2**	**0**	**0**	**1**	**5**	**20.0**	**–1**	....	....	....	**5**	**0**	**0**	**0**	**4**	**0**	**0**	**0**	....
1998-99	**Pittsburgh**	**NHL**	**2**	**0**	**0**	**0**	**0**	**0**	**0**	**0**	**3**	**0.0**	**0**	**4**	**75.0**	**8:48**	....	....	....	....	....	....	....	....	....
	Houston Aeros	IHL	16	11	7	18	32	....	....	....	....	....	....	....	....	....	....	....	....	....	....	....	....	....	....
	NY Rangers	**NHL**	**14**	**0**	**3**	**3**	**4**	**0**	**0**	**0**	**3**	**0.0**	**–3**	**15**	**20.0**	**6:28**	....	....	....	....	....	....	....	....	....
	Los Angeles	**NHL**	**13**	**0**	**1**	**1**	**4**	**0**	**0**	**0**	**8**	**0.0**	**2**	**20**	**35.0**	**11:00**	....	....	....	....	....	....	....	....	....
99-2000	**Boston**	**NHL**	**11**	**0**	**1**	**1**	**13**	**0**	**0**	**0**	**7**	**0.0**	**–4**	**116**	**46.6**	**10:47**	....	....	....	....	....	....	....	....	....
	Providence Bruins	AHL	51	11	18	29	26	....	....	....	....	....	....	....	....	....	....	....	....	....	....	....	....	....	....
	Manitoba Moose	IHL	14	3	5	8	21	....	....	....	....	....	....	....	....	....	2	0	1	1	2	....	....	....	....
2000-01	Manitoba Moose	IHL	82	18	21	39	85	....	....	....	....	....	....	....	....	....	13	3	6	9	2	....	....	....	....
2001-02	**Columbus**	**NHL**	**26**	**3**	**1**	**4**	**4**	**0**	**0**	**0**	**25**	**12.0**	**–4**	**167**	**52.1**	**11:26**	....	....	....	....	....	....	....	....	....
	Syracuse Crunch	AHL	54	23	26	49	53	....	....	....	....	....	....	....	....	....	8	4	1	5	10	....	....	....	....
2002-03	**Columbus**	**NHL**	**78**	**7**	**6**	**13**	**72**	**1**	**0**	**0**	**67**	**10.4**	**–26**	**655**	**49.5**	**11:32**	....	....	....	....	....	....	....	....	....
	NHL Totals		**257**	**23**	**35**	**58**	**155**	**3**	**0**	**4**	**232**	**9.9**		**977**	**48.9**	**10:52**	**14**	**0**	**2**	**2**	**8**	**0**	**0**	**0**	....

Signed as a free agent by **Anaheim**, February 14, 1995. Traded to **Pittsburgh** by **Anaheim** for the rights to Patrick Lalime, March 24, 1998. Traded to **NY Rangers** by **Pittsburgh** with Chris Tamer and Petr Nedved for Alex Kovalev and Harry York, November 25, 1998. Traded to **Los Angeles** by **NY Rangers** for Eric Lacroix, February 12, 1999. Signed as a free agent by **Boston**, August 25, 1999. Traded to **Manitoba** (IHL) by **Providence** (AHL) with Keith McCambridge for Terry Hollinger, March 16, 2000 with Boston retaining Pronger's NHL rights. Traded to **NY Islanders** by **Boston** for future considerations, December 5, 2000. Claimed on waivers by **Columbus** from **NY Islanders**, May 18, 2001.

PROSPAL, Vaclav (PRAWS-pahl, VAHT-slahv) ANA.

Center. Shoots left. 6'2", 195 lbs. Born, Ceske Budejovice, Czech., February 17, 1975. Philadelphia's 2nd choice, 71st overall, in 1993 Entry Draft.

			Regular Season														Playoffs								
Season	Club	League	GP	G	A	Pts	PIM	PP	SH	GW	S	%	+/-	TF	F%	Min	GP	G	A	Pts	PIM	PP	SH	GW	Min
1991-92	C. Budejovice Jr.	Czech-Jr.	36	16	16	32	12	....	....	....	....	....	....	....	....	....	....	....	....	....	....	....	....	....	....
1992-93	C. Budejovice Jr.	Czech-Jr.	32	26	31	57	24	....	....	....	....	....	....	....	....	....	....	....	....	....	....	....	....	....	....
1993-94	Hershey Bears	AHL	55	14	21	35	38	....	....	....	....	....	....	....	....	....	2	0	0	0	2	....	....	....	....
1994-95	Hershey Bears	AHL	69	13	32	45	36	....	....	....	....	....	....	....	....	....	2	1	0	1	4	....	....	....	....
1995-96	Hershey Bears	AHL	68	15	36	51	59	....	....	....	....	....	....	....	....	....	5	2	4	6	2	....	....	....	....
1996-97	**Philadelphia**	**NHL**	**18**	**5**	**10**	**15**	**4**	**0**	**0**	**0**	**35**	**14.3**	**3**	....	....	....	**5**	**1**	**3**	**4**	**4**	**0**	**0**	**0**	....
	Philadelphia	AHL	63	32	63	95	70	....	....	....	....	....	....	....	....	....	....	....	....	....	....	....	....	....	....
1997-98	**Philadelphia**	**NHL**	**41**	**5**	**13**	**18**	**17**	**4**	**0**	**0**	**60**	**8.3**	**–10**	....	....	....	....	....	....	....	....	....	....	....	....
	Ottawa	**NHL**	**15**	**1**	**6**	**7**	**4**	**0**	**0**	**0**	**28**	**3.6**	**–1**	....	....	....	**6**	**0**	**0**	**0**	**0**	**0**	**0**	**0**	....
1998-99	**Ottawa**	**NHL**	**79**	**10**	**26**	**36**	**58**	**2**	**0**	**3**	**114**	**8.8**	**8**	**997**	**56.2**	**13:03**	**4**	**0**	**0**	**0**	**0**	**0**	**0**	**0**	**12:36**
99-2000	**Ottawa**	**NHL**	**79**	**22**	**33**	**55**	**40**	**5**	**0**	**4**	**204**	**10.8**	**–2**	**1331**	**49.6**	**16:26**	**6**	**0**	**4**	**4**	**4**	**0**	**0**	**0**	**17:40**
2000-01	**Ottawa**	**NHL**	**40**	**1**	**12**	**13**	**12**	**0**	**0**	**0**	**68**	**1.5**	**1**	**501**	**50.1**	**12:57**	....	....	....	....	....	....	....	....	....
	Florida	**NHL**	**34**	**4**	**12**	**16**	**10**	**1**	**0**	**0**	**68**	**5.9**	**–2**	**487**	**54.6**	**16:36**	....	....	....	....	....	....	....	....	....
2001-02	**Tampa Bay**	**NHL**	**81**	**18**	**37**	**55**	**38**	**7**	**0**	**2**	**166**	**10.8**	**–11**	**555**	**52.8**	**17:31**	....	....	....	....	....	....	....	....	....
2002-03	**Tampa Bay**	**NHL**	**80**	**22**	**57**	**79**	**53**	**9**	**0**	**4**	**134**	**16.4**	**9**	**161**	**51.6**	**18:39**	**11**	**4**	**2**	**6**	**8**	**2**	**0**	**0**	**21:15**
	NHL Totals		**467**	**88**	**206**	**294**	**236**	**28**	**0**	**13**	**877**	**10.0**		**4032**	**52.4**	**16:05**	**32**	**5**	**9**	**14**	**16**	**2**	**0**	**0**	**18:35**

AHL First All-Star Team (1997)

Traded to **Ottawa** by **Philadelphia** with Pat Falloon and Dallas' 2nd round choice (previously acquired, Ottawa selected Chris Bala) in 1998 Entry Draft for Alexandre Daigle, January 17, 1998. Traded to **Florida** by **Ottawa** for future considerations, January 20, 2001. Traded to **Tampa Bay** by **Florida** for Ryan Johnson and Tampa Bay's 6th round choice (later traded back to Tampa Bay – Tampa Bay selected Doug O'Brien) in 2003 Entry Draft, July 10, 2001. Signed as a free agent by **Anaheim**, July 17, 2003.

PURINTON, Dale (PUHR-ihn-TOHN, DAYL) NYR

Defense. Shoots left. 6'3", 214 lbs. Born, Fort Wayne, IN, October 11, 1976. NY Rangers' 5th choice, 117th overall, in 1995 Entry Draft.

			Regular Season														Playoffs								
Season	Club	League	GP	G	A	Pts	PIM	PP	SH	GW	S	%	+/-	TF	F%	Min	GP	G	A	Pts	PIM	PP	SH	GW	Min
1992-93	Moose Jaw	SMHL	34	1	16	17	107	....	....	....	....	....	....	....	....	....	....	....	....	....	....	....	....	....	....
	Moose Jaw	WHL	2	0	0	0	2	....	....	....	....	....	....	....	....	....	....	....	....	....	....	....	....	....	....
1993-94	Vernon Vipers	BCJHL	42	1	6	7	194	....	....	....	....	....	....	....	....	....	....	....	....	....	....	....	....	....	....
1994-95	Tacoma Rockets	WHL	65	0	8	8	291	....	....	....	....	....	....	....	....	....	3	0	0	0	13	....	....	....	....
1995-96	Kelowna Rockets	WHL	22	1	4	5	88	....	....	....	....	....	....	....	....	....	....	....	....	....	....	....	....	....	....
	Lethbridge	WHL	37	3	6	9	144	....	....	....	....	....	....	....	....	....	4	1	1	2	25	....	....	....	....
1996-97	Lethbridge	WHL	51	6	26	32	254	....	....	....	....	....	....	....	....	....	18	3	5	8	*88	....	....	....	....
1997-98	Hartford	AHL	17	0	0	0	95	....	....	....	....	....	....	....	....	....	....	....	....	....	....	....	....	....	....
	Charlotte	ECHL	34	3	5	8	186	....	....	....	....	....	....	....	....	....	....	....	....	....	....	....	....	....	....
1998-99	Hartford	AHL	45	1	3	4	306	....	....	....	....	....	....	....	....	....	7	0	2	2	24	....	....	....	....
99-2000	**NY Rangers**	**NHL**	**1**	**0**	**0**	**0**	**7**	**0**	**0**	**0**	**1**	**0.0**	**–1**	**0**	**0.0**	**12:45**	....	....	....	....	....	....	....	....	....
	Hartford	AHL	62	4	4	8	415	....	....	....	....	....	....	....	....	....	23	0	3	3	*87	....	....	....	....
2000-01	**NY Rangers**	**NHL**	**42**	**0**	**2**	**2**	**180**	**0**	**0**	**0**	**13**	**0.0**	**5**	**0**	**0.0**	**9:33**	....	....	....	....	....	....	....	....	....
	Hartford	AHL	11	0	1	1	75	....	....	....	....	....	....	....	....	....	....	....	....	....	....	....	....	....	....
2001-02	**NY Rangers**	**NHL**	**40**	**0**	**4**	**4**	**113**	**0**	**0**	**0**	**11**	**0.0**	**4**	**0**	**0.0**	**7:37**	....	....	....	....	....	....	....	....	....
2002-03	**NY Rangers**	**NHL**	**58**	**3**	**9**	**12**	**161**	**0**	**0**	**0**	**50**	**6.0**	**–2**	**0**	**0.0**	**15:02**	....	....	....	....	....	....	....	....	....
	NHL Totals		**141**	**3**	**15**	**18**	**461**	**0**	**0**	**0**	**75**	**4.0**		**0**	**0.0**	**11:17**	....	....	....	....	....	....	....	....	....

PUSHOR, Jamie

(PUH-shohr, JAY-mee)

Defense. Shoots right. 6'3", 218 lbs. Born, Lethbridge, Alta., February 11, 1973. Detroit's 2nd choice, 32nd overall, in 1991 Entry Draft.

			Regular Season														Playoffs								
Season	Club	League	GP	G	A	Pts	PIM	PP	SH	GW	S	%	+/-	TF	F%	Min	GP	G	A	Pts	PIM	PP	SH	GW	Min
1988-89	Lethbridge	AMHL	37	1	8	9	20	....	....	....	....	....	....	....	....	....	....	....	....	....	....	....	....	....	....
	Lethbridge	WHL	2	0	0	0	0	....	....	....	....	....	....	....	....	....	....	....	....	....	....	....	....	....	....
1989-90	Lethbridge	AMHL	35	6	27	33	92	....	....	....	....	....	....	....	....	....	....	....	....	....	....	....	....	....	....
	Lethbridge	WHL	10	0	2	2	2	....	....	....	....	....	....	....	....	....	16	0	0	0	63	....	....	....	....
1990-91	Lethbridge	WHL	71	1	13	14	202	....	....	....	....	....	....	....	....	....	....	....	....	....	....	....	....	....	....
1991-92	Lethbridge	WHL	49	2	15	17	232	....	....	....	....	....	....	....	....	....	5	0	0	0	33	....	....	....	....
1992-93	Lethbridge	WHL	72	6	22	28	200	....	....	....	....	....	....	....	....	....	4	0	1	1	9	....	....	....	....
1993-94	Adirondack	AHL	73	1	17	18	124	....	....	....	....	....	....	....	....	....	12	0	0	0	22	....	....	....	....
1994-95	Adirondack	AHL	58	2	11	13	129	....	....	....	....	....	....	....	....	....	4	0	1	1	0	....	....	....	....
1995-96	**Detroit**	**NHL**	**5**	**0**	**1**	**1**	**17**	**0**	**0**	**0**	**6**	**0.0**	**2**	....	....	....	....	....	....	....	....	....	....	....	....
	Adirondack	AHL	65	2	16	18	126	....	....	....	....	....	....	....	....	....	3	0	0	0	5	....	....	....	....
1996-97◆	**Detroit**	**NHL**	**75**	**4**	**7**	**11**	**129**	**0**	**0**	**0**	**63**	**6.3**	**1**	....	....	....	**5**	**0**	**1**	**1**	**5**	**0**	**0**	**0**	....
1997-98	**Detroit**	**NHL**	**54**	**2**	**5**	**7**	**71**	**0**	**0**	**0**	**43**	**4.7**	**2**	....	....	....	....	....	....	....	....	....	....	....	....
	Anaheim	**NHL**	**10**	**0**	**2**	**2**	**10**	**0**	**0**	**0**	**8**	**0.0**	**1**	....	....	....	....	....	....	....	....	....	....	....	....
1998-99	**Anaheim**	**NHL**	**70**	**1**	**2**	**3**	**112**	**0**	**0**	**0**	**75**	**1.3**	**–20**	**0**	**0.0**	**19:16**	**4**	**0**	**0**	**0**	**6**	**0**	**0**	**0**	**14:08**
99-2000	**Dallas**	**NHL**	**62**	**0**	**8**	**8**	**53**	**0**	**0**	**0**	**27**	**0.0**	**0**	**0**	**0.0**	**11:36**	**5**	**0**	**0**	**0**	**5**	**0**	**0**	**0**	**10:06**
2000-01	**Columbus**	**NHL**	**75**	**3**	**10**	**13**	**94**	**0**	**1**	**0**	**64**	**4.7**	**7**	**0**	**0.0**	**20:48**	....	....	....	....	....	....	....	....	....
2001-02	**Columbus**	**NHL**	**61**	**0**	**6**	**6**	**54**	**0**	**0**	**0**	**46**	**0.0**	**–10**	**0**	**0.0**	**17:06**	....	....	....	....	....	....	....	....	....
	Pittsburgh	**NHL**	**15**	**0**	**2**	**2**	**30**	**0**	**0**	**0**	**14**	**0.0**	**–3**	**0**	**0.0**	**19:03**	....	....	....	....	....	....	....	....	....
2002-03	**Pittsburgh**	**NHL**	**76**	**3**	**1**	**4**	**76**	**0**	**0**	**0**	**54**	**5.6**	**–28**	**0**	**0.0**	**16:58**	....	....	....	....	....	....	....	....	....
	NHL Totals		**503**	**13**	**44**	**57**	**646**	**0**	**1**	**0**	**400**	**3.3**		**0**	**0.0**	**17:24**	**14**	**0**	**1**	**1**	**16**	**0**	**0**	**0**	**11:53**

Traded to **Anaheim** by **Detroit** with Detroit's 4th round choice (Viktor Wallin) in 1998 Entry Draft for Dmitri Mironov, March 24, 1998. Claimed by **Atlanta** from **Anaheim** in Expansion Draft, June 25, 1999. Traded to **Dallas** by **Atlanta** for Jason Botterill, July 15, 1999. Selected by **Columbus** from **Dallas** in Expansion Draft, June 23, 2000. Traded to **Pittsburgh** by **Columbus** for Pittsburgh's 4th round choice (Kevin Jarman) in 2003 Entry Draft, March 15, 2002.

PYATT, Taylor

(PIGH-at, TAY-lohr) **BUF.**

Left wing. Shoots left. 6'4", 222 lbs. Born, Thunder Bay, Ont., August 19, 1981. NY Islanders' 2nd choice, 8th overall, in 1999 Entry Draft.

			Regular Season														Playoffs								
Season	Club	League	GP	G	A	Pts	PIM	PP	SH	GW	S	%	+/-	TF	F%	Min	GP	G	A	Pts	PIM	PP	SH	GW	Min
1996-97	Thunder Bay	TBAHA	60	52	61	113	72	....	....	....	....	....	....	....	....	....	....	....	....	....	....	....	....	....	....
1997-98	Sudbury Wolves	OHL	58	14	17	31	104	....	....	....	....	....	....	....	....	....	10	3	1	4	8	....	....	....	....
1998-99	Sudbury Wolves	OHL	68	37	38	75	95	....	....	....	....	....	....	....	....	....	4	0	4	4	6	....	....	....	....
99-2000	Sudbury Wolves	OHL	68	40	49	89	98	....	....	....	....	....	....	....	....	....	12	8	7	15	25	....	....	....	....
2000-01	**NY Islanders**	**NHL**	**78**	**4**	**14**	**18**	**39**	**1**	**0**	**2**	**86**	**4.7**	**–17**	**1**	**0.0**	**12:14**	....	....	....	....	....	....	....	....	....
2001-02	**Buffalo**	**NHL**	**48**	**10**	**10**	**20**	**35**	**0**	**0**	**0**	**61**	**16.4**	**4**	**0**	**0.0**	**13:30**	....	....	....	....	....	....	....	....	....
	Rochester	AHL	27	6	4	10	36	....	....	....	....	....	....	....	....	....	....	....	....	....	....	....	....	....	....
2002-03	**Buffalo**	**NHL**	**78**	**14**	**14**	**28**	**38**	**2**	**0**	**0**	**110**	**12.7**	**–8**	**8**	**25.0**	**14:06**	....	....	....	....	....	....	....	....	....
	NHL Totals		**204**	**28**	**38**	**66**	**112**	**3**	**0**	**2**	**257**	**10.9**		**9**	**22.2**	**13:14**	....	....	....	....	....	....	....	....	....

OHL First All-Star Team (2000)

Traded to **Buffalo** by **NY Islanders** with Tim Connolly for Michael Peca, June 24, 2001.

QUINT, Deron

(KWIHNT, DAIR-ohn) **CHI.**

Defense. Shoots left. 6'2", 219 lbs. Born, Durham, NH, March 12, 1976. Winnipeg's 1st choice, 30th overall, in 1994 Entry Draft.

			Regular Season														Playoffs								
Season	Club	League	GP	G	A	Pts	PIM	PP	SH	GW	S	%	+/-	TF	F%	Min	GP	G	A	Pts	PIM	PP	SH	GW	Min
1990-91	Cardigan High	Hi-School	31	67	54	121	....	....	....	....	....	....	....	....	....	....	....	....	....	....	....	....	....	....	....
1991-92	Cardigan High	Hi-School	21	111	58	169	....	....	....	....	....	....	....	....	....	....	....	....	....	....	....	....	....	....	....
1992-93	Tabor Academy	Hi-School	28	15	26	41	30	....	....	....	....	....	....	....	....	....	1	0	2	2	0	....	....	....	....
1993-94	Seattle	WHL	63	15	29	44	47	....	....	....	....	....	....	....	....	....	9	4	12	16	8	....	....	....	....
1994-95	Seattle	WHL	65	29	60	89	82	....	....	....	....	....	....	....	....	....	3	1	2	3	6	....	....	....	....
1995-96	**Winnipeg**	**NHL**	**51**	**5**	**13**	**18**	**22**	**2**	**0**	**0**	**97**	**5.2**	**–2**	....	....	....	....	....	....	....	....	....	....	....	....
	Springfield	AHL	11	2	3	5	4	....	....	....	....	....	....	....	....	....	10	2	3	5	6	....	....	....	....
	Seattle	WHL	....	....	....	....	....	....	....	....	....	....	....	....	....	....	5	4	1	5	6	....	....	....	....
1996-97	**Phoenix**	**NHL**	**27**	**3**	**11**	**14**	**4**	**1**	**0**	**0**	**63**	**4.8**	**–4**	....	....	....	**7**	**0**	**2**	**2**	**0**	**0**	**0**	**0**	....
	Springfield	AHL	43	6	18	24	20	....	....	....	....	....	....	....	....	....	12	2	7	9	4	....	....	....	....
1997-98	**Phoenix**	**NHL**	**32**	**4**	**7**	**11**	**16**	**1**	**0**	**1**	**61**	**6.6**	**–6**	....	....	....	....	....	....	....	....	....	....	....	....
	Springfield	AHL	8	1	7	8	10	....	....	....	....	....	....	....	....	....	1	0	0	0	0	....	....	....	....
1998-99	**Phoenix**	**NHL**	**60**	**5**	**8**	**13**	**20**	**2**	**0**	**0**	**94**	**5.3**	**–10**	**0**	**0.0**	**16:12**	....	....	....	....	....	....	....	....	....
99-2000	**Phoenix**	**NHL**	**50**	**3**	**7**	**10**	**22**	**0**	**0**	**1**	**88**	**3.4**	**0**	**0**	**0.0**	**16:39**	....	....	....	....	....	....	....	....	....
	New Jersey	**NHL**	**4**	**1**	**0**	**1**	**2**	**0**	**0**	**0**	**6**	**16.7**	**–2**	**0**	**0.0**	**16:26**	....	....	....	....	....	....	....	....	....
2000-01	**Columbus**	**NHL**	**57**	**7**	**16**	**23**	**16**	**3**	**0**	**0**	**148**	**4.7**	**–19**	**1**	**100.0**	**24:06**	....	....	....	....	....	....	....	....	....
	Syracuse Crunch	AHL	21	5	15	20	30	....	....	....	....	....	....	....	....	....	....	....	....	....	....	....	....	....	....
2001-02	**Columbus**	**NHL**	**75**	**7**	**18**	**25**	**26**	**3**	**0**	**1**	**169**	**4.1**	**–34**	**0**	**0.0**	**22:01**	....	....	....	....	....	....	....	....	....
2002-03	Springfield	AHL	4	1	2	3	4	....	....	....	....	....	....	....	....	....	....	....	....	....	....	....	....	....	....
	Phoenix	**NHL**	**51**	**7**	**10**	**17**	**20**	**2**	**0**	**0**	**85**	**8.2**	**–5**	**0**	**0.0**	**15:51**	....	....	....	....	....	....	....	....	....
	NHL Totals		**407**	**42**	**90**	**132**	**148**	**14**	**0**	**3**	**811**	**5.2**		**1**	**100.0**	**19:12**	**7**	**0**	**2**	**2**	**0**	**0**	**0**	**0**	....

WHL West First All-Star Team (1995)

Transferred to **Phoenix** after **Winnipeg** franchise relocated, July 1, 1996. Traded to **New Jersey** by **Phoenix** with Phoenix's 3rd round choice (later traded back to Phoenix – Phoenix selected Beat Forster) in 2001 Entry Draft for Lyle Odelein, March 7, 2000. Traded to **Columbus** by **New Jersey** to complete transaction that sent Krzysztof Oliwa to Columbus (June 12, 2000) and Turner Stevenson to New Jersey (June 23, 2000), June 23, 2000. Signed to a professional try-out contract by **Springfield** (AHL), October 16, 2002. Signed as a free agent by **Phoenix**, October 26, 2002. Signed as a free agent by **Chicago**, August 5, 2003.

QUINTAL, Stephane

(KAYN-tahl, STEH-fan) **MTL.**

Defense. Shoots right. 6'3", 231 lbs. Born, Boucherville, Que., October 22, 1968. Boston's 2nd choice, 14th overall, in 1987 Entry Draft.

			Regular Season														Playoffs								
Season	Club	League	GP	G	A	Pts	PIM	PP	SH	GW	S	%	+/-	TF	F%	Min	GP	G	A	Pts	PIM	PP	SH	GW	Min
1984-85	Richelieu Riverains	QAAA	41	1	10	11	68	....	....	....	....	....	....	....	....	....	9	0	5	5	27	....	....	....	....
1985-86	Granby Bisons	QMJHL	67	2	17	19	144	....	....	....	....	....	....	....	....	....	....	....	....	....	....	....	....	....	....
1986-87	Granby Bisons	QMJHL	67	13	41	54	178	....	....	....	....	....	....	....	....	....	8	0	9	9	10	....	....	....	....
1987-88	Hull Olympiques	QMJHL	38	13	23	36	138	....	....	....	....	....	....	....	....	....	19	7	12	19	30	....	....	....	....
1988-89	**Boston**	**NHL**	**26**	**0**	**1**	**1**	**29**	**0**	**0**	**0**	**23**	**0.0**	**–5**	....	....	....	....	....	....	....	....	....	....	....	....
	Maine Mariners	AHL	16	4	10	14	28	....	....	....	....	....	....	....	....	....	....	....	....	....	....	....	....	....	....
1989-90	**Boston**	**NHL**	**38**	**2**	**2**	**4**	**22**	**0**	**0**	**0**	**43**	**4.7**	**–11**	....	....	....	....	....	....	....	....	....	....	....	....
	Maine Mariners	AHL	37	4	16	20	27	....	....	....	....	....	....	....	....	....	....	....	....	....	....	....	....	....	....
1990-91	**Boston**	**NHL**	**45**	**2**	**6**	**8**	**89**	**1**	**0**	**0**	**54**	**3.7**	**2**	....	....	....	**3**	**0**	**1**	**1**	**7**	**0**	**0**	**0**	....
	Maine Mariners	AHL	23	1	5	6	30	....	....	....	....	....	....	....	....	....	....	....	....	....	....	....	....	....	....
1991-92	**Boston**	**NHL**	**49**	**4**	**10**	**14**	**77**	**0**	**0**	**0**	**52**	**7.7**	**–8**	....	....	....	....	....	....	....	....	....	....	....	....
	St. Louis	**NHL**	**26**	**0**	**6**	**6**	**32**	**0**	**0**	**0**	**19**	**0.0**	**–3**	....	....	....	**4**	**1**	**2**	**3**	**6**	**1**	**0**	**0**	....
1992-93	**St. Louis**	**NHL**	**75**	**1**	**10**	**11**	**100**	**0**	**1**	**0**	**81**	**1.2**	**–6**	....	....	....	**9**	**0**	**0**	**0**	**8**	**0**	**0**	**0**	....
1993-94	**Winnipeg**	**NHL**	**81**	**8**	**18**	**26**	**119**	**1**	**1**	**1**	**154**	**5.2**	**–25**	....	....	....	....	....	....	....	....	....	....	....	....
1994-95	**Winnipeg**	**NHL**	**43**	**6**	**17**	**23**	**78**	**3**	**0**	**2**	**107**	**5.6**	**0**	....	....	....	....	....	....	....	....	....	....	....	....
1995-96	**Montreal**	**NHL**	**68**	**2**	**14**	**16**	**117**	**0**	**1**	**1**	**104**	**1.9**	**–4**	....	....	....	**6**	**0**	**1**	**1**	**6**	**0**	**0**	**0**	....
1996-97	**Montreal**	**NHL**	**71**	**7**	**15**	**22**	**100**	**1**	**0**	**0**	**139**	**5.0**	**1**	....	....	....	**5**	**0**	**1**	**1**	**6**	**0**	**0**	**0**	....
1997-98	**Montreal**	**NHL**	**71**	**6**	**10**	**16**	**97**	**0**	**0**	**0**	**88**	**6.8**	**13**	....	....	....	**9**	**0**	**2**	**2**	**4**	**0**	**0**	**0**	....
1998-99	**Montreal**	**NHL**	**82**	**8**	**19**	**27**	**84**	**1**	**1**	**4**	**159**	**5.0**	**–23**	**0**	**0.0**	**22:06**	....	....	....	....	....	....	....	....	....
99-2000	**NY Rangers**	**NHL**	**75**	**2**	**14**	**16**	**77**	**0**	**0**	**1**	**102**	**2.0**	**–10**	**0**	**0.0**	**19:04**	....	....	....	....	....	....	....	....	....
2000-01	**Chicago**	**NHL**	**72**	**1**	**18**	**19**	**60**	**0**	**0**	**0**	**109**	**0.9**	**–9**	**0**	**0.0**	**22:30**	....	....	....	....	....	....	....	....	....
2001-02	**Montreal**	**NHL**	**75**	**6**	**10**	**16**	**87**	**1**	**0**	**1**	**85**	**7.1**	**–7**	**0**	**0.0**	**18:52**	**12**	**1**	**3**	**4**	**12**	**0**	**0**	**0**	**22:41**
2002-03	**Montreal**	**NHL**	**67**	**5**	**5**	**10**	**70**	**0**	**0**	**0**	**73**	**6.8**	**–4**	**0**	**0.0**	**18:38**	....	....	....	....	....	....	....	....	....
	NHL Totals		**964**	**60**	**175**	**235**	**1238**	**8**	**4**	**10**	**1392**	**4.3**		**0**	**0.0**	**20:17**	**48**	**2**	**10**	**12**	**49**	**1**	**0**	**0**	**22:41**

QMJHL First All-Star Team (1987)

Traded to **St. Louis** by **Boston** with Craig Janney for Adam Oates, February 7, 1992. Traded to **Winnipeg** by **St. Louis** with Nelson Emerson for Phil Housley, September 24, 1993. Traded to **Montreal** by **Winnipeg** for Montreal's 2nd round choice (Jason Doig) in 1995 Entry Draft, July 8, 1995. Signed as a free agent by **NY Rangers**, July 13, 1999. Claimed on waivers by **Chicago** from **NY Rangers**, October 5, 2000. Traded to **Montreal** by **Chicago** for Montreal's 4th round choice (Brent MacLellan) in 2001 Entry Draft, June 23, 2001.

RACHUNEK, Karel
(ra-KHOO-nehk, KAH-rehl) **OTT.**

Defense. Shoots right. 6'2", 211 lbs. Born, Gottwaldov, Czech., August 27, 1979. Ottawa's 8th choice, 229th overall, in 1997 Entry Draft.

			Regular Season														Playoffs								
Season	Club	League	GP	G	A	Pts	PIM	PP	SH	GW	S	%	+/-	TF	F%	Min	GP	G	A	Pts	PIM	PP	SH	GW	Min
1995-96	AC ZPS Zlin Jr.	Czech-Jr.	38	8	11	19	....	....	....	....	....	....	....	....	....	....	....	....	....	....	....	....	....	....	....
1996-97	AC ZPS Zlin Jr.	Czech-Jr.	27	2	11	13	....	....	....	....	....	....	....	....	....	....	....	....	....	....	....	....	....	....	....
1997-98	Zlin	Czech	27	1	2	3	16	....	....	....	....	....	....	....	....	....	....	....	....	....	....	....	....	....	....
1998-99	Zlin	Czech	39	3	9	12	88	....	....	....	....	....	....	....	....	....	6	0	0	0	....	....	....	....	....
99-2000	**Ottawa**	**NHL**	**6**	**0**	**0**	**0**	**2**	**0**	**0**	**0**	**3**	**0.0**	**0**	**0**	**0.0**	**8:03**	....	....	....	....	....	....	....	....	....
	Grand Rapids	IHL	62	6	20	26	64	....	....	....	....	....	....	....	....	....	9	0	5	5	6	....	....	....	....
2000-01	**Ottawa**	**NHL**	**71**	**3**	**30**	**33**	**60**	**3**	**0**	**0**	**77**	**3.9**	**17**	**0**	**0.0**	**20:54**	**3**	**0**	**0**	**0**	**0**	**0**	**0**	**0**	**22:38**
2001-02	**Ottawa**	**NHL**	**51**	**3**	**15**	**18**	**24**	**1**	**0**	**2**	**55**	**5.5**	**7**	**2**	**0.0**	**19:19**	....	....	....	....	....	....	....	....	....
2002-03	Yaroslavl	Russia	9	3	0	3	8	....	....	....	....	....	....	....	....	....	....	....	....	....	....	....	....	....	....
	Ottawa	**NHL**	**58**	**4**	**25**	**29**	**30**	**3**	**0**	**1**	**110**	**3.6**	**23**	**3**	**33.3**	**21:46**	**17**	**1**	**3**	**4**	**14**	**0**	**0**	**0**	**23:14**
	Binghamton	AHL	6	0	2	2	10	....	....	....	....	....	....	....	....	....	....	....	....	....	....	....	....	....	....
	NHL Totals		**186**	**10**	**70**	**80**	**116**	**7**	**0**	**3**	**245**	**4.1**		**5**	**20.0**	**20:19**	**20**	**1**	**3**	**4**	**14**	**0**	**0**	**0**	**23:09**

RADIVOJEVIC, Branko
(ra-dih-VOI-uh-vihch, BRAN-koh) **PHX.**

Right wing. Shoots right. 6'1", 209 lbs. Born, Piestany, Czech., November 24, 1980. Colorado's 3rd choice, 93rd overall, in 1999 Entry Draft.

Season	Club	League	GP	G	A	Pts	PIM	PP	SH	GW	S	%	+/-	TF	F%	Min	GP	G	A	Pts	PIM	PP	SH	GW	Min
1997-98	Dukla Trencin Jr.	Slovak-Jr.	52	30	31	61	50	....	....	....	....	....	....	....	....	....	....	....	....	....	....	....	....	....	....
	Dukla Trencin	Slovakia	1	0	0	0	2	....	....	....	....	....	....	....	....	....	....	....	....	....	....	....	....	....	....
1998-99	Belleville Bulls	OHL	68	20	38	58	61	....	....	....	....	....	....	....	....	....	21	7	17	24	18	....	....	....	....
99-2000	Belleville Bulls	OHL	59	23	49	72	86	....	....	....	....	....	....	....	....	....	16	5	8	13	32	....	....	....	....
2000-01	Belleville Bulls	OHL	61	34	70	104	77	....	....	....	....	....	....	....	....	....	10	6	10	16	18	....	....	....	....
2001-02	**Phoenix**	**NHL**	**18**	**4**	**2**	**6**	**4**	**0**	**0**	**1**	**19**	**21.1**	**1**	**0**	**0.0**	**9:22**	**1**	**0**	**0**	**0**	**2**	**0**	**0**	**0**	**8:07**
	Springfield	AHL	62	18	21	39	64	....	....	....	....	....	....	....	....	....	....	....	....	....	....	....	....	....	....
2002-03	**Phoenix**	**NHL**	**79**	**12**	**15**	**27**	**63**	**1**	**0**	**3**	**109**	**11.0**	**−2**	**20**	**40.0**	**13:18**	....	....	....	....	....	....	....	....	....
	NHL Totals		**97**	**16**	**17**	**33**	**67**	**1**	**0**	**4**	**128**	**12.5**		**20**	**40.0**	**12:34**	**1**	**0**	**0**	**0**	**2**	**0**	**0**	**0**	**8:07**

OHL First All-Star Team (2001)

Signed as a free agent by **Phoenix**, June 19, 2001.

RADULOV, Igor
(rah-DOO-lahf, EE-gohr) **CHI.**

Left wing. Shoots left. 6'1", 186 lbs. Born, Nizhny Tagil, USSR, August 23, 1982. Chicago's 4th choice, 74th overall, in 2000 Entry Draft.

Season	Club	League	GP	G	A	Pts	PIM	PP	SH	GW	S	%	+/-	TF	F%	Min	GP	G	A	Pts	PIM	PP	SH	GW	Min
1997-98	Yaroslavl	Russia	5	0	2	2	4	....	....	....	....	....	....	....	....	....	....	....	....	....	....	....	....	....	....
1998-99	Yaroslavl 2	Russia-3	21	2	3	5	4	....	....	....	....	....	....	....	....	....	....	....	....	....	....	....	....	....	....
99-2000	Yaroslavl 2	Russia-3	31	17	16	33	....	....	....	....	....	....	....	....	....	....	....	....	....	....	....	....	....	....	....
2000-01	Kristall Saratov	Russia-2	4	0	2	2	2	....	....	....	....	....	....	....	....	....	....	....	....	....	....	....	....	....	....
	St. Petersburg	Russia	8	1	0	1	6	....	....	....	....	....	....	....	....	....	....	....	....	....	....	....	....	....	....
2001-02	Mississauga	OHL	62	33	30	63	30	....	....	....	....	....	....	....	....	....	....	....	....	....	....	....	....	....	....
2002-03	**Chicago**	**NHL**	**7**	**5**	**0**	**5**	**4**	**3**	**0**	**0**	**14**	**35.7**	**−3**	**0**	**0.0**	**15:06**	....	....	....	....	....	....	....	....	....
	Norfolk Admirals	AHL	62	18	9	27	26	....	....	....	....	....	....	....	....	....	9	2	2	4	8	....	....	....	....
	NHL Totals		**7**	**5**	**0**	**5**	**4**	**3**	**0**	**0**	**14**	**35.7**		**0**	**0.0**	**15:06**	....	....	....	....	....	....	....	....	....

RAFALSKI, Brian
(ra-FAWL-skee, BRIGH-uhn) **N.J.**

Defense. Shoots right. 5'9", 190 lbs. Born, Dearborn, MI, September 28, 1973.

Season	Club	League	GP	G	A	Pts	PIM	PP	SH	GW	S	%	+/-	TF	F%	Min	GP	G	A	Pts	PIM	PP	SH	GW	Min
1990-91	Madison Capitols	USHL	47	12	11	23	28	....	....	....	....	....	....	....	....	....	....	....	....	....	....	....	....	....	....
1991-92	U. of Wisconsin	WCHA	34	3	14	17	34	....	....	....	....	....	....	....	....	....	....	....	....	....	....	....	....	....	....
1992-93	U. of Wisconsin	WCHA	32	0	13	13	10	....	....	....	....	....	....	....	....	....	....	....	....	....	....	....	....	....	....
1993-94	U. of Wisconsin	WCHA	37	6	17	23	26	....	....	....	....	....	....	....	....	....	....	....	....	....	....	....	....	....	....
1994-95	U. of Wisconsin	WCHA	43	11	34	45	48	....	....	....	....	....	....	....	....	....	....	....	....	....	....	....	....	....	....
1995-96	Brynas IF Gavle	Sweden	40	4	14	18	26	....	....	....	....	....	....	....	....	....	9	0	1	1	2	....	....	....	....
1996-97	HPK Hameenlinna	Finland	49	11	24	35	26	....	....	....	....	....	....	....	....	....	10	6	5	11	4	....	....	....	....
1997-98	HIFK Helsinki	Finland	40	13	10	23	20	....	....	....	....	....	....	....	....	....	9	5	6	11	0	....	....	....	....
1998-99	HIFK Helsinki	Finland	53	19	34	53	18	....	....	....	....	....	....	....	....	....	11	5	*9	*14	4	....	....	....	....
	HIFK Helsinki	EuroHL	6	4	6	10	10	....	....	....	....	....	....	....	....	....	4	1	0	1	2	....	....	....	....
99-2000♦	**New Jersey**	**NHL**	**75**	**5**	**27**	**32**	**28**	**1**	**0**	**1**	**128**	**3.9**	**21**	**1**	**0.0**	**18:51**	**23**	**2**	**6**	**8**	**8**	**0**	**0**	**1**	**21:25**
2000-01	**New Jersey**	**NHL**	**78**	**9**	**43**	**52**	**26**	**6**	**0**	**1**	**142**	**6.3**	**36**	**2**	**100.0**	**21:41**	**25**	**7**	**11**	**18**	**7**	**1**	**0**	**3**	**22:08**
2001-02	**New Jersey**	**NHL**	**76**	**7**	**40**	**47**	**18**	**2**	**0**	**4**	**125**	**5.6**	**15**	**0**	**0.0**	**22:08**	**6**	**3**	**2**	**5**	**4**	**3**	**0**	**0**	**21:45**
	United States	Olympics	6	1	2	3	2	....	....	....	....	....	....	....	....	....	....	....	....	....	....	....	....	....	....
2002-03♦	**New Jersey**	**NHL**	**79**	**3**	**37**	**40**	**14**	**2**	**0**	**0**	**178**	**1.7**	**18**	**1**	**0.0**	**23:09**	**23**	**2**	**9**	**11**	**8**	**2**	**0**	**0**	**25:46**
	NHL Totals		**308**	**24**	**147**	**171**	**86**	**11**	**0**	**6**	**573**	**4.2**		**4**	**50.0**	**21:29**	**77**	**14**	**28**	**42**	**27**	**6**	**0**	**4**	**22:59**

WCHA First All-Star Team (1995) • NCAA West First All-American Team (1995) • NHL All-Rookie Team (2000)

Signed as a free agent by **New Jersey**, May 7, 1999.

RAGNARSSON, Marcus
(RAG-nahr-suhn, MAHR-kuhs) **PHI.**

Defense. Shoots left. 6'1", 215 lbs. Born, Ostervala, Sweden, August 13, 1971. San Jose's 5th choice, 99th overall, in 1992 Entry Draft.

Season	Club	League	GP	G	A	Pts	PIM	PP	SH	GW	S	%	+/-	TF	F%	Min	GP	G	A	Pts	PIM	PP	SH	GW	Min
1986-87	Ostervala IF	Swede-3	28	1	6	7	....	....	....	....	....	....	....	....	....	....	....	....	....	....	....	....	....	....	....
1987-88	Ostervala IF	Swede-3	25	3	12	15	....	....	....	....	....	....	....	....	....	....	....	....	....	....	....	....	....	....	....
1988-89	Ostervala IF	Swede-3	30	15	14	29	....	....	....	....	....	....	....	....	....	....	....	....	....	....	....	....	....	....	....
1989-90	Nacka HK	Swede-2	9	2	3	5	4	....	....	....	....	....	....	....	....	....	....	....	....	....	....	....	....	....	....
	Djurgarden	Sweden	13	0	2	2	0	....	....	....	....	....	....	....	....	....	1	0	0	0	0	....	....	....	....
1990-91	Djurgarden	Sweden	35	4	1	5	12	....	....	....	....	....	....	....	....	....	7	0	0	0	6	....	....	....	....
1991-92	Djurgarden	Sweden	40	8	5	13	14	....	....	....	....	....	....	....	....	....	10	0	1	1	4	....	....	....	....
1992-93	Djurgarden	Sweden	35	3	3	6	53	....	....	....	....	....	....	....	....	....	6	0	3	3	8	....	....	....	....
1993-94	Djurgarden	Sweden	19	0	4	4	24	....	....	....	....	....	....	....	....	....	....	....	....	....	....	....	....	....	....
1994-95	Djurgarden	Sweden	38	7	9	16	20	....	....	....	....	....	....	....	....	....	3	0	0	0	4	....	....	....	....
1995-96	**San Jose**	**NHL**	**71**	**8**	**31**	**39**	**42**	**4**	**0**	**0**	**94**	**8.5**	**−24**	....	....	....	....	....	....	....	....	....	....	....	....
1996-97	**San Jose**	**NHL**	**69**	**3**	**14**	**17**	**63**	**2**	**0**	**0**	**57**	**5.3**	**−18**	....	....	....	....	....	....	....	....	....	....	....	....
1997-98	**San Jose**	**NHL**	**79**	**5**	**20**	**25**	**65**	**3**	**0**	**2**	**91**	**5.5**	**−11**	....	....	....	**6**	**0**	**0**	**0**	**4**	**0**	**0**	**0**	....
	Sweden	Olympics	3	0	1	1	0	....	....	....	....	....	....	....	....	....	....	....	....	....	....	....	....	....	....
1998-99	**San Jose**	**NHL**	**74**	**0**	**13**	**13**	**66**	**0**	**0**	**0**	**87**	**0.0**	**7**	**3**	**66.7**	**21:55**	**6**	**0**	**1**	**1**	**6**	**0**	**0**	**0**	**22:16**
99-2000	**San Jose**	**NHL**	**63**	**3**	**13**	**16**	**38**	**0**	**0**	**0**	**60**	**5.0**	**13**	**0**	**0.0**	**22:52**	**12**	**0**	**3**	**3**	**10**	**0**	**0**	**0**	**22:22**
2000-01	**San Jose**	**NHL**	**68**	**3**	**12**	**15**	**44**	**1**	**0**	**0**	**74**	**4.1**	**2**	**0**	**0.0**	**23:36**	**5**	**0**	**1**	**1**	**8**	**0**	**0**	**0**	**20:24**
2001-02	**San Jose**	**NHL**	**70**	**5**	**15**	**20**	**44**	**2**	**0**	**3**	**68**	**7.4**	**4**	**4**	**25.0**	**22:37**	**12**	**1**	**3**	**4**	**12**	**0**	**0**	**0**	**21:35**
	Sweden	Olympics	4	0	2	2	2	....	....	....	....	....	....	....	....	....	....	....	....	....	....	....	....	....	....
2002-03	**San Jose**	**NHL**	**25**	**1**	**7**	**8**	**30**	**0**	**0**	**0**	**27**	**3.7**	**2**	**2**	**100.0**	**24:56**	....	....	....	....	....	....	....	....	....
	Philadelphia	**NHL**	**43**	**2**	**6**	**8**	**32**	**1**	**0**	**0**	**52**	**3.8**	**5**	**1**	**100.0**	**21:10**	**13**	**0**	**1**	**1**	**6**	**0**	**0**	**0**	**25:23**
	NHL Totals		**562**	**30**	**131**	**161**	**424**	**13**	**0**	**5**	**610**	**4.9**		**10**	**60.0**	**22:42**	**54**	**1**	**9**	**10**	**46**	**0**	**0**	**0**	**22:46**

Played in NHL All-Star Game (2001)

Traded to **Philadelphia** by **San Jose** for Dan McGillis, December 6, 2002.

RALPH, Brad
(RALF, BRAD)

Left wing. Shoots left. 6'2", 206 lbs. Born, Ottawa, Ont., October 17, 1980. Phoenix's 3rd choice, 53rd overall, in 1999 Entry Draft.

Season	Club	League	GP	G	A	Pts	PIM	PP	SH	GW	S	%	+/-	TF	F%	Min	GP	G	A	Pts	PIM	PP	SH	GW	Min
1995-96	Kanata Valley	OCJHL	19	6	1	7	19	....	....	....	....	....	....	....	....	....	....	....	....	....	....	....	....	....	....
1996-97	Kanata Valley	OCJHL	44	13	13	26	63	....	....	....	....	....	....	....	....	....	....	....	....	....	....	....	....	....	....
1997-98	Oshawa Generals	OHL	59	20	17	37	45	....	....	....	....	....	....	....	....	....	7	2	1	3	8	....	....	....	....
1998-99	Oshawa Generals	OHL	67	31	44	75	93	....	....	....	....	....	....	....	....	....	14	7	7	14	10	....	....	....	....
99-2000	Oshawa Generals	OHL	56	28	35	63	68	....	....	....	....	....	....	....	....	....	5	1	1	2	4	....	....	....	....
2000-01	**Phoenix**	**NHL**	**1**	**0**	**0**	**0**	**0**	**0**	**0**	**0**	**0**	**0.0**	**0**	**0**	**0.0**	**5:16**	....	....	....	....	....	....	....	....	....
	Springfield	AHL	50	5	13	18	23	....	....	....	....	....	....	....	....	....	....	....	....	....	....	....	....	....	....
2001-02	Mississippi	ECHL	16	2	3	5	12	....	....	....	....	....	....	....	....	....	....	....	....	....	....	....	....	....	....

Season	Club	League	GP	G	A	Pts	PIM	PP	SH	GW	S	%	+/-	TF	F%	Min	GP	G	A	Pts	PIM	PP	SH	GW	Min
			Regular Season														Playoffs								
2002-03	Augusta Lynx	ECHL	44	11	15	26	80	....	....	....	....	....	....	....	....	....	....	....	....	....	....	....	....	....	....
	Springfield	AHL	16	2	5	7	6	....	....	....	....	....	....	....	....	....	....	....	....	....	....	....	....	....	....
	NHL Totals		1	0	0	0	0	0	0	0	0	0.0		0	0.0	5:16	....	....	....	....	....	....	....	....	....

• Missed majority of 2001-02 season recovering from shoulder injury suffered in game vs. Greenville (ECHL), December 8, 2001.

RANHEIM, Paul

(RAN-highm, PAWL)

Left wing. Shoots right. 6'1", 210 lbs. Born, St. Louis, MO, January 25, 1966. Calgary's 3rd choice, 38th overall, in 1984 Entry Draft.

Season	Club	League	GP	G	A	Pts	PIM	PP	SH	GW	S	%	+/-	TF	F%	Min	GP	G	A	Pts	PIM	PP	SH	GW	Min
1982-83	Edina Hornets	Hi-School	26	12	25	37	4	....	....	....	....	....	....	....	....	....	....	....	....	....	....	....	....	....	....
1983-84	Edina Hornets	Hi-School	26	16	24	40	6	....	....	....	....	....	....	....	....	....	....	....	....	....	....	....	....	....	....
1984-85	U. of Wisconsin	WCHA	42	11	11	22	40	....	....	....	....	....	....	....	....	....	....	....	....	....	....	....	....	....	....
1985-86	U. of Wisconsin	WCHA	33	17	17	34	34	....	....	....	....	....	....	....	....	....	....	....	....	....	....	....	....	....	....
1986-87	U. of Wisconsin	WCHA	42	24	35	59	54	....	....	....	....	....	....	....	....	....	....	....	....	....	....	....	....	....	....
1987-88	U. of Wisconsin	WCHA	44	36	26	62	63	....	....	....	....	....	....	....	....	....	....	....	....	....	....	....	....	....	....
1988-89	**Calgary**	**NHL**	**5**	**0**	**0**	**0**	**0**	**0**	**0**	**0**	**4**	**0.0**	**-3**	....	....	....	....	....	....	....	....	....	....	....	....
	Salt Lake	IHL	75	*68	29	97	16	....	....	....	....	....	....	....	....	....	14	5	5	10	8	....	....	....	....
1989-90	**Calgary**	**NHL**	**80**	**26**	**28**	**54**	**23**	**1**	**3**	**4**	**197**	**13.2**	**27**	....	....	....	**6**	**1**	**3**	**4**	**2**	**0**	**0**	**0**	....
1990-91	**Calgary**	**NHL**	**39**	**14**	**16**	**30**	**4**	**2**	**0**	**2**	**108**	**13.0**	**20**	....	....	....	**7**	**2**	**2**	**4**	**0**	**0**	**0**	**0**	....
1991-92	**Calgary**	**NHL**	**80**	**23**	**20**	**43**	**32**	**1**	**3**	**3**	**159**	**14.5**	**16**	....	....	....	....	....	....	....	....	....	....	....	....
1992-93	**Calgary**	**NHL**	**83**	**21**	**22**	**43**	**26**	**3**	**4**	**1**	**179**	**11.7**	**-4**	....	....	....	**6**	**0**	**1**	**1**	**0**	**0**	**0**	**0**	....
1993-94	**Calgary**	**NHL**	**67**	**10**	**14**	**24**	**20**	**0**	**2**	**2**	**110**	**9.1**	**-7**	....	....	....	....	....	....	....	....	....	....	....	....
	Hartford	**NHL**	**15**	**0**	**3**	**3**	**2**	**0**	**0**	**0**	**21**	**0.0**	**-11**	....	....	....	....	....	....	....	....	....	....	....	....
1994-95	**Hartford**	**NHL**	**47**	**6**	**14**	**20**	**10**	**0**	**0**	**1**	**73**	**8.2**	**-3**	....	....	....	....	....	....	....	....	....	....	....	....
1995-96	**Hartford**	**NHL**	**73**	**10**	**20**	**30**	**14**	**0**	**1**	**1**	**126**	**7.9**	**-2**	....	....	....	....	....	....	....	....	....	....	....	....
1996-97	**Hartford**	**NHL**	**67**	**10**	**11**	**21**	**18**	**0**	**3**	**1**	**96**	**10.4**	**-13**	....	....	....	....	....	....	....	....	....	....	....	....
1997-98	**Carolina**	**NHL**	**73**	**5**	**9**	**14**	**28**	**0**	**1**	**2**	**77**	**6.5**	**-11**	....	....	....	....	....	....	....	....	....	....	....	....
1998-99	**Carolina**	**NHL**	**78**	**9**	**10**	**19**	**39**	**0**	**2**	**1**	**67**	**13.4**	**4**	**10**	**50.0**	**9:02**	**6**	**0**	**0**	**0**	**2**	**0**	**0**	**0**	**9:22**
99-2000	**Carolina**	**NHL**	**79**	**9**	**13**	**22**	**6**	**0**	**0**	**2**	**98**	**9.2**	**-14**	**78**	**46.2**	**11:19**	....	....	....	....	....	....	....	....	....
2000-01	**Philadelphia**	**NHL**	**80**	**10**	**7**	**17**	**14**	**0**	**2**	**0**	**123**	**8.1**	**2**	**18**	**55.6**	**12:57**	**6**	**0**	**2**	**2**	**2**	**0**	**0**	**0**	**12:50**
2001-02	**Philadelphia**	**NHL**	**79**	**5**	**4**	**9**	**36**	**1**	**0**	**0**	**75**	**6.7**	**5**	**40**	**40.0**	**9:15**	**5**	**0**	**0**	**0**	**0**	**0**	**0**	**0**	**8:56**
2002-03	**Philadelphia**	**NHL**	**28**	**0**	**4**	**4**	**6**	**0**	**0**	**0**	**37**	**0.0**	**-4**	**14**	**57.1**	**11:56**	....	....	....	....	....	....	....	....	....
	Phoenix	**NHL**	**40**	**3**	**4**	**7**	**10**	**0**	**0**	**0**	**34**	**8.8**	**-4**	**39**	**48.7**	**11:59**	....	....	....	....	....	....	....	....	....
	NHL Totals		**1013**	**161**	**199**	**360**	**288**	**8**	**21**	**20**	**1584**	**10.2**		**199**	**47.2**	**10:53**	**36**	**3**	**8**	**11**	**6**	**0**	**0**	**0**	**10:28**

WCHA Second All-Star Team (1987) • WCHA First All-Star Team (1988) • NCAA West First All-American Team (1988) • IHL Second All-Star Team (1989) • Ken McKenzie Trophy (U.S. Born Rookie of the Year – IHL) (1989) • Garry F. Longman Memorial Trophy (Top Rookie – IHL) (1989)

• Missed majority of 1990-91 season recovering from ankle injury suffered in game vs. Minnesota, December 11, 1990. Traded to **Hartford** by **Calgary** with Gary Suter and Ted Drury for James Patrick, Zarley Zalapski and Michael Nylander, March 10, 1994. Transferred to **Carolina** after **Hartford** franchise relocated, June 25, 1997. Traded to **Philadelphia** by **Carolina** for Philadelphia's 8th round choice (later traded to Tampa Bay – Tampa Bay selected Darren Reid) in 2002 Entry Draft, May 31, 2000. Traded to **Phoenix** by **Philadelphia** for future consiserations, December 19, 2002.

RASMUSSEN, Erik

(RAS-moo-suhn, AIR-ihk) **N.J.**

Left wing/Center. Shoots left. 6'3", 210 lbs. Born, Minneapolis, MN, March 28, 1977. Buffalo's 1st choice, 7th overall, in 1996 Entry Draft.

Season	Club	League	GP	G	A	Pts	PIM	PP	SH	GW	S	%	+/-	TF	F%	Min	GP	G	A	Pts	PIM	PP	SH	GW	Min
1992-93	St. Louis Park	Hi-School	23	16	24	40	50	....	....	....	....	....	....	....	....	....	....	....	....	....	....	....	....	....	....
1993-94	St. Louis Park	Hi-School	18	25	18	43	80	....	....	....	....	....	....	....	....	....	....	....	....	....	....	....	....	....	....
1994-95	St. Louis Park	Hi-School	23	19	33	52	80	....	....	....	....	....	....	....	....	....	....	....	....	....	....	....	....	....	....
1995-96	U. of Minnesota	WCHA	40	16	32	48	55	....	....	....	....	....	....	....	....	....	....	....	....	....	....	....	....	....	....
1996-97	U. of Minnesota	WCHA	34	15	12	27	*123	....	....	....	....	....	....	....	....	....	....	....	....	....	....	....	....	....	....
1997-98	**Buffalo**	**NHL**	**21**	**2**	**3**	**5**	**14**	**0**	**0**	**0**	**28**	**7.1**	**2**	....	....	....	....	....	....	....	....	....	....	....	....
	Rochester	AHL	53	9	14	23	83	....	....	....	....	....	....	....	....	....	1	0	0	0	5	....	....	....	....
1998-99	**Buffalo**	**NHL**	**42**	**3**	**7**	**10**	**37**	**0**	**0**	**0**	**40**	**7.5**	**6**	**67**	**40.3**	**12:22**	**21**	**2**	**4**	**6**	**18**	**0**	**0**	**1**	**12:51**
	Rochester	AHL	37	12	14	26	47	....	....	....	....	....	....	....	....	....	....	....	....	....	....	....	....	....	....
99-2000	**Buffalo**	**NHL**	**67**	**8**	**6**	**14**	**43**	**0**	**0**	**2**	**76**	**10.5**	**1**	**130**	**44.6**	**11:27**	**3**	**0**	**0**	**0**	**4**	**0**	**0**	**0**	**8:59**
2000-01	**Buffalo**	**NHL**	**82**	**12**	**19**	**31**	**51**	**1**	**0**	**3**	**95**	**12.6**	**0**	**565**	**43.7**	**13:47**	**3**	**0**	**1**	**1**	**0**	**0**	**0**	**0**	**16:26**
2001-02	**Buffalo**	**NHL**	**69**	**8**	**11**	**19**	**34**	**0**	**0**	**2**	**89**	**9.0**	**-1**	**236**	**39.8**	**13:03**	....	....	....	....	....	....	....	....	....
2002-03	**Los Angeles**	**NHL**	**57**	**4**	**12**	**16**	**28**	**0**	**0**	**1**	**75**	**5.3**	**-1**	**278**	**44.6**	**13:39**	....	....	....	....	....	....	....	....	....
	NHL Totals		**338**	**37**	**58**	**95**	**207**	**1**	**0**	**8**	**403**	**9.2**		**1276**	**43.1**	**12:55**	**27**	**2**	**5**	**7**	**22**	**0**	**0**	**1**	**12:49**

Minnesota High School Player of the Year (1995)

Traded to **Los Angeles** by **Buffalo** for Adam Mair and Los Angeles' 5th round choice (Thomas Morrow) in 2003 Entry Draft, July 24, 2002. Signed as a free agent by **New Jersey**, July 25, 2003.

RATCHUK, Peter

(RAT-chuhk, PEE-tuhr)

Defense. Shoots left. 6'1", 185 lbs. Born, Buffalo, NY, September 10, 1977. Colorado's 1st choice, 25th overall, in 1996 Entry Draft.

Season	Club	League	GP	G	A	Pts	PIM	PP	SH	GW	S	%	+/-	TF	F%	Min	GP	G	A	Pts	PIM	PP	SH	GW	Min
1994-95	Lawrence School	Hi-School	31	8	15	23	18	....	....	....	....	....	....	....	....	....	....	....	....	....	....	....	....	....	....
1995-96	Shattuck High	Hi-School	35	22	28	50	24	....	....	....	....	....	....	....	....	....	....	....	....	....	....	....	....	....	....
1996-97	Bowling Green	CCHA	35	9	12	21	14	....	....	....	....	....	....	....	....	....	....	....	....	....	....	....	....	....	....
1997-98	Hull Olympiques	QMJHL	60	23	31	54	34	....	....	....	....	....	....	....	....	....	11	3	6	9	8	....	....	....	....
1998-99	**Florida**	**NHL**	**24**	**1**	**1**	**2**	**10**	**0**	**0**	**0**	**34**	**2.9**	**-1**	**0**	**0.0**	**13:55**	....	....	....	....	....	....	....	....	....
	New Haven	AHL	53	7	20	27	44	....	....	....	....	....	....	....	....	....	....	....	....	....	....	....	....	....	....
99-2000	Louisville Panthers	AHL	76	9	17	26	64	....	....	....	....	....	....	....	....	....	4	1	2	3	0	....	....	....	....
2000-01	**Florida**	**NHL**	**8**	**0**	**0**	**0**	**0**	**0**	**0**	**0**	**11**	**0.0**	**-1**	**1**	**100.0**	**13:09**	....	....	....	....	....	....	....	....	....
	Louisville Panthers	AHL	64	5	13	18	85	....	....	....	....	....	....	....	....	....	....	....	....	....	....	....	....	....	....
2001-02	Wilkes-Barre	AHL	75	16	23	39	55	....	....	....	....	....	....	....	....	....	....	....	....	....	....	....	....	....	....
2002-03	Rochester	AHL	70	11	21	32	64	....	....	....	....	....	....	....	....	....	3	0	1	1	6	....	....	....	....
	NHL Totals		**32**	**1**	**1**	**2**	**10**	**0**	**0**	**0**	**45**	**2.2**		**1**	**100.0**	**13:43**	....	....	....	....	....	....	....	....	....

Signed as a free agent by **Florida**, June 15, 1998. Signed as a free agent by **Pittsburgh**, August 14, 2001. Signed as a free agent by **Buffalo**, August 7, 2002.

RATHJE, Mike

(RATH-jee, MIGHK) **S.J.**

Defense. Shoots left. 6'5", 245 lbs. Born, Mannville, Alta., May 11, 1974. San Jose's 1st choice, 3rd overall, in 1992 Entry Draft.

Season	Club	League	GP	G	A	Pts	PIM	PP	SH	GW	S	%	+/-	TF	F%	Min	GP	G	A	Pts	PIM	PP	SH	GW	Min
1989-90	Sherwood Park	AMHL	33	6	11	17	30	....	....	....	....	....	....	....	....	....	6	1	1	2	2	....	....	....	....
1990-91	Medicine Hat	WHL	64	1	16	17	28	....	....	....	....	....	....	....	....	....	12	0	4	4	2	....	....	....	....
1991-92	Medicine Hat	WHL	67	11	23	34	99	....	....	....	....	....	....	....	....	....	4	0	1	1	2	....	....	....	....
1992-93	Medicine Hat	WHL	57	12	37	49	103	....	....	....	....	....	....	....	....	....	10	3	3	6	12	....	....	....	....
	Kansas City	IHL	....	....	....	....	....	....	....	....	....	....	....	....	....	....	5	0	0	0	12	....	....	....	....
1993-94	**San Jose**	**NHL**	**47**	**1**	**9**	**10**	**59**	**1**	**0**	**0**	**30**	**3.3**	**-9**	....	....	....	**1**	**0**	**0**	**0**	**0**	**0**	**0**	**0**	....
	Kansas City	IHL	6	0	2	2	0	....	....	....	....	....	....	....	....	....	....	....	....	....	....	....	....	....	....
1994-95	Kansas City	IHL	6	0	1	1	7	....	....	....	....	....	....	....	....	....	....	....	....	....	....	....	....	....	....
	San Jose	**NHL**	**42**	**2**	**7**	**9**	**29**	**0**	**0**	**0**	**38**	**5.3**	**-1**	....	....	....	**11**	**5**	**2**	**7**	**4**	**5**	**0**	**0**	....
1995-96	**San Jose**	**NHL**	**27**	**0**	**7**	**7**	**14**	**0**	**0**	**0**	**26**	**0.0**	**-16**	....	....	....	....	....	....	....	....	....	....	....	....
	Kansas City	IHL	36	6	11	17	34	....	....	....	....	....	....	....	....	....	....	....	....	....	....	....	....	....	....
1996-97	**San Jose**	**NHL**	**31**	**0**	**8**	**8**	**21**	**0**	**0**	**0**	**22**	**0.0**	**-1**	....	....	....	....	....	....	....	....	....	....	....	....
1997-98	**San Jose**	**NHL**	**81**	**3**	**12**	**15**	**59**	**1**	**0**	**0**	**61**	**4.9**	**-4**	....	....	....	**6**	**1**	**0**	**1**	**6**	**1**	**0**	**0**	....
1998-99	**San Jose**	**NHL**	**82**	**5**	**9**	**14**	**36**	**2**	**0**	**1**	**67**	**7.5**	**15**	**0**	**0.0**	**20:07**	**6**	**0**	**0**	**0**	**4**	**0**	**0**	**0**	**22:08**
99-2000	**San Jose**	**NHL**	**66**	**2**	**14**	**16**	**31**	**0**	**0**	**0**	**46**	**4.3**	**-2**	**0**	**0.0**	**22:11**	**12**	**1**	**3**	**4**	**8**	**0**	**0**	**0**	**21:32**
2000-01	**San Jose**	**NHL**	**81**	**0**	**11**	**11**	**48**	**0**	**0**	**0**	**89**	**0.0**	**7**	**0**	**0.0**	**22:20**	**6**	**0**	**1**	**1**	**4**	**0**	**0**	**0**	**24:20**
2001-02	**San Jose**	**NHL**	**52**	**5**	**12**	**17**	**48**	**4**	**0**	**0**	**56**	**8.9**	**23**	**0**	**0.0**	**21:31**	**12**	**1**	**3**	**4**	**6**	**1**	**0**	**0**	**23:29**
2002-03	**San Jose**	**NHL**	**82**	**7**	**22**	**29**	**48**	**3**	**0**	**1**	**147**	**4.8**	**-19**	**1**	**0.0**	**24:07**	....	....	....	....	....	....	....	....	....
	NHL Totals		**591**	**25**	**111**	**136**	**393**	**11**	**0**	**2**	**582**	**4.3**		**1**	**0.0**	**22:06**	**54**	**8**	**9**	**17**	**32**	**7**	**0**	**0**	**22:45**

WHL East Second All-Star Team (1992, 1993)

• Missed majority of 1996-97 season recovering from groin injury suffered in game vs. Dallas, November 8, 1996.

RAY, Rob (RAY, RAWB)

Right wing. Shoots left. 6', 217 lbs. Born, Stirling, Ont., June 8, 1968. Buffalo's 5th choice, 97th overall, in 1988 Entry Draft.

			Regular Season														Playoffs								
Season	Club	League	GP	G	A	Pts	PIM	PP	SH	GW	S	%	+/-	TF	F%	Min	GP	G	A	Pts	PIM	PP	SH	GW	Min
1983-84	Trenton Bobcats	OJHL-B	40	11	10	21	57	....	....	....	....	....	....	....	....	....	....	....	....	....	....	....	....	....	....
1984-85	Whitby Lawmen	OPJHL	35	5	10	15	318	....	....	....	....	....	....	....	....	....	....	....	....	....	....	....	....	....	....
1985-86	Cornwall Royals	OHL	53	6	13	19	253	....	....	....	....	....	....	....	....	....	6	0	0	0	26	....	....	....	....
1986-87	Cornwall Royals	OHL	46	17	20	37	158	....	....	....	....	....	....	....	....	....	5	1	1	2	16	....	....	....	....
1987-88	Cornwall Royals	OHL	61	11	41	52	179	....	....	....	....	....	....	....	....	....	11	2	3	5	33	....	....	....	....
1988-89	Rochester	AHL	74	11	18	29	*446	....	....	....	....	....	....	....	....	....	....	....	....	....	....	....	....	....	....
1989-90	**Buffalo**	**NHL**	**27**	**2**	**1**	**3**	**99**	**0**	**0**	**0**	**20**	**10.0**	**–2**	....	....	....	....	....	....	....	....	....	....	....	....
	Rochester	AHL	43	2	13	15	335	....	....	....	....	....	....	....	....	....	17	1	3	4	115	....	....	....	....
1990-91	**Buffalo**	**NHL**	**66**	**8**	**8**	**16**	***350**	**0**	**0**	**1**	**54**	**14.8**	**–11**	....	....	....	**6**	**1**	**1**	**2**	**56**	**0**	**0**	**1**	....
	Rochester	AHL	8	1	1	2	15	....	....	....	....	....	....	....	....	....	....	....	....	....	....	....	....	....	....
1991-92	**Buffalo**	**NHL**	**63**	**5**	**3**	**8**	**354**	**0**	**0**	**0**	**29**	**17.2**	**–9**	....	....	....	**7**	**0**	**0**	**0**	**2**	**0**	**0**	**0**	....
1992-93	**Buffalo**	**NHL**	**68**	**3**	**2**	**5**	**211**	**1**	**0**	**0**	**28**	**10.7**	**–3**	....	....	....	....	....	....	....	....	....	....	....	....
1993-94	**Buffalo**	**NHL**	**82**	**3**	**4**	**7**	**274**	**0**	**0**	**0**	**34**	**8.8**	**2**	....	....	....	**7**	**1**	**0**	**1**	**43**	**0**	**0**	**0**	....
1994-95	**Buffalo**	**NHL**	**47**	**0**	**3**	**3**	**173**	**0**	**0**	**0**	**7**	**0.0**	**–4**	....	....	....	**5**	**0**	**0**	**0**	**14**	**0**	**0**	**0**	....
1995-96	**Buffalo**	**NHL**	**71**	**3**	**6**	**9**	**287**	**0**	**0**	**0**	**21**	**14.3**	**–8**	....	....	....	....	....	....	....	....	....	....	....	....
1996-97	**Buffalo**	**NHL**	**82**	**7**	**3**	**10**	**286**	**0**	**0**	**1**	**45**	**15.6**	**3**	....	....	....	**12**	**0**	**1**	**1**	**28**	**0**	**0**	**0**	....
1997-98	**Buffalo**	**NHL**	**63**	**2**	**4**	**6**	**234**	**1**	**0**	**1**	**19**	**10.5**	**2**	....	....	....	**10**	**0**	**0**	**0**	**24**	**0**	**0**	**0**	....
1998-99	**Buffalo**	**NHL**	**76**	**0**	**4**	**4**	***261**	**0**	**0**	**0**	**23**	**0.0**	**–2**	**0**	**0.0**	**5:11**	**5**	**1**	**0**	**1**	**0**	**0**	**0**	**1**	**3:11**
99-2000	**Buffalo**	**NHL**	**69**	**1**	**3**	**4**	**158**	**0**	**0**	**0**	**17**	**5.9**	**0**	**0**	**0.0**	**4:13**	....	....	....	....	....	....	....	....	....
2000-01	**Buffalo**	**NHL**	**63**	**4**	**6**	**10**	**210**	**0**	**0**	**1**	**33**	**12.1**	**2**	**1**	**100.0**	**5:38**	**3**	**0**	**0**	**0**	**2**	**0**	**0**	**0**	**1:05**
2001-02	**Buffalo**	**NHL**	**71**	**2**	**3**	**5**	**200**	**0**	**0**	**0**	**23**	**8.7**	**–3**	**0**	**0.0**	**5:08**	....	....	....	....	....	....	....	....	....
2002-03	**Buffalo**	**NHL**	**41**	**0**	**0**	**0**	**92**	**0**	**0**	**0**	**14**	**0.0**	**–5**	**3**	**33.3**	**4:24**	....	....	....	....	....	....	....	....	....
	Ottawa	**NHL**	**5**	**0**	**0**	**0**	**4**	**0**	**0**	**0**	**0**	**0.0**	**0**	**0**	**0.0**	**4:53**	....	....	....	....	....	....	....	....	....
	NHL Totals		**894**	**40**	**50**	**90**	**3193**	**2**	**0**	**4**	**367**	**10.9**		**4**	**50.0**	**4:57**	**55**	**3**	**2**	**5**	**169**	**0**	**0**	**2**	**2:24**

King Clancy Memorial Trophy (1999)

Traded to **Ottawa** by **Buffalo** for future considerations, March 10, 2003.

REASONER, Marty (REE-sohn-uhr, MAHR-tee) EDM.

Center. Shoots left. 6'1", 190 lbs. Born, Honeoye Falls, NY, February 26, 1977. St. Louis' 1st choice, 14th overall, in 1996 Entry Draft.

			Regular Season														Playoffs								
Season	Club	League	GP	G	A	Pts	PIM	PP	SH	GW	S	%	+/-	TF	F%	Min	GP	G	A	Pts	PIM	PP	SH	GW	Min
1993-94	Deerfield	Hi-School	22	27	25	52	....	....	....	....	....	....	....	....	....	....	....	....	....	....	....	....	....	....	....
1994-95	Deerfield	Hi-School	26	25	32	57	14	....	....	....	....	....	....	....	....	....	....	....	....	....	....	....	....	....	....
1995-96	Boston College	H-East	34	16	29	45	32	....	....	....	....	....	....	....	....	....	....	....	....	....	....	....	....	....	....
1996-97	Boston College	H-East	35	20	24	44	31	....	....	....	....	....	....	....	....	....	....	....	....	....	....	....	....	....	....
1997-98	Boston College	H-East	42	*33	40	*73	56	....	....	....	....	....	....	....	....	....	....	....	....	....	....	....	....	....	....
1998-99	**St. Louis**	**NHL**	**22**	**3**	**7**	**10**	**8**	**1**	**0**	**0**	**33**	**9.1**	**2**	**224**	**53.6**	**13:55**	....	....	....	....	....	....	....	....	....
	Worcester IceCats	AHL	44	17	22	39	24	....	....	....	....	....	....	....	....	....	4	2	1	3	6	....	....	....	....
99-2000	**St. Louis**	**NHL**	**32**	**10**	**14**	**24**	**20**	**3**	**0**	**0**	**51**	**19.6**	**9**	**379**	**49.6**	**15:20**	**7**	**2**	**1**	**3**	**4**	**1**	**0**	**0**	**13:12**
	Worcester IceCats	AHL	44	23	28	51	39	....	....	....	....	....	....	....	....	....	....	....	....	....	....	....	....	....	....
2000-01	**St. Louis**	**NHL**	**41**	**4**	**9**	**13**	**14**	**0**	**0**	**0**	**65**	**6.2**	**–5**	**454**	**53.1**	**14:00**	**10**	**3**	**1**	**4**	**0**	**0**	**0**	**1**	**12:21**
	Worcester IceCats	AHL	34	17	18	35	25	....	....	....	....	....	....	....	....	....	....	....	....	....	....	....	....	....	....
2001-02	**Edmonton**	**NHL**	**52**	**6**	**5**	**11**	**41**	**3**	**0**	**2**	**66**	**9.1**	**0**	**470**	**55.5**	**11:44**	....	....	....	....	....	....	....	....	....
2002-03	**Edmonton**	**NHL**	**70**	**11**	**20**	**31**	**28**	**2**	**2**	**0**	**102**	**10.8**	**19**	**968**	**53.5**	**14:50**	**6**	**1**	**0**	**1**	**2**	**1**	**0**	**0**	**14:22**
	Hamilton	AHL	2	0	2	2	2	....	....	....	....	....	....	....	....	....	....	....	....	....	....	....	....	....	....
	NHL Totals		**217**	**34**	**55**	**89**	**111**	**9**	**2**	**2**	**317**	**10.7**		**2495**	**53.2**	**13:55**	**23**	**6**	**2**	**8**	**6**	**2**	**0**	**1**	**13:08**

Hockey East Rookie of the Year (1996) • Hockey East First All-Star Team (1997, 1998) • NCAA East First All-American Team (1998) • NCAA Championship All-Tournament Team (1998)

Traded to **Edmonton** by **St. Louis** with Jochen Hecht and Jan Horacek for Doug Weight and Michel Riesen, July 1, 2001.

RECCHI, Mark (REH-kee, MAHRK) PHI.

Right wing. Shoots left. 5'10", 185 lbs. Born, Kamloops, B.C., February 1, 1968. Pittsburgh's 4th choice, 67th overall, in 1988 Entry Draft.

			Regular Season														Playoffs								
Season	Club	League	GP	G	A	Pts	PIM	PP	SH	GW	S	%	+/-	TF	F%	Min	GP	G	A	Pts	PIM	PP	SH	GW	Min
1984-85	Langley Eagles	BCJHL	51	26	39	65	39	....	....	....	....	....	....	....	....	....	....	....	....	....	....	....	....	....	....
	New Westminster	WHL	4	1	0	1	0	....	....	....	....	....	....	....	....	....	....	....	....	....	....	....	....	....	....
1985-86	New Westminster	WHL	72	21	40	61	55	....	....	....	....	....	....	....	....	....	....	....	....	....	....	....	....	....	....
1986-87	Kamloops Blazers	WHL	40	26	50	76	63	....	....	....	....	....	....	....	....	....	13	3	16	19	17	....	....	....	....
1987-88	Kamloops Blazers	WHL	62	61	*93	154	75	....	....	....	....	....	....	....	....	....	17	10	*21	*31	18	....	....	....	....
1988-89	**Pittsburgh**	**NHL**	**15**	**1**	**1**	**2**	**0**	**0**	**0**	**0**	**11**	**9.1**	**–2**	....	....	....	....	....	....	....	....	....	....	....	....
	Muskegon	IHL	63	50	49	99	86	....	....	....	....	....	....	....	....	....	14	7	*14	*21	28	....	....	....	....
1989-90	**Pittsburgh**	**NHL**	**74**	**30**	**37**	**67**	**44**	**6**	**2**	**4**	**143**	**21.0**	**6**	....	....	....	....	....	....	....	....	....	....	....	....
	Muskegon	IHL	4	7	4	11	2	....	....	....	....	....	....	....	....	....	....	....	....	....	....	....	....	....	....
1990-91♦	**Pittsburgh**	**NHL**	**78**	**40**	**73**	**113**	**48**	**12**	**0**	**9**	**184**	**21.7**	**0**	....	....	....	**24**	**10**	**24**	**34**	**33**	**5**	**0**	**2**	....
1991-92	**Pittsburgh**	**NHL**	**58**	**33**	**37**	**70**	**78**	**16**	**1**	**4**	**156**	**21.2**	**–16**	....	....	....	....	....	....	....	....	....	....	....	....
	Philadelphia	**NHL**	**22**	**10**	**17**	**27**	**18**	**4**	**0**	**1**	**54**	**18.5**	**–5**	....	....	....	....	....	....	....	....	....	....	....	....
1992-93	**Philadelphia**	**NHL**	**84**	**53**	**70**	**123**	**95**	**15**	**4**	**6**	**274**	**19.3**	**1**	....	....	....	....	....	....	....	....	....	....	....	....
1993-94	**Philadelphia**	**NHL**	**84**	**40**	**67**	**107**	**46**	**11**	**0**	**5**	**217**	**18.4**	**–2**	....	....	....	....	....	....	....	....	....	....	....	....
1994-95	**Philadelphia**	**NHL**	**10**	**2**	**3**	**5**	**12**	**1**	**0**	**2**	**17**	**11.8**	**–6**	....	....	....	....	....	....	....	....	....	....	....	....
	Montreal	**NHL**	**39**	**14**	**29**	**43**	**16**	**8**	**0**	**1**	**104**	**13.5**	**–3**	....	....	....	....	....	....	....	....	....	....	....	....
1995-96	**Montreal**	**NHL**	**82**	**28**	**50**	**78**	**69**	**11**	**2**	**6**	**191**	**14.7**	**20**	....	....	....	**6**	**3**	**3**	**6**	**0**	**3**	**0**	**0**	....
1996-97	**Montreal**	**NHL**	**82**	**34**	**46**	**80**	**58**	**7**	**2**	**3**	**202**	**16.8**	**–1**	....	....	....	**5**	**4**	**2**	**6**	**2**	**0**	**0**	**0**	....
1997-98	**Montreal**	**NHL**	**82**	**32**	**42**	**74**	**51**	**9**	**1**	**6**	**216**	**14.8**	**11**	....	....	....	**10**	**4**	**8**	**12**	**6**	**0**	**0**	**2**	....
	Canada	Olympics	5	0	2	2	0	....	....	....	....	....	....	....	....	....	....	....	....	....	....	....	....	....	....
1998-99	**Montreal**	**NHL**	**61**	**12**	**35**	**47**	**28**	**3**	**0**	**2**	**152**	**7.9**	**–4**	**239**	**44.8**	**20:37**	....	....	....	....	....	....	....	....	....
	Philadelphia	**NHL**	**10**	**4**	**2**	**6**	**6**	**0**	**0**	**0**	**19**	**21.1**	**–3**	**4**	**25.0**	**19:30**	**6**	**0**	**1**	**1**	**2**	**0**	**0**	**0**	**19:35**
99-2000	**Philadelphia**	**NHL**	**82**	**28**	***63**	**91**	**50**	**7**	**1**	**5**	**223**	**12.6**	**20**	**353**	**49.6**	**21:43**	**18**	**6**	**12**	**18**	**6**	**2**	**0**	**1**	**23:10**
2000-01	**Philadelphia**	**NHL**	**69**	**27**	**50**	**77**	**33**	**7**	**1**	**8**	**191**	**14.1**	**15**	**138**	**42.8**	**21:40**	**6**	**2**	**2**	**4**	**2**	**1**	**0**	**1**	**23:00**
2001-02	**Philadelphia**	**NHL**	**80**	**22**	**42**	**64**	**46**	**7**	**2**	**4**	**205**	**10.7**	**5**	**82**	**53.7**	**20:40**	**4**	**0**	**0**	**0**	**2**	**0**	**0**	**0**	**21:10**
2002-03	**Philadelphia**	**NHL**	**79**	**20**	**32**	**52**	**35**	**8**	**1**	**3**	**171**	**11.7**	**0**	**168**	**52.4**	**18:50**	**13**	**7**	**3**	**10**	**2**	**1**	**0**	**1**	**18:00**
	NHL Totals		**1091**	**430**	**696**	**1126**	**733**	**132**	**17**	**69**	**2730**	**15.8**		**984**	**48.2**	**20:39**	**92**	**36**	**55**	**91**	**55**	**12**	**0**	**7**	**21:05**

WHL West First All-Star Team (1988) • IHL Second All-Star Team (1989) • NHL Second All-Star Team (1992)

Played in NHL All-Star Game (1991, 1993, 1994, 1997, 1998, 1999, 2000)

Traded to **Philadelphia** by **Pittsburgh** with Brian Benning and Los Angeles' 1st round choice (previously acquired, Philadelphia selected Jason Bowen) in 1992 Entry Draft for Rick Tocchet, Kjell Samuelsson, Ken Wregget and Philadelphia's 3rd round choice (Dave Roche) in 1993 Entry Draft, February 19, 1992. Traded to **Montreal** by **Philadelphia** with Philadelphia's 3rd round choice (Martin Hohenberger) in 1995 Entry Draft for Eric Desjardins, Gilbert Dionne and John LeClair, February 9, 1995. Traded to **Philadelphia** by **Montreal** for Danius Zubrus, Philadelphia's 2nd round choice (Matt Carkner) in 1999 Entry Draft and NY Islanders' 6th round choice (previously acquired, Montreal selected Scott Selig) in 2000 Entry Draft, March 10, 1999.

REDDEN, Wade (REH-duhn, WAYD) OTT.

Defense. Shoots left. 6'2", 205 lbs. Born, Lloydminster, Sask., June 12, 1977. NY Islanders' 1st choice, 2nd overall, in 1995 Entry Draft.

			Regular Season														Playoffs								
Season	Club	League	GP	G	A	Pts	PIM	PP	SH	GW	S	%	+/-	TF	F%	Min	GP	G	A	Pts	PIM	PP	SH	GW	Min
1992-93	Lloydminster	AJHL	34	4	11	15	64	....	....	....	....	....	....	....	....	....	....	....	....	....	....	....	....	....	....
1993-94	Brandon	WHL	63	4	35	39	98	....	....	....	....	....	....	....	....	....	14	2	4	6	10	....	....	....	....
1994-95	Brandon	WHL	64	14	46	60	83	....	....	....	....	....	....	....	....	....	18	5	10	15	8	....	....	....	....
1995-96	Brandon	WHL	51	9	45	54	55	....	....	....	....	....	....	....	....	....	19	5	10	15	19	....	....	....	....
1996-97	**Ottawa**	**NHL**	**82**	**6**	**24**	**30**	**41**	**2**	**0**	**1**	**102**	**5.9**	**1**	....	....	....	**7**	**1**	**3**	**4**	**2**	**0**	**0**	**0**	....
1997-98	**Ottawa**	**NHL**	**80**	**8**	**14**	**22**	**27**	**3**	**0**	**2**	**103**	**7.8**	**17**	....	....	....	**9**	**0**	**2**	**2**	**2**	**0**	**0**	**0**	....
1998-99	**Ottawa**	**NHL**	**72**	**8**	**21**	**29**	**54**	**3**	**0**	**1**	**127**	**6.3**	**7**	**0**	**0.0**	**23:27**	**4**	**1**	**2**	**3**	**2**	**1**	**0**	**0**	**26:39**
99-2000	**Ottawa**	**NHL**	**81**	**10**	**26**	**36**	**49**	**3**	**0**	**2**	**163**	**6.1**	**–1**	**0**	**0.0**	**23:43**	....	....	....	....	....	....	....	....	....
2000-01	**Ottawa**	**NHL**	**78**	**10**	**37**	**47**	**49**	**4**	**0**	**0**	**159**	**6.3**	**22**	**0**	**0.0**	**25:17**	**4**	**0**	**0**	**0**	**0**	**0**	**0**	**0**	**27:29**
2001-02	**Ottawa**	**NHL**	**79**	**9**	**25**	**34**	**48**	**4**	**1**	**1**	**156**	**5.8**	**22**	**1**	**0.0**	**25:06**	**12**	**3**	**2**	**5**	**6**	**1**	**0**	**1**	**27:56**
2002-03	**Ottawa**	**NHL**	**76**	**10**	**35**	**45**	**70**	**4**	**0**	**3**	**154**	**6.5**	**23**	**0**	**0.0**	**25:24**	**18**	**1**	**8**	**9**	**10**	**0**	**0**	**1**	**25:28**
	NHL Totals		**548**	**61**	**182**	**243**	**338**	**23**	**1**	**10**	**964**	**6.3**		**1**	**0.0**	**24:36**	**54**	**6**	**17**	**23**	**22**	**2**	**0**	**2**	**26:35**

WHL Rookie of the Year (1994) • WHL East Second All-Star Team (1995) • WHL East First All-Star Team (1996) • Memorial Cup All-Star Team (1996)

Played in NHL All-Star Game (2002)

Traded to **Ottawa** by **NY Islanders** with Damian Rhodes for Don Beaupre, Martin Straka and Bryan Berard, January 23, 1996.

REGEHR, Robyn

(reh-GUHR, RAW-bihn) **CGY.**

Defense. Shoots left. 6'2", 226 lbs. Born, Recife, Brazil, April 19, 1980. Colorado's 3rd choice, 19th overall, in 1998 Entry Draft.

			Regular Season														Playoffs								
Season	Club	League	GP	G	A	Pts	PIM	PP	SH	GW	S	%	+/-	TF	F%	Min	GP	G	A	Pts	PIM	PP	SH	GW	Min
1995-96	Prince Albert	SMHL	59	8	24	32	157																		
1996-97	Kamloops Blazers	WHL	64	4	19	23	96										5	0	1	1	18				
1997-98	Kamloops Blazers	WHL	65	4	10	14	120										5	0	3	3	8				
1998-99	Kamloops Blazers	WHL	54	12	20	32	130										12	1	4	5	21				
99-2000	**Calgary**	**NHL**	**57**	**5**	**7**	**12**	**46**	**2**	**0**	**0**	**64**	**7.8**	**–2**	**0**	**0.0**	**18:24**									
	Saint John Flames	AHL	5	0	0	0	0																		
2000-01	**Calgary**	**NHL**	**71**	**1**	**3**	**4**	**70**	**0**	**0**	**0**	**62**	**1.6**	**–7**	**1**	**0.0**	**19:43**									
2001-02	**Calgary**	**NHL**	**77**	**2**	**6**	**8**	**93**	**0**	**0**	**0**	**82**	**2.4**	**–24**	**0**	**0.0**	**20:54**									
2002-03	**Calgary**	**NHL**	**76**	**0**	**12**	**12**	**87**	**0**	**0**	**0**	**109**	**0.0**	**–9**	**1**	**100.0**	**22:45**									
	NHL Totals		**281**	**8**	**28**	**36**	**296**	**2**	**0**	**0**	**317**	**2.5**		**2**	**50.0**	**20:36**									

WHL West First All-Star Team (1999)

Traded to **Calgary** by **Colorado** with Rene Corbet, Wade Belak and Colorado's 2nd round compensatory choice (Jarret Stoll) in 2000 Entry Draft for Theoren Fleury and Chris Dingman, February 28, 1999.

REICHEL, Robert

(RIGH-khul, RAW-buhrt) **TOR.**

Center. Shoots left. 5'10", 180 lbs. Born, Litvinov, Czech., June 25, 1971. Calgary's 5th choice, 70th overall, in 1989 Entry Draft.

			Regular Season														Playoffs								
Season	Club	League	GP	G	A	Pts	PIM	PP	SH	GW	S	%	+/-	TF	F%	Min	GP	G	A	Pts	PIM	PP	SH	GW	Min
1987-88	CHZ Litvinov	Czech	36	17	10	27	8																		
1988-89	CHZ Litvinov	Czech	44	23	25	48	32																		
1989-90	CHZ Litvinov	Czech	44	*43	28	*71											8	6	6	12					
1990-91	**Calgary**	**NHL**	**66**	**19**	**22**	**41**	**22**	**3**	**0**	**3**	**131**	**14.5**	**17**				**6**	**1**	**1**	**2**	**0**	**1**	**0**	**0**	
1991-92	**Calgary**	**NHL**	**77**	**20**	**34**	**54**	**32**	**8**	**0**	**3**	**181**	**11.0**	**1**												
1992-93	**Calgary**	**NHL**	**80**	**40**	**48**	**88**	**54**	**12**	**0**	**5**	**238**	**16.8**	**25**				**6**	**2**	**4**	**6**	**2**	**2**	**0**	**0**	
1993-94	**Calgary**	**NHL**	**84**	**40**	**53**	**93**	**58**	**14**	**0**	**6**	**249**	**16.1**	**20**				**7**	**0**	**5**	**5**	**0**	**0**	**0**	**0**	
1994-95	Frankfurt Lions	Germany	21	19	24	43	41																		
	Calgary	**NHL**	**48**	**18**	**17**	**35**	**28**	**5**	**0**	**2**	**160**	**11.3**	**–2**				**7**	**2**	**4**	**6**	**4**	**0**	**0**	**1**	
1995-96	Frankfurt Lions	Germany	46	47	54	101	84										3	1	3	4	0				
1996-97	**Calgary**	**NHL**	**70**	**16**	**27**	**43**	**22**	**6**	**0**	**3**	**181**	**8.8**	**–2**												
	NY Islanders	**NHL**	**12**	**5**	**14**	**19**	**4**	**0**	**1**	**0**	**33**	**15.2**	**7**												
1997-98	**NY Islanders**	**NHL**	**82**	**25**	**40**	**65**	**32**	**8**	**0**	**2**	**201**	**12.4**	**–11**												
	Czech Republic	Olympics	6	3	0	3	0																		
1998-99	**NY Islanders**	**NHL**	**70**	**19**	**37**	**56**	**50**	**5**	**1**	**1**	**186**	**10.2**	**–15**	**1241**	**51.7**	**19:36**									
	Phoenix	**NHL**	**13**	**7**	**6**	**13**	**4**	**3**	**0**	**3**	**50**	**14.0**	**2**	**241**	**48.5**	**20:03**	**7**	**1**	**3**	**4**	**2**	**0**	**0**	**0**	**18:56**
99-2000	Litvinov	Czech	45	25	32	57	24										7	3	4	7	2				
2000-01	Litvinov	Czech	49	23	33	56	72										5	1	2	3	4				
2001-02	**Toronto**	**NHL**	**78**	**20**	**31**	**51**	**26**	**1**	**0**	**3**	**152**	**13.2**	**7**	**1045**	**49.6**	**15:11**	**18**	**0**	**3**	**3**	**4**	**0**	**0**	**0**	**12:40**
	Czech Republic	Olympics	4	1	0	1	2																		
2002-03	**Toronto**	**NHL**	**81**	**12**	**30**	**42**	**26**	**1**	**1**	**1**	**111**	**10.8**	**7**	**1123**	**52.2**	**14:33**	**7**	**2**	**1**	**3**	**0**	**0**	**0**	**0**	**20:54**
	NHL Totals		**761**	**241**	**359**	**600**	**358**	**66**	**3**	**32**	**1873**	**12.9**		**3650**	**51.0**	**16:30**	**58**	**8**	**21**	**29**	**12**	**3**	**0**	**1**	**15:50**

Traded to **NY Islanders** by **Calgary** for Marty McInnis, Tyrone Garner and Calgary's 6th round choice (previously acquired, Calgary selected Ilja Demidov) in 1997 Entry Draft, March 18, 1997. Traded to **Phoenix** by **NY Islanders** with NY Islanders' 3rd round choice (Jason Jaspers) in 1999 Entry Draft and Ottawa's 4th round choice (previously acquired, Phoenix selected Preston Mizzi) in 1999 Entry Draft for Brad Isbister and Phoenix's 3rd round choice (Brian Collins) in 1999 Entry Draft, March 20, 1999. Traded to **Toronto** by **Phoenix** with Travis Green and Craig Mills for Danny Markov, June 12, 2001.

REID, Brandon

(REED, BRAN-duhn) **VAN.**

Center. Shoots right. 5'8", 165 lbs. Born, Kirkland, Que., March 9, 1981. Vancouver's 5th choice, 208th overall, in 2000 Entry Draft.

			Regular Season														Playoffs								
Season	Club	League	GP	G	A	Pts	PIM	PP	SH	GW	S	%	+/-	TF	F%	Min	GP	G	A	Pts	PIM	PP	SH	GW	Min
1996-97	Lac-St-Louis Lions	QAAA	44	17	34	51											7	2	3	5					
1997-98	Halifax	QMJHL	67	13	21	36	6										5	1	0	1	15				
1998-99	Halifax	QMJHL	70	32	25	57	33										5	2	2	4	0				
99-2000	Halifax	QMJHL	62	44	80	124	10										10	7	11	18	4				
2000-01	Val-d'Or Foreurs	QMJHL	57	45	81	126	18										21	13	29	42	14				
2001-02	Manitoba Moose	AHL	60	18	19	37	6										7	0	3	3	0				
2002-03	**Vancouver**	**NHL**	**7**	**2**	**3**	**5**	**0**	**0**	**0**	**0**	**15**	**13.3**	**4**	**69**	**55.1**	**9:47**	**9**	**0**	**1**	**1**	**0**	**0**	**0**	**0**	**9:36**
	Manitoba Moose	AHL	73	18	36	54	18										1	1	1	2	0				
	NHL Totals		**7**	**2**	**3**	**5**	**0**	**0**	**0**	**0**	**15**	**13.3**		**69**	**55.1**	**9:47**	**9**	**0**	**1**	**1**	**0**	**0**	**0**	**0**	**9:36**

QMJHL Second All-Star Team (2000) • George Parsons Trophy (Memorial Cup Most Sportsmanlike Player) (2000, 2001) • QMJHL First All-Star Team (2001)

REINPRECHT, Steve

(REIGHN-prehkt, STEEV) **CGY.**

Center. Shoots left. 6', 190 lbs. Born, Edmonton, Alta., May 7, 1976.

			Regular Season														Playoffs								
Season	Club	League	GP	G	A	Pts	PIM	PP	SH	GW	S	%	+/-	TF	F%	Min	GP	G	A	Pts	PIM	PP	SH	GW	Min
1993-94	Edmonton SSAC	AMHL	71	48	77	125																			
1994-95	St. Albert Saints	AJHL	56	35	44	79	14																		
1995-96	St. Albert Saints	AJHL	32	24	36	60																			
1996-97	U. of Wisconsin	WCHA	38	11	9	20	12																		
1997-98	U. of Wisconsin	WCHA	41	19	24	43	18																		
1998-99	U. of Wisconsin	WCHA	38	16	17	33	14																		
99-2000	U. of Wisconsin	WCHA	37	26	40	*66	14																		
	Los Angeles	**NHL**	**1**	**0**	**0**	**0**	**2**	**0**	**0**	**0**	**0**	**0.0**	**0**	**6**	**50.0**	**6:01**									
2000-01	**Los Angeles**	**NHL**	**59**	**12**	**17**	**29**	**12**	**3**	**2**	**3**	**72**	**16.7**	**11**	**676**	**41.4**	**12:39**									
	♦ **Colorado**	**NHL**	**21**	**3**	**4**	**7**	**2**	**0**	**0**	**0**	**28**	**10.7**	**–1**	**209**	**51.2**	**15:38**	**22**	**2**	**3**	**5**	**2**	**0**	**0**	**0**	**12:09**
2001-02	**Colorado**	**NHL**	**67**	**19**	**27**	**46**	**18**	**4**	**0**	**3**	**111**	**17.1**	**14**	**413**	**52.1**	**16:32**	**21**	**7**	**5**	**12**	**8**	**0**	**0**	**2**	**16:23**
2002-03	**Colorado**	**NHL**	**77**	**18**	**33**	**51**	**18**	**2**	**1**	**1**	**146**	**12.3**	**–6**	**928**	**46.4**	**17:22**	**7**	**1**	**2**	**3**	**0**	**0**	**0**	**0**	**15:32**
	NHL Totals		**225**	**52**	**81**	**133**	**52**	**9**	**3**	**7**	**357**	**14.6**		**2232**	**46.4**	**15:40**	**50**	**10**	**10**	**20**	**10**	**0**	**0**	**2**	**14:24**

WCHA Second All-Star Team (1998) • WCHA First All-Star Team (2000) • WCHA Player of the Year (2000) • NCAA West First All-American Team (2000)

Signed as a free agent by **Los Angeles**, March 31, 2000. Traded to **Colorado** by **Los Angeles** with Rob Blake for Adam Deadmarsh, Aaron Miller, a player to be named later (Jared Aulin, March 22, 2001), and Colorado's 1st round choices in 2001 (Dave Steckel) and 2003 (Brian Boyle) Entry Drafts, February 21, 2001. Traded to **Buffalo** by **Colorado** for Keith Ballard, July 3, 2003. Traded to **Calgary** by **Buffalo** with Rhett Warrener for Chris Drury and Steve Begin, July 3, 2003.

REIRDEN, Todd

(REER-dehn, TAWD) **ANA.**

Defense. Shoots left. 6'5", 225 lbs. Born, Deerfield, IL, June 25, 1971. New Jersey's 14th choice, 242nd overall, in 1990 Entry Draft.

			Regular Season														Playoffs								
Season	Club	League	GP	G	A	Pts	PIM	PP	SH	GW	S	%	+/-	TF	F%	Min	GP	G	A	Pts	PIM	PP	SH	GW	Min
1987-88	Deerfield	Hi-School	22	19	32	51																			
1988-89	Tabor Academy	Hi-School	22	6	16	22																			
1989-90	Tabor Academy	Hi-School	22	10	28	38																			
1990-91	Bowling Green	CCHA	28	1	5	6	22																		
1991-92	Bowling Green	CCHA	33	8	7	15	34																		
1992-93	Bowling Green	CCHA	41	8	17	25	48																		
1993-94	Bowling Green	CCHA	38	7	23	30	56																		
1994-95	Albany River Rats	AHL	2	0	1	1	2																		
	Raleigh Icecaps	ECHL	26	2	13	15	33																		
	Tallahassee	ECHL	43	5	25	30	61										13	2	5	7	40				
1995-96	Tallahassee	ECHL	7	1	3	4	10																		
	Jacksonville	ECHL	15	1	10	11	41										1	0	2	2	4				
	Chicago Wolves	IHL	31	0	2	2	39										9	0	2	2	16				
1996-97	Chicago Wolves	IHL	57	3	10	13	108																		
	San Antonio	IHL	23	2	5	7	51										9	0	1	1	17				
1997-98	San Antonio	IHL	70	5	14	19	132																		
	Fort Wayne	IHL	11	2	2	4	16										4	0	2	2	4				
1998-99	**Edmonton**	**NHL**	**17**	**2**	**3**	**5**	**20**	**0**	**0**	**0**	**26**	**7.7**	**–1**	**0**	**0.0**	**17:17**									
	Hamilton	AHL	58	9	25	34	84										11	0	5	5	6				
99-2000	**St. Louis**	**NHL**	**56**	**4**	**21**	**25**	**32**	**0**	**0**	**1**	**77**	**5.2**	**18**	**1**	**0.0**	**18:18**	**4**	**0**	**1**	**1**	**0**	**0**	**0**	**0**	**13:43**
2000-01	**St. Louis**	**NHL**	**38**	**2**	**4**	**6**	**43**	**1**	**0**	**0**	**58**	**3.4**	**–2**	**2**	**50.0**	**16:50**	**1**	**0**	**0**	**0**	**0**	**0**	**0**	**0**	**2:52**
	Worcester IceCats	AHL	7	2	6	8	20																		

			Regular Season														Playoffs								
Season	Club	League	GP	G	A	Pts	PIM	PP	SH	GW	S	%	+/-	TF	F%	Min	GP	G	A	Pts	PIM	PP	SH	GW	Min
2001-02	Atlanta	NHL	65	3	5	8	82	1	0	0	85	3.5	–25	1	0.0	18:02	....	....	....	....	....	....	....	....	....
2002-03	Cincinnati	AHL	58	7	13	20	97	....	....	....	....	....	....	....	....	....	....	....	....	....	....	....	....	....	....
	NHL Totals		176	11	33	44	177	2	0	1	246	4.5	....	4	25.0	17:47	5	0	1	1	0	0	0	0	11:33

Signed as a free agent by **Edmonton**, September 17, 1998. Claimed on waivers by **St. Louis** from **Edmonton**, September 30, 1999. Signed as a free agent by **Atlanta**, July 16, 2001. Signed as a free agent by **Anaheim**, July 17, 2002.

RENBERG, Mikael (REHN-buhrg, MIGH-kuhl) TOR.

Right wing. Shoots left. 6'2", 235 lbs. Born, Pitea, Sweden, May 5, 1972. Philadelphia's 3rd choice, 40th overall, in 1990 Entry Draft.

Season	Club	League	GP	G	A	Pts	PIM	PP	SH	GW	S	%	+/-	TF	F%	Min	GP	G	A	Pts	PIM	PP	SH	GW	Min
1988-89	Pitea HC	Swede-2	12	6	3	9	....	....	....	....	....	....	....	....	....	....	....	....	....	....	....	....	....	....	....
1989-90	Pitea HC	Swede-2	29	15	19	34	....	....	....	....	....	....	....	....	....	....	....	....	....	....	....	....	....	....	....
1990-91	Lulea HF	Sweden	29	11	6	17	12	....	....	....	....	....	....	....	....	....	5	1	1	2	4	....	....	....	....
1991-92	Lulea HF	Sweden	38	8	15	23	20	....	....	....	....	....	....	....	....	....	2	0	0	0	0	....	....	....	....
1992-93	Lulea HF	Sweden	39	19	13	32	61	....	....	....	....	....	....	....	....	....	11	4	4	8	4	....	....	....	....
1993-94	Philadelphia	NHL	83	38	44	82	36	9	0	1	195	19.5	8	....	....	....	....	....	....	....	....	....	....	....	....
1994-95	Lulea HF	Sweden	10	9	4	13	16	....	....	....	....	....	....	....	....	....	....	....	....	....	....	....	....	....	....
	Philadelphia	NHL	47	26	31	57	20	8	0	4	143	18.2	20	....	....	....	15	6	7	13	6	2	0	0	....
1995-96	Philadelphia	NHL	51	23	20	43	45	9	0	4	198	11.6	8	....	....	....	11	3	6	9	14	1	0	0	....
1996-97	Philadelphia	NHL	77	22	37	59	65	1	0	4	249	8.8	36	....	....	....	18	5	6	11	4	2	0	0	....
1997-98	Tampa Bay	NHL	68	16	22	38	34	6	3	0	175	9.1	–37	....	....	....	....	....	....	....	....	....	....	....	....
	Sweden	Olympics	4	1	2	3	4	....	....	....	....	....	....	....	....	....	....	....	....	....	....	....	....	....	....
1998-99	Tampa Bay	NHL	20	4	8	12	4	2	0	0	42	9.5	–2	2	100.0	15:32	....	....	....	....	....	....	....	....	....
	Philadelphia	NHL	46	11	15	26	14	4	0	2	112	9.8	7	1	0.0	16:00	6	0	1	1	0	0	0	0	13:26
99-2000	Philadelphia	NHL	62	8	21	29	30	3	0	1	106	7.5	–1	3	33.3	13:27	....	....	....	....	....	....	....	....	....
	Phoenix	NHL	10	2	4	6	2	0	0	0	16	12.5	0	0	0.0	15:31	5	1	2	3	4	0	0	1	15:02
2000-01	Lulea HF	Sweden	48	22	32	54	36	....	....	....	....	....	....	....	....	....	11	6	5	11	35	....	....	....	....
2001-02	Toronto	NHL	71	14	38	52	36	4	0	3	130	10.8	11	6	33.3	14:35	3	0	0	0	2	0	0	0	12:16
	Sweden	Olympics	4	1	0	1	4	....	....	....	....	....	....	....	....	....	....	....	....	....	....	....	....	....	....
2002-03	Toronto	NHL	67	14	21	35	36	7	0	1	137	10.2	5	9	33.3	13:32	7	1	0	1	8	1	0	1	14:39
	NHL Totals		602	178	261	439	322	53	3	20	1503	11.8		21	38.1	14:25	65	16	22	38	38	6	0	2	14:03

NHL All-Rookie Team (1994)

Traded to **Tampa Bay** by **Philadelphia** with Karl Dykhuis for Philadelphia's 1st round choices (previously acquired) in 1998 (Philadelphia selected Simon Gagne), 1999 (Philadelphia selected Maxime Ouellet), 2000 (Philadelphia selected Justin Williams) and 2001 (later traded to Ottawa – Ottawa selected Tim Gleason) Entry Drafts, August 20, 1997. Traded to **Philadelphia** by **Tampa Bay** with Daymond Langkow for Chris Gratton and Mike Sillinger, December 12, 1998. Traded to **Phoenix** by **Philadelphia** for Rick Tocchet, March 8, 2000. Traded to **Toronto** by **Phoenix** for Sergei Berezin, June 23, 2001.

RHEAUME, Pascal (RAY-awm, PAS-kal)

Center. Shoots left. 6'1", 220 lbs. Born, Quebec City, Que., June 21, 1973.

Season	Club	League	GP	G	A	Pts	PIM	PP	SH	GW	S	%	+/-	TF	F%	Min	GP	G	A	Pts	PIM	PP	SH	GW	Min
1990-91	Ste-Foy	QAAA	37	20	38	58	25	....	....	....	....	....	....	....	....	....	7	7	1	8	6	....	....	....	....
1991-92	Trois-Rivieres	QMJHL	65	17	20	37	84	....	....	....	....	....	....	....	....	....	14	5	4	9	23	....	....	....	....
1992-93	Sherbrooke	QMJHL	65	28	34	62	88	....	....	....	....	....	....	....	....	....	14	6	5	11	31	....	....	....	....
1993-94	Albany River Rats	AHL	55	17	18	35	43	....	....	....	....	....	....	....	....	....	5	0	1	1	0	....	....	....	....
1994-95	Albany River Rats	AHL	78	19	25	44	46	....	....	....	....	....	....	....	....	....	14	3	6	9	19	....	....	....	....
1995-96	Albany River Rats	AHL	68	26	42	68	50	....	....	....	....	....	....	....	....	....	4	1	2	3	2	....	....	....	....
1996-97	New Jersey	NHL	2	1	0	1	0	0	0	0	5	20.0	1	....	....	....	....	....	....	....	....	....	....	....	....
	Albany River Rats	AHL	51	22	23	45	40	....	....	....	....	....	....	....	....	....	16	2	8	10	16	....	....	....	....
1997-98	St. Louis	NHL	48	6	9	15	35	1	0	0	45	13.3	4	....	....	....	10	1	3	4	8	1	0	0	....
1998-99	St. Louis	NHL	60	9	18	27	24	2	0	0	85	10.6	10	21	71.4	13:19	5	1	0	1	4	0	0	0	11:36
99-2000	St. Louis	NHL	7	1	1	2	6	0	0	0	5	20.0	–2	2	0.0	10:08	....	....	....	....	....	....	....	....	....
	Worcester IceCats	AHL	7	1	1	2	4	....	....	....	....	....	....	....	....	....	....	....	....	....	....	....	....	....	....
2000-01	St. Louis	NHL	8	2	0	2	5	2	0	0	16	12.5	–1	7	42.9	11:56	3	0	1	1	0	0	0	0	11:30
	Worcester IceCats	AHL	56	23	35	58	63	....	....	....	....	....	....	....	....	....	11	2	4	6	2	....	....	....	....
2001-02	Chicago	NHL	19	0	2	2	4	0	0	0	19	0.0	–1	165	51.5	9:22	....	....	....	....	....	....	....	....	....
	Atlanta	NHL	42	11	9	20	25	6	0	2	61	18.0	–3	510	45.9	14:27	....	....	....	....	....	....	....	....	....
2002-03	Atlanta	NHL	56	4	9	13	24	0	2	1	70	5.7	–8	602	46.8	12:17	....	....	....	....	....	....	....	....	....
	♦ New Jersey	NHL	21	4	1	5	8	0	1	1	23	17.4	3	248	51.6	11:50	24	1	2	3	13	0	0	0	13:32
	NHL Totals		263	38	49	87	131	11	3	4	329	11.6		1555	48.0	12:37	42	3	6	9	25	1	0	0	13:03

Signed as a free agent by **New Jersey**, October 1, 1993. Claimed by **St. Louis** from **New Jersey** in Waiver Draft, September 28, 1997. • Missed majority of 1999-2000 season recovering from shoulder surgery, August, 1999. Signed as a free agent by **Chicago**, July 31, 2001. Claimed on waivers by **Atlanta** from **Chicago**, November 14, 2001. Traded to **New Jersey** by **Atlanta** for future considerations, February 24, 2003.

RIBEIRO, Mike (rih-bee-AIR-roh, MIGHK) MTL.

Center. Shoots left. 6', 177 lbs. Born, Montreal, Que., February 10, 1980. Montreal's 2nd choice, 45th overall, in 1998 Entry Draft.

Season	Club	League	GP	G	A	Pts	PIM	PP	SH	GW	S	%	+/-	TF	F%	Min	GP	G	A	Pts	PIM	PP	SH	GW	Min
1996-97	Mtl-Bourassa	QAAA	43	32	57	89	48	....	....	....	....	....	....	....	....	....	16	15	23	38	14	....	....	....	....
1997-98	Rouyn-Noranda	QMJHL	67	40	*85	125	55	....	....	....	....	....	....	....	....	....	6	3	1	4	0	....	....	....	....
1998-99	Rouyn-Noranda	QMJHL	69	*67	*100	*167	137	....	....	....	....	....	....	....	....	....	11	5	11	16	12	....	....	....	....
	Fredericton	AHL	....	....	....	....	....	....	....	....	....	....	....	....	....	....	5	0	1	1	2	....	....	....	....
99-2000	Montreal	NHL	19	1	1	2	2	1	0	0	18	5.6	–6	95	34.7	10:40	....	....	....	....	....	....	....	....	....
	Quebec Citadelles	AHL	3	0	0	0	2	....	....	....	....	....	....	....	....	....	....	....	....	....	....	....	....	....	....
	Rouyn-Noranda	QMJHL	2	1	3	4	0	....	....	....	....	....	....	....	....	....	....	....	....	....	....	....	....	....	....
	Quebec Remparts	QMJHL	21	17	28	45	30	....	....	....	....	....	....	....	....	....	11	3	20	23	38	....	....	....	....
2000-01	Montreal	NHL	2	0	0	0	2	0	0	0	3	0.0	0	11	18.2	10:38	....	....	....	....	....	....	....	....	....
	Quebec Citadelles	AHL	74	26	40	66	44	....	....	....	....	....	....	....	....	....	9	1	5	6	23	....	....	....	....
2001-02	Montreal	NHL	43	8	10	18	12	3	0	0	48	16.7	–11	141	44.0	13:55	....	....	....	....	....	....	....	....	....
	Quebec Citadelles	AHL	23	9	14	23	36	....	....	....	....	....	....	....	....	....	3	0	3	3	0	....	....	....	....
2002-03	Montreal	NHL	52	5	12	17	6	2	0	0	57	8.8	–3	358	50.3	11:07	....	....	....	....	....	....	....	....	....
	Hamilton	AHL	3	0	1	1	0	....	....	....	....	....	....	....	....	....	....	....	....	....	....	....	....	....	....
	NHL Totals		116	14	23	37	22	6	0	0	126	11.1		605	45.8	12:05	....	....	....	....	....	....	....	....	....

QMJHL Second All-Star Team (1998) • QMJHL First All-Star Team (1999) • Canadian Major Junior First All-Star Team (1999)

RICCI, Mike (REE-CHEE, MIGHK) S.J.

Center. Shoots left. 6', 185 lbs. Born, Scarborough, Ont., October 27, 1971. Philadelphia's 1st choice, 4th overall, in 1990 Entry Draft.

Season	Club	League	GP	G	A	Pts	PIM	PP	SH	GW	S	%	+/-	TF	F%	Min	GP	G	A	Pts	PIM	PP	SH	GW	Min
1986-87	Toronto Marlies	MTHL	38	39	42	81	27	....	....	....	....	....	....	....	....	....	....	....	....	....	....	....	....	....	....
1987-88	Peterborough	OHL	41	24	37	61	20	....	....	....	....	....	....	....	....	....	8	5	5	10	4	....	....	....	....
1988-89	Peterborough	OHL	60	54	52	106	43	....	....	....	....	....	....	....	....	....	17	19	16	35	18	....	....	....	....
1989-90	Peterborough	OHL	60	52	64	116	39	....	....	....	....	....	....	....	....	....	12	5	7	12	26	....	....	....	....
1990-91	Philadelphia	NHL	68	21	20	41	64	9	0	4	121	17.4	–8	....	....	....	....	....	....	....	....	....	....	....	....
1991-92	Philadelphia	NHL	78	20	36	56	93	11	2	0	149	13.4	–10	....	....	....	....	....	....	....	....	....	....	....	....
1992-93	Quebec	NHL	77	27	51	78	123	12	1	10	142	19.0	8	....	....	....	6	0	6	6	8	0	0	0	....
1993-94	Quebec	NHL	83	30	21	51	113	13	3	6	138	21.7	–9	....	....	....	....	....	....	....	....	....	....	....	....
1994-95	Quebec	NHL	48	15	21	36	40	9	0	1	73	20.5	5	....	....	....	6	1	3	4	8	0	0	0	....
1995-96♦	Colorado	NHL	62	6	21	27	52	3	0	1	73	8.2	1	....	....	....	22	6	11	17	18	3	0	1	....
1996-97	Colorado	NHL	63	13	19	32	59	5	0	3	74	17.6	–3	....	....	....	17	2	4	6	17	0	0	1	....
1997-98	Colorado	NHL	6	0	4	4	2	0	0	0	5	0.0	0	....	....	....	....	....	....	....	....	....	....	....	....
	San Jose	NHL	59	9	14	23	30	5	0	2	86	10.5	–4	....	....	....	6	1	3	4	6	0	0	0	....
1998-99	San Jose	NHL	82	13	26	39	68	2	1	2	98	13.3	1	1465	49.6	15:23	6	2	3	5	10	1	0	0	16:53
99-2000	San Jose	NHL	82	20	24	44	60	10	0	5	134	14.9	14	1522	50.7	16:52	12	5	1	6	2	3	0	1	17:37
2000-01	San Jose	NHL	81	22	22	44	60	9	2	4	141	15.6	3	1631	51.4	17:60	6	0	3	3	0	0	0	0	19:44
2001-02	San Jose	NHL	79	19	34	53	44	5	2	0	115	16.5	9	1501	49.0	17:04	12	4	6	10	4	0	0	1	19:51
2002-03	San Jose	NHL	75	11	23	34	53	5	1	2	101	10.9	–12	1152	51.6	16:31	....	....	....	....	....	....	....	....	....
	NHL Totals		943	226	336	562	861	98	12	40	1450	15.6		7271	50.4	16:46	93	21	40	61	73	7	0	4	18:36

OHL Second All-Star Team (1989) • OHL First All-Star Team (1990) • OHL MVP (1990) • Canadian Major Junior Player of the Year (1990) • OHL First All-Star Team (1990)

Traded to **Quebec** by **Philadelphia** with Steve Duchesne, Peter Forsberg, Kerry Huffman, Ron Hextall, Philadelphia's 1st round choice (Jocelyn Thibault) in 1993 Entry Draft, $15,000,000 and future considerations (Chris Simon and Philadelphia's 1st round choice (later traded to Toronto – later traded to Washington – Washington selected Nolan Baumgartner) in 1994 Entry Draft, July 21, 1992) for Eric Lindros, June 30, 1992. Transferred to **Colorado** after **Quebec** franchise relocated, June 21, 1995. Traded to **San Jose** by **Colorado** with Colorado's 2nd round choice (later traded to Buffalo – Buffalo selected Jaroslav Kristek) in 1998 Entry Draft for Shean Donovan and San Jose's 1st round choice (Alex Tanguay) in 1998 Entry Draft, November 21, 1997.

RICHARDS, Brad

(RIH-chahrds, BRAD) **T.B.**

Center. Shoots left. 6'1", 198 lbs. Born, Murray Harbour, P.E.I., May 2, 1980. Tampa Bay's 2nd choice, 64th overall, in 1998 Entry Draft.

			Regular Season														Playoffs								
Season	Club	League	GP	G	A	Pts	PIM	PP	SH	GW	S	%	+/-	TF	F%	Min	GP	G	A	Pts	PIM	PP	SH	GW	Min
1996-97	Notre Dame	SJHL	63	39	48	87	73	....	....	....	....	....	....	....	....	....	....	....	....	....	....	....	....	....	....
1997-98	Rimouski Oceanic	QMJHL	68	33	82	115	44	....	....	....	....	....	....	....	....	....	19	8	24	32	2	....	....	....	....
1998-99	Rimouski Oceanic	QMJHL	59	39	92	131	55	....	....	....	....	....	....	....	....	....	11	9	12	21	6	....	....	....	....
99-2000	Rimouski Oceanic	QMJHL	63	*71	*115	*186	69	....	....	....	....	....	....	....	....	....	12	13	*24	*37	16	....	....	....	....
2000-01	**Tampa Bay**	**NHL**	**82**	**21**	**41**	**62**	**14**	**7**	**0**	**3**	**179**	**11.7**	**-10**	**955**	**41.4**	**16:54**	....	....	....	....	....	....	....	....	....
2001-02	**Tampa Bay**	**NHL**	**82**	**20**	**42**	**62**	**13**	**5**	**0**	**0**	**251**	**8.0**	**-18**	**911**	**41.2**	**19:48**	....	....	....	....	....	....	....	....	....
2002-03	**Tampa Bay**	**NHL**	**80**	**17**	**57**	**74**	**24**	**4**	**0**	**2**	**277**	**6.1**	**3**	**1007**	**47.5**	**19:56**	**11**	**0**	**5**	**5**	**12**	**0**	**0**	**0**	**22:21**
	NHL Totals		**244**	**58**	**140**	**198**	**51**	**16**	**0**	**5**	**707**	**8.2**		**2873**	**43.4**	**18:52**	**11**	**0**	**5**	**5**	**12**	**0**	**0**	**0**	**22:21**

SJHL Rookie of the Year (1997) • QMJHL First All-Star Team (2000) • Canadian Major Junior First All-Star Team (2000) • Canadian Major Junior Player of the Year (2000) • Memorial Cup All-Star Team (2000) • Stafford Smythe Memorial Trophy (Memorial Cup MVP) (2000) • NHL All-Rookie Team (2001)

RICHARDS, Travis

(RIH-chuhrds, TRA-vihs)

Defense. Shoots left. 6'1", 195 lbs. Born, Crystal, MN, March 22, 1970. Minnesota's 6th choice, 169th overall, in 1988 Entry Draft.

			Regular Season														Playoffs								
Season	Club	League	GP	G	A	Pts	PIM	PP	SH	GW	S	%	+/-	TF	F%	Min	GP	G	A	Pts	PIM	PP	SH	GW	Min
1986-87	Armstrong	Hi-School	22	6	16	22	20	....	....	....	....	....	....	....	....	....	....	....	....	....	....	....	....	....	....
1987-88	Armstrong	Hi-School	24	14	14	28	....	....	....	....	....	....	....	....	....	....	....	....	....	....	....	....	....	....	....
1988-89	Armstrong	Hi-School	STATISTICS NOT AVAILABLE					....	....	....	....	....	....	....	....	....	....	....	....	....	....	....	....	....	....
1989-90	U. of Minnesota	WCHA	45	4	24	28	38	....	....	....	....	....	....	....	....	....	....	....	....	....	....	....	....	....	....
1990-91	U. of Minnesota	WCHA	45	9	25	34	28	....	....	....	....	....	....	....	....	....	....	....	....	....	....	....	....	....	....
1991-92	U. of Minnesota	WCHA	41	10	22	32	65	....	....	....	....	....	....	....	....	....	....	....	....	....	....	....	....	....	....
1992-93	U. of Minnesota	WCHA	42	12	26	38	52	....	....	....	....	....	....	....	....	....	....	....	....	....	....	....	....	....	....
1993-94	Team USA	Nat-Tm	51	1	11	12	38	....	....	....	....	....	....	....	....	....	....	....	....	....	....	....	....	....	....
	United States	Olympics	8	0	0	0	2	....	....	....	....	....	....	....	....	....	....	....	....	....	....	....	....	....	....
	Kalamazoo Wings	IHL	19	2	10	12	20	....	....	....	....	....	....	....	....	....	4	1	1	2	0	....	....	....	....
1994-95	Kalamazoo Wings	IHL	63	4	16	20	53	....	....	....	....	....	....	....	....	....	15	1	5	6	12	....	....	....	....
	Dallas	**NHL**	**2**	**0**	**0**	**0**	**0**	**0**	**0**	**0**	**1**	**0.0**	**0**	....	....	....	....	....	....	....	....	....	....	....	....
1995-96	**Dallas**	**NHL**	**1**	**0**	**0**	**0**	**2**	**0**	**0**	**0**	**0**	**0.0**	**-1**	....	....	....	....	....	....	....	....	....	....	....	....
	Michigan	IHL	65	8	15	23	55	....	....	....	....	....	....	....	....	....	9	2	2	4	4	....	....	....	....
1996-97	Grand Rapids	IHL	77	10	13	23	83	....	....	....	....	....	....	....	....	....	5	1	3	4	2	....	....	....	....
1997-98	Grand Rapids	IHL	81	12	20	32	70	....	....	....	....	....	....	....	....	....	3	1	1	2	4	....	....	....	....
1998-99	Grand Rapids	IHL	82	9	23	32	84	....	....	....	....	....	....	....	....	....	....	....	....	....	....	....	....	....	....
99-2000	Grand Rapids	IHL	71	5	23	28	47	....	....	....	....	....	....	....	....	....	17	1	7	8	18	....	....	....	....
2000-01	Grand Rapids	IHL	75	5	30	35	42	....	....	....	....	....	....	....	....	....	10	0	5	5	8	....	....	....	....
2001-02	Grand Rapids	AHL	72	6	23	29	36	....	....	....	....	....	....	....	....	....	5	0	1	1	2	....	....	....	....
2002-03	Grand Rapids	AHL	73	6	21	27	52	....	....	....	....	....	....	....	....	....	15	0	4	4	6	....	....	....	....
	NHL Totals		**3**	**0**	**0**	**0**	**2**	**0**	**0**	**0**	**1**	**0.0**		....	....	....	....	....	....	....	....	....	....	....	....

WCHA Second All-Star Team (1992, 1993) • IHL First All-Star Team (1995, 1996) • Governors' Trophy (Outstanding Defenseman – IHL) (1995) • IHL Second All-Star Team (2001)

Rights transferred to **Dallas** after **Minnesota** franchise relocated, June 9, 1993. Signed as a free agent by **Ottawa**, July 13, 2001.

RICHARDSON, Luke

(RIH-chahrd-sohn, LEWK) **CBJ**

Defense. Shoots left. 6'4", 210 lbs. Born, Ottawa, Ont., March 26, 1969. Toronto's 1st choice, 7th overall, in 1987 Entry Draft.

			Regular Season														Playoffs								
Season	Club	League	GP	G	A	Pts	PIM	PP	SH	GW	S	%	+/-	TF	F%	Min	GP	G	A	Pts	PIM	PP	SH	GW	Min
1984-85	Ottawa Knights	OMHA	35	5	26	31	72	....	....	....	....	....	....	....	....	....	....	....	....	....	....	....	....	....	....
1985-86	Peterborough	OHL	63	6	18	24	57	....	....	....	....	....	....	....	....	....	16	2	1	3	50	....	....	....	....
1986-87	Peterborough	OHL	59	13	32	45	70	....	....	....	....	....	....	....	....	....	12	0	5	5	24	....	....	....	....
1987-88	**Toronto**	**NHL**	**78**	**4**	**6**	**10**	**90**	**0**	**0**	**0**	**49**	**8.2**	**-25**	....	....	....	**2**	**0**	**0**	**0**	**0**	**0**	**0**	**0**	....
1988-89	**Toronto**	**NHL**	**55**	**2**	**7**	**9**	**106**	**0**	**0**	**0**	**59**	**3.4**	**-15**	....	....	....	....	....	....	....	....	....	....	....	....
1989-90	**Toronto**	**NHL**	**67**	**4**	**14**	**18**	**122**	**0**	**0**	**0**	**80**	**5.0**	**-1**	....	....	....	**5**	**0**	**0**	**0**	**22**	**0**	**0**	**0**	....
1990-91	**Toronto**	**NHL**	**78**	**1**	**9**	**10**	**238**	**0**	**0**	**0**	**68**	**1.5**	**-28**	....	....	....	....	....	....	....	....	....	....	....	....
1991-92	**Edmonton**	**NHL**	**75**	**2**	**19**	**21**	**118**	**0**	**0**	**0**	**85**	**2.4**	**-9**	....	....	....	**16**	**0**	**5**	**5**	**45**	**0**	**0**	**0**	....
1992-93	**Edmonton**	**NHL**	**82**	**3**	**10**	**13**	**142**	**0**	**2**	**0**	**78**	**3.8**	**-18**	....	....	....	....	....	....	....	....	....	....	....	....
1993-94	**Edmonton**	**NHL**	**69**	**2**	**6**	**8**	**131**	**0**	**0**	**0**	**92**	**2.2**	**-13**	....	....	....	....	....	....	....	....	....	....	....	....
1994-95	**Edmonton**	**NHL**	**46**	**3**	**10**	**13**	**40**	**1**	**1**	**1**	**51**	**5.9**	**-6**	....	....	....	....	....	....	....	....	....	....	....	....
1995-96	**Edmonton**	**NHL**	**82**	**2**	**9**	**11**	**108**	**0**	**0**	**0**	**61**	**3.3**	**-27**	....	....	....	....	....	....	....	....	....	....	....	....
1996-97	**Edmonton**	**NHL**	**82**	**1**	**11**	**12**	**91**	**0**	**0**	**0**	**67**	**1.5**	**9**	....	....	....	**12**	**0**	**2**	**2**	**14**	**0**	**0**	**0**	....
1997-98	**Philadelphia**	**NHL**	**81**	**2**	**3**	**5**	**139**	**2**	**0**	**0**	**57**	**3.5**	**7**	....	....	....	**5**	**0**	**0**	**0**	**0**	**0**	**0**	**0**	....
1998-99	**Philadelphia**	**NHL**	**78**	**0**	**6**	**6**	**106**	**0**	**0**	**0**	**49**	**0.0**	**-3**	**0**	**0.0**	**16:33**	....	....	....	....	....	....	....	....	....
99-2000	**Philadelphia**	**NHL**	**74**	**2**	**5**	**7**	**140**	**0**	**0**	**1**	**50**	**4.0**	**14**	**0**	**0.0**	**16:11**	**18**	**0**	**1**	**1**	**41**	**0**	**0**	**0**	**21:58**
2000-01	**Philadelphia**	**NHL**	**82**	**2**	**6**	**8**	**131**	**0**	**1**	**0**	**75**	**2.7**	**23**	**1**	**0.0**	**20:42**	**6**	**0**	**0**	**0**	**4**	**0**	**0**	**0**	**24:39**
2001-02	**Philadelphia**	**NHL**	**72**	**1**	**8**	**9**	**102**	**0**	**0**	**0**	**65**	**1.5**	**18**	**0**	**0.0**	**18:17**	**5**	**0**	**0**	**0**	**4**	**0**	**0**	**0**	**19:18**
2002-03	**Columbus**	**NHL**	**82**	**0**	**13**	**13**	**73**	**0**	**0**	**0**	**56**	**0.0**	**-16**	**2**	**50.0**	**23:31**	....	....	....	....	....	....	....	....	....
	NHL Totals		**1183**	**31**	**142**	**173**	**1877**	**3**	**4**	**2**	**1042**	**3.0**		**3**	**33.3**	**19:09**	**69**	**0**	**8**	**8**	**130**	**0**	**0**	**0**	**22:04**

Traded to **Edmonton** by **Toronto** with Vincent Damphousse, Peter Ing and Scott Thornton for Grant Fuhr, Glenn Anderson and Craig Berube, September 19, 1991. Signed as a free agent by **Philadelphia**, July 23, 1997. Signed as a free agent by **Columbus**, July 4, 2002.

RICHTER, Barry

(RIHK-tuhr, BAIR-ree)

Defense. Shoots left. 6'2", 200 lbs. Born, Madison, WI, September 11, 1970. Hartford's 2nd choice, 32nd overall, in 1988 Entry Draft.

			Regular Season														Playoffs								
Season	Club	League	GP	G	A	Pts	PIM	PP	SH	GW	S	%	+/-	TF	F%	Min	GP	G	A	Pts	PIM	PP	SH	GW	Min
1986-87	Culver Eagles	Hi-School	39	15	30	45	....	....	....	....	....	....	....	....	....	....	....	....	....	....	....	....	....	....	....
1987-88	Culver Eagles	Hi-School	35	24	29	53	18	....	....	....	....	....	....	....	....	....	....	....	....	....	....	....	....	....	....
1988-89	Culver Eagles	Hi-School	19	21	29	50	16	....	....	....	....	....	....	....	....	....	....	....	....	....	....	....	....	....	....
1989-90	U. of Wisconsin	WCHA	42	13	23	36	36	....	....	....	....	....	....	....	....	....	....	....	....	....	....	....	....	....	....
1990-91	U. of Wisconsin	WCHA	43	15	20	35	42	....	....	....	....	....	....	....	....	....	....	....	....	....	....	....	....	....	....
1991-92	U. of Wisconsin	WCHA	39	10	25	35	62	....	....	....	....	....	....	....	....	....	....	....	....	....	....	....	....	....	....
1992-93	U. of Wisconsin	WCHA	42	14	32	46	74	....	....	....	....	....	....	....	....	....	....	....	....	....	....	....	....	....	....
1993-94	Team USA	Nat-Tm	56	7	16	23	50	....	....	....	....	....	....	....	....	....	....	....	....	....	....	....	....	....	....
	United States	Olympics	8	0	3	3	4	....	....	....	....	....	....	....	....	....	....	....	....	....	....	....	....	....	....
	Binghamton	AHL	21	0	9	9	12	....	....	....	....	....	....	....	....	....	....	....	....	....	....	....	....	....	....
1994-95	Binghamton	AHL	73	15	41	56	54	....	....	....	....	....	....	....	....	....	11	4	5	9	12	....	....	....	....
1995-96	**NY Rangers**	**NHL**	**4**	**0**	**1**	**1**	**0**	**0**	**0**	**0**	**3**	**0.0**	**2**	....	....	....	....	....	....	....	....	....	....	....	....
	Binghamton	AHL	69	20	61	81	64	....	....	....	....	....	....	....	....	....	3	0	3	3	0	....	....	....	....
1996-97	**Boston**	**NHL**	**50**	**5**	**13**	**18**	**32**	**1**	**0**	**0**	**79**	**6.3**	**-7**	....	....	....	....	....	....	....	....	....	....	....	....
	Providence Bruins	AHL	19	2	6	8	4	....	....	....	....	....	....	....	....	....	10	4	4	8	4	....	....	....	....
1997-98	Providence Bruins	AHL	75	16	29	45	47	....	....	....	....	....	....	....	....	....	....	....	....	....	....	....	....	....	....
1998-99	**NY Islanders**	**NHL**	**72**	**6**	**18**	**24**	**34**	**0**	**0**	**2**	**111**	**5.4**	**-4**	**0**	**0.0**	**21:08**	....	....	....	....	....	....	....	....	....
99-2000	**Montreal**	**NHL**	**23**	**0**	**2**	**2**	**8**	**0**	**0**	**0**	**13**	**0.0**	**-5**	**1**	**100.0**	**12:15**	....	....	....	....	....	....	....	....	....
	Quebec Citadelles	AHL	2	0	0	0	0	....	....	....	....	....	....	....	....	....	....	....	....	....	....	....	....	....	....
	Manitoba Moose	IHL	19	5	4	9	6	....	....	....	....	....	....	....	....	....	2	1	1	2	0	....	....	....	....
2000-01	**Montreal**	**NHL**	**2**	**0**	**0**	**0**	**2**	**0**	**0**	**0**	**0**	**0.0**	**-1**	**0**	**0.0**	**10:44**	....	....	....	....	....	....	....	....	....
	Quebec Citadelles	AHL	68	4	47	51	45	....	....	....	....	....	....	....	....	....	6	0	3	3	2	....	....	....	....
2001-02	Linkopings HC	Sweden	44	5	12	17	82	....	....	....	....	....	....	....	....	....	....	....	....	....	....	....	....	....	....
2002-03	Linkopings HC	Sweden	44	6	10	16	74	....	....	....	....	....	....	....	....	....	....	....	....	....	....	....	....	....	....
	HC Lugano	Swiss	....	....	....	....	....	....	....	....	....	....	....	....	....	....	9	2	6	8	10	....	....	....	....
	NHL Totals		**151**	**11**	**34**	**45**	**76**	**1**	**0**	**2**	**206**	**5.3**		**1**	**100.0**	**18:49**									

NCAA Championship All-Tournament Team (1992) • WCHA First All-Star Team (1993) • NCAA West First All-American Team (1993) • AHL First All-Star Team (1996) • Eddie Shore Award (Top Defenseman – AHL) (1996)

Traded to **NY Rangers** by **Hartford** with Steve Larmer, Nick Kypreos and Hartford's 6th round choice (Yuri Litvinov) in 1994 Entry Draft for Darren Turcotte and James Patrick, November 2, 1993. Signed as a free agent by **Boston**, July 19, 1996. Signed as a free agent by **NY Islanders**, August 17, 1998. Signed as a free agent by **Montreal**, August 20, 1999. Loaned to **Manitoba** (IHL) by **Montreal** for loan of Patrice Tardif to **Quebec** (AHL), March 3, 2000.

RIESEN, Michel
(REE-sehn, MEE-shehl)

Right wing. Shoots right. 6'2", 190 lbs. Born, Oberbalm, Switz., April 11, 1979. Edmonton's 1st choice, 14th overall, in 1997 Entry Draft.

Season	Club	League	GP	G	A	Pts	PIM	PP	SH	GW	S	%	+/-	TF	F%	Min	Playoffs GP	G	A	Pts	PIM	PP	SH	GW	Min
1994-95	EHC Biel-Bienne	Swiss	12	0	2	2	0										6	2	0	2	0				
1995-96	EHC Biel-Bienne	Swiss-2	34	9	6	15	2										3	1	0	1	0				
1996-97	EHC Biel-Bienne	Swiss-2	38	16	16	32	49																		
1997-98	HC Davos	Swiss	32	16	9	25	8										18	5	5	10	4				
1998-99	Hamilton	AHL	60	6	17	23	6										3	0	0	0	0				
99-2000	Hamilton	AHL	73	29	31	60	20										10	3	5	8	4				
2000-01	**Edmonton**	**NHL**	**12**	**0**	**1**	**1**	**4**	**0**	**0**	**0**	**16**	**0.0**	**2**	**0**	**0.0**	**9:54**									
	Hamilton	AHL	69	26	28	54	14																		
2001-02	HC Davos	Swiss	35	12	12	24	28										16	7	8	15	*52				
2002-03	HC Davos	Swiss	44	17	17	34	32										17	3	6	9	8				
	NHL Totals		**12**	**0**	**1**	**1**	**4**	**0**	**0**	**0**	**16**	**0.0**		**0**	**0.0**	**9:54**									

Traded to **St. Louis** by **Edmonton** with Doug Weight for Marty Reasoner, Jochen Hecht and Jan Horacek, July 1, 2001. Signed as a free agent by **HC Davos** (Swiss), October 2, 2001.

RITA, Jani
(REETA, YA-nee) **EDM.**

Left wing. Shoots left. 6'1", 206 lbs. Born, Helsinki, Finland, July 25, 1981. Edmonton's 1st choice, 13th overall, in 1999 Entry Draft.

Season	Club	League	GP	G	A	Pts	PIM	PP	SH	GW	S	%	+/-	TF	F%	Min	Playoffs GP	G	A	Pts	PIM	PP	SH	GW	Min
1994-95	Jokerit Helsinki-C	Finn-Jr.	7	3	0	3	0										6	1	0	1	0				
1995-96	Jokerit Helsinki-C	Finn-Jr.	12	10	3	13	2																		
	Jokerit Helsinki-B	Finn-Jr.	5	0	0	0	0																		
1996-97	Jokerit Helsinki-B	Finn-Jr.	27	22	7	29	4																		
1997-98	Jokerit Helsinki-B	Finn-Jr.	7	7	4	11	2																		
	Jokerit Helsinki Jr.	Finn-Jr.	36	15	9	24	2										8	4	1	5	0				
	Jokerit Helsinki	Finland															1	0	0	0	0				
1998-99	Jokerit Helsinki Jr.	Finn-Jr.	20	9	13	22	8																		
	Jokerit Helsinki	Finland	41	3	2	5	39																		
	Jokerit Helsinki	EuroHL	3	0	0	0	0																		
99-2000	Jokerit Helsinki Jr.	Finn-Jr.	1	1	0	1	0																		
	Jokerit Helsinki	Finland	49	6	3	9	10										11	1	0	1	0				
2000-01	Jokerit Helsinki Jr.	Finn-Jr.	3	3	2	5	0																		
	Jokerit Helsinki	Finland	50	5	10	15	18										5	0	0	0	2				
2001-02	**Edmonton**	**NHL**	**1**	**0**	**0**	**0**	**0**	**0**	**0**	**0**	**0**	**0.0**	**0**	**0**	**0.0**	**6:09**									
	Hamilton	AHL	76	25	17	42	32										15	8	4	12	0				
2002-03	**Edmonton**	**NHL**	**12**	**3**	**1**	**4**	**0**	**0**	**0**	**0**	**18**	**16.7**	**2**	**1**	**0.0**	**9:32**									
	Hamilton	AHL	64	21	27	48	18										23	3	4	7	2				
	NHL Totals		**13**	**3**	**1**	**4**	**0**	**0**	**0**	**0**	**18**	**16.7**		**1**	**0.0**	**9:17**									

RITCHIE, Byron
(RIHT-chee, BIGH-rohn) **FLA.**

Center. Shoots left. 5'10", 195 lbs. Born, Burnaby, B.C., April 24, 1977. Hartford's 6th choice, 165th overall, in 1995 Entry Draft.

Season	Club	League	GP	G	A	Pts	PIM	PP	SH	GW	S	%	+/-	TF	F%	Min	Playoffs GP	G	A	Pts	PIM	PP	SH	GW	Min
1992-93	North Delta	BCAHA	60	102	151	253	147																		
1993-94	Lethbridge	WHL	44	4	11	15	44										6	0	0	0	14				
1994-95	Lethbridge	WHL	58	22	28	50	132																		
1995-96	Lethbridge	WHL	66	55	51	106	163										4	0	2	2	4				
	Springfield	AHL	6	2	1	3	4										8	0	3	3	0				
1996-97	Lethbridge	WHL	63	50	76	126	115										18	*16	12	*28	28				
1997-98	New Haven	AHL	65	13	18	31	97																		
1998-99	**Carolina**	**NHL**	**3**	**0**	**0**	**0**	**0**	**0**	**0**	**0**	**0**	**0.0**	**0**	**5**	**20.0**	**3:25**									
	New Haven	AHL	66	24	33	57	139																		
99-2000	**Carolina**	**NHL**	**26**	**0**	**2**	**2**	**17**	**0**	**0**	**0**	**13**	**0.0**	**–10**	**155**	**49.7**	**7:24**									
	Cincinnati	IHL	34	8	13	21	81										10	1	6	7	32				
2000-01	Cincinnati	IHL	77	31	35	66	166										5	3	2	5	10				
2001-02	**Carolina**	**NHL**	**4**	**0**	**0**	**0**	**2**	**0**	**0**	**0**	**5**	**0.0**	**0**	**9**	**44.4**	**11:30**									
	Lowell	AHL	43	25	30	55	38																		
	Florida	**NHL**	**31**	**5**	**6**	**11**	**34**	**2**	**0**	**0**	**55**	**9.1**	**–2**	**324**	**50.9**	**12:26**									
2002-03	**Florida**	**NHL**	**30**	**0**	**3**	**3**	**19**	**0**	**0**	**0**	**29**	**0.0**	**–4**	**251**	**48.2**	**9:18**									
	San Antonio	AHL	26	3	14	17	68										3	1	0	1	0				
	NHL Totals		**94**	**5**	**11**	**16**	**72**	**2**	**0**	**0**	**102**	**4.9**		**744**	**49.5**	**9:43**									

WHL East Second All-Star Team (1996, 1997)

Rights transferred to **Carolina** after **Hartford** franchise relocated, June 25, 1997. Traded to **Florida** by **Carolina** with Sandis Ozolinsh for Bret Hedican, Kevyn Adams, Tomas Malec and a conditional 2nd round choice in 2003 Entry Draft, January 16, 2002.

RIVERS, Jamie
(RIH-vuhrs, JAY-mee) **DET.**

Defense. Shoots left. 6', 195 lbs. Born, Ottawa, Ont., March 16, 1975. St. Louis' 2nd choice, 63rd overall, in 1993 Entry Draft.

Season	Club	League	GP	G	A	Pts	PIM	PP	SH	GW	S	%	+/-	TF	F%	Min	Playoffs GP	G	A	Pts	PIM	PP	SH	GW	Min
1989-90	Ottawa South	ODMHA	50	26	46	72	46																		
1990-91	Ottawa Jr. Sens	OCJHL	55	4	30	34	74																		
1991-92	Sudbury Wolves	OHL	55	3	13	16	20										8	0	0	0	0				
1992-93	Sudbury Wolves	OHL	62	12	43	55	20										14	7	19	26	4				
1993-94	Sudbury Wolves	OHL	65	32	*89	121	58										10	1	9	10	14				
1994-95	Sudbury Wolves	OHL	46	9	56	65	30										18	7	26	33	22				
1995-96	**St. Louis**	**NHL**	**3**	**0**	**0**	**0**	**2**	**0**	**0**	**0**	**5**	**0.0**	**–1**												
	Worcester IceCats	AHL	75	7	45	52	130										4	0	1	1	4				
1996-97	**St. Louis**	**NHL**	**15**	**2**	**5**	**7**	**6**	**1**	**0**	**0**	**9**	**22.2**	**–4**												
	Worcester IceCats	AHL	63	8	35	43	83										5	1	2	3	14				
1997-98	**St. Louis**	**NHL**	**59**	**2**	**4**	**6**	**36**	**1**	**0**	**1**	**53**	**3.8**	**5**												
1998-99	**St. Louis**	**NHL**	**76**	**2**	**5**	**7**	**47**	**1**	**0**	**0**	**78**	**2.6**	**–3**	**0**	**0.0**	**14:10**	**9**	**1**	**1**	**2**	**2**	**1**	**0**	**1**	**6:29**
99-2000	**NY Islanders**	**NHL**	**75**	**1**	**16**	**17**	**84**	**1**	**0**	**0**	**95**	**1.1**	**–4**	**0**	**0.0**	**19:39**									
2000-01	**Ottawa**	**NHL**	**45**	**2**	**4**	**6**	**44**	**0**	**0**	**0**	**41**	**4.9**	**6**	**0**	**0.0**	**14:01**	**1**	**0**	**0**	**0**	**4**	**0**	**0**	**0**	**12:45**
	Grand Rapids	IHL	2	0	0	0	2																		
2001-02	**Ottawa**	**NHL**	**2**	**0**	**0**	**0**	**4**	**0**	**0**	**0**	**3**	**0.0**	**–3**	**0**	**0.0**	**11:37**									
	Boston	**NHL**	**64**	**4**	**2**	**6**	**45**	**1**	**0**	**1**	**48**	**8.3**	**6**	**39**	**33.3**	**8:27**	**3**	**0**	**0**	**0**	**0**	**0**	**0**	**0**	**4:57**
2002-03	**Florida**	**NHL**	**1**	**0**	**0**	**0**	**2**	**0**	**0**	**0**	**2**	**0.0**	**–2**	**0**	**0.0**	**18:27**									
	San Antonio	AHL	50	6	19	25	68										3	0	1	1	10				
	NHL Totals		**340**	**13**	**36**	**49**	**270**	**5**	**0**	**2**	**334**	**3.9**		**39**	**33.3**	**14:19**	**13**	**1**	**1**	**2**	**6**	**1**	**0**	**1**	**6:37**

OHL First All-Star Team (1994) • Canadian Major Junior Second All-Star Team (1994) • OHL Second All-Star Team (1995) • AHL Second All-Star Team (1997)

Claimed by **NY Islanders** from **St. Louis** in Waiver Draft, September 27, 1999. Signed as a free agent by **Ottawa**, November 30, 2000. Claimed on waivers by **Boston** from **Ottawa**, October 13, 2001. Signed as a free agent by **San Antonio** (AHL), November 2, 2002. Signed as a free agent by **Florida**, December 16, 2002. Signed as a free agent by **Detroit**, July 29, 2003.

RIVET, Craig
(rih-VAY, KRAYG) **MTL.**

Defense. Shoots right. 6'2", 207 lbs. Born, North Bay, Ont., September 13, 1974. Montreal's 4th choice, 68th overall, in 1992 Entry Draft.

Season	Club	League	GP	G	A	Pts	PIM	PP	SH	GW	S	%	+/-	TF	F%	Min	Playoffs GP	G	A	Pts	PIM	PP	SH	GW	Min
1990-91	Barrie Colts	OJHL-B	42	9	17	26	55																		
1991-92	Kingston	OHL	66	5	21	26	97																		
1992-93	Kingston	OHL	64	19	55	74	117										16	5	7	12	39				
1993-94	Kingston	OHL	61	12	52	64	100										6	0	3	3	6				
	Fredericton	AHL	4	0	2	2	2																		
1994-95	Fredericton	AHL	78	5	27	32	126										12	0	4	4	17				
	Montreal	**NHL**	**5**	**0**	**1**	**1**	**5**	**0**	**0**	**0**	**2**	**0.0**	**2**												
1995-96	**Montreal**	**NHL**	**19**	**1**	**4**	**5**	**54**	**0**	**0**	**0**	**9**	**11.1**	**4**												
	Fredericton	AHL	49	5	18	23	189										6	0	0	0	12				
1996-97	**Montreal**	**NHL**	**35**	**0**	**4**	**4**	**54**	**0**	**0**	**0**	**24**	**0.0**	**7**				**5**	**0**	**1**	**1**	**14**	**0**	**0**	**0**	
	Fredericton	AHL	23	3	12	15	99																		
1997-98	**Montreal**	**NHL**	**61**	**0**	**2**	**2**	**93**	**0**	**0**	**0**	**26**	**0.0**	**–3**				**5**	**0**	**0**	**0**	**2**	**0**	**0**	**0**	
1998-99	**Montreal**	**NHL**	**66**	**2**	**8**	**10**	**66**	**0**	**0**	**0**	**39**	**5.1**	**–3**	**0**	**0.0**	**14:20**									
99-2000	**Montreal**	**NHL**	**61**	**3**	**14**	**17**	**76**	**0**	**0**	**1**	**71**	**4.2**	**11**	**0**	**0.0**	**19:03**									
2000-01	**Montreal**	**NHL**	**26**	**1**	**2**	**3**	**36**	**0**	**0**	**0**	**22**	**4.5**	**–8**	**0**	**0.0**	**19:04**									

			Regular Season														Playoffs								
Season	Club	League	GP	G	A	Pts	PIM	PP	SH	GW	S	%	+/-	TF	F%	Min	GP	G	A	Pts	PIM	PP	SH	GW	Min
2001-02	**Montreal**	**NHL**	**82**	**8**	**17**	**25**	**76**	**0**	**0**	**0**	**90**	**8.9**	**1**	**1**	**0.0**	**19:00**	**12**	**0**	**3**	**3**	**4**	**0**	**0**	**0**	**21:26**
2002-03	**Montreal**	**NHL**	**82**	**7**	**15**	**22**	**71**	**3**	**0**	**2**	**118**	**5.9**	**1**	**0**	**0.0**	**21:60**	....	....	....	....	....	....	....	....	....
	NHL Totals		**437**	**22**	**67**	**89**	**531**	**3**	**0**	**3**	**401**	**5.5**		**1**	**0.0**	**18:49**	**22**	**0**	**4**	**4**	**20**	**0**	**0**	**0**	**21:26**

• Missed majority of 2000-01 season recovering from shoulder injury suffered in game vs. Vancouver, October 30, 2000.

ROBERTS, Gary

(RAW-buhrts, GAIR-ree) **TOR.**

Left wing. Shoots left. 6'2", 215 lbs. Born, North York, Ont., May 23, 1966. Calgary's 1st choice, 12th overall, in 1984 Entry Draft.

Season	Club	League	GP	G	A	Pts	PIM	PP	SH	GW	S	%	+/-	TF	F%	Min	GP	G	A	Pts	PIM	PP	SH	GW	Min
1980-81	Hamilton Kilty B's	OHA-B	3	0	1	1	0	....	....	....	....	....	....	....	....	....	....	....	....	....	....	....	....	....	....
1981-82	Whitby	OMHA	44	55	31	86	133	....	....	....	....	....	....	....	....	....	....	....	....	....	....	....	....	....	....
1982-83	Ottawa 67's	OHL	53	12	8	20	83	....	....	....	....	....	....	....	....	....	5	1	0	1	19	....	....	....	....
1983-84	Ottawa 67's	OHL	48	27	30	57	144	....	....	....	....	....	....	....	....	....	13	10	7	17	62	....	....	....	....
1984-85	Ottawa 67's	OHL	59	44	62	106	186	....	....	....	....	....	....	....	....	....	5	2	8	10	10	....	....	....	....
	Moncton	AHL	7	4	2	6	7	....	....	....	....	....	....	....	....	....	....	....	....	....	....	....	....	....	....
1985-86	Ottawa 67's	OHL	24	26	25	51	83	....	....	....	....	....	....	....	....	....	....	....	....	....	....	....	....	....	....
	Guelph Platers	OHL	23	18	15	33	65	....	....	....	....	....	....	....	....	....	20	18	13	31	43	....	....	....	....
1986-87	**Calgary**	**NHL**	**32**	**5**	**10**	**15**	**85**	**0**	**0**	**0**	**38**	**13.2**	**6**	....	....	....	**2**	**0**	**0**	**0**	**4**	**0**	**0**	**0**	....
	Moncton	AHL	38	20	18	38	72	....	....	....	....	....	....	....	....	....	....	....	....	....	....	....	....	....	....
1987-88	**Calgary**	**NHL**	**74**	**13**	**15**	**28**	**282**	**0**	**0**	**1**	**118**	**11.0**	**24**	....	....	....	**9**	**2**	**3**	**5**	**29**	**0**	**0**	**0**	....
1988-89♦	**Calgary**	**NHL**	**71**	**22**	**16**	**38**	**250**	**0**	**1**	**2**	**123**	**17.9**	**32**	....	....	....	**22**	**5**	**7**	**12**	**57**	**0**	**0**	**0**	....
1989-90	**Calgary**	**NHL**	**78**	**39**	**33**	**72**	**222**	**5**	**0**	**5**	**175**	**22.3**	**31**	....	....	....	**6**	**2**	**5**	**7**	**41**	**0**	**0**	**0**	....
1990-91	**Calgary**	**NHL**	**80**	**22**	**31**	**53**	**252**	**0**	**0**	**3**	**132**	**16.7**	**15**	....	....	....	**7**	**1**	**3**	**4**	**18**	**0**	**0**	**0**	....
1991-92	**Calgary**	**NHL**	**76**	**53**	**37**	**90**	**207**	**15**	**0**	**2**	**196**	**27.0**	**32**	....	....	....	....	....	....	....	....	....	....	....	....
1992-93	**Calgary**	**NHL**	**58**	**38**	**41**	**79**	**172**	**8**	**3**	**4**	**166**	**22.9**	**32**	....	....	....	**5**	**1**	**6**	**7**	**43**	**1**	**0**	**0**	....
1993-94	**Calgary**	**NHL**	**73**	**41**	**43**	**84**	**145**	**12**	**3**	**5**	**202**	**20.3**	**37**	....	....	....	**7**	**2**	**6**	**8**	**24**	**1**	**0**	**1**	....
1994-95	**Calgary**	**NHL**	**8**	**2**	**2**	**4**	**43**	**2**	**0**	**0**	**20**	**10.0**	**1**	....	....	....	....	....	....	....	....	....	....	....	....
1995-96	**Calgary**	**NHL**	**35**	**22**	**20**	**42**	**78**	**9**	**0**	**5**	**84**	**26.2**	**15**	....	....	....	....	....	....	....	....	....	....	....	....
1996-97	**Calgary**	**NHL**	DID NOT PLAY – INJURED																						
1997-98	**Carolina**	**NHL**	**61**	**20**	**29**	**49**	**103**	**4**	**0**	**2**	**106**	**18.9**	**3**	....	....	....	....	....	....	....	....	....	....	....	....
1998-99	**Carolina**	**NHL**	**77**	**14**	**28**	**42**	**178**	**1**	**1**	**4**	**138**	**10.1**	**2**	**15**	**46.7**	**19:36**	**6**	**1**	**1**	**2**	**8**	**0**	**0**	**0**	**21:01**
99-2000	**Carolina**	**NHL**	**69**	**23**	**30**	**53**	**62**	**12**	**0**	**1**	**150**	**15.3**	**–10**	**7**	**28.6**	**18:31**	....	....	....	....	....	....	....	....	....
2000-01	**Toronto**	**NHL**	**82**	**29**	**24**	**53**	**109**	**8**	**2**	**3**	**138**	**21.0**	**16**	**13**	**46.2**	**17:08**	**11**	**2**	**9**	**11**	**0**	**0**	**0**	**0**	**19:49**
2001-02	**Toronto**	**NHL**	**69**	**21**	**27**	**48**	**63**	**6**	**2**	**2**	**122**	**17.2**	**–4**	**6**	**33.3**	**17:23**	**19**	**7**	**12**	**19**	**56**	**3**	**0**	**1**	**19:28**
2002-03	**Toronto**	**NHL**	**14**	**5**	**3**	**8**	**10**	**3**	**0**	**0**	**22**	**22.7**	**–2**	**4**	**50.0**	**15:35**	**7**	**1**	**1**	**2**	**8**	**0**	**0**	**0**	**21:04**
	NHL Totals		**957**	**369**	**389**	**758**	**2261**	**85**	**12**	**39**	**1930**	**19.1**		**45**	**42.2**	**18:02**	**101**	**24**	**53**	**77**	**288**	**5**	**0**	**2**	**20:02**

OHL Second All-Star Team (1985, 1986) • Bill Masterton Memorial Trophy (1996)

Played in NHL All-Star Game (1992, 1993)

• Missed remainder of 1994-95 and majority of 1995-96 seasons recovering from neck injury suffered in game vs. Toronto, February 4, 1995. • Missed remainder of 1995-96 and entire 1996-97 seasons recovering from neck injury suffered in game vs. Vancouver, April 3, 1996. Traded to **Carolina** by **Calgary** with Trevor Kidd for Andrew Cassels and Jean-Sebastien Giguere, August 25, 1997. Signed as a free agent by **Toronto**, July 4, 2000. • Missed majority of 2002-03 season recovering from off-season shoulder surgery, August 13, 2002.

ROBIDAS, Stephane

(ROH-bih-dah, STEH-fan) **DAL.**

Defense. Shoots right. 5'11", 189 lbs. Born, Sherbrooke, Que., March 3, 1977. Montreal's 7th choice, 164th overall, in 1995 Entry Draft.

Season	Club	League	GP	G	A	Pts	PIM	PP	SH	GW	S	%	+/-	TF	F%	Min	GP	G	A	Pts	PIM	PP	SH	GW	Min
1992-93	Magog	QAAA	41	3	12	15	16	....	....	....	....	....	....	....	....	....	5	1	1	2	2	....	....	....	....
1993-94	Shawinigan	QMJHL	67	3	18	21	33	....	....	....	....	....	....	....	....	....	1	0	0	0	0	....	....	....	....
1994-95	Shawinigan	QMJHL	71	13	56	69	44	....	....	....	....	....	....	....	....	....	15	7	12	19	4	....	....	....	....
1995-96	Shawinigan	QMJHL	67	23	56	79	53	....	....	....	....	....	....	....	....	....	6	1	5	6	10	....	....	....	....
1996-97	Shawinigan	QMJHL	67	24	51	75	59	....	....	....	....	....	....	....	....	....	7	4	6	10	14	....	....	....	....
1997-98	Fredericton	AHL	79	10	21	31	50	....	....	....	....	....	....	....	....	....	4	0	2	2	0	....	....	....	....
1998-99	Fredericton	AHL	79	8	33	41	59	....	....	....	....	....	....	....	....	....	15	1	5	6	10	....	....	....	....
99-2000	**Montreal**	**NHL**	**1**	**0**	**0**	**0**	**0**	**0**	**0**	**0**	**0**	**0.0**	**0**	**0**	**0.0**	**15:54**	....	....	....	....	....	....	....	....	....
	Quebec Citadelles	AHL	76	14	31	45	36	....	....	....	....	....	....	....	....	....	3	0	1	1	0	....	....	....	....
2000-01	**Montreal**	**NHL**	**65**	**6**	**6**	**12**	**14**	**1**	**0**	**0**	**77**	**7.8**	**0**	**1**	**100.0**	**20:44**	....	....	....	....	....	....	....	....	....
2001-02	**Montreal**	**NHL**	**56**	**1**	**10**	**11**	**14**	**1**	**0**	**0**	**68**	**1.5**	**–25**	**3**	**33.3**	**18:58**	**2**	**0**	**0**	**0**	**4**	**0**	**0**	**0**	**13:07**
2002-03	**Dallas**	**NHL**	**76**	**3**	**7**	**10**	**35**	**0**	**0**	**1**	**47**	**6.4**	**15**	**1**	**100.0**	**12:54**	**12**	**0**	**1**	**1**	**20**	**0**	**0**	**0**	**13:54**
	NHL Totals		**198**	**10**	**23**	**33**	**63**	**2**	**0**	**1**	**192**	**5.2**		**5**	**60.0**	**17:12**	**14**	**0**	**1**	**1**	**24**	**0**	**0**	**0**	**13:47**

QMJHL First All-Star Team (1996, 1997)

Claimed by **Atlanta** from **Montreal** in Waiver Draft, October 4, 2002. Traded to **Dallas** by **Atlanta** for Atlanta's 6th round choice in 2003 Entry Draft, October 4, 2002.

ROBITAILLE, Luc

(ROH-buh-tigh, LEWK) **L.A.**

Left wing. Shoots left. 6'1"; 215 lbs. Born, Montreal, Que., February 17, 1966. Los Angeles' 9th choice, 171st overall, in 1984 Entry Draft.

Season	Club	League	GP	G	A	Pts	PIM	PP	SH	GW	S	%	+/-	TF	F%	Min	GP	G	A	Pts	PIM	PP	SH	GW	Min
1982-83	Mtl-Bourassa	QAAA	48	36	57	93	28	....	....	....	....	....	....	....	....	....	7	9	6	15	14	....	....	....	....
1983-84	Hull Olympiques	QMJHL	70	32	53	85	48	....	....	....	....	....	....	....	....	....	....	....	....	....	....	....	....	....	....
1984-85	Hull Olympiques	QMJHL	64	55	94	149	115	....	....	....	....	....	....	....	....	....	5	4	2	6	27	....	....	....	....
1985-86	Hull Olympiques	QMJHL	63	68	123	191	91	....	....	....	....	....	....	....	....	....	15	17	27	44	28	....	....	....	....
1986-87	**Los Angeles**	**NHL**	**79**	**45**	**39**	**84**	**28**	**18**	**0**	**3**	**199**	**22.6**	**–18**	....	....	....	**5**	**1**	**4**	**5**	**2**	**0**	**0**	**0**	....
1987-88	**Los Angeles**	**NHL**	**80**	**53**	**58**	**111**	**82**	**17**	**0**	**6**	**220**	**24.1**	**–9**	....	....	....	**5**	**2**	**5**	**7**	**18**	**2**	**0**	**1**	....
1988-89	**Los Angeles**	**NHL**	**78**	**46**	**52**	**98**	**65**	**10**	**0**	**4**	**237**	**19.4**	**5**	....	....	....	**11**	**2**	**6**	**8**	**10**	**0**	**0**	**1**	....
1989-90	**Los Angeles**	**NHL**	**80**	**52**	**49**	**101**	**38**	**20**	**0**	**7**	**210**	**24.8**	**8**	....	....	....	**10**	**5**	**5**	**10**	**12**	**1**	**0**	**1**	....
1990-91	**Los Angeles**	**NHL**	**76**	**45**	**46**	**91**	**68**	**11**	**0**	**5**	**229**	**19.7**	**28**	....	....	....	**12**	**12**	**4**	**16**	**22**	**5**	**0**	**2**	....
1991-92	**Los Angeles**	**NHL**	**80**	**44**	**63**	**107**	**95**	**26**	**0**	**6**	**240**	**18.3**	**–4**	....	....	....	**6**	**3**	**4**	**7**	**12**	**1**	**0**	**1**	....
1992-93	**Los Angeles**	**NHL**	**84**	**63**	**62**	**125**	**100**	**24**	**2**	**8**	**265**	**23.8**	**18**	....	....	....	**24**	**9**	**13**	**22**	**28**	**4**	**0**	**2**	....
1993-94	**Los Angeles**	**NHL**	**83**	**44**	**42**	**86**	**86**	**24**	**0**	**3**	**267**	**16.5**	**–20**	....	....	....	....	....	....	....	....	....	....	....	....
1994-95	**Pittsburgh**	**NHL**	**46**	**23**	**19**	**42**	**37**	**5**	**0**	**3**	**109**	**21.1**	**10**	....	....	....	**12**	**7**	**4**	**11**	**26**	**0**	**0**	**2**	....
1995-96	**NY Rangers**	**NHL**	**77**	**23**	**46**	**69**	**80**	**11**	**0**	**4**	**223**	**10.3**	**13**	....	....	....	**11**	**1**	**5**	**6**	**8**	**0**	**0**	**0**	....
1996-97	**NY Rangers**	**NHL**	**69**	**24**	**24**	**48**	**48**	**5**	**0**	**4**	**200**	**12.0**	**16**	....	....	....	**15**	**4**	**7**	**11**	**4**	**0**	**0**	**0**	....
1997-98	**Los Angeles**	**NHL**	**57**	**16**	**24**	**40**	**66**	**5**	**0**	**7**	**130**	**12.3**	**5**	....	....	....	**4**	**1**	**2**	**3**	**6**	**0**	**0**	**0**	....
1998-99	**Los Angeles**	**NHL**	**82**	**39**	**35**	**74**	**54**	**11**	**0**	**7**	**292**	**13.4**	**–1**	**7**	**57.1**	**19:11**	....	....	....	....	....	....	....	....	....
99-2000	**Los Angeles**	**NHL**	**71**	**36**	**38**	**74**	**68**	**13**	**0**	**7**	**221**	**16.3**	**11**	**10**	**30.0**	**18:34**	**4**	**2**	**2**	**4**	**6**	**0**	**0**	**0**	**20:25**
2000-01	**Los Angeles**	**NHL**	**82**	**37**	**51**	**88**	**66**	**16**	**1**	**4**	**235**	**15.7**	**10**	**12**	**33.3**	**18:42**	**13**	**4**	**3**	**7**	**10**	**1**	**0**	**1**	**18:19**
2001-02♦	**Detroit**	**NHL**	**81**	**30**	**20**	**50**	**38**	**13**	**0**	**5**	**190**	**15.8**	**–2**	**12**	**41.7**	**14:51**	**23**	**4**	**5**	**9**	**10**	**1**	**0**	**1**	**13:16**
2002-03	**Detroit**	**NHL**	**81**	**11**	**20**	**31**	**50**	**3**	**0**	**0**	**148**	**7.4**	**4**	**18**	**50.0**	**12:49**	**4**	**1**	**0**	**1**	**0**	**0**	**0**	**0**	**11:30**
	NHL Totals		**1286**	**631**	**688**	**1319**	**1069**	**232**	**3**	**83**	**3615**	**17.5**		**59**	**42.4**	**16:47**	**159**	**58**	**69**	**127**	**174**	**15**	**0**	**12**	**15:15**

QMJHL Second All-Star Team (1985) • QMJHL First All-Star Team (1986) • Canadian Major Junior Player of the Year (1986) • NHL All-Rookie Team (1987) • NHL Second All-Star Team (1987, 1992, 2001) • Calder Memorial Trophy (1987) • NHL First All-Star Team (1988, 1989, 1990, 1991, 1993)

Played in NHL All-Star Game (1988, 1989, 1990, 1991, 1992, 1993, 1999, 2001)

Traded to **Pittsburgh** by **Los Angeles** for Rick Tocchet and Pittsburgh's 2nd round choice (Pavel Rosa) in 1995 Entry Draft, July 29, 1994. Traded to **NY Rangers** by **Pittsburgh** with Ulf Samuelsson for Petr Nedved and Sergei Zubov, August 31, 1995. Traded to **Los Angeles** by **NY Rangers** for Kevin Stevens, August 28, 1997. Signed as a free agent by **Detroit**, July 5, 2001. Signed as a free agent by **Los Angeles**, July 25, 2003.

ROBITAILLE, Randy

(ROH-buh-tigh, RAN-dee) **ATL.**

Center. Shoots left. 5'11", 200 lbs. Born, Ottawa, Ont., October 12, 1975.

Season	Club	League	GP	G	A	Pts	PIM	PP	SH	GW	S	%	+/-	TF	F%	Min	GP	G	A	Pts	PIM	PP	SH	GW	Min
1993-94	Ottawa Jr. Sens	OCJHL	57	33	55	88	31	....	....	....	....	....	....	....	....	....	....	....	....	....	....	....	....	....	....
1994-95	Ottawa Jr. Sens	OCJHL	54	48	77	*125	111	....	....	....	....	....	....	....	....	....	....	....	....	....	....	....	....	....	....
1995-96	Miami-Ohio	CCHA	36	14	31	45	26	....	....	....	....	....	....	....	....	....	....	....	....	....	....	....	....	....	....
1996-97	Miami-Ohio	CCHA	39	27	34	61	44	....	....	....	....	....	....	....	....	....	....	....	....	....	....	....	....	....	....
	Boston	**NHL**	**1**	**0**	**0**	**0**	**0**	**0**	**0**	**0**	**0**	**0.0**	**0**	....	....	....	....	....	....	....	....	....	....	....	....
1997-98	**Boston**	**NHL**	**4**	**0**	**0**	**0**	**0**	**0**	**0**	**0**	**5**	**0.0**	**–2**	....	....	....	....	....	....	....	....	....	....	....	....
	Providence Bruins	AHL	48	15	29	44	16	....	....	....	....	....	....	....	....	....	....	....	....	....	....	....	....	....	....
1998-99	**Boston**	**NHL**	**4**	**0**	**2**	**2**	**0**	**0**	**0**	**0**	**5**	**0.0**	**–1**	**24**	**25.0**	**10:11**	**1**	**0**	**0**	**0**	**0**	**0**	**0**	**0**	**7:14**
	Providence Bruins	AHL	74	28	*74	102	34	....	....	....	....	....	....	....	....	....	19	6	*14	20	20	....	....	....	....
99-2000	**Nashville**	**NHL**	**69**	**11**	**14**	**25**	**10**	**2**	**0**	**1**	**113**	**9.7**	**–13**	**528**	**51.5**	**12:52**	....	....	....	....	....	....	....	....	....
2000-01	**Nashville**	**NHL**	**62**	**9**	**17**	**26**	**12**	**5**	**0**	**0**	**121**	**7.4**	**–11**	**481**	**48.4**	**14:10**	....	....	....	....	....	....	....	....	....
	Milwaukee	IHL	19	10	23	33	4	....	....	....	....	....	....	....	....	....	....	....	....	....	....	....	....	....	....

Season	Club	League	GP	G	A	Pts	PIM	PP	SH	GW	S	%	+/-	TF	F%	Min	GP	G	A	Pts	PIM	PP	SH	GW	Min
			Regular Season														Playoffs								
2001-02	Los Angeles	NHL	18	4	3	7	17	2	0	0	30	13.3	–9	60	65.0	12:54									
	Manchester	AHL	6	7	3	10	0																		
	Pittsburgh	NHL	40	10	20	30	16	3	0	1	91	11.0	–14	599	51.4	18:08									
2002-03	Pittsburgh	NHL	41	5	12	17	8	1	0	2	61	8.2	5	429	55.9	13:58									
	NY Islanders	NHL	10	1	2	3	2	1	0	0	8	12.5	0	68	48.5	12:28	5	1	1	2	0	1	0	0	13:03
	NHL Totals		249	40	70	110	65	14	0	4	434	9.2		2189	51.7	14:11	6	1	1	2	0	1	0	0	12:05

OCJHL First All-Star Team (1995) • CCHA First All-Star Team (1997) • NCAA West First All-American Team (1997) • AHL First All-Star Team (1999) • Les Cunningham Award (MVP – AHL) (1999)

Signed as a free agent by **Boston**, March 27, 1997. Traded to **Atlanta** by **Boston** for Peter Ferraro, June 25, 1999. Traded to **Nashville** by **Atlanta** for Denny Lambert, August 16, 1999. Signed as a free agent by **Los Angeles**, July 6, 2001. Claimed on waivers by **Pittsburgh** from **Los Angeles**, January 4, 2002. Traded to **NY Islanders** by **Pittsburgh** for Philadelphia's 5th round choice (previously acquired, Pittsburgh selected Evgeni Isakov) in 2003 Entry Draft, March 9, 2003. Signed as a free agent by **Atlanta**, August 12, 2003.

ROCHE, Dave

(ROHSH, DAYV)

Left wing. Shoots left. 6'4", 230 lbs. Born, Lindsay, Ont., June 13, 1975. Pittsburgh's 3rd choice, 62nd overall, in 1993 Entry Draft.

Season	Club	League	GP	G	A	Pts	PIM	PP	SH	GW	S	%	+/-	TF	F%	Min	GP	G	A	Pts	PIM	PP	SH	GW	Min
1990-91	Peterborough	OJHL-B	40	22	17	39	86																		
1991-92	Peterborough	OHL	62	10	17	27	134										10	0	0	0	34				
1992-93	Peterborough	OHL	56	40	60	100	105										21	14	15	29	42				
1993-94	Peterborough	OHL	34	15	22	37	127																		
	Windsor Spitfires	OHL	29	14	20	34	73										4	1	1	2	15				
1994-95	Windsor Spitfires	OHL	66	55	59	114	180										10	9	6	15	16				
1995-96	Pittsburgh	NHL	71	7	7	14	130	0	0	1	65	10.8	–5				16	2	7	9	26	0	0	0	
1996-97	Pittsburgh	NHL	61	5	5	10	155	2	0	0	53	9.4	–13												
	Cleveland	IHL	18	5	5	10	25										13	6	3	9	*87				
1997-98	Syracuse Crunch	AHL	73	12	20	32	307										5	2	0	2	10				
1998-99	Calgary	NHL	36	3	3	6	44	1	0	2	30	10.0	–1	0	0.0	7:15									
	Saint John Flames	AHL	7	0	3	3	6																		
99-2000	Calgary	NHL	2	0	0	0	5	0	0	0	3	0.0	–1	0	0.0	8:33									
	Saint John Flames	AHL	67	22	21	43	130										3	0	1	1	8				
2000-01	Saint John Flames	AHL	79	32	26	58	179										19	3	6	9	43				
2001-02	Cincinnati	AHL	29	6	7	13	41																		
	NY Islanders	NHL	1	0	0	0	0	0	0	0	0	0.0	0	1	0.0	2:51									
	Bridgeport	AHL	48	25	14	39	64										20	3	0	3	20				
2002-03	Albany River Rats	AHL	76	21	16	37	89																		
	NHL Totals		171	15	15	30	334	3	0	3	151	9.9		1	0.0	7:12	16	2	7	9	26	0	0	0	

OHL First All-Star Team (1995)

Traded to **Calgary** by **Pittsburgh** with Ken Wregget for German Titov and Todd Hlushko, June 17, 1998. Signed as a free agent by **NY Islanders**, August 17, 2001. Traded to **Anaheim** by **NY Islanders** for Jim Cummins, January 14, 2002. Traded to **NY Islanders** by **Anaheim** for Ben Guite and the rights to Bjorn Mellin, March 19, 2002. Signed as a free agent by **New Jersey**, August 27, 2002.

ROCHE, Travis

(ROHSH, TRA-vihs) **MIN.**

Defense. Shoots right. 6'1", 190 lbs. Born, Grand Cache, Alta, June 17, 1978.

Season	Club	League	GP	G	A	Pts	PIM	PP	SH	GW	S	%	+/-	TF	F%	Min	GP	G	A	Pts	PIM	PP	SH	GW	Min
1996-97	Trail	BCHL	49	17	40	57	159																		
1997-98	Trail	BCHL	38	11	31	42	104										11	0	8	8	21				
1998-99	North Dakota	WCHA	DID NOT PLAY – FRESHMAN																						
99-2000	North Dakota	WCHA	42	6	22	28	60																		
2000-01	North Dakota	WCHA	42	11	38	49	42																		
	Minnesota	NHL	1	0	0	0	0	0	0	0	0	0.0	0	0	0.0	15:22									
2001-02	Minnesota	NHL	4	0	0	0	2	0	0	0	1	0.0	–1	0	0.0	12:30									
	Houston Aeros	AHL	60	13	21	34	107										12	2	3	5	6				
2002-03	Houston Aeros	AHL	65	14	34	48	42										23	3	5	8	26				
	NHL Totals		5	0	0	0	2	0	0	0	1	0.0		0	0.0	13:04									

BCHL Second All-Star Team (1997) • BCHL Rookie of the Year Award (1997) • BCHL Playoff MVP Award (1997) • BCHL First All-Star Team (1998) • BCHL Best Defenseman Award (1998) • WCHA All-Rookie Team (2000) • WCHA First All-Star Team (2001) • NCAA West First All-American Team (2001) • NCAA Championship All-Tournament Team (2001)

Signed as a free agent by **Minnesota**, April 8, 2001.

ROENICK, Jeremy

(ROH-nihk, JAIR-eh-mee) **PHI.**

Center. Shoots right. 6'1", 196 lbs. Born, Boston, MA, January 17, 1970. Chicago's 1st choice, 8th overall, in 1988 Entry Draft.

Season	Club	League	GP	G	A	Pts	PIM	PP	SH	GW	S	%	+/-	TF	F%	Min	GP	G	A	Pts	PIM	PP	SH	GW	Min
1986-87	Thayer Academy	Hi-School	24	31	34	65																			
1987-88	Thayer Academy	Hi-School	24	34	50	84																			
1988-89	Hull Olympiques	QMJHL	28	34	36	70	14																		
	Chicago	NHL	20	9	9	18	4	2	0	0	52	17.3	4				10	1	3	4	7	1	0	1	
1989-90	Chicago	NHL	78	26	40	66	54	6	0	4	173	15.0	2				20	11	7	18	8	4	0	1	
1990-91	Chicago	NHL	79	41	53	94	80	15	4	10	194	21.1	38				6	3	5	8	4	1	0	1	
1991-92	Chicago	NHL	80	53	50	103	98	22	3	13	234	22.6	23				18	12	10	22	12	4	0	3	
1992-93	Chicago	NHL	84	50	57	107	86	22	3	3	255	19.6	15				4	1	2	3	2	0	0	0	
1993-94	Chicago	NHL	84	46	61	107	125	24	5	5	281	16.4	21				6	1	6	7	2	0	0	1	
1994-95	Kolner Haie	Germany	3	3	1	4	2																		
	Chicago	NHL	33	10	24	34	14	5	0	1	93	10.8	5				8	1	2	3	16	0	0	0	
1995-96	Chicago	NHL	66	32	35	67	109	12	4	2	171	18.7	9				10	5	7	12	2	1	0	1	
1996-97	Phoenix	NHL	72	29	40	69	115	10	3	7	228	12.7	–7				6	2	4	6	4	0	0	0	
1997-98	Phoenix	NHL	79	24	32	56	103	6	1	3	182	13.2	5				6	5	3	8	4	2	2	2	
	United States	Olympics	4	0	1	1	6																		
1998-99	Phoenix	NHL	78	24	48	72	130	4	0	3	203	11.8	7	956	47.6	20:10	1	0	0	0	0	0	0	0	26:55
99-2000	Phoenix	NHL	75	34	44	78	102	6	3	12	192	17.7	11	925	50.1	20:51	5	2	2	4	10	1	0	0	19:46
2000-01	Phoenix	NHL	80	30	46	76	114	13	0	7	192	15.6	–1	888	49.1	20:60									
2001-02	Philadelphia	NHL	75	21	46	67	74	5	0	3	167	12.6	32	1329	49.1	18:14	5	0	0	0	14	0	0	0	18:41
	United States	Olympics	6	1	4	5	2																		
2002-03	Philadelphia	NHL	79	27	32	59	75	8	1	6	197	13.7	20	1088	53.0	18:48	13	3	5	8	8	0	0	1	21:07
	NHL Totals		1062	456	617	1073	1283	160	27	79	2814	16.2		5186	49.8	19:49	118	47	56	103	93	14	2	11	20:34

QMJHL Second All-Star Team (1989)

Played in NHL All-Star Game (1991, 1992, 1993, 1994, 1999, 2000, 2002, 2003)

Traded to **Phoenix** by **Chicago** for Alexei Zhamnov, Craig Mills and Phoenix's 1st round choice (Ty Jones) in 1997 Entry Draft, August 16, 1996. Signed as a free agent by **Philadelphia**, July 2, 2001.

ROEST, Stacy

(ROOST, STAY-see)

Right wing. Shoots right. 5'9", 185 lbs. Born, Lethbridge, Alta., March 15, 1974.

Season	Club	League	GP	G	A	Pts	PIM	PP	SH	GW	S	%	+/-	TF	F%	Min	GP	G	A	Pts	PIM	PP	SH	GW	Min
1990-91	Lethbridge	AMHL	34	22	50	72	38																		
	Medicine Hat	WHL	5	1	2	3	0										12	5	5	10	4				
1991-92	Medicine Hat	WHL	72	22	43	65	20										4	2	1	3	0				
1992-93	Medicine Hat	WHL	72	33	73	106	30										10	3	10	13	6				
1993-94	Medicine Hat	WHL	72	48	72	120	48										3	1	0	1	4				
1994-95	Medicine Hat	WHL	69	37	78	115	32										5	2	7	9	2				
	Adirondack	AHL	3	0	0	0	0																		
1995-96	Adirondack	AHL	76	16	39	55	40										3	0	0	0	0				
1996-97	Adirondack	AHL	78	25	41	66	30										4	1	1	2	0				
1997-98	Adirondack	AHL	80	34	58	92	30										3	2	1	3	6				
1998-99	Detroit	NHL	59	4	8	12	14	0	0	1	50	8.0	–7	234	57.3	8:04									
	Adirondack	AHL	2	0	1	1	0																		
99-2000	Detroit	NHL	49	7	9	16	12	1	0	1	56	12.5	–1	397	55.4	9:56	3	0	0	0	0	0	0	0	6:50
2000-01	Minnesota	NHL	76	7	20	27	20	1	0	1	125	5.6	3	731	57.1	14:01									
2001-02	Minnesota	NHL	58	10	11	21	8	1	4	2	98	10.2	–3	504	55.0	15:50									
2002-03	Detroit	NHL	2	0	0	0	0	0	0	0	2	0.0	0	19	63.2	7:19									
	Grand Rapids	AHL	70	24	48	72	28										15	10	6	16	8				
	NHL Totals		244	28	48	76	54	3	4	5	331	8.5		1885	56.2	12:08	3	0	0	0	0	0	0	0	6:50

WHL East First All-Star Team (1994) • WHL East Second All-Star Team (1995)

Signed as a free agent by **Detroit**, June 9, 1997. Selected by **Minnesota** from **Detroit** in Expansion Draft, June 23, 2000. Signed as a free agent by **Detroit**, August 27, 2002.

ROHLOFF, Todd
(ROH-lawf, TAWD)

Defense. Shoots left. 6'3", 213 lbs. Born, Grand Rapids, IL, January 16, 1974.

Season	Club	League	GP	G	A	Pts	PIM	PP	SH	GW	S	%	+/-	TF	F%	Min	Playoffs GP	G	A	Pts	PIM	PP	SH	GW	Min
1993-94	St. Paul Vulcans	USHL	47	4	22	26	....	....	....	....	....	....	....	....	....	....	....	....	....	....	....	....	....	....	....
1994-95	Miami-Ohio	CCHA	38	1	6	7	22	....	....	....	....	....	....	....	....	....	....	....	....	....	....	....	....	....	....
1995-96	Miami-Ohio	CCHA	23	2	4	6	24	....	....	....	....	....	....	....	....	....	....	....	....	....	....	....	....	....	....
1996-97	Miami-Ohio	CCHA	38	2	12	14	48	....	....	....	....	....	....	....	....	....	....	....	....	....	....	....	....	....	....
1997-98	Miami-Ohio	CCHA	17	2	5	7	38	....	....	....	....	....	....	....	....	....	....	....	....	....	....	....	....	....	....
	Indianapolis Ice	IHL	5	0	1	1	6	....	....	....	....	....	....	....	....	....	1	0	0	0	0	....	....	....	....
1998-99	Portland Pirates	AHL	58	1	6	7	58	....	....	....	....	....	....	....	....	....	....	....	....	....	....	....	....	....	....
	Indianapolis Ice	IHL	12	2	0	2	8	....	....	....	....	....	....	....	....	....	5	1	1	2	6	....	....	....	....
99-2000	Cleveland	IHL	77	1	13	14	88	....	....	....	....	....	....	....	....	....	9	0	0	0	6	....	....	....	....
2000-01	Portland Pirates	AHL	58	3	8	11	59	....	....	....	....	....	....	....	....	....	3	0	0	0	2	....	....	....	....
2001-02	**Washington**	**NHL**	**16**	**0**	**1**	**1**	**14**	**0**	**0**	**0**	**6**	**0.0**	**–2**	**0**	**0.0**	**14:11**	....	....	....	....	....	....	....	....	....
	Portland Pirates	AHL	17	1	3	4	22	....	....	....	....	....	....	....	....	....	....	....	....	....	....	....	....	....	....
2002-03	Portland Pirates	AHL	64	2	10	12	65	....	....	....	....	....	....	....	....	....	3	0	0	0	2	....	....	....	....
	NHL Totals		**16**	**0**	**1**	**1**	**14**	**0**	**0**	**0**	**6**	**0.0**		**0**	**0.0**	**14:11**	....	....	....	....	....	....	....	....	....

Signed as a free agent by **Chicago**, March 24, 1998. Signed as a free agent by **Washington**, July 21, 2000. • Missed majority of 2001-02 season recovering from ankle injury suffered in off-season, September, 2001.

ROLSTON, Brian
(ROHL-stuhn, BRIGH-uhn) **BOS.**

Center/Right wing. Shoots left. 6'2", 210 lbs. Born, Flint, MI, February 21, 1973. New Jersey's 2nd choice, 11th overall, in 1991 Entry Draft.

Season	Club	League	GP	G	A	Pts	PIM	PP	SH	GW	S	%	+/-	TF	F%	Min	Playoffs GP	G	A	Pts	PIM	PP	SH	GW	Min
1989-90	Det. Compuware	NAJHL	40	36	37	73	57	....	....	....	....	....	....	....	....	....	....	....	....	....	....	....	....	....	....
1990-91	Det. Compuware	NAJHL	36	49	46	95	14	....	....	....	....	....	....	....	....	....	....	....	....	....	....	....	....	....	....
1991-92	Lake Superior	CCHA	37	14	23	37	14	....	....	....	....	....	....	....	....	....	....	....	....	....	....	....	....	....	....
1992-93	Lake Superior	CCHA	39	33	31	64	20	....	....	....	....	....	....	....	....	....	....	....	....	....	....	....	....	....	....
1993-94	Team USA	Nat-Tm	41	20	28	48	36	....	....	....	....	....	....	....	....	....	....	....	....	....	....	....	....	....	....
	United States	Olympics	8	7	0	7	8	....	....	....	....	....	....	....	....	....	....	....	....	....	....	....	....	....	....
	Albany River Rats	AHL	17	5	5	10	8	....	....	....	....	....	....	....	....	....	5	1	2	3	0	....	....	....	....
1994-95	Albany River Rats	AHL	18	9	11	20	10	....	....	....	....	....	....	....	....	....	....	....	....	....	....	....	....	....	....
	♦ **New Jersey**	**NHL**	**40**	**7**	**11**	**18**	**17**	**2**	**0**	**3**	**92**	**7.6**	**5**	....	....	....	**6**	**2**	**1**	**3**	**4**	**1**	**0**	**0**	....
1995-96	**New Jersey**	**NHL**	**58**	**13**	**11**	**24**	**8**	**3**	**1**	**4**	**139**	**9.4**	**9**	....	....	....	....	....	....	....	....	....	....	....	....
1996-97	**New Jersey**	**NHL**	**81**	**18**	**27**	**45**	**20**	**2**	**2**	**3**	**237**	**7.6**	**6**	....	....	....	**10**	**4**	**1**	**5**	**6**	**1**	**2**	**0**	....
1997-98	**New Jersey**	**NHL**	**76**	**16**	**14**	**30**	**16**	**0**	**2**	**1**	**185**	**8.6**	**7**	....	....	....	**6**	**1**	**0**	**1**	**2**	**0**	**1**	**0**	....
1998-99	**New Jersey**	**NHL**	**82**	**24**	**33**	**57**	**14**	**5**	**5**	**3**	**210**	**11.4**	**11**	**51**	**45.1**	**18:49**	**7**	**1**	**0**	**1**	**2**	**0**	**1**	**0**	**17:36**
99-2000	**New Jersey**	**NHL**	**11**	**3**	**1**	**4**	**0**	**1**	**0**	**2**	**33**	**9.1**	**–2**	**37**	**37.8**	**19:09**	....	....	....	....	....	....	....	....	....
	Colorado	**NHL**	**50**	**8**	**10**	**18**	**12**	**1**	**0**	**3**	**107**	**7.5**	**–6**	**65**	**41.5**	**16:18**	....	....	....	....	....	....	....	....	....
	Boston	**NHL**	**16**	**5**	**4**	**9**	**6**	**3**	**0**	**1**	**66**	**7.6**	**–4**	**265**	**41.1**	**22:13**	....	....	....	....	....	....	....	....	....
2000-01	**Boston**	**NHL**	**77**	**19**	**39**	**58**	**28**	**5**	**0**	**4**	**286**	**6.6**	**6**	**666**	**45.7**	**19:19**	....	....	....	....	....	....	....	....	....
2001-02	**Boston**	**NHL**	**82**	**31**	**31**	**62**	**30**	**6**	**9**	**7**	**331**	**9.4**	**11**	**1289**	**46.6**	**20:24**	**6**	**4**	**1**	**5**	**0**	**1**	**1**	**0**	**20:37**
	United States	Olympics	6	0	3	3	0	....	....	....	....	....	....	....	....	....	....	....	....	....	....	....	....	....	....
2002-03	**Boston**	**NHL**	**81**	**27**	**32**	**59**	**32**	**6**	**5**	**5**	**281**	**9.6**	**1**	**1148**	**47.6**	**20:28**	**5**	**0**	**2**	**2**	**0**	**0**	**0**	**0**	**18:39**
	NHL Totals		**654**	**171**	**213**	**384**	**183**	**34**	**24**	**36**	**1967**	**8.7**		**3521**	**46.1**	**19:24**	**40**	**12**	**5**	**17**	**14**	**3**	**5**	**0**	**18:54**

NCAA Championship All-Tournament Team (1992, 1993) • CCHA First All-Star Team (1993) • NCAA West Second All-American Team (1993)

Traded to **Colorado** by **New Jersey** with New Jersey's 1st round choice (later traded to Boston – Boston selected Martin Samuelsson) in 2000 Entry Draft for Claude Lemieux and Colorado's 1st (David Hale) and 2nd (Matt DeMarchi) round choices in 2000 Entry Draft, November 3, 1999. Traded to **Boston** by **Colorado** with Martin Grenier, Samuel Pahlsson and New Jersey's 1st round choice (previously acquired, Boston selected Martin Samuelsson) in 2000 Entry Draft for Raymond Bourque and Dave Andreychuk, March 6, 2000.

RONNING, Cliff
(RAWN-ihng, KLIHF)

Center. Shoots left. 5'8", 165 lbs. Born, Burnaby, B.C., October 1, 1965. St. Louis' 9th choice, 134th overall, in 1984 Entry Draft.

Season	Club	League	GP	G	A	Pts	PIM	PP	SH	GW	S	%	+/-	TF	F%	Min	Playoffs GP	G	A	Pts	PIM	PP	SH	GW	Min
1982-83	New Westminster	BCJHL	52	83	68	151	22	....	....	....	....	....	....	....	....	....	....	....	....	....	....	....	....	....	....
1983-84	New Westminster	WHL	71	69	67	136	10	....	....	....	....	....	....	....	....	....	9	8	13	21	10	....	....	....	....
1984-85	New Westminster	WHL	70	*89	108	*197	20	....	....	....	....	....	....	....	....	....	11	10	14	24	4	....	....	....	....
1985-86	Team Canada	Nat-Tm	71	*55	*63	*118	53	....	....	....	....	....	....	....	....	....	....	....	....	....	....	....	....	....	....
	St. Louis	**NHL**	....	....	....	....	....	....	....	....	....	....	....	....	....	....	**5**	**1**	**1**	**2**	**2**	**1**	**0**	**0**	....
1986-87	Team Canada	Nat-Tm	26	17	16	33	12	....	....	....	....	....	....	....	....	....	....	....	....	....	....	....	....	....	....
	St. Louis	**NHL**	**42**	**11**	**14**	**25**	**6**	**2**	**0**	**2**	**68**	**16.2**	**–1**	....	....	....	**4**	**0**	**1**	**1**	**0**	**0**	**0**	**0**	....
1987-88	**St. Louis**	**NHL**	**26**	**5**	**8**	**13**	**12**	**1**	**0**	**1**	**38**	**13.2**	**6**	....	....	....	....	....	....	....	....	....	....	....	....
1988-89	**St. Louis**	**NHL**	**64**	**24**	**31**	**55**	**18**	**16**	**0**	**1**	**150**	**16.0**	**3**	....	....	....	**7**	**1**	**3**	**4**	**0**	**1**	**0**	**0**	....
	Peoria Rivermen	IHL	12	11	20	31	8	....	....	....	....	....	....	....	....	....	....	....	....	....	....	....	....	....	....
1989-90	HC Asiago	Italy	36	67	49	116	25	....	....	....	....	....	....	....	....	....	6	7	12	19	4	....	....	....	....
1990-91	**St. Louis**	**NHL**	**48**	**14**	**18**	**32**	**10**	**5**	**0**	**2**	**81**	**17.3**	**2**	....	....	....	....	....	....	....	....	....	....	....	....
	Vancouver	**NHL**	**11**	**6**	**6**	**12**	**0**	**2**	**0**	**0**	**32**	**18.8**	**–2**	....	....	....	**6**	**6**	**3**	**9**	**12**	**2**	**0**	**2**	....
1991-92	**Vancouver**	**NHL**	**80**	**24**	**47**	**71**	**42**	**6**	**0**	**2**	**216**	**11.1**	**18**	....	....	....	**13**	**8**	**5**	**13**	**6**	**1**	**0**	**1**	....
1992-93	**Vancouver**	**NHL**	**79**	**29**	**56**	**85**	**30**	**10**	**0**	**2**	**209**	**13.9**	**19**	....	....	....	**12**	**2**	**9**	**11**	**6**	**0**	**0**	**0**	....
1993-94	**Vancouver**	**NHL**	**76**	**25**	**43**	**68**	**42**	**10**	**0**	**4**	**197**	**12.7**	**7**	....	....	....	**24**	**5**	**10**	**15**	**16**	**2**	**0**	**2**	....
1994-95	**Vancouver**	**NHL**	**41**	**6**	**19**	**25**	**27**	**3**	**0**	**2**	**93**	**6.5**	**–4**	....	....	....	**11**	**3**	**5**	**8**	**2**	**1**	**0**	**2**	....
1995-96	**Vancouver**	**NHL**	**79**	**22**	**45**	**67**	**42**	**5**	**0**	**1**	**187**	**11.8**	**16**	....	....	....	**6**	**0**	**2**	**2**	**6**	**0**	**0**	**0**	....
1996-97	**Phoenix**	**NHL**	**69**	**19**	**32**	**51**	**26**	**8**	**0**	**2**	**171**	**11.1**	**–9**	....	....	....	**7**	**0**	**7**	**7**	**12**	**0**	**0**	**0**	....
1997-98	**Phoenix**	**NHL**	**80**	**11**	**44**	**55**	**36**	**3**	**0**	**0**	**197**	**5.6**	**5**	....	....	....	**6**	**1**	**3**	**4**	**4**	**0**	**0**	**0**	....
1998-99	**Phoenix**	**NHL**	**7**	**2**	**5**	**7**	**2**	**2**	**0**	**1**	**18**	**11.1**	**3**	**81**	**51.9**	**15:22**	....	....	....	....	....	....	....	....	....
	Nashville	**NHL**	**72**	**18**	**35**	**53**	**40**	**8**	**0**	**3**	**239**	**7.5**	**–6**	**1129**	**47.7**	**19:42**	....	....	....	....	....	....	....	....	....
99-2000	**Nashville**	**NHL**	**82**	**26**	**36**	**62**	**34**	**7**	**0**	**2**	**248**	**10.5**	**–13**	**611**	**45.7**	**18:11**	....	....	....	....	....	....	....	....	....
2000-01	**Nashville**	**NHL**	**80**	**19**	**43**	**62**	**28**	**6**	**0**	**4**	**237**	**8.0**	**4**	**331**	**45.0**	**17:23**	....	....	....	....	....	....	....	....	....
2001-02	**Nashville**	**NHL**	**67**	**18**	**31**	**49**	**24**	**4**	**0**	**0**	**164**	**11.0**	**0**	**98**	**51.0**	**16:44**	....	....	....	....	....	....	....	....	....
	Los Angeles	**NHL**	**14**	**1**	**4**	**5**	**8**	**1**	**0**	**0**	**35**	**2.9**	**0**	**14**	**50.0**	**16:53**	**4**	**0**	**1**	**1**	**2**	**0**	**0**	**0**	**11:09**
2002-03	**Minnesota**	**NHL**	**80**	**17**	**31**	**48**	**24**	**8**	**0**	**5**	**171**	**9.9**	**–6**	**566**	**47.0**	**17:25**	**17**	**2**	**7**	**9**	**4**	**1**	**0**	**0**	**16:39**
	NHL Totals		**1097**	**297**	**548**	**845**	**451**	**107**	**0**	**34**	**2751**	**10.8**		**2830**	**47.1**	**17:48**	**122**	**29**	**57**	**86**	**72**	**9**	**0**	**7**	**15:36**

BCJHL Coastal Division First All-Star Team (1983) • WHL Rookie of the Year (1984) • WHL West First All-Star Team (1985) • WHL MVP (1985)

Traded to **Vancouver** by **St. Louis** with Geoff Courtnall, Robert Dirk, Sergio Momesso and St. Louis' 5th round choice (Brian Loney) in 1992 Entry Draft for Dan Quinn and Garth Butcher, March 5, 1991. Signed as a free agent by **Phoenix**, July 1, 1996. Traded to **Nashville** by **Phoenix** with Richard Lintner for future considerations, October 31, 1998. Traded to **Los Angeles** by **Nashville** for Jere Karalahti and Los Angeles' 4th round choice (Teemu Lassila) in 2003 Entry Draft, March 16, 2002. Traded to **Minnesota** by **Los Angeles** for Minnesota's 4th round choice (Aaron Rome) in 2002 Entry Draft, June 22, 2002.

RONNQVIST, Jonas
(RAWN-kvihst, YOH-nuhs)

Right wing. Shoots right. 6'2", 200 lbs. Born, Kalix, Sweden, August 22, 1973. Anaheim's 3rd choice, 98th overall, in 2000 Entry Draft.

Season	Club	League	GP	G	A	Pts	PIM	PP	SH	GW	S	%	+/-	TF	F%	Min	Playoffs GP	G	A	Pts	PIM	PP	SH	GW	Min
1991-92	Bodens IK	Swede-2	6	1	1	2	2	....	....	....	....	....	....	....	....	....	1	0	0	0	0	....	....	....	....
1992-93	Bodens IK	Swede-2	35	10	4	14	16	....	....	....	....	....	....	....	....	....	....	....	....	....	....	....	....	....	....
1993-94	Bodens IK	Swede-2	34	15	10	25	24	....	....	....	....	....	....	....	....	....	9	1	1	2	6	....	....	....	....
1994-95	Bodens IK	Swede-2	35	10	15	5	48	....	....	....	....	....	....	....	....	....	8	1	0	1	0	....	....	....	....
1995-96	Bodens IK	Swede-2	26	12	10	22	26	....	....	....	....	....	....	....	....	....	....	....	....	....	....	....	....	....	....
1996-97	Bodens IK	Swede-2	32	15	14	29	48	....	....	....	....	....	....	....	....	....	....	....	....	....	....	....	....	....	....
1997-98	Lulea HF	Sweden	40	6	8	14	24	....	....	....	....	....	....	....	....	....	3	0	0	0	2	....	....	....	....
	Lulea HF	EuroHL	5	0	1	1	0	....	....	....	....	....	....	....	....	....	....	....	....	....	....	....	....	....	....
1998-99	Lulea HF	Sweden	41	5	8	13	30	....	....	....	....	....	....	....	....	....	3	0	2	2	29	....	....	....	....
99-2000	Lulea HF	Sweden	49	15	24	39	42	....	....	....	....	....	....	....	....	....	8	3	3	6	4	....	....	....	....
2000-01	**Anaheim**	**NHL**	**38**	**0**	**4**	**4**	**14**	**0**	**0**	**0**	**30**	**0.0**	**–7**	**101**	**44.6**	**10:37**	....	....	....	....	....	....	....	....	....
	Cincinnati	AHL	13	3	2	5	6	....	....	....	....	....	....	....	....	....	....	....	....	....	....	....	....	....	....
2001-02	Cincinnati	AHL	74	10	18	28	30	....	....	....	....	....	....	....	....	....	3	0	0	0	0	....	....	....	....
2002-03	Lulea HF	Sweden	46	10	23	33	28	....	....	....	....	....	....	....	....	....	4	0	1	1	0	....	....	....	....
	NHL Totals		**38**	**0**	**4**	**4**	**14**	**0**	**0**	**0**	**30**	**0.0**		**101**	**44.6**	**10:37**	....	....	....	....	....	....	....	....	....

			Regular Season														Playoffs								
Season	Club	League	GP	G	A	Pts	PIM	PP	SH	GW	S	%	+/-	TF	F%	Min	GP	G	A	Pts	PIM	PP	SH	GW	Min

ROSA, Pavel

(ROHZA, PAH-vehl) **L.A.**

Right wing. Shoots right. 5'11", 188 lbs. Born, Most, Czech., June 7, 1977. Los Angeles' 3rd choice, 50th overall, in 1995 Entry Draft.

Season	Club	League	GP	G	A	Pts	PIM	PP	SH	GW	S	%	+/-	TF	F%	Min	GP	G	A	Pts	PIM	PP	SH	GW	Min
1994-95	Litvinov Jr.	Czech-Jr.	40	56	42	98	....	....	....	....	....	....	....	....	....	....	....	....	....	....	....	....	....	....	....
	Litvinov	Czech	2	0	0	0	0	....	....	....	....	....	....	....	....	....	1	0	0	0	0	....	....	....	....
1995-96	Hull Olympiques	QMJHL	61	46	70	116	39	....	....	....	....	....	....	....	....	....	18	14	22	36	25	....	....	....	....
1996-97	Hull Olympiques	QMJHL	68	*63	*90	*153	66	....	....	....	....	....	....	....	....	....	14	18	13	31	16	....	....	....	....
1997-98	Fredericton	AHL	1	0	0	0	0	....	....	....	....	....	....	....	....	....	....	....	....	....	....	....	....	....	....
	Long Beach	IHL	2	0	1	1	0	....	....	....	....	....	....	....	....	....	1	1	1	2	0	....	....	....	....
1998-99	**Los Angeles**	**NHL**	**29**	**4**	**12**	**16**	**6**	**0**	**0**	**0**	**61**	**6.6**	**0**	**0**	**0.0**	**13:34**	....	....	....	....	....	....	....	....	....
	Long Beach	IHL	31	17	13	30	28	....	....	....	....	....	....	....	....	....	6	1	2	3	0	....	....	....	....
99-2000	**Los Angeles**	**NHL**	**3**	**0**	**0**	**0**	**0**	**0**	**0**	**0**	**1**	**0.0**	**–1**	**0**	**0.0**	**11:21**	....	....	....	....	....	....	....	....	....
	Long Beach	IHL	74	22	31	53	76	....	....	....	....	....	....	....	....	....	6	2	2	4	4	....	....	....	....
2000-01	HPK Hameenlinna	Finland	54	25	25	50	53	....	....	....	....	....	....	....	....	....	....	....	....	....	....	....	....	....	....
2001-02	Jokerit Helsinki	Finland	46	21	22	43	37	....	....	....	....	....	....	....	....	....	12	3	5	8	18	....	....	....	....
2002-03	**Los Angeles**	**NHL**	**2**	**0**	**0**	**0**	**0**	**0**	**0**	**0**	**4**	**0.0**	**–1**	**0**	**0.0**	**13:57**	....	....	....	....	....	....	....	....	....
	Manchester	AHL	61	28	35	63	20	....	....	....	....	....	....	....	....	....	3	3	1	4	4	....	....	....	....
	NHL Totals		**34**	**4**	**12**	**16**	**6**	**0**	**0**	**0**	**66**	**6.1**		**0**	**0.0**	**13:24**	....	....	....	....	....	....	....	....	....

QMJHL All-Rookie Team (1996) • QMJHL Offensive Rookie of the Year (1996) • QMJHL First All-Star Team (1997) • Canadian Major Junior First All-Star Team (1997)
• Missed majority of 1997-98 season recovering from head injury suffered in training camp, September, 1997.

ROSSITER, Kyle

(RAWS-ih-tuhr, KIGHL) **FLA.**

Defense. Shoots left. 6'3", 217 lbs. Born, Edmonton, Alta., June 9, 1980. Florida's 1st choice, 30th overall, in 1998 Entry Draft.

Season	Club	League	GP	G	A	Pts	PIM	PP	SH	GW	S	%	+/-	TF	F%	Min	GP	G	A	Pts	PIM	PP	SH	GW	Min
1995-96	Edmonton SSAC	AMHL	34	5	19	24	116	....	....	....	....	....	....	....	....	....	....	....	....	....	....	....	....	....	....
1996-97	Spokane Chiefs	WHL	50	0	2	2	65	....	....	....	....	....	....	....	....	....	9	0	0	0	6	....	....	....	....
1997-98	Spokane Chiefs	WHL	61	6	16	22	190	....	....	....	....	....	....	....	....	....	15	0	3	3	28	....	....	....	....
1998-99	Spokane Chiefs	WHL	71	4	17	21	206	....	....	....	....	....	....	....	....	....	....	....	....	....	....	....	....	....	....
99-2000	Spokane Chiefs	WHL	63	11	22	33	155	....	....	....	....	....	....	....	....	....	15	1	4	5	25	....	....	....	....
2000-01	Louisville Panthers	AHL	78	2	5	7	110	....	....	....	....	....	....	....	....	....	....	....	....	....	....	....	....	....	....
2001-02	**Florida**	**NHL**	**2**	**0**	**0**	**0**	**2**	**0**	**0**	**0**	**0**	**0.0**	**–1**	**0**	**0.0**	**15:27**	....	....	....	....	....	....	....	....	....
	Utah Grizzlies	AHL	74	3	7	10	88	....	....	....	....	....	....	....	....	....	5	0	1	1	0	....	....	....	....
2002-03	**Florida**	**NHL**	**3**	**0**	**0**	**0**	**0**	**0**	**0**	**0**	**0**	**0.0**	**–2**	**0**	**0.0**	**10:09**	....	....	....	....	....	....	....	....	....
	San Antonio	AHL	67	0	7	7	107	....	....	....	....	....	....	....	....	....	3	0	0	0	0	....	....	....	....
	NHL Totals		**5**	**0**	**0**	**0**	**2**	**0**	**0**	**0**	**0**	**0.0**		**0**	**0.0**	**12:16**	....	....	....	....	....	....	....	....	....

Canadian Major Junior Scholastic Player of the Year (1998)

ROY, Andre

(WAH, AHN-dray) **T.B.**

Right wing. Shoots left. 6'4", 213 lbs. Born, Port Chester, NY, February 8, 1975. Boston's 5th choice, 151st overall, in 1994 Entry Draft.

Season	Club	League	GP	G	A	Pts	PIM	PP	SH	GW	S	%	+/-	TF	F%	Min	GP	G	A	Pts	PIM	PP	SH	GW	Min
1992-93	Nord Selects	QAHA	STATISTICS NOT AVAILABLE																						
1993-94	Goulbourn Royals	OJHL-C	9	9	13	22	98	....	....	....	....	....	....	....	....	....	....	....	....	....	....	....	....	....	....
	Beauport	QMJHL	33	6	7	13	125	....	....	....	....	....	....	....	....	....	....	....	....	....	....	....	....	....	....
	Chicoutimi	QMJHL	32	4	14	18	152	....	....	....	....	....	....	....	....	....	25	3	6	9	94	....	....	....	....
1994-95	Chicoutimi	QMJHL	20	15	8	23	90	....	....	....	....	....	....	....	....	....	....	....	....	....	....	....	....	....	....
	Drummondville	QMJHL	34	18	13	31	233	....	....	....	....	....	....	....	....	....	4	2	0	2	34	....	....	....	....
1995-96	**Boston**	**NHL**	**3**	**0**	**0**	**0**	**0**	**0**	**0**	**0**	**0**	**0.0**	**0**	....	....	....	....	....	....	....	....	....	....	....	....
	Providence Bruins	AHL	58	7	8	15	167	....	....	....	....	....	....	....	....	....	1	0	0	0	10	....	....	....	....
1996-97	**Boston**	**NHL**	**10**	**0**	**2**	**2**	**12**	**0**	**0**	**0**	**12**	**0.0**	**–5**	....	....	....	....	....	....	....	....	....	....	....	....
	Providence Bruins	AHL	50	17	11	28	234	....	....	....	....	....	....	....	....	....	....	....	....	....	....	....	....	....	....
1997-98	Providence Bruins	AHL	36	3	11	14	154	....	....	....	....	....	....	....	....	....	....	....	....	....	....	....	....	....	....
	Charlotte	ECHL	27	10	8	18	132	....	....	....	....	....	....	....	....	....	7	2	3	5	34	....	....	....	....
1998-99	Fort Wayne	IHL	65	15	6	21	*395	....	....	....	....	....	....	....	....	....	2	0	0	0	11	....	....	....	....
99-2000	**Ottawa**	**NHL**	**73**	**4**	**3**	**7**	**145**	**0**	**0**	**1**	**39**	**10.3**	**3**	**3**	**33.3**	**6:29**	**5**	**0**	**0**	**0**	**2**	**0**	**0**	**0**	**5:54**
2000-01	**Ottawa**	**NHL**	**64**	**3**	**5**	**8**	**169**	**0**	**0**	**0**	**33**	**9.1**	**1**	**2**	**50.0**	**4:36**	**2**	**0**	**0**	**0**	**16**	**0**	**0**	**0**	**4:16**
2001-02	**Ottawa**	**NHL**	**56**	**6**	**8**	**14**	**148**	**0**	**0**	**0**	**60**	**10.0**	**3**	**1**	**100.0**	**8:23**	....	....	....	....	....	....	....	....	....
	Tampa Bay	**NHL**	**9**	**1**	**1**	**2**	**63**	**0**	**0**	**0**	**6**	**16.7**	**–5**	**0**	**0.0**	**8:58**	....	....	....	....	....	....	....	....	....
2002-03	**Tampa Bay**	**NHL**	**62**	**10**	**7**	**17**	**119**	**0**	**0**	**2**	**85**	**11.8**	**0**	**7**	**57.1**	**10:46**	**5**	**0**	**1**	**1**	**2**	**0**	**0**	**0**	**12:31**
	NHL Totals		**277**	**24**	**26**	**50**	**656**	**0**	**0**	**3**	**235**	**10.2**		**13**	**53.8**	**7:31**	**12**	**0**	**1**	**1**	**20**	**0**	**0**	**0**	**8:23**

Signed as a free agent by **Ottawa**, April 28, 1999. Traded to **Tampa Bay** by **Ottawa** with Ottawa's 6th round choice (Paul Ranger) in 2002 Entry Draft for Juha Ylonen, March 15, 2002.

ROYER, Gaetan

(ROI-ay, GAY-tan)

Right wing. Shoots right. 6'3", 210 lbs. Born, Donnacona, Que., March 13, 1976.

Season	Club	League	GP	G	A	Pts	PIM	PP	SH	GW	S	%	+/-	TF	F%	Min	GP	G	A	Pts	PIM	PP	SH	GW	Min
1994-95	Sherbrooke	QMJHL	65	11	25	36	194	....	....	....	....	....	....	....	....	....	7	0	2	2	6	....	....	....	....
1995-96	Sherbrooke	QMJHL	36	25	26	51	174	....	....	....	....	....	....	....	....	....	....	....	....	....	....	....	....	....	....
	Beauport	QMJHL	25	11	10	21	59	....	....	....	....	....	....	....	....	....	19	5	9	14	47	....	....	....	....
1996-97	Jacksonville	ECHL	28	7	8	15	149	....	....	....	....	....	....	....	....	....	....	....	....	....	....	....	....	....	....
	Indianapolis Ice	IHL	29	2	4	6	60	....	....	....	....	....	....	....	....	....	....	....	....	....	....	....	....	....	....
1997-98	Grand Rapids	IHL	52	12	6	18	177	....	....	....	....	....	....	....	....	....	....	....	....	....	....	....	....	....	....
1998-99	Saint John Flames	AHL	15	1	0	1	36	....	....	....	....	....	....	....	....	....	....	....	....	....	....	....	....	....	....
99-2000	Michigan	IHL	20	6	2	8	64	....	....	....	....	....	....	....	....	....	7	0	1	1	8	....	....	....	....
2000-01	Saint John Flames	AHL	58	8	4	12	134	....	....	....	....	....	....	....	....	....	14	0	0	0	16	....	....	....	....
2001-02	Muskegon Fury	UHL	1	0	0	0	7	....	....	....	....	....	....	....	....	....	....	....	....	....	....	....	....	....	....
	Tampa Bay	**NHL**	**3**	**0**	**0**	**0**	**2**	**0**	**0**	**0**	**0**	**0.0**	**–1**	**0**	**0.0**	**4:57**	....	....	....	....	....	....	....	....	....
	Pensacola	ECHL	33	13	10	23	129	....	....	....	....	....	....	....	....	....	....	....	....	....	....	....	....	....	....
	Springfield	AHL	40	6	4	10	112	....	....	....	....	....	....	....	....	....	....	....	....	....	....	....	....	....	....
2002-03	Jackson Bandits	ECHL	11	3	6	9	58	....	....	....	....	....	....	....	....	....	....	....	....	....	....	....	....	....	....
	Pensacola	ECHL	20	3	10	13	60	....	....	....	....	....	....	....	....	....	....	....	....	....	....	....	....	....	....
	Springfield	AHL	33	2	5	7	50	....	....	....	....	....	....	....	....	....	6	2	0	2	15	....	....	....	....
	NHL Totals		**3**	**0**	**0**	**0**	**2**	**0**	**0**	**0**	**0**	**0.0**		**0**	**0.0**	**4:57**	....	....	....	....	....	....	....	....	....

Signed as a free agent by **Calgary**, September 12, 2000. Signed as a free agent by **Tampa Bay**, October 23, 2001. Signed as a free agent by **Florida**, September 12, 2002.

ROZSIVAL, Michal

(roh-ZIH-vahl, mee-KHUHL) **PIT.**

Defense. Shoots right. 6'1", 212 lbs. Born, Vlasim, Czech., September 3, 1978. Pittsburgh's 5th choice, 105th overall, in 1996 Entry Draft.

Season	Club	League	GP	G	A	Pts	PIM	PP	SH	GW	S	%	+/-	TF	F%	Min	GP	G	A	Pts	PIM	PP	SH	GW	Min
1994-95	Dukla Jihlava Jr.	Czech-Jr.	31	8	13	21	....																		
1995-96	HC Dukla Jihlava	Czech	36	3	4	7	....	....	....	....	....	....	....	....	....	....	....	....	....	....	....	....	....	....	....
1996-97	Swift Current	WHL	63	8	31	39	80	....	....	....	....	....	....	....	....	....	10	0	6	6	15	....	....	....	....
1997-98	Swift Current	WHL	71	14	55	69	122	....	....	....	....	....	....	....	....	....	12	0	5	5	33	....	....	....	....
1998-99	Syracuse Crunch	AHL	49	3	22	25	72	....	....	....	....	....	....	....	....	....	....	....	....	....	....	....	....	....	....
99-2000	**Pittsburgh**	**NHL**	**75**	**4**	**17**	**21**	**48**	**1**	**0**	**1**	**73**	**5.5**	**11**	**1**	**0.0**	**19:01**	**2**	**0**	**0**	**0**	**4**	**0**	**0**	**0**	**30:56**
2000-01	**Pittsburgh**	**NHL**	**30**	**1**	**4**	**5**	**26**	**0**	**0**	**0**	**17**	**5.9**	**3**	**1**	**100.0**	**17:06**	....	....	....	....	....	....	....	....	....
	Wilkes-Barre	AHL	29	8	8	16	32	....	....	....	....	....	....	....	....	....	21	3	*19	22	23	....	....	....	....
2001-02	**Pittsburgh**	**NHL**	**79**	**9**	**20**	**29**	**47**	**4**	**0**	**4**	**89**	**10.1**	**–6**	**0**	**0.0**	**20:01**	....	....	....	....	....	....	....	....	....
2002-03	**Pittsburgh**	**NHL**	**53**	**4**	**6**	**10**	**40**	**1**	**0**	**0**	**61**	**6.6**	**–5**	**0**	**0.0**	**20:25**	....	....	....	....	....	....	....	....	....
	NHL Totals		**237**	**18**	**47**	**65**	**161**	**6**	**0**	**5**	**240**	**7.5**		**2**	**50.0**	**19:25**	**2**	**0**	**0**	**0**	**4**	**0**	**0**	**0**	**30:56**

WHL East First All-Star Team (1998)

RUCCHIN, Steve

(ROO-chihn, STEEV) **ANA.**

Center. Shoots left. 6'2", 211 lbs. Born, Thunder Bay, Ont., July 4, 1971. Anaheim's 1st choice, 2nd overall, in 1994 Supplemental Draft.

Season	Club	League	GP	G	A	Pts	PIM	PP	SH	GW	S	%	+/-	TF	F%	Min	GP	G	A	Pts	PIM	PP	SH	GW	Min
1989-90	Banting High	Hi-School	STATISTICS NOT AVAILABLE																						
	Thamesford	OJHL-D	2	1	2	3	0	....	....	....	....	....	....	....	....	....	....	....	....	....	....	....	....	....	....
1990-91	Western Ontario	OUAA	34	13	16	29	14	....	....	....	....	....	....	....	....	....	....	....	....	....	....	....	....	....	....
1991-92	Western Ontario	OUAA	37	28	34	62	36	....	....	....	....	....	....	....	....	....	....	....	....	....	....	....	....	....	....
1992-93	Western Ontario	OUAA	34	22	26	48	16	....	....	....	....	....	....	....	....	....	....	....	....	....	....	....	....	....	....
1993-94	Western Ontario	OUAA	35	30	23	53	30	....	....	....	....	....	....	....	....	....	....	....	....	....	....	....	....	....	....

			Regular Season														Playoffs								
Season	Club	League	GP	G	A	Pts	PIM	PP	SH	GW	S	%	+/-	TF	F%	Min	GP	G	A	Pts	PIM	PP	SH	GW	Min
1994-95	San Diego Gulls	IHL	41	11	15	26	14	....	....	....	....	....	....	....	....	....	....	....	....	....	....	....	....	....	....
	Anaheim	**NHL**	**43**	**6**	**11**	**17**	**23**	**0**	**0**	**1**	**59**	**10.2**	**7**	....	....	....	....	....	....	....	....	....	....	....	....
1995-96	**Anaheim**	**NHL**	**64**	**19**	**25**	**44**	**12**	**8**	**1**	**4**	**113**	**16.8**	**3**	....	....	....	....	....	....	....	....	....	....	....	....
1996-97	**Anaheim**	**NHL**	**79**	**19**	**48**	**67**	**24**	**6**	**1**	**2**	**153**	**12.4**	**26**	....	....	....	**8**	**1**	**2**	**3**	**10**	**0**	**0**	**0**	....
1997-98	**Anaheim**	**NHL**	**72**	**17**	**36**	**53**	**13**	**8**	**1**	**3**	**131**	**13.0**	**8**	....	....	....	....	....	....	....	....	....	....	....	....
1998-99	**Anaheim**	**NHL**	**69**	**23**	**39**	**62**	**22**	**5**	**1**	**5**	**145**	**15.9**	**11**	**1845**	**52.3**	**22:33**	**4**	**0**	**3**	**3**	**0**	**0**	**0**	**0**	**21:55**
99-2000	**Anaheim**	**NHL**	**71**	**19**	**38**	**57**	**16**	**10**	**0**	**2**	**131**	**14.5**	**9**	**1996**	**53.4**	**22:12**	....	....	....	....	....	....	....	....	....
2000-01	**Anaheim**	**NHL**	**16**	**3**	**5**	**8**	**0**	**2**	**0**	**0**	**19**	**15.8**	**–5**	**289**	**51.6**	**18:47**	....	....	....	....	....	....	....	....	....
2001-02	**Anaheim**	**NHL**	**38**	**7**	**16**	**23**	**6**	**4**	**0**	**1**	**57**	**12.3**	**–3**	**808**	**52.2**	**19:17**	....	....	....	....	....	....	....	....	....
2002-03	**Anaheim**	**NHL**	**82**	**20**	**38**	**58**	**12**	**6**	**1**	**4**	**194**	**10.3**	**–14**	**1613**	**54.2**	**21:05**	**21**	**7**	**3**	**10**	**2**	**1**	**0**	**2**	**23:35**
	NHL Totals		**534**	**133**	**256**	**389**	**128**	**49**	**5**	**22**	**1002**	**13.3**		**6551**	**53.1**	**21:21**	**33**	**8**	**8**	**16**	**12**	**1**	**0**	**2**	**23:19**

• Missed majority of 2000-01 season recovering from jaw injury suffered in game vs. Colorado, November 15, 2000. • Missed majority of 2001-02 season recovering from leg injury suffered in game vs. San Jose, November 16, 2001.

RUCINSKY, Martin

(roo-SHIHN-skee, MAHR-tihn)

Left wing. Shoots left. 6'1", 205 lbs. Born, Most, Czech., March 11, 1971. Edmonton's 2nd choice, 20th overall, in 1991 Entry Draft.

Season	Club	League	GP	G	A	Pts	PIM	PP	SH	GW	S	%	+/-	TF	F%	Min	GP	G	A	Pts	PIM	PP	SH	GW	Min
1988-89	CHZ Litvinov	Czech	3	1	0	1	2	....	....	....	....	....	....	....	....	....	....	....	....	....	....	....	....	....	....
1989-90	CHZ Litvinov	Czech	39	12	6	18	....	....	....	....	....	....	....	....	....	....	8	5	3	8	....	....	....	....	....
1990-91	CHZ Litvinov	Czech	56	24	20	44	69	....	....	....	....	....	....	....	....	....	....	....	....	....	....	....	....	....	....
1991-92	**Edmonton**	**NHL**	**2**	**0**	**0**	**0**	**0**	**0**	**0**	**0**	**1**	**0.0**	**–3**	....	....	....	....	....	....	....	....	....	....	....	....
	Cape Breton	AHL	35	11	12	23	34	....	....	....	....	....	....	....	....	....	....	....	....	....	....	....	....	....	....
	Quebec	**NHL**	**4**	**1**	**1**	**2**	**2**	**0**	**0**	**0**	**4**	**25.0**	**1**	....	....	....	....	....	....	....	....	....	....	....	....
	Halifax Citadels	AHL	7	1	1	2	6	....	....	....	....	....	....	....	....	....	....	....	....	....	....	....	....	....	....
1992-93	**Quebec**	**NHL**	**77**	**18**	**30**	**48**	**51**	**4**	**0**	**1**	**133**	**13.5**	**16**	....	....	....	**6**	**1**	**1**	**2**	**4**	**1**	**0**	**0**	....
1993-94	**Quebec**	**NHL**	**60**	**9**	**23**	**32**	**58**	**4**	**0**	**1**	**96**	**9.4**	**4**	....	....	....	....	....	....	....	....	....	....	....	....
1994-95	Litvinov	Czech	13	12	10	22	54	....	....	....	....	....	....	....	....	....	....	....	....	....	....	....	....	....	....
	Quebec	**NHL**	**20**	**3**	**6**	**9**	**14**	**0**	**0**	**0**	**32**	**9.4**	**5**	....	....	....	....	....	....	....	....	....	....	....	....
1995-96	HC Petra Vsetin	Czech	1	1	1	2	0	....	....	....	....	....	....	....	....	....	....	....	....	....	....	....	....	....	....
	Colorado	**NHL**	**22**	**4**	**11**	**15**	**14**	**0**	**0**	**1**	**39**	**10.3**	**10**	....	....	....	....	....	....	....	....	....	....	....	....
	Montreal	**NHL**	**56**	**25**	**35**	**60**	**54**	**9**	**2**	**3**	**142**	**17.6**	**8**	....	....	....	....	....	....	....	....	....	....	....	....
1996-97	**Montreal**	**NHL**	**70**	**28**	**27**	**55**	**62**	**6**	**3**	**3**	**172**	**16.3**	**1**	....	....	....	**5**	**0**	**0**	**0**	**4**	**0**	**0**	**0**	....
1997-98	**Montreal**	**NHL**	**78**	**21**	**32**	**53**	**84**	**5**	**3**	**3**	**192**	**10.9**	**13**	....	....	....	**10**	**3**	**0**	**3**	**4**	**1**	**0**	**0**	....
	Czech Republic	Olympics	6	3	1	4	4	....	....	....	....	....	....	....	....	....	....	....	....	....	....	....	....	....	....
1998-99	Litvinov	Czech	3	2	2	4	0	....	....	....	....	....	....	....	....	....	....	....	....	....	....	....	....	....	....
	Montreal	**NHL**	**73**	**17**	**17**	**34**	**50**	**5**	**0**	**1**	**180**	**9.4**	**–25**	**12**	**50.0**	**18:12**	....	....	....	....	....	....	....	....	....
99-2000	**Montreal**	**NHL**	**80**	**25**	**24**	**49**	**70**	**7**	**1**	**4**	**242**	**10.3**	**1**	**31**	**54.8**	**18:54**	....	....	....	....	....	....	....	....	....
2000-01	**Montreal**	**NHL**	**57**	**16**	**22**	**38**	**66**	**5**	**1**	**4**	**141**	**11.3**	**–5**	**5**	**40.0**	**19:11**	....	....	....	....	....	....	....	....	....
2001-02	**Montreal**	**NHL**	**18**	**2**	**6**	**8**	**12**	**1**	**0**	**0**	**41**	**4.9**	**–1**	**5**	**80.0**	**16:15**	....	....	....	....	....	....	....	....	....
	Dallas	**NHL**	**42**	**6**	**11**	**17**	**24**	**2**	**0**	**1**	**63**	**9.5**	**3**	**7**	**57.1**	**14:33**	....	....	....	....	....	....	....	....	....
	Czech Republic	Olympics	4	0	3	3	2	....	....	....	....	....	....	....	....	....	....	....	....	....	....	....	....	....	....
	NY Rangers	**NHL**	**15**	**3**	**10**	**13**	**6**	**0**	**0**	**1**	**24**	**12.5**	**6**	**3**	**33.3**	**16:39**	....	....	....	....	....	....	....	....	....
2002-03	Litvinov	Czech	2	1	0	1	2	....	....	....	....	....	....	....	....	....	....	....	....	....	....	....	....	....	....
	St. Louis	**NHL**	**61**	**16**	**14**	**30**	**38**	**4**	**4**	**3**	**135**	**11.9**	**–1**	**19**	**57.9**	**16:55**	**7**	**4**	**2**	**6**	**4**	**0**	**0**	**0**	**16:52**
	NHL Totals		**735**	**194**	**269**	**463**	**605**	**52**	**14**	**26**	**1637**	**11.9**		**82**	**54.9**	**17:41**	**28**	**8**	**3**	**11**	**16**	**2**	**0**	**0**	**16:52**

Played in NHL All-Star Game (2000)

Traded to **Quebec** by **Edmonton** for Ron Tugnutt and Brad Zavisha, March 10, 1992. Transferred to **Colorado** after **Quebec** franchise relocated, June 21, 1995. Traded to **Montreal** by **Colorado** with Andrei Kovalenko and Jocelyn Thibault for Patrick Roy and Mike Keane, December 6, 1995. Traded to **Dallas** by **Montreal** with Benoit Brunet for Donald Audette and Shaun Van Allen, November 21, 2001. Traded to **NY Rangers** by **Dallas** with Roman Lyashenko for Manny Malhotra and Barrett Heisten, March 12, 2002. Signed as a free agent by **St. Louis**, October 30, 2002.

RUMBLE, Darren

(RUHM-buhl, DAIR-rehn) **T.B.**

Defense. Shoots left. 6'1", 200 lbs. Born, Barrie, Ont., January 23, 1969. Philadelphia's 1st choice, 20th overall, in 1987 Entry Draft.

Season	Club	League	GP	G	A	Pts	PIM	PP	SH	GW	S	%	+/-	TF	F%	Min	GP	G	A	Pts	PIM	PP	SH	GW	Min
1985-86	Barrie Colts	OJHL-B	46	14	32	46	91	....	....	....	....	....	....	....	....	....	....	....	....	....	....	....	....	....	....
1986-87	Kitchener Rangers	OHL	64	11	32	43	44	....	....	....	....	....	....	....	....	....	4	0	1	1	9	....	....	....	....
1987-88	Kitchener Rangers	OHL	55	15	50	65	64	....	....	....	....	....	....	....	....	....	....	....	....	....	....	....	....	....	....
1988-89	Kitchener Rangers	OHL	46	11	28	39	25	....	....	....	....	....	....	....	....	....	5	1	0	1	2	....	....	....	....
1989-90	Hershey Bears	AHL	57	2	13	15	31	....	....	....	....	....	....	....	....	....	....	....	....	....	....	....	....	....	....
1990-91	**Philadelphia**	**NHL**	**3**	**1**	**0**	**1**	**0**	**0**	**0**	**0**	**2**	**50.0**	**1**	....	....	....	....	....	....	....	....	....	....	....	....
	Hershey Bears	AHL	73	6	35	41	48	....	....	....	....	....	....	....	....	....	3	0	5	5	2	....	....	....	....
1991-92	Hershey Bears	AHL	79	12	54	66	118	....	....	....	....	....	....	....	....	....	6	0	3	3	2	....	....	....	....
1992-93	**Ottawa**	**NHL**	**69**	**3**	**13**	**16**	**61**	**0**	**0**	**0**	**92**	**3.3**	**–24**	....	....	....	....	....	....	....	....	....	....	....	....
	New Haven	AHL	2	1	0	1	0	....	....	....	....	....	....	....	....	....	....	....	....	....	....	....	....	....	....
1993-94	**Ottawa**	**NHL**	**70**	**6**	**9**	**15**	**116**	**0**	**0**	**0**	**95**	**6.3**	**–50**	....	....	....	....	....	....	....	....	....	....	....	....
	P.E.I. Senators	AHL	3	2	0	2	0	....	....	....	....	....	....	....	....	....	....	....	....	....	....	....	....	....	....
1994-95	P.E.I. Senators	AHL	70	7	46	53	77	....	....	....	....	....	....	....	....	....	11	0	6	6	4	....	....	....	....
1995-96	**Philadelphia**	**NHL**	**5**	**0**	**0**	**0**	**4**	**0**	**0**	**0**	**7**	**0.0**	**0**	....	....	....	....	....	....	....	....	....	....	....	....
	Hershey Bears	AHL	58	13	37	50	83	....	....	....	....	....	....	....	....	....	5	0	0	0	6	....	....	....	....
1996-97	**Philadelphia**	**NHL**	**10**	**0**	**0**	**0**	**0**	**0**	**0**	**0**	**9**	**0.0**	**–2**	....	....	....	....	....	....	....	....	....	....	....	....
	Philadelphia	AHL	72	18	44	62	83	....	....	....	....	....	....	....	....	....	7	0	3	3	19	....	....	....	....
1997-98	Adler Mannheim	Germany	21	2	7	9	18	....	....	....	....	....	....	....	....	....	....	....	....	....	....	....	....	....	....
	Adler Mannheim	EuroHL	4	0	1	1	4	....	....	....	....	....	....	....	....	....	....	....	....	....	....	....	....	....	....
	San Antonio	IHL	46	7	22	29	47	....	....	....	....	....	....	....	....	....	....	....	....	....	....	....	....	....	....
1998-99	Utah Grizzlies	IHL	10	1	4	5	10	....	....	....	....	....	....	....	....	....	....	....	....	....	....	....	....	....	....
	Grand Rapids	IHL	53	6	22	28	44	....	....	....	....	....	....	....	....	....	....	....	....	....	....	....	....	....	....
99-2000	Grand Rapids	IHL	29	3	10	13	20	....	....	....	....	....	....	....	....	....	....	....	....	....	....	....	....	....	....
	Worcester IceCats	AHL	39	0	17	17	31	....	....	....	....	....	....	....	....	....	9	0	2	2	6	....	....	....	....
2000-01	**St. Louis**	**NHL**	**12**	**0**	**4**	**4**	**27**	**0**	**0**	**0**	**11**	**0.0**	**7**	**0**	**0.0**	**18:12**	....	....	....	....	....	....	....	....	....
	Worcester IceCats	AHL	53	6	24	30	65	....	....	....	....	....	....	....	....	....	8	0	1	1	10	....	....	....	....
2001-02	Worcester IceCats	AHL	60	3	29	32	48	....	....	....	....	....	....	....	....	....	3	0	4	4	2	....	....	....	....
2002-03	**Tampa Bay**	**NHL**	**19**	**0**	**0**	**0**	**6**	**0**	**0**	**0**	**10**	**0.0**	**–2**	**0**	**0.0**	**11:07**	....	....	....	....	....	....	....	....	....
	Springfield	AHL	33	5	17	22	18	....	....	....	....	....	....	....	....	....	....	....	....	....	....	....	....	....	....
	NHL Totals		**188**	**10**	**26**	**36**	**214**	**0**	**0**	**0**	**226**	**4.4**		**0**	**0.0**	**13:52**	....	....	....	....	....	....	....	....	....

AHL Second All-Star Team (1995) • AHL First All-Star Team (1997) • Eddie Shore Award (Top Defenseman – AHL) (1997)

Claimed by **Ottawa** from **Philadelphia** in Expansion Draft, June 18, 1992. Signed as a free agent by **Philadelphia**, July 31, 1995. Signed as a free agent by **St. Louis**, February 1, 2000. Signed as a free agent by **Tampa Bay**, September 11, 2002.

RUPP, Mike

(RUHP, MIGHK) **N.J.**

Right wing. Shoots left. 6'5", 230 lbs. Born, Cleveland, OH, January 13, 1980. New Jersey's 7th choice, 76th overall, in 2000 Entry Draft.

Season	Club	League	GP	G	A	Pts	PIM	PP	SH	GW	S	%	+/-	TF	F%	Min	GP	G	A	Pts	PIM	PP	SH	GW	Min
1996-97	St. Edward's	Hi-School	20	26	24	50	....	....	....	....	....	....	....	....	....	....	....	....	....	....	....	....	....	....	....
1997-98	Windsor Spitfires	OHL	38	9	8	17	60	....	....	....	....	....	....	....	....	....	....	....	....	....	....	....	....	....	....
	Erie Otters	OHL	26	7	3	10	57	....	....	....	....	....	....	....	....	....	7	3	1	4	6	....	....	....	....
1998-99	Erie Otters	OHL	63	22	25	47	102	....	....	....	....	....	....	....	....	....	5	0	2	2	25	....	....	....	....
99-2000	Erie Otters	OHL	58	32	21	53	134	....	....	....	....	....	....	....	....	....	13	5	5	10	22	....	....	....	....
2000-01	Albany River Rats	AHL	71	10	10	20	63	....	....	....	....	....	....	....	....	....	....	....	....	....	....	....	....	....	....
2001-02	Albany River Rats	AHL	78	13	17	30	90	....	....	....	....	....	....	....	....	....	....	....	....	....	....	....	....	....	....
2002-03♦	**New Jersey**	**NHL**	**26**	**5**	**3**	**8**	**21**	**2**	**0**	**3**	**34**	**14.7**	**0**	**150**	**44.7**	**11:39**	**4**	**1**	**3**	**4**	**0**	**0**	**0**	**1**	**11:28**
	Albany River Rats	AHL	47	8	11	19	74	....	....	....	....	....	....	....	....	....	....	....	....	....	....	....	....	....	....
	NHL Totals		**26**	**5**	**3**	**8**	**21**	**2**	**0**	**3**	**34**	**14.7**		**150**	**44.7**	**11:39**	**4**	**1**	**3**	**4**	**0**	**0**	**0**	**1**	**11:28**

• Re-entered NHL Entry Draft. Originally NY Islanders' 1st choice, 9th overall, in 1998 Entry Draft.

RUUTU, Jarkko
(ROO-too, YAHR-koh) **VAN.**

Right wing. Shoots left. 6'2", 194 lbs. Born, Vantaa, Finland, August 23, 1975. Vancouver's 3rd choice, 68th overall, in 1998 Entry Draft.

			Regular Season														Playoffs								
Season	Club	League	GP	G	A	Pts	PIM	PP	SH	GW	S	%	+/-	TF	F%	Min	GP	G	A	Pts	PIM	PP	SH	GW	Min
1991-92	HIFK Helsinki Jr.	Finn-Jr.	1	0	0	0	0																		
1992-93	HIFK Helsinki-B	Finn-Jr.	33	26	21	47	53																		
	HIFK Helsinki Jr.	Finn-Jr.	1	0	0	0	0																		
1993-94	HIFK Helsinki Jr.	Finn-Jr.	19	9	12	21	44																		
1994-95	HIFK Helsinki Jr.	Finn-Jr.	35	26	22	48	117																		
1995-96	Michigan Tech	WCHA	39	12	10	22	96																		
1996-97	HIFK Helsinki	Finland	48	11	10	21	*155																		
1997-98	HIFK Helsinki	Finland	37	10	10	20	87										8	*7	4	11	10				
1998-99	HIFK Helsinki	Finland	25	10	4	14	136										9	0	2	2	43				
	HIFK Helsinki	EuroHL	5	1	2	3	8																		
99-2000	**Vancouver**	**NHL**	**8**	**0**	**1**	**1**	**6**	**0**	**0**	**0**	**4**	**0.0**	**–1**	**0**	**0.0**	**8:47**									
	Syracuse Crunch	AHL	65	26	32	58	164										4	3	1	4	8				
2000-01	**Vancouver**	**NHL**	**21**	**3**	**3**	**6**	**32**	**0**	**1**	**0**	**23**	**13.0**	**1**	**0**	**0.0**	**10:39**	**4**	**0**	**1**	**1**	**8**	**0**	**0**	**0**	**10:18**
	Kansas City	IHL	46	11	18	29	111																		
2001-02	**Vancouver**	**NHL**	**49**	**2**	**7**	**9**	**74**	**0**	**0**	**0**	**37**	**5.4**	**–1**	**5**	**0.0**	**10:11**	**1**	**0**	**0**	**0**	**0**	**0**	**0**	**0**	**8:53**
	Finland	Olympics	4	0	0	0	4																		
2002-03	**Vancouver**	**NHL**	**36**	**2**	**2**	**4**	**66**	**0**	**0**	**1**	**36**	**5.6**	**–7**	**6**	**16.7**	**8:58**	**13**	**0**	**2**	**2**	**14**	**0**	**0**	**0**	**11:59**
	NHL Totals		**114**	**7**	**13**	**20**	**178**	**0**	**1**	**1**	**100**	**7.0**		**11**	**9.1**	**9:48**	**18**	**0**	**3**	**3**	**22**	**0**	**0**	**0**	**11:26**

• Spent majority of 2002-03 season as a healthy reserve.

RYCROFT, Mark
(RIGH-krawft, MAHRK) **ST.L.**

Right wing. Shoots right. 5'11", 192 lbs. Born, Penticton, B.C., July 12, 1978.

Season	Club	League	GP	G	A	Pts	PIM	PP	SH	GW	S	%	+/-	TF	F%	Min	GP	G	A	Pts	PIM	PP	SH	GW	Min
1993-94	Penticton Ice	BCAHA	60	47	65	112	100																		
1994-95	Penticton Ice	BCAHA	43	33	43	76	90																		
1995-96	Nanaimo Clippers	BCHL	60	17	28	45	28																		
1996-97	Nanaimo Clippers	BCHL	58	32	35	67	79																		
1997-98	U. of Denver	WCHA	35	15	17	32	28																		
1998-99	U. of Denver	WCHA	41	19	18	37	36																		
99-2000	U. of Denver	WCHA	41	17	17	34	87																		
2000-01	Worcester IceCats	AHL	71	24	26	50	68										11	2	5	7	4				
2001-02	**St. Louis**	**NHL**	**9**	**0**	**3**	**3**	**4**	**0**	**0**	**0**	**14**	**0.0**	**0**	**1**	**0.0**	**9:50**									
	Worcester IceCats	AHL	66	12	19	31	68										3	0	1	1	0				
2002-03	Worcester IceCats	AHL	45	8	18	26	35										1	0	0	0	0				
	NHL Totals		**9**	**0**	**3**	**3**	**4**	**0**	**0**	**0**	**14**	**0.0**		**1**	**0.0**	**9:50**									

WCHA All-Rookie Team (1998)

Signed as a free agent by **St. Louis**, May 15, 2000.

SACCO, Joe
(SAK-oh, JOH)

Right wing. Shoots left. 6'1", 190 lbs. Born, Medford, MA, February 4, 1969. Toronto's 4th choice, 71st overall, in 1987 Entry Draft.

Season	Club	League	GP	G	A	Pts	PIM	PP	SH	GW	S	%	+/-	TF	F%	Min	GP	G	A	Pts	PIM	PP	SH	GW	Min
1985-86	Medford	Hi-School	20	30	30	60																			
1986-87	Medford	Hi-School	21	22	32	54																			
1987-88	Boston University	H-East	34	16	20	36	40																		
1988-89	Boston University	H-East	33	21	19	40	66																		
1989-90	Boston University	H-East	44	28	24	52	70																		
1990-91	**Toronto**	**NHL**	**20**	**0**	**5**	**5**	**2**	**0**	**0**	**0**	**20**	**0.0**	**–5**												
	Newmarket Saints	AHL	49	18	17	35	24																		
1991-92	Team USA	Nat-Tm	50	11	26	37	61																		
	United States	Olympics	8	0	2	2	0																		
	Toronto	**NHL**	**17**	**7**	**4**	**11**	**4**	**0**	**0**	**1**	**40**	**17.5**	**8**												
	St. John's	AHL															1	1	1	2	0				
1992-93	**Toronto**	**NHL**	**23**	**4**	**4**	**8**	**8**	**0**	**0**	**0**	**38**	**10.5**	**–4**												
	St. John's	AHL	37	14	16	30	45										7	6	4	10	2				
1993-94	**Anaheim**	**NHL**	**84**	**19**	**18**	**37**	**61**	**3**	**1**	**2**	**206**	**9.2**	**–11**												
1994-95	**Anaheim**	**NHL**	**41**	**10**	**8**	**18**	**23**	**2**	**0**	**0**	**77**	**13.0**	**–8**												
1995-96	**Anaheim**	**NHL**	**76**	**13**	**14**	**27**	**40**	**1**	**2**	**2**	**132**	**9.8**													
1996-97	**Anaheim**	**NHL**	**77**	**12**	**17**	**29**	**35**	**1**	**1**	**2**	**131**	**9.2**	**1**				**11**	**2**	**0**	**2**	**2**	**0**	**0**	**0**	
1997-98	**Anaheim**	**NHL**	**55**	**8**	**11**	**19**	**24**	**0**	**2**	**2**	**90**	**8.9**	**–1**												
	NY Islanders	**NHL**	**25**	**3**	**3**	**6**	**10**	**0**	**0**	**0**	**32**	**9.4**	**1**												
1998-99	**NY Islanders**	**NHL**	**73**	**3**	**0**	**3**	**45**	**0**	**1**	**2**	**84**	**3.6**	**–24**	**32**	**56.3**	**9:59**									
99-2000	**Washington**	**NHL**	**79**	**7**	**16**	**23**	**50**	**0**	**0**	**1**	**117**	**6.0**	**7**	**9**	**33.3**	**11:51**	**5**	**0**	**0**	**0**	**4**	**0**	**0**	**0**	**12:08**
2000-01	**Washington**	**NHL**	**69**	**7**	**7**	**14**	**48**	**0**	**0**	**0**	**81**	**8.6**	**4**	**1**	**100.0**	**11:10**	**6**	**0**	**0**	**0**	**2**	**0**	**0**	**0**	**10:54**
2001-02	**Washington**	**NHL**	**65**	**0**	**7**	**7**	**51**	**0**	**0**	**0**	**57**	**0.0**	**–13**	**12**	**16.7**	**7:38**									
2002-03	**Philadelphia**	**NHL**	**34**	**1**	**5**	**6**	**20**	**0**	**0**	**1**	**48**	**2.1**	**0**	**3**	**0.0**	**12:27**	**4**	**0**	**0**	**0**	**0**	**0**	**0**	**0**	**7:56**
	Philadelphia	AHL	6	4	3	7	4																		
	NHL Totals		**738**	**94**	**119**	**213**	**421**	**7**	**7**	**13**	**1153**	**8.2**		**57**	**42.1**	**10:29**	**26**	**2**	**0**	**2**	**8**	**0**	**0**	**0**	**10:31**

Claimed by **Anaheim** from **Toronto** in Expansion Draft, June 24, 1993. Traded to **NY Islanders** by **Anaheim** with J.J. Daigneault and Mark Janssens for Travis Green, Doug Houda and Tony Tuzzolino, February 6, 1998. Signed as a free agent by **Washington**, August 9, 1999. Signed as a free agent by **Philadelphia** (AHL), January 2, 2003. Signed as a free agent by **Philadelphia**, January 15, 2003.

SAFRONOV, Kirill
(sah-FRAW-nawf, kih-RIHL) **ATL.**

Defense. Shoots left. 6'2", 215 lbs. Born, Leningrad, USSR, February 26, 1981. Phoenix's 2nd choice, 19th overall, in 1999 Entry Draft.

Season	Club	League	GP	G	A	Pts	PIM	PP	SH	GW	S	%	+/-	TF	F%	Min	GP	G	A	Pts	PIM	PP	SH	GW	Min
1996-97	St. Petersburg 2	Russia-3	9	0	0	0	6																		
	St. Petersburg	Russia	1	0	0	0	0																		
1997-98	St. Petersburg 2	Russia-3	34	4	3	7	36																		
	St. Petersburg	Russia	9	0	1	1	4										1	0	0	0	0				
1998-99	St. Petersburg 2	Russia-4	4	2	1	3	2																		
	St. Petersburg	Russia	45	1	3	4	32																		
99-2000	Quebec Remparts	QMJHL	55	11	32	43	95										11	2	4	6	14				
2000-01	Springfield	AHL	65	5	13	18	77																		
2001-02	**Phoenix**	**NHL**	**1**	**0**	**0**	**0**	**0**	**0**	**0**	**0**	**0**	**0.0**	**–2**	**0**	**0.0**	**6:08**									
	Springfield	AHL	68	3	19	22	26																		
	Atlanta	**NHL**	**2**	**0**	**0**	**0**	**2**	**0**	**0**	**0**	**2**	**0.0**	**–3**	**0**	**0.0**	**21:11**									
	Chicago Wolves	AHL	8	0	2	2	2										25	2	6	8	8				
2002-03	**Atlanta**	**NHL**	**32**	**2**	**2**	**4**	**14**	**0**	**0**	**0**	**21**	**9.5**	**–10**	**1**	**0.0**	**15:02**									
	Chicago Wolves	AHL	44	4	15	19	29										9	1	2	3	4				
	NHL Totals		**35**	**2**	**2**	**4**	**16**	**0**	**0**	**0**	**23**	**8.7**		**1**	**0.0**	**15:08**									

Traded to **Atlanta** by **Phoenix** with the rights to Ruslan Zainullin and Phoenix's 5th round choice (Patrick Dwyer) in 2002 Entry Draft for Darcy Hordichuk and Atlanta's 4th (Lance Monych) and 5th (John Zeiler) round choices in 2002 Entry Draft, March 19, 2002.

ST. JACQUES, Bruno
(SAINT ZHAWK, BREW-noh) **CAR.**

Defense. Shoots left. 6'2", 204 lbs. Born, Montreal, Que., August 22, 1980. Philadelphia's 12th choice, 253rd overall, in 1998 Entry Draft.

Season	Club	League	GP	G	A	Pts	PIM	PP	SH	GW	S	%	+/-	TF	F%	Min	GP	G	A	Pts	PIM	PP	SH	GW	Min
1996-97	Mtl-Bourassa	QAAA	40	5	8	13											16	0	7	7					
1997-98	Baie-Comeau	QMJHL	63	1	11	12	140																		
1998-99	Baie-Comeau	QMJHL	49	8	13	21	85																		
99-2000	Baie-Comeau	QMJHL	60	8	28	36	120										6	0	2	2	10				
	Philadelphia	AHL	3	0	1	1	0										1	0	0	0	0				
2000-01	Philadelphia	AHL	45	1	16	17	83										10	1	0	1	16				
2001-02	**Philadelphia**	**NHL**	**7**	**0**	**0**	**0**	**2**	**0**	**0**	**0**	**4**	**0.0**	**4**	**0**	**0.0**	**13:51**									
	Philadelphia	AHL	55	3	11	14	59										4	0	0	0	0				

Season	Club	League	GP	G	A	Pts	PIM	PP	SH	GW	S	%	+/-	TF	F%	Min	GP	G	A	Pts	PIM	PP	SH	GW	Min
			Regular Season														Playoffs								
2002-03	**Philadelphia**	**NHL**	**6**	**0**	**0**	**0**	**2**	**0**	**0**	**0**	**5**	**0.0**	**–1**	**0**	**0.0**	**14:35**	....	....	....	....	....	....	....	....	....
	Philadelphia	AHL	30	0	7	7	46	....	....	....	....	....	....	....	....	....	....	....	....	....	....	....	....	....	....
	Carolina	**NHL**	**18**	**2**	**5**	**7**	**12**	**0**	**0**	**0**	**14**	**14.3**	**–3**	**0**	**0.0**	**18:15**	....	....	....	....	....	....	....	....	....
	Lowell	AHL	8	1	1	2	8	....	....	....	....	....	....	....	....	....	....	....	....	....	....	....	....	....	....
	NHL Totals		**31**	**2**	**5**	**7**	**16**	**0**	**0**	**0**	**23**	**8.7**		**0**	**0.0**	**16:33**	....	....	....	....	....	....	....	....	....

Traded to **Carolina** by **Philadelphia** with Pavel Brendl for Sami Kapanen and Ryan Bast, February 7, 2003.

ST. LOUIS, Martin (sehn-loo-EE, mahr-TEHN) T.B.

Right wing. Shoots left. 5'9", 185 lbs. Born, Laval, Que., June 18, 1975.

Season	Club	League	GP	G	A	Pts	PIM	PP	SH	GW	S	%	+/-	TF	F%	Min	GP	G	A	Pts	PIM	PP	SH	GW	Min
1991-92	Laval Laurentide	QAAA	42	29	*74	*103	38										12	7	15	22	16				
1992-93	Hawkesbury	OCJHL	31	37	50	87	70																		
1993-94	U. of Vermont	ECAC	33	15	36	51	24																		
1994-95	U. of Vermont	ECAC	35	23	48	71	36																		
1995-96	U. of Vermont	ECAC	35	29	56	85	38																		
1996-97	U. of Vermont	ECAC	36	24	*36	60	65																		
1997-98	Cleveland	IHL	56	16	34	50	24																		
	Saint John Flames	AHL	25	15	11	26	20										20	5	15	20	16				
1998-99	**Calgary**	**NHL**	**13**	**1**	**1**	**2**	**10**	**0**	**0**	**0**	**14**	**7.1**	**–2**	**0**	**0.0**	**8:15**									
	Saint John Flames	AHL	53	28	34	62	30										7	4	4	8	2				
99-2000	**Calgary**	**NHL**	**56**	**3**	**15**	**18**	**22**	**0**	**0**	**1**	**73**	**4.1**	**–5**	**3**	**0.0**	**14:41**									
	Saint John Flames	AHL	17	15	11	26	14																		
2000-01	**Tampa Bay**	**NHL**	**78**	**18**	**22**	**40**	**12**	**3**	**3**	**4**	**141**	**12.8**	**–4**	**48**	**41.7**	**15:14**									
2001-02	**Tampa Bay**	**NHL**	**53**	**16**	**19**	**35**	**20**	**6**	**1**	**2**	**105**	**15.2**	**4**	**33**	**39.4**	**18:41**									
2002-03	**Tampa Bay**	**NHL**	**82**	**33**	**37**	**70**	**32**	**12**	**3**	**5**	**201**	**16.4**	**10**	**37**	**37.8**	**19:43**	**11**	**7**	**5**	**12**	**0**	**1**	**2**	**3**	**22:21**
	NHL Totals		**282**	**71**	**94**	**165**	**96**	**21**	**7**	**12**	**534**	**13.3**		**121**	**38.8**	**16:45**	**11**	**7**	**5**	**12**	**0**	**1**	**2**	**3**	**22:21**

ECAC First All-Star Team (1995, 1996, 1997) • ECAC Player of the Year (1995) • NCAA East First All-American Team (1995, 1996, 1997) • NCAA Championship All-Tournament Team (1996)

Played in NHL All-Star Game (2003)

Signed as a free agent by **Calgary**, February 19, 1998. Signed as a free agent by **Tampa Bay**, July 31, 2000.

SAKIC, Joe (SAK-ihk, JOH) COL.

Center. Shoots left. 5'11", 195 lbs. Born, Burnaby, B.C., July 7, 1969. Quebec's 2nd choice, 15th overall, in 1987 Entry Draft.

Season	Club	League	GP	G	A	Pts	PIM	PP	SH	GW	S	%	+/-	TF	F%	Min	GP	G	A	Pts	PIM	PP	SH	GW	Min
1985-86	Burnaby	BCAHA	80	83	73	156	96																		
	Lethbridge	WHL	3	0	0	0	0																		
1986-87	Swift Current	WHL	72	60	73	133	31										4	0	1	1	0				
1987-88	Swift Current	WHL	64	*78	82	*160	64										10	11	13	24	12				
1988-89	**Quebec**	**NHL**	**70**	**23**	**39**	**62**	**24**	**10**	**0**	**2**	**148**	**15.5**	**–36**												
1989-90	**Quebec**	**NHL**	**80**	**39**	**63**	**102**	**27**	**8**	**1**	**2**	**234**	**16.7**	**–40**												
1990-91	**Quebec**	**NHL**	**80**	**48**	**61**	**109**	**24**	**12**	**3**	**7**	**245**	**19.6**	**–26**												
1991-92	**Quebec**	**NHL**	**69**	**29**	**65**	**94**	**20**	**6**	**3**	**1**	**217**	**13.4**	**5**												
1992-93	**Quebec**	**NHL**	**78**	**48**	**57**	**105**	**40**	**20**	**2**	**4**	**264**	**18.2**	**–3**				**6**	**3**	**3**	**6**	**2**	**1**	**0**	**0**	
1993-94	**Quebec**	**NHL**	**84**	**28**	**64**	**92**	**18**	**10**	**1**	**9**	**279**	**10.0**	**–8**												
1994-95	**Quebec**	**NHL**	**47**	**19**	**43**	**62**	**30**	**3**	**2**	**5**	**157**	**12.1**	**7**				**6**	**4**	**1**	**5**	**0**	**1**	**1**	**1**	
1995-96♦	**Colorado**	**NHL**	**82**	**51**	**69**	**120**	**44**	**17**	**6**	**7**	**339**	**15.0**	**14**				**22**	***18**	**16**	***34**	**14**	**6**	**0**	**6**	
1996-97	**Colorado**	**NHL**	**65**	**22**	**52**	**74**	**34**	**10**	**2**	**5**	**261**	**8.4**	**–10**				**17**	**8**	***17**	**25**	**14**	**3**	**0**	**0**	
1997-98	**Colorado**	**NHL**	**64**	**27**	**36**	**63**	**50**	**12**	**1**	**2**	**254**	**10.6**	**0**				**6**	**2**	**3**	**5**	**6**	**0**	**1**	**2**	
	Canada	Olympics	4	1	2	3	4																		
1998-99	**Colorado**	**NHL**	**73**	**41**	**55**	**96**	**29**	**12**	**5**	**6**	**255**	**16.1**	**23**	**1723**	**51.4**	**25:35**	**19**	**6**	**13**	**19**	**8**	**1**	**1**	**1**	**25:01**
99-2000	**Colorado**	**NHL**	**60**	**28**	**53**	**81**	**28**	**5**	**1**	**5**	**242**	**11.6**	**30**	**1392**	**53.8**	**23:16**	**17**	**2**	**7**	**9**	**8**	**2**	**0**	**0**	**23:50**
2000-01♦	**Colorado**	**NHL**	**82**	**54**	**64**	**118**	**30**	**19**	**3**	**12**	**332**	**16.3**	**45**	**2292**	**53.0**	**23:01**	**21**	***13**	**13**	***26**	**6**	**5**	**0**	**3**	**21:33**
2001-02	**Colorado**	**NHL**	**82**	**26**	**53**	**79**	**18**	**9**	**1**	**4**	**260**	**10.0**	**12**	**2148**	**52.2**	**22:00**	**21**	**9**	**10**	**19**	**4**	**4**	**0**	**1**	**22:44**
	Canada	Olympics	6	4	3	7	0																		
2002-03	**Colorado**	**NHL**	**58**	**26**	**32**	**58**	**24**	**8**	**0**	**1**	**190**	**13.7**	**4**	**1359**	**50.8**	**21:12**	**7**	**6**	**3**	**9**	**2**	**2**	**0**	**1**	**22:29**
	NHL Totals		**1074**	**509**	**806**	**1315**	**440**	**161**	**31**	**72**	**3677**	**13.8**		**8914**	**52.3**	**23:03**	**142**	**71**	**86**	**157**	**64**	**25**	**3**	**15**	**23:09**

WHL East Second All-Star Team (1987) • WHL East Rookie of the Year (1987) • WHL East MVP (1987) • WHL East First All-Star Team (1988) • WHL MVP (1988) • Canadian Major Junior Player of the Year (1988) • Conn Smythe Trophy (1996) • NHL First All-Star Team (2001, 2002) • Lady Byng Trophy (2001) • Lester B. Pearson Award (2001) • Hart Trophy (2001)

Played in NHL All-Star Game (1990, 1991, 1992, 1993, 1994, 1996, 1998, 2000, 2001, 2002)

Transferred to **Colorado** after **Quebec** franchise relocated, June 21, 1995.

SALEI, Ruslan (sah-LAY, roos-LAHN) ANA.

Defense. Shoots left. 6'1", 205 lbs. Born, Minsk, USSR, November 2, 1974. Anaheim's 1st choice, 9th overall, in 1996 Entry Draft.

Season	Club	League	GP	G	A	Pts	PIM	PP	SH	GW	S	%	+/-	TF	F%	Min	GP	G	A	Pts	PIM	PP	SH	GW	Min
1992-93	Dynamo Minsk	CIS	9	1	0	1	10																		
1993-94	Tivali Minsk	CIS	39	2	3	5	50																		
1994-95	Tivali Minsk	CIS	51	4	2	6	44																		
1995-96	Las Vegas	IHL	76	7	23	30	123										15	3	7	10	18				
1996-97	**Anaheim**	**NHL**	**30**	**0**	**1**	**1**	**37**	**0**	**0**	**0**	**14**	**0.0**	**–8**												
	Baltimore Bandits	AHL	12	1	4	5	12																		
	Las Vegas	IHL	8	0	2	2	24										3	2	1	3	6				
1997-98	**Anaheim**	**NHL**	**66**	**5**	**10**	**15**	**70**	**1**	**0**	**0**	**104**	**4.8**	**7**												
	Cincinnati	AHL	6	3	6	9	14																		
	Belarus	Olympics	7	1	0	1	4																		
1998-99	**Anaheim**	**NHL**	**74**	**2**	**14**	**16**	**65**	**1**	**0**	**0**	**123**	**1.6**	**1**	**0**	**0.0**	**22:03**	**3**	**0**	**0**	**0**	**4**	**0**	**0**	**0**	**15:40**
99-2000	**Anaheim**	**NHL**	**71**	**5**	**5**	**10**	**94**	**1**	**0**	**0**	**116**	**4.3**	**3**	**0**	**0.0**	**20:21**									
2000-01	**Anaheim**	**NHL**	**50**	**1**	**5**	**6**	**70**	**0**	**0**	**0**	**73**	**1.4**	**–14**	**0**	**0.0**	**20:40**									
2001-02	**Anaheim**	**NHL**	**82**	**4**	**7**	**11**	**97**	**0**	**0**	**1**	**96**	**4.2**	**–10**	**0**	**0.0**	**21:25**									
	Belarus	Olympics	6	2	1	3	4																		
2002-03	**Anaheim**	**NHL**	**61**	**4**	**8**	**12**	**78**	**0**	**0**	**0**	**93**	**4.3**	**2**	**0**	**0.0**	**21:53**	**21**	**2**	**3**	**5**	**26**	**0**	**0**	**1**	**26:05**
	NHL Totals		**434**	**21**	**50**	**71**	**511**	**3**	**0**	**1**	**619**	**3.4**		**0**	**0.0**	**21:18**	**24**	**2**	**3**	**5**	**30**	**0**	**0**	**1**	**24:47**

SALO, Sami (SA-loh, SA-mee) VAN.

Defense. Shoots right. 6'3", 215 lbs. Born, Turku, Finland, September 2, 1974. Ottawa's 7th choice, 239th overall, in 1996 Entry Draft.

Season	Club	League	GP	G	A	Pts	PIM	PP	SH	GW	S	%	+/-	TF	F%	Min	GP	G	A	Pts	PIM	PP	SH	GW	Min
1991-92	Kiekko-67 Jr.	Finn-Jr.	23	4	5	9	26																		
1992-93	Kiekko-67-B	Finn-Jr.	21	9	4	13	4																		
	Kiekko-67 Jr.	Finn-Jr.	13	6	2	8	2																		
1993-94	TPS Turku Jr.	Finn-Jr.	36	7	13	20	16										7	0	1	1	10				
1994-95	TPS Turku Jr.	Finn-Jr.	14	1	3	4	6																		
	Kiekko-67 Turku	Finland-2	19	4	2	6	4																		
	TPS Turku	Finland	7	1	2	3	8										1	0	0	0	0				
1995-96	TPS Turku	Finland	47	7	14	21	32										11	1	3	4	8				
1996-97	TPS Turku	Finland	48	9	6	15	10										10	2	3	5	4				
	TPS Turku	EuroHL	6	0	2	2	6										2	0	0	0	2				
1997-98	Jokerit Helsinki	Finland	35	3	5	8	10										8	0	1	1	2				
	Jokerit Helsinki	EuroHL	6	1	1	2	2																		
1998-99	**Ottawa**	**NHL**	**61**	**7**	**12**	**19**	**24**	**2**	**0**	**1**	**106**	**6.6**	**20**	**0**	**0.0**	**19:42**	**4**	**0**	**0**	**0**	**0**	**0**	**0**	**0**	**21:32**
	Detroit Vipers	IHL	5	0	2	2	0																		
99-2000	**Ottawa**	**NHL**	**37**	**6**	**8**	**14**	**2**	**3**	**0**	**1**	**85**	**7.1**	**6**	**0**	**0.0**	**20:18**	**6**	**1**	**1**	**2**	**0**	**1**	**0**	**0**	**24:11**
2000-01	**Ottawa**	**NHL**	**31**	**2**	**16**	**18**	**10**	**1**	**0**	**0**	**61**	**3.3**	**9**	**0**	**0.0**	**19:44**	**4**	**0**	**0**	**0**	**0**	**0**	**0**	**0**	**22:30**
2001-02	**Ottawa**	**NHL**	**66**	**4**	**14**	**18**	**14**	**1**	**1**	**2**	**122**	**3.3**	**1**	**0**	**0.0**	**19:52**	**12**	**2**	**1**	**3**	**4**	**0**	**0**	**0**	**20:22**
	Finland	Olympics	4	0	0	0	0																		
2002-03	**Vancouver**	**NHL**	**79**	**9**	**21**	**30**	**10**	**4**	**0**	**1**	**126**	**7.1**	**9**	**0**	**0.0**	**20:08**	**12**	**1**	**3**	**4**	**0**	**0**	**0**	**0**	**20:52**
	NHL Totals		**274**	**28**	**71**	**99**	**60**	**11**	**1**	**5**	**500**	**5.6**		**0**	**0.0**	**19:57**	**38**	**4**	**5**	**9**	**4**	**1**	**0**	**0**	**21:29**

NHL All-Rookie Team (1999)

• Missed majority of 1999-2000 season recovering from wrist injury suffered in game vs. Philadelphia, November 28, 1999. • Missed majority of 2000-01 season recovering from shoulder injury suffered in game vs. Atlanta, December 14, 2000. Traded to **Vancouver** by **Ottawa** for Peter Schaefer, September 21, 2002.

SALOMONSSON, Andreas

(sal-oh-MAWN-suhn, an-DRAY-uhs) **WSH.**

Right wing. Shoots left. 6'1", 200 lbs. Born, Ornskoldsvik, Sweden, December 19, 1973. New Jersey's 8th choice, 163rd overall, in 2001 Entry Draft.

Season	Club	League	GP	G	A	Pts	PIM	PP	SH	GW	S	%	+/-	TF	F%	Min	GP	G	A	Pts	PIM	PP	SH	GW	Min
			Regular Season														Playoffs								
1990-91	MoDo	Sweden	2	0	0	0	0	....	....	....	....	....	....	....	....	....	....	....	....	....	....	....	....	....	....
1991-92	MoDo	Sweden	20	1	1	2	26	....	....	....	....	....	....	....	....	....	....	....	....	....	....	....	....	....	....
1992-93	MoDo Jr.	Swede-Jr.	10	4	16	20	8	....	....	....	....	....	....	....	....	....	....	....	....	....	....	....	....	....	....
	MoDo	Sweden	33	1	1	2	0	....	....	....	....	....	....	....	....	....	....	....	....	....	....	....	....	....	....
1993-94	MoDo	Sweden	38	15	8	23	33	....	....	....	....	....	....	....	....	....	11	1	2	3	4	....	....	....	....
1994-95	MoDo	Sweden	40	5	9	14	34	....	....	....	....	....	....	....	....	....	....	....	....	....	....	....	....	....	....
1995-96	MoDo	Sweden	38	13	6	19	22	....	....	....	....	....	....	....	....	....	7	0	4	4	8	....	....	....	....
1996-97	MoDo	Sweden	23	6	6	12	22	....	....	....	....	....	....	....	....	....	....	....	....	....	....	....	....	....	....
	Ratingen	Germany	21	5	1	6	49	....	....	....	....	....	....	....	....	....	....	....	....	....	....	....	....	....	....
1997-98	MoDo	Sweden	45	6	15	21	69	....	....	....	....	....	....	....	....	....	8	4	3	7	4	....	....	....	....
1998-99	MoDo	Sweden	46	13	13	26	60	....	....	....	....	....	....	....	....	....	13	4	5	9	12	....	....	....	....
99-2000	MoDo	EuroHL	5	2	2	4	4	....	....	....	....	....	....	....	....	....	3	1	1	2	4	....	....	....	....
	MoDo	Sweden	48	9	15	24	38	....	....	....	....	....	....	....	....	....	12	0	4	4	12	....	....	....	....
2000-01	Djurgarden	Sweden	48	10	12	22	46	....	....	....	....	....	....	....	....	....	13	3	4	7	31	....	....	....	....
2001-02	**New Jersey**	**NHL**	**39**	**4**	**5**	**9**	**22**	**1**	**0**	**1**	**58**	**6.9**	**–12**	**6**	**33.3**	**13:30**	**4**	**0**	**1**	**1**	**0**	**0**	**0**	**0**	**12:15**
	Albany River Rats	AHL	19	3	10	13	6	....	....	....	....	....	....	....	....	....	....	....	....	....	....	....	....	....	....
2002-03	**Washington**	**NHL**	**32**	**1**	**4**	**5**	**14**	**0**	**0**	**0**	**20**	**5.0**	**–1**	**29**	**37.9**	**8:50**	....	....	....	....	....	....	....	....	....
	Portland Pirates	AHL	31	7	17	24	23	....	....	....	....	....	....	....	....	....	3	4	0	4	0	....	....	....	....
	NHL Totals		**71**	**5**	**9**	**14**	**36**	**1**	**0**	**1**	**78**	**6.4**		**35**	**37.1**	**11:24**	**4**	**0**	**1**	**1**	**0**	**0**	**0**	**0**	**12:15**

Claimed on waivers by **Washington** from **New Jersey**, October 15, 2002.

SALVADOR, Bryce

(SAL-vuh-dohr, BRIGHS) **ST.L.**

Defense. Shoots left. 6'2", 215 lbs. Born, Brandon, Man., February 11, 1976. Tampa Bay's 6th choice, 138th overall, in 1994 Entry Draft.

Season	Club	League	GP	G	A	Pts	PIM	PP	SH	GW	S	%	+/-	TF	F%	Min	GP	G	A	Pts	PIM	PP	SH	GW	Min
1991-92	Brandon	MAHA	52	6	23	29	38	....	....	....	....	....	....	....	....	....	....	....	....	....	....	....	....	....	....
1992-93	Lethbridge	WHL	64	1	4	5	29	....	....	....	....	....	....	....	....	....	4	0	0	0	0	....	....	....	....
1993-94	Lethbridge	WHL	61	4	14	18	36	....	....	....	....	....	....	....	....	....	9	0	1	1	2	....	....	....	....
1994-95	Lethbridge	WHL	67	1	9	10	88	....	....	....	....	....	....	....	....	....	....	....	....	....	....	....	....	....	....
1995-96	Lethbridge	WHL	56	4	12	16	75	....	....	....	....	....	....	....	....	....	3	0	1	1	2	....	....	....	....
1996-97	Lethbridge	WHL	63	8	32	40	81	....	....	....	....	....	....	....	....	....	19	0	7	7	14	....	....	....	....
1997-98	Worcester IceCats	AHL	46	2	8	10	74	....	....	....	....	....	....	....	....	....	11	0	1	1	45	....	....	....	....
1998-99	Worcester IceCats	AHL	69	5	13	18	129	....	....	....	....	....	....	....	....	....	4	0	1	1	2	....	....	....	....
99-2000	Worcester IceCats	AHL	55	0	13	13	53	....	....	....	....	....	....	....	....	....	9	0	1	1	2	....	....	....	....
2000-01	**St. Louis**	**NHL**	**75**	**2**	**8**	**10**	**69**	**0**	**0**	**1**	**60**	**3.3**	**–4**	**1**	**0.0**	**16:38**	**14**	**2**	**0**	**2**	**18**	**0**	**0**	**1**	**14:41**
2001-02	**St. Louis**	**NHL**	**66**	**5**	**7**	**12**	**78**	**1**	**0**	**2**	**37**	**13.5**	**3**	**0**	**0.0**	**16:55**	**10**	**0**	**1**	**1**	**4**	**0**	**0**	**0**	**12:34**
2002-03	**St. Louis**	**NHL**	**71**	**2**	**8**	**10**	**95**	**1**	**0**	**0**	**73**	**2.7**	**7**	**0**	**0.0**	**18:57**	**7**	**0**	**0**	**0**	**2**	**0**	**0**	**0**	**17:17**
	NHL Totals		**212**	**9**	**23**	**32**	**242**	**2**	**0**	**3**	**170**	**5.3**		**1**	**0.0**	**17:30**	**31**	**2**	**1**	**3**	**24**	**0**	**0**	**1**	**14:35**

Signed as a free agent by **St. Louis**, December 16, 1996.

SAMSONOV, Sergei

(sam-SAWN-nahf, SAIR-gay) **BOS.**

Left wing. Shoots right. 5'8", 194 lbs. Born, Moscow, USSR, October 27, 1978. Boston's 2nd choice, 8th overall, in 1997 Entry Draft.

Season	Club	League	GP	G	A	Pts	PIM	PP	SH	GW	S	%	+/-	TF	F%	Min	GP	G	A	Pts	PIM	PP	SH	GW	Min
1994-95	CSKA Moscow Jr.	CIS-Jr.	50	110	72	182		....	....	....	....	....	....	....	....	....	....	....	....	....	....	....	....	....	....
	CSKA Moscow	CIS	13	2	2	4	14	....	....	....	....	....	....	....	....	....	2	0	0	0	0	....	....	....	....
1995-96	CSKA Moscow	CIS	51	21	17	38	12	....	....	....	....	....	....	....	....	....	3	1	1	2	4	....	....	....	....
1996-97	Detroit Vipers	IHL	73	29	35	64	18	....	....	....	....	....	....	....	....	....	19	8	4	12	12	....	....	....	....
1997-98	**Boston**	**NHL**	**81**	**22**	**25**	**47**	**8**	**7**	**0**	**3**	**159**	**13.8**	**9**	....	....	....	**6**	**2**	**5**	**7**	**0**	**0**	**0**	**1**	....
1998-99	**Boston**	**NHL**	**79**	**25**	**26**	**51**	**18**	**6**	**0**	**8**	**160**	**15.6**	**–6**	**0**	**0.0**	**16:23**	**11**	**3**	**1**	**4**	**0**	**0**	**0**	**0**	**16:11**
99-2000	**Boston**	**NHL**	**77**	**19**	**26**	**45**	**4**	**6**	**0**	**3**	**145**	**13.1**	**–6**	**3**	**0.0**	**16:32**	....	....	....	....	....	....	....	....	....
2000-01	**Boston**	**NHL**	**82**	**29**	**46**	**75**	**18**	**3**	**0**	**3**	**215**	**13.5**	**6**	**14**	**42.9**	**19:23**	....	....	....	....	....	....	....	....	....
2001-02	**Boston**	**NHL**	**74**	**29**	**41**	**70**	**27**	**3**	**0**	**4**	**192**	**15.1**	**21**	**1**	**0.0**	**18:47**	**6**	**2**	**2**	**4**	**0**	**0**	**0**	**0**	**17:41**
	Russia	Olympics	6	1	2	3	4	....	....	....	....	....	....	....	....	....	....	....	....	....	....	....	....	....	....
2002-03	**Boston**	**NHL**	**8**	**5**	**6**	**11**	**2**	**1**	**0**	**3**	**23**	**21.7**	**8**	**0**	**0.0**	**20:20**	**5**	**0**	**2**	**2**	**0**	**0**	**0**	**0**	**17:07**
	NHL Totals		**401**	**129**	**170**	**299**	**77**	**26**	**0**	**24**	**894**	**14.4**		**18**	**33.3**	**17:50**	**28**	**7**	**10**	**17**	**0**	**0**	**0**	**1**	**16:48**

Garry F. Longman Memorial Trophy (Top Rookie – IHL) (1997) • NHL All-Rookie Team (1998) • Calder Memorial Trophy (1998)

Played in NHL All-Star Game (2001)

• Missed majority of 2002-03 season recovering from wrist injury suffered in game vs. Columbus, October 18, 2002.

SAMUELSSON, Martin

(SAM-yuhl-suhn, MAHR-tihn) **BOS.**

Right wing. Shoots left. 6'2", 200 lbs. Born, Upplands Vasby, Sweden, January 25, 1982. Boston's 2nd choice, 27th overall, in 2000 Entry Draft.

Season	Club	League	GP	G	A	Pts	PIM	PP	SH	GW	S	%	+/-	TF	F%	Min	GP	G	A	Pts	PIM	PP	SH	GW	Min
1996-97	Hammarby Jr.	Swede-Jr.	6	1	1	2	0	....	....	....	....	....	....	....	....	....	....	....	....	....	....	....	....	....	....
1997-98	Hammarby Jr.	Swede-Jr.	20	13	12	25	....	....	....	....	....	....	....	....	....	....	....	....	....	....	....	....	....	....	....
	Hammarby	Swede-2	2	0	0	0	0	....	....	....	....	....	....	....	....	....	....	....	....	....	....	....	....	....	....
1998-99	MoDo Jr.	Swede-Jr.	31	18	13	31	10	....	....	....	....	....	....	....	....	....	....	....	....	....	....	....	....	....	....
99-2000	MoDo-18	Swede-Jr.	6	3	0	3	4	....	....	....	....	....	....	....	....	....	....	....	....	....	....	....	....	....	....
	MoDo Jr.	Swede-Jr.	19	9	8	17	18	....	....	....	....	....	....	....	....	....	2	1	0	1	2	....	....	....	....
2000-01	Hammarby	Swede-Q	14	2	2	4	10	....	....	....	....	....	....	....	....	....	....	....	....	....	....	....	....	....	....
	Hammarby	Swede-2	24	13	4	17	8	....	....	....	....	....	....	....	....	....	5	0	0	0	2	....	....	....	....
	Hammarby Jr.	Swede-Jr.	1	0	1	1	0	....	....	....	....	....	....	....	....	....	....	....	....	....	....	....	....	....	....
2001-02	Hammarby Jr.	Swede-Jr.	2	5	2	7	2	....	....	....	....	....	....	....	....	....	....	....	....	....	....	....	....	....	....
	Hammarby	Swede-2	44	13	10	23	45	....	....	....	....	....	....	....	....	....	2	0	0	0	2	....	....	....	....
	Hammarby	Swede-Q	10	3	1	4	10	....	....	....	....	....	....	....	....	....	....	....	....	....	....	....	....	....	....
2002-03	**Boston**	**NHL**	**8**	**0**	**1**	**1**	**2**	**0**	**0**	**0**	**3**	**0.0**	**–1**	**0**	**0.0**	**11:42**	....	....	....	....	....	....	....	....	....
	Providence Bruins	AHL	64	24	15	39	34	....	....	....	....	....	....	....	....	....	4	0	0	0	0	....	....	....	....
	NHL Totals		**8**	**0**	**1**	**1**	**2**	**0**	**0**	**0**	**3**	**0.0**		**0**	**0.0**	**11:42**	....	....	....	....	....	....	....	....	....

SAMUELSSON, Mikael

(SAM-yuhl-suhn, MIH-kigh-ehl) **FLA.**

Right wing. Shoots left. 6'2", 211 lbs. Born, Mariefred, Sweden, December 23, 1976. San Jose's 7th choice, 145th overall, in 1998 Entry Draft.

Season	Club	League	GP	G	A	Pts	PIM	PP	SH	GW	S	%	+/-	TF	F%	Min	GP	G	A	Pts	PIM	PP	SH	GW	Min
1994-95	Sodertalje SK Jr.	Swede-Jr.	30	8	6	14	12	....	....	....	....	....	....	....	....	....	....	....	....	....	....	....	....	....	....
1995-96	Sodertalje SK Jr.	Swede-Jr.	22	13	12	25	20	....	....	....	....	....	....	....	....	....	....	....	....	....	....	....	....	....	....
	Sodertalje SK	Swede-2	18	5	1	6	0	....	....	....	....	....	....	....	....	....	4	0	0	0	0	....	....	....	....
1996-97	Sodertalje SK Jr.	Swede-Jr.	2	2	1	3	....	....	....	....	....	....	....	....	....	....	....	....	....	....	....	....	....	....	....
	Sodertalje SK	Sweden	29	3	2	5	10	....	....	....	....	....	....	....	....	....	10	0	0	0	4	....	....	....	....
1997-98	IK Nykopings	Swede-2	10	5	1	6	14	....	....	....	....	....	....	....	....	....	....	....	....	....	....	....	....	....	....
	Sodertalje SK	Sweden	41	11	9	20	66	....	....	....	....	....	....	....	....	....	....	....	....	....	....	....	....	....	....
1998-99	Sodertalje SK	Swede-2	18	13	10	23	26	....	....	....	....	....	....	....	....	....	10	2	2	4	12	....	....	....	....
	Vastra Frolunda	Sweden	27	0	5	5	10	....	....	....	....	....	....	....	....	....	....	....	....	....	....	....	....	....	....
99-2000	Brynas IF Gavle	Sweden	40	4	3	7	76	....	....	....	....	....	....	....	....	....	11	7	2	9	6	....	....	....	....
	Brynas IF Gavle	EuroHL	4	0	2	2	4	....	....	....	....	....	....	....	....	....	....	....	....	....	....	....	....	....	....
2000-01	**San Jose**	**NHL**	**4**	**0**	**0**	**0**	**0**	**0**	**0**	**0**	**3**	**0.0**	**0**	**0**	**0.0**	**4:41**	....	....	....	....	....	....	....	....	....
	Kentucky	AHL	66	32	46	78	58	....	....	....	....	....	....	....	....	....	3	1	0	1	0	....	....	....	....
2001-02	**NY Rangers**	**NHL**	**67**	**6**	**10**	**16**	**23**	**1**	**2**	**1**	**94**	**6.4**	**10**	**5**	**40.0**	**11:52**	....	....	....	....	....	....	....	....	....
	Hartford	AHL	8	3	6	9	12	....	....	....	....	....	....	....	....	....	....	....	....	....	....	....	....	....	....
2002-03	**NY Rangers**	**NHL**	**58**	**8**	**14**	**22**	**32**	**1**	**1**	**2**	**118**	**6.8**	**0**	**35**	**42.9**	**15:32**	....	....	....	....	....	....	....	....	....
	Pittsburgh	**NHL**	**22**	**2**	**0**	**2**	**8**	**1**	**0**	**0**	**36**	**5.6**	**–21**	**8**	**75.0**	**14:04**	....	....	....	....	....	....	....	....	....
	NHL Totals		**151**	**16**	**24**	**40**	**63**	**3**	**3**	**3**	**251**	**6.4**		**48**	**47.9**	**13:24**	....	....	....	....	....	....	....	....	....

Traded to **NY Rangers** by **San Jose** with Christian Gosselin for Adam Graves and future considerations, June 24, 2001. Traded to **Pittsburgh** by **NY Rangers** with Joel Bouchard, Richard Lintner and Rico Fata for Mike Wilson, Alex Kovalev, Janne Laukkanen and Dan LaCouture, February 10, 2003. Traded to **Florida** by **Pittsburgh** with Pittsburgh's 1st round choice (Nathan Horton) and 2nd round compensatory choice (Stefan Meyer) in 2003 Entry Draft for Florida's 1st (Marc-Andre Fleury) and 3rd (Daniel Carcillo) round choices in 2003 Entry Draft, June 21, 2003.

			Regular Season														Playoffs								
Season	Club	League	GP	G	A	Pts	PIM	PP	SH	GW	S	%	+/-	TF	F%	Min	GP	G	A	Pts	PIM	PP	SH	GW	Min

SANDERSON, Geoff

(SAN-duhr-sohn, JEHF) **CBJ**

Left wing. Shoots left. 6', 190 lbs. Born, Hay River, N.W.T., February 1, 1972. Hartford's 2nd choice, 36th overall, in 1990 Entry Draft.

Season	Club	League	GP	G	A	Pts	PIM	PP	SH	GW	S	%	+/-	TF	F%	Min	GP	G	A	Pts	PIM	PP	SH	GW	Min
1987-88	St. Albert Royals	AMHL	45	65	55	120	175	....	....	....	....	....	....	....	....	....	....	....	....	....	....	....	....	....	....
1988-89	Swift Current	WHL	58	17	11	28	16	....	....	....	....	....	....	....	....	....	12	3	5	8	6	....	....	....	....
1989-90	Swift Current	WHL	70	32	62	94	56	....	....	....	....	....	....	....	....	....	4	1	4	5	8	....	....	....	....
1990-91	Swift Current	WHL	70	62	50	112	57	....	....	....	....	....	....	....	....	....	3	1	2	3	4	....	....	....	....
	Hartford	**NHL**	**2**	**1**	**0**	**1**	**0**	**0**	**0**	**0**	**2**	**50.0**	**–2**	....	....	....	**3**	**0**	**0**	**0**	**0**	**0**	**0**	**0**	....
	Springfield	AHL	....	....	....	....	....	....	....	....	....	....	....	....	....	....	1	0	0	0	2	....	....	....	....
1991-92	**Hartford**	**NHL**	**64**	**13**	**18**	**31**	**18**	**2**	**0**	**1**	**98**	**13.3**	**5**	....	....	....	**7**	**1**	**0**	**1**	**2**	**0**	**0**	**0**	....
1992-93	**Hartford**	**NHL**	**82**	**46**	**43**	**89**	**28**	**21**	**2**	**4**	**271**	**17.0**	**–21**	....	....	....	....	....	....	....	....	....	....	....	....
1993-94	**Hartford**	**NHL**	**82**	**41**	**26**	**67**	**42**	**15**	**1**	**6**	**266**	**15.4**	**–13**	....	....	....	....	....	....	....	....	....	....	....	....
1994-95	HPK Hameenlinna	Finland	12	6	4	10	24	....	....	....	....	....	....	....	....	....	....	....	....	....	....	....	....	....	....
	Hartford	**NHL**	**46**	**18**	**14**	**32**	**24**	**4**	**0**	**4**	**170**	**10.6**	**–10**	....	....	....	....	....	....	....	....	....	....	....	....
1995-96	**Hartford**	**NHL**	**81**	**34**	**31**	**65**	**40**	**6**	**0**	**7**	**314**	**10.8**	**0**	....	....	....	....	....	....	....	....	....	....	....	....
1996-97	**Hartford**	**NHL**	**82**	**36**	**31**	**67**	**29**	**12**	**1**	**4**	**297**	**12.1**	**–9**	....	....	....	....	....	....	....	....	....	....	....	....
1997-98	**Carolina**	**NHL**	**40**	**7**	**10**	**17**	**14**	**2**	**0**	**0**	**96**	**7.3**	**–4**	....	....	....	....	....	....	....	....	....	....	....	....
	Vancouver	**NHL**	**9**	**0**	**3**	**3**	**4**	**0**	**0**	**0**	**29**	**0.0**	**–1**	....	....	....	....	....	....	....	....	....	....	....	....
	Buffalo	**NHL**	**26**	**4**	**5**	**9**	**20**	**0**	**0**	**2**	**72**	**5.6**	**6**	....	....	....	**14**	**3**	**1**	**4**	**4**	**1**	**0**	**1**	....
1998-99	**Buffalo**	**NHL**	**75**	**12**	**18**	**30**	**22**	**1**	**0**	**1**	**155**	**7.7**	**8**	**4**	**50.0**	**12:55**	**19**	**4**	**6**	**10**	**14**	**0**	**0**	**1**	**13:52**
99-2000	**Buffalo**	**NHL**	**67**	**13**	**13**	**26**	**22**	**4**	**0**	**3**	**136**	**9.6**	**4**	**3**	**100.0**	**12:54**	**5**	**0**	**2**	**2**	**8**	**0**	**0**	**0**	**12:16**
2000-01	**Columbus**	**NHL**	**68**	**30**	**26**	**56**	**46**	**9**	**0**	**7**	**199**	**15.1**	**4**	**726**	**49.0**	**16:37**	....	....	....	....	....	....	....	....	....
2001-02	**Columbus**	**NHL**	**42**	**11**	**5**	**16**	**12**	**5**	**0**	**2**	**112**	**9.8**	**–15**	**322**	**42.9**	**16:50**	....	....	....	....	....	....	....	....	....
2002-03	**Columbus**	**NHL**	**82**	**34**	**33**	**67**	**34**	**15**	**2**	**2**	**286**	**11.9**	**–4**	**96**	**41.7**	**18:44**	....	....	....	....	....	....	....	....	....
	NHL Totals		**848**	**300**	**276**	**576**	**355**	**96**	**6**	**43**	**2503**	**12.0**		**1151**	**46.8**	**15:35**	**48**	**8**	**9**	**17**	**28**	**1**	**0**	**2**	**13:32**

Played in NHL All-Star Game (1994, 1997)

Transferred to **Carolina** after **Hartford** franchise relocated, June 25, 1997. Traded to **Vancouver** by **Carolina** with Sean Burke and Enrico Ciccone for Kirk McLean and Martin Gelinas, January 3, 1998. Traded to **Buffalo** by **Vancouver** for Brad May and Buffalo's 3rd round choice (later traded to Tampa Bay – Tampa Bay selected Jimmie Olvestad) in 1999 Entry Draft, February 4, 1998. Selected by **Columbus** from **Buffalo** in Expansion Draft, June 23, 2000.

SAPRYKIN, Oleg

(sah-PRIH-kihn, OH-lehg) **CGY.**

Left wing. Shoots left. 6', 195 lbs. Born, Moscow, USSR, February 12, 1981. Calgary's 1st choice, 11th overall, in 1999 Entry Draft.

Season	Club	League	GP	G	A	Pts	PIM	PP	SH	GW	S	%	+/-	TF	F%	Min	GP	G	A	Pts	PIM	PP	SH	GW	Min
1997-98	HC CSKA 2	Russia-3	15	0	3	3	6	....	....	....	....	....	....	....	....	....	....	....	....	....	....	....	....	....	....
	HC CSKA	Russia	20	0	2	2	8	....	....	....	....	....	....	....	....	....	....	....	....	....	....	....	....	....	....
1998-99	Seattle	WHL	66	47	46	93	107	....	....	....	....	....	....	....	....	....	11	5	11	16	36	....	....	....	....
99-2000	**Calgary**	**NHL**	**4**	**0**	**1**	**1**	**2**	**0**	**0**	**0**	**2**	**0.0**	**–4**	**0**	**0.0**	**12:35**	....	....	....	....	....	....	....	....	....
	Seattle	WHL	48	30	36	66	91	....	....	....	....	....	....	....	....	....	6	3	3	6	37	....	....	....	....
2000-01	**Calgary**	**NHL**	**59**	**9**	**14**	**23**	**43**	**2**	**0**	**0**	**95**	**9.5**	**4**	**2**	**50.0**	**12:10**	....	....	....	....	....	....	....	....	....
2001-02	**Calgary**	**NHL**	**3**	**0**	**0**	**0**	**0**	**0**	**0**	**0**	**9**	**0.0**	**–2**	**0**	**0.0**	**13:25**	....	....	....	....	....	....	....	....	....
	Saint John Flames	AHL	52	5	19	24	53	....	....	....	....	....	....	....	....	....	....	....	....	....	....	....	....	....	....
2002-03	**Calgary**	**NHL**	**52**	**8**	**15**	**23**	**46**	**1**	**0**	**1**	**116**	**6.9**	**5**	**1**	**0.0**	**11:53**	....	....	....	....	....	....	....	....	....
	Saint John Flames	AHL	21	12	9	21	22	....	....	....	....	....	....	....	....	....	....	....	....	....	....	....	....	....	....
	NHL Totals		**118**	**17**	**30**	**47**	**91**	**3**	**0**	**1**	**222**	**7.7**		**3**	**33.3**	**12:06**	....	....	....	....	....	....	....	....	....

WHL West Second All-Star Team (1999, 2000)

SARAULT, Yves

(sah-ROH, EEV)

Left wing. Shoots left. 6'1", 190 lbs. Born, Valleyfield, Que., December 23, 1972. Montreal's 4th choice, 61st overall, in 1991 Entry Draft.

Season	Club	League	GP	G	A	Pts	PIM	PP	SH	GW	S	%	+/-	TF	F%	Min	GP	G	A	Pts	PIM	PP	SH	GW	Min
1987-88	Lac St-Louis Lions	QAAA	4	0	0	0	4	....	....	....	....	....	....	....	....	....	....	....	....	....	....	....	....	....	....
1988-89	Lac St-Louis Lions	QAAA	42	23	30	53	64	....	....	....	....	....	....	....	....	....	3	2	3	5	4	....	....	....	....
1989-90	Victoriaville Tigres	QMJHL	70	12	28	40	140	....	....	....	....	....	....	....	....	....	16	0	3	3	26	....	....	....	....
1990-91	St-Jean Lynx	QMJHL	56	22	24	46	113	....	....	....	....	....	....	....	....	....	....	....	....	....	....	....	....	....	....
1991-92	St-Jean Lynx	QMJHL	50	28	38	66	96	....	....	....	....	....	....	....	....	....	....	....	....	....	....	....	....	....	....
	Trois-Rivieres	QMJHL	18	15	14	29	12	....	....	....	....	....	....	....	....	....	15	10	10	20	18	....	....	....	....
1992-93	Fredericton	AHL	59	14	17	31	41	....	....	....	....	....	....	....	....	....	3	0	1	1	2	....	....	....	....
	Wheeling	ECHL	2	1	3	4	0	....	....	....	....	....	....	....	....	....	....	....	....	....	....	....	....	....	....
1993-94	Fredericton	AHL	60	13	14	27	72	....	....	....	....	....	....	....	....	....	....	....	....	....	....	....	....	....	....
1994-95	Fredericton	AHL	69	24	21	45	96	....	....	....	....	....	....	....	....	....	13	2	1	3	33	....	....	....	....
	Montreal	**NHL**	**8**	**0**	**1**	**1**	**0**	**0**	**0**	**0**	**9**	**0.0**	**–1**	....	....	....	....	....	....	....	....	....	....	....	....
1995-96	**Montreal**	**NHL**	**14**	**0**	**0**	**0**	**4**	**0**	**0**	**0**	**14**	**0.0**	**–7**	....	....	....	....	....	....	....	....	....	....	....	....
	Calgary	**NHL**	**11**	**2**	**1**	**3**	**4**	**0**	**0**	**1**	**12**	**16.7**	**–2**	....	....	....	....	....	....	....	....	....	....	....	....
	Saint John Flames	AHL	26	10	12	22	34	....	....	....	....	....	....	....	....	....	16	6	2	8	33	....	....	....	....
1996-97	**Colorado**	**NHL**	**28**	**2**	**1**	**3**	**6**	**0**	**0**	**0**	**41**	**4.9**	**0**	....	....	....	**5**	**0**	**0**	**0**	**2**	**0**	**0**	**0**	....
	Hershey Bears	AHL	6	2	3	5	8	....	....	....	....	....	....	....	....	....	....	....	....	....	....	....	....	....	....
1997-98	**Colorado**	**NHL**	**2**	**1**	**0**	**1**	**0**	**0**	**0**	**0**	**1**	**100.0**	**1**	....	....	....	....	....	....	....	....	....	....	....	....
	Hershey Bears	AHL	63	23	36	59	43	....	....	....	....	....	....	....	....	....	7	1	2	3	14	....	....	....	....
1998-99	**Ottawa**	**NHL**	**11**	**0**	**1**	**1**	**4**	**0**	**0**	**0**	**7**	**0.0**	**1**	**0**	**0.0**	**7:15**	....	....	....	....	....	....	....	....	....
	Detroit Vipers	IHL	36	11	12	23	52	....	....	....	....	....	....	....	....	....	11	7	2	9	40	....	....	....	....
99-2000	**Ottawa**	**NHL**	**11**	**0**	**2**	**2**	**7**	**0**	**0**	**0**	**13**	**0.0**	**–3**	**1**	**0.0**	**9:03**	....	....	....	....	....	....	....	....	....
	Grand Rapids	IHL	62	17	26	43	77	....	....	....	....	....	....	....	....	....	17	7	4	11	32	....	....	....	....
2000-01	**Atlanta**	**NHL**	**20**	**5**	**4**	**9**	**26**	**2**	**0**	**0**	**44**	**11.4**	**–9**	**2**	**50.0**	**13:08**	....	....	....	....	....	....	....	....	....
	Orlando	IHL	35	17	17	34	42	....	....	....	....	....	....	....	....	....	....	....	....	....	....	....	....	....	....
2001-02	**Nashville**	**NHL**	**1**	**0**	**0**	**0**	**0**	**0**	**0**	**0**	**0**	**0.0**	**0**	**0**	**0.0**	**5:15**	....	....	....	....	....	....	....	....	....
	Milwaukee	AHL	27	5	5	10	24	....	....	....	....	....	....	....	....	....	....	....	....	....	....	....	....	....	....
	Philadelphia	AHL	7	0	2	2	9	....	....	....	....	....	....	....	....	....	5	0	0	0	6	....	....	....	....
2002-03	Springfield	AHL	4	1	1	2	10	....	....	....	....	....	....	....	....	....	....	....	....	....	....	....	....	....	....
	Thetford Mines	QSPHL	7	4	9	13	6	....	....	....	....	....	....	....	....	....	....	....	....	....	....	....	....	....	....
	SC Bern	Swiss	14	4	10	14	59	....	....	....	....	....	....	....	....	....	13	4	6	10	26	....	....	....	....
	NHL Totals		**106**	**10**	**10**	**20**	**51**	**2**	**0**	**1**	**141**	**7.1**		**3**	**33.3**	**10:24**	**5**	**0**	**0**	**0**	**2**	**0**	**0**	**0**	....

QMJHL Second All-Star Team (1992)

Traded to **Calgary** by **Montreal** with Craig Ferguson for Calgary's 8th round choice (Petr Kubos) in 1997 Entry Draft, November 26, 1995. Signed as a free agent by **Colorado**, September 13, 1996. Signed as a free agent by **Ottawa**, August 7, 1998. Signed as a free agent by **Atlanta**, July 20, 2000. Claimed on waivers by **Nashville** from **Atlanta**, June 19, 2001. Traded to **Philadelphia** by **Nashville** for Petr Hubacek and Jason Beckett, January 11, 2002. Signed as a free agent by **Thetford Mines** (QSPHL) following release by Springfield (AHL), November 10, 2002. Signed as a free agent by **HC Bern** (Swiss), January 19, 2003.

SARICH, Cory

(SAHR-ihch, KOH-ree) **T.B.**

Defense. Shoots right. 6'3", 204 lbs. Born, Saskatoon, Sask., August 16, 1978. Buffalo's 2nd choice, 27th overall, in 1996 Entry Draft.

Season	Club	League	GP	G	A	Pts	PIM	PP	SH	GW	S	%	+/-	TF	F%	Min	GP	G	A	Pts	PIM	PP	SH	GW	Min
1994-95	Sask. Contacts	SMHL	31	5	22	27	99	....	....	....	....	....	....	....	....	....	....	....	....	....	....	....	....	....	....
	Saskatoon Blades	WHL	6	0	0	0	4	....	....	....	....	....	....	....	....	....	3	0	1	1	0	....	....	....	....
1995-96	Saskatoon Blades	WHL	59	5	18	23	54	....	....	....	....	....	....	....	....	....	3	0	0	0	4	....	....	....	....
1996-97	Saskatoon Blades	WHL	58	6	27	33	158	....	....	....	....	....	....	....	....	....	....	....	....	....	....	....	....	....	....
1997-98	Saskatoon Blades	WHL	33	5	24	29	90	....	....	....	....	....	....	....	....	....	....	....	....	....	....	....	....	....	....
	Seattle	WHL	13	3	16	19	47	....	....	....	....	....	....	....	....	....	....	....	....	....	....	....	....	....	....
1998-99	**Buffalo**	**NHL**	**4**	**0**	**0**	**0**	**0**	**0**	**0**	**0**	**2**	**0.0**	**3**	**0**	**0.0**	**13:11**	....	....	....	....	....	....	....	....	....
	Rochester	AHL	77	3	26	29	82	....	....	....	....	....	....	....	....	....	20	2	4	6	14	....	....	....	....
99-2000	**Buffalo**	**NHL**	**42**	**0**	**4**	**4**	**35**	**0**	**0**	**0**	**49**	**0.0**	**2**	**0**	**0.0**	**17:42**	....	....	....	....	....	....	....	....	....
	Rochester	AHL	15	0	6	6	44	....	....	....	....	....	....	....	....	....	....	....	....	....	....	....	....	....	....
	Tampa Bay	**NHL**	**17**	**0**	**2**	**2**	**42**	**0**	**0**	**0**	**20**	**0.0**	**–8**	**0**	**0.0**	**20:42**	....	....	....	....	....	....	....	....	....
2000-01	**Tampa Bay**	**NHL**	**73**	**1**	**8**	**9**	**106**	**0**	**0**	**1**	**66**	**1.5**	**–25**	**3**	**0.0**	**18:44**	....	....	....	....	....	....	....	....	....
	Detroit Vipers	IHL	3	0	2	2	2	....	....	....	....	....	....	....	....	....	....	....	....	....	....	....	....	....	....
2001-02	**Tampa Bay**	**NHL**	**72**	**0**	**11**	**11**	**105**	**0**	**0**	**0**	**55**	**0.0**	**–4**	**2**	**50.0**	**16:06**	....	....	....	....	....	....	....	....	....
	Springfield	AHL	2	0	0	0	0	....	....	....	....	....	....	....	....	....	....	....	....	....	....	....	....	....	....
2002-03	**Tampa Bay**	**NHL**	**82**	**5**	**9**	**14**	**63**	**0**	**0**	**2**	**79**	**6.3**	**–3**	**3**	**0.0**	**19:36**	**11**	**0**	**2**	**2**	**6**	**0**	**0**	**0**	**21:18**
	NHL Totals		**290**	**6**	**34**	**40**	**351**	**0**	**0**	**3**	**271**	**2.2**		**8**	**12.5**	**18:13**	**11**	**0**	**2**	**2**	**6**	**0**	**0**	**0**	**21:18**

WHL West Second All-Star Team (1998)

Traded to **Tampa Bay** by **Buffalo** with Wayne Primeau, Brian Holzinger and Buffalo's 3rd round choice (Alexander Kharitonov) in 2000 Entry Draft for Chris Gratton and Tampa Bay's 2nd round choice (Derek Roy) in 2001 Entry Draft, March 9, 2000.

SATAN, Miroslav
(SHA-tuhn, MEER-oh-slahv) **BUF.**

Left wing. Shoots left. 6'3", 190 lbs. Born, Topolcany, Czech., October 22, 1974. Edmonton's 6th choice, 111th overall, in 1993 Entry Draft.

			Regular Season														Playoffs								
Season	Club	League	GP	G	A	Pts	PIM	PP	SH	GW	S	%	+/-	TF	F%	Min	GP	G	A	Pts	PIM	PP	SH	GW	Min
1991-92	VTJ Topolcany Jr.	Czech-Jr.	31	30	22	52	....	....	....	....	....	....	....	....	....	....	....	....	....	....	....	....	....	....	....
	VTJ Topolcany	Czech-2	9	2	1	3	6	....	....	....	....	....	....	....	....	....	....	....	....	....	....	....	....	....	....
1992-93	Dukla Trencin	Czech	38	11	6	17	....	....	....	....	....	....	....	....	....	....	....	....	....	....	....	....	....	....	....
1993-94	Dukla Trencin	Slovakia	30	32	16	48	16	....	....	....	....	....	....	....	....	....	....	....	....	....	....	....	....	....	....
	Slovakia	Olympics	8	*9	0	9	0	....	....	....	....	....	....	....	....	....	....	....	....	....	....	....	....	....	....
1994-95	Cape Breton	AHL	25	24	16	40	15	....	....	....	....	....	....	....	....	....	....	....	....	....	....	....	....	....	....
	Detroit Vipers	IHL	8	1	3	4	4	....	....	....	....	....	....	....	....	....	....	....	....	....	....	....	....	....	....
	San Diego Gulls	IHL	6	0	2	2	6	....	....	....	....	....	....	....	....	....	....	....	....	....	....	....	....	....	....
1995-96	**Edmonton**	**NHL**	**62**	**18**	**17**	**35**	**22**	**6**	**0**	**4**	**113**	**15.9**	**0**	....	....	....	....	....	....	....	....	....	....	....	....
1996-97	**Edmonton**	**NHL**	**64**	**17**	**11**	**28**	**22**	**5**	**0**	**2**	**90**	**18.9**	**–4**	....	....	....	....	....	....	....	....	....	....	....	....
	Buffalo	**NHL**	**12**	**8**	**2**	**10**	**4**	**2**	**0**	**1**	**29**	**27.6**	**1**	....	....	....	**7**	**0**	**0**	**0**	**0**	**0**	**0**	**0**	....
1997-98	**Buffalo**	**NHL**	**79**	**22**	**24**	**46**	**34**	**9**	**0**	**4**	**139**	**15.8**	**2**	....	....	....	**14**	**5**	**4**	**9**	**4**	**4**	**0**	**1**	....
1998-99	**Buffalo**	**NHL**	**81**	**40**	**26**	**66**	**44**	**13**	**3**	**6**	**208**	**19.2**	**24**	**9**	**55.6**	**20:49**	**12**	**3**	**5**	**8**	**2**	**1**	**0**	**1**	**21:18**
99-2000	Dukla Trencin	Slovakia	3	2	8	10	2	....	....	....	....	....	....	....	....	....	....	....	....	....	....	....	....	....	....
	Buffalo	**NHL**	**81**	**33**	**34**	**67**	**32**	**5**	**3**	**5**	**265**	**12.5**	**16**	**7**	**14.3**	**20:35**	**5**	**3**	**2**	**5**	**0**	**0**	**0**	**0**	**19:52**
2000-01	**Buffalo**	**NHL**	**82**	**29**	**33**	**62**	**36**	**8**	**2**	**4**	**206**	**14.1**	**5**	**11**	**36.4**	**19:56**	**13**	**3**	**10**	**13**	**8**	**1**	**0**	**0**	**21:18**
2001-02	**Buffalo**	**NHL**	**82**	**37**	**36**	**73**	**33**	**15**	**5**	**5**	**267**	**13.9**	**14**	**4**	**50.0**	**21:10**	....	....	....	....	....	....	....	....	....
	Slovakia	Olympics	2	0	1	1	0	....	....	....	....	....	....	....	....	....	....	....	....	....	....	....	....	....	....
2002-03	**Buffalo**	**NHL**	**79**	**26**	**49**	**75**	**20**	**11**	**1**	**3**	**240**	**10.8**	**–3**	**10**	**20.0**	**21:23**	....	....	....	....	....	....	....	....	....
	NHL Totals		**622**	**230**	**232**	**462**	**247**	**74**	**14**	**34**	**1557**	**14.8**		**41**	**34.1**	**20:46**	**51**	**14**	**21**	**35**	**14**	**6**	**0**	**2**	**21:04**

Played in NHL All-Star Game (2000, 2003)

Traded to **Buffalo** by **Edmonton** for Barrie Moore and Craig Millar, March 18, 1997.

SAUER, Kurt
(SAW-uhr, KUHRT) **ANA.**

Defense. Shoots left. 6'4", 225 lbs. Born, St. Cloud, MN, January 16, 1981. Colorado's 5th choice, 88th overall, in 2000 Entry Draft.

Season	Club	League	GP	G	A	Pts	PIM	PP	SH	GW	S	%	+/-	TF	F%	Min	GP	G	A	Pts	PIM	PP	SH	GW	Min
1998-99	North Iowa	USHL	52	1	4	5	67	....	....	....	....	....	....	....	....	....	....	....	....	....	....	....	....	....	....
99-2000	Spokane Chiefs	WHL	71	3	12	15	48	....	....	....	....	....	....	....	....	....	15	2	1	3	8	....	....	....	....
2000-01	Spokane Chiefs	WHL	48	5	10	15	85	....	....	....	....	....	....	....	....	....	3	1	0	1	2	....	....	....	....
2001-02	Spokane Chiefs	WHL	61	4	20	24	73	....	....	....	....	....	....	....	....	....	11	0	3	3	12	....	....	....	....
2002-03	**Anaheim**	**NHL**	**80**	**1**	**2**	**3**	**74**	**0**	**0**	**0**	**50**	**2.0**	**–23**	**0**	**0.0**	**18:33**	**21**	**1**	**1**	**2**	**6**	**0**	**1**	**1**	**20:45**
	NHL Totals		**80**	**1**	**2**	**3**	**74**	**0**	**0**	**0**	**50**	**2.0**		**0**	**0.0**	**18:33**	**21**	**1**	**1**	**2**	**6**	**0**	**1**	**1**	**20:45**

WHL West First All-Star Team (2002)

Signed as a free agent by **Anaheim**, June 6, 2002.

SAVAGE, Andre
(SA-vahj, AWN-dray) **PHI.**

Center. Shoots right. 6', 195 lbs. Born, Ottawa, Ont., May 27, 1975.

Season	Club	League	GP	G	A	Pts	PIM	PP	SH	GW	S	%	+/-	TF	F%	Min	GP	G	A	Pts	PIM	PP	SH	GW	Min
1992-93	Gloucester	OCJHL	54	34	34	68	38	....	....	....	....	....	....	....	....	....	....	....	....	....	....	....	....	....	....
1993-94	Gloucester	OCJHL	57	43	74	117	44	....	....	....	....	....	....	....	....	....	....	....	....	....	....	....	....	....	....
1994-95	Michigan Tech	WCHA	39	7	17	24	56	....	....	....	....	....	....	....	....	....	....	....	....	....	....	....	....	....	....
1995-96	Michigan Tech	WCHA	38	13	27	40	42	....	....	....	....	....	....	....	....	....	....	....	....	....	....	....	....	....	....
1996-97	Michigan Tech	WCHA	37	18	20	38	34	....	....	....	....	....	....	....	....	....	....	....	....	....	....	....	....	....	....
1997-98	Michigan Tech	WCHA	33	14	27	41	34	....	....	....	....	....	....	....	....	....	....	....	....	....	....	....	....	....	....
1998-99	**Boston**	**NHL**	**6**	**1**	**0**	**1**	**0**	**0**	**0**	**0**	**8**	**12.5**	**2**	**32**	**65.6**	**9:31**	....	....	....	....	....	....	....	....	....
	Providence Bruins	AHL	63	27	42	69	54	....	....	....	....	....	....	....	....	....	5	0	1	1	0	....	....	....	....
99-2000	**Boston**	**NHL**	**43**	**7**	**13**	**20**	**10**	**2**	**0**	**1**	**70**	**10.0**	**–8**	**619**	**55.1**	**14:40**	....	....	....	....	....	....	....	....	....
	Providence Bruins	AHL	30	15	17	32	22	....	....	....	....	....	....	....	....	....	14	6	7	13	22	....	....	....	....
2000-01	**Boston**	**NHL**	**1**	**0**	**0**	**0**	**0**	**0**	**0**	**0**	**1**	**0.0**	**0**	**3**	**100.0**	**4:38**	....	....	....	....	....	....	....	....	....
	Providence Bruins	AHL	35	13	15	28	47	....	....	....	....	....	....	....	....	....	17	3	4	7	18	....	....	....	....
2001-02	Manitoba Moose	AHL	76	35	26	61	115	....	....	....	....	....	....	....	....	....	6	2	3	5	16	....	....	....	....
2002-03	**Philadelphia**	**NHL**	**16**	**2**	**1**	**3**	**4**	**0**	**0**	**1**	**13**	**15.4**	**2**	**74**	**55.4**	**7:49**	....	....	....	....	....	....	....	....	....
	Philadelphia	AHL	64	11	31	42	66	....	....	....	....	....	....	....	....	....	....	....	....	....	....	....	....	....	....
	NHL Totals		**66**	**10**	**14**	**24**	**14**	**2**	**0**	**2**	**92**	**10.9**		**728**	**55.8**	**12:23**	....	....	....	....	....	....	....	....	....

WCHA First All-Star Team (1998)

Signed as a free agent by **Boston**, June 18, 1998. Signed as a free agent by **Vancouver**, August 2, 2001. Signed as a free agent by **Philadelphia**, August 20, 2002.

SAVAGE, Brian
(SA-vuhj, BRIGH-uhn) **PHX.**

Left wing. Shoots left. 6'1", 200 lbs. Born, Sudbury, Ont., February 24, 1971. Montreal's 11th choice, 171st overall, in 1991 Entry Draft.

Season	Club	League	GP	G	A	Pts	PIM	PP	SH	GW	S	%	+/-	TF	F%	Min	GP	G	A	Pts	PIM	PP	SH	GW	Min
1989-90	Sud. Cub Wolves	NOJHA	32	45	40	85	61	....	....	....	....	....	....	....	....	....	....	....	....	....	....	....	....	....	....
1990-91	Miami-Ohio	CCHA	28	5	6	11	26	....	....	....	....	....	....	....	....	....	....	....	....	....	....	....	....	....	....
1991-92	Miami-Ohio	CCHA	40	24	16	40	43	....	....	....	....	....	....	....	....	....	....	....	....	....	....	....	....	....	....
1992-93	Miami-Ohio	CCHA	38	*37	21	58	44	....	....	....	....	....	....	....	....	....	....	....	....	....	....	....	....	....	....
1993-94	Team Canada	Nat-Tm	51	20	26	46	38	....	....	....	....	....	....	....	....	....	....	....	....	....	....	....	....	....	....
	Canada	Olympics	8	2	2	4	6	....	....	....	....	....	....	....	....	....	....	....	....	....	....	....	....	....	....
	Montreal	**NHL**	**3**	**1**	**0**	**1**	**0**	**0**	**0**	**0**	**3**	**33.3**	**0**	....	....	....	**3**	**0**	**2**	**2**	**0**	**0**	**0**	**0**	....
	Fredericton	AHL	17	12	15	27	4	....	....	....	....	....	....	....	....	....	....	....	....	....	....	....	....	....	....
1994-95	**Montreal**	**NHL**	**37**	**12**	**7**	**19**	**27**	**0**	**0**	**0**	**64**	**18.8**	**5**	....	....	....	....	....	....	....	....	....	....	....	....
1995-96	**Montreal**	**NHL**	**75**	**25**	**8**	**33**	**28**	**4**	**0**	**4**	**150**	**16.7**	**–8**	....	....	....	**6**	**0**	**2**	**2**	**2**	**0**	**0**	**0**	....
1996-97	**Montreal**	**NHL**	**81**	**23**	**37**	**60**	**39**	**5**	**0**	**2**	**219**	**10.5**	**–14**	....	....	....	**5**	**1**	**1**	**2**	**0**	**0**	**0**	**0**	....
1997-98	**Montreal**	**NHL**	**64**	**26**	**17**	**43**	**36**	**8**	**0**	**7**	**152**	**17.1**	**11**	....	....	....	**9**	**0**	**2**	**2**	**6**	**0**	**0**	**0**	....
1998-99	**Montreal**	**NHL**	**54**	**16**	**10**	**26**	**20**	**5**	**0**	**4**	**124**	**12.9**	**–14**	**70**	**44.3**	**16:30**	....	....	....	....	....	....	....	....	....
99-2000	**Montreal**	**NHL**	**38**	**17**	**12**	**29**	**19**	**6**	**1**	**5**	**107**	**15.9**	**–4**	**67**	**47.8**	**17:56**	....	....	....	....	....	....	....	....	....
2000-01	**Montreal**	**NHL**	**62**	**21**	**24**	**45**	**26**	**12**	**0**	**1**	**172**	**12.2**	**–13**	**30**	**56.7**	**18:50**	....	....	....	....	....	....	....	....	....
2001-02	**Montreal**	**NHL**	**47**	**14**	**15**	**29**	**30**	**7**	**0**	**2**	**117**	**12.0**	**–14**	**3**	**0.0**	**18:12**	....	....	....	....	....	....	....	....	....
	Phoenix	**NHL**	**30**	**6**	**6**	**12**	**8**	**2**	**0**	**2**	**47**	**12.8**	**1**	**4**	**50.0**	**15:02**	**5**	**0**	**0**	**0**	**0**	**0**	**0**	**0**	**11:13**
2002-03	**Phoenix**	**NHL**	**43**	**6**	**10**	**16**	**22**	**1**	**0**	**1**	**68**	**8.8**	**–4**	**14**	**35.7**	**13:22**	....	....	....	....	....	....	....	....	....
	NHL Totals		**534**	**167**	**146**	**313**	**255**	**50**	**1**	**28**	**1223**	**13.7**		**188**	**46.3**	**16:52**	**28**	**1**	**7**	**8**	**8**	**0**	**0**	**0**	**11:13**

CCHA First All-Star Team (1993) • CCHA Player of the Year (1993) • NCAA West Second All-American Team (1993)

• Missed majority of 1999-2000 season recovering from neck injury suffered in game vs. Los Angeles, November 20, 1999. Traded to **Phoenix** by **Montreal** with Montreal's 3rd round choice (Matt Jones) in 2002 Entry Draft and future considerations for Sergei Berezin, January 25, 2002.

SAVARD, Marc
(sa-VAHR, MAHRK) **ATL.**

Center. Shoots left. 5'10", 190 lbs. Born, Ottawa, Ont., July 17, 1977. NY Rangers' 3rd choice, 91st overall, in 1995 Entry Draft.

Season	Club	League	GP	G	A	Pts	PIM	PP	SH	GW	S	%	+/-	TF	F%	Min	GP	G	A	Pts	PIM	PP	SH	GW	Min
1992-93	Metcalfe Jets	OJHL-B	36	*44	55	*99	38	....	....	....	....	....	....	....	....	....	....	....	....	....	....	....	....	....	....
1993-94	Oshawa Generals	OHL	61	18	39	57	20	....	....	....	....	....	....	....	....	....	5	4	3	7	8	....	....	....	....
1994-95	Oshawa Generals	OHL	66	43	96	*139	78	....	....	....	....	....	....	....	....	....	7	5	6	11	8	....	....	....	....
1995-96	Oshawa Generals	OHL	48	28	59	87	77	....	....	....	....	....	....	....	....	....	5	4	5	9	6	....	....	....	....
1996-97	Oshawa Generals	OHL	64	43	*87	*130	94	....	....	....	....	....	....	....	....	....	18	13	*24	*37	20	....	....	....	....
1997-98	**NY Rangers**	**NHL**	**28**	**1**	**5**	**6**	**4**	**0**	**0**	**0**	**32**	**3.1**	**–4**	....	....	....	....	....	....	....	....	....	....	....	....
	Hartford	AHL	58	21	53	74	66	....	....	....	....	....	....	....	....	....	15	8	19	27	24	....	....	....	....
1998-99	**NY Rangers**	**NHL**	**70**	**9**	**36**	**45**	**38**	**4**	**0**	**1**	**116**	**7.8**	**–7**	**956**	**48.4**	**14:35**	....	....	....	....	....	....	....	....	....
	Hartford	AHL	9	3	10	13	16	....	....	....	....	....	....	....	....	....	7	1	12	13	16	....	....	....	....
99-2000	**Calgary**	**NHL**	**78**	**22**	**31**	**53**	**56**	**4**	**0**	**3**	**184**	**12.0**	**–2**	**1021**	**49.6**	**16:36**	....	....	....	....	....	....	....	....	....
2000-01	**Calgary**	**NHL**	**77**	**23**	**42**	**65**	**46**	**10**	**1**	**5**	**197**	**11.7**	**–12**	**1050**	**53.1**	**19:13**	....	....	....	....	....	....	....	....	....
2001-02	**Calgary**	**NHL**	**56**	**14**	**19**	**33**	**48**	**7**	**0**	**3**	**140**	**10.0**	**–18**	**577**	**54.8**	**17:20**	....	....	....	....	....	....	....	....	....
2002-03	**Calgary**	**NHL**	**10**	**1**	**2**	**3**	**8**	**0**	**0**	**0**	**21**	**4.8**	**–3**	**89**	**52.8**	**14:41**	....	....	....	....	....	....	....	....	....
	Atlanta	**NHL**	**57**	**16**	**31**	**47**	**77**	**6**	**0**	**4**	**127**	**12.6**	**–11**	**1247**	**50.9**	**19:50**	....	....	....	....	....	....	....	....	....
	NHL Totals		**376**	**86**	**166**	**252**	**277**	**31**	**1**	**16**	**817**	**10.5**		**4940**	**51.1**	**17:22**	....	....	....	....	....	....	....	....	....

OHL Second All-Star Team (1995)

Traded to **Calgary** by **NY Rangers** with NY Rangers 1st round choice (Oleg Saprykin) in 1999 Entry Draft for the rights to Jan Hlavac and Calgary's 1st (Jamie Lundmark) and 3rd (later traded back to Calgary – Calgary selected Craig Andersson) round choices in 1999 Entry Draft, June 26, 1999. Traded to **Atlanta** by **Calgary** for Ruslan Zainullin, November 15, 2002.

SAWYER, Kevin
(SOI-yuhr, KEH-vihn)

Left wing. Shoots left. 6'2", 212 lbs. Born, Christina Lake, B.C., February 21, 1974.

Season	Club	League	GP	G	A	Pts	PIM	PP	SH	GW	S	%	+/-	TF	F%	Min	Playoffs GP	G	A	Pts	PIM	PP	SH	GW	Min
1991-92	Grand Forks	KIJHL	24	9	11	20	200																		
	Kelowna Spartans	BCJHL	3	0	0	0	9																		
	Vernon Lakers	BCJHL	12	0	1	1	18																		
	Penticton	BCJHL	3	0	0	0	13																		
1992-93	Spokane Chiefs	WHL	62	4	3	7	274										8	1	1	2	13				
1993-94	Spokane Chiefs	WHL	60	10	15	25	350										3	0	1	1	6				
1994-95	Spokane Chiefs	WHL	54	7	9	16	365										11	2	0	2	58				
	Peoria Rivermen	IHL															2	0	0	0	12				
1995-96	**St. Louis**	**NHL**	**6**	**0**	**0**	**0**	**23**	**0**	**0**	**0**	**1**	**0.0**	**-2**												
	Worcester IceCats	AHL	41	3	4	7	268																		
	Boston	**NHL**	**2**	**0**	**0**	**0**	**5**	**0**	**0**	**0**	**0**	**0.0**	**1**												
	Providence Bruins	AHL	4	0	0	0	29										4	0	1	1	9				
1996-97	**Boston**	**NHL**	**2**	**0**	**0**	**0**	**0**	**0**	**0**	**0**	**0**	**0.0**	**0**												
	Providence Bruins	AHL	60	8	9	17	367										6	0	0	0	32				
1997-98	Michigan	IHL	60	2	5	7	*398										3	0	0	0	23				
1998-99	Worcester IceCats	AHL	70	8	14	22	299										4	0	1	1	4				
99-2000	**Phoenix**	**NHL**	**3**	**0**	**0**	**0**	**12**	**0**	**0**	**0**	**0**	**0.0**	**1**	**0**	**0.0**	**2:20**									
	Springfield	AHL	56	4	8	12	321										4	0	0	0	6				
2000-01	**Anaheim**	**NHL**	**9**	**0**	**1**	**1**	**27**	**0**	**0**	**0**	**6**	**0.0**	**-1**	**0**	**0.0**	**6:31**									
	Cincinnati	AHL	41	2	12	14	211																		
2001-02	**Anaheim**	**NHL**	**57**	**1**	**1**	**2**	**221**	**0**	**0**	**0**	**29**	**3.4**	**-4**	**3**	**0.0**	**5:47**									
2002-03	**Anaheim**	**NHL**	**31**	**2**	**1**	**3**	**115**	**0**	**0**	**0**	**11**	**18.2**	**-2**	**1**	**0.0**	**6:06**									
	NHL Totals		**110**	**3**	**3**	**6**	**403**	**0**	**0**	**0**	**47**	**6.4**		**4**	**0.0**	**5:51**									

Signed as a free agent by **St. Louis**, February 28, 1995. Traded to **Boston** by **St. Louis** with Steve Staios for Steve Leach, March 8, 1996. Signed as a free agent by **Dallas**, August 19, 1997. Signed as a free agent by **St. Louis**, September 4, 1998. Signed as a free agent by **Phoenix**, August 15, 1999. Signed as a free agent by **Anaheim**, July 13, 2000. • Missed majority of 2002-03 season recovering from head injury suffered in game vs. Los Angeles, December 19, 2002.

SCATCHARD, Dave
(SKAT-chuhrd, DAYV) **NYI**

Center. Shoots right. 6'2", 224 lbs. Born, Hinton, Alta., February 20, 1976. Vancouver's 3rd choice, 42nd overall, in 1994 Entry Draft.

Season	Club	League	GP	G	A	Pts	PIM	PP	SH	GW	S	%	+/-	TF	F%	Min	Playoffs GP	G	A	Pts	PIM	PP	SH	GW	Min
1991-92	Salmon Arm	BCAHA	65	98	100	198	167																		
1992-93	Kimberley	RMJHL	51	20	23	43	61																		
1993-94	Portland	WHL	47	9	11	20	46										10	2	1	3	4				
1994-95	Portland	WHL	71	20	30	50	148										8	0	3	3	21				
1995-96	Portland	WHL	59	19	28	47	146										7	1	8	9	14				
	Syracuse Crunch	AHL	1	0	0	0	0										15	2	5	7	29				
1996-97	Syracuse Crunch	AHL	26	8	7	15	65																		
1997-98	**Vancouver**	**NHL**	**76**	**13**	**11**	**24**	**165**	**0**	**0**	**1**	**85**	**15.3**	**-4**												
1998-99	**Vancouver**	**NHL**	**82**	**13**	**13**	**26**	**140**	**0**	**2**	**2**	**130**	**10.0**	**-12**	**1007**	**56.3**	**13:46**									
99-2000	**Vancouver**	**NHL**	**21**	**0**	**4**	**4**	**24**	**0**	**0**	**0**	**25**	**0.0**	**-3**	**190**	**59.5**	**10:12**									
	NY Islanders	**NHL**	**44**	**12**	**14**	**26**	**93**	**0**	**1**	**1**	**103**	**11.7**	**0**	**710**	**55.8**	**13:42**									
2000-01	**NY Islanders**	**NHL**	**81**	**21**	**24**	**45**	**114**	**4**	**0**	**5**	**176**	**11.9**	**-9**	**1322**	**55.1**	**16:50**									
2001-02	**NY Islanders**	**NHL**	**80**	**12**	**15**	**27**	**111**	**3**	**1**	**4**	**117**	**10.3**	**-4**	**788**	**53.8**	**12:31**	**7**	**1**	**1**	**2**	**22**	**0**	**0**	**0**	**12:38**
2002-03	**NY Islanders**	**NHL**	**81**	**27**	**18**	**45**	**108**	**5**	**0**	**2**	**165**	**16.4**	**9**	**1147**	**52.7**	**14:30**	**5**	**1**	**0**	**1**	**6**	**0**	**0**	**1**	**15:58**
	NHL Totals		**465**	**98**	**99**	**197**	**755**	**12**	**4**	**15**	**801**	**12.2**		**5164**	**54.9**	**14:06**	**12**	**2**	**1**	**3**	**28**	**0**	**0**	**1**	**14:01**

Traded to **NY Islanders** by **Vancouver** with Kevin Weekes and Bill Muckalt for Felix Potvin, NY Islanders' compensatory 2nd round choice (later traded to New Jersey – New Jersey selected Teemu Laine) in 2000 Entry Draft and NY Islanders' 3rd round choice (Thatcher Bell) in 2000 Entry Draft, December 19, 1999.

SCHAEFER, Peter
(SHAY-fuhr, PEE-tuhr) **OTT.**

Left wing. Shoots left. 5'11", 195 lbs. Born, Yellow Grass, Sask., July 12, 1977. Vancouver's 3rd choice, 66th overall, in 1995 Entry Draft.

Season	Club	League	GP	G	A	Pts	PIM	PP	SH	GW	S	%	+/-	TF	F%	Min	Playoffs GP	G	A	Pts	PIM	PP	SH	GW	Min
1993-94	Yorkton Mallers	SMHL	32	27	14	41	133																		
	Brandon	WHL	2	1	0	1	0																		
1994-95	Brandon	WHL	68	27	32	59	34										18	5	3	8	18				
1995-96	Brandon	WHL	69	47	61	108	53										19	10	13	23	5				
1996-97	Brandon	WHL	61	49	74	123	85										6	1	4	5	4				
	Syracuse Crunch	AHL	5	0	3	3	0										3	1	3	4	14				
1997-98	Syracuse Crunch	AHL	73	19	44	63	41										5	2	1	3	2				
1998-99	**Vancouver**	**NHL**	**25**	**4**	**4**	**8**	**8**	**1**	**0**	**1**	**24**	**16.7**	**-1**	**6**	**0.0**	**13:21**									
	Syracuse Crunch	AHL	41	10	19	29	66																		
99-2000	**Vancouver**	**NHL**	**71**	**16**	**15**	**31**	**20**	**2**	**2**	**4**	**101**	**15.8**	**0**	**21**	**19.1**	**15:28**									
	Syracuse Crunch	AHL	2	0	0	0	2																		
2000-01	**Vancouver**	**NHL**	**82**	**16**	**20**	**36**	**22**	**3**	**4**	**2**	**163**	**9.8**	**4**	**25**	**32.0**	**16:18**	**3**	**0**	**0**	**0**	**0**	**0**	**0**	**0**	**13:08**
2001-02	TPS Turku	Finland	33	16	15	31	93										8	1	2	3	2				
2002-03	**Ottawa**	**NHL**	**75**	**6**	**17**	**23**	**32**	**0**	**0**	**1**	**93**	**6.5**	**11**	**44**	**20.5**	**14:59**	**16**	**2**	**3**	**5**	**6**	**0**	**1**	**0**	**11:51**
	NHL Totals		**253**	**42**	**56**	**98**	**82**	**6**	**6**	**8**	**381**	**11.0**		**96**	**21.9**	**15:23**	**19**	**2**	**3**	**5**	**6**	**0**	**1**	**0**	**12:03**

WHL East First All-Star Team (1996, 1997) • Canadian Major Junior First All-Star Team (1997)

Signed as a free agent by **TPS Turku** (Finland) with Vancouver retaining NHL rights, October 18, 2001. Traded to **Ottawa** by **Vancouver** for Sami Salo, September 21, 2002.

SCHASTLIVY, Petr
(schust-LEE-vee, PEH-tuhr) **OTT.**

Left wing. Shoots left. 6'1", 204 lbs. Born, Angarsk, USSR, April 18, 1979. Ottawa's 5th choice, 101st overall, in 1998 Entry Draft.

Season	Club	League	GP	G	A	Pts	PIM	PP	SH	GW	S	%	+/-	TF	F%	Min	Playoffs GP	G	A	Pts	PIM	PP	SH	GW	Min
1997-98	Yaroslavl	Russia	47	15	9	24	34																		
	Yaroslavl	Russia	4	0	0	0	0																		
1998-99	Yaroslavl	Russia	40	6	1	7	28										6	0	0	0	2				
99-2000	**Ottawa**	**NHL**	**13**	**2**	**5**	**7**	**2**	**1**	**0**	**1**	**22**	**9.1**	**4**	**0**	**0.0**	**12:18**	**1**	**0**	**0**	**0**	**0**	**0**	**0**	**0**	**13:09**
	Grand Rapids	IHL	46	16	12	28	10										17	8	7	15	6				
2000-01	**Ottawa**	**NHL**	**17**	**3**	**2**	**5**	**6**	**0**	**0**	**0**	**32**	**9.4**	**-1**	**0**	**0.0**	**11:20**									
	Grand Rapids	IHL	43	10	14	24	10										7	4	4	8	0				
2001-02	**Ottawa**	**NHL**	**1**	**0**	**1**	**1**	**0**	**0**	**0**	**0**	**0**	**0.0**	**1**	**0**	**0.0**	**3:21**									
	Grand Rapids	AHL	31	22	13	35	10																		
2002-03	**Ottawa**	**NHL**	**33**	**9**	**10**	**19**	**4**	**5**	**0**	**2**	**68**	**13.2**	**3**	**2**	**0.0**	**13:21**									
	NHL Totals		**64**	**14**	**18**	**32**	**12**	**6**	**0**	**3**	**122**	**11.5**		**2**	**0.0**	**12:27**	**1**	**0**	**0**	**0**	**0**	**0**	**0**	**0**	**13:09**

• Missed majority of 2001-02 season recovering from knee injury suffered in game vs. Chicago, December 31, 2001. • Missed majority of 2002-03 season recovering from groin injury suffered in practice, October 5, 2002.

SCHMIDT, Chris
(SHMIHT, KRIHS) **L.A.**

Center. Shoots left. 6'3", 212 lbs. Born, Beaver Lodge, Alta., March 1, 1976. Los Angeles' 4th choice, 111th overall, in 1994 Entry Draft.

Season	Club	League	GP	G	A	Pts	PIM	PP	SH	GW	S	%	+/-	TF	F%	Min	Playoffs GP	G	A	Pts	PIM	PP	SH	GW	Min
1992-93	Seattle	WHL	61	6	7	13	17										5	0	1	1	0				
1993-94	Seattle	WHL	68	7	17	24	26										9	3	1	4	2				
1994-95	Seattle	WHL	61	21	11	32	31										3	0	0	0	0				
1995-96	Seattle	WHL	61	39	23	62	135										5	1	5	6	9				
1996-97	Mississippi	ECHL	18	7	7	14	35																		
	Phoenix	IHL	37	3	6	9	60																		
1997-98	Fredericton	AHL	69	8	5	13	67										4	0	0	0	2				
1998-99	Springfield	AHL	17	3	2	5	19										1	0	0	0	0				
	Mississippi	ECHL	6	1	0	1	2										18	6	8	14	10				
99-2000	Team Canada	Nat-Tm	33	1	9	10	28																		
	Lowell	AHL	38	8	10	18	38										7	2	1	3	8				
2000-01	Lowell	AHL	79	21	32	53	84										4	2	2	4	2				
2001-02	Manchester	AHL	62	9	12	21	43										5	0	2	2	0				
2002-03	**Los Angeles**	**NHL**	**10**	**0**	**2**	**2**	**5**	**0**	**0**	**0**	**10**	**0.0**	**-1**	**2**	**100.0**	**10:01**									
	Manchester	AHL	53	12	13	25	58										2	0	1	1	4				
	NHL Totals		**10**	**0**	**2**	**2**	**5**	**0**	**0**	**0**	**10**	**0.0**		**2**	**100.0**	**10:01**									

SCHNABEL, Robert

(SHNAH-buhl, RAW-buhrt) **NSH.**

Defense. Shoots left. 6'5", 230 lbs. Born, Prague, Czech., November 10, 1978. Phoenix's 7th choice, 129th overall, in 1998 Entry Draft.

			Regular Season														Playoffs								
Season	Club	League	GP	G	A	Pts	PIM	PP	SH	GW	S	%	+/-	TF	F%	Min	GP	G	A	Pts	PIM	PP	SH	GW	Min
1994-95	Slavia Praha Jr.	Czech-Jr.	35	11	6	17	14																		
1995-96	Slavia Praha Jr.	Czech-Jr.	38	3	5	8																			
1996-97	Slavia Praha Jr.	Czech-Jr.	36	5	2	7																			
	HC Slavia Praha	Czech	4	0	0	0	4										1	0	0	0	0				
1997-98	Red Deer Rebels	WHL	61	1	22	23	143										5	0	0	0	16				
1998-99	Red Deer Rebels	WHL	1	0	0	0	2																		
	Springfield	AHL	77	1	7	8	155										3	1	0	1	4				
99-2000	Springfield	AHL	40	2	8	10	133										5	0	0	0	4				
2000-01	Springfield	AHL	22	1	2	3	38																		
	Timra IK	Sweden	16	0	2	2	72																		
2001-02	**Nashville**	**NHL**	**1**	**0**	**0**	**0**	**0**	**0**	**0**	**0**	**0**	**0.0**	**0**	**0**	**0.0**	**7:16**									
	Milwaukee	AHL	67	2	7	9	130																		
2002-03	**Nashville**	**NHL**	**1**	**0**	**0**	**0**	**0**	**0**	**0**	**0**	**0**	**0.0**	**0**	**0**	**0.0**	**4:28**									
	Milwaukee	AHL	62	3	6	9	178										6	0	0	0	34				
	NHL Totals		**2**	**0**	**0**	**0**	**0**	**0**	**0**	**0**	**0**	**0.0**		**0**	**0.0**	**5:52**									

• Re-entered NHL Entry Draft. Originally NY Islanders' 5th choice, 79th overall, in 1997 Entry Draft.

Claimed on waivers by **Nashville** from **Phoenix**, January 2, 2001.

SCHNEIDER, Mathieu

(SHNIGH-duhr, MA-thew) **DET.**

Defense. Shoots left. 5'10", 192 lbs. Born, New York, NY, June 12, 1969. Montreal's 4th choice, 44th overall, in 1987 Entry Draft.

Season	Club	League	GP	G	A	Pts	PIM	PP	SH	GW	S	%	+/-	TF	F%	Min	GP	G	A	Pts	PIM	PP	SH	GW	Min
1985-86	Mount St. Charles	Hi-School	19	3	27	30																			
1986-87	Cornwall Royals	OHL	63	7	29	36	75										5	0	0	0	22				
1987-88	Cornwall Royals	OHL	48	21	40	61	83										11	2	6	8	14				
	Montreal	**NHL**	**4**	**0**	**0**	**0**	**2**	**0**	**0**	**0**	**2**	**0.0**	**–1**												
	Sherbrooke	AHL															3	0	3	3	12				
1988-89	Cornwall Royals	OHL	59	16	57	73	96										18	7	20	27	30				
1989-90	**Montreal**	**NHL**	**44**	**7**	**14**	**21**	**25**	**5**	**0**	**1**	**84**	**8.3**	**2**				**9**	**1**	**3**	**4**	**31**	**1**	**0**	**0**	
	Sherbrooke	AHL	28	6	13	19	20																		
1990-91	**Montreal**	**NHL**	**69**	**10**	**20**	**30**	**63**	**5**	**0**	**3**	**164**	**6.1**	**7**				**13**	**2**	**7**	**9**	**18**	**1**	**0**	**0**	
1991-92	**Montreal**	**NHL**	**78**	**8**	**24**	**32**	**72**	**2**	**0**	**1**	**194**	**4.1**	**10**				**10**	**1**	**4**	**5**	**6**	**1**	**0**	**0**	
1992-93♦	**Montreal**	**NHL**	**60**	**13**	**31**	**44**	**91**	**3**	**0**	**2**	**169**	**7.7**	**8**				**11**	**1**	**2**	**3**	**16**	**0**	**0**	**0**	
1993-94	**Montreal**	**NHL**	**75**	**20**	**32**	**52**	**62**	**11**	**0**	**4**	**193**	**10.4**	**15**				**1**	**0**	**0**	**0**	**0**	**0**	**0**	**0**	
1994-95	**Montreal**	**NHL**	**30**	**5**	**15**	**20**	**49**	**2**	**0**	**0**	**82**	**6.1**	**–3**												
	NY Islanders	**NHL**	**13**	**3**	**6**	**9**	**30**	**1**	**0**	**2**	**36**	**8.3**	**–5**												
1995-96	**NY Islanders**	**NHL**	**65**	**11**	**36**	**47**	**93**	**7**	**0**	**1**	**155**	**7.1**	**–18**												
	Toronto	**NHL**	**13**	**2**	**5**	**7**	**10**	**0**	**0**	**0**	**36**	**5.6**	**–2**				**6**	**0**	**4**	**4**	**8**	**0**	**0**	**0**	
1996-97	**Toronto**	**NHL**	**26**	**5**	**7**	**12**	**20**	**1**	**0**	**1**	**63**	**7.9**	**3**												
1997-98	**Toronto**	**NHL**	**76**	**11**	**26**	**37**	**44**	**4**	**1**	**1**	**181**	**6.1**	**–12**												
	United States	Olympics	4	0	0	0	6																		
1998-99	**NY Rangers**	**NHL**	**75**	**10**	**24**	**34**	**71**	**5**	**0**	**2**	**159**	**6.3**	**–19**	**0**	**0.0**	**24:35**									
99-2000	**NY Rangers**	**NHL**	**80**	**10**	**20**	**30**	**78**	**3**	**0**	**1**	**228**	**4.4**	**–6**	**0**	**0.0**	**22:31**									
2000-01	**Los Angeles**	**NHL**	**73**	**16**	**35**	**51**	**56**	**7**	**1**	**2**	**183**	**8.7**	**0**	**0**	**0.0**	**23:04**	**13**	**0**	**9**	**9**	**10**	**0**	**0**	**0**	**25:51**
2001-02	**Los Angeles**	**NHL**	**55**	**7**	**23**	**30**	**68**	**4**	**0**	**0**	**123**	**5.7**	**3**	**0**	**0.0**	**22:25**	**7**	**0**	**1**	**1**	**18**	**0**	**0**	**0**	**22:52**
2002-03	**Los Angeles**	**NHL**	**65**	**14**	**29**	**43**	**57**	**10**	**0**	**1**	**162**	**8.6**	**0**	**0**	**0.0**	**22:20**									
	Detroit	**NHL**	**13**	**2**	**5**	**7**	**16**	**1**	**0**	**0**	**37**	**5.4**	**2**	**0**	**0.0**	**22:42**	**4**	**0**	**0**	**0**	**6**	**0**	**0**	**0**	**28:15**
	NHL Totals		**914**	**154**	**352**	**506**	**907**	**71**	**2**	**22**	**2251**	**6.8**		**0**	**0.0**	**23:01**	**74**	**5**	**30**	**35**	**113**	**3**	**0**	**0**	**25:23**

OHL First All-Star Team (1988, 1989)

Played in NHL All-Star Game (1996, 2003)

Traded to **NY Islanders** by **Montreal** with Kirk Muller and Craig Darby for Pierre Turgeon and Vladimir Malakhov, April 5, 1995. Traded to **Toronto** by **NY Islanders** with Wendel Clark and D.J. Smith for Darby Hendrickson, Sean Haggerty, Kenny Jonsson and Toronto's 1st round choice (Roberto Luongo) in 1997 Entry Draft, March 13, 1996. • Missed majority of 1996-97 season recovering from groin injury suffered in game vs. St. Louis, December 27, 1996. Rights traded to **NY Rangers** by **Toronto** for Alexander Karpovtsev and NY Rangers' 4th round choice (Mirko Murovic) in 1999 Entry Draft, October 14, 1998. Selected by **Columbus** from **NY Rangers** in Expansion Draft, June 23, 2000. Signed as a free agent by **Los Angeles**, August 14, 2000. Traded to **Detroit** by **Los Angeles** for Sean Avery, Maxim Kuznetsov, Detroit's 1st round choice (Jeff Tambellini) in 2003 Entry Draft and Detroit's 2nd round choice in 2004 Entry Draft, March 11, 2003.

SCHULTZ, Nick

(SHULTZ, NIHK) **MIN.**

Defense. Shoots left. 6'1", 207 lbs. Born, Strasbourg, Sask., August 25, 1982. Minnesota's 2nd choice, 33rd overall, in 2000 Entry Draft.

Season	Club	League	GP	G	A	Pts	PIM	PP	SH	GW	S	%	+/-	TF	F%	Min	GP	G	A	Pts	PIM	PP	SH	GW	Min
1997-98	Yorkton Mallers	SMHL	59	10	30	40	74																		
1998-99	Prince Albert	WHL	58	5	18	23	37										14	0	7	7	0				
99-2000	Prince Albert	WHL	72	11	33	44	38										6	0	3	3	2				
2000-01	Prince Albert	WHL	59	17	30	47	120																		
	Cleveland	IHL	4	1	1	2	2										3	0	1	1	0				
2001-02	**Minnesota**	**NHL**	**52**	**4**	**6**	**10**	**14**	**1**	**0**	**1**	**47**	**8.5**	**0**	**0**	**0.0**	**16:08**									
	Houston Aeros	AHL															14	1	5	6	2				
2002-03	**Minnesota**	**NHL**	**75**	**3**	**7**	**10**	**23**	**0**	**0**	**1**	**70**	**4.3**	**11**	**0**	**0.0**	**18:28**	**18**	**0**	**1**	**1**	**10**	**0**	**0**	**0**	**19:39**
	NHL Totals		**127**	**7**	**13**	**20**	**37**	**1**	**0**	**2**	**117**	**6.0**		**0**	**0.0**	**17:31**	**18**	**0**	**1**	**1**	**10**	**0**	**0**	**0**	**19:39**

SCHULTZ, Ray

(SHUHLTZ, RAY) **NSH.**

Defense. Shoots left. 6'2", 215 lbs. Born, Red Deer, Alta., November 14, 1976. Ottawa's 8th choice, 184th overall, in 1995 Entry Draft.

Season	Club	League	GP	G	A	Pts	PIM	PP	SH	GW	S	%	+/-	TF	F%	Min	GP	G	A	Pts	PIM	PP	SH	GW	Min
1993-94	Edmonton SSAC	AMHL	31	3	24	27	94																		
	Tri-City	WHL	3	0	0	0	11																		
1994-95	Tri-City	WHL	63	1	8	9	209										11	0	0	0	16				
1995-96	Calgary Hitmen	WHL	66	3	17	20	282																		
1996-97	Calgary Hitmen	WHL	32	3	17	20	141																		
	Kelowna Rockets	WHL	23	3	11	14	63										6	0	2	2	12				
1997-98	**NY Islanders**	**NHL**	**13**	**0**	**1**	**1**	**45**	**0**	**0**	**0**	**4**	**0.0**	**3**												
	Kentucky	AHL	51	2	4	6	179										1	0	0	0	25				
1998-99	**NY Islanders**	**NHL**	**4**	**0**	**0**	**0**	**7**	**0**	**0**	**0**	**2**	**0.0**	**–2**	**1**	**0.0**	**15:21**									
	Lowell	AHL	54	0	3	3	184										1	0	0	0	4				
99-2000	**NY Islanders**	**NHL**	**9**	**0**	**1**	**1**	**30**	**0**	**0**	**0**	**2**	**0.0**	**1**	**0**	**0.0**	**14:18**									
	Kansas City	IHL	65	5	5	10	208																		
2000-01	**NY Islanders**	**NHL**	**13**	**0**	**2**	**2**	**40**	**0**	**0**	**0**	**3**	**0.0**	**–1**	**0**	**0.0**	**10:50**									
	Lowell	AHL	13	0	1	1	33																		
	Cleveland	IHL	44	3	5	8	127										3	1	0	1	16				
2001-02	**NY Islanders**	**NHL**	**2**	**0**	**0**	**0**	**5**	**0**	**0**	**0**	**0**	**0.0**	**–1**	**0**	**0.0**	**3:22**	**2**	**0**	**0**	**0**	**2**	**0**	**0**	**0**	**9:11**
	Bridgeport	AHL	69	0	15	15	205										19	1	3	4	18				
2002-03	**NY Islanders**	**NHL**	**4**	**0**	**0**	**0**	**28**	**0**	**0**	**0**	**1**	**0.0**	**–1**	**0**	**0.0**	**5:23**									
	Bridgeport	AHL	51	2	8	10	105										9	1	0	1	14				
	NHL Totals		**45**	**0**	**4**	**4**	**155**	**0**	**0**	**0**	**12**	**0.0**		**1**	**0.0**	**11:13**	**2**	**0**	**0**	**0**	**2**	**0**	**0**	**0**	**9:11**

Signed as a free agent by **NY Islanders**, June 9, 1997. Signed as a free agent by **Nashville**, July 17, 2003.

SCOTT, Richard

(SKAWT, RIH-churd) **NYR**

Left wing. Shoots left. 6'2", 195 lbs. Born, Orillia, Ont., August 1, 1978.

Season	Club	League	GP	G	A	Pts	PIM	PP	SH	GW	S	%	+/-	TF	F%	Min	GP	G	A	Pts	PIM	PP	SH	GW	Min
1996-97	Orillia Terriers	OPJHL	10	0	0	0	23																		
1997-98	Couchiching	OPJHL	45	13	19	32	166																		
1998-99	Oshawa Generals	OHL	54	12	12	24	193																		
99-2000	Charlotte	ECHL	55	1	5	6	317																		
2000-01	Charlotte	ECHL	4	1	1	2	22																		
	Hartford	AHL	64	2	5	7	320										1	0	0	0	0				
2001-02	**NY Rangers**	**NHL**	**5**	**0**	**0**	**0**	**5**	**0**	**0**	**0**	**1**	**0.0**	**0**	**0**	**0.0**	**2:25**									
	Hartford	AHL	39	2	3	5	211																		

			Regular Season														Playoffs								
Season	Club	League	GP	G	A	Pts	PIM	PP	SH	GW	S	%	+/-	TF	F%	Min	GP	G	A	Pts	PIM	PP	SH	GW	Min
2002-03	Hartford	AHL	32	0	5	5	150										2	0	0	0	16				
	Charlotte	ECHL	3	0	1	1	4																		
	NHL Totals		**5**	**0**	**0**	**0**	**5**	**0**	**0**	**0**	**1**	**0.0**		**0**	**0.0**	**2:25**									

Signed as a free agent by **NY Rangers**, May 8, 2001.

SCOVILLE, Darrel

(SKO-vihl, DAIR-uhl) **CBJ**

Defense. Shoots left. 6'3", 215 lbs. Born, Swift Current, Sask., October 13, 1975.

Season	Club	League	GP	G	A	Pts	PIM	PP	SH	GW	S	%	+/-	TF	F%	Min	GP	G	A	Pts	PIM	PP	SH	GW	Min
1994-95	Lebret Eagles	SJHL	STATISTICS NOT AVAILABLE																						
1995-96	Merrimack	H-East	34	6	20	26	54																		
1996-97	Merrimack	H-East	35	7	16	23	71																		
1997-98	Merrimack	H-East	38	4	26	30	84																		
1998-99	Saint John Flames	AHL	61	1	7	8	66										7	1	2	3	13				
99-2000	**Calgary**	**NHL**	**6**	**0**	**0**	**0**	**2**	**0**	**0**	**0**	**1**	**0.0**	**1**	**0**	**0.0**	**9:18**									
	Saint John Flames	AHL	64	11	25	36	99										3	1	2	3	0				
2000-01	Saint John Flames	AHL	76	11	32	47	125										11	2	6	8	8				
2001-02	Syracuse Crunch	AHL	51	5	16	21	60										10	0	0	0	6				
2002-03	**Columbus**	**NHL**	**2**	**0**	**0**	**0**	**4**	**0**	**0**	**0**	**1**	**0.0**	**0**	**0**	**0.0**	**14:31**									
	Syracuse Crunch	AHL	24	4	9	13	26																		
	NHL Totals		**8**	**0**	**0**	**0**	**6**	**0**	**0**	**0**	**2**	**0.0**		**0**	**0.0**	**10:36**									

Hockey East All-Rookie Team (1996)

Signed as a free agent by **Calgary**, June 12, 1998. Signed as a free agent by **Columbus**, July 10, 2001. • Spent majority of 2002-03 season with Norfolk (AHL) as a healthy reserve.

SEDIN, Daniel

(suh-DEEN, DAN-yehl) **VAN.**

Left wing. Shoots left. 6'1", 200 lbs. Born, Ornskoldsvik, Sweden, September 26, 1980. Vancouver's 1st choice, 2nd overall, in 1999 Entry Draft.

Season	Club	League	GP	G	A	Pts	PIM	PP	SH	GW	S	%	+/-	TF	F%	Min	GP	G	A	Pts	PIM	PP	SH	GW	Min
1996-97	MoDo Jr.	Swede-Jr.	26	26	14	40																			
1997-98	MoDo Jr.	Swede-Jr.	4	3	3	6	4																		
	MoDo	Sweden	45	4	8	12	26										9	0	0	0	2				
1998-99	MoDo	Sweden	50	21	21	42	20										13	4	8	12	14				
99-2000	MoDo	Sweden	50	19	26	45	28										13	*8	6	14	18				
	MoDo	EuroHL	4	3	3	6	0										2	0	0	0	0				
2000-01	**Vancouver**	**NHL**	**75**	**20**	**14**	**34**	**24**	**10**	**0**	**3**	**127**	**15.7**	**−3**	**10**	**60.0**	**12:60**	**4**	**1**	**2**	**3**	**0**	**0**	**0**	**0**	**16:15**
2001-02	**Vancouver**	**NHL**	**79**	**9**	**23**	**32**	**32**	**4**	**0**	**2**	**117**	**7.7**	**1**	**18**	**33.3**	**12:22**	**6**	**0**	**1**	**1**	**0**	**0**	**0**	**0**	**10:44**
2002-03	**Vancouver**	**NHL**	**79**	**14**	**17**	**31**	**34**	**4**	**0**	**2**	**134**	**10.4**	**8**	**24**	**45.8**	**12:26**	**14**	**1**	**5**	**6**	**8**	**1**	**0**	**1**	**12:23**
	NHL Totals		**233**	**43**	**54**	**97**	**90**	**18**	**0**	**7**	**378**	**11.4**		**52**	**44.2**	**12:35**	**24**	**2**	**8**	**10**	**8**	**1**	**0**	**1**	**12:37**

SEDIN, Henrik

(suh-DEEN, HEHN-rihk) **VAN.**

Center. Shoots left. 6'2", 200 lbs. Born, Ornskoldsvik, Sweden, September 26, 1980. Vancouver's 2nd choice, 3rd overall, in 1999 Entry Draft.

Season	Club	League	GP	G	A	Pts	PIM	PP	SH	GW	S	%	+/-	TF	F%	Min	GP	G	A	Pts	PIM	PP	SH	GW	Min
1996-97	MoDo Jr.	Swede-Jr.	26	14	22	36																			
1997-98	MoDo Jr.	Swede-Jr.	8	4	7	11	6																		
	MoDo	Sweden	39	1	4	5	8										7	0	0	0	0				
1998-99	MoDo	Sweden	49	12	22	34	32										13	2	8	10	6				
99-2000	MoDo	Sweden	50	9	38	47	22										13	5	9	14	2				
2000-01	**Vancouver**	**NHL**	**82**	**9**	**20**	**29**	**38**	**2**	**0**	**1**	**98**	**9.2**	**−2**	**1020**	**44.1**	**13:31**	**4**	**0**	**4**	**4**	**0**	**0**	**0**	**0**	**16:31**
2001-02	**Vancouver**	**NHL**	**82**	**16**	**20**	**36**	**36**	**3**	**0**	**1**	**78**	**20.5**	**9**	**785**	**47.4**	**12:48**	**6**	**3**	**0**	**3**	**0**	**0**	**0**	**1**	**11:55**
2002-03	**Vancouver**	**NHL**	**78**	**8**	**31**	**39**	**38**	**4**	**1**	**1**	**81**	**9.9**	**9**	**995**	**48.2**	**13:58**	**14**	**3**	**2**	**5**	**8**	**1**	**0**	**0**	**13:01**
	NHL Totals		**242**	**33**	**71**	**104**	**112**	**9**	**1**	**3**	**257**	**12.8**		**2800**	**46.5**	**13:25**	**24**	**6**	**6**	**12**	**8**	**1**	**0**	**1**	**13:20**

SEIDENBERG, Dennis

(ZIGH-dehn-buhrg, DEH-nihs) **PHI.**

Defense. Shoots left. 6', 200 lbs. Born, Schwenningen, West Germany, July 18, 1981. Philadelphia's 6th choice, 172nd overall, in 2001 Entry Draft.

Season	Club	League	GP	G	A	Pts	PIM	PP	SH	GW	S	%	+/-	TF	F%	Min	GP	G	A	Pts	PIM	PP	SH	GW	Min
99-2000	Mannheim Jr.	Ger.-Jr.	52	12	28	40	28																		
	Adler Mannheim	Germany	3	0	0	0	0																		
2000-01	Mannheim Jr.	Ger.-Jr.	9	3	8	11	20																		
	Adler Mannheim	Germany	55	2	5	7	6										12	0	1	1	10				
2001-02	Adler Mannheim	Germany	55	7	13	20	56										8	0	0	0	2				
2002-03	**Philadelphia**	**NHL**	**58**	**4**	**9**	**13**	**20**	**1**	**0**	**0**	**123**	**3.3**	**8**	**1**	**0.0**	**16:50**									
	Philadelphia	AHL	19	5	6	11	17																		
	NHL Totals		**58**	**4**	**9**	**13**	**20**	**1**	**0**	**0**	**123**	**3.3**		**1**	**0.0**	**16:50**									

SEJNA, Peter

(SHAY-nah, PEE-tuhr) **ST.L.**

Left wing. Shoots left. 5'11", 198 lbs. Born, Liptovski Mikulas, Czech., October 5, 1979.

Season	Club	League	GP	G	A	Pts	PIM	PP	SH	GW	S	%	+/-	TF	F%	Min	GP	G	A	Pts	PIM	PP	SH	GW	Min
1998-99	Des Moines	USHL	52	40	23	63	26										14	11	6	17	8				
99-2000	Des Moines	USHL	58	41	53	94	36										9	4	5	9	4				
2000-01	Colorado College	WCHA	41	29	29	58	10																		
2001-02	Colorado College	WCHA	43	26	24	50	16																		
2002-03	Colorado College	WCHA	42	*36	46	*82	12																		
	St. Louis	**NHL**	**1**	**1**	**0**	**1**	**0**	**1**	**0**	**0**	**3**	**33.3**	**0**	**0**	**0.0**	**15:22**									
	NHL Totals		**1**	**1**	**0**	**1**	**0**	**1**	**0**	**0**	**3**	**33.3**		**0**	**0.0**	**15:22**									

WCHA First All-Star Team (2003) • WCHA Player of the Year (2003) • NCAA West First All-American Team (2003) • Hobey Baker Memorial Award (Top U.S. Collegiate Player) (2003)

Signed as a free agent by **St. Louis**, April 6, 2003.

SEKERAS, Lubomir

(SHE-kuhr-ahsh, LOO-boh-mihr)

Defense. Shoots left. 6', 183 lbs. Born, Trencin, Czech., November 18, 1968. Minnesota's 8th choice, 232nd overall, in 2000 Entry Draft.

Season	Club	League	GP	G	A	Pts	PIM	PP	SH	GW	S	%	+/-	TF	F%	Min	GP	G	A	Pts	PIM	PP	SH	GW	Min
1987-88	Dukla Trencin Jr.	Czech-Jr.	STATISTICS NOT AVAILABLE																						
	Dukla Trencin	Czech															9	0	0	0	0				
1988-89	Dukla Trencin	Czech	16	2	5	7	22										11	0	4	4	0				
1989-90	Dukla Trencin	Czech	44	6	8	14											9	0	2	2					
1990-91	Dukla Trencin	Czech	52	6	16	22											6	0	1	1					
1991-92	Dukla Trencin	Czech	30	2	6	8	32										13	1	1	2	0				
1992-93	Dukla Trencin	Czech	40	5	19	24	48										11	4	9	13	0				
1993-94	Dukla Trencin	Slovakia	36	9	12	21	46										9	2	4	6	10				
1994-95	Dukla Trencin	Slovakia	36	11	11	22	24										9	2	7	9	8				
1995-96	Trinec	Czech	40	11	13	24	44										3	0	0	0	0				
1996-97	Trinec	Czech	52	14	21	35	56										4	1	0	1	2				
1997-98	Trinec	Czech	50	11	33	44	42										13	2	10	12	4				
1998-99	Trinec	Czech	50	8	15	23	38										10	2	6	8					
99-2000	HC Ocelari Trinec	Czech	52	7	24	31	36										4	0	2	2	2				
2000-01	**Minnesota**	**NHL**	**80**	**11**	**23**	**34**	**52**	**4**	**0**	**2**	**102**	**10.8**	**−8**	**0**	**0.0**	**21:13**									
2001-02	**Minnesota**	**NHL**	**69**	**4**	**20**	**24**	**38**	**4**	**0**	**1**	**82**	**4.9**	**−7**	**0**	**0.0**	**22:37**									
2002-03	**Minnesota**	**NHL**	**60**	**2**	**9**	**11**	**30**	**1**	**0**	**1**	**50**	**4.0**	**−12**	**3**	**100.0**	**18:52**	**15**	**1**	**1**	**2**	**6**	**1**	**0**	**1**	**16:51**
	NHL Totals		**209**	**17**	**52**	**69**	**120**	**9**	**0**	**4**	**234**	**7.3**		**3**	**100.0**	**21:00**	**15**	**1**	**1**	**2**	**6**	**1**	**0**	**1**	**16:51**

SELANNE, Teemu

(SEH-lahn-nay, TEE-moo) **COL.**

Right wing. Shoots right. 6', 204 lbs. Born, Helsinki, Finland, July 3, 1970. Winnipeg's 1st choice, 10th overall, in 1988 Entry Draft.

Season	Club	League	GP	G	A	Pts	PIM	PP	SH	GW	S	%	+/-	TF	F%	Min	GP	G	A	Pts	PIM	PP	SH	GW	Min
1986-87	Jokerit Helsinki Jr.	Finn-Jr.	33	10	12	22	8																		
1987-88	Jokerit Helsinki Jr.	Finn-Jr.	33	*43	23	*66	18										5	4	3	7	2				
	Jokerit Helsinki	Finland-2	5	1	1	2	0																		
1988-89	Army Jr.	Finn-Jr.	3	3	1	4	2																		
	Jokerit Helsinki Jr.	Finn-Jr.	3	8	8	16	4																		
	Jokerit Helsinki	Finland-2	34	35	33	68	12										5	7	3	10	4				
1989-90	Jokerit Helsinki	Finland	11	4	8	12	0																		

			Regular Season														Playoffs								
Season	Club	League	GP	G	A	Pts	PIM	PP	SH	GW	S	%	+/-	TF	F%	Min	GP	G	A	Pts	PIM	PP	SH	GW	Min
1990-91	Jokerit Helsinki Jr.	Finn-Jr.	1	0	0	0	0	....	....	....	....	....	....	....	....	....	....	....	....	....	....	....	....	....	....
	Jokerit Helsinki	Finland	42	33	25	58	12	....	....	....	....	....	....	....	....	....	....	....	....	....	....	....	....	....	....
1991-92	Jokerit Helsinki	Finland	44	*39	23	62	20	....	....	....	....	....	....	....	....	....	10	*10	7	*17	18	....	....	....	....
	Finland	Olympics	8	7	4	11	6	....	....	....	....	....	....	....	....	....	....	....	....	....	....	....	....	....	....
1992-93	**Winnipeg**	**NHL**	84	*76	56	132	45	24	0	7	387	19.6	8	....	....	....	6	4	2	6	2	2	0	2	....
1993-94	**Winnipeg**	**NHL**	51	25	29	54	22	11	0	2	191	13.1	–23	....	....	....	....	....	....	....	....	....	....	....	....
1994-95	Jokerit Helsinki	Finland	20	7	12	19	6	....	....	....	....	....	....	....	....	....	....	....	....	....	....	....	....	....	....
	Winnipeg	**NHL**	45	22	26	48	2	8	2	1	167	13.2	1	....	....	....	....	....	....	....	....	....	....	....	....
1995-96	**Winnipeg**	**NHL**	51	24	48	72	18	6	1	4	163	14.7	3	....	....	....	....	....	....	....	....	....	....	....	....
	Anaheim	**NHL**	28	16	20	36	4	3	0	1	104	15.4	2	....	....	....	....	....	....	....	....	....	....	....	....
1996-97	**Anaheim**	**NHL**	78	51	58	109	34	11	1	8	273	18.7	28	....	....	....	11	7	3	10	4	3	0	1	....
1997-98	**Anaheim**	**NHL**	73	*52	34	86	30	10	1	10	268	19.4	12	....	....	....	....	....	....	....	....	....	....	....	....
	Finland	Olympics	5	4	6	*10	8	....	....	....	....	....	....	....	....	....	....	....	....	....	....	....	....	....	....
1998-99	**Anaheim**	**NHL**	75	*47	60	107	30	25	0	7	281	16.7	18	5	20.0	22:47	4	2	2	4	2	1	0	0	22:23
99-2000	**Anaheim**	**NHL**	79	33	52	85	12	8	0	6	236	14.0	6	13	23.1	22:44	....	....	....	....	....	....	....	....	....
2000-01	**Anaheim**	**NHL**	61	26	33	59	36	10	0	5	202	12.9	–8	4	50.0	21:51	....	....	....	....	....	....	....	....	....
	San Jose	**NHL**	12	7	6	13	0	2	0	2	31	22.6	1	4	75.0	18:14	6	0	2	2	2	0	0	0	17:13
2001-02	**San Jose**	**NHL**	82	29	25	54	40	9	1	8	202	14.4	–11	12	25.0	16:58	12	5	3	8	2	2	0	1	16:51
	Finland	Olympics	4	3	0	3	2	....	....	....	....	....	....	....	....	....	....	....	....	....	....	....	....	....	....
2002-03	**San Jose**	**NHL**	82	28	36	64	30	7	0	5	253	11.1	–6	107	42.1	19:14	....	....	....	....	....	....	....	....	....
	NHL Totals		**801**	**436**	**483**	**919**	**303**	**134**	**6**	**66**	**2758**	**15.8**		**145**	**39.3**	**20:31**	**39**	**18**	**12**	**30**	**12**	**8**	**0**	**4**	**17:57**

NHL All-Rookie Team (1993) • NHL First All-Star Team (1993, 1997) • Calder Memorial Trophy (1993) • NHL Second All-Star Team (1998, 1999) • Maurice "Rocket" Richard Trophy (1999)

Played in NHL All-Star Game (1993, 1994, 1996, 1997, 1998, 1999, 2000, 2002, 2003)

• Missed majority of 1989-90 season recovering from leg injury suffered in game vs. HIFK Helsinki (Finland), October 19, 1989. Traded to **Anaheim** by **Winnipeg** with Marc Chouinard and Winnipeg's 4th round choice (later traded to Toronto – later traded to Montreal – Montreal selected Kim Staal) in 1996 Entry Draft for Chad Kilger, Oleg Tverdovsky and Anaheim's 3rd round choice (Per-Anton Lundstrom) in 1996 Entry Draft, February 7, 1996. Traded to **San Jose** by **Anaheim** for Jeff Friesen, Steve Shields and San Jose's 2nd round choice (later traded to Dallas – Dallas selected Vojtech Polak) in 2003 Entry Draft, March 5, 2001. Signed as a free agent by **Colorado**, July 3, 2003.

SELLARS, Luke (SEHL-lahrs, LEWK) ATL.

Defense. Shoots left. 6'1", 205 lbs. Born, Toronto, Ont., May 21, 1981. Atlanta's 2nd choice, 30th overall, in 1999 Entry Draft.

Season	Club	League	GP	G	A	Pts	PIM	PP	SH	GW	S	%	+/-	TF	F%	Min	GP	G	A	Pts	PIM	PP	SH	GW	Min
1997-98	Wexford Raiders	MTJHL	46	2	18	20	155	....	....	....	....	....	....	....	....	....	....	....	....	....	....	....	....	....	....
1998-99	Ottawa 67's	OHL	56	4	19	23	87	....	....	....	....	....	....	....	....	....	9	1	2	3	7	....	....	....	....
	Ottawa 67's	M-Cup	4	1	0	1	6	....	....	....	....	....	....	....	....	....	....	....	....	....	....	....	....	....	....
99-2000	Ottawa 67's	OHL	56	8	34	42	147	....	....	....	....	....	....	....	....	....	11	4	6	10	28	....	....	....	....
2000-01	Ottawa 67's	OHL	59	9	21	30	136	....	....	....	....	....	....	....	....	....	18	4	10	14	47	....	....	....	....
2001-02	**Atlanta**	**NHL**	1	0	0	0	2	0	0	0	0	0.0	0	0	0.0	3:27	....	....	....	....	....	....	....	....	....
	Chicago Wolves	AHL	31	2	4	6	87	....	....	....	....	....	....	....	....	....	....	....	....	....	....	....	....	....	....
	Greenville	ECHL	21	2	6	8	61	....	....	....	....	....	....	....	....	....	17	7	6	13	44	....	....	....	....
2002-03	Chicago Wolves	AHL	42	4	11	15	117	....	....	....	....	....	....	....	....	....	....	....	....	....	....	....	....	....	....
	Greenville	ECHL	4	2	2	4	6	....	....	....	....	....	....	....	....	....	....	....	....	....	....	....	....	....	....
	NHL Totals		**1**	**0**	**0**	**0**	**2**	**0**	**0**	**0**	**0**	**0.0**		**0**	**0.0**	**3:27**	....	....	....	....	....	....	....	....	....

OHL All-Rookie Team (1999)

SEMENOV, Alexei (seh-MEH-nahv, al-EHX-ay) EDM.

Defense. Shoots left. 6'6", 210 lbs. Born, Murmansk, USSR, April 10, 1981. Edmonton's 2nd choice, 36th overall, in 1999 Entry Draft.

Season	Club	League	GP	G	A	Pts	PIM	PP	SH	GW	S	%	+/-	TF	F%	Min	GP	G	A	Pts	PIM	PP	SH	GW	Min
1997-98	Krylja Sovetov 2	Russia-3	52	1	2	3	48	....	....	....	....	....	....	....	....	....	....	....	....	....	....	....	....	....	....
1998-99	St. Petersburg 2	Russia-4	19	0	1	1	20	....	....	....	....	....	....	....	....	....	....	....	....	....	....	....	....	....	....
	Sudbury Wolves	OHL	28	0	3	3	28	....	....	....	....	....	....	....	....	....	2	0	0	0	4	....	....	....	....
99-2000	Sudbury Wolves	OHL	65	9	35	44	135	....	....	....	....	....	....	....	....	....	12	1	3	4	23	....	....	....	....
	Hamilton	AHL	....	....	....	....	....	....	....	....	....	....	....	....	....	....	3	0	0	0	0	....	....	....	....
2000-01	Sudbury Wolves	OHL	65	21	42	63	106	....	....	....	....	....	....	....	....	....	12	4	13	17	17	....	....	....	....
2001-02	Hamilton	AHL	78	5	11	16	67	....	....	....	....	....	....	....	....	....	....	....	....	....	....	....	....	....	....
2002-03	**Edmonton**	**NHL**	46	1	6	7	58	0	0	0	33	3.0	–7	0	0.0	19:41	6	0	0	0	0	0	0	0	13:05
	Hamilton	AHL	37	4	3	7	45	....	....	....	....	....	....	....	....	....	....	....	....	....	....	....	....	....	....
	NHL Totals		**46**	**1**	**6**	**7**	**58**	**0**	**0**	**0**	**33**	**3.0**		**0**	**0.0**	**19:41**	**6**	**0**	**0**	**0**	**0**	**0**	**0**	**0**	**13:05**

OHL First All-Star Team (2001)

SEVERSON, Cam (SEH-vuhr-SOHN, KAM) ANA.

Left wing. Shoots left. 6'1", 215 lbs. Born, Canora, Sask., January 15, 1978. San Jose's 6th choice, 192nd overall, in 1997 Entry Draft.

Season	Club	League	GP	G	A	Pts	PIM	PP	SH	GW	S	%	+/-	TF	F%	Min	GP	G	A	Pts	PIM	PP	SH	GW	Min
1996-97	Lethbridge	WHL	45	12	13	25	169	....	....	....	....	....	....	....	....	....	....	....	....	....	....	....	....	....	....
	Prince Albert	WHL	16	5	13	18	54	....	....	....	....	....	....	....	....	....	4	4	0	4	8	....	....	....	....
1997-98	Prince Albert	WHL	41	23	25	48	129	....	....	....	....	....	....	....	....	....	....	....	....	....	....	....	....	....	....
	Spokane Chiefs	WHL	23	9	11	20	88	....	....	....	....	....	....	....	....	....	18	11	4	15	51	....	....	....	....
1998-99	Spokane Chiefs	WHL	46	16	17	33	190	....	....	....	....	....	....	....	....	....	....	....	....	....	....	....	....	....	....
	Oklahoma City	CHL	5	6	3	9	4	....	....	....	....	....	....	....	....	....	10	4	0	4	26	....	....	....	....
99-2000	Louisiana	ECHL	7	0	2	2	22	....	....	....	....	....	....	....	....	....	....	....	....	....	....	....	....	....	....
	Peoria Rivermen	ECHL	56	19	8	27	138	....	....	....	....	....	....	....	....	....	18	3	4	7	41	....	....	....	....
2000-01	Portland Pirates	AHL	8	0	0	0	11	....	....	....	....	....	....	....	....	....	....	....	....	....	....	....	....	....	....
	Cincinnati	AHL	20	4	7	11	60	....	....	....	....	....	....	....	....	....	3	1	1	2	0	....	....	....	....
2001-02	Hartford	AHL	65	11	10	21	116	....	....	....	....	....	....	....	....	....	5	0	0	0	7	....	....	....	....
2002-03	**Anaheim**	**NHL**	2	0	0	0	8	0	0	0	1	0.0	0	0	0.0	6:44	1	0	0	0	0	0	0	0	2:24
	Cincinnati	AHL	71	12	9	21	156	....	....	....	....	....	....	....	....	....	....	....	....	....	....	....	....	....	....
	NHL Totals		**2**	**0**	**0**	**0**	**8**	**0**	**0**	**0**	**1**	**0.0**		**0**	**0.0**	**6:44**	**1**	**0**	**0**	**0**	**0**	**0**	**0**	**0**	**2:24**

Signed as a free agent by **Hartford** (AHL), September 24, 2001. Signed as a free agent by **Anaheim**, August 22, 2002.

SHANAHAN, Brendan (SHAN-na-HAN, BREHN-duhn) DET.

Left wing. Shoots right. 6'3", 218 lbs. Born, Mimico, Ont., January 23, 1969. New Jersey's 1st choice, 2nd overall, in 1987 Entry Draft.

Season	Club	League	GP	G	A	Pts	PIM	PP	SH	GW	S	%	+/-	TF	F%	Min	GP	G	A	Pts	PIM	PP	SH	GW	Min
1984-85	Mississauga Reps	MTHL	36	20	21	41	26	....	....	....	....	....	....	....	....	....	....	....	....	....	....	....	....	....	....
	Dixie Beehives	MTJHL	1	0	0	0	0	....	....	....	....	....	....	....	....	....	....	....	....	....	....	....	....	....	....
1985-86	London Knights	OHL	59	28	34	62	70	....	....	....	....	....	....	....	....	....	5	5	5	10	5	....	....	....	....
1986-87	London Knights	OHL	56	39	53	92	92	....	....	....	....	....	....	....	....	....	....	....	....	....	....	....	....	....	....
1987-88	**New Jersey**	**NHL**	65	7	19	26	131	2	0	2	72	9.7	–20	....	....	....	12	2	1	3	44	1	0	0	....
1988-89	**New Jersey**	**NHL**	68	22	28	50	115	9	0	0	152	14.5	2	....	....	....	....	....	....	....	....	....	....	....	....
1989-90	**New Jersey**	**NHL**	73	30	42	72	137	8	0	5	196	15.3	15	....	....	....	6	3	3	6	20	1	0	1	....
1990-91	**New Jersey**	**NHL**	75	29	37	66	141	7	0	2	195	14.9	4	....	....	....	7	3	5	8	12	2	0	0	....
1991-92	**St. Louis**	**NHL**	80	33	36	69	171	13	0	2	215	15.3	–3	....	....	....	6	2	3	5	14	1	0	0	....
1992-93	**St. Louis**	**NHL**	71	51	43	94	174	18	0	8	232	22.0	10	....	....	....	11	4	3	7	18	2	0	0	....
1993-94	**St. Louis**	**NHL**	81	52	50	102	211	15	7	8	397	13.1	–9	....	....	....	4	2	5	7	4	0	0	0	....
1994-95	Dusseldorfer EG	Germany	3	5	3	8	4	....	....	....	....	....	....	....	....	....	....	....	....	....	....	....	....	....	....
	St. Louis	**NHL**	45	20	21	41	136	6	2	6	153	13.1	7	....	....	....	5	4	5	9	14	1	0	1	....
1995-96	**Hartford**	**NHL**	74	44	34	78	125	17	2	6	280	15.7	2	....	....	....	....	....	....	....	....	....	....	....	....
1996-97	**Hartford**	**NHL**	2	1	0	1	0	0	1	0	13	7.7	1	....	....	....	....	....	....	....	....	....	....	....	....
	♦ **Detroit**	**NHL**	79	46	41	87	131	20	2	7	323	14.2	31	....	....	....	20	9	8	17	43	2	0	2	....
1997-98	♦ **Detroit**	**NHL**	75	28	29	57	154	15	1	9	266	10.5	6	....	....	....	20	5	4	9	22	3	0	2	....
	Canada	Olympics	6	2	0	2	0	....	....	....	....	....	....	....	....	....	....	....	....	....	....	....	....	....	....
1998-99	**Detroit**	**NHL**	81	31	27	58	123	5	0	5	288	10.8	2	18	44.4	17:31	10	3	7	10	6	1	0	1	18:31
99-2000	**Detroit**	**NHL**	78	41	37	78	105	13	1	9	283	14.5	24	24	50.0	18:35	9	3	2	5	10	0	0	0	17:36
2000-01	**Detroit**	**NHL**	81	31	45	76	81	15	1	7	278	11.2	9	115	43.5	18:22	2	2	2	4	0	0	0	1	21:01

Season	Club	League	Regular Season GP	G	A	Pts	PIM	PP	SH	GW	S	%	+/-	TF	F%	Min	Playoffs GP	G	A	Pts	PIM	PP	SH	GW	Min
2001-02 ♦	Detroit	NHL	80	37	38	75	118	12	3	7	277	13.4	23	70	47.1	18:55	23	8	11	19	20	1	0	2	19:06
	Canada	Olympics	6	0	1	1	0																		
2002-03	Detroit	NHL	78	30	38	68	103	13	0	6	260	11.5	5	28	60.7	18:38	4	1	1	2	4	1	0	0	22:03
	NHL Totals		**1186**	**533**	**565**	**1098**	**2156**	**188**	**20**	**89**	**3880**	**13.7**		**255**	**47.1**	**18:24**	**139**	**51**	**60**	**111**	**231**	**16**	**0**	**10**	**19:02**

NHL First All-Star Team (1994, 2000) • NHL Second All-Star Team (2002) • King Clancy Memorial Trophy (2003)

Played in NHL All-Star Game (1994, 1996, 1997, 1998, 1999, 2000, 2002)

Signed as a free agent by **St. Louis**, July 25, 1991. Traded to **Hartford** by **St. Louis** for Chris Pronger, July 27, 1995. Traded to **Detroit** by **Hartford** with Brian Glynn for Paul Coffey, Keith Primeau and Detroit's 1st round choice (Nikos Tselios) in 1997 Entry Draft, October 9, 1996.

SHANTZ, Jeff

(SHAWNTS, JEHF)

Center. Shoots right. 6', 195 lbs. Born, Duchess, Alta., October 10, 1973. Chicago's 2nd choice, 36th overall, in 1992 Entry Draft.

Season	Club	League	GP	G	A	Pts	PIM	PP	SH	GW	S	%	+/-	TF	F%	Min	GP	G	A	Pts	PIM	PP	SH	GW	Min
1989-90	Medicine Hat	AMHL	36	18	31	49	30																		
	Regina Pats	WHL	1	0	0	0	0																		
1990-91	Regina Pats	WHL	69	16	21	37	22										8	2	2	4	2				
1991-92	Regina Pats	WHL	72	39	50	89	35																		
1992-93	Regina Pats	WHL	64	29	54	83	75										13	2	12	14	14				
1993-94	**Chicago**	**NHL**	**52**	**3**	**13**	**16**	**30**	**0**	**0**	**0**	**56**	**5.4**	**–14**				**6**	**0**	**0**	**0**	**6**	**0**	**0**	**0**	
	Indianapolis Ice	IHL	19	5	9	14	20																		
1994-95	Indianapolis Ice	IHL	32	9	15	24	20																		
	Chicago	**NHL**	**45**	**6**	**12**	**18**	**33**	**0**	**2**	**0**	**58**	**10.3**	**11**				**16**	**3**	**1**	**4**	**2**	**0**	**0**	**0**	
1995-96	**Chicago**	**NHL**	**78**	**6**	**14**	**20**	**24**	**1**	**2**	**0**	**72**	**8.3**	**12**				**10**	**2**	**3**	**5**	**6**	**0**	**0**	**0**	
1996-97	**Chicago**	**NHL**	**69**	**9**	**21**	**30**	**28**	**0**	**1**	**1**	**86**	**10.5**	**11**				**6**	**0**	**4**	**4**	**6**	**0**	**0**	**0**	
1997-98	**Chicago**	**NHL**	**61**	**11**	**20**	**31**	**36**	**1**	**2**	**2**	**69**	**15.9**	**0**												
1998-99	**Chicago**	**NHL**	**7**	**1**	**0**	**1**	**4**	**0**	**0**	**0**	**5**	**20.0**	**–1**	**72**	**38.9**	**15:14**									
	Calgary	**NHL**	**69**	**12**	**17**	**29**	**40**	**1**	**1**	**3**	**77**	**15.6**	**15**	**1112**	**48.4**	**16:47**									
99-2000	**Calgary**	**NHL**	**74**	**13**	**18**	**31**	**30**	**6**	**0**	**1**	**112**	**11.6**	**–13**	**1576**	**51.1**	**18:15**									
2000-01	**Calgary**	**NHL**	**73**	**5**	**15**	**20**	**58**	**0**	**0**	**0**	**88**	**5.7**	**–7**	**876**	**53.5**	**14:51**									
2001-02	**Calgary**	**NHL**	**40**	**3**	**3**	**6**	**23**	**2**	**0**	**0**	**37**	**8.1**	**–3**	**298**	**53.0**	**11:26**									
	Saint John Flames	AHL	2	0	1	1	0																		
2002-03	**Colorado**	**NHL**	**74**	**3**	**6**	**9**	**35**	**0**	**0**	**2**	**68**	**4.4**	**–12**	**874**	**52.1**	**11:28**	**6**	**0**	**0**	**0**	**4**	**0**	**0**	**0**	**9:42**
	NHL Totals		**642**	**72**	**139**	**211**	**341**	**11**	**8**	**9**	**728**	**9.9**		**4808**	**51.0**	**14:51**	**44**	**5**	**8**	**13**	**24**	**0**	**0**	**0**	**9:42**

WHL East First All-Star Team (1993)

Traded to **Calgary** by **Chicago** with Steve Dubinsky for Marty McInnis, Jamie Allison and Eric Andersson, October 27, 1998. Traded to **Colorado** by **Calgary** with Derek Morris and Dean McAmmond for Chris Drury and Stephane Yelle, October 1, 2002.

SHARP, Patrick

(SHAHRP, PAT-rihk) **PHI.**

Center. Shoots right. 6', 197 lbs. Born, Thunder Bay, Ont., December 27, 1981. Philadelphia's 2nd choice, 95th overall, in 2001 Entry Draft.

Season	Club	League	GP	G	A	Pts	PIM	PP	SH	GW	S	%	+/-	TF	F%	Min	GP	G	A	Pts	PIM	PP	SH	GW	Min
1998-99	Thunder Bay	USHL	55	19	24	43	48										3	1	1	2	0				
99-2000	Thunder Bay	USHL	56	20	35	55	41																		
2000-01	U. of Vermont	ECAC	34	12	15	27	36																		
2001-02	U. of Vermont	ECAC	31	13	13	26	50																		
2002-03	**Philadelphia**	**NHL**	**3**	**0**	**0**	**0**	**2**	**0**	**0**	**0**	**3**	**0.0**	**0**	**7**	**42.9**	**5:59**									
	Philadelphia	AHL	53	14	19	33	39																		
	NHL Totals		**3**	**0**	**0**	**0**	**2**	**0**	**0**	**0**	**3**	**0.0**		**7**	**42.9**	**5:59**									

SHELLEY, Jody

(SHEH-lee, JOH-dee) **CBJ**

Left wing. Shoots left. 6'4", 225 lbs. Born, Thompson, Man., February 7, 1976.

Season	Club	League	GP	G	A	Pts	PIM	PP	SH	GW	S	%	+/-	TF	F%	Min	GP	G	A	Pts	PIM	PP	SH	GW	Min
1994-95	Halifax	QMJHL	72	10	12	22	194										7	0	1	1	12				
1995-96	Halifax	QMJHL	50	13	19	32	319										6	0	2	2	36				
1996-97	Halifax	QMJHL	58	25	19	44	*448										17	6	6	12	*123				
1997-98	Dalhousie	AUAA	19	6	11	17	145																		
	Saint John Flames	AHL	18	1	1	2	50																		
1998-99	Saint John Flames	AHL	8	0	0	0	46																		
	Johnstown Chiefs	ECHL	52	12	17	29	325																		
99-2000	Johnstown Chiefs	ECHL	36	9	17	26	256																		
	Saint John Flames	AHL	22	1	4	5	93										3	0	0	0	2				
2000-01	Syracuse Crunch	AHL	69	1	7	8	*357										5	0	0	0	21				
	Columbus	**NHL**	**1**	**0**	**0**	**0**	**10**	**0**	**0**	**0**	**0**	**0.0**	**0**	**0**	**0.0**	**1:33**									
2001-02	**Columbus**	**NHL**	**52**	**3**	**3**	**6**	**206**	**0**	**0**	**0**	**35**	**8.6**	**1**	**0**	**0.0**	**6:32**									
	Syracuse Crunch	AHL	22	3	5	8	165																		
2002-03	**Columbus**	**NHL**	**68**	**1**	**4**	**5**	***249**	**0**	**0**	**0**	**39**	**2.6**	**–5**	**1**	**0.0**	**6:08**									
	NHL Totals		**121**	**4**	**7**	**11**	**465**	**0**	**0**	**0**	**74**	**5.4**		**1**	**0.0**	**6:16**									

Signed as a free agent by **Calgary**, September 1, 1998. Signed as a free agent by **Syracuse** (AHL), September 15, 2000. Signed as a free agent by **Columbus**, January 31, 2001.

SHVIDKI, Denis

(SHVIHD-kee, DEH-nihs) **FLA.**

Right wing. Shoots left. 6', 195 lbs. Born, Kharkov, USSR, November 21, 1980. Florida's 1st choice, 12th overall, in 1999 Entry Draft.

Season	Club	League	GP	G	A	Pts	PIM	PP	SH	GW	S	%	+/-	TF	F%	Min	GP	G	A	Pts	PIM	PP	SH	GW	Min
1996-97	Yaroslavl 2	Russia-3	35	21	12	33	32																		
	Yaroslavl	Russia	17	3	2	5	6																		
1997-98	Yaroslavl 2	Russia-2	32	20	13	33	20																		
	Yaroslavl	Russia	15	1	1	2	2																		
1998-99	Barrie Colts	OHL	61	35	59	94	8										12	7	9	16	2				
99-2000	Barrie Colts	OHL	61	41	65	106	55										9	3	1	4	2				
2000-01	**Florida**	**NHL**	**43**	**6**	**10**	**16**	**16**	**0**	**0**	**1**	**28**	**21.4**	**6**	**4**	**50.0**	**10:21**									
	Louisville Panthers	AHL	34	15	11	26	20																		
2001-02	**Florida**	**NHL**	**8**	**1**	**2**	**3**	**2**	**0**	**0**	**0**	**11**	**9.1**	**–4**	**1**	**0.0**	**11:57**									
	Utah Grizzlies	AHL	8	2	4	6	2																		
2002-03	**Florida**	**NHL**	**23**	**4**	**2**	**6**	**12**	**2**	**0**	**1**	**29**	**13.8**	**–7**	**5**	**60.0**	**14:14**									
	San Antonio	AHL	54	8	18	26	28																		
	NHL Totals		**74**	**11**	**14**	**25**	**30**	**2**	**0**	**2**	**68**	**16.2**		**10**	**50.0**	**11:44**									

OHL All-Rookie Team (1999) • OHL Second All-Star Team (1999)

• Missed majority of 2001-02 season recovering from head injury suffered in game vs. Philadelphia, October 4, 2001.

SIKLENKA, Mike

(sih-KLEHN-kuh, MIGHK) **PHI.**

Right wing. Shoots right. 6'5", 224 lbs. Born, Meadow Lake, Sask., December 18, 1979. Washington's 5th choice, 118th overall, in 1998 Entry Draft.

Season	Club	League	GP	G	A	Pts	PIM	PP	SH	GW	S	%	+/-	TF	F%	Min	GP	G	A	Pts	PIM	PP	SH	GW	Min
1997-98	Lloydminster	AJHL	54	10	17	27	120																		
1998-99	Seattle	WHL	68	19	13	32	115										11	6	6	12	24				
99-2000	Portland Pirates	AHL	9	0	0	0	14																		
	Hampton Roads	ECHL	58	7	4	11	62										8	1	0	1	15				
2000-01	Richmond	ECHL	65	19	18	37	117										4	0	0	0	34				
	Portland Pirates	AHL	3	0	0	0	0																		
2001-02	Richmond	ECHL	55	13	21	34	111																		
	Portland Pirates	AHL	8	1	0	1	2																		
2002-03	**Philadelphia**	**NHL**	**1**	**0**	**0**	**0**	**0**	**0**	**0**	**0**	**1**	**0.0**	**0**	**0**	**0.0**	**4:26**									
	Philadelphia	AHL	64	6	6	12	169																		
	NHL Totals		**1**	**0**	**0**	**0**	**0**	**0**	**0**	**0**	**1**	**0.0**		**0**	**0.0**	**4:26**									

Signed as a free agent by **Philadelphia**, January 27, 2002.

SILLINGER, Mike

(sih-LIHN-juhr, MIGHK) **PHX.**

Center. Shoots right. 5'11", 196 lbs. Born, Regina, Sask., June 29, 1971. Detroit's 1st choice, 11th overall, in 1989 Entry Draft.

			Regular Season														Playoffs								
Season	Club	League	GP	G	A	Pts	PIM	PP	SH	GW	S	%	+/-	TF	F%	Min	GP	G	A	Pts	PIM	PP	SH	GW	Min
1986-87	Regina Kings	SMHL	31	83	51	134	....	....	....	....	....	....	....	....	....	....	....	....	....	....	....	....	....	....	....
1987-88	Regina Pats	WHL	67	18	25	43	17	....	....	....	....	....	....	....	....	....	4	2	2	4	0	....	....	....	....
1988-89	Regina Pats	WHL	72	53	78	131	52	....	....	....	....	....	....	....	....	....	....	....	....	....	....	....	....	....	....
1989-90	Regina Pats	WHL	70	57	72	129	41	....	....	....	....	....	....	....	....	....	11	12	10	22	2	....	....	....	....
	Adirondack	AHL	....	....	....	....	....	....	....	....	....	....	....	....	....	....	1	0	0	0	0	....	....	....	....
1990-91	Regina Pats	WHL	57	50	66	116	42	....	....	....	....	....	....	....	....	....	8	6	9	15	4	....	....	....	....
	Detroit	**NHL**	**3**	**0**	**1**	**1**	**0**	**0**	**0**	**0**	**6**	**0.0**	**–2**	....	....	....	**3**	**0**	**1**	**1**	**0**	**0**	**0**	**0**	....
1991-92	Adirondack	AHL	64	25	41	66	26	....	....	....	....	....	....	....	....	....	15	9	*19	*28	12	....	....	....	....
	Detroit	**NHL**	....	....	....	....	....	....	....	....	....	....	....	....	....	....	**8**	**2**	**2**	**4**	**2**	**0**	**0**	**0**	....
1992-93	**Detroit**	**NHL**	**51**	**4**	**17**	**21**	**16**	**0**	**0**	**0**	**47**	**8.5**	**0**	....	....	....	....	....	....	....	....	....	....	....	....
	Adirondack	AHL	15	10	20	30	31	....	....	....	....	....	....	....	....	....	11	5	13	18	10	....	....	....	....
1993-94	**Detroit**	**NHL**	**62**	**8**	**21**	**29**	**10**	**0**	**1**	**1**	**91**	**8.8**	**2**	....	....	....	....	....	....	....	....	....	....	....	....
1994-95	CE Wien	Austria	13	13	14	27	10	....	....	....	....	....	....	....	....	....	....	....	....	....	....	....	....	....	....
	Detroit	**NHL**	**13**	**2**	**6**	**8**	**2**	**0**	**0**	**0**	**11**	**18.2**	**3**	....	....	....	....	....	....	....	....	....	....	....	....
	Anaheim	**NHL**	**15**	**2**	**5**	**7**	**6**	**2**	**0**	**0**	**28**	**7.1**	**1**	....	....	....	....	....	....	....	....	....	....	....	....
1995-96	**Anaheim**	**NHL**	**62**	**13**	**21**	**34**	**32**	**7**	**0**	**2**	**143**	**9.1**	**–20**	....	....	....	....	....	....	....	....	....	....	....	....
	Vancouver	**NHL**	**12**	**1**	**3**	**4**	**6**	**0**	**1**	**0**	**16**	**6.3**	**2**	....	....	....	**6**	**0**	**0**	**0**	**2**	**0**	**0**	**0**	....
1996-97	**Vancouver**	**NHL**	**78**	**17**	**20**	**37**	**25**	**3**	**3**	**2**	**112**	**15.2**	**–3**	....	....	....	....	....	....	....	....	....	....	....	....
1997-98	**Vancouver**	**NHL**	**48**	**10**	**9**	**19**	**34**	**1**	**2**	**1**	**56**	**17.9**	**–14**	....	....	....	....	....	....	....	....	....	....	....	....
	Philadelphia	**NHL**	**27**	**11**	**11**	**22**	**16**	**1**	**2**	**0**	**40**	**27.5**	**3**	....	....	....	**3**	**1**	**0**	**1**	**0**	**0**	**0**	**0**	....
1998-99	**Philadelphia**	**NHL**	**25**	**0**	**3**	**3**	**8**	**0**	**0**	**0**	**23**	**0.0**	**–9**	**229**	**62.9**	**10:42**	....	....	....	....	....	....	....	....	....
	Tampa Bay	**NHL**	**54**	**8**	**2**	**10**	**28**	**0**	**2**	**0**	**69**	**11.6**	**–20**	**320**	**57.8**	**13:57**	....	....	....	....	....	....	....	....	....
99-2000	**Tampa Bay**	**NHL**	**67**	**19**	**25**	**44**	**86**	**6**	**3**	**1**	**126**	**15.1**	**–29**	**493**	**56.0**	**19:42**	....	....	....	....	....	....	....	....	....
	Florida	**NHL**	**13**	**4**	**4**	**8**	**16**	**2**	**0**	**1**	**20**	**20.0**	**–1**	**248**	**61.3**	**19:33**	**4**	**2**	**1**	**3**	**2**	**0**	**0**	**0**	**20:24**
2000-01	**Florida**	**NHL**	**55**	**13**	**21**	**34**	**44**	**1**	**0**	**2**	**100**	**13.0**	**–12**	**1028**	**59.7**	**18:52**	....	....	....	....	....	....	....	....	....
	Ottawa	**NHL**	**13**	**3**	**4**	**7**	**4**	**0**	**0**	**0**	**19**	**15.8**	**1**	**215**	**63.3**	**14:31**	**4**	**0**	**0**	**0**	**2**	**0**	**0**	**0**	**13:40**
2001-02	**Columbus**	**NHL**	**80**	**20**	**23**	**43**	**54**	**8**	**0**	**5**	**150**	**13.3**	**–35**	**2024**	**57.0**	**20:51**	....	....	....	....	....	....	....	....	....
2002-03	**Columbus**	**NHL**	**75**	**18**	**25**	**43**	**52**	**9**	**3**	**3**	**128**	**14.1**	**–21**	**1490**	**56.5**	**19:08**	....	....	....	....	....	....	....	....	....
	NHL Totals		**753**	**153**	**221**	**374**	**439**	**40**	**17**	**18**	**1185**	**12.9**		**6047**	**57.9**	**18:08**	**28**	**5**	**4**	**9**	**8**	**0**	**0**	**0**	**17:02**

WHL East Second All-Star Team (1990) • WHL East First All-Star Team (1991)

Traded to **Anaheim** by **Detroit** with Jason York for Stu Grimson, Mark Ferner and Anaheim's 6th round choice (Magnus Nilsson) in 1996 Entry Draft, April 4, 1995. Traded to **Vancouver** by **Anaheim** for Roman Oksiuta, March 15, 1996. Traded to **Philadelphia** by **Vancouver** for Philadelphia's 5th round choice (later traded back to Philadelphia – Philadelphia selected Garrett Prosofsky) in 1998 Entry Draft, February 5, 1998. Traded to **Tampa Bay** by **Philadelphia** with Chris Gratton for Mikael Renberg and Daymond Langkow, December 12, 1998. Traded to **Florida** by **Tampa Bay** for Ryan Johnson and Dwayne Hay, March 14, 2000. Traded to **Ottawa** by **Florida** for future considerations, March 13, 2001. Signed as a free agent by **Columbus**, July 7, 2001. Traded to **Dallas** by **Columbus** with Columbus's 2nd round choice in 2004 Entry Draft for Darryl Sydor, July 22, 2003. Traded to **Phoenix** by **Dallas** with future considerations for Teppo Numminen, July 22, 2003.

SIM, Jon

(SIHM, JAWN) **L.A.**

Left wing. Shoots left. 5'10", 190 lbs. Born, New Glasgow, N.S., September 29, 1977. Dallas' 2nd choice, 70th overall, in 1996 Entry Draft.

			Regular Season														Playoffs								
Season	Club	League	GP	G	A	Pts	PIM	PP	SH	GW	S	%	+/-	TF	F%	Min	GP	G	A	Pts	PIM	PP	SH	GW	Min
1994-95	Laval Titan	QMJHL	9	0	1	1	6	....	....	....	....	....	....	....	....	....	....	....	....	....	....	....	....	....	....
	Sarnia Sting	OHL	25	9	12	21	19	....	....	....	....	....	....	....	....	....	4	3	2	5	2	....	....	....	....
1995-96	Sarnia Sting	OHL	63	56	46	102	130	....	....	....	....	....	....	....	....	....	10	8	7	15	26	....	....	....	....
1996-97	Sarnia Sting	OHL	64	*56	39	95	109	....	....	....	....	....	....	....	....	....	12	9	5	14	32	....	....	....	....
1997-98	Sarnia Sting	OHL	59	44	50	94	95	....	....	....	....	....	....	....	....	....	5	1	4	5	14	....	....	....	....
1998-99♦	**Dallas**	**NHL**	**7**	**1**	**0**	**1**	**12**	**0**	**0**	**0**	**8**	**12.5**	**1**	**6**	**50.0**	**11:26**	**4**	**0**	**0**	**0**	**0**	**0**	**0**	**0**	**6:26**
	Michigan	IHL	68	24	27	51	91	....	....	....	....	....	....	....	....	....	5	3	1	4	18	....	....	....	....
99-2000	**Dallas**	**NHL**	**25**	**5**	**3**	**8**	**10**	**2**	**0**	**1**	**44**	**11.4**	**4**	**4**	**75.0**	**10:51**	**7**	**1**	**0**	**1**	**6**	**0**	**0**	**0**	**11:11**
	Michigan	IHL	35	14	16	30	65	....	....	....	....	....	....	....	....	....	....	....	....	....	....	....	....	....	....
2000-01	**Dallas**	**NHL**	**15**	**0**	**3**	**3**	**6**	**0**	**0**	**0**	**18**	**0.0**	**–2**	**1**	**100.0**	**8:47**	....	....	....	....	....	....	....	....	....
	Utah Grizzlies	IHL	39	16	13	29	44	....	....	....	....	....	....	....	....	....	....	....	....	....	....	....	....	....	....
2001-02	**Dallas**	**NHL**	**26**	**3**	**0**	**3**	**10**	**1**	**0**	**0**	**43**	**7.0**	**–3**	**3**	**0.0**	**9:30**	....	....	....	....	....	....	....	....	....
	Utah Grizzlies	AHL	31	21	6	27	63	....	....	....	....	....	....	....	....	....	....	....	....	....	....	....	....	....	....
2002-03	**Dallas**	**NHL**	**4**	**0**	**0**	**0**	**0**	**0**	**0**	**0**	**7**	**0.0**	**–1**	**2**	**50.0**	**9:10**	....	....	....	....	....	....	....	....	....
	Utah Grizzlies	AHL	42	16	31	47	85	....	....	....	....	....	....	....	....	....	....	....	....	....	....	....	....	....	....
	Nashville	**NHL**	**4**	**1**	**0**	**1**	**0**	**0**	**0**	**0**	**3**	**33.3**	**0**	**14**	**35.7**	**9:18**	....	....	....	....	....	....	....	....	....
	Los Angeles	**NHL**	**14**	**0**	**2**	**2**	**19**	**0**	**0**	**0**	**29**	**0.0**	**–3**	**3**	**33.3**	**12:05**	....	....	....	....	....	....	....	....	....
	NHL Totals		**95**	**10**	**8**	**18**	**57**	**3**	**0**	**1**	**152**	**6.6**		**33**	**42.4**	**10:15**	**11**	**1**	**0**	**1**	**6**	**0**	**0**	**0**	**9:27**

OHL Second All-Star Team (1998)

Traded to **Nashville** by **Dallas** for Bubba Berenzweig and future considerations, February 17, 2003. Claimed on waivers by **Los Angeles** from **Nashville**, March 8, 2003.

SIMICEK, Roman

(SIH-mih-chehk, ROH-muhn)

Center. Shoots left. 6'1", 190 lbs. Born, Ostrava, Czech., November 4, 1971. Pittsburgh's 9th choice, 273rd overall, in 2000 Entry Draft.

			Regular Season														Playoffs								
Season	Club	League	GP	G	A	Pts	PIM	PP	SH	GW	S	%	+/-	TF	F%	Min	GP	G	A	Pts	PIM	PP	SH	GW	Min
1990-91	TJ Vitkovice	Czech	35	2	4	6	....	....	....	....	....	....	....	....	....	....	....	....	....	....	....	....	....	....	....
1991-92	TJ Vitkovice	Czech	33	6	12	18	34	....	....	....	....	....	....	....	....	....	12	2	7	9	....	....	....	....	....
1992-93	TJ Vitkovice	Czech	38	8	11	19	52	....	....	....	....	....	....	....	....	....	14	5	8	13	....	....	....	....	....
1993-94	HC Vitkovice	Czech	40	18	16	34	78	....	....	....	....	....	....	....	....	....	5	0	2	2	....	....	....	....	....
1994-95	HC Vitkovice	Czech	41	11	14	25	100	....	....	....	....	....	....	....	....	....	6	1	3	4	8	....	....	....	....
1995-96	HC Vitkovice	Czech	39	9	11	20	38	....	....	....	....	....	....	....	....	....	4	2	0	2	8	....	....	....	....
1996-97	HC Vitkovice	Czech	49	18	19	37	48	....	....	....	....	....	....	....	....	....	9	4	4	8	22	....	....	....	....
1997-98	HC Vitkovice	Czech	40	16	27	43	71	....	....	....	....	....	....	....	....	....	9	2	4	6	6	....	....	....	....
	HC Vitkovice	EuroHL	4	1	2	3	4	....	....	....	....	....	....	....	....	....	....	....	....	....	....	....	....	....	....
1998-99	HPK Hameenlinna	Finland	49	24	27	51	75	....	....	....	....	....	....	....	....	....	8	2	5	7	18	....	....	....	....
99-2000	HPK Hameenlinna	Finland	23	10	17	27	50	....	....	....	....	....	....	....	....	....	8	2	4	6	10	....	....	....	....
2000-01	**Pittsburgh**	**NHL**	**29**	**3**	**6**	**9**	**30**	**1**	**0**	**1**	**19**	**15.8**	**–5**	**203**	**45.8**	**9:28**	....	....	....	....	....	....	....	....	....
	Minnesota	**NHL**	**28**	**2**	**4**	**6**	**21**	**2**	**0**	**0**	**14**	**14.3**	**–4**	**4**	**0.0**	**12:40**	....	....	....	....	....	....	....	....	....
2001-02	**Minnesota**	**NHL**	**6**	**2**	**0**	**2**	**8**	**0**	**0**	**0**	**4**	**50.0**	**1**	**0**	**0.0**	**13:16**	....	....	....	....	....	....	....	....	....
	Houston Aeros	AHL	49	12	14	26	61	....	....	....	....	....	....	....	....	....	4	1	0	1	2	....	....	....	....
2002-03	HIFK Helsinki	Finland	30	4	11	15	49	....	....	....	....	....	....	....	....	....	....	....	....	....	....	....	....	....	....
	HC Sparta Praha	Czech	11	3	5	8	14	....	....	....	....	....	....	....	....	....	10	2	8	10	10	....	....	....	....
	NHL Totals		**63**	**7**	**10**	**17**	**59**	**3**	**0**	**1**	**37**	**18.9**		**207**	**44.9**	**11:15**	....	....	....	....	....	....	....	....	....

Traded to **Minnesota** by **Pittsburgh** for Steve McKenna, January 13, 2001.

SIMON, Ben

(SIGH-mohn, BEN) **NSH.**

Left wing. Shoots left. 6', 195 lbs. Born, Shaker Heights, OH, June 14, 1978. Chicago's 5th choice, 110th overall, in 1997 Entry Draft.

			Regular Season														Playoffs								
Season	Club	League	GP	G	A	Pts	PIM	PP	SH	GW	S	%	+/-	TF	F%	Min	GP	G	A	Pts	PIM	PP	SH	GW	Min
1992-93	Shaker Heights	Hi-School	25	15	21	36	....	....	....	....	....	....	....	....	....	....	....	....	....	....	....	....	....	....	....
1993-94	Shaker Heights	Hi-School	24	45	41	86	....	....	....	....	....	....	....	....	....	....	....	....	....	....	....	....	....	....	....
1994-95	Shaker Heights	Hi-School	25	61	68	129	....	....	....	....	....	....	....	....	....	....	....	....	....	....	....	....	....	....	....
1995-96	Cleveland Barons	NAJHL	45	38	33	71	....	....	....	....	....	....	....	....	....	....	5	7	13	20	....	....	....	....	....
1996-97	U. of Notre Dame	CCHA	30	4	15	19	79	....	....	....	....	....	....	....	....	....	....	....	....	....	....	....	....	....	....
1997-98	U. of Notre Dame	CCHA	37	9	28	37	91	....	....	....	....	....	....	....	....	....	....	....	....	....	....	....	....	....	....
1998-99	U. of Notre Dame	CCHA	37	18	24	42	65	....	....	....	....	....	....	....	....	....	....	....	....	....	....	....	....	....	....
99-2000	U. of Notre Dame	CCHA	40	13	19	32	53	....	....	....	....	....	....	....	....	....	....	....	....	....	....	....	....	....	....
2000-01	Orlando	IHL	77	8	12	20	47	....	....	....	....	....	....	....	....	....	16	6	5	11	20	....	....	....	....
2001-02	**Atlanta**	**NHL**	**6**	**0**	**0**	**0**	**6**	**0**	**0**	**0**	**7**	**0.0**	**1**	**32**	**40.6**	**9:20**	....	....	....	....	....	....	....	....	....
	Chicago Wolves	AHL	74	11	23	34	56	....	....	....	....	....	....	....	....	....	25	2	3	5	24	....	....	....	....
2002-03	**Atlanta**	**NHL**	**10**	**0**	**1**	**1**	**9**	**0**	**0**	**0**	**7**	**0.0**	**0**	**54**	**31.5**	**9:25**	....	....	....	....	....	....	....	....	....
	Chicago Wolves	AHL	69	15	17	32	78	....	....	....	....	....	....	....	....	....	9	0	0	0	6	....	....	....	....
	NHL Totals		**16**	**0**	**1**	**1**	**15**	**0**	**0**	**0**	**14**	**0.0**		**86**	**34.9**	**9:23**	....	....	....	....	....	....	....	....	....

NAJHL First All-Star Team (1996) • NAJHL Rookie of the Year (1996) • CCHA Second All-Star Team (1999)

Rights traded to **Atlanta** by **Chicago** for Atlanta's 9th round choice (Peter Flache) in 2000 Entry Draft, June 25, 2000. Signed as a free agent by **Nashville**, July 14, 2003.

			Regular Season														Playoffs								
Season	Club	League	GP	G	A	Pts	PIM	PP	SH	GW	S	%	+/-	TF	F%	Min	GP	G	A	Pts	PIM	PP	SH	GW	Min

SIMON, Chris

(SIGH-mohn, KRIHS) **NYR**

Left wing. Shoots left. 6'4", 235 lbs. Born, Wawa, Ont., January 30, 1972. Philadelphia's 2nd choice, 25th overall, in 1990 Entry Draft.

Season	Club	League	GP	G	A	Pts	PIM	PP	SH	GW	S	%	+/-	TF	F%	Min	GP	G	A	Pts	PIM	PP	SH	GW	Min
1986-87	Wawa Flyers	NOHA	36	12	20	32	108																		
1987-88	Soo Thunderbirds	NOJHA	55	42	36	78	172																		
1988-89	Ottawa 67's	OHL	36	4	2	6	31																		
1989-90	Ottawa 67's	OHL	57	36	38	74	146										3	2	1	3	4				
1990-91	Ottawa 67's	OHL	20	16	6	22	69										17	5	9	14	59				
1991-92	Ottawa 67's	OHL	2	1	1	2	24																		
	Sault Ste. Marie	OHL	31	19	25	44	143										11	5	8	13	49				
1992-93	**Quebec**	**NHL**	**16**	**1**	**1**	**2**	**67**	**0**	**0**	**1**	**15**	**6.7**	**–2**				**5**	**0**	**0**	**0**	**26**	**0**	**0**	**0**	
	Halifax Citadels	AHL	36	12	6	18	131																		
1993-94	**Quebec**	**NHL**	**37**	**4**	**4**	**8**	**132**	**0**	**0**	**1**	**39**	**10.3**	**–2**												
1994-95	**Quebec**	**NHL**	**29**	**3**	**9**	**12**	**106**	**0**	**0**	**0**	**33**	**9.1**	**14**				**6**	**1**	**1**	**2**	**19**	**0**	**0**	**1**	
1995-96 ♦	**Colorado**	**NHL**	**64**	**16**	**18**	**34**	**250**	**4**	**0**	**1**	**105**	**15.2**	**10**				**12**	**1**	**2**	**3**	**11**	**0**	**0**	**0**	
1996-97	**Washington**	**NHL**	**42**	**9**	**13**	**22**	**165**	**3**	**0**	**1**	**89**	**10.1**	**–1**												
1997-98	**Washington**	**NHL**	**28**	**7**	**10**	**17**	**38**	**4**	**0**	**1**	**71**	**9.9**	**–1**				**18**	**1**	**0**	**1**	**26**	**0**	**0**	**0**	
1998-99	**Washington**	**NHL**	**23**	**3**	**7**	**10**	**48**	**0**	**0**	**0**	**29**	**10.3**	**–4**	**2**	**50.0**	**12:08**									
99-2000	**Washington**	**NHL**	**75**	**29**	**20**	**49**	**146**	**7**	**0**	**5**	**201**	**14.4**	**11**	**7**	**28.6**	**15:32**	**4**	**2**	**0**	**2**	**24**	**0**	**0**	**0**	**18:07**
2000-01	**Washington**	**NHL**	**60**	**10**	**10**	**20**	**109**	**4**	**0**	**2**	**123**	**8.1**	**–12**	**3**	**33.3**	**14:34**	**6**	**0**	**1**	**1**	**4**	**0**	**0**	**0**	**9:55**
2001-02	**Washington**	**NHL**	**82**	**14**	**17**	**31**	**137**	**1**	**0**	**1**	**121**	**11.6**	**–8**	**7**	**28.6**	**12:11**									
2002-03	**Washington**	**NHL**	**10**	**0**	**2**	**2**	**23**	**0**	**0**	**0**	**16**	**0.0**	**–3**	**0**	**0.0**	**8:53**									
	Chicago	**NHL**	**61**	**12**	**6**	**18**	**125**	**2**	**0**	**2**	**72**	**16.7**	**–4**	**5**	**20.0**	**11:06**									
	NHL Totals		**527**	**108**	**117**	**225**	**1346**	**25**	**0**	**15**	**914**	**11.8**		**24**	**29.2**	**13:08**	**51**	**5**	**4**	**9**	**110**	**0**	**0**	**1**	**13:12**

• Missed majority of 1990-91 season recovering from shoulder surgery, October, 1990. Traded to **Quebec** by **Philadelphia** with Philadelphia's 1st round choice (later traded to Toronto – later traded to Washington – Washington selected Nolan Baumgartner) in 1994 Entry Draft to complete transaction that sent Eric Lindros to Philadelphia (June 30, 1992), July 21, 1992. Transferred to **Colorado** after **Quebec** franchise relocated, June 21, 1995. Traded to **Washington** by **Colorado** with Curtis Leschyshyn for Keith Jones and Washington's 1st (Scott Parker) and 4th (later traded back to Washington – Washington selected Krys Barch) round choices in 1998 Entry Drarft, November 2, 1996. Traded to **Chicago** by **Washington** with Andrei Nikolishin for Michael Nylander, Chicago's 3rd round choice (Stephen Werner) in 2003 Entry Draft and future considerations, November 1, 2002. Signed as a free agent by **NY Rangers**, July 25, 2003.

SIMPSON, Reid

(SIHMP-sohn, REED)

Left wing. Shoots left. 6'2", 216 lbs. Born, Flin Flon, Man., May 21, 1969. Philadelphia's 3rd choice, 72nd overall, in 1989 Entry Draft.

Season	Club	League	GP	G	A	Pts	PIM	PP	SH	GW	S	%	+/-	TF	F%	Min	GP	G	A	Pts	PIM	PP	SH	GW	Min
1984-85	Flin Flon Bombers	MMHL	50	60	70	130	100																		
1985-86	Flin Flon Bombers	MJHL	40	20	21	41	200																		
	New Westminster	WHL	2	0	0	0	0																		
1986-87	Prince Albert	WHL	47	3	8	11	105										8	2	3	5	13				
1987-88	Prince Albert	WHL	72	13	14	27	164										10	1	0	1	43				
1988-89	Prince Albert	WHL	59	26	29	55	264										4	2	1	3	30				
1989-90	Prince Albert	WHL	29	15	17	32	121										14	4	7	11	34				
	Hershey Bears	AHL	28	2	2	4	175																		
1990-91	Hershey Bears	AHL	54	9	15	24	183										1	0	0	0	0				
1991-92	**Philadelphia**	**NHL**	**1**	**0**	**0**	**0**	**0**	**0**	**0**	**0**	**0**	**0.0**	**0**												
	Hershey Bears	AHL	60	11	7	18	145																		
1992-93	**Minnesota**	**NHL**	**1**	**0**	**0**	**0**	**5**	**0**	**0**	**0**	**0**	**0.0**	**0**												
	Kalamazoo Wings	IHL	45	5	5	10	193																		
1993-94	Kalamazoo Wings	IHL	5	0	0	0	16																		
	Albany River Rats	AHL	37	9	5	14	135										5	1	1	2	18				
1994-95	Albany River Rats	AHL	70	18	25	43	268										14	1	8	9	13				
	New Jersey	**NHL**	**9**	**0**	**0**	**0**	**27**	**0**	**0**	**0**	**5**	**0.0**	**–1**												
1995-96	**New Jersey**	**NHL**	**23**	**1**	**5**	**6**	**79**	**0**	**0**	**0**	**8**	**12.5**	**2**												
	Albany River Rats	AHL	6	1	3	4	17																		
1996-97	**New Jersey**	**NHL**	**27**	**0**	**4**	**4**	**60**	**0**	**0**	**0**	**17**	**0.0**	**0**				**5**	**0**	**0**	**0**	**29**	**0**	**0**	**0**	
	Albany River Rats	AHL	3	0	0	0	10																		
1997-98	**New Jersey**	**NHL**	**6**	**0**	**0**	**0**	**16**	**0**	**0**	**0**	**5**	**0.0**	**–2**												
	Chicago	**NHL**	**38**	**3**	**2**	**5**	**102**	**1**	**0**	**0**	**19**	**15.8**	**–1**												
1998-99	**Chicago**	**NHL**	**53**	**5**	**4**	**9**	**145**	**1**	**0**	**0**	**23**	**21.7**	**2**	**5**	**40.0**	**5:56**									
99-2000	Cleveland	IHL	12	2	2	4	56																		
	Tampa Bay	**NHL**	**26**	**1**	**0**	**1**	**103**	**0**	**0**	**0**	**13**	**7.7**	**–3**	**1**	**100.0**	**4:33**									
2000-01	**St. Louis**	**NHL**	**38**	**2**	**1**	**3**	**96**	**0**	**0**	**1**	**23**	**8.7**	**–3**	**1**	**0.0**	**6:57**	**5**	**0**	**0**	**0**	**2**	**0**	**0**	**0**	**6:13**
2001-02	**Montreal**	**NHL**	**25**	**1**	**1**	**2**	**63**	**0**	**0**	**1**	**9**	**11.1**	**0**	**0**	**0.0**	**4:22**									
	Nashville	**NHL**	**26**	**5**	**0**	**5**	**69**	**0**	**0**	**0**	**13**	**38.5**	**–1**	**5**	**60.0**	**5:45**									
	Milwaukee	AHL	2	1	0	1	37																		
2002-03	**Nashville**	**NHL**	**26**	**0**	**1**	**1**	**56**	**0**	**0**	**0**	**11**	**0.0**	**–4**	**1**	**0.0**	**5:04**									
	Milwaukee	AHL	17	6	6	12	40																		
	NHL Totals		**299**	**18**	**18**	**36**	**821**	**2**	**0**	**2**	**146**	**12.3**		**13**	**46.2**	**5:36**	**10**	**0**	**0**	**0**	**31**	**0**	**0**	**0**	**6:13**

Signed as a free agent by **Minnesota**, December 14, 1992. Transferred to **Dallas** after **Minnesota** franchise relocated, June 9, 1993. Traded to **New Jersey** by **Dallas** with Roy Mitchell for future considerations, March 21, 1994. Traded to **Chicago** by **New Jersey** for Chicago's 4th round choice (Mikko Jokela) in 1998 Entry Draft and future considerations, January 8, 1998. Traded to **Tampa Bay** by **Chicago** with Bryan Muir for Michael Nylander, November 12, 1999. • Missed majority of 1999-2000 season recovering from jaw injury suffered in game vs. NY Islanders, January 13, 2000. Signed as a free agent by **St. Louis**, August 24, 2000. • Missed majority of 2000-01 season recovering from groin injury originally suffered in game vs. Nashville, November 24, 2000. Signed as a free agent by **Montreal**, September 10, 2001. Claimed on waivers by **Nashville** from **Montreal**, January 28, 2002.

SIMPSON, Todd

(SIHMP-sohn, TAWD) **PHX.**

Defense. Shoots left. 6'3", 218 lbs. Born, North Vancouver, B.C., May 28, 1973.

Season	Club	League	GP	G	A	Pts	PIM	PP	SH	GW	S	%	+/-	TF	F%	Min	GP	G	A	Pts	PIM	PP	SH	GW	Min
1991-92	Brown U.	ECAC	18	1	4	5	38																		
1992-93	Tri-City	WHL	69	5	18	23	196										4	0	0	0	13				
1993-94	Tri-City	WHL	12	2	3	5	32																		
	Saskatoon Blades	WHL	51	7	19	26	175										16	1	5	6	42				
1994-95	Saint John Flames	AHL	80	3	10	13	321										5	0	0	0	4				
1995-96	**Calgary**	**NHL**	**6**	**0**	**0**	**0**	**32**	**0**	**0**	**0**	**3**	**0.0**	**0**												
	Saint John Flames	AHL	66	4	13	17	277										16	2	3	5	32				
1996-97	**Calgary**	**NHL**	**82**	**1**	**13**	**14**	**208**	**0**	**0**	**0**	**85**	**1.2**	**–14**												
1997-98	**Calgary**	**NHL**	**53**	**1**	**5**	**6**	**109**	**0**	**0**	**1**	**51**	**2.0**	**–10**												
1998-99	**Calgary**	**NHL**	**73**	**2**	**8**	**10**	**151**	**0**	**0**	**0**	**52**	**3.8**	**18**	**1**	**100.0**	**17:19**									
99-2000	**Florida**	**NHL**	**82**	**1**	**6**	**7**	**202**	**0**	**0**	**0**	**50**	**2.0**	**5**	**0**	**0.0**	**16:35**	**4**	**0**	**0**	**0**	**4**	**0**	**0**	**0**	**15:24**
2000-01	**Florida**	**NHL**	**25**	**1**	**3**	**4**	**74**	**0**	**0**	**1**	**26**	**3.8**	**0**	**0**	**0.0**	**16:29**									
	Phoenix	**NHL**	**13**	**0**	**1**	**1**	**12**	**0**	**0**	**0**	**9**	**0.0**	**–4**	**0**	**0.0**	**13:56**									
2001-02	**Phoenix**	**NHL**	**67**	**2**	**13**	**15**	**152**	**0**	**0**	**0**	**51**	**3.9**	**20**	**0**	**0.0**	**17:20**	**5**	**0**	**2**	**2**	**6**	**0**	**0**	**0**	**18:30**
2002-03	**Phoenix**	**NHL**	**66**	**2**	**7**	**9**	**135**	**0**	**0**	**0**	**67**	**3.0**	**7**	**0**	**0.0**	**16:59**									
	NHL Totals		**467**	**10**	**56**	**66**	**1075**	**0**	**0**	**2**	**394**	**2.5**		**1**	**100.0**	**16:52**	**9**	**0**	**2**	**2**	**10**	**0**	**0**	**0**	**17:07**

Signed as free agent by **Calgary**, July 6, 1994. Traded to **Florida** by **Calgary** for Bill Lindsay, September 30, 1999. • Missed majority of 2000-01 season recovering from head injury suffered in game vs. NY Islanders, December 6, 2000. Traded to **Phoenix** by **Florida** for Phoenix's 2nd round choice (later traded to New Jersey – New Jersey selected Tuomas Pihlman) in 2001 Entry Draft, March 13, 2001.

SIVEK, Michal

(sih-VIHK, mee-KHAHL) **PIT.**

Center. Shoots left. 6'3", 213 lbs. Born, Nachod, Czech., January 21, 1981. Washington's 2nd choice, 29th overall, in 1999 Entry Draft.

Season	Club	League	GP	G	A	Pts	PIM	PP	SH	GW	S	%	+/-	TF	F%	Min	GP	G	A	Pts	PIM	PP	SH	GW	Min
1997-98	Sparta Praha Jr.	Czech-Jr.	31	13	8	21	....																		
	HC Sparta Praha	Czech	25	1	1	2	10										5	1	0	1	0				
1998-99	HC Sparta Praha	Czech	1	1	0	1	....																		
	Kladno	Czech	34	3	8	11	24																		
99-2000	Prince Albert	WHL	53	23	37	60	65										6	1	4	5	10				
2000-01	HC Sparta Praha	Czech	32	6	7	13	28										13	4	2	6	8				
2001-02	Wilkes-Barre	AHL	25	4	8	12	30																		
	HC Sparta Praha	Czech	17	5	3	8	20										12	0	1	1	10				
2002-03	**Pittsburgh**	**NHL**	**38**	**3**	**3**	**6**	**14**	**1**	**0**	**0**	**45**	**6.7**	**–5**	**32**	**43.8**	**13:05**									
	Wilkes-Barre	AHL	40	10	17	27	33										6	3	2	5	20				
	NHL Totals		**38**	**3**	**3**	**6**	**14**	**1**	**0**	**0**	**45**	**6.7**		**32**	**43.8**	**13:05**									

Traded to **Pittsburgh** by **Washington** with Kris Beech, Ross Lupaschuk and future considerations for Jaromir Jagr and Frantisek Kucera, July 11, 2001.

SKALDE, Jarrod (SKAHL-dee, JAIR-ruhd) DAL.

Center. Shoots left. 6', 185 lbs. Born, Niagara Falls, Ont., February 26, 1971. New Jersey's 3rd choice, 26th overall, in 1989 Entry Draft.

| | | | Regular Season | | | | | | | | | | | | | | Playoffs | | | | | | | | |
Season	Club	League	GP	G	A	Pts	PIM	PP	SH	GW	S	%	+/-	TF	F%	Min	GP	G	A	Pts	PIM	PP	SH	GW	Min
1986-87	Fort Erie Meteors	OJHL-B	41	27	34	61	36																		
1987-88	Oshawa Generals	OHL	60	12	16	28	24										7	2	1	3	2				
1988-89	Oshawa Generals	OHL	65	38	38	76	36										6	1	5	6	2				
1989-90	Oshawa Generals	OHL	62	40	52	92	66										17	10	7	17	6				
1990-91	Oshawa Generals	OHL	15	8	14	22	14																		
	Belleville Bulls	OHL	40	30	52	82	21										6	9	6	15	10				
	New Jersey	NHL	1	0	1	1	0	0	0	0	2	0.0	0											
	Utica Devils	AHL	3	3	2	5	0																		
1991-92	New Jersey	NHL	15	2	4	6	4	0	0	2	25	8.0	-1											
	Utica Devils	AHL	62	20	20	40	56										4	3	1	4	8				
1992-93	New Jersey	NHL	11	0	2	2	4	0	0	0	11	0.0	-3											
	Utica Devils	AHL	59	21	39	60	76										5	0	2	2	19				
	Cincinnati	IHL	4	1	2	3	4																		
1993-94	Anaheim	NHL	20	5	4	9	10	2	0	2	25	20.0	-3											
	San Diego Gulls	IHL	57	25	38	63	79										9	3	12	15	10				
1994-95	Las Vegas	IHL	74	34	41	75	103										9	2	4	6					
1995-96	Baltimore Bandits	AHL	11	2	6	8	55																		
	Calgary	NHL	1	0	0	0	0	0	0	0	0	0.0	0											
	Saint John Flames	AHL	68	27	40	67	98										16	4	9	13	6				
1996-97	Saint John Flames	AHL	65	32	36	68	94										3	0	0	0	14				
1997-98	San Jose	NHL	22	4	6	10	14	0	0	0	30	13.3	-2											
	Kentucky	AHL	6	2	6	8	10																		
	Chicago	NHL	4	0	1	1	2	0	0	0	4	0.0	0											
	Indianapolis Ice	IHL	2	0	2	2	0																		
	Dallas	NHL	1	0	0	0	0	0	0	0	0	0.0	0											
	Chicago	NHL	3	0	0	0	2	0	0	0	0	0.0	0											
	Kentucky	AHL	17	3	9	12	38										3	3	0	3	6				
1998-99	San Jose	NHL	17	1	1	2	4	0	0	0	17	5.9	-6	191	52.4	10:07								
	Kentucky	AHL	54	17	40	57	75										12	4	5	9	16				
99-2000	Utah Grizzlies	IHL	77	25	54	79	98										5	0	1	1	10				
2000-01	Atlanta	NHL	19	1	2	3	20	0	0	0	24	4.2	-8	291	47.1	13:57								
	Orlando	IHL	60	14	40	54	56										15	3	6	9	20				
2001-02	Chicago Wolves	AHL	64	15	37	52	71																		
	Philadelphia	NHL	1	0	0	0	2	0	0	0	5	0.0	0	15	60.0	12:25								
	Philadelphia	AHL	16	4	4	8	23										4	0	2	2	4				
2002-03	Lausanne HC	Swiss	23	7	8	15	30																		
	NHL Totals		115	13	21	34	62	2	0	4	143	9.1		497	49.5	12:09								

OHL Second All-Star Team (1991) • IHL First All-Star Team (2000)

Claimed by **Anaheim** from **New Jersey** in Expansion Draft, June 24, 1993. Traded to **Calgary** by **Anaheim** for Bobby Marshall, October 30, 1995. Signed as a free agent by **San Jose**, August 14, 1997. Claimed on waivers by **Chicago** from **San Jose**, January 8, 1998. Claimed on waivers by **San Jose** from **Chicago**, January 23, 1998. Claimed on waivers by **Dallas** from **San Jose**, January 27, 1998. Claimed on waivers by **Chicago** from **Dallas**, February 10, 1998. Claimed on waivers by **San Jose** from **Chicago**, March 6, 1998. Signed as a free agent by **Atlanta**, July 21, 2000. Traded to **Philadelphia** by **Atlanta** for Joe DiPenta, March 5, 2002. Signed as a free agent by **Lausanne HC** (Swiss), March 21, 2002. Signed as a free agent by **Dallas**, July 17, 2003.

SKOULA, Martin (SHKOH-la, MAHR-tihn) COL.

Defense. Shoots left. 6'2", 195 lbs. Born, Litomerice, Czech., October 28, 1979. Colorado's 2nd choice, 17th overall, in 1998 Entry Draft.

| | | | Regular Season | | | | | | | | | | | | | | Playoffs | | | | | | | | |
Season	Club	League	GP	G	A	Pts	PIM	PP	SH	GW	S	%	+/-	TF	F%	Min	GP	G	A	Pts	PIM	PP	SH	GW	Min
1995-96	Litvinov Jr.	Czech-Jr.	38	0	4	4											1	0	0	0	0				
	Litvinov	Czech																						
1996-97	Litvinov Jr.	Czech-Jr.	38	2	9	11																			
	Litvinov	Czech	1	0	0	0	0																		
1997-98	Barrie Colts	OHL	66	8	36	44	36										6	1	3	4	4				
1998-99	Barrie Colts	OHL	67	13	46	59	46										12	3	10	13	13				
	Hershey Bears	AHL															1	0	0	0	0				
99-2000	Colorado	NHL	80	3	13	16	20	2	0	0	66	4.5	5	0		18:15	17	0	2	2	4	0	0	0	18:45
2000-01 ♦	Colorado	NHL	82	8	17	25	38	3	0	2	108	7.4	8	1	100.0	20:41	23	1	4	5	8	0	0	0	11:59
2001-02	Colorado	NHL	82	10	21	31	42	5	0	1	100	10.0	-3	0		22:18	21	0	6	6	2	0	0	0	14:37
	Czech Republic	Olympics	4	0	0	0	0																		
2002-03	Colorado	NHL	81	4	21	25	68	2	0	0	93	4.3	11	1	100.0	18:27	7	0	1	1	4	0	0	0	11:05
	NHL Totals		325	25	72	97	168	12	0	3	367	6.8		2	100.0	19:56	68	1	13	14	18	0	0	0	14:24

OHL All-Rookie Team (1998) • OHL Second All-Star Team (1999)

SKRASTINS, Karlis (SKRAS-tinsh, KAR-lihs) COL.

Defense. Shoots left. 6'1", 212 lbs. Born, Riga, USSR, July 9, 1974. Nashville's 8th choice, 230th overall, in 1998 Entry Draft.

| | | | Regular Season | | | | | | | | | | | | | | Playoffs | | | | | | | | |
Season	Club	League	GP	G	A	Pts	PIM	PP	SH	GW	S	%	+/-	TF	F%	Min	GP	G	A	Pts	PIM	PP	SH	GW	Min
1992-93	Pardaugava Riga	CIS	40	3	5	8	16										2	0	0	0	0				
1993-94	Pardaugava Riga	CIS	42	7	5	12	18										2	1	0	1	4				
1994-95	Pardaugava Riga	CIS	52	4	14	18	69																		
1995-96	TPS Turku	Finland	50	4	11	15	32										11	2	2	4	10				
1996-97	TPS Turku	Finland	50	8	12	20	20										12	0	4	4	2				
	TPS Turku	EuroHL	6	0	1	1	4										4	0	0	0	14				
1997-98	TPS Turku	Finland	48	4	15	19	67										4	0	1	1	0				
	TPS Turku	EuroHL	6	0	1	1	6																		
1998-99	Nashville	NHL	2	0	1	1	0	0	0	0	0	0.0	0	0	0.0	11:47	2	0	1	1	2				
	Milwaukee	IHL	75	8	36	44	47																		
99-2000	Nashville	NHL	59	5	6	11	20	1	0	2	51	9.8	-7	0	0.0	20:51									
	Milwaukee	IHL	19	3	8	11	10																		
2000-01	Nashville	NHL	82	1	11	12	30	0	0	1	66	1.5	-12	0	0.0	19:12									
2001-02	Nashville	NHL	82	4	13	17	36	0	0	1	84	4.8	-12	0	0.0	20:29									
	Latvia	Olympics	1	0	0	0	0																		
2002-03	Nashville	NHL	82	3	10	13	44	0	0	1	86	3.5	-18	0	0.0	20:17									
	NHL Totals		307	13	41	54	130	1	1	4	287	4.5		0	0.0	20:06								

Traded to **Colorado** by **Nashville** for Colorado's 3rd round choice in 2004 Entry Draft, July 1, 2003.

SKRBEK, Pavel (SKUHR-behk, PAH-vehl) NSH.

Defense. Shoots left. 6'3", 217 lbs. Born, Kladno, Czech., August 9, 1978. Pittsburgh's 2nd choice, 28th overall, in 1996 Entry Draft.

| | | | Regular Season | | | | | | | | | | | | | | Playoffs | | | | | | | | |
Season	Club	League	GP	G	A	Pts	PIM	PP	SH	GW	S	%	+/-	TF	F%	Min	GP	G	A	Pts	PIM	PP	SH	GW	Min
1994-95	HC Kladno Jr.	Czech-Jr.	29	7	6	13																			
1995-96	Kladno Jr.	Czech-Jr.	29	10	12	22																			
	HC Poldi Kladno	Czech	13	0	1	1											5	0	0	0	0				
1996-97	HC Poldi Kladno	Czech	35	1	5	6	26										3	0	0	0	4				
1997-98	Kladno	Czech	47	4	10	14	126																		
1998-99	Pittsburgh	NHL	4	0	0	0	0	0	0	0	1	0.0	2	0	0.0	14:21									
	Syracuse Crunch	AHL	64	6	16	22	38																		
99-2000	Wilkes-Barre	AHL	51	7	16	23	50																		
	Milwaukee	IHL	6	0	0	0	0																		
2000-01	Nashville	NHL	5	0	0	0	4	0	0	0	2	0.0	1	0	0.0	11:44									
	Milwaukee	IHL	54	2	22	24	55										5	0	0	0	0				
2001-02	Nashville	NHL	3	0	0	0	2	0	0	0	0	0.0	-2	0	0.0	10:18									
	Kladno	Czech	24	2	3	5	30																		
2002-03	Lulea HF	Sweden	39	2	2	4	61										4	0	0	0	10				
	NHL Totals		12	0	0	0	8	0	0	0	3	0.0		0	0.0	12:15								

Traded to **Nashville** by **Pittsburgh** for Bob Boughner, March 13, 2000. Assigned to **Kladno** (Czech) by **Nashville**, October 31, 2001. Signed as a free agent by **Lulea HF** (Sweden), June 20, 2002.

SLANEY, John

(SLAY-nee, JAWN) **PHI.**

Defense. Shoots left. 6', 189 lbs. Born, St. John's, Nfld., February 2, 1972. Washington's 1st choice, 9th overall, in 1990 Entry Draft.

			Regular Season														Playoffs								
Season	Club	League	GP	G	A	Pts	PIM	PP	SH	GW	S	%	+/-	TF	F%	Min	GP	G	A	Pts	PIM	PP	SH	GW	Min
1987-88	St. John's	NFAHA	65	41	69	110	70																		
1988-89	Cornwall Royals	OHL	66	16	43	59	23										18	8	16	24	10				
1989-90	Cornwall Royals	OHL	64	38	59	97	68										6	0	8	8	11				
1990-91	Cornwall Royals	OHL	34	21	25	46	28																		
1991-92	Cornwall Royals	OHL	34	19	41	60	43										6	3	8	11	0				
	Baltimore	AHL	6	2	4	6	0																		
1992-93	Baltimore	AHL	79	20	46	66	60										7	0	7	7	8				
1993-94	**Washington**	**NHL**	**47**	**7**	**9**	**16**	**27**	**3**	**0**	**1**	**70**	**10.0**	**3**				**11**	**1**	**1**	**2**	**2**	**1**	**0**	**0**	
	Portland Pirates	AHL	29	14	13	27	17																		
1994-95	**Washington**	**NHL**	**16**	**0**	**3**	**3**	**6**	**0**	**0**	**0**	**21**	**0.0**	**–3**												
	Portland Pirates	AHL	8	3	10	13	4										7	1	3	4	4				
1995-96	**Colorado**	**NHL**	**7**	**0**	**3**	**3**	**4**	**0**	**0**	**0**	**12**	**0.0**	**2**												
	Cornwall Aces	AHL	5	0	4	4	2																		
	Los Angeles	**NHL**	**31**	**6**	**11**	**17**	**10**	**3**	**1**	**0**	**63**	**9.5**	**5**												
1996-97	**Los Angeles**	**NHL**	**32**	**3**	**11**	**14**	**4**	**1**	**0**	**1**	**60**	**5.0**	**–10**												
	Phoenix	IHL	35	9	25	34	8																		
1997-98	**Phoenix**	**NHL**	**55**	**3**	**14**	**17**	**24**	**1**	**0**	**1**	**74**	**4.1**	**–3**												
	Las Vegas	IHL	5	2	2	4	10																		
1998-99	**Nashville**	**NHL**	**46**	**2**	**12**	**14**	**14**	**0**	**0**	**1**	**84**	**2.4**	**–12**	**0**	**0.0**	**20:39**									
	Milwaukee	IHL	7	0	1	1	0																		
99-2000	**Pittsburgh**	**NHL**	**29**	**1**	**4**	**5**	**10**	**1**	**0**	**0**	**27**	**3.7**	**–10**	**35**	**40.0**	**12:13**	**2**	**1**	**0**	**1**	**2**	**1**	**0**	**0**	**5:42**
	Wilkes-Barre	AHL	49	30	30	60	25																		
2000-01	Wilkes-Barre	AHL	40	12	38	50	4																		
	Philadelphia	AHL	25	6	11	17	10										10	2	6	8	6				
2001-02	**Philadelphia**	**NHL**	**1**	**0**	**0**	**0**	**0**	**0**	**0**	**0**	**1**	**0.0**	**2**	**0**	**0.0**	**23:33**	**1**	**0**	**0**	**0**	**0**	**0**	**0**	**0**	**11:20**
	Philadelphia	AHL	64	20	39	59	26										5	2	1	3	0				
2002-03	Philadelphia	AHL	55	9	33	42	36																		
	NHL Totals		**264**	**22**	**67**	**89**	**99**	**9**	**1**	**4**	**412**	**5.3**		**35**	**40.0**	**17:28**	**14**	**2**	**1**	**3**	**4**	**2**	**0**	**0**	**7:35**

OHL First All-Star Team (1990) • Canadian Major Junior Defenseman of the Year (1990) • OHL Second All-Star Team (1991) • AHL First All-Star Team (2001, 2002) • Eddie Shore Award (Top Defenseman – AHL) (2001, 2002)

Traded to **Colorado** by **Washington** for Philadelphia's 3rd round choice (previously acquired, Washington selected Shawn McNeil) in 1996 Entry Draft, July 12, 1995. Traded to **Los Angeles** by **Colorado** for Winnipeg's 6th round choice (previously acquired, Colorado selected Brian Willsie) in 1996 Entry Draft, December 28, 1995. Signed as a free agent by **Phoenix**, August 19, 1997. Claimed by **Nashville** from **Phoenix** in Expansion Draft, June 26, 1998. Signed as a free agent by **Pittsburgh**, September 30, 1999. Traded to **Philadelphia** by **Pittsburgh** for Kevin Stevens, January 14, 2001.

SLEGR, Jiri

(SLAY-guhr, YEE-ree)

Defense. Shoots left. 6', 216 lbs. Born, Jihlava, Czech., May 30, 1971. Vancouver's 3rd choice, 23rd overall, in 1990 Entry Draft.

1987-88	CHZ Litvinov	Czech	4	1	1	2	0																		
1988-89	CHZ Litvinov	Czech	8	0	0	0	4																		
1989-90	CHZ Litvinov	Czech	51	4	15	19	....																		
1990-91	HC CHZ Litvinov	Czech	47	11	36	47	26																		
1991-92	Litvinov	Czech	42	9	23	32	38																		
	Czechoslovakia	Olympics	8	1	1	2	14																		
1992-93	**Vancouver**	**NHL**	**41**	**4**	**22**	**26**	**109**	**2**	**0**	**0**	**89**	**4.5**	**16**				**5**	**0**	**3**	**3**	**4**	**0**	**0**	**0**	
	Hamilton	AHL	21	4	14	18	42																		
1993-94	**Vancouver**	**NHL**	**78**	**5**	**33**	**38**	**86**	**1**	**0**	**0**	**160**	**3.1**	**0**												
1994-95	Litvinov	Czech	11	3	10	13	80																		
	Vancouver	**NHL**	**19**	**1**	**5**	**6**	**32**	**0**	**0**	**1**	**42**	**2.4**	**0**												
	Edmonton	**NHL**	**12**	**1**	**5**	**6**	**14**	**1**	**0**	**0**	**27**	**3.7**	**–5**												
1995-96	**Edmonton**	**NHL**	**57**	**4**	**13**	**17**	**74**	**0**	**1**	**1**	**91**	**4.4**	**–1**												
	Cape Breton	AHL	4	1	2	3	4																		
1996-97	Litvinov	Czech	1	0	0	0	0																		
	Sodertalje SK	Sweden	30	4	14	18	62										10	4	2	6	32				
1997-98	**Pittsburgh**	**NHL**	**73**	**5**	**12**	**17**	**109**	**1**	**1**	**0**	**131**	**3.8**	**10**				**6**	**0**	**4**	**4**	**2**	**0**	**0**	**0**	
	Czech Republic	Olympics	6	1	0	1	8																		
1998-99	**Pittsburgh**	**NHL**	**63**	**3**	**20**	**23**	**86**	**1**	**0**	**0**	**91**	**3.3**	**13**	**2**	**0.0**	**18:42**	**13**	**1**	**3**	**4**	**12**	**0**	**0**	**1**	**19:50**
99-2000	**Pittsburgh**	**NHL**	**74**	**11**	**20**	**31**	**82**	**0**	**0**	**2**	**144**	**7.6**	**20**	**3**	**66.7**	**21:22**	**10**	**2**	**3**	**5**	**19**	**0**	**0**	**1**	**20:02**
2000-01	**Pittsburgh**	**NHL**	**42**	**5**	**10**	**15**	**60**	**0**	**1**	**1**	**67**	**7.5**	**–9**	**0**	**0.0**	**17:37**									
	Atlanta	**NHL**	**33**	**3**	**16**	**19**	**36**	**2**	**0**	**0**	**78**	**3.8**	**–1**	**1**	**0.0**	**21:34**									
2001-02	**Atlanta**	**NHL**	**38**	**3**	**5**	**8**	**51**	**1**	**0**	**0**	**56**	**5.4**	**–21**	**0**	**0.0**	**21:21**									
	♦ Detroit	**NHL**	**8**	**0**	**1**	**1**	**8**	**0**	**0**	**0**	**11**	**0.0**	**1**	**0**	**0.0**	**19:16**	**1**	**0**	**0**	**0**	**2**	**0**	**0**	**0**	**17:11**
2002-03	Litvinov	Czech	10	2	3	5	14																		
	Avangard Omsk	Russia	6	1	2	3	8										9	0	3	3	*45				
	NHL Totals		**538**	**45**	**162**	**207**	**747**	**9**	**3**	**5**	**987**	**4.6**		**6**	**33.3**	**20:04**	**35**	**3**	**13**	**16**	**39**	**0**	**0**	**2**	**19:48**

Czechoslovakian First All-Star Team (1991)

Traded to **Edmonton** by **Vancouver** for Roman Oksiuta, April 7, 1995. Traded to **Pittsburgh** by **Edmonton** for Pittsburgh's 3rd round choice (later traded to New Jersey – New Jersey selected Brian Gionta) in 1998 Entry Draft, August 12, 1997. Traded to **Atlanta** by **Pittsburgh** for San Jose's 3rd round choice (previously acquired, later traded to Columbus – Columbus selected Aaron Johnson) in 2001 Entry Draft, January 14, 2001. Traded to **Detroit** by **Atlanta** for Yuri Butsayev and Detroit's 3rd round choice (later traded to Columbus – Columbus selected Jeff Genovy) in 2002 Entry Draft, March 19, 2002.

SLOAN, Blake

(SLOHN, BLAYK)

Right wing. Shoots right. 5'10", 196 lbs. Born, Park Ridge, IL, July 27, 1975.

1992-93	Tabor Academy	Hi-School	33	7	15	22	....																		
1993-94	U. of Michigan	CCHA	38	2	4	6	48																		
1994-95	U. of Michigan	CCHA	39	2	15	17	60																		
1995-96	U. of Michigan	CCHA	41	6	24	30	55																		
1996-97	U. of Michigan	CCHA	41	2	15	17	52																		
1997-98	Houston Aeros	IHL	70	2	13	15	86										2	0	0	0	0				
1998-99 ♦	**Dallas**	**NHL**	**14**	**0**	**0**	**0**	**10**	**0**	**0**	**0**	**7**	**0.0**	**–1**	**0**	**0.0**	**9:01**	**19**	**0**	**2**	**2**	**8**	**0**	**0**	**0**	**9:58**
	Houston Aeros	IHL	62	8	10	18	76																		
99-2000	**Dallas**	**NHL**	**67**	**4**	**13**	**17**	**50**	**0**	**0**	**1**	**78**	**5.1**	**11**	**2**	**50.0**	**13:30**	**16**	**0**	**0**	**0**	**12**	**0**	**0**	**0**	**8:54**
2000-01	**Dallas**	**NHL**	**33**	**2**	**2**	**4**	**4**	**0**	**0**	**1**	**29**	**6.9**	**–2**	**4**	**25.0**	**9:56**									
	Houston Aeros	IHL	20	7	4	11	18																		
	Columbus	**NHL**	**14**	**1**	**0**	**1**	**13**	**0**	**0**	**0**	**16**	**6.3**	**–2**	**7**	**28.6**	**13:19**									
2001-02	**Columbus**	**NHL**	**60**	**2**	**7**	**9**	**46**	**0**	**0**	**0**	**49**	**4.1**	**–18**	**3**	**66.7**	**10:56**									
	Calgary	**NHL**	**7**	**0**	**2**	**2**	**4**	**0**	**0**	**0**	**7**	**0.0**	**1**	**2**	**0.0**	**12:16**									
2002-03	**Calgary**	**NHL**	**67**	**2**	**8**	**10**	**28**	**0**	**0**	**0**	**56**	**3.6**	**–5**	**31**	**12.9**	**12:23**									
	NHL Totals		**262**	**11**	**32**	**43**	**155**	**0**	**0**	**2**	**242**	**4.5**		**49**	**20.4**	**11:54**	**35**	**0**	**2**	**2**	**20**	**0**	**0**	**0**	**9:29**

Signed as a free agent by **Dallas**, March 10, 1998. Claimed on waivers by **Columbus** from **Dallas**, March 13, 2001. Traded to **Calgary** by **Columbus** for Jamie Allison, March 19, 2002.

SMEHLIK, Richard

(SHMEH-lihk, RIH-chahrd)

Defense. Shoots left. 6'4", 222 lbs. Born, Ostrava, Czech., January 23, 1970. Buffalo's 3rd choice, 97th overall, in 1990 Entry Draft.

1988-89	TJ Vitkovice	Czech	38	2	5	7	12																		
1989-90	TJ Vitkovice	Czech	44	4	3	7	....										7	1	1	2	....				
1990-91	Dukla Jihlava	Czech	58	4	3	7	22																		
1991-92	TJ Vitkovice	Czech	47	9	10	19	42																		
	Czechoslovakia	Olympics	8	0	1	1	2																		
1992-93	**Buffalo**	**NHL**	**80**	**4**	**27**	**31**	**59**	**0**	**0**	**0**	**82**	**4.9**	**9**				**8**	**0**	**4**	**4**	**2**	**0**	**0**	**0**	
1993-94	**Buffalo**	**NHL**	**84**	**14**	**27**	**41**	**69**	**3**	**3**	**1**	**106**	**13.2**	**22**				**7**	**0**	**2**	**2**	**10**	**0**	**0**	**0**	
1994-95	HC Vitkovice	Czech	13	5	2	7	12																		
	Buffalo	**NHL**	**39**	**4**	**7**	**11**	**46**	**0**	**1**	**1**	**49**	**8.2**	**5**				**5**	**0**	**0**	**0**	**2**	**0**	**0**	**0**	
1995-96	**Buffalo**	**NHL**	DID NOT PLAY – INJURED																						
1996-97	**Buffalo**	**NHL**	**62**	**11**	**19**	**30**	**43**	**2**	**0**	**1**	**100**	**11.0**	**19**				**12**	**0**	**2**	**2**	**4**	**0**	**0**	**0**	
1997-98	**Buffalo**	**NHL**	**72**	**3**	**17**	**20**	**62**	**0**	**1**	**0**	**90**	**3.3**	**11**				**15**	**0**	**2**	**2**	**6**	**0**	**0**	**0**	
	Czech Republic	Olympics	6	0	1	1	4																		
1998-99	**Buffalo**	**NHL**	**72**	**3**	**11**	**14**	**44**	**0**	**0**	**0**	**61**	**4.9**	**–9**	**0**	**0.0**	**21:50**	**21**	**0**	**3**	**3**	**10**	**0**	**0**	**0**	**24:04**
99-2000	**Buffalo**	**NHL**	**64**	**2**	**9**	**11**	**50**	**0**	**0**	**0**	**67**	**3.0**	**13**	**0**	**0.0**	**21:04**	**5**	**1**	**0**	**1**	**0**	**0**	**0**	**0**	**20:20**

			Regular Season														Playoffs								
Season	Club	League	GP	G	A	Pts	PIM	PP	SH	GW	S	%	+/-	TF	F%	Min	GP	G	A	Pts	PIM	PP	SH	GW	Min
2000-01	**Buffalo**	**NHL**	**56**	**3**	**12**	**15**	**4**	**0**	**0**	**1**	**40**	**7.5**	**6**	**0**	**0.0**	**19:25**	**10**	**0**	**1**	**1**	**4**	**0**	**0**	**0**	**19:45**
2001-02	**Buffalo**	**NHL**	**60**	**3**	**6**	**9**	**22**	**0**	**0**	**1**	**52**	**5.8**	**–9**	**0**	**0.0**	**20:22**	....	....	....	....	....	....	....	....	....
	Czech Republic	Olympics	4	0	0	0	0	....	....	....	....	....	....	....	....	....	....	....	....	....	....	....	....	....	....
2002-03	**Atlanta**	**NHL**	**43**	**2**	**9**	**11**	**16**	**0**	**0**	**0**	**38**	**5.3**	**–4**	**0**	**0.0**	**19:42**	....	....	....	....	....	....	....	....	....
	♦ New Jersey	**NHL**	**12**	**0**	**2**	**2**	**0**	**0**	**0**	**0**	**11**	**0.0**	**–1**	**0**	**0.0**	**17:20**	**5**	**0**	**0**	**0**	**2**	**0**	**0**	**0**	**12:58**
	NHL Totals		**644**	**49**	**146**	**195**	**415**	**5**	**5**	**5**	**696**	**7.0**		**0**	**0.0**	**20:28**	**88**	**1**	**14**	**15**	**40**	**0**	**0**	**0**	**21:13**

• Missed entire 1995-96 season recovering from knee surgery, August 11, 1995. Signed as a free agent by **Atlanta**, July 11, 2002. Traded to **New Jersey** by **Atlanta** with New Jersey's 6th and 8th round choices (previously acquired) in 2004 Entry Draft for New Jersey's 4th round choice (Michael Vannelli) in 2003 Entry Draft, March 10, 2003.

SMIRNOV, Alexei

(smihr-NAHV, al-EHX-ay) **ANA.**

Left wing. Shoots left. 6'3", 211 lbs. Born, Tver, USSR, January 28, 1982. Anaheim's 1st choice, 12th overall, in 2000 Entry Draft.

Season	Club	League	GP	G	A	Pts	PIM	PP	SH	GW	S	%	+/-	TF	F%	Min	GP	G	A	Pts	PIM	PP	SH	GW	Min
1997-98	DynamoMoscow2	Russia-2	11	1	1	2	4	....	....	....	....	....	....	....	....	....	....	....	....	....	....	....	....	....	....
1998-99	DynamoMoscow2	Russia-3	27	9	3	12	24	....	....	....	....	....	....	....	....	....	....	....	....	....	....	....	....	....	....
99-2000	DynamoMoscow2	Russia-3	12	5	3	8	34	....	....	....	....	....	....	....	....	....	....	....	....	....	....	....	....	....	....
	THC Tver	Russia-2	35	3	5	8	24	....	....	....	....	....	....	....	....	....	....	....	....	....	....	....	....	....	....
	Dynamo Moscow	Russia	1	0	0	0	0	....	....	....	....	....	....	....	....	....	....	....	....	....	....	....	....	....	....
2000-01	Dynamo Moscow	Russia	29	2	0	2	16	....	....	....	....	....	....	....	....	....	....	....	....	....	....	....	....	....	....
2001-02	CSKA Moscow 2	Russia-3	2	1	0	1	0	....	....	....	....	....	....	....	....	....	....	....	....	....	....	....	....	....	....
	CSKA Moscow	Russia	51	5	11	16	42	....	....	....	....	....	....	....	....	....	....	....	....	....	....	....	....	....	....
2002-03	**Anaheim**	**NHL**	**44**	**3**	**2**	**5**	**18**	**0**	**0**	**1**	**46**	**6.5**	**–1**	**6**	**16.7**	**8:50**	**4**	**0**	**0**	**0**	**2**	**0**	**0**	**0**	**4:22**
	Cincinnati	AHL	19	7	3	10	12	....	....	....	....	....	....	....	....	....	....	....	....	....	....	....	....	....	....
	NHL Totals		**44**	**3**	**2**	**5**	**18**	**0**	**0**	**1**	**46**	**6.5**		**6**	**16.7**	**8:50**	**4**	**0**	**0**	**0**	**2**	**0**	**0**	**0**	**4:22**

SMITH, Brandon

(SMIHTH, BRAN-duhn) **NYI**

Defense. Shoots left. 6'1", 209 lbs. Born, Hazelton, B.C., February 25, 1973.

Season	Club	League	GP	G	A	Pts	PIM	PP	SH	GW	S	%	+/-	TF	F%	Min	GP	G	A	Pts	PIM	PP	SH	GW	Min
1989-90	Portland	WHL	59	2	17	19	16	....	....	....	....	....	....	....	....	....	....	....	....	....	....	....	....	....	....
1990-91	Portland	WHL	17	8	5	13	8	....	....	....	....	....	....	....	....	....	....	....	....	....	....	....	....	....	....
1991-92	Portland	WHL	70	12	32	44	63	....	....	....	....	....	....	....	....	....	....	....	....	....	....	....	....	....	....
1992-93	Portland	WHL	72	20	54	74	38	....	....	....	....	....	....	....	....	....	16	4	9	13	6	....	....	....	....
1993-94	Portland	WHL	72	19	63	82	47	....	....	....	....	....	....	....	....	....	10	2	10	12	8	....	....	....	....
1994-95	Dayton Bombers	ECHL	60	16	49	65	57	....	....	....	....	....	....	....	....	....	4	2	3	5	0	....	....	....	....
	Minnesota Moose	IHL	1	0	0	0	0	....	....	....	....	....	....	....	....	....	....	....	....	....	....	....	....	....	....
	Adirondack	AHL	14	1	2	3	7	....	....	....	....	....	....	....	....	....	3	0	0	0	2	....	....	....	....
1995-96	Adirondack	AHL	48	4	13	17	22	....	....	....	....	....	....	....	....	....	3	0	1	1	2	....	....	....	....
1996-97	Adirondack	AHL	80	8	26	34	30	....	....	....	....	....	....	....	....	....	4	0	0	0	0	....	....	....	....
1997-98	Adirondack	AHL	64	9	27	36	26	....	....	....	....	....	....	....	....	....	1	0	1	1	0	....	....	....	....
1998-99	**Boston**	**NHL**	**5**	**0**	**0**	**0**	**0**	**0**	**0**	**0**	**2**	**0.0**	**2**	**0**	**0.0**	**9:38**	....	....	....	....	....	....	....	....	....
	Providence Bruins	AHL	72	16	46	62	32	....	....	....	....	....	....	....	....	....	19	1	9	10	12	....	....	....	....
99-2000	**Boston**	**NHL**	**22**	**2**	**4**	**6**	**10**	**0**	**0**	**0**	**24**	**8.3**	**–4**	**0**	**0.0**	**19:29**	....	....	....	....	....	....	....	....	....
	Providence Bruins	AHL	55	8	30	38	20	....	....	....	....	....	....	....	....	....	14	1	11	12	2	....	....	....	....
2000-01	**Boston**	**NHL**	**3**	**1**	**0**	**1**	**0**	**1**	**0**	**0**	**2**	**50.0**	**–1**	**0**	**0.0**	**6:46**	....	....	....	....	....	....	....	....	....
	Providence Bruins	AHL	63	11	28	39	30	....	....	....	....	....	....	....	....	....	17	0	5	5	6	....	....	....	....
2001-02	Cleveland Barons	AHL	59	6	29	35	26	....	....	....	....	....	....	....	....	....	....	....	....	....	....	....	....	....	....
2002-03	**NY Islanders**	**NHL**	**3**	**0**	**0**	**0**	**0**	**0**	**0**	**0**	**1**	**0.0**	**–2**	**0**	**0.0**	**9:59**	....	....	....	....	....	....	....	....	....
	Bridgeport	AHL	63	9	32	41	37	....	....	....	....	....	....	....	....	....	9	1	3	4	5	....	....	....	....
	NHL Totals		**33**	**3**	**4**	**7**	**10**	**1**	**0**	**0**	**29**	**10.3**		**0**	**0.0**	**15:58**	....	....	....	....	....	....	....	....	....

WHL West Second All-Star Team (1993, 1994) • ECHL First All-Star Team (1995) • ECHL Top Defenseman Award (1995) • AHL First All-Star Team (1999)

Signed as a free agent by **Detroit**, July 22, 1997. Signed as a free agent by **Boston**, August 5, 1998. Signed as a free agent by **San Jose**, July 23, 2001. Signed as a free agent by **NY Islanders**, August 3, 2002.

SMITH, D.J.

(SMIHTH, DEE-JAY) **COL.**

Defense. Shoots left. 6'2", 205 lbs. Born, Windsor, Ont., May 13, 1977. NY Islanders' 3rd choice, 41st overall, in 1995 Entry Draft.

Season	Club	League	GP	G	A	Pts	PIM	PP	SH	GW	S	%	+/-	TF	F%	Min	GP	G	A	Pts	PIM	PP	SH	GW	Min
1992-93	Belle River	OJHL-C	40	5	18	23	39	....	....	....	....	....	....	....	....	....	....	....	....	....	....	....	....	....	....
	Windsor Bulldogs	OJHL-B	1	0	0	0	0	....	....	....	....	....	....	....	....	....	....	....	....	....	....	....	....	....	....
1993-94	Windsor Bulldogs	OJHL-B	51	8	34	42	267	....	....	....	....	....	....	....	....	....	....	....	....	....	....	....	....	....	....
1994-95	Windsor Spitfires	OHL	61	4	13	17	201	....	....	....	....	....	....	....	....	....	10	1	3	4	41	....	....	....	....
1995-96	Windsor Spitfires	OHL	64	14	45	59	260	....	....	....	....	....	....	....	....	....	7	1	7	8	23	....	....	....	....
	St. John's	AHL	1	0	0	0	0	....	....	....	....	....	....	....	....	....	....	....	....	....	....	....	....	....	....
1996-97	Windsor Spitfires	OHL	63	15	52	67	190	....	....	....	....	....	....	....	....	....	5	1	7	8	11	....	....	....	....
	Toronto	**NHL**	**8**	**0**	**1**	**1**	**7**	**0**	**0**	**0**	**4**	**0.0**	**–5**	....	....	....	....	....	....	....	....	....	....	....	....
	St. John's	AHL	....	....	....	....	....	....	....	....	....	....	....	....	....	....	1	0	0	0	0	....	....	....	....
1997-98	St. John's	AHL	65	4	11	15	237	....	....	....	....	....	....	....	....	....	4	0	0	0	4	....	....	....	....
1998-99	St. John's	AHL	79	7	28	35	216	....	....	....	....	....	....	....	....	....	5	0	1	1	0	....	....	....	....
99-2000	**Toronto**	**NHL**	**3**	**0**	**0**	**0**	**5**	**0**	**0**	**0**	**2**	**0.0**	**–1**	**0**	**0.0**	**12:37**	....	....	....	....	....	....	....	....	....
	St. John's	AHL	74	6	22	28	197	....	....	....	....	....	....	....	....	....	....	....	....	....	....	....	....	....	....
2000-01	St. John's	AHL	59	7	12	19	106	....	....	....	....	....	....	....	....	....	4	0	0	0	11	....	....	....	....
2001-02	St. John's	AHL	59	6	10	16	152	....	....	....	....	....	....	....	....	....	....	....	....	....	....	....	....	....	....
	Hershey Bears	AHL	14	0	3	3	33	....	....	....	....	....	....	....	....	....	8	1	0	1	33	....	....	....	....
2002-03	**Colorado**	**NHL**	**34**	**1**	**0**	**1**	**55**	**0**	**0**	**0**	**7**	**14.3**	**2**	**0**	**0.0**	**3:49**	....	....	....	....	....	....	....	....	....
	Hershey Bears	AHL	2	0	0	0	4	....	....	....	....	....	....	....	....	....	....	....	....	....	....	....	....	....	....
	NHL Totals		**45**	**1**	**1**	**2**	**67**	**0**	**0**	**0**	**13**	**7.7**		**0**	**0.0**	**4:32**	....	....	....	....	....	....	....	....	....

OHL Second All-Star Team (1997)

Traded to **Toronto** by **NY Islanders** with Wendel Clark and Mathieu Schneider for Darby Hendrickson, Sean Haggerty, Kenny Jonsson and Toronto's 1st round choice (Roberto Luongo) in 1997 Entry Draft, March 13, 1996. Traded to **Nashville** by **Toronto** with Marty Wilford for Marc Moro, March 1, 2002. Traded to **Colorado** by **Nashville** for Tampa Bay's 9th round choice (previously acquired, Nashville selected Matt Davis) in 2002 Entry Draft, March 1, 2002. • Missed majority of 2002-03 season recovering from head injury suffered in game vs. San Jose, November 5, 2002.

SMITH, Dan

(SMIHTH, DAN) **EDM.**

Defense. Shoots left. 6'2", 200 lbs. Born, Fernie, B.C., October 19, 1976. Colorado's 7th choice, 181st overall, in 1995 Entry Draft.

Season	Club	League	GP	G	A	Pts	PIM	PP	SH	GW	S	%	+/-	TF	F%	Min	GP	G	A	Pts	PIM	PP	SH	GW	Min
1994-95	U.B.C.	CWUAA	28	1	3	4	26	....	....	....	....	....	....	....	....	....	....	....	....	....	....	....	....	....	....
1995-96	Tri-City	WHL	58	1	21	22	70	....	....	....	....	....	....	....	....	....	11	1	3	4	14	....	....	....	....
1996-97	Tri-City	WHL	72	5	19	24	174	....	....	....	....	....	....	....	....	....	....	....	....	....	....	....	....	....	....
	Hershey Bears	AHL	8	0	1	1	6	....	....	....	....	....	....	....	....	....	15	0	1	1	25	....	....	....	....
1997-98	Hershey Bears	AHL	50	1	2	3	71	....	....	....	....	....	....	....	....	....	6	0	0	0	4	....	....	....	....
1998-99	**Colorado**	**NHL**	**12**	**0**	**0**	**0**	**9**	**0**	**0**	**0**	**6**	**0.0**	**5**	**0**	**0.0**	**12:14**	....	....	....	....	....	....	....	....	....
	Hershey Bears	AHL	54	5	7	12	72	....	....	....	....	....	....	....	....	....	5	0	1	1	0	....	....	....	....
99-2000	**Colorado**	**NHL**	**3**	**0**	**0**	**0**	**0**	**0**	**0**	**0**	**0**	**0.0**	**2**	**0**	**0.0**	**11:03**	....	....	....	....	....	....	....	....	....
	Hershey Bears	AHL	49	7	15	22	56	....	....	....	....	....	....	....	....	....	....	....	....	....	....	....	....	....	....
2000-01	Hershey Bears	AHL	58	2	12	14	34	....	....	....	....	....	....	....	....	....	12	0	1	1	4	....	....	....	....
2001-02	Colorado	WCHL	12	0	2	2	16	....	....	....	....	....	....	....	....	....	....	....	....	....	....	....	....	....	....
	Lukko Rauma	Finland	32	1	2	3	18	....	....	....	....	....	....	....	....	....	....	....	....	....	....	....	....	....	....
2002-03	Springfield	AHL	69	1	14	15	53	....	....	....	....	....	....	....	....	....	6	0	2	2	0	....	....	....	....
	NHL Totals		**15**	**0**	**0**	**0**	**9**	**0**	**0**	**0**	**6**	**0.0**		**0**	**0.0**	**11:60**	....	....	....	....	....	....	....	....	....

Signed as a free agent by **Colorado** (WCHL), October 26, 2001. Signed as a free agent by **Lukko** (Finland) after receiving release from Colorado (WCHL), November 21, 2001. Signed as a free agent by **Edmonton**, August 21, 2003.

SMITH, Jason

(SMIHTH, JAY-suhn) **EDM.**

Defense. Shoots right. 6'3", 212 lbs. Born, Calgary, Alta., November 2, 1973. New Jersey's 1st choice, 18th overall, in 1992 Entry Draft.

Season	Club	League	GP	G	A	Pts	PIM	PP	SH	GW	S	%	+/-	TF	F%	Min	GP	G	A	Pts	PIM	PP	SH	GW	Min
1990-91	Calgary Canucks	AJHL	45	3	15	18	69	....	....	....	....	....	....	....	....	....	....	....	....	....	....	....	....	....	....
	Regina Pats	WHL	2	0	0	0	7	....	....	....	....	....	....	....	....	....	4	0	0	0	2	....	....	....	....
1991-92	Regina Pats	WHL	62	9	29	38	138	....	....	....	....	....	....	....	....	....	....	....	....	....	....	....	....	....	....
1992-93	Regina Pats	WHL	64	14	52	66	175	....	....	....	....	....	....	....	....	....	13	4	8	12	39	....	....	....	....
	Utica Devils	AHL	....	....	....	....	....	....	....	....	....	....	....	....	....	....	1	0	0	0	2	....	....	....	....
1993-94	**New Jersey**	**NHL**	**41**	**0**	**5**	**5**	**43**	**0**	**0**	**0**	**47**	**0.0**	**7**	....	....	....	**6**	**0**	**0**	**0**	**7**	**0**	**0**	**0**	
	Albany River Rats	AHL	20	6	3	9	31	....	....	....	....	....	....	....	....	....	....	....	....	....	....	....	....	....	....

			Regular Season														Playoffs								
Season	Club	League	GP	G	A	Pts	PIM	PP	SH	GW	S	%	+/-	TF	F%	Min	GP	G	A	Pts	PIM	PP	SH	GW	Min
1994-95	Albany River Rats	AHL	7	0	2	2	15	....	....	....	....	....	....	....	....	....	11	2	2	4	19	....	....	....	....
	New Jersey	NHL	2	0	0	0	0	0	0	0	5	0.0	–3	....	....	....	....	....	....	....	....	....	....	....	....
1995-96	New Jersey	NHL	64	2	1	3	86	0	0	0	52	3.8	5	....	....	....	....	....	....	....	....	....	....	....	....
1996-97	New Jersey	NHL	57	1	2	3	38	0	0	0	48	2.1	–8	....	....	....	....	....	....	....	....	....	....	....	....
	Toronto	NHL	21	0	5	5	16	0	0	0	26	0.0	–4	....	....	....	....	....	....	....	....	....	....	....	....
1997-98	Toronto	NHL	81	3	13	16	100	0	0	0	97	3.1	–5	....	....	....	....	....	....	....	....	....	....	....	....
1998-99	Toronto	NHL	60	2	11	13	40	0	0	0	53	3.8	–9	0	0.0	17:31	....	....	....	....	....	....	....	....	....
	Edmonton	NHL	12	1	1	2	11	0	0	0	15	6.7	0	0	0.0	20:26	4	0	1	1	4	0	0	0	26:29
99-2000	Edmonton	NHL	80	3	11	14	60	0	0	1	96	3.1	16	1	100.0	21:15	5	0	1	1	4	0	0	0	21:56
2000-01	Edmonton	NHL	82	5	15	20	120	1	1	0	140	3.6	14	1	0.0	21:40	6	0	2	2	6	0	0	0	25:27
2001-02	Edmonton	NHL	74	5	13	18	103	0	1	1	85	5.9	14	0	0.0	21:00	....	....	....	....	....	....	....	....	....
2002-03	Edmonton	NHL	68	4	8	12	64	0	0	1	93	4.3	5	0	0.0	0:00	6	0	0	0	19	0	0	0	....
	NHL Totals		642	26	85	111	681	1	2	3	757	3.4		2	50.0	16:50	27	0	4	4	40	0	0	0	24:33

WHL East First All-Star Team (1993) • Canadian Major Junior First All-Star Team (1993)

• Missed majority of 1994-95 season recovering from knee injury suffered in practice, November 5, 1994. Traded to **Toronto** by **New Jersey** with Steve Sullivan and the rights to Alyn McCauley for Doug Gilmour, Dave Ellett and New Jersey's 4th round choice (previously acquired, New Jersey selected Andre Lakos) in 1999 Entry Draft, February 25, 1997. Traded to **Edmonton** by **Toronto** for Edmonton's 4th round choice (Jonathon Zion) in 1999 Entry Draft and 2nd round choice (Kris Vernarsky) in 2000 Entry Draft, March 23, 1999.

SMITH, Mark

(SMIHTH, MAHRK) **S.J.**

Center. Shoots left. 5'10", 205 lbs. Born, Edmonton, Alta., October 24, 1977. San Jose's 7th choice, 219th overall, in 1997 Entry Draft.

1993-94	Nipawin Hawks	SJHL	62	14	12	26	44	....	....	....	....	....	....	....	....	....	....	....	....	....	....	....	....	....	....
1994-95	Lethbridge	WHL	49	3	4	7	25	....	....	....	....	....	....	....	....	....	....	....	....	....	....	....	....	....	....
1995-96	Lethbridge	WHL	71	11	24	35	59	....	....	....	....	....	....	....	....	....	4	2	0	2	2	....	....	....	....
1996-97	Lethbridge	WHL	62	19	38	57	125	....	....	....	....	....	....	....	....	....	19	7	13	20	51	....	....	....	....
1997-98	Lethbridge	WHL	70	42	67	109	206	....	....	....	....	....	....	....	....	....	3	0	2	2	18	....	....	....	....
	Kentucky	AHL	2	0	0	0	0	....	....	....	....	....	....	....	....	....	....	....	....	....	....	....	....	....	....
1998-99	Kentucky	AHL	78	18	21	39	101	....	....	....	....	....	....	....	....	....	12	2	7	9	16	....	....	....	....
99-2000	Kentucky	AHL	79	21	45	66	153	....	....	....	....	....	....	....	....	....	9	0	5	5	22	....	....	....	....
2000-01	San Jose	NHL	42	2	2	4	51	0	0	0	39	5.1	2	308	52.9	8:48	....	....	....	....	....	....	....	....	....
	Kentucky	AHL	6	2	6	8	23	....	....	....	....	....	....	....	....	....	....	....	....	....	....	....	....	....	....
2001-02	San Jose	NHL	49	3	3	6	72	0	0	1	40	7.5	–1	368	54.1	8:03	....	....	....	....	....	....	....	....	....
2002-03	San Jose	NHL	75	4	11	15	64	0	0	0	68	5.9	1	632	57.0	9:21	....	....	....	....	....	....	....	....	....
	NHL Totals		166	9	16	25	187	0	0	1	147	6.1		1308	55.2	8:50	....	....	....	....	....	....	....	....	....

WHL East Second All-Star Team (1998)

SMITH, Nick

(SMIHTH, NIHK) **ANA.**

Center. Shoots left. 6'2", 196 lbs. Born, Hamilton, Ont., March 23, 1979. Florida's 4th choice, 74th overall, in 1997 Entry Draft.

1995-96	Shelburne Wolves	MTJHL	42	13	18	31	12	....	....	....	....	....	....	....	....	....	....	....	....	....	....	....	....	....	....
1996-97	Barrie Colts	OHL	63	10	18	28	15	....	....	....	....	....	....	....	....	....	9	3	8	11	13	....	....	....	....
1997-98	Barrie Colts	OHL	63	13	21	34	21	....	....	....	....	....	....	....	....	....	6	1	2	3	4	....	....	....	....
1998-99	Barrie Colts	OHL	68	19	34	53	18	....	....	....	....	....	....	....	....	....	12	3	8	11	8	....	....	....	....
99-2000	Louisville Panthers	AHL	53	8	4	12	8	....	....	....	....	....	....	....	....	....	4	0	0	0	0	....	....	....	....
	Port Huron	UHL	2	1	1	2	0	....	....	....	....	....	....	....	....	....	....	....	....	....	....	....	....	....	....
2000-01	Louisville Panthers	AHL	23	1	2	3	25	....	....	....	....	....	....	....	....	....	....	....	....	....	....	....	....	....	....
2001-02	Florida	NHL	15	0	0	0	0	0	0	0	2	0.0	–1	53	47.2	4:09	....	....	....	....	....	....	....	....	....
	Bridgeport	AHL	22	3	6	9	4	....	....	....	....	....	....	....	....	....	....	....	....	....	....	....	....	....	....
	Saint John Flames	AHL	41	8	9	17	10	....	....	....	....	....	....	....	....	....	....	....	....	....	....	....	....	....	....
2002-03	Cincinnati	AHL	79	12	26	38	28	....	....	....	....	....	....	....	....	....	....	....	....	....	....	....	....	....	....
	NHL Totals		15	0	0	0	0	0	0	0	2	0.0		53	47.2	4:09	....	....	....	....	....	....	....	....	....

• Missed majority of 2000-01 season recovering from knee injury suffered in training camp, September 25, 2000. Signed as a free agent by **Anaheim**, August 22, 2002.

SMITH, Wyatt

(SMIHTH, WIGH-uht) **NSH.**

Center. Shoots left. 5'11", 200 lbs. Born, Thief River Falls, MN, February 13, 1977. Phoenix's 6th choice, 233rd overall, in 1997 Entry Draft.

1994-95	Warroad Warriors	Hi-School	28	29	31	60	28	....	....	....	....	....	....	....	....	....	....	....	....	....	....	....	....	....	....
1995-96	U. of Minnesota	WCHA	32	4	5	9	32	....	....	....	....	....	....	....	....	....	....	....	....	....	....	....	....	....	....
1996-97	U. of Minnesota	WCHA	38	16	14	30	44	....	....	....	....	....	....	....	....	....	....	....	....	....	....	....	....	....	....
1997-98	U. of Minnesota	WCHA	39	24	23	47	62	....	....	....	....	....	....	....	....	....	....	....	....	....	....	....	....	....	....
1998-99	U. of Minnesota	WCHA	43	23	20	43	37	....	....	....	....	....	....	....	....	....	....	....	....	....	....	....	....	....	....
99-2000	Phoenix	NHL	2	0	0	0	0	0	0	0	0	0.0	–2	20	30.0	11:39	....	....	....	....	....	....	....	....	....
	Springfield	AHL	60	14	26	40	26	....	....	....	....	....	....	....	....	....	5	2	3	5	13	....	....	....	....
2000-01	Phoenix	NHL	42	3	7	10	13	0	1	0	40	7.5	7	335	40.9	12:20	....	....	....	....	....	....	....	....	....
	Springfield	AHL	18	5	7	12	11	....	....	....	....	....	....	....	....	....	....	....	....	....	....	....	....	....	....
2001-02	Phoenix	NHL	10	0	0	0	0	0	0	0	4	0.0	–5	81	48.2	10:36	....	....	....	....	....	....	....	....	....
	Springfield	AHL	69	23	32	55	69	....	....	....	....	....	....	....	....	....	....	....	....	....	....	....	....	....	....
2002-03	Nashville	NHL	11	1	0	1	0	0	0	0	8	12.5	–1	123	49.6	11:56	....	....	....	....	....	....	....	....	....
	Milwaukee	AHL	56	24	27	51	89	....	....	....	....	....	....	....	....	....	4	1	0	1	2	....	....	....	....
	NHL Totals		65	4	7	11	13	0	1	0	52	7.7		559	43.5	11:59	....	....	....	....	....	....	....	....	....

Signed as a free agent by **Nashville**, July 15, 2002.

SMITHSON, Jerred

(SMIHTH-suhn, JEHR-rehd) **L.A.**

Center. Shoots right. 6'2", 197 lbs. Born, Vernon, B.C., February 4, 1979.

1994-95	Vernon	BCAHA	64	39	46	85	120	....	....	....	....	....	....	....	....	....	....	....	....	....	....	....	....	....	....
1995-96	Calgary Hitmen	WHL	60	4	2	6	16	....	....	....	....	....	....	....	....	....	....	....	....	....	....	....	....	....	....
1996-97	Calgary Hitmen	WHL	65	3	6	9	49	....	....	....	....	....	....	....	....	....	....	....	....	....	....	....	....	....	....
1997-98	Calgary Hitmen	WHL	65	12	9	21	65	....	....	....	....	....	....	....	....	....	18	0	2	2	25	....	....	....	....
1998-99	Calgary Hitmen	WHL	63	14	22	36	108	....	....	....	....	....	....	....	....	....	21	3	7	10	17	....	....	....	....
99-2000	Calgary Hitmen	WHL	66	14	25	39	111	....	....	....	....	....	....	....	....	....	10	1	1	2	16	....	....	....	....
2000-01	Lowell	AHL	24	1	1	2	10	....	....	....	....	....	....	....	....	....	4	0	0	0	2	....	....	....	....
2001-02	Manchester	AHL	78	5	13	18	45	....	....	....	....	....	....	....	....	....	5	0	1	1	4	....	....	....	....
2002-03	Los Angeles	NHL	22	0	2	2	21	0	0	0	9	0.0	–5	175	48.0	8:50	....	....	....	....	....	....	....	....	....
	Manchester	AHL	38	4	21	25	60	....	....	....	....	....	....	....	....	....	3	0	0	0	4	....	....	....	....
	NHL Totals		22	0	2	2	21	0	0	0	9	0.0		175	48.0	8:50	....	....	....	....	....	....	....	....	....

Signed as a free agent by **Los Angeles**, February 18, 2000.

SMOLINSKI, Bryan

(smoh-LIHN-skee, BRIGH-uhn) **OTT.**

Center. Shoots right. 6'1", 208 lbs. Born, Toledo, OH, December 27, 1971. Boston's 1st choice, 21st overall, in 1990 Entry Draft.

1987-88	Det. Caesars	MNHL	80	43	77	120	....	....	....	....	....	....	....	....	....	....	....	....	....	....	....	....	....	....	....
1988-89	Stratford Cullitons	OJHL-B	46	32	62	94	132	....	....	....	....	....	....	....	....	....	....	....	....	....	....	....	....	....	....
1989-90	Michigan State	CCHA	35	9	13	22	34	....	....	....	....	....	....	....	....	....	....	....	....	....	....	....	....	....	....
1990-91	Michigan State	CCHA	35	9	12	21	24	....	....	....	....	....	....	....	....	....	....	....	....	....	....	....	....	....	....
1991-92	Michigan State	CCHA	41	28	33	61	55	....	....	....	....	....	....	....	....	....	....	....	....	....	....	....	....	....	....
1992-93	Michigan State	CCHA	40	31	37	*68	93	....	....	....	....	....	....	....	....	....	....	....	....	....	....	....	....	....	....
	Boston	NHL	9	1	3	4	0	0	0	0	10	10.0	3	....	....	....	4	1	0	1	2	0	0	0	....
1993-94	Boston	NHL	83	31	20	51	82	4	3	5	179	17.3	4	....	....	....	13	5	4	9	4	2	0	0	....
1994-95	Boston	NHL	44	18	13	31	31	6	0	5	121	14.9	–3	....	....	....	5	0	1	1	4	0	0	0	....
1995-96	Pittsburgh	NHL	81	24	40	64	69	8	2	1	229	10.5	6	....	....	....	18	5	4	9	10	0	0	1	....
1996-97	Detroit Vipers	IHL	6	5	7	12	10	....	....	....	....	....	....	....	....	....	....	....	....	....	....	....	....	....	....
	NY Islanders	NHL	64	28	28	56	25	9	0	1	183	15.3	9	....	....	....	....	....	....	....	....	....	....	....	....
1997-98	NY Islanders	NHL	81	13	30	43	34	3	0	4	203	6.4	–16	....	....	....	....	....	....	....	....	....	....	....	....
1998-99	NY Islanders	NHL	82	16	24	40	49	7	0	3	223	7.2	–7	1011	48.3	19:19	....	....	....	....	....	....	....	....	....
99-2000	Los Angeles	NHL	79	20	36	56	48	2	0	0	160	12.5	2	1545	50.9	18:35	4	0	0	0	2	0	0	0	18:22
2000-01	Los Angeles	NHL	78	27	32	59	40	5	3	5	183	14.8	10	952	48.7	18:32	13	1	5	6	14	0	0	0	20:35
2001-02	Los Angeles	NHL	80	13	25	38	56	4	1	0	187	7.0	7	1316	45.7	19:23	7	2	0	2	2	1	0	0	18:15

			Regular Season														Playoffs								
Season	Club	League	GP	G	A	Pts	PIM	PP	SH	GW	S	%	+/-	TF	F%	Min	GP	G	A	Pts	PIM	PP	SH	GW	Min
2002-03	**Los Angeles**	**NHL**	**58**	**18**	**20**	**38**	**18**	**6**	**1**	**8**	**150**	**12.0**	**–1**	**831**	**46.3**	**19:02**	....	....	....	....	....	....	....	....	....
	Ottawa	**NHL**	**10**	**3**	**5**	**8**	**2**	**0**	**0**	**0**	**26**	**11.5**	**1**	**127**	**46.5**	**15:42**	**18**	**2**	**7**	**9**	**6**	**0**	**0**	**0**	**15:21**
	NHL Totals		**749**	**212**	**276**	**488**	**454**	**54**	**10**	**32**	**1854**	**11.4**		**5782**	**48.1**	**18:53**	**82**	**16**	**21**	**37**	**44**	**3**	**0**	**1**	**17:44**

CCHA First All-Star Team (1993) • NCAA West First All-American Team (1993)

Traded to **Pittsburgh** by **Boston** with Glen Murray and Boston's 3rd round choice (Boyd Kane) in 1996 Entry Draft for Kevin Stevens and Shawn McEachern, August 2, 1995. Traded to **NY Islanders** by **Pittsburgh** for Darius Kasparaitis and Andreas Johansson, November 17, 1996. Traded to **Los Angeles** by **NY Islanders** with Ziggy Palffy, Marcel Cousineau and New Jersey's 4th round choice (previously acquired, Los Angeles selected Daniel Johansson) in 1999 Entry Draft for Olli Jokinen, Josh Green, Mathieu Biron and Los Angeles' 1st round choice (Taylor Pyatt) in 1999 Entry Draft, June 20, 1999. Traded to **Ottawa** by **Los Angeles** for the rights to Tim Gleason and future considerations, March 11, 2003.

SMREK, Peter

(SMUHR-ehk, PEE-tuhr) **OTT.**

Defense. Shoots left. 6'1", 215 lbs. Born, Martin, Czech., February 16, 1979. St. Louis' 2nd choice, 85th overall, in 1999 Entry Draft.

Season	Club	League	GP	G	A	Pts	PIM	PP	SH	GW	S	%	+/-	TF	F%	Min	GP	G	A	Pts	PIM	PP	SH	GW	Min
1996-97	Martin	Slovakia	12	1	0	1	....	....	....	....	....	....	....	....	....	....	3	0	0	0	....	....	....	....	....
1997-98	Martin Jr.	Slovak-Jr.	19	7	6	13	32	....	....	....	....	....	....	....	....	....	....	....	....	....	....	....	....	....	....
	Martin	Slovakia	23	0	5	5	24	....	....	....	....	....	....	....	....	....	1	0	0	0	0	....	....	....	....
1998-99	Des Moines	USHL	52	6	26	32	59	....	....	....	....	....	....	....	....	....	14	2	7	9	8	....	....	....	....
99-2000	Peoria Rivermen	ECHL	4	1	1	2	2	....	....	....	....	....	....	....	....	....	....	....	....	....	....	....	....	....	....
	Worcester IceCats	AHL	64	5	19	24	26	....	....	....	....	....	....	....	....	....	2	0	0	0	4	....	....	....	....
2000-01	**St. Louis**	**NHL**	**6**	**2**	**0**	**2**	**2**	**0**	**0**	**1**	**5**	**40.0**	**1**	**0**	**0.0**	**13:01**	....	....	....	....	....	....	....	....	....
	Worcester IceCats	AHL	50	2	7	9	71	....	....	....	....	....	....	....	....	....	....	....	....	....	....	....	....	....	....
	NY Rangers	**NHL**	**14**	**0**	**3**	**3**	**12**	**0**	**0**	**0**	**9**	**0.0**	**1**	**0**	**0.0**	**16:47**	....	....	....	....	....	....	....	....	....
	Hartford	AHL	....	....	....	....	....	....	....	....	....	....	....	....	....	....	5	0	2	2	2	....	....	....	....
2001-02	**NY Rangers**	**NHL**	**8**	**0**	**1**	**1**	**4**	**0**	**0**	**0**	**2**	**0.0**	**–7**	**0**	**0.0**	**14:28**	....	....	....	....	....	....	....	....	....
	Hartford	AHL	50	2	5	7	36	....	....	....	....	....	....	....	....	....	....	....	....	....	....	....	....	....	....
	Slovakia	Olympics	4	0	0	0	0	....	....	....	....	....	....	....	....	....	....	....	....	....	....	....	....	....	....
	Milwaukee	AHL	8	0	2	2	4	....	....	....	....	....	....	....	....	....	....	....	....	....	....	....	....	....	....
2002-03	Milwaukee	AHL	68	3	20	23	70	....	....	....	....	....	....	....	....	....	5	0	0	0	0	....	....	....	....
	NHL Totals		**28**	**2**	**4**	**6**	**18**	**0**	**0**	**1**	**16**	**12.5**		**0**	**0.0**	**15:19**	....	....	....	....	....	....	....	....	....

Traded to **NY Rangers** by **St. Louis** for Alexei Gusarov, March 5, 2001. Traded to **Nashville** by **NY Rangers** for Richard Lintner, March 19, 2002. Traded to **Ottawa** by **Nashville** for Chris Bala, June 26, 2003.

SMYTH, Brad

(SMIHTH, BRAD)

Right wing. Shoots right. 6', 195 lbs. Born, Ottawa, Ont., March 13, 1973.

Season	Club	League	GP	G	A	Pts	PIM	PP	SH	GW	S	%	+/-	TF	F%	Min	GP	G	A	Pts	PIM	PP	SH	GW	Min
1989-90	Nepean	OMHA	55	53	36	89	105	....	....	....	....	....	....	....	....	....	....	....	....	....	....	....	....	....	....
1990-91	London Knights	OHL	29	2	6	8	22	....	....	....	....	....	....	....	....	....	....	....	....	....	....	....	....	....	....
1991-92	London Knights	OHL	58	17	18	35	93	....	....	....	....	....	....	....	....	....	10	2	0	2	8	....	....	....	....
1992-93	London Knights	OHL	66	54	55	109	118	....	....	....	....	....	....	....	....	....	12	7	8	15	25	....	....	....	....
1993-94	Cincinnati	IHL	30	7	3	10	54	....	....	....	....	....	....	....	....	....	....	....	....	....	....	....	....	....	....
	Birmingham Bulls	ECHL	29	26	30	56	38	....	....	....	....	....	....	....	....	....	10	8	8	16	19	....	....	....	....
1994-95	Springfield	AHL	3	0	0	0	7	....	....	....	....	....	....	....	....	....	....	....	....	....	....	....	....	....	....
	Birmingham Bulls	ECHL	36	33	35	68	52	....	....	....	....	....	....	....	....	....	3	5	2	7	0	....	....	....	....
	Cincinnati	IHL	26	2	11	13	34	....	....	....	....	....	....	....	....	....	1	0	0	0	2	....	....	....	....
1995-96	**Florida**	**NHL**	**7**	**1**	**1**	**2**	**4**	**1**	**0**	**0**	**12**	**8.3**	**–3**	....	....	....	....	....	....	....	....	....	....	....	....
	Carolina	AHL	68	*68	58	*126	80	....	....	....	....	....	....	....	....	....	....	....	....	....	....	....	....	....	....
1996-97	**Florida**	**NHL**	**8**	**1**	**0**	**1**	**2**	**0**	**0**	**0**	**10**	**10.0**	**–3**	....	....	....	....	....	....	....	....	....	....	....	....
	Los Angeles	**NHL**	**44**	**8**	**8**	**16**	**74**	**0**	**0**	**1**	**74**	**10.8**	**–7**	....	....	....	....	....	....	....	....	....	....	....	....
	Phoenix	IHL	3	5	2	7	0	....	....	....	....	....	....	....	....	....	....	....	....	....	....	....	....	....	....
1997-98	**Los Angeles**	**NHL**	**9**	**1**	**3**	**4**	**4**	**0**	**0**	**0**	**12**	**8.3**	**–1**	....	....	....	....	....	....	....	....	....	....	....	....
	NY Rangers	**NHL**	**1**	**0**	**0**	**0**	**0**	**0**	**0**	**0**	**1**	**0.0**	**0**	....	....	....	....	....	....	....	....	....	....	....	....
	Hartford	AHL	57	29	33	62	79	....	....	....	....	....	....	....	....	....	15	12	8	20	11	....	....	....	....
1998-99	**Nashville**	**NHL**	**3**	**0**	**0**	**0**	**6**	**0**	**0**	**0**	**5**	**0.0**	**–1**	**0**	**0.0**	**9:54**	....	....	....	....	....	....	....	....	....
	Milwaukee	IHL	34	11	16	27	21	....	....	....	....	....	....	....	....	....	....	....	....	....	....	....	....	....	....
	Hartford	AHL	36	25	19	44	48	....	....	....	....	....	....	....	....	....	7	6	0	6	14	....	....	....	....
99-2000	Hartford	AHL	80	39	37	76	62	....	....	....	....	....	....	....	....	....	23	*13	10	23	8	....	....	....	....
2000-01	**NY Rangers**	**NHL**	**4**	**1**	**0**	**1**	**4**	**0**	**0**	**0**	**10**	**10.0**	**0**	**0**	**0.0**	**13:57**	....	....	....	....	....	....	....	....	....
	Hartford	AHL	77	*50	29	79	110	....	....	....	....	....	....	....	....	....	5	2	3	5	8	....	....	....	....
2001-02	Hartford	AHL	79	34	48	82	90	....	....	....	....	....	....	....	....	....	10	3	8	11	14	....	....	....	....
2002-03	**Ottawa**	**NHL**	**12**	**3**	**1**	**4**	**15**	**2**	**0**	**0**	**16**	**18.8**	**–2**	**2**	**0.0**	**9:30**	....	....	....	....	....	....	....	....	....
	Binghamton	AHL	69	24	32	56	77	....	....	....	....	....	....	....	....	....	14	7	6	13	12	....	....	....	....
	NHL Totals		**88**	**15**	**13**	**28**	**109**	**3**	**0**	**1**	**140**	**10.7**		**2**	**0.0**	**10:30**	....	....	....	....	....	....	....	....	....

AHL First All-Star Team (1996, 2001, 2002) • John B. Sollenberger Trophy (Top Scorer – AHL) (1996) • Les Cunningham Award (MVP – AHL) (1996)

Signed as a free agent by **Florida**, October 4, 1993. Traded to **Los Angeles** by **Florida** for Los Angeles' 3rd round choice (Vratislav Cech) in 1997 Entry Draft, November 28, 1996. Traded to **NY Rangers** by **Los Angeles** for future considerations, November 14, 1997. Signed as a free agent by **Nashville**, July 16, 1998. Traded to **NY Rangers** by **Nashville** for future considerations, May 3, 1999. Signed as a free agent by **Ottawa**, August 1, 2002.

SMYTH, Ryan

(SMIHTH, RIGH-uhn) **EDM.**

Left wing. Shoots left. 6'1", 190 lbs. Born, Banff, Alta., February 21, 1976. Edmonton's 2nd choice, 6th overall, in 1994 Entry Draft.

Season	Club	League	GP	G	A	Pts	PIM	PP	SH	GW	S	%	+/-	TF	F%	Min	GP	G	A	Pts	PIM	PP	SH	GW	Min
1990-91	Banff Blazers	ABHL	25	100	50	150	....	....	....	....	....	....	....	....	....	....	....	....	....	....	....	....	....	....	....
	Lethbridge	AMHL	34	8	21	29	....	....	....	....	....	....	....	....	....	....	....	....	....	....	....	....	....	....	....
1991-92	Caronport	SMHL	35	55	61	116	98	....	....	....	....	....	....	....	....	....	....	....	....	....	....	....	....	....	....
	Moose Jaw	WHL	2	0	0	0	0	....	....	....	....	....	....	....	....	....	....	....	....	....	....	....	....	....	....
1992-93	Moose Jaw	WHL	64	19	14	33	59	....	....	....	....	....	....	....	....	....	....	....	....	....	....	....	....	....	....
1993-94	Moose Jaw	WHL	72	50	55	105	88	....	....	....	....	....	....	....	....	....	....	....	....	....	....	....	....	....	....
1994-95	Moose Jaw	WHL	50	41	45	86	66	....	....	....	....	....	....	....	....	....	10	6	9	15	22	....	....	....	....
	Edmonton	**NHL**	**3**	**0**	**0**	**0**	**0**	**0**	**0**	**0**	**2**	**0.0**	**–1**	....	....	....	....	....	....	....	....	....	....	....	....
1995-96	**Edmonton**	**NHL**	**48**	**2**	**9**	**11**	**28**	**1**	**0**	**0**	**65**	**3.1**	**–10**	....	....	....	....	....	....	....	....	....	....	....	....
	Cape Breton	AHL	9	6	5	11	4	....	....	....	....	....	....	....	....	....	....	....	....	....	....	....	....	....	....
1996-97	**Edmonton**	**NHL**	**82**	**39**	**22**	**61**	**76**	**20**	**0**	**4**	**265**	**14.7**	**–7**	....	....	....	**12**	**5**	**5**	**10**	**12**	**1**	**0**	**2**	....
1997-98	**Edmonton**	**NHL**	**65**	**20**	**13**	**33**	**44**	**10**	**0**	**2**	**205**	**9.8**	**–24**	....	....	....	**12**	**1**	**3**	**4**	**16**	**1**	**0**	**0**	....
1998-99	**Edmonton**	**NHL**	**71**	**13**	**18**	**31**	**62**	**6**	**0**	**2**	**161**	**8.1**	**0**	**5**	**20.0**	**14:26**	**3**	**3**	**0**	**3**	**0**	**2**	**0**	**0**	**24:35**
99-2000	**Edmonton**	**NHL**	**82**	**28**	**26**	**54**	**58**	**11**	**0**	**4**	**238**	**11.8**	**–2**	**24**	**54.2**	**19:12**	**5**	**1**	**0**	**1**	**6**	**0**	**1**	**0**	**19:18**
2000-01	**Edmonton**	**NHL**	**82**	**31**	**39**	**70**	**58**	**11**	**0**	**6**	**245**	**12.7**	**10**	**17**	**35.3**	**19:58**	**6**	**3**	**4**	**7**	**4**	**0**	**0**	**0**	**24:46**
2001-02	**Edmonton**	**NHL**	**61**	**15**	**35**	**50**	**48**	**7**	**1**	**5**	**150**	**10.0**	**7**	**12**	**41.7**	**19:27**	....	....	....	....	....	....	....	....	....
	Canada	Olympics	6	0	1	1	0	....	....	....	....	....	....	....	....	....	....	....	....	....	....	....	....	....	....
2002-03	**Edmonton**	**NHL**	**66**	**27**	**34**	**61**	**67**	**10**	**0**	**3**	**199**	**13.6**	**5**	**42**	**42.9**	**19:21**	**6**	**2**	**0**	**2**	**16**	**0**	**1**	**0**	**17:39**
	NHL Totals		**560**	**175**	**196**	**371**	**441**	**76**	**1**	**26**	**1530**	**11.4**		**100**	**43.0**	**18:30**	**44**	**15**	**12**	**27**	**54**	**4**	**2**	**2**	**21:15**

WHL East Second All-Star Team (1995)

SNYDER, Dan

(SHNIGH-duhr, DAN) **ATL.**

Center. Shoots left. 6', 190 lbs. Born, Elmira, Ont., February 23, 1978.

Season	Club	League	GP	G	A	Pts	PIM	PP	SH	GW	S	%	+/-	TF	F%	Min	GP	G	A	Pts	PIM	PP	SH	GW	Min
1994-95	Elmira	OJHL-B	43	8	17	25	46	....	....	....	....	....	....	....	....	....	....	....	....	....	....	....	....	....	....
1995-96	Owen Sound	OHL	63	8	17	25	78	....	....	....	....	....	....	....	....	....	6	1	2	3	4	....	....	....	....
1996-97	Owen Sound	OHL	57	17	29	46	96	....	....	....	....	....	....	....	....	....	4	2	3	5	8	....	....	....	....
1997-98	Owen Sound	OHL	46	23	33	56	74	....	....	....	....	....	....	....	....	....	10	2	3	5	16	....	....	....	....
1998-99	Owen Sound	OHL	64	27	67	94	110	....	....	....	....	....	....	....	....	....	16	8	5	13	30	....	....	....	....
99-2000	Orlando	IHL	71	12	13	25	123	....	....	....	....	....	....	....	....	....	6	1	2	3	4	....	....	....	....
2000-01	**Atlanta**	**NHL**	**2**	**0**	**0**	**0**	**0**	**0**	**0**	**0**	**2**	**0.0**	**0**	**12**	**50.0**	**6:55**	....	....	....	....	....	....	....	....	....
	Orlando	IHL	78	13	30	43	127	....	....	....	....	....	....	....	....	....	16	7	3	10	20	....	....	....	....
2001-02	**Atlanta**	**NHL**	**11**	**1**	**1**	**2**	**30**	**0**	**0**	**0**	**7**	**14.3**	**–3**	**122**	**43.4**	**10:57**	....	....	....	....	....	....	....	....	....
	Chicago Wolves	AHL	56	11	24	35	115	....	....	....	....	....	....	....	....	....	22	7	10	17	25	....	....	....	....
2002-03	**Atlanta**	**NHL**	**36**	**10**	**4**	**14**	**34**	**0**	**1**	**1**	**41**	**24.4**	**–4**	**356**	**41.6**	**10:54**	....	....	....	....	....	....	....	....	....
	Chicago Wolves	AHL	35	11	12	23	39	....	....	....	....	....	....	....	....	....	....	....	....	....	....	....	....	....	....
	NHL Totals		**49**	**11**	**5**	**16**	**64**	**0**	**1**	**1**	**50**	**22.0**		**490**	**42.2**	**10:45**	....	....	....	....	....	....	....	....	....

Signed as a free agent by **Atlanta**, June 28, 1999.

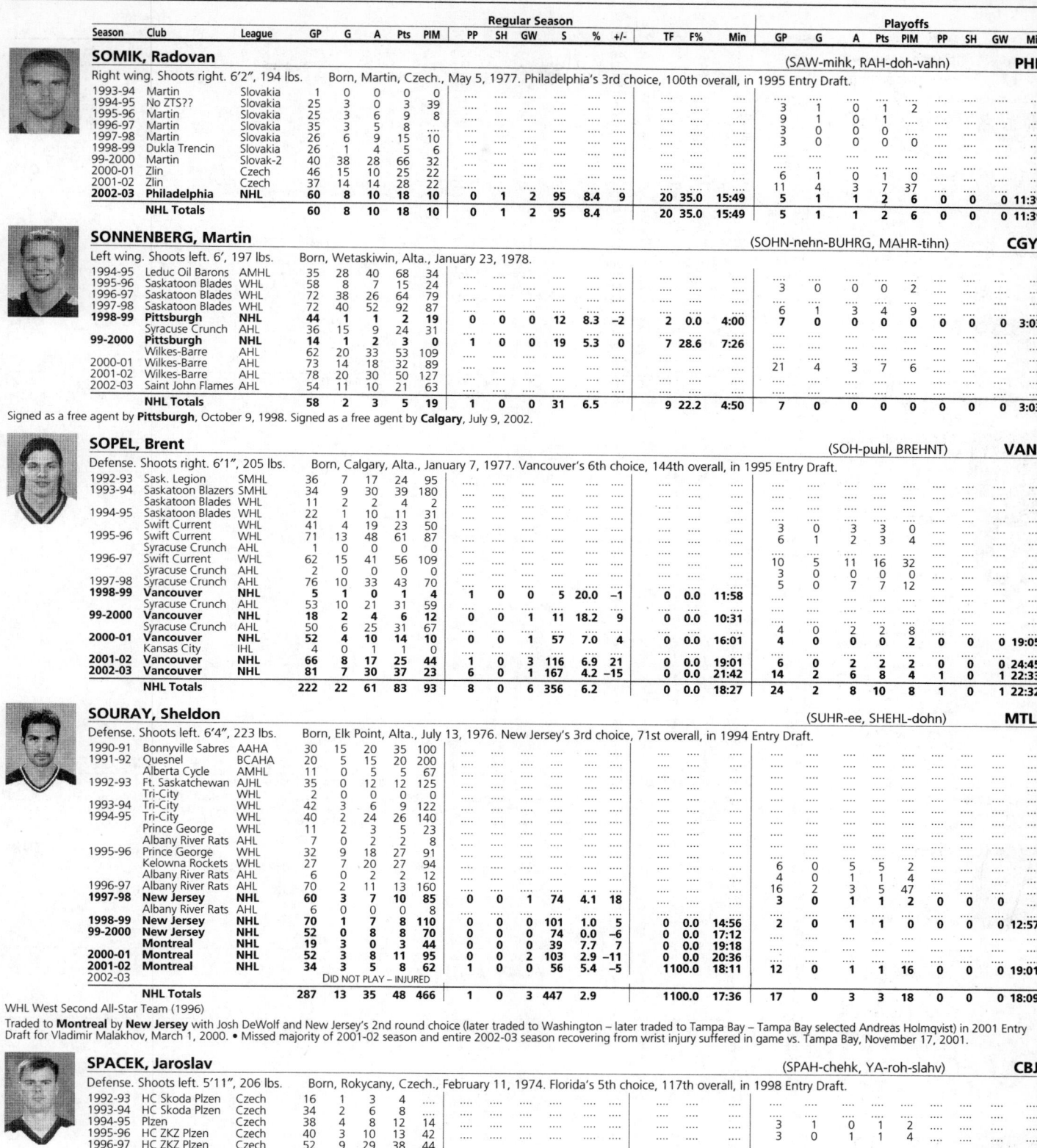

SOMIK, Radovan

(SAW-mihk, RAH-doh-vahn) **PHI.**

Right wing. Shoots right. 6'2", 194 lbs. Born, Martin, Czech., May 5, 1977. Philadelphia's 3rd choice, 100th overall, in 1995 Entry Draft.

			Regular Season														Playoffs								
Season	Club	League	GP	G	A	Pts	PIM	PP	SH	GW	S	%	+/-	TF	F%	Min	GP	G	A	Pts	PIM	PP	SH	GW	Min
1993-94	Martin	Slovakia	1	0	0	0	0	....	....	....	....	....	....	....	....	....	....	....	....	....	....	....	....	....	....
1994-95	No ZTS??	Slovakia	25	3	0	3	39	....	....	....	....	....	....	....	....	....	3	1	0	1	2	....	....	....	....
1995-96	Martin	Slovakia	25	3	6	9	8	....	....	....	....	....	....	....	....	....	9	1	0	1	....	....	....	....	....
1996-97	Martin	Slovakia	35	3	5	8	....	....	....	....	....	....	....	....	....	....	3	0	0	0	....	....	....	....	....
1997-98	Martin	Slovakia	26	6	9	15	10	....	....	....	....	....	....	....	....	....	3	0	0	0	0	....	....	....	....
1998-99	Dukla Trencin	Slovakia	26	1	4	5	6	....	....	....	....	....	....	....	....	....	....	....	....	....	....	....	....	....	....
99-2000	Martin	Slovak-2	40	38	28	66	32	....	....	....	....	....	....	....	....	....	....	....	....	....	....	....	....	....	....
2000-01	Zlin	Czech	46	15	10	25	22	....	....	....	....	....	....	....	....	....	6	1	0	1	0	....	....	....	....
2001-02	Zlin	Czech	37	14	14	28	22	....	....	....	....	....	....	....	....	....	11	4	3	7	37	....	....	....	....
2002-03	**Philadelphia**	**NHL**	**60**	**8**	**10**	**18**	**10**	**0**	**1**	**2**	**95**	**8.4**	**9**	**20**	**35.0**	**15:49**	**5**	**1**	**1**	**2**	**6**	**0**	**0**	**0**	**11:39**
	NHL Totals		**60**	**8**	**10**	**18**	**10**	**0**	**1**	**2**	**95**	**8.4**		**20**	**35.0**	**15:49**	**5**	**1**	**1**	**2**	**6**	**0**	**0**	**0**	**11:39**

SONNENBERG, Martin

(SOHN-nehn-BUHRG, MAHR-tihn) **CGY.**

Left wing. Shoots left. 6', 197 lbs. Born, Wetaskiwin, Alta., January 23, 1978.

Season	Club	League	GP	G	A	Pts	PIM	PP	SH	GW	S	%	+/-	TF	F%	Min	GP	G	A	Pts	PIM	PP	SH	GW	Min
1994-95	Leduc Oil Barons	AMHL	35	28	40	68	34	....	....	....	....	....	....	....	....	....	....	....	....	....	....	....	....	....	....
1995-96	Saskatoon Blades	WHL	58	8	7	15	24	....	....	....	....	....	....	....	....	....	3	0	0	0	2	....	....	....	....
1996-97	Saskatoon Blades	WHL	72	38	26	64	79	....	....	....	....	....	....	....	....	....	....	....	....	....	....	....	....	....	....
1997-98	Saskatoon Blades	WHL	72	40	52	92	87	....	....	....	....	....	....	....	....	....	6	1	3	4	9	....	....	....	....
1998-99	**Pittsburgh**	**NHL**	**44**	**1**	**1**	**2**	**19**	**0**	**0**	**0**	**12**	**8.3**	**–2**	**2**	**0.0**	**4:00**	**7**	**0**	**0**	**0**	**0**	**0**	**0**	**0**	**3:03**
	Syracuse Crunch	AHL	36	15	9	24	31	....	....	....	....	....	....	....	....	....	....	....	....	....	....	....	....	....	....
99-2000	**Pittsburgh**	**NHL**	**14**	**1**	**2**	**3**	**0**	**1**	**0**	**0**	**19**	**5.3**	**0**	**7**	**28.6**	**7:26**	....	....	....	....	....	....	....	....	....
	Wilkes-Barre	AHL	62	20	33	53	109	....	....	....	....	....	....	....	....	....	....	....	....	....	....	....	....	....	....
2000-01	Wilkes-Barre	AHL	73	14	18	32	89	....	....	....	....	....	....	....	....	....	21	4	3	7	6	....	....	....	....
2001-02	Wilkes-Barre	AHL	78	20	30	50	127	....	....	....	....	....	....	....	....	....	....	....	....	....	....	....	....	....	....
2002-03	Saint John Flames	AHL	54	11	10	21	63	....	....	....	....	....	....	....	....	....	....	....	....	....	....	....	....	....	....
	NHL Totals		**58**	**2**	**3**	**5**	**19**	**1**	**0**	**0**	**31**	**6.5**		**9**	**22.2**	**4:50**	**7**	**0**	**0**	**0**	**0**	**0**	**0**	**0**	**3:03**

Signed as a free agent by **Pittsburgh**, October 9, 1998. Signed as a free agent by **Calgary**, July 9, 2002.

SOPEL, Brent

(SOH-puhl, BREHNT) **VAN.**

Defense. Shoots right. 6'1", 205 lbs. Born, Calgary, Alta., January 7, 1977. Vancouver's 6th choice, 144th overall, in 1995 Entry Draft.

Season	Club	League	GP	G	A	Pts	PIM	PP	SH	GW	S	%	+/-	TF	F%	Min	GP	G	A	Pts	PIM	PP	SH	GW	Min
1992-93	Sask. Legion	SMHL	36	7	17	24	95	....	....	....	....	....	....	....	....	....	....	....	....	....	....	....	....	....	....
1993-94	Saskatoon Blazers	SMHL	34	9	30	39	180	....	....	....	....	....	....	....	....	....	....	....	....	....	....	....	....	....	....
	Saskatoon Blades	WHL	11	2	2	4	2	....	....	....	....	....	....	....	....	....	....	....	....	....	....	....	....	....	....
1994-95	Saskatoon Blades	WHL	22	1	10	11	31	....	....	....	....	....	....	....	....	....	....	....	....	....	....	....	....	....	....
	Swift Current	WHL	41	4	19	23	50	....	....	....	....	....	....	....	....	....	3	0	3	3	0	....	....	....	....
1995-96	Swift Current	WHL	71	13	48	61	87	....	....	....	....	....	....	....	....	....	6	1	2	3	4	....	....	....	....
	Syracuse Crunch	AHL	1	0	0	0	0	....	....	....	....	....	....	....	....	....	....	....	....	....	....	....	....	....	....
1996-97	Swift Current	WHL	62	15	41	56	109	....	....	....	....	....	....	....	....	....	10	5	11	16	32	....	....	....	....
	Syracuse Crunch	AHL	2	0	0	0	0	....	....	....	....	....	....	....	....	....	3	0	0	0	0	....	....	....	....
1997-98	Syracuse Crunch	AHL	76	10	33	43	70	....	....	....	....	....	....	....	....	....	5	0	7	7	12	....	....	....	....
1998-99	**Vancouver**	**NHL**	**5**	**1**	**0**	**1**	**4**	**1**	**0**	**0**	**5**	**20.0**	**–1**	**0**	**0.0**	**11:58**	....	....	....	....	....	....	....	....	....
	Syracuse Crunch	AHL	53	10	21	31	59	....	....	....	....	....	....	....	....	....	....	....	....	....	....	....	....	....	....
99-2000	**Vancouver**	**NHL**	**18**	**2**	**4**	**6**	**12**	**0**	**0**	**1**	**11**	**18.2**	**9**	**0**	**0.0**	**10:31**	....	....	....	....	....	....	....	....	....
	Syracuse Crunch	AHL	50	6	25	31	67	....	....	....	....	....	....	....	....	....	4	0	2	2	8	....	....	....	....
2000-01	**Vancouver**	**NHL**	**52**	**4**	**10**	**14**	**10**	**0**	**0**	**1**	**57**	**7.0**	**4**	**0**	**0.0**	**16:01**	**4**	**0**	**0**	**0**	**2**	**0**	**0**	**0**	**19:05**
	Kansas City	IHL	4	0	1	1	0	....	....	....	....	....	....	....	....	....	....	....	....	....	....	....	....	....	....
2001-02	**Vancouver**	**NHL**	**66**	**8**	**17**	**25**	**44**	**1**	**0**	**3**	**116**	**6.9**	**21**	**0**	**0.0**	**19:01**	**6**	**0**	**2**	**2**	**2**	**0**	**0**	**0**	**24:45**
2002-03	**Vancouver**	**NHL**	**81**	**7**	**30**	**37**	**23**	**6**	**0**	**1**	**167**	**4.2**	**–15**	**0**	**0.0**	**21:42**	**14**	**2**	**6**	**8**	**4**	**1**	**0**	**1**	**22:33**
	NHL Totals		**222**	**22**	**61**	**83**	**93**	**8**	**0**	**6**	**356**	**6.2**		**0**	**0.0**	**18:27**	**24**	**2**	**8**	**10**	**8**	**1**	**0**	**1**	**22:32**

SOURAY, Sheldon

(SUHR-ee, SHEHL-dohn) **MTL.**

Defense. Shoots left. 6'4", 223 lbs. Born, Elk Point, Alta., July 13, 1976. New Jersey's 3rd choice, 71st overall, in 1994 Entry Draft.

Season	Club	League	GP	G	A	Pts	PIM	PP	SH	GW	S	%	+/-	TF	F%	Min	GP	G	A	Pts	PIM	PP	SH	GW	Min
1990-91	Bonnyville Sabres	AAHA	30	15	20	35	100	....	....	....	....	....	....	....	....	....	....	....	....	....	....	....	....	....	....
1991-92	Quesnel	BCAHA	20	5	15	20	200	....	....	....	....	....	....	....	....	....	....	....	....	....	....	....	....	....	....
	Alberta Cycle	AMHL	11	0	5	5	67	....	....	....	....	....	....	....	....	....	....	....	....	....	....	....	....	....	....
1992-93	Ft. Saskatchewan	AJHL	35	0	12	12	125	....	....	....	....	....	....	....	....	....	....	....	....	....	....	....	....	....	....
	Tri-City	WHL	2	0	0	0	0	....	....	....	....	....	....	....	....	....	....	....	....	....	....	....	....	....	....
1993-94	Tri-City	WHL	42	3	6	9	122	....	....	....	....	....	....	....	....	....	....	....	....	....	....	....	....	....	....
1994-95	Tri-City	WHL	40	2	24	26	140	....	....	....	....	....	....	....	....	....	....	....	....	....	....	....	....	....	....
	Prince George	WHL	11	2	3	5	23	....	....	....	....	....	....	....	....	....	....	....	....	....	....	....	....	....	....
	Albany River Rats	AHL	7	0	2	2	8	....	....	....	....	....	....	....	....	....	....	....	....	....	....	....	....	....	....
1995-96	Prince George	WHL	32	9	18	27	91	....	....	....	....	....	....	....	....	....	....	....	....	....	....	....	....	....	....
	Kelowna Rockets	WHL	27	7	20	27	94	....	....	....	....	....	....	....	....	....	6	0	5	5	2	....	....	....	....
	Albany River Rats	AHL	6	0	2	2	12	....	....	....	....	....	....	....	....	....	4	0	1	1	4	....	....	....	....
1996-97	Albany River Rats	AHL	70	2	11	13	160	....	....	....	....	....	....	....	....	....	16	2	3	5	47	....	....	....	....
1997-98	**New Jersey**	**NHL**	**60**	**3**	**7**	**10**	**85**	**0**	**0**	**1**	**74**	**4.1**	**18**	....	....	....	**3**	**0**	**1**	**1**	**2**	**0**	**0**	**0**	....
	Albany River Rats	AHL	6	0	0	0	8	....	....	....	....	....	....	....	....	....	....	....	....	....	....	....	....	....	....
1998-99	**New Jersey**	**NHL**	**70**	**1**	**7**	**8**	**110**	**0**	**0**	**0**	**101**	**1.0**	**5**	**0**	**0.0**	**14:56**	**2**	**0**	**1**	**1**	**0**	**0**	**0**	**0**	**12:57**
99-2000	**New Jersey**	**NHL**	**52**	**0**	**8**	**8**	**70**	**0**	**0**	**0**	**74**	**0.0**	**–6**	**0**	**0.0**	**17:12**	....	....	....	....	....	....	....	....	....
	Montreal	**NHL**	**19**	**3**	**0**	**3**	**44**	**0**	**0**	**0**	**39**	**7.7**	**7**	**0**	**0.0**	**19:18**	....	....	....	....	....	....	....	....	....
2000-01	**Montreal**	**NHL**	**52**	**3**	**8**	**11**	**95**	**0**	**0**	**2**	**103**	**2.9**	**–11**	**0**	**0.0**	**20:36**	....	....	....	....	....	....	....	....	....
2001-02	**Montreal**	**NHL**	**34**	**3**	**5**	**8**	**62**	**1**	**0**	**0**	**56**	**5.4**	**–5**	**1**	**100.0**	**18:11**	**12**	**0**	**1**	**1**	**16**	**0**	**0**	**0**	**19:01**
2002-03			DID NOT PLAY – INJURED																						
	NHL Totals		**287**	**13**	**35**	**48**	**466**	**1**	**0**	**3**	**447**	**2.9**		**1**	**100.0**	**17:36**	**17**	**0**	**3**	**3**	**18**	**0**	**0**	**0**	**18:09**

WHL West Second All-Star Team (1996)

Traded to **Montreal** by **New Jersey** with Josh DeWolf and New Jersey's 2nd round choice (later traded to Washington – later traded to Tampa Bay – Tampa Bay selected Andreas Holmqvist) in 2001 Entry Draft for Vladimir Malakhov, March 1, 2000. • Missed majority of 2001-02 season and entire 2002-03 season recovering from wrist injury suffered in game vs. Tampa Bay, November 17, 2001.

SPACEK, Jaroslav

(SPAH-chehk, YA-roh-slahv) **CBJ**

Defense. Shoots left. 5'11", 206 lbs. Born, Rokycany, Czech., February 11, 1974. Florida's 5th choice, 117th overall, in 1998 Entry Draft.

Season	Club	League	GP	G	A	Pts	PIM	PP	SH	GW	S	%	+/-	TF	F%	Min	GP	G	A	Pts	PIM	PP	SH	GW	Min
1992-93	HC Skoda Plzen	Czech	16	1	3	4	....	....	....	....	....	....	....	....	....	....	....	....	....	....	....	....	....	....	....
1993-94	HC Skoda Plzen	Czech	34	2	6	8	....	....	....	....	....	....	....	....	....	....	....	....	....	....	....	....	....	....	....
1994-95	Plzen	Czech	38	4	8	12	14	....	....	....	....	....	....	....	....	....	3	1	0	1	2	....	....	....	....
1995-96	HC ZKZ Plzen	Czech	40	3	10	13	42	....	....	....	....	....	....	....	....	....	3	0	1	1	4	....	....	....	....
1996-97	HC ZKZ Plzen	Czech	52	9	29	38	44	....	....	....	....	....	....	....	....	....	....	....	....	....	....	....	....	....	....
1997-98	Farjestad	Sweden	45	10	16	26	63	....	....	....	....	....	....	....	....	....	12	2	5	7	14	....	....	....	....
	Farjestad	EuroHL	6	2	3	5	2	....	....	....	....	....	....	....	....	....	....	....	....	....	....	....	....	....	....
1998-99	**Florida**	**NHL**	**63**	**3**	**12**	**15**	**28**	**2**	**1**	**0**	**92**	**3.3**	**15**	**1**	**100.0**	**19:27**	....	....	....	....	....	....	....	....	....
	New Haven	AHL	14	4	8	12	15	....	....	....	....	....	....	....	....	....	....	....	....	....	....	....	....	....	....
99-2000	**Florida**	**NHL**	**82**	**10**	**26**	**36**	**53**	**4**	**0**	**1**	**111**	**9.0**	**7**	**1**	**0.0**	**22:40**	**4**	**0**	**0**	**0**	**0**	**0**	**0**	**0**	**20:29**
2000-01	**Florida**	**NHL**	**12**	**2**	**1**	**3**	**8**	**1**	**0**	**0**	**21**	**9.5**	**–4**	**0**	**0.0**	**19:12**	....	....	....	....	....	....	....	....	....
	Chicago	**NHL**	**50**	**5**	**18**	**23**	**20**	**2**	**0**	**1**	**85**	**5.9**	**7**	**0**	**0.0**	**21:31**	....	....	....	....	....	....	....	....	....
2001-02	**Chicago**	**NHL**	**60**	**3**	**10**	**13**	**29**	**0**	**0**	**1**	**64**	**4.7**	**5**	**0**	**0.0**	**16:25**	....	....	....	....	....	....	....	....	....
	Czech Republic	Olympics	4	0	0	0	0	....	....	....	....	....	....	....	....	....	....	....	....	....	....	....	....	....	....
	Columbus	**NHL**	**14**	**2**	**3**	**5**	**24**	**1**	**1**	**1**	**29**	**6.9**	**–9**	**0**	**0.0**	**23:35**	....	....	....	....	....	....	....	....	....
2002-03	**Columbus**	**NHL**	**81**	**9**	**36**	**45**	**70**	**5**	**0**	**1**	**166**	**5.4**	**–23**	**0**	**0.0**	**24:47**	....	....	....	....	....	....	....	....	....
	NHL Totals		**362**	**34**	**106**	**140**	**232**	**15**	**2**	**5**	**568**	**6.0**		**2**	**50.0**	**21:18**	**4**	**0**	**0**	**0**	**0**	**0**	**0**	**0**	**20:29**

Traded to **Chicago** by **Florida** for Anders Eriksson, November 6, 2000. Traded to **Columbus** by **Chicago** with Chicago's 2nd round choice (Dan Fritsche) in 2003 Entry Draft for Lyle Odelein, March 19, 2002.

			Regular Season													Playoffs							
Season	Club	League	GP	G	A	Pts	PIM	PP	SH	GW	S	%	+/-	TF	F%	Min	GP	G	A	Pts	PIM	PP	SH	GW	Min

SPANHEL, Martin (SPAN-hehl, MAHR-tihn) **CBJ**

Left wing. Shoots left. 6'2", 206 lbs. Born, Zlin, Czech., July 1, 1977. Philadelphia's 6th choice, 152nd overall, in 1995 Entry Draft.

Season	Club	League	GP	G	A	Pts	PIM	PP	SH	GW	S	%	+/-	TF	F%	Min	GP	G	A	Pts	PIM	PP	SH	GW	Min
1994-95	AC ZPS Zlin Jr.	Czech-Jr.	33	25	16	41	0	....	....	....	....	....	....	....	....	....	....	....	....	....	....	....	....	....	....
	AC ZPS Zlin	Czech	1	0	0	0	0	....	....	....	....	....	....	....	....	....	....	....	....	....	....	....	....	....	....
1995-96	Lethbridge	WHL	6	1	0	1	0	....	....	....	....	....	....	....	....	....	....	....	....	....	....	....	....	....	....
	Moose Jaw	WHL	61	4	12	16	33	....	....	....	....	....	....	....	....	....	....	....	....	....	....	....	....	....	....
1996-97	AC ZPS Zlin	Czech	22	3	6	9	20	....	....	....	....	....	....	....	....	....	....	....	....	....	....	....	....	....	....
1997-98	Zlin	Czech	40	7	9	16	70	....	....	....	....	....	....	....	....	....	....	....	....	....	....	....	....	....	....
1998-99	Plzen	Czech	49	12	12	24	60	....	....	....	....	....	....	....	....	....	5	2	1	3	27	....	....	....	....
99-2000	Plzen	Czech	52	21	27	48	86	....	....	....	....	....	....	....	....	....	7	1	4	5	12	....	....	....	....
2000-01	**Columbus**	**NHL**	6	1	0	1	2	0	0	0	8	12.5	−1	1	0.0	12:29	....	....	....	....	....	....	....	....	....
	Syracuse Crunch	AHL	67	11	13	24	75	....	....	....	....	....	....	....	....	....	2	0	0	0	8	....	....	....	....
2001-02	**Columbus**	**NHL**	4	1	0	1	2	0	0	0	6	16.7	−2	0	0.0	11:12	....	....	....	....	....	....	....	....	....
	Syracuse Crunch	AHL	50	7	12	19	43	....	....	....	....	....	....	....	....	....	....	....	....	....	....	....	....	....	....
2002-03	HC Sparta Praha	Czech	40	5	5	10	46	....	....	....	....	....	....	....	....	....	8	1	0	1	6	....	....	....	....
	NHL Totals		**10**	**2**	**0**	**2**	**4**	**0**	**0**	**0**	**14**	**14.3**		**1**	**0.0**	**11:58**	....	....	....	....	....	....	....	....	....

Traded to **San Jose** by **Philadelphia** with Philadelphia's 1st round choice (later traded to Buffalo – later traded to Phoenix – Phoenix selected Daniel Briere) in 1996 Entry Draft and Philadelphia's 4th round choice (later traded to Buffalo – Buffalo selected Mike Martone) in 1996 Entry Draft for Pat Falloon, November 16, 1995. Traded to **Buffalo** by **San Jose** with Vaclav Varada and Philadelphia's 1st (previously acquired, later traded to Phoenix – Phoenix selected Daniel Briere) and 4th (previously acquired, Buffalo selected Mike Martone) round choices in 1996 Entry Draft for Doug Bodger, November 16, 1995. Signed as a free agent by **Columbus**, May 30, 2000. Signed as a free agent by **HC Sparta Praha** (Czech) with Columbus retaining NHL rights, July 26, 2002.

SPEZZA, Jason (SPEHT-zah, JAY-suhn) **OTT.**

Center. Shoots right. 6'2", 206 lbs. Born, Mississauga, Ont., June 13, 1983. Ottawa's 1st choice, 2nd overall, in 2001 Entry Draft.

Season	Club	League	GP	G	A	Pts	PIM	PP	SH	GW	S	%	+/-	TF	F%	Min	GP	G	A	Pts	PIM	PP	SH	GW	Min
1997-98	Tor. Marlboros	MTHL	54	53	61	114	42	....	....	....	....	....	....	....	....	....	....	....	....	....	....	....	....	....	....
1998-99	Brampton	OHL	67	22	49	71	18	....	....	....	....	....	....	....	....	....	....	....	....	....	....	....	....	....	....
99-2000	Mississauga	OHL	52	24	37	61	33	....	....	....	....	....	....	....	....	....	....	....	....	....	....	....	....	....	....
2000-01	Mississauga	OHL	15	7	23	30	11	....	....	....	....	....	....	....	....	....	....	....	....	....	....	....	....	....	....
	Windsor Spitfires	OHL	41	36	50	86	32	....	....	....	....	....	....	....	....	....	9	4	5	9	10	....	....	....	....
2001-02	Windsor Spitfires	OHL	27	19	26	45	16	....	....	....	....	....	....	....	....	....	....	....	....	....	....	....	....	....	....
	Belleville Bulls	OHL	26	23	37	60	26	....	....	....	....	....	....	....	....	....	11	5	6	11	18	....	....	....	....
	Grand Rapids	AHL	....	....	....	....	....	....	....	....	....	....	....	....	....	....	3	1	0	1	2	....	....	....	....
2002-03	**Ottawa**	**NHL**	33	7	14	21	8	3	0	0	65	10.8	−3	330	45.8	12:40	3	1	1	2	0	1	0	0	11:34
	Binghamton	AHL	43	22	32	54	71	....	....	....	....	....	....	....	....	....	2	1	2	3	4	....	....	....	....
	NHL Totals		**33**	**7**	**14**	**21**	**8**	**3**	**0**	**0**	**65**	**10.8**		**330**	**45.8**	**12:40**	**3**	**1**	**1**	**2**	**0**	**1**	**0**	**0**	**11:34**

OHL All-Rookie Team (1999) • AHL All-Rookie Team (2003)

STAIOS, Steve (STAY-uhs, STEEV) **EDM.**

Defense. Shoots right. 6'1", 200 lbs. Born, Hamilton, Ont., July 28, 1973. St. Louis' 1st choice, 27th overall, in 1991 Entry Draft.

Season	Club	League	GP	G	A	Pts	PIM	PP	SH	GW	S	%	+/-	TF	F%	Min	GP	G	A	Pts	PIM	PP	SH	GW	Min
1988-89	Hamilton Huskies	OMHA	58	13	39	52	78	....	....	....	....	....	....	....	....	....	....	....	....	....	....	....	....	....	....
1989-90	Hamilton Kilty B's	OJHL-B	40	9	27	36	66	....	....	....	....	....	....	....	....	....	....	....	....	....	....	....	....	....	....
1990-91	Niagara Falls	OHL	66	17	29	46	115	....	....	....	....	....	....	....	....	....	12	2	3	5	10	....	....	....	....
1991-92	Niagara Falls	OHL	65	11	42	53	122	....	....	....	....	....	....	....	....	....	17	7	8	15	27	....	....	....	....
1992-93	Niagara Falls	OHL	12	4	14	18	30	....	....	....	....	....	....	....	....	....	....	....	....	....	....	....	....	....	....
	Sudbury Wolves	OHL	53	13	44	57	67	....	....	....	....	....	....	....	....	....	11	5	6	11	22	....	....	....	....
1993-94	Peoria Rivermen	IHL	38	3	9	12	42	....	....	....	....	....	....	....	....	....	....	....	....	....	....	....	....	....	....
1994-95	Peoria Rivermen	IHL	60	3	13	16	64	....	....	....	....	....	....	....	....	....	6	0	0	0	10	....	....	....	....
1995-96	Peoria Rivermen	IHL	6	0	1	1	14	....	....	....	....	....	....	....	....	....	....	....	....	....	....	....	....	....	....
	Worcester IceCats	AHL	57	1	11	12	114	....	....	....	....	....	....	....	....	....	....	....	....	....	....	....	....	....	....
	Boston	**NHL**	12	0	0	0	4	0	0	0	0	0.0	−5	....	....	....	3	0	0	0	0	0	0	0	0
	Providence Bruins	AHL	7	1	4	5	8	....	....	....	....	....	....	....	....	....	....	....	....	....	....	....	....	....	....
1996-97	**Boston**	**NHL**	54	3	8	11	71	0	0	0	56	5.4	−26	....	....	....	....	....	....	....	....	....	....	....	....
	Vancouver	**NHL**	9	0	6	6	20	0	0	0	10	0.0	2	....	....	....	....	....	....	....	....	....	....	....	....
1997-98	**Vancouver**	**NHL**	77	3	4	7	134	0	0	0	45	6.7	−3	....	....	....	....	....	....	....	....	....	....	....	....
1998-99	**Vancouver**	**NHL**	57	0	2	2	54	0	0	0	33	0.0	−12	4	25.0	6:53	....	....	....	....	....	....	....	....	....
99-2000	**Atlanta**	**NHL**	27	2	3	5	66	0	0	0	38	5.3	−5	2	50.0	13:01	....	....	....	....	....	....	....	....	....
2000-01	**Atlanta**	**NHL**	70	9	13	22	137	4	0	0	156	5.8	−23	1	0.0	21:45	....	....	....	....	....	....	....	....	....
2001-02	**Edmonton**	**NHL**	73	5	5	10	108	0	0	1	101	5.0	10	0	0.0	18:05	....	....	....	....	....	....	....	....	....
2002-03	**Edmonton**	**NHL**	76	5	21	26	96	1	3	0	126	4.0	13	1	0.0	22:17	6	0	0	0	4	0	0	0	23:27
	NHL Totals		**455**	**27**	**62**	**89**	**690**	**5**	**3**	**2**	**569**	**4.7**		**8**	**25.0**	**17:25**	**9**	**0**	**0**	**0**	**4**	**0**	**0**	**0**	**23:27**

Traded to **Boston** by **St. Louis** with Kevin Sawyer for Steve Leach, March 8, 1996. Claimed on waivers by **Vancouver** from **Boston**, March 18, 1997. Claimed by **Atlanta** from **Vancouver** in Expansion Draft, June 25, 1999. • Missed majority of 1999-2000 season recovering from knee injury suffered in game vs. Colorado, October 23, 1999. Traded to **New Jersey** by New Jersey's 9th round choice (Simon Gamache) in 2000 Entry Draft, June 12, 2000. Traded to **Atlanta** by **New Jersey** for future considerations, July 10, 2000. Signed as a free agent by **Edmonton**, July 12, 2001.

STAJAN, Matt (STAY-juhn, MAHT) **TOR.**

Center. Shoots left. 6'1", 180 lbs. Born, Mississauga, Ont., December 19, 1983. Toronto's 2nd choice, 57th overall, in 2002 Entry Draft.

Season	Club	League	GP	G	A	Pts	PIM	PP	SH	GW	S	%	+/-	TF	F%	Min	GP	G	A	Pts	PIM	PP	SH	GW	Min
99-2000	Miss. Senators	GTHL	STATISTICS NOT AVAILABLE					....	....	....	....	....	....	....	....	....	7	1	6	7	5	....	....	....	....
2000-01	Belleville Bulls	OHL	57	9	18	27	27	....	....	....	....	....	....	....	....	....	7	1	6	7	5	....	....	....	....
2001-02	Belleville Bulls	OHL	68	33	52	85	50	....	....	....	....	....	....	....	....	....	11	3	8	11	14	....	....	....	....
2002-03	Belleville Bulls	OHL	57	34	60	94	75	....	....	....	....	....	....	....	....	....	7	5	8	13	16	....	....	....	....
	St. John's	AHL	1	0	1	1	0	....	....	....	....	....	....	....	....	....	....	....	....	....	....	....	....	....	....
	Toronto	**NHL**	1	1	0	1	0	0	0	0	1	100.0	1	12	33.3	11:00	....	....	....	....	....	....	....	....	....
	NHL Totals		**1**	**1**	**0**	**1**	**0**	**0**	**0**	**0**	**1**	**100.0**	**1**	**12**	**33.3**	**11:00**	....	....	....	....	....	....	....	....	....

• Recorded an assist in his first professional game (April 4, 2003 vs. Manitoba-AHL). • One of only four players (Rolly Huard, Dean Morton, Damian Surma) to score a goal in only NHL game (April 5, 2003, at home vs. Ottawa).

STAPLETON, Mike (STAY-puhl-TOHN, MIGHK)

Center. Shoots right. 5'10", 183 lbs. Born, Sarnia, Ont., May 5, 1966. Chicago's 7th choice, 132nd overall, in 1984 Entry Draft.

Season	Club	League	GP	G	A	Pts	PIM	PP	SH	GW	S	%	+/-	TF	F%	Min	GP	G	A	Pts	PIM	PP	SH	GW	Min
1982-83	Strathroy Blades	OJHL-B	40	39	38	77	99	....	....	....	....	....	....	....	....	....	3	1	2	3	4	....	....	....	....
1983-84	Cornwall Royals	OHL	70	24	45	69	94	....	....	....	....	....	....	....	....	....	3	1	2	3	4	....	....	....	....
1984-85	Cornwall Royals	OHL	56	41	44	85	68	....	....	....	....	....	....	....	....	....	9	2	4	6	23	....	....	....	....
1985-86	Cornwall Royals	OHL	56	39	64	103	74	....	....	....	....	....	....	....	....	....	6	2	3	5	2	....	....	....	....
1986-87	Team Canada	Nat-Tm	21	2	4	6	4	....	....	....	....	....	....	....	....	....	....	....	....	....	....	....	....	....	....
	Chicago	**NHL**	39	3	6	9	6	0	0	0	54	5.6	−9	....	....	....	4	0	0	0	2	0	0	0	....
1987-88	**Chicago**	**NHL**	53	2	9	11	59	0	0	1	50	4.0	−10	....	....	....	....	....	....	....	....	....	....	....	....
	Saginaw Hawks	IHL	31	11	19	30	52	....	....	....	....	....	....	....	....	....	10	5	6	11	10	....	....	....	....
1988-89	**Chicago**	**NHL**	7	0	1	1	7	0	0	0	6	0.0	−1	....	....	....	....	....	....	....	....	....	....	....	....
	Saginaw Hawks	IHL	69	21	47	68	162	....	....	....	....	....	....	....	....	....	6	1	3	4	4	....	....	....	....
1989-90	Arvika HC	Swede-3	30	15	18	33	....	....	....	....	....	....	....	....	....	....	....	....	....	....	....	....	....	....	....
	Indianapolis Ice	IHL	16	5	10	15	6	....	....	....	....	....	....	....	....	....	13	9	10	19	38	....	....	....	....
1990-91	**Chicago**	**NHL**	7	0	1	1	2	0	0	0	6	0.0	0	....	....	....	....	....	....	....	....	....	....	....	....
	Indianapolis Ice	IHL	75	29	52	81	76	....	....	....	....	....	....	....	....	....	7	1	4	5	0	....	....	....	....
1991-92	**Chicago**	**NHL**	19	4	4	8	8	1	0	0	32	12.5	−4	....	....	....	....	....	....	....	....	....	....	....	....
	Indianapolis Ice	IHL	59	18	40	58	65	....	....	....	....	....	....	....	....	....	....	....	....	....	....	....	....	....	....
1992-93	**Pittsburgh**	**NHL**	78	4	9	13	10	0	1	1	78	5.1	−8	....	....	....	4	0	0	0	0	0	0	0	....
1993-94	**Pittsburgh**	**NHL**	58	7	4	11	18	3	0	0	59	11.9	−4	....	....	....	....	....	....	....	....	....	....	....	....
	Edmonton	**NHL**	23	5	9	14	28	1	0	0	43	11.6	−1	....	....	....	....	....	....	....	....	....	....	....	....
1994-95	**Edmonton**	**NHL**	46	6	11	17	21	3	0	2	59	10.2	−12	....	....	....	....	....	....	....	....	....	....	....	....
1995-96	**Winnipeg**	**NHL**	58	10	14	24	37	3	1	0	91	11.0	−4	....	....	....	6	0	0	0	21	0	0	0	....
1996-97	**Phoenix**	**NHL**	55	4	11	15	36	2	0	1	74	5.4	−4	....	....	....	7	0	0	0	14	0	0	0	....
1997-98	**Phoenix**	**NHL**	64	5	5	10	36	1	1	1	69	7.2	−4	....	....	....	6	0	0	0	0	0	0	0	....
1998-99	**Phoenix**	**NHL**	76	9	9	18	34	0	2	2	106	8.5	−6	345	46.1	13:40	7	1	0	1	0	0	0	0	10:51
99-2000	**Atlanta**	**NHL**	62	10	12	22	30	4	0	1	146	6.8	−29	717	48.0	17:18	....	....	....	....	....	....	....	....	....
2000-01	**NY Islanders**	**NHL**	34	1	4	5	22	0	0	0	22	4.5	−5	192	45.3	9:09	....	....	....	....	....	....	....	....	....
	Vancouver	**NHL**	18	1	2	3	8	1	0	0	9	11.1	−6	104	41.4	9:58	....	....	....	....	....	....	....	....	....
2001-02	Blues Espoo	Finland	41	18	19	37	42	....	....	....	....	....	....	....	....	....	3	0	0	0	4	....	....	....	....

Season	Club	League	GP	G	A	Pts	PIM	PP	SH	GW	S	%	+/-	TF	F%	Min	GP	G	A	Pts	PIM	PP	SH	GW	Min
			Regular Season														Playoffs								
2002-03	Leksands IF	Sweden	19	5	5	10	10	....	....	....	....	....	....	....	....	....	....	....	....	....	....	....	....	....	....
	Blues Espoo	Finland	33	8	20	28	55	....	....	....	....	....	....	....	....	....	7	1	2	3	10	....	....	....	....
	NHL Totals		**697**	**71**	**111**	**182**	**342**	**19**	**5**	**9**	**904**	**7.9**		**1358**	**46.6**	**13:42**	**34**	**1**	**0**	**1**	**39**	**0**	**0**	**0**	**10:51**

Signed as a free agent by **Pittsburgh**, September 30, 1992. Claimed on waivers by **Edmonton** from **Pittsburgh**, February 19, 1994. Signed as a free agent by **Winnipeg**, August 18, 1995. Transferred to **Phoenix** after **Winnipeg** franchise relocated, July 1, 1996. Claimed by **Atlanta** from **Phoenix** in Expansion Draft, June 25, 1999. Signed as a free agent by **NY Islanders**, July 3, 2000. Traded to **Vancouver** by **NY Islanders** for Vancouver's 9th round choice (later traded to Washington – Washington selected Robert Muller) in 2001 Entry Draft, December 28, 2000. Signed as a free agent by **Blues Espoo** (Finland), October 23, 2001. Signed as a free agent by **Leksands IF** (Sweden), November 11, 2002.

STEFAN, Patrik

(SHTEH-fan, PAT-rihk) **ATL.**

Center. Shoots left. 6'2", 210 lbs. Born, Pribram, Czech., September 16, 1980. Atlanta's 1st choice, 1st overall, in 1999 Entry Draft.

Season	Club	League	GP	G	A	Pts	PIM	PP	SH	GW	S	%	+/-	TF	F%	Min	GP	G	A	Pts	PIM	PP	SH	GW	Min
1996-97	HC Sparta Praha	Czech	5	0	1	1	2	....	....	....	....	....	....	....	....	....	7	1	0	1	0	....	....	....	....
1997-98	HC Sparta Praha	Czech	27	2	6	8	16	....	....	....	....	....	....	....	....	....	....	....	....	....	....	....	....	....	....
	Long Beach	IHL	25	5	10	15	10	....	....	....	....	....	....	....	....	....	10	1	1	2	2	....	....	....	....
1998-99	Long Beach	IHL	33	11	24	35	26	....	....	....	....	....	....	....	....	....	....	....	....	....	....	....	....	....	....
99-2000	**Atlanta**	**NHL**	**72**	**5**	**20**	**25**	**30**	**1**	**0**	**0**	**117**	**4.3**	**–20**	**988**	**41.4**	**14:49**	....	....	....	....	....	....	....	....	....
2000-01	**Atlanta**	**NHL**	**66**	**10**	**21**	**31**	**22**	**0**	**0**	**1**	**93**	**10.8**	**–3**	**834**	**42.9**	**14:07**	....	....	....	....	....	....	....	....	....
2001-02	**Atlanta**	**NHL**	**59**	**7**	**16**	**23**	**22**	**0**	**1**	**0**	**67**	**10.4**	**–4**	**628**	**41.9**	**15:58**	....	....	....	....	....	....	....	....	....
	Chicago Wolves	AHL	5	3	0	3	0	....	....	....	....	....	....	....	....	....	....	....	....	....	....	....	....	....	....
2002-03	**Atlanta**	**NHL**	**71**	**13**	**21**	**34**	**12**	**3**	**0**	**2**	**96**	**13.5**	**–10**	**1125**	**45.7**	**16:50**	....	....	....	....	....	....	....	....	....
	NHL Totals		**268**	**35**	**78**	**113**	**86**	**4**	**1**	**3**	**373**	**9.4**		**3575**	**43.2**	**15:26**	....	....	....	....	....	....	....	....	....

STEPHENS, Charlie

(STEE-vuhns, CHAHR-lee) **COL.**

Center/Right wing. Shoots right. 6'3", 225 lbs. Born, London, Ont., April 5, 1981. Colorado's 9th choice, 196th overall, in 2001 Entry Draft.

Season	Club	League	GP	G	A	Pts	PIM	PP	SH	GW	S	%	+/-	TF	F%	Min	GP	G	A	Pts	PIM	PP	SH	GW	Min
1995-96	Elgin-Middlesex	MHAO	60	25	29	54	60	....	....	....	....	....	....	....	....	....	....	....	....	....	....	....	....	....	....
1996-97	Leamington Flyers	OJHL-B	50	26	36	62	103	....	....	....	....	....	....	....	....	....	....	....	....	....	....	....	....	....	....
1997-98	St. Michael's	OHL	58	9	21	30	38	....	....	....	....	....	....	....	....	....	....	....	....	....	....	....	....	....	....
1998-99	St. Michael's	OHL	7	2	4	6	8	....	....	....	....	....	....	....	....	....	....	....	....	....	....	....	....	....	....
	Guelph Storm	OHL	61	24	28	52	72	....	....	....	....	....	....	....	....	....	11	3	5	8	19	....	....	....	....
99-2000	Guelph Storm	OHL	56	16	34	50	87	....	....	....	....	....	....	....	....	....	6	1	3	4	15	....	....	....	....
2000-01	Guelph Storm	OHL	67	38	38	76	53	....	....	....	....	....	....	....	....	....	4	0	2	2	2	....	....	....	....
2001-02	Guelph Storm	OHL	4	1	2	3	2	....	....	....	....	....	....	....	....	....	....	....	....	....	....	....	....	....	....
	London Knights	OHL	56	23	33	56	55	....	....	....	....	....	....	....	....	....	12	6	10	16	18	....	....	....	....
	Hershey Bears	AHL	....	....	....	....	....	....	....	....	....	....	....	....	....	....	1	0	0	0	0	....	....	....	....
2002-03	**Colorado**	**NHL**	**2**	**0**	**0**	**0**	**0**	**0**	**0**	**0**	**1**	**0.0**	**0**	**0**	**0.0**	**5:20**	....	....	....	....	....	....	....	....	....
	Hershey Bears	AHL	74	17	33	50	38	....	....	....	....	....	....	....	....	....	5	1	1	2	2	....	....	....	....
	NHL Totals		**2**	**0**	**0**	**0**	**0**	**0**	**0**	**0**	**1**	**0.0**		**0**	**0.0**	**5:20**	....	....	....	....	....	....	....	....	....

• Re-entered NHL Entry Draft. Originally Washington's 3rd choice, 31st overall, in 1999 Entry Draft.

STEVENS, Scott

(STEE-vehns, SKAWT) **N.J.**

Defense. Shoots left. 6'2", 215 lbs. Born, Kitchener, Ont., April 1, 1964. Washington's 1st choice, 5th overall, in 1982 Entry Draft.

Season	Club	League	GP	G	A	Pts	PIM	PP	SH	GW	S	%	+/-	TF	F%	Min	GP	G	A	Pts	PIM	PP	SH	GW	Min
1980-81	Kitchener	OHA-B	39	7	33	40	82	....	....	....	....	....	....	....	....	....	....	....	....	....	....	....	....	....	....
	Kitchener Rangers	OMJHL	1	0	0	0	0	....	....	....	....	....	....	....	....	....	....	....	....	....	....	....	....	....	....
1981-82	Kitchener Rangers	OHL	68	6	36	42	158	....	....	....	....	....	....	....	....	....	15	1	10	11	71	....	....	....	....
1982-83	**Washington**	**NHL**	**77**	**9**	**16**	**25**	**195**	**0**	**0**	**0**	**121**	**7.4**	**14**	....	....	....	**4**	**1**	**0**	**1**	**26**	**0**	**0**	**0**	....
1983-84	**Washington**	**NHL**	**78**	**13**	**32**	**45**	**201**	**7**	**0**	**2**	**155**	**8.4**	**26**	....	....	....	**8**	**1**	**8**	**9**	**21**	**1**	**0**	**0**	....
1984-85	**Washington**	**NHL**	**80**	**21**	**44**	**65**	**221**	**16**	**0**	**5**	**170**	**12.4**	**19**	....	....	....	**5**	**0**	**1**	**1**	**20**	**0**	**0**	**0**	....
1985-86	**Washington**	**NHL**	**73**	**15**	**38**	**53**	**165**	**3**	**0**	**2**	**121**	**12.4**	**0**	....	....	....	**9**	**3**	**8**	**11**	**12**	**2**	**0**	**2**	....
1986-87	**Washington**	**NHL**	**77**	**10**	**51**	**61**	**283**	**2**	**0**	**0**	**165**	**6.1**	**13**	....	....	....	**7**	**0**	**5**	**5**	**19**	**0**	**0**	**0**	....
1987-88	**Washington**	**NHL**	**80**	**12**	**60**	**72**	**184**	**5**	**1**	**2**	**231**	**5.2**	**14**	....	....	....	**13**	**1**	**11**	**12**	**46**	**0**	**0**	**0**	....
1988-89	**Washington**	**NHL**	**80**	**7**	**61**	**68**	**225**	**6**	**0**	**3**	**195**	**3.6**	**1**	....	....	....	**6**	**1**	**4**	**5**	**11**	**0**	**0**	**0**	....
1989-90	**Washington**	**NHL**	**56**	**11**	**29**	**40**	**154**	**7**	**0**	**0**	**143**	**7.7**	**1**	....	....	....	**15**	**2**	**7**	**9**	**25**	**1**	**0**	**0**	....
1990-91	**St. Louis**	**NHL**	**78**	**5**	**44**	**49**	**150**	**1**	**0**	**1**	**160**	**3.1**	**23**	....	....	....	**13**	**0**	**3**	**3**	**36**	**0**	**0**	**0**	....
1991-92	**New Jersey**	**NHL**	**68**	**17**	**42**	**59**	**124**	**7**	**1**	**2**	**156**	**10.9**	**24**	....	....	....	**7**	**2**	**1**	**3**	**29**	**2**	**0**	**1**	....
1992-93	**New Jersey**	**NHL**	**81**	**12**	**45**	**57**	**120**	**8**	**0**	**1**	**146**	**8.2**	**14**	....	....	....	**5**	**2**	**2**	**4**	**10**	**1**	**0**	**0**	....
1993-94	**New Jersey**	**NHL**	**83**	**18**	**60**	**78**	**112**	**5**	**1**	**4**	**215**	**8.4**	**53**	....	....	....	**20**	**2**	**9**	**11**	**42**	**2**	**0**	**1**	....
1994-95♦	**New Jersey**	**NHL**	**48**	**2**	**20**	**22**	**56**	**1**	**0**	**1**	**111**	**1.8**	**4**	....	....	....	**20**	**1**	**7**	**8**	**24**	**0**	**0**	**1**	....
1995-96	**New Jersey**	**NHL**	**82**	**5**	**23**	**28**	**100**	**2**	**1**	**1**	**174**	**2.9**	**7**	....	....	....	....	....	....	....	....	....	....	....	....
1996-97	**New Jersey**	**NHL**	**79**	**5**	**19**	**24**	**70**	**0**	**0**	**1**	**166**	**3.0**	**26**	....	....	....	**10**	**0**	**4**	**4**	**2**	**0**	**0**	**0**	....
1997-98	**New Jersey**	**NHL**	**80**	**4**	**22**	**26**	**80**	**1**	**0**	**1**	**94**	**4.3**	**19**	....	....	....	**6**	**1**	**0**	**1**	**8**	**0**	**0**	**0**	....
	Canada	Olympics	6	0	0	0	2	....	....	....	....	....	....	....	....	....	....	....	....	....	....	....	....	....	....
1998-99	**New Jersey**	**NHL**	**75**	**5**	**22**	**27**	**64**	**0**	**0**	**1**	**111**	**4.5**	**29**	**1**	**0.0**	**24:11**	**7**	**2**	**1**	**3**	**10**	**2**	**0**	**0**	**24:28**
99-2000♦	**New Jersey**	**NHL**	**78**	**8**	**21**	**29**	**103**	**0**	**1**	**1**	**133**	**6.0**	**30**	**0**	**0.0**	**23:23**	**23**	**3**	**8**	**11**	**6**	**0**	**0**	**2**	**25:25**
2000-01	**New Jersey**	**NHL**	**81**	**9**	**22**	**31**	**71**	**3**	**0**	**2**	**171**	**5.3**	**40**	**0**	**0.0**	**24:37**	**25**	**1**	**7**	**8**	**37**	**0**	**0**	**0**	**22:37**
2001-02	**New Jersey**	**NHL**	**82**	**1**	**16**	**17**	**44**	**0**	**0**	**1**	**121**	**0.8**	**15**	**0**	**0.0**	**23:19**	**6**	**0**	**0**	**0**	**4**	**0**	**0**	**0**	**22:14**
2002-03♦	**New Jersey**	**NHL**	**81**	**4**	**16**	**20**	**41**	**0**	**0**	**2**	**113**	**3.5**	**18**	**0**	**0.0**	**23:05**	**24**	**3**	**6**	**9**	**14**	**1**	**0**	**1**	**24:44**
	NHL Totals		**1597**	**193**	**703**	**896**	**2763**	**74**	**5**	**33**	**3172**	**6.1**		**1**	**0.0**	**23:43**	**233**	**26**	**92**	**118**	**402**	**12**	**0**	**8**	**24:06**

NHL All-Rookie Team (1983) • NHL First All-Star Team (1988, 1994) • NHL Second All-Star Team (1992, 1997, 2001) • Alka-Seltzer Plus Award (1994) • Conn Smythe Trophy (2000)

Played in NHL All-Star Game (1985, 1989, 1991, 1992, 1993, 1994, 1996, 1997, 1998, 1999, 2000, 2001, 2003)

Signed as a free agent by **St. Louis**, July 16, 1990. Transferred to **New Jersey** from **St. Louis** as compensation for St. Louis' signing of free agent Brendan Shanahan, September 3, 1991.

STEVENSON, Jeremy

(STEE-vehn-suhn, JAIR-eh-mee) **MIN.**

Left wing. Shoots left. 6'1", 215 lbs. Born, San Bernardino, CA, July 28, 1974. Anaheim's 10th choice, 262nd overall, in 1994 Entry Draft.

Season	Club	League	GP	G	A	Pts	PIM	PP	SH	GW	S	%	+/-	TF	F%	Min	GP	G	A	Pts	PIM	PP	SH	GW	Min
1989-90	Elliot Lake Vikings	NOHA	61	39	26	65	203	....	....	....	....	....	....	....	....	....	....	....	....	....	....	....	....	....	....
1990-91	Cornwall Royals	OHL	58	13	20	33	124	....	....	....	....	....	....	....	....	....	....	....	....	....	....	....	....	....	....
1991-92	Cornwall Royals	OHL	63	15	23	38	176	....	....	....	....	....	....	....	....	....	6	3	1	4	4	....	....	....	....
1992-93	Newmarket	OHL	54	28	28	56	144	....	....	....	....	....	....	....	....	....	5	5	1	6	28	....	....	....	....
1993-94	Newmarket	OHL	9	2	4	6	27	....	....	....	....	....	....	....	....	....	....	....	....	....	....	....	....	....	....
	Sault Ste. Marie	OHL	48	18	19	37	183	....	....	....	....	....	....	....	....	....	14	1	1	2	23	....	....	....	....
1994-95	Greensboro	ECHL	43	14	13	27	231	....	....	....	....	....	....	....	....	....	17	6	11	17	64	....	....	....	....
1995-96	**Anaheim**	**NHL**	**3**	**0**	**1**	**1**	**12**	**0**	**0**	**0**	**1**	**0.0**	**1**	....	....	....	....	....	....	....	....	....	....	....	....
	Baltimore Bandits	AHL	60	11	10	21	295	....	....	....	....	....	....	....	....	....	12	4	2	6	23	....	....	....	....
1996-97	**Anaheim**	**NHL**	**5**	**0**	**0**	**0**	**14**	**0**	**0**	**0**	**1**	**0.0**	**–1**	....	....	....	....	....	....	....	....	....	....	....	....
	Baltimore Bandits	AHL	25	8	8	16	125	....	....	....	....	....	....	....	....	....	3	0	0	0	8	....	....	....	....
1997-98	**Anaheim**	**NHL**	**45**	**3**	**5**	**8**	**101**	**0**	**0**	**1**	**43**	**7.0**	**–4**	....	....	....	....	....	....	....	....	....	....	....	....
	Cincinnati	AHL	10	5	0	5	34	....	....	....	....	....	....	....	....	....	....	....	....	....	....	....	....	....	....
1998-99	Cincinnati	AHL	22	4	4	8	83	....	....	....	....	....	....	....	....	....	3	1	0	1	2	....	....	....	....
99-2000	**Anaheim**	**NHL**	**3**	**0**	**0**	**0**	**7**	**0**	**0**	**0**	**2**	**0.0**	**–1**	**0**	**0.0**	**6:50**	....	....	....	....	....	....	....	....	....
	Cincinnati	AHL	41	11	14	25	100	....	....	....	....	....	....	....	....	....	....	....	....	....	....	....	....	....	....
2000-01	**Nashville**	**NHL**	**8**	**1**	**0**	**1**	**39**	**0**	**0**	**0**	**6**	**16.7**	**–1**	**0**	**0.0**	**6:24**	....	....	....	....	....	....	....	....	....
	Milwaukee	IHL	60	16	13	29	262	....	....	....	....	....	....	....	....	....	5	2	0	2	12	....	....	....	....
2001-02	**Nashville**	**NHL**	**4**	**0**	**0**	**0**	**9**	**0**	**0**	**0**	**0**	**0.0**	**0**	**0**	**0.0**	**5:53**	....	....	....	....	....	....	....	....	....
	Milwaukee	AHL	53	12	7	19	192	....	....	....	....	....	....	....	....	....	....	....	....	....	....	....	....	....	....
2002-03	Houston Aeros	AHL	18	6	7	13	77	....	....	....	....	....	....	....	....	....	....	....	....	....	....	....	....	....	....
	Minnesota	**NHL**	**32**	**9**	**6**	**11**	**69**	**1**	**0**	**1**	**29**	**17.2**	**6**	**0**	**0.0**	**10:48**	**14**	**0**	**5**	**5**	**12**	**0**	**0**	**0**	**12:32**
	NHL Totals		**100**	**9**	**12**	**21**	**251**	**1**	**0**	**2**	**82**	**11.0**		**0**	**0.0**	**9:23**	**14**	**0**	**5**	**5**	**12**	**0**	**0**	**0**	**12:32**

• Re-entered NHL Entry Draft. Originally Winnipeg's 3rd choice, 60th overall, in 1992 Entry Draft.

Signed as a free agent by **Nashville**, September 25, 2000. Signed as a free agent by **Minnesota** November 26, 2002.

			Regular Season														Playoffs								
Season	Club	League	GP	G	A	Pts	PIM	PP	SH	GW	S	%	+/-	TF	F%	Min	GP	G	A	Pts	PIM	PP	SH	GW	Min

STEVENSON, Turner   (STEE-vehn-suhn, TUHR-nuhr)   **N.J.**

Right wing. Shoots right. 6'3", 220 lbs.   Born, Prince George, B.C., May 18, 1972. Montreal's 1st choice, 12th overall, in 1990 Entry Draft.

Season	Club	League	GP	G	A	Pts	PIM	PP	SH	GW	S	%	+/-	TF	F%	Min	GP	G	A	Pts	PIM	PP	SH	GW	Min
1987-88	Prince George	BCAHA	53	45	46	91	127	....																	
1988-89	Seattle	WHL	69	15	12	27	84	....																	
1989-90	Seattle	WHL	62	29	32	61	276	....							13	3	2	5	35				
1990-91	Seattle	WHL	57	36	27	63	222	....							6	1	5	6	15				
	Fredericton	AHL	....												4	0	0	0	5				
1991-92	Seattle	WHL	58	20	32	52	264	....							15	9	3	12	55				
1992-93	Montreal	NHL	1	0	0	0	0	0	0	0	1	0.0	-1				....								
	Fredericton	AHL	79	25	34	59	102											5	2	3	5	11			
1993-94	Montreal	NHL	2	0	0	0	2	0	0	0	0	0.0	-2				3	0	2	2	0	0	0	0
	Fredericton	AHL	66	19	28	47	155																		
1994-95	Fredericton	AHL	37	12	12	24	109																		
	Montreal	NHL	41	6	1	7	86	0	0	1	35	17.1	0											
1995-96	Montreal	NHL	80	9	16	25	167	0	0	2	101	8.9	-2				6	0	1	1	2	0	0	0
1996-97	Montreal	NHL	65	8	13	21	97	1	0	0	76	10.5	-14				5	1	1	2	2	0	0	0
1997-98	Montreal	NHL	63	4	6	10	110	1	0	0	43	9.3	-8				10	3	4	7	12	0	0	0
1998-99	Montreal	NHL	69	10	17	27	88	0	0	2	102	9.8	6	29	37.9	12:57								
99-2000	Montreal	NHL	64	8	13	21	61	0	0	2	94	8.5	-1	5	20.0	13:10								
2000-01	New Jersey	NHL	69	8	18	26	97	2	0	1	92	8.7	11	0	0.0	11:00	23	1	3	4	20	0	0	1	9:27
2001-02	New Jersey	NHL	21	0	2	2	25	0	0	0	33	0.0	-3	0	0.0	11:38	1	0	0	0	4	0	0	0	10:13
2002-03♦	New Jersey	NHL	77	7	13	20	115	0	0	0	85	8.2	7	12	41.7	11:53	14	1	1	2	26	0	0	0	13:01
	NHL Totals		552	60	99	159	848	4	0	8	662	9.1		46	37.0	12:11	62	6	12	18	66	0	0	1	10:47

WHL West First All-Star Team (1992) • Memorial Cup All-Star Team (1992).
Selected by **Columbus** from **Montreal** in Expansion Draft, June 23, 2000. Traded to **New Jersey** by **Columbus** to complete transaction that sent Krzysztof Oliwa (June 12, 2000) and Deron Quint (June 23, 2000) to **Columbus**, June 23, 2000. • Missed majority of 2001-02 season recovering from knee injury suffered in game vs. Vancouver, December 29, 2001.

STILLMAN, Cory   (STIHL-mahn, KOHR-ee)   **T.B.**

Left wing. Shoots left. 6', 194 lbs.   Born, Peterborough, Ont., December 20, 1973. Calgary's 1st choice, 6th overall, in 1992 Entry Draft.

Season	Club	League	GP	G	A	Pts	PIM	PP	SH	GW	S	%	+/-	TF	F%	Min	GP	G	A	Pts	PIM	PP	SH	GW	Min
1989-90	Peterboro B's	OJHL-B	41	30	*54	84	76	....																	
1990-91	Windsor Spitfires	OHL	64	31	70	101	31	....							11	3	6	9	8				
1991-92	Windsor Spitfires	OHL	53	29	61	90	59	....							7	2	4	6	8				
1992-93	Peterborough	OHL	61	25	55	80	55	....							18	3	8	11	18				
1993-94	Saint John Flames	AHL	79	35	48	83	52	....							7	2	4	6	16				
1994-95	Saint John Flames	AHL	63	28	53	81	70	....							5	0	2	2	2				
	Calgary	NHL	10	0	2	2	2	0	0	0	7	0.0	1											
1995-96	Calgary	NHL	74	16	19	35	41	4	1	3	132	12.1	-5				2	1	1	2	0	0	0	0
1996-97	Calgary	NHL	58	6	20	26	14	2	0	0	112	5.4	-6											
1997-98	Calgary	NHL	72	27	22	49	40	9	4	1	178	15.2	-9											
1998-99	Calgary	NHL	76	27	30	57	38	9	3	5	175	15.4	7	535	46.5	16:19								
99-2000	Calgary	NHL	37	12	9	21	12	6	0	3	59	20.3	-9	283	54.4	17:45								
2000-01	Calgary	NHL	66	21	24	45	45	7	0	4	148	14.2	-6	346	43.9	18:50								
	St. Louis	NHL	12	3	4	7	6	3	0	0	26	11.5	-2	36	61.1	18:37	15	3	5	8	8	1	0	1	14:58
2001-02	St. Louis	NHL	80	23	22	45	36	6	0	4	140	16.4	8	196	46.4	0:00	9	0	2	2	2	0	0	0
2002-03	St. Louis	NHL	79	24	43	67	56	6	0	4	157	15.3	12	266	41.7	0:00	6	2	2	4	2	2	0	1
	NHL Totals		564	159	195	354	290	52	8	24	1134	14.0		1662	34.7	9:37	32	6	10	16	12	3	0	2	14:58

OHL Rookie of the Year (1991)
• Missed majority of 1999-2000 season recovering from shoulder injury suffered in game vs. Philadelphia, December 27, 1999. Traded to **St. Louis** by **Calgary** for Craig Conroy and St. Louis' 7th round choice (David Moss) in 2001 Entry Draft, March 13, 2001. Traded to **Tampa Bay** by **St. Louis** for Tampa Bay's 2nd round choice (David Backes) in 2003 Entry Draft, June 21, 2003.

STOCK, P.J.   (STAWK, PEE-JAY)   **BOS.**

Center. Shoots left. 5'10", 197 lbs.   Born, Montreal, Que., May 26, 1975.

Season	Club	League	GP	G	A	Pts	PIM	PP	SH	GW	S	%	+/-	TF	F%	Min	GP	G	A	Pts	PIM	PP	SH	GW	Min
1992-93	Pembroke	OCJHL	55	10	38	48	189	....																	
1993-94	Pembroke	OCJHL	52	25	48	73	262	....																	
1994-95	Victoriaville Tigres	QMJHL	70	9	46	55	386	....							4	0	0	0	60				
1995-96	Victoriaville Tigres	QMJHL	67	19	43	62	432	....							12	5	4	9	79				
1996-97	St. FX University	AUAA	27	11	20	31	110	....							3	0	4	4	14				
1997-98	Hartford	AHL	41	8	8	16	202	....							11	1	3	4	79				
	NY Rangers	NHL	38	2	3	5	114	0	0	1	9	22.2	4											
1998-99	NY Rangers	NHL	5	0	0	0	6	0	0	0	0	0.0	-1	8	50.0	2:42								
	Hartford	AHL	55	4	14	18	250											6	0	1	1	35			
99-2000	NY Rangers	NHL	11	0	1	1	11	0	0	0	2	0.0	1	63	31.8	6:13								
	Hartford	AHL	64	13	23	36	290											23	1	11	12	69			
2000-01	Montreal	NHL	20	1	2	3	32	0	0	0	9	11.1	-1	83	53.0	5:31								
	Philadelphia	NHL	31	1	3	4	78	0	0	0	18	5.6	-2	12	50.0	7:48	2	0	0	0	0	0	0	0	4:59
	Philadelphia	AHL	9	1	2	3	37																		
2001-02	Boston	NHL	58	0	3	3	122	0	0	0	12	0.0	-2	120	45.8	5:09	6	1	0	1	19	0	0	0	3:15
2002-03	Boston	NHL	71	1	9	10	160	1	0	0	38	2.6	-5	185	44.9	6:14								
	NHL Totals		234	5	21	26	523	1	0	1	88	5.7		471	45.0	5:60	8	1	0	1	19	0	0	0	3:41

Signed as a free agent by **NY Rangers**, November 18, 1997. Signed as a free agent by **Montreal**, July 7, 2000. Traded to **Philadelphia** by **Montreal** with Montreal's 6th round choice (Dennis Seidenberg) in 2001 Entry Draft for Gino Odjick, December 7, 2000. Signed as a free agent by **NY Rangers**, August 23, 2001. Claimed by **Boston** from **NY Rangers** in Waiver Draft, September 28, 2001.

STOLL, Jarret   (STOHL, JEHR-eht)   **EDM.**

Center. Shoots right. 6'1", 200 lbs.   Born, Melville, Sask., June 25, 1982. Edmonton's 3rd choice, 36th overall, in 2002 Entry Draft.

Season	Club	League	GP	G	A	Pts	PIM	PP	SH	GW	S	%	+/-	TF	F%	Min	GP	G	A	Pts	PIM	PP	SH	GW	Min
1997-98	Saskatoon Blazers	SMHL	44	45	44	*89	78																		
	Edmonton Ice	WHL	8	2	3	5	4																		
1998-99	Kootenay Ice	WHL	57	13	21	34	38	....							4	0	0	0	2				
99-2000	Kootenay Ice	WHL	71	37	38	75	64	....							20	7	9	16	24				
2000-01	Kootenay Ice	WHL	62	40	66	106	105	....							11	5	9	14	22				
2001-02	Kootenay Ice	WHL	47	32	34	66	64	....							22	6	14	20	35				
2002-03	Edmonton	NHL	4	0	1	1	0	0	0	0	5	0.0	-3	30	63.3	7:44								
	Hamilton	AHL	76	21	33	54	86											23	5	8	13	25			
	NHL Totals		4	0	1	1	0	0	0	0	5	0.0		30	63.3	7:44								

• Re-entered NHL Entry Draft. Originally Calgary's 3rd choice, 46th overall, in 2000 Entry Draft.
WHL East First All-Star Team (2001) • Canadian Major Junior First All-Star Team (2001) • WHL West First All-Star Team (2002)

STRAKA, Martin   (STRAH-kuh, MAHR-tihn)   **PIT.**

Center. Shoots left. 5'9", 178 lbs.   Born, Plzen, Czech., September 3, 1972. Pittsburgh's 1st choice, 19th overall, in 1992 Entry Draft.

Season	Club	League	GP	G	A	Pts	PIM	PP	SH	GW	S	%	+/-	TF	F%	Min	GP	G	A	Pts	PIM	PP	SH	GW	Min
1989-90	TJ Skoda Plzen	Czech	1	0	3	3																			
1990-91	HC Skoda Plzen	Czech	47	7	24	31	6																		
1991-92	HC Skoda Plzen	Czech	50	27	28	55	20																		
1992-93	Pittsburgh	NHL	42	3	13	16	29	0	0	1	28	10.7	2				11	2	1	3	2	0	0	0
	Cleveland	IHL	4	4	3	7	0																		
1993-94	Pittsburgh	NHL	84	30	34	64	24	2	0	6	130	23.1	24				6	0	1	1	0	0	0	0
1994-95	Plzen	Czech	19	10	11	21	18																		
	Pittsburgh	NHL	31	4	12	16	16	0	0	0	36	11.1	0											
	Ottawa	NHL	6	1	1	2	0	0	0	0	13	7.7	-1											
1995-96	Ottawa	NHL	43	9	16	25	29	5	0	1	63	14.3	-14											
	NY Islanders	NHL	22	2	10	12	6	0	0	0	18	11.1	-6											
	Florida	NHL	12	2	4	6	4	0	0	0	17	11.8	1				13	2	4	6	0	0	0	0
1996-97	Florida	NHL	55	7	22	29	12	2	0	1	94	7.4	9				4	0	0	0	0	0	0	0
1997-98	Pittsburgh	NHL	75	19	23	42	28	4	3	4	117	16.2	-1				6	2	1	3	0	0	0	0
	Czech Republic	Olympics	6	1	2	3	0																		
1998-99	Pittsburgh	NHL	80	35	48	83	26	5	4	4	177	19.8	12	845	43.6	23:35	13	6	9	15	6	1	0	0	25:00

			Regular Season														Playoffs								
Season	Club	League	GP	G	A	Pts	PIM	PP	SH	GW	S	%	+/-	TF	F%	Min	GP	G	A	Pts	PIM	PP	SH	GW	Min
99-2000	Pittsburgh	NHL	71	20	39	59	26	3	1	2	146	13.7	24	651	42.9	23:58	11	3	9	12	10	1	0	0	24:27
2000-01	Pittsburgh	NHL	82	27	68	95	38	7	1	4	185	14.6	19	331	43.2	23:01	18	5	8	13	8	3	0	2	21:24
2001-02	Pittsburgh	NHL	13	5	4	9	0	1	0	1	33	15.2	3	5	60.0	18:00	....	....	....	....	....	....	....	....	....
2002-03	Pittsburgh	NHL	60	18	28	46	12	7	0	4	136	13.2	–18	115	45.2	20:37	....	....	....	....	....	....	....	....	....
	NHL Totals		676	182	322	504	252	37	9	28	1193	15.3		1947	43.4	22:42	82	21	29	50	32	5	1	2	23:19

Czechoslovakian First All-Star Team (1992)
Played in NHL All-Star Game (1999)

Traded to **Ottawa** by **Pittsburgh** for Troy Murray and Norm Maciver, April 7, 1995. Traded to **NY Islanders** by **Ottawa** with Don Beaupre and Bryan Berard for Damian Rhodes and Wade Redden, January 23, 1996. Claimed on waivers by **Florida** from **NY Islanders**, March 15, 1996. Signed as a free agent by **Pittsburgh**, August 6, 1997. • Missed majority of 2001-02 season recovering from leg injury suffered in game vs. Florida, October 28, 2001.

STRUDWICK, Jason (STRUHD-wihk, JAY-suhn) CHI.

Wing/Defense. Shoots left. 6'3", 210 lbs. Born, Edmonton, Alta., July 17, 1975. NY Islanders' 3rd choice, 63rd overall, in 1994 Entry Draft.

Season	Club	League	GP	G	A	Pts	PIM	PP	SH	GW	S	%	+/-	TF	F%	Min	GP	G	A	Pts	PIM	PP	SH	GW	Min
1991-92	Edmonton Legion	AMHL	35	3	8	11	67	....	....	....	....	....	....	....	....	....	....	....	....	....	....	....	....	....	....
1992-93	Edmonton Pats	AMHL	33	8	20	28	135	....	....	....	....	....	....	....	....	....	....	....	....	....	....	....	....	....	....
1993-94	Kamloops Blazers	WHL	61	6	8	14	118	....	....	....	....	....	....	....	....	....	19	0	4	4	24	....	....	....	....
1994-95	Kamloops Blazers	WHL	72	3	11	14	183	....	....	....	....	....	....	....	....	....	21	1	1	2	39	....	....	....	....
1995-96	NY Islanders	NHL	1	0	0	0	7	0	0	0	0	0.0	0	....	....	....	....	....	....	....	....	....	....	....	....
	Worcester IceCats	AHL	60	2	7	9	119	....	....	....	....	....	....	....	....	....	4	0	1	1	0	....	....	....	....
1996-97	Kentucky	AHL	80	1	9	10	198	....	....	....	....	....	....	....	....	....	4	0	0	0	0	....	....	....	....
1997-98	NY Islanders	NHL	17	0	1	1	36	0	0	0	3	0.0	1	....	....	....	....	....	....	....	....	....	....	....	....
	Kentucky	AHL	39	3	1	4	87	....	....	....	....	....	....	....	....	....	....	....	....	....	....	....	....	....	....
	Vancouver	NHL	11	0	1	1	29	0	0	0	5	0.0	–3	....	....	....	....	....	....	....	....	....	....	....	....
	Syracuse Crunch	AHL	....	....	....	....	....	....	....	....	....	....	....	....	....	....	3	0	0	0	6	....	....	....	....
1998-99	Vancouver	NHL	65	0	3	3	114	0	0	0	25	0.0	–19	0	0.0	12:49	....	....	....	....	....	....	....	....	....
99-2000	Vancouver	NHL	63	1	3	4	64	0	0	0	18	5.6	–13	0	0.0	15:12	....	....	....	....	....	....	....	....	....
2000-01	Vancouver	NHL	60	1	4	5	64	0	0	1	21	4.8	16	0	0.0	9:59	2	0	0	0	0	0	0	0	2:15
2001-02	Vancouver	NHL	44	2	4	6	96	0	0	0	13	15.4	4	0	0.0	9:45	....	....	....	....	....	....	....	....	....
2002-03	Chicago	NHL	48	2	3	5	87	0	0	0	19	10.5	–4	3	0.0	8:32	....	....	....	....	....	....	....	....	....
	NHL Totals		309	6	19	25	497	0	0	1	104	5.8		3	0.0	11:32	2	0	0	0	0	0	0	0	2:15

Traded to **Vancouver** by **NY Islanders** for Gino Odjick, March 23, 1998. Signed as a free agent by **Chicago**, July 15, 2002.

STUART, Brad (STEW-ahrt, BRAD) S.J.

Defense. Shoots left. 6'2", 215 lbs. Born, Rocky Mountain House, Alta., November 6, 1979. San Jose's 1st choice, 3rd overall, in 1998 Entry Draft.

Season	Club	League	GP	G	A	Pts	PIM	PP	SH	GW	S	%	+/-	TF	F%	Min	GP	G	A	Pts	PIM	PP	SH	GW	Min
1995-96	Red Deer	AMHL	35	12	25	37	83	....	....	....	....	....	....	....	....	....	....	....	....	....	....	....	....	....	....
	Regina Pats	WHL	3	0	0	0	0	....	....	....	....	....	....	....	....	....	....	....	....	....	....	....	....	....	....
1996-97	Regina Pats	WHL	57	7	36	43	58	....	....	....	....	....	....	....	....	....	5	0	4	4	14	....	....	....	....
1997-98	Regina Pats	WHL	72	20	45	65	82	....	....	....	....	....	....	....	....	....	9	3	4	7	10	....	....	....	....
1998-99	Regina Pats	WHL	29	10	19	29	43	....	....	....	....	....	....	....	....	....	....	....	....	....	....	....	....	....	....
	Calgary Hitmen	WHL	30	11	22	33	26	....	....	....	....	....	....	....	....	....	21	8	15	23	59	....	....	....	....
99-2000	San Jose	NHL	82	10	26	36	32	5	1	3	133	7.5	3	0	0.0	20:24	12	1	0	1	6	1	0	0	16:30
2000-01	San Jose	NHL	77	5	18	23	56	1	0	2	119	4.2	10	0	0.0	20:06	5	1	0	1	0	0	0	0	20:19
2001-02	San Jose	NHL	82	6	23	29	39	2	0	2	96	6.3	13	0	0.0	21:41	12	0	3	3	8	0	0	0	19:42
2002-03	San Jose	NHL	36	4	10	14	46	2	0	1	63	6.3	–6	0	0.0	20:53	....	....	....	....	....	....	....	....	....
	NHL Totals		277	25	77	102	173	10	1	8	411	6.1		0	0.0	20:46	29	2	3	5	14	1	0	0	18:29

WHL East Second All-Star Team (1998) • WHL East First All-Star Team (1999) • Canadian Major Junior First All-Star Team (1999) • Canadian Major Junior Defenseman of the Year (1999) • NHL All-Rookie Team (2000)

• Missed majority of 2002-03 season recovering from ankle (January 4, 2003 vs. Los Angeles) and head (February 21, 2003 vs. Columbus) injuries.

STUMPEL, Jozef (STUM-puhl, JOH-zehf) L.A.

Center. Shoots right. 6'3", 225 lbs. Born, Nitra, Czech., July 20, 1972. Boston's 2nd choice, 40th overall, in 1991 Entry Draft.

Season	Club	League	GP	G	A	Pts	PIM	PP	SH	GW	S	%	+/-	TF	F%	Min	GP	G	A	Pts	PIM	PP	SH	GW	Min
1989-90	Plastika Nitra	Czech-2	38	12	11	23	....	....	....	....	....	....	....	....	....	....	....	....	....	....	....	....	....	....	....
1990-91	AC Nitra	Czech	49	23	22	45	14	....	....	....	....	....	....	....	....	....	....	....	....	....	....	....	....	....	....
1991-92	Kolner EC	Germany	33	19	18	37	35	....	....	....	....	....	....	....	....	....	4	1	1	2	0	....	....	....	....
	Boston	NHL	4	1	0	1	0	0	0	0	3	33.3	1	....	....	....	....	....	....	....	....	....	....	....	....
1992-93	Boston	NHL	13	1	3	4	4	0	0	0	8	12.5	–3	....	....	....	....	....	....	....	....	....	....	....	....
	Providence Bruins	AHL	56	31	61	92	26	....	....	....	....	....	....	....	....	....	6	4	4	8	0	....	....	....	....
1993-94	Boston	NHL	59	8	15	23	14	0	0	1	62	12.9	4	....	....	....	13	1	7	8	4	0	0	0	....
	Providence Bruins	AHL	17	5	12	17	4	....	....	....	....	....	....	....	....	....	....	....	....	....	....	....	....	....	....
1994-95	Kolner Haie	Germany	25	16	23	39	18	....	....	....	....	....	....	....	....	....	....	....	....	....	....	....	....	....	....
	Boston	NHL	44	5	13	18	8	1	0	2	46	10.9	4	....	....	....	5	0	0	0	0	0	0	0	....
1995-96	Boston	NHL	76	18	36	54	14	5	0	2	158	11.4	–8	....	....	....	5	1	2	3	0	0	0	0	....
1996-97	Boston	NHL	78	21	55	76	14	6	0	1	168	12.5	–22	....	....	....	....	....	....	....	....	....	....	....	....
1997-98	Los Angeles	NHL	77	21	58	79	53	4	0	2	162	13.0	17	....	....	....	4	1	2	3	2	0	0	0	....
1998-99	Los Angeles	NHL	64	13	21	34	10	1	0	1	131	9.9	–18	1484	54.0	19:44	....	....	....	....	....	....	....	....	....
99-2000	Los Angeles	NHL	57	17	41	58	10	3	0	7	126	13.5	23	1088	50.6	19:16	4	0	4	4	8	0	0	0	21:05
2000-01	Slov. Bratislava	Slovakia	9	2	4	6	16	....	....	....	....	....	....	....	....	....	....	....	....	....	....	....	....	....	....
	Los Angeles	NHL	63	16	39	55	14	9	0	6	95	16.8	20	1278	52.7	19:35	13	3	5	8	10	2	0	1	21:56
2001-02	Los Angeles	NHL	9	1	3	4	4	0	0	0	7	14.3	1	164	48.2	20:06	....	....	....	....	....	....	....	....	....
	Boston	NHL	72	7	47	54	14	1	0	3	93	7.5	21	1346	49.7	18:36	6	0	2	2	0	0	0	0	16:43
	Slovakia	Olympics	2	2	1	3	0	....	....	....	....	....	....	....	....	....	....	....	....	....	....	....	....	....	....
2002-03	Boston	NHL	78	14	37	51	12	4	0	2	110	12.7	0	1601	54.7	18:27	5	0	2	2	0	0	0	0	17:31
	NHL Totals		694	143	368	511	171	34	0	27	1169	12.2		6961	52.4	19:06	55	6	24	30	24	2	0	1	19:55

Traded to **Los Angeles** by **Boston** with Sandy Moger and Boston's 4th round choice (later traded to New Jersey – New Jersey selected Pierre Dagenais) in 1998 Entry Draft for Dmitri Kristich and Byron Dafoe, August 29, 1997. Traded to **Boston** by **Los Angeles** with Glen Murray for Jason Allison and Mikko Eloranta, October 24, 2001. Traded to **Los Angeles** by **Boston** with Boston's 7th round choice (later traded to Nashville – Nashville selected Miroslav Hanuljak) in 2003 Entry Draft for Philadelphia's 4th round choice (previously acquired, Boston selected Patrick Valcak) in 2003 Entry Draft and Detroit's 2nd round choice (previously acquired) in 2004 Entry Draft, June 22, 2003.

STURM, Marco (STURHM, MAHR-koh) S.J.

Left wing. Shoots left. 6', 195 lbs. Born, Dingolfing, West Germany, September 8, 1978. San Jose's 2nd choice, 21st overall, in 1996 Entry Draft.

Season	Club	League	GP	G	A	Pts	PIM	PP	SH	GW	S	%	+/-	TF	F%	Min	GP	G	A	Pts	PIM	PP	SH	GW	Min
1995-96	EV Landshut	Germany	47	12	20	32	50	....	....	....	....	....	....	....	....	....	11	1	3	4	18	....	....	....	....
1996-97	EV Landshut	Germany	46	16	27	43	40	....	....	....	....	....	....	....	....	....	7	1	4	5	6	....	....	....	....
1997-98	San Jose	NHL	74	10	20	30	40	2	0	3	118	8.5	–2	....	....	....	2	0	0	0	0	0	0	0	....
	Germany	Olympics	2	0	0	0	0	....	....	....	....	....	....	....	....	....	....	....	....	....	....	....	....	....	....
1998-99	San Jose	NHL	78	16	22	38	52	3	2	3	140	11.4	7	576	45.0	15:23	6	2	2	4	4	0	0	1	14:16
99-2000	San Jose	NHL	74	12	15	27	22	2	4	3	120	10.0	4	183	45.4	14:07	12	1	3	4	6	0	0	0	12:60
2000-01	San Jose	NHL	81	14	18	32	28	2	3	5	153	9.2	9	517	40.2	16:06	6	0	2	2	0	0	0	0	18:18
2001-02	San Jose	NHL	77	21	20	41	32	4	3	5	174	12.1	23	105	47.6	15:39	12	3	2	5	2	0	0	0	15:32
	Germany	Olympics	5	0	1	1	0	....	....	....	....	....	....	....	....	....	....	....	....	....	....	....	....	....	....
2002-03	San Jose	NHL	82	28	20	48	16	6	0	2	208	13.5	9	83	48.2	16:31	....	....	....	....	....	....	....	....	....
	NHL Totals		466	101	115	216	190	19	12	21	913	11.1		1464	43.7	15:35	38	6	9	15	12	0	0	1	14:56

Played in NHL All-Star Game (1999)

SUCHY, Radoslav (soo-KHEE, RAD-oh-slav) PHX.

Defense. Shoots left. 6'2", 204 lbs. Born, Kezmarok, Czech., April 7, 1976.

Season	Club	League	GP	G	A	Pts	PIM	PP	SH	GW	S	%	+/-	TF	F%	Min	GP	G	A	Pts	PIM	PP	SH	GW	Min
1993-94	SKP PS Poprad Jr.	Slovak-Jr.	30	11	12	23	16	....	....	....	....	....	....	....	....	....	....	....	....	....	....	....	....	....	....
	SKP PS Poprad	Slovakia	3	0	0	0	0	....	....	....	....	....	....	....	....	....	....	....	....	....	....	....	....	....	....
1994-95	Sherbrooke	QMJHL	69	12	32	44	30	....	....	....	....	....	....	....	....	....	7	0	3	3	2	....	....	....	....
1995-96	Sherbrooke	QMJHL	68	15	53	68	68	....	....	....	....	....	....	....	....	....	7	0	3	3	2	....	....	....	....
1996-97	Sherbrooke	QMJHL	32	6	34	40	14	....	....	....	....	....	....	....	....	....	....	....	....	....	....	....	....	....	....
	Chicoutimi	QMJHL	28	5	24	29	26	....	....	....	....	....	....	....	....	....	19	6	15	21	12	....	....	....	....
1997-98	Las Vegas	IHL	26	1	4	5	10	....	....	....	....	....	....	....	....	....	....	....	....	....	....	....	....	....	....
	Springfield	AHL	41	6	15	21	16	....	....	....	....	....	....	....	....	....	4	0	1	1	2	....	....	....	....
1998-99	Springfield	AHL	69	4	32	36	10	....	....	....	....	....	....	....	....	....	3	0	1	1	0	....	....	....	....

			Regular Season														Playoffs								
Season	**Club**	**League**	**GP**	**G**	**A**	**Pts**	**PIM**	**PP**	**SH**	**GW**	**S**	**%**	**+/-**	**TF**	**F%**	**Min**	**GP**	**G**	**A**	**Pts**	**PIM**	**PP**	**SH**	**GW**	**Min**
99-2000	**Phoenix**	**NHL**	**60**	**0**	**6**	**6**	**16**	**0**	**0**	**0**	**36**	**0.0**	**2**	**0**	**0.0**	**15:09**	**5**	**0**	**1**	**1**	**0**	**0**	**0**	**0**	**16:18**
	Springfield	AHL	2	0	1	1	0	....	....	....	....	....	....	....	....	....	....	....	....	....	....	....	....	....	....
2000-01	**Phoenix**	**NHL**	**72**	**0**	**10**	**10**	**22**	**0**	**0**	**0**	**33**	**0.0**	**1**	**0**	**0.0**	**17:09**	....	....	....	....	....	....	....	....	....
2001-02	**Phoenix**	**NHL**	**81**	**4**	**13**	**17**	**10**	**1**	**0**	**0**	**49**	**8.2**	**25**	**1**	**100.0**	**18:05**	**5**	**1**	**0**	**1**	**0**	**0**	**0**	**0**	**20:35**
2002-03	**Phoenix**	**NHL**	**77**	**1**	**8**	**9**	**18**	**1**	**0**	**0**	**48**	**2.1**	**2**	**1**	**0.0**	**16:26**	....	....	....	....	....	....	....	....	....
	NHL Totals		**290**	**5**	**37**	**42**	**66**	**2**	**0**	**0**	**166**	**3.0**		**2**	**50.0**	**16:48**	**10**	**1**	**1**	**2**	**0**	**0**	**0**	**0**	**18:27**

QMJHL All-Rookie Team (1995) • QMJHL Second All-Star Team (1997) • George Parsons Trophy (Memorial Cup Most Sportsmanlike Player) (1997)

Signed as a free agent by **Phoenix**, September 26, 1997.

SULLIVAN, Steve (SUH-lih-van, STEEV) CHI.

Right wing. Shoots right. 5'9", 155 lbs. Born, Timmins, Ont., July 6, 1974. New Jersey's 10th choice, 233rd overall, in 1994 Entry Draft.

Season	Club	League	GP	G	A	Pts	PIM	PP	SH	GW	S	%	+/-	TF	F%	Min	GP	G	A	Pts	PIM	PP	SH	GW	Min
1991-92	Timmins	NOJHA	47	66	55	121	141	....	....	....	....	....	....	....	....	....	....	....	....	....	....	....	....	....	....
1992-93	Sault Ste. Marie	OHL	62	36	27	63	44	....	....	....	....	....	....	....	....	....	16	3	8	11	18	....	....	....	....
1993-94	Sault Ste. Marie	OHL	63	51	62	113	82	....	....	....	....	....	....	....	....	....	14	9	16	25	22	....	....	....	....
1994-95	Albany River Rats	AHL	75	31	50	81	124	....	....	....	....	....	....	....	....	....	14	4	7	11	10	....	....	....	....
1995-96	**New Jersey**	**NHL**	**16**	**5**	**4**	**9**	**8**	**2**	**0**	**1**	**23**	**21.7**	**3**	....	....	....	....	....	....	....	....	....	....	....	....
	Albany River Rats	AHL	53	33	42	75	127	....	....	....	....	....	....	....	....	....	4	3	0	3	6	....	....	....	....
1996-97	**New Jersey**	**NHL**	**33**	**8**	**14**	**22**	**14**	**2**	**0**	**2**	**63**	**12.7**	**9**	....	....	....	....	....	....	....	....	....	....	....	....
	Albany River Rats	AHL	15	8	7	15	16	....	....	....	....	....	....	....	....	....	....	....	....	....	....	....	....	....	....
	Toronto	**NHL**	**21**	**5**	**11**	**16**	**23**	**1**	**0**	**1**	**45**	**11.1**	**5**	....	....	....	....	....	....	....	....	....	....	....	....
1997-98	**Toronto**	**NHL**	**63**	**10**	**18**	**28**	**40**	**1**	**0**	**1**	**112**	**8.9**	**–8**	....	....	....	....	....	....	....	....	....	....	....	....
1998-99	**Toronto**	**NHL**	**63**	**20**	**20**	**40**	**28**	**4**	**0**	**5**	**110**	**18.2**	**12**	**685**	**44.4**	**14:12**	**13**	**3**	**3**	**6**	**14**	**2**	**0**	**0**	**16:20**
99-2000	**Toronto**	**NHL**	**7**	**0**	**1**	**1**	**4**	**0**	**0**	**0**	**11**	**0.0**	**–1**	**47**	**48.9**	**11:52**	....	....	....	....	....	....	....	....	....
	Chicago	**NHL**	**73**	**22**	**42**	**64**	**52**	**2**	**1**	**6**	**169**	**13.0**	**20**	**692**	**48.0**	**18:05**	....	....	....	....	....	....	....	....	....
2000-01	**Chicago**	**NHL**	**81**	**34**	**41**	**75**	**54**	**6**	**8**	**3**	**204**	**16.7**	**3**	**649**	**42.4**	**20:32**	....	....	....	....	....	....	....	....	....
2001-02	**Chicago**	**NHL**	**78**	**21**	**39**	**60**	**67**	**3**	**0**	**8**	**155**	**13.5**	**23**	**758**	**48.9**	**19:10**	**5**	**1**	**0**	**1**	**2**	**0**	**0**	**0**	**18:04**
2002-03	**Chicago**	**NHL**	**82**	**26**	**35**	**61**	**42**	**4**	**2**	**3**	**190**	**13.7**	**15**	**382**	**46.1**	**19:15**	....	....	....	....	....	....	....	....	....
	NHL Totals		**517**	**151**	**225**	**376**	**332**	**25**	**11**	**30**	**1082**	**14.0**		**3213**	**46.1**	**18:19**	**18**	**4**	**3**	**7**	**16**	**2**	**0**	**0**	**16:49**

AHL First All-Star Team (1996)

Traded to **Toronto** by **New Jersey** with Jason Smith and the rights to Alyn McCauley for Doug Gilmour, Dave Ellett and New Jersey's 3rd round choice (previously acquired, New Jersey selected Andre Lakos) in 1999 Entry Draft, February 25, 1997. Claimed on waivers by **Chicago** from **Toronto**, October 23, 1999.

SUNDIN, Mats (sahn-DEEN, MATS) TOR.

Center. Shoots right. 6'5", 231 lbs. Born, Bromma, Sweden, February 13, 1971. Quebec's 1st choice, 1st overall, in 1989 Entry Draft.

Season	Club	League	GP	G	A	Pts	PIM	PP	SH	GW	S	%	+/-	TF	F%	Min	GP	G	A	Pts	PIM	PP	SH	GW	Min
1988-89	Nacka HK	Swede-2	25	10	8	18	18	....	....	....	....	....	....	....	....	....	....	....	....	....	....	....	....	....	....
1989-90	Djurgarden	Sweden	34	10	8	18	16	....	....	....	....	....	....	....	....	....	8	7	0	7	4	....	....	....	....
1990-91	**Quebec**	**NHL**	**80**	**23**	**36**	**59**	**58**	**4**	**0**	**0**	**155**	**14.8**	**–24**	....	....	....	....	....	....	....	....	....	....	....	....
1991-92	**Quebec**	**NHL**	**80**	**33**	**43**	**76**	**103**	**8**	**2**	**2**	**231**	**14.3**	**–19**	....	....	....	....	....	....	....	....	....	....	....	....
1992-93	**Quebec**	**NHL**	**80**	**47**	**67**	**114**	**96**	**13**	**4**	**9**	**215**	**21.9**	**21**	....	....	....	**6**	**3**	**1**	**4**	**6**	**1**	**0**	**0**	....
1993-94	**Quebec**	**NHL**	**84**	**32**	**53**	**85**	**60**	**6**	**2**	**4**	**226**	**14.2**	**1**	....	....	....	....	....	....	....	....	....	....	....	....
1994-95	Djurgarden	Sweden	12	7	2	9	14	....	....	....	....	....	....	....	....	....	....	....	....	....	....	....	....	....	....
	Toronto	**NHL**	**47**	**23**	**24**	**47**	**14**	**9**	**0**	**4**	**173**	**13.3**	**–5**	....	....	....	**7**	**5**	**4**	**9**	**4**	**2**	**0**	**1**	....
1995-96	**Toronto**	**NHL**	**76**	**33**	**50**	**83**	**46**	**7**	**6**	**7**	**301**	**11.0**	**8**	....	....	....	**6**	**3**	**1**	**4**	**4**	**2**	**0**	**1**	....
1996-97	**Toronto**	**NHL**	**82**	**41**	**53**	**94**	**59**	**7**	**4**	**8**	**281**	**14.6**	**6**	....	....	....	....	....	....	....	....	....	....	....	....
1997-98	**Toronto**	**NHL**	**82**	**33**	**41**	**74**	**49**	**9**	**1**	**5**	**219**	**15.1**	**–3**	....	....	....	....	....	....	....	....	....	....	....	....
	Sweden	Olympics	4	3	0	3	4	....	....	....	....	....	....	....	....	....	....	....	....	....	....	....	....	....	....
1998-99	**Toronto**	**NHL**	**82**	**31**	**52**	**83**	**58**	**4**	**0**	**6**	**209**	**14.8**	**22**	**1993**	**57.3**	**20:41**	**17**	**8**	**8**	**16**	**16**	**3**	**0**	**2**	**22:46**
99-2000	**Toronto**	**NHL**	**73**	**32**	**41**	**73**	**46**	**10**	**2**	**7**	**184**	**17.4**	**16**	**1619**	**50.8**	**20:11**	**12**	**3**	**5**	**8**	**10**	**0**	**0**	**1**	**21:27**
2000-01	**Toronto**	**NHL**	**82**	**28**	**46**	**74**	**76**	**9**	**0**	**6**	**226**	**12.4**	**15**	**1870**	**56.6**	**19:21**	**11**	**6**	**7**	**13**	**14**	**2**	**1**	**1**	**20:12**
2001-02	**Toronto**	**NHL**	**82**	**41**	**39**	**80**	**94**	**10**	**2**	**9**	**262**	**15.6**	**6**	**1812**	**57.5**	**19:20**	**8**	**2**	**5**	**7**	**4**	**0**	**0**	**0**	**20:07**
	Sweden	Olympics	4	5	4	*9	10	....	....	....	....	....	....	....	....	....	....	....	....	....	....	....	....	....	....
2002-03	**Toronto**	**NHL**	**75**	**37**	**35**	**72**	**58**	**16**	**3**	**8**	**223**	**16.6**	**1**	**1774**	**56.1**	**20:15**	**7**	**1**	**3**	**4**	**6**	**1**	**0**	**0**	**24:17**
	NHL Totals		**1005**	**434**	**580**	**1014**	**817**	**112**	**26**	**75**	**2905**	**14.9**		**9068**	**55.8**	**19:57**	**74**	**31**	**34**	**65**	**64**	**11**	**1**	**6**	**21:46**

NHL Second All-Star Team (2002)

Played in NHL All-Star Game (1996, 1997, 1998, 1999, 2000, 2001, 2002)

Traded to **Toronto** by **Quebec** with Garth Butcher, Todd Warriner and Philadelphia's 1st round choice (previously acquired, later traded to Washington – Washington selected Nolan Baumgartner) in 1994 Entry Draft for Wendel Clark, Sylvain Lefebvre, Landon Wilson and Toronto's 1st round choice (Jeffrey Kealty) in 1994 Entry Draft, June 28, 1994.

SUNDSTROM, Niklas (SUHN-struhm, NIHK-las) MTL.

Right wing. Shoots left. 6', 195 lbs. Born, Ornskoldsvik, Sweden, June 6, 1975. NY Rangers' 1st choice, 8th overall, in 1993 Entry Draft.

Season	Club	League	GP	G	A	Pts	PIM	PP	SH	GW	S	%	+/-	TF	F%	Min	GP	G	A	Pts	PIM	PP	SH	GW	Min
1991-92	MoDo	Sweden	9	1	3	4	0	....	....	....	....	....	....	....	....	....	....	....	....	....	....	....	....	....	....
1992-93	MoDo Jr.	Swede-Jr.	2	3	1	4	0	....	....	....	....	....	....	....	....	....	....	....	....	....	....	....	....	....	....
	MoDo	Sweden	40	7	11	18	18	....	....	....	....	....	....	....	....	....	3	0	0	0	0	....	....	....	....
1993-94	MoDo Jr.	Swede-Jr.	3	3	4	7	2	....	....	....	....	....	....	....	....	....	....	....	....	....	....	....	....	....	....
	MoDo	Sweden	37	7	12	19	28	....	....	....	....	....	....	....	....	....	11	4	3	7	2	....	....	....	....
1994-95	MoDo	Sweden	33	8	13	21	30	....	....	....	....	....	....	....	....	....	....	....	....	....	....	....	....	....	....
1995-96	**NY Rangers**	**NHL**	**82**	**9**	**12**	**21**	**14**	**1**	**1**	**2**	**90**	**10.0**	**2**	....	....	....	**11**	**4**	**3**	**7**	**4**	**1**	**0**	**0**	....
1996-97	**NY Rangers**	**NHL**	**82**	**24**	**28**	**52**	**20**	**5**	**1**	**4**	**132**	**18.2**	**23**	....	....	....	**9**	**0**	**5**	**5**	**2**	**0**	**0**	**0**	....
1997-98	**NY Rangers**	**NHL**	**70**	**19**	**28**	**47**	**24**	**4**	**0**	**1**	**115**	**16.5**	**0**	....	....	....	....	....	....	....	....	....	....	....	....
	Sweden	Olympics	4	1	1	2	2	....	....	....	....	....	....	....	....	....	....	....	....	....	....	....	....	....	....
1998-99	**NY Rangers**	**NHL**	**81**	**13**	**30**	**43**	**20**	**1**	**2**	**3**	**89**	**14.6**	**–2**	**376**	**40.4**	**19:11**	....	....	....	....	....	....	....	....	....
99-2000	**San Jose**	**NHL**	**79**	**12**	**25**	**37**	**22**	**2**	**1**	**2**	**90**	**13.3**	**9**	**10**	**50.0**	**15:10**	**12**	**0**	**2**	**2**	**2**	**0**	**0**	**0**	**15:09**
2000-01	**San Jose**	**NHL**	**82**	**10**	**39**	**49**	**28**	**4**	**1**	**0**	**100**	**10.0**	**10**	**26**	**30.8**	**16:44**	**6**	**0**	**3**	**3**	**2**	**0**	**0**	**0**	**16:40**
2001-02	**San Jose**	**NHL**	**73**	**9**	**30**	**39**	**50**	**0**	**1**	**0**	**74**	**12.2**	**7**	**9**	**33.3**	**15:57**	**12**	**1**	**6**	**7**	**6**	**0**	**0**	**0**	**16:25**
	Sweden	Olympics	4	1	3	4	0	....	....	....	....	....	....	....	....	....	....	....	....	....	....	....	....	....	....
2002-03	**San Jose**	**NHL**	**47**	**2**	**10**	**12**	**22**	**0**	**0**	**0**	**36**	**5.6**	**–4**	**1**	**0.0**	**14:09**	....	....	....	....	....	....	....	....	....
	Montreal	**NHL**	**33**	**5**	**9**	**14**	**8**	**0**	**0**	**1**	**35**	**14.3**	**3**	**10**	**40.0**	**14:26**	....	....	....	....	....	....	....	....	....
	NHL Totals		**629**	**103**	**211**	**314**	**208**	**17**	**7**	**13**	**761**	**13.5**		**432**	**39.8**	**16:17**	**50**	**5**	**19**	**24**	**16**	**1**	**0**	**0**	**15:58**

Traded to **Tampa Bay** by **NY Rangers** with Dan Cloutier and NY Rangers' 1st (Nikita Alexeev) and 3rd (later traded to San Jose – later traded to Chicago – Chicago selected Igor Radulov) round choices in 2000 Entry Draft for Chicago's 1st round choice (previously acquired, NY Rangers selected Pavel Brendl) in 1999 Entry Draft, June 26, 1999. Traded to **San Jose** by **Tampa Bay** with NY Rangers' 3rd round choice (previously acquired, later traded to Chicago – Chicago selected Igor Radulov) in 2000 Entry Draft for Bill Houlder, Andrei Zyuzin, Shawn Burr and Steve Guolla, August 4, 1999. Traded to **Montreal** by **San Jose** with San Jose's 3rd round choice in 2004 Entry Draft for Jeff Hackett, January 23, 2003.

SURMA, Damian (SUHR-ma, DAY-mee-an) CAR.

Center. Shoots left. 5'10", 200 lbs. Born, Lincoln Park, MI, January 22, 1981. Carolina's 5th choice, 174th overall, in 1999 Entry Draft.

Season	Club	League	GP	G	A	Pts	PIM	PP	SH	GW	S	%	+/-	TF	F%	Min	GP	G	A	Pts	PIM	PP	SH	GW	Min
1997-98	Det. Compuware	NAJHL	50	12	17	29	50	....	....	....	....	....	....	....	....	....	6	3	1	4	4	....	....	....	....
1998-99	Plymouth Whalers	OHL	65	17	15	32	62	....	....	....	....	....	....	....	....	....	11	3	6	9	15	....	....	....	....
99-2000	Plymouth Whalers	OHL	66	34	44	78	114	....	....	....	....	....	....	....	....	....	20	9	8	17	10	....	....	....	....
2000-01	Plymouth Whalers	OHL	55	26	34	60	62	....	....	....	....	....	....	....	....	....	19	8	9	17	25	....	....	....	....
2001-02	Plymouth Whalers	OHL	55	28	27	55	68	....	....	....	....	....	....	....	....	....	6	3	0	3	10	....	....	....	....
	Lowell	AHL	1	0	0	0	0	....	....	....	....	....	....	....	....	....	4	0	0	0	0	....	....	....	....
2002-03	**Carolina**	**NHL**	**1**	**1**	**0**	**1**	**0**	**0**	**0**	**0**	**1**	**100.0**	**0**	**0**	**0.0**	**7:15**	....	....	....	....	....	....	....	....	....
	Lowell	AHL	68	11	11	22	46	....	....	....	....	....	....	....	....	....	....	....	....	....	....	....	....	....	....
	NHL Totals		**1**	**1**	**0**	**1**	**0**	**0**	**0**	**0**	**1**	**100.0**		**0**	**0.0**	**7:15**	....	....	....	....	....	....	....	....	....

• One of only four players (Rolly Huard, Dean Morton, Matt Stajan) to score a goal in only NHL game (March 18, 2003, at home vs. Ottawa).

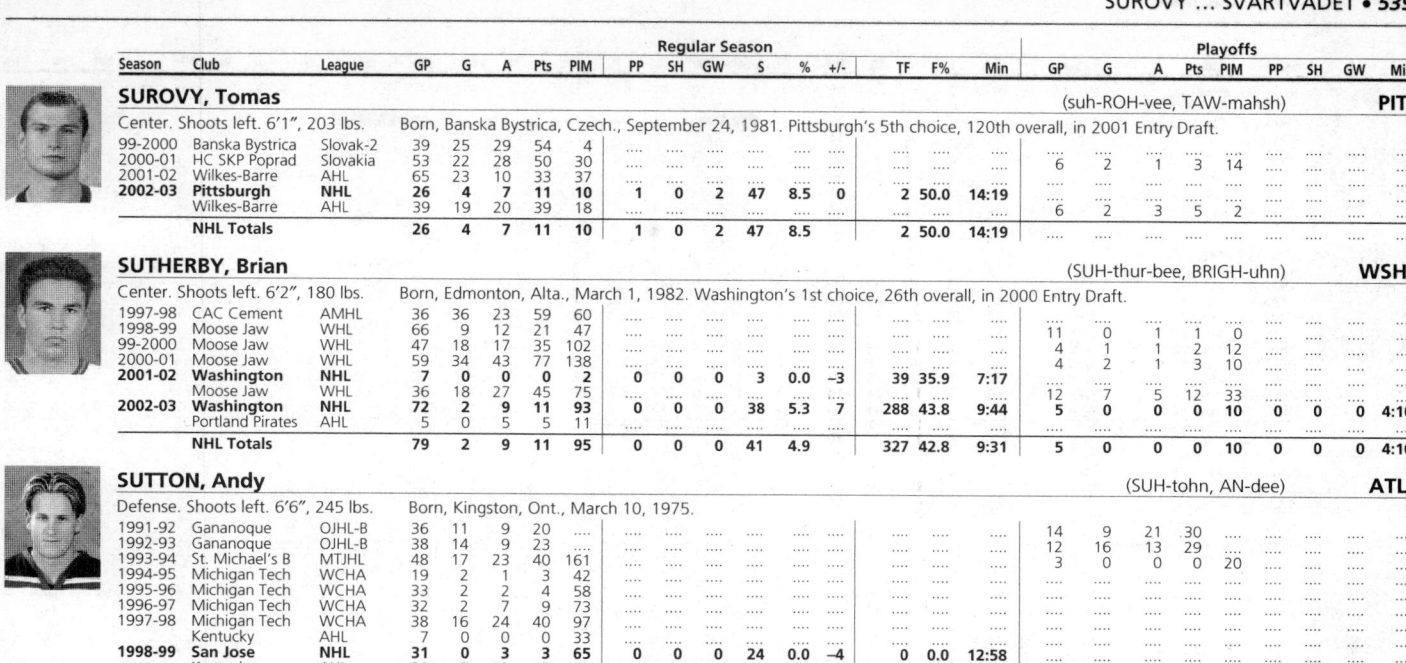

SUROVY, Tomas

(suh-ROH-vee, TAW-mahsh) **PIT.**

Center. Shoots left. 6'1", 203 lbs. Born, Banska Bystrica, Czech., September 24, 1981. Pittsburgh's 5th choice, 120th overall, in 2001 Entry Draft.

Season	Club	League	GP	G	A	Pts	PIM	PP	SH	GW	S	%	+/-	TF	F%	Min	Playoffs GP	G	A	Pts	PIM	PP	SH	GW	Min
99-2000	Banska Bystrica	Slovak-2	39	25	29	54	4																		
2000-01	HC SKP Poprad	Slovakia	53	22	28	50	30										6	2	1	3	14				
2001-02	Wilkes-Barre	AHL	65	23	10	33	37																		
2002-03	**Pittsburgh**	**NHL**	**26**	**4**	**7**	**11**	**10**	**1**	**0**	**2**	**47**	**8.5**	**0**	**2**	**50.0**	**14:19**									
	Wilkes-Barre	AHL	39	19	20	39	18										6	2	3	5	2				
	NHL Totals		**26**	**4**	**7**	**11**	**10**	**1**	**0**	**2**	**47**	**8.5**		**2**	**50.0**	**14:19**									

SUTHERBY, Brian

(SUH-thur-bee, BRIGH-uhn) **WSH.**

Center. Shoots left. 6'2", 180 lbs. Born, Edmonton, Alta., March 1, 1982. Washington's 1st choice, 26th overall, in 2000 Entry Draft.

Season	Club	League	GP	G	A	Pts	PIM	PP	SH	GW	S	%	+/-	TF	F%	Min	Playoffs GP	G	A	Pts	PIM	PP	SH	GW	Min
1997-98	CAC Cement	AMHL	36	36	23	59	60																		
1998-99	Moose Jaw	WHL	66	9	12	21	47										11	0	1	1	0				
99-2000	Moose Jaw	WHL	47	18	17	35	102										4	1	1	2	12				
2000-01	Moose Jaw	WHL	59	34	43	77	138										4	2	1	3	10				
2001-02	**Washington**	**NHL**	**7**	**0**	**0**	**0**	**2**	**0**	**0**	**0**	**3**	**0.0**	**-3**	**39**	**35.9**	**7:17**									
	Moose Jaw	WHL	36	18	27	45	75										12	7	5	12	33				
2002-03	**Washington**	**NHL**	**72**	**2**	**9**	**11**	**93**	**0**	**0**	**0**	**38**	**5.3**	**7**	**288**	**43.8**	**9:44**	**5**	**0**	**0**	**0**	**10**	**0**	**0**	**0**	**4:10**
	Portland Pirates	AHL	5	0	5	5	11																		
	NHL Totals		**79**	**2**	**9**	**11**	**95**	**0**	**0**	**0**	**41**	**4.9**		**327**	**42.8**	**9:31**	**5**	**0**	**0**	**0**	**10**	**0**	**0**	**0**	**4:10**

SUTTON, Andy

(SUH-tohn, AN-dee) **ATL.**

Defense. Shoots left. 6'6", 245 lbs. Born, Kingston, Ont., March 10, 1975.

Season	Club	League	GP	G	A	Pts	PIM	PP	SH	GW	S	%	+/-	TF	F%	Min	Playoffs GP	G	A	Pts	PIM	PP	SH	GW	Min
1991-92	Gananoque	OJHL-B	36	11	9	20	....										14	9	21	30	....				
1992-93	Gananoque	OJHL-B	38	14	9	23	....										12	16	13	29	....				
1993-94	St. Michael's B	MTJHL	48	17	23	40	161										3	0	0	0	20				
1994-95	Michigan Tech	WCHA	19	2	1	3	42																		
1995-96	Michigan Tech	WCHA	33	2	2	4	58																		
1996-97	Michigan Tech	WCHA	32	2	7	9	73																		
1997-98	Michigan Tech	WCHA	38	16	24	40	97																		
	Kentucky	AHL	7	0	0	0	33																		
1998-99	**San Jose**	**NHL**	**31**	**0**	**3**	**3**	**65**	**0**	**0**	**0**	**24**	**0.0**	**-4**	**0**	**0.0**	**12:58**									
	Kentucky	AHL	21	5	10	15	53										5	0	0	0	23				
99-2000	**San Jose**	**NHL**	**40**	**1**	**1**	**2**	**80**	**0**	**0**	**0**	**29**	**3.4**	**-5**	**0**	**0.0**	**12:57**									
	Kentucky	AHL	3	0	1	1	0																		
2000-01	**Minnesota**	**NHL**	**69**	**3**	**4**	**7**	**131**	**2**	**0**	**0**	**64**	**4.7**	**-11**	**3**	**33.3**	**12:55**									
2001-02	**Minnesota**	**NHL**	**19**	**2**	**4**	**6**	**35**	**1**	**0**	**0**	**21**	**9.5**	**-4**	**2**	**0.0**	**10:57**									
	Atlanta	**NHL**	**24**	**0**	**4**	**4**	**46**	**0**	**0**	**0**	**20**	**0.0**	**0**	**0**	**0.0**	**15:25**									
2002-03	**Atlanta**	**NHL**	**53**	**3**	**18**	**21**	**114**	**1**	**1**	**0**	**65**	**4.6**	**-8**	**3**	**33.3**	**18:00**									
	NHL Totals		**236**	**9**	**34**	**43**	**471**	**4**	**1**	**0**	**223**	**4.0**		**8**	**25.0**	**14:10**									

WCHA Second All-Star Team (1998)

Signed as a free agent by **San Jose**, March 20, 1998. Traded to **Minnesota** by **San Jose** with San Jose's 7th round choice (Peter Bartos) in 2000 Entry Draft and 3rd round choice (later traded to Atlanta – later traded to Pittsburgh – later traded to Columbus – Columbus selected Aaron Johnson) in 2001 Entry Draft for Minnesota's 8th round choice (later traded to Calgary – Calgary selected Joe Campbell) in 2001 Entry Draft and future considerations, June 12, 2000. Traded to **Atlanta** by **Minnesota** for Hnat Domenichelli, January 22, 2002.

SUTTON, Ken

(SUH-tohn, KEHN)

Defense. Shoots left. 6'1", 205 lbs. Born, Edmonton, Alta., November 5, 1969. Buffalo's 4th choice, 98th overall, in 1989 Entry Draft.

Season	Club	League	GP	G	A	Pts	PIM	PP	SH	GW	S	%	+/-	TF	F%	Min	Playoffs GP	G	A	Pts	PIM	PP	SH	GW	Min
1987-88	Calgary Canucks	AJHL	53	13	43	56	228																		
1988-89	Saskatoon Blades	WHL	71	22	31	53	104										8	2	5	7	12				
1989-90	Rochester	AHL	57	5	14	19	83										11	1	6	7	15				
1990-91	**Buffalo**	**NHL**	**15**	**3**	**6**	**9**	**13**	**2**	**0**	**0**	**26**	**11.5**	**2**				**6**	**0**	**1**	**1**	**2**	**0**	**0**	**0**	
	Rochester	AHL	62	7	24	31	65										3	1	1	2	14				
1991-92	**Buffalo**	**NHL**	**64**	**2**	**18**	**20**	**71**	**0**	**0**	**0**	**81**	**2.5**	**5**				**7**	**0**	**2**	**2**	**4**	**0**	**0**	**0**	
1992-93	**Buffalo**	**NHL**	**63**	**8**	**14**	**22**	**30**	**1**	**0**	**2**	**77**	**10.4**	**-3**				**8**	**3**	**1**	**4**	**8**	**0**	**0**	**0**	
1993-94	**Buffalo**	**NHL**	**78**	**4**	**20**	**24**	**71**	**1**	**0**	**0**	**95**	**4.2**	**-6**				**4**	**0**	**0**	**0**	**2**	**0**	**0**	**0**	
1994-95	**Buffalo**	**NHL**	**12**	**1**	**2**	**3**	**30**	**0**	**0**	**1**	**12**	**8.3**	**-2**												
	Edmonton	**NHL**	**12**	**3**	**1**	**4**	**12**	**0**	**0**	**0**	**28**	**10.7**	**-1**												
1995-96	**Edmonton**	**NHL**	**32**	**0**	**8**	**8**	**39**	**0**	**0**	**0**	**38**	**0.0**	**-12**												
	St. Louis	**NHL**	**6**	**0**	**0**	**0**	**4**	**0**	**0**	**0**	**3**	**0.0**	**-1**				**1**	**0**	**0**	**0**	**0**	**0**	**0**	**0**	
	Worcester IceCats	AHL	32	4	16	20	60										4	0	2	2	21				
1996-97	Manitoba Moose	IHL	20	3	10	13	48																		
	Albany River Rats	AHL	61	6	13	19	79										16	4	8	12	55				
1997-98	**New Jersey**	**NHL**	**13**	**0**	**0**	**0**	**6**	**0**	**0**	**0**	**5**	**0.0**	**1**												
	Albany River Rats	AHL	10	0	7	7	15																		
	San Jose	**NHL**	**8**	**0**	**0**	**0**	**15**	**0**	**0**	**0**	**7**	**0.0**	**-4**												
1998-99	**New Jersey**	**NHL**	**5**	**1**	**0**	**1**	**0**	**0**	**0**	**0**	**5**	**20.0**	**1**	**0**	**0.0**	**13:02**									
	Albany River Rats	AHL	75	13	42	55	118										5	0	2	2	12				
99-2000♦	**New Jersey**	**NHL**	**6**	**0**	**2**	**2**	**2**	**0**	**0**	**0**	**10**	**0.0**	**2**	**0**	**0.0**	**17:20**									
	Albany River Rats	AHL	57	5	16	21	129																		
2000-01	**New Jersey**	**NHL**	**53**	**1**	**7**	**8**	**37**	**0**	**0**	**0**	**35**	**2.9**	**9**	**0**	**0.0**	**15:44**	**6**	**0**	**0**	**0**	**13**	**0**	**0**	**0**	**16:46**
2001-02	**NY Islanders**	**NHL**	**21**	**0**	**2**	**2**	**8**	**0**	**0**	**0**	**22**	**0.0**	**-5**	**0**	**0.0**	**12:44**									
	Bridgeport	AHL	28	1	10	11	51										20	2	8	10	24				
2002-03	Albany River Rats	AHL	74	6	26	32	70																		
	NHL Totals		**388**	**23**	**80**	**103**	**338**	**4**	**0**	**3**	**444**	**5.2**		**0**	**0.0**	**14:57**	**32**	**3**	**4**	**7**	**29**	**0**	**0**	**0**	**16:46**

Memorial Cup All-Star Team (1989) • AHL First All-Star Team (1999) • Eddie Shore Award (Top Defenseman – AHL) (1999)

Traded to **Edmonton** by **Buffalo** for Scott Pearson, April 7, 1995. Traded to **St. Louis** by **Edmonton** with Igor Kravchuk for Jeff Norton and Donald Dufresne, January 4, 1996. Traded to **New Jersey** by **St. Louis** with St. Louis' 2nd round choice (Brett Clouthier) in 1999 Entry Draft for Mike Peluso and Ricard Persson, November 26, 1996. Traded to **San Jose** by **New Jersey** with John MacLean for Doug Bodger and Dody Wood, December 7, 1997. Traded to **New Jersey** by **San Jose** for future considerations, August 26, 1998. Claimed by **Washington** from **New Jersey** in Waiver Draft, September 27, 1999. Traded to **New Jersey** by **Washington** for future considerations, October 5, 1999. Signed as a free agent by **NY Islanders**, July 5, 2001. Signed as a free agent by **New Jersey**, August 27, 2002.

SVARTVADET, Per

(svahrt-VAH-deht, PAIR)

Center. Shoots left. 6'1", 195 lbs. Born, Sollefteа, Sweden, May 17, 1975. Dallas' 5th choice, 139th overall, in 1993 Entry Draft.

Season	Club	League	GP	G	A	Pts	PIM	PP	SH	GW	S	%	+/-	TF	F%	Min	Playoffs GP	G	A	Pts	PIM	PP	SH	GW	Min
1990-91	Solleftea HK	Swede-2	5	1	0	1	0																		
1991-92	MoDo Jr.	Swede-Jr.	30	17	19	36	36																		
1992-93	MoDo Jr.	Swede-Jr.	14	5	10	15	18																		
	MoDo	Sweden	2	0	0	0	0																		
1993-94	MoDo Jr.	Swede-Jr.	12	7	12	19	6																		
	MoDo	Sweden	36	2	1	3	4										11	0	0	0	6				
1994-95	MoDo	Sweden	40	6	9	15	31																		
1995-96	MoDo	Sweden	40	9	14	23	26										8	2	3	5	0				
1996-97	MoDo	Sweden	50	7	18	25	38																		
1997-98	MoDo	Sweden	46	6	12	18	28										7	3	2	5	2				
1998-99	MoDo	Sweden	50	9	23	32	30										13	3	6	9	6				
99-2000	**Atlanta**	**NHL**	**38**	**3**	**4**	**7**	**6**	**0**	**0**	**0**	**36**	**8.3**	**-8**	**452**	**45.6**	**13:24**									
	Orlando	IHL	27	4	6	10	10										5	0	1	1	0				
2000-01	**Atlanta**	**NHL**	**69**	**10**	**11**	**21**	**20**	**0**	**2**	**1**	**98**	**10.2**	**-6**	**902**	**42.5**	**14:42**									
2001-02	**Atlanta**	**NHL**	**78**	**3**	**12**	**15**	**24**	**0**	**0**	**0**	**80**	**3.8**	**-12**	**347**	**45.0**	**13:22**									
2002-03	**Atlanta**	**NHL**	**62**	**1**	**7**	**8**	**8**	**0**	**0**	**0**	**47**	**2.1**	**-11**	**36**	**38.9**	**11:46**									
	Chicago Wolves	AHL	3	0	0	0	2																		
	NHL Totals		**247**	**17**	**34**	**51**	**58**	**0**	**2**	**1**	**261**	**6.5**		**1737**	**43.7**	**13:21**									

Traded to **Atlanta** by **Dallas** for Ottawa's 6th round choice (previously acquired, Dallas selected Justin Cox) in 1999 Entry Draft, June 26, 1999.

SVEHLA, Robert (SHVEH-lah, RAW-buhrt) TOR.

Defense. Shoots right. 6', 209 lbs. Born, Martin, Czech., January 2, 1969. Calgary's 4th choice, 78th overall, in 1992 Entry Draft.

			Regular Season														Playoffs								
Season	Club	League	GP	G	A	Pts	PIM	PP	SH	GW	S	%	+/-	TF	F%	Min	GP	G	A	Pts	PIM	PP	SH	GW	Min
1989-90	Dukla Trencin	Czech	29	4	3	7	....	....	....	....	....	....	....	....	....	....	....	....	....	....	....	....	....	....	....
1990-91	Dukla Trencin	Czech	52	16	9	25	62	....	....	....	....	....	....	....	....	....	....	....	....	....	....	....	....	....	....
1991-92	Dukla Trencin	Czech	51	23	28	51	74	....	....	....	....	....	....	....	....	....	....	....	....	....	....	....	....	....	....
	Czechoslovakia	Olympics	8	2	1	3	8	....	....	....	....	....	....	....	....	....	....	....	....	....	....	....	....	....	....
1992-93	Malmo IF	Sweden	40	19	10	29	86	....	....	....	....	....	....	....	....	....	6	0	1	1	14	....	....	....	....
1993-94	Malmo IF	Sweden	37	14	25	39	*127	....	....	....	....	....	....	....	....	....	10	5	1	6	23	....	....	....	....
	Slovakia	Olympics	8	2	4	6	26	....	....	....	....	....	....	....	....	....	....	....	....	....	....	....	....	....	....
1994-95	Malmo IF	Sweden	32	11	13	24	83	....	....	....	....	....	....	....	....	....	9	2	3	5	6	....	....	....	....
	Florida	**NHL**	**5**	**1**	**1**	**2**	**0**	**1**	**0**	**0**	**6**	**16.7**	**3**	....	....	....	....	....	....	....	....	....	....	....	....
1995-96	**Florida**	**NHL**	**81**	**8**	**49**	**57**	**94**	**7**	**0**	**0**	**146**	**5.5**	**−3**	....	....	....	**22**	**0**	**6**	**6**	**32**	**0**	**0**	**0**	....
1996-97	**Florida**	**NHL**	**82**	**13**	**32**	**45**	**86**	**5**	**0**	**3**	**159**	**8.2**	**2**	....	....	....	**5**	**1**	**4**	**5**	**4**	**1**	**0**	**0**	....
1997-98	**Florida**	**NHL**	**79**	**9**	**34**	**43**	**113**	**3**	**0**	**0**	**144**	**6.3**	**−3**	....	....	....	....	....	....	....	....	....	....	....	....
	Slovakia	Olympics	2	0	1	1	0	....	....	....	....	....	....	....	....	....	....	....	....	....	....	....	....	....	....
1998-99	**Florida**	**NHL**	**80**	**8**	**29**	**37**	**83**	**4**	**0**	**0**	**157**	**5.1**	**−13**	**2**	**0.0**	**24:45**	....	....	....	....	....	....	....	....	....
99-2000	**Florida**	**NHL**	**82**	**9**	**40**	**49**	**64**	**3**	**0**	**1**	**143**	**6.3**	**23**	**1**	**0.0**	**24:33**	**4**	**0**	**1**	**1**	**4**	**0**	**0**	**0**	**26:08**
2000-01	**Florida**	**NHL**	**82**	**6**	**22**	**28**	**76**	**0**	**0**	**0**	**121**	**5.0**	**−8**	**1**	**0.0**	**25:34**	....	....	....	....	....	....	....	....	....
2001-02	**Florida**	**NHL**	**82**	**7**	**22**	**29**	**87**	**3**	**0**	**0**	**119**	**5.9**	**−19**	**1**	**0.0**	**25:41**	....	....	....	....	....	....	....	....	....
2002-03	**Toronto**	**NHL**	**82**	**7**	**38**	**45**	**46**	**2**	**0**	**1**	**110**	**6.4**	**13**	**0**	**0.0**	**23:44**	**7**	**0**	**3**	**3**	**2**	**0**	**0**	**0**	**28:55**
	NHL Totals		**655**	**68**	**267**	**335**	**649**	**28**	**0**	**5**	**1105**	**6.2**		**5**	**0.0**	**24:51**	**38**	**1**	**14**	**15**	**42**	**1**	**0**	**0**	**27:54**

Czechoslovakian First All-Star Team (1992)

Played in NHL All-Star Game (1997)

Traded to **Florida** by **Calgary** with Magnus Svensson for Florida's 3rd round choice (Dmitri Vlasenkov) in 1996 Entry Draft and Florida's 4th round choice (Ryan Ready) in 1997 Entry Draft, September 29, 1994. Traded to **Toronto** by **Florida** for Dmitry Yushkevich, July 18, 2002.

SVITOV, Alexander (SVEE-tawf, al-ehx-AN-duhr) T.B.

Center. Shoots left. 6'3", 198 lbs. Born, Omsk, USSR, November 3, 1982. Tampa Bay's 1st choice, 3rd overall, in 2001 Entry Draft.

			Regular Season														Playoffs								
Season	Club	League	GP	G	A	Pts	PIM	PP	SH	GW	S	%	+/-	TF	F%	Min	GP	G	A	Pts	PIM	PP	SH	GW	Min
1997-98	Novokuznetsk 2	Russia-3	4	0	0	0	0	....	....	....	....	....	....	....	....	....	....	....	....	....	....	....	....	....	....
1998-99	Omsk 2	Russia-4	27	15	8	23	20	....	....	....	....	....	....	....	....	....	....	....	....	....	....	....	....	....	....
	Avangard Omsk	Russia	....	....	....	....	....	....	....	....	....	....	....	....	....	....	1	0	0	0	0	....	....	....	....
99-2000	Omsk 2	Russia-3	14	13	9	22	62	....	....	....	....	....	....	....	....	....	....	....	....	....	....	....	....	....	....
	Avangard Omsk	Russia	18	3	3	6	45	....	....	....	....	....	....	....	....	....	6	1	0	1	16	....	....	....	....
2000-01	Avangard Omsk	Russia	39	8	6	14	115	....	....	....	....	....	....	....	....	....	14	2	1	3	34	....	....	....	....
2001-02	CSKA Moscow 2	Russia-3	2	1	0	1	2	....	....	....	....	....	....	....	....	....	....	....	....	....	....	....	....	....	....
	Avangard Omsk	Russia	2	0	1	1	2	....	....	....	....	....	....	....	....	....	....	....	....	....	....	....	....	....	....
2002-03	**Tampa Bay**	**NHL**	**63**	**4**	**4**	**8**	**58**	**1**	**0**	**0**	**69**	**5.8**	**−4**	**395**	**42.8**	**8:50**	**7**	**0**	**0**	**0**	**6**	**0**	**0**	**0**	**7:19**
	Springfield	AHL	11	4	5	9	17	....	....	....	....	....	....	....	....	....	....	....	....	....	....	....	....	....	....
	NHL Totals		**63**	**4**	**4**	**8**	**58**	**1**	**0**	**0**	**69**	**5.8**		**395**	**42.8**	**8:50**	**7**	**0**	**0**	**0**	**6**	**0**	**0**	**0**	**7:19**

SVOBODA, Jaroslav (svah-BOH-duh, YAR-oh-slawf) CAR.

Left wing. Shoots left. 6'2", 190 lbs. Born, Cervenka, Czech., June 1, 1980. Carolina's 8th choice, 208th overall, in 1998 Entry Draft.

			Regular Season														Playoffs								
Season	Club	League	GP	G	A	Pts	PIM	PP	SH	GW	S	%	+/-	TF	F%	Min	GP	G	A	Pts	PIM	PP	SH	GW	Min
1995-96	HC Olomouc Jr.	Czech-Jr.	40	13	15	28	....	....	....	....	....	....	....	....	....	....	....	....	....	....	....	....	....	....	....
1996-97	HC Olomouc Jr.	Czech-Jr.	39	19	14	33	....	....	....	....	....	....	....	....	....	....	....	....	....	....	....	....	....	....	....
1997-98	HC Olomouc Jr.	Czech-Jr.	36	14	21	35	....	....	....	....	....	....	....	....	....	....	....	....	....	....	....	....	....	....	....
	HC Olomouc	Czech-2	13	0	1	1	....	....	....	....	....	....	....	....	....	....	....	....	....	....	....	....	....	....	....
1998-99	Kootenay Ice	WHL	54	26	33	59	46	....	....	....	....	....	....	....	....	....	7	2	2	4	11	....	....	....	....
99-2000	Kootenay Ice	WHL	56	23	43	66	97	....	....	....	....	....	....	....	....	....	21	*15	13	*28	51	....	....	....	....
2000-01	Cincinnati	IHL	52	4	10	14	25	....	....	....	....	....	....	....	....	....	....	....	....	....	....	....	....	....	....
2001-02	**Carolina**	**NHL**	**10**	**2**	**2**	**4**	**2**	**0**	**0**	**0**	**12**	**16.7**	**0**	**1**	**0.0**	**9:23**	**23**	**1**	**4**	**5**	**28**	**1**	**0**	**1**	**14:45**
	Lowell	AHL	66	12	16	28	58	....	....	....	....	....	....	....	....	....	....	....	....	....	....	....	....	....	....
2002-03	**Carolina**	**NHL**	**48**	**3**	**11**	**14**	**32**	**1**	**0**	**0**	**63**	**4.8**	**−5**	**25**	**40.0**	**14:33**	....	....	....	....	....	....	....	....	....
	Lowell	AHL	9	1	1	2	10	....	....	....	....	....	....	....	....	....	....	....	....	....	....	....	....	....	....
	NHL Totals		**58**	**5**	**13**	**18**	**34**	**1**	**0**	**0**	**75**	**6.7**		**26**	**38.5**	**13:40**	**23**	**1**	**4**	**5**	**28**	**1**	**0**	**1**	**14:45**

SWANSON, Brian (SWAHN-suhn, BRIGH-uhn) ATL.

Center. Shoots left. 5'10", 185 lbs. Born, Eagle River, AK, March 24, 1976. San Jose's 5th choice, 115th overall, in 1994 Entry Draft.

			Regular Season														Playoffs								
Season	Club	League	GP	G	A	Pts	PIM	PP	SH	GW	S	%	+/-	TF	F%	Min	GP	G	A	Pts	PIM	PP	SH	GW	Min
1991-92	Anchorage	AAHL	50	35	40	75	10	....	....	....	....	....	....	....	....	....	....	....	....	....	....	....	....	....	....
1992-93	Anchorage	AAHL	45	40	50	90	12	....	....	....	....	....	....	....	....	....	....	....	....	....	....	....	....	....	....
1993-94	Omaha Lancers	USHL	47	38	42	80	40	....	....	....	....	....	....	....	....	....	....	....	....	....	....	....	....	....	....
1994-95	Omaha Lancers	USHL	33	14	35	49	12	....	....	....	....	....	....	....	....	....	....	....	....	....	....	....	....	....	....
1995-96	Colorado College	WCHA	40	26	33	59	24	....	....	....	....	....	....	....	....	....	....	....	....	....	....	....	....	....	....
1996-97	Colorado College	WCHA	43	19	32	51	47	....	....	....	....	....	....	....	....	....	....	....	....	....	....	....	....	....	....
1997-98	Colorado College	WCHA	42	18	*38	*56	26	....	....	....	....	....	....	....	....	....	....	....	....	....	....	....	....	....	....
1998-99	Colorado College	WCHA	42	25	*41	66	28	....	....	....	....	....	....	....	....	....	....	....	....	....	....	....	....	....	....
	Hartford	AHL	4	0	0	0	4	....	....	....	....	....	....	....	....	....	....	....	....	....	....	....	....	....	....
99-2000	Hamilton	AHL	69	19	40	59	18	....	....	....	....	....	....	....	....	....	10	2	5	7	6	....	....	....	....
2000-01	**Edmonton**	**NHL**	**16**	**1**	**1**	**2**	**6**	**0**	**0**	**0**	**8**	**12.5**	**−1**	**150**	**44.0**	**10:55**	....	....	....	....	....	....	....	....	....
	Hamilton	AHL	49	18	29	47	20	....	....	....	....	....	....	....	....	....	....	....	....	....	....	....	....	....	....
2001-02	**Edmonton**	**NHL**	**8**	**1**	**1**	**2**	**0**	**0**	**0**	**0**	**7**	**14.3**	**−1**	**59**	**54.2**	**10:10**	....	....	....	....	....	....	....	....	....
	Hamilton	AHL	65	34	39	73	26	....	....	....	....	....	....	....	....	....	15	7	6	13	6	....	....	....	....
2002-03	**Edmonton**	**NHL**	**44**	**2**	**10**	**12**	**10**	**1**	**0**	**1**	**67**	**3.0**	**−7**	**405**	**52.4**	**11:55**	....	....	....	....	....	....	....	....	....
	NHL Totals		**68**	**4**	**12**	**16**	**16**	**1**	**0**	**1**	**82**	**4.9**		**614**	**50.5**	**11:29**	....	....	....	....	....	....	....	....	....

USHL First All-Star Team (1994) • USHL Second Team All-Star (1995) • WCHA Second All-Star Team (1996) • WCHA Rookie of the Year (1996) • WCHA First All-Star Team (1997, 1998, 1999) • NCAA West Second All-American Team (1998) • NCAA West First All-American Team (1999) • AHL Second All-Star Team (2002)

Traded to **NY Rangers** by **San Jose** with Jayson More and San Jose's 4th round choice (later traded back to San Jose – San Jose selected Adam Colagiacomo) in 1997 Entry Draft for Marty McSorley, August 20, 1996. Signed as a free agent by **Edmonton**, August 19, 1999. Signed as a free agent by **Atlanta**, July 24, 2003.

SWEENEY, Don (SWEE-nee, DAWN) DAL.

Defense. Shoots left. 5'10", 185 lbs. Born, St. Stephen, N.B., August 17, 1966. Boston's 8th choice, 166th overall, in 1984 Entry Draft.

			Regular Season														Playoffs								
Season	Club	League	GP	G	A	Pts	PIM	PP	SH	GW	S	%	+/-	TF	F%	Min	GP	G	A	Pts	PIM	PP	SH	GW	Min
1983-84	South St. Paul	Hi-School	22	33	26	59	....	....	....	....	....	....	....	....	....	....	....	....	....	....	....	....	....	....	....
1984-85	Harvard Crimson	ECAC	29	3	7	10	30	....	....	....	....	....	....	....	....	....	....	....	....	....	....	....	....	....	....
1985-86	Harvard Crimson	ECAC	31	4	5	9	12	....	....	....	....	....	....	....	....	....	....	....	....	....	....	....	....	....	....
1986-87	Harvard Crimson	ECAC	34	7	4	11	22	....	....	....	....	....	....	....	....	....	....	....	....	....	....	....	....	....	....
1987-88	Harvard Crimson	ECAC	30	6	23	29	37	....	....	....	....	....	....	....	....	....	....	....	....	....	....	....	....	....	....
	Maine Mariners	AHL	....	....	....	....	....	....	....	....	....	....	....	....	....	....	6	1	3	4	0	....	....	....	....
1988-89	**Boston**	**NHL**	**36**	**3**	**5**	**8**	**20**	**0**	**0**	**0**	**35**	**8.6**	**−6**	....	....	....	....	....	....	....	....	....	....	....	....
	Maine Mariners	AHL	42	8	17	25	24	....	....	....	....	....	....	....	....	....	....	....	....	....	....	....	....	....	....
1989-90	**Boston**	**NHL**	**58**	**3**	**5**	**8**	**58**	**0**	**0**	**0**	**49**	**6.1**	**11**	....	....	....	**21**	**1**	**5**	**6**	**18**	**1**	**0**	**0**	....
	Maine Mariners	AHL	11	0	8	8	8	....	....	....	....	....	....	....	....	....	....	....	....	....	....	....	....	....	....
1990-91	**Boston**	**NHL**	**77**	**8**	**13**	**21**	**67**	**0**	**1**	**3**	**102**	**7.8**	**2**	....	....	....	**19**	**3**	**0**	**3**	**25**	**0**	**0**	**0**	....
1991-92	**Boston**	**NHL**	**75**	**3**	**11**	**14**	**74**	**0**	**0**	**1**	**92**	**3.3**	**−9**	....	....	....	**15**	**0**	**0**	**0**	**10**	**0**	**0**	**0**	....
1992-93	**Boston**	**NHL**	**84**	**7**	**27**	**34**	**68**	**0**	**1**	**0**	**107**	**6.5**	**34**	....	....	....	**4**	**0**	**0**	**0**	**4**	**0**	**0**	**0**	....
1993-94	**Boston**	**NHL**	**75**	**6**	**15**	**21**	**50**	**1**	**2**	**2**	**136**	**4.4**	**29**	....	....	....	**12**	**2**	**1**	**3**	**4**	**0**	**0**	**1**	....
1994-95	**Boston**	**NHL**	**47**	**3**	**19**	**22**	**24**	**1**	**0**	**2**	**102**	**2.9**	**6**	....	....	....	**5**	**0**	**0**	**0**	**4**	**0**	**0**	**0**	....
1995-96	**Boston**	**NHL**	**77**	**4**	**24**	**28**	**42**	**2**	**0**	**3**	**142**	**2.8**	**−4**	....	....	....	**5**	**0**	**2**	**2**	**6**	**0**	**0**	**0**	....
1996-97	**Boston**	**NHL**	**82**	**3**	**23**	**26**	**39**	**0**	**0**	**0**	**113**	**2.7**	**−5**	....	....	....	....	....	....	....	....	....	....	....	....
1997-98	**Boston**	**NHL**	**59**	**1**	**15**	**16**	**24**	**0**	**0**	**0**	**55**	**1.8**	**12**	....	....	....	....	....	....	....	....	....	....	....	....
1998-99	**Boston**	**NHL**	**81**	**2**	**10**	**12**	**64**	**0**	**0**	**0**	**79**	**2.5**	**14**	**0**	**0.0**	**19:31**	**11**	**3**	**0**	**3**	**6**	**1**	**0**	**0**	**21:48**
99-2000	**Boston**	**NHL**	**81**	**1**	**13**	**14**	**48**	**0**	**0**	**0**	**82**	**1.2**	**−14**	**1**	**0.0**	**21:08**	....	....	....	....	....	....	....	....	....
2000-01	**Boston**	**NHL**	**72**	**2**	**10**	**12**	**26**	**1**	**0**	**1**	**60**	**3.3**	**−1**	**0**	**0.0**	**19:16**	....	....	....	....	....	....	....	....	....

Season	Club	League	GP	G	A	Pts	PIM	PP	SH	GW	S	%	+/-	TF	F%	Min	GP	G	A	Pts	PIM	PP	SH	GW	Min
			Regular Season														Playoffs								
2001-02	Boston	NHL	81	3	15	18	35	1	0	0	70	4.3	22	0	0.0	20:09	6	0	1	1	2	0	0	0	17:44
2002-03	Boston	NHL	67	3	5	8	24	0	0	0	55	5.5	−1	0	0.0	13:13	5	0	1	1	0	0	0	0	14:40
	NHL Totals		1052	52	210	262	663	6	4	12	1279	4.1		1	0.0	18:50	103	9	10	19	79	2	0	1	19:04

ECAC First All-Star Team (1988) • NCAA East All-American Team (1988)

Signed as a free agent by **Dallas**, July 14, 2003.

SYDOR, Darryl

(sih-DOHR, DAIR-ihl) **CBJ**

Defense. Shoots left. 6'1", 205 lbs. Born, Edmonton, Alta., May 13, 1972. Los Angeles' 1st choice, 7th overall, in 1990 Entry Draft.

Season	Club	League	GP	G	A	Pts	PIM	PP	SH	GW	S	%	+/-	TF	F%	Min	GP	G	A	Pts	PIM	PP	SH	GW	Min
1985-86	Genstar Cement	AAHA	34	20	17	37	60	....	....	....	....	....	....	....	....	....	....	....	....	....	....	....	....	....	....
1986-87	Genstar Cement	AAHA	36	15	20	35	60	....	....	....	....	....	....	....	....	....	....	....	....	....	....	....	....	....	....
1987-88	Edmonton Mets	AJHL	38	10	11	21	54	....	....	....	....	....	....	....	....	....	....	....	....	....	....	....	....	....	....
1988-89	Kamloops Blazers	WHL	65	12	14	26	86	....	....	....	....	....	....	....	....	....	15	1	4	5	19	....	....	....	....
1989-90	Kamloops Blazers	WHL	67	29	66	95	129	....	....	....	....	....	....	....	....	....	17	2	9	11	28	....	....	....	....
1990-91	Kamloops Blazers	WHL	66	27	78	105	88	....	....	....	....	....	....	....	....	....	12	3	*22	25	10	....	....	....	....
1991-92	Kamloops Blazers	WHL	29	9	39	48	33	....	....	....	....	....	....	....	....	....	17	3	15	18	18	....	....	....	....
	Los Angeles	NHL	18	1	5	6	22	0	0	0	18	5.6	−3	....	....	....	....	....	....	....	....	....	....	....	....
1992-93	Los Angeles	NHL	80	6	23	29	63	0	0	1	112	5.4	−2	....	....	....	24	3	8	11	16	2	0	0	....
1993-94	Los Angeles	NHL	84	8	27	35	94	1	0	0	146	5.5	−9	....	....	....	....	....	....	....	....	....	....	....	....
1994-95	Los Angeles	NHL	48	4	19	23	36	3	0	0	96	4.2	−2	....	....	....	....	....	....	....	....	....	....	....	....
1995-96	Los Angeles	NHL	58	1	11	12	34	1	0	0	84	1.2	−11	....	....	....	....	....	....	....	....	....	....	....	....
	Dallas	NHL	26	2	6	8	41	1	0	0	33	6.1	−1	....	....	....	....	....	....	....	....	....	....	....	....
1996-97	Dallas	NHL	82	8	40	48	51	2	0	2	142	5.6	37	....	....	....	7	0	2	2	0	0	0	0	....
1997-98	Dallas	NHL	79	11	35	46	51	4	1	1	166	6.6	17	....	....	....	17	0	5	5	14	0	0	0	....
1998-99♦	Dallas	NHL	74	14	34	48	50	9	0	2	163	8.6	−1	1	100.0	21:16	23	3	9	12	16	1	0	1	22:20
99-2000	Dallas	NHL	74	8	26	34	32	5	0	1	132	6.1	6	1	0.0	23:09	23	1	6	7	6	0	0	0	20:48
2000-01	Dallas	NHL	81	10	37	47	34	8	0	1	140	7.1	5	1	0.0	21:25	10	1	3	4	0	1	0	0	22:42
2001-02	Dallas	NHL	78	4	29	33	50	2	0	0	183	2.2	3	0	0.0	21:07	....	....	....	....	....	....	....	....	....
2002-03	Dallas	NHL	81	5	31	36	40	2	0	1	132	3.8	22	0	0.0	18:19	12	0	6	6	6	0	0	0	19:14
	NHL Totals		863	82	323	405	598	38	1	9	1547	5.3		3	33.3	21:01	116	8	39	47	58	4	0	1	21:19

WHL West First All-Star Team (1990, 1991, 1992)

Played in NHL All-Star Game (1998, 1999)

Traded to **Dallas** by **Los Angeles** with Los Angeles' 5th round choice (Ryan Christie) in 1996 Entry Draft for Shane Churla and Doug Zmolek, February 17, 1996. Traded to **Columbus** by **Dallas** for Mike Sillinger and Columbus's 2nd round choice in 2004 Entry Draft, July 22, 2003.

SYKORA, Michal

(SEE-koh-ra, MIHK-al)

Defense. Shoots left. 6'5", 225 lbs. Born, Pardubice, Czech., July 5, 1973. San Jose's 6th choice, 123rd overall, in 1992 Entry Draft.

Season	Club	League	GP	G	A	Pts	PIM	PP	SH	GW	S	%	+/-	TF	F%	Min	GP	G	A	Pts	PIM	PP	SH	GW	Min
1990-91	Pardubice Jr.	Czech-Jr.	40	17	26	43	45	....	....	....	....	....	....	....	....	....	....	....	....	....	....	....	....	....	....
	Tesla Pardubice	Czech	2	0	0	0	....	....	....	....	....	....	....	....	....	....	....	....	....	....	....	....	....	....	....
1991-92	Tacoma Rockets	WHL	61	13	23	36	46	....	....	....	....	....	....	....	....	....	4	0	2	2	2	....	....	....	....
1992-93	Tacoma Rockets	WHL	70	23	50	73	73	....	....	....	....	....	....	....	....	....	7	4	8	12	2	....	....	....	....
1993-94	San Jose	NHL	22	1	4	5	14	0	0	0	22	4.5	−4	....	....	....	....	....	....	....	....	....	....	....	....
	Kansas City	IHL	47	5	11	16	30	....	....	....	....	....	....	....	....	....	....	....	....	....	....	....	....	....	....
1994-95	Kansas City	IHL	36	1	10	11	30	....	....	....	....	....	....	....	....	....	....	....	....	....	....	....	....	....	....
	San Jose	NHL	16	0	4	4	10	0	0	0	6	0.0	6	....	....	....	....	....	....	....	....	....	....	....	....
1995-96	San Jose	NHL	79	4	16	20	54	1	0	0	80	5.0	−14	....	....	....	....	....	....	....	....	....	....	....	....
1996-97	San Jose	NHL	35	2	5	7	59	1	0	0	39	5.1	0	....	....	....	....	....	....	....	....	....	....	....	....
	Chicago	NHL	28	1	9	10	10	0	0	0	38	2.6	4	....	....	....	1	0	0	0	0	0	0	0	....
1997-98	Chicago	NHL	28	1	3	4	12	0	0	0	35	2.9	−10	....	....	....	....	....	....	....	....	....	....	....	....
	Indianapolis Ice	IHL	6	0	0	0	4	....	....	....	....	....	....	....	....	....	....	....	....	....	....	....	....	....	....
	Pardubice	Czech	1	1	0	1	2	....	....	....	....	....	....	....	....	....	....	....	....	....	....	....	....	....	....
1998-99	HC Sparta Praha	Czech	26	4	9	13	38	....	....	....	....	....	....	....	....	....	8	2	0	2	....	....	....	....	....
	HC Sparta Praha	EuroHL	2	2	2	4	4	....	....	....	....	....	....	....	....	....	2	2	2	4	0	....	....	....	....
	Tampa Bay	NHL	10	1	2	3	0	0	0	1	24	4.2	−7	0	0.0	16:20	....	....	....	....	....	....	....	....	....
99-2000	HC Sparta Praha	Czech	48	11	14	25	89	....	....	....	....	....	....	....	....	....	9	5	3	8	8	....	....	....	....
2000-01	Philadelphia	NHL	49	5	11	16	26	1	1	1	71	7.0	9	1	0.0	16:27	6	0	1	1	0	0	0	0	18:11
2001-02	Pardubice	Czech	49	7	11	18	111	....	....	....	....	....	....	....	....	....	6	2	2	4	26	....	....	....	....
	Czech Republic	Olympics	4	0	0	0	0	....	....	....	....	....	....	....	....	....	....	....	....	....	....	....	....	....	....
2002-03	Pardubice	Czech	45	6	17	23	58	....	....	....	....	....	....	....	....	....	8	4	5	9	6	....	....	....	....
	NHL Totals		267	15	54	69	185	3	1	2	315	4.8		1	0.0	16:26	7	0	1	1	0	0	0	0	18:11

WHL West First All-Star Team (1993)

Traded to **Chicago** by **San Jose** with Chris Terreri and Ulf Dahlen for Ed Belfour, January 25, 1997. Traded to **Tampa Bay** by **Chicago** for Mark Fitzpatrick and Tampa Bay's 4th round choice (later traded to Montreal – Montreal selected Chris Dyment) in 1999 Entry Draft, July 17, 1998. Signed as a free agent by **Philadelphia**, July 6, 2000.

SYKORA, Petr

(SEE-koh-ra, PEE-tuhr) **WSH.**

Center. Shoots right. 6'3", 206 lbs. Born, Pardubice, Czech., December 21, 1978. Detroit's 2nd choice, 76th overall, in 1997 Entry Draft.

Season	Club	League	GP	G	A	Pts	PIM	PP	SH	GW	S	%	+/-	TF	F%	Min	GP	G	A	Pts	PIM	PP	SH	GW	Min
1994-95	HC Pardubice Jr.	Czech-Jr.	38	35	33	68	....	....	....	....	....	....	....	....	....	....	....	....	....	....	....	....	....	....	....
1995-96	HC Pardubice Jr.	Czech-Jr.	16	26	17	43	....	....	....	....	....	....	....	....	....	....	....	....	....	....	....	....	....	....	....
1996-97	HC Pardubice Jr.	Czech-Jr.	12	14	4	18	....	....	....	....	....	....	....	....	....	....	....	....	....	....	....	....	....	....	....
	Pardubice	Czech	29	1	3	4	4	....	....	....	....	....	....	....	....	....	....	....	....	....	....	....	....	....	....
1997-98	Pardubice	Czech	39	4	5	9	8	....	....	....	....	....	....	....	....	....	3	0	0	0	....	....	....	....	....
1998-99	Nashville	NHL	2	0	0	0	0	0	0	0	2	0.0	−1	11	45.5	8:19	....	....	....	....	....	....	....	....	....
	Milwaukee	IHL	73	14	15	29	50	....	....	....	....	....	....	....	....	....	2	1	1	2	0	....	....	....	....
99-2000	Milwaukee	IHL	3	0	1	1	2	....	....	....	....	....	....	....	....	....	....	....	....	....	....	....	....	....	....
	Pardubice	Czech	36	7	13	20	49	....	....	....	....	....	....	....	....	....	3	0	0	0	2	....	....	....	....
2000-01	Pardubice	Czech	47	26	18	44	42	....	....	....	....	....	....	....	....	....	7	5	3	8	6	....	....	....	....
2001-02	Pardubice	Czech	32	18	8	26	72	....	....	....	....	....	....	....	....	....	6	1	2	3	26	....	....	....	....
2002-03	Pardubice	Czech	45	18	18	36	86	....	....	....	....	....	....	....	....	....	19	7	7	14	39	....	....	....	....
	NHL Totals		2	0	0	0	0	0	0	0	2	0.0		11	45.5	8:19	....	....	....	....	....	....	....	....	....

Traded to **Nashville** by **Detroit** with Detroit's 3rd round choice (later traded to Edmonton – Edmonton selected Mike Comrie) and 4th round compensatory choice (Alexander Krevsun) in 1999 Entry Draft for Doug Brown, July 14, 1998. Traded to **Washington** by **Nashville** for Washington's 3rd round choice (Paul Brown) in 2003 Entry Draft, June 22, 2002.

SYKORA, Petr

(SEE-koh-ra, PEE-tuhr) **ANA.**

Right wing. Shoots left. 6', 190 lbs. Born, Plzen, Czech., November 19, 1976. New Jersey's 1st choice, 18th overall, in 1995 Entry Draft.

Season	Club	League	GP	G	A	Pts	PIM	PP	SH	GW	S	%	+/-	TF	F%	Min	GP	G	A	Pts	PIM	PP	SH	GW	Min
1991-92	Plzen Jr.	Czech-Jr.	30	50	50	100	....	....	....	....	....	....	....	....	....	....	....	....	....	....	....	....	....	....	....
1992-93	HC Skoda Plzen	Czech	19	12	5	17	....	....	....	....	....	....	....	....	....	....	....	....	....	....	....	....	....	....	....
1993-94	HC Skoda Plzen	Czech	37	10	16	26	....	....	....	....	....	....	....	....	....	....	4	0	1	1	....	....	....	....	....
	Cleveland	IHL	13	4	5	9	8	....	....	....	....	....	....	....	....	....	....	....	....	....	....	....	....	....	....
1994-95	Detroit Vipers	IHL	29	12	17	29	16	....	....	....	....	....	....	....	....	....	....	....	....	....	....	....	....	....	....
1995-96	New Jersey	NHL	63	18	24	42	32	8	0	3	128	14.1	7	....	....	....	....	....	....	....	....	....	....	....	....
	Albany River Rats	AHL	5	4	1	5	0	....	....	....	....	....	....	....	....	....	....	....	....	....	....	....	....	....	....
1996-97	New Jersey	NHL	19	1	2	3	4	0	0	0	26	3.8	−8	....	....	....	2	0	0	0	2	0	0	0	....
	Albany River Rats	AHL	43	20	25	45	48	....	....	....	....	....	....	....	....	....	4	1	4	5	2	....	....	....	....
1997-98	New Jersey	NHL	58	16	20	36	22	3	1	4	130	12.3	0	....	....	....	2	0	0	0	0	0	0	0	....
	Albany River Rats	AHL	2	4	1	5	0	....	....	....	....	....	....	....	....	....	....	....	....	....	....	....	....	....	....
1998-99	New Jersey	NHL	80	29	43	72	22	15	0	7	222	13.1	16	33	33.3	16:14	7	3	3	6	4	0	0	1	18:11
99-2000♦	New Jersey	NHL	79	25	43	68	26	5	1	4	222	11.3	24	47	61.7	17:06	23	9	8	17	10	1	0	3	15:20
2000-01	New Jersey	NHL	73	35	46	81	32	9	2	3	249	14.1	36	15	33.3	17:44	25	10	12	22	12	2	2	2	18:40
2001-02	New Jersey	NHL	73	21	27	48	44	4	0	4	194	10.8	12	1	0.0	17:51	4	0	1	1	0	0	0	0	17:57
	Czech Republic	Olympics	4	1	0	1	0	....	....	....	....	....	....	....	....	....	....	....	....	....	....	....	....	....	....
2002-03	Anaheim	NHL	82	34	25	59	24	15	1	5	299	11.4	−7	23	39.1	0:00	21	4	9	13	12	1	0	2	....
	NHL Totals		527	179	230	409	206	59	5	30	1470	12.2		119	37.8	13:34	84	26	33	59	40	4	2	8	17:16

NHL All-Rookie Team (1996)

Traded to **Anaheim** by **New Jersey** with Mike Commodore, Jean-Francois Damphousse and Igor Pohanka for Jeff Friesen, Oleg Tverdovsky and Maxim Balmochnykh, July 6, 2002.

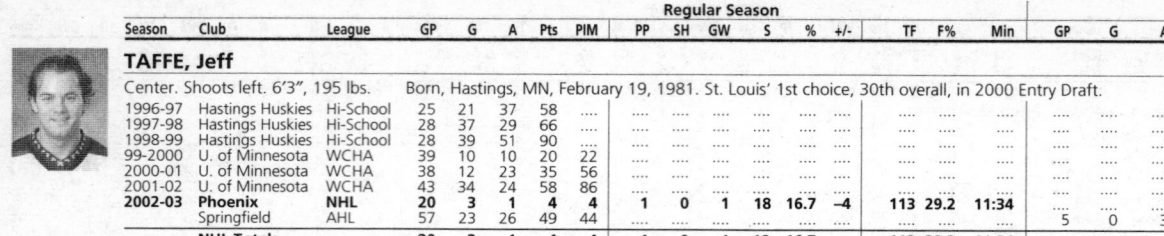

TAFFE, Jeff
(TAYF, JEHF) **PHX.**

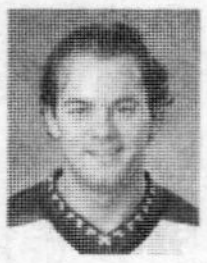

Center. Shoots left. 6'3", 195 lbs. Born, Hastings, MN, February 19, 1981. St. Louis' 1st choice, 30th overall, in 2000 Entry Draft.

			Regular Season														Playoffs								
Season	Club	League	GP	G	A	Pts	PIM	PP	SH	GW	S	%	+/-	TF	F%	Min	GP	G	A	Pts	PIM	PP	SH	GW	Min
1996-97	Hastings Huskies	Hi-School	25	21	37	58	....	....	....	....	....	....	....	....	....	....	....	....	....	....	....	....	....	....	....
1997-98	Hastings Huskies	Hi-School	28	37	29	66	....	....	....	....	....	....	....	....	....	....	....	....	....	....	....	....	....	....	....
1998-99	Hastings Huskies	Hi-School	28	39	51	90	....	....	....	....	....	....	....	....	....	....	....	....	....	....	....	....	....	....	....
99-2000	U. of Minnesota	WCHA	39	10	10	20	22	....	....	....	....	....	....	....	....	....	....	....	....	....	....	....	....	....	....
2000-01	U. of Minnesota	WCHA	38	12	23	35	56	....	....	....	....	....	....	....	....	....	....	....	....	....	....	....	....	....	....
2001-02	U. of Minnesota	WCHA	43	34	24	58	86	....	....	....	....	....	....	....	....	....	....	....	....	....	....	....	....	....	....
2002-03	**Phoenix**	**NHL**	**20**	**3**	**1**	**4**	**4**	**1**	**0**	**1**	**18**	**16.7**	**–4**	**113**	**29.2**	**11:34**	....	....	....	....	....	....	....	....	....
	Springfield	AHL	57	23	26	49	44	....	....	....	....	....	....	....	....	....	5	0	3	3	8	....	....	....	....
	NHL Totals		**20**	**3**	**1**	**4**	**4**	**1**	**0**	**1**	**18**	**16.7**		**113**	**29.2**	**11:34**	....	....	....	....	....	....	....	....	....

Minnesota High School Player of the Year (1999)

Rights traded to **Phoenix** by **St. Louis** with Michal Handzus, Ladislav Nagy and St. Louis' 1st round choice (Ben Eager) in 2002 Entry Draft for Keith Tkachuk, March 13, 2001.

TALLINDER, Henrik
(tah-LIHN-duhr, HEHN-rihk) **BUF.**

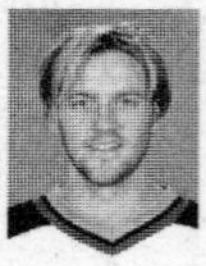

Defense. Shoots left. 6'3", 210 lbs. Born, Stockholm, Sweden, January 10, 1979. Buffalo's 2nd choice, 48th overall, in 1997 Entry Draft.

Season	Club	League	GP	G	A	Pts	PIM	PP	SH	GW	S	%	+/-	TF	F%	Min	GP	G	A	Pts	PIM	PP	SH	GW	Min
1996-97	AIK Solna Jr.	Swede-Jr.	40	4	13	17	55	....	....	....	....	....	....	....	....	....	....	....	....	....	....	....	....	....	....
	AIK Solna	Sweden	1	0	0	0	0	....	....	....	....	....	....	....	....	....	....	....	....	....	....	....	....	....	....
1997-98	AIK Solna	Sweden	34	0	0	0	26	....	....	....	....	....	....	....	....	....	....	....	....	....	....	....	....	....	....
1998-99	AIK Solna	Sweden	36	0	0	0	30	....	....	....	....	....	....	....	....	....	....	....	....	....	....	....	....	....	....
99-2000	AIK Solna	Sweden	50	0	2	2	59	....	....	....	....	....	....	....	....	....	....	....	....	....	....	....	....	....	....
2000-01	TPS Turku	Finland	56	5	9	14	62	....	....	....	....	....	....	....	....	....	10	2	1	3	8	....	....	....	....
2001-02	**Buffalo**	**NHL**	**2**	**0**	**0**	**0**	**0**	**0**	**0**	**0**	**4**	**0.0**	**–1**	**0**	**0.0**	**18:10**	....	....	....	....	....	....	....	....	....
	Rochester	AHL	73	6	14	20	26	....	....	....	....	....	....	....	....	....	2	0	0	0	0	....	....	....	....
2002-03	**Buffalo**	**NHL**	**46**	**3**	**10**	**13**	**28**	**1**	**0**	**0**	**37**	**8.1**	**–3**	**0**	**0.0**	**19:53**	....	....	....	....	....	....	....	....	....
	NHL Totals		**48**	**3**	**10**	**13**	**28**	**1**	**0**	**0**	**41**	**7.3**		**0**	**0.0**	**19:48**	....	....	....	....	....	....	....	....	....

TAMER, Chris
(TAY-muhr, KRIHS) **ATL.**

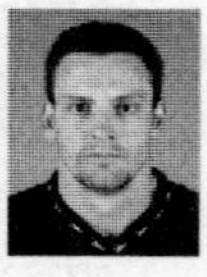

Defense. Shoots left. 6'2", 205 lbs. Born, Dearborn, MI, November 17, 1970. Pittsburgh's 3rd choice, 68th overall, in 1990 Entry Draft.

Season	Club	League	GP	G	A	Pts	PIM	PP	SH	GW	S	%	+/-	TF	F%	Min	GP	G	A	Pts	PIM	PP	SH	GW	Min
1987-88	Redford Royals	NAJHL	40	10	20	30	217	....	....	....	....	....	....	....	....	....	....	....	....	....	....	....	....	....	....
1988-89	Redford Royals	NAJHL	31	6	13	19	79	....	....	....	....	....	....	....	....	....	....	....	....	....	....	....	....	....	....
1989-90	U. of Michigan	CCHA	42	2	7	9	147	....	....	....	....	....	....	....	....	....	....	....	....	....	....	....	....	....	....
1990-91	U. of Michigan	CCHA	45	8	19	27	130	....	....	....	....	....	....	....	....	....	....	....	....	....	....	....	....	....	....
1991-92	U. of Michigan	CCHA	43	4	15	19	125	....	....	....	....	....	....	....	....	....	....	....	....	....	....	....	....	....	....
1992-93	U. of Michigan	CCHA	39	5	18	23	113	....	....	....	....	....	....	....	....	....	....	....	....	....	....	....	....	....	....
1993-94	**Pittsburgh**	**NHL**	**12**	**0**	**0**	**0**	**9**	**0**	**0**	**0**	**10**	**0.0**	**3**	....	....	....	**5**	**0**	**0**	**0**	**2**	**0**	**0**	**0**	....
	Cleveland	IHL	53	1	2	3	160	....	....	....	....	....	....	....	....	....	....	....	....	....	....	....	....	....	....
1994-95	Cleveland	IHL	48	4	10	14	204	....	....	....	....	....	....	....	....	....	....	....	....	....	....	....	....	....	....
	Pittsburgh	**NHL**	**36**	**2**	**0**	**2**	**82**	**0**	**0**	**0**	**26**	**7.7**	**0**	....	....	....	**4**	**0**	**0**	**0**	**18**	**0**	**0**	**0**	....
1995-96	**Pittsburgh**	**NHL**	**70**	**4**	**10**	**14**	**153**	**0**	**0**	**1**	**75**	**5.3**	**20**	....	....	....	**18**	**0**	**7**	**7**	**24**	**0**	**0**	**0**	....
1996-97	**Pittsburgh**	**NHL**	**45**	**2**	**4**	**6**	**131**	**0**	**1**	**0**	**56**	**3.6**	**–25**	....	....	....	**4**	**0**	**0**	**0**	**4**	**0**	**0**	**0**	....
1997-98	**Pittsburgh**	**NHL**	**79**	**0**	**7**	**7**	**181**	**0**	**0**	**0**	**55**	**0.0**	**4**	....	....	....	**6**	**0**	**1**	**1**	**4**	**0**	**0**	**0**	....
1998-99	**Pittsburgh**	**NHL**	**11**	**0**	**0**	**0**	**32**	**0**	**0**	**0**	**2**	**0.0**	**–2**	**0**	**0.0**	**5:59**	....	....	....	....	....	....	....	....	....
	NY Rangers	**NHL**	**52**	**1**	**5**	**6**	**92**	**0**	**0**	**1**	**46**	**2.2**	**–12**	**0**	**0.0**	**15:25**	....	....	....	....	....	....	....	....	....
99-2000	**Atlanta**	**NHL**	**69**	**2**	**8**	**10**	**91**	**0**	**0**	**0**	**61**	**3.3**	**–32**	**5**	**40.0**	**18:29**	....	....	....	....	....	....	....	....	....
2000-01	**Atlanta**	**NHL**	**82**	**4**	**13**	**17**	**128**	**0**	**1**	**1**	**90**	**4.4**	**–1**	**1**	**0.0**	**19:42**	....	....	....	....	....	....	....	....	....
2001-02	**Atlanta**	**NHL**	**78**	**3**	**3**	**6**	**111**	**0**	**1**	**0**	**66**	**4.5**	**–11**	**0**	**0.0**	**18:30**	....	....	....	....	....	....	....	....	....
2002-03	**Atlanta**	**NHL**	**72**	**1**	**9**	**10**	**118**	**0**	**0**	**0**	**53**	**1.9**	**–10**	**0**	**0.0**	**15:41**	....	....	....	....	....	....	....	....	....
	NHL Totals		**606**	**19**	**59**	**78**	**1128**	**0**	**3**	**3**	**540**	**3.5**		**6**	**33.3**	**17:23**	**37**	**0**	**8**	**8**	**52**	**0**	**0**	**0**	....

Traded to **NY Rangers** by **Pittsburgh** with Petr Nedved and Sean Pronger for Alex Kovalev and Harry York, November 25, 1998. Claimed by **Atlanta** from **NY Rangers** in Expansion Draft, June 25, 1999.

TANABE, David
(tuh-NA-bee, DAY-vihd) **PHX.**

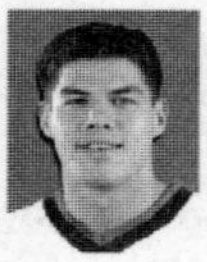

Defense. Shoots right. 6'1", 195 lbs. Born, White Bear Lake, MN, July 19, 1980. Carolina's 1st choice, 16th overall, in 1999 Entry Draft.

Season	Club	League	GP	G	A	Pts	PIM	PP	SH	GW	S	%	+/-	TF	F%	Min	GP	G	A	Pts	PIM	PP	SH	GW	Min
1996-97	Hill-Murray	Hi-School	28	12	14	26	....	....	....	....	....	....	....	....	....	....	....	....	....	....	....	....	....	....	....
1997-98	U.S. National U-18	USDP	73	8	21	29	96	....	....	....	....	....	....	....	....	....	....	....	....	....	....	....	....	....	....
1998-99	U. of Wisconsin	WCHA	35	10	12	22	44	....	....	....	....	....	....	....	....	....	....	....	....	....	....	....	....	....	....
99-2000	**Carolina**	**NHL**	**31**	**4**	**0**	**4**	**14**	**3**	**0**	**0**	**28**	**14.3**	**–4**	**0**	**0.0**	**12:53**	....	....	....	....	....	....	....	....	....
	Cincinnati	IHL	32	0	13	13	14	....	....	....	....	....	....	....	....	....	11	1	4	5	6	....	....	....	....
2000-01	**Carolina**	**NHL**	**74**	**7**	**22**	**29**	**42**	**5**	**0**	**1**	**130**	**5.4**	**–9**	**0**	**0.0**	**17:55**	**6**	**2**	**0**	**2**	**12**	**2**	**0**	**0**	**20:47**
2001-02	**Carolina**	**NHL**	**78**	**1**	**15**	**16**	**35**	**0**	**0**	**0**	**113**	**0.9**	**–13**	**0**	**0.0**	**18:27**	**1**	**0**	**1**	**1**	**0**	**0**	**0**	**0**	**7:31**
2002-03	**Carolina**	**NHL**	**68**	**3**	**10**	**13**	**24**	**2**	**0**	**0**	**104**	**2.9**	**–27**	**0**	**0.0**	**18:12**	....	....	....	....	....	....	....	....	....
	NHL Totals		**251**	**15**	**47**	**62**	**115**	**10**	**0**	**1**	**375**	**4.0**		**0**	**0.0**	**17:32**	**7**	**2**	**1**	**3**	**12**	**2**	**0**	**0**	**18:53**

WCHA All-Rookie Team (1999)

Traded to **Phoenix** by **Carolina** with Igor Knyazev for Danny Markov and future considerations, June 21, 2003.

TANGUAY, Alex
(TAN-guay, AL-ehx) **COL.**

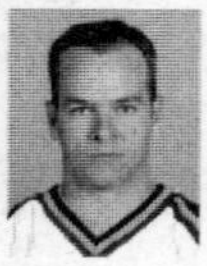

Left wing. Shoots left. 6', 190 lbs. Born, Ste-Justine, Que., November 21, 1979. Colorado's 1st choice, 12th overall, in 1998 Entry Draft.

Season	Club	League	GP	G	A	Pts	PIM	PP	SH	GW	S	%	+/-	TF	F%	Min	GP	G	A	Pts	PIM	PP	SH	GW	Min
1994-95	Cap-d-Madeleine	QAAA	1	0	1	1	0	....	....	....	....	....	....	....	....	....	....	....	....	....	....	....	....	....	....
1995-96	Cap-d-Madeleine	QAAA	44	29	34	63	64	....	....	....	....	....	....	....	....	....	5	2	4	6	14	....	....	....	....
1996-97	Halifax	QMJHL	70	27	41	68	60	....	....	....	....	....	....	....	....	....	12	5	8	13	8	....	....	....	....
1997-98	Halifax	QMJHL	51	47	38	85	32	....	....	....	....	....	....	....	....	....	5	7	6	13	4	....	....	....	....
1998-99	Halifax	QMJHL	31	27	34	61	30	....	....	....	....	....	....	....	....	....	5	1	2	3	2	....	....	....	....
	Hershey Bears	AHL	5	1	2	3	2	....	....	....	....	....	....	....	....	....	5	0	2	2	0	....	....	....	....
99-2000	**Colorado**	**NHL**	**76**	**17**	**34**	**51**	**22**	**5**	**0**	**3**	**74**	**23.0**	**6**	**11**	**45.5**	**15:38**	**17**	**2**	**1**	**3**	**2**	**1**	**0**	**1**	**10:49**
2000-01♦	**Colorado**	**NHL**	**82**	**27**	**50**	**77**	**37**	**7**	**1**	**3**	**135**	**20.0**	**35**	**30**	**43.3**	**17:51**	**23**	**6**	**15**	**21**	**8**	**1**	**0**	**2**	**19:18**
2001-02	**Colorado**	**NHL**	**70**	**13**	**35**	**48**	**36**	**7**	**0**	**2**	**90**	**14.4**	**8**	**37**	**40.5**	**18:20**	**19**	**5**	**8**	**13**	**0**	**3**	**0**	**0**	**17:25**
2002-03	**Colorado**	**NHL**	**82**	**26**	**41**	**67**	**36**	**3**	**0**	**5**	**142**	**18.3**	**34**	**123**	**39.0**	**17:48**	**7**	**1**	**2**	**3**	**4**	**0**	**0**	**1**	**19:06**
	NHL Totals		**310**	**83**	**160**	**243**	**131**	**22**	**1**	**13**	**441**	**18.8**		**201**	**40.3**	**17:24**	**66**	**14**	**26**	**40**	**14**	**5**	**0**	**4**	**16:33**

QMJHL All-Rookie Team (1997)

TAPPER, Brad
(TA-puhr, BRAD) **ATL.**

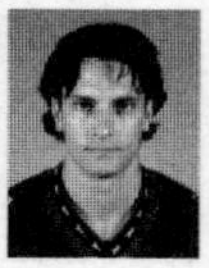

Right wing. Shoots right. 6', 185 lbs. Born, Scarborough, Ont., April 28, 1978.

Season	Club	League	GP	G	A	Pts	PIM	PP	SH	GW	S	%	+/-	TF	F%	Min	GP	G	A	Pts	PIM	PP	SH	GW	Min
1996-97	Wexford Raiders	MTJHL	50	42	70	112	169	....	....	....	....	....	....	....	....	....	....	....	....	....	....	....	....	....	....
1997-98	RPI Engineers	ECAC	34	14	11	25	62	....	....	....	....	....	....	....	....	....	....	....	....	....	....	....	....	....	....
1998-99	RPI Engineers	ECAC	35	20	20	40	60	....	....	....	....	....	....	....	....	....	....	....	....	....	....	....	....	....	....
99-2000	RPI Engineers	ECAC	37	*31	20	51	81	....	....	....	....	....	....	....	....	....	....	....	....	....	....	....	....	....	....
2000-01	**Atlanta**	**NHL**	**16**	**2**	**3**	**5**	**6**	**0**	**0**	**0**	**21**	**9.5**	**1**	**0**	**0.0**	**12:44**	....	....	....	....	....	....	....	....	....
	Orlando	IHL	45	7	9	16	39	....	....	....	....	....	....	....	....	....	2	0	0	0	2	....	....	....	....
2001-02	**Atlanta**	**NHL**	**20**	**2**	**4**	**6**	**43**	**0**	**0**	**0**	**34**	**5.9**	**–3**	**3**	**66.7**	**13:21**	....	....	....	....	....	....	....	....	....
	Chicago Wolves	AHL	50	14	12	26	62	....	....	....	....	....	....	....	....	....	19	3	4	7	42	....	....	....	....
2002-03	**Atlanta**	**NHL**	**35**	**10**	**4**	**14**	**23**	**1**	**0**	**3**	**68**	**14.7**	**2**	**4**	**25.0**	**13:03**	....	....	....	....	....	....	....	....	....
	Chicago Wolves	AHL	28	9	14	23	42	....	....	....	....	....	....	....	....	....	9	1	3	4	10	....	....	....	....
	NHL Totals		**71**	**14**	**11**	**25**	**72**	**1**	**0**	**3**	**123**	**11.4**		**7**	**42.9**	**13:04**	....	....	....	....	....	....	....	....	....

ECAC First All-Star Team (2000) • NCAA East Second All-American Team (2000)

Signed as a free agent by **Atlanta**, April 11, 2000.

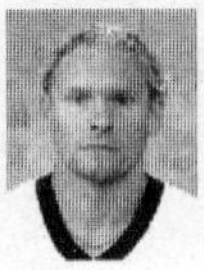

TARNSTROM, Dick

(TAHRN-struhm, DIHK) **PIT.**

Defense. Shoots left. 6'2", 205 lbs. Born, Sundbyberg, Sweden, January 20, 1975. NY Islanders' 12th choice, 272nd overall, in 1994 Entry Draft.

Season	Club	League	GP	G	A	Pts	PIM	PP	SH	GW	S	%	+/-	TF	F%	Min	Playoffs GP	G	A	Pts	PIM	PP	SH	GW	Min
1992-93	AIK Solna	Sweden	3	0	0	0	0																		
1993-94	AIK Solna	Sweden	33	1	4	5																			
1994-95	AIK Solna	Swede-2	37	8	4	12	26																		
1995-96	AIK Solna	Sweden	40	0	5	5	32																		
1996-97	AIK Solna	Sweden	49	5	3	8	38										7	0	1	1	6				
1997-98	AIK Solna	Sweden	45	2	12	14	30																		
1998-99	AIK Solna	Sweden	47	9	14	23	36																		
99-2000	AIK Solna	Sweden	42	7	15	22	20																		
2000-01	AIK Solna	Sweden	50	10	18	28	28										5	0	0	0	8				
2001-02	NY Islanders	NHL	62	3	16	19	38	0	0	0	59	5.1	-12	0	0.0	17:39	5	0	0	0	2	0	0	0	7:13
	Bridgeport	AHL	9	0	2	2	2																		
2002-03	Pittsburgh	NHL	61	7	34	41	50	3	0	0	115	6.1	-11	0	0.0	23:54									
	NHL Totals		123	10	50	60	88	3	0	0	174	5.7		0	0.0	20:45	5	0	0	0	2	0	0	0	7:13

Claimed on waivers by **Pittsburgh** from **NY Islanders**, August 6, 2002.

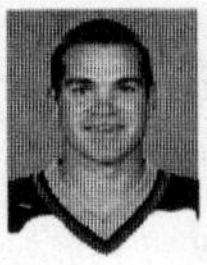

TAYLOR, Chris

(TAY-lohr, KRIHS) **BUF.**

Center. Shoots left. 6'2", 192 lbs. Born, Stratford, Ont., March 6, 1972. NY Islanders' 2nd choice, 27th overall, in 1990 Entry Draft.

Season	Club	League	GP	G	A	Pts	PIM	PP	SH	GW	S	%	+/-	TF	F%	Min	Playoffs GP	G	A	Pts	PIM	PP	SH	GW	Min
1987-88	Stratford Cullitons	OJHL-B	52	28	37	65	112																		
1988-89	London Knights	OHL	62	7	16	23	52										15	0	2	2	15				
1989-90	London Knights	OHL	66	45	60	105	60										6	3	2	5	6				
1990-91	London Knights	OHL	65	50	78	128	50										7	4	8	12	6				
1991-92	London Knights	OHL	66	48	74	122	57										10	8	16	24	9				
1992-93	Capital District	AHL	77	19	43	62	32										4	0	1	1	2				
1993-94	Salt Lake	IHL	79	21	20	41	38																		
1994-95	Denver Grizzlies	IHL	78	38	48	86	47										14	7	6	13	10				
	NY Islanders	NHL	10	0	3	3	2	0	0	0	13	0.0	1												
1995-96	NY Islanders	NHL	11	0	1	1	2	0	0	0	4	0.0	1												
	Utah Grizzlies	IHL	50	18	23	41	60										22	5	11	16	26				
1996-97	NY Islanders	NHL	1	0	0	0	0	0	0	0	1	0.0	0												
	Utah Grizzlies	IHL	71	27	40	67	24										7	1	2	3	0				
1997-98	Utah Grizzlies	IHL	79	28	56	84	66										4	0	2	2	6				
1998-99	Boston	NHL	37	3	5	8	12	0	1	0	60	5.0	-3	512	53.7	14:24									
	Providence Bruins	AHL	21	6	11	17	6																		
	Las Vegas	IHL	14	3	12	15	2																		
99-2000	Buffalo	NHL	11	1	1	2	2	0	0	0	15	6.7	-2	125	45.6	10:54	2	0	0	0	2	0	0	0	10:32
	Rochester	AHL	49	21	28	49	21																		
2000-01	Buffalo	NHL	14	0	2	2	6	0	0	0	21	0.0	1	138	50.7	11:08									
	Rochester	AHL	45	20	24	44	25																		
2001-02	Rochester	AHL	77	21	45	66	66										2	0	1	1	0				
2002-03	Buffalo	NHL	11	1	3	4	2	0	0	0	10	10.0	-1	152	47.4	13:55									
	Rochester	AHL	61	12	55	67	44										3	3	1	4	2				
	NHL Totals		95	5	15	20	26	0	1	0	124	4.0		927	51.1	13:10	2	0	0	0	2	0	0	0	10:32

Signed as a free agent by **Los Angeles**, July 25, 1997. Signed as a free agent by **Boston**, August 5, 1998. Signed as a free agent by **Buffalo**, August 13, 1999.

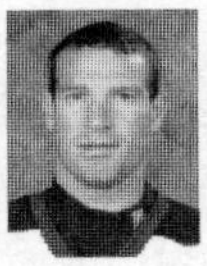

TAYLOR, Tim

(TAY-lohr, TIHM) **T.B.**

Center. Shoots left. 6'1", 189 lbs. Born, Stratford, Ont., February 6, 1969. Washington's 2nd choice, 36th overall, in 1988 Entry Draft.

Season	Club	League	GP	G	A	Pts	PIM	PP	SH	GW	S	%	+/-	TF	F%	Min	Playoffs GP	G	A	Pts	PIM	PP	SH	GW	Min
1985-86	Stratford Cullitons	OJHL-B	1	0	0	0	0																		
1986-87	Stratford Cullitons	OJHL-B	31	25	26	51	51																		
	London Knights	OHL	34	7	9	16	11																		
1987-88	London Knights	OHL	64	46	50	96	66										12	9	9	18	26				
1988-89	London Knights	OHL	61	34	80	114	93										21	*21	25	*46	58				
1989-90	Baltimore	AHL	79	31	36	67	124										9	2	2	4	13				
1990-91	Baltimore	AHL	79	25	42	67	75										5	0	1	1	4				
1991-92	Baltimore	AHL	65	9	18	27	131																		
1992-93	Baltimore	AHL	41	15	16	31	49																		
	Hamilton	AHL	36	15	22	37	37																		
1993-94	Detroit	NHL	1	1	0	1	0	0	0	0	4	25.0	-1												
	Adirondack	AHL	79	36	*81	*117	86										12	2	10	12	12				
1994-95	Detroit	NHL	22	0	4	4	16	0	0	0	21	0.0	3				6	0	1	1	12	0	0	0	
1995-96	Detroit	NHL	72	11	14	25	39	1	1	4	81	13.6	11				18	0	4	4	4	0	0	0	
1996-97♦	Detroit	NHL	44	3	4	7	52	0	1	0	44	6.8	-6				2	0	0	0	0	0	0	0	
1997-98	Boston	NHL	79	20	11	31	57	1	3	0	127	15.7	-16				6	0	0	0	10	0	0	0	
1998-99	Boston	NHL	49	4	7	11	55	0	0	1	76	5.3	-10	834	58.3	15:56	12	0	3	3	8	0	0	0	15:09
99-2000	NY Rangers	NHL	76	9	11	20	72	0	0	2	79	11.4	-4	1276	58.9	14:09									
2000-01	NY Rangers	NHL	38	2	5	7	16	0	0	1	34	5.9	-6	292	59.3	8:57									
2001-02	Tampa Bay	NHL	48	4	4	8	25	0	1	0	50	8.0	-2	559	54.6	13:29									
2002-03	Tampa Bay	NHL	82	4	8	12	38	0	0	1	95	4.2	-13	961	57.9	13:43	11	0	1	1	6	0	0	0	13:54
	NHL Totals		511	58	68	126	370	2	6	9	611	9.5		3922	57.9	13:32	55	0	9	9	40	0	0	0	14:33

AHL First All-Star Team (1994) • John B. Sollenberger Trophy (Top Scorer – AHL) (1994)

Traded to **Vancouver** by **Washington** for Eric Murano, January 29, 1993. Signed as a free agent by **Detroit**, July 28, 1993. Claimed by **Boston** from **Detroit** in Waiver Draft, September 28, 1997. Signed as a free agent by **NY Rangers**, July 30, 1999. • Missed majority of 2000-01 season recovering from abdominal injury suffered in game vs. Phoenix, January 4, 2001. Traded to **Tampa Bay** by **NY Rangers** for Kyle Freadrich and Nils Ekman, June 30, 2001.

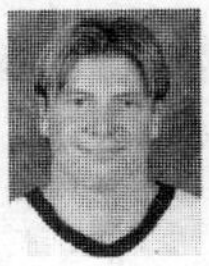

TENKRAT, Petr

(TEHN-krat, PEE-tuhr) **CBJ**

Right wing. Shoots right. 5'11", 200 lbs. Born, Kladno, Czech., May 31, 1977. Anaheim's 6th choice, 230th overall, in 1999 Entry Draft.

Season	Club	League	GP	G	A	Pts	PIM	PP	SH	GW	S	%	+/-	TF	F%	Min	Playoffs GP	G	A	Pts	PIM	PP	SH	GW	Min
1994-95	HC Kladno	Czech	1	0	0	0	0																		
1995-96	HC Poldi Kladno	Czech	20	0	4	4	4										3	0	1	1	0				
1996-97	HC Poldi Kladno	Czech	43	5	9	14	6										3	0	1	1	0				
1997-98	Kladno	Czech	52	9	10	19	24																		
1998-99	Kladno	Czech	50	21	14	35	32																		
99-2000	HPK Hameenlinna	Finland	32	20	9	29	31																		
	Ilves Tampere	Finland	22	15	5	20	44										3	1	1	2	14				
2000-01	Anaheim	NHL	46	5	9	14	16	0	0	2	79	6.3	-11	0	0.0	12:48									
	Cincinnati	AHL	25	9	9	18	24										4	3	2	5	0				
2001-02	Anaheim	NHL	9	0	0	0	6	0	0	0	13	0.0	-6	1	0.0	11:47									
	Cincinnati	AHL	3	2	3	5	2																		
	Nashville	NHL	58	8	16	24	28	0	1	2	82	9.8	-4	7	28.6	11:60									
	Milwaukee	AHL	4	0	0	0	2																		
2002-03	Karpat Oulu	Finland	51	21	19	40	60										14	4	2	6	6				
	NHL Totals		113	13	25	38	50	0	1	4	174	7.5		8	25.0	12:18									

Traded to **Nashville** by **Anaheim** for Patrick Kjellberg, November 1, 2001. Claimed by **Florida** from **Nashville** in Waiver Draft, October 4, 2002. Traded to **Columbus** by **Florida** for Mathieu Biron, October 4, 2002. Signed as a free agent by **Karpat** (Finland), May 15, 2002.

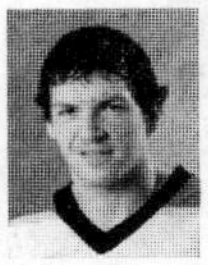

TETARENKO, Joey

(teh-tar-EHN-koh, JOH-ee) **CAR.**

Right wing. Shoots right. 6'2", 215 lbs. Born, Prince Albert, Sask., March 3, 1978. Florida's 4th choice, 82nd overall, in 1996 Entry Draft.

Season	Club	League	GP	G	A	Pts	PIM	PP	SH	GW	S	%	+/-	TF	F%	Min	Playoffs GP	G	A	Pts	PIM	PP	SH	GW	Min
1993-94	North Battleford	SMHL	36	6	13	19	75																		
1994-95	Portland	WHL	59	0	1	1	134										9	0	0	0	8				
1995-96	Portland	WHL	71	4	11	15	190										7	0	1	1	17				
1996-97	Portland	WHL	68	8	18	26	182										2	0	0	0	2				
1997-98	Portland	WHL	49	2	12	14	148										16	0	2	2	30				
1998-99	New Haven	AHL	65	4	10	14	154																		
99-2000	Louisville Panthers	AHL	57	3	11	14	136										4	0	0	0	2				

			Regular Season														Playoffs								
Season	Club	League	GP	G	A	Pts	PIM	PP	SH	GW	S	%	+/-	TF	F%	Min	GP	G	A	Pts	PIM	PP	SH	GW	Min
2000-01	**Florida**	**NHL**	**29**	**3**	**1**	**4**	**44**	**0**	**0**	**0**	**21**	**14.3**	**–1**	**0**	**0.0**	**6:12**	....	....	....	....	....	....	....	....	....
	Louisville Panthers	AHL	29	1	4	5	74	....	....	....	....	....	....	....	....	....	....	....	....	....	....	....	....	....	....
2001-02	**Florida**	**NHL**	**38**	**1**	**0**	**1**	**123**	**0**	**0**	**0**	**10**	**10.0**	**–5**	**0**	**0.0**	**5:08**	....	....	....	....	....	....	....	....	....
2002-03	**Florida**	**NHL**	**2**	**0**	**0**	**0**	**4**	**0**	**0**	**0**	**2**	**0.0**	**–1**	**0**	**0.0**	**6:19**	....	....	....	....	....	....	....	....	....
	San Antonio	AHL	50	4	12	16	123	....	....	....	....	....	....	....	....	....	....	....	....	....	....	....	....	....	....
	Ottawa	**NHL**	**2**	**0**	**0**	**0**	**5**	**0**	**0**	**0**	**1**	**0.0**	**0**	**0**	**0.0**	**6:29**	....	....	....	....	....	....	....	....	....
	Binghamton	AHL	14	2	2	4	33	....	....	....	....	....	....	....	....	....	14	0	0	0	36	....	....	....	....
	NHL Totals		**71**	**4**	**1**	**5**	**176**	**0**	**0**	**0**	**34**	**11.8**		**0**	**0.0**	**5:38**	....	....	....	....	....	....	....	....	....

• Missed majority of 2001-02 season recovering from jaw injury suffered in game vs. NY Rangers, November 3, 2001. Traded to **Ottawa** by **Florida** for Simon Lajeunesse, March 4, 2003. Signed as a free agent by **Carolina**, July 2, 2003.

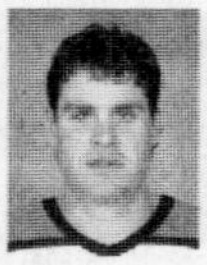

THERIEN, Chris

(TEH-ree-ehn, KRIHS) **PHI.**

Defense. Shoots left. 6'5", 235 lbs. Born, Ottawa, Ont., December 14, 1971. Philadelphia's 7th choice, 47th overall, in 1990 Entry Draft.

Season	Club	League	GP	G	A	Pts	PIM	PP	SH	GW	S	%	+/-	TF	F%	Min	GP	G	A	Pts	PIM	PP	SH	GW	Min
1988-89	Ottawa Jr. Sens	OCJHL	8	3	1	4	22	....	....	....	....	....	....	....	....	....	....	....	....	....	....	....	....	....	....
1989-90	Ottawa Jr. Sens	OCJHL	3	0	2	2	2	....	....	....	....	....	....	....	....	....	....	....	....	....	....	....	....	....	....
	Northfield Prep	Hi-School	31	35	37	72	54	....	....	....	....	....	....	....	....	....	....	....	....	....	....	....	....	....	....
1990-91	Providence	H-East	36	4	18	22	36	....	....	....	....	....	....	....	....	....	....	....	....	....	....	....	....	....	....
1991-92	Providence	H-East	36	16	25	41	38	....	....	....	....	....	....	....	....	....	....	....	....	....	....	....	....	....	....
1992-93	Providence	H-East	33	8	11	19	52	....	....	....	....	....	....	....	....	....	....	....	....	....	....	....	....	....	....
	Team Canada	Nat-Tm	8	1	4	5	8	....	....	....	....	....	....	....	....	....	....	....	....	....	....	....	....	....	....
1993-94	Team Canada	Nat-Tm	59	7	15	22	46	....	....	....	....	....	....	....	....	....	....	....	....	....	....	....	....	....	....
	Canada	Olympics	4	0	0	0	4	....	....	....	....	....	....	....	....	....	....	....	....	....	....	....	....	....	....
	Hershey Bears	AHL	6	0	0	0	2	....	....	....	....	....	....	....	....	....	....	....	....	....	....	....	....	....	....
1994-95	Hershey Bears	AHL	34	3	13	16	27	....	....	....	....	....	....	....	....	....	....	....	....	....	....	....	....	....	....
	Philadelphia	**NHL**	**48**	**3**	**10**	**13**	**38**	**1**	**0**	**0**	**53**	**5.7**	**8**	....	....	....	**15**	**0**	**0**	**0**	**10**	**0**	**0**	**0**	....
1995-96	**Philadelphia**	**NHL**	**82**	**6**	**17**	**23**	**89**	**3**	**0**	**1**	**123**	**4.9**	**16**	....	....	....	**12**	**0**	**0**	**0**	**18**	**0**	**0**	**0**	....
1996-97	**Philadelphia**	**NHL**	**71**	**2**	**22**	**24**	**64**	**0**	**0**	**0**	**107**	**1.9**	**27**	....	....	....	**19**	**1**	**6**	**7**	**6**	**0**	**0**	**1**	....
1997-98	**Philadelphia**	**NHL**	**78**	**3**	**16**	**19**	**80**	**1**	**0**	**1**	**102**	**2.9**	**5**	....	....	....	**5**	**0**	**1**	**1**	**4**	**0**	**0**	**0**	....
1998-99	**Philadelphia**	**NHL**	**74**	**3**	**15**	**18**	**48**	**1**	**0**	**0**	**115**	**2.6**	**16**	**0**	**0.0**	**20:45**	**6**	**0**	**0**	**0**	**6**	**0**	**0**	**0**	**20:23**
99-2000	**Philadelphia**	**NHL**	**80**	**4**	**9**	**13**	**66**	**1**	**0**	**1**	**126**	**3.2**	**11**	**0**	**0.0**	**20:12**	**18**	**0**	**1**	**1**	**12**	**0**	**0**	**0**	**21:40**
2000-01	**Philadelphia**	**NHL**	**73**	**2**	**12**	**14**	**48**	**1**	**0**	**0**	**103**	**1.9**	**22**	**0**	**0.0**	**20:38**	**6**	**1**	**0**	**1**	**8**	**0**	**0**	**0**	**20:55**
2001-02	**Philadelphia**	**NHL**	**77**	**4**	**10**	**14**	**30**	**0**	**2**	**3**	**105**	**3.8**	**16**	**0**	**0.0**	**18:42**	**5**	**0**	**0**	**0**	**2**	**0**	**0**	**0**	**19:50**
2002-03	**Philadelphia**	**NHL**	**67**	**1**	**6**	**7**	**36**	**0**	**0**	**0**	**93**	**1.1**	**10**	**0**	**0.0**	**17:24**	**13**	**0**	**2**	**2**	**2**	**0**	**0**	**0**	**17:51**
	NHL Totals		**650**	**28**	**117**	**145**	**499**	**8**	**2**	**6**	**927**	**3.0**		**0**	**0.0**	**19:35**	**99**	**2**	**10**	**12**	**68**	**0**	**0**	**1**	**20:11**

Hockey East Second All-Star Team (1993) • NHL All-Rookie Team (1995)

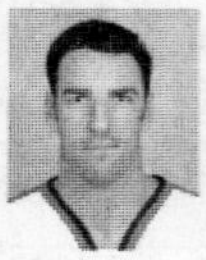

THOMAS, Scott

(TAW-mas, SKAWT)

Right wing. Shoots right. 6'2", 200 lbs. Born, Buffalo, NY, January 18, 1970. Buffalo's 2nd choice, 56th overall, in 1989 Entry Draft.

Season	Club	League	GP	G	A	Pts	PIM	PP	SH	GW	S	%	+/-	TF	F%	Min	GP	G	A	Pts	PIM	PP	SH	GW	Min
1987-88	Nichols High	Hi-School	16	23	39	62	62	....	....	....	....	....	....	....	....	....	....	....	....	....	....	....	....	....	....
1988-89	Nichols High	Hi-School	17	38	52	90	....	....	....	....	....	....	....	....	....	....	....	....	....	....	....	....	....	....	....
1989-90	Clarkson Knights	ECAC	34	19	13	32	95	....	....	....	....	....	....	....	....	....	....	....	....	....	....	....	....	....	....
1990-91	Clarkson Knights	ECAC	40	28	14	42	89	....	....	....	....	....	....	....	....	....	....	....	....	....	....	....	....	....	....
1991-92	Clarkson Knights	ECAC	29	22	20	42	57	....	....	....	....	....	....	....	....	....	....	....	....	....	....	....	....	....	....
	Rochester	AHL	....	....	....	....	....	....	....	....	....	....	....	....	....	....	9	0	1	1	17	....	....	....	....
1992-93	**Buffalo**	**NHL**	**7**	**1**	**1**	**2**	**15**	**0**	**0**	**0**	**4**	**25.0**	**2**	....	....	....	....	....	....	....	....	....	....	....	....
	Rochester	AHL	65	32	27	59	38	....	....	....	....	....	....	....	....	....	17	8	5	13	6	....	....	....	....
1993-94	**Buffalo**	**NHL**	**32**	**2**	**2**	**4**	**8**	**1**	**0**	**0**	**26**	**7.7**	**–6**	....	....	....	....	....	....	....	....	....	....	....	....
	Rochester	AHL	11	4	5	9	0	....	....	....	....	....	....	....	....	....	....	....	....	....	....	....	....	....	....
1994-95	Rochester	AHL	55	21	25	46	115	....	....	....	....	....	....	....	....	....	5	4	0	4	4	....	....	....	....
1995-96	Cincinnati	IHL	78	32	28	60	54	....	....	....	....	....	....	....	....	....	17	*13	2	15	4	....	....	....	....
1996-97	Cincinnati	IHL	71	32	29	61	46	....	....	....	....	....	....	....	....	....	3	0	0	0	0	....	....	....	....
1997-98	Detroit Vipers	IHL	44	11	16	27	18	....	....	....	....	....	....	....	....	....	....	....	....	....	....	....	....	....	....
	Manitoba Moose	IHL	26	12	4	16	8	....	....	....	....	....	....	....	....	....	3	0	1	1	2	....	....	....	....
1998-99	Manitoba Moose	IHL	78	45	25	70	32	....	....	....	....	....	....	....	....	....	5	3	4	7	4	....	....	....	....
99-2000	Long Beach	IHL	52	15	16	31	18	....	....	....	....	....	....	....	....	....	6	2	1	3	6	....	....	....	....
2000-01	**Los Angeles**	**NHL**	**24**	**3**	**1**	**4**	**9**	**0**	**0**	**0**	**16**	**18.8**	**0**	**0**	**0.0**	**8:07**	**12**	**1**	**0**	**1**	**4**	**1**	**0**	**0**	**6:12**
	Manitoba Moose	IHL	22	9	14	23	21	....	....	....	....	....	....	....	....	....	3	1	2	3	0	....	....	....	....
2001-02	Manchester	AHL	56	14	29	43	6	....	....	....	....	....	....	....	....	....	5	1	0	1	4	....	....	....	....
2002-03	Cleveland Barons	AHL	23	7	3	10	6	....	....	....	....	....	....	....	....	....	....	....	....	....	....	....	....	....	....
	NHL Totals		**63**	**6**	**4**	**10**	**32**	**1**	**0**	**0**	**46**	**13.0**		**0**	**0.0**	**8:07**	**12**	**1**	**0**	**1**	**4**	**1**	**0**	**0**	**6:12**

Signed as a free agent by **Los Angeles**, July 30, 1999. Signed as a free agent by **San Jose**, September 5, 2002. • Missed majority of 2002-03 season recovering from leg injury suffered in game vs. Hamilton (AHL), December 8, 2002.

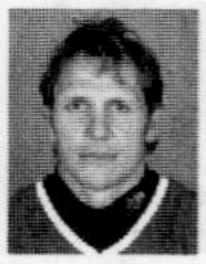

THOMAS, Steve

(TAW-mas, STEEV)

Left wing. Shoots left. 5'10", 185 lbs. Born, Stockport, England, July 15, 1963.

Season	Club	League	GP	G	A	Pts	PIM	PP	SH	GW	S	%	+/-	TF	F%	Min	GP	G	A	Pts	PIM	PP	SH	GW	Min
1980-81	Markham Waxers	OHA-A	42	22	25	47	76	....	....	....	....	....	....	....	....	....	....	....	....	....	....	....	....	....	....
	Toronto	OMJHL	1	0	0	0	0	....	....	....	....	....	....	....	....	....	....	....	....	....	....	....	....	....	....
1981-82	Markham Waxers	OJHL	48	68	57	125	113	....	....	....	....	....	....	....	....	....	....	....	....	....	....	....	....	....	....
	Toronto	OHL	1	0	0	0	0	....	....	....	....	....	....	....	....	....	....	....	....	....	....	....	....	....	....
1982-83	Toronto	OHL	61	18	20	38	42	....	....	....	....	....	....	....	....	....	....	....	....	....	....	....	....	....	....
1983-84	Toronto	OHL	70	51	54	105	77	....	....	....	....	....	....	....	....	....	....	....	....	....	....	....	....	....	....
1984-85	**Toronto**	**NHL**	**18**	**1**	**1**	**2**	**2**	**0**	**0**	**0**	**26**	**3.8**	**–13**	....	....	....	....	....	....	....	....	....	....	....	....
	St. Catharines	AHL	64	42	48	90	56	....	....	....	....	....	....	....	....	....	....	....	....	....	....	....	....	....	....
1985-86	**Toronto**	**NHL**	**65**	**20**	**37**	**57**	**36**	**5**	**0**	**5**	**197**	**10.2**	**–15**	....	....	....	**10**	**6**	**8**	**14**	**9**	**3**	**0**	**0**	....
	St. Catharines	AHL	19	18	14	32	35	....	....	....	....	....	....	....	....	....	....	....	....	....	....	....	....	....	....
1986-87	**Toronto**	**NHL**	**78**	**35**	**27**	**62**	**114**	**3**	**0**	**7**	**245**	**14.3**	**–3**	....	....	....	**13**	**2**	**3**	**5**	**13**	**0**	**0**	**0**	....
1987-88	**Chicago**	**NHL**	**30**	**13**	**13**	**26**	**40**	**5**	**0**	**3**	**69**	**18.8**	**1**	....	....	....	**3**	**1**	**2**	**3**	**6**	**0**	**0**	**0**	....
1988-89	**Chicago**	**NHL**	**45**	**21**	**19**	**40**	**69**	**8**	**0**	**0**	**124**	**16.9**	**–2**	....	....	....	**12**	**3**	**5**	**8**	**10**	**1**	**0**	**2**	....
1989-90	**Chicago**	**NHL**	**76**	**40**	**30**	**70**	**91**	**13**	**0**	**7**	**235**	**17.0**	**–3**	....	....	....	**20**	**7**	**6**	**13**	**33**	**1**	**0**	**3**	....
1990-91	**Chicago**	**NHL**	**69**	**19**	**35**	**54**	**129**	**2**	**0**	**3**	**192**	**9.9**	**8**	....	....	....	**6**	**1**	**2**	**3**	**15**	**0**	**0**	**0**	....
1991-92	**Chicago**	**NHL**	**11**	**2**	**6**	**8**	**26**	**0**	**0**	**1**	**35**	**5.7**	**–3**	....	....	....	....	....	....	....	....	....	....	....	....
	NY Islanders	**NHL**	**71**	**28**	**42**	**70**	**71**	**3**	**0**	**2**	**210**	**13.3**	**11**	....	....	....	....	....	....	....	....	....	....	....	....
1992-93	**NY Islanders**	**NHL**	**79**	**37**	**50**	**87**	**111**	**12**	**0**	**7**	**264**	**14.0**	**3**	....	....	....	**18**	**9**	**8**	**17**	**37**	**0**	**0**	**0**	....
1993-94	**NY Islanders**	**NHL**	**78**	**42**	**33**	**75**	**139**	**17**	**0**	**5**	**249**	**16.9**	**–9**	....	....	....	**4**	**1**	**0**	**1**	**8**	**1**	**0**	**0**	....
1994-95	**NY Islanders**	**NHL**	**47**	**11**	**15**	**26**	**60**	**3**	**0**	**2**	**133**	**8.3**	**–14**	....	....	....	....	....	....	....	....	....	....	....	....
1995-96	**New Jersey**	**NHL**	**81**	**26**	**35**	**61**	**98**	**6**	**0**	**6**	**192**	**13.5**	**–2**	....	....	....	....	....	....	....	....	....	....	....	....
1996-97	**New Jersey**	**NHL**	**57**	**15**	**19**	**34**	**46**	**1**	**0**	**2**	**124**	**12.1**	**9**	....	....	....	**10**	**1**	**1**	**2**	**18**	**0**	**0**	**0**	....
1997-98	**New Jersey**	**NHL**	**55**	**14**	**10**	**24**	**32**	**3**	**0**	**4**	**111**	**12.6**	**4**	....	....	....	**6**	**0**	**3**	**3**	**2**	**0**	**0**	**0**	....
1998-99	**Toronto**	**NHL**	**78**	**28**	**45**	**73**	**33**	**11**	**0**	**7**	**209**	**13.4**	**26**	**4**	**25.0**	**18:23**	**17**	**6**	**3**	**9**	**12**	**2**	**0**	**1**	**20:37**
99-2000	**Toronto**	**NHL**	**81**	**26**	**37**	**63**	**68**	**9**	**0**	**9**	**151**	**17.2**	**1**	**8**	**50.0**	**16:19**	**12**	**6**	**3**	**9**	**10**	**0**	**0**	**1**	**18:21**
2000-01	**Toronto**	**NHL**	**57**	**8**	**26**	**34**	**46**	**1**	**0**	**1**	**140**	**5.7**	**0**	**3**	**33.3**	**16:02**	**11**	**6**	**3**	**9**	**4**	**4**	**0**	**0**	**16:22**
2001-02	**Chicago**	**NHL**	**34**	**11**	**4**	**15**	**17**	**3**	**0**	**0**	**66**	**16.7**	**0**	**0**	**0.0**	**17:21**	**5**	**1**	**1**	**2**	**0**	**0**	**0**	**0**	**15:45**
2002-03	**Chicago**	**NHL**	**69**	**4**	**13**	**17**	**51**	**0**	**0**	**1**	**91**	**4.4**	**0**	**19**	**36.8**	**12:45**	....	....	....	....	....	....	....	....	....
	Anaheim	**NHL**	**12**	**10**	**3**	**13**	**2**	**1**	**0**	**3**	**27**	**37.0**	**10**	**5**	**20.0**	**13:42**	**21**	**4**	**4**	**8**	**8**	**2**	**0**	**3**	**15:13**
	NHL Totals		**1191**	**411**	**500**	**911**	**1281**	**106**	**0**	**75**	**3090**	**13.3**		**39**	**35.9**	**16:01**	**168**	**54**	**52**	**106**	**185**	**14**	**0**	**10**	**17:24**

AHL First All-Star Team (1985) • Dudley "Red" Garrett Memorial Trophy (Top Rookie – AHL) (1985)

Signed as a free agent by **Toronto,** May 12, 1984. Traded to **Chicago** by **Toronto** with Rick Vaive and Bob McGill for Al Secord and Ed Olczyk, September 3, 1987. Traded to **NY Islanders** by **Chicago** with Adam Creighton for Brent Sutter and Brad Lauer, October 25, 1991. Traded to **New Jersey** by **NY Islanders** for Claude Lemieux, October 3, 1995. Signed as a free agent by **Toronto**, July 30, 1998. Signed as a free agent by **Chicago**, July 17, 2001. • Missed majority of 2001-02 season recovering from ankle injury suffered in game vs. Calgary, November 15, 2001. Traded to **Anaheim** by **Chicago** for Anaheim's 5th round choice (Alexei Ivanov) in 2003 Entry Draft, March 11, 2003.

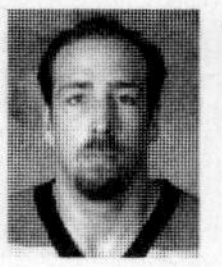

THOMPSON, Brent

(TAWM-suhn, BREHNT)

Defense. Shoots left. 6'2", 205 lbs. Born, Calgary, Alta., January 9, 1971. Los Angeles' 1st choice, 39th overall, in 1989 Entry Draft.

			Regular Season														Playoffs								
Season	Club	League	GP	G	A	Pts	PIM	PP	SH	GW	S	%	+/-	TF	F%	Min	GP	G	A	Pts	PIM	PP	SH	GW	Min
1987-88	Cgy. North Stars	AMHL	25	0	13	13	33	....	....	....	....	....	....	....	....	....	....	....	....	....	....	....	....	....	....
1988-89	Medicine Hat	WHL	72	3	10	13	160	....	....	....	....	....	....	....	....	....	3	0	0	0	2	....	....	....	....
1989-90	Medicine Hat	WHL	68	10	35	45	167	....	....	....	....	....	....	....	....	....	3	0	1	1	14	....	....	....	....
1990-91	Medicine Hat	WHL	51	5	40	45	87	....	....	....	....	....	....	....	....	....	12	1	7	8	16	....	....	....	....
	Phoenix	IHL	....	....	....	....	....	....	....	....	....	....	....	....	....	....	4	0	1	1	6	....	....	....	....
1991-92	**Los Angeles**	**NHL**	**27**	**0**	**5**	**5**	**89**	**0**	**0**	**0**	**18**	**0.0**	**-7**	....	....	....	**4**	**0**	**0**	**0**	**4**	**0**	**0**	**0**	....
	Phoenix	IHL	42	4	13	17	139	....	....	....	....	....	....	....	....	....	....	....	....	....	....	....	....	....	....
1992-93	**Los Angeles**	**NHL**	**30**	**0**	**4**	**4**	**76**	**0**	**0**	**0**	**18**	**0.0**	**-4**	....	....	....	....	....	....	....	....	....	....	....	....
	Phoenix	IHL	22	0	5	5	112	....	....	....	....	....	....	....	....	....	....	....	....	....	....	....	....	....	....
1993-94	**Los Angeles**	**NHL**	**24**	**1**	**0**	**1**	**81**	**0**	**0**	**0**	**9**	**11.1**	**-1**	....	....	....	....	....	....	....	....	....	....	....	....
	Phoenix	IHL	26	1	11	12	118	....	....	....	....	....	....	....	....	....	....	....	....	....	....	....	....	....	....
1994-95	**Winnipeg**	**NHL**	**29**	**0**	**0**	**0**	**78**	**0**	**0**	**0**	**16**	**0.0**	**-17**	....	....	....	....	....	....	....	....	....	....	....	....
1995-96	**Winnipeg**	**NHL**	**10**	**0**	**1**	**1**	**21**	**0**	**0**	**0**	**7**	**0.0**	**-2**	....	....	....	....	....	....	....	....	....	....	....	....
	Springfield	AHL	58	2	10	12	203	....	....	....	....	....	....	....	....	....	10	1	4	5	*55	....	....	....	....
1996-97	**Phoenix**	**NHL**	**1**	**0**	**0**	**0**	**7**	**0**	**0**	**0**	**0**	**0.0**	**-1**	....	....	....	....	....	....	....	....	....	....	....	....
	Springfield	AHL	64	2	15	17	215	....	....	....	....	....	....	....	....	....	17	0	2	2	31	....	....	....	....
	Phoenix	IHL	12	0	1	1	67	....	....	....	....	....	....	....	....	....	....	....	....	....	....	....	....	....	....
1997-98	Hartford	AHL	77	4	15	19	308	....	....	....	....	....	....	....	....	....	15	0	4	4	25	....	....	....	....
1998-99	Hartford	AHL	76	3	15	18	265	....	....	....	....	....	....	....	....	....	7	0	0	0	23	....	....	....	....
99-2000	Louisville Panthers	AHL	67	4	22	26	311	....	....	....	....	....	....	....	....	....	3	0	0	0	11	....	....	....	....
2000-01	Louisville Panthers	AHL	59	1	9	10	170	....	....	....	....	....	....	....	....	....	....	....	....	....	....	....	....	....	....
	Hershey Bears	AHL	15	0	1	1	44	....	....	....	....	....	....	....	....	....	12	0	0	0	10	....	....	....	....
2001-02	Hershey Bears	AHL	79	8	16	24	178	....	....	....	....	....	....	....	....	....	8	0	0	0	21	....	....	....	....
2002-03	Hershey Bears	AHL	61	2	17	19	134	....	....	....	....	....	....	....	....	....	3	0	0	0	7	....	....	....	....
	NHL Totals		**121**	**1**	**10**	**11**	**352**	**0**	**0**	**0**	**68**	**1.5**		....	....	....	**4**	**0**	**0**	**0**	**4**	**0**	**0**	**0**	....

WHL East Second All-Star Team (1991)

Traded to **Winnipeg** by **Los Angeles** with cash for the rights to Ruslan Batyrshin and Winnipeg's 2nd round choice (Marian Cisar) in 1996 Entry Draft, August 8, 1994. Transferred to **Phoenix** after **Winnipeg** franchise relocated, July 1, 1996. Signed as a free agent by **NY Rangers**, August 26, 1997. Signed as a free agent by **Florida**, July 27, 1999. Traded to **Colorado** by **Florida** for future considerations, March 3, 2001.

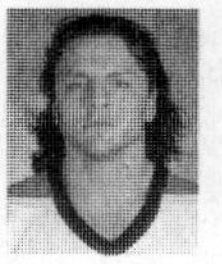

THOMPSON, Rocky

(TAWM-suhn, RAW-kee) **EDM.**

Defense. Shoots right. 6'2", 205 lbs. Born, Calgary, Alta., August 8, 1977. Calgary's 3rd choice, 72nd overall, in 1995 Entry Draft.

			Regular Season														Playoffs								
Season	Club	League	GP	G	A	Pts	PIM	PP	SH	GW	S	%	+/-	TF	F%	Min	GP	G	A	Pts	PIM	PP	SH	GW	Min
1992-93	Spruce Grove	AMHL	65	13	50	63	295	....	....	....	....	....	....	....	....	....	....	....	....	....	....	....	....	....	....
1993-94	Medicine Hat	WHL	68	1	4	5	166	....	....	....	....	....	....	....	....	....	3	0	0	0	2	....	....	....	....
1994-95	Medicine Hat	WHL	63	1	6	7	220	....	....	....	....	....	....	....	....	....	5	0	0	0	17	....	....	....	....
1995-96	Medicine Hat	WHL	71	9	20	29	260	....	....	....	....	....	....	....	....	....	5	2	3	5	26	....	....	....	....
	Saint John Flames	AHL	4	0	0	0	33	....	....	....	....	....	....	....	....	....	....	....	....	....	....	....	....	....	....
1996-97	Medicine Hat	WHL	47	6	9	15	170	....	....	....	....	....	....	....	....	....	....	....	....	....	....	....	....	....	....
	Swift Current	WHL	22	3	5	8	90	....	....	....	....	....	....	....	....	....	10	1	2	3	22	....	....	....	....
1997-98	**Calgary**	**NHL**	**12**	**0**	**0**	**0**	**61**	**0**	**0**	**0**	**3**	**0.0**	**0**	....	....	....	....	....	....	....	....	....	....	....	....
	Saint John Flames	AHL	51	3	0	3	187	....	....	....	....	....	....	....	....	....	18	1	1	2	47	....	....	....	....
1998-99	**Calgary**	**NHL**	**3**	**0**	**0**	**0**	**25**	**0**	**0**	**0**	**0**	**0.0**	**0**	**0**	**0.0**	**2:01**	....	....	....	....	....	....	....	....	....
	Saint John Flames	AHL	27	2	2	4	108	....	....	....	....	....	....	....	....	....	....	....	....	....	....	....	....	....	....
99-2000	Saint John Flames	AHL	53	2	8	10	125	....	....	....	....	....	....	....	....	....	....	....	....	....	....	....	....	....	....
	Louisville Panthers	AHL	3	0	1	1	54	....	....	....	....	....	....	....	....	....	4	0	0	0	4	....	....	....	....
2000-01	**Florida**	**NHL**	**4**	**0**	**0**	**0**	**19**	**0**	**0**	**0**	**0**	**0.0**	**0**	**0**	**0.0**	**1:28**	....	....	....	....	....	....	....	....	....
	Louisville Panthers	AHL	55	3	5	8	193	....	....	....	....	....	....	....	....	....	....	....	....	....	....	....	....	....	....
2001-02	**Florida**	**NHL**	**6**	**0**	**0**	**0**	**12**	**0**	**0**	**0**	**1**	**0.0**	**0**	**1**	**0.0**	**4:03**	....	....	....	....	....	....	....	....	....
	Hershey Bears	AHL	42	0	3	3	143	....	....	....	....	....	....	....	....	....	8	1	0	1	19	....	....	....	....
2002-03	San Antonio	AHL	79	1	11	12	275	....	....	....	....	....	....	....	....	....	3	0	0	0	4	....	....	....	....
	NHL Totals		**25**	**0**	**0**	**0**	**117**	**0**	**0**	**0**	**4**	**0.0**		**1**	**0.0**	**2:47**	....	....	....	....	....	....	....	....	....

Traded to **Florida** by **Calgary** for Filip Kuba, March 16, 2000. Signed as a free agent by **Edmonton**, July 20, 2003.

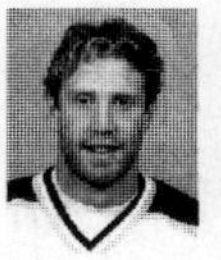

THORNTON, Joe

(THOHRN-tuhn, JOH) **BOS.**

Center. Shoots left. 6'4", 220 lbs. Born, London, Ont., July 2, 1979. Boston's 1st choice, 1st overall, in 1997 Entry Draft.

			Regular Season														Playoffs								
Season	Club	League	GP	G	A	Pts	PIM	PP	SH	GW	S	%	+/-	TF	F%	Min	GP	G	A	Pts	PIM	PP	SH	GW	Min
1993-94	Elgin-Middlesex	OMHA	67	*83	*85	*168	45	....	....	....	....	....	....	....	....	....	....	....	....	....	....	....	....	....	....
	St. Thomas Stars	OJHL-B	6	2	6	8	2	....	....	....	....	....	....	....	....	....	....	....	....	....	....	....	....	....	....
1994-95	St. Thomas Stars	OJHL-B	50	40	64	104	53	....	....	....	....	....	....	....	....	....	....	....	....	....	....	....	....	....	....
1995-96	Sault Ste. Marie	OHL	66	30	46	76	53	....	....	....	....	....	....	....	....	....	4	1	1	2	11	....	....	....	....
1996-97	Sault Ste. Marie	OHL	59	41	81	122	123	....	....	....	....	....	....	....	....	....	11	11	8	19	24	....	....	....	....
1997-98	**Boston**	**NHL**	**55**	**3**	**4**	**7**	**19**	**0**	**0**	**1**	**33**	**9.1**	**-6**	....	....	....	**6**	**0**	**0**	**0**	**9**	**0**	**0**	**0**	....
1998-99	**Boston**	**NHL**	**81**	**16**	**25**	**41**	**69**	**7**	**0**	**1**	**128**	**12.5**	**3**	**1073**	**48.7**	**15:21**	**11**	**3**	**6**	**9**	**4**	**2**	**0**	**2**	**19:52**
99-2000	**Boston**	**NHL**	**81**	**23**	**37**	**60**	**82**	**5**	**0**	**3**	**171**	**13.5**	**-5**	**1861**	**49.5**	**21:18**	....	....	....	....	....	....	....	....	....
2000-01	**Boston**	**NHL**	**72**	**37**	**34**	**71**	**107**	**19**	**1**	**5**	**181**	**20.4**	**-4**	**1651**	**52.1**	**21:45**	....	....	....	....	....	....	....	....	....
2001-02	**Boston**	**NHL**	**66**	**22**	**46**	**68**	**127**	**6**	**0**	**5**	**152**	**14.5**	**7**	**1341**	**49.1**	**19:59**	**6**	**2**	**4**	**6**	**10**	**0**	**0**	**0**	**21:09**
2002-03	**Boston**	**NHL**	**77**	**36**	**65**	**101**	**109**	**12**	**2**	**4**	**196**	**18.4**	**12**	**1766**	**49.5**	**22:33**	**5**	**1**	**2**	**3**	**4**	**1**	**0**	**0**	**20:13**
	NHL Totals		**432**	**137**	**211**	**348**	**513**	**49**	**3**	**19**	**861**	**15.9**		**7692**	**49.9**	**20:08**	**28**	**6**	**12**	**18**	**27**	**3**	**0**	**2**	**20:18**

OHL All-Rookie Team (1996) • OHL Rookie of the Year (1996) • Canadian Major Junior Rookie of the Year (1996) • OHL Second All-Star Team (1997) • NHL Second All-Star Team (2003)

Played in NHL All-Star Game (2002, 2003)

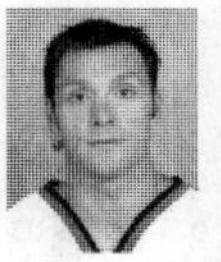

THORNTON, Scott

(THOHRN-tuhn, SKAWT) **S.J.**

Left wing. Shoots left. 6'3", 220 lbs. Born, London, Ont., January 9, 1971. Toronto's 1st choice, 3rd overall, in 1989 Entry Draft.

			Regular Season														Playoffs								
Season	Club	League	GP	G	A	Pts	PIM	PP	SH	GW	S	%	+/-	TF	F%	Min	GP	G	A	Pts	PIM	PP	SH	GW	Min
1986-87	London	OJHL-B	31	10	7	17	10	....	....	....	....	....	....	....	....	....	....	....	....	....	....	....	....	....	....
1987-88	Belleville Bulls	OHL	62	11	19	30	54	....	....	....	....	....	....	....	....	....	6	0	1	1	2	....	....	....	....
1988-89	Belleville Bulls	OHL	59	28	34	62	103	....	....	....	....	....	....	....	....	....	5	1	1	2	6	....	....	....	....
1989-90	Belleville Bulls	OHL	47	21	28	49	91	....	....	....	....	....	....	....	....	....	11	2	10	12	15	....	....	....	....
1990-91	Belleville Bulls	OHL	3	2	1	3	2	....	....	....	....	....	....	....	....	....	6	0	7	7	14	....	....	....	....
	Toronto	**NHL**	**33**	**1**	**3**	**4**	**30**	**0**	**0**	**0**	**31**	**3.2**	**-15**	....	....	....	....	....	....	....	....	....	....	....	....
	Newmarket Saints	AHL	5	1	0	1	4	....	....	....	....	....	....	....	....	....	....	....	....	....	....	....	....	....	....
1991-92	**Edmonton**	**NHL**	**15**	**0**	**1**	**1**	**43**	**0**	**0**	**0**	**11**	**0.0**	**-6**	....	....	....	**1**	**0**	**0**	**0**	**0**	**0**	**0**	**0**	....
	Cape Breton	AHL	49	9	14	23	40	....	....	....	....	....	....	....	....	....	5	1	0	1	8	....	....	....	....
1992-93	**Edmonton**	**NHL**	**9**	**0**	**1**	**1**	**0**	**0**	**0**	**0**	**7**	**0.0**	**-4**	....	....	....	....	....	....	....	....	....	....	....	....
	Cape Breton	AHL	58	23	27	50	102	....	....	....	....	....	....	....	....	....	16	1	2	3	35	....	....	....	....
1993-94	**Edmonton**	**NHL**	**61**	**4**	**7**	**11**	**104**	**0**	**0**	**0**	**65**	**6.2**	**-15**	....	....	....	....	....	....	....	....	....	....	....	....
	Cape Breton	AHL	2	1	1	2	31	....	....	....	....	....	....	....	....	....	....	....	....	....	....	....	....	....	....
1994-95	**Edmonton**	**NHL**	**47**	**10**	**12**	**22**	**89**	**0**	**1**	**1**	**69**	**14.5**	**-4**	....	....	....	....	....	....	....	....	....	....	....	....
1995-96	**Edmonton**	**NHL**	**77**	**9**	**9**	**18**	**149**	**0**	**2**	**3**	**95**	**9.5**	**-25**	....	....	....	....	....	....	....	....	....	....	....	....
1996-97	**Montreal**	**NHL**	**73**	**10**	**10**	**20**	**128**	**1**	**1**	**1**	**110**	**9.1**	**-19**	....	....	....	**5**	**1**	**0**	**1**	**2**	**0**	**0**	**0**	....
1997-98	**Montreal**	**NHL**	**67**	**6**	**9**	**15**	**158**	**1**	**0**	**1**	**51**	**11.8**	**0**	....	....	....	**9**	**0**	**2**	**2**	**10**	**0**	**0**	**0**	....
1998-99	**Montreal**	**NHL**	**47**	**7**	**4**	**11**	**87**	**1**	**0**	**1**	**56**	**12.5**	**-2**	**466**	**52.8**	**12:24**	....	....	....	....	....	....	....	....	....
99-2000	**Montreal**	**NHL**	**35**	**2**	**3**	**5**	**70**	**0**	**0**	**1**	**36**	**5.6**	**-7**	**253**	**51.8**	**12:40**	....	....	....	....	....	....	....	....	....
	Dallas	**NHL**	**30**	**6**	**3**	**9**	**38**	**1**	**0**	**0**	**47**	**12.8**	**-5**	**14**	**14.3**	**13:03**	**23**	**2**	**7**	**9**	**28**	**0**	**0**	**1**	**14:11**
2000-01	**San Jose**	**NHL**	**73**	**19**	**17**	**36**	**114**	**4**	**0**	**1**	**159**	**11.9**	**4**	**29**	**41.4**	**13:54**	**6**	**3**	**0**	**3**	**8**	**0**	**0**	**1**	**15:50**
2001-02	**San Jose**	**NHL**	**77**	**26**	**16**	**42**	**116**	**6**	**0**	**5**	**144**	**18.1**	**11**	**18**	**61.1**	**13:31**	**12**	**3**	**3**	**6**	**6**	**0**	**0**	**0**	**15:51**
2002-03	**San Jose**	**NHL**	**41**	**9**	**12**	**21**	**41**	**4**	**0**	**1**	**64**	**14.1**	**-7**	**6**	**50.0**	**13:53**	....	....	....	....	....	....	....	....	....
	NHL Totals		**685**	**109**	**107**	**216**	**1167**	**18**	**4**	**15**	**945**	**11.5**		**786**	**51.5**	**13:20**	**56**	**9**	**12**	**21**	**54**	**0**	**0**	**2**	**14:55**

Traded to **Edmonton** by **Toronto** with Vincent Damphousse, Peter Ing and Luke Richardson for Grant Fuhr, Glenn Anderson and Craig Berube, September 19, 1991. Traded to **Montreal** by **Edmonton** for Andrei Kovalenko, September 6, 1996. Traded to **Dallas** by **Montreal** for Juha Lind, January 22, 2000. Signed as a free agent by **San Jose**, July 1, 2000. • Missed majority of 2002-03 season recovering from shoulder (October 7, 2002 in training camp) and head (February 21, 2003 vs. Columbus) injuries.

			Regular Season														Playoffs								
Season	Club	League	GP	G	A	Pts	PIM	PP	SH	GW	S	%	+/-	TF	F%	Min	GP	G	A	Pts	PIM	PP	SH	GW	Min

THORNTON, Shawn   (THOHRN-tohn, SHAWN)   **CHI.**

Right wing. Shoots right. 6'1", 203 lbs.   Born, Oshawa, Ont., July 23, 1977. Toronto's 6th choice, 190th overall, in 1997 Entry Draft.

Season	Club	League	GP	G	A	Pts	PIM	PP	SH	GW	S	%	+/-	TF	F%	Min	GP	G	A	Pts	PIM	PP	SH	GW	Min
1995-96	Peterborough	OHL	63	4	10	14	192										24	3	0	3	25				
1996-97	Peterborough	OHL	61	19	10	29	204										11	2	4	6	20				
1997-98	St. John's	AHL	59	0	3	3	225																		
1998-99	St. John's	AHL	78	8	11	19	354										5	0	0	0	9				
99-2000	St. John's	AHL	60	4	12	16	316																		
2000-01	St. John's	AHL	79	5	12	17	320										3	1	2	3	2				
2001-02	Norfolk Admirals	AHL	70	8	14	22	281										4	0	0	0	4				
2002-03	**Chicago**	**NHL**	**13**	**1**	**1**	**2**	**31**	0	0	0	15	6.7	−4	3	66.7	8:30									
	Norfolk Admirals	AHL	50	11	2	13	213										9	0	2	2	28				
	NHL Totals		**13**	**1**	**1**	**2**	**31**	**0**	**0**	**0**	**15**	**6.7**		**3**	**66.7**	**8:30**									

Traded to **Chicago** by **Toronto** for Marty Wilford, September 30, 2001.

TIBBETTS, Billy   (TIH-buhts, BIHL-ee)

Right wing. Shoots right. 6'2", 215 lbs.   Born, Boston, MA, October 14, 1974.

Season	Club	League	GP	G	A	Pts	PIM	PP	SH	GW	S	%	+/-	TF	F%	Min	GP	G	A	Pts	PIM	PP	SH	GW	Min
1992-93	Boston Jr. Bruins	NEJHL	73	60	80	140	150																		
1993-94	Sioux City	USHL	7	1	4	5	27																		
	London Knights	OHL	14	6	6	12	49																		
	Tri-City	WHL	9	0	2	2	39																		
1994-95	Antigonish	MJrHL	30	13	12	25																				
	Birmingham Bulls	ECHL	2	0	1	1	18																		
1995-96	Johnstown Chiefs	ECHL	58	37	31	68	300																		
1996/00					DID NOT PLAY																				
2000-01	**Pittsburgh**	**NHL**	**29**	**1**	**2**	**3**	**79**	0	0	0	16	6.3	−2	115	28.7	7:14									
	Wilkes-Barre	AHL	38	14	24	38	185										12	4	6	10	55				
2001-02	**Pittsburgh**	**NHL**	**33**	**1**	**5**	**6**	**109**	0	0	1	42	2.4	−13	87	36.8	12:05									
	Wilkes-Barre	AHL	24	13	17	30	193																		
	Philadelphia	**NHL**	**9**	**0**	**1**	**1**	**69**	0	0	0	6	0.0	−3	25	32.0	6:41									
2002-03	**NY Rangers**	**NHL**	**11**	**0**	**0**	**0**	**12**	0	0	0	6	0.0	−2	75	41.3	9:58									
	Hartford	AHL	35	7	10	17	172																		
	NHL Totals		**82**	**2**	**8**	**10**	**269**	**0**	**0**	**1**	**70**	**2.9**		**302**	**34.4**	**9:29**									

• Missed 1996-97 through 1999-2000 seasons serving prison sentence that commenced July 12, 1996. Signed as a free agent by **Pittsburgh**, April 10, 2000. Traded to **Philadelphia** by Pittsburgh for Kent Manderville, March 17, 2002. Signed as a free agent by **NY Rangers**, December 16, 2002.

TILEY, Brad   (TIHL-ee, BRAD)

Defense. Shoots left. 6'1", 199 lbs.   Born, Markdale, Ont., July 5, 1971. Boston's 4th choice, 84th overall, in 1991 Entry Draft.

Season	Club	League	GP	G	A	Pts	PIM	PP	SH	GW	S	%	+/-	TF	F%	Min	GP	G	A	Pts	PIM	PP	SH	GW	Min
1987-88	Owen Sound	OJHL-B	45	18	25	43	69																		
1988-89	Sault Ste. Marie	OHL	50	4	11	15	31																		
1989-90	Sault Ste. Marie	OHL	66	9	32	41	47																		
1990-91	Sault Ste. Marie	OHL	66	11	55	66	29										14	4	15	19	12				
1991-92	Maine Mariners	AHL	62	7	22	29	36																		
1992-93	Phoenix	IHL	46	11	27	38	35																		
	Binghamton	AHL	26	6	10	16	19										8	0	1	1	2				
1993-94	Binghamton	AHL	29	6	10	16	6																		
	Phoenix	IHL	35	8	15	23	21																		
1994-95	Detroit Vipers	IHL	56	7	19	26	32										3	1	2	3	0				
	Fort Wayne	IHL	14	1	6	7	2																		
1995-96	Orlando	IHL	69	11	23	34	82										23	2	4	6	16				
1996-97	Phoenix	IHL	66	8	28	36	34																		
	Long Beach	IHL	3	1	0	1	2																		
1997-98	**Phoenix**	**NHL**	**1**	**0**	**0**	**0**	**0**																		
	Springfield	AHL	60	10	31	41	36										4	0	4	4	2				
1998-99	**Phoenix**	**NHL**	**8**	**0**	**0**	**0**	**0**	0	0	0	1	0.0	−1	0	0.0	11:29	1	0	0	0	0	0	0	0	13:11
	Springfield	AHL	69	9	35	44	14										1	0	0	0	0				
99-2000	Springfield	AHL	80	14	54	68	51										5	0	4	4	2				
2000-01	**Philadelphia**	**NHL**	**2**	**0**	**0**	**0**	**0**	0	0	0	1	0.0	−1	0	0.0	15:46									
	Philadelphia	AHL	56	11	19	30	10										10	1	2	3	2				
2001-02	Philadelphia	AHL	56	6	15	21	14																		
2002-03	Philadelphia	AHL	79	8	28	36	28																		
	NHL Totals		**11**	**0**	**0**	**0**	**0**	**0**	**0**	**0**	**2**	**0.0**		**0**	**0.0**	**12:20**	**1**	**0**	**0**	**0**	**0**	**0**	**0**	**0**	**13:11**

Memorial Cup All-Star Team (1991) • AHL First All-Star Team (2000) • Eddie Shore Award (Top Defenseman – AHL) (2000)

Signed as a free agent by **NY Rangers**, September 4, 1992. Traded to **Los Angeles** by NY Rangers for Los Angeles' 11th round choice (Jamie Butt) in 1994 Entry Draft, January 28, 1994. Signed as a free agent by **Phoenix**, September 4, 1997. Signed as a free agent by **Philadelphia**, July 14, 2000.

TIMANDER, Mattias   (tih-MAHN-duhr, MA-tee-uhs)   **NYI**

Defense. Shoots left. 6'2", 230 lbs.   Born, Solleftea, Sweden, April 16, 1974. Boston's 7th choice, 208th overall, in 1992 Entry Draft.

Season	Club	League	GP	G	A	Pts	PIM	PP	SH	GW	S	%	+/-	TF	F%	Min	GP	G	A	Pts	PIM	PP	SH	GW	Min
1992-93	MoDo Jr.	Swede-Jr.	4	0	0	0	0																		
	Husums IF	Swede-2	27	4	9	13	22																		
	MoDo	Sweden	1	0	0	0	0																		
1993-94	MoDo Jr.	Swede-Jr.	3	2	2	4	10																		
	MoDo	Sweden	23	2	2	4	6										11	2	0	2	10				
1994-95	MoDo	Sweden	39	8	9	17	24																		
1995-96	MoDo	Sweden	37	4	10	14	34										7	1	1	2	8				
1996-97	**Boston**	**NHL**	**41**	**1**	**8**	**9**	**14**	0	0	0	62	1.6	−9												
	Providence Bruins	AHL	32	3	11	14	20										10	1	1	2	12				
1997-98	**Boston**	**NHL**	**23**	**1**	**1**	**2**	**6**	0	0	0	17	5.9	−9												
	Providence Bruins	AHL	31	3	7	10	25																		
1998-99	**Boston**	**NHL**	**22**	**0**	**6**	**6**	**10**	0	0	0	22	0.0	4	0	0.0	12:54	4	1	1	2	2	0	0	0	13:03
	Providence Bruins	AHL	43	2	22	24	24																		
99-2000	**Boston**	**NHL**	**60**	**0**	**8**	**8**	**22**	0	0	0	39	0.0	−11	0	0.0	12:29									
	Hershey Bears	AHL	1	0	0	0	2																		
2000-01	**Columbus**	**NHL**	**76**	**2**	**9**	**11**	**24**	0	0	1	68	2.9	−8	2100.0		21:02									
2001-02	**Columbus**	**NHL**	**78**	**4**	**7**	**11**	**44**	1	0	0	68	5.9	−34	1	0.0	19:52									
2002-03	**NY Islanders**	**NHL**	**80**	**3**	**13**	**16**	**24**	0	0	1	83	3.6	−2	0	0.0	17:29	1	0	0	0	0	0	0	0	4:08
	NHL Totals		**380**	**11**	**52**	**63**	**144**	**1**	**0**	**2**	**359**	**3.1**		**3**	**66.7**	**17:40**	**5**	**1**	**1**	**2**	**2**	**0**	**0**	**0**	**11:16**

Selected by **Columbus** from **Boston** in Expansion Draft, June 23, 2000. Traded to **NY Islanders** by **Columbus** for NY Islanders' 4th round choice (Jekabs Redlihs) in 2002 Entry Draft, June 22, 2002.

TIMONEN, Kimmo   (TEEM-oh-nehn, KEE-moh)   **NSH.**

Defense. Shoots left. 5'10", 196 lbs.   Born, Kuopio, Finland, March 18, 1975. Los Angeles' 11th choice, 250th overall, in 1993 Entry Draft.

Season	Club	League	GP	G	A	Pts	PIM	PP	SH	GW	S	%	+/-	TF	F%	Min	GP	G	A	Pts	PIM	PP	SH	GW	Min
1990-91	KalPa Kuopio Jr.	Finn-Jr.	4	0	1	1	2																		
1991-92	KalPa Kuopio Jr.	Finn-Jr.	32	7	10	17	4																		
	KalPa Kuopio	Finland	5	0	0	0	0																		
1992-93	KalPa Kuopio Jr.	Finn-Jr.	16	9	15	24	10																		
	KalPa Kuopio	Finland	33	0	2	2	4																		
1993-94	KalPa Kuopio Jr.	Finn-Jr.	5	4	7	11	0																		
	KalPa Kuopio	Finland	46	6	7	13	55																		
1994-95	TPS Turku Jr.	Finn-Jr.	1	0	0	0	0																		
	TPS Turku	Finland	45	3	4	7	10										13	0	1	1	6				
1995-96	TPS Turku	Finland	48	3	21	24	22										9	1	2	3	12				
1996-97	TPS Turku	Finland	50	10	14	24	18										12	2	7	9	7				
	TPS Turku	EuroHL	6	1	0	1	27										4	0	1	1	0				
1997-98	HIFK Helsinki	Finland	45	10	15	25	59										9	3	4	7	8				
	Finland	Olympics	6	0	2	2	2																		

Season	Club	League	GP	G	A	Pts	PIM	PP	SH	GW	S	%	+/-	TF	F%	Min	GP	G	A	Pts	PIM	PP	SH	GW	Min
			Regular Season														Playoffs								
1998-99	Nashville	NHL	50	4	8	12	30	1	0	0	75	5.3	-4	0	0.0	19:04	....	....	....	....	....	....	....	....	....
	Milwaukee	IHL	29	2	13	15	22	....	....	....	....	....	....	....	....	....	....	....	....	....	....	....	....	....	....
99-2000	Nashville	NHL	51	8	25	33	26	2	1	2	97	8.2	-5	0	0.0	21:06	....	....	....	....	....	....	....	....	....
2000-01	Nashville	NHL	82	12	13	25	50	6	0	3	151	7.9	-6	2	50.0	23:11	....	....	....	....	....	....	....	....	....
2001-02	Nashville	NHL	82	13	29	42	28	9	0	1	154	8.4	2	0	0.0	24:12	....	....	....	....	....	....	....	....	....
	Finland	Olympics	4	0	1	1	2	....	....	....	....	....	....	....	....	....	....	....	....	....	....	....	....	....	....
2002-03	Nashville	NHL	72	6	34	40	46	4	0	0	144	4.2	-3	0	0.0	22:25	....	....	....	....	....	....	....	....	....
	NHL Totals		337	43	109	152	180	22	1	6	621	6.9		2	50.0	22:20	....	....	....	....	....	....	....	....	....

Traded to **Nashville** by **Los Angeles** with Jan Vopat for future considerations, June 26, 1998.

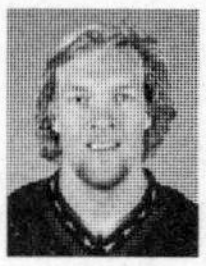

TJARNQVIST, Daniel (TUH-yahrn-kvihst, DAN-yehl) ATL.

Defense. Shoots left. 6'2", 195 lbs. Born, Umea, Sweden, October 14, 1976. Florida's 5th choice, 88th overall, in 1995 Entry Draft.

Season	Club	League	GP	G	A	Pts	PIM	PP	SH	GW	S	%	+/-	TF	F%	Min	GP	G	A	Pts	PIM	PP	SH	GW	Min
1994-95	Rogle	Sweden	18	0	1	1	2	....	....	....	....	....	....	....	....	....	....	....	....	....	....	....	....	....	....
	Rogle	Swede-Q	15	2	3	5	0	....	....	....	....	....	....	....	....	....	....	....	....	....	....	....	....	....	....
1995-96	Rogle	Sweden	22	1	7	8	6	....	....	....	....	....	....	....	....	....	....	....	....	....	....	....	....	....	....
1996-97	Jokerit Helsinki	Finland	44	3	8	11	4	....	....	....	....	....	....	....	....	....	9	0	3	3	4	....	....	....	....
	Jokerit Helsinki	EuroHL	6	1	1	2	2	....	....	....	....	....	....	....	....	....	....	....	....	....	....	....	....	....	....
1997-98	Djurgarden	Sweden	40	5	9	14	12	....	....	....	....	....	....	....	....	....	15	1	1	2	2	....	....	....	....
1998-99	Djurgarden	Sweden	40	4	3	7	16	....	....	....	....	....	....	....	....	....	4	0	0	0	2	....	....	....	....
99-2000	Djurgarden	Sweden	42	3	16	19	8	....	....	....	....	....	....	....	....	....	5	0	0	0	2	....	....	....	....
2000-01	Djurgarden	Sweden	45	9	17	26	26	....	....	....	....	....	....	....	....	....	16	6	5	11	2	....	....	....	....
2001-02	Atlanta	NHL	75	2	16	18	14	1	0	0	68	2.9	-22	4	25.0	21:32	....	....	....	....	....	....	....	....	....
2002-03	Atlanta	NHL	75	3	12	15	26	1	0	0	65	4.6	-20	3	66.7	21:53	....	....	....	....	....	....	....	....	....
	NHL Totals		150	5	28	33	40	2	0	0	133	3.8		7	42.9	21:42	....	....	....	....	....	....	....	....	....

Traded to **Atlanta** by **Florida** with Gord Murphy, Herbert Vasiljevs and Ottawa's 6th round choice (previously acquired, later traded to Dallas – Dallas selected Justin Cox) in 1999 Entry Draft for Trevor Kidd, June 25, 1999.

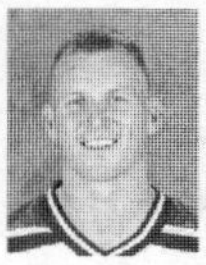

TKACHUK, Keith (kuh-CHUK, KEETH) ST.L.

Left wing. Shoots left. 6'2", 225 lbs. Born, Melrose, MA, March 28, 1972. Winnipeg's 1st choice, 19th overall, in 1990 Entry Draft.

Season	Club	League	GP	G	A	Pts	PIM	PP	SH	GW	S	%	+/-	TF	F%	Min	GP	G	A	Pts	PIM	PP	SH	GW	Min
1988-89	Malden	Hi-School	21	30	16	46	....	....	....	....	....	....	....	....	....	....	....	....	....	....	....	....	....	....	....
1989-90	Malden	Hi-School	6	12	14	26	....	....	....	....	....	....	....	....	....	....	....	....	....	....	....	....	....	....	....
1990-91	Boston University	H-East	36	17	23	40	70	....	....	....	....	....	....	....	....	....	....	....	....	....	....	....	....	....	....
1991-92	Team USA	Nat-Tm	45	10	10	20	141	....	....	....	....	....	....	....	....	....	....	....	....	....	....	....	....	....	....
	United States	Olympics	8	1	1	2	12	....	....	....	....	....	....	....	....	....	....	....	....	....	....	....	....	....	....
	Winnipeg	NHL	17	3	5	8	28	2	0	0	22	13.6	0	....	....	....	7	3	0	3	30	0	0	0	....
1992-93	Winnipeg	NHL	83	28	23	51	201	12	0	2	199	14.1	-13	....	....	....	6	4	0	4	14	1	0	0	....
1993-94	Winnipeg	NHL	84	41	40	81	255	22	3	3	218	18.8	-12	....	....	....	....	....	....	....	....	....	....	....	....
1994-95	Winnipeg	NHL	48	22	29	51	152	7	2	2	129	17.1	-4	....	....	....	....	....	....	....	....	....	....	....	....
1995-96	Winnipeg	NHL	76	50	48	98	156	20	2	6	249	20.1	11	....	....	....	6	1	2	3	22	0	0	0	....
1996-97	Phoenix	NHL	81	*52	34	86	228	9	2	7	296	17.6	-1	....	....	....	7	6	0	6	7	2	0	0	....
1997-98	Phoenix	NHL	69	40	26	66	147	11	0	8	232	17.2	9	....	....	....	6	3	3	6	10	0	0	0	....
	United States	Olympics	4	0	2	2	6	....	....	....	....	....	....	....	....	....	....	....	....	....	....	....	....	....	....
1998-99	Phoenix	NHL	68	36	32	68	151	11	2	7	258	14.0	22	770	47.7	20:59	7	1	3	4	13	1	0	0	25:09
99-2000	Phoenix	NHL	50	22	21	43	82	5	1	1	183	12.0	7	500	50.4	19:21	5	1	1	2	4	1	0	0	18:46
2000-01	Phoenix	NHL	64	29	42	71	108	15	0	4	230	12.6	6	646	51.9	20:11	....	....	....	....	....	....	....	....	....
	St. Louis	NHL	12	6	2	8	14	2	0	1	41	14.6	-3	87	54.0	19:39	15	2	7	9	20	2	0	1	19:17
2001-02	St. Louis	NHL	73	38	37	75	117	13	0	7	244	15.6	21	88	43.2	19:38	10	5	5	10	18	1	0	0	19:24
	United States	Olympics	5	2	0	2	2	....	....	....	....	....	....	....	....	....	....	....	....	....	....	....	....	....	....
2002-03	St. Louis	NHL	56	31	24	55	139	14	0	5	185	16.8	1	346	55.8	19:16	7	1	3	4	14	0	0	0	19:22
	NHL Totals		781	398	363	761	1778	143	12	53	2486	16.0		2437	50.6	19:55	76	27	24	51	152	8	0	1	20:12

NHL Second All-Star Team (1995, 1998)

Played in NHL All-Star Game (1997, 1998, 1999)

Transferred to **Phoenix** after **Winnipeg** franchise relocated, July 1, 1996. Traded to **St. Louis** by **Phoenix** for Michal Handzus, Ladislav Nagy, the rights to Jeff Taffe and St. Louis' 1st round choice (Ben Eager) in 2002 Entry Draft, March 13, 2001.

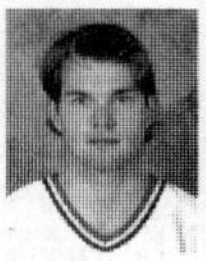

TKACZUK, Daniel (kuh-CHUK, DAN-yehl)

Center. Shoots left. 6'1", 197 lbs. Born, Toronto, Ont., June 10, 1979. Calgary's 1st choice, 6th overall, in 1997 Entry Draft.

Season	Club	League	GP	G	A	Pts	PIM	PP	SH	GW	S	%	+/-	TF	F%	Min	GP	G	A	Pts	PIM	PP	SH	GW	Min
1994-95	Mississauga Reps	MTHL	53	65	66	131	20	....	....	....	....	....	....	....	....	....	....	....	....	....	....	....	....	....	....
1995-96	Barrie Colts	OHL	61	22	39	61	38	....	....	....	....	....	....	....	....	....	7	1	2	3	8	....	....	....	....
1996-97	Barrie Colts	OHL	62	45	48	93	49	....	....	....	....	....	....	....	....	....	9	7	2	9	2	....	....	....	....
1997-98	Barrie Colts	OHL	57	35	40	75	38	....	....	....	....	....	....	....	....	....	6	2	3	5	8	....	....	....	....
1998-99	Barrie Colts	OHL	58	43	62	105	58	....	....	....	....	....	....	....	....	....	12	7	8	15	10	....	....	....	....
99-2000	Saint John Flames	AHL	80	25	41	66	56	....	....	....	....	....	....	....	....	....	3	0	0	0	0	....	....	....	....
2000-01	Calgary	NHL	19	4	7	11	14	1	0	0	34	11.8	1	197	43.2	12:14	....	....	....	....	....	....	....	....	....
	Saint John Flames	AHL	50	15	21	36	48	....	....	....	....	....	....	....	....	....	14	10	9	19	4	....	....	....	....
2001-02	Worcester IceCats	AHL	75	10	27	37	37	....	....	....	....	....	....	....	....	....	3	1	1	2	2	....	....	....	....
2002-03	Bridgeport	AHL	69	9	18	27	44	....	....	....	....	....	....	....	....	....	9	3	7	10	18	....	....	....	....
	NHL Totals		19	4	7	11	14	1	0	0	34	11.8		197	43.1	12:14	....	....	....	....	....	....	....	....	....

OHL First All-Star Team (1999)

Traded to **St. Louis** by **Calgary** with Fred Brathwaite, Sergei Varlamov and Calgary's 9th round choice (Grant Jacobsen) in 2001 Entry Draft for Roman Turek and St. Louis' 4th round choice (Yegor Shastin) in 2001 Entry Draft, June 23, 2001.

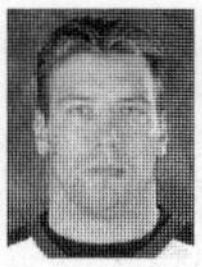

TOBLER, Ryan (TOH-bluhr, RIGH-uhn)

Left wing. Shoots left. 6'3", 227 lbs. Born, Calgary, Alta., May 13, 1976.

Season	Club	League	GP	G	A	Pts	PIM	PP	SH	GW	S	%	+/-	TF	F%	Min	GP	G	A	Pts	PIM	PP	SH	GW	Min
1993-94	Calgary Royals	AJHL	56	32	17	49	195	....	....	....	....	....	....	....	....	....	....	....	....	....	....	....	....	....	....
1994-95	Saskatoon Blades	WHL	61	11	19	30	81	....	....	....	....	....	....	....	....	....	10	1	2	3	8	....	....	....	....
1995-96	Calgary Hitmen	WHL	16	10	3	13	8	....	....	....	....	....	....	....	....	....	....	....	....	....	....	....	....	....	....
	Swift Current	WHL	25	17	11	28	31	....	....	....	....	....	....	....	....	....	6	1	1	2	2	....	....	....	....
1996-97	Swift Current	WHL	39	10	17	27	40	....	....	....	....	....	....	....	....	....	....	....	....	....	....	....	....	....	....
	Moose Jaw	WHL	24	6	15	21	16	....	....	....	....	....	....	....	....	....	12	1	6	7	16	....	....	....	....
1997-98	Lake Charles	WPHL	66	22	34	56	204	....	....	....	....	....	....	....	....	....	4	2	3	5	18	....	....	....	....
	Utah Grizzlies	IHL	3	1	0	1	2	....	....	....	....	....	....	....	....	....	....	....	....	....	....	....	....	....	....
1998-99	Adirondack	AHL	64	9	18	27	157	....	....	....	....	....	....	....	....	....	3	0	0	0	2	....	....	....	....
99-2000	Milwaukee	IHL	78	19	28	47	293	....	....	....	....	....	....	....	....	....	2	0	0	0	0	....	....	....	....
2000-01	Milwaukee	IHL	49	7	9	16	196	....	....	....	....	....	....	....	....	....	....	....	....	....	....	....	....	....	....
	Hartford	AHL	13	1	5	6	71	....	....	....	....	....	....	....	....	....	5	0	0	0	2	....	....	....	....
2001-02	Tampa Bay	NHL	4	0	0	0	5	0	0	0	1	0.0	-2	0	0.0	4:08	....	....	....	....	....	....	....	....	....
	Springfield	AHL	73	17	24	41	215	....	....	....	....	....	....	....	....	....	....	....	....	....	....	....	....	....	....
2002-03	Springfield	AHL	11	0	2	2	44	....	....	....	....	....	....	....	....	....	....	....	....	....	....	....	....	....	....
	Chicago Wolves	AHL	58	13	18	31	143	....	....	....	....	....	....	....	....	....	2	0	0	0	0	....	....	....	....
	NHL Totals		4	0	0	0	5	0	0	0	1	0.0		0	0.0	4:08	....	....	....	....	....	....	....	....	....

Signed as a free agent by **Nashville**, May 1, 2000. Traded to **NY Rangers** by **Nashville** for Bert Robertsson, March 7, 2001. Signed as a free agent by **Tampa Bay**, August 21, 2001.

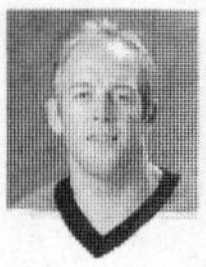

TOMS, Jeff (TAWMS, JEHF) FLA.

Center. Shoots left. 6'5", 200 lbs. Born, Swift Current, Sask., June 4, 1974. New Jersey's 10th choice, 210th overall, in 1992 Entry Draft.

Season	Club	League	GP	G	A	Pts	PIM	PP	SH	GW	S	%	+/-	TF	F%	Min	GP	G	A	Pts	PIM	PP	SH	GW	Min
1990-91	Oakville	OMHA	58	34	47	81	72	....	....	....	....	....	....	....	....	....	....	....	....	....	....	....	....	....	....
1991-92	Sault Ste. Marie	OHL	36	9	5	14	0	....	....	....	....	....	....	....	....	....	16	0	1	1	2	....	....	....	....
1992-93	Sault Ste. Marie	OHL	59	16	23	39	20	....	....	....	....	....	....	....	....	....	16	4	4	8	7	....	....	....	....
1993-94	Sault Ste. Marie	OHL	64	52	45	97	19	....	....	....	....	....	....	....	....	....	14	11	4	15	2	....	....	....	....
1994-95	Atlanta Knights	IHL	40	7	8	15	10	....	....	....	....	....	....	....	....	....	4	0	0	0	4	....	....	....	....
1995-96	Tampa Bay	NHL	1	0	0	0	0	0	0	0	1	0.0	0	....	....	....	....	....	....	....	....	....	....	....	....
	Atlanta Knights	IHL	68	16	18	34	18	....	....	....	....	....	....	....	....	....	1	0	0	0	0	....	....	....	....
1996-97	Tampa Bay	NHL	34	2	8	10	10	0	0	1	53	3.8	2	....	....	....	....	....	....	....	....	....	....	....	....
	Adirondack	AHL	37	11	16	27	8	....	....	....	....	....	....	....	....	....	4	1	2	3	0	....	....	....	....

			Regular Season														Playoffs								
Season	Club	League	GP	G	A	Pts	PIM	PP	SH	GW	S	%	+/-	TF	F%	Min	GP	G	A	Pts	PIM	PP	SH	GW	Min
1997-98	**Tampa Bay**	**NHL**	**13**	**1**	**2**	**3**	**7**	**0**	**0**	**0**	**14**	**7.1**	**–6**	....	....	....	....	....	....	....	....	....	....	....	....
	Washington	**NHL**	**33**	**3**	**4**	**7**	**8**	**0**	**0**	**1**	**55**	**5.5**	**–11**	....	....	....	**1**	**0**	**0**	**0**	**0**	**0**	**0**	**0**	....
1998-99	**Washington**	**NHL**	**21**	**1**	**5**	**6**	**2**	**0**	**0**	**0**	**30**	**3.3**	**0**	**92**	**54.3**	**13:35**	....	....	....	....	....	....	....	....	....
	Portland Pirates	AHL	20	3	7	10	8	....	....	....	....	....	....	....	....	....	....	....	....	....	....	....	....	....	....
99-2000	**Washington**	**NHL**	**20**	**1**	**2**	**3**	**4**	**0**	**0**	**1**	**18**	**5.6**	**–1**	**17**	**52.9**	**8:26**	....	....	....	....	....	....	....	....	....
	Portland Pirates	AHL	33	16	21	37	16	....	....	....	....	....	....	....	....	....	4	1	1	2	2	....	....	....	....
2000-01	**NY Islanders**	**NHL**	**39**	**2**	**4**	**6**	**10**	**0**	**0**	**0**	**37**	**5.4**	**–7**	**172**	**42.4**	**9:44**	....	....	....	....	....	....	....	....	....
	Springfield	AHL	5	6	5	11	0	....	....	....	....	....	....	....	....	....	....	....	....	....	....	....	....	....	....
	NY Rangers	**NHL**	**15**	**1**	**1**	**2**	**0**	**0**	**0**	**0**	**12**	**8.3**	**–3**	**21**	**33.3**	**6:34**	....	....	....	....	....	....	....	....	....
	Hartford	AHL	12	4	9	13	2	....	....	....	....	....	....	....	....	....	5	6	0	6	2	....	....	....	....
2001-02	**NY Rangers**	**NHL**	**38**	**7**	**4**	**11**	**10**	**2**	**0**	**0**	**62**	**11.3**	**–4**	**243**	**45.3**	**10:31**	....	....	....	....	....	....	....	....	....
	Hartford	AHL	9	6	6	12	4	....	....	....	....	....	....	....	....	....	....	....	....	....	....	....	....	....	....
	Pittsburgh	**NHL**	**14**	**2**	**1**	**3**	**4**	**0**	**0**	**0**	**22**	**9.1**	**–5**	**71**	**40.9**	**12:19**	....	....	....	....	....	....	....	....	....
2002-03	**Florida**	**NHL**	**8**	**2**	**2**	**4**	**4**	**0**	**0**	**1**	**12**	**16.7**	**2**	**83**	**53.0**	**11:36**	....	....	....	....	....	....	....	....	....
	San Antonio	AHL	64	30	33	63	28	....	....	....	....	....	....	....	....	....	1	0	0	0	0	....	....	....	....
	NHL Totals		**236**	**22**	**33**	**55**	**59**	**2**	**0**	**4**	**316**	**7.0**		**699**	**46.1**	**10:18**	**1**	**0**	**0**	**0**	**0**	**0**	**0**	**0**	....

Traded to **Tampa Bay** by **New Jersey** for Vancouver's 4th round choice (previously acquired, later traded to New Jersey – later traded to Calgary – Calgary selected Ryan Duthie) in 1994 Entry Draft, May 31, 1994. Claimed by on waivers by **Washington** from **Tampa Bay**, November 19, 1997. Signed as a free agent by **NY Islanders**, July 27, 2000. Claimed on waivers by **NY Rangers** from **NY Islanders**, January 13, 2001. Claimed on waivers by **Pittsburgh** from **NY Rangers**, March 16, 2002. Signed as a free agent by **Florida**, July 11, 2002.

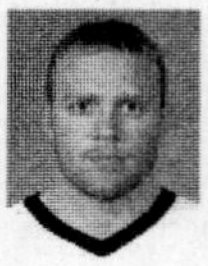

TORRES, Raffi

(TAW-rehs, RA-fee) **EDM.**

Left wing. Shoots left. 6', 210 lbs. Born, Toronto, Ont., October 8, 1981. NY Islanders' 2nd choice, 5th overall, in 2000 Entry Draft.

Season	Club	League	GP	G	A	Pts	PIM	PP	SH	GW	S	%	+/-	TF	F%	Min	GP	G	A	Pts	PIM	PP	SH	GW	Min
1997-98	Thornhill Rattlers	MTJHL	46	17	16	33	90	....	....	....	....	....	....	....	....	....	....	....	....	....	....	....	....	....	....
1998-99	Brampton	OHL	62	35	27	62	32	....	....	....	....	....	....	....	....	....	....	....	....	....	....	....	....	....	....
99-2000	Brampton	OHL	68	43	48	91	40	....	....	....	....	....	....	....	....	....	6	5	2	7	23	....	....	....	....
2000-01	Brampton	OHL	55	33	37	70	76	....	....	....	....	....	....	....	....	....	8	7	4	11	19	....	....	....	....
2001-02	**NY Islanders**	**NHL**	**14**	**0**	**1**	**1**	**6**	**0**	**0**	**0**	**9**	**0.0**	**2**	**0**	**0.0**	**7:35**	....	....	....	....	....	....	....	....	....
	Bridgeport	AHL	59	20	10	30	45	....	....	....	....	....	....	....	....	....	20	8	9	17	26	....	....	....	....
2002-03	**NY Islanders**	**NHL**	**17**	**0**	**5**	**5**	**10**	**0**	**0**	**0**	**12**	**0.0**	**0**	**4**	**25.0**	**7:40**	....	....	....	....	....	....	....	....	....
	Bridgeport	AHL	49	17	15	32	54	....	....	....	....	....	....	....	....	....	....	....	....	....	....	....	....	....	....
	Hamilton	AHL	11	1	7	8	14	....	....	....	....	....	....	....	....	....	23	6	1	7	29	....	....	....	....
	NHL Totals		**31**	**0**	**6**	**6**	**16**	**0**	**0**	**0**	**21**	**0.0**		**4**	**25.0**	**7:38**	....	....	....	....	....	....	....	....	....

OHL All-Rookie Team (1999) • OHL Second All-Star Team (2000, 2001)

Traded to **Edmonton** by **NY Islanders** with Brad Isbister for Janne Niinimaa and Washington's 2nd round choice (previously acquired, NY Islanders selected Evgeni Tunik) in 2003 Entry Draft, March 11, 2003.

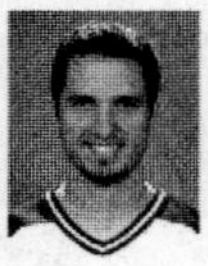

TRAVERSE, Patrick

(tra-VAIRZ, PAT-rihk) **MTL.**

Defense. Shoots left. 6'4", 207 lbs. Born, Montreal, Que., March 14, 1974. Ottawa's 3rd choice, 50th overall, in 1992 Entry Draft.

Season	Club	League	GP	G	A	Pts	PIM	PP	SH	GW	S	%	+/-	TF	F%	Min	GP	G	A	Pts	PIM	PP	SH	GW	Min
1990-91	Mtl-Bourassa	QAAA	42	4	19	23	10	....	....	....	....	....	....	....	....	....	5	0	3	3	2	....	....	....	....
1991-92	Shawinigan	QMJHL	59	3	11	14	12	....	....	....	....	....	....	....	....	....	10	0	0	0	4	....	....	....	....
1992-93	Shawinigan	QMJHL	53	5	24	29	24	....	....	....	....	....	....	....	....	....	....	....	....	....	....	....	....	....	....
	St-Jean Lynx	QMJHL	15	1	6	7	0	....	....	....	....	....	....	....	....	....	4	0	1	1	2	....	....	....	....
	New Haven	AHL	2	0	0	0	2	....	....	....	....	....	....	....	....	....	....	....	....	....	....	....	....	....	....
1993-94	St-Jean Lynx	QMJHL	66	15	37	52	30	....	....	....	....	....	....	....	....	....	5	0	4	4	4	....	....	....	....
	P.E.I. Senators	AHL	3	0	1	1	2	....	....	....	....	....	....	....	....	....	....	....	....	....	....	....	....	....	....
1994-95	P.E.I. Senators	AHL	70	5	13	18	19	....	....	....	....	....	....	....	....	....	7	0	2	2	0	....	....	....	....
1995-96	**Ottawa**	**NHL**	**5**	**0**	**0**	**0**	**2**	**0**	**0**	**0**	**2**	**0.0**	**–1**	....	....	....	....	....	....	....	....	....	....	....	....
	P.E.I. Senators	AHL	55	4	21	25	32	....	....	....	....	....	....	....	....	....	5	1	2	3	2	....	....	....	....
1996-97	Worcester IceCats	AHL	24	0	4	4	23	....	....	....	....	....	....	....	....	....	....	....	....	....	....	....	....	....	....
	Grand Rapids	IHL	10	2	1	3	10	....	....	....	....	....	....	....	....	....	2	0	1	1	2	....	....	....	....
1997-98	Hershey Bears	AHL	71	14	15	29	67	....	....	....	....	....	....	....	....	....	7	1	3	4	4	....	....	....	....
1998-99	**Ottawa**	**NHL**	**46**	**1**	**9**	**10**	**22**	**0**	**0**	**0**	**35**	**2.9**	**12**	**0**	**0.0**	**14:56**	....	....	....	....	....	....	....	....	....
99-2000	**Ottawa**	**NHL**	**66**	**6**	**17**	**23**	**21**	**1**	**0**	**0**	**73**	**8.2**	**17**	**0**	**0.0**	**18:43**	**6**	**0**	**0**	**0**	**2**	**0**	**0**	**0**	**17:49**
2000-01	**Anaheim**	**NHL**	**15**	**1**	**0**	**1**	**6**	**0**	**0**	**0**	**7**	**14.3**	**–6**	**0**	**0.0**	**17:19**	....	....	....	....	....	....	....	....	....
	Boston	**NHL**	**37**	**2**	**6**	**8**	**14**	**1**	**0**	**1**	**39**	**5.1**	**4**	**0**	**0.0**	**16:38**	....	....	....	....	....	....	....	....	....
	Montreal	**NHL**	**19**	**2**	**3**	**5**	**10**	**0**	**0**	**0**	**16**	**12.5**	**–8**	**0**	**0.0**	**21:36**	....	....	....	....	....	....	....	....	....
2001-02	**Montreal**	**NHL**	**25**	**2**	**3**	**5**	**14**	**2**	**0**	**0**	**24**	**8.3**	**–7**	**0**	**0.0**	**18:14**	....	....	....	....	....	....	....	....	....
	Quebec Citadelles	AHL	4	0	2	2	4	....	....	....	....	....	....	....	....	....	....	....	....	....	....	....	....	....	....
2002-03	**Montreal**	**NHL**	**65**	**0**	**13**	**13**	**24**	**0**	**0**	**0**	**63**	**0.0**	**–9**	**0**	**0.0**	**20:12**	....	....	....	....	....	....	....	....	....
	NHL Totals		**278**	**14**	**51**	**65**	**113**	**4**	**0**	**1**	**259**	**5.4**		**0**	**0.0**	**18:14**	**6**	**0**	**0**	**0**	**2**	**0**	**0**	**0**	**17:49**

Traded to **Anaheim** by **Ottawa** for Joel Kwiatkowski, June 12, 2000. Traded to **Boston** by **Anaheim** with Andrei Nazarov for Samuel Pahlsson, November 18, 2000. • Missed majority of 2001-02 season recovering from knee (November 3, 2001 vs. Calgary) and head (January 10, 2002 vs. NY Islanders) injuries. Traded to **Montreal** by **Boston** for Eric Weinrich, February 21, 2001.

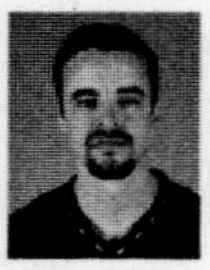

TREMBLAY, Yannick

(TRAHM-blay, YA-nihk) **ATL.**

Defense. Shoots right. 6'2", 200 lbs. Born, Pointe-aux-Trembles, Que., November 15, 1975. Toronto's 4th choice, 145th overall, in 1995 Entry Draft.

Season	Club	League	GP	G	A	Pts	PIM	PP	SH	GW	S	%	+/-	TF	F%	Min	GP	G	A	Pts	PIM	PP	SH	GW	Min
1991-92	Mtl-Bourassa	QAAA	35	2	5	7	55	....	....	....	....	....	....	....	....	....	8	0	4	4	2	....	....	....	....
1992-93	Mtl-Bourassa	CEGEP	21	2	5	7	10	....	....	....	....	....	....	....	....	....	3	0	0	0	2	....	....	....	....
1993-94	St. Thomas	AUAA	25	2	3	5	10	....	....	....	....	....	....	....	....	....	....	....	....	....	....	....	....	....	....
1994-95	Beauport	QMJHL	70	10	32	42	22	....	....	....	....	....	....	....	....	....	17	6	8	14	6	....	....	....	....
1995-96	Beauport	QMJHL	61	12	33	45	42	....	....	....	....	....	....	....	....	....	20	3	16	19	18	....	....	....	....
	St. John's	AHL	3	0	1	1	0	....	....	....	....	....	....	....	....	....	....	....	....	....	....	....	....	....	....
1996-97	**Toronto**	**NHL**	**5**	**0**	**0**	**0**	**0**	**0**	**0**	**0**	**2**	**0.0**	**–4**	....	....	....	....	....	....	....	....	....	....	....	....
	St. John's	AHL	67	7	25	32	34	....	....	....	....	....	....	....	....	....	11	2	9	11	0	....	....	....	....
1997-98	**Toronto**	**NHL**	**38**	**2**	**4**	**6**	**6**	**1**	**0**	**0**	**45**	**4.4**	**–6**	....	....	....	....	....	....	....	....	....	....	....	....
	St. John's	AHL	17	3	7	10	4	....	....	....	....	....	....	....	....	....	4	0	1	1	5	....	....	....	....
1998-99	**Toronto**	**NHL**	**35**	**2**	**7**	**9**	**16**	**0**	**0**	**0**	**37**	**5.4**	**0**	**0**	**0.0**	**17:39**	....	....	....	....	....	....	....	....	....
99-2000	**Atlanta**	**NHL**	**75**	**10**	**21**	**31**	**22**	**4**	**1**	**2**	**139**	**7.2**	**–42**	**3**	**0.0**	**19:27**	....	....	....	....	....	....	....	....	....
2000-01	**Atlanta**	**NHL**	**46**	**4**	**8**	**12**	**30**	**1**	**0**	**1**	**102**	**3.9**	**–6**	**1**	**100.0**	**20:27**	....	....	....	....	....	....	....	....	....
2001-02	**Atlanta**	**NHL**	**66**	**9**	**15**	**24**	**47**	**1**	**0**	**1**	**115**	**7.8**	**–15**	**0**	**0.0**	**21:50**	....	....	....	....	....	....	....	....	....
2002-03	**Atlanta**	**NHL**	**75**	**8**	**22**	**30**	**32**	**5**	**0**	**1**	**151**	**5.3**	**–27**	**1**	**0.0**	**21:45**	....	....	....	....	....	....	....	....	....
	NHL Totals		**340**	**35**	**77**	**112**	**153**	**12**	**1**	**5**	**591**	**5.9**		**5**	**20.0**	**20:30**	....	....	....	....	....	....	....	....	....

Claimed by **Atlanta** from **Toronto** in Expansion Draft, June 25, 1999.

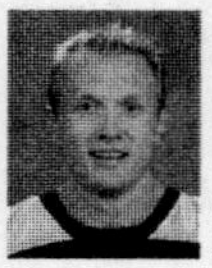

TREPANIER, Pascal

(TREHP-uhn-yay, PAS-kal) **T.B.**

Defense. Shoots right. 6', 210 lbs. Born, Gaspe, Que., September 4, 1973.

Season	Club	League	GP	G	A	Pts	PIM	PP	SH	GW	S	%	+/-	TF	F%	Min	GP	G	A	Pts	PIM	PP	SH	GW	Min
1989-90	Jonquiere Elites	QAAA	40	2	8	10	46	....	....	....	....	....	....	....	....	....	....	....	....	....	....	....	....	....	....
1990-91	Hull Olympiques	QMJHL	46	3	3	6	56	....	....	....	....	....	....	....	....	....	4	0	2	2	7	....	....	....	....
1991-92	Trois-Rivieres	QMJHL	53	4	18	22	125	....	....	....	....	....	....	....	....	....	15	3	5	8	21	....	....	....	....
1992-93	Sherbrooke	QMJHL	59	15	33	48	130	....	....	....	....	....	....	....	....	....	15	5	7	12	36	....	....	....	....
1993-94	Sherbrooke	QMJHL	48	16	41	57	67	....	....	....	....	....	....	....	....	....	12	1	8	9	14	....	....	....	....
1994-95	Dayton Bombers	ECHL	36	16	28	44	113	....	....	....	....	....	....	....	....	....	9	2	4	6	20	....	....	....	....
	Kalamazoo Wings	IHL	14	1	2	3	47	....	....	....	....	....	....	....	....	....	....	....	....	....	....	....	....	....	....
	Cornwall Aces	AHL	4	0	0	0	9	....	....	....	....	....	....	....	....	....	14	2	7	9	32	....	....	....	....
1995-96	Cornwall Aces	AHL	70	13	20	33	142	....	....	....	....	....	....	....	....	....	8	1	2	3	24	....	....	....	....
1996-97	Hershey Bears	AHL	73	14	39	53	151	....	....	....	....	....	....	....	....	....	23	6	13	19	59	....	....	....	....
1997-98	**Colorado**	**NHL**	**15**	**0**	**1**	**1**	**18**	**0**	**0**	**0**	**9**	**0.0**	**–2**	....	....	....	....	....	....	....	....	....	....	....	....
	Hershey Bears	AHL	43	13	18	31	105	....	....	....	....	....	....	....	....	....	7	4	2	6	8	....	....	....	....
1998-99	**Anaheim**	**NHL**	**45**	**2**	**4**	**6**	**48**	**0**	**0**	**1**	**49**	**4.1**	**0**	**1**	**0.0**	**12:42**	....	....	....	....	....	....	....	....	....
99-2000	**Anaheim**	**NHL**	**37**	**0**	**4**	**4**	**54**	**0**	**0**	**0**	**33**	**0.0**	**2**	**1**	**0.0**	**11:18**	....	....	....	....	....	....	....	....	....
2000-01	**Anaheim**	**NHL**	**57**	**6**	**4**	**10**	**73**	**3**	**0**	**0**	**86**	**7.0**	**–12**	**1**	**100.0**	**16:47**	....	....	....	....	....	....	....	....	....
2001-02	**Colorado**	**NHL**	**74**	**4**	**9**	**13**	**59**	**2**	**0**	**0**	**87**	**4.6**	**4**	**0**	**0.0**	**14:37**	**2**	**0**	**0**	**0**	**0**	**0**	**0**	**0**	**5:43**

Season	Club	League	GP	G	A	Pts	PIM	PP	SH	GW	S	%	+/-	TF	F%	Min	GP	G	A	Pts	PIM	PP	SH	GW	Min
						Regular Season														Playoffs					
2002-03	**Nashville**	**NHL**	**1**	**0**	**0**	**0**	**0**	**0**	**0**	**0**	**1**	**0.0**	**0**	**0**	**0.0**	**9:55**	....	....	....	....	....	....	....	....	....
	Milwaukee	AHL	52	9	15	24	33	....	....	....	....	....	....	....	....	....	....	....	....	....	....	....	....	....	....
	San Antonio	AHL	12	4	6	10	10	....	....	....	....	....	....	....	....	....	2	0	0	0	2	....	....	....	....
	NHL Totals		**229**	**12**	**22**	**34**	**252**	**5**	**0**	**1**	**265**	**4.5**		**3**	**33.3**	**14:12**	**2**	**0**	**0**	**0**	**0**	**0**	**0**	**0**	**5:43**

AHL Second All-Star Team (1997)

Signed as a free agent by **Colorado**, August 30, 1995. Claimed by **Anaheim** from **Colorado** in Waiver Draft, October 5, 1998. Signed as a free agent by **Colorado**, September, 2001. Signed as a free agent by **Nashville**, July 16, 2002. Traded to **Florida** by **Nashville** for Wade Flaherty, March 9, 2003. Signed as a free agent by **Tampa Bay**, July 23, 2003.

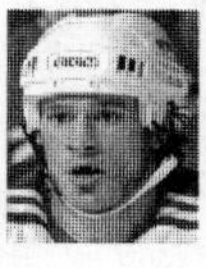

TRIPP, John (TRIHP, JAWN) L.A.

Right wing. Shoots right. 6'2", 215 lbs. Born, Kingston, Ont., May 4, 1977. Calgary's 3rd choice, 42nd overall, in 1997 Entry Draft.

Season	Club	League	GP	G	A	Pts	PIM	PP	SH	GW	S	%	+/-	TF	F%	Min	GP	G	A	Pts	PIM	PP	SH	GW	Min
1993-94	St. Mary's Lincolns	OJHL-B	42	15	29	44	116	....	....	....	....	....	....	....	....	....	....	....	....	....	....	....	....	....	....
1994-95	Oshawa Generals	OHL	58	6	11	17	53	....	....	....	....	....	....	....	....	....	7	0	1	1	4	....	....	....	....
1995-96	Oshawa Generals	OHL	56	13	14	27	95	....	....	....	....	....	....	....	....	....	5	1	1	2	13	....	....	....	....
1996-97	Oshawa Generals	OHL	59	28	20	48	126	....	....	....	....	....	....	....	....	....	18	*16	10	26	42	....	....	....	....
1997-98	Roanoke Express	ECHL	9	0	2	2	22	....	....	....	....	....	....	....	....	....	....	....	....	....	....	....	....	....	....
	Saint John Flames	AHL	61	1	11	12	66	....	....	....	....	....	....	....	....	....	2	0	1	1	0	....	....	....	....
1998-99	Saint John Flames	AHL	2	0	0	0	10	....	....	....	....	....	....	....	....	....	....	....	....	....	....	....	....	....	....
	Johnstown Chiefs	ECHL	7	2	0	2	12	....	....	....	....	....	....	....	....	....	....	....	....	....	....	....	....	....	....
99-2000	Johnstown Chiefs	ECHL	38	13	11	24	64	....	....	....	....	....	....	....	....	....	....	....	....	....	....	....	....	....	....
	Saint John Flames	AHL	29	8	7	15	38	....	....	....	....	....	....	....	....	....	3	0	0	0	2	....	....	....	....
2000-01	Pensacola	ECHL	36	19	14	33	110	....	....	....	....	....	....	....	....	....	....	....	....	....	....	....	....	....	....
	Houston Aeros	IHL	15	0	6	6	14	....	....	....	....	....	....	....	....	....	....	....	....	....	....	....	....	....	....
	Hershey Bears	AHL	5	0	1	1	0	....	....	....	....	....	....	....	....	....	....	....	....	....	....	....	....	....	....
	Milwaukee	IHL	12	0	1	1	31	....	....	....	....	....	....	....	....	....	....	....	....	....	....	....	....	....	....
2001-02	Pensacola	ECHL	49	25	27	52	114	....	....	....	....	....	....	....	....	....	....	....	....	....	....	....	....	....	....
	Hartford	AHL	23	4	9	13	22	....	....	....	....	....	....	....	....	....	10	4	2	6	17	....	....	....	....
2002-03	**NY Rangers**	**NHL**	**9**	**1**	**2**	**3**	**2**	**0**	**0**	**0**	**16**	**6.3**	**1**	**0**	**0.0**	**8:43**	....	....	....	....	....	....	....	....	....
	Hartford	AHL	57	29	21	50	68	....	....	....	....	....	....	....	....	....	2	0	0	0	2	....	....	....	....
	NHL Totals		**9**	**1**	**2**	**3**	**2**	**0**	**0**	**0**	**16**	**6.3**		**0**	**0.0**	**8:43**	....	....	....	....	....	....	....	....	....

• Re-entered NHL Entry Draft. Originally Colorado's 3rd choice, 77th overall, in 1995 Entry Draft.

Signed to tryout contract by **Hartford** (AHL), January 29, 2002. Signed as a free agent by **Hartford** (AHL), September 3, 2002. Signed as a free agent by **Los Angeles**, August 6, 2003.

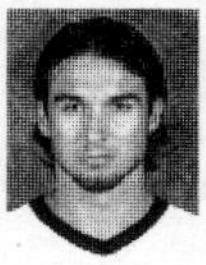

TRNKA, Pavel (truhn-KAH, PAH-vehl) FLA.

Defense. Shoots left. 6'2", 206 lbs. Born, Plzen, Czech., July 27, 1976. Anaheim's 5th choice, 106th overall, in 1994 Entry Draft.

Season	Club	League	GP	G	A	Pts	PIM	PP	SH	GW	S	%	+/-	TF	F%	Min	GP	G	A	Pts	PIM	PP	SH	GW	Min
1993-94	HC Skoda Plzen	Czech	12	0	1	1	....	....	....	....	....	....	....	....	....	....	....	....	....	....	....	....	....	....	....
1994-95	HC Kladno	Czech	28	0	5	5	24	....	....	....	....	....	....	....	....	....	....	....	....	....	....	....	....	....	....
	Plzen	Czech	6	0	0	0	0	....	....	....	....	....	....	....	....	....	....	....	....	....	....	....	....	....	....
1995-96	Baltimore Bandits	AHL	69	2	6	8	44	....	....	....	....	....	....	....	....	....	6	0	0	0	2	....	....	....	....
1996-97	Baltimore Bandits	AHL	69	6	14	20	86	....	....	....	....	....	....	....	....	....	3	0	0	0	2	....	....	....	....
1997-98	**Anaheim**	**NHL**	**48**	**3**	**4**	**7**	**40**	**1**	**0**	**0**	**46**	**6.5**	**–4**	....	....	....	....	....	....	....	....	....	....	....	....
	Cincinnati	AHL	23	3	5	8	28	....	....	....	....	....	....	....	....	....	....	....	....	....	....	....	....	....	....
1998-99	**Anaheim**	**NHL**	**63**	**0**	**4**	**4**	**60**	**0**	**0**	**0**	**50**	**0.0**	**–6**	**0**	**0.0**	**16:06**	**4**	**0**	**1**	**1**	**2**	**0**	**0**	**0**	**21:26**
99-2000	**Anaheim**	**NHL**	**57**	**2**	**15**	**17**	**34**	**0**	**0**	**0**	**54**	**3.7**	**12**	**0**	**0.0**	**19:21**	....	....	....	....	....	....	....	....	....
2000-01	**Anaheim**	**NHL**	**59**	**1**	**7**	**8**	**42**	**0**	**0**	**0**	**59**	**1.7**	**–12**	**0**	**0.0**	**20:07**	....	....	....	....	....	....	....	....	....
2001-02	**Anaheim**	**NHL**	**71**	**2**	**11**	**13**	**66**	**1**	**0**	**0**	**78**	**2.6**	**–5**	**0**	**0.0**	**17:03**	....	....	....	....	....	....	....	....	....
2002-03	**Anaheim**	**NHL**	**24**	**3**	**6**	**9**	**6**	**1**	**0**	**0**	**33**	**9.1**	**2**	**0**	**0.0**	**15:60**	....	....	....	....	....	....	....	....	....
	Florida	**NHL**	**22**	**0**	**3**	**3**	**24**	**0**	**0**	**0**	**25**	**0.0**	**–1**	**0**	**0.0**	**17:24**	....	....	....	....	....	....	....	....	....
	NHL Totals		**344**	**11**	**50**	**61**	**272**	**3**	**0**	**0**	**345**	**3.2**		**0**	**0.0**	**17:51**	**4**	**0**	**1**	**1**	**2**	**0**	**0**	**0**	**21:26**

Traded to **Florida** by **Anaheim** with Matt Cullen and Anaheim's 4th round choice (James Pemberton) in 2003 Entry Draft for Sandis Ozolinsh and Lance Ward, January 30, 2003.

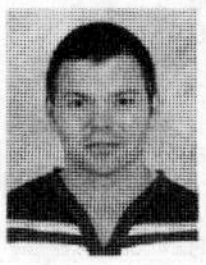

TRUDEL, Jean-Guy (TROO-dehl, zhawn-gee)

Left wing. Shoots left. 5'11", 202 lbs. Born, Sudbury, Ont., October 18, 1975.

Season	Club	League	GP	G	A	Pts	PIM	PP	SH	GW	S	%	+/-	TF	F%	Min	GP	G	A	Pts	PIM	PP	SH	GW	Min
1991-92	Beauport	QMJHL	35	5	7	12	20	....	....	....	....	....	....	....	....	....	....	....	....	....	....	....	....	....	....
1992-93	Beauport	QMJHL	56	1	4	5	20	....	....	....	....	....	....	....	....	....	....	....	....	....	....	....	....	....	....
	Verdun	QMJHL	10	1	0	1	0	....	....	....	....	....	....	....	....	....	2	0	0	0	5	....	....	....	....
1993-94			DID NOT PLAY																						
1994-95	Hull Olympiques	QMJHL	54	29	42	71	76	....	....	....	....	....	....	....	....	....	19	4	13	17	25	....	....	....	....
1995-96	Hull Olympiques	QMJHL	70	50	71	121	96	....	....	....	....	....	....	....	....	....	17	11	18	29	8	....	....	....	....
1996-97	Quad City	ColHL	5	8	7	15	4	....	....	....	....	....	....	....	....	....	....	....	....	....	....	....	....	....	....
	Chicago Wolves	IHL	6	1	2	3	2	....	....	....	....	....	....	....	....	....	....	....	....	....	....	....	....	....	....
	San Antonio	IHL	12	1	5	6	4	....	....	....	....	....	....	....	....	....	....	....	....	....	....	....	....	....	....
	Peoria Rivermen	ECHL	37	25	29	54	47	....	....	....	....	....	....	....	....	....	9	9	10	19	22	....	....	....	....
1997-98	Peoria Rivermen	ECHL	62	39	74	113	147	....	....	....	....	....	....	....	....	....	3	0	0	0	2	....	....	....	....
1998-99	Kansas City	IHL	76	24	25	49	66	....	....	....	....	....	....	....	....	....	3	1	0	1	0	....	....	....	....
99-2000	**Phoenix**	**NHL**	**1**	**0**	**0**	**0**	**0**	**0**	**0**	**0**	**0**	**0.0**	**–1**	**0**	**0.0**	**4:33**	....	....	....	....	....	....	....	....	....
	Springfield	AHL	72	34	39	73	80	....	....	....	....	....	....	....	....	....	3	0	1	1	4	....	....	....	....
2000-01	Springfield	AHL	80	34	65	99	89	....	....	....	....	....	....	....	....	....	....	....	....	....	....	....	....	....	....
2001-02	**Phoenix**	**NHL**	**3**	**0**	**0**	**0**	**2**	**0**	**0**	**0**	**1**	**0.0**	**0**	**0**	**0.0**	**8:42**	....	....	....	....	....	....	....	....	....
	Springfield	AHL	76	22	48	70	83	....	....	....	....	....	....	....	....	....	....	....	....	....	....	....	....	....	....
2002-03	**Minnesota**	**NHL**	**1**	**0**	**0**	**0**	**2**	**0**	**0**	**0**	**0**	**0.0**	**0**	**0**	**0.0**	**5:37**	....	....	....	....	....	....	....	....	....
	Houston Aeros	AHL	79	31	54	85	85	....	....	....	....	....	....	....	....	....	23	7	9	16	22	....	....	....	....
	NHL Totals		**5**	**0**	**0**	**0**	**4**	**0**	**0**	**0**	**1**	**0.0**		**0**	**0.0**	**7:15**	....	....	....	....	....	....	....	....	....

QMJHL Second All-Star Team (1996) • ECHL First All-Star Team (1998) • AHL Second All-Star Team (2000, 2002) • AHL First All-Star Team (2001, 2003)

• Sat out 1993-94 season to regain eligibility for U.S. College scholarship. Signed as a free agent by **Phoenix**, July 17, 1999. Signed as a free agent by **Minnesota**, July 16, 2002.

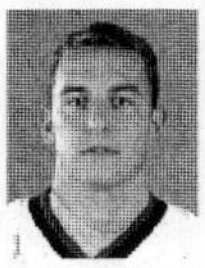

TSELIOS, Nikos (TSEHL-ee-ohs, NEE-kohs) PHX.

Defense. Shoots left. 6'5", 210 lbs. Born, Oak Park, IL, January 20, 1979. Carolina's 1st choice, 22nd overall, in 1997 Entry Draft.

Season	Club	League	GP	G	A	Pts	PIM	PP	SH	GW	S	%	+/-	TF	F%	Min	GP	G	A	Pts	PIM	PP	SH	GW	Min
1995-96	Chicago	MEHL	27	5	8	13	40	....	....	....	....	....	....	....	....	....	....	....	....	....	....	....	....	....	....
1996-97	Belleville Bulls	OHL	64	9	37	46	61	....	....	....	....	....	....	....	....	....	6	1	1	2	2	....	....	....	....
1997-98	Belleville Bulls	OHL	20	2	10	12	16	....	....	....	....	....	....	....	....	....	....	....	....	....	....	....	....	....	....
	Plymouth Whalers	OHL	41	8	20	28	27	....	....	....	....	....	....	....	....	....	15	1	8	9	27	....	....	....	....
1998-99	Plymouth Whalers	OHL	60	21	39	60	60	....	....	....	....	....	....	....	....	....	11	4	10	14	8	....	....	....	....
99-2000	Cincinnati	IHL	80	3	19	22	75	....	....	....	....	....	....	....	....	....	10	0	2	2	4	....	....	....	....
2000-01	Cincinnati	IHL	79	7	18	25	98	....	....	....	....	....	....	....	....	....	5	0	3	3	0	....	....	....	....
2001-02	**Carolina**	**NHL**	**2**	**0**	**0**	**0**	**6**	**0**	**0**	**0**	**3**	**0.0**	**–2**	**0**	**0.0**	**13:13**	....	....	....	....	....	....	....	....	....
	Lowell	AHL	70	3	16	19	64	....	....	....	....	....	....	....	....	....	....	....	....	....	....	....	....	....	....
2002-03	Lowell	AHL	61	4	8	12	65	....	....	....	....	....	....	....	....	....	....	....	....	....	....	....	....	....	....
	Springfield	AHL	13	0	2	2	12	....	....	....	....	....	....	....	....	....	6	0	0	0	4	....	....	....	....
	NHL Totals		**2**	**0**	**0**	**0**	**6**	**0**	**0**	**0**	**3**	**0.0**		**0**	**0.0**	**13:13**	....	....	....	....	....	....	....	....	....

OHL All-Rookie Team (1997)

Signed as a free agent by **Phoenix**, July 21, 2003.

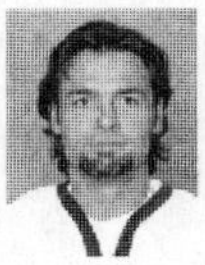

TUCKER, Darcy (TUH-kuhr, DAHR-see) TOR.

Right wing. Shoots left. 5'10", 178 lbs. Born, Castor, Alta., March 15, 1975. Montreal's 8th choice, 151st overall, in 1993 Entry Draft.

Season	Club	League	GP	G	A	Pts	PIM	PP	SH	GW	S	%	+/-	TF	F%	Min	GP	G	A	Pts	PIM	PP	SH	GW	Min
1990-91	Red Deer	AMHL	47	70	90	160	48	....	....	....	....	....	....	....	....	....	....	....	....	....	....	....	....	....	....
1991-92	Kamloops Blazers	WHL	26	3	10	13	32	....	....	....	....	....	....	....	....	....	9	0	1	1	16	....	....	....	....
1992-93	Kamloops Blazers	WHL	67	31	58	89	155	....	....	....	....	....	....	....	....	....	13	7	6	13	34	....	....	....	....
1993-94	Kamloops Blazers	WHL	66	52	88	140	143	....	....	....	....	....	....	....	....	....	19	9	*18	*27	43	....	....	....	....
1994-95	Kamloops Blazers	WHL	64	64	73	137	94	....	....	....	....	....	....	....	....	....	21	*16	15	*31	19	....	....	....	....
1995-96	**Montreal**	**NHL**	**3**	**0**	**0**	**0**	**0**	**0**	**0**	**0**	**1**	**0.0**	**–1**	....	....	....	....	....	....	....	....	....	....	....	....
	Fredericton	AHL	74	29	64	93	174	....	....	....	....	....	....	....	....	....	7	7	3	10	14	....	....	....	....
1996-97	**Montreal**	**NHL**	**73**	**7**	**13**	**20**	**110**	**1**	**0**	**3**	**62**	**11.3**	**–5**	....	....	....	**4**	**0**	**0**	**0**	**0**	**0**	**0**	**0**	....

			Regular Season														Playoffs								
Season	Club	League	GP	G	A	Pts	PIM	PP	SH	GW	S	%	+/-	TF	F%	Min	GP	G	A	Pts	PIM	PP	SH	GW	Min
1997-98	Montreal	NHL	39	1	5	6	57	0	0	0	19	5.3	–6	....	....	....	....	....	....	....	....	....	....	....	....
	Tampa Bay	NHL	35	6	8	14	89	1	1	0	44	13.6	–8	....	....	....	....	....	....	....	....	....	....	....	....
1998-99	Tampa Bay	NHL	82	21	22	43	176	8	2	3	178	11.8	–34	1470	45.6	19:24	....	....	....	....	....	....	....	....	....
99-2000	Tampa Bay	NHL	50	14	20	34	108	1	0	2	98	14.3	–15	152	48.7	19:58	....	....	....	....	....	....	....	....	....
	Toronto	NHL	27	7	10	17	55	0	2	3	40	17.5	3	11	54.6	16:41	12	4	2	6	15	1	0	2	17:23
2000-01	Toronto	NHL	82	16	21	37	141	2	0	4	122	13.1	6	413	47.0	16:09	11	0	2	2	6	0	0	0	13:59
2001-02	Toronto	NHL	77	24	35	59	92	7	0	5	124	19.4	24	138	43.5	16:59	17	4	4	8	38	1	0	1	16:50
2002-03	Toronto	NHL	77	10	26	36	119	4	1	2	108	9.3	–7	68	45.6	15:21	6	0	3	3	6	0	0	0	21:07
	NHL Totals		545	106	160	266	947	24	6	22	796	13.3		2252	46.0	17:21	50	8	11	19	65	2	0	3	16:51

WHL West First All-Star Team (1994, 1995) • Canadian Major Junior First All-Star Team (1994) • Memorial Cup All-Star Team (1994, 1995) • Stafford Smythe Memorial Trophy (Memorial Cup MVP) (1994) • Dudley "Red" Garrett Memorial Trophy (Top Rookie – AHL) (1996)

Traded to **Tampa Bay** by **Montreal** with Stephane Richer and David Wilkie for Patrick Poulin, Mick Vukota and Igor Ulanov, January 15, 1998. Traded to **Toronto** by **Tampa Bay** with Tampa Bay's 4th round choice (Miguel Delisle) in 2000 Entry Draft and future considerations for Mike Johnson, Marek Posmyk, Toronto's 5th (Pavel Sedov) and 6th (Aaron Gionet) round choices in 2000 Entry Draft and future considerations, February 9, 2000.

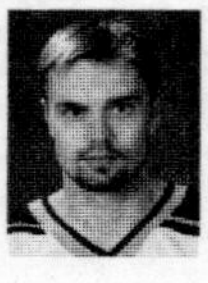

TUOMAINEN, Marko

(TOO-oh-migh-nehn, MAHR-koh)

Right wing. Shoots right. 6'3", 230 lbs. Born, Kuopio, Finland, April 25, 1972. Edmonton's 10th choice, 205th overall, in 1992 Entry Draft.

Season	Club	League	GP	G	A	Pts	PIM	PP	SH	GW	S	%	+/-	TF	F%	Min	GP	G	A	Pts	PIM	PP	SH	GW	Min
1988-89	KalPa Kuopio Jr.	Finn-Jr.	7	6	6	12	4	....	....	....	....	....	....	....	....	....	....	....	....	....	....	....	....	....	....
1989-90	KalPa Kuopio Jr.	Finn-Jr.	36	13	24	37	30	....	....	....	....	....	....	....	....	....	....	....	....	....	....	....	....	....	....
	KalPa Kuopio	Finland	5	0	0	0	0	....	....	....	....	....	....	....	....	....	....	....	....	....	....	....	....	....	....
1990-91	KalPa Kuopio Jr.	Finn-Jr.	35	36	17	53	61	....	....	....	....	....	....	....	....	....	....	....	....	....	....	....	....	....	....
	KalPa Kuopio	Finland	30	2	1	3	2	....	....	....	....	....	....	....	....	....	8	0	0	0	6	....	....	....	....
1991-92	Clarkson Knights	ECAC	28	11	12	23	32	....	....	....	....	....	....	....	....	....	....	....	....	....	....	....	....	....	....
1992-93	Clarkson Knights	ECAC	35	25	30	55	26	....	....	....	....	....	....	....	....	....	....	....	....	....	....	....	....	....	....
1993-94	Clarkson Knights	ECAC	34	23	29	52	60	....	....	....	....	....	....	....	....	....	....	....	....	....	....	....	....	....	....
1994-95	Clarkson Knights	ECAC	37	23	38	61	34	....	....	....	....	....	....	....	....	....	....	....	....	....	....	....	....	....	....
	Edmonton	NHL	4	0	0	0	0	0	0	0	5	0.0	0	....	....	....	....	....	....	....	....	....	....	....	....
1995-96	Cape Breton	AHL	58	25	35	60	71	....	....	....	....	....	....	....	....	....	....	....	....	....	....	....	....	....	....
1996-97	Hamilton	AHL	79	31	21	52	130	....	....	....	....	....	....	....	....	....	22	7	5	12	4	....	....	....	....
1997-98	HIFK Helsinki	Finland	46	13	9	22	20	....	....	....	....	....	....	....	....	....	9	0	3	3	0	....	....	....	....
1998-99	HIFK Helsinki	Finland	48	11	17	28	*173	....	....	....	....	....	....	....	....	....	11	1	3	4	12	....	....	....	....
	HIFK Helsinki	EuroHL	6	0	1	1	8	....	....	....	....	....	....	....	....	....	4	3	0	3	4	....	....	....	....
99-2000	Los Angeles	NHL	63	9	8	17	80	2	1	1	74	12.2	–12	8	25.0	11:30	1	0	0	0	0	0	0	0	5:33
2000-01	Lowell	AHL	59	28	39	67	73	....	....	....	....	....	....	....	....	....	4	3	3	6	10	....	....	....	....
	Los Angeles	NHL	11	0	1	1	4	0	0	0	12	0.0	1	1	100.0	9:22	....	....	....	....	....	....	....	....	....
2001-02	NY Islanders	NHL	1	0	0	0	0	0	0	0	0	0.0	–1	0	0.0	7:11	....	....	....	....	....	....	....	....	....
	Bridgeport	AHL	76	11	34	45	82	....	....	....	....	....	....	....	....	....	20	1	2	3	6	....	....	....	....
2002-03	Blues Espoo	Finland	46	10	11	21	70	....	....	....	....	....	....	....	....	....	7	0	1	1	4	....	....	....	....
	NHL Totals		79	9	9	18	84	2	1	1	91	9.9		9	33.3	11:08	1	0	0	0	0	0	0	0	5:33

ECAC First All-Star Team (1993, 1995) • NCAA East Second All-American Team (1995)

Signed as a free agent by **Los Angeles**, June 20, 1999. Signed as a free agent by **Los Angeles**, January 4, 2001. Signed as a free agent by **NY Islanders**, July 18, 2001. Signed as a free agent by **Blues Espoo** (Finland), June 2, 2002.

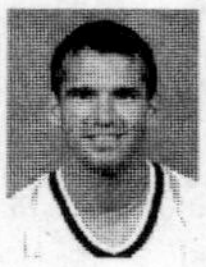

TURGEON, Pierre

(TUHR-zhaw, PEE-air) **DAL.**

Center. Shoots left. 6'1", 199 lbs. Born, Rouyn, Que., August 28, 1969. Buffalo's 1st choice, 1st overall, in 1987 Entry Draft.

Season	Club	League	GP	G	A	Pts	PIM	PP	SH	GW	S	%	+/-	TF	F%	Min	GP	G	A	Pts	PIM	PP	SH	GW	Min
1984-85	Mtl-Bourassa	QAAA	41	49	52	101	26	....	....	....	....	....	....	....	....	....	5	3	8	11	2	....	....	....	....
1985-86	Granby Bisons	QMJHL	69	47	67	114	31	....	....	....	....	....	....	....	....	....	....	....	....	....	....	....	....	....	....
1986-87	Granby Bisons	QMJHL	58	69	85	154	8	....	....	....	....	....	....	....	....	....	7	9	6	15	15	....	....	....	....
1987-88	Buffalo	NHL	76	14	28	42	34	8	0	3	101	13.9	–8	....	....	....	6	4	3	7	4	3	0	0	....
1988-89	Buffalo	NHL	80	34	54	88	26	19	0	5	182	18.7	–2	....	....	....	5	3	5	8	2	1	0	0	....
1989-90	Buffalo	NHL	80	40	66	106	29	17	1	10	193	20.7	10	....	....	....	6	2	4	6	2	0	0	1	....
1990-91	Buffalo	NHL	78	32	47	79	26	13	2	3	174	18.4	14	....	....	....	6	3	1	4	6	1	0	0	....
1991-92	Buffalo	NHL	8	2	6	8	4	0	0	0	14	14.3	–1	....	....	....	....	....	....	....	....	....	....	....	....
	NY Islanders	NHL	69	38	49	87	16	13	0	6	193	19.7	8	....	....	....	....	....	....	....	....	....	....	....	....
1992-93	NY Islanders	NHL	83	58	74	132	26	24	0	10	301	19.3	–1	....	....	....	11	6	7	13	0	0	0	0	....
1993-94	NY Islanders	NHL	69	38	56	94	18	10	4	6	254	15.0	14	....	....	....	4	0	1	1	0	0	0	0	....
1994-95	NY Islanders	NHL	34	13	14	27	10	3	2	2	93	14.0	–12	....	....	....	....	....	....	....	....	....	....	....	....
	Montreal	NHL	15	11	9	20	4	2	0	2	67	16.4	12	....	....	....	....	....	....	....	....	....	....	....	....
1995-96	Montreal	NHL	80	38	58	96	44	17	1	6	297	12.8	19	....	....	....	6	2	4	6	2	0	0	0	....
1996-97	Montreal	NHL	9	1	10	11	2	0	0	0	22	4.5	4	....	....	....	....	....	....	....	....	....	....	....	....
	St. Louis	NHL	69	25	49	74	12	5	0	7	194	12.9	4	....	....	....	5	1	1	2	2	1	0	0	....
1997-98	St. Louis	NHL	60	22	46	68	24	6	0	4	140	15.7	13	....	....	....	10	4	4	8	2	2	0	0	....
1998-99	St. Louis	NHL	67	31	34	65	36	10	0	5	193	16.1	4	1285	50.0	19:07	13	4	9	13	6	0	0	2	19:35
99-2000	St. Louis	NHL	52	26	40	66	8	8	0	3	139	18.7	30	1016	53.2	19:13	7	0	7	7	0	0	0	0	19:45
2000-01	St. Louis	NHL	79	30	52	82	37	11	0	6	171	17.5	14	1569	49.7	18:50	15	5	10	15	2	1	0	0	19:07
2001-02	Dallas	NHL	66	15	32	47	16	7	0	1	121	12.4	–4	822	48.4	16:31	....	....	....	....	....	....	....	....	....
2002-03	Dallas	NHL	65	12	30	42	18	3	0	5	76	15.8	4	290	53.8	14:38	5	0	1	1	0	0	0	0	12:21
	NHL Totals		1139	480	754	1234	390	176	10	84	2925	16.4		4982	50.5	17:39	99	34	57	91	28	9	0	3	18:32

QMJHL Offensive Rookie of the Year) (1986) • Lady Byng Memorial Trophy (1993)

Played in NHL All-Star Game (1990, 1993, 1994, 1996)

Traded to **NY Islanders** by **Buffalo** with Uwe Krupp, Benoit Hogue and Dave McLlwain for Pat LaFontaine, Randy Hillier, Randy Wood and NY Islanders' 4th round choice (Dean Melanson) in 1992 Entry Draft, October 25, 1991. Traded to **Montreal** by **NY Islanders** with Vladimir Malakhov for Kirk Muller, Mathieu Schneider and Craig Darby, April 5, 1995. Traded to **St. Louis** by **Montreal** with Rory Fitzpatrick and Craig Conroy for Murray Baron, Shayne Corson and St. Louis' 5th round choice (Gennady Razin) in 1997 Entry Draft, October 29, 1996. Signed as a free agent by **Dallas**, July 1, 2001.

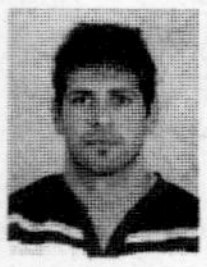

TUZZOLINO, Tony

(too-zuh-LEE-noh, TOH-nee)

Right wing. Shoots right. 6'2", 208 lbs. Born, Buffalo, NY, October 9, 1975. Quebec's 7th choice, 113th overall, in 1994 Entry Draft.

Season	Club	League	GP	G	A	Pts	PIM	PP	SH	GW	S	%	+/-	TF	F%	Min	GP	G	A	Pts	PIM	PP	SH	GW	Min
1989-90	Amherst Knights	NYAHA	29	50	95	145	....	....	....	....	....	....	....	....	....	....	....	....	....	....	....	....	....	....	....
1990-91	Buffalo Regals	NAJHL	55	39	47	86	....	....	....	....	....	....	....	....	....	....	....	....	....	....	....	....	....	....	....
1991-92	Niagara Scenics	NAJHL	45	19	27	46	82	....	....	....	....	....	....	....	....	....	....	....	....	....	....	....	....	....	....
1992-93	Niagara Scenics	NAJHL	50	36	41	77	134	....	....	....	....	....	....	....	....	....	....	....	....	....	....	....	....	....	....
1993-94	Michigan State	CCHA	35	4	3	7	46	....	....	....	....	....	....	....	....	....	....	....	....	....	....	....	....	....	....
1994-95	Michigan State	CCHA	39	9	18	27	81	....	....	....	....	....	....	....	....	....	....	....	....	....	....	....	....	....	....
1995-96	Michigan State	CCHA	41	12	17	29	120	....	....	....	....	....	....	....	....	....	....	....	....	....	....	....	....	....	....
1996-97	Michigan State	CCHA	39	14	18	32	120	....	....	....	....	....	....	....	....	....	....	....	....	....	....	....	....	....	....
1997-98	Kentucky	AHL	35	9	14	23	83	....	....	....	....	....	....	....	....	....	....	....	....	....	....	....	....	....	....
	Anaheim	NHL	1	0	0	0	2	0	0	0	0	0.0	–2	....	....	....	....	....	....	....	....	....	....	....	....
	Cincinnati	AHL	13	3	3	6	6	....	....	....	....	....	....	....	....	....	....	....	....	....	....	....	....	....	....
1998-99	Cincinnati	AHL	50	4	10	14	55	....	....	....	....	....	....	....	....	....	....	....	....	....	....	....	....	....	....
	Cleveland	IHL	15	2	4	6	22	....	....	....	....	....	....	....	....	....	....	....	....	....	....	....	....	....	....
99-2000	Cincinnati	AHL	15	0	3	3	8	....	....	....	....	....	....	....	....	....	....	....	....	....	....	....	....	....	....
	Huntington	ECHL	20	6	13	19	43	....	....	....	....	....	....	....	....	....	....	....	....	....	....	....	....	....	....
	Hartford	AHL	32	3	8	11	41	....	....	....	....	....	....	....	....	....	19	2	2	4	16	....	....	....	....
2000-01	Hartford	AHL	47	12	23	35	136	....	....	....	....	....	....	....	....	....	5	0	2	2	6	....	....	....	....
	NY Rangers	NHL	6	0	0	0	5	0	0	0	3	0.0	–1	1	0.0	3:41	....	....	....	....	....	....	....	....	....
2001-02	Boston	NHL	2	0	0	0	0	0	0	0	1	0.0	–1	3	33.3	5:32	....	....	....	....	....	....	....	....	....
	Providence Bruins	AHL	59	10	19	29	123	....	....	....	....	....	....	....	....	....	1	0	0	0	0	....	....	....	....
2002-03	Louisiana	ECHL	12	8	7	15	47	....	....	....	....	....	....	....	....	....	....	....	....	....	....	....	....	....	....
	Houston Aeros	AHL	50	9	6	15	92	....	....	....	....	....	....	....	....	....	23	4	4	8	43	....	....	....	....
	NHL Totals		9	0	0	0	7	0	0	0	4	0.0		4	25.0	4:09	....	....	....	....	....	....	....	....	....

Rights transferred to **Colorado** after **Quebec** franchise relocated, June 21, 1995. Signed as a free agent by **NY Islanders**, April 26, 1997. Traded to **Anaheim** by **NY Islanders** with Travis Green and Doug Houda for Joe Sacco, J.J. Daigneault and Mark Janssens, February 6, 1998. Loaned to **Hartford** (AHL) by **Anaheim**, January 25, 2000. Signed as a free agent by **NY Rangers**, February 9, 2001. Signed as a free agent by **Boston**, July 23, 2001. Signed as a free agent by **Minnesota**, July 9, 2002.

			Regular Season														Playoffs							
Season	Club	League	GP	G	A	Pts	PIM	PP	SH	GW	S	%	+/-	TF	F%	Min	GP	G	A	Pts	PIM	PP	SH	GW	Min

TVERDOVSKY, Oleg   (tvehr-DOHV-skee, OH-lehg)

Defense. Shoots left. 6'1", 205 lbs.   Born, Donetsk, USSR, May 18, 1976. Anaheim's 1st choice, 2nd overall, in 1994 Entry Draft.

Season	Club	League	GP	G	A	Pts	PIM	PP	SH	GW	S	%	+/-	TF	F%	Min	GP	G	A	Pts	PIM	PP	SH	GW	Min
1992-93	Krylja Sovetov	CIS	21	0	1	1	6	….	….	….	….	….	….				6	0	0	0	0	….	….	….	….
1993-94	Krylja Sovetov	CIS	46	4	10	14	22	….	….	….	….	….	….				3	1	0	1	2	….	….	….	….
1994-95	Brandon	WHL	7	1	4	5	4	….	….	….	….	….	….				….	….	….	….	….	….	….	….	….
	Anaheim	NHL	36	3	9	12	14	1	1	0	26	11.5	-6				….	….	….	….	….	….	….	….	….
1995-96	Anaheim	NHL	51	7	15	22	35	2	0	0	84	8.3	0				….	….	….	….	….	….	….	….	….
	Winnipeg	NHL	31	0	8	8	6	0	0	0	35	0.0	-7				6	0	1	1	0	0	0	0	….
1996-97	Phoenix	NHL	82	10	45	55	30	3	1	2	144	6.9	-5				7	0	1	1	0	0	0	0	….
1997-98	Hamilton	AHL	9	8	6	14	2	….	….	….	….	….	….				….	….	….	….	….	….	….	….	….
	Phoenix	NHL	46	7	12	19	12	4	0	1	83	8.4	1				6	0	7	7	0	0	0	0	….
1998-99	Phoenix	NHL	82	7	18	25	32	2	0	2	117	6.0	11	1	0.0	20:48	6	0	2	2	6	0	0	0	17:43
99-2000	Anaheim	NHL	82	15	36	51	30	5	0	5	153	9.8	5	1	0.0	22:46									
2000-01	Anaheim	NHL	82	14	39	53	32	8	0	3	188	7.4	-11	0	0.0	24:25									
2001-02	Anaheim	NHL	73	6	26	32	31	2	0	1	147	4.1	0	0	0.0	22:50									
	Russia	Olympics	6	1	1	2	0	….	….	….	….	….	….												
2002-03 ◆	New Jersey	NHL	50	5	8	13	22	2	0	1	76	6.6	2	0	0.0	16:48	15	0	3	3	0	0	0	0	15:06
	NHL Totals		**615**	**74**	**216**	**290**	**244**	**29**	**2**	**15**	**1053**	**7.0**		**2**	**0.0**	**21:54**	**40**	**0**	**14**	**14**	**6**	**0**	**0**	**0**	**15:51**

Played in NHL All-Star Game (1997)

Traded to **Winnipeg** by **Anaheim** with Chad Kilger and Anaheim's 3rd round choice (Per-Anton Lundstrom) in 1996 Entry Draft for Teemu Selanne, Marc Chouinard and Winnipeg's 4th round choice (later traded to Toronto – later traded to Montreal – Montreal selected Kim Staal) in 1996 Entry Draft, February 7, 1996. Transferred to **Phoenix** after **Winnipeg** franchise relocated, July 1, 1996. Traded to **Anaheim** by **Phoenix** for Travis Green and Anaheim's 1st round choice (Scott Kelman) in 1999 Entry Draft, June 26, 1999. Traded to **New Jersey** by **Anaheim** with Jeff Friesen and Maxim Balmochnykh for Petr Sykora, Mike Commodore, Jean-Francois Damphousse and Igor Pohanka, July 6, 2002.

ULANOV, Igor   (yoo-LAH-nahf, EE-gohr)

Defense. Shoots left. 6'3", 220 lbs.   Born, Krasnokamsk, USSR, October 1, 1969. Winnipeg's 8th choice, 203rd overall, in 1991 Entry Draft.

Season	Club	League	GP	G	A	Pts	PIM	PP	SH	GW	S	%	+/-	TF	F%	Min	GP	G	A	Pts	PIM	PP	SH	GW	Min
1990-91	Voskresensk	USSR	41	2	2	4	52	….	….	….	….	….	….				….	….	….	….	….	….	….	….	….
1991-92	Voskresensk	CIS	27	1	4	5	24	….	….	….	….	….	….				….	….	….	….	….	….	….	….	….
	Winnipeg	NHL	27	2	9	11	67	0	0	0	23	8.7	5				7	0	0	0	39	0	0	0	….
	Moncton Hawks	AHL	3	0	1	1	16	….	….	….	….	….	….				….	….	….	….	….	….	….	….	….
1992-93	Winnipeg	NHL	56	2	14	16	124	0	0	0	26	7.7	6				4	0	0	0	4	0	0	0	….
	Moncton Hawks	AHL	9	1	3	4	26	….	….	….	….	….	….				….	….	….	….	….	….	….	….	….
	Fort Wayne	IHL	3	0	1	1	29	….	….	….	….	….	….				….	….	….	….	….	….	….	….	….
1993-94	Winnipeg	NHL	74	0	17	17	165	0	0	0	46	0.0	-11				….	….	….	….	….	….	….	….	….
1994-95	Winnipeg	NHL	19	1	3	4	27	0	0	0	13	7.7	-2				….	….	….	….	….	….	….	….	….
	Washington	NHL	3	0	1	1	2	0	0	0	0	0.0	3				2	0	0	0	4	0	0	0	….
1995-96	Chicago	NHL	53	1	8	9	92	0	0	0	24	4.2	12				….	….	….	….	….	….	….	….	….
	Indianapolis Ice	IHL	1	0	0	0	0	….	….	….	….	….	….				….	….	….	….	….	….	….	….	….
	Tampa Bay	NHL	11	2	1	3	24	0	0	1	13	15.4	-1				5	0	0	0	15	0	0	0	….
1996-97	Tampa Bay	NHL	59	1	7	8	108	0	0	0	56	1.8	2				….	….	….	….	….	….	….	….	….
1997-98	Tampa Bay	NHL	45	2	7	9	85	1	0	0	32	6.3	-5				….	….	….	….	….	….	….	….	….
	Montreal	NHL	4	0	1	1	12	0	0	0	4	0.0	-2				10	0	4	4	12	0	0	0	….
1998-99	Montreal	NHL	76	3	9	12	109	0	0	0	55	5.5	-3	0	0.0	17:35	….	….	….	….	….	….	….	….	….
99-2000	Montreal	NHL	43	1	5	6	76	0	0	0	33	3.0	-11	0	0.0	16:33	….	….	….	….	….	….	….	….	….
	Edmonton	NHL	14	0	3	3	10	0	0	0	6	0.0	-3	0	0.0	16:23	5	0	0	0	6	0	0	0	16:59
2000-01	Edmonton	NHL	67	3	20	23	90	1	0	0	74	4.1	15	0	0.0	23:01	6	0	0	0	4	0	0	0	24:25
2001-02	NY Rangers	NHL	39	0	6	6	53	0	0	0	17	0.0	-4	0	0.0	16:19	….	….	….	….	….	….	….	….	….
	Hartford	AHL	6	1	1	2	2	….	….	….	….	….	….				….	….	….	….	….	….	….	….	….
	Florida	NHL	14	0	4	4	11	0	0	0	9	0.0	-3	0	0.0	20:50	….	….	….	….	….	….	….	….	….
2002-03	Florida	NHL	56	1	1	2	39	0	0	0	20	5.0	7	0	0.0	16:42	….	….	….	….	….	….	….	….	….
	San Antonio	AHL	5	1	0	1	4	….	….	….	….	….	….				….	….	….	….	….	….	….	….	….
	NHL Totals		**660**	**19**	**116**	**135**	**1094**	**2**	**0**	**1**	**451**	**4.2**		**0**	**0.0**	**18:24**	**39**	**1**	**4**	**5**	**84**	**0**	**0**	**0**	**21:02**

Traded to **Washington** by **Winnipeg** with Mike Eagles for Washington's 3rd (later traded to Dallas – Dallas selected Sergey Gusev) and 5th (Brian Elder) round choices in 1995 Entry Draft, April 7, 1995. Traded to **Chicago** by **Washington** for Chicago's 3rd round choice (Dave Weninger) in 1996 Entry Draft, October 17, 1995. Traded to **Tampa Bay** by **Chicago** with Patrick Poulin and Chicago's 2nd round choice (later traded to New Jersey – New Jersey selected Pierre Dagenais) in 1996 Entry Draft for Enrico Ciccone and Tampa Bay's 2nd round choice (Jeff Paul) in 1996 Entry Draft, March 20, 1996. Traded to **Montreal** by **Tampa Bay** with Patrick Poulin and Mick Vukota for Stephane Richer, Darcy Tucker and David Wilkie, January 15, 1998. Traded to **Edmonton** by **Montreal** with Alain Nasreddine for Christian Laflamme and Matthieu Descoteaux, March 9, 2000. Signed as a free agent by **NY Rangers**, July 20, 2001. Traded to **Florida** by **NY Rangers** with Filip Novak, NY Rangers' 1st (later traded to Calgary – Calgary selected Eric Nystrom) and 2nd (Rob Globke) round choices in 2002 Entry Draft and NY Rangers' 4th round choice (later traded to Atlanta – Atlanta selected Guillaume Desbiens) in 2003 Entry Draft for Pavel Bure and Florida's 2nd round choice (Lee Falardeau) in 2002 Entry Draft, March 18, 2002.

ULMER, Jeff   (UHL-muhr, JEHF)

Right wing. Shoots right. 5'11", 195 lbs.   Born, Wilcox, Sask., April 27, 1977.

Season	Club	League	GP	G	A	Pts	PIM	PP	SH	GW	S	%	+/-	TF	F%	Min	GP	G	A	Pts	PIM	PP	SH	GW	Min
1994-95	Notre Dame	AJHL	63	25	35	60	….	….	….	….	….	….	….				….	….	….	….	….	….	….	….	….
1995-96	North Dakota	WCHA	29	5	3	8	26	….	….	….	….	….	….				….	….	….	….	….	….	….	….	….
1996-97	North Dakota	WCHA	26	6	11	17	16	….	….	….	….	….	….				….	….	….	….	….	….	….	….	….
1997-98	North Dakota	WCHA	32	12	12	24	44	….	….	….	….	….	….				….	….	….	….	….	….	….	….	….
1998-99	North Dakota	WCHA	38	16	20	36	46	….	….	….	….	….	….				….	….	….	….	….	….	….	….	….
99-2000	Team Canada	Nat-Tm	48	14	25	39	20	….	….	….	….	….	….				11	2	4	6	6				
	Houston Aeros	IHL	5	1	0	1	0	….	….	….	….	….	….				….	….	….	….	….	….	….	….	….
2000-01	NY Rangers	NHL	21	3	0	3	8	0	0	0	22	13.6	-6	16	31.3	10:23	….	….	….	….	….	….	….	….	….
	Hartford	AHL	48	11	14	25	34	….	….	….	….	….	….				5	0	1	1	11				
2001-02	Grand Rapids	AHL	73	9	17	26	65	….	….	….	….	….	….				5	0	1	1	11				
2002-03	Binghamton	AHL	57	8	12	20	40	….	….	….	….	….	….				13	0	1	1	30				
	NHL Totals		**21**	**3**	**0**	**3**	**8**	**0**	**0**	**0**	**22**	**13.6**		**16**	**31.3**	**10:23**									

Signed as a free agent by **Houston** (IHL), March 30, 2000. Signed as a free agent by **NY Rangers**, July 27, 2000. Traded to **Ottawa** by **NY Rangers** with Jason Doig for Sean Gagnon, June 29, 2001.

UPSHALL, Scottie   (UHP-shuhl, SKAW-tee)   **NSH.**

Right wing. Shoots left. 6', 187 lbs.   Born, Fort McMurray, Alta., October 7, 1983. Nashville's 1st choice, 6th overall, in 2002 Entry Draft.

Season	Club	League	GP	G	A	Pts	PIM	PP	SH	GW	S	%	+/-	TF	F%	Min	GP	G	A	Pts	PIM	PP	SH	GW	Min
1998-99	Fort McMurray	AMHL	28	62	40	102	100	….	….	….	….	….	….				….	….	….	….	….	….	….	….	….
99-2000	Fort McMurray	AJHL	52	26	26	52	65	….	….	….	….	….	….				….	….	….	….	….	….	….	….	….
2000-01	Kamloops Blazers	WHL	70	42	45	87	111	….	….	….	….	….	….				4	0	2	2	10				
2001-02	Kamloops Blazers	WHL	61	32	51	83	139	….	….	….	….	….	….				4	1	2	3	21				
2002-03	Nashville	NHL	8	1	0	1	0	0	0	0	6	16.7	2	2	0.0	8:42	….	….	….	….	….	….	….	….	….
	Kamloops Blazers	WHL	42	25	31	56	111	….	….	….	….	….	….				6	0	2	2	34				
	Milwaukee	AHL	2	1	0	1	2	….	….	….	….	….	….				6	0	0	0	2				
	NHL Totals		**8**	**1**	**0**	**1**	**0**	**0**	**0**	**0**	**6**	**16.7**		**2**	**0.0**	**8:42**									

WHL All-Rookie Team (2001) • WHL Rookie of the Year (2001) • CHL All-Rookie Team (2001) • Canadian Major Junior Rookie of the Year (2001) • WHL West Second All-Star Team (2002)

VAANANEN, Ossi   (VAN-ih-nehn, AW-see)   **PHX.**

Defense. Shoots left. 6'4", 215 lbs.   Born, Vantaa, Finland, August 18, 1980. Phoenix's 2nd choice, 43rd overall, in 1998 Entry Draft.

Season	Club	League	GP	G	A	Pts	PIM	PP	SH	GW	S	%	+/-	TF	F%	Min	GP	G	A	Pts	PIM	PP	SH	GW	Min
1994-95	Jokerit Helsinki-C	Finn-Jr.	23	0	1	1	10	….	….	….	….	….	….				6	0	0	0	8	….	….	….	….
1995-96	Jokerit Helsinki-C	Finn-Jr.	12	0	0	0	10	….	….	….	….	….	….				….	….	….	….	….	….	….	….	….
	Jokerit Helsinki-B	Finn-Jr.	1	0	0	0	0	….	….	….	….	….	….				1	0	0	0	0	….	….	….	….
1996-97	Jokerit Helsinki Jr.	Finn-Jr.	17	1	2	3	43	….	….	….	….	….	….				….	….	….	….	….	….	….	….	….
1997-98	Jokerit Helsinki Jr.	Finn-Jr.	31	0	6	6	24	….	….	….	….	….	….				….	….	….	….	….	….	….	….	….
1998-99	Jokerit Helsinki Jr.	Finn-Jr.	12	1	6	7	16	….	….	….	….	….	….				1	0	1	1	0	….	….	….	….
	Jokerit Helsinki	EuroHL	5	0	0	0	2	….	….	….	….	….	….				….	….	….	….	….	….	….	….	….
	Jokerit Helsinki	Finland	48	0	1	1	42	….	….	….	….	….	….				3	0	1	1	2	….	….	….	….
99-2000	Jokerit Helsinki	Finland	49	1	6	7	46	….	….	….	….	….	….				11	1	1	2	5	….	….	….	….
2000-01	Phoenix	NHL	81	4	12	16	90	0	0	2	69	5.8	9	0	0.0	19:09	….	….	….	….	….	….	….	….	….
2001-02	Phoenix	NHL	76	2	12	14	74	0	0	0	41	4.9	6	0	0.0	20:13	5	0	0	0	6	0	0	0	20:33
	Finland	Olympics	2	0	1	1	0	….	….	….	….	….	….												
2002-03	Phoenix	NHL	67	2	7	9	82	0	1	0	49	4.1	1	0	0.0	19:15	….	….	….	….	….	….	….	….	….
	NHL Totals		**224**	**8**	**31**	**39**	**246**	**0**	**1**	**2**	**159**	**5.0**		**0**	**0.0**	**19:32**	**5**	**0**	**0**	**0**	**6**	**0**	**0**	**0**	**20:33**

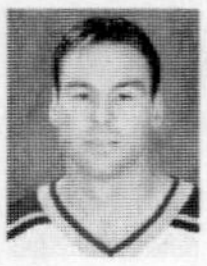

VALICEVIC, Rob

(val-IH-seh-VIK, RAWB)

Right wing. Shoots right. 6'1", 198 lbs. Born, Detroit, MI, January 6, 1971. NY Islanders' 6th choice, 114th overall, in 1991 Entry Draft.

			Regular Season														Playoffs								
Season	Club	League	GP	G	A	Pts	PIM	PP	SH	GW	S	%	+/-	TF	F%	Min	GP	G	A	Pts	PIM	PP	SH	GW	Min
1990-91	Det. Compuware	NAJHL	39	31	44	75	54																		
1991-92	Lake Superior	CCHA	32	8	4	12	12																		
1992-93	Lake Superior	CCHA	43	21	20	41	28																		
1993-94	Lake Superior	CCHA	45	18	20	38	46																		
1994-95	Lake Superior	CCHA	37	10	21	31	40																		
1995-96	Louisiana	ECHL	60	42	20	62	85										5	2	3	5	8				
	Springfield	AHL	2	0	0	0	2																		
1996-97	Louisiana	ECHL	8	7	2	9	21																		
	Houston Aeros	IHL	58	11	12	23	42										12	1	3	4	11				
1997-98	Houston Aeros	IHL	72	29	28	57	47										4	2	0	2	2				
1998-99	**Nashville**	**NHL**	**19**	**4**	**2**	**6**	**2**	**0**	**0**	**2**	**23**	**17.4**	**4**	**17**	**29.4**	**11:01**									
	Houston Aeros	IHL	57	16	33	49	62										19	7	10	17	8				
99-2000	**Nashville**	**NHL**	**80**	**14**	**11**	**25**	**21**	**2**	**1**	**3**	**113**	**12.4**	**–11**	**50**	**44.0**	**14:31**									
2000-01	**Nashville**	**NHL**	**60**	**8**	**6**	**14**	**26**	**1**	**0**	**4**	**62**	**12.9**	**–2**	**35**	**40.0**	**14:06**									
2001-02	**Los Angeles**	**NHL**	**17**	**1**	**1**	**2**	**8**	**0**	**0**	**0**	**9**	**11.1**	**–4**	**166**	**41.6**	**9:34**									
	Manchester	AHL	59	11	23	34	25										5	1	0	1	4				
2002-03	**Anaheim**	**NHL**	**10**	**1**	**0**	**1**	**2**	**0**	**0**	**1**	**7**	**14.3**	**1**	**0**	**0.0**	**8:35**									
	Cincinnati	AHL	69	17	26	43	38																		
	NHL Totals		**186**	**28**	**20**	**48**	**59**	**3**	**1**	**10**	**214**	**13.1**		**268**	**41.0**	**13:15**									

Signed as a free agent by **Nashville**, May 28, 1998. Signed as a free agent by **Los Angeles**, August 16, 2001. Signed as a free agent by **Anaheim**, July 24, 2002.

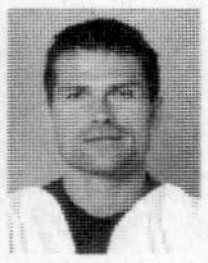

VALK, Garry

(VAHLK, GAIR-ee)

Right wing. Shoots left. 6'1", 200 lbs. Born, Edmonton, Alta., November 27, 1967. Vancouver's 5th choice, 108th overall, in 1987 Entry Draft.

			Regular Season														Playoffs								
Season	Club	League	GP	G	A	Pts	PIM	PP	SH	GW	S	%	+/-	TF	F%	Min	GP	G	A	Pts	PIM	PP	SH	GW	Min
1984-85	Sherwood Park	AJHL	53	20	22	42	66																		
1985-86	Sherwood Park	AJHL	40	20	26	46	116																		
1986-87	Sherwood Park	AJHL	59	42	44	86	204																		
1987-88	North Dakota	WCHA	38	23	12	35	64																		
1988-89	North Dakota	WCHA	40	14	17	31	71																		
1989-90	North Dakota	WCHA	43	22	17	39	92																		
1990-91	**Vancouver**	**NHL**	**59**	**10**	**11**	**21**	**67**	**1**	**0**	**1**	**90**	**11.1**	**–23**				**5**	**0**	**0**	**0**	**20**	**0**	**0**	**0**	
	Milwaukee	IHL	10	12	4	16	13										3	0	0	0	2				
1991-92	**Vancouver**	**NHL**	**65**	**8**	**17**	**25**	**56**	**2**	**1**	**2**	**93**	**8.6**	**3**				**4**	**0**	**0**	**0**	**5**	**0**	**0**	**0**	
1992-93	**Vancouver**	**NHL**	**48**	**6**	**7**	**13**	**77**	**0**	**0**	**2**	**46**	**13.0**	**6**				**7**	**0**	**1**	**1**	**12**	**0**	**0**	**0**	
	Hamilton	AHL	7	3	6	9	6																		
1993-94	**Anaheim**	**NHL**	**78**	**18**	**27**	**45**	**100**	**4**	**1**	**5**	**165**	**10.9**	**8**												
1994-95	**Anaheim**	**NHL**	**36**	**3**	**6**	**9**	**34**	**0**	**0**	**0**	**53**	**5.7**	**–4**												
1995-96	**Anaheim**	**NHL**	**79**	**12**	**12**	**24**	**125**	**1**	**1**	**2**	**108**	**11.1**	**8**												
1996-97	**Anaheim**	**NHL**	**53**	**7**	**7**	**14**	**53**	**0**	**0**	**1**	**68**	**10.3**	**–2**												
	Pittsburgh	**NHL**	**17**	**3**	**4**	**7**	**25**	**0**	**0**	**0**	**32**	**9.4**	**–6**												
1997-98	**Pittsburgh**	**NHL**	**39**	**2**	**1**	**3**	**33**	**0**	**0**	**0**	**32**	**6.3**	**–3**												
1998-99	**Toronto**	**NHL**	**77**	**8**	**21**	**29**	**53**	**1**	**0**	**0**	**93**	**8.6**	**8**	**19**	**36.8**	**13:53**	**17**	**3**	**4**	**7**	**22**	**0**	**0**	**1**	**13:22**
99-2000	**Toronto**	**NHL**	**73**	**10**	**14**	**24**	**44**	**0**	**1**	**1**	**91**	**11.0**	**–2**	**10**	**30.0**	**12:51**	**12**	**1**	**2**	**3**	**14**	**0**	**0**	**0**	**12:58**
2000-01	**Toronto**	**NHL**	**74**	**8**	**18**	**26**	**46**	**1**	**0**	**2**	**87**	**9.2**	**4**	**30**	**33.3**	**11:33**	**5**	**1**	**0**	**1**	**2**	**0**	**0**	**0**	**13:28**
2001-02	**Toronto**	**NHL**	**63**	**5**	**10**	**15**	**28**	**0**	**0**	**0**	**80**	**6.3**	**2**	**6**	**33.3**	**10:48**	**11**	**1**	**0**	**1**	**4**	**0**	**0**	**0**	**11:19**
2002-03	**Chicago**	**NHL**	**16**	**0**	**1**	**1**	**6**	**0**	**0**	**0**	**9**	**0.0**	**0**	**4**	**50.0**	**9:50**									
	Norfolk Admirals	AHL	22	6	5	11	16																		
	NHL Totals		**777**	**100**	**156**	**256**	**747**	**10**	**4**	**16**	**1047**	**9.6**		**69**	**34.8**	**12:12**	**61**	**6**	**7**	**13**	**79**	**0**	**0**	**1**	**12:46**

Claimed by **Anaheim** from **Vancouver** in Waiver Draft, October 3, 1993. Traded to **Pittsburgh** by **Anaheim** for J.J. Daigneault, February 21, 1997. Signed as a free agent by **Toronto**, October 8, 1998. Signed to a professional try-out contract by **Chicago**, September 12, 2002. • Released by **Chicago**, October 8, 2002. Signed as a free agent by **Chicago**, October 9, 2002. • Spent majority of 2002-03 season as a healthy reserve.

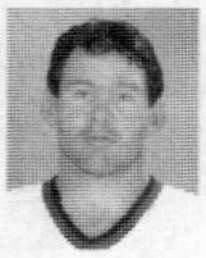

VAN ALLEN, Shaun

(VAN-AL-ehn, SHAWN) **OTT.**

Center. Shoots left. 6'1", 205 lbs. Born, Calgary, Alta., August 29, 1967. Edmonton's 5th choice, 105th overall, in 1987 Entry Draft.

			Regular Season														Playoffs								
Season	Club	League	GP	G	A	Pts	PIM	PP	SH	GW	S	%	+/-	TF	F%	Min	GP	G	A	Pts	PIM	PP	SH	GW	Min
1984-85	Swift Current	SJHL	61	12	20	32	136																		
1985-86	Saskatoon Blades	WHL	55	12	11	23	43										13	4	8	12	28				
1986-87	Saskatoon Blades	WHL	72	38	59	97	116										11	4	6	10	24				
1987-88	Milwaukee	IHL	40	14	28	42	34																		
	Nova Scotia Oilers	AHL	19	4	10	14	17										4	1	1	2	4				
1988-89	Cape Breton	AHL	76	32	42	74	81																		
1989-90	Cape Breton	AHL	61	25	44	69	83										4	0	2	2	8				
1990-91	**Edmonton**	**NHL**	**2**	**0**	**0**	**0**	**0**	**0**	**0**	**0**	**0**	**0.0**	**0**												
	Cape Breton	AHL	76	25	75	100	182										4	0	1	1	8				
1991-92	Cape Breton	AHL	77	29	*84	*113	80										5	3	7	10	14				
1992-93	**Edmonton**	**NHL**	**21**	**1**	**4**	**5**	**6**	**0**	**0**	**0**	**19**	**5.3**	**–2**												
	Cape Breton	AHL	43	14	62	76	68										15	8	9	17	18				
1993-94	**Anaheim**	**NHL**	**80**	**8**	**25**	**33**	**64**	**2**	**2**	**1**	**104**	**7.7**	**0**												
1994-95	**Anaheim**	**NHL**	**45**	**8**	**21**	**29**	**32**	**1**	**1**	**1**	**68**	**11.8**	**–4**												
1995-96	**Anaheim**	**NHL**	**49**	**8**	**17**	**25**	**41**	**0**	**0**	**2**	**78**	**10.3**	**13**												
1996-97	**Ottawa**	**NHL**	**80**	**11**	**14**	**25**	**35**	**1**	**1**	**2**	**123**	**8.9**	**–8**				**7**	**0**	**1**	**1**	**4**	**0**	**0**	**0**	
1997-98	**Ottawa**	**NHL**	**80**	**4**	**15**	**19**	**48**	**0**	**0**	**0**	**104**	**3.8**	**4**				**11**	**0**	**1**	**1**	**10**	**0**	**0**	**0**	
1998-99	**Ottawa**	**NHL**	**79**	**6**	**11**	**17**	**30**	**0**	**1**	**0**	**47**	**12.8**	**3**	**656**	**47.4**	**11:07**	**4**	**0**	**0**	**0**	**0**	**0**	**0**	**0**	**8:42**
99-2000	**Ottawa**	**NHL**	**75**	**9**	**19**	**28**	**37**	**0**	**2**	**4**	**75**	**12.0**	**20**	**911**	**48.6**	**11:49**	**6**	**0**	**1**	**1**	**9**	**0**	**0**	**0**	**12:09**
2000-01	**Dallas**	**NHL**	**59**	**7**	**16**	**23**	**16**	**0**	**2**	**3**	**51**	**13.7**	**5**	**559**	**47.1**	**12:05**	**8**	**0**	**2**	**2**	**8**	**0**	**0**	**0**	**13:56**
2001-02	**Dallas**	**NHL**	**19**	**2**	**4**	**6**	**6**	**0**	**0**	**0**	**20**	**10.0**	**–5**	**177**	**53.1**	**12:57**									
	Montreal	**NHL**	**54**	**6**	**9**	**15**	**20**	**0**	**1**	**1**	**28**	**21.4**	**5**	**381**	**47.8**	**10:08**	**7**	**0**	**1**	**1**	**2**	**0**	**0**	**0**	**9:25**
2002-03	**Ottawa**	**NHL**	**78**	**12**	**20**	**32**	**66**	**2**	**2**	**3**	**53**	**22.6**	**17**	**838**	**45.0**	**12:29**	**18**	**1**	**1**	**2**	**12**	**0**	**0**	**1**	**11:54**
	NHL Totals		**721**	**82**	**175**	**257**	**401**	**6**	**12**	**17**	**770**	**10.6**		**3522**	**47.4**	**11:40**	**61**	**1**	**7**	**8**	**45**	**0**	**0**	**1**	**11:37**

AHL Second All-Star Team (1991) • AHL First All-Star Team (1992) • John B. Sollenberger Trophy (Top Scorer – AHL) (1992)

Signed as a free agent by **Anaheim**, July 22, 1993. Traded to **Ottawa** by **Anaheim** with Jason York for Ted Drury and the rights to Marc Moro, October 1, 1996. Signed as a free agent by **Dallas**, July 12, 2000. Traded to **Montreal** by **Dallas** with Donald Audette for Martin Rucinsky and Benoit Brunet, November 21, 2001. Signed as a free agent by **Ottawa**, July 24, 2002.

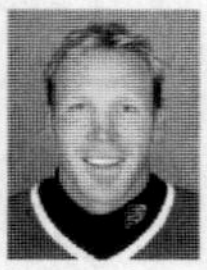

VANDENBUSSCHE, Ryan

(van-dehn-BUHSH, RIGH-yuhn) **CHI.**

Right wing. Shoots right. 6', 200 lbs. Born, Simcoe, Ont., February 28, 1973. Toronto's 9th choice, 173rd overall, in 1992 Entry Draft.

			Regular Season														Playoffs								
Season	Club	League	GP	G	A	Pts	PIM	PP	SH	GW	S	%	+/-	TF	F%	Min	GP	G	A	Pts	PIM	PP	SH	GW	Min
1988-89	Delhi Flames	OJHL-D	3	1	1	2	2																		
1989-90	Norwich	OJHL-C	21	12	10	22	146																		
	Tillsonburg Titans	OJHL-B	24	0	5	5	113																		
1990-91	Massena	OCJHL	10	2	3	5	46																		
	Cornwall Royals	OHL	49	3	8	11	139																		
1991-92	Cornwall Royals	OHL	61	13	15	28	232										6	0	2	2	9				
1992-93	Newmarket	OHL	30	15	12	27	161																		
	Guelph Storm	OHL	29	3	14	17	99										5	1	3	4	13				
	St. John's	AHL	1	0	0	0	0																		
1993-94	St. John's	AHL	44	4	10	14	124																		
	Springfield	AHL	9	1	2	3	29										5	0	0	0	16				
1994-95	St. John's	AHL	53	2	13	15	239										3	0	0	0	17				
1995-96	Binghamton	AHL	68	3	17	20	240										4	0	0	0	9				
1996-97	**NY Rangers**	**NHL**	**11**	**1**	**0**	**1**	**30**	**0**	**0**	**0**	**4**	**25.0**	**–2**												
	Binghamton	AHL	38	8	11	19	133																		
1997-98	**NY Rangers**	**NHL**	**16**	**1**	**0**	**1**	**38**	**0**	**0**	**0**	**2**	**50.0**	**–2**												
	Hartford	AHL	15	2	0	2	45																		
	Chicago	**NHL**	**4**	**0**	**1**	**1**	**5**	**0**	**0**	**0**	**0**	**0.0**	**0**												
	Indianapolis Ice	IHL	3	1	1	2	4																		
1998-99	**Chicago**	**NHL**	**6**	**0**	**0**	**0**	**17**	**0**	**0**	**0**	**3**	**0.0**	**0**	**0**	**0.0**	**9:29**									
	Indianapolis Ice	IHL	34	3	10	13	130																		
	Portland Pirates	AHL	37	4	1	5	119																		

			Regular Season														Playoffs								
Season	Club	League	GP	G	A	Pts	PIM	PP	SH	GW	S	%	+/-	TF	F%	Min	GP	G	A	Pts	PIM	PP	SH	GW	Min
99-2000	Chicago	NHL	52	0	1	1	143	0	0	0	19	0.0	–3	3	0.0	5:37	....	....	....	....	....	....	....	....	....
2000-01	Chicago	NHL	64	2	5	7	146	0	0	0	24	8.3	–8	2	0.0	7:46	....	....	....	....	....	....	....	....	....
2001-02	Chicago	NHL	50	1	2	3	103	0	0	0	22	4.5	–10	2	50.0	6:19	1	0	0	0	0	0	0	0	7:20
2002-03	Chicago	NHL	22	0	0	0	58	0	0	0	7	0.0	0	1	100.0	6:30	....	....	....	....	....	....	....	....	....
	Norfolk Admirals	AHL	4	0	1	1	5	....	....	....	....	....	....	....	....	....	....	....	....	....	....	....	....	....	....
	NHL Totals		225	5	9	14	540	0	0	0	81	6.2		8	25.0	6:44	1	0	0	0	0	0	0	0	7:20

Signed as a free agent by **NY Rangers**, August 22, 1995. Traded to **Chicago** by **NY Rangers** for Ryan Risidore, March 24, 1998. • Missed majority of 2002-03 season recovering from hand injury suffered in game vs. Detroit, January 5, 2003.

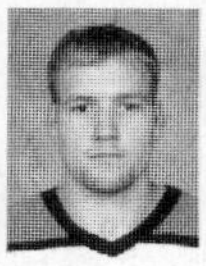

VANDERMEER, Jim

(VAN-duhr-meer, JIHM) **PHI.**

Defense. Shoots left. 6'1", 218 lbs. Born, Caroline, Alta., February 21, 1980.

Season	Club	League	GP	G	A	Pts	PIM	PP	SH	GW	S	%	+/-	TF	F%	Min	GP	G	A	Pts	PIM	PP	SH	GW	Min
1997-98	Red Deer	AMHL	26	4	8	12	51	....	....	....	....	....	....	....	....	....	....	....	....	....	....	....	....	....	....
	Red Deer Rebels	WHL	35	0	3	3	55	....	....	....	....	....	....	....	....	....	2	0	0	0	0	....	....	....	....
1998-99	Red Deer Rebels	WHL	70	5	23	28	258	....	....	....	....	....	....	....	....	....	9	0	1	1	24	....	....	....	....
99-2000	Red Deer Rebels	WHL	71	8	30	38	221	....	....	....	....	....	....	....	....	....	4	0	1	1	16	....	....	....	....
2000-01	Red Deer Rebels	WHL	72	21	44	65	180	....	....	....	....	....	....	....	....	....	22	3	13	16	43	....	....	....	....
2001-02	Philadelphia	AHL	74	1	13	14	88	....	....	....	....	....	....	....	....	....	5	0	2	2	14	....	....	....	....
2002-03	**Philadelphia**	**NHL**	**24**	**2**	**1**	**3**	**27**	**0**	**0**	**0**	**22**	**9.1**	**9**	**0**	**0.0**	**13:42**	**8**	**0**	**1**	**1**	**9**	**0**	**0**	**0**	**12:42**
	Philadelphia	AHL	48	4	8	12	122	....	....	....	....	....	....	....	....	....	....	....	....	....	....	....	....	....	....
	NHL Totals		**24**	**2**	**1**	**3**	**27**	**0**	**0**	**0**	**22**	**9.1**		**0**	**0.0**	**13:42**	**8**	**0**	**1**	**1**	**9**	**0**	**0**	**0**	**12:42**

WHL East First All-Star Team (2001) • Canadian Major Junior Humanitarian Player of the Year (2001)

Signed as a free agent by **Philadelphia**, December 21, 2000.

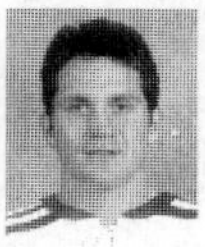

VAN IMPE, Darren

(van-IHMP, DAIR-ehn)

Defense. Shoots left. 6'1", 205 lbs. Born, Saskatoon, Sask., May 18, 1973. NY Islanders' 7th choice, 170th overall, in 1993 Entry Draft.

Season	Club	League	GP	G	A	Pts	PIM	PP	SH	GW	S	%	+/-	TF	F%	Min	GP	G	A	Pts	PIM	PP	SH	GW	Min
1989-90	Prince Albert	SMHL	32	16	31	47	100	....	....	....	....	....	....	....	....	....	....	....	....	....	....	....	....	....	....
	Prince Albert	WHL	1	0	1	1	0	....	....	....	....	....	....	....	....	....	....	....	....	....	....	....	....	....	....
1990-91	Prince Albert	WHL	70	15	45	60	57	....	....	....	....	....	....	....	....	....	3	1	1	2	2	....	....	....	....
1991-92	Prince Albert	WHL	69	9	37	46	89	....	....	....	....	....	....	....	....	....	8	1	5	6	10	....	....	....	....
1992-93	Red Deer Rebels	WHL	54	23	47	70	118	....	....	....	....	....	....	....	....	....	4	2	5	7	16	....	....	....	....
1993-94	Red Deer Rebels	WHL	58	20	64	84	125	....	....	....	....	....	....	....	....	....	4	2	4	6	6	....	....	....	....
1994-95	San Diego Gulls	IHL	76	6	17	23	74	....	....	....	....	....	....	....	....	....	5	0	0	0	0	....	....	....	....
	Anaheim	**NHL**	**1**	**0**	**1**	**1**	**4**	**0**	**0**	**0**	**0**	**0.0**	**0**	....	....	....	....	....	....	....	....	....	....	....	....
1995-96	**Anaheim**	**NHL**	**16**	**1**	**2**	**3**	**14**	**0**	**0**	**1**	**13**	**7.7**	**8**	....	....	....	....	....	....	....	....	....	....	....	....
	Baltimore Bandits	AHL	63	11	47	58	79	....	....	....	....	....	....	....	....	....	....	....	....	....	....	....	....	....	....
1996-97	**Anaheim**	**NHL**	**74**	**4**	**19**	**23**	**90**	**2**	**0**	**0**	**107**	**3.7**	**3**	....	....	....	**9**	**0**	**2**	**2**	**16**	**0**	**0**	**0**	....
1997-98	**Anaheim**	**NHL**	**19**	**1**	**3**	**4**	**4**	**0**	**0**	**0**	**21**	**4.8**	**–10**	....	....	....	....	....	....	....	....	....	....	....	....
	Boston	**NHL**	**50**	**2**	**8**	**10**	**36**	**2**	**0**	**0**	**50**	**4.0**	**4**	....	....	....	**6**	**2**	**1**	**3**	**0**	**1**	**0**	**1**	....
1998-99	**Boston**	**NHL**	**60**	**5**	**15**	**20**	**66**	**4**	**0**	**0**	**92**	**5.4**	**–5**	**0**	**0.0**	**17:54**	**11**	**1**	**2**	**3**	**4**	**1**	**0**	**0**	**17:48**
99-2000	**Boston**	**NHL**	**79**	**5**	**23**	**28**	**73**	**4**	**0**	**0**	**97**	**5.2**	**–19**	**0**	**0.0**	**19:31**	....	....	....	....	....	....	....	....	....
2000-01	**Boston**	**NHL**	**31**	**3**	**10**	**13**	**41**	**2**	**0**	**0**	**40**	**7.5**	**–9**	**0**	**0.0**	**20:11**	....	....	....	....	....	....	....	....	....
2001-02	**NY Rangers**	**NHL**	**17**	**1**	**0**	**1**	**12**	**1**	**0**	**0**	**19**	**5.3**	**3**	**1**	**0.0**	**14:09**	....	....	....	....	....	....	....	....	....
	Florida	**NHL**	**36**	**1**	**6**	**7**	**31**	**1**	**0**	**1**	**27**	**3.7**	**3**	**1**	**0.0**	**19:16**	....	....	....	....	....	....	....	....	....
	NY Islanders	**NHL**	**14**	**1**	**2**	**3**	**16**	**0**	**0**	**0**	**14**	**7.1**	**6**	**0**	**0.0**	**21:36**	**7**	**0**	**4**	**4**	**8**	**0**	**0**	**0**	**17:38**
2002-03	Syracuse Crunch	AHL	6	1	4	5	8	....	....	....	....	....	....	....	....	....	....	....	....	....	....	....	....	....	....
	Columbus	**NHL**	**14**	**1**	**1**	**2**	**10**	**0**	**1**	**0**	**11**	**9.1**	**–6**	**0**	**0.0**	**18:29**	....	....	....	....	....	....	....	....	....
	NHL Totals		**411**	**25**	**90**	**115**	**397**	**16**	**1**	**2**	**491**	**5.1**		**2**	**0.0**	**18:52**	**33**	**3**	**9**	**12**	**28**	**2**	**0**	**1**	**17:44**

WHL East First All-Star Team (1993, 1994)

Traded to **Anaheim** by **NY Islanders** for Anaheim's 8th round choice (Mike Broda) in 1995 Entry Draft, August 31, 1994. Claimed on waivers by **Boston** from **Anaheim**, November 26, 1997. • Missed majority of 2000-01 season recovering from shoulder injury suffered in game vs. Detroit, December 23, 2000. Claimed on waivers by **NY Rangers** from **Boston**, August 7, 2001. Claimed on waivers by **Florida** from **NY Rangers**, December 18, 2001. Traded to **NY Islanders** by **Florida** for NY Islanders' 5th round choice (later traded to Los Angeles – Los Angeles selected Brady Murray) in 2003 Entry Draft, March 19, 2002. Signed to a professional try-out contract by **Syracuse** (AHL), January 9, 2003. Signed as a free agent by **Columbus**, January 20, 2003.

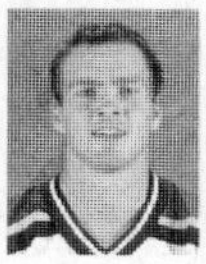

VAN RYN, Mike

(VAN RIHN, MIGHK) **FLA.**

Defense. Shoots right. 6'1", 202 lbs. Born, London, Ont., May 14, 1979. New Jersey's 1st choice, 26th overall, in 1998 Entry Draft.

Season	Club	League	GP	G	A	Pts	PIM	PP	SH	GW	S	%	+/-	TF	F%	Min	GP	G	A	Pts	PIM	PP	SH	GW	Min
1995-96	London Nationals	OJHL-B	44	9	14	23	24	....	....	....	....	....	....	....	....	....	....	....	....	....	....	....	....	....	....
1996-97	London Nationals	OJHL-B	46	14	31	45	32	....	....	....	....	....	....	....	....	....	....	....	....	....	....	....	....	....	....
1997-98	U. of Michigan	CCHA	38	4	14	18	44	....	....	....	....	....	....	....	....	....	....	....	....	....	....	....	....	....	....
1998-99	U. of Michigan	CCHA	37	10	13	23	52	....	....	....	....	....	....	....	....	....	....	....	....	....	....	....	....	....	....
99-2000	Sarnia Sting	OHL	61	6	35	41	34	....	....	....	....	....	....	....	....	....	7	0	5	5	4	....	....	....	....
2000-01	**St. Louis**	**NHL**	**1**	**0**	**0**	**0**	**0**	**0**	**0**	**0**	**1**	**0.0**	**–2**	**0**	**0.0**	**13:43**	....	....	....	....	....	....	....	....	....
	Worcester IceCats	AHL	37	3	10	13	12	....	....	....	....	....	....	....	....	....	7	1	1	2	2	....	....	....	....
2001-02	**St. Louis**	**NHL**	**48**	**2**	**8**	**10**	**18**	**0**	**0**	**1**	**52**	**3.8**	**10**	**0**	**0.0**	**16:23**	**9**	**0**	**0**	**0**	**0**	**0**	**0**	**0**	**16:04**
	Worcester IceCats	AHL	24	2	7	9	17	....	....	....	....	....	....	....	....	....	....	....	....	....	....	....	....	....	....
2002-03	**St. Louis**	**NHL**	**20**	**0**	**3**	**3**	**8**	**0**	**0**	**0**	**21**	**0.0**	**3**	**0**	**0.0**	**15:04**	....	....	....	....	....	....	....	....	....
	Worcester IceCats	AHL	33	2	8	10	16	....	....	....	....	....	....	....	....	....	....	....	....	....	....	....	....	....	....
	San Antonio	AHL	11	0	3	3	20	....	....	....	....	....	....	....	....	....	3	0	0	0	0	....	....	....	....
	NHL Totals		**69**	**2**	**11**	**13**	**26**	**0**	**0**	**1**	**74**	**2.7**		**0**	**0.0**	**15:58**	**9**	**0**	**0**	**0**	**0**	**0**	**0**	**0**	**16:04**

OJHL-B First All-Star Team (1997)

Signed as a free agent by **St. Louis**, June 30, 2000. • Missed majority of 2000-01 season recovering from shoulder injury suffered in game vs. Phoenix, October 5, 2000. Traded to **Florida** by **St. Louis** for Valeri Bure and future considerations, March 11, 2003.

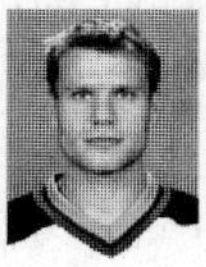

VARADA, Vaclav

(vuh-RA-da, VATS-LAV) **OTT.**

Right wing. Shoots left. 6', 208 lbs. Born, Vsetin, Czech., April 26, 1976. San Jose's 4th choice, 89th overall, in 1994 Entry Draft.

Season	Club	League	GP	G	A	Pts	PIM	PP	SH	GW	S	%	+/-	TF	F%	Min	GP	G	A	Pts	PIM	PP	SH	GW	Min
1993-94	HC Vitkovice	Czech	24	6	7	13	....	....	....	....	....	....	....	....	....	....	5	1	1	2	....	....	....	....	....
1994-95	Tacoma Rockets	WHL	68	50	38	88	108	....	....	....	....	....	....	....	....	....	4	4	3	7	11	....	....	....	....
1995-96	Kelowna Rockets	WHL	59	39	46	85	100	....	....	....	....	....	....	....	....	....	6	3	3	6	16	....	....	....	....
	Buffalo	**NHL**	**1**	**0**	**0**	**0**	**0**	**0**	**0**	**0**	**2**	**0.0**	**0**	....	....	....	....	....	....	....	....	....	....	....	....
	Rochester	AHL	5	3	0	3	4	....	....	....	....	....	....	....	....	....	....	....	....	....	....	....	....	....	....
1996-97	**Buffalo**	**NHL**	**5**	**0**	**0**	**0**	**2**	**0**	**0**	**0**	**2**	**0.0**	**0**	....	....	....	....	....	....	....	....	....	....	....	....
	Rochester	AHL	53	23	25	48	81	....	....	....	....	....	....	....	....	....	10	1	6	7	27	....	....	....	....
1997-98	**Buffalo**	**NHL**	**27**	**5**	**6**	**11**	**15**	**0**	**0**	**1**	**27**	**18.5**	**0**	....	....	....	**15**	**3**	**4**	**7**	**18**	**0**	**0**	**0**	....
	Rochester	AHL	45	30	26	56	74	....	....	....	....	....	....	....	....	....	....	....	....	....	....	....	....	....	....
1998-99	**Buffalo**	**NHL**	**72**	**7**	**24**	**31**	**61**	**1**	**0**	**1**	**123**	**5.7**	**11**	**1**	**0.0**	**14:30**	**21**	**5**	**4**	**9**	**14**	**1**	**0**	**0**	**16:31**
99-2000	HC Vitkovice	Czech	5	2	3	5	12	....	....	....	....	....	....	....	....	....	....	....	....	....	....	....	....	....	....
	Buffalo	**NHL**	**76**	**10**	**27**	**37**	**62**	**0**	**0**	**0**	**140**	**7.1**	**12**	**1**	**0.0**	**14:58**	**5**	**0**	**0**	**0**	**8**	**0**	**0**	**0**	**14:19**
2000-01	**Buffalo**	**NHL**	**75**	**10**	**21**	**31**	**81**	**2**	**0**	**2**	**112**	**8.9**	**–2**	**2**	**0.0**	**15:57**	**13**	**0**	**4**	**4**	**8**	**0**	**0**	**0**	**18:08**
2001-02	**Buffalo**	**NHL**	**76**	**7**	**16**	**23**	**82**	**1**	**0**	**1**	**138**	**5.1**	**–7**	**3**	**0.0**	**16:33**	....	....	....	....	....	....	....	....	....
2002-03	**Buffalo**	**NHL**	**44**	**7**	**4**	**11**	**23**	**1**	**0**	**0**	**64**	**10.9**	**–2**	**13**	**53.9**	**16:07**	....	....	....	....	....	....	....	....	....
	Ottawa	**NHL**	**11**	**2**	**6**	**8**	**8**	**1**	**0**	**0**	**17**	**11.8**	**3**	**8**	**0.0**	**14:57**	**18**	**2**	**4**	**6**	**18**	**0**	**0**	**0**	**13:57**
	NHL Totals		**387**	**48**	**104**	**152**	**334**	**6**	**0**	**5**	**625**	**7.7**		**28**	**25.0**	**15:34**	**72**	**10**	**16**	**26**	**66**	**1**	**0**	**0**	**15:53**

Traded to **Buffalo** by **San Jose** with Martin Spahnel and Philadelphia's 1st (previously acquired, later traded to Phoenix – Phoenix selected Daniel Briere) and 4th (previously acquired, Buffalo selected Mike Martone) round choices in 1996 Entry Draft for Doug Bodger, November 16, 1995. Traded to **Ottawa** by **Buffalo** with Buffalo's 5th round choice (Tim Cook) in 2003 Entry Draft for Jakub Klepis, February 25, 2003.

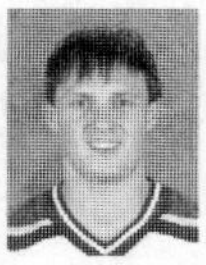

VARLAMOV, Sergei

(vahr-LAHM-uhf, SAIR-gay) **ST.L.**

Left wing. Shoots left. 5'11", 203 lbs. Born, Kiev, USSR, July 21, 1978.

Season	Club	League	GP	G	A	Pts	PIM	PP	SH	GW	S	%	+/-	TF	F%	Min	GP	G	A	Pts	PIM	PP	SH	GW	Min
1994-95	Nelson	RMJHL	26	11	15	26	56	....	....	....	....	....	....	....	....	....	....	....	....	....	....	....	....	....	....
1995-96	Swift Current	WHL	55	23	21	44	65	....	....	....	....	....	....	....	....	....	....	....	....	....	....	....	....	....	....
1996-97	Swift Current	WHL	72	46	39	85	94	....	....	....	....	....	....	....	....	....	10	3	8	11	10	....	....	....	....
	Saint John Flames	AHL	1	0	0	0	0	....	....	....	....	....	....	....	....	....	....	....	....	....	....	....	....	....	....

								Regular Season									Playoffs								
Season	Club	League	GP	G	A	Pts	PIM	PP	SH	GW	S	%	+/-	TF	F%	Min	GP	G	A	Pts	PIM	PP	SH	GW	Min
1997-98	Swift Current	WHL	72	*66	53	*119	132	....	....	....	....	....	....	....	....	....	12	10	5	15	28	....	....	....	....
	Calgary	**NHL**	**1**	**0**	**0**	**0**	**0**	**0**	**0**	**0**	**0**	**0.0**	**0**	....	....	....	....	....	....	....	....	....	....	....	....
	Saint John Flames	AHL	....	....	....	....	....	....	....	....	....	....	....	....	....	....	3	0	0	0	0	....	....	....	....
1998-99	Saint John Flames	AHL	76	24	33	57	66	....	....	....	....	....	....	....	....	....	7	0	4	4	8	....	....	....	....
99-2000	**Calgary**	**NHL**	**7**	**3**	**0**	**3**	**0**	**0**	**0**	**1**	**11**	**27.3**	**0**	**1**	**0.0**	**10:22**	....	....	....	....	....	....	....	....	....
	Saint John Flames	AHL	68	20	21	41	88	....	....	....	....	....	....	....	....	....	3	0	0	0	24	....	....	....	....
2000-01	Saint John Flames	AHL	55	21	30	51	56	....	....	....	....	....	....	....	....	....	19	*15	8	23	10	....	....	....	....
2001-02	**St. Louis**	**NHL**	**52**	**5**	**7**	**12**	**26**	**0**	**0**	**0**	**83**	**6.0**	**4**	**1**	**0.0**	**11:10**	**1**	**0**	**0**	**0**	**2**	**0**	**0**	**0**	**8:45**
	Ukraine	Olympics	2	0	1	1	14	....	....	....	....	....	....	....	....	....	....	....	....	....	....	....	....	....	....
2002-03	**St. Louis**	**NHL**	**3**	**0**	**0**	**0**	**0**	**0**	**0**	**0**	**5**	**0.0**	**1**	**0**	**0.0**	**11:26**	....	....	....	....	....	....	....	....	....
	Worcester IceCats	AHL	72	23	38	61	79	....	....	....	....	....	....	....	....	....	3	2	0	2	0	....	....	....	....
	NHL Totals		**63**	**8**	**7**	**15**	**26**	**0**	**0**	**1**	**99**	**8.1**		**2**	**0.0**	**11:06**	**1**	**0**	**0**	**0**	**2**	**0**	**0**	**0**	**8:45**

WHL East First All-Star Team (1998) • Canadian Major Junior First All-Star Team (1998) • Canadian Major Junior Player of the Year (1998)

Signed as a free agent by **Calgary**, September 18, 1996. Traded to **St. Louis** by **Calgary** with Fred Brathwaite, Daniel Tkaczuk and Calgary's 9th round choice (Grant Jacobsen) in 2001 Entry Draft for Roman Turek and St. Louis' 4th round choice (Yegor Shastin) in 2001 Entry Draft, June 23, 2001.

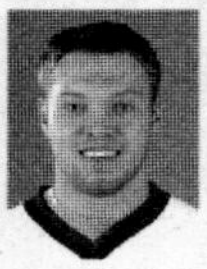

VASICEK, Josef

(VAHSH-ih-chehk, YOH-zehf) **CAR.**

Center. Shoots left. 6'4", 200 lbs. Born, Havlickuv Brod, Czech., September 12, 1980. Carolina's 4th choice, 91st overall, in 1998 Entry Draft.

Season	Club	League	GP	G	A	Pts	PIM	PP	SH	GW	S	%	+/-	TF	F%	Min	GP	G	A	Pts	PIM	PP	SH	GW	Min
1995-96	HavlickuvBrodJr.	Czech-Jr.	36	25	25	50	....	....	....	....	....	....	....	....	....	....	....	....	....	....	....	....	....	....	....
1996-97	Slavia Praha Jr.	Czech-Jr.	37	20	40	60	....	....	....	....	....	....	....	....	....	....	....	....	....	....	....	....	....	....	....
1997-98	Slavia Praha Jr.	Czech-Jr.	34	13	20	33	....	....	....	....	....	....	....	....	....	....	....	....	....	....	....	....	....	....	....
1998-99	Sault Ste. Marie	OHL	66	21	35	56	30	....	....	....	....	....	....	....	....	....	5	3	0	3	10	....	....	....	....
99-2000	Sault Ste. Marie	OHL	54	26	46	72	49	....	....	....	....	....	....	....	....	....	17	5	15	20	8	....	....	....	....
2000-01	**Carolina**	**NHL**	**76**	**8**	**13**	**21**	**53**	**1**	**0**	**0**	**103**	**7.8**	**–8**	**786**	**46.6**	**11:49**	**6**	**2**	**0**	**2**	**0**	**0**	**0**	**0**	**13:56**
	Cincinnati	IHL	....	....	....	....	....	....	....	....	....	....	....	....	....	....	3	0	0	0	0	....	....	....	....
2001-02	**Carolina**	**NHL**	**78**	**14**	**17**	**31**	**53**	**3**	**0**	**3**	**117**	**12.0**	**–7**	**878**	**48.3**	**14:11**	**23**	**3**	**2**	**5**	**12**	**0**	**0**	**1**	**14:50**
2002-03	**Carolina**	**NHL**	**57**	**10**	**10**	**20**	**33**	**4**	**0**	**1**	**87**	**11.5**	**–19**	**652**	**49.5**	**15:57**	....	....	....	....	....	....	....	....	....
	NHL Totals		**211**	**32**	**40**	**72**	**139**	**8**	**0**	**4**	**307**	**10.4**		**2316**	**48.1**	**13:49**	**29**	**5**	**2**	**7**	**12**	**0**	**0**	**1**	**14:39**

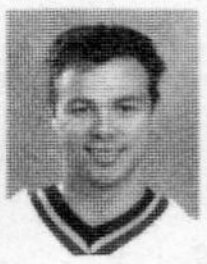

VASILJEVS, Herbert

(vah-SEE-lee-ehf, HUHR-buhrt)

Right wing. Shoots right. 5'11", 180 lbs. Born, Riga, Latvia, May 27, 1976.

Season	Club	League	GP	G	A	Pts	PIM	PP	SH	GW	S	%	+/-	TF	F%	Min	GP	G	A	Pts	PIM	PP	SH	GW	Min
1994-95	Krefelder EV	Germany	42	4	5	9	24	....	....	....	....	....	....	....	....	....	15	1	4	5	10	....	....	....	....
1995-96	Guelph Storm	OHL	65	34	33	67	63	....	....	....	....	....	....	....	....	....	16	6	13	19	6	....	....	....	....
1996-97	Carolina	AHL	54	13	18	31	30	....	....	....	....	....	....	....	....	....	....	....	....	....	....	....	....	....	....
	Port Huron	ColHL	3	3	2	5	4	....	....	....	....	....	....	....	....	....	....	....	....	....	....	....	....	....	....
1997-98	New Haven	AHL	76	36	30	66	60	....	....	....	....	....	....	....	....	....	3	1	0	1	2	....	....	....	....
1998-99	**Florida**	**NHL**	**5**	**0**	**0**	**0**	**2**	**0**	**0**	**0**	**6**	**0.0**	**–1**	**3**	**66.7**	**11:06**	....	....	....	....	....	....	....	....	....
	Kentucky	AHL	76	28	48	76	66	....	....	....	....	....	....	....	....	....	12	2	1	3	4	....	....	....	....
99-2000	**Atlanta**	**NHL**	**7**	**1**	**0**	**1**	**4**	**0**	**0**	**0**	**2**	**50.0**	**–3**	**27**	**48.2**	**9:18**	....	....	....	....	....	....	....	....	....
	Orlando	IHL	73	25	35	60	60	....	....	....	....	....	....	....	....	....	6	2	2	4	6	....	....	....	....
2000-01	**Atlanta**	**NHL**	**21**	**4**	**5**	**9**	**14**	**2**	**0**	**1**	**41**	**9.8**	**–11**	**37**	**40.5**	**16:01**	....	....	....	....	....	....	....	....	....
	Orlando	IHL	58	22	26	48	32	....	....	....	....	....	....	....	....	....	12	8	3	11	14	....	....	....	....
2001-02	**Vancouver**	**NHL**	**18**	**3**	**2**	**5**	**2**	**2**	**0**	**0**	**17**	**17.6**	**0**	**8**	**75.0**	**9:09**	....	....	....	....	....	....	....	....	....
	Manitoba Moose	AHL	31	12	14	26	10	....	....	....	....	....	....	....	....	....	....	....	....	....	....	....	....	....	....
2002-03	Manitoba Moose	AHL	69	10	29	39	30	....	....	....	....	....	....	....	....	....	14	3	5	8	8	....	....	....	....
	NHL Totals		**51**	**8**	**7**	**15**	**22**	**4**	**0**	**1**	**66**	**12.1**		**75**	**48.0**	**12:11**	....	....	....	....	....	....	....	....	....

Signed as a free agent by **Florida**, October 3, 1996. Traded to **Atlanta** by **Florida** with Gord Murphy, Daniel Tjarnqvist and Ottawa's 6th round choice (previously acquired, later traded to Dallas – Dallas selected Justin Cox) in 1999 Entry Draft for Trevor Kidd, June 25, 1999. Signed as a free agent by **Vancouver**, August 11, 2001.

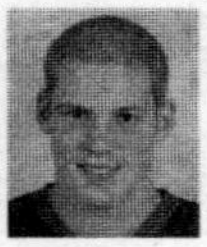

VEILLEUX, Stephane

(VAY-oo, STEH-fan) **MIN.**

Left wing. Shoots left. 6'1", 187 lbs. Born, Beaureville, Que., November 16, 1981. Minnesota's 4th choice, 93rd overall, in 2001 Entry Draft.

Season	Club	League	GP	G	A	Pts	PIM	PP	SH	GW	S	%	+/-	TF	F%	Min	GP	G	A	Pts	PIM	PP	SH	GW	Min
1997-98	Beauce-Amiante	QAAA	21	20	17	37	....	....	....	....	....	....	....	....	....	....	....	....	....	....	....	....	....	....	....
	Levis-Lauzon	QAAA	14	3	5	8	....	....	....	....	....	....	....	....	....	....	1	0	0	0	....	....	....	....	....
1998-99	Victoriaville Tigres	QMJHL	65	6	13	19	35	....	....	....	....	....	....	....	....	....	6	1	3	4	2	....	....	....	....
99-2000	Victoriaville Tigres	QMJHL	22	1	4	5	17	....	....	....	....	....	....	....	....	....	....	....	....	....	....	....	....	....	....
	Val-d'Or Foreurs	QMJHL	50	14	28	42	100	....	....	....	....	....	....	....	....	....	....	....	....	....	....	....	....	....	....
2000-01	Val-d'Or Foreurs	QMJHL	68	48	67	115	90	....	....	....	....	....	....	....	....	....	21	15	18	33	42	....	....	....	....
2001-02	Houston Aeros	AHL	77	13	22	35	113	....	....	....	....	....	....	....	....	....	14	2	4	6	20	....	....	....	....
2002-03	**Minnesota**	**NHL**	**38**	**3**	**2**	**5**	**23**	**1**	**0**	**0**	**52**	**5.8**	**–6**	**13**	**7.7**	**12:08**	....	....	....	....	....	....	....	....	....
	Houston Aeros	AHL	29	8	4	12	43	....	....	....	....	....	....	....	....	....	23	7	11	18	12	....	....	....	....
	NHL Totals		**38**	**3**	**2**	**5**	**23**	**1**	**0**	**0**	**52**	**5.8**		**13**	**7.7**	**12:08**	....	....	....	....	....	....	....	....	....

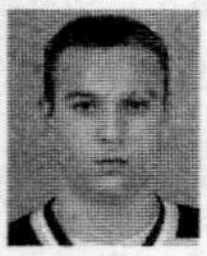

VERNARSKY, Kris

(veh-NAHR-skee, KRIHS) **BOS.**

Center. Shoots left. 6'3", 201 lbs. Born, Detroit, MI, April 5, 1982. Toronto's 2nd choice, 51st overall, in 2000 Entry Draft.

Season	Club	League	GP	G	A	Pts	PIM	PP	SH	GW	S	%	+/-	TF	F%	Min	GP	G	A	Pts	PIM	PP	SH	GW	Min
1997-98	U.S. National U-18	USDP	69	11	18	29	97	....	....	....	....	....	....	....	....	....	....	....	....	....	....	....	....	....	....
1998-99	Plymouth Whalers	OHL	45	3	14	17	30	....	....	....	....	....	....	....	....	....	11	0	0	0	2	....	....	....	....
99-2000	Plymouth Whalers	OHL	64	16	22	38	63	....	....	....	....	....	....	....	....	....	19	3	6	9	24	....	....	....	....
2000-01	Plymouth Whalers	OHL	60	14	21	35	35	....	....	....	....	....	....	....	....	....	19	7	10	17	19	....	....	....	....
2001-02	Plymouth Whalers	OHL	59	19	36	55	98	....	....	....	....	....	....	....	....	....	6	1	2	3	15	....	....	....	....
2002-03	**Boston**	**NHL**	**14**	**1**	**0**	**1**	**2**	**0**	**0**	**0**	**18**	**5.6**	**–2**	**22**	**54.6**	**10:15**	....	....	....	....	....	....	....	....	....
	Providence Bruins	AHL	65	12	15	27	49	....	....	....	....	....	....	....	....	....	4	0	0	0	20	....	....	....	....
	NHL Totals		**14**	**1**	**0**	**1**	**2**	**0**	**0**	**0**	**18**	**5.6**		**22**	**54.5**	**10:15**	....	....	....	....	....	....	....	....	....

Rights traded to **Boston** by **Toronto** for Richard Jackman, May 13, 2002.

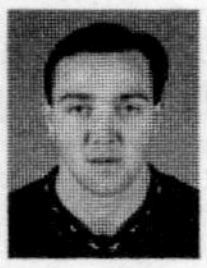

VIGIER, J.P.

(vih-ZHAY, JAY-pee **ATL.**

Right wing. Shoots right. 6', 205 lbs. Born, Notre Dame de Lourdes, Man., September 11, 1976.

Season	Club	League	GP	G	A	Pts	PIM	PP	SH	GW	S	%	+/-	TF	F%	Min	GP	G	A	Pts	PIM	PP	SH	GW	Min
1995-96	Portage Terriers	MJHL	56	32	49	81	....	....	....	....	....	....	....	....	....	....	....	....	....	....	....	....	....	....	....
1996-97	North-Michigan	WCHA	36	10	14	24	54	....	....	....	....	....	....	....	....	....	....	....	....	....	....	....	....	....	....
1997-98	North-Michigan	CCHA	36	12	15	27	60	....	....	....	....	....	....	....	....	....	....	....	....	....	....	....	....	....	....
1998-99	North-Michigan	CCHA	42	21	18	39	80	....	....	....	....	....	....	....	....	....	....	....	....	....	....	....	....	....	....
99-2000	North-Michigan	CCHA	39	18	17	35	72	....	....	....	....	....	....	....	....	....	....	....	....	....	....	....	....	....	....
	Orlando	IHL	3	1	0	1	0	....	....	....	....	....	....	....	....	....	....	....	....	....	....	....	....	....	....
2000-01	**Atlanta**	**NHL**	**2**	**0**	**0**	**0**	**0**	**0**	**0**	**0**	**1**	**0.0**	**–2**	**1**	**100.0**	**9:56**	....	....	....	....	....	....	....	....	....
	Orlando	IHL	78	23	17	40	66	....	....	....	....	....	....	....	....	....	16	6	6	12	14	....	....	....	....
2001-02	**Atlanta**	**NHL**	**15**	**4**	**1**	**5**	**4**	**0**	**0**	**0**	**18**	**22.2**	**–5**	**3**	**66.7**	**13:13**	....	....	....	....	....	....	....	....	....
	Chicago Wolves	AHL	62	25	16	41	26	....	....	....	....	....	....	....	....	....	21	7	7	14	20	....	....	....	....
2002-03	**Atlanta**	**NHL**	**13**	**0**	**0**	**0**	**4**	**0**	**0**	**0**	**21**	**0.0**	**–13**	**1**	**0.0**	**14:07**	....	....	....	....	....	....	....	....	....
	Chicago Wolves	AHL	63	29	27	56	54	....	....	....	....	....	....	....	....	....	9	3	1	4	4	....	....	....	....
	NHL Totals		**30**	**4**	**1**	**5**	**8**	**0**	**0**	**0**	**40**	**10.0**		**5**	**60.0**	**13:23**	....	....	....	....	....	....	....	....	....

CCHA Second All-Star Team (1999) • CCHA All-Tournament Team (1999)

Signed as a free agent by **Atlanta**, April 20, 2000.

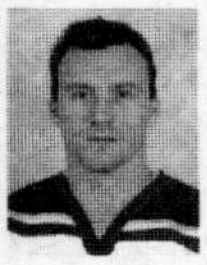

VIRTA, Tony

(VIHR-ta, TON-nee)

Right wing. Shoots left. 5'10", 187 lbs. Born, Hameenlinna, Finland, June 28, 1972. Minnesota's 5th choice, 103rd overall, in 2001 Entry Draft.

Season	Club	League	GP	G	A	Pts	PIM	PP	SH	GW	S	%	+/-	TF	F%	Min	GP	G	A	Pts	PIM	PP	SH	GW	Min
1990-91	HPK Jr.	Finn-Jr.	28	17	34	51	42	....	....	....	....	....	....	....	....	....	....	....	....	....	....	....	....	....	....
1991-92	HPK Hameenlinna	Finland	35	24	31	55	114	....	....	....	....	....	....	....	....	....	....	....	....	....	....	....	....	....	....
1992-93	HPK Jr.	Finn-Jr.	2	1	2	3	2	....	....	....	....	....	....	....	....	....	....	....	....	....	....	....	....	....	....
	HPK Hameenlinna	Finland	48	9	8	17	35	....	....	....	....	....	....	....	....	....	12	1	0	1	0	....	....	....	....
1993-94	HPK Hameenlinna	Finland	47	17	16	33	50	....	....	....	....	....	....	....	....	....	....	....	....	....	....	....	....	....	....
1994-95	HPK Hameenlinna	Finland	43	9	24	33	75	....	....	....	....	....	....	....	....	....	....	....	....	....	....	....	....	....	....
1995-96	HPK Hameenlinna	Finland	48	15	19	34	12	....	....	....	....	....	....	....	....	....	9	1	3	4	31	....	....	....	....
1996-97	Frankfurt Lions	Germany	48	13	13	26	40	....	....	....	....	....	....	....	....	....	8	1	2	3	56	....	....	....	....

			Regular Season														Playoffs								
Season	Club	League	GP	G	A	Pts	PIM	PP	SH	GW	S	%	+/-	TF	F%	Min	GP	G	A	Pts	PIM	PP	SH	GW	Min
1997-98	TPS Turku	EuroHL	6	1	0	1	0	....	....	....	....	....	....	....	....	....	....	....	....	....	....	....	....	....	....
	TPS Turku	Finland	48	17	15	32	26	....	....	....	....	....	....	....	....	....	3	0	0	0	0	....	....	....	....
1998-99	TPS Turku	Finland	54	16	27	43	32	....	....	....	....	....	....	....	....	....	10	6	6	12	8	....	....	....	....
99-2000	TPS Turku	EuroHL	5	1	5	6	2	....	....	....	....	....	....	....	....	....	4	1	2	3	0	....	....	....	....
	TPS Turku	Finland	53	14	37	51	57	....	....	....	....	....	....	....	....	....	11	2	7	9	6	....	....	....	....
2000-01	TPS Turku	Finland	56	27	33	60	24	....	....	....	....	....	....	....	....	....	10	2	5	7	6	....	....	....	....
2001-02	**Minnesota**	**NHL**	**8**	**2**	**3**	**5**	**0**	**0**	**0**	**0**	**15**	**13.3**	**0**	**0**	**0.0**	**13:23**	....	....	....	....	....	....	....	....	....
	Houston Aeros	AHL	67	25	33	58	29	....	....	....	....	....	....	....	....	....	14	1	9	10	10	....	....	....	....
2002-03	Houston Aeros	AHL	39	6	12	18	14	....	....	....	....	....	....	....	....	....	....	....	....	....	....	....	....	....	....
	Sodertalje SK	Sweden	5	2	1	3	31	....	....	....	....	....	....	....	....	....	....	....	....	....	....	....	....	....	....
	NHL Totals		**8**	**2**	**3**	**5**	**0**	**0**	**0**	**0**	**15**	**13.3**		**0**	**0.0**	**13:23**	....	....	....	....	....	....	....	....	....

Finnish League Player of the Year (2001)
• Loaned to **Sodertalje SK** (Sweden), by **Minnesota**, February 6, 2003.

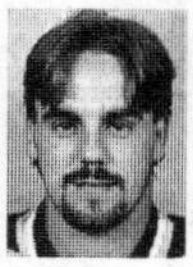

VIRTUE, Terry

(VIR-too, TAIR-ee)

Defense. Shoots right. 6', 207 lbs. Born, Scarborough, Ont., August 12, 1970.

Season	Club	League	GP	G	A	Pts	PIM	PP	SH	GW	S	%	+/-	TF	F%	Min	GP	G	A	Pts	PIM	PP	SH	GW	Min
1988-89	Hobbema Hawks	AJHL	56	6	31	37	339	....	....	....	....	....	....	....	....	....	....	....	....	....	....	....	....	....	....
	Victoria Cougars	WHL	8	1	1	2	13	....	....	....	....	....	....	....	....	....	....	....	....	....	....	....	....	....	....
1989-90	Victoria Cougars	WHL	24	1	9	10	85	....	....	....	....	....	....	....	....	....	....	....	....	....	....	....	....	....	....
	Tri-City	WHL	34	1	10	11	82	....	....	....	....	....	....	....	....	....	6	0	0	0	30	....	....	....	....
1990-91	Tri-City	WHL	11	1	8	9	24	....	....	....	....	....	....	....	....	....	....	....	....	....	....	....	....	....	....
	Portland	WHL	59	9	44	53	127	....	....	....	....	....	....	....	....	....	....	....	....	....	....	....	....	....	....
1991-92	Roanoke Valley	ECHL	38	4	22	26	165	....	....	....	....	....	....	....	....	....	....	....	....	....	....	....	....	....	....
	Louisville	ECHL	23	1	15	16	58	....	....	....	....	....	....	....	....	....	13	0	8	8	49	....	....	....	....
1992-93	Louisville	ECHL	28	0	17	17	84	....	....	....	....	....	....	....	....	....	....	....	....	....	....	....	....	....	....
	Wheeling	ECHL	31	3	15	18	86	....	....	....	....	....	....	....	....	....	16	3	5	8	18	....	....	....	....
1993-94	Wheeling	ECHL	34	5	28	33	61	....	....	....	....	....	....	....	....	....	6	2	2	4	4	....	....	....	....
	Cape Breton	AHL	26	4	6	10	10	....	....	....	....	....	....	....	....	....	5	0	0	0	17	....	....	....	....
1994-95	Worcester IceCats	AHL	73	14	25	39	183	....	....	....	....	....	....	....	....	....	....	....	....	....	....	....	....	....	....
	Atlanta Knights	IHL	1	0	0	0	2	....	....	....	....	....	....	....	....	....	....	....	....	....	....	....	....	....	....
1995-96	Worcester IceCats	AHL	76	7	31	38	234	....	....	....	....	....	....	....	....	....	4	0	0	0	4	....	....	....	....
1996-97	Worcester IceCats	AHL	80	16	26	42	220	....	....	....	....	....	....	....	....	....	5	0	4	4	8	....	....	....	....
1997-98	Worcester IceCats	AHL	74	8	26	34	233	....	....	....	....	....	....	....	....	....	11	1	4	5	41	....	....	....	....
1998-99	**Boston**	**NHL**	**4**	**0**	**0**	**0**	**0**	**0**	**0**	**0**	**2**	**0.0**	**2**	**0**	**0.0**	**9:41**	....	....	....	....	....	....	....	....	....
	Providence Bruins	AHL	76	8	48	56	117	....	....	....	....	....	....	....	....	....	17	2	12	14	29	....	....	....	....
99-2000	**NY Rangers**	**NHL**	**1**	**0**	**0**	**0**	**0**	**0**	**0**	**0**	**2**	**0.0**	**–2**	**0**	**0.0**	**12:32**	....	....	....	....	....	....	....	....	....
	Hartford	AHL	67	5	22	27	166	....	....	....	....	....	....	....	....	....	23	3	7	10	51	....	....	....	....
2000-01	Hartford	AHL	71	5	24	29	166	....	....	....	....	....	....	....	....	....	5	1	0	1	2	....	....	....	....
2001-02	Hartford	AHL	76	4	20	24	117	....	....	....	....	....	....	....	....	....	10	0	1	1	19	....	....	....	....
2002-03	Worcester IceCats	AHL	78	5	30	35	144	....	....	....	....	....	....	....	....	....	....	....	....	....	....	....	....	....	....
	NHL Totals		**5**	**0**	**0**	**0**	**0**	**0**	**0**	**0**	**4**	**0.0**		**0**	**0.0**	**10:15**	....	....	....	....	....	....	....	....	....

AHL Second All-Star Team (1999)
Signed as a free agent by **St. Louis**, January 29, 1996. Signed as a free agent by **Boston**, August 28, 1998. Signed as a free agent by **NY Rangers**, July 29, 1999. Signed as a free agent by **St. Louis**, July 14, 2002.

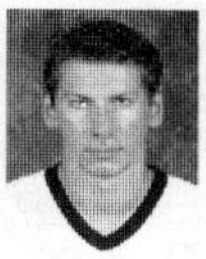

VISHNEVSKI, Vitaly

(vihsh-NEHV-skee, vih-TAL-ee) **ANA.**

Defense. Shoots left. 6'2", 206 lbs. Born, Kharkov, USSR, March 18, 1980. Anaheim's 1st choice, 5th overall, in 1998 Entry Draft.

Season	Club	League	GP	G	A	Pts	PIM	PP	SH	GW	S	%	+/-	TF	F%	Min	GP	G	A	Pts	PIM	PP	SH	GW	Min
1995-96	Yaroslavl	CIS	40	4	4	8	20	....	....	....	....	....	....	....	....	....	....	....	....	....	....	....	....	....	....
1996-97	Yaroslavl 2	Russia-3	45	0	2	2	30	....	....	....	....	....	....	....	....	....	....	....	....	....	....	....	....	....	....
1997-98	Yaroslavl	Russia	47	8	9	17	164	....	....	....	....	....	....	....	....	....	....	....	....	....	....	....	....	....	....
1998-99	Yaroslavl	Russia	34	3	4	7	38	....	....	....	....	....	....	....	....	....	10	0	0	0	4	....	....	....	....
99-2000	**Anaheim**	**NHL**	**31**	**1**	**1**	**2**	**26**	**1**	**0**	**0**	**17**	**5.9**	**0**	**0**	**0.0**	**16:38**	....	....	....	....	....	....	....	....	....
	Cincinnati	AHL	35	1	3	4	45	....	....	....	....	....	....	....	....	....	....	....	....	....	....	....	....	....	....
2000-01	**Anaheim**	**NHL**	**76**	**1**	**10**	**11**	**99**	**0**	**0**	**0**	**49**	**2.0**	**–1**	**0**	**0.0**	**19:14**	....	....	....	....	....	....	....	....	....
2001-02	**Anaheim**	**NHL**	**74**	**0**	**3**	**3**	**60**	**0**	**0**	**0**	**54**	**0.0**	**–10**	**0**	**0.0**	**17:36**	....	....	....	....	....	....	....	....	....
2002-03	**Anaheim**	**NHL**	**80**	**2**	**6**	**8**	**76**	**0**	**1**	**0**	**65**	**3.1**	**–8**	**0**	**0.0**	**14:10**	**21**	**0**	**1**	**1**	**6**	**0**	**0**	**0**	**10:02**
	NHL Totals		**261**	**4**	**20**	**24**	**261**	**1**	**1**	**0**	**185**	**2.2**		**0**	**0.0**	**16:55**	**21**	**0**	**1**	**1**	**6**	**0**	**0**	**0**	**10:02**

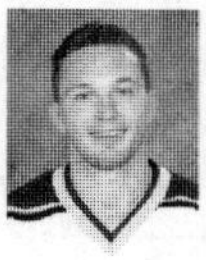

VISNOVSKY, Lubomir

(vihsh-NAWV-skee, LOO-boh-mihr) **L.A.**

Defense. Shoots left. 5'10", 183 lbs. Born, Topolcany, Czech., August 11, 1976. Los Angeles' 4th choice, 118th overall, in 2000 Entry Draft.

Season	Club	League	GP	G	A	Pts	PIM	PP	SH	GW	S	%	+/-	TF	F%	Min	GP	G	A	Pts	PIM	PP	SH	GW	Min
1994-95	Slov. Bratislava	Slovakia	36	11	12	23	10	....	....	....	....	....	....	....	....	....	9	1	3	4	2	....	....	....	....
1995-96	Slov. Bratislava	Slovakia	35	8	6	14	22	....	....	....	....	....	....	....	....	....	13	1	5	6	2	....	....	....	....
1996-97	Slov. Bratislava	Slovakia	44	11	12	23	....	....	....	....	....	....	....	....	....	....	2	0	1	1	....	....	....	....	....
	Slov. Bratislava	EuroHL	6	3	1	4	2	....	....	....	....	....	....	....	....	....	2	0	0	0	6	....	....	....	....
1997-98	Slov. Bratislava	Slovakia	36	7	9	16	16	....	....	....	....	....	....	....	....	....	11	2	4	6	8	....	....	....	....
	Slov. Bratislava	EuroHL	6	1	0	1	4	....	....	....	....	....	....	....	....	....	....	....	....	....	....	....	....	....	....
1998-99	Slov. Bratislava	Slovakia	40	9	10	19	31	....	....	....	....	....	....	....	....	....	10	5	5	10	0	....	....	....	....
	Slov. Bratislava	EuroHL	6	0	3	3	4	....	....	....	....	....	....	....	....	....	....	....	....	....	....	....	....	....	....
99-2000	Slov. Bratislava	Slovakia	52	21	24	45	38	....	....	....	....	....	....	....	....	....	8	5	3	8	16	....	....	....	....
2000-01	**Los Angeles**	**NHL**	**81**	**7**	**32**	**39**	**36**	**3**	**0**	**3**	**105**	**6.7**	**16**	**0**	**0.0**	**16:58**	**8**	**0**	**0**	**0**	**0**	**0**	**0**	**0**	**13:57**
2001-02	**Los Angeles**	**NHL**	**72**	**4**	**17**	**21**	**14**	**1**	**0**	**2**	**95**	**4.2**	**–5**	**0**	**0.0**	**16:15**	**4**	**0**	**1**	**1**	**0**	**0**	**0**	**0**	**8:22**
	Slovakia	Olympics	3	1	2	3	0	....	....	....	....	....	....	....	....	....	....	....	....	....	....	....	....	....	....
2002-03	**Los Angeles**	**NHL**	**57**	**8**	**16**	**24**	**28**	**1**	**0**	**1**	**85**	**9.4**	**2**	**0**	**0.0**	**19:20**	....	....	....	....	....	....	....	....	....
	NHL Totals		**210**	**19**	**65**	**84**	**78**	**5**	**0**	**6**	**285**	**6.7**		**0**	**0.0**	**17:22**	**12**	**0**	**1**	**1**	**0**	**0**	**0**	**0**	**12:05**

NHL All-Rookie Team (2001)

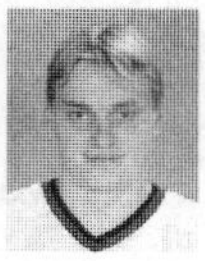

VOLCHENKOV, Anton

(vohl-chen-KAHF, an-TUHN) **OTT.**

Defense. Shoots left. 6'1", 227 lbs. Born, Moscow, USSR, February 25, 1982. Ottawa's 1st choice, 21st overall, in 2000 Entry Draft.

Season	Club	League	GP	G	A	Pts	PIM	PP	SH	GW	S	%	+/-	TF	F%	Min	GP	G	A	Pts	PIM	PP	SH	GW	Min
99-2000	HC CSKA 2	Russia-3	6	0	1	1	10	....	....	....	....	....	....	....	....	....	....	....	....	....	....	....	....	....	....
	HC CSKA	Russia-2	30	2	9	11	36	....	....	....	....	....	....	....	....	....	....	....	....	....	....	....	....	....	....
2000-01	Krylja Sovetov	Russia-2	34	3	4	7	56	....	....	....	....	....	....	....	....	....	....	....	....	....	....	....	....	....	....
2001-02	Krylja Sovetov 2	Russia-3	1	0	0	0	0	....	....	....	....	....	....	....	....	....	....	....	....	....	....	....	....	....	....
	Krylja Sovetov	Russia	47	4	16	20	50	....	....	....	....	....	....	....	....	....	3	0	0	0	29	....	....	....	....
2002-03	**Ottawa**	**NHL**	**57**	**3**	**13**	**16**	**40**	**0**	**0**	**0**	**75**	**4.0**	**–4**	**0**	**0.0**	**15:30**	**17**	**1**	**1**	**2**	**4**	**0**	**0**	**1**	**13:31**
	NHL Totals		**57**	**3**	**13**	**16**	**40**	**0**	**0**	**0**	**75**	**4.0**		**0**	**0.0**	**15:30**	**17**	**1**	**1**	**2**	**4**	**0**	**0**	**1**	**13:31**

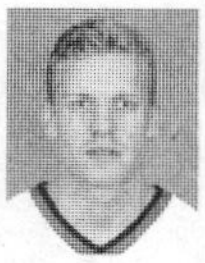

VON ARX, Reto

(VAWN-ARX, RAY-toh)

Center. Shoots left. 5'10", 190 lbs. Born, Egerkingen, Switz., September 13, 1976. Chicago's 14th choice, 271st overall, in 2000 Entry Draft.

Season	Club	League	GP	G	A	Pts	PIM	PP	SH	GW	S	%	+/-	TF	F%	Min	GP	G	A	Pts	PIM	PP	SH	GW	Min
1992-93	SC Langnau	Swiss-2	35	11	4	15	28	....	....	....	....	....	....	....	....	....	5	0	0	0	6	....	....	....	....
1993-94	SC Langnau	Swiss-3	36	35	31	66	42	....	....	....	....	....	....	....	....	....	....	....	....	....	....	....	....	....	....
1994-95	SC Langnau	Swiss-2	36	14	9	23	72	....	....	....	....	....	....	....	....	....	5	1	2	3	27	....	....	....	....
1995-96	HC Davos	Swiss	34	4	6	10	59	....	....	....	....	....	....	....	....	....	5	0	2	2	4	....	....	....	....
1996-97	HC Davos	Swiss	42	10	17	27	78	....	....	....	....	....	....	....	....	....	6	1	3	4	4	....	....	....	....
1997-98	HC Davos	Swiss	39	8	15	23	113	....	....	....	....	....	....	....	....	....	18	10	6	16	18	....	....	....	....
1998-99	HC Davos	Swiss	45	21	20	41	76	....	....	....	....	....	....	....	....	....	6	4	6	10	16	....	....	....	....
99-2000	HC Davos	Swiss	45	19	26	45	70	....	....	....	....	....	....	....	....	....	5	2	0	2	10	....	....	....	....
2000-01	**Chicago**	**NHL**	**19**	**3**	**1**	**4**	**4**	**0**	**0**	**1**	**12**	**25.0**	**–4**	**94**	**42.6**	**11:26**	....	....	....	....	....	....	....	....	....
	Norfolk Admirals	AHL	49	16	26	42	28	....	....	....	....	....	....	....	....	....	9	1	2	3	8	....	....	....	....
2001-02	HC Davos	Swiss	31	6	15	21	95	....	....	....	....	....	....	....	....	....	12	3	8	11	35	....	....	....	....
	Switzerland	Olympics	2	0	1	1	0	....	....	....	....	....	....	....	....	....	....	....	....	....	....	....	....	....	....
2002-03	HC Davos	Swiss	42	10	32	42	73	....	....	....	....	....	....	....	....	....	17	4	8	12	28	....	....	....	....
	NHL Totals		**19**	**3**	**1**	**4**	**4**	**0**	**0**	**1**	**12**	**25.0**		**94**	**42.6**	**11:26**	....	....	....	....	....	....	....	....	....

Signed as a free agent by **HC Davos** (Swiss), October 6, 2001.

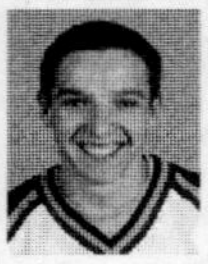

VRBATA, Radim
(vuhr-BA-tuh, ra-DEEM) **CAR.**

Right wing. Shoots right. 6'1", 190 lbs. Born, Mlada Boleslav, Czech., June 13, 1981. Colorado's 10th choice, 212th overall, in 1999 Entry Draft.

			Regular Season														Playoffs								
Season	Club	League	GP	G	A	Pts	PIM	PP	SH	GW	S	%	+/-	TF	F%	Min	GP	G	A	Pts	PIM	PP	SH	GW	Min
1997-98	Mlada Boleslav Jr.	Czech-Jr.	35	42	31	73	4	....	....	....	....	....	....	....	....	....	....	....	....	....	....	....	....	....	....
1998-99	Hull Olympiques	QMJHL	54	22	38	60	16	....	....	....	....	....	....	....	....	....	23	6	13	19	6	....	....	....	....
99-2000	Hull Olympiques	QMJHL	58	29	45	74	26	....	....	....	....	....	....	....	....	....	15	3	9	12	8	....	....	....	....
2000-01	Shawinigan	QMJHL	55	56	64	120	67	....	....	....	....	....	....	....	....	....	10	4	7	11	4	....	....	....	....
	Hershey Bears	AHL	....	....	....	....	....	....	....	....	....	....	....	....	....	....	1	0	1	1	2	....	....	....	....
2001-02	**Colorado**	**NHL**	**52**	**18**	**12**	**30**	**14**	**6**	**0**	**3**	**112**	**16.1**	**7**	**8**	**37.5**	**14:32**	**9**	**0**	**0**	**0**	**0**	**0**	**0**	**0**	**13:05**
	Hershey Bears	AHL	20	8	14	22	8	....	....	....	....	....	....	....	....	....	....	....	....	....	....	....	....	....	....
2002-03	**Colorado**	**NHL**	**66**	**11**	**19**	**30**	**16**	**3**	**0**	**4**	**171**	**6.4**	**0**	**14**	**50.0**	**13:55**	....	....	....	....	....	....	....	....	....
	Carolina	**NHL**	**10**	**5**	**0**	**5**	**2**	**3**	**0**	**0**	**44**	**11.4**	**–7**	**15**	**46.7**	**19:00**	....	....	....	....	....	....	....	....	....
	NHL Totals		**128**	**34**	**31**	**65**	**32**	**12**	**0**	**7**	**327**	**10.4**		**37**	**45.9**	**14:34**	**9**	**0**	**0**	**0**	**0**	**0**	**0**	**0**	**13:05**

QMJHL First All-Star Team (2001)

Traded to **Carolina** by **Colorado** for Bates Battaglia, March 11, 2003.

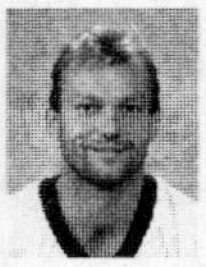

VUJTEK, Vladimir
(VYOO-tehk, VLAD-dih-MEER)

Left wing. Shoots left. 6'2", 200 lbs. Born, Ostrava, Czech., February 17, 1972. Montreal's 5th choice, 73rd overall, in 1991 Entry Draft.

			Regular Season														Playoffs								
Season	Club	League	GP	G	A	Pts	PIM	PP	SH	GW	S	%	+/-	TF	F%	Min	GP	G	A	Pts	PIM	PP	SH	GW	Min
1988-89	TJ Vitkovice	Czech	3	0	1	1	0	....	....	....	....	....	....	....	....	....	....	....	....	....	....	....	....	....	....
1989-90	TJ Vitkovice	Czech	22	3	4	7	....	....	....	....	....	....	....	....	....	....	7	4	3	7	....	....	....	....	....
1990-91	TJ Vitkovice	Czech	27	7	4	11	....	....	....	....	....	....	....	....	....	....	....	....	....	....	....	....	....	....	....
	Tri-City	WHL	37	26	18	44	74	....	....	....	....	....	....	....	....	....	7	2	3	5	4	....	....	....	....
1991-92	Tri-City	WHL	53	41	61	102	114	....	....	....	....	....	....	....	....	....	....	....	....	....	....	....	....	....	....
	Montreal	**NHL**	**2**	**0**	**0**	**0**	**0**	**0**	**0**	**0**	**1**	**0.0**	**–1**	....	....	....	....	....	....	....	....	....	....	....	....
1992-93	**Edmonton**	**NHL**	**30**	**1**	**10**	**11**	**8**	**0**	**0**	**0**	**49**	**2.0**	**–1**	....	....	....	....	....	....	....	....	....	....	....	....
	Cape Breton	AHL	20	10	9	19	14	....	....	....	....	....	....	....	....	....	1	0	0	0	0	....	....	....	....
1993-94	**Edmonton**	**NHL**	**40**	**4**	**15**	**19**	**14**	**1**	**0**	**0**	**66**	**6.1**	**–7**	....	....	....	....	....	....	....	....	....	....	....	....
1994-95	HC Vitkovice	Czech	18	5	7	12	51	....	....	....	....	....	....	....	....	....	....	....	....	....	....	....	....	....	....
	Cape Breton	AHL	30	10	11	21	30	....	....	....	....	....	....	....	....	....	....	....	....	....	....	....	....	....	....
	Las Vegas	IHL	1	0	0	0	0	....	....	....	....	....	....	....	....	....	....	....	....	....	....	....	....	....	....
1995-96	HC Vitkovice	Czech	26	6	7	13	....	....	....	....	....	....	....	....	....	....	4	1	1	2	....	....	....	....	....
1996-97	Assat Pori	Finland	50	27	31	58	48	....	....	....	....	....	....	....	....	....	4	1	2	3	2	....	....	....	....
1997-98	**Tampa Bay**	**NHL**	**30**	**2**	**4**	**6**	**16**	**0**	**0**	**1**	**44**	**4.5**	**–2**	....	....	....	....	....	....	....	....	....	....	....	....
	Adirondack	AHL	2	1	2	3	0	....	....	....	....	....	....	....	....	....	....	....	....	....	....	....	....	....	....
1998-99	HC Vitkovice	Czech	47	20	34	54	77	....	....	....	....	....	....	....	....	....	....	....	....	....	....	....	....	....	....
99-2000	**Atlanta**	**NHL**	**3**	**0**	**0**	**0**	**0**	**0**	**0**	**0**	**2**	**0.0**	**0**	**0**	**0.0**	**10:52**	....	....	....	....	....	....	....	....	....
	HC Sparta Praha	Czech	21	12	19	31	14	....	....	....	....	....	....	....	....	....	8	2	3	5	10	....	....	....	....
2000-01	HC Sparta Praha	Czech	38	11	18	29	28	....	....	....	....	....	....	....	....	....	13	3	6	9	4	....	....	....	....
2001-02	HPK Hameenlinna	Finland	45	19	39	58	38	....	....	....	....	....	....	....	....	....	8	4	7	11	6	....	....	....	....
2002-03	**Pittsburgh**	**NHL**	**5**	**0**	**1**	**1**	**0**	**0**	**0**	**0**	**3**	**0.0**	**–4**	**2**	**0.0**	**7:34**	....	....	....	....	....	....	....	....	....
	HC Vitkovice	Czech	6	1	5	6	4	....	....	....	....	....	....	....	....	....	....	....	....	....	....	....	....	....	....
	Cherepovets	Russia	16	7	14	21	12	....	....	....	....	....	....	....	....	....	12	2	3	5	8	....	....	....	....
	NHL Totals		**110**	**7**	**30**	**37**	**38**	**1**	**0**	**1**	**165**	**4.2**		**2**	**0.0**	**8:48**	....	....	....	....	....	....	....	....	....

WHL West First All-Star Team (1992)

Traded to **Edmonton** by **Montreal** with Shayne Corson and Brent Gilchrist for Vincent Damphousse and Edmonton's 4th round choice (Adam Wiesel) in 1993 Entry Draft, August 27, 1992. Traded to **Tampa Bay** by **Edmonton** with Edmonton's 3rd round choice (Dmitry Afanasenkov) in 1998 Entry Draft for Brantt Myhres and Toronto's 3rd round choice (previously acquired, Edmonton selected Alex Henry) in 1998 Entry Draft, July 16, 1997. • Missed majority of 1997-98 season recovering from Epstein-Barr Virus, December, 1997. Signed as a free agent by **Atlanta**, July 29, 1999. • Missed majority of 1999-2000 season recovering from facial injuries suffered in exhibition game vs. NY Rangers, September 18, 1999. Signed as a free agent by **Pittsburgh**, July 15, 2002. • Signed as a free agent by **HC Vitkovice** (Czech) after securing release from **Pittsburgh**, November 15, 2002.

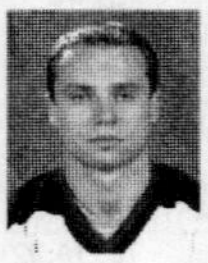

VYBORNY, David
(vih-BOHR-nee, DAY-vihd) **CBJ**

Right wing. Shoots left. 5'10", 189 lbs. Born, Jihlava, Czech., June 2, 1975. Edmonton's 3rd choice, 33rd overall, in 1993 Entry Draft.

			Regular Season														Playoffs								
Season	Club	League	GP	G	A	Pts	PIM	PP	SH	GW	S	%	+/-	TF	F%	Min	GP	G	A	Pts	PIM	PP	SH	GW	Min
1991-92	HC Sparta Praha	Czech	32	6	9	15	2	....	....	....	....	....	....	....	....	....	....	....	....	....	....	....	....	....	....
1992-93	HC Sparta Praha	Czech	52	20	24	44	....	....	....	....	....	....	....	....	....	....	....	....	....	....	....	....	....	....	....
1993-94	HC Sparta Praha	Czech	44	15	20	35	0	....	....	....	....	....	....	....	....	....	6	4	7	11	0	....	....	....	....
1994-95	Cape Breton	AHL	76	23	38	61	30	....	....	....	....	....	....	....	....	....	....	....	....	....	....	....	....	....	....
1995-96	HC Sparta Praha	Czech	40	12	18	30	....	....	....	....	....	....	....	....	....	....	12	6	5	11	....	....	....	....	....
1996-97	HC Sparta Praha	Czech	47	20	29	49	14	....	....	....	....	....	....	....	....	....	10	7	7	14	6	....	....	....	....
1997-98	MoDo	Sweden	45	16	21	37	34	....	....	....	....	....	....	....	....	....	9	0	2	2	2	....	....	....	....
1998-99	HC Sparta Praha	Czech	52	24	*46	*70	22	....	....	....	....	....	....	....	....	....	8	1	3	4	....	....	....	....	....
	Czech Republic	WC-A	12	4	4	8	6	....	....	....	....	....	....	....	....	....	....	....	....	....	....	....	....	....	....
99-2000	HC Sparta Praha	Czech	50	25	38	63	30	....	....	....	....	....	....	....	....	....	9	3	*8	*11	4	....	....	....	....
2000-01	**Columbus**	**NHL**	**79**	**13**	**19**	**32**	**22**	**5**	**0**	**1**	**125**	**10.4**	**–9**	**36**	**44.4**	**15:25**	....	....	....	....	....	....	....	....	....
2001-02	**Columbus**	**NHL**	**75**	**13**	**18**	**31**	**6**	**6**	**0**	**2**	**103**	**12.6**	**–14**	**25**	**44.0**	**15:27**	....	....	....	....	....	....	....	....	....
2002-03	**Columbus**	**NHL**	**79**	**20**	**26**	**46**	**16**	**4**	**1**	**4**	**125**	**16.0**	**12**	**46**	**32.6**	**16:20**	....	....	....	....	....	....	....	....	....
	NHL Totals		**233**	**46**	**63**	**109**	**44**	**15**	**1**	**7**	**353**	**13.0**		**107**	**39.3**	**15:45**	....	....	....	....	....	....	....	....	....

Signed as a free agent by **Columbus**, June 8, 2000.

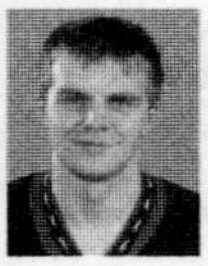

VYSHEDKEVICH, Sergei
(vee-shehd-KAY-vihch, SAIR-gay)

Defense. Shoots left. 6', 195 lbs. Born, Dedovsk, USSR, January 3, 1975. New Jersey's 3rd choice, 70th overall, in 1995 Entry Draft.

			Regular Season														Playoffs								
Season	Club	League	GP	G	A	Pts	PIM	PP	SH	GW	S	%	+/-	TF	F%	Min	GP	G	A	Pts	PIM	PP	SH	GW	Min
1994-95	Dynamo Moscow	CIS	49	6	7	13	67	....	....	....	....	....	....	....	....	....	14	2	0	2	12	....	....	....	....
1995-96	Dynamo Moscow	CIS	49	5	4	9	12	....	....	....	....	....	....	....	....	....	13	1	1	2	6	....	....	....	....
1996-97	Albany River Rats	AHL	65	8	27	35	16	....	....	....	....	....	....	....	....	....	12	0	6	6	0	....	....	....	....
1997-98	Albany River Rats	AHL	54	12	16	28	12	....	....	....	....	....	....	....	....	....	13	0	10	10	4	....	....	....	....
1998-99	Albany River Rats	AHL	79	11	38	49	28	....	....	....	....	....	....	....	....	....	5	0	3	3	0	....	....	....	....
99-2000	**Atlanta**	**NHL**	**7**	**1**	**3**	**4**	**2**	**1**	**0**	**0**	**5**	**20.0**	**–3**	**0**	**0.0**	**23:18**	....	....	....	....	....	....	....	....	....
	Orlando	IHL	69	11	24	35	32	....	....	....	....	....	....	....	....	....	6	3	3	6	8	....	....	....	....
2000-01	**Atlanta**	**NHL**	**23**	**1**	**2**	**3**	**14**	**0**	**0**	**0**	**28**	**3.6**	**–7**	**0**	**0.0**	**20:34**	....	....	....	....	....	....	....	....	....
	Orlando	IHL	10	2	3	5	2	....	....	....	....	....	....	....	....	....	....	....	....	....	....	....	....	....	....
	Cincinnati	AHL	17	3	2	5	2	....	....	....	....	....	....	....	....	....	....	....	....	....	....	....	....	....	....
2001-02	Dynamo Moscow	Russia	50	5	7	12	56	....	....	....	....	....	....	....	....	....	3	0	0	0	0	....	....	....	....
2002-03	Dynamo Moscow	Russia	50	4	8	12	58	....	....	....	....	....	....	....	....	....	5	0	2	2	36	....	....	....	....
	NHL Totals		**30**	**2**	**5**	**7**	**16**	**1**	**0**	**0**	**33**	**6.1**		**0**	**0.0**	**21:13**	....	....	....	....	....	....	....	....	....

Traded to **Atlanta** by **New Jersey** for future considerations, June 25, 1999. Traded to **Anaheim** by **Atlanta** with Scott Langkow for Ladislav Kohn, February 9, 2001.

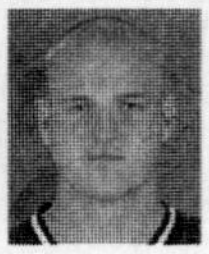

WALKER, Matt
(WAHL-kuhr, MAT) **ST.L.**

Defense. Shoots right. 6'2", 236 lbs. Born, Beaverlodge, Alta., April 7, 1980. St. Louis' 3rd choice, 83rd overall, in 1998 Entry Draft.

			Regular Season														Playoffs								
Season	Club	League	GP	G	A	Pts	PIM	PP	SH	GW	S	%	+/-	TF	F%	Min	GP	G	A	Pts	PIM	PP	SH	GW	Min
1996-97	Grand Prairie	AAHA	68	22	62	74	186	....	....	....	....	....	....	....	....	....	....	....	....	....	....	....	....	....	....
1997-98	Portland	WHL	64	2	13	15	124	....	....	....	....	....	....	....	....	....	16	0	0	0	21	....	....	....	....
1998-99	Portland	WHL	64	1	10	11	151	....	....	....	....	....	....	....	....	....	4	0	1	1	6	....	....	....	....
99-2000	Portland	WHL	38	2	7	9	97	....	....	....	....	....	....	....	....	....	....	....	....	....	....	....	....	....	....
	Kootenay Ice	WHL	31	4	19	23	53	....	....	....	....	....	....	....	....	....	21	5	13	18	24	....	....	....	....
2000-01	Worcester IceCats	AHL	61	4	8	12	131	....	....	....	....	....	....	....	....	....	11	0	0	0	6	....	....	....	....
	Peoria Rivermen	ECHL	8	1	0	1	70	....	....	....	....	....	....	....	....	....	....	....	....	....	....	....	....	....	....
2001-02	Worcester IceCats	AHL	49	2	11	13	164	....	....	....	....	....	....	....	....	....	3	0	0	0	8	....	....	....	....
2002-03	**St. Louis**	**NHL**	**16**	**0**	**1**	**1**	**38**	**0**	**0**	**0**	**13**	**0.0**	**0**	**1**	**100.0**	**11:09**	....	....	....	....	....	....	....	....	....
	Worcester IceCats	AHL	40	1	8	9	58	....	....	....	....	....	....	....	....	....	....	....	....	....	....	....	....	....	....
	NHL Totals		**16**	**0**	**1**	**1**	**38**	**0**	**0**	**0**	**13**	**0.0**		**1**	**100.0**	**11:09**	....	....	....	....	....	....	....	....	....

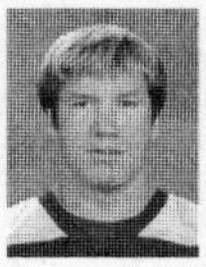

WALKER, Scott

(WAH-kuhr, SKAWT) **NSH.**

Right wing. Shoots right. 5'10", 196 lbs. Born, Cambridge, Ont., July 19, 1973. Vancouver's 4th choice, 124th overall, in 1993 Entry Draft.

Season	Club	League	GP	G	A	Pts	PIM	PP	SH	GW	S	%	+/-	TF	F%	Min	GP	G	A	Pts	PIM	PP	SH	GW	Min
			Regular Season														Playoffs								
1989-90	Kitchener	OJHL-B	6	0	5	5	4																		
	Cambridge	OJHL-B	27	7	22	29	87																		
1990-91	Cambridge	OJHL-B	45	10	27	37	241																		
1991-92	Owen Sound	OHL	53	7	31	38	128										5	0	7	7	8				
1992-93	Owen Sound	OHL	57	23	68	91	110										8	1	5	6	16				
1993-94	Hamilton	AHL	77	10	29	39	272										4	0	1	1	25				
1994-95	Syracuse Crunch	AHL	74	14	38	52	334																		
	Vancouver	**NHL**	**11**	**0**	**1**	**1**	**33**	**0**	**0**	**0**	**8**	**0.0**	**0**												
1995-96	**Vancouver**	**NHL**	**63**	**4**	**8**	**12**	**137**	**0**	**1**	**1**	**45**	**8.9**	**-7**												
	Syracuse Crunch	AHL	15	3	12	15	52										16	9	8	17	39				
1996-97	**Vancouver**	**NHL**	**64**	**3**	**15**	**18**	**132**	**0**	**0**	**0**	**55**	**5.5**	**2**												
1997-98	**Vancouver**	**NHL**	**59**	**3**	**10**	**13**	**164**	**0**	**1**	**1**	**40**	**7.5**	**-8**												
1998-99	**Nashville**	**NHL**	**71**	**15**	**25**	**40**	**103**	**0**	**1**	**2**	**96**	**15.6**	**0**	**265**	**48.3**	**16:21**									
99-2000	**Nashville**	**NHL**	**69**	**7**	**21**	**28**	**90**	**0**	**1**	**0**	**98**	**7.1**	**-16**	**30**	**36.7**	**15:49**									
2000-01	**Nashville**	**NHL**	**74**	**25**	**29**	**54**	**66**	**9**	**3**	**1**	**159**	**15.7**	**-2**	**541**	**51.4**	**19:17**									
2001-02	**Nashville**	**NHL**	**28**	**4**	**5**	**9**	**18**	**1**	**0**	**0**	**46**	**8.7**	**-13**	**149**	**38.9**	**18:38**									
2002-03	**Nashville**	**NHL**	**60**	**15**	**18**	**33**	**58**	**7**	**0**	**5**	**124**	**12.1**	**2**	**336**	**49.1**	**19:50**									
	NHL Totals		**499**	**76**	**132**	**208**	**801**	**17**	**7**	**10**	**671**	**11.3**		**1321**	**48.4**	**17:51**									

OHL Second All-Star Team (1993)

Claimed by **Nashville** from **Vancouver** in Expansion Draft, June 26, 1998.

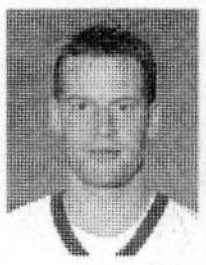

WALLIN, Jesse

(WAHL-ihn, JEH-see) **CGY.**

Defense. Shoots left. 6'2", 190 lbs. Born, Saskatoon, Sask., March 10, 1978. Detroit's 1st choice, 26th overall, in 1996 Entry Draft.

Season	Club	League	GP	G	A	Pts	PIM	PP	SH	GW	S	%	+/-	TF	F%	Min	GP	G	A	Pts	PIM	PP	SH	GW	Min
1993-94	North Battleford	SMHL	32	1	7	8	41																		
1994-95	Red Deer Rebels	WHL	72	4	20	24	72																		
1995-96	Red Deer Rebels	WHL	70	5	19	24	61										9	0	3	3	4				
1996-97	Red Deer Rebels	WHL	59	6	33	39	70										16	1	4	5	10				
1997-98	Red Deer Rebels	WHL	14	1	6	7	17										5	0	1	1	2				
1998-99	Adirondack	AHL	76	4	12	16	34										3	0	2	2	2				
99-2000	**Detroit**	**NHL**	**1**	**0**	**0**	**0**	**0**	**0**	**0**	**0**	**0**	**0.0**	**-2**	**0**	**0.0**	**19:22**									
	Cincinnati	AHL	75	3	14	17	61																		
2000-01	**Detroit**	**NHL**	**1**	**0**	**0**	**0**	**2**	**0**	**0**	**0**	**1**	**0.0**	**0**	**0**	**0.0**	**3:50**									
	Cincinnati	AHL	76	2	15	17	50										4	0	1	1	4				
2001-02	**Detroit**	**NHL**	**15**	**0**	**1**	**1**	**13**	**0**	**0**	**0**	**8**	**0.0**	**-1**	**0**	**0.0**	**10:42**									
	Cincinnati	AHL	5	1	1	2	2																		
2002-03	**Detroit**	**NHL**	**32**	**0**	**1**	**1**	**19**	**0**	**0**	**0**	**23**	**0.0**	**-2**	**0**	**0.0**	**13:16**									
	NHL Totals		**49**	**0**	**2**	**2**	**34**	**0**	**0**	**0**	**32**	**0.0**		**0**	**0.0**	**12:25**									

Canadian Major Junior Humanitarian Player of the Year (1997)

• Missed majority of 1997-98 season recovering from arm injury suffered in automobile accident (September 10, 1997) and foot injury suffered in World Junior Championship game vs. Germany, December 30, 1997 • Missed majority of 2001-02 season recovering from groin injury suffered in training camp, October 1, 2001. • Missed majority of 2002-03 season recovering from elbow (December 17, 2002 vs. NY Islanders), wrist (January 5, 2003 vs. Chicago) and knee (March 16, 2003 vs. Colorado) injuries. Signed as a free agent by **Calgary**, July 31, 2003.

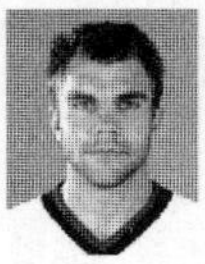

WALLIN, Niclas

(VAH-lihn, NIH-kluhs) **CAR.**

Defense. Shoots left. 6'3", 220 lbs. Born, Boden, Sweden, February 20, 1975. Carolina's 3rd choice, 97th overall, in 2000 Entry Draft.

Season	Club	League	GP	G	A	Pts	PIM	PP	SH	GW	S	%	+/-	TF	F%	Min	GP	G	A	Pts	PIM	PP	SH	GW	Min
1994-95	Bodens IK Jr.	Swede-Jr.	30	2	13	15	125																		
	Bodens IK	Swede-2	13	0	0	0	0										2	0	0	0	0				
1995-96	Bodens IK Jr.	Swede-Jr.	2	2	2	4	0																		
	Bodens IK	Swede-2	30	2	7	9	26										2	0	1	1	2				
1996-97	Brynas IF Gavle	Sweden	47	1	1	2	14																		
1997-98	Brynas IF Gavle	Sweden	44	2	3	5	57										3	0	1	1	4				
1998-99	Brynas IF Gavle	Sweden	46	2	4	6	52										14	0	1	1	8				
99-2000	Brynas IF Gavle	Sweden	48	7	9	16	73										11	2	1	3	14				
	Brynas IF Gavle	EuroHL	5	1	1	2	10																		
2000-01	**Carolina**	**NHL**	**37**	**2**	**3**	**5**	**21**	**0**	**0**	**0**	**19**	**10.5**	**-11**	**0**	**0.0**	**14:57**	**3**	**0**	**0**	**0**	**2**	**0**	**0**	**0**	**19:10**
	Cincinnati	IHL	8	1	2	3	4										3	0	0	0	2				
2001-02	**Carolina**	**NHL**	**52**	**1**	**2**	**3**	**36**	**0**	**0**	**0**	**33**	**3.0**	**1**	**0**	**0.0**	**12:12**	**23**	**2**	**1**	**3**	**12**	**0**	**0**	**2**	**15:26**
2002-03	**Carolina**	**NHL**	**77**	**2**	**8**	**10**	**71**	**0**	**0**	**2**	**69**	**2.9**	**-19**	**0**	**0.0**	**16:12**									
	NHL Totals		**166**	**5**	**13**	**18**	**128**	**0**	**0**	**2**	**121**	**4.1**		**0**	**0.0**	**14:40**	**26**	**2**	**1**	**3**	**14**	**0**	**0**	**2**	**15:52**

• Missed most of 2000-01 season recovering from shoulder injury suffered in game vs. Florida, January 12, 2001.

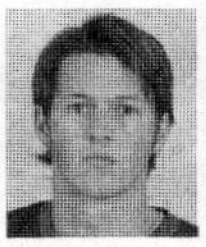

WALLIN, Rickard

(WAHL-in, RIH-kahrd) **MIN.**

Center. Shoots left. 6'2", 185 lbs. Born, Stockholm, Sweden, April 19, 1980. Phoenix's 8th choice, 160th overall, in 1998 Entry Draft.

Season	Club	League	GP	G	A	Pts	PIM	PP	SH	GW	S	%	+/-	TF	F%	Min	GP	G	A	Pts	PIM	PP	SH	GW	Min
1996-97	Vasteras IK Jr.	Swede-Jr.	26	3	3	6																			
1997-98	Farjestad Jr.	Swede-Jr.	29	20	30	50	32										2	1	1	2	2				
1998-99	Farjestad Jr.	Swede-Jr.	21	11	15	26	30																		
	Farjestad	Sweden	5	0	0	0	0																		
99-2000	IF Troja-Ljungby	Swede-2	46	15	22	37	54																		
2000-01	Farjestad	Sweden	47	9	22	31	24										16	11	3	14	4				
2001-02	Farjestad	Sweden	50	12	31	43	56										10	4	9	13	8				
2002-03	**Minnesota**	**NHL**	**4**	**1**	**0**	**1**	**0**	**0**	**0**	**1**	**1**	**100.0**	**1**	**28**	**53.6**	**7:44**									
	Houston Aeros	AHL	52	13	22	35	70										23	4	11	15	22				
	NHL Totals		**4**	**1**	**0**	**1**	**0**	**0**	**0**	**1**	**1**	**100.0**		**28**	**53.6**	**7:44**									

Rights traded to **Minnesota** by **Phoenix** for Joe Juneau, June 23, 2000.

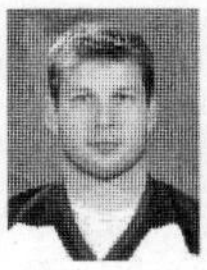

WALSER, Derrick

(WAHL-zuhr, DEHR-rihk) **CBJ**

Defense. Shoots left. 5'10", 196 lbs. Born, New Glasgow, N.S., May 12, 1978.

Season	Club	League	GP	G	A	Pts	PIM	PP	SH	GW	S	%	+/-	TF	F%	Min	GP	G	A	Pts	PIM	PP	SH	GW	Min
1994-95	Beauport	QMJHL	48	4	18	22	34										12	2	5	7	2				
1995-96	Beauport	QMJHL	69	9	31	40	56										20	2	11	13	16				
1996-97	Beauport	QMJHL	37	13	25	38	26																		
	Rimouski Oceanic	QMJHL	31	15	30	45	44										4	2	2	4	6				
1997-98	Rimouski Oceanic	QMJHL	70	41	69	110	135										18	10	*26	36	49				
1998-99	Saint John Flames	AHL	40	3	7	10	24																		
	Johnstown Chiefs	ECHL	24	8	12	20	29																		
99-2000	Saint John Flames	AHL	14	2	3	5	10																		
	Johnstown Chiefs	ECHL	54	17	26	43	104										7	3	3	6	8				
2000-01	Saint John Flames	AHL	76	19	36	55	36										19	7	9	16	14				
2001-02	**Columbus**	**NHL**	**2**	**1**	**0**	**1**	**0**	**0**	**0**	**0**	**2**	**50.0**	**-2**	**0**	**0.0**	**16:18**									
	Syracuse Crunch	AHL	73	23	38	61	70										10	1	5	6	12				
2002-03	**Columbus**	**NHL**	**53**	**4**	**13**	**17**	**34**	**3**	**0**	**2**	**86**	**4.7**	**-9**	**1**	**100.0**	**14:52**									
	Syracuse Crunch	AHL	28	7	14	21	30																		
	NHL Totals		**55**	**5**	**13**	**18**	**34**	**3**	**0**	**2**	**88**	**5.7**		**1**	**100.0**	**14:55**									

QMJHL First All-Star Team (1997) • Emile Bouchard Trophy (Top Defenseman – QMJHL) (1998) • QMJHL First All-Star Team (1998) • Canadian Major Junior First All-Star Team (1998) • Canadian Major Junior Defenseman of the Year (1998)

Signed as a free agent by **Calgary**, October 16, 1998. Signed as a free agent by **Columbus**, September 17, 2001.

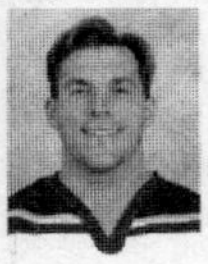

WALZ, Wes

(WAHLZ, WEHS) **MIN.**

Center. Shoots right. 5'10", 180 lbs. Born, Calgary, Alta., May 15, 1970. Boston's 3rd choice, 57th overall, in 1989 Entry Draft.

			Regular Season														Playoffs								
Season	Club	League	GP	G	A	Pts	PIM	PP	SH	GW	S	%	+/-	TF	F%	Min	GP	G	A	Pts	PIM	PP	SH	GW	Min
1987-88	Cgy. North Stars	AMHL	35	47	52	99	72	....	....	....	....	....	....	....	....	....	....	....	....	....	....	....	....	....	....
	Prince Albert	WHL	1	1	1	2	0	....	....	....	....	....	....	....	....	....	....	....	....	....	....	....	....	....	....
1988-89	Lethbridge	WHL	63	29	75	104	32	....	....	....	....	....	....	....	....	....	8	1	5	6	6	....	....	....	....
1989-90	Lethbridge	WHL	56	54	86	140	69	....	....	....	....	....	....	....	....	....	19	13	*24	*37	33	....	....	....	....
	Boston	**NHL**	**2**	**1**	**1**	**2**	**0**	**1**	**0**	**0**	**1**	**100.0**	**–1**	....	....	....	....	....	....	....	....	....	....	....	....
1990-91	**Boston**	**NHL**	**56**	**8**	**8**	**16**	**32**	**1**	**0**	**1**	**57**	**14.0**	**–14**	....	....	....	**2**	**0**	**0**	**0**	**0**	**0**	**0**	**0**	....
	Maine Mariners	AHL	20	8	12	20	19	....	....	....	....	....	....	....	....	....	2	0	0	0	21	....	....	....	....
1991-92	**Boston**	**NHL**	**15**	**0**	**3**	**3**	**12**	**0**	**0**	**0**	**17**	**0.0**	**–3**	....	....	....	....	....	....	....	....	....	....	....	....
	Maine Mariners	AHL	21	13	11	24	38	....	....	....	....	....	....	....	....	....	....	....	....	....	....	....	....	....	....
	Philadelphia	**NHL**	**2**	**1**	**0**	**1**	**0**	**0**	**0**	**1**	**2**	**50.0**	**1**	....	....	....	....	....	....	....	....	....	....	....	....
	Hershey Bears	AHL	41	13	28	41	37	....	....	....	....	....	....	....	....	....	6	1	2	3	0	....	....	....	....
1992-93	Hershey Bears	AHL	78	35	45	80	106	....	....	....	....	....	....	....	....	....	....	....	....	....	....	....	....	....	....
1993-94	**Calgary**	**NHL**	**53**	**11**	**27**	**38**	**16**	**1**	**0**	**0**	**79**	**13.9**	**20**	....	....	....	**6**	**3**	**0**	**3**	**2**	**0**	**0**	**0**	....
	Saint John Flames	AHL	15	6	6	12	14	....	....	....	....	....	....	....	....	....	....	....	....	....	....	....	....	....	....
1994-95	**Calgary**	**NHL**	**39**	**6**	**12**	**18**	**11**	**4**	**0**	**1**	**73**	**8.2**	**7**	....	....	....	**1**	**0**	**0**	**0**	**0**	**0**	**0**	**0**	....
1995-96	**Detroit**	**NHL**	**2**	**0**	**0**	**0**	**0**	**0**	**0**	**0**	**2**	**0.0**	**0**	....	....	....	....	....	....	....	....	....	....	....	....
	Adirondack	AHL	38	20	35	55	58	....	....	....	....	....	....	....	....	....	....	....	....	....	....	....	....	....	....
1996-97	EV Zug	Swiss	41	24	22	46	67	....	....	....	....	....	....	....	....	....	9	5	1	6	39	....	....	....	....
1997-98	EV Zug	Swiss	38	18	34	52	32	....	....	....	....	....	....	....	....	....	20	*16	*12	*28	18	....	....	....	....
	EV Zug	EuroHL	5	1	3	4	10	....	....	....	....	....	....	....	....	....	....	....	....	....	....	....	....	....	....
1998-99	EV Zug	Swiss	42	22	27	49	75	....	....	....	....	....	....	....	....	....	10	3	9	12	2	....	....	....	....
	EV Zug	EuroHL	6	7	5	12	4	....	....	....	....	....	....	....	....	....	2	0	0	0	12	....	....	....	....
99-2000	Long Beach	IHL	6	4	3	7	8	....	....	....	....	....	....	....	....	....	....	....	....	....	....	....	....	....	....
	HC Lugano	Swiss	13	7	11	18	14	....	....	....	....	....	....	....	....	....	5	3	4	7	4	....	....	....	....
2000-01	**Minnesota**	**NHL**	**82**	**18**	**12**	**30**	**37**	**0**	**7**	**3**	**152**	**11.8**	**–8**	**1533**	**47.2**	**16:45**	....	....	....	....	....	....	....	....	....
2001-02	**Minnesota**	**NHL**	**64**	**10**	**20**	**30**	**43**	**0**	**2**	**5**	**97**	**10.3**	**0**	**1231**	**44.8**	**16:42**	....	....	....	....	....	....	....	....	....
2002-03	**Minnesota**	**NHL**	**80**	**13**	**19**	**32**	**63**	**0**	**0**	**4**	**115**	**11.3**	**11**	**1505**	**50.4**	**15:56**	**18**	**7**	**6**	**13**	**14**	**0**	**2**	**2**	**17:24**
	NHL Totals		**395**	**68**	**102**	**170**	**214**	**7**	**9**	**15**	**595**	**11.4**		**4269**	**47.6**	**16:27**	**27**	**10**	**6**	**16**	**16**	**0**	**2**	**2**	**17:24**

WHL Rookie of the Year (1989) • WHL East First All-Star Team (1990)

Traded to **Philadelphia** by **Boston** with Garry Galley and Boston's 3rd round choice (Milos Holan) in 1993 Entry Draft for Gord Murphy, Brian Dobbin, Philadelphia's 3rd round choice (Sergei Zholtok) in 1992 Entry Draft and 4th round choice (Charles Paquette) in 1993 Entry Draft, January 2, 1992. Signed as a free agent by **Calgary**, August 26, 1993. Signed as a free agent by **Detroit**, September 6, 1995. Signed as a free agent by **Long Beach** (IHL), October 12, 1999. Signed as a free agent by **Minnesota**, June 28, 2000.

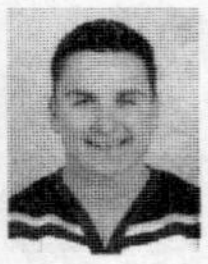

WANVIG, Kyle

(WEHN-vihg, KIGHL) **MIN.**

Right wing. Shoots right. 6'2", 219 lbs. Born, Calgary, Alta., January 29, 1981. Minnesota's 2nd choice, 36th overall, in 2001 Entry Draft.

Season	Club	League	GP	G	A	Pts	PIM	PP	SH	GW	S	%	+/-	TF	F%	Min	GP	G	A	Pts	PIM	PP	SH	GW	Min
1996-97	Calgary Blazers	AMHL	26	31	48	79	85	....	....	....	....	....	....	....	....	....	....	....	....	....	....	....	....	....	....
1997-98	Edmonton Ice	WHL	62	17	12	29	69	....	....	....	....	....	....	....	....	....	....	....	....	....	....	....	....	....	....
1998-99	Kootenay Ice	WHL	71	12	20	32	119	....	....	....	....	....	....	....	....	....	7	1	3	4	18	....	....	....	....
99-2000	Kootenay Ice	WHL	6	2	2	4	12	....	....	....	....	....	....	....	....	....	....	....	....	....	....	....	....	....	....
	Red Deer Rebels	WHL	58	21	18	39	123	....	....	....	....	....	....	....	....	....	4	1	0	1	4	....	....	....	....
2000-01	Red Deer Rebels	WHL	69	55	46	101	202	....	....	....	....	....	....	....	....	....	22	10	12	22	47	....	....	....	....
2001-02	Houston Aeros	AHL	34	6	7	13	43	....	....	....	....	....	....	....	....	....	9	0	1	1	23	....	....	....	....
2002-03	**Minnesota**	**NHL**	**7**	**1**	**0**	**1**	**13**	**0**	**0**	**0**	**5**	**20.0**	**0**	**1**	**100.0**	**9:14**	....	....	....	....	....	....	....	....	....
	Houston Aeros	AHL	57	13	16	29	137	....	....	....	....	....	....	....	....	....	21	6	4	10	27	....	....	....	....
	NHL Totals		**7**	**1**	**0**	**1**	**13**	**0**	**0**	**0**	**5**	**20.0**		**1**	**100.0**	**9:14**	....	....	....	....	....	....	....	....	....

• Re-entered NHL Entry Draft. Originally Boston's 3rd choice, 89th overall, in 1999 Entry Draft.

WHL East Second All-Star Team (2001) • Memorial Cup All-Star Team (2001) • Stafford Smythe Memorial Trophy (Memorial Cup MVP) (2001)

• Missed majority of 2001-02 season recovering from ankle injury suffered in game vs. Grand Rapids (AHL), December 30, 2001.

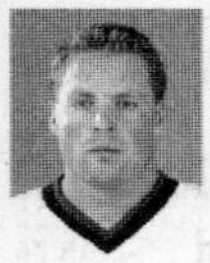

WARD, Aaron

(WOHRD, AIR-ruhn) **CAR.**

Defense. Shoots right. 6'2", 225 lbs. Born, Windsor, Ont., January 17, 1973. Winnipeg's 1st choice, 5th overall, in 1991 Entry Draft.

Season	Club	League	GP	G	A	Pts	PIM	PP	SH	GW	S	%	+/-	TF	F%	Min	GP	G	A	Pts	PIM	PP	SH	GW	Min
1988-89	Nepean Raiders	OCJHL	54	1	14	15	40	....	....	....	....	....	....	....	....	....	....	....	....	....	....	....	....	....	....
1989-90	Nepean Raiders	OCJHL	52	6	33	39	85	....	....	....	....	....	....	....	....	....	....	....	....	....	....	....	....	....	....
1990-91	U. of Michigan	CCHA	46	8	11	19	126	....	....	....	....	....	....	....	....	....	....	....	....	....	....	....	....	....	....
1991-92	U. of Michigan	CCHA	42	7	12	19	64	....	....	....	....	....	....	....	....	....	....	....	....	....	....	....	....	....	....
1992-93	U. of Michigan	CCHA	30	5	8	13	73	....	....	....	....	....	....	....	....	....	....	....	....	....	....	....	....	....	....
1993-94	**Detroit**	**NHL**	**5**	**1**	**0**	**1**	**4**	**0**	**0**	**0**	**3**	**33.3**	**2**	....	....	....	....	....	....	....	....	....	....	....	....
	Adirondack	AHL	58	4	12	16	87	....	....	....	....	....	....	....	....	....	9	2	6	8	6	....	....	....	....
1994-95	Adirondack	AHL	76	11	24	35	87	....	....	....	....	....	....	....	....	....	4	0	1	1	0	....	....	....	....
	Detroit	**NHL**	**1**	**0**	**1**	**1**	**2**	**0**	**0**	**0**	**0**	**0.0**	**1**	....	....	....	....	....	....	....	....	....	....	....	....
1995-96	Adirondack	AHL	74	5	10	15	133	....	....	....	....	....	....	....	....	....	3	0	0	0	6	....	....	....	....
1996-97♦	**Detroit**	**NHL**	**49**	**2**	**5**	**7**	**52**	**0**	**0**	**0**	**40**	**5.0**	**–9**	....	....	....	**19**	**0**	**0**	**0**	**17**	**0**	**0**	**0**	....
1997-98♦	**Detroit**	**NHL**	**52**	**5**	**5**	**10**	**47**	**0**	**0**	**1**	**47**	**10.6**	**–1**	....	....	....	....	....	....	....	....	....	....	....	....
1998-99	**Detroit**	**NHL**	**60**	**3**	**8**	**11**	**52**	**0**	**0**	**0**	**46**	**6.5**	**–5**	**0**	**0.0**	**13:55**	**8**	**0**	**1**	**1**	**8**	**0**	**0**	**0**	**10:15**
99-2000	**Detroit**	**NHL**	**36**	**1**	**3**	**4**	**24**	**0**	**0**	**0**	**25**	**4.0**	**–4**	**0**	**0.0**	**12:36**	**3**	**0**	**0**	**0**	**0**	**0**	**0**	**0**	**7:36**
2000-01	**Detroit**	**NHL**	**73**	**4**	**5**	**9**	**57**	**0**	**0**	**1**	**48**	**8.3**	**–4**	**0**	**0.0**	**16:60**	....	....	....	....	....	....	....	....	....
2001-02	**Carolina**	**NHL**	**79**	**3**	**11**	**14**	**74**	**0**	**0**	**2**	**69**	**4.3**	**0**	**1**	**100.0**	**19:40**	**23**	**1**	**1**	**2**	**22**	**0**	**0**	**0**	**21:12**
2002-03	**Carolina**	**NHL**	**77**	**3**	**6**	**9**	**90**	**0**	**0**	**1**	**66**	**4.5**	**–23**	**0**	**0.0**	**18:43**	....	....	....	....	....	....	....	....	....
	NHL Totals		**432**	**22**	**44**	**66**	**402**	**0**	**0**	**5**	**344**	**6.4**		**1**	**100.0**	**16:60**	**53**	**1**	**2**	**3**	**47**	**0**	**0**	**0**	**17:26**

Traded to **Detroit** by **Winnipeg** with Toronto's 4th round choice (previously acquired, later traded to Detroit – Detroit selected John Jakopin) in 1993 Entry Draft for Paul Ysebaert and future considerations (Alan Kerr, June 18, 1993), June 11, 1993. • Missed majority of 1999-2000 season recovering from shoulder injury suffered in game vs. Vancouver, January 19, 2000. Traded to **Carolina** by **Detroit** for Carolina's 2nd round choice (Jiri Hudler) in 2002 Entry Draft, July 9, 2001.

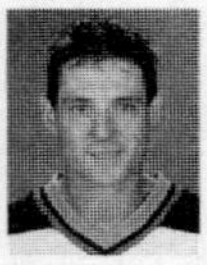

WARD, Dixon

(WOHRD, DIHX-ohn)

Right wing. Shoots right. 6', 200 lbs. Born, Leduc, Alta., September 23, 1968. Vancouver's 6th choice, 128th overall, in 1988 Entry Draft.

Season	Club	League	GP	G	A	Pts	PIM	PP	SH	GW	S	%	+/-	TF	F%	Min	GP	G	A	Pts	PIM	PP	SH	GW	Min
1986-87	Red Deer Rebels	AJHL	59	46	40	86	153	....	....	....	....	....	....	....	....	....	20	11	11	22	16	....	....	....	....
1987-88	Red Deer Rebels	AJHL	51	60	71	131	167	....	....	....	....	....	....	....	....	....	....	....	....	....	....	....	....	....	....
1988-89	North Dakota	WCHA	37	8	9	17	26	....	....	....	....	....	....	....	....	....	....	....	....	....	....	....	....	....	....
1989-90	North Dakota	WCHA	45	35	34	69	44	....	....	....	....	....	....	....	....	....	....	....	....	....	....	....	....	....	....
1990-91	North Dakota	WCHA	43	34	35	69	84	....	....	....	....	....	....	....	....	....	....	....	....	....	....	....	....	....	....
1991-92	North Dakota	WCHA	38	33	31	64	90	....	....	....	....	....	....	....	....	....	....	....	....	....	....	....	....	....	....
1992-93	**Vancouver**	**NHL**	**70**	**22**	**30**	**52**	**82**	**4**	**1**	**0**	**111**	**19.8**	**34**	....	....	....	**9**	**2**	**3**	**5**	**0**	**2**	**0**	**0**	....
1993-94	**Vancouver**	**NHL**	**33**	**6**	**1**	**7**	**37**	**2**	**0**	**1**	**46**	**13.0**	**–14**	....	....	....	....	....	....	....	....	....	....	....	....
	Los Angeles	**NHL**	**34**	**6**	**2**	**8**	**45**	**2**	**0**	**0**	**44**	**13.6**	**–8**	....	....	....	....	....	....	....	....	....	....	....	....
1994-95	**Toronto**	**NHL**	**22**	**0**	**3**	**3**	**31**	**0**	**0**	**0**	**15**	**0.0**	**–4**	....	....	....	....	....	....	....	....	....	....	....	....
	St. John's	AHL	6	3	3	6	19	....	....	....	....	....	....	....	....	....	....	....	....	....	....	....	....	....	....
	Detroit Vipers	IHL	7	3	6	9	7	....	....	....	....	....	....	....	....	....	5	3	0	3	7	....	....	....	....
1995-96	**Buffalo**	**NHL**	**8**	**2**	**2**	**4**	**6**	**0**	**0**	**1**	**12**	**16.7**	**1**	....	....	....	....	....	....	....	....	....	....	....	....
	Rochester	AHL	71	38	56	94	74	....	....	....	....	....	....	....	....	....	19	11	*24	*35	8	....	....	....	....
1996-97	**Buffalo**	**NHL**	**79**	**13**	**32**	**45**	**36**	**1**	**2**	**4**	**93**	**14.0**	**17**	....	....	....	**12**	**2**	**3**	**5**	**6**	**0**	**0**	**1**	....
1997-98	**Buffalo**	**NHL**	**71**	**10**	**13**	**23**	**42**	**0**	**2**	**3**	**99**	**10.1**	**9**	....	....	....	**15**	**3**	**8**	**11**	**6**	**0**	**0**	**0**	....
1998-99	**Buffalo**	**NHL**	**78**	**20**	**24**	**44**	**44**	**2**	**1**	**4**	**101**	**19.8**	**10**	**11**	**54.5**	**15:47**	**21**	**7**	**5**	**12**	**32**	**0**	**2**	**3**	**16:07**
99-2000	**Buffalo**	**NHL**	**71**	**11**	**9**	**20**	**41**	**1**	**2**	**2**	**101**	**10.9**	**1**	**8**	**50.0**	**13:58**	**5**	**0**	**1**	**1**	**2**	**0**	**0**	**0**	**14:43**
2000-01	**Boston**	**NHL**	**63**	**5**	**13**	**18**	**65**	**0**	**0**	**0**	**88**	**5.7**	**–1**	**108**	**48.2**	**12:38**	....	....	....	....	....	....	....	....	....
2001-02	Langnau	Swiss	23	8	19	27	38	....	....	....	....	....	....	....	....	....	9	3	6	9	2	....	....	....	....
2002-03	**NY Rangers**	**NHL**	**8**	**0**	**0**	**0**	**2**	**0**	**0**	**0**	**7**	**0.0**	**–2**	**11**	**54.6**	**8:45**	....	....	....	....	....	....	....	....	....
	Hartford	AHL	67	23	41	64	108	....	....	....	....	....	....	....	....	....	....	....	....	....	....	....	....	....	....
	NHL Totals		**537**	**95**	**129**	**224**	**431**	**12**	**8**	**15**	**717**	**13.2**		**138**	**49.3**	**14:02**	**62**	**14**	**20**	**34**	**46**	**2**	**2**	**4**	**15:51**

WCHA Second All-Star Team (1991, 1992) • Jack A. Butterfield Trophy (Playoff MVP – AHL) (1996)

Traded to **Los Angeles** by **Vancouver** for Jimmy Carson, January 8, 1994. Traded to **Toronto** by **Los Angeles** with Guy Leveque, Kelly Fairchild and Shayne Toporowski for Eric Lacroix, Chris Snell and Toronto's 4th round choice (Eric Belanger) in 1996 Entry Draft, October 3, 1994. Signed as a free agent by **Buffalo**, September 20, 1995. Signed as a free agent by **Boston**, November 8, 2000. Signed as a free agent by **NY Rangers**, October 1, 2002.

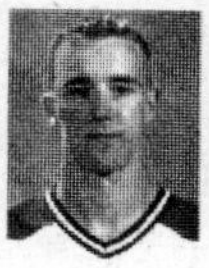

WARD, Jason

(WOHRD, JAY-suhn) **MTL.**

Right wing. Shoots right. 6'3", 200 lbs. Born, Chapleau, Ont., January 16, 1979. Montreal's 1st choice, 11th overall, in 1997 Entry Draft.

			Regular Season														Playoffs								
Season	Club	League	GP	G	A	Pts	PIM	PP	SH	GW	S	%	+/-	TF	F%	Min	GP	G	A	Pts	PIM	PP	SH	GW	Min
1994-95	Oshawa	OJHL-B	47	30	31	61	75	....	....	....	....	....	....	....	....	....	....	....	....	....	....	....	....	....	....
1995-96	Niagara Falls	OHL	64	15	35	50	139	....	....	....	....	....	....	....	....	....	10	6	4	10	23	....	....	....	....
1996-97	Erie Otters	OHL	58	25	39	64	137	....	....	....	....	....	....	....	....	....	5	1	2	3	2	....	....	....	....
1997-98	Erie Otters	OHL	21	7	9	16	42	....	....	....	....	....	....	....	....	....	....	....	....	....	....	....	....	....	....
	Windsor Spitfires	OHL	26	19	27	46	34	....	....	....	....	....	....	....	....	....	....	....	....	....	....	....	....	....	....
	Fredericton	AHL	7	1	0	1	2	....	....	....	....	....	....	....	....	....	1	0	0	0	2	....	....	....	....
1998-99	Windsor Spitfires	OHL	12	8	11	19	25	....	....	....	....	....	....	....	....	....	....	....	....	....	....	....	....	....	....
	Plymouth Whalers	OHL	23	14	13	27	28	....	....	....	....	....	....	....	....	....	11	6	8	14	12	....	....	....	....
	Fredericton	AHL	....	....	....	....	....	....	....	....	....	....	....	....	....	....	10	4	2	6	22	....	....	....	....
99-2000	**Montreal**	**NHL**	32	2	1	3	10	1	0	0	24	8.3	−1	86	44.2	9:10	....	....	....	....	....	....	....	....	....
	Quebec Citadelles	AHL	40	14	12	26	30	....	....	....	....	....	....	....	....	....	3	2	1	3	4	....	....	....	....
2000-01	**Montreal**	**NHL**	12	0	0	0	12	0	0	0	4	0.0	3	2	50.0	8:16	....	....	....	....	....	....	....	....	....
	Quebec Citadelles	AHL	23	7	12	19	69	....	....	....	....	....	....	....	....	....	....	....	....	....	....	....	....	....	....
2001-02	Quebec Citadelles	AHL	78	24	33	57	128	....	....	....	....	....	....	....	....	....	3	0	0	0	2	....	....	....	....
2002-03	**Montreal**	**NHL**	8	3	2	5	0	0	0	0	10	30.0	3	6	50.0	11:17	....	....	....	....	....	....	....	....	....
	Hamilton	AHL	69	31	41	72	78	....	....	....	....	....	....	....	....	....	23	*12	9	*21	20	....	....	....	....
	NHL Totals		52	5	3	8	22	1	0	0	38	13.2		94	44.7	9:17	....	....	....	....	....	....	....	....	....

AHL First All-Star Team (2003)

• Missed majority of 2000-01 season recovering from knee injury suffered in game vs. Carolina, January 16, 2001.

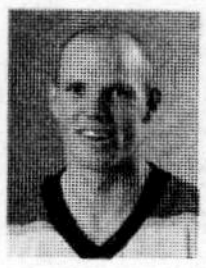

WARD, Lance

(WAWRD, LANTS) **ANA.**

Defense. Shoots left. 6'3", 220 lbs. Born, Lloydminster, Alta., June 2, 1978. Florida's 3rd choice, 63rd overall, in 1998 Entry Draft.

			Regular Season														Playoffs								
Season	Club	League	GP	G	A	Pts	PIM	PP	SH	GW	S	%	+/-	TF	F%	Min	GP	G	A	Pts	PIM	PP	SH	GW	Min
1993-94	Lloydminister	AAHA	20	8	12	20	68	....	....	....	....	....	....	....	....	....	....	....	....	....	....	....	....	....	....
1994-95	Red Deer Rebels	WHL	28	0	0	0	57	....	....	....	....	....	....	....	....	....	....	....	....	....	....	....	....	....	....
1995-96	Red Deer Rebels	WHL	72	4	13	17	127	....	....	....	....	....	....	....	....	....	10	0	4	4	10	....	....	....	....
1996-97	Red Deer Rebels	WHL	70	5	34	39	229	....	....	....	....	....	....	....	....	....	16	0	3	3	36	....	....	....	....
1997-98	Red Deer Rebels	WHL	71	8	25	33	233	....	....	....	....	....	....	....	....	....	5	0	0	0	16	....	....	....	....
1998-99	Miami Matadors	ECHL	6	1	0	1	12	....	....	....	....	....	....	....	....	....	....	....	....	....	....	....	....	....	....
	Fort Wayne	IHL	13	0	2	2	28	....	....	....	....	....	....	....	....	....	....	....	....	....	....	....	....	....	....
	New Haven	AHL	43	2	5	7	51	....	....	....	....	....	....	....	....	....	....	....	....	....	....	....	....	....	....
99-2000	Louisville Panthers	AHL	80	4	16	20	190	....	....	....	....	....	....	....	....	....	4	0	0	0	6	....	....	....	....
2000-01	**Florida**	**NHL**	30	0	2	2	45	0	0	0	17	0.0	−3	0	0.0	15:50	....	....	....	....	....	....	....	....	....
	Louisville Panthers	AHL	35	3	2	5	78	....	....	....	....	....	....	....	....	....	....	....	....	....	....	....	....	....	....
2001-02	**Florida**	**NHL**	68	1	4	5	131	0	0	0	39	2.6	−20	1	0.0	14:31	....	....	....	....	....	....	....	....	....
2002-03	**Florida**	**NHL**	36	3	1	4	78	0	0	1	34	8.8	−4	0	0.0	9:07	....	....	....	....	....	....	....	....	....
	Anaheim	**NHL**	29	0	1	1	43	0	0	0	18	0.0	−2	0	0.0	7:08	....	....	....	....	....	....	....	....	....
	NHL Totals		163	4	8	12	297	0	0	1	108	3.7		1	0.0	12:15	....	....	....	....	....	....	....	....	....

• Re-entered NHL Entry Draft. Originally New Jersey's 1st choice, 10th overall, in 1996 Entry Draft.

Traded to **Anaheim** by **Florida** with Sandis Ozolinsh for Pavel Trnka, Matt Cullen and Anaheim's 4th round choice (James Pemberton) in 2003 Entry Draft, January 30, 2003.

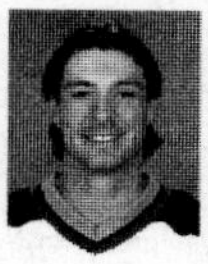

WARRENER, Rhett

(WAHR-ihn-uhr, REHT) **CGY.**

Defense. Shoots right. 6'2", 217 lbs. Born, Shaunavon, Sask., January 27, 1976. Florida's 2nd choice, 27th overall, in 1994 Entry Draft.

			Regular Season														Playoffs								
Season	Club	League	GP	G	A	Pts	PIM	PP	SH	GW	S	%	+/-	TF	F%	Min	GP	G	A	Pts	PIM	PP	SH	GW	Min
1991-92	Saskatoon Blazers	SMHL	33	6	5	11	71	....	....	....	....	....	....	....	....	....	....	....	....	....	....	....	....	....	....
	Saskatoon Blades	WHL	2	0	0	0	0	....	....	....	....	....	....	....	....	....	....	....	....	....	....	....	....	....	....
1992-93	Saskatoon Blades	WHL	68	2	17	19	100	....	....	....	....	....	....	....	....	....	9	0	0	0	14	....	....	....	....
1993-94	Saskatoon Blades	WHL	61	7	19	26	131	....	....	....	....	....	....	....	....	....	16	0	5	5	33	....	....	....	....
1994-95	Saskatoon Blades	WHL	66	13	26	39	137	....	....	....	....	....	....	....	....	....	10	0	3	3	6	....	....	....	....
1995-96	**Florida**	**NHL**	28	0	3	3	46	0	0	0	19	0.0	4	....	....	....	21	0	1	1	0	0	0	0	....
	Carolina	AHL	9	0	0	0	4	....	....	....	....	....	....	....	....	....	....	....	....	....	....	....	....	....	....
1996-97	**Florida**	**NHL**	62	4	9	13	88	1	0	1	58	6.9	20	....	....	....	5	0	0	0	0	0	0	0	....
1997-98	**Florida**	**NHL**	79	0	4	4	99	0	0	0	66	0.0	−16	....	....	....	....	....	....	....	....	....	....	....	....
1998-99	**Florida**	**NHL**	48	0	7	7	64	0	0	0	33	0.0	−1	0	0.0	19:01	....	....	....	....	....	....	....	....	....
	Buffalo	**NHL**	13	1	0	1	20	0	0	0	11	9.1	3	0	0.0	18:13	20	1	3	4	32	0	0	0	22:08
99-2000	**Buffalo**	**NHL**	61	0	3	3	89	0	0	0	68	0.0	18	0	0.0	19:51	5	0	0	0	2	0	0	0	21:42
2000-01	**Buffalo**	**NHL**	77	3	16	19	78	0	0	2	103	2.9	10	0	0.0	20:24	13	0	2	2	4	0	0	0	22:37
2001-02	**Buffalo**	**NHL**	65	5	5	10	113	0	0	1	66	7.6	15	0	0.0	19:39	....	....	....	....	....	....	....	....	....
2002-03	**Buffalo**	**NHL**	50	0	9	9	63	0	0	0	47	0.0	1	0	0.0	18:14	....	....	....	....	....	....	....	....	....
	NHL Totals		483	13	56	69	660	1	0	4	471	2.8		0	0.0	19:29	64	1	6	7	38	0	0	0	22:14

Traded to **Buffalo** by **Florida** with Florida's 5th round choice (Ryan Miller) in 1999 Entry Draft for Mike Wilson, March 23, 1999. Traded to **Calgary** by **Buffalo** with Steve Reinprecht for Chris Drury and Steve Begin, July 3, 2003.

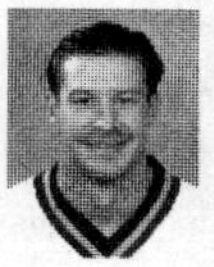

WARRINER, Todd

(WAHR-ihn-uhr, TAWD)

Left wing. Shoots left. 6'1", 200 lbs. Born, Blenheim, Ont., January 3, 1974. Quebec's 1st choice, 4th overall, in 1992 Entry Draft.

			Regular Season														Playoffs								
Season	Club	League	GP	G	A	Pts	PIM	PP	SH	GW	S	%	+/-	TF	F%	Min	GP	G	A	Pts	PIM	PP	SH	GW	Min
1988-89	Blenheim Blades	OJHL-C	10	1	4	5	0	....	....	....	....	....	....	....	....	....	....	....	....	....	....	....	....	....	....
1989-90	Chatham	OJHL-B	40	24	21	45	12	....	....	....	....	....	....	....	....	....	....	....	....	....	....	....	....	....	....
1990-91	Windsor Spitfires	OHL	57	36	28	64	26	....	....	....	....	....	....	....	....	....	11	5	6	11	12	....	....	....	....
1991-92	Windsor Spitfires	OHL	50	41	41	82	64	....	....	....	....	....	....	....	....	....	7	5	4	9	6	....	....	....	....
1992-93	Windsor Spitfires	OHL	23	13	21	34	29	....	....	....	....	....	....	....	....	....	....	....	....	....	....	....	....	....	....
	Kitchener Rangers	OHL	32	19	24	43	35	....	....	....	....	....	....	....	....	....	7	5	14	19	14	....	....	....	....
1993-94	Team Canada	Nat-Tm	50	11	20	31	33	....	....	....	....	....	....	....	....	....	....	....	....	....	....	....	....	....	....
	Canada	Olympics	4	1	1	2	0	....	....	....	....	....	....	....	....	....	....	....	....	....	....	....	....	....	....
	Kitchener Rangers	OHL	....	....	....	....	....	....	....	....	....	....	....	....	....	....	1	0	1	1	0	....	....	....	....
	Cornwall Aces	AHL	....	....	....	....	....	....	....	....	....	....	....	....	....	....	10	1	4	5	4	....	....	....	....
1994-95	St. John's	AHL	46	8	10	18	22	....	....	....	....	....	....	....	....	....	4	1	0	1	2	....	....	....	....
	Toronto	**NHL**	5	0	0	0	0	0	0	0	1	0.0	−3	....	....	....	....	....	....	....	....	....	....	....	....
1995-96	**Toronto**	**NHL**	57	7	8	15	26	1	0	0	79	8.9	−11	....	....	....	6	1	1	2	2	0	0	0	....
	St. John's	AHL	11	5	6	11	16	....	....	....	....	....	....	....	....	....	....	....	....	....	....	....	....	....	....
1996-97	**Toronto**	**NHL**	75	12	21	33	41	2	2	0	146	8.2	−3	....	....	....	....	....	....	....	....	....	....	....	....
1997-98	**Toronto**	**NHL**	45	5	8	13	20	0	0	1	73	6.8	5	....	....	....	....	....	....	....	....	....	....	....	....
1998-99	**Toronto**	**NHL**	53	9	10	19	28	1	0	1	96	9.4	−6	579	47.8	14:06	9	0	0	0	2	0	0	0	13:56
99-2000	**Toronto**	**NHL**	18	3	1	4	2	0	0	0	33	9.1	6	33	45.5	12:33	....	....	....	....	....	....	....	....	....
	Tampa Bay	**NHL**	55	11	13	24	34	3	1	0	100	11.0	−14	175	52.0	16:28	....	....	....	....	....	....	....	....	....
2000-01	**Tampa Bay**	**NHL**	64	10	11	21	46	3	2	1	99	10.1	−13	400	50.5	14:43	....	....	....	....	....	....	....	....	....
2001-02	**Phoenix**	**NHL**	18	0	3	3	8	0	0	0	10	0.0	−3	16	62.5	10:53	....	....	....	....	....	....	....	....	....
	Springfield	AHL	2	0	0	0	0	....	....	....	....	....	....	....	....	....	....	....	....	....	....	....	....	....	....
	Vancouver	**NHL**	14	2	4	6	12	0	0	0	18	11.1	4	4	100.0	9:01	6	1	0	1	2	0	0	0	11:28
	Manitoba Moose	AHL	30	7	13	20	32	....	....	....	....	....	....	....	....	....	....	....	....	....	....	....	....	....	....
2002-03	**Vancouver**	**NHL**	30	4	6	10	22	0	0	0	53	7.5	0	29	41.4	11:41	....	....	....	....	....	....	....	....	....
	Philadelphia	**NHL**	13	2	3	5	6	0	0	1	13	15.4	2	0	0.0	8:30	....	....	....	....	....	....	....	....	....
	Nashville	**NHL**	6	0	1	1	4	0	0	0	6	0.0	−1	5	60.0	11:16	....	....	....	....	....	....	....	....	....
	NHL Totals		453	65	89	154	249	10	5	4	727	8.9		1241	49.5	13:33	21	2	1	3	6	0	0	0	12:57

OHL First All-Star Team (1992)

Traded to **Toronto** by **Quebec** with Mats Sundin, Garth Butcher and Philadelphia's 1st round choice (previously acquired, later traded to Washington – Washington selected Nolan Baumgartner) in 1994 Entry Draft for Wendel Clark, Sylvain Lefebvre, Landon Wilson and Toronto's 1st round choice (Jeffrey Kealty) in 1994 Entry Draft, June 28, 1994. Traded to **Tampa Bay** by **Toronto** for Tampa Bay's 3rd round choice (Mikael Tellqvist) in 2000 Entry Draft, November 29, 1999. Traded to **Phoenix** by **Tampa Bay** for Juha Ylonen, June 18, 2001. Traded to **Vancouver** by **Phoenix** with Trevor Letowski, Tyler Bouck and Phoenix's 3rd round choice (later traded back to Phoenix – Phoenix selected Dimitri Pestunov) in 2003 Entry Draft for Drake Berehowsky and Denis Pederson, December 28, 2001. Traded to **Philadelphia** by **Vancouver** for future considerations, February 5, 2003. Claimed on waivers by **Nashville** from **Philadelphia**, March 11, 2003.

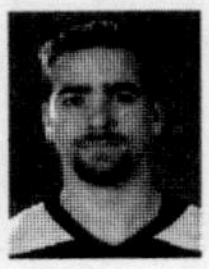

WASHBURN, Steve

(WAWSH-buhrn, STEEV)

Center. Shoots left. 6'2", 198 lbs. Born, Ottawa, Ont., April 10, 1975. Florida's 5th choice, 78th overall, in 1993 Entry Draft.

			Regular Season														Playoffs								
Season	Club	League	GP	G	A	Pts	PIM	PP	SH	GW	S	%	+/-	TF	F%	Min	GP	G	A	Pts	PIM	PP	SH	GW	Min
1990-91	Gloucester	OCJHL	56	21	30	51	47	....	....	....	....	....	....	....	....	....	....	....	....	....	....	....	....	....	....
1991-92	Ottawa 67's	OHL	59	5	17	22	10	....	....	....	....	....	....	....	....	....	11	2	3	5	4	....	....	....	....
1992-93	Ottawa 67's	OHL	66	20	38	58	54	....	....	....	....	....	....	....	....	....	....	....	....	....	....	....	....	....	....
1993-94	Ottawa 67's	OHL	65	30	50	80	88	....	....	....	....	....	....	....	....	....	17	7	16	23	10	....	....	....	....
1994-95	Ottawa 67's	OHL	63	43	63	106	72	....	....	....	....	....	....	....	....	....	....	....	....	....	....	....	....	....	....
	Cincinnati	IHL	6	3	1	4	0	....	....	....	....	....	....	....	....	....	9	1	3	4	4	....	....	....	....
1995-96	**Florida**	**NHL**	**1**	**0**	**1**	**1**	**0**	**0**	**0**	**0**	**1**	**0.0**	**1**	....	....	....	**1**	**0**	**1**	**1**	**0**	**0**	**0**	**0**	....
	Carolina	AHL	78	29	54	83	45	....	....	....	....	....	....	....	....	....	....	....	....	....	....	....	....	....	....
1996-97	**Florida**	**NHL**	**18**	**3**	**6**	**9**	**4**	**1**	**0**	**0**	**21**	**14.3**	**2**	....	....	....	....	....	....	....	....	....	....	....	....
	Carolina	AHL	60	23	40	63	66	....	....	....	....	....	....	....	....	....	....	....	....	....	....	....	....	....	....
1997-98	**Florida**	**NHL**	**58**	**11**	**8**	**19**	**32**	**4**	**0**	**2**	**61**	**18.0**	**-6**	....	....	....	....	....	....	....	....	....	....	....	....
	New Haven	AHL	6	3	5	8	4	....	....	....	....	....	....	....	....	....	3	2	0	2	15	....	....	....	....
1998-99	**Florida**	**NHL**	**4**	**0**	**0**	**0**	**4**	**0**	**0**	**0**	**0**	**0.0**	**-1**	**21**	**38.1**	**6:17**	....	....	....	....	....	....	....	....	....
	New Haven	AHL	10	4	3	7	6	....	....	....	....	....	....	....	....	....	....	....	....	....	....	....	....	....	....
	Vancouver	**NHL**	**8**	**0**	**0**	**0**	**2**	**0**	**0**	**0**	**6**	**0.0**	**0**	**30**	**40.0**	**8:05**	....	....	....	....	....	....	....	....	....
	Syracuse Crunch	AHL	13	1	6	7	6	....	....	....	....	....	....	....	....	....	....	....	....	....	....	....	....	....	....
99-2000	Milwaukee	IHL	12	0	4	4	16	....	....	....	....	....	....	....	....	....	....	....	....	....	....	....	....	....	....
	Philadelphia	**NHL**	**1**	**0**	**0**	**0**	**0**	**0**	**0**	**0**	**1**	**0.0**	**0**	**8**	**12.5**	**14:26**	....	....	....	....	....	....	....	....	....
	Philadelphia	AHL	61	19	52	71	93	....	....	....	....	....	....	....	....	....	5	0	2	2	8	....	....	....	....
2000-01	EHC Kloten	Swiss	8	0	6	6	16	....	....	....	....	....	....	....	....	....	....	....	....	....	....	....	....	....	....
	Philadelphia	**NHL**	**3**	**0**	**0**	**0**	**0**	**0**	**0**	**0**	**0**	**0.0**	**0**	**16**	**50.0**	**7:04**	....	....	....	....	....	....	....	....	....
	Philadelphia	AHL	46	12	16	28	52	....	....	....	....	....	....	....	....	....	2	0	0	0	2	....	....	....	....
2001-02	Iserlohn Roosters	Germany	38	7	14	21	59	....	....	....	....	....	....	....	....	....	....	....	....	....	....	....	....	....	....
2002-03	Iserlohn Roosters	Germany	51	12	18	30	40	....	....	....	....	....	....	....	....	....	....	....	....	....	....	....	....	....	....
	NHL Totals		**93**	**14**	**15**	**29**	**42**	**5**	**0**	**2**	**90**	**15.6**		**75**	**38.7**	**7:50**	**1**	**0**	**1**	**1**	**0**	**0**	**0**	**0**	....

Claimed on waivers by **Vancouver** from **Florida**, February 18, 1999. Signed as a free agent by **Nashville**, August 11, 1999. Traded to **Philadelphia** by **Nashville** for future considerations, November 16, 1999. Signed as a free agent by **EHC Kloten** (Swiss), July 26, 2000. Signed as a free agent by **Philadelphia**, November 21, 2000.

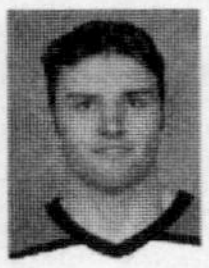

WATT, Mike

(WAHT, MIGHK)

Left wing. Shoots left. 6'2", 212 lbs. Born, Seaforth, Ont., March 31, 1976. Edmonton's 3rd choice, 32nd overall, in 1994 Entry Draft.

			Regular Season														Playoffs								
Season	Club	League	GP	G	A	Pts	PIM	PP	SH	GW	S	%	+/-	TF	F%	Min	GP	G	A	Pts	PIM	PP	SH	GW	Min
1990-91	Seaforth	OJHL-D	39	15	23	38	43	....	....	....	....	....	....	....	....	....	....	....	....	....	....	....	....	....	....
1991-92	Stratford Cullitons	OJHL-B	40	5	21	26	103	....	....	....	....	....	....	....	....	....	....	....	....	....	....	....	....	....	....
1992-93	Stratford Cullitons	OJHL-B	45	20	35	55	100	....	....	....	....	....	....	....	....	....	....	....	....	....	....	....	....	....	....
1993-94	Stratford Cullitons	OJHL-B	48	34	34	68	165	....	....	....	....	....	....	....	....	....	....	....	....	....	....	....	....	....	....
1994-95	Michigan State	CCHA	39	12	6	18	64	....	....	....	....	....	....	....	....	....	....	....	....	....	....	....	....	....	....
1995-96	Michigan State	CCHA	37	17	22	39	60	....	....	....	....	....	....	....	....	....	....	....	....	....	....	....	....	....	....
1996-97	Michigan State	CCHA	39	24	17	41	109	....	....	....	....	....	....	....	....	....	....	....	....	....	....	....	....	....	....
1997-98	**Edmonton**	**NHL**	**14**	**1**	**2**	**3**	**4**	**0**	**0**	**1**	**14**	**7.1**	**-4**	....	....	....	....	....	....	....	....	....	....	....	....
	Hamilton	AHL	63	24	25	49	65	....	....	....	....	....	....	....	....	....	9	2	2	4	8	....	....	....	....
1998-99	**NY Islanders**	**NHL**	**75**	**8**	**17**	**25**	**12**	**0**	**0**	**4**	**75**	**10.7**	**-2**	**180**	**50.6**	**11:15**	....	....	....	....	....	....	....	....	....
99-2000	**NY Islanders**	**NHL**	**45**	**5**	**6**	**11**	**17**	**0**	**1**	**0**	**49**	**10.2**	**-8**	**81**	**48.2**	**12:02**	....	....	....	....	....	....	....	....	....
	Lowell	AHL	16	6	11	17	6	....	....	....	....	....	....	....	....	....	7	1	1	2	4	....	....	....	....
2000-01	**Nashville**	**NHL**	**18**	**1**	**1**	**2**	**8**	**0**	**0**	**1**	**18**	**5.6**	**-2**	**2**	**50.0**	**11:02**	....	....	....	....	....	....	....	....	....
	Milwaukee	IHL	60	20	20	40	48	....	....	....	....	....	....	....	....	....	5	1	2	3	6	....	....	....	....
2001-02	Philadelphia	AHL	53	11	13	24	38	....	....	....	....	....	....	....	....	....	5	2	1	3	6	....	....	....	....
2002-03	**Carolina**	**NHL**	**5**	**0**	**0**	**0**	**0**	**0**	**0**	**0**	**2**	**0.0**	**-1**	**19**	**47.4**	**7:30**	....	....	....	....	....	....	....	....	....
	Lowell	AHL	61	9	14	23	35	....	....	....	....	....	....	....	....	....	....	....	....	....	....	....	....	....	....
	NHL Totals		**157**	**15**	**26**	**41**	**41**	**0**	**1**	**6**	**158**	**9.5**		**282**	**49.6**	**11:20**	....	....	....	....	....	....	....	....	....

Traded to **NY Islanders** by **Edmonton** for Eric Fichaud, June 18, 1998. Claimed on waivers by **Nashville** from **NY Islanders**, May 23, 2000. Traded to **Philadelphia** by **Nashville** for Mikhail Chernov, May 24, 2001. Signed as a free agent by **Carolina**, August 7, 2002.

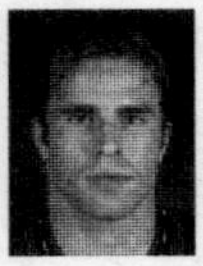

WEAVER, Mike

(WEE-vuhr, MIGHK) **ATL.**

Defense. Shoots right. 5'9", 180 lbs. Born, Bramalea, Ont., May 2, 1978.

			Regular Season														Playoffs								
Season	Club	League	GP	G	A	Pts	PIM	PP	SH	GW	S	%	+/-	TF	F%	Min	GP	G	A	Pts	PIM	PP	SH	GW	Min
1995-96	Bramalea Blues	OPJHL	48	10	39	49	103	....	....	....	....	....	....	....	....	....	....	....	....	....	....	....	....	....	....
1996-97	Michigan State	CCHA	39	0	7	7	46	....	....	....	....	....	....	....	....	....	....	....	....	....	....	....	....	....	....
1997-98	Michigan State	CCHA	44	4	22	26	68	....	....	....	....	....	....	....	....	....	....	....	....	....	....	....	....	....	....
1998-99	Michigan State	CCHA	42	1	6	7	54	....	....	....	....	....	....	....	....	....	....	....	....	....	....	....	....	....	....
99-2000	Michigan State	CCHA	26	0	7	7	20	....	....	....	....	....	....	....	....	....	....	....	....	....	....	....	....	....	....
2000-01	Orlando	IHL	68	0	8	8	34	....	....	....	....	....	....	....	....	....	16	0	2	2	8	....	....	....	....
2001-02	**Atlanta**	**NHL**	**16**	**0**	**1**	**1**	**10**	**0**	**0**	**0**	**9**	**0.0**	**0**	**0**	**0.0**	**13:54**	....	....	....	....	....	....	....	....	....
	Chicago Wolves	AHL	58	2	8	10	67	....	....	....	....	....	....	....	....	....	25	1	3	4	21	....	....	....	....
2002-03	**Atlanta**	**NHL**	**40**	**0**	**5**	**5**	**20**	**0**	**0**	**0**	**21**	**0.0**	**-5**	**0**	**0.0**	**18:38**	....	....	....	....	....	....	....	....	....
	Chicago Wolves	AHL	33	2	2	4	32	....	....	....	....	....	....	....	....	....	9	0	3	3	4	....	....	....	....
	NHL Totals		**56**	**0**	**6**	**6**	**30**	**0**	**0**	**0**	**30**	**0.0**		**0**	**0.0**	**17:17**	....	....	....	....	....	....	....	....	....

OPJHL Defenseman of the Year (1996) • CCHA All-Tournament Team (1997) • CCHA First All-Star Team (1999, 2000) • CCHA Best Defensive Defenseman Award (1999, 2000) • NCAA West Second All-American Team (1999, 2000)

Signed as a free agent by **Atlanta**, June 15, 2000.

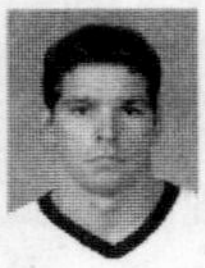

WEBB, Steve

(WEHB, STEEV)

Right wing. Shoots right. 6', 211 lbs. Born, Peterborough, Ont., April 30, 1975. Buffalo's 8th choice, 176th overall, in 1994 Entry Draft.

			Regular Season														Playoffs								
Season	Club	League	GP	G	A	Pts	PIM	PP	SH	GW	S	%	+/-	TF	F%	Min	GP	G	A	Pts	PIM	PP	SH	GW	Min
1991-92	Peterborough	OJHL-B	37	9	9	18	195	....	....	....	....	....	....	....	....	....	....	....	....	....	....	....	....	....	....
1992-93	Windsor Spitfires	OHL	63	14	25	39	184	....	....	....	....	....	....	....	....	....	....	....	....	....	....	....	....	....	....
1993-94	Windsor Spitfires	OHL	2	0	1	1	9	....	....	....	....	....	....	....	....	....	....	....	....	....	....	....	....	....	....
	Peterborough	OHL	33	6	15	21	117	....	....	....	....	....	....	....	....	....	6	1	1	2	20	....	....	....	....
1994-95	Peterborough	OHL	42	8	16	24	109	....	....	....	....	....	....	....	....	....	11	3	3	6	22	....	....	....	....
1995-96	Muskegon Fury	ColHL	58	18	24	42	263	....	....	....	....	....	....	....	....	....	5	1	2	3	22	....	....	....	....
	Detroit Vipers	IHL	4	0	0	0	24	....	....	....	....	....	....	....	....	....	....	....	....	....	....	....	....	....	....
1996-97	**NY Islanders**	**NHL**	**41**	**1**	**4**	**5**	**144**	**1**	**0**	**0**	**21**	**4.8**	**-10**	....	....	....	....	....	....	....	....	....	....	....	....
	Kentucky	AHL	25	6	6	12	103	....	....	....	....	....	....	....	....	....	2	0	0	0	19	....	....	....	....
1997-98	**NY Islanders**	**NHL**	**20**	**0**	**0**	**0**	**35**	**0**	**0**	**0**	**6**	**0.0**	**-2**	....	....	....	....	....	....	....	....	....	....	....	....
	Kentucky	AHL	37	5	13	18	139	....	....	....	....	....	....	....	....	....	3	0	1	1	10	....	....	....	....
1998-99	**NY Islanders**	**NHL**	**45**	**0**	**0**	**0**	**32**	**0**	**0**	**0**	**18**	**0.0**	**-10**	**0**	**0.0**	**4:13**	....	....	....	....	....	....	....	....	....
	Lowell	AHL	23	2	4	6	80	....	....	....	....	....	....	....	....	....	....	....	....	....	....	....	....	....	....
99-2000	**NY Islanders**	**NHL**	**65**	**1**	**3**	**4**	**103**	**0**	**0**	**0**	**27**	**3.7**	**-4**	**1**	**0.0**	**7:00**	....	....	....	....	....	....	....	....	....
2000-01	**NY Islanders**	**NHL**	**31**	**0**	**2**	**2**	**35**	**0**	**0**	**0**	**8**	**0.0**	**1**	**0**	**0.0**	**6:26**	....	....	....	....	....	....	....	....	....
2001-02	**NY Islanders**	**NHL**	**60**	**2**	**4**	**6**	**104**	**0**	**0**	**0**	**31**	**6.5**	**0**	**1**	**100.0**	**6:29**	**7**	**0**	**0**	**0**	**12**	**0**	**0**	**0**	**6:52**
2002-03	**NY Islanders**	**NHL**	**49**	**1**	**0**	**1**	**75**	**0**	**0**	**0**	**27**	**3.7**	**-5**	**0**	**0.0**	**6:02**	**5**	**0**	**0**	**0**	**10**	**0**	**0**	**0**	**6:46**
	NHL Totals		**311**	**5**	**13**	**18**	**528**	**1**	**0**	**0**	**138**	**3.6**		**2**	**50.0**	**6:07**	**12**	**0**	**0**	**0**	**22**	**0**	**0**	**0**	**6:50**

Signed as a free agent by **NY Islanders**, October 10, 1996. • Missed majority of 2000-01 season recovering from knee injury suffered in game vs. Anaheim, November 19, 2000.

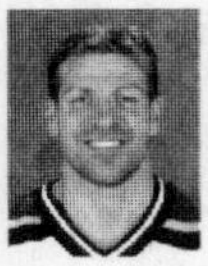

WEIGHT, Doug

(WAYT, DUHG) **ST.L.**

Center. Shoots left. 5'11", 200 lbs. Born, Warren, MI, January 21, 1971. NY Rangers' 2nd choice, 34th overall, in 1990 Entry Draft.

			Regular Season														Playoffs								
Season	Club	League	GP	G	A	Pts	PIM	PP	SH	GW	S	%	+/-	TF	F%	Min	GP	G	A	Pts	PIM	PP	SH	GW	Min
1988-89	Bloomfield Jets	NAJHL	34	26	53	79	105	....	....	....	....	....	....	....	....	....	....	....	....	....	....	....	....	....	....
1989-90	Lake Superior	CCHA	46	21	48	69	44	....	....	....	....	....	....	....	....	....	....	....	....	....	....	....	....	....	....
1990-91	Lake Superior	CCHA	42	29	46	75	86	....	....	....	....	....	....	....	....	....	....	....	....	....	....	....	....	....	....
	NY Rangers	**NHL**	....	....	....	....	....	....	....	....	....	....	....	....	....	....	**1**	**0**	**0**	**0**	**0**	**0**	**0**	**0**	....
1991-92	**NY Rangers**	**NHL**	**53**	**8**	**22**	**30**	**23**	**0**	**0**	**2**	**72**	**11.1**	**-3**	....	....	....	**7**	**2**	**2**	**4**	**0**	**1**	**0**	**0**	....
	Binghamton	AHL	9	3	14	17	2	....	....	....	....	....	....	....	....	....	4	1	4	5	6	....	....	....	....
1992-93	**NY Rangers**	**NHL**	**65**	**15**	**25**	**40**	**55**	**3**	**0**	**1**	**90**	**16.7**	**4**	....	....	....	....	....	....	....	....	....	....	....	....
	Edmonton	**NHL**	**13**	**2**	**6**	**8**	**10**	**0**	**0**	**0**	**35**	**5.7**	**-2**	....	....	....	....	....	....	....	....	....	....	....	....
1993-94	**Edmonton**	**NHL**	**84**	**24**	**50**	**74**	**47**	**4**	**1**	**1**	**188**	**12.8**	**-22**	....	....	....	....	....	....	....	....	....	....	....	....
1994-95	Rosenheim	Germany	8	2	3	5	18	....	....	....	....	....	....	....	....	....	....	....	....	....	....	....	....	....	....
	Edmonton	**NHL**	**48**	**7**	**33**	**40**	**69**	**1**	**0**	**1**	**104**	**6.7**	**-17**	....	....	....	....	....	....	....	....	....	....	....	....

Season	Club	League	GP	G	A	Pts	PIM	PP	SH	GW	S	%	+/-	TF	F%	Min	GP	G	A	Pts	PIM	PP	SH	GW	Min
			Regular Season														Playoffs								
1995-96	Edmonton	NHL	82	25	79	104	95	9	0	2	204	12.3	-19	....	....	....	....	....	....	....	....	....	....	....	....
1996-97	Edmonton	NHL	80	21	61	82	80	4	0	2	235	8.9	1	....	....	....	12	3	8	11	8	0	0	0	....
1997-98	Edmonton	NHL	79	26	44	70	69	9	0	4	205	12.7	1	....	....	....	12	2	7	9	14	2	0	1	....
	United States	Olympics	4	0	2	2	2	....	....	....	....	....	....	....	....	....	....	....	....	....	....	....	....	....	....
1998-99	Edmonton	NHL	43	6	31	37	12	1	0	0	79	7.6	-8	853	49.5	19:51	4	1	1	2	15	0	0	0	14:43
99-2000	Edmonton	NHL	77	21	51	72	54	3	1	4	167	12.6	6	1588	50.4	20:35	5	3	2	5	4	2	0	1	21:05
2000-01	Edmonton	NHL	82	25	65	90	91	8	0	3	188	13.3	12	1514	51.3	22:08	6	1	5	6	17	0	0	0	22:45
2001-02	St. Louis	NHL	61	15	34	49	40	3	0	1	131	11.5	20	1123	49.2	19:48	10	1	1	2	4	1	0	1	16:26
	United States	Olympics	6	0	3	3	4	....	....	....	....	....	....	....	....	....	....	....	....	....	....	....	....	....	....
2002-03	St. Louis	NHL	70	15	52	67	52	7	0	3	182	8.2	-6	1048	50.4	20:23	7	5	8	13	2	5	0	1	22:26
	NHL Totals		837	210	553	763	697	52	2	24	1880	11.2		6126	50.3	20:41	64	18	34	52	64	11	0	4	19:26

CCHA First All-Star Team (1991) • NCAA West Second All-American Team (1991)
Played in NHL All-Star Game (1996, 1998, 2001, 2003)
Traded to **Edmonton** by **NY Rangers** for Esa Tikkanen, March 17, 1993. Traded to **St. Louis** by **Edmonton** with Michel Riesen for Marty Reasoner, Jochen Hecht and Jan Horacek, July 1, 2001.

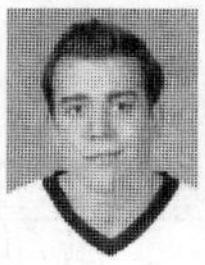

WEINHANDL, Mattias

(vayn-hanh-duhl, mah-TEE-uhs) **NYI**

Right wing. Shoots right. 6', 183 lbs. Born, Ljungby, Sweden, June 1, 1980. NY Islanders' 5th choice, 78th overall, in 1999 Entry Draft.

Season	Club	League	GP	G	A	Pts	PIM	PP	SH	GW	S	%	+/-	TF	F%	Min	GP	G	A	Pts	PIM	PP	SH	GW	Min
1995-96	Troja-Ljungby Jr.	Swede-Jr.	28	38	40	78	....	....	....	....	....	....	....	....	....	....	....	....	....	....	....	....	....	....	....
1996-97	Troja-Ljungby Jr.	Swede-Jr.	48	61	69	130	46	....	....	....	....	....	....	....	....	....	....	....	....	....	....	....	....	....	....
1997-98	IF Troja-Ljungby	Swede-2	28	3	2	5	2	....	....	....	....	....	....	....	....	....	5	0	0	0	2	....	....	....	....
1998-99	IF Troja-Ljungby	Swede-2	38	20	20	40	30	....	....	....	....	....	....	....	....	....	5	4	3	7	4	....	....	....	....
99-2000	MoDo Jr.	Swede-Jr.	1	2	2	4	2	....	....	....	....	....	....	....	....	....	....	....	....	....	....	....	....	....	....
	MoDo	Sweden	32	15	9	24	6	....	....	....	....	....	....	....	....	....	13	5	3	8	8	....	....	....	....
2000-01	MoDo	Sweden	48	16	16	32	14	....	....	....	....	....	....	....	....	....	6	1	3	4	6	....	....	....	....
2001-02	MoDo	Sweden	50	18	16	34	10	....	....	....	....	....	....	....	....	....	14	4	*11	*15	4	....	....	....	....
2002-03	NY Islanders	NHL	47	6	17	23	10	1	0	0	66	9.1	-2	5	60.0	13:52	....	....	....	....	....	....	....	....	....
	Bridgeport	AHL	23	9	12	21	14	....	....	....	....	....	....	....	....	....	....	....	....	....	....	....	....	....	....
	NHL Totals		47	6	17	23	10	1	0	0	66	9.1		5	60.0	13:52	....	....	....	....	....	....	....	....	....

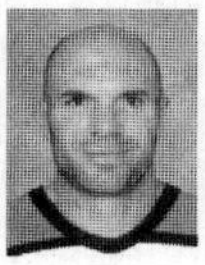

WEINRICH, Eric

(WIGHN-rihch, AIR-ihk) **PHI.**

Defense. Shoots left. 6'1", 207 lbs. Born, Roanoke, VA, December 19, 1966. New Jersey's 3rd choice, 32nd overall, in 1985 Entry Draft.

Season	Club	League	GP	G	A	Pts	PIM	PP	SH	GW	S	%	+/-	TF	F%	Min	GP	G	A	Pts	PIM	PP	SH	GW	Min
1983-84	N. Yarmouth	Hi-School	17	23	33	56	....	....	....	....	....	....	....	....	....	....	....	....	....	....	....	....	....	....	....
1984-85	N. Yarmouth	Hi-School	20	6	21	27	....	....	....	....	....	....	....	....	....	....	....	....	....	....	....	....	....	....	....
1985-86	U. of Maine	H-East	34	0	14	14	26	....	....	....	....	....	....	....	....	....	....	....	....	....	....	....	....	....	....
1986-87	U. of Maine	H-East	41	12	32	44	59	....	....	....	....	....	....	....	....	....	....	....	....	....	....	....	....	....	....
1987-88	U. of Maine	H-East	8	4	7	11	22	....	....	....	....	....	....	....	....	....	....	....	....	....	....	....	....	....	....
	Team USA	Nat-Tm	38	3	9	12	24	....	....	....	....	....	....	....	....	....	....	....	....	....	....	....	....	....	....
	United States	Olympics	3	0	0	0	0	....	....	....	....	....	....	....	....	....	....	....	....	....	....	....	....	....	....
1988-89	New Jersey	NHL	2	0	0	0	0	0	0	0	3	0.0	-1	....	....	....	....	....	....	....	....	....	....	....	....
	Utica Devils	AHL	80	17	27	44	70	....	....	....	....	....	....	....	....	....	5	0	1	1	4	....	....	....	....
1989-90	New Jersey	NHL	19	2	7	9	11	1	0	1	16	12.5	1	....	....	....	6	1	3	4	17	0	0	0	....
	Utica Devils	AHL	57	12	48	60	38	....	....	....	....	....	....	....	....	....	....	....	....	....	....	....	....	....	....
1990-91	New Jersey	NHL	76	4	34	38	48	1	0	0	96	4.2	10	....	....	....	7	1	2	3	6	1	0	0	....
1991-92	New Jersey	NHL	76	7	25	32	55	5	0	0	97	7.2	10	....	....	....	7	0	2	2	4	0	0	0	....
1992-93	Hartford	NHL	79	7	29	36	76	0	2	2	104	6.7	-11	....	....	....	....	....	....	....	....	....	....	....	....
1993-94	Hartford	NHL	8	1	1	2	2	1	0	0	10	10.0	-5	....	....	....	....	....	....	....	....	....	....	....	....
	Chicago	NHL	54	3	23	26	31	1	0	2	105	2.9	6	....	....	....	6	0	2	2	6	0	0	0	....
1994-95	Chicago	NHL	48	3	10	13	33	1	0	2	50	6.0	1	....	....	....	16	1	5	6	4	0	0	0	....
1995-96	Chicago	NHL	77	5	10	15	65	0	0	0	76	6.6	14	....	....	....	10	1	4	5	10	1	0	0	....
1996-97	Chicago	NHL	81	7	25	32	62	1	0	0	115	6.1	19	....	....	....	6	0	1	1	4	0	0	0	....
1997-98	Chicago	NHL	82	2	21	23	106	0	0	0	85	2.4	10	....	....	....	....	....	....	....	....	....	....	....	....
1998-99	Chicago	NHL	14	1	3	4	12	0	0	0	24	4.2	-13	0	0.0	20:12	....	....	....	....	....	....	....	....	....
	Montreal	NHL	66	6	12	18	77	4	0	1	95	6.3	-12	0	0.0	24:44	....	....	....	....	....	....	....	....	....
99-2000	Montreal	NHL	77	4	25	29	39	2	0	0	120	3.3	4	0	0.0	25:21	....	....	....	....	....	....	....	....	....
2000-01	Montreal	NHL	60	6	19	25	34	2	0	1	81	7.4	-1	1	100.0	24:27	....	....	....	....	....	....	....	....	....
	Boston	NHL	22	1	5	6	10	1	0	1	28	3.6	-8	0	0.0	25:52	....	....	....	....	....	....	....	....	....
2001-02	Philadelphia	NHL	80	4	20	24	26	0	0	2	102	3.9	27	0	0.0	21:53	5	0	0	0	4	0	0	0	18:42
2002-03	Philadelphia	NHL	81	2	18	20	40	1	1	0	103	1.9	16	1	0.0	21:24	13	2	3	5	12	1	0	0	24:59
	NHL Totals		1002	65	287	352	727	21	3	12	1310	5.0		2	50.0	23:28	76	6	22	28	67	3	0	0	23:14

Hockey East First All-Star Team (1987) • NCAA East Second All-American Team (1987) • AHL First All-Star Team (1990) • Eddie Shore Award (Top Defenseman – AHL) (1990) • NHL All-Rookie Team (1991)
Traded to **Hartford** by **New Jersey** with Sean Burke for Bobby Holik and Hartford's 2nd round choice (Jay Pandolfo) in 1993 Entry Draft, August 28, 1992. Traded to **Chicago** by **Hartford** with Patrick Poulin for Steve Larmer and Bryan Marchment, November 2, 1993. Traded to **Montreal** by **Chicago** with Jeff Hackett, Alain Nasreddine and Tampa Bay's 4th round choice (previously acquired, Montreal selected Chris Dyment) in 1999 Entry Draft for Jocelyn Thibault, Dave Manson and Brad Brown, November 16, 1998. Traded to **Boston** by **Montreal** for Patrick Traverse, February 21, 2001. Signed as a free agent by **Philadelphia**, July 5, 2001.

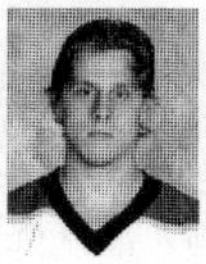

WEISS, Stephen

(WIGHS, STEEV-ehn) **FLA.**

Center. Shoots left. 5'11", 185 lbs. Born, Toronto, Ont., April 3, 1983. Florida's 1st choice, 4th overall, in 2001 Entry Draft.

Season	Club	League	GP	G	A	Pts	PIM	PP	SH	GW	S	%	+/-	TF	F%	Min	GP	G	A	Pts	PIM	PP	SH	GW	Min
1997-98	Tor. Young Nats	MTHL	48	51	58	109	....	....	....	....	....	....	....	....	....	....	....	....	....	....	....	....	....	....	....
1998-99	North York	OPJHL	35	15	22	37	10	....	....	....	....	....	....	....	....	....	....	....	....	....	....	....	....	....	....
99-2000	Plymouth Whalers	OHL	64	24	42	66	35	....	....	....	....	....	....	....	....	....	23	8	18	26	18	....	....	....	....
2000-01	Plymouth Whalers	OHL	62	40	47	87	45	....	....	....	....	....	....	....	....	....	18	7	16	23	10	....	....	....	....
2001-02	Florida	NHL	7	1	1	2	0	1	0	0	15	6.7	0	107	52.3	16:14	....	....	....	....	....	....	....	....	....
	Plymouth Whalers	OHL	46	25	45	70	69	....	....	....	....	....	....	....	....	....	6	2	7	9	13	....	....	....	....
2002-03	Florida	NHL	77	6	15	21	17	0	0	2	87	6.9	-13	1065	46.3	14:17	....	....	....	....	....	....	....	....	....
	NHL Totals		84	7	16	23	17	1	0	2	102	6.9		1172	46.8	14:27	....	....	....	....	....	....	....	....	....

OHL All-Rookie Team (2000)

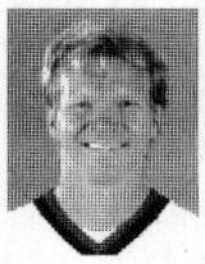

WESLEY, Glen

(WEH-slee, GLEHN) **CAR.**

Defense. Shoots left. 6'1", 205 lbs. Born, Red Deer, Alta., October 2, 1968. Boston's 1st choice, 3rd overall, in 1987 Entry Draft.

Season	Club	League	GP	G	A	Pts	PIM	PP	SH	GW	S	%	+/-	TF	F%	Min	GP	G	A	Pts	PIM	PP	SH	GW	Min
1983-84	Red Deer Rustlers	AJHL	57	9	20	29	40	....	....	....	....	....	....	....	....	....	....	....	....	....	....	....	....	....	....
	Portland	WHL	3	1	2	3	0	....	....	....	....	....	....	....	....	....	....	....	....	....	....	....	....	....	....
1984-85	Portland	WHL	67	16	52	68	76	....	....	....	....	....	....	....	....	....	6	1	6	7	8	....	....	....	....
1985-86	Portland	WHL	69	16	75	91	96	....	....	....	....	....	....	....	....	....	15	3	11	14	29	....	....	....	....
1986-87	Portland	WHL	63	16	46	62	72	....	....	....	....	....	....	....	....	....	20	8	18	26	27	....	....	....	....
1987-88	Boston	NHL	79	7	30	37	69	1	2	0	158	4.4	21	....	....	....	23	6	8	14	22	4	1	0	....
1988-89	Boston	NHL	77	19	35	54	61	8	1	1	181	10.5	23	....	....	....	10	0	2	2	4	0	0	0	....
1989-90	Boston	NHL	78	9	27	36	48	5	0	4	166	5.4	6	....	....	....	21	2	6	8	36	0	0	1	....
1990-91	Boston	NHL	80	11	32	43	78	5	1	1	199	5.5	0	....	....	....	19	2	9	11	19	2	0	0	....
1991-92	Boston	NHL	78	9	37	46	54	4	0	1	211	4.3	-9	....	....	....	15	2	4	6	16	0	0	0	....
1992-93	Boston	NHL	64	8	25	33	47	4	1	0	183	4.4	-2	....	....	....	4	0	0	0	0	0	0	0	....
1993-94	Boston	NHL	81	14	44	58	64	6	1	1	265	5.3	1	....	....	....	13	3	3	6	12	1	0	0	....
1994-95	Hartford	NHL	48	2	14	16	50	1	0	1	125	1.6	-6	....	....	....	....	....	....	....	....	....	....	....	....
1995-96	Hartford	NHL	68	8	16	24	88	6	0	1	129	6.2	-9	....	....	....	....	....	....	....	....	....	....	....	....
1996-97	Hartford	NHL	68	6	26	32	40	3	1	0	126	4.8	0	....	....	....	....	....	....	....	....	....	....	....	....
1997-98	Carolina	NHL	82	6	19	25	36	1	0	1	121	5.0	7	....	....	....	....	....	....	....	....	....	....	....	....
1998-99	Carolina	NHL	74	7	17	24	44	0	0	2	112	6.3	14	1	0.0	22:31	6	0	0	0	2	0	0	0	28:21
99-2000	Carolina	NHL	78	7	15	22	38	1	0	0	99	7.1	-4	0	0.0	21:32	....	....	....	....	....	....	....	....	....
2000-01	Carolina	NHL	71	5	16	21	42	3	0	0	92	5.4	-2	0	0.0	22:21	6	0	0	0	0	0	0	0	22:07
2001-02	Carolina	NHL	77	5	13	18	56	1	0	0	88	5.7	-8	0	0.0	20:13	22	0	2	2	12	0	0	0	21:04

Season	Club	League	GP	G	A	Pts	PIM	PP	SH	GW	S	%	+/-	TF	F%	Min	GP	G	A	Pts	PIM	PP	SH	GW	Min
			Regular Season														Playoffs								
2002-03	**Carolina**	**NHL**	**63**	**1**	**7**	**8**	**40**	**1**	**0**	**0**	**72**	**1.4**	**–5**	**0**	**0.0**	**21:24**	....	....	....	....	....	....	....	....	....
	Toronto	**NHL**	**7**	**0**	**3**	**3**	**4**	**0**	**0**	**0**	**5**	**0.0**	**3**	**0**	**0.0**	**20:41**	**5**	**0**	**1**	**1**	**2**	**0**	**0**	**0**	**27:39**
	NHL Totals		**1173**	**124**	**376**	**500**	**859**	**50**	**7**	**13**	**2332**	**5.3**		**1**	**0.0**	**21:35**	**144**	**15**	**35**	**50**	**125**	**7**	**1**	**1**	**23:11**

WHL West First All-Star Team (1986, 1987) • NHL All-Rookie Team (1988)

Played in NHL All-Star Game (1989)

Traded to **Hartford** by **Boston** for Hartford's 1st round choices in 1995 (Kyle McLaren), 1996 (Johnathan Aitken) and 1997 (Sergei Samsonov) Entry Drafts, August 26, 1994. Transferred to **Carolina** after **Hartford** franchise relocated, June 25, 1997. Traded to **Toronto** by **Carolina** for Toronto's 2nd round choice in 2004 Entry Draft, March 9, 2003. Signed as a free agent by **Carolina**, July 8, 2003.

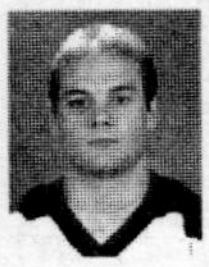

WESTCOTT, Duvie

(WEST-coht, DOO-vee) **CBJ**

Defense. Shoots right. 5'11", 192 lbs. Born, Winnipeg, Man., October 30, 1977.

Season	Club	League	GP	G	A	Pts	PIM	PP	SH	GW	S	%	+/-	TF	F%	Min	GP	G	A	Pts	PIM	PP	SH	GW	Min
1996-97	Winnipeg South	MJHL	52	12	47	59	....	....	....	....	....	....	....	....	....	....	....	....	....	....	....	....	....	....	....
1997-98	Alaska-Anchorage	WCHA	25	3	5	8	43	....	....	....	....	....	....	....	....	....	....	....	....	....	....	....	....	....	....
	Omaha Lancers	USHL	12	3	3	6	31	....	....	....	....	....	....	....	....	....	14	0	8	8	84	....	....	....	....
1998-99	St. Cloud State	WCHA	DID NOT PLAY – TRANSFERRED COLLEGES																						
99-2000	St. Cloud State	WCHA	36	1	18	19	67	....	....	....	....	....	....	....	....	....	....	....	....	....	....	....	....	....	....
2000-01	St. Cloud State	WCHA	38	10	24	34	116	....	....	....	....	....	....	....	....	....	....	....	....	....	....	....	....	....	....
2001-02	**Columbus**	**NHL**	**4**	**0**	**0**	**0**	**2**	**0**	**0**	**0**	**3**	**0.0**	**–2**	**0**	**0.0**	**15:08**	....	....	....	....	....	....	....	....	....
	Syracuse Crunch	AHL	68	4	29	33	99	....	....	....	....	....	....	....	....	....	10	0	1	1	12	....	....	....	....
2002-03	**Columbus**	**NHL**	**39**	**0**	**7**	**7**	**77**	**0**	**0**	**0**	**27**	**0.0**	**–3**	**0**	**0.0**	**18:41**	....	....	....	....	....	....	....	....	....
	Syracuse Crunch	AHL	22	1	10	11	54	....	....	....	....	....	....	....	....	....	....	....	....	....	....	....	....	....	....
	NHL Totals		**43**	**0**	**7**	**7**	**79**	**0**	**0**	**0**	**30**	**0.0**		**0**	**0.0**	**18:21**	....	....	....	....	....	....	....	....	....

WCHA Second All-Star Team (2001)

Signed as a free agent by **Columbus**, May 10, 2001.

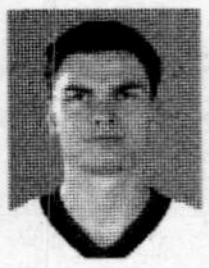

WESTLUND, Tommy

(WEHST-luhnd, TOHM-mee)

Right wing. Shoots right. 6', 210 lbs. Born, Fors, Sweden, December 29, 1974. Carolina's 5th choice, 93rd overall, in 1998 Entry Draft.

Season	Club	League	GP	G	A	Pts	PIM	PP	SH	GW	S	%	+/-	TF	F%	Min	GP	G	A	Pts	PIM	PP	SH	GW	Min
1991-92	Avesta BK	Swede-3	27	11	9	20	8	....	....	....	....	....	....	....	....	....	....	....	....	....	....	....	....	....	....
1992-93	Avesta BK	Swede-2	32	9	5	14	32	....	....	....	....	....	....	....	....	....	....	....	....	....	....	....	....	....	....
1993-94	Avesta BK	Swede-2	31	20	11	31	34	....	....	....	....	....	....	....	....	....	....	....	....	....	....	....	....	....	....
1994-95	Avesta BK	Swede-2	32	17	13	30	22	....	....	....	....	....	....	....	....	....	....	....	....	....	....	....	....	....	....
1995-96	Brynas IF Gavle	Sweden	18	2	1	3	2	....	....	....	....	....	....	....	....	....	....	....	....	....	....	....	....	....	....
	Brynas IF Gavle	Swede-Q	18	10	10	20	4	....	....	....	....	....	....	....	....	....	8	1	0	1	4	....	....	....	....
1996-97	Brynas IF Gavle	Sweden	50	21	13	34	16	....	....	....	....	....	....	....	....	....	....	....	....	....	....	....	....	....	....
1997-98	Brynas IF Gavle	Sweden	46	29	9	38	45	....	....	....	....	....	....	....	....	....	3	0	1	1	0	....	....	....	....
1998-99	New Haven	AHL	50	8	18	26	31	....	....	....	....	....	....	....	....	....	....	....	....	....	....	....	....	....	....
99-2000	**Carolina**	**NHL**	**81**	**4**	**8**	**12**	**19**	**0**	**1**	**0**	**67**	**6.0**	**–10**	**336**	**52.7**	**10:23**	....	....	....	....	....	....	....	....	....
2000-01	**Carolina**	**NHL**	**79**	**5**	**3**	**8**	**23**	**0**	**0**	**1**	**47**	**10.6**	**–9**	**340**	**50.9**	**9:22**	**6**	**0**	**0**	**0**	**17**	**0**	**0**	**0**	**14:28**
2001-02	**Carolina**	**NHL**	**40**	**0**	**2**	**2**	**6**	**0**	**0**	**0**	**29**	**0.0**	**–8**	**118**	**56.8**	**10:38**	**19**	**1**	**0**	**1**	**0**	**0**	**0**	**0**	**8:37**
2002-03	**Carolina**	**NHL**	**3**	**0**	**0**	**0**	**0**	**0**	**0**	**0**	**0**	**0.0**	**0**	**8**	**62.5**	**6:29**	....	....	....	....	....	....	....	....	....
	Lowell	AHL	22	1	3	4	12	....	....	....	....	....	....	....	....	....	....	....	....	....	....	....	....	....	....
	NHL Totals		**203**	**9**	**13**	**22**	**48**	**0**	**1**	**1**	**143**	**6.3**		**802**	**52.6**	**9:59**	**25**	**1**	**0**	**1**	**17**	**0**	**0**	**0**	**10:01**

• Missed majority of 2001-02 season recovering from back injury suffered in game vs. Columbus, November 19, 2001. • Spent majority of 2002-03 season with Lowell (AHL) as a healthy reserve. Signed as a free agent by **Leksands IF** (Sweden), April 3, 2003.

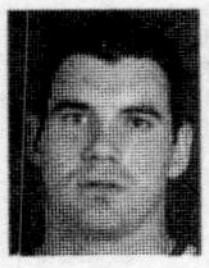

WHITE, Brian

(WHIGHT, BRIGH-uhn)

Defense. Shoots right. 6'1", 195 lbs. Born, Winchester, MA, February 7, 1976. Tampa Bay's 11th choice, 268th overall, in 1994 Entry Draft.

Season	Club	League	GP	G	A	Pts	PIM	PP	SH	GW	S	%	+/-	TF	F%	Min	GP	G	A	Pts	PIM	PP	SH	GW	Min
1993-94	Arlington	Hi-School	40	14	18	32	81	....	....	....	....	....	....	....	....	....	....	....	....	....	....	....	....	....	....
1994-95	U. of Maine	H-East	28	1	1	2	16	....	....	....	....	....	....	....	....	....	....	....	....	....	....	....	....	....	....
1995-96	U. of Maine	H-East	39	0	4	4	18	....	....	....	....	....	....	....	....	....	....	....	....	....	....	....	....	....	....
1996-97	U. of Maine	H-East	35	4	12	16	36	....	....	....	....	....	....	....	....	....	....	....	....	....	....	....	....	....	....
1997-98	U. of Maine	H-East	33	0	12	12	45	....	....	....	....	....	....	....	....	....	....	....	....	....	....	....	....	....	....
	Long Beach	IHL	1	0	0	0	0	....	....	....	....	....	....	....	....	....	....	....	....	....	....	....	....	....	....
1998-99	**Colorado**	**NHL**	**2**	**0**	**0**	**0**	**0**	**0**	**0**	**0**	**0**	**0.0**	**0**	**0**	**0.0**	**0:40**	....	....	....	....	....	....	....	....	....
	Hershey Bears	AHL	71	4	8	12	41	....	....	....	....	....	....	....	....	....	4	0	1	1	2	....	....	....	....
99-2000	Hershey Bears	AHL	79	3	19	22	78	....	....	....	....	....	....	....	....	....	14	0	3	3	21	....	....	....	....
2000-01	Hershey Bears	AHL	75	2	9	11	44	....	....	....	....	....	....	....	....	....	9	0	1	1	12	....	....	....	....
2001-02	Cincinnati	AHL	73	0	8	8	32	....	....	....	....	....	....	....	....	....	3	0	0	0	2	....	....	....	....
2002-03	Providence Bruins	AHL	51	2	5	7	34	....	....	....	....	....	....	....	....	....	4	0	1	1	8	....	....	....	....
	NHL Totals		**2**	**0**	**0**	**0**	**0**	**0**	**0**	**0**	**0**	**0.0**		**0**	**0.0**	**0:40**	....	....	....	....	....	....	....	....	....

Signed as a free agent by **Colorado**, July 7, 1998. Signed as a free agent by **Anaheim**, August 14, 2001. Signed as a free agent by **Providence** (AHL), September 23, 2002.

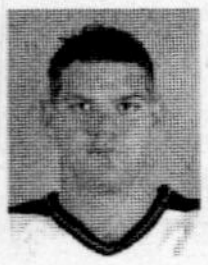

WHITE, Colin

(WHIGHT, CAWI-ihn) **N.J.**

Defense. Shoots left. 6'4", 215 lbs. Born, New Glasgow, N.S., December 12, 1977. New Jersey's 5th choice, 49th overall, in 1996 Entry Draft.

Season	Club	League	GP	G	A	Pts	PIM	PP	SH	GW	S	%	+/-	TF	F%	Min	GP	G	A	Pts	PIM	PP	SH	GW	Min
1994-95	Laval Titan	QMJHL	7	0	1	1	32	....	....	....	....	....	....	....	....	....	....	....	....	....	....	....	....	....	....
	Hull Olympiques	QMJHL	5	0	1	1	4	....	....	....	....	....	....	....	....	....	12	0	0	0	23	....	....	....	....
1995-96	Hull Olympiques	QMJHL	62	2	8	10	303	....	....	....	....	....	....	....	....	....	18	0	4	4	42	....	....	....	....
1996-97	Hull Olympiques	QMJHL	63	3	12	15	297	....	....	....	....	....	....	....	....	....	14	3	12	15	65	....	....	....	....
1997-98	Albany River Rats	AHL	76	3	13	16	235	....	....	....	....	....	....	....	....	....	13	0	0	0	55	....	....	....	....
1998-99	Albany River Rats	AHL	77	2	12	14	265	....	....	....	....	....	....	....	....	....	5	0	1	1	8	....	....	....	....
99-2000♦	**New Jersey**	**NHL**	**21**	**2**	**1**	**3**	**40**	**0**	**0**	**1**	**29**	**6.9**	**3**	**0**	**0.0**	**14:45**	**23**	**1**	**5**	**6**	**18**	**0**	**0**	**1**	**14:25**
	Albany River Rats	AHL	52	5	21	26	176	....	....	....	....	....	....	....	....	....	....	....	....	....	....	....	....	....	....
2000-01	**New Jersey**	**NHL**	**82**	**1**	**19**	**20**	**155**	**0**	**0**	**1**	**114**	**0.9**	**32**	**0**	**0.0**	**19:06**	**25**	**0**	**3**	**3**	**42**	**0**	**0**	**0**	**16:45**
2001-02	**New Jersey**	**NHL**	**73**	**2**	**3**	**5**	**133**	**0**	**0**	**0**	**81**	**2.5**	**6**	**0**	**0.0**	**20:06**	**6**	**0**	**0**	**0**	**2**	**0**	**0**	**0**	**21:50**
2002-03♦	**New Jersey**	**NHL**	**72**	**5**	**8**	**13**	**98**	**0**	**0**	**1**	**81**	**6.2**	**19**	**0**	**0.0**	**19:41**	**24**	**0**	**5**	**5**	**29**	**0**	**0**	**0**	**22:02**
	NHL Totals		**248**	**10**	**31**	**41**	**426**	**0**	**0**	**3**	**305**	**3.3**		**0**	**0.0**	**19:12**	**78**	**1**	**13**	**14**	**91**	**0**	**0**	**1**	**18:05**

QMJHL All-Rookie Team (1996) • NHL All-Rookie Team (2001)

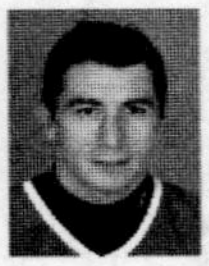

WHITE, Peter

(WHIGHT, PEE-tuhr) **PHI.**

Center. Shoots left. 5'11", 200 lbs. Born, Montreal, Que., March 15, 1969. Edmonton's 4th choice, 92nd overall, in 1989 Entry Draft.

Season	Club	League	GP	G	A	Pts	PIM	PP	SH	GW	S	%	+/-	TF	F%	Min	GP	G	A	Pts	PIM	PP	SH	GW	Min
1984-85	Lac St-Louis Lions	QAAA	42	16	32	48	18	....	....	....	....	....	....	....	....	....	11	4	3	7	4	....	....	....	....
1985-86	Lac St-Louis Lions	QAAA	42	38	62	100	28	....	....	....	....	....	....	....	....	....	2	3	1	4	2	....	....	....	....
1986-87	Pembroke	OCJHL	55	20	34	54	20	....	....	....	....	....	....	....	....	....	....	....	....	....	....	....	....	....	....
1987-88	Pembroke	OCJHL	56	*90	*136	*226	32	....	....	....	....	....	....	....	....	....	....	....	....	....	....	....	....	....	....
1988-89	Michigan State	CCHA	46	20	33	53	17	....	....	....	....	....	....	....	....	....	....	....	....	....	....	....	....	....	....
1989-90	Michigan State	CCHA	45	22	40	62	6	....	....	....	....	....	....	....	....	....	....	....	....	....	....	....	....	....	....
1990-91	Michigan State	CCHA	37	7	31	38	28	....	....	....	....	....	....	....	....	....	....	....	....	....	....	....	....	....	....
1991-92	Michigan State	CCHA	41	26	49	75	32	....	....	....	....	....	....	....	....	....	....	....	....	....	....	....	....	....	....
1992-93	Cape Breton	AHL	64	12	28	40	10	....	....	....	....	....	....	....	....	....	16	3	3	6	12	....	....	....	....
1993-94	**Edmonton**	**NHL**	**26**	**3**	**5**	**8**	**2**	**0**	**0**	**0**	**17**	**17.6**	**1**	....	....	....	....	....	....	....	....	....	....	....	....
	Cape Breton	AHL	45	21	49	70	12	....	....	....	....	....	....	....	....	....	5	2	3	5	2	....	....	....	....
1994-95	Cape Breton	AHL	65	36	*69	*105	30	....	....	....	....	....	....	....	....	....	....	....	....	....	....	....	....	....	....
	Edmonton	**NHL**	**9**	**2**	**4**	**6**	**0**	**2**	**0**	**0**	**13**	**15.4**	**1**	....	....	....	....	....	....	....	....	....	....	....	....
1995-96	**Edmonton**	**NHL**	**26**	**5**	**3**	**8**	**0**	**1**	**0**	**0**	**34**	**14.7**	**–14**	....	....	....	....	....	....	....	....	....	....	....	....
	Toronto	**NHL**	**1**	**0**	**0**	**0**	**0**	**0**	**0**	**0**	**0**	**0.0**	**0**	....	....	....	....	....	....	....	....	....	....	....	....
	St. John's	AHL	17	6	7	13	6	....	....	....	....	....	....	....	....	....	....	....	....	....	....	....	....	....	....
	Atlanta Knights	IHL	36	21	20	41	4	....	....	....	....	....	....	....	....	....	3	0	3	3	2	....	....	....	....
1996-97	Philadelphia	AHL	80	*44	61	*105	28	....	....	....	....	....	....	....	....	....	10	6	8	14	6	....	....	....	....
1997-98	Philadelphia	AHL	80	27	*78	*105	28	....	....	....	....	....	....	....	....	....	20	9	9	18	6	....	....	....	....
1998-99	**Philadelphia**	**NHL**	**3**	**0**	**0**	**0**	**0**	**0**	**0**	**0**	**0**	**0.0**	**0**	**8**	**37.5**	**2:02**	....	....	....	....	....	....	....	....	....
	Philadelphia	AHL	77	31	59	90	20	....	....	....	....	....	....	....	....	....	16	4	13	17	12	....	....	....	....
99-2000	**Philadelphia**	**NHL**	**21**	**1**	**5**	**6**	**6**	**0**	**0**	**0**	**24**	**4.2**	**1**	**277**	**54.5**	**13:04**	**16**	**0**	**2**	**2**	**0**	**0**	**0**	**0**	**11:54**
	Philadelphia	AHL	62	20	41	61	38	....	....	....	....	....	....	....	....	....	....	....	....	....	....	....	....	....	....
2000-01	**Philadelphia**	**NHL**	**77**	**9**	**16**	**25**	**16**	**1**	**0**	**1**	**68**	**13.2**	**1**	**1038**	**54.3**	**12:56**	**3**	**0**	**0**	**0**	**0**	**0**	**0**	**0**	**11:47**

			Regular Season														Playoffs								
Season	Club	League	GP	G	A	Pts	PIM	PP	SH	GW	S	%	+/-	TF	F%	Min	GP	G	A	Pts	PIM	PP	SH	GW	Min
2001-02	**Chicago**	**NHL**	**48**	**3**	**3**	**6**	**10**	**1**	**0**	**1**	**21**	**14.3**	**–8**	**513**	**53.0**	**10:31**									
	Norfolk Admirals	AHL	24	4	19	23	18										4	0	1	1	0				
2002-03	**Chicago**	**NHL**	**6**	**0**	**1**	**1**	**0**	**0**	**0**	**0**	**2**	**0.0**	**0**	**58**	**39.7**	**9:01**									
	Norfolk Admirals	AHL	31	6	17	23	21																		
	Philadelphia	AHL	47	17	26	43	16										9	2	4	6	5				
	NHL Totals		**217**	**23**	**37**	**60**	**34**	**5**	**0**	**2**	**179**	**12.8**		**1894**	**53.5**	**11:50**	**19**	**0**	**2**	**2**	**0**	**0**	**0**	**0**	**11:53**

AHL Second All-Star Team (1995, 1997) • John B. Sollenberger Trophy (Top Scorer – AHL) (1995, 1997, 1998)

Traded to **Toronto** by **Edmonton** with Edmonton's 4th round choice (Jason Sessa) in 1996 Entry Draft for Kent Manderville, December 4, 1995. Signed as a free agent by **Philadelphia**, August 19, 1996. Signed as a free agent by **Chicago**, September 10, 2001. Traded to **Philadelphia** by **Chicago** for future considerations, March 11, 2003.

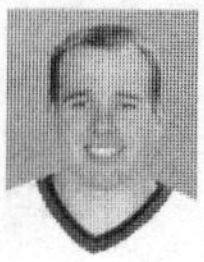

WHITE, Todd

(WHIGHT, TAWD) **OTT.**

Center. Shoots left. 5'10", 194 lbs. Born, Kanata, Ont., May 21, 1975.

Season	Club	League	GP	G	A	Pts	PIM	PP	SH	GW	S	%	+/-	TF	F%	Min	GP	G	A	Pts	PIM	PP	SH	GW	Min
1990-91	Powassan Hawks	NOJHA	38	34	38	72	118																		
1991-92	Kanata Valley	OCJHL	55	39	49	88	30																		
1992-93	Kanata Valley	OCJHL	49	51	87	138	46																		
1993-94	Clarkson Knights	ECAC	33	10	12	22	28																		
1994-95	Clarkson Knights	ECAC	34	13	16	29	44																		
1995-96	Clarkson Knights	ECAC	38	29	43	72	36																		
1996-97	Clarkson Knights	ECAC	37	*38	*36	*74	22																		
1997-98	**Chicago**	**NHL**	**7**	**1**	**0**	**1**	**2**	**0**	**0**	**0**	**3**	**33.3**	**0**												
	Indianapolis Ice	IHL	65	46	36	82	28										5	2	3	5	4				
1998-99	**Chicago**	**NHL**	**35**	**5**	**8**	**13**	**20**	**2**	**0**	**0**	**43**	**11.6**	**–1**	**452**	**46.0**	**13:39**									
	Chicago Wolves	IHL	25	11	13	24	8										10	1	4	5	8				
99-2000	**Chicago**	**NHL**	**1**	**0**	**0**	**0**	**0**	**0**	**0**	**0**	**0**	**0.0**	**0**	**9**	**55.6**	**13:02**									
	Cleveland	IHL	42	21	30	51	32																		
	Philadelphia	**NHL**	**3**	**1**	**0**	**1**	**0**	**0**	**0**	**0**	**4**	**25.0**	**–1**	**25**	**40.0**	**10:29**									
	Philadelphia	AHL	32	19	24	43	12										5	2	1	3	8				
2000-01	**Ottawa**	**NHL**	**16**	**4**	**1**	**5**	**4**	**0**	**0**	**0**	**12**	**33.3**	**5**	**133**	**57.1**	**8:33**	**2**	**0**	**0**	**0**	**0**	**0**	**0**	**0**	**7:28**
	Grand Rapids	IHL	64	22	32	54	20										10	4	4	8	10				
2001-02	**Ottawa**	**NHL**	**81**	**20**	**30**	**50**	**24**	**4**	**0**	**1**	**147**	**13.6**	**12**	**1508**	**50.5**	**18:22**	**12**	**2**	**2**	**4**	**6**	**0**	**0**	**0**	**18:57**
2002-03	**Ottawa**	**NHL**	**80**	**25**	**35**	**60**	**28**	**8**	**1**	**5**	**144**	**17.4**	**19**	**1396**	**50.5**	**17:58**	**18**	**5**	**1**	**6**	**6**	**1**	**1**	**2**	**16:59**
	NHL Totals		**223**	**56**	**74**	**130**	**78**	**14**	**1**	**6**	**353**	**15.9**		**3523**	**50.1**	**16:35**	**32**	**7**	**3**	**10**	**12**	**1**	**1**	**2**	**17:08**

ECAC Second All-Star Team (1996) • NCAA East Second All-American Team (1996) • ECAC First All-Star Team (1997) • NCAA East First All-American Team (1997) • Garry F. Longman Memorial Trophy (Top Rookie – IHL) (1998)

Signed as a free agent by **Chicago**, August 27, 1997. Traded to **Philadelphia** by **Chicago** for future considerations, January 26, 2000. Signed as a free agent by **Ottawa**, July 12, 2000.

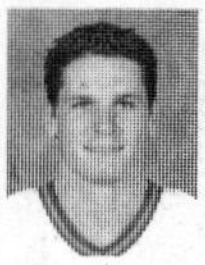

WHITFIELD, Trent

(WHIHT-feeld, TREHNT) **WSH.**

Center. Shoots left. 5'11", 204 lbs. Born, Estevan, Sask., June 17, 1977. Boston's 5th choice, 100th overall, in 1996 Entry Draft.

Season	Club	League	GP	G	A	Pts	PIM	PP	SH	GW	S	%	+/-	TF	F%	Min	GP	G	A	Pts	PIM	PP	SH	GW	Min
1993-94	Saskatoon Blazers	SMHL	36	26	22	48	42																		
	Spokane Chiefs	WHL	5	1	1	2	0																		
1994-95	Spokane Chiefs	WHL	48	8	17	25	26										11	7	6	13	5				
1995-96	Spokane Chiefs	WHL	72	33	51	84	75										18	8	10	18	10				
1996-97	Spokane Chiefs	WHL	58	34	42	76	74										9	5	7	12	10				
1997-98	Spokane Chiefs	WHL	65	38	44	82	97										18	9	10	19	15				
1998-99	Portland Pirates	AHL	50	10	8	18	20																		
	Hampton Roads	ECHL	19	13	12	25	12										4	2	0	2	14				
99-2000	Portland Pirates	AHL	79	18	35	53	52										3	1	1	2	2				
	Washington	**NHL**															**3**	**0**	**0**	**0**	**0**	**0**	**0**	**0**	**5:47**
2000-01	**Washington**	**NHL**	**61**	**2**	**4**	**6**	**35**	**0**	**0**	**0**	**47**	**4.3**	**3**	**520**	**51.9**	**9:39**	**5**	**0**	**0**	**0**	**2**	**0**	**0**	**0**	**7:07**
	Portland Pirates	AHL	19	9	11	20	27																		
2001-02	**Washington**	**NHL**	**24**	**0**	**1**	**1**	**28**	**0**	**0**	**0**	**15**	**0.0**	**–3**	**189**	**54.0**	**7:06**									
	Portland Pirates	AHL	10	4	4	8	8																		
	NY Rangers	**NHL**	**1**	**0**	**0**	**0**	**0**	**0**	**0**	**0**	**0**	**0.0**	**1**	**18**	**50.0**	**12:44**									
	Portland Pirates	AHL	24	10	16	26	16																		
2002-03	**Washington**	**NHL**	**14**	**1**	**1**	**2**	**6**	**0**	**0**	**1**	**4**	**25.0**	**1**	**124**	**57.3**	**8:30**	**6**	**0**	**0**	**0**	**10**	**0**	**0**	**0**	**11:01**
	Portland Pirates	AHL	64	27	34	61	42																		
	NHL Totals		**100**	**3**	**6**	**9**	**69**	**0**	**0**	**1**	**66**	**4.5**		**851**	**53.1**	**8:55**	**14**	**0**	**0**	**0**	**12**	**0**	**0**	**0**	**8:30**

WHL West First All-Star Team (1997) • WHL West Second All-Star Team (1998)

Signed as a free agent by **Washington**, September 1, 1998. Claimed on waivers by **NY Rangers** from **Washington**, January 16, 2002. Claimed on waivers by **Washington** from **NY Rangers**, February 1, 2002.

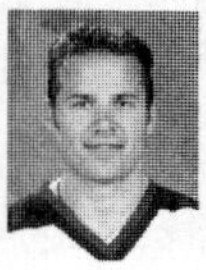

WHITNEY, Ray

(WHIHT-nee, RAY) **DET.**

Left wing. Shoots right. 5'10", 175 lbs. Born, Fort Saskatchewan, Alta., May 8, 1972. San Jose's 2nd choice, 23rd overall, in 1991 Entry Draft.

Season	Club	League	GP	G	A	Pts	PIM	PP	SH	GW	S	%	+/-	TF	F%	Min	GP	G	A	Pts	PIM	PP	SH	GW	Min
1987-88	Ft. Saskatchewan	AMHL	71	80	155	235	119																		
1988-89	Spokane Chiefs	WHL	71	17	33	50	16																		
1989-90	Spokane Chiefs	WHL	71	57	56	113	50										6	3	4	7	6				
1990-91	Spokane Chiefs	WHL	72	67	118	*185	36										15	13	18	*31	12				
1991-92	Kolner EC	Germany	10	3	6	9	4																		
	Team Canada	Nat-Tm	5	1	0	1	6																		
	San Jose	**NHL**	**2**	**0**	**3**	**3**	**0**	**0**	**0**	**0**	**4**	**0.0**	**–1**												
	San Diego Gulls	IHL	63	36	54	90	12										4	0	0	0	0				
1992-93	**San Jose**	**NHL**	**26**	**4**	**6**	**10**	**4**	**1**	**0**	**0**	**24**	**16.7**	**–14**												
	Kansas City	IHL	46	20	33	53	14										12	5	7	12	2				
1993-94	**San Jose**	**NHL**	**61**	**14**	**26**	**40**	**14**	**1**	**0**	**0**	**82**	**17.1**	**2**				**14**	**0**	**4**	**4**	**8**	**0**	**0**	**0**	
1994-95	**San Jose**	**NHL**	**39**	**13**	**12**	**25**	**14**	**4**	**0**	**1**	**67**	**19.4**	**–7**				**11**	**4**	**4**	**8**	**2**	**0**	**0**	**1**	
1995-96	**San Jose**	**NHL**	**60**	**17**	**24**	**41**	**16**	**4**	**2**	**2**	**106**	**16.0**	**–23**												
1996-97	**San Jose**	**NHL**	**12**	**0**	**2**	**2**	**4**	**0**	**0**	**0**	**24**	**0.0**	**–6**												
	Kentucky	AHL	9	1	7	8	2																		
	Utah Grizzlies	IHL	43	13	35	48	34										7	3	1	4	6				
1997-98	**Edmonton**	**NHL**	**9**	**1**	**3**	**4**	**0**	**0**	**0**	**0**	**19**	**5.3**	**–1**												
	Florida	**NHL**	**68**	**32**	**29**	**61**	**28**	**12**	**0**	**2**	**156**	**20.5**	**10**												
1998-99	**Florida**	**NHL**	**81**	**26**	**38**	**64**	**18**	**7**	**0**	**6**	**193**	**13.5**	**–3**	**144**	**43.8**	**18:20**									
99-2000	**Florida**	**NHL**	**81**	**29**	**42**	**71**	**35**	**5**	**0**	**3**	**198**	**14.6**	**16**	**198**	**49.0**	**18:41**	**4**	**1**	**0**	**1**	**4**	**0**	**0**	**0**	**18:13**
2000-01	**Florida**	**NHL**	**43**	**10**	**21**	**31**	**28**	**5**	**0**	**0**	**117**	**8.5**	**–16**	**38**	**39.5**	**17:41**									
	Columbus	**NHL**	**3**	**0**	**3**	**3**	**2**	**0**	**0**	**0**	**3**	**0.0**	**–1**	**19**	**36.8**	**20:17**									
2001-02	**Columbus**	**NHL**	**67**	**21**	**40**	**61**	**12**	**6**	**0**	**3**	**210**	**10.0**	**–22**	**21**	**47.6**	**20:13**									
2002-03	**Columbus**	**NHL**	**81**	**24**	**52**	**76**	**22**	**8**	**2**	**2**	**235**	**10.2**	**–26**	**29**	**44.8**	**21:00**									
	NHL Totals		**633**	**191**	**301**	**492**	**197**	**53**	**4**	**19**	**1438**	**13.3**		**449**	**45.7**	**19:19**	**29**	**5**	**8**	**13**	**14**	**0**	**0**	**1**	**18:13**

WHL West First All-Star Team (1991) • WHL MVP (1991) • Memorial Cup All-Star Team (1991) • George Parsons Trophy (Memorial Cup Most Sportsmanlike Player) (1991)

Played in NHL All-Star Game (2000, 2003)

Signed as a free agent by **Edmonton**, October 1, 1997. Claimed on waivers by **Florida** from **Edmonton**, November 6, 1997. Traded to **Columbus** by **Florida** with future considerations for Kevyn Adams and Coliumbus's 4th round choice (Michael Woodford) in 2001 Entry Draft, March 13, 2001. Signed as a free agent by **Detroit**, July 30, 2003.

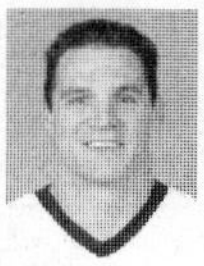

WIEMER, Jason

(WEE-muhr, JAY-suhn) **NYI**

Center. Shoots left. 6'1", 225 lbs. Born, Kimberley, B.C., April 14, 1976. Tampa Bay's 1st choice, 8th overall, in 1994 Entry Draft.

Season	Club	League	GP	G	A	Pts	PIM	PP	SH	GW	S	%	+/-	TF	F%	Min	GP	G	A	Pts	PIM	PP	SH	GW	Min
1991-92	Kimberley	RMJHL	45	33	33	66	211																		
	Portland	WHL	2	0	1	1	0																		
1992-93	Portland	WHL	68	18	34	52	159										16	7	3	10	27				
1993-94	Portland	WHL	72	45	51	96	236										10	4	4	8	32				
1994-95	Portland	WHL	16	10	14	24	63																		
	Tampa Bay	**NHL**	**36**	**1**	**4**	**5**	**44**	**0**	**0**	**0**	**10**	**10.0**	**–2**												
1995-96	**Tampa Bay**	**NHL**	**66**	**9**	**9**	**18**	**81**	**4**	**0**	**1**	**89**	**10.1**	**–9**				**6**	**1**	**0**	**1**	**28**	**1**	**0**	**0**	
1996-97	**Tampa Bay**	**NHL**	**63**	**9**	**5**	**14**	**134**	**2**	**0**	**0**	**103**	**8.7**	**–13**												
	Adirondack	AHL	4	1	0	1	7																		

			Regular Season														Playoffs								
Season	Club	League	GP	G	A	Pts	PIM	PP	SH	GW	S	%	+/-	TF	F%	Min	GP	G	A	Pts	PIM	PP	SH	GW	Min
1997-98	Tampa Bay	NHL	67	8	9	17	132	2	0	0	106	7.5	–9	....	....	....	....	....	....	....	....	....	....	....	....
	Calgary	NHL	12	4	1	5	28	1	0	2	16	25.0	–1	....	....	....	....	....	....	....	....	....	....	....	....
1998-99	Calgary	NHL	78	8	13	21	177	1	0	1	128	6.3	–12	867	40.9	13:17	....	....	....	....	....	....	....	....	....
99-2000	Calgary	NHL	64	11	11	22	120	2	0	3	104	10.6	–10	955	47.6	14:41	....	....	....	....	....	....	....	....	....
2000-01	Calgary	NHL	65	10	5	15	177	3	0	1	76	13.2	–15	599	51.1	13:56	....	....	....	....	....	....	....	....	....
2001-02	Florida	NHL	70	11	20	31	178	5	1	1	115	9.6	–4	1241	44.1	17:09	....	....	....	....	....	....	....	....	....
2002-03	NY Islanders	NHL	81	9	19	28	116	0	1	2	139	6.5	5	347	49.0	12:26	5	0	0	0	23	0	0	0	13:37
	NHL Totals		602	80	96	176	1187	20	2	11	886	9.0		4009	45.7	14:13	11	1	0	1	51	1	0	0	13:37

Traded to **Calgary** by **Tampa Bay** for Sandy McCarthy and Calgary's 3rd (Brad Richards) and 5th (Curtis Rich) round choices in 1998 Entry Draft, March 24, 1998. Traded to **Florida** by **Calgary** with Valeri Bure for Rob Neidermayer and Philadelphia's 2nd round choice (previously acquired, Calgary selected Andrei Medvedev) in 2001 Entry Draft, June 24, 2001. Traded to **NY Islanders** by **Florida** for Branislav Mezei, July 3, 2002.

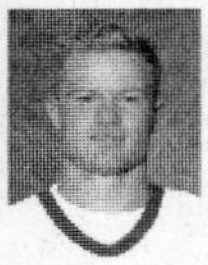

WILLIAMS, Jason
(WIHL-yuhms, JAY-suhn) **DET.**

Center. Shoots right. 5'11", 185 lbs. Born, London, Ont., August 11, 1980.

1995-96	Mount Brydges	OJHL-D	36	31	28	59	18	....	....	....	....	....	....	....	....	....	....	....	....	....	....	....	....	....	....
1996-97	Peterborough	OHL	60	4	8	12	8	....	....	....	....	....	....	....	....	....	10	1	0	1	2	....	....	....	....
1997-98	Peterborough	OHL	55	8	27	35	31	....	....	....	....	....	....	....	....	....	4	0	1	1	2	....	....	....	....
1998-99	Peterborough	OHL	68	26	48	74	42	....	....	....	....	....	....	....	....	....	5	1	2	3	2	....	....	....	....
99-2000	Peterborough	OHL	66	36	37	75	64	....	....	....	....	....	....	....	....	....	5	2	1	3	2	....	....	....	....
2000-01	Detroit	NHL	5	0	3	3	2	0	0	0	7	0.0	1	56	39.3	12:24	2	0	0	0	0	0	0	0	11:45
	Cincinnati	AHL	76	24	45	69	48	....	....	....	....	....	....	....	....	....	1	0	0	0	2	....	....	....	....
2001-02 ♦	Detroit	NHL	25	8	2	10	4	4	0	0	32	25.0	2	208	47.6	10:50	9	0	0	0	2	0	0	0	6:12
	Cincinnati	AHL	52	23	27	50	27	....	....	....	....	....	....	....	....	....	3	0	1	1	6	....	....	....	....
2002-03	Detroit	NHL	16	3	3	6	2	1	0	0	20	15.0	3	78	51.3	10:43	....	....	....	....	....	....	....	....	....
	Grand Rapids	AHL	45	23	22	45	18	....	....	....	....	....	....	....	....	....	15	1	7	8	16	....	....	....	....
	NHL Totals		46	11	8	19	8	5	0	0	59	18.6		342	47.1	10:58	11	0	0	0	2	0	0	0	7:13

OHL Third Team All-Star (2000)

Signed as a free agent by **Detroit**, September 18, 2000.

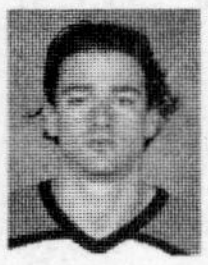

WILLIAMS, Justin
(WIHL-yuhms, JUHS-tihn) **PHI.**

Right wing. Shoots right. 6'1", 190 lbs. Born, Cobourg, Ont., October 4, 1981. Philadelphia's 1st choice, 28th overall, in 2000 Entry Draft.

1997-98	Colborne Colts	OJHL-C	36	32	35	67	26	....	....	....	....	....	....	....	....	....	....	....	....	....	....	....	....	....	....
	Cobourg Cougars	OPJHL	17	0	3	3	5	....	....	....	....	....	....	....	....	....	....	....	....	....	....	....	....	....	....
1998-99	Plymouth Whalers	OHL	47	4	8	12	28	....	....	....	....	....	....	....	....	....	7	1	2	3	0	....	....	....	....
99-2000	Plymouth Whalers	OHL	68	37	46	83	46	....	....	....	....	....	....	....	....	....	23	*14	16	*30	10	....	....	....	....
2000-01	Philadelphia	NHL	63	12	13	25	22	0	0	0	99	12.1	6	13	53.9	12:31	....	....	....	....	....	....	....	....	....
2001-02	Philadelphia	NHL	75	17	23	40	32	0	0	1	162	10.5	11	16	25.0	14:27	5	0	0	0	4	0	0	0	16:42
2002-03	Philadelphia	NHL	41	8	16	24	22	0	0	2	105	7.6	15	16	50.0	15:57	12	1	5	6	8	0	0	1	14:11
	NHL Totals		179	37	52	89	76	0	0	3	366	10.1		45	42.2	14:07	17	1	5	6	12	0	0	1	14:56

• Missed majority of 2002-03 season recovering from shoulder (November 15, 2002 vs. Carolina) and knee (January 18, 2003 vs. Tampa Bay) injuries.

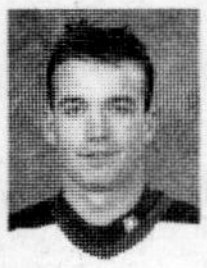

WILLIS, Shane
(WIH-lihs, SHAYN) **T.B.**

Right wing. Shoots right. 6'1", 190 lbs. Born, Edmonton, Alta., June 13, 1977. Carolina's 4th choice, 88th overall, in 1997 Entry Draft.

1992-93	Red Deer	ABHL	36	32	18	50	88	....	....	....	....	....	....	....	....	....	....	....	....	....	....	....	....	....	....
1993-94	Red Deer	AMHL	34	40	26	66	103	....	....	....	....	....	....	....	....	....	....	....	....	....	....	....	....	....	....
1994-95	Prince Albert	WHL	65	24	19	43	38	....	....	....	....	....	....	....	....	....	13	3	4	7	6	....	....	....	....
1995-96	Prince Albert	WHL	69	41	40	81	47	....	....	....	....	....	....	....	....	....	18	11	10	21	18	....	....	....	....
1996-97	Prince Albert	WHL	41	34	22	56	63	....	....	....	....	....	....	....	....	....	....	....	....	....	....	....	....	....	....
	Lethbridge	WHL	26	22	17	39	24	....	....	....	....	....	....	....	....	....	19	13	11	24	20	....	....	....	....
1997-98	Lethbridge	WHL	64	58	54	112	73	....	....	....	....	....	....	....	....	....	4	2	3	5	6	....	....	....	....
	New Haven	AHL	1	0	1	1	2	....	....	....	....	....	....	....	....	....	....	....	....	....	....	....	....	....	....
1998-99	Carolina	NHL	7	0	0	0	0	0	0	0	1	0.0	–2	0	0.0	2:14	....	....	....	....	....	....	....	....	....
	New Haven	AHL	73	31	50	81	49	....	....	....	....	....	....	....	....	....	....	....	....	....	....	....	....	....	....
99-2000	Carolina	NHL	2	0	0	0	0	0	0	0	1	0.0	–1	0	0.0	5:50	....	....	....	....	....	....	....	....	....
	Cincinnati	IHL	80	35	25	60	64	....	....	....	....	....	....	....	....	....	11	5	3	8	8	....	....	....	....
2000-01	Carolina	NHL	73	20	24	44	45	9	0	6	172	11.6	–6	10	20.0	15:58	2	0	0	0	0	0	0	0	12:56
2001-02	Carolina	NHL	59	7	10	17	24	2	0	0	126	5.6	–8	10	50.0	12:60	....	....	....	....	....	....	....	....	....
	Tampa Bay	NHL	21	4	3	7	6	0	0	0	29	13.8	0	12	8.3	11:18	....	....	....	....	....	....	....	....	....
2002-03	Springfield	AHL	56	16	16	32	26	....	....	....	....	....	....	....	....	....	6	4	2	6	4	....	....	....	....
	NHL Totals		162	31	37	68	75	11	0	6	329	9.4		32	25.0	13:34	2	0	0	0	0	0	0	0	12:56

• Re-entered NHL Entry Draft. Originally Tampa Bay's 3rd choice, 56th overall, in 1995 Entry Draft.

WHL East First All-Star Team (1997, 1998) • AHL First All-Star Team (1999) • Dudley "Red" Garrett Memorial Trophy (Top Rookie – AHL) (1999) • NHL All-Rookie Team (2001)

Traded to **Tampa Bay** by **Carolina** with Chris Dingman for Kevin Weekes, March 5, 2002.

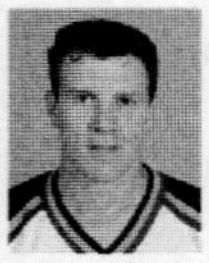

WILLSIE, Brian
(WIHL-see, BRIGH-uhn) **COL.**

Right wing. Shoots right. 6'1", 195 lbs. Born, London, Ont., March 16, 1978. Colorado's 7th choice, 146th overall, in 1996 Entry Draft.

1993-94	Belmont Bombers	OJHL-D	13	9	5	14	14	....	....	....	....	....	....	....	....	....	....	....	....	....	....	....	....	....	....
1994-95	St. Thomas Stars	OJHL-B	45	35	47	82	47	....	....	....	....	....	....	....	....	....	....	....	....	....	....	....	....	....	....
1995-96	Guelph Storm	OHL	65	13	21	34	18	....	....	....	....	....	....	....	....	....	16	4	2	6	6	....	....	....	....
1996-97	Guelph Storm	OHL	64	37	31	68	37	....	....	....	....	....	....	....	....	....	18	15	4	19	10	....	....	....	....
1997-98	Guelph Storm	OHL	57	45	31	76	41	....	....	....	....	....	....	....	....	....	12	9	5	14	18	....	....	....	....
1998-99	Hershey Bears	AHL	72	19	10	29	28	....	....	....	....	....	....	....	....	....	3	1	0	1	0	....	....	....	....
99-2000	Colorado	NHL	1	0	0	0	0	0	0	0	1	0.0	0	0	0.0	8:16	....	....	....	....	....	....	....	....	....
	Hershey Bears	AHL	78	20	39	59	44	....	....	....	....	....	....	....	....	....	12	2	6	8	8	....	....	....	....
2000-01	Hershey Bears	AHL	48	18	23	41	20	....	....	....	....	....	....	....	....	....	12	7	2	9	14	....	....	....	....
2001-02	Colorado	NHL	56	7	7	14	14	2	0	1	66	10.6	4	8	12.5	11:24	4	0	1	1	2	0	0	0	11:54
2002-03	Colorado	NHL	12	0	1	1	15	0	0	0	12	0.0	0	7	14.3	9:36	6	1	0	1	2	0	0	1	10:48
	Hershey Bears	AHL	59	29	28	57	49	....	....	....	....	....	....	....	....	....	....	....	....	....	....	....	....	....	....
	NHL Totals		69	7	8	15	29	2	0	1	79	8.9		15	13.3	11:02	10	1	1	2	4	0	0	1	11:14

OHL First All-Star Team (1998)

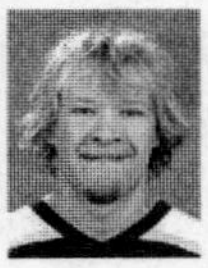

WILM, Clarke
(WIHLM, KLAHRK)

Center. Shoots left. 6', 202 lbs. Born, Central Butte, Sask., October 24, 1976. Calgary's 5th choice, 150th overall, in 1995 Entry Draft.

1991-92	Saskatoon Blazers	SMHL	36	18	28	46	16	....	....	....	....	....	....	....	....	....	....	....	....	....	....	....	....	....	....
	Saskatoon Blades	WHL	....	....	....	....	....	....	....	....	....	....	....	....	....	....	1	0	0	0	0	....	....	....	....
1992-93	Saskatoon Blades	WHL	69	14	19	33	71	....	....	....	....	....	....	....	....	....	9	4	2	6	13	....	....	....	....
1993-94	Saskatoon Blades	WHL	70	18	32	50	181	....	....	....	....	....	....	....	....	....	16	0	9	9	19	....	....	....	....
1994-95	Saskatoon Blades	WHL	71	20	39	59	179	....	....	....	....	....	....	....	....	....	10	6	1	7	21	....	....	....	....
1995-96	Saskatoon Blades	WHL	72	49	61	110	83	....	....	....	....	....	....	....	....	....	4	1	1	2	4	....	....	....	....
1996-97	Saint John Flames	AHL	62	9	19	28	107	....	....	....	....	....	....	....	....	....	5	2	0	2	15	....	....	....	....
1997-98	Saint John Flames	AHL	68	13	26	39	112	....	....	....	....	....	....	....	....	....	21	5	9	14	8	....	....	....	....
1998-99	Calgary	NHL	78	10	8	18	53	2	2	0	94	10.6	11	609	40.9	11:32	....	....	....	....	....	....	....	....	....
99-2000	Calgary	NHL	78	10	12	22	67	1	3	0	81	12.3	–6	872	44.4	12:38	....	....	....	....	....	....	....	....	....
2000-01	Calgary	NHL	81	7	8	15	69	2	0	0	85	8.2	–11	992	51.9	14:11	....	....	....	....	....	....	....	....	....
2001-02	Calgary	NHL	66	4	14	18	61	0	1	0	83	4.8	–1	995	51.1	15:00	....	....	....	....	....	....	....	....	....
2002-03	Nashville	NHL	82	5	11	16	36	0	0	0	108	4.6	–11	339	50.4	11:58	....	....	....	....	....	....	....	....	....
	NHL Totals		385	36	53	89	286	5	6	0	451	8.0		3807	48.1	12:60	....	....	....	....	....	....	....	....	....

Signed as a free agent by **Nashville**, July 11, 2002.

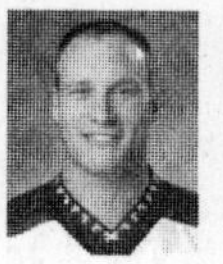

WILSON, Landon
(WIHL-sohn, LAN-duhn) **PHX.**

Right wing. Shoots right. 6'3", 226 lbs. Born, St. Louis, MO, March 13, 1975. Toronto's 2nd choice, 19th overall, in 1993 Entry Draft.

			Regular Season														Playoffs								
Season	Club	League	GP	G	A	Pts	PIM	PP	SH	GW	S	%	+/-	TF	F%	Min	GP	G	A	Pts	PIM	PP	SH	GW	Min
1991-92	California	WSJHL	38	50	42	92	135	....	....	....	....	....	....	....	....	....	....	....	....	....	....	....	....	....	....
1992-93	Dubuque	USHL	43	29	36	65	284	....	....	....	....	....	....	....	....	....	....	....	....	....	....	....	....	....	....
1993-94	North Dakota	WCHA	35	18	15	33	*147	....	....	....	....	....	....	....	....	....	....	....	....	....	....	....	....	....	....
1994-95	North Dakota	WCHA	31	7	16	23	141	....	....	....	....	....	....	....	....	....	....	....	....	....	....	....	....	....	....
	Cornwall Aces	AHL	8	4	4	8	25	....	....	....	....	....	....	....	....	....	13	3	4	7	68	....	....	....	....
1995-96	**Colorado**	**NHL**	**7**	**1**	**0**	**1**	**6**	**0**	**0**	**0**	**6**	**16.7**	**3**	....	....	....	....	....	....	....	....	....	....	....	....
	Cornwall Aces	AHL	53	21	13	34	154	....	....	....	....	....	....	....	....	....	8	1	3	4	22	....	....	....	....
1996-97	**Colorado**	**NHL**	**9**	**1**	**2**	**3**	**23**	**0**	**0**	**0**	**7**	**14.3**	**1**	....	....	....	....	....	....	....	....	....	....	....	....
	Boston	**NHL**	**40**	**7**	**10**	**17**	**49**	**0**	**0**	**0**	**76**	**9.2**	**–6**	....	....	....	....	....	....	....	....	....	....	....	....
	Providence Bruins	AHL	2	2	1	3	2	....	....	....	....	....	....	....	....	....	10	3	4	7	16	....	....	....	....
1997-98	**Boston**	**NHL**	**28**	**1**	**5**	**6**	**7**	**0**	**0**	**0**	**26**	**3.8**	**3**	....	....	....	**1**	**0**	**0**	**0**	**0**	**0**	**0**	**0**	....
	Providence Bruins	AHL	42	18	10	28	146	....	....	....	....	....	....	....	....	....	....	....	....	....	....	....	....	....	....
1998-99	**Boston**	**NHL**	**22**	**3**	**3**	**6**	**17**	**0**	**0**	**0**	**32**	**9.4**	**0**	**3**	**0.0**	**10:04**	**8**	**1**	**1**	**2**	**8**	**1**	**0**	**1**	**13:41**
	Providence Bruins	AHL	48	31	22	53	89	....	....	....	....	....	....	....	....	....	11	7	1	8	19	....	....	....	....
99-2000	**Boston**	**NHL**	**40**	**1**	**3**	**4**	**18**	**0**	**0**	**0**	**67**	**1.5**	**–6**	**14**	**42.9**	**10:09**	....	....	....	....	....	....	....	....	....
	Providence Bruins	AHL	17	5	5	10	45	....	....	....	....	....	....	....	....	....	9	2	3	5	38	....	....	....	....
2000-01	**Phoenix**	**NHL**	**70**	**18**	**13**	**31**	**92**	**2**	**0**	**3**	**123**	**14.6**	**3**	**13**	**46.2**	**11:26**	....	....	....	....	....	....	....	....	....
2001-02	Springfield	AHL	2	2	1	3	2	....	....	....	....	....	....	....	....	....	....	....	....	....	....	....	....	....	....
	Phoenix	**NHL**	**47**	**7**	**12**	**19**	**46**	**1**	**0**	**0**	**100**	**7.0**	**4**	**15**	**53.3**	**12:51**	**4**	**0**	**0**	**0**	**12**	**0**	**0**	**0**	**12:03**
2002-03	**Phoenix**	**NHL**	**31**	**6**	**8**	**14**	**26**	**0**	**0**	**3**	**92**	**6.5**	**1**	**35**	**54.3**	**12:11**	....	....	....	....	....	....	....	....	....
	NHL Totals		**294**	**45**	**56**	**101**	**284**	**3**	**0**	**6**	**529**	**8.5**		**80**	**48.8**	**11:28**	**13**	**1**	**1**	**2**	**20**	**1**	**0**	**1**	**13:08**

WCHA Rookie of the Year (1994) • AHL First All-Star Team (1999)

Traded to **Quebec** by **Toronto** with Wendel Clark, Sylvain Lefebvre and Toronto's 1st round choice (Jeffrey Kealty) in 1994 Entry Draft for Mats Sundin, Garth Butcher, Todd Warriner and Philadelphia's 1st round choice (previously acquired, later traded to Washington – Washington selected Nolan Baumgartner) in 1994 Entry Draft, June 28, 1994. Transferred to **Colorado** after **Quebec** franchise relocated, June 21, 1995. Traded to **Boston** by **Colorado** with Anders Myrvold for Boston's 1st round choice (Robyn Regehr) in 1998 Entry Draft, November 22, 1996. Signed as a free agent by **Phoenix**, July 7, 2000. • Missed majority of 2002-03 season recovering from eye injury suffered in game vs. Los Angeles, December 26, 2002.

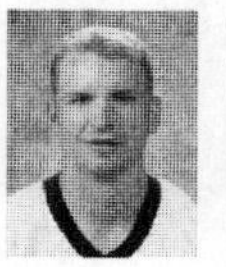

WILSON, Mike
(WIHL-sohn, MIGHK)

Defense. Shoots left. 6'6", 229 lbs. Born, Brampton, Ont., February 26, 1975. Vancouver's 1st choice, 20th overall, in 1993 Entry Draft.

Season	Club	League	GP	G	A	Pts	PIM	PP	SH	GW	S	%	+/-	TF	F%	Min	GP	G	A	Pts	PIM	PP	SH	GW	Min
1991-92	Georgetown	OJHL-B	41	9	13	22	65	....	....	....	....	....	....	....	....	....	....	....	....	....	....	....	....	....	....
1992-93	Sudbury Wolves	OHL	53	6	7	13	58	....	....	....	....	....	....	....	....	....	14	1	1	2	2	....	....	....	....
1993-94	Sudbury Wolves	OHL	60	4	22	26	62	....	....	....	....	....	....	....	....	....	9	1	3	4	8	....	....	....	....
1994-95	Sudbury Wolves	OHL	64	13	34	47	46	....	....	....	....	....	....	....	....	....	18	1	8	9	10	....	....	....	....
1995-96	**Buffalo**	**NHL**	**58**	**4**	**8**	**12**	**41**	**1**	**0**	**1**	**52**	**7.7**	**13**	....	....	....	....	....	....	....	....	....	....	....	....
	Rochester	AHL	15	0	5	5	38	....	....	....	....	....	....	....	....	....	....	....	....	....	....	....	....	....	....
1996-97	**Buffalo**	**NHL**	**77**	**2**	**9**	**11**	**51**	**0**	**0**	**1**	**57**	**3.5**	**13**	....	....	....	**10**	**0**	**1**	**1**	**2**	**0**	**0**	**0**	....
1997-98	**Buffalo**	**NHL**	**66**	**4**	**4**	**8**	**48**	**0**	**0**	**1**	**52**	**7.7**	**13**	....	....	....	**15**	**0**	**1**	**1**	**13**	**0**	**0**	**0**	....
1998-99	Las Vegas	IHL	6	3	1	4	6	....	....	....	....	....	....	....	....	....	....	....	....	....	....	....	....	....	....
	Buffalo	**NHL**	**30**	**1**	**2**	**3**	**47**	**0**	**0**	**1**	**40**	**2.5**	**10**	**0**	**0.0**	**16:40**	....	....	....	....	....	....	....	....	....
	Florida	**NHL**	**4**	**0**	**0**	**0**	**0**	**0**	**0**	**0**	**8**	**0.0**	**2**	**0**	**0.0**	**19:23**	....	....	....	....	....	....	....	....	....
99-2000	**Florida**	**NHL**	**60**	**4**	**16**	**20**	**35**	**0**	**0**	**2**	**65**	**6.2**	**10**	**0**	**0.0**	**18:07**	**4**	**0**	**0**	**0**	**0**	**0**	**0**	**0**	**18:52**
2000-01	**Florida**	**NHL**	**19**	**0**	**1**	**1**	**25**	**0**	**0**	**0**	**26**	**0.0**	**–7**	**0**	**0.0**	**13:20**	....	....	....	....	....	....	....	....	....
	Louisville Panthers	AHL	4	0	2	2	5	....	....	....	....	....	....	....	....	....	....	....	....	....	....	....	....	....	....
2001-02	Wilkes-Barre	AHL	46	3	9	12	59	....	....	....	....	....	....	....	....	....	....	....	....	....	....	....	....	....	....
	Pittsburgh	**NHL**	**21**	**1**	**1**	**2**	**17**	**0**	**0**	**0**	**14**	**7.1**	**–12**	**0**	**0.0**	**14:51**	....	....	....	....	....	....	....	....	....
2002-03	Wilkes-Barre	AHL	45	4	5	9	89	....	....	....	....	....	....	....	....	....	....	....	....	....	....	....	....	....	....
	NY Rangers	**NHL**	**1**	**0**	**0**	**0**	**0**	**0**	**0**	**0**	**0**	**0.0**	**1**	**0**	**0.0**	**12:41**	....	....	....	....	....	....	....	....	....
	Hartford	AHL	5	1	2	3	5	....	....	....	....	....	....	....	....	....	....	....	....	....	....	....	....	....	....
	NHL Totals		**336**	**16**	**41**	**57**	**264**	**1**	**0**	**6**	**314**	**5.1**		**0**	**0.0**	**16:37**	**29**	**0**	**2**	**2**	**15**	**0**	**0**	**0**	**18:52**

OHL All-Rookie Team (1993)

Traded to **Buffalo** by **Vancouver** with Michael Peca and Vancouver's 1st round choice (Jay McKee) in 1995 Entry Draft for Alexander Mogilny and Buffalo's 5th round choice (Todd Norman) in 1995 Entry Draft, July 8, 1995. Traded to **Florida** by **Buffalo** for Rhett Warrener and Florida's 5th round choice (Ryan Miller) in 1999 Entry Draft, March 23, 1999. • Missed majority of 2000-01 season recovering from shoulder injury suffered in game vs. New Jersey, October 25, 2000. Signed as a free agent by **Pittsburgh**, July 5, 2001. Traded to **NY Rangers** by **Pittsburgh** with Alex Kovalev, Janne Laukkanen and Dan LaCouture for Joel Bouchard, Richard Lintner, Rico Fata, Mikael Samuelsson and future considerations, February 10, 2003.

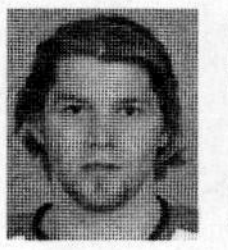

WISEMAN, Chad
(WIGHZ-man, CHAD) **NYR**

Left wing. Shoots left. 6', 190 lbs. Born, Burlington, Ont., March 25, 1981. San Jose's 8th choice, 246th overall, in 2000 Entry Draft.

Season	Club	League	GP	G	A	Pts	PIM	PP	SH	GW	S	%	+/-	TF	F%	Min	GP	G	A	Pts	PIM	PP	SH	GW	Min
1997-98	Burlington	OPJHL	50	28	36	64	31	....	....	....	....	....	....	....	....	....	....	....	....	....	....	....	....	....	....
1998-99	Mississauga	OHL	64	11	25	36	29	....	....	....	....	....	....	....	....	....	....	....	....	....	....	....	....	....	....
99-2000	Mississauga	OHL	68	23	45	68	53	....	....	....	....	....	....	....	....	....	....	....	....	....	....	....	....	....	....
2000-01	Mississauga	OHL	30	15	29	44	22	....	....	....	....	....	....	....	....	....	....	....	....	....	....	....	....	....	....
	Plymouth Whalers	OHL	32	11	16	27	12	....	....	....	....	....	....	....	....	....	19	12	8	20	22	....	....	....	....
2001-02	Cleveland Barons	AHL	76	21	29	50	61	....	....	....	....	....	....	....	....	....	....	....	....	....	....	....	....	....	....
2002-03	**San Jose**	**NHL**	**4**	**0**	**0**	**0**	**4**	**0**	**0**	**0**	**1**	**0.0**	**–2**	**0**	**0.0**	**9:19**	....	....	....	....	....	....	....	....	....
	Cleveland Barons	AHL	77	17	35	52	44	....	....	....	....	....	....	....	....	....	....	....	....	....	....	....	....	....	....
	NHL Totals		**4**	**0**	**0**	**0**	**4**	**0**	**0**	**0**	**1**	**0.0**		**0**	**0.0**	**9:19**	....	....	....	....	....	....	....	....	....

Traded to **NY Rangers** by **San Jose** for Nils Ekman, August 12, 2003.

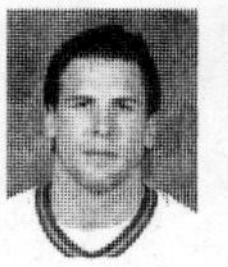

WITT, Brendan
(WIHT, BREHN-duhn) **WSH.**

Defense. Shoots left. 6'2", 229 lbs. Born, Humboldt, Sask., February 20, 1975. Washington's 1st choice, 11th overall, in 1993 Entry Draft.

Season	Club	League	GP	G	A	Pts	PIM	PP	SH	GW	S	%	+/-	TF	F%	Min	GP	G	A	Pts	PIM	PP	SH	GW	Min
1990-91	Saskatoon Blazers	SMHL	31	5	13	18	42	....	....	....	....	....	....	....	....	....	....	....	....	....	....	....	....	....	....
	Seattle	WHL	....	....	....	....	....	....	....	....	....	....	....	....	....	....	1	0	0	0	0	....	....	....	....
1991-92	Seattle	WHL	67	3	9	12	212	....	....	....	....	....	....	....	....	....	15	1	1	2	84	....	....	....	....
1992-93	Seattle	WHL	70	2	26	28	239	....	....	....	....	....	....	....	....	....	5	1	2	3	30	....	....	....	....
1993-94	Seattle	WHL	56	8	31	39	235	....	....	....	....	....	....	....	....	....	9	3	8	11	23	....	....	....	....
1994-95			DID NOT PLAY																						
1995-96	**Washington**	**NHL**	**48**	**2**	**3**	**5**	**85**	**0**	**0**	**1**	**44**	**4.5**	**–4**	....	....	....	....	....	....	....	....	....	....	....	....
1996-97	**Washington**	**NHL**	**44**	**3**	**2**	**5**	**88**	**0**	**0**	**0**	**41**	**7.3**	**–20**	....	....	....	....	....	....	....	....	....	....	....	....
	Portland Pirates	AHL	30	2	4	6	56	....	....	....	....	....	....	....	....	....	5	1	0	1	30	....	....	....	....
1997-98	**Washington**	**NHL**	**64**	**1**	**7**	**8**	**112**	**0**	**0**	**0**	**68**	**1.5**	**–11**	....	....	....	**16**	**1**	**0**	**1**	**14**	**0**	**0**	**0**	....
1998-99	**Washington**	**NHL**	**54**	**2**	**5**	**7**	**87**	**0**	**0**	**0**	**51**	**3.9**	**–6**	**0**	**0.0**	**15:50**	....	....	....	....	....	....	....	....	....
99-2000	**Washington**	**NHL**	**77**	**1**	**7**	**8**	**114**	**0**	**0**	**0**	**64**	**1.6**	**5**	**2**	**50.0**	**20:56**	**3**	**0**	**0**	**0**	**0**	**0**	**0**	**0**	**20:52**
2000-01	**Washington**	**NHL**	**72**	**3**	**3**	**6**	**101**	**0**	**0**	**0**	**87**	**3.4**	**2**	**1**	**100.0**	**20:41**	**6**	**2**	**0**	**2**	**12**	**1**	**0**	**0**	**20:49**
2001-02	**Washington**	**NHL**	**68**	**3**	**7**	**10**	**78**	**0**	**0**	**0**	**81**	**3.7**	**–1**	**1**	**100.0**	**20:03**	....	....	....	....	....	....	....	....	....
2002-03	**Washington**	**NHL**	**69**	**2**	**9**	**11**	**106**	**0**	**0**	**0**	**80**	**2.5**	**12**	**0**	**0.0**	**20:55**	**6**	**1**	**0**	**1**	**0**	**0**	**0**	**0**	**23:33**
	NHL Totals		**496**	**17**	**43**	**60**	**771**	**0**	**0**	**1**	**516**	**3.3**		**4**	**75.0**	**19:53**	**31**	**4**	**0**	**4**	**26**	**1**	**0**	**0**	**21:55**

WHL West First All-Star Team (1993, 1994) • Canadian Major Junior First All-Star Team (1994)

• Missed entire 1994-95 season after failing to come to contract terms with **Washington**.

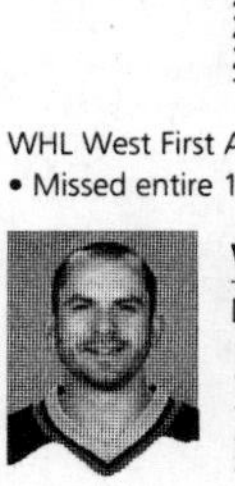

WOOLLEY, Jason
(WU-lee, JAY-suhn) **DET.**

Defense. Shoots left. 6', 203 lbs. Born, Toronto, Ont., July 27, 1969. Washington's 4th choice, 61st overall, in 1989 Entry Draft.

Season	Club	League	GP	G	A	Pts	PIM	PP	SH	GW	S	%	+/-	TF	F%	Min	GP	G	A	Pts	PIM	PP	SH	GW	Min
1986-87	St. Michael's B	OJHL-B	35	13	22	35	40	....	....	....	....	....	....	....	....	....	....	....	....	....	....	....	....	....	....
1987-88	St. Michael's B	OJHL-B	31	19	37	56	22	....	....	....	....	....	....	....	....	....	....	....	....	....	....	....	....	....	....
1988-89	Michigan State	CCHA	47	12	25	37	26	....	....	....	....	....	....	....	....	....	....	....	....	....	....	....	....	....	....
1989-90	Michigan State	CCHA	45	10	38	48	26	....	....	....	....	....	....	....	....	....	....	....	....	....	....	....	....	....	....
1990-91	Michigan State	CCHA	40	15	44	59	24	....	....	....	....	....	....	....	....	....	....	....	....	....	....	....	....	....	....
1991-92	Team Canada	Nat-Tm	60	14	30	44	36	....	....	....	....	....	....	....	....	....	....	....	....	....	....	....	....	....	....
	Canada	Olympics	8	0	5	5	4	....	....	....	....	....	....	....	....	....	....	....	....	....	....	....	....	....	....
	Washington	**NHL**	**1**	**0**	**0**	**0**	**0**	**0**	**0**	**0**	**2**	**0.0**	**1**	....	....	....	....	....	....	....	....	....	....	....	....
	Baltimore	AHL	15	1	10	11	6	....	....	....	....	....	....	....	....	....	....	....	....	....	....	....	....	....	....
1992-93	**Washington**	**NHL**	**26**	**0**	**2**	**2**	**10**	**0**	**0**	**0**	**11**	**0.0**	**3**	....	....	....	....	....	....	....	....	....	....	....	....
	Baltimore	AHL	29	14	27	41	22	....	....	....	....	....	....	....	....	....	1	0	2	2	0	....	....	....	....

			Regular Season														Playoffs								
Season	Club	League	GP	G	A	Pts	PIM	PP	SH	GW	S	%	+/-	TF	F%	Min	GP	G	A	Pts	PIM	PP	SH	GW	Min
1993-94	Washington	NHL	10	1	2	3	4	0	0	0	15	6.7	2				4	1	0	1	4	0	0	1	
	Portland Pirates	AHL	41	12	29	41	14										9	2	2	4	4				
1994-95	Detroit Vipers	IHL	48	8	28	36	38																		
	Florida	NHL	34	4	9	13	18	1	0	0	76	5.3	−1												
1995-96	Florida	NHL	52	6	28	34	32	3	0	0	98	6.1	−9				13	2	6	8	14	1	0	1	
1996-97	Florida	NHL	3	0	0	0	2	0	0	0	7	0.0	1												
	Pittsburgh	NHL	57	6	30	36	28	2	0	1	79	7.6	3				5	0	3	3	0	0	0	0	
1997-98	Buffalo	NHL	71	9	26	35	35	3	0	2	129	7.0	8				15	2	9	11	12	1	0	1	
1998-99	Buffalo	NHL	80	10	33	43	62	4	0	2	154	6.5	16	0	0.0	18:43	21	4	11	15	10	2	0	1	17:54
99-2000	Buffalo	NHL	74	8	25	33	52	2	0	2	113	7.1	14	0	0.0	17:51	5	0	2	2	2	0	0	0	18:06
2000-01	Buffalo	NHL	67	5	18	23	46	4	0	3	92	5.4	0	0	0.0	17:22	8	1	5	6	2	0	0	1	18:30
2001-02	Buffalo	NHL	59	8	20	28	34	6	0	2	90	8.9	−6	0	0.0	17:11									
2002-03	Buffalo	NHL	14	0	3	3	29	0	0	0	29	0.0	−1	0	0.0	15:59									
	Detroit	NHL	62	6	17	23	22	1	0	2	52	11.5	12	0	0.0	16:59	4	1	0	1	0	0	0	0	15:25
	NHL Totals		610	63	213	276	374	26	0	14	947	6.7		0	0.0	17:37	75	11	36	47	44	4	0	5	17:47

CCHA First All-Star Team (1991) • NCAA West First All-American Team (1991)

Signed as a free agent by **Florida**, February 15, 1995. Traded to **Pittsburgh** by **Florida** with Stu Barnes for Chris Wells, November 19, 1996. Traded to **Buffalo** by **Pittsburgh** for Buffalo's 5th round choice (Robert Scuderi) in 1998 Entry Draft, September 24, 1997. Traded to **Detroit** by **Buffalo** for future considerations, November 16, 2002.

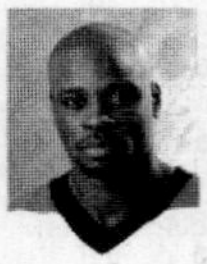

WORRELL, Peter (woh-REHL, PEE-tuhr) COL.

Left wing. Shoots left. 6'6", 235 lbs. Born, Pierrefonds, Que., August 18, 1977. Florida's 7th choice, 166th overall, in 1995 Entry Draft.

Season	Club	League	GP	G	A	Pts	PIM	PP	SH	GW	S	%	+/-	TF	F%	Min	GP	G	A	Pts	PIM	PP	SH	GW	Min
1993-94	Lac St-Louis Lions	QAAA	1	0	0	0	0										1	0	0	0	0				
1994-95	Hull Olympiques	QMJHL	56	1	8	9	243										21	0	1	1	91				
1995-96	Hull Olympiques	QMJHL	63	23	36	59	464										18	11	8	19	81				
1996-97	Hull Olympiques	QMJHL	62	17	46	63	437										14	3	13	16	83				
1997-98	Florida	NHL	19	0	0	0	153	0	0	0	15	0.0	−4												
	New Haven	AHL	50	15	12	27	309										1	0	1	1	6				
1998-99	Florida	NHL	62	4	5	9	258	0	0	2	50	8.0	0	0	0.0	6:15									
	New Haven	AHL	10	3	1	4	65																		
99-2000	Florida	NHL	48	3	6	9	169	2	0	1	45	6.7	−7	1	100.0	8:25	4	1	0	1	8	0	0	0	11:17
2000-01	Florida	NHL	71	3	7	10	248	0	0	0	86	3.5	−10	3	33.3	9:28									
2001-02	Florida	NHL	79	4	5	9	*354	0	0	1	65	6.2	−15	9	0.0	8:45									
2002-03	Florida	NHL	63	2	3	5	193	0	0	0	52	3.8	−14	13	15.4	9:16									
	NHL Totals		342	16	26	42	1375	2	0	4	313	5.1		26	15.4	8:29	4	1	0	1	8	0	0	0	11:17

Traded to **Colorado** by **Florida** with Florida's 2nd round choice in 2004 Entry Draft for Eric Messier and Vaclav Nedorost, July 19, 2003.

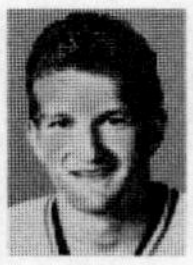

WOTTON, Mark (WAH-tuhn, MAHRK) DAL.

Defense. Shoots left. 6'1", 195 lbs. Born, Foxwarren, Man., November 16, 1973. Vancouver's 11th choice, 237th overall, in 1992 Entry Draft.

Season	Club	League	GP	G	A	Pts	PIM	PP	SH	GW	S	%	+/-	TF	F%	Min	GP	G	A	Pts	PIM	PP	SH	GW	Min
1988-89	Foxwarren Blades	MAHA	60	10	30	40	70																		
1989-90	Saskatoon Blades	WHL	51	2	3	5	31										7	1	1	2	15				
1990-91	Saskatoon Blades	WHL	45	4	11	15	37																		
1991-92	Saskatoon Blades	WHL	64	11	25	36	62										21	2	6	8	22				
1992-93	Saskatoon Blades	WHL	71	15	51	66	90										9	6	5	11	18				
1993-94	Saskatoon Blades	WHL	65	12	34	46	108										16	3	12	15	32				
1994-95	Syracuse Crunch	AHL	75	12	29	41	50																		
	Vancouver	NHL	1	0	0	0	0	0	0	0	2	0.0	1				5	0	0	0	4	0	0	0	
1995-96	Syracuse Crunch	AHL	80	10	35	45	96										15	1	12	13	20				
1996-97	Vancouver	NHL	36	3	6	9	19	0	1	0	41	7.3	8												
	Syracuse Crunch	AHL	27	2	8	10	25										2	0	0	0	4				
1997-98	Vancouver	NHL	5	0	0	0	6	0	0	0	3	0.0	−2												
	Syracuse Crunch	AHL	56	12	21	33	80										5	0	0	0	12				
1998-99	Syracuse Crunch	AHL	72	4	31	35	74																		
99-2000	Michigan	IHL	70	3	7	10	72																		
2000-01	Dallas	NHL	1	0	0	0	0	0	0	0	0	0.0	0	0	0.0	13:45									
	Utah Grizzlies	IHL	63	2	2	4	64																		
2001-02	Utah Grizzlies	AHL	57	9	18	27	68										4	0	1	1	6				
2002-03	Utah Grizzlies	AHL	69	8	26	34	68										2	0	0	0	2				
	NHL Totals		43	3	6	9	25	0	1	0	46	6.5		0	0.0	13:45	5	0	0	0	4	0	0	0	

WHL East Second All-Star Team (1994)

Signed as a free agent by **Dallas**, July 9, 1999.

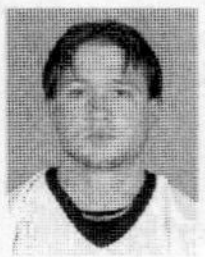

WREN, Bob (REHN, BAWB)

Center. Shoots left. 5'10", 185 lbs. Born, Preston, Ont., September 16, 1974. Los Angeles' 3rd choice, 94th overall, in 1993 Entry Draft.

Season	Club	League	GP	G	A	Pts	PIM	PP	SH	GW	S	%	+/-	TF	F%	Min	GP	G	A	Pts	PIM	PP	SH	GW	Min
1989-90	Guelph Jr. B's	OJHL-B	48	24	36	60	82																		
1990-91	Guelph Jr. B's	OJHL-B	18	17	13	30	51																		
	Kingston	OCJHL	14	10	15	25	34																		
1991-92	Detroit	OHL	62	13	36	49	58										7	3	4	7	19				
1992-93	Detroit	OHL	63	57	88	145	91										15	4	11	15	20				
1993-94	Detroit	OHL	57	45	64	109	81										17	12	18	30	20				
1994-95	Springfield	AHL	61	16	15	31	118																		
	Richmond	ECHL	2	0	1	1	0																		
1995-96	Detroit Vipers	IHL	1	0	0	0	0																		
	Knoxville	ECHL	50	21	35	56	257										8	4	11	15	32				
1996-97	Baltimore Bandits	AHL	72	23	36	59	97										3	1	1	2	0				
1997-98	Anaheim	NHL	3	0	0	0	0	0	0	0	4	0.0	0												
	Cincinnati	AHL	77	*42	58	100	151																		
1998-99	Cincinnati	AHL	73	27	43	70	102										3	1	2	3	8				
99-2000	Cincinnati	AHL	57	24	38	62	61																		
2000-01	Anaheim	NHL	1	0	0	0	0	0	0	0	0	0.0	−1	0	0.0	11:41									
	Cincinnati	AHL	70	20	47	67	103										4	4	2	6	2				
2001-02	Toronto	NHL	1	0	0	0	0	0	0	0	0	0.0	1	0	0.0	9:33	1	0	0	0	0	0	0	0	9:09
	St. John's	AHL	69	24	49	73	83										11	5	7	12	6				
2002-03	St. John's	AHL	27	8	11	19	25																		
	Milwaukee	AHL	16	1	6	7	17																		
	Binghamton	AHL	14	2	12	14	23										14	2	8	10	31				
	NHL Totals		5	0	0	0	0	0	0	0	4	0.0		0	0.0	10:37	1	0	0	0	0	0	0	0	9:09

OHL Second All-Star Team (1993, 1994)

Signed as a free agent by **Hartford**, September 6, 1994. Signed as a free agent by **Anaheim**, August 1, 1997. Signed as a free agent by **Toronto**, July 24, 2001. Traded to **Nashville** by **Toronto** for Nathan Perrott, December 31, 2002. Traded to **Ottawa** by **Nashville** for future considerations, March 10, 2003.

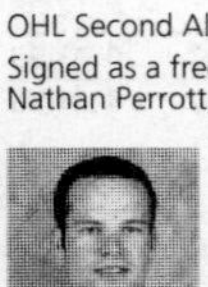

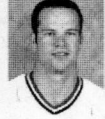

WRIGHT, Jamie (RIGHT, JAY-mee) EDM.

Left wing. Shoots left. 6', 195 lbs. Born, Kitchener, Ont., May 13, 1976. Dallas' 3rd choice, 98th overall, in 1994 Entry Draft.

Season	Club	League	GP	G	A	Pts	PIM	PP	SH	GW	S	%	+/-	TF	F%	Min	GP	G	A	Pts	PIM	PP	SH	GW	Min
1991-92	Elmira	OJHL-B	44	17	11	28	46																		
1992-93	Elmira	OJHL-B	47	22	32	54	52																		
1993-94	Guelph Storm	OHL	65	17	15	32	34										8	2	1	3	10				
1994-95	Guelph Storm	OHL	65	43	39	82	36										14	6	8	14	6				
1995-96	Guelph Storm	OHL	55	30	36	66	45										16	10	12	22	35				
1996-97	Michigan	IHL	60	6	8	14	34										1	0	0	0	0				
1997-98	Dallas	NHL	21	4	2	6	2	0	0	2	15	26.7	8				5	0	0	0	0	0	0	0	
	Michigan	IHL	53	15	11	26	31																		
1998-99	Dallas	NHL	11	0	0	0	0	0	0	0	10	0.0	−3	0	0.0	7:37									
	Michigan	IHL	64	16	15	31	92										2	0	0	0	2				
99-2000	Dallas	NHL	23	1	4	5	16	0	0	0	15	6.7	4	2	50.0	9:50									
	Michigan	IHL	49	12	4	16	64																		
2000-01	Dallas	NHL	2	1	0	1	0	0	0	0	4	25.0	−3	1	0.0	10:45									
	Utah Grizzlies	IHL	74	25	27	52	126																		

Season	Club	League	GP	G	A	Pts	PIM	PP	SH	GW	S	%	+/-	TF	F%	Min	Playoffs GP	G	A	Pts	PIM	PP	SH	GW	Min
			Regular Season														Playoffs								
2001-02	**Calgary**	**NHL**	**44**	**4**	**12**	**16**	**20**	**0**	**0**	**0**	**64**	**6.3**	**6**	**10**	**60.0**	**13:44**									
	Saint John Flames	AHL	34	11	13	24	34																		
2002-03	**Calgary**	**NHL**	**19**	**2**	**2**	**4**	**12**	**0**	**0**	**0**	**16**	**12.5**	**1**	**14**	**42.9**	**11:43**									
	Saint John Flames	AHL	3	2	1	3	0																		
	Philadelphia	**NHL**	**4**	**0**	**0**	**0**	**4**	**0**	**0**	**0**	**2**	**0.0**	**–1**	**0**	**0.0**	**9:27**									
	Philadelphia	AHL	33	10	14	24	31																		
	NHL Totals		**124**	**12**	**20**	**32**	**54**	**0**	**0**	**2**	**126**	**9.5**		**27**	**48.1**	**11:37**	**5**	**0**	**0**	**0**	**0**	**0**	**0**	**0**	....

Signed as a free agent by **Calgary**, August 2, 2001. Traded to **Philadelphia** by **Calgary** for future considerations, January 22, 2003. Signed as a free agent by **Edmonton**, August 8, 2003.

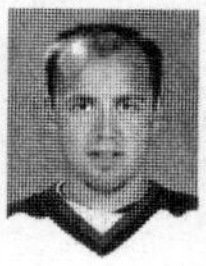

WRIGHT, Tyler

(RIGHT, TIGH-luhr) **CBJ**

Center. Shoots right. 6', 190 lbs. Born, Kamsack, Sask., April 6, 1973. Edmonton's 1st choice, 12th overall, in 1991 Entry Draft.

Season	Club	League	GP	G	A	Pts	PIM	PP	SH	GW	S	%	+/-	TF	F%	Min	Playoffs GP	G	A	Pts	PIM	PP	SH	GW	Min
1988-89	Swift Current	SMHL	36	20	13	33	102																		
1989-90	Swift Current	WHL	67	14	18	32	119										4	0	0	0	12				
1990-91	Swift Current	WHL	66	41	51	92	157										3	0	0	0	6				
1991-92	Swift Current	WHL	63	36	46	82	185										8	2	5	7	16				
1992-93	Swift Current	WHL	37	24	41	65	76										17	9	17	26	*49				
	Edmonton	**NHL**	**7**	**1**	**1**	**2**	**19**	**0**	**0**	**0**	**7**	**14.3**	**–4**												
1993-94	**Edmonton**	**NHL**	**5**	**0**	**0**	**0**	**4**	**0**	**0**	**0**	**2**	**0.0**	**–3**												
	Cape Breton	AHL	65	14	27	41	160										5	2	0	2	11				
1994-95	Cape Breton	AHL	70	16	15	31	184																		
	Edmonton	**NHL**	**6**	**1**	**0**	**1**	**14**	**0**	**0**	**0**	**6**	**16.7**	**1**												
1995-96	**Edmonton**	**NHL**	**23**	**1**	**0**	**1**	**33**	**0**	**0**	**0**	**18**	**5.6**	**–7**												
	Cape Breton	AHL	31	6	12	18	158																		
1996-97	**Pittsburgh**	**NHL**	**45**	**2**	**2**	**4**	**70**	**0**	**0**	**2**	**30**	**6.7**	**–7**												
	Cleveland	IHL	10	4	3	7	34										14	4	2	6	44				
1997-98	**Pittsburgh**	**NHL**	**82**	**3**	**4**	**7**	**112**	**1**	**0**	**0**	**46**	**6.5**	**–3**				**6**	**0**	**1**	**1**	**4**	**0**	**0**	**0**	
1998-99	**Pittsburgh**	**NHL**	**61**	**0**	**0**	**0**	**90**	**0**	**0**	**0**	**16**	**0.0**	**–2**	**122**	**46.7**	**3:46**	**13**	**0**	**0**	**0**	**19**	**0**	**0**	**0**	**3:22**
99-2000	**Pittsburgh**	**NHL**	**50**	**12**	**10**	**22**	**45**	**0**	**0**	**1**	**68**	**17.6**	**4**	**698**	**47.1**	**13:24**	**11**	**3**	**1**	**4**	**17**	**0**	**0**	**0**	**16:12**
	Wilkes-Barre	AHL	25	5	15	20	86																		
2000-01	**Columbus**	**NHL**	**76**	**16**	**16**	**32**	**140**	**4**	**1**	**2**	**141**	**11.3**	**–9**	**999**	**45.1**	**17:41**									
2001-02	**Columbus**	**NHL**	**77**	**13**	**11**	**24**	**100**	**4**	**0**	**1**	**120**	**10.8**	**–40**	**1036**	**43.9**	**17:12**									
2002-03	**Columbus**	**NHL**	**70**	**19**	**11**	**30**	**113**	**3**	**2**	**3**	**108**	**17.6**	**–25**	**760**	**41.3**	**16:07**									
	NHL Totals		**502**	**68**	**55**	**123**	**740**	**12**	**3**	**9**	**562**	**12.1**		**3615**	**44.4**	**14:04**	**30**	**3**	**2**	**5**	**40**	**0**	**0**	**0**	**9:15**

Traded to **Pittsburgh** by **Edmonton** for Pittsburgh's 7th round choice (Brandon Lafrance) in 1996 Entry Draft, June 22, 1996. Selected by **Columbus** from **Pittsburgh** in Expansion Draft, June 23, 2000.

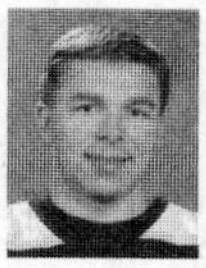

YACHMENEV, Vitali

(YATCH-muh-nehv, VIH-tal-ee)

Left wing. Shoots left. 5'11", 200 lbs. Born, Chelyabinsk, USSR, January 8, 1975. Los Angeles' 3rd choice, 59th overall, in 1994 Entry Draft.

Season	Club	League	GP	G	A	Pts	PIM	PP	SH	GW	S	%	+/-	TF	F%	Min	Playoffs GP	G	A	Pts	PIM	PP	SH	GW	Min
1990-91	Chelyabinsk Jr.	CIS-Jr.	80	88	60	148	72																		
1991-92	Chelyabinsk Jr.	CIS-Jr.	80	82	70	152	20																		
1992-93	Chelyabinsk	CIS	51	23	20	43	12																		
1993-94	North Bay	OHL	66	*61	52	113	18										18	13	19	32	12				
1994-95	North Bay	OHL	59	53	52	105	8										6	1	8	9	2				
	Phoenix	IHL															4	1	0	1	0				
1995-96	**Los Angeles**	**NHL**	**80**	**19**	**34**	**53**	**16**	**6**	**1**	**2**	**133**	**14.3**	**–3**												
1996-97	**Los Angeles**	**NHL**	**65**	**10**	**22**	**32**	**10**	**2**	**0**	**2**	**97**	**10.3**	**–9**												
1997-98	**Los Angeles**	**NHL**	**4**	**0**	**1**	**1**	**4**	**0**	**0**	**0**	**4**	**0.0**	**1**												
	Long Beach	IHL	59	23	28	51	14										17	8	9	17	4				
1998-99	**Nashville**	**NHL**	**55**	**7**	**10**	**17**	**10**	**0**	**1**	**2**	**83**	**8.4**	**–10**	**0**	**0.0**	**15:06**									
	Milwaukee	IHL	16	7	6	13	0																		
99-2000	**Nashville**	**NHL**	**68**	**16**	**16**	**32**	**12**	**1**	**1**	**3**	**120**	**13.3**	**5**	**8**	**25.0**	**15:26**									
2000-01	**Nashville**	**NHL**	**78**	**15**	**19**	**34**	**10**	**4**	**1**	**4**	**123**	**12.2**	**–5**	**29**	**37.9**	**17:52**									
2001-02	**Nashville**	**NHL**	**75**	**11**	**16**	**27**	**14**	**1**	**2**	**0**	**103**	**10.7**	**–16**	**42**	**33.3**	**17:33**									
2002-03	**Nashville**	**NHL**	**62**	**5**	**15**	**20**	**12**	**0**	**0**	**1**	**68**	**7.4**	**7**	**24**	**20.8**	**16:38**									
	NHL Totals		**487**	**83**	**133**	**216**	**88**	**14**	**6**	**14**	**731**	**11.4**		**103**	**31.1**	**16:38**									

OHL All-Rookie Team (1994) • OHL Rookie of the Year (1994) • Canadian Major Junior Rookie of the Year (1994)

Traded to **Nashville** by **Los Angeles** for future considerations, July 7, 1998.

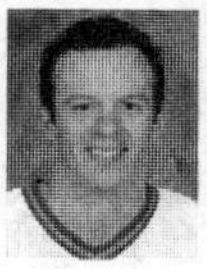

YAKE, Terry

(YAYK, TAIR-ee)

Center. Shoots right. 5'11", 190 lbs. Born, New Westminster, B.C., October 22, 1968. Hartford's 3rd choice, 81st overall, in 1987 Entry Draft.

Season	Club	League	GP	G	A	Pts	PIM	PP	SH	GW	S	%	+/-	TF	F%	Min	Playoffs GP	G	A	Pts	PIM	PP	SH	GW	Min
1984-85	Brandon	WHL	11	1	1	2	0																		
1985-86	Brandon	WHL	72	26	26	52	49																		
1986-87	Brandon	WHL	71	44	58	102	64																		
1987-88	Brandon	WHL	72	55	85	140	59										4	5	6	11	12				
1988-89	**Hartford**	**NHL**	**2**	**0**	**0**	**0**	**0**	**0**	**0**	**0**	**0**	**0.0**	**1**												
	Binghamton	AHL	75	39	56	95	57																		
1989-90	**Hartford**	**NHL**	**2**	**0**	**1**	**1**	**0**	**0**	**0**	**0**	**2**	**0.0**	**–1**												
	Binghamton	AHL	77	13	42	55	37																		
1990-91	**Hartford**	**NHL**	**19**	**1**	**4**	**5**	**10**	**0**	**0**	**1**	**19**	**5.3**	**–3**				**6**	**1**	**1**	**2**	**16**	**0**	**1**	**0**	
	Springfield	AHL	60	35	42	77	56										15	9	9	18	10				
1991-92	**Hartford**	**NHL**	**15**	**1**	**1**	**2**	**4**	**0**	**0**	**0**	**12**	**8.3**	**–2**												
	Springfield	AHL	53	21	34	55	63										8	3	4	7	2				
1992-93	**Hartford**	**NHL**	**66**	**22**	**31**	**53**	**46**	**4**	**1**	**2**	**98**	**22.4**	**3**												
	Springfield	AHL	16	8	14	22	27																		
1993-94	**Anaheim**	**NHL**	**82**	**21**	**31**	**52**	**44**	**5**	**0**	**2**	**188**	**11.2**	**2**												
1994-95	**Toronto**	**NHL**	**19**	**3**	**2**	**5**	**2**	**1**	**0**	**2**	**26**	**11.5**	**1**												
	Denver Grizzlies	IHL	2	0	3	3	2										17	4	11	15	16				
1995-96	Milwaukee	IHL	70	32	56	88	70										5	3	6	9	4				
1996-97	Rochester	AHL	78	34	*67	101	77										10	8	8	16	2				
1997-98	**St. Louis**	**NHL**	**65**	**10**	**15**	**25**	**38**	**3**	**1**	**4**	**60**	**16.7**	**1**				**10**	**2**	**1**	**3**	**6**	**2**	**0**	**1**	
1998-99	**St. Louis**	**NHL**	**60**	**9**	**18**	**27**	**34**	**3**	**0**	**4**	**59**	**15.3**	**–9**	**453**	**48.1**	**14:50**	**13**	**1**	**2**	**3**	**14**	**1**	**0**	**0**	**13:47**
	Worcester IceCats	AHL	24	8	11	19	26																		
99-2000	**St. Louis**	**NHL**	**26**	**4**	**9**	**13**	**22**	**2**	**0**	**2**	**26**	**15.4**	**2**	**129**	**55.8**	**13:51**									
	Washington	**NHL**	**35**	**6**	**5**	**11**	**12**	**1**	**0**	**1**	**29**	**20.7**	**2**	**219**	**51.1**	**12:36**	**3**	**0**	**0**	**0**	**0**	**0**	**0**	**0**	**7:55**
2000-01	**Washington**	**NHL**	**12**	**0**	**3**	**3**	**8**	**0**	**0**	**0**	**13**	**0.0**	**0**	**32**	**65.6**	**12:11**									
	Portland Pirates	AHL	55	11	38	49	47										3	0	1	1	12				
2001-02	Moskitos Essen	Germany	51	19	30	49	78																		
2002-03	Nurnberg	Germany	50	14	32	46	111										5	0	3	3	4				
	NHL Totals		**403**	**77**	**120**	**197**	**220**	**19**	**2**	**18**	**532**	**14.5**		**833**	**50.8**	**13:49**	**32**	**4**	**4**	**8**	**36**	**3**	**1**	**1**	**12:41**

Claimed by **Anaheim** from **Hartford** in Expansion Draft, June 24, 1993. Traded to **Toronto** by **Anaheim** for David Sacco, September 28, 1994. Loaned to **Denver** (IHL) by **Toronto**, April 5, 1995. Signed as a free agent by **Buffalo**, September 17, 1996. Signed as a free agent by **St. Louis**, July 24, 1997. Claimed by **Atlanta** from **St. Louis** in Expansion Draft, June 25, 1999. Claimed by **St. Louis** from **Atlanta** in Waiver Draft, September 27, 1999. Claimed on waivers by **Washington** from **St. Louis**, January 18, 2000.

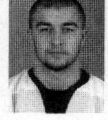

YAKUSHIN, Dmitri

(yah-KOO-shihn. DIH-mee-TREE)

Defense. Shoots left. 6', 200 lbs. Born, Kharkov, USSR, January 21, 1978. Toronto's 9th choice, 140th overall, in 1996 Entry Draft.

Season	Club	League	GP	G	A	Pts	PIM	PP	SH	GW	S	%	+/-	TF	F%	Min	Playoffs GP	G	A	Pts	PIM	PP	SH	GW	Min
1995-96	Pembroke	OCJHL	31	8	5	13	62																		
1996-97	Edmonton Ice	WHL	63	3	14	17	103																		
1997-98	Edmonton Ice	WHL	29	1	10	11	41																		
	Regina Pats	WHL	13	0	14	14	16										9	2	8	10	12				
1998-99	St. John's	AHL	71	2	6	8	65										4	0	0	0	0				
99-2000	**Toronto**	**NHL**	**2**	**0**	**0**	**0**	**2**	**0**	**0**	**0**	**1**	**0.0**	**0**	**0**	**0.0**	**10:03**									
	St. John's	AHL	64	1	13	14	106																		
2000-01	St. John's	AHL	45	2	0	2	61										1	0	0	0	0				

			Regular Season														Playoffs								
Season	Club	League	GP	G	A	Pts	PIM	PP	SH	GW	S	%	+/-	TF	F%	Min	GP	G	A	Pts	PIM	PP	SH	GW	Min
2001-02	Sokol Kiev	EEHL	14	1	3	4	54																		
	Sokol Kiev	Ukraine	3	1	0	1	4																		
	Donbass Donetsk	Ukraine	8	3	8	11	6																		
2002-03	St. John's	AHL	29	1	2	3	23																		
	NHL Totals		**2**	**0**	**0**	**0**	**2**	**0**	**0**	**0**	**1**	**0.0**		**0**	**0.0**	**10:03**									

• Spent majority of 2002-03 season with St. John's (AHL) as a healthy reserve.

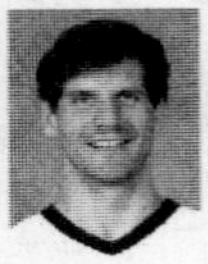

YASHIN, Alexei

(YAH-shin, al-EHX-ay) **NYI**

Center. Shoots right. 6'3", 225 lbs. Born, Sverdlovsk, USSR, November 5, 1973. Ottawa's 1st choice, 2nd overall, in 1992 Entry Draft.

1990-91	Sverdlovsk	USSR	26	2	1	3	10																		
1991-92	Dynamo Moscow	CIS	35	7	5	12	19																		
1992-93	Dynamo Moscow	CIS	27	10	12	22	18										10	7	3	10	18				
1993-94	**Ottawa**	**NHL**	**83**	**30**	**49**	**79**	**22**	**11**	**2**	**3**	**232**	**12.9**	**-49**												
1994-95	Las Vegas	IHL	24	15	20	35	32																		
	Ottawa	**NHL**	**47**	**21**	**23**	**44**	**20**	**11**	**0**	**1**	**154**	**13.6**	**-20**												
1995-96	CSKA Moscow	CIS	4	2	2	4	4																		
	Ottawa	**NHL**	**46**	**15**	**24**	**39**	**28**	**8**	**0**	**1**	**143**	**10.5**	**-15**												
1996-97	**Ottawa**	**NHL**	**82**	**35**	**40**	**75**	**44**	**10**	**0**	**5**	**291**	**12.0**	**-7**				**7**	**1**	**5**	**6**	**2**	**1**	**0**	**0**	
1997-98	**Ottawa**	**NHL**	**82**	**33**	**39**	**72**	**24**	**5**	**0**	**6**	**291**	**11.3**	**6**				**11**	**5**	**3**	**8**	**8**	**3**	**0**	**2**	
	Russia	Olympics	6	3	3	6	0																		
1998-99	**Ottawa**	**NHL**	**82**	**44**	**50**	**94**	**54**	**19**	**0**	**5**	**337**	**13.1**	**16**	**1428**	**41.9**	**22:05**	**4**	**0**	**0**	**0**	**10**	**0**	**0**	**0**	**26:06**
99-2000	**Ottawa**	**NHL**	DID NOT PLAY – SUSPENDED																						
2000-01	**Ottawa**	**NHL**	**82**	**40**	**48**	**88**	**30**	**13**	**2**	**10**	**263**	**15.2**	**10**	**1414**	**43.1**	**20:24**	**4**	**0**	**1**	**1**	**0**	**0**	**0**	**0**	**24:53**
2001-02	**NY Islanders**	**NHL**	**78**	**32**	**43**	**75**	**25**	**15**	**0**	**5**	**239**	**13.4**	**-3**	**828**	**46.7**	**20:37**	**7**	**3**	**4**	**7**	**2**	**1**	**0**	**0**	**21:54**
	Russia	Olympics	6	1	1	2	0																		
2002-03	**NY Islanders**	**NHL**	**81**	**26**	**39**	**65**	**32**	**14**	**0**	**7**	**274**	**9.5**	**-12**	**1074**	**47.2**	**18:32**	**5**	**2**	**2**	**4**	**2**	**0**	**0**	**0**	**21:06**
	NHL Totals		**663**	**276**	**355**	**631**	**279**	**106**	**4**	**43**	**2224**	**12.4**		**4744**	**44.3**	**20:25**	**38**	**11**	**15**	**26**	**24**	**5**	**0**	**2**	**23:08**

NHL Second All-Star Team (1999)

Played in NHL All-Star Game (1994, 1999, 2002)

• Suspended for entire 1999-2000 season by **Ottawa** for refusing to report to team, November 9, 1999. Traded to **NY Islanders** by **Ottawa** for Bill Muckalt, Zdeno Chara and NY Islanders' 1st round choice (Jason Spezza) in 2001 Entry Draft, June 23, 2001.

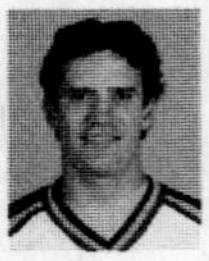

YELLE, Stephane

(YEHL, STEH-fan) **CGY.**

Center. Shoots left. 6'1", 190 lbs. Born, Ottawa, Ont., May 9, 1974. New Jersey's 9th choice, 186th overall, in 1992 Entry Draft.

1990-91	Cumberland	OJHL-B	33	20	30	50	16																		
1991-92	Oshawa Generals	OHL	55	12	14	26	20										7	2	0	2	2				
1992-93	Oshawa Generals	OHL	66	24	50	74	20										10	2	4	6	4				
1993-94	Oshawa Generals	OHL	66	35	69	104	22										5	1	7	8	2				
1994-95	Cornwall Aces	AHL	40	18	15	33	22										13	7	7	14	8				
1995-96♦	**Colorado**	**NHL**	**71**	**13**	**14**	**27**	**30**	**0**	**2**	**1**	**93**	**14.0**	**15**				**22**	**1**	**4**	**5**	**8**	**0**	**1**	**0**	
1996-97	**Colorado**	**NHL**	**79**	**9**	**17**	**26**	**38**	**0**	**1**	**1**	**89**	**10.1**	**1**				**12**	**1**	**6**	**7**	**2**	**0**	**0**	**0**	
1997-98	**Colorado**	**NHL**	**81**	**7**	**15**	**22**	**48**	**0**	**1**	**0**	**93**	**7.5**	**-10**				**7**	**1**	**0**	**1**	**12**	**0**	**0**	**0**	
1998-99	**Colorado**	**NHL**	**72**	**8**	**7**	**15**	**40**	**1**	**0**	**0**	**99**	**8.1**	**-8**	**1201**	**51.2**	**15:15**	**10**	**0**	**1**	**1**	**6**	**0**	**0**	**0**	**15:13**
99-2000	**Colorado**	**NHL**	**79**	**8**	**14**	**22**	**28**	**0**	**1**	**1**	**90**	**8.9**	**9**	**1294**	**52.2**	**15:51**	**17**	**1**	**2**	**3**	**4**	**0**	**0**	**0**	**15:38**
2000-01♦	**Colorado**	**NHL**	**50**	**4**	**10**	**14**	**20**	**0**	**1**	**0**	**54**	**7.4**	**-3**	**736**	**56.4**	**14:28**	**23**	**1**	**2**	**3**	**8**	**0**	**0**	**1**	**13:52**
2001-02	**Colorado**	**NHL**	**73**	**5**	**12**	**17**	**48**	**0**	**1**	**1**	**71**	**7.0**	**1**	**1036**	**51.8**	**14:02**	**20**	**0**	**2**	**2**	**14**	**0**	**0**	**0**	**13:26**
2002-03	**Calgary**	**NHL**	**82**	**10**	**15**	**25**	**50**	**3**	**0**	**3**	**121**	**8.3**	**-10**	**1494**	**53.4**	**18:06**									
	NHL Totals		**587**	**64**	**104**	**168**	**302**	**4**	**7**	**7**	**710**	**9.0**		**5761**	**52.8**	**15:41**	**111**	**5**	**17**	**22**	**54**	**0**	**1**	**1**	**14:22**

Traded to **Quebec** by **New Jersey** with New Jersey's 11th round choice (Steven Low) in 1994 Entry Draft for Quebec's 11th round choice (Mike Hanson) in 1994 Entry Draft, June 1, 1994. Transferred to **Colorado** after **Quebec** franchise relocated, June 21, 1995. Traded to **Calgary** by **Colorado** with Chris Drury for Derek Morris, Jeff Shantz and Dean McAmmond, October 1, 2002.

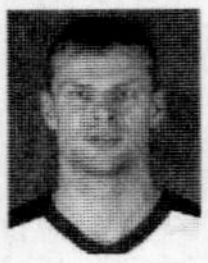

YLONEN, Juha

(YOO-lih-nehn, YOO-hah)

Center. Shoots left. 6'1", 189 lbs. Born, Helsinki, Finland, February 13, 1972. Winnipeg's 3rd choice, 91st overall, in 1991 Entry Draft.

1988-89	Kiekko Espoo Jr.	Finn-Jr.	31	9	14	23	8																		
1989-90	Kiekko Espoo Jr.	Finn-Jr.	4	1	5	6	0										5	1	5	6	0				
	Kiekko Espoo	Finland-2	38	10	17	27	12																		
1990-91	Kiekko Espoo Jr.	Finn-Jr.	5	3	1	4	2																		
	Kiekko Espoo	Finland-2	40	12	21	33	4																		
1991-92	HPK Jr.	Finn-Jr.	2	1	2	3	0																		
	HPK Hameenlinna	Finland-2	9	8	14	22	0																		
	HPK Hameenlinna	Finland	43	7	11	18	8																		
1992-93	HPK Hameenlinna	Finland	48	8	18	26	22										12	3	5	8	2				
	HPK Jr.	Finn-Jr.	2	2	1	3	0										1	0	0	0	0				
1993-94	Jokerit Helsinki	Finland	37	5	11	16	2										12	1	3	4	8				
1994-95	Jokerit Helsinki	Finland	50	13	15	28	10										11	3	2	5	0				
1995-96	Jokerit Helsinki	Finland	24	3	13	16	20										11	4	5	9	4				
1996-97	**Phoenix**	**NHL**	**2**	**0**	**0**	**0**	**0**	**0**	**0**	**0**	**2**	**0.0**	**0**												
	Springfield	AHL	70	20	41	61	6										17	5	*16	21	4				
1997-98	**Phoenix**	**NHL**	**55**	**1**	**11**	**12**	**10**	**0**	**1**	**0**	**60**	**1.7**	**-3**												
	Finland	Olympics	6	0	0	0	8																		
1998-99	**Phoenix**	**NHL**	**59**	**6**	**17**	**23**	**20**	**2**	**0**	**1**	**66**	**9.1**	**18**	**297**	**46.5**	**15:55**	**2**	**0**	**2**	**2**	**2**	**0**	**0**	**0**	**15:26**
99-2000	**Phoenix**	**NHL**	**76**	**6**	**23**	**29**	**12**	**0**	**1**	**1**	**82**	**7.3**	**-6**	**753**	**45.6**	**16:43**	**1**	**0**	**0**	**0**	**0**	**0**	**0**	**0**	**8:54**
2000-01	**Phoenix**	**NHL**	**69**	**9**	**14**	**23**	**38**	**0**	**1**	**1**	**72**	**12.5**	**10**	**163**	**41.1**	**14:18**									
2001-02	**Tampa Bay**	**NHL**	**65**	**3**	**10**	**13**	**8**	**0**	**0**	**0**	**75**	**4.0**	**-10**	**427**	**39.8**	**15:45**									
	Finland	Olympics	4	0	1	1	2																		
	Ottawa	**NHL**	**15**	**1**	**1**	**2**	**2**	**0**	**1**	**0**	**22**	**4.5**	**-1**	**221**	**49.8**	**15:17**	**12**	**0**	**5**	**5**	**2**	**0**	**0**	**0**	**12:43**
2002-03	Blues Espoo	Finland	54	4	19	23	59										4	1	1	2	27				
	NHL Totals		**341**	**26**	**76**	**102**	**90**	**2**	**4**	**3**	**379**	**6.9**		**1861**	**44.5**	**15:40**	**15**	**0**	**7**	**7**	**4**	**0**	**0**	**0**	**12:49**

Rights transferred to **Phoenix** after **Winnipeg** franchise relocated, July 1, 1996. Traded to **Tampa Bay** by **Phoenix** for Todd Warriner, June 18, 2001. Traded to **Ottawa** by **Tampa Bay** for Andre Roy and Ottawa's 6th round choice (Paul Ranger) in 2002 Entry Draft, March 15, 2002.

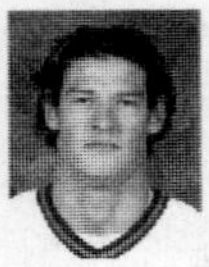

YONKMAN, Nolan

(YAWK-man, NOH-lan) **WSH.**

Defense. Shoots right. 6'6", 236 lbs. Born, Punnichy, Sask., April 1, 1981. Washington's 5th choice, 37th overall, in 1999 Entry Draft.

1996-97	Naicam Vikings	SAHA	64	15	23	38	36																		
	Kelowna Rockets	WHL	4	0	0	0	0																		
1997-98	Kelowna Rockets	WHL	65	0	2	2	36										7	0	0	0	2				
1998-99	Kelowna Rockets	WHL	61	1	6	7	129										6	0	0	0	6				
99-2000	Kelowna Rockets	WHL	71	5	7	12	153										5	0	0	0	8				
2000-01	Kelowna Rockets	WHL	7	0	1	1	19																		
	Brandon	WHL	51	6	10	16	94										6	0	1	1	12				
2001-02	**Washington**	**NHL**	**11**	**1**	**0**	**1**	**4**	**0**	**0**	**0**	**7**	**14.3**	**3**	**0**	**0.0**	**12:44**									
	Portland Pirates	AHL	59	4	3	7	116																		
2002-03	Portland Pirates	AHL	24	1	4	5	40										3	0	1	1	2				
	NHL Totals		**11**	**1**	**0**	**1**	**4**	**0**	**0**	**0**	**7**	**14.3**		**0**	**0.0**	**12:44**									

• Missed majority of 2002-03 season recovering from abdominal injury suffered in training camp, September 25, 2002.

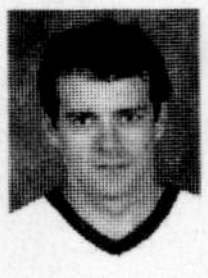

YORK, Jason

(YOHRK, JAY-suhn) **NSH.**

Defense. Shoots right. 6'1", 208 lbs. Born, Nepean, Ont., May 20, 1970. Detroit's 6th choice, 129th overall, in 1990 Entry Draft.

1986-87	Smiths Falls Bears	OCJHL	46	6	13	19	86																		
1987-88	Hamilton	OHL	58	4	9	13	110																		
1988-89	Windsor Spitfires	OHL	65	19	44	63	105																		
1989-90	Windsor Spitfires	OHL	39	9	30	39	38																		
	Kitchener Rangers	OHL	25	11	25	36	17										17	3	19	22	10				
1990-91	Windsor Spitfires	OHL	66	13	80	93	40										11	3	10	13	12				

Season	Club	League	Regular Season														Playoffs								
			GP	G	A	Pts	PIM	PP	SH	GW	S	%	+/-	TF	F%	Min	GP	G	A	Pts	PIM	PP	SH	GW	Min
1991-92	Adirondack	AHL	49	4	20	24	32	....	....	....	....	....	....	....	....	....	5	0	1	1	0	....	....	....	....
1992-93	**Detroit**	**NHL**	**2**	**0**	**0**	**0**	**0**	**0**	**0**	**0**	**1**	**0.0**	**0**	....	....	....	....	....	....	....	....	....	....	....	....
	Adirondack	AHL	77	15	40	55	86	....	....	....	....	....	....	....	....	....	11	0	3	3	18	....	....	....	....
1993-94	**Detroit**	**NHL**	**7**	**1**	**2**	**3**	**2**	**0**	**0**	**0**	**9**	**11.1**	**0**	....	....	....	....	....	....	....	....	....	....	....	....
	Adirondack	AHL	74	10	56	66	98	....	....	....	....	....	....	....	....	....	12	3	11	14	22	....	....	....	....
1994-95	**Detroit**	**NHL**	**10**	**1**	**2**	**3**	**2**	**0**	**0**	**0**	**6**	**16.7**	**0**	....	....	....	....	....	....	....	....	....	....	....	....
	Adirondack	AHL	5	1	3	4	4	....	....	....	....	....	....	....	....	....	....	....	....	....	....	....	....	....	....
	Anaheim	**NHL**	**15**	**0**	**8**	**8**	**12**	**0**	**0**	**0**	**22**	**0.0**	**4**	....	....	....	....	....	....	....	....	....	....	....	....
1995-96	**Anaheim**	**NHL**	**79**	**3**	**21**	**24**	**88**	**0**	**0**	**0**	**106**	**2.8**	**–7**	....	....	....	....	....	....	....	....	....	....	....	....
1996-97	**Ottawa**	**NHL**	**75**	**4**	**17**	**21**	**67**	**1**	**0**	**0**	**121**	**3.3**	**–8**	....	....	....	**7**	**0**	**0**	**0**	**4**	**0**	**0**	**0**	....
1997-98	**Ottawa**	**NHL**	**73**	**3**	**13**	**16**	**62**	**0**	**0**	**0**	**109**	**2.8**	**8**	....	....	....	**7**	**1**	**1**	**2**	**7**	**1**	**0**	**0**	....
1998-99	**Ottawa**	**NHL**	**79**	**4**	**31**	**35**	**48**	**2**	**0**	**0**	**177**	**2.3**	**17**	**2**	**0.0**	**23:49**	**4**	**1**	**1**	**2**	**4**	**0**	**0**	**0**	**24:59**
99-2000	**Ottawa**	**NHL**	**79**	**8**	**22**	**30**	**60**	**1**	**0**	**1**	**159**	**5.0**	**–3**	**0**	**0.0**	**23:20**	**6**	**0**	**2**	**2**	**2**	**0**	**0**	**0**	**25:30**
2000-01	**Ottawa**	**NHL**	**74**	**6**	**16**	**22**	**72**	**3**	**0**	**2**	**133**	**4.5**	**7**	**0**	**0.0**	**23:49**	**4**	**0**	**0**	**0**	**4**	**0**	**0**	**0**	**20:58**
2001-02	**Anaheim**	**NHL**	**74**	**5**	**20**	**25**	**60**	**3**	**0**	**2**	**104**	**4.8**	**–11**	**0**	**0.0**	**19:19**	....	....	....	....	....	....	....	....	....
2002-03	**Nashville**	**NHL**	**74**	**4**	**15**	**19**	**52**	**2**	**0**	**0**	**107**	**3.7**	**13**	**0**	**0.0**	**19:57**	....	....	....	....	....	....	....	....	....
	Cincinnati	AHL	4	3	2	5	8	....	....	....	....	....	....	....	....	....	....	....	....	....	....	....	....	....	....
	NHL Totals		**641**	**39**	**167**	**206**	**525**	**12**	**0**	**5**	**1054**	**3.7**		**2**	**0.0**	**22:05**	**28**	**2**	**4**	**6**	**21**	**1**	**0**	**0**	**24:03**

AHL First All-Star Team (1994)

Traded to **Anaheim** by **Detroit** with Mike Sillinger for Stu Grimson, Mark Ferner and Anaheim's 6th round choice (Magnus Nilsson) in 1996 Entry Draft, April 4, 1995. Traded to **Ottawa** by **Anaheim** with Shaun Van Allen for Ted Drury and the rights to Marc Moro, October 1, 1996. Signed as a free agent by **Anaheim**, July 3, 2001. Traded to **Nashville** by **Anaheim** for future considerations, October 23, 2002.

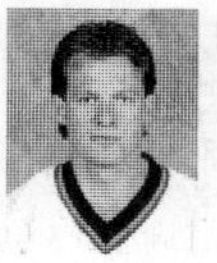

YORK, Mike

(YOHRK, MIGHK) **EDM.**

Left wing. Shoots right. 5'10", 185 lbs. Born, Waterford, MI, January 3, 1978. NY Rangers' 7th choice, 136th overall, in 1997 Entry Draft.

Season	Club	League	GP	G	A	Pts	PIM	PP	SH	GW	S	%	+/-	TF	F%	Min	GP	G	A	Pts	PIM	PP	SH	GW	Min
1992-93	Michigan	MNHL	50	45	50	95	....	....	....	....	....	....	....	....	....	....	....	....	....	....	....	....	....	....	....
1993-94	Det. Compuware	MNHL	85	136	140	276	....	....	....	....	....	....	....	....	....	....	....	....	....	....	....	....	....	....	....
1994-95	Thornhill Islanders	MTJHL	49	39	54	*93	44	....	....	....	....	....	....	....	....	....	11	7	6	13	0	....	....	....	....
1995-96	Michigan State	CCHA	39	12	27	39	20	....	....	....	....	....	....	....	....	....	....	....	....	....	....	....	....	....	....
1996-97	Michigan State	CCHA	37	18	29	47	42	....	....	....	....	....	....	....	....	....	....	....	....	....	....	....	....	....	....
1997-98	Michigan State	CCHA	40	27	34	61	38	....	....	....	....	....	....	....	....	....	....	....	....	....	....	....	....	....	....
1998-99	Michigan State	CCHA	42	22	32	*54	41	....	....	....	....	....	....	....	....	....	....	....	....	....	....	....	....	....	....
	Hartford	AHL	3	2	2	4	0	....	....	....	....	....	....	....	....	....	6	3	1	4	0	....	....	....	....
99-2000	**NY Rangers**	**NHL**	**82**	**26**	**24**	**50**	**18**	**8**	**0**	**4**	**177**	**14.7**	**–17**	**1131**	**48.1**	**1:35**	....	....	....	....	....	....	....	....	....
2000-01	**NY Rangers**	**NHL**	**79**	**14**	**17**	**31**	**20**	**3**	**2**	**4**	**171**	**8.2**	**1**	**1098**	**46.9**	**17:45**	....	....	....	....	....	....	....	....	....
2001-02	**NY Rangers**	**NHL**	**69**	**18**	**39**	**57**	**16**	**2**	**0**	**5**	**188**	**9.6**	**8**	**267**	**43.1**	**20:24**	....	....	....	....	....	....	....	....	....
	United States	Olympics	6	0	1	1	0	....	....	....	....	....	....	....	....	....	....	....	....	....	....	....	....	....	....
	Edmonton	**NHL**	**12**	**2**	**2**	**4**	**0**	**1**	**0**	**1**	**30**	**6.7**	**–1**	**100**	**56.0**	**16:35**	....	....	....	....	....	....	....	....	....
2002-03	**Edmonton**	**NHL**	**71**	**22**	**29**	**51**	**10**	**7**	**2**	**4**	**177**	**12.4**	**–8**	**390**	**43.9**	**19:04**	**6**	**0**	**2**	**2**	**2**	**0**	**0**	**0**	**14:20**
	NHL Totals		**313**	**82**	**111**	**193**	**64**	**21**	**4**	**18**	**743**	**11.0**		**2986**	**46.9**	**14:21**	**6**	**0**	**2**	**2**	**2**	**0**	**0**	**0**	**14:20**

MTJHL Bauer Divison All-Star Team (1995) • MTJHL Bauer Divison Rookie of the Year (1995) • CCHA Second All-Star Team (1998) • NCAA West First All-American Team (1998, 1999) • CCHA First All-Star Team (1999) • CCHA Player of the Year (1999) • NHL All-Rookie Team (2000)

Played in NHL All-Star Game (2002)

Traded to **Edmonton** by **NY Rangers** with NY Rangers' 4th round choice (Ivan Koltsov) in 2002 Entry Draft for Tom Poti and Rem Murray, March 19, 2002.

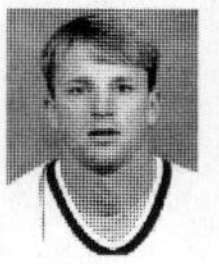

YOUNG, Scott

(YUHNG, SKAWT) **DAL.**

Right wing. Shoots right. 6'1", 200 lbs. Born, Clinton, MA, October 1, 1967. Hartford's 1st choice, 11th overall, in 1986 Entry Draft.

Season	Club	League	GP	G	A	Pts	PIM	PP	SH	GW	S	%	+/-	TF	F%	Min	GP	G	A	Pts	PIM	PP	SH	GW	Min
1984-85	St. Mark's	Hi-School	23	28	41	69	....	....	....	....	....	....	....	....	....	....	....	....	....	....	....	....	....	....	....
1985-86	Boston University	H-East	38	16	13	29	31	....	....	....	....	....	....	....	....	....	....	....	....	....	....	....	....	....	....
1986-87	Boston University	H-East	33	15	21	36	24	....	....	....	....	....	....	....	....	....	....	....	....	....	....	....	....	....	....
1987-88	Team USA	Nat-Tm	56	11	47	58	31	....	....	....	....	....	....	....	....	....	....	....	....	....	....	....	....	....	....
	United States	Olympics	6	2	6	8	4	....	....	....	....	....	....	....	....	....	....	....	....	....	....	....	....	....	....
	Hartford	**NHL**	**7**	**0**	**0**	**0**	**2**	**0**	**0**	**0**	**6**	**0.0**	**–6**	....	....	....	**4**	**1**	**0**	**1**	**0**	**0**	**0**	**0**	....
1988-89	**Hartford**	**NHL**	**76**	**19**	**40**	**59**	**27**	**6**	**0**	**2**	**203**	**9.4**	**–21**	....	....	....	**4**	**2**	**0**	**2**	**4**	**0**	**0**	**0**	....
1989-90	**Hartford**	**NHL**	**80**	**24**	**40**	**64**	**47**	**10**	**2**	**5**	**239**	**10.0**	**–24**	....	....	....	**7**	**2**	**0**	**2**	**2**	**0**	**0**	**0**	....
1990-91	**Hartford**	**NHL**	**34**	**6**	**9**	**15**	**8**	**3**	**1**	**2**	**94**	**6.4**	**–9**	....	....	....	....	....	....	....	....	....	....	....	....
	♦ **Pittsburgh**	**NHL**	**43**	**11**	**16**	**27**	**33**	**3**	**1**	**3**	**116**	**9.5**	**3**	....	....	....	**17**	**1**	**6**	**7**	**2**	**1**	**0**	**0**	....
1991-92	HC Bolzano	Alpenliga	15	19	11	30	14	....	....	....	....	....	....	....	....	....	....	....	....	....	....	....	....	....	....
	HC Bolzano	Italy	18	22	17	39	6	....	....	....	....	....	....	....	....	....	5	4	3	7	7	....	....	....	....
	Team USA	Nat-Tm	10	2	4	6	21	....	....	....	....	....	....	....	....	....	....	....	....	....	....	....	....	....	....
	United States	Olympics	8	2	1	3	2	....	....	....	....	....	....	....	....	....	....	....	....	....	....	....	....	....	....
1992-93	**Quebec**	**NHL**	**82**	**30**	**30**	**60**	**20**	**9**	**6**	**5**	**225**	**13.3**	**5**	....	....	....	**6**	**4**	**1**	**5**	**0**	**0**	**0**	**2**	....
1993-94	**Quebec**	**NHL**	**76**	**26**	**25**	**51**	**14**	**6**	**1**	**1**	**236**	**11.0**	**–4**	....	....	....	....	....	....	....	....	....	....	....	....
1994-95	EV Landshut	Germany	4	6	1	7	6	....	....	....	....	....	....	....	....	....	....	....	....	....	....	....	....	....	....
	Frankfurt Lions	Germany	1	1	0	1	0	....	....	....	....	....	....	....	....	....	....	....	....	....	....	....	....	....	....
	Quebec	**NHL**	**48**	**18**	**21**	**39**	**14**	**3**	**3**	**0**	**167**	**10.8**	**9**	....	....	....	**6**	**3**	**3**	**6**	**2**	**0**	**1**	**0**	....
1995-96 ♦	**Colorado**	**NHL**	**81**	**21**	**39**	**60**	**50**	**7**	**0**	**5**	**229**	**9.2**	**2**	....	....	....	**22**	**3**	**12**	**15**	**10**	**0**	**0**	**0**	....
1996-97	**Colorado**	**NHL**	**72**	**18**	**19**	**37**	**14**	**7**	**0**	**0**	**164**	**11.0**	**–5**	....	....	....	**17**	**4**	**2**	**6**	**14**	**2**	**0**	**0**	....
1997-98	**Anaheim**	**NHL**	**73**	**13**	**20**	**33**	**22**	**4**	**2**	**1**	**187**	**7.0**	**–13**	....	....	....	....	....	....	....	....	....	....	....	....
1998-99	**St. Louis**	**NHL**	**75**	**24**	**28**	**52**	**27**	**8**	**0**	**4**	**205**	**11.7**	**8**	**4**	**25.0**	**15:14**	**13**	**4**	**7**	**11**	**10**	**1**	**0**	**1**	**17:56**
99-2000	**St. Louis**	**NHL**	**75**	**24**	**15**	**39**	**18**	**6**	**1**	**7**	**244**	**9.8**	**12**	**2**	**50.0**	**16:06**	**6**	**6**	**2**	**8**	**8**	**3**	**0**	**0**	**17:18**
2000-01	**St. Louis**	**NHL**	**81**	**40**	**33**	**73**	**30**	**14**	**3**	**7**	**321**	**12.5**	**15**	**4**	**25.0**	**19:18**	**15**	**6**	**7**	**13**	**2**	**0**	**2**	**3**	**20:34**
2001-02	**St. Louis**	**NHL**	**67**	**19**	**22**	**41**	**26**	**5**	**0**	**1**	**210**	**9.0**	**11**	**4**	**0.0**	**18:31**	**10**	**3**	**0**	**3**	**2**	**1**	**1**	**0**	**17:40**
	United States	Olympics	6	4	0	4	2	....	....	....	....	....	....	....	....	....	....	....	....	....	....	....	....	....	....
2002-03	**Dallas**	**NHL**	**79**	**23**	**19**	**42**	**30**	**5**	**1**	**4**	**237**	**9.7**	**24**	**8**	**37.5**	**16:08**	**10**	**4**	**3**	**7**	**6**	**2**	**0**	**1**	**19:12**
	NHL Totals		**1049**	**316**	**376**	**692**	**382**	**96**	**21**	**47**	**3083**	**10.2**		**22**	**27.3**	**17:03**	**137**	**43**	**43**	**86**	**62**	**10**	**4**	**7**	**18:47**

Hockey East Rookie of the Year (1986) (co-winner - Al Loring)

Traded to **Pittsburgh** by **Hartford** for Rob Brown, December 21, 1990. Traded to **Quebec** by **Pittsburgh** for Bryan Fogarty, March 10, 1992. Transferred to **Colorado** after **Quebec** franchise relocated, June 21, 1995. Traded to **Anaheim** by **Colorado** for Anaheim's 3rd round choice (later traded to Florida – Florida selected Lance Ward) in 1998 Entry Draft, September 17, 1997. Signed as a free agent by **St. Louis**, July 28, 1998. Signed as a free agent by **Dallas**, July 5, 2002.

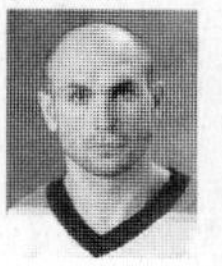

YUSHKEVICH, Dmitry

(yoosh-KAY-vihch, dih-MEE-tree)

Defense. Shoots right. 5'11", 208 lbs. Born, Cherepovets, USSR, November 19, 1971. Philadelphia's 6th choice, 122nd overall, in 1991 Entry Draft.

Season	Club	League	GP	G	A	Pts	PIM	PP	SH	GW	S	%	+/-	TF	F%	Min	GP	G	A	Pts	PIM	PP	SH	GW	Min
1988-89	Yaroslavl	USSR	23	2	1	3	8	....	....	....	....	....	....	....	....	....	....	....	....	....	....	....	....	....	....
1989-90	Yaroslavl	USSR	41	2	3	5	39	....	....	....	....	....	....	....	....	....	....	....	....	....	....	....	....	....	....
1990-91	Yaroslavl	USSR	41	10	4	14	22	....	....	....	....	....	....	....	....	....	....	....	....	....	....	....	....	....	....
1991-92	Dynamo Moscow	CIS	35	5	7	12	14	....	....	....	....	....	....	....	....	....	....	....	....	....	....	....	....	....	....
	Russia	Olympics	8	1	2	3	4	....	....	....	....	....	....	....	....	....	....	....	....	....	....	....	....	....	....
1992-93	**Philadelphia**	**NHL**	**82**	**5**	**27**	**32**	**71**	**1**	**0**	**1**	**155**	**3.2**	**12**	....	....	....	....	....	....	....	....	....	....	....	....
1993-94	**Philadelphia**	**NHL**	**75**	**5**	**25**	**30**	**86**	**1**	**0**	**2**	**136**	**3.7**	**–8**	....	....	....	....	....	....	....	....	....	....	....	....
1994-95	Yaroslavl	CIS	10	3	4	7	8	....	....	....	....	....	....	....	....	....	....	....	....	....	....	....	....	....	....
	Philadelphia	**NHL**	**40**	**5**	**9**	**14**	**47**	**3**	**1**	**1**	**80**	**6.3**	**–4**	....	....	....	**15**	**1**	**5**	**6**	**12**	**0**	**0**	**0**	....
1995-96	**Toronto**	**NHL**	**69**	**1**	**10**	**11**	**54**	**1**	**0**	**0**	**96**	**1.0**	**–14**	....	....	....	**4**	**0**	**0**	**0**	**0**	**0**	**0**	**0**	....
1996-97	**Toronto**	**NHL**	**74**	**4**	**10**	**14**	**56**	**1**	**1**	**1**	**99**	**4.0**	**–24**	....	....	....	....	....	....	....	....	....	....	....	....
1997-98	**Toronto**	**NHL**	**72**	**0**	**12**	**12**	**78**	**0**	**0**	**0**	**92**	**0.0**	**–13**	....	....	....	....	....	....	....	....	....	....	....	....
	Russia	Olympics	6	0	0	0	2	....	....	....	....	....	....	....	....	....	....	....	....	....	....	....	....	....	....
1998-99	**Toronto**	**NHL**	**78**	**6**	**22**	**28**	**88**	**2**	**1**	**0**	**95**	**6.3**	**25**	**0**	**0.0**	**22:20**	**17**	**1**	**5**	**6**	**22**	**1**	**0**	**0**	**23:13**
99-2000	Yaroslavl	Russia	7	2	3	5	2	....	....	....	....	....	....	....	....	....	....	....	....	....	....	....	....	....	....
	Toronto	**NHL**	**77**	**3**	**24**	**27**	**55**	**2**	**1**	**1**	**103**	**2.9**	**2**	**0**	**0.0**	**23:18**	**12**	**1**	**1**	**2**	**4**	**0**	**0**	**0**	**24:45**
2000-01	**Toronto**	**NHL**	**81**	**5**	**19**	**24**	**52**	**1**	**0**	**0**	**110**	**4.5**	**–2**	**0**	**0.0**	**24:14**	**11**	**0**	**4**	**4**	**12**	**0**	**0**	**0**	**25:18**
2001-02	**Toronto**	**NHL**	**55**	**6**	**13**	**19**	**26**	**3**	**0**	**0**	**79**	**7.6**	**14**	**1**	**100.0**	**23:25**	....	....	....	....	....	....	....	....	....

			Regular Season														Playoffs								
Season	Club	League	GP	G	A	Pts	PIM	PP	SH	GW	S	%	+/-	TF	F%	Min	GP	G	A	Pts	PIM	PP	SH	GW	Min
2002-03	Florida	NHL	23	1	6	7	14	0	0	0	23	4.3	-12	3	33.3	23:40									
	Los Angeles	NHL	42	0	3	3	24	0	0	0	36	0.0	-4	2	0.0	19:57									
	Philadelphia	NHL	18	2	2	4	8	0	0	0	16	12.5	7	0	0.0	18:05	13	1	4	5	2	0	0	1	24:20
	NHL Totals		786	43	182	225	659	15	4	6	1120	3.8		6	33.3	22:43	72	4	19	23	52	1	0	1	24:16

Played in NHL All-Star Game (2000)

Traded to **Toronto** by **Philadelphia** with Philadelphia's 2nd round choice (Francis Larivee) in 1996 Entry Draft for Toronto's 1st round choice (Dainius Zubrus) in 1996 Entry Draft, 2nd round choice (Jean-Marc Pelletier) in 1997 Entry Draft and Los Angeles' 4th round choice (previously acquired, later traded to Los Angeles – Los Angeles selected Mikael Simons) in 1996 Entry Draft, August 30, 1995. Traded to **Florida** by **Toronto** for Robert Svehla, July 18, 2002. Traded to **Los Angeles** by **Florida** with NY Islanders' 5th round choice (previously acquired, Los Angeles selected Brady Murray) in 2003 Entry Draft for Jaroslav Bednar and Andreas Lilja, November 26, 2002. Traded to **Philadelphia** by **Los Angeles** for Philadelphia's 4th round choice (later traded to Boston – Boston selected Patrick Valcak) in 2003 Entry Draft and Philadelphia's 7th round choice in 2004 Entry Draft, March 1, 2003.

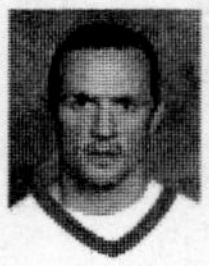

YZERMAN, Steve

(IGH-zuhr-muhn, STEEV) **DET.**

Center. Shoots right. 5'11", 185 lbs. Born, Cranbrook, B.C., May 9, 1965. Detroit's 1st choice, 4th overall, in 1983 Entry Draft.

Season	Club	League	GP	G	A	Pts	PIM	PP	SH	GW	S	%	+/-	TF	F%	Min	GP	G	A	Pts	PIM	PP	SH	GW	Min
1980-81	Nepean Raiders	OCJHL	50	38	*54	92	44																		
1981-82	Peterborough	OHL	58	21	43	64	65										6	0	1	1	16				
1982-83	Peterborough	OHL	56	42	49	91	33										4	1	4	5	0				
1983-84	Detroit	NHL	80	39	48	87	33	13	0	2	177	22.0	-17				4	3	3	6	0	1	0	1	
1984-85	Detroit	NHL	80	30	59	89	58	9	0	3	231	13.0	-17				3	2	1	3	2	0	0	0	
1985-86	Detroit	NHL	51	14	28	42	16	3	0	3	132	10.6	-24												
1986-87	Detroit	NHL	80	31	59	90	43	9	1	2	217	14.3	-1				16	5	13	18	8	1	0	0	
1987-88	Detroit	NHL	64	50	52	102	44	10	6	6	242	20.7	30				3	1	3	4	6	0	0	0	
1988-89	Detroit	NHL	80	65	90	155	61	17	3	7	388	16.8	17				6	5	5	10	2	2	0	0	
1989-90	Detroit	NHL	79	62	65	127	79	16	7	8	332	18.7	-6												
1990-91	Detroit	NHL	80	51	57	108	34	12	6	4	326	15.6	-2				7	3	3	6	4	1	0	0	
1991-92	Detroit	NHL	79	45	58	103	64	9	8	9	295	15.3	26				11	3	5	8	12	0	1	1	
1992-93	Detroit	NHL	84	58	79	137	44	13	7	6	307	18.9	33				7	4	3	7	4	1	1	1	
1993-94	Detroit	NHL	58	24	58	82	36	7	3	3	217	11.1	11				3	1	3	4	0	0	0	0	
1994-95	Detroit	NHL	47	12	26	38	40	4	0	1	134	9.0	6				15	4	8	12	0	2	0	1	
1995-96	Detroit	NHL	80	36	59	95	64	16	2	8	220	16.4	29				18	8	12	20	4	4	0	1	
1996-97♦	Detroit	NHL	81	22	63	85	78	8	0	3	232	9.5	22				20	7	6	13	4	3	0	2	
1997-98♦	Detroit	NHL	75	24	45	69	46	6	2	0	188	12.8	3				22	6	*18	*24	22	3	1	0	
	Canada	Olympics	6	1	1	2	10																		
1998-99	Detroit	NHL	80	29	45	74	42	13	2	4	231	12.6	8	1600	56.9	21:35	10	9	4	13	0	4	0	2	21:49
99-2000	Detroit	NHL	78	35	44	79	34	15	2	6	234	15.0	28	1868	56.8	21:07	8	0	4	4	0	0	0	0	22:39
2000-01	Detroit	NHL	54	18	34	52	18	5	0	7	155	11.6	4	1197	59.6	22:14	1	0	0	0	0	0	0	0	5:58
2001-02♦	Detroit	NHL	52	13	35	48	18	5	1	5	104	12.5	11	1182	58.4	20:35	23	6	17	23	10	4	0	2	21:22
	Canada	Olympics	6	2	4	6	2																		
2002-03	Detroit	NHL	16	2	6	8	8	1	0	1	13	15.4	6	134	56.0	15:35	4	0	1	1	2	0	0	0	20:33
	NHL Totals		1378	660	1010	1670	860	191	50	88	4375	15.1		5981	57.7	21:03	181	67	109	176	80	26	3	11	21:17

NHL All-Rookie Team (1984) • Lester B. Pearson Award (1989) • Conn Smythe Trophy (1998) • NHL First All-Star Team (2000) • Frank J. Selke Trophy (2000) • Bill Masterton Memorial Trophy (2003)

Played in NHL All-Star Game (1984, 1988, 1989, 1990, 1991, 1992, 1993, 1997, 2000)

♦ Missed majority of 2002-03 season recovering from off-season knee surgery, August 2, 2002.

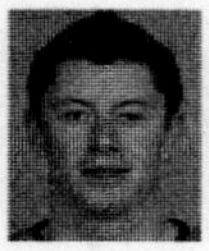

ZALESAK, Miroslav

(zah-LIH-sahk, MEER-oh-slav) **S.J.**

Right wing. Shoots left. 6', 185 lbs. Born, Skalica, Czech., January 2, 1980. San Jose's 5th choice, 104th overall, in 1998 Entry Draft.

Season	Club	League	GP	G	A	Pts	PIM	PP	SH	GW	S	%	+/-	TF	F%	Min	GP	G	A	Pts	PIM	PP	SH	GW	Min
1995-96	HC Nitra Jr.	Slovak-Jr.	49	53	29	82	....																		
1996-97	HC Nitra Jr.	Slovak-Jr.	58	51	31	82	....																		
1997-98	Nitra Jr.	Slovak-Jr.	27	32	29	61	30																		
	Nitra	Slovakia	30	8	6	14	0																		
1998-99	Nitra	Slovakia	15	4	3	7	10																		
	Drummondville	QMJHL	45	24	27	51	18																		
99-2000	Drummondville	QMJHL	60	50	61	111	40										16	7	11	18	4				
2000-01	Kentucky	AHL	60	14	11	25	26										3	0	1	1	4				
2001-02	Cleveland Barons	AHL	74	22	20	42	44																		
2002-03	San Jose	NHL	10	1	2	3	0	0	0	0	8	12.5	-2	1	0.0	9:28									
	Cleveland Barons	AHL	50	27	22	49	35																		
	NHL Totals		10	1	2	3	0	0	0	0	8	12.5		1	0.0	9:28									

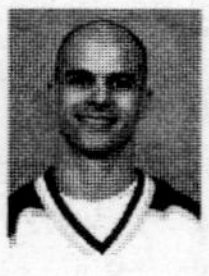

ZAMUNER, Rob

(ZAM-nuhr, RAWB) **BOS.**

Left wing. Shoots left. 6'3", 203 lbs. Born, Oakville, Ont., September 17, 1969. NY Rangers' 3rd choice, 45th overall, in 1989 Entry Draft.

Season	Club	League	GP	G	A	Pts	PIM	PP	SH	GW	S	%	+/-	TF	F%	Min	GP	G	A	Pts	PIM	PP	SH	GW	Min
1985-86	Oakville Oaks	OMHA	48	43	50	93	66																		
1986-87	Guelph Jr. B's	OJHL-B	3	6	7	13	15																		
	Guelph Platers	OHL	62	6	15	21	8																		
1987-88	Guelph Platers	OHL	58	20	41	61	18																		
1988-89	Guelph Platers	OHL	66	46	65	111	38										7	5	5	10	9				
1989-90	Flint Spirits	IHL	77	44	35	79	32										4	1	0	1	6				
1990-91	Binghamton	AHL	80	25	58	83	50										9	7	6	13	35				
1991-92	NY Rangers	NHL	9	1	2	3	2	0	0	0	11	9.1	0												
	Binghamton	AHL	61	19	53	72	42										11	8	9	17	8				
1992-93	Tampa Bay	NHL	84	15	28	43	74	1	0	0	183	8.2	-25												
1993-94	Tampa Bay	NHL	59	6	6	12	42	0	0	1	109	5.5	-9												
1994-95	Tampa Bay	NHL	43	9	6	15	24	0	3	1	74	12.2	-3												
1995-96	Tampa Bay	NHL	72	15	20	35	62	0	3	4	152	9.9	11				6	2	3	5	10	0	1	0	
1996-97	Tampa Bay	NHL	82	17	33	50	56	0	4	3	216	7.9	3												
1997-98	Tampa Bay	NHL	77	14	12	26	41	0	3	4	126	11.1	-31												
	Canada	Olympics	6	1	0	1	8																		
1998-99	Tampa Bay	NHL	58	8	11	19	24	1	1	2	89	9.0	-15	34	47.1	16:26									
99-2000	Ottawa	NHL	57	9	12	21	32	0	1	0	103	8.7	-6	29	37.9	14:56	6	2	0	2	2	0	0	1	12:58
2000-01	Ottawa	NHL	79	19	18	37	52	1	2	4	123	15.4	7	162	35.8	14:46	4	0	0	0	6	0	0	0	13:51
2001-02	Boston	NHL	66	12	13	25	24	1	2	0	98	12.2	6	192	41.7	13:13	6	0	2	2	4	0	0	0	12:35
2002-03	Boston	NHL	55	10	6	16	18	3	0	1	94	10.6	2	97	45.4	12:08	5	0	0	0	4	0	0	0	9:23
	NHL Totals		741	135	167	302	451	7	19	20	1378	9.8		514	40.7	14:19	27	4	5	9	26	0	1	1	12:11

Signed as a free agent by **Tampa Bay**, July 13, 1992. Traded to **Ottawa** by **Tampa Bay** with Tampa Bay's 2nd round choice (later traded to Philadelphia – later traded back to Tampa Bay – later traded to Dallas – Dallas selected Tobias Stephan) in 2002 Entry Draft for Andreas Johansson, June 29, 1999. Signed as a free agent by **Boston**, July 6, 2001.

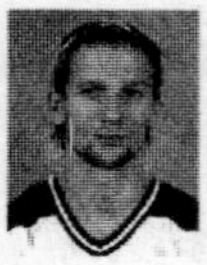

ZEDNIK, Richard

(ZEHD-nihk, REE-khahrd) **MTL.**

Right wing. Shoots left. 6', 200 lbs. Born, Bystrica, Czech., January 6, 1976. Washington's 10th choice, 249th overall, in 1994 Entry Draft.

Season	Club	League	GP	G	A	Pts	PIM	PP	SH	GW	S	%	+/-	TF	F%	Min	GP	G	A	Pts	PIM	PP	SH	GW	Min
1993-94	Banska Bystrica	Slovak-2	25	3	6	9	....																		
1994-95	Portland	WHL	65	35	51	86	89										9	5	5	10	20				
1995-96	Portland	WHL	61	44	37	81	154										7	8	4	12	23				
	Washington	NHL	1	0	0	0	0	0	0	0	0	0.0	0												
	Portland Pirates	AHL	1	1	1	2	0										21	4	5	9	26				
1996-97	Washington	NHL	11	2	1	3	4	1	0	0	21	9.5	-5												
	Portland Pirates	AHL	56	15	20	35	70										5	1	0	1	6				
1997-98	Washington	NHL	65	17	9	26	28	2	0	2	148	11.5	-2				17	7	3	10	16	2	0	0	
1998-99	Washington	NHL	49	9	8	17	50	1	0	2	115	7.8	-6	2	0.0	15:08									
99-2000	Washington	NHL	69	19	16	35	54	1	0	2	179	10.6	6	1	100.0	15:34	5	0	0	0	5	0	0	0	16:57
2000-01	Washington	NHL	62	16	19	35	61	4	0	3	155	10.3	-2	1	0.0	15:32									
	Montreal	NHL	12	3	6	9	10	1	0	0	23	13.0	-2	0	0.0	18:29									
2001-02	Montreal	NHL	82	22	22	44	59	4	0	3	249	8.8	-3	10	30.0	17:39	4	4	4	8	6	2	0	0	21:19
2002-03	Montreal	NHL	80	31	19	50	79	9	0	2	250	12.4	4	10	30.0	18:25									
	NHL Totals		431	119	100	219	345	23	0	14	1140	10.4		24	29.2	16:44	26	11	7	18	27	4	0	0	18:53

WHL West Second All-Star Team (1996)

Traded to **Montreal** by **Washington** with Jan Bulis and Washington's 1st round choice (Alexander Perezhogin) in 2001 Entry Draft for Trevor Linden, Dainius Zubrus and New Jersey's 2nd round choice (previously acquired, later traded to Tampa Bay – Tampa Bay selected Andreas Holmqvist) in 2001 Entry Draft, March 13, 2001.

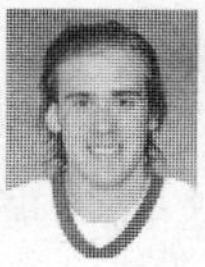

ZETTERBERG, Henrik

(ZEH-tuhr-buhrg, HEHN-rihk) **DET.**

Left wing. Shoots left. 5'11", 176 lbs. Born, Njurunda, Sweden, October 9, 1980. Detroit's 4th choice, 210th overall, in 1999 Entry Draft.

			Regular Season														Playoffs								
Season	Club	League	GP	G	A	Pts	PIM	PP	SH	GW	S	%	+/-	TF	F%	Min	GP	G	A	Pts	PIM	PP	SH	GW	Min
1997-98	Timra IK Jr.	Swede-Jr.	18	9	5	14	4																		
	Timra IK	Swede-2	16	1	2	3	4										4	0	1	1	0				
1998-99	Timra IK	Swede-2	37	15	13	28	2										4	2	1	3	2				
99-2000	Timra IK	Swede-2	32	20	14	34	20										10	10	4	14	4				
2000-01	Timra IK	Sweden	47	15	31	46	24																		
2001-02	Timra IK	Sweden	48	10	22	32	20																		
	Sweden	Olympics	4	0	1	1	0																		
2002-03	**Detroit**	**NHL**	**79**	**22**	**22**	**44**	**8**	**5**	**1**	**4**	**135**	**16.3**	**6**	**401**	**46.1**	**16:19**	**4**	**1**	**0**	**1**	**0**	**0**	**0**	**0**	**18:19**
	NHL Totals		**79**	**22**	**22**	**44**	**8**	**5**	**1**	**4**	**135**	**16.3**		**401**	**46.1**	**16:19**	**4**	**1**	**0**	**1**	**0**	**0**	**0**	**0**	**18:19**

Swedish Elite League Rookie of the Year (2001) • NHL All-Rookie Team (2003)

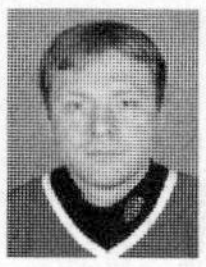

ZHAMNOV, Alexei

(ZHAHM-nahf, al-EHX-ay) **CHI.**

Center. Shoots left. 6'1", 204 lbs. Born, Moscow, USSR, October 1, 1970. Winnipeg's 5th choice, 77th overall, in 1990 Entry Draft.

			Regular Season														Playoffs								
Season	Club	League	GP	G	A	Pts	PIM	PP	SH	GW	S	%	+/-	TF	F%	Min	GP	G	A	Pts	PIM	PP	SH	GW	Min
1988-89	Dynamo Moscow	USSR	4	0	0	0	0																		
1989-90	Dynamo Moscow	USSR	43	11	6	17	21																		
1990-91	Dynamo Moscow	USSR	46	16	12	28	24																		
1991-92	Dynamo Moscow	CIS	39	15	21	36	28																		
	Russia	Olympics	8	0	3	3	8																		
1992-93	**Winnipeg**	**NHL**	**68**	**25**	**47**	**72**	**58**	**6**	**1**	**4**	**163**	**15.3**	**7**				**6**	**0**	**2**	**2**	**2**	**0**	**0**	**0**	
1993-94	**Winnipeg**	**NHL**	**61**	**26**	**45**	**71**	**62**	**7**	**0**	**1**	**196**	**13.3**	**–20**												
1994-95	**Winnipeg**	**NHL**	**48**	**30**	**35**	**65**	**20**	**9**	**0**	**4**	**155**	**19.4**	**5**												
1995-96	**Winnipeg**	**NHL**	**58**	**22**	**37**	**59**	**65**	**5**	**0**	**2**	**199**	**11.1**	**–4**				**6**	**2**	**1**	**3**	**8**	**0**	**0**	**0**	
1996-97	**Chicago**	**NHL**	**74**	**20**	**42**	**62**	**56**	**6**	**1**	**2**	**208**	**9.6**	**18**												
1997-98	**Chicago**	**NHL**	**70**	**21**	**28**	**49**	**61**	**6**	**2**	**3**	**193**	**10.9**	**16**												
	Russia	Olympics	6	2	1	3	2																		
1998-99	**Chicago**	**NHL**	**76**	**20**	**41**	**61**	**50**	**8**	**1**	**2**	**200**	**10.0**	**–10**	**1299**	**48.9**	**21:30**									
99-2000	**Chicago**	**NHL**	**71**	**23**	**37**	**60**	**61**	**5**	**0**	**7**	**175**	**13.1**	**7**	**1171**	**45.8**	**22:08**									
2000-01	**Chicago**	**NHL**	**63**	**13**	**36**	**49**	**40**	**3**	**1**	**3**	**117**	**11.1**	**–12**	**1486**	**48.1**	**21:15**									
2001-02	**Chicago**	**NHL**	**77**	**22**	**45**	**67**	**67**	**6**	**0**	**3**	**173**	**12.7**	**8**	**1634**	**50.0**	**22:19**	**5**	**0**	**0**	**0**	**0**	**0**	**0**	**0**	**21:16**
	Russia	Olympics	6	1	0	1	4																		
2002-03	**Chicago**	**NHL**	**74**	**15**	**43**	**58**	**70**	**2**	**3**	**1**	**166**	**9.0**	**0**	**1345**	**51.3**	**21:06**									
	NHL Totals		**740**	**237**	**436**	**673**	**610**	**63**	**9**	**32**	**1945**	**12.2**		**6935**	**48.9**	**21:40**	**17**	**2**	**3**	**5**	**10**	**0**	**0**	**0**	**21:16**

NHL Second All-Star Team (1995)

Played in NHL All-Star Game (2002)

Traded to **Chicago** by **Phoenix** with Craig Mills and Phoenix's 1st round choice (Ty Jones) in 1997 Entry Draft for Jeremy Roenick, August 16, 1996.

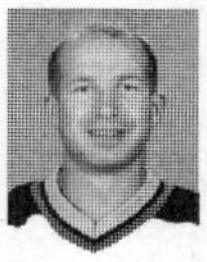

ZHITNIK, Alexei

(ZHIHT-nihk, al-EHX-ay) **BUF.**

Defense. Shoots left. 5'11", 215 lbs. Born, Kiev, USSR, October 10, 1972. Los Angeles' 3rd choice, 81st overall, in 1991 Entry Draft.

			Regular Season														Playoffs								
Season	Club	League	GP	G	A	Pts	PIM	PP	SH	GW	S	%	+/-	TF	F%	Min	GP	G	A	Pts	PIM	PP	SH	GW	Min
1989-90	Sokol Kiev	USSR	31	3	4	7	16																		
1990-91	Sokol Kiev	USSR	46	1	4	5	46																		
1991-92	CSKA Moscow	CIS	44	2	7	9	52																		
	Russia	Olympics	8	1	0	1	0																		
1992-93	**Los Angeles**	**NHL**	**78**	**12**	**36**	**48**	**80**	**5**	**0**	**2**	**136**	**8.8**	**–3**				**24**	**3**	**9**	**12**	**26**	**2**	**0**	**1**	
1993-94	**Los Angeles**	**NHL**	**81**	**12**	**40**	**52**	**101**	**11**	**0**	**1**	**227**	**5.3**	**–11**												
1994-95	**Los Angeles**	**NHL**	**11**	**2**	**5**	**7**	**27**	**2**	**0**	**0**	**33**	**6.1**	**–3**												
	Buffalo	**NHL**	**21**	**2**	**5**	**7**	**34**	**1**	**0**	**0**	**33**	**6.1**	**–3**				**5**	**0**	**1**	**1**	**14**	**0**	**0**	**0**	
1995-96	**Buffalo**	**NHL**	**80**	**6**	**30**	**36**	**58**	**5**	**0**	**0**	**193**	**3.1**	**–25**												
1996-97	**Buffalo**	**NHL**	**80**	**7**	**28**	**35**	**95**	**3**	**1**	**0**	**170**	**4.1**	**10**				**12**	**1**	**0**	**1**	**16**	**0**	**0**	**0**	
1997-98	**Buffalo**	**NHL**	**78**	**15**	**30**	**45**	**102**	**2**	**3**	**3**	**191**	**7.9**	**19**				**15**	**0**	**3**	**3**	**36**	**0**	**0**	**0**	
	Russia	Olympics	6	0	2	2	2																		
1998-99	**Buffalo**	**NHL**	**81**	**7**	**26**	**33**	**96**	**3**	**1**	**2**	**185**	**3.8**	**–6**	**0**	**0.0**	**25:39**	**21**	**4**	**11**	**15**	***52**	**4**	**0**	**2**	**27:07**
99-2000	**Buffalo**	**NHL**	**74**	**2**	**11**	**13**	**95**	**1**	**0**	**0**	**139**	**1.4**	**–6**	**0**	**0.0**	**24:48**	**4**	**0**	**0**	**0**	**8**	**0**	**0**	**0**	**25:50**
2000-01	**Buffalo**	**NHL**	**78**	**8**	**29**	**37**	**75**	**5**	**0**	**1**	**149**	**5.4**	**–3**	**0**	**0.0**	**24:15**	**13**	**1**	**6**	**7**	**12**	**0**	**0**	**0**	**25:38**
2001-02	**Buffalo**	**NHL**	**82**	**1**	**33**	**34**	**80**	**1**	**0**	**0**	**150**	**0.7**	**–1**	**0**	**0.0**	**25:36**									
2002-03	**Buffalo**	**NHL**	**70**	**3**	**18**	**21**	**85**	**0**	**0**	**1**	**138**	**2.2**	**–5**	**1**	**0.0**	**26:33**									
	NHL Totals		**814**	**77**	**291**	**368**	**928**	**39**	**5**	**10**	**1744**	**4.4**		**1**	**0.0**	**25:21**	**94**	**9**	**30**	**39**	**164**	**6**	**0**	**3**	**26:29**

Played in NHL All-Star Game (1999, 2002)

Traded to **Buffalo** by **Los Angeles** with Robb Stauber, Charlie Huddy and Los Angeles' 5th round choice (Marian Menhart) in 1995 Entry Draft for Philippe Boucher, Denis Tsygurov and Grant Fuhr, February 14, 1995.

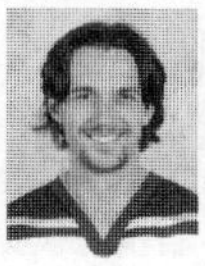

ZHOLTOK, Sergei

(ZHOL-tok, SAIR-gay) **MIN.**

Center. Shoots right. 6'2", 197 lbs. Born, Riga, Latvia, December 2, 1972. Boston's 2nd choice, 55th overall, in 1992 Entry Draft.

			Regular Season														Playoffs								
Season	Club	League	GP	G	A	Pts	PIM	PP	SH	GW	S	%	+/-	TF	F%	Min	GP	G	A	Pts	PIM	PP	SH	GW	Min
1990-91	Dynamo Riga	USSR	39	4	0	4	16																		
1991-92	Riga Stars	CIS	27	6	3	9	6																		
1992-93	**Boston**	**NHL**	**1**	**0**	**1**	**1**	**0**	**0**	**0**	**0**	**2**	**0.0**	**1**												
	Providence Bruins	AHL	64	31	35	66	57										6	3	5	8	4				
1993-94	**Boston**	**NHL**	**24**	**2**	**1**	**3**	**2**	**1**	**0**	**0**	**25**	**8.0**	**–7**												
	Providence Bruins	AHL	54	29	33	62	16																		
1994-95	Providence Bruins	AHL	78	23	35	58	42										13	8	5	13	6				
1995-96	Las Vegas	IHL	82	51	50	101	30										15	7	13	20	6				
1996-97	**Ottawa**	**NHL**	**57**	**12**	**16**	**28**	**19**	**5**	**0**	**0**	**96**	**12.5**	**2**				**7**	**1**	**1**	**2**	**0**	**1**	**0**	**0**	
	Las Vegas	IHL	19	13	14	27	20																		
1997-98	**Ottawa**	**NHL**	**78**	**10**	**13**	**23**	**16**	**7**	**0**	**1**	**127**	**7.9**	**–7**				**11**	**0**	**2**	**2**	**0**	**0**	**0**	**0**	
1998-99	**Montreal**	**NHL**	**70**	**7**	**15**	**22**	**6**	**2**	**0**	**3**	**102**	**6.9**	**–12**	**522**	**49.0**	**11:11**									
	Fredericton	AHL	7	3	4	7	0																		
99-2000	**Montreal**	**NHL**	**68**	**26**	**12**	**38**	**28**	**9**	**0**	**7**	**163**	**16.0**	**2**	**914**	**48.9**	**17:17**									
	Quebec Citadelles	AHL	1	0	1	1	2																		
2000-01	**Montreal**	**NHL**	**32**	**1**	**10**	**11**	**8**	**0**	**0**	**0**	**78**	**1.3**	**–15**	**318**	**52.2**	**15:38**									
	Edmonton	**NHL**	**37**	**4**	**16**	**20**	**22**	**1**	**0**	**0**	**61**	**6.6**	**8**	**109**	**60.6**	**12:55**	**3**	**0**	**0**	**0**	**0**	**0**	**0**	**0**	**9:23**
2001-02	**Minnesota**	**NHL**	**73**	**19**	**20**	**39**	**28**	**10**	**0**	**2**	**146**	**13.0**	**–10**	**823**	**45.6**	**16:04**									
2002-03	**Minnesota**	**NHL**	**78**	**16**	**26**	**42**	**18**	**3**	**0**	**2**	**153**	**10.5**	**1**	**998**	**45.2**	**16:36**	**18**	**2**	**11**	**13**	**0**	**1**	**0**	**0**	**15:43**
	NHL Totals		**518**	**97**	**130**	**227**	**147**	**38**	**0**	**15**	**953**	**10.2**		**3684**	**47.8**	**15:06**	**39**	**3**	**14**	**17**	**0**	**2**	**0**	**0**	**14:49**

Signed as a free agent by **Las Vegas** (IHL), August 5, 1995. Signed as a free agent by **Ottawa**, July 10, 1996. Signed as a free agent by **Montreal**, September 9, 1998. Traded to **Edmonton** by **Montreal** for Chad Kilger, December 18, 2000. Traded to **Minnesota** by **Edmonton** for Minnesota's 7th round choice (J.F. Dufort) in 2002 Entry Draft, June 29, 2001.

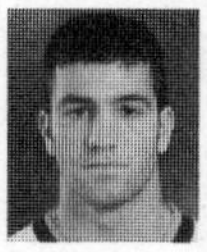

ZIGOMANIS, Mike

(zih-goh-MAN-his, MIGHK) **CAR.**

Center. Shoots right. 6'1", 189 lbs. Born, North York, Ont., January 17, 1981. Carolina's 2nd choice, 46th overall, in 2001 Entry Draft.

			Regular Season														Playoffs								
Season	Club	League	GP	G	A	Pts	PIM	PP	SH	GW	S	%	+/-	TF	F%	Min	GP	G	A	Pts	PIM	PP	SH	GW	Min
1996-97	Wexford Raiders	MTHL	40	37	48	85	23																		
	Wexford Raiders	MTJHL	8	2	5	7	2																		
1997-98	Kingston	OHL	62	23	51	74	30										12	1	6	7	2				
1998-99	Kingston	OHL	67	29	56	85	36										5	1	7	8	2				
99-2000	Kingston	OHL	59	40	54	94	49										5	0	4	4	0				
2000-01	Kingston	OHL	52	40	37	77	44																		
2001-02	Lowell	AHL	79	18	30	48	24										5	1	1	2	2				
2002-03	**Carolina**	**NHL**	**19**	**2**	**1**	**3**	**0**	**1**	**1**	**0**	**19**	**10.5**	**–4**	**147**	**59.2**	**9:43**									
	Lowell	AHL	38	13	18	31	19																		
	NHL Totals		**19**	**2**	**1**	**3**	**0**	**1**	**1**	**0**	**19**	**10.5**		**147**	**59.2**	**9:43**									

• Re-entered NHL Entry Draft. Originally Buffalo's 4th choice, 64th overall, in 1999 Entry Draft.

ZIZKA, Tomas
(ZHIHZH-kuh, TAW-mahsh) **L.A.**

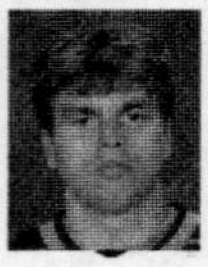

Defense. Shoots left. 6'1", 198 lbs. Born, Sternberk, Czech., October 10, 1979. Los Angeles' 6th choice, 163rd overall, in 1998 Entry Draft.

			Regular Season														Playoffs								
Season	Club	League	GP	G	A	Pts	PIM	PP	SH	GW	S	%	+/-	TF	F%	Min	GP	G	A	Pts	PIM	PP	SH	GW	Min
1994-95	AC ZPS Zlin Jr.	Czech-Jr.	39	1	10	11	....	....	....	....	....	....	....	....	....	....	....	....	....	....	....	....	....	....	....
1995-96	AC ZPS Zlin Jr.	Czech-Jr.	47	2	8	10	....	....	....	....	....	....	....	....	....	....	....	....	....	....	....	....	....	....	....
1996-97	AC ZPS Zlin Jr.	Czech-Jr.	14	1	0	1	....	....	....	....	....	....	....	....	....	....	....	....	....	....	....	....	....	....	....
1997-98	Zlin Jr.	Czech-Jr.	11	3	4	7	....	....	....	....	....	....	....	....	....	....	....	....	....	....	....	....	....	....	....
	Zlin	Czech	33	0	3	3	2	....	....	....	....	....	....	....	....	....	....	....	....	....	....	....	....	....	....
1998-99	Zlin	Czech	44	3	7	10	14	....	....	....	....	....	....	....	....	....	11	1	2	3	....	....	....	....	....
99-2000	Zlin	Czech	46	4	6	10	30	....	....	....	....	....	....	....	....	....	4	1	0	1	4	....	....	....	....
2000-01	Zlin	Czech	43	2	11	13	16	....	....	....	....	....	....	....	....	....	6	0	0	0	6	....	....	....	....
2001-02	Manchester	AHL	58	4	17	21	22	....	....	....	....	....	....	....	....	....	4	1	0	1	14	....	....	....	....
2002-03	**Los Angeles**	**NHL**	**10**	**0**	**3**	**3**	**4**	**0**	**0**	**0**	**12**	**0.0**	**-4**	**0**	**0.0**	**15:24**	....	....	....	....	....	....	....	....	....
	Manchester	AHL	61	13	30	43	50	....	....	....	....	....	....	....	....	....	3	0	2	2	2	....	....	....	....
	NHL Totals		**10**	**0**	**3**	**3**	**4**	**0**	**0**	**0**	**12**	**0.0**		**0**	**0.0**	**15:24**	....	....	....	....	....	....	....	....	....

ZUBOV, Sergei
(ZOO-bahf, SAIR-gay) **DAL.**

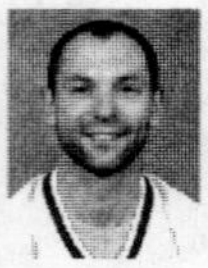

Defense. Shoots right. 6'1", 200 lbs. Born, Moscow, USSR, July 22, 1970. NY Rangers' 6th choice, 85th overall, in 1990 Entry Draft.

			Regular Season														Playoffs								
Season	Club	League	GP	G	A	Pts	PIM	PP	SH	GW	S	%	+/-	TF	F%	Min	GP	G	A	Pts	PIM	PP	SH	GW	Min
1988-89	CSKA Moscow	USSR	29	1	4	5	10	....	....	....	....	....	....	....	....	....	....	....	....	....	....	....	....	....	....
1989-90	CSKA Moscow	USSR	48	6	2	8	16	....	....	....	....	....	....	....	....	....	....	....	....	....	....	....	....	....	....
1990-91	CSKA Moscow	USSR	41	6	5	11	12	....	....	....	....	....	....	....	....	....	....	....	....	....	....	....	....	....	....
1991-92	CSKA Moscow	CIS	44	4	7	11	8	....	....	....	....	....	....	....	....	....	....	....	....	....	....	....	....	....	....
	Russia	Olympics	8	0	1	1	0	....	....	....	....	....	....	....	....	....	....	....	....	....	....	....	....	....	....
1992-93	CSKA Moscow	CIS	1	0	1	1	0	....	....	....	....	....	....	....	....	....	....	....	....	....	....	....	....	....	....
	NY Rangers	**NHL**	**49**	**8**	**23**	**31**	**4**	**3**	**0**	**0**	**93**	**8.6**	**-1**	....	....	....	....	....	....	....	....	....	....	....	....
	Binghamton	AHL	30	7	29	36	14	....	....	....	....	....	....	....	....	....	11	5	5	10	2	....	....	....	....
1993-94♦	**NY Rangers**	**NHL**	**78**	**12**	**77**	**89**	**39**	**9**	**0**	**1**	**222**	**5.4**	**20**	....	....	....	**22**	**5**	**14**	**19**	**0**	**2**	**0**	**0**	....
	Binghamton	AHL	2	1	2	3	0	....	....	....	....	....	....	....	....	....	....	....	....	....	....	....	....	....	....
1994-95	**NY Rangers**	**NHL**	**38**	**10**	**26**	**36**	**18**	**6**	**0**	**0**	**116**	**8.6**	**-2**	....	....	....	**10**	**3**	**8**	**11**	**2**	**1**	**0**	**0**	....
1995-96	**Pittsburgh**	**NHL**	**64**	**11**	**55**	**66**	**22**	**3**	**2**	**1**	**141**	**7.8**	**28**	....	....	....	**18**	**1**	**14**	**15**	**26**	**1**	**0**	**0**	....
1996-97	**Dallas**	**NHL**	**78**	**13**	**30**	**43**	**24**	**1**	**0**	**3**	**133**	**9.8**	**19**	....	....	....	**7**	**0**	**3**	**3**	**2**	**0**	**0**	**0**	....
1997-98	**Dallas**	**NHL**	**73**	**10**	**47**	**57**	**16**	**5**	**1**	**2**	**148**	**6.8**	**16**	....	....	....	**17**	**4**	**5**	**9**	**2**	**3**	**0**	**1**	....
1998-99♦	**Dallas**	**NHL**	**81**	**10**	**41**	**51**	**20**	**5**	**0**	**3**	**155**	**6.5**	**9**	**0**	**0.0**	**24:14**	**23**	**1**	**12**	**13**	**4**	**0**	**0**	**0**	**30:16**
99-2000	**Dallas**	**NHL**	**77**	**9**	**33**	**42**	**18**	**3**	**1**	**3**	**179**	**5.0**	**-2**	**0**	**0.0**	**28:50**	**18**	**2**	**7**	**9**	**6**	**1**	**1**	**0**	**26:28**
2000-01	**Dallas**	**NHL**	**79**	**10**	**41**	**51**	**24**	**6**	**0**	**1**	**173**	**5.8**	**22**	**0**	**0.0**	**26:37**	**10**	**1**	**5**	**6**	**4**	**0**	**0**	**0**	**30:37**
2001-02	**Dallas**	**NHL**	**80**	**12**	**32**	**44**	**22**	**8**	**0**	**2**	**198**	**6.1**	**-4**	**0**	**0.0**	**26:46**	....	....	....	....	....	....	....	....	....
2002-03	**Dallas**	**NHL**	**82**	**11**	**44**	**55**	**26**	**8**	**0**	**2**	**158**	**7.0**	**21**	**0**	**0.0**	**25:50**	**12**	**4**	**10**	**14**	**4**	**2**	**0**	**0**	**30:45**
	NHL Totals		**779**	**116**	**449**	**565**	**233**	**57**	**4**	**18**	**1716**	**6.8**		**0**	**0.0**	**26:26**	**137**	**21**	**78**	**99**	**50**	**10**	**1**	**1**	**29:20**

Played in NHL All-Star Game (1998, 1999, 2000)

Traded to **Pittsburgh** by **NY Rangers** with Petr Nedved for Luc Robitaille and Ulf Samuelsson, August 31, 1995. Traded to **Dallas** by **Pittsburgh** for Kevin Hatcher, June 22, 1996.

ZUBRUS, Dainius
(ZOO-bruhs, DAYN-ihs) **WSH.**

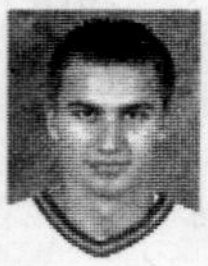

Right wing. Shoots left. 6'4", 231 lbs. Born, Elektrenai, USSR, June 16, 1978. Philadelphia's 1st choice, 15th overall, in 1996 Entry Draft.

			Regular Season														Playoffs								
Season	Club	League	GP	G	A	Pts	PIM	PP	SH	GW	S	%	+/-	TF	F%	Min	GP	G	A	Pts	PIM	PP	SH	GW	Min
1995-96	Pembroke	OCJHL	28	19	13	32	73	....	....	....	....	....	....	....	....	....	....	....	....	....	....	....	....	....	....
	Caledon	MTJHL	7	3	7	10	2	....	....	....	....	....	....	....	....	....	17	11	12	23	4	....	....	....	....
1996-97	**Philadelphia**	**NHL**	**68**	**8**	**13**	**21**	**22**	**1**	**0**	**2**	**71**	**11.3**	**3**	....	....	....	**19**	**5**	**4**	**9**	**12**	**1**	**0**	**1**	....
1997-98	**Philadelphia**	**NHL**	**69**	**8**	**25**	**33**	**42**	**1**	**0**	**5**	**101**	**7.9**	**29**	....	....	....	**5**	**0**	**1**	**1**	**2**	**0**	**0**	**0**	....
1998-99	**Philadelphia**	**NHL**	**63**	**3**	**5**	**8**	**25**	**0**	**1**	**0**	**49**	**6.1**	**-5**	**29**	**51.7**	**11:00**	....	....	....	....	....	....	....	....	....
	Montreal	**NHL**	**17**	**3**	**5**	**8**	**4**	**0**	**0**	**1**	**31**	**9.7**	**-3**	**2**	**50.0**	**16:53**	....	....	....	....	....	....	....	....	....
99-2000	**Montreal**	**NHL**	**73**	**14**	**28**	**42**	**54**	**3**	**0**	**1**	**139**	**10.1**	**-1**	**212**	**39.2**	**17:37**	....	....	....	....	....	....	....	....	....
2000-01	**Montreal**	**NHL**	**49**	**12**	**12**	**24**	**30**	**3**	**0**	**0**	**70**	**17.1**	**-7**	**190**	**41.1**	**18:30**	....	....	....	....	....	....	....	....	....
	Washington	**NHL**	**12**	**1**	**1**	**2**	**7**	**1**	**0**	**0**	**13**	**7.7**	**-4**	**0**	**0.0**	**13:05**	**6**	**0**	**0**	**0**	**2**	**0**	**0**	**0**	**17:23**
2001-02	**Washington**	**NHL**	**71**	**17**	**26**	**43**	**38**	**4**	**0**	**3**	**138**	**12.3**	**5**	**131**	**37.4**	**18:52**	....	....	....	....	....	....	....	....	....
2002-03	**Washington**	**NHL**	**63**	**13**	**22**	**35**	**43**	**2**	**0**	**0**	**104**	**12.5**	**15**	**565**	**50.3**	**16:26**	**6**	**2**	**2**	**4**	**4**	**1**	**0**	**0**	**21:30**
	NHL Totals		**485**	**79**	**137**	**216**	**265**	**15**	**1**	**12**	**716**	**11.0**		**1129**	**45.2**	**16:23**	**36**	**7**	**7**	**14**	**20**	**2**	**0**	**1**	**19:27**

Traded to **Montreal** by **Philadelphia** with Philadelphia's 2nd round choice (Matt Carkner) in 1999 Entry Draft and NY Islanders' 6th round choice (previously acquired, Montreal selected Scott Selig) in 2000 Entry Draft for Mark Recchi, March 10, 1999. Traded to **Washington** by **Montreal** with Trevor Linden and New Jersey's 2nd round choice (previously acquired, later traded to Tampa Bay – Tampa Bay selected Andreas Holmqvist) in 2001 Entry Draft for Richard Zednik, Jan Bulis and Washington's 1st round choice (Alexander Perezhogin) in 2001 Entry Draft, March 13, 2001.

ZYUZIN, Andrei
(ZYOO-zin, AWN-dray) **MIN.**

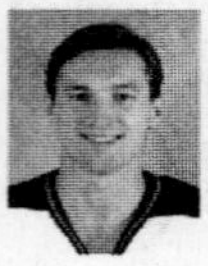

Defense. Shoots left. 6'1", 215 lbs. Born, Ufa, USSR, January 21, 1978. San Jose's 1st choice, 2nd overall, in 1996 Entry Draft.

			Regular Season														Playoffs								
Season	Club	League	GP	G	A	Pts	PIM	PP	SH	GW	S	%	+/-	TF	F%	Min	GP	G	A	Pts	PIM	PP	SH	GW	Min
1994-95	Ufa	CIS	30	3	0	3	16	....	....	....	....	....	....	....	....	....	....	....	....	....	....	....	....	....	....
1995-96	Ufa	CIS	41	6	3	9	24	....	....	....	....	....	....	....	....	....	....	....	....	....	....	....	....	....	....
1996-97	Ufa	Russia	32	7	10	17	28	....	....	....	....	....	....	....	....	....	7	1	1	2	4	....	....	....	....
1997-98	**San Jose**	**NHL**	**56**	**6**	**7**	**13**	**66**	**2**	**0**	**2**	**72**	**8.3**	**8**	....	....	....	**6**	**1**	**0**	**1**	**14**	**0**	**0**	**1**	....
	Kentucky	AHL	17	4	5	9	28	....	....	....	....	....	....	....	....	....	....	....	....	....	....	....	....	....	....
1998-99	**San Jose**	**NHL**	**25**	**3**	**1**	**4**	**38**	**2**	**0**	**0**	**44**	**6.8**	**5**	**0**	**0.0**	**15:56**	....	....	....	....	....	....	....	....	....
	Kentucky	AHL	23	2	12	14	42	....	....	....	....	....	....	....	....	....	....	....	....	....	....	....	....	....	....
99-2000	**Tampa Bay**	**NHL**	**34**	**2**	**9**	**11**	**33**	**0**	**0**	**0**	**47**	**4.3**	**-11**	**0**	**0.0**	**20:28**	....	....	....	....	....	....	....	....	....
2000-01	**Tampa Bay**	**NHL**	**64**	**4**	**16**	**20**	**76**	**2**	**1**	**1**	**92**	**4.3**	**-8**	**0**	**0.0**	**18:39**	....	....	....	....	....	....	....	....	....
	Detroit Vipers	IHL	2	0	1	1	0	....	....	....	....	....	....	....	....	....	....	....	....	....	....	....	....	....	....
2001-02	**Tampa Bay**	**NHL**	**9**	**0**	**2**	**2**	**6**	**0**	**0**	**0**	**14**	**0.0**	**-6**	**0**	**0.0**	**19:41**	....	....	....	....	....	....	....	....	....
	New Jersey	**NHL**	**38**	**1**	**2**	**3**	**25**	**1**	**0**	**0**	**47**	**2.1**	**1**	**0**	**0.0**	**15:04**	....	....	....	....	....	....	....	....	....
	Albany River Rats	AHL	3	0	1	1	2	....	....	....	....	....	....	....	....	....	....	....	....	....	....	....	....	....	....
2002-03	**New Jersey**	**NHL**	**1**	**0**	**1**	**1**	**2**	**0**	**0**	**0**	**0**	**0.0**	**-1**	**0**	**0.0**	**20:03**	....	....	....	....	....	....	....	....	....
	Minnesota	**NHL**	**66**	**4**	**12**	**16**	**34**	**2**	**0**	**0**	**113**	**3.5**	**-7**	**4**	**25.0**	**21:38**	**18**	**0**	**1**	**1**	**14**	**0**	**0**	**0**	**23:07**
	NHL Totals		**293**	**20**	**50**	**70**	**280**	**9**	**1**	**3**	**429**	**4.7**		**4**	**25.0**	**18:56**	**24**	**1**	**1**	**2**	**28**	**0**	**0**	**1**	**23:07**

• Suspended for remainder of 1998-99 season by **San Jose** for leaving team without permission, April 1, 1999. Traded to **Tampa Bay** by **San Jose** with Bill Houlder, Shawn Burr and Steve Guolla for Niklas Sundstrom and NY Rangers' 3rd round choice (previously acquired, later traded to Chicago – Chicago selected Igor Radulov) in 2000 Entry Draft, August 4, 1999. • Missed majority of 1999-2000 season recovering from shoulder injury suffered in game vs. NY Islanders, January 13, 2000. Traded to **New Jersey** by **Tampa Bay** for Josef Boumedienne, Sascha Goc and the rights to Anton But, November 9, 2001. Claimed on waivers by **Minnesota** from **New Jersey**, November 2, 2002.

NHL Goaltenders

David Aebischer	Jean-Sebastien Aubin	Alexander Auld	Ed Belfour	Zac Bierk	Martin Biron	Dan Blackburn	Brian Boucher	Fred Brathwaite	Martin Brochu
Martin Brodeur	Ilja Bryzgalov	Sean Burke	Sebastian Caron	Frederic Cassivi	Roman Cechmanek	Sebastien Centomo	Sebastien Charpentier	Scott Clemmensen	Dan Cloutier
Ty Conklin	Byron Dafoe	Jean-Francois Damphousse	Marc Denis	Patrick DesRochers	Rick DiPietro	Reinhard Divis	Mike Dunham	Robert Esche	Manny Fernandez
Wade Flaherty	Mathieu Garon	Jean-Sebastien Giguere	John Grahame	Jeff Hackett	Dominik Hasek	Johan Hedberg	Corey Hirsch	Milan Hnilicka	Jani Hurme
Arturs Irbe	Brent Johnson	Curtis Joseph	Nikolai Khabibulin	Trevor Kidd	Miika Kiprusoff	Olaf Kolzig	Jean-Francois Labbe	Simon Lajeunesse	Patrick Lalime
Marc Lamothe	Jan Lasak	Manny Legace	Michael Leighton	Neil Little	Roberto Luongo	Norm Maracle	Jussi Markkanen	Jamie McLennan	Alfie Michaud
Olivier Michaud	Ryan Miller	Tyler Moss	Evgeni Nabokov	Mika Noronen	Pasi Nurminen	Chris Osgood	Maxime Ouellet	Steve Passmore	Felix Potvin
Martin Prusek	Andrew Raycroft	Damian Rhodes	Mike Richter	Dwayne Roloson	Tommy Salo	Philippe Sauve	Corey Schwab	Steve Shields	Peter Skudra
Garth Snow	Jamie Storr	Jose Theodore	Jocelyn Thibault	Vesa Toskala	Ron Tugnutt	Marty Turco	Roman Turek	Tomas Vokoun	Kevin Weekes

2003-04 Goaltender Register

Note: The 2003-04 Goaltender Register lists every goaltender who appeared in an NHL game in the 2002-03 season, every goaltender drafted in the first five rounds of the 2003 Entry Draft, goaltenders on NHL Reserve Lists and other goaltenders. Trades and roster changes are current as of August 25, 2003.

To calculate a goaltender's goals-against per game average **(Avg)**, divide goals against **(GA)** by minutes played **(Mins)** and multiply this result by **60**.

Abbreviations: GP – games played; **W** – wins; **L** – losses; **T** – ties; **GA** – goals against; **SO** – shutouts; **Avg** – goals-against per game average.
♦ – member of Stanley Cup-winning team.

NHL Player Register begins on page 336.
Prospect Register begins on page 267.
League Abbreviations are listed on page 335.

AEBISCHER, David   (A-bih-shuhr, DAY-vihd)   COL.
Goaltender. Catches left. 6'1", 190 lbs.   Born, Fribourg, Switz., February 7, 1978.
(Colorado's 7th choice, 161st overall, in 1997 Entry Draft).

| | | | | | | Regular Season | | | | | | Playoffs | | | |
Season	Club	League	GP	W	L	T	Mins	GA	SO	Avg	GP	W	L	Mins	GA	SO	Avg
1996-97	Fribourg	Swiss	10	....	....	....	577	34	0	3.54	3	1	2	184	13	0	4.24
1997-98	Chesapeake	ECHL	17	5	7	2	930	52	0	3.35							
	Wheeling Nailers	ECHL	10	5	3	1	564	30	1	3.19							
	Hershey Bears	AHL	2	0	0	1	79	5	0	3.76							
	Fribourg	Swiss	1	1	0	0	60	1	0	1.00	4	....	....	240	17	0	4.25
1998-99	Hershey Bears	AHL	38	17	10	5	1932	79	2	2.45	3	1	2	152	6	0	2.37
99-2000	Hershey Bears	AHL	58	29	23	2	3259	180	1	3.31	14	7	6	788	40	2	3.05
2000-01♦	**Colorado**	**NHL**	26	12	7	3	1393	52	3	2.24	1	0	0	1	0	0	0.00
2001-02	**Colorado**	**NHL**	21	13	6	0	1184	37	2	1.88	1	0	0	34	1	0	1.76
	Switzerland	Olympics	2	1	0	0	81	6	0	4.43							
2002-03	**Colorado**	**NHL**	22	7	12	0	1235	50	1	2.43							
	NHL Totals		**69**	**32**	**25**	**3**	**3812**	**139**	**6**	**2.19**	**2**	**0**	**0**	**35**	**1**	**0**	**1.71**

AHONEN, Ari   (ah-HOH-nuhn, AH-ree)   N.J.
Goaltender. Catches left. 6'1", 195 lbs.   Born, Jyvaskyla, Finland, February 6, 1981.
(New Jersey's 1st choice, 27th overall, in 1999 Entry Draft).

| | | | | | | Regular Season | | | | | | Playoffs | | | |
Season	Club	League	GP	W	L	T	Mins	GA	SO	Avg	GP	W	L	Mins	GA	SO	Avg
1997-98	JYP Jyvaskyla Jr.	Finn-Jr.	31	....	....	....	1853	64	....	2.09							
1998-99	JYP Jyvaskyla Jr.	Finn-Jr.	24	....	....	....	1447	70	....	2.90							
99-2000	HIFK Helsinki	Finland	24	11	7	1	1347	70	1	3.12	2	0	2	119	7	0	3.53
	HIFK Helsinki	EuroHL	5	4	1	0	285	15	1	3.16							
2000-01	HIFK Helsinki	Finland	37	18	13	4	2101	97	2	2.77	7	4	3	395	9	1	1.37
2001-02	Albany River Rats	AHL	36	6	22	6	2106	106	0	3.02							
2002-03	Albany River Rats	AHL	38	13	20	3	2171	110	1	3.04							

ANDERSON, Craig   (AN-duhr-suhn, KRAYG)   CHI.
Goaltender. Catches left. 6'2", 174 lbs.   Born, Park Ridge, IL, May 21, 1981.
(Chicago's 4th choice, 73rd overall, in 2001 Entry Draft).

| | | | | | | Regular Season | | | | | | Playoffs | | | |
Season	Club	League	GP	W	L	T	Mins	GA	SO	Avg	GP	W	L	Mins	GA	SO	Avg
1997-98	Chicago Jets	MEHL	50	....	....	....	2991	143	2	2.86							
1998-99	Chicago Freeze	NAJHL	14	11	3	0	840	40	0	2.56							
	Guelph Storm	OHL	21	12	5	1	1006	52	1	3.10	3	0	2	114	9	0	4.74
99-2000	Guelph Storm	OHL	38	12	17	2	1955	117	0	3.59	3	0	1	110	5	0	2.73
2000-01	Guelph Storm	OHL	59	30	19	9	3555	156	3	2.63	4	0	4	240	17	0	4.25
2001-02	Norfolk Admirals	AHL	28	9	13	4	1568	77	2	2.95	1	0	1	21	1	0	2.83
2002-03	**Chicago**	**NHL**	6	0	3	2	270	18	0	4.00							
	Norfolk Admirals	AHL	32	15	11	5	1795	58	4	1.94	5	2	3	345	15	0	2.61
	NHL Totals		**6**	**0**	**3**	**2**	**270**	**18**	**0**	**4.00**							

• Re-entered NHL Entry Draft. Originally Calgary's 3rd choice, 77th overall, in 1999 Entry Draft.
OHL First All-Star Team (2001)

ANDERSSON, Andreas   (AN-duhr-suhn, AN-dree-as)   ANA.
Goaltender. Catches left. 6', 180 lbs.   Born, Jonkoping, Sweden, April 4, 1979.
(Anaheim's 8th choice, 245th overall, in 1998 Entry Draft).

| | | | | | | Regular Season | | | | | | Playoffs | | | |
Season	Club	League	GP	W	L	T	Mins	GA	SO	Avg	GP	W	L	Mins	GA	SO	Avg
1997-98	HV 71 Jr.	Swede-Jr.	10	....	....	....	600	31	....	3.10							
	HV 71 Jonkoping	Sweden	7	....	....	....	420	20	....	2.86							
1998-99	Mora IK Jr.	Swede-Jr.	12	....	....	....	720	28	0	1.92							
	HV 71 Jonkoping	Sweden	12	....	....	....	633	35	0	3.32							
99-2000	Tranas AIF	Swede-2	5	....	....	....	297	17	0	3.44							
	HV 71 Jonkoping	Sweden	1	....	....	....	51	5	0	5.88							
2000-01	IF Troja-Ljungby	Swede-2	19	....	....	....	1076	66	0	3.68	2	1	1	120	5	0	2.50
2001-02	IF Troja-Ljungby	Swede-2	6	....	....	....	360	27	0	4.50							
2002-03	IF Troja-Ljungby	Swede-2	7	....	....	....	419	20	0	2.86	2	....	....	116	3	0	1.55

ANTILA, Kristian   (AN-tih-luh, KRIHS-tan)   EDM.
Goaltender. Catches left. 6'3", 207 lbs.   Born, Vammala, Finland, January 10, 1980.
(Edmonton's 4th choice, 113th overall, in 1998 Entry Draft).

| | | | | | | Regular Season | | | | | | Playoffs | | | |
Season	Club	League	GP	W	L	T	Mins	GA	SO	Avg	GP	W	L	Mins	GA	SO	Avg
1997-98	Ilves Tampere Jr.	Finn-Jr.	11	....	....	....	564	28	0	2.97							
1998-99	Ilves Tampere Jr.	Finn-Jr.	18	8	8	1	1080	48	0	2.63	5	....	....	300	11	....	2.22
	Ilves Tampere	Finland	5	....	....	....	207	12	0	3.48							
99-2000	Ilves Tampere Jr.	Finn-Jr.	6	4	2	0	360	21	0	3.56							
	Diskos Jyvaskyla	Finland-2	5	1	4	0	300	23	0	4.67							
	Ilves Tampere	Finland	25	4	11	4	1239	74	1	3.58	1	0	1	20	4	0	12.00
2000-01	Assat Pori	Finland	42	9	27	7	2417	146	1	3.62							
2001-02	Assat Pori	Finland	35	7	22	3	1951	112	3	3.44							
2002-03	Hamilton Bulldogs	AHL	2	1	1	0	97	6	0	3.71							
	Wichita Thunder	CHL	21	10	7	2	1147	70	0	3.66							

ASKEY, Tom   (AS-kee, TAWM)   BUF.
Goaltender. Catches left. 6'1", 195 lbs.   Born, Kenmore, NY, October 4, 1974.
(Anaheim's 8th choice, 186th overall, in 1993 Entry Draft).

| | | | | | | Regular Season | | | | | | Playoffs | | | |
Season	Club	League	GP	W	L	T	Mins	GA	SO	Avg	GP	W	L	Mins	GA	SO	Avg
1992-93	Ohio State	CCHA	25	2	19	0	1235	125	0	6.07							
1993-94	Ohio State	CCHA	27	3	19	4	1488	103	0	4.15							
1994-95	Ohio State	CCHA	26	4	19	2	1387	121	0	5.23							
1995-96	Ohio State	CCHA	26	8	11	4	1340	68	0	3.05							
1996-97	Baltimore Bandits	AHL	40	17	18	2	2238	140	1	3.75	3	0	3	137	11	0	4.79
1997-98	**Anaheim**	**NHL**	7	0	1	2	273	12	0	2.64							
	Cincinnati	AHL	32	10	16	4	1753	104	3	3.56							
1998-99	Cincinnati	AHL	53	21	22	3	2893	131	3	2.72	3	0	3	178	13	0	4.38
	Anaheim	**NHL**									1	0	1	30	2	0	4.00
99-2000	Kansas City Blades	IHL	13	3	5	3	658	43	0	3.92							
	Houston Aeros	IHL	13	4	7	1	727	33	0	2.55							
2000-01	Rochester	AHL	29	15	8	4	1671	71	1	2.55							
2001-02	Rochester	AHL	34	16	15	3	2048	86	3	2.52	1	0	1	58	4	0	4.11
2002-03	Rochester	AHL	16	3	8	4	895	49	0	3.28							
	NHL Totals		**7**	**0**	**1**	**2**	**273**	**12**	**0**	**2.64**	**1**	**0**	**1**	**30**	**2**	**0**	**4.00**

CCHA Second All-Star Team (1996) • Shared Harry "Hap" Holmes Memorial Trophy (fewest goals against – AHL) (2001) with Mika Noronen
Signed as a free agent by **Rochester** (AHL), September 29, 2000. Signed as a free agent by **Buffalo**, August 10, 2001.

ASPLUND, Johan   (AS-pluhnd, YOH-hahn)   NYR
Goaltender. Catches left. 6'1", 180 lbs.   Born, Slutskar, Sweden, December 15, 1980.
(NY Rangers' 4th choice, 79th overall, in 1999 Entry Draft).

| | | | | | | Regular Season | | | | | | Playoffs | | | |
Season	Club	League	GP	W	L	T	Mins	GA	SO	Avg	GP	W	L	Mins	GA	SO	Avg
1998-99	Brynas IF Gavle	Sweden	12	....	....	....	646	32	0	2.97							
99-2000	Mora IK	Swede-2	3	3	0	0	180	6	0	2.00							
	Brynas IF Gavle	Sweden	10	....	....	....	622	30	0	2.89							
2000-01	Brynas IF Gavle	Sweden	29	....	....	....	1761	79	2	2.69	3	0	3	177	11	0	3.73
2001-02	Brynas IF Gavle	Sweden	34	....	....	....	2069	102	1	2.96	3	0	3	188	16	0	5.11
2002-03	Brynas IF Gavle	Sweden	13	....	....	....	680	43	0	3.79							

AUBIN, Jean-Sebastien   (OH-behn, ZHAWN-suh-BAS-tee-yeh)   PIT.
Goaltender. Catches right. 5'11", 180 lbs.   Born, Montreal, Que., July 19, 1977.
(Pittsburgh's 2nd choice, 76th overall, in 1995 Entry Draft).

| | | | | | | Regular Season | | | | | | Playoffs | | | |
Season	Club	League	GP	W	L	T	Mins	GA	SO	Avg	GP	W	L	Mins	GA	SO	Avg
1993-94	Montreal-Bourassa	QAAA	27	14	13	0	1524	96	1	3.74	4	1	3	222	19	0	5.14
1994-95	Sherbrooke	QMJHL	27	13	10	1	1287	73	1	3.40	4	1	2	185	11	0	3.57
1995-96	Sherbrooke	QMJHL	40	18	14	2	2140	127	0	3.57	4	1	3	238	23	0	5.55
1996-97	Sherbrooke	QMJHL	4	....	....	....	249	8	0	1.93	1	0	1	60	4	0	4.00
	Moncton Wildcats	QMJHL	22	9	12	0	1252	67	1	3.21							
	Laval Titan	QMJHL	11	2	6	1	532	41	0	4.62							
1997-98	Syracuse Crunch	AHL	8	2	4	1	380	26	0	4.10							
	Dayton Bombers	ECHL	21	15	2	2	1177	59	1	3.01	3	1	1	142	4	0	1.69
1998-99	**Pittsburgh**	**NHL**	17	4	3	6	756	28	2	2.22							
	Kansas City Blades	IHL	13	5	7	1	751	41	0	3.28							
99-2000	**Pittsburgh**	**NHL**	51	23	21	3	2789	120	2	2.58							
	Wilkes-Barre	AHL	11	2	8	0	538	39	0	4.35							
2000-01	**Pittsburgh**	**NHL**	36	20	14	1	2050	107	0	3.13	1	0	0	1	0	0	0.00
2001-02	**Pittsburgh**	**NHL**	21	3	12	1	1094	65	0	3.56							
2002-03	**Pittsburgh**	**NHL**	21	6	13	0	1132	59	1	3.13							
	Wilkes-Barre	AHL	16	8	6	1	919	29	3	1.89	6	3	3	356	12	0	2.02
	NHL Totals		**146**	**56**	**63**	**11**	**7821**	**379**	**5**	**2.91**	**1**	**0**	**0**	**1**	**0**	**0**	**0.00**

AULD, Alexander (AWLD, al-ehx-AN-duhr) VAN.

Goaltender. Catches left. 6'4", 197 lbs. Born, Cold Lake, Alta., January 7, 1981.
(Florida's 2nd choice, 40th overall, in 1999 Entry Draft).

			Regular Season								Playoffs						
Season	**Club**	**League**	**GP**	**W**	**L**	**T**	**Mins**	**GA**	**SO**	**Avg**	**GP**	**W**	**L**	**Mins**	**GA**	**SO**	**Avg**
1996-97	Thunder Bay Kings	TBMHL	35	....	....	....	2100	46	10	1.35	....	....	....	....	....	....	....
1997-98	Sturgeon Falls Lynx	NOJHA	11	4	6	0	611	46	0	4.52	....	....	....	....	....	....	....
	North Bay	OHL	6	0	4	0	206	17	0	4.95	....	....	....	....	....	....	....
1998-99	North Bay	OHL	37	9	20	1	1894	106	1	3.36	3	0	3	170	10	0	3.53
99-2000	North Bay	OHL	55	21	26	6	3047	167	2	3.29	6	2	4	374	12	0	*1.93
2000-01	North Bay	OHL	40	22	11	5	2319	98	1	2.54	4	0	4	240	15	0	3.75
2001-02	**Vancouver**	**NHL**	**1**	**1**	**0**	**0**	**60**	**2**	**0**	**2.00**	....	....	....	....	....	....	....
	Columbia Inferno	ECHL	6	3	1	2	375	12	0	1.92	....	....	....	....	....	....	....
	Manitoba Moose	AHL	21	11	9	0	1104	65	1	3.53	1	0	0	20	0	0	0.00
2002-03	**Vancouver**	**NHL**	**7**	**3**	**3**	**0**	**382**	**10**	**1**	**1.57**	**1**	**0**	**0**	**20**	**1**	**0**	**3.00**
	Manitoba Moose	AHL	37	15	19	3	2209	97	3	2.64	....	....	....	....	....	....	....
	NHL Totals		**8**	**4**	**3**	**0**	**442**	**12**	**1**	**1.63**	**1**	**0**	**0**	**20**	**1**	**0**	**3.00**

Rights traded to **Vancouver** by **Florida** for Vancouver's compensatory 2nd round choice (later traded to New Jersey – New Jersey selected Tuomas Pihlman) in 2001 Entry Draft and Vancouver's 3rd round choice (later traded to Atlanta – later traded to Buffalo – Buffalo selected John Adams) in 2002 Entry Draft, May 31, 2001.

AYERS, Michael (AY-uhrs, MIGH-kuhl) CHI.

Goaltender. Catches left. 5'11", 188 lbs. Born, Weymouth, MA, January 16, 1980.
(Chicago's 8th choice, 177th overall, in 2000 Entry Draft).

			Regular Season								Playoffs						
Season	**Club**	**League**	**GP**	**W**	**L**	**T**	**Mins**	**GA**	**SO**	**Avg**	**GP**	**W**	**L**	**Mins**	**GA**	**SO**	**Avg**
1998-99	Trinity Pawling	H.S.					STATISTICS NOT AVAILABLE										
99-2000	Dubuque	USHL	55	16	35	3	3188	196	0	3.69	....	....	....	....	....	....	....
2000-01	New Hampshire	H-East	4	0	0	0	26	2	0	4.68	....	....	....	....	....	....	....
2001-02	New Hampshire	H-East	20	14	3	1	1129	46	1	2.44	....	....	....	....	....	....	....
2002-03	New Hampshire	H-East	*41	*27	8	6	*2499	91	*7	2.18	....	....	....	....	....	....	....

Hockey East Second All-Star Team (2002) • Hockey East First All-Star Team (2003) • Hockey East Player of the Year (2003) (co-winner - Ben Eaves) • NCAA East Second All-American Team (2003)

BACASHIHUA, Jason (bak-ah-SHIH-hu-ah, JAY-suhn) DAL.

Goaltender. Catches left. 5'11", 175 lbs. Born, Garden City, MI, September 20, 1982.
(Dallas' 1st choice, 26th overall, in 2001 Entry Draft).

			Regular Season								Playoffs						
Season	**Club**	**League**	**GP**	**W**	**L**	**T**	**Mins**	**GA**	**SO**	**Avg**	**GP**	**W**	**L**	**Mins**	**GA**	**SO**	**Avg**
99-2000	Chicago Freeze	NAJHL	41	20	19	2	2432	118	2	2.91	2	0	2	103	12	0	6.97
2000-01	Chicago Freeze	NAJHL	39	24	14	0	2246	121	1	3.23	3	1	2	190	12	0	3.79
2001-02	Plymouth Whalers	OHL	46	26	12	7	2688	105	*5	2.34	6	2	4	360	15	0	2.50
	Utah Grizzlies	AHL	1	0	1	0	61	3	0	2.97	....	....	....	....	....	....	....
2002-03	Utah Grizzlies	AHL	39	18	18	2	2245	118	3	3.15	1	0	1	59	2	0	2.05

BARRASSO, Tom (buh-RAH-soh, TAWM)

Goaltender. Catches right. 6'3", 210 lbs. Born, Boston, MA, March 31, 1965.
(Buffalo's 1st choice, 5th overall, in 1983 Entry Draft).

			Regular Season								Playoffs						
Season	**Club**	**League**	**GP**	**W**	**L**	**T**	**Mins**	**GA**	**SO**	**Avg**	**GP**	**W**	**L**	**Mins**	**GA**	**SO**	**Avg**
1981-82	Acton-Boxborough	H.S.	23	....	....	....	1035	32	7	1.86	....	....	....	....	....	....	....
1982-83	Acton-Boxborough	H.S.	23	22	0	1	1035	17	10	0.99	....	....	....	....	....	....	....
1983-84	**Buffalo**	**NHL**	**42**	**26**	**12**	**3**	**2475**	**117**	**2**	**2.84**	**3**	**0**	**2**	**139**	**8**	**0**	**3.45**
1984-85	**Buffalo**	**NHL**	**54**	**25**	**18**	**10**	**3248**	**144**	***5**	***2.66**	**5**	**2**	**3**	**300**	**22**	**0**	**4.40**
	Rochester	AHL	5	3	1	1	267	6	1	1.35	....	....	....	....	....	....	....
1985-86	**Buffalo**	**NHL**	**60**	**29**	**24**	**5**	**3561**	**214**	**2**	**3.61**	....	....	....	....	....	....	....
1986-87	**Buffalo**	**NHL**	**46**	**17**	**23**	**2**	**2501**	**152**	**2**	**3.65**	....	....	....	....	....	....	....
1987-88	**Buffalo**	**NHL**	**54**	**25**	**18**	**8**	**3133**	**173**	**2**	**3.31**	**4**	**1**	**3**	**224**	**16**	**0**	**4.29**
1988-89	**Buffalo**	**NHL**	**10**	**2**	**7**	**0**	**545**	**45**	**0**	**4.95**	....	....	....	....	....	....	....
	Pittsburgh	**NHL**	**44**	**18**	**15**	**7**	**2406**	**162**	**0**	**4.04**	**11**	**7**	**4**	**631**	**40**	**0**	**3.80**
1989-90	**Pittsburgh**	**NHL**	**24**	**7**	**12**	**3**	**1294**	**101**	**0**	**4.68**	....	....	....	....	....	....	....
1990-91♦	**Pittsburgh**	**NHL**	**48**	**27**	**16**	**3**	**2754**	**165**	**1**	**3.59**	**20**	**12**	**7**	**1175**	**51**	***1**	***2.60**
1991-92♦	**Pittsburgh**	**NHL**	**57**	**25**	**22**	**9**	**3329**	**196**	**1**	**3.53**	***21**	***16**	**5**	***1233**	**58**	**1**	**2.82**
1992-93	**Pittsburgh**	**NHL**	**63**	***43**	**14**	**5**	**3702**	**186**	**4**	**3.01**	**12**	**7**	**5**	**722**	**35**	***2**	**2.91**
1993-94	**Pittsburgh**	**NHL**	**44**	**22**	**15**	**5**	**2482**	**139**	**2**	**3.36**	**6**	**2**	**4**	**356**	**17**	**0**	**2.87**
1994-95	**Pittsburgh**	**NHL**	**2**	**0**	**1**	**1**	**125**	**8**	**0**	**3.84**	**2**	**0**	**1**	**80**	**8**	**0**	**6.00**
1995-96	**Pittsburgh**	**NHL**	**49**	**29**	**16**	**2**	**2799**	**160**	**2**	**3.43**	**10**	**4**	**5**	**558**	**26**	**1**	**2.80**
1996-97	**Pittsburgh**	**NHL**	**5**	**0**	**5**	**0**	**270**	**26**	**0**	**5.78**	....	....	....	....	....	....	....
1997-98	**Pittsburgh**	**NHL**	**63**	**31**	**14**	**13**	**3542**	**122**	**7**	**2.07**	**6**	**2**	**4**	**376**	**17**	**0**	**2.71**
1998-99	**Pittsburgh**	**NHL**	**43**	**19**	**16**	**3**	**2306**	**98**	**4**	**2.55**	**13**	**6**	**7**	**787**	**35**	**1**	**2.67**
99-2000	**Pittsburgh**	**NHL**	**18**	**5**	**7**	**2**	**870**	**46**	**1**	**3.17**	....	....	....	....	....	....	....
	Ottawa	**NHL**	**7**	**3**	**4**	**0**	**418**	**22**	**0**	**3.16**	**6**	**2**	**4**	**372**	**16**	**0**	**2.58**
2000-01							DID NOT PLAY										
2001-02	**Carolina**	**NHL**	**34**	**13**	**12**	**5**	**1908**	**83**	**2**	**2.61**	....	....	....	....	....	....	....
	United States	Olympics	1	1	0	0	60	1	0	1.00	....	....	....	....	....	....	....
	Toronto	**NHL**	**4**	**2**	**2**	**0**	**219**	**10**	**0**	**2.74**	....	....	....	....	....	....	....
2002-03	**St. Louis**	**NHL**	**6**	**1**	**4**	**0**	**293**	**16**	**1**	**3.28**	....	....	....	....	....	....	....
	NHL Totals		**777**	**369**	**277**	**86**	**44180**	**2385**	**38**	**3.24**	**119**	**61**	**54**	**6953**	**349**	**6**	**3.01**

NHL All-Rookie Team (1984) • NHL First All-Star Team (1984) • Calder Memorial Trophy (1984) • Vezina Trophy (1984) • NHL Second All-Star Team (1985, 1993) • Shared William M. Jennings Trophy (1985) with Bob Sauve

Played in NHL All-Star Game (1985)

Traded to **Pittsburgh** by **Buffalo** with Buffalo's 3rd round choice (Joe Dziedzic) in 1990 Entry Draft for Doug Bodger and Darrin Shannon, November 12, 1988. • Missed majority of 1994-95 season recovering from wrist surgery, January 20, 1995. • Missed majority of 1996-97 season recovering from shoulder injury suffered in game vs. Montreal, February 5, 1996. Traded to **Ottawa** by **Pittsburgh** for Ron Tugnutt and Janne Laukkanen, March 14, 2000. • Missed entire 2000-01 season for personal reasons. Signed as a free agent by **Carolina**, July 17, 2001. Traded to **Toronto** by **Carolina** for Toronto's 4th round choice (Kevin Nastiuk) in 2003 Entry Draft, March 15, 2002. Signed as a free agent by **St. Louis**, November 1, 2002. Signed as a free agent by **Pittsburgh**, June 18, 2003. • Officially announced retirement, June 18, 2003.

BARULIN, Konstantin (bah-ROO-lihn, kawn-stuhn-TIHN) ST.L.

Goaltender. Catches left. 6', 180 lbs. Born, Karaganda, USSR, September 4, 1984.
(St. Louis' 3rd choice, 84th overall, in 2003 Entry Draft).

			Regular Season								Playoffs						
Season	**Club**	**League**	**GP**	**W**	**L**	**T**	**Mins**	**GA**	**SO**	**Avg**	**GP**	**W**	**L**	**Mins**	**GA**	**SO**	**Avg**
2001-02	Gazovik Tyumen	Russia-2	4	....	....	....	188	15	0	4.79	....	....	....	....	....	....	....
2002-03	Gazovik Tyumen	Russia-2	28	....	....	....	1672	47	5	1.69	....	....	....	....	....	....	....

BECKFORD-TSEU, Chris (BEHK-fuhrd-TSEW, KRIHS) ST.L.

Goaltender. Catches left. 6'3", 196 lbs. Born, Toronto, Ont., June 22, 1984.
(St. Louis' 8th choice, 159th overall, in 2003 Entry Draft).

			Regular Season								Playoffs						
Season	**Club**	**League**	**GP**	**W**	**L**	**T**	**Mins**	**GA**	**SO**	**Avg**	**GP**	**W**	**L**	**Mins**	**GA**	**SO**	**Avg**
2000-01	St. Michael's	OJHL-B	26	....	....	....	1506	121	0	4.83	....	....	....	....	....	....	....
2001-02	Guelph Storm	OHL	5	2	0	0	207	16	0	4.64	....	....	....	....	....	....	....
	Oshawa Generals	OHL	7	2	3	0	341	19	0	3.34	5	1	4	310	16	0	3.10
	Oshawa	OPJHL					STATISTICS NOT AVAILABLE										
2002-03	Oshawa Generals	OHL	54	25	26	2	2978	157	4	3.16	13	6	7	727	48	1	3.96

BELFOUR, Ed (BEHL-fohr, EHD) TOR.

Goaltender. Catches left. 5'11", 202 lbs. Born, Carman, Man., April 21, 1965.

			Regular Season								Playoffs						
Season	**Club**	**League**	**GP**	**W**	**L**	**T**	**Mins**	**GA**	**SO**	**Avg**	**GP**	**W**	**L**	**Mins**	**GA**	**SO**	**Avg**
1983-84	Winkler Flyers	MJHL	14	....	....	....	818	68	0	4.99	....	....	....	....	....	....	....
1984-85	Winkler Flyers	MJHL	34	....	....	....	1973	145	1	4.41	7	3	4	528	41	0	4.66
1985-86	Winkler Flyers	MJHL	33	....	....	....	1943	124	1	3.83	....	....	....	....	....	....	....
1986-87	North Dakota	WCHA	34	29	4	0	2049	81	3	2.37	....	....	....	....	....	....	....
1987-88	Saginaw Hawks	IHL	61	32	25	0	*3446	183	3	3.19	9	4	5	561	33	0	3.53
1988-89	**Chicago**	**NHL**	**23**	**4**	**12**	**3**	**1148**	**74**	**0**	**3.87**	....	....	....	....	....	....	....
	Saginaw Hawks	IHL	29	12	10	0	1760	92	0	3.14	5	2	3	298	14	0	2.82
1989-90	Canada	Nat-Tm	33	13	12	6	1808	93	0	3.09	....	....	....	....	....	....	....
	Chicago	**NHL**	....	....	....	....	....	....	....	....	**9**	**4**	**2**	**409**	**17**	**0**	**2.49**
1990-91	**Chicago**	**NHL**	***74**	***43**	**19**	**7**	***4127**	**170**	**4**	***2.47**	**6**	**2**	**4**	**295**	**20**	**0**	**4.07**
1991-92	**Chicago**	**NHL**	**52**	**21**	**18**	**10**	**2928**	**132**	***5**	**2.70**	**18**	**12**	**4**	**949**	**39**	**1**	***2.47**
1992-93	**Chicago**	**NHL**	***71**	**41**	**18**	**11**	***4106**	**177**	***7**	**2.59**	**4**	**0**	**4**	**249**	**13**	**0**	**3.13**
1993-94	**Chicago**	**NHL**	**70**	**37**	**24**	**6**	**3998**	**178**	***7**	**2.67**	**6**	**2**	**4**	**360**	**15**	**0**	**2.50**
1994-95	**Chicago**	**NHL**	**42**	**22**	**15**	**3**	**2450**	**93**	***5**	**2.28**	**16**	**9**	**7**	**1014**	**37**	**1**	**2.19**
1995-96	**Chicago**	**NHL**	**50**	**22**	**17**	**10**	**2956**	**135**	**1**	**2.74**	**9**	**6**	**3**	**666**	**23**	**1**	***2.07**
1996-97	**Chicago**	**NHL**	**33**	**11**	**15**	**6**	**1966**	**88**	**1**	**2.69**	....	....	....	....	....	....	....
	San Jose	**NHL**	**13**	**3**	**9**	**0**	**757**	**43**	**1**	**3.41**	....	....	....	....	....	....	....
1997-98	**Dallas**	**NHL**	**61**	**37**	**12**	**10**	**3581**	**112**	**9**	***1.88**	**17**	**10**	**7**	**1039**	**31**	**1**	***1.79**
1998-99♦	**Dallas**	**NHL**	**61**	**35**	**15**	**9**	**3536**	**117**	**5**	**1.99**	***23**	***16**	**7**	***1544**	**43**	***3**	***1.67**
99-2000	**Dallas**	**NHL**	**62**	**32**	**21**	**7**	**3620**	**127**	**4**	**2.10**	***23**	**14**	**9**	**1443**	**45**	***4**	**1.87**
2000-01	**Dallas**	**NHL**	**63**	**35**	**20**	**7**	**3687**	**144**	**8**	**2.34**	**10**	**4**	**6**	**671**	**25**	**0**	**2.24**
2001-02	**Dallas**	**NHL**	**60**	**21**	**27**	**11**	**3467**	**153**	**1**	**2.65**	....	....	....	....	....	....	....
	Canada	Olympics					DID NOT PLAY – SPARE GOALTENDER										
2002-03	**Toronto**	**NHL**	**62**	**37**	**20**	**5**	**3738**	**141**	**7**	**2.26**	**7**	**3**	**4**	**532**	**24**	**0**	**2.71**
	NHL Totals		**797**	**401**	**262**	**105**	**46065**	**1884**	**65**	**2.45**	**148**	**82**	**61**	**9171**	**332**	**11**	**2.17**

WCHA First All-Star Team (1987) • NCAA Championship All-Tournament Team (1987) • IHL First All-Star Team (1988) • Garry F. Longman Memorial Trophy (Top Rookie – IHL) (1988) (co-winner - John Cullen) • NHL All-Rookie Team (1991) • NHL First All-Star Team (1991, 1993) • Trico Goaltender Award (1991) • Calder Memorial Trophy (1991) • William M. Jennings Trophy (1991, 1993, 1995) • Vezina Trophy (1991, 1993) • NHL Second All-Star Team (1995) • Shared William M. Jennings Trophy (1999) with Roman Turek • MBNA Roger Crozier Saving Grace Award (2000)

Played in NHL All-Star Game (1992, 1993, 1996, 1998, 1999)

Signed as a free agent by **Chicago**, September 25, 1987. Traded to **San Jose** by **Chicago** for Chris Terreri, Ulf Dahlen and Michal Sykora, January 25, 1997. Signed as a free agent by **Dallas**, July 2, 1997. Traded to **Nashville** by **Dallas** with Cameron Mann for David Gosselin and Nashville's 5th round choice (Eero Kilpelainen) in 2003 Entry Draft, June 29, 2002. Signed as a free agent by **Toronto**, July 2, 2002.

BENDERA, Shane (behn-DEHR-ah, SHAYN) CBJ

Goaltender. Catches left. 5'11", 170 lbs. Born, St. Albert, Alta., July 13, 1982.
(Columbus' 6th choice, 169th overall, in 2000 Entry Draft).

			Regular Season								Playoffs						
Season	**Club**	**League**	**GP**	**W**	**L**	**T**	**Mins**	**GA**	**SO**	**Avg**	**GP**	**W**	**L**	**Mins**	**GA**	**SO**	**Avg**
1997-98	Edmonton KC Pats	AMHL	22	8	10	2	1284	82	0	3.84	....	....	....	....	....	....	....
	Red Deer Rebels	WHL	1	0	0	0	8	0	0	0.00	....	....	....	....	....	....	....
1998-99	Bonnyville Pontiacs	AJHL	20	....	....	....	956	70	0	4.38	....	....	....	....	....	....	....
	Red Deer Rebels	WHL	2	0	1	0	72	7	0	5.83	....	....	....	....	....	....	....
99-2000	Red Deer Rebels	WHL	*69	31	27	9	*4003	202	0	3.03	3	0	2	76	15	0	11.84
2000-01	Red Deer Rebels	WHL	45	32	8	2	2603	108	*5	*2.49	*22	*16	6	*1404	43	*4	1.84
2001-02	Red Deer Rebels	WHL	20	11	6	3	1211	46	1	2.28	....	....	....	....	....	....	....
	Kelowna Rockets	WHL	30	13	9	8	1816	79	0	2.61	15	9	6	918	29	*2	*1.90
2002-03	Dayton Bombers	ECHL	39	13	19	5	2243	106	1	2.84	....	....	....	....	....	....	....

WHL East Second All-Star Team (2001) • WHL West Second All-Star Team (2002)

BERKHOEL, Adam (BUHRK-uhl, A-duhm) CHI.

Goaltender. Catches left. 5'11", 173 lbs. Born, St. Paul, MN, May 16, 1981.
(Chicago's 12th choice, 240th overall, in 2000 Entry Draft).

			Regular Season								Playoffs						
Season	**Club**	**League**	**GP**	**W**	**L**	**T**	**Mins**	**GA**	**SO**	**Avg**	**GP**	**W**	**L**	**Mins**	**GA**	**SO**	**Avg**
1998-99	Stillwater Ponies	H.S.					STATISTICS NOT AVAILABLE										
99-2000	Twin Cities	USHL	49	25	15	7	2848	129	0	2.72	13	7	6	797	43	0	3.24
2000-01	U. of Denver	WCHA	15	7	6	1	745	38	1	3.06	....	....	....	....	....	....	....
2001-02	U. of Denver	WCHA	18	12	4	1	1026	40	1	2.34	....	....	....	....	....	....	....
2002-03	U. of Denver	WCHA	26	12	6	4	1436	55	3	*2.30	....	....	....	....	....	....	....

USHL All-Rookie Team (2000) • USHL Second All-Star Team (2000)

BIERK, Zac (BUHRK, ZAK) PHX.

Goaltender. Catches left. 6'4", 205 lbs. Born, Peterborough, Ont., September 17, 1976.
(Tampa Bay's 8th choice, 212th overall, in 1995 Entry Draft).

			Regular Season								Playoffs						
Season	**Club**	**League**	**GP**	**W**	**L**	**T**	**Mins**	**GA**	**SO**	**Avg**	**GP**	**W**	**L**	**Mins**	**GA**	**SO**	**Avg**
1993-94	Peterborough	OPJHL	4	....	....	....	205	17	0	4.98	....	....	....	....	....	....	....
	Peterborough	OHL	9	0	4	2	423	37	0	5.22	1	0	0	33	7	0	12.70
1994-95	Peterborough	OHL	35	11	15	5	1779	117	0	3.95	6	2	3	301	24	0	4.78
1995-96	Peterborough	OHL	58	31	16	6	3292	174	2	3.17	*22	*14	7	*1383	83	0	3.60
1996-97	Peterborough	OHL	49	*28	16	0	2744	151	2	3.30	11	6	5	666	35	0	3.15
1997-98	**Tampa Bay**	**NHL**	**13**	**1**	**4**	**1**	**433**	**30**	**0**	**4.16**	....	....	....	....	....	....	....
	Adirondack	AHL	12	1	6	1	557	36	0	3.87	....	....	....	....	....	....	....
1998-99	**Tampa Bay**	**NHL**	**1**	**0**	**1**	**0**	**59**	**2**	**0**	**2.03**	....	....	....	....	....	....	....
	Cleveland	IHL	27	11	12	4	1556	79	0	3.05	....	....	....	....	....	....	....
99-2000	**Tampa Bay**	**NHL**	**12**	**4**	**4**	**1**	**509**	**31**	**0**	**3.65**	....	....	....	....	....	....	....
	Detroit Vipers	IHL	15	4	8	2	846	46	1	3.26	....	....	....	....	....	....	....
2000-01	**Minnesota**	**NHL**	**1**	**0**	**1**	**0**	**60**	**6**	**0**	**6.00**	....	....	....	....	....	....	....
	Cleveland	IHL	49	24	18	5	2785	134	6	2.89	4	0	3	182	10	0	3.29
2001-02	Augusta Lynx	ECHL	30	16	9	3	1748	68	1	2.33	....	....	....	....	....	....	....
	Springfield Falcons	AHL	1	0	1	0	20	4	0	12.00	....	....	....	....	....	....	....
2002-03	**Phoenix**	**NHL**	**16**	**4**	**9**	**1**	**884**	**32**	**1**	**2.17**	....	....	....	....	....	....	....
	Springfield Falcons	AHL	13	6	4	1	685	33	0	2.89	....	....	....	....	....	....	....
	NHL Totals		**43**	**9**	**19**	**3**	**1945**	**101**	**1**	**3.12**	....	....	....	....	....	....	....

CHL Second All-Star Team (1997) • OHL First All-Star Team (1997)

• Missed remainder of 1998-99 season recovering from Meniere's Disease which was diagnosed on March 25, 1999. Claimed by **Minnesota** from **Tampa Bay** in Expansion Draft, June 23, 2000. Signed as a free agent by **Phoenix**, August 30, 2001.

BILLINGTON, Craig (BIHL-lihng-tohn, KRAYG)

Goaltender. Catches left. 5'10", 170 lbs. Born, London, Ont., September 11, 1966.
(New Jersey's 2nd choice, 23rd overall, in 1984 Entry Draft).

			Regular Season								Playoffs						
Season	**Club**	**League**	**GP**	**W**	**L**	**T**	**Mins**	**GA**	**SO**	**Avg**	**GP**	**W**	**L**	**Mins**	**GA**	**SO**	**Avg**
1982-83	London Diamonds	OJHL-B	23	....	....	....	1338	76	0	3.41	....	....	....	....	....	....	....
1983-84	Belleville Bulls	OHL	44	20	19	0	2335	162	1	4.16	1	0	0	30	3	0	6.00
1984-85	Belleville Bulls	OHL	47	26	19	0	2544	180	1	4.25	14	7	5	761	47	1	3.71
1985-86	Belleville Bulls	OHL	3	2	1	0	180	11	0	3.67	20	9	6	1133	68	0	3.60
	New Jersey	**NHL**	**18**	**4**	**9**	**1**	**901**	**77**	**0**	**5.13**	....	....	....	....	....	....	....
1986-87	**New Jersey**	**NHL**	**22**	**4**	**13**	**2**	**1114**	**89**	**0**	**4.79**	....	....	....	....	....	....	....
	Maine Mariners	AHL	20	9	8	2	1151	70	0	3.65	....	....	....	....	....	....	....
1987-88	Utica Devils	AHL	*59	22	27	8	*3404	208	1	3.67	....	....	....	....	....	....	....

1988-89	New Jersey	NHL	3	1	1	0	140	11	0	4.71							
	Utica Devils	AHL	41	17	18	6	2432	150	2	3.70	4	1	3	220	18	0	4.91
1989-90	Utica Devils	AHL	38	20	13	1	2087	138	0	3.97							
1990-91	Canada	Nat-Tm	34	17	14	2	1879	110	2	3.51							
1991-92	New Jersey	NHL	26	13	7	1	1363	69	2	3.04							
1992-93	New Jersey	NHL	42	21	16	4	2389	146	2	3.67	2	0	1	78	5	0	3.85
1993-94	Ottawa	NHL	63	11	41	4	3319	254	0	4.59							
1994-95	Ottawa	NHL	9	0	6	2	472	32	0	4.07							
	Boston	NHL	8	5	1	0	373	19	0	3.06	1	0	0	25	1	0	2.40
1995-96	Boston	NHL	27	10	13	3	1380	79	1	3.43	1	0	1	60	6	0	6.00
1996-97	Colorado	NHL	23	11	8	2	1200	53	1	2.65	1	0	0	20	1	0	3.00
1997-98	Colorado	NHL	23	8	7	4	1162	45	1	2.32	1	0	0	1	0	0	0.00
1998-99	Colorado	NHL	21	11	8	1	1086	52	0	2.87	1	0	0	9	1	0	6.67
99-2000	Washington	NHL	13	3	6	1	611	28	2	2.75	1	0	0	20	1	0	3.00
2000-01	Washington	NHL	12	3	5	2	660	27	0	2.45							
2001-02	Washington	NHL	17	4	5	3	710	36	0	3.04							
2002-03	Washington	NHL	5	1	3	1	217	17	0	4.70							
	NHL Totals		332	110	149	31	17097	1034	9	3.63	8	0	2	213	15	0	4.23

OHL First All-Star Team (1985)

Played in NHL All-Star Game (1993)

Traded to **Ottawa** by **New Jersey** with Troy Mallette and New Jersey's 4th round choice (Cosmo Dupaul) in 1993 Entry Draft for Peter Sidorkiewicz and future considerations (Mike Peluso, June 26, 1993), June 20, 1993. Traded to **Boston** by **Ottawa** for NY Islanders' 8th round choice (previously acquired, Ottawa selected Ray Schultz) in 1995 Entry Draft, April 7, 1995. Signed as a free agent by **Florida**, September 5, 1996. Claimed by **Colorado** from **Florida** in Waiver Draft, September 30, 1996. Traded to **Washington** by **Colorado** for future considerations, July 16, 1999. • Officially announced retirement, January 7, 2003.

BIRON, Martin (BIH-rohn, MAHR-tihn) BUF.

Goaltender. Catches left. 6'2", 168 lbs. Born, Lac-St-Charles, Que., August 15, 1977.
(Buffalo's 2nd choice, 16th overall, in 1995 Entry Draft).

							Regular Season							Playoffs			
Season	Club	League	GP	W	L	T	Mins	GA	SO	Avg	GP	W	L	Mins	GA	SO	Avg
1993-94	Trois-Rivieres	QAAA	23	14	8	1	1412	80	1	3.40	2	1	1	112	7	0	3.73
1994-95	Beauport Harfangs	QMJHL	56	29	16	9	3193	132	3	*2.48	16	8	7	900	37	*4	2.47
1995-96	Beauport Harfangs	QMJHL	55	29	17	7	3201	152	1	2.85	*19	*12	7	1134	64	0	3.39
	Buffalo	NHL	3	0	2	0	119	10	0	5.04							
1996-97	Beauport Harfangs	QMJHL	18	6	9	1	928	61	1	3.94							
	Hull Olympiques	QMJHL	16	11	4	1	974	43	2	2.65	6	3	1	325	19	0	3.51
1997-98	South Carolina	ECHL	2	0	1	1	86	3	0	2.09							
	Rochester	AHL	41	14	18	6	2312	113	*5	2.93	4	1	3	239	16	0	4.01
1998-99	Buffalo	NHL	6	1	2	1	281	10	0	2.14							
	Rochester	AHL	52	36	13	3	3129	108	*6	*2.07	*20	12	8	1167	42	1	*2.16
99-2000	Buffalo	NHL	41	19	18	2	2229	90	5	2.42							
	Rochester	AHL	6	6	0	0	344	12	1	2.09							
2000-01	Buffalo	NHL	18	7	7	1	918	39	2	2.55							
	Rochester	AHL	4	3	1	0	239	4	1	1.00							
2001-02	Buffalo	NHL	72	31	28	10	4085	151	4	2.22							
2002-03	Buffalo	NHL	54	17	28	6	3170	135	4	2.56							
	NHL Totals		194	75	85	20	10802	435	15	2.42							

QMJHL All-Rookie Team (1995) • QMJHL Defensive Rookie of the Year (1995) • Canadian Major Junior First All-Star Team (1995) • Canadian Major Junior Goaltender of the Year (1995) • AHL First All-Star Team (1999) • Shared Harry "Hap" Holmes Memorial Trophy (fewest goals against – AHL) (1999) with Tom Draper • Baz Bastien Memorial Trophy (Top Goaltender – AHL) (1999)

BLACKBURN, Dan (BLAK-buhrn, DAN) NYR

Goaltender. Catches left. 6', 180 lbs. Born, Montreal, Que., May 20, 1983.
(NY Rangers' 1st choice, 10th overall, in 2001 Entry Draft).

							Regular Season							Playoffs			
Season	Club	League	GP	W	L	T	Mins	GA	SO	Avg	GP	W	L	Mins	GA	SO	Avg
1997-98	Bow Valley Eagles	AJHL	20	9	6	1	1039	58	1	3.35	3	0	0	97	8	0	4.95
1998-99	Bow Valley Eagles	AJHL	38	7	19	6	1941	146	0	4.51	2	0	2	118	8	0	4.07
99-2000	Kootenay Ice	WHL	51	34	8	7	3004	126	3	2.52	*21	*16	5	*1272	43	2	*2.03
2000-01	Kootenay Ice	WHL	50	*33	14	2	2922	135	1	2.77	11	7	4	706	23	1	1.95
2001-02	NY Rangers	NHL	31	12	16	0	1737	95	0	3.28							
	Hartford Wolf Pack	AHL	4	2	1	1	244	11	0	2.71							
2002-03	NY Rangers	NHL	32	8	16	4	1762	93	1	3.17							
	NHL Totals		63	20	32	4	3499	188	1	3.22							

AJHL Scholastic Player of the Year (1998, 1999) • WHL East First All-Star Team (2001) • Canadian Major Junior First All-Star Team (2001) • Canadian Major Junior Goaltender of the Year (2001) • NHL All-Rookie Team (2002)

BOISCLAIR, Daniel (BWUH-klair, DAN-yehl) CAR.

Goaltender. Catches left. 6'2", 180 lbs. Born, St. Ang. de Desmaures, Que., November 2, 1982.
(Carolina's 5th choice, 181st overall, in 2001 Entry Draft).

							Regular Season							Playoffs			
Season	Club	League	GP	W	L	T	Mins	GA	SO	Avg	GP	W	L	Mins	GA	SO	Avg
1998-99	Charles-Lemoyne	QAAA	25	14	7	2	1360	69	0	3.04							
99-2000	Cape Breton	QMJHL	29	7	14	1	1421	95	0	4.01	3	0	1	86	6	0	4.21
2000-01	Cape Breton	QMJHL	47	16	23	2	2426	161	0	3.98	12	5	6	685	36	0	3.16
2001-02	Cape Breton	QMJHL	25	9	10	2	1151	73	1	3.81							
	Victoriaville Tigres	QMJHL	15	5	5	3	780	42	0	3.23	*19	*13	6	*1107	53	0	2.87
2002-03	Florida Everblades	ECHL	4	0	2	1	224	15	0	4.03							

• Missed majority of 2002-03 season after being diagnosed with anemia, November 19, 2002.

BOUCHER, Brian (BOO-shay, BRIGH-uhn) PHX.

Goaltender. Catches left. 6'2", 190 lbs. Born, Woonsocket, RI, January 2, 1977.
(Philadelphia's 1st choice, 22nd overall, in 1995 Entry Draft).

							Regular Season							Playoffs			
Season	Club	League	GP	W	L	T	Mins	GA	SO	Avg	GP	W	L	Mins	GA	SO	Avg
1993-94	Mount St. Charles	H.S.	15	*14	0	1	*504	*8	*9	*0.57	4	*4	0	*180	*6	*1	*1.20
1994-95	Wexford Raiders	MTJHL	8	....	....	....	425	23	0	3.25							
	Tri-City Americans	WHL	35	17	11	2	1969	108	1	3.29	13	6	5	795	50	0	3.77
1995-96	Tri-City Americans	WHL	55	33	19	2	3183	181	1	3.41	11	6	5	653	37	*2	3.40
1996-97	Tri-City Americans	WHL	41	10	24	6	2458	149	1	3.64							
1997-98	Philadelphia	AHL	34	16	12	3	1901	101	0	3.19	2	0	0	30	1	0	1.95
1998-99	Philadelphia	AHL	36	20	8	5	2061	89	2	2.59	16	9	7	947	45	0	2.85
99-2000	Philadelphia	NHL	35	20	10	3	2038	65	4	*1.91	18	11	7	1183	40	1	2.03
	Philadelphia	AHL	1	0	0	1	65	3	0	2.77							
2000-01	Philadelphia	NHL	27	8	12	5	1470	80	1	3.27	1	0	0	37	3	0	4.86
2001-02	Philadelphia	NHL	41	18	16	4	2295	92	2	2.41	2	0	1	88	2	0	1.36
2002-03	Phoenix	NHL	45	15	20	8	2544	128	0	3.02							
	NHL Totals		148	61	58	20	8347	365	7	2.62	21	11	8	1308	45	1	2.06

WHL West Second All-Star Team (1996) • WHL West First All-Star Team (1997) • NHL All-Rookie Team (2000)

Traded to **Phoenix** by **Philadelphia** with Nashville's 3rd round choice (previously acquired, Phoenix selected Joe Callahan) in 2002 Entry Draft for Michal Handzus and Robert Esche, June 12, 2002.

BOUCHER, Nick (BOO-shay, NIHK) PIT.

Goaltender. Catches left. 5'11", 175 lbs. Born, Leduc, Alta., December 29, 1980.
(Pittsburgh's 10th choice, 280th overall, in 2000 Entry Draft).

							Regular Season							Playoffs			
Season	Club	League	GP	W	L	T	Mins	GA	SO	Avg	GP	W	L	Mins	GA	SO	Avg
1997-98	Cowichan	BCHL	20	6	7	0	918	65	0	4.25							
1998-99	Cowichan	BCHL	10	3	5	0	464	40	0	5.17							
	Ft. Saskatchewan	AJHL	22	11	9	2	1243	70	1	3.38	7	3	4	420	24	3	3.43
99-2000	Dartmouth	ECAC	24	8	12	3	1378	66	1	2.87							
2000-01	Dartmouth	ECAC	*33	*16	12	4	*1966	84	1	2.56							
2001-02	Dartmouth	ECAC	21	9	7	4	1187	57	1	2.88							
2002-03	Dartmouth	ECAC	27	17	9	0	1602	80	0	3.00							

BOUTIN, Jonathan (boo-TEHN, JAWN-ah-thun) T.B.

Goaltender. Catches left. 6'1", 200 lbs. Born, Granby, Que., March 28, 1985.
(Tampa Bay's 3rd choice, 96th overall, in 2003 Entry Draft).

							Regular Season							Playoffs			
Season	Club	League	GP	W	L	T	Mins	GA	SO	Avg	GP	W	L	Mins	GA	SO	Avg
2001-02	Halifax	QMJHL	11	4	1	1	459	18	0	2.35	2	0	0	15	0	0	0.00
2002-03	Halifax	QMJHL	47	22	11	2	2190	106	4	2.90	1	0	0	27	0	0	0.00

BRATHWAITE, Fred (BRAYTH-wayt, FREHD) CBJ

Goaltender. Catches left. 5'7", 175 lbs. Born, Ottawa, Ont., November 24, 1972.

							Regular Season							Playoffs			
Season	Club	League	GP	W	L	T	Mins	GA	SO	Avg	GP	W	L	Mins	GA	SO	Avg
1988-89	Smiths Falls Bears	COJHL	38	16	18	1	2130	187	0	5.27							
1989-90	Orillia Terriers	OJHL-B	15	....	....	....	782	47	0	3.61							
	Oshawa Generals	OHL	20	11	2	1	886	43	1	2.91	10	4	2	451	22	0	*2.93
1990-91	Oshawa Generals	OHL	39	25	6	3	1986	112	1	3.38	13	*9	2	677	43	0	3.81
1991-92	Oshawa Generals	OHL	24	12	7	2	1248	81	0	3.89							
	London Knights	OHL	23	15	6	2	1325	61	*4	2.76	10	5	5	615	36	0	3.51
1992-93	Detroit	OHL	37	23	10	4	2192	134	0	3.67	15	9	6	858	48	1	3.36
1993-94	Edmonton	NHL	19	3	10	3	982	58	0	3.54							
	Cape Breton Oilers	AHL	2	1	1	0	119	6	0	3.04							
1994-95	Edmonton	NHL	14	2	5	1	601	40	0	3.99							
1995-96	Edmonton	NHL	7	0	2	0	293	12	0	2.46							
	Cape Breton Oilers	AHL	31	12	16	0	1699	110	1	3.88							
1996-97	Manitoba Moose	IHL	58	22	22	5	2945	167	1	3.40							
1997-98	Manitoba Moose	IHL	51	23	18	4	2736	138	1	3.03	2	0	1	72	4	0	3.30
1998-99	Canada	Nat-Tm	24	6	8	3	989	47	2	2.85							
	Calgary	NHL	28	11	9	7	1663	68	1	2.45							
99-2000	Calgary	NHL	61	25	25	7	3448	158	5	2.75							
	Saint John Flames	AHL	2	2	0	0	120	4	0	2.00							
2000-01	Calgary	NHL	49	15	17	10	2742	106	5	2.32							
2001-02	St. Louis	NHL	25	9	11	4	1446	54	2	2.24	1	0	0	1	0	0	0.00
2002-03	St. Louis	NHL	30	12	9	4	1615	74	2	2.75							
	NHL Totals		233	77	88	36	12790	570	15	2.67	1	0	0	1	0	0	0.00

• Scored a goal while with Detroit (OHL), April 20, 1993. • Scored a goal while with Manitoba (IHL), November 9, 1996.Signed as a free agent by **Edmonton**, October 6, 1993. Signed as a free agent by **Calgary**, January 6, 1999. Traded to **St. Louis** by **Calgary** with Daniel Tkaczuk, Sergei Varlamov and Calgary's 9th round choice (Grant Jacobsen) in 2001 Entry Draft for Roman Turek and St. Louis' 4th round choice (Yegor Shastin) in 2001 Entry Draft, June 23, 2001. • Played 6 seconds of playoff game vs. Detroit, May 4, 2002. Signed as a free agent by **Columbus**, June 2, 2003.

BROCHU, Martin (broh-SHOO, MAHR-tihn) PIT.

Goaltender. Catches left. 6', 199 lbs. Born, Anjou, Que., March 10, 1973.

							Regular Season							Playoffs			
Season	Club	League	GP	W	L	T	Mins	GA	SO	Avg	GP	W	L	Mins	GA	SO	Avg
1989-90	Montreal-Bourassa	QAAA	27	11	14	1	1471	103	3	4.20	3	1	2	193	10	1	3.10
1990-91	Granby Bisons	QMJHL	16	6	5	0	622	39	....	3.76							
1991-92	Granby Bisons	QMJHL	52	15	29	2	2772	278	0	4.72							
1992-93	Hull Olympiques	QMJHL	29	9	15	1	1453	137	0	5.66	2	0	1	69	7	0	6.07
1993-94	Fredericton	AHL	32	10	11	3	1505	76	2	3.03							
1994-95	Fredericton	AHL	44	18	18	4	2475	145	0	3.51							
1995-96	Fredericton	AHL	17	6	8	2	986	70	0	4.26							
	Wheeling	ECHL	19	10	6	2	1060	51	1	2.89							
	Portland Pirates	AHL	5	2	2	1	287	15	0	3.14	12	7	4	700	28	*2	*2.40
1996-97	Portland Pirates	AHL	55	23	17	7	2962	150	2	3.04	5	2	3	324	13	0	2.41
1997-98	Portland Pirates	AHL	37	16	14	1	1926	96	2	2.99	6	3	2	296	16	0	3.24
1998-99	Washington	NHL	2	0	2	0	120	6	0	3.00							
	Portland Pirates	AHL	20	6	10	3	1164	57	2	2.94							
	Utah Grizzlies	IHL	5	1	3	1	298	13	0	2.62							
99-2000	Portland Pirates	AHL	54	32	15	6	3192	116	4	2.18	2	0	2	80	7	0	5.27
2000-01	Saint John Flames	AHL	55	27	19	5	3049	132	2	2.60	19	*14	4	1148	39	*4	2.04
2001-02	Vancouver	NHL	6	0	3	0	216	15	0	4.17							
	Manitoba Moose	AHL	29	10	14	3	1625	91	1	3.36							
2002-03	Verdun Dragons	QSPHL	1	1	0	0	60	2	0	2.00							
	Cherepovets	Russia	8	....	....	....	480	15	2	1.88							
	NHL Totals		8	0	5	0	336	21	0	3.75							

AHL First All-Star Team (2000) • Baz Bastien Memorial Trophy (Top Goaltender – AHL) (2000) • Les Cunningham Award (MVP – AHL) (2000)

Signed as a free agent by **Montreal**, September 22, 1992. Traded to **Washington** by **Montreal** for future considerations, March 15, 1996. Signed as a free agent by **Calgary**, August 25, 2000. Signed as a free agent by **Minnesota**, July 17, 2001. Claimed by **Vancouver** from **Minnesota** in Waiver Draft, September 28, 2001. Signed as a free agent by **Verdun** (QSPHL), October 22, 2002.Signed as a free agent by **Pittsburgh**, August 22, 2003.

BRODEUR, Martin (broh-DOOR, MAHR-tihn) N.J.

Goaltender. Catches left. 6'2", 210 lbs. Born, Montreal, Que., May 6, 1972.
(New Jersey's 1st choice, 20th overall, in 1990 Entry Draft).

							Regular Season							Playoffs			
Season	Club	League	GP	W	L	T	Mins	GA	SO	Avg	GP	W	L	Mins	GA	SO	Avg
1988-89	Montreal-Bourassa	QAAA	27	13	12	1	1580	98	0	3.72	3	0	3	210	14	0	3.99
1989-90	St-Hyacinthe Laser	QMJHL	42	23	13	2	2333	156	0	4.01	12	5	7	678	46	0	4.07
1990-91	St-Hyacinthe Laser	QMJHL	52	22	24	4	2946	162	2	3.30	4	0	4	232	16	0	4.14
1991-92	St-Hyacinthe Laser	QMJHL	48	27	16	4	2846	161	2	3.39	5	2	3	317	14	0	2.65
	New Jersey	NHL	4	2	1	0	179	10	0	3.35	1	0	1	32	3	0	5.63
1992-93	Utica Devils	AHL	32	14	13	5	1952	131	0	4.03	4	1	3	258	18	0	4.19
1993-94	New Jersey	NHL	47	27	11	8	2625	105	3	2.40	17	8	9	1171	38	1	1.95
1994-95♦	New Jersey	NHL	40	19	11	6	2184	89	3	2.45	*20	*16	4	*1222	34	*3	*1.67
1995-96	New Jersey	NHL	77	34	30	12	*4433	173	6	2.34							
1996-97	New Jersey	NHL	67	37	14	13	3838	120	*10	*1.88	10	5	5	659	19	2	*1.73
1997-98	New Jersey	NHL	70	*43	17	8	4128	130	10	1.89	6	2	4	366	12	0	1.97
1998-99	New Jersey	NHL	*70	*39	21	10	*4239	162	4	2.29	7	3	4	425	20	0	2.82
99-2000♦	New Jersey	NHL	72	*43	20	8	4312	161	6	2.24	*23	*16	7	*1450	39	2	*1.61
2000-01	New Jersey	NHL	72	*42	17	11	4297	166	9	2.32	*25	15	10	*1505	52	*4	2.07

2001-02	**New Jersey**	**NHL**	***73**	**38**	**26**	**9**	***4347**	**156**	**4**	**2.15**	**6**	**2**	**4**	**381**	**9**	**1**	**1.42**
	Canada	Olympics	5	*4	0	1	300	9	0	*1.80	....	....	....	....	....	....	....
2002-03 ♦	**New Jersey**	**NHL**	**73**	***41**	**23**	**9**	**4374**	**147**	***9**	**2.02**	***24**	***16**	**8**	***1491**	**41**	***7**	**1.65**
	NHL Totals		**665**	**365**	**191**	**94**	**38956**	**1419**	**64**	**2.19**	**139**	**83**	**56**	**8702**	**267**	**20**	**1.84**

QMJHL All-Rookie Team (1990) • QMJHL Second All-Star Team (1992) • NHL All-Rookie Team (1994) • Calder Memorial Trophy (1994) • NHL Second All-Star Team (1997, 1998) • Shared William M. Jennings Trophy (1997) with Mike Dunham • William M. Jennings Trophy (1998) • NHL First All-Star Team (2003) • William M. Jennings Trophy (2003) (tied with Roman Cechmanek/Robert Esche) • Vezina Trophy (2003)

Played in NHL All-Star Game (1996, 1997, 1998, 1999, 2000, 2001, 2003)

• Scored a goal in playoffs vs. Montreal, April 17, 1997.

BROWN, Mike (BROWN, MIGHK) BOS.

Goaltender. Catches left. 6', 177 lbs. Born, Syracuse, NY, March 4, 1985.
(Boston's 7th choice, 153rd overall, in 2003 Entry Draft).

			Regular Season								Playoffs						
Season	**Club**	**League**	**GP**	**W**	**L**	**T**	**Mins**	**GA**	**SO**	**Avg**	**GP**	**W**	**L**	**Mins**	**GA**	**SO**	**Avg**
2001-02	Baldwinsville Bees	Hi-School	7	....	....	....	420	8	4	0.86	5	3	2	300	6	1	1.20
2002-03	Saginaw Spirit	OHL	39	8	23	3	2186	134	0	3.68	....	....	....	....	....	....	....

BRUCKLER, Bernd (BRUK-luhr, BUHRND) PHI.

Goaltender. Catches left. 6'1", 180 lbs. Born, Graz, Austria, September 26, 1981.
(Philadelphia's 4th choice, 150th overall, in 2001 Entry Draft).

			Regular Season								Playoffs						
Season	**Club**	**League**	**GP**	**W**	**L**	**T**	**Mins**	**GA**	**SO**	**Avg**	**GP**	**W**	**L**	**Mins**	**GA**	**SO**	**Avg**
1997-98	EC Graz	Austria	2	....	....	....	61	11	0	10.82	....	....	....	....	....	....	....
1998-99	Ponoka	HJHL					STATISTICS NOT AVAILABLE										
99-2000	EC Graz	Austria-Jr.					STATISTICS NOT AVAILABLE										
2000-01	Tri-City Storm	USHL	28	15	8	3	1624	67	2	2.48	7	3	4	459	21	1	2.75
2001-02	U. of Wisconsin	WCHA	18	6	8	2	973	50	1	3.08	....	....	....	....	....	....	....
2002-03	U. of Wisconsin	WCHA	24	9	11	3	1358	64	0	2.83	....	....	....	....	....	....	....

USHL Second All-Star Team (2001) • WCHA All-Rookie Team (2002)

BRUST, Barry (BRUHST, BAIR-ree) MIN.

Goaltender. Catches left. 6'2", 221 lbs. Born, Swan River, Man., August 8, 1983.
(Minnesota's 4th choice, 73rd overall, in 2002 Entry Draft).

			Regular Season								Playoffs						
Season	**Club**	**League**	**GP**	**W**	**L**	**T**	**Mins**	**GA**	**SO**	**Avg**	**GP**	**W**	**L**	**Mins**	**GA**	**SO**	**Avg**
99-2000	Swan Valley	MJHL	19	10	9	0	1140	67	0	3.50	....	....	....	....	....	....	....
2000-01	Spokane Chiefs	WHL	16	4	6	1	777	42	0	3.24	....	....	....	....	....	....	....
2001-02	Spokane Chiefs	WHL	60	28	21	10	3540	152	1	2.58	11	6	5	677	23	0	2.04
2002-03	Spokane Chiefs	WHL	*59	22	31	4	*3385	194	0	3.44	11	4	7	722	37	0	3.07

WHL West First All-Star Team (2002)

BRYZGALOV, Ilya (breez-GAH-lahf, ihl-YUH) ANA.

Goaltender. Catches left. 6'3", 198 lbs. Born, Togliatti, USSR, June 22, 1980.
(Anaheim's 2nd choice, 44th overall, in 2000 Entry Draft).

			Regular Season								Playoffs						
Season	**Club**	**League**	**GP**	**W**	**L**	**T**	**Mins**	**GA**	**SO**	**Avg**	**GP**	**W**	**L**	**Mins**	**GA**	**SO**	**Avg**
1997-98	Lada Togliatti 2	Russia-3	8	....	....	....	480	28	....	3.50	....	....	....	....	....	....	....
1998-99	Lada Togliatti 2	Russia-4	20	....	....	....	1200	43	....	2.15	....	....	....	....	....	....	....
99-2000	Spartak Moscow	Russia-2	9	....	....	....	500	21	....	2.52	....	....	....	....	....	....	....
	Lada Togliatti	Russia	14	....	....	....	796	18	3	1.36	7	....	....	407	10	1	1.47
2000-01	Lada Togliatti	Russia	34	....	....	....	1992	61	*8	1.84	5	....	....	249	8	0	1.93
2001-02	**Anaheim**	**NHL**	**1**	**0**	**0**	**0**	**32**	**1**	**0**	**1.88**	....	....	....	....	....	....	....
	Cincinnati	AHL	45	20	16	4	2399	99	4	2.48	....	....	....	....	....	....	....
	Russia	Olympics					DID NOT PLAY – SPARE GOALTENDER										
2002-03	Cincinnati	AHL	54	12	26	9	3020	142	1	2.82	....	....	....	....	....	....	....
	NHL Totals		**1**	**0**	**0**	**0**	**32**	**1**	**0**	**1.88**	....	....	....	....	....	....	....

BUDAJ, Peter (BOO-digh, PEE-tuhr) COL.

Goaltender. Catches left. 6', 200 lbs. Born, Bystrica, Czech., September 18, 1982.
(Colorado's 1st choice, 63rd overall, in 2001 Entry Draft).

			Regular Season								Playoffs						
Season	**Club**	**League**	**GP**	**W**	**L**	**T**	**Mins**	**GA**	**SO**	**Avg**	**GP**	**W**	**L**	**Mins**	**GA**	**SO**	**Avg**
99-2000	St. Michael's	OHL	34	6	18	1	1676	112	1	4.01	....	....	....	....	....	....	....
2000-01	St. Michael's	OHL	37	17	12	3	1996	95	3	2.86	11	6	4	621	26	1	2.51
2001-02	St. Michael's	OHL	42	26	9	5	2329	89	2	*2.29	12	5	6	620	34	*1	3.29
2002-03	Hershey Bears	AHL	28	10	10	2	1467	65	2	2.66	1	0	0	6	2	0	20.81

OHL Second All-Star Team (2002)

BURKE, Sean (BUHRK, SHAWN) PHX.

Goaltender. Catches left. 6'4", 211 lbs. Born, Windsor, Ont., January 29, 1967.
(New Jersey's 2nd choice, 24th overall, in 1985 Entry Draft).

			Regular Season								Playoffs						
Season	**Club**	**League**	**GP**	**W**	**L**	**T**	**Mins**	**GA**	**SO**	**Avg**	**GP**	**W**	**L**	**Mins**	**GA**	**SO**	**Avg**
1983-84	St. Michael's B	MTJHL	25	....	....	....	1482	120	0	4.86	....	....	....	....	....	....	....
1984-85	Toronto Marlboros	OHL	49	25	21	3	2987	211	0	4.24	5	1	3	266	25	0	5.64
1985-86	Toronto Marlboros	OHL	47	16	27	3	2840	233	0	4.92	4	0	4	238	24	0	6.05
1986-87	Canada	Nat-Tm	42	27	13	2	2550	130	0	3.05	....	....	....	....	....	....	....
1987-88	Canada	Nat-Tm	37	19	9	2	1962	92	1	2.81	....	....	....	....	....	....	....
	Canada	Olympics	4	1	2	1	238	12	0	3.02	....	....	....	....	....	....	....
	New Jersey	**NHL**	**13**	**10**	**1**	**0**	**689**	**35**	**1**	**3.05**	**17**	**9**	**8**	**1001**	**57**	***1**	**3.42**
1988-89	**New Jersey**	**NHL**	**62**	**22**	**31**	**9**	**3590**	**230**	**3**	**3.84**	....	....	....	....	....	....	....
1989-90	**New Jersey**	**NHL**	**52**	**22**	**22**	**6**	**2914**	**175**	**0**	**3.60**	**2**	**0**	**2**	**125**	**8**	**0**	**3.84**
1990-91	**New Jersey**	**NHL**	**35**	**8**	**12**	**8**	**1870**	**112**	**0**	**3.59**	....	....	....	....	....	....	....
1991-92	Canada	Nat-Tm	31	18	6	4	1721	75	1	2.61	....	....	....	....	....	....	....
	Canada	Olympics	7	5	2	0	429	17	0	2.37	....	....	....	....	....	....	....
	San Diego Gulls	IHL	7	4	2	1	424	17	0	2.41	3	0	3	160	13	0	4.88
1992-93	**Hartford**	**NHL**	**50**	**16**	**27**	**3**	**2656**	**184**	**0**	**4.16**	....	....	....	....	....	....	....
1993-94	**Hartford**	**NHL**	**47**	**17**	**24**	**5**	**2750**	**137**	**2**	**2.99**	....	....	....	....	....	....	....
1994-95	**Hartford**	**NHL**	**42**	**17**	**19**	**4**	**2418**	**108**	**0**	**2.68**	....	....	....	....	....	....	....
1995-96	**Hartford**	**NHL**	**66**	**28**	**28**	**6**	**3669**	**190**	**4**	**3.11**	....	....	....	....	....	....	....
1996-97	**Hartford**	**NHL**	**51**	**22**	**22**	**6**	**2985**	**134**	**4**	**2.69**	....	....	....	....	....	....	....
1997-98	**Carolina**	**NHL**	**25**	**7**	**11**	**5**	**1415**	**66**	**1**	**2.80**	....	....	....	....	....	....	....
	Vancouver	**NHL**	**16**	**2**	**9**	**4**	**838**	**49**	**0**	**3.51**	....	....	....	....	....	....	....
	Philadelphia	**NHL**	**11**	**7**	**3**	**0**	**632**	**27**	**1**	**2.56**	**5**	**1**	**4**	**283**	**17**	**0**	**3.60**
1998-99	**Florida**	**NHL**	**59**	**21**	**24**	**14**	**3402**	**151**	**3**	**2.66**	....	....	....	....	....	....	....
99-2000	**Florida**	**NHL**	**7**	**2**	**5**	**0**	**418**	**18**	**0**	**2.58**	....	....	....	....	....	....	....
	Phoenix	**NHL**	**35**	**17**	**14**	**3**	**2074**	**88**	**3**	**2.55**	**5**	**1**	**4**	**296**	**16**	**0**	**3.24**
2000-01	**Phoenix**	**NHL**	**62**	**25**	**22**	**13**	**3644**	**138**	**4**	**2.27**	....	....	....	....	....	....	....
2001-02	**Phoenix**	**NHL**	**60**	**33**	**21**	**6**	**3587**	**137**	**5**	**2.29**	**5**	**1**	**4**	**297**	**13**	**0**	**2.63**
2002-03	**Phoenix**	**NHL**	**22**	**12**	**6**	**2**	**1248**	**44**	**2**	**2.12**	....	....	....	....	....	....	....
	NHL Totals		**715**	**288**	**301**	**94**	**40799**	**2023**	**33**	**2.98**	**34**	**12**	**22**	**2002**	**111**	**1**	**3.33**

Played in NHL All-Star Game (1989, 2001, 2002)

Traded to **Hartford** by **New Jersey** with Eric Weinrich for Bobby Holik and Hartford's 2nd round choice (Jay Pandolfo) in 1993 Entry Draft, August 28, 1992. Transferred to **Carolina** after **Hartford** franchise relocated, June 25, 1997. Traded to **Vancouver** by **Carolina** with Geoff Sanderson and Enrico Ciccone for Kirk McLean and Martin Gelinas, January 3, 1998. Traded to **Philadelphia** by **Vancouver** for Garth Snow, March 4, 1998. Signed as a free agent by **Florida**, September 12, 1998. Traded to **Phoenix** by **Florida** with Florida's 5th round choice (Nate Kiser) in 2000 Entry Draft for Mikhail Shtalenkov and Phoenix's 4th round choice (Chris Eade) in 2000 Entry Draft, November 18, 1999.

CARON, Sebastian (KAIR-aw, suh-BAS-tee-yeh) PIT.

Goaltender. Catches left. 6'1", 170 lbs. Born, Amqui, Que., June 25, 1980.
(Pittsburgh's 4th choice, 86th overall, in 1999 Entry Draft).

			Regular Season								Playoffs						
Season	**Club**	**League**	**GP**	**W**	**L**	**T**	**Mins**	**GA**	**SO**	**Avg**	**GP**	**W**	**L**	**Mins**	**GA**	**SO**	**Avg**
1997-98	TGV Pentagone	QAHA	17	....	....	....	762	48	1	2.84	....	....	....	....	....	....	....
1998-99	Rimouski Oceanic	QMJHL	30	13	10	3	1570	85	0	3.25	2	1	0	68	0	0	0.00
99-2000	Rimouski Oceanic	QMJHL	54	*38	11	3	3040	179	1	3.53	14	*12	2	828	50	0	3.62
2000-01	Wilkes-Barre	AHL	30	12	14	3	1746	103	4	3.54	....	....	....	....	....	....	....
2001-02	Wilkes-Barre	AHL	46	14	22	8	2671	139	1	3.12	....	....	....	....	....	....	....
2002-03	**Pittsburgh**	**NHL**	**24**	**7**	**14**	**2**	**1408**	**62**	**2**	**2.64**	....	....	....	....	....	....	....
	Wilkes-Barre	AHL	27	12	14	1	1561	81	1	3.11	....	....	....	....	....	....	....
	NHL Totals		**24**	**7**	**14**	**2**	**1408**	**62**	**2**	**2.64**	....	....	....	....	....	....	....

Memorial Cup All-Star Team (2000) • Hap Emms Memorial Trophy (Memorial Cup Top Goaltender) (2000) • NHL All-Rookie Team (2003)

CASSIVI, Frederic (KASS-ih-vee, FREHD-uhr-ihk) ATL.

Goaltender. Catches left. 6'4", 215 lbs. Born, Sorel, Que., June 12, 1975.
(Ottawa's 7th choice, 210th overall, in 1994 Entry Draft).

			Regular Season								Playoffs						
Season	**Club**	**League**	**GP**	**W**	**L**	**T**	**Mins**	**GA**	**SO**	**Avg**	**GP**	**W**	**L**	**Mins**	**GA**	**SO**	**Avg**
1991-92	Abitibi Forestiers	QAAA	22	5	17	0	1320	106	0	4.84	3	1	2	180	15	0	5.06
1992-93							STATISTICS NOT AVAILABLE										
1993-94	St-Hyacinthe Laser	QMJHL	35	15	13	3	1751	127	1	4.35	....	....	....	....	....	....	....
1994-95	Halifax	QMJHL	24	9	12	1	1362	105	0	4.63	....	....	....	....	....	....	....
	St-Jean Lynx	QMJHL	19	12	6	0	1021	55	1	3.23	5	2	3	258	18	0	4.19
1995-96	Thunder Bay	ColHL	12	6	4	2	715	51	0	4.28	....	....	....	....	....	....	....
	P.E.I. Senators	AHL	41	20	14	3	2347	128	1	3.27	5	2	3	317	24	0	4.54
1996-97	Syracuse Crunch	AHL	55	23	22	8	3069	164	2	3.21	1	0	1	60	3	0	3.01
1997-98	Worcester IceCats	AHL	45	20	22	2	2593	140	1	3.24	6	3	3	326	18	0	3.31
1998-99	Cincinnati	IHL	44	21	17	2	2418	123	1	3.05	3	1	2	139	6	0	2.59
99-2000	Hershey Bears	AHL	31	14	9	3	1554	78	1	3.01	2	0	1	63	5	0	4.75
2000-01	Hershey Bears	AHL	49	17	24	3	2620	124	2	2.84	9	7	2	564	14	1	*1.49
2001-02	Hershey Bears	AHL	21	6	10	4	1201	50	0	2.50	....	....	....	....	....	....	....
	Atlanta	**NHL**	**6**	**2**	**3**	**0**	**307**	**17**	**0**	**3.32**	....	....	....	....	....	....	....
	Chicago Wolves	AHL	12	6	2	1	625	26	0	2.50	5	2	2	264	11	0	2.50
2002-03	Chicago Wolves	AHL	21	10	8	1	1171	62	0	3.18	2	0	2	90	3	0	2.00
	Atlanta	**NHL**	**2**	**1**	**1**	**0**	**123**	**11**	**0**	**5.37**	....	....	....	....	....	....	....
	NHL Totals		**8**	**3**	**4**	**0**	**430**	**28**	**0**	**3.91**	....	....	....	....	....	....	....

Signed as a free agent by **Colorado**, August 17, 1999. Traded to **Atlanta** by **Colorado** for Brett Clark, January 24, 2002.

CECHMANEK, Roman (chehkh-MAN-ehk, ROH-muhn) L.A.

Goaltender. Catches left. 6'3", 187 lbs. Born, Gottwaldov, Czech., March 2, 1971.
(Philadelphia's 3rd choice, 171st overall, in 2000 Entry Draft).

			Regular Season								Playoffs						
Season	**Club**	**League**	**GP**	**W**	**L**	**T**	**Mins**	**GA**	**SO**	**Avg**	**GP**	**W**	**L**	**Mins**	**GA**	**SO**	**Avg**
1988-89	TJ Gottwaldov	Czech	1	0	0	0	13	0	0	0.00	....	....	....	....	....	....	....
1989-90	TJ Zlin	Czech	2	0	0	0	89	5	0	3.37	....	....	....	....	....	....	....
1990-91	Dukla Jihlava	Czech	9	....	....	....	447	18	2	2.42	....	....	....	....	....	....	....
1991-92	DS Olomouc	Czech	13	....	....	....	731	54	0	4.43	....	....	....	....	....	....	....
	AC ZPS Zlin	Czech	2	0	1	0	67	8	0	7.73	....	....	....	....	....	....	....
1992-93	Banik Hodonin	Czech-2					STATISTICS NOT AVAILABLE										
1993-94	HC Zbojovka Vsetin	Czech-2					STATISTICS NOT AVAILABLE										
1994-95	HC Dadak Vsetin	Czech	41	....	....	....	2413	98	5	2.44	11	....	....	619	23	1	2.23
1995-96	HC Petra Vsetin	Czech	36	....	....	....	2142	77	4	2.16	13	....	....	783	17	2	1.30
1996-97	HC Petra Vsetin	Czech	48	....	....	....	2762	98	3	2.13	10	....	....	602	11	2	1.10
1997-98	HC Petra Vsetin	Czech	41	....	....	....	2306	76	....	*1.98	10	....	....	600	16	1	*1.60
1998-99	HC Slovnaft Vsetin	Czech	45	....	....	....	2696	77	5	*1.71	12	8	4	*747	23	1	1.85
99-2000	HC Slovnaft Vsetin	Czech	37	....	....	....	2141	88	0	2.47	9	5	4	545	15	3	1.65
2000-01	**Philadelphia**	**NHL**	**59**	**35**	**15**	**6**	**3431**	**115**	**10**	**2.01**	**6**	**2**	**4**	**347**	**18**	**0**	**3.11**
	Philadelphia	AHL	3	1	1	0	160	3	0	1.12	....	....	....	....	....	....	....
2001-02	**Philadelphia**	**NHL**	**46**	**24**	**13**	**6**	**2603**	**89**	**4**	**2.05**	**4**	**1**	**3**	**227**	**7**	**1**	**1.85**
	Czech Republic	Olympics					DID NOT PLAY – SPARE GOALTENDER										
2002-03	**Philadelphia**	**NHL**	**58**	**33**	**15**	**10**	**3350**	**102**	**6**	**1.83**	**13**	**6**	**7**	**867**	**31**	**2**	**2.15**
	NHL Totals		**163**	**92**	**43**	**22**	**9384**	**306**	**20**	**1.96**	**23**	**9**	**14**	**1441**	**56**	**3**	**2.33**

NHL Second All-Star Team (2001) • Shared William M. Jennings Trophy (2003) with Robert Esche (tied with Martin Brodeur)

Played in NHL All-Star Game (2001)

Traded to **Los Angeles** by **Philadelphia** for Los Angeles' 2nd round choice in 2004 Entry Draft, May 28, 2003.

CENTOMO, Sebastien (sehn-TOH-moh, suh-BAS-tee-yeh) TOR.

Goaltender. Catches right. 6'1", 200 lbs. Born, Montreal, Que., March 26, 1981.

			Regular Season								Playoffs						
Season	**Club**	**League**	**GP**	**W**	**L**	**T**	**Mins**	**GA**	**SO**	**Avg**	**GP**	**W**	**L**	**Mins**	**GA**	**SO**	**Avg**
1997-98	Laval Laurentide	QAAA	30	16	11	2	1696	87	0	2.86	....	....	....	....	....	....	....
1998-99	Rouyn-Noranda	QMJHL	32	14	9	4	1658	104	1	3.76	2	0	1	28	5	0	10.71
99-2000	Rouyn-Noranda	QMJHL	50	24	17	3	2758	160	1	3.48	11	6	5	695	41	0	3.54
2000-01	Rouyn-Noranda	QMJHL	46	25	14	4	2599	158	3	3.65	1	0	1	60	4	0	4.00
2001-02	**Toronto**	**NHL**	**1**	**0**	**0**	**0**	**40**	**3**	**0**	**4.50**	....	....	....	....	....	....	....
	Memphis	CHL	19	16	1	0	1035	36	1	2.09	....	....	....	....	....	....	....
	St. John's	AHL	25	12	7	4	1429	60	2	2.52	11	4	6	691	29	2	2.52
2002-03	St. John's	AHL	19	7	10	1	1045	68	0	3.90	....	....	....	....	....	....	....
	Greensboro	ECHL	10	3	3	3	565	24	1	2.55	....	....	....	....	....	....	....
	NHL Totals		**1**	**0**	**0**	**0**	**40**	**3**	**0**	**4.50**	....	....	....	....	....	....	....

CHL Rookie of the Year (2002)

Signed as a free agent by **Toronto**, September 10, 1999.

CHARPENTIER, Sebastien (shahr-PUHNT-yay, suh-BAS-tee-yeh) WSH.

Goaltender. Catches left. 5'9", 177 lbs. Born, Drummondville, Que., April 18, 1977.
(Washington's 4th choice, 93rd overall, in 1995 Entry Draft).

			Regular Season								Playoffs						
Season	**Club**	**League**	**GP**	**W**	**L**	**T**	**Mins**	**GA**	**SO**	**Avg**	**GP**	**W**	**L**	**Mins**	**GA**	**SO**	**Avg**
1991-92	Drummondville	QAHA	14	....	....	....	840	34	2	2.42	....	....	....	....	....	....	....
1992-93	Drummondville	QAHA	20	....	....	....	1215	37	*7	*1.80	....	....	....	....	....	....	....
1993-94	Magog	QAAA	24	14	5	1	1443	75	1	3.16	....	....	....	....	....	....	....

1994-95	Laval Titan	QMJHL	41	25	12	1	2152	99	2	2.76	16	9	4	886	45	0	3.05
1995-96	Laval Titan	QMJHL	18	4	10	0	938	97	0	6.20	....	....	....	....	....	....	....
	Val-d'Or Foreurs	QMJHL	33	21	9	1	1906	87	1	2.74	13	7	5	740	45	0	3.64
1996-97	Shawinigan	QMJHL	*62	*37	17	4	*3480	177	1	3.05	4	2	1	196	13	0	3.98
1997-98	Portland Pirates	AHL	4	1	3	0	229	10	0	2.61	....	....	....	....	....	....	....
	Hampton Roads	ECHL	43	20	16	6	2388	114	0	2.86	18	*14	4	*1183	38	1	*1.93
1998-99	Quad City Mallards	UHL	6	0	0	0	4	0	0	0.00	....	....	....	....	....	....	....
	Portland Pirates	AHL	3	0	3	0	180	10	0	3.34	....	....	....	....	....	....	....
99-2000	Portland Pirates	AHL	18	10	4	3	1041	48	0	2.77	3	1	1	183	9	0	2.96
2000-01	Portland Pirates	AHL	34	16	16	1	1978	113	1	3.43	1	0	1	102	3	0	1.76
2001-02	**Washington**	**NHL**	**2**	**1**	**1**	**0**	**122**	**5**	**0**	**2.46**	....	....	....	....	....	....	....
	Portland Pirates	AHL	49	20	18	10	2941	131	3	2.67	....	....	....	....	....	....	....
2002-03	**Washington**	**NHL**	**17**	**5**	**7**	**1**	**859**	**40**	**0**	**2.79**	....	....	....	....	....	....	....
	Porland Pirates	AHL	12	3	7	2	727	28	2	2.31	....	....	....	....	....	....	....
	NHL Totals		**19**	**6**	**8**	**1**	**981**	**45**	**0**	**2.75**	....	....	....	....	....	....	....

ECHL Playoff MVP (1998)

CHIODO, Andy (KEE-aw-doh, AN-dee) PIT.

Goaltender. Catches left. 5'11", 201 lbs. Born, Toronto, Ont., April 25, 1983.
(Pittsburgh's 8th choice, 199th overall, in 2003 Entry Draft).

			Regular Season								Playoffs						
Season	Club	League	GP	W	L	T	Mins	GA	SO	Avg	GP	W	L	Mins	GA	SO	Avg
1998-99	Wexford Raiders	OPJHL	26	....	....	....	1519	105	0	4.05	....	....	....	....	....	....	....
99-2000	Wexford Raiders	OPJHL	24	....	....	....	1389	89	0	3.84	....	....	....	....	....	....	....
2000-01	St. Michael's	OHL	38	18	12	5	2069	86	*4	2.49	9	2	6	479	30	0	3.76
2001-02	St. Michael's	OHL	33	14	10	3	1743	79	2	2.72	7	3	1	288	17	*1	3.54
2002-03	St. Michael's	OHL	57	26	18	6	3065	154	3	3.01	18	10	8	1021	56	1	3.29

• Re-entered NHL Entry Draft. Originally NY Islanders' 3rd choice, 166th overall, in 2001 Entry Draft.

OHL First All-Star Team (2003)

CHOUINARD, Mathieu (SHWEE-nuhr, ma-TEW) L.A.

Goaltender. Catches left. 6'1", 211 lbs. Born, Laval, Que., April 11, 1980.
(Ottawa's 2nd choice, 45th overall, in 2000 Entry Draft).

			Regular Season								Playoffs						
Season	Club	League	GP	W	L	T	Mins	GA	SO	Avg	GP	W	L	Mins	GA	SO	Avg
1995-96	Amos Forestiers	QAAA	31	14	14	1	1613	114	1	4.24	1	1	2	190	11	0	3.48
1996-97	Shawinigan	QMJHL	17	4	7	1	795	51	0	3.85	4	1	3	264	15	0	3.41
1997-98	Shawinigan	QMJHL	55	*32	18	3	3055	142	2	2.79	6	2	4	348	24	0	4.14
1998-99	Shawinigan	QMJHL	56	36	16	4	3288	150	*5	2.74	6	2	4	392	27	0	4.13
99-2000	Shawinigan	QMJHL	*59	32	20	5	*3339	186	4	3.34	13	7	6	769	41	0	3.20
2000-01	Grand Rapids	IHL	28	17	7	1	1567	69	1	2.64	3	1	1	135	4	0	1.78
2001-02	Grand Rapids	AHL	25	11	12	1	1404	58	2	2.48	....	....	....	....	....	....	....
2002-03	Binghamton	AHL	4	2	0	0	152	5	0	1.98	1	0	0	2	0	0	0.00
	Peoria Rivermen	ECHL	15	12	2	0	820	29	3	2.12	....	....	....	....	....	....	....

• Re-entered NHL Entry Draft. Originally Ottawa's 1st choice, 15th overall, in 1998 Entry Draft.

QMJHL First All-Star Team (1999) • Shared Harry "Hap" Holmes Memorial Trophy (fewest goals against – AHL) (2002) with Martin Prusek and Simon Lajeunesse

Signed as a free agent by **Los Angeles**, July 7, 2003.

CLEMMENSEN, Scott (KLEH-mehn-sehn, SKAWT) N.J.

Goaltender. Catches left. 6'2", 205 lbs. Born, Des Moines, IA, July 23, 1977.
(New Jersey's 7th choice, 215th overall, in 1997 Entry Draft).

			Regular Season								Playoffs						
Season	Club	League	GP	W	L	T	Mins	GA	SO	Avg	GP	W	L	Mins	GA	SO	Avg
1995-96	Des Moines	USHL	20	10	7	1	1082	62	0	3.44	....	....	....	....	....	....	....
1996-97	Des Moines	USHL	36	22	9	2	2042	111	1	3.26	4	1	2	200	9	1	2.70
1997-98	Boston College	H-East	37	24	9	4	2205	102	*4	2.78	....	....	....	....	....	....	....
1998-99	Boston College	H-East	*42	26	12	4	*2507	120	1	2.87	....	....	....	....	....	....	....
99-2000	Boston College	H-East	29	19	7	0	1610	59	*5	2.20	....	....	....	....	....	....	....
2000-01	Boston College	H-East	*39	*30	7	2	*2312	82	3	2.13	....	....	....	....	....	....	....
2001-02	**New Jersey**	**NHL**	**2**	**0**	**0**	**0**	**20**	**1**	**0**	**3.00**	....	....	....	....	....	....	....
	Albany River Rats	AHL	29	5	19	4	1677	92	0	3.29	....	....	....	....	....	....	....
2002-03	Albany River Rats	AHL	47	12	24	8	2694	119	1	2.65	....	....	....	....	....	....	....
	NHL Totals		**2**	**0**	**0**	**0**	**20**	**1**	**0**	**3.00**	....	....	....	....	....	....	....

NCAA Championship All-Tournament Team (2001)

CLOUTIER, Dan (KLOO-tyay, DAN) VAN.

Goaltender. Catches left. 6'1", 182 lbs. Born, Mont-Laurier, Que., April 22, 1976.
(NY Rangers' 1st choice, 26th overall, in 1994 Entry Draft).

			Regular Season								Playoffs						
Season	Club	League	GP	W	L	T	Mins	GA	SO	Avg	GP	W	L	Mins	GA	SO	Avg
1991-92	St. Thomas Stars	OJHL-B	14	....	....	....	823	80	0	5.83	....	....	....	....	....	....	....
1992-93	Timmins	NOJHA	5	4	0	0	255	10	0	2.35	....	....	....	....	....	....	....
	Sault Ste. Marie	OHL	12	4	6	0	572	44	0	4.62	4	1	2	231	12	0	3.12
1993-94	Sault Ste. Marie	OHL	55	28	14	6	2934	174	*2	3.56	14	*10	4	833	52	0	3.75
1994-95	Sault Ste. Marie	OHL	45	15	26	2	2518	185	1	4.41	....	....	....	....	....	....	....
1995-96	Sault Ste. Marie	OHL	13	9	3	0	641	43	0	4.02	....	....	....	....	....	....	....
	Guelph Storm	OHL	17	12	2	2	1004	35	2	2.09	16	11	5	993	52	*2	3.14
1996-97	Binghamton	AHL	60	23	28	8	3367	199	3	3.55	4	1	3	236	13	0	3.31
1997-98	**NY Rangers**	**NHL**	**12**	**4**	**5**	**1**	**551**	**23**	**0**	**2.50**	....	....	....	....	....	....	....
	Hartford Wolf Pack	AHL	24	12	8	3	1417	62	0	2.63	8	5	3	478	24	0	3.01
1998-99	**NY Rangers**	**NHL**	**22**	**6**	**8**	**3**	**1097**	**49**	**0**	**2.68**	....	....	....	....	....	....	....
99-2000	**Tampa Bay**	**NHL**	**52**	**9**	**30**	**3**	**2492**	**145**	**0**	**3.49**	....	....	....	....	....	....	....
2000-01	**Tampa Bay**	**NHL**	**24**	**3**	**13**	**3**	**1005**	**59**	**1**	**3.52**	....	....	....	....	....	....	....
	Detroit Vipers	IHL	1	0	1	0	59	3	0	3.05	....	....	....	....	....	....	....
	Vancouver	**NHL**	**16**	**4**	**6**	**5**	**914**	**37**	**0**	**2.43**	**2**	**0**	**2**	**117**	**9**	**0**	**4.62**
2001-02	**Vancouver**	**NHL**	**62**	**31**	**22**	**5**	**3502**	**142**	**7**	**2.43**	**6**	**2**	**3**	**273**	**16**	**0**	**3.52**
2002-03	**Vancouver**	**NHL**	**57**	**33**	**16**	**7**	**3376**	**136**	**2**	**2.42**	**14**	**7**	**7**	**833**	**45**	**0**	**3.24**
	NHL Totals		**245**	**90**	**100**	**27**	**12937**	**591**	**10**	**2.74**	**22**	**9**	**12**	**1223**	**70**	**0**	**3.43**

OHL Second All-Star Team (1996)

Traded to **Tampa Bay** by **NY Rangers** with Niklas Sundstrom and NY Rangers' 1st (Nikita Alexeev) and 3rd (later traded to San Jose – later traded to Chicago – Chicago selected Igor Radulov) round choices in 2000 Entry Draft for Chicago's 1st round choice (previously acquired, NY Rangers selected Pavel Brendl) in 1999 Entry Draft, June 26, 1999. Traded to **Vancouver** by **Tampa Bay** for Adrian Aucoin and Vancouver's 2nd round choice (Alexander Polushin) in 2001 Entry Draft, February 7, 2001.

CLOUTIER, Frederic (KLOO-tyay, FREHD-uhr-ihk) MIN.

Goaltender. Catches right. 6', 165 lbs. Born, St-Georges, Que., May 14, 1981.

			Regular Season								Playoffs						
Season	Club	League	GP	W	L	T	Mins	GA	SO	Avg	GP	W	L	Mins	GA	SO	Avg
1996-97	Cap-d-Madeleine	QAAA	24	5	16	2	1400	105	0	4.37	....	....	....	....	....	....	....
1997-98	Levis	QAAA	28	18	9	1	1680	106	0	3.77	3	0	3	180	10	0	3.72
1998-99	Acadie-Bathurst	QMJHL	8	2	3	0	383	30	0	4.70	....	....	....	....	....	....	....
99-2000	Acadie-Bathurst	QMJHL	58	16	34	6	3262	208	3	3.83	....	....	....	....	....	....	....
2000-01	Acadie-Bathurst	QMJHL	58	*42	8	2	3270	136	*6	*2.50	9	5	2	467	24	1	3.08
2001-02	Louisiana	ECHL	36	28	5	3	2155	66	*7	*1.84	1	0	1	115	5	0	2.60
2002-03	Louisiana	ECHL	26	16	6	4	1578	80	1	3.04	....	....	....	....	....	....	....
	Houston Aeros	AHL	12	4	3	2	586	24	0	2.46	....	....	....	....	....	....	....

QMJHL First All-Star Team (2001) • QMJHL Top Goaltender (2001) • ECHL All-Rookie Team (2002) • ECHL First All-Star Team (2002) • ECHL Rookie of the Year (2002) • ECHL Top Goaltender (2002) • ECHL MVP (2002)

Signed as a free agent by **Minnesota**, November 23, 2001.

CONKLIN, Ty (KAWN-klihn, TIGH) EDM.

Goaltender. Catches left. 6', 180 lbs. Born, Anchorage, AK, March 30, 1976.

			Regular Season								Playoffs						
Season	Club	League	GP	W	L	T	Mins	GA	SO	Avg	GP	W	L	Mins	GA	SO	Avg
1995-96	Green Bay	USHL	30	....	....	....	1727	82	1	2.85	....	....	....	....	....	....	....
1996-97	Alaska-Anchorage	WCHA	DID NOT PLAY – FRESHMAN														
	Green Bay	USHL	30	19	7	1	1609	86	1	3.21	17	8	9	980	56	1	3.43
1997-98	New Hampshire	H-East	DID NOT PLAY – TRANSFERRED COLLEGES														
1998-99	New Hampshire	H-East	22	18	3	1	1338	41	0	*1.84	....	....	....	....	....	....	....
99-2000	New Hampshire	H-East	*37	*22	8	6	*2194	91	2	2.49	....	....	....	....	....	....	....
2000-01	New Hampshire	H-East	34	17	12	5	2048	70	*5	*2.05	....	....	....	....	....	....	....
2001-02	**Edmonton**	**NHL**	**4**	**2**	**0**	**0**	**148**	**4**	**0**	**1.62**	....	....	....	....	....	....	....
	Hamilton Bulldogs	AHL	37	13	12	8	2043	89	1	2.61	7	4	2	416	18	0	2.60
2002-03	Hamilton Bulldogs	AHL	38	19	13	3	2140	91	4	2.55	17	9	6	1024	38	1	2.23
	NHL Totals		**4**	**2**	**0**	**0**	**148**	**4**	**0**	**1.62**	....	....	....	....	....	....	....

USHL Second All-Star Team (1996) • Hockey East All-Rookie Team (1999) • Hockey East Second All-Star Team (1999) • Hockey East First All-Star Team (2000, 2001) • Hockey East Player of the Year (2000) (co-winner - Mike Mottau) • NCAA East Second All-American Team (2000) • NCAA East First All-American Team (2001) • Walter Brown Award (New England's Outstanding American-born College player) (2001) (co-winner - Brian Gionta)

• Left **Alaska-Anchorage** (WCHA) and returned to **Green Bay** (USHL), November 14, 1996. • First goaltender to be named captain of **New Hampshire** (H-East) since 1961, October 5, 2000. Signed as a free agent by **Edmonton**, April 18, 2001.

CRAWFORD, Corey (KRAW-fohrd, KOHR-ee) CHI.

Goaltender. Catches left. 6'2", 178 lbs. Born, Montreal, Que., December 31, 1984.
(Chicago's 2nd choice, 52nd overall, in 2003 Entry Draft).

			Regular Season								Playoffs						
Season	Club	League	GP	W	L	T	Mins	GA	SO	Avg	GP	W	L	Mins	GA	SO	Avg
2000-01	Gatineau Intrepide	QAAA	21	17	3	1	1260	40	2	1.92	....	....	....	....	....	....	....
2001-02	Moncton Wildcats	QMJHL	38	9	20	3	1863	116	1	3.74	....	....	....	....	....	....	....
2002-03	Moncton Wildcats	QMJHL	50	24	17	6	2855	130	2	2.73	6	2	3	303	20	0	3.97

CRAWFORD-WEST, Brandon (KRAW-fohrd-WEHST, BRAN-duhn) PIT.

Goaltender. Catches right. 5'11", 185 lbs. Born, San Diego, CA, July 1, 1982.
(Pittsburgh's 9th choice, 250th overall, in 2001 Entry Draft).

			Regular Season								Playoffs						
Season	Club	League	GP	W	L	T	Mins	GA	SO	Avg	GP	W	L	Mins	GA	SO	Avg
99-2000	Ventura Marines	WSHL	STATISTICS NOT AVAILABLE														
2000-01	Texas Tornado	NAJHL	43	30	9	3	2534	110	4	2.60	7	6	1	452	6	3	0.80
2001-02	Texas Tornado	NAJHL	50	35	11	2	2825	109	4	2.32	6	3	3	389	13	0	2.01
2002-03	Tri-City Storm	USHL	22	7	12	1	1207	61	0	3.03	....	....	....	....	....	....	....
	Bozeman Icedogs	AWHL	15	7	7	1	825	47	0	3.42	5	2	3	309	14	0	2.71

NAJHL All-Rookie Team (2001) • NAJHL Second All-Star Team (2001)

• Signed Letter of Intent to attend **Miami University** (CCHA), November 18, 2002. Signed as a free agent by **Bozeman** (AWHL) after securing release from **Tri-City** (USHL), December 22, 2002.

DAFOE, Byron (duh-FOH, BIGH-ruhn) ATL.

Goaltender. Catches left. 5'11", 200 lbs. Born, Sussex, England, February 25, 1971.
(Washington's 2nd choice, 35th overall, in 1989 Entry Draft).

			Regular Season								Playoffs						
Season	Club	League	GP	W	L	T	Mins	GA	SO	Avg	GP	W	L	Mins	GA	SO	Avg
1987-88	Juan de Fuca	BCJHL	32	....	....	....	1716	129	0	4.51	....	....	....	....	....	....	....
1988-89	Portland	WHL	59	29	24	3	3279	291	1	5.32	*18	10	8	*1091	81	*1	4.45
1989-90	Portland	WHL	40	14	21	3	2265	193	0	5.11	....	....	....	....	....	....	....
1990-91	Portland	WHL	8	1	5	1	414	41	0	5.94	....	....	....	....	....	....	....
	Prince Albert	WHL	32	13	12	4	1839	124	0	4.05	....	....	....	....	....	....	....
1991-92	Baltimore Skipjacks	AHL	33	12	16	4	1847	119	0	3.87	....	....	....	....	....	....	....
	New Haven	AHL	7	3	2	1	364	22	0	3.63	....	....	....	....	....	....	....
	Hampton Roads	ECHL	10	6	4	0	562	26	0	2.78	....	....	....	....	....	....	....
1992-93	**Washington**	**NHL**	**1**	**0**	**0**	**0**	**1**	**0**	**0**	**0.00**	....	....	....	....	....	....	....
	Baltimore Skipjacks	AHL	48	16	20	7	2617	191	1	4.38	5	2	3	241	22	0	5.48
1993-94	**Washington**	**NHL**	**5**	**2**	**2**	**0**	**230**	**13**	**0**	**3.39**	**2**	**0**	**2**	**118**	**5**	**0**	**2.54**
	Portland Pirates	AHL	47	24	16	4	2661	148	1	3.34	1	0	0	9	1	0	6.79
1994-95	**Washington**	**NHL**	**4**	**1**	**1**	**1**	**187**	**11**	**0**	**3.53**	**1**	**0**	**0**	**20**	**1**	**0**	**3.00**
	Phoenix	IHL	49	25	16	6	2743	169	2	3.70	....	....	....	....	....	....	....
	Portland Pirates	AHL	6	5	0	0	330	16	0	2.91	7	3	4	416	29	0	4.18
1995-96	**Los Angeles**	**NHL**	**47**	**14**	**24**	**8**	**2666**	**172**	**1**	**3.87**	....	....	....	....	....	....	....
1996-97	**Los Angeles**	**NHL**	**40**	**13**	**17**	**5**	**2162**	**112**	**0**	**3.11**	....	....	....	....	....	....	....
1997-98	**Boston**	**NHL**	**65**	**30**	**25**	**9**	**3693**	**138**	**6**	**2.24**	**6**	**2**	**4**	**422**	**14**	**1**	**1.99**
1998-99	**Boston**	**NHL**	**68**	**32**	**23**	**11**	**4001**	**133**	***10**	**1.99**	**12**	**6**	**6**	**768**	**26**	**2**	**2.03**
99-2000	**Boston**	**NHL**	**41**	**13**	**16**	**10**	**2307**	**114**	**3**	**2.96**	....	....	....	....	....	....	....
2000-01	**Boston**	**NHL**	**45**	**22**	**14**	**7**	**2536**	**101**	**2**	**2.39**	....	....	....	....	....	....	....
2001-02	**Boston**	**NHL**	**64**	**35**	**26**	**3**	**3827**	**141**	**4**	**2.21**	**6**	**2**	**4**	**358**	**19**	**0**	**3.18**
2002-03	**Atlanta**	**NHL**	**17**	**5**	**11**	**1**	**895**	**65**	**0**	**4.36**	....	....	....	....	....	....	....
	NHL Totals		**397**	**167**	**159**	**55**	**22505**	**1000**	**26**	**2.67**	**27**	**10**	**16**	**1686**	**65**	**3**	**2.31**

AHL First All-Star Team (1994) • Shared Harry "Hap" Holmes Memorial Trophy (fewest goals against – AHL) (1994) with Olaf Kolzig • NHL Second All-Star Team (1999)

Traded to **Los Angeles** by **Washington** with Dmitri Khristich for Los Angeles' 1st round choice (Alexandre Volchkov) in 1996 Entry Draft and Dallas' 4th round choice (previously acquired, Washington selected Justin Davis) in 1996 Entry Draft, July 8, 1995. Traded to **Boston** by **Los Angeles** with Dimitri Khristich for Jozef Stumpel, Sandy Moger and Boston's 4th round choice (later traded to New Jersey – New Jersey selected Pierre Dagenais) in 1998 Entry Draft, August 29, 1997. Signed as a free agent by **Atlanta**, November 19, 2002.

DAIGNEAULT, Maxime (DAYN-yoh, mahx-EEM) WSH.

Goaltender. Catches left. 6'1", 185 lbs. Born, St-Jacques-le-Mineur, Que., January 23, 1984.
(Washington's 4th choice, 59th overall, in 2002 Entry Draft).

			Regular Season								Playoffs						
Season	Club	League	GP	W	L	T	Mins	GA	SO	Avg	GP	W	L	Mins	GA	SO	Avg
99-2000	Cap-d-Madeleine	QAAA	19	12	3	3	1108	53	3	2.87	18	12	5	945	42	1	2.67
2000-01	Val-d'Or Foreurs	QMJHL	28	14	8	1	1386	82	0	3.55	10	8	1	504	21	0	2.50
2001-02	Val-d'Or Foreurs	QMJHL	61	25	27	5	3270	184	3	3.38	7	3	4	431	23	0	3.20
2002-03	Val-d'Or Foreurs	QMJHL	48	23	18	3	2694	138	2	3.07	8	4	3	487	23	1	2.83

Memorial Cup All-Star Team (2002) • Hap Emms Memorial Trophy (Memorial Cup Top Goaltender) (2002)

DAMPHOUSSE, Jean-Francois (DAHM-fooz, ZHAWN-fran-SWUH) MTL.

Goaltender. Catches left. 6', 180 lbs. Born, St-Alexis-des-Monts, Que., July 21, 1979.
(New Jersey's 1st choice, 24th overall, in 1997 Entry Draft).

			Regular Season								Playoffs						
Season	**Club**	**League**	**GP**	**W**	**L**	**T**	**Mins**	**GA**	**SO**	**Avg**	**GP**	**W**	**L**	**Mins**	**GA**	**SO**	**Avg**
1993-94	Ste-Foy	QAHA	18	10	1	0	1078	53	0	2.95	14	10	4	842	50	0	3.52
1994-95	Ste-Foy	QAHA	16	....	....	....	958	48	0	3.01	....	....	....	....	....	....	....
	Ste-Foy	QAAA	2	1	0	1	120	8	0	3.84	....	....	....	....	....	....	....
1995-96	Ste-Foy	QAAA	32	18	10	1	1629	83	2	3.06	....	....	....	....	....	....	....
1996-97	Moncton Wildcats	QMJHL	39	6	25	2	2063	190	0	5.53	....	....	....	....	....	....	....
1997-98	Moncton Wildcats	QMJHL	59	24	26	6	3400	174	1	3.07	10	5	5	595	28	0	2.82
1998-99	Moncton Wildcats	QMJHL	40	19	17	2	2163	121	1	3.36	4	0	4	200	12	0	3.60
	Albany River Rats	AHL	1	0	1	0	59	3	0	3.06	....	....	....	....	....	....	....
99-2000	Augusta Lynx	ECHL	14	4	7	0	676	49	0	4.35	....	....	....	....	....	....	....
	Albany River Rats	AHL	26	9	11	2	1326	62	0	2.81	2	0	1	62	4	0	3.86
2000-01	Albany River Rats	AHL	55	24	23	3	2963	141	1	2.86	....	....	....	....	....	....	....
2001-02	**New Jersey**	**NHL**	**6**	**1**	**3**	**0**	**294**	**12**	**0**	**2.45**	....	....	....	....	....	....	....
	Albany River Rats	AHL	18	3	11	2	1001	57	0	3.42	....	....	....	....	....	....	....
2002-03	Cincinnati	AHL	31	12	14	4	1669	87	0	3.13	....	....	....	....	....	....	....
	Saint John Flames	AHL	10	5	5	0	591	23	0	2.33	....	....	....	....	....	....	....
	NHL Totals		**6**	**1**	**3**	**0**	**294**	**12**	**0**	**2.45**	....	....	....	....	....	....	....

Traded to **Anaheim** by **New Jersey** with Petr Sykora, Mike Commodore and Igor Pohanka for Jeff Friesen, Oleg Tverdovsky and Maxim Balmochnykh, July 6, 2002. Traded to **Calgary** by **Anaheim** with Mike Commodore for Rob Niedermayer, March 11, 2003. Signed as a free agent by **Montreal**, July 4, 2003.

DAVIS, Matt (DAY-vihs, MAT) NSH.

Goaltender. Catches left. 6'1", 198 lbs. Born, Harvey, N.B., April 28, 1984.
(Nashville's choice, 264th overall, in 2002 Entry Draft).

			Regular Season								Playoffs						
Season	**Club**	**League**	**GP**	**W**	**L**	**T**	**Mins**	**GA**	**SO**	**Avg**	**GP**	**W**	**L**	**Mins**	**GA**	**SO**	**Avg**
2000-01	Moncton Wildcats	QMJHL	18	0	9	2	776	75	0	5.80	....	....	....	....	....	....	....
2001-02	Moncton Wildcats	QMJHL	34	6	19	1	1617	102	1	3.78	....	....	....	....	....	....	....
2002-03	Moncton Wildcats	QMJHL	32	13	8	4	1524	82	1	3.23	1	0	1	54	3	0	3.33

DENIKE, Terry (deh-NIGHK, TEHR-ee) L.A.

Goaltender. Catches left. 6'2", 190 lbs. Born, Mississauga, Ont., April 16, 1981.
(Los Angeles' 7th choice, 152nd overall, in 2001 Entry Draft).

			Regular Season								Playoffs						
Season	**Club**	**League**	**GP**	**W**	**L**	**T**	**Mins**	**GA**	**SO**	**Avg**	**GP**	**W**	**L**	**Mins**	**GA**	**SO**	**Avg**
99-2000	Weyburn	SJHL	38	25	7	5	2171	108	2	2.99	....	....	....	....	....	....	....
2000-01	Weyburn	SJHL	43	28	14	0	2528	107	*6	*2.54	17	13	4	1005	47	0	2.81
2001-02	Lake Superior State	CCHA	16	3	10	0	700	42	0	3.60	....	....	....	....	....	....	....
2002-03	Lake Superior State	CCHA	19	2	5	1	704	45	0	3.84	....	....	....	....	....	....	....

SJHL Second All-Star Team (2001) • SJHL Dedication and Sportsmanship Award (2001) • SJHL Top Goaltender (2001)

DENIS, Marc (deh-NEE, MAHRK) CBJ

Goaltender. Catches left. 6'1", 190 lbs. Born, Montreal, Que., August 1, 1977.
(Colorado's 1st choice, 25th overall, in 1995 Entry Draft).

			Regular Season								Playoffs						
Season	**Club**	**League**	**GP**	**W**	**L**	**T**	**Mins**	**GA**	**SO**	**Avg**	**GP**	**W**	**L**	**Mins**	**GA**	**SO**	**Avg**
1992-93	Montreal-Bourassa	QAAA	26	....	....	....	1559	74	5	2.87	....	....	....	....	....	....	....
1993-94	Trois-Rivieres	QAAA	36	10	22	3	2093	158	0	4.53	4	1	3	249	20	0	4.83
1994-95	Chicoutimi	QMJHL	32	17	9	1	1688	98	0	3.48	6	4	2	372	19	1	3.06
1995-96	Chicoutimi	QMJHL	51	23	21	4	2951	157	2	3.19	16	8	8	957	69	0	4.33
1996-97	Chicoutimi	QMJHL	41	22	15	2	2323	104	4	*2.69	*21	*11	10	*1229	70	*1	3.42
	Colorado	**NHL**	**1**	**0**	**1**	**0**	**60**	**3**	**0**	**3.00**	....	....	....	....	....	....	....
	Hershey Bears	AHL	....	....	....	....	....	....	....	....	4	1	0	56	1	0	1.08
1997-98	Hershey Bears	AHL	47	17	23	4	2588	125	1	2.90	6	3	3	346	15	0	2.59
1998-99	**Colorado**	**NHL**	**4**	**1**	**1**	**1**	**217**	**9**	**0**	**2.49**	....	....	....	....	....	....	....
	Hershey Bears	AHL	52	20	23	5	2908	137	4	2.83	3	1	1	143	7	0	2.93
99-2000	**Colorado**	**NHL**	**23**	**9**	**8**	**3**	**1203**	**51**	**3**	**2.54**	....	....	....	....	....	....	....
2000-01	**Columbus**	**NHL**	**32**	**6**	**20**	**4**	**1830**	**99**	**0**	**3.25**	....	....	....	....	....	....	....
2001-02	**Columbus**	**NHL**	**42**	**9**	**24**	**5**	**2335**	**121**	**1**	**3.11**	....	....	....	....	....	....	....
2002-03	**Columbus**	**NHL**	***77**	**27**	**41**	**8**	***4511**	**232**	**5**	**3.09**	....	....	....	....	....	....	....
	NHL Totals		**179**	**52**	**95**	**21**	**10156**	**515**	**9**	**3.04**	....	....	....	....	....	....	....

QMJHL First All-Star Team (1997) • Canadian Major Junior First All-Star Team (1997) • Canadian Major Junior Goaltender of the Year (1997)

Traded to **Columbus** by **Colorado** for Columbus' 2nd round choice (later traded to Carolina – Carolina selected Tomas Kurka) in 2000 Entry Draft, June 7, 2000.

DESLAURIERS, Jeff (duh-LAW-ree-yay, JEHF) EDM.

Goaltender. Catches right. 6'3", 175 lbs. Born, St-Jean-Richelieu, Que., May 15, 1984.
(Edmonton's 2nd choice, 31st overall, in 2002 Entry Draft).

			Regular Season								Playoffs						
Season	**Club**	**League**	**GP**	**W**	**L**	**T**	**Mins**	**GA**	**SO**	**Avg**	**GP**	**W**	**L**	**Mins**	**GA**	**SO**	**Avg**
2000-01	Gatineau Intrepide	QAAA	22	10	9	2	1194	61	2	3.07	2	1	0	125	6	0	2.89
2001-02	Chicoutimi	QMJHL	51	28	20	1	2909	170	1	3.51	4	0	3	197	20	0	6.11
2002-03	Chicoutimi	QMJHL	54	18	24	1	2582	164	0	3.81	4	0	4	240	15	0	9.00

DesROCHERS, Patrick (duh-RAWSH-ay, PAT-rihk) CAR.

Goaltender. Catches left. 6'3", 209 lbs. Born, Penetanguishene, Ont., October 27, 1979.
(Phoenix's 1st choice, 14th overall, in 1998 Entry Draft).

			Regular Season								Playoffs						
Season	**Club**	**League**	**GP**	**W**	**L**	**T**	**Mins**	**GA**	**SO**	**Avg**	**GP**	**W**	**L**	**Mins**	**GA**	**SO**	**Avg**
1994-95	Barrie Colts	OPJHL	26	....	....	....	3205	179	3	3.08	....	....	....	....	....	....	....
1995-96	Sarnia Sting	OHL	29	12	6	2	1265	96	0	4.55	3	0	1	71	5	0	4.23
1996-97	Sarnia Sting	OHL	50	22	17	4	2667	154	*4	3.46	11	6	5	576	42	0	4.38
1997-98	Sarnia Sting	OHL	56	26	17	11	3205	179	1	3.35	4	1	2	160	12	0	4.50
1998-99	Sarnia Sting	OHL	8	3	5	0	425	26	0	3.67	....	....	....	....	....	....	....
	Kingston	OHL	44	14	22	3	2389	177	1	4.45	5	1	4	323	21	0	3.90
99-2000	Springfield Falcons	AHL	52	21	17	7	2710	137	1	3.03	2	1	1	120	7	1	3.50
2000-01	Springfield Falcons	AHL	50	17	24	5	2807	156	0	3.33	....	....	....	....	....	....	....
2001-02	Springfield Falcons	AHL	34	12	18	1	1864	94	2	3.03	....	....	....	....	....	....	....
	Phoenix	**NHL**	**5**	**1**	**2**	**1**	**243**	**15**	**0**	**3.70**	....	....	....	....	....	....	....
2002-03	**Phoenix**	**NHL**	**4**	**0**	**3**	**0**	**175**	**11**	**0**	**3.77**	....	....	....	....	....	....	....
	Springfield Falcons	AHL	8	2	4	1	454	20	0	2.64	....	....	....	....	....	....	....
	Carolina	**NHL**	**2**	**1**	**1**	**0**	**122**	**7**	**0**	**3.44**	....	....	....	....	....	....	....
	Lowell	AHL	17	4	12	1	1030	48	0	2.80	....	....	....	....	....	....	....
	NHL Totals		**11**	**2**	**6**	**1**	**540**	**33**	**0**	**3.67**	....	....	....	....	....	....	....

Traded to **Carolina** by **Phoenix** for Jean-Marc Pelletier and future considerations, December 31, 2002.

DiPIETRO, Rick (dee-pee-EHT-roh, RIHK) NYI

Goaltender. Catches right. 5'11", 185 lbs. Born, Winthrop, MA, September 19, 1981.
(NY Islanders' 1st choice, 1st overall, in 2000 Entry Draft).

			Regular Season								Playoffs						
Season	**Club**	**League**	**GP**	**W**	**L**	**T**	**Mins**	**GA**	**SO**	**Avg**	**GP**	**W**	**L**	**Mins**	**GA**	**SO**	**Avg**
1997-98	U.S. National U-18	USDP	46	21	19	0	2526	131	2	3.11	....	....	....	....	....	....	....
1998-99	U.S. National U-18	USDP	46	31	11	2	2760	113	2	2.46	....	....	....	....	....	....	....
99-2000	Boston University	H-East	29	18	5	5	1790	73	2	2.45	....	....	....	....	....	....	....
2000-01	**NY Islanders**	**NHL**	**20**	**3**	**15**	**1**	**1083**	**63**	**0**	**3.49**	....	....	....	....	....	....	....
	Chicago Wolves	IHL	14	4	5	2	778	44	0	3.39	....	....	....	....	....	....	....
2001-02	Bridgeport	AHL	59	*30	22	7	3472	134	4	2.32	20	12	8	*1270	45	*3	2.13
2002-03	Bridgeport	AHL	34	16	10	8	2044	73	3	2.14	5	2	3	299	10	1	2.01
	NY Islanders	**NHL**	**10**	**2**	**5**	**2**	**585**	**29**	**0**	**2.97**	**1**	**0**	**0**	**15**	**0**	**0**	**0.00**
	NHL Totals		**30**	**5**	**20**	**3**	**1668**	**92**	**0**	**3.31**	**1**	**0**	**0**	**15**	**0**	**0**	**0.00**

Hockey East Second All-Star Team (2000) • Hockey East Rookie of the Year (2000)

DIVIS, Reinhard (DIH-vihs, RIGHN-hard) ST.L.

Goaltender. Catches left. 5'11", 200 lbs. Born, Vienna, Austria, July 4, 1975.
(St. Louis' 8th choice, 261st overall, in 2000 Entry Draft).

			Regular Season								Playoffs						
Season	**Club**	**League**	**GP**	**W**	**L**	**T**	**Mins**	**GA**	**SO**	**Avg**	**GP**	**W**	**L**	**Mins**	**GA**	**SO**	**Avg**
1995-96	VEU Feldkirch	Austria	37	....	....	....	2200	85	0	2.32	....	....	....	....	....	....	....
1996-97	VEU Feldkirch	Alpenliga	45	....	....	....	2738	105	0	2.30	....	....	....	....	....	....	....
	VEU Feldkirch	Austria	....	....	....	....	....	....	....	....	11	....	....	620	27	0	2.61
1997-98	VEU Feldkirch	Alpenliga	13	....	....	....	779	22	0	1.69	....	....	....	....	....	....	....
	VEU Feldkirch	Austria	27	....	....	....	1620	55	0	2.07	....	....	....	....	....	....	....
1998-99	VEU Feldkirch	Austria	15	....	....	....	900	58	0	3.86	....	....	....	....	....	....	....
99-2000	Leksands IF	Sweden	48	....	....	....	2839	160	3	3.38	....	....	....	....	....	....	....
2000-01	Leksands IF	Sweden	41	....	....	....	2451	141	3	3.45	....	....	....	....	....	....	....
2001-02	**St. Louis**	**NHL**	**1**	**0**	**0**	**0**	**25**	**0**	**0**	**0.00**	....	....	....	....	....	....	....
	Worcester IceCats	AHL	55	28	20	5	3173	137	3	2.59	3	1	2	205	8	0	2.34
	Austria	Olympics	4	1	1	2	238	12	0	3.02	....	....	....	....	....	....	....
2002-03	**St. Louis**	**NHL**	**2**	**2**	**0**	**0**	**83**	**1**	**0**	**0.72**	....	....	....	....	....	....	....
	Worcester IceCats	AHL	9	6	1	0	453	17	0	2.25	....	....	....	....	....	....	....
	NHL Totals		**3**	**2**	**0**	**0**	**108**	**1**	**0**	**0.56**	....	....	....	....	....	....	....

DUBA, Tomas (DOO-bah, TAW-mash) PIT.

Goaltender. Catches left. 6', 176 lbs. Born, Prague, Czech., July 2, 1981.
(Pittsburgh's 8th choice, 217th overall, in 2001 Entry Draft).

			Regular Season								Playoffs						
Season	**Club**	**League**	**GP**	**W**	**L**	**T**	**Mins**	**GA**	**SO**	**Avg**	**GP**	**W**	**L**	**Mins**	**GA**	**SO**	**Avg**
1998-99	Sparta Praha Jr.	Czech-Jr.	34	....	....	....	1850	95	....	3.08	....	....	....	....	....	....	....
99-2000	Sparta Praha Jr.	Czech-Jr.	30	....	....	....	1670	73	....	2.62	....	....	....	....	....	....	....
	HC CKD Slany	Czech-3	1	0	1	0	60	5	0	5.00	....	....	....	....	....	....	....
2000-01	Sparta Praha Jr.	Czech-Jr.	14	....	....	....	774	41	0	3.18	2	....	....	60	6	0	6.00
	Beroun	Czech-2	8	....	....	....	426	18	....	2.54	....	....	....	....	....	....	....
2001-02	SaiPa	Finland	47	10	31	4	2755	152	3	3.31	....	....	....	....	....	....	....
2002-03	SaiPa	Finland	34	9	17	5	1888	86	3	2.73	....	....	....	....	....	....	....

DUBIELEWICZ, Wade (DOO-bih-wihtz, WAYD) NYI

Goaltender. Catches left. 5'10", 178 lbs. Born, Invermere, B.C., January 30, 1978.

			Regular Season								Playoffs						
Season	**Club**	**League**	**GP**	**W**	**L**	**T**	**Mins**	**GA**	**SO**	**Avg**	**GP**	**W**	**L**	**Mins**	**GA**	**SO**	**Avg**
99-2000	U. of Denver	WCHA	13	3	5	1	596	27	1	2.72	....	....	....	....	....	....	....
2000-01	U. of Denver	WCHA	29	12	9	3	1542	59	2	2.30	....	....	....	....	....	....	....
2001-02	U. of Denver	WCHA	24	20	4	0	1431	41	2	*1.72	....	....	....	....	....	....	....
2002-03	U. of Denver	WCHA	19	9	8	2	1060	43	3	2.43	....	....	....	....	....	....	....

WCHA Second All-Star Team (2003)

Signed as a free agent by **NY Islanders**, May 25, 2003.

DUNHAM, Mike (DUHN-uhm, MIGHK) NYR

Goaltender. Catches left. 6'3", 200 lbs. Born, Johnson City, NY, June 1, 1972.
(New Jersey's 4th choice, 53rd overall, in 1990 Entry Draft).

			Regular Season								Playoffs						
Season	**Club**	**League**	**GP**	**W**	**L**	**T**	**Mins**	**GA**	**SO**	**Avg**	**GP**	**W**	**L**	**Mins**	**GA**	**SO**	**Avg**
1987-88	Canterbury School	H.S.	29	....	....	....	1740	69	4	2.38	....	....	....	....	....	....	....
1988-89	Canterbury School	H.S.	25	....	....	....	1500	63	2	2.52	....	....	....	....	....	....	....
1989-90	Canterbury School	H.S.	32	....	....	....	1558	68	3	1.96	....	....	....	....	....	....	....
1990-91	University of Maine	H-East	23	14	5	2	1275	63	0	*2.96	....	....	....	....	....	....	....
1991-92	University of Maine	H-East	7	6	0	0	382	14	1	2.20	....	....	....	....	....	....	....
	United States	Nat-Tm	3	0	1	1	157	10	0	3.82	....	....	....	....	....	....	....
1992-93	University of Maine	H-East	25	*21	1	1	1429	63	0	2.65	....	....	....	....	....	....	....
1993-94	United States	Nat-Tm	33	22	9	2	1983	125	2	3.78	....	....	....	....	....	....	....
	United States	Olympics	3	0	1	2	180	15	0	5.00	....	....	....	....	....	....	....
	Albany River Rats	AHL	5	2	2	1	304	26	0	5.12	....	....	....	....	....	....	....
1994-95	Albany River Rats	AHL	35	20	7	8	2120	99	1	2.80	7	6	1	419	20	1	2.86
1995-96	Albany River Rats	AHL	44	30	10	2	2592	109	1	2.52	3	1	2	182	5	1	1.65
1996-97	**New Jersey**	**NHL**	**26**	**8**	**7**	**1**	**1013**	**43**	**2**	**2.55**	....	....	....	....	....	....	....
	Albany River Rats	AHL	3	1	1	1	184	12	0	3.91	....	....	....	....	....	....	....
1997-98	**New Jersey**	**NHL**	**15**	**5**	**5**	**3**	**773**	**29**	**1**	**2.25**	....	....	....	....	....	....	....
1998-99	**Nashville**	**NHL**	**44**	**16**	**23**	**3**	**2472**	**127**	**1**	**3.08**	....	....	....	....	....	....	....
99-2000	**Nashville**	**NHL**	**52**	**19**	**27**	**6**	**3077**	**146**	**0**	**2.85**	....	....	....	....	....	....	....
	Milwaukee	IHL	1	1	0	0	60	1	0	1.00	....	....	....	....	....	....	....
2000-01	**Nashville**	**NHL**	**48**	**21**	**21**	**4**	**2810**	**107**	**4**	**2.28**	....	....	....	....	....	....	....
2001-02	**Nashville**	**NHL**	**58**	**23**	**24**	**9**	**3316**	**144**	**3**	**2.61**	....	....	....	....	....	....	....
	United States	Olympics	1	1	0	0	60	0	*1	0.00	....	....	....	....	....	....	....
2002-03	**Nashville**	**NHL**	**15**	**2**	**9**	**2**	**819**	**43**	**0**	**3.15**	....	....	....	....	....	....	....
	NY Rangers	**NHL**	**43**	**19**	**17**	**5**	**2467**	**94**	**5**	**2.29**	....	....	....	....	....	....	....
	NHL Totals		**301**	**113**	**133**	**33**	**16747**	**733**	**16**	**2.63**	....	....	....	....	....	....	....

Hockey East First All-Star Team (1993) • NCAA East First All-American Team (1993) • Shared Harry "Hap" Holmes Memorial Trophy (fewest goals against – AHL) (1995) with Corey Schwab • Jack A. Butterfield Trophy (Playoff MVP – AHL) (1995) (co-winner - Corey Schwab) • AHL Second All-Star Team (1996) • Shared William M. Jennings Trophy (1997) with Martin Brodeur

Claimed by **Nashville** from **New Jersey** in Expansion Draft, June 26, 1998. Traded to **NY Rangers** by **Nashville** for Rem Murray, Tomas Kloucek and Marek Zidlicky, December 12, 2002.

EHELECHNER, Patrick (eh-heh-LEHCH-nuhr, PAT-rihk) S.J.

Goaltender. Catches left. 6'2", 169 lbs. Born, Rosenheim, West Germany, September 23, 1984.
(San Jose's 5th choice, 139th overall, in 2003 Entry Draft).

			Regular Season								Playoffs						
Season	**Club**	**League**	**GP**	**W**	**L**	**T**	**Mins**	**GA**	**SO**	**Avg**	**GP**	**W**	**L**	**Mins**	**GA**	**SO**	**Avg**
2000-01	Mannheim	German-4	40	....	....	....	2423	171	2	4.23	....	....	....	....	....	....	....
2001-02	EV Landshut	German-3	2	....	....	....	130	6	0	2.77	....	....	....	....	....	....	....
	Hannover	Germany	8	....	....	....	475	24	0	3.03	....	....	....	....	....	....	....
2002-03	ESC Wedemark	German-4					STATISTICS NOT AVAILABLE										
	Hannover	Germany	4	....	....	....	162	16	0	5.90	....	....	....	....	....	....	....

EKLUND, Brian (EHK-luhnd, BRIGH-uhn) T.B.

Goaltender. Catches left. 6'5", 200 lbs. Born, Quincy, MA, May 24, 1980.
(Tampa Bay's 8th choice, 226th overall, in 2000 Entry Draft).

			Regular Season								Playoffs						
Season	**Club**	**League**	**GP**	**W**	**L**	**T**	**Mins**	**GA**	**SO**	**Avg**	**GP**	**W**	**L**	**Mins**	**GA**	**SO**	**Avg**
1997-98	Archbishop Prep	H.S.	22	....	....	....	1320	40	*6	*1.84	....	....	....	....	....	....	....
1998-99	Brown U.	ECAC	8	1	3	0	299	17	0	3.41	....	....	....	....	....	....	....
99-2000	Brown U.	ECAC	12	1	6	2	569	28	1	2.95	....	....	....	....	....	....	....
2000-01	Brown U.	ECAC	19	2	13	3	1084	62	0	3.43	....	....	....	....	....	....	....
2001-02	Brown U.	ECAC	9	3	5	0	454	30	0	3.97	....	....	....	....	....	....	....

2002-03	Pensacola Ice Pilots	ECHL	19	10	6	0	999	61	0	3.66	....	....	....	....	....	....	....
	Springfield Falcons	AHL	1	1	0	0	60	1	0	1.00	....	....	....	....	....	....	....

School Sports Hockey Player of the Year (1998) • HNIB Division 1 Goalie of the Year (1998)

ELLIS, Dan (EHL-ihs, DAN) DAL.

Goaltender. Catches left. 6', 185 lbs. Born, Saskatoon, Sask., June 19, 1980.
(Dallas' 2nd choice, 60th overall, in 2000 Entry Draft).

			Regular Season								Playoffs						
Season	Club	League	GP	W	L	T	Mins	GA	SO	Avg	GP	W	L	Mins	GA	SO	Avg
1998-99	Newmarket	OPJHL	28	24	3	1	1670	63	3	2.25	....	....	....	....	....	....	....
99-2000	Omaha Lancers	USHL	55	*34	16	4	*3274	123	*11	*2.25	4	1	3	238	10	0	2.52
2000-01	Nebraska-Omaha	CCHA	40	21	14	3	2285	95	2	2.49	....	....	....	....	....	....	....
2001-02	Nebraska-Omaha	CCHA	40	20	15	4	2405	97	3	2.42	....	....	....	....	....	....	....
2002-03	Nebraska-Omaha	CCHA	39	11	21	5	2211	117	3	3.18	....	....	....	....	....	....	....

USHL First All-Star Team (2000) • USHL Goaltender of the Year (2000) • USHL Player of the Year (2000) • CCHA Second All-Star Team (2002)

EMERY, Ray (EH-muhr-ee, RAY) OTT.

Goaltender. Catches left. 6'3", 198 lbs. Born, Cayuga, Ont., September 28, 1982.
(Ottawa's 4th choice, 99th overall, in 2001 Entry Draft).

			Regular Season								Playoffs						
Season	Club	League	GP	W	L	T	Mins	GA	SO	Avg	GP	W	L	Mins	GA	SO	Avg
1998-99	Dunnville Terriers	OJHL-C	22	3	19	0	1320	140	0	6.37	....	....	....	....	....	....	....
99-2000	Welland Cougars	OJHL-B	23	13	10	1	1323	62	1	2.68	....	....	....	....	....	....	....
	Sault Ste. Marie	OHL	16	9	3	0	716	36	1	3.02	15	8	7	883	33	*3	2.24
2000-01	Sault Ste. Marie	OHL	52	18	29	2	2938	174	1	3.55	....	....	....	....	....	....	....
2001-02	Sault Ste. Marie	OHL	*59	*33	17	9	*3477	158	4	2.73	6	2	4	360	19	*1	3.17
2002-03	**Ottawa**	**NHL**	**3**	**1**	**0**	**0**	**85**	**2**	**0**	**1.41**	....	....	....	....	....	....	....
	Binghamton	AHL	50	27	17	6	2924	118	*7	2.42	14	8	6	848	40	*2	2.83
	NHL Totals		**3**	**1**	**0**	**0**	**85**	**2**	**0**	**1.41**	....	....	....	....	....	....	....

OHL First All-Star Team (2002) • Canadian Major Junior First All-Star Team (2002) • Canadian Major Junior Goaltender of the Year (2002) • AHL All-Rookie Team (2003)

ESCHE, Robert (EHSH, RAW-buhrt) PHI.

Goaltender. Catches left. 6'1", 210 lbs. Born, Whitesboro, NY, January 22, 1978.
(Phoenix's 5th choice, 139th overall, in 1996 Entry Draft).

			Regular Season								Playoffs						
Season	Club	League	GP	W	L	T	Mins	GA	SO	Avg	GP	W	L	Mins	GA	SO	Avg
1994-95	Gloucester	COJHL	20	10	6	0	1034	70	0	4.06	....	....	....	....	....	....	....
1995-96	Detroit Jr. Whalers	OHL	23	13	6	0	1219	76	1	3.74	3	0	2	105	4	0	2.29
1996-97	Detroit Jr. Whalers	OHL	58	24	28	2	3241	206	2	3.81	5	1	4	317	19	0	3.60
1997-98	Plymouth Whalers	OHL	48	29	13	4	2810	135	3	2.88	15	8	7	869	45	0	3.11
1998-99	**Phoenix**	**NHL**	**3**	**0**	**1**	**0**	**130**	**7**	**0**	**3.23**	....	....	....	....	....	....	....
	Springfield Falcons	AHL	55	24	20	6	2957	138	1	2.80	1	0	1	60	4	0	4.02
99-2000	**Phoenix**	**NHL**	**8**	**2**	**5**	**0**	**408**	**23**	**0**	**3.38**	....	....	....	....	....	....	....
	Houston Aeros	IHL	7	4	2	1	419	16	2	2.29	....	....	....	....	....	....	....
	Springfield Falcons	AHL	21	9	9	2	1207	61	2	3.03	3	1	2	180	12	0	4.01
2000-01	**Phoenix**	**NHL**	**25**	**10**	**8**	**4**	**1350**	**68**	**2**	**3.02**	....	....	....	....	....	....	....
2001-02	**Phoenix**	**NHL**	**22**	**6**	**10**	**2**	**1145**	**52**	**1**	**2.72**	....	....	....	....	....	....	....
	Springfield Falcons	AHL	1	1	0	0	60	0	1	0.00	....	....	....	....	....	....	....
2002-03	**Philadelphia**	**NHL**	**30**	**12**	**9**	**3**	**1638**	**60**	**2**	**2.20**	**1**	**0**	**0**	**30**	**1**	**0**	**2.00**
	NHL Totals		**88**	**30**	**33**	**9**	**4671**	**210**	**5**	**2.70**	**1**	**0**	**0**	**30**	**1**	**0**	**2.00**

OHL Second All-Star Team (1998) • Shared William M. Jennings Trophy (2003) with Roman Cechmanek (tied with Martin Brodeur)

Traded to **Philadelphia** by **Phoenix** with Michal Handzus for Brian Boucher and Nashville's 3rd round choice (previously acquired, Phoenix selected Joe Callahan) in 2002 Entry Draft, June 12, 2002.

FANKHOUSER, Scott (FANK-how-suhr, SKAWT)

Goaltender. Catches left. 6'2", 205 lbs. Born, Bismark, ND, July 1, 1975.
(St. Louis' 8th choice, 276th overall, in 1994 Entry Draft).

			Regular Season								Playoffs						
Season	Club	League	GP	W	L	T	Mins	GA	SO	Avg	GP	W	L	Mins	GA	SO	Avg
1993-94	Loomis-Chaffe	H.S.					STATISTICS NOT AVAILABLE										
1994-95	U. Mass-Lowell	H-East	11	4	4	1	499	37	0	4.44	....	....	....	....	....	....	....
1995-96	Melfort Mustangs	SJHL	45	31	9	4	2544	109	3	2.57	....	....	....	....	....	....	....
1996-97	U. Mass-Lowell	H-East	11	2	4	1	517	38	0	4.41	....	....	....	....	....	....	....
1997-98	U. Mass-Lowell	H-East	16	4	7	2	798	48	0	3.61	....	....	....	....	....	....	....
1998-99	U. Mass-Lowell	H-East	32	16	14	0	1729	80	1	2.78	....	....	....	....	....	....	....
99-2000	**Atlanta**	**NHL**	**16**	**2**	**11**	**2**	**920**	**49**	**0**	**3.20**	....	....	....	....	....	....	....
	Greenville Grrrowl	ECHL	7	6	1	0	419	18	0	2.58	....	....	....	....	....	....	....
	Orlando	IHL	6	2	2	1	320	14	0	2.63	....	....	....	....	....	....	....
	Louisville Panthers	AHL	1	0	1	0	59	3	0	3.05	....	....	....	....	....	....	....
2000-01	**Atlanta**	**NHL**	**7**	**2**	**1**	**0**	**260**	**16**	**0**	**3.69**	....	....	....	....	....	....	....
	Orlando	IHL	28	13	12	3	1603	69	1	2.58	1	0	0	37	3	0	4.83
2001-02	Chicago Wolves	AHL	2	1	0	1	125	4	0	1.92	....	....	....	....	....	....	....
	Greenville Grrrowl	ECHL	3	1	2	0	180	11	0	3.67	....	....	....	....	....	....	....
	Hershey Bears	AHL	8	5	2	1	487	19	1	2.34	3	0	0	41	3	0	4.44
2002-03	Reading Royals	ECHL	26	11	12	1	1463	94	0	3.86	....	....	....	....	....	....	....
	Arkansas	ECHL	19	11	5	2	1110	49	1	2.65	3	0	3	177	7	0	2.38
	NHL Totals		**23**	**4**	**12**	**2**	**1180**	**65**	**0**	**3.31**	....	....	....	....	....	....	....

SJHL First All-Star Team (1996) • SJHL Playoff MVP (1996) • Shared James Norris Memorial Trophy (fewest goals against – IHL) (2001) with Norm Maracle

Signed as a free agent by **Atlanta**, August 24, 1999. • Loaned to **Hershey** (AHL) by **Atlanta** for remainder of 2001-02 season, January 24, 2002.

FERHI, Eddie (feh-REE, EH-dee) ANA.

Goaltender. Catches left. 6'3", 181 lbs. Born, Charenton, France, November 26, 1979.

			Regular Season								Playoffs						
Season	Club	League	GP	W	L	T	Mins	GA	SO	Avg	GP	W	L	Mins	GA	SO	Avg
99-2000	Sacred Heart	MAAC	7	2	4	0	367	19	0	3.11	....	....	....	....	....	....	....
2000-01	Sacred Heart	MAAC	21	9	7	4	1248	50	2	*2.40	....	....	....	....	....	....	....
2001-02	Sacred Heart	MAAC	31	13	12	4	1775	90	2	3.04	....	....	....	....	....	....	....
2002-03	Sacred Heart	MAAC	29	12	12	5	1770	67	3	*2.27	....	....	....	....	....	....	....
	Cincinnati	AHL	1	1	0	0	60	2	0	2.00	....	....	....	....	....	....	....

MAAC Second All-Star Team (2002)

Signed to amateur tryout contract by **Cincinnati** (AHL), April 3, 2003. Signed as a free agent by **Anaheim**, July 23, 2003.

FERNANDEZ, Manny (fuhr-NAN-dehz, MAN-ee) MIN.

Goaltender. Catches left. 6', 180 lbs. Born, Etobicoke, Ont., August 27, 1974.
(Quebec's 4th choice, 52nd overall, in 1992 Entry Draft).

			Regular Season								Playoffs						
Season	Club	League	GP	W	L	T	Mins	GA	SO	Avg	GP	W	L	Mins	GA	SO	Avg
1990-91	Lac St-Louis Lions	QAAA	20	13	5	0	1176	69	*3	3.52	3	2	1	181	12	0	3.98
1991-92	Laval Titan	QMJHL	31	14	13	2	1593	99	1	3.73	9	3	5	468	39	0	5.00
1992-93	Laval Titan	QMJHL	43	26	14	2	2347	141	1	3.60	13	*12	1	818	42	0	3.08
1993-94	Laval Titan	QMJHL	51	29	14	1	2776	143	*5	3.09	19	14	5	1116	49	*1	*2.63
1994-95	Kalamazoo Wings	IHL	46	21	10	9	2470	115	2	2.79	14	10	2	753	34	1	2.71
	Dallas	**NHL**	**1**	**0**	**1**	**0**	**59**	**3**	**0**	**3.05**	....	....	....	....	....	....	....
1995-96	**Dallas**	**NHL**	**5**	**0**	**1**	**1**	**249**	**19**	**0**	**4.58**	....	....	....	....	....	....	....
	Michigan K-Wings	IHL	47	22	15	9	2664	133	*4	3.00	6	5	1	372	14	0	*2.26
1996-97	Michigan K-Wings	IHL	48	20	24	2	2720	142	2	3.13	4	1	3	277	15	0	3.25
1997-98	**Dallas**	**NHL**	**2**	**1**	**0**	**0**	**69**	**2**	**0**	**1.74**	**1**	**0**	**0**	**2**	**0**	**0**	**0.00**
	Michigan K-Wings	IHL	55	27	17	5	3022	139	5	2.76	2	0	2	88	7	0	4.73
1998-99	**Dallas**	**NHL**	**1**	**0**	**1**	**0**	**60**	**2**	**0**	**2.00**	....	....	....	....	....	....	....
	Houston Aeros	IHL	50	34	6	9	2949	116	2	2.36	*19	*11	8	*1126	49	1	2.61
99-2000	**Dallas**	**NHL**	**24**	**11**	**8**	**3**	**1353**	**48**	**1**	**2.13**	**1**	**0**	**0**	**17**	**1**	**0**	**3.53**
2000-01	**Minnesota**	**NHL**	**42**	**19**	**17**	**4**	**2461**	**92**	**4**	**2.24**	....	....	....	....	....	....	....
2001-02	**Minnesota**	**NHL**	**44**	**12**	**24**	**5**	**2463**	**125**	**1**	**3.05**	....	....	....	....	....	....	....
2002-03	**Minnesota**	**NHL**	**35**	**19**	**13**	**2**	**1979**	**74**	**2**	**2.24**	**9**	**3**	**4**	**552**	**18**	**0**	**1.96**
	NHL Totals		**154**	**62**	**65**	**15**	**8693**	**365**	**8**	**2.52**	**11**	**3**	**4**	**571**	**19**	**0**	**2.00**

QMJHL First All-Star Team (1994) • QMJHL MVP (1994) • IHL Second All-Star Team (1995)

Rights traded to **Dallas** by **Quebec** for Tommy Sjodin and Dallas' 3rd round choice (Chris Drury) in 1994 Entry Draft, February 13, 1994. Traded to **Minnesota** by **Dallas** with Brad Lukowich for Minnesota's 3rd round choice (Joel Lundqvist) in 2000 Entry Draft and Minnesota's 4th round choice (later traded back to Minnesota – later traded to Los Angeles – Los Angeles selected Aaron Rome) in 2002 Entry Draft, June 12, 2000.

FICHAUD, Eric (FEE-shoh, AIR-ihk) MTL.

Goaltender. Catches left. 5'11", 179 lbs. Born, Anjou, Que., November 4, 1975.
(Toronto's 1st choice, 16th overall, in 1994 Entry Draft).

			Regular Season								Playoffs						
Season	Club	League	GP	W	L	T	Mins	GA	SO	Avg	GP	W	L	Mins	GA	SO	Avg
1991-92	Montreal-Bourassa	QAAA	28	12	15	1	1678	110	0	3.95	9	5	4	567	32	0	3.39
1992-93	Chicoutimi	QMJHL	43	18	13	1	2039	149	0	4.38	....	....	....	....	....	....	....
1993-94	Chicoutimi	QMJHL	*63	*37	21	3	*3493	192	4	3.30	*26	*16	10	*1560	86	*1	3.31
1994-95	Chicoutimi	QMJHL	46	21	19	4	2637	151	4	3.44	7	2	5	428	20	0	2.80
1995-96	**NY Islanders**	**NHL**	**24**	**7**	**12**	**2**	**1234**	**68**	**1**	**3.31**	....	....	....	....	....	....	....
	Worcester IceCats	AHL	34	13	15	6	1989	97	1	2.93	2	1	1	127	7	0	3.30
1996-97	**NY Islanders**	**NHL**	**34**	**9**	**14**	**4**	**1759**	**91**	**0**	**3.10**	....	....	....	....	....	....	....
1997-98	**NY Islanders**	**NHL**	**17**	**3**	**8**	**3**	**807**	**40**	**0**	**2.97**	....	....	....	....	....	....	....
	Utah Grizzlies	IHL	1	0	0	0	40	3	0	4.45	....	....	....	....	....	....	....
1998-99	**Nashville**	**NHL**	**9**	**0**	**6**	**0**	**447**	**24**	**0**	**3.22**	....	....	....	....	....	....	....
	Milwaukee	IHL	8	5	2	1	480	25	0	3.13	....	....	....	....	....	....	....
99-2000	**Carolina**	**NHL**	**9**	**3**	**5**	**1**	**490**	**24**	**1**	**2.94**	....	....	....	....	....	....	....
	Quebec Citadelles	AHL	6	4	1	1	368	17	0	2.77	3	0	3	177	10	0	3.39
2000-01	**Montreal**	**NHL**	**2**	**0**	**2**	**0**	**62**	**4**	**0**	**3.87**	....	....	....	....	....	....	....
	Quebec Citadelles	AHL	42	19	19	2	2441	127	1	3.12	2	0	1	98	3	0	1.84
2001-02	Manitoba Moose	AHL	5	2	3	0	279	13	1	2.80	....	....	....	....	....	....	....
	Krefeld Pinguine	Germany	9	....	....	....	401	11	0	1.65	3	....	....	197	8	0	2.44
2002-03	Hamilton Bulldogs	AHL	27	14	7	3	1447	55	4	2.28	8	5	3	472	17	0	2.16
	NHL Totals		**95**	**22**	**47**	**10**	**4799**	**251**	**2**	**3.14**	....	....	....	....	....	....	....

Canadian Major Junior Second All-Star Team (1994) • Memorial Cup All-Star Team (1994) • Hap Emms Memorial Trophy (Memorial Cup Top Goaltender) (1994) • QMJHL First All-Star Team (1995)

Traded to **NY Islanders** by **Toronto** for Benoit Hogue, NY Islanders' 3rd round choice (Ryan Pepperall) in 1995 Entry Draft and NY Islanders' 5th round choice (Brandon Sugden) in 1996 Entry Draft, April 6, 1995. Traded to **Edmonton** by **NY Islanders** for Mike Watt, June 18, 1998. Traded to **Nashville** by **Edmonton** with Drake Berehowsky and Greg de Vries for Mikhail Shtalenkov and Jim Dowd, October 1, 1998. Traded to **Carolina** by **Nashville** for Toronto's 4th round choice (previously acquired, Nashville selected Yevgeny Pavlov) in 1999 Entry Draft and future considerations, June 26, 1999. Claimed on waivers by **Montreal** from **Carolina**, February 11, 2000. Signed as a free agent by **Krefeld** (Germany) following release by **Manitoba** (AHL), January 11, 2002. Signed as a free agent by **Montreal**, September 10, 2002.

FINLEY, Brian (FIHN-lee, BRIGH-uhn) NSH.

Goaltender. Catches right. 6'3", 205 lbs. Born, Sault Ste. Marie, Ont., July 13, 1981.
(Nashville's 1st choice, 6th overall, in 1999 Entry Draft).

			Regular Season								Playoffs						
Season	Club	League	GP	W	L	T	Mins	GA	SO	Avg	GP	W	L	Mins	GA	SO	Avg
1996-97	Soo Carlucci's	NOBHL	45	....	....	....	1943	109	3	2.38	....	....	....	....	....	....	....
1997-98	Barrie Colts	OHL	41	23	14	1	2154	105	3	2.92	5	1	3	260	13	0	3.00
1998-99	Barrie Colts	OHL	52	*36	10	4	3063	136	3	2.66	5	4	1	323	15	0	2.79
99-2000	Barrie Colts	OHL	47	24	12	6	2540	130	2	3.07	*23	14	8	1353	58	1	2.57
2000-01	Barrie Colts	OHL	16	5	8	0	818	42	0	3.08	....	....	....	....	....	....	....
	Brampton Battalion	OHL	11	7	3	1	631	31	0	2.95	9	5	4	503	26	1	3.10
2001-02							DID NOT PLAY – INJURED										
2002-03	**Nashville**	**NHL**	**1**	**0**	**0**	**0**	**47**	**3**	**0**	**3.83**	....	....	....	....	....	....	....
	Milwaukee	AHL	22	7	11	2	1207	59	2	2.93	....	....	....	....	....	....	....
	Toledo Storm	ECHL	7	4	2	0	305	12	0	2.36	1	0	1	60	4	0	4.00
	NHL Totals		**1**	**0**	**0**	**0**	**47**	**3**	**0**	**3.83**	....	....	....	....	....	....	....

NOBHL Top Goaltender (1997) • OHL All-Rookie Team (1998) • OHL First All-Star Team (1999) • OHL Playoff MVP (2000)

• Missed entire 2001-02 season recovering from groin injury suffered during 2000-01 season and re-injured in training camp, October 3, 2001.

FISHER, Glenn (FIH-shuhr, GLEHN) EDM.

Goaltender. Catches left. 6'1", 160 lbs. Born, Edmonton, Alta., April 25, 1983.
(Edmonton's 9th choice, 148th overall, in 2002 Entry Draft).

			Regular Season								Playoffs						
Season	Club	League	GP	W	L	T	Mins	GA	SO	Avg	GP	W	L	Mins	GA	SO	Avg
99-2000	Edm. Leafs	AMBHL	16	9	5	2	944	62	0	3.94	....	....	....	....	....	....	....
2000-01	Edm. Leafs	AMHL	19	6	9	3	1116	77	0	4.14	....	....	....	....	....	....	....
2001-02	Ft. Saskatchewan	AJHL	47	....	....	....	2649	196	2	4.44	....	....	....	....	....	....	....
2002-03	Ft. Saskatchewan	AJHL	41	15	21	5	2401	159	0	3.97	....	....	....	....	....	....	....

AJHL Rookie of the Year (2002)

Signed Letter of Intent to attend **U. of Denver** (WCHA), February 12, 2002.

FLAHERTY, Wade (FLAY-uhr-tee, WAYD) NSH.

Goaltender. Catches left. 6', 185 lbs. Born, Terrace, B.C., January 11, 1968.
(Buffalo's 10th choice, 181st overall, in 1988 Entry Draft).

			Regular Season								Playoffs						
Season	Club	League	GP	W	L	T	Mins	GA	SO	Avg	GP	W	L	Mins	GA	SO	Avg
1984-85	Kelowna Wings	WHL	1	0	0	0	55	5	0	5.45	....	....	....	....	....	....	....
1985-86	Seattle	WHL	9	1	3	0	271	36	0	7.97	....	....	....	....	....	....	....
	Spokane Chiefs	WHL	5	0	3	0	161	21	0	7.83	....	....	....	....	....	....	....
1986-87	Nanaimo Clippers	BCJHL	15	....	....	....	830	53	0	3.83	....	....	....	....	....	....	....
	Victoria Cougars	WHL	3	0	2	0	127	16	0	7.56	....	....	....	....	....	....	....
1987-88	Victoria Cougars	WHL	36	20	15	0	2052	135	0	3.95	5	2	3	300	18	0	3.60
1988-89	Victoria Cougars	WHL	42	21	19	0	2408	180	4	4.49	....	....	....	....	....	....	....
1989-90	Greensboro	ECHL	27	12	10	0	1308	96	0	4.40	....	....	....	....	....	....	....
1990-91	Kansas City Blades	IHL	*56	16	31	4	2990	224	0	4.49	....	....	....	....	....	....	....
1991-92	**San Jose**	**NHL**	**3**	**0**	**3**	**0**	**178**	**13**	**0**	**4.38**	....	....	....	....	....	....	....
	Kansas City Blades	IHL	43	26	14	3	2603	140	1	3.23	1	0	0	1	0	0	0.00
1992-93	**San Jose**	**NHL**	**1**	**0**	**1**	**0**	**60**	**5**	**0**	**5.00**	....	....	....	....	....	....	....
	Kansas City Blades	IHL	*61	*34	19	7	*3642	195	2	3.21	*12	6	6	733	34	*1	2.78
1993-94	Kansas City Blades	IHL	*60	32	19	9	*3564	202	0	3.40	....	....	....	....	....	....	....
1994-95	**San Jose**	**NHL**	**18**	**5**	**6**	**1**	**852**	**44**	**1**	**3.10**	**7**	**2**	**3**	**377**	**31**	**0**	**4.93**
1995-96	**San Jose**	**NHL**	**24**	**3**	**12**	**1**	**1137**	**92**	**0**	**4.85**	....	....	....	....	....	....	....
1996-97	**San Jose**	**NHL**	**7**	**2**	**4**	**0**	**359**	**31**	**0**	**5.18**	....	....	....	....	....	....	....
	Kentucky	AHL	19	8	6	2	1032	54	1	3.14	3	1	2	200	11	0	3.30

1997-98	NY Islanders	NHL	16	4	4	3	694	23	3	1.99	....	....	....	....	....	....	....
	Utah Grizzlies	IHL	24	16	5	3	1341	40	3	1.79	....	....	....	....	....	....	....
1998-99	NY Islanders	NHL	20	5	11	2	1048	53	0	3.03	....	....	....	....	....	....	....
	Lowell	AHL	5	1	3	1	305	16	0	3.15	....	....	....	....	....	....	....
99-2000	NY Islanders	NHL	4	0	1	1	182	7	0	2.31	....	....	....	....	....	....	....
2000-01	NY Islanders	NHL	20	6	10	0	1017	56	1	3.30	....	....	....	....	....	....	....
	Tampa Bay	NHL	2	0	2	0	118	8	0	4.07	....	....	....	....	....	....	....
2001-02	Florida	NHL	4	2	1	1	245	12	0	2.94	....	....	....	....	....	....	....
	Utah Grizzlies	AHL	45	22	13	5	2351	92	2	2.35	5	2	3	312	11	0	2.12
2002-03	Nashville	NHL	1	0	1	0	51	4	0	4.71	....	....	....	....	....	....	....
	San Antonio	AHL	30	11	13	5	1791	86	1	2.88	....	....	....	....	....	....	....
	NHL Totals		120	27	56	9	5941	348	5	3.51	7	2	3	377	31	0	4.93

WHL West Second All-Star Team (1988) • ECHL Playoff MVP (1990) • Shared James Norris Memorial Trophy (fewest goals against – IHL) (1992) with Arturs Irbe • IHL Second All-Star Team (1993, 1994)

Signed as a free agent by **San Jose**, September 3, 1991. Signed as a free agent by **NY Islanders**, July 22, 1997. Traded to **Tampa Bay** by **NY Islanders** for future considerations, February 16, 2001. Signed as a free agent by **Florida**, August 2, 2001. Traded to **Nashville** by **Florida** for Pascal Trepanier, March 9, 2003.

FLEURY, Marc-Andre (fluh-REE, MAHRK-AWN-dray) PIT.

Goaltender. Catches left. 6'1", 172 lbs. Born, Sorel, Que., November 28, 1984.
(Pittsburgh's 1st choice, 1st overall, in 2003 Entry Draft).

			Regular Season								Playoffs						
Season	Club	League	GP	W	L	T	Mins	GA	SO	Avg	GP	W	L	Mins	GA	SO	Avg
99-2000	Charles-Lemoyne	QAAA	15	4	9	0	780	36	1	2.77	....	....	....	....	....	....	....
2000-01	Cape Breton	QMJHL	35	12	13	2	1705	115	0	4.05	2	0	1	32	4	0	7.50
2001-02	Cape Breton	QMJHL	55	26	14	8	3043	141	2	2.78	16	9	7	1003	55	0	3.29
2002-03	Cape Breton	QMJHL	51	17	24	6	2889	162	2	3.36	4	0	4	228	17	0	4.47

QMJHL Second All-Star Team (2003)

FORD, Todd (FOHRD, TAWD) TOR.

Goaltender. Catches left. 6'4", 176 lbs. Born, Calgary, Alta., May 1, 1984.
(Toronto's 3rd choice, 74th overall, in 2002 Entry Draft).

			Regular Season								Playoffs						
Season	Club	League	GP	W	L	T	Mins	GA	SO	Avg	GP	W	L	Mins	GA	SO	Avg
2000-01	Swift Current	WHL	20	12	4	2	1066	53	0	2.98	1	0	0	26	2	0	4.62
2001-02	Swift Current	WHL	37	18	12	3	2003	99	2	2.97	10	5	5	603	28	0	2.79
2002-03	Swift Current	WHL	28	12	9	5	1588	71	2	2.68	....	....	....	....	....	....	....
	Prince George	WHL	17	4	9	2	936	70	0	4.49	1	0	1	60	7	0	7.00

FOUNTAIN, Mike (FOWN-tehn, MIGHK)

Goaltender. Catches left. 6'1", 180 lbs. Born, North York, Ont., January 26, 1972.
(Vancouver's 3rd choice, 45th overall, in 1992 Entry Draft).

			Regular Season								Playoffs						
Season	Club	League	GP	W	L	T	Mins	GA	SO	Avg	GP	W	L	Mins	GA	SO	Avg
1988-89	Huntsville	OJHL-C	22	*18	3	2	1306	82	0	3.77	....	....	....	....	....	....	....
1989-90	Chatham Maroons	OJHL-B	21	....	....	....	1249	76	0	3.65	....	....	....	....	....	....	....
1990-91	Sault Ste. Marie	OHL	7	5	2	0	380	19	0	3.00	....	....	....	....	....	....	....
	Oshawa Generals	OHL	30	17	5	1	1483	84	0	3.40	8	1	4	292	26	0	5.34
1991-92	Oshawa Generals	OHL	40	18	13	6	2260	149	1	3.96	7	3	4	429	26	0	3.64
1992-93	Canada	Nat-Tm	13	7	5	1	745	37	1	2.98	....	....	....	....	....	....	....
	Hamilton Canucks	AHL	12	2	8	0	618	46	0	4.47	....	....	....	....	....	....	....
1993-94	Hamilton Canucks	AHL	*70	*34	28	6	*4005	241	*4	3.61	3	0	2	146	12	0	4.92
1994-95	Syracuse Crunch	AHL	61	25	29	7	3618	225	2	3.73	....	....	....	....	....	....	....
1995-96	Syracuse Crunch	AHL	54	21	27	3	3060	184	1	3.61	15	8	7	915	57	*2	3.74
1996-97	Vancouver	NHL	6	2	2	0	245	14	1	3.43	....	....	....	....	....	....	....
	Syracuse Crunch	AHL	25	8	14	2	1462	78	1	3.20	2	0	2	120	12	0	6.02
1997-98	Carolina	NHL	3	0	3	0	163	10	0	3.68	....	....	....	....	....	....	....
	New Haven	AHL	50	25	19	5	2922	139	3	2.85	....	....	....	....	....	....	....
1998-99	New Haven	AHL	51	23	24	3	2989	150	2	3.01	....	....	....	....	....	....	....
99-2000	Ottawa	NHL	1	0	0	0	16	1	0	3.75	....	....	....	....	....	....	....
	Grand Rapids	IHL	36	21	7	4	1851	77	3	2.50	1	0	0	20	4	0	12.00
2000-01	Ottawa	NHL	1	0	1	0	59	3	0	3.05	....	....	....	....	....	....	....
	Grand Rapids	IHL	*52	*34	10	6	*3005	104	6	2.08	8	5	3	522	21	1	2.41
2001-02	Lada Togliatti	Russia	43	....	....	....	2591	59	*14	*1.37	4	....	....	249	7	0	1.69
2002-03	Lada Togliatti	Russia	21	....	....	....	1028	31	5	1.81	3	....	....	40	2	0	3.00
	NHL Totals		11	2	6	0	483	28	1	3.48	....	....	....	....	....	....	....

OHL First All-Star Team (1992) • AHL Second All-Star Team (1994) • IHL Second All-Star Team (2001)

• Recorded shutout (3-0) in NHL debut vs. **New Jersey**, November 14, 1996. Signed as a free agent by **Carolina**, August 19, 1997. Signed as a free agent by **Ottawa**, July 30, 1999.

FRANEK, Petr (FRAH-nehk, PEE-tuhr) COL.

Goaltender. Catches left. 5'11", 185 lbs. Born, Most, Czech., April 6, 1975.
(Quebec's 10th choice, 205th overall, in 1993 Entry Draft).

			Regular Season								Playoffs						
Season	Club	League	GP	W	L	T	Mins	GA	SO	Avg	GP	W	L	Mins	GA	SO	Avg
1992-93	Litvinov	Czech	5	....	....	....	273	15	0	3.29	....	....	....	....	....	....	....
1993-94	Litvinov	Czech	11	....	....	....	535	34	0	3.81	2	0	1	61	10	0	9.83
1994-95	Litvinov	Czech	12	....	....	....	657	47	0	4.29	1	0	0	16	0	0	0.00
1995-96	Litvinov	Czech	36	....	....	....	2096	85	3	2.43	16	....	....	948	47	1	2.97
1996-97	Hershey Bears	AHL	15	4	1	0	457	23	3	3.02	....	....	....	....	....	....	....
	Brantford Smoke	ColHL	6	4	1	0	321	14	0	2.61	....	....	....	....	....	....	....
	Quebec Rafales	IHL	6	3	3	0	357	18	0	3.02	1	0	1	40	4	0	6.00
1997-98	Hershey Bears	AHL	43	19	14	2	2169	98	2	2.71	1	0	1	60	4	0	4.00
1998-99	Utah Grizzlies	IHL	8	1	6	1	446	26	0	3.50	....	....	....	....	....	....	....
	Las Vegas Thunder	IHL	37	17	13	2	1879	107	0	3.42	....	....	....	....	....	....	....
99-2000	Nurnberg	Germany	30	....	....	....	1603	73	2	2.73	....	....	....	....	....	....	....
2000-01	HC Karlovy Vary	Czech	44	....	....	....	2507	121	....	2.90	....	....	....	....	....	....	....
2001-02	HC Karlovy Vary	Czech	40	....	....	....	2189	109	....	2.99	....	....	....	....	....	....	....
2002-03	HC Karlovy Vary	Czech	45	....	....	....	2570	107	5	2.50	....	....	....	....	....	....	....

Rights transferred to **Colorado** after **Quebec** franchise relocated, June 21, 1995.

GARNER, Tyrone (GAHR-nuhr, TIGH-rohn)

Goaltender. Catches left. 6'1", 200 lbs. Born, Stoney Creek, Ont., July 27, 1978.
(NY Islanders' 4th choice, 83rd overall, in 1996 Entry Draft).

			Regular Season								Playoffs						
Season	Club	League	GP	W	L	T	Mins	GA	SO	Avg	GP	W	L	Mins	GA	SO	Avg
1994-95	Stoney Creek Spirit	OJHL-B	10	2	7	1	589	62	0	6.32	....	....	....	....	....	....	....
	Hamilton Kilty B's	OPJHL	8	....	....	....	419	28	0	4.01	....	....	....	....	....	....	....
1995-96	Oshawa Generals	OHL	32	11	15	4	1697	112	0	3.96	....	....	....	....	....	....	....
1996-97	Oshawa Generals	OHL	9	6	1	0	434	20	0	2.76	3	1	0	88	6	0	4.09
1997-98	Oshawa Generals	OHL	54	23	17	8	2946	162	1	3.30	7	3	4	450	25	0	3.33
1998-99	Oshawa Generals	OHL	44	24	15	3	2496	124	4	2.98	15	9	6	901	57	0	3.80
	Calgary	NHL	3	0	2	0	139	12	0	5.18	....	....	....	....	....	....	....
99-2000	Saint John Flames	AHL	19	4	8	4	940	70	0	4.47	....	....	....	....	....	....	....
	Dayton Bombers	ECHL	3	0	2	0	113	11	0	5.86	....	....	....	....	....	....	....
	Johnstown Chiefs	ECHL	17	8	6	3	971	48	0	2.97	1	0	1	59	2	0	2.03
2000-01	Johnstown Chiefs	ECHL	5	3	1	1	306	15	0	2.94	....	....	....	....	....	....	....
	Greenville Grrrowl	ECHL	35	17	15	3	2114	99	3	2.81	....	....	....	....	....	....	....
2001-02	Greenville Grrrowl	ECHL	29	12	12	5	1763	74	0	2.52	*14	*12	2	803	33	0	2.47
2002-03	San Antonio	AHL	1	0	1	0	60	5	0	5.00	....	....	....	....	....	....	....
	Jackson Bandits	ECHL	39	18	17	4	2351	106	4	2.71	1	0	1	76	3	0	2.35
	NHL Totals		3	0	2	0	139	12	0	5.18	....	....	....	....	....	....	....

OHL Second All-Star Team (1999) • ECHL Playoff MVP Award (2002) (co-winner - Simon Gamache)

Traded to **Calgary** by **NY Islanders** with Marty McInnis and Calgary's 6th round choice (previously acquired, Calgary selected Ilja Demidov) in 1997 Entry Draft for Robert Reichel, March 18, 1997. Signed as a free agent by **Florida**, July 31, 2002.

GARNETT, Michael (gahr-NEHT, MIGHK-uhl) ATL.

Goaltender. Catches left. 6'1", 200 lbs. Born, Saskatoon, Sask., November 25, 1982.
(Atlanta's 2nd choice, 80th overall, in 2001 Entry Draft).

			Regular Season								Playoffs						
Season	Club	League	GP	W	L	T	Mins	GA	SO	Avg	GP	W	L	Mins	GA	SO	Avg
1997-98	Sask. Contacts	SMHL	3	1	1	0	82	8	0	5.85	....	....	....	....	....	....	....
1998-99	Sask. Contacts	SMHL	STATISTICS NOT AVAILABLE														
99-2000	Kindersley Klippers	SJHL	36	....	....	....	2067	140	1	3.57	....	....	....	....	....	....	....
	Red Deer Rebels	WHL	1	0	0	0	14	0	0	0.00	....	....	....	....	....	....	....
2000-01	Red Deer Rebels	WHL	21	14	5	1	1133	39	3	2.07	....	....	....	....	....	....	....
	Saskatoon Blades	WHL	28	7	17	2	1501	83	1	3.32	....	....	....	....	....	....	....
2001-02	Saskatoon Blades	WHL	*67	27	34	4	*3738	205	2	3.29	7	3	4	450	15	0	2.00
2002-03	Greenville Grrrowl	ECHL	38	16	15	3	2092	119	0	3.41	3	1	2	178	13	0	4.38
	Chicago Wolves	AHL	2	0	1	0	33	2	0	3.64	....	....	....	....	....	....	....

GARON, Mathieu (gah-ROHN, MAT-yoo) MTL.

Goaltender. Catches right. 6'2", 192 lbs. Born, Chandler, Que., January 9, 1978.
(Montreal's 2nd choice, 44th overall, in 1996 Entry Draft).

			Regular Season								Playoffs						
Season	Club	League	GP	W	L	T	Mins	GA	SO	Avg	GP	W	L	Mins	GA	SO	Avg
1993-94	Jonquiere Elites	QAAA	17	0	13	0	834	88	0	6.33	....	....	....	....	....	....	....
1994-95	Jonquiere Elites	QAAA	27	13	13	1	1554	94	0	3.63	9	6	2	467	26	0	3.34
1995-96	Victoriaville Tigres	QMJHL	51	18	27	0	2709	189	1	4.19	12	7	4	676	38	1	3.39
1996-97	Victoriaville Tigres	QMJHL	53	29	18	3	3032	150	*6	2.97	6	2	4	330	23	0	4.18
1997-98	Victoriaville Tigres	QMJHL	47	27	18	2	2802	125	5	2.68	6	2	4	345	22	0	3.82
1998-99	Fredericton	AHL	40	14	22	2	2222	114	3	3.08	6	1	1	208	12	0	3.47
99-2000	Quebec Citadelles	AHL	53	17	28	3	2884	149	2	3.10	1	0	0	20	3	0	8.82
2000-01	Montreal	NHL	11	4	5	1	589	24	2	2.44	....	....	....	....	....	....	....
	Quebec Citadelles	AHL	31	16	13	1	1768	86	1	2.92	8	4	4	459	22	1	2.88
2001-02	Montreal	NHL	5	1	4	0	261	19	0	4.37	....	....	....	....	....	....	....
	Quebec Citadelles	AHL	50	21	15	12	2988	136	2	2.73	3	0	3	198	12	0	3.63
2002-03	Montreal	NHL	8	3	5	0	482	16	2	1.99	....	....	....	....	....	....	....
	Hamilton Bulldogs	AHL	20	15	2	2	1150	34	4	1.77	....	....	....	....	....	....	....
	NHL Totals		24	8	14	1	1332	59	4	2.66	....	....	....	....	....	....	....

QMJHL All-Rookie Team (1996) • QMJHL Defensive Rookie of the Year (1996) • QMJHL First All-Star Team (1998) • Canadian Major Junior First All-Star Team (1998) • Canadian Major Junior Goaltender of the Year (1998)

GERBER, Martin (GUHR-buhr, MAHR-tihn) ANA.

Goaltender. Catches left. 6', 185 lbs. Born, Burgdorf, Switz., September 3, 1974.
(Anaheim's 10th choice, 232nd overall, in 2001 Entry Draft).

			Regular Season								Playoffs						
Season	Club	League	GP	W	L	T	Mins	GA	SO	Avg	GP	W	L	Mins	GA	SO	Avg
1996-97	SC Langnau Tigers	Swiss-2	38	....	....	....	2286	121	0	3.18	8	....	....	488	29	0	3.57
1997-98	SC Langnau Tigers	Swiss-2	40	....	....	....	2430	141	2	3.48	16	....	....	961	42	0	2.62
1998-99	SC Langnau Tigers	Swiss	42	....	....	....	2521	203	1	4.83	11	....	....	664	50	0	4.52
99-2000	SC Langnau Tigers	Swiss	44	....	....	....	2652	161	3	3.64	6	....	....	360	13	*2	*2.17
2000-01	SC Langnau Tigers	Swiss	*44	....	....	....	2671	114	3	2.56	5	....	....	319	7	1	1.32
2001-02	Farjestad	Sweden	44	....	....	....	2664	87	*4	*1.96	*10	....	....	*657	18	*2	*1.64
	Switzerland	Olympics	3	1	1	1	158	4	0	1.52	....	....	....	....	....	....	....
2002-03	Anaheim	NHL	22	6	11	3	1203	39	1	1.95	2	0	0	20	1	0	3.00
	Cincinnati	AHL	1	1	0	0	60	2	0	2.00	....	....	....	....	....	....	....
	NHL Totals		22	6	11	3	1203	39	1	1.95	2	0	0	20	1	0	3.00

GHERSON, Rob (GAIR-suhn, RAWB) WSH.

Goaltender. Catches left. 6'1", 155 lbs. Born, Toronto, Ont., October 8, 1983.
(Washington's 9th choice, 145th overall, in 2002 Entry Draft).

			Regular Season								Playoffs						
Season	Club	League	GP	W	L	T	Mins	GA	SO	Avg	GP	W	L	Mins	GA	SO	Avg
99-2000	Wellington Dukes	MTJHL	31	....	....	....	1810	80	3	2.65	....	....	....	....	....	....	....
2000-01	Sarnia Sting	OHL	41	11	22	5	2230	136	1	3.66	4	0	2	158	9	0	3.42
2001-02	Sarnia Sting	OHL	55	20	28	4	3098	183	1	3.54	5	1	3	270	17	0	3.78
2002-03	Sarnia Sting	OHL	49	26	12	7	2631	122	3	2.78	5	1	3	251	13	1	3.11

GIGUERE, Jean-Sebastien (ZHEE-gair, ZHAWN-suh-BAS-tee-yeh) ANA.

Goaltender. Catches left. 6'1", 199 lbs. Born, Montreal, Que., May 16, 1977.
(Hartford's 1st choice, 13th overall, in 1995 Entry Draft).

			Regular Season								Playoffs						
Season	Club	League	GP	W	L	T	Mins	GA	SO	Avg	GP	W	L	Mins	GA	SO	Avg
1992-93	Laval Laurentide	QAAA	25	12	11	2	1498	76	0	3.02	11	6	5	654	38	0	3.49
1993-94	Verdun	QMJHL	25	13	5	2	1234	66	1	3.21	....	....	....	....	....	....	....
1994-95	Halifax	QMJHL	47	14	27	5	2755	181	2	3.94	7	3	4	417	17	1	*2.45
1995-96	Halifax	QMJHL	55	26	23	2	3230	185	1	3.44	6	1	5	354	24	0	4.07
1996-97	Hartford	NHL	8	1	4	0	394	24	0	3.65	....	....	....	....	....	....	....
	Halifax	QMJHL	50	28	19	3	3014	170	2	3.38	16	9	7	954	58	0	3.65
1997-98	Saint John Flames	AHL	31	16	10	3	1758	72	2	2.46	10	5	3	536	27	0	3.02
1998-99	Calgary	NHL	15	6	7	1	860	46	0	3.21	....	....	....	....	....	....	....
	Saint John Flames	AHL	39	18	16	3	2145	123	3	3.44	7	3	2	304	21	0	4.14
99-2000	Calgary	NHL	7	1	3	1	330	15	0	2.73	....	....	....	....	....	....	....
	Saint John Flames	AHL	41	17	17	3	2243	114	0	3.05	3	0	3	178	9	0	3.03
2000-01	Anaheim	NHL	34	11	17	5	2031	87	4	2.57	....	....	....	....	....	....	....
	Cincinnati	AHL	23	12	7	2	1306	53	0	2.43	....	....	....	....	....	....	....
2001-02	Anaheim	NHL	53	20	25	6	3127	111	4	2.13	....	....	....	....	....	....	....
2002-03	Anaheim	NHL	65	34	22	6	3775	145	8	2.30	21	15	6	1407	38	5	*1.62
	NHL Totals		182	73	78	19	10517	428	16	2.44	21	15	6	1407	38	5	1.62

QMJHL Second All-Star Team (1997) • Shared Harry "Hap" Holmes Memorial Trophy (fewest goals against – AHL) (1998) with Tyler Moss • Conn Smythe Trophy (2003)

Transferred to **Carolina** after **Hartford** franchise relocated, June 25, 1997. Traded to **Calgary** by **Carolina** with Andrew Cassels for Gary Roberts and Trevor Kidd, August 25, 1997. Traded to **Anaheim** by **Calgary** for Anaheim's 2nd round choice (later traded to Washington – Washington selected Matt Pettinger) in 2000 Entry Draft, June 10, 2000.

GOEHRING, Karl (GAIR-ihng, KAHRL) CBJ

Goaltender. Catches left. 5'8", 160 lbs. Born, Apple Valley, MN, August 23, 1978.

			Regular Season								Playoffs						
Season	Club	League	GP	W	L	T	Mins	GA	SO	Avg	GP	W	L	Mins	GA	SO	Avg
1996-97	Fargo-Moorhead	USHL	32	13	18	1	1909	79	*4	*2.48	5	2	3	251	15	1	3.58
1997-98	North Dakota	WCHA	27	23	3	1	1504	57	1	*2.27	....	....	....	....	....	....	....
1998-99	North Dakota	WCHA	31	22	5	2	1774	71	3	2.40	....	....	....	....	....	....	....
99-2000	North Dakota	WCHA	30	19	6	4	1747	55	*8	*1.89	....	....	....	....	....	....	....
2000-01	North Dakota	WCHA	30	16	6	6	1662	66	*3	2.38	....	....	....	....	....	....	....

			Regular Season								Playoffs						
2001-02	Syracuse Crunch	AHL	15	5	6	3	891	37	1	2.49	....	....	....	....	....	....	....
	Dayton Bombers	ECHL	23	11	9	3	1393	52	2	2.24	*14	9	5	*866	35	1	2.43
2002-03	Syracuse Crunch	AHL	49	18	21	4	2608	116	4	2.67	....	....	....	....	....	....	....

WCHA First All-Star Team (1998, 2000) • WCHA Rookie of the Year (1998) • NCAA West First All-American Team (1998, 2000) • WCHA Second All-Star Team (1999)

Signed as a free agent by **Columbus**, May 7, 2001.

GOEPFERT, Robert — PIT.

Goaltender. Catches left. 5'10", 170 lbs. Born, Ozone Park, NY, May 9, 1983.
(Pittsburgh's choice, 171st overall, in 2002 Entry Draft).

			Regular Season								Playoffs						
Season	Club	League	GP	W	L	T	Mins	GA	SO	Avg	GP	W	L	Mins	GA	SO	Avg
99-2000	Suffolk PAL	Metro-Jr.	38	....	....	....	2280	87	....	2.36	....	....	....	....	....	....	....
2000-01	Cedar Rapids	USHL	41	25	12	4	2565	125	1	2.92	4	1	3	188	18	0	5.73
2001-02	Cedar Rapids	USHL	51	27	16	5	2918	99	8	2.04	8	4	4	581	19	0	1.97
2002-03	Providence College	H-East	13	6	6	1	754	30	1	2.39	....	....	....	....	....	....	....

GRAHAME, John (GRAY-ham, JAWN) — T.B.

Goaltender. Catches left. 6'2", 214 lbs. Born, Denver, CO, August 31, 1975.
(Boston's 7th choice, 229th overall, in 1994 Entry Draft).

			Regular Season								Playoffs						
Season	Club	League	GP	W	L	T	Mins	GA	SO	Avg	GP	W	L	Mins	GA	SO	Avg
1993-94	Sioux City	USHL	20	....	....	....	1200	73	0	3.70	....	....	....	....	....	....	....
1994-95	Lake Superior State	CCHA	28	16	7	3	1616	75	2	2.79	....	....	....	....	....	....	....
1995-96	Lake Superior State	CCHA	29	21	4	2	1558	66	2	2.54	....	....	....	....	....	....	....
1996-97	Lake Superior State	CCHA	37	19	13	4	2197	134	3	3.66	....	....	....	....	....	....	....
1997-98	Providence Bruins	AHL	55	15	31	4	3053	164	3	3.22	....	....	....	....	....	....	....
1998-99	Providence Bruins	AHL	48	*37	9	1	2771	134	3	2.90	19	*15	4	*1209	48	1	2.38
99-2000	Boston	NHL	24	7	10	5	1344	55	2	2.46	....	....	....	....	....	....	....
	Providence Bruins	AHL	27	11	13	2	1528	86	1	3.38	13	10	3	839	35	0	2.50
2000-01	Boston	NHL	10	3	4	0	471	28	0	3.57	....	....	....	....	....	....	....
	Providence Bruins	AHL	16	4	7	3	893	47	0	3.16	17	8	9	1043	46	2	2.65
2001-02	Boston	NHL	19	8	7	2	1079	52	1	2.89	....	....	....	....	....	....	....
2002-03	Boston	NHL	23	11	9	2	1352	61	1	2.71	....	....	....	....	....	....	....
	Tampa Bay	NHL	17	6	5	4	914	34	2	2.23	1	0	1	111	2	0	1.08
	NHL Totals		93	35	35	13	5160	230	6	2.67	1	0	1	111	2	0	1.08

Traded to **Tampa Bay** by **Boston** for Tampa Bay's 4th round choice in 2004 Entry Draft, January 13, 2003.

GRAHN, Carl (GRAHN, KARL) — L.A.

Goaltender. Catches left. 6', 175 lbs. Born, Koupolo, Finland, January 8, 1981.
(Los Angeles' 11th choice, 282nd overall, in 2000 Entry Draft).

			Regular Season								Playoffs						
Season	Club	League	GP	W	L	T	Mins	GA	SO	Avg	GP	W	L	Mins	GA	SO	Avg
1998-99	KalPa Kuopio Jr.	Finn-Jr.	20	7	10	1	1153	63	1	3.28	....	....	....	....	....	....	....
	KalPa Kuopio	Finland	3	0	2	0	126	16	0	7.63	....	....	....	....	....	....	....
99-2000	KooKoo Jr.	Finn-Jr.	38	....	....	....	2165	124	1	3.44	....	....	....	....	....	....	....
2000-01	KalPa Kuopio	Finland-2	39	20	15	4	2340	105	2	2.69	....	....	....	....	....	....	....
2001-02	KooKoo Kouvola	Finland-2	36	....	....	....	2160	92	0	2.56	10	....	....	600	31	0	3.09
2002-03	KooKoo Kouvola	Finland-2	21	....	....	....	1268	49	0	2.30	8	....	....	465	21	0	2.71

GRUMET-MORRIS, Dov (groo-MAY-MAW-rihs, DAWV) — PHI.

Goaltender. Catches left. 6'2", 190 lbs. Born, Evanston, IL, February 28, 1982.
(Philadelphia's 4th choice, 161st overall, in 2002 Entry Draft).

			Regular Season								Playoffs						
Season	Club	League	GP	W	L	T	Mins	GA	SO	Avg	GP	W	L	Mins	GA	SO	Avg
2000-01	Danville Wings	NAJHL	27	19	5	2	1547	57	3	2.21	5	2	2	300	17	0	3.40
2001-02	Harvard Crimson	ECAC	21	10	8	1	1226	58	1	2.84	....	....	....	....	....	....	....
2002-03	Harvard Crimson	ECAC	29	18	9	2	1741	69	1	2.38	....	....	....	....	....	....	....

GUSTAFSON, Derek (GUHST-ahf-suhn, DEH-rihk)

Goaltender. Catches left. 5'11", 210 lbs. Born, Gresham, OR, June 21, 1979.

			Regular Season								Playoffs						
Season	Club	League	GP	W	L	T	Mins	GA	SO	Avg	GP	W	L	Mins	GA	SO	Avg
1995-96	Seattle Ironmen	BCAHA	16	....	....	....	913	46	0	3.02	....	....	....	....	....	....	....
1996-97	Vernon Vipers	BCHL	23	....	....	....	1241	70	0	3.38	....	....	....	....	....	....	....
1997-98	Vernon Vipers	BCHL	42	27	13	2	2270	144	1	3.81	6	2	1	257	13	0	3.04
1998-99	Vernon Vipers	BCHL	42	39	3	0	2505	94	3	2.25	....	....	....	....	....	....	....
99-2000	St. Lawrence	ECAC	24	17	4	2	1475	51	2	2.07	....	....	....	....	....	....	....
2000-01	Minnesota	NHL	4	1	3	0	239	10	0	2.51	....	....	....	....	....	....	....
	Jackson Bandits	ECHL	7	4	3	0	404	15	1	2.23	....	....	....	....	....	....	....
	Cleveland	IHL	24	14	7	1	1293	59	2	2.74	2	0	1	53	5	0	5.64
2001-02	Minnesota	NHL	1	0	0	0	26	0	0	0.00	....	....	....	....	....	....	....
	Houston Aeros	AHL	38	14	13	6	2016	92	4	2.74	2	0	0	25	1	0	2.37
2002-03	Louisiana	ECHL	2	1	1	0	118	8	0	4.07	....	....	....	....	....	....	....
	Houston Aeros	AHL	41	23	14	2	2301	108	2	2.82	....	....	....	....	....	....	....
	NHL Totals		5	1	3	0	265	10	0	2.26	....	....	....	....	....	....	....

BCHL First All-Star Team (1999) • BCHL Interior Top Goaltender (1999) • ECAC Second All-Star Team (2000) • ECAC Rookie of the Year (2000)

Signed as a free agent by **Minnesota**, June 9, 2000.

HACKETT, Jeff (HA-keht, JEHF) — PHI.

Goaltender. Catches left. 6'1", 198 lbs. Born, London, Ont., June 1, 1968.
(NY Islanders' 2nd choice, 34th overall, in 1987 Entry Draft).

			Regular Season								Playoffs						
Season	Club	League	GP	W	L	T	Mins	GA	SO	Avg	GP	W	L	Mins	GA	SO	Avg
1984-85	London Diamonds	OJHL-B	18	....	....	....	1078	73	1	4.06	....	....	....	....	....	....	....
1985-86	London Diamonds	OJHL-B	19	....	....	....	1150	66	0	3.43	....	....	....	....	....	....	....
1986-87	Oshawa Generals	OHL	31	18	9	2	1672	85	2	3.05	15	8	7	895	40	0	2.68
1987-88	Oshawa Generals	OHL	53	30	21	2	3165	205	0	3.89	7	3	4	438	31	0	4.25
1988-89	NY Islanders	NHL	13	4	7	0	662	39	0	3.53	....	....	....	....	....	....	....
	Springfield Indians	AHL	29	12	14	2	1677	116	0	4.15	....	....	....	....	....	....	....
1989-90	Springfield Indians	AHL	54	24	25	3	3045	187	1	3.68	*17	*10	5	934	60	0	3.85
1990-91	NY Islanders	NHL	30	5	18	1	1508	91	0	3.62	....	....	....	....	....	....	....
1991-92	San Jose	NHL	42	11	27	1	2314	148	0	3.84	....	....	....	....	....	....	....
1992-93	San Jose	NHL	36	2	30	1	2000	176	0	5.28	....	....	....	....	....	....	....
1993-94	Chicago	NHL	22	2	12	3	1084	62	0	3.43	....	....	....	....	....	....	....
1994-95	Chicago	NHL	7	1	3	2	328	13	0	2.38	2	0	0	26	1	0	2.31
1995-96	Chicago	NHL	35	18	11	4	2000	80	4	2.40	1	0	1	60	5	0	5.00
1996-97	Chicago	NHL	41	19	18	4	2473	89	2	2.16	6	2	4	345	25	0	4.35
1997-98	Chicago	NHL	58	21	25	11	3441	126	8	2.20	....	....	....	....	....	....	....
1998-99	Chicago	NHL	10	2	6	1	524	33	0	3.78	....	....	....	....	....	....	....
	Montreal	NHL	53	24	20	9	3091	117	5	2.27	....	....	....	....	....	....	....
99-2000	Montreal	NHL	56	23	25	7	3301	132	3	2.40	....	....	....	....	....	....	....
2000-01	Montreal	NHL	19	4	10	2	998	54	0	3.25	....	....	....	....	....	....	....
2001-02	Montreal	NHL	15	5	5	2	717	38	0	3.18	....	....	....	....	....	....	....
2002-03	Montreal	NHL	18	7	8	2	1063	45	0	2.54	....	....	....	....	....	....	....
	Boston	NHL	18	8	9	0	991	53	1	3.21	3	1	2	179	5	0	1.68
	NHL Totals		473	156	234	50	26495	1296	23	2.93	12	3	7	610	36	0	3.54

Jack A. Butterfield Trophy (Playoff MVP – AHL) (1990)

Claimed by **San Jose** from **NY Islanders** in Expansion Draft, May 30, 1991. Traded to **Chicago** by **San Jose** for Chicago's 3rd round choice (Alexei Yegorov) in 1994 Entry Draft, July 13, 1993. Traded to **Montreal** by **Chicago** with Eric Weinrich, Alain Nasreddine and Tampa Bay's 4th round choice (previously acquired, Montreal selected Chris Dyment) in 1999 Entry Draft for Jocelyn Thibault, Dave Manson and Brad Brown, November 16, 1998. • Missed majority of 2000-01 season recovering from hand injury suffered in game vs. Minnesota, October 24, 2000. • Missed majority of 2001-02 season recovering from shoulder injury suffered in game vs. Buffalo, October 20, 2001. Traded to **San Jose** by **Montreal** for Niklas Sundstrom and San Jose's 3rd round choice in 2004 Entry Draft, January 23, 2003. Traded to **Boston** by **San Jose** with Jeff Jillson for Kyle McLaren and Boston's 4th round choice in 2004 Entry Draft, January 23, 2003. Signed as a free agent by **Philadelphia**, July 1, 2003.

HAMERLIK, Peter (HAHM-ehr-lik, PEE-tuhr) — BOS.

Goaltender. Catches left. 6'1", 194 lbs. Born, Myjava, Czech., January 2, 1982.
(Boston's 4th choice, 153rd overall, in 2002 Entry Draft).

			Regular Season								Playoffs						
Season	Club	League	GP	W	L	T	Mins	GA	SO	Avg	GP	W	L	Mins	GA	SO	Avg
1997-98	HK-36 Skalica Jr.	Slovak-Jr.	49	....	....	....	2969	168	....	3.40	....	....	....	....	....	....	....
1998-99	HK 36 Skalica	Slovakia	1	0	1	0	24	3	0	7.50	....	....	....	....	....	....	....
99-2000	HK 36 Skalica Jr.	Slovak-Jr.	37	....	....	....	1850	121	....	3.92	....	....	....	....	....	....	....
	HK-36 Skalica	Slovakia	7	....	....	....	286	16	....	3.36	....	....	....	....	....	....	....
2000-01	Kingston	OHL	56	21	21	8	3026	153	*4	3.03	3	0	2	131	13	0	5.95
2001-02	Kingston	OHL	43	12	21	6	2371	144	1	3.64	1	0	1	60	6	0	6.00
2002-03	Kingston	OHL	47	19	22	2	2566	153	3	3.58	....	....	....	....	....	....	....
	Providence Bruins	AHL	1	0	0	1	65	4	0	3.69	....	....	....	....	....	....	....
	Cincinnati	ECHL	5	2	1	1	250	14	0	3.35	6	3	1	308	12	0	2.34

• Re-entered NHL Entry Draft. Originally Pittsburgh's 3rd choice, 84th overall, in 2000 Entry Draft.

HARDING, Josh (HAHR-dihng, JAWSH) — MIN.

Goaltender. Catches right. 6'1", 180 lbs. Born, Regina, Sask., June 18, 1984.
(Minnesota's 2nd choice, 38th overall, in 2002 Entry Draft).

			Regular Season								Playoffs						
Season	Club	League	GP	W	L	T	Mins	GA	SO	Avg	GP	W	L	Mins	GA	SO	Avg
2000-01	Regina Pat Cdns.	SMHL	36	....	....	....	2000	81	3	2.41	....	....	....	....	....	....	....
2001-02	Regina Pats	WHL	42	27	13	1	2389	95	*4	2.39	6	2	4	325	16	0	2.95
2002-03	Regina Pats	WHL	57	18	24	13	*3385	155	3	2.75	5	1	4	321	13	0	2.43

WHL East Second All-Star Team (2002) • WHL East First All-Star Team (2003)

HASEK, Dominik (HAH-shihk, DOHM-ihn-ihk) — DET.

Goaltender. Catches left. 5'11", 180 lbs. Born, Pardubice, Czech., January 29, 1965.
(Chicago's 11th choice, 207th overall, in 1983 Entry Draft).

			Regular Season								Playoffs						
Season	Club	League	GP	W	L	T	Mins	GA	SO	Avg	GP	W	L	Mins	GA	SO	Avg
1981-82	HC Pardubice	Czech	12	....	....	....	661	34	....	3.09	....	....	....	....	....	....	....
1982-83	HC Pardubice	Czech	42	....	....	....	2358	105	....	2.67	....	....	....	....	....	....	....
1983-84	HC Pardubice	Czech	40	....	....	....	2304	108	....	2.81	....	....	....	....	....	....	....
1984-85	HC Pardubice	Czech	42	....	....	....	2419	131	....	3.25	....	....	....	....	....	....	....
1985-86	HC Pardubice	Czech	45	....	....	....	2689	138	....	3.08	....	....	....	....	....	....	....
1986-87	HC Pardubice	Czech	43	....	....	....	2515	103	....	2.46	....	....	....	....	....	....	....
1987-88	HC Pardubice	Czech	31	....	....	....	1862	93	....	3.00	....	....	....	....	....	....	....
	Czechoslovakia	Olympics	5	3	2	0	217	18	1	4.98	....	....	....	....	....	....	....
1988-89	HC Pardubice	Czech	42	....	....	....	2507	114	....	2.73	....	....	....	....	....	....	....
1989-90	Dukla Jihlava	Czech	40	....	....	....	2251	80	....	2.13	....	....	....	....	....	....	....
1990-91	Chicago	NHL	5	3	0	1	195	8	0	2.46	3	0	0	69	3	0	2.61
	Indianapolis Ice	IHL	33	20	11	1	1903	80	*5	*2.52	1	1	0	60	3	0	3.00
1991-92	Chicago	NHL	20	10	4	1	1014	44	1	2.60	3	0	2	158	8	0	3.04
	Indianapolis Ice	IHL	20	7	10	3	1162	69	1	3.56	....	....	....	....	....	....	....
1992-93	Buffalo	NHL	28	11	10	4	1429	75	0	3.15	1	1	0	45	1	0	1.33
1993-94	Buffalo	NHL	58	30	20	6	3358	109	*7	*1.95	7	3	4	484	13	2	*1.61
1994-95	HC Pardubice	Czech	2	1	0	1	124	6	0	2.90	....	....	....	....	....	....	....
	Buffalo	NHL	41	19	14	7	2416	85	*5	*2.11	5	1	4	309	18	0	3.50
1995-96	Buffalo	NHL	59	22	30	6	3417	161	2	2.83	....	....	....	....	....	....	....
1996-97	Buffalo	NHL	67	37	20	10	4037	153	5	2.27	3	1	1	153	5	0	1.96
1997-98	Buffalo	NHL	*72	33	23	13	*4220	147	*13	2.09	15	10	5	948	32	1	2.03
	Czech Republic	Olympics	6	*5	1	0	*369	6	*2	*0.97	....	....	....	....	....	....	....
1998-99	Buffalo	NHL	64	30	18	14	3817	119	9	1.87	19	13	6	1217	36	2	1.77
99-2000	Buffalo	NHL	35	15	11	6	2066	76	3	2.21	5	1	4	301	12	0	2.39
2000-01	Buffalo	NHL	67	37	24	4	3904	137	*11	2.11	13	7	6	833	29	1	2.09
2001-02 ◆	Detroit	NHL	65	*41	15	8	3872	140	5	2.17	*23	*16	7	*1455	45	*6	1.86
	Czech Republic	Olympics	4	1	2	1	239	8	0	2.01	....	....	....	....	....	....	....
2002-03	OUT OF HOCKEY – RETIRED																
	NHL Totals		581	288	189	80	33745	1254	61	2.23	97	53	39	5972	202	12	2.03

Czechoslovakian Goaltender of the Year (1986, 1987, 1988, 1989, 1990) • Czechoslovakian Player of the Year (1987, 1989, 1990) • Czechoslovakian First All-Star Team (1988, 1989, 1990) • IHL First All-Star Team (1991) • NHL All-Rookie Team (1992) • NHL First All-Star Team (1994, 1995, 1997, 1998, 1999, 2001) • Shared William M. Jennings Trophy (1994) with Grant Fuhr • Vezina Trophy (1994, 1995, 1997, 1998, 1999, 2001) • Lester B. Pearson Award (1997, 1998) • Hart Trophy (1997, 1998) • William M. Jennings Trophy (2001)

Played in NHL All-Star Game (1996, 1997, 1998, 1999, 2001, 2002)

Traded to **Buffalo** by **Chicago** for Stephane Beauregard and Buffalo's 4th round choice (Eric Daze) in 1993 Entry Draft, August 7, 1992. Traded to **Detroit** by **Buffalo** for Vyacheslav Kozlov, Detroit's 1st round choice (later traded to Columbus – later traded to Atlanta – Atlanta selected Jim Slater) in 2002 Entry Draft and future considerations, July 1, 2001. • Officially announced retirement, June 25, 2002. • **Detroit** picked up the option on his contract, July 1, 2003.

HAUSER, Adam (HOW-suhr, A-duhm)

Goaltender. Catches left. 6'2", 195 lbs. Born, Bovey, MN, May 27, 1980.
(Edmonton's 4th choice, 81st overall, in 1999 Entry Draft).

			Regular Season								Playoffs						
Season	Club	League	GP	W	L	T	Mins	GA	SO	Avg	GP	W	L	Mins	GA	SO	Avg
1996-97	Greenway High	H.S.	25	....	....	....	1496	63	0	2.54	....	....	....	....	....	....	....
1997-98	U.S. National U-18	USDP	38	19	10	7	2110	94	4	2.67	....	....	....	....	....	....	....
1998-99	U. of Minnesota	WCHA	*40	14	18	8	*2350	136	3	3.47	....	....	....	....	....	....	....
99-2000	U. of Minnesota	WCHA	36	20	14	2	2114	104	1	2.95	....	....	....	....	....	....	....
2000-01	U. of Minnesota	WCHA	40	*26	12	2	2366	101	*3	2.56	....	....	....	....	....	....	....
2001-02	U. of Minnesota	WCHA	35	*23	6	4	2003	80	1	2.40	....	....	....	....	....	....	....
2002-03	Jackson Bandits	ECHL	34	20	9	4	2021	83	*5	2.46	....	....	....	....	....	....	....
	Providence Bruins	AHL	1	0	0	1	64	3	0	2.80	....	....	....	....	....	....	....

NCAA Championship All-Tournament Team (2002) • ECHL All-Rookie Team (2003)

HEDBERG, Johan (HEHD-buhrg, YO-han) — VAN.

Goaltender. Catches left. 6', 184 lbs. Born, Leksand, Sweden, May 3, 1973.
(Philadelphia's 8th choice, 218th overall, in 1994 Entry Draft).

			Regular Season								Playoffs						
Season	Club	League	GP	W	L	T	Mins	GA	SO	Avg	GP	W	L	Mins	GA	SO	Avg
1992-93	Leksands IF	Sweden	10	....	....	....	600	24	....	2.40	....	....	....	....	....	....	....
1993-94	Leksands IF	Sweden	17	....	....	....	1020	48	....	2.82	....	....	....	....	....	....	....
1994-95	Leksands IF	Sweden	17	....	....	....	986	58	....	3.53	....	....	....	....	....	....	....

Season	Club	League	GP	W	L	T	Mins	GA	SO	Avg	GP	W	L	Mins	GA	SO	Avg
1995-96	Leksands IF	Sweden	34	....	....	....	2013	95	....	2.83	4	....	....	240	13	....	3.25
1996-97	Leksands IF	Sweden	38	....	....	....	2260	95	3	2.52	8	....	....	581	18	1	1.86
1997-98	Baton Rouge	ECHL	2	1	1	0	100	7	0	4.20	....	....	....	....	....	....	....
	Detroit Vipers	IHL	16	7	2	2	726	32	1	2.64	....	....	....	....	....	....	....
	Manitoba Moose	IHL	14	8	4	1	745	32	1	2.58	2	0	2	105	6	0	3.40
1998-99	Leksands IF	Sweden	*48	....	....	....	*2940	140	0	2.86	4	....	....	255	15	0	3.53
99-2000	Kentucky	AHL	33	18	9	5	1973	88	3	2.68	5	3	2	311	10	1	1.93
2000-01	Manitoba Moose	IHL	46	23	13	7	2697	115	1	2.56	....	....	....	....	....	....	....
	Pittsburgh	**NHL**	**9**	**7**	**1**	**1**	**545**	**24**	**0**	**2.64**	**18**	**9**	**9**	**1123**	**43**	**2**	**2.30**
2001-02	**Pittsburgh**	**NHL**	**66**	**25**	**34**	**7**	**3877**	**178**	**6**	**2.75**	....	....	....	....	....	....	....
	Sweden	Olympics	1	1	0	0	60	1	0	1.00	....	....	....	....	....	....	....
2002-03	**Pittsburgh**	**NHL**	**41**	**14**	**22**	**4**	**2410**	**126**	**1**	**3.14**	....	....	....	....	....	....	....
	NHL Totals		**116**	**46**	**57**	**12**	**6832**	**328**	**7**	**2.88**	**18**	**9**	**9**	**1123**	**43**	**2**	**2.30**

Rights traded to **San Jose** by **Philadelphia** for San Jose's 7th round choice (Pavel Kasparik) in 1999 Entry Draft, August 6, 1998. Traded to **Pittsburgh** by **San Jose** with Bobby Dallas for Jeff Norton, March 12, 2001. Traded to **Vancouver** by **Pittsburgh** for Vancouver's 2nd round choice in 2004 Entry Draft, August 25, 2003.

HIRSCH, Corey (HUHRSH, KOHR-ee)

Goaltender. Catches left. 5'10", 175 lbs. Born, Medicine Hat, Alta., August 10, 1972.
(NY Rangers' 7th choice, 169th overall, in 1991 Entry Draft).

			Regular Season								Playoffs						
Season	Club	League	GP	W	L	T	Mins	GA	SO	Avg	GP	W	L	Mins	GA	SO	Avg
1987-88	Calgary Canucks	AJHL	32	22	5	0	1538	91	1	3.55	....	....	....	....	....	....	....
1988-89	Kamloops Blazers	WHL	32	11	12	2	1516	106	2	4.20	5	3	2	245	19	0	4.65
1989-90	Kamloops Blazers	WHL	*63	*48	13	0	3608	230	*3	3.82	*17	*14	3	*1043	60	0	*3.45
1990-91	Kamloops Blazers	WHL	38	26	7	1	1970	100	3	*3.05	11	5	6	623	42	0	4.04
1991-92	Kamloops Blazers	WHL	48	35	10	2	2732	124	*5	*2.72	*16	*11	5	954	35	*2	*2.20
1992-93	**NY Rangers**	**NHL**	**4**	**1**	**2**	**1**	**224**	**14**	**0**	**3.75**	....	....	....	....	....	....	....
	Binghamton	AHL	46	*35	4	5	2692	125	1	*2.79	14	7	7	831	46	0	3.32
1993-94	Canada	Nat-Tm	45	24	17	3	2653	124	0	2.80	....	....	....	....	....	....	....
	Canada	Olympics	8	5	2	1	495	18	0	2.18	....	....	....	....	....	....	....
	Binghamton	AHL	10	5	4	1	610	38	0	3.73	....	....	....	....	....	....	....
1994-95	Binghamton	AHL	57	31	20	5	3371	175	0	3.11	....	....	....	....	....	....	....
1995-96	**Vancouver**	**NHL**	**41**	**17**	**14**	**6**	**2338**	**114**	**1**	**2.93**	**6**	**2**	**3**	**338**	**21**	**0**	**3.73**
1996-97	**Vancouver**	**NHL**	**39**	**12**	**20**	**4**	**2127**	**116**	**2**	**3.27**	....	....	....	....	....	....	....
1997-98	**Vancouver**	**NHL**	**1**	**0**	**0**	**0**	**50**	**5**	**0**	**6.00**	....	....	....	....	....	....	....
	Syracuse Crunch	AHL	60	30	22	6	3512	187	1	3.19	5	2	3	297	10	1	*2.02
1998-99	**Vancouver**	**NHL**	**20**	**3**	**8**	**3**	**919**	**48**	**1**	**3.13**	....	....	....	....	....	....	....
	Syracuse Crunch	AHL	5	2	3	0	300	14	0	2.80	....	....	....	....	....	....	....
99-2000	Milwaukee	IHL	19	9	8	1	1098	49	0	2.68	....	....	....	....	....	....	....
	Utah Grizzlies	IHL	17	9	5	1	937	42	3	2.69	2	0	2	121	4	0	1.99
2000-01	Albany River Rats	AHL	4	0	4	0	199	19	0	5.72	....	....	....	....	....	....	....
	Washington	**NHL**	**1**	**1**	**0**	**0**	**20**	**0**	**0**	**0.00**	....	....	....	....	....	....	....
	Cincinnati	IHL	13	11	2	0	783	28	1	2.15	....	....	....	....	....	....	....
	Portland Pirates	AHL	36	17	17	2	2142	104	1	2.91	2	0	2	118	7	0	3.55
2001-02	Portland Pirates	AHL	23	6	12	5	1395	62	1	2.67	....	....	....	....	....	....	....
	Philadelphia	AHL	5	2	3	0	299	14	1	2.81	....	....	....	....	....	....	....
2002-03	**Dallas**	**NHL**	**2**	**0**	**1**	**0**	**97**	**4**	**0**	**2.47**	....	....	....	....	....	....	....
	Utah Grizzlies	AHL	35	14	16	2	1953	86	0	2.64	1	0	1	60	5	0	5.00
	NHL Totals		**108**	**34**	**45**	**14**	**5775**	**301**	**4**	**3.13**	**6**	**2**	**3**	**338**	**21**	**0**	**3.73**

WHL West Second All-Star Team (1990) • WHL West First All-Star Team (1991, 1992) • Canadian Major Junior Goaltender of the Year (1992) • Memorial Cup All-Star Team (1992) • Hap Emms Memorial Trophy (Memorial Cup Top Goaltender) (1992) • AHL First All-Star Team (1993) • Dudley "Red" Garrett Memorial Trophy (Top Rookie – AHL) (1993) • Shared Harry "Hap" Holmes Memorial Trophy (fewest goals against – AHL) (1993) with Boris Rousson • NHL All-Rookie Team (1996)

Traded to **Vancouver** by **NY Rangers** for Nathan LaFayette, April 7, 1995. Signed as a free agent by **Nashville**, August 10, 1999. Traded to **Anaheim** by **Nashville** for future considerations, March 14, 2000. Signed as a free agent by **Washington**, October 27, 2000. Signed as a free agent by **Dallas**, August 14, 2002.

HNILICKA, Milan (huh-LEETCH-kuh, MEE-lan) ATL.

Goaltender. Catches left. 6'1", 190 lbs. Born, Pardubice, Czech., June 25, 1973.
(NY Islanders' 4th choice, 70th overall, in 1991 Entry Draft).

			Regular Season								Playoffs						
Season	Club	League	GP	W	L	T	Mins	GA	SO	Avg	GP	W	L	Mins	GA	SO	Avg
1989-90	Poldi Kladno	Czech	24	....	....	....	1113	70	....	3.77	....	....	....	....	....	....	....
1990-91	Poldi Kladno	Czech	40	....	....	....	2122	98	0	2.80	....	....	....	....	....	....	....
1991-92	Poldi Kladno	Czech	38	....	....	....	2066	128	0	3.73	....	....	....	....	....	....	....
1992-93	Swift Current	WHL	*65	*46	12	2	3679	206	2	3.36	*17	*12	5	*1017	54	*2	3.19
1993-94	Richmond	ECHL	43	18	16	5	2299	155	4	4.05	....	....	....	....	....	....	....
	Salt Lake	IHL	8	5	1	0	378	25	0	3.97	....	....	....	....	....	....	....
1994-95	Denver Grizzlies	IHL	15	9	4	1	798	47	1	3.53	....	....	....	....	....	....	....
1995-96	HC Poldi Kladno	Czech	33	....	....	....	1959	93	1	2.84	8	....	....	493	24	....	2.92
1996-97	HC Poldi Kladno	Czech	48	....	....	....	2736	120	*4	2.63	3	....	....	151	14	0	5.56
1997-98	HC Sparta Praha	Czech	49	....	....	....	2847	99	....	2.09	11	....	....	632	31	....	3.00
1998-99	HC Sparta Praha	Czech	*50	....	....	....	*2877	109	....	2.27	8	....	....	507	13	....	*1.54
99-2000	**NY Rangers**	**NHL**	**2**	**0**	**1**	**0**	**86**	**5**	**0**	**3.49**	....	....	....	....	....	....	....
	Hartford Wolf Pack	AHL	36	22	11	0	1979	71	5	*2.15	3	0	1	99	6	0	3.64
2000-01	**Atlanta**	**NHL**	**36**	**12**	**19**	**2**	**1879**	**105**	**2**	**3.35**	....	....	....	....	....	....	....
2001-02	**Atlanta**	**NHL**	**60**	**13**	**33**	**10**	**3367**	**179**	**3**	**3.19**	....	....	....	....	....	....	....
2002-03	**Atlanta**	**NHL**	**21**	**4**	**13**	**1**	**1097**	**65**	**0**	**3.56**	....	....	....	....	....	....	....
	Chicago Wolves	AHL	15	11	2	1	838	33	1	2.36	....	....	....	....	....	....	....
	NHL Totals		**119**	**29**	**66**	**13**	**6429**	**354**	**5**	**3.30**	....	....	....	....	....	....	....

Shared Harry "Hap" Holmes Memorial Trophy (fewest goals against – AHL) (2000) with Jean-Francois Labbe

Signed as a free agent by **NY Rangers**, July 15, 1999. Signed as a free agent by **Atlanta**, July 28, 2000.

HODSON, Jamie (HAWD-suhn, JAY-mee) TOR.

Goaltender. Catches left. 6'2", 205 lbs. Born, Brandon, Man., April 8, 1980.
(Toronto's 3rd choice, 69th overall, in 1998 Entry Draft).

			Regular Season								Playoffs						
Season	Club	League	GP	W	L	T	Mins	GA	SO	Avg	GP	W	L	Mins	GA	SO	Avg
1996-97	Yellowhead Chiefs	MMHL	12	....	....	....	720	58	1	4.83	....	....	....	....	....	....	....
1997-98	Brandon	WHL	20	12	2	2	964	52	2	3.24	6	5	0	337	16	0	2.85
1998-99	Brandon	WHL	43	23	12	3	2295	123	4	3.22	5	1	4	275	26	0	5.67
99-2000	Brandon	WHL	39	13	22	3	2321	130	2	3.36	....	....	....	....	....	....	....
2000-01	St. John's	AHL	4	0	2	0	137	13	0	5.71	....	....	....	....	....	....	....
	Brandon	WHL	29	9	17	1	1587	92	0	3.48	1	0	1	59	3	0	3.05
2001-02	South Carolina	ECHL	36	20	9	3	1996	100	1	3.01	1	0	1	60	3	0	3.01
2002-03	St. John's	AHL	22	8	7	2	1136	64	1	3.38	....	....	....	....	....	....	....
	Greensboro	ECHL	14	9	4	1	816	33	0	2.43	....	....	....	....	....	....	....

HODSON, Kevin (HAWD-suhn, KEH-vihn)

Goaltender. Catches left. 6', 182 lbs. Born, Winnipeg, Man., March 27, 1972.

			Regular Season								Playoffs						
Season	Club	League	GP	W	L	T	Mins	GA	SO	Avg	GP	W	L	Mins	GA	SO	Avg
1989-90	Winnipeg South	MJHL	35	....	....	....	1900	115	2	3.40	....	....	....	....	....	....	....
1990-91	Sault Ste. Marie	OHL	30	18	11	0	1638	88	*2	*3.22	10	*9	1	581	28	0	*2.89
1991-92	Sault Ste. Marie	OHL	50	28	12	4	2722	151	0	3.33	18	12	6	1116	54	1	2.90
1992-93	Sault Ste. Marie	OHL	26	18	5	2	1470	76	1	*3.10	14	11	2	755	34	0	2.70
	Indianapolis Ice	IHL	14	5	9	0	777	53	0	4.09	....	....	....	....	....	....	....
1993-94	Adirondack	AHL	37	20	10	5	2082	102	2	2.94	3	0	2	89	10	0	6.77
1994-95	Adirondack	AHL	51	19	22	8	2731	161	1	3.54	4	0	4	237	14	0	3.53
1995-96	**Detroit**	**NHL**	**4**	**2**	**0**	**0**	**163**	**3**	**1**	**1.10**	....	....	....	....	....	....	....
	Adirondack	AHL	32	13	13	2	1654	87	0	3.16	3	0	2	150	8	0	3.21
1996-97♦	**Detroit**	**NHL**	**6**	**2**	**2**	**1**	**294**	**8**	**1**	**1.63**	....	....	....	....	....	....	....
	Quebec Rafales	IHL	2	1	1	0	118	7	0	3.54	....	....	....	....	....	....	....
1997-98♦	**Detroit**	**NHL**	**21**	**9**	**3**	**3**	**988**	**44**	**2**	**2.67**	**1**	**0**	**0**	**1**	**0**	**0**	**0.00**
1998-99	**Detroit**	**NHL**	**4**	**0**	**2**	**0**	**175**	**9**	**0**	**3.09**	....	....	....	....	....	....	....
	Adirondack	AHL	6	1	3	2	349	19	0	3.27	....	....	....	....	....	....	....
	Tampa Bay	**NHL**	**5**	**2**	**1**	**1**	**238**	**11**	**0**	**2.77**	....	....	....	....	....	....	....
99-2000	**Tampa Bay**	**NHL**	**24**	**2**	**7**	**4**	**769**	**47**	**0**	**3.67**	....	....	....	....	....	....	....
	Detroit Vipers	IHL	9	2	6	0	505	22	0	2.61	....	....	....	....	....	....	....
2000-01			OUT OF HOCKEY – RETIRED														
2001-02	Sault Ste. Marie	OHL	DID NOT PLAY – ASSISTANT COACH														
2002-03	**Tampa Bay**	**NHL**	**7**	**0**	**3**	**1**	**283**	**12**	**0**	**2.54**	....	....	....	....	....	....	....
	NHL Totals		**71**	**17**	**18**	**10**	**2910**	**134**	**4**	**2.76**	**1**	**0**	**0**	**1**	**0**	**0**	**0.00**

Memorial Cup All-Star Team (1993) • Hap Emms Memorial Trophy (Memorial Cup Top Goaltender) (1993)

Signed as a free agent by **Chicago**, August 17, 1992. Signed as a free agent by **Detroit**, June 16, 1993. • Played 16 seconds in playoff game vs. St. Louis, May 17, 1998. Traded to **Tampa Bay** by **Detroit** with San Jose's 2nd round choice (previously acquired, Tampa Bay selected Sheldon Keefe) in 1999 Entry Draft for Wendel Clark and Detroit's 6th round choice (previously acquired, Detroit selected Kent McDonell) in 1999 Entry Draft, March 23, 1999. Traded to **Montreal** by **Tampa Bay** for Montreal's 7th round choice (later traded to Philadelphia – Philadelphia selected John Eichelberger) in 2000 Entry Draft, June 2, 2000. Signed as a free agent by **Tampa Bay**, May 28, 2002. • Officially announced retirement, January 16, 2003.

HOLMQVIST, Johan (HOHLM-kvihst, YOH-han) MIN.

Goaltender. Catches left. 6'3", 195 lbs. Born, Tolfta, Sweden, May 24, 1978.
(NY Rangers' 9th choice, 175th overall, in 1997 Entry Draft).

			Regular Season								Playoffs						
Season	Club	League	GP	W	L	T	Mins	GA	SO	Avg	GP	W	L	Mins	GA	SO	Avg
1996-97	Brynas IF Gavle	Sweden	2	0	0	0	80	4	0	3.00	....	....	....	....	....	....	....
1997-98	Brynas IF Gavle	Sweden	33	....	....	....	1897	82	....	2.59	3	0	3	180	14	....	4.67
1998-99	Brynas IF Gavle	Sweden	41	....	....	....	2383	111	4	2.79	*14	9	5	*855	34	0	2.39
99-2000	Brynas IF Gavle	Sweden	41	....	....	....	2402	104	4	2.60	11	....	....	671	30	1	2.68
2000-01	**NY Rangers**	**NHL**	**2**	**0**	**2**	**0**	**119**	**10**	**0**	**5.04**	....	....	....	....	....	....	....
	Hartford Wolf Pack	AHL	43	19	14	4	2305	111	2	2.89	5	2	3	314	13	0	2.48
2001-02	**NY Rangers**	**NHL**	**1**	**0**	**0**	**0**	**9**	**0**	**0**	**0.00**	....	....	....	....	....	....	....
	Hartford Wolf Pack	AHL	48	26	12	6	2734	140	1	3.07	4	1	2	163	12	0	4.41
2002-03	**NY Rangers**	**NHL**	**1**	**0**	**1**	**0**	**39**	**2**	**0**	**3.08**	....	....	....	....	....	....	....
	Hartford Wolf Pack	AHL	35	14	13	5	1904	84	2	2.65	....	....	....	....	....	....	....
	Charlotte Checkers	ECHL	1	1	0	0	60	2	0	2.00	....	....	....	....	....	....	....
	Houston Aeros	AHL	8	5	3	0	479	23	1	2.88	*23	*15	8	*1499	50	1	2.00
	NHL Totals		**4**	**0**	**3**	**0**	**167**	**12**	**0**	**4.31**	....	....	....	....	....	....	....

Jack A. Butterfield Trophy (Playoff MVP – AHL) (2003)

Traded to **Minnesota** by **NY Rangers** for Lawrence Nycholat, March 11, 2003.

HOLT, Chris (HOHLT, KRIHS) NYR

Goaltender. Catches left. 6'2", 218 lbs. Born, Vancouver, B.C., June 5, 1985.
(NY Rangers' 8th choice, 180th overall, in 2003 Entry Draft).

			Regular Season								Playoffs						
Season	Club	League	GP	W	L	T	Mins	GA	SO	Avg	GP	W	L	Mins	GA	SO	Avg
2001-02	Billings Bulls	AWHL	24	13	7	1	1184	59	2	2.99	....	....	....	....	....	....	....
2002-03	U.S. National U-18	USDP	32	9	15	2	1774	95	1	3.21	....	....	....	....	....	....	....

HOWARD, James (HOW-uhrd, JAYMZ) DET.

Goaltender. Catches left. 6', 218 lbs. Born, Syracuse, NY, March 26, 1984.
(Detroit's 1st choice, 64th overall, in 2003 Entry Draft).

			Regular Season								Playoffs						
Season	Club	League	GP	W	L	T	Mins	GA	SO	Avg	GP	W	L	Mins	GA	SO	Avg
2001-02	U.S. National U-17	USDP	9	6	3	0	484	29	1	3.67	....	....	....	....	....	....	....
	U.S. National U-18	USDP	26	16	8	1	1492	47	3	1.89	....	....	....	....	....	....	....
2002-03	University of Maine	H-East	21	14	6	0	1151	47	3	2.45	....	....	....	....	....	....	....

USA Hockey Goaltender of the Year (2002) • Hockey East All-Rookie Team (2003) • Hockey East Rookie of the Year (2003)

HUET, Cristobal (oo-AY, KRIHS-toh-bahl) L.A.

Goaltender. Catches left. 6', 194 lbs. Born, St. Martin D'Heres, France, September 3, 1975.
(Los Angeles' 9th choice, 214th overall, in 2001 Entry Draft).

			Regular Season								Playoffs						
Season	Club	League	GP	W	L	T	Mins	GA	SO	Avg	GP	W	L	Mins	GA	SO	Avg
1994/98	CSG Grenoble	France	STATISTICS NOT AVAILABLE														
1997-98	France	Olympics	2	1	1	0	120	5	0	2.50	....	....	....	....	....	....	....
1998-99	HC Lugano	Swiss	21	....	....	....	1275	58	1	2.73	10	....	....	628	18	1	*1.72
99-2000	HC Lugano	Swiss	31	....	....	....	1886	50	*8	*1.59	13	....	....	783	29	0	2.22
2000-01	HC Lugano	Swiss	39	....	....	....	2365	77	*6	*1.95	*18	....	....	*1141	39	2	2.05
2001-02	HC Lugano	Swiss	39	....	....	....	2313	107	*4	2.78	1	0	1	60	3	0	3.00
	France	Olympics	3	0	2	1	179	10	0	3.36	....	....	....	....	....	....	....
2002-03	**Los Angeles**	**NHL**	**12**	**4**	**4**	**1**	**541**	**21**	**1**	**2.33**	....	....	....	....	....	....	....
	Manchester	AHL	30	16	8	5	1784	68	1	2.29	1	0	1	30	4	0	8.08
	NHL Totals		**12**	**4**	**4**	**1**	**541**	**21**	**1**	**2.33**	....	....	....	....	....	....	....

HURME, Jani (HOOR-meh, YAN-ee) FLA.

Goaltender. Catches left. 6', 180 lbs. Born, Turku, Finland, January 7, 1975.
(Ottawa's 2nd choice, 58th overall, in 1997 Entry Draft).

			Regular Season								Playoffs						
Season	Club	League	GP	W	L	T	Mins	GA	SO	Avg	GP	W	L	Mins	GA	SO	Avg
1992-93	TPS Turku Jr.	Finn-Jr.	12	....	....	....	669	47	0	4.22	1	....	....	60	0	1	0.00
1993-94	Kiekko-67 Jr.	Finn-Jr.	18	....	....	....	1082	57	0	3.16	....	....	....	....	....	....	....
	Kiekko-67 Turku	Finland-2	3	....	....	....	190	7	0	2.21	....	....	....	....	....	....	....
	TPS Turku	Finland	1	....	....	....	2	0	0	0.00	....	....	....	....	....	....	....
1994-95	TPS Turku Jr.	Finn-Jr.	2	....	....	....	125	5	0	2.40	....	....	....	....	....	....	....
	Kiekko-67 Jr.	Finn-Jr.	9	....	....	....	540	47	....	5.22	....	....	....	....	....	....	....
	Kiekko-67 Turku	Finland-2	19	....	....	....	1049	53	....	3.03	3	....	....	180	6	....	2.00
1995-96	TPS Turku Jr.	Finn-Jr.	13	....	....	....	777	34	1	2.63	....	....	....	....	....	....	....
	Kiekko-67 Turku	Finland-2	16	....	....	....	968	39	1	2.42	....	....	....	....	....	....	....
	TPS Turku	Finland	16	....	....	....	946	34	2	2.16	10	....	....	545	22	2	2.42
1996-97	TPS Turku	Finland	48	*31	11	6	*2917	101	*6	*2.08	*12	6	6	*722	39	0	3.24
1997-98	Detroit Vipers	IHL	6	2	2	2	290	20	0	4.13	....	....	....	....	....	....	....
	Indianapolis Ice	IHL	29	11	11	3	1506	83	1	3.30	3	1	0	129	10	0	4.62
1998-99	Detroit Vipers	IHL	12	7	3	1	643	26	1	2.43	....	....	....	....	....	....	....
	Cincinnati	IHL	26	14	9	2	1428	81	0	3.40	....	....	....	....	....	....	....
99-2000	**Ottawa**	**NHL**	**1**	**1**	**0**	**0**	**60**	**2**	**0**	**2.00**	....	....	....	....	....	....	....
	Grand Rapids	IHL	52	29	15	4	2948	107	4	2.18	*17	*10	7	*1028	37	1	2.16
2000-01	**Ottawa**	**NHL**	**22**	**12**	**5**	**4**	**1296**	**54**	**2**	**2.50**	....	....	....	....	....	....	....

2001-02	Ottawa	NHL	25	12	9	1	1309	54	3	2.48	....	....	....	....	....	....	....
	Finland	Olympics	3	1	2	0	179	9	0	3.01	....	....	....	....	....	....	....
2002-03	Florida	NHL	28	4	11	6	1376	66	1	2.88	....	....	....	....	....	....	....
	NHL Totals		76	29	25	11	4041	176	6	2.61	....	....	....	....	....	....	....

Finnish Elite League Rookie of the Year (1996) • Finnish Elite League Player of the Year (1997) • IHL Second All-Star Team (2000)

Traded to **Florida** by **Ottawa** for Billy Thompson and Greg Watson, October 1, 2002.

IRBE, Arturs (UHR-bay, AHR-tuhrs) CAR.

Goaltender. Catches left. 5'8", 190 lbs. Born, Riga, Latvia, February 2, 1967.
(Minnesota's 11th choice, 196th overall, in 1989 Entry Draft).

			Regular Season								Playoffs						
Season	Club	League	GP	W	L	T	Mins	GA	SO	Avg	GP	W	L	Mins	GA	SO	Avg
1986-87	Dynamo Riga	USSR	2	....	....	....	27	1	0	2.22	....	....	....	....	....	....	....
1987-88	Dynamo Riga	USSR	34	....	....	....	1870	86	4	2.76	....	....	....	....	....	....	....
1988-89	Dynamo Riga	USSR	40	....	....	....	2460	116	4	2.83	....	....	....	....	....	....	....
1989-90	Dynamo Riga	USSR	48	....	....	....	2880	115	2	2.40	....	....	....	....	....	....	....
1990-91	Dynamo Riga	USSR	46	....	....	....	2713	133	5	2.94	....	....	....	....	....	....	....
1991-92	**San Jose**	**NHL**	**13**	**2**	**6**	**3**	**645**	**48**	**0**	**4.47**	....	....	....	....	....	....	....
	Kansas City Blades	IHL	32	24	7	1	1955	80	0	*2.46	*15	*12	3	914	44	0	*2.89
1992-93	**San Jose**	**NHL**	**36**	**7**	**26**	**0**	**2074**	**142**	**1**	**4.11**	....	....	....	....	....	....	....
	Kansas City Blades	IHL	6	3	3	0	364	20	0	3.30	....	....	....	....	....	....	....
1993-94	**San Jose**	**NHL**	***74**	**30**	**28**	**16**	***4412**	**209**	**3**	**2.84**	**14**	**7**	**7**	**806**	**50**	**0**	**3.72**
1994-95	**San Jose**	**NHL**	**38**	**14**	**19**	**3**	**2043**	**111**	**4**	**3.26**	**6**	**2**	**4**	**316**	**27**	**0**	**5.13**
1995-96	**San Jose**	**NHL**	**22**	**4**	**12**	**4**	**1112**	**85**	**0**	**4.59**	....	....	....	....	....	....	....
	Kansas City Blades	IHL	4	1	2	1	226	16	0	4.24	....	....	....	....	....	....	....
1996-97	**Dallas**	**NHL**	**35**	**17**	**12**	**3**	**1965**	**88**	**3**	**2.69**	**1**	**0**	**0**	**13**	**0**	**0**	**0.00**
1997-98	**Vancouver**	**NHL**	**41**	**14**	**11**	**6**	**1999**	**91**	**2**	**2.73**	....	....	....	....	....	....	....
1998-99	**Carolina**	**NHL**	**62**	**27**	**20**	**12**	**3643**	**135**	**6**	**2.22**	**6**	**2**	**4**	**408**	**15**	**0**	**2.21**
99-2000	**Carolina**	**NHL**	***75**	**34**	**28**	**9**	**4345**	**175**	**5**	**2.42**	....	....	....	....	....	....	....
2000-01	**Carolina**	**NHL**	***77**	**37**	**29**	**9**	***4406**	**180**	**6**	**2.45**	**6**	**2**	**4**	**360**	**20**	**0**	**3.33**
2001-02	**Carolina**	**NHL**	**51**	**20**	**19**	**11**	**2974**	**126**	**3**	**2.54**	**18**	**10**	**8**	**1078**	**30**	**1**	**1.67**
	Latvia	Olympics	1	0	1	0	60	4	0	4.00	....	....	....	....	....	....	....
2002-03	**Carolina**	**NHL**	**34**	**7**	**24**	**2**	**1884**	**100**	**0**	**3.18**	....	....	....	....	....	....	....
	Lowell	AHL	7	3	3	1	427	21	0	2.95	....	....	....	....	....	....	....
	NHL Totals		**558**	**213**	**234**	**78**	**31502**	**1490**	**33**	**2.84**	**51**	**23**	**27**	**2981**	**142**	**1**	**2.86**

IHL First All-Star Team (1992) • Shared James Norris Memorial Trophy (fewest goals against – IHL) (1992) with Wade Flaherty

Played in NHL All-Star Game (1994, 1999)

Claimed by **San Jose** from **Minnesota** in Dispersal Draft, May 30, 1991. Signed as a free agent by **Dallas**, August 19, 1996. Signed as a free agent by **Vancouver**, August 25, 1997. Signed as a free agent by **Carolina**, September 14, 1998.

JOHNSON, Brent (JAWN-suhn, BREHNT) ST.L.

Goaltender. Catches left. 6'2", 200 lbs. Born, Farmington, MI, March 12, 1977.
(Colorado's 5th choice, 129th overall, in 1995 Entry Draft).

			Regular Season								Playoffs						
Season	Club	League	GP	W	L	T	Mins	GA	SO	Avg	GP	W	L	Mins	GA	SO	Avg
1993-94	Det. Compuware	NAJHL	18	....	....	....	1024	49	1	3.52	....	....	....	....	....	....	....
1994-95	Owen Sound	OHL	18	3	9	1	904	75	0	4.98	....	....	....	....	....	....	....
1995-96	Owen Sound	OHL	58	24	28	1	3211	243	1	4.54	6	2	4	371	29	0	4.69
1996-97	Owen Sound	OHL	50	20	28	1	2798	201	1	4.31	4	0	4	253	24	0	5.69
1997-98	Worcester IceCats	AHL	42	14	15	7	2240	119	0	3.19	6	3	2	332	19	0	3.43
1998-99	**St. Louis**	**NHL**	**6**	**3**	**2**	**0**	**286**	**10**	**0**	**2.10**	....	....	....	....	....	....	....
	Worcester IceCats	AHL	49	22	22	4	2925	146	2	2.99	4	1	3	238	12	0	3.02
99-2000	Worcester IceCats	AHL	58	24	27	5	3319	161	3	2.91	9	4	5	561	23	1	2.46
2000-01	**St. Louis**	**NHL**	**31**	**19**	**9**	**2**	**1744**	**63**	**4**	**2.17**	**2**	**0**	**1**	**62**	**2**	**0**	**1.94**
2001-02	**St. Louis**	**NHL**	**58**	**34**	**20**	**4**	**3491**	**127**	**5**	**2.18**	**10**	**5**	**5**	**590**	**18**	**3**	**1.83**
2002-03	**St. Louis**	**NHL**	**38**	**16**	**13**	**5**	**2042**	**84**	**2**	**2.47**	....	....	....	....	....	....	....
	Worcester IceCats	AHL	2	0	1	1	125	8	0	3.84	....	....	....	....	....	....	....
	NHL Totals		**133**	**72**	**44**	**11**	**7563**	**284**	**11**	**2.25**	**12**	**5**	**6**	**652**	**20**	**3**	**1.84**

Traded to **St. Louis** by **Colorado** for San Jose's 3rd round choice (previously acquired, Colorado selected Rick Berry) in 1997 Entry Draft, May 30, 1997.

JOKELA, Antti (YOH-keh-luh, AHN-tee) CAR.

Goaltender. Catches left. 5'11", 175 lbs. Born, Rauma, Finland, May 7, 1981.
(Carolina's 8th choice, 237th overall, in 1999 Entry Draft).

			Regular Season								Playoffs						
Season	Club	League	GP	W	L	T	Mins	GA	SO	Avg	GP	W	L	Mins	GA	SO	Avg
1998-99	Lukko Rauma-B	Finn-Jr.	8	....	....	....	480	26	0	3.25	....	....	....	....	....	....	....
	Lukko Rauma Jr.	Finn-Jr.	18	....	....	....	1038	66	1	3.81	....	....	....	....	....	....	....
99-2000	Lukko Rauma Jr.	Finn-Jr.	21	....	....	....	1196	71	0	3.56	....	....	....	....	....	....	....
2000-01	Jaa-Kotkat	Finn-Jr.	42	20	20	2	2520	100	4	2.38	....	....	....	....	....	....	....
	Lukko Rauma	Finland	1	0	0	0	19	2	0	6.32	....	....	....	....	....	....	....
2001-02	Jaa-Kotkat	Finland-2	28	....	....	....	1680	100	0	3.51	....	....	....	....	....	....	....
	Jaa-Kotkat Jr.	Finn-Jr.	....	....	....	....	....	....	....	....	4	1	3	240	14	0	3.46
2002-03	Assat Pori	Finland	10	3	1	3	510	28	0	3.29	....	....	....	....	....	....	....
	Ahmat	Finland-2	1	0	1	0	59	5	0	5.02	....	....	....	....	....	....	....

JOSEPH, Curtis (JOH-sehf, KUR-tihs) DET.

Goaltender. Catches left. 5'11", 190 lbs. Born, Keswick, Ont., April 29, 1967.

			Regular Season								Playoffs						
Season	Club	League	GP	W	L	T	Mins	GA	SO	Avg	GP	W	L	Mins	GA	SO	Avg
1984-85	King City Dukes	OJHL-B	18	....	....	....	947	76	0	4.82	....	....	....	....	....	....	....
	Newmarket Flyers	OPJHL	2	1	1	0	120	16	0	8.00	....	....	....	....	....	....	....
1985-86	Richmond Hill	OPJHL	33	12	18	0	1716	156	1	5.45	....	....	....	....	....	....	....
1986-87	Richmond Hill	OPJHL	30	14	7	6	1764	128	1	4.35	....	....	....	....	....	....	....
1987-88	Notre Dame	SJHL	36	25	4	7	2174	94	1	2.59	....	....	....	....	....	....	....
1988-89	U. of Wisconsin	WCHA	38	21	11	5	2267	94	1	2.49	....	....	....	....	....	....	....
1989-90	Peoria Rivermen	IHL	23	10	8	2	1241	80	0	3.87	....	....	....	....	....	....	....
	St. Louis	**NHL**	**15**	**9**	**5**	**1**	**852**	**48**	**0**	**3.38**	**6**	**4**	**1**	**327**	**18**	**0**	**3.30**
1990-91	**St. Louis**	**NHL**	**30**	**16**	**10**	**2**	**1710**	**89**	**0**	**3.12**	....	....	....	....	....	....	....
1991-92	**St. Louis**	**NHL**	**60**	**27**	**20**	**10**	**3494**	**175**	**2**	**3.01**	**6**	**2**	**4**	**379**	**23**	**0**	**3.64**
1992-93	**St. Louis**	**NHL**	**68**	**29**	**28**	**9**	**3890**	**196**	**1**	**3.02**	**11**	**7**	**4**	**715**	**27**	***2**	**2.27**
1993-94	**St. Louis**	**NHL**	**71**	**36**	**23**	**11**	**4127**	**213**	**1**	**3.10**	**4**	**0**	**4**	**246**	**15**	**0**	**3.66**
1994-95	**St. Louis**	**NHL**	**36**	**20**	**10**	**1**	**1914**	**89**	**1**	**2.79**	**7**	**3**	**3**	**392**	**24**	**0**	**3.67**
1995-96	Las Vegas Thunder	IHL	15	12	2	1	874	29	1	1.99	....	....	....	....	....	....	....
	Edmonton	**NHL**	**34**	**15**	**16**	**2**	**1936**	**111**	**0**	**3.44**	....	....	....	....	....	....	....
1996-97	**Edmonton**	**NHL**	**72**	**32**	**29**	**9**	**4100**	**200**	**6**	**2.93**	**12**	**5**	**7**	**767**	**36**	**2**	**2.82**
1997-98	**Edmonton**	**NHL**	**71**	**29**	**31**	**9**	**4132**	**181**	**8**	**2.63**	**12**	**5**	**7**	**716**	**23**	**3**	**1.93**
1998-99	**Toronto**	**NHL**	**67**	**35**	**24**	**7**	**4001**	**171**	**3**	**2.56**	**17**	**9**	**8**	**1011**	**41**	**1**	**2.43**
99-2000	**Toronto**	**NHL**	**63**	**36**	**20**	**7**	**3801**	**158**	**4**	**2.49**	**12**	**6**	**6**	**729**	**25**	**1**	**2.06**
2000-01	**Toronto**	**NHL**	**68**	**33**	**27**	**8**	**4100**	**163**	**6**	**2.39**	**11**	**7**	**4**	**685**	**24**	**3**	**2.10**
2001-02	**Toronto**	**NHL**	**51**	**29**	**17**	**5**	**3065**	**114**	**4**	**2.23**	**20**	**10**	**10**	**1253**	**48**	**3**	**2.30**
	Canada	Olympics	1	0	1	0	60	5	0	5.00	....	....	....	....	....	....	....
2002-03	**Detroit**	**NHL**	**61**	**34**	**19**	**6**	**3566**	**148**	**5**	**2.49**	**4**	**0**	**4**	**289**	**10**	**0**	**2.08**
	NHL Totals		**767**	**380**	**279**	**87**	**44688**	**2056**	**41**	**2.76**	**122**	**58**	**62**	**7509**	**314**	**15**	**2.51**

WCHA First All-Star Team (1989) • WCHA Freshman of the Year (1989) • WCHA Player of the Year (1989) • NCAA West Second All-American Team (1989) • King Clancy Memorial Trophy (2000)

Played in NHL All-Star Game (1994, 2000)

Signed as a free agent by **St. Louis**, June 16, 1989. Traded to **Edmonton** by **St. Louis** with the rights to Mike Grier for St. Louis' 1st round choices (previously acquired) in 1996 (Marty Reasoner) and 1997 (later traded to Los Angeles – Los Angeles selected Matt Zultek) Entry Drafts, August 4, 1995. Signed as a free agent by **Toronto**, July 15, 1998. Traded to **Calgary** by **Toronto** for Calgary's 3rd round choice (later traded to Minnesota – Minnesota selected Danny Irmen) in 2003 Entry Draft and future considerations, June 30, 2002. Signed as a free agent by **Detroit**, July 2, 2002.

KALTIAINEN, Matti (kal-tee-AY-nehn, MAT-tee) BOS.

Goaltender. Catches left. 6'2", 216 lbs. Born, Espoo, Finland, April 30, 1982.
(Boston's 3rd choice, 111th overall, in 2001 Entry Draft).

			Regular Season								Playoffs						
Season	Club	League	GP	W	L	T	Mins	GA	SO	Avg	GP	W	L	Mins	GA	SO	Avg
1998-99	Blues Espoo Jr.	Finn-Jr.	4	....	....	....	258	10	0	2.33	....	....	....	....	....	....	....
99-2000	Blues Espoo Jr.	Finn-Jr.	23	....	....	....	1337	56	0	2.51	4	2	2	244	15	0	3.93
2000-01	Blues Espoo Jr.	Finn-Jr.	25	....	....	....	1500	65	0	2.60	....	....	....	....	....	....	....
2001-02	Boston College	H-East	18	8	10	0	1080	48	1	2.67	....	....	....	....	....	....	....
2002-03	Boston College	H-East	30	18	9	3	1843	68	1	2.21	....	....	....	....	....	....	....

KELLERMAN, Tyson (KEHL-uhr-man, TIGH-suhn) CHI.

Goaltender. Catches left. 6'3", 180 lbs. Born, Kingston, Ont., January 18, 1984.
(Chicago's 7th choice, 219th overall, in 2002 Entry Draft).

			Regular Season								Playoffs						
Season	Club	League	GP	W	L	T	Mins	GA	SO	Avg	GP	W	L	Mins	GA	SO	Avg
2000-01	Gloucester	CJHL	25	....	....	....	1174	90	0	4.60	....	....	....	....	....	....	....
2001-02	North Bay	OHL	41	11	22	1	2103	122	0	3.48	4	1	3	243	17	0	4.20
2002-03	Saginaw Spirit	OHL	35	3	29	2	1891	132	0	4.19	....	....	....	....	....	....	....

KETTLES, Kyle (KEH-tuhls, KIGHL) MIN.

Goaltender. Catches left. 6'3", 180 lbs. Born, Lac du Bonnet, Man., February 19, 1981.
(Nashville's 13th choice, 205th overall, in 1999 Entry Draft).

			Regular Season								Playoffs						
Season	Club	League	GP	W	L	T	Mins	GA	SO	Avg	GP	W	L	Mins	GA	SO	Avg
1997-98	Selkirk Steelers	MJHL	32	9	19	1	1613	119	0	4.43	....	....	....	....	....	....	....
	Brandon	WHL	....	....	....	....	....	....	....	....	1	0	0	10	2	0	12.00
1998-99	Selkirk Steelers	MJHL	17	7	8	0	939	65	0	4.15	....	....	....	....	....	....	....
	Neepawa Natives	MJHL	6	2	4	0	361	27	0	4.49	....	....	....	....	....	....	....
99-2000	Medicine Hat	WHL	57	16	33	5	3260	215	1	3.96	....	....	....	....	....	....	....
2000-01	Medicine Hat	WHL	47	15	24	2	2586	183	0	4.25	....	....	....	....	....	....	....
2001-02	Medicine Hat	WHL	5	1	4	0	274	23	0	5.04	....	....	....	....	....	....	....
	Moose Jaw	WHL	54	24	25	4	3089	160	*4	3.11	12	6	6	735	29	1	2.37
2002-03	Louisiana	ECHL	41	21	12	7	2439	106	*5	2.61	6	3	3	359	13	1	2.17

Signed as a free agent by **Minnesota**, April 23, 2002.

KHABIBULIN, Nikolai (khah-bee-BOO-lihn, NIH-koh-ligh) T.B.

Goaltender. Catches left. 6'1", 203 lbs. Born, Sverdlovsk, USSR, January 13, 1973.
(Winnipeg's 8th choice, 204th overall, in 1992 Entry Draft).

			Regular Season								Playoffs						
Season	Club	League	GP	W	L	T	Mins	GA	SO	Avg	GP	W	L	Mins	GA	SO	Avg
1991-92	CSKA Moscow	CIS	2	0	0	0	34	2	0	3.53	....	....	....	....	....	....	....
1992-93	CSKA Moscow	CIS	13	....	....	....	491	27	....	3.29	....	....	....	....	....	....	....
1993-94	CSKA Moscow	CIS	46	....	....	....	2625	116	....	2.65	3	....	....	193	11	....	3.42
	Russian Penguins	IHL	12	2	7	2	639	47	0	4.41	....	....	....	....	....	....	....
1994-95	Springfield Falcons	AHL	23	9	9	3	1240	80	0	3.87	....	....	....	....	....	....	....
	Winnipeg	**NHL**	**26**	**8**	**9**	**4**	**1339**	**76**	**0**	**3.41**	....	....	....	....	....	....	....
1995-96	**Winnipeg**	**NHL**	**53**	**26**	**20**	**3**	**2914**	**152**	**2**	**3.13**	**6**	**2**	**4**	**359**	**19**	**0**	**3.18**
1996-97	**Phoenix**	**NHL**	**72**	**30**	**33**	**6**	**4091**	**193**	**7**	**2.83**	**7**	**3**	**4**	**426**	**15**	**1**	**2.11**
1997-98	**Phoenix**	**NHL**	**70**	**30**	**28**	**10**	**4026**	**184**	**4**	**2.74**	**4**	**2**	**1**	**185**	**13**	**0**	**4.22**
1998-99	**Phoenix**	**NHL**	**63**	**32**	**23**	**7**	**3657**	**130**	**8**	**2.13**	**7**	**3**	**4**	**449**	**18**	**0**	**2.41**
99-2000	Long Beach	IHL	33	21	11	1	1936	59	5	*1.83	5	2	3	321	15	0	2.81
2000-01	**Tampa Bay**	**NHL**	**2**	**1**	**1**	**0**	**123**	**6**	**0**	**2.93**	....	....	....	....	....	....	....
2001-02	**Tampa Bay**	**NHL**	**70**	**24**	**32**	**10**	**3896**	**153**	**7**	**2.36**	....	....	....	....	....	....	....
	Russia	Olympics	6	3	2	1	*359	14	*1	2.34	....	....	....	....	....	....	....
2002-03	**Tampa Bay**	**NHL**	**65**	**30**	**22**	**11**	**3787**	**156**	**4**	**2.47**	**10**	**5**	**5**	**644**	**26**	**0**	**2.42**
	NHL Totals		**421**	**181**	**168**	**51**	**23833**	**1050**	**32**	**2.64**	**34**	**15**	**18**	**2063**	**91**	**1**	**2.65**

James Gatschene Memorial Trophy (MVP – IHL) (2000) (co-winner - Frederic Chabot)

Played in NHL All-Star Game (1998, 1999, 2002, 2003)

Transferred to **Phoenix** after **Winnipeg** franchise relocated, July 1, 1996. • Missed entire 1999-2000 NHL season and majority of 2000-01 season after failing to come to contract terms with **Phoenix**. Signed as a free agent by **Long Beach** (IHL) with **Phoenix** retaining NHL rights, January 14, 2000. Traded to **Tampa Bay** by **Phoenix** with Stan Neckar for Mike Johnson, Paul Mara, Ruslan Zainullin and NY Islanders' 2nd round choice (previously acquired, Phoenix selected Matthew Spiller) in 2001 Entry Draft, March 5, 2001.

KHLOPTONOV, Denis (khloh-POHT-nahv, DEH-nihs) FLA.

Goaltender. Catches left. 6'4", 198 lbs. Born, Moscow, USSR, January 27, 1978.
(Florida's 8th choice, 209th overall, in 1996 Entry Draft).

			Regular Season								Playoffs						
Season	Club	League	GP	W	L	T	Mins	GA	SO	Avg	GP	W	L	Mins	GA	SO	Avg
1996-97	HC CSKA	Russia	21	....	....	....	1260	42	0	2.00	....	....	....	....	....	....	....
1997-98	HC CSKA	Russia	20	....	....	....	987	58	....	3.53	....	....	....	....	....	....	....
1998-99	Muskegon Fury	UHL	37	21	8	2	1950	98	1	3.02	4	1	1	166	9	0	3.25
99-2000	CSKA Moscow	Russia	10	....	....	....	540	22	1	2.44	2	....	....	119	7	0	3.53
2000-01	CSKA Moscow	Russia	14	....	....	....	753	26	1	2.07	....	....	....	....	....	....	....
2001-02	Magnitogorsk	Russia	14	....	....	....	572	36	0	3.78	....	....	....	....	....	....	....
2002-03	CSKA Moscow	Russia	DID NOT PLAY – INJURED														

KIDD, Trevor (KIHD, TREH-vohr) TOR.

Goaltender. Catches left. 6'2", 213 lbs. Born, Dugald, Man., March 26, 1972.
(Calgary's 1st choice, 11th overall, in 1990 Entry Draft).

			Regular Season								Playoffs						
Season	Club	League	GP	W	L	T	Mins	GA	SO	Avg	GP	W	L	Mins	GA	SO	Avg
1987-88	Eastman Selects	MAHA	14	....	....	....	840	66	0	4.72	....	....	....	....	....	....	....
1988-89	Brandon	WHL	32	11	13	1	1509	102	0	4.06	....	....	....	....	....	....	....
1989-90	Brandon	WHL	*63	24	32	2	*3676	254	2	4.15	....	....	....	....	....	....	....
1990-91	Brandon	WHL	30	10	19	1	1730	117	0	4.06	....	....	....	....	....	....	....
	Spokane Chiefs	WHL	14	8	3	0	749	44	0	3.52	15	*14	1	926	32	2	*2.07
1991-92	Canada	Nat-Tm	28	18	4	4	1349	79	2	3.51	....	....	....	....	....	....	....
	Canada	Olympics	1	1	0	0	60	0	1	0.00	....	....	....	....	....	....	....
	Calgary	**NHL**	**2**	**1**	**1**	**0**	**120**	**8**	**0**	**4.00**	....	....	....	....	....	....	....
1992-93	Salt Lake	IHL	29	10	16	1	1696	111	1	3.93	....	....	....	....	....	....	....
1993-94	**Calgary**	**NHL**	**31**	**13**	**7**	**6**	**1614**	**85**	**0**	**3.16**	....	....	....	....	....	....	....
1994-95	**Calgary**	**NHL**	***43**	**22**	**14**	**6**	***2463**	**107**	**3**	**2.61**	**7**	**3**	**4**	**434**	**26**	**1**	**3.59**
1995-96	**Calgary**	**NHL**	**47**	**15**	**21**	**8**	**2570**	**119**	**3**	**2.78**	**2**	**0**	**1**	**83**	**9**	**0**	**6.51**

Season	Club	League	GP	W	L	T	Mins	GA	SO	Avg	GP	W	L	Mins	GA	SO	Avg
1996-97	**Calgary**	**NHL**	**55**	**21**	**23**	**6**	**2979**	**141**	**4**	**2.84**	....	....	....	....	....	....	....
1997-98	**Carolina**	**NHL**	**47**	**21**	**21**	**3**	**2685**	**97**	**3**	**2.17**	....	....	....	....	....	....	....
1998-99	**Carolina**	**NHL**	**25**	**7**	**10**	**6**	**1358**	**61**	**2**	**2.70**	....	....	....	....	....	....	....
99-2000	**Florida**	**NHL**	**28**	**14**	**11**	**2**	**1574**	**69**	**1**	**2.63**	....	....	....	....	....	....	....
	Louisville Panthers	AHL	1	0	1	0	60	5	0	5.04	....	....	....	....	....	....	....
2000-01	**Florida**	**NHL**	**42**	**10**	**23**	**6**	**2354**	**130**	**1**	**3.31**	....	....	....	....	....	....	....
2001-02	**Florida**	**NHL**	**33**	**4**	**16**	**5**	**1683**	**90**	**1**	**3.21**	....	....	....	....	....	....	....
2002-03	**Toronto**	**NHL**	**19**	**6**	**10**	**2**	**1143**	**59**	**0**	**3.10**	....	....	....	....	....	....	....
	NHL Totals		**372**	**134**	**157**	**50**	**20543**	**966**	**18**	**2.82**	**9**	**3**	**5**	**517**	**35**	**1**	**4.06**

WHL East First All-Star Team (1990) • Canadian Major Junior Goaltender of the Year (1990)

Traded to **Carolina** by **Calgary** with Gary Roberts for Andrew Cassels and Jean-Sebastien Giguere, August 25, 1997. Claimed by **Atlanta** from **Carolina** in Expansion Draft, June 25, 1999. Traded to **Florida** by **Atlanta** for Gord Murphy, Herbert Vasiljevs, Daniel Tjarnqvist and Ottawa's 6th round choice (previously acquired, later traded to Dallas – Dallas selected Justin Cox) in 1999 Entry Draft, June 25, 1999. Signed as a free agent by **Toronto**, August 26, 2002.

KILPELAINEN, Eero (kih-pehl-AI-nehn, EE-roh) DAL.

Goaltender. Catches left. 5'11", 152 lbs. Born, Juva, Finland, May 7, 1985.
(Dallas' 6th choice, 144th overall, in 2003 Entry Draft).

			Regular Season								Playoffs						
Season	Club	League	GP	W	L	T	Mins	GA	SO	Avg	GP	W	L	Mins	GA	SO	Avg
2001-02	KalPa Kuopio Jr.	Finn-Jr.	STATISTICS NOT AVAILABLE														
2002-03	KalPa Kuopio Jr.	Finn-Jr.	20	8	6	1	991	57	0	3.45	....	....	....	....	....	....	....
	KalPa Kuopio	Finland-2	1	0	0	0	17	4	0	14.12	....	....	....	....	....	....	....

KIPRUSOFF, Miikka (KIHP-ruh-sohf, MEE-kah) S.J.

Goaltender. Catches left. 6'2", 190 lbs. Born, Turku, Finland, October 26, 1976.
(San Jose's 5th choice, 116th overall, in 1995 Entry Draft).

			Regular Season								Playoffs						
Season	Club	League	GP	W	L	T	Mins	GA	SO	Avg	GP	W	L	Mins	GA	SO	Avg
1994-95	TPS Turku Jr.	Finn-Jr.	31	....	....	....	1896	92	....	2.91	....	....	....	....	....	....	....
	TPS Turku	Finland	4	....	....	....	240	12	0	3.00	2	....	....	120	7	....	3.50
1995-96	TPS Turku Jr.	Finn-Jr.	3	....	....	....	180	9	....	3.00	....	....	....	....	....	....	....
	Kiekko-67 Turku	Finland-2	5	....	....	....	300	7	....	1.40	....	....	....	....	....	....	....
	TPS Turku	Finland	12	....	....	....	550	38	0	4.14	3	....	....	114	4	....	2.11
1996-97	AIK Solna	Sweden	42	....	....	....	2466	104	3	2.53	7	....	....	420	23	0	3.28
1997-98	AIK Solna	Sweden	42	....	....	....	2457	110	....	2.69	....	....	....	....	....	....	....
1998-99	TPS Turku	Finland	39	*26	6	6	2259	70	4	1.86	10	*9	1	580	15	*3	*1.55
99-2000	Kentucky	AHL	47	23	19	4	2759	114	3	2.48	5	1	3	239	13	0	3.27
2000-01	**San Jose**	**NHL**	**5**	**2**	**1**	**0**	**154**	**5**	**0**	**1.95**	**3**	**1**	**1**	**149**	**5**	**0**	**2.01**
	Kentucky	AHL	36	19	9	6	2038	76	2	2.24	....	....	....	....	....	....	....
2001-02	**San Jose**	**NHL**	**20**	**7**	**6**	**3**	**1037**	**43**	**2**	**2.49**	**1**	**0**	**0**	**8**	**0**	**0**	**0.00**
	Cleveland Barons	AHL	4	4	0	0	242	7	0	1.73	....	....	....	....	....	....	....
2002-03	**San Jose**	**NHL**	**22**	**5**	**14**	**0**	**1199**	**65**	**1**	**3.25**	....	....	....	....	....	....	....
	NHL Totals		**47**	**14**	**21**	**3**	**2390**	**113**	**3**	**2.84**	**4**	**1**	**1**	**157**	**5**	**0**	**1.91**

KOCHAN, Dieter (KAH-kuhn, DEE-tuhr) NYI

Goaltender. Catches left. 6'1", 180 lbs. Born, Saskatoon, Sask., May 11, 1974.
(Vancouver's 3rd choice, 98th overall, in 1993 Entry Draft).

			Regular Season								Playoffs						
Season	Club	League	GP	W	L	T	Mins	GA	SO	Avg	GP	W	L	Mins	GA	SO	Avg
1991-92	Sioux City	USHL	23	7	10	0	1131	100	0	5.31	....	....	....	....	....	....	....
1992-93	Kelowna Spartans	BCJHL	44	34	8	0	2582	137	1	3.18	15	12	3	927	48	1	3.10
1993-94	Northern Michigan	WCHA	20	9	7	0	985	57	2	3.47	....	....	....	....	....	....	....
1994-95	Northern Michigan	WCHA	29	8	17	3	1512	107	0	4.25	....	....	....	....	....	....	....
1995-96	Northern Michigan	WCHA	31	7	21	2	1627	123	0	4.54	....	....	....	....	....	....	....
1996-97	Northern Michigan	WCHA	26	8	15	2	1528	99	0	3.89	....	....	....	....	....	....	....
1997-98	Louisville	ECHL	18	7	9	2	980	61	1	3.73	....	....	....	....	....	....	....
1998-99	Binghamton	UHL	40	18	16	5	2322	115	2	2.97	4	1	2	208	9	0	2.60
99-2000	Binghamton	UHL	43	29	11	3	2544	110	4	2.59	....	....	....	....	....	....	....
	Orlando	IHL	4	4	0	0	240	4	1	1.00	....	....	....	....	....	....	....
	Springfield Falcons	AHL	2	1	1	0	120	5	1	2.50	....	....	....	....	....	....	....
	Tampa Bay	**NHL**	**5**	**1**	**4**	**0**	**238**	**17**	**0**	**4.29**	....	....	....	....	....	....	....
	Grand Rapids	IHL	2	1	0	1	93	1	0	0.64	....	....	....	....	....	....	....
2000-01	**Tampa Bay**	**NHL**	**10**	**0**	**3**	**0**	**314**	**18**	**0**	**3.44**	....	....	....	....	....	....	....
	Detroit Vipers	IHL	49	13	28	3	2606	154	0	3.55	....	....	....	....	....	....	....
2001-02	**Tampa Bay**	**NHL**	**5**	**0**	**3**	**1**	**237**	**16**	**0**	**4.05**	....	....	....	....	....	....	....
	Springfield Falcons	AHL	45	21	20	1	2518	112	2	2.67	....	....	....	....	....	....	....
2002-03	**Minnesota**	**NHL**	**1**	**0**	**1**	**0**	**60**	**5**	**0**	**5.00**	....	....	....	....	....	....	....
	Houston Aeros	AHL	25	15	6	3	1447	61	1	2.53	2	0	0	20	0	0	0.00
	NHL Totals		**21**	**1**	**11**	**1**	**849**	**56**	**0**	**3.96**	....	....	....	....	....	....	....

UHL Second All-Star Team (2000)

• Scored a goal vs. Winston-Salem (UHL), January 5, 1999. Signed as a free agent by **Tampa Bay**, March 27, 2000. Signed as a free agent by **Minnesota**, August 5, 2002. Signed as a free agent by **NY Islanders**, August 7, 2003.

KOLZIG, Olie (KOHL-zihg, OH-lee) WSH.

Goaltender. Catches left. 6'3", 225 lbs. Born, Johannesburg, South Africa, April 9, 1970.
(Washington's 1st choice, 19th overall, in 1989 Entry Draft).

			Regular Season								Playoffs						
Season	Club	League	GP	W	L	T	Mins	GA	SO	Avg	GP	W	L	Mins	GA	SO	Avg
1986-87	Abbotsford Pilots	BCAHA	17	5	9	0	857	81	0	5.67	....	....	....	....	....	....	....
1987-88	New Westminster	WHL	15	6	5	0	650	48	1	4.43	3	0	3	149	11	0	4.43
1988-89	Tri-City Americans	WHL	30	16	10	2	1671	97	1	*3.48	....	....	....	....	....	....	....
1989-90	**Washington**	**NHL**	**2**	**0**	**2**	**0**	**120**	**12**	**0**	**6.00**	....	....	....	....	....	....	....
	Tri-City Americans	WHL	48	27	27	3	2504	187	1	4.48	6	4	0	318	27	0	5.09
1990-91	Baltimore Skipjacks	AHL	26	10	12	1	1367	72	0	3.16	....	....	....	....	....	....	....
	Hampton Roads	ECHL	21	11	9	1	1248	71	2	3.41	3	1	2	180	14	0	4.66
1991-92	Baltimore Skipjacks	AHL	28	5	17	2	1503	105	1	4.19	....	....	....	....	....	....	....
	Hampton Roads	ECHL	14	11	3	0	847	41	0	2.90	....	....	....	....	....	....	....
1992-93	**Washington**	**NHL**	**1**	**0**	**0**	**0**	**20**	**2**	**0**	**6.00**	....	....	....	....	....	....	....
	Rochester	AHL	49	25	16	4	2737	168	0	3.68	*17	9	8	*1040	61	0	3.52
1993-94	**Washington**	**NHL**	**7**	**0**	**3**	**0**	**224**	**20**	**0**	**5.36**	....	....	....	....	....	....	....
	Portland Pirates	AHL	29	16	8	5	1725	88	3	3.06	17	*12	5	1035	44	0	*2.55
1994-95	**Washington**	**NHL**	**14**	**2**	**8**	**2**	**724**	**30**	**0**	**2.49**	**2**	**1**	**0**	**44**	**1**	**0**	**1.36**
	Portland Pirates	AHL	2	1	0	1	125	3	0	1.44	....	....	....	....	....	....	....
1995-96	**Washington**	**NHL**	**18**	**4**	**8**	**2**	**897**	**46**	**0**	**3.08**	**5**	**2**	**3**	**341**	**11**	**0**	***1.94**
	Portland Pirates	AHL	5	5	0	0	300	7	1	1.40	....	....	....	....	....	....	....
1996-97	**Washington**	**NHL**	**29**	**8**	**15**	**4**	**1645**	**71**	**2**	**2.59**	....	....	....	....	....	....	....
1997-98	**Washington**	**NHL**	**64**	**33**	**18**	**10**	**3788**	**139**	**5**	**2.20**	**21**	**12**	**9**	**1351**	**44**	***4**	**1.95**
	Germany	Olympics	2	0	2	0	120	2	1	1.00	....	....	....	....	....	....	....
1998-99	**Washington**	**NHL**	**64**	**26**	**31**	**3**	**3586**	**154**	**4**	**2.58**	....	....	....	....	....	....	....
99-2000	**Washington**	**NHL**	**73**	**41**	**20**	**11**	***4371**	**163**	**5**	**2.24**	**5**	**1**	**4**	**284**	**16**	**0**	**3.38**
2000-01	**Washington**	**NHL**	**72**	**37**	**26**	**8**	**4279**	**177**	**5**	**2.48**	**6**	**2**	**4**	**375**	**14**	**1**	**2.24**
2001-02	**Washington**	**NHL**	**71**	**31**	**29**	**8**	**4131**	**192**	**6**	**2.79**	....	....	....	....	....	....	....
2002-03	**Washington**	**NHL**	**66**	**33**	**25**	**6**	**3894**	**156**	**4**	**2.40**	**6**	**2**	**4**	**404**	**14**	**1**	**2.08**
	NHL Totals		**481**	**215**	**185**	**54**	**27679**	**1162**	**31**	**2.52**	**45**	**20**	**24**	**2799**	**100**	**6**	**2.14**

WHL West Second All-Star Team (1989) • Shared Harry "Hap" Holmes Memorial Trophy (fewest goals against – AHL) (1994) with Byron Dafoe • Jack A. Butterfield Trophy (Playoff MVP – AHL) (1994) • NHL First All-Star Team (2000) • Vezina Trophy (2000)

Played in NHL All-Star Game (1998, 2000)

• Scored a goal while with Tri-City (WHL), November 29, 1989.

KONSTANTINOV, Evgeny (kohn-stahn-TEE-nahf, EHV-jeh-nee) T.B.

Goaltender. Catches left. 6', 176 lbs. Born, Kazan, USSR, March 29, 1981.
(Tampa Bay's 2nd choice, 67th overall, in 1999 Entry Draft).

			Regular Season								Playoffs						
Season	Club	League	GP	W	L	T	Mins	GA	SO	Avg	GP	W	L	Mins	GA	SO	Avg
1997-98	Ak Bars Kazan 2	Russia-3	34	....	....	....	2040	129	....	3.79	....	....	....	....	....	....	....
1998-99	Ak Bars Kazan 2	Russia-4	17	....	....	....	1020	38	....	2.24	....	....	....	....	....	....	....
99-2000	Leninogorsk	Russia-2	STATISTICS NOT AVAILABLE														
	Ak Bars Kazan	Russia	2	....	....	....	59	5	0	5.08	....	....	....	....	....	....	....
2000-01	Detroit Vipers	IHL	27	4	15	2	1197	85	0	4.26	....	....	....	....	....	....	....
	Tampa Bay	**NHL**	**1**	**0**	**0**	**0**	**1**	**0**	**0**	**0.00**	....	....	....	....	....	....	....
	Louisiana	ECHL	8	4	4	0	458	21	0	2.75	12	5	6	637	32	0	3.01
2001-02	Pensacola Ice Pilots	ECHL	24	10	10	0	1229	71	0	3.47	....	....	....	....	....	....	....
	Springfield Falcons	AHL	3	1	2	0	178	5	0	1.69	....	....	....	....	....	....	....
2002-03	**Tampa Bay**	**NHL**	**1**	**0**	**0**	**0**	**20**	**1**	**0**	**3.00**	....	....	....	....	....	....	....
	Springfield Falcons	AHL	39	13	23	1	2188	118	1	3.24	....	....	....	....	....	....	....
	NHL Totals		**2**	**0**	**0**	**0**	**21**	**1**	**0**	**2.86**	....	....	....	....	....	....	....

• Played 24 seconds of game vs. Colorado, December 8, 2000.

KOOPMANS, Logan (KOOP-manz, LOH-guhn) DET.

Goaltender. Catches left. 6'2", 182 lbs. Born, Cranbrook, B.C., May 18, 1984.
(Detroit's 5th choice, 166th overall, in 2002 Entry Draft).

			Regular Season								Playoffs						
Season	Club	League	GP	W	L	T	Mins	GA	SO	Avg	GP	W	L	Mins	GA	SO	Avg
99-2000	Lethbridge	WHL	5	1	3	0	282	19	0	4.04	....	....	....	....	....	....	....
2000-01	Columbia Valley	KIJHL	37	....	....	....	2140	144	1	3.90	....	....	....	....	....	....	....
2001-02	Lethbridge	WHL	37	20	12	2	2057	97	3	2.83	4	0	4	237	14	0	3.54
2002-03	Lethbridge	WHL	34	9	17	0	1628	131	1	4.83	....	....	....	....	....	....	....

KOSTUR, Matus (KAW-stuhr, ma-TOOSH) N.J.

Goaltender. Catches left. 6'1", 190 lbs. Born, Banska Bystrica, Czech., March 28, 1980.
(New Jersey's 10th choice, 164th overall, in 2000 Entry Draft).

			Regular Season								Playoffs						
Season	Club	League	GP	W	L	T	Mins	GA	SO	Avg	GP	W	L	Mins	GA	SO	Avg
1997-98	B. Bystrica Jr.	Slovak-Jr.	36	....	....	....	2152	120	0	3.35	....	....	....	....	....	....	....
1998-99	Banska Bystrica	Slovak-2	3	....	....	....	133	9	0	4.06	....	....	....	....	....	....	....
99-2000	HKm Zvolen	Slovak-2	10	....	....	....	538	32	0	3.57	....	....	....	....	....	....	....
	HKm Zvolen	Slovakia	20	....	....	....	768	36	0	2.81	2	0	0	41	3	0	4.39
2000-01	HC Nitra	Slovak-2	20	18	1	1	1132	24	4	1.53	....	....	....	....	....	....	....
	HKm Zvolen	Slovakia	3	....	....	....	110	11	0	6.00	....	....	....	....	....	....	....
2001-02	HKm Zvolen	Slovakia	39	....	....	....	2163	78	5	2.16	2	....	....	99	5	0	3.03
2002-03	Columbus	ECHL	44	16	21	2	2422	150	1	3.72	....	....	....	....	....	....	....

KOTYK, Seamus (koh-TIHK, SHAY-muhs) S.J.

Goaltender. Catches left. 5'11", 180 lbs. Born, London, Ont., October 7, 1980.
(Boston's 5th choice, 147th overall, in 1999 Entry Draft).

			Regular Season								Playoffs						
Season	Club	League	GP	W	L	T	Mins	GA	SO	Avg	GP	W	L	Mins	GA	SO	Avg
1996-97	Stratford Cullitons	OJHL-B	28	....	....	....	1615	105	0	3.82	....	....	....	....	....	....	....
1997-98	Ottawa 67's	OHL	31	13	5	5	1422	63	4	2.66	7	3	2	332	11	0	1.99
1998-99	Ottawa 67's	OHL	41	26	7	4	2314	92	5	2.39	5	3	2	338	13	0	*2.31
	Ottawa 67's	M-Cup	5	3	1	0	297	14	0	2.83	....	....	....	....	....	....	....
99-2000	Ottawa 67's	OHL	26	12	6	2	1241	65	1	3.14	....	....	....	....	....	....	....
2000-01	Ottawa 67's	OHL	55	24	20	7	3087	141	2	2.74	*20	*16	4	*1157	46	*3	2.39
2001-02	Cleveland Barons	AHL	24	6	11	0	981	61	1	3.73	....	....	....	....	....	....	....
2002-03	Cleveland Barons	AHL	34	7	22	2	1838	118	2	3.85	....	....	....	....	....	....	....

• Missed majority of 1999-2000 season recovering from surgery for cardiac arrhythmia, October 18, 1999. Signed as a free agent by **San Jose**, July 23, 2001.

KOWALSKI, Craig (koh-WAHL-skee, KRAYG) CAR.

Goaltender. Catches left. 5'10", 190 lbs. Born, Warren, MI, January 15, 1981.
(Carolina's 6th choice, 235th overall, in 2000 Entry Draft).

			Regular Season								Playoffs						
Season	Club	League	GP	W	L	T	Mins	GA	SO	Avg	GP	W	L	Mins	GA	SO	Avg
1998-99	Det. Compuware	NAJHL	42	*34	7	6	2733	96	3	*2.10	7	*7	0	420	13	1	*1.86
99-2000	Det. Compuware	NAJHL	49	33	12	3	2850	113	4	2.38	5	2	3	334	13	0	2.34
2000-01	Northern Michigan	CCHA	19	7	8	4	1078	49	1	2.73	....	....	....	....	....	....	....
2001-02	Northern Michigan	CCHA	38	24	11	2	2271	89	4	2.35	....	....	....	....	....	....	....
2002-03	Northern Michigan	CCHA	38	20	16	2	2213	104	3	2.82	....	....	....	....	....	....	....

NAJHL First All-Star Team (1998, 1999) • NAJHL Goaltender of the Year (1999)

KRAHN, Brent (KRAWN, BREHNT) CGY.

Goaltender. Catches left. 6'4", 200 lbs. Born, Winnipeg, Man., April 2, 1982.
(Calgary's 1st choice, 9th overall, in 2000 Entry Draft).

			Regular Season								Playoffs						
Season	Club	League	GP	W	L	T	Mins	GA	SO	Avg	GP	W	L	Mins	GA	SO	Avg
1997-98	Pembina Valley	MMHL	22	20	0	1	1265	40	3	1.90	2	2	0	120	2	1	1.00
1998-99	Pembina Valley	MMHL	13	10	3	0	770	30	2	2.34	....	....	....	....	....	....	....
99-2000	Calgary Hitmen	WHL	39	33	6	0	2315	92	4	2.38	5	2	2	266	13	0	2.93
2000-01	Calgary Hitmen	WHL	37	22	10	3	2087	104	1	2.99	....	....	....	....	....	....	....
2001-02	Calgary Hitmen	WHL	18	8	6	2	1033	61	0	3.54	2	1	1	119	6	0	3.03
2002-03	Calgary Hitmen	WHL	23	11	10	2	1343	72	2	3.22	....	....	....	....	....	....	....
	Seattle	WHL	5	5	0	0	302	9	2	1.79	15	9	6	960	38	2	2.38

• Missed majority of 2001-02 season recovering from off-season knee surgery, June, 2001.

LABARBERA, Jason (lah-BAR-buhr-uh, JAY-suhn) NYR

Goaltender. Catches left. 6'2", 205 lbs. Born, Prince George, B.C., January 18, 1980.
(NY Rangers' 3rd choice, 66th overall, in 1998 Entry Draft).

			Regular Season								Playoffs						
Season	Club	League	GP	W	L	T	Mins	GA	SO	Avg	GP	W	L	Mins	GA	SO	Avg
1995-96	Prince George	BCAHA	31	....	....	....	1860	83	0	2.68	....	....	....	....	....	....	....
1996-97	Tri-City Americans	WHL	2	1	0	0	63	4	0	3.81	....	....	....	....	....	....	....
	Portland	WHL	9	5	1	1	443	18	0	2.44	....	....	....	....	....	....	....
1997-98	Portland	WHL	23	18	4	0	1305	72	1	3.31	....	....	....	....	....	....	....
1998-99	Portland	WHL	51	18	23	9	2991	170	4	3.41	4	0	4	252	19	0	4.52
99-2000	Portland	WHL	34	8	24	2	2005	123	1	3.68	....	....	....	....	....	....	....
	Spokane Chiefs	WHL	21	12	6	2	1146	50	0	2.62	9	6	1	435	18	1	2.48
2000-01	**NY Rangers**	**NHL**	**1**	**0**	**0**	**0**	**10**	**0**	**0**	**0.00**	....	....	....	....	....	....	....
	Hartford Wolf Pack	AHL	4	1	1	0	156	12	0	4.61	....	....	....	....	....	....	....
	Charlotte Checkers	ECHL	35	18	10	7	2100	112	1	3.20	2	1	1	143	5	0	2.09
2001-02	Charlotte Checkers	ECHL	13	9	3	1	744	29	0	2.34	4	2	2	212	12	0	3.39
	Hartford Wolf Pack	AHL	20	7	11	1	1058	55	0	3.12	....	....	....	....	....	....	....
2002-03	Hartford Wolf Pack	AHL	46	18	17	6	2452	105	2	2.57	2	0	2	117	6	0	3.07
	NHL Totals		**1**	**0**	**0**	**0**	**10**	**0**	**0**	**0.00**	....	....	....	....	....	....	....

LABBE, Jean-Francois (lah-BAY, ZHAWN-fran-SWUH)

Goaltender. Catches left. 5'10", 175 lbs. Born, Sherbrooke, Que., June 15, 1972.

			Regular Season								Playoffs						
Season	Club	League	GP	W	L	T	Mins	GA	SO	Avg	GP	W	L	Mins	GA	SO	Avg
1988-89	L'est Cantonniers	QAAA	29	*22	7	0	1764	94	1	3.20	5	1	4	333	19	0	3.42
1989-90	Trois-Rivieres	QMJHL	28	13	10	0	1499	106	1	4.24	3	1	1	132	8	0	3.64

1990-91	Trois-Rivieres	QMJHL	54	*35	14	0	2870	158	5	3.30	5	1	4	230	19	0	4.96
1991-92	Trois-Rivieres	QMJHL	48	*31	13	3	2749	142	1	3.10	*15	*10	3	791	33	*1	*2.50
1992-93	Hull Olympiques	QMJHL	46	26	18	2	2701	156	2	3.46	10	6	3	518	24	*1	*2.78
1993-94	Thunder Bay	ColHL	52	*35	11	4	*2900	150	*2	*3.10	8	7	1	493	18	*2	*2.19
	P.E.I. Senators	AHL	7	4	3	0	389	22	0	3.39	....	....	....	....	....	....	....
1994-95	P.E.I. Senators	AHL	32	13	14	3	1817	94	2	3.10	....	....	....	....	....	....	....
1995-96	Cornwall Aces	AHL	55	25	21	5	2972	144	3	2.91	8	3	5	471	21	1	2.68
1996-97	Hershey Bears	AHL	66	*34	22	9	3811	160	*6	*2.52	*23	*14	8	*1364	59	1	2.60
1997-98	Hamilton Bulldogs	AHL	52	24	17	11	3138	149	2	2.85	7	3	4	413	20	0	2.90
1998-99	Hartford Wolf Pack	AHL	*59	28	26	3	*3392	182	2	3.22	7	3	4	447	22	0	2.95
99-2000	**NY Rangers**	**NHL**	**1**	**0**	**1**	**0**	**60**	**3**	**0**	**3.00**	....	....	....	....	....	....	....
	Hartford Wolf Pack	AHL	49	27	13	7	2853	120	1	2.52	*22	*15	7	*1320	48	3	2.18
2000-01	Hartford Wolf Pack	AHL	8	4	2	1	394	20	0	3.04	....	....	....	....	....	....	....
	Syracuse Crunch	AHL	37	15	15	5	2201	105	2	2.86	5	2	3	323	18	0	3.34
2001-02	**Columbus**	**NHL**	**3**	**1**	**1**	**0**	**117**	**6**	**0**	**3.08**	....	....	....	....	....	....	....
	Syracuse Crunch	AHL	51	27	16	7	2993	109	*9	2.18	10	6	4	596	19	2	*1.91
2002-03	**Columbus**	**NHL**	**11**	**2**	**4**	**0**	**451**	**27**	**0**	**3.59**	....	....	....	....	....	....	....
	Syracuse Crunch	AHL	4	1	2	1	247	11	0	2.68	....	....	....	....	....	....	....
	NHL Totals		**15**	**3**	**6**	**0**	**628**	**36**	**0**	**3.44**	....	....	....	....	....	....	....

QMJHL First All-Star Team (1992) • ColHL First All-Star Team (1994) • ColHL Rookie of the Year (1994) • ColHL Outstanding Goaltender (1994) • ColHL Playoff MVP (1994) • AHL First All-Star Team (1997) • Harry ''Hap'' Holmes Memorial Trophy (fewest goals against – AHL) (1997) • Baz Bastien Memorial Trophy (Top Goaltender – AHL) (1997) • Les Cunningham Award (MVP – AHL) (1997) • Shared Harry "Hap" Holmes Memorial Trophy (fewest goals against – AHL) (2000) with Milan Hnilicka • AHL Second All-Star Team (2002)

• Scored a goal vs. Quebec (AHL), February 5, 2000. Signed as a free agent by **Ottawa**, May 12, 1994. Traded to **Colorado** by **Ottawa** for future considerations, September 20, 1995. Signed as a free agent by **Edmonton**, September 2, 1997. Signed as a free agent by **NY Rangers**, July 30, 1998. Traded to **Columbus** by **NY Rangers** for Bert Robertsson, November 9, 2000.

LABROSSE, Dwight (LAB-raw-say, DWIGHT) PIT.

Goaltender. Catches left. 6'1", 167 lbs. Born, McMurray, PA, October 6, 1983.
(Pittsburgh's 11th choice, 265th overall, in 2002 Entry Draft).

			Regular Season								Playoffs						
Season	Club	League	GP	W	L	T	Mins	GA	SO	Avg	GP	W	L	Mins	GA	SO	Avg
99-2000	Pittsburgh Hornets	MWEML	39	29	10	0	2350	83	4	2.10	....	....	....	....	....	....	....
2000-01	U.S. National U-18	USDP	10	4	3	3	613	36	0	3.52	....	....	....	....	....	....	....
2001-02	Guelph Storm	OHL	31	15	11	2	1658	89	2	3.22	2	0	0	32	1	0	1.88
2002-03	Guelph Storm	OHL	5	2	1	1	266	18	0	4.06	....	....	....	....	....	....	....
	Sault Ste. Marie	OHL	10	2	6	1	494	42	0	5.10	....	....	....	....	....	....	....
	Kingston	OHL	12	1	6	0	520	37	0	4.27	....	....	....	....	....	....	....

LAJEUNESSE, Simon (lah-ZHUH-nehs, SIGH-mohn) FLA.

Goaltender. Catches left. 6'1", 178 lbs. Born, Quebec City, Que., January 22, 1981.
(Ottawa's 2nd choice, 48th overall, in 1999 Entry Draft).

			Regular Season								Playoffs						
Season	Club	League	GP	W	L	T	Mins	GA	SO	Avg	GP	W	L	Mins	GA	SO	Avg
1996-97	Cap-d-Madeleine	QAAA	23	15	5	1	1300	89	0	4.11	4	1	3	240	26	0	4.72
1997-98	Moncton Wildcats	QMJHL	19	5	6	3	925	51	1	3.31	2	0	0	1	0	0	0.00
1998-99	Moncton Wildcats	QMJHL	36	18	9	3	1993	98	1	2.95	1	0	0	43	2	0	2.79
99-2000	Moncton Wildcats	QMJHL	55	31	15	1	2922	127	6	2.61	16	9	6	910	56	1	3.69
2000-01	Acadie-Bathurst	QMJHL	36	10	19	2	1879	121	1	3.86	....	....	....	....	....	....	....
	Val-d'Or Foreurs	QMJHL	21	16	3	1	1159	54	1	2.80	14	8	4	760	52	0	4.10
2001-02	**Ottawa**	**NHL**	**1**	**0**	**0**	**0**	**24**	**0**	**0**	**0.00**	....	....	....	....	....	....	....
	Mobile Mysticks	ECHL	13	7	2	3	755	36	2	2.86	....	....	....	....	....	....	....
	Grand Rapids	AHL	26	13	7	5	1534	54	3	2.11	2	0	0	21	1	0	2.82
2002-03	Peoria Rivermen	ECHL	4	2	2	0	239	8	0	2.01	....	....	....	....	....	....	....
	Binghamton	AHL	19	7	7	1	966	47	1	2.92	....	....	....	....	....	....	....
	San Antonio	AHL	2	0	1	0	78	6	0	4.60	....	....	....	....	....	....	....
	NHL Totals		**1**	**0**	**0**	**0**	**24**	**0**	**0**	**0.00**	....	....	....	....	....	....	....

QMJHL First All-Star Team (2000) • Shared Harry "Hap" Holmes Memorial Trophy (fewest goals against – AHL) (2002) with Martin Prusek and Mathieu Chouinard

Traded to **Florida** by **Ottawa** for Joey Tetarenko, March 4, 2003.

LALIME, Patrick (lah-LEEM, PAT-rihk) OTT.

Goaltender. Catches left. 6'3", 185 lbs. Born, St-Bonaventure, Que., July 7, 1974.
(Pittsburgh's 6th choice, 156th overall, in 1993 Entry Draft).

			Regular Season								Playoffs						
Season	Club	League	GP	W	L	T	Mins	GA	SO	Avg	GP	W	L	Mins	GA	SO	Avg
1990-91	Abitibi Forestiers	QAAA	26	9	17	0	1595	151	0	5.81	....	....	....	....	....	....	....
1991-92	Shawinigan	QMJHL	6	....	....	....	272	25	0	5.50	....	....	....	....	....	....	....
1992-93	Shawinigan	QMJHL	44	10	24	4	2467	192	0	4.67	....	....	....	....	....	....	....
1993-94	Shawinigan	QMJHL	48	22	20	0	2733	192	1	4.22	5	1	3	223	25	0	6.73
1994-95	Hampton Roads	ECHL	26	15	7	3	1470	82	2	3.35	....	....	....	....	....	....	....
	Cleveland	IHL	23	7	10	4	1230	91	0	4.44	....	....	....	....	....	....	....
1995-96	Cleveland	IHL	41	20	12	7	2314	149	0	3.86	....	....	....	....	....	....	....
1996-97	**Pittsburgh**	**NHL**	**39**	**21**	**12**	**2**	**2058**	**101**	**3**	**2.94**	....	....	....	....	....	....	....
	Cleveland	IHL	14	6	6	2	834	45	1	3.24	....	....	....	....	....	....	....
1997-98	Grand Rapids	IHL	31	10	10	9	1749	76	2	2.61	1	0	1	77	4	0	3.11
1998-99	Kansas City Blades	IHL	*66	*39	20	4	*3789	190	2	3.01	3	1	2	179	6	1	2.01
99-2000	**Ottawa**	**NHL**	**38**	**19**	**14**	**3**	**2038**	**79**	**3**	**2.33**	....	....	....	....	....	....	....
2000-01	**Ottawa**	**NHL**	**60**	**36**	**19**	**5**	**3607**	**141**	**7**	**2.35**	**4**	**0**	**4**	**251**	**10**	**0**	**2.39**
2001-02	**Ottawa**	**NHL**	**61**	**27**	**24**	**8**	**3583**	**148**	**7**	**2.48**	**12**	**7**	**5**	**778**	**18**	**4**	***1.39**
2002-03	**Ottawa**	**NHL**	**67**	**39**	**20**	**7**	**3943**	**142**	**8**	**2.16**	**18**	**11**	**7**	**1122**	**34**	**1**	**1.82**
	NHL Totals		**265**	**142**	**89**	**25**	**15229**	**611**	**28**	**2.41**	**34**	**18**	**16**	**2151**	**62**	**5**	**1.73**

NHL All-Rookie Team (1997) • IHL First All-Star Team (1999)

Played in NHL All-Star Game (2003)

Rights traded to **Anaheim** by **Pittsburgh** for Sean Pronger, March 24, 1998. Traded to **Ottawa** by **Anaheim** for Ted Donato and the rights to Antti-Jussi Niemi, June 18, 1999.

LAMOTHE, Marc (luh-MAWTH, MAHRK) DET.

Goaltender. Catches left. 6'2", 210 lbs. Born, New Liskeard, Ont., February 27, 1974.
(Montreal's 6th choice, 92nd overall, in 1992 Entry Draft).

			Regular Season								Playoffs						
Season	Club	League	GP	W	L	T	Mins	GA	SO	Avg	GP	W	L	Mins	GA	SO	Avg
1990-91	Ottawa Jr. Sens	OCJHL	25	13	7	0	1220	82	1	4.03	....	....	....	....	....	....	....
1991-92	Kingston	OHL	42	10	25	2	2378	189	1	4.77	....	....	....	....	....	....	....
1992-93	Kingston	OHL	45	23	12	6	2489	162	1	3.91	15	8	5	753	48	1	3.82
1993-94	Kingston	OHL	48	23	20	5	2828	177	*2	3.76	6	2	2	224	12	0	3.21
1994-95	Fredericton	AHL	9	2	5	0	428	32	0	4.48	....	....	....	....	....	....	....
	Wheeling	ECHL	13	9	2	1	737	38	0	3.10	....	....	....	....	....	....	....
1995-96	Fredericton	AHL	23	5	9	3	1166	73	1	3.76	3	1	2	161	9	0	3.36
1996-97	Indianapolis Ice	IHL	38	20	14	4	2271	100	1	2.64	1	0	0	20	1	0	3.00
1997-98	Indianapolis Ice	IHL	31	18	10	2	1772	72	3	2.44	4	1	3	177	10	0	3.38
1998-99	Indianapolis Ice	IHL	32	9	16	6	1823	115	1	3.78	6	3	3	338	10	*2	1.78
99-2000	**Chicago**	**NHL**	**2**	**1**	**1**	**0**	**116**	**10**	**0**	**5.17**	....	....	....	....	....	....	....
	Cleveland	IHL	44	19	18	4	2455	112	2	2.74	4	2	2	325	12	0	2.21
2000-01	Syracuse Crunch	AHL	42	17	15	7	2323	112	2	2.89	....	....	....	....	....	....	....
2001-02	Hamilton Bulldogs	AHL	45	22	19	2	2569	102	3	2.38	9	6	3	551	18	0	1.96
2002-03	Grand Rapids	AHL	*60	*33	18	8	*3438	122	6	2.13	15	10	5	945	29	1	1.84
	NHL Totals		**2**	**1**	**1**	**0**	**116**	**10**	**0**	**5.17**	....	....	....	....	....	....	....

AHL First All-Star Team (2003) • Baz Bastien Memorial Trophy (Top Goaltender – AHL) (2003)

Signed as a free agent by **Chicago**, September 26, 1996. Signed as a free agent by **Edmonton**, August 16, 2001. Signed as a free agent by **Detroit**, August 5, 2002.

LANGKOW, Scott (LAING-kow, SKAWT)

Goaltender. Catches left. 5'11", 190 lbs. Born, Sherwood Park, Alta., April 21, 1975.
(Winnipeg's 2nd choice, 31st overall, in 1993 Entry Draft).

			Regular Season								Playoffs						
Season	Club	League	GP	W	L	T	Mins	GA	SO	Avg	GP	W	L	Mins	GA	SO	Avg
1990-91	Sherwood Park	AMHL	32	....	....	....	1920	128	0	4.00	....	....	....	....	....	....	....
1991-92	Abbotsford Pilots	PIJHL					STATISTICS NOT AVAILABLE										
	Portland	WHL	1	0	0	0	33	2	0	3.46	....	....	....	....	....	....	....
1992-93	Portland	WHL	34	24	8	2	2064	119	2	3.46	9	6	3	535	31	0	3.48
1993-94	Portland	WHL	39	27	9	1	2302	121	2	3.15	10	6	4	600	34	0	3.40
1994-95	Portland	WHL	63	20	36	5	*3638	240	1	3.96	8	3	5	510	30	0	3.53
1995-96	**Winnipeg**	**NHL**	**1**	**0**	**0**	**0**	**6**	**0**	**0**	**0.00**	....	....	....	....	....	....	....
	Springfield Falcons	AHL	39	18	15	6	2329	116	3	2.99	7	4	2	393	23	0	3.51
1996-97	Springfield Falcons	AHL	33	15	9	7	1929	85	0	2.64	....	....	....	....	....	....	....
1997-98	**Phoenix**	**NHL**	**3**	**0**	**1**	**1**	**137**	**10**	**0**	**4.38**	....	....	....	....	....	....	....
	Springfield Falcons	AHL	51	30	13	5	2874	128	3	2.67	4	1	3	216	14	0	3.88
1998-99	**Phoenix**	**NHL**	**1**	**0**	**0**	**0**	**35**	**3**	**0**	**5.14**	....	....	....	....	....	....	....
	Las Vegas Thunder	IHL	27	7	14	2	1402	97	1	4.15	....	....	....	....	....	....	....
	Utah Grizzlies	IHL	21	10	9	2	1227	59	1	2.89	....	....	....	....	....	....	....
99-2000	**Atlanta**	**NHL**	**15**	**3**	**11**	**0**	**765**	**55**	**0**	**4.31**	....	....	....	....	....	....	....
	Orlando	IHL	27	14	8	2	1487	57	4	2.30	6	2	3	381	16	0	2.52
2000-01	Orlando	IHL	4	1	1	1	187	9	0	2.88	....	....	....	....	....	....	....
	Mobile Mysticks	ECHL	6	2	4	0	358	23	0	3.86	....	....	....	....	....	....	....
	Cincinnati	AHL	15	6	4	4	838	44	1	3.15	3	1	1	142	7	0	2.95
2001-02	Kalamazoo Wings	UHL	53	20	24	7	3021	165	1	3.28	....	....	....	....	....	....	....
2002-03	Assat Pori	Finland	50	14	24	10	2886	123	3	2.56	....	....	....	....	....	....	....
	NHL Totals		**20**	**3**	**12**	**1**	**943**	**68**	**0**	**4.33**	....	....	....	....	....	....	....

WHL West Second All-Star Team (1994, 1995) • Shared Harry ''Hap'' Holmes Memorial Trophy (fewest goals against – AHL) (1996) with Manny Legace • AHL First All-Star Team (1998) • Baz Bastien Memorial Trophy (Top Goaltender – AHL) (1998)

Transferred to **Phoenix** after **Winnipeg** franchise relocated, July 1, 1996. Traded to **Atlanta** by **Phoenix** for future considerations, June 25, 1999. Traded to **Anaheim** by **Atlanta** with Sergei Vyshedkevich for Ladislav Kohn, February 9, 2001.

LASAK, Jan (LA-shak, YAN) NSH.

Goaltender. Catches left. 6'1", 200 lbs. Born, Zvolen, Czech., April 10, 1979.
(Nashville's 6th choice, 65th overall, in 1999 Entry Draft).

			Regular Season								Playoffs						
Season	Club	League	GP	W	L	T	Mins	GA	SO	Avg	GP	W	L	Mins	GA	SO	Avg
1996-97	HKm Zvolen Jr.	Slovak-Jr.	49	....	....	....	2940	111	....	2.27	....	....	....	....	....	....	....
1997-98	HKm Zvolen Jr.	Slovak-Jr.	48	....	....	....	2881	119	....	2.48	....	....	....	....	....	....	....
	HK SKP Zilina	Slovak-2	4	....	....	....	208	12	....	3.46	....	....	....	....	....	....	....
1998-99	HKm Zvolen Jr.	Slovak-Jr.	43	....	....	....	2580	91	....	2.12	....	....	....	....	....	....	....
	HKm Zvolen	Slovakia	8	....	....	....	387	29	....	4.50	....	....	....	....	....	....	....
99-2000	Hampton Roads	ECHL	*59	*36	17	4	*3409	145	0	2.55	10	5	5	610	28	1	2.75
2000-01	Milwaukee	IHL	43	23	17	2	2439	106	1	2.61	3	0	1	60	5	0	4.97
2001-02	**Nashville**	**NHL**	**3**	**0**	**3**	**0**	**177**	**13**	**0**	**4.41**	....	....	....	....	....	....	....
	Milwaukee	AHL	34	12	18	3	1981	79	2	2.39	....	....	....	....	....	....	....
	Slovakia	Olympics	2	0	1	0	94	6	0	3.81	....	....	....	....	....	....	....
2002-03	**Nashville**	**NHL**	**3**	**0**	**1**	**0**	**90**	**5**	**0**	**3.33**	....	....	....	....	....	....	....
	Milwaukee	AHL	40	18	14	7	2378	113	1	2.85	6	2	4	366	19	0	3.12
	NHL Totals		**6**	**0**	**4**	**0**	**267**	**18**	**0**	**4.04**	....	....	....	....	....	....	....

ECHL First All-Star Team (2000) • ECHL Rookie of the Year (2000) • ECHL Top Goaltender (2000)

LASSILA, Teemu (la-SIHL-uh, TEE-moo) NSH.

Goaltender. Catches left. 5'11", 180 lbs. Born, Helsinki, Finland, March 26, 1983.
(Nashville's 9th choice, 117th overall, in 2003 Entry Draft).

			Regular Season								Playoffs						
Season	Club	League	GP	W	L	T	Mins	GA	SO	Avg	GP	W	L	Mins	GA	SO	Avg
2001-02	TPS Turku Jr.	Finn-Jr.	43	....	....	....	2577	77	5	1.79	9	....	....	571	21	1	2.21
2002-03	Hermes Kokkola	Finland-2	21	9	5	6	1268	45	2	2.13	....	....	....	....	....	....	....
	TPS Turku	Finland	21	12	6	1	1190	38	*6	1.92	7	3	4	416	21	1	3.03

LAWSON, Tom (LAW-suhn, TAWM) COL.

Goaltender. Catches left. 6'5", 200 lbs. Born, Whitby, Ont., August 15, 1979.

			Regular Season								Playoffs						
Season	Club	League	GP	W	L	T	Mins	GA	SO	Avg	GP	W	L	Mins	GA	SO	Avg
1998-99	Markham Waxers	OPJHL	32	19	10	2	1793	101	....	3.38	....	....	....	....	....	....	....
99-2000	Bowling Green	CCHA	3	0	3	0	173	14	0	4.86	....	....	....	....	....	....	....
2000-01	Knoxville Speed	UHL	35	16	16	2	2002	116	0	3.48	....	....	....	....	....	....	....
	Cincinnati	AHL	1	0	0	0	23	1	0	2.58	....	....	....	....	....	....	....
2001-02	Anchorage Aces	WCHL	1	1	0	0	54	2	0	2.22	....	....	....	....	....	....	....
2002-03	Fort Wayne	UHL	56	29	15	10	3178	106	*7	*2.00	12	*11	1	750	21	*2	*1.68

UHL First All-Star Team (2003)

Signed as a free agent by **Knoxville** (UHL) after leaving Bowling Green University (CCHA), September 30, 2000. • Missed majority of 2001-02 season recovering from leg injury suffered in game vs. Colorado (WCHL), October 13, 2001. Signed as a free agent by **Fort Wayne** (UHL), October 13, 2002. Signed as a free agent by **Colorado**, June 3, 2003.

LECLAIRE, Pascal (lah-CLAIR, pas-CAL) CBJ

Goaltender. Catches left. 6'2", 185 lbs. Born, Repentigny, Que., November 7, 1982.
(Columbus' 1st choice, 8th overall, in 2001 Entry Draft).

			Regular Season								Playoffs						
Season	Club	League	GP	W	L	T	Mins	GA	SO	Avg	GP	W	L	Mins	GA	SO	Avg
1997-98	Cap-d-Madeleine	QAAA	26	6	17	3	1580	127	0	4.90	....	....	....	....	....	....	....
1998-99	Halifax	QMJHL	33	19	11	1	1828	96	2	3.15	1	0	0	17	2	0	7.06
99-2000	Halifax	QMJHL	31	16	8	4	1729	103	1	3.57	5	1	2	198	12	0	3.65
2000-01	Halifax	QMJHL	35	14	16	5	2111	126	1	3.58	2	0	2	109	10	0	5.49
2001-02	Montreal Rocket	QMJHL	45	15	23	4	2513	138	1	3.29	7	3	4	441	15	0	*2.04
2002-03	Syracuse Crunch	AHL	36	8	21	3	1886	112	0	3.56	....	....	....	....	....	....	....

LEGACE, Manny (LEH-gah-see, MAN-nee) DET.

Goaltender. Catches left. 5'9", 162 lbs. Born, Toronto, Ont., February 4, 1973.
(Hartford's 5th choice, 188th overall, in 1993 Entry Draft).

			Regular Season								Playoffs						
Season	Club	League	GP	W	L	T	Mins	GA	SO	Avg	GP	W	L	Mins	GA	SO	Avg
1987-88	Alliston Hornets	OJHL-C	16	7	9	0	960	83	0	5.17	....	....	....	....	....	....	....
1988-89	Vaughan Raiders	MTJHL	23	....	....	....	1303	92	1	4.24	....	....	....	....	....	....	....
1989-90	Vaughan Raiders	MTJHL	21	8	11	1	1180	89	1	4.53	....	....	....	....	....	....	....
	Thornhill	MTJHL	8	3	3	2	480	30	0	3.75	....	....	....	....	....	....	....
1990-91	Niagara Falls	OHL	30	13	11	2	1515	107	0	4.24	4	1	1	119	10	0	5.04
1991-92	Niagara Falls	OHL	43	21	16	3	2384	143	0	3.60	14	8	5	791	56	0	4.25
1992-93	Niagara Falls	OHL	48	22	19	3	2630	171	0	3.90	4	0	4	240	18	0	4.50
1993-94	Canada	Nat-Tm	16	8	6	0	859	36	2	2.51	....	....	....	....	....	....	....

1994-95	Springfield Falcons	AHL	39	12	17	6	2169	128	2	3.54	....	....	....	....	....	....	....
1995-96	Springfield Falcons	AHL	37	20	12	4	2196	83	*5	*2.27	4	1	3	220	18	0	4.91
1996-97	Springfield Falcons	AHL	36	17	14	5	2119	107	1	3.03	12	9	3	745	25	*2	2.01
	Richmond	ECHL	3	2	1	0	157	8	0	3.05	....	....	....	....	....	....	....
1997-98	Springfield Falcons	AHL	6	4	2	0	345	16	0	2.78	....	....	....	....	....	....	....
	Las Vegas Thunder	IHL	41	18	16	4	2106	111	1	3.16	4	1	3	237	16	0	4.05
1998-99	**Los Angeles**	**NHL**	**17**	**2**	**9**	**2**	**899**	**39**	**0**	**2.60**	....	....	....	....	....	....	....
	Long Beach	IHL	33	22	8	1	1796	67	2	2.24	6	4	2	338	9	0	*1.60
99-2000	**Detroit**	**NHL**	**4**	**4**	**0**	**0**	**240**	**11**	**0**	**2.75**	....	....	....	....	....	....	....
	Manitoba Moose	IHL	42	17	18	5	2409	104	2	2.59	2	0	2	141	7	0	2.97
2000-01	**Detroit**	**NHL**	**39**	**24**	**5**	**5**	**2136**	**73**	**2**	**2.05**	....	....	....	....	....	....	....
2001-02 ♦	**Detroit**	**NHL**	**20**	**10**	**6**	**2**	**1117**	**45**	**1**	**2.42**	**1**	**0**	**0**	**11**	**1**	**0**	**5.45**
2002-03	**Detroit**	**NHL**	**25**	**14**	**5**	**4**	**1406**	**51**	**0**	**2.18**	....	....	....	....	....	....	....
	NHL Totals		**105**	**54**	**25**	**13**	**5798**	**219**	**3**	**2.27**	**1**	**0**	**0**	**11**	**1**	**0**	**5.45**

OHL First All-Star Team (1993) • AHL First All-Star Team (1996) • Shared Harry "Hap" Holmes Memorial Trophy (fewest goals against – AHL) (1996) with Scott Langkow • Baz Bastien Memorial Trophy (Top Goaltender – AHL) (1996)

Rights transferred to **Carolina** after **Hartford** franchise relocated, June 25, 1997. Traded to **Los Angeles** by **Carolina** for future considerations, July 31, 1998. Signed as a free agent by **Detroit**, August 9, 1999. Claimed on waivers by **Vancouver** from **Detroit**, September 30, 1999. Claimed on waivers by **Detroit** from **Vancouver**, October 13, 1999.

LEHTO, Mika (leh-TOH, MEE-kuh) PIT.

Goaltender. Catches left. 5'11", 172 lbs. Born, Vammala, Finland, April 12, 1979.
(Pittsburgh's 8th choice, 224th overall, in 1998 Entry Draft).

			Regular Season								Playoffs						
Season	Club	League	GP	W	L	T	Mins	GA	SO	Avg	GP	W	L	Mins	GA	SO	Avg
1997-98	Assat Pori Jr.	Finn-Jr.	36	16	14	6	2160	103	2	2.86	....	....	....	....	....	....	....
	Assat Pori	Finland	1	0	0	0	35	1	0	1.71	1	0	0	17	0	0	0.00
1998-99	Assat Pori Jr.	Finn-Jr.	20	7	10	3	1202	68	....	3.39	....	....	....	....	....	....	....
	Assat Pori	Finland	15	4	6	1	773	38	1	2.95	....	....	....	....	....	....	....
99-2000	Assat Pori	Finland	23	4	11	3	1099	87	0	4.75	....	....	....	....	....	....	....
	Hermes	Finland-2	6	3	2	1	339	19	1	3.36	....	....	....	....	....	....	....
	Assat Pori Jr.	Finn-Jr.	2	0	0	2	118	8	0	4.05	....	....	....	....	....	....	....
2000-01	JYP Jyvaskyla	Finland	41	12	20	8	2384	126	1	3.17	....	....	....	....	....	....	....
2001-02	JYP Jyvaskyla	Finland	37	10	17	10	2167	107	6	2.96	....	....	....	....	....	....	....
2002-03	Tappara Tampere	Finland	27	12	11	4	1512	45	3	*1.79	14	*10	3	928	23	*2	*1.49

LEHTONEN, Kari (LEH-tuh-nehn, KAH-ree) ATL.

Goaltender. Catches left. 6'3", 190 lbs. Born, Helsinki, Finland, November 16, 1983.
(Atlanta's 1st choice, 2nd overall, in 2002 Entry Draft).

			Regular Season								Playoffs						
Season	Club	League	GP	W	L	T	Mins	GA	SO	Avg	GP	W	L	Mins	GA	SO	Avg
1998-99	Jokerit Helsinki-C	Finn-Jr.	17	....	....	....	1020	61	0	3.61	....	....	....	....	....	....	....
	Jokerit Helsinki-B	Finn-Jr.	....	....	....	....	....	....	....	....	4	2	2	240	7	0	1.75
99-2000	Jokerit Helsinki Jr.	Finn-Jr.	33	21	9	3	1974	86	2	2.61	12	9	3	758	14	4	1.11
2000-01	Jokerit Helsinki	Finn-Jr.	31	20	9	1	1799	71	3	2.37	1	0	1	54	4	0	4.44
	Jokerit Helsinki	Finland	4	3	0	0	189	6	0	1.90	....	....	....	....	....	....	....
2001-02	Jokerit Helsinki Jr.	Finn-Jr.	6	5	1	0	360	11	1	1.83	....	....	....	....	....	....	....
	Jokerit Helsinki	Finland	23	13	5	3	1242	37	4	1.79	*11	*8	3	*623	18	*3	1.73
2002-03	Jokerit Helsinki	Finland	45	*23	14	6	2635	87	5	1.98	10	6	4	626	17	*2	1.63

LEIGHTON, Michael (LAY-tohn, MIGH-kuhl) CHI.

Goaltender. Catches left. 6'2", 175 lbs. Born, Petrolia, Ont., May 19, 1981.
(Chicago's 5th choice, 165th overall, in 1999 Entry Draft).

			Regular Season								Playoffs						
Season	Club	League	GP	W	L	T	Mins	GA	SO	Avg	GP	W	L	Mins	GA	SO	Avg
1997-98	Petrolia Jets	OJHL-B	30	....	....	....	1583	87	2	3.30	....	....	....	....	....	....	....
1998-99	Windsor Spitfires	OHL	28	4	17	2	1389	112	0	4.84	3	0	1	80	10	0	7.50
99-2000	Windsor Spitfires	OHL	42	17	17	2	2272	118	1	3.12	12	5	6	616	32	0	3.12
2000-01	Windsor Spitfires	OHL	54	32	13	5	3035	138	2	2.73	9	4	5	519	27	1	3.12
2001-02	Norfolk Admirals	AHL	52	27	16	8	3114	111	6	2.14	4	1	2	238	8	0	2.02
2002-03	**Chicago**	**NHL**	**8**	**2**	**3**	**2**	**447**	**21**	**1**	**2.82**	....	....	....	....	....	....	....
	Norfolk Admirals	AHL	36	18	13	5	2184	91	4	2.50	4	3	1	240	7	1	1.75
	NHL Totals		**8**	**2**	**3**	**2**	**447**	**21**	**1**	**2.82**	....	....	....	....	....	....	....

AHL All-Rookie Team (2002)

LENEVEU, David (LEH-neh-voo, DAY-vihd) PHX.

Goaltender. Catches left. 6'1", 170 lbs. Born, Fernie, B.C., May 23, 1983.
(Phoenix's 3rd choice, 46th overall, in 2002 Entry Draft).

			Regular Season								Playoffs						
Season	Club	League	GP	W	L	T	Mins	GA	SO	Avg	GP	W	L	Mins	GA	SO	Avg
99-2000	Fernie Ghostriders	AWJHL	22	15	2	0	1140	48	0	2.49	....	....	....	....	....	....	....
2000-01	Nanaimo Clippers	BCHL	41	....	....	....	2330	127	6	3.29	....	....	....	....	....	....	....
2001-02	Cornell Big Red	ECAC	14	11	2	1	842	21	2	*1.50	....	....	....	....	....	....	....
2002-03	Cornell Big Red	ECAC	32	*28	3	1	1946	39	*9	*1.20	....	....	....	....	....	....	....

ECAC All-Rookie Team (2002) • ECAC First All-Star Team (2003) • ECAC Player of the Year (2003) (co-winner - Christopher Higgins) • NCAA East First All-American Team (2003)

LITTLE, Neil (LIH-tuhl, NEEL) PHI.

Goaltender. Catches left. 6'1", 193 lbs. Born, Medicine Hat, Alta., December 18, 1971.
(Philadelphia's 10th choice, 226th overall, in 1991 Entry Draft).

			Regular Season								Playoffs						
Season	Club	League	GP	W	L	T	Mins	GA	SO	Avg	GP	W	L	Mins	GA	SO	Avg
1989-90	Estevan Bruins	SJHL	46	21	19	4	2707	150	1	3.32	....	....	....	....	....	....	....
1990-91	RPI Engineers	ECAC	18	9	8	0	1032	71	0	4.13	....	....	....	....	....	....	....
1991-92	RPI Engineers	ECAC	28	11	11	3	1532	96	0	3.76	....	....	....	....	....	....	....
1992-93	RPI Engineers	ECAC	*31	*19	9	3	*1801	88	0	2.93	....	....	....	....	....	....	....
1993-94	RPI Engineers	ECAC	27	16	7	4	1570	88	0	3.36	....	....	....	....	....	....	....
	Hershey Bears	AHL	1	0	0	0	18	1	0	3.33	....	....	....	....	....	....	....
1994-95	Hershey Bears	AHL	19	5	7	3	919	60	0	3.91	....	....	....	....	....	....	....
	Johnstown Chiefs	ECHL	16	7	6	1	897	55	0	3.68	3	0	2	145	11	0	4.55
1995-96	Hershey Bears	AHL	48	21	18	6	2680	149	0	3.34	1	0	1	60	4	0	4.02
1996-97	Philadelphia	AHL	54	31	12	7	3007	145	0	2.89	10	6	4	620	20	1	*1.94
1997-98	Philadelphia	AHL	51	*31	11	7	2960	145	0	2.94	*20	*15	5	*1193	48	*3	2.41
1998-99	Grand Rapids	IHL	50	18	21	5	2740	144	3	3.15	....	....	....	....	....	....	....
99-2000	Philadelphia	AHL	51	26	18	2	2830	143	1	3.03	5	2	3	298	15	0	3.02
2000-01	Philadelphia	AHL	*58	22	27	4	3117	148	2	2.85	10	5	5	631	23	1	2.19
2001-02	**Philadelphia**	**NHL**	**1**	**0**	**1**	**0**	**60**	**4**	**0**	**4.00**	....	....	....	....	....	....	....
	Philadelphia	AHL	35	13	15	7	2079	70	2	2.02	5	2	3	298	13	0	2.62
2002-03	Philadelphia	AHL	42	18	19	4	2478	103	4	2.49	....	....	....	....	....	....	....
	NHL Totals		**1**	**0**	**1**	**0**	**60**	**4**	**0**	**4.00**	....	....	....	....	....	....	....

ECAC First All-Star Team (1993) • NCAA East Second All-American Team (1993)

LIV, Stefan (LIHV, STEH-fuhn) DET.

Goaltender. Catches left. 6', 172 lbs. Born, Jonkoping, Sweden, December 21, 1980.
(Detroit's 3rd choice, 102nd overall, in 2000 Entry Draft).

			Regular Season								Playoffs						
Season	Club	League	GP	W	L	T	Mins	GA	SO	Avg	GP	W	L	Mins	GA	SO	Avg
1997-98	HV 71 Jr.	Swede-Jr.	17	....	....	....	1020	47	....	2.76	....	....	....	....	....	....	....
1998-99	HV 71 Jonkoping	Sweden	DID NOT PLAY – SPARE GOALTENDER														
99-2000	HV 71 Jr.	Swede-Jr.	10	....	....	....	600	17	2	1.70	....	....	....	....	....	....	....
	Tranas AIF	Swede-2	9	....	....	....	541	20	0	2.17	....	....	....	....	....	....	....
	HV 71 Jonkoping	Sweden	12	....	....	....	716	24	1	2.01	3	....	....	178	12	0	4.04
2000-01	HV 71 Jonkoping	Sweden	*46	....	....	....	*2752	127	4	2.77	....	....	....	....	....	....	....
2001-02	HV 71 Jonkoping	Sweden	38	....	....	....	2184	95	*4	2.61	8	....	....	517	27	0	3.13
2002-03	HV 71 Jonkoping	Sweden	46	....	....	....	2723	124	3	2.73	7	....	....	391	17	1	2.61

LUNDQVIST, Henrik (LUHND-kvihst, HEHN-rihk) NYR

Goaltender. Catches left. 5'11", 167 lbs. Born, Are, Sweden, March 2, 1982.
(NY Rangers' 7th choice, 205th overall, in 2000 Entry Draft).

			Regular Season								Playoffs						
Season	Club	League	GP	W	L	T	Mins	GA	SO	Avg	GP	W	L	Mins	GA	SO	Avg
1998-99	V. Frolunda Jr.	Swede-Jr.	35	....	....	....	2100	95	0	2.73	....	....	....	....	....	....	....
99-2000	V. Frolunda Jr.	Swede-Jr.	30	....	....	....	1726	73	0	2.54	5	4	1	300	7	2	1.40
2000-01	V. Frolunda-18	Swede-Jr.	2	....	....	....	120	5	0	2.50	3	2	1	182	5	0	1.62
	V. Frolunda Jr.	Swede-Jr.	19	....	....	....	1140	50	2	2.64	....	....	....	....	....	....	....
	Molndals IF	Swede-2	7	....	....	....	420	29	0	4.22	....	....	....	....	....	....	....
	Vastra Frolunda	Sweden	4	....	....	....	190	11	0	3.47	....	....	....	....	....	....	....
2001-02	Vastra Frolunda	Sweden	20	....	....	....	1152	52	2	2.71	8	8	0	489	18	*2	2.21
2002-03	Vastra Frolunda	Sweden	28	....	....	....	1650	40	*6	*1.45	12	....	....	739	26	*2	2.11
	V. Frolunda Jr.	Swede-Jr.	1	1	0	0	60	4	0	4.00	....	....	....	....	....	....	....

LUONGO, Roberto (loo-WAHN-goh, roh-BUHR-toh) FLA.

Goaltender. Catches left. 6'3", 205 lbs. Born, Montreal, Que., April 4, 1979.
(NY Islanders' 1st choice, 4th overall, in 1997 Entry Draft).

			Regular Season								Playoffs						
Season	Club	League	GP	W	L	T	Mins	GA	SO	Avg	GP	W	L	Mins	GA	SO	Avg
1994-95	Montreal-Bourassa	QAAA	25	10	14	0	94	1465	0	3.85	....	....	....	....	....	....	....
1995-96	Val-d'Or Foreurs	QMJHL	23	6	11	4	1201	74	0	3.70	3	0	1	68	5	0	4.41
1996-97	Val-d'Or Foreurs	QMJHL	60	32	22	2	3305	171	2	3.10	13	8	5	777	44	0	3.40
1997-98	Val-d'Or Foreurs	QMJHL	54	27	20	5	3046	157	*7	3.09	*17	*14	3	*1019	37	*2	*2.18
1998-99	Val-d'Or Foreurs	QMJHL	21	6	10	2	1176	77	1	3.93	....	....	....	....	....	....	....
	Acadie-Bathurst	QMJHL	22	14	7	1	1340	74	0	3.31	*23	*16	6	*1400	64	0	2.74
99-2000	**NY Islanders**	**NHL**	**24**	**7**	**14**	**1**	**1292**	**70**	**1**	**3.25**	....	....	....	....	....	....	....
	Lowell	AHL	26	10	12	4	1517	74	1	2.93	6	3	3	359	18	0	3.01
2000-01	**Florida**	**NHL**	**47**	**12**	**24**	**7**	**2628**	**107**	**5**	**2.44**	....	....	....	....	....	....	....
	Louisville Panthers	AHL	3	1	2	0	178	10	0	3.38	....	....	....	....	....	....	....
2001-02	**Florida**	**NHL**	**58**	**16**	**33**	**4**	**3030**	**140**	**4**	**2.77**	....	....	....	....	....	....	....
2002-03	**Florida**	**NHL**	**65**	**20**	**34**	**7**	**3627**	**164**	**6**	**2.71**	....	....	....	....	....	....	....
	NHL Totals		**194**	**55**	**105**	**19**	**10577**	**481**	**16**	**2.73**	....	....	....	....	....	....	....

Traded to **Florida** by **NY Islanders** with Olli Jokinen for Mark Parrish and Oleg Kvasha, June 24, 2000.

MacINTYRE, Drew (MAK-ihn-tighr, DROO) DET.

Goaltender. Catches left. 6', 173 lbs. Born, Charlottetown, P.E.I., June 24, 1983.
(Detroit's 2nd choice, 121st overall, in 2001 Entry Draft).

			Regular Season								Playoffs						
Season	Club	League	GP	W	L	T	Mins	GA	SO	Avg	GP	W	L	Mins	GA	SO	Avg
1998-99	Trenton Sting	OPJHL	20	....	....	....	1173	71	2	3.63	....	....	....	....	....	....	....
99-2000	Sherbrooke	QMJHL	24	10	7	2	1253	67	0	3.21	....	....	....	....	....	....	....
2000-01	Sherbrooke	QMJHL	48	17	22	3	2552	139	4	3.27	4	0	4	238	19	0	4.78
2001-02	Sherbrooke	QMJHL	55	15	34	3	3028	201	1	3.98	....	....	....	....	....	....	....
2002-03	Sherbrooke	QMJHL	*61	31	24	5	*3515	161	2	2.75	12	5	7	767	52	0	4.07

MAGERS, Marty (MAY-juhrs, MAHR-tee) BUF.

Goaltender. Catches left. 6'1", 180 lbs. Born, Maywood, IL, June 7, 1983.
(Buffalo's 6th choice, 121st overall, in 2002 Entry Draft).

			Regular Season								Playoffs						
Season	Club	League	GP	W	L	T	Mins	GA	SO	Avg	GP	W	L	Mins	GA	SO	Avg
99-2000	Fort Erie Meteors	OJHL-B	26	8	10	2	1546	113	0	4.27	....	....	....	....	....	....	....
2000-01	Omaha Lancers	USHL	27	16	5	3	1502	58	3	2.32	2	0	0	71	6	0	5.04
2001-02	Omaha Lancers	USHL	30	21	7	2	1780	48	*10	*1.62	5	2	3	276	11	0	2.39
2002-03	Owen Sound	OHL	26	6	15	2	1394	94	0	4.05	....	....	....	....	....	....	....
	Sudbury Wolves	OHL	13	1	10	1	645	46	0	4.28	....	....	....	....	....	....	....

USHL Top Goaltender (2001) • USHL Second All-Star Team (2002)

MALEK, Roman (MAHL-ehk, ROH-muhn) PHI.

Goaltender. Catches left. 5'11", 161 lbs. Born, Prague, Czech., September 25, 1977.
(Philadelphia's 5th choice, 158th overall, in 2001 Entry Draft).

			Regular Season								Playoffs						
Season	Club	League	GP	W	L	T	Mins	GA	SO	Avg	GP	W	L	Mins	GA	SO	Avg
1998-99	HC Slavia Praha	Czech	18	....	....	....	830	51	....	3.69	....	....	....	....	....	....	....
99-2000	HC Slavia Praha	Czech	25	....	....	....	1342	59	....	2.64	....	....	....	....	....	....	....
2000-01	HC Slavia Praha	Czech	46	....	....	....	2550	100	....	2.35	11	....	....	665	28	....	2.53
2001-02	HC Slavia Praha	Czech	33	....	....	....	1967	80	....	2.44	9	....	....	485	22	....	2.72
2002-03	HC Slavia Praha	Czech	50	....	....	....	2844	77	*11	*1.62	17	....	....	1064	28	*5	1.58

MANZATO, Daniel (man-ZA-toh, DAN-yehl) CAR.

Goaltender. Catches left. 6', 178 lbs. Born, Fribourg, Switz., January 17, 1984.
(Carolina's 3rd choice, 160th overall, in 2002 Entry Draft).

			Regular Season								Playoffs						
Season	Club	League	GP	W	L	T	Mins	GA	SO	Avg	GP	W	L	Mins	GA	SO	Avg
99-2000	Fribourg Jr.	Swiss-Jr.	STATISTICS NOT AVAILABLE														
2000-01	Fribourg Jr.	Swiss-Jr.	36	....	....	....	2160	32	6	0.91	....	....	....	....	....	....	....
2001-02	Victoriaville Tigres	QMJHL	36	20	8	2	1894	102	0	3.23	6	3	0	249	17	0	4.09
2002-03	Victoriaville Tigres	QMJHL	48	23	18	5	2756	155	3	3.37	3	0	3	125	11	0	5.27

MARACLE, Norm (MAHR-ah-kuhl, NOHRM)

Goaltender. Catches left. 5'9", 195 lbs. Born, Belleville, Ont., October 2, 1974.
(Detroit's 6th choice, 126th overall, in 1993 Entry Draft).

			Regular Season								Playoffs						
Season	Club	League	GP	W	L	T	Mins	GA	SO	Avg	GP	W	L	Mins	GA	SO	Avg
1990-91	Cgy. North Stars	AMHL	29	....	....	....	1740	99	0	3.43	....	....	....	....	....	....	....
1991-92	Saskatoon Blades	WHL	29	13	6	3	1529	87	1	3.41	15	9	5	860	37	0	3.38
1992-93	Saskatoon Blades	WHL	53	27	18	3	1939	160	1	3.27	9	4	5	569	33	0	3.48
1993-94	Saskatoon Blades	WHL	56	*41	13	1	3219	148	2	2.76	16	*11	5	940	48	*1	3.06
1994-95	Adirondack	AHL	39	12	15	2	1997	119	0	3.57	....	....	....	....	....	....	....
1995-96	Adirondack	AHL	54	24	18	6	2949	135	2	2.75	1	0	1	30	4	0	8.11
1996-97	Adirondack	AHL	*68	*34	22	9	*3843	173	5	2.70	4	1	3	192	10	1	3.13
1997-98	**Detroit**	**NHL**	**4**	**2**	**0**	**1**	**178**	**6**	**0**	**2.02**	....	....	....	....	....	....	....
	Adirondack	AHL	*66	27	29	8	*3709	190	1	3.07	3	0	3	180	10	0	3.33
1998-99	**Detroit**	**NHL**	**16**	**6**	**5**	**2**	**821**	**31**	**0**	**2.27**	**2**	**0**	**0**	**58**	**3**	**0**	**3.10**
	Adirondack	AHL	6	3	3	0	359	18	0	3.01	....	....	....	....	....	....	....
99-2000	**Atlanta**	**NHL**	**32**	**4**	**19**	**2**	**1618**	**94**	**1**	**3.49**	....	....	....	....	....	....	....

2000-01	Atlanta	NHL	13	2	8	3	753	43	0	3.43	....	....	....	....	....	....	....
	Orlando	IHL	51	33	13	3	2963	100	*8	*2.02	*16	*12	4	*1003	37	1	2.21
2001-02	Atlanta	NHL	1	0	1	0	60	3	0	3.00	....	....	....	....	....	....	....
	Chicago Wolves	AHL	51	21	25	4	2919	141	3	2.90	2	0	1	55	4	0	4.36
2002-03	Chicago Wolves	AHL	49	22	18	6	2795	134	2	2.88	8	3	4	462	17	1	2.21
	NHL Totals		66	14	33	8	3430	177	1	3.10	2	0	0	58	3	0	3.10

Warwick Trophy (MVP – AMHL) (1991) • WHL East Second All-Star Team (1993) • WHL East First All-Star Team (1994) • Canadian Major Junior First All-Star Team (1994) • Canadian Major Junior Goaltender of the Year (1994) • AHL Second All-Star Team (1997, 1998) • IHL First All-Star Team (2001) • Shared James Norris Memorial Trophy (fewest goals against – IHL) (2001) with Scott Fankhouser • James Gatschene Memorial Trophy (MVP – IHL) (2001) • "Bud" Poile Trophy (Playoff MVP – IHL) (2001)

Claimed by **Atlanta** from **Detroit** in Expansion Draft, June 25, 1999.

MARKKANEN, Jussi (MAHR-kah-nehn, YOO-see) NYR

Goaltender. Catches left. 5'11", 183 lbs. Born, Imatra, Finland, May 8, 1975.
(Edmonton's 5th choice, 133rd overall, in 2001 Entry Draft).

			Regular Season								Playoffs						
Season	Club	League	GP	W	L	T	Mins	GA	SO	Avg	GP	W	L	Mins	GA	SO	Avg
1991-92	SaiPa Jr.	Finn-Jr.	2	....	....	....	120	11	0	5.50	....	....	....	....	....	....	....
1992-93	SaiPa Jr.	Finn-Jr.	7	....	....	....	367	28	....	4.58	....	....	....	....	....	....	....
	SaiPa	Finland-2	16	....	....	....	798	60	....	4.51	....	....	....	....	....	....	....
1993-94	SaiPa	Finland-2	30	....	....	....	1726	97	....	3.37	....	....	....	....	....	....	....
1994-95	SaiPa	Finland-2	43	....	....	....	2493	122	....	2.94	3	....	....	179	5	....	1.68
1995-96	Tappara Jr.	Finn-Jr.	5	....	....	....	298	21	....	4.23	....	....	....	....	....	....	....
	Tappara Tampere	Finland	23	11	8	2	1238	59	1	2.86	....	....	....	....	....	....	....
1996-97	SaiPa	Finland	41	9	24	7	2340	132	0	3.38	....	....	....	....	....	....	....
1997-98	SaiPa	Finland	*48	21	20	5	*2870	138	4	2.89	3	0	3	164	11	0	4.02
1998-99	SaiPa	Finland	48	21	19	4	2633	105	4	2.39	7	3	3	366	21	0	3.44
99-2000	SaiPa	Finland	48	4	23	9	2794	150	2	3.22	....	....	....	....	....	....	....
2000-01	Tappara Tampere	Finland	52	*30	17	5	3076	107	*9	2.09	*10	7	3	*608	18	1	1.78
2001-02	Edmonton	NHL	14	6	4	2	784	24	2	1.84	....	....	....	....	....	....	....
	Hamilton Bulldogs	AHL	4	2	2	0	239	9	0	2.26	....	....	....	....	....	....	....
	Finland	Olympics	DID NOT PLAY – SPARE GOALTENDER														
2002-03	Edmonton	NHL	22	7	8	3	1180	51	3	2.59	1	0	0	14	1	0	4.29
	NHL Totals		36	13	12	5	1964	75	5	2.29	1	0	0	14	1	0	4.29

Traded to **NY Rangers** by **Edmonton** with future considerations for the rights to Brian Leetch, June 30, 2003.

MARSTERS, Nathan (MAHR-stuhrs, NAY-thuhn) L.A.

Goaltender. Catches left. 6'4", 190 lbs. Born, Burlington, Ont., January 28, 1980.
(Los Angeles' 5th choice, 165th overall, in 2000 Entry Draft).

			Regular Season								Playoffs						
Season	Club	League	GP	W	L	T	Mins	GA	SO	Avg	GP	W	L	Mins	GA	SO	Avg
1997-98	Bramalea Blues	OPJHL	12	....	....	....	539	25	2	2.78	....	....	....	....	....	....	....
1998-99	Bramalea Blues	OPJHL	29	....	....	....	1711	91	3	3.19	....	....	....	....	....	....	....
99-2000	Bramalea Blues	OPJHL	28	....	....	....	1668	98	2	3.53	....	....	....	....	....	....	....
	Chilliwack Chiefs	BCHL	15	9	6	0	825	63	0	4.58	20	15	5	1187	62	0	3.13
2000-01	RPI Engineers	ECAC	28	14	13	1	1631	64	*4	2.35	....	....	....	....	....	....	....
2001-02	RPI Engineers	ECAC	28	15	9	3	1627	70	1	2.58	....	....	....	....	....	....	....
2002-03	RPI Engineers	ECAC	24	7	15	1	1286	73	0	3.41	....	....	....	....	....	....	....

MASON, Chris (MAY-sohn, KRIHS) FLA.

Goaltender. Catches left. 6', 195 lbs. Born, Red Deer, Alta., April 20, 1976.
(New Jersey's 7th choice, 122nd overall, in 1995 Entry Draft).

			Regular Season								Playoffs						
Season	Club	League	GP	W	L	T	Mins	GA	SO	Avg	GP	W	L	Mins	GA	SO	Avg
1992-93	Red Deer Chiefs	AMHL	20	....	....	....	1280	76	0	3.35	....	....	....	....	....	....	....
1993-94	Victoria Cougars	WHL	5	1	4	0	237	27	0	6.84	....	....	....	....	....	....	....
1994-95	Prince George	WHL	44	8	30	1	2288	192	1	5.03	....	....	....	....	....	....	....
1995-96	Prince George	WHL	59	16	37	1	3289	236	1	4.31	....	....	....	....	....	....	....
1996-97	Prince George	WHL	50	19	24	4	2851	172	2	3.62	15	9	6	938	44	*1	2.81
1997-98	Cincinnati	AHL	47	13	19	7	2368	136	0	3.45	....	....	....	....	....	....	....
1998-99	Nashville	NHL	3	0	0	0	69	6	0	5.22	....	....	....	....	....	....	....
	Milwaukee	IHL	34	15	12	6	1901	92	1	2.90	....	....	....	....	....	....	....
99-2000	Milwaukee	IHL	53	20	21	8	2952	137	2	2.78	3	1	2	252	11	0	2.62
2000-01	Nashville	NHL	1	0	1	0	59	2	0	2.03	....	....	....	....	....	....	....
	Milwaukee	IHL	37	17	14	5	2226	87	5	2.35	4	1	3	239	12	0	3.02
2001-02	Milwaukee	AHL	48	17	21	7	2755	116	2	2.53	....	....	....	....	....	....	....
2002-03	San Antonio	AHL	50	25	18	6	2914	122	1	2.51	3	0	3	195	9	0	2.77
	NHL Totals		4	0	1	0	128	8	0	3.75	....	....	....	....	....	....	....

Signed as a free agent by **Anaheim**, June 27, 1997. Traded to **Nashville** by **Anaheim** with Marc Moro for Dominic Roussel, October 5, 1998. Signed as a free agent by **Florida**, August 20, 2002.

McELHINNEY, Curtis (MAK-IHL-ehn-ee, KUHR-this) CGY.

Goaltender. Catches left. 6'2", 185 lbs. Born, London, Ont., May 23, 1983.
(Calgary's 9th choice, 176th overall, in 2002 Entry Draft).

			Regular Season								Playoffs						
Season	Club	League	GP	W	L	T	Mins	GA	SO	Avg	GP	W	L	Mins	GA	SO	Avg
2001-02	Colorado College	WCHA	9	6	0	1	441	15	1	2.04	....	....	....	....	....	....	....
2002-03	Colorado College	WCHA	*37	*25	6	5	*2147	85	*4	2.37	....	....	....	....	....	....	....

WCHA First All-Star Team (2003) • NCAA West Second All-American Team (2003)

McKENNA, Mike NSH.

Goaltender. Catches right. 6'2", 195 lbs. Born, St. Louis, MO, April 11, 1983.
(Nashville's 4th choice, 172nd overall, in 2002 Entry Draft).

			Regular Season								Playoffs						
Season	Club	League	GP	W	L	T	Mins	GA	SO	Avg	GP	W	L	Mins	GA	SO	Avg
99-2000	Springfield	NAJHL	16	6	8	0	879	48	0	3.28	....	....	....	....	....	....	....
2000-01	Springfield	NAJHL	48	18	28	0	2743	209	0	4.57	2	0	2	120	11	0	5.50
2001-02	St. Lawrence	ECAC	20	7	10	1	1121	59	0	3.16	....	....	....	....	....	....	....
2002-03	St. Lawrence	ECAC	15	1	7	2	618	38	0	3.69	....	....	....	....	....	....	....

McLENNAN, Jamie (muh-KLEH-nuhn, JAY-mee) CGY.

Goaltender. Catches left. 6', 190 lbs. Born, Edmonton, Alta., June 30, 1971.
(NY Islanders' 3rd choice, 48th overall, in 1991 Entry Draft).

			Regular Season								Playoffs						
Season	Club	League	GP	W	L	T	Mins	GA	SO	Avg	GP	W	L	Mins	GA	SO	Avg
1987-88	St. Albert Royals	AMHL	21	....	....	....	1224	80	0	3.92	....	....	....	....	....	....	....
1988-89	Spokane Chiefs	WHL	11	....	....	....	578	63	0	6.54	....	....	....	....	....	....	....
	Lethbridge	WHL	7	....	....	....	368	22	0	3.59	....	....	....	....	....	....	....
1989-90	Lethbridge	WHL	34	20	4	2	1690	110	1	3.91	13	6	5	677	44	0	3.90
1990-91	Lethbridge	WHL	56	32	18	4	3230	205	0	3.81	*16	8	8	*970	56	0	3.46
1991-92	Capital District	AHL	18	4	10	2	952	60	1	3.78	....	....	....	....	....	....	....
	Richmond	ECHL	32	16	12	2	1837	114	0	3.72	....	....	....	....	....	....	....
1992-93	Capital District	AHL	38	17	14	6	2171	117	1	3.23	1	0	1	20	5	0	15.00
1993-94	NY Islanders	NHL	22	8	7	6	1287	61	0	2.84	2	0	1	82	6	0	4.39
	Salt Lake	IHL	24	8	12	2	1320	80	0	3.64	....	....	....	....	....	....	....
1994-95	NY Islanders	NHL	21	6	11	2	1185	67	0	3.39	....	....	....	....	....	....	....
	Denver Grizzlies	IHL	4	3	0	1	239	12	0	3.00	11	8	2	640	23	1	*2.15
1995-96	NY Islanders	NHL	13	3	9	1	636	39	0	3.68	....	....	....	....	....	....	....
	Utah Grizzlies	IHL	14	9	2	2	728	29	0	2.39	....	....	....	....	....	....	....
	Worcester IceCats	AHL	22	14	7	1	1216	57	0	2.81	2	0	2	119	8	0	4.04
1996-97	Worcester IceCats	AHL	39	18	13	4	2152	100	2	2.79	4	2	2	262	16	0	3.67
1997-98	St. Louis	NHL	30	16	8	2	1658	60	2	2.17	1	0	0	14	1	0	4.29
1998-99	St. Louis	NHL	33	13	14	4	1763	70	3	2.38	1	0	1	37	0	0	0.00
99-2000	St. Louis	NHL	19	9	5	2	1009	33	2	1.96	....	....	....	....	....	....	....
2000-01	Minnesota	NHL	38	5	23	9	2230	98	2	2.64	....	....	....	....	....	....	....
2001-02	Houston Aeros	AHL	51	25	18	4	2852	130	3	2.74	14	8	6	880	31	2	2.11
2002-03	Calgary	NHL	22	2	11	4	1165	58	0	2.99	....	....	....	....	....	....	....
	NHL Totals		198	62	88	30	10933	486	9	2.67	4	0	2	133	7	0	3.16

WHL East First All-Star Team (1991) • Bill Masterton Memorial Trophy (1998)

Signed as a free agent by **St. Louis**, July 15, 1996. Claimed by **Minnesota** from **St. Louis** in Expansion Draft, June 23, 2000. Traded to **Calgary** by **Minnesota** for Calgary's 9th round choice (Mika Hannula) in 2002 Entry Draft, June 22, 2002.

McVICAR, Rob (mihk-VIH-kuhr, RAWB) VAN.

Goaltender. Catches left. 6'4", 195 lbs. Born, Hay River, NWT, January 15, 1982.
(Vancouver's 6th choice, 151st overall, in 2002 Entry Draft).

			Regular Season								Playoffs						
Season	Club	League	GP	W	L	T	Mins	GA	SO	Avg	GP	W	L	Mins	GA	SO	Avg
1998-99	Brandon Kings	MMMHL	21	....	....	....	1217	69	0	3.40	....	....	....	....	....	....	....
99-2000	Brandon	WHL	14	5	6	0	687	43	0	3.76	....	....	....	....	....	....	....
2000-01	Brandon	WHL	27	12	10	2	1537	76	0	2.97	5	2	3	324	13	1	2.41
2001-02	Brandon	WHL	55	*33	18	2	3276	151	1	2.77	19	11	8	1255	44	1	2.10
2002-03	Brandon	WHL	51	31	14	5	3027	136	2	2.70	13	6	7	737	32	0	2.61

MEDVEDEV, Andrei (mehd-VEH-dehv, AN-dray) CGY.

Goaltender. Catches left. 6', 211 lbs. Born, Moscow, USSR, April 1, 1983.
(Calgary's 3rd choice, 56th overall, in 2001 Entry Draft).

			Regular Season								Playoffs						
Season	Club	League	GP	W	L	T	Mins	GA	SO	Avg	GP	W	L	Mins	GA	SO	Avg
1998-99	Spartak Moscow	Russia	2	....	....	....	80	2	1	1.50	....	....	....	....	....	....	....
99-2000	Spartak Moscow	Russia-2	STATISTICS NOT AVAILABLE														
2000-01	Spartak Moscow	Russia-2	11	....	....	....	208	8	0	2.31	....	....	....	....	....	....	....
2001-02	Spartak Moscow 2	Russia-3	STATISTICS NOT AVAILABLE														
	Spartak Moscow	Russia	2	....	....	....	61	4	0	3.93	....	....	....	....	....	....	....
2002-03	Spartak Moscow	Russia	17	....	....	....	810	28	1	2.07	....	....	....	....	....	....	....

MENSATOR, Lukas (MEHN-suh-tohr, loo-KAHSH) VAN.

Goaltender. Catches left. 5'8", 167 lbs. Born, Sokolov, Czech., August 18, 1984.
(Vancouver's 4th choice, 83rd overall, in 2002 Entry Draft).

			Regular Season								Playoffs						
Season	Club	League	GP	W	L	T	Mins	GA	SO	Avg	GP	W	L	Mins	GA	SO	Avg
99-2000	HC Karlovy Vary 18	Czech-Jr.	42	....	....	....	2406	160	0	3.99	....	....	....	....	....	....	....
	Karlovy Vary Jr.	Czech-Jr.	1	1	0	0	60	3	0	3.00	....	....	....	....	....	....	....
2000-01	HC Karlovy Vary 18	Czech-Jr.	6	....	....	....	360	15	0	2.50	....	....	....	....	....	....	....
	Karlovy Vary Jr.	Czech-Jr.	19	....	....	....	1085	60	0	3.32	....	....	....	....	....	....	....
2001-02	Karlovy Vary Jr.	Czech-Jr.	31	....	....	....	1809	93	0	3.08	9	....	....	459	17	0	2.22
	Banik CHZ Sokolov	Czech-3	3	....	....	....	180	12	0	4.00	....	....	....	....	....	....	....
2002-03	Ottawa 67's	OHL	42	26	8	5	2395	122	0	3.06	*23	13	8	*1381	63	*2	2.74

MEYER, Scott (MIGH-uhr, SKAWT) NYR

Goaltender. Catches left. 6', 185 lbs. Born, White Bear Lake, MN, April 10, 1976.

			Regular Season								Playoffs						
Season	Club	League	GP	W	L	T	Mins	GA	SO	Avg	GP	W	L	Mins	GA	SO	Avg
1995-96	Fargo-Moorhead	USHL	27	....	....	....	1620	82	1	3.04	....	....	....	....	....	....	....
1996-97	St. Cloud State	WCHA	1	0	0	0	29	1	0	2.07	....	....	....	....	....	....	....
1997-98	St. Cloud State	WCHA	2	0	1	0	75	4	0	3.21	....	....	....	....	....	....	....
1998-99	St. Cloud State	WCHA	9	2	5	1	464	23	0	2.97	....	....	....	....	....	....	....
99-2000	St. Cloud State	WCHA	32	20	8	3	1922	76	7	2.37	....	....	....	....	....	....	....
2000-01	St. Cloud State	WCHA	36	25	8	1	2096	78	2	2.23	....	....	....	....	....	....	....
2001-02	Charlotte Checkers	ECHL	30	14	10	5	1720	78	1	2.72	....	....	....	....	....	....	....
	Hartford Wolf Pack	AHL	13	4	4	2	646	23	0	2.14	8	3	4	505	21	0	2.50
2002-03	Hartford Wolf Pack	AHL	9	1	5	1	498	36	0	4.34	....	....	....	....	....	....	....
	Charlotte Checkers	ECHL	27	20	5	0	1494	65	2	2.61	....	....	....	....	....	....	....

WCHA Second All-Star Team (2000) • WCHA First All-Star Team (2001) • NCAA West Second All-American Team (2001)

Signed as a free agent by **NY Rangers**, July 5, 2001.

MICHAUD, Alfie (mee-SHOH, AL-fee)

Goaltender. Catches left. 5'10", 177 lbs. Born, Selkirk, Man., November 6, 1976.

			Regular Season								Playoffs						
Season	Club	League	GP	W	L	T	Mins	GA	SO	Avg	GP	W	L	Mins	GA	SO	Avg
1995-96	Lebret Eagles	SJHL	44	....	....	....	2547	121	2	2.85	....	....	....	....	....	....	....
1996-97	University of Maine	H-East	29	*17	8	1	1515	78	1	3.09	....	....	....	....	....	....	....
1997-98	University of Maine	H-East	32	15	12	4	1794	94	2	3.14	....	....	....	....	....	....	....
1998-99	University of Maine	H-East	37	*28	6	3	2147	83	3	2.32	....	....	....	....	....	....	....
99-2000	Vancouver	NHL	2	0	1	0	69	5	0	4.35	....	....	....	....	....	....	....
	Syracuse Crunch	AHL	38	10	17	5	2052	132	0	3.86	....	....	....	....	....	....	....
2000-01	Kansas City Blades	IHL	32	14	14	2	1778	93	1	3.14	....	....	....	....	....	....	....
2001-02	Manitoba Moose	AHL	32	16	10	1	1749	78	4	2.68	7	3	4	424	19	0	2.69
	Reading Royals	ECHL	11	5	3	2	606	26	2	2.58	....	....	....	....	....	....	....
2002-03	Tappara Tampere	Finland	4	0	2	1	160	11	0	4.12	....	....	....	....	....	....	....
	Ahmat	Finland-2	5	4	1	0	357	10	2	2.19	....	....	....	....	....	....	....
	Peoria Rivermen	ECHL	30	20	4	4	1685	59	1	*2.10	2	0	2	141	8	0	3.40
	NHL Totals		2	0	1	0	69	5	0	4.35	....	....	....	....	....	....	....

NCAA Championship All-Tournament Team (1999) • NCAA Championship Tournament MVP (1999) • ECHL First All-Star Team (2003) • Top Goaltender – ECHL (2003)

Signed as a free agent by **Vancouver**, July 12, 1999. Signed as a free agent by **Peoria** (ECHL), August 18, 2002. Signed as a free agent by **Tampere** (Finland) with **Peoria** (ECHL) retaining rights, November 5, 2002. • Returned to **Peoria** (ECHL) by **Tampere** (Finland), December 28, 2002.

MICHAUD, Olivier (MEE-shoh, OH-lihv-ee-ay) MTL.

Goaltender. Catches left. 5'11", 160 lbs. Born, Beloeil, Que., September 14, 1983.

			Regular Season								Playoffs						
Season	Club	League	GP	W	L	T	Mins	GA	SO	Avg	GP	W	L	Mins	GA	SO	Avg
1998-99	Eclaireur Bantams	QAHA	23	14	4	5	1380	58	....	2.50	....	....	....	....	....	....	....
99-2000	Antoine-Girourd	QAAA	7	6	1	0	420	15	1	2.14	....	....	....	....	....	....	....
	Charles Lemonthe	QAAA	16	8	4	2	886	57	0	3.86	16	8	8	1015	29	2	1.71
	Shawinigan	QMJHL	1	0	1	0	49	2	0	2.44	....	....	....	....	....	....	....
2000-01	Shawinigan	QMJHL	21	12	4	4	1096	54	1	2.96	3	1	2	150	6	0	2.41
2001-02	Montreal	NHL	1	0	0	0	18	0	0	0.00	....	....	....	....	....	....	....
	Shawinigan	QMJHL	46	29	11	3	2650	108	3	*2.45	12	7	5	744	36	0	2.91
2002-03	Shawinigan	QMJHL	27	8	13	3	1497	82	1	3.29	....	....	....	....	....	....	....
	Baie-Comeau	QMJHL	31	23	5	2	1775	90	3	3.04	12	7	5	748	38	0	3.05
	NHL Totals		1	0	0	0	18	0	0	0.00	....	....	....	....	....	....	....

Signed as a free agent by **Montreal**, September 18, 2001. • Promoted to **Montreal** from **Shawinigan** (QMJHL) and replaced injured Jose Theodore, October 26, 2001. • Returned to **Shawinigan** (QMJHL) by **Montreal**, November 5, 2001.

MILLER, Ryan (MIHL-luhr, RIGH-uhn) BUF.

Goaltender. Catches left. 6'2", 150 lbs. Born, East Lansing, MI, July 17, 1980.
(Buffalo's 7th choice, 138th overall, in 1999 Entry Draft).

			Regular Season								Playoffs						
Season	**Club**	**League**	**GP**	**W**	**L**	**T**	**Mins**	**GA**	**SO**	**Avg**	**GP**	**W**	**L**	**Mins**	**GA**	**SO**	**Avg**
1997-98	Sault Ste. Marie	NAJHL	31	17	13	0	1804	72	1	2.39	6	2	4	311	10	0	1.93
1998-99	Sault Ste. Marie	NAJHL	47	31	14	1	2711	104	8	2.30	4	2	2	218	10	1	2.76
99-2000	Michigan State	CCHA	26	16	5	3	1525	39	*8	*1.53	....	....	....	....	....	....	....
2000-01	Michigan State	CCHA	40	*31	5	4	2447	54	*10	*1.32	....	....	....	....	....	....	....
2001-02	Michigan State	CCHA	40	26	9	5	2411	71	*8	*1.77	....	....	....	....	....	....	....
2002-03	**Buffalo**	**NHL**	**15**	**6**	**8**	**1**	**912**	**40**	**1**	**2.63**	....	....	....	....	....	....	....
	Rochester	AHL	47	23	18	5	2817	110	2	2.34	3	1	2	190	13	0	4.11
	NHL Totals		**15**	**6**	**8**	**1**	**912**	**40**	**1**	**2.63**	....	....	....	....	....	....	....

CCHA Second All-Star Team (2000) • CCHA First All-Star Team (2001, 2002) • NCAA West First All-American Team (2001, 2002) • Hobey Baker Memorial Award (Top U.S. Collegiate Player) (2001) • CCHA Player of the Year (2002)

MINARD, Mike (mih-NAHRD, MIGHK) TOR.

Goaltender. Catches left. 6'2", 200 lbs. Born, Owen Sound, Ont., November 1, 1976.
(Edmonton's 4th choice, 83rd overall, in 1995 Entry Draft).

			Regular Season								Playoffs						
Season	**Club**	**League**	**GP**	**W**	**L**	**T**	**Mins**	**GA**	**SO**	**Avg**	**GP**	**W**	**L**	**Mins**	**GA**	**SO**	**Avg**
1992-93	St. Marys Lincolns	OJHL-B	23	....	....	....	1374	162	0	3.10	....	....	....	....	....	....	....
1993-94	St. Marys Lincolns	OJHL-B	31	*25	5	0	1710	78	1	*2.74	....	....	....	....	....	....	....
1994-95	Chilliwack Chiefs	BCJHL	40	....	....	....	2330	136	0	3.50	....	....	....	....	....	....	....
1995-96	Barrie Colts	OHL	1	0	1	0	52	8	0	9.23	....	....	....	....	....	....	....
	Detroit Jr. Whalers	OHL	42	25	10	4	2314	128	2	3.32	17	9	6	922	55	1	3.58
1996-97	Hamilton Bulldogs	AHL	3	1	1	0	100	7	0	4.20	....	....	....	....	....	....	....
	Wheeling Nailers	ECHL	23	3	7	1	899	69	0	4.60	3	0	2	148	16	0	6.47
1997-98	Hamilton Bulldogs	AHL	2	1	0	0	80	2	0	1.50	....	....	....	....	....	....	....
	Brantford Smoke	UHL	2	1	1	0	74	7	0	5.63	....	....	....	....	....	....	....
	New Orleans Brass	ECHL	11	6	2	0	429	30	0	4.19	....	....	....	....	....	....	....
	Milwaukee	IHL	8	2	2	0	362	19	0	3.15	....	....	....	....	....	....	....
1998-99	Dayton Bombers	ECHL	15	8	5	2	788	42	1	3.20	....	....	....	....	....	....	....
	Milwaukee	IHL	10	3	5	0	531	27	0	3.05	....	....	....	....	....	....	....
	Hamilton Bulldogs	AHL	11	8	3	0	645	30	1	2.79	1	0	0	20	0	0	0.00
99-2000	**Edmonton**	**NHL**	**1**	**1**	**0**	**0**	**60**	**3**	**0**	**3.00**	....	....	....	....	....	....	....
	Hamilton Bulldogs	AHL	38	16	12	5	1987	102	0	3.08	1	0	0	23	0	0	0.00
2000-01	St. John's	AHL	43	23	10	4	2252	91	1	2.42	4	1	3	252	15	0	3.57
2001-02	St. John's	AHL	35	14	11	7	1936	100	1	3.10	....	....	....	....	....	....	....
2002-03	Manitoba Moose	AHL	1	0	1	0	59	5	0	5.06	5	2	2	282	9	0	1.91
	Reading Royals	ECHL	2	0	2	0	119	17	0	8.55	....	....	....	....	....	....	....
	Toledo Storm	ECHL	19	8	4	5	1093	42	1	2.31	....	....	....	....	....	....	....
	NHL Totals		**1**	**1**	**0**	**0**	**60**	**3**	**0**	**3.00**	....	....	....	....	....	....	....

Signed as a free agent by **Toronto**, March 16, 2001.

MORRISON, Mike (MOHR-rihs-ohn, MIGHK) EDM.

Goaltender. Catches right. 6'3", 194 lbs. Born, Medford, MA, July 11, 1979.
(Edmonton's 8th choice, 186th overall, in 1998 Entry Draft).

			Regular Season								Playoffs						
Season	**Club**	**League**	**GP**	**W**	**L**	**T**	**Mins**	**GA**	**SO**	**Avg**	**GP**	**W**	**L**	**Mins**	**GA**	**SO**	**Avg**
1997-98	Exeter Academy	H.S.	27	15	11	2	1632	64	1	2.35	....	....	....	....	....	....	....
1998-99	University of Maine	H-East	11	3	0	1	347	10	1	1.73	....	....	....	....	....	....	....
99-2000	University of Maine	H-East	12	7	2	1	608	27	1	2.67	....	....	....	....	....	....	....
2000-01	University of Maine	H-East	10	2	3	3	490	16	1	1.96	....	....	....	....	....	....	....
2001-02	University of Maine	H-East	30	20	3	4	1645	60	2	2.19	....	....	....	....	....	....	....
2002-03	Columbus	ECHL	38	9	18	6	1948	113	1	3.48	....	....	....	....	....	....	....

Hockey East First All-Star Team (2002)

MOSS, Tyler (MAWS, TIGH-luhr) VAN.

Goaltender. Catches right. 6', 185 lbs. Born, Ottawa, Ont., June 29, 1975.
(Tampa Bay's 2nd choice, 29th overall, in 1993 Entry Draft).

			Regular Season								Playoffs						
Season	**Club**	**League**	**GP**	**W**	**L**	**T**	**Mins**	**GA**	**SO**	**Avg**	**GP**	**W**	**L**	**Mins**	**GA**	**SO**	**Avg**
1991-92	Nepean Raiders	OCJHL	26	7	12	1	1335	109	0	4.90	....	....	....	....	....	....	....
1992-93	Kingston	OHL	31	13	7	5	1537	97	0	3.79	6	1	2	228	19	0	5.00
1993-94	Kingston	OHL	13	6	4	3	795	42	1	3.17	3	0	2	136	8	0	3.53
1994-95	Kingston	OHL	*57	33	17	5	*3249	164	1	3.03	6	2	4	333	27	0	4.86
1995-96	Atlanta Knights	IHL	40	11	19	4	2030	138	1	4.08	3	0	3	213	11	0	3.10
1996-97	Adirondack	AHL	11	1	5	2	507	42	1	4.97	....	....	....	....	....	....	....
	Grand Rapids	IHL	15	5	6	1	715	35	0	2.94	....	....	....	....	....	....	....
	Muskegon Fury	ColHL	2	1	1	0	119	5	0	2.51	....	....	....	....	....	....	....
	Saint John Flames	AHL	9	6	1	1	534	17	0	1.91	5	2	3	242	15	0	3.72
1997-98	**Calgary**	**NHL**	**6**	**2**	**3**	**1**	**367**	**20**	**0**	**3.27**	....	....	....	....	....	....	....
	Saint John Flames	AHL	39	19	10	7	2194	91	0	2.49	15	8	5	761	37	0	2.91
1998-99	**Calgary**	**NHL**	**11**	**3**	**7**	**0**	**550**	**23**	**0**	**2.51**	....	....	....	....	....	....	....
	Saint John Flames	AHL	9	2	5	1	475	25	0	3.16	....	....	....	....	....	....	....
	Orlando	IHL	9	6	2	1	515	21	1	2.45	17	10	7	1017	53	0	3.13
99-2000	Wilkes-Barre	AHL	4	1	1	1	188	11	0	3.52	....	....	....	....	....	....	....
	Kansas City Blades	IHL	36	18	12	5	2116	105	3	2.98	....	....	....	....	....	....	....
2000-01	Cincinnati	IHL	9	5	3	1	506	24	2	2.85	....	....	....	....	....	....	....
	Carolina	**NHL**	**12**	**1**	**6**	**0**	**557**	**37**	**0**	**3.99**	....	....	....	....	....	....	....
2001-02	Lowell	AHL	43	20	16	7	2572	106	1	2.47	....	....	....	....	....	....	....
2002-03	**Vancouver**	**NHL**	**1**	**0**	**0**	**0**	**22**	**1**	**0**	**2.73**	....	....	....	....	....	....	....
	Manitoba Moose	AHL	42	21	15	5	2502	117	3	2.81	10	6	4	618	23	0	2.23
	NHL Totals		**30**	**6**	**16**	**1**	**1496**	**81**	**0**	**3.25**	....	....	....	....	....	....	....

OHL All-Rookie Team (1993) • OHL First All-Star Team (1995) • Shared Harry "Hap" Holmes Memorial Trophy (fewest goals against – AHL) (1998) with Jean-Sebastien Giguere

Traded to **Calgary** by **Tampa Bay** for Jamie Huscroft, March 18, 1997. Traded to **Pittsburgh** by **Calgary** with Rene Corbet for Brad Werenka, March 14, 2000. Signed as a free agent by **Carolina**, August 9, 2000. Signed as a free agent by **Vancouver**, July 5, 2002.

MULLER, Robert (MEW-luhr, RAW-buhrt) WSH.

Goaltender. Catches left. 5'8", 163 lbs. Born, Rosenheim, West Germany, June 25, 1980.
(Washington's 9th choice, 275th overall, in 2001 Entry Draft).

			Regular Season								Playoffs						
Season	**Club**	**League**	**GP**	**W**	**L**	**T**	**Mins**	**GA**	**SO**	**Avg**	**GP**	**W**	**L**	**Mins**	**GA**	**SO**	**Avg**
1996-97	Rosenheim Jr.	Ger.-Jr.					STATISTICS NOT AVAILABLE										
1997-98	EHC Klostersee	German-3					STATISTICS NOT AVAILABLE										
1998-99	Rosenheim	Germany	33	....	....	....	1863	105	1	3.38	....	....	....	....	....	....	....
99-2000	Rosenheim	Germany	39	....	....	....	2228	131	1	3.53	....	....	....	....	....	....	....
2000-01	Adler Mannheim	Germany	23	....	....	....	1195	49	1	2.46	2	....	....	103	2	0	1.17
2001-02	Adler Mannheim	Germany	15	....	....	....	637	26	1	2.45	....	....	....	....	....	....	....
	Germany	Olympics	2	0	1	0	78	4	0	3.07	....	....	....	....	....	....	....
2002-03	Krefeld Pinguine	Germany	47	....	....	....	2762	107	5	2.32	14	....	....	843	28	*1	*1.99

MUNCE, Ryan (MUNTS, RIGH-uhn) L.A.

Goaltender. Catches left. 6'2", 180 lbs. Born, Mississauga, Ont., April 16, 1985.
(Los Angeles' 5th choice, 82nd overall, in 2003 Entry Draft).

			Regular Season								Playoffs						
Season	**Club**	**League**	**GP**	**W**	**L**	**T**	**Mins**	**GA**	**SO**	**Avg**	**GP**	**W**	**L**	**Mins**	**GA**	**SO**	**Avg**
2001-02	Young Nats	GTHL	27	24	2	1	....	....	....	2.01	17	16	1	....	....	....	1.98
2002-03	Sarnia Sting	OHL	27	15	7	0	1410	62	3	2.64	4	1	1	149	8	1	3.22

NABOKOV, Evgeni (na-BAW-kahv, ehv-GEH-nee) S.J.

Goaltender. Catches left. 6', 200 lbs. Born, Ust-Kamenogorsk, USSR, July 25, 1975.
(San Jose's 9th choice, 219th overall, in 1994 Entry Draft).

			Regular Season								Playoffs						
Season	**Club**	**League**	**GP**	**W**	**L**	**T**	**Mins**	**GA**	**SO**	**Avg**	**GP**	**W**	**L**	**Mins**	**GA**	**SO**	**Avg**
1992-93	Ust-Kamenogorsk	CIS	4	1	0	0	109	5	0	2.75	....	....	....	....	....	....	....
1993-94	Ust-Kamenogorsk	CIS	11	....	....	....	539	29	0	3.23	....	....	....	....	....	....	....
1994-95	Dynamo Moscow	CIS	24	....	....	....	1265	40	....	1.90	13	....	....	810	30	....	2.22
1995-96	Dynamo Moscow	CIS	39	....	....	....	2008	67	5	2.00	6	....	....	298	7	....	1.41
1996-97	Dynamo Moscow	Russia	27	....	....	....	1588	56	2	2.12	4	....	....	255	12	0	2.82
1997-98	Kentucky	AHL	33	10	21	2	1866	122	0	3.92	1	0	0	23	1	0	2.59
1998-99	Kentucky	AHL	43	26	14	1	2429	106	5	2.62	11	6	5	599	30	*2	3.00
99-2000	**San Jose**	**NHL**	**11**	**2**	**2**	**1**	**414**	**15**	**1**	**2.17**	**1**	**0**	**0**	**20**	**0**	**0**	**0.00**
	Cleveland	IHL	20	12	4	3	1164	52	0	2.68	....	....	....	....	....	....	....
	Kentucky	AHL	2	1	1	0	120	3	1	1.50	....	....	....	....	....	....	....
2000-01	**San Jose**	**NHL**	**66**	**32**	**21**	**7**	**3700**	**135**	**6**	**2.19**	**4**	**1**	**3**	**218**	**10**	**1**	**2.75**
2001-02	**San Jose**	**NHL**	**67**	**37**	**24**	**5**	**3901**	**149**	**7**	**2.29**	**12**	**7**	**5**	**712**	**31**	**0**	**2.61**
2002-03	**San Jose**	**NHL**	**55**	**19**	**28**	**8**	**3227**	**146**	**3**	**2.71**	....	....	....	....	....	....	....
	NHL Totals		**199**	**90**	**75**	**21**	**11242**	**445**	**17**	**2.38**	**17**	**8**	**8**	**950**	**41**	**1**	**2.59**

NHL All-Rookie Team (2001) • Calder Memorial Trophy (2001)

Played in NHL All-Star Game (2001)

• Scored a goal vs. Vancouver, March 10, 2002.

NASTIUK, Kevin (NAZ-tee-uhk, KEH-vihn) CAR.

Goaltender. Catches left. 6'2", 176 lbs. Born, Edmonton, Alta., July 20, 1985.
(Carolina's 4th choice, 126th overall, in 2003 Entry Draft).

			Regular Season								Playoffs						
Season	**Club**	**League**	**GP**	**W**	**L**	**T**	**Mins**	**GA**	**SO**	**Avg**	**GP**	**W**	**L**	**Mins**	**GA**	**SO**	**Avg**
2000-01	Inland Cement	AMBHL	20	12	7	1	1233	64	0	3.11	1	1	0	60	2	0	2.00
2001-02	Medicine Hat	WHL	19	4	10	0	877	66	0	4.52	....	....	....	....	....	....	....
2002-03	Medicine Hat	WHL	42	15	20	2	2344	172	0	4.40	11	7	4	693	33	0	2.86

NAUMENKO, Gregg (naw-MEHN-koh, GREHG)

Goaltender. Catches left. 6'1", 201 lbs. Born, Chicago, IL, March 30, 1977.

			Regular Season								Playoffs						
Season	**Club**	**League**	**GP**	**W**	**L**	**T**	**Mins**	**GA**	**SO**	**Avg**	**GP**	**W**	**L**	**Mins**	**GA**	**SO**	**Avg**
1995-96	North Iowa	USHL	27	15	12	0	1649	103	1	3.75	4	1	3	239	15	0	3.77
1996-97	North Iowa	USHL	25	11	11	1	1342	85	1	3.80	6	3	2	284	19	0	4.01
1997-98	North Iowa	USHL	38	23	11	3	2171	80	3	2.21	5	4	1	299	11	0	2.21
1998-99	Alaska-Anchorage	WCHA	29	11	13	5	1691	65	1	*2.31	....	....	....	....	....	....	....
99-2000	Cincinnati	AHL	50	17	25	7	2877	143	2	2.98	....	....	....	....	....	....	....
2000-01	**Anaheim**	**NHL**	**2**	**0**	**1**	**0**	**70**	**7**	**0**	**6.00**	....	....	....	....	....	....	....
	Cincinnati	AHL	39	20	12	3	2079	101	2	2.91	2	0	2	123	10	0	4.90
2001-02	Augusta Lynx	ECHL	10	3	5	2	546	36	0	3.96	....	....	....	....	....	....	....
	Cincinnati	AHL	7	2	4	0	364	15	0	2.47	....	....	....	....	....	....	....
	Dayton Bombers	ECHL	23	14	3	5	1347	58	1	2.58	....	....	....	....	....	....	....
2002-03	Cleveland Barons	AHL	2	0	1	1	125	8	0	3.85	....	....	....	....	....	....	....
	Cincinnati	ECHL	17	6	6	3	913	47	1	3.09	....	....	....	....	....	....	....
	Cincinnati	AHL	2	0	1	0	65	6	0	5.50	....	....	....	....	....	....	....
	NHL Totals		**2**	**0**	**1**	**0**	**70**	**7**	**0**	**6.00**	....	....	....	....	....	....	....

WCHA First All-Star Team (1999) • WCHA Rookie of the Year (1999)

Signed as a free agent by **Anaheim**, March 31, 1999.

NIITTYMAKI, Antero (NEE-too-mah-kee, AN-tehr-oh) PHI.

Goaltender. Catches left. 6', 183 lbs. Born, Turku, Finland, June 18, 1980.
(Philadelphia's 7th choice, 168th overall, in 1998 Entry Draft).

			Regular Season								Playoffs						
Season	**Club**	**League**	**GP**	**W**	**L**	**T**	**Mins**	**GA**	**SO**	**Avg**	**GP**	**W**	**L**	**Mins**	**GA**	**SO**	**Avg**
1998-99	TPS Turku Jr.	Finn-Jr.	35	....	....	....	2095	60	0	1.72	....	....	....	....	....	....	....
99-2000	TPS Turku Jr.	Finn-Jr.	1	1	0	0	60	1	0	1.00	....	....	....	....	....	....	....
	TPS Turku	Finland	32	23	6	2	1899	68	3	2.15	8	6	1	453	13	0	1.72
2000-01	TPS Turku	Finland	21	10	6	1	1112	46	2	2.48	....	....	....	....	....	....	....
2001-02	TPS Turku	Finland	27	16	8	1	1498	46	3	1.84	4	2	2	295	11	0	2.24
2002-03	Philadelphia	AHL	40	14	21	2	2283	98	0	2.58	....	....	....	....	....	....	....

NISSINEN, Tuomas (NIHS-ih-nehn, too-OH-muhs) ST.L.

Goaltender. Catches left. 6'1", 176 lbs. Born, Kuopio, Finland, July 17, 1983.
(St. Louis' 2nd choice, 89th overall, in 2001 Entry Draft).

			Regular Season								Playoffs						
Season	**Club**	**League**	**GP**	**W**	**L**	**T**	**Mins**	**GA**	**SO**	**Avg**	**GP**	**W**	**L**	**Mins**	**GA**	**SO**	**Avg**
2000-01	KalPa Kuopio Jr.	Finn-Jr.	40	15	14	5	2327	125	2	3.22	1	0	1	60	4	0	4.00
2001-02	KalPa Kuopio Jr.	Finn-Jr.	33	20	11	2	1988	81	3	2.44	1	0	1	59	4	0	4.04
	Kalpa Kuopio	Finland-2	4	....	....	....	240	12	0	2.89	....	....	....	....	....	....	....
2002-03	Ilves Tampere	Finland	32	4	23	3	1750	108	1	3.70	....	....	....	....	....	....	....

NORONEN, Mika (NOH-rah-nehn, MEE-kah) BUF.

Goaltender. Catches left. 6'2", 196 lbs. Born, Tampere, Finland, June 17, 1979.
(Buffalo's 1st choice, 21st overall, in 1997 Entry Draft).

			Regular Season								Playoffs						
Season	**Club**	**League**	**GP**	**W**	**L**	**T**	**Mins**	**GA**	**SO**	**Avg**	**GP**	**W**	**L**	**Mins**	**GA**	**SO**	**Avg**
1995-96	Tappara Jr.	Finn-Jr.	16	....	....	....	962	37	2	2.31	....	....	....	....	....	....	....
1996-97	Tappara Tampere	Finland	5	1	3	0	215	17	0	4.73	....	....	....	....	....	....	....
1997-98	Tappara Tampere	Finland	37	14	12	3	1704	83	1	2.92	4	1	2	196	12	0	3.67
1998-99	Tappara Tampere	Finland	43	18	20	5	2494	135	2	3.25	....	....	....	....	....	....	....
99-2000	Rochester	AHL	54	*33	13	4	3089	112	*6	2.18	21	13	8	1235	37	*6	*1.80
2000-01	**Buffalo**	**NHL**	**2**	**2**	**0**	**0**	**108**	**5**	**0**	**2.78**	....	....	....	....	....	....	....
	Rochester	AHL	47	26	15	5	2753	100	4	2.18	4	1	3	250	11	0	2.64
2001-02	**Buffalo**	**NHL**	**10**	**4**	**3**	**1**	**518**	**23**	**0**	**2.66**	....	....	....	....	....	....	....
	Rochester	AHL	45	16	17	12	2764	115	3	2.50	1	0	1	59	3	0	3.06
2002-03	**Buffalo**	**NHL**	**16**	**4**	**9**	**3**	**891**	**36**	**1**	**2.42**	....	....	....	....	....	....	....
	Rochester	AHL	19	5	9	5	1169	55	2	2.82	....	....	....	....	....	....	....
	NHL Totals		**28**	**10**	**12**	**4**	**1517**	**64**	**1**	**2.53**	....	....	....	....	....	....	....

AHL Second All-Star Team (2000, 2001) • Dudley "Red" Garrett Memorial Trophy (Top Rookie – AHL) (2000) • Shared Harry "Hap" Holmes Memorial Trophy (fewest goals against – AHL) (2001) with Tom Askey

NORRENA, Fredrik (noh-REH-nah, FREHD-rihk) T.B.

Goaltender. Catches left. 6', 189 lbs. Born, Pietarsaari, Finland, November 29, 1973.
(Tampa Bay's 8th choice, 213th overall, in 2002 Entry Draft).

			Regular Season								Playoffs						
Season	Club	League	GP	W	L	T	Mins	GA	SO	Avg	GP	W	L	Mins	GA	SO	Avg
1997-98	Lukko Rauma	Finland	48	12	19	4	2174	105	0	2.90	....	....	....	....	....	....	....
1998-99	TPS Turku	Finland	20	11	4	1	1010	35	2	2.08	1	0	0	20	2	0	6.00
99-2000	TPS Turku	Finland	21	15	4	0	1175	35	2	*1.79	4	3	1	234	10	0	2.56
	TuTu Turku	Finland-2	2	1	1	0	118	7	0	3.54	....	....	....	....	....	....	....
2000-01	TPS Turku	Finland	39	26	10	3	2266	66	6	*1.75	*10	*9	1	603	13	*2	*1.29
2001-02	TPS Turku	Finland	32	14	11	5	1877	62	2	1.98	4	1	3	256	7	1	*1.64
2002-03	Vastra Frolunda	Sweden	23	....	....	....	1386	56	1	2.42	4	....	....	287	6	1	*1.25

NURMINEN, Pasi (NUR-mih-nehn, PAS-ee) ATL.

Goaltender. Catches left. 5'10", 210 lbs. Born, Lahti, Finland, December 17, 1975.
(Atlanta's 6th choice, 189th overall, in 2001 Entry Draft).

			Regular Season								Playoffs						
Season	Club	League	GP	W	L	T	Mins	GA	SO	Avg	GP	W	L	Mins	GA	SO	Avg
1993-94	Reipas Lahti Jr.	Finn-Jr.	14	....	....	....	847	58	0	4.11	....	....	....	....	....	....	....
	Reipas Lahti	Finland	1	....	....	....	30	2	0	4.00	....	....	....	....	....	....	....
1994-95	Reipas Lahti Jr.	Finn-Jr.	9	....	....	....	542	22	....	2.44	....	....	....	....	....	....	....
	Reipas Lahti	Finland-2	9	....	....	....	423	44	0	6.24	....	....	....	....	....	....	....
1995-96	Kettera Imatra	Finland-2	38	....	....	....	2204	146	0	3.97	....	....	....	....	....	....	....
1996-97	Pelicans Lahti	Finland-2	30	....	....	....	1726	69	0	2.40	3	....	....	204	8	....	2.35
1997-98	Pelicans Lahti	Finland-2	35	....	....	....	3044	59	....	1.73	3	....	....	180	4	....	1.33
1998-99	HPK Hameenlinna	Finland	*48	24	17	6	*2810	127	2	2.71	7	3	4	425	24	1	3.39
99-2000	Jokerit Helsinki	Finland	48	24	15	8	2770	104	*6	2.25	*11	*7	4	*719	22	*2	1.84
2000-01	Jokerit Helsinki	Finland	52	*30	13	7	2971	107	5	2.16	5	2	3	308	11	1	2.14
2001-02	**Atlanta**	**NHL**	**9**	**2**	**5**	**0**	**465**	**28**	**0**	**3.61**	....	....	....	....	....	....	....
	Chicago Wolves	AHL	20	9	9	1	1165	57	2	2.93	*21	*15	5	1267	41	2	1.94
	Finland	Olympics	1	1	0	0	60	1	0	1.00	....	....	....	....	....	....	....
2002-03	**Atlanta**	**NHL**	**52**	**21**	**19**	**5**	**2856**	**137**	**2**	**2.88**	....	....	....	....	....	....	....
	NHL Totals		**61**	**23**	**24**	**5**	**3321**	**165**	**2**	**2.98**	....	....	....	....	....	....	....

Jack A. Butterfield Trophy (Playoff MVP – AHL) (2002)

OSAER, Phil (OH-shar, FIHL)

Goaltender. Catches left. 6'1", 186 lbs. Born, Dearborn, MI, February 10, 1980.
(St. Louis' 6th choice, 203rd overall, in 1999 Entry Draft).

			Regular Season								Playoffs						
Season	Club	League	GP	W	L	T	Mins	GA	SO	Avg	GP	W	L	Mins	GA	SO	Avg
1997-98	Waterloo	USHL	36	12	20	2	2094	107	2	3.07	5	1	4	295	17	0	3.46
1998-99	Ferris State	CCHA	9	2	2	1	399	10	0	1.51	....	....	....	....	....	....	....
99-2000	Ferris State	CCHA	25	13	8	2	1350	49	3	2.18	....	....	....	....	....	....	....
2000-01	Ferris State	CCHA	25	9	12	3	1449	57	3	2.36	....	....	....	....	....	....	....
2001-02	Peoria Rivermen	ECHL	29	16	11	2	1705	69	2	2.43	4	2	2	222	9	1	2.43
2002-03	Worcester IceCats	AHL	24	9	9	3	1328	64	1	2.89	....	....	....	....	....	....	....
	Trenton Titans	ECHL	2	0	2	0	118	7	0	3.57	....	....	....	....	....	....	....
	Louisiana	ECHL	4	2	1	1	244	9	0	2.21	....	....	....	....	....	....	....

CCHA Second All-Star Team (2001)

OSGOOD, Chris (AWS-gud, KRIHS) ST.L.

Goaltender. Catches left. 5'10", 175 lbs. Born, Peace River, Alta., November 26, 1972.
(Detroit's 3rd choice, 54th overall, in 1991 Entry Draft).

			Regular Season								Playoffs						
Season	Club	League	GP	W	L	T	Mins	GA	SO	Avg	GP	W	L	Mins	GA	SO	Avg
1988-89	Medicine Hat	AMHL	26	....	....	....	1441	88	0	3.66	....	....	....	....	....	....	....
1989-90	Medicine Hat	WHL	57	24	28	2	3094	228	0	4.42	3	0	3	173	17	0	5.91
1990-91	Medicine Hat	WHL	46	23	18	3	2630	173	2	3.95	12	7	5	712	42	0	3.54
1991-92	Medicine Hat	WHL	15	10	3	0	819	44	0	3.22	....	....	....	....	....	....	....
	Brandon	WHL	16	3	10	1	890	60	1	4.04	....	....	....	....	....	....	....
	Seattle	WHL	21	12	7	1	1217	65	1	3.20	15	9	6	904	51	0	3.38
1992-93	Adirondack	AHL	45	19	19	4	2438	159	0	3.91	1	0	1	59	2	0	2.03
1993-94	**Detroit**	**NHL**	**41**	**23**	**8**	**5**	**2206**	**105**	**2**	**2.86**	**6**	**3**	**2**	**307**	**12**	**1**	**2.35**
	Adirondack	AHL	4	3	1	0	239	13	0	3.26	....	....	....	....	....	....	....
1994-95	**Detroit**	**NHL**	**19**	**14**	**5**	**0**	**1087**	**41**	**1**	**2.26**	**2**	**0**	**0**	**68**	**2**	**0**	**1.76**
	Adirondack	AHL	2	1	1	0	120	6	0	3.00	....	....	....	....	....	....	....
1995-96	**Detroit**	**NHL**	**50**	***39**	**6**	**5**	**2933**	**106**	**5**	**2.17**	**15**	**8**	**7**	**936**	**33**	**2**	**2.12**
1996-97♦	**Detroit**	**NHL**	**47**	**23**	**13**	**9**	**2769**	**106**	**6**	**2.30**	**2**	**0**	**0**	**47**	**2**	**0**	**2.55**
1997-98♦	**Detroit**	**NHL**	**64**	**33**	**20**	**11**	**3807**	**140**	**6**	**2.21**	***22**	***16**	**6**	***1361**	**48**	**2**	**2.12**
1998-99	**Detroit**	**NHL**	**63**	**34**	**25**	**4**	**3691**	**149**	**3**	**2.42**	**6**	**4**	**2**	**358**	**14**	**1**	**2.35**
99-2000	**Detroit**	**NHL**	**53**	**30**	**14**	**8**	**3148**	**126**	**6**	**2.40**	**9**	**5**	**4**	**547**	**18**	**2**	**1.97**
2000-01	**Detroit**	**NHL**	**52**	**25**	**19**	**4**	**2834**	**127**	**1**	**2.69**	**6**	**2**	**4**	**365**	**15**	**1**	**2.47**
2001-02	**NY Islanders**	**NHL**	**66**	**32**	**25**	**6**	**3743**	**156**	**4**	**2.50**	**7**	**3**	**4**	**392**	**17**	**0**	**2.60**
2002-03	**NY Islanders**	**NHL**	**37**	**17**	**14**	**4**	**1993**	**97**	**2**	**2.92**	....	....	....	....	....	....	....
	St. Louis	**NHL**	**9**	**4**	**3**	**2**	**532**	**27**	**2**	**3.05**	**7**	**3**	**4**	**417**	**17**	**1**	**2.45**
	NHL Totals		**501**	**274**	**152**	**58**	**28743**	**1180**	**38**	**2.46**	**82**	**44**	**33**	**4798**	**178**	**10**	**2.23**

WHL East Second All-Star Team (1991) • NHL Second All-Star Team (1996) • Shared William M. Jennings Trophy (1996) with Mike Vernon

Played in NHL All-Star Game (1996, 1997, 1998)

• Scored a goal while with Medicine Hat (WHL), January 3, 1991. • Scored a goal vs. Hartford, March 6, 1996. Claimed by **NY Islanders** from **Detroit** in Waiver Draft, September 28, 2001. Traded to **St. Louis** by **NY Islanders** with NY Islanders' 3rd round choice (Konstantin Barulin) in 2003 Entry Draft for Justin Papineau and St. Louis' 2nd round choice (Jeremy Colliton) in 2003 Entry Draft, March 11, 2003.

OUELLET, Maxime (OO-leht, MAX-eem) WSH.

Goaltender. Catches left. 6'2", 195 lbs. Born, Beauport, Que., June 17, 1981.
(Philadelphia's 1st choice, 22nd overall, in 1999 Entry Draft).

			Regular Season								Playoffs						
Season	Club	League	GP	W	L	T	Mins	GA	SO	Avg	GP	W	L	Mins	GA	SO	Avg
1996-97	Ste-Foy	QAAA	29	16	8	0	1470	81	0	2.75	9	4	5	555	31	0	3.37
1997-98	Quebec Remparts	QMJHL	24	12	7	1	1188	66	0	3.33	7	3	1	305	16	0	3.15
1998-99	Quebec Remparts	QMJHL	*59	*40	12	6	*3447	155	3	*2.70	13	6	7	803	41	*1	3.06
99-2000	Quebec Remparts	QMJHL	53	31	16	4	2984	133	2	2.67	11	7	4	638	28	*2	*2.63
2000-01	**Philadelphia**	**NHL**	**2**	**0**	**1**	**0**	**76**	**3**	**0**	**2.37**	....	....	....	....	....	....	....
	Philadelphia	AHL	2	1	0	0	86	4	0	2.78	....	....	....	....	....	....	....
	Rouyn-Noranda	QMJHL	25	18	6	1	1471	65	3	2.65	8	4	4	490	25	0	3.06
2001-02	Philadelphia	AHL	41	16	13	8	2294	104	1	2.72	....	....	....	....	....	....	....
	Portland Pirates	AHL	6	3	3	0	358	17	0	2.85	....	....	....	....	....	....	....
2002-03	Porland Pirates	AHL	42	18	16	7	2773	111	*7	2.40	2	1	1	120	8	0	4.00
	NHL Totals		**2**	**0**	**1**	**0**	**76**	**3**	**0**	**2.37**	....	....	....	....	....	....	....

QMJHL Second All-Star Team (1999, 2000, 2001) • Jacques Plante Trophy (fewest goals against – QMJHL) (1999) • AHL Second All-Star Team (2003)

• Returned to **Rouyn-Noranda** (QMJHL) by **Philadelphia**, October 27, 2000. Traded to **Washington** by **Philadelphia** with Philadelphia's 1st (later traded to Dallas – Dallas selected Martin Vagner), 2nd (Maxime Daigneault) and 3rd (Derek Krestanovich) round choices in 2002 Entry Draft for Adam Oates, March 19, 2002.

PASSMORE, Steve (PAS-mohr, STEEV) CHI.

Goaltender. Catches left. 5'9", 165 lbs. Born, Thunder Bay, Ont., January 29, 1973.
(Quebec's 10th choice, 196th overall, in 1992 Entry Draft).

			Regular Season								Playoffs						
Season	Club	League	GP	W	L	T	Mins	GA	SO	Avg	GP	W	L	Mins	GA	SO	Avg
1988-89	Tri-City Americans	WHL	1	0	1	0	60	6	0	6.00	....	....	....	....	....	....	....
1989-90	West Island Deltas	BCAHA	STATISTICS NOT AVAILABLE														
	Tri-City Americans	WHL	4	....	....	....	215	17	0	4.74	....	....	....	....	....	....	....
1990-91	Victoria Cougars	WHL	35	3	25	1	1838	190	0	6.20	....	....	....	....	....	....	....
1991-92	Victoria Cougars	WHL	*71	15	50	5	*4228	347	0	4.92	....	....	....	....	....	....	....
1992-93	Victoria Cougars	WHL	43	14	24	2	2402	150	1	3.75	....	....	....	....	....	....	....
	Kamloops Blazers	WHL	25	19	6	0	1479	69	1	2.80	7	4	2	401	22	1	3.29
1993-94	Kamloops Blazers	WHL	36	22	9	2	1927	88	1	*2.74	*18	*11	7	*1099	60	0	3.28
1994-95	Cape Breton Oilers	AHL	25	8	13	3	1455	93	0	3.83	....	....	....	....	....	....	....
1995-96	Cape Breton Oilers	AHL	2	1	0	0	90	2	0	1.33	....	....	....	....	....	....	....
1996-97	Hamilton Bulldogs	AHL	27	12	12	3	1568	70	1	2.68	22	12	10	1325	61	*2	2.76
	Raleigh IceCaps	ECHL	2	1	1	0	118	13	0	6.56	....	....	....	....	....	....	....
1997-98	San Antonio	IHL	14	3	8	2	736	56	0	4.56	....	....	....	....	....	....	....
	Hamilton Bulldogs	AHL	27	11	10	6	1655	87	2	3.15	3	0	2	132	14	0	6.33
1998-99	**Edmonton**	**NHL**	**6**	**1**	**4**	**1**	**362**	**17**	**0**	**2.82**	....	....	....	....	....	....	....
	Hamilton Bulldogs	AHL	54	24	21	7	3148	117	4	2.23	11	5	6	680	31	0	2.74
99-2000	**Chicago**	**NHL**	**24**	**7**	**12**	**3**	**1388**	**63**	**1**	**2.72**	....	....	....	....	....	....	....
	Cleveland	IHL	2	1	0	1	120	3	1	1.50	....	....	....	....	....	....	....
2000-01	**Los Angeles**	**NHL**	**14**	**3**	**8**	**1**	**718**	**37**	**1**	**3.09**	....	....	....	....	....	....	....
	Lowell	AHL	6	2	4	0	334	24	0	4.32	....	....	....	....	....	....	....
	Chicago	**NHL**	**6**	**0**	**4**	**1**	**340**	**14**	**0**	**2.47**	....	....	....	....	....	....	....
	Chicago Wolves	IHL	6	2	2	2	340	22	0	3.88	....	....	....	....	....	....	....
2001-02	Norfolk Admirals	AHL	2	2	0	0	120	6	0	3.00	....	....	....	....	....	....	....
	Chicago	**NHL**	**23**	**8**	**5**	**4**	**1142**	**43**	**0**	**2.26**	**3**	**0**	**2**	**138**	**6**	**0**	**2.61**
2002-03	**Chicago**	**NHL**	**11**	**2**	**5**	**2**	**617**	**38**	**0**	**3.70**	....	....	....	....	....	....	....
	Norfolk Admirals	AHL	14	4	7	2	832	33	2	2.38	....	....	....	....	....	....	....
	NHL Totals		**84**	**21**	**38**	**12**	**4567**	**212**	**2**	**2.79**	**3**	**0**	**2**	**138**	**6**	**0**	**2.61**

WHL West First All-Star Team (1993, 1994) • Fred Hunt Memorial Trophy (Sportsmanship – AHL) (1997) • AHL Second All-Star Team (1999)

Traded to **Edmonton** by **Quebec** for Brad Werenka, March 21, 1994. • Missed majority of the 1995-96 season recovering from blood disorder, October, 1995. Signed as a free agent by **Chicago**, July 8, 1999. Traded to **Los Angeles** by **Chicago** for Los Angeles' 4th round choice (Olli Malmivaara) in 2000 Entry Draft, May 1, 2000. Traded to **Chicago** by **Los Angeles** for Chicago's 8th round choice (Mike Gabinet) in 2001 Entry Draft, February 28, 2001.

PATZOLD, Dimitri (PATZ-ohld, dih-MEE-tree) S.J.

Goaltender. Catches left. 6', 190 lbs. Born, Ust-Kamenogorsk, USSR, February 3, 1983.
(San Jose's 3rd choice, 107th overall, in 2001 Entry Draft).

			Regular Season								Playoffs						
Season	Club	League	GP	W	L	T	Mins	GA	SO	Avg	GP	W	L	Mins	GA	SO	Avg
99-2000	Kolner Haie Jr.	Ger-Jr.	38	....	....	....	2131	73	0	2.06	....	....	....	....	....	....	....
	Kolner Haie-2	German5	16	....	....	....	896	58	0	3.88	....	....	....	....	....	....	....
2000-01	EV Duisburg	German2	6	....	....	....	360	17	0	2.83	....	....	....	....	....	....	....
	TSV Erding Jets	German2	24	....	....	....	1378	89	0	3.88	....	....	....	....	....	....	....
2001-02	Kolner Haie	Germany	7	....	....	....	260	16	0	3.69	....	....	....	....	....	....	....
	EV Duisburg	German2	6	....	....	....	360	17	0	2.83	....	....	....	....	....	....	....
2002-03	Adler Mannheim	Germany	15	....	....	....	817	35	0	2.57	2	....	....	34	2	0	3.53

PEARCE, Joseph (PEERS-JOH-sehf) T.B.

Goaltender. Catches left. 6'5", 215 lbs. Born, Point Pleasant, NJ, June 29, 1982.
(Tampa Bay's 3rd choice, 135th overall, in 2002 Entry Draft).

			Regular Season								Playoffs						
Season	Club	League	GP	W	L	T	Mins	GA	SO	Avg	GP	W	L	Mins	GA	SO	Avg
2000-01	Bismark Bobcats	AWJHL	17	....	....	....	1020	40	1	2.31	....	....	....	....	....	....	....
2001-02	N.H. Jr. Monarchs	EJHL	32	....	....	....	1885	57	1	1.82	....	....	....	....	....	....	....
2002-03	Chicago Steel	USHL	37	18	12	3	1980	96	1	2.91	....	....	....	....	....	....	....

EJHL First All-Star Team (2002)

• Signed Letter of Intent to attend **Boston College** (H-East), February 14, 2002.

PELLETIER, Jean-Marc (PEHL-tyay, ZHAWN-MAHRK) PHX.

Goaltender. Catches left. 6'3", 200 lbs. Born, Atlanta, GA, March 4, 1978.
(Philadelphia's 1st choice, 30th overall, in 1997 Entry Draft).

			Regular Season								Playoffs						
Season	Club	League	GP	W	L	T	Mins	GA	SO	Avg	GP	W	L	Mins	GA	SO	Avg
1993-94	Richelieu Riverains	QAAA	24	14	8	2	1440	91	0	3.79	2	1	1	104	11	0	6.32
1994-95	Richelieu Riverains	QAAA	21	15	6	0	1260	71	0	3.36	2	1	1	153	11	0	4.32
1995-96	Cornell Big Red	ECAC	5	1	2	0	179	15	0	5.03	....	....	....	....	....	....	....
1996-97	Cornell Big Red	ECAC	11	5	2	3	679	28	1	2.47	....	....	....	....	....	....	....
1997-98	Rimouski Oceanic	QMJHL	34	17	11	3	1913	118	0	3.70	16	11	3	895	51	1	3.42
1998-99	**Philadelphia**	**NHL**	**1**	**0**	**1**	**0**	**60**	**5**	**0**	**5.00**	....	....	....	....	....	....	....
	Philadelphia	AHL	47	25	16	4	2636	122	2	2.78	1	0	0	27	0	0	0.00
99-2000	Philadelphia	AHL	24	14	10	0	1405	58	3	2.48	....	....	....	....	....	....	....
	Cincinnati	IHL	22	14	4	2	1278	52	2	2.44	3	1	1	160	8	1	3.00
2000-01	Cincinnati	IHL	39	18	14	5	2261	119	2	3.16	5	1	4	318	15	0	2.83
2001-02	Lowell	AHL	40	21	12	4	2284	98	2	2.57	5	2	3	298	13	0	2.62
2002-03	Lowell	AHL	17	6	10	0	861	51	1	3.55	....	....	....	....	....	....	....
	Phoenix	**NHL**	**2**	**0**	**2**	**0**	**119**	**6**	**0**	**3.03**	....	....	....	....	....	....	....
	Springfield Falcons	AHL	24	12	7	4	1391	55	2	2.37	6	3	3	368	16	1	2.61
	NHL Totals		**3**	**0**	**3**	**0**	**179**	**11**	**0**	**3.69**	....	....	....	....	....	....	....

Traded to **Carolina** by **Philadelphia** with Rod Brind'Amour and Philadelphia's 2nd round choice (later traded to Colorado – Colorado selected Argis Saviels) in 2000 Entry Draft for Keith Primeau and Carolina's 5th round choice (later traded to NY Islanders – NY Islanders selected Kristofer Ottosson) in 2000 Entry Draft, January 23, 2000. Traded to **Phoenix** by **Carolina** with future considerations for Patrick DesRochers, December 31, 2002.

PENNER, Andrew (PEH-nuhr, AN-droo) CBJ

Goaltender. Catches left. 6'2", 205 lbs. Born, Scarborough, Ont., December 21, 1982.

			Regular Season								Playoffs						
Season	Club	League	GP	W	L	T	Mins	GA	SO	Avg	GP	W	L	Mins	GA	SO	Avg
1998-99	North York	OPJHL	26	....	....	....	1497	107	0	4.29	....	....	....	....	....	....	....
99-2000	North Bay	OHL	22	3	12	0	1070	79	0	4.43	....	....	....	....	....	....	....
2000-01	North Bay	OHL	32	10	19	1	1787	117	1	3.93	....	....	....	....	....	....	....
2001-02	North Bay	OHL	18	4	8	4	917	52	1	3.40	....	....	....	....	....	....	....
	Guelph Storm	OHL	36	18	12	5	2066	107	0	3.11	9	5	4	546	29	0	3.19
2002-03	Guelph Storm	OHL	51	21	21	7	2975	137	0	2.76	11	5	5	665	34	0	3.07

Signed as a free agent by **Columbus**, September 17, 2001.

PETRUK, Randy (PEHT-ruhk, RAN-dee) CAR.

Goaltender. Catches right. 5'9", 175 lbs. Born, Cranbrook, B.C., April 23, 1978.
(Colorado's 5th choice, 107th overall, in 1996 Entry Draft).

			Regular Season								Playoffs						
Season	Club	League	GP	W	L	T	Mins	GA	SO	Avg	GP	W	L	Mins	GA	SO	Avg
1993-94	Cranbrook Colts	RMJHL	21	....	....	....	1158	89	0	4.61	....	....	....	....	....	....	....
1994-95	Kamloops Blazers	WHL	27	16	3	4	1462	71	1	2.91	7	5	2	423	19	0	2.70
1995-96	Kamloops Blazers	WHL	52	34	15	1	3071	181	1	3.54	16	9	6	990	58	0	3.52
1996-97	Kamloops Blazers	WHL	*60	25	28	5	*3475	210	0	3.63	....	....	....	....	....	....	....

1997-98	Kamloops Blazers	WHL	57	31	21	1	3097	157	3	3.04	7	3	4	425	21	0	2.96
1998-99	Florida Everblades	ECHL	25	13	10	2	1441	66	1	2.75	1	0	1	60	5	0	5.00
	New Haven	AHL	1	0	0	1	65	3	0	2.77	....	....	....	....	....	....	....
99-2000	Florida Everblades	ECHL	6	5	0	1	339	19	0	3.36	....	....	....	....	....	....	....
	Cincinnati	IHL	26	13	9	3	1436	84	2	3.51	9	4	5	551	27	1	2.94
2000-01	Cincinnati	IHL	8	4	3	0	420	23	1	3.29	....	....	....	....	....	....	....
	Florida Everblades	ECHL	13	5	7	1	742	41	0	3.31	....	....	....	....	....	....	....
2001-02	Florida Everblades	ECHL	51	27	18	5	3087	140	3	2.72	5	1	3	259	14	0	3.24
2002-03	Lowell	AHL	30	4	20	3	1641	84	1	3.07	....	....	....	....	....	....	....
	Florida Everblades	ECHL	6	3	2	1	365	23	0	3.78	....	....	....	....	....	....	....

WHL West Second All-Star Team (1998)

Traded to **Carolina** by **Colorado** for Carolina's 5th round choice (Will Magnuson) in 1999 Entry Draft, June 1, 1998.

PIETRASIAK, Jeff (peh-TRAZ-ee-ak, JEHF) PHX.

Goaltender. Catches left. 6'1", 180 lbs. Born, Marlboro, MA, April 5, 1983.
(Phoenix's 8th choice, 186th overall, in 2002 Entry Draft).

			Regular Season								Playoffs						
Season	Club	League	GP	W	L	T	Mins	GA	SO	Avg	GP	W	L	Mins	GA	SO	Avg
2000-01	Berkshire High	Hi-School	25	....	....	....	1150	26	8	1.37	....	....	....	....	....	....	....
2001-02	Berkshire High	Hi-School	32	....	....	....	1471	51	5	2.05	....	....	....	....	....	....	....
2002-03	New Hampshire	H-East	2	1	0	0	67	2	0	1.78	....	....	....	....	....	....	....

POTVIN, Felix (PAHT-vihn, FEEL-ihx)

Goaltender. Catches left. 6'1", 190 lbs. Born, Anjou, Que., June 23, 1971.
(Toronto's 2nd choice, 31st overall, in 1990 Entry Draft).

			Regular Season								Playoffs						
Season	Club	League	GP	W	L	T	Mins	GA	SO	Avg	GP	W	L	Mins	GA	SO	Avg
1987-88	Montreal-Bourassa	QAAA	27	15	7	3	1585	103	3	3.90	6	2	4	341	20	0	3.51
1988-89	Chicoutimi	QMJHL	*65	25	31	1	*3489	271	*2	4.66	....	....	....	....	....	....	....
1989-90	Chicoutimi	QMJHL	*62	*31	26	2	*3478	231	*2	3.99	....	....	....	....	....	....	....
1990-91	Chicoutimi	QMJHL	54	33	15	4	3216	145	*6	*2.70	*16	*11	5	*992	46	0	*2.78
1991-92	**Toronto**	**NHL**	**4**	**0**	**2**	**1**	**210**	**8**	**0**	**2.29**	....	....	....	....	....	....	....
	St. John's	AHL	35	18	10	6	2070	101	2	2.93	11	7	4	642	41	0	3.83
1992-93	**Toronto**	**NHL**	**48**	**25**	**15**	**7**	**2781**	**116**	**2**	***2.50**	***21**	**11**	**10**	***1308**	**62**	**1**	**2.84**
	St. John's	AHL	5	3	0	2	309	18	0	3.50	....	....	....	....	....	....	....
1993-94	**Toronto**	**NHL**	**66**	**34**	**22**	**9**	**3883**	**187**	**3**	**2.89**	**18**	**9**	**9**	**1124**	**46**	**3**	**2.46**
1994-95	**Toronto**	**NHL**	**36**	**15**	**13**	**7**	**2144**	**104**	**0**	**2.91**	**7**	**3**	**4**	**424**	**20**	**1**	**2.83**
1995-96	**Toronto**	**NHL**	**69**	**30**	**26**	**11**	**4009**	**192**	**2**	**2.87**	**6**	**2**	**4**	**350**	**19**	**0**	**3.26**
1996-97	**Toronto**	**NHL**	***74**	**27**	**36**	**7**	***4271**	**224**	**0**	**3.15**	....	....	....	....	....	....	....
1997-98	**Toronto**	**NHL**	**67**	**26**	**33**	**7**	**3864**	**176**	**5**	**2.73**	....	....	....	....	....	....	....
1998-99	**Toronto**	**NHL**	**5**	**3**	**2**	**0**	**299**	**19**	**0**	**3.81**	....	....	....	....	....	....	....
	NY Islanders	**NHL**	**11**	**2**	**7**	**1**	**606**	**37**	**0**	**3.66**	....	....	....	....	....	....	....
99-2000	**NY Islanders**	**NHL**	**22**	**5**	**14**	**3**	**1273**	**68**	**1**	**3.21**	....	....	....	....	....	....	....
	Vancouver	**NHL**	**34**	**12**	**13**	**7**	**1966**	**85**	**0**	**2.59**	....	....	....	....	....	....	....
2000-01	**Vancouver**	**NHL**	**35**	**14**	**17**	**3**	**2006**	**103**	**1**	**3.08**	....	....	....	....	....	....	....
	Los Angeles	**NHL**	**23**	**13**	**5**	**5**	**1410**	**46**	**5**	**1.96**	**13**	**7**	**6**	**812**	**33**	**2**	**2.44**
2001-02	**Los Angeles**	**NHL**	**71**	**31**	**27**	**8**	**4071**	**157**	**6**	**2.31**	**7**	**3**	**4**	**417**	**15**	**1**	**2.16**
2002-03	**Los Angeles**	**NHL**	**42**	**17**	**20**	**3**	**2367**	**105**	**3**	**2.66**	....	....	....	....	....	....	....
	NHL Totals		**607**	**254**	**252**	**79**	**35160**	**1627**	**28**	**2.78**	**72**	**35**	**37**	**4435**	**195**	**8**	**2.64**

QMJHL All-Rookie Team (1989) • QMJHL Second All-Star Team (1990) • QMJHL First All-Star Team (1991) • Canadian Major Junior Goaltender of the Year (1991) • Memorial Cup All-Star Team (1991) • Hap Emms Memorial Trophy (Memorial Cup Top Goaltender) (1991) • AHL First All-Star Team (1992) • Dudley "Red" Garrett Memorial Trophy (Top Rookie – AHL) (1992) • Baz Bastien Memorial Trophy (Top Goaltender – AHL) (1992) • NHL All-Rookie Team (1993)

Played in NHL All-Star Game (1994, 1996)

Traded to **NY Islanders** by **Toronto** with Toronto's 6th round choice (later traded to Tampa Bay – Tampa Bay selected Fedor Fedorov) in 1999 Entry Draft for Bryan Berard and NY Islanders' 6th round choice (Jan Sochor) in 1999 Entry Draft, January 9, 1999. Traded to **Vancouver** by **NY Islanders** with NY Islanders' compensatory 2nd round choice (later traded to New Jersey – New Jersey selected Teemu Laine) in 2000 Entry Draft and NY Islanders' 3rd round choice (Thatcher Bell) in 2000 Entry Draft for Kevin Weekes, Dave Scatchard and Bill Muckalt, December 19, 1999. Traded to **Los Angeles** by **Vancouver** for future considerations, February 15, 2001.

PRUSEK, Martin (PREW-sehk, MAHR-tihn) OTT.

Goaltender. Catches left. 6'1", 176 lbs. Born, Ostrava, Czech., December 11, 1975.
(Ottawa's 6th choice, 164th overall, in 1999 Entry Draft).

			Regular Season								Playoffs						
Season	Club	League	GP	W	L	T	Mins	GA	SO	Avg	GP	W	L	Mins	GA	SO	Avg
1994-95	HC Vitkovice	Czech	5	....	....	....	232	18	....	4.65	....	....	....	....	....	....	....
1995-96	HC Vitkovice	Czech	40	....	....	....	2336	113	1	2.90	4	....	....	250	10	1	2.40
1996-97	HC Vitkovice	Czech	49	....	....	....	2841	109	8	2.30	9	....	....	546	19	1	2.08
1997-98	HC Vitkovice	Czech	50	....	....	....	2901	129	....	2.67	9	....	....	529	26	....	3.00
1998-99	HC Vitkovice	Czech	37	....	....	....	1905	85	....	2.68	4	....	....	250	12	....	2.88
99-2000	HC Vitkovice	Czech	50	....	....	....	2647	132	....	2.99	....	....	....	....	....	....	....
2000-01	HC Vitkovice	Czech	30	....	....	....	1679	64	....	2.29	9	....	....	460	25	....	3.26
2001-02	**Ottawa**	**NHL**	**1**	**0**	**1**	**0**	**62**	**3**	**0**	**2.90**	....	....	....	....	....	....	....
	Grand Rapids	AHL	33	18	8	5	1903	58	4	*1.83	5	2	3	278	10	0	2.16
2002-03	**Ottawa**	**NHL**	**18**	**12**	**2**	**1**	**935**	**37**	**0**	**2.37**	....	....	....	....	....	....	....
	Binghamton	AHL	4	1	2	1	243	7	1	1.73	....	....	....	....	....	....	....
	NHL Totals		**19**	**12**	**3**	**1**	**997**	**40**	**0**	**2.41**	....	....	....	....	....	....	....

AHL First All-Star Team (2002) • Shared Harry "Hap" Holmes Memorial Trophy (fewest goals against – AHL) (2002) with Simon Lajeunesse and Mathieu Chouinard • Baz Bastien Memorial Trophy (Top Goaltender – AHL) (2002)

PUURULA, Joni (pu-u-ROO-luh, YOHN-ee) MTL.

Goaltender. Catches left. 5'11", 180 lbs. Born, Kokkola, Finland, August 4, 1982.
(Montreal's 10th choice, 243rd overall, in 2000 Entry Draft).

			Regular Season								Playoffs						
Season	Club	League	GP	W	L	T	Mins	GA	SO	Avg	GP	W	L	Mins	GA	SO	Avg
1998-99	Junkkarit	Finland-2	12	....	....	....	782	37	0	2.84	....	....	....	....	....	....	....
99-2000	Hermes Kokkola	Finland-2	23	8	12	2	1251	81	1	3.88	....	....	....	....	....	....	....
2000-01	FoPS Forssa	Finland-2	39	....	....	....	2263	142	1	3.76	....	....	....	....	....	....	....
	FoPS Forssa Jr.	Finn-Jr.	....	....	....	....	....	....	....	....	4	1	3	240	8	0	2.00
2001-02	HPK Jr.	Finn-Jr.	2	1	1	0	120	11	0	5.52	....	....	....	....	....	....	....
	FPS Fossa	Finland-2	5	....	....	....	300	18	0	3.54	....	....	....	....	....	....	....
	HPK Hameenlinna	Finland	9	8	0	1	515	18	0	2.10	8	4	3	453	13	0	1.72
2002-03	HPK Hameenlinna	Finland	34	19	6	9	1972	71	4	2.16	11	6	5	676	19	1	1.69

RACINE, Jean-Francois (RAY-seen, ZHAWN-fran-SWUH) TOR.

Goaltender. Catches left. 6'3", 194 lbs. Born, St-Hyacinthe, Que., April 27, 1982.
(Toronto's 4th choice, 90th overall, in 2000 Entry Draft).

			Regular Season								Playoffs						
Season	Club	League	GP	W	L	T	Mins	GA	SO	Avg	GP	W	L	Mins	GA	SO	Avg
1998-99	Magog	QAAA	36	19	12	1	2160	107	3	2.98	11	5	6	656	37	0	3.39
99-2000	Moncton Wildcats	QMJHL	10	3	3	1	410	28	0	4.10	....	....	....	....	....	....	....
	Drummondville	QMJHL	20	14	6	0	1152	63	1	3.28	3	0	0	65	5	0	4.60
2000-01	Drummondville	QMJHL	61	27	26	3	3362	189	4	3.37	5	2	3	303	20	0	3.97
2001-02	Drummondville	QMJHL	65	29	30	3	3640	208	2	3.43	12	5	7	720	42	1	3.50
2002-03	Memphis	CHL	35	22	9	3	2050	94	0	2.75	1	0	1	58	5	0	5.14

RAYCROFT, Andrew (RAY-krawft, AN-droo) BOS.

Goaltender. Catches left. 6', 174 lbs. Born, Belleville, Ont., May 4, 1980.
(Boston's 4th choice, 135th overall, in 1998 Entry Draft).

			Regular Season								Playoffs						
Season	Club	League	GP	W	L	T	Mins	GA	SO	Avg	GP	W	L	Mins	GA	SO	Avg
1996-97	Wellington Dukes	MTJHL	27	....	....	....	1402	92	0	3.94	....	....	....	....	....	....	....
1997-98	Sudbury Wolves	OHL	33	8	16	5	1802	125	0	4.16	2	0	1	89	8	0	5.39
1998-99	Sudbury Wolves	OHL	45	17	22	5	2528	173	1	4.11	3	0	2	96	13	0	8.13
99-2000	Kingston	OHL	*61	33	20	5	3340	191	0	3.43	5	1	4	300	21	0	4.20
2000-01	**Boston**	**NHL**	**15**	**4**	**6**	**0**	**649**	**32**	**0**	**2.96**	....	....	....	....	....	....	....
	Providence Bruins	AHL	26	8	14	4	1459	82	1	3.37	....	....	....	....	....	....	....
2001-02	**Boston**	**NHL**	**1**	**0**	**0**	**1**	**65**	**3**	**0**	**2.77**	....	....	....	....	....	....	....
	Providence Bruins	AHL	56	25	24	6	3317	142	4	2.57	2	0	2	119	5	0	2.52
2002-03	**Boston**	**NHL**	**5**	**2**	**3**	**0**	**300**	**12**	**0**	**2.40**	....	....	....	....	....	....	....
	Providence Bruins	AHL	39	23	10	3	2255	94	1	2.50	4	1	3	264	6	1	*1.36
	NHL Totals		**21**	**6**	**9**	**1**	**1014**	**47**	**0**	**2.78**	....	....	....	....	....	....	....

OHL First All-Star Team (2000) • Canadian Major Junior First All-Star Team (2000) • Canadian Major Junior Goaltender of the Year (2000)

RHODES, Damian (ROHDZ, DAY-mee-uhn)

Goaltender. Catches left. 5'11", 195 lbs. Born, St. Paul, MN, May 28, 1969.
(Toronto's 6th choice, 112th overall, in 1987 Entry Draft).

			Regular Season								Playoffs						
Season	Club	League	GP	W	L	T	Mins	GA	SO	Avg	GP	W	L	Mins	GA	SO	Avg
1985-86	Richfield Spartans	H.S.	16	....	....	....	720	56	0	3.50	....	....	....	....	....	....	....
1986-87	Richfield Spartans	H.S.	19	....	....	....	673	51	1	4.55	....	....	....	....	....	....	....
1987-88	Michigan Tech	WCHA	29	16	10	1	1625	114	0	4.20	....	....	....	....	....	....	....
1988-89	Michigan Tech	WCHA	37	15	22	0	2216	163	0	4.41	....	....	....	....	....	....	....
1989-90	Michigan Tech	WCHA	25	6	17	0	1358	119	0	6.26	....	....	....	....	....	....	....
1990-91	**Toronto**	**NHL**	**1**	**1**	**0**	**0**	**60**	**1**	**0**	**1.00**	....	....	....	....	....	....	....
	Newmarket Saints	AHL	38	8	24	3	2154	144	1	4.01	....	....	....	....	....	....	....
1991-92	St. John's	AHL	43	20	16	5	2454	148	0	3.62	6	4	1	331	16	0	2.90
1992-93	St. John's	AHL	*52	27	16	8	*3074	184	1	3.59	9	4	5	538	37	0	4.13
1993-94	**Toronto**	**NHL**	**22**	**9**	**7**	**3**	**1213**	**53**	**0**	**2.62**	**1**	**0**	**0**	**1**	**0**	**0**	**0.00**
1994-95	**Toronto**	**NHL**	**13**	**6**	**6**	**1**	**760**	**34**	**0**	**2.68**	....	....	....	....	....	....	....
1995-96	**Toronto**	**NHL**	**11**	**4**	**5**	**1**	**624**	**29**	**0**	**2.79**	....	....	....	....	....	....	....
	Ottawa	**NHL**	**36**	**10**	**22**	**4**	**2123**	**98**	**2**	**2.77**	....	....	....	....	....	....	....
1996-97	**Ottawa**	**NHL**	**50**	**14**	**20**	**14**	**2934**	**133**	**1**	**2.72**	....	....	....	....	....	....	....
1997-98	**Ottawa**	**NHL**	**50**	**19**	**19**	**7**	**2743**	**107**	**5**	**2.34**	**10**	**5**	**5**	**590**	**21**	**0**	**2.14**
1998-99	**Ottawa**	**NHL**	**45**	**22**	**13**	**7**	**2480**	**101**	**3**	**2.44**	**2**	**0**	**2**	**150**	**6**	**0**	**2.40**
99-2000	**Atlanta**	**NHL**	**28**	**5**	**19**	**3**	**1561**	**101**	**1**	**3.88**	....	....	....	....	....	....	....
2000-01	**Atlanta**	**NHL**	**38**	**7**	**19**	**7**	**2072**	**116**	**0**	**3.36**	....	....	....	....	....	....	....
2001-02	**Atlanta**	**NHL**	**15**	**2**	**10**	**1**	**769**	**47**	**0**	**3.67**	....	....	....	....	....	....	....
2002-03	Lowell	AHL	7	1	4	0	379	26	0	4.12	....	....	....	....	....	....	....
	Greenville Grrrowl	ECHL	12	2	8	2	687	43	1	3.76	1	0	1	60	6	0	6.00
	NHL Totals		**309**	**99**	**140**	**48**	**17339**	**820**	**12**	**2.84**	**13**	**5**	**7**	**741**	**27**	**0**	**2.19**

• Credited with scoring a goal while with Michigan Tech (WCHA), January 21, 1989. • Played 10 seconds of playoff game vs. San Jose, May 6, 1994. • Credited with scoring a goal vs. New Jersey, January 2, 1999.

Traded to **NY Islanders** by **Toronto** with Ken Belanger for future considerations (Kirk Muller and Don Beaupre, January 23, 1996), January 23, 1996. Traded to **Ottawa** by **NY Islanders** with Wade Redden for Don Beaupre, Martin Straka and Bryan Berard, January 23, 1996. Traded to **Atlanta** by **Ottawa** for future considerations, June 18, 1999. • Missed majority of 2002-03 season recovering from hernia surgery, March 26, 2002.

RICHTER, Mike (RIHK-tuhr, MIGHK) NYR

Goaltender. Catches left. 5'11", 185 lbs. Born, Abington, PA, September 22, 1966.
(NY Rangers' 2nd choice, 28th overall, in 1985 Entry Draft).

			Regular Season								Playoffs						
Season	Club	League	GP	W	L	T	Mins	GA	SO	Avg	GP	W	L	Mins	GA	SO	Avg
1983-84	Philadelphia	NEJHL	36	23	10	3	2160	94	0	2.61	....	....	....	....	....	....	....
1984-85	Northwood Prep	H.S.	24	....	....	....	1374	52	2	2.27	....	....	....	....	....	....	....
1985-86	U. of Wisconsin	WCHA	24	14	9	0	1394	92	1	3.96	....	....	....	....	....	....	....
1986-87	U. of Wisconsin	WCHA	36	19	16	1	2136	126	0	3.54	....	....	....	....	....	....	....
1987-88	United States	Nat-Tm	29	17	7	2	1559	86	0	3.31	....	....	....	....	....	....	....
	United States	Olympics	4	2	2	0	230	15	0	3.91	....	....	....	....	....	....	....
	Colorado Rangers	IHL	22	16	5	0	1298	68	1	3.14	10	5	3	536	35	0	3.92
1988-89	Denver Rangers	IHL	*57	23	26	0	3031	217	1	4.30	4	0	4	210	21	0	6.00
	NY Rangers	**NHL**	....	....	....	....	....	....	....	....	**1**	**0**	**1**	**58**	**4**	**0**	**4.14**
1989-90	**NY Rangers**	**NHL**	**23**	**12**	**5**	**5**	**1320**	**66**	**0**	**3.00**	**6**	**3**	**2**	**330**	**19**	**0**	**3.45**
	Flint Spirits	IHL	13	7	4	2	782	49	0	3.76	....	....	....	....	....	....	....
1990-91	**NY Rangers**	**NHL**	**45**	**21**	**13**	**7**	**2596**	**135**	**0**	**3.12**	**6**	**2**	**4**	**313**	**14**	***1**	**2.68**
1991-92	**NY Rangers**	**NHL**	**41**	**23**	**12**	**2**	**2298**	**119**	**3**	**3.11**	**7**	**4**	**2**	**412**	**24**	**1**	**3.50**
1992-93	**NY Rangers**	**NHL**	**38**	**13**	**19**	**3**	**2105**	**134**	**1**	**3.82**	....	....	....	....	....	....	....
	Binghamton	AHL	5	4	0	1	305	6	0	1.18	....	....	....	....	....	....	....
1993-94♦	**NY Rangers**	**NHL**	**68**	***42**	**12**	**6**	**3710**	**159**	**5**	**2.57**	**23**	***16**	**7**	**1417**	**49**	***4**	**2.07**
1994-95	**NY Rangers**	**NHL**	**35**	**14**	**17**	**2**	**1993**	**97**	**2**	**2.92**	**7**	**2**	**5**	**384**	**23**	**0**	**3.59**
1995-96	**NY Rangers**	**NHL**	**41**	**24**	**13**	**3**	**2396**	**107**	**3**	**2.68**	**11**	**5**	**6**	**661**	**36**	**0**	**3.27**
1996-97	**NY Rangers**	**NHL**	**61**	**33**	**22**	**6**	**3598**	**161**	**4**	**2.68**	**15**	**9**	**6**	**939**	**33**	***3**	**2.11**
1997-98	**NY Rangers**	**NHL**	***72**	**21**	**31**	**15**	**4143**	**184**	**0**	**2.66**	....	....	....	....	....	....	....
	United States	Olympics	4	1	3	0	237	14	0	3.54	....	....	....	....	....	....	....
1998-99	**NY Rangers**	**NHL**	**68**	**27**	**30**	**8**	**3878**	**170**	**4**	**2.63**	....	....	....	....	....	....	....
99-2000	**NY Rangers**	**NHL**	**61**	**22**	**31**	**8**	**3622**	**173**	**0**	**2.87**	....	....	....	....	....	....	....
2000-01	**NY Rangers**	**NHL**	**45**	**20**	**21**	**3**	**2635**	**144**	**0**	**3.28**	....	....	....	....	....	....	....
2001-02	**NY Rangers**	**NHL**	**55**	**24**	**26**	**4**	**3195**	**157**	**2**	**2.95**	....	....	....	....	....	....	....
	United States	Olympics	4	2	1	1	240	9	*1	2.25	....	....	....	....	....	....	....
2002-03	**NY Rangers**	**NHL**	**13**	**5**	**6**	**1**	**694**	**34**	**0**	**2.94**	....	....	....	....	....	....	....
	NHL Totals		**666**	**301**	**258**	**73**	**38183**	**1840**	**24**	**2.89**	**76**	**41**	**33**	**4514**	**202**	**9**	**2.68**

WCHA Freshman of the Year (1986) • WCHA Second All-Star Team (1987)

Played in NHL All-Star Game (1992, 1994, 2000)

Claimed by **Nashville** from **NY Rangers** in Expansion Draft, June 26, 1998. Signed as a free agent by **NY Rangers**, July 15, 1998. Traded to **Edmonton** by **NY Rangers** for Edmonton's 4th round choice (Corey Potter) in 2003 Entry Draft, June 30, 2002. Signed as a free agent by **NY Rangers**, July 4, 2002. • Missed majority of 2002-03 season recovering from head injury suffered in game vs. Calgary, November 7, 2002.

ROLOSON, Dwayne (ROH-loh-suhn, DWAYN) MIN.

Goaltender. Catches left. 6'1", 178 lbs. Born, Simcoe, Ont., October 12, 1969.

			Regular Season								Playoffs						
Season	Club	League	GP	W	L	T	Mins	GA	SO	Avg	GP	W	L	Mins	GA	SO	Avg
1984-85	Simcoe Penguins	OJHL-C	3	....	....	....	100	21	0	12.60	....	....	....	....	....	....	....
1985-86	Simcoe Rams	OJHL-C	1	....	....	....	60	6	0	6.00	....	....	....	....	....	....	....
1986-87	Norwich	OJHL-C	19	....	....	....	1091	55	0	*3.03	....	....	....	....	....	....	....
1987-88	Belleville Bobcats	OJHL-B	21	9	6	1	1070	60	*2	3.36	....	....	....	....	....	....	....
1988-89	Thorold	OJHL-B	27	15	6	4	1490	82	0	3.30	....	....	....	....	....	....	....
1989-90	Thorold	OJHL-B	30	18	8	1	1683	108	0	3.85	....	....	....	....	....	....	....
1990-91	U. Mass-Lowell	H-East	15	5	9	0	823	63	0	4.59	....	....	....	....	....	....	....
1991-92	U. Mass-Lowell	H-East	12	3	8	0	660	52	0	4.73	....	....	....	....	....	....	....
1992-93	U. Mass-Lowell	H-East	*39	20	17	2	*2342	150	0	3.84	....	....	....	....	....	....	....
1993-94	U. Mass-Lowell	H-East	*40	*23	10	7	*2305	106	0	2.76	....	....	....	....	....	....	....
1994-95	Saint John Flames	AHL	46	16	21	8	2734	156	1	3.42	5	1	4	298	13	0	2.61
1995-96	Saint John Flames	AHL	67	*33	22	11	4026	190	1	2.83	16	10	6	1027	49	1	2.86

1996-97	Calgary	NHL	31	9	14	3	1618	78	1	2.89	....	....	....	....	....	....	....
	Saint John Flames	AHL	8	6	2	0	481	22	1	2.75	....	....	....	....	....	....	....
1997-98	Calgary	NHL	39	11	16	8	2205	110	0	2.99	....	....	....	....	....	....	....
	Saint John Flames	AHL	4	3	0	1	245	8	0	1.96	....	....	....	....	....	....	....
1998-99	Buffalo	NHL	18	6	8	2	911	42	1	2.77	4	1	1	139	10	0	4.32
	Rochester	AHL	2	2	0	0	120	4	0	2.00	....	....	....	....	....	....	....
99-2000	Buffalo	NHL	14	1	7	3	677	32	0	2.84	....	....	....	....	....	....	....
2000-01	Worcester IceCats	AHL	52	*32	15	5	*3127	113	*6	*2.17	11	6	5	697	23	1	1.98
2001-02	Minnesota	NHL	45	14	20	7	2506	112	5	2.68	....	....	....	....	....	....	....
2002-03	Minnesota	NHL	50	23	16	8	2945	98	4	2.00	11	5	6	579	25	0	2.59
	NHL Totals		197	64	81	31	10862	472	11	2.61	15	6	7	718	35	0	2.92

Hockey East First All-Star Team (1994) • Hockey East Player of the Year (1994) • NCAA East First All-American Team (1994) • AHL First All-Star Team (2001) • Baz Bastien Memorial Trophy (Top Goaltender – AHL) (2001)

Signed as a free agent by **Calgary**, July 4, 1994. Signed as a free agent by **Buffalo**, July 15, 1998. Claimed by **Columbus** from **Buffalo** in Expansion Draft, June 23, 2000. Signed as a free agent by **St. Louis**, July 14, 2000. Signed as a free agent by **Minnesota**, July 2, 2001.

ROY, Patrick (WAH, PAT-rihk)

Goaltender. Catches left. 6'2", 185 lbs. Born, Quebec City, Que., October 5, 1965.
(Montreal's 4th choice, 51st overall, in 1984 Entry Draft).

			Regular Season								Playoffs						
Season	Club	League	GP	W	L	T	Mins	GA	SO	Avg	GP	W	L	Mins	GA	SO	Avg
1981-82	Ste-Foy	QAAA	40	*27	3	10	2400	156	*3	*2.63	2	2	0	114	2	*1	1.05
1982-83	Granby Bisons	QMJHL	54	13	35	1	2808	293	0	6.26	....	....	....	....	....	....	....
1983-84	Granby Bisons	QMJHL	61	29	29	1	3585	265	0	4.44	4	0	4	244	22	0	5.41
1984-85	Granby Bisons	QMJHL	44	16	25	1	2463	228	0	5.55	....	....	....	....	....	....	....
	Montreal	NHL	1	1	0	0	20	0	0	0.00	....	....	....	....	....	....	....
	Sherbrooke	AHL	1	1	0	0	60	4	0	4.00	13	10	3	*769	37	0	*2.89
1985-86 ♦	Montreal	NHL	47	23	18	3	2651	148	1	3.35	20	*15	5	1218	39	*1	1.92
1986-87	Montreal	NHL	46	22	16	6	2686	131	1	2.93	6	4	2	330	22	0	4.00
1987-88	Montreal	NHL	45	23	12	9	2586	125	3	2.90	8	3	4	430	24	0	3.35
1988-89	Montreal	NHL	48	33	5	6	2744	113	4	*2.47	19	13	6	1206	42	2	*2.09
1989-90	Montreal	NHL	54	*31	16	5	3173	134	3	2.53	11	5	6	641	26	1	2.43
1990-91	Montreal	NHL	48	25	15	6	2835	128	1	2.71	13	7	5	785	40	0	3.06
1991-92	Montreal	NHL	67	36	22	8	3935	155	*5	*2.36	11	4	7	686	30	1	2.62
1992-93 ♦	Montreal	NHL	62	31	25	5	3595	192	2	3.20	20	*16	4	1293	46	0	*2.13
1993-94	Montreal	NHL	68	35	17	11	3867	161	*7	2.50	6	3	3	375	16	0	2.56
1994-95	Montreal	NHL	43	17	20	6	2566	127	1	2.97	....	....	....	....	....	....	....
1995-96	Montreal	NHL	22	12	9	1	1260	62	1	2.95	....	....	....	....	....	....	....
	♦ Colorado	NHL	39	22	15	1	2305	103	1	2.68	*22	*16	6	*1454	51	*3	2.10
1996-97	Colorado	NHL	62	*38	15	7	3698	143	7	2.32	17	10	7	1034	38	*3	2.21
1997-98	Colorado	NHL	65	31	19	13	3835	153	4	2.39	7	3	4	430	18	0	2.51
	Canada	Olympics	6	4	2	0	*369	9	1	1.46	....	....	....	....	....	....	....
1998-99	Colorado	NHL	61	32	19	8	3648	139	5	2.29	19	11	8	1173	52	1	2.66
99-2000	Colorado	NHL	63	32	21	8	3704	141	2	2.28	17	11	6	1039	31	3	1.79
2000-01 ♦	Colorado	NHL	62	40	13	7	3585	132	4	2.21	23	*16	7	1451	41	*4	*1.70
2001-02	Colorado	NHL	63	32	23	8	3773	122	*9	*1.94	21	11	10	1241	52	3	2.51
2002-03	Colorado	NHL	63	35	15	13	3769	137	5	2.18	7	3	4	423	16	1	2.27
	NHL Totals		*1029	*551	315	131	*60235	2546	66	2.54	*247	*151	94	*15209	584	*23	2.30

NHL All-Rookie Team (1986) • Conn Smythe Trophy (1986, 1993, 2001) • Shared William M. Jennings Trophy (1987, 1988, 1989) with Brian Hayward • NHL Second All-Star Team (1988, 1991) • NHL First All-Star Team (1989, 1990, 1992, 2002) • Trico Goaltending Award (1989, 1990) • Vezina Trophy (1989, 1990, 1992) • William M. Jennings Trophy (1992, 2002)

Played in NHL All-Star Game (1988, 1990, 1991, 1992, 1993, 1994, 1997, 1998, 2001, 2002, 2003)

Traded to **Colorado** by **Montreal** with Mike Keane for Andrei Kovalenko, Martin Rucinsky and Jocelyn Thibault, December 6, 1995. • Officially announced retirement, May 28, 2003.

RUDKOWSKY, Cody (RUHD-kow-skee, KOH-dee) ST.L.

Goaltender. Catches left. 6'1", 206 lbs. Born, Willingdon, Alta., July 21, 1978.

			Regular Season								Playoffs						
Season	Club	League	GP	W	L	T	Mins	GA	SO	Avg	GP	W	L	Mins	GA	SO	Avg
1995-96	Langley Thunder	BCJHL	23	....	....	....	1172	73	1	3.73	....	....	....	....	....	....	....
	Seattle	WHL	2	0	0	0	21	3	0	8.57	....	....	....	....	....	....	....
1996-97	Seattle	WHL	40	19	16	1	2162	124	0	3.44	1	1	0	30	0	0	0.00
1997-98	Seattle	WHL	53	20	22	3	2805	176	1	3.74	5	1	4	278	18	0	3.88
1998-99	Seattle	WHL	64	34	17	10	3665	177	*7	2.90	11	5	6	637	31	1	2.92
99-2000	Worcester IceCats	AHL	28	9	7	6	1405	75	0	3.20	....	....	....	....	....	....	....
	Peoria Rivermen	ECHL	10	6	4	0	599	32	0	3.20	2	1	1	119	6	0	3.02
2000-01	Worcester IceCats	AHL	25	13	8	3	1477	66	3	2.68	....	....	....	....	....	....	....
2001-02	Worcester IceCats	AHL	21	6	10	2	1108	50	1	2.71	....	....	....	....	....	....	....
	Peoria Rivermen	ECHL	12	5	2	4	709	24	3	2.03	2	0	1	78	4	0	3.08
2002-03	St. Louis	NHL	1	1	0	0	30	0	0	0.00	....	....	....	....	....	....	....
	Worcester IceCats	AHL	10	1	5	3	577	28	0	2.91	....	....	....	....	....	....	....
	Trenton Titans	ECHL	31	17	9	5	1867	85	2	2.73	3	0	3	178	14	0	4.72
	NHL Totals		1	1	0	0	30	0	0	0.00	....	....	....	....	....	....	....

WHL West First All-Star Team (1999) • Canadian Major Junior First All-Star Team (1999) • Canadian Major Junior Goaltender of the Year (1999)

Signed as a free agent by **St. Louis**, March 25, 1999.

SABOURIN, Dany (SA-boo-rihn, DAN-ee) CGY.

Goaltender. Catches left. 6'2", 182 lbs. Born, Val-d'Or, Que., September 2, 1980.
(Calgary's 5th choice, 108th overall, in 1998 Entry Draft).

			Regular Season								Playoffs						
Season	Club	League	GP	W	L	T	Mins	GA	SO	Avg	GP	W	L	Mins	GA	SO	Avg
1996-97	Amos Forestiers	QAAA	24	6	16	0	1440	107	0	4.48	....	....	....	....	....	....	....
1997-98	Sherbrooke	QMJHL	37	15	15	2	1906	128	1	4.03	....	....	....	....	....	....	....
1998-99	Sherbrooke	QMJHL	30	8	13	2	1477	102	1	4.14	1	0	1	49	2	0	2.45
	Saint John Flames	AHL	....	....	....	....	....	....	....	....	1	0	1	57	4	0	4.19
99-2000	Sherbrooke	QMJHL	55	25	22	5	3067	181	1	3.54	5	1	4	324	18	0	3.33
2000-01	Saint John Flames	AHL	1	1	0	0	40	0	0	0.00	....	....	....	....	....	....	....
	Johnstown Chiefs	ECHL	19	4	9	1	903	56	0	3.72	1	0	0	40	2	0	3.00
2001-02	Johnstown Chiefs	ECHL	27	14	10	1	1539	84	0	3.28	3	0	2	137	5	0	2.18
2002-03	Saint John Flames	AHL	41	15	17	4	2220	100	4	2.70	....	....	....	....	....	....	....

SALO, Tommy (SA-loh,TAW-mee) EDM.

Goaltender. Catches left. 5'11", 182 lbs. Born, Surahammar, Sweden, February 1, 1971.
(NY Islanders' 5th choice, 118th overall, in 1993 Entry Draft).

			Regular Season								Playoffs						
Season	Club	League	GP	W	L	T	Mins	GA	SO	Avg	GP	W	L	Mins	GA	SO	Avg
1990-91	Vasteras IK	Sweden	2	....	....	....	100	11	0	6.60	....	....	....	....	....	....	....
1991-92	Vasteras IK Jr.	Swede-Jr.					STATISTICS NOT AVAILABLE										
1992-93	Vasteras IK	Sweden	24	....	....	....	1431	59	2	2.47	2	....	....	120	6	0	3.00
1993-94	Vasteras IK	Sweden	32	....	....	....	1896	106	0	3.35	....	....	....	....	....	....	....
	Sweden	Olympics	6	5	1	0	370	13	1	2.11	....	....	....	....	....	....	....
1994-95	Denver Grizzlies	IHL	*65	*45	14	4	*3810	165	*3	*2.60	8	7	0	390	20	0	3.07
	NY Islanders	NHL	6	1	5	0	358	18	0	3.02	....	....	....	....	....	....	....
1995-96	NY Islanders	NHL	10	1	7	1	523	35	0	4.02	....	....	....	....	....	....	....
	Utah Grizzlies	IHL	45	28	15	2	2695	119	*4	2.65	22	*15	7	1342	51	*3	2.28
1996-97	NY Islanders	NHL	58	20	27	8	3208	151	5	2.82	....	....	....	....	....	....	....
1997-98	NY Islanders	NHL	62	23	29	5	3461	152	4	2.64	....	....	....	....	....	....	....
	Sweden	Olympics	4	2	2	0	238	9	0	2.27	....	....	....	....	....	....	....
1998-99	NY Islanders	NHL	51	17	26	7	3018	132	5	2.62	....	....	....	....	....	....	....
	Edmonton	NHL	13	8	2	2	700	27	0	2.31	4	0	4	296	11	0	2.23
99-2000	Edmonton	NHL	70	27	28	13	4164	162	2	2.33	5	1	4	297	14	0	2.83
2000-01	Edmonton	NHL	73	36	25	12	4364	179	8	2.46	6	2	4	406	15	0	2.22
2001-02	Edmonton	NHL	69	30	28	10	4035	149	6	2.22	....	....	....	....	....	....	....
	Sweden	Olympics	3	2	1	0	179	7	0	2.35	....	....	....	....	....	....	....
2002-03	Edmonton	NHL	65	29	27	8	3814	172	4	2.71	6	2	4	343	18	0	3.15
	NHL Totals		477	192	204	66	27645	1177	34	2.55	21	5	16	1342	58	0	2.59

IHL First All-Star Team (1995) • Garry F. Longman Memorial Trophy (Top Rookie – IHL) (1995) • James Norris Memorial Trophy (fewest goals against – IHL) (1995) • James Gatschene Memorial Trophy (MVP – IHL) (1995) • Shared James Norris Memorial Trophy (fewest goals against – IHL) (1996) with Mark McArthur • ''Bud'' Poile Trophy (Playoff MVP – IHL) (1996)

Played in NHL All-Star Game (2000, 2002)

Traded to **Edmonton** by **NY Islanders** for Mats Lindgren and Edmonton's 8th round choice (Radek Martinek) in 1999 Entry Draft, March 20, 1999.

SANFORD, Curtis (SAN-fohrd, KUHR-this) ST.L.

Goaltender. Catches right. 5'10", 187 lbs. Born, Owen Sound, Ont., October 5, 1979.

			Regular Season								Playoffs						
Season	Club	League	GP	W	L	T	Mins	GA	SO	Avg	GP	W	L	Mins	GA	SO	Avg
1996-97	Owen Sound	OHL	19	4	8	1	847	77	0	5.45	....	....	....	....	....	....	....
1997-98	Owen Sound	OHL	30	13	10	2	1542	114	1	4.44	9	4	4	456	30	1	3.95
1998-99	Owen Sound	OHL	56	30	16	5	2998	191	2	3.82	16	9	7	960	58	0	3.63
99-2000	Owen Sound	OHL	53	18	26	6	3124	198	1	3.80	....	....	....	....	....	....	....
	Missouri	UHL	6	3	1	0	237	6	0	1.52	....	....	....	....	....	....	....
2000-01	Peoria Rivermen	ECHL	27	15	7	4	1511	48	3	*1.91	14	9	4	813	28	*2	2.07
	Worcester IceCats	AHL	5	3	0	1	237	16	0	4.06	....	....	....	....	....	....	....
2001-02	Peoria Rivermen	ECHL	24	13	8	2	1418	58	1	2.45	....	....	....	....	....	....	....
	Worcester IceCats	AHL	9	5	4	0	537	22	0	2.46	....	....	....	....	....	....	....
2002-03	St. Louis	NHL	8	5	1	0	397	13	1	1.96	....	....	....	....	....	....	....
	Worcester IceCats	AHL	41	18	14	8	2317	93	3	2.41	3	0	3	179	8	0	2.68
	NHL Totals		8	5	1	0	397	13	1	1.96	....	....	....	....	....	....	....

Signed as a free agent by **St. Louis**, October 1, 2000.

SAUVE, Philippe (SOH-vay, FIHL-ihp) COL.

Goaltender. Catches left. 6', 180 lbs. Born, Buffalo, NY, February 27, 1980.
(Colorado's 6th choice, 38th overall, in 1998 Entry Draft).

			Regular Season								Playoffs						
Season	Club	League	GP	W	L	T	Mins	GA	SO	Avg	GP	W	L	Mins	GA	SO	Avg
1995-96	Laval Laurentide	QAAA	25	9	10	0	1184	87	1	4.11	15	7	8	900	54	0	3.58
1996-97	Rimouski Oceanic	QMJHL	26	11	9	2	1334	84	0	3.78	1	0	0	14	3	0	12.90
1997-98	Rimouski Oceanic	QMJHL	40	23	16	0	2326	131	1	3.38	7	0	5	262	33	0	7.55
1998-99	Rimouski Oceanic	QMJHL	44	16	19	4	2401	155	0	3.87	11	6	4	595	30	*1	3.03
99-2000	Drummondville	QMJHL	28	12	12	2	1526	106	0	4.17	....	....	....	....	....	....	....
	Hull Olympiques	QMJHL	17	9	7	1	992	57	0	3.45	12	6	6	735	47	0	3.84
2000-01	Hershey Bears	AHL	42	17	18	1	2182	100	3	2.75	3	0	3	218	10	0	2.75
2001-02	Hershey Bears	AHL	55	25	20	6	3130	111	6	2.13	8	3	5	486	21	0	2.59
2002-03	Hershey Bears	AHL	*60	26	20	12	3394	134	5	2.37	5	2	3	295	14	0	2.85

Canadian Major Junior Humanitarian Player of the Year (1999)

SCHAEFER, Nolan (SHAY-fuhr, NOH-luhn) S.J.

Goaltender. Catches left. 6'1", 175 lbs. Born, Yellow Grass, Sask., January 15, 1980.
(San Jose's 4th choice, 166th overall, in 2000 Entry Draft).

			Regular Season								Playoffs						
Season	Club	League	GP	W	L	T	Mins	GA	SO	Avg	GP	W	L	Mins	GA	SO	Avg
1996-97	Yorkton Mallers	SMHL	36	....	....	....	1854	132	0	4.27	....	....	....	....	....	....	....
1997-98	Yorkton Mallers	SMHL	5	....	....	....	239	17	0	4.25	....	....	....	....	....	....	....
	Nipawin Hawks	SJHL	21	12	4	3	1080	42	*3	*2.33	....	....	....	....	....	....	....
1998-99	Nipawin Hawks	SJHL					DID NOT PLAY – INJURED										
99-2000	Providence College	H-East	14	6	5	1	778	42	0	3.24	....	....	....	....	....	....	....
2000-01	Providence College	H-East	25	15	8	2	1529	63	3	2.47	....	....	....	....	....	....	....
2001-02	Providence College	H-East	*35	11	18	5	*2062	113	0	3.29	....	....	....	....	....	....	....
2002-03	Providence College	H-East	25	13	8	2	1440	71	0	2.96	....	....	....	....	....	....	....

SJHL All-Rookie Team (1998) • Hockey East Second All-Star Team (2001) • NCAA East Second All-American Team (2001)

SCHWAB, Corey (SHWAHB, KOHR-ree) N.J.

Goaltender. Catches left. 6', 180 lbs. Born, North Battleford, Sask., November 4, 1970.
(New Jersey's 12th choice, 200th overall, in 1990 Entry Draft).

			Regular Season								Playoffs						
Season	Club	League	GP	W	L	T	Mins	GA	SO	Avg	GP	W	L	Mins	GA	SO	Avg
1988-89	Seattle	WHL	10	2	2	0	386	31	0	4.82	....	....	....	....	....	....	....
1989-90	Seattle	WHL	27	15	2	1	1150	69	1	3.60	3	0	0	49	2	0	2.45
1990-91	Seattle	WHL	*58	32	18	3	*3289	224	0	4.09	6	1	5	382	25	0	3.93
1991-92	Utica Devils	AHL	24	9	12	1	1322	95	0	4.31	....	....	....	....	....	....	....
	Cincinnati	ECHL	8	6	0	1	450	31	0	4.13	9	6	3	540	29	0	3.22
1992-93	Utica Devils	AHL	40	18	16	5	2387	169	*2	4.25	1	0	1	59	6	0	6.10
	Cincinnati	IHL	3	1	2	0	185	17	0	5.51	....	....	....	....	....	....	....
1993-94	Albany River Rats	AHL	51	27	21	3	3058	184	0	3.61	5	1	4	298	20	0	4.02
1994-95	Albany River Rats	AHL	45	25	10	9	2711	117	3	*2.59	7	6	1	425	19	0	2.68
1995-96	New Jersey	NHL	10	0	3	0	331	12	0	2.18	....	....	....	....	....	....	....
	Albany River Rats	AHL	5	3	2	0	299	13	0	2.61	....	....	....	....	....	....	....
1996-97	Tampa Bay	NHL	31	11	12	1	1462	74	2	3.04	....	....	....	....	....	....	....
1997-98	Tampa Bay	NHL	16	2	9	1	821	40	1	2.92	....	....	....	....	....	....	....
1998-99	Tampa Bay	NHL	40	8	25	3	2146	126	0	3.52	....	....	....	....	....	....	....
	Cleveland	IHL	8	1	6	1	477	31	0	3.90	....	....	....	....	....	....	....
99-2000	Orlando	IHL	16	9	4	2	868	31	1	2.14	....	....	....	....	....	....	....
	Vancouver	NHL	6	2	1	1	269	16	0	3.57	....	....	....	....	....	....	....
	Syracuse Crunch	AHL	12	7	5	0	720	42	0	3.50	4	1	3	246	11	1	2.69
2000-01	Kansas City Blades	IHL	50	22	24	1	2866	150	2	3.14	....	....	....	....	....	....	....
2001-02	Toronto	NHL	30	12	10	5	1646	75	1	2.73	1	0	0	12	0	0	0.00
2002-03 ♦	New Jersey	NHL	11	5	3	1	614	15	1	1.47	2	0	0	28	0	0	0.00
	NHL Totals		144	40	63	12	7289	358	5	2.95	3	0	0	40	0	0	0.00

AHL Second All-Star Team (1995) • Shared Harry ''Hap'' Holmes Memorial Trophy (fewest goals against – AHL) (1995) with Mike Dunham • Jack A. Butterfield Trophy (Playoff MVP – AHL) (1995) (co-winner - Mike Dunham)

Traded to **Tampa Bay** by **New Jersey** for Jeff Reese, Chicago's 2nd round choice (previously acquired, New Jersey selected Pierre Dagenais) in 1996 Entry Draft and Tampa Bay's 8th round choice (Jay Bertsch) in 1996 Entry Draft, June 22, 1996. Claimed by **Atlanta** from **Tampa Bay** in Expansion Draft, June 25, 1999. Traded to **Vancouver** by **Atlanta** for Vancouver's 4th round choice (Carl Mallette) in 2000 Entry Draft, October 29, 1999. Signed as a free agent by **Toronto**, October 1, 2001. Signed as a free agent by **New Jersey**, July 8, 2002.

SCOTT, Travis (SKAWT, TRA-vihs) FLA.

Goaltender. Catches left. 6'2", 185 lbs. Born, Kanata, Ont., September 14, 1975.

			Regular Season								Playoffs						
Season	Club	League	GP	W	L	T	Mins	GA	SO	Avg	GP	W	L	Mins	GA	SO	Avg
1991-92	Nepean Raiders	COJHL	19	14	5	0	1065	71	1	4.00	....	....	....	....	....	....	....
1992-93	Nepean Raiders	COJHL	36	19	10	2	1968	133	0	4.05	....	....	....	....	....	....	....
1993-94	Windsor Spitfires	OHL	45	20	18	0	2312	158	1	4.10	4	0	4	240	16	0	4.00
1994-95	Windsor Spitfires	OHL	48	26	14	3	2644	147	3	3.34	3	0	1	94	6	1	3.83

1995-96	Oshawa Generals	OHL	31	15	9	4	1763	78	3	2.65	5	1	4	315	23	0	4.38
1996-97	Baton Rouge	ECHL	10	5	2	1	501	22	0	2.63	....	....	....	....	....	....	....
	Worcester IceCats	AHL	29	14	10	1	1482	75	1	3.04	....	....	....	....	....	....	....
1997-98	Baton Rouge	ECHL	36	14	11	6	1949	96	1	2.96	....	....	....	....	....	....	....
1998-99	Mississippi	ECHL	44	22	12	5	2337	112	1	2.88	*18	*14	4	*1252	42	3	2.01
99-2000	Lowell	AHL	46	15	23	3	2595	126	3	2.91	1	0	1	60	2	0	2.01
2000-01	**Los Angeles**	**NHL**	**1**	**0**	**0**	**0**	**25**	**3**	**0**	**7.20**	....	....	....	....	....	....	....
	Lowell	AHL	34	16	15	1	1977	83	2	2.52	4	1	2	209	7	1	2.01
2001-02	Manchester	AHL	39	21	12	3	2170	83	6	2.30	5	2	3	327	15	0	2.75
2002-03	Manchester	AHL	50	23	19	5	2829	116	4	2.46	3	0	2	148	9	0	3.65
	NHL Totals		**1**	**0**	**0**	**0**	**25**	**3**	**0**	**7.20**	....	....	....	....	....	....	....

ECHL Playoff MVP (1999)

Signed as a free agent by **St. Louis**, December 30, 1996. Signed as a free agent by **Los Angeles**, February 18, 2000. Signed as a free agent by **Florida**, August 12, 2003.

SHIELDS, Steve (SHEELDS, STEEV) BOS.

Goaltender. Catches left. 6'3", 215 lbs. Born, Toronto, Ont., July 19, 1972.
(Buffalo's 5th choice, 101st overall, in 1991 Entry Draft).

			Regular Season								Playoffs						
Season	Club	League	GP	W	L	T	Mins	GA	SO	Avg	GP	W	L	Mins	GA	SO	Avg
1989-90	St. Marys Lincolns	OJHL-B	26	....	....	....	1512	121	0	4.80	....	....	....	....	....	....	....
1990-91	U. of Michigan	CCHA	37	26	6	3	1963	106	0	3.24	....	....	....	....	....	....	....
1991-92	U. of Michigan	CCHA	*37	*27	7	2	*2090	99	1	2.84	....	....	....	....	....	....	....
1992-93	U. of Michigan	CCHA	*39	*30	6	2	2027	75	2	*2.22	....	....	....	....	....	....	....
1993-94	U. of Michigan	CCHA	36	*28	6	1	1961	87	0	2.66	....	....	....	....	....	....	....
1994-95	Rochester	AHL	13	3	8	0	673	53	0	4.72	1	0	0	20	3	0	9.00
	South Carolina	ECHL	21	11	5	2	1158	52	2	2.69	3	0	2	144	11	0	4.58
1995-96	**Buffalo**	**NHL**	**2**	**1**	**0**	**0**	**75**	**4**	**0**	**3.20**	....	....	....	....	....	....	....
	Rochester	AHL	43	20	17	2	2357	140	1	3.56	*19	*15	3	*1127	47	1	2.50
1996-97	**Buffalo**	**NHL**	**13**	**3**	**8**	**2**	**789**	**39**	**0**	**2.97**	**10**	**4**	**6**	**570**	**26**	**1**	**2.74**
	Rochester	AHL	23	14	6	2	1331	60	1	2.70	....	....	....	....	....	....	....
1997-98	**Buffalo**	**NHL**	**16**	**3**	**6**	**4**	**785**	**37**	**0**	**2.83**	....	....	....	....	....	....	....
	Rochester	AHL	1	0	1	0	59	3	0	3.04	....	....	....	....	....	....	....
1998-99	**San Jose**	**NHL**	**37**	**15**	**11**	**8**	**2162**	**80**	**4**	**2.22**	**1**	**0**	**1**	**60**	**6**	**0**	**6.00**
99-2000	**San Jose**	**NHL**	**67**	**27**	**30**	**8**	**3797**	**162**	**4**	**2.56**	**12**	**5**	**7**	**696**	**36**	**0**	**3.10**
2000-01	**San Jose**	**NHL**	**21**	**6**	**8**	**5**	**1135**	**47**	**2**	**2.48**	....	....	....	....	....	....	....
2001-02	**Anaheim**	**NHL**	**33**	**9**	**20**	**2**	**1777**	**79**	**0**	**2.67**	....	....	....	....	....	....	....
2002-03	**Boston**	**NHL**	**36**	**12**	**13**	**9**	**2112**	**97**	**0**	**2.76**	**2**	**0**	**2**	**119**	**6**	**0**	**3.03**
	NHL Totals		**225**	**76**	**96**	**38**	**12632**	**545**	**10**	**2.59**	**25**	**9**	**16**	**1445**	**74**	**1**	**3.07**

CCHA First All-Star Team (1993, 1994) • NCAA West Second All-American Team (1993, 1994)

Traded to **San Jose** by **Buffalo** with Buffalo's 4th round choice (Miroslav Zalesak) in 1998 Entry Draft for Kay Whitmore, Colorado's 2nd round choice (previously acquired, Buffalo selected Jaroslav Kristek) in 1998 Entry Draft and San Jose's 5th round choice (later traded to Columbus – Columbus selected Tyler Kolarik) in 2000 Entry Draft, June 18, 1998. Traded to **Anaheim** by **San Jose** with Jeff Friesen and San Jose's 2nd round choice (later traded to Dallas – Dallas selected Vojtech Polak) in 2003 Entry Draft for Teemu Selanne, March 5, 2001. Traded to **Boston** by **Anaheim** for Boston's 3rd round choice (Shane Hynes) in 2003 Entry Draft, June 25, 2002.

SIDIKOV, Rustam (SIH-dih-kawf, ROOS-tuhm) NSH.

Goaltender. Catches left. 6', 165 lbs. Born, Moscow, USSR, May 7, 1985.
(Nashville's 10th choice, 133rd overall, in 2003 Entry Draft).

			Regular Season								Playoffs						
Season	Club	League	GP	W	L	T	Mins	GA	SO	Avg	GP	W	L	Mins	GA	SO	Avg
2001-02	CSKA Moscow 2	Russia 3	1	....	....	....	60	5	0	5.00	....	....	....	....	....	....	....
2002-03	CSKA Moscow-18	Russia Jr.	22	....	....	....	1173	47	....	2.41	....	....	....	....	....	....	....
	CSKA Moscow 2	Russia 3	5	....	....	....	120	2	0	1.00	....	....	....	....	....	....	....

SIGALET, Jordan (SIH-ga-leht, JOHR-duhn) BOS.

Goaltender. Catches left. 6'1", 180 lbs. Born, New Westminster, B.C., February 19, 1981.
(Boston's 6th choice, 209th overall, in 2001 Entry Draft).

			Regular Season								Playoffs						
Season	Club	League	GP	W	L	T	Mins	GA	SO	Avg	GP	W	L	Mins	GA	SO	Avg
99-2000	Victoria Salsa	BCHL	33	....	....	....	1980	108	0	3.28	....	....	....	....	....	....	....
2000-01	Victoria Salsa	BCHL	48	23	22	0	2820	142	0	3.03	18	12	5	1060	143	0	2.62
2001-02	Bowling Green	CCHA	13	2	6	2	657	38	0	3.47	....	....	....	....	....	....	....
2002-03	Bowling Green	CCHA	20	6	11	2	1208	66	1	3.28	....	....	....	....	....	....	....

BCHL All-Rookie Team (2000) • BCHL Second All-Star Team (2000) • BCHL First All-Star Team (2001)

SKUDRA, Peter (SKOO-druh, PEE-tuhr)

Goaltender. Catches left. 6'1", 189 lbs. Born, Riga, Latvia, April 24, 1973.

			Regular Season								Playoffs						
Season	Club	League	GP	W	L	T	Mins	GA	SO	Avg	GP	W	L	Mins	GA	SO	Avg
1992-93	Pardaugava Riga	CIS	27	....	....	....	1498	74	....	2.96	1	....	....	60	5	0	5.00
1993-94	Pardaugava Riga	CIS	14	....	....	....	783	42	....	3.22	1	....	....	55	4	0	4.36
1994-95	Greensboro	ECHL	33	13	9	5	1612	113	0	4.20	6	2	2	341	28	0	4.92
	Memphis	CHL	2	0	1	0	80	8	0	6.00	....	....	....	....	....	....	....
1995-96	Erie Panthers	ECHL	12	3	8	1	681	47	0	4.14	....	....	....	....	....	....	....
	Johnstown Chiefs	ECHL	30	12	11	4	1657	98	0	3.55	....	....	....	....	....	....	....
1996-97	Hamilton Bulldogs	AHL	32	8	16	2	1615	101	0	3.75	....	....	....	....	....	....	....
	Johnstown Chiefs	ECHL	4	2	1	1	200	11	0	3.30	....	....	....	....	....	....	....
1997-98	**Pittsburgh**	**NHL**	**17**	**6**	**4**	**3**	**851**	**26**	**0**	**1.83**	....	....	....	....	....	....	....
	Houston Aeros	IHL	9	5	3	1	499	23	0	2.77	....	....	....	....	....	....	....
	Kansas City Blades	IHL	13	10	3	0	775	37	0	2.86	8	4	4	512	20	1	*2.34
1998-99	**Pittsburgh**	**NHL**	**37**	**15**	**11**	**5**	**1914**	**89**	**3**	**2.79**	....	....	....	....	....	....	....
99-2000	**Pittsburgh**	**NHL**	**20**	**5**	**7**	**3**	**922**	**48**	**1**	**3.12**	**1**	**0**	**0**	**20**	**1**	**0**	**3.00**
2000-01	**Buffalo**	**NHL**	**1**	**0**	**0**	**0**	**1**	**0**	**0**	**0.00**	....	....	....	....	....	....	....
	Rochester	AHL	2	2	0	0	120	5	0	2.50	....	....	....	....	....	....	....
	Boston	**NHL**	**25**	**6**	**12**	**1**	**1116**	**62**	**0**	**3.33**	....	....	....	....	....	....	....
	Providence Bruins	AHL	3	3	0	0	180	5	0	1.67	....	....	....	....	....	....	....
2001-02	**Vancouver**	**NHL**	**23**	**10**	**8**	**2**	**1166**	**47**	**1**	**2.42**	**2**	**0**	**1**	**96**	**5**	**0**	**3.13**
	Hartford Wolf Pack	AHL	3	2	1	0	179	8	0	2.69	....	....	....	....	....	....	....
2002-03	**Vancouver**	**NHL**	**23**	**9**	**5**	**6**	**1192**	**54**	**1**	**2.72**	....	....	....	....	....	....	....
	Manitoba Moose	AHL	1	1	0	0	60	3	0	3.00	....	....	....	....	....	....	....
	NHL Totals		**146**	**51**	**47**	**20**	**7162**	**326**	**6**	**2.73**	**3**	**0**	**1**	**116**	**6**	**0**	**3.10**

Signed as a free agent by **Pittsburgh**, September 25, 1997. Signed as a free agent by **Boston**, October 3, 2000. Claimed on waivers by **Buffalo** from **Boston**, October 6, 2000. • Played 27 seconds of game vs. Anaheim, October 20, 2000. Claimed on waivers by **Boston** from **Buffalo**, November 14, 2000. Signed as a free agent by **Vancouver**, November 7, 2001.

SMID, Zdenek (SHMIHD, zuh-DEHN-ehk) ATL.

Goaltender. Catches left. 5'10", 172 lbs. Born, Plzen, Czech., February 3, 1980.
(Atlanta's 7th choice, 168th overall, in 2000 Entry Draft).

			Regular Season								Playoffs						
Season	Club	League	GP	W	L	T	Mins	GA	SO	Avg	GP	W	L	Mins	GA	SO	Avg
1996-97	HC ZKZ Plzen Jr.	Czech-Jr.	23	....	....	....	1304	48	....	2.21	....	....	....	....	....	....	....
1997-98	Plzen Jr.	Czech-Jr.	30	....	....	....	1601	91	....	3.41	....	....	....	....	....	....	....
1998-99	Karlovy Vary Jr.	Czech-Jr.					STATISTICS NOT AVAILABLE										
	HC Karlovy Vary	Czech	3	....	....	....	160	11	....	4.13	....	....	....	....	....	....	....
99-2000	Karlovy Vary Jr.	Czech-Jr.	24	....	....	....	1409	54	....	2.30	2	....	....	86	9	....	6.28
	HC Karlovy Vary	Czech	14	....	....	....	650	41	0	3.78	3	....	....	150	8	....	3.20
2000-01	HC Karlovy Vary	Czech	12	....	....	....	630	34	....	3.24	....	....	....	....	....	....	....

2001-02	HPK Hameenlinna	Finland	18	10	4	4	1055	44	2	2.50	....	....	....	....	....	....	....
	Lulea HF	Sweden	1	0	1	0	58	3	0	3.10	1	0	1	40	5	0	7.50
2002-03	Liberec	Czech	2	....	....	....	111	8	0	4.32	....	....	....	....	....	....	....
	HC Keramika Plzen	Czech	15	....	....	....	828	39	0	2.83	....	....	....	....	....	....	....

SMITH, Mike (SMIHTH, MIGHK) DAL.

Goaltender. Catches left. 6'3", 189 lbs. Born, Kingston, Ont., March 22, 1982.
(Dallas' 5th choice, 161st overall, in 2001 Entry Draft).

			Regular Season								Playoffs						
Season	Club	League	GP	W	L	T	Mins	GA	SO	Avg	GP	W	L	Mins	GA	SO	Avg
1998-99	Kingston	OPJHL	16	....	....	....	906	53	0	3.51	....	....	....	....	....	....	....
99-2000	Kingston	OHL	15	4	5	0	666	42	0	3.78	....	....	....	....	....	....	....
2000-01	Kingston	OHL	3	0	0	2	136	8	0	3.53	....	....	....	....	....	....	....
	Sudbury Wolves	OHL	43	22	13	7	2571	108	3	2.52	12	7	5	735	26	2	*2.12
2001-02	Sudbury Wolves	OHL	53	19	28	5	3082	157	3	3.06	5	1	4	302	15	0	2.98
2002-03	Lexington	ECHL	27	11	10	4	1553	66	1	2.55	2	0	1	93	8	0	5.14
	Utah Grizzlies	AHL	11	5	5	0	614	33	0	3.23	....	....	....	....	....	....	....

SNOW, Garth (SNOH, GAHRTH) NYI

Goaltender. Catches left. 6'3", 200 lbs. Born, Wrentham, MA, July 28, 1969.
(Quebec's 6th choice, 114th overall, in 1987 Entry Draft).

			Regular Season								Playoffs						
Season	Club	League	GP	W	L	T	Mins	GA	SO	Avg	GP	W	L	Mins	GA	SO	Avg
1986-87	Mount St. Charles	H.S.	30	....	....	....	1795	53	10	1.77	....	....	....	....	....	....	....
1987-88	Stratford Cullitons	OJHL-B	30	20	6	0	1642	93	2	3.40	....	....	....	....	....	....	....
1988-89	University of Maine	H-East	5	2	2	0	241	14	1	3.49	....	....	....	....	....	....	....
1989-90	University of Maine	H-East					DID NOT PLAY – ACADEMICALLY INELIGIBLE										
1990-91	University of Maine	H-East	25	*18	4	0	1290	64	2	2.98	....	....	....	....	....	....	....
1991-92	University of Maine	H-East	31	*25	4	2	1792	73	*2	*2.44	....	....	....	....	....	....	....
1992-93	University of Maine	H-East	23	*21	0	1	1210	42	1	*2.08	....	....	....	....	....	....	....
1993-94	United States	Nat-Tm	23	13	5	3	1324	71	1	3.22	....	....	....	....	....	....	....
	United States	Olympics	5	1	3	1	299	17	0	3.41	....	....	....	....	....	....	....
	Quebec	**NHL**	**5**	**3**	**2**	**0**	**279**	**16**	**0**	**3.44**	....	....	....	....	....	....	....
	Cornwall Aces	AHL	16	6	5	3	927	51	0	3.30	13	8	5	790	42	0	3.19
1994-95	Cornwall Aces	AHL	*62	*32	20	7	*3558	162	3	2.73	8	4	3	402	14	*2	*2.09
	Quebec	**NHL**	**2**	**1**	**1**	**0**	**119**	**11**	**0**	**5.55**	**1**	**0**	**0**	**9**	**1**	**0**	**6.67**
1995-96	**Philadelphia**	**NHL**	**26**	**12**	**8**	**4**	**1437**	**69**	**0**	**2.88**	**1**	**0**	**0**	**1**	**0**	**0**	**0.00**
1996-97	**Philadelphia**	**NHL**	**35**	**14**	**8**	**8**	**1884**	**79**	**2**	**2.52**	**12**	**8**	**4**	**699**	**33**	**0**	**2.83**
1997-98	**Philadelphia**	**NHL**	**29**	**14**	**9**	**4**	**1651**	**67**	**1**	**2.43**	....	....	....	....	....	....	....
	Vancouver	**NHL**	**12**	**3**	**6**	**0**	**504**	**26**	**0**	**3.10**	....	....	....	....	....	....	....
1998-99	**Vancouver**	**NHL**	**65**	**20**	**31**	**8**	**3501**	**171**	**6**	**2.93**	....	....	....	....	....	....	....
99-2000	**Vancouver**	**NHL**	**32**	**10**	**15**	**3**	**1712**	**76**	**0**	**2.66**	....	....	....	....	....	....	....
2000-01	Wilkes-Barre	AHL	3	2	1	0	178	7	0	2.36	....	....	....	....	....	....	....
	Pittsburgh	**NHL**	**35**	**14**	**15**	**4**	**2032**	**101**	**3**	**2.98**	....	....	....	....	....	....	....
2001-02	**NY Islanders**	**NHL**	**25**	**10**	**7**	**2**	**1217**	**55**	**2**	**2.71**	**1**	**0**	**0**	**26**	**2**	**0**	**4.62**
2002-03	**NY Islanders**	**NHL**	**43**	**16**	**17**	**5**	**2390**	**92**	**1**	**2.31**	**5**	**1**	**4**	**305**	**12**	**1**	**2.36**
	NHL Totals		**309**	**117**	**119**	**38**	**16726**	**763**	**15**	**2.74**	**20**	**9**	**8**	**1040**	**48**	**1**	**2.77**

Hockey East Second All-Star Team (1992, 1993) • NCAA Championship All-Tournament Team (1993)

Transferred to **Colorado** after **Quebec** franchise relocated, June 21, 1995. Traded to **Philadelphia** by **Colorado** for Philadelphia's 3rd (later traded to Washington – Washington selected Shawn McNeil) and 6th (Kai Fischer) round choices in 1996 Entry Draft, July 12, 1995. Traded to **Vancouver** by **Philadelphia** for Sean Burke, March 4, 1998. Signed as a free agent by **Pittsburgh**, October 10, 2000. Signed as a free agent by **NY Islanders**, July 14, 2001.

STANA, Ratislav (STAN-ah, RAH-tih-slahv) WSH.

Goaltender. Catches left. 6'2", 161 lbs. Born, Kosice, Czech., January 10, 1980.
(Washington's 8th choice, 193rd overall, in 1998 Entry Draft).

			Regular Season								Playoffs						
Season	Club	League	GP	W	L	T	Mins	GA	SO	Avg	GP	W	L	Mins	GA	SO	Avg
1997-98	HC Kosice Jr.	Slovak-Jr.	32	....	....	....	1920	56	2	1.75	....	....	....	....	....	....	....
1998-99	Moose Jaw	WHL	36	21	14	1	2131	123	2	3.46	9	4	5	544	30	0	3.31
99-2000	Moose Jaw	WHL	14	4	9	0	730	48	0	3.95	....	....	....	....	....	....	....
	Calgary Hitmen	WHL	16	13	2	1	971	37	1	2.29	9	7	2	526	21	1	2.40
2000-01	Richmond	ECHL	38	15	16	2	2111	90	1	2.56	3	1	2	178	7	1	2.34
2001-02	Richmond	ECHL	36	20	12	3	2098	95	1	2.72	....	....	....	....	....	....	....
	Portland Pirates	AHL	3	1	2	0	180	11	0	3.66	....	....	....	....	....	....	....
	Slovakia	Olympics	1	1	0	0	60	1	0	1.00	....	....	....	....	....	....	....
2002-03	Portland Pirates	AHL	24	8	11	4	1355	49	2	2.17	1	0	1	59	3	0	3.08

STEPHAN, Tobias (STEH-fan, toh-BEE-uhs) DAL.

Goaltender. Catches left. 6'3", 178 lbs. Born, Zurich, Switz., January 21, 1984.
(Dallas' 3rd choice, 34th overall, in 2002 Entry Draft).

			Regular Season								Playoffs						
Season	Club	League	GP	W	L	T	Mins	GA	SO	Avg	GP	W	L	Mins	GA	SO	Avg
2000-01	Kloten Flyers Jr.	Swiss-Jr.					STATISTICS NOT AVAILABLE										
2001-02	EHC Chur	Swiss	23	....	....	....	1396	80	0	3.44	10	....	....	604	39	0	3.87
2002-03	Kloten Flyers	Swiss	*44	....	....	....	2670	125	2	2.81	5	....	....	292	20	0	4.11

STORR, Jamie (STOHR, JAY-mee)

Goaltender. Catches left. 6'2", 195 lbs. Born, Brampton, Ont., December 28, 1975.
(Los Angeles' 1st choice, 7th overall, in 1994 Entry Draft).

			Regular Season								Playoffs						
Season	Club	League	GP	W	L	T	Mins	GA	SO	Avg	GP	W	L	Mins	GA	SO	Avg
1990-91	Brampton Capitals	MTJHL	24	....	....	....	1145	91	0	4.77	15	....	....	885	60	0	4.07
1991-92	Owen Sound	OHL	34	11	16	1	1732	128	0	4.43	5	1	4	299	28	0	5.62
1992-93	Owen Sound	OHL	41	20	17	3	2362	180	0	4.57	8	4	4	454	35	0	4.63
1993-94	Owen Sound	OHL	35	21	11	1	2004	120	1	3.59	9	4	5	547	44	0	4.83
1994-95	Owen Sound	OHL	17	5	9	2	977	64	0	3.93	....	....	....	....	....	....	....
	Los Angeles	**NHL**	**5**	**1**	**3**	**1**	**263**	**17**	**0**	**3.88**	....	....	....	....	....	....	....
	Windsor Spitfires	OHL	4	3	1	0	241	8	1	1.99	10	6	3	520	34	1	3.92
1995-96	**Los Angeles**	**NHL**	**5**	**3**	**1**	**0**	**262**	**12**	**0**	**2.75**	....	....	....	....	....	....	....
	Phoenix	IHL	48	22	20	4	2711	139	2	3.08	2	1	1	118	4	1	2.03
1996-97	**Los Angeles**	**NHL**	**5**	**2**	**1**	**1**	**265**	**11**	**0**	**2.49**	....	....	....	....	....	....	....
	Phoenix	IHL	44	16	22	4	2441	147	0	3.61	....	....	....	....	....	....	....
1997-98	**Los Angeles**	**NHL**	**17**	**9**	**5**	**1**	**920**	**34**	**2**	**2.22**	**3**	**0**	**2**	**145**	**9**	**0**	**3.72**
	Long Beach	IHL	11	7	2	1	629	31	0	2.96	....	....	....	....	....	....	....
1998-99	**Los Angeles**	**NHL**	**28**	**12**	**12**	**2**	**1525**	**61**	**4**	**2.40**	....	....	....	....	....	....	....
99-2000	**Los Angeles**	**NHL**	**42**	**18**	**15**	**5**	**2206**	**93**	**1**	**2.53**	**1**	**0**	**1**	**36**	**2**	**0**	**3.33**
2000-01	**Los Angeles**	**NHL**	**45**	**19**	**18**	**6**	**2498**	**114**	**4**	**2.74**	....	....	....	....	....	....	....
2001-02	**Los Angeles**	**NHL**	**19**	**9**	**4**	**3**	**886**	**28**	**2**	**1.90**	**1**	**0**	**0**	**1**	**0**	**0**	**0.00**
2002-03	**Los Angeles**	**NHL**	**39**	**12**	**19**	**2**	**2027**	**86**	**3**	**2.55**	....	....	....	....	....	....	....
	NHL Totals		**205**	**85**	**78**	**21**	**10852**	**456**	**16**	**2.52**	**5**	**0**	**3**	**182**	**11**	**0**	**3.63**

OHL All-Rookie Team (1992) • OHL First All-Star Team (1994) • NHL All-Rookie Team (1998, 1999)
• Played 8 seconds of playoff game vs. Colorado, April 29, 2002.

SWANSON, Kevin (SWAHN-suhn, KEH-vihn) VAN.

Goaltender. Catches left. 5'10", 170 lbs. Born, Calgary, Alta., April 18, 1980.
(Vancouver's 6th choice, 189th overall, in 1999 Entry Draft).

			Regular Season								Playoffs						
Season	Club	League	GP	W	L	T	Mins	GA	SO	Avg	GP	W	L	Mins	GA	SO	Avg
1996-97	Red Deer Chiefs	AMHL	20	....	....	....	1284	94	0	4.39	....	....	....	....	....	....	....
1997-98	Prince George	WHL	28	14	11	1	1532	93	0	3.64	....	....	....	....	....	....	....
1998-99	Prince George	WHL	4	1	2	0	180	10	0	3.33	....	....	....	....	....	....	....
	Kelowna Rockets	WHL	50	18	23	3	2507	144	2	3.45	6	2	4	355	14	0	2.37
99-2000	Kelowna Rockets	WHL	68	25	40	3	3943	194	*7	2.95	5	1	4	297	16	0	3.23
2000-01	Kelowna Rockets	WHL	49	27	16	5	2854	148	0	3.11	6	2	4	361	17	1	2.83
2001-02	Columbia Inferno	ECHL	19	4	8	4	986	44	0	2.68	1	0	0	20	2	0	5.91
	Manitoba Moose	AHL	1	0	0	0	20	1	0	3.00	....	....	....	....	....	....	....
2002-03	Columbia Inferno	ECHL	5	1	1	0	165	13	0	4.74	....	....	....	....	....	....	....

WHL West First All-Star Team (2000) • WHL West Second All-Star Team (2001)

• Missed majority of 2002-03 season recovering from groin injury suffered in pre-game warm-up, November 27, 2002. Signed as a free agent by **Bentley** (ChSHL) following release by **Columbia** (ECHL), February 1, 2003. • Signed Letter of Intent to attend **U. of British Columbia**, March 20, 2003.

SZUPER, Levente (SHOO-puhr, leh-VEHN-teh)

Goaltender. Catches left. 5'11", 180 lbs. Born, Budapest, Hungary, June 11, 1980.
(Calgary's 4th choice, 116th overall, in 2000 Entry Draft).

			Regular Season								Playoffs						
Season	Club	League	GP	W	L	T	Mins	GA	SO	Avg	GP	W	L	Mins	GA	SO	Avg
1996-97	Ferencvaros Jr.	Hungary	10	....	....	....	600	9	....	0.90	....	....	....	....	....	....	....
	Ferencvaros	Hungary	30	....	....	....	1660	74	3	2.67	....	....	....	....	....	....	....
1997-98	Krefeld Jr.	Ger.-Jr.	40	....	....	....	2300	103	3	2.69	....	....	....	....	....	....	....
1998-99	Ottawa 67's	OHL	32	22	6	3	1800	70	4	2.33	4	2	2	241	11	*1	2.74
99-2000	Ottawa 67's	OHL	53	31	15	2	2862	122	*5	2.56	11	6	5	680	35	1	3.09
2000-01	Saint John Flames	AHL	34	16	10	2	1750	73	2	2.50	1	1	0	36	0	0	0.00
2001-02	Saint John Flames	AHL	43	15	18	5	2429	98	5	2.42	....	....	....	....	....	....	....
2002-03	Saint John Flames	AHL	35	12	18	2	1904	82	1	2.58	....	....	....	....	....	....	....

TALLAS, Robbie (TAL-as, RAW-bee)

Goaltender. Catches left. 6', 170 lbs. Born, Edmonton, Alta., March 20, 1973.

			Regular Season								Playoffs						
Season	Club	League	GP	W	L	T	Mins	GA	SO	Avg	GP	W	L	Mins	GA	SO	Avg
1990-91	Penticton Panthers	BCJHL	37	....	....	....	2055	196	0	5.72	....	....	....	....	....	....	....
1991-92	Seattle	WHL	14	4	7	0	708	52	0	4.41	....	....	....	....	....	....	....
	South Surrey	BCJHL	19	6	12	0	1043	112	1	6.44	....	....	....	....	....	....	....
1992-93	Seattle	WHL	58	24	23	3	3151	194	2	3.69	5	1	4	333	18	0	3.24
1993-94	Seattle	WHL	51	23	21	3	2849	188	0	3.96	9	5	4	567	40	0	4.23
1994-95	Charlotte Checkers	ECHL	36	21	9	3	2011	114	0	3.40	....	....	....	....	....	....	....
	Providence Bruins	AHL	2	1	0	0	82	4	1	2.90	....	....	....	....	....	....	....
1995-96	Boston	NHL	1	1	0	0	60	3	0	3.00	....	....	....	....	....	....	....
	Providence Bruins	AHL	37	12	16	7	2136	117	1	3.29	2	0	2	135	9	0	4.01
1996-97	Boston	NHL	28	8	12	1	1244	69	1	3.33	....	....	....	....	....	....	....
	Providence Bruins	AHL	24	9	14	1	1424	83	0	3.50	....	....	....	....	....	....	....
1997-98	Boston	NHL	14	6	3	3	788	24	1	1.83	....	....	....	....	....	....	....
	Providence Bruins	AHL	10	1	8	1	575	39	0	4.07	....	....	....	....	....	....	....
1998-99	Boston	NHL	17	7	7	2	987	43	1	2.61	....	....	....	....	....	....	....
99-2000	Boston	NHL	27	4	13	4	1363	72	0	3.17	....	....	....	....	....	....	....
2000-01	Chicago	NHL	12	2	7	0	627	35	0	3.35	....	....	....	....	....	....	....
	Chicago Wolves	IHL	3	0	1	0	87	6	0	4.13	....	....	....	....	....	....	....
	Norfolk Admirals	AHL	6	2	2	2	333	12	0	2.16	....	....	....	....	....	....	....
2001-02	Wilkes-Barre	AHL	38	6	25	5	2183	126	0	3.46	....	....	....	....	....	....	....
2002-03	Wilkes-Barre	AHL	33	14	11	3	1763	99	0	3.37	....	....	....	....	....	....	....
	NHL Totals		99	28	42	10	5069	246	3	2.91							

Signed as a free agent by **Boston**, September 13, 1995. Signed as a free agent by **Chicago**, July 31, 2000. Signed as a free agent by **Pittsburgh**, August 14, 2001.

TARASOV, Vadim (ta-RA-sahf, va-DEEM) MTL.

Goaltender. Catches left. 5'11", 187 lbs. Born, Ust-Kamenogorsk, USSR, December 31, 1976.
(Montreal's 9th choice, 196th overall, in 1999 Entry Draft).

			Regular Season								Playoffs						
Season	Club	League	GP	W	L	T	Mins	GA	SO	Avg	GP	W	L	Mins	GA	SO	Avg
1995-96	Novokuznetsk	CIS	26	....	....	....	1355	60	1	2.66	....	....	....	....	....	....	....
1996-97	Novokuznetsk	Russia	34	....	....	....	1971	87	0	2.65	....	....	....	....	....	....	....
1997-98	Novokuznetsk	Russia	23	....	....	....	1364	61	2	2.68	....	....	....	....	....	....	....
1998-99	Novokuznetsk	Russia	*41	....	....	....	*2346	56	*8	1.43	6	....	....	349	16	0	2.75
99-2000	Novokuznetsk	Russia	28	....	....	....	1583	66	1	2.50	14	....	....	791	26	1	1.97
2000-01	Novokuznetsk	Russia	33	....	....	....	1960	69	4	2.11	....	....	....	....	....	....	....
2001-02	Quebec Citadelles	AHL	14	7	4	2	801	42	0	3.15	....	....	....	....	....	....	....
2002-03	Novokuznetsk	Russia	29	....	....	....	1450	64	0	2.65	....	....	....	....	....	....	....

Russian League Best Goaltender (1999, 2000, 2001)

Signed as a free agent by **Novokuznetsk** (Russia) with Montreal retaining NHL rights, July 18, 2002.

TELLQVIST, Mikael (TEHL-kvihst, MIGH-kuhl) TOR.

Goaltender. Catches left. 5'11", 194 lbs. Born, Sundbyberg, Sweden, September 19, 1979.
(Toronto's 3rd choice, 70th overall, in 2000 Entry Draft).

			Regular Season								Playoffs						
Season	Club	League	GP	W	L	T	Mins	GA	SO	Avg	GP	W	L	Mins	GA	SO	Avg
1997-98	Djurgarden Jr.	Swede-Jr.	23	....	....	....	1380	55	....	2.39	2	0	2	120	8	0	4.00
1998-99	Djurgarden	Sweden	3	1	2	0	124	8	0	3.87	4	....	....	240	11	0	2.75
	Djurgarden	EuroHL	3	2	1	0	180	8	....	2.33	....	....	....	....	....	....	....
99-2000	Huddinge IK	Swede-2	11	4	7	0	660	33	....	3.30	....	....	....	....	....	....	....
	Djurgarden	Sweden	30	....	....	....	1909	66	2	*2.07	*13	....	....	*814	21	*3	*1.55
2000-01	Djurgarden	Sweden	43	....	....	....	2622	91	*5	*2.08	*16	....	....	*1006	45	*1	2.68
2001-02	St. John's	AHL	28	8	11	6	1521	79	0	3.12	1	1	0	15	0	0	0.00
	Sweden	Olympics	DID NOT PLAY – SPARE GOALTENDER														
2002-03	Toronto	NHL	3	1	1	0	86	4	0	2.79	....	....	....	....	....	....	....
	St. John's	AHL	47	17	25	3	2651	148	1	3.35	....	....	....	....	....	....	....
	NHL Totals		3	1	1	0	86	4	0	2.79							

THEODORE, Jose (TEE-uh-dohr, joh-SAY) MTL.

Goaltender. Catches right. 5'11", 182 lbs. Born, Laval, Que., September 13, 1976.
(Montreal's 2nd choice, 44th overall, in 1994 Entry Draft).

			Regular Season								Playoffs						
Season	Club	League	GP	W	L	T	Mins	GA	SO	Avg	GP	W	L	Mins	GA	SO	Avg
1990-91	Richelieu	QAHA	42	....	....	....	2520	80	0	1.90	....	....	....	....	....	....	....
1991-92	Richelieu Riverains	QAAA	24	9	13	2	1440	96	0	3.99	5	2	3	295	26	0	5.28
1992-93	St-Jean Lynx	QMJHL	34	12	16	2	1776	112	0	3.78	3	0	2	175	11	0	3.77
1993-94	St-Jean Lynx	QMJHL	57	20	29	6	3225	194	0	3.61	5	1	4	296	18	0	3.65
1994-95	Hull Olympiques	QMJHL	*58	*32	22	2	*3348	193	5	3.46	*21	*15	6	*1263	59	*1	2.80
	Fredericton	AHL	....	....	....	....	....	....	....	....	1	0	1	60	3	0	3.00
1995-96	Montreal	NHL	1	0	0	0	9	1	0	6.67	....	....	....	....	....	....	....
	Hull Olympiques	QMJHL	48	33	11	2	2807	158	0	3.38	5	2	3	299	20	0	4.01
1996-97	Montreal	NHL	16	5	6	2	821	53	0	3.87	2	1	1	168	7	0	2.50
	Fredericton	AHL	26	12	12	0	1469	87	0	3.55	....	....	....	....	....	....	....
1997-98	Fredericton	AHL	53	20	23	8	3053	145	2	2.85	4	1	3	237	13	0	3.28
	Montreal	NHL	....	....	....	....	....	....	....	....	3	0	1	120	1	0	0.50
1998-99	Montreal	NHL	18	4	12	0	913	50	1	3.29	....	....	....	....	....	....	....
	Fredericton	AHL	27	12	13	2	1609	77	2	2.87	13	8	5	694	35	1	3.03
99-2000	Montreal	NHL	30	12	13	2	1655	58	5	2.10	....	....	....	....	....	....	....
2000-01	Montreal	NHL	59	20	29	5	3298	141	2	2.57	....	....	....	....	....	....	....
	Quebec Citadelles	AHL	3	3	0	0	180	9	0	3.00	....	....	....	....	....	....	....
2001-02	Montreal	NHL	67	30	24	10	3864	136	7	2.11	12	6	6	686	35	0	3.06
2002-03	Montreal	NHL	57	20	31	6	3419	165	2	2.90	....	....	....	....	....	....	....
	NHL Totals		248	91	115	25	13979	604	17	2.59	17	7	8	974	43	0	2.65

QMJHL Second All-Star Team (1995, 1996) • NHL Second All-Star Team (2002) • MBNA Roger Crozier Saving Grace Award (2002) • Vezina Trophy (2002) • Hart Trophy (2002)

Played in NHL All-Star Game (2002)

• Scored a goal vs. NY Islanders, January 2, 2001.

THIBAULT, Jocelyn (TEE-boh, JAW-seh-lihn) CHI.

Goaltender. Catches left. 5'11", 170 lbs. Born, Montreal, Que., January 12, 1975.
(Quebec's 1st choice, 10th overall, in 1993 Entry Draft).

			Regular Season								Playoffs						
Season	Club	League	GP	W	L	T	Mins	GA	SO	Avg	GP	W	L	Mins	GA	SO	Avg
1990-91	Laval Laurentide	QAAA	20	14	5	0	1178	78	1	3.94	5	2	3	300	20	0	4.00
1991-92	Trois-Rivieres	QMJHL	30	14	7	1	1496	77	0	3.09	3	1	1	110	4	0	2.19
1992-93	Sherbrooke	QMJHL	56	34	14	5	3190	159	3	2.99	15	9	6	882	57	0	3.87
1993-94	Quebec	NHL	29	8	13	3	1504	83	0	3.31	....	....	....	....	....	....	....
	Cornwall Aces	AHL	4	4	0	0	240	9	1	2.25	....	....	....	....	....	....	....
1994-95	Sherbrooke	QMJHL	13	6	6	1	776	38	1	2.94	....	....	....	....	....	....	....
	Quebec	NHL	18	12	2	2	898	35	1	2.34	3	1	2	148	8	0	3.24
1995-96	Colorado	NHL	10	3	4	2	558	28	0	3.01	....	....	....	....	....	....	....
	Montreal	NHL	40	23	13	3	2334	110	3	2.83	6	2	4	311	18	0	3.47
1996-97	Montreal	NHL	61	22	24	11	3397	164	1	2.90	3	0	3	179	13	0	4.36
1997-98	Montreal	NHL	47	19	15	8	2652	109	2	2.47	2	0	0	43	4	0	5.58
1998-99	Montreal	NHL	10	3	4	2	529	23	1	2.61	....	....	....	....	....	....	....
	Chicago	NHL	52	21	26	5	3014	136	4	2.71	....	....	....	....	....	....	....
99-2000	Chicago	NHL	60	25	26	7	3438	158	3	2.76	....	....	....	....	....	....	....
2000-01	Chicago	NHL	66	27	32	7	3844	180	6	2.81	....	....	....	....	....	....	....
2001-02	Chicago	NHL	67	33	23	9	3838	159	6	2.49	3	1	2	159	7	0	2.64
2002-03	Chicago	NHL	62	26	28	7	3650	144	8	2.37	....	....	....	....	....	....	....
	NHL Totals		522	222	210	66	29656	1329	35	2.69	17	4	11	840	50	0	3.57

QMJHL All-Rookie Team (1992) • QMJHL First All-Star Team (1993) • QMJHL MVP (1993) • Canadian Major Junior First All-Star Team (1993) • Canadian Major Junior Goaltender of the Year (1993)

Played in NHL All-Star Game (2003)

Transferred to **Colorado** after **Quebec** franchise relocated, June 21, 1995. Traded to **Montreal** by **Colorado** with Andrei Kovalenko and Martin Rucinsky for Patrick Roy and Mike Keane, December 6, 1995. Traded to **Chicago** by **Montreal** with Dave Manson and Brad Brown for Jeff Hackett, Eric Weinrich, Alain Nasreddine and Tampa Bay's 4th round choice (previously acquired, Montreal selected Chris Dyment) in 1999 Entry Draft, November 16, 1998.

THOMAS, Tim (TAW-mas, TIHM)

Goaltender. Catches left. 5'11", 181 lbs. Born, Flint, MI, April 15, 1974.
(Quebec's 11th choice, 217th overall, in 1994 Entry Draft).

			Regular Season								Playoffs						
Season	Club	League	GP	W	L	T	Mins	GA	SO	Avg	GP	W	L	Mins	GA	SO	Avg
1992-93	Davison Academy	H.S.	27	....	....	....	1580	87	....	3.30	....	....	....	....	....	....	....
1993-94	U. of Vermont	ECAC	*33	15	12	6	1864	94	0	3.03	....	....	....	....	....	....	....
1994-95	U. of Vermont	ECAC	34	18	13	2	2010	90	*4	*2.69	....	....	....	....	....	....	....
1995-96	U. of Vermont	ECAC	37	*26	7	4	*2254	88	*3	*2.34	....	....	....	....	....	....	....
1996-97	U. of Vermont	ECAC	36	22	11	3	2158	101	2	2.81	....	....	....	....	....	....	....
1997-98	HIFK Helsinki	Finland	18	13	4	1	1035	28	2	*1.62	*9	*9	0	*551	14	*3	*1.52
	Birmingham Bulls	ECHL	6	4	1	1	360	13	1	2.17	....	....	....	....	....	....	....
	Houston Aeros	IHL	1	0	1	0	59	4	0	4.01	....	....	....	....	....	....	....
1998-99	HIFK Helsinki	Finland	14	8	3	3	833	31	2	2.23	*11	7	4	*658	25	0	2.28
	Hamilton Bulldogs	AHL	15	6	8	0	837	45	0	3.23	....	....	....	....	....	....	....
	United States	WC-A	2	....	....	....	98	7	0	4.25	....	....	....	....	....	....	....
99-2000	Detroit Vipers	IHL	36	10	21	3	2020	120	1	3.56	....	....	....	....	....	....	....
2000-01	AIK Solna	Sweden	43	....	....	....	2542	105	3	2.48	5	....	....	299	20	0	4.01
2001-02	Karpat Oulu	Finland	32	15	12	5	1937	79	4	2.45	3	1	2	180	12	0	4.00
2002-03	Boston	NHL	4	3	1	0	220	11	0	3.00	....	....	....	....	....	....	....
	Providence Bruins	AHL	35	18	12	5	2049	98	1	2.87	....	....	....	....	....	....	....
	NHL Totals		4	3	1	0	220	11	0	3.00							

ECAC First All-Star Team (1995, 1996) • NCAA East Second All-American Team (1995) • NCAA East First All-American Team (1996)

Signed as a free agent by **Edmonton**, June 4, 1998. Signed as a free agent by **Boston**, August 8, 2002.

THOMPSON, Billy (TAWMP-suhn, BIHL-lee) OTT.

Goaltender. Catches left. 6'2", 200 lbs. Born, Saskatoon, Sask., September 24, 1982.
(Florida's 7th choice, 136th overall, in 2001 Entry Draft).

			Regular Season								Playoffs						
Season	Club	League	GP	W	L	T	Mins	GA	SO	Avg	GP	W	L	Mins	GA	SO	Avg
1997-98	Sask. Contacts	SMHL	23	14	5	3	1336	65	2	2.92	....	....	....	....	....	....	....
1998-99	Lebret Eagles	SJHL	STATISTICS NOT AVAILABLE														
99-2000	Estevan Bruins	SJHL	31	....	....	....	1763	132	1	4.49	5	1	3	328	17	0	3.11
	Prince George	WHL	1	0	1	0	60	5	0	5.00	....	....	....	....	....	....	....
2000-01	Prince George	WHL	57	24	24	3	3185	178	1	3.35	6	2	4	324	22	0	4.07
2001-02	Prince George	WHL	42	20	17	2	2375	108	2	2.73	7	3	4	402	21	0	3.13
2002-03	Prince George	WHL	50	20	26	0	2776	186	0	4.02	5	1	3	239	12	0	3.01
	Binghamton	AHL	1	1	0	0	60	5	0	5.00	....	....	....	....	....	....	....

WHL West Second All-Star Team (2003)

Traded to **Ottawa** by **Florida** with Greg Watson for Jani Hurme, October 1, 2002.

TOIVONEN, Hannu (TOI-voh-nuhn, HA-noo) BOS.

Goaltender. Catches left. 6'2", 191 lbs. Born, Kalvola, Finland, May 18, 1984.
(Boston's 1st choice, 29th overall, in 2002 Entry Draft).

			Regular Season								Playoffs						
Season	Club	League	GP	W	L	T	Mins	GA	SO	Avg	GP	W	L	Mins	GA	SO	Avg
2000-01	HPK Jr.	Finn-Jr.	STATISTICS NOT AVAILABLE														
2001-02	HPK Jr.	Finn-Jr.	31	15	12	4	1877	103	2	3.29	7	3	4	440	31	0	4.23
	HPK-18	Finn-Jr.	5	4	0	1	300	11	0	2.23	....	....	....	....	....	....	....
2002-03	HPK Hameenlinna	Finland	24	16	2	4	1432	54	2	2.26	2	1	1	118	3	1	1.53

TOPPING, Brad (TAW-pihng, BRAD) NYI

Goaltender. Catches left. 6'1", 186 lbs. Born, London, Ont., June 5, 1984.
(NY Islanders' choice, 220th overall, in 2002 Entry Draft).

			Regular Season								Playoffs						
Season	Club	League	GP	W	L	T	Mins	GA	SO	Avg	GP	W	L	Mins	GA	SO	Avg
99-2000	Lambton	OMHA	30	....	....	....	1352	35	8	1.54	....	....	....	....	....	....	....
2000-01	Brampton Battalion	OHL	31	14	10	4	1800	86	1	2.87	2	0	0	36	2	0	3.33
2001-02	Brampton Battalion	OHL	50	19	25	4	2879	164	1	3.42	....	....	....	....	....	....	....
2002-03	Brampton Battalion	OHL	47	23	17	2	2551	127	4	2.99	11	5	5	568	24	*2	2.54

TOSKALA, Vesa (TAWS-kah-lah, VEH-sa) S.J.

Goaltender. Catches left. 5'10", 190 lbs. Born, Tampere, Finland, May 20, 1977.
(San Jose's 4th choice, 90th overall, in 1995 Entry Draft).

			Regular Season								Playoffs						
Season	Club	League	GP	W	L	T	Mins	GA	SO	Avg	GP	W	L	Mins	GA	SO	Avg
1993-94	Ilves Tampere-2	Finn-Jr.	STATISTICS NOT AVAILABLE														
1994-95	Ilves Tampere	Finn-Jr.	17	....	....	....	956	36	....	2.26	....	....	....	....	....	....	....
1995-96	Ilves Tampere	Finn-Jr.	3	....	....	....	180	3	....	1.00	....	....	....	....	....	....	....
	KooVee Tampere	Finland-2	2	....	....	....	119	5	....	2.51	....	....	....	....	....	....	....
	Ilves Tampere	Finland	37	....	....	....	2073	109	1	3.16	2	....	....	78	11	....	8.49
1996-97	Ilves Tampere	Finland	40	22	12	5	2270	108	0	2.85	8	3	5	479	29	0	3.63
1997-98	Ilves Tampere	Finland	43	*26	13	3	2555	118	1	2.77	*9	6	3	519	18	1	2.08
1998-99	Ilves Tampere	Finland	33	21	12	0	1966	70	*5	2.14	4	1	3	248	14	0	3.39
99-2000	Farjestad	Sweden	44	....	....	....	2652	118	3	2.67	7	....	....	439	19	0	2.60
2000-01	Kentucky	AHL	44	22	13	5	2466	114	2	2.77	3	0	3	197	8	0	2.43
2001-02	**San Jose**	**NHL**	**1**	**0**	**0**	**0**	**10**	**0**	**0**	**0.00**	....	....	....	....	....	....	....
	Cleveland Barons	AHL	*62	19	33	7	*3574	178	3	2.99	....	....	....	....	....	....	....
2002-03	**San Jose**	**NHL**	**11**	**4**	**3**	**1**	**537**	**21**	**1**	**2.35**	....	....	....	....	....	....	....
	Cleveland Barons	AHL	49	15	30	2	2824	151	1	3.21	....	....	....	....	....	....	....
	NHL Totals		**12**	**4**	**3**	**1**	**547**	**21**	**1**	**2.30**	....	....	....	....	....	....	....

TREMBLAY, David (TRAHM-blay, DAY-vihd) PHI.

Goaltender. Catches left. 6'2", 180 lbs. Born, Hull, Que., August 16, 1985.
(Philadelphia's 9th choice, 140th overall, in 2003 Entry Draft).

			Regular Season								Playoffs						
Season	Club	League	GP	W	L	T	Mins	GA	SO	Avg	GP	W	L	Mins	GA	SO	Avg
2001-02	Gatineau Intrepide	QAAA	27	13	8	5	....	....	....	3.02	....	....	....	....	....	....	....
2002-03	Hull Olympiques	QMJHL	30	14	9	2	1513	71	0	2.82	1	0	0	8	0	0	0.00

QMJHL All-Rookie Team (2003)

TUGNUTT, Ron (TUHG-nuht, RAWN) DAL.

Goaltender. Catches left. 5'11", 160 lbs. Born, Scarborough, Ont., October 22, 1967.
(Quebec's 4th choice, 81st overall, in 1986 Entry Draft).

			Regular Season								Playoffs						
Season	Club	League	GP	W	L	T	Mins	GA	SO	Avg	GP	W	L	Mins	GA	SO	Avg
1983-84	Tor. Red Wings	MTHL	34	....	....	....	1690	91	3	2.67	....	....	....	....	....	....	....
	Weston Dukes	MTJHL	1	0	0	0	20	2	0	6.00	....	....	....	....	....	....	....
1984-85	Peterborough	OHL	18	7	4	2	938	59	0	3.77	....	....	....	....	....	....	....
1985-86	Peterborough	OHL	26	18	7	0	1543	74	1	2.88	3	2	0	133	6	0	2.71
1986-87	Peterborough	OHL	31	21	7	2	1891	88	2	*2.79	6	3	3	374	21	1	3.37
1987-88	**Quebec**	**NHL**	**6**	**2**	**3**	**0**	**284**	**16**	**0**	**3.38**	....	....	....	....	....	....	....
	Fredericton Express	AHL	34	20	9	4	1964	118	1	3.60	4	1	2	204	11	0	3.24
1988-89	**Quebec**	**NHL**	**26**	**10**	**10**	**3**	**1367**	**82**	**0**	**3.60**	....	....	....	....	....	....	....
	Halifax Citadels	AHL	24	14	7	2	1368	79	1	3.46	....	....	....	....	....	....	....
1989-90	**Quebec**	**NHL**	**35**	**5**	**24**	**3**	**1978**	**152**	**0**	**4.61**	....	....	....	....	....	....	....
	Halifax Citadels	AHL	6	1	5	0	366	23	0	3.77	....	....	....	....	....	....	....
1990-91	**Quebec**	**NHL**	**56**	**12**	**29**	**10**	**3144**	**212**	**0**	**4.05**	....	....	....	....	....	....	....
	Halifax Citadels	AHL	2	0	1	0	100	8	0	4.80	....	....	....	....	....	....	....
1991-92	**Quebec**	**NHL**	**30**	**6**	**17**	**3**	**1583**	**106**	**1**	**4.02**	....	....	....	....	....	....	....
	Halifax Citadels	AHL	8	3	3	1	447	30	0	4.03	....	....	....	....	....	....	....
	Edmonton	**NHL**	**3**	**1**	**1**	**0**	**124**	**10**	**0**	**4.84**	**2**	**0**	**0**	**60**	**3**	**0**	**3.00**
1992-93	**Edmonton**	**NHL**	**26**	**9**	**12**	**2**	**1338**	**93**	**0**	**4.17**	....	....	....	....	....	....	....
1993-94	**Anaheim**	**NHL**	**28**	**10**	**15**	**1**	**1520**	**76**	**1**	**3.00**	....	....	....	....	....	....	....
	Montreal	**NHL**	**8**	**2**	**3**	**1**	**378**	**24**	**0**	**3.81**	**1**	**0**	**1**	**59**	**5**	**0**	**5.08**
1994-95	**Montreal**	**NHL**	**7**	**1**	**3**	**1**	**346**	**18**	**0**	**3.12**	....	....	....	....	....	....	....
1995-96	Portland Pirates	AHL	58	21	23	6	3068	171	2	3.34	13	7	6	782	36	1	2.76
1996-97	**Ottawa**	**NHL**	**37**	**17**	**15**	**1**	**1991**	**93**	**3**	**2.80**	**7**	**3**	**4**	**425**	**14**	**1**	**1.98**
1997-98	**Ottawa**	**NHL**	**42**	**15**	**14**	**8**	**2236**	**84**	**3**	**2.25**	**2**	**0**	**1**	**74**	**6**	**0**	**4.86**
1998-99	**Ottawa**	**NHL**	**43**	**22**	**10**	**8**	**2508**	**75**	**3**	***1.79**	**2**	**0**	**2**	**118**	**6**	**0**	**3.05**
99-2000	**Ottawa**	**NHL**	**44**	**18**	**12**	**8**	**2435**	**103**	**4**	**2.54**	....	....	....	....	....	....	....
	Pittsburgh	**NHL**	**7**	**4**	**2**	**0**	**374**	**15**	**0**	**2.41**	**11**	**6**	**5**	**746**	**22**	**2**	**1.77**
2000-01	**Columbus**	**NHL**	**53**	**22**	**25**	**5**	**3129**	**127**	**4**	**2.44**	....	....	....	....	....	....	....
2001-02	**Columbus**	**NHL**	**44**	**12**	**27**	**3**	**2502**	**119**	**2**	**2.85**	....	....	....	....	....	....	....
2002-03	**Dallas**	**NHL**	**31**	**15**	**10**	**5**	**1701**	**70**	**4**	**2.47**	....	....	....	....	....	....	....
	NHL Totals		**526**	**183**	**232**	**62**	**28938**	**1475**	**25**	**3.06**	**25**	**9**	**13**	**1482**	**56**	**3**	**2.27**

OHL First All-Star Team (1987)

Played in NHL All-Star Game (1999)

Traded to **Edmonton** by **Quebec** with Brad Zavisha for Martin Rucinsky, March 10, 1992. Claimed by **Anaheim** from **Edmonton** in Expansion Draft, June 24, 1993. Traded to **Montreal** by **Anaheim** for Stephan Lebeau, February 20, 1994. Signed as a free agent by **Washington**, September 25, 1995. Signed as a free agent by **Ottawa**, August 14, 1996. Traded to **Pittsburgh** by **Ottawa** with Janne Laukkanen for Tom Barrasso, March 14, 2000. Signed as a free agent by **Columbus**, July 4, 2000. Traded to **Dallas** by **Columbus** with Columbus' 2nd round choice (Janos Vas) in 2002 Entry Draft for New Jersey's 1st round choice (previously acquired, later traded to Buffalo – Buffalo selected Dan Paille) in 2002 Entry Draft, June 18, 2002.

TURCO, Marty (TUHR-koh, MAHR-tee) DAL.

Goaltender. Catches left. 5'11", 183 lbs. Born, Sault Ste. Marie, Ont., August 13, 1975.
(Dallas' 4th choice, 124th overall, in 1994 Entry Draft).

			Regular Season								Playoffs						
Season	Club	League	GP	W	L	T	Mins	GA	SO	Avg	GP	W	L	Mins	GA	SO	Avg
1993-94	Cambridge	OJHL-B	34	19	10	3	1973	114	0	3.47	....	....	....	....	....	....	....
1994-95	U. of Michigan	CCHA	37	*27	7	1	2063	95	1	2.76	....	....	....	....	....	....	....
1995-96	U. of Michigan	CCHA	*42	*34	7	1	*2335	84	*5	*2.16	....	....	....	....	....	....	....
1996-97	U. of Michigan	CCHA	*41	*33	4	4	*2296	87	*4	*2.27	....	....	....	....	....	....	....
1997-98	U. of Michigan	CCHA	*45	*33	10	1	*2640	95	4	2.16	....	....	....	....	....	....	....
1998-99	Michigan K-Wings	IHL	54	24	17	10	3127	136	1	2.61	5	2	3	300	14	0	2.80
99-2000	Michigan K-Wings	IHL	60	23	27	*7	3399	139	*7	2.45	....	....	....	....	....	....	....
2000-01	**Dallas**	**NHL**	**26**	**13**	**6**	**1**	**1266**	**40**	**3**	***1.90**	....	....	....	....	....	....	....
2001-02	**Dallas**	**NHL**	**31**	**15**	**6**	**2**	**1519**	**53**	**2**	**2.09**	....	....	....	....	....	....	....
2002-03	**Dallas**	**NHL**	**55**	**31**	**10**	**10**	**3203**	**92**	**7**	***1.72**	**12**	**6**	**6**	**798**	**25**	**0**	**1.88**
	NHL Totals		**112**	**59**	**22**	**13**	**5988**	**185**	**12**	**1.85**	**12**	**6**	**6**	**798**	**25**	**0**	**1.88**

CCHA Rookie of the Year (1995) • NCAA Championship All-Tournament Team (1996, 1998) • CCHA First All-Star Team (1997) • NCAA West First All-American Team (1997) • CCHA Second All-Star Team (1998) • NCAA Championship Tournament MVP (1998) • Garry F. Longman Memorial Trophy (Top Rookie – IHL) (1999) • MBNA Roger Crozier Saving Grace Award (2001, 2003) • NHL Second All-Star Team (2003)

Played in NHL All-Star Game (2003)

TUREK, Roman (TOOR-ehk, ROH-muhn) CGY.

Goaltender. Catches right. 6'3", 220 lbs. Born, Strakonice, Czech., May 21, 1970.
(Minnesota's 6th choice, 113th overall, in 1990 Entry Draft).

			Regular Season								Playoffs						
Season	Club	League	GP	W	L	T	Mins	GA	SO	Avg	GP	W	L	Mins	GA	SO	Avg
1990-91	Ceske Budejovice	Czech	26	....	....	....	1244	98	0	4.73	....	....	....	....	....	....	....
1991-92	Ceske Budejovice	Czech-2	STATISTICS NOT AVAILABLE														
1992-93	Ceske Budejovice	Czech	43	....	....	....	2555	121	....	2.84	....	....	....	....	....	....	....
1993-94	Ceske Budejovice	Czech	44	....	....	....	2584	111	....	2.58	3	....	....	180	12	0	4.00
	Czech Republic	Olympics	2	2	0	0	120	3	0	1.50	....	....	....	....	....	....	....
1994-95	Ceske Budejovice	Czech	44	....	....	....	2587	119	....	2.76	9	....	....	498	25	....	3.01
1995-96	Nurnberg	Germany	48	....	....	....	2787	154	....	3.32	5	....	....	338	14	....	2.48
1996-97	**Dallas**	**NHL**	**6**	**3**	**1**	**0**	**263**	**9**	**0**	**2.05**	....	....	....	....	....	....	....
	Michigan K-Wings	IHL	29	8	13	4	1555	77	0	2.97	....	....	....	....	....	....	....
1997-98	**Dallas**	**NHL**	**23**	**11**	**10**	**1**	**1324**	**49**	**1**	**2.22**	....	....	....	....	....	....	....
	Michigan K-Wings	IHL	2	1	1	0	119	5	0	2.52	....	....	....	....	....	....	....
1998-99 ♦	**Dallas**	**NHL**	**26**	**16**	**3**	**3**	**1382**	**48**	**1**	**2.08**	....	....	....	....	....	....	....
99-2000	**St. Louis**	**NHL**	**67**	**42**	**15**	**9**	**3960**	**129**	***7**	**1.95**	**7**	**3**	**4**	**415**	**19**	**0**	**2.75**
2000-01	**St. Louis**	**NHL**	**54**	**24**	**18**	**10**	**3232**	**123**	**6**	**2.28**	**14**	**9**	**5**	**908**	**31**	**0**	**2.05**
2001-02	**Calgary**	**NHL**	**69**	**30**	**28**	**11**	**4081**	**172**	**5**	**2.53**	....	....	....	....	....	....	....
2002-03	**Calgary**	**NHL**	**65**	**27**	**29**	**9**	**3822**	**164**	**4**	**2.57**	....	....	....	....	....	....	....
	NHL Totals		**310**	**153**	**104**	**43**	**18064**	**694**	**24**	**2.31**	**21**	**12**	**9**	**1323**	**50**	**0**	**2.27**

Shared William M. Jennings Trophy (1999) with Ed Belfour • NHL Second All-Star Team (2000) • William M. Jennings Trophy (2000)

Played in NHL All-Star Game (2000)

Rights transferred to **Dallas** after **Minnesota** franchise relocated, June 9, 1993. Traded to **St. Louis** by **Dallas** for St. Louis' compensatory 2nd round choice (Dan Jancevski) in 1999 Entry Draft, June 20, 1999. Traded to **Calgary** by **St. Louis** with St. Louis' 4th round choice (Yegor Shastin) in 2001 Entry Draft for Fred Brathwaite, Daniel Tkaczuk, Sergei Varlamov and Calgary's 9th round choice (Grant Jacobsen) in 2001 Entry Draft, June 23, 2001.

VALIQUETTE, Steve (val-ih-KEHT, STEEV) EDM.

Goaltender. Catches left. 6'5", 205 lbs. Born, Etobicoke, Ont., August 20, 1977.
(Los Angeles' 8th choice, 190th overall, in 1996 Entry Draft).

			Regular Season								Playoffs						
Season	Club	League	GP	W	L	T	Mins	GA	SO	Avg	GP	W	L	Mins	GA	SO	Avg
1993-94	Burlington	OPJHL	30	....	....	....	1663	112	1	4.04	....	....	....	....	....	....	....
1994-95	Rayside-Balfour	NOJHA	2	0	2	0	89	12	0	8.09	....	....	....	....	....	....	....
	Smiths Falls Bears	OCJHL	21	10	8	3	1275	75	0	3.53	....	....	....	....	....	....	....
	Sudbury Wolves	OHL	4	2	0	0	138	6	0	2.61	....	....	....	....	....	....	....
1995-96	Sudbury Wolves	OHL	39	13	16	2	1887	123	0	3.91	....	....	....	....	....	....	....
1996-97	Sudbury Wolves	OHL	*61	21	29	7	3311	232	1	4.20	....	....	....	....	....	....	....
	Dayton Bombers	ECHL	3	1	0	0	89	6	0	4.03	2	1	1	118	5	0	2.54
1997-98	Sudbury Wolves	OHL	14	5	7	1	807	50	0	3.72	....	....	....	....	....	....	....
	Erie Otters	OHL	28	16	7	3	1525	65	3	2.56	7	3	4	467	15	1	1.93
1998-99	Hampton Roads	ECHL	31	18	7	3	1713	84	1	2.94	2	0	1	60	7	0	7.00
	Lowell	AHL	1	0	1	0	59	3	0	3.05	....	....	....	....	....	....	....
99-2000	**NY Islanders**	**NHL**	**6**	**2**	**0**	**0**	**193**	**6**	**0**	**1.87**	....	....	....	....	....	....	....
	Lowell	AHL	14	8	5	0	727	36	0	2.97	....	....	....	....	....	....	....
	Providence Bruins	AHL	1	1	0	0	60	3	0	3.00	....	....	....	....	....	....	....
	Trenton Titans	ECHL	12	5	6	1	692	36	1	3.12	....	....	....	....	....	....	....
2000-01	Springfield Falcons	AHL	20	7	10	1	1066	54	0	3.04	....	....	....	....	....	....	....
2001-02	Bridgeport	AHL	20	10	5	1	1071	45	2	2.52	1	0	0	18	1	0	3.30
2002-03	Bridgeport	AHL	34	15	14	3	1962	86	2	2.63	4	3	1	253	9	0	2.13
	NHL Totals		**6**	**2**	**0**	**0**	**193**	**6**	**0**	**1.87**	....	....	....	....	....	....	....

Signed as a free agent by **NY Islanders**, August 18, 1998. Signed as a free agent by **Edmonton**, July 20, 2003.

VIOLIN, Matt (vigh-oh-LIHN, MAT) VAN.

Goaltender. Catches left. 6'1", 180 lbs. Born, Etobicoke, Ont., February 8, 1982.
(Vancouver's 9th choice, 247th overall, in 2002 Entry Draft).

			Regular Season								Playoffs						
Season	Club	League	GP	W	L	T	Mins	GA	SO	Avg	GP	W	L	Mins	GA	SO	Avg
2001-02	Lake Superior State	CCHA	21	4	11	2	1060	54	0	3.06	....	....	....	....	....	....	....
2002-03	Lake Superior State	CCHA	31	4	23	3	1572	96	1	3.66	....	....	....	....	....	....	....

VOKOUN, Tomas (voh-KOON, TAW-mas) NSH.

Goaltender. Catches right. 6', 195 lbs. Born, Karlovy Vary, Czech., July 2, 1976.
(Montreal's 11th choice, 226th overall, in 1994 Entry Draft).

			Regular Season								Playoffs						
Season	Club	League	GP	W	L	T	Mins	GA	SO	Avg	GP	W	L	Mins	GA	SO	Avg
1993-94	HC Kladno	Czech	1	0	0	0	20	2	0	6.01	....	....	....	....	....	....	....
1994-95	HC Kladno	Czech	26	....	....	....	1368	70	....	3.07	5	....	....	240	19	....	4.75
1995-96	Wheeling	ECHL	35	20	10	2	1912	117	0	3.67	7	4	3	436	19	0	2.61
	Fredericton	AHL	....	....	....	....	....	....	....	....	1	0	1	59	4	0	4.09
1996-97	**Montreal**	**NHL**	**1**	**0**	**0**	**0**	**20**	**4**	**0**	**12.00**	....	....	....	....	....	....	....
	Fredericton	AHL	47	12	26	7	2645	154	2	3.49	....	....	....	....	....	....	....
1997-98	Fredericton	AHL	31	13	13	2	1735	90	0	3.11	....	....	....	....	....	....	....
1998-99	**Nashville**	**NHL**	**37**	**12**	**18**	**4**	**1954**	**96**	**1**	**2.95**	....	....	....	....	....	....	....
	Milwaukee	IHL	9	3	2	4	539	22	1	2.45	2	0	2	149	8	0	3.22
99-2000	**Nashville**	**NHL**	**33**	**9**	**20**	**1**	**1879**	**87**	**1**	**2.78**	....	....	....	....	....	....	....
	Milwaukee	IHL	7	5	2	0	364	17	0	2.80	....	....	....	....	....	....	....
2000-01	**Nashville**	**NHL**	**37**	**13**	**17**	**5**	**2088**	**85**	**2**	**2.44**	....	....	....	....	....	....	....
2001-02	**Nashville**	**NHL**	**29**	**5**	**14**	**4**	**1471**	**66**	**2**	**2.69**	....	....	....	....	....	....	....
2002-03	**Nashville**	**NHL**	**69**	**25**	**31**	**11**	**3974**	**146**	**3**	**2.20**	....	....	....	....	....	....	....
	NHL Totals		**206**	**64**	**100**	**25**	**11386**	**484**	**9**	**2.55**	....	....	....	....	....	....	....

Claimed by **Nashville** from **Montreal** in Expansion Draft, June 26, 1998.

WARD, Cam (WOHRD, KAM) CAR.

Goaltender. Catches left. 6', 176 lbs. Born, Sherwood Park, Alta., February 29, 1984.
(Carolina's 1st choice, 25th overall, in 2002 Entry Draft).

			Regular Season								Playoffs						
Season	Club	League	GP	W	L	T	Mins	GA	SO	Avg	GP	W	L	Mins	GA	SO	Avg
1998-99	Sherwood Park	ABHL	24	13	7	4	1403	85	0	3.64	....	....	....	....	....	....	....
99-2000	Sherwood Park	AMHL	20	9	5	1	1194	71	0	3.57	7	4	3	262	22	0	3.57
2000-01	Sherwood Park	AMHL	25	14	6	3	1449	70	0	2.90	....	....	....	....	....	....	....
	Red Deer Rebels	WHL	1	1	0	0	60	0	1	0.00	....	....	....	....	....	....	....
2001-02	Red Deer Rebels	WHL	46	30	11	4	2694	102	1	*2.27	*23	14	9	*1502	53	*2	2.12
2002-03	Red Deer Rebels	WHL	57	*40	13	3	3368	118	5	2.10	*23	14	9	*1407	49	3	2.09

Bill Ranford Trophy (Top Goaltender – AMHL) (2001) • WHL East First All-Star Team (2002) • WHL East Second All-Star Team (2003)

WEEKES, Kevin (WEEKS, KEH-vihn) CAR.

Goaltender. Catches left. 6', 195 lbs. Born, Toronto, Ont., April 4, 1975.
(Florida's 2nd choice, 41st overall, in 1993 Entry Draft).

			Regular Season								Playoffs						
Season	Club	League	GP	W	L	T	Mins	GA	SO	Avg	GP	W	L	Mins	GA	SO	Avg
1990-91	Tor. Red Wings	MTHL	STATISTICS NOT AVAILABLE														
	St. Michael's B	MTJHL	1	0	0	0	41	1	0	1.46	....	....	....	....	....	....	....
1991-92	Tor. Red Wings	MTHL	35	....	....	....	1575	68	4	1.94	....	....	....	....	....	....	....
	St. Michael's B	MTJHL	2	0	1	1	127	11	0	5.20	4	1	2	214	15	1	4.21
1992-93	Owen Sound	OHL	29	9	12	5	1645	143	0	5.22	1	0	0	26	5	0	11.50
1993-94	Owen Sound	OHL	34	13	19	1	1974	158	0	4.80	....	....	....	....	....	....	....
1994-95	Ottawa 67's	OHL	41	13	23	4	2266	153	1	4.05	....	....	....	....	....	....	....
1995-96	Carolina Monarchs	AHL	60	24	25	8	3404	229	2	4.04	....	....	....	....	....	....	....
1996-97	Carolina Monarchs	AHL	51	17	28	4	2899	172	1	3.56	....	....	....	....	....	....	....
1997-98	**Florida**	**NHL**	**11**	**0**	**5**	**1**	**485**	**32**	**0**	**3.96**	....	....	....	....	....	....	....
	Fort Wayne	IHL	12	9	2	1	719	34	1	2.84	....	....	....	....	....	....	....
1998-99	**Vancouver**	**NHL**	**11**	**0**	**8**	**1**	**532**	**34**	**0**	**3.83**	....	....	....	....	....	....	....
	Detroit Vipers	IHL	33	19	5	7	1857	64	*4	*2.07	....	....	....	....	....	....	....
99-2000	**Vancouver**	**NHL**	**20**	**6**	**7**	**4**	**987**	**47**	**1**	**2.86**	....	....	....	....	....	....	....
	NY Islanders	**NHL**	**36**	**10**	**20**	**4**	**2026**	**115**	**1**	**3.41**	....	....	....	....	....	....	....
2000-01	**Tampa Bay**	**NHL**	**61**	**20**	**33**	**3**	**3378**	**177**	**4**	**3.14**	....	....	....	....	....	....	....

Season	Club	League	GP	W	L	T	Mins	GA	SO	Avg	GP	W	L	Mins	GA	SO	Avg
2001-02	Tampa Bay	NHL	19	3	9	0	830	40	2	2.89	....	..	..	....	...	..	....
	Carolina	NHL	2	2	0	0	120	3	0	1.50	8	3	2	408	11	2	1.62
2002-03	Carolina	NHL	51	14	24	9	2965	126	5	2.55	....	..	..	....	...	..	....
	NHL Totals		211	55	106	22	11323	574	13	3.04	8	3	2	408	11	2	1.62

Shared James Norris Memorial Trophy (fewest goals against – IHL) (1999) with Andrei Trefilov.
Traded to **Vancouver** by **Florida** with Ed Jovanovski, Dave Gagner, Mike Brown and Florida's 1st round choice (Nathan Smith) in 2000 Entry Draft for Pavel Bure, Bret Hedican, Brad Ference and Vancouver's 3rd round choice (Robert Fried) in 2000 Entry Draft, January 17, 1999. Traded to **NY Islanders** by **Vancouver** with Dave Scatchard and Bill Muckalt for Felix Potvin, NY Islanders' compensatory 2nd round choice (later traded to New Jersey – New Jersey selected Teemu Laine) in 2000 Entry Draft and NY Islanders' 3rd round choice (Thatcher Bell) in 2000 Entry Draft, December 19, 1999. Traded to **Tampa Bay** by **NY Islanders** with the rights to Kristian Kudroc and NY Islanders' 2nd round choice (later traded to Phoenix – Phoenix selected Matthew Spiller) in 2001 Entry Draft for Tampa Bay's 1st round choice (Raffi Torres) in 2000 Entry Draft, Calgary's 4th round choice (previously acquired, NY Islanders selected Vladimir Gorbunov) in 2000 Entry Draft and NY Islanders' 7th round choice (previously acquired, NY Islanders selected Ryan Caldwell) in 2000 Entry Draft, June 24, 2000. Traded to **Carolina** by **Tampa Bay** for Shane Willis and Chris Dingman, March 5, 2002.

WEIMAN, Tyler

(WIGH-muhn, TIGH-luhr) **COL.**

Goaltender. Catches left. 5'11", 160 lbs. Born, Saskatoon, Sask., June 5, 1984.
(Colorado's 6th choice, 164th overall, in 2002 Entry Draft).

Season	Club	League	GP	W	L	T	Mins	GA	SO	Avg	GP	W	L	Mins	GA	SO	Avg
99-2000	Ft-Saskatchewan	AMBHL	21	15	4	2	1239	60	0	2.91	....	..	..	....	...	..	....
2000-01	Tri-City Americans	WHL	44	10	25	4	2464	155	0	3.77	....	..	..	....	...	..	....
2001-02	Tri-City Americans	WHL	47	18	17	5	2492	149	2	3.59	5	1	4	300	14	0	2.80
2002-03	Tri-City Americans	WHL	55	16	34	2	3129	207	1	3.97	....	..	..	....	...	..	....

YEATS, Matthew

(YAYTS, MA-thew)

Goaltender. Catches left. 5'11", 165 lbs. Born, Montreal, Que., April 6, 1979.
(Los Angeles' 9th choice, 248th overall, in 1998 Entry Draft).

Season	Club	League	GP	W	L	T	Mins	GA	SO	Avg	GP	W	L	Mins	GA	SO	Avg
1995-96	Lethbridge	WHL	1	0	0	0	20	3	0	9.00	....	..	..	....	...	..	....
1996-97	Olds Grizzlies	AJHL	32	....	....	....	1678	95	1	3.41	....	..	..	....	...	..	....
1997-98	Olds Grizzlies	AJHL	26	12	12	1	1498	96	0	3.85	....	..	..	....	...	..	....

1998-99	University of Maine	H-East						DID NOT PLAY									
99-2000	University of Maine	H-East	32	20	6	4	1821	79	0	2.60	....	..	..	....	...	..	....
2000-01	University of Maine	H-East	33	18	9	4	1897	76	2	2.40	....	..	..	....	...	..	....
2001-02	University of Maine	H-East	20	6	8	3	1048	54	0	3.09	....	..	..	....	...	..	....
2002-03	Philadelphia	AHL	2	1	1	0	90	4	0	2.67	....	..	..	....	...	..	....
	Atlantic City	ECHL	48	23	16	8	2811	141	4	3.01	8	4	1	397	16	1	2.42

• Ruled ineligible to play 1998-99 season by NCAA due to appearance with **Lethbridge** (WHL) in 1995-96.

ZEPP, Rob

(ZEHP, RAWB) **CAR.**

Goaltender. Catches left. 6'1", 181 lbs. Born, Scarborough, Ont., September 7, 1981.
(Carolina's 4th choice, 110th overall, in 2001 Entry Draft).

Season	Club	League	GP	W	L	T	Mins	GA	SO	Avg	GP	W	L	Mins	GA	SO	Avg
1997-98	Newmarket	OPJHL	3	....	....	....	181	13	0	4.31	....	..	..	....	...	..	....
1998-99	Plymouth Whalers	OHL	31	19	3	4	1662	76	3	2.74	3	1	0	100	10	0	6.00
99-2000	Plymouth Whalers	OHL	53	*36	11	3	3005	119	3	*2.38	*23	*15	8	*1374	52	2	2.27
2000-01	Plymouth Whalers	OHL	55	*34	18	3	3246	122	*4	*2.26	19	14	5	1139	51	2	2.69
2001-02	Florida Everblades	ECHL	13	6	5	2	739	41	0	3.33	....	..	..	....	...	..	....
2002-03	Lowell	AHL	5	1	3	1	303	16	1	3.16	....	..	..	....	...	..	....
	Florida Everblades	ECHL	41	20	13	7	2372	112	3	2.83	....	..	..	....	...	..	....

• Re-entered NHL Entry Draft. Originally Atlanta's 5th choice, 99th overall, in 1999 Entry Draft.
Canadian Major Junior Scholastic Player of the Year (1999) • OHL Second All-Star Team (2000, 2001)
• Missed majority of 2001-02 season recovering from groin injury suffered in practice, January 3, 2002.

In Memory of Two Coaching Greats
Herb Brooks and Roger Neilson

Herb Brooks
1937–2003

Roger Neilson
1934–2003

*T*HE SPORT OF HOCKEY LOST TWO FRIENDS IN THE SUMMER OF *2003. On June 21, Roger Neilson passed away after a lengthy battle with cancer. Herb Brooks died on August 11, killed in a car accident on a Minnesota highway.*

Brooks and Neilson first came to the attention of most hockey fans at about the same time: Roger coached the Toronto Maple Leafs from 1977 to 1979 and Herb was the guiding force behind the 1980 Lake Placid "Miracle on Ice" U.S. Olympic hockey team. But both men had extensive accomplishments in hockey by this time.

Herb Brooks (born August 5, 1937) had been the last player cut from the 1960 squad that won the gold medal in hockey at the Squaw Valley Winter Olympics. He later played on U.S. Olympic teams in 1964 and 1968 and U.S. national teams in 1962, 1965, 1967 and 1970. Brooks was a collegiate player at the University of Minnesota from 1955 to 1959, and he became coach there in 1972. He transformed the last-place Gophers into NCAA champions in 1974, 1976 and 1979 before going on to guide the U.S. gold medal team.

Roger Neilson (born June 16, 1934) was already coaching youth baseball and hockey at the time Brooks was winding up his college playing career. Roger taught high school in the suburbs of Toronto and was soon coaching Junior B hockey. In 1966, at the age of 32, he left Toronto to coach the Peterborough Petes of the Ontario Hockey Association. It was only at this time that he finally gave up the paper route he had been operating since he was nine years old! In his ten years in Peterborough, Neilson's Petes finished in third place or better on eight occasions, and reached the Memorial Cup tournament in 1972. He also was a pioneer in the use of video tape as a teaching tool, a technique he would soon introduce to the NHL.

After Lake Placid, there was immediate speculation that Herb Brooks would be hired by the New York Rangers. Instead, he wound up in Switzerland for a year before joining his former Olympic assistant, Craig Patrick, in New York in 1981–82. Brooks recorded 100 wins faster than any Rangers coach before him and is just one of seven men in the team's history to reach that mark. He later coached the Minnesota North Stars, New Jersey Devils and Pittsburgh Penguins, as well as the 1998 French Olympic team and the silver-medal winning 2002 U.S. Olympic team. Herb Brooks was elected to the United States Hockey Hall of Fame in 1990.

Though both Brooks and Neilson were master motivators, Herb was a figure of authority while Roger seemed to be everybody's friend. The two different styles served each man well. Neilson served with 10 different teams during his NHL career, and was the head coach with seven of them. He was working as an assistant with the Ottawa Senators when he was allowed to take over the team for the final two games of the 2000-01 season in order to reach the 1,000-game plateau. He also is one of only 13 coaches to have recorded 400 wins (460-381-159).

Throughout his NHL career, Roger Neilson continued to operate hockey schools for children and run coaching clinics for future leaders of the game. He was elected to the Hockey Hall of Fame as a builder in 2002 and was appointed to the Order of Canada in 2003.

Both men contributed much to hockey, making their players and colleagues better on-ice and off.

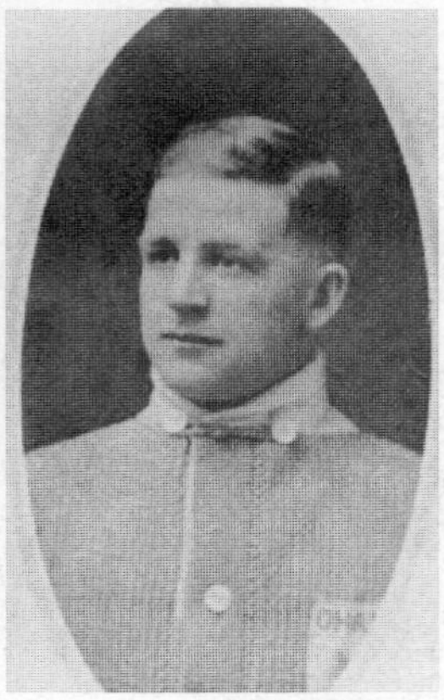

Jack Adams

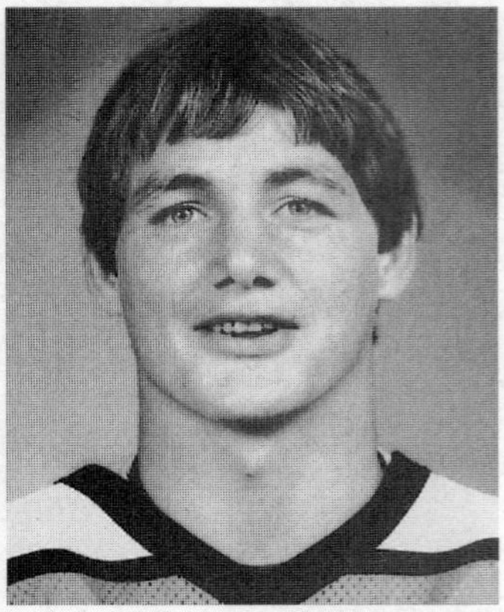

Ray Allison

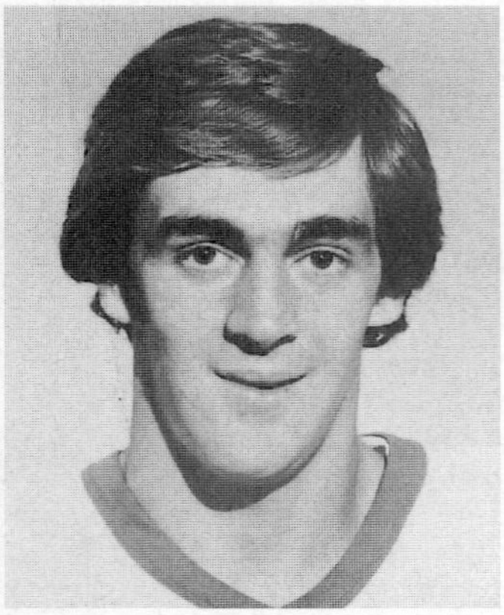

Pierre Aubry

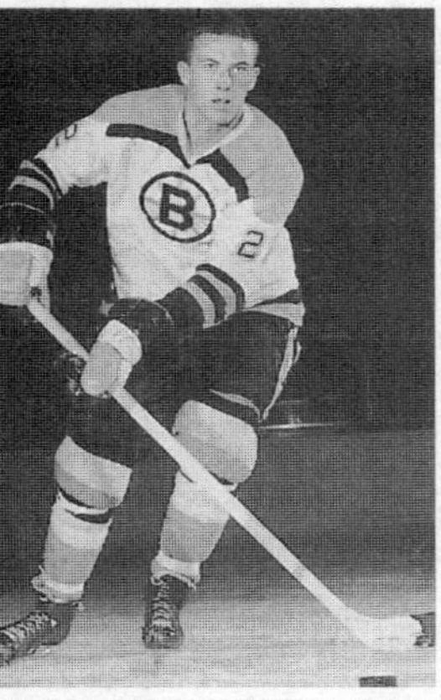

Don Awrey

Retired NHL Player Index

Abbreviations: Teams/Cities: – **Ana.** – Anaheim; **Atl.** – Atlanta; **Bos.** – Boston; **Bro.** – Brooklyn; **Buf.** – Buffalo; **Cal.** – California; **Cgy.** – Calgary; **Cle.** – Cleveland; **Col.** – Colorado; **CBJ** – Columbus; **Dal.** – Dallas; **Det.** – Detroit; **Edm.** – Edmonton; **Fla.** – Florida; **Ham.** – Hamilton; **Hfd.** – Hartford;
K.C. – Kansas City; **L.A.** – Los Angeles; **Min.** – Minnesota; **Mtl.** – Montreal; **Mtl.M.** – Montreal Maroons; **Mtl.W.** – Montreal Wanderers;
N.J. – New Jersey; **NYA** – NY Americans; **NYI** – NY Islanders; **NYR** – New York Rangers; – **Oak.** – Oakland; **Ott.** – Ottawa; – **Phi.** – Philadelphia;
Phx. – Phoenix; **Pit.** – Pittsburgh; **Que.** – Quebec; **St.L.** – St. Louis; **S.J.** – San Jose; **T.B.** – Tampa Bay; **Tor.** – Toronto; **Van.** – Vancouver;
Wpg. – Winnipeg; **Wsh.** – Washington

Total seasons are rounded off to the nearest full season. **A** – assists; **G** – goals; **GP** – games played; **PIM** – penalties in minutes; **TP** – total points.
• – deceased. Assists not recorded during 1917-18 season ‡ – Remains active in other leagues.

A

Name	NHL Teams	NHL Seasons	Regular Schedule GP	G	A	TP	PIM	Playoffs GP	G	A	TP	PIM	NHL Cup Wins	First NHL Season	Last NHL Season
‡ Aalto, Antti	Ana.	4	151	11	17	28	52	4	0	0	0	2	....	1997-98	2000-01
Abbott, Reg	Mtl.	1	3	0	0	0	0	....	....	....	....	....	....	1952-53	1952-53
• Abel, Clarence	NYR, Chi.	8	333	19	18	37	359	38	1	1	2	58	2	1926-27	1933-34
Abel, Gerry	Det.	1	1	0	0	0	0	....	....	....	....	....	....	1966-67	1966-67
• Abel, Sid	Det., Chi.	14	612	189	283	472	376	97	28	30	58	79	3	1938-39	1953-54
Abgrall, Dennis	L.A.	1	13	0	2	2	4	....	....	....	....	....	....	1975-76	1975-76
Abrahamsson, Thommy	Hfd.	1	32	6	11	17	16	....	....	....	....	....	....	1980-81	1980-81
Achtymichuk, Gene	Mtl., Det.	4	32	3	5	8	2	....	....	....	....	....	....	1951-52	1958-59
Acomb, Doug	Tor.	1	2	0	1	1	0	....	....	....	....	....	....	1969-70	1969-70
Acton, Keith	Mtl., Min., Edm., Phi., Wsh., NYI	15	1023	226	358	584	1172	66	12	21	33	88	1	1979-80	1993-94
Adam, Douglas	NYR	1	4	0	1	1	0	....	....	....	....	....	....	1949-50	1949-50
Adam, Russ	Tor.	1	8	1	2	3	11	....	....	....	....	....	....	1982-83	1982-83
Adams, Greg	Phi., Hfd., Wsh., Edm., Van., Que., Det.	10	545	84	143	227	1173	43	2	11	13	153	....	1980-81	1989-90
Adams, Greg	N.J., Van., Dal., Phx., Fla.	17	1056	355	388	743	326	81	20	22	42	16	....	1984-85	2000-01
• Adams, Jack	Tor., Ott.	7	173	83	32	115	366	10	1	0	1	13	2	1917-18	1926-27
Adams, John	Mtl.	1	42	6	12	18	11	3	0	0	0	0	....	1940-41	1940-41
• Adams, Stew	Chi., Tor.	4	95	9	26	35	60	11	3	3	6	14	....	1929-30	1932-33
Adduono, Rick	Bos., Atl.	2	4	0	0	0	2	....	....	....	....	....	....	1975-76	1979-80
Affleck, Bruce	St.L., Van., NYI	7	280	14	66	80	86	8	0	0	0	0	....	1974-75	1983-84
Agnew, Jim	Van., Hfd.	6	81	0	1	1	257	4	0	0	0	6	....	1986-87	1992-93
Ahern, Fred	Cal., Cle., Col.	4	146	31	30	61	130	2	0	1	1	2	....	1974-75	1977-78
Ahlin, Tony	Chi.	1	1	0	0	0	0	....	....	....	....	....	....	1937-38	1937-38
‡ Ahola, Peter	L.A., Pit., S.J., Cgy.	3	123	10	17	27	137	6	0	0	0	2	....	1991-92	1993-94
Ahrens, Chris	Min.	6	52	0	3	3	84	1	0	0	0	0	....	1972-73	1977-78
Ailsby, Lloyd	NYR	1	3	0	0	0	2	....	....	....	....	....	....	1951-52	1951-52
Aitken, Brad	Pit., Edm.	2	14	1	3	4	25	....	....	....	....	....	....	1987-88	1990-91
‡ Aivazoff, Micah	Det., Edm., NYI	3	92	4	6	10	46	....	....	....	....	....	....	1993-94	1995-96
• Albright, Clint	NYR	1	59	14	5	19	19	....	....	....	....	....	....	1948-49	1948-49
Aldcorn, Gary	Tor., Det., Bos.	5	226	41	56	97	78	6	1	2	3	4	....	1956-57	1960-61
‡ Aldridge, Keith	Dal.	1	4	0	0	0	0	....	....	....	....	....	....	1999-00	1999-00
Alexander, Claire	Tor., Van.	4	155	18	47	65	36	16	2	4	6	4	....	1974-75	1977-78
• Alexandre, Art	Mtl.	2	11	0	2	2	8	4	0	0	0	0	....	1931-32	1932-33
Allan, Jeff	Cle.	1	4	0	0	0	2	....	....	....	....	....	....	1977-78	1977-78
‡ Allen, Chris	Fla.	2	2	0	0	0	2	....	....	....	....	....	....	1997-98	1998-99
Allen, George	NYR, Chi., Mtl.	8	339	82	115	197	179	41	9	10	19	32	....	1938-39	1946-47
Allen, Keith	Det.	2	28	0	4	4	8	5	0	0	0	0	1	1953-54	1954-55
‡ Allen, Peter	Pit.	1	8	0	0	0	8	....	....	....	....	....	....	1995-96	1995-96
• Allen, Viv	NYA	1	6	0	1	1	0	....	....	....	....	....	....	1940-41	1940-41
Alley, Steve	Hfd.	2	15	3	3	6	11	3	0	1	1	0	....	1979-80	1980-81
Allison, Dave	Mtl.	1	3	0	0	0	12	....	....	....	....	....	....	1983-84	1983-84
Allison, Mike	NYR, Tor., L.A.	10	499	102	166	268	630	82	9	17	26	135	....	1980-81	1989-90
Allison, Ray	Hfd., Phi.	7	238	64	93	157	223	12	2	3	5	20	....	1979-80	1986-87
• Allum, Bill	NYR	1	1	0	1	1	0	....	....	....	....	....	....	1940-41	1940-41
• Amadio, Dave	Det., L.A.	3	125	5	11	16	163	16	1	2	3	18	....	1957-58	1968-69
‡ Ambroziak, Peter	Buf.	1	12	0	1	1	0	....	....	....	....	....	....	1994-95	1994-95
Amodeo, Mike	Wpg.	1	19	0	0	0	2	....	....	....	....	....	....	1979-80	1979-80
• Anderson, Bill	Bos.	1	....	....	....	....	....	1	0	0	0	0	....	1942-43	1942-43
Anderson, Dale	Det.	1	13	0	0	0	6	2	0	0	0	0	....	1956-57	1956-57
Anderson, Doug	Mtl.	1	....	....	....	....	....	2	0	0	0	0	1	1952-53	1952-53
Anderson, Earl	Det., Bos.	3	109	19	19	38	22	5	0	1	1	0	....	1974-75	1976-77
Anderson, Glenn	Edm., Tor., NYR, St.L.	16	1129	498	601	1099	1120	225	93	121	214	442	6	1980-81	1995-96
Anderson, Jim	L.A.	1	7	1	2	3	2	....	....	....	....	....	....	1967-68	1967-68
Anderson, John	Tor., Que., Hfd.	12	814	282	349	631	263	37	9	18	27	2	....	1977-78	1988-89
Anderson, Murray	Wsh.	1	40	0	1	1	68	....	....	....	....	....	....	1974-75	1974-75
Anderson, Perry	St.L., N.J., S.J.	10	400	50	59	109	1051	36	2	1	3	161	....	1981-82	1991-92
Anderson, Ron	Det., L.A., St.L., Buf.	5	251	28	30	58	146	5	0	0	0	4	....	1967-68	1971-72
Anderson, Ron	Wsh.	1	28	9	7	16	8	....	....	....	....	....	....	1974-75	1974-75
Anderson, Russ	Pit., Hfd., L.A.	9	519	22	99	121	1086	10	0	3	3	28	....	1976-77	1984-85
‡ Anderson, Shawn	Buf., Que., Wsh., Phi.	8	255	11	51	62	117	19	1	1	2	16	....	1986-87	1994-95
• Anderson, Tom	Det., NYA, Bro.	8	319	62	127	189	180	16	2	7	9	8	....	1934-35	1941-42
Andersson, Erik	Cgy.	1	12	2	1	3	8	....	....	....	....	....	....	1997-98	1997-98
Andersson, Kent-Erik	Min., NYR	7	456	72	103	175	78	50	4	11	15	4	....	1977-78	1983-84
‡ Andersson, Mikael	Buf., Hfd., T.B., Phi., NYI	15	761	95	169	264	134	25	2	7	9	10	....	1985-86	1999-00
Andersson, Peter	Wsh., Que.	3	172	10	41	51	81	7	0	2	2	2	....	1983-84	1985-86
‡ Andersson, Peter	NYR, Fla.	2	47	6	13	19	20	....	....	....	....	....	....	1992-93	1993-94
Andrascik, Steve	NYR	1	....	....	....	....	....	1	0	0	0	0	....	1971-72	1971-72
Andrea, Paul	NYR, Pit., Cal., Buf.	4	150	31	49	80	10	....	....	....	....	....	....	1965-66	1970-71
• Andrews, Lloyd	Tor.	4	53	8	5	13	10	2	0	0	0	0	1	1921-22	1924-25
Andrievski, Alexander	Chi.	1	1	0	0	0	0	....	....	....	....	....	....	1992-93	1992-93
Andruff, Ron	Mtl., Col.	5	153	19	36	55	54	2	0	0	0	0	....	1974-75	1978-79
‡ Andrusak, Greg	Pit., Tor.	5	28	0	6	6	16	15	1	0	1	8	....	1993-94	1999-00
Angotti, Lou	NYR, Chi., Phi., Pit., St.L.	10	653	103	186	289	228	65	8	8	16	17	....	1964-65	1973-74
Anholt, Darrel	Chi.	1	1	0	0	0	0	....	....	....	....	....	....	1983-84	1983-84
Anslow, Hub	NYR	1	2	0	0	0	0	....	....	....	....	....	....	1947-48	1947-48
Antonovich, Mike	Min., Hfd., N.J.	5	87	10	15	25	37	....	....	....	....	....	....	1975-76	1983-84
Antoski, Shawn	Van., Phi., Pit., Ana.	8	183	3	5	8	599	36	1	3	4	74	....	1990-91	1997-98
• Apps, Syl	Tor.	10	423	201	231	432	56	69	25	29	54	8	3	1936-37	1947-48
Apps Jr., Syl	NYR, Pit., L.A.	10	727	183	423	606	311	23	5	5	10	23	....	1970-71	1979-80
Arbour, Al	Det., Chi., Tor., St.L.	16	626	12	58	70	617	86	1	8	9	92	4	1953-54	1970-71
• Arbour, Amos	Mtl., Ham., Tor.	6	113	52	20	72	77	....	....	....	....	....	....	1918-19	1923-24
• Arbour, Jack	Det., Tor.	2	47	5	1	6	56	....	....	....	....	....	....	1926-27	1928-29
Arbour, John	Bos., Pit., Van., St.L.	5	106	1	9	10	149	5	0	0	0	0	....	1965-66	1971-72
• Arbour, Ty	Pit., Chi.	5	207	28	28	56	112	11	2	0	2	6	....	1926-27	1930-31
Archambault, Michel	Chi.	1	3	0	0	0	0	....	....	....	....	....	....	1976-77	1976-77
Archibald, Dave	Min., NYR, Ott., NYI	8	323	57	67	124	139	5	0	1	1	0	....	1987-88	1996-97
Archibald, Jim	Min.	3	16	1	2	3	45	....	....	....	....	....	....	1984-85	1986-87
Areshenkoff, Ron	Edm.	1	4	0	0	0	0	....	....	....	....	....	....	1979-80	1979-80
Armstrong, Bill	Phi.	1	1	0	1	1	0	....	....	....	....	....	....	1990-91	1990-91
• Armstrong, Bob	Bos.	12	542	13	86	99	671	42	1	7	8	28	....	1950-51	1961-62
‡ Armstrong, Chris	Min.	1	3	0	0	0	0	....	....	....	....	....	....	2000-01	2000-01
Armstrong, George	Tor.	21	1187	296	417	713	721	110	26	34	60	52	4	1949-50	1970-71
Armstrong, Murray	Tor., NYA, Bro., Det.	8	270	67	121	188	72	30	4	6	10	2	....	1937-38	1945-46
• Armstrong, Norm	Tor.	1	7	1	1	2	2	....	....	....	....	....	....	1962-63	1962-63
Armstrong, Tim	Tor.	1	11	1	0	1	6	....	....	....	....	....	....	1988-89	1988-89
Arnason, Chuck	Mtl., Atl., Pit., K.C., Col., Cle., Min., Wsh.	8	401	109	90	199	122	9	2	4	6	4	....	1971-72	1978-79
Arniel, Scott	Wpg., Buf., Bos.	12	730	149	189	338	599	34	3	3	6	39	....	1981-82	1991-92
Arthur, Fred	Hfd., Phi.	3	80	1	8	9	49	4	0	0	0	2	....	1980-81	1982-83
Arundel, John	Tor.	1	3	0	0	0	9	....	....	....	....	....	....	1949-50	1949-50
• Ashbee, Barry	Bos., Phi.	5	284	15	70	85	291	17	0	4	4	22	1	1965-66	1973-74
• Ashby, Don	Tor., Col., Edm.	6	188	40	56	96	40	12	1	0	1	4	....	1975-76	1980-81
Ashton, Brent	Van., Col., N.J., Min., Que., Det., Wpg., Bos., Cgy.	14	998	284	345	629	635	85	24	25	49	70	....	1979-80	1992-93

Name	NHL Teams	NHL Seasons	Regular Schedule GP	G	A	TP	PIM	Playoffs GP	G	A	TP	PIM	NHL Cup Wins	First NHL Season	Last NHL Season
Ashworth, Frank	Chi.	1	18	5	4	9	2	....	....	....	....	....	....	1946-47	1946-47
Asmundson, Oscar	NYR, Det., St.L., NYA, Mtl.	5	111	11	23	34	30	9	0	2	2	4	1	1932-33	1937-38
‡ Astley, Mark	Buf.	3	75	4	19	23	92	2	0	0	0	0	....	1993-94	1995-96
• Atanas, Walt	NYR	1	49	13	8	21	40	....	....	....	....	....	....	1944-45	1944-45
Atcheynum, Blair	Ott., St.L., Nsh., Chi.	5	196	27	33	60	36	23	1	3	4	8	....	1992-93	2000-01
• Atkinson, Steve	Bos., Buf., Wsh.	6	302	60	51	111	104	1	0	0	0	0	....	1968-69	1974-75
Attwell, Bob	Col.	2	22	1	5	6	0	....	....	....	....	....	....	1979-80	1980-81
Attwell, Ron	St.L., NYR	1	22	1	7	8	8	....	....	....	....	....	....	1967-68	1967-68
Aubin, Norm	Tor.	2	69	18	13	31	30	1	0	0	0	0	....	1981-82	1982-83
Aubry, Pierre	Que., Det.	5	202	24	26	50	133	20	1	1	2	32	....	1980-81	1984-85
Aubuchon, Ossie	Bos., NYR	2	50	20	12	32	4	6	1	0	1	0	....	1942-43	1943-44
‡ Audet, Philippe	Det.	1	4	0	0	0	0	....	....	....	....	....	....	1998-99	1998-99
Auge, Les	Col.	1	6	0	3	3	4	....	....	....	....	....	....	1980-81	1980-81
‡ Augusta, Patrik	Tor., Wsh.	2	4	0	0	0	0	....	....	....	....	....	....	1993-94	1998-99
• Aurie, Larry	Det.	12	489	147	129	276	279	24	6	9	15	10	2	1927-28	1938-39
Awrey, Don	Bos., St.L., Mtl., Pit., NYR, Col.	16	979	31	158	189	1065	71	0	18	18	150	3	1963-64	1978-79
• Ayres, Vern	NYA, Mtl.M., St.L., NYR	6	211	6	11	17	350	....	....	....	....	....	....	1930-31	1935-36

B

Name	NHL Teams	NHL Seasons	Regular Schedule GP	G	A	TP	PIM	Playoffs GP	G	A	TP	PIM	NHL Cup Wins	First NHL Season	Last NHL Season
Babando, Pete	Bos., Det., Chi., NYR	6	351	86	73	159	194	17	3	3	6	6	1	1947-48	1952-53
Babcock, Bobby	Wsh.	2	2	0	0	0	2	....	....	....	....	....	....	1990-91	1992-93
Babe, Warren	Min.	3	21	2	5	7	23	2	0	0	0	0	....	1987-88	1990-91
Babin, Mitch	St.L.	1	8	0	0	0	0	....	....	....	....	....	....	1975-76	1975-76
Baby, John	Cle., Min.	2	26	2	8	10	26	....	....	....	....	....	....	1977-78	1978-79
Babych, Dave	Wpg., Hfd., Van., Phi., L.A.	19	1195	142	581	723	970	114	21	41	62	113	....	1980-81	1998-99
Babych, Wayne	St.L., Pit., Que., Hfd.	9	519	192	246	438	498	41	7	9	16	24	....	1978-79	1986-87
‡ Baca, Jergus	Hfd.	2	10	0	2	2	14	....	....	....	....	....	....	1990-91	1991-92
Backman, Mike	NYR	3	18	1	6	7	18	10	2	2	4	2	....	1981-82	1983-84
• Backor, Pete	Tor.	1	36	4	5	9	6	....	....	....	....	....	1	1944-45	1944-45
Backstrom, Ralph	Mtl., L.A., Chi.	17	1032	278	361	639	386	116	27	32	59	68	6	1956-57	1972-73
• Bailey, Ace	Tor.	8	313	111	82	193	472	21	3	4	7	12	1	1926-27	1933-34
Bailey, Bob	Tor., Det., Chi.	5	150	15	21	36	207	15	0	4	4	22	....	1953-54	1957-58
• Bailey, Garnet	Bos., Det., St.L., Wsh.	10	568	107	171	278	633	15	2	4	6	28	2	1968-69	1977-78
Bailey, Reid	Phi., Tor., Hfd.	4	40	1	3	4	105	16	0	2	2	25	....	1980-81	1983-84
Baillargeon, Joel	Wpg., Que.	3	20	0	2	2	31	....	....	....	....	....	....	1986-87	1988-89
Baird, Ken	Cal.	1	10	0	2	2	15	....	....	....	....	....	....	1971-72	1971-72
Baker, Bill	Mtl., Col., St.L., NYR	3	143	7	25	32	175	6	0	0	0	0	....	1980-81	1982-83
Baker, Jamie	Que., Ott., S.J., Tor.	10	404	71	79	150	271	25	5	4	9	42	....	1989-90	1998-99
Bakovic, Peter	Van.	1	10	2	0	2	48	....	....	....	....	....	....	1987-88	1987-88
Balderis, Helmut	Min.	1	26	3	6	9	2	....	....	....	....	....	....	1989-90	1989-90
Baldwin, Doug	Tor., Det., Chi.	3	24	0	1	1	8	....	....	....	....	....	....	1945-46	1947-48
Balfour, Earl	Tor., Chi.	7	288	30	22	52	78	26	0	3	3	4	1	1951-52	1960-61
• Balfour, Murray	Mtl., Chi., Bos.	8	306	67	90	157	393	40	9	10	19	45	1	1956-57	1964-65
Ball, Terry	Phi., Buf.	4	74	7	19	26	26	....	....	....	....	....	....	1967-68	1971-72
Balon, Dave	NYR, Mtl., Min., Van.	14	776	192	222	414	607	78	14	21	35	109	2	1959-60	1972-73
Baltimore, Bryon	Edm.	1	2	0	0	0	4	....	....	....	....	....	....	1979-80	1979-80
Baluik, Stan	Bos.	1	7	0	0	0	2	....	....	....	....	....	....	1959-60	1959-60
Bandura, Jeff	NYR	1	2	0	1	1	0	....	....	....	....	....	....	1980-81	1980-81
Banks, Darren	Bos.	2	20	2	2	4	73	....	....	....	....	....	....	1992-93	1993-94
Barahona, Ralph	Bos.	2	6	2	2	4	0	....	....	....	....	....	....	1990-91	1991-92
Barbe, Andy	Tor.	1	1	0	0	0	2	....	....	....	....	....	....	1950-51	1950-51
Barber, Bill	Phi.	14	903	420	463	883	623	129	53	55	108	109	2	1972-73	1983-84
Barber, Don	Min., Wpg., Que., S.J.	4	115	25	32	57	64	11	4	4	8	10	....	1988-89	1991-92
• Barilko, Bill	Tor.	5	252	26	36	62	456	47	5	7	12	104	4	1946-47	1950-51
Barkley, Doug	Chi., Det.	6	253	24	80	104	382	30	0	9	9	63	....	1957-58	1965-66
Barlow, Bob	Min.	2	77	16	17	33	10	6	2	2	4	6	....	1969-70	1970-71
Barnes, Blair	L.A.	1	1	0	0	0	0	....	....	....	....	....	....	1982-83	1982-83
Barnes, Norm	Phi., Hfd.	5	156	6	38	44	178	12	0	0	0	8	....	1976-77	1981-82
Baron, Normand	Mtl., St.L.	2	27	2	0	2	51	3	0	0	0	22	....	1983-84	1985-86
Barr, Dave	Bos., NYR, St.L., Hfd., Det., N.J., Dal.	13	614	128	204	332	520	71	12	10	22	70	....	1981-82	1993-94
Barrault, Doug	Min., Fla.	2	4	0	0	0	2	....	....	....	....	....	....	1992-93	1993-94
Barrett, Fred	Min., L.A.	13	745	25	123	148	671	44	0	2	2	60	....	1970-71	1983-84
Barrett, John	Det., Wsh., Min.	8	488	20	77	97	604	16	2	2	4	50	....	1980-81	1987-88
Barrie, Doug	Pit., Buf., L.A.	3	158	10	42	52	268	....	....	....	....	....	....	1968-69	1971-72
‡ Barrie, Len	Phi., Fla., Pit., L.A.	7	184	19	45	64	290	8	1	0	1	8	....	1989-90	2000-01
Barry, Ed	Bos.	1	19	1	3	4	2	....	....	....	....	....	....	1946-47	1946-47
• Barry, Marty	NYA, Bos., Det., Mtl.	12	509	195	192	387	231	43	15	18	33	34	2	1927-28	1939-40
Barry, Ray	Bos.	1	18	1	2	3	6	....	....	....	....	....	....	1951-52	1951-52
Bartel, Robin	Cgy., Van.	2	41	0	1	1	14	6	0	0	0	16	....	1985-86	1986-87
Bartlett, Jim	Mtl., NYR, Bos.	5	191	34	23	57	273	2	0	0	0	0	....	1954-55	1960-61
• Barton, Cliff	Pit., Phi., NYR	3	85	10	9	19	22	....	....	....	....	....	....	1929-30	1939-40
‡ Bartos, Peter	Min.	1	13	4	2	6	6	....	....	....	....	....	....	2000-01	2000-01
‡ Bashkirov, Andrei	Mtl.	3	30	0	3	3	0	....	....	....	....	....	....	1998-99	2000-01
Bassen, Bob	NYI, Chi., St.L., Que., Dal., Cgy.	15	765	88	144	232	1004	93	9	15	24	134	....	1985-86	1999-00
Bathe, Frank	Det., Phi.	9	224	3	28	31	542	27	1	3	4	42	....	1974-75	1983-84
Bathgate, Andy	NYR, Tor., Det., Pit.	17	1069	349	624	973	624	54	21	14	35	76	1	1952-53	1970-71
Bathgate, Frank	NYR	1	2	0	0	0	2	....	....	....	....	....	....	1952-53	1952-53
• Batters, Jeff	St.L.	2	16	0	0	0	28	....	....	....	....	....	....	1993-94	1994-95
‡ Batyrshin, Ruslan	L.A.	1	2	0	0	0	6	....	....	....	....	....	....	1995-96	1995-96
• Bauer, Bobby	Bos.	9	327	123	137	260	36	48	11	8	19	6	2	1936-37	1951-52
Baumgartner, Ken	L.A., NYI, Tor., Ana., Bos.	12	696	13	41	54	2244	51	1	2	3	106	....	1987-88	1998-99
Baumgartner, Mike	K.C.	1	17	0	0	0	0	....	....	....	....	....	....	1974-75	1974-75
Baun, Bob	Tor., Oak., Det.	17	964	37	187	224	1493	96	3	12	15	171	4	1956-57	1972-73
‡ Bautin, Sergei	Wpg., Det., S.J.	3	132	5	25	30	176	6	0	0	0	2	....	1992-93	1995-96
Bawa, Robin	Wsh., Van., S.J., Ana.	4	61	6	1	7	60	1	0	0	0	0	....	1989-90	1993-94
Baxter, Paul	Que., Pit., Cgy.	8	472	48	121	169	1564	40	0	5	5	162	....	1979-80	1986-87
Beadle, Sandy	Wpg.	1	6	1	0	1	2	....	....	....	....	....	....	1980-81	1980-81
Beaton, Frank	NYR	2	25	1	1	2	43	....	....	....	....	....	....	1978-79	1979-80
• Beattie, Red	Bos., Det., NYA	9	334	62	85	147	137	24	4	2	6	8	....	1930-31	1938-39
Beaudin, Norm	St.L., Min.	2	25	1	2	3	4	....	....	....	....	....	....	1967-68	1970-71
Beaudoin, Serge	Atl.	1	3	0	0	0	0	....	....	....	....	....	....	1979-80	1979-80
Beaudoin, Yves	Wsh.	3	11	0	0	0	5	....	....	....	....	....	....	1985-86	1987-88
‡ Beaufait, Mark	S.J.	1	5	1	0	1	0	....	....	....	....	....	....	1992-93	1992-93
Beck, Barry	Col., NYR, L.A.	10	615	104	251	355	1016	51	10	23	33	77	....	1977-78	1989-90
Beckett, Bob	Bos.	4	68	7	6	13	18	....	....	....	....	....	....	1956-57	1963-64
Bedard, James	Chi.	2	22	1	1	2	8	....	....	....	....	....	....	1949-50	1950-51
‡ Beddoes, Clayton	Bos.	2	60	2	8	10	57	....	....	....	....	....	....	1995-96	1996-97
Bednarski, John	NYR, Edm.	4	100	2	18	20	114	1	0	0	0	17	....	1974-75	1979-80
Beers, Bob	Bos., T.B., Edm., NYI	8	258	28	79	107	225	21	1	1	2	22	....	1989-90	1996-97
Beers, Eddy	Cgy., St.L.	5	250	94	116	210	256	41	7	10	17	47	....	1981-82	1985-86
• Behling, Dick	Det.	2	5	1	0	1	2	....	....	....	....	....	....	1940-41	1942-43
Beisler, Frank	NYA	2	2	0	0	0	0	....	....	....	....	....	....	1936-37	1939-40
Belanger, Alain	Tor.	1	9	0	1	1	6	....	....	....	....	....	....	1977-78	1977-78
‡ Belanger, Jesse	Mtl., Fla., Van., Edm., NYI	8	246	59	76	135	56	12	0	3	3	2	1	1991-92	2000-01
Belanger, Roger	Pit.	1	44	3	5	8	32	....	....	....	....	....	....	1984-85	1984-85
Belisle, Danny	NYR	1	4	2	0	2	0	....	....	....	....	....	....	1960-61	1960-61
Beliveau, Jean	Mtl.	20	1125	507	712	1219	1029	162	79	97	176	211	10	1950-51	1970-71
• Bell, Billy	Mtl.W., Mtl., Ott.	6	72	4	2	6	14	5	0	0	0	0	1	1917-18	1923-24
Bell, Bruce	Que., St.L., NYR, Edm.	5	209	12	64	76	113	34	3	5	8	41	....	1984-85	1989-90
Bell, Harry	NYR	1	1	0	1	1	0	....	....	....	....	....	....	1946-47	1946-47
Bell, Joe	NYR	2	62	8	9	17	18	....	....	....	....	....	....	1942-43	1946-47
Belland, Neil	Van., Pit.	6	109	13	32	45	54	21	2	9	11	23	....	1981-82	1986-87
• Bellefeuille, Pete	Tor., Det.	4	92	26	4	30	58	....	....	....	....	....	....	1925-26	1929-30
• Bellemer, Andy	Mtl.M.	1	15	0	0	0	0	....	....	....	....	....	....	1932-33	1932-33
Bellows, Brian	Min., Mtl., T.B., Ana., Wsh.	17	1188	485	537	1022	718	143	51	71	122	143	1	1982-83	1998-99
• Bend, Lin	NYR	1	8	3	1	4	2	....	....	....	....	....	....	1942-43	1942-43
‡ Benda, Jan	Wsh.	1	9	0	3	3	6	....	....	....	....	....	....	1997-98	1997-98
Bennett, Adam	Chi., Edm.	3	69	3	8	11	69	....	....	....	....	....	....	1991-92	1993-94
Bennett, Bill	Bos., Hfd.	2	31	4	7	11	65	....	....	....	....	....	....	1978-79	1979-80
Bennett, Curt	St.L., NYR, Atl.	10	580	152	182	334	347	21	1	1	2	57	....	1970-71	1979-80
Bennett, Frank	Det.	1	7	0	1	1	2	....	....	....	....	....	....	1943-44	1943-44
Bennett Jr., Harvey	Pit., Wsh., Phi., Min., St.L.	5	268	44	46	90	347	4	0	0	0	2	....	1974-75	1978-79
• Bennett, Max	Mtl.	1	1	0	0	0	0	....	....	....	....	....	....	1935-36	1935-36
Bennett, Rick	NYR	3	15	1	1	2	13	....	....	....	....	....	....	1989-90	1991-92
Benning, Brian	St.L., L.A., Phi., Edm., Fla.	11	568	63	233	296	963	48	3	20	23	74	....	1984-85	1994-95

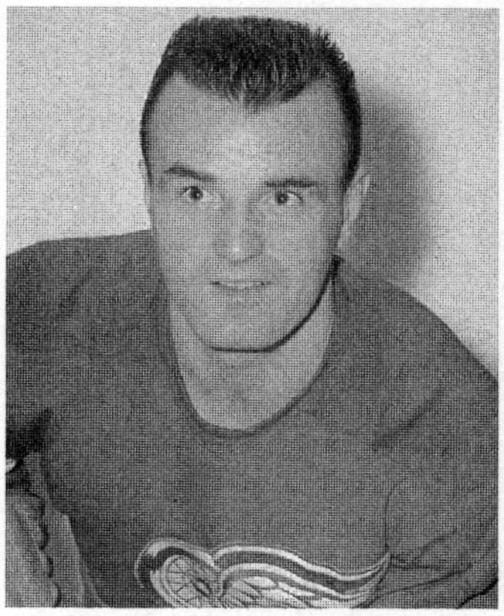

Pete Babando

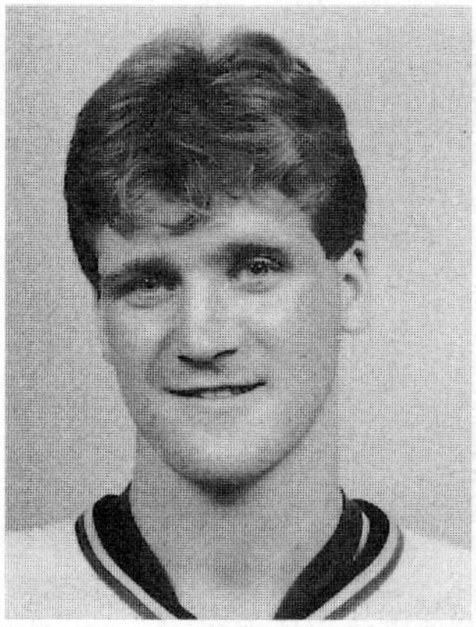

Warren Babe

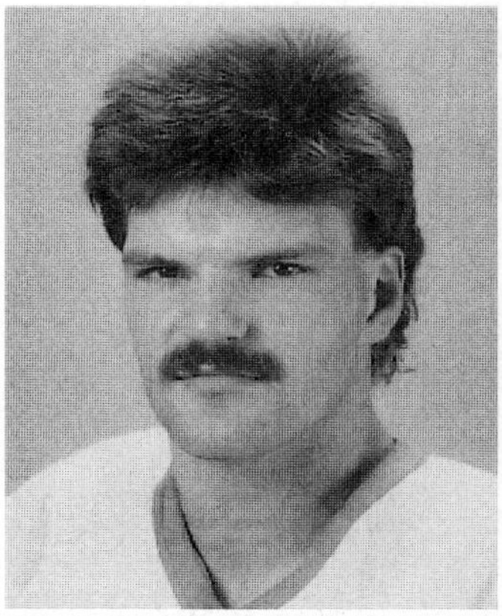

Joel Baillargeon

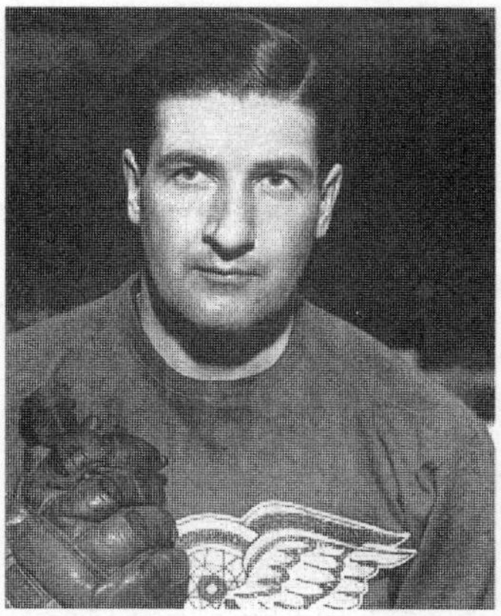

Marty Barry

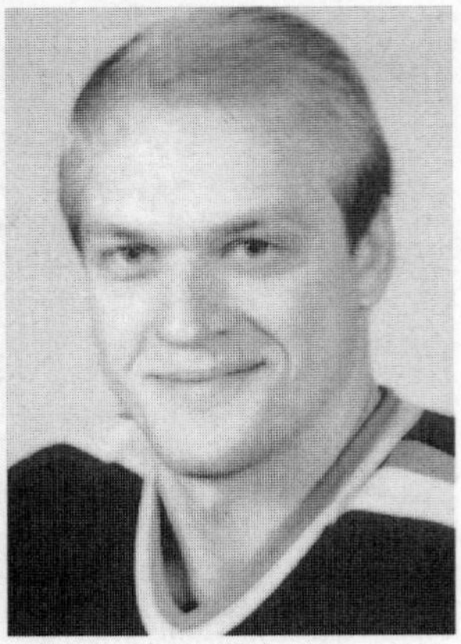

Robin Bartel

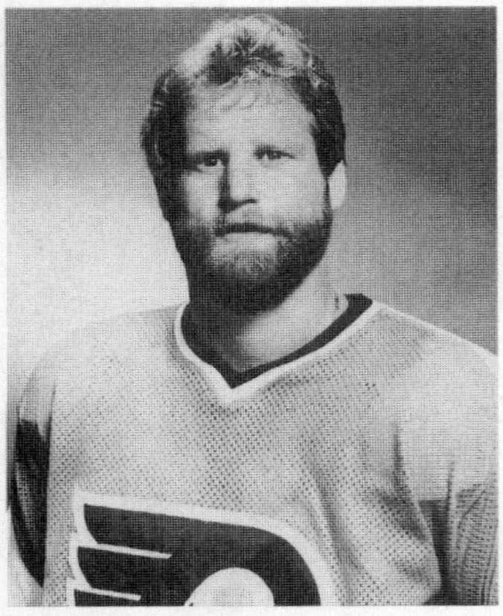

Frank Bathe

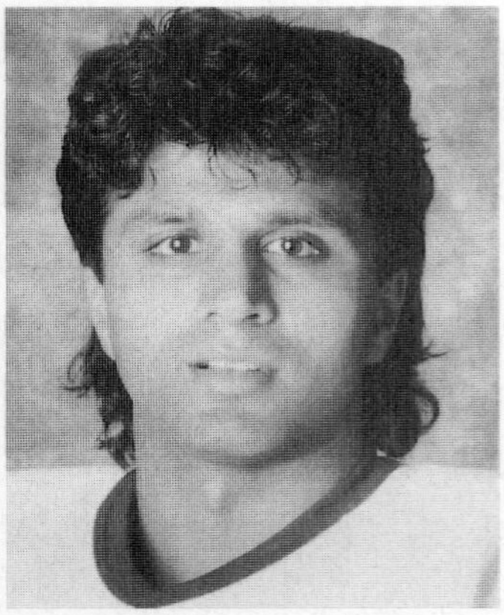

Robin Bawa

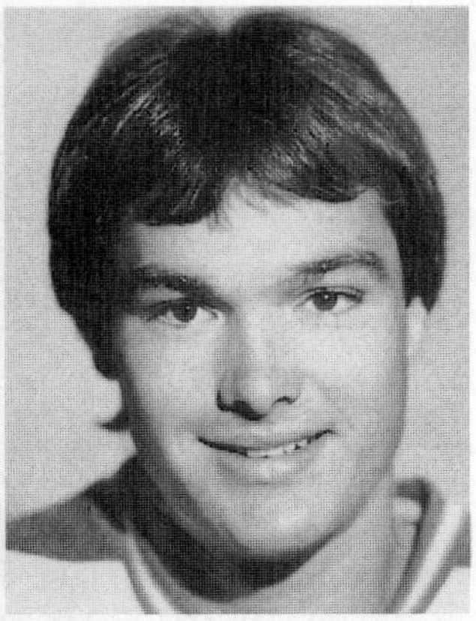

Eddie Beers

			Regular Schedule					Playoffs					NHL	First	Last
Name	NHL Teams	NHL Seasons	GP	G	A	TP	PIM	GP	G	A	TP	PIM	Cup Wins	NHL Season	NHL Season
Benning, Jim	Tor., Van.	9	605	52	191	243	461	7	1	1	2	2	....	1981-82	1989-90
• Benoit, Joe	Mtl.	5	185	75	69	144	94	11	6	3	9	11	1	1940-41	1946-47
Benson, Bill	NYA, Bro.	2	67	11	25	36	35	....	....	....	....	....	....	1940-41	1941-42
• Benson, Bobby	Bos.	1	8	0	1	1	4	....	....	....	....	....	....	1924-25	1924-25
• Bentley, Doug	Chi., NYR	13	566	219	324	543	217	23	9	8	17	12	....	1939-40	1953-54
• Bentley, Max	Chi., Tor., NYR	12	646	245	299	544	179	51	18	27	45	14	3	1940-41	1953-54
Bentley, Reg	Chi.	1	11	1	2	3	2	....	....	....	....	....	....	1942-43	1942-43
Beraldo, Paul	Bos.	2	10	0	0	0	4	....	....	....	....	....	....	1987-88	1988-89
‡ Beranek, Josef	Edm., Phi., Van., Pit.	9	531	118	144	262	398	57	5	8	13	24	....	1991-92	2000-01
Berenson, Red	Mtl., NYR, St.L., Det.	17	987	261	397	658	305	85	23	14	37	49	1	1961-62	1977-78
Berezan, Perry	Cgy., Min., S.J.	9	378	61	75	136	279	31	4	7	11	34	....	1984-85	1992-93
Berg, Bill	NYI, Tor., NYR, Ott.	10	546	55	67	122	488	61	3	4	7	34	....	1988-89	1998-99
• Bergdinon, Fred	Bos.	1	2	0	0	0	0	....	....	....	....	....	....	1925-26	1925-26
Bergen, Todd	Phi.	1	14	11	5	16	4	17	4	9	13	8	....	1984-85	1984-85
‡ Berger, Mike	Min.	2	30	3	1	4	67	....	....	....	....	....	....	1987-88	1988-89
Bergeron, Michel	Det., NYI, Wsh.	5	229	80	58	138	165	....	....	....	....	....	....	1974-75	1978-79
Bergeron, Yves	Pit.	2	3	0	0	0	0	....	....	....	....	....	....	1974-75	1976-77
‡ Bergkvist, Stefan	Pit.	2	7	0	0	0	9	4	0	0	0	2	....	1995-96	1996-97
Bergland, Tim	Wsh., T.B.	5	182	17	26	43	75	26	2	2	4	22	....	1989-90	1993-94
Bergloff, Bob	Min.	1	2	0	0	0	5	....	....	....	....	....	....	1982-83	1982-83
Berglund, Bo	Que., Min., Phi.	3	130	28	39	67	40	9	2	0	2	6	....	1983-84	1985-86
• Bergman, Gary	Det., Min., K.C.	12	838	68	299	367	1249	21	0	5	5	20	....	1964-65	1975-76
Bergman, Thommie	Det.	6	246	21	44	65	243	7	0	2	2	2	....	1972-73	1979-80
Bergqvist, Jonas	Cgy.	1	22	2	5	7	10	....	....	....	....	....	....	1989-90	1989-90
• Berlinquette, Louis	Mtl., Mtl.M., Pit.	8	193	45	33	78	129	11	0	4	4	9	....	1917-18	1925-26
Bernier, Serge	Phi., L.A., Que.	7	302	78	119	197	234	5	1	1	2	0	....	1968-69	1980-81
Berry, Bob	Mtl., L.A.	8	541	159	191	350	344	26	2	6	8	6	....	1968-69	1976-77
Berry, Brad	Wpg., Min., Dal.	8	241	4	28	32	323	13	0	1	1	16	....	1985-86	1993-94
Berry, Doug	Col.	2	121	10	33	43	25	....	....	....	....	....	....	1979-80	1980-81
Berry, Fred	Det.	1	3	0	0	0	0	....	....	....	....	....	....	1976-77	1976-77
Berry, Ken	Edm., Van.	4	55	8	10	18	30	....	....	....	....	....	....	1981-82	1988-89
‡ Bertrand, Eric	N.J., Atl., Mtl.	2	15	0	0	0	4	....	....	....	....	....	....	1999-00	2000-01
• Besler, Phil	Bos., Chi., Det.	2	30	1	4	5	18	....	....	....	....	....	....	1935-36	1938-39
• Bessone, Pete	Det.	1	6	0	1	1	6	....	....	....	....	....	....	1937-38	1937-38
Bethel, John	Wpg.	1	17	0	2	2	4	....	....	....	....	....	....	1979-80	1979-80
‡ Betik, Karel	T.B.	1	3	0	2	2	2	....	....	....	....	....	....	1998-99	1998-99
‡ Bets, Maxim	Ana.	1	3	0	0	0	0	....	....	....	....	....	....	1993-94	1993-94
Bettio, Sam	Bos.	1	44	9	12	21	32	....	....	....	....	....	....	1949-50	1949-50
Beukeboom, Jeff	Edm., NYR	14	804	30	129	159	1890	99	3	16	19	197	4	1985-86	1998-99
Beverley, Nick	Bos., Pit., NYR, Min., L.A., Col.	11	502	18	94	112	156	7	0	1	1	0	....	1966-67	1979-80
Bialowas, Dwight	Atl., Min.	4	164	11	46	57	46	....	....	....	....	....	....	1973-74	1976-77
Bialowas, Frank	Tor.	1	3	0	0	0	12	....	....	....	....	....	....	1993-94	1993-94
Bianchin, Wayne	Pit., Edm.	7	276	68	41	109	137	3	0	1	1	6	....	1973-74	1979-80
Bidner, Todd	Wsh.	1	12	2	1	3	7	....	....	....	....	....	....	1981-82	1981-82
Biggs, Don	Min., Phi.	2	12	2	0	2	8	....	....	....	....	....	....	1984-85	1989-90
Bignell, Larry	Pit.	2	20	0	3	3	2	3	0	0	0	2	....	1973-74	1974-75
Bilodeau, Gilles	Que.	1	9	0	1	1	25	....	....	....	....	....	....	1979-80	1979-80
• Bionda, Jack	Tor., Bos.	4	93	3	9	12	113	11	0	1	1	14	....	1955-56	1958-59
‡ Bissett, Tom	Det.	1	5	0	0	0	0	....	....	....	....	....	....	1990-91	1990-91
Bjugstad, Scott	Min., Pit., L.A.	9	317	76	68	144	144	9	0	1	1	2	....	1983-84	1991-92
‡ Black, James	Hfd., Min., Dal., Buf., Chi., Wsh.	11	352	58	57	115	84	13	2	1	3	4	....	1989-90	2000-01
Black, Steve	Det., Chi.	2	113	11	20	31	77	13	0	0	0	13	1	1949-50	1950-51
Blackburn, Bob	NYR, Pit.	3	135	8	12	20	105	6	0	0	0	4	....	1968-69	1970-71
Blackburn, Don	Bos., Phi., NYR, NYI, Min.	6	185	23	44	67	87	12	3	0	3	10	....	1962-63	1972-73
Blade, Hank	Chi.	2	24	2	3	5	2	....	....	....	....	....	....	1946-47	1947-48
Bladon, Tom	Phi., Pit., Edm., Wpg., Det.	9	610	73	197	270	392	86	8	29	37	70	2	1972-73	1980-81
• Blaine, Garry	Mtl.	1	1	0	0	0	0	....	....	....	....	....	....	1954-55	1954-55
• Blair, Andy	Tor., Chi.	9	402	74	86	160	323	38	6	6	12	32	1	1928-29	1936-37
Blair, Chuck	Tor.	1	1	0	0	0	0	....	....	....	....	....	....	1948-49	1948-49
Blair, Dusty	Tor.	1	2	0	0	0	0	....	....	....	....	....	....	1950-51	1950-51
Blaisdell, Mike	Det., NYR, Pit., Tor.	9	343	70	84	154	166	6	1	2	3	10	....	1980-81	1988-89
Blake, Bob	Bos.	1	12	0	0	0	0	....	....	....	....	....	....	1935-36	1935-36
• Blake, Mickey	Mtl.M., St.L., Tor.	3	10	1	1	2	4	....	....	....	....	....	....	1932-33	1935-36
• Blake, Toe	Mtl.M., Mtl.	14	577	235	292	527	272	58	25	37	62	23	3	1934-35	1947-48
Blight, Rick	Van., L.A.	7	326	96	125	221	170	5	0	5	5	2	....	1975-76	1982-83
• Blinco, Russ	Mtl.M., Chi.	6	268	59	66	125	24	19	3	3	6	4	1	1933-34	1938-39
Block, Ken	Van.	1	1	0	0	0	0	....	....	....	....	....	....	1970-71	1970-71
Bloemberg, Jeff	NYR	4	43	3	6	9	25	7	0	3	3	5	....	1988-89	1991-92
Blomqvist, Timo	Wsh., N.J.	5	243	4	53	57	293	13	0	0	0	24	....	1981-82	1986-87
Blomsten, Arto	Wpg., L.A.	3	25	0	4	4	8	....	....	....	....	....	....	1993-94	1995-96
Bloom, Mike	Wsh., Det.	3	201	30	47	77	215	....	....	....	....	....	....	1974-75	1976-77
Blum, John	Edm., Bos., Wsh., Det.	8	250	7	34	41	610	20	0	2	2	27	....	1982-83	1989-90
Bodak, Bob	Cgy., Hfd.	2	4	0	0	0	29	....	....	....	....	....	....	1987-88	1989-90
Boddy, Gregg	Van.	5	273	23	44	67	263	3	0	0	0	0	....	1971-72	1975-76
Bodger, Doug	Pit., Buf., S.J., N.J., L.A., Van.	16	1071	106	422	528	1007	47	6	18	24	25	....	1984-85	1999-00
Bodnar, Gus	Tor., Chi., Bos.	12	667	142	254	396	207	32	4	3	7	10	2	1943-44	1954-55
Boehm, Ron	Oak.	1	16	2	1	3	10	....	....	....	....	....	....	1967-68	1967-68
• Boesch, Garth	Tor.	4	197	9	28	37	205	34	2	5	7	18	3	1946-47	1949-50
Boh, Rick	Min.	1	8	2	1	3	4	....	....	....	....	....	....	1987-88	1987-88
‡ Bohonos, Lonny	Van., Tor.	4	83	19	16	35	22	9	3	6	9	2	....	1995-96	1998-99
‡ Boikov, Alexandre	Nsh.	2	10	0	0	0	15	....	....	....	....	....	....	1999-00	2000-01
Boileau, Marc	Det.	1	54	5	6	11	8	....	....	....	....	....	....	1961-62	1961-62
Boileau, Rene	NYA	1	7	0	0	0	0	....	....	....	....	....	....	1925-26	1925-26
Boimistruck, Fred	Tor.	2	83	4	14	18	45	....	....	....	....	....	....	1981-82	1982-83
Boisvert, Serge	Tor., Mtl.	5	46	5	7	12	8	23	3	7	10	4	1	1982-83	1987-88
Boivin, Claude	Phi., Ott.	4	132	12	19	31	364	....	....	....	....	....	....	1991-92	1994-95
Boivin, Leo	Tor., Bos., Det., Pit., Min.	19	1150	72	250	322	1192	54	3	10	13	59	....	1951-52	1969-70
Boland, Mike	K.C., Buf.	2	23	1	2	3	29	3	1	0	1	2	....	1974-75	1978-79
Boland, Mike	Phi.	1	2	0	0	0	0	....	....	....	....	....	....	1974-75	1974-75
Boldirev, Ivan	Bos., Cal., Chi., Atl., Van., Det.	15	1052	361	505	866	507	48	13	20	33	14	....	1970-71	1984-85
Bolduc, Danny	Det., Cgy.	3	102	22	19	41	33	1	0	0	0	0	....	1978-79	1983-84
Bolduc, Michel	Que.	2	10	0	0	0	6	....	....	....	....	....	....	1981-82	1982-83
• Boll, Buzz	Tor., NYA, Bro., Bos.	12	437	133	130	263	148	31	7	3	10	13	....	1932-33	1943-44
Bolonchuk, Larry	Van., Wsh.	4	74	3	9	12	97	....	....	....	....	....	....	1972-73	1977-78
• Bolton, Hugh	Tor.	8	235	10	51	61	221	17	0	5	5	14	1	1949-50	1956-57
Bonar, Dan	L.A.	3	170	25	39	64	208	14	3	4	7	22	....	1980-81	1982-83
‡ Bonin, Brian	Pit., Min.	2	12	0	0	0	0	3	0	0	0	0	....	1998-99	2000-01
Bonin, Marcel	Det., Bos., Mtl.	9	454	97	175	272	336	50	11	14	25	51	4	1952-53	1961-62
‡ Bonsignore, Jason	Edm., T.B.	4	79	3	13	16	34	....	....	....	....	....	....	1994-95	1998-99
Boo, Jim	Min.	1	6	0	0	0	22	....	....	....	....	....	....	1977-78	1977-78
• Boone, Buddy	Bos.	2	34	5	3	8	28	22	2	1	3	25	....	1956-57	1957-58
Boothman, George	Tor.	2	58	17	19	36	18	5	2	1	3	2	....	1942-43	1943-44
Bordeleau, Christian	Mtl., St.L., Chi.	4	205	38	65	103	82	19	4	7	11	17	1	1968-69	1971-72
Bordeleau, J.P.	Chi.	10	519	97	126	223	143	48	3	6	9	12	....	1969-70	1979-80
Bordeleau, Paulin	Van.	3	183	33	56	89	47	5	2	1	3	0	....	1973-74	1975-76
Borotsik, Jack	St.L.	1	1	0	0	0	0	....	....	....	....	....	....	1974-75	1974-75
‡ Borsato, Luciano	Wpg.	5	203	35	55	90	113	7	1	0	1	4	....	1990-91	1994-95
Borschevsky, Nikolai	Tor., Cgy., Dal.	4	162	49	73	122	44	31	4	9	13	4	....	1992-93	1995-96
Boschman, Laurie	Tor., Edm., Wpg., N.J., Ott.	14	1009	229	348	577	2265	57	8	13	21	140	....	1979-80	1992-93
Bossy, Mike	NYI	10	752	573	553	1126	210	129	85	75	160	38	4	1977-78	1986-87
• Bostrom, Helge	Chi.	4	96	3	3	6	58	13	0	0	0	16	....	1929-30	1932-33
Botell, Mark	Phi.	1	32	4	10	14	31	....	....	....	....	....	....	1981-82	1981-82
Bothwell, Tim	NYR, St.L., Hfd.	12	502	28	93	121	382	49	0	3	3	56	....	1978-79	1988-89
Botting, Cam	Atl.	1	2	0	1	1	0	....	....	....	....	....	....	1975-76	1975-76
Boucha, Henry	Det., Min., K.C., Col.	6	247	53	49	102	157	....	....	....	....	....	....	1971-72	1976-77
Bouchard, Butch	Mtl.	15	785	49	144	193	863	113	11	21	32	121	4	1941-42	1955-56
Bouchard, Dick	NYR	1	1	0	0	0	0	....	....	....	....	....	....	1954-55	1954-55
• Bouchard, Edmond	Mtl., Ham., NYA, Pit.	8	211	19	21	40	117	....	....	....	....	....	....	1921-22	1928-29
Bouchard, Pierre	Mtl., Wsh.	12	595	24	82	106	433	76	3	10	13	56	5	1970-71	1981-82
• Boucher, Billy	Mtl., Bos., NYA	7	213	93	38	131	409	14	3	0	3	17	1	1921-22	1927-28
• Boucher, Bobby	Mtl.	1	11	1	0	1	0	2	0	0	0	0	1	1923-24	1923-24
• Boucher, Clarence	NYA	2	47	2	2	4	133	....	....	....	....	....	....	1926-27	1927-28
• Boucher, Frank	Ott., NYR	14	557	160	263	423	119	55	16	20	36	12	2	1921-22	1943-44
• Boucher, Georges	Ott., Mtl.M., Chi.	15	449	117	87	204	838	28	5	3	8	88	4	1917-18	1931-32
Boudreau, Bruce	Tor., Chi.	8	141	28	42	70	46	9	2	0	2	0	....	1976-77	1985-86
Boudrias, Andre	Mtl., Min., Chi., St.L., Van.	12	662	151	340	491	216	34	6	10	16	12	....	1963-64	1975-76

Name	NHL Teams	NHL Seasons	Regular Schedule GP	G	A	TP	PIM	Playoffs GP	G	A	TP	PIM	NHL Cup Wins	First NHL Season	Last NHL Season
Boughner, Barry	Oak., Cal.	2	20	0	0	0	11	....	....	....	....	....	....	1969-70	1970-71
Bourbonnais, Dan	Hfd.	2	59	3	25	28	11	....	....	....	....	....	....	1981-82	1983-84
Bourbonnais, Rick	St.L.	3	71	9	15	24	29	4	0	1	1	0	....	1975-76	1977-78
• Bourcier, Conrad	Mtl.	1	6	0	0	0	0	....	....	....	....	....	....	1935-36	1935-36
Bourcier, Jean	Mtl.	1	9	0	1	1	0	....	....	....	....	....	....	1935-36	1935-36
• Bourgeault, Leo	Tor., NYR, Ott., Mtl.	8	307	24	20	44	269	24	1	1	2	18	1	1926-27	1934-35
Bourgeois, Charlie	Cgy., St.L., Hfd.	7	290	16	54	70	788	40	2	3	5	194	....	1981-82	1987-88
Bourne, Bob	NYI, L.A.	14	964	258	324	582	605	139	40	56	96	108	4	1974-75	1987-88
Bourque, Phil	Pit., NYR, Ott.	12	477	88	111	199	516	56	13	12	25	107	2	1983-84	1995-96
Bourque, Raymond	Bos., Col.	22	1612	410	1169	1579	1141	214	41	139	180	171	1	1979-80	2000-01
Boutette, Pat	Tor., Hfd., Pit.	10	756	171	282	453	1354	46	10	14	24	109	....	1975-76	1984-85
Boutilier, Paul	NYI, Bos., Min., NYR, Wpg.	8	288	27	83	110	358	41	1	9	10	45	1	1981-82	1988-89
‡ Bowen, Jason	Phi., Edm.	6	77	2	6	8	109	....	....	....	....	....	....	1992-93	1997-98
‡ Bowler, Bill	CBJ	1	9	0	2	2	8	....	....	....	....	....	....	2000-01	2000-01
Bowman, Kirk	Chi.	3	88	11	17	28	19	7	1	0	1	0	....	1976-77	1978-79
• Bowman, Ralph	Ott., St.L., Det.	7	274	8	17	25	260	22	2	2	4	6	2	1933-34	1939-40
Bownass, Jack	Mtl., NYR	4	80	3	8	11	58	....	....	....	....	....	....	1957-58	1961-62
Bowness, Rick	Atl., Det., St.L., Wpg.	7	173	18	37	55	191	5	0	0	0	2	....	1975-76	1981-82
• Boyd, Bill	NYR, NYA	4	138	15	7	22	72	10	0	0	0	4	1	1926-27	1929-30
Boyd, Irvin	Bos., Det.	4	96	10	10	20	30	5	0	1	1	4	....	1931-32	1943-44
Boyd, Randy	Pit., Chi., NYI, Van.	8	257	20	67	87	328	13	0	2	2	26	....	1981-82	1988-89
Boyer, Wally	Tor., Chi., Oak., Pit.	7	365	54	105	159	163	15	1	3	4	0	....	1965-66	1971-72
‡ Boyer, Zac	Dal.	2	3	0	0	0	0	2	0	0	0	0	....	1994-95	1995-96
Boyko, Darren	Wpg.	1	1	0	0	0	0	....	....	....	....	....	....	1988-89	1988-89
Bozek, Steve	L.A., Cgy., St.L., Van., S.J.	11	641	164	167	331	309	58	12	11	23	69	....	1981-82	1991-92
‡ Bozon, Philippe	St.L.	4	144	16	25	41	101	19	2	0	2	31	....	1991-92	1994-95
• Brackenborough, John	Bos.	1	7	0	0	0	0	....	....	....	....	....	....	1925-26	1925-26
Brackenbury, Curt	Que., Edm., St.L.	4	141	9	17	26	226	2	0	0	0	0	....	1979-80	1982-83
Bradley, Bart	Bos.	1	1	0	0	0	0	....	....	....	....	....	....	1949-50	1949-50
Bradley, Brian	Cgy., Van., Tor., T.B.	13	651	182	321	503	528	13	3	7	10	16	....	1985-86	1997-98
Bradley, Lyle	Cal., Cle.	2	6	1	0	1	2	....	....	....	....	....	....	1973-74	1976-77
Brady, Neil	N.J., Ott., Dal.	5	89	9	22	31	95	....	....	....	....	....	....	1989-90	1993-94
Bragnalo, Rick	Wsh.	4	145	15	35	50	46	....	....	....	....	....	....	1975-76	1978-79
• Branigan, Andy	NYA, Bro.	2	27	1	2	3	31	....	....	....	....	....	....	1940-41	1941-42
Brasar, Per-Olov	Min., Van.	5	348	64	142	206	33	13	1	2	3	0	....	1977-78	1981-82
• Brayshaw, Russ	Chi.	1	43	5	9	14	24	....	....	....	....	....	....	1944-45	1944-45
Breault, Francois	L.A.	3	27	2	4	6	42	....	....	....	....	....	....	1990-91	1992-93
Breitenbach, Ken	Buf.	3	68	1	13	14	49	8	0	1	1	4	....	1975-76	1978-79
Brennan, Dan	L.A.	2	8	0	1	1	9	....	....	....	....	....	....	1983-84	1985-86
Brennan, Doug	NYR	3	123	9	7	16	152	16	1	0	1	21	1	1931-32	1933-34
Brennan, Tom	Bos.	2	12	2	2	4	2	....	....	....	....	....	....	1943-44	1944-45
Brenneman, John	Chi., NYR, Tor., Det., Oak.	5	152	21	19	40	46	....	....	....	....	....	1	1964-65	1968-69
Bretto, Joe	Chi.	1	3	0	0	0	4	....	....	....	....	....	....	1944-45	1944-45
• Brewer, Carl	Tor., Det., St.L.	12	604	25	198	223	1037	72	3	17	20	146	3	1957-58	1979-80
Brickley, Andy	Phi., Pit., N.J., Bos., Wpg.	11	385	82	140	222	81	17	1	4	5	4	....	1982-83	1993-94
• Briden, Archie	Bos., Det., Pit.	2	71	9	5	14	56	....	....	....	....	....	....	1926-27	1929-30
Bridgman, Mel	Phi., Cgy., N.J., Det., Van.	14	977	252	449	701	1625	125	28	39	67	298	....	1975-76	1988-89
• Briere, Michel	Pit.	1	76	12	32	44	20	10	5	3	8	17	....	1969-70	1969-70
Brindley, Doug	Tor.	1	3	0	0	0	0	....	....	....	....	....	....	1970-71	1970-71
• Brink, Milt	Chi.	1	5	0	0	0	0	....	....	....	....	....	....	1936-37	1936-37
Brisson, Gerry	Mtl.	1	4	0	2	2	4	....	....	....	....	....	....	1962-63	1962-63
Britz, Greg	Tor., Hfd.	3	8	0	0	0	4	....	....	....	....	....	....	1983-84	1986-87
• Broadbent, Punch	Ott., Mtl.M., NYA	11	303	121	51	172	564	23	4	5	9	50	4	1918-19	1928-29
Brochu, Stephane	NYR	1	1	0	0	0	0	....	....	....	....	....	....	1988-89	1988-89
Broden, Connie	Mtl.	3	6	2	1	3	2	7	0	1	1	0	2	1955-56	1957-58
Brooke, Bob	NYR, Min., N.J.	7	447	69	97	166	520	34	9	9	18	59	....	1983-84	1989-90
Brooks, Gord	St.L., Wsh.	3	70	7	18	25	37	....	....	....	....	....	....	1971-72	1974-75
• Brophy, Bernie	Mtl.M., Det.	3	62	4	4	8	25	2	0	0	0	2	1	1925-26	1929-30
Brossart, Willie	Phi., Tor., Wsh.	6	129	1	14	15	88	1	0	0	0	0	....	1970-71	1975-76
Broten, Aaron	Col., N.J., Min., Que., Tor., Wpg.	12	748	186	329	515	441	34	7	18	25	40	....	1980-81	1991-92
Broten, Neal	Min., Dal., N.J., L.A.	17	1099	289	634	923	569	135	35	63	98	77	1	1980-81	1996-97
Broten, Paul	NYR, Dal., St.L.	7	322	46	55	101	264	38	4	6	10	18	....	1989-90	1995-96
‡ Brousseau, Paul	Col., T.B., Fla.	4	26	1	3	4	29	....	....	....	....	....	....	1995-96	2000-01
• Brown, Adam	Det., Chi., Bos.	10	391	104	113	217	378	26	2	4	6	14	1	1941-42	1951-52
Brown, Arnie	Tor., NYR, Det., NYI, Atl.	12	681	44	141	185	738	22	0	6	6	23	....	1961-62	1973-74
‡ Brown, Cam	Van.	1	1	0	0	0	7	....	....	....	....	....	....	1990-91	1990-91
• Brown, Connie	Det.	5	73	15	24	39	12	14	2	3	5	0	1	1938-39	1942-43
Brown, Dave	Phi., Edm., S.J.	14	729	45	52	97	1789	80	2	3	5	209	1	1982-83	1995-96
Brown, Doug	N.J., Pit., Det.	15	854	160	214	374	210	109	23	23	46	26	2	1986-87	2000-01
• Brown, Fred	Mtl.M.	1	19	1	0	1	0	9	0	0	0	0	....	1927-28	1927-28
Brown, George	Mtl.	3	79	6	22	28	34	7	0	0	0	2	....	1936-37	1938-39
• Brown, Gerry	Det.	2	23	4	5	9	2	12	2	1	3	4	....	1941-42	1945-46
Brown, Greg	Buf., Pit., Wpg.	4	94	4	14	18	86	6	0	1	1	4	....	1990-91	1994-95
Brown, Harold	NYR	1	13	2	1	3	2	....	....	....	....	....	....	1945-46	1945-46
Brown, Jeff	Que., St.L., Van., Hfd., Car., Tor., Wsh.	13	747	154	430	584	498	87	20	45	65	59	....	1985-86	1997-98
Brown, Jim	L.A.	1	3	0	1	1	5	....	....	....	....	....	....	1982-83	1982-83
Brown, Keith	Chi., Fla.	16	876	68	274	342	916	103	4	32	36	184	....	1979-80	1994-95
‡ Brown, Kevin	L.A., Hfd., Car., Edm.	6	64	7	9	16	28	1	0	0	0	0	....	1994-95	1999-00
Brown, Larry	NYR, Det., Phi., L.A.	9	455	7	53	60	180	35	0	4	4	10	....	1969-70	1977-78
‡ Brown, Rob	Pit., Hfd., Chi., Dal., L.A.	11	543	190	248	438	599	54	12	14	26	45	....	1987-88	1999-00
• Brown, Stan	NYR, Det.	2	48	8	2	10	18	2	0	0	0	0	....	1926-27	1927-28
Brown, Wayne	Bos.	1	....	....	....	....	....	4	0	0	0	2	....	1953-54	1953-54
• Browne, Cecil	Chi.	1	13	2	0	2	4	....	....	....	....	....	....	1927-28	1927-28
Brownschidle, Jack	St.L., Hfd.	9	494	39	162	201	151	26	0	5	5	18	....	1977-78	1985-86
Brownschidle, Jeff	Hfd.	2	7	0	1	1	2	....	....	....	....	....	....	1981-82	1982-83
Brubaker, Jeff	Hfd., Mtl., Cgy., Tor., Edm., NYR, Det.	8	178	16	9	25	512	2	0	0	0	27	....	1979-80	1988-89
Bruce, David	Van., St.L., S.J.	8	234	48	39	87	338	3	0	0	0	2	....	1985-86	1993-94
• Bruce, Gordie	Bos.	3	28	4	9	13	13	7	2	3	5	4	....	1940-41	1945-46
• Bruce, Morley	Ott.	4	71	8	3	11	27	3	0	0	0	2	2	1917-18	1921-22
Brumwell, Murray	Min., N.J.	7	128	12	31	43	70	2	0	0	0	2	....	1980-81	1987-88
Brunet, Benoit	Mtl., Dal., Ott.	13	539	101	161	262	229	54	5	20	25	32	1	1988-89	2001-02
• Bruneteau, Eddie	Det.	7	180	40	42	82	35	31	7	6	13	0	....	1940-41	1948-49
• Bruneteau, Mud	Det.	11	411	139	138	277	80	77	23	14	37	22	3	1935-36	1945-46
• Brydge, Bill	Tor., Det., NYA	9	368	26	52	78	506	2	0	0	0	4	....	1926-27	1935-36
Brydges, Paul	Buf.	1	15	2	2	4	6	....	....	....	....	....	....	1986-87	1986-87
• Brydson, Glenn	Mtl.M., St.L., NYR, Chi.	8	299	56	79	135	203	11	0	0	0	8	....	1930-31	1937-38
• Brydson, Gord	Tor.	1	8	2	0	2	8	....	....	....	....	....	....	1929-30	1929-30
Bubla, Jiri	Van.	5	256	17	101	118	202	6	0	0	0	7	....	1981-82	1985-86
• Buchanan, Al	Tor.	2	4	0	1	1	2	....	....	....	....	....	....	1948-49	1949-50
Buchanan, Bucky	NYR	1	2	0	0	0	0	....	....	....	....	....	....	1948-49	1948-49
Buchanan, Jeff	Col.	1	6	0	0	0	6	....	....	....	....	....	....	1998-99	1998-99
Buchanan, Mike	Chi.	1	1	0	0	0	0	....	....	....	....	....	....	1951-52	1951-52
Buchanan, Ron	Bos., St.L.	2	5	0	0	0	0	....	....	....	....	....	....	1966-67	1969-70
Bucyk, John	Det., Bos.	23	1540	556	813	1369	497	124	41	62	103	42	2	1955-56	1977-78
Bucyk, Randy	Mtl., Cgy.	2	19	4	2	6	8	2	0	0	0	0	....	1985-86	1987-88
Buhr, Doug	K.C.	1	6	0	2	2	4	....	....	....	....	....	....	1974-75	1974-75
Bukovich, Tony	Det.	2	17	7	3	10	6	6	0	1	1	0	....	1943-44	1944-45
‡ Bullard, Mike	Pit., Cgy., St.L., Phi., Tor.	11	727	329	345	674	703	40	11	18	29	44	....	1980-81	1991-92
• Buller, Hy	Det., NYR	5	188	22	58	80	215	....	....	....	....	....	....	1943-44	1953-54
Bulley, Ted	Chi., Wsh., Pit.	8	414	101	113	214	704	29	5	5	10	24	....	1976-77	1983-84
‡ Burakovsky, Robert	Ott.	1	23	2	3	5	6	....	....	....	....	....	....	1993-94	1993-94
• Burch, Billy	Ham., NYA, Bos., Chi.	11	390	137	61	198	255	2	0	0	0	0	....	1922-23	1932-33
• Burchell, Fred	Mtl.	2	4	0	0	0	2	....	....	....	....	....	....	1950-51	1953-54
Burdon, Glen	K.C.	1	11	0	2	2	0	....	....	....	....	....	....	1974-75	1974-75
Bureau, Marc	Cgy., Min., T.B., Mtl., Phi.	11	567	55	83	138	327	50	5	7	12	46	....	1989-90	1999-00
Burega, Bill	Tor.	1	4	0	1	1	4	....	....	....	....	....	....	1955-56	1955-56
• Burke, Eddie	Bos., NYA	4	106	29	20	49	55	....	....	....	....	....	....	1931-32	1934-35
• Burke, Marty	Mtl., Pit., Ott., Chi.	11	494	19	47	66	560	31	2	4	6	44	2	1927-28	1937-38
• Burmeister, Roy	NYA	3	67	4	3	7	2	....	....	....	....	....	....	1929-30	1931-32
Burnett, Kelly	NYR	1	3	1	0	1	0	....	....	....	....	....	....	1952-53	1952-53
• Burns, Bobby	Chi.	3	20	1	0	1	8	....	....	....	....	....	....	1927-28	1929-30
Burns, Charlie	Det., Bos., Oak., Pit., Min.	11	749	106	198	304	252	31	5	4	9	6	....	1958-59	1972-73
Burns, Gary	NYR	2	11	2	2	4	18	5	0	0	0	2	....	1980-81	1981-82
• Burns, Norm	NYR	1	11	0	4	4	2	....	....	....	....	....	....	1941-42	1941-42
Burns, Robin	Pit., K.C.	5	190	31	38	69	139	....	....	....	....	....	....	1970-71	1975-76
Burr, Shawn	Det., T.B., S.J.	16	878	181	259	440	1069	91	16	19	35	95	....	1984-85	1999-00

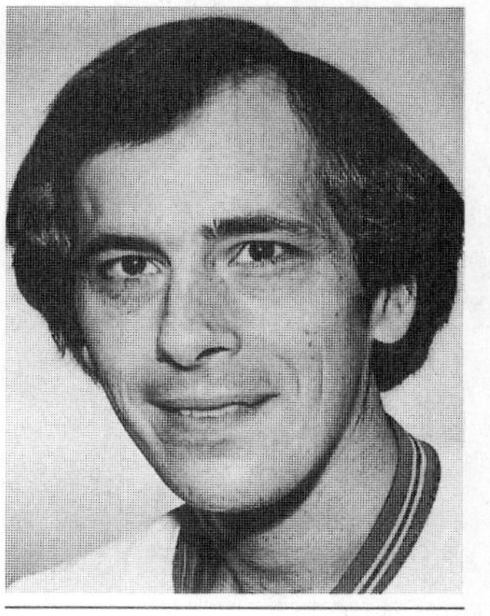

Nick Beverley

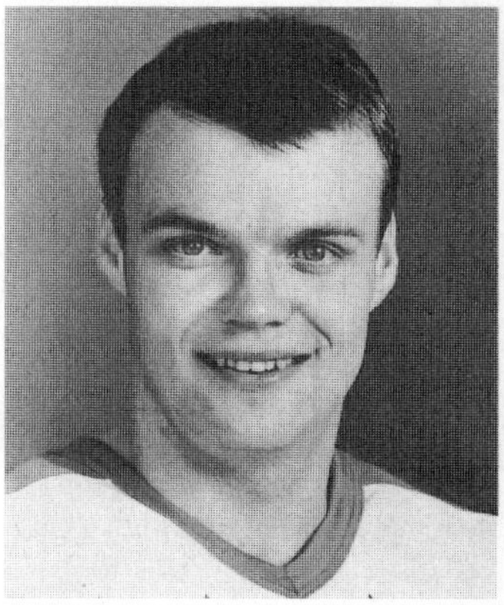

Timo Blomqvist

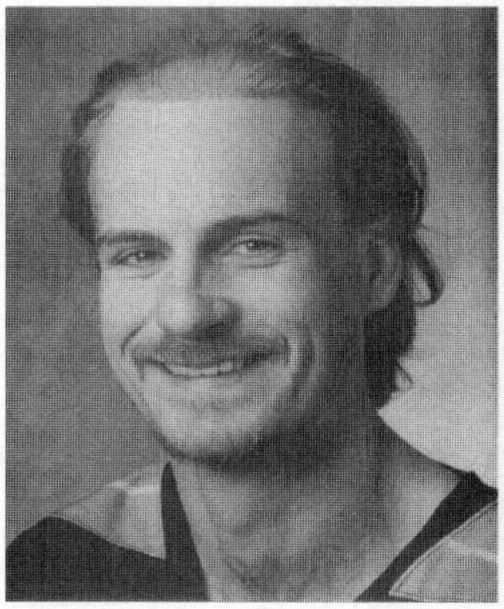

Rob Brown

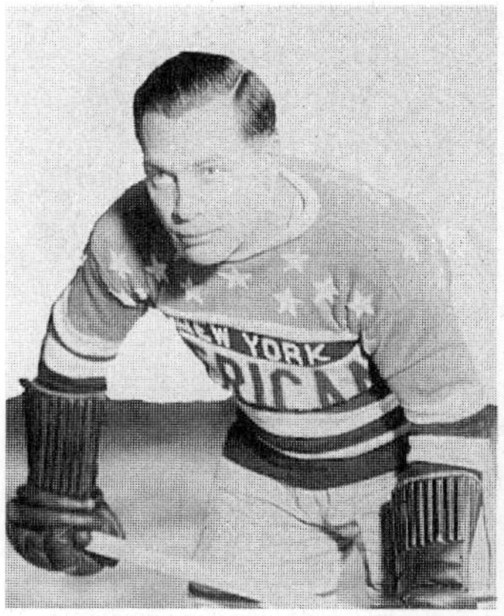

Billy Burch

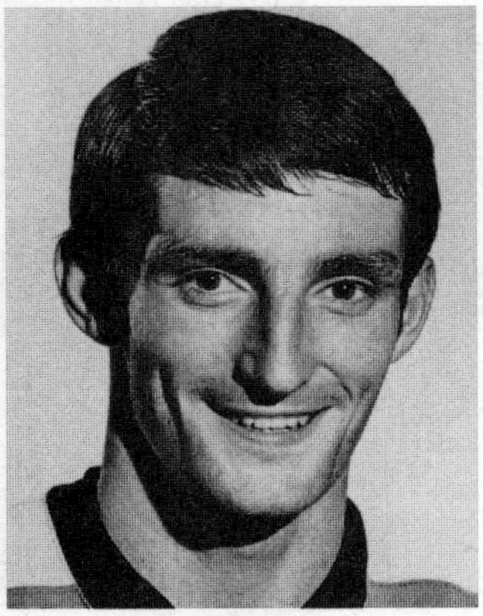

Dave Burrows

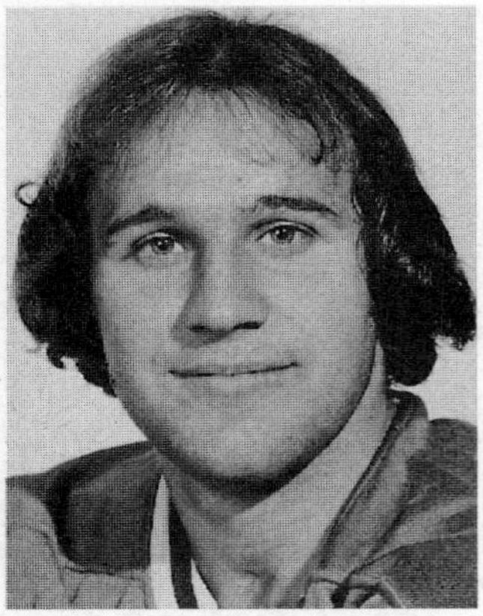

Colin Campbell

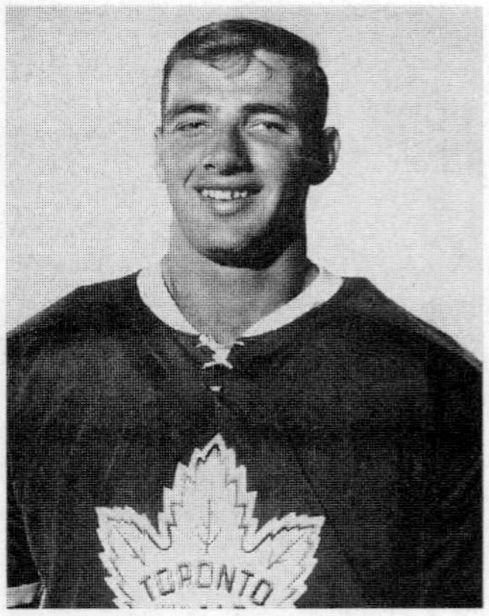

Wayne Carleton

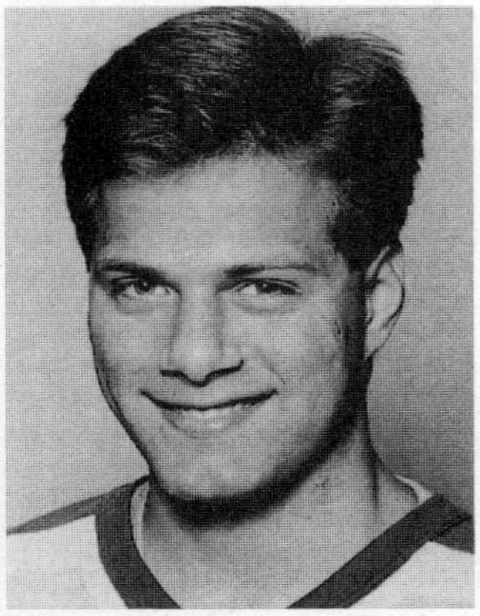

Jimmy Carson

			Regular Schedule					Playoffs					NHL	First	Last
Name	NHL Teams	NHL Seasons	GP	G	A	TP	PIM	GP	G	A	TP	PIM	Cup Wins	NHL Season	NHL Season
Burridge, Randy	Bos., Wsh., L.A., Buf.	13	706	199	251	450	458	107	18	34	52	103	....	1985-86	1997-98
Burrows, Dave	Pit., Tor.	10	724	29	135	164	373	29	1	5	6	25	....	1971-72	1980-81
• Burry, Bert	Ott.	1	4	0	0	0	0	....	....	....	....	....	....	1932-33	1932-33
Burt, Adam	Hfd., Car., Phi., Atl.	13	737	37	115	152	961	21	0	1	1	8	....	1988-89	2000-01
Burton, Cummy	Det.	3	43	0	2	2	21	3	0	0	0	0	....	1955-56	1958-59
Burton, Nelson	Wsh.	2	8	1	0	1	21	....	....	....	....	....	....	1977-78	1978-79
• Bush, Eddie	Det.	2	26	4	6	10	40	11	1	6	7	23	....	1938-39	1941-42
Buskas, Rod	Pit., Van., L.A., Chi.	11	556	19	63	82	1294	18	0	3	3	45	....	1982-83	1992-93
Busniuk, Mike	Phi.	2	143	3	23	26	297	25	2	5	7	34	....	1979-80	1980-81
Busniuk, Ron	Buf.	2	6	0	3	3	13	....	....	....	....	....	....	1972-73	1973-74
• Buswell, Walt	Det., Mtl.	8	368	10	40	50	164	24	2	1	3	10	....	1932-33	1939-40
Butcher, Garth	Van., St.L., Que., Tor.	14	897	48	158	206	2302	50	6	5	11	122	....	1981-82	1994-95
Butler, Dick	Chi.	1	7	2	0	2	0	....	....	....	....	....	....	1947-48	1947-48
Butler, Jerry	NYR, St.L., Tor., Van., Wpg.	11	641	99	120	219	515	48	3	3	6	79	....	1972-73	1982-83
‡ Butsayev, Viacheslav	Phi., S.J., Ana., Fla., Ott., T.B.	6	132	17	26	43	133	....	....	....	....	....	....	1992-93	1999-00
Butters, Bill	Min.	2	72	1	4	5	77	....	....	....	....	....	....	1977-78	1978-79
Buttrey, Gord	Chi.	1	10	0	0	0	0	....	....	....	....	....	....	1943-44	1943-44
Buynak, Gord	St.L.	1	4	0	0	0	2	....	....	....	....	....	....	1974-75	1974-75
‡ Byakin, Ilja	Edm., S.J.	2	57	8	25	33	44	....	....	....	....	....	....	1993-94	1994-95
Byce, John	Bos.	3	21	2	3	5	6	8	2	0	2	2	....	1989-90	1991-92
Byers, Gord	Bos.	1	1	0	1	1	0	....	....	....	....	....	....	1949-50	1949-50
Byers, Jerry	Min., Atl., NYR	4	43	3	4	7	15	....	....	....	....	....	....	1972-73	1977-78
Byers, Lyndon	Bos., S.J.	10	279	28	43	71	1081	37	2	2	4	96	....	1983-84	1992-93
Byers, Mike	Tor., Phi., L.A., Buf.	4	166	42	34	76	39	4	0	1	1	0	....	1967-68	1971-72
‡ Byram, Shawn	NYI, Chi.	2	5	0	0	0	14	....	....	....	....	....	....	1990-91	1991-92
C															
• Caffery, Jack	Tor., Bos.	3	57	3	2	5	22	10	1	0	1	4	....	1954-55	1957-58
Caffery, Terry	Chi., Min.	2	14	0	0	0	0	1	0	0	0	0	....	1969-70	1970-71
• Cahan, Larry	Tor., NYR, Oak., L.A.	13	666	38	92	130	700	29	1	1	2	38	....	1954-55	1970-71
• Cahill, Charles	Bos.	2	32	0	1	1	4	....	....	....	....	....	....	1925-26	1926-27
• Cain, Francis	Mtl.M., Tor.	2	61	4	0	4	35	....	....	....	....	....	....	1924-25	1925-26
• Cain, Herb	Mtl.M., Mtl., Bos.	13	570	206	194	400	178	67	16	13	29	13	2	1933-34	1945-46
Cairns, Don	K.C., Col.	2	9	0	1	1	2	....	....	....	....	....	....	1975-76	1976-77
Calder, Eric	Wsh.	2	2	0	0	0	0	....	....	....	....	....	....	1981-82	1982-83
• Calladine, Norm	Bos.	3	63	19	29	48	8	....	....	....	....	....	....	1942-43	1944-45
Callander, Drew	Phi., Van.	4	39	6	2	8	7	....	....	....	....	....	....	1976-77	1979-80
Callander, Jock	Pit., T.B.	5	109	22	29	51	116	22	3	8	11	12	1	1987-88	1992-93
Callighen, Brett	Edm.	3	160	56	89	145	132	14	4	6	10	8	....	1979-80	1981-82
Callighen, Patsy	NYR	1	36	0	0	0	32	9	0	0	0	0	1	1927-28	1927-28
‡ Caloun, Jan	S.J., CBJ	3	24	8	6	14	2	....	....	....	....	....	....	1995-96	2000-01
‡ Camazzola, James	Chi.	2	3	0	0	0	0	....	....	....	....	....	....	1983-84	1986-87
Camazzola, Tony	Wsh.	1	3	0	0	0	4	....	....	....	....	....	....	1981-82	1981-82
Cameron, Al	Det., Wpg.	6	282	11	44	55	356	7	0	1	1	2	....	1975-76	1980-81
• Cameron, Billy	Mtl., NYA	2	39	0	0	0	2	2	0	0	0	0	1	1923-24	1925-26
Cameron, Craig	Det., St.L., Min., NYI	9	552	87	65	152	196	27	3	1	4	17	....	1966-67	1975-76
Cameron, Dave	Col., N.J.	3	168	25	28	53	238	....	....	....	....	....	....	1981-82	1983-84
• Cameron, Harry	Tor., Ott., Mtl.	6	128	88	51	139	189	11	5	4	9	16	2	1917-18	1922-23
• Cameron, Scotty	NYR	1	35	8	11	19	0	....	....	....	....	....	....	1942-43	1942-43
Campbell, Bryan	L.A., Chi.	5	260	35	71	106	74	22	3	4	7	2	....	1967-68	1971-72
Campbell, Colin	Pit., Col., Edm., Van., Det.	11	636	25	103	128	1292	45	4	10	14	181	....	1974-75	1984-85
• Campbell, Dave	Mtl.	1	2	0	0	0	0	....	....	....	....	....	....	1920-21	1920-21
Campbell, Don	Chi.	1	17	1	3	4	8	....	....	....	....	....	....	1943-44	1943-44
• Campbell, Earl	Ott., NYA	3	76	6	3	9	14	1	0	0	0	6	....	1923-24	1925-26
Campbell, Scott	Wpg., St.L.	3	80	4	21	25	243	....	....	....	....	....	....	1979-80	1981-82
Campbell, Wade	Wpg., Bos.	6	213	9	27	36	305	10	0	0	0	20	....	1982-83	1987-88
Campeau, Tod	Mtl.	3	42	5	9	14	16	1	0	0	0	0	....	1943-44	1948-49
Campedelli, Dom	Mtl.	1	2	0	0	0	0	....	....	....	....	....	....	1985-86	1985-86
Capuano, Dave	Pit., Van., T.B., S.J.	4	104	17	38	55	56	6	1	1	2	5	....	1989-90	1993-94
Capuano, Jack	Tor., Van., Bos.	3	6	0	0	0	0	....	....	....	....	....	....	1989-90	1991-92
Carbol, Leo	Chi.	1	6	0	1	1	4	....	....	....	....	....	....	1942-43	1942-43
Carbonneau, Guy	Mtl., St.L., Dal.	19	1318	260	403	663	820	231	38	55	93	161	3	1980-81	1999-00
Cardin, Claude	St.L.	1	1	0	0	0	0	....	....	....	....	....	....	1967-68	1967-68
Cardwell, Steve	Pit.	3	53	9	11	20	35	4	0	0	0	2	....	1970-71	1972-73
• Carey, George	Que., Ham., Tor.	5	72	21	12	33	20	....	....	....	....	....	....	1919-20	1923-24
Carkner, Terry	NYR, Que., Phi., Det., Fla.	13	858	42	188	230	1588	54	1	9	10	48	....	1986-87	1998-99
Carleton, Wayne	Tor., Bos., Cal.	7	278	55	73	128	172	18	2	4	6	14	1	1965-66	1971-72
Carlin, Brian	L.A.	1	5	1	0	1	0	....	....	....	....	....	....	1971-72	1971-72
Carlson, Jack	Min., St.L.	6	236	30	15	45	417	25	1	2	3	72	....	1978-79	1986-87
Carlson, Kent	Mtl., St.L., Wsh.	5	113	7	11	18	148	8	0	0	0	13	....	1983-84	1988-89
Carlson, Steve	L.A.	1	52	9	12	21	23	4	1	1	2	7	....	1979-80	1979-80
Carlsson, Anders	N.J.	3	104	7	26	33	34	3	1	0	1	2	....	1986-87	1988-89
Carlyle, Randy	Tor., Pit., Wpg.	18	1055	148	499	647	1400	69	9	24	33	120	....	1976-77	1992-93
‡ Carnback, Patrik	Mtl., Ana.	4	154	24	38	62	122	....	....	....	....	....	....	1992-93	1995-96
• Caron, Alain	Oak., Mtl.	2	60	9	13	22	18	....	....	....	....	....	....	1967-68	1968-69
Carpenter, Bob	Wsh., NYR, L.A., Bos., N.J.	19	1178	320	408	728	919	140	21	38	59	136	1	1981-82	1998-99
• Carpenter, Ed	Que., Ham.	2	45	10	5	15	41	....	....	....	....	....	....	1919-20	1920-21
Carr, Gene	St.L., NYR, L.A., Pit., Atl.	8	465	79	136	215	365	35	5	8	13	66	....	1971-72	1978-79
Carr, Lorne	NYR, NYA, Tor.	13	580	204	222	426	132	53	10	9	19	13	2	1933-34	1945-46
Carr, Red	Tor.	1	5	0	1	1	2	....	....	....	....	....	....	1943-44	1943-44
Carriere, Larry	Buf., Atl., Van., L.A., Tor.	7	367	16	74	90	462	27	0	3	3	42	....	1972-73	1979-80
• Carrigan, Gene	NYR, Det., St.L.	3	37	2	1	3	13	4	0	0	0	0	....	1930-31	1934-35
Carroll, Billy	NYI, Edm., Det.	7	322	30	54	84	113	71	6	12	18	18	4	1980-81	1986-87
• Carroll, George	Mtl.M., Bos.	1	16	0	0	0	11	....	....	....	....	....	....	1924-25	1924-25
Carroll, Greg	Wsh., Det., Hfd.	2	131	20	34	54	44	....	....	....	....	....	....	1978-79	1979-80
Carruthers, Dwight	Det., Phi.	2	2	0	0	0	0	....	....	....	....	....	....	1965-66	1967-68
• Carse, Bill	NYR, Chi.	4	124	28	43	71	38	13	3	2	5	0	....	1938-39	1941-42
• Carse, Bob	Chi., Mtl.	5	167	32	55	87	52	10	0	2	2	2	....	1939-40	1947-48
• Carson, Bill	Tor., Bos.	4	159	54	24	78	156	11	3	0	3	14	1	1926-27	1929-30
• Carson, Frank	Mtl.M., NYA, Det.	7	248	42	48	90	166	27	0	2	2	9	1	1925-26	1933-34
• Carson, Gerry	Mtl., NYR, Mtl.M.	6	261	12	11	23	205	22	0	0	0	12	1	1928-29	1936-37
Carson, Jimmy	L.A., Edm., Det., Van., Hfd.	10	626	275	286	561	254	55	17	15	32	22	....	1986-87	1995-96
Carson, Lindsay	Phi., Hfd.	7	373	66	80	146	524	49	4	10	14	56	....	1981-82	1987-88
Carter, Billy	Mtl., Bos.	3	16	0	0	0	6	....	....	....	....	....	....	1957-58	1961-62
Carter, John	Bos., S.J.	8	244	40	50	90	201	31	7	5	12	51	....	1985-86	1992-93
Carter, Ron	Edm.	1	2	0	0	0	0	....	....	....	....	....	....	1979-80	1979-80
• Carveth, Joe	Det., Bos., Mtl.	11	504	150	189	339	81	69	21	16	37	28	2	1940-41	1950-51
Cashman, Wayne	Bos.	17	1027	277	516	793	1041	145	31	57	88	250	2	1964-65	1982-83
‡ Casselman, Mike	Fla.	1	3	0	0	0	0	....	....	....	....	....	....	1995-96	1995-96
Cassidy, Bruce	Chi.	7	36	4	13	17	10	1	0	0	0	0	....	1983-84	1989-90
Cassidy, Tom	Pit.	1	26	3	4	7	15	....	....	....	....	....	....	1977-78	1977-78
Cassolato, Tony	Wsh.	3	23	1	6	7	4	....	....	....	....	....	....	1979-80	1981-82
Caufield, Jay	NYR, Min., Pit.	7	208	5	8	13	759	17	0	0	0	42	2	1986-87	1992-93
Cavallini, Gino	Cgy., St.L., Que.	9	593	114	159	273	507	74	14	19	33	66	....	1984-85	1992-93
Cavallini, Paul	Wsh., St.L., Dal.	10	564	56	177	233	750	69	8	27	35	114	....	1986-87	1995-96
Ceresino, Ray	Tor.	1	12	1	1	2	2	....	....	....	....	....	....	1948-49	1948-49
Cernik, Frantisek	Det.	1	49	5	4	9	13	....	....	....	....	....	....	1984-85	1984-85
Chabot, John	Mtl., Pit., Det.	8	508	84	228	312	85	33	6	20	26	2	....	1983-84	1990-91
• Chad, John	Chi.	3	80	15	22	37	29	10	0	1	1	2	....	1939-40	1945-46
• Chalmers, Chick	NYR	1	1	0	0	0	0	....	....	....	....	....	....	1953-54	1953-54
Chalupa, Milan	Det.	1	14	0	5	5	6	....	....	....	....	....	....	1984-85	1984-85
• Chamberlain, Murph	Tor., Mtl., Bro., Bos.	12	510	100	175	275	769	66	14	17	31	96	2	1937-38	1948-49
Chambers, Shawn	Min., Wsh., T.B., N.J., Dal.	13	625	50	185	235	364	94	7	26	33	72	2	1987-88	1999-00
Champagne, Andre	Tor.	1	2	0	0	0	0	....	....	....	....	....	....	1962-63	1962-63
‡ Chapdelaine, Rene	L.A.	3	32	0	2	2	32	....	....	....	....	....	....	1990-91	1992-93
• Chapman, Art	Bos., NYA	10	438	62	176	238	140	26	1	5	6	9	....	1930-31	1939-40
Chapman, Blair	Pit., St.L.	7	402	106	125	231	158	25	4	6	10	15	....	1976-77	1982-83
Charbonneau, Jose	Mtl., Van.	4	71	9	13	22	67	11	1	0	1	8	....	1987-88	1994-95
Charbonneau, Stephane	Que.	1	2	0	0	0	0	....	....	....	....	....	....	1991-92	1991-92
Charlebois, Bob	Min.	1	7	1	0	1	0	....	....	....	....	....	....	1967-68	1967-68
Charlesworth, Todd	Pit., NYR	6	93	3	9	12	47	....	....	....	....	....	....	1983-84	1989-90
‡ Charron, Eric	Mtl., T.B., Wsh., Cgy.	8	130	2	7	9	127	6	0	0	0	8	....	1992-93	1999-00
Charron, Guy	Mtl., Det., K.C., Wsh.	12	734	221	309	530	146	....	....	....	....	....	....	1969-70	1980-81
Chartier, Dave	Wpg.	1	1	0	0	0	0	....	....	....	....	....	....	1980-81	1980-81
Chartraw, Rick	Mtl., L.A., NYR, Edm.	10	420	28	64	92	399	75	7	9	16	80	4	1974-75	1983-84

Name	NHL Teams	NHL Seasons	Regular Schedule					Playoffs					NHL Cup Wins	First NHL Season	Last NHL Season
			GP	G	A	TP	PIM	GP	G	A	TP	PIM			
Chase, Kelly	St.L., Hfd., Tor.	11	458	17	36	53	2017	27	1	1	2	100	....	1989-90	1999-00
Chasse, Denis	St.L., Wsh., Wpg., Ott.	4	132	11	14	25	292	7	1	7	8	23	....	1993-94	1996-97
Check, Lude	Det., Chi.	2	27	6	2	8	4	....	....	....	....	....	....	1943-44	1944-45
Chernoff, Mike	Min.	1	1	0	0	0	0	....	....	....	....	....	....	1968-69	1968-69
Chernomaz, Rich	Col., N.J., Cgy.	7	51	9	7	16	18	....	....	....	....	....	....	1981-82	1991-92
Cherry, Dick	Bos., Phi.	3	145	12	10	22	45	4	1	0	1	4	....	1956-57	1969-70
Cherry, Don	Bos.	1	....	....	....	....	....	1	0	0	0	0	....	1954-55	1954-55
Chervyakov, Denis	Bos.	1	2	0	0	0	2	....	....	....	....	....	....	1992-93	1992-93
• Chevrefils, Real	Bos., Det.	8	387	104	97	201	185	30	5	4	9	20	....	1951-52	1958-59
• Chiasson, Steve	Det., Cgy., Hfd., Car.	13	751	93	305	398	1107	63	16	19	35	119	....	1986-87	1998-99
‡ Chibirev, Igor	Hfd.	2	45	7	12	19	2	....	....	....	....	....	....	1993-94	1994-95
Chicoine, Dan	Cle., Min.	3	31	1	2	3	12	1	0	0	0	0	....	1977-78	1979-80
Chinnick, Rick	Min.	2	4	0	2	2	0	....	....	....	....	....	....	1973-74	1974-75
Chipperfield, Ron	Edm., Que.	2	83	22	24	46	34	....	....	....	....	....	....	1979-80	1980-81
Chisholm, Art	Bos.	1	3	0	0	0	0	....	....	....	....	....	....	1960-61	1960-61
Chisholm, Colin	Min.	1	1	0	0	0	0	....	....	....	....	....	....	1986-87	1986-87
• Chisholm, Lex	Tor.	2	54	10	8	18	19	3	1	0	1	0	....	1939-40	1940-41
Chorney, Marc	Pit., L.A.	4	210	8	27	35	209	7	0	1	1	2	....	1980-81	1983-84
Chorske, Tom	Mtl., N.J., Ott., NYI, Wsh., Cgy., Pit.	11	596	115	122	237	225	50	5	12	17	10	1	1989-90	1999-00
• Chouinard, Gene	Ott.	1	8	0	0	0	0	....	....	....	....	....	....	1927-28	1927-28
Chouinard, Guy	Atl., Cgy., St.L.	10	578	205	370	575	120	46	9	28	37	12	....	1974-75	1983-84
Christian, Dave	Wpg., Wsh., Bos., St.L., Chi.	15	1009	340	433	773	284	102	32	25	57	27	....	1979-80	1993-94
‡ Christian, Jeff	N.J., Pit., Phx.	5	18	2	2	4	17	....	....	....	....	....	....	1991-92	1997-98
Christie, Mike	Cal., Cle., Col., Van.	7	412	15	101	116	550	2	0	0	0	0	....	1974-75	1980-81
Christoff, Steve	Min., Cgy., L.A.	5	248	77	64	141	108	35	16	12	28	25	....	1979-80	1983-84
Chrystal, Bob	NYR	2	132	11	14	25	112	....	....	....	....	....	....	1953-54	1954-55
‡ Church, Brad	Wsh.	1	2	0	0	0	0	....	....	....	....	....	....	1997-98	1997-98
• Church, Jack	Tor., Bro., Bos.	5	130	4	19	23	154	25	1	1	2	18	....	1938-39	1945-46
Churla, Shane	Hfd., Cgy., Min., Dal., L.A., NYR	11	488	26	45	71	2301	78	5	7	12	282	....	1986-87	1996-97
Chychrun, Jeff	Phi., L.A., Pit., Edm.	8	262	3	22	25	744	19	0	2	2	65	1	1986-87	1993-94
Chynoweth, Dean	NYI, Bos.	9	241	4	18	22	667	6	0	0	0	26	....	1988-89	1997-98
‡ Chyzowski, Dave	NYI, Chi.	6	126	15	16	31	144	2	0	0	0	0	....	1989-90	1996-97
Ciavaglia, Peter	Buf.	2	5	0	0	0	0	....	....	....	....	....	....	1991-92	1992-93
Ciccarelli, Dino	Min., Wsh., Det., T.B., Fla.	19	1232	608	592	1200	1425	141	73	45	118	211	....	1980-81	1998-99
Ciccone, Enrico	Min., Wsh., T.B., Chi., Car., Van., Mtl.	9	374	10	18	28	1469	13	1	0	1	48	....	1991-92	2000-01
Cichocki, Chris	Det., N.J.	4	68	11	12	23	27	....	....	....	....	....	....	1985-86	1988-89
Cierny, Jozef	Edm.	1	1	0	0	0	0	....	....	....	....	....	....	1993-94	1993-94
• Ciesla, Hank	Chi., NYR	4	269	26	51	77	87	6	0	2	2	0	....	1955-56	1958-59
‡ Ciger, Zdeno	N.J., Edm., NYR, T.B.	7	352	94	134	228	101	13	2	6	8	4	....	1990-91	2001-02
Cimellaro, Tony	Ott.	1	2	0	0	0	0	....	....	....	....	....	....	1992-93	1992-93
Cimetta, Rob	Bos., Tor.	4	103	16	16	32	66	1	0	0	0	15	....	1988-89	1991-92
Cirella, Joe	Col., N.J., Que., NYR, Fla., Ott.	15	828	64	211	275	1446	38	0	13	13	98	....	1981-82	1995-96
‡ Cirone, Jason	Wpg.	1	3	0	0	0	2	....	....	....	....	....	....	1991-92	1991-92
Clackson, Kim	Pit., Que.	2	106	0	8	8	370	8	0	0	0	70	....	1979-80	1980-81
• Clancy, King	Ott., Tor.	16	592	136	147	283	914	55	8	8	16	92	3	1921-22	1936-37
Clancy, Terry	Oak., Tor.	4	93	6	6	12	39	....	....	....	....	....	....	1967-68	1972-73
• Clapper, Dit	Bos.	20	833	228	246	474	462	82	13	17	30	50	3	1927-28	1946-47
Clark, Dan	NYR	1	4	0	1	1	6	....	....	....	....	....	....	1978-79	1978-79
Clark, Dean	Edm.	1	1	0	0	0	0	....	....	....	....	....	....	1983-84	1983-84
Clark, Gordie	Bos.	2	8	0	1	1	0	1	0	0	0	0	....	1974-75	1975-76
• Clark, Nobby	Bos.	1	5	0	0	0	0	....	....	....	....	....	....	1927-28	1927-28
Clark, Wendel	Tor., Que., NYI, T.B., Det., Chi.	15	793	330	234	564	1690	95	37	32	69	201	....	1985-86	1999-00
Clarke, Bobby	Phi.	15	1144	358	852	1210	1453	136	42	77	119	152	2	1969-70	1983-84
• Cleghorn, Odie	Mtl., Pit.	10	181	95	34	129	142	12	7	1	8	2	1	1918-19	1927-28
• Cleghorn, Sprague	Ott., Tor., Mtl., Bos.	10	259	83	55	138	538	21	4	2	6	28	2	1918-19	1927-28
Clement, Bill	Phi., Wsh., Atl., Cgy.	11	719	148	208	356	383	50	5	3	8	26	2	1971-72	1981-82
Cline, Bruce	NYR	1	30	2	3	5	10	....	....	....	....	....	....	1956-57	1956-57
Clippingdale, Steve	L.A., Wsh.	2	19	1	2	3	9	1	0	0	0	0	....	1976-77	1979-80
Cloutier, Real	Que., Buf.	6	317	146	198	344	119	25	7	5	12	20	....	1979-80	1984-85
Cloutier, Rejean	Det.	2	5	0	2	2	2	....	....	....	....	....	....	1979-80	1981-82
Cloutier, Roland	Det., Que.	3	34	8	9	17	2	....	....	....	....	....	....	1977-78	1979-80
‡ Cloutier, Sylvain	Chi.	1	7	0	0	0	0	....	....	....	....	....	....	1998-99	1998-99
• Clune, Wally	Mtl.	1	5	0	0	0	6	....	....	....	....	....	....	1955-56	1955-56
Coalter, Gary	Cal., K.C.	2	34	2	4	6	2	....	....	....	....	....	....	1973-74	1974-75
Coates, Steve	Det.	1	5	1	0	1	24	....	....	....	....	....	....	1976-77	1976-77
Cochrane, Glen	Phi., Van., Chi., Edm.	10	411	17	72	89	1556	18	1	1	2	31	....	1978-79	1988-89
Coffey, Paul	Edm., Pit., L.A., Det., Hfd., Phi., Chi., Car., Bos.	21	1409	396	1135	1531	1802	194	59	137	196	264	4	1980-81	2000-01
Coflin, Hugh	Chi.	1	31	0	3	3	33	....	....	....	....	....	....	1950-51	1950-51
Cole, Danton	Wpg., T.B., N.J., NYI, Chi.	7	318	58	60	118	125	1	0	0	0	0	1	1989-90	1995-96
Colley, Tom	Min.	1	1	0	0	0	2	....	....	....	....	....	....	1974-75	1974-75
Collings, Norm	Mtl.	1	1	0	1	1	0	....	....	....	....	....	....	1934-35	1934-35
Collins, Bill	Min., Mtl., Det., St.L., NYR, Phi., Wsh.	11	768	157	154	311	415	18	3	5	8	12	....	1967-68	1977-78
Collins, Gary	Tor.	1	....	....	....	....	....	2	0	0	0	0	....	1958-59	1958-59
Collyard, Bob	St.L.	1	10	1	3	4	4	....	....	....	....	....	....	1973-74	1973-74
• Colman, Michael	S.J.	1	15	0	1	1	32	....	....	....	....	....	....	1991-92	1991-92
• Colville, Mac	NYR	9	353	71	104	175	130	40	9	10	19	14	1	1935-36	1946-47
• Colville, Neil	NYR	12	464	99	166	265	213	46	7	19	26	32	1	1935-36	1948-49
Colwill, Les	NYR	1	69	7	6	13	16	....	....	....	....	....	....	1958-59	1958-59
Comeau, Rey	Mtl., Atl., Col.	9	564	98	141	239	175	9	2	1	3	8	....	1971-72	1979-80
Comrie, Paul	Edm.	1	15	1	2	3	4	....	....	....	....	....	....	1999-00	1999-00
Conacher, Brian	Tor., Det.	5	155	28	28	56	84	12	3	2	5	21	1	1961-62	1971-72
• Conacher, Charlie	Tor., Det., NYA	12	459	225	173	398	523	49	17	18	35	49	1	1929-30	1940-41
Conacher, Jim	Det., Chi., NYR	8	328	85	117	202	91	19	5	2	7	4	....	1945-46	1952-53
• Conacher, Lionel	Pit., NYA, Mtl.M., Chi.	12	498	80	105	185	882	35	2	2	4	34	2	1925-26	1936-37
Conacher, Pat	NYR, Edm., N.J., L.A., Cgy., NYI	13	521	63	76	139	235	66	11	10	21	40	1	1979-80	1995-96
Conacher, Pete	Chi., NYR, Tor.	6	229	47	39	86	57	7	0	0	0	0	....	1951-52	1957-58
• Conacher, Roy	Bos., Det., Chi.	11	490	226	200	426	90	42	15	15	30	14	2	1938-39	1951-52
• Conn, Red	NYA	2	96	9	28	37	22	....	....	....	....	....	....	1933-34	1934-35
Conn, Rob	Chi., Buf.	2	30	2	5	7	20	....	....	....	....	....	....	1991-92	1995-96
• Connelly, Bert	NYR, Chi.	3	87	13	15	28	37	14	1	0	1	0	1	1934-35	1937-38
Connelly, Wayne	Mtl., Bos., Min., Det., St.L., Van.	10	543	133	174	307	156	24	11	7	18	4	....	1960-61	1971-72
Connor, Cam	Mtl., Edm., NYR	5	89	9	22	31	256	20	5	0	5	6	1	1978-79	1982-83
• Connor, Harry	Bos., NYA, Ott.	4	134	16	5	21	149	10	0	0	0	2	....	1927-28	1930-31
• Connors, Bob	NYA, Det.	3	78	17	10	27	110	2	0	0	0	10	....	1926-27	1929-30
Conroy, Al	Phi.	3	114	9	14	23	156	....	....	....	....	....	....	1991-92	1993-94
Contini, Joe	Col., Min.	3	68	17	21	38	34	2	0	0	0	0	....	1977-78	1980-81
‡ Convery, Brandon	Tor., Van., L.A.	4	72	9	19	28	36	5	0	0	0	2	....	1995-96	1998-99
• Convey, Eddie	NYA	3	36	1	1	2	33	....	....	....	....	....	....	1930-31	1932-33
• Cook, Bill	NYR	11	474	229	138	367	386	46	13	11	24	68	2	1926-27	1936-37
• Cook, Bob	Van., Det., NYI, Min.	4	72	13	9	22	22	....	....	....	....	....	....	1970-71	1974-75
• Cook, Bud	Bos., Ott., St.L.	3	50	5	4	9	22	....	....	....	....	....	....	1931-32	1934-35
• Cook, Bun	NYR, Bos.	11	473	158	144	302	444	46	15	3	18	50	2	1926-27	1936-37
• Cook, Lloyd	Bos.	1	4	1	0	1	0	....	....	....	....	....	....	1924-25	1924-25
• Cook, Tom	Chi., Mtl.M.	9	349	77	98	175	184	24	2	4	6	19	1	1929-30	1937-38
• Cooper, Carson	Bos., Mtl., Det.	8	294	110	57	167	111	7	0	0	0	2	....	1924-25	1931-32
‡ Cooper, David	Tor.	3	30	3	7	10	24	....	....	....	....	....	....	1996-97	2000-01
Cooper, Ed	Col.	2	49	8	7	15	46	....	....	....	....	....	....	1980-81	1981-82
• Cooper, Hal	NYR	1	8	0	0	0	2	....	....	....	....	....	....	1944-45	1944-45
• Cooper, Joe	NYR, Chi.	11	420	30	66	96	442	35	3	5	8	58	....	1935-36	1946-47
Copp, Bob	Tor.	2	40	3	9	12	26	....	....	....	....	....	....	1942-43	1950-51
• Corbeau, Bert	Mtl., Ham., Tor.	10	258	63	49	112	629	9	2	2	4	38	....	1917-18	1926-27
Corbet, Rene	Que., Col., Cgy., Pit.	8	362	58	74	132	420	53	7	6	13	52	1	1993-94	2000-01
• Corbett, Mike	L.A.	1	....	....	....	....	....	2	0	1	1	2	....	1967-68	1967-68
Corcoran, Norm	Bos., Det., Chi.	4	29	1	3	4	21	4	0	0	0	6	....	1949-50	1955-56
Corkum, Bob	Buf., Ana., Phi., Phx., L.A., N.J., Atl.	12	720	97	103	200	281	62	7	7	14	24	....	1989-90	2001-02
• Cormier, Roger	Mtl.	1	1	0	0	0	0	....	....	....	....	....	....	1925-26	1925-26
Cornforth, Mark	Bos.	1	6	0	0	0	4	....	....	....	....	....	....	1995-96	1995-96
Corrigan, Chuck	Tor., NYA	2	19	2	2	4	2	....	....	....	....	....	....	1937-38	1940-41
Corrigan, Mike	L.A., Van., Pit.	10	594	152	195	347	698	17	2	3	5	20	....	1967-68	1977-78
• Corriveau, Andre	Mtl.	1	3	0	1	1	0	....	....	....	....	....	....	1953-54	1953-54
‡ Corriveau, Yvon	Wsh., Hfd., S.J.	9	280	48	40	88	310	29	5	7	12	50	....	1985-86	1993-94
Cory, Ross	Wpg.	2	51	2	10	12	41	....	....	....	....	....	....	1979-80	1980-81
Cossette, Jacques	Pit.	3	64	8	6	14	29	3	0	1	1	4	....	1975-76	1978-79
• Costello, Les	Tor.	3	15	2	3	5	11	6	2	2	4	2	1	1947-48	1949-50
Costello, Murray	Chi., Bos., Det.	4	162	13	19	32	54	5	0	0	0	2	....	1953-54	1956-57

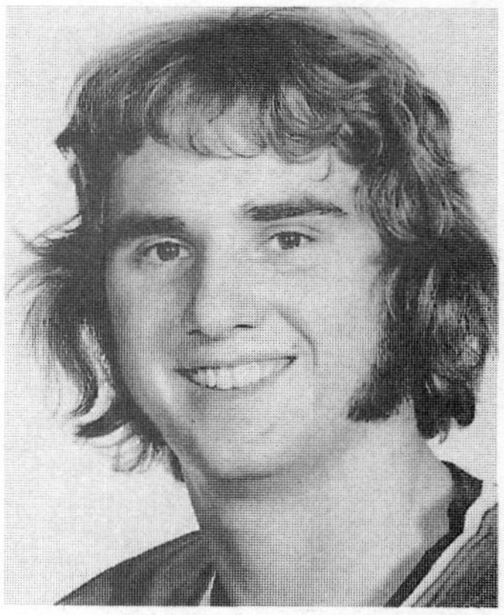

Blair Chapman

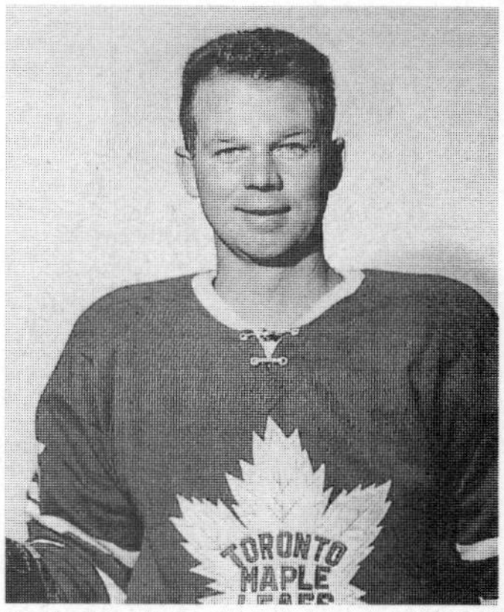

Don Cherry

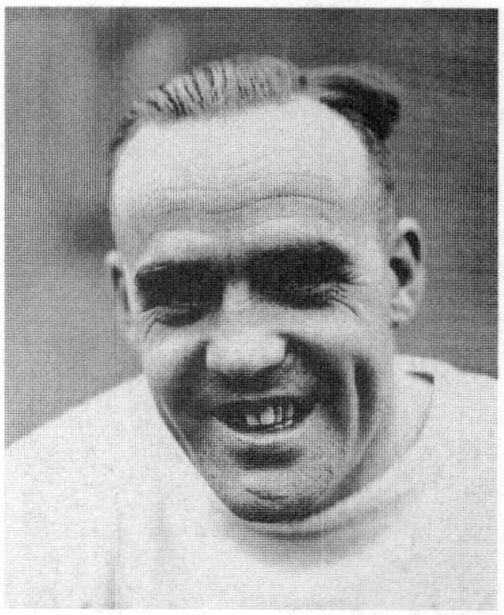

King Clancy

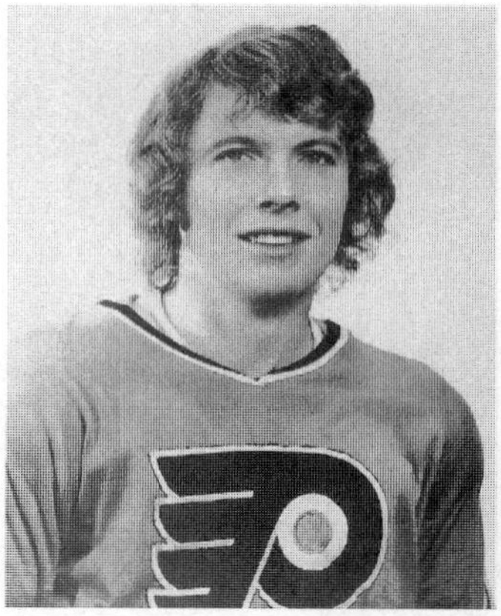

Bobby Clarke

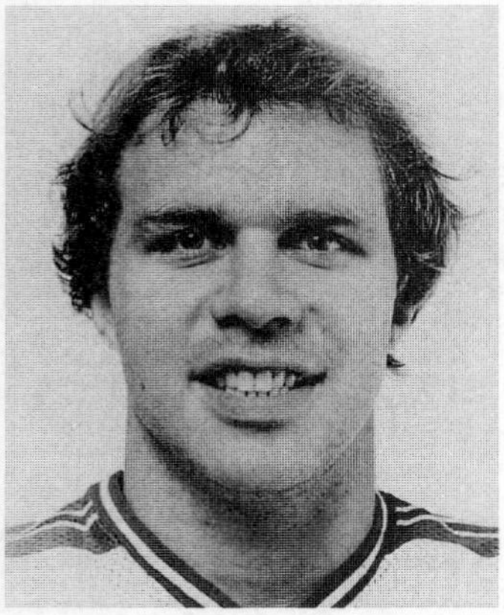
Cam Connor

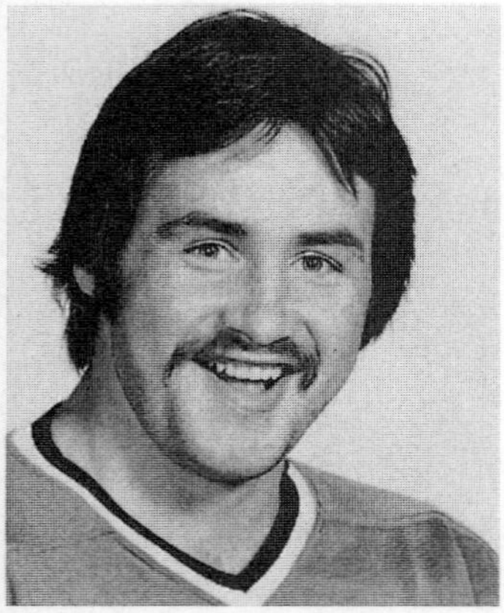
Jacques Cossette

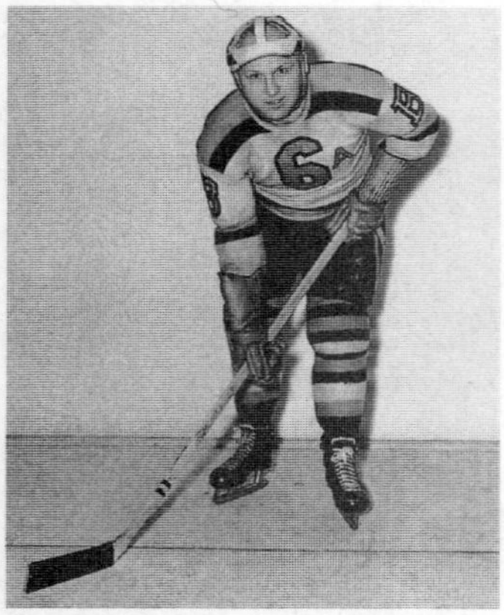
Jack Crawford

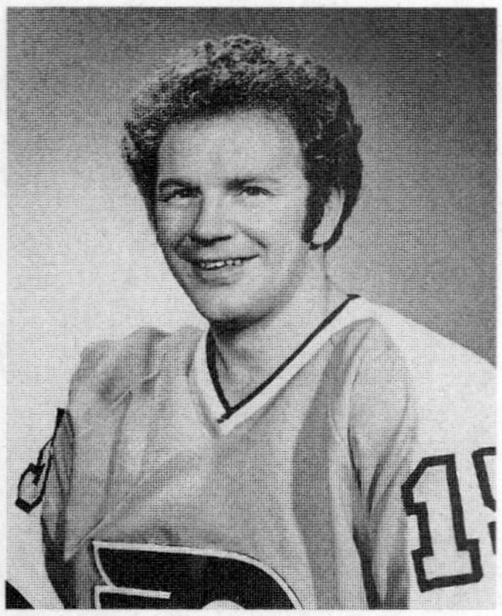
Terry Crisp

Name	NHL Teams	NHL Seasons	Regular Schedule GP	G	A	TP	PIM	Playoffs GP	G	A	TP	PIM	NHL Cup Wins	First NHL Season	Last NHL Season
Costello, Rich	Tor.	2	12	2	2	4	2	....	....	....	....	....	....	1983-84	1985-86
• Cotch, Charlie	Ham., Tor.	1	12	1	0	1	0	....	....	....	....	....	....	1924-25	1924-25
Cote, Alain	Que.	10	696	103	190	293	383	67	9	15	24	44	....	1979-80	1988-89
‡ Cote, Alain	Bos., Wsh., Mtl., T.B., Que.	9	119	2	18	20	124	11	0	2	2	26	....	1985-86	1993-94
‡ Cote, Patrick	Dal., Nsh., Edm.	6	105	1	2	3	377	....	....	....	....	....	....	1995-96	2000-01
Cote, Ray	Edm.	3	15	0	0	0	4	14	3	2	5	0	....	1982-83	1984-85
• Cotton, Baldy	Pit., Tor., NYA	12	503	101	103	204	419	43	4	9	13	46	1	1925-26	1936-37
• Coughlin, Jack	Tor., Que., Mtl., Ham.	3	19	2	0	2	3	....	....	....	....	....	1	1917-18	1920-21
Coulis, Tim	Wsh., Min.	4	47	4	5	9	138	3	1	0	1	2	....	1979-80	1985-86
Coulson, D'arcy	Phi.	1	28	0	0	0	103	....	....	....	....	....	....	1930-31	1930-31
• Coulter, Art	Chi., NYR	11	465	30	82	112	543	49	4	5	9	61	2	1931-32	1941-42
Coulter, Neal	NYI	3	26	5	5	10	11	....	....	....	....	....	....	1985-86	1987-88
Cournoyer, Yvan	Mtl.	16	968	428	435	863	255	147	64	63	127	47	10	1963-64	1978-79
Courteau, Yves	Cgy., Hfd.	3	22	2	5	7	4	1	0	0	0	0	....	1984-85	1986-87
‡ Courtenay, Ed	S.J.	2	44	7	13	20	10	....	....	....	....	....	....	1991-92	1992-93
Courtnall, Geoff	Bos., Edm., Wsh., St.L., Van.	17	1048	367	432	799	1465	156	39	70	109	262	1	1983-84	1999-00
Courtnall, Russ	Tor., Mtl., Min., Dal., Van., NYR, L.A.	16	1029	297	447	744	557	129	39	44	83	83	....	1983-84	1998-99
‡ Courville, Larry	Van.	3	33	1	2	3	16	....	....	....	....	....	....	1995-96	1997-98
• Coutu, Billy	Mtl., Ham., Bos.	10	244	33	21	54	478	19	1	1	2	35	1	1917-18	1926-27
• Couture, Gerry	Det., Mtl., Chi.	10	385	86	70	156	89	45	9	7	16	4	1	1944-45	1953-54
• Couture, Rosie	Chi., Mtl.	8	309	48	56	104	184	23	1	5	6	15	1	1928-29	1935-36
Couturier, Sylvain	L.A.	3	33	4	5	9	4	....	....	....	....	....	....	1988-89	1991-92
Cowick, Bruce	Phi., Wsh., St.L.	3	70	5	6	11	43	8	0	0	0	9	1	1973-74	1975-76
‡ Cowie, Rob	L.A.	2	78	7	12	19	52	....	....	....	....	....	....	1994-95	1995-96
• Cowley, Bill	St.L., Bos.	13	549	195	353	548	143	64	12	34	46	22	2	1934-35	1946-47
• Cox, Danny	Tor., Ott., Det., NYR	8	319	47	49	96	128	10	0	1	1	6	....	1926-27	1933-34
Coxe, Craig	Van., Cgy., St.L., S.J.	8	235	14	31	45	713	5	1	0	1	18	....	1984-85	1991-92
Craigwell, Dale	S.J.	3	98	11	18	29	28	....	....	....	....	....	....	1991-92	1993-94
Crashley, Bart	Det., K.C., L.A.	6	140	7	36	43	50	....	....	....	....	....	....	1965-66	1975-76
Craven, Murray	Det., Phi., Hfd., Van., Chi., S.J.	18	1071	266	493	759	524	118	27	43	70	64	....	1982-83	1999-00
Crawford, Bob	St.L., Hfd., NYR, Wsh.	7	246	71	71	142	72	11	0	1	1	8	....	1979-80	1986-87
Crawford, Bobby	Col., Det.	2	16	1	3	4	6	....	....	....	....	....	....	1980-81	1982-83
• Crawford, Jack	Bos.	13	548	38	140	178	202	66	3	13	16	36	2	1937-38	1949-50
Crawford, Lou	Bos.	2	26	2	1	3	29	1	0	0	0	0	....	1989-90	1991-92
Crawford, Marc	Van.	6	176	19	31	50	229	20	1	2	3	44	....	1981-82	1986-87
• Crawford, Rusty	Ott., Tor.	2	38	10	8	18	117	2	2	1	3	9	1	1917-18	1918-19
Creighton, Adam	Buf., Chi., NYI, T.B., St.L.	14	708	187	216	403	1077	61	11	14	25	137	....	1983-84	1996-97
Creighton, Dave	Bos., Tor., Chi., NYR	12	616	140	174	314	223	51	11	13	24	20	....	1948-49	1959-60
• Creighton, Jimmy	Det.	1	11	1	0	1	2	....	....	....	....	....	....	1930-31	1930-31
Cressman, Dave	Min.	2	85	6	8	14	37	....	....	....	....	....	....	1974-75	1975-76
Cressman, Glen	Mtl.	1	4	0	0	0	2	....	....	....	....	....	....	1956-57	1956-57
Crisp, Terry	Bos., St.L., NYI, Phi.	11	536	67	134	201	135	110	15	28	43	40	2	1965-66	1976-77
Cristofoli, Ed	Mtl.	1	9	0	1	1	4	....	....	....	....	....	....	1989-90	1989-90
• Croghan, Maurice	Mtl.M.	1	16	0	0	0	4	....	....	....	....	....	....	1937-38	1937-38
Crombeen, Mike	Cle., St.L., Hfd.	8	475	55	68	123	218	27	6	2	8	32	....	1977-78	1984-85
Cronin, Shawn	Wsh., Wpg., Phi., S.J.	7	292	3	18	21	877	32	1	0	1	38	....	1988-89	1994-95
• Crossett, Stan	Phi.	1	21	0	0	0	10	....	....	....	....	....	....	1930-31	1930-31
Crossman, Doug	Chi., Phi., L.A., NYI, Hfd., Det., T.B., St.L.	14	914	105	359	464	534	97	12	39	51	105	....	1980-81	1993-94
Croteau, Gary	L.A., Det., Cal., K.C., Col.	12	684	144	175	319	143	11	3	2	5	8	....	1968-69	1979-80
Crowder, Bruce	Bos., Pit.	4	243	47	51	98	156	31	8	4	12	41	....	1981-82	1984-85
Crowder, Keith	Bos., L.A.	10	662	223	271	494	1354	85	14	22	36	218	....	1980-81	1989-90
Crowder, Troy	N.J., Det., L.A., Van.	7	150	9	7	16	433	4	0	0	0	22	....	1987-88	1996-97
‡ Crowe, Phil	L.A., Phi., Ott., Nsh.	6	94	4	5	9	173	3	0	0	0	16	....	1993-94	1999-00
‡ Crowley, Mike	Ana.	3	67	5	15	20	44	....	....	....	....	....	....	1997-98	2000-01
‡ Crowley, Ted	Hfd., Col., NYI	2	34	2	4	6	12	....	....	....	....	....	....	1993-94	1998-99
Crozier, Joe	Tor.	1	5	0	3	3	2	....	....	....	....	....	....	1959-60	1959-60
• Crutchfield, Nels	Mtl.	1	41	5	5	10	20	2	0	1	1	22	....	1934-35	1934-35
Culhane, Jim	Hfd.	1	6	0	1	1	4	....	....	....	....	....	....	1989-90	1989-90
Cullen, Barry	Tor., Det.	5	219	32	52	84	111	6	0	0	0	2	....	1955-56	1959-60
Cullen, Brian	Tor., NYR	7	326	56	100	156	92	19	3	0	3	2	....	1954-55	1960-61
Cullen, John	Pit., Hfd., Tor., T.B.	11	621	187	363	550	898	53	12	22	34	58	....	1988-89	1998-99
Cullen, Ray	NYR, Det., Min., Van.	6	313	92	123	215	120	20	3	10	13	2	....	1965-66	1970-71
Cummins, Barry	Cal.	1	36	1	2	3	39	....	....	....	....	....	....	1973-74	1973-74
Cummins, Jim	Det., Phi., T.B., Chi., Phx., Mtl., Ana., NYI	11	456	23	34	57	1391	37	1	2	3	43	....	1991-92	2001-02
Cunneyworth, Randy	Buf., Pit., Wpg., Hfd., Chi., Ott.	16	866	189	225	414	1280	45	7	7	14	61	....	1980-81	1998-99
Cunningham, Bob	NYR	2	4	0	1	1	0	....	....	....	....	....	....	1960-61	1961-62
Cunningham, Jim	Phi.	1	1	0	0	0	4	....	....	....	....	....	....	1977-78	1977-78
• Cunningham, Les	NYA, Chi.	2	60	7	19	26	21	1	0	0	0	0	....	1936-37	1939-40
Cupolo, Bill	Bos.	1	47	11	13	24	10	7	1	2	3	0	....	1944-45	1944-45
Curran, Brian	Bos., NYI, Tor., Buf., Wsh.	10	381	7	33	40	1461	24	0	1	1	122	....	1983-84	1993-94
‡ Currie, Dan	Edm., L.A.	4	22	2	1	3	4	....	....	....	....	....	....	1990-91	1993-94
Currie, Glen	Wsh., L.A.	8	326	39	79	118	100	12	1	3	4	4	....	1979-80	1987-88
Currie, Hugh	Mtl.	1	1	0	0	0	0	....	....	....	....	....	....	1950-51	1950-51
Currie, Tony	St.L., Van., Hfd.	8	290	92	119	211	83	16	4	12	16	14	....	1977-78	1984-85
Curry, Floyd	Mtl.	11	601	105	99	204	147	91	23	17	40	38	4	1947-48	1957-58
Curtale, Tony	Cgy.	1	2	0	0	0	0	....	....	....	....	....	....	1980-81	1980-81
Curtis, Paul	Mtl., L.A., St.L.	4	185	3	34	37	161	5	0	0	0	2	....	1969-70	1972-73
Cushenan, Ian	Chi., Mtl., NYR, Det.	5	129	3	11	14	134	....	....	....	....	....	1	1956-57	1963-64
Cusson, Jean	Oak.	1	2	0	0	0	0	....	....	....	....	....	....	1967-68	1967-68
Cyr, Denis	Cgy., Chi., St.L.	6	193	41	43	84	36	4	0	0	0	0	....	1980-81	1985-86
Cyr, Paul	Buf., NYR, Hfd.	9	470	101	140	241	623	24	4	6	10	31	....	1982-83	1991-92

D

Name	NHL Teams	NHL Seasons	Regular Schedule GP	G	A	TP	PIM	Playoffs GP	G	A	TP	PIM	NHL Cup Wins	First NHL Season	Last NHL Season
‡ Dahl, Kevin	Cgy., Phx., Tor., CBJ	8	188	7	22	29	153	16	0	2	2	12	....	1992-93	2000-01
Dahlin, Kjell	Mtl.	3	166	57	59	116	10	35	6	11	17	6	1	1985-86	1987-88
Dahlquist, Chris	Pit., Min., Cgy., Ott.	11	532	19	71	90	488	39	4	7	11	30	....	1985-86	1995-96
• Dahlstrom, Cully	Chi.	8	342	88	118	206	58	29	6	8	14	4	1	1937-38	1944-45
Daigle, Alain	Chi.	6	389	56	50	106	122	17	0	1	1	0	....	1974-75	1979-80
‡ Daigneault, J.J.	Van., Phi., Mtl., St.L., Pit., Ana., NYI, Nsh., Phx., Min.	16	899	53	197	250	687	99	5	26	31	100	1	1984-85	2000-01
Dailey, Bob	Van., Phi.	9	561	94	231	325	814	63	12	34	46	105	....	1973-74	1981-82
• Daley, Frank	Det.	1	5	0	0	0	0	2	0	0	0	0	....	1928-29	1928-29
Daley, Pat	Wpg.	2	12	1	0	1	13	....	....	....	....	....	....	1979-80	1980-81
Dalgarno, Brad	NYI	10	321	49	71	120	332	27	2	4	6	37	....	1985-86	1995-96
Dallman, Marty	Tor.	2	6	0	1	1	0	....	....	....	....	....	....	1987-88	1988-89
Dallman, Rod	NYI, Phi.	4	6	1	0	1	26	1	0	1	1	0	....	1987-88	1991-92
Dame, Bunny	Mtl.	1	34	2	5	7	4	....	....	....	....	....	....	1941-42	1941-42
Damore, Hank	NYR	1	4	1	0	1	2	....	....	....	....	....	....	1943-44	1943-44
‡ Daniels, Kimbi	Phi.	2	27	1	2	3	4	....	....	....	....	....	....	1990-91	1991-92
Daniels, Scott	Hfd., Phi., N.J.	6	149	8	12	20	667	1	0	0	0	0	....	1992-93	1998-99
Daoust, Dan	Mtl., Tor.	8	522	87	167	254	544	32	7	5	12	83	....	1982-83	1989-90
Dark, Michael	St.L.	2	43	5	6	11	14	....	....	....	....	....	....	1986-87	1987-88
• Darragh, Harold	Pit., Phi., Bos., Tor.	8	308	68	49	117	50	16	1	3	4	4	1	1925-26	1932-33
• Darragh, Jack	Ott.	6	121	66	46	112	113	11	3	0	3	9	3	1917-18	1923-24
David, Richard	Que.	3	31	4	4	8	10	1	0	0	0	0	....	1979-80	1982-83
• Davidson, Bob	Tor.	12	491	94	160	254	398	79	5	17	22	76	2	1934-35	1945-46
• Davidson, Gord	NYR	2	51	3	6	9	8	....	....	....	....	....	....	1942-43	1943-44
• Davie, Bob	Bos.	3	41	0	1	1	25	....	....	....	....	....	....	1933-34	1935-36
Davies, Buck	NYR	1	....	....	....	....	....	1	0	0	0	0	....	1947-48	1947-48
• Davis, Bob	Det.	1	3	0	0	0	0	....	....	....	....	....	....	1932-33	1932-33
Davis, Kim	Pit., Tor.	4	36	5	7	12	51	4	0	0	0	0	....	1977-78	1980-81
Davis, Lorne	Mtl., Chi., Det., Bos.	6	95	8	12	20	20	18	3	1	4	10	1	1951-52	1959-60
Davis, Mal	Det., Buf.	6	100	31	22	53	34	7	1	0	1	0	....	1978-79	1985-86
• Davison, Murray	Bos.	1	1	0	0	0	0	....	....	....	....	....	....	1965-66	1965-66
Davydov, Evgeny	Wpg., Fla., Ott.	4	155	40	39	79	120	11	2	2	4	2	....	1991-92	1994-95
Dawes, Bob	Tor., Mtl.	4	32	2	7	9	6	10	0	0	0	2	1	1946-47	1950-51
• Day, Hap	Tor., NYA	14	581	86	116	202	601	53	4	7	11	56	1	1924-25	1937-38
Day, Joe	Hfd., NYI	3	72	1	10	11	87	....	....	....	....	....	....	1991-92	1993-94
Dea, Billy	NYR, Det., Chi., Pit.	8	397	67	54	121	44	11	2	1	3	6	....	1953-54	1970-71
• Deacon, Don	Det.	3	30	6	4	10	6	2	2	1	3	0	....	1936-37	1939-40
Deadmarsh, Butch	Buf., Atl., K.C.	5	137	12	5	17	155	4	0	0	0	17	....	1970-71	1974-75
Dean, Barry	Col., Phi.	3	165	25	56	81	146	....	....	....	....	....	....	1976-77	1978-79
Dean, Kevin	N.J., Atl., Dal., Chi.	7	331	7	48	55	138	16	2	2	4	2	1	1994-95	2000-01

			Regular Schedule					Playoffs					NHL	First	Last
Name	NHL Teams	NHL Seasons	GP	G	A	TP	PIM	GP	G	A	TP	PIM	Cup Wins	NHL Season	NHL Season
Debenedet, Nelson	Det., Pit.	2	46	10	4	14	13	....	....	....	....	....	....	1973-74	1974-75
DeBlois, Lucien	NYR, Col., Wpg., Mtl., Que., Tor.	15	993	249	276	525	814	52	7	6	13	38	1	1977-78	1991-92
Debol, Dave	Hfd.	2	92	26	26	52	4	3	0	0	0	0	....	1979-80	1980-81
Defazio, Dean	Pit.	1	22	0	2	2	28	....	....	....	....	....	....	1983-84	1983-84
DeGray, Dale	Cgy., Tor., L.A., Buf.	5	153	18	47	65	195	13	1	3	4	28	....	1985-86	1989-90
‡ Delisle, Jonathan	Mtl.	1	1	0	0	0	0	....	....	....	....	....	....	1998-99	1998-99
‡ Delisle, Xavier	T.B., Mtl.	2	16	3	2	5	6	....	....	....	....	....	....	1998-99	2000-01
• Delmonte, Armand	Bos.	1	1	0	0	0	0	....	....	....	....	....	....	1945-46	1945-46
Delorme, Gilbert	Mtl., St.L., Que., Det., Pit.	9	541	31	92	123	520	56	1	9	10	56	....	1981-82	1989-90
Delorme, Ron	Col., Van.	9	524	83	83	166	667	25	1	2	3	59	....	1976-77	1984-85
Delory, Val	NYR	1	1	0	0	0	0	....	....	....	....	....	....	1948-49	1948-49
Delparte, Guy	Col.	1	48	1	8	9	18	....	....	....	....	....	....	1976-77	1976-77
Delvecchio, Alex	Det.	24	1549	456	825	1281	383	121	35	69	104	29	3	1950-51	1973-74
• DeMarco, Ab	Chi., Tor., Bos., NYR	7	209	72	93	165	53	11	3	0	3	2	....	1938-39	1946-47
DeMarco Jr., Ab	NYR, St.L., Pit., Van., L.A., Bos.	9	344	44	80	124	75	25	1	2	3	17	....	1969-70	1978-79
• Demers, Tony	Mtl., NYR	6	83	20	22	42	23	2	0	0	0	0	....	1937-38	1943-44
Denis, Jean-Paul	NYR	2	10	0	2	2	2	....	....	....	....	....	....	1946-47	1949-50
Denis, Lulu	Mtl.	2	3	0	1	1	0	....	....	....	....	....	....	1949-50	1950-51
• Denneny, Corb	Tor., Ham., Chi.	9	176	103	42	145	148	6	1	0	1	4	2	1917-18	1927-28
• Denneny, Cy	Ott., Bos.	12	328	248	85	333	301	25	16	2	18	17	5	1917-18	1928-29
Dennis, Norm	St.L.	4	12	3	0	3	11	5	0	0	0	2	....	1968-69	1971-72
• Denoird, Gerry	Tor.	1	17	0	1	1	0	....	....	....	....	....	....	1922-23	1922-23
DePalma, Larry	Min., S.J., Pit.	7	148	21	20	41	408	3	0	0	0	6	....	1985-86	1993-94
Derlago, Bill	Van., Tor., Bos., Wpg., Que.	9	555	189	227	416	247	13	5	0	5	8	....	1978-79	1986-87
• Desaulniers, Gerard	Mtl.	3	8	0	2	2	4	....	....	....	....	....	....	1950-51	1953-54
• Desilets, Joffre	Mtl., Chi.	5	192	37	45	82	57	7	1	0	1	7	....	1935-36	1939-40
Desjardins, Martin	Mtl.	1	8	0	2	2	2	....	....	....	....	....	....	1989-90	1989-90
• Desjardins, Vic	Chi., NYR	2	87	6	15	21	27	16	0	0	0	0	....	1930-31	1931-32
Deslauriers, Jacques	Mtl.	1	2	0	0	0	0	....	....	....	....	....	....	1955-56	1955-56
Deuling, Jarrett	NYI	2	15	0	1	1	11	....	....	....	....	....	....	1995-96	1996-97
Devine, Kevin	NYI	1	2	0	1	1	8	....	....	....	....	....	....	1982-83	1982-83
• Dewar, Tom	NYR	1	9	0	2	2	4	....	....	....	....	....	....	1943-44	1943-44
Dewsbury, Al	Det., Chi.	9	347	30	78	108	365	14	1	5	6	16	1	1946-47	1955-56
Deziel, Michel	Buf.	1	....	....	....	....	....	1	0	0	0	0	....	1974-75	1974-75
Dheere, Marcel	Mtl.	1	11	1	2	3	2	5	0	0	0	6	....	1942-43	1942-43
‡ Di Pietro, Paul	Mtl., Tor., L.A.	6	192	31	49	80	96	31	11	10	21	10	1	1991-92	1996-97
Diachuk, Edward	Det.	1	12	0	0	0	19	....	....	....	....	....	....	1960-61	1960-61
Dick, Harry	Chi.	1	12	0	1	1	12	....	....	....	....	....	....	1946-47	1946-47
Dickens, Ernie	Tor., Chi.	6	278	12	44	56	98	13	0	0	0	4	1	1941-42	1950-51
Dickenson, Herb	NYR	2	48	18	17	35	10	....	....	....	....	....	....	1951-52	1952-53
Diduck, Gerald	NYI, Mtl., Van., Chi., Hfd., Phx., Tor., Dal.	17	932	56	156	212	1612	114	8	16	24	212	....	1984-85	2000-01
Dietrich, Don	Chi., N.J.	2	28	0	7	7	10	....	....	....	....	....	....	1983-84	1985-86
• Dill, Bob	NYR	2	76	15	15	30	135	....	....	....	....	....	....	1943-44	1944-45
• Dillabough, Bob	Det., Bos., Pit., Oak.	9	283	32	54	86	76	17	3	0	3	0	....	1961-62	1969-70
• Dillon, Cecil	NYR, Det.	10	453	167	131	298	105	43	14	9	23	14	1	1930-31	1939-40
Dillon, Gary	Col.	1	13	1	1	2	29	....	....	....	....	....	....	1980-81	1980-81
Dillon, Wayne	NYR, Wpg.	4	229	43	66	109	60	3	0	1	1	0	....	1975-76	1979-80
Dineen, Bill	Det., Chi.	5	323	51	44	95	122	37	1	1	2	18	2	1953-54	1957-58
Dineen, Gary	Min.	1	4	0	1	1	0	....	....	....	....	....	....	1968-69	1968-69
Dineen, Gord	NYI, Min., Pit., Ott.	13	528	16	90	106	695	40	1	7	8	68	....	1982-83	1994-95
Dineen, Peter	L.A., Det.	2	13	0	2	2	13	....	....	....	....	....	....	1986-87	1989-90
• Dinsmore, Chuck	Mtl.M.	4	100	6	2	8	50	8	1	0	1	2	1	1924-25	1929-30
‡ Dionne, Gilbert	Mtl., Phi., Fla.	6	223	61	79	140	108	39	10	12	22	34	1	1990-91	1995-96
Dionne, Marcel	Det., L.A., NYR	18	1348	731	1040	1771	600	49	21	24	45	17	....	1971-72	1988-89
Dirk, Robert	St.L., Van., Chi., Ana., Mtl.	9	402	13	29	42	786	39	0	1	1	56	....	1987-88	1995-96
Djoos, Per	Det., NYR	3	82	2	31	33	58	....	....	....	....	....	....	1990-91	1992-93
Doak, Gary	Det., Bos., Van., NYR	16	789	23	107	130	908	78	2	4	6	121	1	1965-66	1980-81
Dobbin, Brian	Phi., Bos.	5	63	7	8	15	61	2	0	0	0	17	....	1986-87	1991-92
Dobson, Jim	Min., Col., Que.	4	12	0	0	0	6	....	....	....	....	....	....	1979-80	1983-84
• Doherty, Fred	Mtl.	1	1	0	0	0	0	....	....	....	....	....	....	1918-19	1918-19
‡ Dollas, Bobby	Wpg., Que., Det., Ana., Edm., Pit., Cgy., Ott., S.J.	16	646	42	96	138	467	47	2	1	3	41	....	1983-84	2000-01
Donaldson, Gary	Chi.	1	1	0	0	0	0	....	....	....	....	....	....	1973-74	1973-74
Donatelli, Clark	Min., Bos.	2	35	3	4	7	39	2	0	0	0	0	....	1989-90	1991-92
• Donnelly, Babe	Mtl.M.	1	34	0	1	1	14	2	0	0	0	0	....	1926-27	1926-27
Donnelly, Dave	Bos., Chi., Edm.	5	137	15	24	39	150	5	0	0	0	0	....	1983-84	1987-88
Donnelly, Gord	Que., Wpg., Buf., Dal.	12	554	28	41	69	2069	26	0	2	2	61	....	1983-84	1994-95
Donnelly, Mike	NYR, Buf., L.A., Dal., NYI	11	465	114	121	235	255	47	12	12	24	30	....	1986-87	1996-97
• Doran, John	NYA, Det., Mtl.	5	98	5	10	15	110	3	0	0	0	0	....	1933-34	1939-40
Doran, Lloyd	Det.	1	24	3	2	5	10	....	....	....	....	....	....	1946-47	1946-47
• Doraty, Ken	Chi., Tor., Det.	5	103	15	26	41	24	15	7	2	9	2	....	1926-27	1937-38
Dore, Andre	NYR, St.L., Que.	7	257	14	81	95	261	23	1	2	3	32	....	1978-79	1984-85
Dore, Daniel	Que.	2	17	2	3	5	59	....	....	....	....	....	....	1989-90	1990-91
Dorey, Jim	Tor., NYR	4	232	25	74	99	553	11	0	2	2	40	....	1968-69	1971-72
Dorion, Dan	N.J.	2	4	1	1	2	2	....	....	....	....	....	....	1985-86	1987-88
Dornhoefer, Gary	Bos., Phi.	14	787	214	328	542	1291	80	17	19	36	203	2	1963-64	1977-78
Dorohoy, Eddie	Mtl.	1	16	0	0	0	6	....	....	....	....	....	....	1948-49	1948-49
Douglas, Jordy	Hfd., Min., Wpg.	6	268	76	62	138	160	6	0	0	0	4	....	1979-80	1984-85
Douglas, Kent	Tor., Oak., Det.	7	428	33	115	148	631	19	1	3	4	33	3	1962-63	1968-69
• Douglas, Les	Det.	4	52	6	12	18	8	10	3	2	5	2	1	1940-41	1946-47
‡ Douris, Peter	Wpg., Bos., Ana., Dal.	11	321	54	67	121	80	27	3	5	8	14	....	1985-86	1997-98
• Downie, Dave	Tor.	1	11	0	1	1	2	....	....	....	....	....	....	1932-33	1932-33
‡ Doyon, Mario	Chi., Que.	3	28	3	4	7	16	....	....	....	....	....	....	1988-89	1990-91
• Draper, Bruce	Tor.	1	1	0	0	0	0	....	....	....	....	....	....	1962-63	1962-63
• Drillon, Gordie	Tor., Mtl.	7	311	155	139	294	56	50	26	15	41	10	1	1936-37	1942-43
Driscoll, Peter	Edm.	2	60	3	8	11	97	3	0	0	0	0	....	1979-80	1980-81
Driver, Bruce	N.J., NYR	15	922	96	390	486	670	108	10	40	50	64	1	1983-84	1997-98
Drolet, Rene	Phi., Det.	2	2	0	0	0	0	....	....	....	....	....	....	1971-72	1974-75
‡ Droppa, Ivan	Chi.	2	19	0	1	1	14	....	....	....	....	....	....	1993-94	1995-96
• Drouillard, Clarence	Det.	1	10	0	1	1	0	....	....	....	....	....	....	1937-38	1937-38
Drouin, Jude	Mtl., Min., NYI, Wpg.	12	666	151	305	456	346	72	27	41	68	33	....	1968-69	1980-81
‡ Drouin, P.C.	Bos.	1	3	0	0	0	0	....	....	....	....	....	....	1996-97	1996-97
• Drouin, Polly	Mtl.	7	160	23	50	73	80	5	0	1	1	5	....	1934-35	1940-41
Druce, John	Wsh., Wpg., L.A., Phi.	10	531	113	126	239	347	53	17	6	23	38	....	1988-89	1997-98
Drulia, Stan	T.B.	3	126	15	27	42	52	....	....	....	....	....	....	1992-93	2000-01
• Drummond, Jim	NYR	1	2	0	0	0	0	....	....	....	....	....	....	1944-45	1944-45
• Drury, Herb	Pit., Phi.	6	213	24	13	37	203	4	1	1	2	0	....	1925-26	1930-31
‡ Drury, Ted	Cgy., Hfd., Ott., Ana., NYI, CBJ	8	414	41	52	93	367	14	1	0	1	4	....	1993-94	2000-01
‡ Dube, Christian	NYR	2	33	1	1	2	4	3	0	0	0	0	....	1996-97	1998-99
Dube, Gilles	Mtl., Det.	2	12	1	2	3	2	2	0	0	0	0	1	1949-50	1953-54
Dube, Norm	K.C.	2	57	8	10	18	54	....	....	....	....	....	....	1974-75	1975-76
Duberman, Justin	Pit.	1	4	0	0	0	0	....	....	....	....	....	....	1993-94	1993-94
Duchesne, Gaetan	Wsh., Que., Min., S.J., Fla.	14	1028	179	254	433	617	84	14	13	27	97	....	1981-82	1994-95
Duchesne, Steve	L.A., Phi., Que., St.L., Ott., Det.	16	1113	227	525	752	824	121	16	61	77	96	1	1986-87	2001-02
Dudley, Rick	Buf., Wpg.	6	309	75	99	174	292	25	7	2	9	69	....	1972-73	1980-81
‡ Duerden, Dave	Fla.	1	2	0	0	0	0	....	....	....	....	....	....	1999-00	1999-00
Duff, Dick	Tor., NYR, Mtl., L.A., Buf.	18	1030	283	289	572	743	114	30	49	79	78	6	1954-55	1971-72
Dufour, Luc	Bos., Que., St.L.	3	167	23	21	44	199	18	1	0	1	32	....	1982-83	1984-85
Dufour, Marc	NYR, L.A.	3	14	1	0	1	2	....	....	....	....	....	....	1963-64	1968-69
Dufresne, Donald	Mtl., T.B., L.A., St.L., Edm.	9	268	6	36	42	258	34	1	3	4	47	1	1988-89	1996-97
• Duggan, John	Ott.	1	27	0	0	0	0	2	0	0	0	0	....	1925-26	1925-26
Duggan, Ken	Min.	1	1	0	0	0	0	....	....	....	....	....	....	1987-88	1987-88
Duguay, Ron	NYR, Det., Pit., L.A.	12	864	274	346	620	582	89	31	22	53	118	....	1977-78	1988-89
• Duguid, Lorne	Mtl.M., Det., Bos.	6	135	9	15	24	57	4	1	0	1	6	....	1931-32	1936-37
• Dukowski, Duke	Chi., NYA, NYR	5	200	16	30	46	172	6	0	0	0	6	....	1926-27	1933-34
• Dumart, Woody	Bos.	16	772	211	218	429	99	88	12	15	27	23	2	1935-36	1953-54
Dunbar, Dale	Van., Bos.	2	2	0	0	0	2	....	....	....	....	....	....	1985-86	1988-89
• Duncan, Art	Det., Tor.	5	156	18	16	34	225	5	0	0	0	4	....	1926-27	1930-31
Duncan, Iain	Wpg.	4	127	34	55	89	149	11	0	3	3	6	....	1986-87	1990-91
Duncanson, Craig	L.A., Wpg., NYR	7	38	5	4	9	61	....	....	....	....	....	....	1985-86	1992-93
Dundas, Rocky	Tor.	1	5	0	0	0	14	....	....	....	....	....	....	1989-90	1989-90
• Dunlap, Frank	Tor.	1	15	0	1	1	2	....	....	....	....	....	....	1943-44	1943-44
Dunlop, Blake	Min., Phi., St.L., Det.	11	550	130	274	404	172	40	4	10	14	18	....	1973-74	1983-84
Dunn, Dave	Van., Tor.	3	184	14	41	55	313	10	1	1	2	41	....	1973-74	1975-76
Dunn, Richie	Buf., Cgy., Hfd.	12	483	36	140	176	314	36	3	15	18	24	....	1977-78	1988-89

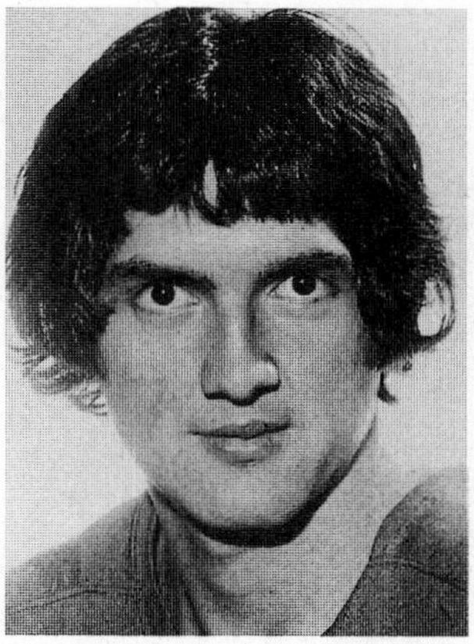
Ron Delorme

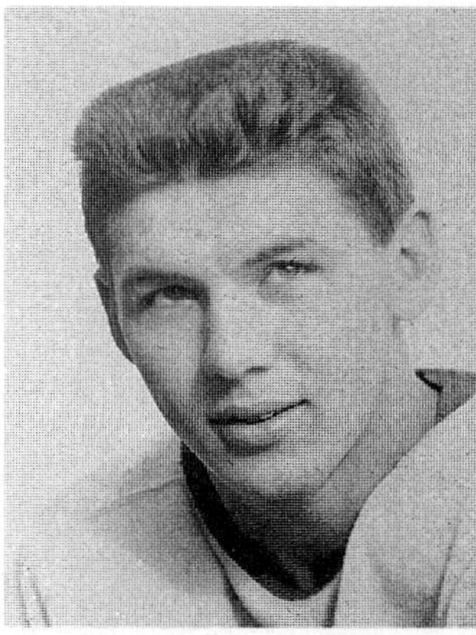
Alex Delvecchio

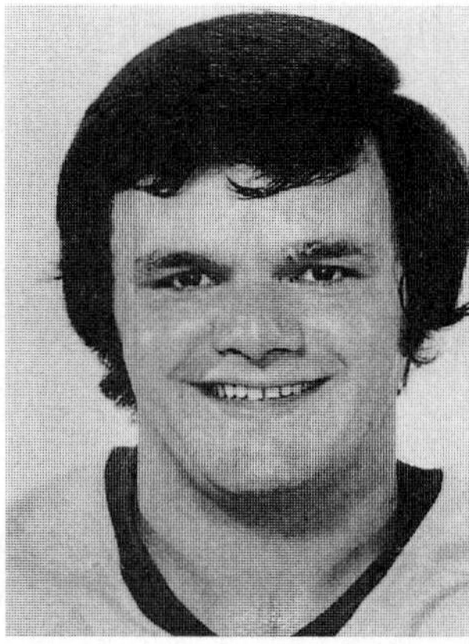
Marcel Dionne

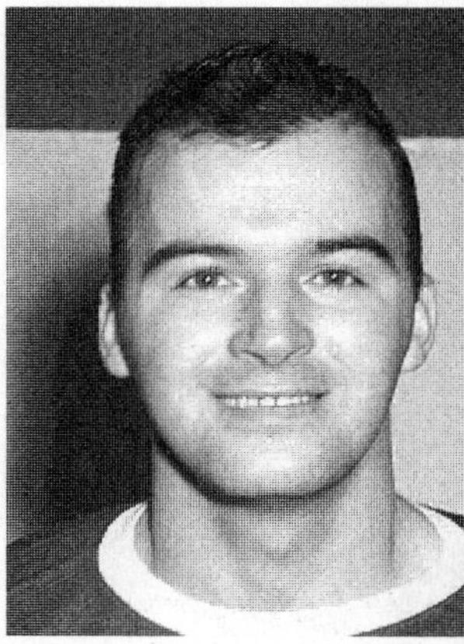
Gordie Drillon

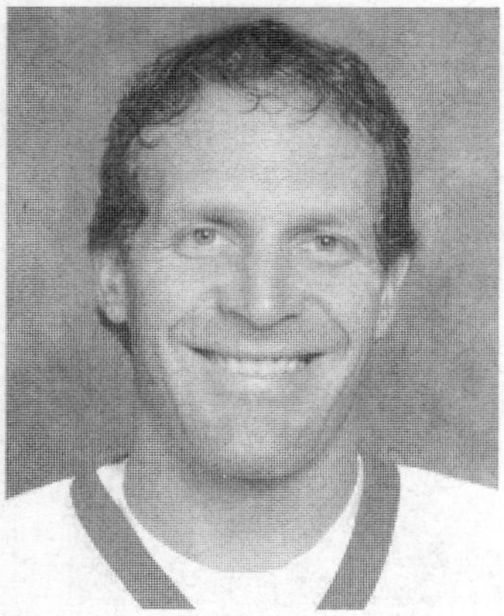

Steve Duchesne

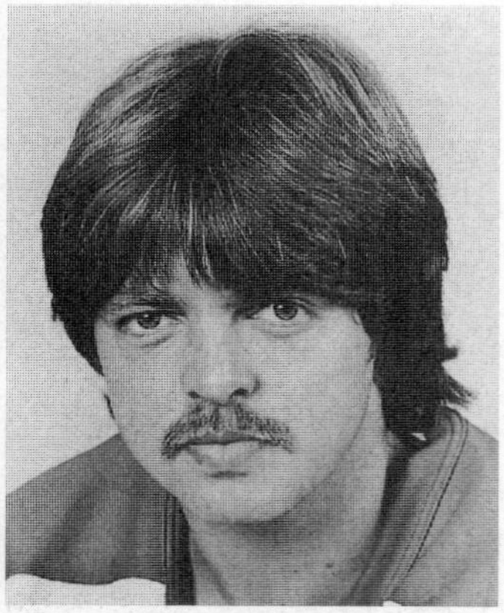

Rolf Edberg

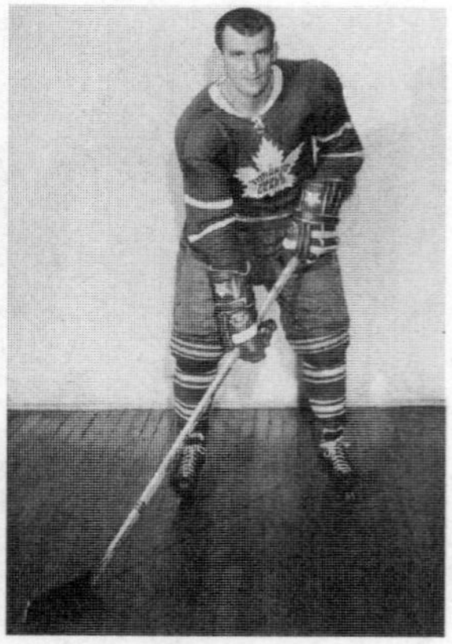

Gerry Ehman

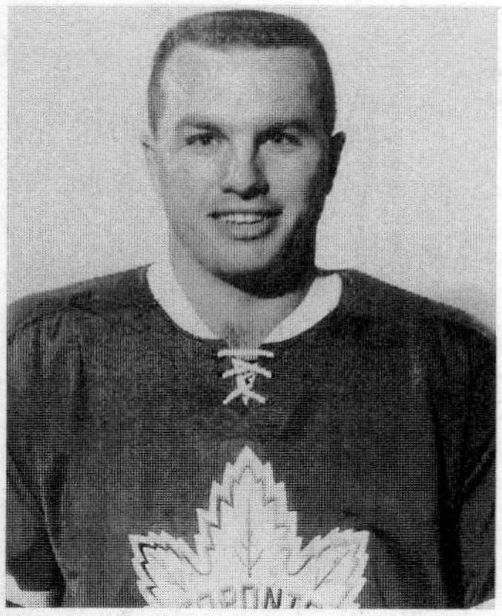

Ron Ellis

			Regular Schedule					Playoffs							
Name	NHL Teams	NHL Seasons	GP	G	A	TP	PIM	GP	G	A	TP	PIM	NHL Cup Wins	First NHL Season	Last NHL Season
Dupere, Denis	Tor., Wsh., St.L., K.C., Col.	8	421	80	99	179	66	16	1	0	1	0	....	1970-71	1977-78
Dupont, Andre	NYR, St.L., Phi., Que.	13	800	59	185	244	1986	140	14	18	32	352	2	1970-71	1982-83
Dupont, Jerome	Chi., Tor.	6	214	7	29	36	468	20	0	2	2	56	....	1981-82	1986-87
Dupont, Norm	Mtl., Wpg., Hfd.	5	256	55	85	140	52	13	4	2	6	0	....	1979-80	1983-84
• Dupre, Yanick	Phi.	3	35	2	0	2	16	....	....	....	....	....	....	1991-92	1995-96
• Durbano, Steve	St.L., Pit., K.C., Col.	6	220	13	60	73	1127	5	0	2	2	8	....	1972-73	1978-79
Duris, Vitezslav	Tor.	2	89	3	20	23	62	3	0	1	1	2	....	1980-81	1982-83
Dussault, Norm	Mtl.	4	206	31	62	93	47	7	3	1	4	0	....	1947-48	1950-51
• Dutton, Red	Mtl.M., NYA	10	449	29	67	96	871	18	1	0	1	33	....	1926-27	1935-36
Dvorak, Miroslav	Phi.	3	193	11	74	85	51	18	0	2	2	6	....	1982-83	1984-85
Dwyer, Mike	Col., Cgy.	4	31	2	6	8	25	1	1	0	1	0	....	1978-79	1981-82
• Dyck, Henry	NYR	1	1	0	0	0	0	....	....	....	....	....	....	1943-44	1943-44
• Dye, Babe	Tor., Ham., Chi., NYA	11	271	201	47	248	221	10	2	0	2	11	1	1919-20	1930-31
Dykstra, Steve	Buf., Edm., Pit., Hfd.	5	217	8	32	40	545	1	0	0	0	2	....	1985-86	1989-90
Dyte, Jack	Chi.	1	27	1	0	1	31	....	....	....	....	....	....	1943-44	1943-44
Dziedzic, Joe	Pit., Phx.	3	130	14	14	28	131	21	1	3	4	23	....	1995-96	1998-99
E															
Eagles, Mike	Que., Chi., Wpg., Wsh.	16	853	74	122	196	928	44	2	6	8	34	....	1982-83	1999-00
Eakin, Bruce	Cgy., Det.	4	13	2	2	4	4	....	....	....	....	....	....	1981-82	1985-86
Eatough, Jeff	Buf.	1	1	0	0	0	0	....	....	....	....	....	....	1981-82	1981-82
Eaves, Mike	Min., Cgy.	8	324	83	143	226	80	43	7	10	17	14	....	1978-79	1985-86
Eaves, Murray	Wpg., Det.	8	57	4	13	17	9	4	0	1	1	2	....	1980-81	1989-90
Ecclestone, Tim	St.L., Det., Tor., Atl.	11	692	126	233	359	344	48	6	11	17	76	....	1967-68	1977-78
Edberg, Rolf	Wsh.	3	184	45	58	103	24	....	....	....	....	....	....	1978-79	1980-81
• Eddolls, Frank	Mtl., NYR	8	317	23	43	66	114	31	0	2	2	10	1	1944-45	1951-52
Edestrand, Darryl	St.L., Phi., Pit., Bos., L.A.	10	455	34	90	124	404	42	3	9	12	57	....	1967-68	1978-79
Edmundson, Garry	Mtl., Tor.	3	43	4	6	10	49	11	0	1	1	8	....	1951-52	1960-61
Edur, Tom	Col., Pit.	2	158	17	70	87	67	....	....	....	....	....	....	1976-77	1977-78
Egan, Pat	NYA, Bro., Det., Bos., NYR	11	554	77	153	230	776	46	9	4	13	48	....	1939-40	1950-51
‡ Egeland, Allan	T.B.	3	17	0	0	0	16	....	....	....	....	....	....	1995-96	1997-98
Egers, Jack	NYR, St.L., Wsh.	7	284	64	69	133	154	32	5	6	11	32	....	1969-70	1975-76
Ehman, Gerry	Bos., Det., Tor., Oak., Cal.	9	429	96	118	214	100	41	10	10	20	12	1	1957-58	1970-71
‡ Eisenhut, Neil	Van., Cgy.	2	16	1	3	4	21	....	....	....	....	....	....	1993-94	1994-95
Eklund, Pelle	Phi., Dal.	9	594	120	335	455	109	66	10	36	46	8	....	1985-86	1993-94
Eldebrink, Anders	Van., Que.	2	55	3	11	14	29	14	0	0	0	10	....	1981-82	1982-83
‡ Elich, Matt	T.B.	2	16	1	1	2	0	....	....	....	....	....	....	1999-00	2000-01
Elik, Bo	Det.	1	3	0	0	0	0	....	....	....	....	....	....	1962-63	1962-63
‡ Elik, Todd	L.A., Min., Edm., S.J., St.L., Bos.	8	448	110	219	329	453	52	15	27	42	48	....	1989-90	1996-97
Ellett, Dave	Wpg., Tor., N.J., Bos., St.L.	16	1129	153	415	568	985	116	11	46	57	87	....	1984-85	1999-00
• Elliott, Fred	Ott.	1	43	2	0	2	6	....	....	....	....	....	....	1928-29	1928-29
Ellis, Ron	Tor.	16	1034	332	308	640	207	70	18	8	26	20	1	1963-64	1980-81
‡ Elomo, Miika	Wsh.	1	2	0	1	1	2	....	....	....	....	....	....	1999-00	1999-00
Eloranta, Kari	Cgy., St.L.	5	267	13	103	116	155	26	1	7	8	19	....	1981-82	1986-87
Elynuik, Pat	Wpg., Wsh., T.B., Ott.	9	506	154	188	342	459	20	6	9	15	25	....	1987-88	1995-96
Emberg, Eddie	Mtl.	1	....	....	....	....	....	2	1	0	1	0	....	1944-45	1944-45
Emerson, Nelson	St.L., Wpg., Hfd., Car., Chi., Ott., Atl., L.A.	12	771	195	293	488	575	40	7	15	22	33	....	1990-91	2001-02
Emma, David	N.J., Bos., Fla.	5	34	5	6	11	2	....	....	....	....	....	....	1992-93	2000-01
Emmons, Gary	S.J.	1	3	1	0	1	0	....	....	....	....	....	....	1993-94	1993-94
• Emms, Hap	Mtl.M., NYA, Det., Bos.	10	320	36	53	89	311	14	0	0	0	12	....	1926-27	1937-38
Endean, Craig	Wpg.	1	2	0	1	1	0	....	....	....	....	....	....	1986-87	1986-87
Engblom, Brian	Mtl., Wsh., L.A., Buf., Cgy.	11	659	29	177	206	599	48	3	9	12	43	3	1976-77	1986-87
Engele, Jerry	Min.	3	100	2	13	15	162	2	0	1	1	0	....	1975-76	1977-78
English, John	L.A.	1	3	1	3	4	4	1	0	0	0	0	....	1987-88	1987-88
Ennis, Jim	Edm.	1	5	1	0	1	10	....	....	....	....	....	....	1987-88	1987-88
Erickson, Aut	Bos., Chi., Tor., Oak.	7	226	7	24	31	182	7	0	0	0	2	1	1959-60	1969-70
Erickson, Bryan	Wsh., L.A., Pit., Wpg.	9	351	80	125	205	141	14	3	4	7	7	....	1983-84	1993-94
Erickson, Grant	Bos., Min.	2	6	1	0	1	0	....	....	....	....	....	....	1968-69	1969-70
Eriksson, Peter	Edm.	1	20	3	3	6	24	....	....	....	....	....	....	1989-90	1989-90
Eriksson, Roland	Min., Van.	3	193	48	95	143	26	2	1	0	1	0	....	1976-77	1978-79
Eriksson, Thomas	Phi.	5	208	22	76	98	107	19	0	3	3	12	....	1980-81	1985-86
Erixon, Jan	NYR	10	556	57	159	216	167	58	7	7	14	16	....	1983-84	1992-93
Errey, Bob	Pit., Buf., S.J., Det., Dal., NYR	15	895	170	212	382	1005	99	13	16	29	109	2	1983-84	1997-98
Esau, Len	Tor., Que., Cgy., Edm.	4	27	0	10	10	24	....	....	....	....	....	....	1991-92	1994-95
Esposito, Phil	Chi., Bos., NYR	18	1282	717	873	1590	910	130	61	76	137	138	2	1963-64	1980-81
• Evans, Chris	Tor., Buf., St.L., Det., K.C.	5	241	19	42	61	143	12	1	1	2	8	....	1969-70	1974-75
Evans, Daryl	L.A., Wsh., Tor.	6	113	22	30	52	25	11	5	8	13	12	....	1981-82	1986-87
Evans, Doug	St.L., Wpg., Phi.	8	355	48	87	135	502	22	3	4	7	38	....	1985-86	1992-93
• Evans, Jack	NYR, Chi.	14	752	19	80	99	989	56	2	2	4	97	1	1948-49	1962-63
Evans, John Paul	Phi.	3	103	14	25	39	34	1	0	0	0	0	....	1978-79	1982-83
Evans, Kevin	Min., S.J.	2	9	0	1	1	44	....	....	....	....	....	....	1990-91	1991-92
Evans, Paul	Tor.	2	11	1	1	2	21	2	0	0	0	0	....	1976-77	1977-78
Evans, Shawn	St.L., NYI	2	9	1	0	1	2	....	....	....	....	....	....	1985-86	1989-90
• Evans, Stewart	Det., Mtl.M., Mtl.	8	367	28	49	77	425	26	0	0	0	20	1	1930-31	1938-39
Evason, Dean	Wsh., Hfd., S.J., Dal., Cgy.	13	803	139	233	372	1002	55	9	20	29	132	....	1983-84	1995-96
Ewen, Todd	St.L., Mtl., Ana., S.J.	11	518	36	40	76	1911	26	0	0	0	87	1	1986-87	1996-97
Ezinicki, Bill	Tor., Bos., NYR	9	368	79	105	184	713	40	5	8	13	87	3	1944-45	1954-55
F															
Fahey, Trevor	NYR	1	1	0	0	0	0	....	....	....	....	....	....	1964-65	1964-65
Fairbairn, Bill	NYR, Min., St.L.	11	658	162	261	423	173	54	13	22	35	42	....	1968-69	1978-79
Falkenberg, Bob	Det.	5	54	1	5	6	26	....	....	....	....	....	....	1966-67	1971-72
‡ Falloon, Pat	S.J., Phi., Ott., Edm., Pit.	9	575	143	179	322	141	66	11	7	18	16	....	1991-92	1999-00
Farrant, Walt	Chi.	1	1	0	0	0	0	....	....	....	....	....	....	1943-44	1943-44
Farrish, Dave	NYR, Que., Tor.	7	430	17	110	127	440	14	0	2	2	24	....	1976-77	1983-84
Fashoway, Gordie	Chi.	1	13	3	2	5	14	....	....	....	....	....	....	1950-51	1950-51
Faubert, Mario	Pit.	7	231	21	90	111	292	10	2	2	4	6	....	1974-75	1981-82
Faulkner, Alex	Tor., Det.	3	101	15	17	32	15	12	5	0	5	2	....	1961-62	1963-64
Fauss, Ted	Tor.	2	28	0	2	2	15	....	....	....	....	....	....	1986-87	1987-88
‡ Faust, Andre	Phi.	2	47	10	7	17	14	....	....	....	....	....	....	1992-93	1993-94
Feamster, Dave	Chi.	4	169	13	24	37	154	33	3	5	8	61	....	1981-82	1984-85
Featherstone, Glen	St.L., Bos., NYR, Hfd., Cgy.	9	384	19	61	80	939	28	0	2	2	103	....	1988-89	1996-97
Featherstone, Tony	Oak., Cal., Min.	3	130	17	21	38	65	2	0	0	0	0	....	1969-70	1973-74
Federko, Bernie	St.L., Det.	14	1000	369	761	1130	487	91	35	66	101	83	....	1976-77	1989-90
Fedotov, Anatoli	Wpg., Ana.	2	4	0	2	2	0	....	....	....	....	....	....	1992-93	1993-94
Fedyk, Brent	Det., Phi., Dal., NYR	10	470	97	112	209	308	16	3	2	5	12	....	1987-88	1998-99
‡ Felix, Chris	Wsh.	4	35	1	12	13	10	2	0	1	1	0	....	1987-88	1990-91
‡ Felsner, Brian	Chi.	1	12	1	3	4	12	....	....	....	....	....	....	1997-98	1997-98
Felsner, Denny	St.L.	4	18	1	4	5	6	10	2	3	5	2	....	1991-92	1994-95
Feltrin, Tony	Pit., NYR	4	48	3	3	6	65	....	....	....	....	....	....	1980-81	1985-86
Fenton, Paul	Hfd., NYR, L.A., Wpg., Tor., Cgy., S.J.	8	411	100	83	183	198	17	4	1	5	27	....	1984-85	1991-92
Fenyves, David	Buf., Phi.	9	206	3	32	35	119	11	0	0	0	9	....	1982-83	1990-91
Fergus, Tom	Bos., Tor., Van.	12	726	235	346	581	499	65	21	17	38	48	....	1981-82	1992-93
‡ Ferguson, Craig	Mtl., Cgy., Fla.	5	27	1	1	2	6	....	....	....	....	....	....	1993-94	1999-00
Ferguson, George	Tor., Pit., Min.	12	797	160	238	398	431	86	14	23	37	44	....	1972-73	1983-84
Ferguson, John	Mtl.	8	500	145	158	303	1214	85	20	18	38	260	5	1963-64	1970-71
Ferguson, Lorne	Bos., Det., Chi.	8	422	82	80	162	193	31	6	3	9	24	....	1949-50	1958-59
Ferguson, Norm	Oak., Cal.	4	279	73	66	139	72	10	1	4	5	7	....	1968-69	1971-72
Ferner, Mark	Buf., Wsh., Ana., Det.	6	91	3	10	13	51	....	....	....	....	....	....	1986-87	1994-95
Ferraro, Ray	Hfd., NYI, NYR, L.A., Atl., St.L.	18	1258	408	490	898	1288	68	21	22	43	54	....	1984-85	2001-02
Fetisov, Viacheslav	N.J., Det.	9	546	36	192	228	656	116	2	26	28	147	2	1989-90	1997-98
Fidler, Mike	Cle., Min., Hfd., Chi.	7	271	84	97	181	124	....	....	....	....	....	....	1976-77	1982-83
• Field, Wilf	NYA, Bro., Mtl., Chi.	6	219	17	25	42	151	2	0	0	0	2	....	1936-37	1944-45
Fielder, Guyle	Chi., Det., Bos.	4	9	0	0	0	2	6	0	0	0	2	....	1950-51	1957-58
‡ Filimonov, Dmitri	Ott.	1	30	1	4	5	18	....	....	....	....	....	....	1993-94	1993-94
Fillion, Bob	Mtl.	7	327	42	61	103	84	33	7	4	11	10	2	1943-44	1949-50
• Fillion, Marcel	Bos.	1	1	0	0	0	0	....	....	....	....	....	....	1944-45	1944-45
• Filmore, Tommy	Det., NYA, Bos.	4	117	15	12	27	33	....	....	....	....	....	....	1930-31	1933-34
• Finkbeiner, Lloyd	NYA	1	2	0	0	0	0	....	....	....	....	....	....	1940-41	1940-41
Finn, Steven	Que., T.B., L.A.	12	725	34	78	112	1724	23	0	4	4	39	....	1985-86	1996-97
Finney, Sid	Chi.	3	59	10	7	17	4	7	0	2	2	0	....	1951-52	1953-54
• Finnigan, Ed	St.L., Bos.	2	15	1	1	2	2	....	....	....	....	....	....	1934-35	1935-36
• Finnigan, Frank	Ott., Tor., St.L.	14	553	115	88	203	407	38	6	9	15	22	2	1923-24	1936-37

Name	NHL Teams	NHL Seasons	Regular Schedule GP	G	A	TP	PIM	Playoffs GP	G	A	TP	PIM	NHL Cup Wins	First NHL Season	Last NHL Season
Fiorentino, Peter	NYR	1	1	0	0	0	0	....	....	....	....	....	....	1991-92	1991-92
Fischer, Ron	Buf.	2	18	0	7	7	6	....	....	....	....	....	....	1981-82	1982-83
● Fisher, Alvin	Tor.	1	9	1	0	1	4	....	....	....	....	....	....	1924-25	1924-25
Fisher, Craig	Phi., Wpg., Fla.	4	12	0	0	0	2	....	....	....	....	....	....	1989-90	1996-97
Fisher, Dunc	NYR, Bos., Det.	7	275	45	70	115	104	21	4	4	8	14	....	1947-48	1958-59
● Fisher, Joe	Det.	4	65	8	12	20	13	12	2	1	3	6	1	1939-40	1942-43
Fitchner, Bob	Que.	2	78	12	20	32	59	3	0	0	0	10	....	1979-80	1980-81
‡ Fitzgerald, Rusty	Pit.	2	25	2	2	4	12	5	0	0	0	4	....	1994-95	1995-96
Fitzpatrick, Ross	Phi.	4	20	5	2	7	0	....	....	....	....	....	....	1982-83	1985-86
Fitzpatrick, Sandy	NYR, Min.	2	22	3	6	9	8	12	0	0	0	0	....	1964-65	1967-68
Flaman, Fern	Bos., Tor.	17	910	34	174	208	1370	63	4	8	12	93	1	1944-45	1960-61
Flatley, Pat	NYI, NYR	14	780	170	340	510	686	70	18	15	33	75	....	1983-84	1996-97
Fleming, Gerry	Mtl.	2	11	0	0	0	42	....	....	....	....	....	....	1993-94	1994-95
Fleming, Reggie	Mtl., Chi., Bos., NYR, Phi., Buf.	12	749	108	132	240	1468	50	3	6	9	106	1	1959-60	1970-71
Flesch, John	Min., Pit., Col.	4	124	18	23	41	117	....	....	....	....	....	....	1974-75	1979-80
Fletcher, Steven	Mtl., Wpg.	2	3	0	0	0	5	1	0	0	0	5	....	1987-88	1988-89
● Flett, Bill	L.A., Phi., Tor., Atl., Edm.	11	689	202	215	417	501	52	7	16	23	42	1	1967-68	1979-80
Flichel, Todd	Wpg.	3	6	0	1	1	4	....	....	....	....	....	....	1987-88	1989-90
Flockhart, Rob	Van., Min.	5	55	2	5	7	14	1	1	0	1	2	....	1976-77	1980-81
Flockhart, Ron	Phi., Pit., Mtl., St.L., Bos.	9	453	145	183	328	208	19	4	6	10	14	....	1980-81	1988-89
Floyd, Larry	N.J.	2	12	2	3	5	9	....	....	....	....	....	....	1982-83	1983-84
● Fogarty, Bryan	Que., Pit., Mtl.	6	156	22	52	74	119	....	....	....	....	....	....	1989-90	1994-95
● Fogolin, Lee	Det., Chi.	9	427	10	48	58	575	28	0	2	2	30	1	1947-48	1955-56
Fogolin Jr., Lee	Buf., Edm.	13	924	44	195	239	1318	108	5	19	24	173	2	1974-75	1986-87
Folco, Peter	Van.	1	2	0	0	0	0	....	....	....	....	....	....	1973-74	1973-74
Foley, Gerry	Tor., NYR, L.A.	4	142	9	14	23	99	9	0	1	1	2	....	1954-55	1968-69
Foley, Rick	Chi., Phi., Det.	3	67	11	26	37	180	4	0	1	1	4	....	1970-71	1973-74
Foligno, Mike	Det., Buf., Tor., Fla.	15	1018	355	372	727	2049	57	15	17	32	185	....	1979-80	1993-94
Folk, Bill	Det.	2	12	0	0	0	4	....	....	....	....	....	....	1951-52	1952-53
Fontaine, Len	Det.	2	46	8	11	19	10	....	....	....	....	....	....	1972-73	1973-74
Fontas, Jon	Min.	2	2	0	0	0	0	....	....	....	....	....	....	1979-80	1980-81
Fonteyne, Val	Det., NYR, Pit.	13	820	75	154	229	26	59	3	10	13	8	....	1959-60	1971-72
Fontinato, Lou	NYR, Mtl.	9	535	26	78	104	1247	21	0	2	2	42	....	1954-55	1962-63
Forbes, Dave	Bos., Wsh.	6	363	64	64	128	341	45	1	4	5	13	....	1973-74	1978-79
Forbes, Mike	Bos., Edm.	3	50	1	11	12	41	....	....	....	....	....	....	1977-78	1981-82
Forey, Connie	St.L.	1	4	0	0	0	2	....	....	....	....	....	....	1973-74	1973-74
● Forsey, Jack	Tor.	1	19	7	9	16	10	3	0	1	1	0	....	1942-43	1942-43
● Forslund, Gus	Ott.	1	48	4	9	13	2	....	....	....	....	....	....	1932-33	1932-33
Forslund, Tomas	Cgy.	2	44	5	11	16	12	....	....	....	....	....	....	1991-92	1992-93
Forsyth, Alex	Wsh.	1	1	0	0	0	0	....	....	....	....	....	....	1976-77	1976-77
Fortier, Dave	Tor., NYI, Van.	4	205	8	21	29	335	20	0	2	2	33	....	1972-73	1976-77
‡ Fortier, Marc	Que., Ott., L.A.	6	212	42	60	102	135	....	....	....	....	....	....	1987-88	1992-93
Fortin, Ray	St.L.	3	92	2	6	8	33	6	0	0	0	8	....	1967-68	1969-70
‡ Foster, Corey	N.J., Phi., Pit., NYI	4	45	5	6	11	24	3	0	0	0	4	....	1988-89	1996-97
Foster, Dwight	Bos., Col., N.J., Det.	10	541	111	163	274	420	35	5	12	17	4	....	1977-78	1986-87
Foster, Herb	NYR	2	6	1	0	1	5	....	....	....	....	....	....	1940-41	1947-48
● Foster, Yip	NYR, Bos., Det.	4	83	3	2	5	32	....	....	....	....	....	....	1929-30	1934-35
Fotiu, Nick	NYR, Hfd., Cgy., Phi., Edm.	13	646	60	77	137	1362	38	0	4	4	67	....	1976-77	1988-89
● Fowler, Jimmy	Tor.	3	135	18	29	47	39	18	0	3	3	2	....	1936-37	1938-39
Fowler, Tom	Chi.	1	24	0	1	1	18	....	....	....	....	....	....	1946-47	1946-47
Fox, Greg	Atl., Chi., Pit.	8	494	14	92	106	637	44	1	9	10	67	....	1977-78	1984-85
Fox, Jim	L.A.	9	578	186	293	479	143	22	4	8	12	0	....	1980-81	1989-90
● Foyston, Frank	Det.	2	64	17	7	24	32	....	....	....	....	....	....	1926-27	1927-28
Frampton, Bob	Mtl.	1	2	0	0	0	0	3	0	0	0	0	....	1949-50	1949-50
Franceschetti, Lou	Wsh., Tor., Buf.	10	459	59	81	140	747	44	3	2	5	111	....	1981-82	1991-92
Francis, Bobby	Det.	1	14	2	0	2	0	....	....	....	....	....	....	1982-83	1982-83
● Fraser, Archie	NYR	1	3	0	1	1	0	....	....	....	....	....	....	1943-44	1943-44
● Fraser, Charles	Ham.	1	1	0	0	0	0	....	....	....	....	....	....	1923-24	1923-24
Fraser, Curt	Van., Chi., Min.	12	704	193	240	433	1306	65	15	18	33	198	....	1978-79	1989-90
● Fraser, Gord	Chi., Det., Mtl., Pit., Phi.	5	144	24	12	36	224	2	1	0	1	6	....	1926-27	1930-31
Fraser, Harvey	Chi.	1	21	5	4	9	0	....	....	....	....	....	....	1944-45	1944-45
‡ Fraser, Iain	NYI, Que., Dal., Edm., Wpg., S.J.	5	94	23	23	46	31	4	0	0	0	0	....	1992-93	1996-97
Fraser, Scott	Mtl., Edm., NYR	3	72	16	15	31	24	11	1	1	2	0	....	1995-96	1998-99
Frawley, Dan	Chi., Pit.	6	273	37	40	77	674	1	0	0	0	0	....	1983-84	1988-89
Freadrich, Kyle	T.B.	2	23	0	1	1	75	....	....	....	....	....	....	1999-00	2000-01
● Fredrickson, Frank	Det., Bos., Pit.	5	161	39	34	73	206	10	2	3	5	24	....	1926-27	1930-31
‡ Freer, Mark	Phi., Ott., Cgy.	7	124	16	23	39	61	....	....	....	....	....	....	1986-87	1993-94
● Frew, Irv	Mtl.M., St.L., Mtl.	3	96	2	5	7	146	4	0	0	0	6	....	1933-34	1935-36
Friday, Tim	Det.	1	23	0	3	3	6	....	....	....	....	....	....	1985-86	1985-86
Fridgen, Dan	Hfd.	2	13	2	3	5	2	....	....	....	....	....	....	1981-82	1982-83
Friedman, Doug	Edm., Nsh.	2	18	0	1	1	34	....	....	....	....	....	....	1997-98	1998-99
Friest, Ron	Min.	3	64	7	7	14	191	6	1	0	1	7	....	1980-81	1982-83
Frig, Len	Chi., Cal., Cle., St.L.	7	311	13	51	64	479	14	2	1	3	0	....	1972-73	1979-80
Frost, Harry	Bos.	1	4	0	0	0	0	1	0	0	0	0	1	1938-39	1938-39
Frycer, Miroslav	Que., Tor., Det., Edm.	8	415	147	183	330	486	17	3	8	11	16	....	1981-82	1988-89
Fryday, Bob	Mtl.	2	5	1	0	1	0	....	....	....	....	....	....	1949-50	1951-52
Ftorek, Robbie	Det., Que., NYR	8	334	77	150	227	262	19	9	6	15	28	....	1972-73	1984-85
Fullan, Larry	Wsh.	1	4	1	0	1	0	....	....	....	....	....	....	1974-75	1974-75
Fusco, Mark	Hfd.	2	80	3	12	15	42	....	....	....	....	....	....	1983-84	1984-85

G

Name	NHL Teams	NHL Seasons	Regular Schedule GP	G	A	TP	PIM	Playoffs GP	G	A	TP	PIM	NHL Cup Wins	First NHL Season	Last NHL Season
Gadsby, Bill	Chi., NYR, Det.	20	1248	130	438	568	1539	67	4	23	27	92	....	1946-47	1965-66
‡ Gaetz, Link	Min., S.J.	3	65	6	8	14	412	....	....	....	....	....	....	1988-89	1991-92
Gage, Jody	Det., Buf.	6	68	14	15	29	26	....	....	....	....	....	....	1980-81	1991-92
● Gagne, Art	Mtl., Bos., Ott., Det.	6	228	67	33	100	257	11	2	1	3	20	....	1926-27	1931-32
Gagne, Paul	Col., N.J., Tor., NYI	8	390	110	101	211	127	....	....	....	....	....	....	1980-81	1989-90
Gagne, Pierre	Bos.	1	2	0	0	0	0	....	....	....	....	....	....	1959-60	1959-60
Gagner, Dave	NYR, Min., Dal., Tor., Cgy., Fla., Van.	15	946	318	401	719	1018	57	22	26	48	64	....	1984-85	1998-99
Gagnon, Germain	Mtl., NYI, Chi., K.C.	5	259	40	101	141	72	19	2	3	5	2	....	1971-72	1975-76
● Gagnon, Johnny	Mtl., Bos., NYA	10	454	120	141	261	295	32	12	12	24	37	1	1930-31	1939-40
Gainey, Bob	Mtl.	16	1160	239	262	501	585	182	25	48	73	151	5	1973-74	1988-89
● Gainor, Dutch	Bos., NYR, Ott., Mtl.M.	7	246	51	56	107	129	22	2	1	3	14	2	1927-28	1934-35
‡ Galanov, Maxim	NYR, Pit., Atl., T.B.	4	122	8	12	20	44	1	0	0	0	0	....	1997-98	2000-01
Galarneau, Michel	Hfd.	3	78	7	10	17	34	....	....	....	....	....	....	1980-81	1982-83
● Galbraith, Percy	Bos., Ott.	8	347	29	31	60	224	31	4	7	11	24	1	1926-27	1933-34
● Gallagher, John	Mtl.M., Det., NYA	7	205	14	19	33	153	24	2	3	5	27	1	1930-31	1938-39
Gallant, Gerard	Det., T.B.	11	615	211	269	480	1674	58	18	21	39	178	....	1984-85	1994-95
Galley, Garry	L.A., Wsh., Bos., Phi., Buf., NYI	17	1149	125	475	600	1218	89	7	23	30	119	....	1984-85	2000-01
Gallimore, Jamie	Min.	1	2	0	0	0	0	....	....	....	....	....	....	1977-78	1977-78
● Gallinger, Don	Bos.	5	222	65	88	153	89	23	5	5	10	19	....	1942-43	1947-48
Gamble, Dick	Mtl., Chi., Tor.	8	195	41	41	82	66	14	1	2	3	4	1	1950-51	1966-67
Gambucci, Gary	Min.	2	51	2	7	9	9	....	....	....	....	....	....	1971-72	1973-74
Ganchar, Perry	St.L., Mtl., Pit.	4	42	3	7	10	36	7	3	1	4	0	....	1983-84	1988-89
Gans, Dave	L.A.	2	6	0	0	0	2	....	....	....	....	....	....	1982-83	1985-86
● Gardiner, Herb	Mtl., Chi.	3	108	10	9	19	52	9	0	1	1	16	....	1926-27	1928-29
Gardner, Bill	Chi., Hfd.	9	380	73	115	188	68	45	3	8	11	17	....	1980-81	1988-89
● Gardner, Cal	NYR, Tor., Chi., Bos.	12	696	154	238	392	517	61	7	10	17	20	2	1945-46	1956-57
Gardner, Dave	Mtl., St.L., Cal., Cle., Phi.	7	350	75	115	190	41	....	....	....	....	....	....	1972-73	1979-80
Gardner, Paul	Col., Tor., Pit., Wsh., Buf.	10	447	201	201	402	207	16	2	6	8	14	....	1976-77	1985-86
Gare, Danny	Buf., Det., Edm.	13	827	354	331	685	1285	64	25	21	46	195	....	1974-75	1986-87
Gariepy, Ray	Bos., Tor.	2	36	1	6	7	43	....	....	....	....	....	....	1953-54	1955-56
● Garland, Scott	Tor., L.A.	3	91	13	24	37	115	7	1	2	3	35	....	1975-76	1978-79
Garner, Rob	Pit.	1	1	0	0	0	0	....	....	....	....	....	....	1982-83	1982-83
Garpenlov, Johan	Det., S.J., Fla., Atl.	10	609	114	197	311	276	44	10	9	19	22	....	1990-91	1999-00
● Garrett, Red	NYR	1	23	1	1	2	18	....	....	....	....	....	....	1942-43	1942-43
Gartner, Mike	Wsh., Min., NYR, Tor., Phx.	19	1432	708	627	1335	1159	122	43	50	93	125	....	1979-80	1997-98
● Gassoff, Bob	St.L.	4	245	11	47	58	866	9	0	1	1	16	....	1973-74	1976-77
Gassoff, Brad	Van.	4	122	19	17	36	163	3	0	0	0	0	....	1975-76	1978-79
Gatzos, Steve	Pit.	4	89	15	20	35	83	1	0	0	0	0	....	1981-82	1984-85
Gaudreau, Rob	S.J., Ott.	4	231	51	54	105	69	14	2	0	2	0	....	1992-93	1995-96
Gaudreault, Armand	Bos.	1	44	15	9	24	27	7	0	2	2	8	....	1944-45	1944-45
● Gaudreault, Leo	Mtl.	3	67	8	4	12	30	....	....	....	....	....	....	1927-28	1932-33
‡ Gaul, Mike	Col., CBJ	2	3	0	0	0	4	....	....	....	....	....	....	1998-99	2000-01
Gaulin, Jean-Marc	Que.	4	26	4	3	7	8	1	0	0	0	0	....	1982-83	1985-86
Gaume, Dallas	Hfd.	1	4	1	1	2	0	....	....	....	....	....	....	1988-89	1988-89

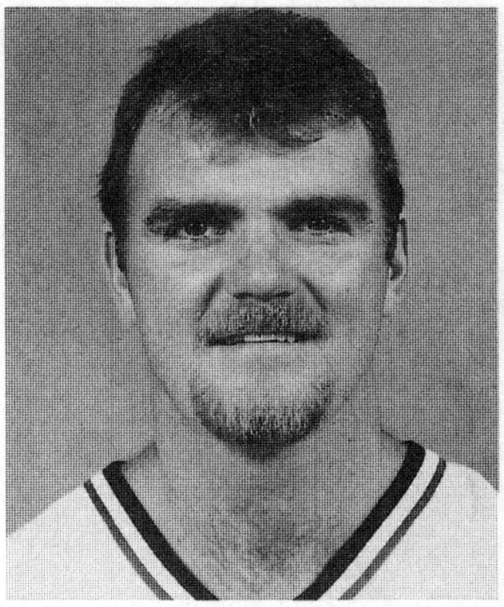
Glen Featherstone

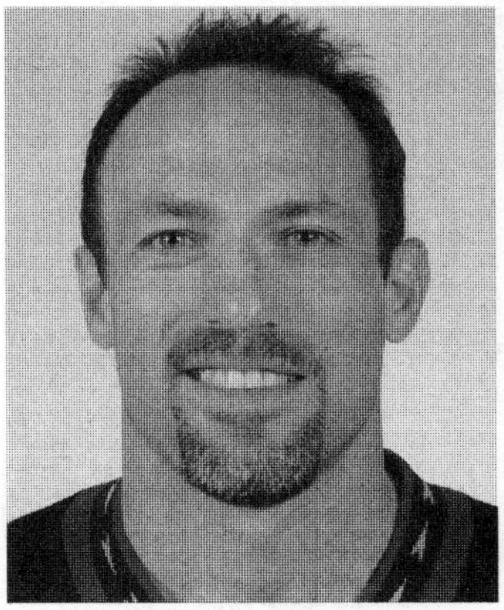
Ray Ferraro

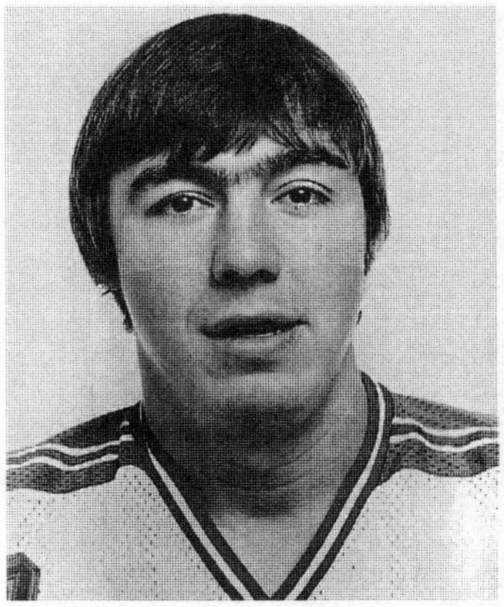
Nick Fotiu

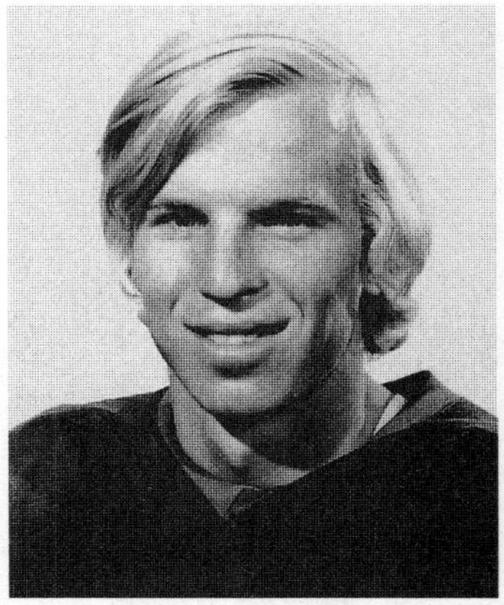
Robbie Ftorek

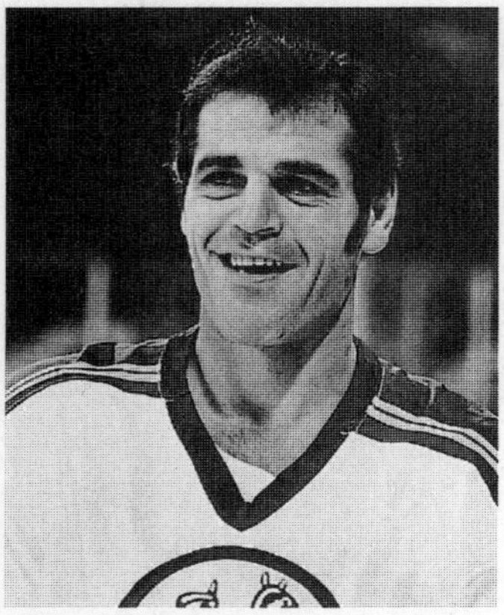

Germain Gagnon

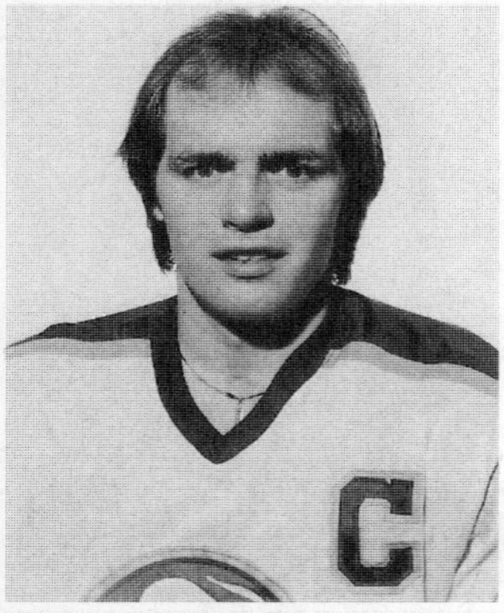

Danny Gare

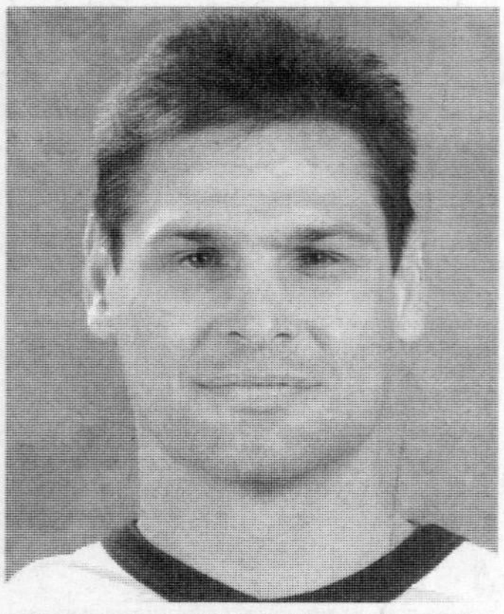

Stu Grimson

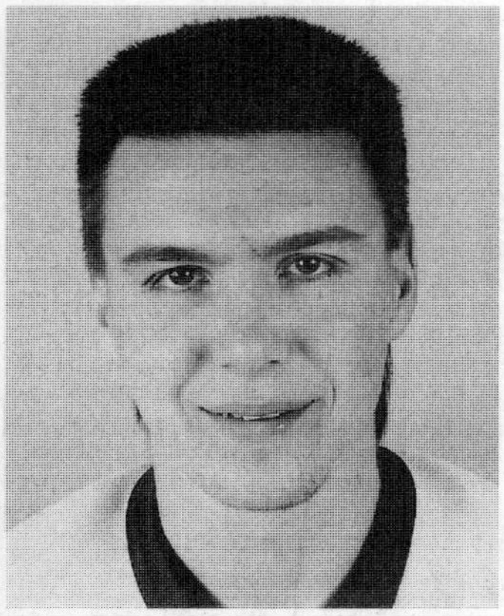

Jari Gronstrand

Name	NHL Teams	NHL Seasons	Regular Schedule GP	G	A	TP	PIM	Playoffs GP	G	A	TP	PIM	NHL Cup Wins	First NHL Season	Last NHL Season
● Gauthier, Art	Mtl.	1	13	0	0	0	0	1	0	0	0	0	....	1926-27	1926-27
‡ Gauthier, Daniel	Chi.	1	5	0	0	0	0	....	....	....	....	....	....	1994-95	1994-95
● Gauthier, Fern	NYR, Mtl., Det.	6	229	46	50	96	35	22	5	1	6	7	....	1943-44	1948-49
Gauthier, Jean	Mtl., Phi., Bos.	10	166	6	29	35	150	14	1	3	4	22	1	1960-61	1969-70
Gauthier, Luc	Mtl.	1	3	0	0	0	2	....	....	....	....	....	....	1990-91	1990-91
Gauvreau, Jocelyn	Mtl.	1	2	0	0	0	0	....	....	....	....	....	....	1983-84	1983-84
Gavin, Stew	Tor., Hfd., Min.	13	768	130	155	285	584	66	14	20	34	75	....	1980-81	1992-93
Geale, Bob	Pit.	1	1	0	0	0	2	....	....	....	....	....	....	1984-85	1984-85
● Gee, George	Chi., Det.	9	551	135	183	318	345	41	6	13	19	32	1	1945-46	1953-54
Geldart, Gary	Min.	1	4	0	0	0	5	....	....	....	....	....	....	1970-71	1970-71
Gendron, Jean-Guy	NYR, Bos., Mtl., Phi.	14	863	182	201	383	701	42	7	4	11	47	....	1955-56	1971-72
‡ Gendron, Martin	Wsh., Chi.	3	30	4	2	6	10	....	....	....	....	....	....	1994-95	1997-98
Geoffrion, Bernie	Mtl., NYR	16	883	393	429	822	689	132	58	60	118	88	6	1950-51	1967-68
Geoffrion, Danny	Mtl., Wpg.	3	111	20	32	52	99	2	0	0	0	7	....	1979-80	1981-82
● Geran, Gerry	Mtl.W., Bos.	2	37	5	1	6	6	....	....	....	....	....	....	1917-18	1925-26
● Gerard, Eddie	Ott.	6	128	50	48	98	108	11	4	0	4	17	3	1917-18	1922-23
Germain, Eric	L.A.	1	4	0	1	1	13	1	0	0	0	4	....	1987-88	1987-88
Getliffe, Ray	Bos., Mtl.	10	393	136	137	273	250	45	9	10	19	30	2	1935-36	1944-45
Giallonardo, Mario	Col.	2	23	0	3	3	6	....	....	....	....	....	....	1979-80	1980-81
Gibbs, Barry	Bos., Min., Atl., St.L., L.A.	13	797	58	224	282	945	36	4	2	6	67	....	1967-68	1979-80
Gibson, Don	Van.	1	14	0	3	3	20	....	....	....	....	....	....	1990-91	1990-91
Gibson, Doug	Bos., Wsh.	3	63	9	19	28	0	1	0	0	0	0	....	1973-74	1977-78
Gibson, John	L.A., Tor., Wpg.	3	48	0	2	2	120	....	....	....	....	....	....	1980-81	1983-84
Giesebrecht, Gus	Det.	4	135	27	51	78	13	17	2	3	5	0	....	1938-39	1941-42
Giffin, Lee	Pit.	2	27	1	3	4	9	....	....	....	....	....	....	1986-87	1987-88
Gilbert, Ed	K.C., Pit.	3	166	21	31	52	22	....	....	....	....	....	....	1974-75	1976-77
Gilbert, Greg	NYI, Chi., NYR, St.L.	15	837	150	228	378	576	133	17	33	50	162	3	1981-82	1995-96
Gilbert, Jeannot	Bos.	2	9	0	1	1	4	....	....	....	....	....	....	1962-63	1964-65
Gilbert, Rod	NYR	18	1065	406	615	1021	508	79	34	33	67	43	....	1960-61	1977-78
Gilbertson, Stan	Cal., St.L., Wsh., Pit.	6	428	85	89	174	148	3	1	1	2	2	....	1971-72	1976-77
Giles, Curt	Min., NYR, St.L.	14	895	43	199	242	733	103	6	16	22	118	....	1979-80	1992-93
Gilhen, Randy	Hfd., Wpg., Pit., L.A., NYR, T.B., Fla.	11	457	55	60	115	314	33	3	2	5	26	1	1982-83	1995-96
Gillen, Don	Phi., Hfd.	2	35	2	4	6	22	....	....	....	....	....	....	1979-80	1981-82
● Gillie, Farrand	Det.	1	1	0	0	0	0	....	....	....	....	....	....	1928-29	1928-29
Gillies, Clark	NYI, Buf.	14	958	319	378	697	1023	164	47	47	94	287	4	1974-75	1987-88
Gillis, Jere	Van., NYR, Que., Buf., Phi.	9	386	78	95	173	230	19	4	7	11	9	....	1977-78	1986-87
Gillis, Mike	Col., Bos.	6	246	33	43	76	186	27	2	5	7	10	....	1978-79	1983-84
Gillis, Paul	Que., Chi., Hfd.	11	624	88	154	242	1498	42	3	14	17	156	....	1982-83	1992-93
Gingras, Gaston	Mtl., Tor., St.L.	10	476	61	174	235	161	52	6	18	24	20	1	1979-80	1988-89
Girard, Bob	Cal., Cle., Wsh.	5	305	45	69	114	140	....	....	....	....	....	....	1975-76	1979-80
Girard, Kenny	Tor.	3	7	0	1	1	2	....	....	....	....	....	....	1956-57	1959-60
● Giroux, Art	Mtl., Bos., Det.	3	54	6	4	10	14	2	0	0	0	0	....	1932-33	1935-36
Giroux, Larry	St.L., K.C., Det., Hfd.	7	274	15	74	89	333	5	0	0	0	4	....	1973-74	1979-80
Giroux, Pierre	L.A.	1	6	1	0	1	17	....	....	....	....	....	....	1982-83	1982-83
Gladney, Bob	L.A., Pit.	2	14	1	5	6	4	....	....	....	....	....	....	1982-83	1983-84
Gladu, Jean-Paul	Bos.	1	40	6	14	20	2	7	2	2	4	0	....	1944-45	1944-45
Glennie, Brian	Tor., L.A.	10	572	14	100	114	621	32	0	1	1	66	....	1969-70	1978-79
Glennon, Matt	Bos.	1	3	0	0	0	2	....	....	....	....	....	....	1991-92	1991-92
Gloeckner, Lorry	Det.	1	13	0	2	2	6	....	....	....	....	....	....	1978-79	1978-79
Gloor, Dan	Van.	1	2	0	0	0	0	....	....	....	....	....	....	1973-74	1973-74
● Glover, Fred	Det., Chi.	5	92	13	11	24	62	8	0	0	0	0	1	1948-49	1952-53
Glover, Howie	Chi., Det., NYR, Mtl.	5	144	29	17	46	101	11	1	2	3	2	....	1958-59	1968-69
Glynn, Brian	Cgy., Min., Edm., Ott., Van., Hfd.	10	431	25	79	104	410	57	6	10	16	40	....	1987-88	1996-97
Godden, Ernie	Tor.	1	5	1	1	2	6	....	....	....	....	....	....	1981-82	1981-82
● Godfrey, Warren	Bos., Det.	16	786	32	125	157	752	52	1	4	5	42	....	1952-53	1967-68
Godin, Eddy	Wsh.	2	27	3	6	9	12	....	....	....	....	....	....	1977-78	1978-79
● Godin, Sam	Ott., Mtl.	3	83	4	3	7	36	....	....	....	....	....	....	1927-28	1933-34
Godynyuk, Alexander	Tor., Cgy., Fla., Hfd.	7	223	10	39	49	224	....	....	....	....	....	....	1990-91	1996-97
Goegan, Pete	Det., NYR, Min.	11	383	19	67	86	365	33	1	3	4	61	....	1957-58	1967-68
Goertz, Dave	Pit.	1	2	0	0	0	2	....	....	....	....	....	....	1987-88	1987-88
● Goldham, Bob	Tor., Chi., Det.	12	650	28	143	171	400	66	3	14	17	53	5	1941-42	1955-56
‡ Goldmann, Erich	Ott.	1	1	0	0	0	0	....	....	....	....	....	....	1999-00	1999-00
● Goldsworthy, Bill	Bos., Min., NYR	14	771	283	258	541	793	40	18	19	37	30	....	1964-65	1977-78
● Goldsworthy, Leroy	NYR, Det., Chi., Mtl., Bos., NYA	10	336	66	57	123	79	24	1	0	1	4	1	1928-29	1938-39
Goldup, Glenn	Mtl., L.A.	9	291	52	67	119	303	16	4	3	7	22	....	1973-74	1981-82
Goldup, Hank	Tor., NYR	6	202	63	80	143	97	26	5	1	6	6	1	1939-40	1945-46
‡ Golubovsky, Yan	Det., Fla.	4	56	1	7	8	32	....	....	....	....	....	....	1997-98	2000-01
‡ Goneau, Daniel	NYR	3	53	12	3	15	14	....	....	....	....	....	....	1996-97	1999-00
● Gooden, Bill	NYR	2	53	9	11	20	15	....	....	....	....	....	....	1942-43	1943-44
Goodenough, Larry	Phi., Van.	6	242	22	77	99	179	22	3	15	18	10	1	1974-75	1979-80
● Goodfellow, Ebbie	Det.	14	557	134	190	324	511	45	8	8	16	65	3	1929-30	1942-43
Gordiouk, Viktor	Buf.	2	26	3	8	11	0	....	....	....	....	....	....	1992-93	1994-95
Gordon, Fred	Det., Bos.	2	81	8	7	15	68	2	0	0	0	0	....	1926-27	1927-28
Gordon, Jack	NYR	3	36	3	10	13	0	9	1	1	2	7	....	1948-49	1950-51
Gordon, Robb	Van.	1	4	0	0	0	2	....	....	....	....	....	....	1998-99	1998-99
Gorence, Tom	Phi., Edm.	6	303	58	53	111	89	37	9	6	15	47	....	1978-79	1983-84
Goring, Butch	L.A., NYI, Bos.	16	1107	375	513	888	102	134	38	50	88	32	4	1969-70	1984-85
Gorman, Dave	Atl.	1	3	0	0	0	0	....	....	....	....	....	....	1979-80	1979-80
● Gorman, Ed	Ott., Tor.	4	111	14	6	20	108	8	0	0	0	2	1	1924-25	1927-28
Gosselin, Benoit	NYR	1	7	0	0	0	33	....	....	....	....	....	....	1977-78	1977-78
Gosselin, Guy	Wpg.	1	5	0	0	0	6	....	....	....	....	....	....	1987-88	1987-88
Gotaas, Steve	Pit., Min.	3	49	6	9	15	53	3	0	1	1	5	....	1987-88	1990-91
● Gottselig, Johnny	Chi.	16	589	176	195	371	203	43	13	13	26	18	2	1928-29	1944-45
Gould, Bobby	Atl., Cgy., Wsh., Bos.	11	697	145	159	304	572	78	15	13	28	58	....	1979-80	1989-90
Gould, John	Buf., Van., Atl.	9	504	131	138	269	113	14	3	2	5	4	....	1971-72	1979-80
Gould, Larry	Van.	1	2	0	0	0	0	....	....	....	....	....	....	1973-74	1973-74
Goulet, Michel	Que., Chi.	15	1089	548	604	1152	825	92	39	39	78	110	....	1979-80	1993-94
Goupille, Red	Mtl.	8	222	12	28	40	256	8	2	0	2	6	....	1935-36	1942-43
Govedaris, Chris	Hfd., Tor.	4	45	4	6	10	24	4	0	0	0	2	....	1989-90	1993-94
Goyer, Gerry	Chi.	1	40	1	2	3	4	3	0	0	0	2	....	1967-68	1967-68
Goyette, Phil	Mtl., NYR, St.L., Buf.	16	941	207	467	674	131	94	17	29	46	26	4	1956-57	1971-72
Graboski, Tony	Mtl.	3	66	6	10	16	24	3	0	0	0	6	....	1940-41	1942-43
● Gracie, Bob	Tor., Bos., NYA, Mtl.M., Mtl., Chi.	9	379	82	109	191	205	33	4	7	11	4	2	1930-31	1938-39
Gradin, Thomas	Van., Bos.	9	677	209	384	593	298	42	17	25	42	20	....	1978-79	1986-87
Graham, Dirk	Min., Chi.	12	772	219	270	489	917	90	17	27	44	92	....	1983-84	1994-95
● Graham, Leth	Ott., Ham.	6	27	3	0	3	0	1	0	0	0	0	1	1920-21	1925-26
Graham, Pat	Pit., Tor.	3	103	11	17	28	136	4	0	0	0	2	....	1981-82	1983-84
Graham, Rod	Bos.	1	14	2	1	3	7	....	....	....	....	....	....	1974-75	1974-75
● Graham, Ted	Chi., Mtl.M., Det., St.L., Bos., NYA	9	346	14	25	39	300	24	3	1	4	30	....	1927-28	1936-37
Granato, Tony	NYR, L.A., S.J.	14	773	248	244	492	1425	79	16	27	43	141	....	1988-89	2000-01
Grant, Danny	Mtl., Min., Det., L.A.	13	736	263	273	536	239	43	10	14	24	19	1	1965-66	1978-79
Gratton, Dan	L.A.	1	7	1	0	1	5	....	....	....	....	....	....	1987-88	1987-88
Gratton, Norm	NYR, Atl., Buf., Min.	5	201	39	44	83	64	6	0	1	1	2	....	1971-72	1975-76
Gravelle, Leo	Mtl., Det.	5	223	44	34	78	42	17	4	1	5	2	....	1946-47	1950-51
Graves, Hilliard	Cal., Atl., Van., Wpg.	9	556	118	163	281	209	2	0	0	0	0	....	1970-71	1979-80
Graves, Steve	Edm.	3	35	5	4	9	10	....	....	....	....	....	....	1983-84	1987-88
● Gray, Alex	NYR, Tor.	2	50	7	0	7	32	13	1	0	1	0	1	1927-28	1928-29
Gray, Terry	Bos., Mtl., L.A., St.L.	6	147	26	28	54	64	35	5	5	10	22	....	1961-62	1970-71
● Green, Red	Ham., NYA, Bos., Det.	6	195	59	26	85	290	1	0	0	0	0	1	1923-24	1928-29
Green, Rick	Wsh., Mtl., Det., NYI	15	845	43	220	263	588	100	3	16	19	73	1	1976-77	1991-92
● Green, Shorty	Ham., NYA	4	103	33	20	53	151	....	....	....	....	....	....	1923-24	1926-27
Green, Ted	Bos.	11	620	48	206	254	1029	31	4	8	12	54	1	1960-61	1971-72
Greenlaw, Jeff	Wsh., Fla.	6	57	3	6	9	108	2	0	0	0	21	....	1986-87	1993-94
Gregg, Randy	Edm., Van.	10	474	41	152	193	333	137	13	38	51	127	5	1981-82	1991-92
Greig, Bruce	Cal.	2	9	0	1	1	46	....	....	....	....	....	....	1973-74	1974-75
Grenier, Lucien	Mtl., L.A.	4	151	14	14	28	18	2	0	0	0	0	1	1968-69	1971-72
Grenier, Richard	NYI	1	10	1	1	2	2	....	....	....	....	....	....	1972-73	1972-73
Greschner, Ron	NYR	16	982	179	431	610	1226	84	17	32	49	106	....	1974-75	1989-90
‡ Gretzky, Brent	T.B.	2	13	1	3	4	2	....	....	....	....	....	....	1993-94	1994-95
Gretzky, Wayne	Edm., L.A., St.L., NYR	20	1487	894	1963	2857	577	208	122	260	382	66	4	1979-80	1998-99
Grieve, Brent	NYI, Edm., Chi., L.A.	4	97	20	16	36	87	....	....	....	....	....	....	1993-94	1996-97
Grigor, George	Chi.	1	2	1	0	1	0	1	0	0	0	0	....	1943-44	1943-44
Grimson, Stu	Cgy., Chi., Ana., Det., Hfd., Car., L.A., Nsh.	14	729	17	22	39	2113	42	1	1	2	120	....	1988-89	2001-02
Grisdale, John	Tor., Van.	6	250	4	39	43	346	10	0	1	1	15	....	1972-73	1978-79
‡ Groleau, Francois	Mtl.	3	8	0	1	1	6	....	....	....	....	....	....	1995-96	1997-98

Name	NHL Teams	NHL Seasons	Regular Schedule GP	G	A	TP	PIM	Playoffs GP	G	A	TP	PIM	NHL Cup Wins	First NHL Season	Last NHL Season
‡ Gron, Stanislav	N.J.	1	1	0	0	0	0	....	....	....	....	....	....	2000-01	2000-01
‡ Gronman, Tuomas	Chi., Pit.	2	38	1	3	4	38	1	0	0	0	0	....	1996-97	1997-98
Gronsdahl, Lloyd	Bos.	1	10	1	2	3	0	....	....	....	....	....	....	1941-42	1941-42
Gronstrand, Jari	Min., NYR, Que., NYI	5	185	8	26	34	135	3	0	0	0	4	....	1986-87	1990-91
Gross, Lloyd	Tor., NYA, Bos., Det.	3	62	11	5	16	20	1	0	0	0	0	....	1926-27	1934-35
• Grosso, Don	Det., Chi., Bos.	9	336	87	117	204	90	48	15	14	29	63	1	1938-39	1946-47
Grosvenor, Len	Ott., NYA, Mtl.	6	149	9	11	20	78	4	0	0	0	2	....	1927-28	1932-33
Groulx, Wayne	Que.	1	1	0	0	0	0	....	....	....	....	....	....	1984-85	1984-85
Gruen, Danny	Det., Col.	3	49	9	13	22	19	....	....	....	....	....	....	1972-73	1976-77
Gruhl, Scott	L.A., Pit.	3	20	3	3	6	6	....	....	....	....	....	....	1981-82	1987-88
Gryp, Bob	Bos., Wsh.	3	74	11	13	24	33	....	....	....	....	....	....	1973-74	1975-76
Guay, Francois	Buf.	1	1	0	0	0	0	....	....	....	....	....	....	1989-90	1989-90
Guay, Paul	Phi., L.A., Bos., NYI	7	117	11	23	34	92	9	0	1	1	12	....	1983-84	1990-91
‡ Guerard, Daniel	Ott.	1	2	0	0	0	0	....	....	....	....	....	....	1994-95	1994-95
Guerard, Stephane	Que.	2	34	0	0	0	40	....	....	....	....	....	....	1987-88	1989-90
Guevremont, Jocelyn	Van., Buf., NYR	9	571	84	223	307	319	40	4	17	21	18	....	1971-72	1979-80
Guidolin, Aldo	NYR	4	182	9	15	24	117	....	....	....	....	....	....	1952-53	1955-56
Guidolin, Bep	Bos., Det., Chi.	9	519	107	171	278	606	24	5	7	12	35	....	1942-43	1951-52
Guindon, Bobby	Wpg.	1	6	0	1	1	0	....	....	....	....	....	....	1979-80	1979-80
Gusarov, Alexei	Que., Col., NYR, St.L.	11	607	39	128	167	313	68	0	14	14	38	1	1990-91	2000-01
‡ Gusev, Sergey	Dal., T.B.	4	89	4	10	14	34	....	....	....	....	....	....	1997-98	2000-01
‡ Gusmanov, Ravil	Wpg.	1	4	0	0	0	0	....	....	....	....	....	....	1995-96	1995-96
Gustafsson, Bengt-Ake	Wsh.	9	629	196	359	555	196	32	9	19	28	16	....	1979-80	1988-89
‡ Gustafsson, Per	Fla., Tor., Ott.	2	89	8	27	35	38	1	0	0	0	0	....	1996-97	1997-98
Gustavsson, Peter	Col.	1	2	0	0	0	0	....	....	....	....	....	....	1981-82	1981-82
Guy, Kevan	Cgy., Van.	6	156	5	20	25	138	5	0	1	1	23	....	1986-87	1991-92

H

Name	NHL Teams	NHL Seasons	Regular Schedule GP	G	A	TP	PIM	Playoffs GP	G	A	TP	PIM	NHL Cup Wins	First NHL Season	Last NHL Season
Haanpaa, Ari	NYI	3	60	6	11	17	37	6	0	0	0	10	....	1985-86	1987-88
‡ Haas, David	Edm., Cgy.	2	7	2	1	3	7	....	....	....	....	....	....	1990-91	1993-94
Habscheid, Marc	Edm., Min., Det., Cgy.	11	345	72	91	163	171	12	1	3	4	13	....	1981-82	1991-92
Hachborn, Len	Phi., L.A.	3	102	20	39	59	29	7	0	3	3	7	....	1983-84	1985-86
Haddon, Lloyd	Det.	1	8	0	0	0	2	1	0	0	0	0	....	1959-60	1959-60
Hadfield, Vic	NYR, Pit.	16	1002	323	389	712	1154	73	27	21	48	117	....	1961-62	1976-77
• Haggarty, Jim	Mtl.	1	5	1	1	2	0	3	2	1	3	0	....	1941-42	1941-42
‡ Haggerty, Sean	Tor., NYI, Nsh.	4	14	1	2	3	4	....	....	....	....	....	....	1995-96	2000-01
• Hagglund, Roger	Que.	1	3	0	0	0	0	....	....	....	....	....	....	1984-85	1984-85
Hagman, Matti	Bos., Edm.	4	237	56	89	145	36	20	5	2	7	6	....	1976-77	1981-82
Haidy, Gord	Det.	1	....	....	....	....	....	1	0	0	0	0	1	1949-50	1949-50
Hajdu, Richard	Buf.	2	5	0	0	0	4	....	....	....	....	....	....	1985-86	1986-87
Hajt, Bill	Buf.	14	854	42	202	244	433	80	2	16	18	70	....	1973-74	1986-87
Hakansson, Anders	Min., Pit., L.A.	5	330	52	46	98	141	6	0	0	0	2	....	1981-82	1985-86
• Halderson, Harold	Det., Tor.	1	44	3	2	5	65	....	....	....	....	....	....	1926-27	1926-27
Hale, Larry	Phi.	4	196	5	37	42	90	8	0	0	0	12	....	1968-69	1971-72
Haley, Len	Det.	2	30	2	2	4	14	6	1	3	4	6	....	1959-60	1960-61
Halkidis, Bob	Buf., L.A., Tor., Det., T.B., NYI	11	256	8	32	40	825	20	0	1	1	51	....	1984-85	1995-96
• Hall, Bob	NYA	1	8	0	0	0	0	....	....	....	....	....	....	1925-26	1925-26
Hall, Del	Cal.	3	9	2	0	2	2	....	....	....	....	....	....	1971-72	1973-74
• Hall, Joe	Mtl.	2	38	15	8	23	189	7	0	1	1	29	....	1917-18	1918-19
Hall, Murray	Chi., Det., Min., Van.	9	164	35	48	83	46	6	0	0	0	0	....	1961-62	1971-72
Hall, Taylor	Van., Bos.	5	41	7	9	16	29	....	....	....	....	....	....	1983-84	1987-88
Hall, Wayne	NYR	1	4	0	0	0	0	....	....	....	....	....	....	1960-61	1960-61
Haller, Kevin	Buf., Mtl., Phi., Hfd., Car., Ana., NYI	13	642	41	97	138	907	64	7	16	23	71	1	1989-90	2001-02
• Halliday, Milt	Ott.	3	67	1	0	1	4	6	0	0	0	0	1	1926-27	1928-29
Hallin, Mats	NYI, Min.	5	152	17	14	31	193	15	1	0	1	13	1	1982-83	1986-87
Halverson, Trevor	Wsh.	1	17	0	4	4	28	....	....	....	....	....	....	1998-99	1998-99
Halward, Doug	Bos., L.A., Van., Det., Edm.	14	653	69	224	293	774	47	7	10	17	113	....	1975-76	1988-89
Hamel, Gilles	Buf., Wpg., L.A.	9	519	127	147	274	276	27	4	5	9	10	....	1980-81	1988-89
• Hamel, Herb	Tor.	1	2	0	0	0	4	....	....	....	....	....	....	1930-31	1930-31
Hamel, Jean	St.L., Det., Que., Mtl.	12	699	26	95	121	766	33	0	2	2	44	....	1972-73	1983-84
• Hamill, Red	Bos., Chi.	12	419	128	94	222	160	24	1	2	3	20	1	1937-38	1950-51
Hamilton, Al	NYR, Buf., Edm.	7	257	10	78	88	258	7	0	0	0	2	....	1965-66	1979-80
Hamilton, Chuck	Mtl., St.L.	2	4	0	2	2	2	....	....	....	....	....	....	1961-62	1972-73
• Hamilton, Jack	Tor.	3	102	28	32	60	20	11	2	1	3	0	....	1942-43	1945-46
Hamilton, Jim	Pit.	8	95	14	18	32	28	6	3	0	3	0	....	1977-78	1984-85
• Hamilton, Reg	Tor., Chi.	12	424	21	87	108	412	64	3	8	11	46	2	1935-36	1946-47
Hammarstrom, Inge	Tor., St.L.	6	427	116	123	239	86	13	2	3	5	4	....	1973-74	1978-79
Hammond, Ken	L.A., Edm., NYR, Tor., Bos., S.J., Van., Ott.	8	193	18	29	47	290	15	0	0	0	24	....	1984-85	1992-93
Hampson, Gord	Cgy.	1	4	0	0	0	5	....	....	....	....	....	....	1982-83	1982-83
Hampson, Ted	Tor., NYR, Det., Oak., Cal., Min.	14	676	108	245	353	94	35	7	10	17	2	....	1959-60	1971-72
Hampton, Rick	Cal., Cle., L.A.	6	337	59	113	172	147	2	0	0	0	0	....	1974-75	1979-80
‡ Hamr, Radek	Ott.	2	11	0	0	0	0	....	....	....	....	....	....	1992-93	1993-94
Hamway, Mark	NYI	3	53	5	13	18	9	1	0	0	0	0	....	1984-85	1986-87
Handy, Ron	NYI, St.L.	2	14	0	3	3	0	....	....	....	....	....	....	1984-85	1987-88
Hangsleben, Al	Hfd., Wsh., L.A.	3	185	21	48	69	396	....	....	....	....	....	....	1979-80	1981-82
Hankinson, Ben	N.J., T.B.	3	43	3	3	6	45	2	1	0	1	4	....	1992-93	1994-95
Hanna, John	NYR, Mtl., Phi.	5	198	6	26	32	206	....	....	....	....	....	....	1958-59	1967-68
Hannan, Dave	Pit., Edm., Tor., Buf., Col., Ott.	16	841	114	191	305	942	63	6	7	13	46	2	1981-82	1996-97
• Hannigan, Gord	Tor.	4	161	29	31	60	117	9	2	0	2	8	....	1952-53	1955-56
Hannigan, Pat	Tor., NYR, Phi.	5	182	30	39	69	116	11	1	2	3	11	....	1959-60	1968-69
Hannigan, Ray	Tor.	1	3	0	0	0	2	....	....	....	....	....	....	1948-49	1948-49
Hansen, Richie	NYI, St.L.	4	20	2	8	10	4	....	....	....	....	....	....	1976-77	1981-82
Hanson, Dave	Det., Min.	2	33	1	1	2	65	....	....	....	....	....	....	1978-79	1979-80
• Hanson, Emil	Det.	1	7	0	0	0	6	....	....	....	....	....	....	1932-33	1932-33
Hanson, Keith	Cgy.	1	25	0	2	2	77	....	....	....	....	....	....	1983-84	1983-84
• Hanson, Oscar	Chi.	1	8	0	0	0	0	....	....	....	....	....	....	1937-38	1937-38
Harbaruk, Nick	Pit., St.L.	5	364	45	75	120	273	14	3	1	4	20	....	1969-70	1973-74
Harding, Jeff	Phi.	2	15	0	0	0	47	....	....	....	....	....	....	1988-89	1989-90
Hardy, Joe	Oak., Cal.	2	63	9	14	23	51	4	0	0	0	0	....	1969-70	1970-71
Hardy, Mark	L.A., NYR, Min.	15	915	62	306	368	1293	67	5	16	21	158	....	1979-80	1993-94
Hargreaves, Jim	Van.	2	66	1	7	8	105	....	....	....	....	....	....	1970-71	1972-73
‡ Harkins, Brett	Bos., Fla., CBJ	4	78	6	30	36	22	....	....	....	....	....	....	1994-95	2001-02
Harkins, Todd	Cgy., Hfd.	3	48	3	3	6	78	....	....	....	....	....	....	1991-92	1993-94
Harlow, Scott	St.L.	1	1	0	1	1	0	....	....	....	....	....	....	1987-88	1987-88
Harmon, Glen	Mtl.	9	452	50	96	146	334	53	5	10	15	37	2	1942-43	1950-51
Harms, John	Chi.	2	44	5	5	10	21	4	3	0	3	2	....	1943-44	1944-45
• Harnott, Walter	Bos.	1	6	0	0	0	2	....	....	....	....	....	....	1933-34	1933-34
Harper, Terry	Mtl., L.A., Det., St.L., Col.	19	1066	35	221	256	1362	112	4	13	17	140	5	1962-63	1980-81
Harrer, Tim	Cgy.	1	3	0	0	0	2	....	....	....	....	....	....	1982-83	1982-83
• Harrington, Hago	Bos., Mtl.	3	72	9	3	12	15	4	1	0	1	2	....	1925-26	1932-33
• Harris, Billy	Tor., Det., Oak., Pit.	13	769	126	219	345	205	62	8	10	18	30	3	1955-56	1968-69
Harris, Billy	NYI, L.A., Tor.	12	897	231	327	558	394	71	19	19	38	48	....	1972-73	1983-84
Harris, Duke	Min., Tor.	1	26	1	4	5	4	....	....	....	....	....	....	1967-68	1967-68
• Harris, Henry	Bos.	1	32	2	4	6	20	....	....	....	....	....	....	1930-31	1930-31
Harris, Hugh	Buf.	1	60	12	26	38	17	3	0	0	0	0	....	1972-73	1972-73
Harris, Ron	Det., Oak., Atl., NYR	11	476	20	91	111	474	28	4	3	7	33	....	1962-63	1975-76
• Harris, Smokey	Bos.	1	6	3	1	4	8	....	....	....	....	....	....	1924-25	1924-25
Harris, Ted	Mtl., Min., Det., St.L., Phi.	12	788	30	168	198	1000	100	1	22	23	230	5	1963-64	1974-75
Harrison, Ed	Bos., NYR	4	194	27	24	51	53	9	1	0	1	2	....	1947-48	1950-51
Harrison, Jim	Bos., Tor., Chi., Edm.	8	324	67	86	153	435	13	1	1	2	43	....	1968-69	1979-80
Hart, Gerry	Det., NYI, Que., St.L.	15	730	29	150	179	1240	78	3	12	15	175	....	1968-69	1982-83
• Hart, Gizzy	Det., Mtl.	3	104	6	8	14	12	8	0	1	1	0	....	1926-27	1932-33
Hartman, Mike	Buf., Wpg., T.B., NYR	9	397	43	35	78	1388	21	0	0	0	106	1	1986-87	1994-95
Hartsburg, Craig	Min.	10	570	98	315	413	818	61	15	27	42	70	....	1979-80	1988-89
Harvey, Buster	Min., Atl., K.C., Det.	7	407	90	118	208	131	14	0	2	2	8	....	1970-71	1976-77
• Harvey, Doug	Mtl., NYR, Det., St.L.	20	1113	88	452	540	1216	137	8	64	72	152	6	1947-48	1968-69
Harvey, Hugh	K.C.	2	18	1	1	2	4	....	....	....	....	....	....	1974-75	1975-76
Hassard, Bob	Tor., Chi.	5	126	9	28	37	22	....	....	....	....	....	1	1949-50	1954-55
Hatcher, Kevin	Wsh., Dal., Pit., NYR, Car.	17	1157	227	450	677	1392	118	22	37	59	252	....	1984-85	2000-01
Hatoum, Ed	Det., Van.	3	47	3	6	9	25	....	....	....	....	....	....	1968-69	1970-71
Hawerchuk, Dale	Wpg., Buf., St.L., Phi.	16	1188	518	891	1409	730	97	30	69	99	67	....	1981-82	1996-97
‡ Hawkins, Todd	Van., Tor.	3	10	0	0	0	15	....	....	....	....	....	....	1988-89	1991-92
Haworth, Alan	Buf., Wsh., Que.	8	524	189	211	400	425	42	12	16	28	28	....	1980-81	1987-88
Haworth, Gord	NYR	1	2	0	1	1	0	....	....	....	....	....	....	1952-53	1952-53

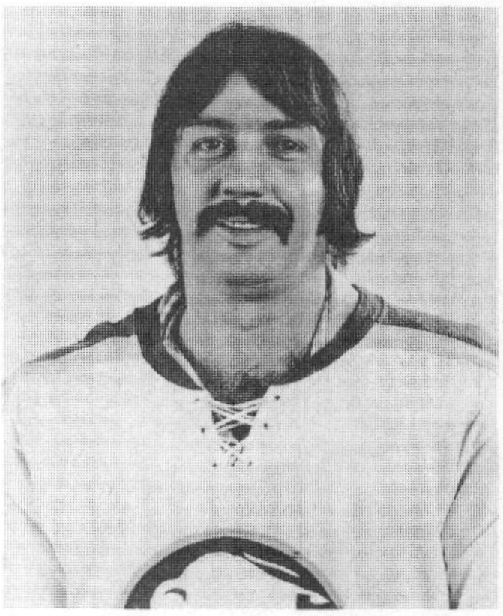
Jocelyn Guevremont

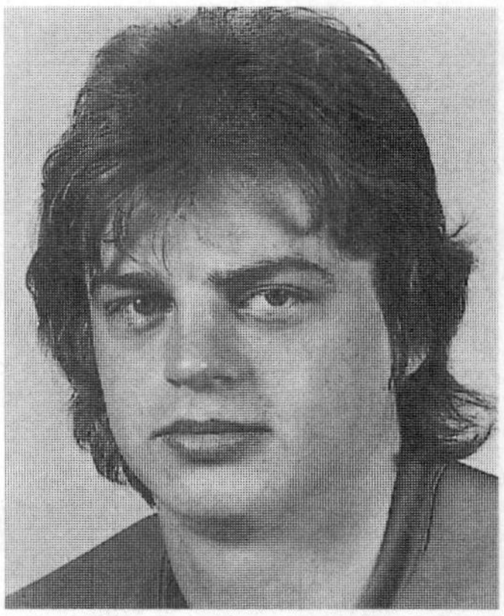
Bengt-Ake Gustafsson

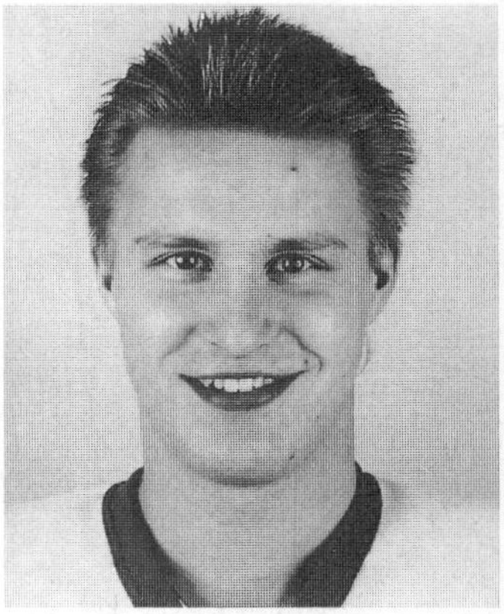
Ari Haanpaa

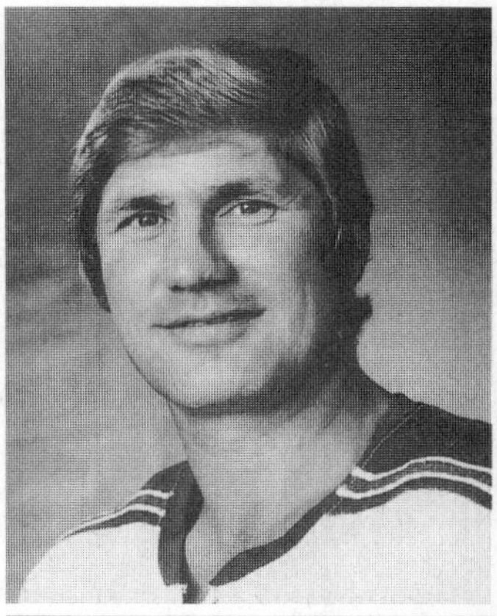
Vic Hadfield

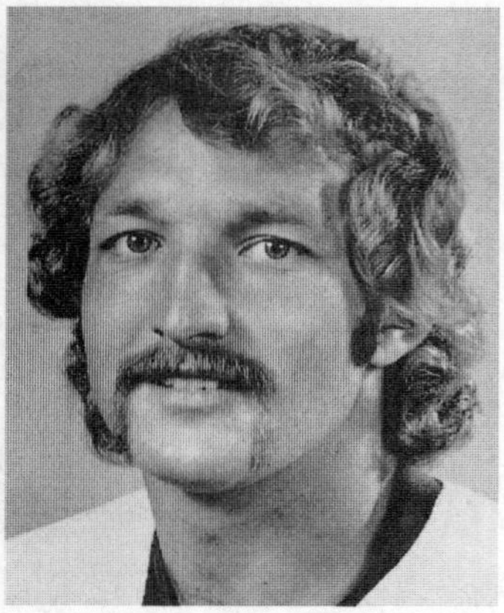
Gerry Hart

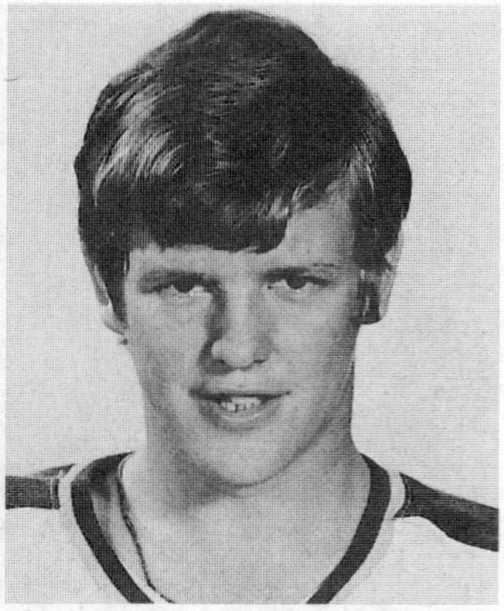
Buster Harvey

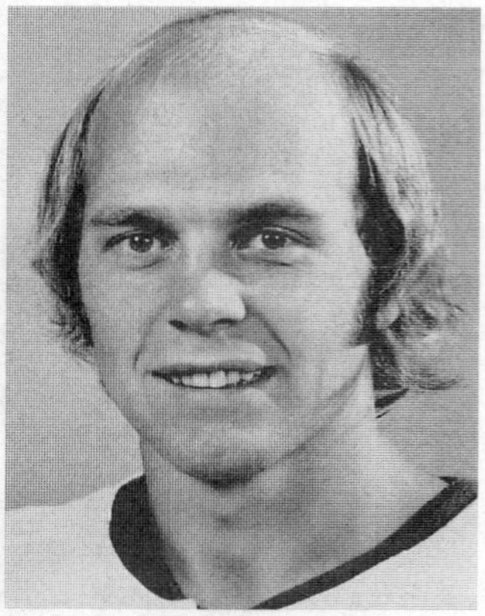
Lorne Henning

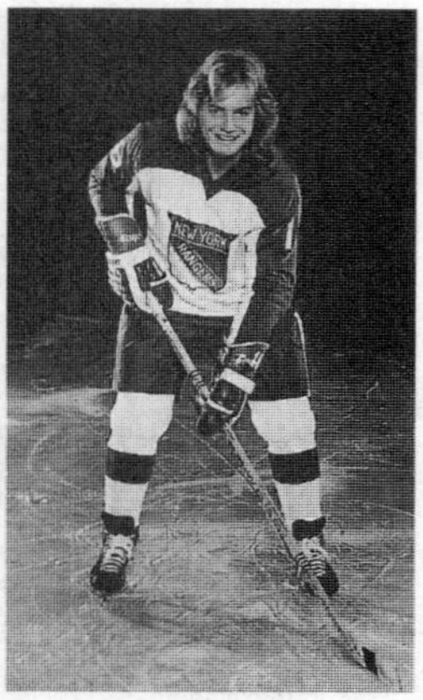
Pat Hickey

			Regular Schedule					Playoffs					NHL	First	Last
Name	NHL Teams	NHL Seasons	GP	G	A	TP	PIM	GP	G	A	TP	PIM	Cup Wins	NHL Season	NHL Season
Hawryliw, Neil	NYI	1	1	0	0	0	0	....	....	....	....	....	....	1981-82	1981-82
Hay, Bill	Chi.	8	506	113	273	386	244	67	15	21	36	62	1	1959-60	1966-67
• Hay, George	Chi., Det.	7	239	74	60	134	84	8	2	3	5	2	....	1926-27	1933-34
Hay, Jim	Det.	3	75	1	5	6	22	9	1	0	1	2	1	1952-53	1954-55
Hayek, Peter	Min.	1	1	0	0	0	0	....	....	....	....	....	....	1981-82	1981-82
Hayes, Chris	Bos.	1	....	....	....	....	....	1	0	0	0	0	1	1971-72	1971-72
• Haynes, Paul	Mtl.M., Bos., Mtl.	11	391	61	134	195	164	24	2	8	10	13	....	1930-31	1940-41
Hayward, Rick	L.A.	1	4	0	0	0	5	....	....	....	....	....	....	1990-91	1990-91
Hazlett, Steve	Van.	1	1	0	0	0	0	....	....	....	....	....	....	1979-80	1979-80
Head, Galen	Det.	1	1	0	0	0	0	....	....	....	....	....	....	1967-68	1967-68
• Headley, Fern	Bos., Mtl.	1	30	1	3	4	10	1	0	0	0	0	....	1924-25	1924-25
Healey, Rich	Det.	1	1	0	0	0	2	....	....	....	....	....	....	1960-61	1960-61
‡ Heaphy, Shawn	Cgy.	1	1	0	0	0	0	....	....	....	....	....	....	1992-93	1992-93
Heaslip, Mark	NYR, L.A.	3	117	10	19	29	110	5	0	0	0	2	....	1976-77	1978-79
Heath, Randy	NYR	2	13	2	4	6	15	....	....	....	....	....	....	1984-85	1985-86
Hebenton, Andy	NYR, Bos.	9	630	189	202	391	83	22	6	5	11	8	....	1955-56	1963-64
Hedberg, Anders	NYR	7	465	172	225	397	144	58	22	24	46	31	....	1978-79	1984-85
• Heffernan, Frank	Tor.	1	19	0	1	1	10	....	....	....	....	....	....	1919-20	1919-20
Heffernan, Gerry	Mtl.	3	83	33	35	68	27	11	3	3	6	8	1	1941-42	1943-44
Heidt, Mike	L.A.	1	6	0	1	1	7	....	....	....	....	....	....	1983-84	1983-84
• Heindl, Bill	Min., NYR	3	18	2	1	3	0	....	....	....	....	....	....	1970-71	1972-73
Heinrich, Lionel	Bos.	1	35	1	1	2	33	....	....	....	....	....	....	1955-56	1955-56
Heiskala, Earl	Phi.	3	127	13	11	24	294	....	....	....	....	....	....	1968-69	1970-71
Helander, Peter	L.A.	1	7	0	1	1	0	....	....	....	....	....	....	1982-83	1982-83
• Heller, Ott	NYR	15	647	55	176	231	465	61	6	8	14	61	2	1931-32	1945-46
Helman, Harry	Ott.	3	44	1	0	1	7	2	0	0	0	0	1	1922-23	1924-25
‡ Helminen, Raimo	NYR, Min., NYI	3	117	13	46	59	16	2	0	0	0	0	....	1985-86	1988-89
• Hemmerling, Tony	NYA	2	22	3	3	6	4	....	....	....	....	....	....	1935-36	1936-37
Henderson, Archie	Wsh., Min., Hfd.	3	23	3	1	4	92	....	....	....	....	....	....	1980-81	1982-83
Henderson, Murray	Bos.	8	405	24	62	86	305	41	2	3	5	23	....	1944-45	1951-52
Henderson, Paul	Det., Tor., Atl.	13	707	236	241	477	304	56	11	14	25	28	....	1962-63	1979-80
Hendrickson, John	Det.	3	5	0	0	0	4	....	....	....	....	....	....	1957-58	1961-62
Henning, Lorne	NYI	9	544	73	111	184	102	81	7	7	14	8	2	1972-73	1980-81
• Henry, Camille	NYR, Chi., St.L.	14	727	279	249	528	88	47	6	12	18	7	....	1953-54	1969-70
‡ Henry, Dale	NYI	6	132	13	26	39	263	14	1	0	1	19	....	1984-85	1989-90
Hepple, Alan	N.J.	3	3	0	0	0	7	....	....	....	....	....	....	1983-84	1985-86
‡ Herbers, Ian	Edm., T.B., NYI	2	65	0	5	5	79	....	....	....	....	....	....	1993-94	1999-00
• Herberts, Jimmy	Bos., Tor., Det.	6	206	83	31	114	253	9	3	0	3	10	....	1924-25	1929-30
Herchenratter, Art	Det.	1	10	1	2	3	2	....	....	....	....	....	....	1940-41	1940-41
Hergerts, Fred	NYA	2	20	2	4	6	2	....	....	....	....	....	....	1934-35	1935-36
Hergesheimer, Phil	Chi., Bos.	4	125	21	41	62	19	6	0	0	0	2	....	1939-40	1942-43
Hergesheimer, Wally	NYR, Chi.	7	351	114	85	199	106	5	1	0	1	0	....	1951-52	1958-59
• Heron, Red	Tor., Bro., Mtl.	4	106	21	19	40	38	21	2	2	4	6	....	1938-39	1941-42
Heroux, Yves	Que.	1	1	0	0	0	0	....	....	....	....	....	....	1986-87	1986-87
‡ Herter, Jason	NYI	1	1	0	1	1	0	....	....	....	....	....	....	1995-96	1995-96
Hervey, Matt	Wpg., Bos., T.B.	3	35	0	5	5	97	5	0	0	0	6	....	1988-89	1992-93
Hess, Bob	St.L., Buf., Hfd.	8	329	27	95	122	178	4	1	1	2	2	....	1974-75	1983-84
• Heximer, Obs	NYR, Bos., NYA	3	84	13	7	20	16	5	0	0	0	2	....	1929-30	1934-35
• Hextall, Bryan	NYR	11	449	187	175	362	227	37	8	9	17	19	1	1936-37	1947-48
Hextall Jr., Bryan	NYR, Pit., Atl., Det., Min.	8	549	99	161	260	738	18	0	4	4	59	....	1962-63	1975-76
Hextall, Dennis	NYR, L.A., Cal., Min., Det., Wsh.	13	681	153	350	503	1398	22	3	3	6	45	....	1967-68	1979-80
Heyliger, Vic	Chi.	2	33	2	3	5	2	....	....	....	....	....	....	1937-38	1943-44
Hicke, Bill	Mtl., NYR, Oak., Cal., Pit.	14	729	168	234	402	395	42	3	10	13	41	2	1958-59	1971-72
Hicke, Ernie	Cal., Atl., NYI, Min., L.A.	8	520	132	140	272	407	2	1	0	1	0	....	1970-71	1977-78
Hickey, Greg	NYR	1	1	0	0	0	0	....	....	....	....	....	....	1977-78	1977-78
Hickey, Pat	NYR, Col., Tor., Que., St.L.	10	646	192	212	404	351	55	5	11	16	37	....	1975-76	1984-85
‡ Hicks, Alex	Ana., Pit., S.J., Fla.	5	258	25	54	79	247	15	0	2	2	8	....	1995-96	1999-00
Hicks, Doug	Min., Chi., Edm., Wsh.	9	561	37	131	168	442	18	2	1	3	15	....	1974-75	1982-83
Hicks, Glenn	Det.	2	108	6	12	18	127	....	....	....	....	....	....	1979-80	1980-81
• Hicks, Henry	Mtl.M., Det.	3	96	7	2	9	72	....	....	....	....	....	....	1928-29	1930-31
Hicks, Wayne	Chi., Bos., Mtl., Phi., Pit.	5	115	13	23	36	22	2	0	1	1	2	1	1959-60	1967-68
Hidi, Andre	Wsh.	2	7	2	1	3	9	2	0	0	0	0	....	1983-84	1984-85
Hiemer, Uli	N.J.	3	143	19	54	73	176	....	....	....	....	....	....	1984-85	1986-87
Higgins, Paul	Tor.	2	25	0	0	0	152	1	0	0	0	0	....	1981-82	1982-83
Higgins, Tim	Chi., N.J., Det.	11	706	154	198	352	719	65	5	8	13	77	....	1978-79	1988-89
Hildebrand, Ike	NYR, Chi.	2	41	7	11	18	16	....	....	....	....	....	....	1953-54	1954-55
Hill, Al	Phi.	8	221	40	55	95	227	51	8	11	19	43	....	1976-77	1987-88
Hill, Brian	Hfd.	1	19	1	1	2	4	....	....	....	....	....	....	1979-80	1979-80
• Hill, Mel	Bos., Bro., Tor.	9	324	89	109	198	128	43	12	7	19	18	3	1937-38	1945-46
Hiller, Dutch	NYR, Det., Bos., Mtl.	9	383	91	113	204	163	48	9	8	17	21	2	1937-38	1945-46
‡ Hiller, Jim	L.A., Det., NYR	2	63	8	12	20	116	2	0	0	0	4	....	1992-93	1993-94
Hillier, Randy	Bos., Pit., NYI, Buf.	11	543	16	110	126	906	28	0	2	2	93	1	1981-82	1991-92
Hillman, Floyd	Bos.	1	6	0	0	0	10	....	....	....	....	....	....	1956-57	1956-57
Hillman, Larry	Det., Bos., Tor., Min., Mtl., Phi., L.A., Buf.	19	790	36	196	232	579	74	2	9	11	30	6	1954-55	1972-73
• Hillman, Wayne	Chi., NYR, Min., Phi.	13	691	18	86	104	534	28	0	3	3	19	1	1960-61	1972-73
Hilworth, John	Det.	3	57	1	1	2	89	....	....	....	....	....	....	1977-78	1979-80
• Himes, Normie	NYA	9	402	106	113	219	127	2	0	0	0	0	....	1926-27	1934-35
Hindmarch, Dave	Cgy.	4	99	21	17	38	25	10	0	0	0	6	....	1980-81	1983-84
Hinse, Andre	Tor.	1	4	0	0	0	0	....	....	....	....	....	....	1967-68	1967-68
Hinton, Dan	Chi.	1	14	0	0	0	16	....	....	....	....	....	....	1976-77	1976-77
Hirsch, Tom	Min.	3	31	1	7	8	30	12	0	0	0	6	....	1983-84	1987-88
• Hirschfeld, Bert	Mtl.	2	33	1	4	5	2	5	1	0	1	0	....	1949-50	1950-51
Hislop, Jamie	Que., Cgy.	5	345	75	103	178	86	28	3	2	5	11	....	1979-80	1983-84
• Hitchman, Lionel	Ott., Bos.	12	417	28	34	62	523	35	3	1	4	73	2	1922-23	1933-34
Hlinka, Ivan	Van.	2	137	42	81	123	28	16	3	10	13	8	....	1981-82	1982-83
‡ Hlushko, Todd	Phi., Cgy., Pit.	6	79	8	13	21	84	3	0	0	0	2	....	1993-94	1998-99
‡ Hocking, Justin	L.A.	1	1	0	0	0	0	....	....	....	....	....	....	1993-94	1993-94
Hodge, Ken	Chi., Bos., NYR	14	881	328	472	800	779	97	34	47	81	120	2	1964-65	1977-78
Hodge, Ken	Min., Bos., T.B.	4	142	39	48	87	32	15	4	6	10	6	....	1988-89	1992-93
‡ Hodgson, Dan	Tor., Van.	4	114	29	45	74	64	....	....	....	....	....	....	1985-86	1988-89
Hodgson, Rick	Hfd.	1	6	0	0	0	6	1	0	0	0	0	....	1979-80	1979-80
Hodgson, Ted	Bos.	1	4	0	0	0	0	....	....	....	....	....	....	1966-67	1966-67
Hoekstra, Cec	Mtl.	1	4	0	0	0	0	....	....	....	....	....	....	1959-60	1959-60
Hoekstra, Ed	Phi.	1	70	15	21	36	6	7	0	1	1	0	....	1967-68	1967-68
Hoene, Phil	L.A.	3	37	2	4	6	22	....	....	....	....	....	....	1972-73	1974-75
Hoffinger, Val	Chi.	2	28	0	1	1	30	....	....	....	....	....	....	1927-28	1928-29
Hoffman, Mike	Hfd.	3	9	1	3	4	2	....	....	....	....	....	....	1982-83	1985-86
Hoffmeyer, Bob	Chi., Phi., N.J.	6	198	14	52	66	325	3	0	1	1	25	....	1977-78	1984-85
Hofford, Jim	Buf., L.A.	3	18	0	0	0	47	....	....	....	....	....	....	1985-86	1988-89
Hogaboam, Bill	Atl., Det., Min.	8	332	80	109	189	100	2	0	0	0	0	....	1972-73	1979-80
Hoganson, Dale	L.A., Mtl., Que.	7	343	13	77	90	186	11	0	3	3	12	....	1969-70	1981-82
Hogue, Benoit	Buf., NYI, Tor., Dal., T.B., Phx., Bos., Wsh.	15	863	222	321	543	877	92	17	16	33	124	1	1987-88	2001-02
Holan, Milos	Phi., Ana.	3	49	5	11	16	42	....	....	....	....	....	....	1993-94	1995-96
Holbrook, Terry	Min.	2	43	3	6	9	4	6	0	0	0	0	....	1972-73	1973-74
Holland, Jerry	NYR	2	37	8	4	12	6	....	....	....	....	....	....	1974-75	1975-76
• Hollett, Flash	Tor., Ott., Bos., Det.	13	562	132	181	313	358	79	8	26	34	38	2	1933-34	1945-46
‡ Hollinger, Terry	St.L.	2	7	0	0	0	2	....	....	....	....	....	....	1993-94	1994-95
• Hollingworth, Gord	Chi., Det.	4	163	4	14	18	201	3	0	0	0	2	....	1954-55	1957-58
Holloway, Bruce	Van.	1	2	0	0	0	0	....	....	....	....	....	....	1984-85	1984-85
• Holmes, Bill	Mtl., NYA	3	52	6	4	10	35	....	....	....	....	....	....	1925-26	1929-30
Holmes, Chuck	Det.	2	23	1	3	4	10	....	....	....	....	....	....	1958-59	1961-62
Holmes, Lou	Chi.	2	59	1	4	5	6	2	0	0	0	2	....	1931-32	1932-33
Holmes, Warren	L.A.	3	45	8	18	26	7	....	....	....	....	....	....	1981-82	1983-84
Holmgren, Paul	Phi., Min.	10	527	144	179	323	1684	82	19	32	51	195	....	1975-76	1984-85
• Holota, John	Det.	2	15	2	0	2	0	....	....	....	....	....	....	1942-43	1945-46
Holst, Greg	NYR	3	11	0	0	0	0	....	....	....	....	....	....	1975-76	1977-78
Holt, Gary	Cal., Cle., St.L.	5	101	13	11	24	133	....	....	....	....	....	....	1973-74	1977-78
Holt, Randy	Chi., Cle., Van., L.A., Cgy., Wsh., Phi.	10	395	4	37	41	1438	21	2	3	5	83	....	1974-75	1983-84
• Holway, Albert	Tor., Mtl.M., Pit.	5	112	7	2	9	48	6	0	0	0	0	1	1923-24	1928-29
Homenuke, Ron	Van.	1	1	0	0	0	0	....	....	....	....	....	....	1972-73	1972-73
Hoover, Ron	Bos., St.L.	3	18	4	0	4	31	8	0	0	0	18	....	1989-90	1991-92
Hopkins, Dean	L.A., Edm., Que.	6	223	23	51	74	306	18	1	5	6	29	....	1979-80	1988-89
Hopkins, Larry	Tor., Wpg.	4	60	13	16	29	26	6	0	0	0	2	....	1977-78	1982-83
Horacek, Tony	Phi., Chi.	5	154	10	19	29	316	2	1	0	1	2	....	1989-90	1994-95

Name	NHL Teams	NHL Seasons	Regular Schedule					Playoffs					NHL Cup Wins	First NHL Season	Last NHL Season
			GP	G	A	TP	PIM	GP	G	A	TP	PIM			
Horava, Miloslav	NYR	3	80	5	17	22	38	2	0	1	1	0	....	1988-89	1990-91
Horbul, Doug	K.C.	1	4	1	0	1	2	....	....	....	....	....	....	1974-75	1974-75
Hordy, Mike	NYI	2	11	0	0	0	7	....	....	....	....	....	....	1978-79	1979-80
Horeck, Pete	Chi., Det., Bos.	8	426	106	118	224	340	34	6	8	14	43	....	1944-45	1951-52
• Horne, George	Mtl.M., Tor.	3	54	9	3	12	34	4	0	0	0	4	1	1925-26	1928-29
Horner, Red	Tor.	12	490	42	110	152	1254	71	7	10	17	170	1	1928-29	1939-40
• Hornung, Larry	St.L.	2	48	2	9	11	10	11	0	2	2	2	....	1970-71	1971-72
• Horton, Tim	Tor., NYR, Pit., Buf.	24	1446	115	403	518	1611	126	11	39	50	183	4	1949-50	1973-74
Horvath, Bronco	NYR, Mtl., Bos., Chi., Tor., Min.	9	434	141	185	326	319	36	12	9	21	18	....	1955-56	1967-68
Hospodar, Ed	NYR, Hfd., Phi., Min., Buf.	9	450	17	51	68	1314	44	4	1	5	208	....	1979-80	1987-88
Hostak, Martin	Phi.	2	55	3	11	14	24	....	....	....	....	....	....	1990-91	1991-92
Hotham, Greg	Tor., Pit.	6	230	15	74	89	139	5	0	3	3	6	....	1979-80	1984-85
Houck, Paul	Min.	3	16	1	2	3	2	....	....	....	....	....	....	1985-86	1987-88
Houde, Claude	K.C.	2	59	3	6	9	40	....	....	....	....	....	....	1974-75	1975-76
‡ Houde, Eric	Mtl.	3	30	2	3	5	4	....	....	....	....	....	....	1996-97	1998-99
Hough, Mike	Que., Fla., NYI	13	707	100	156	256	675	42	5	5	10	38	....	1986-87	1998-99
Houle, Rejean	Mtl.	11	635	161	247	408	395	90	14	34	48	66	5	1969-70	1982-83
Houston, Ken	Atl., Cgy., Wsh., L.A.	9	570	161	167	328	624	35	10	9	19	66	....	1975-76	1983-84
Howard, Jack	Tor.	1	2	0	0	0	0	....	....	....	....	....	....	1936-37	1936-37
Howatt, Garry	NYI, Hfd., N.J.	12	720	112	156	268	1836	87	12	14	26	289	2	1972-73	1983-84
Howe, Gordie	Det., Hfd.	26	1767	801	1049	1850	1685	157	68	92	160	220	4	1946-47	1979-80
Howe, Mark	Hfd., Phi., Det.	16	929	197	545	742	455	101	10	51	61	34	....	1979-80	1994-95
Howe, Marty	Hfd., Bos.	6	197	2	29	31	99	15	1	2	3	9	....	1979-80	1984-85
• Howe, Syd	Ott., Phi., Tor., St.L., Det.	17	698	237	291	528	212	70	17	27	44	10	3	1929-30	1945-46
Howe, Vic	NYR	3	33	3	4	7	10	....	....	....	....	....	....	1950-51	1954-55
Howell, Harry	NYR, Oak., Cal., L.A.	21	1411	94	324	418	1298	38	3	3	6	32	....	1952-53	1972-73
• Howell, Ron	NYR	2	4	0	0	0	0	....	....	....	....	....	....	1954-55	1955-56
Howse, Don	L.A.	1	33	2	5	7	6	2	0	0	0	0	....	1979-80	1979-80
Howson, Scott	NYI	2	18	5	3	8	4	....	....	....	....	....	....	1984-85	1985-86
Hoyda, Dave	Phi., Wpg.	4	132	6	17	23	299	12	0	0	0	17	....	1977-78	1980-81
Hrdina, Jiri	Cgy., Pit.	5	250	45	85	130	92	46	2	5	7	24	3	1987-88	1991-92
Hrechkosy, Dave	Cal., St.L.	4	140	42	24	66	41	3	1	0	1	2	....	1973-74	1976-77
Hrycuik, Jim	Wsh.	1	21	5	5	10	12	....	....	....	....	....	....	1974-75	1974-75
Hrymnak, Steve	Chi., Det.	2	18	2	1	3	4	2	0	0	0	0	....	1951-52	1952-53
Hrynewich, Tim	Pit.	2	55	6	8	14	82	....	....	....	....	....	....	1982-83	1983-84
Huard, Bill	Bos., Ott., Que., Dal., Edm., L.A.	8	223	16	18	34	594	5	0	0	0	2	....	1992-93	1999-00
Huard, Rolly	Tor.	1	1	1	0	1	0	....	....	....	....	....	....	1930-31	1930-31
Huber, Willie	Det., NYR, Van., Phi.	10	655	104	217	321	950	33	5	5	10	35	....	1978-79	1987-88
Hubick, Greg	Tor., Van.	2	77	6	9	15	10	....	....	....	....	....	....	1975-76	1979-80
Huck, Fran	Mtl., St.L.	3	94	24	30	54	38	11	3	4	7	2	....	1969-70	1972-73
Hucul, Fred	Chi., St.L.	5	164	11	30	41	113	6	1	0	1	10	....	1950-51	1967-68
Huddy, Charlie	Edm., L.A., Buf., St.L.	17	1017	99	354	453	785	183	19	66	85	135	5	1980-81	1996-97
Hudson, Dave	NYI, K.C., Col.	6	409	59	124	183	89	2	1	1	2	0	....	1972-73	1977-78
Hudson, Lex	Pit.	1	2	0	0	0	0	2	0	0	0	0	....	1978-79	1978-79
Hudson, Mike	Chi., Edm., NYR, Pit., Tor., St.L., Phx.	9	416	49	87	136	414	49	4	10	14	64	1	1988-89	1996-97
Hudson, Ron	Det.	2	33	5	2	7	2	....	....	....	....	....	....	1937-38	1939-40
Huffman, Kerry	Phi., Que., Ott.	10	401	37	108	145	361	11	0	0	0	2	....	1986-87	1995-96
Huggins, Al	Mtl.M.	1	20	1	1	2	2	....	....	....	....	....	....	1930-31	1930-31
Hughes, Albert	NYA	2	60	6	8	14	22	....	....	....	....	....	....	1930-31	1931-32
Hughes, Brent	L.A., Phi., St.L., Det., K.C.	8	435	15	117	132	440	22	1	3	4	53	....	1967-68	1974-75
Hughes, Brent	Wpg., Bos., Buf., NYI	8	357	41	39	80	831	29	4	1	5	53	....	1988-89	1996-97
Hughes, Frank	Cal.	1	5	0	0	0	0	....	....	....	....	....	....	1971-72	1971-72
Hughes, Howie	L.A.	3	168	25	32	57	30	14	2	0	2	2	....	1967-68	1969-70
Hughes, Jack	Col.	2	46	2	5	7	104	....	....	....	....	....	....	1980-81	1981-82
Hughes, James	Det.	1	40	0	1	1	48	....	....	....	....	....	....	1929-30	1929-30
Hughes, John	Van., Edm., NYR	2	70	2	14	16	211	7	0	1	1	16	....	1979-80	1980-81
Hughes, Pat	Mtl., Pit., Edm., Buf., St.L., Hfd.	10	573	130	128	258	646	71	8	25	33	77	3	1977-78	1986-87
Hughes, Ryan	Bos.	1	3	0	0	0	0	....	....	....	....	....	....	1995-96	1995-96
Hull, Bobby	Chi., Wpg., Hfd.	16	1063	610	560	1170	640	119	62	67	129	102	1	1957-58	1979-80
Hull, Dennis	Chi., Det.	14	959	303	351	654	261	104	33	34	67	30	....	1964-65	1977-78
• Hunt, Fred	NYA, NYR	2	59	15	14	29	6	....	....	....	....	....	....	1940-41	1944-45
Hunter, Dale	Que., Wsh., Col.	19	1407	323	697	1020	3565	186	42	76	118	729	....	1980-81	1998-99
Hunter, Dave	Edm., Pit., Wpg.	10	746	133	190	323	918	105	16	24	40	211	3	1979-80	1988-89
Hunter, Mark	Mtl., St.L., Cgy., Hfd., Wsh.	12	628	213	171	384	1426	79	18	20	38	230	1	1981-82	1992-93
Hunter, Tim	Cgy., Que., Van., S.J.	16	815	62	76	138	3146	132	5	7	12	426	1	1981-82	1996-97
Huras, Larry	NYR	1	2	0	0	0	0	....	....	....	....	....	....	1976-77	1976-77
Hurlburt, Bob	Van.	1	1	0	0	0	2	....	....	....	....	....	....	1974-75	1974-75
Hurlbut, Mike	NYR, Que., Buf.	5	29	1	8	9	20	....	....	....	....	....	....	1992-93	1999-00
Hurley, Paul	Bos.	1	1	0	1	1	0	....	....	....	....	....	....	1968-69	1968-69
Hurst, Ron	Tor.	2	64	9	7	16	70	3	0	2	2	4	....	1955-56	1956-57
Huscroft, Jamie	N.J., Bos., Cgy., T.B., Van., Phx., Wsh.	10	352	5	33	38	1065	21	0	1	1	46	....	1988-89	1999-00
Huska, Ryan	Chi.	1	1	0	0	0	0	....	....	....	....	....	....	1997-98	1997-98
Huston, Ron	Cal.	2	79	15	31	46	8	....	....	....	....	....	....	1973-74	1974-75
Hutchinson, Ron	NYR	1	9	0	0	0	0	....	....	....	....	....	....	1960-61	1960-61
Hutchison, Dave	L.A., Tor., Chi., N.J.	10	584	19	97	116	1550	48	2	12	14	149	....	1974-75	1983-84
• Hutton, Bill	Bos., Ott., Phi.	2	64	3	2	5	8	2	0	0	0	0	....	1929-30	1930-31
• Hyland, Harry	Mtl.W., Ott.	1	17	14	2	16	65	....	....	....	....	....	....	1917-18	1917-18
Hynes, Dave	Bos.	2	22	4	0	4	2	....	....	....	....	....	....	1973-74	1974-75
Hynes, Gord	Bos., Phi.	2	52	3	9	12	22	12	1	2	3	6	....	1991-92	1992-93

I

Name	NHL Teams	NHL Seasons	GP	G	A	TP	PIM	GP	G	A	TP	PIM	NHL Cup Wins	First NHL Season	Last NHL Season
Iafrate, Al	Tor., Wsh., Bos., S.J.	12	799	152	311	463	1301	71	19	16	35	77	....	1984-85	1997-98
‡ Ignatjev, Victor	Pit.	1	11	0	1	1	6	1	0	0	0	2	....	1998-99	1998-99
‡ Ihnacak, Miroslav	Tor., Det.	3	56	8	9	17	39	1	0	0	0	0	....	1985-86	1988-89
Ihnacak, Peter	Tor.	8	417	102	165	267	175	28	4	10	14	25	....	1982-83	1989-90
Imlach, Brent	Tor.	2	3	0	0	0	0	....	....	....	....	....	....	1965-66	1966-67
Ingarfield, Earl	NYR, Pit., Oak., Cal.	13	746	179	226	405	239	21	9	8	17	10	....	1958-59	1970-71
Ingarfield Jr., Earl	Atl., Cgy., Det.	2	39	4	4	8	22	2	0	1	1	0	....	1979-80	1980-81
Inglis, Billy	L.A., Buf.	3	36	1	3	4	4	11	1	2	3	4	....	1967-68	1970-71
• Ingoldsby, Johnny	Tor.	2	29	5	1	6	15	....	....	....	....	....	....	1942-43	1943-44
Ingram, Frank	Chi.	3	101	24	16	40	69	11	0	1	1	2	....	1929-30	1931-32
• Ingram, John	Bos.	1	1	0	0	0	0	....	....	....	....	....	....	1924-25	1924-25
Ingram, Ron	Chi., Det., NYR	4	114	5	15	20	81	2	0	0	0	0	....	1956-57	1964-65
‡ Intranuovo, Ralph	Edm., Tor.	3	22	2	4	6	4	....	....	....	....	....	....	1994-95	1996-97
• Irvin, Dick	Chi.	3	94	29	23	52	78	2	2	0	2	4	....	1926-27	1928-29
Irvine, Ted	Bos., L.A., NYR, St.L.	11	724	154	177	331	657	83	16	24	40	115	....	1963-64	1976-77
Irwin, Ivan	Mtl., NYR	5	155	2	27	29	214	5	0	0	0	8	....	1952-53	1957-58
Isaksson, Ulf	L.A.	1	50	7	15	22	10	....	....	....	....	....	....	1982-83	1982-83
Issel, Kim	Edm.	1	4	0	0	0	0	....	....	....	....	....	....	1988-89	1988-89

J

Name	NHL Teams	NHL Seasons	GP	G	A	TP	PIM	GP	G	A	TP	PIM	NHL Cup Wins	First NHL Season	Last NHL Season
• Jackson, Art	Tor., Bos., NYA	11	468	123	178	301	144	52	8	12	20	29	2	1934-35	1944-45
• Jackson, Busher	Tor., NYA, Bos.	15	633	241	234	475	437	71	18	12	30	53	1	1929-30	1943-44
Jackson, Don	Min., Edm., NYR	10	311	16	52	68	640	53	4	5	9	147	2	1977-78	1986-87
• Jackson, Harold	Chi., Det.	8	219	17	34	51	208	31	1	2	3	33	2	1936-37	1946-47
Jackson, Jack	Chi.	1	48	2	5	7	38	....	....	....	....	....	....	1946-47	1946-47
Jackson, Jeff	Tor., NYR, Que., Chi.	8	263	38	48	86	313	6	1	1	2	16	....	1984-85	1991-92
Jackson, Jim	Cgy., Buf.	4	112	17	30	47	20	14	3	2	5	6	....	1982-83	1987-88
• Jackson, Lloyd	NYA	1	14	1	1	2	0	....	....	....	....	....	....	1936-37	1936-37
• Jackson, Stan	Tor., Bos., Ott.	5	86	9	6	15	75	....	....	....	....	....	1	1921-22	1926-27
Jackson, Walter	NYA, Bos.	4	84	16	11	27	18	....	....	....	....	....	....	1932-33	1935-36
• Jacobs, Paul	Tor.	1	1	0	0	0	0	....	....	....	....	....	....	1918-19	1918-19
Jacobs, Tim	Cal.	1	46	0	10	10	35	....	....	....	....	....	....	1975-76	1975-76
Jalo, Risto	Edm.	1	3	0	3	3	0	....	....	....	....	....	....	1985-86	1985-86
Jalonen, Kari	Cgy., Edm.	2	37	9	6	15	4	5	1	0	1	0	....	1982-83	1983-84
James, Gerry	Tor.	5	149	14	26	40	257	15	1	0	1	8	....	1954-55	1959-60
James, Val	Buf., Tor.	2	11	0	0	0	30	....	....	....	....	....	....	1981-82	1986-87
Jamieson, Jim	NYR	1	1	0	1	1	0	....	....	....	....	....	....	1943-44	1943-44
Jankowski, Lou	Det., Chi.	4	127	19	18	37	15	1	0	0	0	0	....	1950-51	1954-55
Janney, Craig	Bos., St.L., S.J., Wpg., Phx., T.B., NYI	12	760	188	563	751	170	120	24	86	110	53	....	1987-88	1998-99
Janssens, Mark	NYR, Min., Hfd., Ana., NYI, Phx., Chi.	14	711	40	73	113	1422	27	5	1	6	33	....	1987-88	2000-01
‡ Jantunen, Marko	Cgy.	1	3	0	0	0	0	....	....	....	....	....	....	1996-97	1996-97
Jarrett, Doug	Chi., NYR	13	775	38	182	220	631	99	7	16	23	82	....	1964-65	1976-77
Jarrett, Gary	Tor., Det., Oak., Cal.	7	341	72	92	164	131	11	3	1	4	9	....	1960-61	1971-72

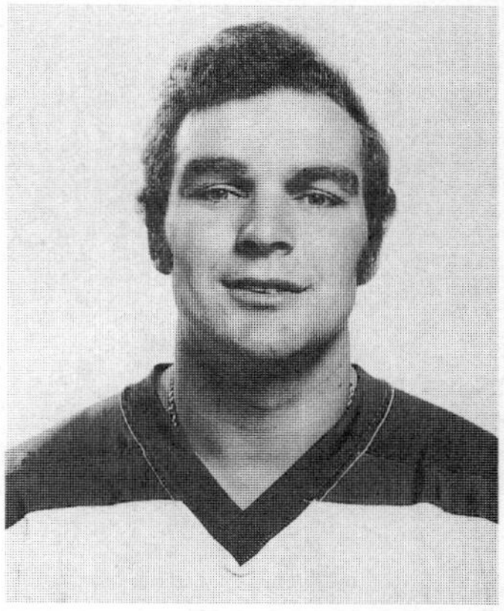

Ken Hodge

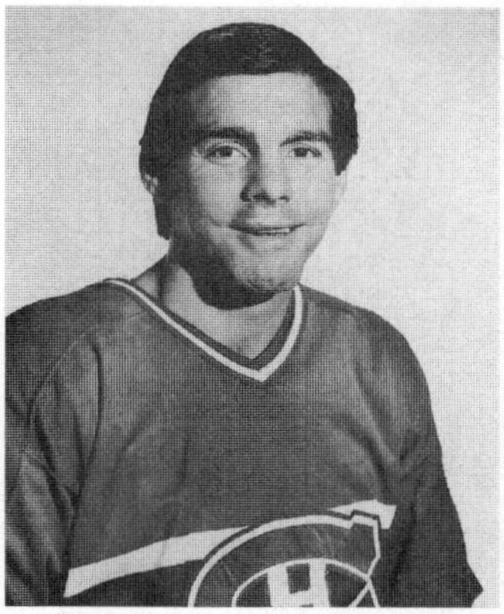

Rejean Houle

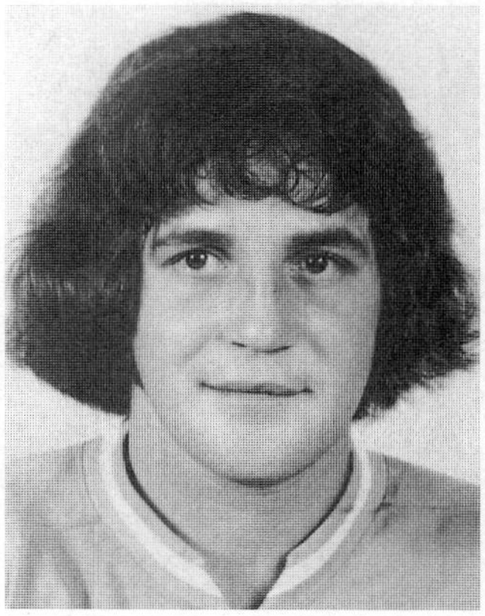

Dave Hrechkosy

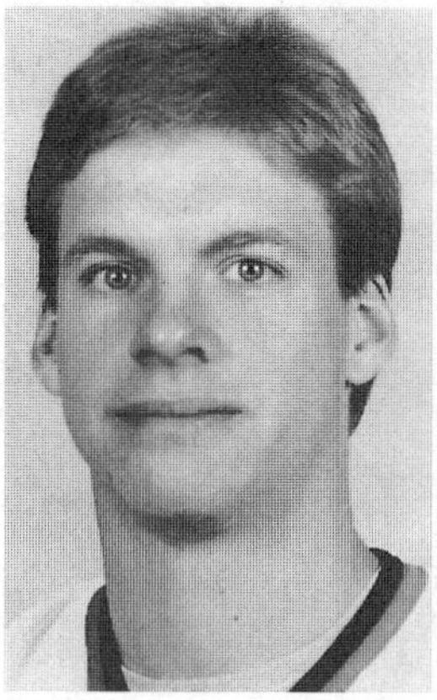

Mike Hudson

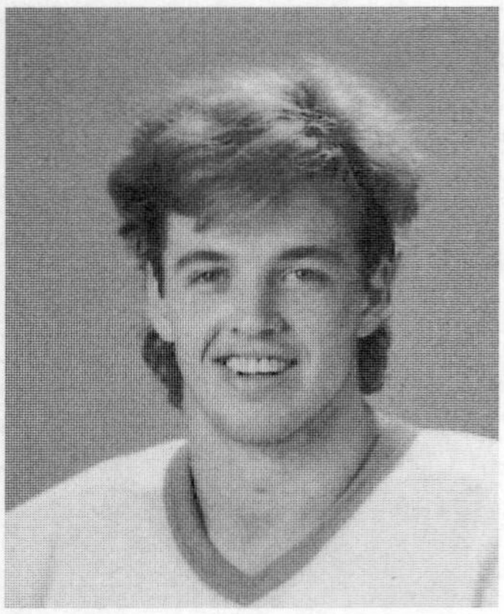

Jeff Jackson

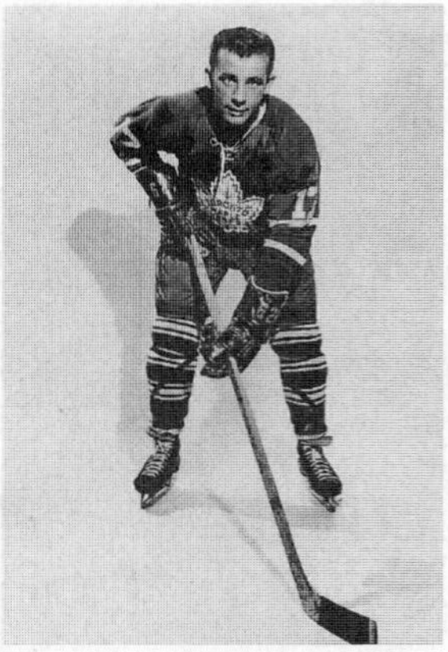

Larry Jeffrey

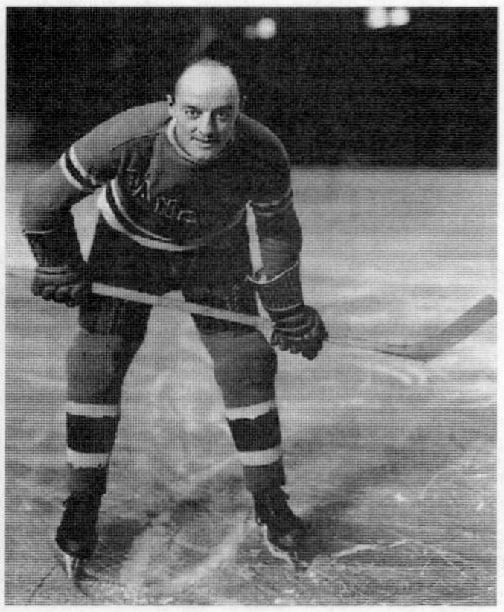

Ching Johnson

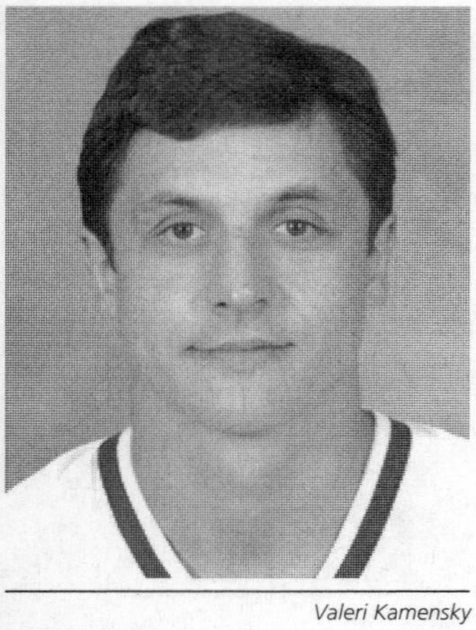

Valeri Kamensky

Name	NHL Teams	NHL Seasons	Regular Schedule GP	G	A	TP	PIM	Playoffs GP	G	A	TP	PIM	NHL Cup Wins	First NHL Season	Last NHL Season
Jarry, Pierre	NYR, Tor., Det., Min.	7	344	88	117	205	142	5	0	1	1	0	....	1971-72	1977-78
Jarvenpaa, Hannu	Wpg.	3	114	11	26	37	83	....	....	....	....	....	....	1986-87	1988-89
‡ Jarventie, Martti	Mtl.	1	1	0	0	0	0	....	....	....	....	....	....	2001-02	2001-02
Jarvi, Iiro	Que.	2	116	18	43	61	58	....	....	....	....	....	....	1988-89	1989-90
Jarvis, Doug	Mtl., Wsh., Hfd.	13	964	139	264	403	263	105	14	27	41	42	4	1975-76	1987-88
• Jarvis, James	Pit., Phi., Tor.	3	112	17	15	32	62	....	....	....	....	....	....	1929-30	1936-37
Jarvis, Wes	Wsh., Min., L.A., Tor.	9	237	31	55	86	98	2	0	0	0	2	....	1979-80	1987-88
Javanainen, Arto	Pit.	1	14	4	1	5	2	....	....	....	....	....	....	1984-85	1984-85
‡ Jay, Bob	L.A.	1	3	0	1	1	0	....	....	....	....	....	....	1993-94	1993-94
Jeffrey, Larry	Det., Tor., NYR	8	368	39	62	101	293	38	4	10	14	42	1	1961-62	1968-69
Jelinek, Tomas	Ott.	1	49	7	6	13	52	....	....	....	....	....	....	1992-93	1992-93
Jenkins, Dean	L.A.	1	5	0	0	0	2	....	....	....	....	....	....	1983-84	1983-84
Jenkins, Roger	Chi., Tor., Mtl., Bos., Mtl.M., NYA	8	325	15	39	54	253	25	1	7	8	12	2	1930-31	1938-39
Jennings, Bill	Det., Bos.	5	108	32	33	65	45	20	4	4	8	6	....	1940-41	1944-45
Jennings, Grant	Wsh., Hfd., Pit., Tor., Buf.	9	389	14	43	57	804	54	2	1	3	68	2	1987-88	1995-96
Jensen, Chris	NYR, Phi.	6	74	9	12	21	27	....	....	....	....	....	....	1985-86	1991-92
Jensen, David	Min.	3	18	0	2	2	11	....	....	....	....	....	....	1983-84	1985-86
Jensen, David	Hfd., Wsh.	4	69	9	13	22	22	11	0	0	0	2	....	1984-85	1987-88
Jensen, Steve	Min., L.A.	7	438	113	107	220	318	12	0	3	3	9	....	1975-76	1981-82
• Jeremiah, Ed	NYA, Bos.	1	15	0	1	1	0	....	....	....	....	....	....	1931-32	1931-32
Jerrard, Paul	Min.	1	5	0	0	0	4	....	....	....	....	....	....	1988-89	1988-89
• Jerwa, Frank	Bos., St.L.	4	81	11	16	27	53	....	....	....	....	....	....	1931-32	1934-35
• Jerwa, Joe	NYR, Bos., NYA	7	234	29	58	87	309	17	2	3	5	16	....	1930-31	1938-39
Jirik, Jaroslav	St.L.	1	3	0	0	0	0	....	....	....	....	....	....	1969-70	1969-70
• Joanette, Rosario	Mtl.	1	2	0	1	1	4	....	....	....	....	....	....	1944-45	1944-45
Jodzio, Rick	Col., Cle.	1	70	2	8	10	71	....	....	....	....	....	....	1977-78	1977-78
Johannesen, Glenn	NYI	1	2	0	0	0	0	....	....	....	....	....	....	1985-86	1985-86
Johannson, John	N.J.	1	5	0	0	0	0	....	....	....	....	....	....	1983-84	1983-84
• Johansen, Bill	Tor.	1	1	0	0	0	0	....	....	....	....	....	....	1949-50	1949-50
Johansen, Trevor	Tor., Col., L.A.	5	286	11	46	57	282	13	0	3	3	21	....	1977-78	1981-82
Johansson, Bjorn	Cle.	2	15	1	1	2	10	....	....	....	....	....	....	1976-77	1977-78
Johansson, Roger	Cgy., Chi.	4	161	9	34	43	163	5	0	1	1	2	....	1989-90	1994-95
Johns, Don	NYR, Mtl., Min.	6	153	2	21	23	76	....	....	....	....	....	....	1960-61	1967-68
Johnson, Allan	Mtl., Det.	4	105	21	28	49	30	11	2	2	4	6	....	1956-57	1962-63
Johnson, Brian	Det.	1	3	0	0	0	5	....	....	....	....	....	....	1983-84	1983-84
• Johnson, Ching	NYR, NYA	12	436	38	48	86	808	61	5	2	7	161	2	1926-27	1937-38
• Johnson, Danny	Tor., Van., Det.	3	121	18	19	37	24	....	....	....	....	....	....	1969-70	1971-72
Johnson, Earl	Det.	1	1	0	0	0	0	....	....	....	....	....	....	1953-54	1953-54
Johnson, Jim	NYR, Phi., L.A.	8	302	75	111	186	73	7	0	2	2	2	....	1964-65	1971-72
Johnson, Jim	Pit., Min., Dal., Wsh., Phx.	13	829	29	166	195	1197	51	1	11	12	132	....	1985-86	1997-98
Johnson, Mark	Pit., Min., Hfd., St.L., N.J.	11	669	203	305	508	260	37	16	12	28	10	....	1979-80	1989-90
Johnson, Norm	Bos., Chi.	3	61	5	20	25	41	14	4	0	4	6	....	1957-58	1959-60
Johnson, Terry	Que., St.L., Cgy., Tor.	9	285	3	24	27	580	38	0	4	4	118	....	1979-80	1987-88
Johnson, Tom	Mtl., Bos.	17	978	51	213	264	960	111	8	15	23	109	6	1947-48	1964-65
• Johnson, Virgil	Chi.	3	75	1	11	12	27	19	0	3	3	4	1	1937-38	1944-45
Johnston, Bernie	Hfd.	2	57	12	24	36	16	3	0	1	1	0	....	1979-80	1980-81
Johnston, George	Chi.	4	58	20	12	32	2	....	....	....	....	....	....	1941-42	1946-47
‡ Johnston, Greg	Bos., Tor.	9	187	26	29	55	124	22	2	1	3	12	....	1983-84	1991-92
Johnston, Jay	Wsh.	2	8	0	0	0	13	....	....	....	....	....	....	1980-81	1981-82
Johnston, Joey	Min., Cal., Chi.	6	331	85	106	191	320	....	....	....	....	....	....	1968-69	1975-76
Johnston, Larry	L.A., Det., K.C., Col.	7	320	9	64	73	580	....	....	....	....	....	....	1967-68	1976-77
Johnston, Marshall	Min., Cal.	7	251	14	52	66	58	6	0	0	0	2	....	1967-68	1973-74
Johnston, Randy	NYI	1	4	0	0	0	4	....	....	....	....	....	....	1979-80	1979-80
Johnstone, Eddie	NYR, Det.	10	426	122	136	258	375	55	13	10	23	83	....	1975-76	1986-87
Johnstone, Ross	Tor.	2	42	5	4	9	14	3	0	0	0	0	1	1943-44	1944-45
• Joliat, Aurel	Mtl.	16	655	270	190	460	771	46	9	13	22	66	3	1922-23	1937-38
• Joliat, Rene	Mtl.	1	1	0	0	0	0	....	....	....	....	....	....	1924-25	1924-25
Joly, Greg	Wsh., Det.	9	365	21	76	97	250	5	0	0	0	8	....	1974-75	1982-83
Joly, Yvan	Mtl.	3	2	0	0	0	0	1	0	0	0	0	....	1979-80	1982-83
‡ Jomphe, Jean-Francois	Ana., Phx., Mtl.	4	111	10	29	39	102	....	....	....	....	....	....	1995-96	1998-99
Jonathan, Stan	Bos., Pit.	8	411	91	110	201	751	63	8	4	12	137	....	1975-76	1982-83
Jones, Bob	NYR	1	2	0	0	0	0	....	....	....	....	....	....	1968-69	1968-69
Jones, Brad	Wpg., L.A., Phi.	6	148	25	31	56	122	9	1	1	2	2	....	1986-87	1991-92
Jones, Buck	Det., Tor.	4	50	2	2	4	36	12	0	1	1	18	....	1938-39	1942-43
Jones, Jim	Cal.	1	2	0	0	0	0	....	....	....	....	....	....	1971-72	1971-72
Jones, Jimmy	Tor.	3	148	13	18	31	68	19	1	5	6	11	....	1977-78	1979-80
Jones, Keith	Wsh., Col., Phi.	9	491	117	141	258	765	63	12	12	24	120	....	1992-93	2000-01
Jones, Ron	Bos., Pit., Wsh.	5	54	1	4	5	31	....	....	....	....	....	....	1971-72	1975-76
‡ Jones, Ty	Chi.	1	8	0	0	0	12	....	....	....	....	....	....	1998-99	1998-99
‡ Jonsson, Jorgen	NYI, Ana.	1	81	12	19	31	16	....	....	....	....	....	....	1999-00	1999-00
Jonsson, Tomas	NYI, Edm.	8	552	85	259	344	482	80	11	26	37	97	2	1981-82	1988-89
‡ Joseph, Chris	Pit., Edm., T.B., Van., Phi., Phx., Atl.	14	510	39	112	151	567	31	3	4	7	24	....	1987-88	2000-01
Joseph, Tony	Wpg.	1	2	1	0	1	0	....	....	....	....	....	....	1988-89	1988-89
Joyal, Eddie	Det., Tor., L.A., Phi.	9	466	128	134	262	103	50	11	8	19	18	....	1962-63	1971-72
Joyce, Bob	Bos., Wsh., Wpg.	6	158	34	49	83	90	46	15	9	24	29	....	1987-88	1992-93
Joyce, Duane	Dal.	1	3	0	0	0	0	....	....	....	....	....	....	1993-94	1993-94
• Juckes, Bing	NYR	2	16	2	1	3	6	....	....	....	....	....	....	1947-48	1949-50
‡ Juhlin, Patrik	Phi.	2	56	7	6	13	23	13	1	0	1	2	....	1994-95	1995-96
Julien, Claude	Que.	2	14	0	1	1	25	....	....	....	....	....	....	1984-85	1985-86
‡ Junker, Steve	NYI	2	5	0	0	0	0	3	0	1	1	0	....	1992-93	1993-94
Jutila, Timo	Buf.	1	10	1	5	6	13	....	....	....	....	....	....	1984-85	1984-85
Juzda, Bill	NYR, Tor.	9	398	14	54	68	398	42	0	3	3	46	2	1940-41	1951-52

K

Name	NHL Teams	NHL Seasons	Regular Schedule GP	G	A	TP	PIM	Playoffs GP	G	A	TP	PIM	NHL Cup Wins	First NHL Season	Last NHL Season
Kabel, Bob	NYR	2	48	5	13	18	34	....	....	....	....	....	....	1959-60	1960-61
Kachowski, Mark	Pit.	3	64	6	5	11	209	....	....	....	....	....	....	1987-88	1989-90
Kachur, Ed	Chi.	2	96	10	14	24	35	....	....	....	....	....	....	1956-57	1957-58
Kaese, Trent	Buf.	1	1	0	0	0	0	....	....	....	....	....	....	1988-89	1988-89
Kaiser, Vern	Mtl.	1	50	7	5	12	33	2	0	0	0	0	....	1950-51	1950-51
• Kalbfleish, Walter	Ott., St.L., NYA, Bos.	4	36	0	4	4	32	5	0	0	0	2	....	1933-34	1936-37
• Kaleta, Alex	Chi., NYR	7	387	92	121	213	190	17	1	6	7	2	....	1941-42	1950-51
Kallur, Anders	NYI	6	383	101	110	211	149	78	12	23	35	32	4	1979-80	1984-85
‡ Kamensky, Valeri	Que., Col., NYR, Dal., N.J.	11	637	200	301	501	383	66	25	35	60	72	1	1991-92	2001-02
Kaminski, Kevin	Min., Que., Wsh.	7	139	3	10	13	528	8	0	0	0	52	....	1988-89	1996-97
• Kaminsky, Max	Ott., Bos., St.L., Mtl.M.	4	130	22	34	56	38	4	0	0	0	0	....	1933-34	1936-37
Kaminsky, Yan	Wpg., NYI	2	26	3	2	5	4	2	0	0	0	4	....	1993-94	1994-95
• Kampman, Bingo	Tor.	5	189	14	30	44	287	47	1	4	5	38	1	1937-38	1941-42
Kane, Francis	Det.	1	2	0	0	0	0	....	....	....	....	....	....	1943-44	1943-44
Kannegiesser, Gord	St.L.	2	23	0	1	1	15	....	....	....	....	....	....	1967-68	1971-72
Kannegiesser, Sheldon	Pit., NYR, L.A., Van.	8	366	14	67	81	292	18	0	2	2	10	....	1970-71	1977-78
‡ Karabin, Ladislav	Pit.	1	9	0	0	0	2	....	....	....	....	....	....	1993-94	1993-94
Karalahti, Jere	L.A., Nsh.	3	149	8	19	27	97	17	0	1	1	20	....	1999-00	2001-02
‡ Karamnov, Vitali	St.L.	3	92	12	20	32	65	2	0	0	0	2	....	1992-93	1994-95
‡ Karjalainen, Kyosti	L.A.	1	28	1	8	9	12	3	0	1	1	2	....	1991-92	1991-92
Karlander, Al	Det.	4	212	36	56	92	70	4	0	1	1	0	....	1969-70	1972-73
‡ Karpov, Valeri	Ana.	3	76	14	15	29	32	....	....	....	....	....	....	1994-95	1996-97
Kasatonov, Alexei	N.J., Ana., St.L., Bos.	7	383	38	122	160	326	33	4	7	11	40	....	1989-90	1995-96
Kasper, Steve	Bos., L.A., Phi., T.B.	13	821	177	291	468	554	94	20	28	48	82	....	1980-81	1992-93
Kastelic, Ed	Wsh., Hfd.	7	220	11	10	21	719	8	1	0	1	32	....	1985-86	1991-92
Kaszycki, Mike	NYI, Wsh., Tor.	5	226	42	80	122	108	19	2	6	8	10	....	1977-78	1982-83
• Kea, Ed	Atl., St.L.	10	583	30	145	175	508	32	2	4	6	39	....	1973-74	1982-83
Kearns, Dennis	Van.	10	677	31	290	321	386	11	1	2	3	8	....	1971-72	1980-81
• Keating, Jack	Det.	2	11	3	0	3	4	....	....	....	....	....	....	1938-39	1939-40
• Keating, John	NYA	2	35	5	5	10	17	....	....	....	....	....	....	1931-32	1932-33
Keating, Mike	NYR	1	1	0	0	0	0	....	....	....	....	....	....	1977-78	1977-78
• Keats, Duke	Bos., Det., Chi.	3	82	30	19	49	113	....	....	....	....	....	....	1926-27	1928-29
Keczmer, Dan	Min., Hfd., Cgy., Dal., Nsh.	10	235	8	38	46	212	12	0	1	1	8	....	1990-91	1999-00
• Keeling, Butch	Tor., NYR	12	525	157	63	220	331	47	11	11	22	34	1	1926-27	1937-38
Keenan, Larry	Tor., St.L., Buf., Phi.	6	233	38	64	102	28	46	15	16	31	12	....	1961-62	1971-72
Kehoe, Rick	Tor., Pit.	14	906	371	396	767	120	39	4	17	21	4	....	1971-72	1984-85
Kekalainen, Jarmo	Bos., Ott.	5	55	5	8	13	28	....	....	....	....	....	....	1989-90	1993-94
Keller, Ralph	NYR	1	3	1	0	1	6	....	....	....	....	....	....	1962-63	1962-63
Kellgren, Christer	Col.	1	5	0	0	0	0	....	....	....	....	....	....	1981-82	1981-82
Kelly, Bob	Phi., Wsh.	12	837	154	208	362	1454	101	9	14	23	172	2	1970-71	1981-82
Kelly, Bob	St.L., Pit., Chi.	6	425	87	109	196	687	23	6	3	9	40	....	1973-74	1978-79

Name	NHL Teams	NHL Seasons	Regular Schedule GP	G	A	TP	PIM	Playoffs GP	G	A	TP	PIM	NHL Cup Wins	First NHL Season	Last NHL Season
Kelly, Dave	Det.	1	16	2	0	2	4	....	....	....	....	....	....	1976-77	1976-77
Kelly, John Paul	L.A.	7	400	54	70	124	366	18	1	1	2	41	....	1979-80	1985-86
● Kelly, Pep	Tor., Chi., Bro.	8	288	74	53	127	105	38	7	6	13	10	....	1934-35	1941-42
Kelly, Pete	St.L., Det., NYA, Bro.	7	177	21	38	59	68	19	3	1	4	2	2	1934-35	1941-42
Kelly, Red	Det., Tor.	20	1316	281	542	823	327	164	33	59	92	51	8	1947-48	1966-67
● Kemp, Kevin	Hfd.	1	3	0	0	0	4	....	....	....	....	....	....	1980-81	1980-81
Kemp, Stan	Tor.	1	1	0	0	0	2	....	....	....	....	....	....	1948-49	1948-49
‡ Kenady, Chris	St.L., NYR	2	7	0	2	2	0	....	....	....	....	....	....	1997-98	1999-00
● Kendall, Bill	Chi., Tor.	5	131	16	10	26	28	6	0	0	0	0	1	1933-34	1937-38
Kennedy, Dean	L.A., NYR, Buf., Wpg., Edm.	12	717	26	108	134	1118	36	1	7	8	59	....	1982-83	1994-95
Kennedy, Forbes	Chi., Det., Bos., Phi., Tor.	11	603	70	108	178	988	12	2	4	6	64	....	1956-57	1968-69
‡ Kennedy, Mike	Dal., Tor., NYI	5	145	16	36	52	112	5	0	0	0	9	....	1994-95	1998-99
Kennedy, Sheldon	Det., Cgy., Bos.	8	310	49	58	107	233	24	6	4	10	20	....	1989-90	1996-97
Kennedy, Ted	Tor.	14	696	231	329	560	432	78	29	31	60	32	5	1942-43	1956-57
● Kenny, Ernest	NYR, Chi.	2	10	0	0	0	18	....	....	....	....	....	....	1930-31	1934-35
Keon, Dave	Tor., Hfd.	18	1296	396	590	986	117	92	32	36	68	6	4	1960-61	1981-82
‡ Kerch, Alexander	Edm.	1	5	0	0	0	2	....	....	....	....	....	....	1993-94	1993-94
Kerr, Alan	NYI, Det., Wpg.	9	391	72	94	166	826	38	5	4	9	70	....	1984-85	1992-93
Kerr, Reg	Cle., Chi., Edm.	6	263	66	94	160	169	7	1	0	1	7	....	1977-78	1983-84
Kerr, Tim	Phi., NYR, Hfd.	13	655	370	304	674	596	81	40	31	71	58	....	1980-81	1992-93
‡ Kesa, Dan	Van., Dal., Pit., T.B.	4	139	8	22	30	66	13	1	0	1	0	....	1993-94	1999-00
Kessell, Rick	Pit., Cal.	5	135	4	24	28	6	....	....	....	....	....	....	1969-70	1973-74
Ketola, Veli-Pekka	Col.	1	44	9	5	14	4	....	....	....	....	....	....	1981-82	1981-82
Ketter, Kerry	Atl.	1	41	0	2	2	58	....	....	....	....	....	....	1972-73	1972-73
Kharin, Sergei	Wpg.	1	7	2	3	5	2	....	....	....	....	....	....	1990-91	1990-91
‡ Kharitonov, Alexander	T.B., NYI	2	71	7	15	22	12	....	....	....	....	....	....	2000-01	2001-02
Khmylev, Yuri	Buf., St.L.	5	263	64	88	152	133	26	8	6	14	24	....	1992-93	1996-97
Kidd, Ian	Van.	2	20	4	7	11	25	....	....	....	....	....	....	1987-88	1988-89
Kiessling, Udo	Min.	1	1	0	0	0	2	....	....	....	....	....	....	1981-82	1981-82
Kilrea, Brian	Det., L.A.	2	26	3	5	8	12	....	....	....	....	....	....	1957-58	1967-68
● Kilrea, Hec	Ott., Det., Tor.	15	633	167	129	296	438	48	8	7	15	18	3	1925-26	1939-40
● Kilrea, Ken	Det.	5	91	16	23	39	8	15	2	2	4	4	....	1938-39	1943-44
● Kilrea, Wally	Ott., Phi., NYA, Mtl.M., Det.	9	329	35	58	93	87	25	2	4	6	6	2	1929-30	1937-38
‡ Kimble, Darin	Que., St.L., Bos., Chi.	7	311	23	20	43	1082	23	0	0	0	52	....	1988-89	1994-95
Kindrachuk, Orest	Phi., Pit., Wsh.	10	508	118	261	379	648	76	20	20	40	53	2	1972-73	1981-82
King, Frank	Mtl.	1	10	1	0	1	2	....	....	....	....	....	....	1950-51	1950-51
King, Kris	Det., NYR, Wpg., Phx., Tor., Chi.	14	849	66	85	151	2030	67	8	5	13	142	....	1987-88	2000-01
King, Steven	NYR, Ana.	3	67	17	8	25	75	....	....	....	....	....	....	1992-93	1995-96
King, Wayne	Cal.	3	73	5	18	23	34	....	....	....	....	....	....	1973-74	1975-76
Kinnear, Geordie	Atl.	1	4	0	0	0	13	....	....	....	....	....	....	1999-00	1999-00
Kinsella, Brian	Wsh.	2	10	0	1	1	0	....	....	....	....	....	....	1975-76	1976-77
● Kinsella, Ray	Ott.	1	14	0	0	0	0	....	....	....	....	....	....	1930-31	1930-31
‡ Kiprusoff, Marko	Mtl., NYI	2	51	0	10	10	12	....	....	....	....	....	....	1995-96	2001-02
● Kirk, Bobby	NYR	1	39	4	8	12	14	....	....	....	....	....	....	1937-38	1937-38
Kirkpatrick, Bob	NYR	1	49	12	12	24	6	....	....	....	....	....	....	1942-43	1942-43
Kirton, Mark	Tor., Det., Van.	6	266	57	56	113	121	4	1	2	3	7	....	1979-80	1984-85
Kisio, Kelly	Det., NYR, S.J., Cgy.	13	761	229	429	658	768	39	6	15	21	52	....	1982-83	1994-95
Kitchen, Bill	Mtl., Tor.	4	41	1	4	5	40	3	0	1	1	0	....	1981-82	1984-85
● Kitchen, Hobie	Mtl.M., Det.	2	47	5	4	9	58	....	....	....	....	....	1	1925-26	1926-27
Kitchen, Mike	Col., N.J.	8	474	12	62	74	370	2	0	0	0	2	....	1976-77	1983-84
Klassen, Ralph	Cal., Cle., Col., St.L.	9	497	52	93	145	120	26	4	2	6	12	....	1975-76	1983-84
● Klein, Lloyd	Bos., NYA	8	164	30	24	54	68	5	0	0	0	2	1	1928-29	1937-38
Kleinendorst, Scot	NYR, Hfd., Wsh.	8	281	12	46	58	452	26	2	7	9	40	....	1982-83	1989-90
‡ Klima, Petr	Det., Edm., T.B., L.A., Pit.	13	786	313	260	573	671	95	28	24	52	83	1	1985-86	1998-99
‡ Klimovich, Sergei	Chi.	1	1	0	0	0	2	....	....	....	....	....	....	1996-97	1996-97
● Klingbeil, Ike	Chi.	1	5	1	2	3	2	....	....	....	....	....	....	1936-37	1936-37
Klukay, Joe	Tor., Bos.	11	566	109	127	236	189	71	13	10	23	23	4	1942-43	1955-56
Kluzak, Gord	Bos.	7	299	25	98	123	543	46	6	13	19	129	....	1982-83	1990-91
Knibbs, Bill	Bos.	1	53	7	10	17	4	....	....	....	....	....	....	1964-65	1964-65
Knipscheer, Fred	Bos., St.L.	3	28	6	3	9	18	16	2	1	3	6	....	1993-94	1995-96
● Knott, Nick	Bro.	1	14	3	1	4	9	....	....	....	....	....	....	1941-42	1941-42
Knox, Paul	Tor.	1	1	0	0	0	0	....	....	....	....	....	....	1954-55	1954-55
Kocur, Joe	Det., NYR, Van.	15	820	80	82	162	2519	118	10	12	22	231	3	1984-85	1998-99
‡ Kolesar, Mark	Tor.	2	28	2	2	4	14	3	1	0	1	2	....	1995-96	1996-97
Kolstad, Dean	Min., S.J.	3	40	1	7	8	69	....	....	....	....	....	....	1988-89	1992-93
Komadoski, Neil	L.A., St.L.	8	502	16	76	92	632	23	0	2	2	47	....	1972-73	1979-80
Konik, George	Pit.	1	52	7	8	15	26	....	....	....	....	....	....	1967-68	1967-68
Konroyd, Steve	Cgy., NYI, Chi., Hfd., Det., Ott.	15	895	41	195	236	863	97	10	15	25	99	....	1980-81	1994-95
Konstantinov, Vladimir	Det.	6	446	47	128	175	838	82	5	14	19	107	1	1991-92	1996-97
Kontos, Chris	NYR, Pit., L.A., T.B.	8	230	54	69	123	103	20	11	0	11	12	....	1982-83	1992-93
● Kopak, Russ	Bos.	1	24	7	9	16	0	....	....	....	....	....	....	1943-44	1943-44
Korab, Jerry	Chi., Van., Buf., L.A.	15	975	114	341	455	1629	93	8	18	26	201	....	1970-71	1984-85
Kordic, Dan	Phi.	6	197	4	8	12	584	12	1	0	1	22	....	1991-92	1998-99
● Kordic, John	Mtl., Tor., Wsh., Que.	7	244	17	18	35	997	41	4	3	7	131	1	1985-86	1991-92
Korn, Jim	Det., Tor., Buf., N.J., Cgy.	10	597	66	122	188	1801	16	1	2	3	109	....	1979-80	1989-90
Korney, Mike	Det., NYR	4	77	9	10	19	59	....	....	....	....	....	....	1973-74	1978-79
Koroll, Cliff	Chi.	11	814	208	254	462	376	85	19	29	48	67	....	1969-70	1979-80
Kortko, Roger	NYI	2	79	7	17	24	28	10	0	3	3	17	....	1984-85	1985-86
Kostynski, Doug	Bos.	2	15	3	1	4	4	....	....	....	....	....	....	1983-84	1984-85
Kotanen, Dick	NYR	1	1	0	0	0	0	....	....	....	....	....	....	1950-51	1950-51
Kotsopoulos, Chris	NYR, Hfd., Tor., Det.	10	479	44	109	153	827	31	1	3	4	91	....	1980-81	1989-90
‡ Kovalenko, Andrei	Que., Col., Mtl., Edm., Phi., Car., Bos.	9	620	173	206	379	389	33	5	6	11	20	....	1992-93	2000-01
Kowal, Joe	Buf.	2	22	0	5	5	13	2	0	0	0	0	....	1976-77	1977-78
Kozak, Don	L.A., Van.	7	437	96	86	182	480	29	7	2	9	69	....	1972-73	1978-79
Kozak, Les	Tor.	1	12	1	0	1	2	....	....	....	....	....	....	1961-62	1961-62
● Kraftcheck, Stephen	Bos., NYR, Tor.	4	157	11	18	29	83	6	0	0	0	7	....	1950-51	1958-59
Krake, Skip	Bos., L.A., Buf.	7	249	23	40	63	182	10	1	0	1	17	....	1963-64	1970-71
Kravets, Mikhail	S.J.	2	2	0	0	0	0	....	....	....	....	....	....	1991-92	1992-93
Krentz, Dale	Det.	3	30	5	3	8	9	2	0	0	0	0	....	1986-87	1988-89
● Krol, Joe	NYR, Bro.	3	26	10	4	14	8	....	....	....	....	....	....	1936-37	1941-42
Kromm, Richard	Cgy., NYI	9	372	70	103	173	138	36	2	6	8	22	....	1983-84	1992-93
‡ Kron, Robert	Van., Hfd., Car., CBJ	12	771	144	194	338	119	16	3	2	5	2	....	1990-91	2001-02
Krook, Kevin	Col.	1	3	0	0	0	2	....	....	....	....	....	....	1978-79	1978-79
‡ Kroupa, Vlastimil	S.J., N.J.	5	105	4	19	23	66	20	1	2	3	25	....	1993-94	1997-98
Krulicki, Jim	NYR, Det.	1	41	0	3	3	6	....	....	....	....	....	....	1970-71	1970-71
Kruppke, Gord	Det.	3	23	0	0	0	32	....	....	....	....	....	....	1990-91	1993-94
‡ Kruse, Paul	Cgy., NYI, Buf., S.J.	11	423	38	33	71	1074	28	5	2	7	36	....	1990-91	2000-01
Krushelnyski, Mike	Bos., Edm., L.A., Tor., Det.	14	897	241	328	569	699	139	29	43	72	106	3	1981-82	1994-95
Krutov, Vladimir	Van.	1	61	11	23	34	20	....	....	....	....	....	....	1989-90	1989-90
Krygier, Todd	Hfd., Wsh., Ana.	9	543	100	143	243	533	48	10	7	17	40	....	1989-90	1997-98
Kryskow, Dave	Chi., Wsh., Det., Atl.	4	231	33	56	89	174	12	2	0	2	4	....	1972-73	1975-76
Kryzanowski, Ed	Bos., Chi.	5	237	15	22	37	65	18	0	1	1	4	....	1948-49	1952-53
‡ Kudashov, Alexei	Tor.	1	25	1	0	1	4	....	....	....	....	....	....	1993-94	1993-94
Kudelski, Bob	L.A., Ott., Fla.	9	442	139	102	241	218	22	4	4	8	4	....	1987-88	1995-96
● Kuhn, Gord	NYA	1	12	1	1	2	4	....	....	....	....	....	....	1932-33	1932-33
Kukulowicz, Aggie	NYR	2	4	1	0	1	0	....	....	....	....	....	....	1952-53	1953-54
Kulak, Stu	Van., Edm., NYR, Que., Wpg.	4	90	8	4	12	130	3	0	0	0	2	....	1982-83	1988-89
● Kullman, Arnie	Bos.	2	13	0	1	1	11	....	....	....	....	....	....	1947-48	1949-50
● Kullman, Eddie	NYR	6	343	56	70	126	298	6	1	0	1	2	....	1947-48	1953-54
Kumpel, Mark	Que., Det., Wpg.	6	288	38	46	84	113	39	6	4	10	14	....	1984-85	1990-91
● Kuntz, Alan	NYR	2	45	10	12	22	12	6	1	0	1	2	....	1941-42	1945-46
Kuntz, Murray	St.L.	1	7	1	2	3	0	....	....	....	....	....	....	1974-75	1974-75
Kurri, Jari	Edm., L.A., NYR, Ana., Col.	17	1251	601	797	1398	545	200	106	127	233	123	5	1980-81	1997-98
Kurtenbach, Orland	NYR, Bos., Tor., Van.	13	639	119	213	332	628	19	2	4	6	70	....	1960-61	1973-74
Kurvers, Tom	Mtl., Buf., N.J., Tor., Van., NYI, Ana.	11	659	93	328	421	350	57	8	22	30	68	1	1984-85	1994-95
Kuryluk, Merv	Chi.	1	....	....	....	....	....	2	0	0	0	0	....	1961-62	1961-62
Kushner, Dale	NYI, Phi.	3	84	10	13	23	215	....	....	....	....	....	....	1989-90	1991-92
Kuzyk, Ken	Cle.	2	41	5	9	14	8	....	....	....	....	....	....	1976-77	1977-78
‡ Kvartalnov, Dmitri	Bos.	2	112	42	49	91	26	4	0	0	0	0	....	1992-93	1993-94
Kwong, Larry	NYR	1	1	0	0	0	0	....	....	....	....	....	....	1947-48	1947-48
● Kyle, Bill	NYR	2	3	0	3	3	0	....	....	....	....	....	....	1949-50	1950-51
● Kyle, Gus	NYR, Bos.	3	203	6	20	26	362	14	1	2	3	34	....	1949-50	1951-52
Kyllonen, Markku	Wpg.	1	9	0	2	2	2	....	....	....	....	....	....	1988-89	1988-89
Kypreos, Nick	Wsh., Hfd., NYR, Tor.	8	442	46	44	90	1210	34	1	3	4	65	1	1989-90	1996-97
Kyte, Jim	Wpg., Pit., Cgy., Ott., S.J.	13	598	17	49	66	1342	42	0	6	6	94	....	1982-83	1995-96

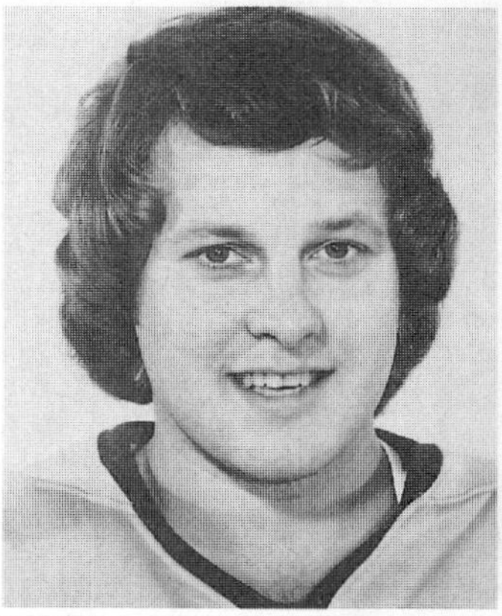

Sheldon Kannegiesser

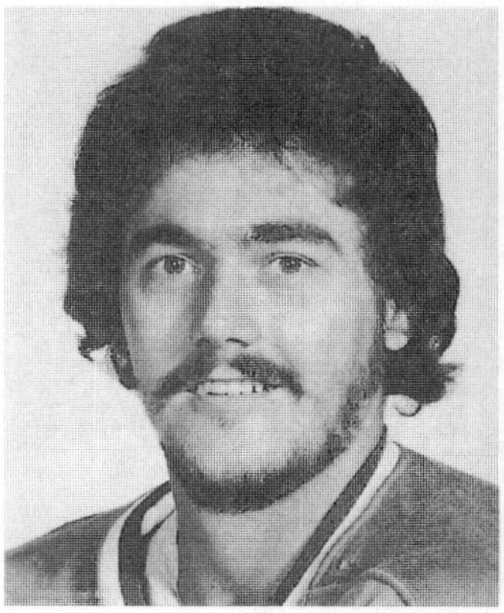

Rick Kehoe

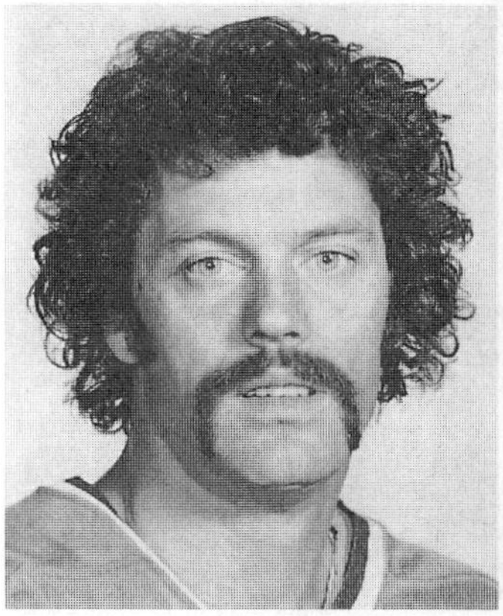

Bob Kelly

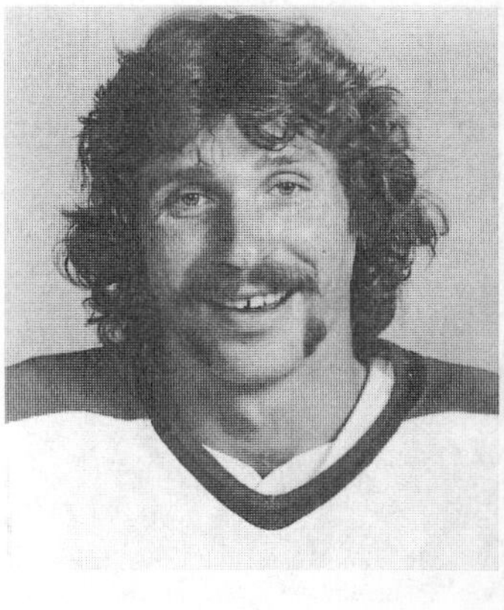

Ralph Klassen

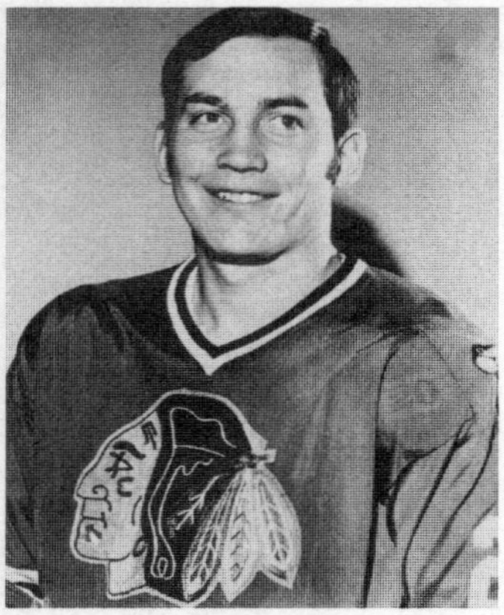

Cliff Koroll

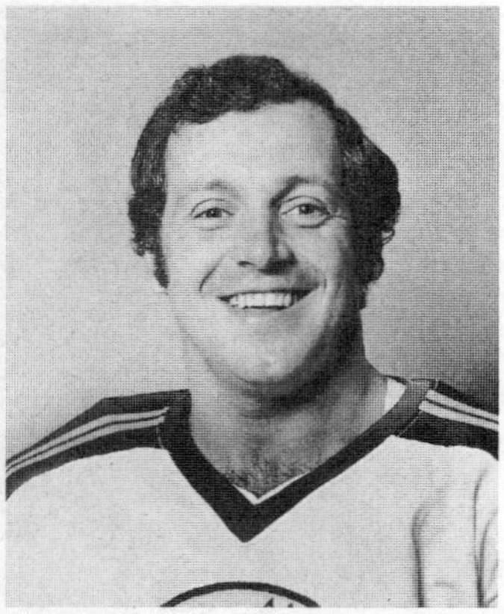

Jean-Guy Lagace

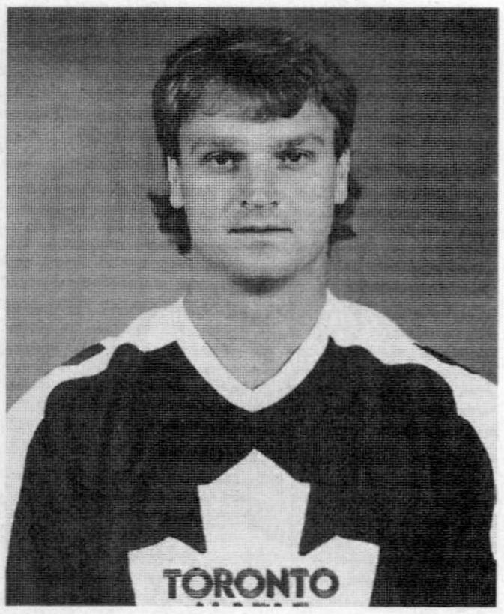

Rick Lanz

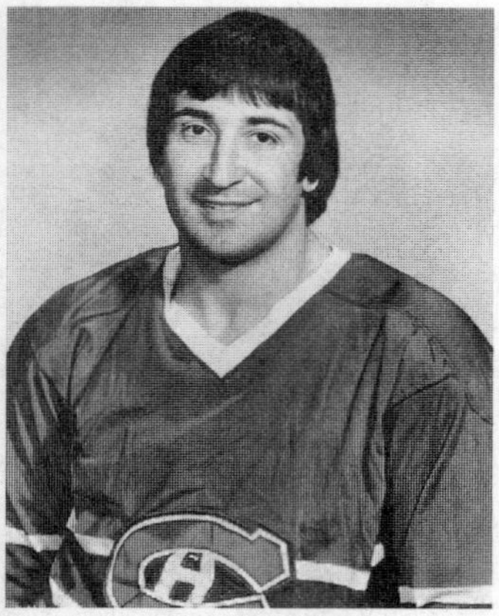

Guy Lapointe

Name	NHL Teams	NHL Seasons	Regular Schedule					Playoffs					NHL Cup Wins	First NHL Season	Last NHL Season
			GP	G	A	TP	PIM	GP	G	A	TP	PIM			
L															
Labadie, Mike	NYR	1	3	0	0	0	0	....	....	....	....	....	....	1952-53	1952-53
Labatte, Neil	St.L.	2	26	0	2	2	19	....	....	....	....	....	....	1978-79	1981-82
L'Abbe, Moe	Chi.	1	5	0	1	1	0	....	....	....	....	....	....	1972-73	1972-73
Labelle, Marc	Dal.	1	9	0	0	0	46	....	....	....	....	....	....	1996-97	1996-97
Labine, Leo	Bos., Det.	11	643	128	193	321	730	60	12	11	23	82	....	1951-52	1961-62
Labossiere, Gord	NYR, L.A., Min.	6	215	44	62	106	75	10	2	3	5	28	....	1963-64	1971-72
Labovitch, Max	NYR	1	5	0	0	0	4	....	....	....	....	....	....	1943-44	1943-44
Labraaten, Dan	Det., Cgy.	4	268	71	73	144	47	8	1	0	1	4	....	1978-79	1981-82
Labre, Yvon	Pit., Wsh.	9	371	14	87	101	788	....	....	....	....	....	....	1970-71	1980-81
Labrie, Guy	Bos., NYR	2	42	4	9	13	16	....	....	....	....	....	....	1943-44	1944-45
Lach, Elmer	Mtl.	14	664	215	408	623	478	76	19	45	64	36	3	1940-41	1953-54
Lachance, Michel	Col.	1	21	0	4	4	22	....	....	....	....	....	....	1978-79	1978-79
Lacombe, Francois	Oak., Buf., Que.	4	78	2	17	19	54	3	1	0	1	0	....	1968-69	1979-80
Lacombe, Normand	Buf., Edm., Phi.	7	319	53	62	115	196	26	5	1	6	49	1	1984-85	1990-91
Lacroix, Andre	Phi., Chi., Hfd.	6	325	79	119	198	44	16	2	5	7	0	....	1967-68	1979-80
‡ Lacroix, Daniel	NYR, Bos., Phi., Edm., NYI	7	188	11	7	18	379	16	0	1	1	26	....	1993-94	1999-00
Lacroix, Eric	Tor., L.A., Col., NYR, Ott.	8	472	67	70	137	361	30	1	5	6	25	....	1993-94	2000-01
Lacroix, Pierre	Que., Hfd.	4	274	24	108	132	197	8	0	2	2	10	....	1979-80	1982-83
Ladouceur, Randy	Det., Hfd., Ana.	14	930	30	126	156	1322	40	5	8	13	59	....	1982-83	1995-96
LaFayette, Nathan	St.L., Van., NYR, L.A.	6	187	17	20	37	103	32	2	7	9	8	....	1993-94	1998-99
Lafleur, Guy	Mtl., NYR, Que.	17	1126	560	793	1353	399	128	58	76	134	67	5	1971-72	1990-91
• Lafleur, Roland	Mtl.	1	1	0	0	0	0	....	....	....	....	....	....	1924-25	1924-25
LaFontaine, Pat	NYI, Buf., NYR	15	865	468	545	1013	552	69	26	36	62	36	....	1983-84	1997-98
Laforce, Ernie	Mtl.	1	1	0	0	0	0	....	....	....	....	....	....	1942-43	1942-43
LaForest, Bob	L.A.	1	5	1	0	1	2	....	....	....	....	....	....	1983-84	1983-84
Laforge, Claude	Mtl., Det., Phi.	8	193	24	33	57	82	5	1	2	3	15	....	1957-58	1968-69
Laforge, Marc	Hfd., Edm.	2	14	0	0	0	64	....	....	....	....	....	....	1989-90	1993-94
Laframboise, Pete	Cal., Wsh., Pit.	4	227	33	55	88	70	9	1	0	1	0	....	1971-72	1974-75
Lafrance, Adie	Mtl.	1	3	0	0	0	2	2	0	0	0	0	....	1933-34	1933-34
• Lafrance, Leo	Mtl., Chi.	2	33	2	0	2	6	....	....	....	....	....	....	1926-27	1927-28
‡ Lafreniere, Jason	Que., NYR, T.B.	5	146	34	53	87	22	15	1	5	6	19	....	1986-87	1993-94
Lafreniere, Roger	Det., St.L.	2	13	0	0	0	4	....	....	....	....	....	....	1962-63	1972-73
Lagace, Jean-Guy	Pit., Buf., K.C.	6	197	9	39	48	251	....	....	....	....	....	....	1968-69	1975-76
Laidlaw, Tom	NYR, L.A.	10	705	25	139	164	717	69	4	17	21	78	....	1980-81	1989-90
Laird, Robbie	Min.	1	1	0	0	0	0	....	....	....	....	....	....	1979-80	1979-80
Lajeunesse, Serge	Det., Phi.	5	103	1	4	5	103	....	....	....	....	....	....	1970-71	1974-75
‡ Lakovic, Sasha	Cgy., N.J.	3	37	0	4	4	118	....	....	....	....	....	....	1996-97	1998-99
Lalande, Hec	Chi., Det.	4	151	21	39	60	120	....	....	....	....	....	....	1953-54	1957-58
Lalonde, Bobby	Van., Atl., Bos., Cgy.	11	641	124	210	334	298	16	4	2	6	6	....	1971-72	1981-82
• Lalonde, Newsy	Mtl., NYA	6	99	124	41	165	183	7	15	4	19	23	....	1917-18	1926-27
Lalonde, Ron	Pit., Wsh.	7	397	45	78	123	106	....	....	....	....	....	....	1972-73	1978-79
Lalor, Mike	Mtl., St.L., Wsh., Wpg., S.J., Dal.	12	687	17	88	105	677	92	5	10	15	167	1	1985-86	1996-97
• Lamb, Joe	Mtl.M., Ott., NYA, Bos., Mtl., St.L., Det.	11	443	108	101	209	601	18	1	1	2	51	....	1927-28	1937-38
Lamb, Mark	Cgy., Det., Edm., Ott., Phi., Mtl.	11	403	46	100	146	291	70	7	19	26	51	1	1985-86	1995-96
‡ Lambert, Dan	Que.	2	29	6	9	15	22	....	....	....	....	....	....	1990-91	1991-92
Lambert, Denny	Ana., Ott., Nsh., Atl.	8	487	27	66	93	1391	17	0	1	1	28	....	1994-95	2001-02
Lambert, Lane	Det., NYR, Que.	6	283	58	66	124	521	17	2	4	6	40	....	1983-84	1988-89
Lambert, Yvon	Mtl., Buf.	10	683	206	273	479	340	90	27	22	49	67	4	1972-73	1981-82
Lamby, Dick	St.L.	3	22	0	5	5	22	....	....	....	....	....	....	1978-79	1980-81
• Lamirande, Jean-Paul	NYR, Mtl.	4	49	5	5	10	26	8	0	0	0	4	....	1946-47	1954-55
Lammens, Hank	Ott.	1	27	1	2	3	22	....	....	....	....	....	....	1993-94	1993-94
• Lamoureux, Leo	Mtl.	6	235	19	79	98	175	28	1	6	7	16	2	1941-42	1946-47
Lamoureux, Mitch	Pit., Phi.	3	73	11	9	20	59	....	....	....	....	....	....	1983-84	1987-88
Lampman, Mike	St.L., Van., Wsh.	4	96	17	20	37	34	....	....	....	....	....	....	1972-73	1976-77
Lancien, Jack	NYR	4	63	1	5	6	35	6	0	1	1	2	....	1946-47	1950-51
Landon, Larry	Mtl., Tor.	2	9	0	0	0	2	....	....	....	....	....	....	1983-84	1984-85
Lane, Gord	Wsh., NYI	10	539	19	94	113	1228	75	3	14	17	214	4	1975-76	1984-85
• Lane, Myles	NYR, Bos.	3	71	4	1	5	41	11	0	0	0	0	1	1928-29	1933-34
Langdon, Steve	Bos.	3	7	0	1	1	2	4	0	0	0	0	....	1974-75	1977-78
Langelle, Pete	Tor.	4	136	22	51	73	11	41	5	9	14	4	1	1938-39	1941-42
Langevin, Chris	Buf.	2	22	3	1	4	22	....	....	....	....	....	....	1983-84	1985-86
Langevin, Dave	NYI, Min., L.A.	8	513	12	107	119	530	87	2	17	19	106	4	1979-80	1986-87
Langlais, Alain	Min.	2	25	4	4	8	10	....	....	....	....	....	....	1973-74	1974-75
Langlois, Albert	Mtl., NYR, Det., Bos.	9	497	21	91	112	488	53	1	5	6	50	3	1957-58	1965-66
• Langlois, Charlie	Ham., NYA, Pit., Mtl.	4	151	22	5	27	189	2	0	0	0	0	....	1924-25	1927-28
Langway, Rod	Mtl., Wsh.	15	994	51	278	329	849	104	5	22	27	97	1	1978-79	1992-93
Lank, Jeff	Phi.	1	2	0	0	0	2	....	....	....	....	....	....	1999-00	1999-00
Lanthier, Jean-Marc	Van.	4	105	16	16	32	29	....	....	....	....	....	....	1983-84	1987-88
Lanyon, Ted	Pit.	1	5	0	0	0	4	....	....	....	....	....	....	1967-68	1967-68
Lanz, Rick	Van., Tor., Chi.	10	569	65	221	286	448	28	3	8	11	35	....	1980-81	1991-92
Laperriere, Daniel	St.L., Ott.	4	48	2	5	7	27	....	....	....	....	....	....	1992-93	1995-96
Laperriere, Jacques	Mtl.	12	691	40	242	282	674	88	9	22	31	101	6	1962-63	1973-74
‡ Laplante, Darryl	Det.	3	35	0	6	6	10	....	....	....	....	....	....	1997-98	1999-00
Lapointe, Guy	Mtl., St.L., Bos.	16	884	171	451	622	893	123	26	44	70	138	6	1968-69	1983-84
• Lapointe, Rick	Det., Phi., St.L., Que., L.A.	11	664	44	176	220	831	46	2	7	9	64	....	1975-76	1985-86
Lappin, Peter	Min., S.J.	2	7	0	0	0	2	....	....	....	....	....	....	1989-90	1991-92
Laprade, Edgar	NYR	10	500	108	172	280	42	18	4	9	13	4	....	1945-46	1954-55
LaPrairie, Benjamin	Chi.	1	7	0	0	0	0	....	....	....	....	....	....	1936-37	1936-37
Lariviere, Garry	Que., Edm.	4	219	6	57	63	167	14	0	5	5	8	....	1979-80	1982-83
Larmer, Jeff	Col., N.J., Chi.	5	158	37	51	88	57	5	1	0	1	2	....	1981-82	1985-86
Larmer, Steve	Chi., NYR	15	1006	441	571	1012	532	140	56	75	131	89	1	1980-81	1994-95
• Larochelle, Wildor	Mtl., Chi.	12	474	92	74	166	211	34	6	4	10	24	2	1925-26	1936-37
Larocque, Denis	L.A.	1	8	0	1	1	18	....	....	....	....	....	....	1987-88	1987-88
‡ Larocque, Mario	T.B.	1	5	0	0	0	16	....	....	....	....	....	....	1998-99	1998-99
• Larose, Bonner	Bos.	1	6	0	0	0	0	....	....	....	....	....	....	1925-26	1925-26
Larose, Claude	Mtl., Min., St.L.	16	943	226	257	483	887	97	14	18	32	143	5	1962-63	1977-78
Larose, Claude	NYR	2	25	4	7	11	2	2	0	0	0	0	....	1979-80	1981-82
‡ Larose, Guy	Wpg., Tor., Cgy., Bos.	6	70	10	9	19	63	4	0	0	0	0	....	1988-89	1994-95
Larouche, Pierre	Pit., Mtl., Hfd., NYR	14	812	395	427	822	237	64	20	34	54	16	2	1974-75	1987-88
‡ Larouche, Steve	Ott., NYR, L.A.	2	26	9	9	18	10	....	....	....	....	....	....	1994-95	1995-96
• Larson, Norm	NYA, Bro., NYR	3	89	25	18	43	12	....	....	....	....	....	....	1940-41	1946-47
Larson, Reed	Det., Bos., Edm., NYI, Min., Buf.	14	904	222	463	685	1391	32	4	7	11	63	....	1976-77	1989-90
Larter, Tyler	Wsh.	1	1	0	0	0	0	....	....	....	....	....	....	1989-90	1989-90
Latal, Jiri	Phi.	3	92	12	36	48	24	....	....	....	....	....	....	1989-90	1991-92
Latos, James	NYR	1	1	0	0	0	0	....	....	....	....	....	....	1988-89	1988-89
Latreille, Phil	NYR	1	4	0	0	0	2	....	....	....	....	....	....	1960-61	1960-61
Latta, David	Que.	4	36	4	8	12	4	....	....	....	....	....	....	1985-86	1990-91
Lauder, Martin	Bos.	1	3	0	0	0	2	....	....	....	....	....	....	1927-28	1927-28
Lauen, Mike	Wpg.	1	4	0	1	1	0	....	....	....	....	....	....	1983-84	1983-84
‡ Lauer, Brad	NYI, Chi., Ott., Pit.	9	323	44	67	111	218	34	7	5	12	24	....	1986-87	1995-96
Laughlin, Craig	Mtl., Wsh., L.A., Tor.	8	549	136	205	341	364	33	6	6	12	20	....	1981-82	1988-89
Laughton, Mike	Oak., Cal.	4	189	39	48	87	101	11	2	4	6	0	....	1967-68	1970-71
Laurence, Don	Atl., St.L.	2	79	15	22	37	14	....	....	....	....	....	....	1978-79	1979-80
LaVallee, Kevin	Cgy., L.A., St.L., Pit.	7	366	110	125	235	85	32	5	8	13	21	....	1980-81	1986-87
LaVarre, Mark	Chi.	3	78	9	16	25	58	1	0	0	0	2	....	1985-86	1987-88
Lavender, Brian	St.L., NYI, Det., Cal.	4	184	16	26	42	174	3	0	0	0	2	....	1971-72	1974-75
‡ Lavigne, Eric	L.A.	1	1	0	0	0	0	....	....	....	....	....	....	1994-95	1994-95
• Laviolette, Jack	Mtl.	1	18	2	1	3	6	2	0	0	0	0	....	1917-18	1917-18
Laviolette, Peter	NYR	1	12	0	0	0	6	....	....	....	....	....	....	1988-89	1988-89
‡ Lavoie, Dominic	St.L., Ott., Bos., L.A.	6	38	5	8	13	32	....	....	....	....	....	....	1988-89	1993-94
Lawless, Paul	Hfd., Phi., Van., Tor.	7	239	49	77	126	54	3	0	2	2	2	....	1982-83	1989-90
‡ Lawrence, Mark	Dal., NYI	6	142	18	26	44	115	....	....	....	....	....	....	1994-95	2000-01
Lawson, Danny	Det., Min., Buf.	5	219	28	29	57	61	16	0	1	1	2	....	1967-68	1971-72
Lawton, Brian	Min., NYR, Hfd., Que., Bos., S.J.	9	483	112	154	266	401	11	1	1	2	12	....	1983-84	1992-93
Laxdal, Derek	Tor., NYI	6	67	12	7	19	88	1	0	2	2	2	....	1984-85	1990-91
• Laycoe, Hal	NYR, Mtl., Bos.	11	531	25	77	102	292	40	2	5	7	39	....	1945-46	1955-56
‡ Lazaro, Jeff	Bos., Ott.	3	102	14	23	37	114	28	3	3	6	32	....	1990-91	1992-93
Leach, Jamie	Pit., Hfd., Fla.	5	81	11	9	20	12	....	....	....	....	....	1	1989-90	1993-94
Leach, Larry	Bos.	3	126	13	29	42	91	7	1	1	2	8	....	1958-59	1961-62
Leach, Reggie	Bos., Cal., Phi., Det.	13	934	381	285	666	387	94	47	22	69	22	1	1970-71	1982-83
Leach, Stephen	Wsh., Bos., St.L., Car., Ott., Phx., Pit.	15	702	130	153	283	978	92	15	11	26	87	....	1985-86	1999-00
Leavins, Jim	Det., NYR	2	41	2	12	14	30	....	....	....	....	....	....	1985-86	1986-87
‡ Lebeau, Patrick	Mtl., Cgy., Fla., Pit.	4	15	3	2	5	6	....	....	....	....	....	....	1990-91	1998-99
Lebeau, Stephan	Mtl., Ana.	7	373	118	159	277	105	30	9	7	16	12	1	1988-89	1994-95

	Name	NHL Teams	NHL Seasons	Regular Schedule GP	G	A	TP	PIM	Playoffs GP	G	A	TP	PIM	NHL Cup Wins	First NHL Season	Last NHL Season
	LeBlanc, Fern	Det.	3	34	5	6	11	0	....	....	....	....	....	....	1976-77	1978-79
	LeBlanc, J.P.	Chi., Det.	5	153	14	30	44	87	2	0	0	0	0	....	1968-69	1978-79
	LeBlanc, John	Van., Edm., Wpg.	7	83	26	13	39	28	1	0	0	0	0	....	1986-87	1994-95
‡	LeBoutillier, Peter	Ana.	2	35	2	1	3	176	....	....	....	....	....	....	1996-97	1997-98
	LeBrun, Al	NYR	2	6	0	2	2	4	....	....	....	....	....	....	1960-61	1965-66
	Lecaine, Bill	Pit.	1	4	0	0	0	0	....	....	....	....	....	....	1968-69	1968-69
	Leclair, Jack	Mtl.	3	160	20	40	60	56	20	6	1	7	6	2	1954-55	1956-57
	Leclerc, Rene	Det.	2	87	10	11	21	105	....	....	....	....	....	....	1968-69	1970-71
	Lecuyer, Doug	Chi., Wpg., Pit.	4	126	11	31	42	178	7	4	0	4	15	....	1978-79	1982-83
	Ledingham, Walt	Chi., NYI	3	15	0	2	2	4	....	....	....	....	....	....	1972-73	1976-77
•	Leduc, Albert	Mtl., Ott., NYR	10	383	57	35	92	614	28	5	6	11	32	2	1925-26	1934-35
	LeDuc, Rich	Bos., Que.	4	130	28	38	66	69	5	0	0	0	9	....	1972-73	1980-81
‡	Ledyard, Grant	NYR, L.A., Wsh., Buf., Dal., Van., Bos., Ott., T.B.	18	1028	90	276	366	766	83	6	12	18	96	....	1984-85	2001-02
•	Lee, Bobby	Mtl.	1	1	0	0	0	0	....	....	....	....	....	....	1942-43	1942-43
	Lee, Edward	Que.	1	2	0	0	0	5	....	....	....	....	....	....	1984-85	1984-85
	Lee, Peter	Pit.	6	431	114	131	245	257	19	0	8	8	4	....	1977-78	1982-83
‡	Leeb, Greg	Dal.	1	2	0	0	0	0	....	....	....	....	....	....	2000-01	2000-01
	Leeman, Gary	Tor., Cgy., Mtl., Van., St.L.	14	667	199	267	466	531	36	8	16	24	36	1	1982-83	1996-97
‡	Lefebvre, Patrice	Wsh.	1	3	0	0	0	2	....	....	....	....	....	....	1998-99	1998-99
•	Lefley, Bryan	NYI, K.C., Col.	5	228	7	29	36	101	2	0	0	0	0	....	1972-73	1977-78
	Lefley, Chuck	Mtl., St.L.	9	407	128	164	292	137	29	5	8	13	10	2	1970-71	1980-81
•	Leger, Roger	NYR, Mtl.	5	187	18	53	71	71	20	0	7	7	14	....	1943-44	1949-50
	Legge, Barry	Que., Wpg.	3	107	1	11	12	144	....	....	....	....	....	....	1979-80	1981-82
	Legge, Randy	NYR	1	12	0	2	2	2	....	....	....	....	....	....	1972-73	1972-73
	Lehman, Tommy	Bos., Edm.	3	36	5	5	10	16	....	....	....	....	....	....	1987-88	1989-90
	Lehto, Petteri	Pit.	1	6	0	0	0	4	....	....	....	....	....	....	1984-85	1984-85
	Lehtonen, Antero	Wsh.	1	65	9	12	21	14	....	....	....	....	....	....	1979-80	1979-80
	Lehvonen, Henri	K.C.	1	4	0	0	0	0	....	....	....	....	....	....	1974-75	1974-75
	Leier, Edward	Chi.	2	16	2	1	3	2	....	....	....	....	....	....	1949-50	1950-51
	Leinonen, Mikko	NYR, Wsh.	4	162	31	78	109	71	20	2	11	13	28	....	1981-82	1984-85
	Leiter, Bobby	Bos., Pit., Atl.	10	447	98	126	224	144	8	3	0	3	2	....	1962-63	1975-76
	Leiter, Ken	NYI, Min.	5	143	14	36	50	62	15	0	6	6	8	....	1984-85	1989-90
	Lemaire, Jacques	Mtl.	12	853	366	469	835	217	145	61	78	139	63	8	1967-68	1978-79
	Lemay, Moe	Van., Edm., Bos., Wpg.	8	317	72	94	166	442	28	6	3	9	55	1	1981-82	1988-89
	Lemelin, Roger	K.C., Col.	4	36	1	2	3	27	....	....	....	....	....	....	1974-75	1977-78
	Lemieux, Alain	St.L., Que., Pit.	6	119	28	44	72	38	19	4	6	10	0	....	1981-82	1986-87
	Lemieux, Bob	Oak.	1	19	0	1	1	12	....	....	....	....	....	....	1967-68	1967-68
	Lemieux, Jacques	L.A.	3	19	0	4	4	8	1	0	0	0	0	....	1967-68	1969-70
	Lemieux, Jean	Atl., Wsh.	5	204	23	63	86	39	3	1	1	2	0	....	1973-74	1977-78
	Lemieux, Jocelyn	St.L., Mtl., Chi., Hfd., N.J., Cgy., Phx.	12	598	80	84	164	740	60	5	10	15	88	....	1986-87	1997-98
•	Lemieux, Real	Det., L.A., NYR, Buf.	8	456	51	104	155	262	18	2	4	6	10	....	1966-67	1973-74
	Lemieux, Rich	Van., K.C., Atl.	5	274	39	82	121	132	2	0	0	0	0	....	1971-72	1975-76
	Lenardon, Tim	N.J., Van.	2	15	2	1	3	4	....	....	....	....	....	....	1986-87	1989-90
•	Lepine, Hec	Mtl.	1	33	5	2	7	2	....	....	....	....	....	....	1925-26	1925-26
•	Lepine, Pit	Mtl.	13	526	143	98	241	392	41	7	5	12	26	2	1925-26	1937-38
	Leroux, Gaston	Mtl.	1	2	0	0	0	0	....	....	....	....	....	....	1935-36	1935-36
‡	Leroux, Jean-Yves	Chi.	5	220	16	22	38	146	....	....	....	....	....	....	1996-97	2000-01
	Lesieur, Art	Mtl., Chi.	4	100	4	2	6	50	14	0	0	0	4	1	1928-29	1935-36
	Lessard, Rick	Cgy., S.J.	3	15	0	4	4	18	....	....	....	....	....	....	1988-89	1991-92
	Lesuk, Bill	Bos., Phi., L.A., Wsh., Wpg.	8	388	44	63	107	368	9	1	0	1	12	1	1968-69	1979-80
•	Leswick, Jack	Chi.	1	37	1	7	8	16	....	....	....	....	....	1	1933-34	1933-34
	Leswick, Pete	NYA, Bos.	2	3	1	0	1	0	....	....	....	....	....	....	1936-37	1944-45
•	Leswick, Tony	NYR, Det., Chi.	12	740	165	159	324	900	59	13	10	23	91	3	1945-46	1957-58
	Levandoski, Joe	NYR	1	8	1	1	2	0	....	....	....	....	....	....	1946-47	1946-47
	Leveille, Normand	Bos.	2	75	17	25	42	49	....	....	....	....	....	....	1981-82	1982-83
	Leveque, Guy	L.A.	2	17	2	2	4	21	....	....	....	....	....	....	1992-93	1993-94
	Lever, Don	Van., Atl., Cgy., Col., N.J., Buf.	15	1020	313	367	680	593	30	7	10	17	26	....	1972-73	1986-87
	Levie, Craig	Wpg., Min., St.L., Van.	6	183	22	53	75	177	16	2	3	5	32	....	1981-82	1986-87
‡	Levins, Scott	Wpg., Fla., Ott., Phx.	5	124	13	20	33	316	....	....	....	....	....	....	1992-93	1997-98
•	Levinsky, Alex	Tor., NYR, Chi.	9	367	19	49	68	307	37	2	1	3	26	2	1930-31	1938-39
	Levo, Tapio	Col., N.J.	2	107	16	53	69	36	....	....	....	....	....	....	1981-82	1982-83
	Lewicki, Danny	Tor., NYR, Chi.	9	461	105	135	240	177	28	0	4	4	8	1	1950-51	1958-59
	Lewis, Dale	NYR	1	8	0	0	0	0	....	....	....	....	....	....	1975-76	1975-76
	Lewis, Dave	NYI, L.A., N.J., Det.	15	1008	36	187	223	953	91	1	20	21	143	....	1973-74	1987-88
•	Lewis, Doug	Mtl.	1	3	0	0	0	0	....	....	....	....	....	....	1946-47	1946-47
•	Lewis, Herbie	Det.	11	483	148	161	309	248	38	13	10	23	6	2	1928-29	1938-39
	Ley, Rick	Tor., Hfd.	6	310	12	72	84	528	14	0	2	2	20	....	1968-69	1980-81
	Liba, Igor	NYR, L.A.	1	37	7	18	25	36	2	0	0	0	2	....	1988-89	1988-89
	Libby, Jeff	NYI	1	1	0	0	0	0	....	....	....	....	....	....	1997-98	1997-98
	Libett, Nick	Det., Pit.	14	982	237	268	505	472	16	6	2	8	2	....	1967-68	1980-81
	Licari, Tony	Det.	1	9	0	1	1	0	....	....	....	....	....	....	1946-47	1946-47
	Liddington, Bob	Tor.	1	11	0	1	1	2	....	....	....	....	....	....	1970-71	1970-71
	Lidster, Doug	Van., NYR, St.L., Dal.	16	897	75	268	343	679	80	6	15	21	64	1	1983-84	1998-99
‡	Lilley, John	Ana.	3	23	3	8	11	13	....	....	....	....	....	....	1993-94	1995-96
‡	Lind, Juha	Dal., Mtl.	3	133	9	13	22	20	15	2	2	4	8	....	1997-98	2000-01
‡	Lindberg, Chris	Cgy., Que.	3	116	17	25	42	47	2	0	1	1	2	....	1991-92	1993-94
	Lindbom, Johan	NYR	1	38	1	3	4	28	....	....	....	....	....	....	1997-98	1997-98
	Linden, Jamie	Fla.	1	4	0	0	0	17	....	....	....	....	....	....	1994-95	1994-95
	Lindgren, Lars	Van., Min.	6	394	25	113	138	325	40	5	6	11	20	....	1978-79	1983-84
	Lindholm, Mikael	L.A.	1	18	2	2	4	2	....	....	....	....	....	....	1989-90	1989-90
‡	Lindquist, Fredrik	Edm.	1	8	0	0	0	2	....	....	....	....	....	....	1998-99	1998-99
	Lindros, Brett	NYI	2	51	2	5	7	147	....	....	....	....	....	....	1994-95	1995-96
	Lindsay, Ted	Det., Chi.	17	1068	379	472	851	1808	133	47	49	96	194	4	1944-45	1964-65
	Lindstrom, Willy	Wpg., Edm., Pit.	8	582	161	162	323	200	57	14	18	32	24	2	1979-80	1986-87
	Linseman, Ken	Phi., Edm., Bos., Tor.	14	860	256	551	807	1727	113	43	77	120	325	1	1978-79	1991-92
‡	Lipuma, Chris	T.B., S.J.	5	72	0	9	9	146	....	....	....	....	....	....	1992-93	1996-97
	Liscombe, Carl	Det.	9	373	137	140	277	117	59	22	19	41	20	1	1937-38	1945-46
	Litzenberger, Ed	Mtl., Chi., Det., Tor.	12	618	178	238	416	283	40	5	13	18	34	4	1952-53	1963-64
‡	Loach, Lonnie	Ott., L.A., Ana.	2	56	10	13	23	29	1	0	0	0	0	....	1992-93	1993-94
•	Locas, Jacques	Mtl.	2	59	7	8	15	66	....	....	....	....	....	....	1947-48	1948-49
	Lochead, Bill	Det., Col., NYR	6	330	69	62	131	180	7	3	0	3	6	....	1974-75	1979-80
•	Locking, Norm	Chi.	2	48	2	6	8	26	....	....	....	....	....	....	1934-35	1935-36
	Loewen, Darcy	Buf., Ott.	5	135	4	8	12	211	....	....	....	....	....	....	1989-90	1993-94
	Lofthouse, Mark	Wsh., Det.	6	181	42	38	80	73	....	....	....	....	....	....	1977-78	1982-83
	Logan, Dave	Chi., Van.	6	218	5	29	34	470	12	0	0	0	10	....	1975-76	1980-81
	Logan, Robert	Buf., L.A.	3	42	10	5	15	0	....	....	....	....	....	....	1986-87	1988-89
	Loiselle, Claude	Det., N.J., Que., Tor., NYI	13	616	92	117	209	1149	41	4	11	15	58	....	1981-82	1993-94
	Lomakin, Andrei	Phi., Fla.	4	215	42	62	104	92	....	....	....	....	....	....	1991-92	1994-95
‡	Loney, Brian	Van.	1	12	2	3	5	6	....	....	....	....	....	....	1995-96	1995-96
	Loney, Troy	Pit., Ana., NYI, NYR	12	624	87	110	197	1091	67	8	14	22	97	2	1983-84	1994-95
	Long, Barry	L.A., Det., Wpg.	5	280	11	68	79	250	5	0	1	1	18	....	1972-73	1981-82
•	Long, Stan	Mtl.	1	....	....	....	....	....	3	0	0	0	0	....	1951-52	1951-52
	Lonsberry, Ross	Bos., L.A., Phi., Pit.	15	968	256	310	566	806	100	21	25	46	87	2	1966-67	1980-81
	Loob, Hakan	Cgy.	6	450	193	236	429	189	73	26	28	54	16	1	1983-84	1988-89
	Loob, Peter	Que.	1	8	1	2	3	0	....	....	....	....	....	....	1984-85	1984-85
	Lorentz, Jim	Bos., St.L., NYR, Buf.	10	659	161	238	399	208	54	12	10	22	30	1	1968-69	1977-78
	Lorimer, Bob	NYI, Col., N.J.	10	529	22	90	112	431	49	3	10	13	83	2	1976-77	1985-86
•	Lorrain, Rod	Mtl.	6	179	28	39	67	30	11	0	3	3	0	....	1935-36	1941-42
•	Loughlin, Clem	Det., Chi.	3	101	8	6	14	77	....	....	....	....	....	....	1926-27	1928-29
•	Loughlin, Wilf	Tor.	1	14	0	0	0	2	....	....	....	....	....	....	1923-24	1923-24
	Lovsin, Ken	Wsh.	1	1	0	0	0	0	....	....	....	....	....	....	1990-91	1990-91
	Lowdermilk, Dwayne	Wsh.	1	2	0	1	1	2	....	....	....	....	....	....	1980-81	1980-81
	Lowe, Darren	Pit.	1	8	1	2	3	0	....	....	....	....	....	....	1983-84	1983-84
	Lowe, Kevin	Edm., NYR	19	1254	84	347	431	1498	214	10	48	58	192	6	1979-80	1997-98
	Lowe, Odie	NYR	1	4	1	1	2	0	....	....	....	....	....	....	1949-50	1949-50
•	Lowe, Ross	Bos., Mtl.	3	77	6	8	14	82	2	0	0	0	0	....	1949-50	1951-52
•	Lowrey, Ed	Ott., Ham.	3	27	2	2	4	6	....	....	....	....	....	....	1917-18	1920-21
•	Lowrey, Fred	Mtl.M., Pit.	2	53	1	1	2	10	2	0	0	0	....	....	1924-25	1925-26
•	Lowrey, Gerry	Tor., Pit., Phi., Chi., Ott.	6	211	48	48	96	148	2	1	0	1	2	....	1927-28	1932-33
	Lucas, Danny	Phi.	1	6	1	0	1	0	....	....	....	....	....	....	1978-79	1978-79
	Lucas, Dave	Det.	1	1	0	0	0	0	....	....	....	....	....	....	1962-63	1962-63
	Luce, Don	NYR, Det., Buf., L.A., Tor.	13	894	225	329	554	364	71	17	22	39	52	....	1969-70	1981-82
‡	Ludvig, Jan	N.J., Buf.	7	314	54	87	141	418	....	....	....	....	....	....	1982-83	1988-89
	Ludwig, Craig	Mtl., NYI, Min., Dal.	17	1256	38	184	222	1437	177	4	25	29	244	2	1982-83	1998-99
	Ludzik, Steve	Chi., Buf.	9	424	46	93	139	333	44	4	8	12	70	....	1981-82	1989-90

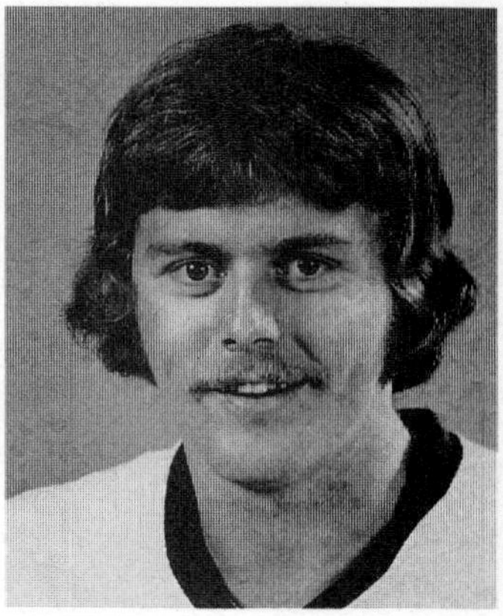

Walt Ledingham

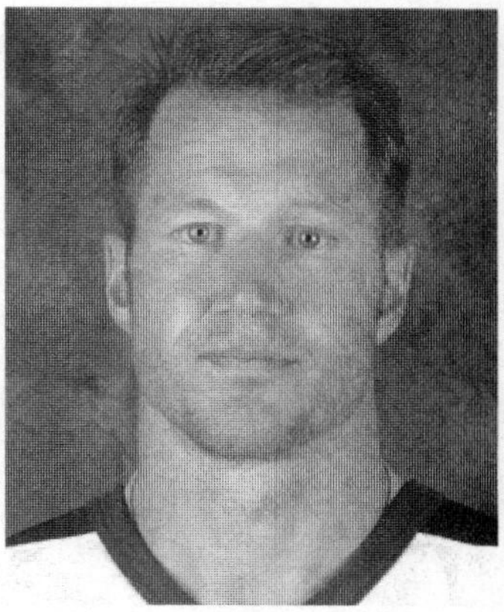

Grant Ledyard

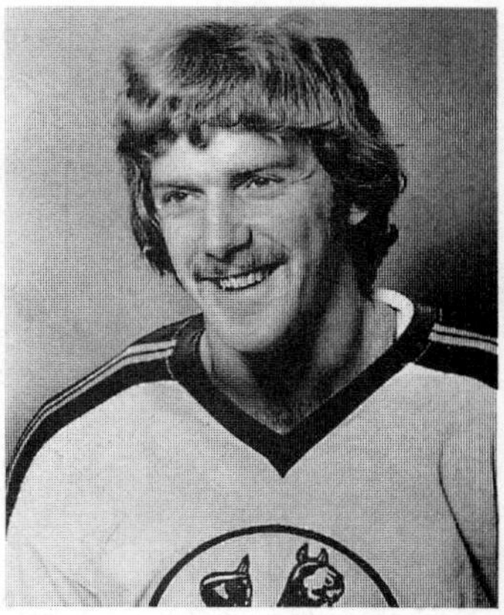

Roger Lemelin

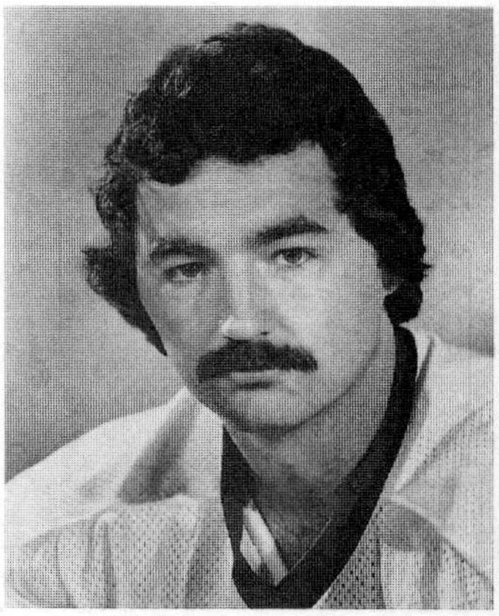

Bob Lorimer

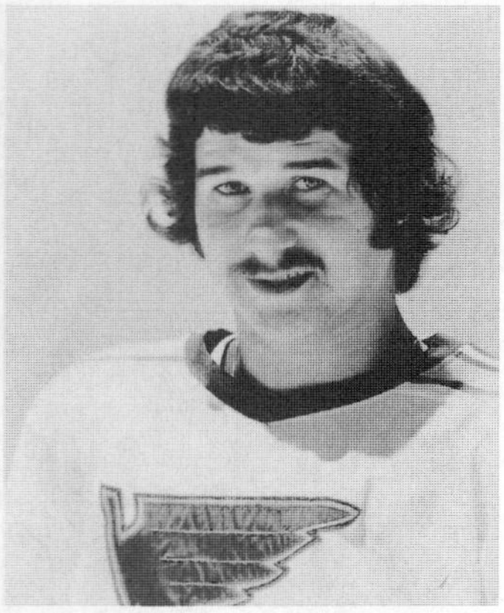

Bernie Lukowich

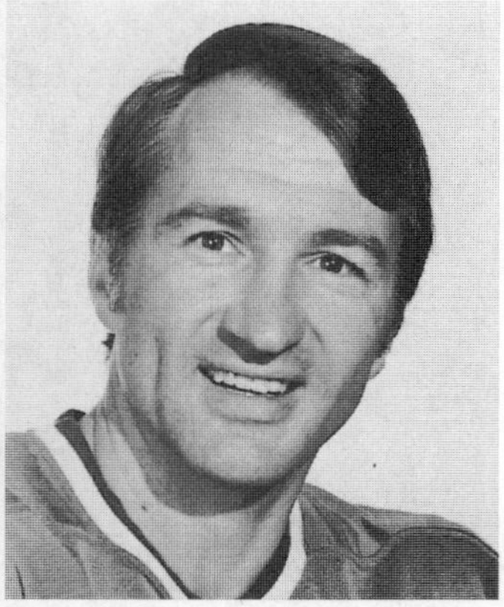

Lowell MacDonald

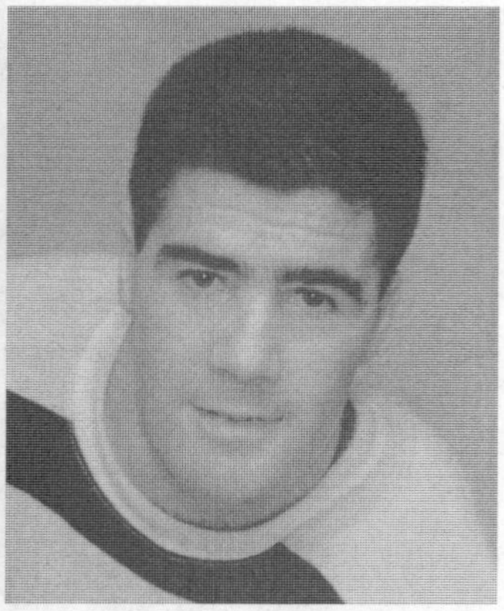

Fleming MacKell

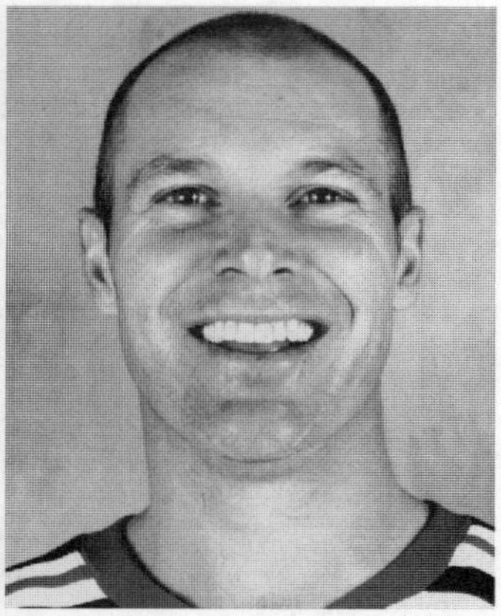

John MacLean

			Regular Schedule					Playoffs					NHL	First	Last
Name	NHL Teams	NHL Seasons	GP	G	A	TP	PIM	GP	G	A	TP	PIM	Cup Wins	NHL Season	NHL Season
Luhning, Warren	NYI, Dal.	3	29	0	1	1	21	....	....	....	....	....	....	1997-98	1999-00
Lukowich, Bernie	Pit., St.L.	2	79	13	15	28	34	2	0	0	0	0	....	1973-74	1974-75
Lukowich, Morris	Wpg., Bos., L.A.	8	582	199	219	418	584	11	0	2	2	24	....	1979-80	1986-87
Luksa, Charlie	Hfd.	1	8	0	1	1	4	....	....	....	....	....	....	1979-80	1979-80
Lumley, Dave	Mtl., Edm., Hfd.	9	437	98	160	258	680	61	6	8	14	131	2	1978-79	1986-87
Lund, Pentti	Bos., NYR	7	259	44	55	99	40	19	7	5	12	0	....	1946-47	1952-53
Lundberg, Brian	Pit.	1	1	0	0	0	2	....	....	....	....	....	....	1982-83	1982-83
Lunde, Len	Det., Chi., Min., Van.	8	321	39	83	122	75	20	3	2	5	2	....	1958-59	1970-71
Lundholm, Bengt	Wpg.	5	275	48	95	143	72	14	3	4	7	14	....	1981-82	1985-86
Lundrigan, Joe	Tor., Wsh.	2	52	2	8	10	22	....	....	....	....	....	....	1972-73	1974-75
Lundstrom, Tord	Det.	1	11	1	1	2	0	....	....	....	....	....	....	1973-74	1973-74
• Lundy, Pat	Det., Chi.	5	150	37	32	69	31	16	2	2	4	2	....	1945-46	1950-51
Luongo, Chris	Det., Ott., NYI	5	218	8	23	31	176	....	....	....	....	....	....	1990-91	1995-96
Lupien, Gilles	Mtl., Pit., Hfd.	5	226	5	25	30	416	25	0	0	0	21	2	1977-78	1981-82
Lupul, Gary	Van.	7	293	70	75	145	243	25	4	7	11	11	....	1979-80	1985-86
Lyle, George	Det., Hfd.	4	99	24	38	62	51	....	....	....	....	....	....	1979-80	1982-83
Lynch, Jack	Pit., Det., Wsh.	7	382	24	106	130	336	....	....	....	....	....	....	1972-73	1978-79
Lynn, Vic	NYR, Det., Mtl., Tor., Bos., Chi.	11	327	49	76	125	274	47	7	10	17	46	3	1942-43	1953-54
Lyon, Steve	Pit.	1	3	0	0	0	2	....	....	....	....	....	....	1976-77	1976-77
Lyons, Ron	Bos., Phi.	1	36	2	4	6	27	5	0	0	0	0	....	1930-31	1930-31
Lysiak, Tom	Atl., Chi.	13	919	292	551	843	567	76	25	38	63	49	....	1973-74	1985-86
M															
MacAdam, Al	Phi., Cal., Cle., Min., Van.	12	864	240	351	591	509	64	20	24	44	21	1	1973-74	1984-85
MacDermid, Paul	Hfd., Wpg., Wsh., Que.	14	690	116	142	258	1303	43	5	11	16	116	....	1981-82	1994-95
MacDonald, Blair	Edm., Van.	4	219	91	100	191	65	11	0	6	6	2	....	1979-80	1982-83
MacDonald, Brett	Van.	1	1	0	0	0	0	....	....	....	....	....	....	1987-88	1987-88
‡ MacDonald, Doug	Buf.	3	11	1	0	1	2	....	....	....	....	....	....	1992-93	1994-95
MacDonald, Kevin	Ott.	1	1	0	0	0	2	....	....	....	....	....	....	1993-94	1993-94
• MacDonald, Kilby	NYR	4	151	36	34	70	47	15	1	2	3	4	1	1939-40	1944-45
MacDonald, Lowell	Det., L.A., Pit.	13	506	180	210	390	92	30	11	11	22	12	....	1961-62	1977-78
MacDonald, Parker	Tor., NYR, Det., Bos., Min.	14	676	144	179	323	253	75	14	14	28	20	....	1952-53	1968-69
MacDougall, Kim	Min.	1	1	0	0	0	0	....	....	....	....	....	....	1974-75	1974-75
MacEachern, Shane	St.L.	1	1	0	0	0	0	....	....	....	....	....	....	1987-88	1987-88
Macey, Hub	NYR, Mtl.	3	30	6	9	15	0	8	0	0	0	0	....	1941-42	1946-47
MacGregor, Bruce	Det., NYR	14	893	213	257	470	217	107	19	28	47	44	....	1960-61	1973-74
MacGregor, Randy	Hfd.	1	2	1	1	2	2	....	....	....	....	....	....	1981-82	1981-82
MacGuigan, Garth	NYI	2	5	0	1	1	2	....	....	....	....	....	....	1979-80	1983-84
MacIntosh, Ian	NYR	1	4	0	0	0	4	....	....	....	....	....	....	1952-53	1952-53
MacIver, Don	Wpg.	1	6	0	0	0	2	....	....	....	....	....	....	1979-80	1979-80
Maciver, Norm	NYR, Hfd., Edm., Ott., Pit., Wpg., Phx.	12	500	55	230	285	350	56	3	11	14	32	....	1986-87	1997-98
MacKasey, Blair	Tor.	1	1	0	0	0	2	....	....	....	....	....	....	1976-77	1976-77
• MacKay, Calum	Det., Mtl.	8	237	50	55	105	214	38	5	13	18	20	1	1946-47	1954-55
MacKay, Dave	Chi.	1	29	3	0	3	26	5	0	1	1	2	....	1940-41	1940-41
• MacKay, Mickey	Chi., Pit., Bos.	4	147	44	19	63	79	11	0	0	0	6	1	1926-27	1929-30
• MacKay, Murdo	Mtl.	4	19	0	3	3	0	15	1	2	3	0	....	1945-46	1948-49
Mackell, Fleming	Tor., Bos.	13	665	149	220	369	562	80	22	41	63	75	2	1947-48	1959-60
• MacKell, Jack	Ott.	2	45	4	2	6	59	2	0	0	0	0	2	1919-20	1920-21
MacKenzie, Barry	Min.	1	6	0	1	1	6	....	....	....	....	....	....	1968-69	1968-69
• MacKenzie, Bill	Chi., Mtl.M., NYR, Mtl.	7	264	15	14	29	145	21	1	1	2	11	1	1932-33	1939-40
Mackey, David	Chi., Min., St.L.	6	126	8	12	20	305	3	0	0	0	2	....	1987-88	1993-94
• Mackey, Reg	NYR	1	34	0	0	0	16	1	0	0	0	0	....	1926-27	1926-27
• Mackie, Howie	Det.	2	20	1	0	1	4	8	0	0	0	0	1	1936-37	1937-38
MacKinnon, Paul	Wsh.	5	147	5	23	28	91	....	....	....	....	....	....	1979-80	1983-84
‡ MacLean, John	N.J., S.J., NYR, Dal.	18	1194	413	429	842	1328	104	35	48	83	152	1	1983-84	2001-02
MacLean, Paul	St.L., Wpg., Det.	11	719	324	349	673	968	53	21	14	35	110	....	1980-81	1990-91
MacLeish, Rick	Phi., Hfd., Pit., Det.	14	846	349	410	759	434	114	54	53	107	38	2	1970-71	1983-84
MacLellan, Brian	L.A., NYR, Min., Cgy., Det.	10	606	172	241	413	551	47	5	9	14	42	1	1982-83	1991-92
MacLeod, Pat	Min., S.J., Dal.	4	53	5	13	18	14	....	....	....	....	....	....	1990-91	1995-96
MacMillan, Billy	Tor., Atl., NYI	7	446	74	77	151	184	53	6	6	12	40	....	1970-71	1976-77
MacMillan, Bob	NYR, St.L., Atl., Cgy., Col., N.J., Chi.	11	753	228	349	577	260	31	8	11	19	16	....	1974-75	1984-85
MacMillan, John	Tor., Det.	5	104	5	10	15	32	12	0	1	1	2	2	1960-61	1964-65
MacNeil, Al	Tor., Mtl., Chi., NYR, Pit.	11	524	17	75	92	617	37	0	4	4	67	....	1955-56	1967-68
MacNeil, Bernie	St.L.	1	4	0	0	0	0	....	....	....	....	....	....	1973-74	1973-74
Macoun, Jamie	Cgy., Tor., Det.	16	1128	76	282	358	1208	159	10	32	42	169	2	1982-83	1998-99
• MacPherson, Bud	Mtl.	7	259	5	33	38	233	29	0	3	3	21	1	1948-49	1956-57
• MacSweyn, Ralph	Phi.	5	47	0	5	5	10	8	0	0	0	6	....	1967-68	1971-72
MacTavish, Craig	Bos., Edm., NYR, Phi., St.L.	17	1093	213	267	480	891	193	20	38	58	218	4	1979-80	1996-97
MacWilliam, Mike	NYI	1	6	0	0	0	14	....	....	....	....	....	....	1995-96	1995-96
Madigan, Connie	St.L.	1	20	0	3	3	25	5	0	0	0	4	....	1972-73	1972-73
Madill, Jeff	N.J.	1	14	4	0	4	46	7	0	2	2	8	....	1990-91	1990-91
Magee, Dean	Min.	1	7	0	0	0	4	....	....	....	....	....	....	1977-78	1977-78
Maggs, Daryl	Chi., Cal., Tor.	3	135	14	19	33	54	4	0	0	0	0	....	1971-72	1979-80
Magnan, Marc	Tor.	1	4	0	1	1	5	....	....	....	....	....	....	1982-83	1982-83
Magnuson, Keith	Chi.	11	589	14	125	139	1442	68	3	9	12	164	....	1969-70	1979-80
Maguire, Kevin	Tor., Buf., Phi.	6	260	29	30	59	782	11	0	0	0	86	....	1986-87	1991-92
Mahaffy, John	Mtl., NYR	3	37	11	25	36	4	1	0	1	1	0	....	1942-43	1944-45
Mahovlich, Frank	Tor., Det., Mtl.	18	1181	533	570	1103	1056	137	51	67	118	163	6	1956-57	1973-74
Mahovlich, Pete	Det., Mtl., Pit.	16	884	288	485	773	916	88	30	42	72	134	4	1965-66	1980-81
Mailhot, Jacques	Que.	1	5	0	0	0	33	....	....	....	....	....	....	1988-89	1988-89
Mailley, Frank	Mtl.	1	1	0	0	0	0	....	....	....	....	....	....	1942-43	1942-43
Mair, Jim	Phi., NYI, Van.	5	76	4	15	19	49	3	1	2	3	4	....	1970-71	1974-75
• Majeau, Fern	Mtl.	2	56	22	24	46	43	1	0	0	0	0	1	1943-44	1944-45
Major, Bruce	Que.	1	4	0	0	0	0	....	....	....	....	....	....	1990-91	1990-91
‡ Major, Mark	Det.	1	2	0	0	0	5	....	....	....	....	....	....	1996-97	1996-97
Makarov, Sergei	Cgy., S.J., Dal.	7	424	134	250	384	317	34	12	11	23	8	....	1989-90	1996-97
Makela, Mikko	NYI, L.A., Buf., Bos.	7	423	118	147	265	139	18	3	8	11	14	....	1985-86	1994-95
Maki, Chico	Chi.	15	841	143	292	435	345	113	17	36	53	43	1	1960-61	1975-76
• Maki, Wayne	Chi., St.L., Van.	6	246	57	79	136	184	2	1	0	1	2	....	1967-68	1972-73
Makkonen, Kari	Edm.	1	9	2	2	4	0	....	....	....	....	....	....	1979-80	1979-80
Maley, David	Mtl., N.J., Edm., S.J., NYI	9	466	43	81	124	1043	46	5	5	10	111	1	1985-86	1993-94
‡ Malgunas, Stewart	Phi., Wpg., Wsh., Cgy.	7	129	1	5	6	144	....	....	....	....	....	....	1993-94	1999-00
Malinowski, Merlin	Col., N.J., Hfd.	5	282	54	111	165	121	....	....	....	....	....	....	1978-79	1982-83
Malkoc, Dean	Van., Bos., NYI	4	116	1	3	4	299	....	....	....	....	....	....	1995-96	1998-99
Mallette, Troy	NYR, Edm., N.J., Ott., Bos., T.B.	9	456	51	68	119	1226	15	2	2	4	99	....	1989-90	1997-98
Malone, Cliff	Mtl.	1	3	0	0	0	0	....	....	....	....	....	....	1951-52	1951-52
Malone, Greg	Pit., Hfd., Que.	11	704	191	310	501	661	20	3	5	8	32	....	1976-77	1986-87
• Malone, Joe	Mtl., Que., Ham.	7	126	143	32	175	57	9	6	0	6	3	1	1917-18	1923-24
Maloney, Dan	Chi., L.A., Det., Tor.	11	737	192	259	451	1489	40	4	7	11	35	....	1970-71	1981-82
Maloney, Dave	NYR, Buf.	11	657	71	246	317	1154	49	7	17	24	91	....	1974-75	1984-85
Maloney, Don	NYR, Hfd., NYI	13	765	214	350	564	815	94	22	35	57	101	....	1978-79	1990-91
Maloney, Phil	Bos., Tor., Chi.	5	158	28	43	71	16	6	0	0	0	0	....	1949-50	1959-60
Maluta, Ray	Bos.	2	25	2	3	5	6	2	0	0	0	0	....	1975-76	1976-77
Manastersky, Tom	Mtl.	1	6	0	0	0	11	....	....	....	....	....	....	1950-51	1950-51
Mancuso, Gus	Mtl., NYR	4	42	7	9	16	17	....	....	....	....	....	....	1937-38	1942-43
Mandich, Dan	Min.	4	111	5	11	16	303	7	0	0	0	2	....	1982-83	1985-86
‡ Maneluk, Mike	Phi., Chi., NYR, CBJ	3	85	11	10	21	57	....	....	....	....	....	....	1998-99	2000-01
Manery, Kris	Cle., Min., Van., Wpg.	4	250	63	64	127	91	....	....	....	....	....	....	1977-78	1980-81
Manery, Randy	Det., Atl., L.A.	10	582	50	206	256	415	13	0	2	2	12	....	1970-71	1979-80
Mann, Jack	NYR	2	9	3	4	7	0	....	....	....	....	....	....	1943-44	1944-45
Mann, Jimmy	Wpg., Que., Pit.	8	293	10	20	30	895	22	0	0	0	89	....	1979-80	1987-88
Mann, Ken	Det.	1	1	0	0	0	0	....	....	....	....	....	....	1975-76	1975-76
• Mann, Norm	Tor.	3	31	0	3	3	4	2	0	0	0	0	....	1935-36	1940-41
• Manners, Rennison	Pit., Phi.	2	37	3	2	5	14	....	....	....	....	....	....	1929-30	1930-31
Manno, Bob	Van., Tor., Det.	8	371	41	131	172	274	17	2	4	6	12	....	1976-77	1984-85
Manson, Dave	Chi., Edm., Wpg., Phx., Mtl., Dal., Tor.	16	1103	102	288	390	2792	112	7	24	31	343	....	1986-87	2001-02
Manson, Ray	Bos., NYR	2	2	0	1	1	0	....	....	....	....	....	....	1947-48	1948-49
• Mantha, Georges	Mtl.	13	488	89	102	191	148	36	6	2	8	24	2	1928-29	1940-41
Mantha, Moe	Wpg., Pit., Edm., Min., Phi.	12	656	81	289	370	501	17	5	10	15	18	....	1980-81	1991-92
• Mantha, Sylvio	Mtl., Bos.	14	542	63	78	141	671	39	5	5	10	64	3	1923-24	1936-37
• Maracle, Bud	NYR	1	11	1	3	4	4	4	0	0	0	0	....	1930-31	1930-31
Marcetta, Milan	Tor., Min.	3	54	7	15	22	10	17	7	7	14	4	1	1966-67	1968-69
• March, Mush	Chi.	17	759	153	230	383	540	45	12	15	27	41	2	1928-29	1944-45
Marchinko, Brian	Tor., NYI	4	47	2	6	8	0	....	....	....	....	....	....	1970-71	1973-74
Marcinyshyn, Dave	N.J., Que., NYR	3	16	0	1	1	49	....	....	....	....	....	....	1990-91	1992-93

			Regular Schedule					Playoffs					NHL	First	Last
Name	NHL Teams	NHL Seasons	GP	G	A	TP	PIM	GP	G	A	TP	PIM	Cup Wins	NHL Season	NHL Season
Marcon, Lou	Det.	3	60	0	4	4	42	....	....	....	....	....	....	1958-59	1962-63
Marcotte, Don	Bos.	15	868	230	254	484	317	132	34	27	61	81	2	1965-66	1981-82
Marini, Hector	NYI, N.J.	5	154	27	46	73	246	10	3	6	9	14	2	1978-79	1983-84
‡ Marinucci, Chris	NYI, L.A.	2	13	1	4	5	2	....	....	....	....	....	....	1994-95	1996-97
● Mario, Frank	Bos.	2	53	9	19	28	24	....	....	....	....	....	....	1941-42	1944-45
● Mariucci, John	Chi.	5	223	11	34	45	308	12	0	3	3	26	....	1940-41	1947-48
Mark, Gordon	N.J., Edm.	4	85	3	10	13	187	....	....	....	....	....	....	1986-87	1994-95
Markell, John	Wpg., St.L., Min.	4	55	11	10	21	36	....	....	....	....	....	....	1979-80	1984-85
● Marker, Gus	Det., Mtl.M., Tor., Bro.	10	322	64	69	133	133	46	5	7	12	36	1	1932-33	1941-42
Markham, Ray	NYR	1	14	1	1	2	21	7	1	0	1	24	....	1979-80	1979-80
● Markle, Jack	Tor.	1	8	0	1	1	0	....	....	....	....	....	....	1935-36	1935-36
● Marks, Jack	Mtl.W., Tor., Que.	2	7	0	0	0	4	....	....	....	....	....	1	1917-18	1919-20
Marks, John	Chi.	10	657	112	163	275	330	57	5	9	14	60	....	1972-73	1981-82
Markwart, Nevin	Bos., Cgy.	8	309	41	68	109	794	19	1	0	1	33	....	1983-84	1991-92
‡ Marois, Daniel	Tor., NYI, Bos., Dal.	8	350	117	93	210	419	19	3	3	6	28	....	1987-88	1995-96
Marois, Mario	NYR, Van., Que., Wpg., St.L.	15	955	76	357	433	1746	100	4	34	38	182	....	1977-78	1991-92
Marotte, Gilles	Bos., Chi., L.A., NYR, St.L.	12	808	56	265	321	919	29	3	3	6	26	....	1965-66	1976-77
Marquess, Mark	Bos.	1	27	5	4	9	6	4	0	0	0	0	....	1946-47	1946-47
Marsh, Brad	Atl., Cgy., Phi., Tor., Det., Ott.	15	1086	23	175	198	1241	97	6	18	24	124	....	1978-79	1992-93
Marsh, Gary	Det., Tor.	2	7	1	3	4	4	....	....	....	....	....	....	1967-68	1968-69
Marsh, Peter	Wpg., Chi.	5	278	48	71	119	224	26	1	5	6	33	....	1979-80	1983-84
Marshall, Bert	Det., Oak., Cal., NYR, NYI	14	868	17	181	198	926	72	4	22	26	99	....	1965-66	1978-79
Marshall, Don	Mtl., NYR, Buf., Tor.	19	1176	265	324	589	127	94	8	15	23	14	5	1951-52	1971-72
Marshall, Paul	Pit., Tor., Hfd.	4	95	15	18	33	17	1	0	0	0	0	....	1979-80	1982-83
Marshall, Willie	Tor.	4	33	1	5	6	2	....	....	....	....	....	....	1952-53	1958-59
Marson, Mike	Wsh., L.A.	6	196	24	24	48	233	....	....	....	....	....	....	1974-75	1979-80
● Martin, Clare	Bos., Det., Chi., NYR	6	237	12	28	40	78	27	0	2	2	6	1	1941-42	1951-52
‡ Martin, Craig	Wpg., Fla.	2	21	0	1	1	24	....	....	....	....	....	....	1994-95	1996-97
Martin, Frank	Bos., Chi.	6	282	11	46	57	122	10	0	2	2	2	....	1952-53	1957-58
Martin, Grant	Van., Wsh.	4	44	0	4	4	55	1	1	0	1	2	....	1983-84	1986-87
Martin, Jack	Tor.	1	1	0	0	0	0	....	....	....	....	....	....	1960-61	1960-61
Martin, Matt	Tor.	4	76	0	5	5	71	....	....	....	....	....	....	1993-94	1996-97
Martin, Pit	Det., Bos., Chi., Van.	17	1101	324	485	809	609	100	27	31	58	56	....	1961-62	1978-79
Martin, Rick	Buf., L.A.	11	685	384	317	701	477	63	24	29	53	74	....	1971-72	1981-82
● Martin, Ron	NYA	2	94	13	16	29	36	....	....	....	....	....	....	1932-33	1933-34
Martin, Terry	Buf., Que., Tor., Edm., Min.	10	479	104	101	205	202	21	4	2	6	26	....	1975-76	1984-85
Martin, Tom	Tor.	1	3	1	0	1	0	....	....	....	....	....	....	1967-68	1967-68
Martin, Tom	Wpg., Hfd., Min.	6	92	12	11	23	249	4	0	0	0	6	....	1984-85	1989-90
Martineau, Don	Atl., Min., Det.	4	90	6	10	16	63	....	....	....	....	....	....	1973-74	1976-77
‡ Martini, Darcy	Edm.	1	2	0	0	0	0	....	....	....	....	....	....	1993-94	1993-94
Martinson, Steve	Det., Mtl., Min.	4	49	2	1	3	244	1	0	0	0	10	....	1987-88	1991-92
Maruk, Dennis	Cal., Cle., Min., Wsh.	14	888	356	522	878	761	34	14	22	36	26	....	1975-76	1988-89
Masnick, Paul	Mtl., Chi., Tor.	6	232	18	41	59	139	33	4	5	9	27	1	1950-51	1957-58
● Mason, Charley	NYR, NYA, Det., Chi.	4	95	7	18	25	44	4	0	1	1	0	....	1934-35	1938-39
● Massecar, George	NYA	3	100	12	11	23	46	....	....	....	....	....	....	1929-30	1931-32
Masters, Jamie	St.L.	3	33	1	13	14	2	2	0	0	0	0	....	1975-76	1978-79
● Masterton, Bill	Min.	1	38	4	8	12	4	....	....	....	....	....	....	1967-68	1967-68
Mathers, Frank	Tor.	3	23	1	3	4	4	....	....	....	....	....	....	1948-49	1951-52
Mathiasen, Dwight	Pit.	3	33	1	7	8	18	....	....	....	....	....	....	1985-86	1987-88
Mathieson, Jim	Wsh.	1	2	0	0	0	4	....	....	....	....	....	....	1989-90	1989-90
‡ Mathieu, Marquis	Bos.	3	16	0	2	2	14	....	....	....	....	....	....	1998-99	2000-01
● Matte, Joe	Tor., Ham., Bos., Mtl.	4	68	17	15	32	54	....	....	....	....	....	....	1919-20	1925-26
● Matte, Joe	Det., Chi.	2	24	0	3	3	8	....	....	....	....	....	....	1929-30	1942-43
Mattiussi, Dick	Pit., Oak., Cal.	4	200	8	31	39	124	8	0	1	1	6	....	1967-68	1970-71
● Matz, Johnny	Mtl.	1	30	2	3	5	0	1	0	0	0	0	....	1924-25	1924-25
Maxner, Wayne	Bos.	2	62	8	9	17	48	....	....	....	....	....	....	1964-65	1965-66
Maxwell, Brad	Min., Que., Tor., Van., NYR	10	612	98	270	368	1292	79	12	49	61	178	....	1977-78	1986-87
Maxwell, Bryan	Min., St.L., Wpg., Pit.	8	331	18	77	95	745	15	1	1	2	86	....	1977-78	1984-85
Maxwell, Kevin	Min., Col., N.J.	3	66	6	15	21	61	16	3	4	7	24	....	1980-81	1983-84
Maxwell, Wally	Tor.	1	2	0	0	0	0	....	....	....	....	....	....	1952-53	1952-53
May, Alan	Bos., Edm., Wsh., Dal., Cgy.	8	393	31	45	76	1348	40	1	2	3	80	....	1987-88	1994-95
‡ Mayer, Derek	Ott.	1	17	2	2	4	8	....	....	....	....	....	....	1993-94	1993-94
Mayer, Jim	NYR	1	4	0	0	0	0	....	....	....	....	....	....	1979-80	1979-80
Mayer, Pat	Pit.	1	1	0	0	0	4	....	....	....	....	....	....	1987-88	1987-88
Mayer, Shep	Tor.	1	12	1	2	3	4	....	....	....	....	....	....	1942-43	1942-43
● Mazur, Eddie	Mtl., Chi.	6	107	8	20	28	120	25	4	5	9	22	1	1950-51	1956-57
Mazur, Jay	Van.	4	47	11	7	18	20	6	0	1	1	8	....	1988-89	1991-92
McAdam, Gary	Buf., Pit., Det., Cgy., Wsh., N.J., Tor.	11	534	96	132	228	243	30	6	5	11	16	....	1975-76	1985-86
● McAdam, Sam	NYR	1	5	0	0	0	0	....	....	....	....	....	....	1930-31	1930-31
● McAndrew, Hazen	Bro.	1	7	0	1	1	6	....	....	....	....	....	....	1941-42	1941-42
McAneeley, Ted	Cal.	3	158	8	35	43	141	....	....	....	....	....	....	1972-73	1974-75
McAtee, Jud	Det.	3	46	15	13	28	6	14	2	1	3	0	....	1942-43	1944-45
McAtee, Norm	Bos.	1	13	0	1	1	0	....	....	....	....	....	....	1946-47	1946-47
● McAvoy, George	Mtl.	1	....	....	....	....	....	4	0	0	0	0	....	1954-55	1954-55
McBain, Andrew	Wpg., Pit., Van., Ott.	11	608	129	172	301	633	24	5	7	12	39	....	1983-84	1993-94
‡ McBain, Jason	Hfd.	2	9	0	0	0	0	....	....	....	....	....	....	1995-96	1996-97
‡ McBain, Mike	T.B.	2	64	0	7	7	22	....	....	....	....	....	....	1997-98	1998-99
McBean, Wayne	L.A., NYI, Wpg.	6	211	10	39	49	168	2	1	1	2	0	....	1987-88	1993-94
McBride, Cliff	Mtl.M., Tor.	2	2	0	0	0	0	....	....	....	....	....	....	1928-29	1929-30
McBurney, Jim	Chi.	1	1	0	1	1	0	....	....	....	....	....	....	1952-53	1952-53
● McCabe, Stan	Det., Mtl.M.	4	78	9	4	13	49	....	....	....	....	....	....	1929-30	1933-34
● McCaffrey, Bert	Tor., Pit., Mtl.	7	260	43	30	73	202	8	2	1	3	10	1	1924-25	1930-31
McCahill, John	Col.	1	1	0	0	0	0	....	....	....	....	....	....	1977-78	1977-78
● McCaig, Doug	Det., Chi.	7	263	8	21	29	255	7	0	1	1	10	....	1941-42	1950-51
● McCallum, Dunc	NYR, Pit.	5	187	14	35	49	230	10	1	2	3	12	....	1965-66	1970-71
● McCalmon, Eddie	Chi., Phi.	2	39	5	0	5	14	....	....	....	....	....	....	1927-28	1930-31
McCann, Rick	Det.	6	43	1	4	5	6	....	....	....	....	....	....	1967-68	1974-75
McCarthy, Dan	NYR	1	5	4	0	4	4	....	....	....	....	....	....	1980-81	1980-81
McCarthy, Kevin	Phi., Van., Pit.	10	537	67	191	258	527	21	2	3	5	20	....	1977-78	1986-87
● McCarthy, Thomas	Que., Ham.	2	35	22	7	29	10	....	....	....	....	....	....	1919-20	1920-21
McCarthy, Tom	Det., Bos.	4	60	8	9	17	8	....	....	....	....	....	....	1956-57	1960-61
McCarthy, Tom	Min., Bos.	9	460	178	221	399	330	68	12	26	38	67	....	1979-80	1987-88
● McCartney, Walt	Mtl.	1	2	0	0	0	0	....	....	....	....	....	....	1932-33	1932-33
McCaskill, Ted	Min.	1	4	0	2	2	0	....	....	....	....	....	....	1967-68	1967-68
McClanahan, Rob	Buf., Hfd., NYR	5	224	38	63	101	126	34	4	12	16	31	....	1979-80	1983-84
McCleary, Trent	Ott., Bos., Mtl.	4	192	8	15	23	134	....	....	....	....	....	....	1995-96	1999-00
McClelland, Kevin	Pit., Edm., Det., Tor., Wpg.	12	588	68	112	180	1672	98	11	18	29	281	4	1981-82	1993-94
McCord, Bob	Bos., Det., Min., St.L.	7	316	10	58	68	262	14	2	5	7	10	....	1963-64	1972-73
McCord, Dennis	Van.	1	3	0	0	0	6	....	....	....	....	....	....	1973-74	1973-74
McCormack, John	Tor., Mtl., Chi.	8	311	25	49	74	35	22	1	1	2	0	2	1947-48	1954-55
McCosh, Shawn	L.A., NYR	2	9	1	0	1	6	....	....	....	....	....	....	1991-92	1994-95
McCourt, Dale	Det., Buf., Tor.	7	532	194	284	478	124	21	9	7	16	6	....	1977-78	1983-84
McCreary, Bill	NYR, Det., Mtl., St.L.	8	309	53	62	115	108	48	6	16	22	14	....	1953-54	1970-71
McCreary Jr., Bill	Tor.	1	12	1	0	1	4	....	....	....	....	....	....	1980-81	1980-81
McCreary, Keith	Mtl., Pit., Atl.	10	532	131	112	243	294	16	0	4	4	6	....	1961-62	1974-75
● McCreedy, John	Tor.	2	64	17	12	29	25	21	4	3	7	16	2	1941-42	1944-45
McCrimmon, Brad	Bos., Phi., Cgy., Det., Hfd., Phx.	18	1222	81	322	403	1416	116	11	18	29	176	1	1979-80	1996-97
McCrimmon, Jim	St.L.	1	2	0	0	0	0	....	....	....	....	....	....	1974-75	1974-75
McCulley, Bob	Mtl.	1	1	0	0	0	0	....	....	....	....	....	....	1934-35	1934-35
● McCurry, Duke	Pit.	4	148	21	11	32	119	4	0	2	2	4	....	1925-26	1928-29
McCutcheon, Brian	Det.	3	37	3	1	4	7	....	....	....	....	....	....	1974-75	1976-77
McCutcheon, Darwin	Tor.	1	1	0	0	0	2	....	....	....	....	....	....	1981-82	1981-82
McDill, Jeff	Chi.	1	1	0	0	0	0	....	....	....	....	....	....	1976-77	1976-77
McDonagh, Bill	NYR	1	4	0	0	0	2	....	....	....	....	....	....	1949-50	1949-50
McDonald, Ab	Mtl., Chi., Bos., Det., Pit., St.L.	15	762	182	248	430	200	84	21	29	50	42	4	1957-58	1971-72
McDonald, Brian	Chi., Buf.	2	12	0	0	0	29	8	0	0	0	2	....	1967-68	1970-71
● McDonald, Bucko	Det., Tor., NYR	11	446	35	88	123	206	50	6	1	7	24	3	1934-35	1944-45
McDonald, Butch	Det., Chi.	2	66	8	20	28	2	5	0	2	2	10	....	1939-40	1944-45
McDonald, Gerry	Hfd.	2	8	0	0	0	4	....	....	....	....	....	....	1981-82	1983-84
● McDonald, Jack	Mtl.W., Mtl., Que., Tor.	5	69	26	14	40	30	7	1	1	2	3	....	1917-18	1921-22
McDonald, Jack	NYR	1	43	10	9	19	6	....	....	....	....	....	....	1943-44	1943-44
McDonald, Lanny	Tor., Col., Cgy.	16	1111	500	506	1006	899	117	44	40	84	120	1	1973-74	1988-89
McDonald, Robert	NYR	1	1	0	0	0	0	....	....	....	....	....	....	1943-44	1943-44
McDonald, Terry	K.C.	1	8	0	1	1	6	....	....	....	....	....	....	1975-76	1975-76
McDonnell, Joe	Van., Pit.	3	50	2	10	12	34	....	....	....	....	....	....	1981-82	1985-86
● McDonnell, Moylan	Ham.	1	22	1	2	3	2	....	....	....	....	....	....	1920-21	1920-21

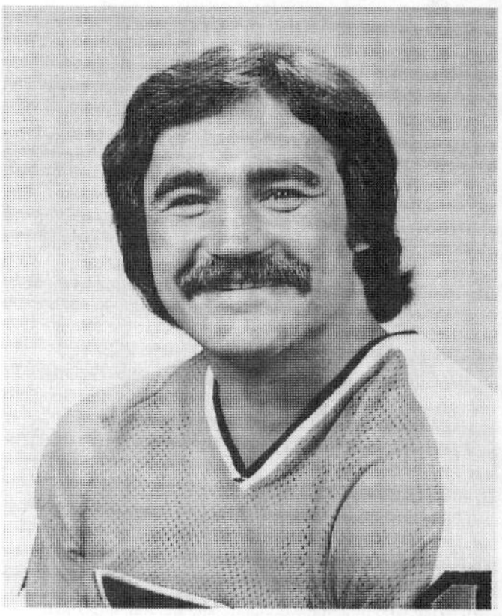
Rick MacLeish

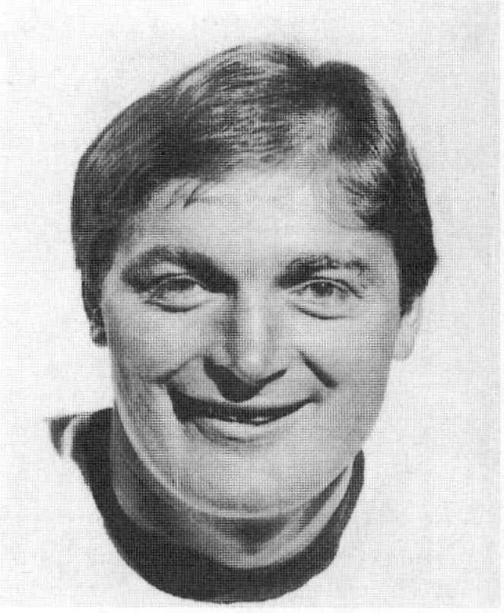
Pete Mahovlich

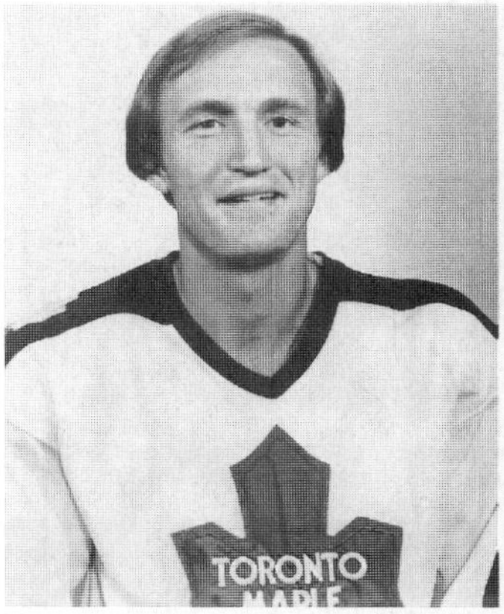

Dan Maloney

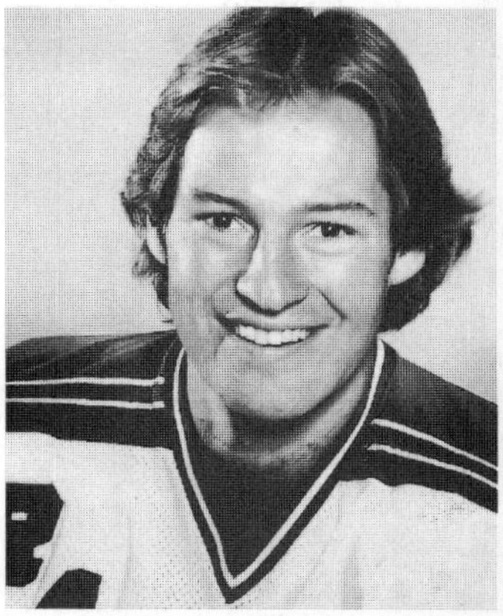
Don Maloney

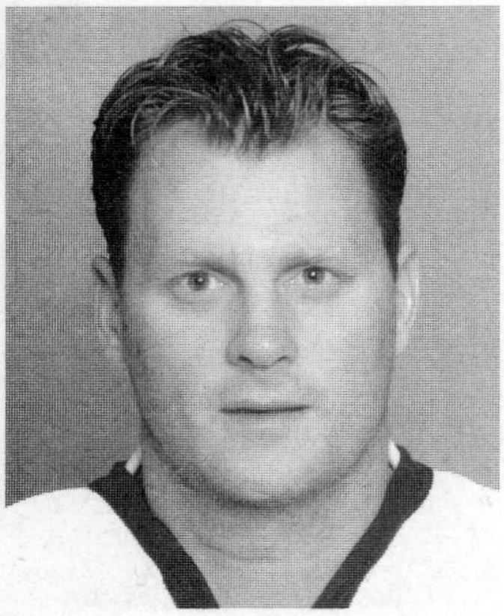

Dave Manson

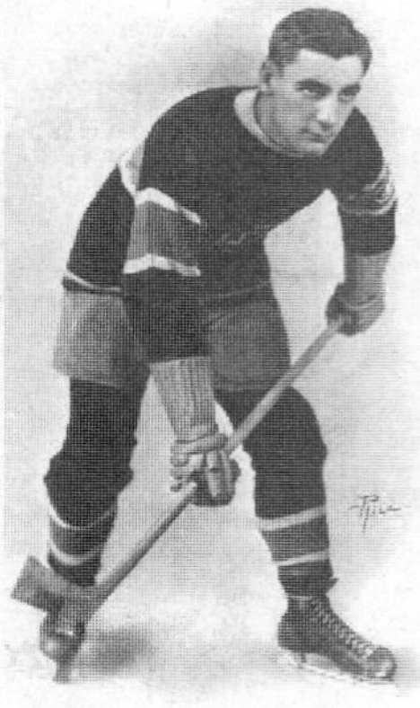

Sylvio Mantha

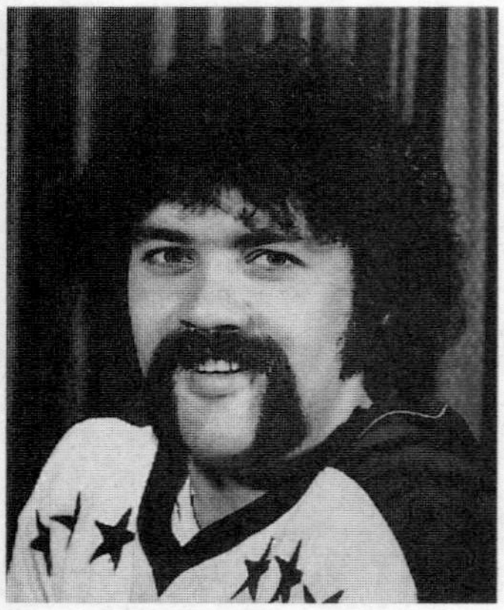

Dennis Maruk

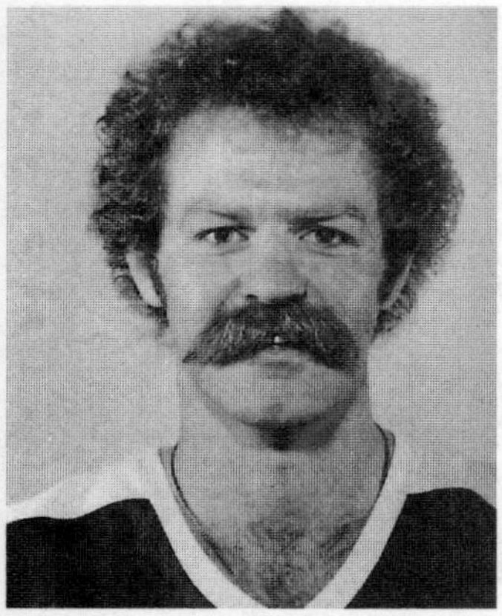

Lanny McDonald

Name	NHL Teams	NHL Seasons	Regular Schedule					Playoffs					NHL Cup Wins	First NHL Season	Last NHL Season
			GP	G	A	TP	PIM	GP	G	A	TP	PIM			
McDonough, Al	L.A., Pit., Atl., Det.	5	237	73	88	161	73	8	0	1	1	2	....	1970-71	1977-78
‡ McDonough, Hubie	L.A., NYI, S.J.	5	195	40	26	66	67	5	1	0	1	4	....	1988-89	1992-93
McDougal, Mike	NYR, Hfd.	4	61	8	10	18	43	....	....	....	....	....	....	1978-79	1982-83
‡ McDougall, Bill	Det., Edm., T.B.	3	28	5	5	10	12	1	0	0	0	0	....	1990-91	1993-94
McElmury, Jim	Min., K.C., Col.	5	180	14	47	61	49	....	....	....	....	....	....	1972-73	1977-78
McEwen, Mike	NYR, Col., NYI, L.A., Wsh., Det., Hfd.	12	716	108	296	404	460	78	12	36	48	48	3	1976-77	1987-88
McFadden, Jim	Det., Chi.	8	412	100	126	226	89	49	10	9	19	30	1	1946-47	1953-54
McFadyen, Don	Chi.	4	179	12	33	45	77	11	2	2	4	5	1	1932-33	1935-36
McFall, Dan	Wpg.	2	9	0	1	1	0	....	....	....	....	....	....	1984-85	1985-86
• McFarlane, Gord	Chi.	1	2	0	0	0	0	....	....	....	....	....	....	1926-27	1926-27
McGeough, Jim	Wsh., Pit.	4	57	7	10	17	32	....	....	....	....	....	....	1981-82	1986-87
• McGibbon, Irv	Mtl.	1	1	0	0	0	2	....	....	....	....	....	....	1942-43	1942-43
McGill, Bob	Tor., Chi., S.J., Det., NYI, Hfd.	13	705	17	55	72	1766	49	0	0	0	88	....	1981-82	1993-94
• McGill, Jack	Mtl.	3	134	27	10	37	71	3	2	0	2	0	....	1934-35	1936-37
• McGill, Jack	Bos.	4	97	23	36	59	42	27	7	4	11	17	....	1941-42	1946-47
McGill, Ryan	Chi., Phi., Edm.	4	151	4	15	19	391	....	....	....	....	....	....	1991-92	1994-95
McGregor, Sandy	NYR	1	2	0	0	0	2	....	....	....	....	....	....	1963-64	1963-64
• McGuire, Mickey	Pit.	2	36	3	0	3	6	....	....	....	....	....	....	1926-27	1927-28
McHugh, Mike	Min., S.J.	4	20	1	0	1	16	....	....	....	....	....	....	1988-89	1991-92
McIlhargey, Jack	Phi., Van., Hfd.	8	393	11	36	47	1102	27	0	3	3	68	....	1974-75	1981-82
• McInenly, Bert	Det., NYA, Ott., Bos.	6	166	19	15	34	144	4	0	0	0	2	....	1930-31	1935-36
McIntosh, Bruce	Min.	1	2	0	0	0	0	....	....	....	....	....	....	1972-73	1972-73
McIntosh, Paul	Buf.	2	48	0	2	2	66	2	0	0	0	7	....	1974-75	1975-76
• McIntyre, Jack	Bos., Chi., Det.	11	499	109	102	211	173	29	7	6	13	4	....	1949-50	1959-60
McIntyre, John	Tor., L.A., NYR, Van.	6	351	24	54	78	516	44	0	6	6	54	....	1989-90	1994-95
McIntyre, Larry	Tor.	2	41	0	3	3	26	....	....	....	....	....	....	1969-70	1972-73
McKay, Doug	Det.	1	....	....	....	....	....	1	0	0	0	0	1	1949-50	1949-50
McKay, Ray	Chi., Buf., Cal.	6	140	2	16	18	102	....	....	....	....	....	....	1968-69	1973-74
McKay, Scott	Ana.	1	1	0	0	0	0	....	....	....	....	....	....	1993-94	1993-94
McKechnie, Walt	Min., Cal., Bos., Det., Wsh., Cle., Tor., Col.	16	955	214	392	606	469	15	7	5	12	7	....	1967-68	1982-83
McKee, Mike	Que.	1	48	3	12	15	41	....	....	....	....	....	....	1993-94	1993-94
McKegney, Ian	Chi.	1	3	0	0	0	2	....	....	....	....	....	....	1976-77	1976-77
McKegney, Tony	Buf., Que., Min., NYR, St.L., Det., Chi.	13	912	320	319	639	517	79	24	23	47	56	....	1978-79	1990-91
McKendry, Alex	NYI, Cgy.	4	46	3	6	9	21	6	2	2	4	0	1	1977-78	1980-81
McKenna, Sean	Buf., L.A., Tor.	9	414	82	80	162	181	15	1	2	3	2	....	1981-82	1989-90
McKenney, Don	Bos., NYR, Tor., Det., St.L.	13	798	237	345	582	211	58	18	29	47	10	1	1954-55	1967-68
McKenny, Jim	Tor., Min.	14	604	82	247	329	294	37	7	9	16	10	....	1965-66	1978-79
McKenzie, Brian	Pit.	1	6	1	1	2	4	....	....	....	....	....	....	1971-72	1971-72
McKenzie, John	Chi., Det., NYR, Bos.	12	691	206	268	474	917	69	15	32	47	133	2	1958-59	1971-72
McKim, Andrew	Bos., Det.	3	38	1	4	5	6	....	....	....	....	....	....	1992-93	1994-95
• McKinnon, Alex	Ham., NYA, Chi.	5	193	19	11	30	237	....	....	....	....	....	....	1924-25	1928-29
• McKinnon, John	Mtl., Pit., Phi.	6	208	28	11	39	224	2	0	0	0	4	....	1925-26	1930-31
McLean, Don	Wsh.	1	9	0	0	0	6	....	....	....	....	....	....	1975-76	1975-76
• McLean, Fred	Que., Ham.	2	8	0	0	0	2	....	....	....	....	....	....	1919-20	1920-21
McLean, Jack	Tor.	3	67	14	24	38	76	13	2	2	4	8	1	1942-43	1944-45
McLean, Jeff	S.J.	1	6	1	0	1	0	....	....	....	....	....	....	1993-94	1993-94
• McLellan, John	Tor.	1	2	0	0	0	0	....	....	....	....	....	....	1951-52	1951-52
McLellan, Scott	Bos.	1	2	0	0	0	0	....	....	....	....	....	....	1982-83	1982-83
McLellan, Todd	NYI	1	5	1	1	2	0	....	....	....	....	....	....	1987-88	1987-88
• McLenahan, Rollie	Det.	1	9	2	1	3	10	2	0	0	0	0	....	1945-46	1945-46
McLeod, Al	Det.	1	26	2	2	4	24	....	....	....	....	....	....	1973-74	1973-74
McLeod, Jackie	NYR	5	106	14	23	37	12	7	0	0	0	0	....	1949-50	1954-55
‡ McLlwain, Dave	Pit., Wpg., Buf., NYI, Tor., Ott.	10	501	100	107	207	292	20	0	2	2	2	....	1987-88	1996-97
• McMahon, Mike	Mtl., Bos.	3	57	7	18	25	102	13	1	2	3	30	1	1942-43	1945-46
McMahon Jr., Mike	NYR, Min., Chi., Det., Pit., Buf.	8	224	15	68	83	171	14	3	7	10	4	....	1963-64	1971-72
McManama, Bob	Pit.	3	99	11	25	36	28	8	0	1	1	6	....	1973-74	1975-76
• McManus, Sammy	Mtl.M., Bos.	2	26	0	1	1	8	1	0	0	0	0	1	1934-35	1936-37
McMurchy, Tom	Chi., Edm.	4	55	8	4	12	65	....	....	....	....	....	....	1983-84	1987-88
McNab, Max	Det.	4	128	16	19	35	24	25	1	0	1	4	1	1947-48	1950-51
McNab, Peter	Buf., Bos., Van., N.J.	14	954	363	450	813	179	107	40	42	82	20	....	1973-74	1986-87
• McNabney, Sid	Mtl.	1	....	....	....	....	....	5	0	1	1	2	....	1950-51	1950-51
• McNamara, Howard	Mtl.	1	10	1	0	1	4	....	....	....	....	....	....	1919-20	1919-20
• McNaughton, George	Que.	1	1	0	0	0	0	....	....	....	....	....	....	1919-20	1919-20
McNeill, Billy	Det.	6	257	21	46	67	142	4	1	1	2	4	....	1956-57	1963-64
McNeill, Mike	Chi., Que.	2	63	5	11	16	18	....	....	....	....	....	....	1990-91	1991-92
McNeill, Stu	Det.	3	10	1	1	2	2	....	....	....	....	....	....	1957-58	1959-60
McPhee, George	NYR, N.J.	7	115	24	25	49	257	29	5	3	8	69	....	1982-83	1988-89
McPhee, Mike	Mtl., Min., Dal.	11	744	200	199	399	661	134	28	27	55	193	1	1983-84	1993-94
McRae, Basil	Que., Tor., Det., Min., T.B., St.L., Chi.	16	576	53	83	136	2457	78	8	4	12	349	....	1981-82	1996-97
McRae, Chris	Tor., Det.	3	21	1	0	1	122	....	....	....	....	....	....	1987-88	1989-90
McRae, Ken	Que., Tor.	7	137	14	21	35	364	6	0	0	0	4	....	1987-88	1993-94
• McReavy, Pat	Bos., Det.	4	55	5	10	15	4	22	3	3	6	9	1	1938-39	1941-42
McReynolds, Brian	Wpg., NYR, L.A.	3	30	1	5	6	8	....	....	....	....	....	....	1989-90	1993-94
McSheffrey, Bryan	Van., Buf.	3	90	13	7	20	44	....	....	....	....	....	....	1972-73	1974-75
‡ McSorley, Marty	Pit., Edm., L.A., NYR, S.J., Bos.	17	961	108	251	359	3381	115	10	19	29	374	2	1983-84	1999-00
McSween, Don	Buf., Ana.	5	47	3	10	13	55	....	....	....	....	....	....	1987-88	1995-96
McTaggart, Jim	Wsh.	2	71	3	10	13	205	....	....	....	....	....	....	1980-81	1981-82
‡ McTavish, Dale	Cgy.	1	9	1	2	3	2	....	....	....	....	....	....	1996-97	1996-97
McTavish, Gord	St.L., Wpg.	2	11	1	3	4	2	....	....	....	....	....	....	1978-79	1979-80
• McVeigh, Charley	Chi., NYA	9	397	84	88	172	138	4	0	0	0	2	....	1926-27	1934-35
• McVicar, Jack	Mtl.M.	2	88	2	4	6	63	6	0	0	0	2	....	1930-31	1931-32
Meagher, Rick	Mtl., Hfd., N.J., St.L.	12	691	144	165	309	383	62	8	7	15	41	....	1979-80	1990-91
Meehan, Gerry	Tor., Phi., Buf., Van., Atl., Wsh.	10	670	180	243	423	111	10	0	1	1	0	....	1968-69	1978-79
Meeke, Brent	Cal., Cle.	5	75	9	22	31	8	....	....	....	....	....	....	1972-73	1976-77
Meeker, Howie	Tor.	8	346	83	102	185	329	42	6	9	15	50	4	1946-47	1953-54
Meeker, Mike	Pit.	1	4	0	0	0	5	....	....	....	....	....	....	1978-79	1978-79
• Meeking, Harry	Tor., Det., Bos.	3	64	18	12	30	66	9	3	0	3	6	....	1917-18	1926-27
Meger, Paul	Mtl.	6	212	39	52	91	118	35	3	8	11	16	1	1949-50	1954-55
Meighan, Ron	Min., Pit.	2	48	3	7	10	18	....	....	....	....	....	....	1981-82	1982-83
Meissner, Barrie	Min.	2	6	0	1	1	4	....	....	....	....	....	....	1967-68	1968-69
Meissner, Dick	Bos., NYR	5	171	11	15	26	37	....	....	....	....	....	....	1959-60	1964-65
Melametsa, Anssi	Wpg.	1	27	0	3	3	2	....	....	....	....	....	....	1985-86	1985-86
Melin, Roger	Min.	2	3	0	0	0	0	....	....	....	....	....	....	1980-81	1981-82
Mellor, Tom	Det.	2	26	2	4	6	25	....	....	....	....	....	....	1973-74	1974-75
• Melnyk, Gerry	Det., Chi., St.L.	6	269	39	77	116	34	53	6	6	12	6	....	1955-56	1967-68
Melnyk, Larry	Bos., Edm., NYR, Van.	10	432	11	63	74	686	66	2	9	11	127	2	1980-81	1989-90
Melrose, Barry	Wpg., Tor., Det.	6	300	10	23	33	728	7	0	2	2	38	....	1979-80	1985-86
Menard, Hillary	Chi.	1	1	0	0	0	0	....	....	....	....	....	....	1953-54	1953-54
Menard, Howie	Det., L.A., Chi., Oak.	4	151	23	42	65	87	19	3	7	10	36	....	1963-64	1969-70
Mercredi, Vic	Atl.	1	2	0	0	0	0	....	....	....	....	....	....	1974-75	1974-75
Meredith, Greg	Cgy.	2	38	6	4	10	8	5	3	1	4	4	....	1980-81	1982-83
Merkosky, Glenn	Hfd., N.J., Det.	5	66	5	12	17	22	....	....	....	....	....	....	1981-82	1989-90
• Meronek, Bill	Mtl.	2	19	5	8	13	0	1	0	0	0	0	....	1939-40	1942-43
Merrick, Wayne	St.L., Cal., Cle., NYI	12	774	191	265	456	303	102	19	30	49	30	4	1972-73	1983-84
• Merrill, Horace	Ott.	2	8	0	0	0	3	....	....	....	....	....	1	1917-18	1919-20
‡ Mertzig, Jan	NYR	1	23	0	2	2	8	....	....	....	....	....	....	1998-99	1998-99
Messier, Joby	NYR	3	25	0	4	4	24	....	....	....	....	....	....	1992-93	1994-95
Messier, Mitch	Min.	4	20	0	2	2	11	....	....	....	....	....	....	1987-88	1990-91
Messier, Paul	Col.	1	9	0	0	0	4	....	....	....	....	....	....	1978-79	1978-79
‡ Metcalfe, Scott	Edm., Buf.	3	19	1	2	3	18	....	....	....	....	....	....	1987-88	1989-90
Metz, Don	Tor.	9	172	20	35	55	42	42	7	8	15	12	5	1938-39	1948-49
• Metz, Nick	Tor.	12	518	131	119	250	149	76	19	20	39	31	4	1934-35	1947-48
Michaluk, Art	Chi.	1	5	0	0	0	0	....	....	....	....	....	....	1947-48	1947-48
Michaluk, John	Chi.	1	1	0	0	0	0	....	....	....	....	....	....	1950-51	1950-51
Michayluk, Dave	Phi., Pit.	3	14	2	6	8	8	7	1	1	2	0	1	1981-82	1991-92
Micheletti, Joe	St.L., Col.	3	158	11	60	71	114	11	1	11	12	10	....	1979-80	1981-82
Micheletti, Pat	Min.	1	12	2	0	2	8	....	....	....	....	....	....	1987-88	1987-88
• Mickey, Larry	Chi., NYR, Tor., Mtl., L.A., Phi., Buf.	11	292	39	53	92	160	9	1	0	1	10	....	1964-65	1974-75
• Mickoski, Nick	NYR, Chi., Det., Bos.	13	703	158	185	343	319	18	1	6	7	6	....	1947-48	1959-60
Middendorf, Max	Que., Edm.	4	13	2	4	6	6	....	....	....	....	....	....	1986-87	1990-91
Middleton, Rick	NYR, Bos.	14	1005	448	540	988	157	114	45	55	100	19	....	1974-75	1987-88
‡ Miehm, Kevin	St.L.	2	22	1	4	5	8	2	0	1	1	0	....	1992-93	1993-94
Migay, Rudy	Tor.	10	418	59	92	151	293	15	1	0	1	20	....	1949-50	1959-60
‡ Mika, Petr	NYI	1	3	0	0	0	0	....	....	....	....	....	....	1999-00	1999-00
Mikita, Stan	Chi.	22	1394	541	926	1467	1270	155	59	91	150	169	1	1958-59	1979-80

			Regular Schedule					Playoffs							
Name	NHL Teams	NHL Seasons	GP	G	A	TP	PIM	GP	G	A	TP	PIM	NHL Cup Wins	First NHL Season	Last NHL Season
Mikkelson, Bill	L.A., NYI, Wsh.	4	147	4	18	22	105	....	....	....	....	....	....	1971-72	1976-77
Mikol, Jim	Tor., NYR	2	34	1	4	5	8	....	....	....	....	....	....	1962-63	1964-65
Mikulchik, Oleg	Wpg., Ana.	3	37	0	3	3	33	....	....	....	....	....	....	1993-94	1995-96
Milbury, Mike	Bos.	12	754	49	189	238	1552	86	4	24	28	219	....	1975-76	1986-87
● Milks, Hib	Pit., Phi., NYR, Ott.	8	317	87	41	128	179	11	0	0	0	2	....	1925-26	1932-33
‡ Millar, Craig	Edm., Nsh., T.B.	5	114	8	14	22	73	....	....	....	....	....	....	1996-97	2000-01
● Millar, Hugh	Det.	1	4	0	0	0	0	1	0	0	0	0	....	1946-47	1946-47
‡ Millar, Mike	Hfd., Wsh., Bos., Tor.	5	78	18	18	36	12	....	....	....	....	....	....	1986-87	1990-91
‡ Millen, Corey	NYR, L.A., N.J., Dal., Cgy.	8	335	90	119	209	236	47	5	7	12	22	....	1989-90	1996-97
● Miller, Bill	Mtl.M., Mtl.	3	95	7	3	10	16	12	0	0	0	0	1	1934-35	1936-37
Miller, Bob	Bos., Col., L.A.	6	404	75	119	194	220	36	4	7	11	27	....	1977-78	1984-85
Miller, Brad	Buf., Ott., Cgy.	6	82	1	5	6	321	....	....	....	....	....	....	1988-89	1993-94
● Miller, Earl	Chi., Tor.	5	109	19	14	33	124	10	1	0	1	6	1	1927-28	1931-32
Miller, Jack	Chi.	2	17	0	0	0	4	....	....	....	....	....	....	1949-50	1950-51
‡ Miller, Jason	N.J.	3	6	0	0	0	0	....	....	....	....	....	....	1990-91	1992-93
Miller, Jay	Bos., L.A.	7	446	40	44	84	1723	48	2	3	5	243	....	1985-86	1991-92
Miller, Kelly	NYR, Wsh.	15	1057	181	282	463	512	119	20	34	54	65	....	1984-85	1998-99
Miller, Paul	Col.	1	3	0	3	3	0	....	....	....	....	....	....	1981-82	1981-82
Miller, Perry	Det.	4	217	10	51	61	387	....	....	....	....	....	....	1977-78	1980-81
Miller, Tom	Det., NYI	4	118	16	25	41	34	....	....	....	....	....	....	1970-71	1974-75
Miller, Warren	NYR, Hfd.	4	262	40	50	90	137	6	1	0	1	0	....	1979-80	1982-83
Miner, John	Edm.	1	14	2	3	5	16	....	....	....	....	....	....	1987-88	1987-88
Minor, Gerry	Van.	5	140	11	21	32	173	12	1	3	4	25	....	1979-80	1983-84
Mironov, Dmitri	Tor., Pit., Ana., Det., Wsh.	11	556	54	206	260	568	75	10	26	36	48	1	1991-92	2001-02
Miszuk, John	Det., Chi., Phi., Min.	6	237	7	39	46	232	19	0	3	3	19	....	1963-64	1969-70
Mitchell, Bill	Det.	1	1	0	0	0	0	....	....	....	....	....	....	1963-64	1963-64
● Mitchell, Herb	Bos.	2	44	6	0	6	36	....	....	....	....	....	....	1924-25	1925-26
‡ Mitchell, Jeff	Dal.	1	7	0	0	0	7	....	....	....	....	....	....	1997-98	1997-98
Mitchell, Red	Chi.	3	83	4	5	9	67	....	....	....	....	....	....	1941-42	1944-45
Mitchell, Roy	Min.	1	3	0	0	0	0	....	....	....	....	....	....	1992-93	1992-93
● Moe, Bill	NYR	5	261	11	42	53	163	1	0	0	0	0	....	1944-45	1948-49
Moffat, Lyle	Tor., Wpg.	3	97	12	16	28	51	....	....	....	....	....	....	1972-73	1979-80
● Moffat, Ron	Det.	3	37	1	1	2	8	7	0	0	0	0	....	1932-33	1934-35
‡ Moger, Sandy	Bos., L.A.	5	236	41	38	79	212	5	2	2	4	12	....	1994-95	1998-99
Moher, Mike	N.J.	1	9	0	1	1	28	....	....	....	....	....	....	1982-83	1982-83
Mohns, Doug	Bos., Chi., Min., Atl., Wsh.	22	1390	248	462	710	1250	94	14	36	50	122	....	1953-54	1974-75
Mohns, Lloyd	NYR	1	1	0	0	0	0	....	....	....	....	....	....	1943-44	1943-44
Mokosak, Carl	Cgy., L.A., Phi., Pit., Bos.	6	83	11	15	26	170	1	0	0	0	0	....	1981-82	1988-89
Mokosak, John	Det.	2	41	0	2	2	96	....	....	....	....	....	....	1988-89	1989-90
Molin, Lars	Van.	3	172	33	65	98	37	19	2	9	11	7	....	1981-82	1983-84
Moller, Mike	Buf., Edm.	7	134	15	28	43	41	3	0	1	1	0	....	1980-81	1986-87
Moller, Randy	Que., NYR, Buf., Fla.	14	815	45	180	225	1692	78	6	16	22	197	....	1981-82	1994-95
Molloy, Mitch	Buf.	1	2	0	0	0	10	....	....	....	....	....	....	1989-90	1989-90
● Molyneaux, Larry	NYR	2	45	0	1	1	20	10	0	0	0	8	....	1937-38	1938-39
‡ Momesso, Sergio	Mtl., St.L., Van., Tor., NYR	13	710	152	193	345	1557	119	18	26	44	311	....	1983-84	1996-97
Monahan, Garry	Mtl., Det., L.A., Tor., Van.	12	748	116	169	285	484	22	3	1	4	13	....	1967-68	1978-79
Monahan, Hartland	Cal., NYR, Wsh., Pit., L.A., St.L.	7	334	61	80	141	163	6	0	0	0	4	....	1973-74	1980-81
● Mondou, Armand	Mtl.	12	386	47	71	118	99	32	3	5	8	12	2	1928-29	1939-40
Mondou, Pierre	Mtl.	9	548	194	262	456	179	69	17	28	45	26	3	1976-77	1984-85
‡ Mongeau, Michel	St.L., T.B.	4	54	6	19	25	10	2	0	1	1	0	....	1989-90	1992-93
Mongrain, Bob	Buf., L.A.	6	81	13	14	27	14	11	1	2	3	2	....	1979-80	1985-86
Monteith, Hank	Det.	3	77	5	12	17	6	4	0	0	0	0	....	1968-69	1970-71
‡ Moore, Barrie	Buf., Edm., Wsh.	3	39	2	6	8	18	....	....	....	....	....	....	1995-96	1999-00
Moore, Dickie	Mtl., Tor., St.L.	14	719	261	347	608	652	135	46	64	110	122	6	1951-52	1967-68
● Moran, Amby	Mtl., Chi.	2	35	1	1	2	24	....	....	....	....	....	....	1926-27	1927-28
More, Jay	NYR, Min., S.J., Phx., Chi., Nsh.	10	406	18	54	72	702	31	0	6	6	45	....	1988-89	1998-99
● Morenz, Howie	Mtl., Chi., NYR	14	550	271	201	472	546	39	13	9	22	58	3	1923-24	1936-37
Moretto, Angelo	Cle.	1	5	1	2	3	2	....	....	....	....	....	....	1976-77	1976-77
● Morin, Pete	Mtl.	1	31	10	12	22	7	1	0	0	0	0	....	1941-42	1941-42
● Morin, Stephane	Que., Van.	5	90	16	39	55	52	....	....	....	....	....	....	1989-90	1993-94
Morissette, Dave	Mtl.	2	11	0	0	0	57	....	....	....	....	....	....	1998-99	1999-00
● Morris, Bernie	Bos.	1	6	1	0	1	0	....	....	....	....	....	....	1924-25	1924-25
Morris, Jon	N.J., S.J., Bos.	6	103	16	33	49	47	11	1	7	8	25	....	1988-89	1993-94
● Morris, Moe	Tor., NYR	4	135	13	29	42	58	18	4	2	6	16	1	1943-44	1948-49
Morrison, Dave	L.A., Van.	4	39	3	3	6	4	....	....	....	....	....	....	1980-81	1984-85
Morrison, Don	Det., Chi.	3	112	18	28	46	12	3	0	1	1	0	....	1947-48	1950-51
Morrison, Doug	Bos.	4	23	7	3	10	15	....	....	....	....	....	....	1979-80	1984-85
Morrison, Gary	Phi.	3	43	1	15	16	70	5	0	1	1	2	....	1979-80	1981-82
Morrison, George	St.L.	2	115	17	21	38	13	3	0	0	0	0	....	1970-71	1971-72
Morrison, Jim	Bos., Tor., Det., NYR, Pit.	12	704	40	160	200	542	36	0	12	12	38	....	1951-52	1970-71
● Morrison, John	NYA	1	18	0	0	0	0	....	....	....	....	....	....	1925-26	1925-26
Morrison, Kevin	Col.	1	41	4	11	15	23	....	....	....	....	....	....	1979-80	1979-80
Morrison, Lew	Phi., Atl., Wsh., Pit.	9	564	39	52	91	107	17	0	0	0	2	....	1969-70	1977-78
Morrison, Mark	NYR	2	10	1	1	2	0	....	....	....	....	....	....	1981-82	1983-84
● Morrison, Rod	Det.	1	34	8	7	15	4	3	0	0	0	0	....	1947-48	1947-48
Morrow, Ken	NYI	10	550	17	88	105	309	127	11	22	33	97	4	1979-80	1988-89
‡ Morrow, Scott	Cgy.	1	4	0	0	0	0	....	....	....	....	....	....	1994-95	1994-95
Morton, Dean	Det.	1	1	1	0	1	2	....	....	....	....	....	....	1989-90	1989-90
Mortson, Gus	Tor., Chi., Det.	13	797	46	152	198	1380	54	5	8	13	68	4	1946-47	1958-59
Mosdell, Ken	Bro., Mtl., Chi.	16	693	141	168	309	475	80	16	13	29	48	4	1941-42	1958-59
● Mosienko, Bill	Chi.	14	711	258	282	540	121	22	10	4	14	15	....	1941-42	1954-55
Mott, Morris	Cal.	3	199	18	32	50	49	....	....	....	....	....	....	1972-73	1974-75
● Motter, Alex	Bos., Det.	8	255	39	64	103	135	41	3	9	12	41	1	1934-35	1942-43
Moxey, Jim	Cal., Cle., L.A.	3	127	22	27	49	59	....	....	....	....	....	....	1974-75	1976-77
Mulhern, Richard	Atl., L.A., Tor., Wpg.	6	303	27	93	120	217	7	0	3	3	5	....	1975-76	1980-81
Mulhern, Ryan	Wsh.	1	3	0	0	0	0	....	....	....	....	....	....	1997-98	1997-98
Mullen, Brian	Wpg., NYR, S.J., NYI	11	832	260	362	622	414	62	12	18	30	30	....	1982-83	1992-93
Mullen, Joe	St.L., Cgy., Pit., Bos.	17	1062	502	561	1063	241	143	60	46	106	42	3	1979-80	1996-97
Muloin, Wayne	Det., Oak., Cal., Min.	3	147	3	21	24	93	11	0	0	0	2	....	1963-64	1970-71
Mulvenna, Glenn	Pit., Phi.	2	2	0	0	0	4	....	....	....	....	....	....	1991-92	1992-93
Mulvey, Grant	Chi., N.J.	10	586	149	135	284	816	42	10	5	15	70	....	1974-75	1983-84
Mulvey, Paul	Wsh., Pit., L.A.	4	225	30	51	81	613	....	....	....	....	....	....	1978-79	1981-82
● Mummery, Harry	Tor., Que., Mtl., Ham.	6	106	33	19	52	226	2	1	1	2	17	1	1917-18	1922-23
Muni, Craig	Tor., Edm., Chi., Buf., Wpg., Pit., Dal.	16	819	28	119	147	775	113	0	17	17	108	3	1981-82	1997-98
● Munro, Dunc	Mtl.M., Mtl.	8	239	28	18	46	172	21	2	2	4	18	1	1924-25	1931-32
● Munro, Gerry	Mtl.M., Tor.	2	34	1	0	1	37	....	....	....	....	....	....	1924-25	1925-26
Murdoch, Bob	Mtl., L.A., Atl., Cgy.	12	757	60	218	278	764	69	4	18	22	92	2	1970-71	1981-82
Murdoch, Bob	Cal., Cle., St.L.	4	260	72	85	157	127	....	....	....	....	....	....	1975-76	1978-79
Murdoch, Don	NYR, Edm., Det.	6	320	121	117	238	155	24	10	8	18	16	....	1976-77	1981-82
● Murdoch, Murray	NYR	11	508	84	108	192	197	55	9	12	21	28	2	1926-27	1936-37
Murphy, Brian	Det.	1	1	0	0	0	0	....	....	....	....	....	....	1974-75	1974-75
Murphy, Gord	Phi., Bos., Fla., Atl.	14	862	85	238	323	668	53	3	16	19	35	....	1988-89	2001-02
Murphy, Joe	Det., Edm., Chi., St.L., S.J., Bos., Wsh.	15	779	233	295	528	810	120	34	43	77	185	1	1986-87	2000-01
Murphy, Larry	L.A., Wsh., Min., Pit., Tor., Det.	21	1615	287	929	1216	1084	215	37	115	152	201	4	1980-81	2000-01
Murphy, Mike	St.L., NYR, L.A.	12	831	238	318	556	514	66	13	23	36	54	....	1971-72	1982-83
‡ Murphy, Rob	Van., Ott., L.A.	7	125	9	12	21	152	4	0	0	0	2	....	1987-88	1993-94
Murphy, Ron	NYR, Chi., Det., Bos.	18	889	205	274	479	460	53	7	8	15	26	1	1952-53	1969-70
Murray, Allan	NYA	7	271	5	9	14	163	14	0	0	0	10	....	1933-34	1939-40
Murray, Bob	Atl., Van.	4	194	6	16	22	98	10	1	1	2	15	....	1973-74	1976-77
Murray, Bob	Chi.	15	1008	132	382	514	873	112	19	37	56	106	....	1975-76	1989-90
Murray, Chris	Mtl., Hfd., Car., Ott., Chi., Dal.	6	242	16	18	34	550	15	1	0	1	12	....	1994-95	1999-00
Murray, Jim	L.A.	1	30	0	2	2	14	....	....	....	....	....	....	1967-68	1967-68
Murray, Ken	Tor., NYI, Det., K.C.	5	106	1	10	11	135	....	....	....	....	....	....	1969-70	1975-76
● Murray, Leo	Mtl.	1	6	0	0	0	2	....	....	....	....	....	....	1932-33	1932-33
‡ Murray, Mike	Phi.	1	1	0	0	0	0	....	....	....	....	....	....	1987-88	1987-88
Murray, Pat	Phi.	2	25	3	1	4	15	....	....	....	....	....	....	1990-91	1991-92
Murray, Randy	Tor.	1	3	0	0	0	2	....	....	....	....	....	....	1969-70	1969-70
‡ Murray, Rob	Wsh., Wpg., Phx.	8	107	4	15	19	111	9	0	0	0	18	....	1989-90	1998-99
Murray, Terry	Cal., Phi., Det., Wsh.	8	302	4	76	80	199	18	2	2	4	10	....	1972-73	1981-82
Murray, Troy	Chi., Wpg., Ott., Pit., Col.	15	915	230	354	584	875	113	17	26	43	145	1	1981-82	1995-96
Murzyn, Dana	Hfd., Cgy., Van.	14	838	52	152	204	1571	82	9	10	19	166	1	1985-86	1998-99
‡ Musil, Frantisek	Min., Cgy., Ott., Edm.	15	797	34	106	140	1241	42	2	4	6	47	....	1986-87	2000-01
Myers, Hap	Buf.	1	13	0	0	0	6	....	....	....	....	....	....	1970-71	1970-71
Myhres, Brantt	T.B., Phi., S.J., Nsh., Wsh., Bos.	7	154	6	2	8	687	....	....	....	....	....	....	1994-95	2002-03
Myles, Vic	NYR	1	45	6	9	15	57	....	....	....	....	....	....	1942-43	1942-43
‡ Myrvold, Anders	Col., Bos., NYI	3	25	0	4	4	10	....	....	....	....	....	....	1995-96	2000-01

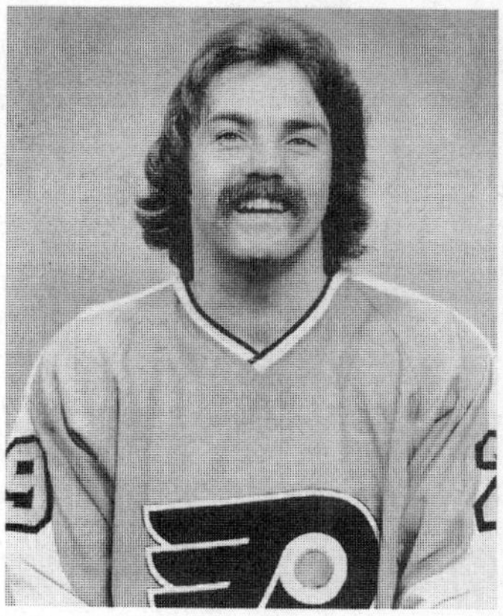
Jack McIlhargey

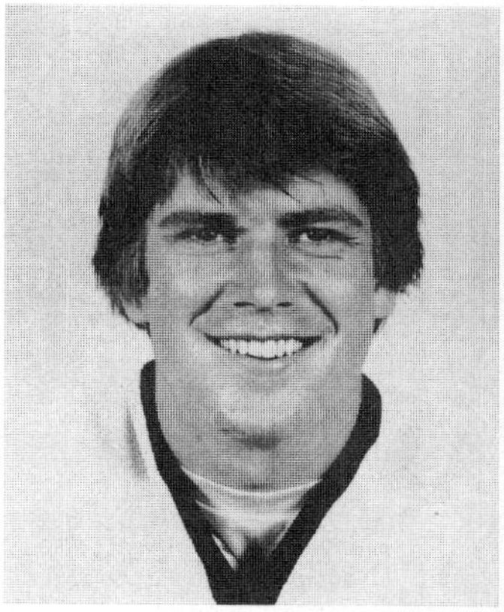
Peter McNab

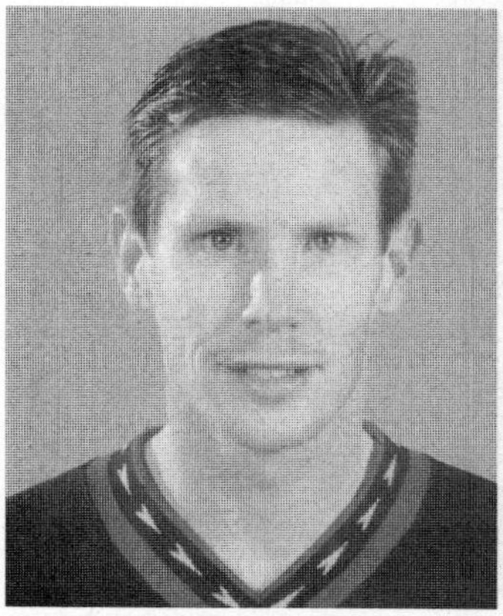
Gord Murphy

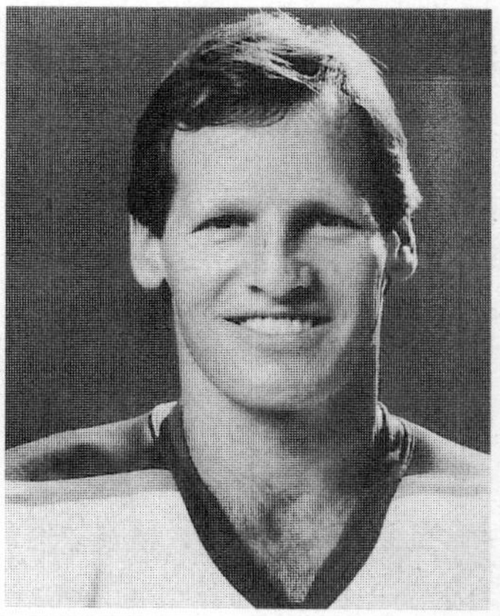
Mark Napier

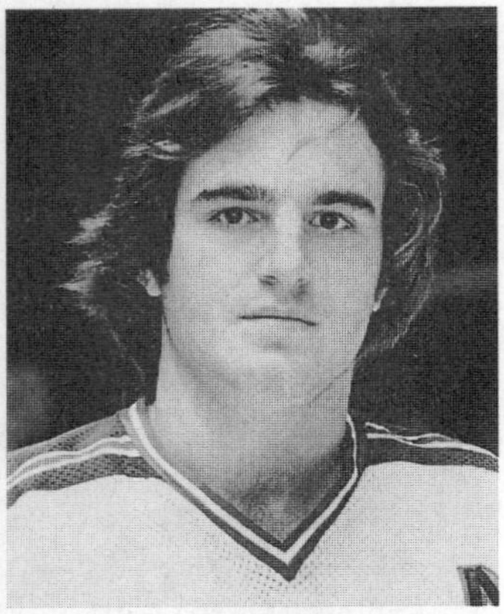

Lance Nethery

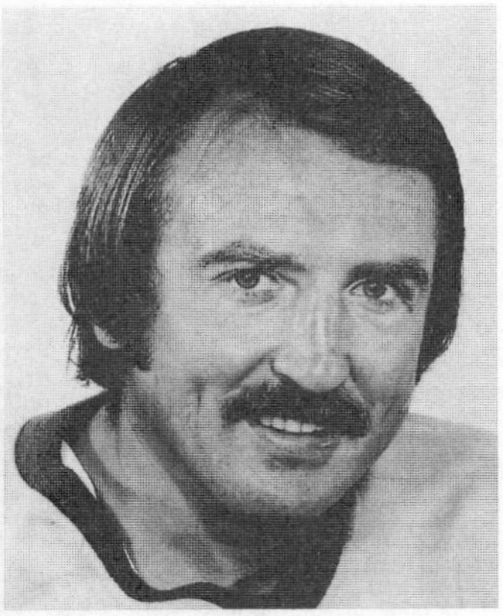

Bob Nevin

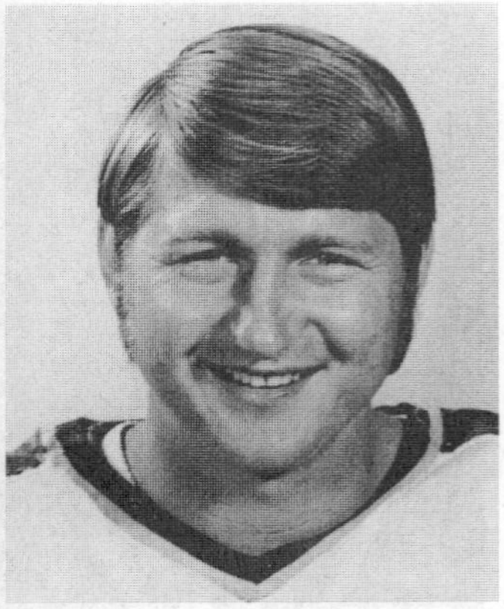

Dennis O'Brien

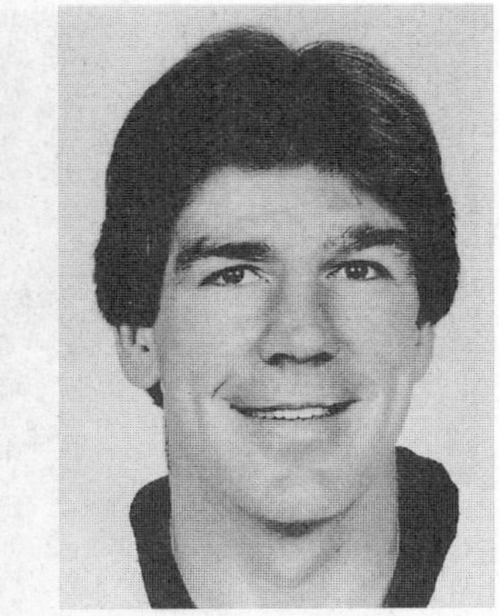

Terry O'Reilly

Name	NHL Teams	NHL Seasons	Regular Schedule					Playoffs					NHL Cup Wins	First NHL Season	Last NHL Season
			GP	G	A	TP	PIM	GP	G	A	TP	PIM			
N															
‡ Nabokov, Dmitri	Chi., NYI	3	55	11	13	24	28	....	....	....	....	....	....	1997-98	1999-00
Nachbaur, Don	Hfd., Edm., Phi.	8	223	23	46	69	465	11	1	1	2	24	....	1980-81	1989-90
Nahrgang, Jim	Det.	3	57	5	12	17	34	....	....	....	....	....	....	1974-75	1976-77
‡ Namestnikov, John	Van., NYI, Nsh.	6	43	0	9	9	24	2	0	0	0	2	....	1993-94	1999-00
Nanne, Lou	Min.	11	635	68	157	225	356	32	4	10	14	8	....	1967-68	1977-78
Nantais, Rich	Min.	3	63	5	4	9	79	....	....	....	....	....	....	1974-75	1976-77
Napier, Mark	Mtl., Min., Edm., Buf.	11	767	235	306	541	157	82	18	24	42	11	2	1978-79	1988-89
Naslund, Mats	Mtl., Bos.	9	651	251	383	634	111	102	35	57	92	33	1	1982-83	1994-95
Nattrass, Ralph	Chi.	4	223	18	38	56	308	....	....	....	....	....	....	1946-47	1949-50
Nattress, Ric	Mtl., St.L., Cgy., Tor., Phi.	11	536	29	135	164	377	67	5	10	15	60	1	1982-83	1992-93
Natyshak, Mike	Que.	1	4	0	0	0	0	....	....	....	....	....	....	1987-88	1987-88
‡ Ndur, Rumun	Buf., NYR, Atl.	4	69	2	3	5	137	....	....	....	....	....	....	1996-97	1999-00
‡ Neaton, Pat	Pit.	1	9	1	1	2	12	....	....	....	....	....	....	1993-94	1993-94
Nechayev, Viktor	L.A.	1	3	1	0	1	0	....	....	....	....	....	....	1982-83	1982-83
Nedomansky, Vaclav	Det., NYR, St.L.	6	421	122	156	278	88	7	3	5	8	0	....	1977-78	1982-83
‡ Nedved, Zdenek	Tor.	3	31	4	6	10	14	....	....	....	....	....	....	1994-95	1996-97
Needham, Mike	Pit., Dal.	3	86	9	5	14	16	14	2	0	2	4	1	1991-92	1993-94
Neely, Bob	Tor., Col.	5	283	39	59	98	266	26	5	7	12	15	....	1973-74	1977-78
Neely, Cam	Van., Bos.	13	726	395	299	694	1241	93	57	32	89	168	....	1983-84	1995-96
Neilson, Jim	NYR, Cal., Cle.	16	1023	69	299	368	904	65	1	17	18	61	....	1962-63	1977-78
Nelson, Gordie	Tor.	1	3	0	0	0	11	....	....	....	....	....	....	1969-70	1969-70
‡ Nelson, Todd	Pit., Wsh.	2	3	1	0	1	2	4	0	0	0	0	....	1991-92	1993-94
Nemeth, Steve	NYR	1	12	2	0	2	2	....	....	....	....	....	....	1987-88	1987-88
‡ Nemirovsky, David	Fla.	4	91	16	22	38	42	3	1	0	1	0	....	1995-96	1998-99
Nesterenko, Eric	Tor., Chi.	21	1219	250	324	574	1273	124	13	24	37	127	1	1951-52	1971-72
Nethery, Lance	NYR, Edm.	2	41	11	14	25	14	14	5	3	8	9	....	1980-81	1981-82
Neufeld, Ray	Hfd., Wpg., Bos.	11	595	157	200	357	816	28	8	6	14	55	....	1979-80	1989-90
• Neville, Mike	Tor., NYA	3	65	5	5	10	14	2	0	0	0	0	....	1924-25	1930-31
Nevin, Bob	Tor., NYR, Min., L.A.	18	1128	307	419	726	211	84	16	18	34	24	2	1957-58	1975-76
Newberry, John	Mtl., Hfd.	4	22	0	4	4	6	2	0	0	0	0	....	1982-83	1985-86
Newell, Rick	Det.	2	6	0	0	0	0	....	....	....	....	....	....	1972-73	1973-74
Newman, Dan	NYR, Mtl., Edm.	4	126	17	24	41	63	3	0	0	0	4	....	1976-77	1979-80
• Newman, John	Det.	1	8	1	1	2	0	....	....	....	....	....	....	1930-31	1930-31
Nicholls, Bernie	L.A., NYR, Edm., N.J., Chi., S.J.	18	1127	475	734	1209	1292	118	42	72	114	164	....	1981-82	1998-99
Nicholson, Al	Bos.	2	19	0	1	1	4	....	....	....	....	....	....	1955-56	1956-57
• Nicholson, Ed	Det.	1	1	0	0	0	0	....	....	....	....	....	....	1947-48	1947-48
• Nicholson, Hickey	Chi.	1	2	1	0	1	0	....	....	....	....	....	....	1937-38	1937-38
Nicholson, Neil	Oak., NYI	4	39	3	1	4	23	2	0	0	0	0	....	1969-70	1977-78
Nicholson, Paul	Wsh.	3	62	4	8	12	18	....	....	....	....	....	....	1974-75	1976-77
Nicolson, Graeme	Bos., Col., NYR	3	52	2	7	9	60	....	....	....	....	....	....	1978-79	1982-83
‡ Nieckar, Barry	Hfd., Cgy., Ana.	4	8	0	0	0	21	....	....	....	....	....	....	1992-93	1997-98
Niekamp, Jim	Det.	2	29	0	2	2	37	....	....	....	....	....	....	1970-71	1971-72
Nielsen, Jeff	NYR, Ana., Min.	5	252	20	27	47	70	4	0	0	0	2	....	1996-97	2000-01
Nielsen, Kirk	Bos.	1	6	0	0	0	0	....	....	....	....	....	....	1997-98	1997-98
Nienhuis, Kraig	Bos.	3	87	20	16	36	39	2	0	0	0	14	....	1985-86	1987-88
• Nighbor, Frank	Ott., Tor.	13	349	139	98	237	249	20	4	9	13	13	4	1917-18	1929-30
Nigro, Frank	Tor.	2	68	8	18	26	39	3	0	0	0	2	....	1982-83	1983-84
‡ Nikulin, Igor	Ana.	1	....	....	....	....	....	1	0	0	0	0	....	1996-97	1996-97
Nilan, Chris	Mtl., NYR, Bos.	13	688	110	115	225	3043	111	8	9	17	541	1	1979-80	1991-92
Nill, Jim	St.L., Van., Bos., Wpg., Det.	9	524	58	87	145	854	59	10	5	15	203	....	1981-82	1989-90
Nilsson, Kent	Atl., Cgy., Min., Edm.	9	553	264	422	686	116	59	11	41	52	14	1	1979-80	1994-95
Nilsson, Ulf	NYR	4	170	57	112	169	85	25	8	14	22	27	....	1978-79	1982-83
Nistico, Lou	Col.	1	3	0	0	0	0	....	....	....	....	....	....	1977-78	1977-78
• Noble, Reg	Tor., Mtl.M., Det.	16	510	168	106	274	916	18	2	2	4	33	3	1917-18	1932-33
Noel, Claude	Wsh.	1	7	0	0	0	0	....	....	....	....	....	....	1979-80	1979-80
• Nolan, Paddy	Tor.	1	2	0	0	0	0	....	....	....	....	....	....	1921-22	1921-22
Nolan, Ted	Det., Pit.	3	78	6	16	22	105	....	....	....	....	....	....	1981-82	1985-86
Nolet, Simon	Phi., K.C., Pit., Col.	10	562	150	182	332	187	34	6	3	9	8	1	1967-68	1976-77
Noonan, Brian	Chi., NYR, St.L., Van., Phx.	12	629	116	159	275	518	71	17	19	36	77	1	1987-88	1998-99
Nordmark, Robert	St.L., Van.	4	236	13	70	83	254	7	3	2	5	8	....	1987-88	1990-91
Noris, Joe	Pit., St.L., Buf.	3	55	2	5	7	22	....	....	....	....	....	....	1971-72	1973-74
‡ Norris, Dwayne	Que., Ana.	3	20	2	4	6	8	....	....	....	....	....	....	1993-94	1995-96
Norrish, Rod	Min.	2	21	3	3	6	2	....	....	....	....	....	....	1973-74	1974-75
• Northcott, Baldy	Mtl.M., Chi.	11	446	133	112	245	273	31	8	5	13	14	1	1928-29	1938-39
Norton, Jeff	NYI, S.J., St.L., Edm., T.B., Fla., Pit., Bos.	15	799	52	332	384	615	65	4	21	25	89	....	1987-88	2001-02
Norwich, Craig	Wpg., St.L., Col.	2	104	17	58	75	60	....	....	....	....	....	....	1979-80	1980-81
Norwood, Lee	Que., Wsh., St.L., Det., N.J., Hfd., Cgy.	12	503	58	153	211	1099	65	6	22	28	171	....	1980-81	1993-94
Novy, Milan	Wsh.	1	73	18	30	48	16	2	0	0	0	0	....	1982-83	1982-83
Nowak, Hank	Pit., Det., Bos.	4	180	26	29	55	161	13	1	0	1	8	....	1973-74	1976-77
‡ Nurminen, Kai	L.A., Min.	2	69	17	11	28	24	....	....	....	....	....	....	1996-97	2000-01
Nykoluk, Mike	Tor.	1	32	3	1	4	20	....	....	....	....	....	....	1956-57	1956-57
Nylund, Gary	Tor., Chi., NYI	11	608	32	139	171	1235	24	0	6	6	63	....	1982-83	1992-93
• Nyrop, Bill	Mtl., Min.	4	207	12	51	63	101	35	1	7	8	22	3	1975-76	1981-82
Nystrom, Bob	NYI	14	900	235	278	513	1248	157	39	44	83	236	4	1972-73	1985-86
O															
• Oatman, Russell	Det., Mtl.M., NYR	3	120	20	9	29	100	15	1	0	1	18	....	1926-27	1928-29
O'Brien, Dennis	Min., Col., Cle., Bos.	10	592	31	91	122	1017	34	1	2	3	101	....	1970-71	1979-80
O'Brien, Ellard	Bos.	1	2	0	0	0	0	....	....	....	....	....	....	1955-56	1955-56
O'Callahan, Jack	Chi., N.J.	7	389	27	104	131	541	32	4	11	15	41	....	1982-83	1988-89
O'Connell, Mike	Chi., Bos., Det.	13	860	105	334	439	605	82	8	24	32	64	....	1977-78	1989-90
• O'Connor, Buddy	Mtl., NYR	10	509	140	257	397	34	53	15	21	36	6	2	1941-42	1950-51
O'Connor, Myles	N.J., Ana.	4	43	3	4	7	69	....	....	....	....	....	....	1990-91	1993-94
Oddleifson, Chris	Bos., Van.	9	524	95	191	286	464	14	1	6	7	8	....	1972-73	1980-81
Odelein, Selmar	Edm.	3	18	0	2	2	35	....	....	....	....	....	....	1985-86	1988-89
Odjick, Gino	Van., NYI, Phi., Mtl.	12	605	64	73	137	2567	44	4	1	5	142	....	1990-91	2001-02
O'Donnell, Fred	Bos.	2	115	15	11	26	98	5	0	1	1	5	....	1972-73	1973-74
O'Donoghue, Don	Oak., Cal.	3	125	18	17	35	35	3	0	0	0	0	....	1969-70	1971-72
Odrowski, Gerry	Det., Oak., St.L.	6	309	12	19	31	111	30	0	1	1	16	....	1960-61	1971-72
O'Dwyer, Bill	L.A., Bos.	5	120	9	13	22	108	10	0	0	0	2	....	1983-84	1989-90
O'Flaherty, Gerry	Tor., Van., Atl.	8	438	99	95	194	168	7	2	2	4	6	....	1971-72	1978-79
O'Flaherty, Peanuts	NYA, Bro.	2	21	5	1	6	0	....	....	....	....	....	....	1940-41	1941-42
Ogilvie, Brian	Chi., St.L.	6	90	15	21	36	29	....	....	....	....	....	....	1972-73	1978-79
• O'Grady, George	Mtl.W.	1	4	0	0	0	0	....	....	....	....	....	....	1917-18	1917-18
Ogrodnick, John	Det., Que., NYR	14	928	402	425	827	260	41	18	8	26	6	....	1979-80	1992-93
‡ Ojanen, Janne	N.J.	4	98	21	23	44	28	3	0	2	2	0	....	1988-89	1992-93
Okerlund, Todd	NYI	1	4	0	0	0	2	....	....	....	....	....	....	1987-88	1987-88
Oksiuta, Roman	Edm., Van., Ana., Pit.	4	153	46	41	87	100	10	2	3	5	0	....	1993-94	1996-97
Olczyk, Ed	Chi., Tor., Wpg., NYR, L.A., Pit.	16	1031	342	452	794	874	57	19	15	34	57	1	1984-85	1999-00
• Oliver, Harry	Bos., NYA	11	463	127	85	212	147	35	10	6	16	24	1	1926-27	1936-37
Oliver, Murray	Det., Bos., Tor., Min.	17	1127	274	454	728	320	35	9	16	25	10	....	1957-58	1974-75
Olmstead, Bert	Chi., Mtl., Tor.	14	848	181	421	602	884	115	16	43	59	101	5	1948-49	1961-62
Olsen, Darryl	Cgy.	1	1	0	0	0	0	....	....	....	....	....	....	1991-92	1991-92
Olson, Dennis	Det.	1	4	0	0	0	0	....	....	....	....	....	....	1957-58	1957-58
‡ Olsson, Christer	St.L., Ott.	2	56	4	12	16	24	3	0	0	0	0	....	1995-96	1996-97
• O'Neil, Jim	Bos., Mtl.	6	156	6	30	36	109	9	1	1	2	13	....	1933-34	1941-42
O'Neil, Paul	Van., Bos.	2	6	0	0	0	0	....	....	....	....	....	....	1973-74	1975-76
• O'Neill, Tom	Tor.	2	66	10	12	22	53	4	0	0	0	6	1	1943-44	1944-45
Orban, Bill	Chi., Min.	3	114	8	15	23	67	3	0	0	0	0	....	1967-68	1969-70
O'Ree, Willie	Bos.	2	45	4	10	14	26	....	....	....	....	....	....	1957-58	1960-61
O'Regan, Tom	Pit.	3	61	5	12	17	10	....	....	....	....	....	....	1983-84	1985-86
O'Reilly, Terry	Bos.	14	891	204	402	606	2095	108	25	42	67	335	....	1971-72	1984-85
Orlando, Gates	Buf.	3	98	18	26	44	51	5	0	4	4	14	....	1984-85	1986-87
• Orlando, Jimmy	Det.	6	199	6	25	31	375	36	0	9	9	105	1	1936-37	1942-43
Orleski, Dave	Mtl.	2	2	0	0	0	0	....	....	....	....	....	....	1980-81	1981-82
Orr, Bobby	Bos., Chi.	12	657	270	645	915	953	74	26	66	92	107	2	1966-67	1978-79
Osborne, Keith	St.L., T.B.	2	16	1	3	4	16	....	....	....	....	....	....	1989-90	1992-93
Osborne, Mark	Det., NYR, Tor., Wpg.	14	919	212	319	531	1152	87	12	16	28	141	....	1981-82	1994-95
Osburn, Randy	Tor., Phi.	2	27	0	2	2	0	....	....	....	....	....	....	1972-73	1974-75
O'Shea, Danny	Min., Chi., St.L.	5	369	64	115	179	265	39	3	7	10	61	....	1968-69	1972-73
O'Shea, Kevin	Buf., St.L.	3	134	13	18	31	85	12	2	1	3	10	....	1970-71	1972-73

Name	NHL Teams	NHL Seasons	Regular Schedule GP	G	A	TP	PIM	Playoffs GP	G	A	TP	PIM	NHL Cup Wins	First NHL Season	Last NHL Season
Osiecki, Mark	Cgy., Ott., Wpg., Min.	2	93	3	11	14	43	....	....	....	....	....	....	1991-92	1992-93
Otevrel, Jaroslav	S.J.	2	16	3	4	7	2	....	....	....	....	....	....	1992-93	1993-94
Otto, Joel	Cgy., Phi.	14	943	195	313	508	1934	122	27	47	74	207	1	1984-85	1997-98
Ouellette, Eddie	Chi.	1	43	3	2	5	11	1	0	0	0	0	....	1935-36	1935-36
Ouellette, Gerry	Bos.	1	34	5	4	9	0	....	....	....	....	....	....	1960-61	1960-61
Owchar, Dennis	Pit., Col.	6	288	30	85	115	200	10	1	1	2	8	....	1974-75	1979-80
● Owen, George	Bos.	5	183	44	33	77	151	21	2	5	7	25	1	1928-29	1932-33

P

Name	NHL Teams	NHL Seasons	Regular Schedule GP	G	A	TP	PIM	Playoffs GP	G	A	TP	PIM	NHL Cup Wins	First NHL Season	Last NHL Season
Pachal, Clayton	Bos., Col.	3	35	2	3	5	95	....	....	....	....	....	....	1976-77	1978-79
Paddock, John	Wsh., Phi., Que.	5	87	8	14	22	86	5	2	0	2	0	....	1975-76	1982-83
‡ Paek, Jim	Pit., L.A., Ott.	5	217	5	29	34	155	27	1	4	5	8	2	1990-91	1994-95
Paiement, Rosaire	Phi., Van.	5	190	48	52	100	343	3	3	0	3	0	....	1967-68	1971-72
Paiement, Wilf	K.C., Col., Tor., Que., NYR, Buf., Pit.	14	946	356	458	814	1757	69	18	17	35	185	....	1974-75	1987-88
Palangio, Pete	Mtl., Det., Chi.	5	71	13	10	23	28	7	0	0	0	0	1	1926-27	1937-38
Palazzari, Aldo	Bos., NYR	1	35	8	3	11	4	....	....	....	....	....	....	1943-44	1943-44
Palazzari, Doug	St.L.	4	108	18	20	38	23	2	0	0	0	0	....	1974-75	1978-79
Palmer, Brad	Min., Bos.	3	168	32	38	70	58	29	9	5	14	16	....	1980-81	1982-83
Palmer, Rob	Chi.	3	16	0	3	3	2	....	....	....	....	....	....	1973-74	1975-76
Palmer, Robert	L.A., N.J.	7	320	9	101	110	115	8	1	2	3	6	....	1977-78	1983-84
● Panagabko, Ed	Bos.	2	29	0	3	3	38	....	....	....	....	....	....	1955-56	1956-57
‡ Pankewicz, Greg	Ott., Cgy.	2	21	0	3	3	22	....	....	....	....	....	....	1993-94	1998-99
‡ Panteleev, Grigori	Bos., NYI	4	54	8	6	14	12	....	....	....	....	....	....	1992-93	1995-96
● Papike, Joe	Chi.	3	20	3	3	6	4	5	0	2	2	0	....	1940-41	1944-45
Pappin, Jim	Tor., Chi., Cal., Cle.	14	767	278	295	573	667	92	33	34	67	101	2	1963-64	1976-77
Paradise, Bob	Min., Atl., Pit., Wsh.	8	368	8	54	62	393	12	0	1	1	19	....	1971-72	1978-79
Pargeter, George	Mtl.	1	4	0	0	0	0	....	....	....	....	....	....	1946-47	1946-47
Parise, J.P.	Bos., Tor., Min., NYI, Cle.	14	890	238	356	594	706	86	27	31	58	87	....	1965-66	1978-79
Parizeau, Michel	St.L., Phi.	1	58	3	14	17	18	....	....	....	....	....	....	1971-72	1971-72
Park, Brad	NYR, Bos., Det.	17	1113	213	683	896	1429	161	35	90	125	217	....	1968-69	1984-85
Parker, Jeff	Buf., Hfd.	5	141	16	19	35	163	5	0	0	0	26	....	1986-87	1990-91
● Parkes, Ernie	Mtl.M.	1	17	0	0	0	2	....	....	....	....	....	....	1924-25	1924-25
‡ Parks, Greg	NYI	3	23	1	2	3	6	2	0	0	0	0	....	1990-91	1992-93
● Parsons, George	Tor.	3	78	12	13	25	20	7	3	2	5	11	....	1936-37	1938-39
● Pasek, Dusan	Min.	1	48	4	10	14	30	2	1	0	1	0	....	1988-89	1988-89
Pasin, Dave	Bos., L.A.	2	76	18	19	37	50	3	0	1	1	0	....	1985-86	1988-89
Paslawski, Greg	Mtl., St.L., Wpg., Buf., Que., Phi., Cgy.	11	650	187	185	372	169	60	19	13	32	25	....	1983-84	1993-94
‡ Patera, Pavel	Dal., Min.	2	32	2	7	9	8	....	....	....	....	....	....	1999-00	2000-01
Paterson, Joe	Det., Phi., L.A., NYR	9	291	19	37	56	829	22	3	4	7	77	....	1980-81	1988-89
Paterson, Mark	Hfd.	4	29	3	3	6	33	....	....	....	....	....	....	1982-83	1985-86
Paterson, Rick	Chi.	9	430	50	43	93	136	61	7	10	17	51	....	1978-79	1986-87
Patey, Doug	Wsh.	3	45	4	2	6	8	....	....	....	....	....	....	1976-77	1978-79
Patey, Larry	Cal., St.L., NYR	12	717	153	163	316	631	40	8	10	18	57	....	1973-74	1984-85
Patrick, Craig	Cal., St.L., K.C., Wsh.	8	401	72	91	163	61	2	0	1	1	0	....	1971-72	1978-79
Patrick, Glenn	St.L., Cal., Cle.	4	38	2	3	5	72	....	....	....	....	....	....	1973-74	1976-77
● Patrick, Lester	NYR	1	1	0	0	0	2	....	....	....	....	....	....	1926-27	1926-27
● Patrick, Lynn	NYR	10	455	145	190	335	240	44	10	6	16	22	1	1934-35	1945-46
● Patrick, Muzz	NYR	5	166	5	26	31	133	25	4	0	4	34	1	1937-38	1945-46
Patrick, Steve	Buf., NYR, Que.	6	250	40	68	108	242	12	0	1	1	12	....	1980-81	1985-86
Patterson, Colin	Cgy., Buf.	10	504	96	109	205	239	85	12	17	29	57	1	1983-84	1992-93
Patterson, Dennis	K.C., Phi.	3	138	6	22	28	67	....	....	....	....	....	....	1974-75	1979-80
‡ Patterson, Ed	Pit.	3	68	3	3	6	56	....	....	....	....	....	....	1993-94	1996-97
● Patterson, George	Tor., Mtl., NYA, Bos., Det., St.L.	9	284	51	27	78	218	3	0	0	0	2	....	1926-27	1934-35
● Paul, Butch	Det.	1	3	0	0	0	0	....	....	....	....	....	....	1964-65	1964-65
● Paulhus, Rollie	Mtl.	1	33	0	0	0	0	....	....	....	....	....	....	1925-26	1925-26
Pavelich, Mark	NYR, Min., S.J.	7	355	137	192	329	340	23	7	17	24	14	....	1981-82	1991-92
Pavelich, Marty	Det.	10	634	93	159	252	454	91	13	15	28	74	4	1947-48	1956-57
Pavese, Jim	St.L., NYR, Det., Hfd.	8	328	13	44	57	689	34	0	6	6	81	....	1981-82	1988-89
● Payer, Evariste	Mtl.	1	1	0	0	0	0	....	....	....	....	....	....	1917-18	1917-18
Payne, Davis	Bos.	2	22	0	1	1	14	....	....	....	....	....	....	1995-96	1996-97
Payne, Steve	Min.	10	613	228	238	466	435	71	35	35	70	60	....	1978-79	1987-88
Paynter, Kent	Chi., Wsh., Wpg., Ott.	7	37	1	3	4	69	4	0	0	0	10	....	1987-88	1993-94
Peake, Pat	Wsh.	5	134	28	41	69	105	13	2	2	4	20	....	1993-94	1997-98
● Pearson, Mel	NYR, Pit.	5	38	2	6	8	25	....	....	....	....	....	....	1959-60	1967-68
‡ Pearson, Rob	Tor., Wsh., St.L.	6	269	56	54	110	645	33	4	2	6	94	....	1991-92	1996-97
Pearson, Scott	Tor., Que., Edm., Buf., NYI	10	292	56	42	98	615	10	2	0	2	14	....	1988-89	1999-00
Pedersen, Allen	Bos., Min., Hfd.	8	428	5	36	41	487	64	0	0	0	91	....	1986-87	1993-94
Pederson, Barry	Bos., Van., Pit., Hfd.	12	701	238	416	654	472	34	22	30	52	25	1	1980-81	1991-92
‡ Pederson, Mark	Mtl., Phi., S.J., Det.	5	169	35	50	85	77	2	0	0	0	0	....	1989-90	1993-94
Pederson, Tom	S.J., Tor.	5	240	20	49	69	142	24	1	11	12	10	....	1992-93	1996-97
● Peer, Bert	Det.	1	1	0	0	0	0	....	....	....	....	....	....	1939-40	1939-40
Peirson, Johnny	Bos.	11	545	153	173	326	315	49	10	16	26	26	....	1946-47	1957-58
Pelensky, Perry	Chi.	1	4	0	0	0	5	....	....	....	....	....	....	1983-84	1983-84
Pelletier, Roger	Phi.	1	1	0	0	0	0	....	....	....	....	....	....	1967-68	1967-68
Peloffy, Andre	Wsh.	1	9	0	0	0	0	....	....	....	....	....	....	1974-75	1974-75
Peluso, Mike	Chi., Ott., N.J., St.L., Cgy.	9	458	38	52	90	1951	62	3	4	7	107	1	1989-90	1997-98
Pelyk, Mike	Tor.	9	441	26	88	114	566	40	0	3	3	41	....	1967-68	1977-78
Penney, Chad	Ott.	1	3	0	0	0	2	....	....	....	....	....	....	1993-94	1993-94
Pennington, Cliff	Mtl., Bos.	3	101	17	42	59	6	....	....	....	....	....	....	1960-61	1962-63
Peplinski, Jim	Cgy.	11	711	161	263	424	1467	99	15	31	46	382	1	1980-81	1994-95
Perlini, Fred	Tor.	2	8	2	3	5	0	....	....	....	....	....	....	1981-82	1983-84
Perreault, Fern	NYR	2	3	0	0	0	0	....	....	....	....	....	....	1947-48	1949-50
Perreault, Gilbert	Buf.	17	1191	512	814	1326	500	90	33	70	103	44	....	1970-71	1986-87
Perry, Brian	Oak., Buf.	3	96	16	29	45	24	8	1	1	2	4	....	1968-69	1970-71
Persson, Stefan	NYI	9	622	52	317	369	574	102	7	50	57	69	4	1977-78	1985-86
Pesut, George	Cal.	2	92	3	22	25	130	....	....	....	....	....	....	1974-75	1975-76
● Peters, Frank	NYR	1	43	0	0	0	59	4	0	0	0	2	....	1930-31	1930-31
Peters, Garry	Mtl., NYR, Phi., Bos.	8	311	34	34	68	261	9	2	2	4	31	1	1964-65	1971-72
Peters, Jimmy	Mtl., Bos., Det., Chi.	9	574	125	150	275	186	60	5	9	14	22	3	1945-46	1953-54
Peters Jr., Jimmy	Det., L.A.	9	309	37	36	73	48	11	0	2	2	2	....	1964-65	1974-75
Peters, Steve	Col.	1	2	0	1	1	0	....	....	....	....	....	....	1979-80	1979-80
Peterson, Brent	Det., Buf., Van., Hfd.	11	620	72	141	213	484	31	4	4	8	65	....	1978-79	1988-89
‡ Peterson, Brent	T.B.	3	56	9	1	10	6	....	....	....	....	....	....	1996-97	1998-99
‡ Petit, Michel	Van., NYR, Que., Tor., Cgy., L.A., T.B., Edm., Phi., Phx.	16	827	90	238	328	1839	19	0	2	2	61	....	1982-83	1997-98
‡ Petrenko, Sergei	Buf.	1	14	0	4	4	0	....	....	....	....	....	....	1993-94	1993-94
‡ Petrovicky, Robert	Hfd., Dal., St.L., T.B., NYI	8	208	27	38	65	118	2	0	0	0	0	....	1992-93	2000-01
Pettersson, Jorgen	St.L., Hfd., Wsh.	6	435	174	192	366	117	44	15	12	27	4	....	1980-81	1985-86
● Pettinger, Eric	Bos., Tor., Ott.	3	98	7	12	19	83	4	1	0	1	8	....	1928-29	1930-31
● Pettinger, Gord	NYR, Det., Bos.	8	292	42	74	116	77	47	4	5	9	11	4	1932-33	1939-40
Phair, Lyle	L.A.	3	48	6	7	13	12	1	0	0	0	0	....	1985-86	1987-88
Phillipoff, Harold	Atl., Chi.	3	141	26	57	83	267	6	0	2	2	9	....	1977-78	1979-80
● Phillips, Bill	Mtl.M.	1	27	1	1	2	6	4	0	0	0	2	....	1929-30	1929-30
Phillips, Charlie	Mtl.	1	17	0	0	0	6	....	....	....	....	....	....	1942-43	1942-43
● Phillips, Merlyn	Mtl.M., NYA	8	302	52	31	83	232	24	5	1	6	19	1	1925-26	1932-33
Picard, Noel	Mtl., St.L., Atl.	7	335	12	63	75	616	50	2	11	13	167	1	1964-65	1972-73
Picard, Robert	Wsh., Tor., Mtl., Wpg., Que., Det.	13	899	104	319	423	1025	36	5	15	20	39	....	1977-78	1989-90
Picard, Roger	St.L.	1	15	2	2	4	21	....	....	....	....	....	....	1967-68	1967-68
Pichette, Dave	Que., St.L., N.J., NYR	7	322	41	140	181	348	28	3	7	10	54	....	1980-81	1987-88
Picketts, Hal	NYA	1	48	3	1	4	32	....	....	....	....	....	....	1933-34	1933-34
Pidhirny, Harry	Bos.	1	2	0	0	0	0	....	....	....	....	....	....	1957-58	1957-58
Pierce, Randy	Col., N.J., Hfd.	8	277	62	76	138	223	2	0	0	0	0	....	1977-78	1984-85
Pike, Alf	NYR	6	234	42	77	119	145	21	4	2	6	12	1	1939-40	1946-47
Pilon, Rich	NYI, NYR, St.L.	14	631	8	69	77	1745	15	0	0	0	50	....	1988-89	2001-02
Pilote, Pierre	Chi., Tor.	14	890	80	418	498	1251	86	8	53	61	102	1	1955-56	1968-69
Pinder, Gerry	Chi., Cal.	3	223	55	69	124	135	17	0	4	4	6	....	1969-70	1971-72
Pirus, Alex	Min., Det.	4	159	30	28	58	94	2	0	1	1	2	....	1976-77	1979-80
Pitlick, Lance	Ott., Fla.	8	393	16	33	49	298	24	0	2	2	21	....	1994-95	2001-02
● Pitre, Didier	Mtl.	6	127	64	34	98	84	9	2	4	6	16	....	1917-18	1922-23
Pivonka, Michal	Wsh.	13	825	181	418	599	478	95	19	36	55	86	....	1986-87	1998-99
● Plager, Barclay	St.L.	10	614	44	187	231	1115	68	3	20	23	182	....	1967-68	1976-77
Plager, Bill	Min., St.L., Atl.	9	263	4	34	38	294	31	0	2	2	26	....	1967-68	1975-76
Plager, Bob	NYR, St.L.	14	644	20	126	146	802	74	2	17	19	195	....	1964-65	1977-78
Plamondon, Gerry	Mtl.	5	74	7	13	20	10	11	5	2	7	2	1	1945-46	1950-51
Plante, Cam	Tor.	1	2	0	0	0	0	....	....	....	....	....	....	1984-85	1984-85

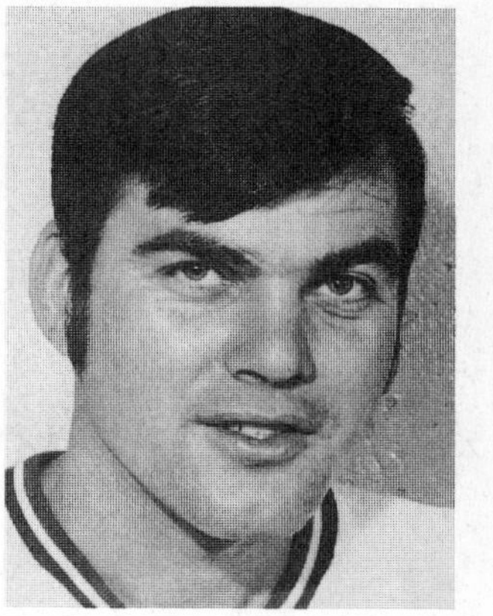
Rosaire Paiement

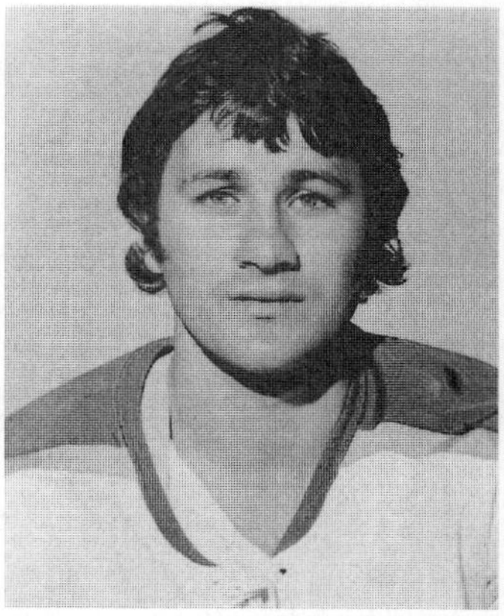
Gilbert Perreault

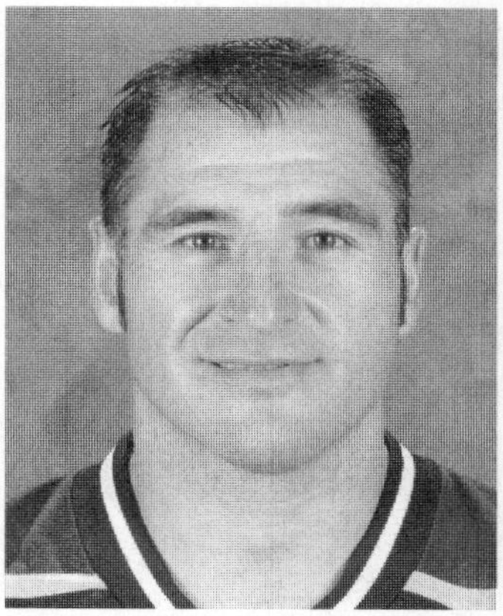
Rich Pilon

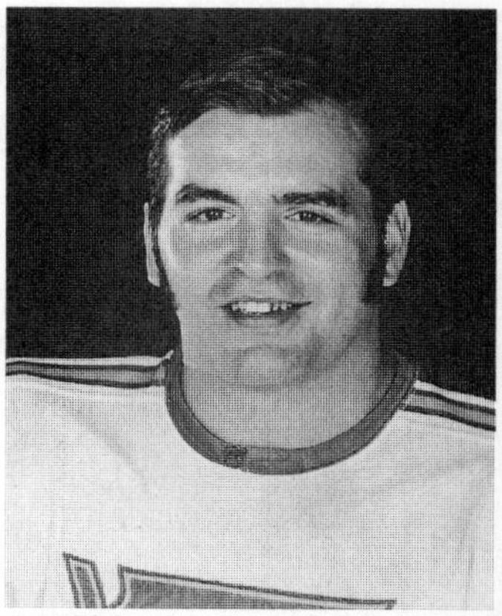
Bob Plager

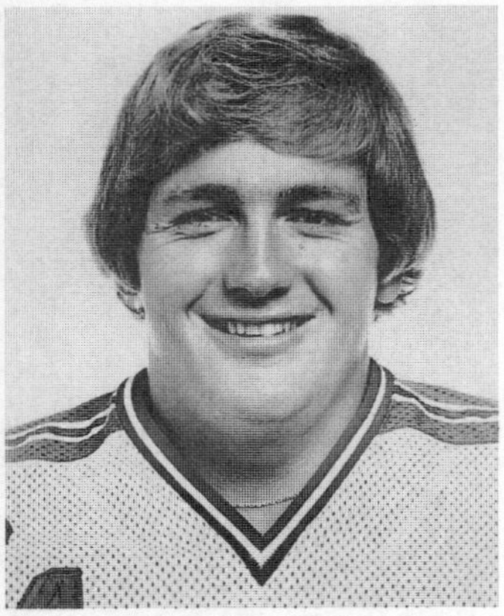

Greg Polis

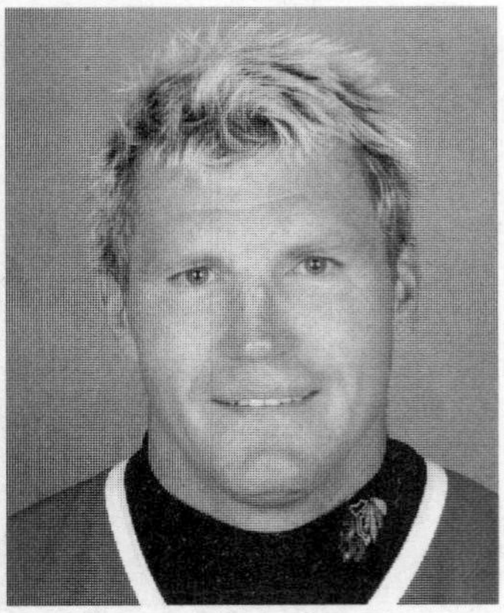

Bob Probert

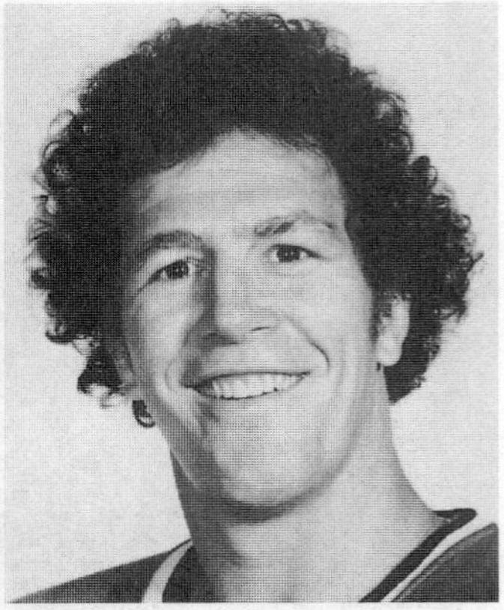

Jean Pronovost

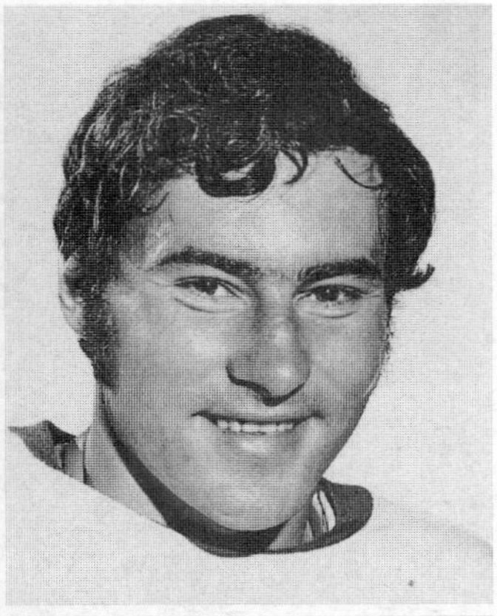

Mickey Redmond

			Regular Schedule					Playoffs							
Name	**NHL Teams**	**NHL Seasons**	**GP**	**G**	**A**	**TP**	**PIM**	**GP**	**G**	**A**	**TP**	**PIM**	**NHL Cup Wins**	**First NHL Season**	**Last NHL Season**
Plante, Dan	NYI	4	159	9	14	23	135	1	1	0	1	2	....	1993-94	1997-98
‡ Plante, Derek	Buf., Dal., Chi., Phi.	8	450	96	152	248	138	41	6	10	16	18	1	1993-94	2000-01
Plante, Pierre	Phi., St.L., Chi., NYR, Que.	9	599	125	172	297	599	33	2	6	8	51	....	1971-72	1979-80
Plantery, Mark	Wpg.	1	25	1	5	6	14	....	....	....	....	....	....	1980-81	1980-81
‡ Plavsic, Adrien	St.L., Van., T.B., Ana.	8	214	16	56	72	161	13	1	7	8	4	....	1989-90	1996-97
• Plaxton, Hugh	Mtl.M.	1	15	1	2	3	4	....	....	....	....	....	....	1932-33	1932-33
Playfair, Jim	Edm., Chi.	3	21	2	4	6	51	....	....	....	....	....	....	1983-84	1988-89
Playfair, Larry	Buf., L.A.	12	688	26	94	120	1812	43	0	6	6	111	....	1978-79	1989-90
Pleau, Larry	Mtl.	3	94	9	15	24	27	4	0	0	0	0	....	1969-70	1971-72
• Pletsch, Charles	Ham.	1	1	0	0	0	0	....	....	....	....	....	....	1920-21	1920-21
Plett, Willi	Atl., Cgy., Min., Bos.	13	834	222	215	437	2572	83	24	22	46	466	....	1975-76	1987-88
Plumb, Rob	Det.	2	14	3	2	5	2	....	....	....	....	....	....	1977-78	1978-79
Plumb, Ron	Hfd.	1	26	3	4	7	14	....	....	....	....	....	....	1979-80	1979-80
Pocza, Harvie	Wsh.	2	3	0	0	0	2	....	....	....	....	....	....	1979-80	1981-82
Poddubny, Walt	Edm., Tor., NYR, Que., N.J.	11	468	184	238	422	454	19	7	2	9	12	....	1981-82	1991-92
‡ Podloski, Ray	Bos.	1	8	0	1	1	17	....	....	....	....	....	....	1988-89	1988-89
Podolsky, Nels	Det.	1	1	0	0	0	0	7	0	0	0	4	....	1948-49	1948-49
Poeschek, Rudy	NYR, Wpg., T.B., St.L.	12	364	6	25	31	817	5	0	0	0	18	....	1987-88	1999-00
Poeta, Tony	Chi.	1	1	0	0	0	0	....	....	....	....	....	....	1951-52	1951-52
Poile, Bud	Tor., Chi., Det., NYR, Bos.	7	311	107	122	229	91	23	4	5	9	8	1	1942-43	1949-50
Poile, Don	Det.	2	66	7	9	16	12	4	0	0	0	0	....	1954-55	1957-58
Poirier, Gordie	Mtl.	1	10	0	0	0	0	....	....	....	....	....	....	1939-40	1939-40
Polanic, Tom	Min.	2	19	0	2	2	53	5	1	1	2	4	....	1969-70	1970-71
• Polich, John	NYR	2	3	0	1	1	0	....	....	....	....	....	....	1939-40	1940-41
Polich, Mike	Mtl., Min.	5	226	24	29	53	57	23	2	1	3	2	1	1976-77	1980-81
Polis, Greg	Pit., St.L., NYR, Wsh.	10	615	174	169	343	391	7	0	2	2	6	....	1970-71	1979-80
Poliziani, Dan	Bos.	1	1	0	0	0	0	3	0	0	0	0	....	1958-59	1958-59
Polonich, Dennis	Det.	8	390	59	82	141	1242	7	1	0	1	19	....	1974-75	1982-83
Pooley, Paul	Wpg.	2	15	0	3	3	0	....	....	....	....	....	....	1984-85	1985-86
Popein, Larry	NYR, Oak.	8	449	80	141	221	162	16	1	4	5	6	....	1954-55	1967-68
Popiel, Poul	Bos., L.A., Det., Van., Edm.	7	224	13	41	54	210	4	1	0	1	4	....	1965-66	1979-80
‡ Popovic, Peter	Mtl., NYR, Pit., Bos.	8	485	10	63	73	291	35	1	4	5	18	....	1993-94	2000-01
• Portland, Jack	Mtl., Bos., Chi.	10	381	15	56	71	323	33	1	3	4	25	1	1933-34	1942-43
Porvari, Jukka	Col., N.J.	2	39	3	9	12	4	....	....	....	....	....	....	1981-82	1982-83
Posa, Victor	Chi.	1	2	0	0	0	2	....	....	....	....	....	....	1985-86	1985-86
Posavad, Mike	St.L.	2	8	0	0	0	0	....	....	....	....	....	....	1985-86	1986-87
Potomski, Barry	L.A., S.J.	3	68	6	5	11	227	....	....	....	....	....	....	1995-96	1997-98
Potvin, Denis	NYI	15	1060	310	742	1052	1356	185	56	108	164	253	4	1973-74	1987-88
Potvin, Jean	L.A., Phi., NYI, Cle., Min.	11	613	63	224	287	478	39	2	9	11	17	1	1970-71	1980-81
Potvin, Marc	Det., L.A., Hfd., Bos.	6	121	3	5	8	456	13	0	1	1	50	....	1990-91	1995-96
‡ Poudrier, Daniel	Que.	3	25	1	5	6	10	....	....	....	....	....	....	1985-86	1987-88
Poulin, Daniel	Min.	1	3	1	1	2	2	....	....	....	....	....	....	1981-82	1981-82
Poulin, Dave	Phi., Bos., Wsh.	13	724	205	325	530	482	129	31	42	73	132	....	1982-83	1994-95
Poulin, Patrick	Hfd., Chi., T.B., Mtl.	11	634	101	134	235	299	32	6	2	8	8	....	1991-92	2001-02
Pouzar, Jaroslav	Edm.	4	186	34	48	82	135	29	6	4	10	16	3	1982-83	1986-87
• Powell, Ray	Chi.	1	31	7	15	22	2	....	....	....	....	....	....	1950-51	1950-51
Powis, Geoff	Chi.	1	2	0	0	0	0	....	....	....	....	....	....	1967-68	1967-68
Powis, Lynn	Chi., K.C.	2	130	19	33	52	25	1	0	0	0	0	....	1973-74	1974-75
Prajsler, Petr	L.A., Bos.	4	46	3	10	13	51	4	0	0	0	0	....	1987-88	1991-92
• Pratt, Babe	NYR, Tor., Bos.	12	517	83	209	292	463	63	12	17	29	90	2	1935-36	1946-47
Pratt, Jack	Bos.	2	37	2	0	2	42	4	0	0	0	0	....	1930-31	1931-32
Pratt, Kelly	Pit.	1	22	0	6	6	15	....	....	....	....	....	....	1974-75	1974-75
Pratt, Tracy	Oak., Pit., Buf., Van., Col., Tor.	10	580	17	97	114	1026	25	0	1	1	62	....	1967-68	1976-77
Prentice, Dean	NYR, Bos., Det., Pit., Min.	22	1378	391	469	860	484	54	13	17	30	38	....	1952-53	1973-74
Prentice, Eric	Tor.	1	5	0	0	0	4	....	....	....	....	....	....	1943-44	1943-44
Presley, Wayne	Chi., S.J., Buf., NYR, Tor.	12	684	155	147	302	953	83	26	17	43	142	....	1984-85	1995-96
Preston, Rich	Chi., N.J.	8	580	127	164	291	348	47	4	18	22	56	....	1979-80	1986-87
Preston, Yves	Phi.	2	28	7	3	10	4	....	....	....	....	....	....	1978-79	1980-81
Priakin, Sergei	Cgy.	3	46	3	8	11	2	1	0	0	0	0	....	1988-89	1990-91
Price, Jack	Chi.	3	57	4	6	10	24	4	0	0	0	0	....	1951-52	1953-54
Price, Noel	Tor., NYR, Det., Mtl., Pit., L.A., Atl.	14	499	14	114	128	333	12	0	1	1	8	1	1957-58	1975-76
Price, Pat	NYI, Edm., Pit., Que., NYR, Min.	13	726	43	218	261	1456	74	2	10	12	195	....	1975-76	1987-88
Price, Tom	Cal., Cle., Pit.	5	29	0	2	2	12	....	....	....	....	....	....	1974-75	1978-79
Priestlay, Ken	Buf., Pit.	6	168	27	34	61	63	14	0	0	0	21	1	1986-87	1991-92
• Primeau, Joe	Tor.	9	310	66	177	243	105	38	5	18	23	12	1	1927-28	1935-36
Primeau, Kevin	Van.	1	2	0	0	0	4	....	....	....	....	....	....	1980-81	1980-81
• Pringle, Ellie	NYA	1	6	0	0	0	0	....	....	....	....	....	....	1930-31	1930-31
Probert, Bob	Det., Chi.	16	935	163	221	384	3300	81	16	32	48	274	....	1985-86	2001-02
‡ Prochazka, Martin	Tor., Atl.	2	32	2	5	7	8	....	....	....	....	....	....	1997-98	1999-00
• Prodgers, Goldie	Tor., Ham.	6	111	63	29	92	39	....	....	....	....	....	....	1919-20	1924-25
Prokhorov, Vitali	St.L.	3	83	19	11	30	35	4	0	0	0	0	....	1992-93	1994-95
Prokopec, Mike	Chi.	2	15	0	0	0	11	....	....	....	....	....	....	1995-96	1996-97
Pronovost, Andre	Mtl., Bos., Det., Min.	10	556	94	104	198	408	70	11	11	22	58	4	1956-57	1967-68
Pronovost, Jean	Pit., Atl., Wsh.	14	998	391	383	774	413	35	11	9	20	14	....	1968-69	1981-82
Pronovost, Marcel	Det., Tor.	21	1206	88	257	345	851	134	8	23	31	104	5	1949-50	1969-70
Propp, Brian	Phi., Bos., Min., Hfd.	15	1016	425	579	1004	830	160	64	84	148	151	....	1979-80	1993-94
‡ Proulx, Christian	Mtl.	1	7	1	2	3	20	....	....	....	....	....	....	1993-94	1993-94
• Provost, Claude	Mtl.	15	1005	254	335	589	469	126	25	38	63	86	9	1955-56	1969-70
Prpic, Joel	Bos., Col.	3	18	0	3	3	4	....	....	....	....	....	....	1997-98	2000-01
Pryor, Chris	Min., NYI	6	82	1	4	5	122	....	....	....	....	....	....	1984-85	1989-90
Prystai, Metro	Chi., Det.	11	674	151	179	330	231	43	12	14	26	8	2	1947-48	1957-58
• Pudas, Al	Tor.	1	4	0	0	0	0	....	....	....	....	....	....	1926-27	1926-27
Pulford, Bob	Tor., L.A.	16	1079	281	362	643	792	89	25	26	51	126	4	1956-57	1971-72
Pulkkinen, Dave	NYI	1	2	0	0	0	0	....	....	....	....	....	....	1972-73	1972-73
• Purpur, Fido	St.L., Chi., Det.	5	144	25	35	60	46	16	1	2	3	4	....	1934-35	1944-45
‡ Purves, John	Wsh.	1	7	1	0	1	0	....	....	....	....	....	....	1990-91	1990-91
• Pusie, Jean	Mtl., NYR, Bos.	5	61	1	4	5	28	7	0	0	0	0	1	1930-31	1935-36
Pyatt, Nelson	Det., Wsh., Col.	7	296	71	63	134	69	....	....	....	....	....	....	1973-74	1979-80
Q															
• Quackenbush, Bill	Det., Bos.	14	774	62	222	284	95	80	2	19	21	8	....	1942-43	1955-56
Quackenbush, Max	Bos., Chi.	2	61	4	7	11	30	6	0	0	0	4	....	1950-51	1951-52
Quenneville, Joel	Tor., Col., N.J., Hfd., Wsh.	13	803	54	136	190	705	32	0	8	8	22	....	1978-79	1990-91
• Quenneville, Leo	NYR	1	25	0	3	3	10	3	0	0	0	0	....	1929-30	1929-30
• Quilty, John	Mtl., Bos.	4	125	36	34	70	81	13	3	5	8	9	....	1940-41	1947-48
Quinn, Dan	Cgy., Pit., Van., St.L., Phi., Min., Ott., L.A.	14	805	266	419	685	533	65	22	26	48	62	....	1983-84	1996-97
Quinn, Pat	Tor., Van., Atl.	9	606	18	113	131	950	11	0	1	1	21	....	1968-69	1976-77
Quinney, Ken	Que.	3	59	7	13	20	23	....	....	....	....	....	....	1986-87	1990-91
‡ Quintin, Jean-Francois	S.J.	2	22	5	5	10	4	....	....	....	....	....	....	1991-92	1992-93
R															
‡ Racine, Yves	Det., Phi., Mtl., S.J., Cgy., T.B.	9	508	37	194	231	439	25	5	4	9	37	....	1989-90	1997-98
• Radley, Yip	NYA, Mtl.M.	2	18	0	1	1	13	....	....	....	....	....	....	1930-31	1936-37
Raglan, Herb	St.L., Que., T.B., Ott.	9	343	33	56	89	775	32	3	6	9	50	....	1985-86	1993-94
Raglan, Rags	Det., Chi.	3	100	4	9	13	52	3	0	0	0	0	....	1950-51	1952-53
Raleigh, Don	NYR	10	535	101	219	320	96	18	6	5	11	6	....	1943-44	1955-56
Ramage, Rob	Col., St.L., Cgy., Tor., Min., T.B., Mtl., Phi.	15	1044	139	425	564	2226	84	8	42	50	218	2	1979-80	1993-94
• Ramsay, Beattie	Tor.	1	43	0	2	2	10	....	....	....	....	....	....	1927-28	1927-28
Ramsay, Craig	Buf.	14	1070	252	420	672	201	89	17	31	48	27	....	1971-72	1984-85
Ramsay, Les	Chi.	1	11	2	2	4	2	....	....	....	....	....	....	1944-45	1944-45
Ramsey, Mike	Buf., Pit., Det.	18	1070	79	266	345	1012	115	8	29	37	176	....	1979-80	1996-97
Ramsey, Wayne	Buf.	1	2	0	0	0	0	....	....	....	....	....	....	1977-78	1977-78
• Randall, Ken	Tor., Ham., NYA	10	218	68	50	118	533	6	2	1	3	27	2	1917-18	1926-27
Ranieri, George	Bos.	1	2	0	0	0	0	....	....	....	....	....	....	1956-57	1956-57
Ratelle, Jean	NYR, Bos.	21	1281	491	776	1267	276	123	32	66	98	24	....	1960-61	1980-81
Rathwell, Jake	Bos.	1	1	0	0	0	0	....	....	....	....	....	....	1974-75	1974-75
Ratushny, Dan	Van.	1	1	0	1	1	2	....	....	....	....	....	....	1992-93	1992-93
Rausse, Errol	Wsh.	3	31	7	3	10	0	....	....	....	....	....	....	1979-80	1981-82
Rautakallio, Pekka	Atl., Cgy.	3	235	33	121	154	122	23	2	5	7	8	....	1979-80	1981-82
Ravlich, Matt	Bos., Chi., Det., L.A.	10	410	12	78	90	364	24	1	5	6	16	....	1962-63	1972-73
• Raymond, Armand	Mtl.	2	22	0	2	2	10	....	....	....	....	....	....	1937-38	1939-40
• Raymond, Paul	Mtl.	4	76	2	3	5	6	5	0	0	0	2	....	1932-33	1938-39

Name	NHL Teams	NHL Seasons	Regular Schedule GP	G	A	TP	PIM	Playoffs GP	G	A	TP	PIM	NHL Cup Wins	First NHL Season	Last NHL Season
Read, Mel	NYR	1	1	0	0	0	0	....	....	....	....	....	....	1946-47	1946-47
Reardon, Ken	Mtl.	7	341	26	96	122	604	31	2	5	7	62	1	1940-41	1949-50
• Reardon, Terry	Bos., Mtl.	7	193	47	53	100	73	30	8	10	18	12	1	1938-39	1946-47
Reaume, Marc	Tor., Det., Mtl., Van.	9	344	8	43	51	273	21	0	2	2	8	....	1954-55	1970-71
Reay, Billy	Det., Mtl.	10	479	105	162	267	202	63	13	16	29	43	2	1943-44	1952-53
Redahl, Gord	Bos.	1	18	0	1	1	2	....	....	....	....	....	....	1958-59	1958-59
• Redding, George	Bos.	2	55	3	2	5	23	....	....	....	....	....	....	1924-25	1925-26
Redmond, Craig	L.A., Edm.	5	191	16	68	84	134	3	1	0	1	2	....	1984-85	1988-89
Redmond, Dick	Min., Cal., Chi., St.L., Atl., Bos.	13	771	133	312	445	504	66	9	22	31	27	....	1969-70	1981-82
Redmond, Keith	L.A.	1	12	1	0	1	20	....	....	....	....	....	....	1993-94	1993-94
Redmond, Mickey	Mtl., Det.	9	538	233	195	428	219	16	2	3	5	2	2	1967-68	1975-76
Reeds, Mark	St.L., Hfd.	8	365	45	114	159	135	53	8	9	17	23	....	1981-82	1988-89
Reekie, Joe	Buf., NYI, T.B., Wsh., Chi.	17	902	25	139	164	1326	51	3	4	7	63	....	1985-86	2001-02
• Regan, Bill	NYR, NYA	3	67	3	2	5	67	8	0	0	0	2	....	1929-30	1932-33
Regan, Larry	Bos., Tor.	5	280	41	95	136	71	42	7	14	21	18	....	1956-57	1960-61
Regier, Darcy	Cle., NYI	3	26	0	2	2	35	....	....	....	....	....	....	1977-78	1983-84
Reibel, Dutch	Det., Chi., Bos.	6	409	84	161	245	75	39	6	14	20	4	2	1953-54	1958-59
Reichert, Craig	Ana.	1	3	0	0	0	0	....	....	....	....	....	....	1996-97	1996-97
• Reid, Dave	Tor.	3	7	0	0	0	0	....	....	....	....	....	....	1952-53	1955-56
Reid, Dave	Bos., Tor., Dal., Col.	18	961	165	204	369	253	118	9	26	35	34	2	1983-84	2000-01
Reid, Gerry	Det.	1	....	....	....	....	....	2	0	0	0	2	....	1948-49	1948-49
Reid, Gord	NYA	1	1	0	0	0	2	....	....	....	....	....	....	1936-37	1936-37
• Reid, Reg	Tor.	2	39	1	0	1	4	2	0	0	0	0	....	1924-25	1925-26
Reid, Tom	Chi., Min.	11	701	17	113	130	654	42	1	13	14	49	....	1967-68	1977-78
Reierson, Dave	Cgy.	1	2	0	0	0	2	....	....	....	....	....	....	1988-89	1988-89
Reigle, Ed	Bos.	1	17	0	2	2	25	....	....	....	....	....	....	1950-51	1950-51
Reinhart, Paul	Atl., Cgy., Van.	11	648	133	426	559	277	83	23	54	77	42	....	1979-80	1989-90
• Reinikka, Ollie	NYR	1	16	0	0	0	0	....	....	....	....	....	....	1926-27	1926-27
• Reise, Leo	Ham., NYA, NYR	8	241	43	43	86	187	6	0	0	0	16	....	1920-21	1929-30
Reise Jr., Leo	Chi., Det., NYR	9	494	28	81	109	399	52	8	5	13	68	2	1945-46	1953-54
Renaud, Mark	Hfd., Buf.	5	152	6	50	56	86	....	....	....	....	....	....	1979-80	1983-84
‡ Reynolds, Bobby	Tor.	1	7	1	1	2	0	....	....	....	....	....	....	1989-90	1989-90
Ribble, Pat	Atl., Chi., Tor., Wsh., Cgy.	8	349	19	60	79	365	8	0	1	1	12	....	1975-76	1982-83
Rice, Steven	NYR, Edm., Hfd., Car.	8	329	64	61	125	275	2	2	1	3	6	....	1990-91	1997-98
Richard, Henri	Mtl.	20	1256	358	688	1046	928	180	49	80	129	181	11	1955-56	1974-75
• Richard, Jacques	Atl., Buf., Que.	10	556	160	187	347	307	35	5	5	10	34	....	1972-73	1982-83
‡ Richard, Jean-Marc	Que.	2	5	2	1	3	2	....	....	....	....	....	....	1987-88	1989-90
• Richard, Maurice	Mtl.	18	978	544	421	965	1285	133	82	44	126	188	8	1942-43	1959-60
‡ Richard, Mike	Wsh.	2	7	0	2	2	0	....	....	....	....	....	....	1987-88	1989-90
‡ Richards, Todd	Hfd.	2	8	0	4	4	4	11	0	3	3	6	....	1990-91	1991-92
Richardson, Dave	NYR, Chi., Det.	4	45	3	2	5	27	....	....	....	....	....	....	1963-64	1967-68
Richardson, Glen	Van.	1	24	3	6	9	19	....	....	....	....	....	....	1975-76	1975-76
Richardson, Ken	St.L.	3	49	8	13	21	16	....	....	....	....	....	....	1974-75	1978-79
Richer, Bob	Buf.	1	3	0	0	0	0	....	....	....	....	....	....	1972-73	1972-73
Richer, Stephane	Mtl., N.J., T.B., St.L., Pit.	17	1054	421	398	819	614	134	53	45	98	61	2	1984-85	2001-02
‡ Richer, Stephane	T.B., Bos., Fla.	3	27	1	5	6	20	3	0	0	0	0	....	1992-93	1994-95
Richmond, Steve	NYR, Det., N.J., L.A.	5	159	4	23	27	514	4	0	0	0	12	....	1983-84	1988-89
Richter, Dave	Min., Phi., Van., St.L.	9	365	9	40	49	1030	22	1	0	1	80	....	1981-82	1989-90
Ridley, Mike	NYR, Wsh., Tor., Van.	12	866	292	466	758	424	104	28	50	78	70	....	1985-86	1996-97
Riley, Bill	Wsh., Wpg.	5	139	31	30	61	320	....	....	....	....	....	....	1974-75	1979-80
Riley, Jack	Det., Mtl., Bos.	4	104	10	22	32	8	4	0	3	3	0	....	1932-33	1935-36
• Riley, Jim	Chi., Det.	1	9	0	2	2	14	....	....	....	....	....	....	1926-27	1926-27
Riopelle, Rip	Mtl.	3	169	27	16	43	73	8	1	1	2	2	....	1947-48	1949-50
Rioux, Gerry	Wpg.	1	8	0	0	0	6	....	....	....	....	....	....	1979-80	1979-80
Rioux, Pierre	Cgy.	1	14	1	2	3	4	....	....	....	....	....	....	1982-83	1982-83
• Ripley, Vic	Chi., Bos., NYR, St.L.	7	278	51	49	100	173	20	4	1	5	10	....	1928-29	1934-35
Risebrough, Doug	Mtl., Cgy.	13	740	185	286	471	1542	124	21	37	58	238	4	1974-75	1986-87
Rissling, Gary	Wsh., Pit.	7	221	23	30	53	1008	5	0	1	1	4	....	1978-79	1984-85
Ritchie, Bob	Phi., Det.	2	29	8	4	12	10	....	....	....	....	....	....	1976-77	1977-78
• Ritchie, Dave	Mtl.W., Ott., Tor., Que., Mtl.	6	58	15	6	21	50	1	0	0	0	0	....	1917-18	1925-26
Ritson, Alex	NYR	1	1	0	0	0	0	....	....	....	....	....	....	1944-45	1944-45
Rittinger, Alan	Bos.	1	19	3	7	10	0	....	....	....	....	....	....	1943-44	1943-44
Rivard, Bob	Pit.	1	27	5	12	17	4	....	....	....	....	....	....	1967-68	1967-68
• Rivers, Gus	Mtl.	3	88	4	5	9	12	16	2	0	2	2	2	1929-30	1931-32
Rivers, Shawn	T.B.	1	4	0	2	2	2	....	....	....	....	....	....	1992-93	1992-93
Rivers, Wayne	Det., Bos., St.L., NYR	7	108	15	30	45	94	....	....	....	....	....	....	1961-62	1968-69
Rizzuto, Garth	Van.	1	37	3	4	7	16	....	....	....	....	....	....	1970-71	1970-71
• Roach, Mickey	Tor., Ham., NYA	8	211	77	34	111	54	....	....	....	....	....	....	1919-20	1926-27
‡ Roberge, Mario	Mtl.	5	112	7	7	14	314	15	0	0	0	24	1	1990-91	1994-95
‡ Roberge, Serge	Que.	1	9	0	0	0	24	....	....	....	....	....	....	1990-91	1990-91
Robert, Claude	Mtl.	1	23	1	0	1	9	....	....	....	....	....	....	1950-51	1950-51
Robert, Rene	Tor., Pit., Buf., Col.	12	744	284	418	702	597	50	22	19	41	73	....	1970-71	1981-82
Roberto, Phil	Mtl., St.L., Det., K.C., Col., Cle.	8	385	75	106	181	464	31	9	8	17	69	1	1969-70	1976-77
‡ Roberts, David	St.L., Edm., Van.	5	125	20	33	53	85	9	0	0	0	16	....	1993-94	1997-98
Roberts, Doug	Det., Oak., Cal., Bos.	10	419	43	104	147	342	16	2	3	5	46	....	1965-66	1974-75
Roberts, Gordie	Hfd., Min., Phi., St.L., Pit., Bos.	15	1097	61	359	420	1582	153	10	47	57	273	2	1979-80	1993-94
Roberts, Jim	Min.	3	106	17	23	40	33	2	0	0	0	0	....	1976-77	1978-79
Roberts, Jimmy	Mtl., St.L.	15	1006	126	194	320	621	153	20	16	36	160	5	1963-64	1977-78
• Robertson, Fred	Tor., Det.	2	34	1	0	1	35	7	0	0	0	0	1	1931-32	1933-34
Robertson, Geordie	Buf.	1	5	1	2	3	7	....	....	....	....	....	....	1982-83	1982-83
Robertson, George	Mtl.	2	31	2	5	7	6	....	....	....	....	....	....	1947-48	1948-49
Robertson, Torrie	Wsh., Hfd., Det.	10	442	49	99	148	1751	22	2	1	3	90	....	1980-81	1989-90
‡ Robertsson, Bert	Van., Edm., NYR	4	123	4	10	14	75	5	0	0	0	0	....	1997-98	2000-01
Robidoux, Florent	Chi.	3	52	7	4	11	75	....	....	....	....	....	....	1980-81	1983-84
Robinson, Doug	Chi., NYR, L.A.	7	239	44	67	111	34	11	4	3	7	0	....	1963-64	1970-71
• Robinson, Earl	Mtl.M., Chi., Mtl.	11	417	83	98	181	133	25	5	4	9	0	1	1928-29	1939-40
Robinson, Larry	Mtl., L.A.	20	1384	208	750	958	793	227	28	116	144	211	6	1972-73	1991-92
Robinson, Moe	Mtl.	1	1	0	0	0	0	....	....	....	....	....	....	1979-80	1979-80
Robinson, Rob	St.L.	1	22	0	1	1	8	....	....	....	....	....	....	1991-92	1991-92
Robinson, Scott	Min.	1	1	0	0	0	2	....	....	....	....	....	....	1989-90	1989-90
Robitaille, Mike	NYR, Det., Buf., Van.	8	382	23	105	128	280	13	0	1	1	4	....	1969-70	1976-77
• Roche, Des	Mtl.M., Ott., St.L., Mtl., Det.	4	113	20	18	38	44	....	....	....	....	....	....	1930-31	1934-35
• Roche, Earl	Mtl.M., Bos., Ott., St.L., Det.	4	147	25	27	52	48	2	0	0	0	0	....	1930-31	1934-35
Roche, Ernie	Mtl.	1	4	0	0	0	2	....	....	....	....	....	....	1950-51	1950-51
Rochefort, Dave	Det.	1	1	0	0	0	0	....	....	....	....	....	....	1966-67	1966-67
Rochefort, Leon	NYR, Mtl., Phi., L.A., Det., Atl., Van.	15	617	121	147	268	93	39	4	4	8	16	2	1960-61	1975-76
Rochefort, Normand	Que., NYR, T.B.	13	598	39	119	158	570	69	7	5	12	82	....	1980-81	1993-94
• Rockburn, Harvey	Det., Ott.	3	94	4	2	6	254	....	....	....	....	....	....	1929-30	1932-33
• Rodden, Eddie	Chi., Tor., Bos., NYR	4	97	6	14	20	60	2	0	1	1	0	....	1926-27	1930-31
‡ Rodgers, Marc	Det.	1	21	1	1	2	10	....	....	....	....	....	....	1999-00	1999-00
Rogers, John	Min.	2	14	2	4	6	0	....	....	....	....	....	....	1973-74	1974-75
Rogers, Mike	Hfd., NYR, Edm.	7	484	202	317	519	184	17	1	13	14	6	....	1979-80	1985-86
Rohlicek, Jeff	Van.	2	9	0	0	0	8	....	....	....	....	....	....	1987-88	1988-89
‡ Rohlin, Leif	Van.	2	96	8	24	32	40	5	0	0	0	0	....	1995-96	1996-97
Rohloff, Jon	Bos.	3	150	7	25	32	129	10	1	2	3	8	....	1994-95	1996-97
Rolfe, Dale	Bos., L.A., Det., NYR	9	509	25	125	150	556	71	5	24	29	89	....	1959-60	1974-75
Romanchych, Larry	Chi., Atl.	6	298	68	97	165	102	7	2	2	4	4	....	1970-71	1976-77
‡ Romaniuk, Russell	Wpg., Phi.	5	102	13	14	27	63	2	0	0	0	0	....	1991-92	1995-96
Rombough, Doug	Buf., NYI, Min.	4	150	24	27	51	80	....	....	....	....	....	....	1972-73	1975-76
Rominski, Dale	T.B.	1	3	0	1	1	2	....	....	....	....	....	....	1999-00	1999-00
• Romnes, Doc	Chi., Tor., NYA	10	360	68	136	204	42	45	7	18	25	4	2	1930-31	1939-40
Ronan, Ed	Mtl., Wpg., Buf.	6	182	13	23	36	101	27	4	3	7	16	1	1991-92	1996-97
• Ronan, Skene	Ott.	1	11	0	0	0	6	....	....	....	....	....	....	1918-19	1918-19
Ronson, Len	NYR, Oak.	2	18	2	1	3	10	....	....	....	....	....	....	1960-61	1968-69
Ronty, Paul	Bos., NYR, Mtl.	8	488	101	211	312	103	21	1	7	8	6	....	1947-48	1954-55
Rooney, Steve	Mtl., Wpg., N.J.	5	154	15	13	28	496	25	3	2	5	86	1	1984-85	1988-89
Root, Bill	Mtl., Tor., St.L., Phi.	6	247	11	23	34	180	22	1	2	3	25	....	1982-83	1987-88
• Ross, Art	Mtl.W.	1	3	1	0	1	12	....	....	....	....	....	....	1917-18	1917-18
Ross, Jim	NYR	2	62	2	11	13	29	....	....	....	....	....	....	1951-52	1952-53
Rossignol, Roly	Det., Mtl.	3	14	3	5	8	6	1	0	0	0	2	....	1943-44	1945-46
Rota, Darcy	Chi., Atl., Van.	11	794	256	239	495	973	60	14	7	21	147	....	1973-74	1983-84
Rota, Randy	Mtl., L.A., K.C., Col.	5	212	38	39	77	60	5	0	1	1	0	....	1972-73	1976-77
• Rothschild, Sam	Mtl.M., Pit., NYA	4	100	8	6	14	25	6	0	0	0	0	1	1924-25	1927-28
• Roulston, Rolly	Det.	3	24	0	6	6	10	....	....	....	....	....	1	1935-36	1937-38
Roulston, Tom	Edm., Pit.	5	195	47	49	96	74	21	2	2	4	2	....	1980-81	1985-86
Roupe, Magnus	Phi.	2	40	3	5	8	42	....	....	....	....	....	....	1987-88	1988-89

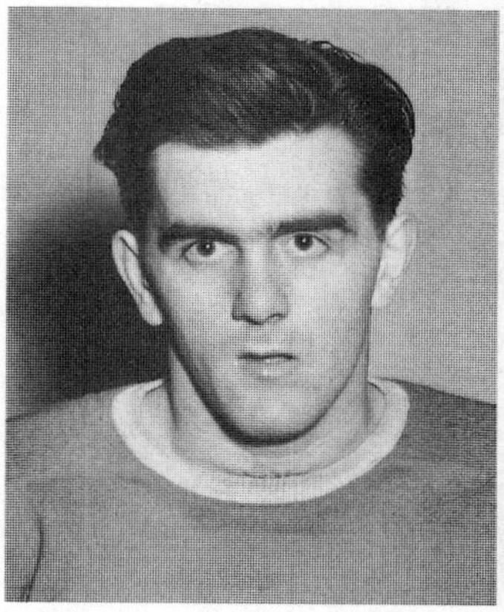

Maurice Richard

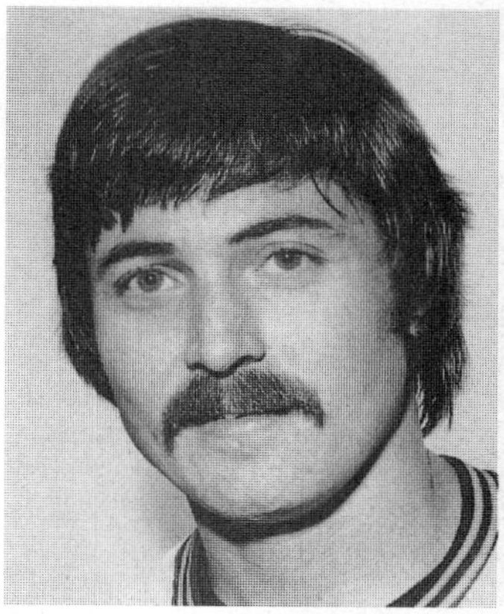

Rene Robert

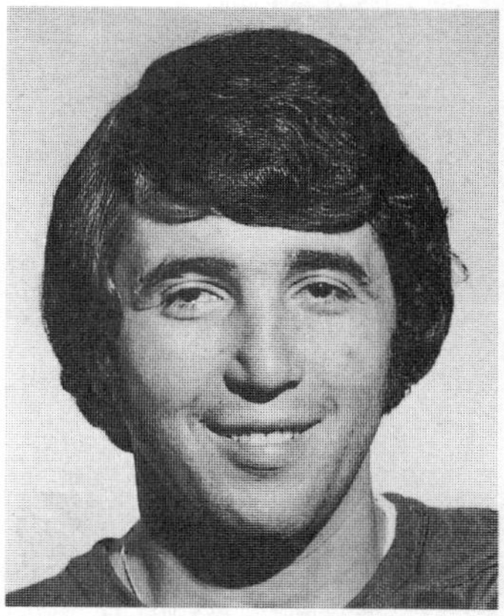

Phil Roberto

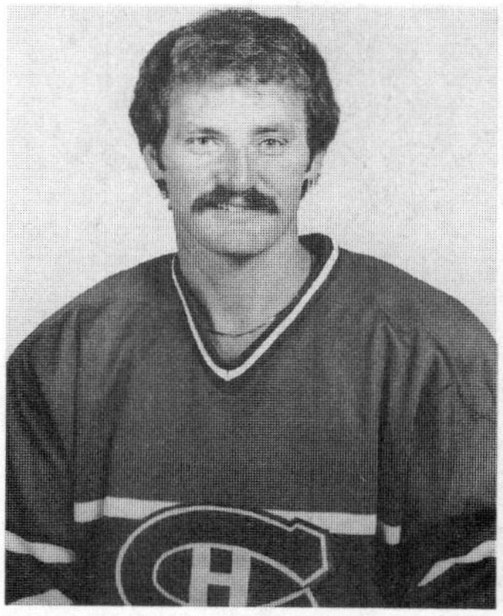

Larry Robinson

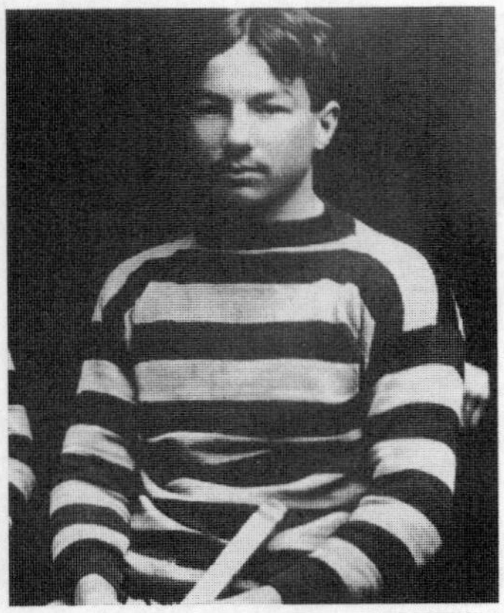

Art Ross

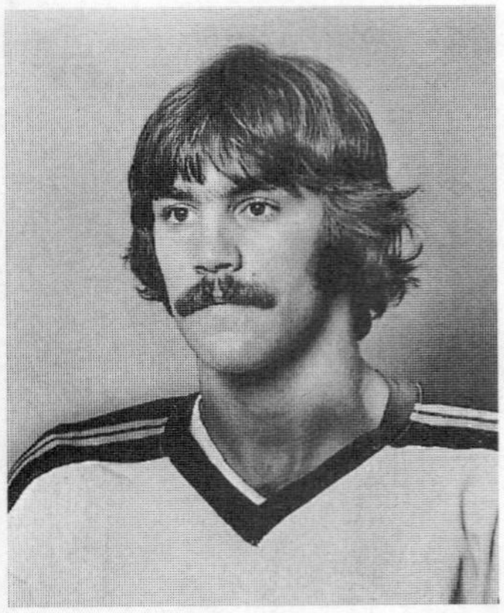

Randy Rota

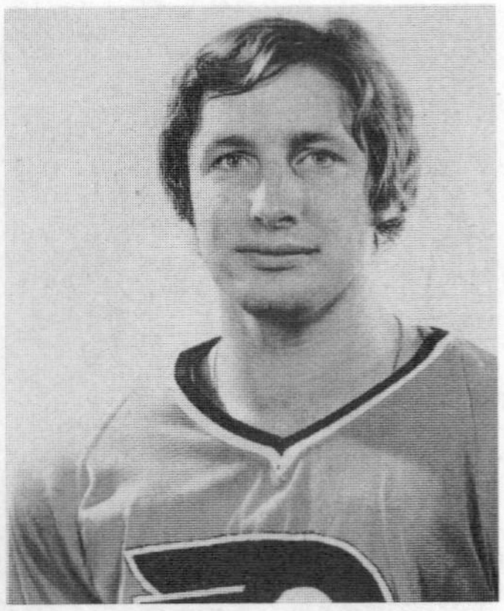

Don Saleski

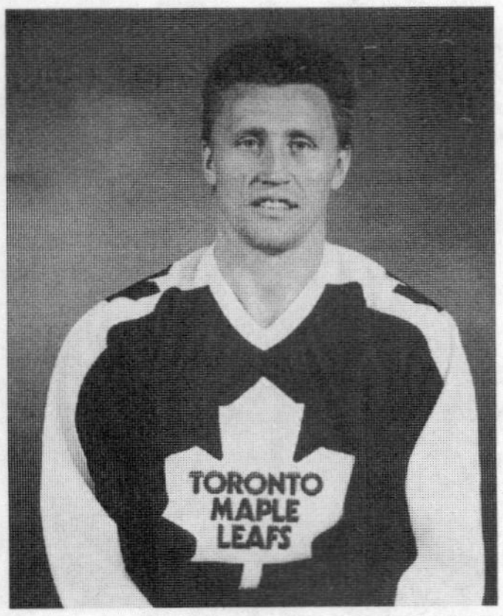

Borje Salming

			Regular Schedule					Playoffs					NHL	First	Last
Name	NHL Teams	NHL Seasons	GP	G	A	TP	PIM	GP	G	A	TP	PIM	Cup Wins	NHL Season	NHL Season
Rouse, Bob	Min., Wsh., Tor., Det., S.J.	17	1061	37	181	218	1559	136	7	21	28	198	2	1983-84	1999-00
Rousseau, Bobby	Mtl., Min., NYR	15	942	245	458	703	359	128	27	57	84	69	4	1960-61	1974-75
Rousseau, Guy	Mtl.	2	4	0	1	1	0	....	....	....	....	....	....	1954-55	1956-57
Rousseau, Roland	Mtl.	1	2	0	0	0	0	....	....	....	....	....	....	1952-53	1952-53
Routhier, Jean-Marc	Que.	1	8	0	0	0	9	....	....	....	....	....	....	1989-90	1989-90
• Rowe, Bobby	Bos.	1	4	1	0	1	0	....	....	....	....	....	....	1924-25	1924-25
Rowe, Mike	Pit.	3	11	0	0	0	11	....	....	....	....	....	....	1984-85	1986-87
Rowe, Ron	NYR	1	5	1	0	1	0	....	....	....	....	....	....	1947-48	1947-48
Rowe, Tom	Wsh., Hfd., Det.	7	357	85	100	185	615	3	2	0	2	0	....	1976-77	1982-83
‡ Roy, Jean-Yves	NYR, Ott., Bos.	4	61	12	16	28	26	....	....	....	....	....	....	1994-95	1997-98
Roy, Stephane	Min.	1	12	1	0	1	0	....	....	....	....	....	....	1987-88	1987-88
‡ Royer, Remi	Chi.	1	18	0	0	0	67	....	....	....	....	....	....	1998-99	1998-99
Rozzini, Gino	Bos.	1	31	5	10	15	20	6	1	2	3	6	....	1944-45	1944-45
Rucinski, Mike	Chi.	2	1	0	0	0	0	2	0	0	0	0	....	1987-88	1988-89
Rucinski, Mike	Car.	3	26	0	2	2	10	....	....	....	....	....	....	1997-98	2000-01
Ruelle, Bernie	Det.	1	2	1	0	1	0	....	....	....	....	....	....	1943-44	1943-44
‡ Ruff, Jason	St.L., T.B.	2	14	3	3	6	10	....	....	....	....	....	....	1992-93	1993-94
Ruff, Lindy	Buf., NYR	12	691	105	195	300	1264	52	11	13	24	193	....	1979-80	1990-91
Ruhnke, Kent	Bos.	1	2	0	1	1	0	....	....	....	....	....	....	1975-76	1975-76
Rundqvist, Thomas	Mtl.	1	2	0	1	1	0	....	....	....	....	....	....	1984-85	1984-85
• Runge, Paul	Bos., Mtl.M., Mtl.	7	140	18	22	40	57	7	0	0	0	6	....	1930-31	1937-38
Ruotsalainen, Reijo	NYR, Edm., N.J.	7	446	107	237	344	180	86	15	32	47	44	2	1981-82	1989-90
Rupp, Duane	NYR, Tor., Min., Pit.	10	374	24	93	117	220	10	2	2	4	8	....	1962-63	1972-73
Ruskowski, Terry	Chi., L.A., Pit., Min.	10	630	113	313	426	1354	21	1	6	7	86	....	1979-80	1988-89
Russell, Cam	Chi., Col.	10	396	9	21	30	872	44	0	5	5	16	....	1989-90	1998-99
• Russell, Church	NYR	3	90	20	16	36	12	....	....	....	....	....	....	1945-46	1947-48
Russell, Phil	Chi., Atl., Cgy., N.J., Buf.	15	1016	99	325	424	2038	73	4	22	26	202	....	1972-73	1986-87
Ruuttu, Christian	Buf., Chi., Van.	9	621	134	298	432	714	42	4	9	13	49	....	1986-87	1994-95
Ruzicka, Vladimir	Edm., Bos., Ott.	5	233	82	85	167	129	30	4	14	18	2	....	1989-90	1993-94
‡ Ryan, Terry	Mtl.	3	8	0	0	0	36	....	....	....	....	....	....	1996-97	1998-99
Rychel, Warren	Chi., L.A., Tor., Col., Ana.	9	406	38	39	77	1422	70	8	13	21	121	1	1988-89	1998-99
Rymsha, Andy	Que.	1	6	0	0	0	23	....	....	....	....	....	....	1991-92	1991-92

S

Saarinen, Simo	NYR	1	8	0	0	0	0	....	....	....	....	....	....	1984-85	1984-85
Sabol, Shaun	Phi.	1	2	0	0	0	0	....	....	....	....	....	....	1989-90	1989-90
Sabourin, Bob	Tor.	1	1	0	0	0	2	....	....	....	....	....	....	1951-52	1951-52
Sabourin, Gary	St.L., Tor., Cal., Cle.	10	627	169	188	357	397	62	19	11	30	58	....	1967-68	1976-77
Sabourin, Ken	Cgy., Wsh.	4	74	2	8	10	201	12	0	0	0	34	....	1988-89	1991-92
Sacco, David	Tor., Ana.	3	35	5	13	18	22	....	....	....	....	....	....	1993-94	1995-96
Sacharuk, Larry	NYR, St.L.	5	151	29	33	62	42	2	1	1	2	2	....	1972-73	1976-77
Saganiuk, Rocky	Tor., Pit.	6	259	57	65	122	201	6	1	0	1	15	....	1978-79	1983-84
Saleski, Don	Phi., Col.	9	543	128	125	253	629	82	13	17	30	131	2	1971-72	1979-80
Salming, Borje	Tor., Det.	17	1148	150	637	787	1344	81	12	37	49	91	....	1973-74	1989-90
Salovaara, Barry	Det.	2	90	2	13	15	70	....	....	....	....	....	....	1974-75	1975-76
Salvian, Dave	NYI	1	....	....	....	....	....	1	0	1	1	2	....	1976-77	1976-77
Samis, Phil	Tor.	2	2	0	0	0	0	5	0	1	1	2	1	1947-48	1949-50
Sampson, Gary	Wsh.	4	105	13	22	35	25	12	1	0	1	0	....	1983-84	1986-87
Samuelsson, Kjell	NYR, Phi., Pit., T.B.	14	813	48	138	186	1225	123	4	20	24	178	1	1985-86	1998-99
Samuelsson, Ulf	Hfd., Pit., NYR, Det., Phi.	16	1080	57	275	332	2453	132	7	27	34	272	2	1984-85	1999-00
Sandelin, Scott	Mtl., Phi., Min.	4	25	0	4	4	2	....	....	....	....	....	....	1986-87	1991-92
Sanderson, Derek	Bos., NYR, St.L., Van., Pit.	13	598	202	250	452	911	56	18	12	30	187	2	1965-66	1977-78
Sandford, Ed	Bos., Det., Chi.	9	502	106	145	251	355	42	13	11	24	27	....	1947-48	1955-56
Sandlak, Jim	Van., Hfd.	11	549	110	119	229	821	33	7	10	17	30	....	1985-86	1995-96
• Sands, Charlie	Tor., Bos., Mtl., NYR	12	427	99	109	208	58	34	6	6	12	4	1	1932-33	1943-44
‡ Sandstrom, Tomas	NYR, L.A., Pit., Det., Ana.	15	983	394	462	856	1193	139	32	49	81	183	1	1984-85	1998-99
‡ Sandwith, Terran	Edm.	1	8	0	0	0	6	....	....	....	....	....	....	1997-98	1997-98
Sanipass, Everett	Chi., Que.	5	164	25	34	59	358	5	2	0	2	4	....	1986-87	1990-91
Sargent, Gary	L.A., Min.	8	402	61	161	222	273	20	5	7	12	8	....	1975-76	1982-83
Sarner, Craig	Bos.	1	7	0	0	0	0	....	....	....	....	....	....	1974-75	1974-75
Sarrazin, Dick	Phi.	3	100	20	35	55	22	4	0	0	0	0	....	1968-69	1971-72
Sasakamoose, Fred	Chi.	1	11	0	0	0	6	....	....	....	....	....	....	1953-54	1953-54
Sasser, Grant	Pit.	1	3	0	0	0	0	....	....	....	....	....	....	1983-84	1983-84
Sather, Glen	Bos., Pit., NYR, St.L., Mtl., Min.	10	658	80	113	193	724	72	1	5	6	86	....	1966-67	1975-76
Saunders, Bernie	Que.	2	10	0	1	1	8	....	....	....	....	....	....	1979-80	1980-81
Saunders, David	Van.	1	56	7	13	20	10	....	....	....	....	....	....	1987-88	1987-88
• Saunders, Ted	Ott.	1	18	1	3	4	4	....	....	....	....	....	....	1933-34	1933-34
Sauve, Jean-Francois	Buf., Que.	7	290	65	138	203	114	36	9	12	21	10	....	1980-81	1986-87
‡ Savage, Joel	Buf.	1	3	0	1	1	0	....	....	....	....	....	....	1990-91	1990-91
‡ Savage, Reggie	Wsh., Que.	3	34	5	7	12	28	....	....	....	....	....	....	1990-91	1993-94
• Savage, Tony	Bos., Mtl.	1	49	1	5	6	6	2	0	0	0	0	....	1934-35	1934-35
Savard, Andre	Bos., Buf., Que.	12	790	211	271	482	411	85	13	18	31	77	....	1973-74	1984-85
Savard, Denis	Chi., Mtl., T.B.	17	1196	473	865	1338	1336	169	66	109	175	256	1	1980-81	1996-97
Savard, Jean	Chi., Hfd.	3	43	7	12	19	29	....	....	....	....	....	....	1977-78	1979-80
Savard, Serge	Mtl., Wpg.	17	1040	106	333	439	592	130	19	49	68	88	8	1966-67	1982-83
‡ Savoia, Ryan	Pit.	1	3	0	0	0	0	....	....	....	....	....	....	1998-99	1998-99
Scamurra, Peter	Wsh.	4	132	8	25	33	59	....	....	....	....	....	....	1975-76	1979-80
Sceviour, Darin	Chi.	1	1	0	0	0	0	....	....	....	....	....	....	1986-87	1986-87
Schaeffer, Butch	Chi.	1	5	0	0	0	6	....	....	....	....	....	....	1936-37	1936-37
Schamehorn, Kevin	Det., L.A.	3	10	0	0	0	17	....	....	....	....	....	....	1976-77	1980-81
Schella, John	Van.	2	115	2	18	20	224	....	....	....	....	....	....	1970-71	1971-72
Scherza, Chuck	Bos., NYR	2	36	6	6	12	35	....	....	....	....	....	....	1943-44	1944-45
Schinkel, Ken	NYR, Pit.	12	636	127	198	325	163	19	7	2	9	4	....	1959-60	1972-73
‡ Schlegel, Brad	Wsh., Cgy.	3	48	1	8	9	10	7	0	1	1	2	....	1991-92	1993-94
Schliebener, Andy	Van.	3	84	2	11	13	74	6	0	0	0	0	....	1981-82	1984-85
Schmautz, Bobby	Chi., Van., Bos., Edm., Col.	13	764	271	286	557	988	84	28	33	61	92	....	1967-68	1980-81
• Schmautz, Cliff	Buf., Phi.	1	56	13	19	32	33	....	....	....	....	....	....	1970-71	1970-71
• Schmidt, Clarence	Bos.	1	7	1	0	1	2	....	....	....	....	....	....	1943-44	1943-44
Schmidt, Jackie	Bos.	1	45	6	7	13	6	5	0	0	0	0	....	1942-43	1942-43
Schmidt, Milt	Bos.	16	776	229	346	575	466	86	24	25	49	60	2	1936-37	1954-55
Schmidt, Norm	Pit.	4	125	23	33	56	73	....	....	....	....	....	....	1983-84	1987-88
Schmidt, Otto	Bos.	1	2	0	0	0	0	....	....	....	....	....	....	1943-44	1943-44
• Schnarr, Werner	Bos.	2	26	0	0	0	0	....	....	....	....	....	....	1924-25	1925-26
‡ Schneider, Andy	Ott.	1	10	0	0	0	15	....	....	....	....	....	....	1993-94	1993-94
Schock, Danny	Bos., Phi.	2	20	1	2	3	0	1	0	0	0	0	1	1969-70	1970-71
Schock, Ron	Bos., St.L., Pit., Buf.	15	909	166	351	517	260	55	4	16	20	29	....	1963-64	1977-78
Schoenfeld, Jim	Buf., Det., Bos.	13	719	51	204	255	1132	75	3	13	16	151	....	1972-73	1984-85
Schofield, Dwight	Det., Mtl., St.L., Wsh., Pit., Wpg.	7	211	8	22	30	631	9	0	0	0	55	....	1976-77	1987-88
Schreiber, Wally	Min.	2	41	8	10	18	12	....	....	....	....	....	....	1987-88	1988-89
• Schriner, Sweeney	NYA, Tor.	11	484	201	204	405	148	59	18	11	29	54	2	1934-35	1945-46
‡ Schulte, Paxton	Que., Cgy.	2	2	0	0	0	4	....	....	....	....	....	....	1993-94	1996-97
Schultz, Dave	Phi., L.A., Pit., Buf.	9	535	79	121	200	2294	73	8	12	20	412	2	1971-72	1979-80
Schurman, Maynard	Hfd.	1	7	0	0	0	0	....	....	....	....	....	....	1979-80	1979-80
Schutt, Rod	Mtl., Pit., Tor.	8	286	77	92	169	177	22	8	6	14	26	....	1977-78	1985-86
Scissons, Scott	NYI	3	2	0	0	0	0	1	0	0	0	0	....	1990-91	1993-94
Sclisizzi, Enio	Det., Chi.	6	81	12	11	23	26	13	0	0	0	6	....	1946-47	1952-53
• Scott, Ganton	Tor., Ham., Mtl.M.	3	57	1	1	2	0	....	....	....	....	....	....	1922-23	1924-25
• Scott, Laurie	NYA, NYR	2	62	6	3	9	28	....	....	....	....	....	....	1926-27	1927-28
Scremin, Claudio	S.J.	2	17	0	1	1	29	....	....	....	....	....	....	1991-92	1992-93
Scruton, Howard	L.A.	1	4	0	4	4	9	....	....	....	....	....	....	1982-83	1982-83
Seabrooke, Glen	Phi.	3	19	1	6	7	4	....	....	....	....	....	....	1986-87	1988-89
Secord, Al	Bos., Chi., Tor., Phi.	12	766	273	222	495	2093	102	21	34	55	382	....	1978-79	1989-90
Sedlbauer, Ron	Van., Chi., Tor.	7	430	143	86	229	210	19	1	3	4	27	....	1974-75	1980-81
Seftel, Steve	Wsh.	1	4	0	0	0	2	....	....	....	....	....	....	1990-91	1990-91
Seguin, Dan	Min., Van.	2	37	2	6	8	50	....	....	....	....	....	....	1970-71	1973-74
Seguin, Steve	L.A.	1	5	0	0	0	9	....	....	....	....	....	....	1984-85	1984-85
• Seibert, Earl	NYR, Chi., Det.	15	645	89	187	276	746	66	11	8	19	76	2	1931-32	1945-46
Seiling, Ric	Buf., Det.	10	738	179	208	387	573	62	14	14	28	36	....	1977-78	1986-87
Seiling, Rod	Tor., NYR, Wsh., St.L., Atl.	17	979	62	269	331	601	77	4	8	12	55	....	1962-63	1978-79
Sejba, Jiri	Buf.	1	11	0	2	2	8	....	....	....	....	....	....	1990-91	1990-91
Selby, Brit	Tor., Phi., St.L.	8	350	55	62	117	163	16	1	1	2	8	....	1964-65	1971-72
Self, Steve	Wsh.	1	3	0	0	0	0	....	....	....	....	....	....	1976-77	1976-77
‡ Selivanov, Alex	T.B., Edm., CBJ	7	459	121	114	235	379	13	2	3	5	16	....	1994-95	2000-01
‡ Selmser, Sean	CBJ	1	1	0	0	0	5	....	....	....	....	....	....	2000-01	2000-01
Selwood, Brad	Tor., L.A.	3	163	7	40	47	153	6	0	0	0	4	....	1970-71	1979-80

Name	NHL Teams	NHL Seasons	Regular Schedule GP	G	A	TP	PIM	Playoffs GP	G	A	TP	PIM	NHL Cup Wins	First NHL Season	Last NHL Season
‡ Semak, Alexander	N.J., T.B., NYI, Van.	6	289	83	91	174	187	8	1	1	2	0	....	1991-92	1996-97
Semchuk, Brandy	L.A.	1	1	0	0	0	2	....	....	....	....	....	....	1992-93	1992-93
Semenko, Dave	Edm., Hfd., Tor.	9	575	65	88	153	1175	73	6	6	12	208	2	1979-80	1987-88
Semenov, Anatoli	Edm., T.B., Van., Ana., Phi., Buf.	8	362	68	126	194	122	49	9	13	22	12	....	1989-90	1996-97
Senick, George	NYR	1	13	2	3	5	8	....	....	....	....	....	....	1952-53	1952-53
Seppa, Jyrki	Wpg.	1	13	0	2	2	6	....	....	....	....	....	....	1983-84	1983-84
Serafini, Ron	Cal.	1	2	0	0	0	2	....	....	....	....	....	....	1973-74	1973-74
Serowik, Jeff	Tor., Bos., Pit.	4	28	0	6	6	16	....	....	....	....	....	....	1990-91	1999-00
Servinis, George	Min.	1	5	0	0	0	0	....	....	....	....	....	....	1987-88	1987-88
Sevcik, Jaroslav	Que.	1	13	0	2	2	2	....	....	....	....	....	....	1989-90	1989-90
Severyn, Brent	Que., Fla., NYI, Col., Ana., Dal.	7	328	10	30	40	825	8	0	0	0	12	....	1989-90	1998-99
‡ Sevigny, Pierre	Mtl., NYR	4	78	4	5	9	64	3	0	1	1	0	....	1993-94	1997-98
Shack, Eddie	NYR, Tor., Bos., L.A., Buf., Pit.	17	1047	239	226	465	1437	74	6	7	13	151	4	1958-59	1974-75
• Shack, Joe	NYR	2	70	9	27	36	20	....	....	....	....	....	....	1942-43	1944-45
Shafranov, Konstantin	St.L.	1	5	2	1	3	0	....	....	....	....	....	....	1996-97	1996-97
Shakes, Paul	Cal.	1	21	0	4	4	12	....	....	....	....	....	....	1973-74	1973-74
Shaldybin, Yevgeny	Bos.	1	3	1	0	1	0	....	....	....	....	....	....	1996-97	1996-97
Shanahan, Sean	Mtl., Col., Bos.	3	40	1	3	4	47	....	....	....	....	....	....	1975-76	1977-78
Shand, Dave	Atl., Tor., Wsh.	8	421	19	84	103	544	26	1	2	3	83	....	1976-77	1984-85
‡ Shank, Daniel	Det., Hfd.	3	77	13	14	27	175	5	0	0	0	22	....	1989-90	1991-92
Shannon, Chuck	NYA	1	4	0	0	0	2	....	....	....	....	....	....	1939-40	1939-40
Shannon, Darrin	Buf., Wpg., Phx.	10	506	87	163	250	344	45	7	10	17	38	....	1988-89	1997-98
‡ Shannon, Darryl	Tor., Wpg., Buf., Atl., Cgy., Mtl.	13	544	28	111	139	523	29	4	7	11	16	....	1988-89	2000-01
• Shannon, Gerry	Ott., St.L., Bos., Mtl.M.	5	180	23	29	52	80	9	0	1	1	2	....	1933-34	1937-38
‡ Sharifijanov, Vadim	N.J., Van.	3	92	16	21	37	50	4	0	0	0	0	....	1996-97	1999-00
Sharples, Jeff	Det.	3	105	14	35	49	70	7	0	3	3	6	....	1986-87	1988-89
Sharpley, Glen	Min., Chi.	6	389	117	161	278	199	27	7	11	18	24	....	1976-77	1981-82
Shaunessy, Scott	Que.	2	7	0	0	0	23	....	....	....	....	....	....	1986-87	1988-89
Shaw, Brad	Hfd., Ott., Wsh., St.L.	11	377	22	137	159	208	23	4	8	12	6	....	1985-86	1998-99
Shaw, David	Que., NYR, Edm., Min., Bos., T.B.	16	769	41	153	194	906	45	3	9	12	81	....	1982-83	1997-98
• Shay, Norm	Bos., Tor.	2	53	5	3	8	34	....	....	....	....	....	....	1924-25	1925-26
• Shea, Pat	Chi.	1	10	1	0	1	0	....	....	....	....	....	....	1931-32	1931-32
‡ Shearer, Rob	Col.	1	2	0	0	0	0	....	....	....	....	....	....	2000-01	2000-01
Shedden, Doug	Pit., Det., Que., Tor.	8	416	139	186	325	176	....	....	....	....	....	....	1981-82	1990-91
Sheehan, Bobby	Mtl., Cal., Chi., Det., NYR, Col., L.A.	9	310	48	63	111	40	25	4	3	7	8	1	1969-70	1981-82
Sheehy, Neil	Cgy., Hfd., Wsh.	9	379	18	47	65	1311	54	0	3	3	241	....	1983-84	1991-92
Sheehy, Tim	Det., Hfd.	2	27	2	1	3	0	....	....	....	....	....	....	1977-78	1979-80
Shelton, Doug	Chi.	1	5	0	1	1	2	....	....	....	....	....	....	1967-68	1967-68
• Sheppard, Frank	Det.	1	8	1	1	2	0	....	....	....	....	....	....	1927-28	1927-28
Sheppard, Gregg	Bos., Pit.	10	657	205	293	498	243	82	32	40	72	31	....	1972-73	1981-82
• Sheppard, Johnny	Det., NYA, Bos., Chi.	8	308	68	58	126	224	10	0	0	0	0	1	1926-27	1933-34
Sheppard, Ray	Buf., NYR, Det., S.J., Fla., Car.	13	817	357	300	657	212	81	30	20	50	21	....	1987-88	1999-00
• Sherf, John	Det.	5	19	0	0	0	8	8	0	1	1	2	1	1935-36	1943-44
• Shero, Fred	NYR	3	145	6	14	20	137	13	0	2	2	8	....	1947-48	1949-50
Sherritt, Gordon	Det.	1	8	0	0	0	12	....	....	....	....	....	....	1943-44	1943-44
Sherven, Gord	Edm., Min., Hfd.	5	97	13	22	35	33	3	0	0	0	0	....	1983-84	1987-88
‡ Shevalier, Jeff	L.A., T.B.	3	32	5	9	14	8	....	....	....	....	....	....	1994-95	1999-00
• Shewchuk, Jack	Bos.	6	187	9	19	28	160	20	0	1	1	19	1	1938-39	1944-45
Shibicky, Alex	NYR	8	324	110	91	201	161	39	12	12	24	12	1	1935-36	1945-46
• Shields, Al	Ott., Phi., NYA, Mtl.M., Bos.	11	459	42	46	88	637	17	0	1	1	14	1	1927-28	1937-38
Shill, Bill	Bos.	3	79	21	13	34	18	7	1	2	3	2	....	1942-43	1946-47
• Shill, Jack	Tor., Bos., NYA, Chi.	6	160	15	20	35	70	25	1	6	7	23	1	1933-34	1938-39
Shinske, Rick	Cle., St.L.	3	63	5	16	21	10	....	....	....	....	....	....	1976-77	1978-79
Shires, Jim	Det., St.L., Pit.	3	56	3	6	9	32	....	....	....	....	....	....	1970-71	1972-73
Shmyr, Paul	Chi., Cal., Min., Hfd.	7	343	13	72	85	528	34	3	3	6	44	....	1968-69	1981-82
Shoebottom, Bruce	Bos.	4	35	1	4	5	53	14	1	2	3	77	....	1987-88	1990-91
• Shore, Eddie	Bos., NYA	14	550	105	179	284	1047	55	6	13	19	181	2	1926-27	1939-40
• Shore, Hamby	Ott.	1	18	3	8	11	51	....	....	....	....	....	....	1917-18	1917-18
Short, Steve	L.A., Det.	2	6	0	0	0	2	....	....	....	....	....	....	1977-78	1978-79
‡ Shuchuk, Gary	Det., L.A.	5	142	13	26	39	70	20	2	2	4	12	....	1990-91	1995-96
‡ Shudra, Ron	Edm.	1	10	0	5	5	6	....	....	....	....	....	....	1987-88	1987-88
Shutt, Steve	Mtl., L.A.	13	930	424	393	817	410	99	50	48	98	65	5	1972-73	1984-85
• Siebert, Babe	Mtl.M., NYR, Bos., Mtl.	14	592	140	156	296	982	49	7	5	12	62	2	1925-26	1938-39
Silk, Dave	NYR, Bos., Det., Wpg.	7	249	54	59	113	271	13	2	4	6	13	....	1979-80	1985-86
Siltala, Mike	Wsh., NYR	3	7	1	0	1	2	....	....	....	....	....	....	1981-82	1987-88
Siltanen, Risto	Edm., Hfd., Que.	8	562	90	265	355	266	32	6	12	18	30	....	1979-80	1986-87
Sim, Trevor	Edm.	1	3	0	1	1	2	....	....	....	....	....	....	1989-90	1989-90
Simard, Martin	Cgy., T.B.	3	44	1	5	6	183	....	....	....	....	....	....	1990-91	1992-93
Simmer, Charlie	Cal., Cle., L.A., Bos., Pit.	14	712	342	369	711	544	24	9	9	18	32	....	1974-75	1987-88
Simmons, Al	Cal., Bos.	3	11	0	1	1	21	1	0	0	0	0	....	1971-72	1975-76
• Simon, Cully	Det., Chi.	3	130	4	11	15	121	14	1	0	1	6	1	1942-43	1944-45
‡ Simon, Jason	NYI, Phx.	2	5	0	0	0	34	....	....	....	....	....	....	1993-94	1996-97
Simon, Thain	Det.	1	3	0	0	0	0	....	....	....	....	....	....	1946-47	1946-47
‡ Simon, Todd	Buf.	1	15	0	1	1	0	5	1	0	1	0	....	1993-94	1993-94
Simonetti, Frank	Bos.	4	115	5	8	13	76	12	0	1	1	8	....	1984-85	1987-88
Simpson, Bobby	Atl., St.L., Pit.	5	175	35	29	64	98	6	0	1	1	2	....	1976-77	1982-83
• Simpson, Cliff	Det.	2	6	0	1	1	0	2	0	0	0	2	....	1946-47	1947-48
Simpson, Craig	Pit., Edm., Buf.	10	634	247	250	497	659	67	36	32	68	56	2	1985-86	1994-95
• Simpson, Joe	NYA	6	228	21	19	40	156	2	0	0	0	0	....	1925-26	1930-31
Sims, Al	Bos., Hfd., L.A.	10	475	49	116	165	286	41	0	2	2	14	....	1973-74	1982-83
Sinclair, Reg	NYR, Det.	3	208	49	43	92	139	3	1	0	1	0	....	1950-51	1952-53
• Singbush, Alex	Mtl.	1	32	0	5	5	15	3	0	0	0	4	....	1940-41	1940-41
Sinisalo, Ilkka	Phi., Min., L.A.	11	582	204	222	426	208	68	21	11	32	6	....	1981-82	1991-92
Siren, Ville	Pit., Min.	5	290	14	68	82	276	7	0	0	0	6	....	1985-86	1989-90
Sirois, Bob	Phi., Wsh.	6	286	92	120	212	42	....	....	....	....	....	....	1974-75	1979-80
Sittler, Darryl	Tor., Phi., Det.	15	1096	484	637	1121	948	76	29	45	74	137	....	1970-71	1984-85
• Sjoberg, Lars-Erik	Wpg.	1	79	7	27	34	48	....	....	....	....	....	....	1979-80	1979-80
‡ Sjodin, Tommy	Min., Dal., Que.	2	106	8	40	48	52	....	....	....	....	....	....	1992-93	1993-94
• Skaare, Bjorn	Det.	1	1	0	0	0	0	....	....	....	....	....	....	1978-79	1978-79
Skarda, Randy	St.L.	2	26	0	5	5	11	....	....	....	....	....	....	1989-90	1991-92
• Skilton, Raymie	Mtl.W.	1	1	0	0	0	0	....	....	....	....	....	....	1917-18	1917-18
• Skinner, Alf	Tor., Bos., Mtl.M., Pit.	4	71	26	10	36	87	2	0	1	1	9	1	1917-18	1925-26
Skinner, Larry	Col.	4	47	10	12	22	8	2	0	0	0	0	....	1976-77	1979-80
‡ Skopintsev, Andrei	T.B., Atl.	3	40	2	4	6	32	....	....	....	....	....	....	1998-99	2000-01
Skov, Glen	Det., Chi., Mtl.	12	650	106	136	242	413	53	7	7	14	48	3	1949-50	1960-61
Skriko, Petri	Van., Bos., Wpg., S.J.	9	541	183	222	405	246	28	5	9	14	4	....	1984-85	1992-93
Skrudland, Brian	Mtl., Cgy., Fla., NYR, Dal.	15	881	124	219	343	1107	164	15	46	61	323	2	1985-86	1999-00
Sleaver, John	Chi.	2	13	1	0	1	6	....	....	....	....	....	....	1953-54	1956-57
Sleigher, Louis	Que., Bos.	6	194	46	53	99	146	17	1	1	2	64	....	1979-80	1985-86
Sloan, Tod	Tor., Chi.	13	745	220	262	482	831	47	9	12	21	47	2	1947-48	1960-61
• Slobodian, Peter	NYA	1	41	3	2	5	54	....	....	....	....	....	....	1940-41	1940-41
• Slowinski, Ed	NYR	6	291	58	74	132	63	16	2	6	8	6	....	1947-48	1952-53
Sly, Darryl	Tor., Min., Van.	4	79	1	2	3	20	....	....	....	....	....	....	1965-66	1970-71
Smail, Doug	Wpg., Min., Que., Ott.	13	845	210	249	459	602	42	9	2	11	49	....	1980-81	1992-93
Smart, Alex	Mtl.	1	8	5	2	7	0	....	....	....	....	....	....	1942-43	1942-43
Smedsmo, Dale	Tor.	1	4	0	0	0	0	....	....	....	....	....	....	1972-73	1972-73
Smillie, Don	Bos.	1	12	2	2	4	4	....	....	....	....	....	....	1933-34	1933-34
• Smith, Alex	Ott., Det., Bos., NYA	11	443	41	50	91	645	19	0	2	2	28	1	1924-25	1934-35
• Smith, Art	Tor., Ott.	4	144	15	10	25	249	4	1	1	2	8	....	1927-28	1930-31
Smith, Barry	Bos., Col.	3	114	7	7	14	10	....	....	....	....	....	....	1975-76	1980-81
Smith, Bobby	Min., Mtl.	15	1077	357	679	1036	917	184	64	96	160	245	1	1978-79	1992-93
Smith, Brad	Van., Atl., Cgy., Det., Tor.	9	222	28	34	62	591	20	3	3	6	49	....	1978-79	1986-87
Smith, Brian	Det.	3	61	2	8	10	12	5	0	0	0	0	....	1957-58	1960-61
• Smith, Brian	L.A., Min.	2	67	10	10	20	33	7	0	0	0	0	....	1967-68	1968-69
• Smith, Carl	Det.	1	7	1	1	2	2	....	....	....	....	....	....	1943-44	1943-44
Smith, Clint	NYR, Chi.	11	483	161	236	397	24	42	10	14	24	2	1	1936-37	1946-47
Smith, Dallas	Bos., NYR	16	890	55	252	307	959	86	3	29	32	128	2	1959-60	1977-78
Smith, Dennis	Wsh., L.A.	2	8	0	0	0	4	....	....	....	....	....	....	1989-90	1990-91
Smith, Derek	Buf., Det.	8	335	78	116	194	60	30	9	14	23	13	....	1975-76	1982-83
Smith, Derrick	Phi., Min., Dal.	10	537	82	92	174	373	82	14	11	25	79	....	1984-85	1993-94
• Smith, Des	Mtl.M., Mtl., Chi., Bos.	5	196	22	25	47	236	25	1	4	5	18	1	1937-38	1941-42
• Smith, Don	Mtl.	1	12	1	0	1	6	....	....	....	....	....	....	1919-20	1919-20
Smith, Don	NYR	1	11	1	1	2	0	1	0	0	0	0	....	1949-50	1949-50
Smith, Doug	L.A., Buf., Edm., Van., Pit.	9	535	115	138	253	624	18	4	2	6	21	....	1981-82	1989-90
Smith, Floyd	Bos., NYR, Det., Tor., Buf.	13	616	129	178	307	207	48	12	11	23	16	....	1954-55	1971-72
Smith, Geoff	Edm., Fla., NYR	10	462	18	73	91	282	13	0	1	1	8	1	1989-90	1998-99

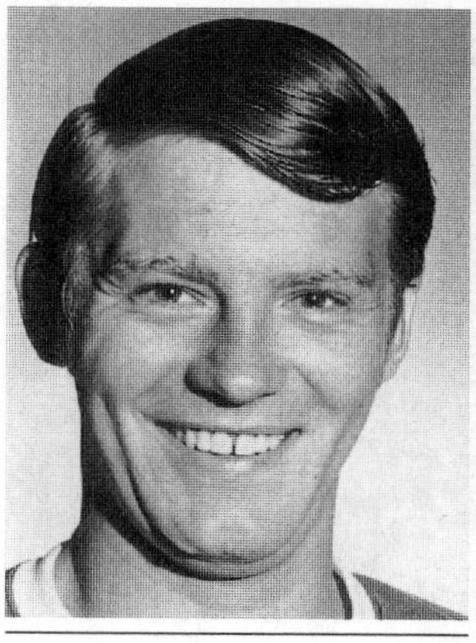

Brad Selwood

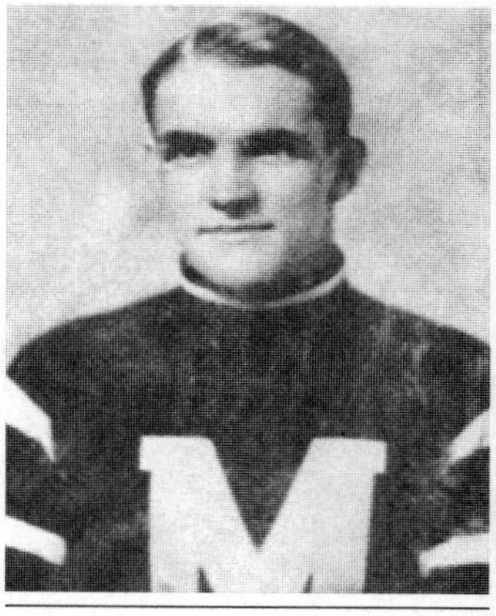

Babe Siebert

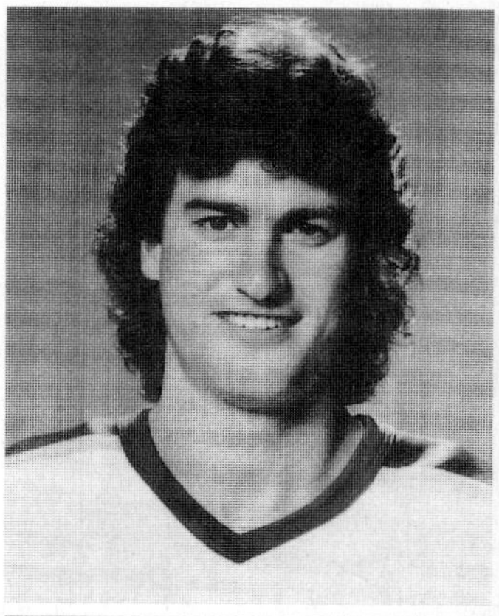

Dave Snuggerud

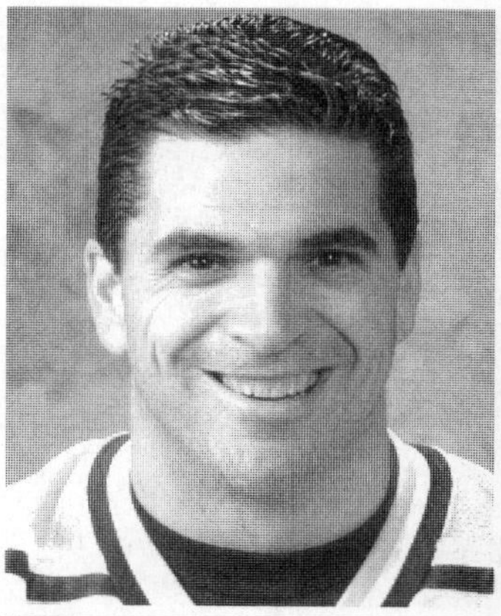

Kevin Stevens

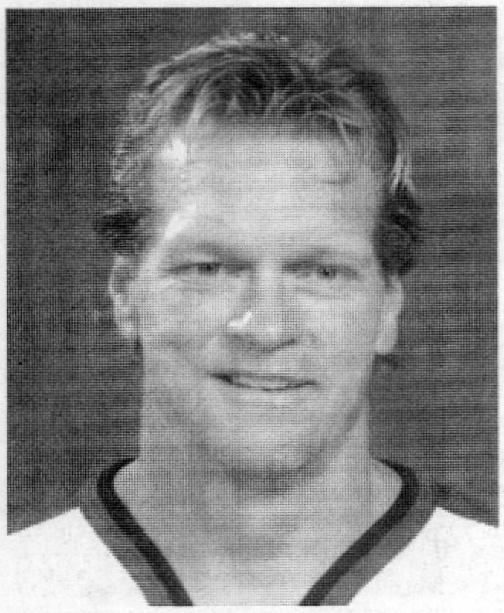
Gary Suter

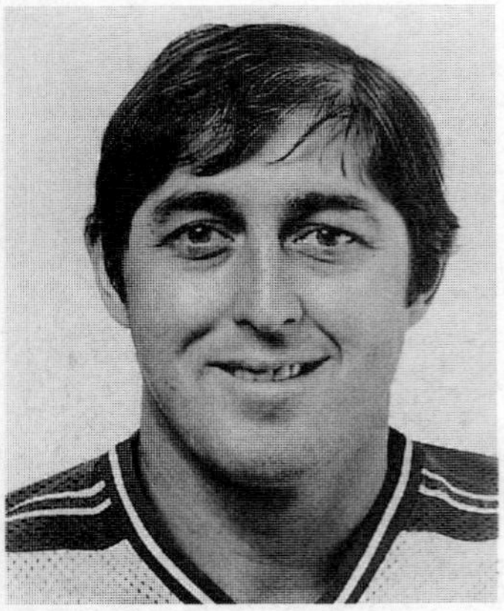
Walt Tkaczuk

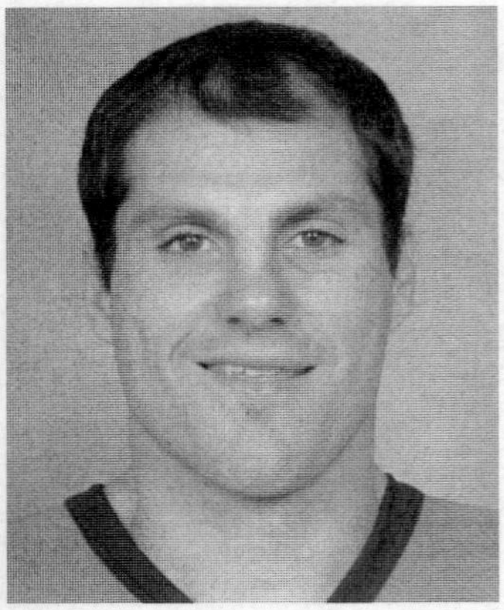
Rick Tocchet

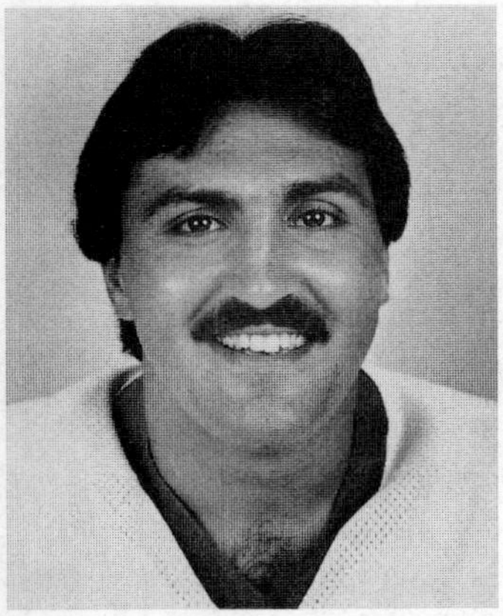
John Tonelli

			Regular Schedule					Playoffs							
Name	NHL Teams	NHL Seasons	GP	G	A	TP	PIM	GP	G	A	TP	PIM	NHL Cup Wins	First NHL Season	Last NHL Season
Smith, Glen	Chi.	1	2	0	0	0	0	....	....	....	....	....	....	1950-51	1950-51
• Smith, Glenn	Tor.	1	9	0	0	0	0	....	....	....	....	....	....	1921-22	1921-22
Smith, Gord	Wsh., Wpg.	6	299	9	30	39	284	....	....	....	....	....	....	1974-75	1979-80
Smith, Greg	Cal., Cle., Min., Det., Wsh.	13	829	56	232	288	1110	63	4	7	11	106	....	1975-76	1987-88
• Smith, Hooley	Ott., Mtl.M., Bos., NYA	17	715	200	225	425	1013	54	11	8	19	109	2	1924-25	1940-41
• Smith, Ken	Bos.	7	331	78	93	171	49	30	8	13	21	6	....	1944-45	1950-51
Smith, Nakina	Det.	1	10	1	2	3	0	....	....	....	....	....	....	1943-44	1943-44
Smith, Randy	Min.	2	3	0	0	0	0	....	....	....	....	....	....	1985-86	1986-87
Smith, Rick	Bos., Cal., St.L., Det., Wsh.	11	687	52	167	219	560	78	3	23	26	73	1	1968-69	1980-81
• Smith, Rodger	Pit., Phi.	6	210	20	4	24	172	4	3	0	3	0	....	1925-26	1930-31
Smith, Ron	NYI	1	11	1	1	2	14	....	....	....	....	....	....	1972-73	1972-73
Smith, Sid	Tor.	12	601	186	183	369	94	44	17	10	27	2	3	1946-47	1957-58
Smith, Stan	NYR	2	9	2	1	3	0	1	0	0	0	0	1	1939-40	1940-41
Smith, Steve	Phi., Buf.	6	18	0	1	1	15	....	....	....	....	....	....	1981-82	1988-89
Smith, Steve	Edm., Chi., Cgy.	16	804	72	303	375	2139	134	11	41	52	288	3	1984-85	2000-01
Smith, Stu	Mtl.	2	4	2	2	4	2	1	0	0	0	0	....	1940-41	1941-42
Smith, Stu	Hfd.	4	77	2	10	12	95	....	....	....	....	....	....	1979-80	1982-83
• Smith, Tommy	Que.	1	10	0	1	1	11	....	....	....	....	....	....	1919-20	1919-20
Smith, Vern	NYI	1	1	0	0	0	0	....	....	....	....	....	....	1984-85	1984-85
Smith, Wayne	Chi.	1	2	1	1	2	2	1	0	0	0	0	....	1966-67	1966-67
Smrke, John	St.L., Que.	3	103	11	17	28	33	....	....	....	....	....	....	1977-78	1979-80
• Smrke, Stan	Mtl.	2	9	0	3	3	0	....	....	....	....	....	....	1956-57	1957-58
Smyl, Stan	Van.	13	896	262	411	673	1556	41	16	17	33	64	....	1978-79	1990-91
• Smylie, Rod	Tor., Ott.	6	74	4	2	6	12	4	0	0	0	2	1	1920-21	1925-26
Smyth, Greg	Phi., Que., Cgy., Fla., Tor., Chi.	10	229	4	16	20	783	12	0	0	0	40	....	1986-87	1996-97
Smyth, Kevin	Hfd.	3	58	6	8	14	31	....	....	....	....	....	....	1993-94	1995-96
‡ Snell, Chris	Tor., L.A.	2	34	2	7	9	24	....	....	....	....	....	....	1993-94	1994-95
Snell, Ron	Pit.	2	7	3	2	5	6	....	....	....	....	....	....	1968-69	1969-70
Snell, Ted	Pit., K.C., Det.	2	104	7	18	25	22	....	....	....	....	....	....	1973-74	1974-75
Snepsts, Harold	Van., Min., Det., St.L.	17	1033	38	195	233	2009	93	1	14	15	231	....	1974-75	1990-91
Snow, Sandy	Det.	1	3	0	0	0	2	....	....	....	....	....	....	1968-69	1968-69
Snuggerud, Dave	Buf., S.J., Phi.	4	265	30	54	84	127	12	1	3	4	6	....	1989-90	1992-93
Sobchuk, Dennis	Det., Que.	2	35	5	6	11	2	....	....	....	....	....	....	1979-80	1982-83
• Sobchuk, Gene	Van.	1	1	0	0	0	0	....	....	....	....	....	....	1973-74	1973-74
Solheim, Ken	Chi., Min., Det., Edm.	5	135	19	20	39	34	3	1	1	2	2	....	1980-81	1985-86
Solinger, Bob	Tor., Det.	5	99	10	11	21	19	....	....	....	....	....	....	1951-52	1959-60
• Somers, Art	Chi., NYR	6	222	33	56	89	189	30	1	5	6	20	1	1929-30	1934-35
Sommer, Roy	Edm.	1	3	1	0	1	7	....	....	....	....	....	....	1980-81	1980-81
Songin, Tom	Bos.	3	43	5	5	10	22	....	....	....	....	....	....	1978-79	1980-81
Sonmor, Glen	NYR	2	28	2	0	2	21	....	....	....	....	....	....	1953-54	1954-55
‡ Sorochan, Lee	Cgy.	2	3	0	0	0	0	....	....	....	....	....	....	1998-99	1999-00
• Sorrell, John	Det., NYA	11	490	127	119	246	100	42	12	15	27	10	2	1930-31	1940-41
• Sparrow, Emory	Bos.	1	8	0	0	0	4	....	....	....	....	....	....	1924-25	1924-25
Speck, Fred	Det., Van.	3	28	1	2	3	2	....	....	....	....	....	....	1968-69	1971-72
• Speer, Bill	Pit., Bos.	4	130	5	20	25	79	8	1	0	1	4	1	1967-68	1970-71
Speers, Ted	Det.	1	4	1	1	2	0	....	....	....	....	....	....	1985-86	1985-86
• Spence, Gordon	Tor.	1	3	0	0	0	0	....	....	....	....	....	....	1925-26	1925-26
• Spencer, Brian	Tor., NYI, Buf., Pit.	10	553	80	143	223	634	37	1	5	6	29	....	1969-70	1978-79
Spencer, Irv	NYR, Bos., Det.	8	230	12	38	50	127	16	0	0	0	8	....	1959-60	1967-68
• Speyer, Chris	Tor., NYA	3	14	0	0	0	0	....	....	....	....	....	....	1923-24	1933-34
‡ Spring, Corey	T.B.	2	16	1	1	2	12	....	....	....	....	....	....	1997-98	1998-99
Spring, Don	Wpg.	4	259	1	54	55	80	6	0	0	0	10	....	1980-81	1983-84
Spring, Frank	Bos., St.L., Cal., Cle.	5	61	14	20	34	12	....	....	....	....	....	....	1969-70	1976-77
• Spring, Jesse	Ham., Pit., Tor., NYA	6	133	11	4	15	74	2	0	2	2	2	....	1923-24	1929-30
Spruce, Andy	Van., Col.	3	172	31	42	73	111	2	0	2	2	0	....	1976-77	1978-79
‡ Srsen, Tomas	Edm.	1	2	0	0	0	0	....	....	....	....	....	....	1990-91	1990-91
‡ St. Amour, Martin	Ott.	1	1	0	0	0	2	....	....	....	....	....	....	1992-93	1992-93
St. Laurent, Andre	NYI, Det., L.A., Pit.	11	644	129	187	316	749	59	8	12	20	48	....	1973-74	1983-84
St. Laurent, Dollard	Mtl., Chi.	12	652	29	133	162	496	92	2	22	24	87	5	1950-51	1961-62
St. Marseille, Frank	St.L., L.A.	10	707	140	285	425	242	88	20	25	45	18	....	1967-68	1976-77
St. Sauveur, Claude	Atl.	1	79	24	24	48	23	2	0	0	0	0	....	1975-76	1975-76
Stackhouse, Ron	Cal., Det., Pit.	12	889	87	372	459	824	32	5	8	13	38	....	1970-71	1981-82
• Stackhouse, Ted	Tor.	1	13	0	0	0	2	1	0	0	0	0	1	1921-22	1921-22
• Stahan, Butch	Mtl.	1	....	....	....	....	....	3	0	1	1	2	....	1944-45	1944-45
Stajduhar, Nick	Edm.	1	2	0	0	0	4	....	....	....	....	....	....	1995-96	1995-96
Staley, Al	NYR	1	1	0	1	1	0	....	....	....	....	....	....	1948-49	1948-49
Stamler, Lorne	L.A., Tor., Wpg.	4	116	14	11	25	16	....	....	....	....	....	....	1976-77	1979-80
Standing, George	Min.	1	2	0	0	0	0	....	....	....	....	....	....	1967-68	1967-68
Stanfield, Fred	Chi., Bos., Min., Buf.	14	914	211	405	616	134	106	21	35	56	10	2	1964-65	1977-78
Stanfield, Jack	Chi.	1	....	....	....	....	....	1	0	0	0	0	....	1965-66	1965-66
Stanfield, Jim	L.A.	3	7	0	1	1	0	....	....	....	....	....	....	1969-70	1971-72
Stankiewicz, Ed	Det.	2	6	0	0	0	2	....	....	....	....	....	....	1953-54	1955-56
Stankiewicz, Myron	St.L., Phi.	1	35	0	7	7	36	1	0	0	0	0	....	1968-69	1968-69
Stanley, Allan	NYR, Chi., Bos., Tor., Phi.	21	1244	100	333	433	792	109	7	36	43	80	4	1948-49	1968-69
• Stanley, Barney	Chi.	1	1	0	0	0	0	....	....	....	....	....	....	1927-28	1927-28
Stanley, Daryl	Phi., Van.	6	189	8	17	25	408	17	0	0	0	30	....	1983-84	1989-90
Stanowski, Wally	Tor., NYR	10	428	23	88	111	160	60	3	14	17	13	4	1939-40	1950-51
‡ Stanton, Paul	Pit., Bos., NYI	5	295	14	49	63	262	44	2	10	12	66	2	1990-91	1994-95
Stapleton, Brian	Wsh.	1	1	0	0	0	0	....	....	....	....	....	....	1975-76	1975-76
Stapleton, Pat	Bos., Chi.	10	635	43	294	337	353	65	10	39	49	38	....	1961-62	1972-73
Starikov, Sergei	N.J.	1	16	0	1	1	8	....	....	....	....	....	....	1989-90	1989-90
• Starr, Harold	Ott., Mtl.M., Mtl., NYR	7	205	6	5	11	186	15	1	0	1	4	....	1929-30	1935-36
Starr, Wilf	NYA, Det.	4	87	8	6	14	25	7	0	2	2	2	....	1932-33	1935-36
Stasiuk, Vic	Chi., Det., Bos.	14	745	183	254	437	669	69	16	18	34	40	3	1949-50	1962-63
Stastny, Anton	Que.	9	650	252	384	636	150	66	20	32	52	31	....	1980-81	1988-89
Stastny, Marian	Que., Tor.	5	322	121	173	294	110	32	5	17	22	7	....	1981-82	1985-86
Stastny, Peter	Que., N.J., St.L.	15	977	450	789	1239	824	93	33	72	105	123	....	1980-81	1994-95
Staszak, Ray	Det.	1	4	0	1	1	7	....	....	....	....	....	....	1985-86	1985-86
• Steele, Frank	Det.	1	1	0	0	0	0	....	....	....	....	....	....	1930-31	1930-31
Steen, Anders	Wpg.	1	42	5	11	16	22	....	....	....	....	....	....	1980-81	1980-81
Steen, Thomas	Wpg.	14	950	264	553	817	753	56	12	32	44	62	....	1981-82	1994-95
Stefaniw, Morris	Atl.	1	13	1	1	2	2	....	....	....	....	....	....	1972-73	1972-73
Stefanski, Bud	NYR	1	1	0	0	0	0	....	....	....	....	....	....	1977-78	1977-78
Stemkowski, Pete	Tor., Det., NYR, L.A.	15	967	206	349	555	866	83	25	29	54	136	1	1963-64	1977-78
Stenlund, Vern	Cle.	1	4	0	0	0	0	....	....	....	....	....	....	1976-77	1976-77
Stephenson, Bob	Hfd., Tor.	1	18	2	3	5	4	....	....	....	....	....	....	1979-80	1979-80
Stern, Ron	Van., Cgy., S.J.	12	638	75	86	161	2077	43	7	7	14	119	....	1987-88	1999-00
Sterner, Ulf	NYR	1	4	0	0	0	0	....	....	....	....	....	....	1964-65	1964-65
Stevens, John	Phi., Hfd.	5	53	0	10	10	48	....	....	....	....	....	....	1986-87	1993-94
‡ Stevens, Kevin	Pit., Bos., L.A., NYR, Phi.	15	874	329	397	726	1470	103	46	60	106	170	2	1987-88	2001-02
‡ Stevens, Mike	Van., Bos., NYI, Tor.	4	23	1	4	5	29	....	....	....	....	....	....	1984-85	1989-90
• Stevens, Phil	Mtl.W., Mtl., Bos.	3	25	1	0	1	3	....	....	....	....	....	....	1917-18	1925-26
Stevenson, Shayne	Bos., T.B.	3	27	0	2	2	35	....	....	....	....	....	....	1990-91	1992-93
Stewart, Allan	N.J., Bos.	6	64	6	4	10	243	....	....	....	....	....	....	1985-86	1991-92
Stewart, Bill	Buf., St.L., Tor., Min.	8	261	7	64	71	424	13	1	3	4	11	....	1977-78	1985-86
Stewart, Blair	Det., Wsh., Que.	7	229	34	44	78	326	....	....	....	....	....	....	1973-74	1979-80
Stewart, Bob	Bos., Cal., Cle., St.L., Pit.	9	575	27	101	128	809	5	1	1	2	2	....	1971-72	1979-80
Stewart, Cam	Bos., Fla., Min.	6	202	16	23	39	120	13	1	3	4	9	....	1993-94	2000-01
Stewart, Gaye	Tor., Chi., Det., NYR, Mtl.	11	502	185	159	344	274	25	2	9	11	16	2	1941-42	1953-54
• Stewart, Jack	Det., Chi.	12	565	31	84	115	765	80	5	14	19	143	2	1938-39	1951-52
Stewart, John	Pit., Atl., Cal.	5	258	58	60	118	158	4	0	0	0	10	....	1970-71	1974-75
Stewart, John	Que.	1	2	0	0	0	0	....	....	....	....	....	....	1979-80	1979-80
Stewart, Ken	Chi.	1	6	1	1	2	2	....	....	....	....	....	....	1941-42	1941-42
• Stewart, Nels	Mtl.M., Bos., NYA	15	650	324	191	515	953	50	9	12	21	47	1	1925-26	1939-40
Stewart, Paul	Que.	1	21	2	0	2	74	....	....	....	....	....	....	1979-80	1979-80
Stewart, Ralph	Van., NYI	7	252	57	73	130	28	19	4	4	8	2	....	1970-71	1977-78
Stewart, Ron	Tor., Bos., St.L., NYR, Van., NYI	21	1353	276	253	529	560	119	14	21	35	60	3	1952-53	1972-73
Stewart, Ryan	Wpg.	1	3	1	0	1	0	....	....	....	....	....	....	1985-86	1985-86
Stienburg, Trevor	Que.	4	71	8	4	12	161	1	0	0	0	0	....	1985-86	1988-89
Stiles, Tony	Cgy.	1	30	2	7	9	20	....	....	....	....	....	....	1983-84	1983-84
Stoddard, Jack	NYR	2	80	16	15	31	31	....	....	....	....	....	....	1951-52	1952-53
‡ Stojanov, Alek	Van., Pit.	3	107	2	5	7	222	14	0	0	0	21	....	1994-95	1996-97
Stoltz, Roland	Wsh.	1	14	2	2	4	14	....	....	....	....	....	....	1981-82	1981-82
Stone, Steve	Van.	1	2	0	0	0	0	....	....	....	....	....	....	1973-74	1973-74
Storm, Jim	Hfd., Dal.	3	84	7	15	22	44	....	....	....	....	....	....	1993-94	1995-96
Stothers, Mike	Phi., Tor.	4	30	0	2	2	65	5	0	0	0	11	....	1984-85	1987-88

Name	NHL Teams	NHL Seasons	Regular Schedule GP	G	A	TP	PIM	Playoffs GP	G	A	TP	PIM	NHL Cup Wins	First NHL Season	Last NHL Season
Stoughton, Blaine	Pit., Tor., Hfd., NYR	8	526	258	191	449	204	8	4	2	6	2	....	1973-74	1983-84
Stoyanovich, Steve	Hfd.	1	23	3	5	8	11	....	....	....	....	....	....	1983-84	1983-84
• Strain, Neil	NYR	1	52	11	13	24	12	....	....	....	....	....	....	1952-53	1952-53
Strate, Gord	Det.	3	61	0	0	0	34	....	....	....	....	....	....	1956-57	1958-59
Stratton, Art	NYR, Det., Chi., Pit., Phi.	4	95	18	33	51	24	5	0	0	0	0	....	1959-60	1967-68
Strobel, Art	NYR	1	7	0	0	0	0	....	....	....	....	....	....	1943-44	1943-44
Strong, Ken	Tor.	3	15	2	2	4	6	....	....	....	....	....	....	1982-83	1984-85
‡ Struch, David	Cgy.	1	4	0	0	0	4	....	....	....	....	....	....	1993-94	1993-94
Strueby, Todd	Edm.	3	5	0	1	1	2	....	....	....	....	....	....	1981-82	1983-84
• Stuart, Billy	Tor., Bos.	7	195	30	20	50	151	12	1	1	2	6	1	1920-21	1926-27
Stumpf, Bob	St.L., Pit.	1	10	1	1	2	20	....	....	....	....	....	....	1974-75	1974-75
Sturgeon, Peter	Col.	2	6	0	1	1	2	....	....	....	....	....	....	1979-80	1980-81
Suikkanen, Kai	Buf.	2	2	0	0	0	0	....	....	....	....	....	....	1981-82	1982-83
Sulliman, Doug	NYR, Hfd., N.J., Phi.	11	631	160	168	328	175	16	1	3	4	2	....	1979-80	1989-90
Sullivan, Barry	Det.	1	1	0	0	0	0	....	....	....	....	....	....	1947-48	1947-48
Sullivan, Bob	Hfd.	1	62	18	19	37	18	....	....	....	....	....	....	1982-83	1982-83
Sullivan, Brian	N.J.	1	2	0	1	1	0	....	....	....	....	....	....	1992-93	1992-93
Sullivan, Frank	Tor., Chi.	4	8	0	0	0	2	....	....	....	....	....	....	1949-50	1955-56
Sullivan, Mike	S.J., Cgy., Bos., Phx.	11	709	54	82	136	203	34	4	8	12	14	....	1991-92	2001-02
Sullivan, Peter	Wpg.	2	126	28	54	82	40	....	....	....	....	....	....	1979-80	1980-81
Sullivan, Red	Bos., Chi., NYR	11	557	107	239	346	441	18	1	2	3	6	....	1949-50	1960-61
Summanen, Raimo	Edm., Van.	5	151	36	40	76	35	10	2	5	7	0	....	1983-84	1987-88
• Summerhill, Bill	Mtl., Bro.	4	72	14	17	31	70	3	0	0	0	2	....	1937-38	1941-42
‡ Sundblad, Niklas	Cgy.	1	2	0	0	0	0	....	....	....	....	....	....	1995-96	1995-96
‡ Sundin, Ronnie	NYR	1	1	0	0	0	0	....	....	....	....	....	....	1997-98	1997-98
Sundstrom, Patrik	Van., N.J.	10	679	219	369	588	349	37	9	17	26	25	....	1982-83	1991-92
Sundstrom, Peter	NYR, Wsh., N.J.	6	338	61	83	144	120	23	3	3	6	8	....	1983-84	1989-90
• Suomi, Al	Chi.	1	5	0	0	0	0	....	....	....	....	....	....	1936-37	1936-37
‡ Sushinsky, Maxim	Min.	1	30	7	4	11	29	....	....	....	....	....	....	2000-01	2000-01
‡ Suter, Gary	Cgy., Chi., S.J.	17	1145	203	641	844	1349	108	17	56	73	120	1	1985-86	2001-02
Sutherland, Bill	Mtl., Phi., Tor., St.L., Det.	6	250	70	58	128	99	14	2	4	6	0	....	1962-63	1971-72
• Sutherland, Max	Bos.	1	2	0	0	0	0	....	....	....	....	....	....	1931-32	1931-32
Sutter, Brent	NYI, Chi.	18	1111	363	466	829	1054	144	30	44	74	164	2	1980-81	1997-98
Sutter, Brian	St.L.	12	779	303	333	636	1786	65	21	21	42	249	....	1976-77	1987-88
Sutter, Darryl	Chi.	8	406	161	118	279	288	51	24	19	43	26	....	1979-80	1986-87
Sutter, Duane	NYI, Chi.	11	731	139	203	342	1333	161	26	32	58	405	4	1979-80	1989-90
Sutter, Rich	Pit., Phi., Van., St.L., Chi., T.B., Tor.	13	874	149	166	315	1411	78	13	5	18	133	....	1982-83	1994-95
Sutter, Ron	Phi., St.L., Que., NYI, Bos., S.J., Cgy.	19	1093	205	329	534	1352	104	8	32	40	193	....	1982-83	2000-01
Suzor, Mark	Phi., Col.	2	64	4	16	20	60	....	....	....	....	....	....	1976-77	1977-78
‡ Svejkovsky, Jaroslav	Wsh., T.B.	4	113	23	19	42	56	1	0	0	0	2	....	1996-97	1999-00
Svensson, Leif	Wsh.	2	121	6	40	46	49	....	....	....	....	....	....	1978-79	1979-80
‡ Svensson, Magnus	Fla.	2	46	4	14	18	31	....	....	....	....	....	....	1994-95	1995-96
Svoboda, Petr	Mtl., Buf., Phi., T.B.	17	1028	58	341	399	1605	127	4	45	49	140	1	1984-85	2000-01
‡ Svoboda, Petr	Tor.	1	18	1	2	3	10	....	....	....	....	....	....	2000-01	2000-01
Swain, Garry	Pit.	1	9	1	1	2	0	....	....	....	....	....	....	1968-69	1968-69
Swarbrick, George	Oak., Pit., Phi.	4	132	17	25	42	173	....	....	....	....	....	....	1967-68	1970-71
• Sweeney, Bill	NYR	1	4	1	0	1	0	....	....	....	....	....	....	1959-60	1959-60
Sweeney, Bob	Bos., Buf., NYI, Cgy.	10	639	125	163	288	799	103	15	18	33	197	....	1986-87	1995-96
Sweeney, Tim	Cgy., Bos., Ana., NYR	8	291	55	83	138	123	4	0	0	0	2	....	1990-91	1997-98
Sykes, Bob	Tor.	1	2	0	0	0	0	....	....	....	....	....	....	1974-75	1974-75
Sykes, Phil	L.A., Wpg.	10	456	79	85	164	519	26	0	3	3	29	....	1982-83	1991-92
Sylvester, Dean	Buf., Atl.	3	96	21	16	37	32	4	0	0	0	0	....	1998-99	2000-01
Szura, Joe	Oak.	2	90	10	15	25	30	7	2	3	5	2	....	1967-68	1968-69
T															
Taft, John	Det.	1	15	0	2	2	4	....	....	....	....	....	....	1978-79	1978-79
Taglianetti, Peter	Wpg., Min., Pit., T.B.	11	451	18	74	92	1106	53	2	8	10	103	2	1984-85	1994-95
Talafous, Dean	Atl., Min., NYR	8	497	104	154	258	163	21	4	7	11	11	....	1974-75	1981-82
Talakoski, Ron	NYR	2	9	0	1	1	33	....	....	....	....	....	....	1986-87	1987-88
Talbot, Jean-Guy	Mtl., Min., Det., St.L., Buf.	17	1056	43	242	285	1006	150	4	26	30	142	7	1954-55	1970-71
Tallon, Dale	Van., Chi., Pit.	10	642	98	238	336	568	33	2	10	12	45	....	1970-71	1979-80
Tambellini, Steve	NYI, Col., N.J., Cgy., Van.	10	553	160	150	310	105	2	0	1	1	0	1	1978-79	1987-88
‡ Tancill, Chris	Hfd., Det., Dal., S.J.	8	134	17	32	49	54	11	1	1	2	8	....	1990-91	1997-98
Tanguay, Christian	Que.	1	2	0	0	0	0	....	....	....	....	....	....	1981-82	1981-82
Tannahill, Don	Van.	2	111	30	33	63	25	....	....	....	....	....	....	1972-73	1973-74
Tanti, Tony	Chi., Van., Pit., Buf.	11	697	287	273	560	661	30	3	12	15	27	....	1981-82	1991-92
Tardif, Marc	Mtl., Que.	8	517	194	207	401	443	62	13	15	28	75	2	1969-70	1982-83
‡ Tardif, Patrice	St.L., L.A.	2	65	7	11	18	78	....	....	....	....	....	....	1994-95	1995-96
Tatarinov, Mikhail	Wsh., Que., Bos.	4	161	21	48	69	184	....	....	....	....	....	....	1990-91	1993-94
Tatchell, Spence	NYR	1	1	0	0	0	0	....	....	....	....	....	....	1942-43	1942-43
• Taylor, Billy	Tor., Det., Bos., NYR	7	323	87	180	267	120	33	6	18	24	13	1	1939-40	1947-48
• Taylor, Bob	Bos.	1	8	0	0	0	6	....	....	....	....	....	....	1929-30	1929-30
Taylor, Dave	L.A.	17	1111	431	638	1069	1589	92	26	33	59	145	....	1977-78	1993-94
Taylor, Harry	Tor., Chi.	3	66	5	10	15	30	1	0	0	0	0	1	1946-47	1951-52
Taylor, Mark	Phi., Pit., Wsh.	5	209	42	68	110	73	6	0	0	0	0	....	1981-82	1985-86
• Taylor, Ralph	Chi., NYR	3	99	4	1	5	169	4	0	0	0	10	....	1927-28	1929-30
Taylor, Ted	NYR, Det., Min., Van.	6	166	23	35	58	181	....	....	....	....	....	....	1964-65	1971-72
Taylor Jr., Billy	NYR	1	2	0	0	0	0	....	....	....	....	....	....	1964-65	1964-65
Teal, Jeff	Mtl.	1	6	0	1	1	0	....	....	....	....	....	....	1984-85	1984-85
Teal, Skip	Bos.	1	1	0	0	0	0	....	....	....	....	....	....	1954-55	1954-55
Teal, Vic	NYI	1	1	0	0	0	0	....	....	....	....	....	....	1973-74	1973-74
Tebbutt, Greg	Que., Pit.	2	26	0	3	3	35	....	....	....	....	....	....	1979-80	1983-84
Tepper, Stephen	Chi.	1	1	0	0	0	0	....	....	....	....	....	....	1992-93	1992-93
Terbenche, Paul	Chi., Buf.	5	189	5	26	31	28	12	0	0	0	0	....	1967-68	1973-74
Terrion, Greg	L.A., Tor.	8	561	93	150	243	339	35	2	9	11	41	....	1980-81	1987-88
Terry, Bill	Min.	1	5	0	0	0	0	....	....	....	....	....	....	1987-88	1987-88
• Tertyshny, Dmitri	Phi.	1	62	2	8	10	30	1	0	0	0	0	....	1998-99	1998-99
Tessier, Orval	Mtl., Bos.	3	59	5	7	12	6	....	....	....	....	....	....	1954-55	1960-61
‡ Tezikov, Alexei	Wsh., Van.	3	30	1	1	2	2	....	....	....	....	....	....	1998-99	2001-02
Theberge, Greg	Wsh.	5	153	15	63	78	73	4	0	1	1	0	....	1979-80	1983-84
Thelin, Mats	Bos.	3	163	8	19	27	107	5	0	0	0	6	....	1984-85	1986-87
Thelven, Michael	Bos.	5	207	20	80	100	217	34	4	10	14	34	....	1985-86	1989-90
Therrien, Gaston	Que.	3	22	0	8	8	12	9	0	1	1	4	....	1980-81	1982-83
Thibaudeau, Gilles	Mtl., NYI, Tor.	5	119	25	37	62	40	8	3	3	6	2	....	1986-87	1990-91
Thibeault, Lorrain	Det., Mtl.	2	5	0	2	2	2	....	....	....	....	....	....	1944-45	1945-46
Thiffault, Leo	Min.	1	....	....	....	....	....	5	0	0	0	0	....	1967-68	1967-68
Thomas, Cy	Chi., Tor.	1	14	2	2	4	12	....	....	....	....	....	....	1947-48	1947-48
Thomas, Reg	Que.	1	39	9	7	16	6	....	....	....	....	....	....	1979-80	1979-80
Thomlinson, Dave	St.L., Bos., L.A.	5	42	1	3	4	50	9	3	1	4	4	....	1989-90	1994-95
• Thompson, Cliff	Bos.	2	13	0	1	1	2	....	....	....	....	....	....	1941-42	1948-49
Thompson, Errol	Tor., Det., Pit.	10	599	208	185	393	184	34	7	5	12	11	....	1970-71	1980-81
• Thompson, Ken	Mtl.W.	1	1	0	0	0	0	....	....	....	....	....	....	1917-18	1917-18
• Thompson, Paul	NYR, Chi.	13	582	153	179	332	336	48	11	11	22	54	3	1926-27	1938-39
• Thoms, Bill	Tor., Chi., Bos.	13	548	135	206	341	154	44	6	10	16	6	....	1932-33	1944-45
• Thomson, Bill	Det.	2	9	2	2	4	0	2	0	0	0	0	....	1938-39	1943-44
Thomson, Floyd	St.L.	8	411	56	97	153	341	10	0	2	2	6	....	1971-72	1979-80
Thomson, Jim	Wsh., Hfd., N.J., L.A., Ott., Ana.	7	115	4	3	7	416	1	0	0	0	0	....	1986-87	1993-94
• Thomson, Jimmy	Tor., Chi.	13	787	19	215	234	920	63	2	13	15	135	4	1945-46	1957-58
• Thomson, Rhys	Mtl., Tor.	2	25	0	2	2	38	....	....	....	....	....	....	1939-40	1942-43
Thornbury, Tom	Pit.	1	14	1	8	9	16	....	....	....	....	....	....	1983-84	1983-84
• Thorsteinson, Joe	NYA	1	4	0	0	0	0	....	....	....	....	....	....	1932-33	1932-33
• Thurier, Fred	NYA, Bro., NYR	3	80	25	27	52	18	....	....	....	....	....	....	1940-41	1944-45
Thurlby, Tom	Oak.	1	20	1	1	2	4	....	....	....	....	....	....	1967-68	1967-68
Thyer, Mario	Min.	1	5	0	0	0	0	1	0	0	0	2	....	1989-90	1989-90
Tichy, Milan	Chi., NYI	3	23	0	5	5	40	....	....	....	....	....	....	1992-93	1995-96
Tidey, Alex	Buf., Edm.	3	9	0	0	0	8	2	0	0	0	0	....	1976-77	1979-80
Tikkanen, Esa	Edm., NYR, St.L., N.J., Van., Fla., Wsh.	15	877	244	386	630	1077	186	72	60	132	275	5	1984-85	1998-99
Tilley, Tom	St.L.	4	174	4	38	42	89	14	1	3	4	19	....	1988-89	1993-94
• Timgren, Ray	Tor., Chi.	6	251	14	44	58	70	30	3	9	12	6	2	1948-49	1954-55
Tinordi, Mark	NYR, Min., Dal., Wsh.	12	663	52	148	200	1514	70	7	11	18	165	....	1987-88	1998-99
Tippett, Dave	Hfd., Wsh., Pit., Phi.	12	721	93	169	262	317	62	6	16	22	34	....	1983-84	1993-94
Titanic, Morris	Buf.	2	19	0	0	0	0	....	....	....	....	....	....	1974-75	1975-76
Titov, German	Cgy., Pit., Edm., Ana.	9	624	157	220	377	311	34	11	12	23	18	....	1993-94	2001-02
Tkaczuk, Walt	NYR	14	945	227	451	678	556	93	19	32	51	119	....	1967-68	1980-81
Toal, Mike	Edm.	1	3	0	0	0	0	....	....	....	....	....	....	1979-80	1979-80

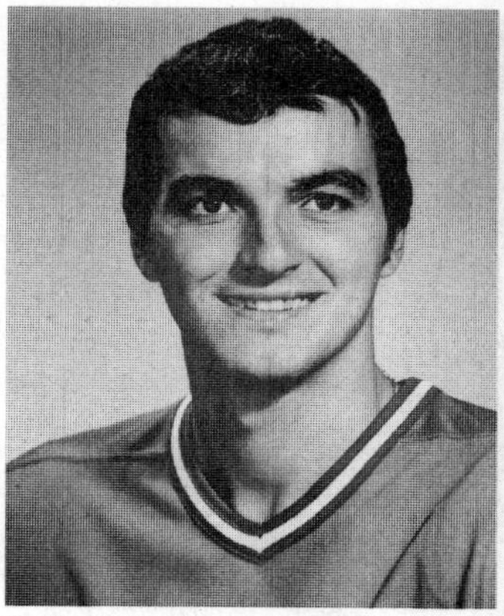

Mario Tremblay

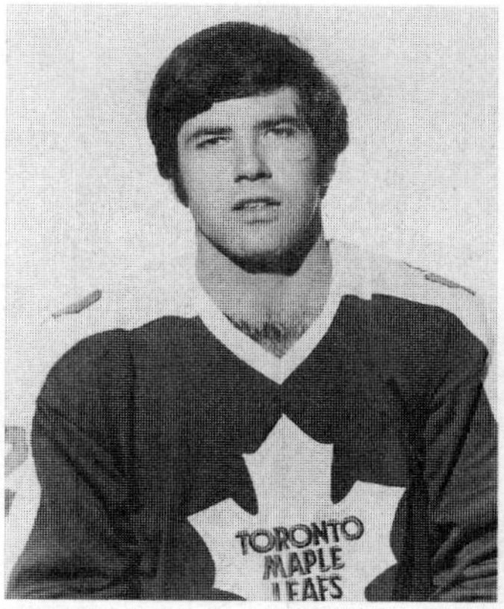

Ian Turnbull

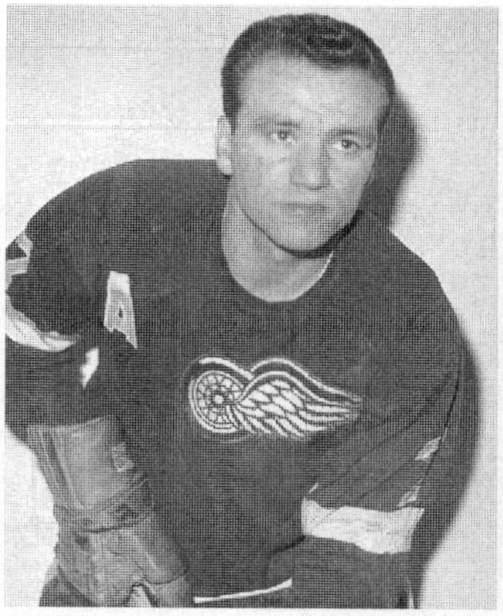

Norm Ullman

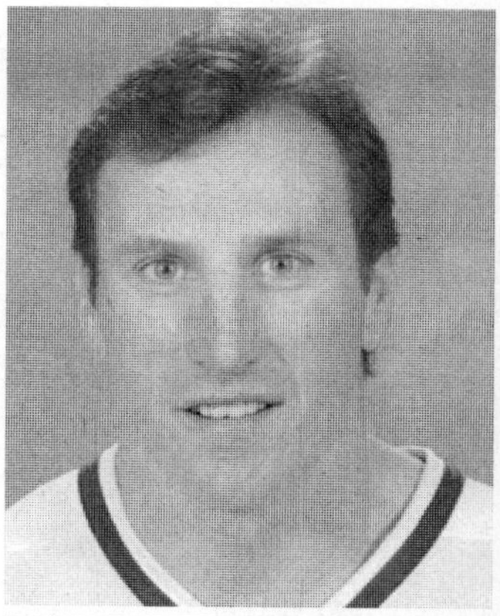

Pat Verbeek

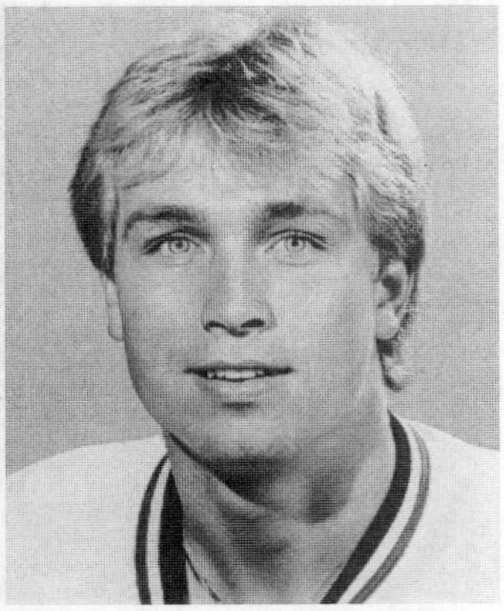

Randy Velischek

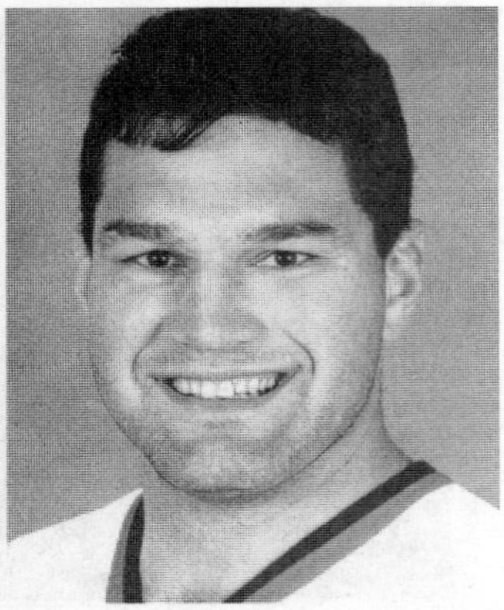

Dennis Vial

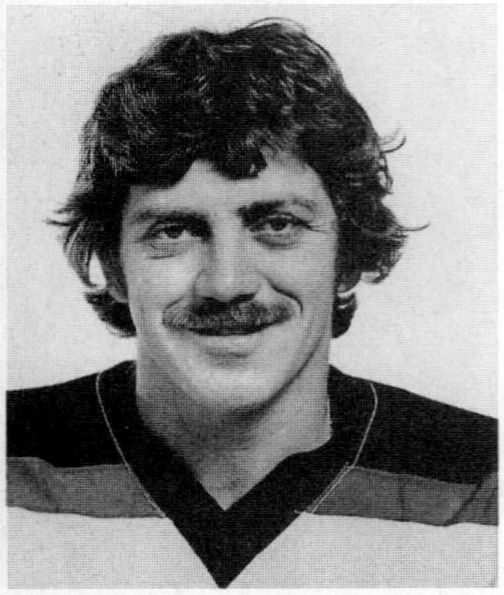

Steve Vickers

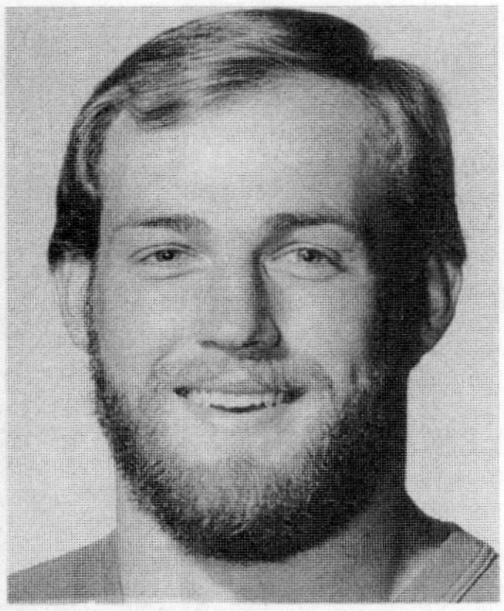

Jay Wells

Name	NHL Teams	NHL Seasons	Regular Schedule GP	G	A	TP	PIM	Playoffs GP	G	A	TP	PIM	NHL Cup Wins	First NHL Season	Last NHL Season
‡ Tocchet, Rick	Phi., Pit., L.A., Bos., Wsh., Phx.	18	1144	440	512	952	2972	145	52	60	112	471	1	1984-85	2001-02
Todd, Kevin	N.J., Edm., Chi., L.A., Ana.	9	383	70	133	203	225	12	3	2	5	16	....	1988-89	1997-98
Tomalty, Glenn	Wpg.	1	1	0	0	0	0	....	....	....	....	....	....	1979-80	1979-80
Tomlak, Mike	Hfd.	4	141	15	22	37	103	10	0	1	1	4	....	1989-90	1993-94
‡ Tomlinson, Dave	Tor., Wpg., Fla.	4	42	1	3	4	28	....	....	....	....	....	....	1991-92	1994-95
Tomlinson, Kirk	Min.	1	1	0	0	0	0	....	....	....	....	....	....	1987-88	1987-88
• Tomson, Jack	NYA	3	15	1	1	2	0	2	0	0	0	0	....	1938-39	1940-41
Tonelli, John	NYI, Cgy., L.A., Chi., Que.	14	1028	325	511	836	911	172	40	75	115	200	4	1978-79	1991-92
Tookey, Tim	Wsh., Que., Pit., Phi., L.A.	7	106	22	36	58	71	10	1	3	4	2	....	1980-81	1988-89
Toomey, Sean	Min.	1	1	0	0	0	0	....	....	....	....	....	....	1986-87	1986-87
‡ Toporowski, Shayne	Tor.	1	3	0	0	0	7	....	....	....	....	....	....	1996-97	1996-97
Toppazzini, Jerry	Bos., Chi., Det.	12	783	163	244	407	436	40	13	9	22	13	....	1952-53	1963-64
• Toppazzini, Zellio	Bos., NYR, Chi.	5	123	21	22	43	49	2	0	0	0	0	....	1948-49	1956-57
Torgaev, Pavel	Cgy., T.B.	2	55	6	14	20	20	1	0	0	0	0	....	1995-96	1999-00
‡ Torkki, Jari	Chi.	1	4	1	0	1	0	....	....	....	....	....	....	1988-89	1988-89
‡ Tormanen, Antti	Ott.	1	50	7	8	15	28	....	....	....	....	....	....	1995-96	1995-96
• Touhey, Bill	Mtl.M., Ott., Bos.	7	280	65	40	105	107	2	1	0	1	0	....	1927-28	1933-34
• Toupin, Jacques	Chi.	1	8	1	2	3	0	4	0	0	0	0	....	1943-44	1943-44
• Townsend, Art	Chi.	1	5	0	0	0	0	....	....	....	....	....	....	1926-27	1926-27
Townshend, Graeme	Bos., NYI, Ott.	5	45	3	7	10	28	....	....	....	....	....	....	1989-90	1993-94
Trader, Larry	Det., St.L., Mtl.	4	91	5	13	18	74	3	0	0	0	0	....	1982-83	1987-88
• Trainor, Wes	NYR	1	17	1	2	3	6	....	....	....	....	....	....	1948-49	1948-49
• Trapp, Bob	Chi.	2	82	4	4	8	129	2	0	0	0	4	....	1926-27	1927-28
Trapp, Doug	Buf.	1	2	0	0	0	0	....	....	....	....	....	....	1986-87	1986-87
• Traub, Percy	Chi., Det.	3	130	3	3	6	217	4	0	0	0	6	....	1926-27	1928-29
‡ Trebil, Dan	Ana., Pit., St.L.	5	85	4	4	8	32	10	0	1	1	8	....	1996-97	2000-01
Tredway, Brock	L.A.	1	....	....	....	....	....	1	0	0	0	0	....	1981-82	1981-82
Tremblay, Brent	Wsh.	2	10	1	0	1	6	....	....	....	....	....	....	1978-79	1979-80
Tremblay, Gilles	Mtl.	9	509	168	162	330	161	48	9	14	23	4	3	1960-61	1968-69
• Tremblay, J.C.	Mtl.	13	794	57	306	363	204	108	14	51	65	58	5	1959-60	1971-72
Tremblay, Marcel	Mtl.	1	10	0	2	2	0	....	....	....	....	....	....	1938-39	1938-39
Tremblay, Mario	Mtl.	12	852	258	326	584	1043	101	20	29	49	187	5	1974-75	1985-86
• Tremblay, Nils	Mtl.	2	3	0	1	1	0	2	0	0	0	0	....	1944-45	1945-46
Trimper, Tim	Chi., Wpg., Min.	6	190	30	36	66	153	2	0	0	0	2	....	1979-80	1984-85
Trottier, Bryan	NYI, Pit.	18	1279	524	901	1425	912	221	71	113	184	277	6	1975-76	1993-94
• Trottier, Dave	Mtl.M., Det.	11	446	121	113	234	517	31	4	3	7	39	1	1928-29	1938-39
Trottier, Guy	NYR, Tor.	3	115	28	17	45	37	9	1	0	1	16	....	1968-69	1971-72
Trottier, Rocky	N.J.	2	38	6	4	10	2	....	....	....	....	....	....	1983-84	1984-85
• Trudel, Lou	Chi., Mtl.	8	306	49	69	118	122	24	1	3	4	4	2	1933-34	1940-41
Trudell, Rene	NYR	3	129	24	28	52	72	5	0	0	0	2	....	1945-46	1947-48
‡ Tsulygin, Nikolai	Ana.	1	22	0	1	1	8	....	....	....	....	....	....	1996-97	1996-97
Tsygurov, Denis	Buf., L.A.	3	51	1	5	6	45	....	....	....	....	....	....	1993-94	1995-96
‡ Tsyplakov, Vladimir	L.A., Buf.	6	331	69	101	170	90	18	1	2	3	16	....	1995-96	2000-01
Tucker, John	Buf., Wsh., NYI, T.B.	12	656	177	259	436	285	31	10	18	28	24	....	1983-84	1995-96
• Tudin, Connie	Mtl.	1	4	0	1	1	4	....	....	....	....	....	....	1941-42	1941-42
Tudor, Rob	Van., St.L.	3	28	4	4	8	19	3	0	0	0	0	....	1978-79	1982-83
Tuer, Allan	L.A., Min., Hfd.	4	57	1	1	2	208	....	....	....	....	....	....	1985-86	1989-90
Turcotte, Alfie	Mtl., Wpg., Wsh.	7	112	17	29	46	49	5	0	0	0	0	....	1983-84	1990-91
Turcotte, Darren	NYR, Hfd., Wpg., S.J., St.L., Nsh.	12	635	195	216	411	301	35	6	8	14	12	....	1988-89	1999-00
‡ Turgeon, Sylvain	Hfd., N.J., Mtl., Ott.	12	669	269	226	495	691	36	4	7	11	22	....	1983-84	1994-95
Turlick, Gord	Bos.	1	2	0	0	0	2	....	....	....	....	....	....	1959-60	1959-60
Turnbull, Ian	Tor., L.A., Pit.	10	628	123	317	440	736	55	13	32	45	94	....	1973-74	1982-83
Turnbull, Perry	St.L., Mtl., Wpg.	9	608	188	163	351	1245	34	6	7	13	86	....	1979-80	1987-88
Turnbull, Randy	Cgy.	1	1	0	0	0	2	....	....	....	....	....	....	1981-82	1981-82
Turner, Bob	Mtl., Chi.	8	478	19	51	70	307	68	1	4	5	44	5	1955-56	1962-63
Turner, Brad	NYI	1	3	0	0	0	0	....	....	....	....	....	....	1991-92	1991-92
Turner, Dean	NYR, Col., L.A.	4	35	1	0	1	59	....	....	....	....	....	....	1978-79	1982-83
• Tustin, Norm	NYR	1	18	2	4	6	0	....	....	....	....	....	....	1941-42	1941-42
Tuten, Aud	Chi.	2	39	4	8	12	48	....	....	....	....	....	....	1941-42	1942-43
Tutt, Brian	Wsh.	1	7	1	0	1	2	....	....	....	....	....	....	1989-90	1989-90
Tuttle, Steve	St.L.	3	144	28	28	56	12	17	1	6	7	2	....	1988-89	1990-91
Twist, Tony	St.L., Que.	10	445	10	18	28	1121	18	1	1	2	22	....	1989-90	1998-99

U V

Name	NHL Teams	NHL Seasons	Regular Schedule GP	G	A	TP	PIM	Playoffs GP	G	A	TP	PIM	NHL Cup Wins	First NHL Season	Last NHL Season
Ubriaco, Gene	Pit., Oak., Chi.	3	177	39	35	74	50	11	2	0	2	4	....	1967-68	1969-70
Ullman, Norm	Det., Tor.	20	1410	490	739	1229	712	106	30	53	83	67	....	1955-56	1974-75
Unger, Garry	Tor., Det., St.L., Atl., L.A., Edm.	16	1105	413	391	804	1075	52	12	18	30	105	....	1967-68	1982-83
‡ Ustorf, Stefan	Wsh.	2	54	7	10	17	16	5	0	0	0	0	....	1995-96	1996-97
Vachon, Nick	NYI	1	1	0	0	0	0	....	....	....	....	....	....	1996-97	1996-97
Vadnais, Carol	Mtl., Oak., Cal., Bos., NYR, N.J.	17	1087	169	418	587	1813	106	10	40	50	185	2	1966-67	1982-83
‡ Vaic, Lubomir	Van.	2	9	1	1	2	2	....	....	....	....	....	....	1997-98	1999-00
Vail, Eric	Atl., Cgy., Det.	9	591	216	260	476	281	20	5	6	11	6	....	1973-74	1981-82
• Vail, Sparky	NYR	2	50	4	1	5	18	10	0	0	0	2	....	1928-29	1929-30
‡ Vaive, Rick	Van., Tor., Chi., Buf.	13	876	441	347	788	1445	54	27	16	43	111	....	1979-80	1991-92
Valentine, Chris	Wsh.	3	105	43	52	95	127	2	0	0	0	4	....	1981-82	1983-84
Valiquette, Jack	Tor., Col.	7	350	84	134	218	79	23	3	6	9	4	....	1974-75	1980-81
Vallis, Lindsay	Mtl.	1	1	0	0	0	0	....	....	....	....	....	....	1993-94	1993-94
Van Boxmeer, John	Mtl., Col., Buf., Que.	11	588	84	274	358	465	38	5	15	20	37	1	1973-74	1983-84
Van Dorp, Wayne	Edm., Pit., Chi., Que.	6	125	12	12	24	565	27	0	1	1	42	....	1986-87	1991-92
‡ Van Drunen, David	Ott.	1	1	0	0	0	0	....	....	....	....	....	....	1999-00	1999-00
Van Impe, Ed	Chi., Phi., Pit.	11	700	27	126	153	1025	66	1	12	13	131	2	1966-67	1976-77
‡ Varis, Petri	Chi.	1	1	0	0	0	0	....	....	....	....	....	....	1997-98	1997-98
‡ Varvio, Jarkko	Dal.	2	13	3	4	7	4	....	....	....	....	....	....	1993-94	1994-95
‡ Vasilevski, Alexander	St.L.	2	4	0	0	0	2	....	....	....	....	....	....	1995-96	1996-97
‡ Vasiliev, Alexei	NYR	1	1	0	0	0	2	....	....	....	....	....	....	1999-00	1999-00
‡ Vasilyev, Andrei	NYI, Phx.	4	16	2	5	7	6	....	....	....	....	....	....	1994-95	1998-99
Vaske, Dennis	NYI, Bos.	9	235	5	41	46	253	22	0	7	7	16	....	1990-91	1998-99
• Vasko, Moose	Chi., Min.	13	786	34	166	200	719	78	2	7	9	73	1	1956-57	1969-70
Vasko, Rick	Det.	3	31	3	7	10	29	....	....	....	....	....	....	1977-78	1980-81
Vautour, Yvon	NYI, Col., N.J., Que.	6	204	26	33	59	401	....	....	....	....	....	....	1979-80	1984-85
Vaydik, Greg	Chi.	1	5	0	0	0	0	....	....	....	....	....	....	1976-77	1976-77
Veitch, Darren	Wsh., Det., Tor.	10	511	48	209	257	296	33	4	11	15	33	....	1980-81	1990-91
Velischek, Randy	Min., N.J., Que.	10	509	21	76	97	401	44	2	5	7	32	....	1982-83	1991-92
Vellucci, Mike	Hfd.	1	2	0	0	0	11	....	....	....	....	....	....	1987-88	1987-88
Venasky, Vic	L.A.	7	430	61	101	162	66	21	1	5	6	12	....	1972-73	1978-79
Veneruzzo, Gary	St.L.	2	7	1	1	2	0	9	0	2	2	2	....	1967-68	1971-72
Verbeek, Pat	N.J., Hfd., NYR, Dal., Det.	20	1424	522	541	1063	2905	117	26	36	62	225	1	1982-83	2001-02
Vermette, Mark	Que.	4	67	5	13	18	33	....	....	....	....	....	....	1988-89	1991-92
Verret, Claude	Buf.	2	14	2	5	7	2	....	....	....	....	....	....	1983-84	1984-85
Verstraete, Leigh	Tor.	3	8	0	1	1	14	....	....	....	....	....	....	1982-83	1987-88
Ververgaert, Dennis	Van., Phi., Wsh.	8	583	176	216	392	247	8	1	2	3	6	....	1973-74	1980-81
Vesey, Jim	St.L., Bos.	3	15	1	2	3	7	....	....	....	....	....	....	1988-89	1991-92
Veysey, Sid	Van.	1	1	0	0	0	0	....	....	....	....	....	....	1977-78	1977-78
‡ Vial, Dennis	NYR, Det., Ott.	8	242	4	15	19	794	....	....	....	....	....	....	1990-91	1997-98
Vickers, Steve	NYR	10	698	246	340	586	330	68	24	25	49	58	....	1972-73	1981-82
Vigneault, Alain	St.L.	2	42	2	5	7	82	4	0	1	1	26	....	1981-82	1982-83
‡ Viitakoski, Vesa	Cgy.	3	23	2	4	6	8	....	....	....	....	....	....	1993-94	1995-96
‡ Vilgrain, Claude	Van., N.J., Phi.	5	89	21	32	53	78	11	1	1	2	17	....	1987-88	1993-94
Vincelette, Dan	Chi., Que.	6	193	20	22	42	351	12	0	0	0	4	....	1986-87	1991-92
Vipond, Pete	Cal.	1	3	0	0	0	0	....	....	....	....	....	....	1972-73	1972-73
Virta, Hannu	Buf.	5	245	25	101	126	66	17	1	3	4	6	....	1981-82	1985-86
Visheau, Mark	Wpg., L.A.	2	29	1	3	4	107	....	....	....	....	....	....	1993-94	1998-99
‡ Vitolinsh, Harijs	Wpg.	1	8	0	0	0	4	....	....	....	....	....	....	1993-94	1993-94
‡ Viveiros, Emanuel	Min.	3	29	1	11	12	6	....	....	....	....	....	....	1985-86	1987-88
‡ Vlasak, Tomas	L.A.	1	10	1	3	4	2	....	....	....	....	....	....	2000-01	2000-01
• Vokes, Ed	Chi.	1	5	0	0	0	0	....	....	....	....	....	....	1930-31	1930-31
Volcan, Mickey	Hfd., Cgy.	4	162	8	33	41	146	....	....	....	....	....	....	1980-81	1983-84
Volchkov, Alexandre	Wsh.	1	3	0	0	0	0	....	....	....	....	....	....	1999-00	1999-00
Volek, David	NYI	6	396	95	154	249	201	15	5	5	10	2	....	1988-89	1993-94
Volmar, Doug	Det., L.A.	4	62	13	8	21	26	2	1	0	1	0	....	1969-70	1972-73
‡ Von Stefenelli, Phil	Bos., Ott.	2	33	0	5	5	23	....	....	....	....	....	....	1995-96	1996-97
Vopat, Jan	L.A., Nsh.	5	126	11	20	31	70	2	0	1	1	2	....	1995-96	1999-00
‡ Vopat, Roman	St.L., L.A., Chi., Phi.	4	133	6	14	20	253	....	....	....	....	....	....	1995-96	1998-99
Vorobiev, Vladimir	NYR, Edm.	3	33	9	7	16	14	1	0	0	0	0	....	1996-97	1998-99

Name	NHL Teams	NHL Seasons	Regular Schedule GP	G	A	TP	PIM	Playoffs GP	G	A	TP	PIM	NHL Cup Wins	First NHL Season	Last NHL Season
• Voss, Carl	Tor., NYR, Det., Ott., St.L., NYA, Mtl.M., Chi.	8	261	34	70	104	50	24	5	3	8	0	1	1926-27	1937-38
Vukota, Mick	NYI, T.B., Mtl.	11	574	17	29	46	2071	23	0	0	0	73	....	1987-88	1997-98
Vyazmikin, Igor	Edm.	1	4	1	0	1	0	....	....	....	....	....	....	1990-91	1990-91

W

Name	NHL Teams	NHL Seasons	Regular Schedule GP	G	A	TP	PIM	Playoffs GP	G	A	TP	PIM	NHL Cup Wins	First NHL Season	Last NHL Season
Waddell, Don	L.A.	1	1	0	0	0	0	....	....	....	....	....	....	1980-81	1980-81
• Waite, Frank	NYR	1	17	1	3	4	4	....	....	....	....	....	....	1930-31	1930-31
Walker, Gord	NYR, L.A.	4	31	3	4	7	23	....	....	....	....	....	....	1986-87	1989-90
Walker, Howard	Wsh., Cgy.	3	83	2	13	15	133	....	....	....	....	....	....	1980-81	1982-83
• Walker, Jack	Det.	2	80	5	8	13	18	....	....	....	....	....	....	1926-27	1927-28
Walker, Kurt	Tor.	3	71	4	5	9	142	16	0	0	0	34	....	1975-76	1977-78
Walker, Russ	L.A.	2	17	1	0	1	41	....	....	....	....	....	....	1976-77	1977-78
Wall, Bob	Det., L.A., St.L.	8	322	30	55	85	155	22	0	3	3	2	....	1964-65	1971-72
Wallin, Peter	NYR	2	52	3	14	17	14	14	2	6	8	6	....	1980-81	1981-82
Walsh, Jim	Buf.	1	4	0	1	1	4	....	....	....	....	....	....	1981-82	1981-82
Walsh, Mike	NYI	2	14	2	0	2	4	....	....	....	....	....	....	1987-88	1988-89
Walter, Ryan	Wsh., Mtl., Van.	15	1003	264	382	646	946	113	16	35	51	62	1	1978-79	1992-93
• Walton, Bobby	Mtl.	1	4	0	0	0	0	....	....	....	....	....	....	1943-44	1943-44
Walton, Mike	Tor., Bos., Van., St.L., Chi.	12	588	201	247	448	357	47	14	10	24	45	2	1965-66	1978-79
Wappel, Gord	Atl., Cgy.	3	20	1	1	2	10	2	0	0	0	4	....	1979-80	1981-82
Ward, Don	Chi., Bos.	2	34	0	1	1	16	....	....	....	....	....	....	1957-58	1959-60
‡ Ward, Ed	Que., Cgy., Atl., Ana., N.J.	8	278	23	26	49	354	....	....	....	....	....	....	1993-94	2000-01
• Ward, Jimmy	Mtl.M., Mtl.	12	527	147	127	274	455	36	4	4	8	26	1	1927-28	1938-39
Ward, Joe	Col.	1	4	0	0	0	2	....	....	....	....	....	....	1980-81	1980-81
Ward, Ron	Tor., Van.	2	89	2	5	7	6	....	....	....	....	....	....	1969-70	1971-72
‡ Ware, Jeff	Tor., Fla.	3	21	0	1	1	12	....	....	....	....	....	....	1996-97	1998-99
‡ Ware, Michael	Edm.	2	5	0	1	1	15	....	....	....	....	....	....	1988-89	1989-90
• Wares, Eddie	NYR, Det., Chi.	9	321	60	102	162	161	45	5	7	12	34	1	1936-37	1946-47
Warner, Bob	Tor.	2	10	1	1	2	4	4	0	0	0	0	....	1975-76	1976-77
Warner, Jim	Hfd.	1	32	0	3	3	10	....	....	....	....	....	....	1979-80	1979-80
Warwick, Bill	NYR	2	14	3	3	6	16	....	....	....	....	....	....	1942-43	1943-44
• Warwick, Grant	NYR, Bos., Mtl.	9	395	147	142	289	220	16	2	4	6	6	....	1941-42	1949-50
• Wasnie, Nick	Chi., Mtl., NYA, Ott., St.L.	7	248	57	34	91	176	20	6	3	9	20	2	1927-28	1934-35
Watson, Bill	Chi.	4	115	23	36	59	12	6	0	2	2	0	....	1985-86	1988-89
Watson, Bryan	Mtl., Det., Oak., Pit., St.L., Wsh.	16	878	17	135	152	2212	32	2	0	2	70	....	1963-64	1978-79
Watson, Dave	Col.	2	18	0	1	1	10	....	....	....	....	....	....	1979-80	1980-81
• Watson, Harry	Bro., Det., Tor., Chi.	14	809	236	207	443	150	62	16	9	25	27	5	1941-42	1956-57
Watson, Jim	Det., Buf.	8	221	4	19	23	345	....	....	....	....	....	....	1963-64	1971-72
Watson, Jimmy	Phi.	10	613	38	148	186	492	101	5	34	39	89	2	1972-73	1981-82
Watson, Joe	Bos., Phi., Col.	14	835	38	178	216	447	84	3	12	15	82	2	1964-65	1978-79
• Watson, Phil	NYR, Mtl.	13	590	144	265	409	532	54	10	25	35	67	2	1935-36	1947-48
Watters, Tim	Wpg., L.A.	14	741	26	151	177	1289	82	1	5	6	115	....	1981-82	1994-95
Watts, Brian	Det.	1	4	0	0	0	0	....	....	....	....	....	....	1975-76	1975-76
• Webster, Aubrey	Phi., Mtl.M.	2	5	0	0	0	0	....	....	....	....	....	....	1930-31	1934-35
• Webster, Don	Tor.	1	27	7	6	13	28	5	0	0	0	12	....	1943-44	1943-44
Webster, John	NYR	1	14	0	0	0	4	....	....	....	....	....	....	1949-50	1949-50
Webster, Tom	Bos., Det., Cal.	5	102	33	42	75	61	1	0	0	0	0	....	1968-69	1979-80
• Weiland, Cooney	Bos., Ott., Det.	11	509	173	160	333	147	45	12	10	22	12	2	1928-29	1938-39
Weir, Stan	Cal., Tor., Edm., Col., Det.	10	642	139	207	346	183	37	6	5	11	4	....	1972-73	1982-83
Weir, Wally	Que., Hfd., Pit.	6	320	21	45	66	625	23	0	1	1	96	....	1979-80	1984-85
• Wellington, Alex	Que.	1	1	0	0	0	0	....	....	....	....	....	....	1919-20	1919-20
‡ Wells, Chris	Pit., Fla.	5	195	9	20	29	193	3	0	0	0	0	....	1995-96	1999-00
Wells, Jay	L.A., Phi., Buf., NYR, St.L., T.B.	18	1098	47	216	263	2359	114	3	14	17	213	1	1979-80	1996-97
Wensink, John	St.L., Bos., Que., Col., N.J.	8	403	70	68	138	840	43	2	6	8	86	....	1973-74	1982-83
• Wentworth, Cy	Chi., Mtl.M., Mtl.	13	575	39	68	107	355	35	5	6	11	20	1	1927-28	1939-40
Werenka, Brad	Edm., Que., Chi., Pit., Cgy.	7	320	19	61	80	299	19	2	1	3	14	....	1992-93	2000-01
Wesenberg, Brian	Phi.	1	1	0	0	0	5	....	....	....	....	....	....	1998-99	1998-99
Wesley, Blake	Phi., Hfd., Que., Tor.	7	298	18	46	64	486	19	2	2	4	30	....	1979-80	1985-86
Westfall, Ed	Bos., NYI	18	1220	231	394	625	544	95	22	37	59	41	2	1961-62	1978-79
Wharram, Kenny	Chi.	14	766	252	281	533	222	80	16	27	43	38	1	1951-52	1968-69
Wharton, Len	NYR	1	1	0	0	0	0	....	....	....	....	....	....	1944-45	1944-45
‡ Wheeldon, Simon	NYR, Wpg.	3	15	0	2	2	10	....	....	....	....	....	....	1987-88	1990-91
• Wheldon, Don	St.L.	1	2	0	0	0	0	....	....	....	....	....	....	1974-75	1974-75
Whelton, Bill	Wpg.	1	2	0	0	0	0	....	....	....	....	....	....	1980-81	1980-81
Whistle, Rob	NYR, St.L.	2	51	7	5	12	16	4	0	0	0	2	....	1985-86	1987-88
White, Bill	L.A., Chi.	9	604	50	215	265	495	91	7	32	39	76	....	1967-68	1975-76
White, Moe	Mtl.	1	4	0	1	1	2	....	....	....	....	....	....	1945-46	1945-46
• White, Sherman	NYR	2	4	0	2	2	0	....	....	....	....	....	....	1946-47	1949-50
• White, Tex	Pit., NYA, Phi.	6	203	33	12	45	141	4	0	0	0	4	....	1925-26	1930-31
White, Tony	Wsh., Min.	5	164	37	28	65	104	....	....	....	....	....	....	1974-75	1979-80
Whitelaw, Bob	Det.	2	32	0	2	2	2	8	0	0	0	0	....	1940-41	1941-42
Whitlock, Bob	Min.	1	1	0	0	0	0	....	....	....	....	....	....	1969-70	1969-70
Whyte, Sean	L.A.	2	21	0	2	2	12	....	....	....	....	....	....	1991-92	1992-93
• Wickenheiser, Doug	Mtl., St.L., Van., NYR, Wsh.	10	556	111	165	276	286	41	4	7	11	18	....	1980-81	1989-90
• Widing, Juha	NYR, L.A., Cle.	8	575	144	226	370	208	8	1	2	3	2	....	1969-70	1976-77
Widmer, Jason	NYI, S.J.	3	7	0	1	1	7	....	....	....	....	....	....	1994-95	1996-97
• Wiebe, Art	Chi.	11	414	14	27	41	201	31	1	3	4	10	1	1932-33	1943-44
Wiemer, Jim	Buf., NYR, Edm., L.A., Bos.	11	325	29	72	101	378	62	5	8	13	63	....	1982-83	1993-94
• Wilcox, Archie	Mtl.M., Bos., St.L.	6	208	8	14	22	158	12	1	0	1	8	....	1929-30	1934-35
Wilcox, Barry	Van.	2	33	3	2	5	15	....	....	....	....	....	....	1972-73	1974-75
Wilder, Arch	Det.	1	18	0	2	2	2	....	....	....	....	....	....	1940-41	1940-41
Wiley, Jim	Pit., Van.	5	63	4	10	14	8	....	....	....	....	....	....	1972-73	1976-77
Wilkie, Bob	Det., Phi.	2	18	2	5	7	10	....	....	....	....	....	....	1990-91	1993-94
Wilkie, David	Mtl., T.B., NYR	6	167	10	26	36	165	8	1	2	3	14	....	1994-95	2000-01
Wilkins, Barry	Bos., Van., Pit.	9	418	27	125	152	663	6	0	1	1	4	....	1966-67	1975-76
• Wilkinson, John	Bos.	1	9	0	0	0	6	....	....	....	....	....	....	1943-44	1943-44
Wilkinson, Neil	Min., S.J., Chi., Wpg., Pit.	10	460	16	67	83	813	53	3	6	9	41	....	1989-90	1998-99
Wilks, Brian	L.A.	4	48	4	8	12	27	....	....	....	....	....	....	1984-85	1988-89
Willard, Rod	Tor.	1	1	0	0	0	0	....	....	....	....	....	....	1982-83	1982-83
• Williams, Burr	Det., St.L., Bos.	3	19	0	1	1	28	7	0	0	0	8	....	1933-34	1936-37
Williams, Butch	St.L., Cal.	3	108	14	35	49	131	....	....	....	....	....	....	1973-74	1975-76
Williams, Darryl	L.A.	1	2	0	0	0	10	....	....	....	....	....	....	1992-93	1992-93
Williams, David	S.J., Ana.	4	173	11	53	64	157	....	....	....	....	....	....	1991-92	1994-95
Williams, Fred	Det.	1	44	2	5	7	10	....	....	....	....	....	....	1976-77	1976-77
Williams, Gord	Phi.	2	2	0	0	0	2	....	....	....	....	....	....	1981-82	1982-83
Williams, Sean	Chi.	1	2	0	0	0	4	....	....	....	....	....	....	1991-92	1991-92
Williams, Tiger	Tor., Van., Det., L.A., Hfd.	14	962	241	272	513	3966	83	12	23	35	455	....	1974-75	1987-88
Williams, Tom	NYR, L.A.	8	397	115	138	253	73	29	8	7	15	4	....	1971-72	1978-79
• Williams, Tommy	Bos., Min., Cal., Wsh.	13	663	161	269	430	177	10	2	5	7	2	....	1961-62	1975-76
Willson, Don	Mtl.	2	22	2	7	9	0	3	0	0	0	0	....	1937-38	1938-39
Wilson, Behn	Phi., Chi.	9	601	98	260	358	1480	67	12	29	41	190	....	1978-79	1987-88
• Wilson, Bert	NYR, St.L., L.A., Cgy.	8	478	37	44	81	646	21	0	2	2	42	....	1973-74	1980-81
Wilson, Bob	Chi.	1	1	0	0	0	0	....	....	....	....	....	....	1953-54	1953-54
Wilson, Carey	Cgy., Hfd., NYR	10	552	169	258	427	314	52	11	13	24	14	....	1983-84	1992-93
• Wilson, Cully	Tor., Mtl., Ham., Chi.	5	127	59	28	87	243	2	1	0	1	6	....	1919-20	1926-27
Wilson, Doug	Chi., S.J.	16	1024	237	590	827	830	95	19	61	80	88	....	1977-78	1992-93
Wilson, Gord	Bos.	1	....	....	....	....	....	2	0	0	0	0	....	1954-55	1954-55
Wilson, Hub	NYA	1	2	0	0	0	0	....	....	....	....	....	....	1931-32	1931-32
Wilson, Jerry	Mtl.	1	3	0	0	0	2	....	....	....	....	....	....	1956-57	1956-57
Wilson, Johnny	Det., Chi., Tor., NYR	13	688	161	171	332	190	66	14	13	27	11	4	1949-50	1961-62
• Wilson, Larry	Det., Chi.	6	152	21	48	69	75	4	0	0	0	0	1	1949-50	1955-56
Wilson, Mitch	N.J., Pit.	2	26	2	3	5	104	....	....	....	....	....	....	1984-85	1986-87
Wilson, Murray	Mtl., L.A.	7	386	94	95	189	162	53	5	14	19	32	4	1972-73	1978-79
Wilson, Rick	Mtl., St.L., Det.	4	239	6	26	32	165	3	0	0	0	0	....	1973-74	1976-77
Wilson, Rik	St.L., Cgy., Chi.	6	251	25	65	90	220	22	0	4	4	23	....	1981-82	1987-88
Wilson, Roger	Chi.	1	7	0	2	2	6	....	....	....	....	....	....	1974-75	1974-75
Wilson, Ron	Tor., Min.	7	177	26	67	93	68	20	4	13	17	8	....	1977-78	1987-88
Wilson, Ron	Wpg., St.L., Mtl.	14	832	110	216	326	415	63	10	12	22	64	....	1979-80	1993-94
Wilson, Wally	Bos.	1	53	11	8	19	18	1	0	0	0	0	....	1947-48	1947-48
Wing, Murray	Det.	1	1	0	1	1	0	....	....	....	....	....	....	1973-74	1973-74
‡ Winnes, Chris	Bos., Phi.	4	33	1	6	7	6	1	0	0	0	0	....	1990-91	1993-94
Wiseman, Brian	Tor.	1	3	0	0	0	0	....	....	....	....	....	....	1996-97	1996-97
• Wiseman, Eddie	Det., NYA, Bos.	10	456	115	165	280	136	43	10	10	20	16	1	1932-33	1941-42
Wiste, Jim	Chi., Van.	3	52	1	10	11	8	....	....	....	....	....	....	1968-69	1970-71

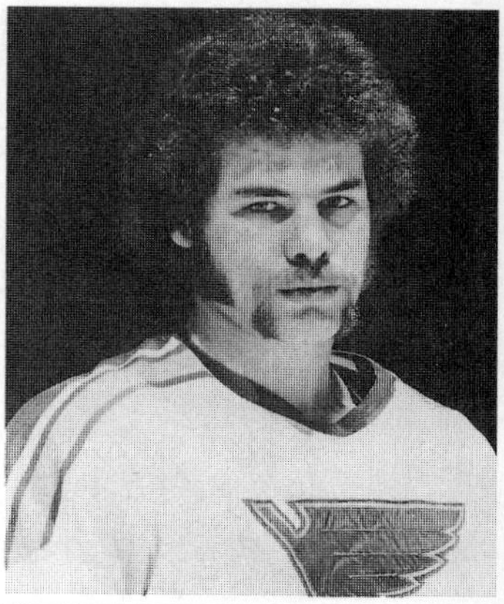
John Wensink

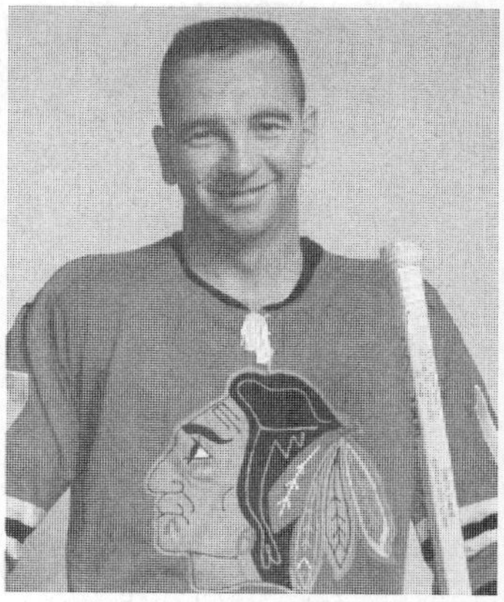
Ken Wharram

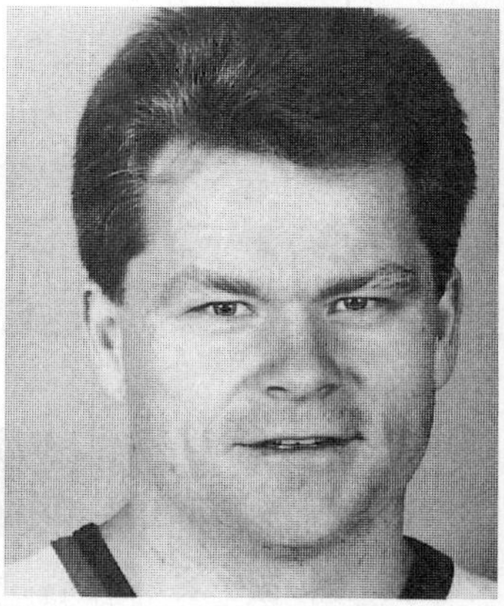
Behn Wilson

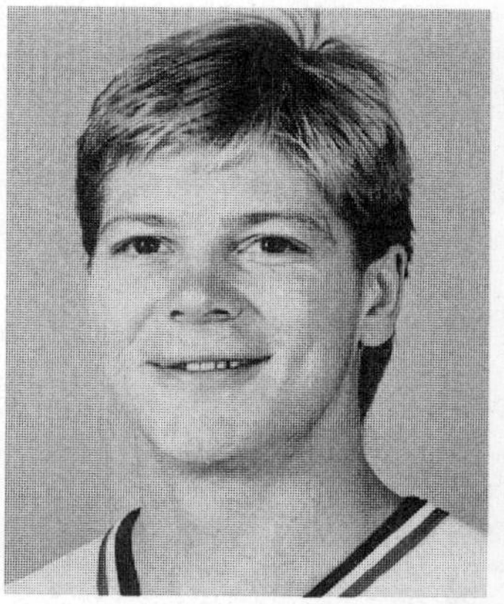
Carey Wilson

Rob Zettler

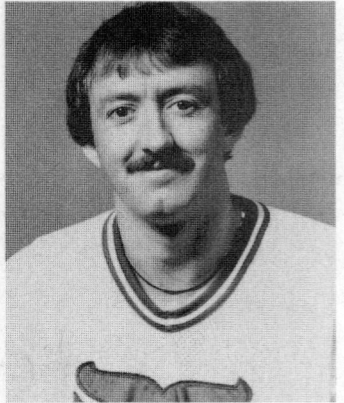

Mike Zuke

Name	NHL Teams	NHL Seasons	Regular Schedule					Playoffs					NHL Cup Wins	First NHL Season	Last NHL Season
			GP	G	A	TP	PIM	GP	G	A	TP	PIM			
‡ Witehall, Johan	NYR, Mtl.	3	54	2	5	7	16	....	....	....	....	....	....	1998-99	2000-01
Witherspoon, Jim	L.A.	1	2	0	0	0	2	....	....	....	....	....	....	1975-76	1975-76
Witiuk, Steve	Chi.	1	33	3	8	11	14	....	....	....	....	....	....	1951-52	1951-52
Woit, Benny	Det., Chi.	7	334	7	26	33	170	41	2	6	8	18	3	1950-51	1956-57
Wojciechowski, Steve	Det.	2	54	19	20	39	17	6	0	1	1	0	....	1944-45	1946-47
Wolanin, Craig	N.J., Que., Col., T.B., Tor.	13	695	40	133	173	894	35	4	6	10	67	1	1985-86	1997-98
Wolf, Bennett	Pit.	3	30	0	1	1	133	....	....	....	....	....	....	1980-81	1982-83
Wong, Mike	Det.	1	22	1	1	2	12	....	....	....	....	....	....	1975-76	1975-76
‡ Wood, Dody	S.J.	5	106	8	10	18	471	....	....	....	....	....	....	1992-93	1997-98
Wood, Randy	NYI, Buf., Tor., Dal.	11	741	175	159	334	603	51	8	9	17	40	....	1986-87	1996-97
Wood, Robert	NYR	1	1	0	0	0	0	....	....	....	....	....	....	1950-51	1950-51
Woodley, Dan	Van.	1	5	2	0	2	17	....	....	....	....	....	....	1987-88	1987-88
Woods, Paul	Det.	7	501	72	124	196	276	7	0	5	5	4	....	1977-78	1983-84
‡ Wortman, Kevin	Cgy.	1	5	0	0	0	2	....	....	....	....	....	....	1993-94	1993-94
• Woytowich, Bob	Bos., Min., Pit., L.A.	8	503	32	126	158	352	24	1	3	4	20	....	1964-65	1971-72
Wright, John	Van., St.L., K.C.	3	127	16	36	52	67	....	....	....	....	....	....	1972-73	1974-75
Wright, Keith	Phi.	1	1	0	0	0	0	....	....	....	....	....	....	1967-68	1967-68
Wright, Larry	Phi., Cal., Det.	5	106	4	8	12	19	....	....	....	....	....	....	1971-72	1977-78
Wycherley, Ralph	NYA, Bro.	2	28	4	7	11	6	....	....	....	....	....	....	1940-41	1941-42
Wylie, Bill	NYR	1	1	0	0	0	0	....	....	....	....	....	....	1950-51	1950-51
Wylie, Duane	Chi.	2	14	3	3	6	2	....	....	....	....	....	....	1974-75	1976-77
Wyrozub, Randy	Buf.	4	100	8	10	18	10	....	....	....	....	....	....	1970-71	1973-74

Y Z

Name	NHL Teams	NHL Seasons	Regular Schedule					Playoffs					NHL Cup Wins	First NHL Season	Last NHL Season
			GP	G	A	TP	PIM	GP	G	A	TP	PIM			
• Yackel, Ken	Bos.	1	6	0	0	0	2	2	0	0	0	2	....	1958-59	1958-59
Yaremchuk, Gary	Tor.	4	34	1	4	5	28	....	....	....	....	....	....	1981-82	1984-85
Yaremchuk, Ken	Chi., Tor.	6	235	36	56	92	106	31	6	8	14	49	....	1983-84	1988-89
Yates, Ross	Hfd.	1	7	1	1	2	4	....	....	....	....	....	....	1983-84	1983-84
Yawney, Trent	Chi., Cgy., St.L.	12	593	27	102	129	783	60	9	17	26	81	....	1987-88	1998-99
• Yegorov, Alexei	S.J.	2	11	3	3	6	2	....	....	....	....	....	....	1995-96	1996-97
York, Harry	St.L., NYR, Pit., Van.	4	244	29	46	75	99	5	0	0	0	2	....	1996-97	1999-00
‡ Young, B.J.	Det.	1	1	0	0	0	0	....	....	....	....	....	....	1999-00	1999-00
Young, Brian	Chi.	1	8	0	2	2	6	....	....	....	....	....	....	1980-81	1980-81
Young, C.J.	Cgy., Bos.	1	43	7	7	14	32	....	....	....	....	....	....	1992-93	1992-93
• Young, Doug	Det., Mtl.	10	388	35	45	80	303	28	1	5	6	16	2	1931-32	1940-41
• Young, Howie	Det., Chi., Van.	8	336	12	62	74	851	19	2	4	6	46	....	1960-61	1970-71
Young, Tim	Min., Wpg., Phi.	10	628	195	341	536	438	36	7	24	31	27	....	1975-76	1984-85
Young, Warren	Min., Pit., Det.	7	236	72	77	149	472	....	....	....	....	....	....	1981-82	1987-88
Younghans, Tom	Min., NYR	6	429	44	41	85	373	24	2	1	3	21	....	1976-77	1981-82
Ysebaert, Paul	N.J., Det., Wpg., Chi., T.B.	11	532	149	187	336	217	30	4	3	7	20	....	1988-89	1998-99
‡ Zabransky, Libor	St.L.	2	40	1	6	7	50	....	....	....	....	....	....	1996-97	1997-98
Zaharko, Miles	Atl., Chi.	4	129	5	32	37	84	3	0	0	0	0	....	1977-78	1981-82
Zaine, Rod	Pit., Buf.	2	61	10	6	16	25	....	....	....	....	....	....	1970-71	1971-72
‡ Zalapski, Zarley	Pit., Hfd., Cgy., Mtl., Phi.	12	637	99	285	384	684	48	4	23	27	47	....	1987-88	1999-00
Zanussi, Joe	NYR, Bos., St.L.	3	87	1	13	14	46	4	0	1	1	2	....	1974-75	1976-77
Zanussi, Ron	Min., Tor.	5	299	52	83	135	373	17	0	4	4	17	....	1977-78	1981-82
Zavisha, Brad	Edm.	1	2	0	0	0	0	....	....	....	....	....	....	1993-94	1993-94
‡ Zehr, Jeff	Bos.	1	4	0	0	0	2	....	....	....	....	....	....	1999-00	1999-00
Zeidel, Larry	Det., Chi., Phi.	5	158	3	16	19	198	12	0	1	1	12	1	1951-52	1968-69
Zelepukin, Valeri	N.J., Edm., Phi., Chi.	10	595	117	177	294	527	85	13	13	26	48	1	1991-92	2000-01
Zemlak, Richard	Que., Min., Pit., Cgy.	5	132	2	12	14	587	1	0	0	0	10	....	1986-87	1991-92
Zeniuk, Ed	Det.	1	2	0	0	0	0	....	....	....	....	....	....	1954-55	1954-55
Zent, Jason	Ott., Phi.	3	27	3	3	6	13	....	....	....	....	....	....	1996-97	1998-99
Zetterstrom, Lars	Van.	1	14	0	1	1	2	....	....	....	....	....	....	1978-79	1978-79
Zettler, Rob	Min., S.J., Phi., Tor., Nsh., Wsh.	14	569	5	65	70	920	14	0	0	0	4	....	1988-89	2001-02
Zezel, Peter	Phi., St.L., Wsh., Tor., Dal., N.J., Van.	15	873	219	389	608	435	131	25	39	64	83	....	1984-85	1998-99
‡ Ziegler, Thomas	T.B.	1	5	0	0	0	0	....	....	....	....	....	....	2000-01	2000-01
Zmolek, Doug	S.J., Dal., L.A., Chi.	8	467	11	53	64	905	14	0	1	1	16	....	1992-93	1999-00
Zoborosky, Marty	Chi.	1	1	0	0	0	2	....	....	....	....	....	....	1944-45	1944-45
Zombo, Rick	Det., St.L., Bos.	12	652	24	130	154	728	60	1	11	12	127	....	1984-85	1995-96
Zuke, Mike	St.L., Hfd.	8	455	86	196	282	220	26	6	6	12	12	....	1978-79	1985-86
Zunich, Rudy	Det.	1	2	0	0	0	2	....	....	....	....	....	....	1943-44	1943-44

Retired Players, Goaltenders and Coaches Research Project

Throughout the Retired Players and Retired Goaltenders sections of this book, you will notice many players with a bullet (•) by their names. These players, according to our records, are deceased. The editors recognize that our information on the death dates of NHLers is incomplete. If you have documented information on the passing of any player not marked with a bullet (•) in this edition, we would like to hear from you. We also welcome information on deceased NHL head coaches. Please send this information to:

Retired Player Research Project
c/o NHL Publishing
194 Dovercourt Road
Toronto, Ontario
M6J 3C8   Canada
Fax: 416/531-3939

Many thanks to the following contributors in 2002-03:

Tim Bateman, Corey Bryant, Paul R. Carroll, Jr., Bob Duff, Peter Fillman, Ernie Fitzsimmons, Gary J. Pearce, Drew "Whitey" White.

Patrick Roy

PATRICK ROY HELPED TO REDEFINE THE POSITION OF GOALTENDER, *playing a perfect butterfly style that allowed him to cover the bottom portion of the net, leaving his sharp reflexes and great glove hand to deal with the top corners. He made goaltending a "glamor" position, and inspired many young hockey players to become goaltenders, particularly in his home province of Quebec. His durability was such that he played against the best of his "disciples" as they reached the NHL.*

Roy made his NHL debut with the Montreal Canadiens on February 23, 1985. He became a regular during the 1985-86 season and led the club to a surprising Stanley Cup victory that spring. He was superb in leading the Canadiens to another Stanley Cup title in 1993. His 16-4 postseason record included 10 consecutive overtime victories. He won the Conn Smythe Trophy as playoff MVP in both of these Cup-winning years.

Traded to the Colorado Avalanche on December 6, 1995, Roy helped his new team win the Stanley Cup that season. He would go on to surpass Terry Sawchuk as the NHL goaltender with the most regular-season wins with his 448th career victory on October 17, 2000. That season, he led Colorado to the Stanley Cup title and was rewarded with the Conn Smythe Trophy for a record third time.

Roy became the first goaltender in NHL history to play in 1,000 regular-season games on January 20, 2003. He retired at season's end with 551 career victories. Always at his best when it mattered most, Roy's total of 151 postseason wins is the best in NHL history, and he is the League's all-time leader with 247 postseason games played.

Retired NHL Goaltender Index

Abbreviations: Teams/Cities: – **Ana.** – Anaheim; **Atl.** – Atlanta; **Bos.** – Boston; **Bro.** – Brooklyn; **Buf.** – Buffalo; **Cal.** – California; **Cgy.** – Calgary; **Cle.** – Cleveland; **Col.** – Colorado; **CBJ** – Columbus; **Dal.** – Dallas; **Det.** – Detroit; **Edm.** – Edmonton; **Fla.** – Florida; **Ham.** – Hamilton; **Hfd.** – Hartford; **K.C.** – Kansas City; **L.A.** – Los Angeles; **Min.** – Minnesota; **Mtl.** – Montreal; **Mtl.M.** – Montreal Maroons; **Mtl.W.** – Montreal Wanderers; **N.J.** – New Jersey; **NYA** – NY Americans; **NYI** – NY Islanders; **NYR** – New York Rangers; – **Oak.** – Oakland; **Ott.** – Ottawa; – **Phi.** – Philadelphia; **Phx.** – Phoenix; **Pit.** – Pittsburgh; **Que.** – Quebec; **St.L.** – St. Louis; **S.J.** – San Jose; **T.B.** – Tampa Bay; **Tor.** – Toronto; **Van.** – Vancouver; **Wpg.** – Winnipeg; **Wsh.** – Washington

Avg. – goals against per 60 minutes played; **GA** – goals agains; **GP** – games played; **Mins** – minutes played; **SO** – shutouts.
• – deceased. § – Forward, defenseman or coach who appeared in goal. For complete career, see Retired Player Index. ‡ – Remains active in other leagues.

			Regular Schedule								Playoffs										
Name	NHL Teams	NHL Seasons	GP	W	L	T	Mins	GA	SO	Avg	GP	W	L	T	Mins	GA	SO	Avg	NHL Cup Wins	First NHL Season	Last NHL Season
Abbott, George	Bos.	1	1	0	1	0	60	7	0	7.00	....	....	....	....	....	....	....	....		1943-44	1943-44
Adams, John	Bos., Wsh.	2	22	9	10	1	1180	85	1	4.32	....	....	....	....	....	....	....	....		1972-73	1974-75
Aiken, Don	Mtl.	1	1	0	1	0	34	6	0	10.59	....	....	....	....	....	....	....	....		1957-58	1957-58
• Aitkenhead, Andy	NYR	3	106	47	43	16	6570	257	11	2.35	10	6	2	2	608	15	3	1.48	1	1932-33	1934-35
• Almas, Red	Det., Chi.	3	3	0	2	1	180	13	0	4.33	5	1	3	....	263	13	0	2.97		1946-47	1952-53
• Anderson, Lorne	NYR	1	3	1	2	0	180	18	0	6.00	....	....	....	....	....	....	....	....		1951-52	1951-52
Astrom, Hardy	NYR, Col.	3	83	17	44	12	4456	278	0	3.74	....	....	....	....	....	....	....	....		1977-78	1980-81
‡ Bach, Ryan	L.A.	1	3	0	3	0	108	8	0	4.44	....	....	....	....	....	....	....	....		1998-99	1998-99
‡ Bailey, Scott	Bos.	2	19	6	6	2	965	55	0	3.42	....	....	....	....	....	....	....	....		1995-96	1996-97
Baker, Steve	NYR	4	57	20	20	11	3081	190	3	3.70	14	7	7	....	826	55	0	4.00		1979-80	1982-83
‡ Bales, Mike	Bos., Ott.	4	23	2	15	1	1120	77	0	4.13	....	....	....	....	....	....	....	....		1992-93	1996-97
Bannerman, Murray	Van., Chi.	8	289	116	125	33	16470	1051	8	3.83	40	20	18	....	2322	165	0	4.26		1977-78	1986-87
Baron, Marco	Bos., L.A., Edm.	6	86	34	38	9	4822	292	1	3.63	1	0	1	....	20	3	0	9.00		1979-80	1984-85
Bassen, Hank	Chi., Det., Pit.	9	156	46	66	31	8759	434	5	2.97	5	1	3	....	274	11	0	2.41		1954-55	1967-68
• Bastien, Baz	Tor.	1	5	0	4	1	300	20	0	4.00	....	....	....	....	....	....	....	....		1945-46	1945-46
Bauman, Gary	Mtl., Min.	3	35	6	18	6	1718	102	0	3.56	....	....	....	....	....	....	....	....		1966-67	1968-69
Beaupre, Don	Min., Wsh., Ott., Tor.	17	667	268	277	75	37396	2151	17	3.45	72	33	31	....	3943	220	3	3.35		1980-81	1996-97
Beauregard, Stephane	Wpg., Phi.	5	90	19	39	11	4402	268	2	3.65	4	1	3	....	238	12	0	3.03		1989-90	1993-94
Bedard, Jim	Wsh.	2	73	17	40	13	4232	278	1	3.94	....	....	....	....	....	....	....	....		1977-78	1978-79
Behrend, Marc	Wpg.	3	39	12	19	3	1991	160	1	4.82	7	1	3	0	312	19	0	3.65		1983-84	1985-86
Belanger, Yves	St.L., Atl., Bos.	6	78	29	33	6	4134	259	2	3.76	....	....	....	....	....	....	....	....		1974-75	1979-80
Belhumeur, Michel	Phi., Wsh.	3	65	9	36	7	3306	254	0	4.61	1	0	0	....	10	1	0	6.00		1972-73	1975-76
• Bell, Gordie	Tor., NYR	2	8	3	5	0	480	31	0	3.88	2	1	1	....	120	9	0	4.50		1945-46	1955-56
• Benedict, Clint	Ott., Mtl.M.	13	362	190	143	28	22367	863	58	2.32	28	11	12	5	1707	53	9	1.86	4	1917-18	1929-30
Bennett, Harvey	Bos.	1	25	10	12	2	1470	103	0	4.20	....	....	....	....	....	....	....	....		1944-45	1944-45
Bergeron, Jean-Claude	Mtl., T.B., L.A.	6	72	21	33	7	3772	232	1	3.69	....	....	....	....	....	....	....	....		1990-91	1996-97
Bernhardt, Tim	Cgy., Tor.	4	67	17	36	7	3748	267	0	4.27	....	....	....	....	....	....	....	....		1982-83	1986-87
‡ Berthiaume, Daniel	Wpg., Min., L.A., Bos., Ott.	9	215	81	90	21	11662	714	5	3.67	14	5	9	....	807	50	0	3.72		1985-86	1993-94
Bester, Allan	Tor., Det., Dal.	10	219	73	99	17	11773	786	7	4.01	11	2	6	....	508	37	0	4.37		1983-84	1995-96
• Beveridge, Bill	Det., Ott., St.L., Mtl.M., NYR	9	297	87	166	42	18375	879	18	2.87	5	2	3	....	300	11	0	2.20		1929-30	1942-43
• Bibeault, Paul	Mtl., Tor., Bos., Chi.	7	214	81	107	25	12890	785	10	3.65	20	6	14	....	1237	71	2	3.44		1940-41	1946-47
Binette, Andre	Mtl.	1	1	1	0	0	60	4	0	4.00	....	....	....	....	....	....	....	....		1954-55	1954-55
Binkley, Les	Pit.	5	196	58	94	34	11046	575	11	3.12	7	5	2	....	428	15	0	2.10		1967-68	1971-72
Bittner, Richard	Bos.	1	1	0	0	1	60	3	0	3.00	....	....	....	....	....	....	....	....		1949-50	1949-50
Blake, Mike	L.A.	3	40	13	15	5	2117	150	0	4.25	....	....	....	....	....	....	....	....		1981-82	1983-84
Blue, John	Bos., Buf.	3	46	16	18	7	2521	126	1	3.00	2	0	1	....	96	5	0	3.13		1992-93	1995-96
Boisvert, Gilles	Det.	1	3	0	3	0	180	9	0	3.00	....	....	....	....	....	....	....	....		1959-60	1959-60
Bouchard, Dan	Atl., Cgy., Que., Wpg.	14	655	286	232	113	37919	2061	27	3.26	43	13	30	....	2549	147	1	3.46		1972-73	1985-86
• Bourque, Claude	Mtl., Det.	2	62	16	38	8	3830	193	4	3.02	3	1	2	....	188	8	1	2.55		1938-39	1939-40
Boutin, Rollie	Wsh.	3	22	7	10	1	1137	75	0	3.96	....	....	....	....	....	....	....	....		1978-79	1980-81
• Bouvrette, Lionel	NYR	1	1	0	1	0	60	6	0	6.00	....	....	....	....	....	....	....	....		1942-43	1942-43
Bower, Johnny	NYR, Tor.	15	552	250	195	90	32016	1340	37	2.51	74	35	34	....	4378	180	5	2.47	4	1953-54	1969-70
§ • Branigan, Andy	NYA	1	1	0	0	0	7	0	0	0.00	....	....	....	....	....	....	....	....		1940-41	1940-41
• Brimsek, Frank	Bos., Chi.	10	514	252	182	80	31210	1404	40	2.70	68	32	36	....	4395	186	2	2.54	2	1938-39	1949-50
• Broda, Turk	Tor.	14	629	302	224	101	38167	1609	62	2.53	101	60	39	....	6389	211	13	1.98	5	1936-37	1951-52
Broderick, Ken	Min., Bos.	3	27	11	12	1	1464	74	1	3.03	....	....	....	....	....	....	....	....		1969-70	1974-75
Broderick, Len	Mtl.	1	1	1	0	0	60	2	0	2.00	....	....	....	....	....	....	....	....		1957-58	1957-58
Brodeur, Richard	NYI, Van., Hfd.	9	385	131	175	62	21968	1410	6	3.85	33	13	20	....	2009	111	1	3.32		1979-80	1987-88
Bromley, Gary	Buf., Van.	6	136	54	44	28	7427	425	7	3.43	7	2	5	....	360	25	0	4.17		1973-74	1980-81
• Brooks, Art	Tor.	1	4	2	2	0	220	23	0	6.27	....	....	....	....	....	....	....	....		1917-18	1917-18
Brooks, Ross	Bos.	3	54	37	7	6	3047	134	4	2.64	1	0	0	....	20	3	0	9.00		1972-73	1974-75
• Brophy, Frank	Que.	1	21	3	18	0	1249	148	0	7.11	....	....	....	....	....	....	....	....		1919-20	1919-20
Brown, Andy	Det., Pit.	3	62	22	26	9	3373	213	1	3.79	....	....	....	....	....	....	....	....		1971-72	1973-74
Brown, Ken	Chi.	1	1	0	0	0	18	1	0	3.33	....	....	....	....	....	....	....	....		1970-71	1970-71
‡ Brunetta, Mario	Que.	3	40	12	17	1	1967	128	0	3.90	....	....	....	....	....	....	....	....		1987-88	1989-90
Bullock, Bruce	Van.	3	16	3	9	3	927	74	0	4.79	....	....	....	....	....	....	....	....		1972-73	1976-77
• Buzinski, Steve	NYR	1	9	2	6	1	560	55	0	5.89	....	....	....	....	....	....	....	....		1942-43	1942-43
Caley, Don	St.L.	1	1	0	0	0	30	3	0	6.00	....	....	....	....	....	....	....	....		1967-68	1967-68
Caprice, Frank	Van.	6	102	31	46	11	5589	391	1	4.20	....	....	....	....	....	....	....	....		1982-83	1987-88
Carey, Jim	Wsh., Bos., St.L.	5	172	79	65	16	9668	416	16	2.58	10	2	5	....	455	35	0	4.62		1994-95	1998-99
Caron, Jacques	L.A., St.L., Van.	5	72	24	29	11	3846	211	2	3.29	12	4	7	....	639	34	0	3.19		1967-68	1973-74
Carter, Lyle	Cal.	1	15	4	7	0	721	50	0	4.16	....	....	....	....	....	....	....	....		1971-72	1971-72
Casey, Jon	Min., Bos., St.L.	12	425	170	157	55	23255	1246	16	3.21	66	32	31	....	3743	192	3	3.08		1983-84	1996-97
‡ Chabot, Frederic	Mtl., Phi., L.A.	5	32	4	8	4	1262	62	0	2.95	....	....	....	....	....	....	....	....		1990-91	1998-99
• Chabot, Lorne	NYR, Tor., Mtl., Chi., Mtl.M., NYA	11	411	201	148	62	25307	860	73	2.04	37	13	17	6	2498	64	5	1.54	2	1926-27	1936-37
Chadwick, Ed	Tor., Bos.	6	184	57	92	35	11040	541	14	2.94	....	....	....	....	....	....	....	....		1955-56	1961-62
Champoux, Bob	Det., Cal.	2	17	2	11	3	923	80	0	5.20	1	1	0	....	55	4	0	4.36		1963-64	1973-74
Cheevers, Gerry	Tor., Bos.	13	418	230	102	74	24394	1174	26	2.89	88	53	34	....	5396	242	8	2.69	2	1961-62	1979-80
Cheveldae, Tim	Det., Wpg., Bos.	9	340	149	136	37	19172	1116	10	3.49	25	9	15	....	1418	71	2	3.00		1988-89	1996-97
Chevrier, Alain	N.J., Wpg., Chi., Pit., Det.	6	234	91	100	14	12202	845	2	4.16	16	9	7	....	1013	44	0	2.61		1985-86	1990-91
§ • Clancy, King	Ott., Tor.	2	2	0	0	0	3	1	0	20.00	....	....	....	....	....	....	....	....		1924-25	1931-32
§ • Cleghorn, Odie	Pit.	1	1	1	0	0	60	2	0	2.00	....	....	....	....	....	....	....	....		1925-26	1925-26
§ • Cleghorn, Sprague	Ott., Mtl.	2	2	0	0	0	5	0	0	0.00	....	....	....	....	....	....	....	....		1918-19	1921-22
Clifford, Chris	Chi.	2	2	0	0	0	24	0	0	0.00	....	....	....	....	....	....	....	....		1984-85	1988-89
Cloutier, Jacques	Buf., Chi., Que.	12	255	82	102	24	12826	778	3	3.64	8	1	5	....	413	18	1	2.62		1981-82	1993-94
Colvin, Les	Bos.	1	1	0	1	0	60	4	0	4.00	....	....	....	....	....	....	....	....		1948-49	1948-49
§ • Conacher, Charlie	Tor., Det.	3	4	0	0	0	10	0	0	0.00	....	....	....	....	....	....	....	....		1932-33	1938-39
• Connell, Alex	Ott., Det., NYA, Mtl.M.	12	417	193	156	67	26050	830	81	1.91	21	8	5	8	1309	26	4	1.19	2	1924-25	1936-37
Corsi, Jim	Edm.	1	26	8	14	3	1366	83	0	3.65	....	....	....	....	....	....	....	....		1979-80	1979-80
Courteau, Maurice	Bos.	1	6	2	4	0	360	33	0	5.50	....	....	....	....	....	....	....	....		1943-44	1943-44
‡ Cousineau, Marcel	Tor., NYI, L.A.	4	26	4	10	1	1047	51	1	2.92	....	....	....	....	....	....	....	....		1996-97	1999-00
Cowley, Wayne	Edm.	1	1	0	1	0	57	3	0	3.16	....	....	....	....	....	....	....	....		1993-94	1993-94
Cox, Abbie	Mtl.M., NYA, Det., Mtl.	3	5	1	1	2	263	11	0	2.51	....	....	....	....	....	....	....	....		1929-30	1935-36
Craig, Jim	Atl., Bos., Min.	3	30	11	10	7	1588	100	0	3.78	....	....	....	....	....	....	....	....		1979-80	1983-84
Crha, Jiri	Tor.	2	69	28	27	11	3942	261	0	3.97	5	0	4	....	186	21	0	6.77		1979-80	1980-81
• Crozier, Roger	Det., Buf., Wsh.	14	518	206	197	70	28567	1446	30	3.04	32	14	16	....	1789	82	1	2.75		1963-64	1976-77
• Cude, Wilf	Phi., Bos., Chi., Mtl., Det.	10	282	100	132	49	17586	798	24	2.72	19	7	11	1	1257	51	1	2.43		1930-31	1940-41
Cutts, Don	Edm.	1	6	1	2	1	269	16	0	3.57	....	....	....	....	....	....	....	....		1979-80	1979-80
• Cyr, Claude	Mtl.	1	1	0	0	0	20	1	0	3.00	....	....	....	....	....	....	....	....		1958-59	1958-59
Dadswell, Doug	Cgy.	2	27	8	8	3	1346	99	0	4.41	....	....	....	....	....	....	....	....		1986-87	1987-88
D'Alessio, Corrie	Hfd.	1	1	0	0	0	11	0	0	0.00	....	....	....	....	....	....	....	....		1992-93	1992-93
Daley, Joe	Pit., Buf., Det.	4	105	34	44	19	5836	326	3	3.35	....	....	....	....	....	....	....	....		1968-69	1971-72
Damore, Nick	Bos.	1	1	1	0	0	60	3	0	3.00	....	....	....	....	....	....	....	....		1941-42	1941-42
D'Amour, Marc	Cgy., Phi.	2	16	2	4	2	579	32	0	3.32	....	....	....	....	....	....	....	....		1985-86	1988-89
§ • Darragh, Jack	Ott.	1	1	0	0	0	2	0	0	0.00	....	....	....	....	....	....	....	....		1919-20	1919-20
Daskalakis, Cleon	Bos.	3	12	3	4	1	506	41	0	4.86	....	....	....	....	....	....	....	....		1984-85	1986-87
Davidson, John	St.L., NYR	10	301	123	124	39	17109	1004	7	3.52	31	16	14	....	1862	77	1	2.48		1973-74	1982-83

			Regular Schedule								Playoffs										
Name	NHL Teams	NHL Seasons	GP	W	L	T	Mins	GA	SO	Avg	GP	W	L	T	Mins	GA	SO	Avg	NHL Cup Wins	First NHL Season	Last NHL Season
Decourcy, Bob	NYR	1	1	0	1	0	29	6	0	12.41	....	....	....	....	....	....	....	....		1947-48	1947-48
Defelice, Norm	Bos.	1	10	3	5	2	600	30	0	3.00	....	....	....	....	....	....	....	....		1956-57	1956-57
DeJordy, Denis	Chi., L.A., Mtl., Det.	12	316	124	128	51	17798	929	15	3.13	18	6	9	....	946	55	0	3.49	1	1960-61	1973-74
DelGuidice, Matt	Bos.	2	11	2	5	1	434	28	0	3.87	....	....	....	....	....	....	....	....		1990-91	1991-92
‡ DeRouville, Philippe	Pit.	2	3	1	2	0	171	9	0	3.16	....	....	....	....	....	....	....	....		1994-95	1996-97
Desjardins, Gerry	L.A., Chi., NYI, Buf.	10	331	122	153	44	19014	1042	12	3.29	35	15	15	....	1874	108	0	3.46		1968-69	1977-78
• Dickie, Bill	Chi.	1	1	1	0	0	60	3	0	3.00	....	....	....	....	....	....	....	....		1941-42	1941-42
Dion, Connie	Det.	2	38	23	11	4	2280	119	1	3.13	5	1	4	....	300	17	0	3.40		1943-44	1944-45
Dion, Michel	Que., Wpg., Pit.	6	227	60	118	32	12695	898	2	4.24	5	2	3	....	304	22	0	4.34		1979-80	1984-85
Dolson, Dolly	Det.	3	93	35	41	17	5820	192	16	1.98	2	0	2	0	120	7	0	3.50		1928-29	1930-31
‡ Dopson, Rob	Pit.	1	2	0	0	0	45	3	0	4.00	....	....	....	....	....	....	....	....		1993-94	1993-94
Dowie, Bruce	Tor.	1	2	0	1	0	72	4	0	3.33	....	....	....	....	....	....	....	....		1983-84	1983-84
‡ Draper, Tom	Wpg., Buf., NYI	6	53	19	23	5	2807	173	1	3.70	7	3	4	....	433	19	1	2.63		1988-89	1995-96
Dryden, Dave	NYR, Chi., Buf., Edm.	9	203	66	76	31	10424	555	9	3.19	3	0	2	....	133	9	0	4.06		1961-62	1979-80
Dryden, Ken	Mtl.	8	397	258	57	74	23352	870	46	2.24	112	80	32	....	6846	274	10	2.40	6	1970-71	1978-79
‡ Duffus, Parris	Phx.	1	1	0	0	0	29	1	0	2.07	....	....	....	....	....	....	....	....		1996-97	1996-97
Dumas, Michel	Chi.	3	8	2	1	2	362	24	0	3.98	1	0	0	....	19	1	0	3.16		1974-75	1976-77
Dupuis, Bob	Edm.	1	1	0	1	0	60	4	0	4.00	....	....	....	....	....	....	....	....		1979-80	1979-80
• Durnan, Bill	Mtl.	7	383	208	112	62	22945	901	34	2.36	45	27	18	....	2871	99	2	2.07	2	1943-44	1949-50
Dyck, Ed	Van.	3	49	8	28	5	2453	178	1	4.35	....	....	....	....	....	....	....	....		1971-72	1973-74
Edwards, Don	Buf., Cgy., Tor.	10	459	208	155	74	26181	1449	16	3.32	42	16	21	....	2302	132	1	3.44		1976-77	1985-86
Edwards, Gary	St.L., L.A., Cle., Min., Edm., Pit.	13	286	88	125	51	16002	973	10	3.65	11	5	4	....	537	34	0	3.80		1968-69	1981-82
Edwards, Marv	Pit., Tor., Cal.	4	61	15	34	7	3467	218	2	3.77	....	....	....	....	....	....	....	....		1968-69	1973-74
• Edwards, Roy	Det., Pit.	7	236	97	88	38	13109	637	12	2.92	4	0	3	....	206	11	0	3.20		1967-68	1973-74
Eliot, Darren	L.A., Det., Buf.	5	89	25	41	12	4931	377	1	4.59	1	0	0	....	40	7	0	10.50		1984-85	1988-89
Ellacott, Ken	Van.	1	12	2	3	4	555	41	0	4.43	....	....	....	....	....	....	....	....		1982-83	1982-83
Erickson, Chad	N.J.	1	2	1	1	0	120	9	0	4.50	....	....	....	....	....	....	....	....		1991-92	1991-92
Esposito, Tony	Mtl., Chi.	16	886	423	306	151	52585	2563	76	2.92	99	45	53	....	6017	308	6	3.07	1	1968-69	1983-84
‡ Essensa, Bob	Wpg., Det., Edm., Phx., Van., Buf.	12	446	173	176	47	24215	1270	18	3.15	16	4	9	0	864	51	0	3.54		1988-89	2001-02
• Evans, Claude	Mtl., Bos.	2	5	1	2	1	260	16	0	3.69	....	....	....	....	....	....	....	....		1954-55	1957-58
Exelby, Randy	Mtl., Edm.	2	2	0	1	0	63	5	0	4.76	....	....	....	....	....	....	....	....		1988-89	1989-90
Farr, Rocky	Buf.	3	19	2	6	3	722	42	0	3.49	....	....	....	....	....	....	....	....		1972-73	1974-75
Favell, Doug	Phi., Tor., Col.	12	373	123	153	69	20771	1096	18	3.17	21	6	15	....	1270	66	1	3.12		1967-68	1978-79
Fiset, Stephane	Que., Col., L.A., Mtl.	13	390	164	153	44	21785	1114	16	3.07	14	1	7	0	563	37	0	3.94	1	1989-90	2001-02
Fitzpatrick, Mark	L.A., NYI, Fla., T.B., Chi., Car.	12	329	113	136	49	18329	953	8	3.12	9	0	3	....	289	23	0	4.78		1988-89	1999-00
• Forbes, Jake	Tor., Ham., NYA, Phi.	13	210	85	114	11	12922	594	19	2.76	2	0	2	0	120	7	0	3.50		1919-20	1932-33
Ford, Brian	Que., Pit.	2	11	3	7	0	580	61	0	6.31	....	....	....	....	....	....	....	....		1983-84	1984-85
Foster, Norm	Bos., Edm.	2	13	7	4	0	623	34	0	3.27	....	....	....	....	....	....	....	....		1990-91	1991-92
• Fowler, Hec	Bos.	1	7	1	6	0	409	42	0	6.16	....	....	....	....	....	....	....	....		1924-25	1924-25
Francis, Emile	Chi., NYR	6	95	31	52	11	5660	355	1	3.76	....	....	....	....	....	....	....	....		1946-47	1951-52
• Franks, Jimmy	Det., NYR, Bos.	4	42	12	23	7	2520	181	1	4.31	1	0	1	....	30	2	0	4.00	1	1936-37	1943-44
Frederick, Ray	Chi.	1	5	0	4	1	300	22	0	4.40	....	....	....	....	....	....	....	....		1954-55	1954-55
Friesen, Karl	N.J.	1	4	0	2	1	130	16	0	7.38	....	....	....	....	....	....	....	....		1986-87	1986-87
Froese, Bob	Phi., NYR	8	242	128	72	20	13451	694	13	3.10	18	3	9	....	830	55	0	3.98		1982-83	1989-90
Fuhr, Grant	Edm., Tor., Buf., L.A., St.L., Cgy.	19	868	403	295	114	48945	2756	25	3.38	150	92	50	....	8834	430	6	2.92	5	1981-82	1999-00
‡ Gage, Joaquin	Edm.	3	23	4	12	1	1076	67	0	3.74	....	....	....	....	....	....	....	....		1994-95	2000-01
Gagnon, David	Det.	1	2	0	1	0	35	6	0	10.29	....	....	....	....	....	....	....	....		1990-91	1990-91
• Gamble, Bruce	NYR, Bos., Tor., Phi.	10	327	110	150	46	18442	988	22	3.21	5	0	4	....	206	25	0	7.28	1	1958-59	1971-72
Gamble, Troy	Van.	4	72	22	29	9	3804	229	1	3.61	4	1	3	....	249	16	0	3.86		1986-87	1991-92
• Gardiner, Bert	NYR, Mtl., Chi., Bos.	6	144	49	68	27	8760	554	4	3.79	9	4	5	....	647	20	0	1.85		1935-36	1943-44
• Gardiner, Charlie	Chi.	7	316	112	152	52	19687	664	42	2.02	21	12	6	3	1472	35	5	1.43	1	1927-28	1933-34
Gardner, George	Det., Van.	5	66	16	30	6	3313	207	0	3.75	....	....	....	....	....	....	....	....		1965-66	1971-72
Garrett, John	Hfd., Que., Van.	6	207	68	91	37	11763	837	1	4.27	9	4	3	....	461	33	0	4.30		1979-80	1984-85
Gatherum, Dave	Det.	1	3	2	0	1	180	3	1	1.00	....	....	....	....	....	....	....	....	1	1953-54	1953-54
Gauthier, Paul	Mtl.	1	1	0	0	1	70	2	0	1.71	....	....	....	....	....	....	....	....		1937-38	1937-38
‡ Gauthier, Sean	S.J.	1	1	0	0	0	3	0	0	0.00	....	....	....	....	....	....	....	....		1998-99	1998-99
• Gelineau, Jack	Bos., Chi.	4	143	46	64	33	8580	447	7	3.13	4	1	2	....	260	7	1	1.62		1948-49	1953-54
Giacomin, Ed	NYR, Det.	13	609	289	209	96	35633	1672	54	2.82	65	29	35	....	3838	180	1	2.81		1965-66	1977-78
Gilbert, Gilles	Min., Bos., Det.	14	416	192	143	60	23677	1290	18	3.27	32	17	15	....	1919	97	3	3.03		1969-70	1982-83
Gill, Andre	Bos.	1	5	3	2	0	270	13	1	2.89	....	....	....	....	....	....	....	....		1967-68	1967-68
• Goodman, Paul	Chi.	3	52	23	20	9	3240	117	6	2.17	3	0	3	....	187	10	0	3.21	1	1937-38	1940-41
Gordon, Scott	Que.	2	23	2	16	0	1082	101	0	5.60	....	....	....	....	....	....	....	....		1989-90	1990-91
Gosselin, Mario	Que., L.A., Hfd.	9	241	91	107	14	12857	801	6	3.74	32	16	15	....	1816	99	0	3.27		1983-84	1993-94
‡ Goverde, David	L.A.	3	5	1	4	0	278	29	0	6.26	....	....	....	....	....	....	....	....		1991-92	1993-94
Grahame, Ron	Bos., L.A., Que.	4	114	50	43	15	6472	409	5	3.79	4	2	1	....	202	7	0	2.08		1977-78	1980-81
• Grant, Benny	Tor., NYA, Bos.	6	50	17	26	4	2990	187	4	3.75	....	....	....	....	....	....	....	....		1928-29	1943-44
Grant, Doug	Det., St.L.	7	77	27	34	8	4199	280	2	4.00	....	....	....	....	....	....	....	....		1973-74	1979-80
Gratton, Gilles	St.L., NYR	2	47	13	18	9	2299	154	0	4.02	....	....	....	....	....	....	....	....		1975-76	1976-77
Gray, Gerry	Det., NYI	2	8	1	5	1	440	35	0	4.77	....	....	....	....	....	....	....	....		1970-71	1972-73
Gray, Harrison	Det.	1	1	0	1	0	40	5	0	7.50	....	....	....	....	....	....	....	....		1963-64	1963-64
Greenlay, Mike	Edm.	1	2	0	0	0	20	4	0	12.00	....	....	....	....	....	....	....	....		1989-90	1989-90
Guenette, Steve	Pit., Cgy.	5	35	19	16	0	1958	122	1	3.74	....	....	....	....	....	....	....	....		1986-87	1990-91
• Hainsworth, George	Mtl., Tor.	11	465	246	145	74	29087	937	94	1.93	52	22	25	5	3486	112	8	1.93	2	1926-27	1936-37
Hall, Glenn	Det., Chi., St.L.	19	906	407	326	163	53484	2222	84	2.49	115	49	65	....	6899	320	6	2.78	2	1951-52	1970-71
Hamel, Pierre	Tor., Wpg.	4	69	13	41	7	3766	276	0	4.40	....	....	....	....	....	....	....	....		1974-75	1980-81
Hanlon, Glen	Van., St.L., NYR, Det.	15	477	167	202	61	26037	1561	13	3.60	35	11	15	....	1756	92	4	3.14		1977-78	1990-91
Harrison, Paul	Min., Tor., Pit., Buf.	7	109	28	59	9	5806	408	2	4.22	4	0	1	....	157	9	0	3.44		1975-76	1981-82
Hayward, Brian	Wpg., Mtl., Min., S.J.	11	357	143	156	37	20025	1242	8	3.72	37	11	18	....	1803	104	0	3.46		1982-83	1992-93
Head, Don	Bos.	1	38	9	26	3	2280	158	2	4.16	....	....	....	....	....	....	....	....		1961-62	1961-62
Healy, Glenn	L.A., NYI, NYR, Tor.	15	437	166	190	47	24256	1361	13	3.37	37	13	15	....	1930	108	0	3.36	1	1985-86	2000-01
Hebert, Guy	St.L., Ana., NYR	10	491	191	222	56	27889	1307	28	2.81	14	4	7	....	744	33	1	2.66		1991-92	2000-01
• Hebert, Sammy	Tor., Ott.	2	4	2	1	0	200	19	0	5.70	....	....	....	....	....	....	....	....	1	1917-18	1923-24
Heinz, Rick	St.L., Van.	5	49	14	19	5	2356	159	2	4.05	1	0	0	....	8	1	0	7.50		1980-81	1984-85
Henderson, John	Bos.	2	46	15	15	15	2688	113	5	2.52	2	0	2	....	120	8	0	4.00		1954-55	1955-56
• Henry, Gord	Bos.	4	3	1	2	0	180	5	1	1.67	5	0	4	....	283	21	0	4.45		1948-49	1952-53
Henry, Jim	NYR, Chi., Bos.	9	406	161	173	70	24355	1166	27	2.87	29	11	18	....	1741	81	2	2.79		1941-42	1954-55
Herron, Denis	Pit., K.C., Mtl.	14	462	146	203	76	25608	1579	10	3.70	15	5	10	....	901	50	0	3.33		1972-73	1985-86
Hextall, Ron	Phi., Que., NYI	13	608	296	214	69	34750	1723	23	2.97	93	47	43	....	5456	276	2	3.04		1986-87	1998-99
Highton, Hec	Chi.	1	24	10	14	0	1440	108	0	4.50	....	....	....	....	....	....	....	....		1943-44	1943-44
§ • Himes, Normie	NYA	2	2	0	1	0	79	3	0	2.28	....	....	....	....	....	....	....	....		1927-28	1928-29
Hodge, Charlie	Mtl., Oak., Van.	14	358	150	125	61	20573	925	24	2.70	16	7	8	....	804	32	2	2.39	5	1954-55	1970-71
Hoffort, Bruce	Phi.	2	9	4	0	3	368	22	0	3.59	....	....	....	....	....	....	....	....		1989-90	1990-91
Hoganson, Paul	Pit.	1	2	0	1	0	57	7	0	7.37	....	....	....	....	....	....	....	....		1970-71	1970-71
Hogosta, Goran	NYI, Que.	2	22	5	12	3	1208	83	1	4.12	....	....	....	....	....	....	....	....		1977-78	1979-80
Holden, Mark	Mtl., Wpg.	4	8	2	2	1	372	25	0	4.03	....	....	....	....	....	....	....	....		1981-82	1984-85
Holland, Ken	Hfd., Det.	2	4	0	2	1	206	17	0	4.95	....	....	....	....	....	....	....	....		1980-81	1983-84
Holland, Robbie	Pit.	2	44	11	22	9	2513	171	1	4.08	....	....	....	....	....	....	....	....		1979-80	1980-81
• Holmes, Hap	Tor., Det.	4	103	39	54	10	6510	264	17	2.43	2	1	1	0	120	7	0	3.50	1	1917-18	1927-28
§ Horner, Red	Tor.	1	1	0	0	0	1	1	0	60.00	....	....	....	....	....	....	....	....		1931-32	1931-32
Hrivnak, Jim	Wsh., Wpg., St.L.	5	85	34	30	3	4217	262	0	3.73	....	....	....	....	....	....	....	....		1989-90	1993-94
Hrudey, Kelly	NYI, L.A., S.J.	15	677	271	265	88	38084	2174	17	3.43	85	36	46	....	5163	283	0	3.29		1983-84	1997-98
Ing, Peter	Tor., Edm., Det.	4	74	20	37	9	3941	266	1	4.05	....	....	....	....	....	....	....	....		1989-90	1993-94
Inness, Gary	Pit., Phi., Wsh.	7	162	58	61	27	8710	494	2	3.40	9	5	4	....	540	24	0	2.67		1973-74	1980-81
Ireland, Randy	Buf.	1	2	0	0	0	30	3	0	6.00	....	....	....	....	....	....	....	....		1978-79	1978-79
Irons, Robbie	St.L.	1	1	0	0	0	3	0	0	0.00	....	....	....	....	....	....	....	....		1968-69	1968-69
• Ironstone, Joe	Ott., NYA, Tor.	3	2	0	0	1	110	3	1	1.64	....	....	....	....	....	....	....	....		1924-25	1927-28
Jablonski, Pat	St.L., T.B., Mtl., Phx., Car.	8	128	28	62	18	6634	413	1	3.74	4	0	0	....	139	6	0	2.59		1989-90	1997-98
Jackson, Doug	Chi.	1	6	2	3	1	360	42	0	7.00	....	....	....	....	....	....	....	....		1947-48	1947-48
Jackson, Percy	Bos., NYA, NYR	4	7	1	3	1	392	26	0	3.98	....	....	....	....	....	....	....	....		1931-32	1935-36

Name	NHL Teams	NHL Seasons	Regular Schedule GP	W	L	T	Mins	GA	SO	Avg	Playoffs GP	W	L	T	Mins	GA	SO	Avg	NHL Cup Wins	First NHL Season	Last NHL Season
‡ Jaks, Pauli	L.A.	1	1	0	0	0	40	2	0	3.00	....	....	....	....	....	....	....	....		1994-95	1994-95
Janaszak, Steve	Min., Col.	2	3	0	1	1	160	15	0	5.63	....	....	....	....	....	....	....	....		1979-80	1981-82
Janecyk, Bob	Chi., L.A.	6	110	43	47	13	6250	432	2	4.15	3	0	3	....	184	10	0	3.26		1983-84	1988-89
§ Jenkins, Roger	NYA	1	1	0	1	0	30	7	0	14.00	....	....	....	....	....	....	....	....		1938-39	1938-39
Jensen, Al	Det., Wsh., L.A.	7	179	95	53	18	9974	557	8	3.35	12	5	5	....	598	32	0	3.21		1980-81	1986-87
Jensen, Darren	Phi.	2	30	15	10	1	1496	95	2	3.81	....	....	....	....	....	....	....	....		1984-85	1985-86
Johnson, Bob	St.L., Pit.	2	24	9	9	1	1059	66	0	3.74	....	....	....	....	....	....	....	....		1972-73	1974-75
Johnston, Eddie	Bos., Tor., St.L., Chi.	16	592	234	257	80	34216	1852	32	3.25	18	7	10	....	1023	57	1	3.34	2	1962-63	1977-78
Junkin, Joe	Bos.	1	1	0	0	0	8	0	0	0.00	....	....	....	....	....	....	....	....		1968-69	1968-69
Kaarela, Jari	Col.	1	5	2	2	0	220	22	0	6.00	....	....	....	....	....	....	....	....		1980-81	1980-81
Kamppuri, Hannu	N.J.	1	13	1	10	1	645	54	0	5.02	....	....	....	....	....	....	....	....		1984-85	1984-85
• Karakas, Mike	Chi., Mtl.	8	336	114	169	53	20616	1002	28	2.92	23	11	12	0	1434	72	3	3.01	1	1935-36	1945-46
Keans, Doug	L.A., Bos.	9	210	96	64	26	11388	666	4	3.51	9	2	6	....	432	34	0	4.72		1979-80	1987-88
Keenan, Don	Bos.	1	1	0	1	0	60	4	0	4.00	....	....	....	....	....	....	....	....		1958-59	1958-59
• Kerr, Dave	Mtl.M., NYA, NYR	11	427	203	148	75	26639	954	51	2.15	40	18	19	3	2616	76	8	1.74	1	1930-31	1940-41
King, Scott	Det.	2	2	0	0	0	61	3	0	2.95	....	....	....	....	....	....	....	....		1990-91	1991-92
Kleisinger, Terry	NYR	1	4	0	2	0	191	14	0	4.40	....	....	....	....	....	....	....	....		1985-86	1985-86
Klymkiw, Julian	NYR	1	1	0	0	0	19	2	0	6.32	....	....	....	....	....	....	....	....		1958-59	1958-59
Knickle, Rick	L.A.	2	14	7	6	0	706	44	0	3.74	....	....	....	....	....	....	....	....		1992-93	1993-94
Kuntar, Les	Mtl.	1	6	2	2	0	302	16	0	3.18	....	....	....	....	....	....	....	....		1993-94	1993-94
Kurt, Gary	Cal.	1	16	1	7	5	838	60	0	4.30	....	....	....	....	....	....	....	....		1971-72	1971-72
‡ Labrecque, Patrick	Mtl.	1	2	0	1	0	98	7	0	4.29	....	....	....	....	....	....	....	....		1995-96	1995-96
Lacher, Blaine	Bos.	2	47	22	16	4	2636	123	4	2.80	5	1	4	....	283	12	0	2.54		1994-95	1995-96
• Lacroix, Frenchy	Mtl.	2	5	1	4	0	280	16	0	3.43	....	....	....	....	....	....	....	....		1925-26	1926-27
LaFerriere, Rick	Col.	1	1	0	0	0	20	1	0	3.00	....	....	....	....	....	....	....	....		1981-82	1981-82
LaForest, Mark	Det., Phi., Tor., Ott.	6	103	25	54	4	5032	354	2	4.22	2	1	0	....	48	1	0	1.25		1985-86	1993-94
• Larocque, Michel	Mtl., Tor., Phi., St.L.	11	312	160	89	45	17615	978	17	3.33	14	6	6	....	759	37	1	2.92	4	1973-74	1983-84
‡ Larocque, Michel	Chi.	1	3	0	2	0	152	9	0	3.55	....	....	....	....	....	....	....	....		2000-01	2000-01
Laskowski, Gary	L.A.	2	59	19	27	5	2942	228	0	4.65	....	....	....	....	....	....	....	....		1982-83	1983-84
Laxton, Gord	Pit.	4	17	4	9	0	800	74	0	5.55	....	....	....	....	....	....	....	....		1975-76	1978-79
LeBlanc, Ray	Chi.	1	1	1	0	0	60	1	0	1.00	....	....	....	....	....	....	....	....		1991-92	1991-92
§ • Leduc, Albert	Mtl.	1	1	0	0	0	2	1	0	30.00	....	....	....	....	....	....	....	....		1931-32	1931-32
Legris, Claude	Det.	2	4	0	1	1	91	4	0	2.64	....	....	....	....	....	....	....	....		1980-81	1981-82
• Lehman, Hugh	Chi.	2	48	20	24	4	3047	136	6	2.68	2	0	1	1	120	10	0	5.00		1926-27	1927-28
Lemelin, Reggie	Atl., Cgy., Bos.	15	507	236	162	63	28006	1613	12	3.46	59	23	25	....	3119	186	2	3.58		1978-79	1992-93
Lenarduzzi, Mike	Hfd.	2	4	1	1	1	189	10	0	3.17	....	....	....	....	....	....	....	....		1992-93	1993-94
Lessard, Mario	L.A.	6	240	92	97	39	13529	843	9	3.74	20	6	12	....	1136	83	0	4.38		1978-79	1983-84
Levasseur, Jean-Louis	Min.	1	1	0	1	0	60	7	0	7.00	....	....	....	....	....	....	....	....		1979-80	1979-80
§ • Levinsky, Alex	Tor.	1	1	0	0	0	1	1	0	60.00	....	....	....	....	....	....	....	....		1931-32	1931-32
• Lindbergh, Pelle	Phi.	5	157	87	49	15	9150	503	7	3.30	23	12	10	....	1214	63	3	3.11		1981-82	1985-86
• Lindsay, Bert	Mtl.W., Tor.	2	20	6	14	0	1238	118	0	5.72	....	....	....	....	....	....	....	....		1917-18	1918-19
Littman, David	Buf., T.B.	3	3	0	2	0	141	14	0	5.96	....	....	....	....	....	....	....	....		1990-91	1992-93
Liut, Mike	St.L., Hfd., Wsh.	13	664	294	271	74	38215	2221	25	3.49	67	29	32	....	3814	215	2	3.38		1979-80	1991-92
Lockett, Ken	Van.	2	55	13	15	8	2348	131	2	3.35	1	0	1	....	60	6	0	6.00		1974-75	1975-76
• Lockhart, Howard	Tor., Que., Ham., Bos.	5	59	16	41	0	3413	287	1	5.05	....	....	....	....	....	....	....	....		1919-20	1924-25
LoPresti, Pete	Min., Edm.	6	175	43	102	20	9858	668	5	4.07	2	0	2	....	77	6	0	4.68		1974-75	1980-81
• LoPresti, Sam	Chi.	2	74	30	38	6	4530	236	4	3.13	8	3	5	....	530	17	1	1.92		1940-41	1941-42
‡ Lorenz, Danny	NYI	3	8	1	5	0	357	25	0	4.20	....	....	....	....	....	....	....	....		1990-91	1992-93
Loustel, Ron	Wpg.	1	1	0	1	0	60	10	0	10.00	....	....	....	....	....	....	....	....		1980-81	1980-81
Low, Ron	Tor., Wsh., Det., Que., Edm., N.J.	11	382	102	203	38	20502	1463	4	4.28	7	1	6	....	452	29	0	3.85		1972-73	1984-85
Lozinski, Larry	Det.	1	30	6	11	7	1459	105	0	4.32	....	....	....	....	....	....	....	....		1980-81	1980-81
• Lumley, Harry	Det., NYR, Chi., Tor., Bos.	16	803	330	329	142	48044	2206	71	2.75	76	29	47	....	4778	198	7	2.49	1	1943-44	1959-60
MacKenzie, Shawn	N.J.	1	4	0	1	0	130	15	0	6.92	....	....	....	....	....	....	....	....		1982-83	1982-83
Madeley, Darrin	Ott.	3	39	4	23	5	1928	140	0	4.36	....	....	....	....	....	....	....	....		1992-93	1994-95
Malarchuk, Clint	Que., Wsh., Buf.	11	338	141	130	45	19030	1100	12	3.47	15	2	9	0	781	56	0	4.30		1981-82	1991-92
Maneluk, George	NYI	1	4	1	1	0	140	15	0	6.43	....	....	....	....	....	....	....	....		1990-91	1990-91
Maniago, Cesare	Tor., Mtl., NYR, Min., Van.	15	568	189	257	97	32570	1773	30	3.27	36	15	21	....	2245	100	3	2.67		1960-61	1977-78
Marois, Jean	Tor., Chi.	2	3	1	2	0	180	15	0	5.00	....	....	....	....	....	....	....	....		1943-44	1953-54
Martin, Seth	St.L.	1	30	8	10	7	1552	67	1	2.59	2	0	0	....	73	5	0	4.11		1967-68	1967-68
Mason, Bob	Wsh., Chi., Que., Van.	8	145	55	65	16	7988	500	1	3.76	5	2	3	....	369	12	1	1.95		1983-84	1990-91
Mattsson, Markus	Wpg., Min., L.A.	4	92	21	46	14	5007	343	6	4.11	....	....	....	....	....	....	....	....		1979-80	1983-84
May, Darrell	St.L.	2	6	1	5	0	364	31	0	5.11	....	....	....	....	....	....	....	....		1985-86	1987-88
Mayer, Gilles	Tor.	4	9	2	6	1	540	24	0	2.67	....	....	....	....	....	....	....	....		1949-50	1955-56
• McAuley, Ken	NYR	2	96	17	64	15	5740	537	1	5.61	....	....	....	....	....	....	....	....		1943-44	1944-45
McCartan, Jack	NYR	2	12	2	7	3	680	42	1	3.71	....	....	....	....	....	....	....	....		1959-60	1960-61
• McCool, Frank	Tor.	2	72	34	31	7	4320	242	4	3.36	13	8	5	....	807	30	4	2.23	1	1944-45	1945-46
McDuffe, Peter	St.L., NYR, K.C., Det.	5	57	11	36	6	3207	218	0	4.08	1	0	1	....	60	7	0	7.00		1971-72	1975-76
McGrattan, Tom	Det.	1	1	0	0	0	8	1	0	7.50	....	....	....	....	....	....	....	....		1947-48	1947-48
McKay, Ross	Hfd.	1	1	0	0	0	35	3	0	5.14	....	....	....	....	....	....	....	....		1990-91	1990-91
McKenzie, Bill	Det., K.C., Col.	6	91	18	49	13	4776	326	2	4.10	....	....	....	....	....	....	....	....		1973-74	1979-80
McKichan, Steve	Van.	1	1	0	0	0	20	2	0	6.00	....	....	....	....	....	....	....	....		1990-91	1990-91
McLachlan, Murray	Tor.	1	2	0	1	0	25	4	0	9.60	....	....	....	....	....	....	....	....		1970-71	1970-71
McLean, Kirk	N.J., Van., Car., Fla., NYR	16	612	245	262	72	35090	1904	22	3.26	68	34	34	....	4189	198	6	2.84		1985-86	2000-01
McLelland, Dave	Van.	1	2	1	1	0	120	10	0	5.00	....	....	....	....	....	....	....	....		1972-73	1972-73
McLeod, Don	Det., Phi.	2	18	3	10	1	879	74	0	5.05	....	....	....	....	....	....	....	....		1970-71	1971-72
McLeod, Jim	St.L.	1	16	6	6	4	880	44	0	3.00	....	....	....	....	....	....	....	....		1971-72	1971-72
McNamara, Gerry	Tor.	2	7	2	2	1	323	14	0	2.60	....	....	....	....	....	....	....	....		1960-61	1969-70
McNeil, Gerry	Mtl.	8	276	119	105	52	16535	649	28	2.36	35	17	18	....	2284	72	5	1.89	3	1947-48	1957-58
McRae, Gord	Tor.	5	71	30	22	10	3799	221	1	3.49	8	2	5	....	454	22	0	2.91		1972-73	1977-78
Melanson, Roland	NYI, Min., L.A., N.J., Mtl.	11	291	129	106	33	16452	995	6	3.63	23	4	9	....	801	59	0	4.42	3	1980-81	1991-92
Meloche, Gilles	Chi., Cal., Cle., Min., Pit.	18	788	270	351	131	45401	2756	20	3.64	45	21	19	....	2464	143	2	3.48		1970-71	1987-88
‡ Micalef, Corrado	Det.	5	113	26	59	15	5794	409	2	4.24	3	0	0	....	49	8	0	9.80		1981-82	1985-86
Middlebrook, Lindsay	Wpg., Min., N.J., Edm.	4	37	3	23	6	1845	152	0	4.94	....	....	....	....	....	....	....	....		1979-80	1982-83
• Millar, Al	Bos.	1	6	1	4	1	360	25	0	4.17	....	....	....	....	....	....	....	....		1957-58	1957-58
Millen, Greg	Pit., Hfd., St.L., Que., Chi., Det.	14	604	215	284	89	35377	2281	17	3.87	59	27	29	....	3383	193	0	3.42		1978-79	1991-92
• Miller, Joe	NYA, NYR, Pit., Phi.	4	127	24	87	16	7871	383	16	2.92	3	2	1	0	180	3	1	1.00	1	1927-28	1930-31
Mio, Eddie	Edm., NYR, Det.	7	192	64	73	30	10428	705	4	4.06	17	9	7	....	986	63	0	3.83		1979-80	1985-86
• Mitchell, Ivan	Tor.	3	22	10	9	0	1190	88	0	4.44	....	....	....	....	....	....	....	....	1	1919-20	1921-22
Moffat, Mike	Bos.	3	19	7	7	2	979	70	0	4.29	11	6	5	....	663	38	0	3.44		1981-82	1983-84
Moog, Andy	Edm., Bos., Dal., Mtl.	18	713	372	209	88	40151	2097	28	3.13	132	68	57	....	7452	377	4	3.04	3	1980-81	1997-98
Moore, Alfie	NYA, Chi., Det.	4	21	7	14	0	1290	81	1	3.77	3	1	2	....	180	7	0	2.33	1	1936-37	1939-40
Moore, Robbie	Phi., Wsh.	2	6	3	1	1	257	8	2	1.87	5	3	2	....	268	18	0	4.03		1978-79	1982-83
Morissette, Jean-Guy	Mtl.	1	1	0	1	0	36	4	0	6.67	....	....	....	....	....	....	....	....		1963-64	1963-64
• Mowers, Johnny	Det.	4	152	65	61	26	9350	399	15	2.56	32	19	13	....	2000	85	2	2.55	1	1940-41	1946-47
Mrazek, Jerome	Phi.	1	1	0	0	0	6	1	0	10.00	....	....	....	....	....	....	....	....		1975-76	1975-76
§ • Mummery, Harry	Que., Ham.	2	4	2	1	0	192	20	0	6.25	....	....	....	....	....	....	....	....		1919-20	1921-22
§ • Munro, Dunc	Mtl.M.	1	1	0	0	0	2	0	0	0.00	....	....	....	....	....	....	....	....		1924-25	1924-25
• Murphy, Hal	Mtl.	1	1	1	0	0	60	4	0	4.00	....	....	....	....	....	....	....	....		1952-53	1952-53
• Murray, Mickey	Mtl.	1	1	0	1	0	60	4	0	4.00	....	....	....	....	....	....	....	....		1929-30	1929-30
‡ Muzzatti, Jason	Cgy., Hfd., NYR, S.J.	5	62	13	25	10	3014	167	1	3.32	....	....	....	....	....	....	....	....		1993-94	1997-98
‡ Myllys, Jarmo	Min., S.J.	4	39	4	27	1	1846	161	0	5.23	....	....	....	....	....	....	....	....		1988-89	1991-92
Mylnikov, Sergei	Que.	1	10	1	7	2	568	47	0	4.96	....	....	....	....	....	....	....	....		1989-90	1989-90
Myre, Phil	Mtl., Atl., St.L., Phi., Col., Buf.	14	439	149	198	76	25220	1482	14	3.53	12	6	5	....	747	41	1	3.29	1	1969-70	1982-83
Newton, Cam	Pit.	2	16	4	7	1	814	51	0	3.76	....	....	....	....	....	....	....	....		1970-71	1972-73
Norris, Jack	Bos., Chi., L.A.	4	58	20	25	4	3119	202	2	3.89	....	....	....	....	....	....	....	....		1964-65	1970-71
Oleschuk, Bill	K.C., Col.	4	55	7	28	10	2835	188	1	3.98	....	....	....	....	....	....	....	....		1975-76	1979-80
• Olesevich, Dan	NYR	1	1	0	0	1	29	2	0	4.14	....	....	....	....	....	....	....	....		1961-62	1961-62
O'Neill, Mike	Wpg., Ana.	4	21	0	9	2	855	61	0	4.28	....	....	....	....	....	....	....	....		1991-92	1996-97
Ouimet, Ted	St.L.	1	1	0	1	0	60	2	0	2.00	....	....	....	....	....	....	....	....		1968-69	1968-69

Name	NHL Teams	NHL Seasons	Regular Schedule GP	W	L	T	Mins	GA	SO	Avg	Playoffs GP	W	L	T	Mins	GA	SO	Avg	NHL Cup Wins	First NHL Season	Last NHL Season
Pageau, Paul	L.A.	1	1	0	1	0	60	8	0	8.00	....	....	....	....	....	....	....	....		1980-81	1980-81
Paille, Marcel	NYR	7	107	32	52	22	6342	362	2	3.42	....	....	....	....	....	....	....	....		1957-58	1964-65
Palmateer, Mike	Tor., Wsh.	8	356	149	138	52	20131	1183	17	3.53	29	12	17	....	1765	89	2	3.03		1976-77	1983-84
Pang, Darren	Chi.	3	81	27	35	7	4252	287	0	4.05	6	1	3	....	250	18	0	4.32		1984-85	1988-89
Parent, Bernie	Bos., Phi., Tor.	13	608	271	198	121	35136	1493	54	2.55	71	38	33	....	4302	174	6	2.43	2	1965-66	1978-79
Parent, Bob	Tor.	2	3	0	2	0	160	15	0	5.63	....	....	....	....	....	....	....	....		1981-82	1982-83
‡ Parent, Rich	St.L., T.B., Pit.	4	32	7	11	5	1561	82	1	3.15	....	....	....	....	....	....	....	....		1997-98	2000-01
Parro, Dave	Wsh.	4	77	21	36	10	4015	274	2	4.09	....	....	....	....	....	....	....	....		1980-81	1983-84
§ • Patrick, Lester	NYR	1	....	....	....	....	....	....	....	....	1	1	0	0	46	1	0	1.30	1	1927-28	1927-28
Peeters, Pete	Phi., Bos., Wsh.	13	489	246	155	51	27699	1424	21	3.08	71	35	35	....	4200	232	2	3.31		1978-79	1990-91
Pelletier, Marcel	Chi., NYR	2	8	1	6	0	395	32	0	4.86	....	....	....	....	....	....	....	....		1950-51	1962-63
Penney, Steve	Mtl., Wpg.	5	91	35	38	12	5194	313	1	3.62	27	15	12	....	1604	72	4	2.69		1983-84	1987-88
• Perreault, Bob	Mtl., Det., Bos.	3	31	8	16	7	1827	103	3	3.38	....	....	....	....	....	....	....	....		1955-56	1962-63
Pettie, Jim	Bos.	3	21	9	7	2	1157	71	1	3.68	....	....	....	....	....	....	....	....		1976-77	1978-79
Pietrangelo, Frank	Pit., Hfd.	7	141	46	59	6	7141	490	1	4.12	12	7	5	....	713	34	1	2.86	1	1987-88	1993-94
• Plante, Jacques	Mtl., NYR, St.L., Tor., Bos.	18	837	437	246	145	49533	1964	82	2.38	112	71	36	....	6651	237	14	2.14	6	1952-53	1972-73
Plasse, Michel	St.L., Mtl., K.C., Pit., Col., Que.	11	299	92	136	54	16760	1058	2	3.79	4	1	2	....	195	9	1	2.77	1	1970-71	1981-82
§ • Plaxton, Hugh	Mtl.M.	1	1	0	1	0	57	5	0	5.26	....	....	....	....	....	....	....	....		1932-33	1932-33
Pronovost, Claude	Bos., Mtl.	2	3	1	1	0	120	7	1	3.50	....	....	....	....	....	....	....	....		1955-56	1958-59
Puppa, Daren	Buf., Tor., T.B.	15	429	179	161	54	23819	1204	19	3.03	16	4	9	....	786	51	0	3.89		1985-86	1999-00
Pusey, Chris	Det.	1	1	0	0	0	40	3	0	4.50	....	....	....	....	....	....	....	....		1985-86	1985-86
‡ Racicot, Andre	Mtl.	5	68	26	23	8	3357	196	2	3.50	4	0	1	....	31	4	0	7.74	1	1989-90	1993-94
‡ Racine, Bruce	St.L.	1	11	0	3	0	230	12	0	3.13	1	0	0	....	1	0	0	0.00		1995-96	1995-96
‡ Ram, Jamie	NYR	1	1	0	0	0	27	0	0	0.00	....	....	....	....	....	....	....	....		1995-96	1995-96
Ranford, Bill	Bos., Edm., Wsh., T.B., Det.	15	647	240	279	76	35936	2042	15	3.41	53	28	25	....	3110	159	4	3.07	2	1985-86	1999-00
Raymond, Alain	Wsh.	1	1	0	1	0	40	2	0	3.00	....	....	....	....	....	....	....	....		1987-88	1987-88
• Rayner, Chuck	NYA, Bro., NYR	10	424	138	208	77	25491	1294	25	3.05	18	9	9	....	1135	46	1	2.43		1940-41	1952-53
Reaugh, Daryl	Edm., Hfd.	3	27	8	9	1	1246	72	1	3.47	....	....	....	....	....	....	....	....		1984-85	1990-91
‡ Reddick, Pokey	Wpg., Edm., Fla.	6	132	46	58	16	7162	443	0	3.71	4	0	2	....	168	10	0	3.57	1	1986-87	1993-94
§ • Redding, George	Bos.	1	1	0	0	0	11	1	0	5.45	....	....	....	....	....	....	....	....		1924-25	1924-25
Redquest, Greg	Pit.	1	1	0	0	0	13	3	0	13.85	....	....	....	....	....	....	....	....		1977-78	1977-78
Reece, Dave	Bos.	1	14	7	5	2	777	43	2	3.32	....	....	....	....	....	....	....	....		1975-76	1975-76
Reese, Jeff	Tor., Cgy., Hfd., T.B., N.J.	11	174	53	65	17	8667	529	5	3.66	11	3	5	....	515	35	0	4.08		1987-88	1998-99
Resch, Glenn	NYI, Col., N.J., Phi.	14	571	231	224	82	32279	1761	26	3.27	41	17	17	....	2044	85	2	2.50	1	1973-74	1986-87
• Rheaume, Herb	Mtl.	1	31	10	20	1	1889	92	0	2.92	....	....	....	....	....	....	....	....		1925-26	1925-26
Ricci, Nick	Pit.	4	19	7	12	0	1087	79	0	4.36	....	....	....	....	....	....	....	....		1979-80	1982-83
Richardson, Terry	Det., St.L.	5	20	3	11	0	906	85	0	5.63	....	....	....	....	....	....	....	....		1973-74	1978-79
Ridley, Curt	NYR, Van., Tor.	6	104	27	47	16	5498	355	1	3.87	2	0	2	....	120	8	0	4.00		1974-75	1980-81
Riendeau, Vincent	Mtl., St.L., Det., Bos.	8	184	85	65	20	10423	573	5	3.30	25	11	12	....	1277	71	1	3.34		1987-88	1994-95
Riggin, Dennis	Det.	2	18	6	10	2	999	52	1	3.12	....	....	....	....	....	....	....	....		1959-60	1962-63
Riggin, Pat	Atl., Cgy., Wsh., Bos., Pit.	9	350	153	120	52	19872	1135	11	3.43	25	8	13	....	1336	72	0	3.23		1979-80	1987-88
Ring, Bob	Bos.	1	1	0	0	0	33	4	0	7.27	....	....	....	....	....	....	....	....		1965-66	1965-66
Rivard, Fern	Min.	4	55	9	26	11	2865	190	2	3.98	....	....	....	....	....	....	....	....		1968-69	1974-75
• Roach, John Ross	Tor., NYR, Det.	14	492	219	204	68	30444	1246	58	2.46	29	12	14	3	1901	60	7	1.89	1	1921-22	1934-35
• Roberts, Moe	Bos., NYA, Chi.	4	10	3	5	0	501	31	0	3.71	....	....	....	....	....	....	....	....		1925-26	1951-52
• Robertson, Earl	Det., NYA, Bro.	6	190	60	95	34	11820	575	16	2.92	15	7	7	....	995	29	2	1.75	1	1936-37	1941-42
• Rollins, Al	Tor., Chi., NYR	9	430	141	205	83	25723	1192	28	2.78	13	6	7	....	755	30	0	2.38	1	1949-50	1959-60
Romano, Roberto	Pit., Bos.	6	126	46	63	8	7111	471	4	3.97	....	....	....	....	....	....	....	....		1982-83	1993-94
‡ Rosati, Mike	Wsh.	1	1	1	0	0	28	0	0	0.00	....	....	....	....	....	....	....	....		1998-99	1998-99
‡ Roussel, Dominic	Phi., Wpg., Ana., Edm.	8	205	77	70	23	10665	555	7	3.12	1	0	0	....	23	0	0	0.00		1991-92	2000-01
Rupp, Pat	Det.	1	1	0	1	0	60	4	0	4.00	....	....	....	....	....	....	....	....		1963-64	1963-64
Rutherford, Jim	Det., Pit., Tor., L.A.	13	457	151	227	59	25895	1576	14	3.65	8	2	5	....	440	28	0	3.82		1970-71	1982-83
Rutledge, Wayne	L.A.	3	82	28	37	9	4325	241	2	3.34	8	2	4	....	378	20	0	3.17		1967-68	1969-70
St. Croix, Rick	Phi., Tor.	8	130	49	54	18	7295	451	2	3.71	11	4	6	....	562	29	1	3.10		1977-78	1984-85
St. Laurent, Sam	N.J., Det.	5	34	7	12	4	1572	92	1	3.51	1	0	0	....	10	1	0	6.00		1985-86	1989-90
§ • Sands, Charlie	Mtl.	1	1	0	0	0	25	5	0	12.00	....	....	....	....	....	....	....	....		1939-40	1939-40
Sands, Mike	Min.	2	6	0	5	0	302	26	0	5.17	....	....	....	....	....	....	....	....		1984-85	1986-87
Sarjeant, Geoff	St.L., S.J.	2	8	1	2	1	291	20	0	4.12	....	....	....	....	....	....	....	....		1994-95	1995-96
Sauve, Bob	Buf., Det., Chi., N.J.	13	420	182	154	54	23711	1377	8	3.48	34	15	16	....	1850	95	4	3.08		1976-77	1988-89
• Sawchuk, Terry	Det., Bos., Tor., L.A., NYR	21	971	447	330	172	57194	2389	103	2.51	106	54	48	....	6290	266	12	2.54	4	1949-50	1969-70
• Schaefer, Joe	NYR	2	2	0	2	0	86	8	0	5.58	....	....	....	....	....	....	....	....		1959-60	1960-61
‡ Schafer, Paxton	Bos.	1	3	0	0	0	77	6	0	4.68	....	....	....	....	....	....	....	....		1996-97	1996-97
Scott, Ron	NYR, L.A.	5	28	8	13	4	1450	91	0	3.77	1	0	0	....	32	4	0	7.50		1983-84	1989-90
Sevigny, Richard	Mtl., Que.	9	176	80	54	20	9485	507	5	3.21	4	0	3	....	208	13	0	3.75	1	1978-79	1986-87
Sharples, Scott	Cgy.	1	1	0	0	1	65	4	0	3.69	....	....	....	....	....	....	....	....		1991-92	1991-92
§ • Shields, Al	NYA	1	2	0	0	0	41	9	0	13.17	....	....	....	....	....	....	....	....		1931-32	1931-32
‡ Shtalenkov, Mikhail	Ana., Edm., Phx., Fla.	7	190	62	82	19	9966	480	8	2.89	4	0	3	....	211	10	0	2.84		1993-94	1999-00
‡ Shulmistra, Richard	N.J., Fla.	2	2	1	1	0	122	3	0	1.48	....	....	....	....	....	....	....	....		1997-98	1999-00
Sidorkiewicz, Peter	Hfd., Ott., N.J.	8	246	79	128	27	13884	832	8	3.60	15	5	10	....	912	55	0	3.62		1987-88	1997-98
Simmons, Don	Bos., Tor., NYR	11	249	101	101	41	14555	701	20	2.89	24	13	11	....	1436	62	3	2.59	3	1956-57	1968-69
Simmons, Gary	Cal., Cle., L.A.	4	107	30	57	15	6162	366	5	3.56	1	0	0	....	20	1	0	3.00		1974-75	1977-78
Skidmore, Paul	St.L.	1	2	1	1	0	120	6	0	3.00	....	....	....	....	....	....	....	....		1981-82	1981-82
Skorodenski, Warren	Chi., Edm.	5	35	12	11	4	1732	100	2	3.46	2	0	0	....	33	6	0	10.91		1981-82	1987-88
• Smith, Al	Tor., Pit., Det., Buf., Hfd., Col.	10	233	74	99	36	12752	735	10	3.46	6	1	4	....	317	21	0	3.97		1965-66	1980-81
Smith, Billy	L.A., NYI	18	680	305	233	105	38431	2031	22	3.17	132	88	36	....	7645	348	5	2.73	4	1971-72	1988-89
Smith, Gary	Tor., Oak., Cal., Chi., Van., Min., Wsh., Wpg.	14	532	173	261	74	29619	1675	26	3.39	20	5	13	....	1153	62	1	3.23		1965-66	1979-80
• Smith, Normie	Mtl.M., Det.	8	199	81	83	35	12357	479	17	2.33	12	9	2	0	820	18	3	1.32	2	1931-32	1944-45
Sneddon, Bob	Cal.	1	5	0	2	0	225	21	0	5.60	....	....	....	....	....	....	....	....		1970-71	1970-71
Soderstrom, Tommy	Phi., NYI	5	156	45	69	19	8189	496	10	3.63	....	....	....	....	....	....	....	....		1992-93	1996-97
Soetaert, Doug	NYR, Wpg., Mtl.	12	284	110	104	42	15583	1030	6	3.97	5	1	2	....	180	14	0	4.67	1	1975-76	1986-87
‡ Soucy, Christian	Chi.	1	1	0	0	0	3	0	0	0.00	....	....	....	....	....	....	....	....		1993-94	1993-94
• Spooner, Red	Pit.	1	1	0	1	0	60	6	0	6.00	....	....	....	....	....	....	....	....		1929-30	1929-30
§ • Spring, Jesse	Ham.	1	1	0	0	0	2	0	0	0.00	....	....	....	....	....	....	....	....		1924-25	1924-25
Staniowski, Ed	St.L., Wpg., Hfd.	10	219	67	104	21	12075	818	2	4.06	8	1	6	....	428	28	0	3.93		1975-76	1984-85
§ • Starr, Harold	Mtl.M.	1	1	0	0	0	3	0	0	0.00	....	....	....	....	....	....	....	....		1931-32	1931-32
Stauber, Robb	L.A., Buf.	4	62	21	23	9	3295	209	1	3.81	4	3	1	....	240	16	0	4.00		1989-90	1994-95
Stefan, Greg	Det.	9	299	115	127	30	16333	1068	5	3.92	30	12	17	....	1681	99	1	3.53		1981-82	1989-90
Stein, Phil	Tor.	1	1	0	0	1	70	2	0	1.71	....	....	....	....	....	....	....	....		1939-40	1939-40
Stephenson, Wayne	St.L., Phi., Wsh.	10	328	146	103	49	18343	937	14	3.06	26	11	12	....	1522	79	2	3.11	1	1971-72	1980-81
Stevenson, Doug	NYR, Chi.	3	8	2	6	0	480	39	0	4.88	....	....	....	....	....	....	....	....		1944-45	1945-46
Stewart, Charles	Bos.	3	77	30	41	5	4742	194	10	2.45	....	....	....	....	....	....	....	....		1924-25	1926-27
Stewart, Jim	Bos.	1	1	0	1	0	20	5	0	15.00	....	....	....	....	....	....	....	....		1979-80	1979-80
• Stuart, Herb	Det.	1	3	1	2	0	180	5	0	1.67	....	....	....	....	....	....	....	....		1926-27	1926-27
Sylvestri, Don	Bos.	1	3	0	0	2	102	6	0	3.53	....	....	....	....	....	....	....	....		1984-85	1984-85
Tabaracci, Rick	Pit., Wpg., Wsh., Cgy., T.B., Atl., Col.	11	286	93	125	30	15255	760	15	2.99	17	4	12	....	1025	53	0	3.10		1988-89	1999-00
Takko, Kari	Min., Edm.	6	142	37	71	14	7317	475	1	3.90	4	0	1	....	109	7	0	3.85		1985-86	1990-91
Tanner, John	Que.	3	21	2	11	5	1084	65	1	3.60	....	....	....	....	....	....	....	....		1989-90	1991-92
Tataryn, Dave	NYR	1	2	1	1	0	80	10	0	7.50	....	....	....	....	....	....	....	....		1976-77	1976-77
Taylor, Bobby	Phi., Pit.	5	46	15	17	6	2268	155	0	4.10	....	....	....	....	....	....	....	....	1	1971-72	1975-76
• Teno, Harvey	Det.	1	5	2	3	0	300	15	0	3.00	....	....	....	....	....	....	....	....		1938-39	1938-39
Terreri, Chris	N.J., S.J., Chi., NYI	14	406	151	172	43	22369	1143	9	3.07	29	12	12	....	1523	86	0	3.39	2	1986-87	2000-01
Thomas, Wayne	Mtl., Tor., NYR	9	243	103	93	34	13768	766	10	3.34	15	6	8	....	849	50	1	3.53		1972-73	1980-81
• Thompson, Tiny	Bos., Det.	12	553	284	194	75	34175	1183	81	2.08	44	20	24	0	2974	93	7	1.88	1	1928-29	1939-40
§ Toppazzini, Jerry	Bos.	1	1	0	0	0	1	0	0	0.00	....	....	....	....	....	....	....	....		1960-61	1960-61
‡ Torchia, Mike	Dal.	1	6	3	2	1	327	18	0	3.30	....	....	....	....	....	....	....	....		1994-95	1994-95
‡ Trefilov, Andrei	Cgy., Buf., Chi.	7	54	12	25	4	2663	153	2	3.45	1	0	0	....	5	0	0	0.00		1992-93	1998-99
Tremblay, Vincent	Tor., Pit.	5	58	12	26	8	2785	223	1	4.80	....	....	....	....	....	....	....	....		1979-80	1983-84
Tucker, Ted	Cal.	1	5	1	1	1	177	10	0	3.39	....	....	....	....	....	....	....	....		1973-74	1973-74
• Turner, Joe	Det.	1	1	0	0	1	70	3	0	2.57	....	....	....	....	....	....	....	....		1941-42	1941-42

Name	NHL Teams	NHL Seasons	GP	W	L	T	Mins	GA	SO	Avg	GP	W	L	T	Mins	GA	SO	Avg	NHL Cup Wins	First NHL Season	Last NHL Season
			Regular Schedule								**Playoffs**										
Vachon, Rogie	Mtl., L.A., Det., Bos.	16	795	355	291	127	46298	2310	51	2.99	48	23	23	....	2876	133	2	2.77	3	1966-67	1981-82
‡ Vanbiesbrouck, John	NYR, Fla., Phi., NYI, N.J.	20	882	374	346	119	50475	2503	40	2.98	71	28	38	....	3969	177	5	2.68		1981-82	2001-02
Veisor, Mike	Chi., Hfd., Wpg.	10	139	41	62	26	7806	532	5	4.09	4	0	2	....	180	15	0	5.00		1973-74	1983-84
‡ Vernon, Mike	Cgy., Det., S.J., Fla.	19	781	385	273	92	44449	2206	27	2.98	138	77	56	....	8214	367	6	2.68	2	1982-83	2001-02
● Vezina, Georges	Mtl.	9	190	103	81	5	11592	633	13	3.28	13	10	3	1	780	35	2	2.69	1	1917-18	1925-26
Villemure, Gilles	NYR, Chi.	10	205	100	64	29	11581	542	13	2.81	14	5	5	....	656	32	0	2.93		1963-64	1976-77
‡ Waite, Jimmy	Chi., S.J., Phx.	11	106	28	41	12	5253	293	4	3.35	6	0	3	....	211	14	0	3.98		1988-89	1998-99
Wakaluk, Darcy	Buf., Min., Dal., Phx.	8	191	67	75	21	9756	524	9	3.22	8	4	2	....	364	18	0	2.97		1988-89	1996-97
Wakely, Ernie	Mtl., St.L.	5	113	41	42	17	6244	290	8	2.79	10	2	6	....	509	37	1	4.36		1962-63	1971-72
Walsh, Flat	Mtl.M., NYA	7	108	48	43	16	6641	256	12	2.31	8	2	4	2	570	16	2	1.68		1926-27	1932-33
Wamsley, Rick	Mtl., St.L., Cgy., Tor.	13	407	204	131	46	23123	1287	12	3.34	27	7	18	....	1397	81	0	3.48	1	1980-81	1992-93
Watt, Jim	St.L.	1	1	0	0	0	20	2	0	6.00	....	....	....					....		1973-74	1973-74
Weeks, Steve	NYR, Hfd., Van., NYI, L.A., Ott.	18	290	111	119	33	15879	989	5	3.74	12	3	5	....	486	27	0	3.33		1980-81	1992-93
Wetzel, Carl	Det., Min.	2	7	1	3	1	301	22	0	4.39	....	....	....					....		1964-65	1967-68
‡ Whitmore, Kay	Hfd., Van., Bos., Cgy.	9	155	60	64	16	8596	508	4	3.55	4	0	2	....	174	13	0	4.48		1988-89	2001-02
Wilkinson, Derek	T.B.	4	22	3	12	3	933	57	0	3.67	....	....	....					....		1995-96	1998-99
‡ Willis, Jordan	Dal.	1	1	0	1	0	19	1	0	3.16	....	....	....					....		1995-96	1995-96
Wilson, Dunc	Phi., Van., Tor., NYR, Pit.	10	287	80	150	33	15851	988	8	3.74	....	....	....					....		1969-70	1978-79
Wilson, Lefty	Det., Tor., Bos.	3	3	0	0	1	81	1	0	0.74	....	....	....					....		1953-54	1957-58
● Winkler, Hal	NYR, Bos.	2	75	35	26	14	4739	126	21	1.60	10	2	3	5	640	18	2	1.69		1926-27	1927-28
Wolfe, Bernie	Wsh.	4	120	20	61	21	6104	424	1	4.17	....	....	....					....		1975-76	1978-79
Wood, Alex	NYA	1	1	0	1	0	70	3	0	2.57	....	....	....					....		1936-37	1936-37
Worsley, Gump	NYR, Mtl., Min.	21	861	335	352	150	50183	2407	43	2.88	70	40	26	....	4084	189	5	2.78	4	1952-53	1973-74
Worters, Roy	Pit., NYA, Mtl.	12	484	171	229	83	30175	1143	67	2.27	11	3	6	2	690	24	3	2.09		1925-26	1936-37
Worthy, Chris	Oak., Cal.	3	26	5	10	4	1326	98	0	4.43	....	....	....					....		1968-69	1970-71
Wregget, Ken	Tor., Phi., Pit., Cgy., Det.	17	575	225	248	53	31663	1917	9	3.63	56	28	25	....	3341	160	3	2.87	1	1983-84	1999-00
‡ Yeremeyev, Vitali	NYR	1	4	0	0	0	212	16	0	4.53	....	....	....					....		2000-01	2000-01
§ Young, Doug	Det.	1	1	0	0	0	21	1	0	2.86	....	....	....					....		1933-34	1933-34
Young, Wendell	Van., Phi., Pit., T.B.	10	187	59	86	12	9410	618	2	3.94	2	0	1	....	99	6	0	3.64	2	1985-86	1994-95
Zanier, Mike	Edm.	1	3	1	1	1	185	12	0	3.89	....	....	....					....		1984-85	1984-85

Frank Brimsek

Doug Favell

Ken McAuley

John Vanbiesbrouck

Lorne Chabot

George Hainsworth

Dave Reece

Mike Vernon

Bob Essensa

Cesare Maniago

Glenn Resch

Kay Whitmore

2002-03 NHL Player Transactions

(listed in chronological order)

September 2002

4 – Vancouver traded **Brad Leeb** to Toronto for **Tomas Mojzis**.

10 – Detroit traded **Ladislav Kohn** to Calgary for future considerations.

21 – Ottawa traded **Sami Salo** to Vancouver for **Peter Schaefer**.

October 2002

1 – Ottawa traded Jani Hurme to Florida for **Billy Thompson** and **Greg Watson**.

1 – Colorado traded **Chris Drury** and **Stephane Yelle** to Calgary for **Derek Morris**, **Jeff Shantz** and **Dean McAmmond**.

4 – **NHL Waiver Draft**

Pos.	Player	Claimed By	Claimed From
D	**Stephane Robidas**	Atlanta	Montreal
D	**Mathieu Biron**	Columbus	Tampa Bay
RW	**Petr Tenkrat**	Florida	Nashville
D	**Francis Bouillon**	Nashville	Montreal
RW	**Ronald Petrovicky**	NY Rangers	Calgary
D	**Rick Berry**	Washington	Pittsburgh

4 – Atlanta traded **Stephane Robidas** to Dallas for its 6th-round choice (later traded back to Dallas – Dallas selected **Drew Bagnall**) in 2003.

4 – Columbus traded **Mathieu Biron** to Florida for **Petr Tenkrat**.

7 – Edmonton traded **Mike Grier** to Washington for its 2nd-round choice (later traded to NY Islanders – NY Islanders selected **Evgeni Tunik**) in 2003 and Vancouver's 3rd-round choice (previously acquired, **Zachary Stortini**) in 2003.

10 – NY Rangers traded **Boyd Kane** to Tampa Bay for **Gordie Dwyer**.

11 – NY Islanders traded **Juraj Kolnik** and its 9th-round choice (later traded to San Jose – San Jose selected **Carter Lee**) in 2003 to Florida for **Sven Butenschon**.

23 – Anaheim traded **Jason York** to Nashville for future considerations.

31 – Minnesota traded **Sylvain Blouin** to Montreal for its 7th-round choice (**Grigory Misharin**) in 2003.

November 2002

1 – Carolina traded **Darren Langdon** and **Marek Malik** to Vancouver for **Jan Hlavac** and **Harold Druken**.

1 – Washington traded **Chris Simon** and **Andrei Nikolishin** to Chicago for **Michael Nylander**, its 3rd-round choice (**Stephen Werner**) in 2003 and future considerations.

15 – Calgary traded **Marc Savard** to Atlanta for **Ruslan Zainullin**.

16 – Buffalo traded **Jason Woolley** to Detroit for future considerations.

26 – Florida traded **Dmitry Yushkevich** and NY Islanders' 5th-round choice (previously acquired, **Brady Murray**) in 2003 to Los Angeles for **Jaroslav Bednar** and **Andreas Lilja**.

December 2002

2 – Columbus traded **Chris Nielsen** and **Petteri Nummelin** to Atlanta for **Tomi Kallio** and **Pauli Levokari**.

5 – St. Louis traded **Dale Clarke** to Colorado for future considerations.

6 – San Jose traded **Marcus Ragnarsson** to Philadelphia for **Dan McGillis**.

12 – Edmonton traded **Josh Green** to NY Rangers for a conditional choice in 2004.

12 – Nashville traded **Mike Dunham** to NY Rangers for **Rem Murray**, **Tomas Kloucek** and **Marek Zidlicky**.

16 – Washington traded **Dean Melanson** to Ottawa for **Josef Boumedienne**.

19 – Philadelphia traded **Paul Ranheim** to Phoenix for a conditional choice in 2004.

31 – Phoenix traded **Patrick DesRochers** to Carolina for **Jean-Marc Pelletier** and a conditional choice in 2004.

31 – Nashville traded **Nathan Perrott** to Toronto for **Bob Wren**.

January 2003

6 – NY Rangers traded **Krzysztof Oliwa** to Boston for a 9th-round choice in 2004.

8 – Chicago traded **Boris Mironov** to NY Rangers for a conditional choice in 2004.

13 – Boston traded **John Grahame** to Tampa Bay for a 4th-round choice in 2004.

15 – Ottawa traded **Joel Kwiatkowski** to Washington for its 9th-round choice (later traded back to Washington – Washington selected **Mark Olafson**) in 2003.

16 – Phoenix traded **Claude Lemieux** to Dallas for **Scott Pellerin** and a conditional choice in 2004.

17 – Boston traded **Jay Henderson** to NY Rangers for a 9th-round choice in 2004.

20 – Atlanta traded **Chris Herperger** and **Chris Nielsen** to Vancouver for **Jeff Farkas**.

22 – Calgary traded **Jamie Wright** to Philadelphia for future considerations.

22 – NY Rangers traded **Mike Mottau** to Calgary for its 6th-round choice (**Ivan Dornic**) in 2003 and future considerations.

23 – Montreal traded **Jeff Hackett** to San Jose for **Niklas Sundstrom** and a 3rd-round choice in 2004.

23 – San Jose traded **Jeff Hackett** and **Jeff Jillson** to Boston for **Kyle McLaren** and a 4th-round choice in 2004.

24 – Vancouver traded **Steve Kariya** to New Jersey for **Mikko Jokela**.

29 – Montreal traded **Eric Chouinard** to Philadelphia for its 2nd-round choice (**Maxim Lapierre**) in 2003.

30 – Florida traded **Sandis Ozolinsh** and **Lance Ward** to Anaheim for **Pavel Trnka**, **Matt Cullen** and its 4th-round choice (**James Pemberton**) in 2003.

February 2003

4 – Nashville traded **Greg Koehler** to Los Angeles for future considerations.

5 – Philadelphia traded **Chris McAllister** to Colorado for its 6th-round choice (**Ville Hostikka**) in 2003.

5 – Vancouver traded **Todd Warriner** to Philadelphia for future considerations.

7 – Carolina traded **Sami Kapanen** and **Ryan Bast** to Philadelphia for **Pavel Brendl** and **Bruno St. Jacques**.

9 – San Jose traded **Shawn Heins** and a conditional choice in 2004 to Pittsburgh for its 5th-round choice (**Patrick Ehelechner**) in 2003.

9 – Pittsburgh traded **Andrew Ference** to Calgary for future considerations.

10 – NY Rangers traded **Joel Bouchard**, **Richard Lintner**, **Rico Fata**, **Mikael Samuelsson** and future considerations to Pittsburgh for **Mike Wilson**, **Alex Kovalev**, **Janne Laukkanen** and **Dan LaCouture**.

17 – Dallas traded **Jon Sim** to Nashville for **Bubba Berenzweig** and a conditional choice in 2004.

20 – Minnesota traded **Cory Larose** to NY Rangers for **Jay Henderson**.

24 – Atlanta traded **Pascal Rheaume** to New Jersey for a conditional choice in 2004.

25 – Buffalo traded **Vaclav Varada** and its 5th-round choice (**Tim Cook**) in 2003 to Ottawa for **Jakub Klepis**.

March 2003

1 – Los Angeles traded **Dmitry Yushkevich** to Philadelphia for its 4th-round choice (later traded to Boston – Boston selected **Patrick Valcak**) in 2003 and a 7th-round choice in 2004.

3 – Montreal traded **Oleg Petrov** to Nashville for its 4th-round choice (later traded to Washington – Washington selected **Andreas Valdix**) in 2003.

4 – Florida traded **Joey Tetarenko** to Ottawa for **Simon Lajeunesse**.

5 – San Jose traded **Owen Nolan** to Toronto for **Alyn McCauley**, **Brad Boyes** and its 1st-round choice (later traded to Boston – Boston selected **Mark Stuart**) in 2003.

8 – Florida traded **Brad Ference** to Phoenix for **Darcy Hordichuk** and its 2nd-round choice (later traded to Tampa Bay – Tampa Bay selected **Matt Smaby**) in 2003.

8 – San Jose traded **Bryan Marchment** to Colorado for its 3rd-round choice (later traded to Calgary – Calgary selected **Ryan Donally**) and 5th-round choice (later traded back to Colorado – Colorado selected **Brad Richardson**) in 2003.

9 – Carolina traded **Glen Wesley** to Toronto for a 2nd-round choice in 2004.

9 – NY Islanders trade **Claude Lapointe** to Philadelphia for its 5th-round choice (later traded to Pittsburgh – Pittsburgh selected **Evgeni Isakov**) in 2003.

9 – Pittsburgh traded **Randy Robitaille** to NY Islanders for Philadelphia's 5th-round choice (previously acquired, **Evgeni Isakov**) in 2003.

9 – Florida traded **Wade Flaherty** to Nashville for **Pascal Trepanier**.

10 – Buffalo traded **Rob Ray** to Ottawa for future considerations.

10 – Buffalo traded **Stu Barnes** to Dallas for **Michael Ryan** and its 2nd-round choice (**Branislav Fabry**) in 2003.

10 – Chicago traded **Lyle Odelein** to Dallas for **Sami Helenius** and a 7th-round choice in 2004.

10 – Columbus traded **Grant Marshall** to New Jersey for a conditional choice in 2004.

10 – Atlanta traded **Richard Smehlik** and a conditional choice in 2004 to New Jersey for its 4th-round choice (**Michael Vannelli**) in 2003.

10 – Nashville traded **Bob Wren** to Ottawa for future considerations.

10 – Phoenix traded **Tony Amonte** to Philadelphia for **Guillaume Lefebvre**, Atlanta's 3rd-round choice (previously acquired, **Tyler Redenbach**) in 2003 and a 2nd-round choice in 2004.

10 – Buffalo traded **Chris Gratton** and a 4th-round choice in 2004 to Phoenix for **Daniel Briere** and a 3rd-round choice in 2004.

11 – Anaheim traded **Mike Commodore** and **Jean-Francois Damphousse** to Calgary for **Rob Niedermayer**.

11 – Calgary traded **Micki DuPont** and **Mathias Johansson** to Pittsburgh for **Shean Donovan**.

11 – Carolina traded **Bates Battaglia** to Colorado for **Radim Vrbata**.

11 – Chicago traded **Steve Thomas** to Anaheim for Anaheim's 5th-round choice (**Alexei Ivanov**) in 2003.

11 – Chicago traded **Peter White** to Philadelphia for future considerations.

11 – Chicago traded **Phil Housley** to Toronto for its 9th-round choice (**Chris Porter**) in 2003 and a 4th-round choice in 2004.

11 – Chicago traded **Sergei Berezin** to Washington for a 4th-round choice in 2004.

11 – Colorado traded **Alexander Riazantsev** to Nashville for its 7th-round choice (**Linus Videll**) in 2003.

11 – Colorado traded **Dean McAmmond** to Calgary for its 5th-round choice (**Mark McCutcheon**) in 2003.

11 – Dallas traded the rights to **Anthony Aquino** to Atlanta for Dallas' 6th-round choice (previously acquired, **Drew Bagnall**) in 2003 and a conditional choice in 2006.

11 – Edmonton traded **Anson Carter** and **Ales Pisa** to NY Rangers for **Radek Dvorak** and **Cory Cross**.

11 – Edmonton traded **Janne Niinimaa** and Washington's 2nd-round choice (previous acquired, **Evgeni Tunik**) in 2003 to NY Islanders for **Brad Isbister** and **Raffi Torres**.

11 – Florida traded **Valeri Bure** and a conditional choice in 2004 to St. Louis for **Mike Van Ryn**.

11 – Los Angeles traded **Mathieu Schneider** to Detroit for **Sean Avery**, **Maxim Kuznetsov**, its 1st-round choice (**Jeff Tambellini**) in 2003 and a 2nd-round choice in 2004.

11 – Los Angeles traded **Bryan Smolinski** to Ottawa for the rights to **Tim Gleason** and future considerations.

11 – Minnesota traded **Lawrence Nycholat** to NY Rangers for **Johan Holmqvist**.

11 – Montreal traded **Doug Gilmour** to Toronto for its 6th-round choice (**Mark Flood**) in 2003.

11 – NY Islanders traded **Chris Osgood** and its 3rd-round choice (**Konstantin Barulin**) in 2003 to St. Louis for **Justin Papineau** and its 2nd-round choice (**Jeremy Colliton**) in 2003.

11 – Phoenix traded **Brad May** to Vancouver for Phoenix's 3rd-round choice (previously acquired, **Dimitri Prestunov**) in 2003.

11 – Phoenix traded **Ramzi Abid**, **Dan Focht** and **Guillaume Lefebvre** to Pittsburgh for **Jan Hrdina** and **Francois Leroux**.

11 – Pittsburgh traded **Wayne Primeau** to San Jose for **Matt Bradley**.

11 – Pittsburgh traded **Marc Bergevin** to Tampa Bay for **Brian Holzinger**.

11 – Pittsburgh traded **Ian Moran** to Boston for its 4th-round choice (**Paul Bissonnette**) in 2003.

11 – San Jose traded **Dan McGillis** to Boston for its 2nd-round choice (**Masi Marjamaki**) in 2003.

May 2003

12 – Tampa Bay traded **Marc Bergevin** to Pittsburgh for NY Rangers' 9th-round choice (previously acquired, **Albert Vishnyakov**) in 2003.

28 – Philadelphia traded **Roman Cechmanek** to Los Angeles for a 2nd-round choice in 2004.

29 – Toronto traded **Allan Rourke** to Carolina for **Harold Druken**.

30 – Boston traded **Darren McLachlan** to Phoenix for a 5th-round choice in 2004.

June 2003

21 – Florida traded its 1st-round choice (**Marc-Andre Fleury**) and 3rd-round choice (**Daniel Carcillo**) in 2003 to Pittsburgh for **Mikael Samuelsson** and Pittsburgh's 1st-round choice (**Nathan Horton**) and 2nd-round compensatory choice (**Stefan Meyer**) in 2003.

21 – Boston traded its 1st-round choice (**Steve Bernier**) in 2003 to San Jose for Toronto's 1st-round choice (previously acquired, **Mark Stuart**), San Jose's 2nd-round compensatory choice (**Masi Marjamaki**) and San Jose's 4th-round choice (**Byron Bitz**) in 2003.

21 – Edmonton traded its 1st-round choice (**Zach Parise**) in 2003 to New Jersey for its 2nd-round choice (**Jean-Francoise Jacques**) and St. Louis' 1st-round choice (previously acquired, **Marc-Antoine Pouliot**) in 2003.

21 – Tampa Bay traded its 1st-round choice (**Anthony Stewart**) in 2003 to Florida for its 2nd-round choice (**Mike Egener**), Phoenix's 2nd-round choice (previously acquired, **Matt Smaby**) and Tampa Bay's 6th-round choice (previously acquired, **Doug O'Brien**) in 2003.

21 – Dallas traded its 1st-round choice (**Corey Perry**) in 2003 to Anaheim for San Jose's 2nd-round choice (previously acquired, **Vojtek Polak**) and its 2nd-round choice (**Brandon Crombeen**) in 2003.

21 – Colorado traded **Scott Parker** to San Jose for Colorado's 5th-round choice (previously acquired, **Brad Richardson**) in 2003.

21 – Chicago traded **Andrei Nikolishin** to Colorado for future considerations.

21 – Florida traded **Ivan Majesky** to Atlanta for its 2nd-round choice (**Kamil Kreps**) in 2003.

21 – Calgary traded its 2nd-round compensatory choice (**Matthew Carle**) in 2003 to San Jose for Colorado's 3rd-round choice (previously acquired, **Ryan Donally**), its 5th-round choice (**Greg Moore**) and its 6th-round choice (**Tyler Johnson**) in 2003.

21 – NY Rangers traded its 2nd-round choice (**Joshua Hennessy**) in 2003 to San Jose for Boston's 2nd-round choice (previously acquired, **Ivan Baranka**) and its 3rd-round choice (**Ken Roche**) in 2003.

21 – St. Louis traded **Cory Stillman** to Tampa Bay for its 2nd-round choice (**David Backes**) in 2003.

21 – Toronto traded Calgary's 3rd-round choice (previously acquired, **Danny Irmen**) in 2003 to Minnesota for its 3rd-round choice (**Martin Sagat**) and 4th-round choice (**Konstantin Volkov**) in 2003.

21 – St. Louis traded its 3rd-round choice (**Ivan Khomutov**) in 2003 to New Jersey for **Mike Danton** and its 3rd-round choice (**Konstantin Zakharov**) in 2003.

21 – St. Louis traded **Tyson Nash** to Phoenix for its 5th-round choice (**Lee Stempniak**) in 2003.

21 – Colorado traded **Sergei Soin** to Nashville for **Tomas Slovak**.

22 – Montreal traded Nashville's 4th-round choice (previously acquired, **Andreas Valdix**) in 2003 to Washington for its 4th-round choice (**Danny Stewart**) and 7th-round choice (**Oskari Korpikari**) in 2003.

22 – Carolina traded its 5th-round choice (**Arsi Piispanen**) and 6th-round choice (**Marc Methot**) in 2003 to Columbus for New Jersey's 4th-round choice (previously acquired) in 2004.

22 – Nashville traded Chicago's 4th-round choice (previously acquired, **Nathan Saunders**) in 2003 to Anaheim for its 4th- and 5th-round choices in 2004.

22 – Los Angeles traded its 9th-round compensatory choice (**Trevor Hendrikx**) in 2003 to Columbus for a 9th-round choice in 2004.

22 – Nashville traded its 6th-round choice (**Esa Pirnes**) in 2003 to Los Angeles for its 7th-round choice (**Andrei Mukhachev**) and Boston's 7th-round choice (previously acquired, **Miroslav Hanuljak**) in 2003.

22 – Ottawa traded Washington's 9th-round choice (previously acquired, **Mark Olafson**) in 2003 to Washington for future considerations.

22 – Philadelphia traded Atlanta's 6th-round choice (previously acquired, **Joe Pavelski**) in 2003 to San Jose for a 6th-round choice in 2004.

22 – Florida traded NY Islanders' 9th-round choice (previously acquired, later traded to San Jose – San Jose selected **Carter Lee**) in 2003 to Chicago for **Dmitri Tolkunov**.

22 – Philadelphia traded **Marty Murray** to Carolina for a 6th-round choice in 2004.

22 – Philadelphia traded its 7th-round choice (**Dany Roussin**) in 2003 to Florida for a 6th-round choice in 2004.

22 – Philadelphia traded its 8th-round choice (**Raimonds Danilics**) in 2003 to Tampa Bay for a 7th-round choice in 2004.

22 – Dallas traded its 9th-round choice (**Loic Burkhalter**) in 2003 to Phoenix for an 8th-round choice in 2004.

22 – Chicago traded NY Islanders' 9th-round choice (previously acquired, **Carter Lee**) in 2003 to San Jose for an 8th-round choice in 2004.

22 – Philadelphia traded its 9th-round choice (**Zbynek Hrdel**) in 2003 to Tampa Bay for a 9th-round choice in 2004.

26 – Ottawa traded **Chris Bala** to Nashville for **Peter Smrek**.

26 – Nashville traded **Chris Bala** to Minnesota for **Curtis Murphy**.

27 – Nashville traded **Andy Delmore** to Buffalo for a 3rd-round choice in 2004.

30 – Philadelphia traded **Dmitry Yushkevich** to Washington for a 7th-round choice in 2004.

30 – Nashville traded **Karlis Skrastins** to Colorado for future considerations.

30 – NY Rangers traded **Mark Messier** to San Jose for future considerations.

30 – NY Rangers traded **Brian Leetch** to Edmonton for **Jussi Markkanen** and a 4th-round choice in 2004.

July 2003

3 – Colorado traded **Steve Reinprecht** to Buffalo for **Keith Ballard**.

3 – Buffalo traded **Steve Reinprecht** and **Rhett Warrener** to Calgary for **Chris Drury** and **Steve Begin**.

14 – Washington traded **Mike Farrell** to Nashville for **Alexander Riazantsev**.

16 – Calgary traded **Bob Boughner** to Carolina for a 4th-round choice in 2004 and future considerations.

18 – Colorado traded **Eric Messier** and **Vaclav Nedorost** to Florida for **Peter Worrell** and a 2nd-round choice in 2004.

22 – Dallas traded **Darryl Sydor** to Columbus for **Mike Sillinger** and a 2nd-round choice in 2004.

22 – Dallas traded **Mike Sillinger** and a conditional 4th-round choice to Phoenix for **Teppo Numminen**.

25 – Vancouver traded **Bryan Helmer** to Phoenix for **Martin Grenier**.

August 2003

12 – San Jose traded **Chad Wiseman** to NY Rangers for **Nils Ekman**.

12 – Anaheim traded **Travis Brigley** to Colorado for future considerations.

25 – Pittsburgh traded **Johan Hedberg** to Vancouver for a 2nd-round choice in 2004.

Trades and free agent signings that occurred after August 25, 2003 are listed on page 335.

Hockey Fights Cancer is a joint initiative created by the National Hockey League and the National Hockey League Players' Association that honors those in the hockey community who have struggled, or continue to struggle, with the disease.

The goal of Hockey Fights Cancer is to raise money and visibility for local cancer care or research, as well as to support the American Cancer Society and Canadian Cancer Society national organizations. Founded by the NHL and the NHLPA, Hockey Fights Cancer is supported by NHL member clubs, NHL Alumni, the NHL Officials Association, Professional Hockey Trainers and Equipment Managers, corporate marketing partners, broadcast partners and fans throughout North America.

Join the Fight! If you would like to make a contribution to Hockey Fights Cancer, please forward a check made payable to Hockey Fights Cancer to one of the following addresses:

For Canadian Residents:
Hockey Fights Cancer
P.O. Box 1282, Station B
Montreal, Quebec H3B 3K9

For U.S. Residents:
Hockey Fights Cancer
P.O. Box 5037
New York, NY 10185-5037

Please include your name and current address so that your donation can be acknowledged. All donations are tax-deductible.

For more information, log-on to www.hockeyfightscancer.com or call 1-800-540-6500.

THREE STAR SELECTION...